W9-CEW-315

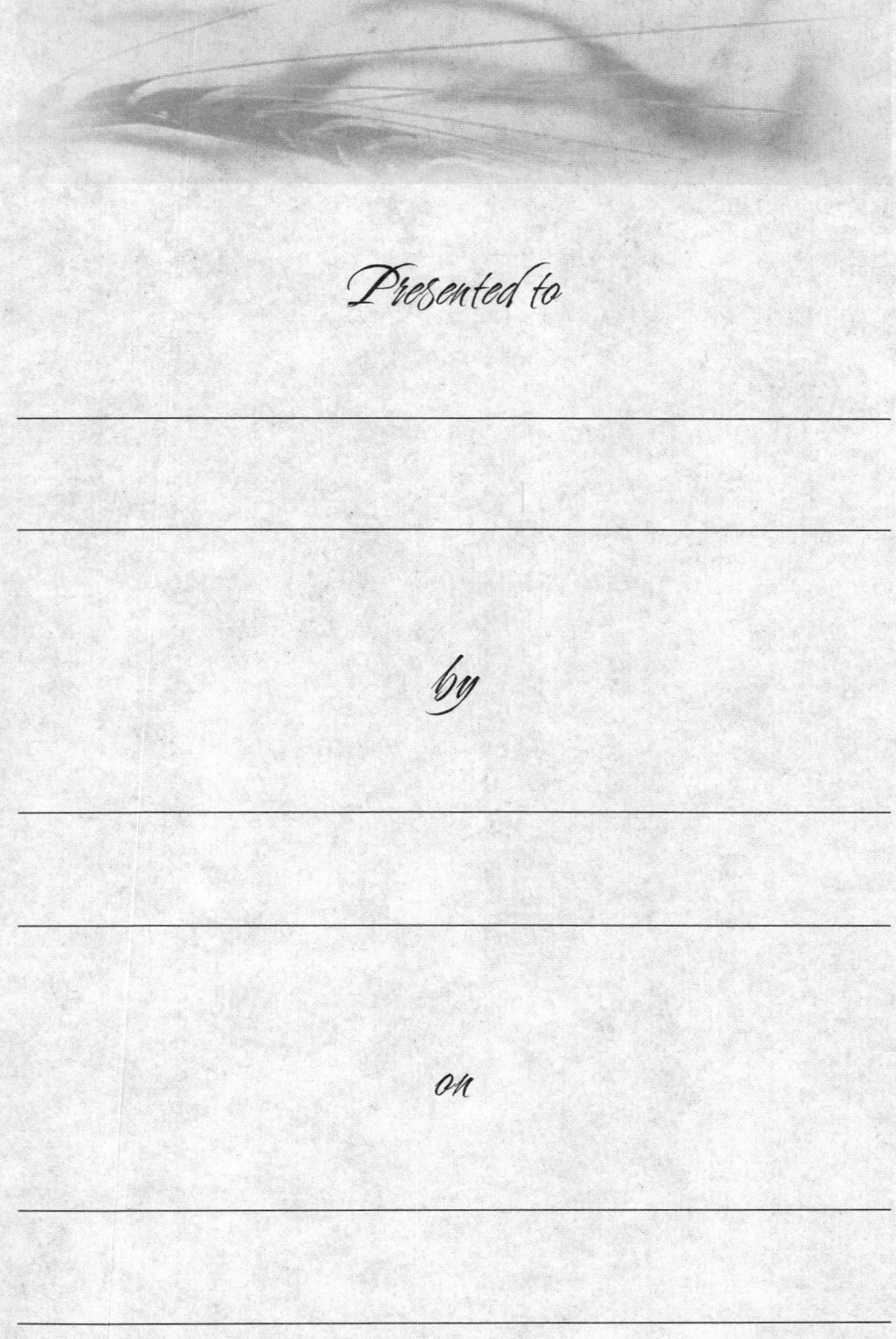

Presented to

_____

_____

by

_____

_____

on

_____

_____

THE DISCIPLESHIP STUDY BIBLE

The Discipleship Study Bible

THE DISCIPLESHIP
STUDY BIBLE

New Revised Standard Version including Apocrypha

EDITORIAL BOARD

Bruce C. Birch

Brian K. Blount

Thomas G. Long

Gail R. O'Day

W. Sibley Towner

Westminster John Knox Press
Louisville / London

© 2008 Westminster John Knox Press

All rights reserved. No part of this book may be reproduced or transmitted in any form or by any means, electronic or mechanical, including photocopying, recording, or by any information storage or retrieval system, without permission in writing from the publisher. For information, address Westminster John Knox Press, 100 Witherspoon Street, Louisville, Kentucky 40202-1396.

The Scripture quotations contained herein are from the New Revised Standard Version of the Bible, copyright © 1989 by the Division of Christian Education of the National Council of the Churches of Christ in the U.S.A., and are used by permission. The NRSV is published by arrangement with HarperOne, an imprint of HarperCollins Publishers. All rights reserved.

Please note: Up to five hundred (500) verses of The New Revised Standard Version (NRSV) Bible text may be quoted or reprinted without the express written permission of the publisher, provided that the verses quoted neither amount to a complete book of the Bible nor account for 50% or more of the written text of the total work in which they are quoted. When the NRSV text is quoted, notice of copyright must appear on the title or copyright page of the work as follows:

> The Scripture quotations contained herein are from the New Revised Standard Version Bible, copyright © 1989 by the Division of Christian Education of the National Council of the Churches of Christ in the U.S.A., and are used by permission. All rights reserved.

When quotations from the NRSV text are used in non-saleable media, such as church bulletins, orders of service, posters, transparencies, or similar media, the initials (NRSV) may be used at the end of each quotation.

Quotations or reprints in excess of five hundred (500) verses (as well as other permissions requests) must be approved in writing by the NRSV Permissions Office, The National Council of the Churches of Christ in the U.S.A., 475 Riverside Drive, New York, NY 10115-0050. For more information regarding licensing and permissions, please visit the Web site nrsv.net.

Portions of the introduction and notes for the books of Hebrews and James were published in an earlier form in Frances Taylor Gench, *Hebrews and James,* Westminster Bible Companion, and are used by permission of Westminster John Knox Press.

Maps © 2008 CHK America 805-682-8900
Concordance provided by Oxford University Press and Blue Heron Bookcraft, Inc. Used by permission.

Produced with the assistance of The Livingstone Corporation (www.Livingstonecorp.com). Production staff includes Jake Barton, Ashley Taylor, Andy Culbertson, Will Reaves, Mary Horner Collins, Tom Ristow, and Kathleen Ristow. Proofread by Peachtree Editorial Service.

Book design by The Livingstone Corporation
Cover design by designpointinc.com
Cover photograph: © Lance Nelson/CORBIS

First edition
Published by Westminster John Knox Press
Louisville, Kentucky

This book is printed on acid-free paper that meets the American National Standards Institute Z39.48 standard.

PRINTED IN THE UNITED STATES OF AMERICA

08 09 10 11 12 13 14 15 16 17 — 10 9 8 7 6 5 4 3 2 1

Library of Congress Cataloging-in-Publication Data

Bible. English. New Revised Standard. 2008
   The discipleship study Bible: New Revised Standard Version, including apocrypha. — 1st ed.
     p. cm.
   ISBN 978-0-664-22371-7 (alk. paper)
1.   Bible—Criticism, interpretation, etc.   I. Title.
   BS191.5.A12008 L68
   220.5′20434—dc22

Contents

THE OLD TESTAMENT

THE APOCRYPHAL OR DEUTEROCANONICAL BOOKS

THE NEW TESTAMENT

Contributors

Bruce C. Birch, Wesley Theological Seminary, Washington, DC (1–2 Samuel)

Brian K. Blount, Union Theological Seminary and Presbyterian School of Christian Education, Richmond, VA (Matthew, Mark)

Nancy R. Bowen, Earlham School of Religion, Richmond, IN (Exodus, Deuteronomy)

John M. Bracke, Eden Theological Seminary, St. Louis, MO (Jeremiah)

William P. Brown, Columbia Theological Seminary, Decatur, GA (Joel, Obadiah, Haggai, Zechariah, Malachi)

Allen Callahan, Brown University, Providence, Rhode Island, and the Seminário Teológico Batista de Nordeste in Baha, Brazil (Philemon)

Warren Carter, Brite Divinity School, Texas Christian University, Fort Worth, TX (John, 1–3 John)

Linda Day, Pittsburgh, PA (Ruth, Esther, Jonah, Additions to Esther)

Kathleen Farmer, United Theological Seminary, Dayton, OH (Proverbs, Song of Solomon)

Mary F. Foskett, Wake Forest University, Winston-Salem, NC (Luke)

Terence Fretheim, Luther Seminary, St. Paul, MN (Genesis)

Julie Galambush, College of William and Mary, Williamsburg, VA (Ezekiel)

Frances Taylor Gench, Union Theological Seminary and Presbyterian School of Christian Education, Richmond, VA (Hebrews, James, 1–2 Peter, Jude)

Frank H. Gorman Jr., Muncie, IN (Leviticus, Numbers)

David Hay † (Romans, 1–2 Corinthians, Galatians)

John C. Holbert, Perkins School of Theology, Southern Methodist University, Dallas, TX (Job, Ecclesiastes)

Denise Dombkowski Hopkins, Wesley Theological Seminary, Washington, DC (Judith, 1–4 Maccabees)

W. Lee Humphreys, Dalton, GA (1–2 Kings)

Deborah Krause, Eden Theological Seminary, St. Louis, MO (1–2 Timothy, Titus)

Jeffrey Kuan, Pacific School of Religion, Berkeley, CA (Micah, Nahum, Habakkuk, Zephaniah)

Nancy C. Lee, Niebuhr Center, Elmhurst College, Elmhurst, IL (Lamentations)

Gary Light, Cayce, GA (Wisdom of Solomon)

Clint McCann, Eden Theological Seminary, St. Louis, MO (Psalms, Prayer of Manasseh, Psalm 151)

Jefferson H. McCrory Jr., Fuller Theological Seminary, Pasadena, CA (Hosea, Amos)

Gail R. O'Day, Candler School of Theology, Emory University, Atlanta, GA (Revelation)

Paul L. Redditt, Georgetown College, Georgetown, KY (Baruch, 1–2 Esdras)

Stephen Breck Reid, Bethany Theological Seminary, Richmond, IN (Daniel, Additions to Daniel)

Edesio Sanchez, Miami, FL (Joshua, Judges)

Stanley Saunders, Columbia Theological Seminary, Decatur, GA (Ephesians, Philippians, Colossians, 1–2 Thessalonians)

Vincent Skemp, College of St. Catherine, St. Paul, MN (Tobit)

Beth L. Tanner, New Brunswick Theological Seminary, New Brunswick, NJ (Letter of Jeremiah)

Mark A. Throntveit, Luther Seminary, St. Paul, MN (1–2 Chronicles, Ezra, Nehemiah)

W. Sibley Towner, Union Theological Seminary and Presbyterian School of Christian Education, Richmond, VA (Isaiah)

Robert W. Wall, Seattle Pacific University, Seattle, WA (Acts)

Benjamin G. Wright III, Lehigh University, Bethlehem, PA (Sirach)

Introduction

Why do we need another study Bible? When we scan the shelves of bookstores that carry a wide selection of Bibles, we may find the array of translations, study editions, and annotated Bibles aimed at particular groups of readers to be bewildering and overwhelming. There is a very positive aspect to this situation. People are hungry to read and study the Bible, seeking to find there the resources that can ground their own journeys of life and faith. It is a marvelous development that various editions of the Bible should seek to make connections with the needs and identities of those who seek biblical wisdom.

Study Bibles fall into two main groupings. On the one hand, there are Bibles that give us additional help in understanding these ancient texts in their own terms. After all, the Bible comes out of a world vastly different from our own. The customs, history, geography, and expressions of that world are often unfamiliar to us. Some study Bibles attempt to help us with this understanding by providing maps, charts, introductions to the biblical books, and notes that explain the meaning and background of texts that might not be immediately understandable to the modern reader. Although aimed at general church readership, these study Bibles are more academic in character.

More recently, some new study Bibles have tried to provide the Bible reader with help in moving from the meaning of the text to the ways in which the text might address and prove applicable to the lives of contemporary people of faith. The notes in such study Bibles place a stress on making connections with contemporary issues of faith in ways that help make connections between ancient witness and modern practice. In an effort to be helpful to particular groups, some Bible editions have notes that focus on age groups (teens, the elderly), ethnic traditions (African American, Asian, Hispanic), gender (men and women), or an aspect of Christian life (spirituality, prayer). The hope is that readers will pick up an edition of the Bible that directly addresses their own identity and needs and in so doing make a more direct biblical connection to their lives.

The *Discipleship Study Bible* developed as an effort to address two needs within today's churches. First, it did not seem necessary to choose as sharply as most available study Bibles do between annotations that assist the reader in the fuller understanding of the text in its own particular terms and ancient contexts and annotations that assist the reader in connecting biblical witness to the living of contemporary lives of faith. Could not one study Bible bring together in fuller measure these two ways of commenting upon the biblical text and its role as Scripture in the lives of people of faith? Could there not be a study Bible that illumined both our understanding and our discipleship?

The *Discipleship Study Bible* also sought to address a second circumstance. Although admirable in intent, Bibles whose notes address only a particular group or a particular area of Christian life suggest that we can selectively read the Bible, and so we may miss the Bible's broader challenges to our identities and interests. Most of these approaches tend to be individualistic, as if the life of faith could

be lived out of our own identity as individuals, rather than as members of a connected community of faith. The Bible challenges us to move beyond individual piety to connection with a community of God's people, called to discipleship in the world. There may be a place for study Bibles that help particular groups or interests make connection to the biblical witness. However, the *Discipleship Study Bible* is intended to highlight the Bible's comprehensive witness to those who wish biblical guidance in living a life of discipleship amid all the diversity and challenge that our world presents. The Bible's witness addresses our personal faith and devotional practices, but also our social commitment, responsibility, and action. It challenges us as persons, as churches, and as members of local and global communities. The Bible can give new depth to our faith, but sometimes confronts that faith with issues that discomfort and challenge our assumptions and practices.

The *Discipleship Study Bible* is intended to provide a study Bible addressed to the entire range of Christian discipleship in its need to be both grounded and challenged by the biblical witness. This study Bible includes

♦ *Comments by an outstanding team of internationally known biblical scholars.* They have been chosen for both their biblical expertise and their commitment to make the biblical witness accessible to the life of Christian discipleship in the world.

♦ *Features common to most study Bibles, with basic information that helps make the ancient witness understandable to modern readers.* Introductions to each of the biblical books will acquaint readers with essential historical, sociocultural, literary, and theological issues valuable in understanding the book in question. The introductions may also indicate areas of ongoing scholarly discussion. A number of study aids, including maps and a chart, are available at the back of the book.

♦ *Notes that attempt to make connection with the entire range of the Christian life.* Both personal and corporate discipleship are regarded as important. Both spiritual and social needs are given attention and response. The *Discipleship Study Bible* will help readers recognize that Christian faith makes claims upon every aspect of our lives, both as persons and communities of faith. The notes will invite the reader to see, in the biblical witness, God's invitation to live faithfully and redemptively in the world. At times the notes may help open us to new avenues of inspiration and insight. But at other times the notes may help highlight a biblical mandate to confront a difficult issue or to take up a sacrificial practice for the sake of God's challenge "to do justice, and to love kindness, and to walk humbly with your God" (Mic. 6:8). The *Discipleship Study Bible* will attempt to avoid simplistic or easy responses to the tensions and complexities of the biblical witness, and it will invite the reader to genuine encounter with the implications of the text for the whole life of Christian discipleship.

♦ *The use of the New Revised Standard Version translation of the biblical text.* The *Discipleship Study Bible* will include all of the deuterocanonical or apocryphal writings found in the NRSV, in the order used by that translation. The NRSV is one of the most widely used translations of the biblical text and is known for its clarity and readability, as well as its use of inclusive expressions.

The editorial team responsible for the preparation of the *Discipleship Study Bible* felt strongly that, in spite of the many study Bibles available, there was a place and a need for a Bible that could assist the serious Christian reader to deepen understanding of the Bible while opening to its claims on every aspect of our lives as Christian disciples. God's word is comprehensive, challenging, transforming, and renewing. Our hope is that the *Discipleship Study Bible* will assist and encourage you on this path of biblical discipleship.

Bruce C. Birch for the Editorial Board

Preface to the
NRSV

To the Reader

This preface is addressed to you by the Committee of translators, who wish to explain, as briefly as possible, the origin and character of our work. The publication of our revision is yet another step in the long, continual process of making the Bible available m the form of the English language that is most widely current in our day. To summarize in a single sentence: the New Revised Standard Version of the Bible is an authorized revision of the Revised Standard Version, published m 1952, which was a revision of the American Standard Version, published in 1901, which, in turn, embodied earlier revisions of the King James Version, published in 1611.

In the course of time, the King James Version came to be regarded as "the Authorized Version." With good reason it has been termed "the noblest monument of English prose," and it has entered, as no other book has, into the making of the personal character and the public institutions of the English-speaking peoples. We owe to it an incalculable debt.

Yet the King James Version has serious defects. By the middle of the nineteenth century, the development of biblical studies and the discovery of many biblical manuscripts more ancient than those on which the King James Version was based made it apparent that these defects were so many as to call for revision. The task was begun, by authority of the Church of England, in 1870. The (British) Revised Version of the Bible was published in 1881–1885; and the American Standard Version, its variant embodying the preferences of the American scholars associated with the work, was published, as was mentioned above, in 1901. In 1928 the copyright of the latter was acquired by the International Council of Religious Education and thus passed into the ownership of the Churches of the United States and Canada that were associated in this Council through their boards of education and publication.

The Council appointed a committee of scholars to have charge of the text of the American Standard Version and to undertake inquiry concerning the need for further revision. After studying the questions whether or not revision should be undertaken, and if so, what its nature and extent should be, in 1937 the Council authorized a revision. The scholars who served as members of the Committee worked in two sections, one dealing with the Old Testament and one with the New Testament. In 1946 the Revised Standard Version of the New Testament was published. The publication of the Revised Standard Version of the Bible, containing the Old and New Testaments, took place on September 30, 1952.

A translation of the Apocryphal/Deuterocanonical Books of the Old Testament followed in 1957. In 1977 this collection was issued m an expanded edition, containing three additional texts received by Eastern Orthodox communions (3 and 4 Maccabees and Psalm 151). Thereafter the Revised Standard Version gained the distinction of being officially authorized for use by all major Christian churches: Protestant, Anglican, Roman Catholic, and Eastern Orthodox.

The Revised Standard Version Bible Committee is a continuing body, comprising about thirty members, both men and women. Ecumenical in representation, it includes scholars affiliated with various Protestant denominations, as well as several Roman Catholic members, an Eastern Orthodox member, and a Jewish member who serves in the Old Testament section. For a period of time the Committee included several members from Canada and from England.

Because no translation of the Bible is perfect or is acceptable to all groups of readers, and because discoveries of older manuscripts and further investigation of linguistic features of the text continue to become available, renderings of the Bible have proliferated. During the years following the publication of the Revised Standard Version, twenty-six other English translations and revisions of the Bible were produced by committees and by individual scholars—not to mention twenty-five other translations and revisions of the New Testament alone. One of the latter was the second edition of the RSV New Testament, issued in 1971, twenty-five years after its initial publication.

Following the publication of the RSV Old Testament in 1952, significant advances were made in the discovery and interpretation of documents in Semitic languages related to Hebrew. In addition to the information that had become available in the late 1940s from the Dead Sea texts of Isaiah and Habakkuk, subsequent acquisitions from the same area brought to light many other early copies of all the books of the Hebrew Scriptures (except Esther), though most of these copies are fragmentary. During the same period early Greek manuscript copies of books of the New Testament also became available.

In order to take these discoveries into account, along with recent studies of documents in Semitic languages related to Hebrew, in 1974 the Policies Committee of the Revised Standard Version, which is a standing committee of the National Council of the Churches of Christ in the U.S.A., authorized the preparation of a revision of the entire RSV Bible.

For the Old Testament the Committee has made use of the *Biblia Hebraica Stuttgartensia* (1977; ed. sec. emendata, 1983). This is an edition of the Hebrew and Aramaic text as current early in the Christian era and fixed by Jewish scholars (the "Masoretes") of the sixth to the ninth centuries. The vowel signs, which were added by the Masoretes, are accepted in the main, but where a more probable and convincing reading can be obtained by assuming different vowels, this has been done. No notes are given in such cases, because the vowel points are less ancient and reliable than the consonants. When an alternative reading given by the Masoretes is translated in a footnote, this is identified by the words "Another reading is."

Departures from the consonantal text of the best manuscripts have been made only where it seems clear that errors in copying had been made before the text was standardized. Most of the corrections adopted are based on the ancient versions (translations into Greek, Aramaic, Syriac, and Latin), which were made prior to the time of the work of the Masoretes and which therefore may reflect earlier forms of the Hebrew text. In such instances a footnote specifies the ver-

sion or versions from which the correction has been derived and also gives a translation of the Masoretic Text. Where it was deemed appropriate to do so, information is supplied in footnotes from subsidiary Jewish traditions concerning other textual readings (the *Tiqqune Sopherim,* "emendations of the scribes"). These are identified in the footnotes as "Ancient Heb tradition."

Occasionally it is evident that the text has suffered in transmission and that none of the versions provides a satisfactory restoration. Here we can only follow the best judgment of competent scholars as to the most probable reconstruction of the original text. Such reconstructions are indicated in footnotes by the abbreviation Cn ("Correction"), and a translation of the Masoretic Text is added.

For the Apocryphal/Deuterocanonical Books of the Old Testament the Committee has made use of a number of texts. For most of these books the basic Greek text from which the present translation was made is the edition of the Septuagint prepared by Alfred Rahlfs and published by the Württemberg Bible Society (Stuttgart, 1935). For several of the books the more recently published individual volumes of the Göttingen Septuagint project were utilized. For the book of Tobit it was decided to follow the form of the Greek text found in codex Sinaiticus (supported as it is by evidence from Qumran); where this text is defective, it was supplemented and corrected by other Greek manuscripts. For the three Additions to Daniel (namely, Susanna, the Prayer of Azariah and the Song of the Three Jews, and Bel and the Dragon) the Committee continued to use the Greek version attributed to Theodotion (the so-called "Theodotion-Daniel"). In translating Ecclesiasticus (Sirach), while constant reference was made to the Hebrew fragments of a large portion of this book (those discovered at Qumran and Masada as well as those recovered from the Cairo Geniza), the Committee generally followed the Greek text (including verse numbers) published by Joseph Ziegler in the Göttingen Septuagint (1965). But in many places the Committee has translated the Hebrew text when this provides a reading that is clearly superior to the Greek; the Syriac and Latin versions were also consulted throughout and occasionally adopted. The basic text adopted in rendering 2 Esdras is the Latin version given in *Biblia Sacra,* edited by Robert Weber (Stuttgart, 1971). This was supplemented by consulting the Latin text as edited by R. L. Bensly (1895) and by Bruno Violet (1910), as well as by taking into account the several Oriental versions of 2 Esdras, namely, the Syriac, Ethiopic, Arabic (two forms, referred to as Arabic 1 and Arabic 2), Armenian, and Georgian versions. Finally, since the Additions to the Book of Esther are disjointed and quite unintelligible as they stand in most editions of the Apocrypha, we have provided them with their original context by translating the whole of the Greek version of Esther from Robert Hanhart's Göttingen edition (1983).

For the New Testament the Committee has based its work on the most recent edition of *The Greek New Testament,* prepared by an interconfessional and international committee and published by the United Bible Societies (1966; 3rd ed. corrected, 1983; information concerning changes to be introduced into the critical apparatus of the forthcoming 4th edition was available to the Committee). As in that edition, double brackets are used to enclose a few passages that are generally regarded to be later additions to the text, but which we have retained because of their evident antiquity and their importance in the textual tradition. Only in very rare instances have we replaced the text or the punctuation of the Bible Societies' edition by an alternative that seemed to us to be superior. Here and there in the footnotes the phrase, "Other ancient authorities read," identifies

alternative readings preserved by Greek manuscripts and early versions. In both Testaments, alternative renderings of the text are indicated by the word "Or."

As for the style of English adopted for the present revision, among the mandates given to the Committee in 1980 by the Division of Education and Ministry of the National Council of Churches of Christ (which now holds the copyright of the RSV Bible) was the directive to continue in the tradition of the King James Bible, but to introduce such changes as are warranted on the basis of accuracy, clarity, euphony, and current English usage. Within the constraints set by the original texts and by the mandates of the Division, the Committee has followed the maxim, "As literal as possible, as free as necessary." As a consequence, the New Revised Standard Version (NRSV) remains essentially a literal translation. Paraphrastic renderings have been adopted only sparingly, and then chiefly to compensate for a deficiency in the English language—the lack of a common gender third person singular pronoun.

During the almost half a century since the publication of the RSV, many in the churches have become sensitive to the danger of linguistic sexism arising from the inherent bias of the English language towards the masculine gender, a bias that in the case of the Bible has often restricted or obscured the meaning of the original text. The mandates from the Division specified that, in references to men and women, masculine-oriented language should be eliminated as far as this can be done without altering passages that reflect the historical situation of ancient patriarchal culture. As can be appreciated, more than once the Committee found that the several mandates stood in tension and even in conflict. The various concerns had to be balanced case by case in order to provide a faithful and acceptable rendering without using contrived English. Only very occasionally has the pronoun "he" or "him" been retained in passages where the reference may have been to a woman as well as to a man; for example, in several legal texts in Leviticus and Deuteronomy. In such instances of formal, legal language, the options of either putting the passage in the plural or of introducing additional nouns to avoid masculine pronouns in English seemed to the Committee to obscure the historic structure and literary character of the original. In the vast majority of cases, however, inclusiveness has been attained by simple rephrasing or by introducing plural forms when this does not distort the meaning of the passage. Of course, in narrative and in parable no attempt was made to generalize the sex of individual persons.

Another aspect of style will be detected by readers who compare the more stately English rendering of the Old Testament with the less formal rendering adopted for the New Testament. For example, the traditional distinction between *shall* and *will* in English has been retained in the Old Testament as appropriate in rendering a document that embodies what may be termed the classic form of Hebrew, while in the New Testament the abandonment of such distinctions in the usage of the future tense in English reflects the more colloquial nature of the koine Greek used by most New Testament authors except when they are quoting the Old Testament.

Careful readers will notice that here and there in the Old Testament the word LORD (or in certain cases GOD) is printed in capital letters. This represents the traditional manner in English versions of rendering the Divine Name, the "Tetragrammaton" (see the notes on Exodus 3.14, 15), following the precedent of the ancient Greek and Latin translators and the long established practice in the reading of the Hebrew Scriptures in the synagogue. While it is almost if

not quite certain that the Name was originally pronounced "Yahweh," this pronunciation was not indicated when the Masoretes added vowel sounds to the consonantal Hebrew text. To the four consonants YHWH of the Name, which had come to be regarded as too sacred to be pronounced, they attached vowel signs indicating that in its place should be read the Hebrew word *Adonai* meaning "Lord" (or *Elohim* meaning "God"). Ancient Greek translators employed the word *Kyrios* ("Lord") for the Name. The Vulgate likewise used the Latin word *Dominus* ("Lord"). The form "Jehovah" is of late medieval origin; it is a combination of the consonants of the Divine Name and the vowels attached to it by the Masoretes but belonging to an entirely different word. Although the American Standard Version (1901) had used "Jehovah" to render the Tetragrammaton (the sound of Y being represented by J and the sound of W by V, as in Latin), for two reasons the Committees that produced the RSV and the NRSV returned to the more familiar usage of the King James Version. (1) The word "Jehovah" does not accurately represent any form of the Name ever used in Hebrew. (2) The use of any proper name for the one and only God, as though there were other gods from whom the true God had to be distinguished, began to be discontinued in Judaism before the Christian era and is inappropriate for the universal faith of the Christian Church.

It will be seen that in the Psalms and in other prayers addressed to God the archaic second person singular pronouns (*thee, thou, thine*) and verb forms (*art, hast, hadst*) are no longer used. Although some readers may regret this change, it should be pointed out that in the original languages neither the Old Testament nor the New makes any linguistic distinction between addressing a human being and addressing the Deity. Furthermore, in the tradition of the King James Version one will not expect to find the use of capital letters for pronouns that refer to the Deity—such capitalization is an unnecessary innovation that has only recently been introduced into a few English translations of the Bible. Finally, we have left to the discretion of the licensed publishers such matters as section headings, cross-references, and clues to the pronunciation of proper names.

This new version seeks to preserve all that is best in the English Bible as it has been known and used through the years. It is intended for use in public reading and congregational worship, as well as in private study, instruction, and meditation. We have resisted the temptation to introduce terms and phrases that merely reflect current moods, and have tried to put the message of the Scriptures in simple, enduring words and expressions that are worthy to stand m the great tradition of the King James Bible and its predecessors.

In traditional Judaism and Christianity, the Bible has been more than a historical document to be preserved or a classic of literature to be cherished and admired; it is recognized as the unique record of God's dealings with people over the ages. The Old Testament sets forth the call of a special people to enter into covenant relation with the God of justice and steadfast love and to bring God's law to the nations. The New Testament records the life and work of Jesus Christ, the one in whom "the Word became flesh," as well as describes the rise and spread of the early Christian Church. The Bible carries its full message, not to those who regard it simply as a noble literary heritage of the past or who wish to use it to enhance political purposes and advance otherwise desirable goals, but to all persons and communities who read it so that they may discern and understand what God is saying to them. That message must not be disguised in phrases that are no longer clear, or hidden under words that have changed

or lost their meaning; it must be presented in language that is direct and plain and meaningful to people today. It is the hope and prayer of the translators that this version of the Bible may continue to hold a large place in congregational life and to speak to all readers, young and old alike, helping them to understand and believe and respond to its message.

For the Committee,
BRUCE M. METZGER

Alphabetical List of Biblical Books

Abbreviations

THE OLD TESTAMENT

Gen.	Genesis	Eccl.	Ecclesiastes
Exod.	Exodus	Song	Song of Solomon
Lev.	Leviticus	Isa.	Isaiah
Num.	Numbers	Jer.	Jeremiah
Deut.	Deuteronomy	Lam.	Lamentations
Josh.	Joshua	Ezek.	Ezekiel
Judg.	Judges	Dan.	Daniel
Ruth	Ruth	Hos.	Hosea
1 Sam.	1 Samuel	Joel	Joel
2 Sam.	2 Samuel	Amos	Amos
1 Kgs.	1 Kings	Obad.	Obadiah
2 Kgs.	2 Kings	Jonah	Jonah
1 Chr.	1 Chronicles	Mic.	Micah
2 Chr.	2 Chronicles	Nah.	Nahum
Ezra	Ezra	Hab.	Habakkuk
Neh.	Nehemiah	Zeph.	Zephaniah
Esth.	Esther	Hag.	Haggai
Job	Job	Zech.	Zechariah
Ps./Pss.	Psalms	Mal.	Malachi
Prov.	Proverbs		

THE APOCRYPHA

Tob.	Tobit	Sus.	Susanna
Jdt.	Judith	Bel	Bel and the Dragon
Add. Esth.	Additions to Esther	1 Macc.	1 Maccabees
Wis.	Wisdom of Solomon	2 Macc.	2 Maccabees
Sir.	Sirach (or Ecclesiasticus)	1 Esd.	1 Esdras
Bar.	Baruch	Pr. Man.	The Prayer of Manasseh
Ep. Jer.	Letter (Epistle) of Jeremiah	Ps. 151	Psalm 151
Add. Dan.	Additions to Daniel	3 Macc.	3 Maccabees
Pr. Azar.	Prayer of Azariah	2 Esd.	2 Esdras
Sg. Three	Song of the Three Jews	4 Macc.	4 Maccabees

THE NEW TESTAMENT

Matt. Matthew	1 Tim. . . . . .1 Timothy
Mark . . . . Mark	2 Tim. . . . . .2 Timothy
Luke. . . . . Luke	Titus . . . . Titus
John .John	Phlm. . . . . Philemon
Acts . . . . .Acts	Heb. . . . . Hebrews
Rom. . . . . .Romans	Jas. . . . . .James
1 Cor. . . . . .1 Corinthians	1 Pet. . . . . .1 Peter
2 Cor. . . . . .2 Corinthians	2 Pet. . . . . .2 Peter
Gal. . . . . Galatians	1 John . . . . 1 John
Eph. . . . . Ephesians	2 John . . . . 2 John
Phil. . . . . .Philippians	3 John . . . . 3 John
Col. . . . . Colossians	Jude . . . . .Jude
1 Thess. . . . . .1 Thessalonians	Rev. . . . . Revelation
2 Thess. . . . . .2 Thessalonians	

In the notes to the books of the Old Testament the following abbreviations
are used:

Ant.	Josephus, *Antiquities of the Jews*
Aram	Aramaic
Ch, chs.	Chapter, chapters
Cn	Correction; made where the text has suffered in transmission and the versions provide no satisfactory restoration but where the Standard Bible Committee agrees with the judgment of competent scholars as to the most probable reconstruction of the original text.
Gk	Septuagint, Greek version of the Old Testament
Heb	Hebrew of the consonantal Masoretic Text of the Old Testament
Josephus	Flavius Josephus (Jewish historian, about A.D. 37 to about 95)
Macc.	The book(s) of the Maccabees
Ms(s)	Manuscript(s)
MT.	The Hebrew of the pointed Masoretic Text of the Old Testament
OL	Old Latin
Q Ms(s)	Manuscript(s) found at Qumran by the Dead Sea
Sam	Samaritan Hebrew text of the Old Testament
Syr	Syriac Version of the Old Testament
Tg.	Targum
Vg	Vulgate, Latin Version of the Old Testament

The
OLD TESTAMENT

THE HEBREW SCRIPTURES
COMMONLY CALLED
THE OLD TESTAMENT

New Revised Standard Version

The Book of
GENESIS

G enesis is a book about beginnings. Genesis moves from the morning of the world to the world of the ordering of families and nations to the birthing of the fathers and mothers of Israel. While God was there "in the beginning," Genesis also testifies to the beginnings of God's activity in the world. It is a new day for God, too. And, given the divine commitment to the creation, God will never be the same again.

But creation is more than chronology. Genesis stands at the beginning because creation is such a basic theological category for understanding all that follows. All of creation, from the least to the greatest, is shaped in decisive ways by the life-giving, life-enhancing work of the Creator. Creation provides the matrix within which God acts; creatures are born, mature, and die; and the God-creature relationship develops.

Genesis also witnesses to the beginning of sin and evil in the world, bringing in its train a remarkable range of disastrous effects upon individuals, families, and nations. The good creation that God brought into being was now in need of redemption. This development in creation greatly complicated God's work in the world and necessitated a new divine strategy for the sake of the world's future. That strategy is most clearly seen in God's choice of the family of Abraham and Sarah. This initially exclusive divine move has the objective of a maximally inclusive end, namely, the redemption of all creatures. Only in relation to God's work in creation can God's actions in and through Israel be seen to be universal in scope. To this end, Genesis has a remarkable and salutary interest in those families and peoples that are not the progenitors of Israel. Among others, readers will encounter individuals such as Melchizedek, Hagar and Ishmael, Abimelech, and Esau, as well as peoples from Egypt, Aram, Philistia, Shechem, Sodom and Gomorrah, and "all the world" (41:57). God's promise to Abraham embraces "all the families of the earth" (12:3).

The structure of the book of Genesis is relatively straightforward in terms of both form and content. Regarding literary form, Genesis is basically an admixture of narratives and genealogies (e.g., 1:1–2:4a; 5:1–32), with an occasional poetic piece (e.g., Gen. 3:14–19; 49:2–27). The genealogies constitute a kind of framework for the book as a whole (from 2:4 to 37:2), testifying to God's ongoing creative work within Israel and without. The form of the narratives is difficult to determine. They are not historical narratives as such, though they are not historically disinterested and no doubt carry some authentic memories of Israel's pre-exodus religious and cultural heritage. The designation "story," understood as an admixture of the story of God and that of humankind, is probably the best we can do. As such, the narratives provide an ongoing means by which Israel's identity as the people of God is revealed and shaped.

In terms of content, Genesis begins with the so-called primeval history (story), with its universal concerns for families and nations (1:1–11:26). The balance of Genesis may be divided into three cycles, focused on the progenitors of Israel: Abraham and

Sarah (11:27–25:18), Jacob and Esau (25:19–36:43), and the family of Jacob, with a special interest in the character of Joseph (37:1–50:26).

Genesis is a composite work; it grew in stages over a period of many centuries and was probably not finally completed until the postexilic period. The sources for Genesis have usually been considered along with other books in the Pentateuch. The classical formulation of the sources for the Pentateuch included the Yahwist (J), the Elohist (E), the Deuteronomist (D), and the Priestly (P) writer. These sources, from persons with different institutional bases and theological commitments, were commonly dated from the ninth to the fifth century BCE. They were gradually interwoven over this period of time by a series of redactors. The important role given to oral tradition, from the earliest stages of the tradition to the latest, complicated this formulation but did not finally dislodge it. In more recent decades, however, this hypothesis has been thrown into disarray from various perspectives; yet, its testimony to Genesis as a composite work remains firmly in place.

At the same time, increasingly common literary approaches have insisted on reading the book as a (finally) unified whole. These holistic readings have greatly enriched the study of Genesis. These readings include studies of individual texts as well as efforts to discern linkages across the book as a whole. Regarding the latter, links between chapters 1–11 and 37–50 have been noted, including family discord/harmony, fertility (1:28 and 47:27), the extension of life to a flood/famine-filled world (41:57), and the "good" that God works in creation and in the family (50:20). To some extent Joseph functions as a new Adam (41:38), though sin and evil and their devastating effects upon family and national life remain stubbornly in place.

These commonalities are accompanied by important literary developments. The narratives become less and less episodic, with more sustained plot lines and more complex portrayals of family life, moving finally to a novel-like form in the Joseph story. God's actions are portrayed more and more in terms that are less direct and obtrusive (for example, God does not appear to Joseph). Correlative with this development is the increasingly prominent role given to human action, climaxing in the social and economic leadership of Joseph.

The high place given to the human being in God's world is remarkable. Human beings are presented as good and responsible creatures. Created in the image of God, as well as from the dust of the ground, they are given creative powers by God and called to care for the earth and its creatures (1:28). Inasmuch as all human beings are created in the divine image, every one of them—each gender, every race, regardless of social status—is given the same stature in God's world. They become sinful, and this reality colors everything they say and do, but they remain God's good creatures, still created in the divine image (9:6), with the same call to responsibility as before the time sin entered their life (3:22–24; 9:1–7).

The portrayal of God in Genesis is remarkably wide ranging. God is the creator and makes choices in the furtherance of the creation-wide divine purpose (see above). God is the judge of human sin, but is also the savior of both the human and the nonhuman family in the face of the flood, and makes covenant promises that include both human beings and nonhuman creatures (9:8–17). What readers today call "the environment" is decisively included within God's salvific and promissory activity. This creation-wide divine promise provides the foundation for God's covenant promises to Israel's progenitors (12:1–3; 15; 17). God as one who blesses all creatures—human

and nonhuman, chosen and nonchosen—is a prominent feature of these narratives. The pervasive divine concern for kinship and family, an order of creation, manifests itself in the growth of families and the reconciliation of dysfunctional families. God's concern for the life of the nation, also an order of creation, is evident especially in the Joseph story, but God's blessing is active throughout the narratives regarding matters of economics, agriculture, and, more generally, the dynamics of political and governmental life.

Readers of Genesis are given a universal frame of reference within which to read the rest of the Bible. It will be wise to read Genesis with this lens in place, so that not only the progenitors of Israel come into view, but all the peoples of the world and all creatures, human and nonhuman.

—**Terence Fretheim**

Six Days of Creation and the Sabbath

1 In the beginning when God created[a] the heavens and the earth, [2] the earth was a formless void and darkness covered the face of the deep, while a wind from God[b] swept over the face of the waters. [3] Then God said, "Let there be light"; and there was light. [4] And God saw that the light was good; and God separated the light from the darkness.

[5] God called the light Day, and the darkness he called Night. And there was evening and there was morning, the first day.

6 And God said, "Let there be a dome in the midst of the waters, and let it separate the waters from the waters." [7] So God made the dome and separated the

[a] Or when God began to create or In the beginning God created   [b] Or while the spirit of God or while a mighty wind

---

1:1–2:4a The Opening Creation Account

1:1 *In the beginning*—Does not refer to the absolute beginning of all things, but to the beginning of the ordered creation, including the temporal order. NRSV reads v. 1 as a temporal clause, subordinate to the main clause in v. 2. The RSV translation of v. 1 as an independent sentence (see NRSV footnote) is more likely, in view of the pattern of other genealogies (5:1; 6:9; 10:1; 11:10).

1:2 *Formless void*—Neither "nothing" nor an undifferentiated mass—as the *earth, darkness,* and *waters* (=*deep*) are discrete realities—but that which is desolate and unproductive. Verse 2 describes the conditions before God began to order the cosmos, in the origins of which the author betrays no interest. *A wind from God*—Often (and better) translated "spirit"; its link to God suggests purposeful, creative activity (as in Ps. 104:30) preparing for the ordering process to follow.

1:3 *Then God said*—God's speaking is a personal, deliberate divine act, expressing what God intends. Yet God's speaking does not stand isolated from God's making (e.g., vv. 6–7, 14–16); hence the word is not a sufficient way of speaking of God's creative activity. God often speaks in this chapter with that which is *already* created (vv. 11, 20, 24, 28) so the creature participates in the creative activity initiated by God. *Let there be light*—Inasmuch as the sun had not yet been cre-

ated, light was probably thought to have another source (see Job 38:19).

1:4 *And God saw that the light was good*—The recurring divine evaluation of God's own work in this chapter implies an ongoing process, within which improvement was considered possible (see 2:18). The "subdue" language of 1:28 implies that the word "good" does not mean perfect or static or in no need of further development, but carries the sense of beauty, appropriateness, and purposefulness.

1:5 *God called the light Day*—God's name-giving in vv. 5–10 is a part of the creative process in discerning the place of the creature among others in the creation (parallel to the human naming in 2:20). *And there was evening and there was morning, the first day*—In view of the evening and morning reference throughout the chapter, and the citing of this text in Exod. 20:11; 31:17, it seems likely that an actual seven-day week is envisaged here. This work/rest temporal ordering is part of God's creative activity. Modern discoveries have moved our understandings regarding temporal origins of the world to ever-new vistas.

1:6 *A dome*—A solid, curved sky, held up by pillars (Job 26:11), over a flat earth; it provided living space between waters above (the source of rain and snow, flowing through windows, Gen. 7:11) and the waters on and below the earth.

waters that were under the dome from the waters that were above the dome. And it was so. ⁸God called the dome Sky. And there was evening and there was morning, the second day.

9 And God said, "Let the waters under the sky be gathered together into one place, and let the dry land appear." And it was so. ¹⁰God called the dry land Earth, and the waters that were gathered together he called Seas. And God saw that it was good. ¹¹Then God said, "Let the earth put forth vegetation: plants yielding seed, and fruit trees of every kind on earth that bear fruit with the seed in it." And it was so. ¹²The earth brought forth vegetation: plants yielding seed of every kind, and trees of every kind bearing fruit with the seed in it. And God saw that it was good. ¹³And there was evening and there was morning, the third day.

14 And God said, "Let there be lights in the dome of the sky to separate the day from the night; and let them be for signs and for seasons and for days and years, ¹⁵and let them be lights in the dome of the sky to give light upon the earth." And it was so. ¹⁶God made the two great lights—the greater light to rule the day and the lesser light to rule the night—and the stars. ¹⁷God set them in the dome of the sky to give light upon the earth, ¹⁸to rule over the day and over the night, and to separate the light from the darkness. And God

saw that it was good. ¹⁹And there was evening and there was morning, the fourth day.

20 And God said, "Let the waters bring forth swarms of living creatures, and let birds fly above the earth across the dome of the sky." ²¹So God created the great sea monsters and every living creature that moves, of every kind, with which the waters swarm, and every winged bird of every kind. And God saw that it was good. ²²God blessed them, saying, "Be fruitful and multiply and fill the waters in the seas, and let birds multiply on the earth." ²³And there was evening and there was morning, the fifth day.

24 And God said, "Let the earth bring forth living creatures of every kind: cattle and creeping things and wild animals of the earth of every kind." And it was so. ²⁵God made the wild animals of the earth of every kind, and the cattle of every kind, and everything that creeps upon the ground of every kind. And God saw that it was good.

26 Then God said, "Let us make humankind *a* in our image, according to our likeness; and let them have dominion over the fish of the sea, and over the birds of the air, and over the cattle, and over all the wild animals of the earth, *b* and over every creeping thing that creeps upon the earth."

a Heb *adam*   *b* Syr: Heb *and over all the earth*

1:9 *Let the dry land appear*—The earth, already present in v. 2, now appears when the waters have been gathered into oceans and seas.

1:12 *The earth brought forth*—God's creatures participate in the creative activity (cf. vv. 20, 24, 28). The description of plants and trees with their capacity to reproduce evidences a kind of "natural science" (see 1 Kgs. 4:33).

1:14 *Let there be lights*—These creatures serve as *signs*, that is, markers of time. The absence of reference to sun, moon, and stars may constitute an antiastrological polemic against views that considered them divine.

1:22 *God blessed them*—God gives power to creatures to reproduce themselves.

1:26 *Let us make*—The plural probably refers to the divine council (see Jer. 23:18–23). God here consults with other divine beings; the creation of humankind thus is the result of a dialogical act. Again, God chooses to share the creative process with those who are not God. *In our image*—The pattern according to which human beings are fashioned is to be sought outside the sphere of the created. They are given such gifts as to communicate with God and take up the God-given responsibilities specified in v. 28, namely, to be an extension of God's dominion over the creatures. All human beings, regardless of gender, race, and station in life, are here declared equal and given commensurable responsibilities.

²⁷ So God created humankind[a] in his
    image,
        in the image of God he created
        them;[b]
        male and female he created them.
²⁸ God blessed them, and God said to
them, "Be fruitful and multiply, and fill
the earth and subdue it; and have dominion over the fish of the sea and over the
birds of the air and over every living
thing that moves upon the earth." ²⁹ God
said, "See, I have given you every plant
yielding seed that is upon the face of all
the earth, and every tree with seed in its
fruit; you shall have them for food. ³⁰ And
to every beast of the earth, and to every
bird of the air, and to everything that
creeps on the earth, everything that has
the breath of life, I have given every green
plant for food." And it was so. ³¹ God saw
everything that he had made, and indeed,
it was very good. And there was evening
and there was morning, the sixth day.
2 Thus the heavens and the earth
    were finished, and all their multi-
tude. ² And on the seventh day God finished the work that he had done, and he
rested on the seventh day from all the
work that he had done. ³ So God blessed
the seventh day and hallowed it, because

on it God rested from all the work that
he had done in creation.
    4 These are the generations of the
heavens and the earth when they were
created.

Another Account of the Creation

    In the day that the LORD[c] God made
the earth and the heavens, ⁵ when no
plant of the field was yet in the earth
and no herb of the field had yet sprung
up—for the LORD God had not caused
it to rain upon the earth, and there was
no one to till the ground; ⁶ but a stream
would rise from the earth, and water the
whole face of the ground—⁷ then the
LORD God formed man from the dust
of the ground,[d] and breathed into his
nostrils the breath of life; and the man
became a living being. ⁸ And the LORD
God planted a garden in Eden, in the
east; and there he put the man whom
he had formed. ⁹ Out of the ground the
LORD God made to grow every tree that
is pleasant to the sight and good for food,
the tree of life also in the midst of the
garden, and the tree of the knowledge of
good and evil.

a Heb *adam*   *b* Heb *him*   *c* Heb *YHWH*, as in other places where "LORD"
is spelled with capital letters (see also Exod 3.14–15 with notes).   *d* Or
formed a man (Heb *adam*) *of dust from the ground* (Heb *adamah*)

1:28 *Subdue . . . have dominion*—God shares
power with the human, choosing not to be the
only one who has creative and ruling capacities. Having dominion is understood in terms
of caregiving, not exploitation; it has its roots
in the ideal conception of royal dominion (see
Ps. 72:8–14; Ezek. 34:1–4) and focuses on the
animals. The command to "subdue" relates to the
earth, particularly the difficult task of cultivation. While the verb may have a coercive aspect
in interhuman relationships (Num. 32:22, 29),
no enemies are in view here. More generally,
these verbs assume ongoing development in the
created order, rather than a finished product. So
God's world is not a static state of affairs.

1:29–30—God intended that human beings have
a vegetarian diet (see 9:2–3).

2:2 *On the seventh day God finished the work*—
This implies that God's resting concludes the
creative process, that is, Sabbath belongs to the
very created order of things. At the same time,
continuing creative work will be needed, as the
balance of chap. 2 implies (see above at 1:5).

2:4b–25 Another Look at Creation

2:5 *There was no one to till the ground*—Future
developments in the created order are dependent
on human activity (see v. 15).

2:7 *The man became a living being*—The one
who is created in the image of God is also made
from the dust of the ground (='*adamah*, a play
on '*adam*) and animated by the very breath of
God. The phrase "living being" also describes the
animals, created from the ground as well, in
v. 19 (see 1:20–30; 7:22).

2:8 *A garden in Eden*—Eden, probably meaning
"luxuriant," is of uncertain location (see 13:10).
As developments in this chapter indicate, Eden
is a dynamic place, not a static paradise. Eden is
the center of the then-known world, out of which
flow major rivers (2:10).

2:9 *The tree of life*—Mentioned only here and in
3:22–24; in view of the latter text, eating its fruit
conferred immortality (probably continued eating,
not just once). This tree shows that human beings
were not created immortal, but could continue

10 A river flows out of Eden to water the garden, and from there it divides and becomes four branches. ¹¹ The name of the first is Pishon; it is the one that flows around the whole land of Havilah, where there is gold; ¹² and the gold of that land is good; bdellium and onyx stone are there. ¹³ The name of the second river is Gihon; it is the one that flows around the whole land of Cush. ¹⁴ The name of the third river is Tigris, which flows east of Assyria. And the fourth river is the Euphrates.

15 The LORD God took the man and put him in the garden of Eden to till it and keep it. ¹⁶ And the LORD God commanded the man, "You may freely eat of every tree of the garden; ¹⁷ but of the tree of the knowledge of good and evil you shall not eat, for in the day that you eat of it you shall die."

18 Then the LORD God said, "It is not good that the man should be alone; I will make him a helper as his partner." ¹⁹ So out of the ground the LORD God formed every animal of the field and every bird of the air, and brought them to the man to see what he would call them; and whatever the man called every living creature, that was its name. ²⁰ The man gave names to all cattle, and to the birds of the air, and to every animal of the field; but for the man *a* there was not found a helper as his partner. ²¹ So the LORD God caused a deep sleep to fall upon the man, and he slept; then he took one of his ribs and closed up its place with flesh. ²² And the rib that the LORD God had taken from the man he made into a woman and brought her to the man. ²³ Then the man said,

"This at last is bone of my bones
    and flesh of my flesh;
this one shall be called Woman, *b*
    for out of Man *c* this one was
       taken."

²⁴ Therefore a man leaves his father and his mother and clings to his wife, and they become one flesh. ²⁵ And the man and his wife were both naked, and were not ashamed.

a Or *for Adam*   *b* Heb *ishshah*   *c* Heb *ish*

---

to live through eating its fruit. *The tree of the knowledge of good and evil*—God has this "knowledge" (3:22), recognized by the serpent (3:5), which the humans gain through eating, but do not have the wherewithal to handle very well. The words "good and evil" do not have their usual meanings (the existence of evil is not in view), but specify a deciding/knowing of what is in the best interests of human life, a divine prerogative.

2:10–14 *A river . . . becomes four branches*—Rivers and places no longer known to us (*Pishon, Havilah, Gihon,* and *Cush*) combine with the known (*Assyria* and the *Tigris-Euphrates* valley). Significant continuities in blessing exist between Eden and the rest of the world (where Adam and Eve will shortly live).

2:15 *To till it and keep it*—Human responsibility for the care of the earth is closely specified ("till" could be translated "serve"), and v. 5 has stated that this caregiving is crucial for the future of the land (so also post-sin, 3:23).

2:17 *You shall die*—Apparently, since the humans do not soon die, death has reference to a pervasive breakdown in relationships.

2:18 *I will make him a helper*—Inasmuch as God is often called a helper (e.g., Ps. 121:1–2), this designation does not imply a hierarchical relationship between man and woman. Procreation does not seem to be in view in this pericope; the issue addressed is companionship, intimate and otherwise.

2:19 *Whatever the man called every living creature, that was its name*—God delegates to the human the prerogative of naming the creatures (as God had named others in 1:5–10) and accepts whatever creative ordering of the animal world the human naming implies.

2:22 *The rib*—Perhaps to be translated "side." That woman is made out of part of the man no more entails subordination than the man's creation from the ground (v. 7) entails his subordination to it.

2:23 *Bone of my bones . . . this one shall be called Woman*—Naming does not entail subordination (here or in 3:20), any more than does Hagar's naming of God (16:13). As with all naming heretofore, the task involves discernment regarding the nature of the relationships involved. The man's poetic reference to the woman implies total equality.

2:24 *One flesh*—Probably a reference to sexual intimacy as part of a close relationship (and not to a child produced). The text does not imply that one must be married in order to be human (i.e.,

The First Sin and Its Punishment

3 Now the serpent was more crafty than any other wild animal that the LORD God had made. He said to the woman, "Did God say, 'You shall not eat from any tree in the garden'?" ² The woman said to the serpent, "We may eat of the fruit of the trees in the garden; ³ but God said, 'You shall not eat of the fruit of the tree that is in the middle of the garden, nor shall you touch it, or you shall die.'" ⁴ But the serpent said to the woman, "You will not die; ⁵ for God knows that when you eat of it your eyes will be opened, and you will be like God,ᵃ knowing good and evil." ⁶ So when the woman saw that the tree was good for food, and that it was a delight to the eyes, and that the tree was to be desired to make one wise, she took of its fruit and ate; and she also gave some to her husband, who was with her, and he ate. ⁷ Then the eyes of both were opened, and they knew that they were naked; and they sewed fig leaves together and made loincloths for themselves.

8 They heard the sound of the LORD God walking in the garden at the time of the evening breeze, and the man and his wife hid themselves from the presence of the LORD God among the trees of the garden. ⁹ But the LORD God called to the man, and said to him, "Where are you?"

¹⁰ He said, "I heard the sound of you in the garden, and I was afraid, because I was naked; and I hid myself." ¹¹ He said, "Who told you that you were naked? Have you eaten from the tree of which I commanded you not to eat?" ¹² The man said, "The woman whom you gave to be with me, she gave me fruit from the tree, and I ate." ¹³ Then the LORD God said to the woman, "What is this that you have done?" The woman said, "The serpent tricked me, and I ate." ¹⁴ The LORD God said to the serpent,

"Because you have done this,
    cursed are you among all
        animals
    and among all wild creatures;
upon your belly you shall go,
    and dust you shall eat
    all the days of your life.
¹⁵ I will put enmity between you and
        the woman,
    and between your offspring and
        hers;
he will strike your head,
    and you will strike his heel."
¹⁶ To the woman he said,
"I will greatly increase your pangs in
        childbearing;
    in pain you shall bring forth
        children,

ᵃ Or gods

---

single persons are fully human), but marriage is deemed an especially appropriate relationship, leading to the establishment of a home.

3:1–24 The Intrusion of Sin

3:1 The serpent—Though traditionally associated with the devil, the serpent is explicitly said to be an animal God made ("wild animal" is a translation of the same Hebrew as "animal of the field" in 2:19). It is nowhere said to be evil and may be a neutral figure. As such, the serpent represents anything in God's good creation that could present tempting options to human beings.

3:3 Nor shall you touch it—Not a part of the divine command to the man in 2:16–17; the man may have exaggerated the command when he told the woman.

3:4–5 You will not die—NIV and RSV offer a more likely translation, "You will not surely die." Thus (in view of v. 22) the serpent never lies; he

does not tell the full truth either (if he knew it), but neither does God. God's withholding knowledge from the humans (**for God knows**) becomes the key point of temptation, inviting trust or mistrust. Mistrust follows and is the primal sin, not disobedience.

3:6 To her husband, who was with her—Note that the man was silently present during the entire conversation (the "you" in vv. 1–5 is plural) and hence bears as much responsibility for what happens as the woman, who seduces no one.

3:16 He shall rule over you—Following upon the inquest (vv. 8–13), God announces, not prescribes, the consequences of the sin: disruptions in every relationship (vv. 14–19). The serpent (and its seed) becomes a symbol for the ongoing struggle with temptation, with no victory in sight (v. 15). The "rule" of the man over the woman is

yet your desire shall be for your
husband,
and he shall rule over you."
¹⁷And to the man*a* he said,
"Because you have listened to the
voice of your wife,
and have eaten of the tree
about which I commanded you,
'You shall not eat of it,'
cursed is the ground because of you;
in toil you shall eat of it all the
days of your life;
¹⁸ thorns and thistles it shall bring
forth for you;
and you shall eat the plants of the
field.
¹⁹ By the sweat of your face
you shall eat bread
until you return to the ground,
for out of it you were taken;
you are dust,
and to dust you shall return."

20 The man named his wife Eve,*b* because she was the mother of all living. ²¹And the LORD God made garments of skins for the man*c* and for his wife, and clothed them.

22 Then the LORD God said, "See, the man has become like one of us, knowing good and evil; and now, he might reach out his hand and take also from the tree of life, and eat, and live forever"— ²³therefore the LORD God sent him forth from the garden of Eden, to till the ground from which he was taken. ²⁴He drove out the man; and at the east of the garden of Eden he placed the cherubim, and a sword flaming and turning to guard the way to the tree of life.

Cain Murders Abel

4 Now the man knew his wife Eve, and she conceived and bore Cain, saying, "I have produced*d* a man with the help of the LORD." ²Next she bore his brother Abel. Now Abel was a keeper of sheep, and Cain a tiller of the ground. ³In the course of time Cain brought to the LORD an offering of the fruit of the ground, ⁴and Abel for his part brought of the firstlings of his flock, their fat portions. And the LORD had regard for Abel and his offering, ⁵but for Cain and his offering he had no regard. So Cain was very angry, and his countenance fell. ⁶The LORD said to Cain, "Why are you angry, and why has your countenance fallen? ⁷If you do well, will you not be accepted? And if you do not do well, sin is lurking at the door; its desire is for you, but you must master it."

8 Cain said to his brother Abel, "Let us go out to the field."*e* And when they were in the field, Cain rose up against his brother Abel, and killed him. ⁹Then the LORD said to Cain, "Where is your brother Abel?" He said, "I do not know; am I my brother's keeper?" ¹⁰And the LORD said, "What have you done? Listen; your brother's blood is crying out to me from the ground! ¹¹And now you are cursed from the ground, which has opened its mouth to receive your brother's blood from your hand. ¹²When you till the ground, it will no longer yield to you its strength; you will be a fugitive

a Or to Adam *b* In Heb Eve resembles the word for *living* *c* Or for Adam *d* The verb in Heb resembles the word for *Cain* *e* Sam Gk Syr Compare Vg: MT lacks *Let us go out to the field*

---

seen as a consequence of sin, contrary to God's intention in creation, not a prescription for their future relationship. Both will experience hardship in their primary roles in that culture.

3:24 *Cherubim*—A human/animal/bird composite, usually functioning symbolically as a guardian of sanctuaries in Israel and the ancient Near East. Eden, the place of the near presence of God, now becomes inaccessible to human beings. There can be no return to Eden.

4:1–26 Cain and Abel
4:1 *I have produced a man with the help of the*

LORD—This word from Eve implies divine-human cooperation in the fulfillment of 1:28.

4:5 *For Cain and his offering God had no regard*—The offerings of Cain and Abel both seem appropriate. The reason for God's rejection of Cain's offering is uncertain; it may be rooted in Cain's motivation or be simply an arbitrary divine choice (as with the choice of the second-born, e.g., Isaac and Jacob, elsewhere in Genesis).

4:9 *Am I my brother's keeper?*—Only God "keeps" human beings in the Old Testament

and a wanderer on the earth." [13] Cain said to the LORD, "My punishment is greater than I can bear! [14] Today you have driven me away from the soil, and I shall be hidden from your face; I shall be a fugitive and a wanderer on the earth, and anyone who meets me may kill me." [15] Then the LORD said to him, "Not so! [a] Whoever kills Cain will suffer a sevenfold vengeance." And the LORD put a mark on Cain, so that no one who came upon him would kill him. [16] Then Cain went away from the presence of the LORD, and settled in the land of Nod, [b] east of Eden.

Beginnings of Civilization

[17] Cain knew his wife, and she conceived and bore Enoch; and he built a city, and named it Enoch after his son Enoch. [18] To Enoch was born Irad; and Irad was the father of Mehujael, and Mehujael the father of Methushael, and Methushael the father of Lamech. [19] Lamech took two wives; the name of the one was Adah, and the name of the other Zillah. [20] Adah bore Jabal; he was the ancestor of those who live in tents and have livestock. [21] His brother's name was Jubal; he was the ancestor of all those who play the lyre and pipe. [22] Zillah bore Tubal-cain, who made all kinds of bronze and iron tools. The sister of Tubal-cain was Naamah.

23 Lamech said to his wives:
"Adah and Zillah, hear my voice;
   you wives of Lamech, listen to
     what I say:
I have killed a man for wounding
   me,
   a young man for striking me.
[24] If Cain is avenged sevenfold,
   truly Lamech seventy-sevenfold."

25 Adam knew his wife again, and she bore a son and named him Seth, for she said, "God has appointed [c] for me another child instead of Abel, because Cain killed him." [26] To Seth also a son was born, and he named him Enosh. At that time people began to invoke the name of the LORD.

Adam's Descendants to Noah and His Sons

5 This is the list of the descendants of Adam. When God created humankind, [d] he made them [e] in the likeness of God. [2] Male and female he created them, and he blessed them and named them "Humankind" [d] when they were created.

3 When Adam had lived one hundred thirty years, he became the father of a son in his likeness, according to his image, and named him Seth. [4] The days of Adam after he became the father of Seth were eight hundred years; and he

a Gk Syr Vg: Heb *Therefore*   *b* That is *Wandering*   *c* The verb in Heb resembles the word for *Seth*   *d* Heb *adam*   *e* Heb *him*

(e.g., Ps. 121:3–8); hence Cain focuses on *God's* responsibility for (not) keeping Abel safe.

4:13 *My punishment is greater than I can bear*—The word translated "punishment" is the same word commonly translated "iniquity" in the Old Testament, specifying an act-consequence continuum. God's statement that Cain is **cursed** (v. 11) is thus an announcement of consequence rather than the imposition of a penalty.

4:15–16 *The LORD put a mark on Cain . . . the land of Nod*—An uncertain external sign designed by a gracious God to protect Cain from those who would take vengeance. The land of Nod, a name that plays on the word "wander," is of uncertain location.

4:17 *Cain knew his wife*—The long-asked questions about who endangered Cain, where he got his wife, and for whom he built his city

are difficult. As with 2:24, these references may collapse the setting of the story into the author's own time, thus enabling the story to function as a mirror for human experience in every age.

4:18–22—The names in Cain's genealogy closely resemble those in 5:1–32. The cultural developments for which these persons are responsible should be viewed positively. They stand as a salutary development in God's good creation alongside the negative development evident in Lamech's revengeful response to an injury (4:23–24).

4:26 *Seth*—Through this son of Adam and Eve the human line will move into the future. His importance is signaled by the reference to the worship of God under the name YHWH (LORD), which is testimony to a pre-Israel worship of Israel's God.

5:1–32 Adam's Family Tree

had other sons and daughters. ⁵Thus all the days that Adam lived were nine hundred thirty years; and he died.

6 When Seth had lived one hundred five years, he became the father of Enosh. ⁷Seth lived after the birth of Enosh eight hundred seven years, and had other sons and daughters. ⁸Thus all the days of Seth were nine hundred twelve years; and he died.

9 When Enosh had lived ninety years, he became the father of Kenan. ¹⁰Enosh lived after the birth of Kenan eight hundred fifteen years, and had other sons and daughters. ¹¹Thus all the days of Enosh were nine hundred five years; and he died.

12 When Kenan had lived seventy years, he became the father of Mahalalel. ¹³Kenan lived after the birth of Mahalalel eight hundred and forty years, and had other sons and daughters. ¹⁴Thus all the days of Kenan were nine hundred and ten years; and he died.

15 When Mahalalel had lived sixty-five years, he became the father of Jared. ¹⁶Mahalalel lived after the birth of Jared eight hundred thirty years, and had other sons and daughters. ¹⁷Thus all the days of Mahalalel were eight hundred ninety-five years; and he died.

18 When Jared had lived one hundred sixty-two years he became the father of Enoch. ¹⁹Jared lived after the birth of Enoch eight hundred years, and had other sons and daughters. ²⁰Thus all the days of Jared were nine hundred sixty-two years; and he died.

21 When Enoch had lived sixty-five years, he became the father of Methuselah. ²²Enoch walked with God after the birth of Methuselah three hundred years, and had other sons and daughters. ²³Thus all the days of Enoch were three hundred sixty-five years. ²⁴Enoch walked with God; then he was no more, because God took him.

25 When Methuselah had lived one hundred eighty-seven years, he became the father of Lamech. ²⁶Methuselah lived after the birth of Lamech seven hundred eighty-two years, and had other sons and daughters. ²⁷Thus all the days of Methuselah were nine hundred sixty-nine years; and he died.

28 When Lamech had lived one hundred eighty-two years, he became the father of a son; ²⁹he named him Noah, saying, "Out of the ground that the LORD has cursed this one shall bring us relief from our work and from the toil of our hands." ³⁰Lamech lived after the birth of Noah five hundred ninety-five years, and had other sons and daughters. ³¹Thus all the days of Lamech were seven hundred seventy-seven years; and he died.

32 After Noah was five hundred years old, Noah became the father of Shem, Ham, and Japheth.

The Wickedness of Humankind

6 When people began to multiply on the face of the ground, and daughters were born to them, ²the sons of God saw that they were fair; and they took wives for themselves of all that they chose. ³Then the LORD said, "My spirit

---

5:24 *Enoch . . . was no more, because God took him*—The meaning of the phrase is uncertain; it could mean that he died prematurely or disappeared unexpectedly and is often linked with the "taking" of Elijah in 2 Kgs. 2:1.

5:27 *Methuselah . . . nine hundred sixty-nine years*—The Bible's longest-lived person. The long ages of these preflood patriarchs (with parallels in ancient Near Eastern literature) were probably understood literally. The decreasing life spans evident in this list (969–777 years, except Enoch), compared to those in 11:10–32 (600–200 years),

may witness to the effects of sin over time (see also 6:3, 120 years).

6:1–4 Sin Becomes Cosmic

6:2, 4 *Sons of God . . . Nephilim*—A difficult text, suggesting sin's devastating effects beyond the human sphere; the cosmic flood is the consequence. The "sons of God" are probably divine beings who breach the earth-heaven boundary by taking human wives. Their offspring are *warriors of renown* (see the violence in vv. 11–13), to whom the Nephilim, probably persons of giant stature known to Israel, are compared.

shall not abide[a] in mortals forever, for they are flesh; their days shall be one hundred twenty years." [4] The Nephilim were on the earth in those days—and also afterward—when the sons of God went in to the daughters of humans, who bore children to them. These were the heroes that were of old, warriors of renown.

5 The LORD saw that the wickedness of humankind was great in the earth, and that every inclination of the thoughts of their hearts was only evil continually. [6] And the LORD was sorry that he had made humankind on the earth, and it grieved him to his heart. [7] So the LORD said, "I will blot out from the earth the human beings I have created—people together with animals and creeping things and birds of the air, for I am sorry that I have made them." [8] But Noah found favor in the sight of the LORD.

Noah Pleases God

9 These are the descendants of Noah. Noah was a righteous man, blameless in his generation; Noah walked with God. [10] And Noah had three sons, Shem, Ham, and Japheth.

11 Now the earth was corrupt in God's sight, and the earth was filled with violence. [12] And God saw that the earth was corrupt; for all flesh had corrupted its ways upon the earth. [13] And God said to Noah, "I have determined to make an end of all flesh, for the earth is filled with violence because of them; now I am going to destroy them along with the earth. [14] Make yourself an ark of cypress[a] wood; make rooms in the ark, and cover it inside and out with pitch. [15] This is how you are to make it: the length of the ark three hundred cubits, its width fifty cubits, and its height thirty cubits. [16] Make a roof[b] for the ark, and finish it to a cubit above; and put the door of the ark in its side; make it with lower, second, and third decks. [17] For my part, I am going to bring a flood of waters on the earth, to destroy from under heaven all flesh in which is the breath of life; everything that is on the earth shall die. [18] But I will establish my covenant with you; and you shall come into the ark, you, your sons, your wife, and your sons' wives with you. [19] And of every living thing, of all flesh, you shall bring two of every kind into the ark, to keep them alive with you; they shall be male and female. [20] Of the birds according to their kinds, and of the animals according to their kinds, of every creeping thing of the ground according to its kind, two of every kind shall come in to you, to keep them alive. [21] Also take with you every kind of food that is eaten, and store it up; and it shall serve as food for you and for them." [22] Noah did this; he did all that God commanded him.

The Great Flood

7 Then the LORD said to Noah, "Go into the ark, you and all your household,

---

[a] Meaning of Heb uncertain [b] Or *window*

6:5–8:22 The Flood: the Great Divide

6:5—This statement of the universal sinful condition of human beings is essentially repeated after the flood (8:21), indicating that the flood did not rid the world of sin. The sinful human heart manifests itself especially in violence (6:11–13), the devastating consequences of which affect the entire created order. These chapters witness to an environmental catastrophe; the disastrous effect on the animal world is given special notice in 7:21–23.

6:6 *The LORD was sorry . . . and it grieved him to his heart*—God's sorrowful response to the sinful human situation and the anticipated consequences portray a God whose heart is deeply pained. This divine agony leads God to the decision to choose Noah and save some.

6:15 *Cubits*—About eighteen inches, the distance from elbow to fingertips; the dimensions of the multidecked ark would be approximately 450 x 75 x 45 feet.

6:19 *Two of every kind*—This number may refer to pairs generally, while the command to take seven pairs of clean animals in 7:2–3 (necessary in view of the need for clean animals in 8:20) is a subset within that general directive. Note that God determines to save both human beings and animals.

for I have seen that you alone are righteous before me in this generation. ² Take with you seven pairs of all clean animals, the male and its mate; and a pair of the animals that are not clean, the male and its mate; ³ and seven pairs of the birds of the air also, male and female, to keep their kind alive on the face of all the earth. ⁴ For in seven days I will send rain on the earth for forty days and forty nights; and every living thing that I have made I will blot out from the face of the ground." ⁵ And Noah did all that the LORD had commanded him.

6 Noah was six hundred years old when the flood of waters came on the earth. ⁷ And Noah with his sons and his wife and his sons' wives went into the ark to escape the waters of the flood. ⁸ Of clean animals, and of animals that are not clean, and of birds, and of everything that creeps on the ground, ⁹ two and two, male and female, went into the ark with Noah, as God had commanded Noah. ¹⁰ And after seven days the waters of the flood came on the earth.

11 In the six hundredth year of Noah's life, in the second month, on the seventeenth day of the month, on that day all the fountains of the great deep burst forth, and the windows of the heavens were opened. ¹² The rain fell on the earth forty days and forty nights. ¹³ On the very same day Noah with his sons, Shem and Ham and Japheth, and Noah's wife and the three wives of his sons entered the ark, ¹⁴ they and every wild animal of every kind, and all domestic animals of every kind, and every creeping thing that creeps on the earth, and every bird of every kind—every bird, every winged creature. ¹⁵ They went into the ark with Noah, two and two of all flesh in which there was the breath of life. ¹⁶ And those that entered, male and female of all flesh, went in as God had commanded him; and the LORD shut him in.

17 The flood continued forty days on the earth; and the waters increased, and bore up the ark, and it rose high above the earth. ¹⁸ The waters swelled and increased greatly on the earth; and the ark floated on the face of the waters. ¹⁹ The waters swelled so mightily on the earth that all the high mountains under the whole heaven were covered; ²⁰ the waters swelled above the mountains, covering them fifteen cubits deep. ²¹ And all flesh died that moved on the earth, birds, domestic animals, wild animals, all swarming creatures that swarm on the earth, and all human beings; ²² everything on dry land in whose nostrils was the breath of life died. ²³ He blotted out every living thing that was on the face of the ground, human beings and animals and creeping things and birds of the air; they were blotted out from the earth. Only Noah was left, and those that were with him in the ark. ²⁴ And the waters swelled on the earth for one hundred fifty days.

The Flood Subsides

8 But God remembered Noah and all the wild animals and all the domestic animals that were with him in the ark. And God made a wind blow over the earth, and the waters subsided; ² the fountains of the deep and the windows of the heavens were closed, the rain from the heavens was restrained, ³ and the waters gradually receded from the earth. At the end of one hundred fifty days the waters had abated; ⁴ and in the seventh month, on the seventeenth day of the month, the ark came to rest on the mountains of Ararat. ⁵ The waters con-

---

8:1 *God remembered Noah and all the . . . animals*—This notice constitutes the turning point in the story; the water now begins to subside. Especially to be noted is God's remembrance of the animals, both wild and domestic, not just human beings. God's concern for the future of the animal world is also lifted up in vv. 17–19 and 9:8–17. A special touch is the return of the dove with an olive branch in its beak (8:11), long a symbol for peace.

8:4 *The mountains of Ararat*—Not one specific mountain, but a range in northeastern Turkey.

tinued to abate until the tenth month; in the tenth month, on the first day of the month, the tops of the mountains appeared.

6 At the end of forty days Noah opened the window of the ark that he had made [7] and sent out the raven; and it went to and fro until the waters were dried up from the earth. [8] Then he sent out the dove from him, to see if the waters had subsided from the face of the ground; [9] but the dove found no place to set its foot, and it returned to him to the ark, for the waters were still on the face of the whole earth. So he put out his hand and took it and brought it into the ark with him. [10] He waited another seven days, and again he sent out the dove from the ark; [11] and the dove came back to him in the evening, and there in its beak was a freshly plucked olive leaf; so Noah knew that the waters had subsided from the earth. [12] Then he waited another seven days, and sent out the dove; and it did not return to him any more.

13 In the six hundred first year, in the first month, on the first day of the month, the waters were dried up from the earth; and Noah removed the covering of the ark, and looked, and saw that the face of the ground was drying. [14] In the second month, on the twenty-seventh day of the month, the earth was dry. [15] Then God said to Noah, [16] "Go out of the ark, you and your wife, and your sons and your sons' wives with you. [17] Bring out with you every living thing that is with you of all flesh—birds and animals and every creeping thing that creeps on the earth—so that they may abound on the earth, and be fruitful and multiply on the earth." [18] So Noah went out with his sons and his wife and his sons' wives. [19] And every animal, every creeping thing, and every bird, everything that moves on the earth, went out of the ark by families.

God's Promise to Noah

20 Then Noah built an altar to the LORD, and took of every clean animal and of every clean bird, and offered burnt offerings on the altar. [21] And when the LORD smelled the pleasing odor, the LORD said in his heart, "I will never again curse the ground because of humankind, for the inclination of the human heart is evil from youth; nor will I ever again destroy every living creature as I have done.

[22] As long as the earth endures,
    seedtime and harvest, cold and
      heat,
  summer and winter, day and night,
    shall not cease."

The Covenant with Noah

9 God blessed Noah and his sons, and said to them, "Be fruitful and multiply, and fill the earth. [2] The fear and dread of you shall rest on every animal of the earth, and on every bird of the air, on everything that creeps on the ground, and on all the fish of the sea; into your hand they are delivered. [3] Every moving thing that lives shall be food for you; and just as I gave you the green plants, I give you everything. [4] Only, you shall not eat flesh with its life, that is, its blood. [5] For your own lifeblood I will surely

---

8:21–22—Given the divine faithfulness, this promise is an eternal divine self-limitation never to respond to human sin and evil in floodlike ways again. The promise focuses on matters environmental, involving agricultural life, climate, seasons, and the daily rhythm. Come what may, the cosmic order will remain steady and regular (see Jer. 31:35–37; 33:20, 25).

9:1–17 God's Covenant with Noah in a New World Order

9:2–5—God extends the vegetarian diet of 1:29–30 to include meat (except for *blood*=life, Lev. 17:11). This permission is not a license for exploitation, but a concession in a famine-ridden world. The restriction regarding blood stands as a sharp reminder that killing animals is not to be taken lightly, for God is the source of their life. The animals have become fearful of human beings and violence against humans by animals also takes place (Gen. 9:5). The prophets envisage a return to God's initial plan (Isa. 11:6–9; Hos. 2:17–18).

require a reckoning: from every animal I will require it and from human beings, each one for the blood of another, I will require a reckoning for human life.
6   Whoever sheds the blood of a
            human,
      by a human shall that person's
            blood be shed;
      for in his own image
      God made humankind.
7 And you, be fruitful and multiply, abound on the earth and multiply in it."

8 Then God said to Noah and to his sons with him, 9 "As for me, I am establishing my covenant with you and your descendants after you, 10 and with every living creature that is with you, the birds, the domestic animals, and every animal of the earth with you, as many as came out of the ark. a 11 I establish my covenant with you, that never again shall all flesh be cut off by the waters of a flood, and never again shall there be a flood to destroy the earth." 12 God said, "This is the sign of the covenant that I make between me and you and every living creature that is with you, for all future generations: 13 I have set my bow in the clouds, and it shall be a sign of the covenant between me and the earth. 14 When I bring clouds over the earth and the bow is seen in the clouds, 15 I will remember my covenant that is between me and you and every living creature of all flesh; and the waters shall never again become a flood to destroy all flesh. 16 When the bow is in the clouds, I will see it and remember the everlasting covenant between God and every living creature of all flesh that is on the earth." 17 God said to Noah, "This is the sign of the covenant that I have established between me and all flesh that is on the earth."

Noah and His Sons

18 The sons of Noah who went out of the ark were Shem, Ham, and Japheth. Ham was the father of Canaan. 19 These three were the sons of Noah; and from these the whole earth was peopled.

20 Noah, a man of the soil, was the first to plant a vineyard. 21 He drank some of the wine and became drunk, and he lay uncovered in his tent. 22 And Ham, the father of Canaan, saw the nakedness of his father, and told his two brothers outside. 23 Then Shem and Japheth took a garment, laid it on both their shoulders, and walked backward and covered the nakedness of their father; their faces were turned away, and they did not see their father's nakedness. 24 When Noah awoke from his wine and knew what his youngest son had done to him, 25 he said,
      "Cursed be Canaan;
            lowest of slaves shall he be to his
                  brothers."
26 He also said,
      "Blessed by the LORD my God be
            Shem;
            and let Canaan be his slave.
27   May God make space for b Japheth,
            and let him live in the tents of
                  Shem;
            and let Canaan be his slave."

a Gk: Heb adds *every animal of the earth* b Heb *yapht*, a play on *Japheth*

9:8–17—The promise that God "said in his heart" (8:21) is now made public to Noah and his family. This unilateral, unconditional promise, which stands forever, is made to both human beings and *every living creature* (*all flesh*). The rainbow is a sign of God's ongoing commitment to the preservation of the created order. What does it mean for our environmental considerations that God has made commitments to nonhuman creatures?

9:18–29 Noah's Dysfunctional Family

9:25–27 Canaan . . . slave—The details of this text are unclear, but seem to be focused on issues of familial respect and harmony (no sexual act is explicitly in view), which in turn affect national life (Noah's sons are understood in both individual and eponymous terms). Inasmuch as Canaan is not the father of a Negroid people (see 10:15–19, where all the peoples in his genealogy are Semitic or Indo-European), any attempt to justify the slavery of African peoples is a gross misuse of this text. The enslavement of Canaan probably reflects their later subjugation by other peoples, including Israel, rather than any practice of slavery as such.

28 After the flood Noah lived three hundred fifty years. 29 All the days of Noah were nine hundred fifty years; and he died.

Nations Descended from Noah

10 These are the descendants of Noah's sons, Shem, Ham, and Japheth; children were born to them after the flood.

2 The descendants of Japheth: Gomer, Magog, Madai, Javan, Tubal, Meshech, and Tiras. 3 The descendants of Gomer: Ashkenaz, Riphath, and Togarmah. 4 The descendants of Javan: Elishah, Tarshish, Kittim, and Rodanim.a 5 From these the coastland peoples spread. These are the descendants of Japhethb in their lands, with their own language, by their families, in their nations.

6 The descendants of Ham: Cush, Egypt, Put, and Canaan. 7 The descendants of Cush: Seba, Havilah, Sabtah, Raamah, and Sabteca. The descendants of Raamah: Sheba and Dedan. 8 Cush became the father of Nimrod; he was the first on earth to become a mighty warrior. 9 He was a mighty hunter before the LORD; therefore it is said, "Like Nimrod a mighty hunter before the LORD." 10 The beginning of his kingdom was Babel, Erech, and Accad, all of them in the land of Shinar. 11 From that land he went into Assyria, and built Nineveh, Rehoboth-ir, Calah, and 12 Resen between Nineveh and Calah; that is the great city. 13 Egypt became the father of Ludim, Anamim, Lehabim, Naphtuhim, 14 Pathrusim, Casluhim, and Caphtorim, from which the Philistines come.c

15 Canaan became the father of Sidon his firstborn, and Heth, 16 and the Jebusites, the Amorites, the Girgashites, 17 the Hivites, the Arkites, the Sinites, 18 the Arvadites, the Zemarites, and the Hamathites. Afterward the families of the Canaanites spread abroad. 19 And the territory of the Canaanites extended from Sidon, in the direction of Gerar, as far as Gaza, and in the direction of Sodom, Gomorrah, Admah, and Zeboiim, as far as Lasha. 20 These are the descendants of Ham, by their families, their languages, their lands, and their nations.

21 To Shem also, the father of all the children of Eber, the elder brother of Japheth, children were born. 22 The descendants of Shem: Elam, Asshur, Arpachshad, Lud, and Aram. 23 The descendants of Aram: Uz, Hul, Gether, and Mash. 24 Arpachshad became the father of Shelah; and Shelah became the father of Eber. 25 To Eber were born two sons: the name of the one was Peleg,d for in his days the earth was divided, and his brother's name was Joktan. 26 Joktan became the father of Almodad, Sheleph, Hazarmaveth, Jerah, 27 Hadoram, Uzal, Diklah, 28 Obal, Abimael, Sheba, 29 Ophir, Havilah, and Jobab; all these were the descendants of Joktan. 30 The territory in which they lived extended from Mesha in the direction of Sephar, the hill country of the east. 31 These are the descendants of Shem, by their families, their languages, their lands, and their nations.

32 These are the families of Noah's sons, according to their genealogies, in their nations; and from these the nations spread abroad on the earth after the flood.

The Tower of Babel

11 Now the whole earth had one language and the same words. 2 And as they migrated from the east,e they came upon a plain in the land of Shinar

---

a Heb Mss Sam Gk See 1 Chr 1.7: MT *Dodanim*   b Compare verses 20, 31. Heb lacks *These are the descendants of Japheth*   c Cn: Heb *Casluhim, from which the Philistines come, and Caphtorim*   d That is *Division*   e Or *migrated eastward*

10:1–32 The Table of Nations

10:5, 20, 31 *Families*—This genealogy of Noah's sons gathers all the peoples in the world known at that time. This threefold reference to "families" links this text to the call of Abram, through whom all the families of the earth will be blessed (12:3).

11:1–9 The City of Babel

and settled there. ³ And they said to one another, "Come, let us make bricks, and burn them thoroughly." And they had brick for stone, and bitumen for mortar. ⁴ Then they said, "Come, let us build ourselves a city, and a tower with its top in the heavens, and let us make a name for ourselves; otherwise we shall be scattered abroad upon the face of the whole earth." ⁵ The LORD came down to see the city and the tower, which mortals had built. ⁶ And the LORD said, "Look, they are one people, and they have all one language; and this is only the beginning of what they will do; nothing that they propose to do will now be impossible for them. ⁷ Come, let us go down, and confuse their language there, so that they will not understand one another's speech." ⁸ So the LORD scattered them abroad from there over the face of all the earth, and they left off building the city. ⁹ Therefore it was called Babel, because there the LORD confused ᵃ the language of all the earth; and from there the LORD scattered them abroad over the face of all the earth.

Descendants of Shem

10 These are the descendants of Shem. When Shem was one hundred years old, he became the father of Arpachshad two years after the flood; ¹¹ and Shem lived after the birth of Arpachshad five hundred years, and had other sons and daughters.

12 When Arpachshad had lived thirty-five years, he became the father of Shelah; ¹³ and Arpachshad lived after the birth of Shelah four hundred three years, and had other sons and daughters.

14 When Shelah had lived thirty years, he became the father of Eber; ¹⁵ and Shelah lived after the birth of Eber four hundred three years, and had other sons and daughters.

16 When Eber had lived thirty-four years, he became the father of Peleg; ¹⁷ and Eber lived after the birth of Peleg four hundred thirty years, and had other sons and daughters.

18 When Peleg had lived thirty years, he became the father of Reu; ¹⁹ and Peleg lived after the birth of Reu two hundred nine years, and had other sons and daughters.

20 When Reu had lived thirty-two years, he became the father of Serug; ²¹ and Reu lived after the birth of Serug two hundred seven years, and had other sons and daughters.

22 When Serug had lived thirty years, he became the father of Nahor; ²³ and Serug lived after the birth of Nahor two hundred years, and had other sons and daughters.

24 When Nahor had lived twenty-nine years, he became the father of Terah; ²⁵ and Nahor lived after the birth of Terah one hundred nineteen years, and had other sons and daughters.

26 When Terah had lived seventy years, he became the father of Abram, Nahor, and Haran.

Descendants of Terah

27 Now these are the descendants of Terah. Terah was the father of Abram,

ᵃ Heb balal, meaning to confuse

11:4 *Otherwise we shall be scattered abroad*—How peoples of common origin had come to speak various languages is ascribed to a divine judgment on those who are concerned not to "be scattered abroad," seeking to keep their community intact. This move constitutes a challenge to the divine command to fill the earth (1:28). Only if people are spread abroad can they fulfill the charge to be caretakers of the earth. God's action thus challenges an isolationist perspective and promotes diver-

sity for the sake of the care of the earth and its creatures.

11:9 *Babel*—A play on the word "confuse"; it seems to have no particular relation to the later Babylon, though some polemic may be in view (see 10:8–10).

11:10–26 From Shem to Abram

11:26 *Terah*—This variation of the genealogy in 10:21–31 is designed to lead up to the family of Terah, one of whose sons is Abram.

11:27–12:9 The Call of Abram

Nahor, and Haran; and Haran was the father of Lot. [28] Haran died before his father Terah in the land of his birth, in Ur of the Chaldeans. [29] Abram and Nahor took wives; the name of Abram's wife was Sarai, and the name of Nahor's wife was Milcah. She was the daughter of Haran the father of Milcah and Iscah. [30] Now Sarai was barren; she had no child.

31 Terah took his son Abram and his grandson Lot son of Haran, and his daughter-in-law Sarai, his son Abram's wife, and they went out together from Ur of the Chaldeans to go into the land of Canaan; but when they came to Haran, they settled there. [32] The days of Terah were two hundred five years; and Terah died in Haran.

The Call of Abram

12 Now the LORD said to Abram, "Go from your country and your kindred and your father's house to the land that I will show you. [2] I will make of you a great nation, and I will bless you, and make your name great, so that you will be a blessing. [3] I will bless those who bless you, and the one who curses you I will curse; and in you all the families of the earth shall be blessed." [a]

4 So Abram went, as the LORD had told him; and Lot went with him. Abram was seventy-five years old when he departed from Haran. [5] Abram took his wife Sarai and his brother's son Lot,

and all the possessions that they had gathered, and the persons whom they had acquired in Haran; and they set forth to go to the land of Canaan. When they had come to the land of Canaan, [6] Abram passed through the land to the place at Shechem, to the oak [b] of Moreh. At that time the Canaanites were in the land. [7] Then the LORD appeared to Abram, and said, "To your offspring [c] I will give this land." So he built there an altar to the LORD, who had appeared to him. [8] From there he moved on to the hill country on the east of Bethel, and pitched his tent, with Bethel on the west and Ai on the east; and there he built an altar to the LORD and invoked the name of the LORD. [9] And Abram journeyed on by stages toward the Negeb.

Abram and Sarai in Egypt

10 Now there was a famine in the land. So Abram went down to Egypt to reside there as an alien, for the famine was severe in the land. [11] When he was about to enter Egypt, he said to his wife Sarai, "I know well that you are a woman beautiful in appearance; [12] and when the Egyptians see you, they will say, 'This is his wife'; then they will kill me, but they will let you live. [13] Say you are my sister, so that it may go well with me because of you, and that my life may be spared on

[a] Or by you all the families of the earth shall bless themselves [b] Or terebinth [c] Heb seed

---

11:30 *Barren*—A theme in Genesis, describing Sarai, Rebekah, and Rachel. The word refers to childlessness, not necessarily infertility.

11:31 *Ur; Haran*—Ur is most likely a city south of Babylon, from which Terah and his family departed for the land of **Canaan**. They stopped for a period of time in Haran (a city in southeastern Turkey), where Abram received his call and from which he departed for Canaan. If Abram received his call in Ur (so Acts 7:2–4; see Gen. 15:7), then 11:1–3 are a renewal of that call (note that God does not identify God's self). Abram obediently goes to Canaan (already the destination in v. 31) and worshipfully passes through the entire land that he and his descendants are promised. Shechem, Bethel, and Negeb (12:6–9) are locations in Canaan moving from north to south, eventually to Egypt.

12:1–3—Interpreters universally understand that the six divine promises in vv. 1–3, 7 provide an interpretive key, as its phrasings regularly punctuate the texts that follow (e.g., 28:13–14). This divine choice of one individual also looks back to previous chapters: Abram is chosen for the sake of **all the families of the earth**. Also, the centrality of **blessing** in the promises links back to the divine blessing of 1:28; in and through this family, God's original intention in creation is to be brought forward in the lives of all people.

12:10–20 Abram and Sarai in Egypt

12:13 *Say you are my sister*—This pericope, parallel in many ways to Israel's later experience in Egypt (e.g., plagues), casts Abram in a poor light in relation to both Sarai and the Egyptians as he endangers the promise (see the parallels

your account." **14** When Abram entered Egypt the Egyptians saw that the woman was very beautiful. **15** When the officials of Pharaoh saw her, they praised her to Pharaoh. And the woman was taken into Pharaoh's house. **16** And for her sake he dealt well with Abram; and he had sheep, oxen, male donkeys, male and female slaves, female donkeys, and camels.

17 But the LORD afflicted Pharaoh and his house with great plagues because of Sarai, Abram's wife. **18** So Pharaoh called Abram, and said, "What is this you have done to me? Why did you not tell me that she was your wife? **19** Why did you say, 'She is my sister,' so that I took her for my wife? Now then, here is your wife, take her, and be gone." **20** And Pharaoh gave his men orders concerning him; and they set him on the way, with his wife and all that he had.

Abram and Lot Separate

13 So Abram went up from Egypt, he and his wife, and all that he had, and Lot with him, into the Negeb.

2 Now Abram was very rich in livestock, in silver, and in gold. **3** He journeyed on by stages from the Negeb as far as Bethel, to the place where his tent had been at the beginning, between Bethel and Ai, **4** to the place where he had made an altar at the first; and there Abram called on the name of the LORD. **5** Now Lot, who went with Abram, also had flocks and herds and tents, **6** so that the land could not support both of them

living together; for their possessions were so great that they could not live together, **7** and there was strife between the herders of Abram's livestock and the herders of Lot's livestock. At that time the Canaanites and the Perizzites lived in the land.

8 Then Abram said to Lot, "Let there be no strife between you and me, and between your herders and my herders; for we are kindred. **9** Is not the whole land before you? Separate yourself from me. If you take the left hand, then I will go to the right; or if you take the right hand, then I will go to the left." **10** Lot looked about him, and saw that the plain of the Jordan was well watered everywhere like the garden of the LORD, like the land of Egypt, in the direction of Zoar; this was before the LORD had destroyed Sodom and Gomorrah. **11** So Lot chose for himself all the plain of the Jordan, and Lot journeyed eastward; thus they separated from each other. **12** Abram settled in the land of Canaan, while Lot settled among the cities of the Plain and moved his tent as far as Sodom. **13** Now the people of Sodom were wicked, great sinners against the LORD.

14 The LORD said to Abram, after Lot had separated from him, "Raise your eyes now, and look from the place where you are, northward and southward and eastward and westward; **15** for all the land that you see I will give to you and to your offspring*a* forever. **16** I will

a Heb *seed*

---

in 20:1–18; 26:1–11). His fearful presentation of Sarai as his sister assumes a situation where adultery is forbidden, but a murder might be arranged (cf. David and Bathsheba). His life is preserved, and he becomes a wealthy man, but his ruse costs Sarai, who has no voice in the narrative, her honor and dignity as she becomes Pharaoh's "wife" (12:19). God's action redeems the situation, and Pharaoh's gracious response serves God's purposes.

13:1–18 Abram and Lot

13:8 *Let there be no strife*—Blessings (land, in this case) can create problems as well as possibilities. The strife between the households of

Abram and Lot occasions a decision regarding land and economic realities with wide-ranging effects. Lot's choice of land moves his household into the Jordan Valley region. Choices people make regarding issues of land and economics can have a negative environmental impact (cf. 21:22–34 and 23:1–20 for other negotiations regarding land). Abram's choice leads to a closer specification of earlier promises (13:14–17).

13:10 *Sodom and Gomorrah*—These wicked cities (v. 13) probably lay southeast of the Dead Sea (vv. 10, 13), and their behaviors in turn lead to environmental disaster for that region and Lot's family (chaps. 18–19).

make your offspring like the dust of the earth; so that if one can count the dust of the earth, your offspring also can be counted. ¹⁷ Rise up, walk through the length and the breadth of the land, for I will give it to you." ¹⁸ So Abram moved his tent, and came and settled by the oaks*ᵃ* of Mamre, which are at Hebron; and there he built an altar to the LORD.

Lot's Captivity and Rescue

14 In the days of King Amraphel of Shinar, King Arioch of Ellasar, King Chedorlaomer of Elam, and King Tidal of Goiim, ² these kings made war with King Bera of Sodom, King Birsha of Gomorrah, King Shinab of Admah, King Shemeber of Zeboiim, and the king of Bela (that is, Zoar). ³ All these joined forces in the Valley of Siddim (that is, the Dead Sea).*ᵇ* ⁴ Twelve years they had served Chedorlaomer, but in the thirteenth year they rebelled. ⁵ In the fourteenth year Chedorlaomer and the kings who were with him came and subdued the Rephaim in Ashteroth-karnaim, the Zuzim in Ham, the Emim in Shaveh-kiriathaim, ⁶ and the Horites in the hill country of Seir as far as El-paran on the edge of the wilderness; ⁷ then they turned back and came to En-mishpat (that is, Kadesh), and subdued all the country of the Amalekites, and also the Amorites who lived in Hazazon-tamar. ⁸ Then the king of Sodom, the king of Gomorrah, the king of Admah, the king of Zeboiim, and the king of Bela (that is, Zoar) went out, and they joined battle in the Valley of Siddim ⁹ with King Ched-orlaomer of Elam, King Tidal of Goiim, King Amraphel of Shinar, and King Arioch of Ellasar, four kings against five. ¹⁰ Now the Valley of Siddim was full of bitumen pits; and as the kings of Sodom and Gomorrah fled, some fell into them, and the rest fled to the hill country. ¹¹ So the enemy took all the goods of Sodom and Gomorrah, and all their provisions, and went their way; ¹² they also took Lot, the son of Abram's brother, who lived in Sodom, and his goods, and departed.

13 Then one who had escaped came and told Abram the Hebrew, who was living by the oaks*ᵃ* of Mamre the Amorite, brother of Eshcol and of Aner; these were allies of Abram. ¹⁴ When Abram heard that his nephew had been taken captive, he led forth his trained men, born in his house, three hundred eighteen of them, and went in pursuit as far as Dan. ¹⁵ He divided his forces against them by night, he and his servants, and routed them and pursued them to Hobah, north of Damascus. ¹⁶ Then he brought back all the goods, and also brought back his nephew Lot with his goods, and the women and the people.

Abram Blessed by Melchizedek

17 After his return from the defeat of Chedorlaomer and the kings who were with him, the king of Sodom went out to meet him at the Valley of Shaveh (that is, the King's Valley). ¹⁸ And King Melchizedek of Salem brought out bread and wine; he was priest of God Most High.*ᶜ* ¹⁹ He blessed him and said,

ᵃ Or terebinths   *ᵇ* Heb Salt Sea   *ᶜ* Heb El Elyon

14:1–24 Abram and Melchizedek

14:1–17—An unusual portrayal of Abram as a military leader on the world stage, engaged in an act of deliverance similar to that of the later judges (e.g., Gideon). Readers are faced with numerous names of persons and places, many of them unknown or of uncertain reference. The setting is a war between four kings from the Mesopotamian region (**Shinar** is Babylon, 10:10) and five kings from the area around Sodom and Gomorrah, during which Lot is captured. Abram marshals his trained men and with the help of al-lies defeats the four kings (!), rescues Lot and the booty, and liberates the region around Sodom. The net effect of Abram's action is that he gains control over much of the promised land.

14:18–20 *Melchizedek*—The king of Salem (probably Jerusalem, Ps. 76:2), who serves as a priest of **God Most High** (=El Elyon), perhaps the name of a pre-Israelite god. Abram identifies El Elyon with his god YHWH as the creator of the world (v. 22). Melchizedek blesses Abram in the name of this God and blesses (=praises) Abram's God for this deliverance, to which Abram

"Blessed be Abram by God Most
    High, *a*
maker of heaven and earth;
20 and blessed be God Most High, *a*
    who has delivered your enemies
        into your hand!"
And Abram gave him one-tenth of everything. 21 Then the king of Sodom said to
Abram, "Give me the persons, but take
the goods for yourself." 22 But Abram
said to the king of Sodom, "I have sworn
to the LORD, God Most High, *a* maker
of heaven and earth, 23 that I would not
take a thread or a sandal-thong or anything that is yours, so that you might not
say, 'I have made Abram rich.' 24 I will
take nothing but what the young men
have eaten, and the share of the men
who went with me—Aner, Eshcol, and
Mamre. Let them take their share."

God's Covenant with Abram

15 After these things the word of
the LORD came to Abram in a
vision, "Do not be afraid, Abram, I am
your shield; your reward shall be very
great." 2 But Abram said, "O Lord GOD,
what will you give me, for I continue
childless, and the heir of my house is Eliezer of Damascus?" *b* 3 And Abram said,
"You have given me no offspring, and
so a slave born in my house is to be my

heir." 4 But the word of the LORD came to
him, "This man shall not be your heir;
no one but your very own issue shall be
your heir." 5 He brought him outside and
said, "Look toward heaven and count
the stars, if you are able to count them."
Then he said to him, "So shall your
descendants be." 6 And he believed the
LORD; and the LORD *c* reckoned it to him
as righteousness.

7 Then he said to him, "I am the LORD
who brought you from Ur of the Chaldeans, to give you this land to possess."
8 But he said, "O Lord GOD, how am I to
know that I shall possess it?" 9 He said
to him, "Bring me a heifer three years
old, a female goat three years old, a ram
three years old, a turtledove, and a young
pigeon." 10 He brought him all these and
cut them in two, laying each half over
against the other; but he did not cut the
birds in two. 11 And when birds of prey
came down on the carcasses, Abram
drove them away.

12 As the sun was going down, a deep
sleep fell upon Abram, and a deep and
terrifying darkness descended upon
him. 13 Then the LORD *c* said to Abram,
"Know this for certain, that your offspring shall be aliens in a land that is
not theirs, and shall be slaves there,

a Heb *El Elyon*   *b* Meaning of Heb uncertain   *c* Heb *he*

---

responds with a tithe of the booty. Melchizedek
is a mysterious figure, but was probably considered a precursor of the royal and priestly lines
in the Davidic empire (see Ps. 110:4; hence the
messianic link in Heb. 5–7); this narrative may
represent efforts to legitimate the later Davidic
monarchy in Jerusalem.

14:24 I will take nothing—Abram, perceiving
that an issue of justice is at stake, refuses to
enrich himself by taking booty from a region that
he had agreed belonged to Lot (13:6–12).

15:1–21 The Covenant with Abram

15:2 I continue childless—Abram responds to
God's reassuring word (v. 1) about reward for his
faithful actions in chap. 14 by wondering what
use it will be if he cannot pass it on to his own
children (**Eliezer** may be his steward). God has
not fulfilled the promise of posterity. In response
God promises him offspring as numerous as the
stars.

**15:6 He believed the LORD; and the LORD reck-
oned it . . . as righteousness**—In response to this
promise, Abram trusts in the promise-giver. In
response to Abram's faith, God formally declares
that Abram is righteous, that is, in a right relationship with God (see Rom. 4:3, 20–24; Gal.
3:6; Jas. 2:23).

**15:8 How am I to know that I shall possess
it?**—Once again in response to a divine promise
(v. 7), Abram asks a question to be reassured.
God's response is a ritual for which Abram prepares (vv. 9–11) and in which God, but not the
sleeping Abram, participates—in both word (vv.
13–16, 18–21) and deed (v. 17).

15:13–16 Know this for certain—God reassures
Abram by sketching a glimpse of the long journey his offspring will take before they take up life
in the land. It includes being oppressed aliens
in Egypt for 400 years (cf. 430 years in Exod.
12:40), the judgment of plagues, the exodus, and

and they shall be oppressed for four hundred years; [14] but I will bring judgment on the nation that they serve, and afterward they shall come out with great possessions. [15] As for yourself, you shall go to your ancestors in peace; you shall be buried in a good old age. [16] And they shall come back here in the fourth generation; for the iniquity of the Amorites is not yet complete."

17 When the sun had gone down and it was dark, a smoking fire pot and a flaming torch passed between these pieces. [18] On that day the LORD made a covenant with Abram, saying, "To your descendants I give this land, from the river of Egypt to the great river, the river Euphrates, [19] the land of the Kenites, the Kenizzites, the Kadmonites, [20] the Hittites, the Perizzites, the Rephaim, [21] the Amorites, the Canaanites, the Girgashites, and the Jebusites."

The Birth of Ishmael

16 Now Sarai, Abram's wife, bore him no children. She had an Egyptian slave-girl whose name was Hagar, [2] and Sarai said to Abram, "You see that the LORD has prevented me from bearing children; go in to my slave-girl; it may be that I shall obtain children by her." And Abram listened to the voice of Sarai. [3] So, after Abram had lived ten years in the land of Canaan, Sarai, Abram's wife, took Hagar the Egyptian, her slave-girl, and gave her to her husband Abram as a wife. [4] He went in to Hagar, and she conceived; and when she saw that she had conceived, she looked with contempt on her mistress. [5] Then Sarai said to Abram, "May the wrong done to me be on you! I gave my slave-girl to your embrace, and when she saw that she had conceived, she looked on me with contempt. May the LORD judge between you and me!" [6] But Abram said to Sarai, "Your slave-girl is in your power; do to her as you please." Then Sarai dealt harshly with her, and she ran away from her.

7 The angel of the LORD found her by a spring of water in the wilderness, the spring on the way to Shur. [8] And he said, "Hagar, slave-girl of Sarai, where have you come from and where are you going?" She said, "I am running away from my mistress Sarai." [9] The angel of the LORD said to her, "Return to your mistress, and submit to her." [10] The angel of the LORD also said to her, "I will so greatly multiply your offspring that they cannot be counted for multitude." [11] And the angel of the LORD said to her,

---

the return to Canaan in the fourth generation (perhaps four one-hundred-year periods). The sin of the *Amorites* (=Canaanites) had not yet built up to the point where its disastrous effects would redound on their head.

15:17 *A smoking fire pot and a flaming torch*—These are symbols for the presence of God, who alone passes through the cut animals (see Jer. 34:18–20). This concrete way in which God's promise is, in effect, written in blood, constitutes the making of the covenant with Abram, which is a unilateral, unconditional promise (detailed in 15:18–21). Note that the covenant does not establish the relationship with Abram; it ratifies the divine promises.

16:1–16 Hagar and Sarai

16:2 *The LORD has prevented me from bearing children*—This is Sarai's opinion, leading her to obtain an heir for Abram through her slave-girl, Hagar (a common custom, see 30:3–13). The promise to Abram did not specify the identity of the mother (15:4).

16:6 *Sarai dealt harshly with her*—Literally, Sarai oppressed Hagar, an Egyptian. God recognizes this oppression in v. 11; this act is parallel to the Egyptians' oppression of Israel in Egypt (Exod. 1:11).

16:7 *The angel of the LORD*—Not a member of the divine council, but God in human form (see v. 13; 18:1–8). God appears to this "outsider" at the point of her exclusion, showers her with promises regarding her posterity (cf. 15:5), and commands that she return to settle things with Sarai (having treated Sarai with contempt, she stood under the curse of 12:3). That God makes promises to these "outsiders" shows that God is graciously at work apart from the chosen community. *Shur*—A wilderness area between Canaan and Egypt. Hence, Hagar was on her way home.

"Now you have conceived and shall
   bear a son;
   you shall call him Ishmael, *a*
   for the LORD has given heed to
      your affliction.
12 He shall be a wild ass of a man,
   with his hand against everyone,
      and everyone's hand against him;
   and he shall live at odds with all his
      kin."

13 So she named the LORD who spoke
to her, "You are El-roi"; *b* for she said,
"Have I really seen God and remained
alive after seeing him?" *c* 14 Therefore the
well was called Beer-lahai-roi; *d* it lies
between Kadesh and Bered.

15 Hagar bore Abram a son; and
Abram named his son, whom Hagar
bore, Ishmael. 16 Abram was eighty-
six years old when Hagar bore him *e*
Ishmael.

The Sign of the Covenant

17 When Abram was ninety-nine
years old, the LORD appeared
to Abram, and said to him, "I am God
Almighty; *f* walk before me, and be
blameless. 2 And I will make my covenant
between me and you, and will make you
exceedingly numerous." 3 Then Abram
fell on his face; and God said to him,
4 "As for me, this is my covenant with
you: You shall be the ancestor of a multitude of nations. 5 No longer shall your
name be Abram, *g* but your name shall

be Abraham; *h* for I have made you the
ancestor of a multitude of nations. 6 I
will make you exceedingly fruitful; and
I will make nations of you, and kings
shall come from you. 7 I will establish
my covenant between me and you, and
your offspring after you throughout
their generations, for an everlasting
covenant, to be God to you and to your
offspring *i* after you. 8 And I will give to
you, and to your offspring after you, the
land where you are now an alien, all the
land of Canaan, for a perpetual holding;
and I will be their God."

9 God said to Abraham, "As for you,
you shall keep my covenant, you and
your offspring after you throughout
their generations. 10 This is my covenant,
which you shall keep, between me and
you and your offspring after you: Every
male among you shall be circumcised.
11 You shall circumcise the flesh of
your foreskins, and it shall be a sign
of the covenant between me and you.
12 Throughout your generations every
male among you shall be circumcised
when he is eight days old, including
the slave born in your house and the
one bought with your money from any
foreigner who is not of your offspring.
13 Both the slave born in your house and

---

a That is *God hears* *b* Perhaps *God of seeing* or *God who sees* *c* Meaning
of Heb uncertain *d* That is *the Well of the Living One who sees me*
e Heb *Abram* *f* Traditional rendering of Heb *El Shaddai* *g* That is *exalted
ancestor* *h* Here taken to mean *ancestor of a multitude* *i* Heb *seed*

16:13 *She named the LORD . . . El-roi*—Hagar is
the only human being in the Old Testament to
give God a new name—based on her experience
and theological reflection after remaining alive
upon having seen God.

16:14 *Beer-lahai-roi*—Hagar's name for the
well where God had appeared to her (see NRSV
footnote). It is later associated with Isaac (24:62;
25:11).

17:1–27 Covenant and Circumcision

17:1–2 *I will make my covenant*—This revision
of the covenant of chap. 15 in view of a new
situation includes a new name for God (**God
Almighty**), new names (Sarah and Abraham), the
specification of Sarah as the mother of the child
of promise and as full partner in the covenant
(17:15–16), the everlastingness of the covenant

(v. 7) with Isaac (v. 19), still more promises for
Ishmael (v. 20), and the institution of the rite of
circumcision.

17:10 *This is my covenant*—Verses 10 and 13 do
not actually identify the covenant with circumcision (see v. 4). This is an instance of synec-
doche—circumcision as a sign of faithfulness
refers to the covenant as a whole. Breaking the
covenant by not circumcising is a sign of human
unfaithfulness to the covenant and would result
in excommunication from the community (v. 14).
God's promise is unconditional, but people could
remove themselves from the sphere of the promise by being unfaithful, one sign of which was
circumcision. Circumcision was common among
Israel's neighbors; so being circumcised in itself
does not guarantee a keeping of the covenant.

the one bought with your money must be circumcised. So shall my covenant be in your flesh an everlasting covenant. **14** Any uncircumcised male who is not circumcised in the flesh of his foreskin shall be cut off from his people; he has broken my covenant."

15 God said to Abraham, "As for Sarai your wife, you shall not call her Sarai, but Sarah shall be her name. **16** I will bless her, and moreover I will give you a son by her. I will bless her, and she shall give rise to nations; kings of peoples shall come from her." **17** Then Abraham fell on his face and laughed, and said to himself, "Can a child be born to a man who is a hundred years old? Can Sarah, who is ninety years old, bear a child?" **18** And Abraham said to God, "O that Ishmael might live in your sight!" **19** God said, "No, but your wife Sarah shall bear you a son, and you shall name him Isaac.ᵃ I will establish my covenant with him as an everlasting covenant for his offspring after him. **20** As for Ishmael, I have heard you; I will bless him and make him fruitful and exceedingly numerous; he shall be the father of twelve princes, and I will make him a great nation. **21** But my covenant I will establish with Isaac, whom Sarah shall bear to you at this season next year." **22** And when he had finished talking with him, God went up from Abraham.

23 Then Abraham took his son Ishmael and all the slaves born in his house or bought with his money, every male among the men of Abraham's house, and he circumcised the flesh of their foreskins that very day, as God had said to him. **24** Abraham was ninety-nine years old when he was circumcised in the flesh of his foreskin. **25** And his son Ishmael was thirteen years old when he was circumcised in the flesh of his

foreskin. **26** That very day Abraham and his son Ishmael were circumcised; **27** and all the men of his house, slaves born in the house and those bought with money from a foreigner, were circumcised with him.

A Son Promised to Abraham and Sarah

18 The Lord appeared to Abrahamᵇ by the oaksᶜ of Mamre, as he sat at the entrance of his tent in the heat of the day. **2** He looked up and saw three men standing near him. When he saw them, he ran from the tent entrance to meet them, and bowed down to the ground. **3** He said, "My lord, if I find favor with you, do not pass by your servant. **4** Let a little water be brought, and wash your feet, and rest yourselves under the tree. **5** Let me bring a little bread, that you may refresh yourselves, and after that you may pass on—since you have come to your servant." So they said, "Do as you have said." **6** And Abraham hastened into the tent to Sarah, and said, "Make ready quickly three measuresᵈ of choice flour, knead it, and make cakes." **7** Abraham ran to the herd, and took a calf, tender and good, and gave it to the servant, who hastened to prepare it. **8** Then he took curds and milk and the calf that he had prepared, and set it before them; and he stood by them under the tree while they ate.

9 They said to him, "Where is your wife Sarah?" And he said, "There, in the tent." **10** Then one said, "I will surely return to you in due season, and your wife Sarah shall have a son." And Sarah was listening at the tent entrance behind him. **11** Now Abraham and Sarah were old, advanced in age; it had ceased to be with Sarah after the manner of women.

ᵃ *That is he laughs* ᵇ Heb *him* ᶜ Or *terebinths* ᵈ Heb *seahs*

18:1–15 God Visits Abraham and Sarah

18:1–2 *The Lord appeared . . . three men*—Two points of view are presented regarding the three visitors, the narrator's (v. 1) and Abraham's (v. 2). It is not clear that Abraham recognizes the

presence of YHWH at any point in this segment. YHWH has assumed human form (16:7) and appears as one of the three; the other two are angelic attendants (see 19:1).

[12] So Sarah laughed to herself, saying, "After I have grown old, and my husband is old, shall I have pleasure?" [13] The LORD said to Abraham, "Why did Sarah laugh, and say, 'Shall I indeed bear a child, now that I am old?' [14] Is anything too wonderful for the LORD? At the set time I will return to you, in due season, and Sarah shall have a son." [15] But Sarah denied, saying, "I did not laugh"; for she was afraid. He said, "Oh yes, you did laugh."

Judgment Pronounced on Sodom

[16] Then the men set out from there, and they looked toward Sodom; and Abraham went with them to set them on their way. [17] The LORD said, "Shall I hide from Abraham what I am about to do, [18] seeing that Abraham shall become a great and mighty nation, and all the nations of the earth shall be blessed in him?[a] [19] No, for I have chosen[b] him, that he may charge his children and his household after him to keep the way of the LORD by doing righteousness and justice; so that the LORD may bring about for Abraham what he has promised him." [20] Then the LORD said, "How great is the outcry against Sodom and Gomorrah and how very grave their sin! [21] I must go down and see whether they have done altogether according to the outcry that has come to me; and if not, I will know."

22 So the men turned from there, and went toward Sodom, while Abraham remained standing before the LORD.[c] [23] Then Abraham came near and said, "Will you indeed sweep away the righteous with the wicked? [24] Suppose there are fifty righteous within the city; will you then sweep away the place and not forgive it for the fifty righteous who are in it? [25] Far be it from you to do such a thing, to slay the righteous with the wicked, so that the righteous fare as the wicked! Far be that from you! Shall not the Judge of all the earth do what is just?" [26] And the LORD said, "If I find at Sodom fifty righteous in the city, I will forgive the whole place for their sake." [27] Abraham answered, "Let me take it upon myself to speak to the Lord, I who am but dust and ashes. [28] Suppose five of the fifty righteous are lacking? Will you destroy the whole city for lack of five?" And he said, "I will not destroy it if I find forty-five there." [29] Again he spoke to him, "Suppose forty are found there." He answered, "For the sake of forty I will not do it." [30] Then he said, "Oh do not let the Lord be angry if I speak. Suppose

[a] Or *and all the nations of the earth shall bless themselves by him*
[b] Heb *known*   [c] Another ancient tradition reads *while the* LORD *remained standing before Abraham*

18:14 *Is anything too wonderful for the* LORD?—It is not clear whether "wonderful" refers to God's competence (Deut. 17:8), power (Deut. 28:59), or marvelousness (Ps. 118:23). The force of the verse has to do with claiming that God's promises will not fail; God will always find a way into the future.

18:16–33 Abraham Intercedes for Sodom

18:17 *Shall I hide from Abraham*—God consults with Abraham regarding a matter of injustice in Sodom because God does not want to keep him ignorant of God's ways in the world, has chosen him to have a role among the nations (12:3), and has charged him to teach his children in matters of justice.

18:21 *I must go down and see whether*—God knows the situation of injustice in Sodom (*outcry*, see Exod. 3:7), but determines to consult with Abraham about it before making a final decision. God admits the possibility of an "if not," and hence the future of Sodom is at least somewhat open, pending the consultation with Abraham.

18:24–32 *Suppose there are fifty righteous*—The issue relates to critical mass; are there enough righteous in the city to outweigh the effects of the wicked? It is finally determined (v. 32) that if there are not at least ten such people, there is an insufficient number to turn the situation around, and judgment must fall.

18:25 *Shall not the Judge of all the earth do what is just?*—Abraham's question assumes that, if God would be just, God must do justice to divinely established relationships (=righteousness) in order to remain faithful. This entails attending to the differences between the righteous and the wicked.

thirty are found there." He answered, "I will not do it, if I find thirty there." [31] He said, "Let me take it upon myself to speak to the Lord. Suppose twenty are found there." He answered, "For the sake of twenty I will not destroy it." [32] Then he said, "Oh do not let the Lord be angry if I speak just once more. Suppose ten are found there." He answered, "For the sake of ten I will not destroy it." [33] And the LORD went his way, when he had finished speaking to Abraham; and Abraham returned to his place.

The Depravity of Sodom

19 The two angels came to Sodom in the evening, and Lot was sitting in the gateway of Sodom. When Lot saw them, he rose to meet them, and bowed down with his face to the ground. [2] He said, "Please, my lords, turn aside to your servant's house and spend the night, and wash your feet; then you can rise early and go on your way." They said, "No; we will spend the night in the square." [3] But he urged them strongly; so they turned aside to him and entered his house; and he made them a feast, and baked unleavened bread, and they ate. [4] But before they lay down, the men of the city, the men of Sodom, both young and old, all the people to the last man, surrounded the house; [5] and they called to Lot, "Where are the men who came to you tonight? Bring them out to us, so that we may know them." [6] Lot went out of the door to the men, shut the door after him, [7] and said, "I beg you, my brothers, do not act so wickedly. [8] Look, I have two daughters who have not known a man; let me bring them out to you, and do to them as you please; only do nothing to these men, for they have come under the shelter of my roof." [9] But they replied, "Stand back!" And they said, "This fellow came here as an alien, and he would play the judge! Now we will deal worse with you than with them." Then they pressed hard against the man Lot, and came near the door to break it down. [10] But the men inside reached out their hands and brought Lot into the house with them, and shut the door. [11] And they struck with blindness the men who were at the door of the house, both small and great, so that they were unable to find the door.

Sodom and Gomorrah Destroyed

12 Then the men said to Lot, "Have you anyone else here? Sons-in-law, sons, daughters, or anyone you have in the city—bring them out of the place. [13] For we are about to destroy this place, because the outcry against its people has become great before the LORD, and the LORD has sent us to destroy it." [14] So Lot went out and said to his sons-in-law, who were to marry his daughters, "Up, get out of this place; for the LORD is about to destroy the city." But he seemed to his sons-in-law to be jesting.

15 When morning dawned, the angels urged Lot, saying, "Get up, take your wife and your two daughters who are here, or else you will be consumed in the punishment of the city." [16] But he lingered; so the men seized him and his wife and his two daughters by the hand, the LORD being merciful to him, and

---

19:1–38 Sodom and Gomorrah

19:1–9—These verses provide an illustration of the wickedness of Sodom. That *every* male in town was involved in this threat to the visitors (v. 4) is important for assessing the sin involved: inhospitality through sexual abuse and violence. The verb *know* (v. 5) refers to sexual activity, whether heterosexual or homosexual; with every man in town involved, the result would have been gang rape of every sexual sort. Sexual abuse of strangers in that culture was a way of demonstrating who was in charge (as it often is in our prisons). The sins of Sodom are mentioned elsewhere most explicitly in Ezek. 16:49: pride, excess of food, prosperous ease, and not aiding the poor and needy (cf. Jesus' use of this text in Matt. 10:14–15). That Lot would substitute his betrothed (!) daughters for sexual activity is another sign of the depravity of Sodom (in Gen. 19:30–38 Lot himself is sexually abused in a "what goes around, comes around" understanding).

they brought him out and left him outside the city. [17] When they had brought them outside, they[a] said, "Flee for your life; do not look back or stop anywhere in the Plain; flee to the hills, or else you will be consumed." [18] And Lot said to them, "Oh, no, my lords; [19] your servant has found favor with you, and you have shown me great kindness in saving my life; but I cannot flee to the hills, for fear the disaster will overtake me and I die. [20] Look, that city is near enough to flee to, and it is a little one. Let me escape there—is it not a little one?—and my life will be saved!" [21] He said to him, "Very well, I grant you this favor too, and will not overthrow the city of which you have spoken. [22] Hurry, escape there, for I can do nothing until you arrive there." Therefore the city was called Zoar.[b] [23] The sun had risen on the earth when Lot came to Zoar.

24 Then the LORD rained on Sodom and Gomorrah sulfur and fire from the LORD out of heaven; [25] and he overthrew those cities, and all the Plain, and all the inhabitants of the cities, and what grew on the ground. [26] But Lot's wife, behind him, looked back, and she became a pillar of salt.

27 Abraham went early in the morning to the place where he had stood before the LORD; [28] and he looked down toward Sodom and Gomorrah and toward all the land of the Plain and saw the smoke of the land going up like the smoke of a furnace.

29 So it was that, when God destroyed the cities of the Plain, God remembered Abraham, and sent Lot out of the midst of the overthrow, when he overthrew the cities in which Lot had settled.

The Shameful Origin of Moab and Ammon

30 Now Lot went up out of Zoar and settled in the hills with his two daughters, for he was afraid to stay in Zoar; so he lived in a cave with his two daughters. [31] And the firstborn said to the younger, "Our father is old, and there is not a man on earth to come in to us after the manner of all the world. [32] Come, let us make our father drink wine, and we will lie with him, so that we may preserve offspring through our father." [33] So they made their father drink wine that night; and the firstborn went in, and lay with her father; he did not know when she lay down or when she rose. [34] On the next day, the firstborn said to the younger, "Look, I lay last night with my father; let us make him drink wine tonight also; then you go in and lie with him, so that we may preserve offspring through our father." [35] So they made their father drink wine that night also; and the younger rose, and lay with him; and he did not know when she lay down or when she rose. [36] Thus both the daughters of Lot became pregnant by their father. [37] The firstborn bore a son, and named him Moab; he is the ancestor of the Moabites to this day. [38] The younger also bore a son and named him Ben-ammi; he is the ancestor of the Ammonites to this day.

Abraham and Sarah at Gerar

20 From there Abraham journeyed toward the region of the Negeb,

a Gk Syr Vg: Heb he b That is Little

19:24–26—The devastation of the cities may have been caused by an earthquake with associated fires that ignited the extensive sulfur and bitumen deposits and petrochemical springs in the area (see 14:10). Lot's hesitant wife may well have been engulfed in the resultant explosion. The environmental disaster changing the area from garden (13:10) to wasteland is laid at the feet of *human* wickedness, a linkage that moderns know all too well (e.g., the depletion of the ozone layer).

19:37–38 *Moabites . . . Ammonites*—These Transjordanian peoples often come into contact with Israel. One remarkable result of these incestuous relationships is that Ruth, whose descendants include David and Jesus, comes from the line of Moab (Ruth 4:18–22; Matt. 1:5). Even from the worst of family situations, God can bring blessing to the world.

20:1–18 Abraham, Sarah, and Abimelech

20:1–2 *King Abimelech of Gerar*—Gerar, a city

and settled between Kadesh and Shur. While residing in Gerar as an alien, [2] Abraham said of his wife Sarah, "She is my sister." And King Abimelech of Gerar sent and took Sarah. [3] But God came to Abimelech in a dream by night, and said to him, "You are about to die because of the woman whom you have taken; for she is a married woman." [4] Now Abimelech had not approached her; so he said, "Lord, will you destroy an innocent people? [5] Did he not himself say to me, 'She is my sister'? And she herself said, 'He is my brother.' I did this in the integrity of my heart and the innocence of my hands." [6] Then God said to him in the dream, "Yes, I know that you did this in the integrity of your heart; furthermore it was I who kept you from sinning against me. Therefore I did not let you touch her. [7] Now then, return the man's wife; for he is a prophet, and he will pray for you and you shall live. But if you do not restore her, know that you shall surely die, you and all that are yours."

8 So Abimelech rose early in the morning, and called all his servants and told them all these things; and the men were very much afraid. [9] Then Abimelech called Abraham, and said to him, "What have you done to us? How have I sinned against you, that you have brought such great guilt on me and my kingdom? You have done things to me that ought not to be done." [10] And Abimelech said to Abraham, "What were you thinking of, that you did this thing?" [11] Abraham said, "I did it because I thought, There is no fear of God at all in this place, and they will kill me because of my wife. [12] Besides, she is indeed my sister, the daughter of my father but not the daughter of my mother; and she became my wife. [13] And when God caused me to wander from my father's house, I said to her, 'This is the kindness you must do me: at every place to which we come, say of me, He is my brother.' " [14] Then Abimelech took sheep and oxen, and male and female slaves, and gave them to Abraham, and restored his wife Sarah to him. [15] Abimelech said, "My land is before you; settle where it pleases you." [16] To Sarah he said, "Look, I have given your brother a thousand pieces of silver; it is your exoneration before all who are with you; you are completely vindicated." [17] Then Abraham prayed to God; and God healed Abimelech, and also healed his wife and female slaves so that they bore children. [18] For the LORD had closed fast all the wombs of the house of Abimelech because of Sarah, Abraham's wife.

The Birth of Isaac

21 The LORD dealt with Sarah as he had said, and the LORD did for Sarah as he had promised. [2] Sarah conceived and bore Abraham a son in his old age, at the time of which God had spoken to him. [3] Abraham gave the

---

of uncertain location, was probably in south of Canaan (the Negev), where Isaac settled (26:6), in what later became Philistine territory (see 21:32–34; 26:1). The king of Gerar, Abimelech, has several dealings with Abraham's family in these chapters (21:22–34; 26:1–11).

20:3 *God came to Abimelech in a dream*—Dreams, commonly considered a medium of divine revelation, were the vehicle by which God communicated with Abimelech, an "outsider," in order to protect Sarah. God also acknowledges his innocence in this matter, but death will be his fate (objective guilt) if he does not restore Sarah (vv. 3, 7).

20:7 *He is a prophet*—This sole reference to

Abraham as a prophet is an anachronism, but appropriate in view of his experience (see 15:1), including his role as a successful intercessor (see 1 Sam. 12:23).

20:9 *What have you done to us?*—Remarkably, this outsider calls God's chosen one to account for his behavior and for the ill effects he has let loose on his community (specified in vv. 17–18). Persons not a part of the chosen community can have a strong sense of justice! Abraham's rationalizing response is self-serving and cannot be trusted for the information it conveys (e.g., there *was* a fear of God in this place).

21:1–7 The Birth of Isaac

name Isaac to his son whom Sarah bore him. ⁴ And Abraham circumcised his son Isaac when he was eight days old, as God had commanded him. ⁵ Abraham was a hundred years old when his son Isaac was born to him. ⁶ Now Sarah said, "God has brought laughter for me; everyone who hears will laugh with me." ⁷ And she said, "Who would ever have said to Abraham that Sarah would nurse children? Yet I have borne him a son in his old age."

Hagar and Ishmael Sent Away

8 The child grew, and was weaned; and Abraham made a great feast on the day that Isaac was weaned. ⁹ But Sarah saw the son of Hagar the Egyptian, whom she had borne to Abraham, playing with her son Isaac. *a* ¹⁰ So she said to Abraham, "Cast out this slave woman with her son; for the son of this slave woman shall not inherit along with my son Isaac." ¹¹ The matter was very distressing to Abraham on account of his son. ¹² But God said to Abraham, "Do not be distressed because of the boy and because of your slave woman; whatever Sarah says to you, do as she tells you, for it is through Isaac that offspring shall be named for you. ¹³ As for the son of the slave woman, I will make a nation of him also, because he is your offspring." ¹⁴ So Abraham rose early in the morning, and took bread and a skin of water, and gave it to Hagar, putting it on her shoulder, along with the child, and sent her away. And she departed, and wandered about in the wilderness of Beer-sheba.

15 When the water in the skin was gone, she cast the child under one of the bushes. ¹⁶ Then she went and sat down opposite him a good way off, about the distance of a bowshot; for she said, "Do not let me look on the death of the child." And as she sat opposite him, she lifted up her voice and wept. ¹⁷ And God heard the voice of the boy; and the angel of God called to Hagar from heaven, and said to her, "What troubles you, Hagar? Do not be afraid; for God has heard the voice of the boy where he is. ¹⁸ Come, lift up the boy and hold him fast with your hand, for I will make a great nation of him." ¹⁹ Then God opened her eyes and she saw a well of water. She went, and filled the skin with water, and gave the boy a drink.

20 God was with the boy, and he grew up; he lived in the wilderness, and became an expert with the bow. ²¹ He lived in the wilderness of Paran; and his mother got a wife for him from the land of Egypt.

Abraham and Abimelech Make a Covenant

22 At that time Abimelech, with Phicol the commander of his army, said to Abraham, "God is with you in all that you do; ²³ now therefore swear to me here by God that you will not deal falsely with me or with my offspring or with my posterity, but as I have dealt loyally with you, you will deal with me and with the land where you have resided as an alien." ²⁴ And Abraham said, "I swear it."

25 When Abraham complained to Abimelech about a well of water that Abimelech's servants had seized, ²⁶ Abimelech said, "I do not know who has done

a Gk Vg: Heb lacks *with her son Isaac*

21:6 *God has brought laughter*—Isaac is born as God had promised (17:19; 18:14). Isaac's name is a play on the word "laughter," in view of both the joy at his birth and his parents' incredulous laughter at God's promise (17:17; 18:12).

21:8–21 Hagar and Ishmael

21:10 *Cast out this slave woman with her son*—Isaac's birth raises a problem regarding his relationship to Ishmael (see 16:1–16; 17:15–21),

both of whom had received promises from God. Sarah, concerned about Isaac's inheritance, successfully urges that Ishmael be sent away, with God's support. Yet Ishmael is not forgotten, as *God was with the boy* (21:20) and reiterates promises regarding his future (vv. 13, 18; see note on 25:12–18). Given that God keeps promises, what might this mean for our understanding of the growth of Islam?

21:22–34 Abraham and Abimelech (Again)

this; you did not tell me, and I have not heard of it until today." ²⁷So Abraham took sheep and oxen and gave them to Abimelech, and the two men made a covenant. ²⁸Abraham set apart seven ewe lambs of the flock. ²⁹And Abimelech said to Abraham, "What is the meaning of these seven ewe lambs that you have set apart?" ³⁰He said, "These seven ewe lambs you shall accept from my hand, in order that you may be a witness for me that I dug this well." ³¹Therefore that place was called Beer-sheba;^a because there both of them swore an oath. ³²When they had made a covenant at Beer-sheba, Abimelech, with Phicol the commander of his army, left and returned to the land of the Philistines. ³³Abraham^b planted a tamarisk tree in Beer-sheba, and called there on the name of the LORD, the Everlasting God.^c ³⁴And Abraham resided as an alien many days in the land of the Philistines.

The Command to Sacrifice Isaac

22 After these things God tested Abraham. He said to him, "Abraham!" And he said, "Here I am." ²He said, "Take your son, your only son Isaac, whom you love, and go to the land of Moriah, and offer him there as a burnt offering on one of the mountains that I shall show you." ³So Abraham rose early in the morning, saddled his donkey, and took two of his young men with him, and his son Isaac; he cut the wood for the burnt offering, and set out and went to the place in the distance that God had shown him. ⁴On the third day Abraham looked up and saw the place far away. ⁵Then Abraham said to his young men, "Stay here with the donkey; the boy and I will go over there; we will worship, and then we will come back to you." ⁶Abraham took the wood of the burnt offering and laid it on his son Isaac, and he himself carried the fire and the knife. So the two of them walked on together. ⁷Isaac said to his father Abraham, "Father!" And he said, "Here I am, my son." He said, "The fire and the wood are here, but where is the lamb for a burnt offering?" ⁸Abraham said, "God himself will provide the lamb for a burnt offering, my son." So the two of them walked on together.

⁹When they came to the place that God had shown him, Abraham built an altar there and laid the wood in order. He bound his son Isaac, and laid him on the altar, on top of the wood. ¹⁰Then Abraham reached out his hand and took

^a That is *Well of seven* or *Well of the oath* ^b Heb *He* ^c Or *the* LORD, *El Olam*

21:31 Beer-sheba—The name of a well in southern Judah commemorating the covenant between Abraham and Abimelech (it later became an important city). Isaac has a comparable experience with Abimelech in 26:12–33.

21:32, 34 The Philistines—An anachronistic reference to these sea people (see 26:1); they settled in Canaan somewhat later (about 1200 BCE) and were often in conflict with the Israelites (see Josh. 13:2).

22:1–19 The Testing of Abraham

22:1 God tested Abraham—The narrator informs readers that this is a test; Abraham is not informed. Testing serves God's purposes, not to kill Isaac, but so that God may know (v. 12)—there is no word about teaching Abraham—that Abraham will be faithful and that the future can be entrusted to him (see Deut. 8:2). Abraham's obedient response, *"Here I am,"* is rooted in his long-standing trust of God (Gen. 15:6) and highlights basic moments of the narrative (22:1, 7, 11). The test confirms a fact: Abraham trusts God unreservedly.

22:2 Your only son Isaac—These words, which also structure the account (vv. 2, 12, 16), indirectly recall Abraham's loss of his other son, Ishmael (21:8–21 closely parallels this chapter). *The land of Moriah*—Its location is uncertain, but this God-chosen place may refer to Jerusalem and is traditionally associated with the Temple Mount (2 Chr. 3:1). *Offer him there as a burnt offering*—God places the test within the context of the sacrificial system (note Abraham's understanding that he is to *worship*, v. 5), so it is not a command to murder. As such, it may reflect a point of origin for the firstborn ritual, where God required the life of the firstborn (Exod. 22:29), but, as in this text, made provision for their redemption (Exod. 13:13). God's providing is a central feature of the text (Gen. 22:8, 14).

the knife to kill[a] his son. **11** But the angel of the LORD called to him from heaven, and said, "Abraham, Abraham!" And he said, "Here I am." **12** He said, "Do not lay your hand on the boy or do anything to him; for now I know that you fear God, since you have not withheld your son, your only son, from me." **13** And Abraham looked up and saw a ram, caught in a thicket by its horns. Abraham went and took the ram and offered it up as a burnt offering instead of his son. **14** So Abraham called that place "The LORD will provide";[b] as it is said to this day, "On the mount of the LORD it shall be provided."[c]

15 The angel of the LORD called to Abraham a second time from heaven, **16** and said, "By myself I have sworn, says the LORD: Because you have done this, and have not withheld your son, your only son, **17** I will indeed bless you, and I will make your offspring as numerous as the stars of heaven and as the sand that is on the seashore. And your offspring shall possess the gate of their enemies, **18** and by your offspring shall all the nations of the earth gain blessing for themselves, because you have obeyed my voice." **19** So Abraham returned to his young men, and they arose and went together to Beer-sheba; and Abraham lived at Beer-sheba.

The Children of Nahor

20 Now after these things it was told Abraham, "Milcah also has borne children, to your brother Nahor: **21** Uz the firstborn, Buz his brother, Kemuel the father of Aram, **22** Chesed, Hazo, Pildash, Jidlaph, and Bethuel." **23** Bethuel became the father of Rebekah. These eight Milcah bore to Nahor, Abraham's brother. **24** Moreover, his concubine, whose name was Reumah, bore Tebah, Gaham, Tahash, and Maacah.

Sarah's Death and Burial

23 Sarah lived one hundred twenty-seven years; this was the length of Sarah's life. **2** And Sarah died at Kiriath-arba (that is, Hebron) in the land of Canaan; and Abraham went in to mourn for Sarah and to weep for her. **3** Abraham rose up from beside his dead, and said to the Hittites, **4** "I am a stranger and an alien residing among you; give me property among you for a burying place, so that I may bury my dead out of my sight." **5** The Hittites answered Abraham, **6** "Hear us, my lord; you are a mighty prince among us. Bury your dead in the choicest of our burial places; none of us will withhold from you any burial ground for burying your dead." **7** Abraham rose and bowed to the Hittites, the people of the land. **8** He said to them, "If you are willing that I should bury my dead out of my sight, hear me, and entreat for me Ephron son of Zohar, **9** so that he may give me the cave of Machpelah, which he owns; it is at the end of his field. For the full price let him give it to me in your presence as a possession for

---

a Or *to slaughter*   *b* Or *will see*; Heb traditionally transliterated *Jehovah Jireh*   *c* Or *he shall be seen*

22:16 *Because you have done this*—Does this language make God's prior promises to Abraham conditional? The original promises were made independent of Abraham's faith (12:1–3), and then God's unconditional promises create Abraham's faith (15:5–6). That point is not reversed here, so that Abraham's faith creates the promises. God's promises will always remain intact, but Abraham could reject God and remove himself from the sphere of the promise. Here the promises are reiterated (with an oath, for the first time) to a trusting Abraham.

22:20–24 *Rebekah's Family*
This text, linked to 11:29, begins to make concrete God's promise of posterity to Abraham. Rebekah is a grandniece of Abraham.

23:1–20 *Abraham Buys Land in Canaan*

23:3 *Hittites*—Probably not the people settled in Anatolia, unless in an extended sense, but one of the pre-Israelite peoples living in Canaan (27:46–28:1 seems to equate them with Canaanites). Ephron was the landowner with whom Abraham dealt.

23:9 *Machpelah*—A cave in southern Canaan near Mamre that became the burial place of Sarah and Abraham (25:9), as well as Isaac, Rebekah, Jacob, and Leah. Ephron offers the

a burying place." **10** Now Ephron was sitting among the Hittites; and Ephron the Hittite answered Abraham in the hearing of the Hittites, of all who went in at the gate of his city, **11** "No, my lord, hear me; I give you the field, and I give you the cave that is in it; in the presence of my people I give it to you; bury your dead." **12** Then Abraham bowed down before the people of the land. **13** He said to Ephron in the hearing of the people of the land, "If you only will listen to me! I will give the price of the field; accept it from me, so that I may bury my dead there." **14** Ephron answered Abraham, **15** "My lord, listen to me; a piece of land worth four hundred shekels of silver—what is that between you and me? Bury your dead." **16** Abraham agreed with Ephron; and Abraham weighed out for Ephron the silver that he had named in the hearing of the Hittites, four hundred shekels of silver, according to the weights current among the merchants.

17 So the field of Ephron in Machpelah, which was to the east of Mamre, the field with the cave that was in it and all the trees that were in the field, throughout its whole area, passed **18** to Abraham as a possession in the presence of the Hittites, in the presence of all who went in at the gate of his city. **19** After this, Abraham buried Sarah his wife in the cave of the field of Machpelah facing Mamre (that is, Hebron) in the land of Canaan. **20** The field and the cave that is in it passed from the Hittites into Abraham's possession as a burying place.

The Marriage of Isaac and Rebekah

24 Now Abraham was old, well advanced in years; and the LORD had blessed Abraham in all things. **2** Abraham said to his servant, the oldest of his house, who had charge of all that he had, "Put your hand under my thigh **3** and I will make you swear by the LORD, the God of heaven and earth, that you will not get a wife for my son from the daughters of the Canaanites, among whom I live, **4** but will go to my country and to my kindred and get a wife for my son Isaac." **5** The servant said to him, "Perhaps the woman may not be willing to follow me to this land; must I then take your son back to the land from which you came?" **6** Abraham said to him, "See to it that you do not take my son back there. **7** The LORD, the God of heaven, who took me from my father's house and from the land of my birth, and who spoke to me and swore to me, 'To your offspring I will give this land,' he will send his angel before you, and you shall take a wife for my son from there. **8** But if the woman is not willing to follow you, then you will be free from this oath of mine; only you must not take my son back there." **9** So the servant put his hand under the thigh of Abraham his master and swore to him concerning this matter.

10 Then the servant took ten of his master's camels and departed, taking all kinds of choice gifts from his master; and he set out and went to Aram-naharaim, to the city of Nahor. **11** He made the camels kneel down outside the city by the well of water; it was toward evening, the time when women go out to draw water. **12** And he said, "O LORD, God of my master Abraham, please grant me success today and show steadfast love to my

---

cave and its environs as a gift, but Abraham, for legal reasons, insists on buying it. This purchase signals the beginning of the acquisition of the promised land for Israel's descendants (cf. Jer. 32:1–15).

24:1–67 The Wooing of Rebekah

24:2 *Under my thigh*—Abraham, in commissioning his servant to procure a wife for Isaac and hence begin to secure his line through them, binds the servant with an oath, which entails placing his hand near the genitals, the seat of procreation.

24:10 *Aram-naharaim . . . city of Nahor*— The city of Nahor, Abraham's brother, is Haran (11:31) in the region of Mesopotamian Aram (southeastern Turkey). Abraham's family remained in Haran after he set out for Canaan.

master Abraham. ¹³ I am standing here by the spring of water, and the daughters of the townspeople are coming out to draw water. ¹⁴ Let the girl to whom I shall say, 'Please offer your jar that I may drink,' and who shall say, 'Drink, and I will water your camels'—let her be the one whom you have appointed for your servant Isaac. By this I shall know that you have shown steadfast love to my master."

15 Before he had finished speaking, there was Rebekah, who was born to Bethuel son of Milcah, the wife of Nahor, Abraham's brother, coming out with her water jar on her shoulder. ¹⁶ The girl was very fair to look upon, a virgin, whom no man had known. She went down to the spring, filled her jar, and came up. ¹⁷ Then the servant ran to meet her and said, "Please let me sip a little water from your jar." ¹⁸ "Drink, my lord," she said, and quickly lowered her jar upon her hand and gave him a drink. ¹⁹ When she had finished giving him a drink, she said, "I will draw for your camels also, until they have finished drinking." ²⁰ So she quickly emptied her jar into the trough and ran again to the well to draw, and she drew for all his camels. ²¹ The man gazed at her in silence to learn whether or not the Lord had made his journey successful.

22 When the camels had finished drinking, the man took a gold nose-ring weighing a half shekel, and two bracelets for her arms weighing ten gold shekels, ²³ and said, "Tell me whose daughter you are. Is there room in your father's house for us to spend the night?" ²⁴ She said to him, "I am the daughter of Bethuel son of Milcah, whom she bore to Nahor." ²⁵ She added, "We have plenty of straw and fodder and a place to spend the night." ²⁶ The man bowed his head and worshiped the Lord ²⁷ and said, "Blessed be the Lord, the God of my master Abraham, who has not forsaken his steadfast love and his faithfulness toward my master. As for me, the Lord has led me on the way to the house of my master's kin."

28 Then the girl ran and told her mother's household about these things. ²⁹ Rebekah had a brother whose name was Laban; and Laban ran out to the man, to the spring. ³⁰ As soon as he had seen the nose-ring, and the bracelets on his sister's arms, and when he heard the words of his sister Rebekah, "Thus the man spoke to me," he went to the man; and there he was, standing by the camels at the spring. ³¹ He said, "Come in, O blessed of the Lord. Why do you stand outside when I have prepared the house and a place for the camels?" ³² So the man came into the house; and Laban unloaded the camels, and gave him straw and fodder for the camels, and water to wash his feet and the feet of the men who were with him. ³³ Then food was set before him to eat; but he said, "I will not eat until I have told my errand." He said, "Speak on."

34 So he said, "I am Abraham's servant. ³⁵ The Lord has greatly blessed my master, and he has become wealthy; he has given him flocks and herds, silver and gold, male and female slaves, camels and donkeys. ³⁶ And Sarah my master's wife bore a son to my master when she was old; and he has given him all that he has. ³⁷ My master made me swear, saying, 'You shall not take a wife for my son from the daughters of the Canaanites, in whose land I live; ³⁸ but you shall

24:21 *The Lord had made his journey successful*—The theme of divine guidance is prominent in this story (vv. 7, 12–14, 21, 26–27, 35, 40, 42–44, 48, 50–52, 56), evident in the narrator's comments but especially in the servant's remarkable prayers. While success depends on God, it is important to note the numerous instances where human decisions and actions could further or frustrate the divine plans (e.g., vv. 8, 41).

24:29 *Laban*—Rebekah's brother, who assumes a more prominent role in this story than her father Bethuel (perhaps anticipating Laban's role in chaps. 29–31).

go to my father's house, to my kindred, and get a wife for my son.' [39] I said to my master, 'Perhaps the woman will not follow me.' [40] But he said to me, 'The LORD, before whom I walk, will send his angel with you and make your way successful. You shall get a wife for my son from my kindred, from my father's house. [41] Then you will be free from my oath, when you come to my kindred; even if they will not give her to you, you will be free from my oath.'

[42] "I came today to the spring, and said, 'O LORD, the God of my master Abraham, if now you will only make successful the way I am going! [43] I am standing here by the spring of water; let the young woman who comes out to draw, to whom I shall say, "Please give me a little water from your jar to drink," [44] and who will say to me, "Drink, and I will draw for your camels also"—let her be the woman whom the LORD has appointed for my master's son.'

[45] "Before I had finished speaking in my heart, there was Rebekah coming out with her water jar on her shoulder; and she went down to the spring, and drew. I said to her, 'Please let me drink.' [46] She quickly let down her jar from her shoulder, and said, 'Drink, and I will also water your camels.' So I drank, and she also watered the camels. [47] Then I asked her, 'Whose daughter are you?' She said, 'The daughter of Bethuel, Nahor's son, whom Milcah bore to him.' So I put the ring on her nose, and the bracelets on her arms. [48] Then I bowed my head and worshiped the LORD, and blessed the LORD, the God of my master Abraham, who had led me by the right way to obtain the daughter of my master's kinsman for his son. [49] Now then, if you will deal loyally and truly with my master, tell me; and if not, tell me, so that I may turn either to the right hand or to the left."

[50] Then Laban and Bethuel answered, "The thing comes from the LORD; we cannot speak to you anything bad or good. [51] Look, Rebekah is before you, take her and go, and let her be the wife of your master's son, as the LORD has spoken."

[52] When Abraham's servant heard their words, he bowed himself to the ground before the LORD. [53] And the servant brought out jewelry of silver and of gold, and garments, and gave them to Rebekah; he also gave to her brother and to her mother costly ornaments. [54] Then he and the men who were with him ate and drank, and they spent the night there. When they rose in the morning, he said, "Send me back to my master." [55] Her brother and her mother said, "Let the girl remain with us a while, at least ten days; after that she may go." [56] But he said to them, "Do not delay me, since the LORD has made my journey successful; let me go that I may go to my master." [57] They said, "We will call the girl, and ask her." [58] And they called Rebekah, and said to her, "Will you go with this man?" She said, "I will." [59] So they sent away their sister Rebekah and her nurse along with Abraham's servant and his men. [60] And they blessed Rebekah and said to her,

"May you, our sister, become
    thousands of myriads;
may your offspring gain possession
    of the gates of their foes."

[61] Then Rebekah and her maids rose up, mounted the camels, and followed the man; thus the servant took Rebekah, and went his way.

[62] Now Isaac had come from[a] Beer-lahai-roi, and was settled in the Negeb. [63] Isaac went out in the evening to walk[b] in the field; and looking up, he saw camels coming. [64] And Rebekah looked up, and when she saw Isaac, she slipped quickly from the camel, [65] and said to

[a] Syr Tg: Heb *from coming to* [b] Meaning of Heb word is uncertain

24:65 *It is my master*—This comment from the servant signals the transition from Abraham to Isaac. Rebekah's presence in *Sarah's tent* (v. 67) also signals this passage.

the servant, "Who is the man over there, walking in the field to meet us?" The servant said, "It is my master." So she took her veil and covered herself. ⁶⁶ And the servant told Isaac all the things that he had done. ⁶⁷ Then Isaac brought her into his mother Sarah's tent. He took Rebekah, and she became his wife; and he loved her. So Isaac was comforted after his mother's death.

Abraham Marries Keturah

25 Abraham took another wife, whose name was Keturah. ² She bore him Zimran, Jokshan, Medan, Midian, Ishbak, and Shuah. ³ Jokshan was the father of Sheba and Dedan. The sons of Dedan were Asshurim, Letushim, and Leummim. ⁴ The sons of Midian were Ephah, Epher, Hanoch, Abida, and Eldaah. All these were the children of Keturah. ⁵ Abraham gave all he had to Isaac. ⁶ But to the sons of his concubines Abraham gave gifts, while he was still living, and he sent them away from his son Isaac, eastward to the east country.

The Death of Abraham

7 This is the length of Abraham's life, one hundred seventy-five years. ⁸ Abraham breathed his last and died in a good old age, an old man and full of years, and was gathered to his people. ⁹ His sons Isaac and Ishmael buried him in the cave of Machpelah, in the field of Ephron son of Zohar the Hittite, east of Mamre, ¹⁰ the field that Abraham purchased from the Hittites. There Abraham was buried,

with his wife Sarah. ¹¹ After the death of Abraham God blessed his son Isaac. And Isaac settled at Beer-lahai-roi.

Ishmael's Descendants

12 These are the descendants of Ishmael, Abraham's son, whom Hagar the Egyptian, Sarah's slave-girl, bore to Abraham. ¹³ These are the names of the sons of Ishmael, named in the order of their birth: Nebaioth, the firstborn of Ishmael; and Kedar, Adbeel, Mibsam, ¹⁴ Mishma, Dumah, Massa, ¹⁵ Hadad, Tema, Jetur, Naphish, and Kedemah. ¹⁶ These are the sons of Ishmael and these are their names, by their villages and by their encampments, twelve princes according to their tribes. ¹⁷ (This is the length of the life of Ishmael, one hundred thirty-seven years; he breathed his last and died, and was gathered to his people.) ¹⁸ They settled from Havilah to Shur, which is opposite Egypt in the direction of Assyria; he settled down*a* alongside of*b* all his people.

The Birth and Youth of Esau and Jacob

19 These are the descendants of Isaac, Abraham's son: Abraham was the father of Isaac, ²⁰ and Isaac was forty years old when he married Rebekah, daughter of Bethuel the Aramean of Paddan-aram, sister of Laban the Aramean. ²¹ Isaac prayed to the LORD for his wife, because she was barren; and the LORD granted his prayer, and his wife Rebekah conceived. ²² The children struggled together within her; and she said, "If it

a Heb *he fell* *b* Or *down in opposition to*

25:1–18 The Death of Abraham and the Family of Ishmael

25:1–2 Keturah . . . Midian—Abraham's wife after the death of Sarah, Keturah bore Abraham six more sons, progenitors of various Arabian groups, the most prominent of which is Midian (see 37:28, 36), a progenitor of Moses' wife Zipporah (Exod. 2:15–22). As with Ishmael, these sons are sent away with appropriate gifts (Gen. 25:6), securing Isaac's line.

25:9 Isaac and Ishmael—Remarkably, Ishmael returns at the death of Abraham; he and Isaac bury their father next to Sarah.

25:12–18 The descendants of Ishmael—The many descendants of Ishmael (twelve tribes mirror the twelve tribes of Israel), progenitors of various Arabian tribal groups to the east and south of Canaan, testify to the fulfillment of God's promises, both to Hagar (17:20; 21:13, 18) and to Abraham. Ishmael too has a future that has been blessed by God.

25:19–34 Jacob and Esau

25:20 Paddan-aram—A variation of Aram-naharaim (see note at 24:10).

is to be this way, why do I live?"*a* So she went to inquire of the LORD. ²³ And the LORD said to her,

"Two nations are in your womb,
    and two peoples born of you shall be divided;
the one shall be stronger than the other,
    the elder shall serve the younger."
²⁴ When her time to give birth was at hand, there were twins in her womb. ²⁵ The first came out red, all his body like a hairy mantle; so they named him Esau. ²⁶ Afterward his brother came out, with his hand gripping Esau's heel; so he was named Jacob.*b* Isaac was sixty years old when she bore them.

27 When the boys grew up, Esau was a skillful hunter, a man of the field, while Jacob was a quiet man, living in tents. ²⁸ Isaac loved Esau, because he was fond of game; but Rebekah loved Jacob.

Esau Sells His Birthright

29 Once when Jacob was cooking a stew, Esau came in from the field, and he was famished. ³⁰ Esau said to Jacob, "Let me eat some of that red stuff, for I am famished!" (Therefore he was called Edom.*c*) ³¹ Jacob said, "First sell me your birthright." ³² Esau said, "I am about to die; of what use is a birthright to me?"

³³ Jacob said, "Swear to me first."*d* So he swore to him, and sold his birthright to Jacob. ³⁴ Then Jacob gave Esau bread and lentil stew, and he ate and drank, and rose and went his way. Thus Esau despised his birthright.

Isaac and Abimelech

26 Now there was a famine in the land, besides the former famine that had occurred in the days of Abraham. And Isaac went to Gerar, to King Abimelech of the Philistines. ² The LORD appeared to Isaac*e* and said, "Do not go down to Egypt; settle in the land that I shall show you. ³ Reside in this land as an alien, and I will be with you, and will bless you; for to you and to your descendants I will give all these lands, and I will fulfill the oath that I swore to your father Abraham. ⁴ I will make your offspring as numerous as the stars of heaven, and will give to your offspring all these lands; and all the nations of the earth shall gain blessing for themselves through your offspring, ⁵ because Abraham obeyed my voice and kept my charge, my commandments, my statutes, and my laws."

6 So Isaac settled in Gerar. ⁷ When the men of the place asked him about

---

a Syr: Meaning of Heb uncertain   *b* That is *He takes by the heel* or *He supplants*   *c* That is *Red*   *d* Heb *today*   *e* Heb *him*

25:23—The divine oracle, sought by Rebekah, *interprets* the struggle of the twins in her womb. The **two nations** reference Edom and Israel, of which Esau and Jacob are the progenitors. The divine description anticipates but does not absolutely determine their later (conflicted) relationship. The oracle establishes a certain *direction* for the future, but Rebekah's actions on behalf of Jacob are important as to what occurs. Esau is the elder and probably the **stronger** (at least initially), but he **shall serve** the weaker and the **younger**. This oracle may reflect Israel's dominance over Edom in the time of David and Solomon (2 Sam. 8:13–14), but is certainly not the case throughout their relationship (see Obadiah).

25:25–26—The Hebrew words *red* and *hairy* play on the names Edom and Seir (the Edomite region, see 33:14). The name *Jacob* plays on the Hebrew words for heel and supplant.

25:32–34 *Birthright*—Normally the right of the eldest son, it entails the leadership position in the family and inheritance rights (two-thirds, see Deut. 21:17 and NRSV footnote).

26:1–33 Stories about Isaac

26:5 *Because Abraham obeyed my voice*—God repeats the promise to Isaac twice (vv. 5, 24) because of *Abraham's* faithfulness, not his own. Through the centuries the community of faith has received God's promises because of the faith of the fathers and mothers who have come before. *My commandments . . . my laws*—These terms are usually thought to reference the law given at Sinai and hence are considered anachronistic. Yet they reinforce a claim that the law is a creational reality (e.g., 1:28; 9:2–6) and that Sinai law provides greater specification with respect to law that is already known in many cultures, including among Israel's pre-Sinai ancestors.

26:7 *She is my sister*—Isaac's experience mirrors that of Abraham; see 12:10–20; 20:1–18.

his wife, he said, "She is my sister"; for he was afraid to say, "My wife," thinking, "or else the men of the place might kill me for the sake of Rebekah, because she is attractive in appearance." [8] When Isaac had been there a long time, King Abimelech of the Philistines looked out of a window and saw him fondling his wife Rebekah. [9] So Abimelech called for Isaac, and said, "So she is your wife! Why then did you say, 'She is my sister'?" Isaac said to him, "Because I thought I might die because of her." [10] Abimelech said, "What is this you have done to us? One of the people might easily have lain with your wife, and you would have brought guilt upon us." [11] So Abimelech warned all the people, saying, "Whoever touches this man or his wife shall be put to death."

[12] Isaac sowed seed in that land, and in the same year reaped a hundredfold. The LORD blessed him, [13] and the man became rich; he prospered more and more until he became very wealthy. [14] He had possessions of flocks and herds, and a great household, so that the Philistines envied him. [15] (Now the Philistines had stopped up and filled with earth all the wells that his father's servants had dug in the days of his father Abraham.) [16] And Abimelech said to Isaac, "Go away from us; you have become too powerful for us."

[17] So Isaac departed from there and camped in the valley of Gerar and settled there. [18] Isaac dug again the wells of water that had been dug in the days of his father Abraham; for the Philistines had stopped them up after the death of Abraham; and he gave them the names that his father had given them. [19] But when Isaac's servants dug in the valley and found there a well of spring water, [20] the herders of Gerar quarreled with Isaac's herders, saying, "The water is ours." So he called the well Esek,[a] because they contended with him. [21] Then they dug another well, and they quarreled over that one also; so he called it Sitnah.[b] [22] He moved from there and dug another well, and they did not quarrel over it; so he called it Rehoboth,[c] saying, "Now the LORD has made room for us, and we shall be fruitful in the land."

23 From there he went up to Beersheba. [24] And that very night the LORD appeared to him and said, "I am the God of your father Abraham; do not be afraid, for I am with you and will bless you and make your offspring numerous for my servant Abraham's sake." [25] So he built an altar there, called on the name of the LORD, and pitched his tent there. And there Isaac's servants dug a well.

26 Then Abimelech went to him from Gerar, with Ahuzzath his adviser and Phicol the commander of his army. [27] Isaac said to them, "Why have you come to me, seeing that you hate me and have sent me away from you?" [28] They said, "We see plainly that the LORD has been with you; so we say, let there be an oath between you and us, and let us make a covenant with you [29] so that you will do us no harm, just as we have not touched you and have done to you nothing but good and have sent you away in peace. You are now the blessed of the LORD." [30] So he made them a feast, and they ate and drank. [31] In the morning they rose early and exchanged oaths; and Isaac set them on their way, and they departed from him in peace. [32] That same day Isaac's servants came and told him about

a That is Contention b That is Enmity c That is Broad places or Room

---

26:8 *Abimelech . . . Philistines*—Probably the same person (and people) as in 20:1–18; 21:22–34.

26:12–33—This narrative about Isaac's disputes with Abimelech regarding land mirrors that of Abraham in 21:22–34, including the establishing of peaceful relationships with a nonchosen

people and the naming of Beer-sheba. Isaac/Israel is portrayed as an instrument of peace.

26:24 *The God of your father*—The first mention of this personal epithet now becomes common in specifying the singularity of this deity and the continuity of God's promise across the generations (e.g., 28:13).

the well that they had dug, and said to him, "We have found water!" [33] He called it Shibah;[a] therefore the name of the city is Beer-sheba[b] to this day.

Esau's Hittite Wives

34 When Esau was forty years old, he married Judith daughter of Beeri the Hittite, and Basemath daughter of Elon the Hittite; [35] and they made life bitter for Isaac and Rebekah.

Isaac Blesses Jacob

27 When Isaac was old and his eyes were dim so that he could not see, he called his elder son Esau and said to him, "My son"; and he answered, "Here I am." [2] He said, "See, I am old; I do not know the day of my death. [3] Now then, take your weapons, your quiver and your bow, and go out to the field, and hunt game for me. [4] Then prepare for me savory food, such as I like, and bring it to me to eat, so that I may bless you before I die."

5 Now Rebekah was listening when Isaac spoke to his son Esau. So when Esau went to the field to hunt for game and bring it, [6] Rebekah said to her son Jacob, "I heard your father say to your brother Esau, [7] 'Bring me game, and prepare for me savory food to eat, that I may bless you before the LORD before I die.' [8] Now therefore, my son, obey my word as I command you. [9] Go to the flock, and get me two choice kids, so that I may prepare from them savory food for your father, such as he likes; [10] and you shall take it to your father to eat, so that he may bless you before he dies." [11] But Jacob said to his mother Rebekah, "Look, my brother Esau is a hairy man, and I am a man of smooth skin. [12] Perhaps my father will feel me,

and I shall seem to be mocking him, and bring a curse on myself and not a blessing." [13] His mother said to him, "Let your curse be on me, my son; only obey my word, and go, get them for me." [14] So he went and got them and brought them to his mother; and his mother prepared savory food, such as his father loved. [15] Then Rebekah took the best garments of her elder son Esau, which were with her in the house, and put them on her younger son Jacob; [16] and she put the skins of the kids on his hands and on the smooth part of his neck. [17] Then she handed the savory food, and the bread that she had prepared, to her son Jacob.

18 So he went in to his father, and said, "My father"; and he said, "Here I am; who are you, my son?" [19] Jacob said to his father, "I am Esau your firstborn. I have done as you told me; now sit up and eat of my game, so that you may bless me." [20] But Isaac said to his son, "How is it that you have found it so quickly, my son?" He answered, "Because the LORD your God granted me success." [21] Then Isaac said to Jacob, "Come near, that I may feel you, my son, to know whether you are really my son Esau or not." [22] So Jacob went up to his father Isaac, who felt him and said, "The voice is Jacob's voice, but the hands are the hands of Esau." [23] He did not recognize him, because his hands were hairy like his brother Esau's hands; so he blessed him. [24] He said, "Are you really my son Esau?" He answered, "I am." [25] Then he said, "Bring it to me, that I may eat of my son's game and bless you." So he brought it to him, and he ate; and he brought him wine, and he drank. [26] Then his father Isaac said to him, "Come near and kiss me, my son."

[a] A word resembling the word for *oath*   [b] That is *Well of the oath* or *Well of seven*

26:34–28:9 Jacob, Esau, and the Blessing

26:34–35; 27:46 *Hittite*—Also called Canaanite in 28:1, 6–8; see chap. 23.

27:4 *That I may bless you before I die*—This personal blessing of the father to the son is a departure blessing; it is not the birthright (see

v. 36), nor is it to be equated with "the blessing of Abraham" (28:4), which is the constitutive or community-creating blessing for this family. *God* gave the latter to Isaac (26:3–4, 24), and Isaac cannot give it to Jacob; he can only *commend* Jacob to God (which he does in 28:3–4).

[27] So he came near and kissed him; and he smelled the smell of his garments, and blessed him, and said,

"Ah, the smell of my son
    is like the smell of a field that the
    LORD has blessed.
[28] May God give you of the dew of
        heaven,
    and of the fatness of the earth,
    and plenty of grain and wine.
[29] Let peoples serve you,
    and nations bow down to you.
Be lord over your brothers,
    and may your mother's sons bow
        down to you.
Cursed be everyone who curses you,
    and blessed be everyone who
        blesses you!"

Esau's Lost Blessing

30 As soon as Isaac had finished blessing Jacob, when Jacob had scarcely gone out from the presence of his father Isaac, his brother Esau came in from his hunting. [31] He also prepared savory food, and brought it to his father. And he said to his father, "Let my father sit up and eat of his son's game, so that you may bless me." [32] His father Isaac said to him, "Who are you?" He answered, "I am your firstborn son, Esau." [33] Then Isaac trembled violently, and said, "Who was it then that hunted game and brought it to me, and I ate it all[a] before you came, and I have blessed him?—yes, and blessed he shall be!" [34] When Esau heard his father's words, he cried out with an exceedingly great and bitter cry, and said to his father, "Bless me, me also, father!" [35] But he said, "Your brother came deceitfully, and he has taken away your blessing." [36] Esau said, "Is he not rightly named Jacob?[b] For he

has supplanted me these two times. He took away my birthright; and look, now he has taken away my blessing." Then he said, "Have you not reserved a blessing for me?" [37] Isaac answered Esau, "I have already made him your lord, and I have given him all his brothers as servants, and with grain and wine I have sustained him. What then can I do for you, my son?" [38] Esau said to his father, "Have you only one blessing, father? Bless me, me also, father!" And Esau lifted up his voice and wept.

39 Then his father Isaac answered him:

"See, away from[c] the fatness of the
        earth shall your home be,
    and away from[d] the dew of heaven
        on high.
[40] By your sword you shall live,
    and you shall serve your brother;
but when you break loose,[e]
    you shall break his yoke from your
        neck."

Jacob Escapes Esau's Fury

41 Now Esau hated Jacob because of the blessing with which his father had blessed him, and Esau said to himself, "The days of mourning for my father are approaching; then I will kill my brother Jacob." [42] But the words of her elder son Esau were told to Rebekah; so she sent and called her younger son Jacob and said to him, "Your brother Esau is consoling himself by planning to kill you. [43] Now therefore, my son, obey my voice; flee at once to my brother Laban in Haran, [44] and stay with him a while, until your brother's fury turns away— [45] until your brother's anger against you

a Cn: Heb of all b That is He supplants or He takes by the heel c Or See, of
d Or and of e Meaning of Heb uncertain

27:27–29—Isaac's blessing of Jacob centers on fertility of the land and dominion (note the lack of reference to progeny and land; cf. 28:4).

27:35–38—It is sometimes thought that Isaac's (or any) *blessing*, once given, could not be retracted. That is not the case. Isaac was so certain in what he had done that retraction was out of the question. Note that the curse could be transferred (v. 13).

27:39–40—Isaac responds to Esau's pleas with a secondary blessing (it is not clear how positive it is; note the footnotes to v. 39 in NRSV). At the least, this blessing qualifies the blessing given to Jacob. Jacob may be *lord over* his brother (v. 29), but at times Esau will *break loose* (v. 40).

turns away, and he forgets what you have done to him; then I will send, and bring you back from there. Why should I lose both of you in one day?"

46 Then Rebekah said to Isaac, "I am weary of my life because of the Hittite women. If Jacob marries one of the Hittite women such as these, one of the women of the land, what good will my life be to me?"

28 Then Isaac called Jacob and blessed him, and charged him, "You shall not marry one of the Canaanite women. ² Go at once to Paddan-aram to the house of Bethuel, your mother's father; and take as wife from there one of the daughters of Laban, your mother's brother. ³ May God Almighty*a* bless you and make you fruitful and numerous, that you may become a company of peoples. ⁴ May he give to you the blessing of Abraham, to you and to your offspring with you, so that you may take possession of the land where you now live as an alien—land that God gave to Abraham." ⁵ Thus Isaac sent Jacob away; and he went to Paddan-aram, to Laban son of Bethuel the Aramean, the brother of Rebekah, Jacob's and Esau's mother.

Esau Marries Ishmael's Daughter

6 Now Esau saw that Isaac had blessed Jacob and sent him away to Paddan-aram to take a wife from there, and that as he blessed him he charged him, "You shall not marry one of the Canaanite women," ⁷ and that Jacob had obeyed his father and his mother and gone to Paddan-aram. ⁸ So when Esau saw that the Canaanite women did not please his father Isaac, ⁹ Esau went to Ishmael and took Mahalath daughter of Abraham's son Ishmael, and sister of Nebaioth, to be his wife in addition to the wives he had.

Jacob's Dream at Bethel

10 Jacob left Beer-sheba and went toward Haran. ¹¹ He came to a certain place and stayed there for the night, because the sun had set. Taking one of the stones of the place, he put it under his head and lay down in that place. ¹² And he dreamed that there was a ladder*b* set up on the earth, the top of it reaching to heaven; and the angels of God were ascending and descending on it. ¹³ And the Lord stood beside him*c* and said, "I am the Lord, the God of Abraham your father and the God of Isaac; the land on which you lie I will give to you and to your offspring; ¹⁴ and your offspring shall be like the dust of the earth, and you shall spread abroad to the west and to the east and to the north and to the south; and all the families of the earth shall be blessed*d* in you and in your offspring. ¹⁵ Know that I am with you and will keep you wherever you go, and will bring you back to this land; for I will not leave you until I have done what I have promised you." ¹⁶ Then Jacob woke from his sleep and said, "Surely the Lord is in this place—and I did not know it!" ¹⁷ And he was afraid, and said, "How awesome is this place! This is none other than the house of God, and this is the gate of heaven."

a Traditional rendering of Heb *El Shaddai*   *b* Or *stairway* or *ramp*
c Or *stood above it*   *d* Or *shall bless themselves*

28:4 *The blessing of Abraham*—See note at 27:4.

28:10–22 Jacob's Dream at Bethel

28:12 *A ladder* (NRSV footnote: *stairway*)—This feature of temples in that world linked the earthly world to the abode of the gods at the top of the tower; priests mediated between the two worlds by the stairway. This text challenges that ritual world by claiming God's very presence with Jacob without the need of intermediaries. On dreams, see note at 20:3.

28:13–15—A remarkable series of eight promises, four of them standing in line with the "blessing of Abraham" (vv. 13–14; see v. 4); the other four are personal promises associated with his journey (v. 15).

28:17 *House of God*—A play on the Hebrew word "Bethel," later the name of an important city north of Jerusalem (v. 19). Jacob poured oil on the stone in order to stain it for later ease in recognizing the place where God appeared (see v. 22; 35:1).

18 So Jacob rose early in the morning, and he took the stone that he had put under his head and set it up for a pillar and poured oil on the top of it. ¹⁹ He called that place Bethel;ᵃ but the name of the city was Luz at the first. ²⁰ Then Jacob made a vow, saying, "If God will be with me, and will keep me in this way that I go, and will give me bread to eat and clothing to wear, ²¹ so that I come again to my father's house in peace, then the Lᴏʀᴅ shall be my God, ²² and this stone, which I have set up for a pillar, shall be God's house; and of all that you give me I will surely give one-tenth to you."

Jacob Meets Rachel

29 Then Jacob went on his journey, and came to the land of the people of the east. ² As he looked, he saw a well in the field and three flocks of sheep lying there beside it; for out of that well the flocks were watered. The stone on the well's mouth was large, ³ and when all the flocks were gathered there, the shepherds would roll the stone from the mouth of the well, and water the sheep, and put the stone back in its place on the mouth of the well.

4 Jacob said to them, "My brothers, where do you come from?" They said, "We are from Haran." ⁵ He said to them, "Do you know Laban son of Nahor?" They said, "We do." ⁶ He said to them, "Is it well with him?" "Yes," they replied, "and here is his daughter Rachel, coming with the sheep." ⁷ He said, "Look, it is still broad daylight; it is not time for the animals to be gathered together. Water the sheep, and go, pasture them." ⁸ But they said, "We cannot until all the flocks are gathered together, and the stone is rolled from the mouth of the well; then we water the sheep."

9 While he was still speaking with them, Rachel came with her father's sheep; for she kept them. ¹⁰ Now when Jacob saw Rachel, the daughter of his mother's brother Laban, and the sheep of his mother's brother Laban, Jacob went up and rolled the stone from the well's mouth, and watered the flock of his mother's brother Laban. ¹¹ Then Jacob kissed Rachel, and wept aloud. ¹² And Jacob told Rachel that he was her father's kinsman, and that he was Rebekah's son; and she ran and told her father.

13 When Laban heard the news about his sister's son Jacob, he ran to meet him; he embraced him and kissed him, and brought him to his house. Jacobᵇ told Laban all these things, ¹⁴ and Laban said to him, "Surely you are my bone and my flesh!" And he stayed with him a month.

Jacob Marries Laban's Daughters

15 Then Laban said to Jacob, "Because you are my kinsman, should you therefore serve me for nothing? Tell me, what shall your wages be?" ¹⁶ Now Laban had two daughters; the name of the elder was Leah, and the name of the younger was Rachel. ¹⁷ Leah's eyes were lovely,ᶜ and Rachel was graceful and beautiful. ¹⁸ Jacob loved Rachel; so he said, "I will serve you seven years for your younger daughter Rachel." ¹⁹ Laban said, "It is better that I give her to you than that I should give her to any other man; stay with me." ²⁰ So Jacob served seven years for Rachel, and they seemed to him but a few days because of the love he had for her.

21 Then Jacob said to Laban, "Give me my wife that I may go in to her, for my time is completed." ²² So Laban gathered together all the people of the place, and made a feast. ²³ But in the evening he took his daughter Leah and

---

ᵃ That is House of God   ᵇ Heb He   ᶜ Meaning of Heb uncertain

---

28:20–22—Jacob's vow should not be interpreted as a bargaining theology, but holding God accountable for promises made.

29:1–31:55 The Birth of Jacob's Children
29:1 *People of the east*—People from the desert regions northeast of Canaan (see 25:6).

brought her to Jacob; and he went in to her. **24** (Laban gave his maid Zilpah to his daughter Leah to be her maid.) **25** When morning came, it was Leah! And Jacob said to Laban, "What is this you have done to me? Did I not serve with you for Rachel? Why then have you deceived me?" **26** Laban said, "This is not done in our country—giving the younger before the firstborn. **27** Complete the week of this one, and we will give you the other also in return for serving me another seven years." **28** Jacob did so, and completed her week; then Laban gave him his daughter Rachel as a wife. **29** (Laban gave his maid Bilhah to his daughter Rachel to be her maid.) **30** So Jacob went in to Rachel also, and he loved Rachel more than Leah. He served Laban*a* for another seven years.

31 When the LORD saw that Leah was unloved, he opened her womb; but Rachel was barren. **32** Leah conceived and bore a son, and she named him Reuben;*b* for she said, "Because the LORD has looked on my affliction; surely now my husband will love me." **33** She conceived again and bore a son, and said, "Because the LORD has heard*c* that I am hated, he has given me this son also"; and she named him Simeon. **34** Again she conceived and bore a son, and said, "Now this time my husband will be joined*d* to me, because I have borne him three sons"; therefore he was named Levi. **35** She conceived again and bore a son, and said, "This time I will praise*e* the LORD"; therefore she named him Judah; then she ceased bearing.

30 When Rachel saw that she bore Jacob no children, she envied her sister; and she said to Jacob, "Give me children, or I shall die!" **2** Jacob became very angry with Rachel and said, "Am I in the place of God, who has withheld from you the fruit of the womb?" **3** Then she said, "Here is my maid Bilhah; go in to her, that she may bear upon my knees and that I too may have children through her." **4** So she gave him her maid Bilhah as a wife; and Jacob went in to her. **5** And Bilhah conceived and bore Jacob a son. **6** Then Rachel said, "God has judged me, and has also heard my voice and given me a son"; therefore she named him Dan.*f* **7** Rachel's maid Bilhah conceived again and bore Jacob a second son. **8** Then Rachel said, "With mighty wrestlings I have wrestled*g* with my sister, and have prevailed"; so she named him Naphtali.

9 When Leah saw that she had ceased bearing children, she took her maid Zilpah and gave her to Jacob as a wife. **10** Then Leah's maid Zilpah bore Jacob a son. **11** And Leah said, "Good fortune!" so she named him Gad.*h* **12** Leah's maid Zilpah bore Jacob a second son. **13** And Leah said, "Happy am I! For the women will call me happy"; so she named him Asher.*i*

14 In the days of wheat harvest Reuben went and found mandrakes in the field, and brought them to his mother Leah. Then Rachel said to Leah, "Please give me some of your son's mandrakes." **15** But she said to her, "Is it a small matter that you have taken away my husband? Would you take away my son's mandrakes also?" Rachel said, "Then he may lie with you tonight for your son's mandrakes." **16** When Jacob came from the field in the evening, Leah went out to meet him, and said, "You must come

a Heb *him* *b* That is *See, a son* *c* Heb *shama* *d* Heb *lawah* *e* Heb *hodah*
f That is *He judged* *g* Heb *niphtal* *h* That is *Fortune* *i* That is *Happy*

29:31–30:24—These verses constitute the heart of this long narrative, shown not least by the pervasive God-talk; they describe the births of twelve of Jacob's thirteen children (except Benjamin, 35:18). Leah and Rachel name their children (and the children of their slave-girls) in terms of their own experience, which includes no little theological reflection (see the wordplays in NRSV footnotes). Note that the only daughter (Dinah, v. 21) is given the briefest of notices (see chap. 34).

30:14–16 *Mandrakes*—An herb thought to promote fertility. For all the mothers' God-talk, they think that nondivine action is important.

in to me; for I have hired you with my son's mandrakes." So he lay with her that night. ¹⁷ And God heeded Leah, and she conceived and bore Jacob a fifth son. ¹⁸ Leah said, "God has given me my hire *a* because I gave my maid to my husband"; so she named him Issachar. ¹⁹ And Leah conceived again, and she bore Jacob a sixth son. ²⁰ Then Leah said, "God has endowed me with a good dowry; now my husband will honor *b* me, because I have borne him six sons"; so she named him Zebulun. ²¹ Afterwards she bore a daughter, and named her Dinah.

22 Then God remembered Rachel, and God heeded her and opened her womb. ²³ She conceived and bore a son, and said, "God has taken away my reproach"; ²⁴ and she named him Joseph, *c* saying, "May the Lord add to me another son!"

Jacob Prospers at Laban's Expense

25 When Rachel had borne Joseph, Jacob said to Laban, "Send me away, that I may go to my own home and country. ²⁶ Give me my wives and my children for whom I have served you, and let me go; for you know very well the service I have given you." ²⁷ But Laban said to him, "If you will allow me to say so, I have learned by divination that the LORD has blessed me because of you; ²⁸ name your wages, and I will give it." ²⁹ Jacob said to him, "You yourself know how I have served you, and how your cattle have fared with me. ³⁰ For you had little before I came, and it has increased abundantly; and the LORD has blessed you wherever I turned. But now when shall I provide for my own household also?" ³¹ He said, "What shall I give you?" Jacob said, "You shall not give me anything; if you will do this for me, I will again feed your flock and keep it: ³² let me pass through all your flock

today, removing from it every speckled and spotted sheep and every black lamb, and the spotted and speckled among the goats; and such shall be my wages. ³³ So my honesty will answer for me later, when you come to look into my wages with you. Every one that is not speckled and spotted among the goats and black among the lambs, if found with me, shall be counted stolen." ³⁴ Laban said, "Good! Let it be as you have said." ³⁵ But that day Laban removed the male goats that were striped and spotted, and all the female goats that were speckled and spotted, every one that had white on it, and every lamb that was black, and put them in charge of his sons; ³⁶ and he set a distance of three days' journey between himself and Jacob, while Jacob was pasturing the rest of Laban's flock.

37 Then Jacob took fresh rods of poplar and almond and plane, and peeled white streaks in them, exposing the white of the rods. ³⁸ He set the rods that he had peeled in front of the flocks in the troughs, that is, the watering places, where the flocks came to drink. And since they bred when they came to drink, ³⁹ the flocks bred in front of the rods, and so the flocks produced young that were striped, speckled, and spotted. ⁴⁰ Jacob separated the lambs, and set the faces of the flocks toward the striped and the completely black animals in the flock of Laban; and he put his own droves apart, and did not put them with Laban's flock. ⁴¹ Whenever the stronger of the flock were breeding, Jacob laid the rods in the troughs before the eyes of the flock, that they might breed among the rods, ⁴² but for the feebler of the flock he did not lay them there; so the feebler were Laban's, and the stronger Jacob's. ⁴³ Thus the man grew exceedingly rich, and had large

a Heb *sakar* *b* Heb *zabal* *c* That is He adds

30:27 *Divination*—A method of (supposedly) discerning information regarding the divine realm, through many devices (e.g., examination of entrails), condemned in the Old Testament (see 2 Kgs. 21:6).

30:37–42—Jacob's strategy (divinely suggested, 31:7–12) assumes that what the animals see during mating determines the coloration of their offspring. The net effect is that Jacob's animals are stronger than Laban's.

flocks, and male and female slaves, and camels and donkeys.

Jacob Flees with Family and Flocks

31 Now Jacob heard that the sons of Laban were saying, "Jacob has taken all that was our father's; he has gained all this wealth from what belonged to our father." ²And Jacob saw that Laban did not regard him as favorably as he did before. ³Then the LORD said to Jacob, "Return to the land of your ancestors and to your kindred, and I will be with you." ⁴So Jacob sent and called Rachel and Leah into the field where his flock was, ⁵and said to them, "I see that your father does not regard me as favorably as he did before. But the God of my father has been with me. ⁶You know that I have served your father with all my strength; ⁷yet your father has cheated me and changed my wages ten times, but God did not permit him to harm me. ⁸If he said, 'The speckled shall be your wages,' then all the flock bore speckled; and if he said, 'The striped shall be your wages,' then all the flock bore striped. ⁹Thus God has taken away the livestock of your father, and given them to me.

10 "During the mating of the flock I once had a dream in which I looked up and saw that the male goats that leaped upon the flock were striped, speckled, and mottled. ¹¹Then the angel of God said to me in the dream, 'Jacob,' and I said, 'Here I am!' ¹²And he said, 'Look up and see that all the goats that leap on the flock are striped, speckled, and mottled; for I have seen all that Laban is doing to you. ¹³I am the God of Bethel,ᵃ where you anointed a pillar and made a vow to me. Now leave this land at once and return to the land of your birth.'" ¹⁴Then Rachel and Leah answered him,

"Is there any portion or inheritance left to us in our father's house? ¹⁵Are we not regarded by him as foreigners? For he has sold us, and he has been using up the money given for us. ¹⁶All the property that God has taken away from our father belongs to us and to our children; now then, do whatever God has said to you."

17 So Jacob arose, and set his children and his wives on camels; ¹⁸and he drove away all his livestock, all the property that he had gained, the livestock in his possession that he had acquired in Paddan-aram, to go to his father Isaac in the land of Canaan.

19 Now Laban had gone to shear his sheep, and Rachel stole her father's household gods. ²⁰And Jacob deceived Laban the Aramean, in that he did not tell him that he intended to flee. ²¹So he fled with all that he had; starting out he crossed the Euphrates,ᵇ and set his face toward the hill country of Gilead.

Laban Overtakes Jacob

22 On the third day Laban was told that Jacob had fled. ²³So he took his kinsfolk with him and pursued him for seven days until he caught up with him in the hill country of Gilead. ²⁴But God came to Laban the Aramean in a dream by night, and said to him, "Take heed that you say not a word to Jacob, either good or bad."

25 Laban overtook Jacob. Now Jacob had pitched his tent in the hill country, and Laban with his kinsfolk camped in the hill country of Gilead. ²⁶Laban said to Jacob, "What have you done? You have deceived me, and carried away my daughters like captives of the sword. ²⁷Why did you flee secretly and deceive me and not tell me? I would have sent

---

ᵃ Cn: Meaning of Heb uncertain ᵇ Heb *the river*

31:14–15—This strong, public stand on the part of Jacob's wives against the abuse they had suffered from their father is remarkable.

31:19 *Household gods*—Small human-shaped figurines (common in that world) that were

symbols of Laban's authority in the household, perhaps tokens of inheritance rights.

31:21 *Gilead*—A region on the northeast edge of Canaan.

you away with mirth and songs, with tambourine and lyre. ²⁸ And why did you not permit me to kiss my sons and my daughters farewell? What you have done is foolish. ²⁹ It is in my power to do you harm; but the God of your father spoke to me last night, saying, 'Take heed that you speak to Jacob neither good nor bad.' ³⁰ Even though you had to go because you longed greatly for your father's house, why did you steal my gods?" ³¹ Jacob answered Laban, "Because I was afraid, for I thought that you would take your daughters from me by force. ³² But anyone with whom you find your gods shall not live. In the presence of our kinsfolk, point out what I have that is yours, and take it." Now Jacob did not know that Rachel had stolen the gods. ^a

33 So Laban went into Jacob's tent, and into Leah's tent, and into the tent of the two maids, but he did not find them. And he went out of Leah's tent, and entered Rachel's. ³⁴ Now Rachel had taken the household gods and put them in the camel's saddle, and sat on them. Laban felt all about in the tent, but did not find them. ³⁵ And she said to her father, "Let not my lord be angry that I cannot rise before you, for the way of women is upon me." So he searched, but did not find the household gods.

36 Then Jacob became angry, and upbraided Laban. Jacob said to Laban, "What is my offense? What is my sin, that you have hotly pursued me? ³⁷ Although you have felt about through all my goods, what have you found of all your household goods? Set it here before my kinsfolk and your kinsfolk, so that they may decide between us two. ³⁸ These twenty years I have been with

you; your ewes and your female goats have not miscarried, and I have not eaten the rams of your flocks. ³⁹ That which was torn by wild beasts I did not bring to you; I bore the loss of it myself; of my hand you required it, whether stolen by day or stolen by night. ⁴⁰ It was like this with me: by day the heat consumed me, and the cold by night, and my sleep fled from my eyes. ⁴¹ These twenty years I have been in your house; I served you fourteen years for your two daughters, and six years for your flock, and you have changed my wages ten times. ⁴² If the God of my father, the God of Abraham and the Fear ^b of Isaac, had not been on my side, surely now you would have sent me away empty-handed. God saw my affliction and the labor of my hands, and rebuked you last night."

Laban and Jacob Make a Covenant

43 Then Laban answered and said to Jacob, "The daughters are my daughters, the children are my children, the flocks are my flocks, and all that you see is mine. But what can I do today about these daughters of mine, or about their children whom they have borne? ⁴⁴ Come now, let us make a covenant, you and I; and let it be a witness between you and me." ⁴⁵ So Jacob took a stone, and set it up as a pillar. ⁴⁶ And Jacob said to his kinsfolk, "Gather stones," and they took stones, and made a heap; and they ate there by the heap. ⁴⁷ Laban called it Jegar-sahadutha: ^c but Jacob called it Galeed. ^d ⁴⁸ Laban said, "This heap is a witness between you and me today." Therefore he called it Galeed, ⁴⁹ and the pillar ^e Mizpah, ^f for he said, "The LORD

^a Heb them   ^b Meaning of Heb uncertain   ^c In Aramaic The heap of witness   ^d In Hebrew The heap of witness   ^e Compare Sam: MT lacks the pillar   ^f That is Watchpost

---

31:35 *The way of women*—Her menstrual period.

31:42, 53 *The Fear of Isaac*—An uncertain translation of an epithet for the God of Isaac (perhaps "Kinsman").

31:47 *Galeed*—Probably a variation of Gilead (see v. 21).

31:49 *Mizpah*—The site in Gilead of the covenant between Jacob and Laban ("Mizpah Benediction"—that God keep Jacob honest when Laban was not around to do so!).

watch between you and me, when we are absent one from the other. ⁵⁰ If you ill-treat my daughters, or if you take wives in addition to my daughters, though no one else is with us, remember that God is witness between you and me."

51 Then Laban said to Jacob, "See this heap and see the pillar, which I have set between you and me. ⁵² This heap is a witness, and the pillar is a witness, that I will not pass beyond this heap to you, and you will not pass beyond this heap and this pillar to me, for harm. ⁵³ May the God of Abraham and the God of Nahor"—the God of their father—"judge between us." So Jacob swore by the Fear*ᵃ* of his father Isaac, ⁵⁴ and Jacob offered a sacrifice on the height and called his kinsfolk to eat bread; and they ate bread and tarried all night in the hill country.

55*ᵇ* Early in the morning Laban rose up, and kissed his grandchildren and his daughters and blessed them; then he departed and returned home.

32 Jacob went on his way and the angels of God met him; ² and when Jacob saw them he said, "This is God's camp!" So he called that place Mahanaim.*ᶜ*

Jacob Sends Presents to Appease Esau

3 Jacob sent messengers before him to his brother Esau in the land of Seir, the country of Edom, ⁴ instructing them, "Thus you shall say to my lord Esau: Thus says your servant Jacob, 'I have lived with Laban as an alien, and stayed until now; ⁵ and I have oxen, donkeys, flocks, male and female slaves; and I have sent to tell my lord, in order that I may find favor in your sight.'"

6 The messengers returned to Jacob, saying, "We came to your brother Esau, and he is coming to meet you, and four hundred men are with him." ⁷ Then Jacob was greatly afraid and distressed; and he divided the people that were with him, and the flocks and herds and camels, into two companies, ⁸ thinking, "If Esau comes to the one company and destroys it, then the company that is left will escape."

9 And Jacob said, "O God of my father Abraham and God of my father Isaac, O Lᴏʀᴅ who said to me, 'Return to your country and to your kindred, and I will do you good,' ¹⁰ I am not worthy of the least of all the steadfast love and all the faithfulness that you have shown to your servant, for with only my staff I crossed this Jordan; and now I have become two companies. ¹¹ Deliver me, please, from the hand of my brother, from the hand of Esau, for I am afraid of him; he may come and kill us all, the mothers with the children. ¹² Yet you have said, 'I will surely do you good, and make your offspring as the sand of the sea, which cannot be counted because of their number.'"

13 So he spent that night there, and from what he had with him he took a present for his brother Esau, ¹⁴ two hundred female goats and twenty male goats, two hundred ewes and twenty rams, ¹⁵ thirty milch camels and their colts, forty cows and ten bulls, twenty female donkeys and ten male donkeys. ¹⁶ These he delivered into the hand of his servants, every drove by itself, and said to his servants, "Pass on ahead of

---

ᵃ Meaning of Heb uncertain   *ᵇ* Ch 32.1 in Heb   *ᶜ* Here taken to mean *Two camps*

32:1–21 Jacob Prepares to Meet Esau

32:1 *Angels of God*—The Hebrew word is the same as the word for *messenger* in v. 3. Jacob *saw them* (v. 2), that is, human figures (see 18:2; 19:1) that he interprets as God's messengers accompanying him on his journey (for their protective function, see Ps. 34:7).

32:2 *Mahanaim*—The word means "two camps";

its location is uncertain. It may refer to two camps of angels; their presence anticipates the dividing of Jacob's retinue into two camps to prepare to meet Esau, one camp of angels for each of his companies (vv. 7, 10).

32:9–12—Jacob's prayer has been interpreted as manipulative, but it need not be so; he claims God's earlier promises to him (28:13–15).

me, and put a space between drove and drove." [17] He instructed the foremost, "When Esau my brother meets you, and asks you, 'To whom do you belong? Where are you going? And whose are these ahead of you?' [18] then you shall say, 'They belong to your servant Jacob; they are a present sent to my lord Esau; and moreover he is behind us.' " [19] He likewise instructed the second and the third and all who followed the droves, "You shall say the same thing to Esau when you meet him, [20] and you shall say, 'Moreover your servant Jacob is behind us.' " For he thought, "I may appease him with the present that goes ahead of me, and afterwards I shall see his face; perhaps he will accept me." [21] So the present passed on ahead of him; and he himself spent that night in the camp.

Jacob Wrestles at Peniel

22 The same night he got up and took his two wives, his two maids, and his eleven children, and crossed the ford of the Jabbok. [23] He took them and sent them across the stream, and likewise everything that he had. [24] Jacob was left alone; and a man wrestled with him until daybreak. [25] When the man saw that he did not prevail against Jacob, he struck him on the hip socket; and Jacob's hip was put out of joint as he wrestled with him. [26] Then he said, "Let me go, for the day is breaking." But Jacob said, "I will not let you go, unless you bless me." [27] So he said to him, "What is your name?" And he said, "Jacob." [28] Then the man[a] said, "You shall no longer be called Jacob, but Israel,[b] for you have striven with God and with humans,[c] and have prevailed." [29] Then Jacob asked him, "Please tell me your name." But he said, "Why is it that you ask my name?" And there he blessed him. [30] So Jacob called the place Peniel,[d] saying, "For I have seen God face to face, and yet my life is preserved." [31] The sun rose upon him as he passed Penuel, limping because of his hip. [32] Therefore to this day the Israelites do not eat the thigh muscle that is on the hip socket, because he struck Jacob on the hip socket at the thigh muscle.

Jacob and Esau Meet

33 Now Jacob looked up and saw Esau coming, and four hundred men with him. So he divided the children among Leah and Rachel and the two maids. [2] He put the maids with their children in front, then Leah with her children, and Rachel and Joseph last of all. [3] He himself went on ahead of them,

---

[a] Heb *he*   [b] That is *The one who strives with God* or *God strives*   [c] Or *with divine and human beings*   [d] That is *The face of God*

32:18–20—Jacob's referring to himself as *servant* and Esau as *lord* reverses earlier claims (25:23; 27:29) in the interests of reconciliation (continued in chap. 33).

32:22–33 Jacob Wrestles with God

32:22 *Jabbok*—An eastern tributary of the Jordan river. Jacob was at or near the border of the promised land. The word is a play on Jacob and the Hebrew word for "wrestle."

32:24 *A man wrestled with him*—Probably God appearing in human form (see 16:7), as suggested by both God (32:28) and Jacob (v. 30; see Hos. 12:3–4). As such, the *physical* wrestling is no game for either participant; it is a genuine match during which the man strikes Jacob and Jacob holds on to the man (Gen. 32:25–26). The concern about the dawn pertains to the issue of Jacob seeing God (v. 30). It is not clear why God initiates the wrestling, but the new name suggests a concern for shaping and sharpening Jacob for what lies ahead (see 33:10). Intense wrestling will be characteristic of Israel's life with God through the centuries (e.g., see the lament psalms).

32:28 *Israel*—God gives this name, probably meaning "one who strives with God," to the progenitor of the twelve tribes as a sign of his *success* (see 35:10 for another version).

32:30–31 *Peniel/Penuel*—Meaning "the face of God," these are variants of the name Jacob gives to the place, in view of his experience of having seen God and remaining alive (see 16:13; Exod. 33:20).

33:1–17 Jacob's Meeting with Esau

33:2—Jacob places Rachel and Joseph in the least vulnerable position, reflecting his preferences. Such precautions turn out to be unnecessary in view of Esau's positive reception of Jacob and his family.

bowing himself to the ground seven times, until he came near his brother.

4 But Esau ran to meet him, and embraced him, and fell on his neck and kissed him, and they wept. 5 When Esau looked up and saw the women and children, he said, "Who are these with you?" Jacob said, "The children whom God has graciously given your servant." 6 Then the maids drew near, they and their children, and bowed down; 7 Leah likewise and her children drew near and bowed down; and finally Joseph and Rachel drew near, and they bowed down. 8 Esau said, "What do you mean by all this company that I met?" Jacob answered, "To find favor with my lord." 9 But Esau said, "I have enough, my brother; keep what you have for yourself." 10 Jacob said, "No, please; if I find favor with you, then accept my present from my hand; for truly to see your face is like seeing the face of God—since you have received me with such favor. 11 Please accept my gift that is brought to you, because God has dealt graciously with me, and because I have everything I want." So he urged him, and he took it.

12 Then Esau said, "Let us journey on our way, and I will go alongside you." 13 But Jacob said to him, "My lord knows that the children are frail and that the flocks and herds, which are nursing, are a care to me; and if they are overdriven for one day, all the flocks will die. 14 Let my lord pass on ahead of his servant, and I will lead on slowly, according to the pace of the cattle that are before me and according to the pace of the children, until I come to my lord in Seir."

15 So Esau said, "Let me leave with you some of the people who are with me." But he said, "Why should my lord be so kind to me?" 16 So Esau returned that day on his way to Seir. 17 But Jacob journeyed to Succoth, a and built himself a house, and made booths for his cattle; therefore the place is called Succoth.

Jacob Reaches Shechem

18 Jacob came safely to the city of Shechem, which is in the land of Canaan, on his way from Paddan-aram; and he camped before the city. 19 And from the sons of Hamor, Shechem's father, he bought for one hundred pieces of money b the plot of land on which he had pitched his tent. 20 There he erected an altar and called it El-Elohe-Israel. c

The Rape of Dinah

34 Now Dinah the daughter of Leah, whom she had borne to Jacob, went out to visit the women of the region. 2 When Shechem son of Hamor the Hivite, prince of the region, saw her, he seized her and lay with her by force. 3 And his soul was drawn to Dinah daughter of Jacob; he loved the girl, and

a That is Booths b Heb one hundred qesitah c That is God, the God of Israel

33:10 *Like seeing the face of God*—Jacob, having been appropriately deferential to Esau, recalls God's graciousness (v. 11) in allowing him to see God's face and live (32:30) in the way in which Esau has graciously received him. The gifts Jacob had designed for appeasement become gifts of gratitude.

33:14–17—Jacob says he will come to Esau in his home in *Seir* (Edom), but this proves to be misleading, as he moves toward Canaan (*Succoth* is on the east side of the Jordan Valley). Jacob is still capable of his old tricks.

33:18–34:31 The Rape of Dinah
33:18–19 *Shechem*—This is both the name of a city in central Canaan (later an important Israelite center, Josh. 24) and the name of the son of a leading citizen named *Hamor*, from whom Jacob buys land.

34:1–2 *Dinah*—The only daughter of Jacob ever mentioned in the text (30:21). Her visiting suggests congenial relations between Israelites and *Hivites* (=Canaanites) at this time. On one such visit she is raped by Shechem (34:2). The narrator never gives Dinah a voice, so we don't hear the story from her perspective.

34:3—Shechem's expressed love for Dinah is difficult to understand, but it is a prominent feature of the narrative (vv. 3–4, 8, 11–12, 18). Such a development was not unusual in view of Israel's laws (see Deut. 22:28–29). Their relationship became such that Dinah had gone to live in Shechem's house (Gen. 34:26), from where she is once again "taken."

spoke tenderly to her. ⁴So Shechem spoke to his father Hamor, saying, "Get me this girl to be my wife."

5 Now Jacob heard that Shechem[a] had defiled his daughter Dinah; but his sons were with his cattle in the field, so Jacob held his peace until they came. ⁶And Hamor the father of Shechem went out to Jacob to speak with him, ⁷just as the sons of Jacob came in from the field. When they heard of it, the men were indignant and very angry, because he had committed an outrage in Israel by lying with Jacob's daughter, for such a thing ought not to be done.

8 But Hamor spoke with them, saying, "The heart of my son Shechem longs for your daughter; please give her to him in marriage. ⁹Make marriages with us; give your daughters to us, and take our daughters for yourselves. ¹⁰You shall live with us; and the land shall be open to you; live and trade in it, and get property in it." ¹¹Shechem also said to her father and to her brothers, "Let me find favor with you, and whatever you say to me I will give. ¹²Put the marriage present and gift as high as you like, and I will give whatever you ask me; only give me the girl to be my wife."

13 The sons of Jacob answered Shechem and his father Hamor deceitfully, because he had defiled their sister Dinah. ¹⁴They said to them, "We cannot do this thing, to give our sister to one who is uncircumcised, for that would be a disgrace to us. ¹⁵Only on this condition will we consent to you: that you will become as we are and every male among you be circumcised. ¹⁶Then we will give our daughters to you, and we will take your daughters for ourselves, and we will live among you and become one people. ¹⁷But if you will not listen to us and be circumcised, then we will take our daughter and be gone."

18 Their words pleased Hamor and Hamor's son Shechem. ¹⁹And the young man did not delay to do the thing, because he was delighted with Jacob's daughter. Now he was the most honored of all his family. ²⁰So Hamor and his son Shechem came to the gate of their city and spoke to the men of their city, saying, ²¹"These people are friendly with us; let them live in the land and trade in it, for the land is large enough for them; let us take their daughters in marriage, and let us give them our daughters. ²²Only on this condition will they agree to live among us, to become one people: that every male among us be circumcised as they are circumcised. ²³Will not their livestock, their property, and all their animals be ours? Only let us agree with them, and they will live among us." ²⁴And all who went out of the city gate heeded Hamor and his son Shechem; and every male was circumcised, all who went out of the gate of his city.

Dinah's Brothers Avenge Their Sister

25 On the third day, when they were still in pain, two of the sons of Jacob, Simeon and Levi, Dinah's brothers, took their swords and came against the city unawares, and killed all the males. ²⁶They killed Hamor and his son Shechem with the sword, and took Dinah out of Shechem's house, and went away. ²⁷And the other sons of Jacob came upon the slain, and plundered the city, because their sister had been defiled. ²⁸They took their flocks and their herds, their donkeys, and whatever was in the city and in the field. ²⁹All their wealth, all their little ones and their wives, all that was in the houses, they captured and made their prey. ³⁰Then Jacob said to Simeon and Levi, "You have brought trouble on me by making me odious to the inhabitants

---

a Heb *he*

34:7—Dinah's brothers' indignation and anger (and honor, v. 31!) moves to deceitful planning (v. 13), using circumcision as a ruse (vv. 24–25). That in turn leads to gratuitous levels of vio-lence against Shechem's family, spearheaded by Simeon and Levi (vv. 27–29), a move that Jacob condemns, both for practical reasons (v. 30) and for the anger and cruelty involved (49:5–7).

of the land, the Canaanites and the Perizzites; my numbers are few, and if they gather themselves against me and attack me, I shall be destroyed, both I and my household." ³¹ But they said, "Should our sister be treated like a whore?"

Jacob Returns to Bethel

35 God said to Jacob, "Arise, go up to Bethel, and settle there. Make an altar there to the God who appeared to you when you fled from your brother Esau." ²So Jacob said to his household and to all who were with him, "Put away the foreign gods that are among you, and purify yourselves, and change your clothes; ³then come, let us go up to Bethel, that I may make an altar there to the God who answered me in the day of my distress and has been with me wherever I have gone." ⁴So they gave to Jacob all the foreign gods that they had, and the rings that were in their ears; and Jacob hid them under the oak that was near Shechem.

5 As they journeyed, a terror from God fell upon the cities all around them, so that no one pursued them. ⁶Jacob came to Luz (that is, Bethel), which is in the land of Canaan, he and all the people who were with him, ⁷and there he built an altar and called the place El-bethel,ᵃ because it was there that God had revealed himself to him when he fled from his brother. ⁸And Deborah, Rebekah's nurse, died, and she was buried under an oak below Bethel. So it was called Allon-bacuth.ᵇ

9 God appeared to Jacob again when he came from Paddan-aram, and he blessed him. ¹⁰God said to him, "Your name is Jacob; no longer shall you be called Jacob, but Israel shall be your name." So he was called Israel. ¹¹God said to him, "I am God Almighty:ᶜ be fruitful and multiply; a nation and a company of nations shall come from you, and kings shall spring from you. ¹²The land that I gave to Abraham and Isaac I will give to you, and I will give the land to your offspring after you." ¹³Then God went up from him at the place where he had spoken with him. ¹⁴Jacob set up a pillar in the place where he had spoken with him, a pillar of stone; and he poured out a drink offering on it, and poured oil on it. ¹⁵So Jacob called the place where God had spoken with him Bethel.

The Birth of Benjamin and the Death of Rachel

16 Then they journeyed from Bethel; and when they were still some distance from Ephrath, Rachel was in childbirth, and she had hard labor. ¹⁷When she was in her hard labor, the midwife said to her, "Do not be afraid; for now you will have another son." ¹⁸As her soul was departing (for she died), she named him Ben-oni;ᵈ but his father called him Benjamin.ᵉ ¹⁹So Rachel died, and she was buried on the way to Ephrath (that is, Bethlehem), ²⁰and Jacob set up a pillar at her grave; it is the pillar of Rachel's tomb, which is there to this day.

ᵃ That is *God of Bethel* ᵇ That is *Oak of weeping* ᶜ Traditional rendering of Heb *El Shaddai* ᵈ That is *Son of my sorrow* ᵉ That is *Son of the right hand* or *Son of the South*

35:1–29 The Journeys of Jacob

35:2–4 *Put away the foreign gods*—This snippet of text embeds the first commandment in the heart of the ancestral story. The command may refer to the household gods of 31:19, as well as the gods of nonfamily members of his retinue. Jacob here becomes a paradigm for all Israel regarding idolatrous practices (see Josh. 24:14–15, 23).

35:5 *A terror from God*—In view of Jacob's fears in 34:30, this may refer to a God-inspired fear in those who threatened Jacob and his family.

35:10 *Israel*—Once again (in view of Jacob's obedience in vv. 1–4?), this time at Bethel, God renames Jacob Israel and extends to him the constitutive promises of Abraham (vv. 11–12). Jacob's response (v. 14) recalls his vow at Bethel (28:16–22; 31:13).

35:16–20 *Ephrath*—Another name for Bethlehem, near which Rachel died while giving birth to Ben-oni/Benjamin (see NRSV footnotes). The image of Rachel's weeping lives on to refer to the suffering and death of children in the fall of Jerusalem (Jer. 31:15–17) and the slaughter of the innocents in Matt. 2:17–18.

21 Israel journeyed on, and pitched his tent beyond the tower of Eder.

22 While Israel lived in that land, Reuben went and lay with Bilhah his father's concubine; and Israel heard of it.

Now the sons of Jacob were twelve. 23 The sons of Leah: Reuben (Jacob's firstborn), Simeon, Levi, Judah, Issachar, and Zebulun. 24 The sons of Rachel: Joseph and Benjamin. 25 The sons of Bilhah, Rachel's maid: Dan and Naphtali. 26 The sons of Zilpah, Leah's maid: Gad and Asher. These were the sons of Jacob who were born to him in Paddan-aram.

The Death of Isaac

27 Jacob came to his father Isaac at Mamre, or Kiriath-arba (that is, Hebron), where Abraham and Isaac had resided as aliens. 28 Now the days of Isaac were one hundred eighty years. 29 And Isaac breathed his last; he died and was gathered to his people, old and full of days; and his sons Esau and Jacob buried him.

Esau's Descendants

36 These are the descendants of Esau (that is, Edom). 2 Esau took his wives from the Canaanites: Adah daughter of Elon the Hittite, Oholibamah daughter of Anah son[a] of Zibeon the Hivite, 3 and Basemath, Ishmael's daughter, sister of Nebaioth. 4 Adah bore Eliphaz to Esau; Basemath bore Reuel; 5 and Oholibamah bore Jeush, Jalam, and Korah. These are the sons of Esau who were born to him in the land of Canaan.

6 Then Esau took his wives, his sons, his daughters, and all the members of his household, his cattle, all his livestock, and all the property he had acquired in the land of Canaan; and he moved to a land some distance from his brother Jacob. 7 For their possessions were too great for them to live together; the land where they were staying could not support them because of their livestock. 8 So Esau settled in the hill country of Seir; Esau is Edom.

9 These are the descendants of Esau, ancestor of the Edomites, in the hill country of Seir. 10 These are the names of Esau's sons: Eliphaz son of Adah the wife of Esau; Reuel, the son of Esau's wife Basemath. 11 The sons of Eliphaz were Teman, Omar, Zepho, Gatam, and Kenaz. 12 (Timna was a concubine of Eliphaz, Esau's son; she bore Amalek to Eliphaz.) These were the sons of Adah, Esau's wife. 13 These were the sons of Reuel: Nahath, Zerah, Shammah, and Mizzah. These were the sons of Esau's wife, Basemath. 14 These were the sons of Esau's wife Oholibamah, daughter of Anah son[b] of Zibeon: she bore to Esau Jeush, Jalam, and Korah.

Clans and Kings of Edom

15 These are the clans[c] of the sons of Esau. The sons of Eliphaz the firstborn of Esau: the clans[c] Teman, Omar, Zepho, Kenaz, 16 Korah, Gatam, and Amalek; these are the clans[c] of Eliphaz in the land of Edom; they are the sons of Adah. 17 These are the sons of Esau's son Reuel: the clans[c] Nahath, Zerah, Shammah, and Mizzah; these are the clans[c] of Reuel in the land of Edom; they are the sons of Esau's wife Basemath. 18 These are the sons of Esau's wife Oholibamah: the clans[c] Jeush, Jalam, and Korah; these are the clans[c] born of Esau's wife Oholibamah, the daughter of Anah. 19 These are the sons of Esau (that is, Edom), and these are their clans.[c]

---

a Sam Gk Syr: Heb *daughter* *b* Gk Syr: Heb *daughter* *c* Or *chiefs*

36:1–43 The Future of Esau

36:1 *The descendants of Esau*—This genealogy is filled with numerous names that are no longer identifiable. Verses 6–8 read like an expansion of 33:16 and Esau's departure from Jacob. The remarkable growth of Esau's family (evident in the genealogy) as well as his wealth confirm that Isaac's blessing in 27:39–40 had a basically positive cast. Once again (see 25:12–18), the story pays detailed attention to the life of nonchosen peoples. God the Creator is at work bringing blessings independent of the chosen people.

20 These are the sons of Seir the Horite, the inhabitants of the land: Lotan, Shobal, Zibeon, Anah, ²¹ Dishon, Ezer, and Dishan; these are the clans*a* of the Horites, the sons of Seir in the land of Edom. ²² The sons of Lotan were Hori and Heman; and Lotan's sister was Timna. ²³ These are the sons of Shobal: Alvan, Manahath, Ebal, Shepho, and Onam. ²⁴ These are the sons of Zibeon: Aiah and Anah; he is the Anah who found the springs*b* in the wilderness, as he pastured the donkeys of his father Zibeon. ²⁵ These are the children of Anah: Dishon and Oholibamah daughter of Anah. ²⁶ These are the sons of Dishon: Hemdan, Eshban, Ithran, and Cheran. ²⁷ These are the sons of Ezer: Bilhan, Zaavan, and Akan. ²⁸ These are the sons of Dishan: Uz and Aran. ²⁹ These are the clans*a* of the Horites: the clans*a* Lotan, Shobal, Zibeon, Anah, ³⁰ Dishon, Ezer, and Dishan; these are the clans*a* of the Horites, clan by clan*c* in the land of Seir.

31 These are the kings who reigned in the land of Edom, before any king reigned over the Israelites. ³² Bela son of Beor reigned in Edom, the name of his city being Dinhabah. ³³ Bela died, and Jobab son of Zerah of Bozrah succeeded him as king. ³⁴ Jobab died, and Husham of the land of the Temanites succeeded him as king. ³⁵ Husham died, and Hadad son of Bedad, who defeated Midian in the country of Moab, succeeded him as king, the name of his city being Avith. ³⁶ Hadad died, and Samlah of Masrekah succeeded him as king. ³⁷ Samlah died, and Shaul of Rehoboth on the Euphrates succeeded him as king. ³⁸ Shaul died, and Baal-hanan son of Achbor succeeded

him as king. ³⁹ Baal-hanan son of Achbor died, and Hadar succeeded him as king, the name of his city being Pau; his wife's name was Mehetabel, the daughter of Matred, daughter of Me-zahab.

40 These are the names of the clans*a* of Esau, according to their families and their localities by their names: the clans*a* Timna, Alvah, Jetheth, ⁴¹ Oholibamah, Elah, Pinon, ⁴² Kenaz, Teman, Mibzar, ⁴³ Magdiel, and Iram; these are the clans*a* of Edom (that is, Esau, the father of Edom), according to their settlements in the land that they held.

Joseph Dreams of Greatness

37 Jacob settled in the land where his father had lived as an alien, the land of Canaan. ² This is the story of the family of Jacob.

Joseph, being seventeen years old, was shepherding the flock with his brothers; he was a helper to the sons of Bilhah and Zilpah, his father's wives; and Joseph brought a bad report of them to their father. ³ Now Israel loved Joseph more than any other of his children, because he was the son of his old age; and he had made him a long robe with sleeves.*d* ⁴ But when his brothers saw that their father loved him more than all his brothers, they hated him, and could not speak peaceably to him.

5 Once Joseph had a dream, and when he told it to his brothers, they hated him even more. ⁶ He said to them, "Listen to this dream that I dreamed. ⁷ There we were, binding sheaves in the field. Suddenly my sheaf rose and stood upright; then your sheaves gathered around it,

a Or *chiefs* *b* Meaning of Heb uncertain *c* Or *chief by chief* *d* Traditional rendering (compare Gk): *a coat of many colors; meaning of Heb uncertain*

37:1–36 Joseph and His Brothers

37:3 *Long robe with sleeves*—Perhaps a striped coat, see NRSV footnote. Clothing plays an important role throughout the narrative, suggesting status (e.g., 3:7, 21; 37:23, 32; 38:14, 19; 39:12; 41:14, 42).

37:5–11 *Once Joseph had a dream*—The Joseph story contains three dream narratives, each with

two dreams (also 40:5–23; 41:1–36). This first narrative is often thought to prophesy events of chaps. 42–50 regarding Joseph's authority (in 37:9 the **sun** and **moon** are his parents and the **eleven stars** his brothers), but this is only partially the case. Jacob never does bow before him, and Joseph will finally deny his dreams' continuing applicability for shaping the future with his brothers (50:15–21).

and bowed down to my sheaf." ⁸ His brothers said to him, "Are you indeed to reign over us? Are you indeed to have dominion over us?" So they hated him even more because of his dreams and his words.

9 He had another dream, and told it to his brothers, saying, "Look, I have had another dream: the sun, the moon, and eleven stars were bowing down to me." ¹⁰ But when he told it to his father and to his brothers, his father rebuked him, and said to him, "What kind of dream is this that you have had? Shall we indeed come, I and your mother and your brothers, and bow to the ground before you?" ¹¹ So his brothers were jealous of him, but his father kept the matter in mind.

Joseph Is Sold by His Brothers

12 Now his brothers went to pasture their father's flock near Shechem. ¹³ And Israel said to Joseph, "Are not your brothers pasturing the flock at Shechem? Come, I will send you to them." He answered, "Here I am." ¹⁴ So he said to him, "Go now, see if it is well with your brothers and with the flock; and bring word back to me." So he sent him from the valley of Hebron.

He came to Shechem, ¹⁵ and a man found him wandering in the fields; the man asked him, "What are you seeking?" ¹⁶ "I am seeking my brothers," he said; "tell me, please, where they are pasturing the flock." ¹⁷ The man said, "They have gone away, for I heard them say, 'Let us go to Dothan.'" So Joseph went after his brothers, and found them at Dothan. ¹⁸ They saw him from a distance, and before he came near to them, they conspired to kill him. ¹⁹ They said to one another, "Here comes this dreamer. ²⁰ Come now, let us kill him and throw

him into one of the pits; then we shall say that a wild animal has devoured him, and we shall see what will become of his dreams." ²¹ But when Reuben heard it, he delivered him out of their hands, saying, "Let us not take his life." ²² Reuben said to them, "Shed no blood; throw him into this pit here in the wilderness, but lay no hand on him"—that he might rescue him out of their hand and restore him to his father. ²³ So when Joseph came to his brothers, they stripped him of his robe, the long robe with sleeves ᵃ that he wore; ²⁴ and they took him and threw him into a pit. The pit was empty; there was no water in it.

25 Then they sat down to eat; and looking up they saw a caravan of Ishmaelites coming from Gilead, with their camels carrying gum, balm, and resin, on their way to carry it down to Egypt. ²⁶ Then Judah said to his brothers, "What profit is it if we kill our brother and conceal his blood? ²⁷ Come, let us sell him to the Ishmaelites, and not lay our hands on him, for he is our brother, our own flesh." And his brothers agreed. ²⁸ When some Midianite traders passed by, they drew Joseph up, lifting him out of the pit, and sold him to the Ishmaelites for twenty pieces of silver. And they took Joseph to Egypt.

29 When Reuben returned to the pit and saw that Joseph was not in the pit, he tore his clothes. ³⁰ He returned to his brothers, and said, "The boy is gone; and I, where can I turn?" ³¹ Then they took Joseph's robe, slaughtered a goat, and dipped the robe in the blood. ³² They had the long robe with sleeves ᵃ taken to their father, and they said, "This we have found; see now whether it is your son's robe or not." ³³ He recognized it, and said, "It is my son's robe! A wild ani-

ᵃ See note on 37.3

37:15 *A man*—Unidentified, but he could be a divine messenger.

37:17 *Dothan*—A town fifteen miles north of Shechem, even farther from home.

37:28 *Midianite traders . . . Ishmaelites*—The text is not clear about their role, as both groups are said to sell Joseph to Egypt (v. 36; 19:1; cf. 37:28); the story may be purposely ambiguous, destabilizing the brothers' plans.

mal has devoured him; Joseph is without doubt torn to pieces." **34** Then Jacob tore his garments, and put sackcloth on his loins, and mourned for his son many days. **35** All his sons and all his daughters sought to comfort him; but he refused to be comforted, and said, "No, I shall go down to Sheol to my son, mourning." Thus his father bewailed him. **36** Meanwhile the Midianites had sold him in Egypt to Potiphar, one of Pharaoh's officials, the captain of the guard.

Judah and Tamar

38 It happened at that time that Judah went down from his brothers and settled near a certain Adullamite whose name was Hirah. **2** There Judah saw the daughter of a certain Canaanite whose name was Shua; he married her and went in to her. **3** She conceived and bore a son; and he named him Er. **4** Again she conceived and bore a son whom she named Onan. **5** Yet again she bore a son, and she named him Shelah. She*a* was in Chezib when she bore him. **6** Judah took a wife for Er his firstborn; her name was Tamar. **7** But Er, Judah's firstborn, was wicked in the sight of the LORD, and the LORD put him to death. **8** Then Judah said to Onan, "Go in to your brother's wife and perform the duty of a brother-in-law to her; raise up offspring for your brother." **9** But since Onan knew that the offspring would not be his, he spilled his

semen on the ground whenever he went in to his brother's wife, so that he would not give offspring to his brother. **10** What he did was displeasing in the sight of the LORD, and he put him to death also. **11** Then Judah said to his daughter-in-law Tamar, "Remain a widow in your father's house until my son Shelah grows up"—for he feared that he too would die, like his brothers. So Tamar went to live in her father's house.

12 In course of time the wife of Judah, Shua's daughter, died; when Judah's time of mourning was over,*b* he went up to Timnah to his sheepshearers, he and his friend Hirah the Adullamite. **13** When Tamar was told, "Your father-in-law is going up to Timnah to shear his sheep," **14** she put off her widow's garments, put on a veil, wrapped herself up, and sat down at the entrance to Enaim, which is on the road to Timnah. She saw that Shelah was grown up, yet she had not been given to him in marriage. **15** When Judah saw her, he thought her to be a prostitute, for she had covered her face. **16** He went over to her at the roadside, and said, "Come, let me come in to you," for he did not know that she was his daughter-in-law. She said, "What will you give me, that you may come in to me?" **17** He answered, "I will send you a kid from the flock." And she said, "Only if you give me a pledge, until you send

a Gk: Heb He *b* Heb when Judah was comforted

37:35 *Go down to Sheol*—The realm of all dead, a shadowy, silent existence—neither heaven nor hell (cf. 42:38).

38:1–30 Tamar and Judah

38:1 *Adullamite*—A Canaanite clan.

38:6 *Tamar*—The wife of Er, apparently a Canaanite, as was Er's mother, the daughter of Shua (v. 2). The generation of Jacob's sons begins to take wives from outside the family (see 41:45).

38:7, 10 *The LORD put him to death*—Both *Er* and *Onan* are uncommon names in the Old Testament for individuals; one factor here is that the line leading to David is at risk (*Perez*, v. 29). The narrator does not specify the means God uses (this language is used for Saul in

1 Chr. 10:14, and we are told that he committed suicide, 10:4).

38:8 *The duty of a brother-in-law*—Also known as the levirate law (Deut. 25:5–10; Ruth 4), wherein the brother is obligated to marry the wife of the deceased to carry on his name and inheritance (an heir for Er). Onan shirks his responsibility by refusing to let his semen enter her (*coitus interruptus*, not masturbation). Judah sends her home, where her future welfare is in jeopardy, rather than put his remaining son (*Shelah*, v. 5) at risk, though he makes a (failed) promise (vv. 11, 14). Seeing this, a resourceful Tamar takes the situation into her own hands in order to fulfill the law, even at the cost of her honor.

38:12, 14 *Timnah . . . Enaim*—Towns near Bethlehem.

it." ¹⁸ He said, "What pledge shall I give you?" She replied, "Your signet and your cord, and the staff that is in your hand." So he gave them to her, and went in to her, and she conceived by him. ¹⁹ Then she got up and went away, and taking off her veil she put on the garments of her widowhood.

20 When Judah sent the kid by his friend the Adullamite, to recover the pledge from the woman, he could not find her. ²¹ He asked the townspeople, "Where is the temple prostitute who was at Enaim by the wayside?" But they said, "No prostitute has been here." ²² So he returned to Judah, and said, "I have not found her; moreover the townspeople said, 'No prostitute has been here.'" ²³ Judah replied, "Let her keep the things as her own, otherwise we will be laughed at; you see, I sent this kid, and you could not find her."

24 About three months later Judah was told, "Your daughter-in-law Tamar has played the whore; moreover she is pregnant as a result of whoredom." And Judah said, "Bring her out, and let her be burned." ²⁵ As she was being brought out, she sent word to her father-in-law, "It was the owner of these who made me pregnant." And she said, "Take note, please, whose these are, the signet and the cord and the staff." ²⁶ Then Judah acknowledged them and said, "She is more in the right than I, since I did not give her to my son Shelah." And he did not lie with her again.

27 When the time of her delivery came, there were twins in her womb. ²⁸ While she was in labor, one put out a hand; and the midwife took and bound on his hand a crimson thread, saying, "This one came out first." ²⁹ But just then he drew back his hand, and out came his brother; and she said, "What a breach you have made for yourself!" Therefore he was named Perez. ᵃ ³⁰ Afterward his brother came out with the crimson thread on his hand; and he was named Zerah. ᵇ

Joseph and Potiphar's Wife

39 Now Joseph was taken down to Egypt, and Potiphar, an officer of Pharaoh, the captain of the guard, an Egyptian, bought him from the Ishmaelites who had brought him down there. ² The LORD was with Joseph, and he became a successful man; he was in the house of his Egyptian master. ³ His master saw that the LORD was with him, and that the LORD caused all that he did to prosper in his hands. ⁴ So Joseph found

ᵃ That is A breach   ᵇ That is Brightness; perhaps alluding to the crimson thread

---

38:18 *Signet . . . cord . . . staff*—A seal (suspended on a neck cord) and a specially marked staff are possessions of Judah that could readily be identified as his. A clever move by Tamar—they later prove that Judah is the father of her children (v. 25).

38:21 *Temple prostitute*—Tamar is not so identified, so this is probably an effort to be discreet. The people of the town indirectly witness to Tamar's integrity; they have not seen a prostitute. While Judah's friends claim she is a harlot (v. 24), the narrator never so identifies her.

38:26 *She is more in the right than I*—Judah's use of the Hebrew word for "more in the right" testifies to Tamar's doing justice to the law in a way that he had not. Tamar's resourceful, anti-establishment commitment to justice and social responsibility stands as an important witness (cf. Jesus' Sabbath-breaking, Mark 2:27, for another instance of discerning a higher law).

38:29 *Perez*—The son of Judah that continues the line of promise to David (Ruth 4:18) and Jesus (Matt. 1:3).

39:1–23 Joseph, Pharaoh, and Success

39:1 *Pharaoh*—A generic term for Egypt's king, never named.

39:2 *The LORD was with Joseph*—The nine references to God that bracket this chapter (vv. 2–3, 21–23) strike the key theme. In his isolation from family and homeland, even in prison, the witness is clear: God has not abandoned him. God's presence is a more unobtrusive, behind-the-scenes type of presence than is common up to this point in Genesis, but it is effective for good for both Joseph and those among whom he lives. God does not act alone, but works in and through Joseph and his considerable competence in the political sphere to bring blessing (see v. 5).

favor in his sight and attended him; he made him overseer of his house and put him in charge of all that he had. ⁵ From the time that he made him overseer in his house and over all that he had, the LORD blessed the Egyptian's house for Joseph's sake; the blessing of the LORD was on all that he had, in house and field. ⁶ So he left all that he had in Joseph's charge; and, with him there, he had no concern for anything but the food that he ate.

Now Joseph was handsome and good-looking. ⁷ And after a time his master's wife cast her eyes on Joseph and said, "Lie with me." ⁸ But he refused and said to his master's wife, "Look, with me here, my master has no concern about anything in the house, and he has put everything that he has in my hand. ⁹ He is not greater in this house than I am, nor has he kept back anything from me except yourself, because you are his wife. How then could I do this great wickedness, and sin against God?" ¹⁰ And although she spoke to Joseph day after day, he would not consent to lie beside her or to be with her. ¹¹ One day, however, when he went into the house to do his work, and while no one else was in the house, ¹² she caught hold of his garment, saying, "Lie with me!" But he left his garment in her hand, and fled and ran outside. ¹³ When she saw that he had left his garment in her hand and had fled outside, ¹⁴ she called out to the members of her household and said to them, "See, my husband[a] has brought among us a Hebrew to insult us! He came in to me to lie with me, and I cried out with a loud voice; ¹⁵ and when he heard me raise my voice and cry out, he left his garment beside me, and fled outside." ¹⁶ Then she kept his garment by her until his master came home, ¹⁷ and she told him the same story, saying, "The Hebrew servant, whom you have brought among us, came in to me to insult me; ¹⁸ but as soon as I raised my voice and cried out, he left his garment beside me, and fled outside."

19 When his master heard the words that his wife spoke to him, saying, "This is the way your servant treated me," he became enraged. ²⁰ And Joseph's master took him and put him into the prison, the place where the king's prisoners were confined; he remained there in prison. ²¹ But the LORD was with Joseph and showed him steadfast love; he gave him favor in the sight of the chief jailer. ²² The chief jailer committed to Joseph's care all the prisoners who were in the prison, and whatever was done there, he was the one who did it. ²³ The chief jailer paid no heed to anything that was in Joseph's care, because the LORD was with him; and whatever he did, the LORD made it prosper.

The Dreams of Two Prisoners

40 Some time after this, the cupbearer of the king of Egypt and his baker offended their lord the king of Egypt. ² Pharaoh was angry with his two officers, the chief cupbearer and the chief baker, ³ and he put them in custody in the house of the captain of the guard, in the prison where Joseph was confined. ⁴ The captain of the guard charged Joseph with them, and he waited on them; and they continued for some time in custody. ⁵ One night they both dreamed—the cupbearer and the baker of the king of Egypt, who were confined in the prison—each his own dream, and each dream with its own meaning. ⁶ When Joseph came to them in the morning, he saw that they were troubled. ⁷ So he asked Pharaoh's officers, who were with him in custody in his master's house, "Why are your faces

a Heb *he*

39:9 *Sin against God*—Joseph resists the temptations of Potiphar's (unnamed) wife. That this sin would have been "against God" shows that God's will does not always get done in human life.

40:1–23 Joseph, Interpreter of Dreams

downcast today?" [8]They said to him, "We have had dreams, and there is no one to interpret them." And Joseph said to them, "Do not interpretations belong to God? Please tell them to me."

[9]So the chief cupbearer told his dream to Joseph, and said to him, "In my dream there was a vine before me, [10]and on the vine there were three branches. As soon as it budded, its blossoms came out and the clusters ripened into grapes. [11]Pharaoh's cup was in my hand; and I took the grapes and pressed them into Pharaoh's cup, and placed the cup in Pharaoh's hand." [12]Then Joseph said to him, "This is its interpretation: the three branches are three days; [13]within three days Pharaoh will lift up your head and restore you to your office; and you shall place Pharaoh's cup in his hand, just as you used to do when you were his cupbearer. [14]But remember me when it is well with you; please do me the kindness to make mention of me to Pharaoh, and so get me out of this place. [15]For in fact I was stolen out of the land of the Hebrews; and here also I have done nothing that they should have put me into the dungeon."

[16]When the chief baker saw that the interpretation was favorable, he said to Joseph, "I also had a dream: there were three cake baskets on my head, [17]and in the uppermost basket there were all sorts of baked food for Pharaoh, but the birds were eating it out of the basket on my head." [18]And Joseph answered, "This is its interpretation: the three baskets are three days; [19]within three days Pharaoh will lift up your head—from you!—and hang you on a pole; and the birds will eat the flesh from you."

[20]On the third day, which was Pharaoh's birthday, he made a feast for all his servants, and lifted up the head of the chief cupbearer and the head of the chief baker among his servants. [21]He restored the chief cupbearer to his cupbearing, and he placed the cup in Pharaoh's hand; [22]but the chief baker he hanged, just as Joseph had interpreted to them. [23]Yet the chief cupbearer did not remember Joseph, but forgot him.

Joseph Interprets Pharaoh's Dream

41 After two whole years, Pharaoh dreamed that he was standing by the Nile, [2]and there came up out of the Nile seven sleek and fat cows, and they grazed in the reed grass. [3]Then seven other cows, ugly and thin, came up out of the Nile after them, and stood by the other cows on the bank of the Nile. [4]The ugly and thin cows ate up the seven sleek and fat cows. And Pharaoh awoke. [5]Then he fell asleep and dreamed a second time; seven ears of grain, plump and good, were growing on one stalk. [6]Then seven ears, thin and blighted by the east wind, sprouted after them. [7]The thin ears swallowed up the seven plump and full ears. Pharaoh awoke, and it was a dream. [8]In the morning his spirit was troubled; so he sent and called for all the magicians of Egypt and all its wise men. Pharaoh told them his dreams, but there was no one who could interpret them to Pharaoh.

40:8 *Do not interpretations belong to God?*— While the servant's dreams are not said to come from God, the interpretation, which Joseph himself will now give, does; at the same time, Joseph's gifts are important (see note at 41:16). God works in and through the dreams of the nonchosen to develop the future of the chosen. While Joseph's own dreams (37:5–9) resulted in his slavery, the dreams of others now become the means for his release from slavery.

40:13, 19, 20 *Lift up the head*—This expression does double duty in these verses, from elevat-

ing one's status (v. 13) to beheading (v. 19), both senses of which appear in v. 20, where both dreams are realized. Notably, Joseph's dream interpretation is crucial for the dreams themselves being realized; their fulfillment is not automatic.

40:14–15 *Remember me*—Here Joseph speaks for the first time about his own experiences and, notably, for all his reliance on God, he still expresses the need for *human* help, which is delayed (v. 23; see 41:9–13).

41:1–57 *Joseph's Elevation to Power*

9 Then the chief cupbearer said to Pharaoh, "I remember my faults today. 10 Once Pharaoh was angry with his servants, and put me and the chief baker in custody in the house of the captain of the guard. 11 We dreamed on the same night, he and I, each having a dream with its own meaning. 12 A young Hebrew was there with us, a servant of the captain of the guard. When we told him, he interpreted our dreams to us, giving an interpretation to each according to his dream. 13 As he interpreted to us, so it turned out; I was restored to my office, and the baker was hanged."

14 Then Pharaoh sent for Joseph, and he was hurriedly brought out of the dungeon. When he had shaved himself and changed his clothes, he came in before Pharaoh. 15 And Pharaoh said to Joseph, "I have had a dream, and there is no one who can interpret it. I have heard it said of you that when you hear a dream you can interpret it." 16 Joseph answered Pharaoh, "It is not I; God will give Pharaoh a favorable answer." 17 Then Pharaoh said to Joseph, "In my dream I was standing on the banks of the Nile; 18 and seven cows, fat and sleek, came up out of the Nile and fed in the reed grass. 19 Then seven other cows came up after them, poor, very ugly, and thin. Never had I seen such ugly ones in all the land of Egypt. 20 The thin and ugly cows ate up the first seven fat cows, 21 but when they had eaten them no one would have known that they had done so, for they were still as ugly as before. Then I awoke. 22 I fell asleep a second time*a* and I saw in my dream seven ears of grain, full and good, growing on one stalk, 23 and seven ears, withered, thin,

and blighted by the east wind, sprouting after them; 24 and the thin ears swallowed up the seven good ears. But when I told it to the magicians, there was no one who could explain it to me."

25 Then Joseph said to Pharaoh, "Pharaoh's dreams are one and the same; God has revealed to Pharaoh what he is about to do. 26 The seven good cows are seven years, and the seven good ears are seven years; the dreams are one. 27 The seven lean and ugly cows that came up after them are seven years, as are the seven empty ears blighted by the east wind. They are seven years of famine. 28 It is as I told Pharaoh; God has shown to Pharaoh what he is about to do. 29 There will come seven years of great plenty throughout all the land of Egypt. 30 After them there will arise seven years of famine, and all the plenty will be forgotten in the land of Egypt; the famine will consume the land. 31 The plenty will no longer be known in the land because of the famine that will follow, for it will be very grievous. 32 And the doubling of Pharaoh's dream means that the thing is fixed by God, and God will shortly bring it about. 33 Now therefore let Pharaoh select a man who is discerning and wise, and set him over the land of Egypt. 34 Let Pharaoh proceed to appoint overseers over the land, and take one-fifth of the produce of the land of Egypt during the seven plenteous years. 35 Let them gather all the food of these good years that are coming, and lay up grain under the authority of Pharaoh for food in the cities, and let them keep it. 36 That food shall be a reserve for the land against the

a Gk Syr Vg: Heb lacks *I fell asleep a second time*

41:16 *God will give Pharaoh a favorable answer*—Note Joseph's confidence; he has not yet heard Pharaoh's dreams. It is not that Joseph does not interpret dreams; he does indeed (see 40:12, 16; 41:12–13). But God gives him the insight to interpret them properly (see 40:8). Ironically, after he has heard Joseph's interpretation (41:25–36), Pharaoh gets the theology right (vv. 38–39): God, yes, but Joseph's wisdom and

discernment as well, for his gifts are not irrelevant. Yet he does not boast, but gives the glory to God (note God as the subject in vv. 16, 25, 28). Agency is both divine and human.

41:32 *The thing is fixed by God*—God has firmly established the future to which the dreams point, but within that future human decisions will remain very important in the shape developments take.

seven years of famine that are to befall the land of Egypt, so that the land may not perish through the famine."

Joseph's Rise to Power

37 The proposal pleased Pharaoh and all his servants. 38 Pharaoh said to his servants, "Can we find anyone else like this—one in whom is the spirit of God?" 39 So Pharaoh said to Joseph, "Since God has shown you all this, there is no one so discerning and wise as you. 40 You shall be over my house, and all my people shall order themselves as you command; only with regard to the throne will I be greater than you." 41 And Pharaoh said to Joseph, "See, I have set you over all the land of Egypt." 42 Removing his signet ring from his hand, Pharaoh put it on Joseph's hand; he arrayed him in garments of fine linen, and put a gold chain around his neck. 43 He had him ride in the chariot of his second-in-command; and they cried out in front of him, "Bow the knee!" a Thus he set him over all the land of Egypt. 44 Moreover Pharaoh said to Joseph, "I am Pharaoh, and without your consent no one shall lift up hand or foot in all the land of Egypt." 45 Pharaoh gave Joseph the name Zaphenath-paneah; and he gave him Asenath daughter of Potiphera, priest of On, as his wife. Thus Joseph gained authority over the land of Egypt.

46 Joseph was thirty years old when he entered the service of Pharaoh king of Egypt. And Joseph went out from the presence of Pharaoh, and went through all the land of Egypt. 47 During the seven plenteous years the earth produced abundantly. 48 He gathered up all the food of the seven years when there was plenty b in the land of Egypt, and stored up food in the cities; he stored up in every city the food from the fields around it. 49 So Joseph stored up grain in such abundance—like the sand of the sea—that he stopped measuring it; it was beyond measure.

50 Before the years of famine came, Joseph had two sons, whom Asenath daughter of Potiphera, priest of On, bore to him. 51 Joseph named the firstborn Manasseh, c "For," he said, "God has made me forget all my hardship and all my father's house." 52 The second he named Ephraim, d "For God has made me fruitful in the land of my misfortunes."

53 The seven years of plenty that prevailed in the land of Egypt came to an end; 54 and the seven years of famine began to come, just as Joseph had said. There was famine in every country, but throughout the land of Egypt there was bread. 55 When all the land of Egypt was famished, the people cried to Pharaoh for bread. Pharaoh said to all the Egyptians, "Go to Joseph; what he says to you, do." 56 And since the famine had spread over all the land, Joseph opened all the storehouses, e and sold to the Egyptians, for the famine was severe in the land of Egypt. 57 Moreover, all the world came to Joseph in Egypt to buy grain, because the famine became severe throughout the world.

a Abrek, apparently an Egyptian word similar in sound to the Hebrew word meaning to kneel b Sam Gk: MT the seven years that were c That is Making to forget d From a Hebrew word meaning to be fruitful e Gk Vg Compare Syr: Heb opened all that was in (or, among) them

---

41:38 *One in whom is the spirit of God*—Joseph has divinely given gifts suitable for the task at hand (see v. 16; Exod. 31:3; 35:31).

41:45 *Zaphenath-paneah*—A new name for Joseph, to signify his new status; perhaps means "God speaks and lives."

41:45 *Asenath*—The name of Joseph's Egyptian wife, the daughter of a priest of the sun god Re in the city of On (=Heliopolis).

41:50–52 *Manasseh . . . Ephraim*—Joseph's two sons, whose names summarize his recent experiences, namely, God's preserving and prospering amid great hardship. The sons are two of the twelve tribes of Israel (see chap. 48).

41:57 *All the world*—Due to Joseph's social, political, and economic wisdom, everyone from the known world, including Jacob's family (the subject of the next three chapters), can buy grain from Egypt for relief from the famine. This statement links this text back to Gen. 12:3.

Joseph's Brothers Go to Egypt

42 When Jacob learned that there was grain in Egypt, he said to his sons, "Why do you keep looking at one another? ²I have heard," he said, "that there is grain in Egypt; go down and buy grain for us there, that we may live and not die." ³So ten of Joseph's brothers went down to buy grain in Egypt. ⁴But Jacob did not send Joseph's brother Benjamin with his brothers, for he feared that harm might come to him. ⁵Thus the sons of Israel were among the other people who came to buy grain, for the famine had reached the land of Canaan.

6 Now Joseph was governor over the land; it was he who sold to all the people of the land. And Joseph's brothers came and bowed themselves before him with their faces to the ground. ⁷When Joseph saw his brothers, he recognized them, but he treated them like strangers and spoke harshly to them. "Where do you come from?" he said. They said, "From the land of Canaan, to buy food." ⁸Although Joseph had recognized his brothers, they did not recognize him. ⁹Joseph also remembered the dreams that he had dreamed about them. He said to them, "You are spies; you have come to see the nakedness of the land!" ¹⁰They said to him, "No, my lord; your servants have come to buy food. ¹¹We are all sons of one man; we are honest men; your servants have never been spies." ¹²But he said to them, "No, you have come to see the nakedness of the land!" ¹³They said, "We, your servants, are twelve brothers, the sons of a certain man in the land of Canaan; the youngest, however, is now with our father, and one is no more." ¹⁴But Joseph said to them, "It is just as I have said to you; you are spies! ¹⁵Here is how you shall be tested: as Pharaoh lives, you shall not leave this place unless your youngest brother comes here! ¹⁶Let one of you go and bring your brother, while the rest of you remain in prison, in order that your words may be tested, whether there is truth in you; or else, as Pharaoh lives, surely you are spies." ¹⁷And he put them all together in prison for three days.

18 On the third day Joseph said to them, "Do this and you will live, for I fear God: ¹⁹if you are honest men, let one of your brothers stay here where you are imprisoned. The rest of you shall go and carry grain for the famine of your households, ²⁰and bring your youngest brother to me. Thus your words will be verified, and you shall not die." And they agreed to do so. ²¹They said to one another, "Alas, we are paying the penalty for what we did to our brother; we saw his anguish when he pleaded with us, but we would not listen. That is why this anguish has come upon us." ²²Then Reuben answered them, "Did I not tell you not to wrong the boy? But you would not listen. So now there comes a reckoning for his blood." ²³They did not know that Joseph understood them, since he spoke with them through an interpreter. ²⁴He turned away from them and wept; then he returned and spoke to them. And he picked out Simeon and had him bound before their eyes. ²⁵Joseph then gave orders to fill their bags with grain,

---

42:1–38 Joseph Meets His Brothers

42:6 Bowed themselves—With the brothers' lord/servant language, a partial fulfillment of Joseph's dream (37:5–9), which Joseph now remembers (42:9).

42:9, 12 The nakedness of the land—A reference to Egypt's exposed borders. Turning the tables on his brothers, Joseph exposes their defenselessness and tests their integrity. Have they changed or not? The brothers must be tested for reconciliation to be possible.

42:13 One is no more—The brothers omit any role they had in Joseph's disappearance.

42:21 Anguish—The brothers see what they have done from Joseph's perspective and confess their crime.

42:24 Wept—Joseph weeps several times in the narrative, signaling a new development in his relationship with his brothers and revealing his true feelings, which soften the harsh façade (43:30; 45:1–2, 14–15; 46:29; 50:1, 17).

to return every man's money to his sack, and to give them provisions for their journey. This was done for them.

Joseph's Brothers Return to Canaan

26 They loaded their donkeys with their grain, and departed. 27 When one of them opened his sack to give his donkey fodder at the lodging place, he saw his money at the top of the sack. 28 He said to his brothers, "My money has been put back; here it is in my sack!" At this they lost heart and turned trembling to one another, saying, "What is this that God has done to us?"

29 When they came to their father Jacob in the land of Canaan, they told him all that had happened to them, saying, 30 "The man, the lord of the land, spoke harshly to us, and charged us with spying on the land. 31 But we said to him, 'We are honest men, we are not spies. 32 We are twelve brothers, sons of our father; one is no more, and the youngest is now with our father in the land of Canaan.' 33 Then the man, the lord of the land, said to us, 'By this I shall know that you are honest men: leave one of your brothers with me, take grain for the famine of your households, and go your way. 34 Bring your youngest brother to me, and I shall know that you are not spies but honest men. Then I will release your brother to you, and you may trade in the land.'"

35 As they were emptying their sacks, there in each one's sack was his bag of money. When they and their father saw their bundles of money, they were dismayed. 36 And their father Jacob said to them, "I am the one you have bereaved of children: Joseph is no more, and Simeon is no more, and now you would take Benjamin. All this has happened to me!" 37 Then Reuben said to his father, "You may kill my two sons if I do not

bring him back to you. Put him in my hands, and I will bring him back to you." 38 But he said, "My son shall not go down with you, for his brother is dead, and he alone is left. If harm should come to him on the journey that you are to make, you would bring down my gray hairs with sorrow to Sheol."

The Brothers Come Again, Bringing Benjamin

43 Now the famine was severe in the land. 2 And when they had eaten up the grain that they had brought from Egypt, their father said to them, "Go again, buy us a little more food." 3 But Judah said to him, "The man solemnly warned us, saying, 'You shall not see my face unless your brother is with you.' 4 If you will send our brother with us, we will go down and buy you food; 5 but if you will not send him, we will not go down, for the man said to us, 'You shall not see my face, unless your brother is with you.'" 6 Israel said, "Why did you treat me so badly as to tell the man that you had another brother?" 7 They replied, "The man questioned us carefully about ourselves and our kindred, saying, 'Is your father still alive? Have you another brother?' What we told him was in answer to these questions. Could we in any way know that he would say, 'Bring your brother down'?" 8 Then Judah said to his father Israel, "Send the boy with me, and let us be on our way, so that we may live and not die—you and we and also our little ones. 9 I myself will be surety for him; you can hold me accountable for him. If I do not bring him back to you and set him before you, then let me bear the blame forever. 10 If we had not delayed, we would now have returned twice."

11 Then their father Israel said to them, "If it must be so, then do this:

42:38 *Sheol*—See note at 37:35.

43:1–34 The Second Journey to Egypt

43:3 *Judah*—Judah is the chief spokesperson for

the brothers through the balance of the story, risking his honor (vv. 8–9; 44:32). This narrative is also a story about Judah, who is the brother in the Davidic line (49:8–12).

take some of the choice fruits of the land in your bags, and carry them down as a present to the man—a little balm and a little honey, gum, resin, pistachio nuts, and almonds. 12 Take double the money with you. Carry back with you the money that was returned in the top of your sacks; perhaps it was an oversight. 13 Take your brother also, and be on your way again to the man; 14 may God Almighty[a] grant you mercy before the man, so that he may send back your other brother and Benjamin. As for me, if I am bereaved of my children, I am bereaved." 15 So the men took the present, and they took double the money with them, as well as Benjamin. Then they went on their way down to Egypt, and stood before Joseph.

16 When Joseph saw Benjamin with them, he said to the steward of his house, "Bring the men into the house, and slaughter an animal and make ready, for the men are to dine with me at noon." 17 The man did as Joseph said, and brought the men to Joseph's house. 18 Now the men were afraid because they were brought to Joseph's house, and they said, "It is because of the money, replaced in our sacks the first time, that we have been brought in, so that he may have an opportunity to fall upon us, to make slaves of us and take our donkeys." 19 So they went up to the steward of Joseph's house and spoke with him at the entrance to the house. 20 They said, "Oh, my lord, we came down the first time to buy food; 21 and when we came to the lodging place we opened our sacks, and there was each one's money in the top of his sack, our money in full weight. So we have brought it back with us. 22 Moreover we have brought down with us additional money to buy food. We do not know who put our money in

our sacks." 23 He replied, "Rest assured, do not be afraid; your God and the God of your father must have put treasure in your sacks for you; I received your money." Then he brought Simeon out to them. 24 When the steward[b] had brought the men into Joseph's house, and given them water, and they had washed their feet, and when he had given their donkeys fodder, 25 they made the present ready for Joseph's coming at noon, for they had heard that they would dine there.

26 When Joseph came home, they brought him the present that they had carried into the house, and bowed to the ground before him. 27 He inquired about their welfare, and said, "Is your father well, the old man of whom you spoke? Is he still alive?" 28 They said, "Your servant our father is well; he is still alive." And they bowed their heads and did obeisance. 29 Then he looked up and saw his brother Benjamin, his mother's son, and said, "Is this your youngest brother, of whom you spoke to me? God be gracious to you, my son!" 30 With that, Joseph hurried out, because he was overcome with affection for his brother, and he was about to weep. So he went into a private room and wept there. 31 Then he washed his face and came out; and controlling himself he said, "Serve the meal." 32 They served him by himself, and them by themselves, and the Egyptians who ate with him by themselves, because the Egyptians could not eat with the Hebrews, for that is an abomination to the Egyptians. 33 When they were seated before him, the firstborn according to his birthright and the youngest according to his youth, the men looked at one another in amazement. 34 Portions were taken to them from Joseph's table,

a Traditional rendering of Heb *El Shaddai*   b Heb *the man*

43:23 God . . . must have put treasure in your sacks—This "nonchosen" steward offers a word of comfort and peace to the brothers and gives a theological interpretation. It was not that God directly placed the money in their sacks (see 42:25); but because this human action was in tune with God's purposes, God was the decisive agent in the action (see 45:8).

43:26 Bowed to the ground—The second fulfillment of Joseph's double dream in 37:5–9.

but Benjamin's portion was five times as much as any of theirs. So they drank and were merry with him.

Joseph Detains Benjamin

44 Then he commanded the steward of his house, "Fill the men's sacks with food, as much as they can carry, and put each man's money in the top of his sack. ² Put my cup, the silver cup, in the top of the sack of the youngest, with his money for the grain." And he did as Joseph told him. ³ As soon as the morning was light, the men were sent away with their donkeys. ⁴ When they had gone only a short distance from the city, Joseph said to his steward, "Go, follow after the men; and when you overtake them, say to them, 'Why have you returned evil for good? Why have you stolen my silver cup?*a* ⁵ Is it not from this that my lord drinks? Does he not indeed use it for divination? You have done wrong in doing this.'"

6 When he overtook them, he repeated these words to them. ⁷ They said to him, "Why does my lord speak such words as these? Far be it from your servants that they should do such a thing! ⁸ Look, the money that we found at the top of our sacks, we brought back to you from the land of Canaan; why then would we steal silver or gold from your lord's house? ⁹ Should it be found with any one of your servants, let him die; moreover the rest of us will become my lord's slaves." ¹⁰ He said, "Even so; in accordance with your words, let it be: he with whom it is found shall become my slave, but the rest of you shall go free." ¹¹ Then each one quickly lowered his sack to the ground, and each opened his sack. ¹² He

searched, beginning with the eldest and ending with the youngest; and the cup was found in Benjamin's sack. ¹³ At this they tore their clothes. Then each one loaded his donkey, and they returned to the city.

14 Judah and his brothers came to Joseph's house while he was still there; and they fell to the ground before him. ¹⁵ Joseph said to them, "What deed is this that you have done? Do you not know that one such as I can practice divination?" ¹⁶ And Judah said, "What can we say to my lord? What can we speak? How can we clear ourselves? God has found out the guilt of your servants; here we are then, my lord's slaves, both we and also the one in whose possession the cup has been found." ¹⁷ But he said, "Far be it from me that I should do so! Only the one in whose possession the cup was found shall be my slave; but as for you, go up in peace to your father."

Judah Pleads for Benjamin's Release

18 Then Judah stepped up to him and said, "O my lord, let your servant please speak a word in my lord's ears, and do not be angry with your servant; for you are like Pharaoh himself. ¹⁹ My lord asked his servants, saying, 'Have you a father or a brother?' ²⁰ And we said to my lord, 'We have a father, an old man, and a young brother, the child of his old age. His brother is dead; he alone is left of his mother's children, and his father loves him.' ²¹ Then you said to your servants, 'Bring him down to me, so that I may set my eyes on him.' ²² We said to my lord, 'The boy cannot leave his father, for if he

a Gk Compare Vg: Heb lacks *Why have you stolen my silver cup?*

44:1–34 Joseph's Final Test of His Brothers

44:5, 15 *Divination*—See note at 30:27.

44:16 *God has found out*—The brothers' treatment of Joseph has now come full circle (*my lord's slaves*, often noted). Before, the brothers had confessed their guilt to one another (42:21); here, they confess it to Joseph. They also use God language positively (cf. 42:29), bringing together their guilt and God, witnessing to God's activity

to expose their guilt. To say that God has "found out" their guilt witnesses to that activity of both God and Joseph in exposing it (see 41:16; 43:23; 45:8).

44:18–34—This speech of Judah provides the turning point in the narrative (see 43:3). Note the poignancy of his final remark, which prompts Joseph's emotional response in chap. 45.

should leave his father, his father would die.' ²³ Then you said to your servants, 'Unless your youngest brother comes down with you, you shall see my face no more.' ²⁴ When we went back to your servant my father we told him the words of my lord. ²⁵ And when our father said, 'Go again, buy us a little food,' ²⁶ we said, 'We cannot go down. Only if our youngest brother goes with us, will we go down; for we cannot see the man's face unless our youngest brother is with us.' ²⁷ Then your servant my father said to us, 'You know that my wife bore me two sons; ²⁸ one left me, and I said, Surely he has been torn to pieces; and I have never seen him since. ²⁹ If you take this one also from me, and harm comes to him, you will bring down my gray hairs in sorrow to Sheol.' ³⁰ Now therefore, when I come to your servant my father and the boy is not with us, then, as his life is bound up in the boy's life, ³¹ when he sees that the boy is not with us, he will die; and your servants will bring down the gray hairs of your servant our father with sorrow to Sheol. ³² For your servant became surety for the boy to my father, saying, 'If I do not bring him back to you, then I will bear the blame in the sight of my father all my life.' ³³ Now therefore, please let your servant remain as a slave to my lord in place of the boy; and let the boy go back with his brothers. ³⁴ For how can I go back to my father if the boy is not with me? I fear to see the suffering that would come upon my father."

Joseph Reveals Himself to His Brothers

45 Then Joseph could no longer control himself before all those who stood by him, and he cried out, "Send everyone away from me." So no one stayed with him when Joseph made himself known to his brothers. ² And he wept so loudly that the Egyptians heard it, and the household of Pharaoh heard it. ³ Joseph said to his brothers, "I am Joseph. Is my father still alive?" But his brothers could not answer him, so dismayed were they at his presence.

4 Then Joseph said to his brothers, "Come closer to me." And they came closer. He said, "I am your brother, Joseph, whom you sold into Egypt. ⁵ And now do not be distressed, or angry with yourselves, because you sold me here; for God sent me before you to preserve life. ⁶ For the famine has been in the land these two years; and there are five more years in which there will be neither plowing nor harvest. ⁷ God sent me before you to preserve for you a remnant on earth, and to keep alive for you many survivors. ⁸ So it was not

---

45:1–28 Joseph Makes Himself Known

45:1–2, 14–15 *Wept*—See note at 42:24. While some level of reconciliation occurs between Joseph and his brothers at this point, it is not complete until 50:15–21, which shows that the brothers still have a lord/slave mentality; only there does Joseph deal with that issue. Notably, Joseph does not seek to shame his brothers (45:5), and he himself exhibits a character that sets aside royal trappings and vulnerably enters into the pathos of the situation.

45:4, 8 *Whom you sold . . . So it was not you who sent me here, but God*—This seems contradictory, but the force of it is similar to prior formulations (see 41:16; 43:23; 44:16) wherein both human and divine agency are in evidence; however, the decisive action is divine. In this context, God has in effect "taken over" what they in fact have done and used their evil (50:20) to

bring about this good end. Their actions have *become* God's by being woven into the divine life-giving purposes. Even more, *Pharaoh's* actions—elevating Joseph as ruler—have become God's! God's actions are independent of any repentance on the part of the brothers.

45:5 *God sent me . . . to preserve life*—An important theme in the Joseph story is repeated here (e.g., 46:30; 50:20). God's concern is life, especially for this family, but finally for the whole world (see 41:57).

45:7 *A remnant on earth*—Another Genesis theme, which can be tracked back to the saving of the family of Noah (6:8) and on through the prophets (e.g., Isa. 10–11). God is concerned with the survival of this family.

45:8 *A father to Pharaoh*—One whose policies protected Pharaoh.

you who sent me here, but God; he has made me a father to Pharaoh, and lord of all his house and ruler over all the land of Egypt. ⁹Hurry and go up to my father and say to him, 'Thus says your son Joseph, God has made me lord of all Egypt; come down to me, do not delay. ¹⁰You shall settle in the land of Goshen, and you shall be near me, you and your children and your children's children, as well as your flocks, your herds, and all that you have. ¹¹I will provide for you there—since there are five more years of famine to come—so that you and your household, and all that you have, will not come to poverty.' ¹²And now your eyes and the eyes of my brother Benjamin see that it is my own mouth that speaks to you. ¹³You must tell my father how greatly I am honored in Egypt, and all that you have seen. Hurry and bring my father down here." ¹⁴Then he fell upon his brother Benjamin's neck and wept, while Benjamin wept upon his neck. ¹⁵And he kissed all his brothers and wept upon them; and after that his brothers talked with him.

16 When the report was heard in Pharaoh's house, "Joseph's brothers have come," Pharaoh and his servants were pleased. ¹⁷Pharaoh said to Joseph, "Say to your brothers, 'Do this: load your animals and go back to the land of Canaan. ¹⁸Take your father and your households and come to me, so that I may give you the best of the land of Egypt, and you may enjoy the fat of the land.' ¹⁹You are further charged to say, 'Do this: take wagons from the land of Egypt for your little ones and for your wives, and bring your father, and come. ²⁰Give no thought to your possessions, for the best of all the land of Egypt is yours.'"

21 The sons of Israel did so. Joseph gave them wagons according to the instruction of Pharaoh, and he gave them provisions for the journey. ²²To each one of them he gave a set of garments; but to Benjamin he gave three hundred pieces of silver and five sets of garments. ²³To his father he sent the following: ten donkeys loaded with the good things of Egypt, and ten female donkeys loaded with grain, bread, and provision for his father on the journey. ²⁴Then he sent his brothers on their way, and as they were leaving he said to them, "Do not quarrel ᵃ along the way."

25 So they went up out of Egypt and came to their father Jacob in the land of Canaan. ²⁶And they told him, "Joseph is still alive! He is even ruler over all the land of Egypt." He was stunned; he could not believe them. ²⁷But when they told him all the words of Joseph that he had said to them, and when he saw the wagons that Joseph had sent to carry him, the spirit of their father Jacob revived. ²⁸Israel said, "Enough! My son Joseph is still alive. I must go and see him before I die."

Jacob Brings His Whole Family to Egypt

46 When Israel set out on his journey with all that he had and came to Beer-sheba, he offered sacrifices to the God of his father Isaac. ²God spoke to Israel in visions of the night, and said, "Jacob, Jacob." And he said, "Here I am." ³Then he said, "I am God, ᵇ the God of your father; do not be afraid to go down to Egypt, for I will make of you a great nation there. ⁴I myself will go down with you to Egypt, and I will also bring you up again; and Joseph's own hand shall close your eyes."

ᵃ Or be agitated　ᵇ Heb the God

45:10 *The land of Goshen*—A region in the northeastern Nile delta (nearest to Canaan), especially suitable for grazing animals, where the Israelites are settled in Exodus.

45:22 *Benjamin*—Joseph's only full brother receives special gifts.

45:28 *Enough!*—Shorthand for putting the past behind and getting on with new possibilities.

46:1–47:26 The Descent into Egypt

46:1–4—God comes to Jacob with an assuring word, to which Jacob is obediently attentive (cf. Abraham, 22:1). God quells his fear about the

5 Then Jacob set out from Beer-sheba; and the sons of Israel carried their father Jacob, their little ones, and their wives, in the wagons that Pharaoh had sent to carry him. 6 They also took their livestock and the goods that they had acquired in the land of Canaan, and they came into Egypt, Jacob and all his offspring with him, 7 his sons, and his sons' sons with him, his daughters, and his sons' daughters; all his offspring he brought with him into Egypt.

8 Now these are the names of the Israelites, Jacob and his offspring, who came to Egypt. Reuben, Jacob's firstborn, 9 and the children of Reuben: Hanoch, Pallu, Hezron, and Carmi. 10 The children of Simeon: Jemuel, Jamin, Ohad, Jachin, Zohar, and Shaul,*a* the son of a Canaanite woman. 11 The children of Levi: Gershon, Kohath, and Merari. 12 The children of Judah: Er, Onan, Shelah, Perez, and Zerah (but Er and Onan died in the land of Canaan); and the children of Perez were Hezron and Hamul. 13 The children of Issachar: Tola, Puvah, Jashub,*b* and Shimron. 14 The children of Zebulun: Sered, Elon, and Jahleel 15 (these are the sons of Leah, whom she bore to Jacob in Paddan-aram, together with his daughter Dinah; in all his sons and his daughters numbered thirty-three). 16 The children of Gad: Ziphion, Haggi, Shuni, Ezbon, Eri, Arodi, and Areli. 17 The children of Asher: Imnah, Ishvah, Ishvi, Beriah, and their sister Serah. The children of Beriah: Heber and Malchiel 18 (these are the children of Zilpah, whom Laban gave to his daughter Leah; and these she bore to Jacob—six-

teen persons). 19 The children of Jacob's wife Rachel: Joseph and Benjamin. 20 To Joseph in the land of Egypt were born Manasseh and Ephraim, whom Asenath daughter of Potiphera, priest of On, bore to him. 21 The children of Benjamin: Bela, Becher, Ashbel, Gera, Naaman, Ehi, Rosh, Muppim, Huppim, and Ard 22 (these are the children of Rachel, who were born to Jacob—fourteen persons in all). 23 The children of Dan: Hashum.*c* 24 The children of Naphtali: Jahzeel, Guni, Jezer, and Shillem 25 (these are the children of Bilhah, whom Laban gave to his daughter Rachel, and these she bore to Jacob—seven persons in all). 26 All the persons belonging to Jacob who came into Egypt, who were his own offspring, not including the wives of his sons, were sixty-six persons in all. 27 The children of Joseph, who were born to him in Egypt, were two; all the persons of the house of Jacob who came into Egypt were seventy.

Jacob Settles in Goshen

28 Israel*d* sent Judah ahead to Joseph to lead the way before him into Goshen. When they came to the land of Goshen, 29 Joseph made ready his chariot and went up to meet his father Israel in Goshen. He presented himself to him, fell on his neck, and wept on his neck a good while. 30 Israel said to Joseph, "I can die now, having seen for myself that you are still alive." 31 Joseph said to his brothers and to his father's household, "I will go up and tell Pharaoh, and will

a Or *Saul* *b* Compare Sam Gk Num 26.24; 1 Chr 7.1: MT *Iob* *c* Gk: Heb *Hushim* *d* Heb *He*

journey (see 26:24), assuring him of the divine presence; indeed this will be a journey for *God* (46:4). God reiterates the promise of *a great nation* (see 12:2), which will happen in *Egypt*. The move from family to people is now clearly in view and continues through the balance of Genesis.

46:7 *His daughters*—Includes his daughters-in-law (see v. 15; 37:35). The word *children* (46:22) may also include grandchildren.

46:21 *The children of Benjamin*—This reference

indicates that the list of Jacob's descendants assumes a later time.

46:26–27 *Sixty-six persons . . . seventy*—This list constitutes the family of Israel with which the book of Exodus begins (Exod. 1:5). The numbers in vv. 15, 18, 22, and 25 total seventy; the number sixty-six assumes that Er and Onan (v. 12) and Joseph's sons never made the trip.

46:28 *Goshen*—See note at 45:10.

46:29 *Wept*—See 42:24; 45:1–2.

say to him, 'My brothers and my father's household, who were in the land of Canaan, have come to me. ³²The men are shepherds, for they have been keepers of livestock; and they have brought their flocks, and their herds, and all that they have.' ³³When Pharaoh calls you, and says, 'What is your occupation?' ³⁴you shall say, 'Your servants have been keepers of livestock from our youth even until now, both we and our ancestors'—in order that you may settle in the land of Goshen, because all shepherds are abhorrent to the Egyptians."

47 So Joseph went and told Pharaoh, "My father and my brothers, with their flocks and herds and all that they possess, have come from the land of Canaan; they are now in the land of Goshen." ²From among his brothers he took five men and presented them to Pharaoh. ³Pharaoh said to his brothers, "What is your occupation?" And they said to Pharaoh, "Your servants are shepherds, as our ancestors were." ⁴They said to Pharaoh, "We have come to reside as aliens in the land; for there is no pasture for your servants' flocks because the famine is severe in the land of Canaan. Now, we ask you, let your servants settle in the land of Goshen." ⁵Then Pharaoh said to Joseph, "Your father and your brothers have come to you. ⁶The land of Egypt is before you; settle your father and your brothers in the best part of the land; let them live in the land of Goshen; and if you know that there are capable men among them, put them in charge of my livestock."

7 Then Joseph brought in his father Jacob, and presented him before Pharaoh, and Jacob blessed Pharaoh. ⁸Pharaoh said to Jacob, "How many are the years of your life?" ⁹Jacob said to Pharaoh, "The years of my earthly sojourn are one hundred thirty; few and hard have been the years of my life. They do not compare with the years of the life of my ancestors during their long sojourn." ¹⁰Then Jacob blessed Pharaoh, and went out from the presence of Pharaoh. ¹¹Joseph settled his father and his brothers, and granted them a holding in the land of Egypt, in the best part of the land, in the land of Rameses, as Pharaoh had instructed. ¹²And Joseph provided his father, his brothers, and all his father's household with food, according to the number of their dependents.

The Famine in Egypt

13 Now there was no food in all the land, for the famine was very severe. The land of Egypt and the land of Canaan languished because of the famine. ¹⁴Joseph collected all the money to be found in the land of Egypt and in the land of Canaan, in exchange for the grain that they bought; and Joseph brought the money into Pharaoh's house. ¹⁵When the money from the land of Egypt and from the land of Canaan was spent, all the Egyptians came to Joseph, and said, "Give us food! Why should we die before your eyes? For our money is gone." ¹⁶And Joseph answered, "Give me your livestock, and I will give you food in exchange for your livestock, if your money is gone." ¹⁷So they brought their livestock to Joseph; and Joseph gave them food in exchange for the horses, the flocks, the herds, and the donkeys. That year he supplied them with food in exchange for all their livestock. ¹⁸When

---

46:34 *All shepherds are abhorrent*—The reference may be to foreign shepherds. In any case, to stress this point would assure that, given Joseph's position, Pharaoh would be pleased to have his family at some distance from the general populace (and also for ease of escape?).

47:7, 10 *Jacob blessed Pharaoh*—A recurring theme from 12:3.

47:11 *Land of Rameses*—The land of Goshen. The name is anachronistic, referencing the later Pharaoh of the exodus (see Exod. 1:11).

47:13–26—This segment seeks to show Joseph's administrative wisdom (see 41:46–57). Yet the harsh emergency measures concentrating property and power in the crown, with which the Egyptians are pleased (47:25), could become tyrannical under a less benevolent leader.

that year was ended, they came to him the following year, and said to him, "We can not hide from my lord that our money is all spent; and the herds of cattle are my lord's. There is nothing left in the sight of my lord but our bodies and our lands. ¹⁹ Shall we die before your eyes, both we and our land? Buy us and our land in exchange for food. We with our land will become slaves to Pharaoh; just give us seed, so that we may live and not die, and that the land may not become desolate."

20 So Joseph bought all the land of Egypt for Pharaoh. All the Egyptians sold their fields, because the famine was severe upon them; and the land became Pharaoh's. ²¹ As for the people, he made slaves of them *a* from one end of Egypt to the other. ²² Only the land of the priests he did not buy; for the priests had a fixed allowance from Pharaoh, and lived on the allowance that Pharaoh gave them; therefore they did not sell their land. ²³ Then Joseph said to the people, "Now that I have this day bought you and your land for Pharaoh, here is seed for you; sow the land. ²⁴ And at the harvests you shall give one-fifth to Pharaoh, and four-fifths shall be your own, as seed for the field and as food for yourselves and your households, and as food for your little ones." ²⁵ They said, "You have saved our lives; may it please my lord, we will be slaves to Pharaoh." ²⁶ So Joseph made it a statute concerning the land of Egypt, and it stands to this day, that Pharaoh should have the fifth. The land of the priests alone did not become Pharaoh's.

The Last Days of Jacob

27 Thus Israel settled in the land of Egypt, in the region of Goshen; and they gained possessions in it, and were fruitful and multiplied exceedingly. ²⁸ Jacob lived in the land of Egypt seventeen years; so the days of Jacob, the years of his life, were one hundred forty-seven years.

29 When the time of Israel's death drew near, he called his son Joseph and said to him, "If I have found favor with you, put your hand under my thigh and promise to deal loyally and truly with me. Do not bury me in Egypt. ³⁰ When I lie down with my ancestors, carry me out of Egypt and bury me in their burial place." He answered, "I will do as you have said." ³¹ And he said, "Swear to me"; and he swore to him. Then Israel bowed himself on the head of his bed.

Jacob Blesses Joseph's Sons

48 After this Joseph was told, "Your father is ill." So he took with him his two sons, Manasseh and Ephraim. ² When Jacob was told, "Your son Joseph has come to you," he *b* summoned his strength and sat up in bed. ³ And Jacob said to Joseph, "God Almighty *c* appeared to me at Luz in the land of Canaan, and he blessed me, ⁴ and said to me, 'I am going to make you fruitful and increase your numbers; I will make of you a company of peoples, and will give this land to your offspring after you for a perpetual holding.' ⁵ Therefore your two sons, who were born to you in the land of Egypt before I came to you

a Sam Gk Compare Vg: MT *He removed them to the cities*   *b* Heb *Israel*
c Traditional rendering of Heb *El Shaddai*

47:27–48:22 Joseph and His Sons

47:27—This summary verse emphasizes the growth of Israel in Egypt in fulfillment of the divine promise (35:11) and links up with Exod. 1:7.

47:29 *Hand under my thigh*—See note at 24:2.

47:30 *Lie down with my ancestors*—An idiom for death, not an afterlife. *Their burial place*—The cave of Machpelah, where Jacob's ancestors were buried (see 23:9; 49:29–32).

47:31 *Bowed himself*—An approval of the burial arrangements.

48:5 *Ephraim and Manasseh shall be mine*—Jacob confers on Joseph's two sons (grandchildren of his favorite wife, Rachel) full status as his own children. This explains their later status as (prominent) Israelite tribes (in place of Joseph; that Levi is a nonterritorial tribe keeps the number of tribes at twelve). If Joseph has other children, they shall not be accorded this status (v. 6).

in Egypt, are now mine; Ephraim and Manasseh shall be mine, just as Reuben and Simeon are. [6] As for the offspring born to you after them, they shall be yours. They shall be recorded under the names of their brothers with regard to their inheritance. [7] For when I came from Paddan, Rachel, alas, died in the land of Canaan on the way, while there was still some distance to go to Ephrath; and I buried her there on the way to Ephrath" (that is, Bethlehem).

[8] When Israel saw Joseph's sons, he said, "Who are these?" [9] Joseph said to his father, "They are my sons, whom God has given me here." And he said, "Bring them to me, please, that I may bless them." [10] Now the eyes of Israel were dim with age, and he could not see well. So Joseph brought them near him; and he kissed them and embraced them. [11] Israel said to Joseph, "I did not expect to see your face; and here God has let me see your children also." [12] Then Joseph removed them from his father's knees,[a] and he bowed himself with his face to the earth. [13] Joseph took them both, Ephraim in his right hand toward Israel's left, and Manasseh in his left hand toward Israel's right, and brought them near him. [14] But Israel stretched out his right hand and laid it on the head of Ephraim, who was the younger, and his left hand on the head of Manasseh, crossing his hands, for Manasseh was the firstborn. [15] He blessed Joseph, and said,

"The God before whom my
    ancestors Abraham and Isaac
    walked,

the God who has been my shepherd
    all my life to this day,
[16] the angel who has redeemed me
    from all harm, bless the boys;
and in them let my name be
    perpetuated, and the name of
    my ancestors Abraham and
    Isaac;
and let them grow into a multitude
    on the earth."

[17] When Joseph saw that his father laid his right hand on the head of Ephraim, it displeased him; so he took his father's hand, to remove it from Ephraim's head to Manasseh's head. [18] Joseph said to his father, "Not so, my father! Since this one is the firstborn, put your right hand on his head." [19] But his father refused, and said, "I know, my son, I know; he also shall become a people, and he also shall be great. Nevertheless his younger brother shall be greater than he, and his offspring shall become a multitude of nations." [20] So he blessed them that day, saying,

"By you[b] Israel will invoke blessings,
    saying,
'God make you[b] like Ephraim and
    like Manasseh.'"

So he put Ephraim ahead of Manasseh. [21] Then Israel said to Joseph, "I am about to die, but God will be with you and will bring you again to the land of your ancestors. [22] I now give to you one portion[c] more than to your brothers, the portion[c] that I took from the hand of the Amorites with my sword and with my bow."

---

[a] Heb from his knees   [b] you here is singular in Heb   [c] Or mountain slope (Heb shekem, a play on the name of the town and district of Shechem)

48:7 *Paddan* —Paddan-aram (see 25:20). *Ephrath*—See 35:16.

48:13–19—Joseph places Manasseh on the right of Jacob, the favored position, but Jacob crosses his hands (over Joseph's objection, vv. 17–18), so that his right hand is laid on Ephraim and gives him the favored position (once again, the second born). Jacob proceeds to bless their father Joseph (which includes his sons) with a remarkable confessional statement regarding God's role in his life. Jacob blesses Manasseh in terms

not unlike those given Ishmael by Abraham (see 17:20; 21:13). The growth of these two tribes is sharply evident already in Num. 26:28–37. Among Israel's leaders, Joshua and Samuel were descendants of Ephraim, Gideon of Manasseh.

48:20 *By you*—The "you" is singular. The first "you" probably refers to Joseph (see v. 15) and the second "you" refers to the one being blessed: May you be blessed as Joseph's two sons were.

48:22—The elevation of Joseph's sons entails an elevation of Joseph to the status of firstborn, who

Jacob's Last Words to His Sons

49 Then Jacob called his sons, and said: "Gather around, that I may tell you what will happen to you in days to come.

2 Assemble and hear, O sons of Jacob;
   listen to Israel your father.

3 Reuben, you are my firstborn,
      my might and the first fruits of my vigor,
      excelling in rank and excelling in power.
4 Unstable as water, you shall no longer excel
   because you went up onto your father's bed;
   then you defiled it—you[a] went up onto my couch!

5 Simeon and Levi are brothers;
      weapons of violence are their swords.
6 May I never come into their council;
   may I not be joined to their company—
   for in their anger they killed men,
   and at their whim they hamstrung oxen.
7 Cursed be their anger, for it is fierce,
   and their wrath, for it is cruel!

I will divide them in Jacob,
   and scatter them in Israel.

8 Judah, your brothers shall praise you;
   your hand shall be on the neck of your enemies;
   your father's sons shall bow down before you.
9 Judah is a lion's whelp;
   from the prey, my son, you have gone up.
He crouches down, he stretches out like a lion,
   like a lioness—who dares rouse him up?
10 The scepter shall not depart from Judah,
   nor the ruler's staff from between his feet,
until tribute comes to him;[b]
   and the obedience of the peoples is his.
11 Binding his foal to the vine
      and his donkey's colt to the choice vine,
   he washes his garments in wine
      and his robe in the blood of grapes;

a Gk Syr Tg: Heb *he*   *b* Or *until Shiloh comes* or *until he comes to Shiloh* or (with Syr) *until he comes to whom it belongs*

---

in his sons receives the double inheritance of the firstborn (Josh. 17:14–18; see Deut. 21:15–17). The word *portion* is a play on the town of Shechem, a central city in the tribal territory of Ephraim.

49:1–33 The Last Words of Jacob

49:1–28—See the comparable poem in Deut. 33:1–29. The poetry is difficult, and translations are often proximate (see NRSV footnotes). The differences in the form and content of the various sayings suggests that they come from disparate times and places. The *blessing* of Jacob on his sons assumes the later tribal units (Gen. 49:28) and probably reflects later tribal history in part. Moreover, the poem includes curse and censure (vv. 4–7) and hence is not simply a blessing (v. 28), but the overall perspective is positive. Judah (vv. 8–12) and Joseph (vv. 22–26) receive the most extensive and most positive blessings, reflecting their dominance in the narrative and in later tribal history.

49:3–4 *Your father's bed*—See 35:22. The tribe of Reuben was later absorbed by the Moabites.

49:5–7 *Weapons of violence*—Based on their actions in 34:25–29. Their dividing and scattering corresponds to Simeon's absorption into Judah (Josh. 19:9) and Levi's priestly landlessness (Num. 18:20–24).

49:8–10—Judah's blessing, at the heart of which is a promise (esp. v. 10), anticipates the Davidic monarchy (see 38:27–30). Its images are used in royal and messianic texts (see Num. 24:17; "the lion of Judah," Rev. 5:5).

49:10 *Until tribute comes to him*—A difficult text (see NRSV footnote). It could be a reference to a unified Israel (Shiloh was a northern center) or, more likely, a person, whose rule (=*scepter*/staff) will continue until a glorious and fertile future is assured (vv. 11–12).

12 his eyes are darker than wine,
  and his teeth whiter than milk.

13 Zebulun shall settle at the shore of
    the sea;
  he shall be a haven for ships,
    and his border shall be at Sidon.

14 Issachar is a strong donkey,
  lying down between the
    sheepfolds;
15 he saw that a resting place was
    good,
  and that the land was pleasant;
    so he bowed his shoulder to the
    burden,
  and became a slave at forced labor.

16 Dan shall judge his people
  as one of the tribes of Israel.
17 Dan shall be a snake by the roadside,
  a viper along the path,
    that bites the horse's heels
  so that its rider falls backward.

18 I wait for your salvation, O LORD.

19 Gad shall be raided by raiders,
  but he shall raid at their heels.

20 Asher's[a] food shall be rich,
  and he shall provide royal
    delicacies.

21 Naphtali is a doe let loose
  that bears lovely fawns.[b]

22 Joseph is a fruitful bough,
  a fruitful bough by a spring;
    his branches run over the wall.[c]
23 The archers fiercely attacked him;
  they shot at him and pressed him
    hard.
24 Yet his bow remained taut,
  and his arms[d] were made agile
    by the hands of the Mighty One of
    Jacob,
  by the name of the Shepherd, the
    Rock of Israel,
25 by the God of your father, who will
    help you,

by the Almighty[e] who will bless
    you
  with blessings of heaven above,
blessings of the deep that lies
    beneath,
  blessings of the breasts and of the
    womb.
26 The blessings of your father
  are stronger than the blessings of
    the eternal mountains,
  the bounties[f] of the everlasting
    hills;
may they be on the head of Joseph,
  on the brow of him who was set
    apart from his brothers.

27 Benjamin is a ravenous wolf,
  in the morning devouring the
    prey,
  and at evening dividing the spoil."

28 All these are the twelve tribes of
Israel, and this is what their father said
to them when he blessed them, blessing each one of them with a suitable
blessing.

Jacob's Death and Burial

29 Then he charged them, saying to
them, "I am about to be gathered to my
people. Bury me with my ancestors—in
the cave in the field of Ephron the Hittite, 30 in the cave in the field at Machpelah, near Mamre, in the land of Canaan,
in the field that Abraham bought from
Ephron the Hittite as a burial site.
31 There Abraham and his wife Sarah
were buried; there Isaac and his wife
Rebekah were buried; and there I buried
Leah— 32 the field and the cave that is
in it were purchased from the Hittites."
33 When Jacob ended his charge to his
sons, he drew up his feet into the bed,
breathed his last, and was gathered to
his people.

---

a Gk Vg Syr: Heb *From Asher*   *b* Or *that gives beautiful words*   *c* Meaning
of Heb uncertain   *d* Heb *the arms of his hands*   *e* Traditional rendering of
Heb *Shaddai*   *f* Cn Compare Gk: Heb *of my progenitors to the boundaries*

49:22–26—The sixfold use of the word *blessing*
makes this segment about Joseph and his sons
especially optimistic.

49:29–33—A variant of 47:29–31, this time ending with Jacob's death.

50

Then Joseph threw himself on his father's face and wept over him and kissed him. ² Joseph commanded the physicians in his service to embalm his father. So the physicians embalmed Israel; ³ they spent forty days in doing this, for that is the time required for embalming. And the Egyptians wept for him seventy days.

4 When the days of weeping for him were past, Joseph addressed the household of Pharaoh, "If now I have found favor with you, please speak to Pharaoh as follows: ⁵ My father made me swear an oath; he said, 'I am about to die. In the tomb that I hewed out for myself in the land of Canaan, there you shall bury me.' Now therefore let me go up, so that I may bury my father; then I will return." ⁶ Pharaoh answered, "Go up, and bury your father, as he made you swear to do."

7 So Joseph went up to bury his father. With him went up all the servants of Pharaoh, the elders of his household, and all the elders of the land of Egypt, ⁸ as well as all the household of Joseph, his brothers, and his father's household. Only their children, their flocks, and their herds were left in the land of Goshen. ⁹ Both chariots and charioteers went up with him. It was a very great company. ¹⁰ When they came to the threshing floor of Atad, which is beyond the Jordan, they held there a very great and sorrowful lamentation; and he observed a time of mourning for his father seven days. ¹¹ When the Canaanite inhabitants of the land saw the mourning on the threshing floor of Atad, they said, "This is a grievous mourning on the part of the Egyptians." Therefore the place was named Abel-mizraim;ᵃ it is beyond the Jordan. ¹² Thus his sons did for him as he had instructed them. ¹³ They carried him to the land of Canaan and buried him in the cave of the field at Machpelah, the field near Mamre, which Abraham bought as a burial site from Ephron the Hittite. ¹⁴ After he had buried his father, Joseph returned to Egypt with his brothers and all who had gone up with him to bury his father.

Joseph Forgives His Brothers

15 Realizing that their father was dead, Joseph's brothers said, "What if Joseph still bears a grudge against us and pays us back in full for all the wrong that we did to him?" ¹⁶ So they approachedᵇ Joseph, saying, "Your father gave this instruction before he died, ¹⁷ 'Say to Joseph: I beg you, forgive the crime of your brothers and the wrong they did in harming you.' Now therefore please forgive the crime of the servants of the God of your father." Joseph wept when they spoke to him. ¹⁸ Then his brothers also wept,ᶜ fell down before him, and said, "We are here as your slaves." ¹⁹ But Joseph said to them, "Do not be afraid! Am I in the place of God?

ᵃ That is *mourning* (or *meadow*) *of Egypt*   ᵇ Gk Syr: Heb *they commanded*
ᶜ Cn: Heb *also came*

50:1–14 The Burial of Jacob

50:1–14—The mourning of the Egyptians for the Israelite Jacob is elaborate and remarkable, especially given the conflict to come in Exodus.

50:11 *Atad*—An unknown site, aptly renamed *Abel-mizraim* ("mourning of Egypt").

50:15–21 The Full Reconciliation of Israel's Sons

50:16 *Your father gave this instruction*—This instruction is not recorded elsewhere; it could be a self-serving effort on the part of the brothers, but is probably truthful. They have a high consciousness of the crime they have committed, evident in their repetitive words about sin and forgiveness.

50:17 *Joseph wept*—See 42:24; 45:1–2.

50:18 *His brothers . . . fell down before him*—This gesture does not fulfill Joseph's dream of 37:7 (as it does in 42:6; 43:26; 44:14), for Joseph rejects such a status as finally inappropriate.

50:19 *Am I in the place of God?*—Probably has reference both to their request for forgiveness and their offer to become slaves. Joseph is not God, and hence he will not be a Pharaoh to them; they will be servants of God alone. Also, though he is highly conciliatory, Joseph rejects a guilt-and-forgiveness approach, leaving that matter up to God.

[20] Even though you intended to do harm to me, God intended it for good, in order to preserve a numerous people, as he is doing today. [21] So have no fear; I myself will provide for you and your little ones." In this way he reassured them, speaking kindly to them.

Joseph's Last Days and Death

22 So Joseph remained in Egypt, he and his father's household; and Joseph lived one hundred ten years. [23] Joseph saw Ephraim's children of the third generation; the children of Machir son of Manasseh were also born on Joseph's knees.

24 Then Joseph said to his brothers, "I am about to die; but God will surely come to you, and bring you up out of this land to the land that he swore to Abraham, to Isaac, and to Jacob." [25] So Joseph made the Israelites swear, saying, "When God comes to you, you shall carry up my bones from here." [26] And Joseph died, being one hundred ten years old; he was embalmed and placed in a coffin in Egypt.

50:20 *Though you intended to do harm to me, God intended it for good*—Joseph names the brothers' actions evil (see 44:4–5), but God has drawn their actions into God's larger purposes for goodness, and these have come to prevail (see 45:4–8). Working from within their very evil plans, God has been working for good. The theme of goodness and life returns to that of the creation story; Joseph serves God's purposes in creation. Sin and evil, with all of their consequences, do not have the last word. God's good will for life perseveres through everything.

50:22–26 The Promise Transmitted

50:23 *Born on Joseph's knees*—That is, claimed as his descendants.

50:24—Joseph transmits the promises of God to Abraham, Isaac, and Jacob to all the brothers. Anticipating the exodus, he assures them that, while God will indeed visit them in Egypt, God will bring them up from there to the land of promise.

EXODUS

T he title of the book derives from the Greek word for "exit," because it is literally about *exiting*. The first part of the story (chaps. 1–15) tells how a group of
slaves exits from their situation of oppression to freedom. The second part of the
story (chaps. 16–40) tells how a "mixed crowd" (12:38) exits from estrangement to
covenant community. The movement from oppression to freedom is what has made
Exodus the authorizing document for so many movements of liberation.

Who God Is

   Though the theme of liberation is central to Exodus, there are also other interests.
One interest is in the identity of God. Who is God? What does God do? Here are
some of the ways Exodus identifies God.

   A. *God who calls.* God calls Moses to lead the people out of bondage (3:1–4:17; cf.
Judg. 6:11–24; Isa. 6:1–13; Jer. 1:4–19). God calls the people to be holy (Exod. 19:6).

   B. *God who is "I AM."* The divine name is revealed to Moses in Exodus 3:14. Linguistically the Hebrew of 3:14 can be translated a number of ways: "I am who/what
I am"; "I will be who/what I will be"; "I create who/what I create"; "I bring into
being who/what I bring into being"; "I cause to be who/what I cause to be." The latter
translations assert the creative character of God. This God will be able to create a
new nation out of a group of slaves. The ambiguous and indeterminate nature of the
translation asserts that God is beyond human control and understanding. If God is so
beyond, then can God also be near? God's name is also linguistically related to God's
promise "I will be with you" (3:12). "I will be" is the same first person form as "I AM."
Thus "I AM" is also Immanuel (God with us). Exodus makes clear what it means to
declare "God with us."

   C. *God who delivers.* Like the Hebrews and the Egyptians, we will know who God
is by witnessing what God does in the world (6:7; 7:5, 17; 8:10, 22; 9:14; 10:2; 14:4,
18; 16:6, 12; 29:46). What God does is bring the Hebrews out of Egypt. What matters is not that slaves are free, but that God frees slaves. In the end, God's identity is
revealed in acts of liberation.

   D. *God who fights.* Exodus 15 is one of the earliest traditions of holy or divine war
theology. God claims to be a warrior because it is *God's* decisive act of liberation, not
the people's. God fights, not the people. At the sea, the Hebrews are not called to do
battle in the usual sense of the word, but to respond to and trust in God as the sole
warrior against the military might of Egypt (14:14). God as warrior answers a particular, if you will, "historical" question, namely, how do you explain the victory of some
slaves over the might (political, military, theological) of Pharaoh and Egypt? The only
plausible explanation is that (a) it was a miracle and (b) it was because God fought for
the Hebrews.

   E. *God who is incomprehensible.* God is not merely mysterious, but perverse. In

Exodus God promises an already populated land to the Hebrew slaves (3:8, 17; 13:5), attempts to kill Moses (4:24–26), hardens Pharaoh's heart (7:3; 9:12; 10:1, 20, 27; 11:10; 14:4, 8), and kills all the Egyptian firstborn (4:21–23; 11:5; 12:12, 29: 13:15). Exodus recognizes that even these seemingly objectionable acts are a part of who God is.

Who Israel Is

Exodus is also interested in the identity of the people. Who are they as the people of God? How will they be in the world? Here are some of the ways Exodus identifies the people.

A. *A free people.* Israel's primary identity is as *former* slaves. They are *out of* Egypt (13:3, 8, 9, 14, 16; 18:1; 23:15). This identity is fundamental for Israel (Deut. 5:6; 6:20–24; 26:5–9; Josh. 24:4–7; 1 Sam. 10:18; 12:6–8; 1 Kgs. 8:51, 53; Pss. 81:5–10; 105:23–45; 136:10–16; Hos. 11:1). It is so central to Israel's identity that the exilic prophet in Isaiah 40–55 will declare the return from exile in the language of the book of Exodus. The return becomes a new exodus, God's new act of deliverance (Isa. 42:13; 43:2–3, 15–21; 48:20–21; 51:9–11; 52:11–12).

B. *A covenant people.* Much of the discussion on the Mosaic or Sinaitic covenant in the twentieth century focused on how the covenant paralleled various treaties found in other western Asian states. The treaty parallel identifies the divine/human relationship as that of *king and vassal.* Thus, when the people enter into covenant relationship with God, the treatylike nature of the covenant suggests that the people be identified as God's subjects. One of the issues in Exodus is whom the people will *serve.* In its noun form, one who serves can be a slave. The question for the people's identity is whether they will be slaves of Pharaoh or of YHWH. Covenant gives the former slaves their true identity: they are *God's treasured possession* and a *holy nation* (19:5–6). The covenant will make them God's people, and they will be set apart as mediators of God's way to the world.

The way Israel lives out its covenant life can be seen as the beginning of the reign of God (cf. Matt. 6:33; Mk. 1:15; Luke 4:43). To know what that realm looks like, you need only to examine the Decalogue (Exod. 20:1–17) and the Covenant Code (20:22–23:33). The legal materials are the Ruler's instruction of the way in which the divine reign is to be manifested in the human community. In other words, it's about God's will being done on earth, as it is in heaven.

It is important to see the formation of a covenant people as a response to God's gracious acts in Exodus. *Because* God brought the people out from Egypt and bore them on eagle's wings, *therefore* they would live in gracious and joyous response to that (19:4–5; 20:2–17). Law has *always* followed gospel. The impetus for obedience to the law is grounded in God's grace. Obedience to the law *is not* a means to right relationship with God. The people are *already* in relationship with God.

Other Themes

Other central interests in Exodus are the legal materials, the wilderness, the tabernacle, and the role of women.

A. *Legal material.* The main point of the legal material is *to structure covenant life.* There are numerous types of law. *Apodictic or absolute laws* (e.g., Decalogue; 20:1–17) are laws that focus on the requirement, not the penalty. They prohibit broad

forms of behavior. These laws derive from a family or clan ethos in the form of direct instruction. Just as today when we talk about capital punishment, *capital laws* are laws where the death penalty or its equivalent (to be cut off from the community) is required for violation of the law (21:12, 15–17; 31:14–15; 35:2). Capital punishment is associated with the fundamental laws that guard the things that matter most. *Casuistic or case laws* are structured around "If . . . then . . . ." These laws are usually in mind when the tradition refers to "statutes and ordinances." This kind of law develops as guidelines based on community experience. Thus, precedents are set that guide the community in its future. These laws derive from the regular, judicial process that is common to all communities. Some of the main themes of the laws are justice (21:2, 13, 18, 22–24, 33–36), God's compassion for those in need (22:21–27; 23:1–12), and worship (23:14–19; chaps. 25–31).

B. *The wilderness.* The theme of wandering in the wilderness begins at Exodus 15:22 and continues through Numbers. One theme of this narrative is failure. The people rebel against the God who delivered them. The main stories of complaint over resources are repeated (manna/quail: Exod. 16 and Num. 11; water: Exod. 17:1–7 and Num. 20). The overall message seems to be that the people have complained from beginning to end. Other acts of rebellion in the wilderness include the golden calf (Exod. 32–34), dispute over prophetic leadership (Num. 12), refusal to enter the land (Num. 13–14), and dispute over priestly leadership (Num. 16–17). This failure lends the narrative its most acute sense of God's providential care for the people. Even in the face of their stubborn resistance, God does not abandon them. In the wilderness the people learn the necessity of trust in God for fulfilling their mission as the people of God.

Another wilderness theme is life in the transition between slavery and freedom. This theme is about change and living in the transition from one paradigm to another. Israel was in slavery. Now they are free, but they don't know where they are going. They will wander in the wilderness for forty years. How do they survive? God will lead and guide—the pillar of fire and cloud moving ahead; and God will provide—food, water, leadership.

Why are these themes emphasized? The various materials in Exodus were probably finally edited in the period of exile (587–540 BCE) when the people found themselves outside of the promised land as they had been in the wilderness. By telling the story of the wilderness during the exile, the people recalled their disobedience *and* God's faithfulness—despite their disobedience. That God hadn't rejected the people in the wilderness would have provided comfort and motivation for the folk in exile.

C. *The tabernacle.* The tradition of the tabernacle (chaps. 25–40) is about God's immanence and transcendence. One of the concerns of this tradition is to understand how a holy God can come into the midst of an unclean people. This mediating between God's transcendence and immanence is accomplished via the tabernacle.

The tabernacle uses the traditions of the ark of the covenant and the tent of meeting. Until the building of the temple in Jerusalem (1 Kgs. 6–8), the ark was understood to be the portable meeting place of heaven and earth. The ark was where God would be present to the people, that is, the location of God's perpetual presence (Exod. 25:22; Num. 10:33–36; 1 Sam. 3:3; 4:3–4). The theological problem with the ark was the danger of confining God; it downplayed God's freedom and transcendence.

The tent of meeting was the place of the occasional immanence of God. The tent

was a shrine for receiving oracles. The divine presence did not reside there permanently but was manifested occasionally, in the form of a pillar of cloud, whenever Moses entered the tent to inquire of God (Exod. 33:7–11). The tent emphasized God's hiddenness and mobility. God is essentially transcendent but would occasionally appear. The theological problem with the tent is the uncertainty of when or where God will be present.

The tabernacle maintained this tension by putting *the ark in the tent*, which leads to God's sure presence and sure freedom (25:16; 26:33; 36:14; 40:2–3, 18–22). This combination led to the creation of a new term, *tabernacle*. As both noun and verb this word maintains the tension.

D. *Women.* Women play a prominent role in the book of Exodus, especially at the beginning. The midwives Shiphrah and Puah are biblical paradigms for civil disobedience (1:15–21). Moses' mother and sister are slaves who subvert the power of the overlord (2:1–4, 7–10). Pharaoh's daughter is inside the courts of power and commits an act of treason in defying her father's command (2:5–10). Zipporah, Moses' wife, acts to save Moses from the anger of God, thereby helping Moses to emerge as leader (4:24–26). Later Miriam plays an important leadership role in the new community (15:20–21), and women assist in the building of the tabernacle (35:21–26, 29).

For all this, they are relatively absent from the legal materials. This absence reflects the patriarchal bias of biblical communities. You may read somewhere or hear from someone that in the Old Testament "women are property." Exodus 20:17 is often cited in support of this view. However, that statement is not true. An examination of the laws that deal with women makes clear that women could not be treated in an arbitrary and capricious manner. The fact that there is gender inequity in the laws does not justify the conclusion that women are property.

Historicity

A final consideration is the question of historicity. Whenever a movie about an historical event is made, a reviewer can ask, "But is it true to history?" The same can be asked about movies that portray biblical history. But another question also has to be asked, "Is it true to the story in the text?" In regard to the first question, there is no definitive answer. The only record of the event is the book of Exodus. There are no records in Egyptian archives that tell this tale. Scholars don't even agree. There are generally two accepted ranges of dates for the exodus, the "early" date (approximately 1400s BCE) and the "late" date (approximately 1200s BCE). In addition to the lack of nonbiblical witnesses to the event, the discrepancy arises because the Pharaoh of 1:8 is not identified, the sites of the two cities (1:11) are disputed, and the Bible is inconsistent about the dating of the event (Gen. 15:13, 16; Exod. 12:40; 1 Kgs. 6:1). Not only can't we be sure of when the exodus happened, nobody is sure about Mount Sinai's location, and there are three proposals for the route through the wilderness! All this doesn't mean that it didn't happen the way it says; it just means it can't be proven. As to the second question, you will just have to read the story and see the movies and decide for yourself.

—Nancy R. Bowen

1 These are the names of the sons of Israel who came to Egypt with Jacob, each with his household: ² Reuben, Simeon, Levi, and Judah, ³ Issachar, Zebulun, and Benjamin, ⁴ Dan and Naphtali, Gad and Asher. ⁵ The total number of people born to Jacob was seventy. Joseph was already in Egypt. ⁶ Then Joseph died, and all his brothers, and that whole generation. ⁷ But the Israelites were fruitful and prolific; they multiplied and grew exceedingly strong, so that the land was filled with them.

The Israelites Are Oppressed

8 Now a new king arose over Egypt, who did not know Joseph. ⁹ He said to his people, "Look, the Israelite people are more numerous and more powerful than we. ¹⁰ Come, let us deal shrewdly with them, or they will increase and, in the event of war, join our enemies and fight against us and escape from the land." ¹¹ Therefore they set taskmasters over them to oppress them with forced labor. They built supply cities, Pithom and Rameses, for Pharaoh. ¹² But the more they were oppressed, the more they multiplied and spread, so that the Egyptians came to dread the Israelites. ¹³ The Egyptians became ruthless in imposing tasks on the Israelites, ¹⁴ and made their lives bitter with hard service in mortar and brick and in every kind of field labor. They were ruthless in all the tasks that they imposed on them.

15 The king of Egypt said to the Hebrew midwives, one of whom was named Shiphrah and the other Puah, ¹⁶ "When you act as midwives to the Hebrew women, and see them on the birthstool, if it is a boy, kill him; but if it is a girl, she shall live." ¹⁷ But the midwives feared God; they did not do as the king of Egypt commanded them, but they let the boys live. ¹⁸ So the king of Egypt summoned the midwives and said to them, "Why have you done this, and allowed the boys to live?" ¹⁹ The midwives said to Pharaoh, "Because the Hebrew women are not like the Egyptian women; for they are vigorous and give birth before the midwife comes to them." ²⁰ So God dealt well with the

---

1:1–15:27 A Group of Slaves Finds Freedom

1:8—The *new king* is not identified. This permits us to see how others, including ourselves, also act as Pharaoh. Throughout this story, identify with the Egyptians, as well as with the Hebrew slaves.

Egypt means "narrow straits." The Hebrew can mean "straits," "distress," or "adversary, foe." Traditionally Egypt has been understood to mean a spiritual state, the *narrow place* of confusion, fragmentation, and spiritual disconnection. But as Exodus makes clear, "narrow straits" is also a physical, social, and political place of hostility and adversity.

Oppression begins silently and unobtrusively because Pharaoh does **not know Joseph**. *Knowing* has profound consequences for *doing* (see note at 2:24–25).

1:9–10—In Hebrew "shrewd" has overtones of wisdom. But here wisdom is perverted by this plan for *ethnic cleansing*. There is no evidence the Hebrews posed a real threat to Pharaoh. The notion that a group is a *threat to vital security interests* is a matter of perception. History has no shortage of methods for dealing shrewdly with those we think may be inclined to fight against

us, especially if one day they might outnumber us. Any country receiving a large influx of immigrants asks how it will deal with this new, unknown group. How might we act differently than Pharaoh towards the increasing Asian, Hispanic, and Muslim populations in the U.S.?

1:11—Oppression in Exodus is focused on political and economic exploitation. Exodus does not deal with other forms of oppression such as sexism or racism.

1:15–2:10—Women play a central role in the story. The acts of the midwives (1:15–21), Moses' mother and sister (2:1–4), and Pharaoh's daughter (2:5–10) all make liberation possible by working to save the life of Moses. Each woman uses the limited power she has to thwart the plan of Pharaoh. We must each use the limited power we have to thwart the powers of oppression.

1:17—To *fear God* is to have a profound and deep knowledge of God and to act in harmony with it (cf. Prov. 2:5–15). The midwives participate in nonviolent resistance to oppression by refusing to carry out Pharaoh's edict to kill baby boys. They refuse to act in ways that are not in harmony with God's activity in the world.

midwives; and the people multiplied and became very strong. ²¹ And because the midwives feared God, he gave them families. ²² Then Pharaoh commanded all his people, "Every boy that is born to the Hebrews*ᵃ* you shall throw into the Nile, but you shall let every girl live."

Birth and Youth of Moses

2 Now a man from the house of Levi went and married a Levite woman. ² The woman conceived and bore a son; and when she saw that he was a fine baby, she hid him three months. ³ When she could hide him no longer she got a papyrus basket for him, and plastered it with bitumen and pitch; she put the child in it and placed it among the reeds on the bank of the river. ⁴ His sister stood at a distance, to see what would happen to him.

5 The daughter of Pharaoh came down to bathe at the river, while her attendants walked beside the river. She saw the basket among the reeds and sent her maid to bring it. ⁶ When she opened it, she saw the child. He was crying, and she took pity on him. "This must be one of the Hebrews' children," she said. ⁷ Then his sister said to Pharaoh's daughter, "Shall I go and get you a nurse from the Hebrew women to nurse the child for you?" ⁸ Pharaoh's daughter said to her, "Yes." So the girl went and called the child's mother. ⁹ Pharaoh's daughter said to her, "Take this child and nurse it for me, and I will give you your wages." So the woman took the child and nursed it. ¹⁰ When the child grew up, she brought him to Pharaoh's daughter, and she took him as her son. She named him Moses,*ᵇ* "because," she said, "I drew him out*ᶜ* of the water."

Moses Flees to Midian

11 One day, after Moses had grown up, he went out to his people and saw their forced labor. He saw an Egyptian beating a Hebrew, one of his kinsfolk. ¹² He looked this way and that, and seeing no one he killed the Egyptian and hid him in the sand. ¹³ When he went out the next day, he saw two Hebrews fighting; and he said to the one who was in the wrong, "Why do you strike your fellow Hebrew?" ¹⁴ He answered, "Who made you a ruler and judge over us? Do you mean to kill me as you killed the Egyptian?" Then Moses was afraid and thought, "Surely the thing is known." ¹⁵ When Pharaoh heard of it, he sought to kill Moses.

ᵃ Sam Gk Tg: Heb lacks *to the Hebrews* *ᵇ* Heb *Mosheh* *ᶜ* Heb *mashah*

2:3—Who is such a woman that she would give up her baby and then stand back to see what would happen? Incarcerated women can identify with Moses' mother. They understand that when you are in bondage (in jail) it may be best to give up your baby to someone else who can love, nurture, and care for it when you can't.

2:5—Pharaoh's daughter demonstrates the resistance of one who is a part of the system of domination and oppression. She can be seen as an early biblical example of a group of people who will be known in later Judaism as *righteous Gentiles*, like Oskar Schindler, who rescued Jews from the Nazi death camps. Righteous Gentiles are those who have learned to love their enemies. Just as Schindler was not the only righteous Gentile during WWII, perhaps there were other Egyptian daughters who rescued other Hebrew sons. Consider how we might love our enemies.

2:10—The liberator, Moses, is someone who belongs to two worlds. As the son of Pharaoh's daughter, he belongs to the world of the oppressor. As the son of a Levite's daughter, he belongs to the world of the oppressed. An effective leader is one who knows *both* sides of a situation.

2:12—Moses intervenes to prevent the injustice of a Hebrew slave being beaten to death by committing another injustice, killing the Egyptian. This future liberator is also a fugitive from justice, at least the justice of Pharaoh. Many leaders, from the perspective of the oppressed, have engaged in a justified act of violence but, from the perspective of the oppressors, are lawbreakers needing to be brought to justice. One group's liberator is another group's terrorist.

2:17—Moses' *defense* of the women is the Hebrew word used in 14:30 to describe God's saving activity at the Reed Sea and is the root from which the names Joshua, Isaiah, and Jesus are derived. Here salvation means access to the well and the water so necessary to life in the desert. Then, as now, water rights and access to water

But Moses fled from Pharaoh. He settled in the land of Midian, and sat down by a well. ¹⁶ The priest of Midian had seven daughters. They came to draw water, and filled the troughs to water their father's flock. ¹⁷ But some shepherds came and drove them away. Moses got up and came to their defense and watered their flock. ¹⁸ When they returned to their father Reuel, he said, "How is it that you have come back so soon today?" ¹⁹ They said, "An Egyptian helped us against the shepherds; he even drew water for us and watered the flock." ²⁰ He said to his daughters, "Where is he? Why did you leave the man? Invite him to break bread." ²¹ Moses agreed to stay with the man, and he gave Moses his daughter Zipporah in marriage. ²² She bore a son, and he named him Gershom; for he said, "I have been an alien[a] residing in a foreign land."

23 After a long time the king of Egypt died. The Israelites groaned under their slavery, and cried out. Out of the slavery their cry for help rose up to God. ²⁴ God heard their groaning, and God remembered his covenant with Abraham, Isaac, and Jacob. ²⁵ God looked upon the Israelites, and God took notice of them.

Moses at the Burning Bush

3 Moses was keeping the flock of his father-in-law Jethro, the priest of Midian; he led his flock beyond the wilderness, and came to Horeb, the mountain of God. ² There the angel of the

[a] Heb ger

---

are crucial political and social issues. To deprive someone of water is an act of injustice.

2:19—Help is another word used in Exodus to describe God's deliverance (cf. 3:8; 6:6; 18:8–10). It means to snatch away from one place/situation and put in another. Sometimes deliverance comes in the form of being removed from a situation of distress and being placed in a situation of calm. This kind of help would be like helping a battered woman to leave her batterer and go to a shelter.

2:22—Gershom means "an alien there." The name of Moses' and Zipporah's son reflects Moses' own status as an alien or outsider (see note at 22:21).

2:23–24—In the theology of this twofold movement, the crying out of the oppressed and God's hearing, the catalyst for divine deliverance is the outcry. Only now in the story does Israel find its voice. So only now does God enter the story. From the beginning of the story until now, oppression continues unabated, and God doesn't appear to do anything about it. This is the world in which most of us are engaged in acts for peace and justice. Oppression continues unabated and God appears absent. In such a world, how can we make a dent or make a difference? The story of the women of Exodus tells us that in the face of Pharaoh, we can still save one baby. We can do what we have the power and ability to do. We must also discover ways for the oppressed to find their voice and cry out their pain and outrage. Together these may not make a bit of difference to the Pharaohs of the world, but the story tells us that these seemingly insignificant acts are really the beginning of salvation.

2:24–25—The activity that God now engages in is described by four verbs. First, God *hears* the people. Then God *remembers* the covenant with the ancestors. God's remembering reminds us that this is a politically engaged text. God takes sides. In this instance, God is on the side of the people with whom God has made a covenant. Next God *looks upon* the people. Seeing means to strike a responsive chord, to begin to move toward the other with kindness or sympathy (3:7, 9; 4:31; cf. Gen. 31:42). To *take notice* is literally *to know*. Knowing someone is so to share an experience with another that the other's experience can be called one's own. This is why knowing someone has such profound implications for our doing (cf. Exod. 1:8). It is remarkable that God suggests a divine experience (knowing) of suffering.

3:1—The place where God appears to Moses says something about places where we might encounter God. We can highlight its *ordinariness*—it is Moses' customary place as a shepherd. We can encounter God as we go about our daily work. Or we can focus on its *extraordinariness*—it is the place of exile after the plushness of palace life. Ensconced in the world of privilege, we can be blind and deaf to God's presence. Both are possibilities, and the text does not force us to choose one or the other. There are many places we can encounter God.

3:2—Angel comes from the Greek translation of the Hebrew word for "messenger." Messengers can be human (cf. Gen. 32:3; Num. 24:12; Judg. 11:12–14; 1 Sam. 16:19; 19:14–26) as well as divine (cf. Gen. 16:7–11; 22:11; Exod. 14:19; Num. 22:22–35; Judg. 13:3). Messengers deliver a message or carry out a task. Biblical divine

LORD appeared to him in a flame of fire out of a bush; he looked, and the bush was blazing, yet it was not consumed. ³Then Moses said, "I must turn aside and look at this great sight, and see why the bush is not burned up." ⁴When the LORD saw that he had turned aside to see, God called to him out of the bush, "Moses, Moses!" And he said, "Here I am." ⁵Then he said, "Come no closer! Remove the sandals from your feet, for the place on which you are standing is holy ground." ⁶He said further, "I am the God of your father, the God of Abraham, the God of Isaac, and the God of Jacob." And Moses hid his face, for he was afraid to look at God.

⁷Then the LORD said, "I have observed the misery of my people who are in Egypt; I have heard their cry on account of their taskmasters. Indeed, I know their sufferings, ⁸and I have come down to deliver them from the Egyptians, and to bring them up out of that land to a good and broad land, a land flowing with milk and honey, to the country of the Canaanites, the Hittites, the Amorites, the Perizzites, the Hivites, and the Jebusites. ⁹The cry of the Israelites has now come to me; I have also seen how the Egyptians oppress them. ¹⁰So come, I will send you to Pharaoh to bring my people, the Israelites, out of Egypt." ¹¹But Moses said to God, "Who

---

messengers do not always resemble contemporary depictions of angels.

The literary convention of a "call narrative" (cf. Judg. 6; Isa. 6) tells of God's commissioning a person for a particular task. The *first* step is God's appearance (see notes at vv. 4, 10, 11, 12).

Much is made of the miraculous nature of this bush. But what does it take to get our attention? Hearing the people's cry and seeing their oppression gets God's attention. Will that also get our attention, or only something more miraculous? After all, we hear cries and see oppression every day, and that hardly earns our attention.

3:4—The *second* step of the divine call is an introductory word explaining the circumstances necessitating the call (vv. 4b–9; see notes at vv. 2, 10, 11, 12).

3:6—Much of Exod. 1–15 is about *who* God is. This verse tells us that the God Moses encounters is the same God encountered by Moses' ancestors. What's important here is that Moses has his *own* encounter with God. We must at some point have our own encounter with God, or faith becomes fossilized.

Are we *afraid* of God? Contemporary society has a tendency to tame experiences of God and make them conform more to a light, therapeutic expectation, as something friendly, centering, and comforting. But God in Exodus can be wild, mysterious, violent, and a powerful enemy. How do we decide what is the true nature of God?

3:7—God states in the first person that God observes, hears, and knows the situation of oppression, which leads to God's action of deliverance (see note at 2:24–25). Similarly, it is when we see oppression and hear the stories of pain firsthand that we set ourselves to do something about it.

3:8—This is a pivotal verse in the story. The first half rings exuberantly with the sounds of hope and promise. The people will be brought out of the land of oppression and slave labor and be brought to a good land, a land more akin to Eden than to Egypt. We are not just delivered *from* something but also *to* something. But there is a dark side to this deliverance. The land to which the Israelites will go is an occupied land. What is going to happen to all those –ites? Only later do we discover that the divine plan is to forcibly remove the prior inhabitants in order to make room for the Israelites (23:23–33). This verse has very real political, social, and economic consequences. Jews in Europe during WWII, African Americans in the United States from the Civil War to the civil rights movement, peasants in base communities in Latin America have all seen this story and the hopeful promise of the first half of this verse as inspiration for their struggle against injustice. However, it has been viewed by Palestinians and Native Americans as biblical warrant for forcibly removing them from their land. This raises the question as to the cost of liberation. Will we assume the fortunes of liberated slaves without being concerned about whom we might, at the same time, be dispossessing?

3:10—The *third* step of a call narrative (see notes at vv. 2, 4, 11, 12) is the specific commission. God sends Moses to Pharaoh to demand the release of the slaves. The process of liberation requires human as well as divine action.

3:11—The *fourth* step of a call narrative (see notes at vv. 2, 4, 10, 12) is a protest by the person being commissioned. Moses' first protest seems to be that he is a person of no account. This may be the case, but God has a long history of choosing those who are foolish, weak, low, and

am I that I should go to Pharaoh, and bring the Israelites out of Egypt?" [12] He said, "I will be with you; and this shall be the sign for you that it is I who sent you: when you have brought the people out of Egypt, you shall worship God on this mountain."

The Divine Name Revealed

13 But Moses said to God, "If I come to the Israelites and say to them, 'The God of your ancestors has sent me to you,' and they ask me, 'What is his name?' what shall I say to them?" [14] God said to Moses, "I AM WHO I AM."[a] He said further, "Thus you shall say to the Israelites, 'I AM has sent me to you.'" [15] God also said to Moses, "Thus you shall say to the Israelites, 'The LORD,[b] the God of your ancestors, the God of Abraham, the God of Isaac, and the God of Jacob, has sent me to you':

This is my name forever,
and this my title for all generations.
[16] Go and assemble the elders of Israel, and say to them, 'The LORD, the God of your ancestors, the God of Abraham, of Isaac, and of Jacob, has appeared to me, saying: I have given heed to you and to what has been done to you in Egypt. [17] I declare that I will bring you up out of the misery of Egypt, to the land of the Canaanites, the Hittites, the Amorites, the Perizzites, the Hivites, and the Jebusites, a land flowing with milk and honey.' [18] They will listen to your voice; and you and the elders of Israel shall go to the king of Egypt and say to him, 'The LORD, the God of the Hebrews, has met with us; let us now go a three days' journey into the wilderness, so that we may sacrifice to the LORD our God.' [19] I know, however, that the king of Egypt will not let you go unless compelled by a mighty hand.[c] [20] So I will stretch out my hand and strike Egypt with all my wonders that I will perform in it; after that he will let you go. [21] I will bring this people into such favor with the Egyptians that, when you go, you will not go empty-handed; [22] each woman shall ask her neighbor and any woman living in the neighbor's house for jewelry of silver

[a] Or I AM WHAT I AM or I WILL BE WHAT I WILL BE   [b] The word "LORD" when spelled with capital letters stands for the divine name, YHWH, which is here connected with the verb *hayah*, "to be"   [c] Gk Vg: Heb *no, not by a mighty hand*

---

despised to accomplish divine purposes (1 Cor. 1:27–28).

3:12—The *fifth* step in a call narrative is God's response to the protest in a form of divine assurance. Moses can go to Pharaoh because *God will be with him* (a form of "Immanuel"; cf. Isa. 7:14; Matt. 1:23). Only with God's presence will any of us be able to accomplish what God calls us to do.

The *sixth* and final step in a call narrative is a sign: the people will worship God on this mountain. Only when Moses' task was done would he truly know that God had sent him. Sometimes it is only at the end that we can look back and know that God was with us in our endeavors for peace and justice.

3:13—Moses has more than one objection to God's command to go to Pharaoh (see 3:11; 4:1, 10, 13). It is one thing to go to the oppressor; going to one's own people has its own problems. Moses ponders whether the people will question his authority by questioning God's authority. Organizing for political action isn't always easy. It is easy to be discounted as leader when others question one's call.

3:14—What's in a name? God's name, YHWH, is a wordplay in Hebrew on God's answer to Moses. There is no one precise way to translate the Hebrew. Some possibilities are "I am who/what I am," "I will be who I will be," "I create/cause to be who/what I create/cause to be." The last testifies to God's creative character, as God is about to create a new people. The ambiguity is an answer, but not an answer. We can know some of the Divine, but never the totality. There is always a part of God that remains free, elusive, and transcendent from our attempts to contain God (see notes at 3:6 and 40:1). To limit how we name God is antithetical to God's nature.

3:19—Oppressors do not easily or willingly give up or let go, for the oppression benefits them in some way (see note at 4:21). We should consider various ways to compel the relinquishment of oppressive and abusive power.

3:22—A reiteration of this episode (11:2) shows that women approached Egyptian women and men approached Egyptian men. This may indicate that some kind of gender-specific informal network existed between slaves and oppressors,

and of gold, and clothing, and you shall put them on your sons and on your daughters; and so you shall plunder the Egyptians."

Moses' Miraculous Power

4 Then Moses answered, "But suppose they do not believe me or listen to me, but say, 'The LORD did not appear to you.'" ² The LORD said to him, "What is that in your hand?" He said, "A staff." ³ And he said, "Throw it on the ground." So he threw the staff on the ground, and it became a snake; and Moses drew back from it. ⁴ Then the LORD said to Moses, "Reach out your hand, and seize it by the tail"—so he reached out his hand and grasped it, and it became a staff in his hand— ⁵ "so that they may believe that the LORD, the God of their ancestors, the God of Abraham, the God of Isaac, and the God of Jacob, has appeared to you."

6 Again, the LORD said to him, "Put your hand inside your cloak." He put his hand into his cloak; and when he took it out, his hand was leprous,ᵃ as white as snow. ⁷ Then God said, "Put your hand back into your cloak"—so he put his hand back into his cloak, and when he took it out, it was restored like the rest of his body— ⁸ "If they will not believe you or heed the first sign, they may believe the second sign. ⁹ If they will not believe even these two signs or heed you, you shall take some water from the Nile and pour it on the dry ground; and the water that you shall take from the Nile will become blood on the dry ground."

10 But Moses said to the LORD, "O my Lord, I have never been eloquent, neither in the past nor even now that you have spoken to your servant; but I am slow of speech and slow of tongue." ¹¹ Then the LORD said to him, "Who gives speech to mortals? Who makes them mute or deaf, seeing or blind? Is it not I, the LORD? ¹² Now go, and I will be with your mouth and teach you what you are to speak." ¹³ But he said, "O my Lord, please send someone else." ¹⁴ Then the anger of the LORD was kindled against Moses and he said, "What of your brother Aaron the Levite? I know that he can speak fluently; even now he is coming out to meet you, and when he sees you his heart will be glad. ¹⁵ You shall speak to him and put the words in his mouth; and I will be with your mouth and with his mouth, and will teach you what you shall do. ¹⁶ He indeed shall speak for you to the people; he shall serve as a mouth for you, and you shall serve as God for him. ¹⁷ Take in your hand this staff, with which you shall perform the signs."

Moses Returns to Egypt

18 Moses went back to his father-in-law Jethro and said to him, "Please let me go back to my kindred in Egypt and see whether they are still living." And Jethro said to Moses, "Go in peace." ¹⁹ The LORD said to Moses in Midian, "Go back to Egypt; for all those who were seeking your life are dead." ²⁰ So Moses took his wife and his sons, put them on a donkey, and went back to the land of Egypt; and Moses carried the staff of God in his hand.

21 And the LORD said to Moses, "When you go back to Egypt, see that

ᵃ A term for several skin diseases; precise meaning uncertain

---

outside of official channels, that permitted the slaves to request and receive these valuable items. Similar networks, whether or not they are gender specific, can assist in well-being, even between groups that are hostile to each other.

4:1—Moses offers yet another objection to God's call (see 3:11, 13; 4:10, 13). Moses' objections are not frivolous. He has legitimate concerns. The people do respond, as Moses fears (6:9). It is legitimate to question our call and express our fears and concerns.

4:13–14—Moses still objects; God finally has had enough and gets angry with Moses. At some point, even with our objections, fears, and concerns, we must finally accept God's call.

4:21—God's hardening of Pharaoh's heart presents a theological conundrum. Sometimes Pharaoh hardens his own heart (8:15, 32; 9:34); sometimes God is responsible (7:3; 9:12; 10:1,

you perform before Pharaoh all the wonders that I have put in your power; but I will harden his heart, so that he will not let the people go. ²²Then you shall say to Pharaoh, 'Thus says the LORD: Israel is my firstborn son. ²³I said to you, "Let my son go that he may worship me." But you refused to let him go; now I will kill your firstborn son.'"

24 On the way, at a place where they spent the night, the LORD met him and tried to kill him. ²⁵But Zipporah took a flint and cut off her son's foreskin, and touched Moses'[a] feet with it, and said, "Truly you are a bridegroom of blood to me!" ²⁶So he let him alone. It was then she said, "A bridegroom of blood by circumcision."

27 The LORD said to Aaron, "Go into the wilderness to meet Moses." So he went; and he met him at the mountain of God and kissed him. ²⁸Moses told Aaron all the words of the LORD with which he had sent him, and all the signs with which he had charged him. ²⁹Then Moses and Aaron went and assembled all the elders of the Israelites. ³⁰Aaron spoke all the words that the LORD had spoken to Moses, and performed the signs in the sight of the people. ³¹The people believed; and when they heard that the LORD had given heed to the Israelites and that he had seen their misery, they bowed down and worshiped.

Bricks without Straw

5 Afterward Moses and Aaron went to Pharaoh and said, "Thus says the LORD, the God of Israel, 'Let my people go, so that they may celebrate a festival to me in the wilderness.'" ²But Pharaoh said, "Who is the LORD, that I should heed him and let Israel go? I do not know the LORD, and I will not let Israel go." ³Then they said, "The God of the Hebrews has revealed himself to us; let us go a three days' journey into the wilderness to sacrifice to the LORD our God, or he will fall upon us with pestilence or sword." ⁴But the king of Egypt said to them, "Moses and Aaron, why are you taking the people away from their work? Get to your labors!" ⁵Pharaoh continued, "Now they are more numerous than the people of the land[b] and yet you want them to stop working!" ⁶That same day Pharaoh commanded the taskmasters of the people, as well as their supervisors, ⁷"You shall no longer give the people straw to make bricks, as before; let them go and gather straw for themselves. ⁸But you shall require of them the same quantity of bricks as they have made previously; do not diminish

[a] Heb *his*   [b] Sam: Heb *The people of the land are now many*

20, 27; 11:10; 14:4, 8). This troubling view of God reminds us that God is the God of all people, including our enemy. God's hardening Pharaoh's heart suggests God's involvement in the lives of oppressors as well as oppressed. God knows that the cost to oppressors is going to be loss of power, prestige, status, and wealth. God knows that Pharaoh's hard heart and increased repression are a step along the way of liberation. God understands that liberation comes only when enough pressure is exerted on the system to compel liberation. Liberation in Exodus is messy business. Can liberation happen in other ways?

4:24—This verse generates endless speculation. Who is this God who, having commissioned Moses to bring the Israelites out of Egypt, tries to kill him (see also note at 15:26)? No reason is given for the attack, but his wife Zipporah rescues him, joining the other women of Exod. 1–2 who rescue Moses. Although women are central to the beginning of the story of Exodus, they disappear as Moses and Aaron take center stage. This is likely a consequence of the patriarchal bias of the biblical communities. Women are allowed supporting roles but seldom the leading roles. Consider how women might take the stage as leaders against oppression in their own right and not only as rescuers of male leaders.

5:7–9—Moses' first attempt to bring the Israelites out of Egypt is a disaster. Not only does Pharaoh reject Moses' plea; he immediately institutes measures to make life that much more difficult. This shows that the process of liberation is not smooth. The *powers that be* will resist any attempt to alter the status quo. Often the response to cries for justice is to increase the demands and restrictions on peoples' lives in the belief that more repression is a solution to the problem.

it, for they are lazy; that is why they cry, 'Let us go and offer sacrifice to our God.' [9] Let heavier work be laid on them; then they will labor at it and pay no attention to deceptive words."

10 So the taskmasters and the supervisors of the people went out and said to the people, "Thus says Pharaoh, 'I will not give you straw. [11] Go and get straw yourselves, wherever you can find it; but your work will not be lessened in the least.'" [12] So the people scattered throughout the land of Egypt, to gather stubble for straw. [13] The taskmasters were urgent, saying, "Complete your work, the same daily assignment as when you were given straw." [14] And the supervisors of the Israelites, whom Pharaoh's taskmasters had set over them, were beaten, and were asked, "Why did you not finish the required quantity of bricks yesterday and today, as you did before?"

15 Then the Israelite supervisors came to Pharaoh and cried, "Why do you treat your servants like this? [16] No straw is given to your servants, yet they say to us, 'Make bricks!' Look how your servants are beaten! You are unjust to your own people."[a] [17] He said, "You are lazy, lazy; that is why you say, 'Let us go and sacrifice to the LORD.' [18] Go now, and work; for no straw shall be given you, but you shall still deliver the same number of bricks." [19] The Israelite supervisors saw that they were in trouble when they were told, "You shall not lessen your daily number of bricks." [20] As they left Pharaoh, they came upon Moses and Aaron who were waiting to meet them. [21] They said to them, "The LORD look upon you and judge! You have brought us into bad odor with Pharaoh and his officials, and have put a sword in their hand to kill us."

22 Then Moses turned again to the LORD and said, "O LORD, why have you mistreated this people? Why did you ever send me? [23] Since I first came to Pharaoh to speak in your name, he has mistreated this people, and you have done nothing at all to deliver your people."

Israel's Deliverance Assured

6 Then the LORD said to Moses, "Now you shall see what I will do to Pharaoh: Indeed, by a mighty hand he will let them go; by a mighty hand he will drive them out of his land."

2 God also spoke to Moses and said to him: "I am the LORD. [3] I appeared to Abraham, Isaac, and Jacob as God Almighty,[b] but by my name 'The LORD'[c] I did not make myself known to them. [4] I also established my covenant with them, to give them the land of Canaan, the land in which they resided as aliens. [5] I have also heard the groaning of the Israelites whom the Egyptians are holding as slaves, and I have remembered my covenant. [6] Say therefore to the Israelites, 'I am the LORD, and I will free you from the burdens of the Egyptians and deliver you from slavery to them.

[a] Gk Compare Syr Vg: Heb beaten, and the sin of your people   [b] Traditional rendering of Heb El Shaddai   [c] Heb YHWH; see note at 3.15

5:17—(Cf. v. 8). How often do we say something like this about those who are economically disadvantaged? It is the social policies of the wealthy that make the lives of the poor so difficult. And yet we blame the victim. When we call them *welfare queens* or *druggies* or *wetbacks* or *lazy,* we misplace responsibility from where it rightly belongs.

5:23—Needless to say, the Israelites are unhappy with Moses' attempts to garner their freedom (v. 21). Moses feels quite free to pass that unhappiness along to God. The theological question is: What is God doing for Israel? However we might wish it, the text is clear that God is no Superman who swoops in and saves the day faster than a speeding bullet.

6:3—Two names of God are given. *El Shaddai* (=**God Almighty**) can also be translated "God of Breasts" or "Breasted God." In Genesis, *El Shaddai* occurs in contexts of blessing and promises of offspring (Gen. 17:1; 28:3; 35:11; 43:14; 48:3; 49:25). This is a female image of God who concerns herself with fertility and abundance. Exodus associates the Lord (=YHWH) as the God who saves. God is known differently in different contexts. The ancestors needed the God of

I will redeem you with an outstretched arm and with mighty acts of judgment. [7] I will take you as my people, and I will be your God. You shall know that I am the LORD your God, who has freed you from the burdens of the Egyptians. [8] I will bring you into the land that I swore to give to Abraham, Isaac, and Jacob; I will give it to you for a possession. I am the LORD.'" [9] Moses told this to the Israelites; but they would not listen to Moses, because of their broken spirit and their cruel slavery.

10 Then the LORD spoke to Moses, [11] "Go and tell Pharaoh king of Egypt to let the Israelites go out of his land." [12] But Moses spoke to the LORD, "The Israelites have not listened to me; how then shall Pharaoh listen to me, poor speaker that I am?"[a] [13] Thus the LORD spoke to Moses and Aaron, and gave them orders regarding the Israelites and Pharaoh king of Egypt, charging them to free the Israelites from the land of Egypt.

The Genealogy of Moses and Aaron

14 The following are the heads of their ancestral houses: the sons of Reuben, the firstborn of Israel: Hanoch, Pallu, Hezron, and Carmi; these are the families of Reuben. [15] The sons of Simeon: Jemuel, Jamin, Ohad, Jachin, Zohar, and Shaul,[b] the son of a Canaanite woman; these are the families of Simeon. [16] The following are the names of the sons of Levi according to their genealogies: Gershon,[c] Kohath, and Merari, and the length of Levi's life was one hundred thirty-seven years. [17] The sons of Gershon:[c] Libni and Shimei, by their families. [18] The sons of Kohath: Amram, Izhar, Hebron, and Uzziel, and the length of Kohath's life was one hundred thirty-three years. [19] The sons of Merari: Mahli and Mushi. These are the families of the Levites according to their genealogies. [20] Amram married Jochebed his father's sister and she bore him Aaron and Moses, and the length of Amram's life was one hundred thirty-seven years. [21] The sons of Izhar: Korah, Nepheg, and Zichri. [22] The sons of Uzziel: Mishael, Elzaphan, and Sithri. [23] Aaron married Elisheba, daughter of Amminadab and sister of Nahshon, and she bore him Nadab, Abihu, Eleazar, and Ithamar. [24] The sons of Korah: Assir, Elkanah, and Abiasaph; these are the families of the Korahites. [25] Aaron's son Eleazar married one of the daughters of Putiel, and she bore him Phinehas. These are the heads of the ancestral houses of the Levites by their families.

26 It was this same Aaron and Moses to whom the LORD said, "Bring the

[a] Heb me? I am uncircumcised of lips [b] Or Saul [c] Also spelled Gershom; see 2.22

---

fertility. In Exodus the people need the God who delivers from slavery. God is experienced in more than one way.

6:7—The theme of *knowing* God is central to Exodus. Sometimes those who know are the Hebrews (6:7; 10:2; 16:12; 29:48), sometimes Pharaoh and the Egyptians (7:5, 17; 14:4, 18). Knowledge comes through observing and participating in what God *does*. In our day, when God so often appears to be absent, all we have to do is look for moments when people are freed from their burdens, to be able to say that we too know *I AM*. But Israel comes to know God not only in liberation. Later Israel will know "that I am the LORD" when God judges them, destroys them, and takes them into exile (cf. Ezek. 6:7, 10, 13–14; 12:15–16, 20). Both liberation and exile can reveal divine activity.

6:9—Moses was right to question whether the people would listen to him (4:1), but their resistance is not because they don't believe God sent him. They don't listen because of their broken spirits. When one is in slavery, it can be hard to believe that liberation is possible, just as resurrection is unbelievable when one is dead. Broken spirits as well as slavery are a challenge for liberation.

6:20—The Septuagint and Samaritan Pentateuch add "and Miriam" to the list of Jochebed's children. But no other daughters are listed in this genealogy, whose concern is with legitimating Aaron and Moses as part of the priestly line of Levi (vv. 14–26). A question might be why it wasn't important to legitimate Miriam as part of the priestly line. Her omission here may reflect the tensions among the leaders of the exodus (see Num. 12), as well as the patriarchal bias of the text. Whose names are left out of our records of liberation? Why?

Israelites out of the land of Egypt, company by company." ²⁷ It was they who spoke to Pharaoh king of Egypt to bring the Israelites out of Egypt, the same Moses and Aaron.

Moses and Aaron Obey God's Commands

28 On the day when the LORD spoke to Moses in the land of Egypt, ²⁹ he said to him, "I am the LORD; tell Pharaoh king of Egypt all that I am speaking to you." ³⁰ But Moses said in the LORD's presence, "Since I am a poor speaker,*a* why would Pharaoh listen to me?"

7 The LORD said to Moses, "See, I have made you like God to Pharaoh, and your brother Aaron shall be your prophet. ² You shall speak all that I command you, and your brother Aaron shall tell Pharaoh to let the Israelites go out of his land. ³ But I will harden Pharaoh's heart, and I will multiply my signs and wonders in the land of Egypt. ⁴ When Pharaoh does not listen to you, I will lay my hand upon Egypt and bring my people the Israelites, company by company, out of the land of Egypt by great acts of judgment. ⁵ The Egyptians shall know that I am the LORD, when I stretch out my hand against Egypt and bring the Israelites out from among them." ⁶ Moses and Aaron did so; they did just as the LORD commanded them. ⁷ Moses was eighty years old and Aaron eighty-three when they spoke to Pharaoh.

Aaron's Miraculous Rod

8 The LORD said to Moses and Aaron, ⁹ "When Pharaoh says to you, 'Perform a wonder,' then you shall say to Aaron, 'Take your staff and throw it down before Pharaoh, and it will become a snake.'" ¹⁰ So Moses and Aaron went to Pharaoh and did as the LORD had commanded; Aaron threw down his staff before Pharaoh and his officials, and it became a snake. ¹¹ Then Pharaoh summoned the wise men and the sorcerers; and they also, the magicians of Egypt, did the same by their secret arts. ¹² Each one threw down his staff, and they became snakes; but Aaron's staff swallowed up theirs. ¹³ Still Pharaoh's heart was hardened, and he would not listen to them, as the LORD had said.

The First Plague: Water Turned to Blood

14 Then the LORD said to Moses, "Pharaoh's heart is hardened; he refuses to let the people go. ¹⁵ Go to Pharaoh in the morning, as he is going out to the water; stand by at the river bank to meet him, and take in your hand the staff that was turned into a snake. ¹⁶ Say to him, 'The LORD, the God of the Hebrews, sent me to you to say, "Let my people go, so that they may worship me in the wilderness." But until now you have not listened. ¹⁷ Thus says the LORD, "By this you shall know that I am the LORD." See, with the staff that is in my hand I will strike the water that is in the Nile, and it shall be turned to blood. ¹⁸ The fish in the river shall die, the river itself shall stink, and the Egyptians shall be unable to drink water from the Nile.'" ¹⁹ The LORD said to Moses, "Say to Aaron, 'Take your staff and stretch out your hand over the waters of Egypt—over its rivers, its canals, and its ponds, and all its pools of water—so that they may become blood; and there shall be blood throughout the

a Heb *am uncircumcised of lips;* see 6.12

7:7—The ages of Moses and Aaron are surprising. Elders in the Old Testament are seen as having wisdom. Today, with more people living into their eighties and beyond, the problem of *elder abuse* is rapidly growing. We need to take advantage of the wisdom of elders, instead of seeing them as *disposable*. Perhaps their wisdom will help lead us out of other forms of bondage.

7:11—The first time Moses and Aaron go to

Pharaoh they use only words, which fail. Now they try to persuade with signs. Here and with the first two plagues Pharaoh's religious officials are able to match the signs performed by Moses and Aaron (7:22; 8:7). This is a contest between the power of Pharaoh (oppression) and the power of God (freedom). At first the power is evenly matched, and the force of oppression counters the force for liberation.

whole land of Egypt, even in vessels of wood and in vessels of stone.'"

20 Moses and Aaron did just as the LORD commanded. In the sight of Pharaoh and of his officials he lifted up the staff and struck the water in the river, and all the water in the river was turned into blood, ²¹ and the fish in the river died. The river stank so that the Egyptians could not drink its water, and there was blood throughout the whole land of Egypt. ²² But the magicians of Egypt did the same by their secret arts; so Pharaoh's heart remained hardened, and he would not listen to them, as the LORD had said. ²³ Pharaoh turned and went into his house, and he did not take even this to heart. ²⁴ And all the Egyptians had to dig along the Nile for water to drink, for they could not drink the water of the river.

25 Seven days passed after the LORD had struck the Nile.

The Second Plague: Frogs

8 ª Then the LORD said to Moses, "Go to Pharaoh and say to him, 'Thus says the LORD: Let my people go, so that they may worship me. ² If you refuse to let them go, I will plague your whole country with frogs. ³ The river shall swarm with frogs; they shall come up into your palace, into your bedchamber and your bed, and into the houses of your officials and of your people,ᵇ and into your ovens and your kneading bowls. ⁴ The frogs shall come up on you and on your people and on all your officials.'"
⁵ᶜ And the LORD said to Moses, "Say to Aaron, 'Stretch out your hand with your staff over the rivers, the canals, and the pools, and make frogs come up on the land of Egypt.'" ⁶ So Aaron stretched out his hand over the waters of Egypt; and the frogs came up and covered the land of Egypt. ⁷ But the magicians did the same by their secret arts, and brought frogs up on the land of Egypt.

8 Then Pharaoh called Moses and Aaron, and said, "Pray to the LORD to take away the frogs from me and my people, and I will let the people go to sacrifice to the LORD." ⁹ Moses said to Pharaoh, "Kindly tell me when I am to pray for you and for your officials and for your people, that the frogs may be removed from you and your houses and be left only in the Nile." ¹⁰ And he said, "Tomorrow." Moses said, "As you say! So that you may know that there is no one like the LORD our God, ¹¹ the frogs shall leave you and your houses and your officials and your people; they shall be left only in the Nile." ¹² Then Moses and Aaron went out from Pharaoh; and Moses cried out to the LORD concerning the frogs that he had brought upon Pharaoh.ᵈ ¹³ And the LORD did as Moses requested: the frogs died in the houses, the courtyards, and the fields. ¹⁴ And they gathered them together in heaps, and the land stank. ¹⁵ But when Pharaoh saw that there was a respite, he hardened his heart, and would not listen to them, just as the LORD had said.

The Third Plague: Gnats

16 Then the LORD said to Moses, "Say to Aaron, 'Stretch out your staff and strike the dust of the earth, so that it may become gnats throughout the whole land of Egypt.'" ¹⁷ And they did so; Aaron stretched out his hand with his staff and struck the dust of the earth, and gnats came on humans and animals alike; all the dust of the earth turned into gnats throughout the whole land of Egypt. ¹⁸ The magicians tried to produce gnats by their secret arts, but they could not. There were gnats on both humans and animals. ¹⁹ And the magicians said to Pharaoh, "This is the finger of God!" But Pharaoh's heart was hardened, and he would not listen to them, just as the LORD had said.

The Fourth Plague: Flies

20 Then the LORD said to Moses, "Rise early in the morning and present

ªCh 7.26 in Heb ᵇGk: Heb upon your people ᶜCh 8.1 in Heb ᵈOr frogs, as he had agreed with Pharaoh

yourself before Pharaoh, as he goes out to the water, and say to him, 'Thus says the LORD: Let my people go, so that they may worship me. ²¹ For if you will not let my people go, I will send swarms of flies on you, your officials, and your people, and into your houses; and the houses of the Egyptians shall be filled with swarms of flies; so also the land where they live. ²² But on that day I will set apart the land of Goshen, where my people live, so that no swarms of flies shall be there, that you may know that I the LORD am in this land. ²³ Thus I will make a distinction*a* between my people and your people. This sign shall appear tomorrow.'" ²⁴ The LORD did so, and great swarms of flies came into the house of Pharaoh and into his officials' houses; in all of Egypt the land was ruined because of the flies.

25 Then Pharaoh summoned Moses and Aaron, and said, "Go, sacrifice to your God within the land." ²⁶ But Moses said, "It would not be right to do so; for the sacrifices that we offer to the LORD our God are offensive to the Egyptians. If we offer in the sight of the Egyptians sacrifices that are offensive to them, will they not stone us? ²⁷ We must go a three days' journey into the wilderness and sacrifice to the LORD our God as he commands us." ²⁸ So Pharaoh said, "I will let you go to sacrifice to the LORD your God in the wilderness, provided you do not go very far away. Pray for me." ²⁹ Then Moses said, "As soon as I leave you, I will pray to the LORD that the swarms of flies may depart tomorrow from Pharaoh, from his officials, and from his people; only do not let Pharaoh again deal falsely by not letting the people go to sacrifice to the LORD."

30 So Moses went out from Pharaoh and prayed to the LORD. ³¹ And the LORD did as Moses asked: he removed the swarms of flies from Pharaoh, from his officials, and from his people; not one remained. ³² But Pharaoh hardened his heart this time also, and would not let the people go.

The Fifth Plague: Livestock Diseased

9 Then the LORD said to Moses, "Go to Pharaoh, and say to him, 'Thus says the LORD, the God of the Hebrews: Let my people go, so that they may worship me. ² For if you refuse to let them go and still hold them, ³ the hand of the LORD will strike with a deadly pestilence your livestock in the field: the horses, the donkeys, the camels, the herds, and the flocks. ⁴ But the LORD will make a distinction between the livestock of Israel and the livestock of Egypt, so that nothing shall die of all that belongs to the Israelites.'" ⁵ The LORD set a time, saying, "Tomorrow the LORD will do this thing in the land." ⁶ And on the next day the LORD did so; all the livestock of the Egyptians died, but of the livestock of the Israelites not one died. ⁷ Pharaoh inquired and found that not one of the livestock of the Israelites was dead. But the heart of Pharaoh was hardened, and he would not let the people go.

The Sixth Plague: Boils

8 Then the LORD said to Moses and Aaron, "Take handfuls of soot from the kiln, and let Moses throw it in the air in the sight of Pharaoh. ⁹ It shall become fine dust all over the land of Egypt, and shall cause festering boils on humans and animals throughout the whole land of Egypt." ¹⁰ So they took soot from the kiln, and stood before Pharaoh, and Moses threw it in the air, and it caused festering boils on humans and animals. ¹¹ The magicians could not stand before

a Gk Vg: Heb *will set redemption*

8:22—To this point the plagues have affected everyone equally. Now God makes a distinction. This *setting apart* shows that this is not a socially disinterested text (see note at 2:24–25). God cares for those on the social and economic margins. Each side experiences God differently. The Hebrews experience God's care and protection. The Egyptians experience God's judgment and terror. God is experienced differently by the various parties in the story (see note at 6:3).

Moses because of the boils, for the boils afflicted the magicians as well as all the Egyptians. **12** But the LORD hardened the heart of Pharaoh, and he would not listen to them, just as the LORD had spoken to Moses.

The Seventh Plague: Thunder and Hail

13 Then the LORD said to Moses, "Rise up early in the morning and present yourself before Pharaoh, and say to him, 'Thus says the LORD, the God of the Hebrews: Let my people go, so that they may worship me. **14** For this time I will send all my plagues upon you yourself, and upon your officials, and upon your people, so that you may know that there is no one like me in all the earth. **15** For by now I could have stretched out my hand and struck you and your people with pestilence, and you would have been cut off from the earth. **16** But this is why I have let you live: to show you my power, and to make my name resound through all the earth. **17** You are still exalting yourself against my people, and will not let them go. **18** Tomorrow at this time I will cause the heaviest hail to fall that has ever fallen in Egypt from the day it was founded until now. **19** Send, therefore, and have your livestock and everything that you have in the open field brought to a secure place; every human or animal that is in the open field and is not brought under shelter will die when the hail comes down upon them.' " **20** Those officials of Pharaoh who feared the word of the LORD hurried their slaves and livestock off to a secure place. **21** Those who did not regard the word of the LORD left their slaves and livestock in the open field.

22 The LORD said to Moses, "Stretch out your hand toward heaven so that hail may fall on the whole land of Egypt, on humans and animals and all the plants of the field in the land of Egypt." **23** Then Moses stretched out his staff toward heaven, and the LORD sent thunder and hail, and fire came down on the earth.

And the LORD rained hail on the land of Egypt; **24** there was hail with fire flashing continually in the midst of it, such heavy hail as had never fallen in all the land of Egypt since it became a nation. **25** The hail struck down everything that was in the open field throughout all the land of Egypt, both human and animal; the hail also struck down all the plants of the field, and shattered every tree in the field. **26** Only in the land of Goshen, where the Israelites were, there was no hail.

27 Then Pharaoh summoned Moses and Aaron, and said to them, "This time I have sinned; the LORD is in the right, and I and my people are in the wrong. **28** Pray to the LORD! Enough of God's thunder and hail! I will let you go; you need stay no longer." **29** Moses said to him, "As soon as I have gone out of the city, I will stretch out my hands to the LORD; the thunder will cease, and there will be no more hail, so that you may know that the earth is the LORD's. **30** But as for you and your officials, I know that you do not yet fear the LORD God." **31** (Now the flax and the barley were ruined, for the barley was in the ear and the flax was in bud. **32** But the wheat and the spelt were not ruined, for they are late in coming up.) **33** So Moses left Pharaoh, went out of the city, and stretched out his hands to the LORD; then the thunder and the hail ceased, and the rain no longer poured down on the earth. **34** But when Pharaoh saw that the rain and the hail and the thunder had ceased, he sinned once more and hardened his heart, he and his officials. **35** So the heart of Pharaoh was hardened, and he would not let the Israelites go, just as the LORD had spoken through Moses.

The Eighth Plague: Locusts

10 Then the LORD said to Moses, "Go to Pharaoh; for I have hardened his heart and the heart of his officials, in order that I may show these signs of mine among them, **2** and that

you may tell your children and grand-children how I have made fools of the Egyptians and what signs I have done among them—so that you may know that I am the LORD."

3 So Moses and Aaron went to Pharaoh, and said to him, "Thus says the LORD, the God of the Hebrews, 'How long will you refuse to humble yourself before me? Let my people go, so that they may worship me. ⁴ For if you refuse to let my people go, tomorrow I will bring locusts into your country. ⁵ They shall cover the surface of the land, so that no one will be able to see the land. They shall devour the last remnant left you after the hail, and they shall devour every tree of yours that grows in the field. ⁶ They shall fill your houses, and the houses of all your officials and of all the Egyptians—something that neither your parents nor your grandparents have seen, from the day they came on earth to this day.'" Then he turned and went out from Pharaoh.

7 Pharaoh's officials said to him, "How long shall this fellow be a snare to us? Let the people go, so that they may worship the LORD their God; do you not yet understand that Egypt is ruined?" ⁸ So Moses and Aaron were brought back to Pharaoh, and he said to them, "Go, worship the LORD your God! But which ones are to go?" ⁹ Moses said, "We will go with our young and our old; we will go with our sons and daughters and with our flocks and herds, because we have the LORD's festival to celebrate." ¹⁰ He said to them, "The LORD indeed will be with you, if ever I let your little ones go with you! Plainly, you have some evil purpose in mind. ¹¹ No, never! Your men may go and worship the LORD, for that is what you are asking." And they were

driven out from Pharaoh's presence.

12 Then the LORD said to Moses, "Stretch out your hand over the land of Egypt, so that the locusts may come upon it and eat every plant in the land, all that the hail has left." ¹³ So Moses stretched out his staff over the land of Egypt, and the LORD brought an east wind upon the land all that day and all that night; when morning came, the east wind had brought the locusts. ¹⁴ The locusts came upon all the land of Egypt and settled on the whole country of Egypt, such a dense swarm of locusts as had never been before, nor ever shall be again. ¹⁵ They covered the surface of the whole land, so that the land was black; and they ate all the plants in the land and all the fruit of the trees that the hail had left; nothing green was left, no tree, no plant in the field, in all the land of Egypt. ¹⁶ Pharaoh hurriedly summoned Moses and Aaron and said, "I have sinned against the LORD your God, and against you. ¹⁷ Do forgive my sin just this once, and pray to the LORD your God that at the least he remove this deadly thing from me." ¹⁸ So he went out from Pharaoh and prayed to the LORD. ¹⁹ The LORD changed the wind into a very strong west wind, which lifted the locusts and drove them into the Red Sea;ᵃ not a single locust was left in all the country of Egypt. ²⁰ But the LORD hardened Pharaoh's heart, and he would not let the Israelites go.

The Ninth Plague: Darkness

21 Then the LORD said to Moses, "Stretch out your hand toward heaven so that there may be darkness over the land of Egypt, a darkness that can be felt." ²² So Moses stretched out his hand

ᵃ Or Sea of Reeds

10:7—The system of oppression begins to collapse when people refuse to support it, especially those who have previously benefited from it. They now understand that loyalty to oppressive systems is not worth it and that they will gain more by changing the system.

10:22—There is escalation in the violence and destructiveness of the plagues and a sense of overkill. Overall, the plagues are nothing short of an appalling environmental disaster. This disaster affects not only the responsible parties, but also the peasants who had nothing to say about the

toward heaven, and there was dense darkness in all the land of Egypt for three days. 23 People could not see one another, and for three days they could not move from where they were; but all the Israelites had light where they lived. 24 Then Pharaoh summoned Moses, and said, "Go, worship the LORD. Only your flocks and your herds shall remain behind. Even your children may go with you." 25 But Moses said, "You must also let us have sacrifices and burnt offerings to sacrifice to the LORD our God. 26 Our livestock also must go with us; not a hoof shall be left behind, for we must choose some of them for the worship of the LORD our God, and we will not know what to use to worship the LORD until we arrive there." 27 But the LORD hardened Pharaoh's heart, and he was unwilling to let them go. 28 Then Pharaoh said to him, "Get away from me! Take care that you do not see my face again, for on the day you see my face you shall die." 29 Moses said, "Just as you say! I will never see your face again."

Warning of the Final Plague

11 The LORD said to Moses, "I will bring one more plague upon Pharaoh and upon Egypt; afterwards he will let you go from here; indeed, when he lets you go, he will drive you away. 2 Tell the people that every man is to ask his neighbor and every woman is to ask her neighbor for objects of silver and gold." 3 The LORD gave the people favor in the sight of the Egyptians. Moreover, Moses himself was a man of great importance in the land of Egypt, in the sight of Pharaoh's officials and in the sight of the people.

4 Moses said, "Thus says the LORD: About midnight I will go out through Egypt. 5 Every firstborn in the land of Egypt shall die, from the firstborn of Pharaoh who sits on his throne to the firstborn of the female slave who is behind the handmill, and all the firstborn of the livestock. 6 Then there will be a loud cry throughout the whole land of Egypt, such as has never been or will ever be again. 7 But not a dog shall growl at any of the Israelites—not at people, not at animals—so that you may know that the LORD makes a distinction between Egypt and Israel. 8 Then all these officials of yours shall come down to me, and bow low to me, saying, 'Leave us, you and all the people who follow you.' After that I will leave." And in hot anger he left Pharaoh.

---

system in which they lived. The plagues end up polluting the water supply, the earth, and the air. Not only are people affected but also animals and plants as well. Oppression and the struggle for liberation are not just about people, but also about the earth and our resources. Injustice and oppression also affects the nonhuman world (cf. Isa. 24:1–13, 19–20; Jer. 4:23–28; Joel 1:4, 10–12, 17–20). On the other hand, the rewards of peace and justice extend also to the earth (cf. Isa. 30:23–26; 43:18–21; 44:3; Joel 2:22–26). Human rights and the environment are issues that are joined together.

10:27—In the *realpolitik* of this story the plagues function to calcify everyone's position. With each plague Pharaoh becomes less and less willing to negotiate, and Moses' (God's?) position is equally rigid and uncompromising. There is no negotiation, no possibility of a *peaceful* settlement. This story of liberation ends up being bloody and costly for everyone. Is this just the nature of the struggle for liberation, or can we envision an alternative exodus that also brings about justice but without the rigidity and subsequent violence? Oppressors bring additional suffering by their tenacious clinging to power. Where do we need to let go of structures that are unjust?

11:1—The final plague won't occur until 12:29. Within the story God's promise of deliverance seems to be constantly delayed. The reader wonders if God is ever going to make good on this promise. It may often seem within our own story that God's deliverance is long delayed.

11:5—We know as early as 4:21–23 that the death of Egypt's firstborn will eventually occur. Deliverance happens as a direct consequence of this event (12:12–13, 31, 41, 51). The text hints that this event is an *eye for an eye*. The deaths of Egyptian baby boys correspond to the deaths of Hebrew baby boys (1:16, 22). But what does it mean that innocent children must die for our deliverance? Perhaps there were Hebrews who saved the lives of Egyptian babies that night (see note at 2:5).

9 The LORD said to Moses, "Pharaoh will not listen to you, in order that my wonders may be multiplied in the land of Egypt." ¹⁰ Moses and Aaron performed all these wonders before Pharaoh; but the LORD hardened Pharaoh's heart, and he did not let the people of Israel go out of his land.

The First Passover Instituted

12 The LORD said to Moses and Aaron in the land of Egypt: ² This month shall mark for you the beginning of months; it shall be the first month of the year for you. ³ Tell the whole congregation of Israel that on the tenth of this month they are to take a lamb for each family, a lamb for each household. ⁴ If a household is too small for a whole lamb, it shall join its closest neighbor in obtaining one; the lamb shall be divided in proportion to the number of people who eat of it. ⁵ Your lamb shall be without blemish, a year-old male; you may take it from the sheep or from the goats. ⁶ You shall keep it until the fourteenth day of this month; then the whole assembled congregation of Israel shall slaughter it at twilight. ⁷ They shall take some of the blood and put it on the two doorposts and the lintel of the houses in which they eat it. ⁸ They shall eat the lamb that same night; they shall eat it roasted over the fire with unleavened bread and bitter herbs. ⁹ Do not eat any of it raw or boiled in water, but roasted over the fire, with its head, legs, and inner organs. ¹⁰ You shall let none of it remain until the morning; anything that remains until the morning you shall burn. ¹¹ This is how you shall eat it: your loins girded, your sandals on your feet, and your staff in your hand; and you shall eat it hurriedly. It is the passover of the LORD. ¹² For I will pass through the land of Egypt that night, and I will strike down every firstborn in the land of Egypt, both human beings and animals; on all the gods of Egypt I will execute judgments: I am the LORD. ¹³ The blood shall be a sign for you on the houses where you live: when I see the blood, I will pass over you, and no plague shall destroy you when I strike the land of Egypt.

14 This day shall be a day of remembrance for you. You shall celebrate it as a festival to the LORD; throughout your generations you shall observe it as a perpetual ordinance. ¹⁵ Seven days you shall eat unleavened bread; on the first day you shall remove leaven from your houses, for whoever eats leavened bread from the first day until the seventh day shall be cut off from Israel. ¹⁶ On the first

---

12:2—The exodus is a divine act of new creation, remembered by the beginning of the year marking the beginning of Israel's new life. In the same way Christians mark their calendar from Jesus' birth and Muslims from Mohammed's journey from Mecca to Medina (Hijira). Such divine acts are so momentous that they require the reordering and recreating of time.

12:4—The cost of a lamb would be prohibitive to many, so the corporate community comes together to ensure that the needs of all are met.

12:2, 3, 6—*Congregation* is in-group/out-group language. The directions are for *this* group of slaves. This suggests that not all of God's acts of deliverance are the same and that one deliverance may not look like another deliverance. This should caution us about applying the exodus paradigm to all situations of oppression. Just because God chose to deliver *this* group in *this* manner, does not mean that all God's acts of deliverance will look the same.

12:8—In addition to all the symbolic and theological significance associated with Passover, it also had the rather commonplace practicality of providing the people with a solid meal before hitting the road. Just as God will provide the manna and water the people need for sustenance in the wilderness, God now provides the sustenance they need to begin their journey. Sometimes in our quest for liberation we can forget that something as practical as a solid meal is needed to sustain us on the way.

12:14—The festival of Passover remembers an event that occurred in the past. However, it looks also to the future, since this day will come around each year on the calendar. Thus the day creates the hope for fresh acts of salvation. Deliverance by God is not just a single act in the past but an ongoing reality.

day you shall hold a solemn assembly, and on the seventh day a solemn assembly; no work shall be done on those days; only what everyone must eat, that alone may be prepared by you. 17 You shall observe the festival of unleavened bread, for on this very day I brought your companies out of the land of Egypt: you shall observe this day throughout your generations as a perpetual ordinance. 18 In the first month, from the evening of the fourteenth day until the evening of the twenty-first day, you shall eat unleavened bread. 19 For seven days no leaven shall be found in your houses; for whoever eats what is leavened shall be cut off from the congregation of Israel, whether an alien or a native of the land. 20 You shall eat nothing leavened; in all your settlements you shall eat unleavened bread.

21 Then Moses called all the elders of Israel and said to them, "Go, select lambs for your families, and slaughter the passover lamb. 22 Take a bunch of hyssop, dip it in the blood that is in the basin, and touch the lintel and the two doorposts with the blood in the basin. None of you shall go outside the door of your house until morning. 23 For the LORD will pass through to strike down the Egyptians; when he sees the blood on the lintel and on the two doorposts, the LORD will pass over that door and will not allow the destroyer to enter your houses to strike you down. 24 You shall observe this rite as a perpetual ordinance for you and your children. 25 When you come to the land that the LORD will give you, as he has promised, you shall keep this observance. 26 And when your children ask you, 'What do you mean by this observance?' 27 you shall say, 'It is the passover sacrifice to the LORD, for he passed over the houses of the Israelites in Egypt, when he struck down the Egyptians but spared our houses.'" And the people bowed down and worshiped.

28 The Israelites went and did just as the LORD had commanded Moses and Aaron.

The Tenth Plague: Death of the Firstborn

29 At midnight the LORD struck down all the firstborn in the land of Egypt, from the firstborn of Pharaoh who sat on his throne to the firstborn of the prisoner who was in the dungeon, and all the firstborn of the livestock. 30 Pharaoh arose in the night, he and all his officials and all the Egyptians; and there was a loud cry in Egypt, for there was not a house without someone dead. 31 Then he summoned Moses and Aaron in the night, and said, "Rise up, go away from my people, both you and the Israelites! Go, worship the LORD, as you said. 32 Take your flocks and your herds, as you said, and be gone. And bring a blessing on me too!"

The Exodus: From Rameses to Succoth

33 The Egyptians urged the people to hasten their departure from the land, for they said, "We shall all be dead." 34 So the people took their dough before it was leavened, with their kneading bowls wrapped up in their cloaks on their shoulders. 35 The Israelites had done as Moses told them; they had asked the Egyptians for jewelry of silver and gold, and for clothing, 36 and the LORD had given the people favor in the sight of the Egyptians, so that they let them have what they asked. And so they plundered the Egyptians.

37 The Israelites journeyed from

12:26—An event has lasting significance only if it is passed on to the next generation. Each generation must appropriate the story for itself in a meaningful way. Telling the stories of the deliverance of our ancestors is not enough. Otherwise the exodus is only a pleasant memory of the past.

To know that on this night we have been freed, we must tell our own stories of deliverance.

12:37—Free at last! Free at last! Thank God Almighty, free at last!" Martin Luther King Jr.'s words are appropriate at this point. After lifetimes of slavery the Hebrews are on their way out of

Rameses to Succoth, about six hundred thousand men on foot, besides children. **38** A mixed crowd also went up with them, and livestock in great numbers, both flocks and herds. **39** They baked unleavened cakes of the dough that they had brought out of Egypt; it was not leavened, because they were driven out of Egypt and could not wait, nor had they prepared any provisions for themselves.

40 The time that the Israelites had lived in Egypt was four hundred thirty years. **41** At the end of four hundred thirty years, on that very day, all the companies of the LORD went out from the land of Egypt. **42** That was for the LORD a night of vigil, to bring them out of the land of Egypt. That same night is a vigil to be kept for the LORD by all the Israelites throughout their generations.

Directions for the Passover

43 The LORD said to Moses and Aaron: This is the ordinance for the passover: no foreigner shall eat of it, **44** but any slave who has been purchased may eat of it after he has been circumcised; **45** no bound or hired servant may eat of it. **46** It shall be eaten in one house; you shall not take any of the animal outside the house, and you shall not break any of its bones. **47** The whole congregation of Israel shall celebrate it. **48** If an alien who resides with you wants to celebrate the passover to the LORD, all his males shall be circumcised; then he may draw near to celebrate it; he shall be regarded as a native of the land. But no uncircumcised person shall eat of it; **49** there shall be one law for the native and for the alien who resides among you.

50 All the Israelites did just as the LORD had commanded Moses and Aaron. **51** That very day the LORD brought the Israelites out of the land of Egypt, company by company.

13 The LORD said to Moses: **2** Consecrate to me all the firstborn; whatever is the first to open the womb among the Israelites, of human beings and animals, is mine.

The Festival of Unleavened Bread

3 Moses said to the people, "Remember this day on which you came out of Egypt, out of the house of slavery, because the LORD brought you out from there by strength of hand; no leavened bread shall be eaten. **4** Today, in the month of Abib, you are going out. **5** When the LORD brings you into the land of the Canaanites, the Hittites, the Amorites, the Hivites, and the Jebusites, which he swore to your ancestors to give you, a land flowing with milk and honey, you shall keep this observance in this month. **6** Seven days you shall eat unleavened bread, and on the seventh day there shall be a festival to the LORD. **7** Unleavened bread shall be eaten for seven days; no leavened bread shall be seen in your possession, and no leaven shall be seen among you in all your territory. **8** You shall tell your child on that day, 'It is because of what the LORD did for me when I came out of Egypt.' **9** It shall serve for you as a sign on your hand and as a reminder on your forehead, so that the teaching of the LORD may be on your lips; for with a strong hand the LORD brought you out of Egypt. **10** You shall keep this ordinance at its proper time from year to year.

The Consecration of the Firstborn

11 "When the LORD has brought you into the land of the Canaanites, as he swore to you and your ancestors, and has given it to you, **12** you shall set apart to the LORD all that first opens the womb. All the firstborn of your livestock that are males shall be the LORD's. **13** But every firstborn donkey you shall redeem with a sheep; if you

---

Egypt. But liberation is not a simple process. This is but the first step on the journey toward

freedom (see notes at 14:10; 15:24; 16:3; 17:8; 20:1).

do not redeem it, you must break its neck. Every firstborn male among your children you shall redeem. [14] When in the future your child asks you, 'What does this mean?' you shall answer, 'By strength of hand the LORD brought us out of Egypt, from the house of slavery. [15] When Pharaoh stubbornly refused to let us go, the LORD killed all the firstborn in the land of Egypt, from human firstborn to the firstborn of animals. Therefore I sacrifice to the LORD every male that first opens the womb, but every firstborn of my sons I redeem.' [16] It shall serve as a sign on your hand and as an emblem[a] on your forehead that by strength of hand the LORD brought us out of Egypt."

The Pillars of Cloud and Fire

[17] When Pharaoh let the people go, God did not lead them by way of the land of the Philistines, although that was nearer; for God thought, "If the people face war, they may change their minds and return to Egypt." [18] So God led the people by the roundabout way of the wilderness toward the Red Sea.[b] The Israelites went up out of the land of Egypt prepared for battle. [19] And Moses took with him the bones of Joseph who had required a solemn oath of the Israelites, saying, "God will surely take notice of you, and then you must carry my bones with you from here." [20] They set out from Succoth, and camped at Etham, on the edge of the wilderness. [21] The LORD went in front of them in a pillar of cloud by day, to lead them along the way, and in a pillar of fire by night, to give them light, so that they might travel by day and by night. [22] Neither the pillar of cloud by day nor the pillar of fire by night left its place in front of the people.

Crossing the Red Sea

14 Then the LORD said to Moses: [2] Tell the Israelites to turn back and camp in front of Pi-hahiroth, between Migdol and the sea, in front of Baal-zephon; you shall camp opposite it, by the sea. [3] Pharaoh will say of the Israelites, "They are wandering aimlessly in the land; the wilderness has closed in on them." [4] I will harden Pharaoh's heart, and he will pursue them, so that I will gain glory for myself over Pharaoh and all his army; and the Egyptians shall know that I am the LORD. And they did so.

[5] When the king of Egypt was told that the people had fled, the minds of Pharaoh and his officials were changed toward the people, and they said, "What have we done, letting Israel leave our service?" [6] So he had his chariot made ready, and took his army with him; [7] he took six hundred picked chariots and all the other chariots of Egypt with officers over all of them. [8] The LORD hardened the heart of Pharaoh king of Egypt and he pursued the Israelites, who were going out boldly. [9] The Egyptians pursued them, all Pharaoh's horses and chariots, his chariot drivers and his army; they overtook them camped by the sea, by Pi-hahiroth, in front of Baal-zephon.

[10] As Pharaoh drew near, the Israelites

---

[a] Or as a frontlet; meaning of Heb uncertain   [b] Or Sea of Reeds

---

13:19—Rabbinic tradition credits Serah, daughter of Asher (Gen. 46:17; Num. 26:46; 1 Chr. 7:30), for ensuring that Joseph's bones are taken to Canaan (cf. Gen. 50:25). The tradition developed that not only was Serah alive when Israel went into Egypt, but she was still alive when Israel left and was therefore the only one who knew where Joseph's bones were hidden. Sometimes wisdom and leadership arise from the most unexpected of sources.

13:21—God is present in the pillars of cloud and fire as guide and protector (see also 13:22; 14:19, 20, 24; 40:36–38). Keep in mind that these slaves had never been to Canaan. How would they know when they got there? Moses won't have to stop to ask for directions, since God provides a means of guidance through the wilderness. God will not abandon us in the wilderness but will guide us through.

14:10—Of course the Israelites were afraid. There was an angry Egyptian army on one side and an impassable sea on the other. Liberation is not

looked back, and there were the Egyptians advancing on them. In great fear the Israelites cried out to the LORD. [11] They said to Moses, "Was it because there were no graves in Egypt that you have taken us away to die in the wilderness? What have you done to us, bringing us out of Egypt? [12] Is this not the very thing we told you in Egypt, 'Let us alone and let us serve the Egyptians'? For it would have been better for us to serve the Egyptians than to die in the wilderness." [13] But Moses said to the people, "Do not be afraid, stand firm, and see the deliverance that the LORD will accomplish for you today; for the Egyptians whom you see today you shall never see again. [14] The LORD will fight for you, and you have only to keep still."

15 Then the LORD said to Moses, "Why do you cry out to me? Tell the Israelites to go forward. [16] But you lift up your staff, and stretch out your hand over the sea and divide it, that the Israelites may go into the sea on dry ground. [17] Then I will harden the hearts of the Egyptians so that they will go in after them; and so I will gain glory for myself over Pharaoh and all his army, his chariots, and his chariot drivers. [18] And the Egyptians shall know that I am the LORD, when I have gained glory for myself over Pharaoh, his chariots, and his chariot drivers."

19 The angel of God who was going before the Israelite army moved and went behind them; and the pillar of cloud moved from in front of them and took its place behind them. [20] It came between the army of Egypt and the army of Israel. And so the cloud was there with the darkness, and it lit up the night; one did not come near the other all night.

21 Then Moses stretched out his hand over the sea. The LORD drove the sea back by a strong east wind all night, and turned the sea into dry land; and the waters were divided. [22] The Israelites went into the sea on dry ground, the waters forming a wall for them on their right and on their left. [23] The Egyptians pursued, and went into the sea after them, all of Pharaoh's horses, chariots, and chariot drivers. [24] At the morning watch the LORD in the pillar of fire and cloud looked down upon the Egyptian army, and threw the Egyptian army into panic. [25] He clogged[a] their chariot wheels so that they turned with difficulty. The Egyptians said, "Let us flee from the Israelites, for the LORD is fighting for them against Egypt."

The Pursuers Drowned

26 Then the LORD said to Moses, "Stretch out your hand over the sea, so that the water may come back upon the Egyptians, upon their chariots and chariot drivers." [27] So Moses stretched out his hand over the sea, and at dawn the sea returned to its normal depth. As the Egyptians fled before it, the LORD

[a] Sam Gk Syr: MT *removed*

---

easy and does not happen all at once. There will be setbacks along the way and even times when slavery seems preferable (see notes at 15:24; 16:3; 17:8; 20:1).

14:13—Moses' response is a command to the people to not fear and to be still. Why? Because the Lord will fight for them and will deliver them. Then, as now, this is easier said than done. Our usual impulse is to leap into action and do *something*. Yet, when standing between enemies and impassable seas, we are called to be still (cf. Isa. 7:4). We do not have leap into the fray, fight back, or struggle if deliverance is something not accomplished on our own (see note at Exod. 15:3).

14:21—God's deliverance involved this miracle of the parting of the waters. This verse suggests that in addition to divine activity this miracle involved human activity (Moses stretched out his hand) and the activity of the natural world (a strong east wind). God uses humans and the natural world to accomplish divine purposes (cf. Jonah).

14:22—Do we ever wonder who it was who took that first step onto the dry land between the walls of water? To step into such an unknown takes trust and courage. To step into the unknown world of freedom also takes trust and courage.

tossed the Egyptians into the sea. **28** The waters returned and covered the chariots and the chariot drivers, the entire army of Pharaoh that had followed them into the sea; not one of them remained. **29** But the Israelites walked on dry ground through the sea, the waters forming a wall for them on their right and on their left.

30 Thus the LORD saved Israel that day from the Egyptians; and Israel saw the Egyptians dead on the seashore. **31** Israel saw the great work that the LORD did against the Egyptians. So the people feared the LORD and believed in the LORD and in his servant Moses.

The Song of Moses

15 Then Moses and the Israelites sang this song to the LORD:

"I will sing to the LORD, for he has triumphed gloriously;
  horse and rider he has thrown into the sea.
2 The LORD is my strength and my might,*a*
  and he has become my salvation;
this is my God, and I will praise him,
  my father's God, and I will exalt him.
3 The LORD is a warrior;
  the LORD is his name.

4 "Pharaoh's chariots and his army he cast into the sea;
  his picked officers were sunk in the Red Sea.*b*

5 The floods covered them;
  they went down into the depths like a stone.
6 Your right hand, O LORD, glorious in power—
  your right hand, O LORD, shattered the enemy.
7 In the greatness of your majesty you overthrew your adversaries;
  you sent out your fury, it consumed them like stubble.
8 At the blast of your nostrils the waters piled up,
  the floods stood up in a heap;
  the deeps congealed in the heart of the sea.
9 The enemy said, 'I will pursue, I will overtake,
  I will divide the spoil, my desire shall have its fill of them.
  I will draw my sword, my hand shall destroy them.'
10 You blew with your wind, the sea covered them;
  they sank like lead in the mighty waters.

11 "Who is like you, O LORD, among the gods?
  Who is like you, majestic in holiness,
  awesome in splendor, doing wonders?
12 You stretched out your right hand, the earth swallowed them.

a Or song   *b* Or Sea of Reeds

14:30—Once again Israel's deliverance comes at tremendous cost (see notes at 3:8 and 11:5). We need always to remember that there is more than one side to a story. For Egyptians this is a story of tragedy and defeat. Recountings of the American Civil War illustrate the truth that each side has their story to tell. We need to hear the story of the Egyptians *and* the slaves, the South *and* the North, Israelis *and* Palestinians. We must hear even the stories of our enemies. Perhaps, as we consider not only our own inclinations to oppress but also the consequences, we'll be inclined to heed the voices of those crying out to be let go.

15:3—This verse makes clear that God is literally *a man of war*. Those who argue that a God of war leads inexorably to the concept of *holy war* critique this militant image of God. Yet there is a certain attraction to this warring deity. Exodus makes clear that in terms of conventional warfare, there was no war at all. The Hebrews themselves did not fight or engage in battle. In fact, they could not have done so. They had no armament. Think of David and Goliath. The only way to explain this victory of the Hebrews was by divine intervention. Had not God fought on their behalf, they would surely have left Egypt only to die in the wilderness. Whether or not one embraces this image of God, remember that God fights for those who have no other weapons.

13 "In your steadfast love you led the
      people whom you redeemed;
  you guided them by your strength
      to your holy abode.
14 The peoples heard, they trembled;
      pangs seized the inhabitants of
      Philistia.
15 Then the chiefs of Edom were
      dismayed;
      trembling seized the leaders of
      Moab;
      all the inhabitants of Canaan
      melted away.
16 Terror and dread fell upon them;
      by the might of your arm, they
      became still as a stone
  until your people, O LORD, passed
      by,
      until the people whom you
      acquired passed by.
17 You brought them in and planted
      them on the mountain of your
      own possession,
      the place, O LORD, that you made
      your abode,
      the sanctuary, O LORD, that your
      hands have established.
18 The LORD will reign forever and
      ever."

19 When the horses of Pharaoh with
his chariots and his chariot drivers went
into the sea, the LORD brought back the
waters of the sea upon them; but the
Israelites walked through the sea on dry
ground.

The Song of Miriam

20 Then the prophet Miriam, Aaron's
sister, took a tambourine in her hand;
and all the women went out after her
with tambourines and with dancing.
21 And Miriam sang to them:
"Sing to the LORD, for he has
      triumphed gloriously;
  horse and rider he has thrown into
      the sea."

Bitter Water Made Sweet

22 Then Moses ordered Israel to set
out from the Red Sea,[a] and they went
into the wilderness of Shur. They went
three days in the wilderness and found
no water. 23 When they came to Marah,
they could not drink the water of Marah
because it was bitter. That is why it was
called Marah.[b] 24 And the people complained against Moses, saying, "What
shall we drink?" 25 He cried out to the

[a] Or Sea of Reeds   [b] That is Bitterness

15:20–21—Canonically, and maybe historically, Miriam is the first of five specific women in the Old Testament named as a prophet (see Judg. 4:4; 2 Kgs. 22:14; Neh. 6:14; Isa. 8:3). Although the text never attributes the usual prophetic activity to Miriam, the tradition remembers her as having a significant leadership role in the exodus community on a par with Moses and Aaron (see Num. 12:1–15; Mic. 6:4). Miriam is also portrayed as a worship leader. Scholars have noted that Miriam sings only the chorus of the longer song in vv. 1–18. Feminists have questioned whether it was Miriam, rather than Moses, who was the singer of the Song of the Sea, since victory songs in the biblical narrative are sung by women (Judg. 5; 1 Sam. 2). Her leadership challenges the notion that only men can be leaders in the church.

15:20—The translation *tambourine* is anachronistic, since the tambourine cannot be authenticated as a musical instrument before the thirteenth century CE. It was more likely a hand drum. Elsewhere women play drums in celebration of military victory (Judg. 11:34; 1 Sam. 18:6).

This association between women and drums suggests that in other texts where the drum (tambourine) is mentioned, women would be the musicians and central participants in Israel's formal religious celebrations (see 1 Sam. 10:5; 2 Sam. 6:5; Pss. 81:2; 149:3; 150:4; Isa. 5:12; Jer. 31:4).

15:24—The ringing tones of victory have barely faded before the people complain. Elsewhere the wilderness is remembered as a honeymoon period (Jer. 2:2; Hos. 2:14–15) instead of a place of complaint and apostasy. The first complaint is that there is no potable water, which is not a trivial problem in the desert. It threatens their very survival. Want and deprivation show that liberation is a process that moves forward in fits and starts. Leaving Egypt is only one step toward freedom. Along the way there will be many obstacles and setbacks to their freedom (see notes at 14:10; 16:3; 17:8; 20:1).

15:25—In response to their complaint, God provides water. One of the lessons of the wilderness experience is that God provides what is needed for survival.

LORD; and the LORD showed him a piece of wood;*a* he threw it into the water, and the water became sweet.

There the LORD*b* made for them a statute and an ordinance and there he put them to the test. 26 He said, "If you will listen carefully to the voice of the LORD your God, and do what is right in his sight, and give heed to his commandments and keep all his statutes, I will not bring upon you any of the diseases that I brought upon the Egyptians; for I am the LORD who heals you."

27 Then they came to Elim, where there were twelve springs of water and seventy palm trees; and they camped there by the water.

Bread from Heaven

16 The whole congregation of the Israelites set out from Elim; and Israel came to the wilderness of Sin, which is between Elim and Sinai, on the fifteenth day of the second month after they had departed from the land of Egypt. 2 The whole congregation of the Israelites complained against Moses and Aaron in the wilderness. 3 The Israelites said to them, "If only we had died by the hand of the LORD in the land of Egypt, when we sat by the fleshpots and ate our fill of bread; for you have brought us out into this wilderness to kill this whole assembly with hunger."

4 Then the LORD said to Moses, "I am going to rain bread from heaven for you, and each day the people shall go out and gather enough for that day. In that way I will test them, whether they will follow my instruction or not. 5 On the sixth day, when they prepare what they bring in, it will be twice as much as they gather on other days." 6 So Moses and Aaron said to all the Israelites, "In the evening you shall know that it was the LORD who brought you out of the land of Egypt, 7 and in the morning you shall see the glory of the LORD, because he has heard your complaining against the LORD. For what are we, that you complain against us?" 8 And Moses said,

a Or *a tree*   *b* Heb *he*

Just as God tested Abraham (Gen. 22:1), now God tests the people (Exod. 16:4; 20:20) to determine their faithfulness and obedience. This test is whether they will listen carefully to God and keep God's statutes. In 16:4 the manna tests whether they will follow God's instruction to only take enough for each day. In 20:20 God's display of thunder and lightning tests whether their faith is serious. God does not seem to know ahead of time what the people's response will be. There is a long tradition of interpreting difficult circumstances as a divine test. Will we remain faithful to God in those times or not? Not even God knows.

15:26—Even before Sinai, the people discover that their relationship with God is conditional. *If* they are obedient, *then* God will not punish them. Sometimes God's response toward us depends upon our response toward God.

God as healer is a beautiful and comforting image. But in the context of the verse it raises a paradox about the divine nature (see notes at 3:14; 20:5–6; 34:6–7). The same one who heals is also the one who brings disease. This paradox is expressed in Deut. 32:39, "I wound and I heal." In the prophetic literature disease and wounds are a metaphor for God's punishment of the people for their sins, and divine healing a metaphor for restoration (Isa. 30:26; Hos. 6:1;

cf. Job 5:18). What kind of God is this who is responsible for both wounding and healing?

16:1–18:27 Building Community as a Congregation

16:3—The people soon face another threat to their survival—hunger. Some liberation! Without food they will soon be a dead free people. What good is freedom without food? Liberation may look like a good idea in the abstract, but when people are faced with the threat that it may kill, it may look less attractive, and people will resist. The struggle is to continue in faith in the face of such threats (see notes at 14:10; 15:24; 17:8; 20:1).

Whenever the people are faced with some seemingly insurmountable obstacle, instead of seeking to overcome the obstacle and move forward, the initial response is to turn back (14:12) and return to the comforts of the *good old days,* even if those days weren't so good.

16:4—See note at 15:25.

16:8—Though different from 2:23, complaining is also a form of crying out to God. As 2:23–24 and this verse indicate, we must learn to cry out to God in order to receive the gifts God would bestow. It is difficult in a society that advocates self-sufficiency to ask for help when

"When the LORD gives you meat to eat in the evening and your fill of bread in the morning, because the LORD has heard the complaining that you utter against him—what are we? Your complaining is not against us but against the LORD."

9 Then Moses said to Aaron, "Say to the whole congregation of the Israelites, 'Draw near to the LORD, for he has heard your complaining.'" 10 And as Aaron spoke to the whole congregation of the Israelites, they looked toward the wilderness, and the glory of the LORD appeared in the cloud. 11 The LORD spoke to Moses and said, 12 "I have heard the complaining of the Israelites; say to them, 'At twilight you shall eat meat, and in the morning you shall have your fill of bread; then you shall know that I am the LORD your God.'"

13 In the evening quails came up and covered the camp; and in the morning there was a layer of dew around the camp. 14 When the layer of dew lifted, there on the surface of the wilderness was a fine flaky substance, as fine as frost on the ground. 15 When the Israelites saw it, they said to one another, "What is it?"*a* For they did not know what it was. Moses said to them, "It is the bread that the LORD has given you to eat. 16 This is what the LORD has commanded: 'Gather as much of it as each of you needs, an omer to a person according to the number of persons, all providing for those in their own tents.'" 17 The Israelites did so, some gathering more, some less. 18 But when they measured it with an omer, those who gathered much had nothing over, and those who gathered little had no shortage; they gathered as much as each of them needed. 19 And Moses said to them, "Let no one leave any of it over until morning." 20 But they did not listen to Moses; some left part of it until morning, and it bred worms and became foul. And Moses was angry with them. 21 Morning by morning they gathered it, as much as each needed; but when the sun grew hot, it melted.

22 On the sixth day they gathered twice as much food, two omers apiece. When all the leaders of the congregation came and told Moses, 23 he said to them, "This is what the LORD has commanded: 'Tomorrow is a day of solemn rest, a holy sabbath to the LORD; bake what you want to bake and boil what you want to boil, and all that is left over put aside to be kept until morning.'" 24 So they put it aside until morning, as Moses commanded them; and it did not become foul, and there were no worms in it. 25 Moses said, "Eat it today, for today is a sabbath to the LORD; today you will not find it in the field. 26 Six days you shall gather it; but on the seventh day, which is a sabbath, there will be none."

27 On the seventh day some of the people went out to gather, and they found none. 28 The LORD said to Moses, "How long will you refuse to keep my commandments and instructions? 29 See! The LORD has given you the sabbath, therefore on the sixth day he gives you food for two days; each of you stay where you

a Or "It is manna" (Heb man hu, see verse 31)

---

it is needed and then to receive it and trust it will be enough.

16:10—God is frequently imaged as being present in cloud and fire (19:9, 16, 18, etc.). This image highlights God as glorious and as awesome as a storm, but also as hidden, since we don't want to get too near to a storm.

16:15—*"What is it?"* is a possible translation for *manna* (Heb. *man hu*). This sounds like a question we might ask of God's gifts to us. Sometimes God's gifts are not the ones we expect.

16:18—God's provision is remarkably egalitarian. Each has what they need; none are left without, and none can accumulate more than they need. In societies run by capitalism and market forces, is it possible to consider such equitable distribution of resources?

16:21—The provision of the manna reminds us to take one day at a time. What God gives us each day is enough (cf. Matt. 6:11; Luke 11:3; 2 Cor. 12:9).

are; do not leave your place on the seventh day." [30] So the people rested on the seventh day.

31 The house of Israel called it manna; it was like coriander seed, white, and the taste of it was like wafers made with honey. [32] Moses said, "This is what the LORD has commanded: 'Let an omer of it be kept throughout your generations, in order that they may see the food with which I fed you in the wilderness, when I brought you out of the land of Egypt.'" [33] And Moses said to Aaron, "Take a jar, and put an omer of manna in it, and place it before the LORD, to be kept throughout your generations." [34] As the LORD commanded Moses, so Aaron placed it before the covenant,[a] for safekeeping. [35] The Israelites ate manna forty years, until they came to a habitable land; they ate manna, until they came to the border of the land of Canaan. [36] An omer is a tenth of an ephah.

Water from the Rock

17 From the wilderness of Sin the whole congregation of the Israelites journeyed by stages, as the LORD commanded. They camped at Rephidim, but there was no water for the people to drink. [2] The people quarreled with Moses, and said, "Give us water to drink." Moses said to them, "Why do you quarrel with me? Why do you test the LORD?" [3] But the people thirsted there for water; and the people complained against Moses and said, "Why did you bring us out of Egypt, to kill us and our children and livestock with thirst?" [4] So Moses cried out to the LORD, "What shall I do with this people? They are almost ready to stone me." [5] The LORD said to Moses, "Go on ahead of the people, and take some of the elders of Israel with you; take in your hand the staff with which you struck the Nile, and go. [6] I will be standing there in front of you on the rock at Horeb. Strike the rock, and water will come out of it, so that the people may drink." Moses did so, in the sight of the elders of Israel. [7] He called the place Massah[b] and Meribah,[c] because the Israelites quarreled and tested the LORD, saying, "Is the LORD among us or not?"

Amalek Attacks Israel and Is Defeated

8 Then Amalek came and fought with Israel at Rephidim. [9] Moses said to Joshua, "Choose some men for us and go out, fight with Amalek. Tomorrow I will stand on the top of the hill with the staff of God in my hand." [10] So Joshua did as Moses told him, and fought with Amalek, while Moses, Aaron, and Hur went up to the top of the hill. [11] Whenever Moses held up his hand, Israel prevailed; and whenever he lowered his hand, Amalek prevailed. [12] But Moses' hands grew weary; so they took a stone and put it under him, and he sat on it. Aaron and Hur held up his hands, one on one side, and the other on the other side; so his hands were steady until the sun set. [13] And Joshua defeated Amalek and his people with the sword.

[a] Or treaty or testimony; Heb eduth   [b] That is Test   [c] That is Quarrel

16:35—God's provision of food ceases at the border to the promised land. Now the people will be responsible for their own food provisions. An open question is whether the people will follow God's pattern of equitable distribution of resources.

17:1–7—Some suggest that the people complained needlessly—if they only had faith in the One who saved them, they would not need to ask how to survive. But is it so simple? The Israelites were faced with real, life-threatening dangers. When faced with starvation, AIDS, or tanks, an understandable response is the questioning of God's presence and provision.

17:8—Armed attacks by enemies is another threat to the liberation process (see notes at 14:10; 15:24; 16:3; 20:1). In a paradoxical way, a free life *guarantees* hardship—uncertainty about meeting basic needs like food and water and hostile people who threaten us at our most vulnerable. The choice is the risks and hardships of freedom or the security of needs met even at the cost of bondage.

14 Then the LORD said to Moses, "Write this as a reminder in a book and recite it in the hearing of Joshua: I will utterly blot out the remembrance of Amalek from under heaven." 15 And Moses built an altar and called it, The LORD is my banner. 16 He said, "A hand upon the banner of the LORD!ᵃ The LORD will have war with Amalek from generation to generation."

Jethro's Advice

18 Jethro, the priest of Midian, Moses' father-in-law, heard of all that God had done for Moses and for his people Israel, how the LORD had brought Israel out of Egypt. 2 After Moses had sent away his wife Zipporah, his father-in-law Jethro took her back, 3 along with her two sons. The name of the one was Gershom (for he said, "I have been an alienᵇ in a foreign land"), 4 and the name of the other, Eliezerᶜ (for he said, "The God of my father was my help, and delivered me from the sword of Pharaoh"). 5 Jethro, Moses' father-in-law, came into the wilderness where Moses was encamped at the mountain of God, bringing Moses' sons and wife to him. 6 He sent word to Moses, "I, your father-in-law Jethro, am coming to you, with your wife and her two sons." 7 Moses went out to meet his father-in-law; he bowed down and kissed him; each asked after the other's welfare, and they went into the tent. 8 Then Moses told his father-in-law all that the LORD had done to Pharaoh and to the Egyptians for Israel's sake, all the hardship that had beset them on the way, and how the LORD had delivered them. 9 Jethro rejoiced for all the good that the LORD had done to Israel, in delivering them from the Egyptians.

10 Jethro said, "Blessed be the LORD, who has delivered you from the Egyptians and from Pharaoh. 11 Now I know that the LORD is greater than all gods, because he delivered the people from the Egyptians,ᵈ when they dealt arrogantly with them." 12 And Jethro, Moses' father-in-law, brought a burnt offering and sacrifices to God; and Aaron came with all the elders of Israel to eat bread with Moses' father-in-law in the presence of God.

13 The next day Moses sat as judge for the people, while the people stood around him from morning until evening. 14 When Moses' father-in-law saw all that he was doing for the people, he said, "What is this that you are doing for the people? Why do you sit alone, while all the people stand around you from morning until evening?" 15 Moses said to his father-in-law, "Because the people come to me to inquire of God. 16 When they have a dispute, they come to me and I decide between one person and another, and I make known to them the statutes and instructions of God." 17 Moses' father-in-law said to him, "What you are doing is not good.

ᵃ Cn: Meaning of Heb uncertain ᵇ Heb ger ᶜ Heb Eli, my God; ezer, help ᵈ The clause because . . . Egyptians has been transposed from verse 10

17:14–16—The eternal war with Amalek reflects our need for a permanent enemy. We can band together in unity against this enemy, thereby avoiding the tensions and divisions within our own community. Equally problematic is the inability to consider actions that contradict such an all-consuming ideology (1 Sam. 15:1–33). Who can consider compromises or even peaceful coexistence with an enemy we have warred with for generations? The common choice is to continue the violence. Consider ways to break the cycles of violence caused by hatreds that have lasted for generations.

18:2—The text gives no indication of why Moses sent away Zipporah and their sons. Although they come with Jethro, they play no part in the ensuing scene, and there is no indication they then stayed with Moses. Women and children are often incidental or disposable characters. Would the story be different if they were seen as central and necessary? Consider bringing those who are on the edges of the community into the center.

18:13–26—This interchange between Jethro and Moses serves as a warning to all leaders. Burnout is an ever-present danger. Nowhere does the Bible advocate that we should do it all on our own. We need not only God, but also one another.

¹⁸ You will surely wear yourself out, both you and these people with you. For the task is too heavy for you; you cannot do it alone. ¹⁹ Now listen to me. I will give you counsel, and God be with you! You should represent the people before God, and you should bring their cases before God; ²⁰ teach them the statutes and instructions and make known to them the way they are to go and the things they are to do. ²¹ You should also look for able men among all the people, men who fear God, are trustworthy, and hate dishonest gain; set such men over them as officers over thousands, hundreds, fifties, and tens. ²² Let them sit as judges for the people at all times; let them bring every important case to you, but decide every minor case themselves. So it will be easier for you, and they will bear the burden with you. ²³ If you do this, and God so commands you, then you will be able to endure, and all these people will go to their home in peace."

24 So Moses listened to his father-in-law and did all that he had said. ²⁵ Moses chose able men from all Israel and appointed them as heads over the people, as officers over thousands, hundreds, fifties, and tens. ²⁶ And they judged the people at all times; hard cases they brought to Moses, but any minor case they decided themselves. ²⁷ Then Moses let his father-in-law depart, and he went off to his own country.

The Israelites Reach Mount Sinai

19 On the third new moon after the Israelites had gone out of the land of Egypt, on that very day, they came into the wilderness of Sinai. ² They had journeyed from Rephidim, entered the wilderness of Sinai, and camped in the wilderness; Israel camped there in front of the mountain. ³ Then Moses went up to God; the LORD called to him from the mountain, saying, "Thus you shall say to the house of Jacob, and tell the Israelites: ⁴ You have seen what I did to the Egyptians, and how I bore you on eagles' wings and brought you to myself. ⁵ Now therefore, if you obey my voice and keep my covenant, you shall be my treasured possession out of all the peoples. Indeed, the whole earth is mine, ⁶ but you shall be for me a priestly kingdom and a holy nation. These are the words that you shall speak to the Israelites."

7 So Moses came, summoned the elders of the people, and set before them all these words that the LORD had commanded him. ⁸ The people all answered as one: "Everything that the LORD has spoken we will do." Moses reported the words of the people to the LORD. ⁹ Then the LORD said to Moses, "I am going to come to you in a dense cloud, in order that the people may hear when I speak with you and so trust you ever after."

The People Consecrated

When Moses had told the words of the people to the LORD, ¹⁰ the LORD said to Moses: "Go to the people and consecrate them today and tomorrow. Have them wash their clothes ¹¹ and prepare for the third day, because on the third

---

19:1–24:18 The Covenant at Mount Sinai, including the Ten Commandments

19:1–6—These verses begin the chapters (through 24:18) that are the foundation of the Mosaic covenant. Christians need to be reminded that law has always followed gospel. *Because God brought us out from Egypt, therefore* we will live in covenant community as gracious and joyous response. The impetus for obedience to the law is grounded in God's grace and creative activity that forms a new people (see 20:2). Obedience to the law *is not* a means to relationship with God. The people are already in relationship with God, and have been since the creation of male and female.

19:5–6—The language here speaks of Israel's *chosenness* or *election*. There is a tendency to interpret chosenness as deserving God's special blessings. But *being in relationship to God is not about what we get from it. There are tremendous responsibilities that come with being chosen.* Consider ways in which being chosen is not a blessing but a terrible burden with great costs and sacrifices.

day the LORD will come down upon Mount Sinai in the sight of all the people. ¹²You shall set limits for the people all around, saying, 'Be careful not to go up the mountain or to touch the edge of it. Any who touch the mountain shall be put to death. ¹³No hand shall touch them, but they shall be stoned or shot with arrows;*a* whether animal or human being, they shall not live.' When the trumpet sounds a long blast, they may go up on the mountain." ¹⁴So Moses went down from the mountain to the people. He consecrated the people, and they washed their clothes. ¹⁵And he said to the people, "Prepare for the third day; do not go near a woman."

16 On the morning of the third day there was thunder and lightning, as well as a thick cloud on the mountain, and a blast of a trumpet so loud that all the people who were in the camp trembled. ¹⁷Moses brought the people out of the camp to meet God. They took their stand at the foot of the mountain. ¹⁸Now Mount Sinai was wrapped in smoke, because the LORD had descended upon it in fire; the smoke went up like the smoke of a kiln, while the whole mountain shook violently. ¹⁹As the blast of the trumpet grew louder and louder, Moses

would speak and God would answer him in thunder. ²⁰When the LORD descended upon Mount Sinai, to the top of the mountain, the LORD summoned Moses to the top of the mountain, and Moses went up. ²¹Then the LORD said to Moses, "Go down and warn the people not to break through to the LORD to look; otherwise many of them will perish. ²²Even the priests who approach the LORD must consecrate themselves or the LORD will break out against them." ²³Moses said to the LORD, "The people are not permitted to come up to Mount Sinai; for you yourself warned us, saying, 'Set limits around the mountain and keep it holy.'" ²⁴The LORD said to him, "Go down, and come up bringing Aaron with you; but do not let either the priests or the people break through to come up to the LORD; otherwise he will break out against them." ²⁵So Moses went down to the people and told them.

The Ten Commandments

20 Then God spoke all these words: 2 I am the LORD your God, who brought you out of the land of Egypt, out of the house of slavery; ³you shall have no other gods before*b* me.

a Heb lacks *with arrows*   *b* Or *besides*

19:15—Although the text has Moses giving directions to *the people* (v. 14), the command to *not go near a woman* suggests that "the people" is composed only of men. It is important in reading the commandments to consider whether the audience is only men or also includes women. If the covenant is addressed primarily to men, then how are women to be included?

19:23—Holiness is about setting limits. Limits become a problem when they are either too rigid or too porous. When too rigid, what is considered *holy* must be defended even at the expense of human life. When too porous, there is no basis for determining what should be off-limits. A community is holy when limits are defined and negotiated by the whole community.

20:1—The main point of the legal material is to structure covenant life. The problem of building a new social order is another challenge for the liberation process (see notes at 14:10; 15:24; 16:3; 17:8). The community needs to move from an oppressive social order in Egypt to one of life

in freedom. Building and structuring that order is never easy. There may be different, and even conflicting, views on what that order should look like. We still have to consider how to structure covenant life together. Ours will be different from that of our ancestors. But we still, in loving response to God's grace and mercy, ask ourselves how we should live as God's people.

20:3–17—The Ten Commandments (Decalogue) are a type of law known as absolute or apodictic law. Such laws do not consider special cases, circumstances, or the penalty for infraction (see note at 21:12–13). They are similar to contemporary injunctions such as "Just Say No" or "Don't Drink and Drive." The primary ethical issue is how we reappropriate these laws.

20:3—The translation *before me* suggests the recognition of the existence of other gods, and that the Lord should be the primary or chief god on our list of gods to worship. The alternative translation *besides me* is a demand for an exclusive relationship, and the Lord is to be Israel's

4 You shall not make for yourself an idol, whether in the form of anything that is in heaven above, or that is on the earth beneath, or that is in the water under the earth. 5 You shall not bow down to them or worship them; for I the LORD your God am a jealous God, punishing children for the iniquity of parents, to the third and the fourth generation of those who reject me, 6 but showing steadfast love to the thousandth generation*a* of those who love me and keep my commandments.

7 You shall not make wrongful use of the name of the LORD your God, for the LORD will not acquit anyone who misuses his name.

8 Remember the sabbath day, and keep it holy. 9 Six days you shall labor and do all your work. 10 But the seventh day is a sabbath to the LORD your God; you shall not do any work—you, your son or your daughter, your male or female slave, your livestock, or the alien resident in your towns. 11 For in six days the LORD made heaven and earth, the sea, and all that is in them, but rested the seventh day; therefore the LORD blessed the sabbath day and consecrated it.

12 Honor your father and your mother, so that your days may be long in the land that the LORD your God is giving you.

13 You shall not murder.*b*

14 You shall not commit adultery.

a Or to thousands b Or kill

---

only god. Consider what it means for God to be first and only in your life.

20:4—The prohibition against making idols limits our ability to tie God down or to reduce God to something we are comfortable with.

20:5–6—It's bad enough we are tempted to reduce God. It's even worse when we make our limited vision of God the object of adoration. God's reaction to this is jealousy. This may be an image of God that makes some uncomfortable, since in prophetic literature the jealous God can become an abusive God (Jer. 2–3; Ezek. 16, 23; Hos. 1–3). It sounds horrible that God would send punishment that would last for generations. Yet we are familiar with this consequence. Consider the effects of slavery and racism through generations of Americans or the effects of abuse through generations of a family. Sin is not just an individual matter. The sins of parents, or even nations, have far-reaching consequences that we might perhaps interpret as God's judgment. The counterpoint to God's punishing to the third and fourth generation is God's steadfast love to the thousandth generation. God's love far exceeds God's judgment. Yet both are there. This is one of several theological tensions that are scattered throughout Exodus (see notes at 3:14; 15:26; 34:6-7). Problems arise when we lose the tension. On one side we get a God who is only wrathful and vengeful. On the other side we get a God who is indifferent to injustice. This tension is also part of human existence. How do we extend both mercy and justice?

20:7—The Hebrew word for *wrongful use* has associations with divination; therefore misusing God's name means using God's name unnecessarily or abusing it in a ritual way. In other words,

this commandment is not about swear words but about what we do in the Lord's name. Slavery, the Inquisition, the Holocaust, gay bashing—there is an indefinite list of atrocities committed in the Lord's name. Perpetuating injustice in God's name constitutes wrongful use.

20:8–11—The motivation for the keeping of the Sabbath is the story of creation in Gen. 1. Just as God rested from work, so God's creatures should emulate the Creator. Note that the Sabbath is extended to everyone—children, slaves, animals, and resident aliens. (See note on Exod. 19:15 regarding the absence of the wife.) Resting from work is becoming harder and harder in a world that makes full-time demands. How do we emulate our Creator? Note that Deut. 5:15 gives a different justification for the Sabbath.

20:12—Honoring one's parents wasn't just a matter of being nice to them. For the Israelites, there were no retirement homes or Social Security. Care by one's children meant survival past one's productive years. The care of those most vulnerable in society is an overarching theme of Exodus. Even with retirement homes and Social Security, the care of the elderly who are economically vulnerable should still be our concern.

20:13—Although often translated as "you shall not kill," the prohibition is much more restricted. The word elsewhere in the Old Testament occurs only in instances of one-on-one violence such as premeditated murder or manslaughter. This command is not a prohibition against killing in warfare (17:8–12) or capital punishment (see note at 21:12–13).

20:14—*Adultery* meant different things for men and women in the ancient world. A woman's

15 You shall not steal.

16 You shall not bear false witness against your neighbor.

17 You shall not covet your neighbor's house; you shall not covet your neighbor's wife, or male or female slave, or ox, or donkey, or anything that belongs to your neighbor.

18 When all the people witnessed the thunder and lightning, the sound of the trumpet, and the mountain smoking, they were afraid[a] and trembled and stood at a distance, 19 and said to Moses, "You speak to us, and we will listen; but do not let God speak to us, or we will die." 20 Moses said to the people, "Do not be afraid; for God has come only to test you and to put the fear of him upon you so that you do not sin." 21 Then the people stood at a distance, while Moses drew near to the thick darkness where God was.

The Law concerning the Altar

22 The LORD said to Moses: Thus you shall say to the Israelites: "You have seen for yourselves that I spoke with you from heaven. 23 You shall not make gods of silver alongside me, nor shall you make for yourselves gods of gold. 24 You need make for me only an altar of earth and sacrifice on it your burnt offerings and your offerings of well-being, your sheep and your oxen; in every place where I cause my name to be remembered I will come to you and bless you. 25 But if you make for me an altar of stone, do not build it of hewn stones; for if you use a chisel upon it you profane it. 26 You shall not go up by steps to my altar, so that your nakedness may not be exposed on it."

The Law concerning Slaves

21 These are the ordinances that you shall set before them:

2 When you buy a male Hebrew slave, he shall serve six years, but in the seventh he shall go out a free person, without debt. 3 If he comes in single, he

[a] Sam Gk Syr Vg: MT they saw

---

sexual activity was restricted and controlled, first by her father, then by her husband. A woman was guilty of adultery if she had intercourse (consensual or otherwise) with any man other than her husband. A man, however, could have intercourse with a woman who was not another man's wife, e.g., a prostitute. Women have rightly protested this double standard. Sexual fidelity should be a standard for everyone.

20:15—Stealing is taking something (property or persons) from another that is not yours. Theft creates inequity since it increases the goods of one by depleting the goods of another. Stealing is not done only by individuals, but is also practiced by corporations and nations. We should be concerned not only with individual offenses, but also corporate offenses.

20:16—This commandment is not generally about lying but about courtroom practice. In a community created by God, there needs to be an arena where truth is told, a place where spin doctors are not allowed. There is a saying about speaking truth to power. Those who have power are adept at presenting a distorted picture of reality. If our current justice system is not always the place where reality is reliably described, perhaps communities of faith can be places of truthful witness.

20:17—Covet has to do both with wanting and trying to obtain, maybe damaging what is wanted

in the attempt. Perhaps this commandment is last because such coveting usually motivates the breaking of the other commandments. Wanting what someone else has—their possessions, their land, their natural resources—we resort to stealing, false witness, and even murder. (Again, note that the specificity of coveting a neighbor's wife indicates that the audience for this commandment is male.) Our tendency is to want to point out the sins of others. If only they would cease lusting, stealing, lying, and coveting, then the world would be a better place. The world will be a better place only when we address the lust and covetousness of our hearts.

20:20—See note at 15:25.

20:22–23:19—Referred to as the book of the covenant or the Covenant Code, this section is probably the earliest collection of covenant laws. There is no obvious ordering to the laws. They deal with a variety of issues of daily life.

21:1—Ordinances is a translation of the Hebrew word mishpatim, the plural of mishpat, usually translated "justice." These laws are "justices." These are not arbitrary but exist to create a community in which justice prevails.

21:2–6—It is ironic that, in a book devoted to releasing slaves from bondage, there are laws about slavery. Exodus may not be about ending slavery, but considering its conditions. That the

shall go out single; if he comes in married, then his wife shall go out with him. **4** If his master gives him a wife and she bears him sons or daughters, the wife and her children shall be her master's and he shall go out alone. **5** But if the slave declares, "I love my master, my wife, and my children; I will not go out a free person," **6** then his master shall bring him before God.*a* He shall be brought to the door or the doorpost; and his master shall pierce his ear with an awl; and he shall serve him for life.

7 When a man sells his daughter as a slave, she shall not go out as the male slaves do. **8** If she does not please her master, who designated her for himself, then he shall let her be redeemed; he shall have no right to sell her to a foreign people, since he has dealt unfairly with her. **9** If he designates her for his son, he shall deal with her as with a daughter. **10** If he takes another wife to himself, he shall not diminish the food, clothing, or marital rights of the first wife.*b* **11** And if he does not do these three things for her, she shall go out without debt, without payment of money.

The Law concerning Violence

12 Whoever strikes a person mortally shall be put to death. **13** If it was not pre-

meditated, but came about by an act of God, then I will appoint for you a place to which the killer may flee. **14** But if someone willfully attacks and kills another by treachery, you shall take the killer from my altar for execution.

15 Whoever strikes father or mother shall be put to death.

16 Whoever kidnaps a person, whether that person has been sold or is still held in possession, shall be put to death.

17 Whoever curses father or mother shall be put to death.

18 When individuals quarrel and one strikes the other with a stone or fist so that the injured party, though not dead, is confined to bed, **19** but recovers and walks around outside with the help of a staff, then the assailant shall be free of liability, except to pay for the loss of time, and to arrange for full recovery.

20 When a slaveowner strikes a male or female slave with a rod and the slave dies immediately, the owner shall be punished. **21** But if the slave survives a day or two, there is no punishment; for the slave is the owner's property.

22 When people who are fighting injure a pregnant woman so that there is a miscarriage, and yet no further

a Or to the judges *b* Heb of her

---

male slave is to be set free "without debt" suggests that slavery within the Israelite community was an economic problem. Significantly, the laws regarding slaves are set at the beginning of the code. The memory of abuse of debt slaves leads Israel to formulate laws that treat justly those in debt in their own community. Considering the amount of economic debt accumulated by many poor Americans, as well as by many poor countries, we need to remember that they also have the right to live "without debt."

21:7–11—There are separate laws for male and female slaves. The sale of the daughter reinforces that slavery is a condition of those who are economically vulnerable. The master's behavior toward his female slave is restricted. He cannot treat her as property or sexually abuse her (cf. 21:20–21, 26–27). Men and masters are not given a divine mandate to treat women and slaves however they may wish.

21:12–13—The prohibition of murder does not

eliminate capital punishment. This law requires the death penalty for premeditated murder. It is also the penalty for breaking other commandments: honoring parents (21:15, 17); stealing (21:16—kidnapping is stealing a person); keeping the Sabbath (31:14–15; 35:2). But for an accidental death (an act of God) the killer goes free. The intent of such laws is to preclude actions that would destabilize the community. Even if one is against the death penalty, the issue remains how, as a community, we respond to actions that disorder and destabilize the community. What should be the cost to perpetrators of engaging in such behavior?

21:22–25—The principle of retribution in kind is often called by the Latin *lex talionis* ("law of retaliation"; Lev. 24:17–21; Deut. 19:15–21). This law is often seen as harsh, compared to Jesus' command to turn the other cheek (Matt. 5:38–41). However, this law functions to reduce bloodshed by limiting the extent of retaliation.

harm follows, the one responsible shall be fined what the woman's husband demands, paying as much as the judges determine. 23 If any harm follows, then you shall give life for life, 24 eye for eye, tooth for tooth, hand for hand, foot for foot, 25 burn for burn, wound for wound, stripe for stripe.

26 When a slaveowner strikes the eye of a male or female slave, destroying it, the owner shall let the slave go, a free person, to compensate for the eye. 27 If the owner knocks out a tooth of a male or female slave, the slave shall be let go, a free person, to compensate for the tooth.

Laws concerning Property

28 When an ox gores a man or a woman to death, the ox shall be stoned, and its flesh shall not be eaten; but the owner of the ox shall not be liable. 29 If the ox has been accustomed to gore in the past, and its owner has been warned but has not restrained it, and it kills a man or a woman, the ox shall be stoned, and its owner also shall be put to death. 30 If a ransom is imposed on the owner, then the owner shall pay whatever is imposed for the redemption of the victim's life. 31 If it gores a boy or a girl, the owner shall be dealt with according to this same rule. 32 If the ox gores a male or female slave, the owner shall pay to the slaveowner thirty shekels of silver, and the ox shall be stoned.

33 If someone leaves a pit open, or digs a pit and does not cover it, and an ox or a donkey falls into it, 34 the owner of the pit shall make restitution, giving money to its owner, but keeping the dead animal.

35 If someone's ox hurts the ox of another, so that it dies, then they shall sell the live ox and divide the price of it; and the dead animal they shall also divide. 36 But if it was known that the ox was accustomed to gore in the past, and its owner has not restrained it, the owner shall restore ox for ox, but keep the dead animal.

Laws of Restitution

22 *a* When someone steals an ox or a sheep, and slaughters it or sells it, the thief shall pay five oxen for an ox, and four sheep for a sheep.*b* The thief shall make restitution, but if unable to do so, shall be sold for the theft. 4 When the animal, whether ox or donkey or sheep, is found alive in the thief's possession, the thief shall pay double.

2*c* If a thief is found breaking in, and is beaten to death, no bloodguilt is incurred; 3 but if it happens after sunrise, bloodguilt is incurred.

5 When someone causes a field or vineyard to be grazed over, or lets livestock loose to graze in someone else's field, restitution shall be made from the best in the owner's field or vineyard.

6 When fire breaks out and catches in thorns so that the stacked grain or the standing grain or the field is consumed, the one who started the fire shall make full restitution.

7 When someone delivers to a neighbor money or goods for safekeeping, and they are stolen from the neighbor's house, then the thief, if caught, shall pay double. 8 If the thief is not caught, the owner of the house shall be brought

a Ch 21.37 in Heb   *b* Verses 2, 3, and 4 rearranged thus: 3b, 4, 2, 3a
c Ch 22.1 in Heb

If this law is followed, there can be no *blood feuds* that continue for generations, with no end to the retaliation. Nor can *excessive force* be justified.

21:28–22:15—These laws deal with issues regarding various kinds of property. Although reflecting an economic and social world different from our own, we still see echoes of these laws today in cases dealing with deaths and injuries caused by dogs or incurred on someone else's property. The concern with many of these laws is with just and equitable restitution in the case of injury, damage, or loss. Lack of such restitution will inevitably disrupt the larger community. As a covenant people, when we assure that injuries and loss are fairly dealt with, we support the well-being of the people as a whole.

before God,^a to determine whether or not the owner had laid hands on the neighbor's goods.

9 In any case of disputed ownership involving ox, donkey, sheep, clothing, or any other loss, of which one party says, "This is mine," the case of both parties shall come before God;^a the one whom God condemns^b shall pay double to the other.

10 When someone delivers to another a donkey, ox, sheep, or any other animal for safekeeping, and it dies or is injured or is carried off, without anyone seeing it, ¹¹ an oath before the LORD shall decide between the two of them that the one has not laid hands on the property of the other; the owner shall accept the oath, and no restitution shall be made. ¹² But if it was stolen, restitution shall be made to its owner. ¹³ If it was mangled by beasts, let it be brought as evidence; restitution shall not be made for the mangled remains.

14 When someone borrows an animal from another and it is injured or dies, the owner not being present, full restitution shall be made. ¹⁵ If the owner was present, there shall be no restitution; if it was hired, only the hiring fee is due.

Social and Religious Laws

16 When a man seduces a virgin who is not engaged to be married, and lies with her, he shall give the bride-price for her and make her his wife. ¹⁷ But if her father refuses to give her to him, he shall pay an amount equal to the bride-price for virgins.

18 You shall not permit a female sorcerer to live.

19 Whoever lies with an animal shall be put to death.

20 Whoever sacrifices to any god, other than the LORD alone, shall be devoted to destruction.

21 You shall not wrong or oppress a resident alien, for you were aliens in the land of Egypt. ²² You shall not abuse any widow or orphan. ²³ If you do abuse them, when they cry out to me, I will surely heed their cry; ²⁴ my wrath will burn, and I will kill you with the sword, and your wives shall become widows and your children orphans.

25 If you lend money to my people, to

^a Or before the judges   ^b Or the judges condemn

22:16—In today's world we might call this *date rape*. In the patriarchal world of the Bible, the offense is not against the woman, but against her father. He has control over what will happen to her, including giving her in marriage to the offender. We should conclude that such laws are no longer binding on contemporary communities. We have made progress in formulating laws that protect women's right to control their own bodies. We should continue to support such laws.

22:21—The law regarding *resident aliens* is justified by the Hebrews' own alien status in Egypt. A resident alien was an outsider, had no protection in court, and was denied possession of landed property, the possession of which would ensure economic independence. Because Israel knew what it was like to live in such distressed circumstances, the care of aliens became an important sign of the covenanted community (23:9, 12; Deut. 10:17–19; 24:19–21). If we haven't experienced such circumstances, how will we ensure the care of the outsiders in our community?

22:22–24—The *orphan* is literally one who is fatherless. *Widows* and orphans had no male protector and, therefore, remained outside of normal social structures. The resident alien, widow, and orphan represent three of the most economically vulnerable groups within Israel. Thus their care becomes especially important. If they are abused, their cry will arise to God, as did the cry of the slaves (2:23). God hears and is moved by such cries. Community failure to care for the economically vulnerable results in God's judgment upon that community.

22:25–27—*The poor* are a distinct social class from the alien, widow, and orphan. They are landowning members of the community caught in the spiral of debt. Israel was aware that such debt could lead to slavery (see note at 21:2–6). Therefore they were not to contribute further to the poor's economic precariousness. We should put an end to practices that make the poor endlessly indebted and dependent. Ultimately there is something more important than *the bottom line*. Economic gain at the expense of human costs is an abomination (Amos 2:8, Matt. 5:40; Luke 6:29).

the poor among you, you shall not deal with them as a creditor; you shall not exact interest from them. ²⁶ If you take your neighbor's cloak in pawn, you shall restore it before the sun goes down; ²⁷ for it may be your neighbor's only clothing to use as cover; in what else shall that person sleep? And if your neighbor cries out to me, I will listen, for I am compassionate.

28 You shall not revile God, or curse a leader of your people.

29 You shall not delay to make offerings from the fullness of your harvest and from the outflow of your presses.ᵃ

The firstborn of your sons you shall give to me. ³⁰ You shall do the same with your oxen and with your sheep: seven days it shall remain with its mother; on the eighth day you shall give it to me.

31 You shall be people consecrated to me; therefore you shall not eat any meat that is mangled by beasts in the field; you shall throw it to the dogs.

Justice for All

23 You shall not spread a false report. You shall not join hands with the wicked to act as a malicious witness. ² You shall not follow a majority in wrongdoing; when you bear witness in a lawsuit, you shall not side with the majority so as to pervert justice; ³ nor shall you be partial to the poor in a lawsuit.

4 When you come upon your enemy's ox or donkey going astray, you shall bring it back.

5 When you see the donkey of one who hates you lying under its burden and you would hold back from setting it free, you must help to set it free.ᵃ

6 You shall not pervert the justice due to your poor in their lawsuits. ⁷ Keep far from a false charge, and do not kill the innocent and those in the right, for I will not acquit the guilty. ⁸ You shall take no bribe, for a bribe blinds the officials, and subverts the cause of those who are in the right.

9 You shall not oppress a resident alien; you know the heart of an alien, for you were aliens in the land of Egypt.

Sabbatical Year and Sabbath

10 For six years you shall sow your land and gather in its yield; ¹¹ but the seventh year you shall let it rest and lie fallow, so that the poor of your people may eat; and what they leave the wild animals may eat. You shall do the same with your vineyard, and with your olive orchard.

12 Six days you shall do your work, but on the seventh day you shall rest, so that your ox and your donkey may have relief, and your homeborn slave and the resident alien may be refreshed. ¹³ Be

ᵃ Meaning of Heb uncertain

23:2—We are used to a political system where *majority rules*. But as history shows, the **majority** isn't always right. And when siding with the majority serves to pervert justice, it's even worse. The days when African Americans and women had no rights, which was the view of the majority, are not so far behind us.

23:4–5—This is not quite "Love your enemy," but these laws remind us that when someone is in need, the divine response is to offer help and assistance. And we should do so even, and especially, to those whom we are least inclined to want to help. We should do unto others as God has done unto us.

23:6—A persistent problem for the *poor* is having their rights addressed justly in court. It is clear in our own justice system that the poor are the

most likely to end up with a prison sentence. Those who have money buy the best lawyers. Why aren't persons of faith standing up in a mighty chorus to protest this inequity? God will hold us accountable for our injustice, and therefore injustice puts the entire community at risk.

23:11–12—It's not just people who should rest, but also the land and animals. This suggests that exploiting natural resources until they are exhausted displeases God.

23:12—Even God needed to be refreshed (31:17). The word "refresh" is based upon the Hebrew *nephesh* ("soul, self") and literally means "to be souled, to be selfed." The implication is that work drains and diminishes humans, animals, and land. Thus, the purpose of Sabbath is to refill and replenish souls (including the souls of

attentive to all that I have said to you. Do not invoke the names of other gods; do not let them be heard on your lips.

The Annual Festivals

14 Three times in the year you shall hold a festival for me. 15 You shall observe the festival of unleavened bread; as I commanded you, you shall eat unleavened bread for seven days at the appointed time in the month of Abib, for in it you came out of Egypt.

No one shall appear before me empty-handed.

16 You shall observe the festival of harvest, of the first fruits of your labor, of what you sow in the field. You shall observe the festival of ingathering at the end of the year, when you gather in from the field the fruit of your labor. 17 Three times in the year all your males shall appear before the Lord GOD.

18 You shall not offer the blood of my sacrifice with anything leavened, or let the fat of my festival remain until the morning.

19 The choicest of the first fruits of your ground you shall bring into the house of the LORD your God.

You shall not boil a kid in its mother's milk.

The Conquest of Canaan Promised

20 I am going to send an angel in front of you, to guard you on the way and to bring you to the place that I have prepared. 21 Be attentive to him and listen to his voice; do not rebel against him, for he will not pardon your transgression; for my name is in him.

22 But if you listen attentively to his voice and do all that I say, then I will be an enemy to your enemies and a foe to your foes.

23 When my angel goes in front of you, and brings you to the Amorites, the Hittites, the Perizzites, the Canaanites, the Hivites, and the Jebusites, and I blot them out, 24 you shall not bow down to their gods, or worship them, or follow their practices, but you shall utterly demolish them and break their pillars in pieces. 25 You shall worship the LORD your God, and I[a] will bless your bread and your water; and I will take sickness away from among you. 26 No one shall

[a] Gk Vg: Heb *he*

---

animals and land). We literally need to be given more of our self.

23:14–17—There are three mandated festivals—unleavened bread, harvest, and ingathering. They point to a need to "take time to be holy." The laws show that we need to work on our relationship with God, as well as with each other. One way to do this is through gatherings of the faithful in worship. (Again, note the focus on *males*. Women are excluded from this obligation. See note at 19:15.)

23:23—This verse raises the specter of ethnic cleansing and the Holocaust. It also raises the question of what to do with a God who demands the destruction of another people. The tragedy and irony for Israel is that later they will face the same problem, God's determination to blot them out at the hands of another people (cf. Isa. 8:5–8; 10:5–11; Ezek. 5:11–12; 9:3–10). Instead of perpetuating this cycle of violence, let us protest against God's injustice and demand that God consider alternatives to annihilation (see note at 23:33).

23:24—This verse speaks of the forced assimila-

tion of one culture by another. This is similar to traditional European/American Christian attitudes toward nonwhite, non-Christian cultures. It was thought that native populations needed to be Christianized and thereby civilized. The result was the destruction of much of native culture. Israel will later face the same problem—forced assimilation to Babylonian culture and the threat of the destruction of their culture. Are total acceptance and total rejection of another culture the only options? For example, how are Christians and Muslims, Western and Eastern worlds to coexist without each wanting to eliminate the other? Working toward openness to other cultures and religious perspectives without abandoning one's own is the challenge for today.

23:26—In Israel a woman's status was highest and most equal in her role as mother (e.g., 21:15, 17; Deut. 21:18–19; 22:15). Therefore, having children, especially sons, was especially important. This explains why barrenness was so shameful. Even today women go to extraordinary lengths and expense in order to conceive children. Why do some people still consider barrenness or childlessness to be shameful?

miscarry or be barren in your land; I will fulfill the number of your days. ²⁷ I will send my terror in front of you, and will throw into confusion all the people against whom you shall come, and I will make all your enemies turn their backs to you. ²⁸ And I will send the pestilence*a* in front of you, which shall drive out the Hivites, the Canaanites, and the Hittites from before you. ²⁹ I will not drive them out from before you in one year, or the land would become desolate and the wild animals would multiply against you. ³⁰ Little by little I will drive them out from before you, until you have increased and possess the land. ³¹ I will set your borders from the Red Sea*b* to the sea of the Philistines, and from the wilderness to the Euphrates; for I will hand over to you the inhabitants of the land, and you shall drive them out before you. ³² You shall make no covenant with them and their gods. ³³ They shall not live in your land, or they will make you sin against me; for if you worship their gods, it will surely be a snare to you.

The Blood of the Covenant

24 Then he said to Moses, "Come up to the LORD, you and Aaron, Nadab, and Abihu, and seventy of the elders of Israel, and worship at a distance. ² Moses alone shall come near the LORD; but the others shall not come near, and the people shall not come up with him."

3 Moses came and told the people all the words of the LORD and all the ordinances; and all the people answered with one voice, and said, "All the words that the LORD has spoken we will do." ⁴ And Moses wrote down all the words of the LORD. He rose early in the morning, and built an altar at the foot of the mountain, and set up twelve pillars, corresponding to the twelve tribes of Israel. ⁵ He sent young men of the people of Israel, who offered burnt offerings and sacrificed oxen as offerings of well-being to the LORD. ⁶ Moses took half of the blood and put it in basins, and half of the blood he dashed against the altar. ⁷ Then he took the book of the covenant, and read it in the hearing of the people; and they said, "All that the LORD has spoken we will do, and we will be obedient." ⁸ Moses took the blood and dashed it on the people, and said, "See the blood of the covenant that the LORD has made with you in accordance with all these words."

On the Mountain with God

9 Then Moses and Aaron, Nadab, and Abihu, and seventy of the elders of Israel went up, ¹⁰ and they saw the God of Israel. Under his feet there was something like a pavement of sapphire stone, like the very heaven for clearness. ¹¹ God*c* did not lay his hand on the chief men of the people of Israel; also they beheld God, and they ate and drank.

12 The LORD said to Moses, "Come up to me on the mountain, and wait there; and I will give you the tablets of stone, with the law and the commandment, which I have written for their instruc-

a Or *hornets*: Meaning of Heb uncertain   *b* Or *Sea of Reeds*   *c* Heb *He*

23:29—Although God will drive out Israel's enemies, it will take some time. This actually contradicts 23:23. The reason seems strange, but suggests that the elimination of one threat raises another threat. Wiping out towns and cities too quickly will leave insufficient population to defend against or control wild animals. Today we still experience unintended consequences of some actions. An action that at the time seems beneficial can later have a negative impact. Combustion engines lead to air pollution. Security measures lead to violation of civil rights. Can this be avoided?

23:33—God's reason for the drastic measure of wiping out the Canaanites is because they presented a perceived threat to the covenant relationship between God and Israel. Yet this is exactly what happens at the beginning of this story. Pharaoh sees the Hebrews as a threat and decides to wipe them out (see note at 1:9–10). With the Israelites as with Pharaoh, it doesn't matter if it is a real threat or not. It is the potential for danger that must be eliminated. Clearly there are many dangers on the path of faith and life. Are there other ways to face those dangers besides trying to eliminate people?

tion." [13] So Moses set out with his assistant Joshua, and Moses went up into the mountain of God. [14] To the elders he had said, "Wait here for us, until we come to you again; for Aaron and Hur are with you; whoever has a dispute may go to them."

15 Then Moses went up on the mountain, and the cloud covered the mountain. [16] The glory of the LORD settled on Mount Sinai, and the cloud covered it for six days; on the seventh day he called to Moses out of the cloud. [17] Now the appearance of the glory of the LORD was like a devouring fire on the top of the mountain in the sight of the people of Israel. [18] Moses entered the cloud, and went up on the mountain. Moses was on the mountain for forty days and forty nights.

Offerings for the Tabernacle

25 The LORD said to Moses: [2] Tell the Israelites to take for me an offering; from all whose hearts prompt them to give you shall receive the offering for me. [3] This is the offering that you shall receive from them: gold, silver, and bronze, [4] blue, purple, and crimson yarns and fine linen, goats' hair, [5] tanned rams' skins, fine leather,[a] acacia wood, [6] oil for the lamps, spices for the anointing oil and for the fragrant incense, [7] onyx stones and gems to be set in the ephod and for the breastpiece. [8] And have them make me a sanctuary, so that I may dwell among them. [9] In accordance with all that I show you concerning the pattern of the tabernacle and of all its furniture, so you shall make it.

The Ark of the Covenant

10 They shall make an ark of acacia wood; it shall be two and a half cubits long, a cubit and a half wide, and a cubit and a half high. [11] You shall overlay it with pure gold, inside and outside you shall overlay it, and you shall make a molding of gold upon it all around. [12] You shall cast four rings of gold for it and put them on its four feet, two rings on the one side of it, and two rings on the other side. [13] You shall make poles of acacia wood, and overlay them with gold. [14] And you shall put the poles into

[a] Meaning of Heb uncertain

24:16–17—As elsewhere (see 13:21; 19:18) God is imaged as fire. Here God is imaged as the kind of fire that can consume thousands of acres of forest. Forest fires are both destructive and beneficial to the forest. Have you experienced God in this way?

24:18—*Forty days and . . . nights* is a common biblical idiom for "a very long time" (see Gen. 7:12; Exod. 34:28; Deut. 9:9; 1 Kgs. 19:8; Matt. 4:2). But more than that, it is a time of significant encounter with God. This suggests that such an encounter requires a very long time, and thus Lent developed as a time of penitence and preparation.

25:1–31:18 Plans for Constructing the Tabernacle

The command to build the tabernacle and its construction (35:1–40:38) take up thirteen chapters, nearly one-third of the book of Exodus! Yet it is tedious reading and usually ignored. The emphasis in these chapters is on the process of creating—the making, weaving, and joining. It stresses the *process*, not the end product. There is also endless repetition—God lays down the plan, Moses tells the plan to the people, the tabernacle is built according to the plan. This emphasizes the obedience of the people who build the tabernacle according to God's direction (see note at 36:8–39:43). But obedience does not end with the completion of the tabernacle. The people cannot conclude that because they have finished the building project, they are also finished being obedient. No, obedience to God must continue throughout life. Thus the building of the tabernacle models the building of the church. The continued reforming of church and society through two thousand years suggests that we are never finished with being obedient.

25:8—The construction of the tabernacle is a response to the problem of balancing God's immanence and transcendence, namely, how a holy God can come into the midst of a sinful people (see note at 40:1).

25:10—Until the building of Solomon's temple, the ark was understood to be the portable meeting place of heaven and earth. Positively, the ark underscores God's perpetual presence with the people. Negatively, it poses the danger of confining God and downplaying God's freedom and transcendence.

the rings on the sides of the ark, by which to carry the ark. **15** The poles shall remain in the rings of the ark; they shall not be taken from it. **16** You shall put into the ark the covenant[a] that I shall give you.

17 Then you shall make a mercy seat[b] of pure gold; two cubits and a half shall be its length, and a cubit and a half its width. **18** You shall make two cherubim of gold; you shall make them of hammered work, at the two ends of the mercy seat.[c] **19** Make one cherub at the one end, and one cherub at the other; of one piece with the mercy seat[c] you shall make the cherubim at its two ends. **20** The cherubim shall spread out their wings above, overshadowing the mercy seat[c] with their wings. They shall face one to another; the faces of the cherubim shall be turned toward the mercy seat.[c] **21** You shall put the mercy seat[c] on the top of the ark; and in the ark you shall put the covenant[a] that I shall give you. **22** There I will meet with you, and from above the mercy seat,[c] from between the two cherubim that are on the ark of the covenant,[a] I will deliver to you all my commands for the Israelites.

The Table for the Bread of the Presence

23 You shall make a table of acacia wood, two cubits long, one cubit wide, and a cubit and a half high. **24** You shall overlay it with pure gold, and make a molding of gold around it. **25** You shall make around it a rim a handbreadth wide, and a molding of gold around the rim. **26** You shall make for it four rings of gold, and fasten the rings to the four corners at its four legs. **27** The rings that hold the poles used for carrying the table shall be close to the rim. **28** You

shall make the poles of acacia wood, and overlay them with gold, and the table shall be carried with these. **29** You shall make its plates and dishes for incense, and its flagons and bowls with which to pour drink offerings; you shall make them of pure gold. **30** And you shall set the bread of the Presence on the table before me always.

The Lampstand

31 You shall make a lampstand of pure gold. The base and the shaft of the lampstand shall be made of hammered work; its cups, its calyxes, and its petals shall be of one piece with it; **32** and there shall be six branches going out of its sides, three branches of the lampstand out of one side of it and three branches of the lampstand out of the other side of it; **33** three cups shaped like almond blossoms, each with calyx and petals, on one branch, and three cups shaped like almond blossoms, each with calyx and petals, on the other branch—so for the six branches going out of the lampstand. **34** On the lampstand itself there shall be four cups shaped like almond blossoms, each with its calyxes and petals. **35** There shall be a calyx of one piece with it under the first pair of branches, a calyx of one piece with it under the next pair of branches, and a calyx of one piece with it under the last pair of branches— so for the six branches that go out of the lampstand. **36** Their calyxes and their branches shall be of one piece with it, the whole of it one hammered piece of pure gold. **37** You shall make the seven lamps for it; and the lamps shall be set up so as to give light on the space in front of it. **38** Its snuffers and trays shall be of pure

[a] Or treaty, or testimony; Heb eduth　[b] Or a cover　[c] Or the cover

---

25:23–27:21—Since we are not interested in building a tabernacle, what do we do with these texts? Traditional Christian interpretation has allegorized them. For example, the lampstand stands for the light of Christ within us. But these texts could point us in another direction. The furnishings are not meaningless. Each of them held significance for the Israelites. Look at the furnish-

ings where we worship. Consider what each signifies. There is also an aesthetic quality to the furnishings of the tabernacle. They are opulent and finely crafted. Whether it is a tabernacle or a cathedral, the aesthetics of a place of worship are intended to point us to the grandeur and glory of God. Look at the aesthetics where you worship. What of God do they indicate?

gold. [39] It, and all these utensils, shall be made from a talent of pure gold. [40] And see that you make them according to the pattern for them, which is being shown you on the mountain.

The Tabernacle

26 Moreover you shall make the tabernacle with ten curtains of fine twisted linen, and blue, purple, and crimson yarns; you shall make them with cherubim skillfully worked into them. [2] The length of each curtain shall be twenty-eight cubits, and the width of each curtain four cubits; all the curtains shall be of the same size. [3] Five curtains shall be joined to one another; and the other five curtains shall be joined to one another. [4] You shall make loops of blue on the edge of the outermost curtain in the first set; and likewise you shall make loops on the edge of the outermost curtain in the second set. [5] You shall make fifty loops on the one curtain, and you shall make fifty loops on the edge of the curtain that is in the second set; the loops shall be opposite one another. [6] You shall make fifty clasps of gold, and join the curtains to one another with the clasps, so that the tabernacle may be one whole.

7 You shall also make curtains of goats' hair for a tent over the tabernacle; you shall make eleven curtains. [8] The length of each curtain shall be thirty cubits, and the width of each curtain four cubits; the eleven curtains shall be of the same size. [9] You shall join five curtains by themselves, and six curtains by themselves, and the sixth curtain you shall double over at the front of the tent. [10] You shall make fifty loops on the edge of the curtain that is outermost in one set, and fifty loops on the edge of the curtain that is outermost in the second set.

11 You shall make fifty clasps of bronze, and put the clasps into the loops, and join the tent together, so that it may be one whole. [12] The part that remains of the curtains of the tent, the half curtain that remains, shall hang over the back of the tabernacle. [13] The cubit on the one side, and the cubit on the other side, of what remains in the length of the curtains of the tent, shall hang over the sides of the tabernacle, on this side and that side, to cover it. [14] You shall make for the tent a covering of tanned rams' skins and an outer covering of fine leather.[a]

The Framework

15 You shall make upright frames of acacia wood for the tabernacle. [16] Ten cubits shall be the length of a frame, and a cubit and a half the width of each frame. [17] There shall be two pegs in each frame to fit the frames together; you shall make these for all the frames of the tabernacle. [18] You shall make the frames for the tabernacle: twenty frames for the south side; [19] and you shall make forty bases of silver under the twenty frames, two bases under the first frame for its two pegs, and two bases under the next frame for its two pegs; [20] and for the second side of the tabernacle, on the north side twenty frames, [21] and their forty bases of silver, two bases under the first frame, and two bases under the next frame; [22] and for the rear of the tabernacle westward you shall make six frames. [23] You shall make two frames for corners of the tabernacle in the rear; [24] they shall be separate beneath, but joined at the top, at the first ring; it shall be the same with both of them; they shall form the two corners. [25] And so there shall be eight frames, with their bases of silver, sixteen bases; two bases under the first frame, and two bases under the next frame.

26 You shall make bars of acacia wood, five for the frames of the one side of the tabernacle, [27] and five bars for the frames of the other side of the tabernacle, and five bars for the frames of the side of the tabernacle at the rear westward. [28] The middle bar, halfway up the frames, shall

[a] Meaning of Heb uncertain

pass through from end to end. ²⁹ You shall overlay the frames with gold, and shall make their rings of gold to hold the bars; and you shall overlay the bars with gold. ³⁰ Then you shall erect the tabernacle according to the plan for it that you were shown on the mountain.

The Curtain

31 You shall make a curtain of blue, purple, and crimson yarns, and of fine twisted linen; it shall be made with cherubim skillfully worked into it. ³² You shall hang it on four pillars of acacia overlaid with gold, which have hooks of gold and rest on four bases of silver. ³³ You shall hang the curtain under the clasps, and bring the ark of the covenant*a* in there, within the curtain; and the curtain shall separate for you the holy place from the most holy. ³⁴ You shall put the mercy seat*b* on the ark of the covenant*a* in the most holy place. ³⁵ You shall set the table outside the curtain, and the lampstand on the south side of the tabernacle opposite the table; and you shall put the table on the north side.

36 You shall make a screen for the entrance of the tent, of blue, purple, and crimson yarns, and of fine twisted linen, embroidered with needlework. ³⁷ You shall make for the screen five pillars of acacia, and overlay them with gold; their hooks shall be of gold, and you shall cast five bases of bronze for them.

The Altar of Burnt Offering

27 You shall make the altar of acacia wood, five cubits long and five cubits wide; the altar shall be square, and it shall be three cubits high. ² You shall make horns for it on its four corners; its horns shall be of one piece with it, and you shall overlay it with bronze. ³ You shall make pots for it to receive its ashes, and shovels and basins and forks and firepans; you shall make all its utensils of bronze. ⁴ You shall also make for it a grating, a network of bronze; and on the net you shall make four bronze rings at its four corners. ⁵ You shall set it under the ledge of the altar so that the net shall extend halfway down the altar. ⁶ You shall make poles for the altar, poles of acacia wood, and overlay them with bronze; ⁷ the poles shall be put through the rings, so that the poles shall be on the two sides of the altar when it is carried. ⁸ You shall make it hollow, with boards. They shall be made just as you were shown on the mountain.

The Court and Its Hangings

9 You shall make the court of the tabernacle. On the south side the court shall have hangings of fine twisted linen one hundred cubits long for that side; ¹⁰ its twenty pillars and their twenty bases shall be of bronze, but the hooks of the pillars and their bands shall be of silver. ¹¹ Likewise for its length on the north side there shall be hangings one hundred cubits long, their pillars twenty and their bases twenty, of bronze, but the hooks of the pillars and their bands shall be of silver. ¹² For the width of the court on the west side there shall be fifty cubits of hangings, with ten pillars and ten bases. ¹³ The width of the court on the front to the east shall be fifty cubits. ¹⁴ There shall be fifteen cubits of hangings on the one side, with three pillars and three bases. ¹⁵ There shall be fifteen cubits of hangings on the other side, with three pillars and three bases. ¹⁶ For the gate of the court there shall be a screen twenty cubits long, of blue, purple, and crimson yarns, and of fine twisted linen, embroidered with needlework; it shall have four pillars and with them four bases. ¹⁷ All the pillars around the court shall be banded with silver; their hooks shall be of silver, and their bases of bronze. ¹⁸ The length of the court shall be one hundred cubits, the width fifty, and the height five cubits, with hangings of fine twisted linen and bases of bronze. ¹⁹ All the utensils of the tabernacle for every use, and all its pegs

a Or treaty, or testimony; Heb eduth b Or the cover

and all the pegs of the court, shall be of bronze.

The Oil for the Lamp

20 You shall further command the Israelites to bring you pure oil of beaten olives for the light, so that a lamp may be set up to burn regularly. 21 In the tent of meeting, outside the curtain that is before the covenant,*a* Aaron and his sons shall tend it from evening to morning before the Lord. It shall be a perpetual ordinance to be observed throughout their generations by the Israelites.

Vestments for the Priesthood

28 Then bring near to you your brother Aaron, and his sons with him, from among the Israelites, to serve me as priests—Aaron and Aaron's sons, Nadab and Abihu, Eleazar and Ithamar. 2 You shall make sacred vestments for the glorious adornment of your brother Aaron. 3 And you shall speak to all who have ability, whom I have endowed with skill, that they make Aaron's vestments to consecrate him for my priesthood. 4 These are the vestments that they shall make: a breastpiece, an ephod, a robe, a checkered tunic, a turban, and a sash. When they make these sacred vestments for your brother Aaron and his sons to serve me as priests, 5 they shall use gold, blue, purple, and crimson yarns, and fine linen.

The Ephod

6 They shall make the ephod of gold, of blue, purple, and crimson yarns, and of fine twisted linen, skillfully worked. 7 It shall have two shoulder-pieces attached to its two edges, so that it may be joined together. 8 The decorated band on it shall be of the same workmanship and materials, of gold, of blue, purple, and crimson yarns, and of fine twisted linen. 9 You shall take two onyx stones, and engrave on them the names of the sons of Israel, 10 six of their names on the one stone, and the names of the remaining six on the other stone, in the order of their birth. 11 As a gem-cutter engraves signets, so you shall engrave the two stones with the names of the sons of Israel; you shall mount them in settings of gold filigree. 12 You shall set the two stones on the shoulder-pieces of the ephod, as stones of remembrance for the sons of Israel; and Aaron shall bear their names before the Lord on his two shoulders for remembrance. 13 You shall make settings of gold filigree, 14 and two chains of pure gold, twisted like cords; and you shall attach the corded chains to the settings.

The Breastplate

15 You shall make a breastpiece of judgment, in skilled work; you shall make it in the style of the ephod; of gold, of blue and purple and crimson yarns, and of fine twisted linen you shall make it. 16 It shall be square and doubled, a span in length and a span in width. 17 You shall set in it four rows of stones. A row of carnelian,*b* chrysolite, and emerald shall be the first row; 18 and the second row a turquoise, a sapphire,*c* and a moonstone; 19 and the third row a jacinth, an agate, and an amethyst; 20 and the fourth row a beryl, an onyx, and a jasper; they shall be set in gold filigree. 21 There shall be twelve stones with names corresponding to the names

a Or *treaty*, or *testimony*; Heb *eduth*   *b* The identity of several of these stones is uncertain *c* Or *lapis lazuli*

27:21—The *tent of meeting* is a shrine for receiving oracles. God's presence does not reside there permanently (unlike the ark, see 25:10), but is manifested in the form of a cloud whenever Moses enters the tent to inquire of God (33:7–11). Positively, the tent of meeting emphasizes God's hiddenness and mobility. Negatively, the people are left uncertain as to when and where God will be present.

28:1—The descendants of Aaron are appointed to serve as priests. In chaps. 28–29 a great deal is said about the priests' garments and their ordination ceremony, but almost nothing about why priests are needed, what their function is (see 28:43), or why Aaron's family is chosen.

of the sons of Israel; they shall be like signets, each engraved with its name, for the twelve tribes. ²² You shall make for the breastpiece chains of pure gold, twisted like cords; ²³ and you shall make for the breastpiece two rings of gold, and put the two rings on the two edges of the breastpiece. ²⁴ You shall put the two cords of gold in the two rings at the edges of the breastpiece; ²⁵ the two ends of the two cords you shall attach to the two settings, and so attach it in front to the shoulder-pieces of the ephod. ²⁶ You shall make two rings of gold, and put them at the two ends of the breastpiece, on its inside edge next to the ephod. ²⁷ You shall make two rings of gold, and attach them in front to the lower part of the two shoulder-pieces of the ephod, at its joining above the decorated band of the ephod. ²⁸ The breastpiece shall be bound by its rings to the rings of the ephod with a blue cord, so that it may lie on the decorated band of the ephod, and so that the breastpiece shall not come loose from the ephod. ²⁹ So Aaron shall bear the names of the sons of Israel in the breastpiece of judgment on his heart when he goes into the holy place, for a continual remembrance before the LORD. ³⁰ In the breastpiece of judgment you shall put the Urim and the Thummim, and they shall be on Aaron's heart when he goes in before the LORD; thus Aaron shall bear the judgment of the Israelites on his heart before the LORD continually.

Other Priestly Vestments

31 You shall make the robe of the ephod all of blue. ³² It shall have an opening for the head in the middle of it, with a woven binding around the opening, like the opening in a coat of mail,ᵃ so that it may not be torn. ³³ On its lower hem you shall make pomegranates of blue, purple, and crimson yarns, all around the lower hem, with bells of gold between them all around— ³⁴ a golden bell and a pomegranate alternating all around the lower hem of the robe. ³⁵ Aaron shall wear it when he ministers, and its sound shall be heard when he goes into the holy place before the LORD, and when he comes out, so that he may not die.

36 You shall make a rosette of pure gold, and engrave on it, like the engraving of a signet, "Holy to the LORD." ³⁷ You shall fasten it on the turban with a blue cord; it shall be on the front of the turban. ³⁸ It shall be on Aaron's forehead, and Aaron shall take on himself any guilt incurred in the holy offering that the Israelites consecrate as their sacred donations; it shall always be on his forehead, in order that they may find favor before the LORD.

39 You shall make the checkered tunic of fine linen, and you shall make a turban of fine linen, and you shall make a sash embroidered with needlework.

40 For Aaron's sons you shall make tunics and sashes and headdresses; you shall make them for their glorious adornment. ⁴¹ You shall put them on your brother Aaron, and on his sons with him, and shall anoint them and ordain them and consecrate them, so that they may serve me as priests. ⁴² You shall make for them linen undergarments to cover their naked flesh; they shall reach from the hips to the thighs; ⁴³ Aaron and his sons shall wear them when they go into the tent of meeting,

ᵃ Meaning of Heb uncertain

28:30—The Urim and Thummin were apparently lots or dice used as a means of divining God's will (Num. 27:21; 1 Sam. 14:41; 28:6). Elsewhere, various practices of divination are condemned (see Deut. 13:1–2; 18:10–11), which suggests that acceptable means of communicating with God varied over time. There is no one right way to communicate with God.

28:41—The words *"ordain"* and *"ordination"* are literally "to fill the hand." The original sense of this is not evident. Therefore one should consider the question: What do our hands need to be filled with, in order to be holy to God?

or when they come near the altar to minister in the holy place; or they will bring guilt on themselves and die. This shall be a perpetual ordinance for him and for his descendants after him.

The Ordination of the Priests

29 Now this is what you shall do to them to consecrate them, so that they may serve me as priests. Take one young bull and two rams without blemish, ² and unleavened bread, unleavened cakes mixed with oil, and unleavened wafers spread with oil. You shall make them of choice wheat flour. ³ You shall put them in one basket and bring them in the basket, and bring the bull and the two rams. ⁴ You shall bring Aaron and his sons to the entrance of the tent of meeting, and wash them with water. ⁵ Then you shall take the vestments, and put on Aaron the tunic and the robe of the ephod, and the ephod, and the breastpiece, and gird him with the decorated band of the ephod; ⁶ and you shall set the turban on his head, and put the holy diadem on the turban. ⁷ You shall take the anointing oil, and pour it on his head and anoint him. ⁸ Then you shall bring his sons, and put tunics on them, ⁹ and you shall gird them with sashes*a* and tie headdresses on them; and the priesthood shall be theirs by a perpetual ordinance. You shall then ordain Aaron and his sons.

10 You shall bring the bull in front of the tent of meeting. Aaron and his sons shall lay their hands on the head of the bull, ¹¹ and you shall slaughter the bull before the LORD, at the entrance of the tent of meeting, ¹² and shall take some of the blood of the bull and put it on the horns of the altar with your finger, and all the rest of the blood you shall pour out at the base of the altar. ¹³ You shall

take all the fat that covers the entrails, and the appendage of the liver, and the two kidneys with the fat that is on them, and turn them into smoke on the altar. ¹⁴ But the flesh of the bull, and its skin, and its dung, you shall burn with fire outside the camp; it is a sin offering.

15 Then you shall take one of the rams, and Aaron and his sons shall lay their hands on the head of the ram, ¹⁶ and you shall slaughter the ram, and shall take its blood and dash it against all sides of the altar. ¹⁷ Then you shall cut the ram into its parts, and wash its entrails and its legs, and put them with its parts and its head, ¹⁸ and turn the whole ram into smoke on the altar; it is a burnt offering to the LORD; it is a pleasing odor, an offering by fire to the LORD.

19 You shall take the other ram; and Aaron and his sons shall lay their hands on the head of the ram, ²⁰ and you shall slaughter the ram, and take some of its blood and put it on the lobe of Aaron's right ear and on the lobes of the right ears of his sons, and on the thumbs of their right hands, and on the big toes of their right feet, and dash the rest of the blood against all sides of the altar. ²¹ Then you shall take some of the blood that is on the altar, and some of the anointing oil, and sprinkle it on Aaron and his vestments and on his sons and his sons' vestments with him; then he and his vestments shall be holy, as well as his sons and his sons' vestments.

22 You shall also take the fat of the ram, the fat tail, the fat that covers the entrails, the appendage of the liver, the two kidneys with the fat that is on them, and the right thigh (for it is a ram of ordination), ²³ and one loaf of bread, one cake of bread made with oil, and one wafer, out of the basket of unleavened

---

a Gk: Heb *sashes, Aaron and his sons*

29:21—The acts of ordination serve to make Aaron holy or set him apart. Throughout history this holiness is often interpreted as imbuing priests with special qualities and attributes. This has led to all sorts of difficulties (see note at

19:23), including ignoring sins committed by priests. But nowhere in the Bible does being set apart indicate exemption from obedience to God (see Eli and his sons in 1 Sam. 2:12–36).

bread that is before the LORD; ²⁴ and you shall place all these on the palms of Aaron and on the palms of his sons, and raise them as an elevation offering before the LORD. ²⁵ Then you shall take them from their hands, and turn them into smoke on the altar on top of the burnt offering of pleasing odor before the LORD; it is an offering by fire to the LORD.

26 You shall take the breast of the ram of Aaron's ordination and raise it as an elevation offering before the LORD; and it shall be your portion. ²⁷ You shall consecrate the breast that was raised as an elevation offering and the thigh that was raised as an elevation offering from the ram of ordination, from that which belonged to Aaron and his sons. ²⁸ These things shall be a perpetual ordinance for Aaron and his sons from the Israelites, for this is an offering; and it shall be an offering by the Israelites from their sacrifice of offerings of well-being, their offering to the LORD.

29 The sacred vestments of Aaron shall be passed on to his sons after him; they shall be anointed in them and ordained in them. ³⁰ The son who is priest in his place shall wear them seven days, when he comes into the tent of meeting to minister in the holy place.

31 You shall take the ram of ordination, and boil its flesh in a holy place; ³² and Aaron and his sons shall eat the flesh of the ram and the bread that is in the basket, at the entrance of the tent of meeting. ³³ They themselves shall eat the food by which atonement is made, to ordain and consecrate them, but no one else shall eat of them, because they are holy. ³⁴ If any of the flesh for the ordination, or of the bread, remains until the morning, then you shall burn the remainder with fire; it shall not be eaten, because it is holy.

35 Thus you shall do to Aaron and to his sons, just as I have commanded you; through seven days you shall ordain them. ³⁶ Also every day you shall offer a bull as a sin offering for atonement. Also you shall offer a sin offering for the altar, when you make atonement for it, and shall anoint it, to consecrate it. ³⁷ Seven days you shall make atonement for the altar, and consecrate it, and the altar shall be most holy; whatever touches the altar shall become holy.

The Daily Offerings

38 Now this is what you shall offer on the altar: two lambs a year old regularly each day. ³⁹ One lamb you shall offer in the morning, and the other lamb you shall offer in the evening; ⁴⁰ and with the first lamb one-tenth of a measure of choice flour mixed with one-fourth of a hin of beaten oil, and one-fourth of a hin of wine for a drink offering. ⁴¹ And the other lamb you shall offer in the evening, and shall offer with it a grain offering and its drink offering, as in the morning, for a pleasing odor, an offering by fire to the LORD. ⁴² It shall be a regular burnt offering throughout your generations at the entrance of the tent of meeting before the LORD, where I will meet with you, to speak to you there. ⁴³ I will meet with the Israelites there, and it shall be sanctified by my glory; ⁴⁴ I will consecrate the tent of meeting and the altar; Aaron also and his sons I will consecrate, to serve me as priests. ⁴⁵ I will dwell among the Israelites, and I will be their God. ⁴⁶ And they shall know that I am the LORD their God, who brought them out of the land of Egypt that I might dwell among them; I am the LORD their God.

The Altar of Incense

30 You shall make an altar on which to offer incense; you shall make it of acacia wood. ² It shall be one cubit long, and one cubit wide; it shall be square, and shall be two cubits high; its horns shall be of one piece with it. ³ You shall overlay it with pure gold, its top, and its sides all around and its horns; and you shall make for it a mold-

ing of gold all around. ⁴ And you shall make two golden rings for it; under its molding on two opposite sides of it you shall make them, and they shall hold the poles with which to carry it. ⁵ You shall make the poles of acacia wood, and overlay them with gold. ⁶ You shall place it in front of the curtain that is above the ark of the covenant,ᵃ in front of the mercy seatᵇ that is over the covenant,ᵃ where I will meet with you. ⁷ Aaron shall offer fragrant incense on it; every morning when he dresses the lamps he shall offer it, ⁸ and when Aaron sets up the lamps in the evening, he shall offer it, a regular incense offering before the LORD throughout your generations. ⁹ You shall not offer unholy incense on it, or a burnt offering, or a grain offering; and you shall not pour a drink offering on it. ¹⁰ Once a year Aaron shall perform the rite of atonement on its horns. Throughout your generations he shall perform the atonement for it once a year with the blood of the atoning sin offering. It is most holy to the LORD.

The Half Shekel for the Sanctuary

11 The LORD spoke to Moses: ¹² When you take a census of the Israelites to register them, at registration all of them shall give a ransom for their lives to the LORD, so that no plague may come upon them for being registered. ¹³ This is what each one who is registered shall give: half a shekel according to the shekel of the sanctuary (the shekel is twenty gerahs), half a shekel as an offering to the LORD. ¹⁴ Each one who is registered, from twenty years old and upward, shall give the LORD's offering. ¹⁵ The rich shall not give more, and the poor shall not give less, than the half shekel, when you bring this offering to the LORD to make atonement for your lives. ¹⁶ You shall take the atonement money from the Israelites and shall designate it for the service of the tent of meeting; before the LORD it will be a reminder to the Israelites of the ransom given for your lives.

The Bronze Basin

17 The LORD spoke to Moses: ¹⁸ You shall make a bronze basin with a bronze stand for washing. You shall put it between the tent of meeting and the altar, and you shall put water in it; ¹⁹ with the waterᶜ Aaron and his sons shall wash their hands and their feet. ²⁰ When they go into the tent of meeting, or when they come near the altar to minister, to make an offering by fire to the LORD, they shall wash with water, so that they may not die. ²¹ They shall wash their hands and their feet, so that they may not die: it shall be a perpetual ordinance for them, for him and for his descendants throughout their generations.

The Anointing Oil and Incense

22 The LORD spoke to Moses: ²³ Take the finest spices: of liquid myrrh five hundred shekels, and of sweet-smelling cinnamon half as much, that is, two hundred fifty, and two hundred fifty of aromatic cane, ²⁴ and five hundred of cassia—measured by the sanctuary shekel—and a hin of olive oil; ²⁵ and you shall make of these a sacred anointing oil blended as by the perfumer; it shall be a holy anointing oil. ²⁶ With it you shall anoint the tent of meeting and the ark of the covenant,ᵃ ²⁷ and the table and all its utensils, and the lampstand and its utensils, and the altar of incense, ²⁸ and the altar of burnt offering with all its utensils, and the basin with its stand; ²⁹ you shall consecrate them, so that they may be most holy; whatever touches them will become holy. ³⁰ You shall anoint Aaron and his sons, and consecrate them, in order that they may serve me as priests. ³¹ You shall say to the Israelites, "This shall be my holy anointing oil throughout your generations. ³² It shall not be used in any ordinary anointing of the body, and you shall make no other like it in composition; it is holy, and it shall be holy to you. ³³ Whoever

---

ᵃ Or treaty, or testimony; Heb eduth ᵇ Or the cover ᶜ Heb it

compounds any like it or whoever puts any of it on an unqualified person shall be cut off from the people."

34 The LORD said to Moses: Take sweet spices, stacte, and onycha, and galbanum, sweet spices with pure frankincense (an equal part of each), 35 and make an incense blended as by the perfumer, seasoned with salt, pure and holy; 36 and you shall beat some of it into powder, and put part of it before the covenant[a] in the tent of meeting where I shall meet with you; it shall be for you most holy. 37 When you make incense according to this composition, you shall not make it for yourselves; it shall be regarded by you as holy to the LORD. 38 Whoever makes any like it to use as perfume shall be cut off from the people.

Bezalel and Oholiab

31 The LORD spoke to Moses: 2 See, I have called by name Bezalel son of Uri son of Hur, of the tribe of Judah: 3 and I have filled him with divine spirit,[b] with ability, intelligence, and knowledge in every kind of craft, 4 to devise artistic designs, to work in gold, silver, and bronze, 5 in cutting stones for setting, and in carving wood, in every kind of craft. 6 Moreover, I have appointed with him Oholiab son of Ahisamach, of the tribe of Dan; and I have given skill to all the skillful, so that they may make all that I have commanded you: 7 the tent of meeting, and the ark of the covenant,[a] and the mercy seat[c] that is on it, and all the furnishings of the tent, 8 the table and its utensils, and the pure lampstand with all its utensils, and the altar of incense, 9 and the altar of burnt offering with all its utensils, and the basin with its stand, 10 and the finely worked vest-

ments, the holy vestments for the priest Aaron and the vestments of his sons, for their service as priests, 11 and the anointing oil and the fragrant incense for the holy place. They shall do just as I have commanded you.

The Sabbath Law

12 The LORD said to Moses: 13 You yourself are to speak to the Israelites: "You shall keep my sabbaths, for this is a sign between me and you throughout your generations, given in order that you may know that I, the LORD, sanctify you. 14 You shall keep the sabbath, because it is holy for you; everyone who profanes it shall be put to death; whoever does any work on it shall be cut off from among the people. 15 Six days shall work be done, but the seventh day is a sabbath of solemn rest, holy to the LORD; whoever does any work on the sabbath day shall be put to death. 16 Therefore the Israelites shall keep the sabbath, observing the sabbath throughout their generations, as a perpetual covenant. 17 It is a sign forever between me and the people of Israel that in six days the LORD made heaven and earth, and on the seventh day he rested, and was refreshed."

The Two Tablets of the Covenant

18 When God[d] finished speaking with Moses on Mount Sinai, he gave him the two tablets of the covenant,[a] tablets of stone, written with the finger of God.

The Golden Calf

32 When the people saw that Moses delayed to come down from the mountain, the people gathered around Aaron, and said to him, "Come, make gods for us, who shall go before us; as for

---

[a] Or treaty, or testimony; Heb eduth   [b] Or with the spirit of God   [c] Or the cover   [d] Heb he

---

31:18—God is sometimes imaged as a human being (Gen. 3:8; Exod. 24:10; Lev. 1:9; Deut. 7:19; Dan. 7:9–10). Consider the significance of a human image of God versus a nonhuman image, such as fire (see notes at Exod. 16:10; 24:16–17).

32:1–34:35 The Breach and Renewal of the Covenant

32:1—The people ask for a symbol of God's presence in the same way as the ark (see note at 25:10). The failure of the golden calf is not the attempt to worship other (or foreign) gods but to

this Moses, the man who brought us up out of the land of Egypt, we do not know what has become of him." ²Aaron said to them, "Take off the gold rings that are on the ears of your wives, your sons, and your daughters, and bring them to me." ³So all the people took off the gold rings from their ears, and brought them to Aaron. ⁴He took the gold from them, formed it in a mold,ᵃ and cast an image of a calf; and they said, "These are your gods, O Israel, who brought you up out of the land of Egypt!" ⁵When Aaron saw this, he built an altar before it; and Aaron made proclamation and said, "Tomorrow shall be a festival to the LORD." ⁶They rose early the next day, and offered burnt offerings and brought sacrifices of well-being; and the people sat down to eat and drink, and rose up to revel.

7 The LORD said to Moses, "Go down at once! Your people, whom you brought up out of the land of Egypt, have acted perversely; ⁸they have been quick to turn aside from the way that I commanded them; they have cast for themselves an image of a calf, and have worshiped it and sacrificed to it, and said, 'These are your gods, O Israel, who brought you up out of the land of Egypt!'" ⁹The LORD said to Moses, "I have seen this people, how stiff-necked they are. ¹⁰Now let me

alone, so that my wrath may burn hot against them and I may consume them; and of you I will make a great nation."

11 But Moses implored the LORD his God, and said, "O LORD, why does your wrath burn hot against your people, whom you brought out of the land of Egypt with great power and with a mighty hand? ¹²Why should the Egyptians say, 'It was with evil intent that he brought them out to kill them in the mountains, and to consume them from the face of the earth'? Turn from your fierce wrath; change your mind and do not bring disaster on your people. ¹³Remember Abraham, Isaac, and Israel, your servants, how you swore to them by your own self, saying to them, 'I will multiply your descendants like the stars of heaven, and all this land that I have promised I will give to your descendants, and they shall inherit it forever.'" ¹⁴And the LORD changed his mind about the disaster that he planned to bring on his people.

15 Then Moses turned and went down from the mountain, carrying the two tablets of the covenantᵇ in his hands, tablets that were written on both sides, written on the front and on the back. ¹⁶The tablets were the work of God, and the writing was the writing of

ᵃ Or fashioned it with a graving tool; Meaning of Heb uncertain ᵇ Or treaty, or testimony; Heb eduth

---

maintain the tension of God's immanence *and* transcendence. In the dangerous terrain of the wilderness the people wanted *assurance* of God's presence (cf. 17:7) and sought to reduce God to manageable proportion. This sin confronts us daily. When life seems out of control, we cope by reducing God to a manageable proportion. Whether it's a golden calf or a narrow view of God, it is still idolatry.

32:6—Some suggest that in the context of eating and drinking, reveling implies that an orgy took place (see the scene in the movie *The Ten Commandments*). There is some *delightful* ambiguity in the word *revel*. It is the same root upon which the name Isaac ("laughter") is based (Gen. 18:12–15; 21:6). In some contexts it can be translated "play" (Gen. 21:9). In others it has connotations of sexual activity that might lead to laughter (Gen. 26:8). One wonders how, if the same word

were used in the context of worship of the Lord, it might be rendered (cf. Exod. 24:11).

32:9–10—*Stiff-necked* is a good description of these Hebrew slaves. Bending doesn't come naturally. From Moses' resistance to complaining in the wilderness, they have grumbled every step of the way and refused to rely solely on God. God has finally had enough. Just as God's wrath burns hot when the marginalized are oppressed or abused (22:23–24) in violation of God's command, God experiences the calf as disobedience. In the theology of Exodus, disobedience leads to divine punishment.

32:12–14—We don't often think of God changing God's mind (see Num. 23:19; Ps. 110:4). But there is a tradition of God doing such things (see Gen. 6:6–7; Jer. 26:13, 19; Jonah 3:9–10; 4:2). If God can turn away from the intent of destruction, perhaps we also can.

God, engraved upon the tablets. [17] When Joshua heard the noise of the people as they shouted, he said to Moses, "There is a noise of war in the camp." [18] But he said,

"It is not the sound made by victors,
　or the sound made by losers;
it is the sound of revelers that I hear."

[19] As soon as he came near the camp and saw the calf and the dancing, Moses' anger burned hot, and he threw the tablets from his hands and broke them at the foot of the mountain. [20] He took the calf that they had made, burned it with fire, ground it to powder, scattered it on the water, and made the Israelites drink it.

21 Moses said to Aaron, "What did this people do to you that you have brought so great a sin upon them?" [22] And Aaron said, "Do not let the anger of my lord burn hot; you know the people, that they are bent on evil. [23] They said to me, 'Make us gods, who shall go before us; as for this Moses, the man who brought us up out of the land of Egypt, we do not know what has become of him.' [24] So I said to them, 'Whoever has gold, take it off'; so they gave it to me, and I threw it into the fire, and out came this calf!"

25 When Moses saw that the people were running wild (for Aaron had let them run wild, to the derision of their enemies), [26] then Moses stood in the gate of the camp, and said, "Who is on the LORD's side? Come to me!" And all the sons of Levi gathered around him. [27] He said to them, "Thus says the LORD, the God of Israel, 'Put your sword on your side, each of you! Go back and forth from gate to gate throughout the camp, and each of you kill your brother, your friend, and your neighbor.'" [28] The sons

of Levi did as Moses commanded, and about three thousand of the people fell on that day. [29] Moses said, "Today you have ordained yourselves[a] for the service of the LORD, each one at the cost of a son or a brother, and so have brought a blessing on yourselves this day."

30 On the next day Moses said to the people, "You have sinned a great sin. But now I will go up to the LORD; perhaps I can make atonement for your sin." [31] So Moses returned to the LORD and said, "Alas, this people has sinned a great sin; they have made for themselves gods of gold. [32] But now, if you will only forgive their sin—but if not, blot me out of the book that you have written." [33] But the LORD said to Moses, "Whoever has sinned against me I will blot out of my book. [34] But now go, lead the people to the place about which I have spoken to you; see, my angel shall go in front of you. Nevertheless, when the day comes for punishment, I will punish them for their sin."

35 Then the LORD sent a plague on the people, because they made the calf—the one that Aaron made.

The Command to Leave Sinai

33 The LORD said to Moses, "Go, leave this place, you and the people whom you have brought up out of the land of Egypt, and go to the land of which I swore to Abraham, Isaac, and Jacob, saying, 'To your descendants I will give it.' [2] I will send an angel before you, and I will drive out the Canaanites, the Amorites, the Hittites, the Perizzites, the Hivites, and the Jebusites. [3] Go up to a land flowing with milk and honey; but I will not go up among you, or I would

[a] Gk Vg Compare Tg: Heb *Today ordain yourselves*

32:22—Since Adam (Gen. 3:12), when confronted with our transgressions, our first impulse is to blame someone else. Our society has become particularly adept at this. We do need to consider that external forces sometimes impact and influence us (see note at Exod. 20:5–6). However, at some point we need to accept responsibility for our own actions.

32:27–29—This is a problematic text. Kill our brother and it's a blessing. This reflects a tension within God that runs throughout Exodus of the mercy that forgives and the sovereignty that will not be compromised (see notes at 20:5–6; 34:6–7). This is a tension we struggle with at the human level as well.

consume you on the way, for you are a stiff-necked people."

4 When the people heard these harsh words, they mourned, and no one put on ornaments. 5 For the LORD had said to Moses, "Say to the Israelites, 'You are a stiff-necked people; if for a single moment I should go up among you, I would consume you. So now take off your ornaments, and I will decide what to do to you.'" 6 Therefore the Israelites stripped themselves of their ornaments, from Mount Horeb onward.

The Tent outside the Camp

7 Now Moses used to take the tent and pitch it outside the camp, far off from the camp; he called it the tent of meeting. And everyone who sought the LORD would go out to the tent of meeting, which was outside the camp. 8 Whenever Moses went out to the tent, all the people would rise and stand, each of them, at the entrance of their tents and watch Moses until he had gone into the tent. 9 When Moses entered the tent, the pillar of cloud would descend and stand at the entrance of the tent, and the LORD would speak with Moses. 10 When all the people saw the pillar of cloud standing at the entrance of the tent, all the people would rise and bow down, all of them, at the entrance of their tent. 11 Thus the LORD used to speak to Moses face to face, as one speaks to a friend. Then he would return to the camp; but his young assistant, Joshua son of Nun, would not leave the tent.

Moses' Intercession

12 Moses said to the LORD, "See, you have said to me, 'Bring up this people'; but you have not let me know whom you will send with me. Yet you have said, 'I know you by name, and you have also found favor in my sight.' 13 Now if I have found favor in your sight, show me your ways, so that I may know you and find favor in your sight. Consider too that this nation is your people." 14 He said, "My presence will go with you, and I will give you rest." 15 And he said to him, "If your presence will not go, do not carry us up from here. 16 For how shall it be known that I have found favor in your sight, I and your people, unless you go with us? In this way, we shall be distinct, I and your people, from every people on the face of the earth."

17 The LORD said to Moses, "I will do the very thing that you have asked; for you have found favor in my sight, and I know you by name." 18 Moses said, "Show me your glory, I pray." 19 And he said, "I will make all my goodness pass before you, and will proclaim before you the name, 'The LORD';[a] and I will be gracious to whom I will be gracious, and will show mercy on whom I will

[a] Heb YHWH; see note at 3.15

33:11—We can be glad this verse is in the canon. It reflects the intimacy of the relationship between God and Moses (Deut. 34:10). Those with whom we are most intimate are those with whom we are face to face. Face to face, one cannot ignore the other. It images the divine-human relationship as one of friends and friendship (see John 15:15). Imagine relating to God as a friend.

33:12–23—Moses asks to see God's glory (v. 18). First, this request provides a model for prayer. No prayer request is off limits. God permits us to make even the most outrageous and audacious requests. Second, God's response that Moses cannot see God's face contradicts v. 11. Perhaps this reflects the tension between individual and communal. It is possible for an individual to experience God in a direct and intimate way

(v. 11). But Moses' request is in the context of how *the people* will have assurance of God's presence (vv. 12–16). The answer is that God's *face* will go before them and what they will see is God's *back*. In other words, God has always gone on ahead of us. We see God as we are led into the future. Look back on life and identify the places where you can say God was going before you.

33:19—*No human can control God's grace and mercy.* This sounds like such a fundamental truth, but it is one with which we have such difficulty. The reason is because *God so often is gracious and merciful to those whom we think least deserve it* (cf. Jonah; Matt. 9:11; Luke 5:30). Let us learn to be gracious and merciful, as God is.

show mercy. ²⁰ But," he said, "you cannot see my face; for no one shall see me and live." ²¹ And the LORD continued, "See, there is a place by me where you shall stand on the rock; ²² and while my glory passes by I will put you in a cleft of the rock, and I will cover you with my hand until I have passed by; ²³ then I will take away my hand, and you shall see my back; but my face shall not be seen."

Moses Makes New Tablets

34 The LORD said to Moses, "Cut two tablets of stone like the former ones, and I will write on the tablets the words that were on the former tablets, which you broke. ² Be ready in the morning, and come up in the morning to Mount Sinai and present yourself there to me, on the top of the mountain. ³ No one shall come up with you, and do not let anyone be seen throughout all the mountain; and do not let flocks or herds graze in front of that mountain." ⁴ So Moses cut two tablets of stone like the former ones; and he rose early in the morning and went up on Mount Sinai, as the LORD had commanded him, and took in his hand the two tablets of stone. ⁵ The LORD descended in the cloud and stood with him there, and proclaimed the name, "The LORD."*a* ⁶ The LORD passed before him, and proclaimed,

"The LORD, the LORD,
a God merciful and gracious,
slow to anger,
and abounding in steadfast love and
faithfulness,

⁷ keeping steadfast love for the
thousandth generation,*b*
forgiving iniquity and transgression
and sin,
yet by no means clearing the guilty,
but visiting the iniquity of the
parents
upon the children
and the children's children,
to the third and the fourth
generation."

⁸ And Moses quickly bowed his head toward the earth, and worshiped. ⁹ He said, "If now I have found favor in your sight, O Lord, I pray, let the Lord go with us. Although this is a stiff-necked people, pardon our iniquity and our sin, and take us for your inheritance."

The Covenant Renewed

10 He said: I hereby make a covenant. Before all your people I will perform marvels, such as have not been performed in all the earth or in any nation; and all the people among whom you live shall see the work of the LORD; for it is an awesome thing that I will do with you.

11 Observe what I command you today. See, I will drive out before you the Amorites, the Canaanites, the Hittites, the Perizzites, the Hivites, and the Jebusites. ¹² Take care not to make a covenant with the inhabitants of the land to which you are going, or it will become a snare among you. ¹³ You shall tear down their altars, break their pil-

---

a Heb YHWH; see note at 3.15   *b* Or for thousands

34:6–7—It is often said that the God of the Old Testament is vengeful and wrathful. But the One who is merciful and gracious, slow to anger, and abounding in steadfast love and faithfulness is also manifestly present in the Old Testament (Num. 14:18; Neh. 9:17; Pss. 86:15; 103:8; 145:8; Joel 2:13; Jonah 4:2; Nah. 1:3). Christians must affirm that the God of the Old Testament is one God (Deut. 6:4) and the same God who is manifest in Jesus Christ. To suggest that God in the New Testament is somehow a kinder, gentler image of God than that found in the Old Testament leads to interpretations that are anti-Semitic and anti-Jewish (see note at Exod. 19:1–6). These verses manifest a

central theological tension within Scripture. God both judges us for our iniquity and forgives us our transgressions. We tend to want to be recipients of forgiveness and not judgment. Yet Exodus is about God *judging Pharaoh to be guilty* and thereby holding Pharaoh accountable for his actions. For there to be any hope of justice, those who commit an injustice must be judged guilty and held accountable for their actions—even God's own people. The idea of visiting the iniquity of the parents upon their children, even to the third and fourth generations, may sound excessively harsh, but it is also an unmistakable description of reality (see note at 20:5–6).

lars, and cut down their sacred poles[a]
14 (for you shall worship no other god,
because the LORD, whose name is Jealous, is a jealous God). 15 You shall not
make a covenant with the inhabitants of
the land, for when they prostitute themselves to their gods and sacrifice to their
gods, someone among them will invite
you, and you will eat of the sacrifice.
16 And you will take wives from among
their daughters for your sons, and their
daughters who prostitute themselves
to their gods will make your sons also
prostitute themselves to their gods.

17 You shall not make cast idols.

18 You shall keep the festival of
unleavened bread. Seven days you shall
eat unleavened bread, as I commanded
you, at the time appointed in the month
of Abib; for in the month of Abib you
came out from Egypt.

19 All that first opens the womb is
mine, all your male[b] livestock, the firstborn of cow and sheep. 20 The firstborn
of a donkey you shall redeem with a
lamb, or if you will not redeem it you
shall break its neck. All the firstborn of
your sons you shall redeem.

No one shall appear before me
empty-handed.

21 Six days you shall work, but on the
seventh day you shall rest; even in plowing time and in harvest time you shall
rest. 22 You shall observe the festival of
weeks, the first fruits of wheat harvest,
and the festival of ingathering at the
turn of the year. 23 Three times in the
year all your males shall appear before
the LORD God, the God of Israel. 24 For
I will cast out nations before you, and
enlarge your borders; no one shall covet
your land when you go up to appear
before the LORD your God three times
in the year.

25 You shall not offer the blood of my
sacrifice with leaven, and the sacrifice of

the festival of the passover shall not be
left until the morning.

26 The best of the first fruits of your
ground you shall bring to the house of
the LORD your God.

You shall not boil a kid in its mother's
milk.

27 The LORD said to Moses: Write
these words; in accordance with these
words I have made a covenant with you
and with Israel. 28 He was there with the
LORD forty days and forty nights; he
neither ate bread nor drank water. And
he wrote on the tablets the words of the
covenant, the ten commandments.[c]

The Shining Face of Moses

29 Moses came down from Mount
Sinai. As he came down from the
mountain with the two tablets of the
covenant[d] in his hand, Moses did not
know that the skin of his face shone
because he had been talking with God.
30 When Aaron and all the Israelites saw
Moses, the skin of his face was shining,
and they were afraid to come near him.
31 But Moses called to them; and Aaron
and all the leaders of the congregation
returned to him, and Moses spoke with
them. 32 Afterward all the Israelites came
near, and he gave them in commandment all that the LORD had spoken with
him on Mount Sinai. 33 When Moses had
finished speaking with them, he put a
veil on his face; 34 but whenever Moses
went in before the LORD to speak with
him, he would take the veil off, until he
came out; and when he came out, and
told the Israelites what he had been
commanded, 35 the Israelites would see
the face of Moses, that the skin of his
face was shining; and Moses would put
the veil on his face again, until he went
in to speak with him.

[a] Heb *Asherim*   [b] Gk Theodotion Vg Tg: Meaning of Heb uncertain
[c] Heb *words*   [d] Or *treaty,* or *testimony;* Heb *eduth*

34:30–35—There is something transforming
about being in God's presence (see Matt. 17:2;
Mark 9:2). Moses' face becomes God's face,

God's light to the people (cf. Num. 6:25). Spend
time in God's presence. Be transformed. Be God's
face, God's light to the people.

Sabbath Regulations

35 Moses assembled all the congregation of the Israelites and said to them: These are the things that the LORD has commanded you to do:

2 Six days shall work be done, but on the seventh day you shall have a holy sabbath of solemn rest to the LORD; whoever does any work on it shall be put to death. 3 You shall kindle no fire in all your dwellings on the sabbath day.

Preparations for Making the Tabernacle

4 Moses said to all the congregation of the Israelites: This is the thing that the LORD has commanded: 5 Take from among you an offering to the LORD; let whoever is of a generous heart bring the LORD's offering: gold, silver, and bronze; 6 blue, purple, and crimson yarns, and fine linen; goats' hair, 7 tanned rams' skins, and fine leather;*a* acacia wood, 8 oil for the light, spices for the anointing oil and for the fragrant incense, 9 and onyx stones and gems to be set in the ephod and the breastpiece.

10 All who are skillful among you shall come and make all that the LORD has commanded: the tabernacle, 11 its tent and its covering, its clasps and its frames, its bars, its pillars, and its bases; 12 the ark with its poles, the mercy seat,*b* and the curtain for the screen; 13 the table with its poles and all its utensils, and the bread of the Presence; 14 the lampstand also for the light, with its utensils and its lamps, and the oil for the light; 15 and the altar of incense, with its poles, and the anointing oil and the fragrant incense,

and the screen for the entrance, the entrance of the tabernacle; 16 the altar of burnt offering, with its grating of bronze, its poles, and all its utensils, the basin with its stand; 17 the hangings of the court, its pillars and its bases, and the screen for the gate of the court; 18 the pegs of the tabernacle and the pegs of the court, and their cords; 19 the finely worked vestments for ministering in the holy place, the holy vestments for the priest Aaron, and the vestments of his sons, for their service as priests.

Offerings for the Tabernacle

20 Then all the congregation of the Israelites withdrew from the presence of Moses. 21 And they came, everyone whose heart was stirred, and everyone whose spirit was willing, and brought the LORD's offering to be used for the tent of meeting, and for all its service, and for the sacred vestments. 22 So they came, both men and women; all who were of a willing heart brought brooches and earrings and signet rings and pendants, all sorts of gold objects, everyone bringing an offering of gold to the LORD. 23 And everyone who possessed blue or purple or crimson yarn or fine linen or goats' hair or tanned rams' skins or fine leather,*a* brought them. 24 Everyone who could make an offering of silver or bronze brought it as the LORD's offering; and everyone who possessed acacia wood of any use in the work, brought it. 25 All the skillful women spun with their hands, and brought what they had spun

a Meaning of Heb uncertain   b Or the cover

35:1–40:38 The Obedient Construction of the Tabernacle

35:21–24, 29—Apparently men and women could independently own jewelry, as well as yarns, linens, skins, silver, bronze, and acacia wood. They were also able independently to dispose of these possessions. This is important, since it indicates that women could own goods and dispose of them at their own discretion; not all aspects of women's lives were subject to the authority of a male figure. However, although men and women apparently contributed equally

to the construction of the tabernacle, they did not participate equally in worship or leadership.

35:21—(see also 35:5, 22, 29). If we seek to end oppression, it is essential that the oppressed do not themselves become the oppressors. So, having themselves escaped from forced labor, the former slaves do not *force* anyone to give to the offering. And there is no negative consequence for not giving.

35:25–26—The word for *skillful* is from the same Hebrew root as the word for wisdom. Here *wisdom* is associated with the technical abilities

in blue and purple and crimson yarns and fine linen; ²⁶ all the women whose hearts moved them to use their skill spun the goats' hair. ²⁷ And the leaders brought onyx stones and gems to be set in the ephod and the breastpiece, ²⁸ and spices and oil for the light, and for the anointing oil, and for the fragrant incense. ²⁹ All the Israelite men and women whose hearts made them willing to bring anything for the work that the LORD had commanded by Moses to be done, brought it as a freewill offering to the LORD.

Bezalel and Oholiab

30 Then Moses said to the Israelites: See, the LORD has called by name Bezalel son of Uri son of Hur, of the tribe of Judah; ³¹ he has filled him with divine spirit,ᵃ with skill, intelligence, and knowledge in every kind of craft, ³² to devise artistic designs, to work in gold, silver, and bronze, ³³ in cutting stones for setting, and in carving wood, in every kind of craft. ³⁴ And he has inspired him to teach, both him and Oholiab son of Ahisamach, of the tribe of Dan. ³⁵ He has filled them with skill to do every kind of work done by an artisan or by a designer or by an embroiderer in blue, purple, and crimson yarns, and in fine linen, or by a weaver—by any sort of artisan or skilled designer.

36 Bezalel and Oholiab and every skillful one to whom the LORD has given skill and understanding to

know how to do any work in the construction of the sanctuary shall work in accordance with all that the LORD has commanded.

2 Moses then called Bezalel and Oholiab and every skillful one to whom the LORD had given skill, everyone whose heart was stirred to come to do the work; ³ and they received from Moses all the freewill offerings that the Israelites had brought for doing the work on the sanctuary. They still kept bringing him freewill offerings every morning, ⁴ so that all the artisans who were doing every sort of task on the sanctuary came, each from the task being performed, ⁵ and said to Moses, "The people are bringing much more than enough for doing the work that the LORD has commanded us to do." ⁶ So Moses gave command, and word was proclaimed throughout the camp: "No man or woman is to make anything else as an offering for the sanctuary." So the people were restrained from bringing; ⁷ for what they had already brought was more than enough to do all the work.

Construction of the Tabernacle

8 All those with skill among the workers made the tabernacle with ten curtains; they were made of fine twisted linen, and blue, purple, and crimson yarns, with cherubim skillfully worked into them. ⁹ The length of each curtain was twenty-eight cubits, and the width

ᵃ Or *the spirit of God*

---

of artisans. These skillful women were involved in textile production. Although the production of textiles is often associated with women, especially in rural settings, here the production is for ritual purposes. This places women in a public role and setting, which is often unnoticed.

36:1–2—The text suggests that artistic *skill* and ability are gifts from God. Here the gifts of God that are needed are those of builders, weavers, smiths, jewelers, and tanners. The religious community needs more than just *religious* leaders. How can we more fully incorporate the skills of artists to enhance and deepen our religious experience?

36:6—The command to stop is given to both

men and women. Because women are included in this command, terms such as "artisan" (v. 4) or "designer" (35:35), which are grammatically masculine in Hebrew, should be interpreted to include women as well as men who are trained in a particular craft.

36:8–39:43—The construction of the tabernacle is nearly word for word identical to the pattern for the construction (25:10–31:18). The function of this lengthy repetition tells us that the people who had so dismally failed to be obedient to God's commands in chaps. 32–34 now *completely obey* God's command. Exodus draws to a close with a picture of a truly transformed and liberated people.

of each curtain four cubits; all the curtains were of the same size.

10 He joined five curtains to one another, and the other five curtains he joined to one another. [11] He made loops of blue on the edge of the outermost curtain of the first set; likewise he made them on the edge of the outermost curtain of the second set; [12] he made fifty loops on the one curtain, and he made fifty loops on the edge of the curtain that was in the second set; the loops were opposite one another. [13] And he made fifty clasps of gold, and joined the curtains one to the other with clasps; so the tabernacle was one whole.

14 He also made curtains of goats' hair for a tent over the tabernacle; he made eleven curtains. [15] The length of each curtain was thirty cubits, and the width of each curtain four cubits; the eleven curtains were of the same size. [16] He joined five curtains by themselves, and six curtains by themselves. [17] He made fifty loops on the edge of the outermost curtain of the one set, and fifty loops on the edge of the other connecting curtain. [18] He made fifty clasps of bronze to join the tent together so that it might be one whole. [19] And he made for the tent a covering of tanned rams' skins and an outer covering of fine leather.[a]

20 Then he made the upright frames for the tabernacle of acacia wood. [21] Ten cubits was the length of a frame, and a cubit and a half the width of each frame. [22] Each frame had two pegs for fitting together; he did this for all the frames of the tabernacle. [23] The frames for the tabernacle he made in this way: twenty frames for the south side; [24] and he made forty bases of silver under the twenty frames, two bases under the first frame for its two pegs, and two bases under the next frame for its two pegs. [25] For the second side of the tabernacle, on the north side, he made twenty frames [26] and their forty bases of silver, two bases under the first frame and two bases under the next frame. [27] For

the rear of the tabernacle westward he made six frames. [28] He made two frames for corners of the tabernacle in the rear. [29] They were separate beneath, but joined at the top, at the first ring; he made two of them in this way, for the two corners. [30] There were eight frames with their bases of silver: sixteen bases, under every frame two bases.

31 He made bars of acacia wood, five for the frames of the one side of the tabernacle, [32] and five bars for the frames of the other side of the tabernacle, and five bars for the frames of the tabernacle at the rear westward. [33] He made the middle bar to pass through from end to end halfway up the frames. [34] And he overlaid the frames with gold, and made rings of gold for them to hold the bars, and overlaid the bars with gold.

35 He made the curtain of blue, purple, and crimson yarns, and fine twisted linen, with cherubim skillfully worked into it. [36] For it he made four pillars of acacia, and overlaid them with gold; their hooks were of gold, and he cast for them four bases of silver. [37] He also made a screen for the entrance to the tent, of blue, purple, and crimson yarns, and fine twisted linen, embroidered with needlework; [38] and its five pillars with their hooks. He overlaid their capitals and their bases with gold, but their five bases were of bronze.

Making the Ark of the Covenant

37 Bezalel made the ark of acacia wood; it was two and a half cubits long, a cubit and a half wide, and a cubit and a half high. [2] He overlaid it with pure gold inside and outside, and made a molding of gold around it. [3] He cast for it four rings of gold for its four feet, two rings on its one side and two rings on its other side. [4] He made poles of acacia wood, and overlaid them with gold, [5] and put the poles into the rings on the sides of the ark, to carry the ark. [6] He made a mercy seat[b] of pure gold; two cubits and

[a] Meaning of Heb uncertain   [b] Or a cover

a half was its length, and a cubit and a half its width. **7** He made two cherubim of hammered gold; at the two ends of the mercy seat*a* he made them, **8** one cherub at the one end, and one cherub at the other end; of one piece with the mercy seat*a* he made the cherubim at its two ends. **9** The cherubim spread out their wings above, overshadowing the mercy seat*a* with their wings. They faced one another; the faces of the cherubim were turned toward the mercy seat.*a*

Making the Table for the Bread of the Presence

10 He also made the table of acacia wood, two cubits long, one cubit wide, and a cubit and a half high. **11** He overlaid it with pure gold, and made a molding of gold around it. **12** He made around it a rim a handbreadth wide, and made a molding of gold around the rim. **13** He cast for it four rings of gold, and fastened the rings to the four corners at its four legs. **14** The rings that held the poles used for carrying the table were close to the rim. **15** He made the poles of acacia wood to carry the table, and overlaid them with gold. **16** And he made the vessels of pure gold that were to be on the table, its plates and dishes for incense, and its bowls and flagons with which to pour drink offerings.

Making the Lampstand

17 He also made the lampstand of pure gold. The base and the shaft of the lampstand were made of hammered work; its cups, its calyxes, and its petals were of one piece with it. **18** There were six branches going out of its sides, three branches of the lampstand out of one side of it and three branches of the lampstand out of the other side of it; **19** three cups shaped like almond blossoms, each with calyx and petals, on one branch, and three cups shaped like almond blossoms, each with calyx and petals, on the other branch—so for the six branches going out of the lampstand.

20 On the lampstand itself there were four cups shaped like almond blossoms, each with its calyxes and petals. **21** There was a calyx of one piece with it under the first pair of branches, a calyx of one piece with it under the next pair of branches, and a calyx of one piece with it under the last pair of branches. **22** Their calyxes and their branches were of one piece with it, the whole of it one hammered piece of pure gold. **23** He made its seven lamps and its snuffers and its trays of pure gold. **24** He made it and all its utensils of a talent of pure gold.

Making the Altar of Incense

25 He made the altar of incense of acacia wood, one cubit long, and one cubit wide; it was square, and was two cubits high; its horns were of one piece with it. **26** He overlaid it with pure gold, its top, and its sides all around, and its horns; and he made for it a molding of gold all around, **27** and made two golden rings for it under its molding, on two opposite sides of it, to hold the poles with which to carry it. **28** And he made the poles of acacia wood, and overlaid them with gold.

Making the Anointing Oil and the Incense

29 He made the holy anointing oil also, and the pure fragrant incense, blended as by the perfumer.

Making the Altar of Burnt Offering

38 He made the altar of burnt offering also of acacia wood; it was five cubits long, and five cubits wide; it was square, and three cubits high. **2** He made horns for it on its four corners; its horns were of one piece with it, and he overlaid it with bronze. **3** He made all the utensils of the altar, the pots, the shovels, the basins, the forks, and the firepans: all its utensils he made of bronze. **4** He made for the altar a grating, a network of bronze, under its ledge, extending

a Or the cover

halfway down. [5] He cast four rings on the four corners of the bronze grating to hold the poles; [6] he made the poles of acacia wood, and overlaid them with bronze. [7] And he put the poles through the rings on the sides of the altar, to carry it with them; he made it hollow, with boards.

[8] He made the basin of bronze with its stand of bronze, from the mirrors of the women who served at the entrance to the tent of meeting.

Making the Court of the Tabernacle

[9] He made the court; for the south side the hangings of the court were of fine twisted linen, one hundred cubits long; [10] its twenty pillars and their twenty bases were of bronze, but the hooks of the pillars and their bands were of silver. [11] For the north side there were hangings one hundred cubits long; its twenty pillars and their twenty bases were of bronze, but the hooks of the pillars and their bands were of silver. [12] For the west side there were hangings fifty cubits long, with ten pillars and ten bases; the hooks of the pillars and their bands were of silver. [13] And for the front to the east, fifty cubits. [14] The hangings for one side of the gate were fifteen cubits, with three pillars and three bases. [15] And so for the other side; on each side of the gate of the court were hangings of fifteen cubits, with three pillars and three bases. [16] All the hangings around the court were of fine twisted linen. [17] The bases for the pillars were of bronze, but the hooks of the pillars and their bands were of silver; the overlaying of their capitals was also of silver, and all the pillars of the court were banded with silver. [18] The screen for the entrance to the court was embroidered with needlework in blue, purple, and crimson yarns and fine twisted linen. It was twenty cubits long and, along the width of it, five cubits high, corresponding to the hangings of the court. [19] There were four pillars; their four bases were of bronze,

their hooks of silver, and the overlaying of their capitals and their bands of silver. [20] All the pegs for the tabernacle and for the court all around were of bronze.

Materials of the Tabernacle

21 These are the records of the tabernacle, the tabernacle of the covenant,[a] which were drawn up at the commandment of Moses, the work of the Levites being under the direction of Ithamar son of the priest Aaron. [22] Bezalel son of Uri son of Hur, of the tribe of Judah, made all that the LORD commanded Moses; [23] and with him was Oholiab son of Ahisamach, of the tribe of Dan, engraver, designer, and embroiderer in blue, purple, and crimson yarns, and in fine linen.

24 All the gold that was used for the work, in all the construction of the sanctuary, the gold from the offering, was twenty-nine talents and seven hundred thirty shekels, measured by the sanctuary shekel. [25] The silver from those of the congregation who were counted was one hundred talents and one thousand seven hundred seventy-five shekels, measured by the sanctuary shekel; [26] a beka a head (that is, half a shekel, measured by the sanctuary shekel), for everyone who was counted in the census, from twenty years old and upward, for six hundred three thousand, five hundred fifty men. [27] The hundred talents of silver were for casting the bases of the sanctuary, and the bases of the curtain; one hundred bases for the hundred talents, a talent for a base. [28] Of the thousand seven hundred seventy-five shekels he made hooks for the pillars, and overlaid their capitals and made bands for them. [29] The bronze that was contributed was seventy talents, and two thousand four hundred shekels; [30] with it he made the bases for the entrance of the tent of meeting, the bronze altar and the bronze grating for it and all the utensils of the altar, [31] the bases all around the court, and the bases

a Or treaty, or testimony; Heb eduth

of the gate of the court, all the pegs of the tabernacle, and all the pegs around the court.

Making the Vestments for the Priesthood

39 Of the blue, purple, and crimson yarns they made finely worked vestments, for ministering in the holy place; they made the sacred vestments for Aaron; as the LORD had commanded Moses.

2 He made the ephod of gold, of blue, purple, and crimson yarns, and of fine twisted linen. 3 Gold leaf was hammered out and cut into threads to work into the blue, purple, and crimson yarns and into the fine twisted linen, in skilled design. 4 They made for the ephod shoulder-pieces, joined to it at its two edges. 5 The decorated band on it was of the same materials and workmanship, of gold, of blue, purple, and crimson yarns, and of fine twisted linen; as the LORD had commanded Moses.

6 The onyx stones were prepared, enclosed in settings of gold filigree and engraved like the engravings of a signet, according to the names of the sons of Israel. 7 He set them on the shoulder-pieces of the ephod, to be stones of remembrance for the sons of Israel; as the LORD had commanded Moses.

8 He made the breastpiece, in skilled work, like the work of the ephod, of gold, of blue, purple, and crimson yarns, and of fine twisted linen. 9 It was square; the breastpiece was made double, a span in length and a span in width when doubled. 10 They set in it four rows of stones. A row of carnelian,*a* chrysolite, and emerald was the first row; 11 and the second row, a turquoise, a sapphire,*b* and a moonstone; 12 and the third row, a jacinth, an agate, and an amethyst; 13 and the fourth row, a beryl, an onyx, and a jasper; they were enclosed in settings of gold filigree. 14 There were twelve stones with names corresponding to the names of the sons of Israel; they were like sig-

nets, each engraved with its name, for the twelve tribes. 15 They made on the breastpiece chains of pure gold, twisted like cords; 16 and they made two settings of gold filigree and two gold rings, and put the two rings on the two edges of the breastpiece; 17 and they put the two cords of gold in the two rings at the edges of the breastpiece. 18 Two ends of the two cords they had attached to the two settings of filigree; in this way they attached it in front to the shoulder-pieces of the ephod. 19 Then they made two rings of gold, and put them at the two ends of the breastpiece, on its inside edge next to the ephod. 20 They made two rings of gold, and attached them in front to the lower part of the two shoulder-pieces of the ephod, at its joining above the decorated band of the ephod. 21 They bound the breastpiece by its rings to the rings of the ephod with a blue cord, so that it should lie on the decorated band of the ephod, and that the breastpiece should not come loose from the ephod; as the LORD had commanded Moses.

22 He also made the robe of the ephod woven all of blue yarn; 23 and the opening of the robe in the middle of it was like the opening in a coat of mail,*c* with a binding around the opening, so that it might not be torn. 24 On the lower hem of the robe they made pomegranates of blue, purple, and crimson yarns, and of fine twisted linen. 25 They also made bells of pure gold, and put the bells between the pomegranates on the lower hem of the robe all around, between the pomegranates; 26 a bell and a pomegranate, a bell and a pomegranate all around on the lower hem of the robe for ministering; as the LORD had commanded Moses.

27 They also made the tunics, woven of fine linen, for Aaron and his sons, 28 and the turban of fine linen, and the headdresses of fine linen, and the linen undergarments of fine twisted linen,

---

a The identification of several of these stones is uncertain   *b* Or *lapis lazuli*   *c* Meaning of Heb uncertain

²⁹and the sash of fine twisted linen, and of blue, purple, and crimson yarns, embroidered with needlework; as the LORD had commanded Moses.

30 They made the rosette of the holy diadem of pure gold, and wrote on it an inscription, like the engraving of a signet, "Holy to the LORD." ³¹They tied to it a blue cord, to fasten it on the turban above; as the LORD had commanded Moses.

The Work Completed

32 In this way all the work of the tabernacle of the tent of meeting was finished; the Israelites had done everything just as the LORD had commanded Moses. ³³Then they brought the tabernacle to Moses, the tent and all its utensils, its hooks, its frames, its bars, its pillars, and its bases; ³⁴the covering of tanned rams' skins and the covering of fine leather,ᵃ and the curtain for the screen; ³⁵the ark of the covenantᵇ with its poles and the mercy seat;ᶜ ³⁶the table with all its utensils, and the bread of the Presence; ³⁷the pure lampstand with its lamps set on it and all its utensils, and the oil for the light; ³⁸the golden altar, the anointing oil and the fragrant incense, and the screen for the entrance of the tent; ³⁹the bronze altar, and its grating of bronze, its poles, and all its utensils; the basin with its stand; ⁴⁰the hangings of the court, its pillars, and its bases, and the screen for the gate of the court, its cords, and its pegs; and all the utensils for the service of the tabernacle, for the tent of meeting; ⁴¹the finely worked vestments for ministering in the holy place, the sacred vestments for the priest Aaron, and the vestments of his sons to serve as priests. ⁴²The Israelites had done all of the work just as the LORD had commanded Moses. ⁴³When Moses saw that they had done all the work just as the LORD had commanded, he blessed them.

The Tabernacle Erected and Its Equipment Installed

40 The LORD spoke to Moses: ²On the first day of the first month you shall set up the tabernacle of the tent of meeting. ³You shall put in it the ark of the covenant,ᵇ and you shall screen the ark with the curtain. ⁴You shall bring in the table, and arrange its setting; and you shall bring in the lampstand, and set up its lamps. ⁵You shall put the golden altar for incense before the ark of the covenant,ᵇ and set up the screen for the entrance of the tabernacle. ⁶You shall set the altar of burnt offering before the entrance of the tabernacle of the tent of meeting, ⁷and place the basin between the tent of meeting and the altar, and put water in it. ⁸You shall set up the court all around, and hang up the screen for the gate of the court. ⁹Then you shall take the anointing oil, and anoint the tabernacle and all that is in it, and consecrate it and all its furniture, so that it shall become holy. ¹⁰You shall also anoint the altar of burnt offering and all its utensils, and consecrate the altar, so that the altar shall be most holy. ¹¹You shall also anoint the basin with its stand, and consecrate it. ¹²Then you shall bring Aaron and his sons to the entrance of the tent of meeting, and shall wash them with water, ¹³and put on Aaron the sacred vestments, and you shall anoint him and consecrate him, so that he may serve me as priest. ¹⁴You shall bring his sons also

ᵃ Meaning of Heb uncertain   ᵇ Or treaty, or testimony; Heb eduth   ᶜ Or the cover

---

40:1—The tension between God's immanence (see note at 25:10) and transcendence (see note at 27:21) is maintained by spreading the tent over the ark (vv. 2–3, 18–22; also 26:7, 33; 36:14). This maintains both sure presence and sure freedom. The combination of ark and tent leads to the creation of a new term, *tabernacle*, which is both a noun and a verb, as a way of speaking about God's semipermanence. In the New Testament God tabernacles again with people (John 1:14) and provides another way to consider this tension. We are still searching for a way to have the divine as a visible presence. So how do we imagine both God's sure presence and God's sure freedom in today's world? What does that look like? Does it look like the church?

and put tunics on them, [15] and anoint them, as you anointed their father, that they may serve me as priests: and their anointing shall admit them to a perpetual priesthood throughout all generations to come.

16 Moses did everything just as the LORD had commanded him. [17] In the first month in the second year, on the first day of the month, the tabernacle was set up. [18] Moses set up the tabernacle; he laid its bases, and set up its frames, and put in its poles, and raised up its pillars; [19] and he spread the tent over the tabernacle, and put the covering of the tent over it; as the LORD had commanded Moses. [20] He took the covenant[a] and put it into the ark, and put the poles on the ark, and set the mercy seat[b] above the ark; [21] and he brought the ark into the tabernacle, and set up the curtain for screening, and screened the ark of the covenant;[a] as the LORD had commanded Moses. [22] He put the table in the tent of meeting, on the north side of the tabernacle, outside the curtain, [23] and set the bread in order on it before the LORD; as the LORD had commanded Moses. [24] He put the lampstand in the tent of meeting, opposite the table on the south side of the tabernacle, [25] and set up the lamps before the LORD; as the LORD had commanded Moses. [26] He put the golden altar in the tent of meeting before the curtain, [27] and offered fragrant incense on it; as the LORD had commanded Moses. [28] He also put in place the screen for the entrance of the tabernacle. [29] He set the altar of burnt offering at the entrance of the tabernacle of the tent of meeting, and offered on it the burnt offering and the grain offering as the LORD had commanded Moses. [30] He set the basin between the tent of meeting and the altar, and put water in it for washing, [31] with which Moses and Aaron and his sons washed their hands and their feet. [32] When they went into the tent of meeting, and when they approached the altar, they washed; as the LORD had commanded Moses. [33] He set up the court around the tabernacle and the altar, and put up the screen at the gate of the court. So Moses finished the work.

The Cloud and the Glory

34 Then the cloud covered the tent of meeting, and the glory of the LORD filled the tabernacle. [35] Moses was not able to enter the tent of meeting because the cloud settled upon it, and the glory of the LORD filled the tabernacle. [36] Whenever the cloud was taken up from the tabernacle, the Israelites would set out on each stage of their journey; [37] but if the cloud was not taken up, then they did not set out until the day that it was taken up. [38] For the cloud of the LORD was on the tabernacle by day, and fire was in the cloud[c] by night, before the eyes of all the house of Israel at each stage of their journey.

a Or *treaty*, or *testimony*; Heb *eduth* *b* Or *the cover* *c* Heb *it*

40:33—Jesus' cry of "It is finished!" (John 19:30) announces that God's act of liberation in Christ had been achieved. In the completion of the tabernacle, God's act of liberation of Israel has been achieved. But in neither case does **finished** imply being done. God's acts of salvation continue even today.

40:38—See notes at 13:21; 16:10; 33:12–23. With God going before them, leading them on the way, the people are ready to continue their journey. As in our own journeys of faith, one stage comes to a close for Israel as the next stage beckons them on. Take time to reflect on your own journey of faith and where you have experienced God's acts of liberation. Be in God's presence and go boldly on the next stage of the journey.

The Book of
LEVITICUS

Leviticus is the third book of the Pentateuch, the center book in the extended narrative of Israel's national history. Everything in Leviticus takes place at Mount Sinai, the mountain where Israel entered into covenant with YHWH and received the divine instructions for the community. Leviticus, then, has to do with the formation of community in relation to the divine word of instruction. What makes this community distinctive is that the God with whom it enters into covenant, and from whom it receives instructions, is determined to dwell in the midst of and travel with the community through the wilderness. Instructions for community life reflect Israel's belief that YHWH, the creator, redeemer, warrior, covenant maker, and torah speaker, was present with them in their story and that they lived their lives within the context of the divine presence.

The book opens with two sets of instructions concerning the sacrifices and offerings (1:1–6:7; 6:8–7:38), instructions required in order for Moses to undertake the ritual ordination of Aaron and his sons and the consecration of the tabernacle (chap. 8). The narrative-like material that reports these rituals points back to the construction of the tabernacle and the divine glory taking residence in it (Exod. 40). The newly ordained priesthood presents the first sacrifices and offerings of the tabernacle cult (chap. 9), and then two of Aaron's sons, on the very day of the inauguration of the cult, bring strange fire into the holy place and are killed by the fire of YHWH (chap. 10). The two corpses in the holy place provide the context for the purity and impurity instructions central to Israel's identity (chaps. 11–15), as well as the instructions for the observance of the annual day of "atonement" (purification; chap. 16).

The Holiness Code (chaps. 17–26), a block of material that reflects its own development prior to its incorporation in the final text, focuses on a variety of issues relating to the practice and experience of holiness by and in the community. Holiness, in these texts, is understood primarily in terms of social acts of honesty, integrity, and justice. A final chapter (chap. 27) places values on human beings in relation to vows.

The material in Leviticus belongs to the Priestly materials of the Pentateuch, generally thought to have originated in or shortly after the Babylonian exile (sixth century BCE), although a growing number of scholars date the material to earlier periods (from the ninth to the seventh centuries BCE). Does Leviticus report a cultic system that was well known and widely practiced, a reflection of the way things were at the time of writing (a preexilic date)? If so, the tabernacle stands in for the Jerusalem temple. Or does Leviticus provide a proposal for cultic activity to begin if and when those in exile return to Jerusalem (a postexilic date)? If so, the tabernacle is proposed as an alternative possibility for the destroyed temple in Jerusalem.

Efforts to date the material raise a difficult methodological question: How is one to determine the relationship between the origins of the practices reported in the texts and the origins of the composition of Leviticus? Many of the practices may well be

very ancient, but written down and included in "the book of Leviticus" at a much later time. The majority of scholars agree that Leviticus reflects a lengthy and complex history of composition and, because of that, contains material that reflects many different periods in Israel's history. In the case of Leviticus, context might best be thought of in terms of Israel's cultic life and theological reflection on that life, rather than a specific "moment" in history.

An important question on which to reflect: What role might the ritual texts play in the faith community, Jewish and Christian, when neither temple nor altar exists for the enactment of the sacrificial offerings? What is the nature of the worship experience in which sacrificial texts are read and reflected on, but not enacted? Christianity has been quick to let Leviticus be tossed into the dustbins of biblical literature—the rituals are not ours, Jesus was the ultimate sacrifice, so why worry with them? Yet the book has maintained its place within the Christian canon. What theological dynamics might be generated through the reading of these texts within the context of Christian worship? What do these texts suggest about Christian community and Christian life in the contemporary world?

Although Leviticus contains extremely diverse material, a central theological focus found throughout the book concerns the relationship between the community of faith and YHWH. The instructions of Leviticus address a variety of concerns associated with the question of how the faith community is to live its life in the presence of the divine and holy one. Of importance is the recognition that even when an individual enacts a ritual, the individual's enactment is understood to take place within the larger context of the community. Individual actions are an expression of community life and values. A related concern, but one that must be examined on its own, has to do with how YHWH is understood to be present in the midst of the community. Viewed in this way, the book provides guidance for the enactment of human existence within the context of the divine life of YHWH, the Holy One. At the heart of this relationship is the call for Israel to practice holiness and, in doing so, to reflect the divine life of YHWH. The Holiness Code (chaps. 17–26) is characterized in part by the way it weaves together ritual enactment and social practice in terms of its understanding of holiness. The Israelites are called to practice holiness in their relationship with YHWH as well as in their relationships with each other. Thus, at the heart of the theology operative in Leviticus is a concern for community, divine presence, and the enactment of holiness.

—Frank H. Gorman Jr.

The Burnt Offering

1 The LORD summoned Moses and spoke to him from the tent of meeting, saying: ² Speak to the people of Israel and say to them: When any of you bring an offering of livestock to the LORD, you shall bring your offering from the herd or from the flock.

3 If the offering is a burnt offering from the herd, you shall offer a male

---

1:1–6:7 Sacrifices and Offerings: First Series
1:1–2:16 The Burnt Offering and the Grain Offering
The burnt offering and the grain offering reflect the basic ingredients for Israel's sacrificial system: animals and grains. These materials reflect the divine blessing of crops, herds, and flocks. The

Israelites approached the altar of God with the material realities of their day-to-day existence. Both offerings provide a soothing aroma for YHWH, an indication that they are designed to bring about a change in God, from agitation and wrath to peace and rest (see Num. 16:46–50).

without blemish; you shall bring it to the entrance of the tent of meeting, for acceptance in your behalf before the LORD. **4** You shall lay your hand on the head of the burnt offering, and it shall be acceptable in your behalf as atonement for you. **5** The bull shall be slaughtered before the LORD; and Aaron's sons the priests shall offer the blood, dashing the blood against all sides of the altar that is at the entrance of the tent of meeting. **6** The burnt offering shall be flayed and cut up into its parts. **7** The sons of the priest Aaron shall put fire on the altar and arrange wood on the fire. **8** Aaron's sons the priests shall arrange the parts, with the head and the suet, on the wood that is on the fire on the altar; **9** but its entrails and its legs shall be washed with water. Then the priest shall turn the whole into smoke on the altar as a burnt offering, an offering by fire of pleasing odor to the LORD.

10 If your gift for a burnt offering is from the flock, from the sheep or goats, your offering shall be a male without blemish. **11** It shall be slaughtered on the north side of the altar before the LORD, and Aaron's sons the priests shall dash its blood against all sides of the altar. **12** It shall be cut up into its parts, with its head and its suet, and the priest shall arrange them on the wood that is on the fire on the altar; **13** but the entrails and the legs shall be washed with water. Then the priest shall offer the whole and turn it into smoke on the altar; it is a burnt offering, an offering by fire of pleasing odor to the LORD.

14 If your offering to the LORD is a burnt offering of birds, you shall choose your offering from turtledoves or pigeons. **15** The priest shall bring it to the altar and wring off its head, and turn it into smoke on the altar; and its blood shall be drained out against the side of the altar. **16** He shall remove its crop with its contents*a* and throw it at the east side of the altar, in the place for ashes. **17** He shall tear it open by its wings without severing it. Then the priest shall turn it into smoke on the altar, on the wood that is on the fire; it is a burnt offering, an offering by fire of pleasing odor to the LORD.

Grain Offerings

2 When anyone presents a grain offering to the LORD, the offering shall be of choice flour; the worshiper shall pour oil on it, and put frankincense on it, **2** and bring it to Aaron's sons the priests. After taking from it a handful of the choice flour and oil, with all its frankincense, the priest shall turn this token portion into smoke on the altar, an offering by fire of pleasing odor to the LORD. **3** And what is left of the grain offering shall be for Aaron and his sons, a most holy part of the offerings by fire to the LORD.

4 When you present a grain offering baked in the oven, it shall be of choice flour: unleavened cakes mixed with oil, or unleavened wafers spread with oil. **5** If your offering is grain prepared on a griddle, it shall be of choice flour mixed with oil, unleavened; **6** break it in pieces, and pour oil on it; it is a grain offering. **7** If your offering is grain prepared in

---

a Meaning of Heb uncertain

1:4 *Atonement*—"Expiation" is a better translation (see 17:10–12).

1:9, 13, 17—The "soothing aroma" (*pleasing odor*) is primarily concerned to hold back the anger and wrath of God's response to the violation of the divine-human relationship or the disruption of the very good order of creation (Gen. 1:31). YHWH's anger arises when human actions disregard the divine will revealed both in word and creation. Paul draws on the image of the

Creator and the message of creation to argue that no person is able to excuse sinful actions before God for lack of knowledge (Rom. 1).

2:1–16—In this text, the grain offering is probably understood to be a less expensive form of the burnt offering. Two differences exist: the grain offering is not said to accomplish "atonement" (no blood is available; see 17:10–12), and only a "token part" of the grain offering is burned.

a pan, it shall be made of choice flour in oil. ⁸ You shall bring to the LORD the grain offering that is prepared in any of these ways; and when it is presented to the priest, he shall take it to the altar. ⁹ The priest shall remove from the grain offering its token portion and turn this into smoke on the altar, an offering by fire of pleasing odor to the LORD. ¹⁰ And what is left of the grain offering shall be for Aaron and his sons; it is a most holy part of the offerings by fire to the LORD.

11 No grain offering that you bring to the LORD shall be made with leaven, for you must not turn any leaven or honey into smoke as an offering by fire to the LORD. ¹² You may bring them to the LORD as an offering of choice products, but they shall not be offered on the altar for a pleasing odor. ¹³ You shall not omit from your grain offerings the salt of the covenant with your God; with all your offerings you shall offer salt.

14 If you bring a grain offering of first fruits to the LORD, you shall bring as the grain offering of your first fruits coarse new grain from fresh ears, parched with fire. ¹⁵ You shall add oil to it and lay frankincense on it; it is a grain offering. ¹⁶ And the priest shall turn a token portion of it into smoke—some of the coarse grain and oil with all its frankincense; it is an offering by fire to the LORD.

Offerings of Well-Being

3 If the offering is a sacrifice of well-being, if you offer an animal of the herd, whether male or female, you shall offer one without blemish before the LORD. ² You shall lay your hand on the head of the offering and slaughter it at the entrance of the tent of meeting; and

Aaron's sons the priests shall dash the blood against all sides of the altar. ³ You shall offer from the sacrifice of well-being, as an offering by fire to the LORD, the fat that covers the entrails and all the fat that is around the entrails; ⁴ the two kidneys with the fat that is on them at the loins, and the appendage of the liver, which he shall remove with the kidneys. ⁵ Then Aaron's sons shall turn these into smoke on the altar, with the burnt offering that is on the wood on the fire, as an offering by fire of pleasing odor to the LORD.

6 If your offering for a sacrifice of well-being to the LORD is from the flock, male or female, you shall offer one without blemish. ⁷ If you present a sheep as your offering, you shall bring it before the LORD ⁸ and lay your hand on the head of the offering. It shall be slaughtered before the tent of meeting, and Aaron's sons shall dash its blood against all sides of the altar. ⁹ You shall present its fat from the sacrifice of well-being, as an offering by fire to the LORD: the whole broad tail, which shall be removed close to the backbone, the fat that covers the entrails, and all the fat that is around the entrails; ¹⁰ the two kidneys with the fat that is on them at the loins, and the appendage of the liver, which you shall remove with the kidneys. ¹¹ Then the priest shall turn these into smoke on the altar as a food offering by fire to the LORD.

12 If your offering is a goat, you shall bring it before the LORD ¹³ and lay your hand on its head; it shall be slaughtered before the tent of meeting; and the sons of Aaron shall dash its blood against all sides of the altar. ¹⁴ You shall present as your offering from it, as an offering by

---

3:1–17 The Well-Being Offering
Only a portion of the well-being sacrifice is burned on the altar. The one who brings the sacrifice must consume a portion. Although the burning provides a *pleasing odor* for YHWH (v. 5), the sacrificial eating by the offerer suggests a shared meal of sorts (*a food offering by fire,*

vv. 11, 16). Well-being sacrifices are presented as acts of thanksgiving, as payments of vows, or as acts of free will (7:11–18). They enact and express thanksgiving, joy, and gratitude in the presence of YHWH so that the "shared meal" becomes, as it were, an occasion for shared joy and thanksgiving.

fire to the LORD, the fat that covers the entrails, and all the fat that is around the entrails; 15 the two kidneys with the fat that is on them at the loins, and the appendage of the liver, which you shall remove with the kidneys. 16 Then the priest shall turn these into smoke on the altar as a food offering by fire for a pleasing odor.

All fat is the LORD's. 17 It shall be a perpetual statute throughout your generations, in all your settlements: you must not eat any fat or any blood.

Sin Offerings

4 The LORD spoke to Moses, saying, 2 Speak to the people of Israel, saying: When anyone sins unintentionally in any of the LORD's commandments about things not to be done, and does any one of them:

3 If it is the anointed priest who sins, thus bringing guilt on the people, he shall offer for the sin that he has committed a bull of the herd without blemish as a sin offering to the LORD. 4 He shall bring the bull to the entrance of the tent of meeting before the LORD and lay his hand on the head of the bull; the bull shall be slaughtered before the LORD. 5 The anointed priest shall take some of the blood of the bull and bring it into the tent of meeting. 6 The priest shall dip his finger in the blood and sprinkle some of the blood seven times before the LORD in front of the curtain of the sanctuary. 7 The priest shall put some of the blood on the horns of the altar of fragrant incense that is in the tent of meeting before the LORD; and the rest of the blood of the bull he shall pour out at the base of the altar of burnt offering, which is at the entrance of the tent of meeting. 8 He shall remove all the fat from the bull of sin offering: the fat that covers the entrails and all the fat that is around the entrails; 9 the two kidneys with the fat that is on them at the loins; and the appendage of the liver, which he shall remove with the kidneys, 10 just as these are removed from the ox of the sacrifice of well-being. The priest shall turn them into smoke upon the altar of burnt offering. 11 But the skin of the bull and all its flesh, as well as its head, its legs, its entrails, and its dung— 12 all the rest of the bull—he shall carry out to a clean place outside the camp, to the ash heap, and shall burn it on a wood fire; at the ash heap it shall be burned.

13 If the whole congregation of Israel errs unintentionally and the matter escapes the notice of the assembly, and

---

4:1–5:13 The Sin Offering

4:1–35—The "sin" offering is required both when a person sins and when a person experiences certain forms of impurity (see chaps. 11–15). In both situations, the sacrifice purifies the sacred area, normally the outer altar, from the effects of impurity and sin. The sacrifice is better understood as a "purification" sacrifice. When offered because of unintentional sin, the sacrifice also brings about forgiveness.

4:2—The text focuses on actions prohibited by YHWH (*things not to be done*), but done *unintentionally*. When an individual or the community experiences guilt and recognizes the unintentional wrong that was done, the "sin offering" must be presented. The ritual presentation of the sacrifice brings forgiveness (vv. 20, 26, 31). At the same time, the blood placed on the altar cleanses it from the impurity generated by the wrongful act.

The text recognizes different degrees of sin based on status: the high priest and the community have one form of ritual, the ruler and the common person have a different form. Israel recognized the reality and serious nature of community sin. This is important! The modern world focuses so consistently on the individual in reflecting on human existence, that all too often the individual's concrete existence within a variety of communities is forgotten. As a result, the role, the life, and the responsibility of the community are also forgotten.

The actions of human beings, individuals and communities, have significant implications for the presence of God in history and in the midst of the community. Israel took seriously both human existence and human action. Human beings with all of their flaws, weaknesses, and dirty little sins bring their lives into the presence of the sacred and seek through sacrificial ritual to set matters right. The daily mundane realities of human life are at the heart of Israel's sacred engagement with YHWH.

they do any one of the things that by the LORD's commandments ought not to be done and incur guilt; ¹⁴ when the sin that they have committed becomes known, the assembly shall offer a bull of the herd for a sin offering and bring it before the tent of meeting. ¹⁵ The elders of the congregation shall lay their hands on the head of the bull before the LORD, and the bull shall be slaughtered before the LORD. ¹⁶ The anointed priest shall bring some of the blood of the bull into the tent of meeting, ¹⁷ and the priest shall dip his finger in the blood and sprinkle it seven times before the LORD, in front of the curtain. ¹⁸ He shall put some of the blood on the horns of the altar that is before the LORD in the tent of meeting; and the rest of the blood he shall pour out at the base of the altar of burnt offering that is at the entrance of the tent of meeting. ¹⁹ He shall remove all its fat and turn it into smoke on the altar. ²⁰ He shall do with the bull just as is done with the bull of sin offering; he shall do the same with this. The priest shall make atonement for them, and they shall be forgiven. ²¹ He shall carry the bull outside the camp, and burn it as he burned the first bull; it is the sin offering for the assembly.

22 When a ruler sins, doing unintentionally any one of all the things that by commandments of the LORD his God ought not to be done and incurs guilt, ²³ once the sin that he has committed is made known to him, he shall bring as his offering a male goat without blemish. ²⁴ He shall lay his hand on the head of the goat; it shall be slaughtered at the spot where the burnt offering is slaughtered before the LORD; it is a sin offering. ²⁵ The priest shall take some of the blood of the sin offering with his finger and put it on the horns of the altar of burnt offering, and pour out the rest of its blood at the base of the altar of burnt offering. ²⁶ All its fat he shall turn into

smoke on the altar, like the fat of the sacrifice of well-being. Thus the priest shall make atonement on his behalf for his sin, and he shall be forgiven.

27 If anyone of the ordinary people among you sins unintentionally in doing any one of the things that by the LORD's commandments ought not to be done and incurs guilt, ²⁸ when the sin that you have committed is made known to you, you shall bring a female goat without blemish as your offering, for the sin that you have committed. ²⁹ You shall lay your hand on the head of the sin offering; and the sin offering shall be slaughtered at the place of the burnt offering. ³⁰ The priest shall take some of its blood with his finger and put it on the horns of the altar of burnt offering, and he shall pour out the rest of its blood at the base of the altar. ³¹ He shall remove all its fat, as the fat is removed from the offering of well-being, and the priest shall turn it into smoke on the altar for a pleasing odor to the LORD. Thus the priest shall make atonement on your behalf, and you shall be forgiven.

32 If the offering you bring as a sin offering is a sheep, you shall bring a female without blemish. ³³ You shall lay your hand on the head of the sin offering; and it shall be slaughtered as a sin offering at the spot where the burnt offering is slaughtered. ³⁴ The priest shall take some of the blood of the sin offering with his finger and put it on the horns of the altar of burnt offering, and pour out the rest of its blood at the base of the altar. ³⁵ You shall remove all its fat, as the fat of the sheep is removed from the sacrifice of well-being, and the priest shall turn it into smoke on the altar, with the offerings by fire to the LORD. Thus the priest shall make atonement on your behalf for the sin that you have committed, and you shall be forgiven.

5 When any of you sin in that you have heard a public adjuration to

---

5:1–13—Confession forms an important element in the ritual experience of forgiveness. These

instructions address both failure to do something and doing something prohibited. When the

testify and—though able to testify as one who has seen or learned of the matter—do not speak up, you are subject to punishment. ²Or when any of you touch any unclean thing—whether the carcass of an unclean beast or the carcass of unclean livestock or the carcass of an unclean swarming thing—and are unaware of it, you have become unclean, and are guilty. ³Or when you touch human uncleanness—any uncleanness by which one can become unclean—and are unaware of it, when you come to know it, you shall be guilty. ⁴Or when any of you utter aloud a rash oath for a bad or a good purpose, whatever people utter in an oath, and are unaware of it, when you come to know it, you shall in any of these be guilty. ⁵When you realize your guilt in any of these, you shall confess the sin that you have committed. ⁶And you shall bring to the LORD, as your penalty for the sin that you have committed, a female from the flock, a sheep or a goat, as a sin offering; and the priest shall make atonement on your behalf for your sin.

7 But if you cannot afford a sheep, you shall bring to the LORD, as your penalty for the sin that you have committed, two turtledoves or two pigeons, one for a sin offering and the other for a burnt offering. ⁸You shall bring them to the priest, who shall offer first the one for the sin offering, wringing its head at the nape without severing it. ⁹He shall sprinkle some of the blood of the sin offering on the side of the altar, while the rest of the blood shall be drained out at the base of the altar; it is a sin offering. ¹⁰And the second he shall offer for a burnt offering according to the regulation. Thus the priest shall make atonement on your behalf for the sin that you have committed, and you shall be forgiven.

11 But if you cannot afford two turtledoves or two pigeons, you shall bring as your offering for the sin that you have committed one-tenth of an ephah of choice flour for a sin offering; you shall not put oil on it or lay frankincense on it, for it is a sin offering. ¹²You shall bring it to the priest, and the priest shall scoop up a handful of it as its memorial portion, and turn this into smoke on the altar, with the offerings by fire to the LORD; it is a sin offering. ¹³Thus the priest shall make atonement on your behalf for whichever of these sins you have committed, and you shall be forgiven. Like the grain offering, the rest shall be for the priest.

Offerings with Restitution

14 The LORD spoke to Moses, saying: ¹⁵When any of you commit a trespass and sin unintentionally in any of the holy things of the LORD, you shall bring, as your guilt offering to the LORD, a ram without blemish from the flock, convertible into silver by the sanctuary shekel; it is a guilt offering. ¹⁶And you shall make restitution for the holy thing in which you were remiss, and shall add one-fifth to it and give it to the priest. The priest shall make atonement on your behalf with the ram of the guilt offering, and you shall be forgiven.

17 If any of you sin without knowing

---

individual realizes the wrong that has been done and experiences guilt, confession and sacrifice lead to forgiveness. Confession includes, minimally, both the recognition that one has acted wrongly toward God, another human being, or the community, and a willingness to accept responsibility for one's actions through taking steps to set matters right.

The emphasis placed on guilt takes human actions, feelings, and responsibility seriously. When guilt is experienced, a person must take immediate steps to set things right. Importantly, YHWH remains present in the midst of the human community even in the midst of wrong-doing!

5:14–6:7 The Guilt Offering

5:14–16—*Trespass* is viewed as a faithless act that disturbs or violates the integrity of the holy realm. It is a misuse of holy things dedicated to YHWH, e.g., land, clothing, animals, and sacrificial foods. Reparation must be made so that what was misappropriated is restored. The text focuses on the restoration of the sacred realm, rather than punishment of the trespasser.

it, doing any of the things that by the LORD's commandments ought not to be done, you have incurred guilt, and are subject to punishment. [18] You shall bring to the priest a ram without blemish from the flock, or the equivalent, as a guilt offering; and the priest shall make atonement on your behalf for the error that you committed unintentionally, and you shall be forgiven. [19] It is a guilt offering; you have incurred guilt before the LORD.

6 [a] The LORD spoke to Moses, saying: [2] When any of you sin and commit a trespass against the LORD by deceiving a neighbor in a matter of a deposit or a pledge, or by robbery, or if you have defrauded a neighbor, [3] or have found something lost and lied about it—if you swear falsely regarding any of the various things that one may do and sin thereby— [4] when you have sinned and realize your guilt, and would restore what you took by robbery or by fraud or the deposit that was committed to you, or the lost thing that you found, [5] or anything else about which you have sworn falsely, you shall repay the principal amount and shall add one-fifth to it. You shall pay it to its owner when you realize your guilt. [6] And you shall bring to the priest, as your guilt offering to the LORD, a ram without blemish from the flock, or its equivalent, for a guilt offering. [7] The priest shall make atonement on your behalf before the LORD, and you shall be forgiven for any of the

things that one may do and incur guilt thereby.

Instructions concerning Sacrifices

[8b] The LORD spoke to Moses, saying: [9] Command Aaron and his sons, saying: This is the ritual of the burnt offering. The burnt offering itself shall remain on the hearth upon the altar all night until the morning, while the fire on the altar shall be kept burning. [10] The priest shall put on his linen vestments after putting on his linen undergarments next to his body; and he shall take up the ashes to which the fire has reduced the burnt offering on the altar, and place them beside the altar. [11] Then he shall take off his vestments and put on other garments, and carry the ashes out to a clean place outside the camp. [12] The fire on the altar shall be kept burning; it shall not go out. Every morning the priest shall add wood to it, lay out the burnt offering on it, and turn into smoke the fat pieces of the offerings of well-being. [13] A perpetual fire shall be kept burning on the altar; it shall not go out.

14 This is the ritual of the grain offering: The sons of Aaron shall offer it before the LORD, in front of the altar. [15] They shall take from it a handful of the choice flour and oil of the grain offering, with all the frankincense that is on the offering, and they shall turn its memorial portion into smoke on the altar as a pleasing odor to the LORD.

[a] Ch 5.20 in Heb   [b] Ch 6.1 in Heb

6:1–7—Actions against another person that are viewed as a trespass against YHWH have to do with *swearing falsely* (vv. 3, 5). Such oaths were sacred and to swear a false oath was to misuse and violate YHWH's integrity. Deceiving a neighbor, withholding something due another person, lying about finding something lost by another, are viewed as acts of fraud and treachery. The false oath seeks to hide the fraudulent act by invoking the sanctity of YHWH.

Words have power. Dishonest words designed to add to one's own wealth or well-being are sinful because they harm another person. They also constitute a treacherous act against YHWH. YHWH values human relationships of integrity

and honesty. Indeed, they have a significant impact on the sacred realm and the life of YHWH. Human words must reflect the integrity and honesty that are demanded in social relationships.

6:8–7:38 Sacrifices and Offerings: Second Series

6:8–13 The Burnt Offering and the Altar

The holy fire on the outer altar must be kept burning even when the altar is cleaned of its ashes. This fire originates with YHWH (not reported until 9:24) and is the only fire allowed inside the sacred precincts (see the story of Nadab and Abihu in chap. 10).

6:14–23 The Grain Offering (see chap. 2)

¹⁶ Aaron and his sons shall eat what is left of it; it shall be eaten as unleavened cakes in a holy place; in the court of the tent of meeting they shall eat it. ¹⁷ It shall not be baked with leaven. I have given it as their portion of my offerings by fire; it is most holy, like the sin offering and the guilt offering. ¹⁸ Every male among the descendants of Aaron shall eat of it, as their perpetual due throughout your generations, from the LORD's offerings by fire; anything that touches them shall become holy.

19 The LORD spoke to Moses, saying: ²⁰ This is the offering that Aaron and his sons shall offer to the LORD on the day when he is anointed: one-tenth of an ephah of choice flour as a regular offering, half of it in the morning and half in the evening. ²¹ It shall be made with oil on a griddle; you shall bring it well soaked, as a grain offering of baked*a* pieces, and you shall present it as a pleasing odor to the LORD. ²² And so the priest, anointed from among Aaron's descendants as a successor, shall prepare it; it is the LORD's—a perpetual due—to be turned entirely into smoke. ²³ Every grain offering of a priest shall be wholly burned; it shall not be eaten.

24 The LORD spoke to Moses, saying: ²⁵ Speak to Aaron and his sons, saying: This is the ritual of the sin offering. The sin offering shall be slaughtered before the LORD at the spot where the burnt offering is slaughtered; it is most holy. ²⁶ The priest who offers it as a sin offering shall eat of it; it shall be eaten in a holy place, in the court of the tent of meeting. ²⁷ Whatever touches its flesh shall become holy; and when any of its blood is spattered on a garment, you shall wash the bespattered part in a holy place. ²⁸ An earthen vessel in which it was boiled shall be broken; but if it is boiled in a bronze vessel, that shall be scoured and rinsed in water. ²⁹ Every male among the priests shall eat of it; it is most holy. ³⁰ But no sin offering shall be eaten from which any blood is brought into the tent of meeting for atonement in the holy place; it shall be burned with fire.

7 This is the ritual of the guilt offering. It is most holy; ²at the spot where the burnt offering is slaughtered, they shall slaughter the guilt offering, and its blood shall be dashed against all sides of the altar. ³ All its fat shall be offered: the broad tail, the fat that covers the entrails, ⁴ the two kidneys with the fat that is on them at the loins, and the appendage of the liver, which shall be removed with the kidneys. ⁵ The priest shall turn them into smoke on the altar as an offering by fire to the LORD; it is a guilt offering. ⁶ Every male among the priests shall eat of it; it shall be eaten in a holy place; it is most holy.

7 The guilt offering is like the sin offering, there is the same ritual for them; the priest who makes atonement with it shall have it. ⁸ So, too, the priest who offers anyone's burnt offering shall keep the skin of the burnt offering that he has offered. ⁹ And every grain offering baked in the oven, and all that is prepared in a pan or on a griddle, shall belong to the priest who offers it. ¹⁰ But every other grain offering, mixed with

a Meaning of Heb uncertain

6:24–30 The Sin Offering (cf. 4:1–5:13)

The priest who puts the blood of the *sin offering* on the altar must eat a portion of the animal (unless, as in the case of the high priest or the community, its blood is brought inside the tent; see 4:3–31) The "sin" or "impurity" removed from the altar must be eliminated. As "sin eaters" and "impurity eaters" the priests "bear away" the sins and impurities of the Israelites. The importance of bearing the sin of another has played a significant role in Christian theology concerned with the death of Jesus. Such "sin bearing" also has important implications for the daily practice of ministry within the community of faith and in the world. The goal of freedom enacted in the exodus, proclaimed in jubilee, and promised by Jesus generates an image of "bearing" away the sin, guilt, oppression, and suffering of others in a world all too often experienced in terms of judgment, dehumanization, and pain.

7:1–10 The Guilt Offering (see 5:14–6:7)

oil or dry, shall belong to all the sons of Aaron equally.

Further Instructions

11 This is the ritual of the sacrifice of the offering of well-being that one may offer to the LORD. 12 If you offer it for thanksgiving, you shall offer with the thank offering unleavened cakes mixed with oil, unleavened wafers spread with oil, and cakes of choice flour well soaked in oil. 13 With your thanksgiving sacrifice of well-being you shall bring your offering with cakes of leavened bread. 14 From this you shall offer one cake from each offering, as a gift to the LORD; it shall belong to the priest who dashes the blood of the offering of well-being. 15 And the flesh of your thanksgiving sacrifice of well-being shall be eaten on the day it is offered; you shall not leave any of it until morning. 16 But if the sacrifice you offer is a votive offering or a freewill offering, it shall be eaten on the day that you offer your sacrifice, and what is left of it shall be eaten the next day; 17 but what is left of the flesh of the sacrifice shall be burned up on the third day. 18 If any of the flesh of your sacrifice of well-being is eaten on the third day, it shall not be acceptable, nor shall it be credited to the one who offers it; it shall be an abomination, and the one who eats of it shall incur guilt.

19 Flesh that touches any unclean thing shall not be eaten; it shall be burned up. As for other flesh, all who are clean may eat such flesh. 20 But those who eat flesh from the LORD's sacrifice of well-being while in a state of uncleanness shall be cut off from their kin. 21 When any one of you touches any unclean thing—human uncleanness or an unclean animal or any unclean creature—and then eats flesh from the LORD's sacrifice of well-being, you shall be cut off from your kin.

22 The LORD spoke to Moses, saying: 23 Speak to the people of Israel, saying: You shall eat no fat of ox or sheep or goat. 24 The fat of an animal that died or was torn by wild animals may be put to any other use, but you must not eat it. 25 If any one of you eats the fat from an animal of which an offering by fire may be made to the LORD, you who eat it shall be cut off from your kin. 26 You must not eat any blood whatever, either of bird or of animal, in any of your settlements. 27 Any one of you who eats any blood shall be cut off from your kin.

28 The LORD spoke to Moses, saying: 29 Speak to the people of Israel, saying: Any one of you who would offer to the LORD your sacrifice of well-being must yourself bring to the LORD your offering from your sacrifice of well-being. 30 Your own hands shall bring the LORD's offering by fire; you shall bring the fat with the breast, so that the breast may be raised as an elevation offering before the LORD. 31 The priest shall turn the fat into smoke on the altar, but the breast shall belong to Aaron and his sons. 32 And the right thigh from your sacrifices of well-being you shall give to the priest as an offering; 33 the one among the sons of Aaron who offers the blood and fat of the offering of well-being shall have the right thigh for a portion. 34 For I have taken the breast of the elevation offering, and the thigh that is offered, from the people of Israel, from their sacrifices of well-being, and have given them to Aaron the priest and to his sons, as a perpetual due from the people of Israel. 35 This is the portion allotted to Aaron and to his sons from the offerings made by fire to the LORD, once they have been brought forward to serve the LORD as priests; 36 these the LORD commanded to be given them, when he anointed them, as a perpetual

---

7:11–36 The Well-Being Offering (see 3:1–17)

7:22–26—Both the *fat* (cf. 3:16b–17) and the *blood* (see 17:10–13) belong to YHWH, and must be "given" to YHWH on the altar. Although

no explanation is provided for the ruling, both are viewed as "sacred" precisely because they are "set apart" for YHWH.

due from the people of Israel throughout their generations.

37 This is the ritual of the burnt offering, the grain offering, the sin offering,
the guilt offering, the offering of ordination, and the sacrifice of well-being,
38 which the LORD commanded Moses
on Mount Sinai, when he commanded
the people of Israel to bring their offerings to the LORD, in the wilderness of
Sinai.

The Rites of Ordination

8 The LORD spoke to Moses, saying:
2 Take Aaron and his sons with him,
the vestments, the anointing oil, the bull

of sin offering, the two rams, and the basket of unleavened bread; 3 and assemble
the whole congregation at the entrance
of the tent of meeting. 4 And Moses did
as the LORD commanded him. When
the congregation was assembled at the
entrance of the tent of meeting, 5 Moses
said to the congregation, "This is what
the LORD has commanded to be done."

6 Then Moses brought Aaron and his
sons forward, and washed them with
water. 7 He put the tunic on him, fastened the sash around him, clothed him
with the robe, and put the ephod on
him. He then put the decorated band of
the ephod around him, tying the ephod

**7:37–38 The Conclusion of the Sacrificial
Instructions**

These verses locate YHWH's speech with Moses
on Mount Sinai, whereas the introductory verse,
Lev. 1:1, located YHWH's speech in the tent
of meeting. The inclusion of both suggests that
Israel recognized both (1) the ongoing nature
of YHWH's "speaking" with them and (2) the
possibility that such speaking might take place
in a variety of places. No effort is made to limit
the ways in which God might speak to, provide
instruction for, and continue to interact with the
human community. Although the word of YHWH
spoken at Sinai in the past remains foundational,
it did not end YHWH's interaction with the community.

**8:1–10:20 Consecration, Ordination, Sin,
and Death**

The narrative materials in chaps. 8–10 point back
to the instructions for the ordination of the priesthood (Exod. 29:1–37) and the construction of the
tabernacle (Exod. 35–40) and, at the same time,
look forward to the purity instructions in Lev.
11–15 and the annual day of purification in
chap. 16.

The ordination ritual is both a rite of passage
(Aaron and his sons are moved from their ordinary status in Israel into their institutional status
as priests) and a rite of founding (the institution of the priesthood comes into being in, by,
and through this ritual). Status and location are
intertwined through common ritual anointings.
The priests, who are holy, work in the place that
is holy.

**8:1–36 Consecration of the Tabernacle
and the Priests**

8:3–4—The ritual takes place at the door of *the
tent of meeting*, the primary location of the
priestly sacrificial ministry as well as the place in

which they will function as mediators between
YHWH and the community. The priests are lo-
cated institutionally within the ritual space where
Israel meets with and encounters YHWH.

Because the priesthood is a social institution,
the ritual founding of that institution must take
place within the context of and presence of the
whole community. The priests come from the
community and are set apart to represent, to
stand in for, the community.

The priesthood is part of the divine vision for
the Israelite community. Just as the tabernacle
was constructed "as the LORD commanded" (see
Exod. 40:16–33), so also the priesthood must be
"constructed" *as the LORD commanded* (see Lev.
8:5, 9, 13, 17, 21, 29, 34, 36). The "priestly" ministry reflects one of the ways in which YHWH has
chosen to interact with the Israelite community.

8:6—The *water* functions both to "purify" the
priests and to mark their entry into the ritual
process. Water marks both exits out of and
entries into a variety of states and conditions.
For example, passage through the Red Sea marks
Israel's exit out of Egypt (Exod. 14–15), and the
passage through the Jordan River marks the
people's entry into the land of promise (Josh.
3–4). Paul draws on this imagery in his discussion
of baptism (Rom. 6:1–11). For Paul, the water
of baptism marks an exit out of the old life and
entry into the new life in Christ. Ritual and story
often interact to create a way of thinking about
the world, about God, about human existence,
and about redemption.

8:7–12—Aaron's special clothing marks the distinction between the high priest and the ordinary
priest, as does his special anointing (see Exod.
30:22–33). In conjunction with the anointing of
the tabernacle this creates a common status for
Aaron and the tabernacle.

to him with it. [8] He placed the breastpiece on him, and in the breastpiece he put the Urim and the Thummim. [9] And he set the turban on his head, and on the turban, in front, he set the golden ornament, the holy crown, as the LORD commanded Moses.

10 Then Moses took the anointing oil and anointed the tabernacle and all that was in it, and consecrated them. [11] He sprinkled some of it on the altar seven times, and anointed the altar and all its utensils, and the basin and its base, to consecrate them. [12] He poured some of the anointing oil on Aaron's head and anointed him, to consecrate him. [13] And Moses brought forward Aaron's sons, and clothed them with tunics, and fastened sashes around them, and tied headdresses on them, as the LORD commanded Moses.

14 He led forward the bull of sin offering; and Aaron and his sons laid their hands upon the head of the bull of sin offering, [15] and it was slaughtered. Moses took the blood and with his finger put some on each of the horns of the altar, purifying the altar; then he poured out the blood at the base of the altar. Thus he consecrated it, to make atonement for it. [16] Moses took all the fat that was around the entrails, and the appendage of the liver, and the two kidneys with their fat, and turned them into smoke on the altar. [17] But the bull itself, its skin and flesh and its dung, he burned with fire outside the camp, as the LORD commanded Moses.

18 Then he brought forward the ram of burnt offering. Aaron and his sons laid their hands on the head of the ram, [19] and it was slaughtered. Moses dashed the blood against all sides of the altar. [20] The ram was cut into its parts, and Moses turned into smoke the head and the parts and the suet. [21] And after the entrails and the legs were washed with water, Moses turned into smoke the whole ram on the altar; it was a burnt offering for a pleasing odor, an offering by fire to the LORD, as the LORD commanded Moses.

22 Then he brought forward the second ram, the ram of ordination. Aaron and his sons laid their hands on the head of the ram, [23] and it was slaughtered. Moses took some of its blood and put it on the lobe of Aaron's right ear and on the thumb of his right hand and on the big toe of his right foot. [24] After Aaron's sons were brought forward, Moses put some of the blood on the lobes of their right ears and on the thumbs of their right hands and on the big toes of their right feet; and Moses dashed the rest of the blood against all sides of the altar. [25] He took the fat—the broad tail, all the fat that was around the entrails, the appendage of the liver, and the two kidneys with their fat—and the right thigh. [26] From the basket of unleavened bread that was before the LORD, he took one cake of unleavened bread, one cake of bread with oil, and one wafer, and placed them on the fat and on the right thigh. [27] He placed all these on the palms of Aaron and on the palms of his sons, and raised them as an elevation offering before the LORD. [28] Then Moses took them from their hands and turned them into smoke on the altar with the burnt offering. This was an ordination offering

---

8:14–17—Moses places the blood of the sin offering on the horns of the altar in order to "purify" it and then pours out the rest of the blood at the base of the altar in order to "consecrate" it (cf. 4:1–5:13; 6:24–30). The blood on the horns cleanses the altar of impurities, whereas the blood poured at the base restores the integrity of the holy realm ("reconsecrates" it).

8:22–29—Placing the blood on the extremities is found elsewhere only in the ritual to move a person recovered from an unclean skin disorder back into the camp (see 14:12–20). In both cases, the ritual effects passage—for the priests, from the "common" world into the holy (on the dangers of this realm and priestly activity, see Num. 16–17), and for the one recovered from the unclean skin disorder, from life outside the camp and community (a state not unlike death) back into life inside the camp and community.

for a pleasing odor, an offering by fire to the LORD. ²⁹ Moses took the breast and raised it as an elevation offering before the LORD; it was Moses' portion of the ram of ordination, as the LORD commanded Moses.

30 Then Moses took some of the anointing oil and some of the blood that was on the altar and sprinkled them on Aaron and his vestments, and also on his sons and their vestments. Thus he consecrated Aaron and his vestments, and also his sons and their vestments.

31 And Moses said to Aaron and his sons, "Boil the flesh at the entrance of the tent of meeting, and eat it there with the bread that is in the basket of ordination offerings, as I was commanded, 'Aaron and his sons shall eat it'; ³² and what remains of the flesh and the bread you shall burn with fire. ³³ You shall not go outside the entrance of the tent of meeting for seven days, until the day when your period of ordination is completed. For it will take seven days to ordain you; ³⁴ as has been done today, the LORD has commanded to be done to make atonement for you. ³⁵ You shall remain at the entrance of the tent of meeting day and night for seven days, keeping the LORD's charge so that you do not die; for so I am commanded." ³⁶ Aaron and his sons did all the things that the LORD commanded through Moses.

Aaron's Priesthood Inaugurated

9 On the eighth day Moses summoned Aaron and his sons and the elders of Israel. ² He said to Aaron, "Take a bull calf for a sin offering and a ram for a burnt offering, without blemish, and offer them before the LORD. ³ And say to the people of Israel, 'Take a male goat for a sin offering; a calf and a lamb, yearlings without blemish, for a burnt offering; ⁴ and an ox and a ram for an offering of well-being to sacrifice before the LORD; and a grain offering mixed with oil. For today the LORD will appear to you.'" ⁵ They brought what Moses commanded to the front of the tent of meeting; and the whole congregation drew near and stood before the LORD. ⁶ And Moses said, "This is the thing that the LORD commanded you to do, so that the glory of the LORD may appear to you." ⁷ Then Moses said to Aaron, "Draw near to the altar and sacrifice your sin offering and your burnt offering, and make atonement for yourself and for the people; and sacrifice the offering of the people, and make atonement for them; as the LORD has commanded."

8 Aaron drew near to the altar, and slaughtered the calf of the sin offering, which was for himself. ⁹ The sons of Aaron presented the blood to him, and he dipped his finger in the blood and put it on the horns of the altar; and the rest of the blood he poured out at the base of the altar. ¹⁰ But the fat, the kidneys, and the appendage of the liver from the sin offering he turned into smoke on the altar, as the LORD commanded Moses; ¹¹ and the flesh and the skin he burned with fire outside the camp.

12 Then he slaughtered the burnt offering. Aaron's sons brought him the

---

8:30–36—The *seven days* reflect a major rite of passage, e.g., 12:2, for a woman who has given birth to a male child; 14:8–9, for a person recovered from an unclean skin disorder; 15:19, for a woman having her menstrual flow; 15:24, for a man after sexual intercourse with a woman during her menstrual flow; Num. 19:11, for a person defiled by a corpse. Seven is related to the movement toward wholeness expressed, for example, in the creation account in Gen. 1:1–2:4a. These rituals recognize and reflect a view of life as movement and process from one moment to another, from one situation to another.

9:1–24 The Inauguration of the Priestly Cult

9:1–7—On the *eighth day* of the ritual process, the priests perform their sacrificial duties for the first time, as commanded by YHWH. Creation, the community, the tabernacle, and the priesthood all reflect the divine will and word. The world envisioned and spoken by YHWH is concretized by the ritual actions of humans. World construction is understood as the common and shared work of YHWH and the human community.

blood, and he dashed it against all sides of the altar. [13] And they brought him the burnt offering piece by piece, and the head, which he turned into smoke on the altar. [14] He washed the entrails and the legs and, with the burnt offering, turned them into smoke on the altar.

15 Next he presented the people's offering. He took the goat of the sin offering that was for the people, and slaughtered it, and presented it as a sin offering like the first one. [16] He presented the burnt offering, and sacrificed it according to regulation. [17] He presented the grain offering, and, taking a handful of it, he turned it into smoke on the altar, in addition to the burnt offering of the morning.

18 He slaughtered the ox and the ram as a sacrifice of well-being for the people. Aaron's sons brought him the blood, which he dashed against all sides of the altar, [19] and the fat of the ox and of the ram—the broad tail, the fat that covers the entrails, the two kidneys and the fat on them,*a* and the appendage of the liver. [20] They first laid the fat on the breasts, and the fat was turned into smoke on the altar; [21] and the breasts and the right thigh Aaron raised as an elevation offering before the LORD, as Moses had commanded.

22 Aaron lifted his hands toward the people and blessed them; and he came down after sacrificing the sin offering, the burnt offering, and the offering of well-being. [23] Moses and Aaron entered the tent of meeting, and then came out and blessed the people; and the glory of the LORD appeared to all the people. [24] Fire came out from the LORD and consumed the burnt offering and the fat on the altar; and when all the people saw it, they shouted and fell on their faces.

Nadab and Abihu

10 Now Aaron's sons, Nadab and Abihu, each took his censer, put fire in it, and laid incense on it; and they offered unholy fire before the LORD, such as he had not commanded them. [2] And fire came out from the presence of the LORD and consumed them, and they died before the LORD. [3] Then Moses said to Aaron, "This is what the LORD meant when he said,

'Through those who are near me
    I will show myself holy,

a Gk: Heb *the broad tail, and that which covers, and the kidneys*

9:22–23a—(see Num. 6:22–27) Aaron's blessing is related to and reflects the blessing of God at the time of creation (see Gen. 1:28) as well as the blessing promised to the ancestors (e.g., Gen. 12:1–3; 22:15–19; 28:10–17). Divine blessing and promise converge in the formation of community and are experienced most fully in the context of community. Aaron's blessing marks Israel's emergence as a faith community that dwells with and travels through the wilderness with YHWH.

9:23b–24—At the conclusion of the priestly blessing, the divine *glory*, initially seen on top of the mountain by all of Israel (Exod. 24:15–18; cf. Exod. 40:34–38), takes up residence in the tabernacle in the sight of the whole community. YHWH's presence in the tabernacle indicates the divine commitment to the ongoing life of the people. The divine *fire*, a perpetual marker of the divine presence in the midst of the community, ignites the altar (cf. Lev. 6:8–13). The early church saw tongues of fire at Pentecost as a sign that the divine presence had come to dwell in the midst of the worshiping community (Acts 2:1–4).

10:1–20 The Death of Nadab and Abihu
The story takes place later on the same day as the inauguration of the tabernacle cult (chap. 9). A low point in Israel's story immediately follows a high point. This is a common narrative technique, e.g., the worship of the golden calf just after entering into covenant with YHWH (Exod. 19–24 and 32–34); David's affair with Bathsheba shortly after YHWH declares that David's rule has divine backing (2 Sam. 7 and 12). The narrative expresses the interconnectedness of divine hope and human failure. In the face of mercy, grace, and redemption, humans act unfaithfully, without integrity, and with arrogance.

Nadab and Abihu bring "strange" fire into the holy place, fire that did not originate in the holy place (see Lev. 9:24). This violation of boundaries disrupts the holy place and angers YHWH. Their deaths turned the joy and glory of the day into a day of sorrow, mourning, and conflict. The divine presence has taken up residence in the midst of an unfaithful and arrogant group—human beings!

and before all the people
I will be glorified.'"
And Aaron was silent.

4 Moses summoned Mishael and Elzaphan, sons of Uzziel the uncle of Aaron, and said to them, "Come forward, and carry your kinsmen away from the front of the sanctuary to a place outside the camp." **5** They came forward and carried them by their tunics out of the camp, as Moses had ordered. **6** And Moses said to Aaron and to his sons Eleazar and Ithamar, "Do not dishevel your hair, and do not tear your vestments, or you will die and wrath will strike all the congregation; but your kindred, the whole house of Israel, may mourn the burning that the LORD has sent. **7** You shall not go outside the entrance of the tent of meeting, or you will die; for the anointing oil of the LORD is on you." And they did as Moses had ordered.

8 And the LORD spoke to Aaron: **9** Drink no wine or strong drink, neither you nor your sons, when you enter the tent of meeting, that you may not die; it is a statute forever throughout your generations. **10** You are to distinguish between the holy and the common, and between the unclean and the clean; **11** and you are to teach the people of Israel all the statutes that the LORD has spoken to them through Moses.

12 Moses spoke to Aaron and to his remaining sons, Eleazar and Ithamar: Take the grain offering that is left from the LORD's offerings by fire, and eat it unleavened beside the altar, for it is most holy; **13** you shall eat it in a holy place, because it is your due and your sons' due, from the offerings by fire to the LORD; for so I am commanded. **14** But the breast that is elevated and the thigh that is raised, you and your sons and daughters as well may eat in any clean place; for they have been assigned to you and your children from the sacrifices of the offerings of well-being of the people of Israel. **15** The thigh that is raised and the breast that is elevated they shall bring, together with the offerings by fire of the fat, to raise for an elevation offering before the LORD; they are to be your due and that of your children forever, as the LORD has commanded.

16 Then Moses made inquiry about the goat of the sin offering, and—it had already been burned! He was angry with Eleazar and Ithamar, Aaron's remaining sons, and said, **17** "Why did you not eat the sin offering in the sacred area? For it is most holy, and God[a] has given it to you that you may remove the guilt of the congregation, to make atonement on their behalf before the LORD. **18** Its blood was not brought into the inner part of the sanctuary. You should certainly have eaten it in the sanctuary, as I commanded." **19** And Aaron spoke to Moses, "See, today they offered their sin offering and their burnt offering before the LORD; and yet such things as these have befallen me! If I had eaten the sin offering today, would it have been agreeable to the LORD?" **20** And when Moses heard that, he agreed.

a Heb *he*

10:10–11—The priests are to distinguish between (to separate) *the holy and the common, the unclean and the clean*, and to teach (from the same root as "torah") the statutes of YHWH. Just as YHWH separated the basic elements in creation, e.g., sky, earth, water (Gen. 1:1–2:4a), so the priests are to keep separate the holy and common, the clean and the unclean. The "very good" order of creation provides the context for the priestly ministry and the life of the community.

10:16–20 Conflict between Moses and Aaron

Moses is angered because the priests *did not eat the sin offering* as instructed by YHWH (see 6:24–30). Aaron says, in effect, "Are we to do that when we sit in the midst of this catastrophe? We have no idea whether the normal rules are operative or not!" This encounter reflects conflict between prophetic and priestly groups concerning the divinely sanctioned interpreter of the divine will in new and unexpected situations. The text indicates a freedom of interpretation, as Moses and Aaron seek to make sense of the "word of YHWH" *and* a tragic situation. Conflict, disagreement, and conversation are all parts of the process that seeks to discover and understand the will of YHWH for the community.

Clean and Unclean Foods

11 The LORD spoke to Moses and Aaron, saying to them: ² Speak to the people of Israel, saying:

From among all the land animals, these are the creatures that you may eat. ³ Any animal that has divided hoofs and is cleft-footed and chews the cud—such you may eat. ⁴ But among those that chew the cud or have divided hoofs, you shall not eat the following: the camel, for even though it chews the cud, it does not have divided hoofs; it is unclean for you. ⁵ The rock badger, for even though it chews the cud, it does not have divided hoofs; it is unclean for you. ⁶ The hare, for even though it chews the cud, it does not have divided hoofs; it is unclean for you. ⁷ The pig, for even though it has divided hoofs and is cleft-footed, it does not chew the cud; it is unclean for you. ⁸ Of their flesh you shall not eat, and their carcasses you shall not touch; they are unclean for you.

9 These you may eat, of all that are in the waters. Everything in the waters that has fins and scales, whether in the seas or in the streams—such you may eat. ¹⁰ But anything in the seas or the streams that does not have fins and scales, of the swarming creatures in the waters and among all the other living creatures that are in the waters—they are detestable to you ¹¹ and detestable they shall remain. Of their flesh you shall not eat, and their carcasses you shall regard as detestable. ¹² Everything in the waters that does not have fins and scales is detestable to you.

13 These you shall regard as detestable among the birds. They shall not be eaten; they are an abomination: the eagle, the vulture, the osprey, ¹⁴ the buzzard, the kite of any kind; ¹⁵ every raven of any kind; ¹⁶ the ostrich, the nighthawk, the sea gull, the hawk of any kind; ¹⁷ the little owl, the cormorant, the great owl, ¹⁸ the water hen, the desert owl,ᵃ the carrion vulture, ¹⁹ the stork, the heron of any kind, the hoopoe, and the bat.ᵇ

20 All winged insects that walk upon all fours are detestable to you. ²¹ But among the winged insects that walk on all fours you may eat those that have jointed legs above their feet, with which to leap on the ground. ²² Of them you may eat: the locust according to its kind, the bald locust according to its kind, the cricket according to its kind, and the

---

ᵃ Or pelican ᵇ Identification of several of the birds in verses 13-19 is uncertain

---

11:1–16:34 Purity and Impurity Instructions

The purity and impurity instructions play a crucial role in Israel's faith and practice. They are concerned with the construction and maintenance of a community that lives in the presence of YHWH. The issues addressed are real flesh-and-blood issues: food and death, childbirth, flaking skin disorders, and genital flows. Far from being esoteric rules, these instructions locate everyday human realities in the context of the sacred. The practice of holiness takes place within the context of the mundane realities of concrete human existence.

11:1–47 Clean and Unclean Foods

The division of animals reflects, to a degree, the basic categories of creation, i.e., land, air, and water (Gen. 1:1–2:4a). The dietary instructions take shape within the context of creation theology. At the same time, the instructions recognize a relationship between God's altar and the human table. The food rulings are a means by which the Israelite community distinguished (separated) itself from other communities and enacted its distinctive status as the people of God. In observing the rulings, an individual identified with the holy community.

11:2–9—The domesticated bovine provides the basic pattern for edible land animals, defined in this case in terms of *hoofs* that are divided and the chewing of *cud*. The "home" animal, the everyday common domesticated animal, provides a model for engaging the sacred and the holy.

11:9–12—Animals from the water must have both *fins and scales* in order to be eaten. In this case, appearance and means of movement determine "acceptable" and "normal" food.

11:13–19—The prohibited "air" creatures, at least those identified with certainty, are scavengers, likely to have ingested blood (for the prohibition of blood, see 17:10–13; cf. Gen. 9:4–6).

11:20–23—Insects that walk on all four legs are excluded, although those with jointed legs that hop are acceptable. Physical features and means of mobility determine edible insects.

grasshopper according to its kind. ²³ But all other winged insects that have four feet are detestable to you.

Unclean Animals

24 By these you shall become unclean; whoever touches the carcass of any of them shall be unclean until the evening, ²⁵ and whoever carries any part of the carcass of any of them shall wash his clothes and be unclean until the evening. ²⁶ Every animal that has divided hoofs but is not cleft-footed or does not chew the cud is unclean for you; everyone who touches one of them shall be unclean. ²⁷ All that walk on their paws, among the animals that walk on all fours, are unclean for you; whoever touches the carcass of any of them shall be unclean until the evening, ²⁸ and the one who carries the carcass shall wash his clothes and be unclean until the evening; they are unclean for you.

29 These are unclean for you among the creatures that swarm upon the earth: the weasel, the mouse, the great lizard according to its kind, ³⁰ the gecko, the land crocodile, the lizard, the sand lizard, and the chameleon. ³¹ These are unclean for you among all that swarm; whoever touches one of them when they are dead shall be unclean until the evening. ³² And anything upon which any of them falls when they are dead shall be unclean, whether an article of wood or cloth or skin or sacking, any article that is used for any purpose; it shall be

dipped into water, and it shall be unclean until the evening, and then it shall be clean. ³³ And if any of them falls into any earthen vessel, all that is in it shall be unclean, and you shall break the vessel. ³⁴ Any food that could be eaten shall be unclean if water from any such vessel comes upon it; and any liquid that could be drunk shall be unclean if it was in any such vessel. ³⁵ Everything on which any part of the carcass falls shall be unclean; whether an oven or stove, it shall be broken in pieces; they are unclean, and shall remain unclean for you. ³⁶ But a spring or a cistern holding water shall be clean, while whatever touches the carcass in it shall be unclean. ³⁷ If any part of their carcass falls upon any seed set aside for sowing, it is clean; ³⁸ but if water is put on the seed and any part of their carcass falls on it, it is unclean for you.

39 If an animal of which you may eat dies, anyone who touches its carcass shall be unclean until the evening. ⁴⁰ Those who eat of its carcass shall wash their clothes and be unclean until the evening; and those who carry the carcass shall wash their clothes and be unclean until the evening.

41 All creatures that swarm upon the earth are detestable; they shall not be eaten. ⁴² Whatever moves on its belly, and whatever moves on all fours, or whatever has many feet, all the creatures that swarm upon the earth, you shall not eat; for they are detestable. ⁴³ You shall not make yourselves detestable

---

11:24–40—These verses address impurity generated through contact with the corpses of various animals, a reflection of Israel's concern to remain separate from the realm of death.

11:41–45—The prohibition concerning swarming things is conjoined with a call for Israel to *be holy* as YHWH is holy. The call to holiness is related both to the avoidance of prohibited creatures and to YHWH's deliverance of Israel from Egypt. Israel's story of redemption, YHWH's call for community holiness, and the dietary instructions are woven together to shape Israel's beliefs, practices, and community identity.

The convergence of creation theology, the association of altar and table, and the concern

for community practices and identity reflect significant elements of Christian communion. At the communion table, the satisfying of God's hunger for righteousness and the human desire for communion with the divine life come together in the bread and wine.

Jesus is reported to have declared all foods clean (see Mark 7:1–23). However, food is still able to function as one means by which a faith community is able to mark its identity and by which individuals are able to identify with the faith community. The table, the bread, and the wine identify Christian faith, practice, and community.

with any creature that swarms; you shall not defile yourselves with them, and so become unclean. **44** For I am the LORD your God; sanctify yourselves therefore, and be holy, for I am holy. You shall not defile yourselves with any swarming creature that moves on the earth. **45** For I am the LORD who brought you up from the land of Egypt, to be your God; you shall be holy, for I am holy.

46 This is the law pertaining to land animal and bird and every living creature that moves through the waters and every creature that swarms upon the earth, **47** to make a distinction between the unclean and the clean, and between the living creature that may be eaten and the living creature that may not be eaten.

Purification of Women after Childbirth

12 The LORD spoke to Moses, saying: **2** Speak to the people of Israel, saying:

If a woman conceives and bears a male child, she shall be ceremonially unclean seven days; as at the time of her menstruation, she shall be unclean. **3** On the eighth day the flesh of his foreskin shall be circumcised. **4** Her time of blood purification shall be thirty-three days; she shall not touch any holy thing, or come into the sanctuary, until the days of her purification are completed. **5** If she bears a female child, she shall be unclean two weeks, as in her menstruation; her time of blood purification shall be sixty-six days.

6 When the days of her purification are completed, whether for a son or for a daughter, she shall bring to the priest at the entrance of the tent of meeting a lamb in its first year for a burnt offering, and a pigeon or a turtledove for a sin offering. **7** He shall offer it before the LORD, and make atonement on her behalf; then she shall be clean from her flow of blood. This is the law for her who bears a child, male or female. **8** If she cannot afford a sheep, she shall take two turtledoves or two pigeons, one for a burnt offering and the other for a sin offering; and the priest shall make atonement on her behalf, and she shall be clean.

Leprosy, Varieties and Symptoms

13 The LORD spoke to Moses and Aaron, saying:

12:1–8 Childbirth

12:2—The instructions in this chapter are primarily addressed to the women of Israel (*if a woman*), those who would give birth, count the days of impurity, and present the purifying sacrifices. Childbirth was part of God's creative blessing of human beings (Gen. 1:28) and is not a sin that requires forgiveness. These instructions reflect Israel's purity concerns, not Israel's sin concerns. She presents a *purification* sacrifice, not a sin sacrifice (see Lev. 4:1–5:13). In addition, the text indicates what happens "if" and "when" a woman gives birth, not that a woman "must" give birth.

The impurity associated with childbirth is related to menstrual blood (vv. 2, 5; cf. v. 7). The woman's loss of blood through her reproductive organs is viewed as a loss of life ("the life is in the blood"; see Gen. 9:4; Lev. 17:10–13).

12:3—Circumcision provided a means by which the Israelites were able "to mark" their male children as members of the covenant community that God had promised their ancestors (Gen. 17:9–14).

12:4–5—The more extended time of impurity for the birth of a daughter recognizes that the daughter is herself a *female*, who will one day be capable of giving birth. The ruling recognizes power in the ability of women to give birth. This may account, in part, for the efforts of the (male) priests to set ritual boundaries around childbirth, and, as a result, to attempt to control female reproductive power.

13:1–14:57 Unclean Skin Disorders

13:1–44—The list of conditions described in the text is concerned not with determining a medical condition (the conditions described in the text are not clinical characteristics of "leprosy"), but with impurity. The priests are authorized to determine clean and unclean states (10:10). The skin conditions share a flaking away of the skin, as if it is being eaten away ("flaking away" like snow). These conditions reflect the decomposition of dead bodies, viewed as an encroachment of death into the life of the community (cf. Num. 12:10–15). Such disorders were thought to reflect a horror of some sort, possibly a mark of divine punishment or judgment.

2 When a person has on the skin of his body a swelling or an eruption or a spot, and it turns into a leprous[a] disease on the skin of his body, he shall be brought to Aaron the priest or to one of his sons the priests. [3] The priest shall examine the disease on the skin of his body, and if the hair in the diseased area has turned white and the disease appears to be deeper than the skin of his body, it is a leprous[a] disease; after the priest has examined him he shall pronounce him ceremonially unclean. [4] But if the spot is white in the skin of his body, and appears no deeper than the skin, and the hair in it has not turned white, the priest shall confine the diseased person for seven days. [5] The priest shall examine him on the seventh day, and if he sees that the disease is checked and the disease has not spread in the skin, then the priest shall confine him seven days more. [6] The priest shall examine him again on the seventh day, and if the disease has abated and the disease has not spread in the skin, the priest shall pronounce him clean; it is only an eruption; and he shall wash his clothes, and be clean. [7] But if the eruption spreads in the skin after he has shown himself to the priest for his cleansing, he shall appear again before the priest. [8] The priest shall make an examination, and if the eruption has spread in the skin, the priest shall pronounce him unclean; it is a leprous[a] disease.

9 When a person contracts a leprous[a] disease, he shall be brought to the priest. [10] The priest shall make an examination, and if there is a white swelling in the skin that has turned the hair white, and there is quick raw flesh in the swelling, [11] it is a chronic leprous[a] disease in the skin of his body. The priest shall pronounce him unclean; he shall not confine him, for he is unclean. [12] But if the disease breaks out in the skin, so that it covers all the skin of the diseased person from head to foot, so far as the priest can see, [13] then the priest shall make an examina-

tion, and if the disease has covered all his body, he shall pronounce him clean of the disease; since it has all turned white, he is clean. [14] But if raw flesh ever appears on him, he shall be unclean; [15] the priest shall examine the raw flesh and pronounce him unclean. Raw flesh is unclean, for it is a leprous[a] disease. [16] But if the raw flesh again turns white, he shall come to the priest; [17] the priest shall examine him, and if the disease has turned white, the priest shall pronounce the diseased person clean. He is clean.

18 When there is on the skin of one's body a boil that has healed, [19] and in the place of the boil there appears a white swelling or a reddish-white spot, it shall be shown to the priest. [20] The priest shall make an examination, and if it appears deeper than the skin and its hair has turned white, the priest shall pronounce him unclean; this is a leprous[a] disease, broken out in the boil. [21] But if the priest examines it and the hair on it is not white, nor is it deeper than the skin but has abated, the priest shall confine him seven days. [22] If it spreads in the skin, the priest shall pronounce him unclean; it is diseased. [23] But if the spot remains in one place and does not spread, it is the scar of the boil; the priest shall pronounce him clean.

24 Or, when the body has a burn on the skin and the raw flesh of the burn becomes a spot, reddish-white or white, [25] the priest shall examine it. If the hair in the spot has turned white and it appears deeper than the skin, it is a leprous[a] disease; it has broken out in the burn, and the priest shall pronounce him unclean. This is a leprous[a] disease. [26] But if the priest examines it and the hair in the spot is not white, and it is no deeper than the skin but has abated, the priest shall confine him seven days. [27] The priest shall examine him the seventh day; if it is spreading in the skin, the priest shall pronounce him unclean.

[a] A term for several skin diseases; precise meaning uncertain

This is a leprous[a] disease. 28 But if the spot remains in one place and does not spread in the skin but has abated, it is a swelling from the burn, and the priest shall pronounce him clean; for it is the scar of the burn.

29 When a man or woman has a disease on the head or in the beard, 30 the priest shall examine the disease. If it appears deeper than the skin and the hair in it is yellow and thin, the priest shall pronounce him unclean; it is an itch, a leprous[a] disease of the head or the beard. 31 If the priest examines the itching disease, and it appears no deeper than the skin and there is no black hair in it, the priest shall confine the person with the itching disease for seven days. 32 On the seventh day the priest shall examine the itch; if the itch has not spread, and there is no yellow hair in it, and the itch appears to be no deeper than the skin, 33 he shall shave, but the itch he shall not shave. The priest shall confine the person with the itch for seven days more. 34 On the seventh day the priest shall examine the itch; if the itch has not spread in the skin and it appears to be no deeper than the skin, the priest shall pronounce him clean. He shall wash his clothes and be clean. 35 But if the itch spreads in the skin after he was pronounced clean, 36 the priest shall examine him. If the itch has spread in the skin, the priest need not seek for the yellow hair; he is unclean. 37 But if in his eyes the itch is checked, and black hair has grown in it, the itch is healed, he is clean; and the priest shall pronounce him clean.

38 When a man or a woman has spots on the skin of the body, white spots, 39 the priest shall make an examination, and if the spots on the skin of the body are of a dull white, it is a rash that has broken out on the skin; he is clean.

40 If anyone loses the hair from his head, he is bald but he is clean. 41 If he loses the hair from his forehead and temples, he has baldness of the forehead but he is clean. 42 But if there is on the bald head or the bald forehead a reddish-white diseased spot, it is a leprous[a] disease breaking out on his bald head or his bald forehead. 43 The priest shall examine him; if the diseased swelling is reddish-white on his bald head or on his bald forehead, which resembles a leprous[a] disease in the skin of the body, 44 he is leprous,[a] he is unclean. The priest shall pronounce him unclean; the disease is on his head.

45 The person who has the leprous[a] disease shall wear torn clothes and let the hair of his head be disheveled; and he shall cover his upper lip and cry out, "Unclean, unclean." 46 He shall remain unclean as long as he has the disease; he is unclean. He shall live alone; his dwelling shall be outside the camp.

47 Concerning clothing: when a leprous[a] disease appears in it, in woolen or linen cloth, 48 in warp or woof of linen or wool, or in a skin or in anything made of skin, 49 if the disease shows greenish or reddish in the garment, whether in warp or woof or in skin or in anything made of skin, it is a leprous[a] disease and

[a] A term for several skin diseases; precise meaning uncertain

---

13:45–46—The appearance and the banishment from the camp create a state like death, a reflection of the person's condition. Such exile was a form of death because the community was understood as the place within which one experienced life, blessing, and well-being.

It is difficult to read this text and not reflect on AIDS. Initially judged by some to be divine punishment on the gay community, the present reality of AIDS as a global crisis indicates that the "divine judgment" view was misguided (based, in part, on an inconsistent reading of biblical texts, see 18:19–23; 20:10–16). The judgment on the gay community, along with the fear and loathing in which such judgments were couched, were themselves (attempted) forms of community expulsion and death (v. 46 indicates that the unclean person voluntarily withdrew). Contemporary readers must not confuse Israel's purity concerns with medical concerns. Equally important, the contemporary reader must not confuse fear, loathing, and a preference for judgment with the righteousness, mercy, and love of God.

shall be shown to the priest. ⁵⁰ The priest shall examine the disease, and put the diseased article aside for seven days. ⁵¹ He shall examine the disease on the seventh day. If the disease has spread in the cloth, in warp or woof, or in the skin, whatever be the use of the skin, this is a spreading leprous*ᵃ* disease; it is unclean. ⁵² He shall burn the clothing, whether diseased in warp or woof, woolen or linen, or anything of skin, for it is a spreading leprous*ᵃ* disease; it shall be burned in fire.

53 If the priest makes an examination, and the disease has not spread in the clothing, in warp or woof or in anything of skin, ⁵⁴ the priest shall command them to wash the article in which the disease appears, and he shall put it aside seven days more. ⁵⁵ The priest shall examine the diseased article after it has been washed. If the diseased spot has not changed color, though the disease has not spread, it is unclean; you shall burn it in fire, whether the leprous*ᵃ* spot is on the inside or on the outside.

56 If the priest makes an examination, and the disease has abated after it is washed, he shall tear the spot out of the cloth, in warp or woof, or out of skin. ⁵⁷ If it appears again in the garment, in warp or woof, or in anything of skin, it is spreading; you shall burn with fire that in which the disease appears. ⁵⁸ But the cloth, warp or woof, or anything of skin from which the disease disappears when you have washed it, shall then be washed a second time, and it shall be clean.

59 This is the ritual for a leprous*ᵃ* disease in a cloth of wool or linen, either in warp or woof, or in anything of skin, to decide whether it is clean or unclean.

Purification of Lepers and Leprous Houses

14 The LORD spoke to Moses, saying: ² This shall be the ritual for the leprous*ᵃ* person at the time of his cleansing:

He shall be brought to the priest; ³ the priest shall go out of the camp, and the priest shall make an examination. If the disease is healed in the leprous*ᵃ* person, ⁴ the priest shall command that two living clean birds and cedarwood and crimson yarn and hyssop be brought for the one who is to be cleansed. ⁵ The priest shall command that one of the birds be slaughtered over fresh water in an earthen vessel. ⁶ He shall take the living bird with the cedarwood and the crimson yarn and the hyssop, and dip them and the living bird in the blood of the bird that was slaughtered over the fresh water. ⁷ He shall sprinkle it seven times upon the one who is to be cleansed of the leprous*ᵃ* disease; then he shall pronounce him clean, and he shall let the living bird go into the open field. ⁸ The one who is to be cleansed shall wash his clothes, and shave off all his hair, and bathe himself in water, and he shall be clean. After that he shall come into the camp, but shall live outside his tent seven days. ⁹ On the seventh day he shall shave all his hair: of head, beard, eyebrows; he shall shave all his hair. Then he shall wash his clothes, and bathe his body in water, and he shall be clean.

10 On the eighth day he shall take two male lambs without blemish, and one ewe lamb in its first year without blemish, and a grain offering of three-tenths of an ephah of choice flour mixed with oil, and one log*ᵇ* of oil. ¹¹ The priest who cleanses shall set the person to be cleansed, along with these things, before the LORD, at the entrance of the tent of meeting. ¹² The priest shall take one of the lambs, and offer it as a guilt offering, along with the log*ᵇ* of oil, and raise them as an elevation offering before the

ᵃ A term for several skin diseases; precise meaning uncertain *ᵇ* A liquid measure

---

14:1–32—The text clearly indicates that Israel embraced ways for a persons exiled from the community to return to the community. The ritual enacts the movement of the individual from a state of death outside the community to a state of life within the community.

LORD. [13] He shall slaughter the lamb in the place where the sin offering and the burnt offering are slaughtered in the holy place; for the guilt offering, like the sin offering, belongs to the priest: it is most holy. [14] The priest shall take some of the blood of the guilt offering and put it on the lobe of the right ear of the one to be cleansed, and on the thumb of the right hand, and on the big toe of the right foot. [15] The priest shall take some of the log[a] of oil and pour it into the palm of his own left hand, [16] and dip his right finger in the oil that is in his left hand and sprinkle some oil with his finger seven times before the LORD. [17] Some of the oil that remains in his hand the priest shall put on the lobe of the right ear of the one to be cleansed, and on the thumb of the right hand, and on the big toe of the right foot, on top of the blood of the guilt offering. [18] The rest of the oil that is in the priest's hand he shall put on the head of the one to be cleansed. Then the priest shall make atonement on his behalf before the LORD: [19] the priest shall offer the sin offering, to make atonement for the one to be cleansed from his uncleanness. Afterward he shall slaughter the burnt offering; [20] and the priest shall offer the burnt offering and the grain offering on the altar. Thus the priest shall make atonement on his behalf and he shall be clean.

21 But if he is poor and cannot afford so much, he shall take one male lamb for a guilt offering to be elevated, to make atonement on his behalf, and one-tenth of an ephah of choice flour mixed with oil for a grain offering and a log[a] of oil; [22] also two turtledoves or two pigeons, such as he can afford, one for a sin offering and the other for a burnt offering. [23] On the eighth day he shall bring them for his cleansing to the priest, to the entrance of the tent of meeting, before the LORD; [24] and the priest shall take the lamb of the guilt offering and the log[a] of oil, and the priest shall raise them as an elevation offering before the LORD. [25] The priest shall slaughter the lamb of the guilt offering and shall take some of the blood of the guilt offering, and put it on the lobe of the right ear of the one to be cleansed, and on the thumb of the right hand, and on the big toe of the right foot. [26] The priest shall pour some of the oil into the palm of his own left hand, [27] and shall sprinkle with his right finger some of the oil that is in his left hand seven times before the LORD. [28] The priest shall put some of the oil that is in his hand on the lobe of the right ear of the one to be cleansed, and on the thumb of the right hand, and the big toe of the right foot, where the blood of the guilt offering was placed. [29] The rest of the oil that is in the priest's hand he shall put on the head of the one to be cleansed, to make atonement on his behalf before the LORD. [30] And he shall offer, of the turtledoves or pigeons such as he can afford, [31] one[b] for a sin offering and the other for a burnt offering, along with a grain offering; and the priest shall make atonement before the LORD on behalf of the one being cleansed. [32] This is the ritual for the one who has a leprous[c] disease, who cannot afford the offerings for his cleansing.

33 The LORD spoke to Moses and Aaron, saying:

34 When you come into the land of Canaan, which I give you for a possession, and I put a leprous[c] disease in a house in the land of your possession, [35] the owner of the house shall come and tell the priest, saying, "There seems to me to be some sort of disease in my house." [36] The priest shall command that they empty the house before the priest goes to examine the disease, or all that is in the house will become unclean; and afterward the priest shall go in to inspect the house. [37] He shall examine the disease; if the disease is in the walls of the house with greenish or reddish spots, and if it appears to be deeper than

---

[a] A liquid measure [b] Gk Syr: Heb afford, [31]such as he can afford, one [c] A term for several skin diseases; precise meaning uncertain

the surface, ³⁸ the priest shall go out-side to the door of the house and shut up the house seven days. ³⁹ The priest shall come again on the seventh day and make an inspection; if the disease has spread in the walls of the house, ⁴⁰ the priest shall command that the stones in which the disease appears be taken out and thrown into an unclean place out-side the city. ⁴¹ He shall have the inside of the house scraped thoroughly, and the plaster that is scraped off shall be dumped in an unclean place outside the city. ⁴² They shall take other stones and put them in the place of those stones, and take other plaster and plaster the house.

43 If the disease breaks out again in the house, after he has taken out the stones and scraped the house and plas-tered it, ⁴⁴ the priest shall go and make inspection; if the disease has spread in the house, it is a spreading leprous*ᵃ* dis-ease in the house; it is unclean. ⁴⁵ He shall have the house torn down, its stones and timber and all the plaster of the house, and taken outside the city to an unclean place. ⁴⁶ All who enter the house while it is shut up shall be unclean until the eve-ning; ⁴⁷ and all who sleep in the house shall wash their clothes; and all who eat in the house shall wash their clothes.

48 If the priest comes and makes an inspection, and the disease has not spread in the house after the house was plastered, the priest shall pronounce the house clean; the disease is healed. ⁴⁹ For the cleansing of the house he shall take two birds, with cedarwood and crimson yarn and hyssop, ⁵⁰ and shall slaugh-ter one of the birds over fresh water in an earthen vessel, ⁵¹ and shall take the cedarwood and the hyssop and the crim-son yarn, along with the living bird, and dip them in the blood of the slaughtered bird and the fresh water, and sprinkle the house seven times. ⁵² Thus he shall cleanse the house with the blood of the bird, and with the fresh water, and with the living bird, and with the cedarwood and hyssop and crimson yarn; ⁵³ and he shall let the living bird go out of the city into the open field; so he shall make atonement for the house, and it shall be clean.

54 This is the ritual for any leprous*ᵃ* disease: for an itch, ⁵⁵ for leprous*ᵃ* dis-eases in clothing and houses, ⁵⁶ and for a swelling or an eruption or a spot, ⁵⁷ to determine when it is unclean and when it is clean. This is the ritual for leprous*ᵃ* diseases.

Concerning Bodily Discharges

15 The LORD spoke to Moses and Aaron, saying: ² Speak to the people of Israel and say to them:

When any man has a discharge from his member,*ᵇ* his discharge makes him ceremonially unclean. ³ The unclean-ness of his discharge is this: whether his member*ᵇ* flows with his discharge, or his member*ᵇ* is stopped from discharging, it is uncleanness for him. ⁴ Every bed on which the one with the discharge lies shall be unclean; and everything on which he sits shall be unclean. ⁵ Anyone who touches his bed shall wash his clothes, and bathe in water, and be unclean until the evening. ⁶ All who sit on anything on which the one with the discharge has

---

ᵃ A term for several skin diseases; precise meaning uncertain   *ᵇ* Heb *flesh*

15:1–33 Unclean Flows

Unclean bodily fluids are associated with the reproductive organs. Israel thought of these fluids in terms of life and death, fertility and birth. Fertility is an element both of God's blessing of humans at the time of creation (Gen. 1:28) and God's promise to the ancestors (e.g., Gen. 12:2; 15:5; 17:2).

The text raises important questions for the con-temporary world: What is the meaning and sig-nificance of the human body, with all of its flows and flaws, for human existence? What is the role of the body in religious faith and practice? The body has often been viewed as something to be tamed, the home of desires and passions, a prison to be escaped. Christian theology often has focused almost exclusively on the soul or spirit. The body, as these texts suggest, must be taken seriously and "made sense of" in contem-porary theological reflection and discourse.

sat shall wash their clothes, and bathe in water, and be unclean until the evening. 7 All who touch the body of the one with the discharge shall wash their clothes, and bathe in water, and be unclean until the evening. 8 If the one with the discharge spits on persons who are clean, then they shall wash their clothes, and bathe in water, and be unclean until the evening. 9 Any saddle on which the one with the discharge rides shall be unclean. 10 All who touch anything that was under him shall be unclean until the evening, and all who carry such a thing shall wash their clothes, and bathe in water, and be unclean until the evening. 11 All those whom the one with the discharge touches without his having rinsed his hands in water shall wash their clothes, and bathe in water, and be unclean until the evening. 12 Any earthen vessel that the one with the discharge touches shall be broken; and every vessel of wood shall be rinsed in water.

13 When the one with a discharge is cleansed of his discharge, he shall count seven days for his cleansing; he shall wash his clothes and bathe his body in fresh water, and he shall be clean. 14 On the eighth day he shall take two turtledoves or two pigeons and come before the LORD to the entrance of the tent of meeting and give them to the priest. 15 The priest shall offer them, one for a sin offering and the other for a burnt offering; and the priest shall make atonement on his behalf before the LORD for his discharge.

16 If a man has an emission of semen, he shall bathe his whole body in water, and be unclean until the evening. 17 Everything made of cloth or of skin on which the semen falls shall be washed with water, and be unclean until the evening. 18 If a man lies with a woman and has an emission of semen, both of them shall bathe in water, and be unclean until the evening.

19 When a woman has a discharge of blood that is her regular discharge from her body, she shall be in her impurity for seven days, and whoever touches her shall be unclean until the evening. 20 Everything upon which she lies during her impurity shall be unclean; everything also upon which she sits shall be unclean. 21 Whoever touches her bed shall wash his clothes, and bathe in water, and be unclean until the evening. 22 Whoever touches anything upon which she sits shall wash his clothes, and bathe in water, and be unclean until the evening; 23 whether it is the bed or anything upon which she sits, when he touches it he shall be unclean until the evening. 24 If any man lies with her, and her impurity falls on him, he shall be unclean seven days; and every bed on which he lies shall be unclean.

25 If a woman has a discharge of blood for many days, not at the time of her impurity, or if she has a discharge beyond the time of her impurity, all the days of the discharge she shall continue in uncleanness; as in the days of her impurity, she shall be unclean. 26 Every bed on which she lies during all the days of her discharge shall be treated as the bed of her impurity; and everything on which she sits shall be unclean, as in the uncleanness of her impurity. 27 Whoever touches these things shall be unclean, and shall wash his clothes, and bathe in water, and be unclean until the evening. 28 If she is cleansed of her discharge, she shall count seven days, and after that she shall be clean. 29 On the eighth day she shall take two turtledoves or two pigeons and bring them to the priest at the entrance of the tent of meeting. 30 The priest shall offer one for a sin offering and the other for a burnt offering; and the priest shall make atonement on her behalf before the LORD for her unclean discharge.

31 Thus you shall keep the people of Israel separate from their uncleanness, so that they do not die in their uncleanness by defiling my tabernacle that is in their midst.

32 This is the ritual for those who have a discharge: for him who has an emission of semen, becoming unclean thereby, 33 for her who is in the infirmity of her period, for anyone, male or female, who has a discharge, and for the man who lies with a woman who is unclean.

The Day of Atonement

16 The LORD spoke to Moses after the death of the two sons of Aaron, when they drew near before the LORD and died. 2 The LORD said to Moses:

Tell your brother Aaron not to come just at any time into the sanctuary inside the curtain before the mercy seat*a* that is upon the ark, or he will die; for I appear in the cloud upon the mercy seat.*a* 3 Thus shall Aaron come into the holy place: with a young bull for a sin offering and a ram for a burnt offering. 4 He shall put on the holy linen tunic, and shall have the linen undergarments next to his body, fasten the linen sash, and wear the linen turban; these are the holy vestments. He shall bathe his body in water, and then put them on. 5 He shall take from the congregation of the people of Israel two male goats for a sin offering, and one ram for a burnt offering.

6 Aaron shall offer the bull as a sin offering for himself, and shall make atonement for himself and for his house. 7 He shall take the two goats and set them before the LORD at the entrance of the tent of meeting; 8 and Aaron shall cast lots on the two goats, one lot for the LORD and the other lot for Azazel.*b* 9 Aaron shall present the goat on which the lot fell for the LORD, and offer it as a sin offering; 10 but the goat on which the lot fell for Azazel*b* shall be presented alive before the LORD to make atonement over it, that it may be sent away into the wilderness to Azazel.*b*

11 Aaron shall present the bull as a sin offering for himself, and shall make atonement for himself and for his house; he shall slaughter the bull as a sin offering for himself. 12 He shall take a censer full of coals of fire from the altar before the LORD, and two handfuls of crushed sweet incense, and he shall bring it inside the curtain 13 and put the incense on the fire before the LORD, that the cloud of the incense may cover the mercy seat*a* that is upon the covenant,*c* or he will die. 14 He shall take some of the blood of the bull, and sprinkle it with his finger on the front of the mercy seat,*a* and before the mercy seat*a* he shall sprinkle the blood with his finger seven times.

15 He shall slaughter the goat of the sin offering that is for the people and bring its blood inside the curtain, and do with its blood as he did with the blood of the bull, sprinkling it upon the mercy seat*a* and before the mercy seat.*a* 16 Thus he shall make atonement for the sanctuary, because of the uncleannesses of the people of Israel, and because of their transgressions, all their sins; and so he shall do for the tent of meeting, which remains with them in the midst of their uncleannesses. 17 No one shall be in the tent of meeting from the time he enters to make atonement in the sanctuary until he comes out and has made atonement for himself and for his house and for all the assembly of Israel. 18 Then he shall go out to the altar that is before the LORD and make atonement

a Or *the cover*   *b* Traditionally rendered *a scapegoat*   *c* Or *treaty*, or *testament*; Heb *eduth*

16:1–34 The Annual Day of Purification

16:1–19—The annual ritual of purification is associated with the death of Aaron's two sons (see chap. 10) and provides instructions for how Aaron is to enter into the most holy place in order to enact purification rites (vv. 12–17). Aaron sprinkles blood on (to cleanse) and before

(to reconsecrate) the ark inside the Holy of Holies (the only time this happens) and also on the outer altar of burnt offerings, a cleansing of the "tent" from its innermost region to its outermost object (vv. 16, 18). The ritual makes a "clean sweep of things" and brings to mind the themes of renewal and re-creation.

on its behalf, and shall take some of the blood of the bull and of the blood of the goat, and put it on each of the horns of the altar. [19] He shall sprinkle some of the blood on it with his finger seven times, and cleanse it and hallow it from the uncleannesses of the people of Israel.

20 When he has finished atoning for the holy place and the tent of meeting and the altar, he shall present the live goat. [21] Then Aaron shall lay both his hands on the head of the live goat, and confess over it all the iniquities of the people of Israel, and all their transgressions, all their sins, putting them on the head of the goat, and sending it away into the wilderness by means of someone designated for the task.[a] [22] The goat shall bear on itself all their iniquities to a barren region; and the goat shall be set free in the wilderness.

23 Then Aaron shall enter the tent of meeting, and shall take off the linen vestments that he put on when he went into the holy place, and shall leave them there. [24] He shall bathe his body in water in a holy place, and put on his vestments; then he shall come out and offer his burnt offering and the burnt offering of the people, making atonement for himself and for the people. [25] The fat of the sin offering he shall turn into smoke on the altar. [26] The one who sets the goat free for Azazel[b] shall wash his clothes and bathe his body in water, and afterward may come into the camp. [27] The bull of the sin offering and the goat of the sin offering, whose blood was brought in to make atonement in the holy place, shall be taken outside the camp; their skin and their flesh and their dung shall be consumed in fire. [28] The one who burns them shall wash his clothes and bathe his body in water, and afterward may come into the camp.

29 This shall be a statute to you forever: In the seventh month, on the tenth day of the month, you shall deny yourselves,[c] and shall do no work, neither the citizen nor the alien who resides among you. [30] For on this day atonement shall be made for you, to cleanse you; from all your sins you shall be clean before the LORD. [31] It is a sabbath of complete rest to you, and you shall deny yourselves;[c] it is a statute forever. [32] The priest who is anointed and consecrated as priest in his father's place shall make atonement, wearing the linen vestments, the holy vestments. [33] He shall make atonement for the sanctuary, and he shall make atonement for the tent of meeting and for the altar, and he shall make atonement for the priests and for all the people of the assembly. [34] This shall be an everlasting statute for you, to make atonement for the people of Israel once in the year for all their sins. And Moses did as the LORD had commanded him.

The Slaughtering of Animals

17 The LORD spoke to Moses: 2 Speak to Aaron and his sons

[a] Meaning of Heb uncertain   [b] Traditionally rendered a scapegoat   [c] Or shall fast

---

16:21–22—Azazel is viewed as a demonic being associated with the wilderness. The goat bearing the sins of the Israelites removes Israel's sins from the camp. The causes of the impurities that pollute the tabernacle, in this case sin, must be eliminated. The high priest, representing the community, confesses the sins of the people and places them on the head of the goat, which then bears the sins into the wilderness, a dangerous and chaotic place, and "puts things in their place." Sin defiles the tabernacle, and such defilement, if left unattended, would drive YHWH from the tent. The absence of YHWH from the community would be experienced as a form of chaos (the normal order of things would be disrupted), so the sins—one possible cause of such defilement and chaos—are taken from the camp and put in the place of chaos. This is an act of keeping separate the holy and the common, the clean and the unclean.

16:29–34—The people observe the day as a day of humiliation and rest, a community form of confession and sorrow. The enacted "sorrow" associated with purification and confession leads to community renewal and re-creation. The observance is itself a means by which the community practices and enacts holiness.

17:1–26:46 The Holiness Code
The Holiness Code calls for Israel to be holy, just

and to all the people of Israel and say to them: This is what the LORD has commanded. [3] If anyone of the house of Israel slaughters an ox or a lamb or a goat in the camp, or slaughters it outside the camp, [4] and does not bring it to the entrance of the tent of meeting, to present it as an offering to the LORD before the tabernacle of the LORD, he shall be held guilty of bloodshed; he has shed blood, and he shall be cut off from the people. [5] This is in order that the people of Israel may bring their sacrifices that they offer in the open field, that they may bring them to the LORD, to the priest at the entrance of the tent of meeting, and offer them as sacrifices of well-being to the LORD. [6] The priest shall dash the blood against the altar of the LORD at the entrance of the tent of meeting, and turn the fat into smoke as a pleasing odor to the LORD, [7] so that they may no longer offer their sacrifices for goat-demons, to whom they prostitute themselves. This shall be a statute forever to them throughout their generations.

[8] And say to them further: Anyone of the house of Israel or of the aliens who reside among them who offers a burnt offering or sacrifice, [9] and does not bring it to the entrance of the tent of meeting, to sacrifice it to the LORD, shall be cut off from the people.

Eating Blood Prohibited

[10] If anyone of the house of Israel or of the aliens who reside among them eats any blood, I will set my face against that person who eats blood, and will cut that person off from the people. [11] For the life of the flesh is in the blood; and I have given it to you for making atonement for your lives on the altar; for, as life, it is the blood that makes atonement. [12] Therefore I have said to the people of Israel: No person among you shall eat blood, nor shall any alien who resides among you eat blood. [13] And anyone of the people of Israel, or of the aliens who reside among them, who hunts down an animal or bird that may be eaten shall pour out its blood and cover it with earth.

---

as YHWH is holy (e.g., 19:2; 20:26). The instructions focus on the meaning and nature of holiness in terms of life lived in community. Holiness is viewed as relational practices undertaken both in relation to YHWH and in relation to other persons in the community.

17:1–16 Blood, Sacrifice, and Food

17:3–7—The *well-being* sacrifices (v. 5) must be presented at the door of the tent of meeting. Failure to do so is considered "murder"; bloodguilt will be ascribed to the offender. Although a prohibition against offering sacrifices to demons (v. 7), the ruling reflects a concern both for the proper manipulation of sacrificial blood and the bloodless consumption of sacrificial food. To be *cut off* is to be under divine judgment, a judgment that will bring an end to one's life within the community.

17:10–12—These verses provide the most important, although not entirely clear, statement concerning blood (cf. Gen. 9:1–7). No animal blood is to be ingested (the well-being sacrifices remain the primary focus). Three reasons are given for the prohibition: (1) *the life of the flesh is in the blood*; (2) YHWH has given the blood so that it may be poured on the altar to effect expiation; (3) it is the blood, in terms of life, that accom-

plishes expiation (NRSV *atonement*). Although not stated explicitly, the text suggests that the life in the blood is sacred, belonging to YHWH, and, therefore, prohibited for human consumption. Further, YHWH states that the blood, and the life in it, is to be placed on the altar to effect expiation ("because the blood, by the life, will expiate," NRSV *for, as life, it is the blood that makes atonement*, v. 11c).

Expiation addresses a range of problems, e.g., sin and impurity, the disruption of the created order, cheating or defrauding a neighbor, trespass on the sacred, a lack of justice in social relationships. YHWH "set apart" the blood to effect expiation, a way "to set things right" when human actions disrupt the world.

A Christian perspective locates the death of Jesus, his very real flesh-and-blood death, within the context of death and life, sacrifice and slaughter, sin and redemption (e.g., Rom. 3:21–26; Heb. 2:10–18; 9:1–28). At the same time, the Christian mission of the transformation of the world, as opposed to escape from it, requires serious theological reflection on and engagement with the reality of human flesh and human blood in matters relating to redemption and "setting things right."

14 For the life of every creature—its blood is its life; therefore I have said to the people of Israel: You shall not eat the blood of any creature, for the life of every creature is its blood; whoever eats it shall be cut off. 15 All persons, citizens or aliens, who eat what dies of itself or what has been torn by wild animals, shall wash their clothes, and bathe themselves in water, and be unclean until the evening; then they shall be clean. 16 But if they do not wash themselves or bathe their body, they shall bear their guilt.

Sexual Relations

18 The LORD spoke to Moses, saying: 2 Speak to the people of Israel and say to them: I am the LORD your God.

3 You shall not do as they do in the land of Egypt, where you lived, and you shall not do as they do in the land of Canaan, to which I am bringing you. You shall not follow their statutes. 4 My ordinances you shall observe and my statutes you shall keep, following them: I am the LORD your God. 5 You shall keep my statutes and my ordinances; by doing so one shall live: I am the LORD.

6 None of you shall approach anyone near of kin to uncover nakedness: I am the LORD. 7 You shall not uncover the nakedness of your father, which is the nakedness of your mother; she is your mother, you shall not uncover her nakedness. 8 You shall not uncover the nakedness of your father's wife; it is the nakedness of your father. 9 You shall

---

18:1–30 Family and Sexuality

Chapters 18–20 contain a variety of instructions concerning the ways in which the Israelite community was able to practice and experience holiness. Holiness includes the practice of honesty, integrity, and faithfulness in personal, family, and community relationships. To practice justice and integrity in social relationships is to be holy, as YHWH is holy. The divine life and holiness are inseparable from the practice of justice and integrity.

Paraenetic exhortations (18:2–5, 24–30) frame the instructions (vv. 6–18; 19–23). The opening exhortation (vv. 2–5) weaves together three elements. First, the Israelites are not to do things done by the people of Egypt and Canaan; human actions are taken seriously. Second, the specific mention of the Egyptians and Canaanites points to the exodus from Egypt and the entry into Canaan; instruction is significantly related to and grounded in Israel's story of redemption. Third, YHWH's redemptive actions provide a reason for obedience.

The closing exhortation (vv. 24–30) uses the language of defilement to describe the practices of the nations to be driven out of **the land**: they defiled the land, and the land vomited them out. A close relationship exists between people and the land on which they live (Israel recognized a close relationship between "the earth" ['adamah] and "the earth creature" ['adam], Gen. 2:7). The land on which people live reflects the life they live (see Hos. 4:1–3). Although "the land" is not a primary concern for many, the place or space in which we live our lives is shaped in significant ways by the things we do. We must take seriously our responsibility in shaping and mapping the places and spaces in which we live.

The exhortations offer a cautionary tale. Israel characterized the other nations as perverse, in part to construct their own separate community or national identity. Whether historically accurate or not, Israel used such characterizations to justify their story of conquest. Is it possible, in the contemporary world, to construct religious identity and community (a) without justifying violence against "those others" and (b) without characterizing "those others" as morally perverse? How are we to construct our own identity without, at the same time, attempting to deconstruct the identity of others? How are we to experience, appreciate, and affirm diversity without seeking to dehumanize and/or degrade others?

18:6–18—The family is defined, in part, by declaring who is and who is not an acceptable sexual partner in relation to the patriarchal head of the family. Sexual boundaries are constructed primarily in terms of blood relations and marriage relations. The text reflects the reality of an extended family.

The sexual construction of the family is suggestive of significant issues in contemporary society—the matter of abuse, especially sexual abuse, within a variety of domestic situations, and the way we understand family. Although blood and marriage remain significant categories for defining relationships, the contemporary context has generated a number of other categories, e.g., adoption, blended families, single-parent families, families with same-sex parents. Both theological discourse and religious practice must find ways to include and affirm the variety of new family structures and relationships.

not uncover the nakedness of your sister, your father's daughter or your mother's daughter, whether born at home or born abroad. [10] You shall not uncover the nakedness of your son's daughter or of your daughter's daughter, for their nakedness is your own nakedness. [11] You shall not uncover the nakedness of your father's wife's daughter, begotten by your father, since she is your sister. [12] You shall not uncover the nakedness of your father's sister; she is your father's flesh. [13] You shall not uncover the nakedness of your mother's sister, for she is your mother's flesh. [14] You shall not uncover the nakedness of your father's brother, that is, you shall not approach his wife; she is your aunt. [15] You shall not uncover the nakedness of your daughter-in-law: she is your son's wife; you shall not uncover her nakedness. [16] You shall not uncover the nakedness of your brother's wife; it is your brother's nakedness. [17] You shall not uncover the nakedness of a woman and her daughter, and you shall not take[a] her son's daughter or her daughter's daughter to uncover her nakedness; they are your[b] flesh; it is depravity. [18] And you shall not take[a] a woman as a rival to her sister, uncovering her nakedness while her sister is still alive.

19 You shall not approach a woman to uncover her nakedness while she is in her menstrual uncleanness. [20] You shall not have sexual relations with your kinsman's wife, and defile yourself with her. [21] You shall not give any of your offspring to sacrifice them[c] to Molech, and so profane the name of your God: I am the LORD. [22] You shall not lie with a male as with a woman; it is an abomination. [23] You shall not have sexual relations with any animal and defile yourself with it, nor shall any woman give herself to an animal to have sexual relations with it: it is perversion.

24 Do not defile yourselves in any of these ways, for by all these practices the nations I am casting out before you

[a] Or marry   [b] Gk: Heb lacks your   [c] Heb to pass them over

---

18:19–23—These five prohibitions, grouped together as they are, seek to preserve and protect male seed and male lineage. Israel, for a variety of reasons, valued children and viewed them as a family asset. Conditions were such, however, that many babies, in all probability, did not survive. Thus, practices that did not maximize and protect what Israel viewed to be the generative power of the male seed were prohibited. The concern is not so much the "moral" nature of the practices, as a concern for the well-being of the male seed (a reflection of the divine promise and blessing, see Gen. 1:28; 12:1–3; 15:2–6; 17:3–8).

The male seed is "wasted" if it is "lost" or "misused" in any of these five practices (Israel may well have believed that a man had a limited number of generative possibilities). Masturbation is not included, in all probability, because another person is not involved. This reflects the context provided by the adjacent rulings, which are designed to determine acceptable and unacceptable sexual partners.

As suggested above, the primary concern of this ruling is to prohibit the loss of male seed in a nongenerative situation. It is difficult to maintain that it is a blanket statement against homosexual relationships, in that the ruling does not address "a woman with a woman" (additional biblical statements generally included in the discussion

of homosexuality include Gen. 19:4–11 [cf. Judg. 19]; Lev. 20:13; Rom. 1:26–27; 1 Cor. 6:9–10; 1 Tim. 1:9–10). This is important, in that the following verse specifically prohibits both men *and* women having sexual intercourse with an animal.

The writer of this text did not have access to twenty-first-century understandings of same-sex relationships or heterosexual relationships. For example, Lev. 20:10 and 13 prescribe death for adultery (both parties) and male-with-male intercourse. The texts indicate, however, that Israel held not only different understandings of sexual relationships but also different notions of community, guilt, judgment, and punishment. Whether the ruling reflects a concern for wasted male seed, the crossing of boundaries that should not be crossed, or the mixing of fluids that should remain distinct, the social, cultural, and religious contexts for the ruling are radically distinct from social, cultural, and religious contexts of the contemporary world. Just as Israel and the church repeatedly recognized the need for interpretive adaptation of the sacred words, so the contemporary context requires that the faithful community take seriously the challenge to discover again, in new and emerging contexts, the meaning and nature of the mercy, love, and righteousness of God.

have defiled themselves. [25] Thus the land became defiled; and I punished it for its iniquity, and the land vomited out its inhabitants. [26] But you shall keep my statutes and my ordinances and commit none of these abominations, either the citizen or the alien who resides among you [27] (for the inhabitants of the land, who were before you, committed all of these abominations, and the land became defiled); [28] otherwise the land will vomit you out for defiling it, as it vomited out the nation that was before you. [29] For whoever commits any of these abominations shall be cut off from their people. [30] So keep my charge not to commit any of these abominations that were done before you, and not to defile yourselves by them: I am the LORD your God.

Ritual and Moral Holiness

19 The LORD spoke to Moses, saying:

[2] Speak to all the congregation of the people of Israel and say to them: You shall be holy, for I the LORD your God am holy. [3] You shall each revere your mother and father, and you shall keep my sabbaths: I am the LORD your God. [4] Do not turn to idols or make cast images for yourselves: I am the LORD your God.

[5] When you offer a sacrifice of well-being to the LORD, offer it in such a way that it is acceptable in your behalf. [6] It shall be eaten on the same day you offer it, or on the next day; and any-thing left over until the third day shall be consumed in fire. [7] If it is eaten at all on the third day, it is an abomination; it will not be acceptable. [8] All who eat it shall be subject to punishment, because they have profaned what is holy to the LORD; and any such person shall be cut off from the people.

[9] When you reap the harvest of your land, you shall not reap to the very edges of your field, or gather the gleanings of your harvest. [10] You shall not strip your vineyard bare, or gather the fallen grapes of your vineyard; you shall leave them for the poor and the alien: I am the LORD your God.

[11] You shall not steal; you shall not deal falsely; and you shall not lie to one another. [12] And you shall not swear falsely by my name, profaning the name of your God: I am the LORD.

[13] You shall not defraud your neighbor; you shall not steal; and you shall not keep for yourself the wages of a laborer until morning. [14] You shall not revile the deaf or put a stumbling block before the blind; you shall fear your God: I am the LORD.

[15] You shall not render an unjust judgment; you shall not be partial to the poor or defer to the great: with justice you shall judge your neighbor. [16] You shall not go around as a slanderer[a] among your people, and you shall not profit by the blood[b] of your neighbor: I am the LORD.

---

[a] Meaning of Heb uncertain [b] Heb *stand against the blood*

19:1–37 Miscellaneous Instructions

19:2—The instructions are addressed to the whole community and are concerned with the practice of holiness. Issues addressed include worship and cult, family, social practices, relationships, and responsibilities. Holiness is concretely enacted in the context of relationships.

19:9–10—Attending to and providing for *the poor and the alien* (non-Israelites who chose to live with Israel, we might say "the other") are concrete acts of holiness that reflect the divine holiness. *Harvest* becomes an occasion for the practice of justice.

19:11–18—At the heart of these instructions is a profound call to practice integrity and honesty in one's interactions with others: do not deal falsely, do not lie, do not defraud, do not steal, do not withhold the wages of the worker, do not revile the deaf or cause the blind to stumble, do not render unjust judgments, do not slander, do not profit by violence against your neighbor, do not hate your kinfolk, do not take vengeance or bear a grudge. *Love your neighbor as yourself* (cf. Matt. 22:34–40; Mark 12:28–34; Luke 10:25–28; and Jesus' teachings in Matt. 5–8). Community holiness becomes concrete when people act with integrity and justice.

17 You shall not hate in your heart anyone of your kin; you shall reprove your neighbor, or you will incur guilt yourself. ¹⁸ You shall not take vengeance or bear a grudge against any of your people, but you shall love your neighbor as yourself: I am the LORD.

19 You shall keep my statutes. You shall not let your animals breed with a different kind; you shall not sow your field with two kinds of seed; nor shall you put on a garment made of two different materials.

20 If a man has sexual relations with a woman who is a slave, designated for another man but not ransomed or given her freedom, an inquiry shall be held. They shall not be put to death, since she has not been freed; ²¹ but he shall bring a guilt offering for himself to the LORD, at the entrance of the tent of meeting, a ram as guilt offering. ²² And the priest shall make atonement for him with the ram of guilt offering before the LORD for his sin that he committed; and the sin he committed shall be forgiven him.

23 When you come into the land and plant all kinds of trees for food, then you shall regard their fruit as forbidden;ᵃ three years it shall be forbiddenᵃ to you, it must not be eaten. ²⁴ In the fourth year all their fruit shall be set apart for rejoicing in the LORD. ²⁵ But in the fifth year you may eat of their fruit, that their yield may be increased for you: I am the LORD your God.

26 You shall not eat anything with its blood. You shall not practice augury or witchcraft. ²⁷ You shall not round off the hair on your temples or mar the edges of your beard. ²⁸ You shall not make any gashes in your flesh for the dead or tattoo any marks upon you: I am the LORD.

29 Do not profane your daughter by making her a prostitute, that the land not become prostituted and full of depravity. ³⁰ You shall keep my sabbaths and reverence my sanctuary: I am the LORD.

31 Do not turn to mediums or wizards; do not seek them out, to be defiled by them: I am the LORD your God.

32 You shall rise before the aged, and defer to the old; and you shall fear your God: I am the LORD.

33 When an alien resides with you in your land, you shall not oppress the alien. ³⁴ The alien who resides with you shall be to you as the citizen among you; you shall love the alien as yourself, for you were aliens in the land of Egypt: I am the LORD your God.

35 You shall not cheat in measuring length, weight, or quantity. ³⁶ You shall have honest balances, honest weights, an honest ephah, and an honest hin: I am the LORD your God, who brought you out of the land of Egypt. ³⁷ You shall keep all my statutes and all my ordinances, and observe them: I am the LORD.

Penalties for Violations of Holiness

20 The LORD spoke to Moses, saying: ² Say further to the people of Israel:

Any of the people of Israel, or of the aliens who reside in Israel, who give any of their offspring to Molech shall be put to death; the people of the land shall stone them to death. ³ I myself will set my face against them, and will cut them off from the people, because they

ᵃ Heb as their uncircumcision

19:33–34—The *aliens*, non-Israelites who have chosen to live with Israel, must be treated as *citizens*. Israel is reminded of its "alien" status and oppression in Egypt. The ruling weaves together Israel's history, a call for just and equitable social relationships, and the practice of holiness.

20:1–27 Family, Sexuality, and Punishments (cf. chap. 18)

20:2–5—Although the precise nature of *Molech* worship remains unclear, this text associates it with the sacrifice of children. The text weaves together two issues: the importance of the life of Israel's children and the prohibition against worshiping other gods (e.g., Exod. 20:3; 34:14).

have given of their offspring to Molech, defiling my sanctuary and profaning my holy name. [4] And if the people of the land should ever close their eyes to them, when they give of their offspring to Molech, and do not put them to death, [5] I myself will set my face against them and against their family, and will cut them off from among their people, them and all who follow them in prostituting themselves to Molech.

6 If any turn to mediums and wizards, prostituting themselves to them, I will set my face against them, and will cut them off from the people. [7] Consecrate yourselves therefore, and be holy; for I am the LORD your God. [8] Keep my statutes, and observe them; I am the LORD; I sanctify you. [9] All who curse father or mother shall be put to death; having cursed father or mother, their blood is upon them.

10 If a man commits adultery with the wife of[a] his neighbor, both the adulterer and the adulteress shall be put to death. [11] The man who lies with his father's wife has uncovered his father's nakedness; both of them shall be put to death; their blood is upon them. [12] If a man lies with his daughter-in-law, both of them shall be put to death; they have committed perversion, their blood is upon them. [13] If a man lies with a male as with a woman, both of them have committed an abomination; they shall be put to death; their blood is upon them. [14] If a man takes a wife and her mother also, it is depravity; they shall be burned to death, both he and they, that there may be no depravity among you. [15] If a man has sexual relations with an animal, he shall be put to death; and you shall kill the animal. [16] If a woman approaches any animal and has sexual relations with it, you shall kill the woman and the animal; they shall be put to death, their blood is upon them.

17 If a man takes his sister, a daughter of his father or a daughter of his mother, and sees her nakedness, and she sees his nakedness, it is a disgrace, and they shall be cut off in the sight of their people; he has uncovered his sister's nakedness, he shall be subject to punishment. [18] If a man lies with a woman having her sickness and uncovers her nakedness, he has laid bare her flow and she has laid bare her flow of blood; both of them shall be cut off from their people. [19] You shall not uncover the nakedness of your mother's sister or of your father's sister, for that is to lay bare one's own flesh; they shall be subject to punishment. [20] If a man lies with his uncle's wife, he has uncovered his uncle's nakedness; they shall be subject to punishment; they shall die childless. [21] If a man takes his brother's wife, it is impurity; he has uncovered his brother's nakedness; they shall be childless.

22 You shall keep all my statutes and all my ordinances, and observe them, so that the land to which I bring you to settle in may not vomit you out. [23] You shall not follow the practices of the nation that I am driving out before you. Because they did all these things, I abhorred them. [24] But I have said to you: You shall inherit their land, and I will give it to you to possess, a land flowing with milk and honey. I am the LORD your God; I have separated you from the peoples. [25] You shall therefore make a distinction between the clean

---

[a] Heb repeats *if a man commits adultery with the wife of*

20:10–16—These rulings reflect a concern to construct and maintain boundaries and categories believed by Israel to be of foundational importance: family (blood and marriage), gender (male and female), and human (as distinct from animal). See 18:19–23.

20:22–26—A sermonlike conclusion to chaps. 18–20. The text states that the people of the land are **abhorred** by God, a characterization that provides some justification for Israel's reception of the land. God has separated Israel from the other nations and Israel must maintain its "set apartness" through observing and maintaining the separation of the *clean* and the *unclean* (cf. 10:10). On the negative construction of "the other," see notes on 18:2–5, 24–30.

animal and the unclean, and between the unclean bird and the clean; you shall not bring abomination on yourselves by animal or by bird or by anything with which the ground teems, which I have set apart for you to hold unclean. **26** You shall be holy to me; for I the LORD am holy, and I have separated you from the other peoples to be mine.

27 A man or a woman who is a medium or a wizard shall be put to death; they shall be stoned to death, their blood is upon them.

The Holiness of Priests

21 The LORD said to Moses: Speak to the priests, the sons of Aaron, and say to them:

No one shall defile himself for a dead person among his relatives, **2** except for his nearest kin: his mother, his father, his son, his daughter, his brother; **3** likewise, for a virgin sister, close to him because she has had no husband, he may defile himself for her. **4** But he shall not defile himself as a husband among his people and so profane himself. **5** They shall not make bald spots upon their heads, or shave off the edges of their beards, or make any gashes in their flesh. **6** They shall be holy to their God, and not profane the name of their God; for they offer the LORD's offerings by fire, the food of their God; therefore they shall be holy. **7** They shall not marry a prostitute or a woman who has been defiled; neither shall they marry a woman divorced from her husband. For they are holy to their God, **8** and you shall treat them as holy, since they offer the food of your God; they shall be holy to you, for I the LORD, I who sanctify you, am holy. **9** When the daughter of a priest profanes herself through prostitution, she profanes her father; she shall be burned to death.

10 The priest who is exalted above his fellows, on whose head the anointing oil has been poured and who has been consecrated to wear the vestments, shall not dishevel his hair, nor tear his vestments. **11** He shall not go where there is a dead body; he shall not defile himself even for his father or mother. **12** He shall not go outside the sanctuary and thus profane the sanctuary of his God; for the consecration of the anointing oil of his God is upon him: I am the LORD. **13** He shall marry only a woman who is a virgin. **14** A widow, or a divorced woman, or a woman who has been defiled, a prostitute, these he shall not marry. He shall marry a virgin of his own kin, **15** that he may not profane his offspring among his kin; for I am the LORD; I sanctify him.

16 The LORD spoke to Moses, saying: **17** Speak to Aaron and say: No one of

---

21:1–22:33 Instructions for the Priesthood

21:1–15—Ordinary *priests* may draw near to the corpse of immediate family for the purpose of burial, but the high priest is prohibited from all contact (he must remain in the Holy Place). Death was viewed as the primary form of impurity, and great care was taken to keep it separate from the Holy Place (the priests were holy; see chap. 8).

The "set apart" nature of the priests also informs the rulings concerning marriage partners. The purity of the priestly line must be maintained. Hence, any woman who for a variety of reasons might be carrying another man's child was prohibited.

Although reflecting different concerns, the contemporary world is all too familiar with efforts to maintain blood purity through genocide, prejudice and hate, and national borders. Israel's concern for the blood purity of priests was located within Israel's understanding of holiness. Contemporary efforts to maintain blood purity have different political and national contexts and, because of that, different purposes and agendas.

21:16–24—Blemished priests are unable to serve at the altar (see 22:17–30 for blemished animals and sacrifice). The writer of the text viewed the *blemishes* in terms of physical "imperfections" or "abnormalities." In this context, holiness begins to take on the meaning of wholeness (although, "wholeness" is itself an interpretive and, very often, an aesthetic category). The rulings have to do only with Israelite priests who serve at the altar of burnt offerings.

Clearly, instructions for Israel's sacrificial priesthood must not be "translated" into contemporary views of "normal" and "abnormal," "perfect" and "imperfect." The rulings do raise issues, however, for religious communities that seek to exclude persons from full participation in the life

your offspring throughout their generations who has a blemish may approach to offer the food of his God. ¹⁸ For no one who has a blemish shall draw near, one who is blind or lame, or one who has a mutilated face or a limb too long, ¹⁹ or one who has a broken foot or a broken hand, ²⁰ or a hunchback, or a dwarf, or a man with a blemish in his eyes or an itching disease or scabs or crushed testicles. ²¹ No descendant of Aaron the priest who has a blemish shall come near to offer the LORD's offerings by fire; since he has a blemish, he shall not come near to offer the food of his God. ²² He may eat the food of his God, of the most holy as well as of the holy. ²³ But he shall not come near the curtain or approach the altar, because he has a blemish, that he may not profane my sanctuaries; for I am the LORD; I sanctify them. ²⁴ Thus Moses spoke to Aaron and to his sons and to all the people of Israel.

The Use of Holy Offerings

22 The LORD spoke to Moses, saying: ² Direct Aaron and his sons to deal carefully with the sacred donations of the people of Israel, which they dedicate to me, so that they may not profane my holy name; I am the LORD. ³ Say to them: If anyone among all your offspring throughout your generations comes near the sacred donations, which the people of Israel dedicate to the LORD, while he is in a state of uncleanness, that person shall be cut off from my presence: I am the LORD. ⁴ No one of Aaron's offspring who has a leprous*a* disease or suffers a discharge may eat of the sacred donations until he is clean. Whoever touches anything made unclean by a corpse or a man who has had an emission of semen, ⁵ and whoever touches any swarming thing by which he may be made unclean or any human being by whom he may be made unclean—whatever his uncleanness may be— ⁶ the person who touches any such shall be unclean until evening and shall not eat of the sacred donations unless he has washed his body in water. ⁷ When the sun sets he shall be clean; and afterward he may eat of the sacred donations, for they are his food. ⁸ That which died or was torn by wild animals he shall not eat, becoming unclean by it: I am the LORD. ⁹ They shall keep my charge, so that they may not incur guilt and die in the sanctuary *b* for having profaned it: I am the LORD; I sanctify them.

10 No lay person shall eat of the sacred donations. No bound or hired servant of the priest shall eat of the sacred donations; ¹¹ but if a priest acquires anyone by purchase, the person may eat of them; and those that are born in his house may eat of his food. ¹² If a priest's daughter marries a layman, she shall not eat of the offering of the sacred donations; ¹³ but if a priest's daughter is widowed or divorced, without offspring, and returns to her father's house, as in her youth, she may eat of her father's food. No lay person shall eat of it. ¹⁴ If a man eats of the sacred donation unintentionally, he shall add one-fifth of its value to it, and give the sacred donation to the priest. ¹⁵ No one shall profane the sacred donations of the people of Israel, which they offer to the LORD, ¹⁶ causing them to bear guilt requiring a guilt offering, by eating their sacred donations: for I am the LORD; I sanctify them.

a A term for several skin diseases; precise meaning uncertain   *b* Vg: Heb incur guilt for it and die in it

---

of the community. Christian history is filled with battles over who can and who cannot approach and/or serve at the communion table (similar in many ways to the altar of God that stood outside the tabernacle). One must always ask two questions: (1) On what is exclusion based? (2) Who is empowered (and by whom) to draw and enforce the line between included and excluded? Physical attributes or bodily features perceived to be "imperfect," "abnormal," or "different" continue to play a significant role in accepting or rejecting persons both in religious communities and social contexts. From a Christian perspective, one must recall that Jesus seemed willing to accept, affirm, and include everyone (with the exception of religious hypocrites!).

Acceptable Offerings

17 The LORD spoke to Moses, saying: ¹⁸ Speak to Aaron and his sons and all the people of Israel and say to them: When anyone of the house of Israel or of the aliens residing in Israel presents an offering, whether in payment of a vow or as a freewill offering that is offered to the LORD as a burnt offering, ¹⁹ to be acceptable in your behalf it shall be a male without blemish, of the cattle or the sheep or the goats. ²⁰ You shall not offer anything that has a blemish, for it will not be acceptable in your behalf.

21 When anyone offers a sacrifice of well-being to the LORD, in fulfillment of a vow or as a freewill offering, from the herd or from the flock, to be acceptable it must be perfect; there shall be no blemish in it. ²² Anything blind, or injured, or maimed, or having a discharge or an itch or scabs—these you shall not offer to the LORD or put any of them on the altar as offerings by fire to the LORD. ²³ An ox or a lamb that has a limb too long or too short you may present for a freewill offering; but it will not be accepted for a vow. ²⁴ Any animal that has its testicles bruised or crushed or torn or cut, you shall not offer to the LORD; such you shall not do within your land, ²⁵ nor shall you accept any such animals from a foreigner to offer as food to your God; since they are mutilated, with a blemish in them, they shall not be accepted in your behalf.

26 The LORD spoke to Moses, saying: ²⁷ When an ox or a sheep or a goat is born, it shall remain seven days with its mother, and from the eighth day on it shall be acceptable as the LORD's offering by fire. ²⁸ But you shall not slaughter, from the herd or the flock, an animal with its young on the same day. ²⁹ When you sacrifice a thanksgiving offering to the LORD, you shall sacrifice it so that it may be acceptable in your behalf. ³⁰ It shall be eaten on the same day; you shall not leave any of it until morning: I am the LORD.

31 Thus you shall keep my commandments and observe them: I am the LORD. ³² You shall not profane my holy name, that I may be sanctified among the people of Israel: I am the LORD; I sanctify you, ³³ I who brought you out of the land of Egypt to be your God: I am the LORD.

Appointed Festivals

23 The LORD spoke to Moses, saying: ² Speak to the people of Israel and say to them: These are the appointed festivals of the LORD that you shall proclaim as holy convocations, my appointed festivals.

The Sabbath, Passover, and Unleavened Bread

3 Six days shall work be done; but the seventh day is a sabbath of complete rest, a holy convocation; you shall do no work: it is a sabbath to the LORD throughout your settlements.

4 These are the appointed festivals of the LORD, the holy convocations, which you shall celebrate at the time appointed for them. ⁵ In the first month, on the fourteenth day of the month, at twilight,ᵃ there shall be a passover offering to the LORD, ⁶ and on the fifteenth day of the same month is the festival of unleavened bread to the LORD; seven

ᵃ Heb between the two evenings

23:1–25:55 Sacred Days and Festivals

23:2—Israel marked out the year by a regular cycle of sacred observances (sacred times were included in the structure of creation; see Gen. 1:14; 2:2–3). Observing these sacred times is one means of celebrating the wonder of creation. The interweaving of sacred times and mundane times imposes a temporal order on the year and on the life of the Israelite community. The festival calendar indicates both the time of the observances and the types and numbers of sacrifices and offerings to be presented (cf. Num. 28–29).

23:3—The Sabbath provides the model for all the observances. Israel located Sabbath within the context of creation (Gen. 1:1–2:4a; Exod. 16:22–30; 31:12–17). Sabbath was a day set apart for rest, but also, always, a celebration of the very good order of creation.

days you shall eat unleavened bread. [7] On the first day you shall have a holy convocation; you shall not work at your occupations. [8] For seven days you shall present the LORD's offerings by fire; on the seventh day there shall be a holy convocation: you shall not work at your occupations.

The Offering of First Fruits

9 The LORD spoke to Moses: [10] Speak to the people of Israel and say to them: When you enter the land that I am giving you and you reap its harvest, you shall bring the sheaf of the first fruits of your harvest to the priest. [11] He shall raise the sheaf before the LORD, that you may find acceptance; on the day after the sabbath the priest shall raise it. [12] On the day when you raise the sheaf, you shall offer a lamb a year old, without blemish, as a burnt offering to the LORD. [13] And the grain offering with it shall be two-tenths of an ephah of choice flour mixed with oil, an offering by fire of pleasing odor to the LORD; and the drink offering with it shall be of wine, one-fourth of a hin. [14] You shall eat no bread or parched grain or fresh ears until that very day, until you have brought the offering of your God: it is a statute forever throughout your generations in all your settlements.

The Festival of Weeks

15 And from the day after the sabbath, from the day on which you bring the sheaf of the elevation offering, you shall count off seven weeks; they shall be complete. [16] You shall count until the day after the seventh sabbath, fifty days; then you shall present an offering of new grain to the LORD. [17] You shall bring from your settlements two loaves of bread as an elevation offering, each made of two-tenths of an ephah; they shall be of choice flour, baked with leaven, as first fruits to the LORD. [18] You shall present with the bread seven lambs a year old without blemish, one young bull, and two rams; they shall be a burnt offering to the LORD, along with their grain offering and their drink offerings, an offering by fire of pleasing odor to the LORD. [19] You shall also offer one male goat for a sin offering, and two male lambs a year old as a sacrifice of well-being. [20] The priest shall raise them with the bread of the first fruits as an elevation offering before the LORD, together with the two lambs; they shall be holy to the LORD for the priest. [21] On that same day you shall make proclamation; you shall hold a holy convocation; you shall not work at your occupations. This is a statute forever in all your settlements throughout your generations.

22 When you reap the harvest of your land, you shall not reap to the very edges of your field, or gather the gleanings of your harvest; you shall leave them for the poor and for the alien: I am the LORD your God.

The Festival of Trumpets

23 The LORD spoke to Moses, saying: [24] Speak to the people of Israel, saying: In the seventh month, on the first day of the month, you shall observe a day of complete rest, a holy convocation commemorated with trumpet blasts. [25] You shall not work at your occupations; and you shall present the LORD's offering by fire.

The Day of Atonement

26 The LORD spoke to Moses, saying: [27] Now, the tenth day of this seventh month is the day of atonement; it shall be a holy convocation for you: you shall deny yourselves[a] and present the LORD's

[a] Or shall fast

23:9–15—The presentation of the *first fruits* is an act associated with Israel's agricultural existence in the land of Canaan (v. 10), a way of remembering Israel's story of redemption. At the same time, the presentation of first fruits is an act of thanks to YHWH in recognition of the divine blessing of life and sustenance.
23:22—See 19:33–34.

offering by fire; [28] and you shall do no work during that entire day; for it is a day of atonement, to make atonement on your behalf before the LORD your God. [29] For anyone who does not practice self-denial[a] during that entire day shall be cut off from the people. [30] And anyone who does any work during that entire day, such a one I will destroy from the midst of the people. [31] You shall do no work: it is a statute forever throughout your generations in all your settlements. [32] It shall be to you a sabbath of complete rest, and you shall deny yourselves;[b] on the ninth day of the month at evening, from evening to evening you shall keep your sabbath.

The Festival of Booths

33 The LORD spoke to Moses, saying: [34] Speak to the people of Israel, saying: On the fifteenth day of this seventh month, and lasting seven days, there shall be the festival of booths[c] to the LORD. [35] The first day shall be a holy convocation; you shall not work at your occupations. [36] Seven days you shall present the LORD's offerings by fire; on the eighth day you shall observe a holy convocation and present the LORD's offerings by fire; it is a solemn assembly; you shall not work at your occupations.

37 These are the appointed festivals of the LORD, which you shall celebrate as times of holy convocation, for presenting to the LORD offerings by fire—burnt offerings and grain offerings, sacrifices and drink offerings, each on its proper day— [38] apart from the sabbaths of the LORD, and apart from your gifts, and apart from all your votive offerings, and apart from all your freewill offerings, which you give to the LORD.

39 Now, the fifteenth day of the seventh month, when you have gathered in the produce of the land, you shall keep the festival of the LORD, lasting seven days; a complete rest on the first day, and a complete rest on the eighth day. [40] On the first day you shall take the fruit of majestic[d] trees, branches of palm trees, boughs of leafy trees, and willows of the brook; and you shall rejoice before the LORD your God for seven days. [41] You shall keep it as a festival to the LORD seven days in the year; you shall keep it in the seventh month as a statute forever throughout your generations. [42] You shall live in booths for seven days; all that are citizens in Israel shall live in booths, [43] so that your generations may know that I made the people of Israel live in booths when I brought them out of the land of Egypt: I am the LORD your God.

44 Thus Moses declared to the people of Israel the appointed festivals of the LORD.

The Lamp

24 The LORD spoke to Moses, saying: [2] Command the people of Israel to bring you pure oil of beaten olives for the lamp, that a light may be kept burning regularly. [3] Aaron shall set it up in the tent of meeting, outside the curtain of the covenant,[e] to burn from evening to morning before the LORD regularly; it shall be a statute forever throughout your generations. [4] He shall set up the lamps on the lampstand of pure gold ƒ before the LORD regularly.

---

[a] Or does not fast   [b] Or shall fast   [c] Or tabernacles: Heb succoth   [d] Meaning of Heb uncertain   [e] Or treaty, or testament; Heb eduth   ƒ Heb pure lampstand

---

23:39–43—The observance of **booths** reflects Israel's story of and experience of redemption, especially the journey through the wilderness. The festival not only marks the close of harvest, an agricultural observance, but also Israel's journey to freedom, an historical observance. The natural rhythms of planting and harvest are woven together with the experiential events of Israel's history to create one of the sacred observances of the year.

24:1–9—God's instructions concerning the lamp and the loaves.

24:2–4—The **light**, in part, is a symbol of YHWH's presence in the tabernacle. It must burn regularly **before the LORD**.

The Bread for the Tabernacle

5 You shall take choice flour, and bake twelve loaves of it; two-tenths of an ephah shall be in each loaf. 6 You shall place them in two rows, six in a row, on the table of pure gold.*a* 7 You shall put pure frankincense with each row, to be a token offering for the bread, as an offering by fire to the LORD. 8 Every sabbath day Aaron shall set them in order before the LORD regularly as a commitment of the people of Israel, as a covenant forever. 9 They shall be for Aaron and his descendants, who shall eat them in a holy place, for they are most holy portions for him from the offerings by fire to the LORD, a perpetual due.

Blasphemy and Its Punishment

10 A man whose mother was an Israelite and whose father was an Egyptian came out among the people of Israel; and the Israelite woman's son and a certain Israelite began fighting in the camp. 11 The Israelite woman's son blasphemed the Name in a curse. And they brought him to Moses—now his mother's name was Shelomith, daughter of Dibri, of the tribe of Dan— 12 and they put him in custody, until the decision of the LORD should be made clear to them.

13 The LORD said to Moses, saying: 14 Take the blasphemer outside the camp; and let all who were within hearing lay their hands on his head, and let the whole congregation stone him. 15 And speak to the people of Israel, saying: Anyone who curses God shall bear the sin. 16 One who blasphemes the name of the LORD shall be put to death; the whole congregation shall stone the blasphemer. Aliens as well as citizens, when they blaspheme the Name, shall be put to death. 17 Anyone who kills a human being shall be put to death. 18 Anyone who kills an animal shall make restitution for it, life for life. 19 Anyone who maims another shall suffer the same injury in return: 20 fracture for fracture, eye for eye, tooth for tooth; the injury inflicted is the injury to be suffered. 21 One who kills an animal shall make restitution for it; but one who kills a human being shall be

a Heb *pure table*

24:5–9—The *loaves* are a regular presentation to YHWH and an indication of the people's commitment to YHWH and the covenant relationship.

24:10–23—God's instructions concerning a case of blasphemy.

24:11—Two acts take place: the improper use of the divine name and a curse. The man spoke the name of God without regard for its sanctity and in the context of a curse.

24:12—Discovering the will of God was understood as an ongoing process. The *decision of the LORD* is sought in a specific context and with a specific situation in mind. God continues to speak in and to unexpected and suddenly emerging situations.

24:16—The community is responsible to administer the punishment. Responsibility applies both to an individual and to the community (see the community "sin offering" in 4:13–21). Community responsibility need not be limited to punishment, however, but might well be practiced in acts of care, concern, support, and affirmation.

24:16–22—A symmetrical pattern helps understand the text: (A) one law for all (v. 16b);

(B) killing a human being (v. 17); (C) killing an animal (v. 18); (D) the law of equitable retaliation (vv. 19–20); (C′) killing an animal (v. 21a); (B′) killing a human being (v. 21b); (A′) one law for all (v. 22). The law of equitable retribution (the *lex talionis;* see Exod. 21:22–25) is at the heart of the text. The ruling is most likely designed to *restrain* violence in an effort to create an equitable response. If violence leads to violence, even when perceived to be equitable acts of retribution, the escalation of violence remains an ever-present possibility.

The larger context suggests the writers recognized that the call for a communal execution raised questions concerning the nature of "murder." One may think of justice as punishment of the "criminal" or as restoration of the "victim." Generally speaking, Israel's laws focus on the latter. Equitable retribution itself was probably perceived as a way to set things right, rather than a way to punish the wrongdoer. Of particular importance, the text raises questions concerning murder, government-sponsored executions, and justice. Although the text offers some answers, as always, one must ask if its answers (and maybe even its questions!) "make sense" in the modern world.

put to death. ²²You shall have one law for the alien and for the citizen: for I am the LORD your God. ²³Moses spoke thus to the people of Israel; and they took the blasphemer outside the camp, and stoned him to death. The people of Israel did as the LORD had commanded Moses.

The Sabbatical Year

25 The LORD spoke to Moses on Mount Sinai, saying: ²Speak to the people of Israel and say to them: When you enter the land that I am giving you, the land shall observe a sabbath for the LORD. ³Six years you shall sow your field, and six years you shall prune your vineyard, and gather in their yield; ⁴but in the seventh year there shall be a sabbath of complete rest for the land, a sabbath for the LORD: you shall not sow your field or prune your vineyard. ⁵You shall not reap the aftergrowth of your harvest or gather the grapes of your unpruned vine: it shall be a year of complete rest for the land. ⁶You may eat what the land yields during its sabbath—you, your male and female slaves, your hired and your bound laborers who live with you; ⁷for your livestock also, and for the wild animals in your land all its yield shall be for food.

The Year of Jubilee

8 You shall count off seven weeks*a* of years, seven times seven years, so that the period of seven weeks of years gives forty-nine years. ⁹Then you shall have the trumpet sounded loud; on the tenth day of the seventh month—on the day of atonement—you shall have the trumpet sounded throughout all your land. ¹⁰And you shall hallow the fiftieth year and you shall proclaim liberty throughout the land to all its inhabitants. It shall be a jubilee for you: you shall return, every one of you, to your property and every one of you to your family. ¹¹That fiftieth year shall be a jubilee for you: you shall not sow, or reap the aftergrowth, or harvest the unpruned vines. ¹²For it is a jubilee; it shall be holy to you: you shall eat only what the field itself produces.

13 In this year of jubilee you shall return, every one of you, to your property. ¹⁴When you make a sale to your neighbor or buy from your neighbor, you shall not cheat one another. ¹⁵When you buy from your neighbor, you shall pay only for the number of years since the jubilee; the seller shall charge you only for the remaining crop years. ¹⁶If the years are more, you shall increase the price, and if the years are fewer, you shall diminish the price; for it is a certain number of harvests that are being sold to you. ¹⁷You shall not cheat one another, but you shall fear your God; for I am the LORD your God.

18 You shall observe my statutes and faithfully keep my ordinances, so that you may live on the land securely. ¹⁹The land will yield its fruit, and you will eat your fill and live on it securely. ²⁰Should you ask, "What shall we eat in the seventh year, if we may not sow or gather in our crop?" ²¹I will order my blessing for you in the sixth year, so that it will

a Or *sabbaths*

25:1–55—Instructions for sabbatical and jubilee years.

25:1–7—Every seventh year the land must be given a *sabbath of complete rest*. The rhythm of creation, a seventh day of rest after six days of work, is built into the life of the land. In this way, the life of the land reflects the life of the people (see 18:2–5, 24–30).

25:8–24—In the fiftieth year, after counting seven times seven years, Israel is to observe a *jubilee*, a time when every person returns to ancestral property and family (v. 10). This is a time of liberation from poverty, debt, and debt-labor.

The jubilee acknowledges that YHWH, who "owns" the land, gave to each Israelite family a piece of the land of promise, which they care for as *aliens and tenants* (v. 23). The property may be "rented" to another during difficult economic times, but jubilee requires that the land return to the original family. God's promises to the ancestors inform the thinking.

yield a crop for three years. ²² When you sow in the eighth year, you will be eating from the old crop; until the ninth year, when its produce comes in, you shall eat the old. ²³ The land shall not be sold in perpetuity, for the land is mine; with me you are but aliens and tenants. ²⁴ Throughout the land that you hold, you shall provide for the redemption of the land.

25 If anyone of your kin falls into difficulty and sells a piece of property, then the next of kin shall come and redeem what the relative has sold. ²⁶ If the person has no one to redeem it, but then prospers and finds sufficient means to do so, ²⁷ the years since its sale shall be computed and the difference shall be refunded to the person to whom it was sold, and the property shall be returned. ²⁸ But if there are not sufficient means to recover it, what was sold shall remain with the purchaser until the year of jubilee; in the jubilee it shall be released, and the property shall be returned.

29 If anyone sells a dwelling house in a walled city, it may be redeemed until a year has elapsed since its sale; the right of redemption shall be one year. ³⁰ If it is not redeemed before a full year has elapsed, a house that is in a walled city shall pass in perpetuity to the purchaser, throughout the generations; it shall not be released in the jubilee. ³¹ But houses in villages that have no walls around them shall be classed as open country; they may be redeemed, and they shall be released in the jubilee. ³² As for the cities of the Levites, the Levites shall forever have the right of redemption of the houses in the cities belonging to them. ³³ Such property as may be redeemed from the Levites—houses sold in a city belonging to them—shall be released in the jubilee; because the houses in the cities of the Levites are their possession among the people of Israel. ³⁴ But the open land around their cities may not be sold; for that is their possession for all time.

35 If any of your kin fall into difficulty and become dependent on you,ᵃ you shall support them; they shall live with you as though resident aliens. ³⁶ Do not take interest in advance or otherwise make a profit from them, but fear your God; let them live with you. ³⁷ You shall not lend them your money at interest taken in advance, or provide them food at a profit. ³⁸ I am the LORD your God, who brought you out of the land of Egypt, to give you the land of Canaan, to be your God.

39 If any who are dependent on you become so impoverished that they sell themselves to you, you shall not make them serve as slaves. ⁴⁰ They shall remain with you as hired or bound laborers. They shall serve with you until the year of the jubilee. ⁴¹ Then they and their children with them shall be free from your authority; they shall go back to their own family and return to their ancestral property. ⁴² For they are my servants, whom I brought out of the land of Egypt; they shall not be sold as slaves are sold. ⁴³ You shall not rule over them with harshness, but shall fear your God. ⁴⁴ As for the male and female slaves whom you may have, it is from the nations around you that you may acquire male and female slaves. ⁴⁵ You

ᵃ Meaning of Heb uncertain

25:25–55—These verses detail various economic difficulties that an Israelite might experience and how jubilee is to be practiced in such circumstances.

25:25–28—If a person must "sell" land (allow another person to work the land and receive its benefits for a payment of money), the closest kinsperson, if able, is to help buy it back. Such a kinsperson is termed a "redeemer," the one who *redeems* (pays for and buys back) the land. In this context, redemption is an economic concern. A kinsperson has experienced crop failure, poverty, famine, or starvation, and "sells" land for money in order to survive. The extended family has a responsibility to redeem the land if possible. Both economic help and personal restoration are viewed as acts of justice.

may also acquire them from among the aliens residing with you, and from their families that are with you, who have been born in your land; and they may be your property. ⁴⁶ You may keep them as a possession for your children after you, for them to inherit as property. These you may treat as slaves, but as for your fellow Israelites, no one shall rule over the other with harshness.

47 If resident aliens among you prosper, and if any of your kin fall into difficulty with one of them and sell themselves to an alien, or to a branch of the alien's family, ⁴⁸ after they have sold themselves they shall have the right of redemption; one of their brothers may redeem them, ⁴⁹ or their uncle or their uncle's son may redeem them, or anyone of their family who is of their own flesh may redeem them; or if they prosper they may redeem themselves. ⁵⁰ They shall compute with the purchaser the total from the year when they sold themselves to the alien until the jubilee year; the price of the sale shall be applied to the number of years: the time they were with the owner shall be rated as the time of a hired laborer. ⁵¹ If many years remain, they shall pay for their redemption in proportion to the purchase price; ⁵² and if few years remain until the jubilee year, they shall compute thus: according to the years involved they shall make payment for their redemption. ⁵³ As a laborer hired by the year they shall be

under the alien's authority, who shall not, however, rule with harshness over them in your sight. ⁵⁴ And if they have not been redeemed in any of these ways, they and their children with them shall go free in the jubilee year. ⁵⁵ For to me the people of Israel are servants; they are my servants whom I brought out from the land of Egypt: I am the LORD your God.

Rewards for Obedience

26 You shall make for yourselves no idols and erect no carved images or pillars, and you shall not place figured stones in your land, to worship at them; for I am the LORD your God. ² You shall keep my sabbaths and reverence my sanctuary: I am the LORD.

3 If you follow my statutes and keep my commandments and observe them faithfully, ⁴ I will give you your rains in their season, and the land shall yield its produce, and the trees of the field shall yield their fruit. ⁵ Your threshing shall overtake the vintage, and the vintage shall overtake the sowing; you shall eat your bread to the full, and live securely in your land. ⁶ And I will grant peace in the land, and you shall lie down, and no one shall make you afraid; I will remove dangerous animals from the land, and no sword shall go through your land. ⁷ You shall give chase to your enemies, and they shall fall before you by the sword. ⁸ Five of you shall give chase to a hundred, and a hundred of you shall

---

25:55—The people are the *servants* of YHWH, redeemed by YHWH, and are not to become perpetual slaves. Jubilee was a time for all of Israel to experience freedom and liberty. The story of Israel's redemption from Egypt provides the basis for the proclamation of liberty. Story and practice are intimately bound together to give concrete expression to Israel's ongoing experiences of redemption. Poverty and need were real experiences of some, but the community was to make certain that the poverty and need were not continuous.

Israel's jubilee tradition is at the basis of Jesus' "proclamation" at the beginning of his public ministry in Luke 4:16–20. The Isaiah text from which he reads (Isa. 61:1–2; 58:6) draws on and

develops the jubilee tradition in providing a word of hope and encouragement to the Babylonian exiles. The gospel must be enacted in terms of the proclamation of liberation, the practice of acts that liberate, and a vision of the transformation of the world.

26:1–46 Blessings and Curses

26:3–13—Obedience and faithfulness to YHWH lead to blessing: seasonal rains, abundant crops, peace in the land, fertility, and the divine presence walking among them (v. 12). The promise of blessings is related to YHWH's redemption of Israel. The blessings provide insight into Israel's vision of the good life.

give chase to ten thousand; your enemies shall fall before you by the sword. ⁹I will look with favor upon you and make you fruitful and multiply you; and I will maintain my covenant with you. ¹⁰You shall eat old grain long stored, and you shall have to clear out the old to make way for the new. ¹¹I will place my dwelling in your midst, and I shall not abhor you. ¹²And I will walk among you, and will be your God, and you shall be my people. ¹³I am the LORD your God who brought you out of the land of Egypt, to be their slaves no more; I have broken the bars of your yoke and made you walk erect.

Penalties for Disobedience

14 But if you will not obey me, and do not observe all these commandments, ¹⁵if you spurn my statutes, and abhor my ordinances, so that you will not observe all my commandments, and you break my covenant, ¹⁶I in turn will do this to you: I will bring terror on you; consumption and fever that waste the eyes and cause life to pine away. You shall sow your seed in vain, for your enemies shall eat it. ¹⁷I will set my face against you, and you shall be struck down by your enemies; your foes shall rule over you, and you shall flee though no one pursues you. ¹⁸And if in spite of this you will not obey me, I will continue to punish you sevenfold for your sins. ¹⁹I will break your proud glory, and I will make your sky like iron and your earth like copper. ²⁰Your strength shall be spent to no purpose: your land shall not yield its produce, and the trees of the land shall not yield their fruit.

21 If you continue hostile to me, and will not obey me, I will continue to plague you sevenfold for your sins. ²²I will let loose wild animals against you, and they shall bereave you of your children and destroy your livestock; they shall make you few in number, and your roads shall be deserted.

23 If in spite of these punishments you have not turned back to me, but continue hostile to me, ²⁴then I too will continue hostile to you: I myself will strike you sevenfold for your sins. ²⁵I will bring the sword against you, executing vengeance for the covenant; and if you withdraw within your cities, I will send pestilence among you, and you shall be delivered into enemy hands. ²⁶When I break your staff of bread, ten women shall bake your bread in a single oven, and they shall dole out your bread by weight; and though you eat, you shall not be satisfied.

27 But if, despite this, you disobey me, and continue hostile to me, ²⁸I will continue hostile to you in fury; I in turn will punish you myself sevenfold for your sins. ²⁹You shall eat the flesh of your sons, and you shall eat the flesh of your daughters. ³⁰I will destroy your high places and cut down your incense altars; I will heap your carcasses on the carcasses of your idols. I will abhor you. ³¹I will lay your cities waste, will make your sanctuaries desolate, and I will not smell your pleasing odors. ³²I will devastate the land, so that your enemies who come to settle in it shall be appalled at it. ³³And you I will scatter among the nations, and I will unsheathe the sword against you; your land shall be a desolation, and your cities a waste.

34 Then the land shall enjoy*a* its

a Or make up for

26:14–39—If the people are hostile to YHWH and fail to obey, then YHWH will bring curses on them. The list of curses consistently includes the possibility that Israel can change (vv. 18, 21, 23, 27). YHWH takes Israel's actions seriously. The images of destruction reflect the response of YHWH to the lives of the people, not just fate working itself out in history. Human actions and human responsibility must be taken seriously in the construction of the world.

26:31–33—The curses conclude with the destruction and desolation of the land, and the removal of the people from the land. Death and exile reverse the divine promise of a people living on a land.

sabbath years as long as it lies desolate, while you are in the land of your
enemies; then the land shall rest, and
enjoy*a* its sabbath years. ³⁵ As long as it
lies desolate, it shall have the rest it did
not have on your sabbaths when you
were living on it. ³⁶ And as for those of
you who survive, I will send faintness
into their hearts in the lands of their
enemies; the sound of a driven leaf shall
put them to flight, and they shall flee
as one flees from the sword, and they
shall fall though no one pursues. ³⁷ They
shall stumble over one another, as if to
escape a sword, though no one pursues;
and you shall have no power to stand
against your enemies. ³⁸ You shall perish among the nations, and the land of
your enemies shall devour you. ³⁹ And
those of you who survive shall languish
in the land of your enemies because
of their iniquities; also they shall languish because of the iniquities of their
ancestors.

40 But if they confess their iniquity
and the iniquity of their ancestors, in
that they committed treachery against
me and, moreover, that they continued hostile to me— ⁴¹ so that I, in turn,
continued hostile to them and brought
them into the land of their enemies;
if then their uncircumcised heart is
humbled and they make amends for
their iniquity, ⁴² then will I remember
my covenant with Jacob; I will remember also my covenant with Isaac and
also my covenant with Abraham, and I
will remember the land. ⁴³ For the land
shall be deserted by them, and enjoy*a* its
sabbath years by lying desolate without

them, while they shall make amends
for their iniquity, because they dared to
spurn my ordinances, and they abhorred
my statutes. ⁴⁴ Yet for all that, when they
are in the land of their enemies, I will
not spurn them, or abhor them so as
to destroy them utterly and break my
covenant with them; for I am the LORD
their God; ⁴⁵ but I will remember in their
favor the covenant with their ancestors
whom I brought out of the land of Egypt
in the sight of the nations, to be their
God: I am the LORD.

46 These are the statutes and ordinances and laws that the LORD established between himself and the people of
Israel on Mount Sinai through Moses.

Votive Offerings

27 The LORD spoke to Moses, saying: ² Speak to the people of
Israel and say to them: When a person
makes an explicit vow to the LORD
concerning the equivalent for a human
being, ³ the equivalent for a male shall
be: from twenty to sixty years of age the
equivalent shall be fifty shekels of silver
by the sanctuary shekel. ⁴ If the person is
a female, the equivalent is thirty shekels.
⁵ If the age is from five to twenty years of
age, the equivalent is twenty shekels for
a male and ten shekels for a female. ⁶ If
the age is from one month to five years,
the equivalent for a male is five shekels
of silver, and for a female the equivalent
is three shekels of silver. ⁷ And if the person is sixty years old or over, then the
equivalent for a male is fifteen shekels,
and for a female ten shekels. ⁸ If any can-

a Or make up for

26:40–45—Exile is not final. Even then, if the
people will confess and make amends for their
sins, YHWH will remember the ancestral covenants and the land. Hope remains alive even in
the midst of devastation and exile. The text makes
a strong statement concerning the possibility of
change and transformation in human life.

27:1–34 Vows and Payments

27:2–8—*Vows* concerning human beings played
a role in the life of Israel. Jephthah vows to

sacrifice the first person out of his house if given
victory in battle. Unfortunately, his daughter was
the first one out, and he killed her in accordance
with his vow (Judg. 11:29–40). Hannah asks for
a child and vows to dedicate the child to the
sanctuary (1 Sam. 1:10–11). The valuation of
humans is addressed specifically to paying vows
and is not an effort to place ultimate value on
human life.

not afford the equivalent, they shall be brought before the priest and the priest shall assess them; the priest shall assess them according to what each one making a vow can afford.

9 If it concerns an animal that may be brought as an offering to the LORD, any such that may be given to the LORD shall be holy. 10 Another shall not be exchanged or substituted for it, either good for bad or bad for good; and if one animal is substituted for another, both that one and its substitute shall be holy. 11 If it concerns any unclean animal that may not be brought as an offering to the LORD, the animal shall be presented before the priest. 12 The priest shall assess it: whether good or bad, according to the assessment of the priest, so it shall be. 13 But if it is to be redeemed, one-fifth must be added to the assessment.

14 If a person consecrates a house to the LORD, the priest shall assess it: whether good or bad, as the priest assesses it, so it shall stand. 15 And if the one who consecrates the house wishes to redeem it, one-fifth shall be added to its assessed value, and it shall revert to the original owner.

16 If a person consecrates to the LORD any inherited landholding, its assessment shall be in accordance with its seed requirements: fifty shekels of silver to a homer of barley seed. 17 If the person consecrates the field as of the year of jubilee, that assessment shall stand; 18 but if the field is consecrated after the jubilee, the priest shall compute the price for it according to the years that remain until the year of jubilee, and the assessment shall be reduced. 19 And if the one who consecrates the field wishes to redeem it, then one-fifth shall be added to its assessed value, and it shall revert to the original owner; 20 but if the field is not redeemed, or if it has been sold to someone else, it shall no longer be redeemable. 21 But when the field is released in the jubilee, it shall be holy to the LORD as a devoted field; it becomes the priest's holding. 22 If someone consecrates to the LORD a field that has been purchased, which is not a part of the inherited landholding, 23 the priest shall compute for it the proportionate assessment up to the year of jubilee, and the assessment shall be paid as of that day, a sacred donation to the LORD. 24 In the year of jubilee the field shall return to the one from whom it was bought, whose holding the land is. 25 All assessments shall be by the sanctuary shekel: twenty gerahs shall make a shekel.

26 A firstling of animals, however, which as a firstling belongs to the LORD, cannot be consecrated by anyone; whether ox or sheep, it is the LORD's. 27 If it is an unclean animal, it shall be ransomed at its assessment, with one-fifth added; if it is not redeemed, it shall be sold at its assessment.

28 Nothing that a person owns that has been devoted to destruction for the LORD, be it human or animal, or inherited landholding, may be sold or redeemed; every devoted thing is most holy to the LORD. 29 No human beings who have been devoted to destruction can be ransomed; they shall be put to death.

30 All tithes from the land, whether the seed from the ground or the fruit from the tree, are the LORD's; they are holy to the LORD. 31 If persons wish to redeem any of their tithes, they must add one-fifth to them. 32 All tithes of herd and flock, every tenth one that passes under the shepherd's staff, shall be holy to the LORD. 33 Let no one inquire whether it is good or bad, or make substitution for it; if one makes substitution for it, then both it and the substitute shall be holy and cannot be redeemed.

34 These are the commandments that the LORD gave to Moses for the people of Israel on Mount Sinai.

The Book of
NUMBERS

Numbers, the fourth book of the Pentateuch, narrates Israel's journey from Mount Sinai to the borders of the land of promise. As such, the story of Numbers is told primarily in the context of journey. The narrative is particularly interesting because it reflects the struggles of Israel and YHWH as they travel together. The story continuously returns to issues and problems raised because YHWH, the holy one, dwells in the midst of Israel, a sinful, rebellious, unfaithful, complaining, and contentious people. The book provides a profound story of the interweaving and interaction of the life of YHWH and the life of the Israelite community.

The book opens with a census of the people, called for by YHWH, which anticipates Israel's departure and entry into Canaan as an army (chap. 1). The order of the tribes in the march and the duties of the Levites, the ones who are responsible for transporting the tabernacle, receive specific attention (chaps. 2–4). Divine instructions (chaps. 5–6), offerings of the community leaders (chap. 7), the consecration ritual for the Levites (chap. 8), and the observance of Passover (chap. 9) lead up to the departure of Israel from the mountain (10:11).

The central part of the book (chaps. 11–25) reports a series of rebellions by the people against YHWH, Moses, and Aaron. The rebellions are located in the context of journey and movement: from Sinai to Kadesh-barnea (20:1 reports their arrival) and from Kadesh-barnea to the plains of Moab (22:1 reports their arrival). The stories reflect critical concern for the meaning and nature of community leadership. At the same time, the stories reflect the human struggle to live in the present moment, as Israel remembers its distress in Egypt and anxiously anticipates its future life in the land.

A second census of the people (chap. 26) marks a turning point in the larger narrative. This census recalls the first one in chapter 1 and anticipates the people's new life in the land as instructions are given for the division of the land (26:52–56). In terms of the Pentateuch, the movement toward the land recalls the promises of YHWH to the ancestors (Gen. 12:1–9; 15:7–21; 26:1–5; 28:10–15) and locates the wilderness journey in the context of the divine guidance of history through promise.

The remainder of the book (chaps. 27–36) provides the Israelites with instructions for their new life in the land. The narrative demonstrates the emergence of hope in the context of sin, defeat, and despair. Thus, the Israelite journey provides a profound story of human struggle in the context of human weakness.

The book of Numbers reflects, in the traditional view, the editorial activity of the Priestly writers. It certainly is significantly connected to what precedes it and anticipates what follows. It is generally recognized to have achieved something of its present form during or after the Babylonian exile (sixth–fifth centuries BCE). Numbers does, however, include material that is thought to have been part of an earlier narrative of Israel's origins. The Priestly editors drew on and incorporated various parts of this older "epic" tradition in the composition of Numbers.

At the same time, however, Numbers appears to have a structure and narrative integrity of its own. The strongest evidence for this is found in the two reports of a census of the people. The first census (chap. 1) is concerned with the people who came out of Egypt and saw the wonders of God on their behalf. The second census (chap. 26) is concerned with the descendants of the generation that came out of Egypt. In both cases, the census functions to indicate that Israel is turning toward the land of Canaan—the realization of the promise of YHWH to the ancestors that their descendants would dwell on this land.

Numbers is concerned with the construction of community. The desire to compose a "national" story makes sense both in the early moments of the founding of the nation, that is, when the Israelite monarchy first came into being, and in the context of exile and the possible "death" of the nation, that is, when Israel was in Babylon.

Numbers reflects a long and complex history of composition. It reflects traditions that may well be as early as the tribal period and traditions that may well be as late as the exilic or postexilic periods. Because of this history, the book may well reflect a great variety of perspectives concerning the history of Israel, the faith of Israel, and the cultic practices of Israel. In its current location and form, it provides the key narratives of Israel's journey from Mount Sinai to Canaan. Regardless of its history, its contribution to the Pentateuchal story is clear.

—**Frank H. Gorman Jr.**

The First Census of Israel

1 The LORD spoke to Moses in the wilderness of Sinai, in the tent of meeting, on the first day of the second month, in the second year after they had come out of the land of Egypt, saying: ² Take a census of the whole congregation of Israelites, in their clans, by ancestral houses, according to the number of names, every male individually; ³ from twenty years old and upward, everyone in Israel able to go to war. You and Aaron shall enroll them, company by company. ⁴ A man from each tribe shall be with you, each man the head of his ancestral house. ⁵ These are the names of the men who shall assist you:

From Reuben, Elizur son of Shedeur.
⁶ From Simeon, Shelumiel son of Zurishaddai.

1:1–2:34 Numbering the People, Ordering the Camp

1:1—Israel arrived at Mount Sinai on the third new moon following their exit from Egypt (Exod. 19:1). The tabernacle was set up on the first day of the first month of the second year (Exod. 40:17). YHWH tells Moses to take a census of the people on the first day of the second month of the second year, a month after the construction of the tabernacle. Israel will leave the mountain on the twentieth day of the second month of the second year (Num. 10:11). Exodus 19:1 to Num. 10:10 reports events that took place in a bit less than a year. Numbers 10:11 through Num. 36:13 report events that took place over a period of forty years.

1:2—The census marks a turning point in the story. With the covenant made (Exod. 19–24; cf. Exod. 32–34), the divine instructions conveyed to Moses (Exod. 25–Lev. 27), and the divine presence dwelling in the tabernacle in the midst of the community (Exod. 40), the story begins to turn to the journey to the promised land. The census marks YHWH's prompting to prepare for that journey and for entry into Canaan. (See the discussion of the second census in Num. 26 for a discussion of its role in the larger narrative.)

The census includes males twenty years of age or older who are able to go to war. This anticipates Israel's depiction as a conquering army entering the land of Canaan (see Josh. 6–10). The Israelites are led by YHWH, the divine warrior who delivered them from Egypt (see Exod. 15:1–18) and who will lead them on their journey through the wilderness to the land. YHWH is depicted as divine warrior, powerful creator, divine ruler, and the community redeemer.

7 From Judah, Nahshon son of
Amminadab.

8 From Issachar, Nethanel son of Zuar.

9 From Zebulun, Eliab son of Helon.

10 From the sons of Joseph:
from Ephraim, Elishama son of
Ammihud;
from Manasseh, Gamaliel son of
Pedahzur.

11 From Benjamin, Abidan son of
Gideoni.

12 From Dan, Ahiezer son of
Ammishaddai.

13 From Asher, Pagiel son of Ochran.

14 From Gad, Eliasaph son of Deuel.

15 From Naphtali, Ahira son of Enan.

16 These were the ones chosen from the congregation, the leaders of their ancestral tribes, the heads of the divisions of Israel.

17 Moses and Aaron took these men who had been designated by name, 18 and on the first day of the second month they assembled the whole congregation together. They registered themselves in their clans, by their ancestral houses, according to the number of names from twenty years old and upward, individually, 19 as the Lord commanded Moses. So he enrolled them in the wilderness of Sinai.

20 The descendants of Reuben, Israel's firstborn, their lineage, in their clans, by their ancestral houses, according to the number of names, individually, every male from twenty years old and upward, everyone able to go to war: 21 those enrolled of the tribe of Reuben were forty-six thousand five hundred.

22 The descendants of Simeon, their lineage, in their clans, by their ancestral houses, those of them that were numbered, according to the number of names, individually, every male from twenty years old and upward, everyone able to go to war: 23 those enrolled of the tribe of Simeon were fifty-nine thousand three hundred.

24 The descendants of Gad, their lineage, in their clans, by their ancestral houses, according to the number of the names, from twenty years old and upward, everyone able to go to war: 25 those enrolled of the tribe of Gad were forty-five thousand six hundred fifty.

26 The descendants of Judah, their lineage, in their clans, by their ancestral houses, according to the number of names, from twenty years old and upward, everyone able to go to war: 27 those enrolled of the tribe of Judah were seventy-four thousand six hundred.

28 The descendants of Issachar, their lineage, in their clans, by their ancestral houses, according to the number of names, from twenty years old and upward, everyone able to go to war: 29 those enrolled of the tribe of Issachar were fifty-four thousand four hundred.

30 The descendants of Zebulun, their lineage, in their clans, by their ancestral houses, according to the number of names, from twenty years old and upward, everyone able to go to war: 31 those enrolled of the tribe of Zebulun were fifty-seven thousand four hundred.

32 The descendants of Joseph, namely, the descendants of Ephraim, their lineage, in their clans, by their ancestral houses, according to the number of names, from twenty years old and upward, everyone able to go to war: 33 those enrolled of the tribe of Ephraim were forty thousand five hundred.

1:17–19—The census registration takes place according to *clans* and *ancestral houses*. Israel's national story, which is the same as Israel's faith story, begins with a couple (Abraham and Sarah), moves to twelve tribes (the twelve "sons of Israel"), and concludes with a nation. Family, faith, and national concerns converge in Israel's founding story. A contemporary reader may well view this convergence with caution, even skepticism. History includes too many stories of violence, genocide, and colonialism undertaken in the name of religion and national interests. While the separation of one's religion and one's politics is impossible, if and when their convergence causes harm to others, mercy and love require a critical look at one's faith *and* one's politics!

34 The descendants of Manasseh, their lineage, in their clans, by their ancestral houses, according to the number of names, from twenty years old and upward, everyone able to go to war: [35] those enrolled of the tribe of Manasseh were thirty-two thousand two hundred.

36 The descendants of Benjamin, their lineage, in their clans, by their ancestral houses, according to the number of names, from twenty years old and upward, everyone able to go to war: [37] those enrolled of the tribe of Benjamin were thirty-five thousand four hundred.

38 The descendants of Dan, their lineage, in their clans, by their ancestral houses, according to the number of names, from twenty years old and upward, everyone able to go to war: [39] those enrolled of the tribe of Dan were sixty-two thousand seven hundred.

40 The descendants of Asher, their lineage, in their clans, by their ancestral houses, according to the number of names, from twenty years old and upward, everyone able to go to war: [41] those enrolled of the tribe of Asher were forty-one thousand five hundred.

42 The descendants of Naphtali, their lineage, in their clans, by their ancestral houses, according to the number of names, from twenty years old and upward, everyone able to go to war: [43] those enrolled of the tribe of Naphtali were fifty-three thousand four hundred.

44 These are those who were enrolled, whom Moses and Aaron enrolled with the help of the leaders of Israel, twelve men, each representing his ancestral house. [45] So the whole number of the Israelites, by their ancestral houses, from twenty years old and upward, everyone able to go to war in Israel— [46] their whole number was six hundred three thousand five hundred fifty. [47] The Levites, however, were not numbered by their ancestral tribe along with them.

48 The LORD had said to Moses: [49] Only the tribe of Levi you shall not enroll, and you shall not take a census of them with the other Israelites. [50] Rather you shall appoint the Levites over the tabernacle of the covenant,[a] and over all its equipment, and over all that belongs to it; they are to carry the tabernacle and all its equipment, and they shall tend it, and shall camp around the tabernacle. [51] When the tabernacle is to set out, the Levites shall take it down; and when the tabernacle is to be pitched, the Levites shall set it up. And any outsider who comes near shall be put to death. [52] The other Israelites shall camp in their respective regimental camps, by companies; [53] but the Levites shall camp around the tabernacle of the covenant,[a] that there may be no wrath on the congregation of the Israelites; and the Levites shall perform the guard duty of the tabernacle of the covenant.[a] [54] The Israelites did so; they did just as the LORD commanded Moses.

The Order of Encampment and Marching

2 The LORD spoke to Moses and Aaron, saying: [2] The Israelites shall

[a] Or treaty, or testimony; Heb eduth

1:44–47—Some 603,550 males over the age of twenty are counted and registered (2:32; cf. Exod. 12:37). The high numbers indicate that God's promise of a great nation to the ancestors is a reality (cf. Exod. 1:1–7). In addition, the numbers indicate that God the creator is able to sustain and provide for such a large group in the wilderness. Even when reporting census numbers, the text points the reader to YHWH: the creator, the promise maker, the redeemer, and the warrior.

1:48–54—The Levites are excluded from the census because they are assigned responsibilities for the tabernacle. They are to protect the sacred precincts from violation and trespass and, in that way, protect the Israelites from the wrath of YHWH. The tabernacle ministry must protect both YHWH's holy tent from violation and the people from divine wrath. This is a dangerous ministry: they stand between the holy and the sinful.

2:1–34—The location of the tent at the center

camp each in their respective regiments, under ensigns by their ancestral houses; they shall camp facing the tent of meeting on every side. ³ Those to camp on the east side toward the sunrise shall be of the regimental encampment of Judah by companies. The leader of the people of Judah shall be Nahshon son of Amminadab, ⁴ with a company as enrolled of seventy-four thousand six hundred. ⁵ Those to camp next to him shall be the tribe of Issachar. The leader of the Issacharites shall be Nethanel son of Zuar, ⁶ with a company as enrolled of fifty-four thousand four hundred. ⁷ Then the tribe of Zebulun: The leader of the Zebulunites shall be Eliab son of Helon, ⁸ with a company as enrolled of fifty-seven thousand four hundred. ⁹ The total enrollment of the camp of Judah, by companies, is one hundred eighty-six thousand four hundred. They shall set out first on the march.

10 On the south side shall be the regimental encampment of Reuben by companies. The leader of the Reubenites shall be Elizur son of Shedeur, ¹¹ with a company as enrolled of forty-six thousand five hundred. ¹² And those to camp next to him shall be the tribe of Simeon. The leader of the Simeonites shall be Shelumiel son of Zurishaddai, ¹³ with a company as enrolled of fifty-nine thousand three hundred. ¹⁴ Then the tribe of Gad: The leader of the Gadites shall be Eliasaph son of Reuel, ¹⁵ with a company as enrolled of forty-five thousand six hundred fifty. ¹⁶ The total enrollment of the camp of Reuben, by companies, is one hundred fifty-one thousand

four hundred fifty. They shall set out second.

17 The tent of meeting, with the camp of the Levites, shall set out in the center of the camps; they shall set out just as they camp, each in position, by their regiments.

18 On the west side shall be the regimental encampment of Ephraim by companies. The leader of the people of Ephraim shall be Elishama son of Ammihud, ¹⁹ with a company as enrolled of forty thousand five hundred. ²⁰ Next to him shall be the tribe of Manasseh. The leader of the people of Manasseh shall be Gamaliel son of Pedahzur, ²¹ with a company as enrolled of thirty-two thousand two hundred. ²² Then the tribe of Benjamin: The leader of the Benjaminites shall be Abidan son of Gideoni, ²³ with a company as enrolled of thirty-five thousand four hundred. ²⁴ The total enrollment of the camp of Ephraim, by companies, is one hundred eight thousand one hundred. They shall set out third on the march.

25 On the north side shall be the regimental encampment of Dan by companies. The leader of the Danites shall be Ahiezer son of Ammishaddai, ²⁶ with a company as enrolled of sixty-two thousand seven hundred. ²⁷ Those to camp next to him shall be the tribe of Asher. The leader of the Asherites shall be Pagiel son of Ochran, ²⁸ with a company as enrolled of forty-one thousand five hundred. ²⁹ Then the tribe of Naphtali: The leader of the Naphtalites shall be Ahira son of Enan, ³⁰ with a company as enrolled of fifty-three thousand four hundred. ³¹ The total enrollment of the

---

of the people provides a concrete image of the divine presence in the midst of the community. Israel recognized that problems arise when YHWH, the holy one, dwells in the midst of a sinful, obstinate, and faithless people, that is, any human community. Both Judaism and Christianity have struggled to understand the ways in which God might be present in the world and in history. This is an intellectual and theological problem. Christianity recognizes that Jesus was

born a human being, very real flesh and very real blood, into the real world of human suffering and sorrow. He died a real and horrible death. How, in this particular flesh-and-blood human being, did God enter into history in a redemptive way? Equally important, how are we to understand the presence of God in history when for so many history is a continuous story of suffering, pain, oppression, sorrow, and horrors?

camp of Dan is one hundred fifty-seven thousand six hundred. They shall set out last, by companies.*

32 This was the enrollment of the Israelites by their ancestral houses; the total enrollment in the camps by their companies was six hundred three thousand five hundred fifty. ³³ Just as the LORD had commanded Moses, the Levites were not enrolled among the other Israelites.

34 The Israelites did just as the LORD had commanded Moses: They camped by regiments, and they set out the same way, everyone by clans, according to ancestral houses.

The Sons of Aaron

3 This is the lineage of Aaron and Moses at the time when the LORD spoke with Moses on Mount Sinai. ² These are the names of the sons of Aaron: Nadab the firstborn, and Abihu, Eleazar, and Ithamar; ³ these are the names of the sons of Aaron, the anointed priests, whom he ordained to minister as priests. ⁴ Nadab and Abihu died before the LORD when they offered unholy fire before the LORD in the wilderness of Sinai, and they had no children. Eleazar and Ithamar served as priests in the lifetime of their father Aaron.

The Duties of the Levites

5 Then the LORD spoke to Moses, saying: ⁶ Bring the tribe of Levi near, and set them before Aaron the priest, so that they may assist him. ⁷ They shall perform duties for him and for the whole congregation in front of the tent of meeting, doing service at the tabernacle; ⁸ they shall be in charge of all the furnishings of the tent of meeting, and attend to the duties for the Israelites as

they do service at the tabernacle. ⁹ You shall give the Levites to Aaron and his descendants; they are unreservedly given to him from among the Israelites. ¹⁰ But you shall make a register of Aaron and his descendants; it is they who shall attend to the priesthood, and any outsider who comes near shall be put to death.

11 Then the LORD spoke to Moses, saying: ¹² I hereby accept the Levites from among the Israelites as substitutes for all the firstborn that open the womb among the Israelites. The Levites shall be mine, ¹³ for all the firstborn are mine; when I killed all the firstborn in the land of Egypt, I consecrated for my own all the firstborn in Israel, both human and animal; they shall be mine. I am the LORD.

A Census of the Levites

14 Then the LORD spoke to Moses in the wilderness of Sinai, saying: ¹⁵ Enroll the Levites by ancestral houses and by clans. You shall enroll every male from a month old and upward. ¹⁶ So Moses enrolled them according to the word of the LORD, as he was commanded. ¹⁷ The following were the sons of Levi, by their names: Gershon, Kohath, and Merari. ¹⁸ These are the names of the sons of Gershon by their clans: Libni and Shimei. ¹⁹ The sons of Kohath by their clans: Amram, Izhar, Hebron, and Uzziel. ²⁰ The sons of Merari by their clans: Mahli and Mushi. These are the clans of the Levites, by their ancestral houses.

21 To Gershon belonged the clan of the Libnites and the clan of the Shimeites; these were the clans of the Gershonites. ²² Their enrollment, counting

---

*Compare verses 9, 16, 24: Heb *by their regiments*

3:1–4:49 Counting Levites; Different Duties for Different Families

3:5–10—On the duties of the Levites, see Num. 1:48–54.

3:11–13—YHWH accepts the Levites as *substitutes for all the firstborn* of Israel: the firstborn belong to YHWH (cf. Exod. 13:11–16). YHWH's

claim on the Israelite firstborn is related to the death of the Egyptian firstborn (v. 13; see Exod. 11:4–8; 12:29–32). The firstfruits of harvest, animals, and family belong to YHWH. The Levites are dedicated and holy to YHWH because they are substitutes for the firstborn of Israel (see vv. 44–51 as well).

all the males from a month old and upward, was seven thousand five hundred. 23 The clans of the Gershonites were to camp behind the tabernacle on the west, 24 with Eliasaph son of Lael as head of the ancestral house of the Gershonites. 25 The responsibility of the sons of Gershon in the tent of meeting was to be the tabernacle, the tent with its covering, the screen for the entrance of the tent of meeting, 26 the hangings of the court, the screen for the entrance of the court that is around the tabernacle and the altar, and its cords—all the service pertaining to these.

27 To Kohath belonged the clan of the Amramites, the clan of the Izharites, the clan of the Hebronites, and the clan of the Uzzielites; these are the clans of the Kohathites. 28 Counting all the males, from a month old and upward, there were eight thousand six hundred, attending to the duties of the sanctuary. 29 The clans of the Kohathites were to camp on the south side of the tabernacle, 30 with Elizaphan son of Uzziel as head of the ancestral house of the clans of the Kohathites. 31 Their responsibility was to be the ark, the table, the lampstand, the altars, the vessels of the sanctuary with which the priests minister, and the screen—all the service pertaining to these. 32 Eleazar son of Aaron the priest was to be chief over the leaders of the Levites, and to have oversight of those who had charge of the sanctuary.

33 To Merari belonged the clan of the Mahlites and the clan of the Mushites: these are the clans of Merari. 34 Their enrollment, counting all the males from a month old and upward, was six thousand two hundred. 35 The head of the ancestral house of the clans of Merari was Zuriel son of Abihail; they were to camp on the north side of the tabernacle. 36 The responsibility assigned to the sons of Merari was to be the frames of the tabernacle, the bars, the pillars, the bases, and all their accessories—all the service pertaining to these; 37 also the pillars of the court all around, with their bases and pegs and cords.

38 Those who were to camp in front of the tabernacle on the east—in front of the tent of meeting toward the east— were Moses and Aaron and Aaron's sons, having charge of the rites within the sanctuary, whatever had to be done for the Israelites; and any outsider who came near was to be put to death. 39 The total enrollment of the Levites whom Moses and Aaron enrolled at the commandment of the LORD, by their clans, all the males from a month old and upward, was twenty-two thousand.

The Redemption of the Firstborn

40 Then the LORD said to Moses: Enroll all the firstborn males of the Israelites, from a month old and upward, and count their names. 41 But you shall accept the Levites for me—I am the LORD—as substitutes for all the firstborn among the Israelites, and the livestock of the Levites as substitutes for all the firstborn among the livestock of the Israelites. 42 So Moses enrolled all the firstborn among the Israelites, as the LORD commanded him. 43 The total enrollment, all the firstborn males from a month old and upward, counting the number of names, was twenty-two thousand two hundred seventy-three.

44 Then the LORD spoke to Moses, saying: 45 Accept the Levites as substitutes for all the firstborn among the Israelites, and the livestock of the Levites as substitutes for their livestock; and the Levites shall be mine. I am the LORD. 46 As the price of redemption of the two hundred seventy-three of the firstborn of the Israelites, over and above the number of the Levites, 47 you shall accept five shekels apiece, reckoning by the shekel of the sanctuary, a shekel of twenty gerahs. 48 Give to Aaron and his sons the money by which the excess number of them is redeemed. 49 So Moses took the redemption money from those who were over and above those redeemed by

the Levites; [50] from the firstborn of the Israelites he took the money, one thousand three hundred sixty-five shekels, reckoned by the shekel of the sanctuary; [51] and Moses gave the redemption money to Aaron and his sons, according to the word of the LORD, as the LORD had commanded Moses.

The Kohathites

4 The LORD spoke to Moses and Aaron, saying: [2] Take a census of the Kohathites separate from the other Levites, by their clans and their ancestral houses, [3] from thirty years old up to fifty years old, all who qualify to do work relating to the tent of meeting. [4] The service of the Kohathites relating to the tent of meeting concerns the most holy things.

5 When the camp is to set out, Aaron and his sons shall go in and take down the screening curtain, and cover the ark of the covenant[a] with it; [6] then they shall put on it a covering of fine leather,[b] and spread over that a cloth all of blue, and shall put its poles in place. [7] Over the table of the bread of the Presence they shall spread a blue cloth, and put on it the plates, the dishes for incense, the bowls, and the flagons for the drink offering; the regular bread also shall be on it; [8] then they shall spread over them a crimson cloth, and cover it with a covering of fine leather,[b] and shall put its poles in place. [9] They shall take a blue cloth, and cover the lampstand for the light, with its lamps, its snuffers, its trays, and all the vessels for oil with which it is supplied; [10] and they shall put it with all its utensils in a covering of fine leather,[b] and put it on the carrying frame. [11] Over the golden altar they shall spread a blue cloth, and cover it with a covering of fine leather,[b] and shall put its poles in place; [12] and they shall take all the utensils of the service that are used in the sanctuary, and put them in a blue cloth, and cover them with a covering of fine leather,[b] and put them on the carrying frame. [13] They shall take away the ashes from the altar, and spread a purple cloth over it; [14] and they shall put on it all the utensils of the altar, which are used for the service there, the firepans, the forks, the shovels, and the basins, all the utensils of the altar; and they shall spread on it a covering of fine leather,[b] and shall put its poles in place. [15] When Aaron and his sons have finished covering the sanctuary and all the furnishings of the sanctuary, as the camp sets out, after that the Kohathites shall come to carry these, but they must not touch the holy things, or they will die. These are the things of the tent of meeting that the Kohathites are to carry.

16 Eleazar son of Aaron the priest shall have charge of the oil for the light, the fragrant incense, the regular grain offering, and the anointing oil, the oversight of all the tabernacle and all that is in it, in the sanctuary and in its utensils.

17 Then the LORD spoke to Moses and Aaron, saying: [18] You must not let the tribe of the clans of the Kohathites be destroyed from among the Levites. [19] This is how you must deal with them in order that they may live and not die when they come near to the most holy things: Aaron and his sons shall go in

---

[a] Or *treaty,* or *testimony;* Heb *eduth*   [b] Meaning of Heb uncertain

---

4:1–33—The *Kohathites* (vv. 2–15) are assigned the transport of the holy things of the tabernacle. They are not to touch them, however, so the priests place cloths over the holy objects. The Gershonites (vv. 21–28) are assigned the transport of the curtains and covering of the tabernacle. The Merarites (vv. 26–33) transport the frame of the tent.

The instructions reflect a division of labor in the maintenance and moving of the tabernacle.

The mission of transporting the tabernacle is an important and dangerous job and requires a variety of groups undertaking a variety of activities. Paul thought of the body of Christ in much the same way (e.g., Rom. 12). The church is the body of Christ and is called to service in the world. Just as a body has many parts with distinct functions, so the church has many parts with many distinct functions. Ministry is characterized by variety and diversity of activity.

and assign each to a particular task or burden. **20** But the Kohathites*a* must not go in to look on the holy things even for a moment; otherwise they will die.

The Gershonites and Merarites

21 Then the LORD spoke to Moses, saying: **22** Take a census of the Gershonites also, by their ancestral houses and by their clans; **23** from thirty years old up to fifty years old you shall enroll them, all who qualify to do work in the tent of meeting. **24** This is the service of the clans of the Gershonites, in serving and bearing burdens: **25** They shall carry the curtains of the tabernacle, and the tent of meeting with its covering, and the outer covering of fine leather*b* that is on top of it, and the screen for the entrance of the tent of meeting, **26** and the hangings of the court, and the screen for the entrance of the gate of the court that is around the tabernacle and the altar, and their cords, and all the equipment for their service; and they shall do all that needs to be done with regard to them. **27** All the service of the Gershonites shall be at the command of Aaron and his sons, in all that they are to carry, and in all that they have to do; and you shall assign to their charge all that they are to carry. **28** This is the service of the clans of the Gershonites relating to the tent of meeting, and their responsibilities are to be under the oversight of Ithamar son of Aaron the priest.

29 As for the Merarites, you shall enroll them by their clans and their ancestral houses; **30** from thirty years old up to fifty years old you shall enroll them, everyone who qualifies to do the work of the tent of meeting. **31** This is what they are charged to carry, as the whole of their service in the tent of meeting: the frames of the tabernacle, with its bars, pillars, and bases, **32** and the pillars of the court all around with their bases, pegs, and cords, with all their equipment and all their related service; and you shall assign by name the objects that they are

required to carry. **33** This is the service of the clans of the Merarites, the whole of their service relating to the tent of meeting, under the hand of Ithamar son of Aaron the priest.

Census of the Levites

34 So Moses and Aaron and the leaders of the congregation enrolled the Kohathites, by their clans and their ancestral houses, **35** from thirty years old up to fifty years old, everyone who qualified for work relating to the tent of meeting; **36** and their enrollment by clans was two thousand seven hundred fifty. **37** This was the enrollment of the clans of the Kohathites, all who served at the tent of meeting, whom Moses and Aaron enrolled according to the commandment of the LORD by Moses.

38 The enrollment of the Gershonites, by their clans and their ancestral houses, **39** from thirty years old up to fifty years old, everyone who qualified for work relating to the tent of meeting— **40** their enrollment by their clans and their ancestral houses was two thousand six hundred thirty. **41** This was the enrollment of the clans of the Gershonites, all who served at the tent of meeting, whom Moses and Aaron enrolled according to the commandment of the LORD.

42 The enrollment of the clans of the Merarites, by their clans and their ancestral houses, **43** from thirty years old up to fifty years old, everyone who qualified for work relating to the tent of meeting— **44** their enrollment by their clans was three thousand two hundred. **45** This is the enrollment of the clans of the Merarites, whom Moses and Aaron enrolled according to the commandment of the LORD by Moses.

46 All those who were enrolled of the Levites, whom Moses and Aaron and the leaders of Israel enrolled, by their clans and their ancestral houses, **47** from thirty years old up to fifty years old, everyone who qualified to do the

a Heb *they*   *b* Meaning of Heb uncertain

work of service and the work of bearing burdens relating to the tent of meeting, [48] their enrollment was eight thousand five hundred eighty. [49] According to the commandment of the LORD through Moses they were appointed to their several tasks of serving or carrying; thus they were enrolled by him, as the LORD commanded Moses.

Unclean Persons

5 The LORD spoke to Moses, saying: [2] Command the Israelites to put out of the camp everyone who is leprous,[a] or has a discharge, and everyone who is unclean through contact with a corpse; [3] you shall put out both male and female, putting them outside the camp; they must not defile their camp, where I dwell among them. [4] The Israelites did so, putting them outside the camp; as the LORD had spoken to Moses, so the Israelites did.

Confession and Restitution

5 The LORD spoke to Moses, saying: [6] Speak to the Israelites: When a man or a woman wrongs another, breaking faith with the LORD, that person incurs guilt [7] and shall confess the sin that has been committed. The person shall make full restitution for the wrong, adding one-fifth to it, and giving it to the one who was wronged. [8] If the injured party has no next of kin to whom restitution may be made for the wrong, the restitution for wrong shall go to the LORD for the priest, in addition to the ram of atonement with which atonement is made for the guilty party. [9] Among all the sacred donations of the Israelites, every gift that they bring to the priest shall be his. [10] The sacred donations of all are their own; whatever anyone gives to the priest shall be his.

Concerning an Unfaithful Wife

11 The LORD spoke to Moses, saying: [12] Speak to the Israelites and say to them: If any man's wife goes astray and is unfaithful to him, [13] if a man has had intercourse with her but it is hidden from her husband, so that she is undetected though she has defiled herself, and there is no witness against her since she was not caught in the act; [14] if a spirit of jealousy comes on him, and he is jealous of his wife who has defiled herself; or if a spirit of jealousy comes on him, and

[a] A term for several skin diseases; precise meaning uncertain

5:1–6:27 Miscellaneous Rulings: the Holiness of the Camp; Adultery

5:1–4—Persons who have an unclean skin disorder (see the more complete discussion in Lev. 13–14), who have an unclean flow (Lev. 15), or who are unclean because of a corpse are placed outside the camp. Expulsion indicates the severity with which these impure states were viewed, and seeks to protect both the tabernacle and the community from contamination.

5:5–10—To wrong another person is to break faith with YHWH and incur guilt. The wrongdoer must confess, i.e., accept responsibility for the action, and make restitution, i.e., restore the loss to the wronged person plus an additional twenty percent. The ruling emphasizes that the one wronged must be "restored" and "set right." Restoration and restitution take precedence over punishment.

5:11–31—The text is disturbing. Adultery was considered an offense against God and a husband (the ruling reflects the male viewpoint). In this text, the woman appears to be the only one able to be accused of adultery (see, however, Lev. 20:10; cf. John 8:2–11). If the husband even suspects that his wife has been with another man, he is allowed to put her through the ordeal. The text does not view marriage as an equitable relationship, and, because of that, places the woman in a vulnerable position. In addition, the text focuses so strongly on the matter of sexual faithlessness that the reader may forget that the marriage relationship includes emotional, economic, and experiential dynamics as well.

The contemporary reader can recognize Israel's concern for adultery, embrace the importance of the marriage relationship, and recognize the problems that arise when one partner is unfaithful, without at the same time adopting the male-oriented, patriarchal, suspicious, and severe viewpoint of this ruling. Israel's understanding of marriage was very different from modern views. More importantly, the violence against a woman supported by this text must be dismissed for what it is: male violence, generated by and based on male suspicions, against a woman.

he is jealous of his wife, though she has not defiled herself; [15] then the man shall bring his wife to the priest. And he shall bring the offering required for her, one-tenth of an ephah of barley flour. He shall pour no oil on it and put no frankincense on it, for it is a grain offering of jealousy, a grain offering of remembrance, bringing iniquity to remembrance.

[16] Then the priest shall bring her near, and set her before the LORD; [17] the priest shall take holy water in an earthen vessel, and take some of the dust that is on the floor of the tabernacle and put it into the water. [18] The priest shall set the woman before the LORD, dishevel the woman's hair, and place in her hands the grain offering of remembrance, which is the grain offering of jealousy. In his own hand the priest shall have the water of bitterness that brings the curse. [19] Then the priest shall make her take an oath, saying, "If no man has lain with you, if you have not turned aside to uncleanness while under your husband's authority, be immune to this water of bitterness that brings the curse. [20] But if you have gone astray while under your husband's authority, if you have defiled yourself and some man other than your husband has had intercourse with you," [21]—let the priest make the woman take the oath of the curse and say to the woman—"the LORD make you an execration and an oath among your people, when the LORD makes your uterus drop, your womb discharge; [22] now may this water that brings the curse enter your bowels and make your womb discharge, your uterus drop!" And the woman shall say, "Amen. Amen."

[23] Then the priest shall put these curses in writing, and wash them off into the water of bitterness. [24] He shall make the woman drink the water of bitterness that brings the curse, and the water that brings the curse shall enter her and cause bitter pain. [25] The priest shall take the grain offering of jealousy out of the woman's hand, and shall elevate the grain offering before the LORD and bring it to the altar; [26] and the priest shall take a handful of the grain offering, as its memorial portion, and turn it into smoke on the altar, and afterward shall make the woman drink the water. [27] When he has made her drink the water, then, if she has defiled herself and has been unfaithful to her husband, the water that brings the curse shall enter into her and cause bitter pain, and her womb shall discharge, her uterus drop, and the woman shall become an execration among her people. [28] But if the woman has not defiled herself and is clean, then she shall be immune and be able to conceive children.

[29] This is the law in cases of jealousy, when a wife, while under her husband's authority, goes astray and defiles herself, [30] or when a spirit of jealousy comes on a man and he is jealous of his wife; then he shall set the woman before the LORD, and the priest shall apply this entire law to her. [31] The man shall be free from iniquity, but the woman shall bear her iniquity.

The Nazirites

6 The LORD spoke to Moses, saying: [2] Speak to the Israelites and say to them: When either men or women make a special vow, the vow of a nazirite,[a] to

a That is one separated or one consecrated

6:2—The *nazirite* took a vow of dedication to God and entered into a "set apart" status for a specific period of time (see, e.g., Samson, Judg. 13:5; 16:17, and Samuel, 1 Sam. 1:22). The vow was considered holy and absolute and prohibited the person taking the vow from drinking wine or fermented drink, from cutting her or his hair, and from coming into contact with a corpse. Both women and men were able to take this vow.

Occasions arise when individuals may make a vow to God and seek to set themselves apart, in one way or another, for a specific time in order to dedicate themselves to a specific mission. Such a vow need not require withdrawal from the community, but may well be accomplished by aiding, empowering, or supporting the community.

separate themselves to the LORD, [3] they shall separate themselves from wine and strong drink; they shall drink no wine vinegar or other vinegar, and shall not drink any grape juice or eat grapes, fresh or dried. [4] All their days as nazirites[a] they shall eat nothing that is produced by the grapevine, not even the seeds or the skins.

5 All the days of their nazirite vow no razor shall come upon the head; until the time is completed for which they separate themselves to the LORD, they shall be holy; they shall let the locks of the head grow long.

6 All the days that they separate themselves to the LORD they shall not go near a corpse. [7] Even if their father or mother, brother or sister, should die, they may not defile themselves; because their consecration to God is upon the head. [8] All their days as nazirites[a] they are holy to the LORD.

9 If someone dies very suddenly nearby, defiling the consecrated head, then they shall shave the head on the day of their cleansing; on the seventh day they shall shave it. [10] On the eighth day they shall bring two turtledoves or two young pigeons to the priest at the entrance of the tent of meeting, [11] and the priest shall offer one as a sin offering and the other as a burnt offering, and make atonement for them, because they incurred guilt by reason of the corpse. They shall sanctify the head that same day, [12] and separate themselves to the LORD for their days as nazirites,[a] and bring a male lamb a year old as a guilt offering. The former time shall be void, because the consecrated head was defiled.

13 This is the law for the nazirites[a] when the time of their consecration has been completed: they shall be brought to the entrance of the tent of meeting, [14] and

they shall offer their gift to the LORD, one male lamb a year old without blemish as a burnt offering, one ewe lamb a year old without blemish as a sin offering, one ram without blemish as an offering of well-being, [15] and a basket of unleavened bread, cakes of choice flour mixed with oil and unleavened wafers spread with oil, with their grain offering and their drink offerings. [16] The priest shall present them before the LORD and offer their sin offering and burnt offering, [17] and shall offer the ram as a sacrifice of well-being to the LORD, with the basket of unleavened bread; the priest also shall make the accompanying grain offering and drink offering. [18] Then the nazirites[a] shall shave the consecrated head at the entrance of the tent of meeting, and shall take the hair from the consecrated head and put it on the fire under the sacrifice of well-being. [19] The priest shall take the shoulder of the ram, when it is boiled, and one unleavened cake out of the basket, and one unleavened wafer, and shall put them in the palms of the nazirites,[a] after they have shaved the consecrated head. [20] Then the priest shall elevate them as an elevation offering before the LORD; they are a holy portion for the priest, together with the breast that is elevated and the thigh that is offered. After that the nazirites[a] may drink wine.

21 This is the law for the nazirites[a] who take a vow. Their offering to the LORD must be in accordance with the nazirite[b] vow, apart from what else they can afford. In accordance with whatever vow they take, so they shall do, following the law for their consecration.

The Priestly Benediction

22 The LORD spoke to Moses, saying: [23] Speak to Aaron and his sons, saying,

[a] That is *those separated* or *those consecrated*   [b] That is *one separated* or *one consecrated*

6:22–27—Many associate this blessing with the one Aaron said on the day the tabernacle cult was inaugurated (see Lev. 9:22). "Blessing" is understood to be putting the *name* of YHWH on the Israelites (v. 27). The name is one way in

which YHWH is present among the people (see Exod. 3:13–15; 6:2–8; 34:6–7; Num. 14:17–19; 1 Kgs. 8:27–30). Putting the name on the people in blessing is a means by which YHWH will be present with them in order to bless them. Blessing

Thus you shall bless the Israelites: You shall say to them,

24 The LORD bless you and keep you;

25 the LORD make his face to shine
       upon you, and be gracious to
       you;

26 the LORD lift up his countenance
       upon you, and give you peace.

27 So they shall put my name on the Israelites, and I will bless them.

Offerings of the Leaders

7 On the day when Moses had finished setting up the tabernacle, and had anointed and consecrated it with all its furnishings, and had anointed and consecrated the altar with all its utensils, 2 the leaders of Israel, heads of their ancestral houses, the leaders of the tribes, who were over those who were enrolled, made offerings. 3 They brought their offerings before the LORD, six covered wagons and twelve oxen, a wagon for every two of the leaders, and for each one an ox; they presented them before the tabernacle. 4 Then the LORD said to Moses: 5 Accept these from them, that they may be used in doing the service of the tent of meeting, and give them to the Levites, to each according to his service. 6 So Moses took the wagons and the oxen, and gave them to the Levites. 7 Two wagons and four oxen he gave to the Gershonites, according to their service; 8 and four wagons and eight oxen he gave to the Merarites, according to their service, under the direction of Ithamar son of Aaron the priest. 9 But to the Kohathites he gave none, because they were charged with the care of the holy things that had to be carried on the shoulders.

10 The leaders also presented offerings for the dedication of the altar at the time when it was anointed; the leaders presented their offering before the altar. 11 The LORD said to Moses: They shall present their offerings, one leader each day, for the dedication of the altar.

12 The one who presented his offering the first day was Nahshon son of Amminadab, of the tribe of Judah; 13 his offering was one silver plate weighing one hundred thirty shekels, one silver basin weighing seventy shekels, according to the shekel of the sanctuary, both of them full of choice flour mixed with oil for a grain offering; 14 one golden dish weighing ten shekels, full of incense; 15 one young bull, one ram, one male lamb a year old, for a burnt offering; 16 one male goat for a sin offering; 17 and for the sacrifice of well-being, two oxen, five rams, five male goats, and five male lambs a year old. This was the offering of Nahshon son of Amminadab.

18 On the second day Nethanel son of Zuar, the leader of Issachar, presented an offering; 19 he presented for his offering one silver plate weighing one hundred thirty shekels, one silver basin weighing seventy shekels, according to the shekel of the sanctuary, both of them full of choice flour mixed with oil for a grain offering; 20 one golden dish weighing ten shekels, full of incense; 21 one young bull, one ram, one male lamb a year old, as a burnt offering; 22 one male goat as a sin offering; 23 and for the sacrifice of well-being, two oxen, five rams, five

---

has to do with safety, the gracious attentiveness of YHWH, and peace. The emphasis on the divine face expresses the turning of YHWH to Israel with love and grace. Although we may hear these words as if spoken to an individual, they are spoken to and for the community. Israel recognized that the individual always lived concretely within the context of a larger community. Individual and community blessing were interwoven and experienced together.

7:1–89 Offerings by Tribal Leaders

7:1–9—The narrative returns to the day that Moses set up the tabernacle (the first day of the first month; see Exod. 40:1). The community leaders, the heads of the census lists, present offerings both for the tabernacle, presented on one day (vv. 1–9), and the altar, presented on twelve consecutive days (vv. 10–88). The community participates in the maintenance of the tabernacle, the place where the Israelites encounter YHWH in the presentation of sacrifices and offerings. The offerings are substantial.

male goats, and five male lambs a year old. This was the offering of Nethanel son of Zuar.

24 On the third day Eliab son of Helon, the leader of the Zebulunites: [25] his offering was one silver plate weighing one hundred thirty shekels, one silver basin weighing seventy shekels, according to the shekel of the sanctuary, both of them full of choice flour mixed with oil for a grain offering; [26] one golden dish weighing ten shekels, full of incense; [27] one young bull, one ram, one male lamb a year old, for a burnt offering; [28] one male goat for a sin offering; [29] and for the sacrifice of well-being, two oxen, five rams, five male goats, and five male lambs a year old. This was the offering of Eliab son of Helon.

30 On the fourth day Elizur son of Shedeur, the leader of the Reubenites: [31] his offering was one silver plate weighing one hundred thirty shekels, one silver basin weighing seventy shekels, according to the shekel of the sanctuary, both of them full of choice flour mixed with oil for a grain offering; [32] one golden dish weighing ten shekels, full of incense; [33] one young bull, one ram, one male lamb a year old, for a burnt offering; [34] one male goat for a sin offering; [35] and for the sacrifice of well-being, two oxen, five rams, five male goats, and five male lambs a year old. This was the offering of Elizur son of Shedeur.

36 On the fifth day Shelumiel son of Zurishaddai, the leader of the Simeonites: [37] his offering was one silver plate weighing one hundred thirty shekels, one silver basin weighing seventy shekels, according to the shekel of the sanctuary, both of them full of choice flour mixed with oil for a grain offering; [38] one golden dish weighing ten shekels, full of incense; [39] one young bull, one ram, one male lamb a year old, for a burnt offering; [40] one male goat for a sin offering; [41] and for the sacrifice of well-being, two oxen, five rams, five male goats, and five male lambs a year old.

This was the offering of Shelumiel son of Zurishaddai.

42 On the sixth day Eliasaph son of Deuel, the leader of the Gadites: [43] his offering was one silver plate weighing one hundred thirty shekels, one silver basin weighing seventy shekels, according to the shekel of the sanctuary, both of them full of choice flour mixed with oil for a grain offering; [44] one golden dish weighing ten shekels, full of incense; [45] one young bull, one ram, one male lamb a year old, for a burnt offering; [46] one male goat for a sin offering; [47] and for the sacrifice of well-being, two oxen, five rams, five male goats, and five male lambs a year old. This was the offering of Eliasaph son of Deuel.

48 On the seventh day Elishama son of Ammihud, the leader of the Ephraimites: [49] his offering was one silver plate weighing one hundred thirty shekels, one silver basin weighing seventy shekels, according to the shekel of the sanctuary, both of them full of choice flour mixed with oil for a grain offering; [50] one golden dish weighing ten shekels, full of incense; [51] one young bull, one ram, one male lamb a year old, for a burnt offering; [52] one male goat for a sin offering; [53] and for the sacrifice of well-being, two oxen, five rams, five male goats, and five male lambs a year old. This was the offering of Elishama son of Ammihud.

54 On the eighth day Gamaliel son of Pedahzur, the leader of the Manassites: [55] his offering was one silver plate weighing one hundred thirty shekels, one silver basin weighing seventy shekels, according to the shekel of the sanctuary, both of them full of choice flour mixed with oil for a grain offering; [56] one golden dish weighing ten shekels, full of incense; [57] one young bull, one ram, one male lamb a year old, for a burnt offering; [58] one male goat for a sin offering; [59] and for the sacrifice of well-being, two oxen, five rams, five male goats, and five male lambs a year old. This was the offering of Gamaliel son of Pedahzur.

60 On the ninth day Abidan son of Gideoni, the leader of the Benjaminites: 61 his offering was one silver plate weighing one hundred thirty shekels, one silver basin weighing seventy shekels, according to the shekel of the sanctuary, both of them full of choice flour mixed with oil for a grain offering; 62 one golden dish weighing ten shekels, full of incense; 63 one young bull, one ram, one male lamb a year old, for a burnt offering; 64 one male goat for a sin offering; 65 and for the sacrifice of well-being, two oxen, five rams, five male goats, and five male lambs a year old. This was the offering of Abidan son of Gideoni.

66 On the tenth day Ahiezer son of Ammishaddai, the leader of the Danites: 67 his offering was one silver plate weighing one hundred thirty shekels, one silver basin weighing seventy shekels, according to the shekel of the sanctuary, both of them full of choice flour mixed with oil for a grain offering; 68 one golden dish weighing ten shekels, full of incense; 69 one young bull, one ram, one male lamb a year old, for a burnt offering; 70 one male goat for a sin offering; 71 and for the sacrifice of well-being, two oxen, five rams, five male goats, and five male lambs a year old. This was the offering of Ahiezer son of Ammishaddai.

72 On the eleventh day Pagiel son of Ochran, the leader of the Asherites: 73 his offering was one silver plate weighing one hundred thirty shekels, one silver basin weighing seventy shekels, according to the shekel of the sanctuary, both of them full of choice flour mixed with oil for a grain offering; 74 one golden dish weighing ten shekels, full of incense; 75 one young bull, one ram, one male lamb a year old, for a burnt offering; 76 one male goat for a sin offering; 77 and for the sacrifice of well-being, two oxen, five rams, five male goats, and five male lambs a year old. This was the offering of Pagiel son of Ochran.

78 On the twelfth day Ahira son of Enan, the leader of the Naphtalites: 79 his offering was one silver plate weighing one hundred thirty shekels, one silver basin weighing seventy shekels, according to the shekel of the sanctuary, both of them full of choice flour mixed with oil for a grain offering; 80 one golden dish weighing ten shekels, full of incense; 81 one young bull, one ram, one male lamb a year old, for a burnt offering; 82 one male goat for a sin offering; 83 and for the sacrifice of well-being, two oxen, five rams, five male goats, and five male lambs a year old. This was the offering of Ahira son of Enan.

84 This was the dedication offering for the altar, at the time when it was anointed, from the leaders of Israel: twelve silver plates, twelve silver basins, twelve golden dishes, 85 each silver plate weighing one hundred thirty shekels and each basin seventy, all the silver of the vessels two thousand four hundred shekels according to the shekel of the sanctuary, 86 the twelve golden dishes, full of incense, weighing ten shekels apiece according to the shekel of the sanctuary, all the gold of the dishes being one hundred twenty shekels; 87 all the livestock for the burnt offering twelve bulls, twelve rams, twelve male lambs a year old, with their grain offering; and twelve male goats for a sin offering; 88 and all the livestock for the sacrifice of well-being twenty-four bulls, the rams sixty, the male goats sixty, the male lambs a year old sixty. This was the dedication offering for the altar, after it was anointed.

89 When Moses went into the tent of meeting to speak with the LORD,a he would hear the voice speaking to him from above the mercy seatb that was on

a Heb him   b Or the cover

7:89—The ark inside the tent provided the location for Moses to hear the voice of YHWH (see Exod. 29:44–46 for an extended statement on the purpose of the tabernacle and Exod. 25:17–22 for a statement concerning the ark). No one other than Moses is reported to have entered the tent

the ark of the covenant*a* from between the two cherubim; thus it spoke to him.

The Seven Lamps

8 The LORD spoke to Moses, saying: ² Speak to Aaron and say to him: When you set up the lamps, the seven lamps shall give light in front of the lampstand. ³ Aaron did so; he set up its lamps to give light in front of the lampstand, as the LORD had commanded Moses. ⁴ Now this was how the lampstand was made, out of hammered work of gold. From its base to its flowers, it was hammered work; according to the pattern that the LORD had shown Moses, so he made the lampstand.

Consecration and Service of the Levites

5 The LORD spoke to Moses, saying: ⁶ Take the Levites from among the Israelites and cleanse them. ⁷ Thus you shall do to them, to cleanse them: sprinkle the water of purification on them, have them shave their whole body with a razor and wash their clothes, and so cleanse themselves. ⁸ Then let them take a young bull and its grain offering of choice flour mixed with oil, and you shall take another young bull for a sin offering. ⁹ You shall bring the Levites before the tent of meeting, and assemble the whole congregation of the Israelites. ¹⁰ When you bring the Levites before the LORD, the Israelites shall lay their hands on the Levites, ¹¹ and Aaron shall present the Levites before the LORD as an elevation offering from the Israelites, that they may do the service of the LORD. ¹² The Levites shall lay their hands on the heads of the bulls, and he shall offer the one for a sin offering and the other for a burnt offering to the LORD, to make atonement for the Levites. ¹³ Then you shall have the Levites stand before Aaron and his sons, and you shall present them as an elevation offering to the LORD.

14 Thus you shall separate the Levites from among the other Israelites, and the Levites shall be mine. ¹⁵ Thereafter the Levites may go in to do service at the tent of meeting, once you have cleansed them and presented them as an elevation offering. ¹⁶ For they are unreservedly given to me from among the Israelites; I have taken them for myself, in place of all that open the womb, the firstborn of all the Israelites. ¹⁷ For all the firstborn among the Israelites are mine, both human and animal. On the day that I struck down all the firstborn in the land of Egypt I consecrated them for myself, ¹⁸ but I have taken the Levites in place of all the firstborn among the Israelites. ¹⁹ Moreover, I have given the Levites as a gift to Aaron and his sons from among the Israelites, to do the service for the Israelites at the tent of meeting, and to make atonement for the Israelites, in order that there may be no plague among the Israelites for coming too close to the sanctuary.

a Or *treaty,* or *testimony;* Heb *eduth*

---

to speak with YHWH (Aaron entered on "the day of purification" to take blood into the Holy of Holies; see Lev. 16). The text recognizes that YHWH's instructions to and for the community were ongoing. Although YHWH spoke in the past in a way that was foundational for the Israelite community, the word of YHWH was neither finalized in the past nor limited to the past (see Lev. 10:16–20; 24:10–23; Num. 9:1–14 for similar examples).

8:1–26 Lamps and Levites

8:5–26—The text reports the consecration service that sets the Levites apart for their tabernacle duties, i.e., protection of and transportation of the tabernacle (see chap. 4). Although not as elaborate as the consecration service for the priesthood (Lev. 8), the present ritual is also a rite of passage that moves the Levites into their "set apart" status. As such, it serves both as a means of moving them into their new status and as a means of marking their passage. The Levites are a "gift" to Aaron and his descendants. The tabernacle ministry includes a clearly defined hierarchy of status in relation to the holy, and creates a multifaceted ministry—various persons are assigned to a variety of duties.

8:16—YHWH accepts the Levites as a substitute for the *firstborn* of Israel (see the discussion of Num. 3:11–13).

20 Moses and Aaron and the whole congregation of the Israelites did with the Levites accordingly; the Israelites did with the Levites just as the LORD had commanded Moses concerning them. ²¹ The Levites purified themselves from sin and washed their clothes; then Aaron presented them as an elevation offering before the LORD, and Aaron made atonement for them to cleanse them. ²² Thereafter the Levites went in to do their service in the tent of meeting in attendance on Aaron and his sons. As the LORD had commanded Moses concerning the Levites, so they did with them.

23 The LORD spoke to Moses, saying: ²⁴ This applies to the Levites: from twenty-five years old and upward they shall begin to do duty in the service of the tent of meeting; ²⁵ and from the age of fifty years they shall retire from the duty of the service and serve no more. ²⁶ They may assist their brothers in the tent of meeting in carrying out their duties, but they shall perform no service. Thus you shall do with the Levites in assigning their duties.

The Passover at Sinai

9 The LORD spoke to Moses in the wilderness of Sinai, in the first month of the second year after they had come out of the land of Egypt, saying: ² Let the Israelites keep the passover at its appointed time. ³ On the fourteenth day of this month, at twilight,*a* you shall keep it at its appointed time; according to all its statutes and all its regulations you shall keep it. ⁴ So Moses told the Israelites that they should keep the passover. ⁵ They kept the passover in the first month, on the fourteenth day of the month, at twilight,*a* in the wilderness of Sinai. Just as the LORD had commanded Moses, so the Israelites did. ⁶ Now there were certain people who were unclean through touching a corpse, so that they could not keep the passover on that day. They came before Moses and Aaron on that day, ⁷ and said to him, "Although we are unclean through touching a corpse, why must we be kept from presenting the LORD's offering at its appointed time among the Israelites?" ⁸ Moses spoke to them, "Wait, so that I may hear what the LORD will command concerning you."

9 The LORD spoke to Moses, saying: ¹⁰ Speak to the Israelites, saying: Anyone of you or your descendants who is unclean through touching a corpse, or is away on a journey, shall still keep the passover to the LORD. ¹¹ In the second month on the fourteenth day, at twilight,*a* they shall keep it; they shall eat it with unleavened bread and bitter herbs. ¹² They shall leave none of it until morning, nor break a bone of it; according to all the statute for the passover they shall keep it. ¹³ But anyone who is clean and is not on a journey, and yet refrains from keeping the passover, shall be cut off from the people for not presenting the LORD's offering at its appointed time; such a one shall bear the consequences for the sin. ¹⁴ Any alien residing among

a Heb between the two evenings

9:1–23 Passover and Impurity; the Cloud and the Tent

9:1–14—Of particular interest in this story is the fact that Moses waits to hear from YHWH to determine what is to be done in the case of impurity and the observance of Passover. Although Passover must be observed at its established time, ritually impure people are not allowed to participate. The case indicates the serious nature of impurity: impurity prohibits participation in the sacred observances (see Lev. 23; Num. 28–29 for calendars of the sacred observances). The impure must observe Passover at a later date. Although

the divine rulings on Passover have already been stated clearly (see Exod. 12:1–27, 43–49), a new situation gives rise to a new set of questions. Living in the context of the divine presence and seeking to be obedient to the divine will, both individuals and the community must be open to new ways of being in the world, living in community, and practicing holiness.

9:14—The resident Israelite and the resident non-Israelite (the *alien*) have one law. Justice includes fairness, equity, and consistency for everyone in the community. Justice does not discriminate on

you who wishes to keep the passover to the LORD shall do so according to the statute of the passover and according to its regulation; you shall have one statute for both the resident alien and the native.

The Cloud and the Fire

15 On the day the tabernacle was set up, the cloud covered the tabernacle, the tent of the covenant;[a] and from evening until morning it was over the tabernacle, having the appearance of fire. [16] It was always so: the cloud covered it by day[b] and the appearance of fire by night. [17] Whenever the cloud lifted from over the tent, then the Israelites would set out; and in the place where the cloud settled down, there the Israelites would camp. [18] At the command of the LORD the Israelites would set out, and at the command of the LORD they would camp. As long as the cloud rested over the tabernacle, they would remain in camp. [19] Even when the cloud continued over the tabernacle many days, the Israelites would keep the charge of the LORD, and would not set out. [20] Sometimes the cloud would remain a few days over the tabernacle, and according to the command of the LORD they would remain in camp; then according to the command of the LORD they would set out. [21] Sometimes the cloud would remain from evening until morning; and when the cloud lifted in the morning, they would set out, or if it continued for a day and a night, when the cloud lifted they would set out. [22] Whether it was two days, or a month, or a longer time, that the cloud continued over the tabernacle, resting upon it, the Israelites would remain in camp and would not set out; but when it lifted they would set out. [23] At the command of the LORD they would camp, and at the command of the LORD they would set out. They kept the charge of the LORD, at the command of the LORD by Moses.

The Silver Trumpets

10 The LORD spoke to Moses, saying: [2] Make two silver trumpets; you shall make them of hammered work; and you shall use them for summoning the congregation, and for breaking camp. [3] When both are blown, the whole congregation shall assemble before you at the entrance of the tent of meeting. [4] But if only one is blown, then the leaders, the heads of the tribes of Israel, shall assemble before you. [5] When you blow an alarm, the camps on the east side shall set out; [6] when you blow a second alarm, the camps on the south side shall set out. An alarm is to be blown whenever they are to set out. [7] But when the assembly is to be gathered, you shall blow, but you shall not sound an alarm. [8] The sons of Aaron, the priests, shall blow the trumpets; this shall be a perpetual institution for you throughout your generations. [9] When you go to war in your land against the adversary who oppresses you, you shall sound an alarm with the trumpets, so that you may be remembered before the LORD your God and be saved from your enemies. [10] Also on your days of rejoicing, at your

[a] Or treaty, or testimony; Heb eduth   [b] Gk Syr Vg: Heb lacks by day

---

the basis of birth—Israelite as opposed to non-Israelite—but seeks to create a common realm in which all are treated equitably.

9:15–23—These verses look back to Exod. 40:34–38, the report of the divine glory taking up residence in the tabernacle (cf. Exod. 19:16–18; 24:15–18 for similar images associated with Mount Sinai). The cloud and the fire are concrete images of YHWH's presence with the people and indicate that the encounter with YHWH at Sinai now continues as YHWH leads them and travels with them in their journey through the wilderness to the land of promise.

10:1–36 The Trumpets and Departure from Sinai

10:1–10—The blowing of the *trumpets* has several distinct purposes: to alert the people to break *camp* (v. 2), to call the people to *war* (v. 9), and to mark the beginning of a sacred observance (v. 10). The specific purpose is determined by context. Clearly context is crucial for correct interpretation and understanding.

appointed festivals, and at the beginnings of your months, you shall blow the trumpets over your burnt offerings and over your sacrifices of well-being; they shall serve as a reminder on your behalf before the LORD your God: I am the LORD your God.

Departure from Sinai

11 In the second year, in the second month, on the twentieth day of the month, the cloud lifted from over the tabernacle of the covenant.*a* 12 Then the Israelites set out by stages from the wilderness of Sinai, and the cloud settled down in the wilderness of Paran. 13 They set out for the first time at the command of the LORD by Moses. 14 The standard of the camp of Judah set out first, company by company, and over the whole company was Nahshon son of Amminadab. 15 Over the company of the tribe of Issachar was Nethanel son of Zuar; 16 and over the company of the tribe of Zebulun was Eliab son of Helon.

17 Then the tabernacle was taken down, and the Gershonites and the Merarites, who carried the tabernacle, set out. 18 Next the standard of the camp of Reuben set out, company by company; and over the whole company was Elizur son of Shedeur. 19 Over the company of the tribe of Simeon was Shelumiel son of Zurishaddai, 20 and over the company of the tribe of Gad was Eliasaph son of Deuel.

21 Then the Kohathites, who carried the holy things, set out; and the tabernacle was set up before their arrival. 22 Next the standard of the Ephraimite camp set out, company by company, and over the whole company was Elishama son of Ammihud. 23 Over the company of the tribe of Manasseh was Gamaliel son of Pedahzur, 24 and over the company of the tribe of Benjamin was Abidan son of Gideoni.

25 Then the standard of the camp of Dan, acting as the rear guard of all the camps, set out, company by company, and over the whole company was Ahiezer son of Ammishaddai. 26 Over the company of the tribe of Asher was Pagiel son of Ochran, 27 and over the company of the tribe of Naphtali was Ahira son of Enan. 28 This was the order of march of the Israelites, company by company, when they set out.

29 Moses said to Hobab son of Reuel the Midianite, Moses' father-in-law, "We are setting out for the place of which the LORD said, 'I will give it to you'; come with us, and we will treat you well; for the LORD has promised good to Israel." 30 But he said to him, "I will not go, but I will go back to my own land and to my kindred." 31 He said, "Do not leave us, for you know where we should camp in the wilderness, and you will serve as eyes for us. 32 Moreover, if you go with us, whatever good the LORD does for us, the same we will do for you."

33 So they set out from the mount of the LORD three days' journey with the ark of the covenant of the LORD going before them three days' journey, to seek out a resting place for them, 34 the cloud of the LORD being over them by day when they set out from the camp.

35 Whenever the ark set out, Moses would say,

"Arise, O LORD, let your enemies be scattered,

a Or *treaty,* or *testimony;* Heb *eduth*

10:11–36—Israel's sojourn at Mount Sinai comes to an end (the arrival at the mountain is reported in Exod. 19). The mountain has served as the location for Israel to enter into covenant with YHWH (Exod. 19–24; cf. 32–34), to receive the instructions for the tabernacle cult (Exod. 25–Lev. 16), and to receive the instructions for the practice of holiness (Lev. 17–26). The mountain is also the place where Israel worshiped the golden calf and rebelled against YHWH (Exod. 32). The Israelite "army" begins its march to the land of promise, led by YHWH, the divine warrior. Moses' words concerning the ark focus on the image of the divine warrior (vv. 35–36). Israel is both faith community and army; YHWH is both divine warrior and the jealous God who demands their worship (see Num. 1:17–19 for a discussion of Israel's status as faith community and army).

and your foes flee before you."
36 And whenever it came to rest, he would say,

"Return, O Lord of the ten
thousand thousands of Israel."*a*

Complaining in the Desert

11 Now when the people complained in the hearing of the Lord about their misfortunes, the Lord heard it and his anger was kindled. Then the fire of the Lord burned against them, and consumed some outlying parts of the camp. **2** But the people cried out to Moses; and Moses prayed to the Lord, and the fire abated. **3** So that place was called Taberah,*b* because the fire of the Lord burned against them.

4 The rabble among them had a strong craving; and the Israelites also wept again, and said, "If only we had meat to eat! **5** We remember the fish we used to eat in Egypt for nothing, the cucumbers, the melons, the leeks, the onions, and the garlic; **6** but now our strength is dried up, and there is nothing at all but this manna to look at."

7 Now the manna was like coriander seed, and its color was like the color of gum resin. **8** The people went around and gathered it, ground it in mills or beat it in mortars, then boiled it in pots and made cakes of it; and the taste of it was like the taste of cakes baked with oil. **9** When the dew fell on the camp in the night, the manna would fall with it.

10 Moses heard the people weeping throughout their families, all at the entrances of their tents. Then the Lord became very angry, and Moses was displeased. **11** So Moses said to the Lord, "Why have you treated your servant so badly? Why have I not found favor in your sight, that you lay the burden of all this people on me? **12** Did I conceive all this people? Did I give birth to them, that you should say to me, 'Carry them

a Meaning of Heb uncertain *b* That is *Burning*

11:1–25:18 A Series of Rebellions

The journey through the wilderness is marked by a series of complaints, murmurings, and rebellions by the Israelites against Moses, Aaron, and YHWH. The journey provides a story of divine-human struggle (Gen. 32:22–32 reports the change of Jacob's name to Israel, one who strives with God). Wandering between the mountain and the land, Israel struggles to bend YHWH to its will, while YHWH struggles with problems generated because of the divine presence dwelling in the midst of a difficult, angry, and rebellious people. In one sense, the journey through the wilderness may be viewed as a time in which YHWH and Israel discover the nature and meaning of their relationship in the concrete realities of day-to-day existence.

11:1–3 First Rebellion of the People against God

The Israelites begin to complain about their situation immediately after their departure from Sinai. This story sets the tone for the following stories of complaint and rebellion in the wilderness. YHWH is angered and the divine *fire* burns on the perimeters of the camp. The angry and fiery "wrath" of YHWH remains a constant threat in the wilderness. Moses prays and the fire is extinguished. Moses' role as mediator on behalf of the community becomes more and more important as the people's complaints continue and intensify.

The interaction of YHWH, the people, and Moses provides a densely textured image of relational possibilities and dynamics: the faithless and complaining people, the angry and snorting God, the angry and fussy Moses, the merciful and gracious God. This is the nature of human existence lived in the presence of YHWH.

11:4–35—Second Rebellion: YHWH's Provision and Leadership

11:4–11—The people complain that they are tired of the manna (see Exod. 16). The text understands this to be a complaint concerning YHWH's ability to provide. As such, it is an attack on YHWH the creator and redeemer; i.e., our creator and our redeemer should be able to provide for us in a better way than this! The people look back to and long for their lives in Egypt. Although concretely embedded in Israel's story, the longing for slavery in the midst of a journey to freedom also points to the all-too-common failure of human beings to be satisfied and grateful in the present moment of existence. Things all too often seem to have been better "in the old days," or things will surely get better "in the days to come." In both cases, the present moment of life is "just not enough."

11:12–35—Who Is in Charge of These People?

11:12–15—Moses complains to YHWH about having to care for the people. His language is interesting in that it draws on activities associated

in your bosom, as a nurse carries a sucking child, to the land that you promised on oath to their ancestors'? [13] Where am I to get meat to give to all this people? For they come weeping to me and say, 'Give us meat to eat!' [14] I am not able to carry all this people alone, for they are too heavy for me. [15] If this is the way you are going to treat me, put me to death at once—if I have found favor in your sight—and do not let me see my misery."

The Seventy Elders

[16] So the LORD said to Moses, "Gather for me seventy of the elders of Israel, whom you know to be the elders of the people and officers over them; bring them to the tent of meeting, and have them take their place there with you. [17] I will come down and talk with you there; and I will take some of the spirit that is on you and put it on them; and they shall bear the burden of the people along with you so that you will not bear it all by yourself. [18] And say to the people: Consecrate yourselves for tomorrow, and you shall eat meat; for you have wailed in the hearing of the LORD, saying, 'If only we had meat to eat! Surely it was better for us in Egypt.' Therefore the LORD will give you meat, and you shall eat. [19] You shall eat not only one day, or two days, or five days, or ten days, or twenty days, [20] but for a whole month—until it comes out of your nostrils and becomes loathsome to you—because you have rejected the LORD who is among you, and have

wailed before him, saying, 'Why did we ever leave Egypt?'" [21] But Moses said, "The people I am with number six hundred thousand on foot; and you say, 'I will give them meat, that they may eat for a whole month'! [22] Are there enough flocks and herds to slaughter for them? Are there enough fish in the sea to catch for them?" [23] The LORD said to Moses, "Is the LORD's power limited?[a] Now you shall see whether my word will come true for you or not."

[24] So Moses went out and told the people the words of the LORD; and he gathered seventy elders of the people, and placed them all around the tent. [25] Then the LORD came down in the cloud and spoke to him, and took some of the spirit that was on him and put it on the seventy elders; and when the spirit rested upon them, they prophesied. But they did not do so again.

[26] Two men remained in the camp, one named Eldad, and the other named Medad, and the spirit rested on them; they were among those registered, but they had not gone out to the tent, and so they prophesied in the camp. [27] And a young man ran and told Moses, "Eldad and Medad are prophesying in the camp." [28] And Joshua son of Nun, the assistant of Moses, one of his chosen men,[b] said, "My lord Moses, stop them!" [29] But Moses said to him, "Are you jealous for my sake? Would that all the LORD's people were prophets, and

[a] Heb LORD's hand too short?   [b] Or of Moses from his youth

---

with women: "Did I conceive this people? Did I give birth to them? Must I carry them as a nurse and feed them"? Moses raises pointed questions about the people, himself, and YHWH. With regard to the people, he asks why they act so childishly, indeed, like very young children, and why they require so much care. With regard to himself, he states clearly that the situation has become too much for him. He must have help to continue on as the human leader of this group. Finally, Moses somewhat heatedly points out that divine leadership, care, and responsibility are somewhat lacking. Moses' heated interaction with YHWH is typical and provides one of the

more interesting elements of the narrative (e.g., Exod. 5:22–23; 33:12–16). Moses directs his anger and his frustration at YHWH—recognition on Moses' part that YHWH is "the one in charge" and therefore the one with ultimate responsibility!

11:16–35—Both complaints are addressed. YHWH helps Moses establish leaders to help him work with the people and provides quail for the people to eat. The latter is not a happy moment in the story because the promise is that the people will eat quail until it comes out of their nostrils! YHWH is Israel's provider; Israel is YHWH's small child.

that the LORD would put his spirit on them!" ³⁰ And Moses and the elders of Israel returned to the camp.

The Quails

31 Then a wind went out from the LORD, and it brought quails from the sea and let them fall beside the camp, about a day's journey on this side and a day's journey on the other side, all around the camp, about two cubits deep on the ground. ³² So the people worked all that day and night and all the next day, gathering the quails; the least anyone gathered was ten homers; and they spread them out for themselves all around the camp. ³³ But while the meat was still between their teeth, before it was consumed, the anger of the LORD was kindled against the people, and the LORD struck the people with a very great plague. ³⁴ So that place was called Kibroth-hattaavah,ᵃ because there they buried the people who had the craving. ³⁵ From Kibroth-hattaavah the people journeyed to Hazeroth.

Aaron and Miriam Jealous of Moses

12 While they were at Hazeroth, Miriam and Aaron spoke against Moses because of the Cushite woman whom he had married (for he had indeed married a Cushite woman);

² and they said, "Has the LORD spoken only through Moses? Has he not spoken through us also?" And the LORD heard it. ³ Now the man Moses was very humble,ᵇ more so than anyone else on the face of the earth. ⁴ Suddenly the LORD said to Moses, Aaron, and Miriam, "Come out, you three, to the tent of meeting." So the three of them came out. ⁵ Then the LORD came down in a pillar of cloud, and stood at the entrance of the tent, and called Aaron and Miriam; and they both came forward. ⁶ And he said, "Hear my words:

When there are prophets among
      you,
   I the LORD make myself known to
         them in visions;
   I speak to them in dreams.
⁷ Not so with my servant Moses;
      he is entrusted with all my house.
⁸ With him I speak face to face—
         clearly, not in riddles;
      and he beholds the form of the
         LORD.

Why then were you not afraid to speak against my servant Moses?" ⁹ And the anger of the LORD was kindled against them, and he departed.

10 When the cloud went away from over the tent, Miriam had become

ᵃ That is *Graves of craving* ᵇ Or *devout*

12:1–16 Third Rebellion: Miriam and Aaron Question Moses' Authority

12:2—Miriam and Aaron question Moses' leadership. Specifically, they ask if YHWH speaks only through Moses. The text reflects conflict between different groups in Israel concerning who has access to YHWH and who can speak for YHWH (cf. Lev. 10:16–20; Num. 16–17). This is an especially pointed issue in light of Israel's belief that YHWH continues to speak to the community (see Lev. 10:16–20; 24:10–23; Num. 7:89; 9:1–14). Who can speak for YHWH, and how are those in the faith community to know? Both questions remain crucial issues for any religious faith that believes the divine voice is still speaking in the contemporary context.

12:3–9—YHWH calls Moses, Miriam, and Aaron to the tent of meeting and states clearly that Moses has a special status in relation to the divine voice: *"With him I speak face to face"* (cf. Exod.

33:17–23). Moses' status is presented in contrast to the prophets. YHWH speaks to the latter in *visions* and *dreams*. The text emphasizes the peculiar authority and clarity of the words of Moses, without necessarily seeking to question the validity of prophetic speech (cf. Num. 11:24–30; Deut. 13:1–5; 18:15–22).

12:10–16—When YHWH finishes speaking, Miriam is afflicted with "leprosy" (see Lev. 13–14)—a difficult moment in the text, in that only Miriam, not Aaron, is afflicted. The text clearly seeks to emphasize Moses' authority and, at the same time, to preserve Aaron's purity in relation to a defiling skin condition. Aaron asks Moses to pray for Miriam, and Moses asks YHWH to heal her. She is shut out of the camp for seven days (see Lev. 13:45–46; cf. Num. 5:2–4), at the end of which time the Israelites continue their travel through the wilderness.

leprous,*a* as white as snow. And Aaron turned towards Miriam and saw that she was leprous. **11** Then Aaron said to Moses, "Oh, my lord, do not punish us*b* for a sin that we have so foolishly committed. **12** Do not let her be like one stillborn, whose flesh is half consumed when it comes out of its mother's womb." **13** And Moses cried to the LORD, "O God, please heal her." **14** But the LORD said to Moses, "If her father had but spit in her face, would she not bear her shame for seven days? Let her be shut out of the camp for seven days, and after that she may be brought in again." **15** So Miriam was shut out of the camp for seven days; and the people did not set out on the march until Miriam had been brought in again. **16** After that the people set out from Hazeroth, and camped in the wilderness of Paran.

Spies Sent into Canaan

13 The LORD said to Moses, **2** "Send men to spy out the land of Canaan, which I am giving to the Israelites; from each of their ancestral tribes you shall send a man, every one a leader among them." **3** So Moses sent them from the wilderness of Paran, according to the command of the LORD, all of them leading men among the Israelites. **4** These were their names: From the tribe of Reuben, Shammua son of Zaccur; **5** from the tribe of Simeon, Shaphat son of Hori; **6** from the tribe of Judah, Caleb son of Jephunneh; **7** from the tribe of Issachar, Igal son of Joseph; **8** from the tribe of Ephraim, Hoshea son of Nun; **9** from the tribe of Benjamin, Palti son of Raphu; **10** from the tribe of Zebulun, Gaddiel son of Sodi; **11** from the tribe of Joseph (that is, from the tribe of Manasseh), Gaddi son of Susi; **12** from the tribe of Dan, Ammiel son of Gemalli; **13** from the tribe of Asher, Sethur son of Michael; **14** from the tribe of Naphtali, Nahbi son of Vophsi; **15** from the tribe of Gad, Geuel son of Machi. **16** These were the names of the men whom Moses sent to spy out the land. And Moses changed the name of Hoshea son of Nun to Joshua.

17 Moses sent them to spy out the land of Canaan, and said to them, "Go up there into the Negeb, and go up into the hill country, **18** and see what the land is like, and whether the people who live in it are strong or weak, whether they are few or many, **19** and whether the land they live in is good or bad, and whether the towns that they live in are unwalled or fortified, **20** and whether the land is rich or poor, and whether there are trees in it or not. Be bold, and bring some of the fruit of the land." Now it was the season of the first ripe grapes.

21 So they went up and spied out the land from the wilderness of Zin to Rehob, near Lebo-hamath. **22** They went up into the Negeb, and came to Hebron; and Ahiman, Sheshai, and Talmai, the Anakites, were there. (Hebron was built seven years before Zoan in Egypt.) **23** And they came to the Wadi Eshcol, and cut down from there a branch with a single cluster of grapes, and they carried it on a pole between two of them. They also brought some pomegranates and figs. **24** That place was called the Wadi Eshcol,*c* because of the cluster that the Israelites cut down from there.

a A term for several skin diseases; precise meaning uncertain   *b* Heb *do not lay sin upon us*   *c* That is *Cluster*

13:1–14:45 Fourth Rebellion: the Report of the Spies and the Refusal of the People to Enter the Land

The failure of the people at just this point in the narrative marks a dramatic moment in Israel's story and leads to the extension of their time in the wilderness.

13:1–20—The goal of YHWH's redemptive activity for Israel has consistently been life in the land (Exod. 3:7–8; 6:2–9), a land now within their grasp. Twelve spies, one from each of the ancestral tribes, are sent into the land to evaluate both the land and its inhabitants.

13:21–24—The spies enter the land, travel to various places, and secure representative produce that reflects the land's fertility.

The Report of the Spies

25 At the end of forty days they returned from spying out the land. 26 And they came to Moses and Aaron and to all the congregation of the Israelites in the wilderness of Paran, at Kadesh; they brought back word to them and to all the congregation, and showed them the fruit of the land. 27 And they told him, "We came to the land to which you sent us; it flows with milk and honey, and this is its fruit. 28 Yet the people who live in the land are strong, and the towns are fortified and very large; and besides, we saw the descendants of Anak there. 29 The Amalekites live in the land of the Negeb; the Hittites, the Jebusites, and the Amorites live in the hill country; and the Canaanites live by the sea, and along the Jordan."

30 But Caleb quieted the people before Moses, and said, "Let us go up at once and occupy it, for we are well able to overcome it." 31 Then the men who had gone up with him said, "We are not able to go up against this people, for they are stronger than we." 32 So they brought to the Israelites an unfavorable report of the land that they had spied out, saying, "The land that we have gone through as spies is a land that devours its inhabitants; and all the people that we saw in it are of great size. 33 There we saw the Nephilim (the Anakites come from the Nephilim); and to ourselves we seemed like grasshoppers, and so we seemed to them."

The People Rebel

14 Then all the congregation raised a loud cry, and the people wept that night. 2 And all the Israelites complained against Moses and Aaron; the whole congregation said to them, "Would that we had died in the land of Egypt! Or would that we had died in this wilderness! 3 Why is the LORD bringing us into this land to fall by the sword? Our wives and our little ones will become booty; would it not be better for us to go back to Egypt?" 4 So they said to one another, "Let us choose a captain, and go back to Egypt."

5 Then Moses and Aaron fell on their faces before all the assembly of the congregation of the Israelites. 6 And Joshua son of Nun and Caleb son of Jephunneh, who were among those who had spied out the land, tore their clothes 7 and said to all the congregation of the Israelites, "The land that we went through as spies is an exceedingly good land. 8 If the LORD is pleased with us, he will bring us into this land and give it to us, a land that flows with milk and honey. 9 Only, do not rebel against the LORD; and do not fear the people of the land, for they are no more than bread for us; their protection is removed from them, and the LORD is with us; do not fear them." 10 But the whole congregation threatened to stone them.

13:25–33—Reporting back to Moses at Kadesh, all the spies agree that the land is a fertile land flowing *with milk and honey*. Disagreements arise concerning the inhabitants of the land. Ten of the spies—Caleb and Joshua are the exceptions (see 13:30; 14:38)—indicate that the inhabitants of the land are powerful, extremely large (on the Nephilim, ancestors of the Anakim, see Gen. 6:4; Deut. 2:10; Josh. 11:21–22) and dwell in *fortified* cities. According to the ten, Israel will not be able to prevail against the people of the land (v. 31). Caleb, delivering the minority report, calls for the Israelites to go and enter the land immediately. The Israelites fail to trust *wholeheartedly* (14:24) in YHWH, although they have seen the glory of YHWH repeatedly, and, in doing so, fail to believe the promise of land made by YHWH to the ancestors (14:22–24). YHWH has promised the Israelites the land, but they are required to take the necessary steps to make the promise a reality. In this case, the promise of YHWH will be realized in spite of the people.

14:1–4—The people not only refuse to enter the land, they cry out, they weep, they complain, and they wish for death. They decide to choose a new captain and return to Egypt! On the verge of freedom in the land, the people refuse to trust in YHWH and seek to return to the land of slavery.

14:10–25—YHWH tells Moses that the people have gone too far: "I will disinherit them and start over with you, a new ancestor, a new promise." Moses argues on behalf of the people and, as a conclusion to his argument, quotes an earlier

Then the glory of the LORD appeared at the tent of meeting to all the Israelites. [11] And the LORD said to Moses, "How long will this people despise me? And how long will they refuse to believe in me, in spite of all the signs that I have done among them? [12] I will strike them with pestilence and disinherit them, and I will make of you a nation greater and mightier than they."

Moses Intercedes for the People

[13] But Moses said to the LORD, "Then the Egyptians will hear of it, for in your might you brought up this people from among them, [14] and they will tell the inhabitants of this land. They have heard that you, O LORD, are in the midst of this people; for you, O LORD, are seen face to face, and your cloud stands over them and you go in front of them, in a pillar of cloud by day and in a pillar of fire by night. [15] Now if you kill this people all at one time, then the nations who have heard about you will say, [16] 'It is because the LORD was not able to bring this people into the land he swore to give them that he has slaughtered them in the wilderness.' [17] And now, therefore, let the power of the LORD be great in the way that you promised when you spoke, saying,

[18] 'The LORD is slow to anger,
  and abounding in steadfast love,
  forgiving iniquity and transgression,
  but by no means clearing the guilty,
  visiting the iniquity of the parents
  upon the children
  to the third and the fourth
  generation.'

[19] Forgive the iniquity of this people according to the greatness of your steadfast love, just as you have pardoned this people, from Egypt even until now."

20 Then the LORD said, "I do forgive, just as you have asked; [21] nevertheless— as I live, and as all the earth shall be filled with the glory of the LORD— [22] none of the people who have seen my glory and the signs that I did in Egypt and in the wilderness, and yet have tested me these ten times and have not obeyed my voice, [23] shall see the land that I swore to give to their ancestors; none of those who despised me shall see it. [24] But my servant Caleb, because he has a different spirit and has followed me wholeheartedly, I will bring into the land into which he went, and his descendants shall possess it. [25] Now, since the Amalekites and the Canaanites live in the valleys, turn tomorrow and set out for the wilderness by the way to the Red Sea."[a]

An Attempted Invasion is Repulsed

26 And the LORD spoke to Moses and to Aaron, saying: [27] How long shall this wicked congregation complain against me? I have heard the complaints of the Israelites, which they complain against me. [28] Say to them, "As I live," says the LORD, "I will do to you the very things I heard you say: [29] your dead bodies shall fall in this very wilderness; and of all your number, included in the census, from twenty years old and upward, who have complained against me, [30] not one of you shall come into the land in which

[a] Or Sea of Reeds

---

statement of YHWH (YHWH's response to the golden calf, Exod. 34:5–8). YHWH's statement promises love, mercy, and forgiveness. In effect, Moses says: "You said it, now you have to live up to it." As in Exod. 34:5–8, Moses convinces YHWH to turn from wrath and continue with the Israelites. YHWH responds to, adapts to, and interacts with the people in concrete situations. In the same way the people are learning about the nature and ways of their God, YHWH is also learning about the nature and ways of this community.

YHWH promises to forgive, but forgiveness is not without a cost. The Israelites who came out of Egypt and saw the works of YHWH, will die in the wilderness. Only their descendants will enter the land. Divine forgiveness does not mean that YHWH acts as if nothing has happened (note the severity with which the quails are promised Israel in Num. 11:18–20). The reality of Israel's actions remains, and within that context YHWH finds a way to keep alive the story of this community.

I swore to settle you, except Caleb son of Jephunneh and Joshua son of Nun. [31] But your little ones, who you said would become booty, I will bring in, and they shall know the land that you have despised. [32] But as for you, your dead bodies shall fall in this wilderness. [33] And your children shall be shepherds in the wilderness for forty years, and shall suffer for your faithlessness, until the last of your dead bodies lies in the wilderness. [34] According to the number of the days in which you spied out the land, forty days, for every day a year, you shall bear your iniquity, forty years, and you shall know my displeasure." [35] I the LORD have spoken; surely I will do thus to all this wicked congregation gathered together against me: in this wilderness they shall come to a full end, and there they shall die.

36 And the men whom Moses sent to spy out the land, who returned and made all the congregation complain against him by bringing a bad report about the land— [37] the men who brought an unfavorable report about the land died by a plague before the LORD. [38] But Joshua son of Nun and Caleb son of Jephunneh alone remained alive, of those men who went to spy out the land.

39 When Moses told these words to all the Israelites, the people mourned greatly. [40] They rose early in the morning and went up to the heights of the hill country, saying, "Here we are. We will go up to the place that the LORD has promised, for we have sinned." [41] But Moses said, "Why do you continue to transgress the command of the LORD? That will not succeed. [42] Do not go up, for the LORD is not with you; do not let yourselves be struck down before your enemies. [43] For the Amalekites and the Canaanites will confront you there, and you shall fall by the sword; because you have turned back from following the LORD, the LORD will not be with you." [44] But they presumed to go up to the heights of the hill country, even though the ark of the covenant of the LORD, and Moses, had not left the camp. [45] Then the Amalekites and the Canaanites who lived in that hill country came down and defeated them, pursuing them as far as Hormah.

Various Offerings

15 The LORD spoke to Moses, saying: [2] Speak to the Israelites and say to them: When you come into the land you are to inhabit, which I am giving you, [3] and you make an offering by fire to the LORD from the herd or from the flock—whether a burnt offering or a sacrifice, to fulfill a vow or as a freewill offering or at your appointed festivals—to make a pleasing odor for the LORD, [4] then whoever presents such an offering to the LORD shall present also a grain offering, one-tenth of an ephah of choice flour, mixed with one-fourth of a hin of oil. [5] Moreover, you shall offer one-fourth of a hin of wine as a drink offering with the burnt offering or the sacrifice, for each lamb. [6] For a ram, you shall offer a grain offering, two-tenths of an ephah of choice flour mixed with one-third of a hin of oil; [7] and as a drink offering you shall offer one-third of a hin of wine, a pleasing odor to the LORD. [8] When you offer a bull as a burnt offering or a sacrifice, to fulfill a vow or as an offering of well-being to the LORD,

---

14:39–45—Israel now seeks, in light of YHWH's judgment of a forty-year death march, to invade the land. They are defeated and driven back by *the Amalekites and the Canaanites*. YHWH's judgment is final. The forty years of wandering in the wilderness now begin.

15:1–36 Rulings for Life in the Land
YHWH provides instructions for Israel's presen-

tation of sacrifices and offerings in the land. In the context of Israel's refusal to enter the land, YHWH's declaration of judgment, and Israel's defeat, YHWH speaks of Israel's life in the land. Embedded in the context of judgment and defeat, the rulings provide a word of hope. YHWH has not given up on the people. The land remains a reality.

⁹ then you shall present with the bull a grain offering, three-tenths of an ephah of choice flour, mixed with half a hin of oil, ¹⁰ and you shall present as a drink offering half a hin of wine, as an offering by fire, a pleasing odor to the LORD.

11 Thus it shall be done for each ox or ram, or for each of the male lambs or the kids. ¹² According to the number that you offer, so you shall do with each and every one. ¹³ Every native Israelite shall do these things in this way, in presenting an offering by fire, a pleasing odor to the LORD. ¹⁴ An alien who lives with you, or who takes up permanent residence among you, and wishes to offer an offering by fire, a pleasing odor to the LORD, shall do as you do. ¹⁵ As for the assembly, there shall be for both you and the resident alien a single statute, a perpetual statute throughout your generations; you and the alien shall be alike before the LORD. ¹⁶ You and the alien who resides with you shall have the same law and the same ordinance.

17 The LORD spoke to Moses, saying: ¹⁸ Speak to the Israelites and say to them: After you come into the land to which I am bringing you, ¹⁹ whenever you eat of the bread of the land, you shall present a donation to the LORD. ²⁰ From your first batch of dough you shall present a loaf as a donation; you shall present it just as you present a donation from the threshing floor. ²¹ Throughout your generations you shall give to the LORD a donation from the first of your batch of dough.

22 But if you unintentionally fail to observe all these commandments that the LORD has spoken to Moses— ²³ everything that the LORD has commanded you by Moses, from the day the LORD gave commandment and thereafter, throughout your generations— ²⁴ then if it was done unintentionally without the knowledge of the congregation, the whole congregation shall offer one young bull for a burnt offering, a pleasing odor to the LORD, together with its grain offering and its drink offering, according to the ordinance, and one male goat for a sin offering. ²⁵ The priest shall make atonement for all the congregation of the Israelites, and they shall be forgiven; it was unintentional, and they have brought their offering, an offering by fire to the LORD, and their sin offering before the LORD, for their error. ²⁶ All the congregation of the Israelites shall be forgiven, as well as the aliens residing among them, because the whole people was involved in the error.

27 An individual who sins unintentionally shall present a female goat a year old for a sin offering. ²⁸ And the priest shall make atonement before the LORD for the one who commits an error, when it is unintentional, to make atonement for the person, who then shall be forgiven. ²⁹ For both the native among the Israelites and the alien residing among them—you shall have the same law for anyone who acts in error. ³⁰ But whoever acts high-handedly, whether a native or an alien, affronts the LORD, and shall be cut off from among the people. ³¹ Because of having despised the word of the LORD and broken his commandment, such a person shall be utterly cut off and bear the guilt.

Penalty for Violating the Sabbath

32 When the Israelites were in the wilderness, they found a man gathering sticks on the sabbath day. ³³ Those who found him gathering sticks brought him to Moses, Aaron, and to the whole congregation. ³⁴ They put him in custody, because it was not clear what should be done to him. ³⁵ Then the LORD said to Moses, "The man shall be put to death; all the congregation shall stone him outside the camp." ³⁶ The whole congregation brought him outside the camp and stoned him to death, just as the LORD had commanded Moses.

Fringes on Garments

37 The LORD said to Moses: ³⁸ Speak to the Israelites, and tell them to make

fringes on the corners of their garments throughout their generations and to put a blue cord on the fringe at each corner. ³⁹ You have the fringe so that, when you see it, you will remember all the commandments of the LORD and do them, and not follow the lust of your own heart and your own eyes. ⁴⁰ So you shall remember and do all my commandments, and you shall be holy to your God. ⁴¹ I am the LORD your God, who brought you out of the land of Egypt, to be your God: I am the LORD your God.

Revolt of Korah, Dathan, and Abiram

16 Now Korah son of Izhar son of Kohath son of Levi, along with Dathan and Abiram sons of Eliab, and On son of Peleth—descendants of Reuben—took ² two hundred fifty Israelite men, leaders of the congregation, chosen from the assembly, well-known men,ᵃ and they confronted Moses. ³ They assembled against Moses and against Aaron, and said to them, "You have gone too far! All the congregation are holy, every one of them, and the LORD is among them. So why then do you exalt yourselves above the assembly of the LORD?" ⁴ When Moses heard it, he fell on his face. ⁵ Then he said to Korah and all his company, "In the morning the LORD will make known who is his, and who is holy, and who will be allowed to approach him; the one whom he will choose he will allow to approach him. ⁶ Do this: take censers, Korah and all yourᵇ company, ⁷ and tomorrow put fire in them, and lay incense on them before the LORD; and the man whom the LORD chooses shall be the holy one. You Levites have gone too far!" ⁸ Then Moses said to Korah, "Hear now, you Levites! ⁹ Is it too little for you that the God of Israel has separated you from the congregation of Israel, to allow you to approach him in order to perform the duties of the LORD's tabernacle, and to stand before the congregation and serve them? ¹⁰ He has allowed you to approach him, and all your brother Levites with you; yet you seek the priesthood as well! ¹¹ Therefore you and all your company have gathered together against the LORD. What is Aaron that you rail against him?"

12 Moses sent for Dathan and Abiram sons of Eliab; but they said, "We will not come! ¹³ Is it too little that you have brought us up out of a land flowing with milk and honey to kill us in the wilderness, that you must also lord it over us? ¹⁴ It is clear you have not brought us into a land flowing with milk and honey, or given us an inheritance of fields and vineyards. Would you put out the eyes of these men? We will not come!"

15 Moses was very angry and said to the LORD, "Pay no attention to their offering. I have not taken one donkey from them, and I have not harmed any one of them." ¹⁶ And Moses said to Korah, "As for you and all your company, be present tomorrow before the LORD, you and they and Aaron; ¹⁷ and let each one of you take his censer, and put incense on it, and each one of you present his censer before the LORD, two hundred fifty censers; you also, and Aaron, each his censer." ¹⁸ So each man took his censer, and they put fire in the censers and laid incense on them, and they stood at the entrance of the tent of meeting with Moses and Aaron. ¹⁹ Then Korah assembled the whole congregation against

---

ᵃ Cn: Heb *and they confronted Moses, and two hundred fifty men . . . well-known men* ᵇ Heb *his*

16:1–17:13 Fifth Rebellion: Who Is in Charge?

16:1–40—Two distinct rebellions are woven together (and are at times difficult to distinguish). *Korah* questions the subordinate role of the Levites in relation to Aaron and his sons. *Dathan and Abiram* question the special status of Moses and his exclusive right to enter into the presence of the holy one. The text focuses on the latter issue. The holy place cannot be entered by just anyone, just anytime. YHWH decides the issue in favor of Moses and Aaron, but one sees in this story Israel's struggle with the nature of leadership, especially in matters relating to YHWH.

them at the entrance of the tent of meeting. And the glory of the LORD appeared to the whole congregation.

20 Then the LORD spoke to Moses and to Aaron, saying: [21] Separate yourselves from this congregation, so that I may consume them in a moment. [22] They fell on their faces, and said, "O God, the God of the spirits of all flesh, shall one person sin and you become angry with the whole congregation?"

23 And the LORD spoke to Moses, saying: [24] Say to the congregation: Get away from the dwellings of Korah, Dathan, and Abiram. [25] So Moses got up and went to Dathan and Abiram; the elders of Israel followed him. [26] He said to the congregation, "Turn away from the tents of these wicked men, and touch nothing of theirs, or you will be swept away for all their sins." [27] So they got away from the dwellings of Korah, Dathan, and Abiram; and Dathan and Abiram came out and stood at the entrance of their tents, together with their wives, their children, and their little ones. [28] And Moses said, "This is how you shall know that the LORD has sent me to do all these works; it has not been of my own accord: [29] If these people die a natural death, or if a natural fate comes on them, then the LORD has not sent me. [30] But if the LORD creates something new, and the ground opens its mouth and swallows them up, with all that belongs to them, and they go down alive into Sheol, then you shall know that these men have despised the LORD."

31 As soon as he finished speaking all these words, the ground under them was split apart. [32] The earth opened its mouth and swallowed them up, along with their households—everyone who belonged to Korah and all their goods. [33] So they with all that belonged to them went down alive into Sheol; the earth closed over them, and they perished from the midst of the assembly. [34] All Israel around them fled at their outcry, for they said, "The earth will swallow us too!" [35] And fire came out from the LORD and consumed the two hundred fifty men offering the incense.

36[a] Then the LORD spoke to Moses, saying: [37] Tell Eleazar son of Aaron the priest to take the censers out of the blaze; then scatter the fire far and wide. [38] For the censers of these sinners have become holy at the cost of their lives. Make them into hammered plates as a covering for the altar, for they presented them before the LORD and they became holy. Thus they shall be a sign to the Israelites. [39] So Eleazar the priest took the bronze censers that had been presented by those who were burned; and they were hammered out as a covering for the altar— [40] a reminder to the Israelites that no outsider, who is not of the descendants of Aaron, shall approach to offer incense before the LORD, so as not to become like Korah and his company—just as the LORD had said to him through Moses.

41 On the next day, however, the whole congregation of the Israelites rebelled against Moses and against Aaron, saying, "You have killed the people of the LORD." [42] And when the congregation had assembled against them, Moses and Aaron turned toward the tent of meeting; the cloud had covered it and the glory of the LORD appeared. [43] Then Moses and Aaron came to the

[a] Ch 17.1 in Heb

16:41–50—Following the death of the rebels, the people attack Moses and Aaron. YHWH is prepared to destroy the people, and a *plague* is unleashed upon them. The role of Aaron as a mediator between YHWH and the people is graphically depicted as he takes his burning *censer* and stands between "the dead and the living" (v. 48). He stops the plague that YHWH had unleashed and "sets things right" (NRSV *made atonement*) for the people (vv. 47–48). The priestly ministry includes both distinguishing between the holy and the not holy, the clean and the unclean (Lev. 10:10), and the dangerous task of standing between a rebellious and sinful people and an angry God. This is a dangerous place to stand (note the people's response in Num. 17:12–13)!

front of the tent of meeting, **44** and the LORD spoke to Moses, saying, **45** "Get away from this congregation, so that I may consume them in a moment." And they fell on their faces. **46** Moses said to Aaron, "Take your censer, put fire on it from the altar and lay incense on it, and carry it quickly to the congregation and make atonement for them. For wrath has gone out from the LORD; the plague has begun." **47** So Aaron took it as Moses had ordered, and ran into the middle of the assembly, where the plague had already begun among the people. He put on the incense, and made atonement for the people. **48** He stood between the dead and the living; and the plague was stopped. **49** Those who died by the plague were fourteen thousand seven hundred, besides those who died in the affair of Korah. **50** When the plague was stopped, Aaron returned to Moses at the entrance of the tent of meeting.

The Budding of Aaron's Rod

17 *a* The LORD spoke to Moses, saying: **2** Speak to the Israelites, and get twelve staffs from them, one for each ancestral house, from all the leaders of their ancestral houses. Write each man's name on his staff, **3** and write Aaron's name on the staff of Levi. For there shall be one staff for the head of each ancestral house. **4** Place them in the tent of meeting before the covenant,*b*

where I meet with you. **5** And the staff of the man whom I choose shall sprout; thus I will put a stop to the complaints of the Israelites that they continually make against you. **6** Moses spoke to the Israelites; and all their leaders gave him staffs, one for each leader, according to their ancestral houses, twelve staffs; and the staff of Aaron was among theirs. **7** So Moses placed the staffs before the LORD in the tent of the covenant. *b*

8 When Moses went into the tent of the covenant *b* on the next day, the staff of Aaron for the house of Levi had sprouted. It put forth buds, produced blossoms, and bore ripe almonds. **9** Then Moses brought out all the staffs from before the LORD to all the Israelites; and they looked, and each man took his staff. **10** And the LORD said to Moses, "Put back the staff of Aaron before the covenant, *b* to be kept as a warning to rebels, so that you may make an end of their complaints against me, or else they will die." **11** Moses did so; just as the LORD commanded him, so he did.

12 The Israelites said to Moses, "We are perishing; we are lost, all of us are lost! **13** Everyone who approaches the tabernacle of the LORD will die. Are we all to perish?"

Responsibility of Priests and Levites

18 The LORD said to Aaron: You and your sons and your ancestral

a Ch 17.16 in Heb   *b* Or *treaty,* or *testimony;* Heb *eduth*

17:1–11—At the direction of YHWH, Moses acts to determine for the whole community who YHWH has chosen to act as priest. The central question: Who may safely and legitimately "approach" YHWH (see 16:5) in the holy place? A staff representing each tribe is placed in the tent of meeting before the ark of the covenant. The following morning, Aaron's *staff* has sprouted, budded, and produced *ripe almonds*. Aaron's rod is then placed before the ark *as a warning* against further rebellion.

17:12–13—The Israelites, however, are not content. They react in hyperbolic fear: *We are perishing! We are lost!* We will all die! They now argue that *everyone who approaches the tabernacle . . . will die*. Note carefully that the people

do not make a distinction between drawing near to the "tabernacle" and acting as priests "inside" the tabernacle.

18:1–32 Rulings for Aaron and the Levites

18:1—The priests are responsible for offenses committed in relation to the sanctuary. Their ministry includes both danger and responsibility. Although the priests exercised a great deal of power in relation to the community, they also carried a great deal of responsibility to perform their duties faithfully and with integrity. Although contemporary ministry may not be concerned with sacrifices and offerings, or protection of the holy tabernacle, these texts have much to say concerning the responsibility and gravity

house with you shall bear responsibility for offenses connected with the sanctuary, while you and your sons alone shall bear responsibility for offenses connected with the priesthood. ²So bring with you also your brothers of the tribe of Levi, your ancestral tribe, in order that they may be joined to you, and serve you while you and your sons with you are in front of the tent of the covenant. *a* ³They shall perform duties for you and for the whole tent. But they must not approach either the utensils of the sanctuary or the altar, otherwise both they and you will die. ⁴They are attached to you in order to perform the duties of the tent of meeting, for all the service of the tent; no outsider shall approach you. ⁵You yourselves shall perform the duties of the sanctuary and the duties of the altar, so that wrath may never again come upon the Israelites. ⁶It is I who now take your brother Levites from among the Israelites; they are now yours as a gift, dedicated to the LORD, to perform the service of the tent of meeting. ⁷But you and your sons with you shall diligently perform your priestly duties in all that concerns the altar and the area behind the curtain. I give your priesthood as a gift;*b* any outsider who approaches shall be put to death.

The Priests' Portion

8 The LORD spoke to Aaron: I have given you charge of the offerings made to me, all the holy gifts of the Israelites; I have given them to you and your sons as a priestly portion due you in perpetuity. ⁹This shall be yours from the most holy things, reserved from the fire: every offering of theirs that they render to me as a most holy thing, whether grain offering, sin offering, or guilt offering, shall belong to you and your sons. ¹⁰As a most holy thing you shall eat it; every male may eat it; it shall be holy to you. ¹¹This also is yours: I have given to you,

together with your sons and daughters, as a perpetual due, whatever is set aside from the gifts of all the elevation offerings of the Israelites; everyone who is clean in your house may eat them. ¹²All the best of the oil and all the best of the wine and of the grain, the choice produce that they give to the LORD, I have given to you. ¹³The first fruits of all that is in their land, which they bring to the LORD, shall be yours; everyone who is clean in your house may eat of it. ¹⁴Every devoted thing in Israel shall be yours. ¹⁵The first issue of the womb of all creatures, human and animal, which is offered to the LORD, shall be yours; but the firstborn of human beings you shall redeem, and the firstborn of unclean animals you shall redeem. ¹⁶Their redemption price, reckoned from one month of age, you shall fix at five shekels of silver, according to the shekel of the sanctuary (that is, twenty gerahs). ¹⁷But the firstborn of a cow, or the firstborn of a sheep, or the firstborn of a goat, you shall not redeem; they are holy. You shall dash their blood on the altar, and shall turn their fat into smoke as an offering by fire for a pleasing odor to the LORD; ¹⁸but their flesh shall be yours, just as the breast that is elevated and as the right thigh are yours. ¹⁹All the holy offerings that the Israelites present to the LORD I have given to you, together with your sons and daughters, as a perpetual due; it is a covenant of salt forever before the LORD for you and your descendants as well. ²⁰Then the LORD said to Aaron: You shall have no allotment in their land, nor shall you have any share among them; I am your share and your possession among the Israelites.

21 To the Levites I have given every tithe in Israel for a possession in return for the service that they perform, the

---

a Or *treaty*, or *testimony*; Heb *eduth*   *b* Heb *as a service of gift*

---

associated with the priestly ministry. Those who stand as mediators between God and the people must be both faithful to the community in which they live and responsible to the God they serve.

service in the tent of meeting. ²² From now on the Israelites shall no longer approach the tent of meeting, or else they will incur guilt and die. ²³ But the Levites shall perform the service of the tent of meeting, and they shall bear responsibility for their own offenses; it shall be a perpetual statute throughout your generations. But among the Israelites they shall have no allotment, ²⁴ because I have given to the Levites as their portion the tithe of the Israelites, which they set apart as an offering to the LORD. Therefore I have said of them that they shall have no allotment among the Israelites.

25 Then the LORD spoke to Moses, saying: ²⁶ You shall speak to the Levites, saying: When you receive from the Israelites the tithe that I have given you from them for your portion, you shall set apart an offering from it to the LORD, a tithe of the tithe. ²⁷ It shall be reckoned to you as your gift, the same as the grain of the threshing floor and the fullness of the wine press. ²⁸ Thus you also shall set apart an offering to the LORD from all the tithes that you receive from the Israelites; and from them you shall give the LORD's offering to the priest Aaron. ²⁹ Out of all the gifts to you, you shall set apart every offering due to the LORD; the best of all of them is the part to be consecrated. ³⁰ Say also to them: When you have set apart the best of it, then the rest shall be reckoned to the Levites as produce of the threshing floor, and as produce of the wine press. ³¹ You may eat it in any place, you and your households; for it is your payment for your service in the tent of meeting. ³² You shall incur no guilt by reason of it, when you have offered the best of it. But you shall not profane the holy gifts of the Israelites, on pain of death.

Ceremony of the Red Heifer

19 The LORD spoke to Moses and Aaron, saying: ² This is a statute of the law that the LORD has commanded: Tell the Israelites to bring you a red heifer without defect, in which there is no blemish and on which no yoke has been laid. ³ You shall give it to the priest Eleazar, and it shall be taken outside the camp and slaughtered in his presence. ⁴ The priest Eleazar shall take some of its blood with his finger and sprinkle it seven times towards the front of the tent of meeting. ⁵ Then the heifer shall be burned in his sight; its skin, its flesh, and its blood, with its dung, shall be burned. ⁶ The priest shall take cedarwood, hyssop, and crimson material, and throw them into the fire in which the heifer is burning. ⁷ Then the priest shall wash his clothes and bathe his body in water, and afterwards he may come into the camp; but the priest shall remain unclean until evening. ⁸ The one who burns the heifer[a] shall wash his clothes in water and bathe his body in water; he shall remain unclean until evening. ⁹ Then someone who is clean shall gather up the ashes of the heifer, and deposit them outside the camp in a clean place; and they shall be kept for the congregation of the Israelites for the water for cleansing. It is a purification offering. ¹⁰ The one who gathers the ashes of the heifer shall wash his clothes and be unclean until evening.

This shall be a perpetual statute for the Israelites and for the alien residing among them. ¹¹ Those who touch the dead body of any human being shall be unclean seven days. ¹² They shall purify themselves with the water on the third day and on the seventh day, and so be clean; but if they do not purify themselves on the third day and on the

[a] Heb *it*

19:1–22 The Ashes of the Red Heifer
The ashes are used in the ritual to cleanse persons from corpse contamination. Corpse contamination was a major form of impurity and required a seven day cleansing ritual. Death was considered the ultimate form of impurity and was to be avoided and "held back" in any way possible.

seventh day, they will not become clean. [13] All who touch a corpse, the body of a human being who has died, and do not purify themselves, defile the tabernacle of the LORD; such persons shall be cut off from Israel. Since water for cleansing was not dashed on them, they remain unclean; their uncleanness is still on them.

[14] This is the law when someone dies in a tent: everyone who comes into the tent, and everyone who is in the tent, shall be unclean seven days. [15] And every open vessel with no cover fastened on it is unclean. [16] Whoever in the open field touches one who has been killed by a sword, or who has died naturally,[a] or a human bone, or a grave, shall be unclean seven days. [17] For the unclean they shall take some ashes of the burnt purification offering, and running water shall be added in a vessel; [18] then a clean person shall take hyssop, dip it in the water, and sprinkle it on the tent, on all the furnishings, on the persons who were there, and on whoever touched the bone, the slain, the corpse, or the grave. [19] The clean person shall sprinkle the unclean ones on the third day and on the seventh day, thus purifying them on the seventh day. Then they shall wash their clothes and bathe themselves in water, and at evening they shall be clean. [20] Any who are unclean but do not purify themselves, those persons shall be cut off from the assembly, for they have defiled the sanctuary of the LORD. Since the water for cleansing has not been dashed on them, they are unclean.

[21] It shall be a perpetual statute for them. The one who sprinkles the water for cleansing shall wash his clothes, and whoever touches the water for cleansing shall be unclean until evening. [22] Whatever the unclean person touches shall be unclean, and anyone who touches it shall be unclean until evening.

The Waters of Meribah

20 The Israelites, the whole congregation, came into the wilderness of Zin in the first month, and the people stayed in Kadesh. Miriam died there, and was buried there.

[2] Now there was no water for the congregation; so they gathered together against Moses and against Aaron. [3] The people quarreled with Moses and said, "Would that we had died when our kindred died before the LORD! [4] Why have you brought the assembly of the LORD into this wilderness for us and our livestock to die here? [5] Why have you brought us up out of Egypt, to bring us to this wretched place? It is no place for grain, or figs, or vines, or pomegranates; and there is no water to drink." [6] Then Moses and Aaron went away from the assembly to the entrance of the tent of meeting; they fell on their faces, and the glory of the LORD appeared to them. [7] The LORD spoke to Moses, saying: [8] Take the staff, and assemble the congregation, you and your brother Aaron, and command the rock before their eyes to yield its water. Thus you shall bring water out of the rock for them; thus you shall provide drink for the congregation and their livestock.

[a] Heb lacks *naturally*

20:1–29—Moses and Aaron Offend YHWH

20:1–13—In the context of the people's complaint concerning water, Moses disobeys YHWH. YHWH's response addresses Moses' integrity and faithfulness, matters relating to his role as leader of the people. The judgment is harsh: *you shall not bring this assembly into the land* (v. 12). The narrative returns to the question of leadership, its meaning and the responsibilities that go along with it, raised earlier by Moses (11:10–30). Repeatedly in these stories, the question of leadership is addressed. As Israel journeys in the

wilderness, ultimately moving toward life in the land, one of the difficult issues with which they repeatedly struggle has to do with leadership. In a variety of ways, these struggles continue to be important and difficult issues in contemporary faith communities.

Moses and Aaron were called to lead Israel out of Egypt and through the wilderness. Life in the land will require new leadership. There is a time and a place for everything. New times and new places may require new visions and new leadership. Change is part of the divine-human story.

9 So Moses took the staff from before the LORD, as he had commanded him. [10] Moses and Aaron gathered the assembly together before the rock, and he said to them, "Listen, you rebels, shall we bring water for you out of this rock?" [11] Then Moses lifted up his hand and struck the rock twice with his staff; water came out abundantly, and the congregation and their livestock drank. [12] But the LORD said to Moses and Aaron, "Because you did not trust in me, to show my holiness before the eyes of the Israelites, therefore you shall not bring this assembly into the land that I have given them." [13] These are the waters of Meribah,[a] where the people of Israel quarreled with the LORD, and by which he showed his holiness.

Passage through Edom Refused

14 Moses sent messengers from Kadesh to the king of Edom, "Thus says your brother Israel: You know all the adversity that has befallen us: [15] how our ancestors went down to Egypt, and we lived in Egypt a long time; and the Egyptians oppressed us and our ancestors; [16] and when we cried to the LORD, he heard our voice, and sent an angel and brought us out of Egypt; and here we are in Kadesh, a town on the edge of your territory. [17] Now let us pass through your land. We will not pass through field or vineyard, or drink water from any well; we will go along the King's Highway, not turning aside to the right hand or to the left until we have passed through your territory."

18 But Edom said to him, "You shall not pass through, or we will come out with the sword against you." [19] The Israelites said to him, "We will stay on the highway; and if we drink of your water, we and our livestock, then we will pay for it. It is only a small matter; just let us pass through on foot." [20] But he said, "You shall not pass through." And Edom came out against them with a large force, heavily armed. [21] Thus Edom refused to give Israel passage through their territory; so Israel turned away from them.

The Death of Aaron

22 They set out from Kadesh, and the Israelites, the whole congregation, came to Mount Hor. [23] Then the LORD said to Moses and Aaron at Mount Hor, on the border of the land of Edom, [24] "Let Aaron be gathered to his people. For he shall not enter the land that I have given to the Israelites, because you rebelled against my command at the waters of Meribah. [25] Take Aaron and his son Eleazar, and bring them up Mount Hor; [26] strip Aaron of his vestments, and put them on his son Eleazar. But Aaron shall be gathered to his people,[b] and shall die there." [27] Moses did as the LORD had commanded; they went up Mount Hor in the sight of the whole congregation. [28] Moses stripped Aaron of his vestments, and put them on his son Eleazar; and Aaron died there on the top of the mountain. Moses and Eleazar came down from the mountain. [29] When all the congregation saw that Aaron had died, all the house of Israel mourned for Aaron thirty days.

The Bronze Serpent

21 When the Canaanite, the king of Arad, who lived in the Negeb, heard that Israel was coming by the way of Atharim, he fought against Israel and took some of them captive. [2] Then Israel made a vow to the LORD and said, "If you will indeed give this people into our hands, then we will utterly destroy their

[a] That is *Quarrel* [b] Heb lacks *to his people*

20:22–29—Aaron dies on *Mount Hor*, and *Eleazer, his son*, takes his place as the anointed priest.

21:1–3 Israel Defeats Arad

This initial victory over the *Canaanites* (v. 3) continues the theme of hope begun in chap. 15 (instructions for life lived in the land of Canaan). The victory anticipates Israel's conquest and settlement of Canaan.

towns." [3] The LORD listened to the voice of Israel, and handed over the Canaanites; and they utterly destroyed them and their towns; so the place was called Hormah.[a]

[4] From Mount Hor they set out by the way to the Red Sea,[b] to go around the land of Edom; but the people became impatient on the way. [5] The people spoke against God and against Moses, "Why have you brought us up out of Egypt to die in the wilderness? For there is no food and no water, and we detest this miserable food." [6] Then the LORD sent poisonous[c] serpents among the people, and they bit the people, so that many Israelites died. [7] The people came to Moses and said, "We have sinned by speaking against the LORD and against you; pray to the LORD to take away the serpents from us." So Moses prayed for the people. [8] And the LORD said to Moses, "Make a poisonous[d] serpent, and set it on a pole; and everyone who is bitten shall look at it and live." [9] So Moses made a serpent of bronze, and put it upon a pole; and whenever a serpent bit someone, that person would look at the serpent of bronze and live.

The Journey to Moab

[10] The Israelites set out, and camped in Oboth. [11] They set out from Oboth, and camped at Iye-abarim, in the wilderness bordering Moab toward the sunrise. [12] From there they set out, and camped in the Wadi Zered. [13] From there they set out, and camped on the other side of the Arnon, in[e] the wilderness that extends from the boundary of the Amorites; for the Arnon is the boundary of Moab, between Moab and the Amorites. [14] Wherefore it is said in the Book of the Wars of the LORD,

"Waheb in Suphah and the wadis.
　The Arnon [15] and the slopes of the wadis
　that extend to the seat of Ar,
　and lie along the border of Moab."[f]

[16] From there they continued to Beer;[g] that is the well of which the LORD said to Moses, "Gather the people together, and I will give them water." [17] Then Israel sang this song:

"Spring up, O well!—Sing to it!—
[18]　the well that the leaders sank,
　that the nobles of the people dug,
　with the scepter, with the staff."

From the wilderness to Mattanah, [19] from Mattanah to Nahaliel, from Nahaliel to Bamoth, [20] and from Bamoth to the valley lying in the region of Moab by the top of Pisgah that overlooks the wasteland.[h]

King Sihon Defeated

[21] Then Israel sent messengers to King Sihon of the Amorites, saying, [22] "Let me pass through your land; we will not turn aside into field or vineyard; we will not drink the water of any well; we will go by the King's Highway until we have passed through your territory." [23] But Sihon would not allow Israel to pass through his territory. Sihon gathered all his people together, and went out against Israel to the wilderness; he came to Jahaz, and fought against Israel. [24] Israel put him to the sword, and took possession of his land from the Arnon to the Jabbok, as far as to the Ammonites; for the

[a] Heb Destruction　[b] Or Sea of Reeds　[c] Or fiery; Heb seraphim　[d] Or fiery; Heb seraph　[e] Gk: Heb which is in　[f] Meaning of Heb uncertain　[g] That is Well　[h] Or Jeshimon

---

21:4–9 Again, the People Rebel

Again the people refuse to believe in YHWH's provisions. Again they look back to *Egypt*. The people continue to struggle with YHWH, and YHWH continues to respond with punishing wrath. This rebellion story is reported within the emerging context of hope and certainty concerning Israel's life in Canaan. The struggle between YHWH and Israel continues, and the narrative

moves from hope to rebellion, between promise and apostasy, around faith and faithlessness.

21:10–35 Israel on the March

The victories over *Sihon* and *Og* are viewed as signs of hope that Israel is now on the right path. Israel continues its journey to the land of promise even in the midst of rebellion and complaint. And YHWH continues on with them!

boundary of the Ammonites was strong.
25 Israel took all these towns, and Israel
settled in all the towns of the Amorites,
in Heshbon, and in all its villages. 26 For
Heshbon was the city of King Sihon of
the Amorites, who had fought against
the former king of Moab and captured
all his land as far as the Arnon. 27 Therefore the ballad singers say,

"Come to Heshbon, let it be built;
   let the city of Sihon be established.
28 For fire came out from Heshbon,
   flame from the city of Sihon.
It devoured Ar of Moab,
   and swallowed up*a* the heights of
     the Arnon.
29 Woe to you, O Moab!
   You are undone, O people of
     Chemosh!
He has made his sons fugitives,
   and his daughters captives,
   to an Amorite king, Sihon.
30 So their posterity perished
   from Heshbon*b* to Dibon,
   and we laid waste until fire spread
     to Medeba."*c*

31 Thus Israel settled in the land of the
Amorites. 32 Moses sent to spy out Jazer;
and they captured its villages, and dispossessed the Amorites who were there.

King Og Defeated

33 Then they turned and went up the
road to Bashan; and King Og of Bashan
came out against them, he and all his
people, to battle at Edrei. 34 But the LORD
said to Moses, "Do not be afraid of him;
for I have given him into your hand,
with all his people, and all his land. You
shall do to him as you did to King Sihon
of the Amorites, who ruled in Heshbon."
35 So they killed him, his sons, and all his
people, until there was no survivor left;
and they took possession of his land.

Balak Summons Balaam to Curse Israel

22 The Israelites set out, and
camped in the plains of Moab
across the Jordan from Jericho. 2 Now
Balak son of Zippor saw all that Israel
had done to the Amorites. 3 Moab was
in great dread of the people, because
they were so numerous; Moab was overcome with fear of the people of Israel.
4 And Moab said to the elders of Midian, "This horde will now lick up all that
is around us, as an ox licks up the grass
of the field." Now Balak son of Zippor
was king of Moab at that time. 5 He sent

a Gk: Heb *and the lords of* *b* Gk: Heb *we have shot at them; Heshbon has perished* *c* Compare Sam Gk: Meaning of MT uncertain

---

22:1–24:25 Balaam Blesses Israel

This story takes place without Israel's awareness.
Humans make plans, make decisions, undertake
projects, and work diligently at their jobs without
knowing fully all that is going on and having
an impact on them. This is the nature of human
life and history. Even when the Israelites are not
aware that they are being threatened, YHWH is
watching over their story to make certain that it
leads to blessing and life in the land.

Balaam lives at *Pethor, on the Euphrates*
(22:5). Balak, the king of Moab, sends to a region
known for its diviners to seek someone to curse
Israel and bring them to defeat. Balaam, even as
a non-Israelite, becomes the voice of YHWH and
speaks oracles of blessing. The "outsider" may
well be one way in which God speaks. At the
time Israel is not even aware that this non-Israelite Babylonian is shaping a future of blessing for
them as he speaks the word of YHWH. Importantly, Balaam speaks what YHWH speaks, even
in the face of the king who had initially brought
him to the situation to curse Israel. Far from being

simply a religious act, his oracle of blessing is a
political act. Balaam, the outsider, demonstrates
courage, integrity, and conviction as he speaks
the word of YHWH.

The word of the oracle (23:7, 18; 24:3), understood as the word of YHWH, is a word of power
that is able to shape history. Human words also
carry power: the power to shape lives, to harm
lives, to provide joy and comfort, sadness and
sorrow. Human words, even when spoken casu-
ally and without thought, are able to change the
shape of lives and the course of history. The gift
of voice carries with it responsibility—to help or
to harm, to build up or to tear down, to affirm or
to negate.

The story continues to develop the theme of
hope and focuses on YHWH's blessing. YHWH
has promised the Israelites life in the land of
promise, and YHWH watches over that promise
to make certain it will take place. Even when
Israel acts faithlessly, YHWH remains faithful to
the promises and acts to ensure that Israel will
experience the blessing.

messengers to Balaam son of Beor at Pethor, which is on the Euphrates, in the land of Amaw,[a] to summon him, saying, "A people has come out of Egypt; they have spread over the face of the earth, and they have settled next to me. ⁶ Come now, curse this people for me, since they are stronger than I; perhaps I shall be able to defeat them and drive them from the land; for I know that whomever you bless is blessed, and whomever you curse is cursed."

7 So the elders of Moab and the elders of Midian departed with the fees for divination in their hand; and they came to Balaam, and gave him Balak's message. ⁸ He said to them, "Stay here tonight, and I will bring back word to you, just as the LORD speaks to me"; so the officials of Moab stayed with Balaam. ⁹ God came to Balaam and said, "Who are these men with you?" ¹⁰ Balaam said to God, "King Balak son of Zippor of Moab, has sent me this message: ¹¹ 'A people has come out of Egypt and has spread over the face of the earth; now come, curse them for me; perhaps I shall be able to fight against them and drive them out.'" ¹² God said to Balaam, "You shall not go with them; you shall not curse the people, for they are blessed." ¹³ So Balaam rose in the morning, and said to the officials of Balak, "Go to your own land, for the LORD has refused to let me go with you." ¹⁴ So the officials of Moab rose and went to Balak, and said, "Balaam refuses to come with us."

15 Once again Balak sent officials, more numerous and more distinguished than these. ¹⁶ They came to Balaam and said to him, "Thus says Balak son of Zippor: 'Do not let anything hinder you from coming to me; ¹⁷ for I will surely do you great honor, and whatever you say to me I will do; come, curse this people for me.'" ¹⁸ But Balaam replied to the servants of Balak, "Although Balak were to give me his house full of silver and gold, I could not go beyond the command of the LORD my God, to do less or

more. ¹⁹ You remain here, as the others did, so that I may learn what more the LORD may say to me." ²⁰ That night God came to Balaam and said to him, "If the men have come to summon you, get up and go with them; but do only what I tell you to do." ²¹ So Balaam got up in the morning, saddled his donkey, and went with the officials of Moab.

Balaam, the Donkey, and the Angel

22 God's anger was kindled because he was going, and the angel of the LORD took his stand in the road as his adversary. Now he was riding on the donkey, and his two servants were with him. ²³ The donkey saw the angel of the LORD standing in the road, with a drawn sword in his hand; so the donkey turned off the road, and went into the field; and Balaam struck the donkey, to turn it back onto the road. ²⁴ Then the angel of the LORD stood in a narrow path between the vineyards, with a wall on either side. ²⁵ When the donkey saw the angel of the LORD, it scraped against the wall, and scraped Balaam's foot against the wall; so he struck it again. ²⁶ Then the angel of the LORD went ahead, and stood in a narrow place, where there was no way to turn either to the right or to the left. ²⁷ When the donkey saw the angel of the LORD, it lay down under Balaam; and Balaam's anger was kindled, and he struck the donkey with his staff. ²⁸ Then the LORD opened the mouth of the donkey, and it said to Balaam, "What have I done to you, that you have struck me these three times?" ²⁹ Balaam said to the donkey, "Because you have made a fool of me! I wish I had a sword in my hand! I would kill you right now!" ³⁰ But the donkey said to Balaam, "Am I not your donkey, which you have ridden all your life to this day? Have I been in the habit of treating you this way?" And he said, "No."

31 Then the LORD opened the eyes of Balaam, and he saw the angel of the

[a] Or land of his kinsfolk

LORD standing in the road, with his drawn sword in his hand; and he bowed down, falling on his face. [32] The angel of the LORD said to him, "Why have you struck your donkey these three times? I have come out as an adversary, because your way is perverse[a] before me. [33] The donkey saw me, and turned away from me these three times. If it had not turned away from me, surely just now I would have killed you and let it live." [34] Then Balaam said to the angel of the LORD, "I have sinned, for I did not know that you were standing in the road to oppose me. Now therefore, if it is displeasing to you, I will return home." [35] The angel of the LORD said to Balaam, "Go with the men; but speak only what I tell you to speak." So Balaam went on with the officials of Balak.

36 When Balak heard that Balaam had come, he went out to meet him at Ir-moab, on the boundary formed by the Arnon, at the farthest point of the boundary. [37] Balak said to Balaam, "Did I not send to summon you? Why did you not come to me? Am I not able to honor you?" [38] Balaam said to Balak, "I have come to you now, but do I have power to say just anything? The word God puts in my mouth, that is what I must say." [39] Then Balaam went with Balak, and they came to Kiriath-huzoth. [40] Balak sacrificed oxen and sheep, and sent them to Balaam and to the officials who were with him.

Balaam's First Oracle

41 On the next day Balak took Balaam and brought him up to Bamoth-baal; and from there he could see part of the people of Israel.[b] **23** [1] Then Balaam said to Balak, "Build me seven altars here, and prepare seven bulls and seven rams for me." [2] Balak did as Balaam had said; and Balak and Balaam offered a bull and a ram on each altar. [3] Then Balaam said to Balak, "Stay here beside your burnt offerings while I go aside. Perhaps the LORD will come to meet me. Whatever he shows me I will tell you." And he went to a bare height.

4 Then God met Balaam; and Balaam said to him, "I have arranged the seven altars, and have offered a bull and a ram on each altar." [5] The LORD put a word in Balaam's mouth, and said, "Return to Balak, and this is what you must say." [6] So he returned to Balak,[c] who was standing beside his burnt offerings with all the officials of Moab. [7] Then Balaam[d] uttered his oracle, saying:

"Balak has brought me from Aram,
   the king of Moab from the eastern
      mountains:
'Come, curse Jacob for me;
   Come, denounce Israel!'
[8] How can I curse whom God has not
      cursed?
   How can I denounce those whom
      the LORD has not denounced?
[9] For from the top of the crags I see
      him,
   from the hills I behold him.
Here is a people living alone,
   and not reckoning itself among the
      nations!
[10] Who can count the dust of Jacob,
   or number the dust-cloud[e] of
      Israel?
Let me die the death of the
      upright,
   and let my end be like his!"

11 Then Balak said to Balaam, "What have you done to me? I brought you to curse my enemies, but now you have done nothing but bless them." [12] He answered, "Must I not take care to say what the LORD puts into my mouth?"

Balaam's Second Oracle

13 So Balak said to him, "Come with me to another place from which you may see them; you shall see only part of them, and shall not see them all; then curse them for me from there." [14] So he took him to the field of Zophim, to the

---

[a] Meaning of Heb uncertain   [b] Heb lacks *of Israel*   [c] Heb *him*   [d] Heb *he*
[e] Or *fourth part*

23:7–10—First oracle: In this oracle, Balaam does not bless Israel, but refuses to curse them (v. 8b).

top of Pisgah. He built seven altars, and offered a bull and a ram on each altar. [15] Balaam said to Balak, "Stand here beside your burnt offerings, while I meet the LORD over there." [16] The LORD met Balaam, put a word into his mouth, and said, "Return to Balak, and this is what you shall say." [17] When he came to him, he was standing beside his burnt offerings with the officials of Moab. Balak said to him, "What has the LORD said?" [18] Then Balaam uttered his oracle, saying:

"Rise, Balak, and hear;
　　listen to me, O son of Zippor:
[19]　God is not a human being, that he should lie,
　　or a mortal, that he should change his mind.
　Has he promised, and will he not do it?
　　Has he spoken, and will he not fulfill it?
[20]　See, I received a command to bless;
　　he has blessed, and I cannot revoke it.
[21]　He has not beheld misfortune in Jacob;
　　nor has he seen trouble in Israel.
　The LORD their God is with them,
　　acclaimed as a king among them.
[22]　God, who brings them out of Egypt,
　　is like the horns of a wild ox for them.
[23]　Surely there is no enchantment against Jacob,
　　no divination against Israel;
　now it shall be said of Jacob and Israel,
　　'See what God has done!'
[24]　Look, a people rising up like a lioness,
　　and rousing itself like a lion!

It does not lie down until it has eaten the prey
　and drunk the blood of the slain."

25 Then Balak said to Balaam, "Do not curse them at all, and do not bless them at all." [26] But Balaam answered Balak, "Did I not tell you, 'Whatever the LORD says, that is what I must do'?"

27 So Balak said to Balaam, "Come now, I will take you to another place; perhaps it will please God that you may curse them for me from there." [28] So Balak took Balaam to the top of Peor, which overlooks the wasteland.[a] [29] Balaam said to Balak, "Build me seven altars here, and prepare seven bulls and seven rams for me." [30] So Balak did as Balaam had said, and offered a bull and a ram on each altar.

Balaam's Third Oracle

24 Now Balaam saw that it pleased the LORD to bless Israel, so he did not go, as at other times, to look for omens, but set his face toward the wilderness. [2] Balaam looked up and saw Israel camping tribe by tribe. Then the spirit of God came upon him, [3] and he uttered his oracle, saying:

"The oracle of Balaam son of Beor,
　　the oracle of the man whose eye is clear,[b]
[4]　the oracle of one who hears the words of God,
　　who sees the vision of the Almighty,[c]
　who falls down, but with eyes uncovered:
[5]　how fair are your tents, O Jacob,
　　your encampments, O Israel!
[6]　Like palm groves that stretch far away,

[a] Or overlooks Jeshimon　[b] Or closed or open　[c] Traditional rendering of Heb Shaddai

---

23:18–24—Second oracle: Again, Balaam does not "speak a blessing," but notes that he has received a command to bless Israel, and that, since YHWH has blessed Israel, the blessing cannot be revoked (v. 19).

24:3–9—Third oracle: Blessing resonates

throughout this oracle. Power and prosperity belong to Israel. The concluding statement, those who bless Israel will be **blessed**, and those who curse Israel will be **cursed** (v. 9b), reflects the promise that God made to the ancestors (e.g., Gen. 12:3; 22:15–19; 26:1–5).

like gardens beside a river,
  like aloes that the Lord has planted,
  like cedar trees beside the waters.
7 Water shall flow from his buckets,
  and his seed shall have abundant
    water,
  his king shall be higher than Agag,
  and his kingdom shall be
    exalted.
8 God who brings him out of Egypt,
  is like the horns of a wild ox for
    him;
  he shall devour the nations that are
    his foes
  and break their bones.
  He shall strike with his arrows.*a*
9 He crouched, he lay down like a
    lion,
  and like a lioness; who will rouse
    him up?
  Blessed is everyone who blesses you,
  and cursed is everyone who curses
    you."

10 Then Balak's anger was kindled against Balaam, and he struck his hands together. Balak said to Balaam, "I summoned you to curse my enemies, but instead you have blessed them these three times. 11 Now be off with you! Go home! I said, 'I will reward you richly,' but the Lord has denied you any reward." 12 And Balaam said to Balak, "Did I not tell your messengers whom you sent to me, 13 'If Balak should give me his house full of silver and gold, I would not be able to go beyond the word of the Lord, to do either good or bad of my own will; what the Lord says, that is what I will say'? 14 So now, I am going to my people; let me advise you what this people will do to your people in days to come."

Balaam's Fourth Oracle

15 So he uttered his oracle, saying:
"The oracle of Balaam son of Beor,
  the oracle of the man whose eye is
    clear,*b*

16 the oracle of one who hears the
    words of God,
  and knows the knowledge of the
    Most High,*c*
  who sees the vision of the
    Almighty,*d*
  who falls down, but with his eyes
    uncovered:
17 I see him, but not now;
  I behold him, but not near—
  a star shall come out of Jacob,
  and a scepter shall rise out of
    Israel;
  it shall crush the borderlands*e* of
    Moab,
  and the territory*f* of all the
    Shethites.
18 Edom will become a possession,
  Seir a possession of its
    enemies,*g*
  while Israel does valiantly.
19 One out of Jacob shall rule,
  and destroy the survivors of Ir."

20 Then he looked on Amalek, and uttered his oracle, saying:
"First among the nations was
    Amalek,
  but its end is to perish forever."
21 Then he looked on the Kenite, and uttered his oracle, saying:
"Enduring is your dwelling place,
  and your nest is set in the rock;
22 yet Kain is destined for burning.
  How long shall Asshur take you
    away captive?"
23 Again he uttered his oracle, saying:
"Alas, who shall live when God does
    this?
24 But ships shall come from Kittim
  and shall afflict Asshur and Eber;
  and he also shall perish forever."
25 Then Balaam got up and went back to his place, and Balak also went his way.

a Meaning of Heb uncertain *b* Or *closed* or *open* *c* Or of *Elyon*
d Traditional rendering of Heb *Shaddai* *e* Or *forehead* *f* Some Mss read
skull *g* Heb *Seir, its enemies, a possession*

24:15–24—Fourth oracle: The oracle sees power for Israel and the defeat of Moab by the Israelites (v. 17b). Those who seek to curse Israel will be cursed. The promises of God are making their way effectively through history as Israel makes its journey through the wilderness.

Worship of Baal of Peor

25 While Israel was staying at Shittim, the people began to have sexual relations with the women of Moab. ² These invited the people to the sacrifices of their gods, and the people ate and bowed down to their gods. ³ Thus Israel yoked itself to the Baal of Peor, and the LORD's anger was kindled against Israel. ⁴ The LORD said to Moses, "Take all the chiefs of the people, and impale them in the sun before the LORD, in order that the fierce anger of the LORD may turn away from Israel." ⁵ And Moses said to the judges of Israel, "Each of you shall kill any of your people who have yoked themselves to the Baal of Peor."

6 Just then one of the Israelites came and brought a Midianite woman into his family, in the sight of Moses and in the sight of the whole congregation of the Israelites, while they were weeping at the entrance of the tent of meeting. ⁷ When Phinehas son of Eleazar, son of Aaron the priest, saw it, he got up and left the congregation. Taking a spear in his hand, ⁸ he went after the Israelite man into the tent, and pierced the two of them, the Israelite and the woman, through the belly. So the plague was stopped among the people of Israel. ⁹ Nevertheless those that died by the plague were twenty-four thousand.

10 The LORD spoke to Moses, saying: ¹¹ "Phinehas son of Eleazar, son of Aaron the priest, has turned back my wrath from the Israelites by manifesting such zeal among them on my behalf that in my jealousy I did not consume the Israelites. ¹² Therefore say, 'I hereby grant him my covenant of peace. ¹³ It shall be for him and for his descendants after him a covenant of perpetual priesthood, because he was zealous for his God, and made atonement for the Israelites.'"

14 The name of the slain Israelite man, who was killed with the Midianite woman, was Zimri son of Salu, head of an ancestral house belonging to the Simeonites. ¹⁵ The name of the Midianite woman who was killed was Cozbi daughter of Zur, who was the head of a clan, an ancestral house in Midian.

16 The LORD said to Moses, ¹⁷ "Harass the Midianites, and defeat them; ¹⁸ for they have harassed you by the trickery with which they deceived you in the affair of Peor, and in the affair of Cozbi, the daughter of a leader of Midian, their sister; she was killed on the day of the plague that resulted from Peor."

25:1–18 Apostasy with the Baal of Peor

25:1–5—Israelite men have sexual relations with Moabite women and bow down to the gods of the women. YHWH wants Moses to impale the chiefs of the people in order to turn away YHWH's wrath, although Moses opts for an alternative approach. Although contemporary readers may find the graphic violence bound up in YHWH's punishment troubling, Israel's depiction of its God remains consistent: God is jealous, becomes angry, unleashes the divine wrath, violence erupts, people die. These stories reflect Israel's perceptions of their God, perceptions that emerged in the midst of violence, harsh lives, and difficult times. Such views of a violent and angry God are not unknown in the modern world, where genocide, war, and hate are realities.

25:6–18—Phinehas, the son of Eleazar the priest (see 20:22–29), kills an Israelite man and a Midianite woman by running a spear through both of their bellies (an indication that they were having intercourse at the time). YHWH rewards him with a perpetual covenant of peace and priesthood. Obviously, Israel had a variety of traditions concerning the origins and roles of the priesthood. YHWH views apostasy as a "crime" that requires death. The text asks, who better than the priests to search out and punish those guilty?

For the contemporary reader, the image of the priestly executioner may well be distressing and disturbing. Although the text is accurate in its recognition that religion and politics are inseparable in the thinking and practice of an individual, the modern context demands a critical effort to understand how they are related. Religion and politics are both institutions of power and thus are able to use power in both constructive and destructive ways. More than a concern to distinguish "what is religious" from "what is political," critical reflection should raise questions concerning the use of violence by religion or by government.

A Census of the New Generation

26 After the plague the LORD said to Moses and to Eleazar son of Aaron the priest, [2] "Take a census of the whole congregation of the Israelites, from twenty years old and upward, by their ancestral houses, everyone in Israel able to go to war." [3] Moses and Eleazar the priest spoke with them in the plains of Moab by the Jordan opposite Jericho, saying, [4] "Take a census of the people,[a] from twenty years old and upward," as the LORD commanded Moses.

The Israelites, who came out of the land of Egypt, were:

[5] Reuben, the firstborn of Israel. The descendants of Reuben: of Hanoch, the clan of the Hanochites; of Pallu, the clan of the Palluites; [6] of Hezron, the clan of the Hezronites; of Carmi, the clan of the Carmites. [7] These are the clans of the Reubenites; the number of those enrolled was forty-three thousand seven hundred thirty. [8] And the descendants of Pallu: Eliab. [9] The descendants of Eliab: Nemuel, Dathan, and Abiram. These are the same Dathan and Abiram, chosen from the congregation, who rebelled against Moses and Aaron in the company of Korah, when they rebelled against the LORD, [10] and the earth opened its mouth and swallowed them up along with Korah, when that company died, when the fire devoured two hundred fifty men; and they became a warning. [11] Notwithstanding, the sons of Korah did not die.

[12] The descendants of Simeon by their clans: of Nemuel, the clan of the Nemuelites; of Jamin, the clan of the Jaminites; of Jachin, the clan of the Jachinites; [13] of Zerah, the clan of the Zerahites; of Shaul, the clan of the Shaulites.[b] [14] These are the clans of the Simeonites, twenty-two thousand two hundred.

[15] The children of Gad by their clans: of Zephon, the clan of the Zephonites; of Haggi, the clan of the Haggites; of Shuni, the clan of the Shunites; [16] of Ozni, the clan of the Oznites; of Eri, the clan of the Erites; [17] of Arod, the clan of the Arodites; of Areli, the clan of the Arelites. [18] These are the clans of the Gadites: the number of those enrolled was forty thousand five hundred.

[19] The sons of Judah: Er and Onan; Er and Onan died in the land of Canaan. [20] The descendants of Judah by their clans were: of Shelah, the clan of the Shelanites; of Perez, the clan of the Perezites; of Zerah, the clan of the Zerahites. [21] The descendants of Perez were: of Hezron, the clan of the Hezronites; of Hamul, the clan of the Hamulites. [22] These are the clans of Judah: the number of those enrolled was seventy-six thousand five hundred.

[23] The descendants of Issachar by their clans: of Tola, the clan of the Tolaites; of Puvah, the clan of the Punites; [24] of Jashub, the clan of the Jashubites; of Shimron, the clan of the Shimronites. [25] These are the clans of Issachar: sixty-four thousand three hundred enrolled.

[26] The descendants of Zebulun by their clans: of Sered, the clan of the Seredites; of Elon, the clan of the Elonites; of Jahleel, the clan of the Jahleelites. [27] These are the clans of the Zebulunites; the number of those enrolled was sixty thousand five hundred.

[28] The sons of Joseph by their clans: Manasseh and Ephraim. [29] The descendants of Manasseh: of Machir, the clan of the Machirites; and Machir was the father of Gilead; of Gilead, the clan of the Gileadites. [30] These are the descendants of Gilead: of Iezer, the clan of

a Heb lacks *take a census of the people*: Compare verse 2   b Or Saul . . . Saulites

---

26:1–65 The Second Census

The second census marks a turning point in the narrative. The first census marked YHWH's prompting of Israel to prepare for its journey to the land (chap. 1). This census also marks a turn to the land. No more rebellion or complaint stories will be reported. The generation that came out of Egypt is dead, with the exception of Caleb, Joshua, and Moses. The Israelites are ready to enter the land.

the Iezerites; of Helek, the clan of the Helekites; [31] and of Asriel, the clan of the Asrielites; and of Shechem, the clan of the Shechemites; [32] and of Shemida, the clan of the Shemidaites; and of Hepher, the clan of the Hepherites. [33] Now Zelophehad son of Hepher had no sons, but daughters: and the names of the daughters of Zelophehad were Mahlah, Noah, Hoglah, Milcah, and Tirzah. [34] These are the clans of Manasseh; the number of those enrolled was fifty-two thousand seven hundred.

35 These are the descendants of Ephraim according to their clans: of Shuthelah, the clan of the Shuthelahites; of Becher, the clan of the Becherites; of Tahan, the clan of the Tahanites. [36] And these are the descendants of Shuthelah: of Eran, the clan of the Eranites. [37] These are the clans of the Ephraimites: the number of those enrolled was thirty-two thousand five hundred. These are the descendants of Joseph by their clans.

38 The descendants of Benjamin by their clans: of Bela, the clan of the Belaites; of Ashbel, the clan of the Ashbelites; of Ahiram, the clan of the Ahiramites; [39] of Shephupham, the clan of the Shuphamites; of Hupham, the clan of the Huphamites. [40] And the sons of Bela were Ard and Naaman: of Ard, the clan of the Ardites; of Naaman, the clan of the Naamites. [41] These are the descendants of Benjamin by their clans; the number of those enrolled was forty-five thousand six hundred.

42 These are the descendants of Dan by their clans: of Shuham, the clan of the Shuhamites. These are the clans of Dan by their clans. [43] All the clans of the Shuhamites: sixty-four thousand four hundred enrolled.

44 The descendants of Asher by their families: of Imnah, the clan of the Imnites; of Ishvi, the clan of the Ishvites; of Beriah, the clan of the Beriites. [45] Of the descendants of Beriah: of Heber, the clan of the Heberites; of Malchiel, the clan of the Malchielites. [46] And the name of the daughter of Asher was Serah. [47] These are the clans of the Asherites: the number of those enrolled was fifty-three thousand four hundred.

48 The descendants of Naphtali by their clans: of Jahzeel, the clan of the Jahzeelites; of Guni, the clan of the Gunites; [49] of Jezer, the clan of the Jezerites; of Shillem, the clan of the Shillemites. [50] These are the Naphtalites[a] by their clans: the number of those enrolled was forty-five thousand four hundred.

51 This was the number of the Israelites enrolled: six hundred and one thousand seven hundred thirty.

52 The LORD spoke to Moses, saying: [53] To these the land shall be apportioned for inheritance according to the number of names. [54] To a large tribe you shall give a large inheritance, and to a small tribe you shall give a small inheritance; every tribe shall be given its inheritance according to its enrollment. [55] But the land shall be apportioned by lot; according to the names of their ancestral tribes they shall inherit. [56] Their inheritance shall be apportioned according to lot between the larger and the smaller.

57 This is the enrollment of the Levites by their clans: of Gershon, the clan of the Gershonites; of Kohath, the clan of the Kohathites; of Merari, the clan of the Merarites. [58] These are the clans of Levi: the clan of the Libnites, the clan of the Hebronites, the clan of the Mahlites, the clan of the Mushites, the clan of the Korahites. Now Kohath was the father of Amram. [59] The name of Amram's wife was Jochebed daughter of Levi, who was born to Levi in Egypt; and she bore to Amram: Aaron, Moses, and their sister Miriam. [60] To Aaron were born Nadab, Abihu, Eleazar, and

a Heb *clans of Naphtali*

26:57–65—The numbers of the new census are similar to those of the first. In this way, continuity is established with the previous generation. This is a sign of God's continued blessing.

Ithamar. [61] But Nadab and Abihu died when they offered unholy fire before the LORD. [62] The number of those enrolled was twenty-three thousand, every male one month old and upward; for they were not enrolled among the Israelites because there was no allotment given to them among the Israelites.

63 These were those enrolled by Moses and Eleazar the priest, who enrolled the Israelites in the plains of Moab by the Jordan opposite Jericho. [64] Among these there was not one of those enrolled by Moses and Aaron the priest, who had enrolled the Israelites in the wilderness of Sinai. [65] For the LORD had said of them, "They shall die in the wilderness." Not one of them was left, except Caleb son of Jephunneh and Joshua son of Nun.

The Daughters of Zelophehad

27 Then the daughters of Zelophehad came forward. Zelophehad was son of Hepher son of Gilead son of Machir son of Manasseh son of Joseph, a member of the Manassite clans. The names of his daughters were: Mahlah, Noah, Hoglah, Milcah, and Tirzah. [2] They stood before Moses, Eleazar the priest, the leaders, and all the congregation, at the entrance of the tent of meeting, and they said, [3] "Our father died in the wilderness; he was not among the company of those who gathered themselves together against the LORD in the company of Korah, but died for his own sin; and he had no sons. [4] Why should the name of our father be taken away from his clan because he had no son? Give to us a possession among our father's brothers."

5 Moses brought their case before the LORD. [6] And the LORD spoke to Moses, saying: [7] The daughters of Zelophehad are right in what they are saying; you shall indeed let them possess an inheritance among their father's brothers and pass the inheritance of their father on to them. [8] You shall also say to the Israelites, "If a man dies, and has no son, then you shall pass his inheritance on to his daughter. [9] If he has no daughter, then you shall give his inheritance to his brothers. [10] If he has no brothers, then you shall give his inheritance to his father's brothers. [11] And if his father has no brothers, then you shall give his inheritance to the nearest kinsman of his clan, and he shall possess it. It shall be for the Israelites a statute and ordinance, as the LORD commanded Moses."

Joshua Appointed Moses' Successor

12 The LORD said to Moses, "Go up this mountain of the Abarim range,

---

27:1–11 The Daughters of Zelophehad

27:1–4—Zelophehad, the father of five daughters but no son, dies in the wilderness. The daughters are concerned that because they are women, they will not receive an inheritance in the land. Their question raises two issues: (1) What happens to the property of a man who dies without a male heir? (2) What happens to the property of a man who dies without a son but with daughters? The daughters raise the question at the door of the tent, in the presence of Moses, Eleazar, and the whole congregation. This is an official inquiry that Moses takes to YHWH.

27:5–11—YHWH agrees with the women and makes a number of rulings concerning inheritance. This is an important example of Israel's recognition that the will of YHWH is determined along the way, in the process of moving through life, in concrete situations.

The text demonstrates an awareness of the importance of women within the Israelite community. However, the rights of the daughters become operative only in the absence of a son. Male heirs continue to have the primary rights of inheritance. Only when a male heir does not exist does the question of the inheritance of daughters come into play. If neither son nor daughter is alive to inherit, the inheritance passes on to another *male* member of the man's extended family. Thus, even when the text does recognize the validity of women and their claim as part of the community of faith, it does so within the larger context of a patriarchal perspective.

27:12–23 Moses Commissions Joshua

Moses passes his authority to Joshua in the presence of the Eleazar the priest and the whole community. The community that will now have Joshua as its leader assembles to watch the

and see the land that I have given to the Israelites. ¹³ When you have seen it, you also shall be gathered to your people, as your brother Aaron was, ¹⁴ because you rebelled against my word in the wilderness of Zin when the congregation quarreled with me.ᵃ You did not show my holiness before their eyes at the waters." (These are the waters of Meribath-kadesh in the wilderness of Zin.) ¹⁵ Moses spoke to the LORD, saying, ¹⁶ "Let the LORD, the God of the spirits of all flesh, appoint someone over the congregation ¹⁷ who shall go out before them and come in before them, who shall lead them out and bring them in, so that the congregation of the LORD may not be like sheep without a shepherd." ¹⁸ So the LORD said to Moses, "Take Joshua son of Nun, a man in whom is the spirit, and lay your hand upon him; ¹⁹ have him stand before Eleazar the priest and all the congregation, and commission him in their sight. ²⁰ You shall give him some of your authority, so that all the congregation of the Israelites may obey. ²¹ But he shall stand before Eleazar the priest, who shall inquire for him by the decision of the Urim before the LORD; at his word they shall go out, and at his word they shall come in, both he and all the Israelites with him, the whole congregation." ²² So Moses did as the LORD commanded him. He took Joshua and had him stand before Eleazar the priest and the whole congregation; ²³ he laid his hands on him and commissioned him—as the LORD had directed through Moses.

Daily Offerings

28 The LORD spoke to Moses, saying: ² Command the Israelites, and say to them: My offering, the food for my offerings by fire, my pleasing odor, you shall take care to offer to me at its appointed time. ³ And you shall say to them, This is the offering by fire that you shall offer to the LORD: two male lambs a year old without blemish, daily, as a regular offering. ⁴ One lamb you shall offer in the morning, and the other lamb you shall offer at twilight;ᵇ ⁵ also one-tenth of an ephah of choice flour for a grain offering, mixed with one-fourth of a hin of beaten oil. ⁶ It is a regular burnt offering, ordained at Mount Sinai for a pleasing odor, an offering by fire to the LORD. ⁷ Its drink offering shall be one-fourth of a hin for each lamb; in the sanctuary you shall pour out a drink offering of strong drink to the LORD. ⁸ The other lamb you shall offer at twilightᵇ with a grain offering and a drink offering like the one in the morning; you shall offer it as an offering by fire, a pleasing odor to the LORD.

Sabbath Offerings

9 On the sabbath day: two male lambs a year old without blemish, and two-tenths of an ephah of choice flour for a grain offering, mixed with oil, and its drink offering— ¹⁰ this is the burnt offering for every sabbath, in addition to the regular burnt offering and its drink offering.

Monthly Offerings

11 At the beginnings of your months you shall offer a burnt offering to the LORD: two young bulls, one ram, seven male lambs a year old without blemish; ¹² also three-tenths of an ephah of choice flour for a grain offering, mixed with oil, for each bull; and two-tenths of choice flour for a grain offering, mixed with oil, for the one ram; ¹³ and one-tenth of choice flour mixed with oil as

ᵃ Heb lacks *with me*   ᵇ Heb *between the two evenings*

passing of leadership from Moses. Joshua's authority, however, is limited. He must inquire of Eleazar the priest concerning Israel's entry into and conquest of the land. The priest's word will guide them in these matters. Leadership and authority remain ongoing issues for Israel as it draws near to the land.

28:1–29:40 The Sacred Calendar of the Year See the discussion of Lev. 23.

a grain offering for every lamb—a burnt offering of pleasing odor, an offering by fire to the LORD. [14] Their drink offerings shall be half a hin of wine for a bull, one-third of a hin for a ram, and one-fourth of a hin for a lamb. This is the burnt offering of every month throughout the months of the year. [15] And there shall be one male goat for a sin offering to the LORD; it shall be offered in addition to the regular burnt offering and its drink offering.

Offerings at Passover

16 On the fourteenth day of the first month there shall be a passover offering to the LORD. [17] And on the fifteenth day of this month is a festival; seven days shall unleavened bread be eaten. [18] On the first day there shall be a holy convocation. You shall not work at your occupations. [19] You shall offer an offering by fire, a burnt offering to the LORD: two young bulls, one ram, and seven male lambs a year old; see that they are without blemish. [20] Their grain offering shall be of choice flour mixed with oil: three-tenths of an ephah shall you offer for a bull, and two-tenths for a ram; [21] one-tenth shall you offer for each of the seven lambs; [22] also one male goat for a sin offering, to make atonement for you. [23] You shall offer these in addition to the burnt offering of the morning, which belongs to the regular burnt offering. [24] In the same way you shall offer daily, for seven days, the food of an offering by fire, a pleasing odor to the LORD; it shall be offered in addition to the regular burnt offering and its drink offering. [25] And on the seventh day you shall have a holy convocation; you shall not work at your occupations.

Offerings at the Festival of Weeks

26 On the day of the first fruits, when you offer a grain offering of new grain to the LORD at your festival of weeks, you shall have a holy convocation; you shall not work at your occupations. [27] You

shall offer a burnt offering, a pleasing odor to the LORD: two young bulls, one ram, seven male lambs a year old. [28] Their grain offering shall be of choice flour mixed with oil, three-tenths of an ephah for each bull, two-tenths for one ram, [29] one-tenth for each of the seven lambs; [30] with one male goat, to make atonement for you. [31] In addition to the regular burnt offering with its grain offering, you shall offer them and their drink offering. They shall be without blemish.

Offerings at the Festival of Trumpets

29 On the first day of the seventh month you shall have a holy convocation; you shall not work at your occupations. It is a day for you to blow the trumpets, [2] and you shall offer a burnt offering, a pleasing odor to the LORD: one young bull, one ram, seven male lambs a year old without blemish. [3] Their grain offering shall be of choice flour mixed with oil, three-tenths of one ephah for the bull, two-tenths for the ram, [4] and one-tenth for each of the seven lambs; [5] with one male goat for a sin offering, to make atonement for you. [6] These are in addition to the burnt offering of the new moon and its grain offering, and the regular burnt offering and its grain offering, and their drink offerings, according to the ordinance for them, a pleasing odor, an offering by fire to the LORD.

Offerings on the Day of Atonement

7 On the tenth day of this seventh month you shall have a holy convocation, and deny yourselves;[a] you shall do no work. [8] You shall offer a burnt offering to the LORD, a pleasing odor: one young bull, one ram, seven male lambs a year old. They shall be without blemish. [9] Their grain offering shall be of choice flour mixed with oil, three-tenths of an ephah for the bull, two-tenths for the one ram, [10] one-tenth for each of the

a Or and fast

seven lambs; [11] with one male goat for a sin offering, in addition to the sin offering of atonement, and the regular burnt offering and its grain offering, and their drink offerings.

Offerings at the Festival of Booths

12 On the fifteenth day of the seventh month you shall have a holy convocation; you shall not work at your occupations. You shall celebrate a festival to the LORD seven days. [13] You shall offer a burnt offering, an offering by fire, a pleasing odor to the LORD: thirteen young bulls, two rams, fourteen male lambs a year old. They shall be without blemish. [14] Their grain offering shall be of choice flour mixed with oil, three-tenths of an ephah for each of the thirteen bulls, two-tenths for each of the two rams, [15] and one-tenth for each of the fourteen lambs; [16] also one male goat for a sin offering, in addition to the regular burnt offering, its grain offering and its drink offering.

17 On the second day: twelve young bulls, two rams, fourteen male lambs a year old without blemish, [18] with the grain offering and the drink offerings for the bulls, for the rams, and for the lambs, as prescribed in accordance with their number; [19] also one male goat for a sin offering, in addition to the regular burnt offering and its grain offering, and their drink offerings.

20 On the third day: eleven bulls, two rams, fourteen male lambs a year old without blemish, [21] with the grain offering and the drink offerings for the bulls, for the rams, and for the lambs, as prescribed in accordance with their number; [22] also one male goat for a sin offering, in addition to the regular burnt offering and its grain offering and its drink offering.

23 On the fourth day: ten bulls, two rams, fourteen male lambs a year old without blemish, [24] with the grain offering and the drink offerings for the bulls, for the rams, and for the lambs, as pre-scribed in accordance with their number; [25] also one male goat for a sin offering, in addition to the regular burnt offering, its grain offering and its drink offering.

26 On the fifth day: nine bulls, two rams, fourteen male lambs a year old without blemish, [27] with the grain offering and the drink offerings for the bulls, for the rams, and for the lambs, as prescribed in accordance with their number; [28] also one male goat for a sin offering, in addition to the regular burnt offering and its grain offering and its drink offering.

29 On the sixth day: eight bulls, two rams, fourteen male lambs a year old without blemish, [30] with the grain offering and the drink offerings for the bulls, for the rams, and for the lambs, as prescribed in accordance with their number; [31] also one male goat for a sin offering, in addition to the regular burnt offering, its grain offering, and its drink offerings.

32 On the seventh day: seven bulls, two rams, fourteen male lambs a year old without blemish, [33] with the grain offering and the drink offerings for the bulls, for the rams, and for the lambs, as prescribed in accordance with their number; [34] also one male goat for a sin offering, besides the regular burnt offering, its grain offering, and its drink offering.

35 On the eighth day you shall have a solemn assembly; you shall not work at your occupations. [36] You shall offer a burnt offering, an offering by fire, a pleasing odor to the LORD: one bull, one ram, seven male lambs a year old without blemish, [37] and the grain offering and the drink offerings for the bull, for the ram, and for the lambs, as prescribed in accordance with their number; [38] also one male goat for a sin offering, in addition to the regular burnt offering and its grain offering and its drink offering.

39 These you shall offer to the LORD at your appointed festivals, in addition to

your votive offerings and your freewill offerings, as your burnt offerings, your grain offerings, your drink offerings, and your offerings of well-being.

40[a] So Moses told the Israelites everything just as the LORD had commanded Moses.

Vows Made by Women

30 Then Moses said to the heads of the tribes of the Israelites: This is what the LORD has commanded. 2 When a man makes a vow to the LORD, or swears an oath to bind himself by a pledge, he shall not break his word; he shall do according to all that proceeds out of his mouth.

3 When a woman makes a vow to the LORD, or binds herself by a pledge, while within her father's house, in her youth, 4 and her father hears of her vow or her pledge by which she has bound herself, and says nothing to her; then all her vows shall stand, and any pledge by which she has bound herself shall stand. 5 But if her father expresses disapproval to her at the time that he hears of it, no vow of hers, and no pledge by which she has bound herself, shall stand; and the LORD will forgive her, because her father had expressed to her his disapproval.

6 If she marries, while obligated by her vows or any thoughtless utterance of her lips by which she has bound herself, 7 and her husband hears of it and says nothing to her at the time that he hears, then her vows shall stand, and her pledges by which she has bound herself

shall stand. 8 But if, at the time that her husband hears of it, he expresses disapproval to her, then he shall nullify the vow by which she was obligated, or the thoughtless utterance of her lips, by which she bound herself; and the LORD will forgive her. 9 (But every vow of a widow or of a divorced woman, by which she has bound herself, shall be binding upon her.) 10 And if she made a vow in her husband's house, or bound herself by a pledge with an oath, 11 and her husband heard it and said nothing to her, and did not express disapproval to her, then all her vows shall stand, and any pledge by which she bound herself shall stand. 12 But if her husband nullifies them at the time that he hears them, then whatever proceeds out of her lips concerning her vows, or concerning her pledge of herself, shall not stand. Her husband has nullified them, and the LORD will forgive her. 13 Any vow or any binding oath to deny herself,[b] her husband may allow to stand, or her husband may nullify. 14 But if her husband says nothing to her from day to day,[c] then he validates all her vows, or all her pledges, by which she is obligated; he has validated them, because he said nothing to her at the time that he heard of them. 15 But if he nullifies them some time after he has heard of them, then he shall bear her guilt.

16 These are the statutes that the LORD commanded Moses concerning a husband and his wife, and a father and

[a] Ch 30.1 in Heb [b] Or to fast [c] Or from that day to the next

---

30:1–16 Regulations Concerning Vows
Sacred vows were taken seriously in Israel. Most persons are familiar with what is commonly known as "the deal with God" approach to a crisis. Most are also familiar with the failure to give to God what was promised in the midst of crisis. The text suggests that Israel found new negotiations, after the crisis is passed, to be unacceptable. You promised. Now pay up!

A disturbing feature of the text, however, has to do with the way men are given authority over a woman's religious life. A man with socially recognized authority over a woman is able to

invalidate her vows. Viewed from a contemporary perspective, the text allows for the religious life of a woman to be regulated by a man. Although the text reflects the gender relations of the ancient world, the contemporary community of faith must think carefully and critically about any situation in which one person (one gender), has the power to regulate and to determine the religious life of another person (the other gender). The gender relations of ancient Israel are not normative or paradigmatic for gender relations in the contemporary world.

his daughter while she is still young and in her father's house.

War against Midian

31 The LORD spoke to Moses, saying, [2] "Avenge the Israelites on the Midianites; afterward you shall be gathered to your people." [3] So Moses said to the people, "Arm some of your number for the war, so that they may go against Midian, to execute the LORD's vengeance on Midian. [4] You shall send a thousand from each of the tribes of Israel to the war." [5] So out of the thousands of Israel, a thousand from each tribe were conscripted, twelve thousand armed for battle. [6] Moses sent them to the war, a thousand from each tribe, along with Phinehas son of Eleazar the priest,[a] with the vessels of the sanctuary and the trumpets for sounding the alarm in his hand. [7] They did battle against Midian, as the LORD had commanded Moses, and killed every male. [8] They killed the kings of Midian: Evi, Rekem, Zur, Hur, and Reba, the five kings of Midian, in addition to others who were slain by them; and they also killed Balaam son of Beor with the sword. [9] The Israelites took the women of Midian and their little ones captive; and they took all their cattle, their flocks, and all their goods as booty. [10] All their towns where they had settled, and all their encampments, they burned, [11] but they took all the spoil and all the booty, both people and animals. [12] Then they brought the captives and the booty and the spoil to Moses, to Eleazar the priest, and to the congregation of the Israelites, at the camp on the plains of Moab by the Jordan at Jericho.

Return from the War

13 Moses, Eleazar the priest, and all the leaders of the congregation went to meet them outside the camp. [14] Moses became angry with the officers of the army, the commanders of thousands and the commanders of hundreds, who had come from service in the war. [15] Moses said to them, "Have you allowed all the women to live? [16] These women here, on Balaam's advice, made the Israelites act treacherously against the LORD in the affair of Peor, so that the plague came among the congregation of the LORD. [17] Now therefore, kill every male among the little ones, and kill every woman who has known a man by sleeping with him. [18] But all the young girls who have not known a man by sleeping with him, keep alive for yourselves. [19] Camp outside the camp seven days; whoever of you has killed any person or touched a corpse, purify yourselves and your captives on the third and on the seventh day. [20] You shall purify every garment, every article of skin, everything made of goats' hair, and every article of wood."

21 Eleazar the priest said to the troops who had gone to battle: "This is the statute of the law that the LORD has commanded Moses: [22] gold, silver, bronze, iron, tin, and lead— [23] everything that can withstand fire, shall be passed through fire, and it shall be clean. Never-

[a] Gk: Heb adds *to the war*

31:1–54 The Defeat of the Midianites

This is Moses' final act of military leadership. The attack is viewed as an act of vengeance on the Midianites. The attack, the slaughter, and the kidnapping of virgin females and female children (vv. 17–18) anticipate Israel's war with the Canaanites. The text raises crucial issues concerning the nature of justice, military power, violence, and religious beliefs. The contemporary reader must recognize that the original context for the composition of this text included images of YHWH the divine warrior, a strong commitment to a particular understanding of YHWH's promises to Israel concerning the land of the Canaanites, and a notion of conquest as a means to "share" the divine blessing with others. The history of the convergence of violence, conquest, colonialism, and religious faith requires critical reflection on this story. Vengeance, retribution, and justice are words often used to support and sustain violent militaristic attacks that, in the process of "taking care of business," injure and kill innocent men, women, and children. The interweaving of religious beliefs with violent military activity must be viewed carefully, critically, and cautiously.

theless it shall also be purified with the water for purification; and whatever cannot withstand fire, shall be passed through the water. 24 You must wash your clothes on the seventh day, and you shall be clean; afterward you may come into the camp."

Disposition of Captives and Booty

25 The LORD spoke to Moses, saying, 26 "You and Eleazar the priest and the heads of the ancestral houses of the congregation make an inventory of the booty captured, both human and animal. 27 Divide the booty into two parts, between the warriors who went out to battle and all the congregation. 28 From the share of the warriors who went out to battle, set aside as tribute for the LORD, one item out of every five hundred, whether persons, oxen, donkeys, sheep, or goats. 29 Take it from their half and give it to Eleazar the priest as an offering to the LORD. 30 But from the Israelites' half you shall take one out of every fifty, whether persons, oxen, donkeys, sheep, or goats—all the animals— and give them to the Levites who have charge of the tabernacle of the LORD."

31 Then Moses and Eleazar the priest did as the LORD had commanded Moses:

32 The booty remaining from the spoil that the troops had taken totaled six hundred seventy-five thousand sheep, 33 seventy-two thousand oxen, 34 sixty-one thousand donkeys, 35 and thirty-two thousand persons in all, women who had not known a man by sleeping with him.

36 The half-share, the portion of those who had gone out to war, was in number three hundred thirty-seven thousand five hundred sheep and goats, 37 and the LORD's tribute of sheep and goats was six hundred seventy-five. 38 The oxen were thirty-six thousand, of which the LORD's tribute was seventy-two. 39 The donkeys were thirty thousand five hundred, of which the LORD's tribute was

sixty-one. 40 The persons were sixteen thousand, of which the LORD's tribute was thirty-two persons. 41 Moses gave the tribute, the offering for the LORD, to Eleazar the priest, as the LORD had commanded Moses.

42 As for the Israelites' half, which Moses separated from that of the troops, 43 the congregation's half was three hundred thirty-seven thousand five hundred sheep and goats, 44 thirty-six thousand oxen, 45 thirty thousand five hundred donkeys, 46 and sixteen thousand persons. 47 From the Israelites' half Moses took one of every fifty, both of persons and of animals, and gave them to the Levites who had charge of the tabernacle of the LORD; as the LORD had commanded Moses.

48 Then the officers who were over the thousands of the army, the commanders of thousands and the commanders of hundreds, approached Moses, 49 and said to Moses, "Your servants have counted the warriors who are under our command, and not one of us is missing. 50 And we have brought the LORD's offering, what each of us found, articles of gold, armlets and bracelets, signet rings, earrings, and pendants, to make atonement for ourselves before the LORD." 51 Moses and Eleazar the priest received the gold from them, all in the form of crafted articles. 52 And all the gold of the offering that they offered to the LORD, from the commanders of thousands and the commanders of hundreds, was sixteen thousand seven hundred fifty shekels. 53 (The troops had all taken plunder for themselves.) 54 So Moses and Eleazar the priest received the gold from the commanders of thousands and of hundreds, and brought it into the tent of meeting as a memorial for the Israelites before the LORD.

Conquest and Division of Transjordan

32 Now the Reubenites and the Gadites owned a very great

32:1–42 The Request of Reuben and Gad
The reality of the land of promise begins to

emerge as these two tribes ask for land on the eastern side of the Jordan River.

number of cattle. When they saw that the land of Jazer and the land of Gilead was a good place for cattle, [2] the Gadites and the Reubenites came and spoke to Moses, to Eleazar the priest, and to the leaders of the congregation, saying, [3] "Ataroth, Dibon, Jazer, Nimrah, Heshbon, Elealeh, Sebam, Nebo, and Beon— [4] the land that the LORD subdued before the congregation of Israel—is a land for cattle; and your servants have cattle." [5] They continued, "If we have found favor in your sight, let this land be given to your servants for a possession; do not make us cross the Jordan."

[6] But Moses said to the Gadites and to the Reubenites, "Shall your brothers go to war while you sit here? [7] Why will you discourage the hearts of the Israelites from going over into the land that the LORD has given them? [8] Your fathers did this, when I sent them from Kadesh-barnea to see the land. [9] When they went up to the Wadi Eshcol and saw the land, they discouraged the hearts of the Israelites from going into the land that the LORD had given them. [10] The LORD's anger was kindled on that day and he swore, saying, [11] 'Surely none of the people who came up out of Egypt, from twenty years old and upward, shall see the land that I swore to give to Abraham, to Isaac, and to Jacob, because they have not unreservedly followed me— [12] none except Caleb son of Jephunneh the Kenizzite and Joshua son of Nun, for they have unreservedly followed the LORD.' [13] And the LORD's anger was kindled against Israel, and he made them wander in the wilderness for forty years, until all the generation that had done evil in the sight of the LORD had disappeared. [14] And now you, a brood of sinners, have risen in place of your fathers, to increase the LORD's fierce anger against Israel! [15] If you turn away from following him, he will again abandon them in the wilderness; and you will destroy all this people."

[16] Then they came up to him and said, "We will build sheepfolds here for our flocks, and towns for our little ones, [17] but we will take up arms as a vanguard[a] before the Israelites, until we have brought them to their place. Meanwhile our little ones will stay in the fortified towns because of the inhabitants of the land. [18] We will not return to our homes until all the Israelites have obtained their inheritance. [19] We will not inherit with them on the other side of the Jordan and beyond, because our inheritance has come to us on this side of the Jordan to the east."

[20] So Moses said to them, "If you do this—if you take up arms to go before the LORD for the war, [21] and all those of you who bear arms cross the Jordan before the LORD, until he has driven out his enemies from before him [22] and the land is subdued before the LORD—then after that you may return and be free of obligation to the LORD and to Israel, and this land shall be your possession before the LORD. [23] But if you do not do this, you have sinned against the LORD; and be sure your sin will find you out. [24] Build towns for your little ones, and folds for your flocks; but do what you have promised."

[25] Then the Gadites and the Reubenites said to Moses, "Your servants will do as my lord commands. [26] Our little ones, our wives, our flocks, and all our livestock shall remain there in the towns of Gilead; [27] but your servants will cross over, everyone armed for war, to do battle for the LORD, just as my lord orders."

[28] So Moses gave command concerning them to Eleazar the priest, to Joshua son of Nun, and to the heads of the ancestral houses of the Israelite tribes. [29] And Moses said to them, "If the Gadites and the Reubenites, everyone armed for battle before the LORD, will cross over the Jordan with you and the land shall be subdued before you, then

[a] Cn: Heb *hurrying*

you shall give them the land of Gilead for a possession; **30** but if they will not cross over with you armed, they shall have possessions among you in the land of Canaan." **31** The Gadites and the Reubenites answered, "As the LORD has spoken to your servants, so we will do. **32** We will cross over armed before the LORD into the land of Canaan, but the possession of our inheritance shall remain with us on this side of*a* the Jordan."

33 Moses gave to them—to the Gadites and to the Reubenites and to the half-tribe of Manasseh son of Joseph—the kingdom of King Sihon of the Amorites and the kingdom of King Og of Bashan, the land and its towns, with the territories of the surrounding towns. **34** And the Gadites rebuilt Dibon, Ataroth, Aroer, **35** Atroth-shophan, Jazer, Jogbehah, **36** Beth-nimrah, and Beth-haran, fortified cities, and folds for sheep. **37** And the Reubenites rebuilt Heshbon, Elealeh, Kiriathaim, **38** Nebo, and Baal-meon (some names being changed), and Sibmah; and they gave names to the towns that they rebuilt. **39** The descendants of Machir son of Manasseh went to Gilead, captured it, and dispossessed the Amorites who were there; **40** so Moses gave Gilead to Machir son of Manasseh, and he settled there. **41** Jair son of Manasseh went and captured their villages, and renamed them Havvoth-jair.*b* **42** And Nobah went and captured Kenath and its villages, and renamed it Nobah after himself.

The Stages of Israel's Journey from Egypt

33 These are the stages by which the Israelites went out of the land of Egypt in military formation under the leadership of Moses and Aaron. **2** Moses wrote down their starting points, stage by stage, by command of the LORD; and these are their stages according to their starting places. **3** They set out from Rameses in the first month, on the fifteenth day of the first month; on the day after the passover the Israelites went out boldly in the sight of all the Egyptians, **4** while the Egyptians were burying all their firstborn, whom the LORD had struck down among them. The LORD executed judgments even against their gods.

5 So the Israelites set out from Rameses, and camped at Succoth. **6** They set out from Succoth, and camped at Etham, which is on the edge of the wilderness. **7** They set out from Etham, and turned back to Pi-hahiroth, which faces Baal-zephon; and they camped before Migdol. **8** They set out from Pi-hahiroth, passed through the sea into the wilderness, went a three days' journey in the wilderness of Etham, and camped at Marah. **9** They set out from Marah and came to Elim; at Elim there were twelve springs of water and seventy palm trees, and they camped there. **10** They set out from Elim and camped by the Red Sea.*c* **11** They set out from the Red Sea*c* and camped in the wilderness of Sin. **12** They set out from the wilderness of Sin and camped at Dophkah. **13** They set out from Dophkah and camped at Alush. **14** They set out from Alush and camped at Rephidim, where there was no water for the people to drink. **15** They set out from Rephidim and camped in the wilderness of Sinai. **16** They set out from the wilderness of Sinai and camped at Kibroth-hattaavah. **17** They set out from Kibroth-hattaavah and camped at Hazeroth. **18** They set out from Hazeroth

a Heb *beyond* *b* That is *the villages of Jair* *c* Or *Sea of Reeds*

33:1–49 The Stages of Israel's Wilderness Journey

The report of Israel's journey through the wilderness provides a summary of the journey and functions as a marker of the reality of that journey. The itinerary follows Israel's progress and marks the places where Israel camped. More than just an itinerary report, the text provides a "historical" memory of the reality of the wilderness journey. The itinerary report maps the journey from slavery to the promised land.

and camped at Rithmah. ¹⁹ They set out from Rithmah and camped at Rimmon-perez. ²⁰ They set out from Rimmon-perez and camped at Libnah. ²¹ They set out from Libnah and camped at Rissah. ²² They set out from Rissah and camped at Kehelathah. ²³ They set out from Kehelathah and camped at Mount Shepher. ²⁴ They set out from Mount Shepher and camped at Haradah. ²⁵ They set out from Haradah and camped at Makheloth. ²⁶ They set out from Makheloth and camped at Tahath. ²⁷ They set out from Tahath and camped at Terah. ²⁸ They set out from Terah and camped at Mithkah. ²⁹ They set out from Mithkah and camped at Hashmonah. ³⁰ They set out from Hashmonah and camped at Moseroth. ³¹ They set out from Moseroth and camped at Bene-jaakan. ³² They set out from Bene-jaakan and camped at Hor-haggidgad. ³³ They set out from Hor-haggidgad and camped at Jotbathah. ³⁴ They set out from Jotbathah and camped at Abronah. ³⁵ They set out from Abronah and camped at Ezion-geber. ³⁶ They set out from Ezion-geber and camped in the wilderness of Zin (that is, Kadesh). ³⁷ They set out from Kadesh and camped at Mount Hor, on the edge of the land of Edom.

38 Aaron the priest went up Mount Hor at the command of the LORD and died there in the fortieth year after the Israelites had come out of the land of Egypt, on the first day of the fifth month. ³⁹ Aaron was one hundred twenty-three years old when he died on Mount Hor.

40 The Canaanite, the king of Arad, who lived in the Negeb in the land of Canaan, heard of the coming of the Israelites.

41 They set out from Mount Hor and camped at Zalmonah. ⁴² They set out from Zalmonah and camped at Punon. ⁴³ They set out from Punon and camped at Oboth. ⁴⁴ They set out from Oboth and camped at Iye-abarim, in the territory of Moab. ⁴⁵ They set out from Iyim and camped at Dibon-gad. ⁴⁶ They set out from Dibon-gad and camped at Almon-diblathaim. ⁴⁷ They set out from Almon-diblathaim and camped in the mountains of Abarim, before Nebo. ⁴⁸ They set out from the mountains of Abarim and camped in the plains of Moab by the Jordan at Jericho; ⁴⁹ they camped by the Jordan from Beth-jeshimoth as far as Abel-shittim in the plains of Moab.

Directions for the Conquest of Canaan

50 In the plains of Moab by the Jordan at Jericho, the LORD spoke to Moses, saying: ⁵¹ Speak to the Israelites, and say to them: When you cross over the Jordan into the land of Canaan, ⁵² you shall drive out all the inhabitants of the land from before you, destroy all their figured stones, destroy all their cast images, and demolish all their high places. ⁵³ You shall take possession of the land and settle in it, for I have given you the land to possess. ⁵⁴ You shall apportion the land by lot according to your clans; to a large one you shall give a large inheritance, and to a small one you shall give a small inheritance; the inheritance shall belong to the person on whom the lot falls; according to your ancestral tribes you shall inherit. ⁵⁵ But if you do not drive out the inhabitants of the land from before you, then those whom you let remain shall be as barbs in your eyes and thorns in your sides; they shall trouble you in the land where you are settling. ⁵⁶ And I will do to you as I thought to do to them.

33:50–56 Instructions to Drive Out the Canaanites

YHWH's instructions to Israel are clear: drive out the Canaanites, destroy their sacred places and objects, and take their land. The text provides theological justification for conquest and the vio-

lent taking of the land of others. Fights over land and religion remain a very present element of the contemporary world. Will the human desire to destroy and take, defeat and remove, ever be replaced by justice, mercy, and cooperation in creating a life of peace?

The Boundaries of the Land

34 The LORD spoke to Moses, saying: [2] Command the Israelites, and say to them: When you enter the land of Canaan (this is the land that shall fall to you for an inheritance, the land of Canaan, defined by its boundaries), [3] your south sector shall extend from the wilderness of Zin along the side of Edom. Your southern boundary shall begin from the end of the Dead Sea[a] on the east; [4] your boundary shall turn south of the ascent of Akrabbim, and cross to Zin, and its outer limit shall be south of Kadesh-barnea; then it shall go on to Hazar-addar, and cross to Azmon; [5] the boundary shall turn from Azmon to the Wadi of Egypt, and its termination shall be at the Sea.

6 For the western boundary, you shall have the Great Sea and its[b] coast; this shall be your western boundary.

7 This shall be your northern boundary: from the Great Sea you shall mark out your line to Mount Hor; [8] from Mount Hor you shall mark it out to Lebo-hamath, and the outer limit of the boundary shall be at Zedad; [9] then the boundary shall extend to Ziphron, and its end shall be at Hazar-enan; this shall be your northern boundary.

10 You shall mark out your eastern boundary from Hazar-enan to Shepham; [11] and the boundary shall continue down from Shepham to Riblah on the east side of Ain; and the boundary shall go down, and reach the eastern slope of the sea of Chinnereth; [12] and the boundary shall go down to the Jordan, and its end shall be at the Dead Sea.[a] This shall be your land with its boundaries all around.

13 Moses commanded the Israelites, saying: This is the land that you shall inherit by lot, which the LORD has commanded to give to the nine tribes and to the half-tribe; [14] for the tribe of the Reubenites by their ancestral houses and the tribe of the Gadites by their ancestral houses have taken their inheritance, and also the half-tribe of Manasseh; [15] the two tribes and the half-tribe have taken their inheritance beyond the Jordan at Jericho eastward, toward the sunrise.

Tribal Leaders

16 The LORD spoke to Moses, saying: [17] These are the names of the men who shall apportion the land to you for inheritance: the priest Eleazar and Joshua son of Nun. [18] You shall take one leader of every tribe to apportion the land for inheritance. [19] These are the names of the men: Of the tribe of Judah, Caleb son of Jephunneh. [20] Of the tribe of the Simeonites, Shemuel son of Ammihud. [21] Of the tribe of Benjamin, Elidad son of Chislon. [22] Of the tribe of the Danites a leader, Bukki son of Jogli. [23] Of the Josephites: of the tribe of the Manassites a leader, Hanniel son of Ephod, [24] and of the tribe of the Ephraimites a leader, Kemuel son of Shiphtan. [25] Of the tribe of the Zebulunites a leader, Eli-zaphan son of Parnach. [26] Of the tribe of the Issacharites a leader, Paltiel son of Azzan. [27] And of the tribe of the Asherites a leader, Ahihud son of Shelomi. [28] Of the tribe of the Naphtalites a leader, Pedahel son of Ammihud. [29] These were the ones whom the LORD commanded to apportion the inheritance for the Israelites in the land of Canaan.

Cities for the Levites

35 In the plains of Moab by the Jordan at Jericho, the LORD spoke to

a Heb Salt Sea b Syr: Heb lacks its

34:1–29 The Boundaries of the Land
YHWH instructs Moses concerning the boundaries of the land and assigns men to apportion the land.

35:1–34 Cities of Refuge
Identification of the cities of refuge provides the context for a number of rulings on murder and the taking of life (cf. Deut. 19). The role of the blood avenger plays an important role in this discussion. The rulings recognize the difference between murder and accidental homicide. Those responsible for the latter must be protected from the avenger of blood. The cities of refuge provide a safe haven.

Moses, saying: ²Command the Israelites to give, from the inheritance that they possess, towns for the Levites to live in; you shall also give to the Levites pasture lands surrounding the towns. ³The towns shall be theirs to live in, and their pasture lands shall be for their cattle, for their livestock, and for all their animals. ⁴The pasture lands of the towns, which you shall give to the Levites, shall reach from the wall of the town outward a thousand cubits all around. ⁵You shall measure, outside the town, for the east side two thousand cubits, for the south side two thousand cubits, for the west side two thousand cubits, and for the north side two thousand cubits, with the town in the middle; this shall belong to them as pasture land for their towns.

6 The towns that you give to the Levites shall include the six cities of refuge, where you shall permit a slayer to flee, and in addition to them you shall give forty-two towns. ⁷The towns that you give to the Levites shall total forty-eight, with their pasture lands. ⁸And as for the towns that you shall give from the possession of the Israelites, from the larger tribes you shall take many, and from the smaller tribes you shall take few; each, in proportion to the inheritance that it obtains, shall give of its towns to the Levites.

Cities of Refuge

9 The LORD spoke to Moses, saying: ¹⁰Speak to the Israelites, and say to them: When you cross the Jordan into the land of Canaan, ¹¹then you shall select cities to be cities of refuge for you, so that a slayer who kills a person without intent may flee there. ¹²The cities shall be for you a refuge from the avenger, so that the slayer may not die until there is a trial before the congregation.

13 The cities that you designate shall be six cities of refuge for you: ¹⁴you shall designate three cities beyond the Jordan, and three cities in the land of Canaan, to be cities of refuge. ¹⁵These six cities shall serve as refuge for the Israelites, for the resident or transient alien among them, so that anyone who kills a person without intent may flee there.

Concerning Murder and Blood Revenge

16 But anyone who strikes another with an iron object, and death ensues, is a murderer; the murderer shall be put to death. ¹⁷Or anyone who strikes another with a stone in hand that could cause death, and death ensues, is a murderer; the murderer shall be put to death. ¹⁸Or anyone who strikes another with a weapon of wood in hand that could cause death, and death ensues, is a murderer; the murderer shall be put to death. ¹⁹The avenger of blood is the one who shall put the murderer to death; when they meet, the avenger of blood shall execute the sentence. ²⁰Likewise, if someone pushes another from hatred, or hurls something at another, lying in wait, and death ensues, ²¹or in enmity strikes another with the hand, and death ensues, then the one who struck the blow shall be put to death; that person is a murderer; the avenger of blood shall put the murderer to death, when they meet.

22 But if someone pushes another suddenly without enmity, or hurls any object without lying in wait, ²³or, while handling any stone that could cause death, unintentionally*a* drops it on another and death ensues, though they were not enemies, and no harm was intended, ²⁴then the congregation shall judge between the slayer and the avenger of blood, in accordance with these ordinances; ²⁵and the congregation shall rescue the slayer from the avenger of blood. Then the congregation shall send the slayer back to the original city of refuge. The slayer shall live in it until the death of the high priest who was anointed with the holy oil. ²⁶But if the slayer shall at any time go outside the bounds of the original city of refuge,

a Heb *without seeing*

27 and is found by the avenger of blood outside the bounds of the city of refuge, and is killed by the avenger, no blood-guilt shall be incurred. 28 For the slayer must remain in the city of refuge until the death of the high priest; but after the death of the high priest the slayer may return home.

29 These things shall be a statute and ordinance for you throughout your generations wherever you live.

30 If anyone kills another, the murderer shall be put to death on the evidence of witnesses; but no one shall be put to death on the testimony of a single witness. 31 Moreover you shall accept no ransom for the life of a murderer who is subject to the death penalty; a murderer must be put to death. 32 Nor shall you accept ransom for one who has fled to a city of refuge, enabling the fugitive to return to live in the land before the death of the high priest. 33 You shall not pollute the land in which you live; for blood pollutes the land, and no expiation can be made for the land, for the blood that is shed in it, except by the blood of the one who shed it. 34 You shall not defile the land in which you live, in which I also dwell; for I the LORD dwell among the Israelites.

Marriage of Female Heirs

36 The heads of the ancestral houses of the clans of the descendants of Gilead son of Machir son of Manasseh, of the Josephite clans, came forward and spoke in the presence of Moses and the leaders, the heads of the ancestral houses of the Israelites; 2 they said, "The LORD commanded my lord to give the land for inheritance by lot to the Israelites; and my lord was commanded by the LORD to give the inheritance of our brother Zelophehad to his daughters. 3 But if they are married into another Israelite tribe, then their inheritance will be taken from the inheritance of our ancestors and added to the inheritance of the tribe into which they marry; so it will be taken away from the allotted portion of our inheritance. 4 And when the jubilee of the Israelites comes, then their inheritance will be added to the inheritance of the tribe into which they have married; and their inheritance will be taken from the inheritance of our ancestral tribe."

5 Then Moses commanded the Israelites according to the word of the LORD, saying, "The descendants of the tribe of Joseph are right in what they are saying. 6 This is what the LORD commands concerning the daughters of Zelophehad, 'Let them marry whom they think best; only it must be into a clan of their father's tribe that they are married, 7 so that no inheritance of the Israelites shall be transferred from one tribe to another; for all Israelites shall retain the inheritance of their ancestral tribes. 8 Every daughter who possesses an inheritance in any tribe of the Israelites shall marry one from the clan of her father's tribe, so that all Israelites may continue to possess their ancestral inheritance. 9 No inheritance shall be transferred from one tribe to another; for each of the tribes of the Israelites shall retain its own inheritance.'"

10 The daughters of Zelophehad did as the LORD had commanded Moses. 11 Mahlah, Tirzah, Hoglah, Milcah, and Noah, the daughters of Zelophehad, married sons of their father's brothers. 12 They were married into the clans of

---

36:1–13 The Daughters of Zelophehad Revisited
The issues raised by the questions of the daughters of Zelophehad are now resolved. If a woman has inherited, and then decides to marry, she is allowed to marry only within the clan of her father's house. The land must not transfer from one tribe to another (similar concerns are reflected in the regulations concerning the year of jubilee, see Lev. 25:8–25). The division of the land must be equitable and reflect the will of YHWH. Marriage must not violate either the will of YHWH or the equitable division and distribution of the land.

the descendants of Manasseh son of Joseph, and their inheritance remained in the tribe of their father's clan.

13 These are the commandments and the ordinances that the LORD commanded through Moses to the Israelites in the plains of Moab by the Jordan at Jericho.

DEUTERONOMY

The title of the book that is most familiar is from the Greek *deuteronomos*, meaning "second law" or "repetition of the law." This title prepares the reader to consider that Deuteronomy is about *law*. The Hebrew word usually translated "law" is *torah*. The reader should keep in mind that *law* is a narrow definition of *torah*. Deuteronomy uses many words for what is usually thought of as law: commandments, statutes, ordinances, and decrees (see introduction to Exodus for a general discussion on types of laws). More broadly defined, *torah* is *instruction* or *teaching*, that is, what parents pass on to their children. In its broadest meaning *torah* also includes the story of what God has done for Israel and is therefore the name given to the first five books of the Bible. All of these definitions of *torah* are present within Deuteronomy.

The Hebrew title of this book is *devarim* or "words." This also accurately reflects what the book is about, since it consists of a series of speeches given by Moses. The first speech (1:1–4:40) is a memoir of the beginning of Israel's history. The second speech (4:44–28:68) lays out the law (or torah) instructing the people on how they are to live. The third speech (29:1–30:20 [or 32:47]) formalizes the covenant relationship between God and the people. But Moses hasn't yet finished speaking! In addition, just as a song of Moses is sung at the beginning of the wilderness journey (Exod. 15:1–19), another song of Moses is sung at the end of the wilderness journey (Deut. 32:1–47). A final blessing upon Israel are Moses' concluding words (33:1–29). For a man who claimed he couldn't speak so well (Exod. 3:10; 6:12, 30) he sure had a lot to say!

What gives significance and meaning to these laws and words is their setting. Deuteronomy is set on the boundary. Historically it sits on the boundary of the initial settlement of the land. It is presented as Moses' words to all Israel before they entered Canaan. Thus it is on the boundary of Israel's beginning as a people, at a point when they are forming a new nation. Deuteronomy is meant to found a people and to guide them in their ongoing life. This foundation document is presented as given by the original leader of the nation, giving it the weight of the leader's authority, similar to the way Americans give authority to their foundation document, the Constitution.

Origin on the Boundary

Although the book is cast as the words of Moses, some scholars have argued that the earliest traditions and material in Deuteronomy were written long after Moses, in the period of Assyrian domination of Israel and Judah (eighth century BCE; see 2 Kgs. 17–21). These scholars have noted that the structure of the covenant between God and the people in Deuteronomy corresponds to the structure of Neo-Assyrian state treaties. In this historical context Deuteronomy marks the boundary between Assyrian hegemony and Judean autonomy and independence. As a countertreaty,

Deuteronomy demands that the people's oath of loyalty be given to their divine sovereign, not their Assyrian overlord.

Other scholars have noted the striking similarities between the distinctive legal and religious requirements of Deuteronomy and the account of Josiah's major reform of Israel's institutions in 622 BCE (see 2 Kgs. 22–23). These scholars have argued that a copy of Deuteronomy as we basically know it (or at least 4:44–28:28) was found (or planted?) in the temple (see 2 Kgs. 22:3–20). In heeding the words of this "book of the law" (2 Kgs. 22:8) or "book of the covenant" (2 Kgs. 23:2), both of which are apt descriptions of Deuteronomy, Josiah's reform restricted all sacrificial worship of God to Jerusalem and removed foreign elements from the system of worship.

In the contexts of Assyrian domination and Josiah's reform, Deuteronomy was addressed to Israel as a nation, living in the land of promise. Thus, it would have reminded the people afresh of the promise of the land they now enjoyed. It also would have warned the people against the tendencies shown by Israel in the wilderness that threatened the possibility of a long life in a good land—disobedience, idolatry, and faithlessness.

But these laws and words also addressed the Israel of an even later era. Deuteronomy would receive its final form in the period of the exile, when the people had experienced the loss of the land. Thus, it also addressed a people sent back across the boundary into wilderness again. On the one hand, it helped Israel to (re)interpret their history as failure to live by instruction of God. On the other hand, it said afresh that the promise was still good and explained what had to be done to realize and maintain its possibilities.

Literarily Deuteronomy is the boundary document between Genesis–Numbers and Joshua–2 Kings. There are many affinities with the previous four books. Deuteronomy clearly picks up the narrative from the end of Numbers. Moses is still the central character, as he has been since Exodus. It repeats material found elsewhere in the Pentateuch. There are also clear affinities with Joshua–2 Kings. Deuteronomy begins the time of Israel's being settled on the land. The similarity in style, language, and themes between Deuteronomy and Joshua–2 Kings has led scholars to call this literary complex the Deuteronomistic History. Canonically, Deuteronomy is on the boundary between Israel's past and Israel's future.

This implies that, on the one hand, the book is shaped or understood by what has preceded. It summarizes and brings to an end the beginning of the early period of Israel's history. The character of the book as a last will and testament signals the end of an era. The future generation now has in this book the full story of how they came to be and what God wants of them. The foundations are laid. Nothing more is necessary. The Torah of the Lord is complete. It is theologically significant that Torah, that is, the Pentateuch, is complete without God's promises being fulfilled. In the end, Israel can be God's covenant people *without* land, *without* king, and *without* temple. Torah lays out the way for God's people. All the people have is Torah. That is all they need.

On the other hand, Deuteronomy is self-consciously instruction for the future, not simply a record of the past. This book is the standard for the future, the plumb line by which generations to come will be measured. The modern term Deuteronomistic History testifies to Joshua–2 Kings being not merely a reporting of history but an accounting of how well the kings, the leaders, and the people kept torah, that is, the laws. Thus modern readers might consider these laws and words as being what

is needed to know God's ways and as a plumb line by which even our generation is measured.

This notion of Deuteronomy as the means of holding Israel accountable for their keeping of torah is exemplified in its theology. Anyone who has asked the questions, "Why did this bad thing happen to me? What have I done *to deserve* this?" is expressing the essence of Deuteronomic theology. Central to Deuteronomy is the proposition that *if* the people obey the covenant, *then* God will bless them (7:12–16; 11:13–15, 27; 28:1–14). Likewise *if* the people turn away from the covenant, *then* God will punish them (8:11–20; 11:16–17, 28; 28:15–68). In other words, good things happen to good people, and bad things happen to bad people. Indeed, this is Israel's dominant interpretation of suffering (cf. Judg. 2:11–20; 2 Kgs. 17:1–41; 23:26–27; 24:2–4; Pss. 1:1–8; 145:14–20; Prov. 3:33; 10:3, 30; 11:20–21; Jeremiah, Hosea, Amos). Deuteronomy does not consider the limits of this theology (cf. Job; Ecclesiastes; Isa. 52:13–53:12). The truth this theology expresses is that actions have consequences. Deuteronomy recognizes that this is true not only for individuals (24:16), but also for the nation. God's covenant is with *all* the people, so the nation as a whole has to bear the burden of obedience.

Concern with Boundaries

In light of Deuteronomy's position on the boundary, it is not surprising that a central theme of the laws and words is boundaries. The primary boundary Deuteronomy is concerned with is the one that delimits the identity of Israel or the manner in which Israel is to be distinct and separate from its neighbors. As a people just being formed as a nation, or trying to maintain its formation against hegemonic forces, or being reformed in exile—it is not surprising that issues of identity come to the fore. It is at times when identity is threatened—by assimilation to Canaanite, Assyrian, or Babylonian culture—that it is most necessary for Israel to clearly mark the boundaries of their identity. This obsession with Israel's boundaries as a people is clearly seen in these themes:

• Worship of YHWH alone (4:35, 39; 6:4; 7:9) and subsequent warnings against foreign worship (4:16–19; 18:9–11) and idolatry (6:14; 8:19; 11:16, 28)
• Proper Israelite worship (12:1–28; 14:22–29; 16:1–16)
• Proper relationships among Israelites, including the boundary between justice and injustice (15:1–18; 16:18–20; 24:10–22) and proper sexual boundaries (22:13–30; 23:2–6, 10–14; 24:1–4)
• Eating certain foods (14:1–21)
• Concern to utterly destroy the other nations (2:34; 3:6; 7:1–5; 20:10–18)
• Loyalty to the covenant (6:5, 13; 11:1, 26–28; 13:4; 17:2–7, 19; 28:15; 30:15–20)

The maintenance of community identity also places Deuteronomy on another boundary: the ethical boundary between inclusiveness and exclusiveness. On the side of inclusiveness, Deuteronomy is deeply concerned that Israelites demonstrate love and justice toward each other. These concerns are exemplified in the Shema (6:4–5) and the Decalogue (5:1–21). The Shema focuses on how Israel is to love God, and in the Decalogue Israel is told how to live out that love by giving proper regard to others in the covenant community. The themes, emphases, and often the language itself suggest that one proper way of understanding Deuteronomy is as an explication of Jesus' Great Commandment to love God and neighbor (Matt. 22:37–39; Mark

12:29–31; Luke 10:27). The Shema and Decalogue become a center around which everything else revolves.

On the side of exclusiveness, Deuteronomy demonstrates anxiety about those who are other. This is reflected in the emphasis on maintaining patriarchal family structures at the expense of women's interests. But this anxiety is primarily reflected in the Deuteronomic view that the only way to maintain the proper boundaries is by *utterly destroying* (2:34; 3:6; 7:2; 13:15) or *purging the evil from their midst* (13:5; 17:7, 12; 19:13, 19; 21:9, 21; 22:21, 22, 23; 24:7). Thus the laws become not only restrictive, but also destructive. The reader is left with an almost intolerable tension within Deuteronomy between the desire to destroy anyone who violates the boundaries and the desire for love and justice.

Boundaries, identity, the meaning of the past, life in the present, what is at stake for the future, enemies all around, obedience, punishment, blessing, laws, life, death, justice, love—these are all topics that concern Deuteronomy. The words of Deuteronomy's struggle with boundaries for the sake of the well-being of all Israel are to be taught to Israel's children (4:9–10; 6:7, 20; 11:19; 31:12; 31:13; 32:46). The current generation is those children who will hear these words and be instructed by them. This generation too has to struggle with its questions and anxieties about boundaries and identity, faithful living, the well-being of the community, and choosing life.

—Nancy R. Bowen

Events at Horeb Recalled

1 These are the words that Moses spoke to all Israel beyond the Jordan—in the wilderness, on the plain opposite Suph, between Paran and Tophel, Laban, Hazeroth, and Di-zahab. [2] (By the way of Mount Seir it takes eleven days to reach Kadesh-barnea from Horeb.) [3] In the fortieth year, on the first day of the eleventh month, Moses spoke to the Israelites just as the LORD had commanded him to speak to them. [4] This was after he had defeated King Sihon of the Amorites, who reigned in Heshbon, and King Og of Bashan, who reigned in Ashtaroth and[a] in Edri. [5] Beyond the Jordan in the land of Moab, Moses undertook to expound this law as follows:

[6] The LORD our God spoke to us at Horeb, saying, "You have stayed long enough at this mountain. [7] Resume your journey, and go into the hill country of the Amorites as well as into the neighboring regions—the Arabah, the hill country, the Shephelah, the Negeb, and the seacoast—the land of the Canaanites and the Lebanon, as far as the great river, the river Euphrates. [8] See, I have set the land before you; go in and take possession of the land that I[b] swore to your ancestors, to Abraham, to Isaac,

[a] Gk Syr Vg Compare Josh 12.4: Heb lacks *and*   [b] Sam Gk: MT *the LORD*

1:1—Deuteronomy is a boundary document. Literarily, it's on the boundary between the Pentateuch and the rest of the Old Testament canon. Geographically, it's on the boundary between wilderness and promised land. Therefore Deuteronomy reflects boundary issues.

1:6—Here begins what is presented as *Moses' first speech*. Running to 4:43, it is a memoir of Israel's history or confession of faith about what God has done. At the boundary of the river the people look back on what God has done. Before

going in a new direction, it is helpful to know where one has been.

1:8—The phrase about possessing the land is repeated throughout the book. The fulfillment of God's promise of land (Gen. 12:1) is a central theme. Native Americans and Palestinians have experienced the tragic consequences of a literal interpretation of this command in other times. A more nuanced reading notices that remaining in the land is dependent upon obedience, and when the land is lost, any return is conditional

and to Jacob, to give to them and to their descendants after them."

Appointment of Tribal Leaders

9 At that time I said to you, "I am unable by myself to bear you. 10 The LORD your God has multiplied you, so that today you are as numerous as the stars of heaven. 11 May the LORD, the God of your ancestors, increase you a thousand times more and bless you, as he has promised you! 12 But how can I bear the heavy burden of your disputes all by myself? 13 Choose for each of your tribes individuals who are wise, discerning, and reputable to be your leaders." 14 You answered me, "The plan you have proposed is a good one." 15 So I took the leaders of your tribes, wise and reputable individuals, and installed them as leaders over you, commanders of thousands, commanders of hundreds, commanders of fifties, commanders of tens, and officials, throughout your tribes. 16 I charged your judges at that time: "Give the members of your community a fair hearing, and judge rightly between one person and another, whether citizen or resident alien. 17 You must not be partial in judging: hear out the small and the great alike; you shall not be intimidated by anyone, for the judgment is God's. Any case that is too hard for you, bring to me, and I will hear it." 18 So I charged you at that time with all the things that you should do.

Israel's Refusal to Enter the Land

19 Then, just as the LORD our God had ordered us, we set out from Horeb and went through all that great and terrible wilderness that you saw, on the way to the hill country of the Amorites, until we reached Kadesh-barnea. 20 I said to you, "You have reached the hill country of the Amorites, which the LORD our God is giving us. 21 See, the LORD your God has given the land to you; go up, take possession, as the LORD, the God of your ancestors, has promised you; do not fear or be dismayed."

22 All of you came to me and said, "Let us send men ahead of us to explore the land for us and bring back a report to us regarding the route by which we should go up and the cities we will come to." 23 The plan seemed good to me, and I selected twelve of you, one from each tribe. 24 They set out and went up into the hill country, and when they reached the Valley of Eshcol they spied it out 25 and gathered some of the land's produce, which they brought down to us. They brought back a report to us, and said, "It is a good land that the LORD our God is giving us."

26 But you were unwilling to go up. You rebelled against the command of the LORD your God; 27 you grumbled in your tents and said, "It is because the LORD hates us that he has brought us out of the land of Egypt, to hand us over to the Amorites to destroy us. 28 Where are we headed? Our kindred have made our hearts melt by reporting, 'The people are stronger and taller than we; the cities are large and fortified up to heaven! We actually saw there the offspring of the Anakim!'" 29 I said to you, "Have no dread or fear of them. 30 The LORD your God, who goes before you,

---

upon obedience. The land is not ours to do with as we wish.

1:16–17—Mediation of disputes is to be fair regardless of whether one is a *citizen* (insider) or *resident alien* (outsider), *small* (powerless) or *great* (powerful). We should judge fairly because this is how God judges us, without regard to our station or status in society.

1:22–45—Israel faced overwhelming odds in taking possession of the land (cf. 4:38; 7:17; 8:17; 11:23; 20:1). Working for peace and jus-

tice we also face overwhelming odds. We cannot wish those obstacles away. God's promise is to be with us in the struggle against oppressive forces.

1:30—At least fourteen times Deuteronomy reports that something is done before the *eyes* of the people or their eyes have seen something (e.g., 3:21; 4:9, 34). That something is always what God has done for Israel. God's acts are not hidden or mysterious (in contrast to Ecclesiastes) but visible for all to see. Having seen these

is the one who will fight for you, just as he did for you in Egypt before your very eyes, ³¹ and in the wilderness, where you saw how the LORD your God carried you, just as one carries a child, all the way that you traveled until you reached this place. ³² But in spite of this, you have no trust in the LORD your God, ³³ who goes before you on the way to seek out a place for you to camp, in fire by night, and in the cloud by day, to show you the route you should take."

The Penalty for Israel's Rebellion

34 When the LORD heard your words, he was wrathful and swore: ³⁵ "Not one of these—not one of this evil generation—shall see the good land that I swore to give to your ancestors, ³⁶ except Caleb son of Jephunneh. He shall see it, and to him and to his descendants I will give the land on which he set foot, because of his complete fidelity to the LORD." ³⁷ Even with me the LORD was angry on your account, saying, "You also shall not enter there. ³⁸ Joshua son of Nun, your assistant, shall enter there; encourage him, for he is the one who will secure Israel's possession of it. ³⁹ And as for your little ones, who you thought would become booty, your children, who today do not yet know right from wrong, they shall enter there; to them I will give it, and they shall take possession of it. ⁴⁰ But as for you, journey back into the wilderness, in the direction of the Red Sea."ᵃ

41 You answered me, "We have sinned against the LORD! We are ready to go up and fight, just as the LORD our God commanded us." So all of you strapped on your battle gear, and thought it easy to go up into the hill country. ⁴² The LORD said to me, "Say to them, 'Do not go up and do not fight, for I am not in the midst of you; otherwise you will be defeated by your enemies.'" ⁴³ Although I told you, you would not listen. You rebelled against the command of the LORD and presumptuously went up into the hill country. ⁴⁴ The Amorites who lived in that hill country then came out against you and chased you as bees do. They beat you down in Seir as far as Hormah. ⁴⁵ When you returned and wept before the LORD, the LORD would neither heed your voice nor pay you any attention.

The Desert Years

46 After you had stayed at Kadesh as many days as you did, ¹ we journeyed back into the wilderness, in the direction of the Red Sea,ᵃ as the LORD had told me and skirted Mount Seir for many days. ² Then the LORD said to me: ³ "You have been skirting this hill country long enough. Head north, ⁴ and charge the people as follows: You are about to pass through the territory of your kindred, the descendants of Esau, who live in Seir. They will be afraid of you, so, be very careful ⁵ not to engage in battle with them, for I will not give you even so much as a foot's length of their land, since I have given Mount Seir to Esau as a possession. ⁶ You shall purchase food from them for money, so that you may eat; and you shall also buy

ᵃ Or Sea of Reeds

mighty acts, they cannot deny God's presence with or gracious acts toward them. Consider what God has done *before your eyes,* not only for yourself but for your faith community.

1:31—Even though Hebrew uses the masculine "just as *he carries a child,*" imaging a father, the image is also a female, maternal image. The theological point is that as mothers and fathers carry their children over difficult terrain to ease their way, so God has done for the people in the wilderness.

2:5, 9, 19—God also gave land to peoples other than Israel: the Edomites, Moabites, and Ammonites, who are both Israel's enemies and Israel's relatives (Gen. 19:37–38; 25:30). Remember that God cares for *all* the families of the earth, including the families of our enemies. If we are all members of the human family, we are also related to our enemies. One implication would be to consider getting along, instead of continuing family feuds.

water from them for money, so that you may drink. [7] Surely the LORD your God has blessed you in all your undertakings; he knows your going through this great wilderness. These forty years the LORD your God has been with you; you have lacked nothing." [8] So we passed by our kin, the descendants of Esau who live in Seir, leaving behind the route of the Arabah, and leaving behind Elath and Ezion-geber.

When we had headed out along the route of the wilderness of Moab, [9] the LORD said to me: "Do not harass Moab or engage them in battle, for I will not give you any of its land as a possession, since I have given Ar as a possession to the descendants of Lot." [10] (The Emim—a large and numerous people, as tall as the Anakim—had formerly inhabited it. [11] Like the Anakim, they are usually reckoned as Rephaim, though the Moabites call them Emim. [12] Moreover, the Horim had formerly inhabited Seir, but the descendants of Esau dispossessed them, destroying them and settling in their place, as Israel has done in the land that the LORD gave them as a possession.) [13] "Now then, proceed to cross over the Wadi Zered."

So we crossed over the Wadi Zered. [14] And the length of time we had traveled from Kadesh-barnea until we crossed the Wadi Zered was thirty-eight years, until the entire generation of warriors had perished from the camp, as the LORD had sworn concerning them. [15] Indeed, the LORD's own hand was against them, to root them out from the camp, until all had perished.

[16] Just as soon as all the warriors had died off from among the people, [17] the LORD spoke to me, saying, [18] "Today you are going to cross the boundary of Moab at Ar. [19] When you approach the frontier of the Ammonites, do not harass them or engage them in battle, for I will not give the land of the Ammonites to you as a possession, because I have given it to the descendants of Lot." [20] (It also is usually reckoned as a land of Rephaim. Rephaim formerly inhabited it, though the Ammonites call them Zamzummim, [21] a strong and numerous people, as tall as the Anakim. But the LORD destroyed them from before the Ammonites so that they could dispossess them and settle in their place. [22] He did the same for the descendants of Esau, who live in Seir, by destroying the Horim before them so that they could dispossess them and settle in their place even to this day. [23] As for the Avvim, who had lived in settlements in the vicinity of Gaza, the Caphtorim, who came from Caphtor, destroyed them and settled in their place.) [24] "Proceed on your journey and cross the Wadi Arnon. See, I have handed over to you King Sihon the Amorite of Heshbon, and his land. Begin to take possession by engaging him in battle. [25] This day I will begin to put the dread and fear of you upon the peoples everywhere under heaven; when they hear report of you, they will tremble and be in anguish because of you."

Defeat of King Sihon

[26] So I sent messengers from the wilderness of Kedemoth to King Sihon of Heshbon with the following terms of peace: [27] "If you let me pass through your land, I will travel only along the road; I will turn aside neither to the right nor to the left. [28] You shall sell me food for money, so that I may eat, and supply me

---

2:10–12, 20–23—These are asides that indicate that Israel is not the only people to displace prior inhabitants of the land. History has many stories of one group of people successfully occupying the land of another. The new occupiers have the power to rename not only the area, but also the former inhabitants. The result is that occupied people disappear, for they no longer have their own history, their own name, their own voice. There is only the history of those who have replaced them. It is this historical process that native peoples, African Americans, women, and others have resisted. Those who have been dispossessed seek to reclaim their own name and history, even if they can't reclaim the land.

water for money, so that I may drink. Only allow me to pass through on foot—²⁹ just as the descendants of Esau who live in Seir have done for me and likewise the Moabites who live in Ar—until I cross the Jordan into the land that the LORD our God is giving us." ³⁰ But King Sihon of Heshbon was not willing to let us pass through, for the LORD your God had hardened his spirit and made his heart defiant in order to hand him over to you, as he has now done.

31 The LORD said to me, "See, I have begun to give Sihon and his land over to you. Begin now to take possession of his land." ³² So when Sihon came out against us, he and all his people for battle at Jahaz, ³³ the LORD our God gave him over to us; and we struck him down, along with his offspring and all his people. ³⁴ At that time we captured all his towns, and in each town we utterly destroyed men, women, and children. We left not a single survivor. ³⁵ Only the livestock we kept as spoil for ourselves, as well as the plunder of the towns that we had captured. ³⁶ From Aroer on the edge of the Wadi Arnon (including the town that is in the wadi itself) as far as Gilead, there was no citadel too high for us. The LORD our God gave everything to us. ³⁷ You did not encroach, however, on the land of the Ammonites, avoiding the whole upper region of the Wadi Jabbok as well as the towns of the hill country, just as[a] the LORD our God had charged.

Defeat of King Og

3 When we headed up the road to Bashan, King Og of Bashan came out against us, he and all his people, for battle at Edrei. ² The LORD said to me,

"Do not fear him, for I have handed him over to you, along with his people and his land. Do to him as you did to King Sihon of the Amorites, who reigned in Heshbon." ³ So the LORD our God also handed over to us King Og of Bashan and all his people. We struck him down until not a single survivor was left. ⁴ At that time we captured all his towns; there was no citadel that we did not take from them—sixty towns, the whole region of Argob, the kingdom of Og in Bashan. ⁵ All these were fortress towns with high walls, double gates, and bars, besides a great many villages. ⁶ And we utterly destroyed them, as we had done to King Sihon of Heshbon, in each city utterly destroying men, women, and children. ⁷ But all the livestock and the plunder of the towns we kept as spoil for ourselves.

8 So at that time we took from the two kings of the Amorites the land beyond the Jordan, from the Wadi Arnon to Mount Hermon ⁹ (the Sidonians call Hermon Sirion, while the Amorites call it Senir), ¹⁰ all the towns of the tableland, the whole of Gilead, and all of Bashan, as far as Salecah and Edrei, towns of Og's kingdom in Bashan. ¹¹ (Now only King Og of Bashan was left of the remnant of the Rephaim. In fact his bed, an iron bed, can still be seen in Rabbah of the Ammonites. By the common cubit it is nine cubits long and four cubits wide.) ¹² As for the land that we took possession of at that time, I gave to the Reubenites and Gadites the territory north of Aroer,[b] that is on the edge of the Wadi Arnon, as well as half the hill country of Gilead with its towns, ¹³ and I gave to the

[a] Gk Tg: Heb *and all* [b] Heb *territory from Aroer*

2:34; 3:6—Unfortunately, the land that Israel is about to possess is inhabited by others (see Exod. 3:8). One of Deuteronomy's boundary concerns is that if Israel mixes with the inhabitants of the land, they will turn away from God (see notes at 7:1–5; 13:8–17). The solution is genocide. Today we would never condone the utter destruction of men, women, and children in order to maintain racial, ethnic, or religious purity. Why is impurity seen as dangerous to the well-being of a community? Does your community have concerns about persons or objects that must be *utterly destroyed* because they threaten the community? What are the possibilities and difficulties with this solution? What are other responses to the evils that threaten us?

half-tribe of Manasseh the rest of Gilead and all of Bashan, Og's kingdom. (The whole region of Argob: all that portion of Bashan used to be called a land of Rephaim; [14] Jair the Manassite acquired the whole region of Argob as far as the border of the Geshurites and the Maacathites, and he named them—that is, Bashan—after himself, Havvoth-jair,[a] as it is to this day.) [15] To Machir I gave Gilead. [16] And to the Reubenites and the Gadites I gave the territory from Gilead as far as the Wadi Arnon, with the middle of the wadi as a boundary, and up to the Jabbok, the wadi being boundary of the Ammonites; [17] the Arabah also, with the Jordan and its banks, from Chinnereth down to the sea of the Arabah, the Dead Sea,[b] with the lower slopes of Pisgah on the east.

[18] At that time, I charged you as follows: "Although the LORD your God has given you this land to occupy, all your troops shall cross over armed as the vanguard of your Israelite kin. [19] Only your wives, your children, and your livestock—I know that you have much livestock—shall stay behind in the towns that I have given to you. [20] When the LORD gives rest to your kindred, as to you, and they too have occupied the land that the LORD your God is giving them beyond the Jordan, then each of you may return to the property that I have given to you." [21] And I charged Joshua as well at that time, saying: "Your own eyes have seen everything that the LORD your God has done to these two kings; so the LORD will do to all the kingdoms into which you are about to cross. [22] Do not fear them, for it is the LORD your God who fights for you."

Moses Views Canaan from Pisgah

[23] At that time, too, I entreated the LORD, saying: [24] "O Lord GOD, you have only begun to show your servant your greatness and your might; what god in heaven or on earth can perform deeds and mighty acts like yours! [25] Let me cross over to see the good land beyond the Jordan, that good hill country and the Lebanon." [26] But the LORD was angry with me on your account and would not heed me. The LORD said to me, "Enough from you! Never speak to me of this matter again! [27] Go up to the top of Pisgah and look around you to the west, to the north, to the south, and to the east. Look well, for you shall not cross over this Jordan. [28] But charge Joshua, and encourage and strengthen him, because it is he who shall cross over at the head of this people and who shall secure their possession of the land that you will see." [29] So we remained in the valley opposite Beth-peor.

Moses Commands Obedience

4 So now, Israel, give heed to the statutes and ordinances that I am teaching you to observe, so that you may live to enter and occupy the land that the LORD, the God of your ancestors, is giving you. [2] You must neither add anything to what I command you nor take away anything from it, but keep the commandments of the LORD your God with

---

[a] That is *Settlement of Jair* [b] Heb *Salt Sea*

3:22—This militant image of God is critiqued by those who argue that a God of war leads inexorably to the concept of holy war. Yet there is a certain attraction to this fighting deity, for Israel's enemies would always be stronger and mightier—like David versus Goliath. The only way to victory was that God fought on their behalf. However, just as God can fight *for us*, God can fight *against* us when we become the oppressive power (see Isa. 7:18–20; 10:5–6; Jer. 25:29). Remember that God fights for those who have no other weapons.

3:24—Moses' prayer acknowledges that in one lifetime we only begin to experience God's greatness and might. And he lived to be one hundred twenty years old (31:2; 34:7)! One form of idolatry is to think we can know God in totality.

4:1—The Hebrew translated *"give heed"* is really the command "Hear!" Hearing is an important theme in Deuteronomy (5:1; 6:3–4; 9:1; 20:3; 27:9). It involves more than letting the words go in one ear and out the other. Truly hearing God's words means doing God's words.

which I am charging you. ³ You have seen for yourselves what the LORD did with regard to the Baal of Peor—how the LORD your God destroyed from among you everyone who followed the Baal of Peor, ⁴ while those of you who held fast to the LORD your God are all alive today.

5 See, just as the LORD my God has charged me, I now teach you statutes and ordinances for you to observe in the land that you are about to enter and occupy. ⁶ You must observe them diligently, for this will show your wisdom and discernment to the peoples, who, when they hear all these statutes, will say, "Surely this great nation is a wise and discerning people!" ⁷ For what other great nation has a god so near to it as the LORD our God is whenever we call to him? ⁸ And what other great nation has statutes and ordinances as just as this entire law that I am setting before you today?

9 But take care and watch yourselves closely, so as neither to forget the things that your eyes have seen nor to let them slip from your mind all the days of your life; make them known to your children and your children's children— ¹⁰ how you once stood before the LORD your God at Horeb, when the LORD said to me, "Assemble the people for me, and I will let them hear my words, so that they may learn to fear me as long as they live on the earth, and may teach their children so"; ¹¹ you approached and stood at the foot of the mountain while the mountain was blazing up to the very heavens, shrouded in dark clouds. ¹² Then the LORD spoke to you out of the fire. You heard the sound of words but saw no form; there was only a voice. ¹³ He declared to you his covenant, which he charged you to observe, that is, the ten commandments;ᵃ and he wrote them on two stone tablets. ¹⁴ And the LORD charged me at that time to teach you statutes and ordinances for you to observe in the land that you are about to cross into and occupy.

15 Since you saw no form when the LORD spoke to you at Horeb out of the fire, take care and watch yourselves closely, ¹⁶ so that you do not act corruptly by making an idol for yourselves, in the form of any figure—the likeness of male or female, ¹⁷ the likeness of any animal that is on the earth, the likeness of any winged bird that flies in the air, ¹⁸ the likeness of anything that creeps on the ground, the likeness of any fish that is in the water under the earth. ¹⁹ And when you look up to the heavens and see the sun, the moon, and the stars, all the host of heaven, do not be led astray and bow down to them and serve them, things that the LORD your God has allotted to all the peoples everywhere under heaven. ²⁰ But the LORD has taken you and brought you out of the iron-smelter, out of Egypt, to become a people of his very own possession, as you are now.

21 The LORD was angry with me because of you, and he vowed that I should not cross the Jordan and that I should not enter the good land that the LORD your God is giving for your possession. ²² For I am going to die in this

ᵃ Heb *the ten words*

4:6—Do other nations look at us as Americans and see that we are a wise and discerning nation? Do other peoples look at us as Christians and see that we are a wise and discerning people? What would be the evidence for that claim?

4:7—There is perhaps no affirmation of God more moving and powerful than this: God is *so near* when we call. God is not absent or far away or dead. God is near to us, no matter where we are (Ps. 139:7–12) or in what circumstances (Rom. 8:38–39).

4:8—*Law* in Hebrew is *torah*. We often think of torah narrowly as legalism. More broadly, Torah is instruction and refers to the first five books of the Bible. To keep *this entire law* is to be instructed in God's story as well as God's commandments.

4:22—One of the most poignant parts of this narrative is that Moses, who leads the people out of slavery, never realizes the fulfillment of the dream. Moses is not the only person to experience this tragedy. Martin Luther King Jr.'s words,

land without crossing over the Jordan, but you are going to cross over to take possession of that good land. ²³ So be careful not to forget the covenant that the LORD your God made with you, and not to make for yourselves an idol in the form of anything that the LORD your God has forbidden you. ²⁴ For the LORD your God is a devouring fire, a jealous God.

25 When you have had children and children's children, and become complacent in the land, if you act corruptly by making an idol in the form of anything, thus doing what is evil in the sight of the LORD your God, and provoking him to anger, ²⁶ I call heaven and earth to witness against you today that you will soon utterly perish from the land that you are crossing the Jordan to occupy; you will not live long on it, but will be utterly destroyed. ²⁷ The LORD will scatter you among the peoples; only a few of you will be left among the nations where the LORD will lead you. ²⁸ There you will serve other gods made by human hands, objects of wood and stone that neither see, nor hear, nor eat, nor smell. ²⁹ From there you will seek the LORD your God, and you will find him if you search after him with all your heart and soul. ³⁰ In your distress, when all these things have happened to you in time to come, you will return to the LORD your God and heed him. ³¹ Because the LORD your God is a merciful God, he will neither abandon you nor destroy you; he will not forget the covenant with your ancestors that he swore to them.

32 For ask now about former ages, long before your own, ever since the day that God created human beings on the earth; ask from one end of heaven to the other: has anything so great as this ever happened or has its like ever been heard of? ³³ Has any people ever heard the voice of a god speaking out of a fire, as you have heard, and lived? ³⁴ Or has any god ever attempted to go and take a nation for himself from the midst of another nation, by trials, by signs and wonders, by war, by a mighty hand and an outstretched arm, and by terrifying displays of power, as the LORD your God did for you in Egypt before your very eyes? ³⁵ To you it was shown so that you would acknowledge that the LORD is God; there is no other besides him. ³⁶ From heaven he made you hear his voice to discipline you. On earth he showed you his great fire, while you heard his words coming out of the fire. ³⁷ And because he loved your ancestors, he chose their descendants after them. He brought you out of Egypt with his own presence, by his great power, ³⁸ driving out before you nations greater and mightier than yourselves, to bring you in, giving you

---

"I have stood on the mountain and I have seen the promised land," are his recognition that he would not live to see his dream fulfilled. None of us will live to see God's will done on earth as in heaven. God only calls us to the struggle.

4:24—The image of God as *devouring fire* (also 9:3) is a reminder that God is dangerous (see note at 32:39). This kind of fire consumes thousands of acres of forest. There is a tendency in our day to hold a more therapeutic view of God as friendly and focused on our well-being. Does this view help or harm us? What changes for us if we consider a God who can consume us, in wrath as well as in love? The image of a jealous God appears again in the command against idol worship (5:8–9). God's jealousy is invoked as a means to limit Israel to exclusive worship. God does not tolerate rivals. What is troubling is God as jealous husband takes on disturbing and violent tendencies in later prophetic literature (Jer. 2–3; Ezek. 16; Hos. 1–3).

4:25—Moses warns that Israel will be most tempted to turn away from God when they have become complacent in the land. If you and your faith community are complacent in your place, consider how that turns you away from God.

4:32–40—These verses sum up what gave Israel its identity. The language gives attention to Israel's distinctive experience of God and thus to Israel's distinctiveness. Each person and community has their own distinctive experience of God. Instead of thinking that such distinctions make one group better than another, think of how these distinctions all reflect God.

their land for a possession, as it is still today. [39] So acknowledge today and take to heart that the LORD is God in heaven above and on the earth beneath; there is no other. [40] Keep his statutes and his commandments, which I am commanding you today for your own well-being and that of your descendants after you, so that you may long remain in the land that the LORD your God is giving you for all time.

Cities of Refuge East of the Jordan

41 Then Moses set apart on the east side of the Jordan three cities [42] to which a homicide could flee, someone who unintentionally kills another person, the two not having been at enmity before; the homicide could flee to one of these cities and live: [43] Bezer in the wilderness on the tableland belonging to the Reubenites, Ramoth in Gilead belonging to the Gadites, and Golan in Bashan belonging to the Manassites.

Transition to the Second Address

44 This is the law that Moses set before the Israelites. [45] These are the decrees and the statutes and ordinances that Moses spoke to the Israelites when they had come out of Egypt, [46] beyond the Jordan in the valley opposite Beth-peor, in the land of King Sihon of the Amorites, who reigned at Heshbon, whom Moses and the Israelites defeated when they came out of Egypt. [47] They occupied his land and the land of King Og of Bashan, the two kings of the Amorites on the eastern side of the Jordan: [48] from Aroer, which is on the edge of the Wadi Arnon, as far as Mount Sirion[a] (that is, Hermon), [49] together with all the Arabah on the east side of the Jordan as far as the Sea of the Arabah, under the slopes of Pisgah.

The Ten Commandments

5 Moses convened all Israel, and said to them:

Hear, O Israel, the statutes and ordinances that I am addressing to you today; you shall learn them and observe them diligently. [2] The LORD our God made a covenant with us at Horeb. [3] Not with our ancestors did the LORD make this covenant, but with us, who are all of us here alive today. [4] The LORD spoke with you face to face at the mountain, out of the fire. [5] (At that time I was standing between the LORD and you to declare to you the words[b] of the LORD; for you were afraid because of the fire and did not go up the mountain.) And he said:

6 I am the LORD your God, who brought you out of the land of Egypt, out of the house of slavery; [7] you shall have no other gods before[c] me.

[a] Syr: Heb *Sion* [b] Q Mss Sam Gk Syr Vg Tg: MT *word* [c] Or *besides*

4:44—Here begins the heart of the book, *Moses' second speech*, which runs to 28:68. After recounting Israel's history up to their arrival at Mount Horeb (or Sinai), Moses reviews Israel's covenant obligations. These obligations guided Israel in the wilderness. They will now guide Israel in the land. They will guide Israel in the future when they are once again in the wilderness of exile. These words spoke to the people in widely different circumstances. They are a guide whenever we cross into new territory (see note at 1:1).

5:1–21—This is Deuteronomy's version of the Ten Commandments (or Decalogue). The differences from Exodus (Exod. 20:2–17) indicate that law is dynamic and changing, not static. God's commands to us can be altered because God's word to us is ever fresh. God speaks to us in new ways in new situations.

5:1—The main point of legal material is to structure covenant life. The problem is that there may be different, and even conflicting, views on what that order should look like. We still have to consider how to structure covenant life together. Ours will be different from that of our ancestors. But we still, in loving response to God's grace and mercy, ask ourselves how we now live as God's people.

5:7—The phrasing *before me* suggests the recognition of the existence of other gods, and that the Lord should be the *primary* or chief god on one's list of gods to worship. The alternative translation *besides me* is a demand for an exclusive relationship between God and Israel. The Lord is to be Israel's *only* god. Consider what it means for God to be first and only in your life.

8 You shall not make for yourself an idol, whether in the form of anything that is in heaven above, or that is on the earth beneath, or that is in the water under the earth. ⁹ You shall not bow down to them or worship them; for I the LORD your God am a jealous God, punishing children for the iniquity of parents, to the third and fourth generation of those who reject me, ¹⁰ but showing steadfast love to the thousandth generation*a* of those who love me and keep my commandments.

11 You shall not make wrongful use of the name of the LORD your God, for the LORD will not acquit anyone who misuses his name.

12 Observe the sabbath day and keep it holy, as the LORD your God commanded you. ¹³ Six days you shall labor and do all your work. ¹⁴ But the seventh day is a sabbath to the LORD your God; you shall not do any work—you, or your son or your daughter, or your male or female slave, or your ox or your donkey, or any of your livestock, or the resident alien in your towns, so that your male and female slave may rest as well as you. ¹⁵ Remember that you were a slave in the land of Egypt, and the LORD your God brought you out from there with a mighty hand and an outstretched arm; therefore the LORD your God commanded you to keep the sabbath day.

16 Honor your father and your mother, as the LORD your God commanded you, so that your days may be long and that it may go well with you in the land that the LORD your God is giving you.

17 You shall not murder.*b*

18 Neither shall you commit adultery.

a Or to thousands   *b* Or kill

5:8–10—It's bad enough that we are tempted to reduce God. It's even worse when we make our limited vision of God the object of adoration. God's reaction to this is jealousy (see note at 4:24). It sounds horrible that God would send punishment lasting for generations. Yet we are familiar with this consequence. Consider the effects of slavery and racism from generation to generation or the effects of abuse through generations of a family. Sin is not just an individual matter. The sins of parents, or even nations, have far-reaching consequences that we might perhaps interpret as God's judgment. The counterpoint to God's punishing **to the third and fourth generation** is God's steadfast love to the **thousandth generation**. God's love far exceeds God's judgment. Yet both are there. Problems arise when we lose the tension between judgment and love. On one side we get a God who is only wrathful and vengeful. On the other side we get a God who is indifferent to injustice. This tension is also part of human existence. How do we extend both mercy and justice?

5:8—The prohibition against making idols limits our ability to tie God down or to reduce God to something we are comfortable with.

5:11—The Hebrew for **wrongful use** has associations with divination; therefore misusing God's name would be using God's name unnecessarily or abusing it in a ritual way. In other words, this commandment is not about swear words, but about what we do in the Lord's name. Slavery, the Inquisition, the Holocaust, gay bashing—the list could continue indefinitely of atrocities that have been committed in the Lord's name. Perpetuating injustice in God's name constitutes wrongful use.

5:12–15—Here the motivation for Sabbath is the memory of slavery (instead of creation in Exod. 20:10–11). The word for **labor** is the same root in Hebrew as *slave*. Thus, labor and rest is patterned after slavery and release. Resting from work is becoming harder and harder in a society that demands our full time. For many, work may feel like slavery. How can we pattern our lives to include rest and release?

5:16—Honoring one's parents wasn't just a matter of being nice to them. For the Israelites, there were no retirement homes or Social Security. Care by one's children meant survival past one's productive years. The care of those most vulnerable in society is an overarching theme of Deuteronomy. Even with retirement homes and Social Security, the care of the elderly who are economically vulnerable should still be our concern.

5:17—Although often translated "You shall not kill," the prohibition is much more restricted. The word elsewhere in the Old Testament occurs only in instances of one-on-one violence such as premeditated murder or manslaughter. This command is not a prohibition against killing in warfare (cf. 20:10–13) or against capital punishment (cf. 13:5; 17:7; 21:21).

5:18—*Adultery* meant different things for men and women in the ancient world. A woman's sexual activity was restricted and controlled, first

19 Neither shall you steal.

20 Neither shall you bear false witness against your neighbor.

21 Neither shall you covet your neighbor's wife. Neither shall you desire your neighbor's house, or field, or male or female slave, or ox, or donkey, or anything that belongs to your neighbor.

Moses the Mediator of God's Will

22 These words the LORD spoke with a loud voice to your whole assembly at the mountain, out of the fire, the cloud, and the thick darkness, and he added no more. He wrote them on two stone tablets, and gave them to me. 23 When you heard the voice out of the darkness, while the mountain was burning with fire, you approached me, all the heads of your tribes and your elders; 24 and you said, "Look, the LORD our God has shown us his glory and greatness, and we have heard his voice out of the fire. Today we have seen that God may speak to someone and the person may still live. 25 So now why should we die? For this great fire will consume us; if we hear the voice of the LORD our God any longer, we shall die. 26 For who is there of all flesh that has heard the voice of the living God speaking out of fire, as we have, and remained alive? 27 Go near, you yourself, and hear all that the LORD our God will say. Then tell us everything that the LORD our God tells you, and we will listen and do it."

28 The LORD heard your words when you spoke to me, and the LORD said to me: "I have heard the words of this people, which they have spoken to you; they are right in all that they have spoken. 29 If only they had such a mind as this, to fear me and to keep all my commandments always, so that it might go well with them and with their children forever! 30 Go say to them, 'Return to your tents.' 31 But you, stand here by me, and I will tell you all the commandments, the statutes and the ordinances, that you shall teach them, so that they may do them in the land that I am giving them to possess." 32 You must therefore be careful to do as the LORD your God has commanded you; you shall not turn to the right or to the left. 33 You must follow exactly the path that the LORD your God has commanded you, so that you may live, and that it may go well with you, and that you may live long in the land that you are to possess.

---

by her father, then by her husband. A woman was guilty of adultery if she had intercourse (consensual or otherwise) with any man other than her husband. A man, however, could have intercourse with a woman who was not another man's wife, e.g., a prostitute. Women have rightly protested this double standard. Sexual fidelity should be a standard for everyone.

5:19—Stealing is taking something (property or persons) from another that is not yours. Theft creates inequity since it increases the goods of one by depleting the goods of another. Stealing is not done only by individuals, but is also practiced by corporations and nations. We should be concerned not only with individual offenses, but also corporate offenses.

5:20—This commandment is not generally about lying but about courtroom practice. In a community created by God, there needs to be an arena where truth is told, a place where spin doctors are not allowed. There is a saying about "speaking truth to power." Those who have power are adept at presenting a distorted picture of reality. If our current justice system is not always the place where reality is reliably described, perhaps communities of faith can be places of truthful witness.

5:21—Deuteronomy needs two words for the last commandment (cf. Exod. 20:17). *Covet* is about wanting and trying to obtain, maybe damaging what is wanted in the attempt. As in Exodus, it is clear that this command is directed toward men. Here, unlike Exodus, the wife is set apart from other property items, suggesting she not be considered as property (see note at Deut. 22:13–29). *Desire* is about craving, in this instance what someone else owns. Such craving is clearly destructive. The damage to our society from our cravings for what others possess (their fame, stock portfolio, business interests, market share) is bad enough. But the cravings of nations are even more damaging. One nation's craving for another nation's land, oil, minerals inevitably leads to war, since force is the only way to satisfy the craving. What would it mean for governments to follow this commandment?

The Great Commandment

6 Now this is the commandment—the statutes and the ordinances—that the LORD your God charged me to teach you to observe in the land that you are about to cross into and occupy, ²so that you and your children and your children's children may fear the LORD your God all the days of your life, and keep all his decrees and his commandments that I am commanding you, so that your days may be long. ³Hear therefore, O Israel, and observe them diligently, so that it may go well with you, and so that you may multiply greatly in a land flowing with milk and honey, as the LORD, the God of your ancestors, has promised you.

4 Hear, O Israel: The LORD is our God, the LORD alone.*ᵃ* ⁵You shall love the LORD your God with all your heart, and with all your soul, and with all your might. ⁶Keep these words that I am commanding you today in your heart. ⁷Recite them to your children and talk about them when you are at home and when you are away, when you lie down and when you rise. ⁸Bind them as a sign on your hand, fix them as an emblemᵇ on your forehead, ⁹and write them on the doorposts of your house and on your gates.

Caution against Disobedience

10 When the LORD your God has brought you into the land that he swore to your ancestors, to Abraham, to Isaac, and to Jacob, to give you—a land with fine, large cities that you did not build, ¹¹houses filled with all sorts of goods that you did not fill, hewn cisterns that you did not hew, vineyards and olive groves that you did not plant—and when you have eaten your fill, ¹²take care that you do not forget the LORD, who brought you out of the land of Egypt, out of the house of slavery. ¹³The LORD your God you shall fear; him you shall serve, and by his name alone you shall swear. ¹⁴Do not follow other gods, any of the gods of the peoples who are all around you, ¹⁵because the LORD your God, who is present with you, is a jealous God. The

ᵃ Or *The LORD our God is one LORD,* or *The LORD our God, the LORD is one,* or *The LORD is our God, the LORD is one*   ᵇ Or *as a frontlet*

6:4—In Judaism, this verse is known as the Shema, which is the Hebrew word translated *Hear.* It is the masculine singular, so it's possible to interpret the subsequent commands as addressed only to men, making women exempt from covenant responsibilities. Even if women are included within the collective noun "Israel," it is clear that women's concerns are generally absent from the statutes and ordinances. We should consider that our community cannot be well ordered if the concerns of some are absent from the ordering.

There is theological debate regarding the meaning of the phrase *the LORD alone,* literally "YHWH one." Does it suggest the sense of oneness in God's being, that God is not divided in the divine self? Or does it suggest that in the midst of many gods the Israelites should exclusively worship this God alone? The ambiguity means there is no *one* answer. *All* language about God is ambiguous and can never finally have *one* meaning. There are many ways to talk of God.

6:5—Our *love* of God is another central theme in Deuteronomy (5:10; 7:9; 10:12; 11:1, 13, 22; 13:3; 19:9; 30:6, 16, 20). Love is not just about our emotional feelings toward God. Love is cove-

nant or treaty language. It expresses commitment. Thus, the people are to commit themselves to God with all their "heart, soul, and strength." The New Testament adds "all your mind." In Hebrew, "heart" conveys what we associate with "mind." The heart is the center of will, volition, and decision making. To love with one's whole heart is to commit all of one's self to another. The triad of "heart, soul, strength" means there is no part that is not focused and centered on this relationship. This means you cannot separate feelings and actions. You cannot say, "I love God," but then not express that in outward actions.

6:7–9—If one follows these injunctions, there will never be a time when one is not considering God's will. What are the implications of this kind of focus?

6:11—This image about entering the land (cf. Josh. 24:13) will later be inverted and become an image of leaving the land (Amos 5:11).

6:12–13—*Slavery* and *serve* are from the same Hebrew root. A concern is whom the Hebrews will serve, Pharaoh or God. This is similar to Jesus' injunction that one cannot serve two masters (Matt. 6:24; Luke 16:13).

anger of the LORD your God would be kindled against you and he would destroy you from the face of the earth.

16 Do not put the LORD your God to the test, as you tested him at Massah. 17 You must diligently keep the commandments of the LORD your God, and his decrees, and his statutes that he has commanded you. 18 Do what is right and good in the sight of the LORD, so that it may go well with you, and so that you may go in and occupy the good land that the LORD swore to your ancestors to give you, 19 thrusting out all your enemies from before you, as the LORD has promised.

20 When your children ask you in time to come, "What is the meaning of the decrees and the statutes and the ordinances that the LORD our God has commanded you?" 21 then you shall say to your children, "We were Pharaoh's slaves in Egypt, but the LORD brought us out of Egypt with a mighty hand. 22 The LORD displayed before our eyes great and awesome signs and wonders against Egypt, against Pharaoh and all his household. 23 He brought us out from there in order to bring us in, to give us the land that he promised on oath to our ancestors. 24 Then the LORD commanded us to observe all these statutes, to fear the LORD our God, for our lasting good, so as to keep us alive, as is now the case. 25 If we diligently observe this entire commandment before the LORD our God, as he has commanded us, we will be in the right."

A Chosen People

7 When the LORD your God brings you into the land that you are about to enter and occupy, and he clears away many nations before you—the Hittites, the Girgashites, the Amorites, the Canaanites, the Perizzites, the Hivites, and the Jebusites, seven nations mightier and more numerous than you— 2 and when the LORD your God gives them over to you and you defeat them, then you must utterly destroy them. Make no covenant with them and show them no mercy. 3 Do not intermarry with them, giving your daughters to their sons or taking their daughters for your sons, 4 for that would turn away your children from following me, to serve other gods. Then the anger of the LORD would be kindled against you, and he would destroy you quickly. 5 But this is how you must deal with them: break down their altars, smash their pillars, hew down their sacred poles,[a] and burn their idols with fire. 6 For you are a people holy to the LORD your God; the LORD your God has chosen you out of all the peoples on earth to be his people, his treasured possession.

7 It was not because you were more numerous than any other people that the LORD set his heart on you and chose you—for you were the fewest of all peoples. 8 It was because the LORD loved you and kept the oath that he swore to your ancestors, that the LORD has brought you out with a mighty hand, and redeemed

[a] Heb Asherim

7:1–5—The land was not empty when the Hebrews arrived. They are commanded to destroy the centers of worship of the inhabitants of the land. This is similar to traditional European/American Christian attitudes toward nonwhite, non-Christian cultures. It was thought that native populations needed to be Christianized and thereby civilized. The result was the destruction of much of native culture. A tragedy and irony is that Israel will later face the same problem—forced assimilation to Babylonian culture and the threat of the destruction of their culture. Are total acceptance and total rejection of another culture

the only options? For example, how are Christians and Muslims, Western and Eastern worlds, to coexist without each wanting to eliminate the other? Working toward openness to other cultures and religious perspectives without abandoning one's own is the challenge for today (see also notes at 12:2, 3–4).

7:7–8—Just as our love for God is important (see note at 6:5), so is God's love for us (4:37; 5:10; 10:15; 23:5). As elsewhere throughout the Bible, God's love is unmerited. God does not love us because we are wonderful or deserving. In fact,

you from the house of slavery, from the hand of Pharaoh king of Egypt. ⁹Know therefore that the LORD your God is God, the faithful God who maintains covenant loyalty with those who love him and keep his commandments, to a thousand generations, ¹⁰ and who repays in their own person those who reject him. He does not delay but repays in their own person those who reject him. ¹¹ Therefore, observe diligently the commandment—the statutes and the ordinances—that I am commanding you today.

Blessings for Obedience

12 If you heed these ordinances, by diligently observing them, the LORD your God will maintain with you the covenant loyalty that he swore to your ancestors; ¹³ he will love you, bless you, and multiply you; he will bless the fruit of your womb and the fruit of your ground, your grain and your wine and your oil, the increase of your cattle and the issue of your flock, in the land that he swore to your ancestors to give you. ¹⁴ You shall be the most blessed of peoples, with neither sterility nor barrenness among you or your livestock. ¹⁵ The LORD will turn away from you every illness; all the dread diseases of Egypt that you experienced, he will not inflict on you, but he will lay them on all who hate you. ¹⁶ You shall devour all the peoples that the LORD your God is giving over to you, showing them no pity; you shall not serve their gods, for that would be a snare to you.

17 If you say to yourself, "These nations are more numerous than I; how can I dispossess them?" ¹⁸ do not be afraid of them. Just remember what the LORD your God did to Pharaoh and to all Egypt, ¹⁹ the great trials that your eyes saw, the signs and wonders, the mighty hand and the outstretched arm by which the LORD your God brought you out. The LORD your God will do the same to all the peoples of whom you are afraid. ²⁰ Moreover, the LORD your God will send the pestilence*ᵃ* against them, until even the survivors and the fugitives are destroyed. ²¹ Have no dread of them, for the LORD your God, who is present with you, is a great and awesome God. ²² The LORD your God will clear away these nations before you little by little; you will not be able to make a quick end of them, otherwise the wild animals would become too numerous for you. ²³ But the LORD your God will give them over to you, and throw them into great panic, until they are destroyed. ²⁴ He will hand their kings over to you and you shall blot out their name from under heaven; no one will be able to stand against you, until you have destroyed them. ²⁵ The images of their gods you shall burn with fire. Do not covet the silver or the gold that is on them and take it for yourself, because you could be ensnared by it; for it is abhorrent to the LORD your God. ²⁶ Do not bring an abhorrent thing into your house, or you will be set apart for destruction like it. You must utterly detest and abhor it, for it is set apart for destruction.

A Warning Not to Forget God in Prosperity

8 This entire commandment that I command you today you must

ᵃ Or *hornets*: Meaning of Heb uncertain

God's love is often focused on those who are fewest or weakest.

7:9–10—There is always tension between God's mercy and judgment. Note that, as in 5:9–10, the love of God far exceeds (*to the thousandth generation*) God's judgment (*in their own person*). Does our love far exceed our sense of judgment?

7:22—This verse seems to contradict 7:2. The reason seems strange, but suggests that the elimination of one threat raises another. Wiping out towns and cities too quickly will leave insufficient population to defend against or control wild animals. Today we experience unintended consequences of some actions. An action that at the time seems beneficial can later have a negative impact. Combustion engines lead to air pollution. Security measures lead to violation of civil rights. Can this be avoided?

diligently observe, so that you may live and increase, and go in and occupy the land that the LORD promised on oath to your ancestors. ²Remember the long way that the LORD your God has led you these forty years in the wilderness, in order to humble you, testing you to know what was in your heart, whether or not you would keep his commandments. ³He humbled you by letting you hunger, then by feeding you with manna, with which neither you nor your ancestors were acquainted, in order to make you understand that one does not live by bread alone, but by every word that comes from the mouth of the LORD.ᵃ ⁴The clothes on your back did not wear out and your feet did not swell these forty years. ⁵Know then in your heart that as a parent disciplines a child so the LORD your God disciplines you. ⁶Therefore keep the commandments of the LORD your God, by walking in his ways and by fearing him. ⁷For the LORD your God is bringing you into a good land, a land with flowing streams, with springs and underground waters welling up in valleys and hills, ⁸a land of wheat and barley, of vines and fig trees and pomegranates, a land of olive trees and honey, ⁹a land where you may eat bread without scarcity, where you will lack nothing, a land whose stones are iron and from whose hills you may mine copper. ¹⁰You shall eat your fill and bless the LORD your God for the good land that he has given you.

11 Take care that you do not forget the LORD your God, by failing to keep his commandments, his ordinances, and his statutes, which I am commanding you today. ¹²When you have eaten your fill and have built fine houses and live in them, ¹³and when your herds and flocks have multiplied, and your silver and gold is multiplied, and all that you have is multiplied, ¹⁴then do not exalt yourself, forgetting the LORD your God, who brought you out of the land of Egypt, out of the house of slavery, ¹⁵who led you through the great and terrible wilder-

ᵃ Or by anything that the LORD decrees

8:2—The theme of God's testing of individuals or people occurs throughout the Old Testament (Gen. 22:1; Exod. 15:25; Judg. 3:1; Ps. 139:23 and throughout Psalms; Jer. 9:7). Testing usually involves a negative experience, such as cruelty or deprivation. The aim of this test is to know whether or not the people will obey God (see Deut. 6:16; 8:16; 13:3; 33:8). Theologically this suggests we consider the possibility of a divine test when we face negative experiences (see notes at 8:5; 28:1–68). However, this does not suggest that every negative experience be interpreted as a test. Many may find this view of God to be problematic.

8:3—This verse should not be misused to suggest that people therefore don't need bread (Matt. 25:35; Jas. 2:16).

8:4—This verse provides another image of God's care for the people in the wilderness (see note at 1:31). For forty years, not only did God provide food and water, but their clothes did not wear out, nor did their feet swell. What an image for God's sufficient grace (2 Cor. 12:9)! The wilderness is not a place that we can avoid or escape. It is part of the journey. The hope this image offers is that we will not totally be done in by the experience. God gives us what we need in order to survive. In the most extreme circumstances—war, famine, oppression—survival will be reduced to meeting basic needs.

8:5—Remember being disciplined by your parents as a child or disciplining your children as a parent. Now imagine God as the disciplining parent. We might also interpret negative experiences as divine discipline (see notes at 8:2; 28:1–8). However, children who have been abused by their parents may find this image of God problematic.

8:12–20—Prosperity presents its own set of theological difficulties. In adversity we question God's presence with us (see Exod. 17:1–7). In prosperity our sense of self-sufficiency leads us to push God aside (see note at Deut. 4:25). But even the power to accumulate wealth comes from God, and what God has given, God can take away. Does anyone else despair for the U.S., the world's *great superpower*? Surely we have built fine houses and multiplied silver and gold. Have we forgotten God and gone after other gods (e.g., the free market, national self-interest)? Don't we say, individually and corporately, that *My power and the might of my own hand have gotten me this wealth*? Why do we think we are invulnerable? Do we consider that one day God might judge us and cause us to perish?

ness, an arid wasteland with poisonous[a] snakes and scorpions. He made water flow for you from flint rock, 16 and fed you in the wilderness with manna that your ancestors did not know, to humble you and to test you, and in the end to do you good. 17 Do not say to yourself, "My power and the might of my own hand have gotten me this wealth." 18 But remember the LORD your God, for it is he who gives you power to get wealth, so that he may confirm his covenant that he swore to your ancestors, as he is doing today. 19 If you do forget the LORD your God and follow other gods to serve and worship them, I solemnly warn you today that you shall surely perish. 20 Like the nations that the LORD is destroying before you, so shall you perish, because you would not obey the voice of the LORD your God.

The Consequences of Rebelling against God

9 Hear, O Israel! You are about to cross the Jordan today, to go in and dispossess nations larger and mightier than you, great cities, fortified to the heavens, 2 a strong and tall people, the offspring of the Anakim, whom you know. You have heard it said of them, "Who can stand up to the Anakim?" 3 Know then today that the LORD your God is the one who crosses over before you as a devouring fire; he will defeat them and subdue them before you, so that you may dispossess and destroy them quickly, as the LORD has promised you.

4 When the LORD your God thrusts them out before you, do not say to yourself, "It is because of my righteousness that the LORD has brought me in to occupy this land"; it is rather because of the wickedness of these nations that the LORD is dispossessing them before you. 5 It is not because of your righteousness or the uprightness of your heart that you are going in to occupy their land; but because of the wickedness of these nations the LORD your God is dispossessing them before you, in order to fulfill the promise that the LORD made on oath to your ancestors, to Abraham, to Isaac, and to Jacob.

6 Know, then, that the LORD your God is not giving you this good land to occupy because of your righteousness; for you are a stubborn people. 7 Remember and do not forget how you provoked the LORD your God to wrath in the wilderness; you have been rebellious against the LORD from the day you came out of the land of Egypt until you came to this place.

8 Even at Horeb you provoked the LORD to wrath, and the LORD was so angry with you that he was ready to destroy you. 9 When I went up the mountain to receive the stone tablets, the tablets of the covenant that the LORD made with you, I remained on the mountain forty days and forty nights; I neither ate bread nor drank water. 10 And the LORD gave me the two stone tablets written with the finger of God; on them were all the words that the LORD had spoken

[a] Or fiery; Heb seraph

9:4–5—The *wickedness* of the inhabitants is the theological justification for their destruction. We justified our occupation of an inhabited land because of the *wickedness* of the Native Americans. Other countries justify their occupations because of the *wickedness* of the people. It's an appalling ethic and an appalling theological tension. On the one hand, the land is a gift, the fulfillment of a promise, and a practical necessity. But others have paid a great price on our behalf. We can justify such actions by seeing others as damaged or disordered, but only by denying that they are also God's creatures (see note at 2:5).

9:8–10:11—The purpose of this recital is to illustrate that Israel is, in fact, a stubborn people (9:6). There is no way Israel can pass the buck or deny it. We could also list the various sins of the church in the course of two thousand years: Inquisition, slavery, destruction of native cultures, war, oppression, sexual abuse by clergy, just to name a few. Being God's own possession does not mean that we are not at times wicked and stubborn. Consider how the church can confess its sins.

to you at the mountain out of the fire on the day of the assembly. ¹¹ At the end of forty days and forty nights the LORD gave me the two stone tablets, the tablets of the covenant. ¹² Then the LORD said to me, "Get up, go down quickly from here, for your people whom you have brought from Egypt have acted corruptly. They have been quick to turn from the way that I commanded them; they have cast an image for themselves." ¹³ Furthermore the LORD said to me, "I have seen that this people is indeed a stubborn people. ¹⁴ Let me alone that I may destroy them and blot out their name from under heaven; and I will make of you a nation mightier and more numerous than they."

¹⁵ So I turned and went down from the mountain, while the mountain was ablaze; the two tablets of the covenant were in my two hands. ¹⁶ Then I saw that you had indeed sinned against the LORD your God, by casting for yourselves an image of a calf; you had been quick to turn from the way that the LORD had commanded you. ¹⁷ So I took hold of the two tablets and flung them from my two hands, smashing them before your eyes. ¹⁸ Then I lay prostrate before the LORD as before, forty days and forty nights; I neither ate bread nor drank water, because of all the sin you had committed, provoking the LORD by doing what was evil in his sight. ¹⁹ For I was afraid that the anger that the LORD bore against you was so fierce that he would destroy you. But the LORD listened to me that time also. ²⁰ The LORD was so angry with Aaron that he was ready to destroy him, but I interceded also on behalf of Aaron at that same time. ²¹ Then I took the sinful thing you had made, the calf, and burned it with fire and crushed it, grinding it thoroughly, until it was reduced to dust; and I threw the dust of it into the stream that runs down the mountain.

²² At Taberah also, and at Massah, and at Kibroth-hattaavah, you provoked the LORD to wrath. ²³ And when the LORD sent you from Kadesh-barnea, saying, "Go up and occupy the land that I have given you," you rebelled against the command of the LORD your God, neither trusting him nor obeying him. ²⁴ You have been rebellious against the LORD as long as he has[a] known you.

²⁵ Throughout the forty days and forty nights that I lay prostrate before the LORD when the LORD intended to destroy you, ²⁶ I prayed to the LORD and said, "Lord GOD, do not destroy the people who are your very own possession, whom you redeemed in your greatness, whom you brought out of Egypt with a mighty hand. ²⁷ Remember your servants, Abraham, Isaac, and Jacob; pay no attention to the stubbornness of this people, their wickedness and their sin, ²⁸ otherwise the land from which you have brought us might say, 'Because the LORD was not able to bring them into the land that he promised them, and because he hated them, he has brought them out to let them die in the wilderness.' ²⁹ For they are the people of your very own possession, whom you brought out by your great power and by your outstretched arm."

The Second Pair of Tablets

10 At that time the LORD said to me, "Carve out two tablets of stone like the former ones, and come up to me on the mountain, and make an ark of wood. ² I will write on the tablets the words that were on the former tablets, which you smashed, and you shall put them in the ark." ³ So I made an ark of acacia wood, cut two tablets of stone like the former ones, and went up the mountain with the two tablets in my hand. ⁴ Then he wrote on the tablets the same words as before, the ten commandments[b] that the LORD had spoken to you on the mountain out of the fire on the day of the assembly; and

[a] Sam Gk: MT I have   [b] Heb the ten words

the LORD gave them to me. [5] So I turned and came down from the mountain, and put the tablets in the ark that I had made; and there they are, as the LORD commanded me.

[6] (The Israelites journeyed from Beeroth-bene-jaakan[a] to Moserah. There Aaron died, and there he was buried; his son Eleazar succeeded him as priest. [7] From there they journeyed to Gudgodah, and from Gudgodah to Jotbathah, a land with flowing streams. [8] At that time the LORD set apart the tribe of Levi to carry the ark of the covenant of the LORD, to stand before the LORD to minister to him, and to bless in his name, to this day. [9] Therefore Levi has no allotment or inheritance with his kindred; the LORD is his inheritance, as the LORD your God promised him.)

[10] I stayed on the mountain forty days and forty nights, as I had done the first time. And once again the LORD listened to me. The LORD was unwilling to destroy you. [11] The LORD said to me, "Get up, go on your journey at the head of the people, that they may go in and occupy the land that I swore to their ancestors to give them."

The Essence of the Law

[12] So now, O Israel, what does the LORD your God require of you? Only to fear the LORD your God, to walk in all his ways, to love him, to serve the LORD your God with all your heart and with all your soul, [13] and to keep the commandments of the LORD your God[b] and his decrees that I am commanding you today, for your own well-being. [14] Although heaven and the heaven of heavens belong to the LORD your God, the earth with all that is in it, [15] yet the LORD set his heart in love on your ancestors alone and chose you, their descendants after them, out of all the peoples, as it is today. [16] Circumcise, then, the foreskin of your heart, and do not be stubborn any longer. [17] For the LORD your God is God of gods and Lord of lords, the great God, mighty and awesome, who is not partial and takes no bribe, [18] who executes justice for the orphan and the widow, and who loves the strangers, providing them food and clothing. [19] You shall also love the stranger, for you were strangers in the land of Egypt. [20] You shall fear the LORD your God; him alone you shall worship; to him you shall hold fast, and by his name you shall swear. [21] He is your praise; he is your God, who has done for you these great and awesome things that your own eyes have seen. [22] Your ancestors went down to Egypt seventy persons; and now the LORD your God has made you as numerous as the stars in heaven.

a Or the wells of the Bene-jaakan   *b Q Ms Gk Syr: MT lacks your God*

10:12–13—What does God *require* of us? (1) *to fear . . . God*; (2) *to walk in [God's] ways*; (3) *to love [God]* (see note at 6:5); (4) *to serve . . . God* (see note at 6:12–13); (5) *to keep [God's] commandments* (cf. Mic. 6:8). It sounds so simple. But it's not. One of the tricky aspects is defining what each of these words means. Many of the splits within the church have come because of different understandings of what it means to love God or walk in God's ways. What is your understanding of these requirements? How have differences over such definitions affected your faith community? Your own life?

10:16—To have a circumcised heart suggests that a person will fully serve God inwardly as well as outwardly (cf. 30:6; Jer. 4:4; 9:25–26; Ezek. 44:7, 9). However, since only men were circumcised in the flesh, a question is whether only men would be interested in the metaphor. Can this be a helpful image for women, especially in light of the violence against women in some cultures in the form of female genital mutilation? Is there another image that can be meaningful to both men and women?

10:17–18—Two aspects of God are emphasized: (1) God is superlative; (2) God wants perfect justice for those who are most socially and economically disadvantaged. God's greatness is linked with social justice. Therefore, Israel's greatness and our greatness are also linked with social justice.

10:19—Israel's experience of being a stranger was destructive. Instead of being a victim who continues the violence by victimizing others, Israel is to transform fear and hate into love.

Rewards for Obedience

11 You shall love the LORD your God, therefore, and keep his charge, his decrees, his ordinances, and his commandments always. ² Remember today that it was not your children (who have not known or seen the discipline of the LORD your God), but it is you who must acknowledge his greatness, his mighty hand and his outstretched arm, ³ his signs and his deeds that he did in Egypt to Pharaoh, the king of Egypt, and to all his land; ⁴ what he did to the Egyptian army, to their horses and chariots, how he made the water of the Red Sea*a* flow over them as they pursued you, so that the LORD has destroyed them to this day; ⁵ what he did to you in the wilderness, until you came to this place; ⁶ and what he did to Dathan and Abiram, sons of Eliab son of Reuben, how in the midst of all Israel the earth opened its mouth and swallowed them up, along with their households, their tents, and every living being in their company; ⁷ for it is your own eyes that have seen every great deed that the LORD did.

8 Keep, then, this entire commandment that I am commanding you today, so that you may have strength to go in and occupy the land that you are crossing over to occupy, ⁹ and so that you may live long in the land that the LORD swore to your ancestors to give them and to their descendants, a land flowing with milk and honey. ¹⁰ For the land that you are about to enter to occupy is not like the land of Egypt, from which you have come, where you sow your seed and irrigate by foot like a vegetable garden. ¹¹ But the land that you are crossing over to occupy is a land of hills and valleys, watered by rain from the sky, ¹² a land that the LORD your God looks after. The eyes of the LORD your God are always on it, from the beginning of the year to the end of the year.

13 If you will only heed his every commandment*b* that I am commanding you today—loving the LORD your God, and serving him with all your heart and with all your soul— ¹⁴ then he*c* will give the rain for your land in its season, the early rain and the later rain, and you will gather in your grain, your wine, and your oil; ¹⁵ and he*c* will give grass in your fields for your livestock, and you will eat your fill. ¹⁶ Take care, or you will be seduced into turning away, serving other gods and worshiping them, ¹⁷ for then the anger of the LORD will be kindled against you and he will shut up the heavens, so that there will be no rain and the land will yield no fruit; then you will perish quickly off the good land that the LORD is giving you.

18 You shall put these words of mine in your heart and soul, and you shall bind them as a sign on your hand, and fix them as an emblem*d* on your forehead. ¹⁹ Teach them to your children, talking about them when you are at home and

a Or *Sea of Reeds*   *b* Compare Gk: Heb *my commandments*   *c* Sam Gk Vg: MT *I*   *d* Or *as a frontlet*

11:1–7—The repetition of the charge to keep the commandments hints that doing so is neither natural nor easy. If it was hard for Israel, who had seen God's great deeds, how much harder is it for us, for whom other loyalties hide God's activity and self-sufficiency and greed at the expense of others are common.

11:13–17—Obedience is linked with the well-being of the land. If the people are obedient, then God will give the rain. Conversely, drought becomes a sign of God's punishment for disobedience (28:22; 2 Sam. 1:21; 1 Kgs. 8:35; 2 Chr. 6:26; 7:13; Isa. 5:6; Jer. 5:24–25; 14:1–4; Amos 4:7). Injustice and oppression also affect the nonhuman world (cf. Isa. 24:1–13, 19–20;

Jer. 4:23–28; Joel 1:4, 10–12, 17–20), but the rewards of peace and justice also extend to the earth (see Isa. 30:23–26; 43:18–21; 44:3; Joel 2:22–26). Human rights and the environment are issues that must be joined together.

11:18–25—Repetition is a hallmark of Deuteronomic style. The repetition leaves the reader or hearer of the book with a few key items in mind (such as do/keep/observe, listen/hear/obey) and the typical objects of those verbs (law, commandments, statutes, ordinances). This rhetorical effect produces an ethical and theological result: one who really does keep the law, keeps it carefully, and keeps it within the primary time frames of the book: now, today, always.

when you are away, when you lie down and when you rise. ²⁰ Write them on the doorposts of your house and on your gates, ²¹ so that your days and the days of your children may be multiplied in the land that the LORD swore to your ancestors to give them, as long as the heavens are above the earth.

22 If you will diligently observe this entire commandment that I am commanding you, loving the LORD your God, walking in all his ways, and holding fast to him, ²³ then the LORD will drive out all these nations before you, and you will dispossess nations larger and mightier than yourselves. ²⁴ Every place on which you set foot shall be yours; your territory shall extend from the wilderness to the Lebanon and from the River, the river Euphrates, to the Western Sea. ²⁵ No one will be able to stand against you; the LORD your God will put the fear and dread of you on all the land on which you set foot, as he promised you.

26 See, I am setting before you today a blessing and a curse: ²⁷ the blessing, if you obey the commandments of the LORD your God that I am commanding you today; ²⁸ and the curse, if you do not obey the commandments of the LORD your God, but turn from the way that I am commanding you today, to follow other gods that you have not known.

29 When the LORD your God has brought you into the land that you are entering to occupy, you shall set the blessing on Mount Gerizim and the curse on Mount Ebal. ³⁰ As you know, they are beyond the Jordan, some distance to the west, in the land of the Canaanites who live in the Arabah, opposite Gilgal, beside the oak[a] of Moreh.

31 When you cross the Jordan to go in to occupy the land that the LORD your God is giving you, and when you occupy it and live in it, ³² you must diligently observe all the statutes and ordinances that I am setting before you today.

Pagan Shrines to Be Destroyed

12 These are the statutes and ordinances that you must diligently observe in the land that the LORD, the God of your ancestors, has given you to occupy all the days that you live on the earth.

2 You must demolish completely all the places where the nations whom you are about to dispossess served their gods, on the mountain heights, on the hills, and under every leafy tree. ³ Break down their altars, smash their pillars,

[a] Gk Syr: Compare Gen 12.6; Heb oaks or terebinths

11:26–29—Deuteronomy presents a clear choice. *Either* we love God and neighbor *or* destruction awaits. The choice is clear-cut in Deuteronomy. Other traditions suggest that it is not so clear (cf. Job, Ecclesiastes).

12:1—Here begins the core of the *Deuteronomic law code*. It is believed that some form of chaps. 12–26, discovered in the temple and confirmed by Huldah, became the basis of Josiah's reforms (2 Kgs. 22–23). The themes and theology of this expression of the covenant also provide the framework for the Deuteronomistic History (Judges–2 Kings), ultimately as a way to explain the catastrophe of the exile in 587 BCE (see introduction to Deuteronomy).

12:2—A central tenet of Deuteronomic theology is the worship of the Lord alone (5:8–9; 6:4, 13–14). This raises the issue of *syncretism*, or how we are alike and different from our neighbors. Deuteronomy wants to keep cultures totally separate, by creating a tightly drawn and rigid boundary between Israel and everyone else. But a looser and more porous boundary is also possible (see Ruth, Esther). Where do we draw our boundaries? We desire inclusivity. But are there points where we say, "No further"? Some claim that women who use nonmasculine imagery for God have crossed that line; this raises another question: who sets the boundary? How can we be loyal to the Lord and inclusive of diverse experiences of the Lord?

12:3–4—There is now evidence to suggest that these *foreign* practices were once considered legitimate Yahwistic practice. A question in missions and evangelism is how to respond to indigenous worship practices. How does traditional Western Christianity respond to native beliefs and practices from Africa, Asia, the Americas, and the Pacific? Our beliefs and practices will always in some way reflect local context. *Who* decides what are legitimate and illegitimate forms of worship? (See note at 12:2.)

burn their sacred poles[a] with fire, and hew down the idols of their gods, and thus blot out their name from their places. 4 You shall not worship the LORD your God in such ways. 5 But you shall seek the place that the LORD your God will choose out of all your tribes as his habitation to put his name there. You shall go there, 6 bringing there your burnt offerings and your sacrifices, your tithes and your donations, your votive gifts, your freewill offerings, and the firstlings of your herds and flocks. 7 And you shall eat there in the presence of the LORD your God, you and your households together, rejoicing in all the undertakings in which the LORD your God has blessed you.

8 You shall not act as we are acting here today, all of us according to our own desires, 9 for you have not yet come into the rest and the possession that the LORD your God is giving you. 10 When you cross over the Jordan and live in the land that the LORD your God is allotting to you, and when he gives you rest from your enemies all around so that you live in safety, 11 then you shall bring everything that I command you to the place that the LORD your God will choose as a dwelling for his name: your burnt offerings and your sacrifices, your tithes and your donations, and all your choice votive gifts that you vow to the LORD. 12 And you shall rejoice before the LORD your God, you together with your sons and your daughters, your male and female slaves, and the Levites who reside in your towns (since they have no allotment or inheritance with you).

A Prescribed Place of Worship

13 Take care that you do not offer your burnt offerings at any place you happen to see. 14 But only at the place that the LORD will choose in one of your tribes—there you shall offer your burnt offerings and there you shall do everything I command you.

15 Yet whenever you desire you may slaughter and eat meat within any of your towns, according to the blessing that the LORD your God has given you; the unclean and the clean may eat of it, as they would of gazelle or deer. 16 The blood, however, you must not eat; you shall pour it out on the ground like water. 17 Nor may you eat within your towns the tithe of your grain, your wine, and your oil, the firstlings of your herds and your flocks, any of your votive gifts that you vow, your freewill offerings, or your donations; 18 these you shall eat in the presence of the LORD your God at the place that the LORD your God will choose, you together with your son and your daughter, your male and female slaves, and the Levites resident in your towns, rejoicing in the presence of the LORD your God in all your undertakings. 19 Take care that you do not neglect the Levite as long as you live in your land.

20 When the LORD your God enlarges your territory, as he has promised you,

[a] Heb *Asherim*

12:5–7—Another central Deuteronomic theme is the centralization of worship. But if there is a *proper* place or way of worship, other places and practices will be considered *improper*. Israel, of course, figured out that God could be worshiped outside of Jerusalem. But it was a struggle. Contemporary struggles today regarding "contemporary" and "traditional" forms of worship reflect similar concerns.

12:10—Since 9/11/01 the issue of *safety* has taken on new dimensions for Americans. Here and in 33:12, 28, safety results from God's destruction of Israel's enemies. The canon as a whole is clear that Israel's enemies are never totally destroyed and Israel is thus never totally safe. Similarly, today we will never be able to totally destroy our enemies, and thus will never be totally safe. If this is the case, what does it mean to talk about safety? What are different ways to consider what safety means?

12:12, 18—This expression of rejoicing before the Lord is one of the most inclusive statements in the Bible. Here no one is left out of the worship of God. This should be part of our vision of the proper way of worship (see note at 12:5–7).

and you say, "I am going to eat some meat," because you wish to eat meat, you may eat meat whenever you have the desire. ²¹ If the place where the Lord your God will choose to put his name is too far from you, and you slaughter as I have commanded you any of your herd or flock that the Lord has given you, then you may eat within your towns whenever you desire. ²² Indeed, just as gazelle or deer is eaten, so you may eat it; the unclean and the clean alike may eat it. ²³ Only be sure that you do not eat the blood; for the blood is the life, and you shall not eat the life with the meat. ²⁴ Do not eat it; you shall pour it out on the ground like water. ²⁵ Do not eat it, so that all may go well with you and your children after you, because you do what is right in the sight of the Lord. ²⁶ But the sacred donations that are due from you, and your votive gifts, you shall bring to the place that the Lord will choose. ²⁷ You shall present your burnt offerings, both the meat and the blood, on the altar of the Lord your God; the blood of your other sacrifices shall be poured out beside*a* the altar of the Lord your God, but the meat you may eat.

28 Be careful to obey all these words that I command you today,*b* so that it may go well with you and with your children after you forever, because you will be doing what is good and right in the sight of the Lord your God.

Warning against Idolatry

29 When the Lord your God has cut off before you the nations whom you are about to enter to dispossess them, when you have dispossessed them and live in their land, ³⁰ take care that you are not snared into imitating them, after they have been destroyed before you: do not inquire concerning their gods, saying, "How did these nations worship their gods? I also want to do the same." ³¹ You must not do the same for the Lord your God, because every abhorrent thing that the Lord hates they have done for their gods. They would even burn their sons and their daughters in the fire to their gods. ³² *a* You must diligently observe everything that I command you; do not add to it or take anything from it.

13 *d* If prophets or those who divine by dreams appear among you and promise you omens or portents, ² and the omens or the portents declared by them take place, and they say, "Let us follow other gods" (whom you have not known) "and let us serve them," ³ you must not heed the words of those prophets or those who divine by dreams; for the Lord your God is testing you, to know whether you indeed love the Lord your God with all your heart and soul. ⁴ The Lord your God you shall follow, him alone you shall fear, his commandments you shall keep, his voice you shall obey, him you shall serve, and to him you shall hold fast. ⁵ But those prophets or those who divine by dreams shall be put to death for having spoken treason against the Lord your God—who brought you out of the land of Egypt

a Or *on*   *b* Gk Sam Syr: MT lacks *today*   *c* Ch 13.1 in Heb   *d* Ch 13.2 in Heb

---

12:21—The centralization of worship is intended to create uniformity and eliminate deviations and plural forms of worship. Yet Deuteronomy recognized that there were exceptions, and that pragmatic considerations took priority over what might be considered ideal. Ideal worship isn't always good worship.

13:1–7—The problem of how to tell a true from a false prophet was a recurrent problem in the Old Testament (see 1 Kgs. 13, 22; Jer. 23:9–32, 28:1–17; Ezek. 13:1–14:11). This instruction does not provide a definitive solution (see note also at Deut. 18:9–23). For example, here dreams are deemed unreliable, yet elsewhere dreams are a significant means of divine communication (Gen. 28:10–17; 37:5–11; 40:5–19; 41:1–36; 42:9; Dan. 1:17; 2:1–45; 4:1–27; 5:12; 7:1). One significant criterion is that a true prophet will not lead people away from God. But what that means can be differently defined (see note at Deut. 10:12–13). The problem remains of how to determine if a message is from God or not. By what criteria does your faith community authenticate the word of the Lord?

and redeemed you from the house of slavery—to turn you from the way in which the LORD your God commanded you to walk. So you shall purge the evil from your midst.

6 If anyone secretly entices you—even if it is your brother, your father's son or[a] your mother's son, or your own son or daughter, or the wife you embrace, or your most intimate friend—saying, "Let us go worship other gods," whom neither you nor your ancestors have known, 7 any of the gods of the peoples that are around you, whether near you or far away from you, from one end of the earth to the other, 8 you must not yield to or heed any such persons. Show them no pity or compassion and do not shield them. 9 But you shall surely kill them; your own hand shall be first against them to execute them, and afterwards the hand of all the people. 10 Stone them to death for trying to turn you away from the LORD your God, who brought you out of the land of Egypt, out of the house of slavery. 11 Then all Israel shall hear and be afraid, and never again do any such wickedness.

12 If you hear it said about one of the towns that the LORD your God is giving you to live in, 13 that scoundrels from among you have gone out and led the inhabitants of the town astray, saying, "Let us go and worship other gods," whom you have not known, 14 then you shall inquire and make a thorough investigation. If the charge is established that such an abhorrent thing has been done among you, 15 you shall put the inhabi-

tants of that town to the sword, utterly destroying it and everything in it—even putting its livestock to the sword. 16 All of its spoil you shall gather into its public square; then burn the town and all its spoil with fire, as a whole burnt offering to the LORD your God. It shall remain a perpetual ruin, never to be rebuilt. 17 Do not let anything devoted to destruction stick to your hand, so that the LORD may turn from his fierce anger and show you compassion, and in his compassion multiply you, as he swore to your ancestors, 18 if you obey the voice of the LORD your God by keeping all his commandments that I am commanding you today, doing what is right in the sight of the LORD your God.

Pagan Practices Forbidden

14 You are children of the LORD your God. You must not lacerate yourselves or shave your forelocks for the dead. 2 For you are a people holy to the LORD your God; it is you the LORD has chosen out of all the peoples on earth to be his people, his treasured possession.

Clean and Unclean Foods

3 You shall not eat any abhorrent thing. 4 These are the animals you may eat: the ox, the sheep, the goat, 5 the deer, the gazelle, the roebuck, the wild goat, the ibex, the antelope, and the mountain-sheep. 6 Any animal that divides the hoof and has the hoof cleft in two, and chews the cud, among the animals,

a Sam Gk Compare Tg: MT lacks your father's son or

13:8–17—Apostasy was a catastrophe for the Deuteronomists because ultimately such turning away was seen as the cause of the exile. Therefore, any such activity should immediately be purged from the midst of Israel to prevent destruction from recurring (13:5; 17:7, 12; 19:13, 19; 21:9, 21; 22:21, 22, 23; 24:7). It is an unrealistic expectation to think that one can purge all evil from the midst of a community. The dangers are many: one looks for evil where it doesn't exist, the innocent are falsely accused and executed, we become intolerant. Thus the cure becomes as deadly and devastating to the

community as the disease. The challenge is how to respond to dangers that are both real and threatening without creating new threats.

14:3–21—Whatever the reason why various animals are considered clean and unclean, dietary laws end up being a marker of identity. Archaeologists distinguish an Israelite site from a Canaanite site by what animal bones remain—swine remains indicate a non-Israelite presence. Consider today the ways in which foods mark ethnic and religious identity. How does food function in your faith community?

you may eat. ⁷ Yet of those that chew the cud or have the hoof cleft you shall not eat these: the camel, the hare, and the rock badger, because they chew the cud but do not divide the hoof; they are unclean for you. ⁸ And the pig, because it divides the hoof but does not chew the cud, is unclean for you. You shall not eat their meat, and you shall not touch their carcasses.

9 Of all that live in water you may eat these: whatever has fins and scales you may eat. ¹⁰ And whatever does not have fins and scales you shall not eat; it is unclean for you.

11 You may eat any clean birds. ¹² But these are the ones that you shall not eat: the eagle, the vulture, the osprey, ¹³ the buzzard, the kite of any kind; ¹⁴ every raven of any kind; ¹⁵ the ostrich, the nighthawk, the sea gull, the hawk of any kind; ¹⁶ the little owl and the great owl, the water hen ¹⁷ and the desert owl,ᵃ the carrion vulture and the cormorant, ¹⁸ the stork, the heron of any kind; the hoopoe and the bat.ᵇ ¹⁹ And all winged insects are unclean for you; they shall not be eaten. ²⁰ You may eat any clean winged creature.

21 You shall not eat anything that dies of itself; you may give it to aliens residing in your towns for them to eat, or you may sell it to a foreigner. For you are a people holy to the LORD your God.

You shall not boil a kid in its mother's milk.

Regulations concerning Tithes

22 Set apart a tithe of all the yield of your seed that is brought in yearly from the field. ²³ In the presence of the LORD your God, in the place that he will choose as a dwelling for his name, you shall eat the tithe of your grain, your wine, and your oil, as well as the firstlings of your herd and flock, so that you may learn to fear the LORD your God always. ²⁴ But if, when the LORD your God has blessed you, the distance is so great that you are unable to transport it, because the place where the LORD your God will choose to set his name is too far away from you, ²⁵ then you may turn it into money. With the money secure in hand, go to the place that the LORD your God will choose; ²⁶ spend the money for whatever you wish—oxen, sheep, wine, strong drink, or whatever you desire. And you shall eat there in the presence of the LORD your God, you and your household rejoicing together. ²⁷ As for the Levites resident in your towns, do not neglect them, because they have no allotment or inheritance with you.

28 Every third year you shall bring out the full tithe of your produce for that year, and store it within your towns; ²⁹ the Levites, because they have no allotment or inheritance with you, as well as the resident aliens, the orphans, and the widows in your towns, may come and eat their fill so that the LORD your God may bless you in all the work that you undertake.

Laws concerning the Sabbatical Year

15 Every seventh year you shall grant a remission of debts. ² And this is the manner of the remission: every

ᵃ Or *pelican*　ᵇ Identification of several of the birds in verses 12-18 is uncertain

---

14:22–28—Most of us don't want to hear about tithing. But in the first instance, God returns the **tithe** to us to spend on whatever we wish. In the second instance, the tithe benefits the neediest in the community. Why do we find it so difficult to tithe?

15:1–11—Can such an economic vision really work? Can individuals or companies or governments *let fall* (the literal meaning of **remission**) debts when interest on those debts makes the world go round? Will we willingly meet the needs of developing countries? Or will we only view them with hostility and give them nothing? The Jubilee movement to release countries from their crushing burden of debt has not been embraced by the World Bank or the IMF but has been embraced by many church bodies. As the prophecies of Amos, Jeremiah, and Isaiah attest, subordinating moral and ethical interests to commercial interests is ultimately displeasing to God. Consider what it would mean for a free market system to include a Sabbath that considers the

creditor shall remit the claim that is held against a neighbor, not exacting it of a neighbor who is a member of the community, because the LORD's remission has been proclaimed. ³Of a foreigner you may exact it, but you must remit your claim on whatever any member of your community owes you. ⁴There will, however, be no one in need among you, because the LORD is sure to bless you in the land that the LORD your God is giving you as a possession to occupy, ⁵if only you will obey the LORD your God by diligently observing this entire commandment that I command you today. ⁶When the LORD your God has blessed you, as he promised you, you will lend to many nations, but you will not borrow; you will rule over many nations, but they will not rule over you.

7 If there is among you anyone in need, a member of your community in any of your towns within the land that the LORD your God is giving you, do not be hard-hearted or tight-fisted toward your needy neighbor. ⁸You should rather open your hand, willingly lending enough to meet the need, whatever it may be. ⁹Be careful that you do not entertain a mean thought, thinking, "The seventh year, the year of remission, is near," and therefore view your needy neighbor with hostility and give nothing; your neighbor might cry to the LORD against you, and you would incur guilt. ¹⁰Give liberally and be ungrudging when you do so, for on this account the LORD your God will bless you in all your work and in all that you undertake. ¹¹Since there will never cease to be some in need on the earth, I therefore command you, "Open your hand to the poor and needy neighbor in your land."

12 If a member of your community, whether a Hebrew man or a Hebrew woman, is sold*a* to you and works for you six years, in the seventh year you shall set that person free. ¹³And when you send a male slave*b* out from you a free person, you shall not send him out empty-handed. ¹⁴Provide liberally out of your flock, your threshing floor, and your wine press, thus giving to him some of the bounty with which the LORD your God has blessed you. ¹⁵Remember that you were a slave in the land of Egypt, and the LORD your God redeemed you; for this reason I lay this command upon you today. ¹⁶But if he says to you, "I will not go out from you," because he loves you and your household, since he is well off with you, ¹⁷then you shall take an awl and thrust it through his earlobe into the door, and he shall be your slave*c* forever.

You shall do the same with regard to your female slave.*d*

18 Do not consider it a hardship when you send them out from you free persons, because for six years they have given you services worth the wages of hired laborers; and the LORD your God will bless you in all that you do.

The Firstborn of Livestock

19 Every firstling male born of your herd and flock you shall consecrate to the LORD your God; you shall not do work with your firstling ox nor shear the firstling of your flock. ²⁰You shall eat it, you together with your household, in

a Or sells himself or herself　*b* Heb him　*c* Or bondman　*d* Or bondwoman

---

costs of human dignity and well-being, as well as market value share (cf. Matt. 16:26; Mark 8:36; Luke 9:25).

15:12–18—It is ironic that a group of former slaves had laws about slavery. That a Hebrew could be sold suggests that slavery was an economic problem for both men and women. The memory of their own abuse as debt slaves led Israel to formulate laws for the just treatment of those in debt in their own community. Slaves

are to be released in the Sabbath year and given enough resources to ensure survival until they can find other means of support. Current welfare-to-work laws are based upon similar reasoning. Considering the amount of economic debt accumulated by many poor Americans, as well as by many poor countries, we need to consider ways to release them from their burden of debt.

the presence of the LORD your God year by year at the place that the LORD will choose. 21 But if it has any defect—any serious defect, such as lameness or blindness—you shall not sacrifice it to the LORD your God; 22 within your towns you may eat it, the unclean and the clean alike, as you would a gazelle or deer. 23 Its blood, however, you must not eat; you shall pour it out on the ground like water.

The Passover Reviewed

16 Observe the month*a* of Abib by keeping the passover to the LORD your God, for in the month of Abib the LORD your God brought you out of Egypt by night. 2 You shall offer the passover sacrifice to the LORD your God, from the flock and the herd, at the place that the LORD will choose as a dwelling for his name. 3 You must not eat with it anything leavened. For seven days you shall eat unleavened bread with it—the bread of affliction—because you came out of the land of Egypt in great haste, so that all the days of your life you may remember the day of your departure from the land of Egypt. 4 No leaven shall be seen with you in all your territory for seven days; and none of the meat of what you slaughter on the evening of the first day shall remain until morning. 5 You are not permitted to offer the passover sacrifice within any of your towns that the LORD your God is giving you. 6 But at the place that the LORD your God will choose as a dwelling for his name, only there shall you offer the passover sacrifice, in the evening at sunset, the time of day when you departed from Egypt. 7 You shall cook it and eat it at the place that the LORD your God will choose; the next morning you may go back to your tents. 8 For six days you shall continue to eat unleavened bread, and on the seventh day there shall be a solemn assembly for the LORD your God, when you shall do no work.

The Festival of Weeks Reviewed

9 You shall count seven weeks; begin to count the seven weeks from the time the sickle is first put to the standing grain. 10 Then you shall keep the festival of weeks to the LORD your God, contributing a freewill offering in proportion to the blessing that you have received from the LORD your God. 11 Rejoice before the LORD your God— you and your sons and your daughters, your male and female slaves, the Levites resident in your towns, as well as the strangers, the orphans, and the widows who are among you—at the place that the LORD your God will choose as a dwelling for his name. 12 Remember that you were a slave in Egypt, and diligently observe these statutes.

The Festival of Booths Reviewed

13 You shall keep the festival of booths*b* for seven days, when you have gathered in the produce from your threshing floor and your wine press. 14 Rejoice during your festival, you and your sons and your daughters, your male and female slaves, as well as the Levites, the strangers, the orphans, and the widows resident in your towns. 15 Seven days you shall keep the festival to the LORD your God at the place that the LORD will choose; for the LORD your God will bless you in all your produce and in all your undertakings, and you shall surely celebrate.

16 Three times a year all your males shall appear before the LORD your God at the place that he will choose: at the

a Or new moon   *b* Or tabernacles; Heb *succoth*

16:1–17—The legislation for the three mandated festivals names them differently in Exod. 23:14–17 and is much longer. Such differences in legislation show that the laws can be flexible and adapt to changing circumstances. Obedient living does not look the same in every age. Just as the new generation about to enter the land needs to consider what obedient living will look like, each generation needs to consider what obedient living is for their context.

festival of unleavened bread, at the festival of weeks, and at the festival of booths.a They shall not appear before the LORD empty-handed; 17 all shall give as they are able, according to the blessing of the LORD your God that he has given you.

Municipal Judges and Officers

18 You shall appoint judges and officials throughout your tribes, in all your towns that the LORD your God is giving you, and they shall render just decisions for the people. 19 You must not distort justice; you must not show partiality; and you must not accept bribes, for a bribe blinds the eyes of the wise and subverts the cause of those who are in the right. 20 Justice, and only justice, you shall pursue, so that you may live and occupy the land that the LORD your God is giving you.

Forbidden Forms of Worship

21 You shall not plant any tree as a sacred poleb beside the altar that you make for the LORD your God; 22 nor shall you set up a stone pillar—things that the LORD your God hates.

17 You must not sacrifice to the LORD your God an ox or a sheep that has a defect, anything seriously wrong; for that is abhorrent to the LORD your God.

2 If there is found among you, in one of your towns that the LORD your God is giving you, a man or woman who does what is evil in the sight of the LORD your God, and transgresses his covenant 3 by going to serve other gods and worshiping them— whether the sun or the moon or any of the host of heaven, which I have forbidden— 4 and if it is reported to you or you hear of it, and you make a thorough inquiry, and the charge is proved true that such an abhorrent thing has occurred in Israel, 5 then you shall bring out to your gates that man or that woman who has committed this crime and you shall stone the man or woman to death. 6 On the evidence of two or three witnesses the death sentence shall be executed; a person must not be put to death on the evidence of only one witness. 7 The hands of the witnesses shall be the first raised against the person to execute the death penalty, and afterward the hands of all the people. So you shall purge the evil from your midst.

Legal Decisions by Priests and Judges

8 If a judicial decision is too difficult for you to make between one kind of bloodshed and another, one kind of legal right and another, or one kind of assault and another—any such matters of dispute in your towns—then you shall immediately go up to the place that the LORD your God will choose, 9 where you shall consult with the levitical priests and the judge who is in office in those days; they shall announce to you the decision in the case. 10 Carry out exactly the decision that they announce to you from the place that the LORD will choose, diligently observing everything they instruct you. 11 You must carry out fully the law that they interpret for you or the ruling that they announce to you; do not turn aside from the decision that they announce to you, either to the right or to the left. 12 As for anyone who presumes to disobey the priest appointed to minister there to the LORD your God, or the judge, that person shall die. So you shall purge the evil from Israel. 13 All the people will hear and be afraid, and will not act presumptuously again.

a Or tabernacles; Heb succoth b Heb Asherah

16:19–20—Justice, and only justice. These words could summarize what element of the law we must practice in order to live (Luke 10:26–28). Here the well-being of the community is dependent upon a legal system that is impartial and supports those with a just cause. Those who follow God are called to uphold right causes, even if it is not the popular position to take.

Limitations of Royal Authority

14 When you have come into the land that the LORD your God is giving you, and have taken possession of it and settled in it, and you say, "I will set a king over me, like all the nations that are around me," ¹⁵ you may indeed set over you a king whom the LORD your God will choose. One of your own community you may set as king over you; you are not permitted to put a foreigner over you, who is not of your own community. ¹⁶ Even so, he must not acquire many horses for himself, or return the people to Egypt in order to acquire more horses, since the LORD has said to you, "You must never return that way again." ¹⁷ And he must not acquire many wives for himself, or else his heart will turn away; also silver and gold he must not acquire in great quantity for himself. ¹⁸ When he has taken the throne of his kingdom, he shall have a copy of this law written for him in the presence of the levitical priests. ¹⁹ It shall remain with him and he shall read in it all the days of his life, so that he may learn to fear the LORD his God, diligently observing all the words of this law and these statutes, ²⁰ neither exalting himself above other members of the community nor turning aside from the commandment, either to the right or to the left, so that he and his descendants may reign long over his kingdom in Israel.

Privileges of Priests and Levites

18 The levitical priests, the whole tribe of Levi, shall have no allot-ment or inheritance within Israel. They may eat the sacrifices that are the LORD's portion[a] ²but they shall have no inheritance among the other members of the community; the LORD is their inheritance, as he promised them.

3 This shall be the priests' due from the people, from those offering a sacrifice, whether an ox or a sheep: they shall give to the priest the shoulder, the two jowls, and the stomach. ⁴ The first fruits of your grain, your wine, and your oil, as well as the first of the fleece of your sheep, you shall give him. ⁵ For the LORD your God has chosen Levi[b] out of all your tribes, to stand and minister in the name of the LORD, him and his sons for all time.

6 If a Levite leaves any of your towns, from wherever he has been residing in Israel, and comes to the place that the LORD will choose (and he may come whenever he wishes), ⁷ then he may minister in the name of the LORD his God, like all his fellow-Levites who stand to minister there before the LORD. ⁸ They shall have equal portions to eat, even though they have income from the sale of family possessions.[a]

Child-Sacrifice, Divination, and Magic Prohibited

9 When you come into the land that the LORD your God is giving you, you must not learn to imitate the abhorrent practices of those nations. ¹⁰ No one shall be found among you who makes a son or daughter pass through fire, or

[a] Meaning of Heb uncertain [b] Heb him

17:14–19—The law of kings is intended to limit the power and authority of the king. King Solomon violated each of the stipulations: he acquired many horses from Egypt (1 Kgs. 10:26–28); he acquired many wives (1 Kgs. 11:3–4); and he acquired great quantities of silver (1 Kgs. 10:10, 14, 17, 21–22, 27). Samuel may have had such a law in mind when he warned Israel about the danger of kings (1 Sam. 8:11–18). Deuteronomy considers excessive acquisition sinful and a cause of the division of the kingdom. Deuteronomy would consider the excessive acquisition, by companies or individuals, of our consumerist society as a sin that might eventually lead to the downfall of our society.

18:9–14—This section gives further instruction on trustworthy communication from God (see also note on 13:1–7). Although the types of divination listed are considered *foreign*, it is likely that some of them were practiced in Israel and primarily by women (see 1 Sam. 28:5–25; Ezek. 13:17–23). Although they were effective practitioners, their practices were later restricted and considered *unorthodox*. Similarly folk practices in medicine

who practices divination, or is a sooth-sayer, or an augur, or a sorcerer, **11** or one who casts spells, or who consults ghosts or spirits, or who seeks oracles from the dead. **12** For whoever does these things is abhorrent to the LORD; it is because of such abhorrent practices that the LORD your God is driving them out before you. **13** You must remain completely loyal to the LORD your God. **14** Although these nations that you are about to dispossess do give heed to soothsayers and divin-ers, as for you, the LORD your God does not permit you to do so.

A New Prophet Like Moses

15 The LORD your God will raise up for you a prophet*a* like me from among your own people; you shall heed such a prophet.*b* **16** This is what you requested of the LORD your God at Horeb on the day of the assembly when you said: "If I hear the voice of the LORD my God any more, or ever again see this great fire, I will die." **17** Then the LORD replied to me: "They are right in what they have said. **18** I will raise up for them a prophet*a* like you from among their own people; I will put my words in the mouth of the prophet,*c* who shall speak to them everything that I command. **19** Anyone who does not heed the words that the prophet*d* shall speak in my name, I myself will hold accountable. **20** But any prophet who speaks in the name of other gods, or who presumes to speak in my name a word that I have not commanded the prophet to speak—that prophet shall die." **21** You may say to yourself, "How can we recognize a word that the LORD has not spoken?" **22** If a prophet speaks in the name of the LORD but the thing does not take place or prove true, it is a word that the LORD has not spoken. The prophet has spoken it presumptuously; do not be frightened by it.

Laws concerning the Cities of Refuge

19 When the LORD your God has cut off the nations whose land the LORD your God is giving you, and you have dispossessed them and settled in their towns and in their houses, **2** you shall set apart three cities in the land that the LORD your God is giving you to possess. **3** You shall calculate the dis-tances*e* and divide into three regions the land that the LORD your God gives you as a possession, so that any homicide can flee to one of them.

4 Now this is the case of a homicide who might flee there and live, that is, someone who has killed another person unintentionally when the two had not been at enmity before: **5** Suppose some-one goes into the forest with another to cut wood, and when one of them swings the ax to cut down a tree, the head slips from the handle and strikes the other person who then dies; the killer may flee to one of these cities and live. **6** But if the distance is too great, the avenger of blood in hot anger might pursue and overtake and put the killer to death, although a death sentence was not deserved, since the two had not been at enmity before. **7** Therefore I command you: You shall set apart three cities.

a Or prophets *b* Or such prophets *c* Or mouths of the prophets *d* Heb he *e* Or prepare roads to them

---

(often traditionally practiced by women), once central, were displaced by modern medicine. Just as many folk medicines are being proven beneficial, the religious practices of those who are marginal within our communities we might also consider to be legitimate.

18:15–22—The final instruction on trustworthy intermediation uses Moses as a model. The key issues are direct communication with God and whether what is prophesied proved true. This sounds as if it solves the problem of identifying the true prophet. However, there is no external way to verify that God has spoken to someone. Even false prophets can claim that they have spoken only the words God has given them (1 Kgs. 22:6, 20–23; Ezek. 14:9–11). And how long does one wait for something to take place or prove true? A week? A year? A hundred years? A thousand years? Careful consideration needs to be given to how we distinguish between true and false words from God. It is never as simple as we might wish.

Limitations of Royal Authority

14 When you have come into the land that the LORD your God is giving you, and have taken possession of it and settled in it, and you say, "I will set a king over me, like all the nations that are around me," ¹⁵ you may indeed set over you a king whom the LORD your God will choose. One of your own community you may set as king over you; you are not permitted to put a foreigner over you, who is not of your own community. ¹⁶ Even so, he must not acquire many horses for himself, or return the people to Egypt in order to acquire more horses, since the LORD has said to you, "You must never return that way again." ¹⁷ And he must not acquire many wives for himself, or else his heart will turn away; also silver and gold he must not acquire in great quantity for himself. ¹⁸ When he has taken the throne of his kingdom, he shall have a copy of this law written for him in the presence of the levitical priests. ¹⁹ It shall remain with him and he shall read in it all the days of his life, so that he may learn to fear the LORD his God, diligently observing all the words of this law and these statutes, ²⁰ neither exalting himself above other members of the community nor turning aside from the commandment, either to the right or to the left, so that he and his descendants may reign long over his kingdom in Israel.

Privileges of Priests and Levites

18 The levitical priests, the whole tribe of Levi, shall have no allotment or inheritance within Israel. They may eat the sacrifices that are the LORD's portion^a ² but they shall have no inheritance among the other members of the community; the LORD is their inheritance, as he promised them.

3 This shall be the priests' due from the people, from those offering a sacrifice, whether an ox or a sheep: they shall give to the priest the shoulder, the two jowls, and the stomach. ⁴ The first fruits of your grain, your wine, and your oil, as well as the first of the fleece of your sheep, you shall give him. ⁵ For the LORD your God has chosen Levi^b out of all your tribes, to stand and minister in the name of the LORD, him and his sons for all time.

6 If a Levite leaves any of your towns, from wherever he has been residing in Israel, and comes to the place that the LORD will choose (and he may come whenever he wishes), ⁷ then he may minister in the name of the LORD his God, like all his fellow-Levites who stand to minister there before the LORD. ⁸ They shall have equal portions to eat, even though they have income from the sale of family possessions.^a

Child-Sacrifice, Divination, and Magic Prohibited

9 When you come into the land that the LORD your God is giving you, you must not learn to imitate the abhorrent practices of those nations. ¹⁰ No one shall be found among you who makes a son or daughter pass through fire, or

^a Meaning of Heb uncertain   ^b Heb *him*

17:14–19—The law of kings is intended to limit the power and authority of the king. King Solomon violated each of the stipulations: he acquired many horses from Egypt (1 Kgs. 10:26–28); he acquired many wives (1 Kgs. 11:3–4); and he acquired great quantities of silver (1 Kgs. 10:10, 14, 17, 21–22, 27). Samuel may have had such a law in mind when he warned Israel about the danger of kings (1 Sam. 8:11–18). Deuteronomy considers excessive acquisition sinful and a cause of the division of the kingdom. Deuteronomy would consider the excessive acquisition,

by companies or individuals, of our consumerist society as a sin that might eventually lead to the downfall of our society.

18:9–14—This section gives further instruction on trustworthy communication from God (see also note on 13:1–7). Although the types of divination listed are considered *foreign*, it is likely that some of them were practiced in Israel and primarily by women (see 1 Sam. 28:5–25; Ezek. 13:17–23). Although they were effective practitioners, their practices were later restricted and considered *unorthodox*. Similarly folk practices in medicine

who practices divination, or is a sooth-sayer, or an augur, or a sorcerer, **11** or one who casts spells, or who consults ghosts or spirits, or who seeks oracles from the dead. **12** For whoever does these things is abhorrent to the LORD; it is because of such abhorrent practices that the LORD your God is driving them out before you. **13** You must remain completely loyal to the LORD your God. **14** Although these nations that you are about to dispossess do give heed to soothsayers and divin-ers, as for you, the LORD your God does not permit you to do so.

A New Prophet Like Moses

15 The LORD your God will raise up for you a prophet*a* like me from among your own people; you shall heed such a prophet.*b* **16** This is what you requested of the LORD your God at Horeb on the day of the assembly when you said: "If I hear the voice of the LORD my God any more, or ever again see this great fire, I will die." **17** Then the LORD replied to me: "They are right in what they have said. **18** I will raise up for them a prophet*a* like you from among their own people; I will put my words in the mouth of the prophet,*c* who shall speak to them everything that I command. **19** Anyone who does not heed the words that the prophet*d* shall speak in my name, I myself will hold accountable. **20** But any prophet who speaks in the name of other gods, or who presumes to speak in my name a word that I have not commanded the prophet to speak—that prophet shall die." **21** You may say to yourself, "How can we recognize a word that the LORD

has not spoken?" **22** If a prophet speaks in the name of the LORD but the thing does not take place or prove true, it is a word that the LORD has not spoken. The prophet has spoken it presumptuously; do not be frightened by it.

Laws concerning the Cities of Refuge

19 When the LORD your God has cut off the nations whose land the LORD your God is giving you, and you have dispossessed them and settled in their towns and in their houses, **2** you shall set apart three cities in the land that the LORD your God is giving you to possess. **3** You shall calculate the dis-tances*e* and divide into three regions the land that the LORD your God gives you as a possession, so that any homicide can flee to one of them.

4 Now this is the case of a homicide who might flee there and live, that is, someone who has killed another person unintentionally when the two had not been at enmity before: **5** Suppose some-one goes into the forest with another to cut wood, and when one of them swings the ax to cut down a tree, the head slips from the handle and strikes the other person who then dies; the killer may flee to one of these cities and live. **6** But if the distance is too great, the avenger of blood in hot anger might pursue and overtake and put the killer to death, although a death sentence was not deserved, since the two had not been at enmity before. **7** Therefore I command you: You shall set apart three cities.

a Or prophets *b* Or such prophets *c* Or mouths of the prophets *d* Heb he
e Or prepare roads to them

(often traditionally practiced by women), once central, were displaced by modern medicine. Just as many folk medicines are being proven beneficial, the religious practices of those who are marginal within our communities we might also consider to be legitimate.

18:15–22—The final instruction on trustworthy intermediation uses Moses as a model. The key issues are direct communication with God and whether what is prophesied proved true. This sounds as if it solves the problem of identifying

the true prophet. However, there is no external way to verify that God has spoken to someone. Even false prophets can claim that they have spoken only the words God has given them (1 Kgs. 22:6, 20–23; Ezek. 14:9–11). And how long does one wait for something to take place or prove true? A week? A year? A hundred years? A thousand years? Careful consideration needs to be given to how we distinguish between true and false words from God. It is never as simple as we might wish.

8 If the LORD your God enlarges your territory, as he swore to your ancestors—and he will give you all the land that he promised your ancestors to give you, 9 provided you diligently observe this entire commandment that I command you today, by loving the LORD your God and walking always in his ways—then you shall add three more cities to these three, 10 so that the blood of an innocent person may not be shed in the land that the LORD your God is giving you as an inheritance, thereby bringing bloodguilt upon you.

11 But if someone at enmity with another lies in wait and attacks and takes the life of that person, and flees into one of these cities, 12 then the elders of the killer's city shall send to have the culprit taken from there and handed over to the avenger of blood to be put to death. 13 Show no pity; you shall purge the guilt of innocent blood from Israel, so that it may go well with you.

Property Boundaries

14 You must not move your neighbor's boundary marker, set up by former generations, on the property that will be allotted to you in the land that the LORD your God is giving you to possess.

Law concerning Witnesses

15 A single witness shall not suffice to convict a person of any crime or wrong-doing in connection with any offense that may be committed. Only on the evidence of two or three witnesses shall a charge be sustained. 16 If a malicious witness comes forward to accuse someone of wrongdoing, 17 then both parties to the dispute shall appear before the LORD, before the priests and the judges who are in office in those days, 18 and the judges shall make a thorough inquiry. If the witness is a false witness, having testified falsely against another, 19 then you shall do to the false witness just as the false witness had meant to do to the other. So you shall purge the evil from your midst. 20 The rest shall hear and be afraid, and a crime such as this shall never again be committed among you. 21 Show no pity: life for life, eye for eye, tooth for tooth, hand for hand, foot for foot.

Rules of Warfare

20 When you go out to war against your enemies, and see horses and chariots, an army larger than your own, you shall not be afraid of them; for the LORD your God is with you, who brought you up from the land of Egypt. 2 Before you engage in battle, the priest shall come forward and speak to the troops, 3 and shall say to them: "Hear, O Israel! Today you are drawing near

---

19:15–20—This law functions as a safeguard so that innocent persons may not be executed based upon trumped-up charges (see 17:6). The story of Susanna and Daniel in the Apocrypha illustrates the importance of this command. Two witnesses accuse Susanna, but they have conspired falsely and maliciously against her. Justice demands that witnesses be *truthful* witnesses (cf. John 8:7).

19:21—This requirement of retribution in kind is often called by the Latin *lex talionis* ("law of retaliation"; cf. Exod. 21:22–25; Lev. 24:17–21). This law is often seen as harsh compared to Jesus' command to turn the other cheek (Matt. 5:38–41). However, this law functioned to reduce bloodshed by limiting the extent of retaliation. If this law is followed, there can be no blood feuds that continue for generations, nor can the use of excessive force be justified.

20:1—Deuteronomy assumes that enemies and warfare are a part of human existence, and thus a part of the life of the covenant community. Therefore the people are to conduct their warfare in a particular manner. As elsewhere in Deuteronomy, the assumption is that the enemy will be stronger and more powerful (see note at 1:22–45). The call not to fear is rooted in God's previous victory against Pharaoh and Egypt (Exod. 14:13–14).

20:2–4—The participation of a priest makes clear that warfare is a religious act. Although today many decry the concept of jihad in Islam, both Judaism and Christianity have fought their holy wars. Each faith emphasizes that God will fight for them and against their enemies. The reality of war can also be spiritualized in each faith to represent spiritual warfare against principalities and powers or sin or difficult odds (Pss. 55:21; 120; Prov. 28:4; Rom. 7:14–23; Eph. 6:10–17; Rev.

to do battle against your enemies. Do not lose heart, or be afraid, or panic, or be in dread of them; ⁴ for it is the LORD your God who goes with you, to fight for you against your enemies, to give you victory." ⁵ Then the officials shall address the troops, saying, "Has anyone built a new house but not dedicated it? He should go back to his house, or he might die in the battle and another dedicate it. ⁶ Has anyone planted a vineyard but not yet enjoyed its fruit? He should go back to his house, or he might die in the battle and another be first to enjoy its fruit. ⁷ Has anyone become engaged to a woman but not yet married her? He should go back to his house, or he might die in the battle and another marry her." ⁸ The officials shall continue to address the troops, saying, "Is anyone afraid or disheartened? He should go back to his house, or he might cause the heart of his comrades to melt like his own." ⁹ When the officials have finished addressing the troops, then the commanders shall take charge of them.

10 When you draw near to a town to fight against it, offer it terms of peace. ¹¹ If it accepts your terms of peace and surrenders to you, then all the people in it shall serve you at forced labor. ¹² If it does not submit to you peacefully, but makes war against you, then you shall besiege it; ¹³ and when the LORD your God gives it into your hand, you shall put all its males to the sword. ¹⁴ You may,

however, take as your booty the women, the children, livestock, and everything else in the town, all its spoil. You may enjoy the spoil of your enemies, which the LORD your God has given you. ¹⁵ Thus you shall treat all the towns that are very far from you, which are not towns of the nations here. ¹⁶ But as for the towns of these peoples that the LORD your God is giving you as an inheritance, you must not let anything that breathes remain alive. ¹⁷ You shall annihilate them—the Hittites and the Amorites, the Canaanites and the Perizzites, the Hivites and the Jebusites—just as the LORD your God has commanded, ¹⁸ so that they may not teach you to do all the abhorrent things that they do for their gods, and you thus sin against the LORD your God.

19 If you besiege a town for a long time, making war against it in order to take it, you must not destroy its trees by wielding an ax against them. Although you may take food from them, you must not cut them down. Are trees in the field human beings that they should come under siege from you? ²⁰ You may destroy only the trees that you know do not produce food; you may cut them down for use in building siegeworks against the town that makes war with you, until it falls.

Law concerning Murder by Persons Unknown

21 If, in the land that the LORD your God is giving you to possess, a

---

17:14). Consider the image of spiritual warfare. What are the possibilities and the difficulties of this image?

20:5–8—There were other priorities that could exempt someone from battle. Maybe if we had different sets of priorities there would be fewer battles.

20:10–18—This legislation suggests that war is not inevitable. Israel's first step in warfare was to offer peace, except peace was only envisioned as surrender and forced labor, which is hardly peace for those surrendering! Should the enemies resist, then war was the consequence. But the possibility of an alternative to war stands in tension with other places in Deuteronomy, where it is

assumed that Israel's enemies are to be totally destroyed (2:34; 3:6; 7:2; 13:15). We can consider other ways to respond to our enemies besides total destruction or abject submission.

20:19–20—Why must trees be saved? A rabbinic interpretation is that doing so would obliterate their ability to do what they were created for, to produce food. God does not allow the destruction of orchards as a security measure. Even nature has standing in the law.

21:1–9—When there was no known perpetrator to a crime the entire community was held responsible and responded according. For some issues, like violence, that threaten the well-being of our communities, no one cause or person can

body is found lying in open country, and it is not known who struck the person down, [2] then your elders and your judges shall come out to measure the distances to the towns that are near the body. [3] The elders of the town nearest the body shall take a heifer that has never been worked, one that has not pulled in the yoke; [4] the elders of that town shall bring the heifer down to a wadi with running water, which is neither plowed nor sown, and shall break the heifer's neck there in the wadi. [5] Then the priests, the sons of Levi, shall come forward, for the LORD your God has chosen them to minister to him and to pronounce blessings in the name of the LORD, and by their decision all cases of dispute and assault shall be settled. [6] All the elders of that town nearest the body shall wash their hands over the heifer whose neck was broken in the wadi, [7] and they shall declare: "Our hands did not shed this blood, nor were we witnesses to it. [8] Absolve, O LORD, your people Israel, whom you redeemed; do not let the guilt of innocent blood remain in the midst of your people Israel." Then they will be absolved of bloodguilt. [9] So you shall purge the guilt of innocent blood from your midst, because you must do what is right in the sight of the LORD.

Female Captives

10 When you go out to war against your enemies, and the LORD your God hands them over to you and you take them captive, [11] suppose you see among the captives a beautiful woman whom you desire and want to marry, [12] and so you bring her home to your house: she shall shave her head, pare her nails, [13] discard her captive's garb, and shall remain in your house a full month, mourning for her father and mother; after that you may go in to her and be her husband, and she shall be your wife. [14] But if you are not satisfied with her, you shall let her go free and not sell her for money. You must not treat her as a slave, since you have dishonored her.

The Right of the Firstborn

15 If a man has two wives, one of them loved and the other disliked, and if both the loved and the disliked have borne him sons, the firstborn being the son of the one who is disliked, [16] then on the day when he wills his possessions to his sons, he is not permitted to treat the son of the loved as the firstborn in preference to the son of the disliked, who is the firstborn. [17] He must acknowledge as firstborn the son of the one who is disliked, giving him a double portion[a] of all that he has; since he is the first issue of his virility, the right of the firstborn is his.

Rebellious Children

18 If someone has a stubborn and rebellious son who will not obey his father and mother, who does not heed

[a] Heb two-thirds

---

be identified as being responsible. What would happen if the community as a whole were to take responsibility and respond accordingly?

21:10–14—This law reflects patriarchal bias and centers on male interests and concerns. The woman has no say in the matter. But note she does have rights that are indirectly protected. More gratifying is the fact that the law suggests destruction of the enemy is not the only option. Intermarriage happens between even the bitterest enemies. The word *desire* is used elsewhere to speak of Shechem's desire for Dinah (Gen. 34:8), Israel's desire for God (Ps. 91:14), and twice in Deuteronomy of God's desire for Israel (7:7; 10:15). In today's world, perhaps bitter enemies

can consider how they might mutually desire one another.

21:15–17—This law recognizes that fairness doesn't always happen in relationships. Consider Cain and Abel, Sarah and Hagar, Isaac and Ishmael, Jacob and Esau, Rachel and Leah, Hannah and Peninnah. The question is how we will respond when people are treated unfairly. Will we respond destructively or consider a better way?

21:18–21—As mother, a woman shares equal status and authority with men. This *stubborn and rebellious son* disobeys his father *and* his mother. *Both* parents bring the son before the elders. Jesus' parable of the Prodigal Son is clearly

them when they discipline him, ¹⁹ then his father and his mother shall take hold of him and bring him out to the elders of his town at the gate of that place. ²⁰ They shall say to the elders of his town, "This son of ours is stubborn and rebellious. He will not obey us. He is a glutton and a drunkard." ²¹ Then all the men of the town shall stone him to death. So you shall purge the evil from your midst; and all Israel will hear, and be afraid.

Miscellaneous Laws

22 When someone is convicted of a crime punishable by death and is executed, and you hang him on a tree, ²³ his corpse must not remain all night upon the tree; you shall bury him that same day, for anyone hung on a tree is under God's curse. You must not defile the land that the LORD your God is giving you for possession.

22 You shall not watch your neighbor's ox or sheep straying away and ignore them; you shall take them back to their owner. ² If the owner does not reside near you or you do not know who the owner is, you shall bring it to your own house, and it shall remain with you until the owner claims it; then you shall return it. ³ You shall do the same with a neighbor's donkey; you shall do the same with a neighbor's garment; and you shall do the same with anything else that your neighbor loses and you find. You may not withhold your help.

4 You shall not see your neighbor's donkey or ox fallen on the road and ignore it; you shall help to lift it up.

5 A woman shall not wear a man's apparel, nor shall a man put on a woman's garment; for whoever does such things is abhorrent to the LORD your God.

6 If you come on a bird's nest, in any tree or on the ground, with fledglings or eggs, with the mother sitting on the fledglings or on the eggs, you shall not take the mother with the young. ⁷ Let the mother go, taking only the young for yourself, in order that it may go well with you and you may live long.

8 When you build a new house, you shall make a parapet for your roof; otherwise you might have bloodguilt on your house, if anyone should fall from it.

9 You shall not sow your vineyard with a second kind of seed, or the whole yield will have to be forfeited, both the crop that you have sown and the yield of the vineyard itself.

10 You shall not plow with an ox and a donkey yoked together.

11 You shall not wear clothes made of wool and linen woven together.

12 You shall make tassels on the four corners of the cloak with which you cover yourself.

Laws concerning Sexual Relations

13 Suppose a man marries a woman, but after going in to her, he dislikes her ¹⁴ and makes up charges against her,

---

a reinterpretation of this law (Luke 15:11–32). Instead of stoning, the father forgives. But, one has to wonder, where is the *mother* in the story of the Prodigal Son? Were both parents present, as they should have been, we'd also be able to image God as the forgiving mother.

22:1–4—These laws can be seen as the positive expression of the Tenth Commandment. Instead of telling us not to desire what our neighbor has and seek to take it, these laws ask us to consider how we might care for our neighbor's possessions. We can consider this a precursor of "Do unto others as you would have them do unto you." Although we often do not even know our neighbors, Deuteronomy says we have moral duties toward them.

22:5–12—These laws primarily deal with the issue of boundaries. Deuteronomy is concerned that various items should be kept *pure* and not *mixed*, primarily that Israel should not mix with its neighbors. Racial segregation, Nazi Germany, apartheid South Africa, Bosnia, Kosovo, and the Israeli/Palestinian conflict should be sufficient warning that racial or ethnic purity can be maintained only by violence. Verse 5 raises the issue of gender boundaries. Likewise, *pure* gender categories can be maintained only by violence. Is purity in this sense worth the price?

22:13–29—The emphasis on the purity of Israel continues in laws that define adulterous relationships. The gender inequity in the laws places Deuteronomy squarely within a patriarchal

slandering her by saying, "I married this woman; but when I lay with her, I did not find evidence of her virginity." [15] The father of the young woman and her mother shall then submit the evidence of the young woman's virginity to the elders of the city at the gate. [16] The father of the young woman shall say to the elders: "I gave my daughter in marriage to this man but he dislikes her; [17] now he has made up charges against her, saying, 'I did not find evidence of your daughter's virginity.' But here is the evidence of my daughter's virginity." Then they shall spread out the cloth before the elders of the town. [18] The elders of that town shall take the man and punish him; [19] they shall fine him one hundred shekels of silver (which they shall give to the young woman's father) because he has slandered a virgin of Israel. She shall remain his wife; he shall not be permitted to divorce her as long as he lives.

20 If, however, this charge is true, that evidence of the young woman's virginity was not found, [21] then they shall bring the young woman out to the entrance of her father's house and the men of her town shall stone her to death, because she committed a disgraceful act in Israel by prostituting herself in her father's house. So you shall purge the evil from your midst.

22 If a man is caught lying with the wife of another man, both of them shall die, the man who lay with the woman as well as the woman. So you shall purge the evil from Israel.

23 If there is a young woman, a virgin already engaged to be married, and a man meets her in the town and lies with her, [24] you shall bring both of them to the gate of that town and stone them to death, the young woman because she did not cry for help in the town and the man because he violated his neighbor's wife. So you shall purge the evil from your midst.

25 But if the man meets the engaged woman in the open country, and the man seizes her and lies with her, then only the man who lay with her shall die. [26] You shall do nothing to the young woman; the young woman has not committed an offense punishable by death, because this case is like that of someone who attacks and murders a neighbor. [27] Since he found her in the open country, the engaged woman may have cried for help, but there was no one to rescue her.

28 If a man meets a virgin who is not engaged, and seizes her and lies with her, and they are caught in the act, [29] the man who lay with her shall give fifty shekels of silver to the young woman's father, and she shall become his wife. Because he violated her he shall not be permitted to divorce her as long as he lives.

30[a] A man shall not marry his father's wife, thereby violating his father's rights. [b]

Those Excluded from the Assembly

23 No one whose testicles are crushed or whose penis is cut off shall be admitted to the assembly of the LORD.

2 Those born of an illicit union shall not be admitted to the assembly of

[a] Ch 23.1 in Heb   [b] Heb *uncovering his father's skirt*

---

orientation toward women and family. These laws are often seen as evidence that God approves this social ordering. Such a view turns this social structure into an object of idolatry. Even the canon protests the restrictiveness of Deuteronomy. The Song of Songs considers an alternative social ordering. We need to develop alternative social orders of egalitarian, mutual, and just relationships.

23:1–7—The emphasis on the purity of Israel continues in laws that restrict access to the covenant community. However, as much as Israel tried, outsiders kept managing to find their way inside (see Ruth). Matthew's genealogy includes in Jesus' lineage four Old Testament women who can be considered outsiders (Matt. 1:3, 5, 6). Instead of thinking about how to keep undesirable people out of our congregations, we should think about how we are all members of the same family (see note at Deut. 2:5).

the LORD. Even to the tenth generation, none of their descendants shall be admitted to the assembly of the LORD.

3 No Ammonite or Moabite shall be admitted to the assembly of the LORD. Even to the tenth generation, none of their descendants shall be admitted to the assembly of the LORD, [4]because they did not meet you with food and water on your journey out of Egypt, and because they hired against you Balaam son of Beor, from Pethor of Mesopotamia, to curse you. [5](Yet the LORD your God refused to heed Balaam; the LORD your God turned the curse into a blessing for you, because the LORD your God loved you.) [6]You shall never promote their welfare or their prosperity as long as you live.

7 You shall not abhor any of the Edomites, for they are your kin. You shall not abhor any of the Egyptians, because you were an alien residing in their land. [8]The children of the third generation that are born to them may be admitted to the assembly of the LORD.

Sanitary, Ritual, and Humanitarian Precepts

9 When you are encamped against your enemies you shall guard against any impropriety.

10 If one of you becomes unclean because of a nocturnal emission, then he shall go outside the camp; he must not come within the camp. [11]When evening comes, he shall wash himself with water, and when the sun has set, he may come back into the camp.

12 You shall have a designated area outside the camp to which you shall go. [13]With your utensils you shall have a trowel; when you relieve yourself outside, you shall dig a hole with it and then cover up your excrement. [14]Because the LORD your God travels along with your camp, to save you and to hand over your enemies to you, therefore your camp must be holy, so that he may not see anything indecent among you and turn away from you.

15 Slaves who have escaped to you from their owners shall not be given back to them. [16]They shall reside with you, in your midst, in any place they choose in any one of your towns, wherever they please; you shall not oppress them.

17 None of the daughters of Israel shall be a temple prostitute; none of the sons of Israel shall be a temple prostitute. [18]You shall not bring the fee of a prostitute or the wages of a male prostitute[a] into the house of the LORD your God in payment for any vow, for both of these are abhorrent to the LORD your God.

19 You shall not charge interest on loans to another Israelite, interest on money, interest on provisions, interest on anything that is lent. [20]On loans to a foreigner you may charge interest, but on loans to another Israelite you may not charge interest, so that the LORD your God may bless you in all your undertakings in the land that you are about to enter and possess.

21 If you make a vow to the LORD your God, do not postpone fulfilling it; for

[a] Heb a dog

23:15–16—The Underground Railroad before and during the American Civil War recognized that obedience to this divine law took precedence over obedience to civil laws that required the return of runaway slaves. Determining the necessity to violate divine or human law is never easy or clear-cut (see note at 23:21–23).

23:17—*Temple prostitute* reflects the biases of the translators. It is doubtful that these persons engaged in any illicit sexual activity. A more accurate translation is *holy woman* and *holy man.*

They were probably religious leaders whose practices did not conform to strict Deuteronomistic standards (see note at 18:9–14).

23:21–23—Unfortunately the text implies that *any vow* to God *must* be fulfilled. The *content* of a vow must also be considered or we end up with situations such as Jephthah sacrificing his daughter (Judg. 11:30–40) or religious extremists flying airplanes into buildings, just to fulfill a vow. God does not call us to blind obedience.

the LORD your God will surely require it of you, and you would incur guilt. 22 But if you refrain from vowing, you will not incur guilt. 23 Whatever your lips utter you must diligently perform, just as you have freely vowed to the LORD your God with your own mouth.

24 If you go into your neighbor's vineyard, you may eat your fill of grapes, as many as you wish, but you shall not put any in a container.

25 If you go into your neighbor's standing grain, you may pluck the ears with your hand, but you shall not put a sickle to your neighbor's standing grain.

Laws concerning Marriage and Divorce

24 Suppose a man enters into marriage with a woman, but she does not please him because he finds something objectionable about her, and so he writes her a certificate of divorce, puts it in her hand, and sends her out of his house; she then leaves his house 2 and goes off to become another man's wife. 3 Then suppose the second man dislikes her, writes her a bill of divorce, puts it in her hand, and sends her out of his house (or the second man who married her dies); 4 her first husband, who sent her away, is not permitted to take her again to be his wife after she has been defiled; for that would be abhorrent to the LORD, and you shall not bring guilt on the land that the LORD your God is giving you as a possession.

Miscellaneous Laws

5 When a man is newly married, he shall not go out with the army or be charged with any related duty. He shall be free at home one year, to be happy with the wife whom he has married.

6 No one shall take a mill or an upper millstone in pledge, for that would be taking a life in pledge.

7 If someone is caught kidnaping another Israelite, enslaving or selling the Israelite, then that kidnaper shall die. So you shall purge the evil from your midst.

8 Guard against an outbreak of a leprous[a] skin disease by being very careful; you shall carefully observe whatever the levitical priests instruct you, just as I have commanded them. 9 Remember what the LORD your God did to Miriam on your journey out of Egypt.

10 When you make your neighbor a loan of any kind, you shall not go into the house to take the pledge. 11 You shall wait outside, while the person to whom you are making the loan brings the pledge out to you. 12 If the person is poor, you shall not sleep in the garment given you as[b] the pledge. 13 You shall give the pledge back by sunset, so that your neighbor may sleep in the cloak and bless you; and it will be to your credit before the LORD your God.

14 You shall not withhold the wages of poor and needy laborers, whether other Israelites or aliens who reside in your land in one of your towns. 15 You shall pay them their wages daily before sunset, because they are poor and their livelihood depends on them; otherwise they might cry to the LORD against you, and you would incur guilt.

16 Parents shall not be put to death for their children, nor shall children be put to death for their parents; only for

---

[a] A term for several skin diseases; precise meaning uncertain   [b] Heb lacks the garment given you as

---

24:10–13—This law protects someone poor by placing limits on creditors. Some lending practices today exhibit no limits to the capacity to exploit the neediness of others. This is hardly to our credit (cf. Amos 2:8).

24:14—The *poor and needy* are like those today who live from paycheck to paycheck. The need to pay wages promptly is a way of ensuring people didn't go further into debt. Failure to treat workers fairly means they may cry to the Lord. Exodus and Psalms remind us that God's response to those who cry in distress is to punish those guilty of causing the distress. Businesses that treat workers as pawns are warned they fall under divine judgment.

their own crimes may persons be put to death.

17 You shall not deprive a resident alien or an orphan of justice; you shall not take a widow's garment in pledge. ¹⁸ Remember that you were a slave in Egypt and the LORD your God redeemed you from there; therefore I command you to do this.

19 When you reap your harvest in your field and forget a sheaf in the field, you shall not go back to get it; it shall be left for the alien, the orphan, and the widow, so that the LORD your God may bless you in all your undertakings. ²⁰ When you beat your olive trees, do not strip what is left; it shall be for the alien, the orphan, and the widow.

21 When you gather the grapes of your vineyard, do not glean what is left; it shall be for the alien, the orphan, and the widow. ²² Remember that you were a slave in the land of Egypt; therefore I am commanding you to do this.

25 Suppose two persons have a dispute and enter into litigation, and the judges decide between them, declaring one to be in the right and the other to be in the wrong. ² If the one in the wrong deserves to be flogged, the judge shall make that person lie down and be beaten in his presence with the number of lashes proportionate to the offense. ³ Forty lashes may be given but

not more; if more lashes than these are given, your neighbor will be degraded in your sight.

4 You shall not muzzle an ox while it is treading out the grain.

Levirate Marriage

5 When brothers reside together, and one of them dies and has no son, the wife of the deceased shall not be married outside the family to a stranger. Her husband's brother shall go in to her, taking her in marriage, and performing the duty of a husband's brother to her, ⁶ and the firstborn whom she bears shall succeed to the name of the deceased brother, so that his name may not be blotted out of Israel. ⁷ But if the man has no desire to marry his brother's widow, then his brother's widow shall go up to the elders at the gate and say, "My husband's brother refuses to perpetuate his brother's name in Israel; he will not perform the duty of a husband's brother to me." ⁸ Then the elders of his town shall summon him and speak to him. If he persists, saying, "I have no desire to marry her," ⁹ then his brother's wife shall go up to him in the presence of the elders, pull his sandal off his foot, spit in his face, and declare, "This is what is done to the man who does not build up his brother's house." ¹⁰ Throughout Israel his family shall be known as "the house of him whose sandal was pulled off."

24:17—The trio *resident alien, orphan, widow* usually occurs in a fixed series. They have no property and therefore require special social supports (e.g., vv. 19–22). Note that no moral judgment is attached. These are not *bad* people, but folk whose circumstances (residing outside one's country of origin, loss of father, loss of husband) make them vulnerable. Care of these is incumbent upon those in the covenant community who have the resources to provide the needed support. The reason for this care is that Israel has itself experienced the downside of economic vulnerability (see note at 10:19).

24:19–22—The gleaning laws suggest that one way of providing for the economically vulnerable is by providing them with means of obtaining food. Members of the Society of St. Andrew, a contemporary group, obey this law by gleaning

and distributing the food in local communities. Deuteronomy does not consider whether it is better to remedy hunger by providing out of our bounty or by correcting the issues that lead to poverty in the first place.

25:5–10—The law is known as the levirate law, after the Latin *levir*, "brother-in-law." The law demonstrates that a woman's status is not uniform. On the one hand, the law's patriarchal bias makes clear that women could not have lineages of their own. On the other hand, it shows that women had legal rights. *The woman* (not any of her male relations) is the one who goes to the elders to demand that the levirate obligation be fulfilled or that she be released from obligations to her husband's family. This law serves as background for the stories of Tamar (Gen. 38) and Ruth (cf. Matt. 22:23–33).

Various Commands

11 If men get into a fight with one another, and the wife of one intervenes to rescue her husband from the grip of his opponent by reaching out and seizing his genitals, 12 you shall cut off her hand; show no pity.

13 You shall not have in your bag two kinds of weights, large and small. 14 You shall not have in your house two kinds of measures, large and small. 15 You shall have only a full and honest weight; you shall have only a full and honest measure, so that your days may be long in the land that the LORD your God is giving you. 16 For all who do such things, all who act dishonestly, are abhorrent to the LORD your God.

17 Remember what Amalek did to you on your journey out of Egypt, 18 how he attacked you on the way, when you were faint and weary, and struck down all who lagged behind you; he did not fear God. 19 Therefore when the LORD your God has given you rest from all your enemies on every hand, in the land that the LORD your God is giving you as an inheritance to possess, you shall blot out the remembrance of Amalek from under heaven; do not forget.

First Fruits and Tithes

26 When you have come into the land that the LORD your God is giving you as an inheritance to possess, and you possess it, and settle in it, 2 you shall take some of the first of all the fruit of the ground, which you harvest from the land that the LORD your God is giving you, and you shall put it in a basket and go to the place that the LORD your God will choose as a dwelling for his name. 3 You shall go to the priest who is in office at that time, and say to him, "Today I declare to the LORD your God that I have come into the land that the LORD swore to our ancestors to give us." 4 When the priest takes the basket from your hand and sets it down before the altar of the LORD your God, 5 you shall make this response before the LORD your God: "A wandering Aramean was my ancestor; he went down into Egypt and lived there as an alien, few in number, and there he became a great nation, mighty and populous. 6 When the Egyptians treated us harshly and afflicted us, by imposing hard labor on us, 7 we cried to the LORD, the God of our ancestors; the LORD heard our voice and saw our affliction, our toil, and our oppression. 8 The LORD brought us out of Egypt with a mighty hand and an outstretched arm, with a terrifying display of power, and with signs and wonders; 9 and he brought us into this place and gave us this land, a land flowing with milk and honey. 10 So now I bring the first of the fruit of the ground that you, O LORD, have given me." You shall set it down before the LORD your God and bow down before the LORD your God. 11 Then you, together with the Levites and the aliens who reside among you, shall celebrate with all the bounty that the LORD your God has given to you and to your house.

12 When you have finished paying all the tithe of your produce in the third year (which is the year of the tithe), giving it to the Levites, the aliens, the orphans, and the widows, so that they may eat their fill within your towns,

---

25:11–12—One wonders if this was such a social problem that men felt the need to legislate against it (cf. Esth. 1:16–22)!

25:13–16—Deuteronomy clearly articulates that business is also a religious concern and that our business conduct matters to God (see Amos 8:4–6). We have seen the way corporate misconduct has impacted huge groups of ordinary citizens. Deuteronomy states that other moral and social concerns are to override exploitative business practices.

26:5–9—The presentation of the first fruits of the harvest was accompanied by a confession of faith. Neither this confession nor others, such as the Apostles' Creed, are intended to be stifling and meaningless exercises. They are grateful expressions of one's experience of God.

[13] then you shall say before the LORD your God: "I have removed the sacred portion from the house, and I have given it to the Levites, the resident aliens, the orphans, and the widows, in accordance with your entire commandment that you commanded me; I have neither transgressed nor forgotten any of your commandments: [14] I have not eaten of it while in mourning; I have not removed any of it while I was unclean; and I have not offered any of it to the dead. I have obeyed the LORD my God, doing just as you commanded me. [15] Look down from your holy habitation, from heaven, and bless your people Israel and the ground that you have given us, as you swore to our ancestors—a land flowing with milk and honey."

Concluding Exhortation

[16] This very day the LORD your God is commanding you to observe these statutes and ordinances; so observe them diligently with all your heart and with all your soul. [17] Today you have obtained the LORD's agreement: to be your God; and for you to walk in his ways, to keep his statutes, his commandments, and his ordinances, and to obey him. [18] Today the LORD has obtained your agreement: to be his treasured people, as he promised you, and to keep his commandments; [19] for him to set you high above all nations that he has made, in praise and in fame and in honor; and for you to be a people holy to the LORD your God, as he promised.

The Inscribed Stones and Altar on Mount Ebal

27 Then Moses and the elders of Israel charged all the people as follows: Keep the entire commandment that I am commanding you today. [2] On the day that you cross over the Jordan into the land that the LORD your God is giving you, you shall set up large stones and cover them with plaster. [3] You shall write on them all the words of this law when you have crossed over, to enter the land that the LORD your God is giving you, a land flowing with milk and honey, as the LORD, the God of your ancestors, promised you. [4] So when you have crossed over the Jordan, you shall set up these stones, about which I am commanding you today, on Mount Ebal, and you shall cover them with plaster. [5] And you shall build an altar there to the LORD your God, an altar of stones on which you have not used an iron tool. [6] You must build the altar of the LORD your God of unhewn[a] stones. Then offer up burnt offerings on it to the LORD your God, [7] make sacrifices of well-being, and eat them there, rejoicing before the LORD your God. [8] You shall write on the stones all the words of this law very clearly.

[9] Then Moses and the levitical priests spoke to all Israel, saying: Keep silence and hear, O Israel! This very day you have become the people of the LORD your God. [10] Therefore obey the LORD your God, observing his commandments and his statutes that I am commanding you today.

Twelve Curses

[11] The same day Moses charged the people as follows: [12] When you have crossed over the Jordan, these shall stand on Mount Gerizim for the blessing of the people: Simeon, Levi, Judah, Issachar, Joseph, and Benjamin. [13] And

---

a Heb *whole*

26:13–14—The counterpart to confessing what God has done is to confess what we have done. What have you and your community done in response to what God has done for you?

27:1–10—It is not sufficient just to create a monument to the *commandments*; the people must also *obey* the commandments. There is no point to displaying the Ten Commandments if we do not obey them.

27:11–26—One theory is these cursed acts would have occurred "in secret." Yet here they are publicly condemned. Some of our worst sins, such as spouse abuse or sexual abuse of children, are committed in secret. The community is called

these shall stand on Mount Ebal for the curse: Reuben, Gad, Asher, Zebulun, Dan, and Naphtali. **14** Then the Levites shall declare in a loud voice to all the Israelites:

15 "Cursed be anyone who makes an idol or casts an image, anything abhorrent to the LORD, the work of an artisan, and sets it up in secret." All the people shall respond, saying, "Amen!"

16 "Cursed be anyone who dishonors father or mother." All the people shall say, "Amen!"

17 "Cursed be anyone who moves a neighbor's boundary marker." All the people shall say, "Amen!"

18 "Cursed be anyone who misleads a blind person on the road." All the people shall say, "Amen!"

19 "Cursed be anyone who deprives the alien, the orphan, and the widow of justice." All the people shall say, "Amen!"

20 "Cursed be anyone who lies with his father's wife, because he has violated his father's rights."*a* All the people shall say, "Amen!"

21 "Cursed be anyone who lies with any animal." All the people shall say, "Amen!"

22 "Cursed be anyone who lies with his sister, whether the daughter of his father or the daughter of his mother." All the people shall say, "Amen!"

23 "Cursed be anyone who lies with his mother-in-law." All the people shall say, "Amen!"

24 "Cursed be anyone who strikes down a neighbor in secret." All the people shall say, "Amen!"

25 "Cursed be anyone who takes a bribe to shed innocent blood." All the people shall say, "Amen!"

26 "Cursed be anyone who does not uphold the words of this law by observing them." All the people shall say, "Amen!"

Blessings for Obedience

28 If you will only obey the LORD your God, by diligently observing all his commandments that I am commanding you today, the LORD your God will set you high above all the nations of the earth; **2** all these blessings shall come upon you and overtake you, if you obey the LORD your God:

3 Blessed shall you be in the city, and blessed shall you be in the field.

4 Blessed shall be the fruit of your womb, the fruit of your ground, and the fruit of your livestock, both the increase of your cattle and the issue of your flock.

5 Blessed shall be your basket and your kneading bowl.

6 Blessed shall you be when you come in, and blessed shall you be when you go out.

7 The LORD will cause your enemies who rise against you to be defeated before you; they shall come out against you one way, and flee before you seven ways. **8** The LORD will command the blessing upon you in your barns, and in all that you undertake; he will bless you in the land that the LORD your God is giving you. **9** The LORD will establish you as his holy people, as he has sworn to you, if you keep the commandments of the LORD your God and walk in his ways. **10** All the peoples of the earth shall see that you are called by the name of the LORD, and they shall be afraid of

a Heb *uncovered his father's skirt*

---

to name these publicly as sins. Only when secret sins are publicly named can formal action be taken against the perpetrators.

28:1–68—The ideology behind the blessings and curses is that *if* the people are obedient, *then* they will experience blessing, and *if* the people are disobedient, *then* they will experience curses. The truth this ideology expresses is that actions have consequences.

The limits are (1) nothing suggests that what applies to the nation is applicable to individuals or (2) that the equation works in reverse—*if* you are cursed, *then* you have been disobedient. The question of why bad things happen to good people and the book of Job reflect the limits of this ideology. The Bible offers a variety of answers to the question of suffering. The Deuteronomic view is *one* of those answers.

you. [11] The LORD will make you abound in prosperity, in the fruit of your womb, in the fruit of your livestock, and in the fruit of your ground in the land that the LORD swore to your ancestors to give you. [12] The LORD will open for you his rich storehouse, the heavens, to give the rain of your land in its season and to bless all your undertakings. You will lend to many nations, but you will not borrow. [13] The LORD will make you the head, and not the tail; you shall be only at the top, and not at the bottom—if you obey the commandments of the LORD your God, which I am commanding you today, by diligently observing them, [14] and if you do not turn aside from any of the words that I am commanding you today, either to the right or to the left, following other gods to serve them.

Warnings against Disobedience

15 But if you will not obey the LORD your God by diligently observing all his commandments and decrees, which I am commanding you today, then all these curses shall come upon you and overtake you:

16 Cursed shall you be in the city, and cursed shall you be in the field.

17 Cursed shall be your basket and your kneading bowl.

18 Cursed shall be the fruit of your womb, the fruit of your ground, the increase of your cattle and the issue of your flock.

19 Cursed shall you be when you come in, and cursed shall you be when you go out.

20 The LORD will send upon you disaster, panic, and frustration in everything you attempt to do, until you are destroyed and perish quickly, on account of the evil of your deeds, because you have forsaken me. [21] The LORD will make the pestilence cling to you until it has consumed you off the land that you are entering to possess. [22] The LORD will afflict you with consumption, fever, inflammation, with fiery heat and drought, and with blight and mildew; they shall pursue you until you perish. [23] The sky over your head shall be bronze, and the earth under you iron. [24] The LORD will change the rain of your land into powder, and only dust shall come down upon you from the sky until you are destroyed.

25 The LORD will cause you to be defeated before your enemies; you shall go out against them one way and flee before them seven ways. You shall become an object of horror to all the kingdoms of the earth. [26] Your corpses shall be food for every bird of the air and animal of the earth, and there shall be no one to frighten them away. [27] The LORD will afflict you with the boils of Egypt, with ulcers, scurvy, and itch, of which you cannot be healed. [28] The LORD will afflict you with madness, blindness, and confusion of mind; [29] you shall grope about at noon as blind people grope in darkness, but you shall be unable to find your way; and you shall be continually abused and robbed, without anyone to help. [30] You shall become engaged to a woman, but another man shall lie with her. You shall build a house, but not live in it. You shall plant a vineyard, but not enjoy its fruit. [31] Your ox shall be butchered before your eyes, but you shall not eat of it. Your donkey shall be stolen in front of you, and shall not be restored to you. Your sheep shall be given to your enemies, without anyone to help you. [32] Your sons and daughters shall be given to another people, while you look on; you will strain your eyes looking for them all day but be powerless to do anything. [33] A people whom you do not know shall eat up the fruit of your ground and of all your labors; you shall be continually abused and crushed, [34] and driven mad by the sight that your eyes shall see. [35] The LORD will strike you on the knees and on the legs with grievous boils of which you cannot be healed, from the sole of your foot to the crown of your head. [36] The LORD will

bring you, and the king whom you set over you, to a nation that neither you nor your ancestors have known, where you shall serve other gods, of wood and stone. ³⁷ You shall become an object of horror, a proverb, and a byword among all the peoples where the LORD will lead you.

38 You shall carry much seed into the field but shall gather little in, for the locust shall consume it. ³⁹ You shall plant vineyards and dress them, but you shall neither drink the wine nor gather the grapes, for the worm shall eat them. ⁴⁰ You shall have olive trees throughout all your territory, but you shall not anoint yourself with the oil, for your olives shall drop off. ⁴¹ You shall have sons and daughters, but they shall not remain yours, for they shall go into captivity. ⁴² All your trees and the fruit of your ground the cicada shall take over. ⁴³ Aliens residing among you shall ascend above you higher and higher, while you shall descend lower and lower. ⁴⁴ They shall lend to you but you shall not lend to them; they shall be the head and you shall be the tail.

45 All these curses shall come upon you, pursuing and overtaking you until you are destroyed, because you did not obey the LORD your God, by observing the commandments and the decrees that he commanded you. ⁴⁶ They shall be among you and your descendants as a sign and a portent forever.

47 Because you did not serve the LORD your God joyfully and with gladness of heart for the abundance of everything, ⁴⁸ therefore you shall serve your enemies whom the LORD will send against you, in hunger and thirst, in nakedness and lack of everything. He will put an iron yoke on your neck until he has destroyed you. ⁴⁹ The LORD will bring a nation from far away, from the end of the earth, to swoop down on you like an eagle, a nation whose language you do not understand, ⁵⁰ a grim-faced nation showing no respect to the old or favor to the young. ⁵¹ It shall consume the fruit of your livestock and the fruit of your ground until you are destroyed, leaving you neither grain, wine, and oil, nor the increase of your cattle and the issue of your flock, until it has made you perish. ⁵² It shall besiege you in all your towns until your high and fortified walls, in which you trusted, come down throughout your land; it shall besiege you in all your towns throughout the land that the LORD your God has given you. ⁵³ In the desperate straits to which the enemy siege reduces you, you will eat the fruit of your womb, the flesh of your own sons and daughters whom the LORD your God has given you. ⁵⁴ Even the most refined and gentle of men among you will begrudge food to his own brother, to the wife whom he embraces, and to the last of his remaining children, ⁵⁵ giving to none of them any of the flesh of his children whom he is eating, because nothing else remains to him, in the desperate straits to which the enemy siege will reduce you in all your towns. ⁵⁶ She who is the most refined and gentle among you, so gentle and refined that she does not venture to set the sole of her foot on the ground, will begrudge food to the husband whom she embraces, to her own son, and to her own daughter, ⁵⁷ begrudging even the afterbirth that comes out from between her thighs, and the children that she bears, because she is eating them in secret for lack of anything else, in the desperate straits to which the enemy siege will reduce you in your towns.

58 If you do not diligently observe all the words of this law that are written in this book, fearing this glorious and awesome name, the LORD your God, ⁵⁹ then the LORD will overwhelm both

---

28:58–68—As the people are about to enter the promised land, the ultimate curse is that their disobedience can lead them straight back to Egypt.

No matter how much progress we have made toward overcoming oppression in all its forms, we can easily end up back where we started.

you and your offspring with severe and lasting afflictions and grievous and lasting maladies. ⁶⁰ He will bring back upon you all the diseases of Egypt, of which you were in dread, and they shall cling to you. ⁶¹ Every other malady and affliction, even though not recorded in the book of this law, the LORD will inflict on you until you are destroyed. ⁶² Although once you were as numerous as the stars in heaven, you shall be left few in number, because you did not obey the LORD your God. ⁶³ And just as the LORD took delight in making you prosperous and numerous, so the LORD will take delight in bringing you to ruin and destruction; you shall be plucked off the land that you are entering to possess. ⁶⁴ The LORD will scatter you among all peoples, from one end of the earth to the other; and there you shall serve other gods, of wood and stone, which neither you nor your ancestors have known. ⁶⁵ Among those nations you shall find no ease, no resting place for the sole of your foot. There the LORD will give you a trembling heart, failing eyes, and a languishing spirit. ⁶⁶ Your life shall hang in doubt before you; night and day you shall be in dread, with no assurance of your life. ⁶⁷ In the morning you shall say, "If only it were evening!" and at evening you shall say, "If only it were morning!"—because of the dread that your heart shall feel and the sights that your eyes shall see. ⁶⁸ The LORD will bring you back in ships to Egypt, by a route that I promised you would never see again; and there you shall offer yourselves for sale to your enemies as male and female slaves, but there will be no buyer.

29 ᵃ These are the words of the covenant that the LORD commanded Moses to make with the Israelites in the land of Moab, in addition to the covenant that he had made with them at Horeb.

The Covenant Renewed in Moab

2ᵇ Moses summoned all Israel and said to them: You have seen all that the LORD did before your eyes in the land of Egypt, to Pharaoh and to all his servants and to all his land, ³ the great trials that your eyes saw, the signs, and those great wonders. ⁴ But to this day the LORD has not given you a mind to understand, or eyes to see, or ears to hear. ⁵ I have led you forty years in the wilderness. The clothes on your back have not worn out, and the sandals on your feet have not worn out; ⁶ you have not eaten bread, and you have not drunk wine or strong drink—so that you may know that I am the LORD your God. ⁷ When you came to this place, King Sihon of Heshbon and King Og of Bashan came out against us for battle, but we defeated them. ⁸ We took their land and gave it as an inheritance to the Reubenites, the Gadites, and the half-tribe of Manasseh. ⁹ Therefore diligently observe the words of this covenant, in order that you may succeedᶜ in everything that you do.

10 You stand assembled today, all of you, before the LORD your God—the leaders of your tribes,ᵈ your elders, and your officials, all the men of Israel, ¹¹ your children, your women, and the aliens who are in your camp, both those who cut your wood and those who draw your water— ¹² to enter into the covenant of the LORD your God, sworn by an oath, which the LORD your God

ᵃ Ch 28.69 in Heb ᵇ Ch 29.1 in Heb ᶜ Or *deal wisely* ᵈ Gk Syr: Heb *your leaders, your tribes*

29:1—Here begins *Moses' third speech,* which continues to 30:20 or 32:47. Like the other speeches, it is addressed to those who live beyond the boundaries. This farewell address gives encouragement and hope.

29:10–11—Although most of the laws relate to men's concerns, here *everyone* enters into the covenant. This means that even the marginal groups—women, children, and resident aliens—are a part of the covenant community. Who are the marginal groups among us today? How do we ensure their participation in the covenant community?

is making with you today; [13] in order that he may establish you today as his people, and that he may be your God, as he promised you and as he swore to your ancestors, to Abraham, to Isaac, and to Jacob. [14] I am making this covenant, sworn by an oath, not only with you who stand here with us today before the LORD our God, [15] but also with those who are not here with us today. [16] You know how we lived in the land of Egypt, and how we came through the midst of the nations through which you passed. [17] You have seen their detestable things, the filthy idols of wood and stone, of silver and gold, that were among them. [18] It may be that there is among you a man or woman, or a family or tribe, whose heart is already turning away from the LORD our God to serve the gods of those nations. It may be that there is among you a root sprouting poisonous and bitter growth. [19] All who hear the words of this oath and bless themselves, thinking in their hearts, "We are safe even though we go our own stubborn ways" (thus bringing disaster on moist and dry alike)[a]— [20] the LORD will be unwilling to pardon them, for the LORD's anger and passion will smoke against them. All the curses written in this book will descend on them, and the LORD will blot out their names from under heaven. [21] The LORD will single them out from all the tribes of Israel for calamity, in accordance with all the curses of the covenant written in this book of the law. [22] The next generation, your children who rise up after you, as well as the foreigner who comes from a distant country, will see the devastation of that land and the afflictions with which the LORD has afflicted it— [23] all its soil burned out by sulfur and salt, nothing planted, nothing sprouting, unable to support any vegetation, like the destruction of Sodom and Gomorrah, Admah and Zeboiim, which the LORD destroyed in his fierce anger— [24] they and indeed all the nations will wonder, "Why has the LORD done thus to this land? What caused this great display of anger?" [25] They will conclude, "It is because they abandoned the covenant of the LORD, the God of their ancestors, which he made with them when he brought them out of the land of Egypt. [26] They turned and served other gods, worshiping them, gods whom they had not known and whom he had not allotted to them; [27] so the anger of the LORD was kindled against that land, bringing on it every curse written in this book. [28] The LORD uprooted them from their land in anger, fury, and great wrath, and cast them into another land, as is now the case." [29] The secret things belong to the LORD our God, but the revealed things belong to us and to our children forever, to observe all the words of this law.

God's Fidelity Assured

30 When all these things have happened to you, the blessings and the curses that I have set before you, if you call them to mind among all the nations where the LORD your God has driven you, [2] and return to the LORD your God, and you and your children obey him with all your heart and with all your soul, just as I am commanding you today, [3] then the LORD your God will restore your fortunes and have compassion

[a] Meaning of Heb uncertain

29:13—This formula proclaims the essence of covenant relationship—we are God's people and YHWH is our God (see 26:17–19). God and we are bound together in *mutual* relationship. We usually think of our responsibilities toward God. What are God's responsibilities toward us?

30:1–10—It is clear in Deuteronomy that people are sinful and that God judges sinful people. But we must remember that God's judgment is *never* the final word (see notes at 5:8–10; 7:9–10). People in the wilderness and in exile heard these words. Despair of the future is a problem in a traumatized world. In the worst of times we hear God's words of hope to restore and renew (see Ezek. 37). God empowers us to begin again in spite of our failures.

on you, gathering you again from all the peoples among whom the Lord your God has scattered you. [4] Even if you are exiled to the ends of the world,[a] from there the Lord your God will gather you, and from there he will bring you back. [5] The Lord your God will bring you into the land that your ancestors possessed, and you will possess it; he will make you more prosperous and numerous than your ancestors.

[6] Moreover, the Lord your God will circumcise your heart and the heart of your descendants, so that you will love the Lord your God with all your heart and with all your soul, in order that you may live. [7] The Lord your God will put all these curses on your enemies and on the adversaries who took advantage of you. [8] Then you shall again obey the Lord, observing all his commandments that I am commanding you today, [9] and the Lord your God will make you abundantly prosperous in all your undertakings, in the fruit of your body, in the fruit of your livestock, and in the fruit of your soil. For the Lord will again take delight in prospering you, just as he delighted in prospering your ancestors, [10] when you obey the Lord your God by observing his commandments and decrees that are written in this book of the law, because you turn to the Lord your God with all your heart and with all your soul.

Exhortation to Choose Life

[11] Surely, this commandment that I am commanding you today is not too hard for you, nor is it too far away. [12] It is not in heaven, that you should say, "Who will go up to heaven for us, and get it for us so that we may hear it and observe it?" [13] Neither is it beyond the sea, that you should say, "Who will cross to the other side of the sea for us, and get it for us so that we may hear it and observe it?" [14] No, the word is very near to you; it is in your mouth and in your heart for you to observe.

[15] See, I have set before you today life and prosperity, death and adversity. [16] If you obey the commandments of the Lord your God[b] that I am commanding you today, by loving the Lord your God, walking in his ways, and observing his commandments, decrees, and ordinances, then you shall live and become numerous, and the Lord your God will bless you in the land that you are entering to possess. [17] But if your heart turns away and you do not hear, but are led astray to bow down to other gods and serve them, [18] I declare to you today that you shall perish; you shall not live long in the land that you are crossing the Jordan to enter and possess. [19] I call heaven and earth to witness against you today that I have set before you life and death, blessings and curses. Choose life so that you and your descendants may live, [20] loving the Lord your God, obeying him, and holding fast to him; for that means life to you and length of days, so that you may live in the land that the Lord swore to give to your ancestors, to Abraham, to Isaac, and to Jacob.

Joshua Becomes Moses' Successor

31 When Moses had finished speaking all[c] these words to all Israel, [2] he said to them: "I am now one hundred twenty years old. I am no longer able to get about, and the Lord has told me, 'You shall not cross over this Jordan.' [3] The Lord your God himself will

[a] Heb of heaven　[b] Gk: Heb lacks If you obey the commandments of the Lord your God　[c] Q Ms Gk: MT Moses went and spoke

---

30:11–14—New Testament texts such as Matt. 16:1–12; 23:23–28 and Rom. 5:20; 7:5–8 have led to Christian anti-Semitism that considers Jewish obedience to the law as both impossible and undesirable. That is not the view of Deuteronomy. Obedience *is* possible and leads to what we most desire—life.

30:15–20—The primary boundary set before us is that of life and death. Life is radical love of and service to God and neighbor. All around are those who choose not to love, and we can see the deadly results.

cross over before you. He will destroy these nations before you, and you shall dispossess them. Joshua also will cross over before you, as the LORD promised. [4] The LORD will do to them as he did to Sihon and Og, the kings of the Amorites, and to their land, when he destroyed them. [5] The LORD will give them over to you and you shall deal with them in full accord with the command that I have given to you. [6] Be strong and bold; have no fear or dread of them, because it is the LORD your God who goes with you; he will not fail you or forsake you."

7 Then Moses summoned Joshua and said to him in the sight of all Israel: "Be strong and bold, for you are the one who will go with this people into the land that the LORD has sworn to their ancestors to give them; and you will put them in possession of it. [8] It is the LORD who goes before you. He will be with you; he will not fail you or forsake you. Do not fear or be dismayed."

The Law to Be Read Every Seventh Year

9 Then Moses wrote down this law, and gave it to the priests, the sons of Levi, who carried the ark of the covenant of the LORD, and to all the elders of Israel. [10] Moses commanded them: "Every seventh year, in the scheduled year of remission, during the festival of booths,[a] [11] when all Israel comes to appear before the LORD your God at the place that he will choose, you shall read this law before all Israel in their hearing. [12] Assemble the people—men, women, and children, as well as the aliens residing in your towns—so that they may hear and learn to fear the LORD your God and to observe diligently all the words

of this law, [13] and so that their children, who have not known it, may hear and learn to fear the LORD your God, as long as you live in the land that you are crossing over the Jordan to possess."

Moses and Joshua Receive God's Charge

14 The LORD said to Moses, "Your time to die is near; call Joshua and present yourselves in the tent of meeting, so that I may commission him." So Moses and Joshua went and presented themselves in the tent of meeting, [15] and the LORD appeared at the tent in a pillar of cloud; the pillar of cloud stood at the entrance to the tent.

16 The LORD said to Moses, "Soon you will lie down with your ancestors. Then this people will begin to prostitute themselves to the foreign gods in their midst, the gods of the land into which they are going; they will forsake me, breaking my covenant that I have made with them. [17] My anger will be kindled against them in that day. I will forsake them and hide my face from them; they will become easy prey, and many terrible troubles will come upon them. In that day they will say, 'Have not these troubles come upon us because our God is not in our midst?' [18] On that day I will surely hide my face on account of all the evil they have done by turning to other gods. [19] Now therefore write this song, and teach it to the Israelites; put it in their mouths, in order that this song may be a witness for me against the Israelites. [20] For when I have brought them into the land flowing with milk and honey, which I promised on oath to their ancestors, and they have eaten their fill and grown fat, they will turn

a Or tabernacles; Heb succoth

31:6, 8, 23—These weak and fearful slaves (and later exiles) hear that the only way forward to an uncertain future is with strength, boldness, and courage (cf. Josh. 1:9). That is possible only because God is with them. It is also the only way we can face an uncertain future.

31:19–21—God's command to write a song as

a witness shows that most people in the ancient world, like people today, derived their theology from the hymns they sang. In the medieval world illiterate folk learned their theology via stained-glass windows. God's message can be conveyed in many media. Perhaps today God would command Moses to build a Web site.

to other gods and serve them, despising me and breaking my covenant. ²¹ And when many terrible troubles come upon them, this song will confront them as a witness, because it will not be lost from the mouths of their descendants. For I know what they are inclined to do even now, before I have brought them into the land that I promised them on oath." ²² That very day Moses wrote this song and taught it to the Israelites.

23 Then the LORD commissioned Joshua son of Nun and said, "Be strong and bold, for you shall bring the Israelites into the land that I promised them; I will be with you."

24 When Moses had finished writing down in a book the words of this law to the very end, ²⁵ Moses commanded the Levites who carried the ark of the covenant of the LORD, saying, ²⁶ "Take this book of the law and put it beside the ark of the covenant of the LORD your God; let it remain there as a witness against you. ²⁷ For I know well how rebellious and stubborn you are. If you already have been so rebellious toward the LORD while I am still alive among you, how much more after my death! ²⁸ Assemble to me all the elders of your tribes and your officials, so that I may recite these words in their hearing and call heaven and earth to witness against them. ²⁹ For I know that after my death you will surely act corruptly, turning aside from the way that I have commanded you. In time to come trouble will befall you, because you will do what is evil in the sight of the LORD, provoking him to anger through the work of your hands."

The Song of Moses

30 Then Moses recited the words of this song, to the very end, in the hearing of the whole assembly of Israel:

32 Give ear, O heavens, and I will speak;

let the earth hear the words of my
  mouth.
² May my teaching drop like the rain,
  my speech condense like the dew;
like gentle rain on grass,
  like showers on new growth.
³ For I will proclaim the name of the
  LORD;
  ascribe greatness to our God!

⁴ The Rock, his work is perfect,
  and all his ways are just.
A faithful God, without deceit,
  just and upright is he;
⁵ yet his degenerate children have
   dealt falsely with him,ᵃ
  a perverse and crooked
   generation.
⁶ Do you thus repay the LORD,
  O foolish and senseless people?
Is not he your father, who created
   you,
  who made you and established
   you?
⁷ Remember the days of old,
  consider the years long past;
ask your father, and he will inform
   you;
  your elders, and they will tell you.
⁸ When the Most Highᵇ apportioned
   the nations,
  when he divided humankind,
he fixed the boundaries of the
   peoples
  according to the number of the
   gods;ᶜ
⁹ the LORD's own portion was his
   people,
  Jacob his allotted share.

¹⁰ He sustainedᵈ him in a desert land,
  in a howling wilderness waste;
he shielded him, cared for him,
  guarded him as the apple of his
   eye.

ᵃ Meaning of Heb uncertain ᵇ Traditional rendering of Heb *Elyon*
ᶜ Q Ms Compare Gk Tg: MT *the Israelites* ᵈ Sam Gk Compare Tg: MT *found*

31:30–32:43—Moses' songs frame the beginning (Exod. 15:1–19) and the end of the wilderness journey. Singing has often accompanied, and even carried, people on long and tortuous journeys. It can even be a subversive act. What songs carry your community through long journeys?

11 As an eagle stirs up its nest,
    and hovers over its young;
  as it spreads its wings, takes
      them up,
    and bears them aloft on its
        pinions,
12 the LORD alone guided him;
    no foreign god was with him.
13 He set him atop the heights of the
      land,
    and fed him with*a* produce of the
        field;
  he nursed him with honey from the
      crags,
    with oil from flinty rock;
14 curds from the herd, and milk from
      the flock,
    with fat of lambs and rams;
  Bashan bulls and goats,
    together with the choicest wheat—
    you drank fine wine from the
        blood of grapes.
15 Jacob ate his fill;*b*
    Jeshurun grew fat, and kicked.
    You grew fat, bloated, and gorged!
  He abandoned God who made him,
    and scoffed at the Rock of his
        salvation.
16 They made him jealous with strange
      gods,
    with abhorrent things they
        provoked him.
17 They sacrificed to demons, not God,
    to deities they had never known,
  to new ones recently arrived,
    whom your ancestors had not
        feared.
18 You were unmindful of the Rock
      that bore you;*c*
    you forgot the God who gave you
        birth.

19 The LORD saw it, and was jealous;*d*
  he spurned*e* his sons and
      daughters.

20 He said: I will hide my face from
      them,
    I will see what their end will be;
  for they are a perverse generation,
    children in whom there is no
        faithfulness.
21 They made me jealous with what is
      no god,
    provoked me with their idols.
  So I will make them jealous with
      what is no people,
    provoke them with a foolish
        nation.
22 For a fire is kindled by my anger,
    and burns to the depths of
        Sheol;
  it devours the earth and its
      increase,
    and sets on fire the foundations of
        the mountains.
23 I will heap disasters upon them,
    spend my arrows against them:
24 wasting hunger,
    burning consumption,
    bitter pestilence.
  The teeth of beasts I will send
      against them,
    with venom of things crawling in
        the dust.
25 In the street the sword shall
      bereave,
    and in the chambers terror,
  for young man and woman alike,
    nursing child and old gray head.
26 I thought to scatter them*f*
    and blot out the memory of them
        from humankind;
27 but I feared provocation by the
      enemy,
    for their adversaries might
        misunderstand
  and say, "Our hand is triumphant;

a Sam Gk Syr Tg: MT *he ate*   *b* Q Mss Sam Gk: MT lacks *Jacob ate his fill*   *c* Or *that begot you*   *d* Q Mss Gk: MT lacks *was jealous*   *e* Cn: Heb *he spurned because of provocation*   *f* Gk: Meaning of Heb uncertain

---

32:11–14—The mother eagle provides an image of divine care. This can be a way to image God as female (cf. Hos. 13:8; Matt. 23:37).

32:18—The advantage of the NRSV translation is that it places in parallel two feminine images of God: God who bore you and gave you birth. However, the Hebrew pairs masculine and feminine images: God who fathered you and gave you birth. Consider how God is both father and mother.

it was not the LORD who did all
this."

28 They are a nation void of sense;
    there is no understanding in them.
29 If they were wise, they would
        understand this;
    they would discern what the end
        would be.
30 How could one have routed a
        thousand,
    and two put a myriad to flight,
unless their Rock had sold them,
    the LORD had given them up?
31 Indeed their rock is not like our Rock;
    our enemies are fools.*a*
32 Their vine comes from the vinestock
        of Sodom,
    from the vineyards of Gomorrah;
their grapes are grapes of poison,
    their clusters are bitter;
33 their wine is the poison of serpents,
    the cruel venom of asps.

34 Is not this laid up in store with me,
    sealed up in my treasuries?
35 Vengeance is mine, and recompense,
    for the time when their foot shall
        slip;
because the day of their calamity is
        at hand,
    their doom comes swiftly.

36 Indeed the LORD will vindicate his
        people,
    have compassion on his servants,
when he sees that their power is
        gone,
    neither bond nor free remaining.
37 Then he will say: Where are their
        gods,
    the rock in which they took refuge,
38 who ate the fat of their sacrifices,
    and drank the wine of their
        libations?
Let them rise up and help you,
    let them be your protection!

39 See now that I, even I, am he;
    there is no god besides me.
I kill and I make alive;
    I wound and I heal;
    and no one can deliver from my
        hand.
40 For I lift up my hand to heaven,
    and swear: As I live forever,
41 when I whet my flashing sword,
    and my hand takes hold on
        judgment;
I will take vengeance on my
        adversaries,
    and will repay those who
        hate me.
42 I will make my arrows drunk with
        blood,
    and my sword shall devour
        flesh—
with the blood of the slain and the
        captives,
    from the long-haired enemy.

43 Praise, O heavens,*b* his people,
    worship him, all you gods!*c*
For he will avenge the blood of his
        children,*d*
    and take vengeance on his
        adversaries;
he will repay those who hate him,*c*
    and cleanse the land for his
        people.*e*

44 Moses came and recited all the
words of this song in the hearing of
the people, he and Joshua*f* son of Nun.
45 When Moses had finished reciting
all these words to all Israel, 46 he said
to them: "Take to heart all the words
that I am giving in witness against you
today; give them as a command to your
children, so that they may diligently
observe all the words of this law. 47 This
is no trifling matter for you, but rather

a Gk: Meaning of Heb uncertain *b* Q Ms Gk: MT *nations* *c* Q Ms Gk:
MT lacks this line *d* Q Ms Gk: MT *his servants* *e* Q Ms Sam Gk Vg: MT
his land his people *f* Sam Gk Syr Vg: MT *Hoshea*

32:39—This verse is one of the most monotheistic statements in the Bible. In our therapeutic
world we want God to be *nice*. It is nice that God
heals us, but God also wounds. It is nice that
God gives us life, but God also kills. We cannot

have a good God who does all things wonderful
for us, and a bad God (Satan, ourselves) accountable for all things harmful to us. To be truly
monotheistic in our faith, we must wrestle with
this dark side of God (see note at 4:24).

your very life; through it you may live long in the land that you are crossing over the Jordan to possess."

Moses' Death Foretold

48 On that very day the LORD addressed Moses as follows: 49 "Ascend this mountain of the Abarim, Mount Nebo, which is in the land of Moab, across from Jericho, and view the land of Canaan, which I am giving to the Israelites for a possession; 50 you shall die there on the mountain that you ascend and shall be gathered to your kin, as your brother Aaron died on Mount Hor and was gathered to his kin; 51 because both of you broke faith with me among the Israelites at the waters of Meribath-kadesh in the wilderness of Zin, by failing to maintain my holiness among the Israelites. 52 Although you may view the land from a distance, you shall not enter it—the land that I am giving to the Israelites."

Moses' Final Blessing on Israel

33 This is the blessing with which Moses, the man of God, blessed the Israelites before his death. 2 He said:

The LORD came from Sinai,
  and dawned from Seir upon us;*a*
he shone forth from Mount
  Paran.
With him were myriads of holy
  ones;*b*
  at his right, a host of his own.*c*
3 Indeed, O favorite among*d* peoples,
  all his holy ones were in your
    charge;
they marched at your heels,
  accepted direction from you.
4 Moses charged us with the law,

as a possession for the assembly of
  Jacob.
5 There arose a king in Jeshurun,
  when the leaders of the people
    assembled—
  the united tribes of Israel.

6 May Reuben live, and not die out,
  even though his numbers are few.

7 And this he said of Judah:
  O LORD, give heed to Judah,
    and bring him to his people;
  strengthen his hands for him,*e*
  and be a help against his
    adversaries.

8 And of Levi he said:
  Give to Levi*f* your Thummim,
    and your Urim to your loyal one,
  whom you tested at Massah,
    with whom you contended at the
      waters of Meribah;
9 who said of his father and mother,
    "I regard them not";
  he ignored his kin,
    and did not acknowledge his
      children.
  For they observed your word,
    and kept your covenant.
10 They teach Jacob your ordinances,
    and Israel your law;
  they place incense before you,
    and whole burnt offerings on your
      altar.
11 Bless, O LORD, his substance,
    and accept the work of his hands;
  crush the loins of his adversaries,
    of those that hate him, so that they
      do not rise again.

a Gk Syr Vg Compare Tg: Heb *upon them*   *b* Cn Compare Gk Sam Syr Vg: MT *He came from Ribeboth-kodesh,*   *c* Cn Compare Gk: meaning of Heb uncertain   *d* Or *O lover of the*   *e* Cn: Heb *with his hands he contended*   *f* Q Ms Gk: MT lacks *Give to Levi*

33:1–29—Moses' concluding words are a blessing of the twelve tribes as a last will and testament to the people. Even in the modern world we tend toward *tribal* thinking, usually in competition. Yet here the tribes are not in competition but in unity. This can be an ecumenical as well as national vision—churches and nations who have different gifts but are but all one community (1 Cor. 12).

33:5—*Jeshurun* means "upright one." The Hebrew word emphasizes human conduct that is right and honest and does not go *out of bounds.* Deuteronomy calls Israel to stay within certain bounds. The moral dilemma is knowing when a boundary must be honored and when a boundary must be transgressed.

12 Of Benjamin he said:
    The beloved of the LORD rests in
        safety—
    the High God[a] surrounds him all
        day long—
    the beloved[b] rests between his
        shoulders.

13 And of Joseph he said:
    Blessed by the LORD be his land,
        with the choice gifts of heaven
            above,
        and of the deep that lies beneath;
14 with the choice fruits of the sun,
        and the rich yield of the months;
15 with the finest produce of the
            ancient mountains,
        and the abundance of the
            everlasting hills;
16 with the choice gifts of the earth and
            its fullness,
        and the favor of the one who
            dwells on Sinai.[c]
    Let these come on the head of
        Joseph,
        on the brow of the prince among
            his brothers.
17 A firstborn[d] bull—majesty is his!
        His horns are the horns of a wild
            ox;
    with them he gores the peoples,
        driving them to[e] the ends of the
            earth;
    such are the myriads of Ephraim,
        such the thousands of
            Manasseh.

18 And of Zebulun he said:
    Rejoice, Zebulun, in your going out;
        and Issachar, in your tents.
19 They call peoples to the mountain;
        there they offer the right sacrifices;
    for they suck the affluence of the
            seas
        and the hidden treasures of the
            sand.

20 And of Gad he said:
    Blessed be the enlargement of Gad!
        Gad lives like a lion;
        he tears at arm and scalp.

21 He chose the best for himself,
        for there a commander's allotment
            was reserved;
    he came at the head of the people,
        he executed the justice of the
            LORD,
        and his ordinances for Israel.

22 And of Dan he said:
    Dan is a lion's whelp
        that leaps forth from Bashan.

23 And of Naphtali he said:
    O Naphtali, sated with favor,
        full of the blessing of the LORD,
        possess the west and the south.

24 And of Asher he said:
    Most blessed of sons be Asher;
        may he be the favorite of his
            brothers,
        and may he dip his foot in oil.
25 Your bars are iron and bronze;
        and as your days, so is your
            strength.

26 There is none like God, O Jeshurun,
        who rides through the heavens to
            your help,
        majestic through the skies.
27 He subdues the ancient gods,[f]
        shatters[g] the forces of old;[h]
    he drove out the enemy before you,
        and said, "Destroy!"
28 So Israel lives in safety,
        untroubled is Jacob's abode[i]
    in a land of grain and wine,
        where the heavens drop down
            dew.
29 Happy are you, O Israel! Who is like
            you,
        a people saved by the LORD,
    the shield of your help,
        and the sword of your triumph!
    Your enemies shall come fawning to
            you,
        and you shall tread on their
            backs.

a Heb above him b Heb he c Cn: Heb in the bush d Q Ms Gk Syr Vg:
MT His firstborn e Cn: Heb the peoples, together f Or The eternal God
is a dwelling place g Cn: Heb from underneath h Or the everlasting arms
i Or fountain

Moses Dies and Is Buried in the Land of Moab

34 Then Moses went up from the plains of Moab to Mount Nebo, to the top of Pisgah, which is opposite Jericho, and the LORD showed him the whole land: Gilead as far as Dan, [2] all Naphtali, the land of Ephraim and Manasseh, all the land of Judah as far as the Western Sea, [3] the Negeb, and the Plain—that is, the valley of Jericho, the city of palm trees—as far as Zoar. [4] The LORD said to him, "This is the land of which I swore to Abraham, to Isaac, and to Jacob, saying, 'I will give it to your descendants'; I have let you see it with your eyes, but you shall not cross over there." [5] Then Moses, the servant of the LORD, died there in the land of Moab, at the LORD's command. [6] He was buried in a valley in the land of Moab, opposite Beth-peor, but no one knows his burial place to this day. [7] Moses was one hundred twenty years old when he died; his sight was unimpaired and his vigor had not abated. [8] The Israelites wept for Moses in the plains of Moab thirty days; then the period of mourning for Moses was ended.

[9] Joshua son of Nun was full of the spirit of wisdom, because Moses had laid his hands on him; and the Israelites obeyed him, doing as the LORD had commanded Moses.

[10] Never since has there arisen a prophet in Israel like Moses, whom the LORD knew face to face. [11] He was unequaled for all the signs and wonders that the LORD sent him to perform in the land of Egypt, against Pharaoh and all his servants and his entire land, [12] and for all the mighty deeds and all the terrifying displays of power that Moses performed in the sight of all Israel.

34:6—The Hebrew reads, "And he buried him." The antecedent to "he" is God. "And God buried Moses." Human hands did not bury Moses. No, God, the one who was friend to Moses, who spoke with him face to face as with no other, does one final act of care and grace for this good and faithful servant. Because no one else can, God buries Moses on the mountain. What greater love could God show? It is a beautiful and tender moment that should move us to weep with God at the death of God's beloved friend.

It is good that Moses' burial place is unknown, because burial places are nothing but trouble. The sites of greatest conflict between Israelis and Palestinians are the Tomb of the Patriarchs, Rachel's Tomb, and Joseph's Tomb. Or witness the conflict over Jesus' burial place. Muslims were given the key to the Holy Sepulcher because the Christian groups kept fighting and killing each other for control—even though Jesus is not there! The veneration of these burial sites, and thus claims of ownership and possession, led to conflict and death. Such behavior dishonors our mothers and fathers.

The Book of
JOSHUA

From what perspective should the reader view the book of Joshua? Joshua, like all the other books belonging to the Deuteronomic literature (Deuteronomy, Joshua, Judges, 1 and 2 Samuel, 1 and 2 Kings), is written from a theological viewpoint—better yet, from the angle of faith and commitment.

The book interprets the past in light of the present; in other words, what happened with Joshua and the people at the time of the thirteenth-century BCE conquest is viewed and read from the historical context of the community who received the book in its written form, most likely during the exile (sometime after 587 BCE). This helps us understand why certain subjects are emphasized more than others, and why Joshua should not be considered a history-oriented work.

The book was given a theological framework by the Deuteronomic editor. Chapters 1 and 23–24 make up this framework. To this framework, Joshua 21:43–45 was added to form the theological backbone of the book. The main body of the book is divided in two major sections: chapters 2–12 and 13–22. The first section presents the conquest or occupation of the land; in it, the Lord takes the leading role. The second section tells about the distribution of the land to the twelve tribes and to the Levites; in it, Joshua is the main figure.

The first main theme in Joshua is *fidelity*, presented as a tension between what God expects from the people, and what the people are able to do. The book of the law of Moses mostly embodies the will of God. The leader, Joshua, and the people are expected to live by its principles. This explains why in the first major section, God is the leading figure. The people of Israel are able to conquer the land, not because their military strength, but through obedience of God's directions and the Lord's grace.

The wars fought by Israel in Joshua are primarily against the city-states and their kings. These political entities have imperial armies and own most of the land worked by the peasants, who live in the unsecured villages. In some instances the population of those city-states (all of them with massive walls) is said to be "the Anakim" or giants. Thus the enemies of God's people are not all the citizens of Canaan, but those who hold power and wealth. The utter violence found in parts of the book should be seen from this perspective. Those suffering violence are not the weak and vulnerable, or those living in the margins of society, but the powerful who used violence in a systematic way.

What was just said is important for the definition of how the people of God are made up. Neither ethnicity nor race, but fidelity to God's will embodied in the book of the law and the covenant determines membership. Both of these elements accentuate that loyalty to God is concretely shown in acts of justice. In Joshua, the grace of the Lord is made known through the path of justice. Hence the first person who becomes a member of God's people during the conquest is a woman, a foreigner, and

one socially marginalized (Rahab, a harlot). Nor is it a surprise that the first person to receive his portion of land is a foreigner (Caleb; see 14:6).

The grace of the Lord is also shown through the giving of the land. In Joshua the land remains God's property, and thus is a gift from God. From the perspective of the people, land should not be seen in terms of private property but in the viewpoint of stewardship. If Israel fulfils the stipulations of the covenant, the land remains in its hand; but if Israel breaks the covenant, it loses the land and, worse yet, is destroyed just like the other nations. On the other hand, the gift of the land, as result of the grace of God, is an act of justice. The land was taken away from the landowners and given to the poor and vulnerable. This act explains why the land is not received by a commercial transaction but by distribution by lot to families. Everybody in Israel receives land as an inheritance from the Lord.

The other important topic in Joshua is *leadership*. In the book, Joshua's leadership is defined from the model of leadership set by Moses. As the Lord had been with Moses, God will be with Joshua (1:5); as the people obeyed Moses, they will obey Joshua (1:17); as Moses gave the land to the people (1:14–15), Joshua will divide the land among them (1:6; 13:7); as Moses led the people across the water (Exod. 14:15), Joshua is commanded to do the same (Josh. 1:2); and most important, Joshua is commanded by God to perform his leadership "in accordance with all the law that my servant Moses commanded you" (1:7). At the end of the book, when Joshua has faithfully fulfilled his role of leader, following the model of Moses, he is also called "the servant of God" (24:29).

—Edesio Sanchez

God's Commission to Joshua

1 After the death of Moses the servant of the LORD, the LORD spoke to Joshua son of Nun, Moses' assistant, saying, **2** "My servant Moses is dead. Now proceed to cross the Jordan, you and all this people, into the land that I am giving to them, to the Israelites.

1:1–18 The Source of Joshua's Authority

The structure of chap. 1 shows the order of authority through the use of three direct speeches: (a) The Lord commands Joshua (vv. 2–9); (b) Joshua commands the people (vv. 10–15); (c) the people respond to Joshua in submission (vv. 16–18).

1:1 *The servant of the LORD*—An honorary title drawn from the prophetic tradition. In Joshua, Moses' leadership is mostly defined this way, and is directly related to the proclamation of God's word. Thus, in this book leadership is prophetic in character (cf. Deut. 32:10–12), and depends directly on God's authority. *Moses' assistant*—If Moses is "servant (*ebed*) of the LORD," Joshua is named "Moses' assistant" (*mesharet*); with this term the Pentateuch recognizes Joshua (Exod. 24:13; 33:11; Num. 11:28; cf. Deut. 1:38). Only at the end of the book will Joshua be called "servant of the LORD" (24:29), in recognition of his own prophetic leadership.

1:2 *All* (*kol*)—This word, very common in Deuteronomy and the Deuteronomic literature, reflects the theological concept of totality and unity. In this chapter, "all" ("every") is used to affirm the totality and unity of the people of God, of the land about to be conquered, of the presence of God and obedience to the law of Moses, of the promise of a life fully blessed and successful, and of the self-commitment of the people of Israel to obey Joshua.

1:2 *Land . . . giving*—The noun "land" and the verb "to give" are theologically important, both for chap. 1 and for the rest of the book. With them, God functions, nearly every time, as the subject and the people of Israel as the recipient. The possession of the land depends essentially upon God and God's faithfulness to the divine word (v. 6). Following Deuteronomy, Joshua states at the outset that the land is a gift from God, and not a commodity; no Israelite was permitted to hang a sign saying "for sale." The people of Israel were simply stewards of the land. The giving of the land, theologically speaking, responds to God's grace. That explains why the

³ Every place that the sole of your foot will tread upon I have given to you, as I promised to Moses. ⁴ From the wilderness and the Lebanon as far as the great river, the river Euphrates, all the land of the Hittites, to the Great Sea in the west shall be your territory. ⁵ No one shall be able to stand against you all the days of your life. As I was with Moses, so I will be with you; I will not fail you or forsake you. ⁶ Be strong and courageous; for you shall put this people in possession of the land that I swore to their ancestors to give them. ⁷ Only be strong and very courageous, being careful to act in accordance with all the law that my servant Moses commanded you; do not turn from it to the right hand or to the left, so that you may be successful wherever you go. ⁸ This book of the law shall not depart out of your mouth; you shall meditate on it day and night, so that you may be careful to act in accordance with all that is written in it. For then you shall make your way prosperous, and then you shall be successful. ⁹ I hereby command you: Be strong and courageous; do not be frightened or dismayed, for the LORD your God is with you wherever you go."

Preparations for the Invasion

10 Then Joshua commanded the officers of the people, ¹¹ "Pass through the camp, and command the people: 'Prepare your provisions; for in three days you are to cross over the Jordan, to go in to take possession of the land that the LORD your God gives you to possess.'"

12 To the Reubenites, the Gadites, and the half-tribe of Manasseh Joshua said, ¹³ "Remember the word that Moses the servant of the LORD commanded you, saying, 'The LORD your God is providing you a place of rest, and will give you this land.' ¹⁴ Your wives, your little ones, and your livestock shall remain in the land that Moses gave you beyond the Jordan. But all the warriors among you shall cross over armed before your kindred and shall help them, ¹⁵ until the LORD gives rest to your kindred as well as to you, and they too take possession of the land that the LORD your God is giving them. Then you shall return to your own land and take possession of it, the land that Moses the servant of the LORD gave you beyond the Jordan to the east."

16 They answered Joshua: "All that you have commanded us we will do, and wherever you send us we will go. ¹⁷ Just

---

recipients were mostly those living outside the walled cities: former slaves, peasants, and destitute foreigners.

1:3–4—These two verses echo Deut. 11:24–25, thereby indicating the connection between Deuteronomy and Joshua as promise and fulfillment. The extent of the land indicated in v. 4 most likely reflects the geography at the time of the Davidic and Solomonic monarchy (cf. 1 Kgs. 4:21, 24). The promises given by God seem to have posed a great challenge to the people of the covenant; history would show that the people, for the most part, fell short of making fitting response to God's promises.

1:6–9—In these verses, as well as in 5:10–12 and 8:30–35, Joshua is commanded to perform the duties of a king. Several scholars have stated that behind the figure of Joshua stands that of king Josiah. Indeed, Josiah, the Davidic king, could just as well be the one pictured here. Joshua and Josiah are parallel figures: they both lived

in accordance with the law of Moses (2 Kgs. 22:18–20), they both celebrated the Passover (Josh. 5:10–12 = 2 Kgs. 23:21–23) and they both were champions of justice (cf. Jer. 22:15–16).

Living in accordance with God's word (torah) is concomitant with God's very presence. One cannot be separated from the other.

1:12–15—Even though the two and a half tribes had already received from God *a place of rest*, the command is that the warriors may not rest until all other tribes had received from the Lord a place of rest. This principle is part of the Deuteronomic theology of "totality" and "unity." In Joshua, as distinguished from Judges, both the leader and the people act on behalf of the totality of the nation (21:44).

1:14—The leadership of Moses as paradigm for Joshua is so crucial that even though Moses did not enter the promised land, he was able to distribute part of it. By this means, Moses was in a sense able to complete his mission.

as we obeyed Moses in all things, so we will obey you. Only may the LORD your God be with you, as he was with Moses! ¹⁸ Whoever rebels against your orders and disobeys your words, whatever you command, shall be put to death. Only be strong and courageous."

Spies Sent to Jericho

2 Then Joshua son of Nun sent two men secretly from Shittim as spies, saying, "Go, view the land, especially Jericho." So they went, and entered the house of a prostitute whose name was Rahab, and spent the night there. ² The king of Jericho was told, "Some Israelites have come here tonight to search out the land." ³ Then the king of Jericho sent orders to Rahab, "Bring out the men who have come to you, who entered your house, for they have come only to search out the whole land." ⁴ But the woman took the two men and hid them. Then she said, "True, the men came to me, but I did not know where they came from. ⁵ And when it was time to close the gate at dark, the men went out. Where the men went I do not know. Pursue them quickly, for you can overtake them." ⁶ She had, however, brought them up to the roof and hidden them with the stalks of flax that she had laid out on the roof. ⁷ So the men pursued them on the way to the Jordan as far as the fords. As soon as the pursuers had gone out, the gate was shut.

8 Before they went to sleep, she came

2:1–12:24 Wars and Conquest

The first part (chaps. 2–8) tells about the conquest of several city-states; in the second part (chaps. 10–11) we find military campaigns in two major areas of Canaan: the south and the north. Chapter 9 functions as a hinge to unite the parts. It is interesting to note that chap. 2 deals with "foreigners" becoming members of God's people and chap. 12 ends the section by giving the list of the kings defeated by both leaders, Moses and Joshua. In these chaps. (2–12), God is in fact the subject of action; Joshua will be the main actor of chaps. 13–22.

2:1–24 The Good Harlot of Jericho

From a theological perspective it is important that a foreign woman is at the center of the story that opens up the whole historical section of the book. Joshua says at the outset that those marginalized in society are the first to become members of God's kingdom. **Rahab** is the only woman in the list of those who became a paradigm of faith (Heb. 11:31; Jas. 2:25) and is one of the four women in the genealogy of our Savior (Matt. 1:5).

2:1—*Jericho*, like most cities found in Palestine during the so-called conquest period, was a city-state and thus walled ("shut up inside and out," 6:1). According to the archaeological findings, the walled cities were 60–75 percent occupied by public buildings, and only 25–40 percent by housing. This means that those who lived inside them were the few rich and powerful of society. Most of the population lived in the very small, unwalled villages. *A prostitute ... Rahab*—This woman has her house either on top of the wall or as part of it (see 2:15). She belonged to a sector of society considered "outcast." Harlots constituted one of several groups of occupational outcasts whose services were greatly desired but who, because of their demeaning work and the social taboos, codes, and conventions that they breached, bore a scapegoating stigma and worked under decided disabilities. Among those groups were slaves, leatherworkers, butchers, barbers, midwives, prostitutes, entertainers, lepers, and merchants.

2:4–7—At the outset, Rahab was acting as a member of God's people and on behalf of the outsiders. She was a better "spy" than the two men from Israel and smarter than the king and his "intelligence agency."

2:8–11—Rahab's confession of faith follows a concentric structure:

A—Rahab's confession: *"I know that the LORD ..."* (v. 9a)
  B—The fear of the people (v. 9b)
    C—The exodus (v. 10)
  B'—The fear of the people (v. 11a)
A'—Rahab's confession: *"The LORD your God is indeed God ..."* (v. 11b)

Rahab has put her faith in the God of the exodus and sees her liberation and that of her family as an "exodus."

2:8—The Hebrew word for *inhabitants* could be translated as "rulers" (those who sit on a throne). With this translation, a stress is given again to the fact that Rahab's decision to support the "outsiders" was due to the fact that she considered the "insiders" her "enemies." She decided to join the people who had YHWH, the God of exodus, as the liberating God.

up to them on the roof [9] and said to the men: "I know that the LORD has given you the land, and that dread of you has fallen on us, and that all the inhabitants of the land melt in fear before you. [10] For we have heard how the LORD dried up the water of the Red Sea[a] before you when you came out of Egypt, and what you did to the two kings of the Amorites that were beyond the Jordan, to Sihon and Og, whom you utterly destroyed. [11] As soon as we heard it, our hearts melted, and there was no courage left in any of us because of you. The LORD your God is indeed God in heaven above and on earth below. [12] Now then, since I have dealt kindly with you, swear to me by the LORD that you in turn will deal kindly with my family. Give me a sign of good faith [13] that you will spare my father and mother, my brothers and sisters, and all who belong to them, and deliver our lives from death." [14] The men said to her, "Our life for yours! If you do not tell this business of ours, then we will deal kindly and faithfully with you when the LORD gives us the land."

[15] Then she let them down by a rope through the window, for her house was on the outer side of the city wall and she resided within the wall itself. [16] She said to them, "Go toward the hill country, so that the pursuers may not come upon you. Hide yourselves there three days, until the pursuers have returned; then afterward you may go your way." [17] The men said to her, "We will be released from this oath that you have made us swear to you [18] if we invade the land and you do not tie this crimson cord in the window through which you let us down, and you do not gather into your house your father and mother, your brothers, and all your family. [19] If any of you go out of the doors of your house into the street, they shall be responsible for their own death, and we shall be innocent; but if a hand is laid upon any who are with you in the house, we shall bear the responsibility for their death. [20] But if you tell this business of ours, then we shall be released from this oath that you made us swear to you." [21] She said, "According to your words, so be it." She sent them away and they departed. Then she tied the crimson cord in the window.

[22] They departed and went into the hill country and stayed there three days, until the pursuers returned. The pursuers had searched all along the way and found nothing. [23] Then the two men came down again from the hill country. They crossed over, came to Joshua son of Nun, and told him all that had happened to them. [24] They said to Joshua, "Truly the LORD has given all the land into our hands; moreover all the inhabitants of the land melt in fear before us."

Israel Crosses the Jordan

3 Early in the morning Joshua rose and set out from Shittim with all the Israelites, and they came to the Jordan. They camped there before crossing over. [2] At the end of three days the officers went through the camp [3] and commanded the people, "When you

[a] Or Sea of Reeds

2:18—*The crimson cord in the window* of Rahab's house functioned like the blood in the "lintel and the two doorposts" of the Israelites at the time of the exodus (Exod. 12:22).

2:24—The two spies did not need to spy the territory; they believed the word of the single female witness and that was enough for them. Covenant is a matter not only of solidarity, but also of total trust.

3:1–5:1 Liturgical Games: the Crossing of the Jordan River
These two chapters, together with chaps. 5–8, present a narrative with strong liturgical flavor. They remind us of the holy war vocabulary of Deuteronomy (20:1–20; 23:9–14). The priests and the ark of the covenant play a very important role in the crossing of the Jordan River. The Hebrew word translated here mostly with the phrase "crossing over" is repeated twenty-three times. The theme of the crossing of the Jordan interacts with the Hebrew verb for "standing still" to convey the idea that only with the "steadfastness" of the priests and the ark could the people of Israel cross over to the other side of the river.

see the ark of the covenant of the LORD your God being carried by the levitical priests, then you shall set out from your place. Follow it, ⁴ so that you may know the way you should go, for you have not passed this way before. Yet there shall be a space between you and it, a distance of about two thousand cubits; do not come any nearer to it." ⁵ Then Joshua said to the people, "Sanctify yourselves; for tomorrow the LORD will do wonders among you." ⁶ To the priests Joshua said, "Take up the ark of the covenant, and pass on in front of the people." So they took up the ark of the covenant and went in front of the people.

7 The LORD said to Joshua, "This day I will begin to exalt you in the sight of all Israel, so that they may know that I will be with you as I was with Moses. ⁸ You are the one who shall command the priests who bear the ark of the covenant, 'When you come to the edge of the waters of the Jordan, you shall stand still in the Jordan.' " ⁹ Joshua then said to the Israelites, "Draw near and hear the words of the LORD your God." ¹⁰ Joshua said, "By this you shall know that among you is the living God who without fail will drive out from before you the Canaanites, Hittites, Hivites, Perizzites, Girgashites, Amorites, and Jebusites: ¹¹ the ark of the covenant of the Lord of all the earth is going to pass before you into the Jordan. ¹² So now select twelve men from the tribes of Israel, one from each tribe. ¹³ When the soles of the feet of the priests who bear the ark of the LORD, the Lord of all the earth, rest in the waters of the Jordan, the waters of the Jordan flowing from above shall be cut off; they shall stand in a single heap."

14 When the people set out from their tents to cross over the Jordan, the priests bearing the ark of the covenant were in front of the people. ¹⁵ Now the Jordan overflows all its banks throughout the time of harvest. So when those who bore the ark had come to the Jordan, and the feet of the priests bearing the ark were dipped in the edge of the water, ¹⁶ the waters flowing from above stood still, rising up in a single heap far off at Adam, the city that is beside Zarethan, while those flowing toward the sea of the Arabah, the Dead Sea,ᵃ were wholly cut off. Then the people crossed over opposite Jericho. ¹⁷ While all Israel were crossing over on dry ground, the priests who bore the ark of the covenant of the LORD stood on dry ground in the middle of the Jordan, until the entire nation finished crossing over the Jordan.

Twelve Stones Set Up at Gilgal

4 When the entire nation had finished crossing over the Jordan, the LORD said to Joshua: ² "Select twelve men from the people, one from each tribe, ³ and command them, 'Take twelve stones from here out of the middle of the Jordan, from the place where the priests' feet stood, carry them over with you, and lay them down in the place where you camp tonight.' " ⁴ Then Joshua summoned the twelve men from the Israelites, whom he had appointed, one from each tribe. ⁵ Joshua said to them, "Pass on before the ark of the LORD your God into the middle of the Jordan, and each of you take up a stone on his shoulder, one for each of the tribes of the Israelites, ⁶ so that this may be a sign among you. When your children ask in time to come, 'What do those stones mean

ᵃ Heb Salt Sea

3:7—The topic of leadership is considered again, with Moses as the paradigm (see Josh. 1:9; 4:15; Exod. 3:12). For both Moses and Joshua, the success of their ministry depends on the presence of the Lord in their lives. What a way to secure success! "If God is for us, who is against us?" (Rom. 8:31).

4:6, 21 *When your children ask*—Resembling Deut. 6:20–25, these verses convey the catechetical spirit of this chapter. As a pedagogical dialogue between children and parents, this narrative will have perennial value, as did the very act of the exodus.

to you?' [7] then you shall tell them that the waters of the Jordan were cut off in front of the ark of the covenant of the LORD. When it crossed over the Jordan, the waters of the Jordan were cut off. So these stones shall be to the Israelites a memorial forever."

8 The Israelites did as Joshua commanded. They took up twelve stones out of the middle of the Jordan, according to the number of the tribes of the Israelites, as the LORD told Joshua, carried them over with them to the place where they camped, and laid them down there. [9] (Joshua set up twelve stones in the middle of the Jordan, in the place where the feet of the priests bearing the ark of the covenant had stood; and they are there to this day.)

10 The priests who bore the ark remained standing in the middle of the Jordan, until everything was finished that the LORD commanded Joshua to tell the people, according to all that Moses had commanded Joshua. The people crossed over in haste. [11] As soon as all the people had finished crossing over, the ark of the LORD, and the priests, crossed over in front of the people. [12] The Reubenites, the Gadites, and the half-tribe of Manasseh crossed over armed before the Israelites, as Moses had ordered them. [13] About forty thousand armed for war crossed over before the LORD to the plains of Jericho for battle.

14 On that day the LORD exalted Joshua in the sight of all Israel; and they stood in awe of him, as they had stood in awe of Moses, all the days of his life.

15 The LORD said to Joshua, [16] "Command the priests who bear the ark of the covenant,[a] to come up out of the Jordan." [17] Joshua therefore commanded the priests, "Come up out of the Jordan." [18] When the priests bearing the ark of the covenant of the LORD came up from the middle of the Jordan, and the soles of the priests' feet touched dry ground, the waters of the Jordan returned to their place and overflowed all its banks, as before.

19 The people came up out of the Jordan on the tenth day of the first month, and they camped in Gilgal on the east border of Jericho. [20] Those twelve stones, which they had taken out of the Jordan, Joshua set up in Gilgal, [21] saying to the Israelites, "When your children ask their parents in time to come, 'What do these stones mean?' [22] then you shall let your children know, 'Israel crossed over the Jordan here on dry ground.' [23] For the LORD your God dried up the waters of the Jordan for you until you crossed over, as the LORD your God did to the Red Sea,[b] which he dried up for us until we crossed over, [24] so that all the peoples of the earth may know that the hand of the LORD is mighty, and so that you may fear the LORD your God forever."

The New Generation Circumcised

5 When all the kings of the Amorites beyond the Jordan to the west, and all the kings of the Canaanites by the sea, heard that the LORD had dried up the waters of the Jordan for the Israelites until they had crossed over, their hearts melted, and there was no longer any spirit in them, because of the Israelites.

2 At that time the LORD said to Joshua, "Make flint knives and circumcise the Israelites a second time." [3] So Joshua made flint knives, and circumcised the Israelites at Gibeath-haaraloth.[c] [4] This

[a] Or treaty, or testimony; Heb eduth   [b] Or Sea of Reeds   [c] That is the Hill of the Foreskins

---

4:19 *Gilgal*—One of the first religious centers of Israel, the name means "circle," and its location is unknown.

5:2–15 Circumcision, Passover and Encounter with the Angel of the Lord

Like the previous two chapters, chap. 5 has a clear liturgical orientation. Three parts form it:

(a) vv. 1–9, circumcision; (b) vv. 10–12, the Passover; (c) vv. 13–15, the vocation of Joshua.

5:2 *Circumcise*—This act links the people with two key moments in Israel's history: the covenant with Abraham (Gen. 17) and the conquest of the land (Josh. 5:4–6).

is the reason why Joshua circumcised them: all the males of the people who came out of Egypt, all the warriors, had died during the journey through the wilderness after they had come out of Egypt. 5 Although all the people who came out had been circumcised, yet all the people born on the journey through the wilderness after they had come out of Egypt had not been circumcised. 6 For the Israelites traveled forty years in the wilderness, until all the nation, the warriors who came out of Egypt, perished, not having listened to the voice of the LORD. To them the LORD swore that he would not let them see the land that he had sworn to their ancestors to give us, a land flowing with milk and honey. 7 So it was their children, whom he raised up in their place, that Joshua circumcised; for they were uncircumcised, because they had not been circumcised on the way.

8 When the circumcising of all the nation was done, they remained in their places in the camp until they were healed. 9 The LORD said to Joshua, "Today I have rolled away from you the disgrace of Egypt." And so that place is called Gilgal*a* to this day.

The Passover at Gilgal

10 While the Israelites were camped in Gilgal they kept the passover in the evening on the fourteenth day of the month in the plains of Jericho. 11 On the day after the passover, on that very day, they ate the produce of the land, unleavened cakes and parched grain. 12 The manna ceased on the day they ate the produce of the land, and the Israelites no longer had manna; they ate the crops of the land of Canaan that year.

Joshua's Vision

13 Once when Joshua was by Jericho, he looked up and saw a man standing before him with a drawn sword in his hand. Joshua went to him and said to him, "Are you one of us, or one of our adversaries?" 14 He replied, "Neither; but as commander of the army of the LORD I have now come." And Joshua fell on his face to the earth and worshiped, and he said to him, "What do you command your servant, my lord?" 15 The commander of the army of the LORD said to Joshua, "Remove the sandals from your feet, for the place where you stand is holy." And Joshua did so.

a Related to Heb *galal* to roll

5:8—The Hebrew word translated here as *nation* is normally used as reference to "foreign peoples" or "Gentiles." In the context of the circumcision, it is probably used to stress the act by which the generation of the wilderness changed their status from "Gentiles" to members of the covenant people.

5:9—*The disgrace of Egypt* recalls the time of oppression in Egypt. However, this time it is removed not by war, but through a ritual of covenant. In order that the wilderness generation be full participants of the liberated nation, they also need to receive the sign of freedom. Only then can they also participate in the feast of liberation, the Passover. The name *Gilgal* receives a new meaning: "the disgrace has been removed"; it does not recalls a "circle" of stones, but the very event of the exodus.

5:10—The period of the exodus started with the celebration of the Passover festival (Exod. 12–13) and ended with the celebration of the same festival (Josh. 5:10–12). Both when leaving Egypt and when entering the promised land, the people celebrated freedom.

5:11–12—*The produce/crops of the land* is repeated three times in these two verses, signaling the end of the time of wandering. As soon as the people were able to eat from the crops of the promised land, *the manna ceased*. By eating the Passover dinner and the fruits of the land, the people were also, liturgically, celebrating the covenant with the Lord. *Parched grain* was a common food throughout the history of ancient Israel (Lev. 23:14; Ruth 2:14; 1 Sam. 17:17). One of the main ingredients of the liberating feast was an everyday meal!

5:14 *Commander of the army of the LORD*—If, as seems likely, this divine figure is the "angel of the Lord," then through him the Lord has been with Israel from the beginning of the exodus (the killing of the firstborn Egyptian males), during the period of the wandering through the wilderness (Exod. 32:34), and now at the end of the pilgrimage and the beginning of the settlement in the promised land.

Jericho Taken and Destroyed

6 Now Jericho was shut up inside and out because of the Israelites; no one came out and no one went in. ²The LORD said to Joshua, "See, I have handed Jericho over to you, along with its king and soldiers. ³You shall march around the city, all the warriors circling the city once. Thus you shall do for six days, ⁴with seven priests bearing seven trumpets of rams' horns before the ark. On the seventh day you shall march around the city seven times, the priests blowing the trumpets. ⁵When they make a long blast with the ram's horn, as soon as you hear the sound of the trumpet, then all the people shall shout with a great shout; and the wall of the city will fall down flat, and all the people shall charge straight ahead." ⁶So Joshua son of Nun summoned the priests and said to them, "Take up the ark of the covenant, and have seven priests carry seven trumpets of rams' horns in front of the ark of the LORD." ⁷To the people he said, "Go forward and march around the city; have the armed men pass on before the ark of the LORD."

8 As Joshua had commanded the people, the seven priests carrying the seven trumpets of rams' horns before the LORD went forward, blowing the trumpets, with the ark of the covenant of the LORD following them. ⁹And the armed men went before the priests who blew the trumpets; the rear guard came after the ark, while the trumpets blew continually. ¹⁰To the people Joshua gave this command: "You shall not shout or let your voice be heard, nor shall you utter a word, until the day I tell you to shout. Then you shall shout." ¹¹So the ark of the LORD went around the city, circling it once; and they came into the camp, and spent the night in the camp.

12 Then Joshua rose early in the morning, and the priests took up the ark of the LORD. ¹³The seven priests carrying the seven trumpets of rams' horns before the ark of the LORD passed on, blowing the trumpets continually. The armed men went before them, and the rear guard came after the ark of the LORD, while the trumpets blew continually. ¹⁴On the second day they marched around the city once and then returned to the camp. They did this for six days.

15 On the seventh day they rose early, at dawn, and marched around the city in the same manner seven times. It was only on that day that they marched around the city seven times. ¹⁶And at the seventh time, when the priests had blown the trumpets, Joshua said to the people, "Shout! For the LORD has given you the city. ¹⁷The city and all that is in it shall be devoted to the LORD for destruction. Only Rahab the prostitute and all who are with her in her house shall live because she hid the messengers we sent. ¹⁸As for you, keep away

---

6:1–27 The Conquest of Jericho, a Great Liturgy
Liturgy is the key for reading this very well known story—not history or archaeological findings. The whole action belongs to the divine milieu, not to the action of an army with heavy machinery. The triumph over the enemy and the resultant conquest of Jericho belong to the Lord (v. 2), whose property everything in the city becomes.

Two elements need to be stressed here: (1) God's surprising and refreshing way of acting in very important situations; (2) salvation from the fall of Jericho, which came neither to the royal family nor to the powerful or wealthy, but to a prostitute and her family. In the missionary projection of this chapter, it is God's absurdi-

ties—the whole action seems like a group of youngsters following a game leader (see Matt. 21:14–16)—that surprise us, and the locus of salvation becomes a foreigner and prostitute.

6:9 *The armed men*—Just as in Ps. 149:6, weapons are liturgical instruments, and the army is part of a worship act and not of battle.

6:17—Something ***devoted to the LORD*** should be understood as a sacrifice, and in the case of Jericho as a "firstfruit offering." It is part of the elements of holy war (Deut. 20:16–17), and by this law Israel is restrained from assaulting and looting a city just for the sake of material goods. The law, in part, was also given to keep God's people away from idolatry (Deut. 7:1–6, 24–26).

from the things devoted to destruction, so as not to covet[a] and take any of the devoted things and make the camp of Israel an object for destruction, bringing trouble upon it. ¹⁹ But all silver and gold, and vessels of bronze and iron, are sacred to the LORD; they shall go into the treasury of the LORD." ²⁰ So the people shouted, and the trumpets were blown. As soon as the people heard the sound of the trumpets, they raised a great shout, and the wall fell down flat; so the people charged straight ahead into the city and captured it. ²¹ Then they devoted to destruction by the edge of the sword all in the city, both men and women, young and old, oxen, sheep, and donkeys.

22 Joshua said to the two men who had spied out the land, "Go into the prostitute's house, and bring the woman out of it and all who belong to her, as you swore to her." ²³ So the young men who had been spies went in and brought Rahab out, along with her father, her mother, her brothers, and all who belonged to her—they brought all her kindred out—and set them outside the camp of Israel. ²⁴ They burned down the city, and everything in it; only the silver and gold, and the vessels of bronze and iron, they put into the treasury of the house of the LORD. ²⁵ But Rahab the prostitute, with her family and all who belonged to her, Joshua spared. Her family[b] has lived in Israel ever since. For she hid the messengers whom Joshua sent to spy out Jericho.

26 Joshua then pronounced this oath, saying,

"Cursed before the LORD be anyone
        who tries
    to build this city—this Jericho!
At the cost of his firstborn he shall
        lay its foundation,
    and at the cost of his youngest he
        shall set up its gates!"

27 So the LORD was with Joshua; and his fame was in all the land.

The Sin of Achan and Its Punishment

7 But the Israelites broke faith in regard to the devoted things: Achan son of Carmi son of Zabdi son of Zerah, of the tribe of Judah, took some of the devoted things; and the anger of the LORD burned against the Israelites.

2 Joshua sent men from Jericho to Ai, which is near Beth-aven, east of Bethel, and said to them, "Go up and spy out the land." And the men went up and spied out Ai. ³ Then they returned to Joshua and said to him, "Not all the people need go up; about two or three thousand men should go up and attack Ai. Since they are so few, do not make the

[a] Gk: Heb *devote to destruction* Compare 7.21 [b] Heb *She*

6:27—The topic of *fame* is important throughout the book and, indeed, throughout the Deuteronomic literature (Joshua, Judges, Samuel and Kings). The good fame of the leaders goes hand in hand with the Lord's presence with them. What follows gives the other side of the coin (7:9).

7:1–8:29 Results of Disobedience and Obedience; the Conquest of Ai

In both of these chapters, "obedience" is the core of the message. The key to triumph is not having a strong army or a well-planned strategy, but dependence upon God.

7:1–26—The chapter is framed by the theme of the anger of the Lord at Israel's disobedience (vv. 1 and 26). The passage also teaches that the giving of the land, according to God's promises in 1:2–5; 6:2; 8:1, is not automatic. Obedience to God's orders and faithfulness are essential.

7:1–5—In this unit that deals with Israel's plans to take over *Ai*, two items need to be considered besides the sin of *Achan* and the Lord's anger: bad strategy and self-confidence. The Israelites insisted in doing things their own way; there is no word from God giving instructions of what to do (see 9:14); there is no pursuit of Moses' paradigmatic leadership. This whole passage is a reversal of the account in chap. 6. The presence of sin caused the absence of God.

7:1—This verse unites what had been said about *the devoted things* in 6:17, 21 and what follows about why Israel was defeated by its enemies. The devoted things is the motif that gives coherence to the narrative; it appears eight times in the chapter. Even though the sin was that of an individual, all the people of Israel are considered guilty of disloyalty to the Lord.

whole people toil up there." ⁴ So about three thousand of the people went up there; and they fled before the men of Ai. ⁵ The men of Ai killed about thirty-six of them, chasing them from outside the gate as far as Shebarim and killing them on the slope. The hearts of the people melted and turned to water.

6 Then Joshua tore his clothes, and fell to the ground on his face before the ark of the LORD until the evening, he and the elders of Israel; and they put dust on their heads. ⁷ Joshua said, "Ah, Lord GOD! Why have you brought this people across the Jordan at all, to hand us over to the Amorites so as to destroy us? Would that we had been content to settle beyond the Jordan! ⁸ O Lord, what can I say, now that Israel has turned their backs to their enemies! ⁹ The Canaanites and all the inhabitants of the land will hear of it, and surround us, and cut off our name from the earth. Then what will you do for your great name?"

10 The LORD said to Joshua, "Stand up! Why have you fallen upon your face? ¹¹ Israel has sinned; they have transgressed my covenant that I imposed on them. They have taken some of the devoted things; they have stolen, they have acted deceitfully, and they have put them among their own belongings.

¹² Therefore the Israelites are unable to stand before their enemies; they turn their backs to their enemies, because they have become a thing devoted for destruction themselves. I will be with you no more, unless you destroy the devoted things from among you. ¹³ Proceed to sanctify the people, and say, 'Sanctify yourselves for tomorrow; for thus says the LORD, the God of Israel, "There are devoted things among you, O Israel; you will be unable to stand before your enemies until you take away the devoted things from among you." ¹⁴ In the morning therefore you shall come forward tribe by tribe. The tribe that the LORD takes shall come near by clans, the clan that the LORD takes shall come near by households, and the household that the LORD takes shall come near one by one. ¹⁵ And the one who is taken as having the devoted things shall be burned with fire, together with all that he has, for having transgressed the covenant of the LORD, and for having done an outrageous thing in Israel.'"

16 So Joshua rose early in the morning, and brought Israel near tribe by tribe, and the tribe of Judah was taken. ¹⁷ He brought near the clans of Judah, and the clan of the Zerahites was taken; and he brought near the clan of the Zerahites,

---

7:6—*The elders of Israel* are, in the Deuteronomic literature, the representatives of the twelve tribes of Israel, and appear in the context of very important events in the life of Israel.

7:7–9—Joshua's prayer resembles that of Moses in Deut. 9:26–29 (see Exod. 32:11). It poses to the Lord three important questions, dealing with (a) the exodus, (b) the defeat of Israel, and (c) God's great name. The argument about the Lord's *great name* (v. 9) is well known throughout the Scriptures, esp. in the book of Psalms. But here, God's fame depends, according to Joshua, on Israel's fame.

7:10–15—This unit presents an A-B-A structure: The issue about "transgressing God's covenant" appears in verses 11 and 15, and at the center (v. 12) we find the statement, *I will be with you no more*. The phrase *devoted things* appears more in this unit than anywhere else in chap. 7.

By breaking the covenant, Israel becomes

just like the other nations, namely, outside the protective care of the Lord. Thus Israel is, like them, exposed to extermination (v. 12). Again, the difference between being a member of God's people and being an outsider is not a matter of race or ethnicity, but rather of obedience to the stipulations of the covenant. It is instructive to compare this chapter with chap. 2. Here Achan, an "insider," acts as an outsider, and in chap. 2 Rahab, an "outsider," acts as a faithful insider.

7:10—God's answer to Joshua's lament is, "Joshua, the solution of the problem will not come if you remain lamenting. *Stand up!* You need to take an action." (The same Hebrew imperative appears in v. 13, translated here as "proceed.")

7:15—The sin committed by Achan has a double dimension: (1) against the Lord, for *having transgressed the covenant*; (2) against the community, because the whole nation, and especially the family, suffered.

family by family,^a and Zabdi was taken. ¹⁸ And he brought near his household one by one, and Achan son of Carmi son of Zabdi son of Zerah, of the tribe of Judah, was taken. ¹⁹ Then Joshua said to Achan, "My son, give glory to the LORD God of Israel and make confession to him. Tell me now what you have done; do not hide it from me." ²⁰ And Achan answered Joshua, "It is true; I am the one who sinned against the LORD God of Israel. This is what I did: ²¹ when I saw among the spoil a beautiful mantle from Shinar, and two hundred shekels of silver, and a bar of gold weighing fifty shekels, then I coveted them and took them. They now lie hidden in the ground inside my tent, with the silver underneath."

22 So Joshua sent messengers, and they ran to the tent; and there it was, hidden in his tent with the silver underneath. ²³ They took them out of the tent and brought them to Joshua and all the Israelites; and they spread them out before the LORD. ²⁴ Then Joshua and all Israel with him took Achan son of Zerah, with the silver, the mantle, and the bar of gold, with his sons and daughters, with his oxen, donkeys, and sheep, and his tent and all that he had; and they brought them up to the Valley of Achor. ²⁵ Joshua said, "Why did you

bring trouble on us? The LORD is bringing trouble on you today." And all Israel stoned him to death; they burned them with fire, cast stones on them, ²⁶ and raised over him a great heap of stones that remains to this day. Then the LORD turned from his burning anger. Therefore that place to this day is called the Valley of Achor.^b

Ai Captured by a Stratagem and Destroyed

8 Then the LORD said to Joshua, "Do not fear or be dismayed; take all the fighting men with you, and go up now to Ai. See, I have handed over to you the king of Ai with his people, his city, and his land. ² You shall do to Ai and its king as you did to Jericho and its king; only its spoil and its livestock you may take as booty for yourselves. Set an ambush against the city, behind it."

3 So Joshua and all the fighting men set out to go up against Ai. Joshua chose thirty thousand warriors and sent them out by night ⁴ with the command, "You shall lie in ambush against the city, behind it; do not go very far from the city, but all of you stay alert. ⁵ I and all the people who are with me will approach the city. When they come out against us, as before, we shall flee from

^a Mss Syr: MT *man by man*   ^b That is *Trouble*

7:21—The sin of Achan is committed in three steps, following the pattern of Gen. 3:6: *I saw . . . coveted . . . took*. It seems that the author deliberately relates Achan's sin to the original sin.

7:25–26—In Hebrew there is a play on words (pun) with the names of the sinner and the valley, plus the situation created by the sin: *Achan* (in 1 Chr. 2:7 the name is spelled *Achar*)–*Achor*–*achar*. **Trouble** is everywhere. Achan was "troubled" and violated the covenant; that sin created a great "trouble" for the whole nation and for God; God "troubled" Achan and his family by punishing them; the place where the punishment was performed is called *Achor*, "The Trouble."

8:1–29—As in chap. 6, God reappears as the subject of the orders and actions (vv. 1–2, 8, 18), Joshua and the people of Israel as addressees (vv. 3, 9, 18). But in contrast to chap. 7, here the Lord is the giver of the city (vv. 1, 7, 18). The key

concept is not liturgy (chap. 6) but war strategy. The word "ambush" appears eight times in this chapter, and nowhere else in the book.

8:1—Like Jericho, *Ai* is a city-state: it has a king and land belonging to landowners living in the city. According to vv. 17 and 29, the city had a wall. As it has been stated before, the enemies of Israel were the powerful elite of the Canaanite population.

8:2—According to the order of the Lord, Israel should take only goods necessary for subsistence, not implements of war that could make Israel a powerful and oppressive force (see v. 27). It is important to see in 11:6, 9, 13–14 that Israel "hamstrung their horses, and burned their chariots," but did not destroy any of the "towns" (unwalled villages) or the livestock.

them. **6** They will come out after us until we have drawn them away from the city; for they will say, 'They are fleeing from us, as before.' While we flee from them, **7** you shall rise up from the ambush and seize the city; for the LORD your God will give it into your hand. **8** And when you have taken the city, you shall set the city on fire, doing as the LORD has ordered; see, I have commanded you." **9** So Joshua sent them out; and they went to the place of ambush, and lay between Bethel and Ai, to the west of Ai; but Joshua spent that night in the camp.*a*

10 In the morning Joshua rose early and mustered the people, and went up, with the elders of Israel, before the people to Ai. **11** All the fighting men who were with him went up, and drew near before the city, and camped on the north side of Ai, with a ravine between them and Ai. **12** Taking about five thousand men, he set them in ambush between Bethel and Ai, to the west of the city. **13** So they stationed the forces, the main encampment that was north of the city and its rear guard west of the city. But Joshua spent that night in the valley. **14** When the king of Ai saw this, he and all his people, the inhabitants of the city, hurried out early in the morning to the meeting place facing the Arabah to meet Israel in battle; but he did not know that there was an ambush against him behind the city. **15** And Joshua and all Israel made a pretense of being beaten before them, and fled in the direction of the wilderness. **16** So all the people who were in the city were called together to pursue them, and as they pursued Joshua they were drawn away from the city. **17** There was not a man left in Ai or Bethel who did not go out after Israel; they left the city open, and pursued Israel.

18 Then the LORD said to Joshua, "Stretch out the sword that is in your hand toward Ai; for I will give it into your hand." And Joshua stretched out the sword that was in his hand toward

the city. **19** As soon as he stretched out his hand, the troops in ambush rose quickly out of their place and rushed forward. They entered the city, took it, and at once set the city on fire. **20** So when the men of Ai looked back, the smoke of the city was rising to the sky. They had no power to flee this way or that, for the people who fled to the wilderness turned back against the pursuers. **21** When Joshua and all Israel saw that the ambush had taken the city and that the smoke of the city was rising, then they turned back and struck down the men of Ai. **22** And the others came out from the city against them; so they were surrounded by Israelites, some on one side, and some on the other; and Israel struck them down until no one was left who survived or escaped. **23** But the king of Ai was taken alive and brought to Joshua.

24 When Israel had finished slaughtering all the inhabitants of Ai in the open wilderness where they pursued them, and when all of them to the very last had fallen by the edge of the sword, all Israel returned to Ai, and attacked it with the edge of the sword. **25** The total of those who fell that day, both men and women, was twelve thousand—all the people of Ai. **26** For Joshua did not draw back his hand, with which he stretched out the sword, until he had utterly destroyed all the inhabitants of Ai. **27** Only the livestock and the spoil of that city Israel took as their booty, according to the word of the LORD that he had issued to Joshua. **28** So Joshua burned Ai, and made it forever a heap of ruins, as it is to this day. **29** And he hanged the king of Ai on a tree until evening; and at sunset Joshua commanded, and they took his body down from the tree, threw it down at the entrance of the gate of the city, and raised over it a great heap of stones, which stands there to this day.

a Heb *among the people*

8:29—Reflects a law found in Deut. 21:22–23 (see Josh. 10:26–27).

Joshua Renews the Covenant

30 Then Joshua built on Mount Ebal an altar to the LORD, the God of Israel, [31] just as Moses the servant of the LORD had commanded the Israelites, as it is written in the book of the law of Moses, "an altar of unhewn[a] stones, on which no iron tool has been used"; and they offered on it burnt offerings to the LORD, and sacrificed offerings of well-being. [32] And there, in the presence of the Israelites, Joshua[b] wrote on the stones a copy of the law of Moses, which he had written. [33] All Israel, alien as well as citizen, with their elders and officers and their judges, stood on opposite sides of the ark in front of the levitical priests who carried the ark of the covenant of the LORD, half of them in front of Mount Gerizim and half of them in front of Mount Ebal, as Moses the servant of the LORD had commanded at the first, that they should bless the people of Israel. [34] And afterward he read all the words of the law, blessings and curses, according to all that is written in the book of the law. [35] There was not a word of all that Moses commanded that Joshua did not read before all the assembly of Israel, and the women, and the little ones, and the aliens who resided among them.

The Gibeonites Save Themselves by Trickery

9 Now when all the kings who were beyond the Jordan in the hill coun-

try and in the lowland all along the coast of the Great Sea toward Lebanon—the Hittites, the Amorites, the Canaanites, the Perizzites, the Hivites, and the Jebusites—heard of this, [2] they gathered together with one accord to fight Joshua and Israel.

3 But when the inhabitants of Gibeon heard what Joshua had done to Jericho and to Ai, [4] they on their part acted with cunning: they went and prepared provisions,[c] and took worn-out sacks for their donkeys, and wineskins, worn-out and torn and mended, [5] with worn-out, patched sandals on their feet, and worn-out clothes; and all their provisions were dry and moldy. [6] They went to Joshua in the camp at Gilgal, and said to him and to the Israelites, "We have come from a far country; so now make a treaty with us." [7] But the Israelites said to the Hivites, "Perhaps you live among us; then how can we make a treaty with you?" [8] They said to Joshua, "We are your servants." And Joshua said to them, "Who are you? And where do you come from?" [9] They said to him, "Your servants have come from a very far country, because of the name of the LORD your God; for we have heard a report of him, of all that he did in Egypt, [10] and of all that he did to the two kings of the Amorites who were beyond the Jordan, King Sihon of Heshbon, and King Og of Bashan who

[a] Heb whole [b] Heb he [c] Cn: Meaning of Heb uncertain

8:30–35—Theological concern replaces geographical and historical interests. Just after the conquest of Jericho and Ai, the people of Israel find themselves in the area of Shechem (more than twenty-three miles from Gilgal, where they were stationed). The Deuteronomic author wants to leave something clear about the message of Joshua. If the sin of Achan brought "trouble" in the relationship between the Lord and the covenant people, not only was punishment necessary, but so also was a reaffirmation of the strength of the bond between the Lord and Israel. That is why the renewal of the covenant is at the center of these verses.

9:1–27 Saved by Astuteness
Like chap. 2, this chapter tells about the inclu-

sion of foreigners as members of the covenant people of God. Cunning and deceit were the key elements for success. As Rahab tricked the king of Jericho, now the Gibeonites do the same to the leaders of Israel. The final message of the story is one of boundless divine grace and human creativity. According to this and other passages, God's mission is defined as actions in which those on the outside and those at the margins find a place in God's kingdom (2 Sam. 21:1–9 tells part of the subsequent history of the Gibeonites in the midst of Israel).

9:9—The declaration of faith by the Gibeonites is quite similar as the one made by Rahab in 2:9–10.

lived in Ashtaroth. ¹¹ So our elders and all the inhabitants of our country said to us, 'Take provisions in your hand for the journey; go to meet them, and say to them, "We are your servants; come now, make a treaty with us."' ¹² Here is our bread; it was still warm when we took it from our houses as our food for the journey, on the day we set out to come to you, but now, see, it is dry and moldy; ¹³ these wineskins were new when we filled them, and see, they are burst; and these garments and sandals of ours are worn out from the very long journey." ¹⁴ So the leaders*a* partook of their provisions, and did not ask direction from the LORD. ¹⁵ And Joshua made peace with them, guaranteeing their lives by a treaty; and the leaders of the congregation swore an oath to them.

16 But when three days had passed after they had made a treaty with them, they heard that they were their neighbors and were living among them. ¹⁷ So the Israelites set out and reached their cities on the third day. Now their cities were Gibeon, Chephirah, Beeroth, and Kiriath-jearim. ¹⁸ But the Israelites did not attack them, because the leaders of the congregation had sworn to them by the LORD, the God of Israel. Then all the congregation murmured against the leaders. ¹⁹ But all the leaders said to all the congregation, "We have sworn to them by the LORD, the God of Israel, and now we must not touch them. ²⁰ This is what we will do to them: We will let them live, so that wrath may not come upon us, because of the oath that we swore to them." ²¹ The leaders said to them, "Let them live." So they became hewers of wood and drawers of water for all the congregation, as the leaders had decided concerning them.

22 Joshua summoned them, and said to them, "Why did you deceive us, saying, 'We are very far from you,' while in fact you are living among us? ²³ Now therefore you are cursed, and some of you shall always be slaves, hewers of wood and drawers of water for the house of my God." ²⁴ They answered Joshua, "Because it was told to your servants for a certainty that the LORD your God had commanded his servant Moses to give you all the land, and to destroy all the inhabitants of the land before you; so we were in great fear for our lives because of you, and did this thing. ²⁵ And now we are in your hand: do as it seems good and right in your sight to do to us." ²⁶ This is what he did for them: he saved them from the Israelites; and they did not kill them. ²⁷ But on that day Joshua made them hewers of wood and drawers of water for the congregation and for the altar of the LORD, to continue to this day, in the place that he should choose.

The Sun Stands Still

10 When King Adoni-zedek of Jerusalem heard how Joshua had taken Ai, and had utterly destroyed

a Gk: Heb *men*

9:11—From this verse and other implicit information in this chapter and in 10:1, we can conclude that the Gibeonites had no king. Normally the Israelites fought only against walled city-states with kings.

9:14–15—In many biblical texts, partaking of food is a way of concluding a treaty or covenant (see Gen. 31:54).

9:24—The Gibeonites seemed to know the word of God better than the Israelites.

10:1–43 Triumph over the Southern Coalition

This chapter is a concrete example of how a kind of treaty (chap. 9) known in the ancient Near East as a suzerain-vassal treaty works. The strong party, Israel, is committed to assist and protect the weak party, Gibeon. The weak party is committed to serve and be loyal to the strong party.

Joshua 10 is divided in three parts: protection to the Gibeonites (vv. 1–15); defeat of the southern coalition of kings (vv. 16–28); total conquest (vv. 29–43). The war is a holy war: the Lord hands the enemies over to Joshua (v. 8), throws them into panic (v. 10), and uses the power of nature to defeat them (vv. 11–13). In this story, the promises in chap. 1 are kept: the people promised total obedience to Joshua (1:16–18), and God promised to be with Joshua and to make him prosper and succeed (1:5–9).

it, doing to Ai and its king as he had done to Jericho and its king, and how the inhabitants of Gibeon had made peace with Israel and were among them, 2 he a became greatly frightened, because Gibeon was a large city, like one of the royal cities, and was larger than Ai, and all its men were warriors. 3 So King Adoni-zedek of Jerusalem sent a message to King Hoham of Hebron, to King Piram of Jarmuth, to King Japhia of Lachish, and to King Debir of Eglon, saying, 4 "Come up and help me, and let us attack Gibeon; for it has made peace with Joshua and with the Israelites." 5 Then the five kings of the Amorites— the king of Jerusalem, the king of Hebron, the king of Jarmuth, the king of Lachish, and the king of Eglon—gathered their forces, and went up with all their armies and camped against Gibeon, and made war against it.

6 And the Gibeonites sent to Joshua at the camp in Gilgal, saying, "Do not abandon your servants; come up to us quickly, and save us, and help us; for all the kings of the Amorites who live in the hill country are gathered against us." 7 So Joshua went up from Gilgal, he and all the fighting force with him, all the mighty warriors. 8 The LORD said to Joshua, "Do not fear them, for I have handed them over to you; not one of them shall stand before you." 9 So Joshua came upon them suddenly, having marched up all night from Gilgal. 10 And the LORD threw them into a panic before Israel, who inflicted a great slaughter on them at Gibeon, chased them by the way of the ascent of Beth-horon, and struck them down as far as Azekah and Makkedah. 11 As they fled before Israel, while they were going down the slope of Beth-horon, the LORD threw down huge stones from heaven on them as far as Azekah, and they died; there were more who died because of the hailstones than the Israelites killed with the sword.

12 On the day when the LORD gave the Amorites over to the Israelites, Joshua spoke to the LORD; and he said in the sight of Israel,

"Sun, stand still at Gibeon,
    and Moon, in the valley of Aijalon."
13 And the sun stood still, and the
    moon stopped,
    until the nation took vengeance on
        their enemies.

Is this not written in the Book of Jashar? The sun stopped in midheaven, and did not hurry to set for about a whole day. 14 There has been no day like it before or since, when the LORD heeded a human voice; for the LORD fought for Israel.

15 Then Joshua returned, and all Israel with him, to the camp at Gilgal.

Five Kings Defeated

16 Meanwhile, these five kings fled and hid themselves in the cave at Makkedah. 17 And it was told Joshua, "The five kings have been found, hidden in the cave at Makkedah." 18 Joshua said, "Roll large stones against the mouth of the cave, and set men by it to guard them; 19 but do not stay there yourselves; pursue your enemies, and attack them from the rear. Do not let them enter their towns, for the LORD your God has given them into your hand." 20 When Joshua and the Israelites had finished inflicting a very great slaughter on them, until they were wiped out, and when the survivors had entered into the fortified towns, 21 all the people returned safe to Joshua in the camp at Makkedah; no one dared to speak b against any of the Israelites.

22 Then Joshua said, "Open the mouth of the cave, and bring those five kings out to me from the cave." 23 They did so, and brought the five kings out to him from the cave, the king of Jerusalem,

a Heb they   b Heb moved his tongue

10:12–13—A poetic text, quoted from a collection of songs, is used as literary device to explain Joshua's spectacular victory and God's supernatural help.

the king of Hebron, the king of Jarmuth, the king of Lachish, and the king of Eglon. **²⁴** When they brought the kings out to Joshua, Joshua summoned all the Israelites, and said to the chiefs of the warriors who had gone with him, "Come near, put your feet on the necks of these kings." Then they came near and put their feet on their necks. **²⁵** And Joshua said to them, "Do not be afraid or dismayed; be strong and courageous; for thus the LORD will do to all the enemies against whom you fight." **²⁶** Afterward Joshua struck them down and put them to death, and he hung them on five trees. And they hung on the trees until evening. **²⁷** At sunset Joshua commanded, and they took them down from the trees and threw them into the cave where they had hidden themselves; they set large stones against the mouth of the cave, which remain to this very day.

28 Joshua took Makkedah on that day, and struck it and its king with the edge of the sword; he utterly destroyed every person in it; he left no one remaining. And he did to the king of Makkedah as he had done to the king of Jericho.

29 Then Joshua passed on from Makkedah, and all Israel with him, to Libnah, and fought against Libnah. **³⁰** The LORD gave it also and its king into the hand of Israel; and he struck it with the edge of the sword, and every person in it; he left no one remaining in it; and he did to its king as he had done to the king of Jericho.

31 Next Joshua passed on from Libnah, and all Israel with him, to Lachish, and laid siege to it, and assaulted it. **³²** The LORD gave Lachish into the hand of Israel, and he took it on the second day, and struck it with the edge of the sword, and every person in it, as he had done to Libnah.

33 Then King Horam of Gezer came up to help Lachish; and Joshua struck him and his people, leaving him no survivors.

34 From Lachish Joshua passed on with all Israel to Eglon; and they laid siege to it, and assaulted it; **³⁵** and they took it that day, and struck it with the edge of the sword; and every person in it he utterly destroyed that day, as he had done to Lachish.

36 Then Joshua went up with all Israel from Eglon to Hebron; they assaulted it, **³⁷** and took it, and struck it with the edge of the sword, and its king and its towns, and every person in it; he left no one remaining, just as he had done to Eglon, and utterly destroyed it with every person in it.

38 Then Joshua, with all Israel, turned back to Debir and assaulted it, **³⁹** and he took it with its king and all its towns; they struck them with the edge of the sword, and utterly destroyed every person in it; he left no one remaining; just as he had done to Hebron, and, as he had done to Libnah and its king, so he did to Debir and its king.

40 So Joshua defeated the whole land, the hill country and the Negeb and the lowland and the slopes, and all their kings; he left no one remaining, but utterly destroyed all that breathed, as the LORD God of Israel commanded. **⁴¹** And Joshua defeated them from Kadesh-barnea to Gaza, and all the country of Goshen, as far as Gibeon. **⁴²** Joshua took all these kings and their land at one time, because the LORD God of Israel fought for Israel. **⁴³** Then Joshua returned, and all Israel with him, to the camp at Gilgal.

The United Kings of Northern Canaan Defeated

11 When King Jabin of Hazor heard of this, he sent to King Jobab of

---

10:29–43—Saturated with the word **all**, this unit insists that Joshua and the whole people totally conquered the kings of the southern coalition, according to the Lord's command.

11:1–23 Destroy the Imperial Power!
The northern coalition suffers the same fate as the southern coalition. The enemies of Israel are strong imperial armies with countless horses and

Madon, to the king of Shimron, to the king of Achshaph, ² and to the kings who were in the northern hill country, and in the Arabah south of Chinneroth, and in the lowland, and in Naphoth-dor on the west, ³ to the Canaanites in the east and the west, the Amorites, the Hittites, the Perizzites, and the Jebusites in the hill country, and the Hivites under Hermon in the land of Mizpah. ⁴ They came out, with all their troops, a great army, in number like the sand on the seashore, with very many horses and chariots. ⁵ All these kings joined their forces, and came and camped together at the waters of Merom, to fight with Israel.

6 And the LORD said to Joshua, "Do not be afraid of them, for tomorrow at this time I will hand over all of them, slain, to Israel; you shall hamstring their horses, and burn their chariots with fire." ⁷ So Joshua came suddenly upon them with all his fighting force, by the waters of Merom, and fell upon them. ⁸ And the LORD handed them over to Israel, who attacked them and chased them as far as Great Sidon and Misrephoth-maim, and eastward as far as the valley of Mizpeh. They struck them down, until they had left no one remaining. ⁹ And Joshua did to them as the LORD commanded him; he hamstrung their horses, and burned their chariots with fire.

10 Joshua turned back at that time, and took Hazor, and struck its king down with the sword. Before that time Hazor was the head of all those kingdoms. ¹¹ And they put to the sword all who were in it, utterly destroying them; there was no one left who breathed, and he burned Hazor with fire. ¹² And all the towns of those kings, and all their kings, Joshua took, and struck them with the edge of the sword, utterly destroying them, as Moses the servant of the LORD had commanded. ¹³ But Israel burned none of the towns that stood on mounds except Hazor, which Joshua did burn. ¹⁴ All the spoil of these towns, and the livestock, the Israelites took for their booty; but all the people they struck down with the edge of the sword, until they had destroyed them, and they did not leave any who breathed. ¹⁵ As the LORD had commanded his servant Moses, so Moses commanded Joshua, and so Joshua did; he left nothing undone of all that the LORD had commanded Moses.

Summary of Joshua's Conquests

16 So Joshua took all that land: the hill country and all the Negeb and all the land of Goshen and the lowland and the Arabah and the hill country of Israel and its lowland, ¹⁷ from Mount Halak, which rises toward Seir, as far as Baal-gad in the valley of Lebanon below Mount Hermon. He took all their kings, struck them down, and put them to death. ¹⁸ Joshua made war a long time with all those kings. ¹⁹ There was not a town that made peace with the Israelites, except the Hivites, the inhabitants of Gibeon; all were taken in battle. ²⁰ For it was the LORD's doing to harden their hearts so that they would come against Israel in battle, in order that they might be utterly destroyed, and might receive no mercy, but be exterminated, just as the LORD had commanded Moses.

21 At that time Joshua came and wiped out the Anakim from the hill country, from Hebron, from Debir, from Anab, and from all the hill country of Judah, and from all the hill country of Israel;

---

chariots. The Lord's only command is to destroy that military power. The *horses* (vv. 4, 6, 9) are disabled, but the livestock is kept to feed God's people. It is important to see that the destruction of the military equipment not only battered the enemy, but also discouraged Israel from becoming a military power itself. Israel's trust rests in the Lord (Deut. 17:16; Ps. 20:7).

11:21–22 *Anakim*—The giants of ancient times were usually related to city-states. They symbolized every power opposing the Lord and the covenant people. This explains why Joshua is a book overflowing with destruction.

Joshua utterly destroyed them with their towns. ²²None of the Anakim was left in the land of the Israelites; some remained only in Gaza, in Gath, and in Ashdod. ²³So Joshua took the whole land, according to all that the LORD had spoken to Moses; and Joshua gave it for an inheritance to Israel according to their tribal allotments. And the land had rest from war.

The Kings Conquered by Moses

12 Now these are the kings of the land, whom the Israelites defeated, whose land they occupied beyond the Jordan toward the east, from the Wadi Arnon to Mount Hermon, with all the Arabah eastward: ²King Sihon of the Amorites who lived at Heshbon, and ruled from Aroer, which is on the edge of the Wadi Arnon, and from the middle of the valley as far as the river Jabbok, the boundary of the Ammonites, that is, half of Gilead, ³and the Arabah to the Sea of Chinneroth eastward, and in the direction of Beth-jeshimoth, to the sea of the Arabah, the Dead Sea,ᵃ southward to the foot of the slopes of Pisgah; ⁴and King Ogᵇ of Bashan, one of the last of the Rephaim, who lived at Ashtaroth and at Edrei ⁵and ruled over Mount Hermon and Salecah and all Bashan to the boundary of the Geshurites and the Maacathites, and over half of Gilead to the boundary of King Sihon of Heshbon. ⁶Moses, the servant of the LORD, and the Israelites defeated them; and Moses the servant of the LORD gave their land for a possession to the Reubenites and the Gadites and the half-tribe of Manasseh.

The Kings Conquered by Joshua

7 The following are the kings of the land whom Joshua and the Israelites defeated on the west side of the Jordan, from Baal-gad in the valley of Lebanon to Mount Halak, that rises toward Seir (and Joshua gave their land to the tribes of Israel as a possession according to their allotments, ⁸in the hill country, in the lowland, in the Arabah, in the slopes, in the wilderness, and in the Negeb, the land of the Hittites, Amorites, Canaanites, Perizzites, Hivites, and Jebusites):

⁹ the king of Jericho	one
the king of Ai, which is next to Bethel	one
¹⁰ the king of Jerusalem	one
the king of Hebron	one
¹¹ the king of Jarmuth	one
the king of Lachish	one
¹² the king of Eglon	one
the king of Gezer	one
¹³ the king of Debir	one
the king of Geder	one
¹⁴ the king of Hormah	one
the king of Arad	one
¹⁵ the king of Libnah	one
the king of Adullam	one
¹⁶ the king of Makkedah	one
the king of Bethel	one
¹⁷ the king of Tappuah	one
the king of Hepher	one
¹⁸ the king of Aphek	one
the king of Lasharon	one
¹⁹ the king of Madon	one
the king of Hazor	one
²⁰ the king of Shimron-meron	one
the king of Achshaph	one
²¹ the king of Taanach	one
the king of Megiddo	one
²² the king of Kedesh	one
the king of Jokneam in Carmel	one
²³ the king of Dor in Naphath-dor	one
the king of Goiim in Galilee,ᶜ	one
²⁴ the king of Tirzah	one
thirty-one kings in all.	

ᵃHeb Salt Sea ᵇGk: Heb the boundary of King Og ᶜGk: Heb Gilgal

---

11:23 *Inheritance*—This word appears here for the first time in Joshua, but it will appear profusely in chaps. 23–24. This verse is in itself a summary of what follows.

12:1–24 As Moses Conquered, So Does Joshua
Leadership is at the center of this chapter. The figures of Moses (vv. 1–6) and Joshua (vv. 7–24) are parallel. Whatever Moses did, so did Joshua. Kings of city-states make up the list of the defeated. None of them belongs to the list of those protected and saved by Joshua and Israel: Rahab and her family and the Gibeonites. In a way, the wars of the Lord could be defined as wars for justice, for building a society of equals.

The Parts of Canaan Still Unconquered

13 Now Joshua was old and advanced in years; and the LORD said to him, "You are old and advanced in years, and very much of the land still remains to be possessed. ²This is the land that still remains: all the regions of the Philistines, and all those of the Geshurites ³(from the Shihor, which is east of Egypt, northward to the boundary of Ekron, it is reckoned as Canaanite; there are five rulers of the Philistines, those of Gaza, Ashdod, Ashkelon, Gath, and Ekron), and those of the Avvim ⁴in the south; all the land of the Canaanites, and Mearah that belongs to the Sidonians, to Aphek, to the boundary of the Amorites, ⁵and the land of the Gebalites, and all Lebanon, toward the east, from Baal-gad below Mount Hermon to Lebo-hamath, ⁶all the inhabitants of the hill country from Lebanon to Misrephoth-maim, even all the Sidonians. I will myself drive them out from before the Israelites; only allot the land to Israel for an inheritance, as I have commanded you. ⁷Now therefore divide this land for an inheritance to the nine tribes and the half-tribe of Manasseh."

The Territory East of the Jordan

8 With the other half-tribe of Manasseh[a] the Reubenites and the Gadites received their inheritance, which Moses gave them, beyond the Jordan eastward, as Moses the servant of the LORD gave them: ⁹from Aroer, which is on the edge of the Wadi Arnon, and the town that is in the middle of the valley, and all the tableland from[b] Medeba as far as Dibon; ¹⁰and all the cities of King Sihon of the Amorites, who reigned in Heshbon, as far as the boundary of the Ammonites; ¹¹and Gilead, and the region of the Geshurites and Maacathites, and all Mount Hermon, and all Bashan to Salecah; ¹²all the kingdom of Og in Bashan, who reigned in Ashtaroth and in Edrei (he alone was left of the survivors of the Rephaim); these Moses had defeated and driven out. ¹³Yet the Israelites did not drive out the Geshurites or the Maacathites; but Geshur and Maacath live within Israel to this day.

_a_ Cn: Heb _With it_   _b_ Compare Gk: Heb lacks _from_

13:1–21:45 Possessing the Land

The central theme in this second major section of the book is the distribution of the promised land. In the lists the cities appear alone, no longer tagged with the name of the respective king. Most readers find this part of the book rather uninteresting, due to the endless lists of cities and places allotted to one tribe or another. Yet behind these lists are the actions of a God who fulfills promises and of a people challenged to become worthy of receiving those gifts in concrete ways. On the other hand, these detailed lists of borders, cities, and villages show God's justice and equity. All members of the covenant people will have the right to use a portion of land, certain that none other than their family will ever benefit from it. Indeed the ownership of the land belongs to the Lord. No person or group of persons would be able to become owners of extensive portions of land to the detriment of others.

13:1–7 Distribute the Land!

Coming, probably, from the exilic period, this unit talks about distributing the land with an eye on postexilic times. During the monarchy, many kings did not show justice or equity in the dis-

tribution of land; after the exile, the people will need leaders who, like Joshua, will distribute the land with fairness.

With the topic of distribution of the land appears also the theme of undivided loyalty to the Lord. The second cannot become a reality without the first. Thus, in contrast to the spirit of the first section of the book (chaps. 2–12), these chapters clearly show that, as a test to Israel's fidelity, God did not eradicate the pagan nations from the promised land.

13:6

The word *inheritance* is used many times in chaps. 13–21. Its use tells something important about the Lord's attitude towards the land and the people of the covenant. The *land* is not just a piece of soil but is a gift from God. The giving of the land, then, has both social and spiritual aspects. To have a piece of land gives one a sense of security and identity and helps to build a society with relationship based on justice.

13:8–33 Moses' Paradigmatic Leadership

This rather long unit serves a theological purpose: it shows that Moses, the model for Joshua's leadership for the period of the conquest, is also a paradigm for the distribution of the land.

14 To the tribe of Levi alone Moses gave no inheritance; the offerings by fire to the LORD God of Israel are their inheritance, as he said to them.

The Territory of Reuben

15 Moses gave an inheritance to the tribe of the Reubenites according to their clans. ¹⁶ Their territory was from Aroer, which is on the edge of the Wadi Arnon, and the town that is in the middle of the valley, and all the tableland by Medeba; ¹⁷ with Heshbon, and all its towns that are in the tableland; Dibon, and Bamoth-baal, and Beth-baal-meon, ¹⁸ and Jahaz, and Kedemoth, and Mephaath, ¹⁹ and Kiriathaim, and Sibmah, and Zereth-shahar on the hill of the valley, ²⁰ and Beth-peor, and the slopes of Pisgah, and Beth-jeshimoth, ²¹ that is, all the towns of the tableland, and all the kingdom of King Sihon of the Amorites, who reigned in Heshbon, whom Moses defeated with the leaders of Midian, Evi and Rekem and Zur and Hur and Reba, as princes of Sihon, who lived in the land. ²² Along with the rest of those they put to death, the Israelites also put to the sword Balaam son of Beor, who practiced divination. ²³ And the border of the Reubenites was the Jordan and its banks. This was the inheritance of the Reubenites according to their families, with their towns and villages.

The Territory of Gad

24 Moses gave an inheritance also to the tribe of the Gadites, according to their families. ²⁵ Their territory was Jazer, and all the towns of Gilead, and half the land of the Ammonites, to Aroer, which is east of Rabbah, ²⁶ and from Heshbon to Ramath-mizpeh and Betonim, and from Mahanaim to the territory of Debir,ᵃ ²⁷ and in the valley Beth-haram, Beth-nimrah, Succoth, and Zaphon, the rest of the kingdom of King Sihon of Heshbon, the Jordan and its banks, as far as the lower end of the Sea of Chinnereth, eastward beyond the Jordan. ²⁸ This is the inheritance of the Gadites according to their clans, with their towns and villages.

The Territory of the Half-Tribe of Manasseh (East)

29 Moses gave an inheritance to the half-tribe of Manasseh; it was allotted to the half-tribe of the Manassites according to their families. ³⁰ Their territory extended from Mahanaim, through all Bashan, the whole kingdom of King Og of Bashan, and all the settlements of Jair, which are in Bashan, sixty towns, ³¹ and half of Gilead, and Ashtaroth, and Edrei, the towns of the kingdom of Og in Bashan; these were allotted to the people of Machir son of Manasseh according to their clans—for half the Machirites.

32 These are the inheritances that Moses distributed in the plains of Moab, beyond the Jordan east of Jericho. ³³ But to the tribe of Levi Moses gave no inheritance; the LORD God of Israel is their inheritance, as he said to them.

The Distribution of Territory West of the Jordan

14 These are the inheritances that the Israelites received in the land of Canaan, which the priest Eleazar, and Joshua son of Nun, and the heads of the families of the tribes of the Israelites distributed to them. ² Their inheritance was by lot, as the LORD had commanded Moses for the nine and one-half tribes.

ᵃ Gk Syr Vg: Heb *Lidebir*

14:1–5 Summary of Chapters 13–21
The whole section springs out of an order originally given to Moses to which Joshua and the people of Israel should comply.

14:1 *Eleazar and Joshua*—Touching again on the topic of leadership, chaps. 14–21 put two pairs of characters in parallel: Moses-Aaron = Joshua-Eleazar. Since the name Eleazar appears only in priestly texts (postexilic), this tradition gives to the distribution of the land a liturgical flavor.

14:2 *By lot*—Besides the theological significance of this action—the Lord makes the decision—we find a sociological value here: nobody will have an advantage in the distribution of the land.

³ For Moses had given an inheritance to the two and one-half tribes beyond the Jordan; but to the Levites he gave no inheritance among them. ⁴ For the people of Joseph were two tribes, Manasseh and Ephraim; and no portion was given to the Levites in the land, but only towns to live in, with their pasture lands for their flocks and herds. ⁵ The Israelites did as the LORD commanded Moses; they allotted the land.

Hebron Allotted to Caleb

6 Then the people of Judah came to Joshua at Gilgal; and Caleb son of Jephunneh the Kenizzite said to him, "You know what the LORD said to Moses the man of God in Kadesh-barnea concerning you and me. ⁷ I was forty years old when Moses the servant of the LORD sent me from Kadesh-barnea to spy out the land; and I brought him an honest report. ⁸ But my companions who went up with me made the heart of the people melt; yet I wholeheartedly followed the LORD my God. ⁹ And Moses swore on that day, saying, 'Surely the land on which your foot has trodden shall be an inheritance for you and your children forever, because you have wholeheartedly followed the LORD my God.' ¹⁰ And now, as you see, the LORD has kept me alive, as he said, these forty-five years since the time that the LORD spoke this word to Moses, while Israel was journeying through the wilderness; and here I am today, eighty-five years old. ¹¹ I am still as strong today as I was on the day

that Moses sent me; my strength now is as my strength was then, for war, and for going and coming. ¹² So now give me this hill country of which the LORD spoke on that day; for you heard on that day how the Anakim were there, with great fortified cities; it may be that the LORD will be with me, and I shall drive them out, as the LORD said."

13 Then Joshua blessed him, and gave Hebron to Caleb son of Jephunneh for an inheritance. ¹⁴ So Hebron became the inheritance of Caleb son of Jephunneh the Kenizzite to this day, because he wholeheartedly followed the LORD, the God of Israel. ¹⁵ Now the name of Hebron formerly was Kiriath-arba;ᵃ this Arba wasᵇ the greatest man among the Anakim. And the land had rest from war.

The Territory of Judah

15 The lot for the tribe of the people of Judah according to their families reached southward to the boundary of Edom, to the wilderness of Zin at the farthest south. ² And their south boundary ran from the end of the Dead Sea,ᶜ from the bay that faces southward; ³ it goes out southward of the ascent of Akrabbim, passes along to Zin, and goes up south of Kadesh-barnea, along by Hezron, up to Addar, makes a turn to Karka, ⁴ passes along to Azmon, goes out by the Wadi of Egypt, and comes to its end at the sea. This shall be your

---

ᵃ That is *the city of Arba*   ᵇ Heb lacks *this Arba was*   ᶜ Heb *Salt Sea*

14:6–15; 15:13–19 Caleb, a Foreigner, Inherits Part of the Land

Caleb is an Edomite (descendant of Esau). As Rahab was the first to be saved (chap. 6), Caleb was the first to receive his portion of land. Like Rahab in chap. 2, Caleb sets the theological tone of the rest of the section. Thus, again, status is not a matter of ethnicity, but obedience and loyalty to God. In 15:13–19, the member of Caleb's family who specifically received a piece of property is a daughter married to a foreigner, Othniel.

14:12; 15:14 *The Anakim/sons of Anak*—The people driven off the land given to Caleb belong to the group of people defined as "giants." Again,

the enemies are not the vulnerable people of towns and villages, but either kings of city-states or giants, both symbols of power and destruction.

15:1–12 The Boundaries of Judah

Inside the boundaries of Judah are also included the tribe of Simeon and other peoples (Edomites and Amalekites). Historically speaking, these boundaries were reached only at the time of King David. Here again we find a theological lesson: Israel's ideal limits exceeded the historical reality of the people. Thus, there is always room for showing greater loyalty to God, a prerequisite to possess and keep the promised land.

south boundary. ⁵ And the east boundary is the Dead Sea,ᵃ to the mouth of the Jordan. And the boundary on the north side runs from the bay of the sea at the mouth of the Jordan; ⁶ and the boundary goes up to Beth-hoglah, and passes along north of Beth-arabah; and the boundary goes up to the Stone of Bohan, Reuben's son; ⁷ and the boundary goes up to Debir from the Valley of Achor, and so northward, turning toward Gilgal, which is opposite the ascent of Adummim, which is on the south side of the valley; and the boundary passes along to the waters of En-shemesh, and ends at En-rogel; ⁸ then the boundary goes up by the valley of the son of Hinnom at the southern slope of the Jebusites (that is, Jerusalem); and the boundary goes up to the top of the mountain that lies over against the valley of Hinnom, on the west, at the northern end of the valley of Rephaim; ⁹ then the boundary extends from the top of the mountain to the spring of the Waters of Nephtoah, and from there to the towns of Mount Ephron; then the boundary bends around to Baalah (that is, Kiriath-jearim); ¹⁰ and the boundary circles west of Baalah to Mount Seir, passes along to the northern slope of Mount Jearim (that is, Chesalon), and goes down to Beth-shemesh, and passes along by Timnah; ¹¹ the boundary goes out to the slope of the hill north of Ekron, then the boundary bends around to Shikkeron, and passes along to Mount Baalah, and goes out to Jabneel; then the boundary comes to an end at the sea. ¹² And the west boundary was the Mediterranean with its coast. This is the boundary surrounding the people of Judah according to their families.

Caleb Occupies His Portion

13 According to the commandment of the LORD to Joshua, he gave to Caleb son of Jephunneh a portion among the people of Judah, Kiriath-arba,ᵇ that is, Hebron (Arba was the father of Anak). ¹⁴ And Caleb drove out from there the three sons of Anak: Sheshai, Ahiman, and Talmai, the descendants of Anak. ¹⁵ From there he went up against the inhabitants of Debir; now the name of Debir formerly was Kiriath-sepher. ¹⁶ And Caleb said, "Whoever attacks Kiriath-sepher and takes it, to him I will give my daughter Achsah as wife." ¹⁷ Othniel son of Kenaz, the brother of Caleb, took it; and he gave him his daughter Achsah as wife. ¹⁸ When she came to him, she urged him to ask her father for a field. As she dismounted from her donkey, Caleb said to her, "What do you wish?" ¹⁹ She said to him, "Give me a present; since you have set me in the land of the Negeb, give me springs of water as well." So Caleb gave her the upper springs and the lower springs.

The Towns of Judah

20 This is the inheritance of the tribe of the people of Judah according to their families. ²¹ The towns belonging to the tribe of the people of Judah in the extreme south, toward the boundary of Edom, were Kabzeel, Eder, Jagur, ²² Kinah, Dimonah, Adadah, ²³ Kedesh, Hazor, Ithnan, ²⁴ Ziph, Telem, Bealoth, ²⁵ Hazor-hadattah, Kerioth-hezron (that is, Hazor), ²⁶ Amam, Shema, Moladah, ²⁷ Hazar-gaddah, Heshmon, Beth-pelet, ²⁸ Hazar-shual, Beer-sheba, Biziothiah, ²⁹ Baalah, Iim, Ezem, ³⁰ Eltolad, Chesil, Hormah, ³¹ Ziklag, Madmannah, Sansannah, ³² Lebaoth, Shilhim, Ain, and Rim-

ᵃ Heb Salt Sea　ᵇ That is the city of Arba

15:7 Gilgal—This place is not the same one mentioned in the first section of Joshua (chaps. 2–12).

15:20–63 Cities of Judah
The way the land and the society in Israel were structured was quite different from the Canaanite society. The city-states with their kings and imperial armies gave way to a society with the clan as its base. Israel had no city-states, but was an agricultural society formed of hundreds of villages of no more than 150 inhabitants each.

mon: in all, twenty-nine towns, with their villages.

33 And in the lowland, Eshtaol, Zorah, Ashnah, 34 Zanoah, En-gannim, Tappuah, Enam, 35 Jarmuth, Adullam, Socoh, Azekah, 36 Shaaraim, Adithaim, Gederah, Gederothaim: fourteen towns with their villages.

37 Zenan, Hadashah, Migdal-gad, 38 Dilan, Mizpeh, Jokthe-el, 39 Lachish, Bozkath, Eglon, 40 Cabbon, Lahmam, Chitlish, 41 Gederoth, Beth-dagon, Naamah, and Makkedah: sixteen towns with their villages.

42 Libnah, Ether, Ashan, 43 Iphtah, Ashnah, Nezib, 44 Keilah, Achzib, and Mareshah: nine towns with their villages.

45 Ekron, with its dependencies and its villages; 46 from Ekron to the sea, all that were near Ashdod, with their villages.

47 Ashdod, its towns and its villages; Gaza, its towns and its villages; to the Wadi of Egypt, and the Great Sea with its coast.

48 And in the hill country, Shamir, Jattir, Socoh, 49 Dannah, Kiriath-sannah (that is, Debir), 50 Anab, Eshtemoh, Anim, 51 Goshen, Holon, and Giloh: eleven towns with their villages.

52 Arab, Dumah, Eshan, 53 Janim, Beth-tappuah, Aphekah, 54 Humtah, Kiriath-arba (that is, Hebron), and Zior: nine towns with their villages.

55 Maon, Carmel, Ziph, Juttah, 56 Jezreel, Jokdeam, Zanoah, 57 Kain, Gibeah, and Timnah: ten towns with their villages.

58 Halhul, Beth-zur, Gedor, 59 Maarath, Beth-anoth, and Eltekon: six towns with their villages.

60 Kiriath-baal (that is, Kiriath-jearim) and Rabbah: two towns with their villages.

61 In the wilderness, Beth-arabah, Middin, Secacah, 62 Nibshan, the City of Salt, and En-gedi: six towns with their villages.

63 But the people of Judah could not drive out the Jebusites, the inhabitants of Jerusalem; so the Jebusites live with the people of Judah in Jerusalem to this day.

The Territory of Ephraim

16 The allotment of the Josephites went from the Jordan by Jericho, east of the waters of Jericho, into the wilderness, going up from Jericho into the hill country to Bethel; 2 then going from Bethel to Luz, it passes along to Ataroth, the territory of the Archites; 3 then it goes down westward to the territory of the Japhletites, as far as the territory of Lower Beth-horon, then to Gezer, and it ends at the sea.

4 The Josephites—Manasseh and Ephraim—received their inheritance.

5 The territory of the Ephraimites by their families was as follows: the boundary of their inheritance on the east was Ataroth-addar as far as Upper Beth-horon, 6 and the boundary goes from there to the sea; on the north is Michmethath; then on the east the boundary makes a turn toward Taanath-shiloh, and passes along beyond it on the east to Janoah, 7 then it goes down from Janoah to Ataroth and to Naarah, and touches Jericho, ending at the Jordan. 8 From Tappuah the boundary goes westward to the Wadi Kanah, and ends at the sea. Such is the inheritance of the tribe of the Ephraimites by their families, 9 together with the towns that were set apart for the Ephraimites within the inheritance of the Manassites, all those towns with their villages. 10 They did not, however, drive out the Canaanites who lived in Gezer: so the Canaanites have lived within Ephraim to this day but have been made to do forced labor.

The Other Half-Tribe of Manasseh (West)

17 Then allotment was made to the tribe of Manasseh, for he was

the firstborn of Joseph. To Machir the firstborn of Manasseh, the father of Gilead, were allotted Gilead and Bashan, because he was a warrior. ² And allotments were made to the rest of the tribe of Manasseh, by their families, Abiezer, Helek, Asriel, Shechem, Hepher, and Shemida; these were the male descendants of Manasseh son of Joseph, by their families.

3 Now Zelophehad son of Hepher son of Gilead son of Machir son of Manasseh had no sons, but only daughters; and these are the names of his daughters: Mahlah, Noah, Hoglah, Milcah, and Tirzah. ⁴ They came before the priest Eleazar and Joshua son of Nun and the leaders, and said, "The LORD commanded Moses to give us an inheritance along with our male kin." So according to the commandment of the LORD he gave them an inheritance among the kinsmen of their father. ⁵ Thus there fell to Manasseh ten portions, besides the land of Gilead and Bashan, which is on the other side of the Jordan, ⁶ because the daughters of Manasseh received an inheritance along with his sons. The land of Gilead was allotted to the rest of the Manassites.

7 The territory of Manasseh reached from Asher to Michmethath, which is east of Shechem; then the boundary goes along southward to the inhabitants of En-tappuah. ⁸ The land of Tappuah belonged to Manasseh, but the town of Tappuah on the boundary of Manasseh belonged to the Ephraimites. ⁹ Then the boundary went down to the Wadi Kanah. The towns here, to the south of the wadi, among the towns of Manasseh, belong to Ephraim. Then the boundary of Manasseh goes along the north side of the wadi and ends at the sea. ¹⁰ The land to the south is Ephraim's and that to the north is Manasseh's, with the sea forming its boundary; on the north Asher is reached, and on the east Issachar. ¹¹ Within Issachar and Asher, Manasseh had Beth-shean and its villages, Ibleam and its villages, the inhabitants of Dor and its villages, the inhabitants of En-dor and its villages, the inhabitants of Taanach and its villages, and the inhabitants of Megiddo and its villages (the third is Naphath).ᵃ ¹² Yet the Manassites could not take possession of those towns; but the Canaanites continued to live in that land. ¹³ But when the Israelites grew strong, they put the Canaanites to forced labor, but did not utterly drive them out.

The Tribe of Joseph Protests

14 The tribe of Joseph spoke to Joshua, saying, "Why have you given me but one lot and one portion as an inheritance, since we are a numerous people, whom all along the LORD has blessed?" ¹⁵ And Joshua said to them, "If you are a numerous people, go up to the forest, and clear ground there for yourselves in the land of the Perizzites and the Rephaim, since the hill country of Ephraim is too narrow for you." ¹⁶ The tribe of Joseph said, "The hill country is not enough for us; yet all the Canaanites who live in the plain have chariots of iron, both those in Beth-shean and its villages and those in the Valley of Jezreel." ¹⁷ Then Joshua said to the house of Joseph, to Ephraim and Manasseh, "You are indeed a numerous people, and have great power; you shall not have one lot only, ¹⁸ but the hill country shall be yours, for though it is a

ᵃ Meaning of Heb uncertain

17:3–6 *Daughters*—Although found few times in the book of Joshua, the participation of women is very important. In this case the five daughters of Zelophehad remained the leaders of Israel about the time when they, by their bold request, made God and Moses change the law regarding the inheritance of the land (Num. 27:1–11). If we consider the meaning of their names (*Mahlah* "illness," *Noah* "rest," *Hoglah* "fighter," *Milcah* "queen" or "lawyer," *Tirzah* "pleasant"), it seems that they learned to use their abilities, character, and even adversities to achieve their goal.

17:18—*Chariots*, made of wood and covered with iron, were designed for war in the plain.

forest, you shall clear it and possess it to its farthest borders; for you shall drive out the Canaanites, though they have chariots of iron, and though they are strong."

The Territories of the Remaining Tribes

18 Then the whole congregation of the Israelites assembled at Shiloh, and set up the tent of meeting there. The land lay subdued before them.

2 There remained among the Israelites seven tribes whose inheritance had not yet been apportioned. ³ So Joshua said to the Israelites, "How long will you be slack about going in and taking possession of the land that the LORD, the God of your ancestors, has given you? ⁴ Provide three men from each tribe, and I will send them out that they may begin to go throughout the land, writing a description of it with a view to their inheritances. Then come back to me. ⁵ They shall divide it into seven portions, Judah continuing in its territory on the south, and the house of Joseph in their territory on the north. ⁶ You shall describe the land in seven divisions and bring the description here to me; and I will cast lots for you here before the LORD our God. ⁷ The Levites have no portion among you, for the priesthood of the LORD is their heritage; and Gad and Reuben and the half-tribe of Manasseh have received their inheritance beyond the Jordan eastward, which Moses the servant of the LORD gave them."

8 So the men started on their way; and Joshua charged those who went to write the description of the land, saying, "Go throughout the land and write a description of it, and come back to me; and I will cast lots for you here before the LORD in Shiloh." ⁹ So the men went and traversed the land and set down in a book a description of it by towns in seven divisions; then they came back to Joshua in the camp at Shiloh, ¹⁰ and Joshua cast lots for them in Shiloh before the LORD; and there Joshua apportioned the land to the Israelites, to each a portion.

The Territory of Benjamin

11 The lot of the tribe of Benjamin according to its families came up, and the territory allotted to it fell between the tribe of Judah and the tribe of Joseph. ¹² On the north side their boundary began at the Jordan; then the boundary goes up to the slope of Jericho on the north, then up through the hill country westward; and it ends at the wilderness of Beth-aven. ¹³ From there the boundary passes along southward in the direction of Luz, to the slope of Luz (that is, Bethel), then the boundary goes down to Ataroth-addar, on the mountain that lies south of Lower Beth-horon. ¹⁴ Then the boundary goes in another direction, turning on the western side southward from the mountain that lies to the south, opposite Beth-horon, and it ends at Kiriath-baal (that is, Kiriath-jearim), a town belonging to the tribe of Judah. This forms the western side. ¹⁵ The southern side begins at the outskirts of Kiriath-jearim; and the boundary goes

---

The Israelites did not need to fear the Canaanites' chariots, because they were well prepared for battle in the mountains.

18:1–19:51 The Territories of the Remaining Seven Tribes

The apportionment of the territory to the seven remaining tribes is set in an editorial framework (18:1–10 and 19:51): the mention of Shiloh and the tent of meeting (vv. 1 and 51) show that the distribution of the land is a religious matter, not a military one.

18:1 *Shiloh*—The center for the administration of

the tribal confederation has changed from Gilgal to Shiloh. This new center will be the religious center throughout the entire period of the Judges. In the book of Joshua three centers are named. The third one is Shechem, where the renewal of the covenant is celebrated (8:30–35 and chap. 24).

18:3 *Possession of the land*—Like the conquest of the land, its possession is also a double undertaking, of God who gives it (v. 3), and of the people who have to do their "homework" (vv. 4–6). The land is a gift that needs to be "conquered."

from there to Ephron,[a] to the spring of the Waters of Nephtoah; [16] then the boundary goes down to the border of the mountain that overlooks the valley of the son of Hinnom, which is at the north end of the valley of Rephaim; and it then goes down the valley of Hinnom, south of the slope of the Jebusites, and downward to En-rogel; [17] then it bends in a northerly direction going on to En-shemesh, and from there goes to Geliloth, which is opposite the ascent of Adummim; then it goes down to the Stone of Bohan, Reuben's son; [18] and passing on to the north of the slope of Beth-arabah[b] it goes down to the Arabah; [19] then the boundary passes on to the north of the slope of Beth-hoglah; and the boundary ends at the northern bay of the Dead Sea,[c] at the south end of the Jordan: this is the southern border. [20] The Jordan forms its boundary on the eastern side. This is the inheritance of the tribe of Benjamin, according to its families, boundary by boundary all around.

[21] Now the towns of the tribe of Benjamin according to their families were Jericho, Beth-hoglah, Emek-keziz, [22] Beth-arabah, Zemaraim, Bethel, [23] Avvim, Parah, Ophrah, [24] Chephar-ammoni, Ophni, and Geba—twelve towns with their villages: [25] Gibeon, Ramah, Beeroth, [26] Mizpeh, Chephirah, Mozah, [27] Rekem, Irpeel, Taralah, [28] Zela, Haeleph, Jebus[d] (that is, Jerusalem), Gibeah[e] and Kiriath-jearim[f]—fourteen towns with their villages. This is the inheritance of the tribe of Benjamin according to its families.

The Territory of Simeon

19 The second lot came out for Simeon, for the tribe of Simeon, according to its families; its inheritance lay within the inheritance of the tribe of Judah. [2] It had for its inheritance Beersheba, Sheba, Moladah, [3] Hazar-shual, Balah, Ezem, [4] Eltolad, Bethul, Hormah, [5] Ziklag, Beth-marcaboth, Hazar-susah, [6] Beth-lebaoth, and Sharuhen—thirteen towns with their villages; [7] Ain, Rimmon, Ether, and Ashan—four towns with their villages; [8] together with all the villages all around these towns as far as Baalath-beer, Ramah of the Negeb. This was the inheritance of the tribe of Simeon according to its families. [9] The inheritance of the tribe of Simeon formed part of the territory of Judah; because the portion of the tribe of Judah was too large for them, the tribe of Simeon obtained an inheritance within their inheritance.

The Territory of Zebulun

[10] The third lot came up for the tribe of Zebulun, according to its families. The boundary of its inheritance reached as far as Sarid; [11] then its boundary goes up westward, and on to Maralah, and touches Dabbesheth, then the wadi that is east of Jokneam; [12] from Sarid it goes in the other direction eastward toward the sunrise to the boundary of Chisloth-tabor; from there it goes to Daberath, then up to Japhia; [13] from there it passes along on the east toward the sunrise to Gath-hepher, to Eth-kazin, and going on to Rimmon it bends toward Neah; [14] then on the north the boundary makes a turn to Hannathon, and it ends at the valley of Iphtah-el; [15] and Kattath, Nahalal, Shimron, Idalah, and Bethlehem—twelve towns with their villages. [16] This is the inheritance of the tribe of Zebulun, according to its families—these towns with their villages.

The Territory of Issachar

[17] The fourth lot came out for Issachar, for the tribe of Issachar, according to its families. [18] Its territory included Jezreel, Chesulloth, Shunem, [19] Hapharaim, Shion, Anaharath, [20] Rabbith, Kishion, Ebez, [21] Remeth, En-gannim, En-haddah, Beth-pazzez; [22] the boundary also touches Tabor, Shahazumah, and Beth-shemesh, and its boundary ends at the Jordan—sixteen towns with their villages. [23] This

[a] Cn See 15.9. Heb *westward* [b] Gk: Heb *to the slope over against the Arabah* [c] Heb *Salt Sea* [d] Gk Syr Vg: Heb *the Jebusite* [e] Heb *Gibeah* [f] Gk: Heb *Kiriath*

is the inheritance of the tribe of Issachar, according to its families—the towns with their villages.

The Territory of Asher

24 The fifth lot came out for the tribe of Asher according to its families. 25 Its boundary included Helkath, Hali, Beten, Achshaph, 26 Allammelech, Amad, and Mishal; on the west it touches Carmel and Shihor-libnath, 27 then it turns eastward, goes to Beth-dagon, and touches Zebulun and the valley of Iphtah-el northward to Beth-emek and Neiel; then it continues in the north to Cabul, 28 Ebron, Rehob, Hammon, Kanah, as far as Great Sidon; 29 then the boundary turns to Ramah, reaching to the fortified city of Tyre; then the boundary turns to Hosah, and it ends at the sea; Mahalab,*a* Achzib, 30 Ummah, Aphek, and Rehob— twenty-two towns with their villages. 31 This is the inheritance of the tribe of Asher according to its families—these towns with their villages.

The Territory of Naphtali

32 The sixth lot came out for the tribe of Naphtali, for the tribe of Naphtali, according to its families. 33 And its boundary ran from Heleph, from the oak in Zaanannim, and Adami-nekeb, and Jabneel, as far as Lakkum; and it ended at the Jordan; 34 then the boundary turns westward to Aznoth-tabor, and goes from there to Hukkok, touching Zebulun at the south, and Asher on the west, and Judah on the east at the Jordan. 35 The fortified towns are Ziddim, Zer, Hammath, Rakkath, Chinnereth, 36 Adamah, Ramah, Hazor, 37 Kedesh, Edrei, En-hazor, 38 Iron, Migdal-el, Horem, Beth-anath, and Beth-shemesh— nineteen towns with their villages. 39 This is the inheritance of the tribe of

Naphtali according to its families—the towns with their villages.

The Territory of Dan

40 The seventh lot came out for the tribe of Dan, according to its families. 41 The territory of its inheritance included Zorah, Eshtaol, Ir-shemesh, 42 Shaalabbin, Aijalon, Ithlah, 43 Elon, Timnah, Ekron, 44 Eltekeh, Gibbethon, Baalath, 45 Jehud, Bene-berak, Gath-rimmon, 46 Me-jarkon, and Rakkon at the border opposite Joppa. 47 When the territory of the Danites was lost to them, the Danites went up and fought against Leshem, and after capturing it and putting it to the sword, they took possession of it and settled in it, calling Leshem, Dan, after their ancestor Dan. 48 This is the inheritance of the tribe of Dan, according to their families—these towns with their villages.

Joshua's Inheritance

49 When they had finished distributing the several territories of the land as inheritances, the Israelites gave an inheritance among them to Joshua son of Nun. 50 By command of the LORD they gave him the town that he asked for, Timnath-serah in the hill country of Ephraim; he rebuilt the town, and settled in it.

51 These are the inheritances that the priest Eleazar and Joshua son of Nun and the heads of the families of the tribes of the Israelites distributed by lot at Shiloh before the LORD, at the entrance of the tent of meeting. So they finished dividing the land.

The Cities of Refuge

20 Then the LORD spoke to Joshua, saying, 2 "Say to the Israelites, 'Appoint the cities of refuge, of which

a Cn Compare Gk: Heb *Mehebel*

19:49—When Joshua finished distributing the land to the Israelite tribes, the people decided to give Joshua his **inheritance**.

20:1–9 The Cities of Refuge
This passage reflects the justice and humanitar-

ian spirit of Deuteronomy. The action of providing refuge for those whose lives were in danger reminds us of the essential quality of love in the Bible: Love your enemy.

I spoke to you through Moses, ³ so that anyone who kills a person without intent or by mistake may flee there; they shall be for you a refuge from the avenger of blood. ⁴ The slayer shall flee to one of these cities and shall stand at the entrance of the gate of the city, and explain the case to the elders of that city; then the fugitive shall be taken into the city, and given a place, and shall remain with them. ⁵ And if the avenger of blood is in pursuit, they shall not give up the slayer, because the neighbor was killed by mistake, there having been no enmity between them before. ⁶ The slayer shall remain in that city until there is a trial before the congregation, until the death of the one who is high priest at the time: then the slayer may return home, to the town in which the deed was done.'"

7 So they set apart Kedesh in Galilee in the hill country of Naphtali, and Shechem in the hill country of Ephraim, and Kiriath-arba (that is, Hebron) in the hill country of Judah. ⁸ And beyond the Jordan east of Jericho, they appointed Bezer in the wilderness on the tableland, from the tribe of Reuben, and Ramoth in Gilead, from the tribe of Gad, and Golan in Bashan, from the tribe of Manasseh. ⁹ These were the cities designated for all the Israelites, and for the aliens residing among them, that anyone who killed a person without intent could flee there, so as not to die by the hand of the avenger of blood, until there was a trial before the congregation.

Cities Allotted to the Levites

21 Then the heads of the families of the Levites came to the priest Eleazar and to Joshua son of Nun and to the heads of the families of the tribes of the Israelites; ² they said to them at Shiloh in the land of Canaan, "The LORD commanded through Moses that we be given towns to live in, along with their pasture lands for our livestock." ³ So by command of the LORD the Israelites gave to the Levites the following towns and pasture lands out of their inheritance.

4 The lot came out for the families of the Kohathites. So those Levites who were descendants of Aaron the priest received by lot thirteen towns from the tribes of Judah, Simeon, and Benjamin.

5 The rest of the Kohathites received by lot ten towns from the families of the tribe of Ephraim, from the tribe of Dan, and the half-tribe of Manasseh.

6 The Gershonites received by lot thirteen towns from the families of the tribe of Issachar, from the tribe of Asher, from the tribe of Naphtali, and from the half-tribe of Manasseh in Bashan.

7 The Merarites according to their families received twelve towns from the tribe of Reuben, the tribe of Gad, and the tribe of Zebulun.

8 These towns and their pasture lands the Israelites gave by lot to the Levites, as the LORD had commanded through Moses.

9 Out of the tribe of Judah and the tribe of Simeon they gave the following towns mentioned by name, ¹⁰ which went to the descendants of Aaron, one of the families of the Kohathites who belonged to the Levites, since the lot fell to them first. ¹¹ They gave them Kiriath-arba (Arba being the father of Anak), that is Hebron, in the hill country of Judah, along with the pasture lands around it. ¹² But the fields of the town and its villages had been given to Caleb son of Jephunneh as his holding.

13 To the descendants of Aaron the priest they gave Hebron, the city of refuge for the slayer, with its pasture lands, Libnah with its pasture lands, ¹⁴ Jattir with its pasture lands, Eshtemoa with its pasture lands, ¹⁵ Holon with its pas-

---

20:3—*The avenger of blood* could be either a close relative of the slain person or the individual designated by the elders to retaliate for the crime.

21:1–42 The Cities for the Levites
Providing for the Levites cities throughout the territories of the different tribes fulfilled a practical need: all members of the covenant people would have access to the services of a priest or a Levite.

ture lands, Debir with its pasture lands, [16] Ain with its pasture lands, Juttah with its pasture lands, and Beth-shemesh with its pasture lands—nine towns out of these two tribes. [17] Out of the tribe of Benjamin: Gibeon with its pasture lands, Geba with its pasture lands, [18] Anathoth with its pasture lands, and Almon with its pasture lands—four towns. [19] The towns of the descendants of Aaron—the priests— were thirteen in all, with their pasture lands.

20 As to the rest of the Kohathites belonging to the Kohathite families of the Levites, the towns allotted to them were out of the tribe of Ephraim. [21] To them were given Shechem, the city of refuge for the slayer, with its pasture lands in the hill country of Ephraim, Gezer with its pasture lands, [22] Kibzaim with its pasture lands, and Beth-horon with its pasture lands—four towns. [23] Out of the tribe of Dan: Elteke with its pasture lands, Gibbethon with its pasture lands, [24] Aijalon with its pasture lands, Gath-rimmon with its pasture lands—four towns. [25] Out of the half-tribe of Manasseh: Taanach with its pasture lands, and Gath-rimmon with its pasture lands—two towns. [26] The towns of the families of the rest of the Kohath-ites were ten in all, with their pasture lands.

27 To the Gershonites, one of the families of the Levites, were given out of the half-tribe of Manasseh, Golan in Bashan with its pasture lands, the city of refuge for the slayer, and Beeshterah with its pasture lands—two towns. [28] Out of the tribe of Issachar: Kishion with its pasture lands, Daberath with its pasture lands, [29] Jarmuth with its pasture lands, En-gannim with its pasture lands—four towns. [30] Out of the tribe of Asher: Mishal with its pasture lands, Abdon with its pasture lands, [31] Helkath

with its pasture lands, and Rehob with its pasture lands—four towns. [32] Out of the tribe of Naphtali: Kedesh in Galilee with its pasture lands, the city of refuge for the slayer, Hammoth-dor with its pasture lands, and Kartan with its pasture lands—three towns. [33] The towns of the several families of the Gershonites were in all thirteen, with their pasture lands.

34 To the rest of the Levites—the Merarite families—were given out of the tribe of Zebulun: Jokneam with its pasture lands, Kartah with its pasture lands, [35] Dimnah with its pasture lands, Nahalal with its pasture lands—four towns. [36] Out of the tribe of Reuben: Bezer with its pasture lands, Jahzah with its pasture lands, [37] Kedemoth with its pasture lands, and Mephaath with its pasture lands—four towns. [38] Out of the tribe of Gad: Ramoth in Gilead with its pasture lands, the city of refuge for the slayer, Mahanaim with its pasture lands, [39] Heshbon with its pasture lands, Jazer with its pasture lands—four towns in all. [40] As for the towns of the several Merarite families, that is, the remainder of the families of the Levites, those allotted to them were twelve in all.

41 The towns of the Levites within the holdings of the Israelites were in all forty-eight towns with their pasture lands. [42] Each of these towns had its pasture lands around it; so it was with all these towns.

43 Thus the LORD gave to Israel all the land that he swore to their ancestors that he would give them; and having taken possession of it, they settled there. [44] And the LORD gave them rest on every side just as he had sworn to their ancestors; not one of all their enemies had withstood them, for the LORD had given all their enemies into their hands. [45] Not one of all the good promises that the

---

21:43–45 The Lord Has Been Faithful
These verses close the section started in chap. 13. The word *all* is the center of this unit, and provides the main theme: Every word given by God as promise was fulfilled.

LORD had made to the house of Israel had failed; all came to pass.

The Eastern Tribes Return to Their Territory

22 Then Joshua summoned the Reubenites, the Gadites, and the half-tribe of Manasseh, [2] and said to them, "You have observed all that Moses the servant of the LORD commanded you, and have obeyed me in all that I have commanded you; [3] you have not forsaken your kindred these many days, down to this day, but have been careful to keep the charge of the LORD your God. [4] And now the LORD your God has given rest to your kindred, as he promised them; therefore turn and go to your tents in the land where your possession lies, which Moses the servant of the LORD gave you on the other side of the Jordan. [5] Take good care to observe the commandment and instruction that Moses the servant of the LORD commanded you, to love the LORD your God, to walk in all his ways, to keep his commandments, and to hold fast to him, and to serve him with all your heart and with all your soul." [6] So Joshua blessed them and sent them away, and they went to their tents.

[7] Now to the one half of the tribe of Manasseh Moses had given a possession in Bashan; but to the other half Joshua had given a possession beside their fellow Israelites in the land west of the Jordan. And when Joshua sent them away to their tents and blessed them, [8] he said to them, "Go back to your tents with much wealth, and with very much livestock, with silver, gold, bronze, and iron, and with a great quantity of clothing; divide the spoil of your enemies with your kindred." [9] So the Reubenites and the Gadites and the half-tribe of Manasseh returned home, parting from the Israelites at Shiloh, which is in the land of Canaan, to go to the land of Gilead, their own land of which they had taken possession by command of the LORD through Moses.

A Memorial Altar East of the Jordan

[10] When they came to the region[a] near the Jordan that lies in the land of Canaan, the Reubenites and the Gadites and the half-tribe of Manasseh built there an altar by the Jordan, an altar of great size. [11] The Israelites heard that the Reubenites and the Gadites and the half-tribe of Manasseh had built an altar at the frontier of the land of Canaan, in the region[b] near the Jordan, on the side that belongs to the Israelites. [12] And when the people of Israel heard of it, the whole assembly of the Israelites gathered at Shiloh, to make war against them.

[13] Then the Israelites sent the priest Phinehas son of Eleazar to the Reubenites and the Gadites and the half-tribe of Manasseh, in the land of Gilead, [14] and with him ten chiefs, one from each of the tribal families of Israel, every one of them the head of a family among the clans of Israel. [15] They came to the Reubenites, the Gadites, and the half-tribe of Manasseh, in the land of Gilead,

[a] Or to Geliloth   [b] Or at Geliloth

22:1–24:33 Watch Out! You Could Lose the Land

Besides the topic of undivided loyalty to God, these chapters offer a warning: Israel could suffer the same fate as the other nations in the land of Canaan—the loss of the land and destruction. In chap. 22 the danger is the construction of sanctuaries other than the one chosen by the Lord; in chap. 23 the danger is mixed marriages; in chap. 24 the danger is idolatry.

22:1–9 The Eastern Tribes Return to Their Territory

This unit speaks not only about the return of the Reubenites, the Gadites, and the half-tribe of Manasseh, but also about the theological principles they must follow to remain faithful to the Lord. Thus geographical separation is overcome with theological unity.

22:10–34 Avoiding a Civil War

Israel not only fought against foreign enemies (kings and city-states); it also faced the possibility of a civil war. Understanding the others' perspective is the key element for a peaceful solution.

and they said to them, ¹⁶ "Thus says the whole congregation of the LORD, 'What is this treachery that you have committed against the God of Israel in turning away today from following the LORD, by building yourselves an altar today in rebellion against the LORD? ¹⁷ Have we not had enough of the sin at Peor from which even yet we have not cleansed ourselves, and for which a plague came upon the congregation of the LORD, ¹⁸ that you must turn away today from following the LORD! If you rebel against the LORD today, he will be angry with the whole congregation of Israel tomorrow. ¹⁹ But now, if your land is unclean, cross over into the LORD's land where the LORD's tabernacle now stands, and take for yourselves a possession among us; only do not rebel against the LORD, or rebel against us*a* by building yourselves an altar other than the altar of the LORD our God. ²⁰ Did not Achan son of Zerah break faith in the matter of the devoted things, and wrath fell upon all the congregation of Israel? And he did not perish alone for his iniquity!' "

21 Then the Reubenites, the Gadites, and the half-tribe of Manasseh said in answer to the heads of the families of Israel, ²² "The LORD, God of gods! The LORD, God of gods! He knows; and let Israel itself know! If it was in rebellion or in breach of faith toward the LORD, do not spare us today ²³ for building an altar to turn away from following the LORD; or if we did so to offer burnt offerings or grain offerings or offerings of well-being on it, may the LORD himself take vengeance. ²⁴ No! We did it from fear that in time to come your children might say to our children, 'What have you to do with the LORD, the God of Israel? ²⁵ For the LORD has made the Jordan a boundary between us and you, you Reubenites and Gadites; you have no portion in the LORD.' So your children might make our children cease to worship the LORD. ²⁶ Therefore we said, 'Let us now build an altar, not for burnt offering, nor for sacrifice, ²⁷ but to be a witness between us and you, and between the generations after us, that we do perform the service of the LORD in his presence with our burnt offerings and sacrifices and offerings of well-being; so that your children may never say to our children in time to come, "You have no portion in the LORD."' ²⁸ And we thought, If this should be said to us or to our descendants in time to come, we could say, 'Look at this copy of the altar of the LORD, which our ancestors made, not for burnt offerings, nor for sacrifice, but to be a witness between us and you.' ²⁹ Far be it from us that we should rebel against the LORD, and turn away this day from following the LORD by building an altar for burnt offering, grain offering, or sacrifice, other than the altar of the LORD our God that stands before his tabernacle!"

30 When the priest Phinehas and the chiefs of the congregation, the heads of the families of Israel who were with him, heard the words that the Reubenites and the Gadites and the Manassites spoke, they were satisfied. ³¹ The priest Phinehas son of Eleazar said to the Reubenites and the Gadites and the Manassites, "Today we know that the LORD is among us, because you have not committed this treachery against the LORD; now you have saved the Israelites from the hand of the LORD."

32 Then the priest Phinehas son of Eleazar and the chiefs returned from the Reubenites and the Gadites in the land of Gilead to the land of Canaan, to the Israelites, and brought back word to them. ³³ The report pleased the Israelites; and the Israelites blessed God and spoke no more of making war against them, to destroy the land where the Reubenites and the Gadites were settled. ³⁴ The Reubenites and the Gadites called the altar Witness;*b* "For," said they, "it is a witness between us that the LORD is God."

a Or *make rebels of us*   *b* Cn Compare Syr: Heb lacks *Witness*

Joshua Exhorts the People

23 A long time afterward, when the LORD had given rest to Israel from all their enemies all around, and Joshua was old and well advanced in years, ²Joshua summoned all Israel, their elders and heads, their judges and officers, and said to them, "I am now old and well advanced in years; ³and you have seen all that the LORD your God has done to all these nations for your sake, for it is the LORD your God who has fought for you. ⁴I have allotted to you as an inheritance for your tribes those nations that remain, along with all the nations that I have already cut off, from the Jordan to the Great Sea in the west. ⁵The LORD your God will push them back before you, and drive them out of your sight; and you shall possess their land, as the LORD your God promised you. ⁶Therefore be very steadfast to observe and do all that is written in the book of the law of Moses, turning aside from it neither to the right nor to the left, ⁷so that you may not be mixed with these nations left here among you, or make mention of the names of their gods, or swear by them, or serve them, or bow yourselves down to them, ⁸but hold fast to the LORD your God, as you have done to this day. ⁹For the LORD has driven out before you great and strong nations; and as for you, no one has been able to withstand you to this day. ¹⁰One of you puts to flight a thousand, since it is the LORD your God who fights for you, as he promised you. ¹¹Be very careful, therefore, to love the LORD your God. ¹²For if you turn back, and join the survivors of these nations left here among you, and intermarry with them, so that you marry their women and they yours, ¹³know assuredly that the LORD your God will not continue to drive out these nations before you; but they shall be a snare and a trap for you, a scourge on your sides, and thorns in your eyes, until you perish from this good land that the LORD your God has given you.

14 "And now I am about to go the way of all the earth, and you know in your hearts and souls, all of you, that not one thing has failed of all the good things that the LORD your God promised concerning you; all have come to pass for you, not one of them has failed. ¹⁵But just as all the good things that the LORD your God promised concerning you have been fulfilled for you, so the LORD will bring upon you all the bad things, until he has destroyed you from this good land that the LORD your God has given you. ¹⁶If you transgress the covenant of the LORD your God, which he enjoined on you, and go and serve other gods and bow down to them, then the anger of the LORD will be kindled against you, and you shall perish quickly from the good land that he has given to you."

The Tribes Renew the Covenant

24 Then Joshua gathered all the tribes of Israel to Shechem, and summoned the elders, the heads, the judges, and the officers of Israel; and they presented themselves before God. ²And Joshua said to all the people, "Thus says the LORD, the God of Israel: Long

---

23:1–16 Israel's History in a Nutshell
The history of Israel is summarized from the viewpoint of the first two commandments. Reading it from the perspective of the exile, this chapter is an interpretation of the past according to the present.

24:1–28 Choose Whom You Will Serve!
While the people of Israel need the helping hand of God, loyalty to the Lord seems to be a must. But when the people no longer need anything, when they are truly free, the challenge of fidelity is greater. One of the most important teachings of the Bible is that God's commandments are for those living in freedom, not in slavery. The book of Judges will show us how difficult this is.

24:1 *Shechem*—This is the third religious center of the tribes of Israel mentioned in Joshua. Shechem becomes the usual place for covenant renewal. The ceremony described here may mirror the actual cultic practice of covenant renewal connected in later years with a festival such as the Feast of Weeks.

ago your ancestors—Terah and his sons Abraham and Nahor—lived beyond the Euphrates and served other gods. ³Then I took your father Abraham from beyond the River and led him through all the land of Canaan and made his offspring many. I gave him Isaac; ⁴and to Isaac I gave Jacob and Esau. I gave Esau the hill country of Seir to possess, but Jacob and his children went down to Egypt. ⁵Then I sent Moses and Aaron, and I plagued Egypt with what I did in its midst; and afterwards I brought you out. ⁶When I brought your ancestors out of Egypt, you came to the sea; and the Egyptians pursued your ancestors with chariots and horsemen to the Red Sea. ᵃ ⁷When they cried out to the LORD, he put darkness between you and the Egyptians, and made the sea come upon them and cover them; and your eyes saw what I did to Egypt. Afterwards you lived in the wilderness a long time. ⁸Then I brought you to the land of the Amorites, who lived on the other side of the Jordan; they fought with you, and I handed them over to you, and you took possession of their land, and I destroyed them before you. ⁹Then King Balak son of Zippor of Moab, set out to fight against Israel. He sent and invited Balaam son of Beor to curse you, ¹⁰but I would not listen to Balaam; therefore he blessed you; so I rescued you out of his hand. ¹¹When you went over the Jordan and came to Jericho, the citizens of Jericho fought against you, and also the Amorites, the Perizzites, the Canaanites, the Hittites, the Girgashites, the Hivites, and the Jebusites; and I handed them over to you. ¹²I sent the hornet ᵇ ahead of you, which drove out before you the two kings of the Amorites; it was not by your sword or by your bow. ¹³I gave you a land on which you had not labored, and towns that you had not built, and you live in them; you eat the fruit of vineyards and oliveyards that you did not plant.

14 "Now therefore revere the LORD, and serve him in sincerity and in faithfulness; put away the gods that your ancestors served beyond the River and in Egypt, and serve the LORD. ¹⁵Now if you are unwilling to serve the LORD, choose this day whom you will serve, whether the gods your ancestors served in the region beyond the River or the gods of the Amorites in whose land you are living; but as for me and my household, we will serve the LORD."

16 Then the people answered, "Far be it from us that we should forsake the LORD to serve other gods; ¹⁷for it is the LORD our God who brought us and our ancestors up from the land of Egypt, out of the house of slavery, and who did those great signs in our sight. He protected us along all the way that we went, and among all the peoples through whom we passed; ¹⁸and the LORD drove out before us all the peoples, the Amorites who lived in the land. Therefore we also will serve the LORD, for he is our God."

19 But Joshua said to the people, "You cannot serve the LORD, for he is a holy God. He is a jealous God; he will not forgive your transgressions or your sins. ²⁰If you forsake the LORD and serve foreign gods, then he will turn and do you harm, and consume you, after having done you good." ²¹And the people said

ᵃ Or Sea of Reeds ᵇ Meaning of Heb uncertain

24:2–13—Joshua recites to the people a long version of the "little historical credo" that sums up the record of God's mighty acts for the chosen people: promises to the fathers, Egyptian captivity, exodus, wilderness, and now conquest (see shorter versions in Deut. 6:20–25, 26:5–9). In the texts where it is preserved, recitation of this credo is both a pedagogical and liturgical act, perhaps serving Israel as a brief statement of faith to be used in connection with covenant renewal.

24:14–28—In the pattern of the ancient Near Eastern suzerain-vassal treaty (see note on 10:1–43), the ceremony concludes with the public swearing of allegiance and the erection of a memorial stone (stele) as a witness (v. 27). Though no list of sanctions is given here (in contrast to the rewards and punishments appended to the covenant-ratification ceremony in Deut. 27–28), Joshua reminds the people that covenant disobedience has dire consequences (v. 27).

to Joshua, "No, we will serve the LORD!" **22** Then Joshua said to the people, "You are witnesses against yourselves that you have chosen the LORD, to serve him." And they said, "We are witnesses." **23** He said, "Then put away the foreign gods that are among you, and incline your hearts to the LORD, the God of Israel." **24** The people said to Joshua, "The LORD our God we will serve, and him we will obey." **25** So Joshua made a covenant with the people that day, and made statutes and ordinances for them at Shechem. **26** Joshua wrote these words in the book of the law of God; and he took a large stone, and set it up there under the oak in the sanctuary of the LORD. **27** Joshua said to all the people, "See, this stone shall be a witness against us; for it has heard all the words of the LORD that he spoke to us; therefore it shall be a witness against you, if you deal falsely with your God." **28** So Joshua sent the people away to their inheritances.

Death of Joshua and Eleazar

29 After these things Joshua son of Nun, the servant of the LORD, died, being one hundred ten years old. **30** They buried him in his own inheritance at Timnath-serah, which is in the hill country of Ephraim, north of Mount Gaash.

31 Israel served the LORD all the days of Joshua, and all the days of the elders who outlived Joshua and had known all the work that the LORD did for Israel.

32 The bones of Joseph, which the Israelites had brought up from Egypt, were buried at Shechem, in the portion of ground that Jacob had bought from the children of Hamor, the father of Shechem, for one hundred pieces of money;*a* it became an inheritance of the descendants of Joseph.

33 Eleazar son of Aaron died; and they buried him at Gibeah, the town of his son Phinehas, which had been given him in the hill country of Ephraim.

a Heb one hundred qesitah

24:29–33 Farewell to the Great Leaders

24:29 *Servant of the LORD*—Used in the previous chapters for Moses, this title is now bestowed on Joshua himself. No longer just the servant of Moses, Joshua is now the "servant of the LORD."

The Book of JUDGES

The book of Judges speaks about a time in Israel's history marked by disobedience, idolatry, violence, anarchy, and failure. This is recalled in different parts
of the book by different versions of this statement: "In those days there was no
king in Israel; all the people did what was right in their own eyes" (21:25). The sense
of unity and wholeness found in Joshua is lost here. From the point of view of the
book of Deuteronomy, a work that sets the theological perspective for the Deuteronomistic History (Joshua through 2 Kings), in the time of the judges Israel does exactly
the opposite of what it did in the time of Joshua: it sinks into covenant disobedience.
The contrast of the two books may be schematized as follows:

Joshua	Judges
One God	Many gods
United people	Scattered tribes
Obedience to God's precepts	Disobedience to God's precepts
Total distribution of the land	Sharing land with other nations
Worshiping God in one place	Many sanctuaries and altars

Taken together, Joshua and Judges seem to serve as a long narrative illustration of
the two destinies—blessing and curse—set forth in the preaching of Deuteronomy
27–28.

The two main themes, repeated throughout the book of Judges, are violence and
idolatry; in fact, as the two parts (chaps. 17–18 and chaps. 19–21) of the conclusion
of the book show, Israel's total deterioration was exposed both in the social milieu
and in the religious arena. Thus the history of the book of Judges appears to lift up
the names and figures of the enemies, the foreign gods, and the sins of the people of
God as much as the lives of the handful of men and several women who are raised
up by God as deliverers. The latter often appear as flickering lamps, yet they show
how the grace of the Lord will never be overcome by the overwhelming presence of
evil. This divine grace can be concretely measured by comparing the number of years
the people spent in peace with the number of years they lived oppressed by their
enemies. The years of peace, called "rest," are greater in number than those spent
"serving" their enemies.

The book starts by placing the reader at the end of the story of Joshua and the
conquest of the promised land. The author wants to remind the reader that by the
time of the judges the land had not been totally conquered, and an important number
of foreign nations still lived there. There are two introductions: the first (1:1–2:5) is
oriented toward the past; the second (2:6–3:6) toward the future. The first part of the
book (3:7–16:31) has been structured according to a cyclical pattern presented in
2:11–23: the people of Israel sin, the Lord "sells" them into the hand of their enemies,
the people cry out to the Lord, the Lord raises up a deliverer, the land rests a number

of years. The worsening of Israel's life throughout the book becomes evident when one compares how the full pattern is presented in the first deliverers or judges, and how it becomes less and less complete, until it is almost lost as the story of the last judge is reached. At the end of the book (chaps. 17–21) there are no judges, no crying of the people, no presence of the Lord—only idolatry and violence against innocent people, especially against women.

As a matter of fact, the way that women are presented in the book enables us to see how the history of Israel, as presented in Judges, goes from bad to worse. The first women pictured in the book (Achsah, Deborah, Jael) are bold, resolute, brave, and able to take the action into their own hands. As the history moves on, however, women become less proactive and more and more the victims of the egotism, shifting moods, and utter violence of males. The women in the last part of the book are almost all anonymous and at the mercy of men.

In Judges, the phrase "the spirit of the Lord" does not refer to the Holy Spirit of the New Testament, but to an active force that guarantees success, more in terms of power than in the moral sphere (see, e.g., Judg. 6:34; 14:6). It is of course a supernatural gift from God that overtakes the human person and drives him or her like a powerful "wind," as the word in Hebrew suggests. The book also speaks of an evil spirit sent by the Lord to punish and destroy evil people, as in the case of Abimelech and the rulers of the city of Shechem (9:23–57).

The book concludes with the statement: "In those days there was no king in Israel; all the people did what was right in their own eyes" (21:25). For some commentators, this statement closes both the book and the unit started in 17:6, where the same statement is made. Others, however, have pointed out that the statement also functions as a junction between narratives. Thus, the end of the period of the Judges does not conclude at Judges 21:25, but goes on as far as 1 Samuel 12 and covers the leadership of Eli, Samuel, and Saul. (In the Hebrew Bible the books of Samuel immediately follow the book of Judges; Ruth is part of the Writings, the third part of the Hebrew canon.)

What is the intention of the author in recounting the stories of the judges? Much depends on when one thinks the book was written or edited. If the first edition of the book is in place by the beginning of the monarchy (ca. 1000 BCE), then what comes to the fore is its promonarchical attitude. To defeat the main enemies (the Philistines), a unified nation and a strong leader were needed, and these are exactly the assets of a monarchical type of government. As part of the larger block of history writing, the Deuteronomistic History (Joshua–2 Kings), Judges would have undergone the so-called first deuteronomic redaction about the time of King Josiah's reform (ca. 622 BCE). In this larger collection, the promonarchical perspective is still present in part; however, few kings of either Israel or Judah pass muster, but only those considered acceptable in the Lord's eyes, chiefly David and Josiah. In the mind of the Deuteronomist, the driving force is no longer the promonarchical view, but rather faithfulness to the Lord's covenant and the centrality of the sanctuary. Behind the few good kings stand the even greater exemplars of covenant faithfulness, Moses and Joshua. When the exile comes, and Jerusalem, the temple, and the land are lost, the exilic redaction of the Deuteronomistic History sees Judges from a different angle. No longer does it matter what type of government or political institution leads the nation's life. The problem does not rest there, but in the evil and sin that have gotten into the very heart

of the people. If Israel wants to see why the people have suffered the loss of their land and temple, then it should look at the time of the judges. On the other hand, if the people want to prepare for a bright and better future by modeling themselves after an obedient and loyal generation, then Joshua is the book they need to read.

—Edesio Sanchez

Israel's Failure to Complete the Conquest of Canaan

1 After the death of Joshua, the Israelites inquired of the LORD, "Who shall go up first for us against the Canaanites, to fight against them?" ² The LORD said, "Judah shall go up. I hereby give the land into his hand." ³ Judah said to his brother Simeon, "Come up with me into the territory allotted to me, that we may fight against the Canaanites; then I too will go with you into the territory allotted to you." So Simeon went with him. ⁴ Then Judah went up and the LORD gave the Canaanites and the Perizzites into their hand; and they defeated ten thousand of them at Bezek. ⁵ They came upon Adoni-bezek at Bezek, and fought against him, and defeated the Canaanites and the Perizzites. ⁶ Adoni-bezek fled; but they pursued him, and caught him, and cut off his thumbs and big toes. ⁷ Adoni-bezek said, "Seventy kings with their thumbs and big toes cut off used to pick up scraps under my table; as I have done, so God has paid me back." They brought him to Jerusalem, and he died there.

8 Then the people of Judah fought against Jerusalem and took it. They put it to the sword and set the city on fire. ⁹ Afterward the people of Judah went down to fight against the Canaanites who lived in the hill country, in the Negeb, and in the lowland. ¹⁰ Judah went against the Canaanites who lived in Hebron (the name of Hebron was formerly Kiriath-arba); and they defeated Sheshai and Ahiman and Talmai.

11 From there they went against the inhabitants of Debir (the name of Debir was formerly Kiriath-sepher). ¹² Then Caleb said, "Whoever attacks Kiriath-sepher and takes it, I will give him my daughter Achsah as wife." ¹³ And Othniel son of Kenaz, Caleb's younger brother, took it; and he gave him his daughter Achsah as wife. ¹⁴ When she came to

---

1:1–3:6 Who Will Conquer the Land?

The book of Judges seems to have a twofold introduction. Chapters 1:1–2:5 give a linear summary of the conquest just after the death of Joshua, with an evaluation explaining why Israel was unable to drive out the Canaanites. Chapters 2:6–3:6 give an account of what will happen during the time of the judges. The account follows a circular structure that closes (2:20–23) with an evaluation similar to the first part. A closing summary for both introductions in 3:1–6 gives the list of the nations that Israel was unable to drive out of the promised land; it also mentions why God left those nations. The entire introductory section, 1:1–2:23, starts and ends with the invocation of the name of Joshua.

1:1–2:5 Recounting the Conquest Story

This part of the introduction, with the so-called "negative conquest tradition," contradicts the idealism of the book of Joshua. The view of Judges is that Israel was unwilling or unable to conquer all the land. This perspective is accentuated by the constant uses of the phrases *did not/could not drive out*. This unit was written with an eye toward the period of history (after the tenth century BCE) when the tribe of Judah was the most important one and David had already conquered Jerusalem.

1:6 *Cut off his thumbs and big toes*—With this practice the enemy was not only put to shame, but was also disabled for battle.

1:11–15 *Achsah*—Caleb's daughter is a woman who in the world of men begins by being the object of men's actions (vv. 12–13), but who soon takes control of the action (vv. 14–15) and directs and changes the outcome of the story. This, in a way, sets the tone of the whole book. In Judges we learn that history cannot be written by just one gender or race or ethnic group, but by whoever has the courage to grasp "history" in his or her hand. Women, above all, show that this is true.

him, she urged him to ask her father for a field. As she dismounted from her donkey, Caleb said to her, "What do you wish?" 15 She said to him, "Give me a present; since you have set me in the land of the Negeb, give me also Gulloth-mayim."*a* So Caleb gave her Upper Gulloth and Lower Gulloth.

16 The descendants of Hobab*b* the Kenite, Moses' father-in-law, went up with the people of Judah from the city of palms into the wilderness of Judah, which lies in the Negeb near Arad. Then they went and settled with the Amalekites.*c* 17 Judah went with his brother Simeon, and they defeated the Canaanites who inhabited Zephath, and devoted it to destruction. So the city was called Hormah. 18 Judah took Gaza with its territory, Ashkelon with its territory, and Ekron with its territory. 19 The LORD was with Judah, and he took possession of the hill country, but could not drive out the inhabitants of the plain, because they had chariots of iron. 20 Hebron was given to Caleb, as Moses had said; and he drove out from it the three sons of Anak. 21 But the Benjaminites did not drive out the Jebusites who lived in Jerusalem; so the Jebusites have lived in Jerusalem among the Benjaminites to this day.

22 The house of Joseph also went up against Bethel; and the LORD was with them. 23 The house of Joseph sent out spies to Bethel (the name of the city was formerly Luz). 24 When the spies saw a man coming out of the city, they said to him, "Show us the way into the city, and we will deal kindly with you." 25 So he showed them the way into the city; and they put the city to the sword, but they let the man and all his family go. 26 So the man went to the land of the Hittites and built a city, and named it Luz; that is its name to this day.

27 Manasseh did not drive out the inhabitants of Beth-shean and its villages, or Taanach and its villages, or the inhabitants of Dor and its villages, or the inhabitants of Ibleam and its villages, or the inhabitants of Megiddo and its villages; but the Canaanites continued to live in that land. 28 When Israel grew strong, they put the Canaanites to forced labor, but did not in fact drive them out.

29 And Ephraim did not drive out the Canaanites who lived in Gezer; but the Canaanites lived among them in Gezer.

30 Zebulun did not drive out the inhabitants of Kitron, or the inhabitants of Nahalol; but the Canaanites lived among them, and became subject to forced labor.

31 Asher did not drive out the inhabitants of Acco, or the inhabitants of Sidon, or of Ahlab, or of Achzib, or of Helbah, or of Aphik, or of Rehob; 32 but the Asherites lived among the Canaanites, the inhabitants of the land; for they did not drive them out.

33 Naphtali did not drive out the inhabitants of Beth-shemesh, or the inhabitants of Beth-anath, but lived among the Canaanites, the inhabitants of the land; nevertheless the inhabitants of Beth-shemesh and of Beth-anath became subject to forced labor for them.

34 The Amorites pressed the Danites back into the hill country; they did not allow them to come down to the plain. 35 The Amorites continued to live in Har-heres, in Aijalon, and in Shaalbim, but the hand of the house of Joseph rested heavily on them, and they became subject to forced labor. 36 The border of the Amorites ran from the ascent of Akrabbim, from Sela and upward.

a That is *Basins of Water*   *b* Gk: Heb lacks *Hobab*   *c* See 1 Sam 15.6: Heb *people*

1:19 *Chariots of iron*—Most likely these instruments of war either had scythes projecting from their wheels or wheels bound with iron tires.

1:22–26—These verses show important parallels with the story of Rahab in Josh. 2 and 6. As in the case of Rahab, a stranger is saved with his family, and they become members of the people of God.

Israel's Disobedience

2 Now the angel of the LORD went up from Gilgal to Bochim, and said, "I brought you up from Egypt, and brought you into the land that I had promised to your ancestors. I said, 'I will never break my covenant with you. ² For your part, do not make a covenant with the inhabitants of this land; tear down their altars.' But you have not obeyed my command. See what you have done! ³ So now I say, I will not drive them out before you; but they shall become adversaries[a] to you, and their gods shall be a snare to you." ⁴ When the angel of the LORD spoke these words to all the Israelites, the people lifted up their voices and wept. ⁵ So they named that place Bochim,[b] and there they sacrificed to the LORD.

Death of Joshua

6 When Joshua dismissed the people, the Israelites all went to their own inheritances to take possession of the land. ⁷ The people worshiped the LORD all the days of Joshua, and all the days of the elders who outlived Joshua, who had seen all the great work that the LORD had done for Israel. ⁸ Joshua son of Nun, the servant of the LORD, died at the age of one hundred ten years. ⁹ So they buried him within the bounds of his inheritance in Timnath-heres, in the hill country of Ephraim, north of Mount Gaash. ¹⁰ Moreover, that whole generation was gathered to their ancestors, and another generation grew up after them, who did not know the LORD or the work that he had done for Israel.

Israel's Unfaithfulness

11 Then the Israelites did what was evil in the sight of the LORD and worshiped the Baals; ¹² and they abandoned the LORD, the God of their ancestors, who had brought them out of the land of Egypt; they followed other gods, from among the gods of the peoples who were all around them, and bowed down to them; and they provoked the LORD to anger. ¹³ They abandoned the LORD, and worshiped Baal and the Astartes. ¹⁴ So the anger of the LORD was kindled against Israel, and he gave them over to plunderers who plundered them, and he sold them into the power of their enemies all around, so that they could no longer withstand their enemies. ¹⁵ Whenever they marched out, the hand of the LORD was against them to bring misfortune, as the LORD had warned them and sworn to them; and they were in great distress.

16 Then the LORD raised up judges, who delivered them out of the power of

[a] OL Vg Compare Gk: Heb *sides* [b] That is *Weepers*

2:1–5—This small unit is a Deuteronomistic evaluation of chap. 1. It is presented as a manifestation of God in the person of the angel of the Lord. Three basic theological elements of Deuteronomistic theology are listed here: the exodus, the gift of the land, and the covenant. The Lord, as partner of Israel in the making of the covenant, did not break it. Israel was the unfaithful party. Because Israel served other gods, the conquest of the promised land will not be completed.

2:6–23 "Recounting" the Sequel to the Conquest Story
The recurring pattern of sin-oppression-cry-salvation, indicated in this introduction, sets the stage of what will happen in the central section of the book, 3:7–16:31. Thus, the evaluation given in 2:20–23 also asserts that the future history of Israel in the time of the judges will not be better than that of the time of Joshua, but will in fact be worse.

2:6–10—This small unit repeats the idea found in Josh. 24:28–31. Its purpose is to move the story on by showing that the generation that followed the time of Joshua and his contemporaries abandoned the covenant made at Shechem (Josh. 24:27). They no longer knew the Lord and did the terrible things recounted in most of Judges.

2:14—The Lord *sold* Israel to its enemies. The verb is repeated five times in Judges (3:8; 4:2, 9; 10:7) and points to the most radical way God chooses to punish Israel. What has happened to Israel as result of its unfaithfulness is a reversal of the exodus (see v. 12): the Lord has allowed Israel to be a slave people again. This seems to be the best way to deal with a people who have chosen to surround themselves with other gods, forsaking the Lord.

those who plundered them. **17** Yet they did not listen even to their judges; for they lusted after other gods and bowed down to them. They soon turned aside from the way in which their ancestors had walked, who had obeyed the commandments of the LORD; they did not follow their example. **18** Whenever the LORD raised up judges for them, the LORD was with the judge, and he delivered them from the hand of their enemies all the days of the judge; for the LORD would be moved to pity by their groaning because of those who persecuted and oppressed them. **19** But whenever the judge died, they would relapse and behave worse than their ancestors, following other gods, worshiping them and bowing down to them. They would not drop any of their practices or their stubborn ways. **20** So the anger of the LORD was kindled against Israel; and he said, "Because this people have transgressed my covenant that I commanded their ancestors, and have not obeyed my voice, **21** I will no longer drive out before them any of the nations that Joshua left when he died." **22** In order to test Israel, whether or not they would take care to walk in the way of the LORD as their ancestors did, **23** the LORD had left those nations, not driving them out at once, and had not handed them over to Joshua.

Nations Remaining in the Land

3 Now these are the nations that the LORD left to test all those in Israel who had no experience of any war in Canaan **2** (it was only that successive generations of Israelites might know war, to teach those who had no experience of it before): **3** the five lords of the Philistines, and all the Canaanites, and the Sidonians, and the Hivites who lived on Mount Lebanon, from Mount Baal-hermon as far as Lebo-hamath. **4** They were for the testing of Israel, to know whether Israel would obey the commandments of the LORD, which he commanded their ancestors by Moses. **5** So the Israelites lived among the Canaanites, the Hittites, the Amorites, the Perizzites, the Hivites, and the Jebusites; **6** and they took their daughters as wives for themselves, and their own daughters they gave to their sons; and they worshiped their gods.

Othniel

7 The Israelites did what was evil in the sight of the LORD, forgetting the LORD their God, and worshiping the Baals and the Asherahs. **8** Therefore the anger of the LORD was kindled against Israel,

---

2:19—*Worshiping them and bowing down to them,* a stereotyped formula used constantly by the Deuteronomist, has the intention of echoing the two first commandments of the Decalogue. This author chose to write Israel's history with those two commandments in mind.

3:7–16:31 The Judges of Israel

This is the core of the book, the story of the judges of Israel. This is the part that 2:6–3:6 has in mind when giving the circular pattern through which the Deuteronomist evaluates this period. This section is structured to show the deterioration of Israel's conduct in a climactic way. It begins with the stories of Othniel and Ehud, matchless for their show of courage and determination, and ends with the story of Samson, in which courage is mixed with an outburst of a destructive force and an egotistic personality. The deterioration happens by stages. A sequence of judges who show a great deal of courage and

faithfulness (3:7–5:31) is followed by a transitional stage of idolatry and social disunity (6:1–10:5). The final era consists of judges whose erratic and tragic actions demonstrate only personal and family concerns (10:6–16:31). The reader will recognize that the deteriorating conduct does not reach its end even at the conclusion of the book (chaps. 19–21).

This "deterioration" is readily seen when comparing the "all-Israel" point of view in the following three stories. In the Ehud story, the whole of Israel is united (3:12–30); in the story of Deborah and Barak, only about half of the tribes participate (chaps. 4–5); in the story of Gideon, only his own tribe of Manasseh and three neighboring Galilean tribes are initially called out.

3:7–11 Othniel

In this story of the first judge, the circular pattern referred to in 2:11–22 is very visible.

and he sold them into the hand of King Cushan-rishathaim of Aram-naharaim; and the Israelites served Cushan-rishathaim eight years. ⁹But when the Israelites cried out to the LORD, the LORD raised up a deliverer for the Israelites, who delivered them, Othniel son of Kenaz, Caleb's younger brother. ¹⁰The spirit of the LORD came upon him, and he judged Israel; he went out to war, and the LORD gave King Cushan-rishathaim of Aram into his hand; and his hand prevailed over Cushan-rishathaim. ¹¹So the land had rest forty years. Then Othniel son of Kenaz died.

Ehud

12 The Israelites again did what was evil in the sight of the LORD; and the LORD strengthened King Eglon of Moab against Israel, because they had done what was evil in the sight of the LORD. ¹³In alliance with the Ammonites and the Amalekites, he went and defeated Israel; and they took possession of the city of palms. ¹⁴So the Israelites served King Eglon of Moab eighteen years.

15 But when the Israelites cried out to the LORD, the LORD raised up for them a deliverer, Ehud son of Gera, the Benjaminite, a left-handed man. The Israelites sent tribute by him to King Eglon of Moab. ¹⁶Ehud made for himself a sword with two edges, a cubit in length; and he fastened it on his right thigh under his clothes. ¹⁷Then he presented the tribute to King Eglon of Moab. Now Eglon was a very fat man. ¹⁸When Ehud had finished presenting the tribute, he sent the people who carried the tribute on their way. ¹⁹But he himself turned back at the sculptured stones near Gilgal, and said, "I have a secret message for you, O king." So the king said,ª "Silence!" and all his attendants went out from his presence. ²⁰Ehud came to him, while he was sitting alone in his cool roof chamber, and said, "I have a message from God for you." So he rose from his seat. ²¹Then Ehud reached with his left hand, took the sword from his right thigh, and thrust it into Eglon'sᵇ belly; ²²the hilt also went in after the blade, and the fat closed over the blade, for he did not draw the sword out of his belly; and the dirt came out.ᶜ ²³Then Ehud went out into the vestibule,ᶜ and closed the doors

ª Heb *he said* ᵇ Heb *his* ᶜ With Tg Vg: Meaning of Heb uncertain

---

3:9 *Cried*—We should not see in this word an attitude of repentance by Israel, but a recognition of total vulnerability and helplessness. In spite of human sins and faithlessness, God's mercy is also shown by the way the Lord responds to the suffering of the people. As in the time of the oppression in Egypt, God comes to liberate Israel because of its powerlessness, not because of its religious devotion.

3:12–30 Ehud

This is a story full of humor and irony. The man who was unable to use his right hand was able, by shrewdness and his left hand, to kill the powerful king of Moab. The story paints this king as a fatted calf (his name, *Eglon*, sounds in Hebrew as the word for fatted calf) ready for sacrifice. At the end of the story, Eglon's men, also called "fatted ones," were "sacrificed."

Ehud's sagacity is shown in different ways. For instance, when he was close to the king, he told him, "*I have a secret message [or word] for you*" (v. 19). In Hebrew the term for "word" can also mean "thing," "object." Therefore, although the king understood "secret message," Ehud hinted at a "secret object," namely, the sword he had hidden under his clothes.

3:13—*City of palms* refers to Jericho. Israel's sins and God's punishment have pushed the nation back to the time of their wilderness wandering, prior to the conquest of this city by Joshua.

3:15—"Benjamin" means "son of the right hand," and the Hebrew phrase translated here as *left-handed man* literally means, "a man bound [in] his right hand." In later Hebrew the word for "bound" comes to mean "lame." This might suggest that a naturally right-handed Ehud had a crippled arm and was therefore forced to use his left hand. More likely, given that 700 very expert Benjaminite slingers are described in the same way (Judg. 20:16), this is simply the Hebrew idiom for left-handedness. Either way, to be left-handed has often been regarded in traditional cultures as a deviation and even a handicap. Not here, though. From Ehud's story, we conclude that a handicap does not preclude the possibility of performing a great act, as Ehud does on behalf of his people.

of the roof chamber on him, and locked them.

24 After he had gone, the servants came. When they saw that the doors of the roof chamber were locked, they thought, "He must be relieving himself[a] in the cool chamber." 25 So they waited until they were embarrassed. When he still did not open the doors of the roof chamber, they took the key and opened them. There was their lord lying dead on the floor.

26 Ehud escaped while they delayed, and passed beyond the sculptured stones, and escaped to Seirah. 27 When he arrived, he sounded the trumpet in the hill country of Ephraim; and the Israelites went down with him from the hill country, having him at their head. 28 He said to them, "Follow after me; for the LORD has given your enemies the Moabites into your hand." So they went down after him, and seized the fords of the Jordan against the Moabites, and allowed no one to cross over. 29 At that time they killed about ten thousand of the Moabites, all strong, able-bodied men; no one escaped. 30 So Moab was subdued that day under the hand of Israel. And the land had rest eighty years.

Shamgar

31 After him came Shamgar son of Anath, who killed six hundred of the Philistines with an oxgoad. He too delivered Israel.

Deborah and Barak

4 The Israelites again did what was evil in the sight of the LORD, after Ehud died. 2 So the LORD sold them into the hand of King Jabin of Canaan, who reigned in Hazor; the commander of his army was Sisera, who lived in Harosheth-ha-goiim. 3 Then the Israelites cried out to the LORD for help; for he had nine hundred chariots of iron, and had oppressed the Israelites cruelly twenty years.

4 At that time Deborah, a prophetess, wife of Lappidoth, was judging Israel. 5 She used to sit under the palm of Deborah between Ramah and Bethel in the hill country of Ephraim; and the Israelites came up to her for judgment. 6 She sent and summoned Barak son of Abinoam from Kedesh in Naphtali, and said to him, "The LORD, the God of Israel, commands you, 'Go, take position at Mount Tabor, bringing ten thousand from the tribe of Naphtali and the tribe of Zebulun. 7 I will draw out Sisera, the general of Jabin's army, to meet you by the Wadi Kishon with his chariots and his troops; and I will give him into your hand.'" 8 Barak said to her, "If you will

[a] Heb covering his feet

3:31 Shamgar

Question: Why does a practically unknown hero who used an unsophisticated weapon to subdue his enemies become worthy of being mentioned in this book? Answer: This judge did something that put him in the annals of history. He *delivered Israel*, God's people!

4:1–5:31 Deborah, Jael, and Barak

When comparing prose narrative to poetic ballad, one finds that the singer is freer than the chronicler to give a wider role in society to those usually kept in the margin, such as women. That distinction is borne out here when the prose passage (chap. 4) is set alongside the poetic text (chap. 5). In the poem, Deborah is definitely a more important character than Barak; furthermore, Jael, a woman—and a foreigner to boot—is the heroine by whose hand Sisera dies.

The passage has been structured in such a way that the three main human characters (Deborah,

Barak, and Jael) are all good candidates to be the hero of the story. Each time the text seems to suggest a leading role for one of the three, a fourth character takes the lead: the Lord. In fact, according to this passage (4:14, 15, 23), the Lord is the one who leads in the battle and wins. The human characters act under the leadership of God. The fact is, however, that this story conveys the importance of shared leadership. In God's cause, success depends on perspectives that are not blinded by chauvinism, ethnocentrism, and sexism.

4:2—It is quite ironic that Israel suffers oppression under a king, *Jabin*, whom history registers as having been defeated by Joshua (Josh. 11:1–11). It seems that God's people have fallen so far since those glory days that even the defeated and "dead" can overcome them. Or is this a new King Jabin of a rebuilt and reenergized Hazor?

go with me, I will go; but if you will not go with me, I will not go." ⁹ And she said, "I will surely go with you; nevertheless, the road on which you are going will not lead to your glory, for the LORD will sell Sisera into the hand of a woman." Then Deborah got up and went with Barak to Kedesh. ¹⁰ Barak summoned Zebulun and Naphtali to Kedesh; and ten thousand warriors went up behind him; and Deborah went up with him.

11 Now Heber the Kenite had separated from the other Kenites,ᵃ that is, the descendants of Hobab the father-in-law of Moses, and had encamped as far away as Elon-bezaanannim, which is near Kedesh.

12 When Sisera was told that Barak son of Abinoam had gone up to Mount Tabor, ¹³ Sisera called out all his chariots, nine hundred chariots of iron, and all the troops who were with him, from Harosheth-ha-goiim to the Wadi Kishon. ¹⁴ Then Deborah said to Barak, "Up! For this is the day on which the LORD has given Sisera into your hand. The LORD is indeed going out before you." So Barak went down from Mount Tabor with ten thousand warriors following him. ¹⁵ And the LORD threw Sisera and all his chariots and all his army into a panicᵇ before Barak; Sisera got down from his chariot and fled away on foot, ¹⁶ while Barak pursued the chariots and the army to Harosheth-ha-goiim. All the army of Sisera fell by the sword; no one was left.

17 Now Sisera had fled away on foot to the tent of Jael wife of Heber the Kenite; for there was peace between King Jabin of Hazor and the clan of Heber the Kenite. ¹⁸ Jael came out to meet Sisera, and said to him, "Turn aside, my lord, turn aside to me; have no fear." So he turned aside to her into the tent, and she covered him with a rug. ¹⁹ Then he said to her, "Please give me a little water to drink; for I am thirsty." So she opened a skin of milk and gave him a drink and covered him. ²⁰ He said to her, "Stand at the entrance of the tent, and if anybody comes and asks you, 'Is anyone here?' say, 'No.'" ²¹ But Jael wife of Heber took a tent peg, and took a hammer in her hand, and went softly to him and drove the peg into his temple, until it went down into the ground—he was lying fast asleep from weariness—and he died. ²² Then, as Barak came in pursuit of Sisera, Jael went out to meet him, and said to him, "Come, and I will show you the man whom you are seeking." So he went into her tent; and there was Sisera lying dead, with the tent peg in his temple.

23 So on that day God subdued King Jabin of Canaan before the Israelites. ²⁴ Then the hand of the Israelites bore harder and harder on King Jabin of Canaan, until they destroyed King Jabin of Canaan.

The Song of Deborah

5 Then Deborah and Barak son of Abinoam sang on that day, saying:
2   "When locks are long in Israel,
      when the people offer themselves willingly—
      blessᶜ the LORD!

3   "Hear, O kings; give ear,
      O princes;
   to the LORD I will sing,
   I will make melody to the LORD,
      the God of Israel.

4   "LORD, when you went out from Seir,

ᵃ Heb from the Kain ᵇ Heb adds to the sword; compare verse 16 ᶜ Or You who offer yourselves willingly among the people, bless

---

4:17–22 Jael—The name means "mountain goat." If we play with the meaning of the name, Sisera finds his death at the hand of this "wild goat" who first gives him milk and then plunges her "horn" into his temple.

5:1–11—In the midst of Israel's weakness, the Lord is present with divine power and magnificence. It is striking that after vv. 4–5, which speak of God's overwhelming power, the poem sings about the deeds of two people whose weapons were an oxgoad and a tent peg (v. 6).

when you marched from the
region of Edom,
the earth trembled,
and the heavens poured,
the clouds indeed poured water.
5 The mountains quaked before the
Lord, the One of Sinai,
before the Lord, the God of Israel.

6 "In the days of Shamgar son of
Anath,
in the days of Jael, caravans
ceased
and travelers kept to the byways.
7 The peasantry prospered in Israel,
they grew fat on plunder,
because you arose, Deborah,
arose as a mother in Israel.
8 When new gods were chosen,
then war was in the gates.
Was shield or spear to be seen
among forty thousand in Israel?
9 My heart goes out to the
commanders of Israel
who offered themselves willingly
among the people.
Bless the Lord.

10 "Tell of it, you who ride on white
donkeys,
you who sit on rich carpets*a*
and you who walk by the way.
11 To the sound of musicians*a* at the
watering places,
there they repeat the triumphs of
the Lord,
the triumphs of his peasantry in
Israel.

"Then down to the gates marched
the people of the Lord.

12 "Awake, awake, Deborah!
Awake, awake, utter a song!
Arise, Barak, lead away your
captives,
O son of Abinoam.
13 Then down marched the remnant of
the noble;
the people of the Lord marched
down for him*b* against the
mighty.

14 From Ephraim they set out*c* into the
valley,*d*
following you, Benjamin, with
your kin;
from Machir marched down the
commanders,
and from Zebulun those who bear
the marshal's staff;
15 the chiefs of Issachar came with
Deborah,
and Issachar faithful to Barak;
into the valley they rushed out at
his heels.
Among the clans of Reuben
there were great searchings of
heart.
16 Why did you tarry among the
sheepfolds,
to hear the piping for the flocks?
Among the clans of Reuben
there were great searchings of
heart.
17 Gilead stayed beyond the Jordan;
and Dan, why did he abide with
the ships?
Asher sat still at the coast of the sea,
settling down by his landings.
18 Zebulun is a people that scorned
death;
Naphtali too, on the heights of the
field.

19 "The kings came, they fought;
then fought the kings of Canaan,
at Taanach, by the waters of
Megiddo;
they got no spoils of silver.
20 The stars fought from heaven,
from their courses they fought
against Sisera.
21 The torrent Kishon swept them
away,
the onrushing torrent, the torrent
Kishon.
March on, my soul, with might!

22 "Then loud beat the horses' hoofs
with the galloping, galloping of his
steeds.

a Meaning of Heb uncertain *b* Gk: Heb me *c* Cn: Heb From Ephraim their
root *d* Gk: Heb in Amalek

23 "Curse Meroz, says the angel of the
  Lord,
    curse bitterly its inhabitants,
  because they did not come to the
    help of the Lord,
  to the help of the Lord against the
    mighty.

24 "Most blessed of women be Jael,
    the wife of Heber the Kenite,
  of tent-dwelling women most
    blessed.
25 He asked water and she gave him
    milk,
  she brought him curds in a lordly
    bowl.
26 She put her hand to the tent peg
    and her right hand to the
      workmen's mallet;
  she struck Sisera a blow,
    she crushed his head,
  she shattered and pierced his
    temple.
27 He sank, he fell,
    he lay still at her feet;
  at her feet he sank, he fell;
    where he sank, there he fell dead.

28 "Out of the window she peered,
    the mother of Sisera gazed*a*
      through the lattice:
  'Why is his chariot so long in
    coming?
  Why tarry the hoofbeats of his
    chariots?'
29 Her wisest ladies make answer,
    indeed, she answers the question
      herself:

30 'Are they not finding and dividing
      the spoil?—
  A girl or two for every man;
    spoil of dyed stuffs for Sisera,
  spoil of dyed stuffs embroidered,
    two pieces of dyed work
      embroidered for my neck as
        spoil?'
31 "So perish all your enemies,
      O Lord!
  But may your friends be like the
    sun as it rises in its might."

And the land had rest forty years.

The Midianite Oppression

6 The Israelites did what was evil in the sight of the Lord, and the Lord gave them into the hand of Midian seven years. ²The hand of Midian prevailed over Israel; and because of Midian the Israelites provided for themselves hiding places in the mountains, caves and strongholds. ³For whenever the Israelites put in seed, the Midianites and the Amalekites and the people of the east would come up against them. ⁴They would encamp against them and destroy the produce of the land, as far as the neighborhood of Gaza, and leave no sustenance in Israel, and no sheep or ox or donkey. ⁵For they and their livestock would come up, and they would even bring their tents, as thick as locusts; neither they nor their camels could be counted; so they wasted the land as

a Gk Compare Tg: Heb *exclaimed*

5:30 *A girl or two for every man*—Sisera, who expected to get women as spoil of war, was himself spoiled at the hands of a woman.

6:1–8:35 Gideon
The story of this judge is the longest in the book, followed by that of Samson. Unlike the story of Deborah and Barak, in which the enemies were the Canaanites residents of the land, here the enemies come from the east, just as Israel did years before. In this passage, we also read of another enemy Gideon needs to destroy, the god Baal. The development of the story will take us from a fearful and humble Gideon, utterly dependent upon God's reassurance, to a Gideon who takes

matters into his hands like a protomonarch and leaves as a bequest for Israel an "idol" (8:27) and a ruthless and power hungry son.

6:1 *The Israelites did what was evil*—This unit echoes the cyclical structure found in the story of Othniel (3:7–11). However, after hearing the cry of Israel, instead of raising a savior, God sends a prophet (v. 8) to remind Israel about God's loyalty and their own unfaithfulness (see 2:1–5).

6:5—Domesticated *camels* constitute part of the wealth and power of Midian. They were used for carrying goods over great distances, but also for robbery and pillage. Evidently the great herds overgrazed the land.

they came in. 6 Thus Israel was greatly impoverished because of Midian; and the Israelites cried out to the Lord for help.

7 When the Israelites cried to the Lord on account of the Midianites, 8 the Lord sent a prophet to the Israelites; and he said to them, "Thus says the Lord, the God of Israel: I led you up from Egypt, and brought you out of the house of slavery; 9 and I delivered you from the hand of the Egyptians, and from the hand of all who oppressed you, and drove them out before you, and gave you their land; 10 and I said to you, 'I am the Lord your God; you shall not pay reverence to the gods of the Amorites, in whose land you live.' But you have not given heed to my voice."

The Call of Gideon

11 Now the angel of the Lord came and sat under the oak at Ophrah, which belonged to Joash the Abiezrite, as his son Gideon was beating out wheat in the wine press, to hide it from the Midianites. 12 The angel of the Lord appeared to him and said to him, "The Lord is with you, you mighty warrior." 13 Gideon answered him, "But sir, if the Lord is with us, why then has all this happened to us? And where are all his wonderful deeds that our ancestors recounted to us, saying, 'Did not the Lord bring us up from Egypt?' But now the Lord has cast us off, and given us into the hand of Midian." 14 Then the Lord turned to him and said, "Go in this might of yours and deliver Israel from the hand of Midian; I hereby commission you." 15 He responded, "But sir, how can I deliver Israel? My clan is the weakest in

Manasseh, and I am the least in my family." 16 The Lord said to him, "But I will be with you, and you shall strike down the Midianites, every one of them." 17 Then he said to him, "If now I have found favor with you, then show me a sign that it is you who speak with me. 18 Do not depart from here until I come to you, and bring out my present, and set it before you." And he said, "I will stay until you return."

19 So Gideon went into his house and prepared a kid, and unleavened cakes from an ephah of flour; the meat he put in a basket, and the broth he put in a pot, and brought them to him under the oak and presented them. 20 The angel of God said to him, "Take the meat and the unleavened cakes, and put them on this rock, and pour out the broth." And he did so. 21 Then the angel of the Lord reached out the tip of the staff that was in his hand, and touched the meat and the unleavened cakes; and fire sprang up from the rock and consumed the meat and the unleavened cakes; and the angel of the Lord vanished from his sight. 22 Then Gideon perceived that it was the angel of the Lord; and Gideon said, "Help me, Lord God! For I have seen the angel of the Lord face to face." 23 But the Lord said to him, "Peace be to you; do not fear, you shall not die." 24 Then Gideon built an altar there to the Lord, and called it, The Lord is peace. To this day it still stands at Ophrah, which belongs to the Abiezrites.

25 That night the Lord said to him, "Take your father's bull, the second bull seven years old, and pull down the altar of Baal that belongs to your father, and

---

6:11—This story follows the pattern of the call of other leaders like Moses (Exod. 3:1–12) and Jeremiah (Jer. 1:4–10): God promises to be with the hero, in this case Gideon (who considers himself unworthy and unable), and gives him a confirming sign. This text also shows God's freedom to choose the unlikely person, often the least important, the youngest, weakest, and smallest. (Think of David or Mary!) The *angel of the Lord* is God

appearing to Gideon in a visible form, just like a human being.

6:25 *Pull down the altar of Baal*—In the context of the worship of the Lord, there is also an altar in honor of Baal. This mixture of religious practice is called syncretism, and was rejected by the Lord (see v. 10).

cut down the sacred pole*a* that is beside it; **26** and build an altar to the LORD your God on the top of the stronghold here, in proper order; then take the second bull, and offer it as a burnt offering with the wood of the sacred pole*a* that you shall cut down." **27** So Gideon took ten of his servants, and did as the LORD had told him; but because he was too afraid of his family and the townspeople to do it by day, he did it by night.

Gideon Destroys the Altar of Baal

28 When the townspeople rose early in the morning, the altar of Baal was broken down, and the sacred pole*a* beside it was cut down, and the second bull was offered on the altar that had been built. **29** So they said to one another, "Who has done this?" After searching and inquiring, they were told, "Gideon son of Joash did it." **30** Then the townspeople said to Joash, "Bring out your son, so that he may die, for he has pulled down the altar of Baal and cut down the sacred pole*a* beside it." **31** But Joash said to all who were arrayed against him, "Will you contend for Baal? Or will you defend his cause? Whoever contends for him shall be put to death by morning. If he is a god, let him contend for himself, because his altar has been pulled down." **32** Therefore on that day Gideon*b* was called Jerubbaal, that is to say, "Let Baal contend against him," because he pulled down his altar.

33 Then all the Midianites and the Amalekites and the people of the east came together, and crossing the Jordan they encamped in the Valley of Jezreel. **34** But the spirit of the LORD took possession of Gideon; and he sounded the trumpet, and the Abiezrites were called out to follow him. **35** He sent messengers throughout all Manasseh, and they too were called out to follow him. He also sent messengers to Asher, Zebulun, and Naphtali, and they went up to meet them.

The Sign of the Fleece

36 Then Gideon said to God, "In order to see whether you will deliver Israel by my hand, as you have said, **37** I am going to lay a fleece of wool on the threshing floor; if there is dew on the fleece alone, and it is dry on all the ground, then I shall know that you will deliver Israel by my hand, as you have said." **38** And it was so. When he rose early next morning and squeezed the fleece, he wrung enough dew from the fleece to fill a bowl with water. **39** Then Gideon said to God, "Do not let your anger burn against me, let me speak one more time; let me, please, make trial with the fleece just once more; let it be dry only on the fleece, and on all the ground let there be dew." **40** And God did so that night. It was dry on the fleece only, and on all the ground there was dew.

Gideon Surprises and Routs the Midianites

7 Then Jerubbaal (that is, Gideon) and all the troops that were with him rose early and encamped beside the spring of Harod; and the camp of Midian was north of them, below*c* the hill of Moreh, in the valley.

2 The LORD said to Gideon, "The troops with you are too many for me to give the Midianites into their hand.

a Heb *Asherah* *b* Heb *he* *c* Heb *from*

6:34 *Spirit of the LORD*—See introduction.

6:36–40—How great is God's faithfulness, and how small is human confidence in the Lord! Even though the Lord had promised God's presence with Gideon (v. 16), and has proved by way of a miracle the reality of that presence (vv. 19–21), Gideon asks for more proofs.

7:1–18—God's faithfulness is shown once more in giving Gideon the best military strategy to use with the type of enemies he was soon to face. The best time was night; the best use of forces, a small group of watchful people; the best weapon, knowledge of the enemy's fears; the best battle plan, ambush. These would be the ingredients of a definitive victory. This, of course, does not diminish the importance of confidence in and obedience to God's word.

Israel would only take the credit away from me, saying, 'My own hand has delivered me.' ³ Now therefore proclaim this in the hearing of the troops, 'Whoever is fearful and trembling, let him return home.'" Thus Gideon sifted them out;*a* twenty-two thousand returned, and ten thousand remained.

4 Then the LORD said to Gideon, "The troops are still too many; take them down to the water and I will sift them out for you there. When I say, 'This one shall go with you,' he shall go with you; and when I say, 'This one shall not go with you,' he shall not go." ⁵ So he brought the troops down to the water; and the LORD said to Gideon, "All those who lap the water with their tongues, as a dog laps, you shall put to one side; all those who kneel down to drink, putting their hands to their mouths,*b* you shall put to the other side." ⁶ The number of those that lapped was three hundred; but all the rest of the troops knelt down to drink water. ⁷ Then the LORD said to Gideon, "With the three hundred that lapped I will deliver you, and give the Midianites into your hand. Let all the others go to their homes." ⁸ So he took the jars of the troops from their hands,*c* and their trumpets; and he sent all the rest of Israel back to their own tents, but retained the three hundred. The camp of Midian was below him in the valley.

9 That same night the LORD said to him, "Get up, attack the camp; for I have given it into your hand. ¹⁰ But if you fear to attack, go down to the camp with your servant Purah; ¹¹ and you shall hear what they say, and afterward your hands shall be strengthened to attack the camp." Then he went down with his servant Purah to the outposts of the armed men that were in the camp. ¹² The Midianites and the Amalekites and all the people of the east lay along the valley as thick as locusts; and their camels were without number, countless as the sand on the seashore. ¹³ When Gideon arrived, there was a man telling a dream to his comrade; and he said, "I had a dream, and in it a cake of barley bread tumbled into the camp of Midian, and came to the tent, and struck it so that it fell; it turned upside down, and the tent collapsed." ¹⁴ And his comrade answered, "This is no other than the sword of Gideon son of Joash, a man of Israel; into his hand God has given Midian and all the army."

15 When Gideon heard the telling of the dream and its interpretation, he worshiped; and he returned to the camp of Israel, and said, "Get up; for the LORD has given the army of Midian into your hand." ¹⁶ After he divided the three hundred men into three companies, and put trumpets into the hands of all of them, and empty jars, with torches inside the jars, ¹⁷ he said to them, "Look at me, and do the same; when I come to the outskirts of the camp, do as I do. ¹⁸ When I blow the trumpet, I and all who are with me, then you also blow the trumpets around the whole camp, and shout, 'For the LORD and for Gideon!'"

19 So Gideon and the hundred who were with him came to the outskirts of the camp at the beginning of the middle watch, when they had just set the watch; and they blew the trumpets and smashed the jars that were in their hands. ²⁰ So the three companies blew the trumpets and broke the jars, holding in their left hands the torches, and in their right hands the trumpets to blow; and they cried, "A sword for the LORD and for Gideon!" ²¹ Every man stood in his place all around the camp, and all the men in camp ran; they cried out and fled. ²² When they blew the three hundred trumpets, the LORD set every man's sword against his fellow and against all the army; and the army fled as far as Beth-shittah toward Zererah,*d* as far as the border of Abel-meholah, by Tabbath. ²³ And the men of Israel were called out from Naphtali and

---

a Cn: Heb *home, and depart from Mount Gilead'*" *b* Heb places the words *putting their hands to their mouths* after the word *lapped* in verse 6 *c* Cn: Heb *So the people took provisions in their hands* *d* Another reading is *Zeredah*

from Asher and from all Manasseh, and they pursued after the Midianites.

24 Then Gideon sent messengers throughout all the hill country of Ephraim, saying, "Come down against the Midianites and seize the waters against them, as far as Beth-barah, and also the Jordan." So all the men of Ephraim were called out, and they seized the waters as far as Beth-barah, and also the Jordan. ²⁵ They captured the two captains of Midian, Oreb and Zeeb; they killed Oreb at the rock of Oreb, and Zeeb they killed at the wine press of Zeeb, as they pursued the Midianites. They brought the heads of Oreb and Zeeb to Gideon beyond the Jordan.

Gideon's Triumph and Vengeance

8 Then the Ephraimites said to him, "What have you done to us, not to call us when you went to fight against the Midianites?" And they upbraided him violently. ²So he said to them, "What have I done now in comparison with you? Is not the gleaning of the grapes of Ephraim better than the vintage of Abiezer? ³God has given into your hands the captains of Midian, Oreb and Zeeb; what have I been able to do in comparison with you?" When he said this, their anger against him subsided.

4 Then Gideon came to the Jordan and crossed over, he and the three hundred who were with him, exhausted and famished.ᵃ ⁵So he said to the people of Succoth, "Please give some loaves of bread to my followers, for they are exhausted, and I am pursuing Zebah and Zalmunna, the kings of Midian." ⁶But the officials of Succoth said, "Do you already have in your possession the hands of Zebah and Zalmunna, that we should give bread to your army?" ⁷Gideon replied, "Well then, when the LORD has given Zebah

and Zalmunna into my hand, I will trample your flesh on the thorns of the wilderness and on briers." ⁸From there he went up to Penuel, and made the same request of them; and the people of Penuel answered him as the people of Succoth had answered. ⁹So he said to the people of Penuel, "When I come back victorious, I will break down this tower."

10 Now Zebah and Zalmunna were in Karkor with their army, about fifteen thousand men, all who were left of all the army of the people of the east; for one hundred twenty thousand men bearing arms had fallen. ¹¹So Gideon went up by the caravan route east of Nobah and Jogbehah, and attacked the army; for the army was off its guard. ¹²Zebah and Zalmunna fled; and he pursued them and took the two kings of Midian, Zebah and Zalmunna, and threw all the army into a panic.

13 When Gideon son of Joash returned from the battle by the ascent of Heres, ¹⁴he caught a young man, one of the people of Succoth, and questioned him; and he listed for him the officials and elders of Succoth, seventy-seven people. ¹⁵Then he came to the people of Succoth, and said, "Here are Zebah and Zalmunna, about whom you taunted me, saying, 'Do you already have in your possession the hands of Zebah and Zalmunna, that we should give bread to your troops who are exhausted?'" ¹⁶So he took the elders of the city and he took thorns of the wilderness and briers and with them he trampledᵇ the people of Succoth. ¹⁷He also broke down the tower of Penuel, and killed the men of the city.

18 Then he said to Zebah and Zalmunna, "What about the men whom

ᵃ Gk: Heb *pursuing*   ᵇ With verse 7, Compare Gk: Heb *he taught*

8:1–3—Gentle diplomacy is better than violent words or actions (see 12:1–6).

8:4–21—The diplomatic skills and graciousness are over, and Gideon now resorts to vengeance and violence. There has been a change of attitude: Gideon acts more like a king than like a

deliverer or judge; he handles matters by himself, rather than seeking God's guidance. The violence shown here will grow more and more until it reaches catastrophic dimensions at the end of the book.

you killed at Tabor?" They answered, "As you are, so were they, every one of them; they resembled the sons of a king." ¹⁹ And he replied, "They were my brothers, the sons of my mother; as the LORD lives, if you had saved them alive, I would not kill you." ²⁰ So he said to Jether his firstborn, "Go kill them!" But the boy did not draw his sword, for he was afraid, because he was still a boy. ²¹ Then Zebah and Zalmunna said, "You come and kill us; for as the man is, so is his strength." So Gideon proceeded to kill Zebah and Zalmunna; and he took the crescents that were on the necks of their camels.

Gideon's Idolatry

22 Then the Israelites said to Gideon, "Rule over us, you and your son and your grandson also; for you have delivered us out of the hand of Midian." ²³ Gideon said to them, "I will not rule over you, and my son will not rule over you; the LORD will rule over you." ²⁴ Then Gideon said to them, "Let me make a request of you; each of you give me an earring he has taken as booty." (For the enemy*a* had golden earrings, because they were Ishmaelites.) ²⁵ "We will willingly give them," they answered. So they spread a garment, and each threw into it an earring he had taken as booty. ²⁶ The weight of the golden earrings that he requested was one thousand seven hundred shekels of gold (apart from the crescents and the pendants and the purple garments worn by the kings of Midian, and the

collars that were on the necks of their camels). ²⁷ Gideon made an ephod of it and put it in his town, in Ophrah; and all Israel prostituted themselves to it there, and it became a snare to Gideon and to his family. ²⁸ So Midian was subdued before the Israelites, and they lifted up their heads no more. So the land had rest forty years in the days of Gideon.

Death of Gideon

29 Jerubbaal son of Joash went to live in his own house. ³⁰ Now Gideon had seventy sons, his own offspring, for he had many wives. ³¹ His concubine who was in Shechem also bore him a son, and he named him Abimelech. ³² Then Gideon son of Joash died at a good old age, and was buried in the tomb of his father Joash at Ophrah of the Abiezrites.

33 As soon as Gideon died, the Israelites relapsed and prostituted themselves with the Baals, making Baal-berith their god. ³⁴ The Israelites did not remember the LORD their God, who had rescued them from the hand of all their enemies on every side; ³⁵ and they did not exhibit loyalty to the house of Jerubbaal (that is, Gideon) in return for all the good that he had done to Israel.

Abimelech Attempts to Establish a Monarchy

9 Now Abimelech son of Jerubbaal went to Shechem to his mother's kinsfolk and said to them and to the whole clan of his mother's family, ² "Say

a Heb *they*

8:22–28—In this unit too, God seems to be left out. The words expressed in 7:2 have become a reality: the people wanted things their own way. Gideon's apparently pious decision to let the Lord be the "king" of Israel is overshadowed by the making of the ephod. This object took the place of any legitimate divine-human interactions. The veiled idolatry here is just the beginning of what ended up as a terrible religious disintegration of Israel (chaps. 17–18).

8:29–35—This unit serves as a conclusion of the Gideon cycle, as well as an introduction to Abimelech's story. Verses 33–35 echo, in a reverse way, what 6:8–10 say.

8:31—*Abimelech* is the name Gideon gave to his son born to his concubine. The name, meaning "My father is king," seems subtly to reflect Gideon's deeper desire to rule over Israel. The fact that Gideon had many wives and children suggests that he was more like a monarch than a wheat farmer.

9:1–6 Abimelech's Plot

Abimelech's attitude and actions are a normal follow-up of the previous unit: Love of the Lord is displaced by hunger for power, violence, and idolatry. Abimelech's portrait is the antithesis of his father's.

in the hearing of all the lords of Shechem, 'Which is better for you, that all seventy of the sons of Jerubbaal rule over you, or that one rule over you?' Remember also that I am your bone and your flesh." ³ So his mother's kinsfolk spoke all these words on his behalf in the hearing of all the lords of Shechem; and their hearts inclined to follow Abimelech, for they said, "He is our brother." ⁴ They gave him seventy pieces of silver out of the temple of Baal-berith with which Abimelech hired worthless and reckless fellows, who followed him. ⁵ He went to his father's house at Ophrah, and killed his brothers the sons of Jerubbaal, seventy men, on one stone; but Jotham, the youngest son of Jerubbaal, survived, for he hid himself. ⁶ Then all the lords of Shechem and all Beth-millo came together, and they went and made Abimelech king, by the oak of the pillar*a* at Shechem.

The Parable of the Trees

7 When it was told to Jotham, he went and stood on the top of Mount Gerizim, and cried aloud and said to them, "Listen to me, you lords of Shechem, so that God may listen to you.

⁸ The trees once went out
to anoint a king over themselves.
So they said to the olive tree,
'Reign over us.'
⁹ The olive tree answered them,
'Shall I stop producing my rich oil
by which gods and mortals are
honored,
and go to sway over the trees?'
¹⁰ Then the trees said to the fig tree,
'You come and reign over us.'
¹¹ But the fig tree answered them,

'Shall I stop producing my
sweetness
and my delicious fruit,
and go to sway over the trees?'
¹² Then the trees said to the vine,
'You come and reign over us.'
¹³ But the vine said to them,
'Shall I stop producing my wine
that cheers gods and mortals,
and go to sway over the trees?'
¹⁴ So all the trees said to the bramble,
'You come and reign over us.'
¹⁵ And the bramble said to the trees,
'If in good faith you are anointing
me king over you,
then come and take refuge in my
shade;
but if not, let fire come out of the
bramble
and devour the cedars of
Lebanon.'

16 "Now therefore, if you acted in good faith and honor when you made Abimelech king, and if you have dealt well with Jerubbaal and his house, and have done to him as his actions deserved— ¹⁷ for my father fought for you, and risked his life, and rescued you from the hand of Midian; ¹⁸ but you have risen up against my father's house this day, and have killed his sons, seventy men on one stone, and have made Abimelech, the son of his slave woman, king over the lords of Shechem, because he is your kinsman— ¹⁹ if, I say, you have acted in good faith and honor with Jerubbaal and with his house this day, then rejoice in Abimelech, and let him also rejoice in you; ²⁰ but if not, let fire come out from Abimelech, and devour the lords

---

a Cn: Meaning of Heb uncertain

9:3—The men who supported Abimelech's kingship as his "brothers" or *kinsfolk* were killed by him (vv. 34–39).

9:5—The one who killed his brothers on a stone would be killed by a woman with a "millstone" (vv. 53, 56).

9:7–21 The Fable of the Trees
When Jotham, the only son of Gideon to survive

Abimelech's massacre, tells a fable, irony reaches great dimensions. In the story, the mighty trees ultimately choose a lowly bramble to become king over them. Jotham speaks not only as a master of rhetoric, but also as a prophet, for he foretells the destruction of Shechem by fire (9:46–49). The place in which Jotham delivers his speech, Mount Gerizim, overlooking Shechem, provides for the occasion a solemn setting.

of Shechem, and Beth-millo; and let fire come out from the lords of Shechem, and from Beth-millo, and devour Abimelech." [21] Then Jotham ran away and fled, going to Beer, where he remained for fear of his brother Abimelech.

The Downfall of Abimelech

22 Abimelech ruled over Israel three years. [23] But God sent an evil spirit between Abimelech and the lords of Shechem; and the lords of Shechem dealt treacherously with Abimelech. [24] This happened so that the violence done to the seventy sons of Jerubbaal might be avenged[a] and their blood be laid on their brother Abimelech, who killed them, and on the lords of Shechem, who strengthened his hands to kill his brothers. [25] So, out of hostility to him, the lords of Shechem set ambushes on the mountain tops. They robbed all who passed by them along that way; and it was reported to Abimelech.

26 When Gaal son of Ebed moved into Shechem with his kinsfolk, the lords of Shechem put confidence in him. [27] They went out into the field and gathered the grapes from their vineyards, trod them, and celebrated. Then they went into the temple of their god, ate and drank, and ridiculed Abimelech. [28] Gaal son of Ebed said, "Who is Abimelech, and who are we of Shechem, that we should serve him? Did not the son of Jerubbaal and Zebul his officer serve the men of Hamor father of Shechem? Why then should we serve him? [29] If only this people were under my command! Then I would remove Abimelech; I would say[b] to him, 'Increase your army, and come out.'"

30 When Zebul the ruler of the city heard the words of Gaal son of Ebed, his anger was kindled. [31] He sent messengers to Abimelech at Arumah,[c] say-

ing, "Look, Gaal son of Ebed and his kinsfolk have come to Shechem, and they are stirring up[d] the city against you. [32] Now therefore, go by night, you and the troops that are with you, and lie in wait in the fields. [33] Then early in the morning, as soon as the sun rises, get up and rush on the city; and when he and the troops that are with him come out against you, you may deal with them as best you can."

34 So Abimelech and all the troops with him got up by night and lay in wait against Shechem in four companies. [35] When Gaal son of Ebed went out and stood in the entrance of the gate of the city, Abimelech and the troops with him rose from the ambush. [36] And when Gaal saw them, he said to Zebul, "Look, people are coming down from the mountain tops!" And Zebul said to him, "The shadows on the mountains look like people to you." [37] Gaal spoke again and said, "Look, people are coming down from Tabbur-erez, and one company is coming from the direction of Elon-meonenim."[e] [38] Then Zebul said to him, "Where is your boast[f] now, you who said, 'Who is Abimelech, that we should serve him?' Are not these the troops you made light of? Go out now and fight with them." [39] So Gaal went out at the head of the lords of Shechem, and fought with Abimelech. [40] Abimelech chased him, and he fled before him. Many fell wounded, up to the entrance of the gate. [41] So Abimelech resided at Arumah; and Zebul drove out Gaal and his kinsfolk, so that they could not live on at Shechem.

42 On the following day the people went out into the fields. When Abimelech was told, [43] he took his troops and divided them into three companies, and

---

[a] Heb might come [b] Gk: Heb and he said [c] Cn See 9.41. Heb Tormah [d] Cn: Heb are besieging [e] That is Diviners' Oak [f] Heb mouth

---

9:22–49 The Destruction of Shechem
At the beginning of this unit, *an evil spirit* sent by the Lord is the cause of the break between Abimelech and the lords of Shechem. With this

information, the author marks the end of both the self-appointed king and of the people of that city. The rest of the story is told under the shadow of this divine decision.

lay in wait in the fields. When he looked and saw the people coming out of the city, he rose against them and killed them. [44] Abimelech and the company that was[a] with him rushed forward and stood at the entrance of the gate of the city, while the two companies rushed on all who were in the fields and killed them. [45] Abimelech fought against the city all that day; he took the city, and killed the people that were in it; and he razed the city and sowed it with salt.

[46] When all the lords of the Tower of Shechem heard of it, they entered the stronghold of the temple of El-berith. [47] Abimelech was told that all the lords of the Tower of Shechem were gathered together. [48] So Abimelech went up to Mount Zalmon, he and all the troops that were with him. Abimelech took an ax in his hand, cut down a bundle of brushwood, and took it up and laid it on his shoulder. Then he said to the troops with him, "What you have seen me do, do quickly, as I have done." [49] So every one of the troops cut down a bundle and following Abimelech put it against the stronghold, and they set the stronghold on fire over them, so that all the people of the Tower of Shechem also died, about a thousand men and women.

[50] Then Abimelech went to Thebez, and encamped against Thebez, and took it. [51] But there was a strong tower within the city, and all the men and women and all the lords of the city fled to it and shut themselves in; and they went to the roof of the tower. [52] Abimelech came to the tower, and fought against it, and came near to the entrance of the tower to burn it with fire. [53] But a certain woman threw an upper millstone on Abimelech's head, and crushed his skull. [54] Immediately he called to the young man who carried his armor and said to him, "Draw your sword and kill me, so people will not say about me, 'A woman killed him.'" So the young man thrust him through, and he died. [55] When the Israelites saw that Abimelech was dead, they all went home. [56] Thus God repaid Abimelech for the crime he committed against his father in killing his seventy brothers; [57] and God also made all the wickedness of the people of Shechem fall back on their heads, and on them came the curse of Jotham son of Jerubbaal.

Tola and Jair

10 After Abimelech, Tola son of Puah son of Dodo, a man of Issachar, who lived at Shamir in the hill country of Ephraim, rose to deliver Israel. [2] He judged Israel twenty-three years. Then he died, and was buried at Shamir.

[3] After him came Jair the Gileadite, who judged Israel twenty-two years. [4] He had thirty sons who rode on thirty donkeys; and they had thirty towns, which are in the land of Gilead, and are called Havvoth-jair to this day. [5] Jair died, and was buried in Kamon.

Oppression by the Ammonites

[6] The Israelites again did what was evil in the sight of the LORD, worshiping the Baals and the Astartes, the gods of Aram, the gods of Sidon, the gods of

[a] Vg and some Gk Mss: Heb *companies that were*

9:53—The death of Abimelech is as shameful and brutal as that of Sisera. Both die by the hand of a woman. The man who killed his half-brothers on a stone now dies by being struck by a stone.

10:1–5 Tola and Jair
These two minor judges flourish in a peaceful period between times of much trouble. Jair is blessed with a large family and much wealth.

10:6–12:7 Jephthah
This section is unified with the process we may

call "bargaining." In each part of the section there is a "negotiation" going on between two parties, started by the weaker one: the people of Israel with God (10:6–16); the leaders of Israel with Jephthah (10:17–11:11); Jephthah with the Ammonite king (11:12–28); Jephthah with the Lord (11:29–40); the people of the tribe of Ephraim with Jephthah (12:1–7).

10:6–16—In this unit we find some of the components found in the circular pattern presented in 2:6–23: the sin of Israel, the punishment by the

Moab, the gods of the Ammonites, and the gods of the Philistines. Thus they abandoned the LORD, and did not worship him. [7] So the anger of the LORD was kindled against Israel, and he sold them into the hand of the Philistines and into the hand of the Ammonites, [8] and they crushed and oppressed the Israelites that year. For eighteen years they oppressed all the Israelites that were beyond the Jordan in the land of the Amorites, which is in Gilead. [9] The Ammonites also crossed the Jordan to fight against Judah and against Benjamin and against the house of Ephraim; so that Israel was greatly distressed.

10 So the Israelites cried to the LORD, saying, "We have sinned against you, because we have abandoned our God and have worshiped the Baals." [11] And the LORD said to the Israelites, "Did I not deliver you[a] from the Egyptians and from the Amorites, from the Ammonites and from the Philistines? [12] The Sidonians also, and the Amalekites, and the Maonites, oppressed you; and you cried to me, and I delivered you out of their hand. [13] Yet you have abandoned me and worshiped other gods; therefore I will deliver you no more. [14] Go and cry to the gods whom you have chosen; let them deliver you in the time of your distress." [15] And the Israelites said to the LORD, "We have sinned; do to us whatever seems good to you; but deliver us this day!" [16] So they put away the foreign gods from among them and worshiped the LORD; and he could no longer bear to see Israel suffer.

17 Then the Ammonites were called to arms, and they encamped in Gilead; and the Israelites came together, and they encamped at Mizpah. [18] The commanders of the people of Gilead said to one another, "Who will begin the fight against the Ammonites? He shall be head over all the inhabitants of Gilead."

Jephthah

11 Now Jephthah the Gileadite, the son of a prostitute, was a mighty warrior. Gilead was the father of Jephthah. [2] Gilead's wife also bore him sons; and when his wife's sons grew up, they drove Jephthah away, saying to him, "You shall not inherit anything in our father's house; for you are the son of another woman." [3] Then Jephthah fled from his brothers and lived in the land of Tob. Outlaws collected around Jephthah and went raiding with him.

4 After a time the Ammonites made war against Israel. [5] And when the Ammonites made war against Israel, the elders of Gilead went to bring Jephthah from the land of Tob. [6] They said to Jephthah, "Come and be our commander, so that we may fight with the Ammonites." [7] But Jephthah said to the elders of Gilead, "Are you not the very ones who rejected me and drove me out of my father's house? So why do you come to me now when you are in trouble?" [8] The elders of Gilead said to Jephthah, "Nevertheless, we have now turned back to you, so that you may go with us and fight with the Ammonites, and become head over us, over all the inhabitants of Gilead." [9] Jephthah said to the elders of Gilead, "If you bring me home again to fight with the Ammonites, and the LORD gives them over to me, I will be your head." [10] And the elders of Gilead said to Jephthah, "The LORD will be witness between us; we will surely do

---

[a] Heb lacks Did I not deliver you

Lord, and the cry of the people. But there is also a new element, not found before in the book: the people recognize their sins (v. 10). Nevertheless, the Lord will react to the people's request for help only after a second recognition of sin and the actual disposal of the foreign gods (v. 16). As a matter of fact, the text is somewhat ambiguous about God's reaction. It seems that what moves

the Lord to further action on behalf of Israel is the people's suffering, not an action of repentance.

10:17–11:11—The credentials of Jephthah are similar to those of Abimelech: he is the son of a prostitute, an outcast from his family, and the leader of outlaws. In this recruitment, the Lord takes no initiative.

as you say." **11** So Jephthah went with the elders of Gilead, and the people made him head and commander over them; and Jephthah spoke all his words before the LORD at Mizpah.

12 Then Jephthah sent messengers to the king of the Ammonites and said, "What is there between you and me, that you have come to me to fight against my land?" **13** The king of the Ammonites answered the messengers of Jephthah, "Because Israel, on coming from Egypt, took away my land from the Arnon to the Jabbok and to the Jordan; now therefore restore it peaceably." **14** Once again Jephthah sent messengers to the king of the Ammonites **15** and said to him: "Thus says Jephthah: Israel did not take away the land of Moab or the land of the Ammonites, **16** but when they came up from Egypt, Israel went through the wilderness to the Red Sea*a* and came to Kadesh. **17** Israel then sent messengers to the king of Edom, saying, 'Let us pass through your land'; but the king of Edom would not listen. They also sent to the king of Moab, but he would not consent. So Israel remained at Kadesh. **18** Then they journeyed through the wilderness, went around the land of Edom and the land of Moab, arrived on the east side of the land of Moab, and camped on the other side of the Arnon. They did not enter the territory of Moab, for the Arnon was the boundary of Moab. **19** Israel then sent messengers to King Sihon of the Amorites, king of Heshbon; and Israel said to him, 'Let us pass through your land to our country.' **20** But Sihon did not trust Israel to pass through his territory; so Sihon gathered all his people together, and encamped at Jahaz, and fought with Israel. **21** Then the LORD, the God of Israel, gave Sihon and all his people into the hand of Israel, and they defeated them; so Israel occupied all the land of the Amorites, who inhabited that country. **22** They occupied all the territory of the Amorites from the Arnon to the Jabbok and from the wilderness to the Jordan. **23** So now the LORD, the God of Israel, has conquered the Amorites for the benefit of his people Israel. Do you intend to take their place? **24** Should you not possess what your god Chemosh gives you to possess? And should we not be the ones to possess everything that the LORD our God has conquered for our benefit? **25** Now are you any better than King Balak son of Zippor of Moab? Did he ever enter into conflict with Israel, or did he ever go to war with them? **26** While Israel lived in Heshbon and its villages, and in Aroer and its villages, and in all the towns that are along the Arnon, three hundred years, why did you not recover them within that time? **27** It is not I who have sinned against you, but you are the one who does me wrong by making war on me. Let the LORD, who is judge, decide today for the Israelites or for the Ammonites." **28** But the king of the Ammonites did not heed the message that Jephthah sent him.

Jephthah's Vow

29 Then the spirit of the LORD came upon Jephthah, and he passed through Gilead and Manasseh. He passed on to Mizpah of Gilead, and from Mizpah of

a Or Sea of Reeds

11:12–28—During the negotiations between Jephthah and the king of Ammon, Jephthah gives three reasons why Israel should not surrender the territory in dispute: historical reasons (vv. 12–20), theological reasons (vv. 24), and common sense (vv. 25–27).

11:29–40—Empowerment with God's spirit seems not to be enough for Jephthah. Having received the spirit of God as an act of the Lord's grace, Jephthah responds with unfaithfulness. Jephthah uses the vow as a bribe or leverage to influence God in regard to the upcoming war against the Ammonites. Making this vow to God shows two characteristics of Jephthah's personality: (a) his insecurity born out of the rejection by his own people was a deterrent to his full enjoyment of God's empowerment; (b) he was not courageous enough to commit himself, but put the onus on someone else. In the story, it was on his daughter. In fact, he blames her for his own irresponsibility.

Gilead he passed on to the Ammonites. [30] And Jephthah made a vow to the LORD, and said, "If you will give the Ammonites into my hand, [31] then whoever comes out of the doors of my house to meet me, when I return victorious from the Ammonites, shall be the LORD's, to be offered up by me as a burnt offering." [32] So Jephthah crossed over to the Ammonites to fight against them; and the LORD gave them into his hand. [33] He inflicted a massive defeat on them from Aroer to the neighborhood of Minnith, twenty towns, and as far as Abel-keramim. So the Ammonites were subdued before the people of Israel.

Jephthah's Daughter

34 Then Jephthah came to his home at Mizpah; and there was his daughter coming out to meet him with timbrels and with dancing. She was his only child; he had no son or daughter except her. [35] When he saw her, he tore his clothes, and said, "Alas, my daughter! You have brought me very low; you have become the cause of great trouble to me. For I have opened my mouth to the LORD, and I cannot take back my vow." [36] She said to him, "My father, if you have opened your mouth to the LORD, do to me according to what has gone out of your mouth, now that the LORD has given you vengeance against your enemies, the Ammonites." [37] And she said to her father, "Let this thing be done for me: Grant me two months, so that I may go and wander[a] on the mountains, and bewail my virginity, my companions and I." [38] "Go," he said and sent her away for two months. So she departed, she and her companions, and bewailed her virginity on the mountains. [39] At the end of two months, she returned to her father, who did with her according to the vow he had made. She had never slept with a man. So there arose an Israelite custom that [40] for four days every year the daughters of Israel would go out to lament the daughter of Jephthah the Gileadite.

Intertribal Dissension

12 The men of Ephraim were called to arms, and they crossed to Zaphon and said to Jephthah, "Why did you cross over to fight against the Ammonites, and did not call us to go with you? We will burn your house down over you!" [2] Jephthah said to them, "My people and I were engaged in conflict with the Ammonites who oppressed us[b] severely. But when I called you, you did not deliver me from their hand. [3] When I saw that you would not deliver me, I took my life in my hand, and crossed over against the Ammonites, and the LORD gave them into my hand. Why then have you come up to me this day, to fight against me?" [4] Then Jephthah gathered all the men of Gilead and fought with Ephraim; and the men of Gilead defeated Ephraim, because they said, "You are fugitives from Ephraim, you Gileadites—in the heart of Ephraim and Manasseh."[c] [5] Then the Gileadites took the fords of the Jordan against the Ephraimites. Whenever one of the fugitives of Ephraim said, "Let me go over," the men of Gilead would say to him, "Are you an Ephraimite?" When

---

[a] Cn: Heb go down [b] Gk OL, Syr H: Heb lacks who oppressed us [c] Meaning of Heb uncertain: Gk omits because . . . Manasseh

---

11:36—Jephthah's daughter is presented as a figure opposite to her father: she is unselfish, supportive, willing to be sacrificed, responsible for her own role in life.

12:1–7—This last episode in Jephthah's life shows just how the deterioration in the life of the nation has worsened. Now Jephthah's enemy is not people from outside, but a fellow Israelite tribe, Ephraim. As a matter of fact, in Judges the tribe of Ephraim serves as a sort of measuring stick for the cohesion of the nation. In the first part of the book, Ephraim was always ready to give support to the other tribes; by the time of Gideon, the relationship with that tribe shows signs of deterioration. Now, in the third part, with Jephthah, no peaceful solution to the intertribal friction seems to be at hand.

he said, "No," **6** they said to him, "Then say Shibboleth," and he said, "Sibboleth," for he could not pronounce it right. Then they seized him and killed him at the fords of the Jordan. Forty-two thousand of the Ephraimites fell at that time.

7 Jephthah judged Israel six years. Then Jephthah the Gileadite died, and was buried in his town in Gilead. *a*

Ibzan, Elon, and Abdon

8 After him Ibzan of Bethlehem judged Israel. **9** He had thirty sons. He gave his thirty daughters in marriage outside his clan and brought in thirty young women from outside for his sons. He judged Israel seven years. **10** Then Ibzan died, and was buried at Bethlehem.

11 After him Elon the Zebulunite judged Israel; and he judged Israel ten years. **12** Then Elon the Zebulunite died, and was buried at Aijalon in the land of Zebulun.

13 After him Abdon son of Hillel the Pirathonite judged Israel. **14** He had forty sons and thirty grandsons, who rode on seventy donkeys; he judged Israel eight years. **15** Then Abdon son of Hillel the Pirathonite died, and was buried at Pirathon in the land of Ephraim, in the hill country of the Amalekites.

The Birth of Samson

13 The Israelites again did what was evil in the sight of the LORD, and the LORD gave them into the hand of the Philistines forty years.

2 There was a certain man of Zorah, of the tribe of the Danites, whose name was Manoah. His wife was barren, having borne no children. **3** And the angel of the LORD appeared to the woman and said to her, "Although you are barren, having borne no children, you shall conceive and bear a son. **4** Now be careful not to drink wine or strong drink, or to eat anything unclean, **5** for you shall conceive and bear a son. No razor is to come on his head, for the boy shall be a nazirite*b* to God from birth. It is he who shall begin to deliver Israel from the hand of the Philistines." **6** Then the woman came and told her husband, "A man of God came to me, and his appearance was like that of an angel*c* of God, most awe-inspiring; I did not ask him where he came from, and he did not tell me his name; **7** but he said to me, 'You shall conceive and bear a son. So then drink no wine or strong drink, and eat nothing unclean, for the boy shall be a nazirite*b* to God from birth to the day of his death.'"

a Gk: Heb *in the towns of Gilead*   *b* That is *one separated* or *one consecrated*   *c* Or *the angel*

12:8–15 Three Minor Judges: Ibzan, Elon, and Abdon

Nothing new or good is done by these three judges. Their dealings do not have to do with Israel, in whole or part, but are confined to personal or family matters. Ibzan and Abdon are, however, rich and prolific fathers, like Jair before them (10:3–5).

13:1–16:31 Samson

The "hero" to whose life God pays particular and careful attention becomes an "antijudge." How far he has come from the model set by Othniel, the first judge! The expectations raised by the announcement of his birth are disproportionate to the record of the rest of his career. As a matter of fact, mediocrity and failure characterize much of his life. It seems that he chose to do exactly the opposite of what God and his parents expected him to do.

Yet Samson becomes a paradigm of how the

Lord can act on behalf of the covenant people in spite of the obstacles raised by those chosen to be God's instruments. Samson is a good introduction to the last part of the book, which is bracketed by the phrase *all the people did what was right in their own eyes* (17:6; 21:25), for that is exactly what he did.

It is also in Samson that one finds the hard-to-accept idea that the presence of the spirit of God in one's life is not an assurance of good and sound behavior. Human responsibility is a must, because God does not take away one's freedom of action.

More than any other judge, Samson becomes a living paradigm of Israel. In the view of the Deuteronomist, Samson's disobedience, immaturity, and dissipated life mirror the life of Israel, just as his birth, his life consecrated to the Lord, and the presence of God's spirit in his life do. Like Samson, Israel called out to God only in the moment of need and deep crisis.

8 Then Manoah entreated the LORD, and said, "O LORD, I pray, let the man of God whom you sent come to us again and teach us what we are to do concerning the boy who will be born." ⁹God listened to Manoah, and the angel of God came again to the woman as she sat in the field; but her husband Manoah was not with her. ¹⁰So the woman ran quickly and told her husband, "The man who came to me the other day has appeared to me." ¹¹Manoah got up and followed his wife, and came to the man and said to him, "Are you the man who spoke to this woman?" And he said, "I am." ¹²Then Manoah said, "Now when your words come true, what is to be the boy's rule of life; what is he to do?" ¹³The angel of the LORD said to Manoah, "Let the woman give heed to all that I said to her. ¹⁴She may not eat of anything that comes from the vine. She is not to drink wine or strong drink, or eat any unclean thing. She is to observe everything that I commanded her."

15 Manoah said to the angel of the LORD, "Allow us to detain you, and prepare a kid for you." ¹⁶The angel of the LORD said to Manoah, "If you detain me, I will not eat your food; but if you want to prepare a burnt offering, then offer it to the LORD." (For Manoah did not know that he was the angel of the LORD.) ¹⁷Then Manoah said to the angel of the LORD, "What is your name, so that we may honor you when your words come true?" ¹⁸But the angel of the LORD said to him, "Why do you ask my name? It is too wonderful."

19 So Manoah took the kid with the grain offering, and offered it on the rock to the LORD, to him who works*a* wonders.*b* ²⁰When the flame went up toward heaven from the altar, the angel of the LORD ascended in the flame of the altar while Manoah and his wife looked on; and they fell on their faces to the ground. ²¹The angel of the LORD did not appear again to Manoah and his wife. Then Manoah realized that it was the angel of the LORD. ²²And Manoah said to his wife, "We shall surely die, for we have seen God." ²³But his wife said to him, "If the LORD had meant to kill us, he would not have accepted a burnt offering and a grain offering at our hands, or shown us all these things, or now announced to us such things as these."

24 The woman bore a son, and named him Samson. The boy grew, and the LORD blessed him. ²⁵The spirit of the LORD began to stir him in Mahaneh-dan, between Zorah and Eshtaol.

Samson's Marriage

14 Once Samson went down to Timnah, and at Timnah he saw a Philistine woman. ²Then he came up, and told his father and mother, "I saw a Philistine woman at Timnah; now get her for me as my wife." ³But his father and mother said to him, "Is there not a woman among your kin, or among all our*c* people, that you must go to take a wife from the uncircumcised Philistines?" But Samson said to his father, "Get her for me, because she pleases me." ⁴His father and mother did not know that this was from the LORD; for he was seeking a pretext to act against the Philistines. At that time the Philistines had dominion over Israel.

5 Then Samson went down with his father and mother to Timnah. When he came to the vineyards of Timnah, suddenly a young lion roared at him. ⁶The spirit of the LORD rushed on him, and he tore the lion apart barehanded as one might tear apart a kid. But he did not tell his father or his mother what he had done. ⁷Then he went down and talked with the woman, and she pleased Samson. ⁸After a while he returned to marry her, and he turned aside to see the carcass of the lion, and there was a swarm of bees in the body of the lion, and honey. ⁹He scraped it out into his hands, and went on, eating as he went. When he

---

a Gk Vg: Heb *and working* *b* Heb *wonders, while Manoah and his wife looked on* *c* Cn: Heb *my*

came to his father and mother, he gave some to them, and they ate it. But he did not tell them that he had taken the honey from the carcass of the lion.

10 His father went down to the woman, and Samson made a feast there as the young men were accustomed to do. 11 When the people saw him, they brought thirty companions to be with him. 12 Samson said to them, "Let me now put a riddle to you. If you can explain it to me within the seven days of the feast, and find it out, then I will give you thirty linen garments and thirty festal garments. 13 But if you cannot explain it to me, then you shall give me thirty linen garments and thirty festal garments." So they said to him, "Ask your riddle; let us hear it." 14 He said to them,

"Out of the eater came something to
          eat.
Out of the strong came something
          sweet."

But for three days they could not explain the riddle.

15 On the fourth[a] day they said to Samson's wife, "Coax your husband to explain the riddle to us, or we will burn you and your father's house with fire. Have you invited us here to impoverish us?" 16 So Samson's wife wept before him, saying, "You hate me; you do not really love me. You have asked a riddle of my people, but you have not explained it to me." He said to her, "Look, I have not told my father or my mother. Why should I tell you?" 17 She wept before him the seven days that their feast lasted; and because she nagged him, on the seventh day he told her. Then she explained the riddle to her people. 18 The men of the town said to him on the seventh day before the sun went down,

"What is sweeter than honey?
What is stronger than a lion?"

And he said to them,

"If you had not plowed with my
          heifer,

you would not have found out my
          riddle."

19 Then the spirit of the LORD rushed on him, and he went down to Ashkelon. He killed thirty men of the town, took their spoil, and gave the festal garments to those who had explained the riddle. In hot anger he went back to his father's house. 20 And Samson's wife was given to his companion, who had been his best man.

Samson Defeats the Philistines

15 After a while, at the time of the wheat harvest, Samson went to visit his wife, bringing along a kid. He said, "I want to go into my wife's room." But her father would not allow him to go in. 2 Her father said, "I was sure that you had rejected her; so I gave her to your companion. Is not her younger sister prettier than she? Why not take her instead?" 3 Samson said to them, "This time, when I do mischief to the Philistines, I will be without blame." 4 So Samson went and caught three hundred foxes, and took some torches; and he turned the foxes[b] tail to tail, and put a torch between each pair of tails. 5 When he had set fire to the torches, he let the foxes go into the standing grain of the Philistines, and burned up the shocks and the standing grain, as well as the vineyards and[c] olive groves. 6 Then the Philistines asked, "Who has done this?" And they said, "Samson, the son-in-law of the Timnite, because he has taken Samson's wife and given her to his companion." So the Philistines came up, and burned her and her father. 7 Samson said to them, "If this is what you do, I swear I will not stop until I have taken revenge on you." 8 He struck them down hip and thigh with great slaughter; and he went down and stayed in the cleft of the rock of Etam.

9 Then the Philistines came up and encamped in Judah, and made a raid on Lehi. 10 The men of Judah said,

[a] Gk Syr: Heb *seventh*   [b] Heb *them*   [c] Gk Tg Vg: Heb lacks *and*

"Why have you come up against us?"
They said, "We have come up to bind
Samson, to do to him as he did to us."
¹¹ Then three thousand men of Judah
went down to the cleft of the rock of
Etam, and they said to Samson, "Do
you not know that the Philistines are
rulers over us? What then have you
done to us?" He replied, "As they did
to me, so I have done to them." ¹² They
said to him, "We have come down to
bind you, so that we may give you into
the hands of the Philistines." Samson
answered them, "Swear to me that you
yourselves will not attack me." ¹³ They
said to him, "No, we will only bind you
and give you into their hands; we will
not kill you." So they bound him with
two new ropes, and brought him up
from the rock.

14 When he came to Lehi, the Philistines came shouting to meet him; and
the spirit of the LORD rushed on him,
and the ropes that were on his arms
became like flax that has caught fire,
and his bonds melted off his hands.
¹⁵ Then he found a fresh jawbone of a
donkey, reached down and took it, and
with it he killed a thousand men. ¹⁶ And
Samson said,

"With the jawbone of a donkey,
    heaps upon heaps,
with the jawbone of a donkey
    I have slain a thousand men."

¹⁷ When he had finished speaking, he
threw away the jawbone; and that place
was called Ramath-lehi.ᵃ

18 By then he was very thirsty, and he
called on the LORD, saying, "You have
granted this great victory by the hand of
your servant. Am I now to die of thirst,
and fall into the hands of the uncircumcised?" ¹⁹ So God split open the hollow
place that is at Lehi, and water came from
it. When he drank, his spirit returned,
and he revived. Therefore it was named
En-hakkore,ᵇ which is at Lehi to this
day. ²⁰ And he judged Israel in the days
of the Philistines twenty years.

Samson and Delilah

16 Once Samson went to Gaza,
where he saw a prostitute and
went in to her. ² The Gazites were told,ᶜ
"Samson has come here." So they circled
around and lay in wait for him all night
at the city gate. They kept quiet all night,
thinking, "Let us wait until the light of
the morning; then we will kill him." ³ But
Samson lay only until midnight. Then at
midnight he rose up, took hold of the
doors of the city gate and the two posts,
pulled them up, bar and all, put them on
his shoulders, and carried them to the
top of the hill that is in front of Hebron.

4 After this he fell in love with a
woman in the valley of Sorek, whose
name was Delilah. ⁵ The lords of the
Philistines came to her and said to her,
"Coax him, and find out what makes his
strength so great, and how we may over-
power him, so that we may bind him in
order to subdue him; and we will each
give you eleven hundred pieces of silver."
⁶ So Delilah said to Samson, "Please tell
me what makes your strength so great,
and how you could be bound, so that
one could subdue you." ⁷ Samson said to
her, "If they bind me with seven fresh
bowstrings that are not dried out, then
I shall become weak, and be like anyone
else." ⁸ Then the lords of the Philistines
brought her seven fresh bowstrings
that had not dried out, and she bound
him with them. ⁹ While men were lying
in wait in an inner chamber, she said
to him, "The Philistines are upon you,
Samson!" But he snapped the bowstrings, as a strand of fiber snaps when
it touches the fire. So the secret of his
strength was not known.

10 Then Delilah said to Samson, "You
have mocked me and told me lies; please
tell me how you could be bound." ¹¹ He
said to her, "If they bind me with new
ropes that have not been used, then I
shall become weak, and be like anyone
else." ¹² So Delilah took new ropes and

ᵃ That is The Hill of the Jawbone   ᵇ That is The Spring of the One who
Called   ᶜ Gk: Heb lacks were told

bound him with them, and said to him, "The Philistines are upon you, Samson!" (The men lying in wait were in an inner chamber.) But he snapped the ropes off his arms like a thread.

13 Then Delilah said to Samson, "Until now you have mocked me and told me lies; tell me how you could be bound." He said to her, "If you weave the seven locks of my head with the web and make it tight with the pin, then I shall become weak, and be like anyone else." 14 So while he slept, Delilah took the seven locks of his head and wove them into the web,*a* and made them tight with the pin. Then she said to him, "The Philistines are upon you, Samson!" But he awoke from his sleep, and pulled away the pin, the loom, and the web.

15 Then she said to him, "How can you say, 'I love you,' when your heart is not with me? You have mocked me three times now and have not told me what makes your strength so great." 16 Finally, after she had nagged him with her words day after day, and pestered him, he was tired to death. 17 So he told her his whole secret, and said to her, "A razor has never come upon my head; for I have been a nazirite*b* to God from my mother's womb. If my head were shaved, then my strength would leave me; I would become weak, and be like anyone else."

18 When Delilah realized that he had told her his whole secret, she sent and called the lords of the Philistines, saying, "This time come up, for he has told his whole secret to me." Then the lords of the Philistines came up to her, and brought the money in their hands. 19 She let him fall asleep on her lap; and she called a man, and had him shave off the seven locks of his head. He began to weaken,*c* and his strength left him. 20 Then she said, "The Philistines are upon you, Samson!" When he awoke from his sleep, he thought, "I will go out as at other times, and shake myself free." But he did not know that the LORD had

left him. 21 So the Philistines seized him and gouged out his eyes. They brought him down to Gaza and bound him with bronze shackles; and he ground at the mill in the prison. 22 But the hair of his head began to grow again after it had been shaved.

Samson's Death

23 Now the lords of the Philistines gathered to offer a great sacrifice to their god Dagon, and to rejoice; for they said, "Our god has given Samson our enemy into our hand." 24 When the people saw him, they praised their god; for they said, "Our god has given our enemy into our hand, the ravager of our country, who has killed many of us." 25 And when their hearts were merry, they said, "Call Samson, and let him entertain us." So they called Samson out of the prison, and he performed for them. They made him stand between the pillars; 26 and Samson said to the attendant who held him by the hand, "Let me feel the pillars on which the house rests, so that I may lean against them." 27 Now the house was full of men and women; all the lords of the Philistines were there, and on the roof there were about three thousand men and women, who looked on while Samson performed.

28 Then Samson called to the LORD and said, "Lord GOD, remember me and strengthen me only this once, O God, so that with this one act of revenge I may pay back the Philistines for my two eyes."*d* 29 And Samson grasped the two middle pillars on which the house rested, and he leaned his weight against them, his right hand on the one and his left hand on the other. 30 Then Samson said, "Let me die with the Philistines." He strained with all his might; and the house fell on the lords and all the people who were in it. So those he killed at his death were more than those he had

---

a Compare Gk: in verses 13-14, Heb lacks *and make it tight . . . into the web*
b That is *one separated* or *one consecrated*   *c* Gk: Heb *She began to torment him*   *d* Or *so that I may be avenged upon the Philistines for one of my two eyes*

killed during his life. [31] Then his brothers and all his family came down and took him and brought him up and buried him between Zorah and Eshtaol in the tomb of his father Manoah. He had judged Israel twenty years.

Micah and the Levite

17 There was a man in the hill country of Ephraim whose name was Micah. [2] He said to his mother, "The eleven hundred pieces of silver that were taken from you, about which you uttered a curse, and even spoke it in my hearing,—that silver is in my possession; I took it; but now I will return it to you."[a] And his mother said, "May my son be blessed by the LORD!" [3] Then he returned the eleven hundred pieces of silver to his mother; and his mother said, "I consecrate the silver to the LORD from my hand for my son, to make an idol of cast metal." [4] So when he returned the money to his mother, his mother took two hundred pieces of silver, and gave it to the silversmith, who made it into an idol of cast metal; and it was in the house of Micah. [5] This man Micah had a shrine, and he made an ephod and teraphim, and installed one of his sons, who became his priest. [6] In those days there was no king in Israel; all the people did what was right in their own eyes.

[7] Now there was a young man of Bethlehem in Judah, of the clan of Judah. He was a Levite residing there. [8] This man left the town of Bethlehem in Judah, to live wherever he could find a place. He came to the house of Micah in the hill country of Ephraim to carry on his work.[b] [9] Micah said to him, "From where do you come?" He replied, "I am a Levite of Bethlehem in Judah, and I am going to live wherever I can find a place." [10] Then Micah said to him, "Stay with me, and be to me a father and a priest, and I will give you ten pieces of silver a year, a set of clothes, and your living."[c] [11] The Levite agreed to stay with the man; and the young man became to him like one of his sons. [12] So Micah installed the Levite, and the young man became his priest, and was in the house of Micah. [13] Then Micah said, "Now I know that the LORD will prosper me, because the Levite has become my priest."

The Migration of Dan

18 In those days there was no king in Israel. And in those days the tribe of the Danites was seeking for itself a territory to live in; for until then no territory among the tribes of Israel had been allotted to them. [2] So the Danites sent five valiant men from the whole number of their clan, from Zorah and from Eshtaol, to spy out the land and to explore it; and they said to them, "Go, explore the land." When they came to the hill country of Ephraim, to the house

[a] The words *but now I will return it to you* are transposed from the end of verse 3 in Heb　[b] Or *Ephraim, continuing his journey*　[c] Heb *living, and the Levite went*

17:1–21:25 Israel's Total Religious and Social Disintegration

As the book approaches its end, almost every corner of the nation's life reaches new lows. No longer is there any mention of the cyclical pattern referred to in chaps. 3–16. Now everything is bad, and evil is the order of the day. Throughout these chapters, the narratives report a systematic breaking of practically every one of the Ten Commandments.

17:1–18:31 Religious Decay

It is quite ironical to find the name *Micah* ("Who is like the Lord?" 17:1) and the service of a Levite (a member of the tribe selected for the service of the Lord, 17:7) in a clearly idolatrous context.

Both a family and a complete tribe (Dan) fall prey to religious practices rejected by the Lord (see Deut. 4:16; 27:15; 12:2–3).

17:6 *All the people did what was right in their own eyes*—This refrain, which also appears at the end of this section (21:25), serves as a framework for the conclusion of the book of Judges and points to the central theme in these chapters: total disintegration of the nation.

17:10–13—Micah supposes that by his "buying" the service of a priest from the "right" tribe God's favor is guaranteed and that he can manipulate God. Religion of this type is as idolatrous as fabricating an idol (v. 4).

of Micah, they stayed there. ³ While they were at Micah's house, they recognized the voice of the young Levite; so they went over and asked him, "Who brought you here? What are you doing in this place? What is your business here?" ⁴ He said to them, "Micah did such and such for me, and he hired me, and I have become his priest." ⁵ Then they said to him, "Inquire of God that we may know whether the mission we are undertaking will succeed." ⁶ The priest replied, "Go in peace. The mission you are on is under the eye of the LORD."

7 The five men went on, and when they came to Laish, they observed the people who were there living securely, after the manner of the Sidonians, quiet and unsuspecting, lacking*a* nothing on earth, and possessing wealth.*b* Furthermore, they were far from the Sidonians and had no dealings with Aram.*c* ⁸ When they came to their kinsfolk at Zorah and Eshtaol, they said to them, "What do you report?" ⁹ They said, "Come, let us go up against them; for we have seen the land, and it is very good. Will you do nothing? Do not be slow to go, but enter in and possess the land. ¹⁰ When you go, you will come to an unsuspecting people. The land is broad—God has indeed given it into your hands—a place where there is no lack of anything on earth."

11 Six hundred men of the Danite clan, armed with weapons of war, set out from Zorah and Eshtaol, ¹² and went up and encamped at Kiriath-jearim in Judah. On this account that place is called Mahaneh-dan*d* to this day; it is west of Kiriath-jearim. ¹³ From there they passed on to the hill country of Ephraim, and came to the house of Micah.

14 Then the five men who had gone to spy out the land (that is, Laish) said to their comrades, "Do you know that in these buildings there are an ephod, teraphim, and an idol of cast metal? Now therefore consider what you will do." ¹⁵ So they turned in that direction and

came to the house of the young Levite, at the home of Micah, and greeted him. ¹⁶ While the six hundred men of the Danites, armed with their weapons of war, stood by the entrance of the gate, ¹⁷ the five men who had gone to spy out the land proceeded to enter and take the idol of cast metal, the ephod, and the teraphim.*e* The priest was standing by the entrance of the gate with the six hundred men armed with weapons of war. ¹⁸ When the men went into Micah's house and took the idol of cast metal, the ephod, and the teraphim, the priest said to them, "What are you doing?" ¹⁹ They said to him, "Keep quiet! Put your hand over your mouth, and come with us, and be to us a father and a priest. Is it better for you to be priest to the house of one person, or to be priest to a tribe and clan in Israel?" ²⁰ Then the priest accepted the offer. He took the ephod, the teraphim, and the idol, and went along with the people.

21 So they resumed their journey, putting the little ones, the livestock, and the goods in front of them. ²² When they were some distance from the home of Micah, the men who were in the houses near Micah's house were called out, and they overtook the Danites. ²³ They shouted to the Danites, who turned around and said to Micah, "What is the matter that you come with such a company?" ²⁴ He replied, "You take my gods that I made, and the priest, and go away, and what have I left? How then can you ask me, 'What is the matter?'" ²⁵ And the Danites said to him, "You had better not let your voice be heard among us or else hot-tempered fellows will attack you, and you will lose your life and the lives of your household." ²⁶ Then the Danites went their way. When Micah saw that they were too strong for him, he turned and went back to his home.

a Cn Compare 18.10: Meaning of Heb uncertain   *b* Meaning of Heb uncertain   *c* Symmachus: Heb *with anyone*   *d* That is *Camp of Dan*   *e* Compare 17.4, 5; 18.14: Heb *teraphim and the cast metal*

The Danites Settle in Laish

27 The Danites, having taken what Micah had made, and the priest who belonged to him, came to Laish, to a people quiet and unsuspecting, put them to the sword, and burned down the city. 28 There was no deliverer, because it was far from Sidon and they had no dealings with Aram.*a* It was in the valley that belongs to Beth-rehob. They rebuilt the city, and lived in it. 29 They named the city Dan, after their ancestor Dan, who was born to Israel; but the name of the city was formerly Laish. 30 Then the Danites set up the idol for themselves. Jonathan son of Gershom, son of Moses,*b* and his sons were priests to the tribe of the Danites until the time the land went into captivity. 31 So they maintained as their own Micah's idol that he had made, as long as the house of God was at Shiloh.

The Levite's Concubine

19 In those days, when there was no king in Israel, a certain Levite, residing in the remote parts of the hill country of Ephraim, took to himself a concubine from Bethlehem in Judah. 2 But his concubine became angry with*c* him, and she went away from him to her father's house at Bethlehem in Judah, and was there some four months. 3 Then her husband set out after her, to speak tenderly to her and bring her back. He had with him his servant and a couple of donkeys. When he reached*d* her father's house, the girl's father saw him and came with joy to meet him. 4 His father-in-law, the girl's father, made him stay, and he remained with him three days; so they ate and drank, and he*e* stayed there. 5 On the fourth day they got up early in the morning, and he prepared to go; but the girl's father said to his son-in-law, "Fortify yourself with a bit of food, and after that you may go." 6 So the two men sat and ate and drank together; and the girl's father said to the man, "Why not spend the night and enjoy yourself?" 7 When the man got up to go, his father-in-law kept urging him until he spent the night there again. 8 On the fifth day he got up early in the morning to leave; and the girl's father said, "Fortify yourself." So they lingered*f* until the day declined, and the two of them ate and drank.*g* 9 When the man with his concubine and his servant got up to leave, his father-in-law, the girl's father, said to him, "Look, the day has worn on until it is almost evening. Spend the night. See, the day has drawn to a close. Spend the night here and enjoy yourself. Tomorrow you can get up early in the morning for your journey, and go home."

10 But the man would not spend the night; he got up and departed, and arrived opposite Jebus (that is, Jerusalem). He had with him a couple of saddled donkeys, and his concubine was with him. 11 When they were near Jebus, the day was far spent, and the servant said to his master, "Come now, let us turn aside to this city of the Jebusites, and spend the night in it." 12 But his master said to him, "We will not turn aside into a city of foreigners, who do not belong to the people of Israel; but we will continue on to Gibeah." 13 Then he said to his servant, "Come, let us try to reach one of these places, and spend the

a Cn Compare verse 7: Heb *with anyone*   *b* Another reading is *son of Manasseh*   *c* Gk OL: Heb *prostituted herself against*   *d* Gk: Heb *she brought him to*   *e* Compare verse 7 and Gk: Heb *they*   *f* Cn: Heb *Linger*   *g* Gk: Heb *lacks and drank*

19:1–21:25 Social Disintegration
The brutal rape and killing of an unnamed woman opens this second part of the conclusion of the book. The conclusion is as terrifying as the opening of the section. It features the near annihilation of an entire tribe and the kidnapping and raping of young girls. In both cases, the innocent and most vulnerable members of society are those who suffer the most. Indeed, as the concluding verse states, law and order are totally absent from the life of the nation. By ending on this note of godless, leaderless anarchy, the book of Judges sets the stage for the emergence of monarchy and even messiahship in the books of Samuel (see 2 Sam. 7:16).

night at Gibeah or at Ramah." ¹⁴ So they passed on and went their way; and the sun went down on them near Gibeah, which belongs to Benjamin. ¹⁵ They turned aside there, to go in and spend the night at Gibeah. He went in and sat down in the open square of the city, but no one took them in to spend the night.

16 Then at evening there was an old man coming from his work in the field. The man was from the hill country of Ephraim, and he was residing in Gibeah. (The people of the place were Benjaminites.) ¹⁷ When the old man looked up and saw the wayfarer in the open square of the city, he said, "Where are you going and where do you come from?" ¹⁸ He answered him, "We are passing from Bethlehem in Judah to the remote parts of the hill country of Ephraim, from which I come. I went to Bethlehem in Judah; and I am going to my home.ᵃ Nobody has offered to take me in. ¹⁹ We your servants have straw and fodder for our donkeys, with bread and wine for me and the woman and the young man along with us. We need nothing more." ²⁰ The old man said, "Peace be to you. I will care for all your wants; only do not spend the night in the square." ²¹ So he brought him into his house, and fed the donkeys; they washed their feet, and ate and drank.

Gibeah's Crime

22 While they were enjoying themselves, the men of the city, a perverse lot, surrounded the house, and started pounding on the door. They said to the old man, the master of the house, "Bring out the man who came into your house, so that we may have intercourse with him." ²³ And the man, the master of the house, went out to them and said to them, "No, my brothers, do not act so wickedly. Since this man is my guest, do not do this vile thing. ²⁴ Here are my virgin daughter and his concubine; let me bring them out now. Ravish them and do whatever you want to them; but

against this man do not do such a vile thing." ²⁵ But the men would not listen to him. So the man seized his concubine, and put her out to them. They wantonly raped her, and abused her all through the night until the morning. And as the dawn began to break, they let her go. ²⁶ As morning appeared, the woman came and fell down at the door of the man's house where her master was, until it was light.

27 In the morning her master got up, opened the doors of the house, and when he went out to go on his way, there was his concubine lying at the door of the house, with her hands on the threshold. ²⁸ "Get up," he said to her, "we are going." But there was no answer. Then he put her on the donkey; and the man set out for his home. ²⁹ When he had entered his house, he took a knife, and grasping his concubine he cut her into twelve pieces, limb by limb, and sent her throughout all the territory of Israel. ³⁰ Then he commanded the men whom he sent, saying, "Thus shall you say to all the Israelites, 'Has such a thing ever happenedᵇ since the day that the Israelites came up from the land of Egypt until this day? Consider it, take counsel, and speak out.' "

The Other Tribes Attack Benjamin

20 Then all the Israelites came out, from Dan to Beer-sheba, including the land of Gilead, and the congregation assembled in one body before the Lord at Mizpah. ² The chiefs of all the people, of all the tribes of Israel, presented themselves in the assembly of the people of God, four hundred thousand foot-soldiers bearing arms. ³ (Now the Benjaminites heard that the people of Israel had gone up to Mizpah.) And the Israelites said, "Tell us, how did this criminal act come about?" ⁴ The Levite, the husband of the woman who was murdered, answered, "I came to Gibeah that belongs to Benjamin, I and

ᵃ Gk Compare 19.29. Heb *to the house of the Lord*   ᵇ Compare Gk: Heb ³⁰ *And all who saw it said, "Such a thing has not happened or been seen*

my concubine, to spend the night. ⁵ The lords of Gibeah rose up against me, and surrounded the house at night. They intended to kill me, and they raped my concubine until she died. ⁶ Then I took my concubine and cut her into pieces, and sent her throughout the whole extent of Israel's territory; for they have committed a vile outrage in Israel. ⁷ So now, you Israelites, all of you, give your advice and counsel here."

8 All the people got up as one, saying, "We will not any of us go to our tents, nor will any of us return to our houses. ⁹ But now this is what we will do to Gibeah: we will go up*a* against it by lot. ¹⁰ We will take ten men of a hundred throughout all the tribes of Israel, and a hundred of a thousand, and a thousand of ten thousand, to bring provisions for the troops, who are going to repay*b* Gibeah of Benjamin for all the disgrace that they have done in Israel." ¹¹ So all the men of Israel gathered against the city, united as one.

12 The tribes of Israel sent men through all the tribe of Benjamin, saying, "What crime is this that has been committed among you? ¹³ Now then, hand over those scoundrels in Gibeah, so that we may put them to death, and purge the evil from Israel." But the Benjaminites would not listen to their kinsfolk, the Israelites. ¹⁴ The Benjaminites came together out of the towns to Gibeah, to go out to battle against the Israelites. ¹⁵ On that day the Benjaminites mustered twenty-six thousand armed men from their towns, besides the inhabitants of Gibeah. ¹⁶ Of all this force, there were seven hundred picked men who were left-handed; every one could sling a stone at a hair, and not miss. ¹⁷ And the Israelites, apart from Benjamin, mustered four hundred thousand armed men, all of them warriors.

18 The Israelites proceeded to go up to Bethel, where they inquired of God, "Which of us shall go up first to battle against the Benjaminites?" And the LORD answered, "Judah shall go up first."

19 Then the Israelites got up in the morning, and encamped against Gibeah. ²⁰ The Israelites went out to battle against Benjamin; and the Israelites drew up the battle line against them at Gibeah. ²¹ The Benjaminites came out of Gibeah, and struck down on that day twenty-two thousand of the Israelites. ²³ᶜ The Israelites went up and wept before the LORD until the evening; and they inquired of the LORD, "Shall we again draw near to battle against our kinsfolk the Benjaminites?" And the LORD said, "Go up against them." ²² The Israelites took courage, and again formed the battle line in the same place where they had formed it on the first day.

24 So the Israelites advanced against the Benjaminites the second day. ²⁵ Benjamin moved out against them from Gibeah the second day, and struck down eighteen thousand of the Israelites, all of them armed men. ²⁶ Then all the Israelites, the whole army, went back to Bethel and wept, sitting there before the LORD; they fasted that day until evening. Then they offered burnt offerings and sacrifices of well-being before the LORD. ²⁷ And the Israelites inquired of the LORD (for the ark of the covenant of God was there in those days, ²⁸ and Phinehas son of Eleazar, son of Aaron, ministered before it in those days), saying, "Shall we go out once more to battle against our kinsfolk the Benjaminites, or shall we desist?" The LORD answered, "Go up, for tomorrow I will give them into your hand."

29 So Israel stationed men in ambush around Gibeah. ³⁰ Then the Israelites went up against the Benjaminites on the third day, and set themselves in array against Gibeah, as before. ³¹ When the Benjaminites went out against the army, they were drawn away from the city. As before they began to inflict casualties on the troops, along the main roads, one of which goes up to Bethel and the other to

a Gk: Heb lacks we will go up   b Compare Gk: Meaning of Heb uncertain
c Verses 22 and 23 are transposed

Gibeah, as well as in the open country, killing about thirty men of Israel. **32** The Benjaminites thought, "They are being routed before us, as previously." But the Israelites said, "Let us retreat and draw them away from the city toward the roads." **33** The main body of the Israelites drew back its battle line to Baal-tamar, while those Israelites who were in ambush rushed out of their place west*a* of Geba. **34** There came against Gibeah ten thousand picked men out of all Israel, and the battle was fierce. But the Benjaminites did not realize that disaster was close upon them.

35 The LORD defeated Benjamin before Israel; and the Israelites destroyed twenty-five thousand one hundred men of Benjamin that day, all of them armed.

36 Then the Benjaminites saw that they were defeated.*b*

The Israelites gave ground to Benjamin, because they trusted to the troops in ambush that they had stationed against Gibeah. **37** The troops in ambush rushed quickly upon Gibeah. Then they put the whole city to the sword. **38** Now the agreement between the main body of Israel and the men in ambush was that when they sent up a cloud of smoke out of the city **39** the main body of Israel should turn in battle. But Benjamin had begun to inflict casualties on the Israelites, killing about thirty of them; so they thought, "Surely they are defeated before us, as in the first battle." **40** But when the cloud, a column of smoke, began to rise out of the city, the Benjaminites looked behind them—and there was the whole city going up in smoke toward the sky! **41** Then the main body of Israel turned, and the Benjaminites were dismayed, for they saw that disaster was close upon them. **42** Therefore they turned away from the Israelites in the direction of the wilderness; but the battle overtook them, and those who came out of the city*c* were slaughtering them in between.*d* **43** Cutting down*e* the Benjaminites, they

pursued them from Nohah*f* and trod them down as far as a place east of Gibeah. **44** Eighteen thousand Benjaminites fell, all of them courageous fighters. **45** When they turned and fled toward the wilderness to the rock of Rimmon, five thousand of them were cut down on the main roads, and they were pursued as far as Gidom, and two thousand of them were slain. **46** So all who fell that day of Benjamin were twenty-five thousand arms-bearing men, all of them courageous fighters. **47** But six hundred turned and fled toward the wilderness to the rock of Rimmon, and remained at the rock of Rimmon for four months. **48** Meanwhile, the Israelites turned back against the Benjaminites, and put them to the sword—the city, the people, the animals, and all that remained. Also the remaining towns they set on fire.

The Benjaminites Saved from Extinction

21 Now the Israelites had sworn at Mizpah, "No one of us shall give his daughter in marriage to Benjamin." **2** And the people came to Bethel, and sat there until evening before God, and they lifted up their voices and wept bitterly. **3** They said, "O LORD, the God of Israel, why has it come to pass that today there should be one tribe lacking in Israel?" **4** On the next day, the people got up early, and built an altar there, and offered burnt offerings and sacrifices of well-being. **5** Then the Israelites said, "Which of all the tribes of Israel did not come up in the assembly to the LORD?" For a solemn oath had been taken concerning whoever did not come up to the LORD to Mizpah, saying, "That one shall be put to death." **6** But the Israelites had compassion for Benjamin their kin, and said, "One tribe is cut off from Israel this day. **7** What shall we do for wives for those who are left, since we have sworn

a Gk Vg: Heb *in the plain*   *b* This sentence is continued by verse 45.
c Compare Vg and some Gk Mss: Heb *cities*   *d* Compare Syr: Meaning of Heb uncertain   *e* Gk: Heb *Surrounding*   *f* Gk: Heb *pursued them at their resting place*

by the LORD that we will not give them any of our daughters as wives?"

8 Then they said, "Is there anyone from the tribes of Israel who did not come up to the LORD to Mizpah?" It turned out that no one from Jabesh-gilead had come to the camp, to the assembly. 9 For when the roll was called among the people, not one of the inhabitants of Jabesh-gilead was there. 10 So the congregation sent twelve thousand soldiers there and commanded them, "Go, put the inhabitants of Jabesh-gilead to the sword, including the women and the little ones. 11 This is what you shall do; every male and every woman that has lain with a male you shall devote to destruction." 12 And they found among the inhabitants of Jabesh-gilead four hundred young virgins who had never slept with a man and brought them to the camp at Shiloh, which is in the land of Canaan.

13 Then the whole congregation sent word to the Benjaminites who were at the rock of Rimmon, and proclaimed peace to them. 14 Benjamin returned at that time; and they gave them the women whom they had saved alive of the women of Jabesh-gilead; but they did not suffice for them.

15 The people had compassion on Benjamin because the LORD had made a breach in the tribes of Israel. 16 So the elders of the congregation said, "What shall we do for wives for those who are left, since there are no women left in Benjamin?" 17 And they said, "There must be heirs for the survivors of Benjamin, in order that a tribe may not be blotted out from Israel. 18 Yet we cannot give any of our daughters to them as wives." For the Israelites had sworn, "Cursed be anyone who gives a wife to Benjamin." 19 So they said, "Look, the yearly festival of the LORD is taking place at Shiloh, which is north of Bethel, on the east of the highway that goes up from Bethel to Shechem, and south of Lebonah." 20 And they instructed the Benjaminites, saying, "Go and lie in wait in the vineyards, 21 and watch; when the young women of Shiloh come out to dance in the dances, then come out of the vineyards and each of you carry off a wife for himself from the young women of Shiloh, and go to the land of Benjamin. 22 Then if their fathers or their brothers come to complain to us, we will say to them, 'Be generous and allow us to have them; because we did not capture in battle a wife for each man. But neither did you incur guilt by giving your daughters to them.'" 23 The Benjaminites did so; they took wives for each of them from the dancers whom they abducted. Then they went and returned to their territory, and rebuilt the towns, and lived in them. 24 So the Israelites departed from there at that time by tribes and families, and they went out from there to their own territories.

25 In those days there was no king in Israel; all the people did what was right in their own eyes.

The Book of
RUTH

The book of Ruth is a tightly knit gem of a story. Its dialogue is pithy and dramatic, wordplays abound, and the repetition of key words and phrases tie the story together. Themes of emptiness and fullness, food, and fertility are highlighted. The story alludes to ancient Israelite customs: gleaning (Lev. 19:9–10), levirate marriage (Deut. 25:5–10; Gen. 38), and the rights of the next of kin in land redemption (Lev. 25:25).

This is a story of women making their way in a man's world. It represents a radical tradition in the Bible, with two women making their primary commitments to each other rather than to male partners. The book's focus is on three primary characters: Naomi, Ruth, and Boaz. But these individuals are not alone, as the people of the community also play key roles. The story suggests that these three persons would not succeed without the strong support of others.

The book deals with ethnic and class concerns. Ruth is of Moabite ancestry, but the Moabites, especially Moabite women, are typically presented in the Bible as Israel's enemy (see Deut. 23:3–6; Num. 25:1–2). It causes us to reconsider family values, to reassess who is "family" and who are our neighbors. Ruth and Naomi, as childless widows in foreign lands, are the most financially destitute, the poorest of the poor. Yet the story is presented from their perspective, not from that of the wealthy Boaz. Moreover, the world in which they exist is harsh, with famine, death, and barrenness all around.

Ultimately, the story presents a vision of an ideal society. The characters show toward each other the same type of faithfulness and loyalty that God alone usually expresses. The marginalized are included, the elderly are cared for, and the children are valued. Peoples who are different are gladly welcomed into the community; there are no laws against illegal aliens. They enter a society with provisions for the poor. Yet neither are there welfare checks handed out, for people must be willing to take initiative, make sacrifices, and work hard for their own survival.

It is difficult to determine with much certainty when and where the book was composed. Though its concern with King David may suggest that it was composed during the monarchic period, its multiethnic concerns suggest a composition in the postexilic period. Most certainly, however, when the story was used in postexilic times, it would have influenced people's attitudes toward the foreigners with whom they were living. Whereas the exiles may have felt as bereft and bitter as Naomi, they also would have been encouraged by the example of Ruth to work with peoples from other cultures to build new lives for themselves in a strange land.

—Linda Day

Elimelech's Family Goes to Moab

1 In the days when the judges ruled, there was a famine in the land, and a certain man of Bethlehem in Judah went to live in the country of Moab, he and his wife and two sons. ² The name of the man was Elimelech and the name of his wife Naomi, and the names of his two sons were Mahlon and Chilion; they were Ephrathites from Bethlehem in Judah. They went into the country of Moab and remained there. ³ But Elimelech, the husband of Naomi, died, and she was left with her two sons. ⁴ These took Moabite wives; the name of the one was Orpah and the name of the other Ruth. When they had lived there about ten years, ⁵ both Mahlon and Chilion also died, so that the woman was left without her two sons and her husband.

Naomi and Her Moabite Daughters-in-Law

6 Then she started to return with her daughters-in-law from the country of Moab, for she had heard in the country of Moab that the LORD had considered his people and given them food. ⁷ So she set out from the place where she had been living, she and her two daughters-in-law, and they went on their way to go back to the land of Judah. ⁸ But Naomi said to her two daughters-in-law, "Go back each of you to your mother's house. May the LORD deal kindly with you, as you have dealt with the dead and with me. ⁹ The LORD grant that you may find security, each of you in the house of your husband." Then she kissed them, and they wept aloud. ¹⁰ They said to her, "No, we will return with you to your people." ¹¹ But Naomi said, "Turn back, my daughters, why will you go with me? Do I still have sons in my womb that they may become your husbands? ¹² Turn back, my daughters, go your way, for I am too old to have a husband. Even if I thought there was hope for me, even if I should have a husband tonight and bear sons, ¹³ would you then wait until they were grown? Would you then refrain from marrying? No, my daughters, it has been far more bitter for me than for you, because the hand of the LORD has turned against me." ¹⁴ Then they wept aloud again. Orpah kissed her mother-in-law, but Ruth clung to her.

15 So she said, "See, your sister-in-law has gone back to her people and to her gods; return after your sister-in-law." ¹⁶ But Ruth said,

"Do not press me to leave you
　or to turn back from following
　　you!
Where you go, I will go;
　where you lodge, I will lodge;
your people shall be my people,
　and your God my God.
¹⁷ Where you die, I will die—
　there will I be buried.
May the LORD do thus and so to me,
　and more as well,
if even death parts me from you!"

1:1–5 Life in Moab

1:1—The people of Moab prove to be generous to the starving foreigners, sharing their food and their women. This Israelite family survives because of the Moabites' kindness. How often we must learn to swallow our pride and accept help from persons we would not expect to care about us.

1:6–22 Ruth Tags Along

1:9—Naomi suggests that, in a culture focused on men, the only secure future for a young widow would be remarriage. Orpah's and Ruth's career choices are limited.

1:14 *Clung*—This language is reminiscent of a bond between a woman and a man (cf. Gen. 2:24).

1:15–18—Ruth is pledging loyalty primarily to Naomi, rather than to the Israelite God. It is never stated in the story that Ruth herself ever actually converts to the worship of YHWH. Therefore, Ruth serves as a "righteous Gentile" who acts on behalf of the Jews. As people often do things for many reasons simultaneously, Ruth may be choosing to leave with her mother-in-law out of a sense for personal adventure and a desire for a new start in life, in addition to her affection for Naomi.

1:13, 20–21—Naomi laments, citing God as the source of her troubles.

18 When Naomi saw that she was determined to go with her, she said no more to her.

19 So the two of them went on until they came to Bethlehem. When they came to Bethlehem, the whole town was stirred because of them; and the women said, "Is this Naomi?" 20 She said to them,

> "Call me no longer Naomi,*a*
>   call me Mara,*b*
>   for the Almighty*c* has dealt bitterly
>   with me.
21 I went away full,
>   but the LORD has brought me back
>   empty;
> why call me Naomi
>   when the LORD has dealt harshly
>   with*d* me,
>   and the Almighty*c* has brought
>   calamity upon me?"

22 So Naomi returned together with Ruth the Moabite, her daughter-in-law, who came back with her from the country of Moab. They came to Bethlehem at the beginning of the barley harvest.

Ruth Meets Boaz

2 Now Naomi had a kinsman on her husband's side, a prominent rich man, of the family of Elimelech, whose name was Boaz. 2 And Ruth the Moabite said to Naomi, "Let me go to the field and glean among the ears of grain, behind someone in whose sight I may find favor." She said to her, "Go, my daughter." 3 So she went. She came and gleaned in the field behind the reapers. As it happened, she came to the part of the field belonging to Boaz, who was of the family of Elimelech. 4 Just then

Boaz came from Bethlehem. He said to the reapers, "The LORD be with you." They answered, "The LORD bless you." 5 Then Boaz said to his servant who was in charge of the reapers, "To whom does this young woman belong?" 6 The servant who was in charge of the reapers answered, "She is the Moabite who came back with Naomi from the country of Moab. 7 She said, 'Please, let me glean and gather among the sheaves behind the reapers.' So she came, and she has been on her feet from early this morning until now, without resting even for a moment."*e*

8 Then Boaz said to Ruth, "Now listen, my daughter, do not go to glean in another field or leave this one, but keep close to my young women. 9 Keep your eyes on the field that is being reaped, and follow behind them. I have ordered the young men not to bother you. If you get thirsty, go to the vessels and drink from what the young men have drawn." 10 Then she fell prostrate, with her face to the ground, and said to him, "Why have I found favor in your sight, that you should take notice of me, when I am a foreigner?" 11 But Boaz answered her, "All that you have done for your mother-in-law since the death of your husband has been fully told me, and how you left your father and mother and your native land and came to a people that you did not know before. 12 May the LORD reward you for your deeds, and may you have a full reward from the LORD, the God of Israel, under whose wings you have

---

a That is *Pleasant*   *b* That is *Bitter*   *c* Traditional rendering of Heb *Shaddai*   *d* Or *has testified against*   *e* Compare Gk Vg: Meaning of Heb uncertain

---

1:22—Back in Bethlehem, the two women's roles have reversed. Now Ruth is the foreign widow who must learn how to make her way in a new environment.

2:1–23 Ruth in Boaz's Field

2:5—Women in ancient Israelite society were not full individuals in their own right, but the property of a male relative (father, husband, or even son). Ruth, therefore, belongs to no one.

2:8—Both women and men must work together

to produce the harvest. Women's work is important and necessary for survival.

2:9—As an unattached foreign woman might be subject to undesired attention, Boaz is concerned to protect Ruth from sexual harassment.

2:11—Ruth's reputation precedes her. Like Abraham, Ruth has left her family and her country—but without any promise of blessing from God (cf. Gen. 12:1–3).

come for refuge!" [13] Then she said, "May I continue to find favor in your sight, my lord, for you have comforted me and spoken kindly to your servant, even though I am not one of your servants."

[14] At mealtime Boaz said to her, "Come here, and eat some of this bread, and dip your morsel in the sour wine." So she sat beside the reapers, and he heaped up for her some parched grain. She ate until she was satisfied, and she had some left over. [15] When she got up to glean, Boaz instructed his young men, "Let her glean even among the standing sheaves, and do not reproach her. [16] You must also pull out some handfuls for her from the bundles, and leave them for her to glean, and do not rebuke her."

[17] So she gleaned in the field until evening. Then she beat out what she had gleaned, and it was about an ephah of barley. [18] She picked it up and came into the town, and her mother-in-law saw how much she had gleaned. Then she took out and gave her what was left over after she herself had been satisfied. [19] Her mother-in-law said to her, "Where did you glean today? And where have you worked? Blessed be the man who took notice of you." So she told her mother-in-law with whom she had worked, and said, "The name of the man with whom I worked today is Boaz." [20] Then Naomi said to her daughter-in-law, "Blessed be he by the LORD, whose kindness has not forsaken the living or the dead!" Naomi also said to her, "The man is a relative of ours, one of our nearest kin." [a] [21] Then Ruth the Moabite said, "He even said to me, 'Stay close by my servants,

until they have finished all my harvest.'" [22] Naomi said to Ruth, her daughter-in-law, "It is better, my daughter, that you go out with his young women, otherwise you might be bothered in another field." [23] So she stayed close to the young women of Boaz, gleaning until the end of the barley and wheat harvests; and she lived with her mother-in-law.

Ruth and Boaz at the Threshing Floor

3 Naomi her mother-in-law said to her, "My daughter, I need to seek some security for you, so that it may be well with you. [2] Now here is our kinsman Boaz, with whose young women you have been working. See, he is winnowing barley tonight at the threshing floor. [3] Now wash and anoint yourself, and put on your best clothes and go down to the threshing floor; but do not make yourself known to the man until he has finished eating and drinking. [4] When he lies down, observe the place where he lies; then, go and uncover his feet and lie down; and he will tell you what to do." [5] She said to her, "All that you tell me I will do."

[6] So she went down to the threshing floor and did just as her mother-in-law had instructed her. [7] When Boaz had eaten and drunk, and he was in a contented mood, he went to lie down at the end of the heap of grain. Then she came stealthily and uncovered his feet, and lay down. [8] At midnight the man was startled, and turned over, and there, lying at his feet, was a woman! [9] He said, "Who are you?" And she answered, "I am Ruth,

[a] Or one with the right to redeem

2:14–16—Not merely putting a tithe in the collection plate, Boaz's generosity goes far beyond what the law requires him to do.

2:18—Ruth is the family's provider. The one whom Naomi did not want to come along now is the very one to give Naomi life. How often the very thing we do not wish to happen turns out, in hindsight, to have been a blessing in disguise.

3:1–5 Naomi's Plan

3:3–4—The term for *his feet* can be a euphe-

mism for genitals. Ruth's actions are to be sexually suggestive. Naomi's idea is radical and risky. How many mothers would propose that their daughters should dress up and go to a men's bar to find a husband?

3:6–18 Ruth's Encounter with Boaz

3:7–8—Boaz, under the influence of alcohol, does not remember what happened when he awakens.

3:9—Ruth's request to *spread your cloak* is

your servant; spread your cloak over your servant, for you are next-of-kin."[a] [10] He said, "May you be blessed by the LORD, my daughter; this last instance of your loyalty is better than the first; you have not gone after young men, whether poor or rich. [11] And now, my daughter, do not be afraid, I will do for you all that you ask, for all the assembly of my people know that you are a worthy woman. [12] But now, though it is true that I am a near kinsman, there is another kinsman more closely related than I. [13] Remain this night, and in the morning, if he will act as next-of-kin[a] for you, good; let him do it. If he is not willing to act as next-of-kin[a] for you, then, as the LORD lives, I will act as next-of-kin[a] for you. Lie down until the morning."

[14] So she lay at his feet until morning, but got up before one person could recognize another; for he said, "It must not be known that the woman came to the threshing floor." [15] Then he said, "Bring the cloak you are wearing and hold it out." So she held it, and he measured out six measures of barley, and put it on her back; then he went into the city. [16] She came to her mother-in-law, who said, "How did things go with you,[b] my daughter?" Then she told her all that the man had done for her, [17] saying, "He gave me these six measures of barley, for he said, 'Do not go back to your mother-in-law empty-handed.'" [18] She replied, "Wait, my daughter, until you learn how the matter turns out, for the man will not rest, but will settle the matter today."

The Marriage of Boaz and Ruth

4 No sooner had Boaz gone up to the gate and sat down there than the next-of-kin,[a] of whom Boaz had spoken, came passing by. So Boaz said, "Come over, friend; sit down here." And he went over and sat down. [2] Then Boaz took ten men of the elders of the city, and said, "Sit down here"; so they sat down. [3] He then said to the next-of-kin,[a] "Naomi, who has come back from the country of Moab, is selling the parcel of land that belonged to our kinsman Elimelech. [4] So I thought I would tell you of it, and say: Buy it in the presence of those sitting here, and in the presence of the elders of my people. If you will redeem it, redeem it; but if you will not, tell me, so that I may know; for there is no one prior to you to redeem it, and I come after you." So he said, "I will redeem it." [5] Then Boaz said, "The day you acquire the field from the hand of Naomi, you are also acquiring Ruth[c] the Moabite, the widow of the dead man, to maintain the dead man's name on his inheritance." [6] At this, the next-of-kin[a] said, "I cannot redeem it for myself without damaging my own inheritance. Take my right of redemption yourself, for I cannot redeem it."

[7] Now this was the custom in former times in Israel concerning redeeming and exchanging: to confirm a transaction, the one took off a sandal and gave it to the other; this was the manner of attesting in Israel. [8] So when the next-of-kin[a]

[a] Or one with the right to redeem   [b] Or "Who are you,   [c] OL Vg: Heb from the hand of Naomi and from Ruth

---

a marriage proposal. Not following Naomi's suggestion (v. 4), Ruth is the one to tell Boaz what to do. The term *next-of-kin* literally means "the one with the right to redeem." The frequent repetition of this term hints that physical and emotional redemption is an important theme in the story.

3:11—The designation *a worthy woman* is the same as that used to describe Boaz (*a prominent rich man*, 2:1). Boaz is praising Ruth quite highly, like saying that the Spanish-speaking hotel maid is just as important as the city mayor.

3:17—Just as before (2:21), Ruth does not tell Naomi exactly what happened. She acts like a daughter who, though loving her mother, is her own person, with her own ideas and strategies.

4:1–12 Boaz Makes Arrangements

4:3–6—During this entire transaction, Boaz is not entirely straightforward with the other man. The other man acts in good faith and also displays generosity, for he is willing to buy the field until he realizes that he cannot afford it because Ruth is part of the bargain.

said to Boaz, "Acquire it for yourself," he took off his sandal. 9 Then Boaz said to the elders and all the people, "Today you are witnesses that I have acquired from the hand of Naomi all that belonged to Elimelech and all that belonged to Chilion and Mahlon. 10 I have also acquired Ruth the Moabite, the wife of Mahlon, to be my wife, to maintain the dead man's name on his inheritance, in order that the name of the dead may not be cut off from his kindred and from the gate of his native place; today you are witnesses." 11 Then all the people who were at the gate, along with the elders, said, "We are witnesses. May the LORD make the woman who is coming into your house like Rachel and Leah, who together built up the house of Israel. May you produce children in Ephrathah and bestow a name in Bethlehem; 12 and, through the children that the LORD will give you by this young woman, may your house be like the house of Perez, whom Tamar bore to Judah."

The Genealogy of David

13 So Boaz took Ruth and she became his wife. When they came together, the LORD made her conceive, and she bore a son. 14 Then the women said to Naomi, "Blessed be the LORD, who has not left you this day without next-of-kin;a and may his name be renowned in Israel! 15 He shall be to you a restorer of life and a nourisher of your old age; for your daughter-in-law who loves you, who is more to you than seven sons, has borne him." 16 Then Naomi took the child and laid him in her bosom, and became his nurse. 17 The women of the neighborhood gave him a name, saying, "A son has been born to Naomi." They named him Obed; he became the father of Jesse, the father of David.

18 Now these are the descendants of Perez: Perez became the father of Hezron, 19 Hezron of Ram, Ram of Amminadab, 20 Amminadab of Nahshon, Nahshon of Salmon, 21 Salmon of Boaz, Boaz of Obed, 22 Obed of Jesse, and Jesse of David.

a Or one with the right to redeem

4:9–10—Boaz speaks only of the needs of men (himself, Mahlon, and the next of kin), not of the more pressing needs of the two women. In any male-oriented society, women often succeed only to the extent that they are perceived to benefit men.

4:11–12—*Rachel, Leah,* and *Tamar* are all gutsy women who take matters into their own hands to acquire children in unorthodox ways.

4:13–22 A Child Is Born

4:13—God performs only two actions in this story, providing food (1:6) and a baby. Both deeds allow life to continue.

4:14–15—The group of townswomen, here and at the beginning of the story (1:19), act as wise women, or crones, who see issues more clearly than do others. Their statement is very strong praise in a society that tends to more readily value its sons.

4:16—Naomi acts like the typical grandmother who has been forced to wait far too long, in her opinion, for her first grandchild.

4:22—Ruth becomes the great-grandmother of King David and therefore part of the royal lineage. How surprising that the foremother of the most important Israelite king is a foreigner from a despised nation.

Introduction to
1–2 SAMUEL

The oldest Hebrew manuscripts of the books of 1 and 2 Samuel assume they were one book. The oldest of these, from Qumran (4QSamª), included all of 1 and 2 Samuel on a single scroll. Greek translations (Septuagint) divided Samuel and Kings into four books called 1–4 Kingdoms, and Latin translations followed this practice, influencing Roman Catholic Bibles into the current century. Printed editions of the Hebrew Bible and Protestant translations began the practice of division into 1 and 2 Samuel in the sixteenth century. Since many biblical books end with the death of a key figure, it probably made sense to divide the books of Samuel after Saul's death, although the two versions of his death (1 Sam. 31; 2 Sam. 1) are separated by the division. The division into two books of Samuel also creates the oddity that 2 Samuel carries the name of a prophet who does not appear in the book.

Until the discovery of Samuel manuscripts among the Dead Sea Scrolls at Qumran, the Hebrew text used for translations was much shorter than the Greek Septuagint and other ancient versions. The Qumran materials have convinced most translators that the longer text may be more reliable, and most modern English translations, including the one used here, rely heavily on the readings of the Septuagint and ancient versions.

The books of Samuel open in the midst of a profound crisis in the story of Israel. This crisis, both sociopolitical and religious, threatens the very future of Israel. The book of Judges (Ruth was not originally placed prior to the books of Samuel) reflected a tribal society challenged by various enemies and responding without centrally organized governance or military authority. At the end of Judges (see chaps. 13–18) and at the beginning of 1 Samuel (chaps. 4–6) the Philistines present a sustained threat to the future existence of Israel that culminates with the capture of the ark and the occupation of most Israelite tribal territory. This external threat from the militarily superior Philistines provides the context in the story for Israel's demand that the prophet Samuel give them a king (1 Sam. 8:4–5; 9:16). At the same time, the story tells of an internal crisis in Israel's religious life. The sons of Eli, priest at the sanctuary of the ark in Shiloh, are corrupt (1 Sam. 2:11–17), and they seem to reflect a growing state of moral corruption in Israel, signaled at the end of Judges (21:25), where everyone did "what was right in their own eyes." The story of the books of Samuel reflects a remarkable transition in Israel's life. By the end of 2 Samuel, David is king of a growing kingdom free from external domination, and his dynasty is understood as a new expression of divine promise in the midst of Israel, initiated and held accountable by God's prophets. The ark of the covenant is now in David's city, Jerusalem, where his son will soon build the temple on Mount Zion. This dramatic transition is reflected in the present books of Samuel in some of the most dramatic stories in Scripture, filled with some of the most striking characters.

The books of Samuel have undoubtedly gone through a complex history to reach their present form. They include traditions from near the time of the narrated events (ca. 1020–960 BCE) that are both positive and negative in attitude to the institution of kingship and some early collections of stories focused on particular themes: the ark narrative (1 Sam. 4–6), a history of the rise of David (1 Sam. 16:1–2 Sam. 5:10), and a court history of David (2 Sam. 11–20; some would include 2 Sam. 9–10 and 1 Kgs. 1–2). Many scholars believe that many of these stories were edited into a narrative that stresses the role of God's prophet in anointing and holding kings accountable, and regards the king as God's anointed one, subject still to divine sovereignty. The emphases of this prophetic edition can be especially seen in the stories of Samuel's birth (1 Sam. 1–3), Samuel as judge (1 Sam. 7), prophetic initiative in choosing and anointing Saul and David (1 Sam. 8:1–10:16; 16:1–13), Saul's rejection by Samuel (1 Sam. 13 and 15), Nathan's judgment of David (2 Sam. 12), and the confrontation of David by Gad over his census (2 Sam. 24). In its final editorial stage 1 and 2 Samuel became part of the Deuteronomistic History stretching from Joshua through 2 Kings. Looking back from the experience of exile, this great historical work evaluates the experience of Israel from entering the land to leaving it in exile. The hand of the Deuteronomist is not heavy in the books of Samuel but may be seen in the oracle against the house of Eli (1 Sam. 2:27–36), Samuel's farewell speech (1 Sam. 12), and Nathan's oracle of dynastic promise to David (2 Sam. 7).

Whatever their complex literary history, most scholars are agreed that the present form of the books of Samuel fall into seven clearly defined segments:

1. *The story of Samuel* (1 Sam. 1–3; 7). The corruption of the house of Eli is exposed and defines the internal religious crisis of Israel. This, however, is overshadowed by the story of God's response to the urgent plea of a barren woman, Hannah. Her son, dedicated to the Lord's service, becomes the prophet Samuel. Hannah's song (1 Sam. 2:1–10) tells of God's power to bring dramatic reversals and foreshadows the eventual emergence of David as the unlikely eighth son who becomes God's anointed one. The prophet Samuel becomes God's instrument for accomplishing these things, and in chapter 7 leads Israel himself in the crucial interval after Philistine defeat and before kingship.

2. *The ark narrative* (1 Sam. 4–6). These chapters narrate the disastrous events of Israel's defeat by the Philistines, the capture of the ark of the covenant, the occupation of the land, and the death of Eli and his sons. This external crisis threatens Israel's very future. There are no human heroes in this segment, yet it is not solely a tale of defeat. A major theme in these chapters is the "hand of the LORD" that humiliates the Philistines and their god, Dagon, to the point that the ark is returned to Israelite territory. God will soon give Israel kings, but not because God alone could not deal with these crises. Earlier opinion related 2 Samuel 6 to this ark narrative. Although that story involves the ark, it is focused on David and his connecting of the ark with Jerusalem. Recent treatments do not include it in the ark narrative.

3. *The rise of kingship and the reign of Saul* (1 Sam. 8–15). These chapters undoubtedly have a complex literary history and seem sometimes positive to Saul as God's anointed king and at other times negative, regarding kingship as a rejection of God. Although in one sense these are stories of Saul's kingship and reign, they are dominated by the prophet Samuel. Samuel reluctantly agrees to the people's request for a king "like other nations," anoints Saul as a young man, holds Saul accountable to

God's commands, and eventually rejects Saul as God's anointed one. If Israel is to have kings, they must be anointed by God's prophet, receive God's spirit, demonstrate the power of that spirit, and reign in obedience to God's commands (especially as known through God's prophet). When Saul fails on the last count, he is rejected, but this is not a rejection of kingship. The narrative already knows that David will prove to be the man "after [God's] own heart" (1 Sam. 13:14). In many ways Saul's story is a tragic one, and the prophet Samuel seems harsh and judgmental. The story seems to know that David is destined to usher in God's new future for Israel; as a consequence, Saul's story becomes a story of failure in preparation for David. Especially in the stories of David and Saul (next section) Saul's flaws are exposed, but the last word on Saul is in David's tribute to him following his death (2 Sam. 1:17–27).

4. *The rise of David* (1 Sam. 16:1–2 Sam. 5:10). This material, thought by many to be an early collection now incorporated into the books of Samuel, introduces David directly into the story. It is made clear that God's providence is active in designating this unlikely eighth son of an unknown family as God's anointed through the prophet Samuel. The recurring refrain of these chapters and its final conclusion in 2 Samuel 5:10 is "The LORD is with him" (1 Sam. 16:18; 17:37; 18:12, 14, 28; 20:13). David is portrayed as a leader and a warrior who is also a man of piety and prayer (1 Sam. 17:45–47; 23:1–5). By contrast, the flaws and folly of Saul become more evident, leading to his eventual taking of his own life after the defeat at Mount Gilboa (1 Sam. 31; 2 Sam. 1:1–10). A procession of witnesses acknowledge David's claim to the throne throughout these chapters. The telling of the stories seem designed as an apologetic effort to show David as worthy of the throne and untainted by some of the more troubling elements of his story, for example, his life as a fugitive from Saul; his service with the Philistines; the deaths of Saul, Abner, and Ishbaal. After Saul's death David becomes king, first over Judah, then some years later over Israel. At the end of this history of David's rise, he captures Jerusalem and makes it his capital. David and Jerusalem begin the new future toward which God has been moving Israel.

5. *The reign of David* (2 Sam. 5:11–10:19). This section completes the shift from tribal to royal realities in Israel. Family genealogy (2 Sam. 5:13–16) is displaced by court officers (2 Sam. 8:15–18). Relief from Philistine domination (2 Sam. 5:17–25) moves to wars of national expansion (2 Sam. 8:1–14; 10:1–19). The ark, symbol of God's covenant presence, is found and brought to Jerusalem (2 Sam. 6:1–20), but it is superseded by God's new covenant of dynastic promise to David through the prophet Nathan (2 Sam. 7:1–29). The ideology and power of a royal state are fixed firmly in place. Some glimpses of the earlier David are still in view: his enthusiastic dancing before the ark (2 Sam. 6) and his kindness to Mephibosheth, Jonathan's son, out of loyalty to his friendship with Jonathan (2 Sam. 9).

6. *The court history of David* (2 Sam. 11–20). This section has long been recognized as a distinctive literary source now incorporated into the larger story of David. Some argue that its theme is the succession to David's throne, and therefore its proper conclusion is 1 Kings 1–2, with David's deathbed designation of Solomon. This has also led some to argue that its beginning is with 2 Samuel 9 and the perceived co-opting of Mephibosheth as a potential Saulide claimant to the throne. Recent scholarship has not found this argument persuasive and sees instead a tragic family history that portrays the dangers of self-justifying royal power and its consequences. David's story has been described as moving from blessing to curse, from gift to grasp,

from the man after God's own heart to chastened sinner. The key episode is the story of David's own exercise of self-serving authority in his taking of Bathsheba and the murder of her husband Uriah to cover up his adultery (2 Sam. 11). This is followed by the announcement of God's judgment on David through the prophet Nathan and the consequences of violence that will unfold in David's own family as his sons emulate the father's use of power for their own ends (2 Sam. 12). A tragic narrative of rape, murder, exile, treachery, rebellion, civil war, and personal loss unfolds through the remaining chapters of this section (2 Sam. 13–20). David's children Tamar, Amnon, and Absalom all come to tragic ends, and David himself comes close to losing his life and throne. David's retreat from Jerusalem, however, almost has the character of a penitential journey. In the events of this retreat David returns to acknowledgment of his dependence on God's mercy and his recognition of God's sovereignty beyond that of the king (see especially 2 Sam. 15:25–26; 16:12). At the end of these chapters David is still king, but one chastened by suffering and realization of his own limits.

7. *Final Davidic traditions* (2 Sam. 21–24). Until recently, these chapters were treated as a collection of miscellaneous appendices to the books of Samuel that interrupted the flow into 1 Kings 1–2. Many now see a more purposeful conclusion to the books of Samuel in these chapters. They have a symmetrical structure with two great poetic songs at the heart of the section: a psalm of thanksgiving by David for God's deliverance (2 Sam. 22; parallels Ps. 18), and a song in celebration of God's promise to David (2 Sam. 23:1–7). These songs are flanked by notices and stories of David's warriors (2 Sam. 21:15–22; 23:8–39). The section opens with a story of the expiation of Saul's guilt (2 Sam. 21) and closes with a story of the expiation of David's guilt in an act of worship on the eventual site of the temple (2 Sam. 24). Without these chapters David's story would flow from the reestablishment of royal power (2 Sam. 20) to the deathbed vendettas and eventual bloodbath of Solomonic accession (1 Kgs. 1–2). It is persuasive to see these so-called appendices as an intentional conclusion to the books of Samuel. The sovereignty of God, beyond that of the king, is evident in the stories of David's effort to remove guilt from the land and himself (2 Sam. 21; 24), and the poetic songs stress God as the source of all of David's own power or promise. The notices of heroes and their deeds moderate any notion that David alone brought Israel into its new future as a kingdom. The books of Samuel opened with the petition in the prayer of Hannah, which the Lord answered (1 Sam. 1:19), and they end with the prayerful petition of David, which the Lord answered (2 Sam. 24:25).

The books of Samuel have often been treated as historical books with little attention to their theological importance. But these books combine a historically realistic narrative style with theological imagination. Their purpose is not dispassionate historical reporting but witness to the working of divine providence through the events and personalities of a transformative period in Israel's story.

The books of Samuel are filled with the stories of unique and powerful characters. The most obvious of these are Samuel, Saul, and David, but they are surrounded by a dramatic cast of role players who make distinctive contributions to Israel's future: Hannah, Eli, Jonathan, Michal, Joab, Abigail, Abner, Nathan, Mephibosheth, Bathsheba, Absalom, Tamar. Leadership and the distinctive contribution of personality to the course of crucial events is one of the clear themes of the books of Samuel.

Yet the books of Samuel, occupied with issues of power and politics, are clear that power does not arise from the force of personality alone. True power lies in the

realm of God's providence. Behind and through human events and political arenas, God is at working ensuring Israel's future. Hannah's song at the beginning (1 Sam. 2:1–10) and David's song at the end (2 Sam. 22:2–51) make clear that God overturns the usual arrangements of power in the world. A barren woman can, in God's providence, give birth to the prophet who makes kings, and an eighth son, a shepherd boy from an obscure family, can become the man after God's own heart. The books of Samuel present the working of the divine will not as overt interventions into human history, but as a constant working through and in spite of human agency to bring a new and transformed future to Israel. God's providence can initiate, empower, judge and redeem, but God chooses to do so in partnership with human personalities and their potential to contribute to God's purposes. In the arenas of human power, true power still lies with God. "David became greater and greater, for the LORD, the God of hosts, was with him" (2 Sam. 5:10). "The thing that David had done was evil in the eyes of the LORD" (2 Sam. 11:27b, author's translation).

—Bruce C. Birch

The Book of
1 SAMUEL

Samuel's Birth and Dedication

1 There was a certain man of Ramathaim, a Zuphite[a] from the hill country of Ephraim, whose name was Elkanah son of Jeroham son of Elihu son of Tohu son of Zuph, an Ephraimite. [2] He had two wives; the name of the one was Hannah, and the name of the other Peninnah. Peninnah had children, but Hannah had no children.

3 Now this man used to go up year by year from his town to worship and to sacrifice to the LORD of hosts at Shiloh, where the two sons of Eli, Hophni and Phinehas, were priests of the LORD. [4] On the day when Elkanah sacrificed, he would give portions to his wife Peninnah and to all her sons and daughters; [5] but to Hannah he gave a double portion,[b] because he loved her, though the LORD had closed her womb. [6] Her rival used to provoke her severely, to irritate her, because the LORD had closed her womb. [7] So it went on year by year; as often as she went up to the house of the LORD, she used to provoke her. Therefore Hannah wept and would not eat. [8] Her husband Elkanah said to her, "Hannah, why do you weep? Why do you not eat? Why is your heart sad? Am I not more to you than ten sons?"

9 After they had eaten and drunk at Shiloh, Hannah rose and presented herself before the LORD.[c] Now Eli the priest was sitting on the seat beside the doorpost of the temple of the LORD. [10] She was deeply distressed and prayed to the LORD, and wept bitterly. [11] She made this vow: "O LORD of hosts, if only you will look on the misery of your servant, and remember me, and not forget your servant, but will give to your servant a male child, then I will set him before you as a nazirite[d] until the day of his death. He shall drink neither wine nor intoxicants,[e] and no razor shall touch his head."

a Compare Gk and 1 Chr 6.35-36: Heb *Ramathaim-zophim*
b Syr: Meaning of Heb uncertain   c Gk: Heb lacks *and presented herself before the LORD*   d That is *one separated* or *one consecrated*   e Cn Compare Gk Q Ms 1.22: MT *then I will give him to the LORD all the days of his life*

1:1–7:17 The Story of Samuel and the Ark Narrative

This section introduces a dual crisis in Israel toward the end of the eleventh century BCE. One crisis is internal; the priestly family of Eli at the sanctuary in Shiloh has become corrupt. Israel has no clear leadership and people decide for themselves what is right (see Judg. 21:25). The other crisis is external; the Philistines, an aggressive, militaristic enemy, are threatening to expand their control from the coastal plain to the Israelite tribal lands in the hill country. In this context, 1 Samuel begins the story of the establishment of kingship in Israel and introduces Samuel as God's prophet in this crucial time of transition.

1:1–28 Hannah

1:2–8—To begin Israel's transition to new life God chooses Hannah, a barren woman, distraught over her lot and taunted by a rival. God's grace has come through such unlikely channels before (Sarah, Gen. 18; Samson's mother, Judg.

13), and God will choose unlikely candidates in the boys Saul (1 Sam. 9) and David (chap. 16). God often chooses those unacceptable and even rejected by society's standards to become those who mediate God's grace (eventually including Jesus as well).

1:11, 14–17—Hannah's passionate persistence in presenting her need to God is mistaken for drunkenness. The persistent advocates of just needs and causes are often criticized for inappropriate behavior, but we learn from Hannah that God responds to persistence in expressing our needs to God (see Jesus' praise of the persistent widow, Luke 18:1–8). Ironically, when Hannah asks Eli not to consider her **worthless** (1 Sam. 1:16), she uses the same word later used to describe the corrupt sons of Eli (2:12). God sees beyond the surface to the true worth of persons, and the power of God to reverse the status given to persons by the world is the subject of her song in 2:1–10.

12 As she continued praying before the LORD, Eli observed her mouth. 13 Hannah was praying silently; only her lips moved, but her voice was not heard; therefore Eli thought she was drunk. 14 So Eli said to her, "How long will you make a drunken spectacle of yourself? Put away your wine." 15 But Hannah answered, "No, my lord, I am a woman deeply troubled; I have drunk neither wine nor strong drink, but I have been pouring out my soul before the LORD. 16 Do not regard your servant as a worthless woman, for I have been speaking out of my great anxiety and vexation all this time." 17 Then Eli answered, "Go in peace; the God of Israel grant the petition you have made to him." 18 And she said, "Let your servant find favor in your sight." Then the woman went to her quarters,*a* ate and drank with her husband,*b* and her countenance was sad no longer.*c*

19 They rose early in the morning and worshiped before the LORD; then they went back to their house at Ramah. Elkanah knew his wife Hannah, and the LORD remembered her. 20 In due time Hannah conceived and bore a son. She named him Samuel, for she said, "I have asked him of the LORD."

21 The man Elkanah and all his household went up to offer to the LORD the yearly sacrifice, and to pay his vow. 22 But Hannah did not go up, for she said to her husband, "As soon as the child is weaned, I will bring him, that he may appear in the presence of the LORD, and remain there forever; I will offer him as a nazirite*d* for all time."*e* 23 Her husband Elkanah said to her, "Do what seems best to you, wait until you have weaned

him; only—may the LORD establish his word."*f* So the woman remained and nursed her son, until she weaned him. 24 When she had weaned him, she took him up with her, along with a three-year-old bull,*g* an ephah of flour, and a skin of wine. She brought him to the house of the LORD at Shiloh; and the child was young. 25 Then they slaughtered the bull, and they brought the child to Eli. 26 And she said, "Oh, my lord! As you live, my lord, I am the woman who was standing here in your presence, praying to the LORD. 27 For this child I prayed; and the LORD has granted me the petition that I made to him. 28 Therefore I have lent him to the LORD; as long as he lives, he is given to the LORD."

She left him there for*h* the LORD.

Hannah's Prayer

2 Hannah prayed and said,
　"My heart exults in the LORD;
　　my strength is exalted in my God.*i*
　My mouth derides my enemies,
　　because I rejoice in my*j* victory.

2 　"There is no Holy One like the
　　　LORD,
　　no one besides you;
　　there is no Rock like our God.
3 　Talk no more so very proudly,
　　let not arrogance come from your
　　　mouth;
　for the LORD is a God of knowledge,
　　and by him actions are weighed.

a Gk: Heb *went her way*   *b* Gk: Heb lacks *and drank with her husband*
c Gk: Meaning of Heb uncertain   *d* That is *one separated* or *one consecrated*
e Cn Compare Q Ms: MT lacks *I will offer him as a nazirite for all time*
f MT: Q Ms Gk Compare Syr *that which goes out of your mouth*   *g* Q Ms
Gk Syr: MT *three bulls*   *h* Gk (Compare Q Ms) and Gk at 2.11: MT *And
he* (that is, Elkanah) *worshiped there before*   *i* Gk: Heb *the LORD*   *j* Q Ms:
MT *your*

1:20—Hannah relates the name of her child, *Samuel*, to the Hebrew verb *sha'al*, "to ask," which appears seven times in the chapter. This verb is closer to the name of Saul, suggesting that Samuel's future is intertwined with that of Saul.

1:28—Hannah teaches us that the proper response to the gift of God is to give it away. She gives Samuel back to the service of the Lord, and through him gives to all Israel of the grace she has received.

2:1–10 Song of Hannah
Hannah's exultant prayer is a hymn of praise and thanksgiving that has long been recognized as similar in language and theme to Mary's Magnificat in Luke 1:46–55. Both celebrate a birth brought by God's grace, through which God's power can transform the lot of the powerless.

⁴ The bows of the mighty are broken,
  but the feeble gird on strength.
⁵ Those who were full have hired
    themselves out for bread,
  but those who were hungry are fat
    with spoil.
  The barren has borne seven,
    but she who has many children is
      forlorn.
⁶ The LORD kills and brings to life;
  he brings down to Sheol and raises
    up.
⁷ The LORD makes poor and makes
    rich;
  he brings low, he also exalts.
⁸ He raises up the poor from the dust;
  he lifts the needy from the ash
    heap,
  to make them sit with princes
    and inherit a seat of honor.ᵃ
  For the pillars of the earth are the
    LORD's,
    and on them he has set the world.

⁹ "He will guard the feet of his faithful
    ones,
  but the wicked shall be cut off in
    darkness;
  for not by might does one prevail.
¹⁰ The LORD! His adversaries shall be
    shattered;
  the Most Highᵇ will thunder in
    heaven.
  The LORD will judge the ends of the
    earth;
  he will give strength to his king,
    and exalt the power of his
      anointed."

Eli's Wicked Sons

11 Then Elkanah went home to Ramah, while the boy remained to minister to the LORD, in the presence of the priest Eli.

12 Now the sons of Eli were scoundrels; they had no regard for the LORD ¹³ or for the duties of the priests to the people. When anyone offered sacrifice, the priest's servant would come, while the meat was boiling, with a three-pronged fork in his hand, ¹⁴ and he would thrust it into the pan, or kettle, or caldron, or pot; all that the fork brought up the priest would take for himself.ᶜ This is what they did at Shiloh to all the Israelites who came there. ¹⁵ Moreover, before the fat was burned, the priest's servant would come and say to the one who was sacrificing, "Give meat for the priest to roast; for he will not accept boiled meat from you, but only raw." ¹⁶ And if the man said to him, "Let them burn the fat first, and then take whatever you wish," he would say, "No, you must give it now; if not, I will take it by force." ¹⁷ Thus the sin of the young men was very great in the sight of the LORD; for they treated the offerings of the LORD with contempt.

The Child Samuel at Shiloh

18 Samuel was ministering before the LORD, a boy wearing a linen ephod. ¹⁹ His mother used to make for him a little robe and take it to him each year,

ᵃ Gk (Compare Q Ms) adds *He grants the vow of the one who vows, and blesses the years of the just* ᵇ Cn Heb *against him he* ᶜ Gk Syr Vg: Heb *with it*

2:9 *For not by might does one prevail*—This key verse speaks to the reality of God as the true source of transforming power. The stories of Samuel are often concerned with struggles of human power, and Hannah's song reminds us as readers and as persons of faith that God still controls the course of history and through Hannah or Mary can accomplish what entire armies often cannot.

2:10—Hannah's song points to the coming of God's king in Israel, God's *anointed*. But God's promise to the king comes only after singing of God's power that brings low the rich and powerful in behalf of lifting up the weak, the poor, and

the needy. Leadership in God's kingdom must serve these reversals brought by God's grace, which is the genuine source of new life. Such leadership might emulate the resort of Hannah to prayer and the recognition of God's gifts alongside the marshaling of human resources and the attempt to grasp by our own power.

2:11–21 Sons of Eli

The story shifts to the corrupt practices of Eli's sons in the sanctuary at Shiloh and the growing anger of the Lord, contrasted to the growing favor of the Lord toward the boy Samuel.

when she went up with her husband to offer the yearly sacrifice. [20] Then Eli would bless Elkanah and his wife, and say, "May the LORD repay[a] you with children by this woman for the gift that she made to[b] the LORD"; and then they would return to their home.

21 And[c] the LORD took note of Hannah; she conceived and bore three sons and two daughters. And the boy Samuel grew up in the presence of the LORD.

Prophecy against Eli's Household

22 Now Eli was very old. He heard all that his sons were doing to all Israel, and how they lay with the women who served at the entrance to the tent of meeting. [23] He said to them, "Why do you do such things? For I hear of your evil dealings from all these people. [24] No, my sons; it is not a good report that I hear the people of the LORD spreading abroad. [25] If one person sins against another, someone can intercede for the sinner with the LORD;[d] but if someone sins against the LORD, who can make intercession?" But they would not listen to the voice of their father; for it was the will of the LORD to kill them.

26 Now the boy Samuel continued to grow both in stature and in favor with the LORD and with the people.

27 A man of God came to Eli and said to him, "Thus the LORD has said, 'I revealed[e] myself to the family of your ancestor in Egypt when they were slaves[f] to the house of Pharaoh. [28] I chose him out of all the tribes of Israel to be my priest, to go up to my altar, to offer incense, to wear an ephod before me; and I gave to the family of your ancestor all my offerings by fire from the people of Israel. [29] Why then look with greedy eye[g] at my sacrifices and my offerings that I commanded, and honor your sons more than me by fattening yourselves on the choicest parts of every offering of my people Israel?' [30] Therefore the LORD the God of Israel declares: 'I promised that your family and the family of your ancestor should go in and out before me forever'; but now the LORD declares: 'Far be it from me; for those who honor me I will honor, and those who despise me shall be treated with contempt. [31] See, a time is coming when I will cut off your strength and the strength of your ancestor's family, so that no one in your family will live to old age. [32] Then in distress you will look with greedy eye[h] on all the prosperity that shall be bestowed upon Israel; and no one in your family shall ever live to old age. [33] The only one of you whom I shall not cut off from my altar shall be spared to weep out his[i] eyes and grieve his[j] heart; all the members of your household shall die by the sword.[k] [34] The fate of your two sons, Hophni and Phinehas, shall be the sign to you—both of them shall die on the same day. [35] I will raise up for myself a faithful priest, who shall do according to what is in my heart and in my mind. I will build him a sure

a Q Ms Gk: MT *give*　*b* Q Ms Gk: MT *for the petition that she asked of*　*c* Q Ms Gk: MT *When*　*d* Gk Compare Q Ms: MT *another, God will mediate for him*　*e* Gk Tg Syr: Heb *Did I reveal*　*f* Q Ms Gk: MT lacks *slaves*　*g* Q Ms Gk: MT *then kick*　*h* Q Ms Gk: MT *will kick*　*i* Q Ms Gk: MT *your*　*j* Q Ms Gk: Heb *your*　*k* Q Ms See Gk: MT *die like mortals*

2:22–36 Judgment on the House of Eli
Eli is powerless to stop his sons, but we are faced in this story with the inescapability of God's judgment. The statement of v. 25 shocks us, and the words of the prophet to Eli (vv. 27–36) are harsh. Nevertheless, we are reminded that to serve the God of grace is also to serve the God of judgment. Leadership in God's community is not just a task or a job; it is the risky and dangerous service of God's kingdom, and life-and-death issues in the world are at stake. To lead in self-serving or unfaithful ways is to treat God with contempt, and the judgment of God is as real as the grace of God. It is often through God's judgment that things are set right. In this harsh judgment God is also at work, making possible a new future for Israel.

2:33, 35—The one *spared* will be Abiathar, the sole survivor when the remnants of the house of Eli are slaughtered by Saul (22:20–23) and the *faithful priest* will turn out to be Zadok, whose family is made the hereditary priests of the temple built by Solomon. Both were in David's inner circle and served him as high priests, but Abiathar was banished by Solomon (1 Kgs. 2:27).

house, and he shall go in and out before my anointed one forever. **36** Everyone who is left in your family shall come to implore him for a piece of silver or a loaf of bread, and shall say, Please put me in one of the priest's places, that I may eat a morsel of bread.'"

Samuel's Calling and Prophetic Activity

3 Now the boy Samuel was ministering to the LORD under Eli. The word of the LORD was rare in those days; visions were not widespread.

2 At that time Eli, whose eyesight had begun to grow dim so that he could not see, was lying down in his room; ³ the lamp of God had not yet gone out, and Samuel was lying down in the temple of the LORD, where the ark of God was. ⁴ Then the LORD called, "Samuel! Samuel!"*a* and he said, "Here I am!" ⁵ and ran to Eli, and said, "Here I am, for you called me." But he said, "I did not call; lie down again." So he went and lay down. ⁶ The LORD called again, "Samuel!" Samuel got up and went to Eli, and said, "Here I am, for you called me." But he said, "I did not call, my son; lie down again." ⁷ Now Samuel did not yet know the LORD, and the word of the LORD had not yet been revealed to him. ⁸ The LORD called Samuel again, a third time.

And he got up and went to Eli, and said, "Here I am, for you called me." Then Eli perceived that the LORD was calling the boy. ⁹ Therefore Eli said to Samuel, "Go, lie down; and if he calls you, you shall say, 'Speak, LORD, for your servant is listening.'" So Samuel went and lay down in his place.

10 Now the LORD came and stood there, calling as before, "Samuel! Samuel!" And Samuel said, "Speak, for your servant is listening." ¹¹ Then the LORD said to Samuel, "See, I am about to do something in Israel that will make both ears of anyone who hears of it tingle. ¹² On that day I will fulfill against Eli all that I have spoken concerning his house, from beginning to end. ¹³ For I have told him that I am about to punish his house forever, for the iniquity that he knew, because his sons were blaspheming God,*b* and he did not restrain them. ¹⁴ Therefore I swear to the house of Eli that the iniquity of Eli's house shall not be expiated by sacrifice or offering forever."

15 Samuel lay there until morning; then he opened the doors of the house of the LORD. Samuel was afraid to tell the vision to Eli. ¹⁶ But Eli called Samuel

a Q Ms Gk See 3.10: MT *the LORD called Samuel*   *b* Another reading is *for themselves*

3:1–4:1a The Call of Samuel

3:1—This story begins with Samuel as a boy and the absence of God's word in Israel. It ends (vv. 20–21) with Samuel as a prophet who brings God's word to all Israel.

3:4–9—Samuel's failure to recognize God's call to him reminds us of the discernment needed to avoid missing God's call by focusing only on human sources of authority for our lives. However, Eli's recognition of God in Samuel's report shows the important role others may play in helping discern God's call. In this case, the moment is filled with drama. Eli knows that the word of God does not come lightly, and he well might suspect a word of judgment against his house due to the corruption of his sons. Nevertheless, he points Samuel without hesitation to the hearing and speaking of God's truth.

3:10–15—This is not a story of Samuel's general religious awakening. He is only a boy, but he is nevertheless called to the risky business of speaking God's word of judgment in a time of crisis in Israel. The house of Eli is corrupt; the Philistines will soon threaten Israel's survival; the word of God is rare in the land. Samuel's calling is not an end in itself, a mountaintop experience; it is for a task that sets him on the road to becoming God's prophet. The harsh word that Samuel must bring to Eli is a word of ending. God will not allow corruption and oppression to endure in the service of God. But in the very act of bringing this word to Eli, Samuel signals a new beginning. God, in Samuel, is raising up a prophet, and the word of the Lord will return to the land (3:19–4:1a).

3:16–18—Eli models trustful obedience even as he hears the word of judgment upon his house because of his corrupt sons. He is a part of unfaithful institutional structures that he did not desire but has not stopped or rejected. When confronted with his own complicity and judgment, he accepts God's verdict and places himself in trust of God's goodness (v. 18).

and said, "Samuel, my son." He said, "Here I am." [17] Eli said, "What was it that he told you? Do not hide it from me. May God do so to you and more also, if you hide anything from me of all that he told you." [18] So Samuel told him everything and hid nothing from him. Then he said, "It is the LORD; let him do what seems good to him."

19 As Samuel grew up, the LORD was with him and let none of his words fall to the ground. [20] And all Israel from Dan to Beer-sheba knew that Samuel was a trustworthy prophet of the LORD. [21] The LORD continued to appear at Shiloh, for the LORD revealed himself to Samuel at Shiloh by the word of the LORD. 4 [1] And the word of Samuel came to all Israel.

The Ark of God Captured

In those days the Philistines mustered for war against Israel,[a] and Israel went out to battle against them;[b] they encamped at Ebenezer, and the Philistines encamped at Aphek. [2] The Philistines drew up in line against Israel, and when the battle was joined,[c] Israel was defeated by the Philistines, who killed about four thousand men on the field

of battle. [3] When the troops came to the camp, the elders of Israel said, "Why has the LORD put us to rout today before the Philistines? Let us bring the ark of the covenant of the LORD here from Shiloh, so that he may come among us and save us from the power of our enemies." [4] So the people sent to Shiloh, and brought from there the ark of the covenant of the LORD of hosts, who is enthroned on the cherubim. The two sons of Eli, Hophni and Phinehas, were there with the ark of the covenant of God.

5 When the ark of the covenant of the LORD came into the camp, all Israel gave a mighty shout, so that the earth resounded. [6] When the Philistines heard the noise of the shouting, they said, "What does this great shouting in the camp of the Hebrews mean?" When they learned that the ark of the LORD had come to the camp, [7] the Philistines were afraid; for they said, "Gods have[d] come into the camp." They also said, "Woe to us! For nothing like this has happened before. [8] Woe to us! Who can deliver us from the power of these

[a] Gk: Heb lacks In those days the Philistines mustered for war against Israel [b] Gk: Heb against the Philistines [c] Meaning of Heb uncertain [d] Or A god has

3:19–4:1a—It is surely significant that God raises up prophets at the same time as kings. In this story, the word of the Lord is established in the land before the authority of the king is established. The word of God and God's prophet who speaks it have priority. Yet, even though God's word comes to Samuel, it is Samuel's words that come to the people (3:21b–4:1a). This suggests humility in the audacious task of proclamation, as we attempt to render God's word in our own words.

4:1b–7:2 The Ark Narrative

For a time, all human characters recede into the background, and these chapters feature the ark of the covenant and its adventures during a time of Philistine conquest. This ark narrative features the power of the *hand of the LORD* (5:6, 7, 9, 11), even in a time when the failure of human power and traditional religious symbols seem to point to God's defeat or abandonment of Israel. This is a timely reminder of God's sovereignty just ahead of the people's request for an earthly sovereign (chap. 8).

4:1b–2—The Philistines bring out a major army

with the intention of conquering Israel and building a Philistine empire. Israel's volunteer militia is no match for the professional armies of the Philistines.

4:3–4—The elders of Israel respond by bringing out the ark of the covenant of the Lord so that God may *save us from the power of our enemies*. The ark is a sacred object with winged cherubim supporting God's invisible throne. It represents God's presence in the midst of Israel and is carried to the battlefield to ensure victory. But Israel has placed its hope in the symbol of God's rule, while failing to honor God's rule. Significantly, the ark is carried by the corrupt sons of Eli. Trust in the symbols and trappings of religion, rather than in the God to which they point, is idolatry.

4:7–9—Surprisingly, it is the Philistines who give testimony to the God of exodus, who brings life and salvation out of the hopelessness of bondage and death in Egypt. This is an important reminder in a chapter that ends with apparent hopelessness.

mighty gods? These are the gods who struck the Egyptians with every sort of plague in the wilderness. [9] Take courage, and be men, O Philistines, in order not to become slaves to the Hebrews as they have been to you; be men and fight."

[10] So the Philistines fought; Israel was defeated, and they fled, everyone to his home. There was a very great slaughter, for there fell of Israel thirty thousand foot soldiers. [11] The ark of God was captured; and the two sons of Eli, Hophni and Phinehas, died.

Death of Eli

[12] A man of Benjamin ran from the battle line, and came to Shiloh the same day, with his clothes torn and with earth upon his head. [13] When he arrived, Eli was sitting upon his seat by the road watching, for his heart trembled for the ark of God. When the man came into the city and told the news, all the city cried out. [14] When Eli heard the sound of the outcry, he said, "What is this uproar?" Then the man came quickly and told Eli. [15] Now Eli was ninety-eight years old and his eyes were set, so that he could not see. [16] The man said to Eli, "I have just come from the battle; I fled from the battle today." He said, "How did it go, my son?" [17] The messenger replied, "Israel has fled before the Philistines, and there has also been a great slaughter among the troops; your two sons also, Hophni and Phinehas, are dead, and the ark of God has been captured." [18] When he mentioned the ark of God, Eli[a] fell over backward from his seat by the side of the gate; and his neck was broken and he died, for he was an old man, and heavy. He had judged Israel forty years.

[19] Now his daughter-in-law, the wife of Phinehas, was pregnant, about to give birth. When she heard the news that the ark of God was captured, and that her father-in-law and her husband were dead, she bowed and gave birth; for her labor pains overwhelmed her. [20] As she was about to die, the women attending her said to her, "Do not be afraid, for you have borne a son." But she did not answer or give heed. [21] She named the child Ichabod, meaning, "The glory has departed from Israel," because the ark of God had been captured and because of her father-in-law and her husband. [22] She said, "The glory has departed from Israel, for the ark of God has been captured."

The Philistines and the Ark

5 When the Philistines captured the ark of God, they brought it from Ebenezer to Ashdod; [2] then the Philistines took the ark of God and brought it into the house of Dagon and placed it beside Dagon. [3] When the people of Ashdod rose early the next day, there was Dagon, fallen on his face to the ground before the ark of the LORD. So they took Dagon and put him back in his place. [4] But when they rose early on the next morning, Dagon had fallen on his face to the ground before the ark of

[a] Heb *he*

4:9–22—The battle is lost; thirty thousand are killed; the ark is captured; the sons of Eli are killed; Eli falls over dead at the news. The first episode in the ark narrative ends with the deep and troubling theological dilemma of all human times of hopelessness: how do we find hope when **the glory has departed from Israel** (v. 22)? God seems defeated or absent; the ark is captured. Only the Philistines seem to remember the God of exodus deliverance (v. 8)

5:1–12—When the Philistines carry the ark of the covenant to Ashdod in triumph, it is placed in the temple of Dagon. But the idol of Dagon is found fallen, with head and hands broken off. A plague of tumors breaks out in Ashdod, and, as the ark is hastily moved from one Philistine city to another, the plague follows. Israel is defeated and without leadership. Philistine power seems supreme. In human terms the issue is decided, but not in God's terms. On the brink of an unfolding story of human leadership through kings in Israel, this story makes clear that the ultimate power for life, in Israel or in the wider world of Philistia, belongs to God. It is the **hand of the LORD** (vv. 6, 7, 9, 11) that makes a difference, and the idols and enemies to which we attribute power are rendered handless (v. 4).

the LORD, and the head of Dagon and both his hands were lying cut off upon the threshold; only the trunk of[a] Dagon was left to him. 5 This is why the priests of Dagon and all who enter the house of Dagon do not step on the threshold of Dagon in Ashdod to this day.

6 The hand of the LORD was heavy upon the people of Ashdod, and he terrified and struck them with tumors, both in Ashdod and in its territory. 7 And when the inhabitants of Ashdod saw how things were, they said, "The ark of the God of Israel must not remain with us; for his hand is heavy on us and on our god Dagon." 8 So they sent and gathered together all the lords of the Philistines, and said, "What shall we do with the ark of the God of Israel?" The inhabitants of Gath replied, "Let the ark of God be moved on to us."[b] So they moved the ark of the God of Israel to Gath.[c] 9 But after they had brought it to Gath,[c] the hand of the LORD was against the city, causing a very great panic; he struck the inhabitants of the city, both young and old, so that tumors broke out on them. 10 So they sent the ark of the God of Israel[d] to Ekron. But when the ark of God came to Ekron, the people of Ekron cried out, "Why[e] have they brought around to us[f] the ark of the God of Israel to kill us[f] and our[g] people?" 11 They sent therefore and gathered together all the lords of the Philistines, and said, "Send away the ark of the God of Israel, and let it return to its own place, that it may not kill us and our people." For there was a deathly panic[h] throughout the whole city. The hand of God was very heavy there; 12 those who did not die were stricken with tumors, and the cry of the city went up to heaven.

The Ark Returned to Israel

6 The ark of the LORD was in the country of the Philistines seven months. 2 Then the Philistines called for the priests and the diviners and said, "What shall we do with the ark of the LORD? Tell us what we should send with it to its place." 3 They said, "If you send away the ark of the God of Israel, do not send it empty, but by all means return him a guilt offering. Then you will be healed and will be ransomed;[i] will not his hand then turn from you?" 4 And they said, "What is the guilt offering that we shall return to him?" They answered, "Five gold tumors and five gold mice, according to the number of the lords of the Philistines; for the same plague was upon all of you and upon your lords. 5 So you must make images of your tumors and images of your mice that ravage the land, and give glory to the God of Israel; perhaps he will lighten his hand on you and your gods and your land. 6 Why should you harden your hearts as the Egyptians and Pharaoh hardened their hearts? After he had made fools of them, did they not let the people go, and they departed? 7 Now then, get ready a new cart and two milch cows that have never borne a yoke, and yoke the cows to the cart, but take their calves home, away from them. 8 Take the ark of the LORD and place it on the cart, and put in a box at its side the figures of gold, which you are returning to him as a guilt offering. Then send it off, and let it go its way. 9 And watch; if it goes up on the way to its own land, to Bethshemesh, then it is he who has done us this great harm; but if not, then we shall

a Heb lacks the trunk of　b Gk Compare Q Ms: MT They answered, "Let the ark of the God of Israel be brought around to Gath."　c Gk: Heb lacks to Gath　d Q Ms Gk: MT lacks of Israel　e Q Ms Gk: MT lacks Why　f Heb me　g Heb my　h Q Ms reads a panic from the LORD　i Q Ms Gk: MT and it will be known to you

---

6:1–3—The Philistines recognize that they cannot hold and control the power of God simply by possessing the ark, so they determine to send it back to Israel with offerings. Perhaps they are still mistakenly trying to control God by these strange offerings, which are attempts to send the diseases that plagued them back to Israel with Israel's God.

6:6—Once again, it is the Philistines who remember the exodus events and testify to the power of God in opposition to human power (cf. 4:8).

know that it is not his hand that struck us; it happened to us by chance."

10 The men did so; they took two milch cows and yoked them to the cart, and shut up their calves at home. ¹¹ They put the ark of the LORD on the cart, and the box with the gold mice and the images of their tumors. ¹² The cows went straight in the direction of Beth-shemesh along one highway, lowing as they went; they turned neither to the right nor to the left, and the lords of the Philistines went after them as far as the border of Beth-shemesh.

13 Now the people of Beth-shemesh were reaping their wheat harvest in the valley. When they looked up and saw the ark, they went with rejoicing to meet it.ᵃ ¹⁴ The cart came into the field of Joshua of Beth-shemesh, and stopped there. A large stone was there; so they split up the wood of the cart and offered the cows as a burnt offering to the LORD. ¹⁵ The Levites took down the ark of the LORD and the box that was beside it, in which were the gold objects, and set them upon the large stone. Then the people of Beth-shemesh offered burnt offerings and presented sacrifices on that day to the LORD. ¹⁶ When the five lords of the Philistines saw it, they returned that day to Ekron.

17 These are the gold tumors, which the Philistines returned as a guilt offering to the LORD: one for Ashdod, one for Gaza, one for Ashkelon, one for Gath, one for Ekron; ¹⁸ also the gold mice, according to the number of all the cities of the Philistines belonging to the five lords, both fortified cities and unwalled villages. The great stone, beside which they set down the ark of the LORD, is a witness to this day in the field of Joshua of Beth-shemesh.

The Ark at Kiriath-jearim

19 The descendants of Jeconiah did not rejoice with the people of Beth-shemesh when they greetedᵇ the ark of the LORD; and he killed seventy men of them.ᶜ The people mourned because the LORD had made a great slaughter among the people. ²⁰ Then the people of Beth-shemesh said, "Who is able to stand before the LORD, this holy God? To whom shall he go so that we may be rid of him?" ²¹ So they sent messengers to the inhabitants of Kiriath-jearim, saying, "The Philistines have returned the ark of the LORD. Come down and take it up to you." ¹ And the people of Kiriath-jearim came and took up the ark of the LORD, and brought it to the house of Abinadab on the hill. They consecrated his son, Eleazar, to have charge of the ark of the LORD.

2 From the day that the ark was lodged at Kiriath-jearim, a long time passed, some twenty years, and all the house of Israel lamentedᵈ after the LORD.

Samuel as Judge

3 Then Samuel said to all the house of Israel, "If you are returning to the

---

ᵃ Gk: Heb *rejoiced to see it* ᵇ Gk: Heb *And he killed some of the people of Beth-shemesh, because they looked into* ᶜ Heb *killed seventy men, fifty thousand men* ᵈ Meaning of Heb uncertain

---

6:13–21—On an untended cart drawn by two cows, the ark and the Philistine offerings return to Israelite territory at Beth-shemesh. When some of the men disrespect the ark and do not acknowledge the holy presence of God, they are struck down. This is not a warm, friendly deity who can be managed or handled. This text requires us to recognize that the holiness of God is mysterious and dangerous. Israel's failure to honor the holiness of God led to the Philistine defeat and the capture of the ark in the first place. The ark of God's presence will not return to Israel only to be dishonored again.

7:1—It is not yet time for the ark to return to its place of honor in Israel. The people of Kiriath-jearim take it under their care. They are Gibeonites and not Israelites. The ark will not return to the center of Israel's life until David brings it to Jerusalem (2 Sam. 6).

7:3–17 Samuel as Judge

7:3–4—Between the story of reliance on the ark and reliance on a king, Samuel challenges the people to focus on God only. Our sacred symbols and material things and our human leaders are idols if they do not point to our reliance on God. False security results from the belief that

LORD with all your heart, then put away the foreign gods and the Astartes from among you. Direct your heart to the LORD, and serve him only, and he will deliver you out of the hand of the Philistines." ⁴So Israel put away the Baals and the Astartes, and they served the LORD only.

5 Then Samuel said, "Gather all Israel at Mizpah, and I will pray to the LORD for you." ⁶So they gathered at Mizpah, and drew water and poured it out before the LORD. They fasted that day, and said, "We have sinned against the LORD." And Samuel judged the people of Israel at Mizpah.

7 When the Philistines heard that the people of Israel had gathered at Mizpah, the lords of the Philistines went up against Israel. And when the people of Israel heard of it they were afraid of the Philistines. ⁸The people of Israel said to Samuel, "Do not cease to cry out to the LORD our God for us, and pray that he may save us from the hand of the Philistines." ⁹So Samuel took a sucking lamb and offered it as a whole burnt offering to the LORD; Samuel cried out to the LORD for Israel, and the LORD answered him. ¹⁰As Samuel was offering up the burnt offering, the Philistines drew near to attack Israel; but the LORD thundered with a mighty voice that day against the Philistines and threw them into confusion; and they were routed before Israel. ¹¹And the men of Israel went out of Mizpah and pursued the Philistines, and struck them down as far as beyond Beth-car.

12 Then Samuel took a stone and set it up between Mizpah and Jeshanah,ᵃ and named it Ebenezer;ᵇ for he said, "Thus far the LORD has helped us." ¹³So the Philistines were subdued and did not again enter the territory of Israel; the hand of the LORD was against the Philistines all the days of Samuel. ¹⁴The towns that the Philistines had taken from Israel were restored to Israel, from Ekron to Gath; and Israel recovered their territory from the hand of the Philistines. There was peace also between Israel and the Amorites.

15 Samuel judged Israel all the days of his life. ¹⁶He went on a circuit year by year to Bethel, Gilgal, and Mizpah; and he judged Israel in all these places. ¹⁷Then he would come back to Ramah, for his home was there; he administered justice there to Israel, and built there an altar to the LORD.

Israel Demands a King

8 When Samuel became old, he made his sons judges over Israel. ²The

---

ᵃ Gk Syr: Heb *Shen*   ᵇ That is *Stone of Help*

---

power lies in the things we control; this is a story of true security in the *thunder* of God (v. 10).

7:8–9—The verbs of these verses point out alternatives to idolatrous loyalties. What focuses the community on God is when we **cry out** to God, address *prayer* to God, and wait confidently for God's *answer*. Earlier, *confession* and *fasting* (v. 6) and later, the *administration of justice* (v. 17) bracket this story of God's deliverance. These speak of covenant focus on God alone and this is the key to true power, able to meet even Philistine power.

7:10–11—This is the language of holy war, where it is clear that God wins the victory. In our time it is mainly the marginal who can place their hope in the thunder of God, because they have no access to human power. Most of us claim to trust God but marshal our resources and rely on our leadership just in case. Here, on the eve of the story of kingship, this story reminds us that true security still rests in God.

7:13–17—The claims are exaggerated because, of course, the Philistines continue to invade and threaten through most of the rest of the books of Samuel. But in the meantime, it is clear that God's prophet, Samuel, keeps the covenant traditions alive by traveling a circuit in the midst of Philistine occupation.

8:1–15:35 The Rise of Kingship and the Reign of Saul

These chapters introduce the main issue for which chaps. 1–7 have been preparing us—the beginning of kingship in Israel. In response to the people's demand (chap. 8) Samuel makes Saul Israel's first king, although there are multiple stories on how this took place (9:1–10:16; 10:17–27; 11:1–15). But after limited success at the challenges facing him, Saul comes into conflict

name of his firstborn son was Joel, and the name of his second, Abijah; they were judges in Beer-sheba. ³ Yet his sons did not follow in his ways, but turned aside after gain; they took bribes and perverted justice.

4 Then all the elders of Israel gathered together and came to Samuel at Ramah, ⁵ and said to him, "You are old and your sons do not follow in your ways; appoint for us, then, a king to govern us, like other nations." ⁶ But the thing displeased Samuel when they said, "Give us a king to govern us." Samuel prayed to the LORD, ⁷ and the LORD said to Samuel, "Listen to the voice of the people in all that they say to you; for they have not rejected you, but they have rejected me from being king over them. ⁸ Just as they have done to me,ᵃ from the day I brought them up out of Egypt to this day, forsaking me and serving other gods, so also they are doing to you. ⁹ Now then, listen to their voice; only—you shall solemnly warn them, and show them the ways of the king who shall reign over them."

10 So Samuel reported all the words of the LORD to the people who were asking him for a king. ¹¹ He said, "These will be the ways of the king who will reign over you: he will take your sons and appoint them to his chariots and to be his horsemen, and to run before his chariots; ¹² and he will appoint for himself commanders of thousands and commanders of fifties, and some to plow his ground and to reap his harvest, and to make his implements of war and the equipment of his chariots. ¹³ He will take your daughters to be perfumers and cooks and bakers. ¹⁴ He will take the best of your fields and vineyards and olive orchards and give them to his courtiers. ¹⁵ He will take one-tenth of your grain and of your vineyards and give it to his officers and his courtiers. ¹⁶ He will take your male and female slaves, and the best of your cattleᵇ and donkeys, and put them to his work. ¹⁷ He will take one-tenth of your flocks, and you shall be his slaves. ¹⁸ And in that day you will cry out because of your king, whom you have chosen for yourselves; but the LORD will not answer you in that day."

Israel's Request for a King Granted

19 But the people refused to listen to the voice of Samuel; they said, "No! but

ᵃ Gk: Heb lacks *to me*   ᵇ Gk: Heb *young men*

---

with Samuel and is rejected as king (13:1–23; 15:1–35), and the stage is set for David to make his entry (16:1–13).

8:1–22 Request for a King

8:1–3—Ironically, Samuel's own sons become corrupt judges, recalling the situation with Eli's sons (2:11–36). Faithful leadership in the public arena has not found a counterpart in Samuel's own family.

8:4–5—Although the corruption of Samuel's sons is an immediate factor, the people desire a king *like other nations*. This is expanded in v. 19 to the desire for a military leader, perhaps reflecting the Philistine danger, which is not explicitly mentioned. The internal and external crisis of Israel is genuine, but the temptation to meet the crisis "like other nations" is an expression of failed trust in God. The community of God's covenant people is never like the communities of the world around us, but like the elders of Israel we are often tempted to abandon our identity as God's people for the cultural identities that are so appealing. Accommodation is a constant danger in the effort to be relevant to the challenges of the time.

8:6–8—Trust in human power can become a rejection of divine power. Samuel feels put aside, but God reminds the prophet that the real danger is that in seeking new leadership the people have forgotten that the source of power for faithful leadership in the covenant community rests in God. This chapter forces us to think deeply about the relationship between human authority and divine authority. Where does our discipleship loyalty go beyond our citizenship loyalty?

8:10–18—The key word in Samuel's warning about the dangers of kings is *take*. If the source of true power in God is ignored, then kings (or any earthly political authority) simply become self-justified centers of power and "take" for their own needs and desires. Many think this reaches fulfillment in the corruption of Solomon's kingship, but when David "takes" Bathsheba for his own desires and kills her husband, Uriah (2 Sam. 11), Samuel's dire warning has begun to become reality.

we are determined to have a king over us, 20 so that we also may be like other nations, and that our king may govern us and go out before us and fight our battles." 21 When Samuel had heard all the words of the people, he repeated them in the ears of the LORD. 22 The LORD said to Samuel, "Listen to their voice and set a king over them." Samuel then said to the people of Israel, "Each of you return home."

Saul Chosen to Be King

9 There was a man of Benjamin whose name was Kish son of Abiel son of Zeror son of Becorath son of Aphiah, a Benjaminite, a man of wealth. 2 He had a son whose name was Saul, a handsome young man. There was not a man among the people of Israel more handsome than he; he stood head and shoulders above everyone else.

3 Now the donkeys of Kish, Saul's father, had strayed. So Kish said to his son Saul, "Take one of the boys with you; go and look for the donkeys." 4 He passed through the hill country of Ephraim and passed through the land of Shalishah, but they did not find them. And they passed through the land of Shaalim, but they were not there. Then he passed through the land of Benjamin, but they did not find them.

5 When they came to the land of Zuph, Saul said to the boy who was with him, "Let us turn back, or my father will stop worrying about the donkeys and worry about us." 6 But he said to him, "There is a man of God in this town; he is a man held in honor. Whatever he says always comes true. Let us go there now; perhaps he will tell us about the journey on which we have set out." 7 Then Saul replied to the boy, "But if we go, what can we bring the man? For the bread in our sacks is gone, and there is no present to bring to the man of God. What have we?" 8 The boy answered Saul again, "Here, I have with me a quarter shekel of silver; I will give it to the man of God, to tell us our way." 9 (Formerly in Israel, anyone who went to inquire of God would say, "Come, let us go to the seer"; for the one who is now called a prophet was formerly called a seer.) 10 Saul said to the boy, "Good; come, let us go." So they went to the town where the man of God was.

11 As they went up the hill to the town, they met some girls coming out to draw water, and said to them, "Is the seer here?" 12 They answered, "Yes, there he is just ahead of you. Hurry; he has come just now to the town, because the people have a sacrifice today at the shrine. 13 As soon as you enter the town, you will find him, before he goes up to the shrine to eat. For the people will not eat until he comes, since he must bless the sacrifice; afterward those eat who are invited. Now go up, for you will meet him immediately." 14 So they went up to the town. As they were entering the town, they saw Samuel coming out toward them on his way up to the shrine.

15 Now the day before Saul came, the

8:22—The desire for a king may be a rejection of God's sovereignty, but God will not abandon Israel's future. If there is to be a king, God will establish him. God claims our future even through our own sinful choices.

9:1–10:16 Samuel Anoints Saul

9:1–4—This story is part of a common biblical theme: God makes surprising and unexpected choices for those who carry out God's mission in the world. In this case, the choice is a young man looking for his father's lost donkeys. By the end of the story, this adolescent youth is God's anointed instrument to deliver Israel from the

hands of the Philistines and to rule as Israel's first king.

9:5–9—This story comes from a time when the role of prophet was just emerging. Samuel turns out to be man of God, seer, and prophet in this story; the terms seem to overlap in this early time in Israel. Many would count Samuel the first to embody fully the role of prophet in the biblical story.

9:15–17—In a kind of flashback we learn that God had told Samuel in a vision that Saul would come. In the process we learn that God has surprisingly chosen this boy to deliver Israel from

LORD had revealed to Samuel: [16] "Tomorrow about this time I will send to you a man from the land of Benjamin, and you shall anoint him to be ruler over my people Israel. He shall save my people from the hand of the Philistines; for I have seen the suffering of[a] my people, because their outcry has come to me." [17] When Samuel saw Saul, the LORD told him, "Here is the man of whom I spoke to you. He it is who shall rule over my people." [18] Then Saul approached Samuel inside the gate, and said, "Tell me, please, where is the house of the seer?" [19] Samuel answered Saul, "I am the seer; go up before me to the shrine, for today you shall eat with me, and in the morning I will let you go and will tell you all that is on your mind. [20] As for your donkeys that were lost three days ago, give no further thought to them, for they have been found. And on whom is all Israel's desire fixed, if not on you and on all your ancestral house?" [21] Saul answered, "I am only a Benjaminite, from the least of the tribes of Israel, and my family is the humblest of all the families of the tribe of Benjamin. Why then have you spoken to me in this way?"

22 Then Samuel took Saul and his servant-boy and brought them into the hall, and gave them a place at the head of those who had been invited, of whom there were about thirty. [23] And Samuel said to the cook, "Bring the portion I gave you, the one I asked you to put aside." [24] The cook took up the thigh and what went with it[b] and set them before Saul. Samuel said, "See, what was kept is set before you. Eat; for it is set[c] before you at the appointed time, so that you might eat with the guests."[d]

So Saul ate with Samuel that day. [25] When they came down from the shrine into the town, a bed was spread for Saul[e] on the roof, and he lay down to sleep.[f] [26] Then at the break of dawn[g] Samuel called to Saul upon the roof, "Get up, so that I may send you on your way." Saul got up, and both he and Samuel went out into the street.

Samuel Anoints Saul

27 As they were going down to the outskirts of the town, Samuel said to Saul, "Tell the boy to go on before us, and when he has passed on, stop here yourself for a while, that I may make known to you the word of God."

10 [1] Samuel took a vial of oil and poured it on his head, and kissed him; he said, "The LORD has anointed you ruler over his people Israel. You shall reign over the people of the LORD and you will save them from the hand of their enemies all around. Now this shall be the sign to you that the LORD has anointed you ruler[h] over his heritage: [2] When you depart from me today you will meet two men by Rachel's tomb in the territory of Benjamin at Zelzah; they will say to you, 'The donkeys that you went to seek are found, and now your father has stopped worrying about

[a] Gk: Heb lacks *the suffering of*   [b] Meaning of Heb uncertain   [c] Q Ms Gk: MT *it was kept*   [d] Cn: Heb *it was kept for you, saying, I have invited the people*   [e] Gk: Heb *and he spoke with Saul*   [f] Gk: Heb lacks *and he lay down to sleep*   [g] Heb *and they arose early and at break of dawn*   [h] Gk: Heb lacks *over his people Israel. You shall . . . anointed you ruler*

---

the hand of the Philistines in language that is very reminiscent of God's response to Israel's outcry in Egypt. This makes Saul's call parallel to the call of Moses (another surprising choice, since he was a fugitive at the time).

9:21—When Samuel hints to Saul of a larger destiny in store for him (v. 20), Saul objects that he is not worthy of such a calling. This is part of a common pattern in call stories, where persons (Moses, Gideon, Isaiah, Jeremiah, Ezekiel) object that they could not possibly be the person God needs. But calling is a matter of God's initia-tive, not a rational calculation of career goals or formal qualifications.

10:1—Samuel anoints Saul with oil and commissions him to *save* Israel from the Philistines. Commissioning is a common part of call stories in the Bible, but anointing is reserved for kings (e.g., 1 Sam. 16:12–13; 2 Kgs. 9:3, 6; 11:12; 23:30). This gives rise to designation of God's king as "anointed one," for which the Hebrew term is *mashiach*. When earthly kings seem to have failed with the Babylonian exile, the hope for a messiah is projected into the future.

them and is worrying about you, saying: What shall I do about my son?' ³Then you shall go on from there further and come to the oak of Tabor; three men going up to God at Bethel will meet you there, one carrying three kids, another carrying three loaves of bread, and another carrying a skin of wine. ⁴They will greet you and give you two loaves of bread, which you shall accept from them. ⁵After that you shall come to Gibeath-elohim,ª at the place where the Philistine garrison is; there, as you come to the town, you will meet a band of prophets coming down from the shrine with harp, tambourine, flute, and lyre playing in front of them; they will be in a prophetic frenzy. ⁶Then the spirit of the LORD will possess you, and you will be in a prophetic frenzy along with them and be turned into a different person. ⁷Now when these signs meet you, do whatever you see fit to do, for God is with you. ⁸And you shall go down to Gilgal ahead of me; then I will come down to you to present burnt offerings and offer sacrifices of well-being. Seven days you shall wait, until I come to you and show you what you shall do."

Saul Prophesies

9 As he turned away to leave Samuel, God gave him another heart; and all these signs were fulfilled that day. ¹⁰When they were going from thereᵇ to Gibeah,ᶜ a band of prophets met him; and the spirit of God possessed him, and he fell into a prophetic frenzy along with them. ¹¹When all who knew him before saw how he prophesied with the prophets, the people said to one another, "What has come over the son of Kish? Is Saul also among the prophets?" ¹²A man of the place answered, "And who is their father?" Therefore it became a proverb, "Is Saul also among the prophets?" ¹³When his prophetic frenzy had ended, he went home.ᵈ

14 Saul's uncle said to him and to the boy, "Where did you go?" And he replied, "To seek the donkeys; and when we saw they were not to be found, we went to Samuel." ¹⁵Saul's uncle said, "Tell me what Samuel said to you." ¹⁶Saul said to his uncle, "He told us that the donkeys had been found." But about the matter of the kingship, of which Samuel had spoken, he did not tell him anything.

Saul Proclaimed King

17 Samuel summoned the people to the LORD at Mizpah ¹⁸and said to them,ᵉ "Thus says the LORD, the God of Israel, 'I brought up Israel out of Egypt, and I rescued you from the hand of the Egyptians and from the hand of all the kingdoms that were oppressing you.' ¹⁹But today you have rejected your God, who saves you from all your calamities and your distresses; and you have said, 'No! but set a king over us.' Now therefore present yourselves before the LORD by your tribes and by your clans."

20 Then Samuel brought all the tribes

ᵃOr the Hill of God   ᵇGk: Heb they came there   ᶜOr the hill   ᵈCn: Heb he came to the shrine   ᵉHeb to the people of Israel

---

10:5–6, 10—In the stories of Saul and David (16:13), anointing by God's prophet is accompanied by the receiving of God's spirit. This reminds us also of Jesus' baptism by John the Baptist and the receiving of God's spirit at the start of Jesus' public ministry (Matt. 3:13–17; Mark 1:9–11; Luke 3:21–22). All of these stories remind us that God not only initiates the call to participate in God's mission but empowers us to do so as well. Part of Saul's challenge, and our own, is to follow the leading of God's spirit rather than relying on our own gifts alone. For those who are called to God's service, the focus should be on the one who calls. Whatever our gifts, we, like Saul, are transformed (v. 6, *turned into a different person*; v. 9, *gave him another heart*) by the initiative of God's call and the empowerment of God's spirit. Openness to this may take us into experiences we might not have chosen on our own initiative and power (*Is Saul also among the prophets?* v. 12).

10:17–27 A Second Account of How Saul Was Designated as King

10:19—This account, unlike the preceding story, assumes that kingship is a sinful thing in Israel, and a rejection of God.

10:20–24—The people may have rejected God,

of Israel near, and the tribe of Benjamin was taken by lot. ²¹ He brought the tribe of Benjamin near by its families, and the family of the Matrites was taken by lot. Finally he brought the family of the Matrites near man by man,ᵃ and Saul the son of Kish was taken by lot. But when they sought him, he could not be found. ²² So they inquired again of the LORD, "Did the man come here?"ᵇ and the LORD said, "See, he has hidden himself among the baggage." ²³ Then they ran and brought him from there. When he took his stand among the people, he was head and shoulders taller than any of them. ²⁴ Samuel said to all the people, "Do you see the one whom the LORD has chosen? There is no one like him among all the people." And all the people shouted, "Long live the king!"

25 Samuel told the people the rights and duties of the kingship; and he wrote them in a book and laid it up before the LORD. Then Samuel sent all the people back to their homes. ²⁶ Saul also went to his home at Gibeah, and with him went warriors whose hearts God had touched. ²⁷ But some worthless fellows said, "How can this man save us?" They despised him and brought him no present. But he held his peace.

Now Nahash, king of the Ammonites, had been grievously oppressing the Gadites and the Reubenites. He would gouge out the right eye of each of them and would not grant Israel a deliverer. No one was left of the Israelites across the Jordan whose right eye Nahash, king of the Ammonites, had not gouged out. But there were seven thousand men who had escaped from the Ammonites and had entered Jabesh-gilead.ᶜ

Saul Defeats the Ammonites

11 About a month later,ᵈ Nahash the Ammonite went up and besieged Jabesh-gilead; and all the men of Jabesh said to Nahash, "Make a treaty with us, and we will serve you." ² But Nahash the Ammonite said to them, "On this condition I will make a treaty with you, namely that I gouge out everyone's right eye, and thus put disgrace upon all Israel." ³ The elders of Jabesh said to him, "Give us seven days' respite that we may send messengers through all the territory of Israel. Then, if there is no one to save us, we will give ourselves up to you." ⁴ When the messengers came to Gibeah of Saul, they reported the matter in the hearing of the people; and all the people wept aloud.

ᵃ Gk: Heb lacks *Finally . . . man by man* ᵇ Gk: Heb *Is there yet a man to come here?* ᶜ Q Ms Compare Josephus, *Antiquities* VI.v.1 (68-71): MT lacks *Now Nahash . . . entered Jabesh-gilead.* ᵈ Q Ms Gk: MT lacks *About a month later*

---

but God will not reject them even in the matter of a king. Saul is presented as **the one whom the LORD has chosen** (v. 24). Like many of us, Saul hides his gifts until the insistence of God's call to serve brings him out of the baggage. This is the second story of Saul's designation to kingship but serves in the present arrangement as his public debut.

10:27—It is **worthless fellows** who voice a crucial question in their skepticism about Saul: Who can save? In the story that lies ahead, Saul and David can save only by trusting in God's power, the true source of saving. When they turn to their own power alone, they cannot save. Those dismissed as worthless among us often see clearly where true power lies. In Jesus' ministry outcasts and even demons often recognized him as Messiah before the disciples saw this clearly. Chapter 11 goes on to demonstrate that Saul can save only through the power of God's spirit.

11:1–15 A Third Account of Saul's Becoming King
Saul is introduced as a deliverer in time of crisis. The episode is much likes the stories of heroes in the book of Judges who save through the empowerment by God's spirit. This account serves in the present arrangement as a public demonstration of the spirit of God that came upon Saul after his anointing by Samuel (10:10).

11:3—This is a story about salvation. The people of Jabesh-gilead are in a desperate crisis at the hands of Nahash the Ammonite, who has besieged their city, threatening atrocities. The people of Jabesh-gilead fear that no one can **save** them (v. 3). Samuel had already claimed that Israel had rejected the God who saves them, and worthless fellows had wondered if Saul could save them (10:27). Now word is sent that Saul will save them (11:9), and afterward Saul claims that it was God who saved them (v. 13).

5 Now Saul was coming from the field behind the oxen; and Saul said, "What is the matter with the people, that they are weeping?" So they told him the message from the inhabitants of Jabesh. ⁶ And the spirit of God came upon Saul in power when he heard these words, and his anger was greatly kindled. ⁷ He took a yoke of oxen, and cut them in pieces and sent them throughout all the territory of Israel by messengers, saying, "Whoever does not come out after Saul and Samuel, so shall it be done to his oxen!" Then the dread of the LORD fell upon the people, and they came out as one. ⁸ When he mustered them at Bezek, those from Israel were three hundred thousand, and those from Judah seventy*a* thousand. ⁹ They said to the messengers who had come, "Thus shall you say to the inhabitants of Jabesh-gilead: 'Tomorrow, by the time the sun is hot, you shall have deliverance.'" When the messengers came and told the inhabitants of Jabesh, they rejoiced. ¹⁰ So the inhabitants of Jabesh said, "Tomorrow we will give ourselves up to you, and you may do to us whatever seems good to you." ¹¹ The next day Saul put the people in three companies. At the morning watch they came into the camp and cut down the Ammonites until the heat of the day; and those who survived were scattered, so that no two of them were left together.

12 The people said to Samuel, "Who is it that said, 'Shall Saul reign over us?'

Give them to us so that we may put them to death." ¹³ But Saul said, "No one shall be put to death this day, for today the LORD has brought deliverance to Israel."

14 Samuel said to the people, "Come, let us go to Gilgal and there renew the kingship." ¹⁵ So all the people went to Gilgal, and there they made Saul king before the LORD in Gilgal. There they sacrificed offerings of well-being before the LORD, and there Saul and all the Israelites rejoiced greatly.

Samuel's Farewell Address

12 Samuel said to all Israel, "I have listened to you in all that you have said to me, and have set a king over you. ² See, it is the king who leads you now; I am old and gray, but my sons are with you. I have led you from my youth until this day. ³ Here I am; testify against me before the LORD and before his anointed. Whose ox have I taken? Or whose donkey have I taken? Or whom have I defrauded? Whom have I oppressed? Or from whose hand have I taken a bribe to blind my eyes with it? Testify against me*b* and I will restore it to you." ⁴ They said, "You have not defrauded us or oppressed us or taken anything from the hand of anyone." ⁵ He said to them, "The LORD is witness against you, and his anointed is witness this day, that you have not found

a Q Ms Gk: MT *thirty*　*b* Gk: Heb lacks *Testify against me*

11:5–11—Like the deliverers in the book of Judges, Saul is seized by the spirit of the Lord; empowered by the spirit, he wins a mighty victory over Nahash the Ammonite, and the people of Jabesh-gilead are saved. Such salvation is clearly brought by God's power but it is also clear that the power of God's spirit works through a human agent, Saul. As with Moses, and the judges before him, Saul acts in the power of God, not his own power. Losing sight of this later leads to his rejection as king (chaps. 13; 15). God's spirit rouses Saul first to anger (11:6), then to action. The salvation of God and its human agents cannot stay passive in the face of human suffering. But God's salvation is not without cost, and the violence of the oppressor is answered by violence in Saul's

defeat of Nahash. This is troubling, but to do nothing to oppose brutality and injustice would be a greater violence.

11:15—This is the third time Saul is made king, but v. 14 tries to make sense of this in the present arrangement by suggesting this is a "renewal" of his kingship.

12:1–25 Samuel's Farewell

Samuel's farewell address to Israel marks the end of the era of the judges and the start of the time of kings.

12:1–5—Samuel accepts the establishment of a new order he has helped bring by setting a king before Israel, and he steps aside with a testimony to his own integrity of leadership.

anything in my hand." And they said, "He is witness."

6 Samuel said to the people, "The LORD is witness, who[a] appointed Moses and Aaron and brought your ancestors up out of the land of Egypt. 7 Now therefore take your stand, so that I may enter into judgment with you before the LORD, and I will declare to you[b] all the saving deeds of the LORD that he performed for you and for your ancestors. 8 When Jacob went into Egypt and the Egyptians oppressed them,[c] then your ancestors cried to the LORD and the LORD sent Moses and Aaron, who brought forth your ancestors out of Egypt, and settled them in this place. 9 But they forgot the LORD their God; and he sold them into the hand of Sisera, commander of the army of King Jabin of[d] Hazor, and into the hand of the Philistines, and into the hand of the king of Moab; and they fought against them. 10 Then they cried to the LORD, and said, 'We have sinned, because we have forsaken the LORD, and have served the Baals and the Astartes; but now rescue us out of the hand of our enemies, and we will serve you.' 11 And the LORD sent Jerubbaal and Barak,[e] and Jephthah, and Samson,[f] and rescued you out of the hand of your enemies on every side; and you lived in safety. 12 But when you saw that King Nahash of the Ammonites came against you, you said to me, 'No, but a king shall reign over us,' though the LORD your God was your king. 13 See, here is the king whom you have chosen, for whom you have asked; see, the LORD has set a king over you. 14 If you will fear the LORD and serve

him and heed his voice and not rebel against the commandment of the LORD, and if both you and the king who reigns over you will follow the LORD your God, it will be well; 15 but if you will not heed the voice of the LORD, but rebel against the commandment of the LORD, then the hand of the LORD will be against you and your king.[g] 16 Now therefore take your stand and see this great thing that the LORD will do before your eyes. 17 Is it not the wheat harvest today? I will call upon the LORD, that he may send thunder and rain; and you shall know and see that the wickedness that you have done in the sight of the LORD is great in demanding a king for yourselves." 18 So Samuel called upon the LORD, and the LORD sent thunder and rain that day; and all the people greatly feared the LORD and Samuel.

19 All the people said to Samuel, "Pray to the LORD your God for your servants, so that we may not die; for we have added to all our sins the evil of demanding a king for ourselves." 20 And Samuel said to the people, "Do not be afraid; you have done all this evil, yet do not turn aside from following the LORD, but serve the LORD with all your heart; 21 and do not turn aside after useless things that cannot profit or save, for they are useless. 22 For the LORD will not cast away his people, for his great name's sake, because it has pleased the LORD to make you a people for himself. 23 Moreover as for me, far be it from me that I

[a] Gk: Heb lacks is witness, who [b] Gk: Heb lacks and I will declare to you [c] Gk: Heb lacks and the Egyptians oppressed them [d] Gk: Heb lacks King Jabin of [e] Gk Syr: Heb Bedan [f] Gk: Heb Samuel [g] Gk: Heb and your ancestors

---

12:6–22—In a long speech that includes a recital of God's acts of salvation toward Israel, Samuel reminds Israel that even when political institutions and realities change, the moral reality of God's demand for covenant obedience does not change. We often mistake external change as occasion to leave behind supposedly outmoded values, but Samuel reminds Israel and us that God's moral challenge to obedience endures. Further, it is an equal challenge to both king and people. Leaders are not held to a different standard than the people, nor are leaders above such standards. True leadership understands that the fates of leader and people are intertwined and that service to God falls as a responsibility on both leader and people. This speech still suggests that the request for a king was sinful (vv. 17, 19), but that God's grace (v. 22) and the people's obedience (vv. 20, 21) still gives them a hopeful future. The reality of sin cannot have the last word when God's grace is received and acted upon.

12:23—When the time comes for Samuel to give

should sin against the LORD by ceasing to pray for you; and I will instruct you in the good and the right way. ²⁴ Only fear the LORD, and serve him faithfully with all your heart; for consider what great things he has done for you. ²⁵ But if you still do wickedly, you shall be swept away, both you and your king."

Saul's Unlawful Sacrifice

13 Saul was . . .ª years old when he began to reign; and he reigned . . . and twoᵇ years over Israel.

2 Saul chose three thousand out of Israel; two thousand were with Saul in Michmash and the hill country of Bethel, and a thousand were with Jonathan in Gibeah of Benjamin; the rest of the people he sent home to their tents. ³ Jonathan defeated the garrison of the Philistines that was at Geba; and the Philistines heard of it. And Saul blew the trumpet throughout all the land, saying, "Let the Hebrews hear!" ⁴ When all Israel heard that Saul had defeated the garrison of the Philistines, and also that Israel had become odious to the Philistines, the people were called out to join Saul at Gilgal.

5 The Philistines mustered to fight with Israel, thirty thousand chariots, and six thousand horsemen, and troops like the sand on the seashore in multitude; they came up and encamped at Michmash, to the east of Beth-aven. ⁶ When the Israelites saw that they were in distress (for the troops were hard pressed), the people hid themselves in caves and in holes and in rocks and in tombs and in cisterns. ⁷ Some Hebrews crossed the Jordan to the land of Gad and Gilead. Saul was still at Gilgal, and all the people followed him trembling.

8 He waited seven days, the time appointed by Samuel; but Samuel did not come to Gilgal, and the people began to slip away from Saul.ᶜ ⁹ So Saul said, "Bring the burnt offering here to me, and the offerings of well-being." And he offered the burnt offering. ¹⁰ As soon as he had finished offering the burnt offering, Samuel arrived; and Saul went out to meet him and salute him. ¹¹ Samuel said, "What have you done?" Saul replied, "When I saw that the people were slipping away from me, and that you did not come within the days appointed, and that the Philistines were mustering at Michmash, ¹² I said, 'Now

---

ª The number is lacking in the Heb text (the verse is lacking in the Septuagint).   ᵇ *Two* is not the entire number; something has dropped out.   ᶜ Heb *him*

---

way in his office to the new reality of kingship, he does not just abandon his ties to the people, or even to the new king of whom he does not entirely approve. He vows to be active in prayer and instruction. Such a model for transitions in leadership would serve well in any generation.

12:25—This final dire warning may reflect a perspective of the historian responsible for the work from Joshua through 2 Kings. He may already know that Israel and its king have been tragically *swept away* in Babylonian exile.

13:1–15 Samuel's First Rejection of Saul

This is the first of two stories in which Samuel rejects Saul. Saul's offense is that he took upon himself the authority to offer the sacrifices before battle that would normally be offered by a prophet or priest. Samuel appears just after Saul has done this and harshly pronounces judgment on Saul's legitimacy as king, particularly rejecting the notion that a dynasty might come from Saul's own family. In Samuel's reference to God's choosing *a man after [God's] own heart*

we see a foreshadowing of David, who will replace Saul as God's anointed king. Many feel Saul's offense is too trivial to justify such a harsh rejection by Samuel. At issue here are the arenas of power and authority in a time of transition. Many of these issues are still with us. Should the governing authority take on the right to exercise and control religious rituals and practices? Historically Americans have felt government and church were best maintained as separate arenas of authority and responsibility, but this is not the accepted practice in many parts of the world. Readers often have a hard time deciding who is in the right here. Samuel seems harsh; Saul seems naive. Yet the issues here are important ones for the future of Israel. In the harsh realities of history, important choices are often made in complex situations by real persons with all their flaws. Saul chooses his own immediate need over the honoring of legitimate religious authority and practice. This is the beginning of a tragedy for Saul, but God is still at work bringing a new future for God's people.

the Philistines will come down upon me at Gilgal, and I have not entreated the favor of the LORD'; so I forced myself, and offered the burnt offering." [13] Samuel said to Saul, "You have done foolishly; you have not kept the commandment of the LORD your God, which he commanded you. The LORD would have established your kingdom over Israel forever, [14] but now your kingdom will not continue; the LORD has sought out a man after his own heart; and the LORD has appointed him to be ruler over his people, because you have not kept what the LORD commanded you." [15] And Samuel left and went on his way from Gilgal.[a] The rest of the people followed Saul to join the army; they went up from Gilgal toward Gibeah of Benjamin.[b]

Preparations for Battle

Saul counted the people who were present with him, about six hundred men. [16] Saul, his son Jonathan, and the people who were present with them stayed in Geba of Benjamin; but the Philistines encamped at Michmash. [17] And raiders came out of the camp of the Philistines in three companies; one company turned toward Ophrah, to the land of Shual, [18] another company turned toward Beth-horon, and another company turned toward the mountain[c] that looks down upon the valley of Zeboim toward the wilderness.

[19] Now there was no smith to be found throughout all the land of Israel;

for the Philistines said, "The Hebrews must not make swords or spears for themselves"; [20] so all the Israelites went down to the Philistines to sharpen their plowshares, mattocks, axes, or sickles;[d] [21] The charge was two-thirds of a shekel[e] for the plowshares and for the mattocks, and one-third of a shekel for sharpening the axes and for setting the goads.[f] [22] So on the day of the battle neither sword nor spear was to be found in the possession of any of the people with Saul and Jonathan; but Saul and his son Jonathan had them.

Jonathan Surprises and Routs the Philistines

[23] Now a garrison of the Philistines had gone out to the pass of Michmash.

14 [1] One day Jonathan son of Saul said to the young man who carried his armor, "Come, let us go over to the Philistine garrison on the other side." But he did not tell his father. [2] Saul was staying in the outskirts of Gibeah under the pomegranate tree that is at Migron; the troops that were with him were about six hundred men, [3] along with Ahijah son of Ahitub, Ichabod's brother, son of Phinehas son of Eli, the priest of the LORD in Shiloh, carrying an ephod. Now the people did not know that Jonathan had gone. [4] In the pass,[g] by which Jonathan tried to go over to the Philis-

[a] Gk: Heb *went up from Gilgal to Gibeah of Benjamin* [b] Gk: Heb lacks *The rest . . . of Benjamin* [c] Cn Compare Gk: Heb *toward the border* [d] Gk: Heb *plowshare* [e] Heb *was a pim* [f] Cn: Meaning of Heb uncertain [g] Heb *Between the passes*

13:19–22 Philistine Threat
This brief notice makes clear the extensive and serious nature of Philistine occupation of Israel. They control territory, weapons, and strategic routes. The odds against Israel's survival are great.

14:1–52 Jonathan
This episode presents a great contrast between father and son—Saul and Jonathan. On the surface the story is about military action and heroic deeds. Below the surface is a tale of contrasting styles of leadership and the role of true piety in leadership. Jonathan seems pragmatic, efficient, and bold as a military leader. Yet he takes action trusting that *it may be that the LORD will act*. It

is God who can save *by many or by few*. When he is successful he gives God credit for the victory. Piety is not a substitute for action but is a recognition of God's power beyond our actions. By contrast, Saul is hesitant and uncertain about taking action. He wants assurances from God before he begins and surrounds himself with priest and ephod. He swears a rash oath seeking divine favor, but the oath actually weakens his troops and ultimately threatens his son's life. In the end, it is Jonathan who understands that piety is no substitute for wisdom, discernment, and responsible action. Nor can it guarantee an outcome. True piety arises out of trust, not ritual assurance.

tine garrison, there was a rocky crag on one side and a rocky crag on the other; the name of the one was Bozez, and the name of the other Seneh. ⁵ One crag rose on the north in front of Michmash, and the other on the south in front of Geba.

6 Jonathan said to the young man who carried his armor, "Come, let us go over to the garrison of these uncircumcised; it may be that the LORD will act for us; for nothing can hinder the LORD from saving by many or by few." ⁷ His armor-bearer said to him, "Do all that your mind inclines to.ª I am with you; as your mind is, so is mine."ᵇ ⁸ Then Jonathan said, "Now we will cross over to those men and will show ourselves to them. ⁹ If they say to us, 'Wait until we come to you,' then we will stand still in our place, and we will not go up to them. ¹⁰ But if they say, 'Come up to us,' then we will go up; for the LORD has given them into our hand. That will be the sign for us." ¹¹ So both of them showed themselves to the garrison of the Philistines; and the Philistines said, "Look, Hebrews are coming out of the holes where they have hidden themselves." ¹² The men of the garrison hailed Jonathan and his armor-bearer, saying, "Come up to us, and we will show you something." Jonathan said to his armor-bearer, "Come up after me; for the LORD has given them into the hand of Israel." ¹³ Then Jonathan climbed up on his hands and feet, with his armor-bearer following after him. The Philistinesᶜ fell before Jonathan, and his armor-bearer, coming after him, killed them. ¹⁴ In that first slaughter Jonathan and his armor-bearer killed about twenty men within an area about half a furrow long in an acreᵈ of land. ¹⁵ There was a panic in the camp, in the field, and among all the people; the garrison and even the raiders trembled; the earth quaked; and it became a very great panic.

16 Saul's lookouts in Gibeah of Benjamin were watching as the multitude was surging back and forth.ᵉ ¹⁷ Then Saul said to the troops that were with him, "Call the roll and see who has gone from us." When they had called the roll, Jonathan and his armor-bearer were not there. ¹⁸ Saul said to Ahijah, "Bring the arkᶠ of God here." For at that time the arkᶠ of God went with the Israelites. ¹⁹ While Saul was talking to the priest, the tumult in the camp of the Philistines increased more and more; and Saul said to the priest, "Withdraw your hand." ²⁰ Then Saul and all the people who were with him rallied and went into the battle; and every sword was against the other, so that there was very great confusion. ²¹ Now the Hebrews who previously had been with the Philistines and had gone up with them into the camp turned and joined the Israelites who were with Saul and Jonathan. ²² Likewise, when all the Israelites who had gone into hiding in the hill country of Ephraim heard that the Philistines were fleeing, they too followed closely after them in the battle. ²³ So the LORD gave Israel the victory that day.

The battle passed beyond Beth-aven, and the troops with Saul numbered altogether about ten thousand men. The battle spread out over the hill country of Ephraim.

Saul's Rash Oath

24 Now Saul committed a very rash act on that day.ᵍ He had laid an oath on the troops, saying, "Cursed be anyone who eats food before it is evening and I have been avenged on my enemies." So none of the troops tasted food. ²⁵ All the troopsʰ came upon a honeycomb; and there was honey on the ground. ²⁶ When the troops came upon the honeycomb, the honey was dripping out; but they did not put their hands to their mouths, for they feared the oath. ²⁷ But Jonathan had not heard his father charge the troops with the oath; so he extended the staff

ª Gk: Heb *Do all that is in your mind. Turn*   ᵇ Gk: Heb lacks *so is mine*
ᶜ Heb *They*   ᵈ Heb *yoke*   ᵉ Gk: Heb *they went and there*   ᶠ Gk: the ephod
ᵍ Gk: Heb *The Israelites were distressed that day*   ʰ Heb *land*

that was in his hand, and dipped the tip of it in the honeycomb, and put his hand to his mouth; and his eyes brightened. ²⁸ Then one of the soldiers said, "Your father strictly charged the troops with an oath, saying, 'Cursed be anyone who eats food this day.' And so the troops are faint." ²⁹ Then Jonathan said, "My father has troubled the land; see how my eyes have brightened because I tasted a little of this honey. ³⁰ How much better if today the troops had eaten freely of the spoil taken from their enemies; for now the slaughter among the Philistines has not been great."

31 After they had struck down the Philistines that day from Michmash to Aijalon, the troops were very faint; ³² so the troops flew upon the spoil, and took sheep and oxen and calves, and slaughtered them on the ground; and the troops ate them with the blood. ³³ Then it was reported to Saul, "Look, the troops are sinning against the LORD by eating with the blood." And he said, "You have dealt treacherously; roll a large stone before me here."ᵃ ³⁴ Saul said, "Disperse yourselves among the troops, and say to them, 'Let all bring their oxen or their sheep, and slaughter them here, and eat; and do not sin against the LORD by eating with the blood.'" So all of the troops brought their oxen with them that night, and slaughtered them there. ³⁵ And Saul built an altar to the LORD; it was the first altar that he built to the LORD.

Jonathan in Danger of Death

36 Then Saul said, "Let us go down after the Philistines by night and despoil them until the morning light; let us not leave one of them." They said, "Do whatever seems good to you." But the priest said, "Let us draw near to God here." ³⁷ So Saul inquired of God, "Shall I go down after the Philistines? Will you give them into the hand of Israel?" But he did not answer him that day. ³⁸ Saul said, "Come here, all you leaders of the people; and let us find out how this sin has arisen

today. ³⁹ For as the LORD lives who saves Israel, even if it is in my son Jonathan, he shall surely die!" But there was no one among all the people who answered him. ⁴⁰ He said to all Israel, "You shall be on one side, and I and my son Jonathan will be on the other side." The people said to Saul, "Do what seems good to you." ⁴¹ Then Saul said, "O LORD God of Israel, why have you not answered your servant today? If this guilt is in me or in my son Jonathan, O LORD God of Israel, give Urim; but if this guilt is in your people Israel,ᵇ give Thummim." And Jonathan and Saul were indicated by the lot, but the people were cleared. ⁴² Then Saul said, "Cast the lot between me and my son Jonathan." And Jonathan was taken.

43 Then Saul said to Jonathan, "Tell me what you have done." Jonathan told him, "I tasted a little honey with the tip of the staff that was in my hand; here I am, I will die." ⁴⁴ Saul said, "God do so to me and more also; you shall surely die, Jonathan!" ⁴⁵ Then the people said to Saul, "Shall Jonathan die, who has accomplished this great victory in Israel? Far from it! As the LORD lives, not one hair of his head shall fall to the ground; for he has worked with God today." So the people ransomed Jonathan, and he did not die. ⁴⁶ Then Saul withdrew from pursuing the Philistines; and the Philistines went to their own place.

Saul's Continuing Wars

47 When Saul had taken the kingship over Israel, he fought against all his enemies on every side—against Moab, against the Ammonites, against Edom, against the kings of Zobah, and against the Philistines; wherever he turned he routed them. ⁴⁸ He did valiantly, and struck down the Amalekites, and rescued Israel out of the hands of those who plundered them.

49 Now the sons of Saul were Jonathan, Ishvi, and Malchishua; and the

---

ᵃ Gk: Heb *me this day*   ᵇ Vg Compare Gk: Heb ⁴¹*Saul said to the* LORD, *the God of Israel*

names of his two daughters were these: the name of the firstborn was Merab, and the name of the younger, Michal. **50** The name of Saul's wife was Ahinoam daughter of Ahimaaz. And the name of the commander of his army was Abner son of Ner, Saul's uncle; **51** Kish was the father of Saul, and Ner the father of Abner was the son of Abiel.

52 There was hard fighting against the Philistines all the days of Saul; and when Saul saw any strong or valiant warrior, he took him into his service.

Saul Defeats the Amalekites but Spares Their King

15 Samuel said to Saul, "The LORD sent me to anoint you king over his people Israel; now therefore listen to the words of the LORD. **2** Thus says the LORD of hosts, 'I will punish the Amalekites for what they did in opposing the Israelites when they came up out of Egypt. **3** Now go and attack Amalek, and utterly destroy all that they have; do not spare them, but kill both man and woman, child and infant, ox and sheep, camel and donkey.'"

4 So Saul summoned the people, and numbered them in Telaim, two hundred thousand foot soldiers, and ten thousand soldiers of Judah. **5** Saul came to the city of the Amalekites and lay in wait in the valley. **6** Saul said to the Kenites, "Go! Leave! Withdraw from among the Amalekites, or I will destroy you with them; for you showed kindness to all the people of Israel when they came up out of Egypt." So the Kenites withdrew from the Amalekites. **7** Saul defeated

the Amalekites, from Havilah as far as Shur, which is east of Egypt. **8** He took King Agag of the Amalekites alive, but utterly destroyed all the people with the edge of the sword. **9** Saul and the people spared Agag, and the best of the sheep and of the cattle and of the fatlings, and the lambs, and all that was valuable, and would not utterly destroy them; all that was despised and worthless they utterly destroyed.

Saul Rejected as King

10 The word of the LORD came to Samuel: **11** "I regret that I made Saul king, for he has turned back from following me, and has not carried out my commands." Samuel was angry; and he cried out to the LORD all night. **12** Samuel rose early in the morning to meet Saul, and Samuel was told, "Saul went to Carmel, where he set up a monument for himself, and on returning he passed on down to Gilgal." **13** When Samuel came to Saul, Saul said to him, "May you be blessed by the LORD; I have carried out the command of the LORD." **14** But Samuel said, "What then is this bleating of sheep in my ears, and the lowing of cattle that I hear?" **15** Saul said, "They have brought them from the Amalekites; for the people spared the best of the sheep and the cattle, to sacrifice to the LORD your God; but the rest we have utterly destroyed." **16** Then Samuel said to Saul, "Stop! I will tell you what the LORD said to me last night." He replied, "Speak."

17 Samuel said, "Though you are little in your own eyes, are you not the head of the tribes of Israel? The LORD anointed

---

15:1–35 Samuel's Second Rejection of Saul

15:1–24—This is a turning point in the story because it makes clear that the future of Israel cannot lie with Saul or his household. The story is building up to God's choice of David as the *man after [God's] own heart* (13:14). Saul is rejected for disobeying the word of the Lord as given to him by Samuel, the prophet. Modern readers find this story difficult, because Saul is commanded to submit the Amalekites to the holy war ban and destroy all the people and plunder taken in this

military campaign. We find this policy repugnant, although in ancient times it was no doubt intended to limit the use of war for gain. People are treated like property to be disposed of. Saul preserves the king of the Amalekites to parade for his own glory, and keeps choice goods from the campaign for his own use. He does not refuse the holy war command on principle. We cannot approve the holy war policy; however, we can as how often we, like Saul, alter God's comman for our own purposes.

you king over Israel. [18] And the LORD sent you on a mission, and said, 'Go, utterly destroy the sinners, the Amalekites, and fight against them until they are consumed.' [19] Why then did you not obey the voice of the LORD? Why did you swoop down on the spoil, and do what was evil in the sight of the LORD?" [20] Saul said to Samuel, "I have obeyed the voice of the LORD, I have gone on the mission on which the LORD sent me, I have brought Agag the king of Amalek, and I have utterly destroyed the Amalekites. [21] But from the spoil the people took sheep and cattle, the best of the things devoted to destruction, to sacrifice to the LORD your God in Gilgal." [22] And Samuel said,

"Has the LORD as great delight in
       burnt offerings and
       sacrifices,
   as in obedience to the voice of the
       LORD?
Surely, to obey is better than
       sacrifice,
   and to heed than the fat of rams.
[23]   For rebellion is no less a sin than
       divination,
   and stubbornness is like iniquity
       and idolatry.
Because you have rejected the word
       of the LORD,
   he has also rejected you from
       being king."

[24] Saul said to Samuel, "I have sinned; for I have transgressed the commandment of the LORD and your words, because I feared the people and obeyed their voice. [25] Now therefore, I pray, pardon my sin, and return with me, so that I may worship the LORD." [26] Samuel said to Saul, "I will not return with you; for you have rejected the word of the LORD, and the LORD has rejected you from being king over Israel." [27] As Samuel turned to go away, Saul caught hold of the hem of his robe, and it tore. [28] And Samuel said to him, "The LORD has torn the kingdom of Israel from you this very day, and has given it to a neighbor of yours, who is better than you. [29] Moreover the Glory of Israel will not recant[a] or change his mind; for he is not a mortal, that he should change his mind." [30] Then Saul[b] said, "I have sinned; yet honor me now before the elders of my people and before Israel, and return with me, so that I may worship the LORD your God." [31] So Samuel turned back after Saul; and Saul worshiped the LORD.

[32] Then Samuel said, "Bring Agag king of the Amalekites here to me." And Agag came to him haltingly.[c] Agag said, "Surely this is the bitterness of death."[d] [33] But Samuel said,

"As your sword has made women
       childless,
   so your mother shall be childless
       among women."

And Samuel hewed Agag in pieces before the LORD in Gilgal.

[34] Then Samuel went to Ramah; and Saul went up to his house in Gibeah of Saul. [35] Samuel did not see Saul again until the day of his death, but Samuel grieved over Saul. And the LORD was sorry that he had made Saul king over Israel.

[a] Q Ms Gk: MT *deceive*   [b] Heb *he*   [c] Cn Compare Gk: Meaning of Heb uncertain   [d] Q Ms Gk: MT *Surely the bitterness of death is past*

15:24–35—Saul is often regarded as a tragic figure because the harshness of Samuel's judgment seems out of proportion to Saul's offense. It is well to remember that this final rejection of Saul is based not on one event but on the accumulation of events and decisions reflected in chaps. 13–15. It is becoming clear that Saul cannot be king in Israel's future. Later events confirm this judgment. The scene will shift soon to focus on David. Saul is a tragic figure in many ways, but like most tragic figures he is flawed. He is not inclined to trust in God as the source of his leadership, and he increasingly lets his own self-serving agenda get in the way of Israel's best interests. Samuel seems harsh and is sometimes accused of vested interests—wanting to return to an old order of things. Samuel is required to take harsh action, but the text tells us he grieves greatly over it (v. 35) to the point that God has to command him to stop mourning (16:1). He is not allowed to return to some old order but is sent on to anoint David as king—an even more radical choice than Saul.

David Anointed as King

16 The LORD said to Samuel, "How long will you grieve over Saul? I have rejected him from being king over Israel. Fill your horn with oil and set out; I will send you to Jesse the Bethlehemite, for I have provided for myself a king among his sons." ² Samuel said, "How can I go? If Saul hears of it, he will kill me." And the LORD said, "Take a heifer with you, and say, 'I have come to sacrifice to the LORD.' ³ Invite Jesse to the sacrifice, and I will show you what you shall do; and you shall anoint for me the one whom I name to you." ⁴ Samuel did what the LORD commanded, and came to Bethlehem. The elders of the city came to meet him trembling, and said, "Do you come peaceably?" ⁵ He said, "Peaceably; I have come to sacrifice to the LORD; sanctify yourselves and come with me to the sacrifice." And he sanctified Jesse and his sons and invited them to the sacrifice.

6 When they came, he looked on Eliab and thought, "Surely the LORD's anointed is now before the LORD."*a* ⁷ But the LORD said to Samuel, "Do not look on his appearance or on the height of his stature, because I have rejected him; for the LORD does not see as mortals see; they look on the outward appearance, but the LORD looks on the heart." ⁸ Then Jesse called Abinadab, and made him pass before Samuel. He said, "Neither has the LORD chosen this one." ⁹ Then Jesse made Shammah pass by. And he said, "Neither has the LORD chosen this one." ¹⁰ Jesse made seven of his sons pass before Samuel, and Samuel said to Jesse, "The LORD has not chosen any of these." ¹¹ Samuel said to Jesse, "Are all your sons here?" And he said, "There remains yet the youngest, but he is keeping the sheep." And Samuel said to Jesse, "Send and bring him; for we will not sit down until he comes here." ¹² He sent and brought him in. Now he was ruddy, and had beautiful eyes, and was handsome. The LORD said, "Rise and anoint him; for this is the one." ¹³ Then Samuel took the horn of oil, and anointed him in the presence of his brothers; and the spirit of the LORD came mightily upon David from that day forward. Samuel then set out and went to Ramah.

David Plays the Lyre for Saul

14 Now the spirit of the LORD departed from Saul, and an evil spirit from the

a Heb *him*

16:1–2 Sam. 5:10 The Rise of David

The focus of the books of Samuel now shifts to David. Saul is still a part of the story until his death at the end of 1 Samuel, but only as the failed contrast to the rise of David. Many scholars see a connected history of the rise of David beginning with 1 Sam. 16 and concluding with 2 Sam. 5:10. The overall theme of this material is that God is with David, while David in return is a man of great gifts for leadership but also of piety and prayer in recognition of God.

16:1–13 Samuel Anoints David

16:7—Samuel has been sent by God to the house of Jesse in Bethlehem to choose and anoint a new king in place of Saul. When Jesse presents his oldest and most promising son, even Samuel thinks this must be the one, but the Lord reveals to Samuel that the Lord has a different standard for those called. God looks on the heart, not the outward appearance—a sobering reminder to those who have responsibilities for choosing leadership in the church.

16:11–13—Seven of Jesse's sons are presented but are not chosen. The eighth, David, is considered so young and so unlikely that he is still out tending the sheep. Yet, when he is brought before Samuel, the Lord says *he* is the one. When he is anointed, the spirit of God comes upon him as it had upon Saul (chap. 10). This choosing of the eighth son becomes another example of God's ability to use those who seem unlikely by common human standards.

16:14–23 David at Saul's Court

David is introduced into the court of Saul as a musician whose music can soothe Saul when he is tormented by an evil spirit from the Lord. In biblical times, all things were thought to come from God, so we should not be surprised that Saul's turbulent moods are also considered a part of God's plan. Saul appears increasingly unbalanced and dangerous to those around him. David is introduced as a musician, but also as one with many other gifts, including the presence of God with him (v. 18). We are told that Saul loved

LORD tormented him. [15] And Saul's servants said to him, "See now, an evil spirit from God is tormenting you. [16] Let our lord now command the servants who attend you to look for someone who is skillful in playing the lyre; and when the evil spirit from God is upon you, he will play it, and you will feel better." [17] So Saul said to his servants, "Provide for me someone who can play well, and bring him to me." [18] One of the young men answered, "I have seen a son of Jesse the Bethlehemite who is skillful in playing, a man of valor, a warrior, prudent in speech, and a man of good presence; and the LORD is with him." [19] So Saul sent messengers to Jesse, and said, "Send me your son David who is with the sheep." [20] Jesse took a donkey loaded with bread, a skin of wine, and a kid, and sent them by his son David to Saul. [21] And David came to Saul, and entered his service. Saul loved him greatly, and he became his armor-bearer. [22] Saul sent to Jesse, saying, "Let David remain in my service, for he has found favor in my sight." [23] And whenever the evil spirit from God came upon Saul, David took the lyre and played it with his hand, and Saul would be relieved and feel better, and the evil spirit would depart from him.

David and Goliath

17 Now the Philistines gathered their armies for battle; they were gathered at Socoh, which belongs to Judah, and encamped between Socoh and Azekah, in Ephes-dammim. [2] Saul and the Israelites gathered and encamped in the valley of Elah, and formed ranks against the Philistines. [3] The Philistines stood on the mountain on the one side, and Israel stood on the mountain on the other side, with a valley between them. [4] And there came out from the camp of the Philistines a champion named Goliath, of Gath, whose height was six[a] cubits and a span. [5] He had a helmet of bronze on his head, and he was armed with a coat of mail; the weight of the coat was five thousand shekels of bronze. [6] He had greaves of bronze on his legs and a javelin of bronze slung between his shoulders. [7] The shaft of his spear was like a weaver's beam, and his spear's head weighed six hundred shekels of iron; and his shield-bearer went before him. [8] He stood and shouted to the ranks of Israel, "Why have you come out to draw up for battle? Am I not a Philistine, and are you not servants of Saul? Choose a man for yourselves, and let him come down to me. [9] If he is able to fight with me and kill me, then we will be your servants; but if I prevail against him and kill him, then you shall be our servants and serve us." [10] And the Philistine said, "Today I defy the ranks of Israel! Give me a man, that we may fight together." [11] When Saul and all Israel heard these words of the Philistine, they were dismayed and greatly afraid.

12 Now David was the son of an Eph-

[a] MT: Q Ms Gk *four*

(v. 21), but Saul does not prove capable of maintaining such love, even toward his own children.

17:1–58 David and Goliath
Surely the story of David's conquest of Goliath is the best known of David's stories and from very early times defined David in the tradition, as seen in Sir. 47:4–5 in the hymn in praise of famous men. Some have raised historical questions about this episode, since 2 Sam. 21:19 reports that Elhanan of Bethlehem killed Goliath. Nevertheless, David's deed in 1 Sam. 17 establishes David's bravery even as a young man and provides a second introduction into Saul's court, since this chapter does not seem to know the tradition of David as Saul's musician and armor-bearer.

17:1–11—The description of Goliath serves well as representative of all-powerful and oppressive forces that appear impossible to overcome. This is a story revered by the weak, the powerless, and the oppressed who despair at the overwhelming and evil forces that seem undefeatable before them.

17:12–40—The courage of David, a mere boy, in standing up to the Philistine champion appeals to our love of the underdog, but this story is much deeper than this impulse. David, brought before Saul, volunteers to face Goliath because

rathite of Bethlehem in Judah, named Jesse, who had eight sons. In the days of Saul the man was already old and advanced in years.[a] 13 The three eldest sons of Jesse had followed Saul to the battle; the names of his three sons who went to the battle were Eliab the first-born, and next to him Abinadab, and the third Shammah. 14 David was the youngest; the three eldest followed Saul, 15 but David went back and forth from Saul to feed his father's sheep at Bethlehem. 16 For forty days the Philistine came forward and took his stand, morning and evening.

17 Jesse said to his son David, "Take for your brothers an ephah of this parched grain and these ten loaves, and carry them quickly to the camp to your brothers; 18 also take these ten cheeses to the commander of their thousand. See how your brothers fare, and bring some token from them."

19 Now Saul, and they, and all the men of Israel, were in the valley of Elah, fighting with the Philistines. 20 David rose early in the morning, left the sheep with a keeper, took the provisions, and went as Jesse had commanded him. He came to the encampment as the army was going forth to the battle line, shouting the war cry. 21 Israel and the Philistines drew up for battle, army against army. 22 David left the things in charge of the keeper of the baggage, ran to the ranks, and went and greeted his brothers. 23 As he talked with them, the champion, the Philistine of Gath, Goliath by name, came up out of the ranks of the Philistines, and spoke the same words as before. And David heard him.

24 All the Israelites, when they saw the man, fled from him and were very much afraid. 25 The Israelites said, "Have you seen this man who has come up? Surely

he has come up to defy Israel. The king will greatly enrich the man who kills him, and will give him his daughter and make his family free in Israel." 26 David said to the men who stood by him, "What shall be done for the man who kills this Philistine, and takes away the reproach from Israel? For who is this uncircumcised Philistine that he should defy the armies of the living God?" 27 The people answered him in the same way, "So shall it be done for the man who kills him."

28 His eldest brother Eliab heard him talking to the men; and Eliab's anger was kindled against David. He said, "Why have you come down? With whom have you left those few sheep in the wilderness? I know your presumption and the evil of your heart; for you have come down just to see the battle." 29 David said, "What have I done now? It was only a question." 30 He turned away from him toward another and spoke in the same way; and the people answered him again as before.

31 When the words that David spoke were heard, they repeated them before Saul; and he sent for him. 32 David said to Saul, "Let no one's heart fail because of him; your servant will go and fight with this Philistine." 33 Saul said to David, "You are not able to go against this Philistine to fight with him; for you are just a boy, and he has been a warrior from his youth." 34 But David said to Saul, "Your servant used to keep sheep for his father; and whenever a lion or a bear came, and took a lamb from the flock, 35 I went after it and struck it down, rescuing the lamb from its mouth; and if it turned against me, I would catch it by the jaw, strike it down, and kill it. 36 Your servant has killed both lions and bears; and this uncircumcised Philistine shall

[a] Gk Syr: Heb among men

of his confidence that the Lord is with him. David expresses the confidence that in the power of the Lord evil power can be faced, but it cannot be faced on its own terms. Saul tries to dress David in his own battle armor, but David cannot go

onto the field as a second-rate representative of the power of kingdoms. It is only trust in God that imagines a well-placed stone can defeat th armored power of kingdoms.

be like one of them, since he has defied the armies of the living God." ³⁷ David said, "The LORD, who saved me from the paw of the lion and from the paw of the bear, will save me from the hand of this Philistine." So Saul said to David, "Go, and may the LORD be with you!"

38 Saul clothed David with his armor; he put a bronze helmet on his head and clothed him with a coat of mail. ³⁹ David strapped Saul's sword over the armor, and he tried in vain to walk, for he was not used to them. Then David said to Saul, "I cannot walk with these; for I am not used to them." So David removed them. ⁴⁰ Then he took his staff in his hand, and chose five smooth stones from the wadi, and put them in his shepherd's bag, in the pouch; his sling was in his hand, and he drew near to the Philistine.

41 The Philistine came on and drew near to David, with his shield-bearer in front of him. ⁴² When the Philistine looked and saw David, he disdained him, for he was only a youth, ruddy and handsome in appearance. ⁴³ The Philistine said to David, "Am I a dog, that you come to me with sticks?" And the Philistine cursed David by his gods. ⁴⁴ The Philistine said to David, "Come to me, and I will give your flesh to the birds of the air and to the wild animals of the field." ⁴⁵ But David said to the Philistine, "You come to me with sword and spear and javelin; but I come to you in the name of the LORD of hosts, the God of the armies of Israel, whom you have defied. ⁴⁶ This very day the LORD will deliver you into my hand, and I will strike you down and cut off your head; and I will give the dead bodies of the Philistine army this very day to the birds of the air and to the wild animals of the earth, so that all the earth may know that there is a God in Israel, ⁴⁷ and that all this assembly may know that the LORD does not save by sword and spear; for the battle is the LORD's and he will give you into our hand."

48 When the Philistine drew nearer to meet David, David ran quickly toward the battle line to meet the Philistine. ⁴⁹ David put his hand in his bag, took out a stone, slung it, and struck the Philistine on his forehead; the stone sank into his forehead, and he fell face down on the ground.

50 So David prevailed over the Philistine with a sling and a stone, striking down the Philistine and killing him; there was no sword in David's hand. ⁵¹ Then David ran and stood over the Philistine; he grasped his sword, drew it out of its sheath, and killed him; then he cut off his head with it.

When the Philistines saw that their champion was dead, they fled. ⁵² The troops of Israel and Judah rose up with a shout and pursued the Philistines as far as Gathᵃ and the gates of Ekron, so that the wounded Philistines fell on the way from Shaaraim as far as Gath and Ekron. ⁵³ The Israelites came back from chasing the Philistines, and they plundered their camp. ⁵⁴ David took the head of the Philistine and brought it to Jerusalem; but he put his armor in his tent.

ᵃ Gk Syr: Heb Gai

17:41–58—David meets the armor of the Philistine with trust *in the name of the LORD of hosts* (v. 45) and a declaration *that the LORD does not save by sword and spear* (v. 47). An accurately thrown stone brings down the giant champion, and Israel wins an improbable victory on that day. David stands bravely in opposition to oppressive power, not because he can match its power, but because he trusts God can find a way into the future, using the improbable resources of the weak but faithful who dare to stand with God in opposition to evil and oppression. This is a story that urges us to trustful and imaginative use of the resources we have, with the confidence that God can with them bring down giant structures of oppression, violence, and injustice. Note that David speaks boldly as well as acts with courage. It is often in the courageous naming of God's power that we find our own unlikely power in facing the powers of violence, injustice, and corrupting influence in our own time. By God's grace a well-placed stone can bring down seemingly undefeatable systems of power in surprising ways. The end of Soviet and apartheid systems with astonishing suddenness in our lifetimes suggests that Goliaths can still fall.

55 When Saul saw David go out against the Philistine, he said to Abner, the commander of the army, "Abner, whose son is this young man?" Abner said, "As your soul lives, O king, I do not know." ⁵⁶ The king said, "Inquire whose son the stripling is." ⁵⁷ On David's return from killing the Philistine, Abner took him and brought him before Saul, with the head of the Philistine in his hand. ⁵⁸ Saul said to him, "Whose son are you, young man?" And David answered, "I am the son of your servant Jesse the Bethlehemite."

Jonathan's Covenant with David

18 When David*ᵃ* had finished speaking to Saul, the soul of Jonathan was bound to the soul of David, and Jonathan loved him as his own soul. ² Saul took him that day and would not let him return to his father's house. ³ Then Jonathan made a covenant with David, because he loved him as his own soul. ⁴ Jonathan stripped himself of the robe that he was wearing, and gave it to David, and his armor, and even his sword and his bow and his belt. ⁵ David went out and was successful wherever Saul sent him; as a result, Saul set him over the army. And all the people, even the servants of Saul, approved.

6 As they were coming home, when David returned from killing the Philistine, the women came out of all the towns of Israel, singing and dancing, to meet King Saul, with tambourines, with songs of joy, and with musical instruments.*ᵇ* ⁷ And the women sang to one another as they made merry,

"Saul has killed his thousands,
  and David his ten thousands."
⁸ Saul was very angry, for this saying displeased him. He said, "They have ascribed to David ten thousands, and to me they have ascribed thousands; what more can he have but the kingdom?" ⁹ So Saul eyed David from that day on.

Saul Tries to Kill David

10 The next day an evil spirit from God rushed upon Saul, and he raved within his house, while David was playing the lyre, as he did day by day. Saul had his spear in his hand; ¹¹ and Saul threw the spear, for he thought, "I will pin David to the wall." But David eluded him twice.

12 Saul was afraid of David, because the LORD was with him but had departed from Saul. ¹³ So Saul removed him from his presence, and made him a commander of a thousand; and David

ᵃ Heb he   *ᵇ* Or triangles, or three-stringed instruments

18:1–30 David's Success and Saul's Jealousy

David seems to have inspired the love of others. Six times we are told in this chapter of those who loved David (Saul's children, Jonathan, vv. 1, 3; Michal, vv. 22, 28; Saul's servants, v. 22; and all of Israel and Judah, v. 16). David becomes the friend of Jonathan (see chap. 20), he marries Michal, and he serves the people and his king by becoming a successful warrior against the Philistines. We were told in 16:21 that Saul loved David too, but his love is eclipsed by new and darker emotions that will be his undoing.

18:6–11—When the people praise David, Saul responds in anger (v. 8), jealousy (*Saul eyed David*, v. 9), and fear (vv. 12, 29). Saul has other options; his own children love David. David could be a beloved son-in-law, a trusted warrior, Saul's right hand, but Saul responds with violence and even tries to kill David. No wonder he is described as plagued by an evil spirit (v. 10). He

throws his spear at David (v. 11) and then plots to have David killed in battle.

18:12–30—Using his own daughters, Merab and Michal, as bait, Saul conspires to send David into battle to win marriage, thinking that David will be killed. Merab is married to another (v. 19) but Michal herself loves David (vv. 20, 28), and Saul sets a bride price in Philistine foreskins. But David meets the price and becomes part of Saul's family (v. 27). The ominous concluding comment of the story is that *Saul was David's enemy from that time forward* (v. 29). This chapter is tragic, because it is filled with success against Israel's enemies, love for David, David's loyalty to Saul, and yet Saul chooses the path of anger, jealousy, and fear. One would fear for David's future, but this chapter also tells us three times that *the LORD was with him* (vv. 12, 14, 28), and the final time Saul realized it as well. Tragically Saul will choose in the chapters ahead to oppose divine providence.

marched out and came in, leading the army. ¹⁴ David had success in all his undertakings; for the LORD was with him. ¹⁵ When Saul saw that he had great success, he stood in awe of him. ¹⁶ But all Israel and Judah loved David; for it was he who marched out and came in leading them.

David Marries Michal

17 Then Saul said to David, "Here is my elder daughter Merab; I will give her to you as a wife; only be valiant for me and fight the LORD's battles." For Saul thought, "I will not raise a hand against him; let the Philistines deal with him." ¹⁸ David said to Saul, "Who am I and who are my kinsfolk, my father's family in Israel, that I should be son-in-law to the king?" ¹⁹ But at the time when Saul's daughter Merab should have been given to David, she was given to Adriel the Meholathite as a wife.

20 Now Saul's daughter Michal loved David. Saul was told, and the thing pleased him. ²¹ Saul thought, "Let me give her to him that she may be a snare for him and that the hand of the Philistines may be against him." Therefore Saul said to David a second time,ᵃ "You shall now be my son-in-law." ²² Saul commanded his servants, "Speak to David in private and say, 'See, the king is delighted with you, and all his servants love you; now then, become the king's son-in-law.'" ²³ So Saul's servants reported these words to David in private. And David said, "Does it seem to you a little thing to become the king's son-in-law, seeing that I am a poor man and of no repute?" ²⁴ The servants of Saul told him, "This is what David said." ²⁵ Then Saul said, "Thus shall you say to David, 'The king desires no marriage present except a hundred foreskins of the Philistines,

that he may be avenged on the king's enemies.'" Now Saul planned to make David fall by the hand of the Philistines. ²⁶ When his servants told David these words, David was well pleased to be the king's son-in-law. Before the time had expired, ²⁷ David rose and went, along with his men, and killed one hundredᵇ of the Philistines; and David brought their foreskins, which were given in full number to the king, that he might become the king's son-in-law. Saul gave him his daughter Michal as a wife. ²⁸ But when Saul realized that the LORD was with David, and that Saul's daughter Michal loved him, ²⁹ Saul was still more afraid of David. So Saul was David's enemy from that time forward.

30 Then the commanders of the Philistines came out to battle; and as often as they came out, David had more success than all the servants of Saul, so that his fame became very great.

Jonathan Intercedes for David

19 Saul spoke with his son Jonathan and with all his servants about killing David. But Saul's son Jonathan took great delight in David. ² Jonathan told David, "My father Saul is trying to kill you; therefore be on guard tomorrow morning; stay in a secret place and hide yourself. ³ I will go out and stand beside my father in the field where you are, and I will speak to my father about you; if I learn anything I will tell you." ⁴ Jonathan spoke well of David to his father Saul, saying to him, "The king should not sin against his servant David, because he has not sinned against you, and because his deeds have been of good service to you; ⁵ for he took his life in his hand when he attacked the Philistine, and the

ᵃ Heb by two ᵇ Gk Compare 2 Sam 3.14: Heb two hundred

19:1–17 Saul's Attempt to Kill David

This chapter is the sad picture of Saul becoming obsessed with his desire to kill David, while his real tasks of governing Israel and fighting the Philistines go neglected. At first Jonathan intercedes for David and seems successful (vv. 2–7),

but soon David's success as a warrior leads to Saul's attack on David with his spear in one of his tormented moods (vv. 8–10). Michal helps David escape in the night and incurs the wrath of her father (vv. 11–17).

LORD brought about a great victory for all Israel. You saw it, and rejoiced; why then will you sin against an innocent person by killing David without cause?" ⁶ Saul heeded the voice of Jonathan; Saul swore, "As the LORD lives, he shall not be put to death." ⁷ So Jonathan called David and related all these things to him. Jonathan then brought David to Saul, and he was in his presence as before.

Michal Helps David Escape from Saul

8 Again there was war, and David went out to fight the Philistines. He launched a heavy attack on them, so that they fled before him. ⁹ Then an evil spirit from the LORD came upon Saul, as he sat in his house with his spear in his hand, while David was playing music. ¹⁰ Saul sought to pin David to the wall with the spear; but he eluded Saul, so that he struck the spear into the wall. David fled and escaped that night.

11 Saul sent messengers to David's house to keep watch over him, planning to kill him in the morning. David's wife Michal told him, "If you do not save your life tonight, tomorrow you will be killed." ¹² So Michal let David down through the window; he fled away and escaped. ¹³ Michal took an idol*a* and laid it on the bed; she put a net*b* of goats' hair on its head, and covered it with the clothes. ¹⁴ When Saul sent messengers to take David, she said, "He is sick." ¹⁵ Then Saul sent the messengers to see David for themselves. He said, "Bring him up to me in the bed, that I may kill him." ¹⁶ When the messengers came in, the idol*c* was in the bed, with the covering*b* of goats' hair on its head. ¹⁷ Saul said to Michal, "Why have you deceived me

like this, and let my enemy go, so that he has escaped?" Michal answered Saul, "He said to me, 'Let me go; why should I kill you?'"

David Joins Samuel in Ramah

18 Now David fled and escaped; he came to Samuel at Ramah, and told him all that Saul had done to him. He and Samuel went and settled at Naioth. ¹⁹ Saul was told, "David is at Naioth in Ramah." ²⁰ Then Saul sent messengers to take David. When they saw the company of the prophets in a frenzy, with Samuel standing in charge of*b* them, the spirit of God came upon the messengers of Saul, and they also fell into a prophetic frenzy. ²¹ When Saul was told, he sent other messengers, and they also fell into a frenzy. Saul sent messengers again the third time, and they also fell into a frenzy. ²² Then he himself went to Ramah. He came to the great well that is in Secu;*d* he asked, "Where are Samuel and David?" And someone said, "They are at Naioth in Ramah." ²³ He went there, toward Naioth in Ramah; and the spirit of God came upon him. As he was going, he fell into a prophetic frenzy, until he came to Naioth in Ramah. ²⁴ He too stripped off his clothes, and he too fell into a frenzy before Samuel. He lay naked all that day and all that night. Therefore it is said, "Is Saul also among the prophets?"

The Friendship of David and Jonathan

20 David fled from Naioth in Ramah. He came before Jonathan and said, "What have I done? What is

---

a Heb took the teraphim *b* Meaning of Heb uncertain *c* Heb the teraphim *d* Gk reads to the well of the threshing floor on the bare height

---

19:18–24 David Takes Refuge
David takes refuge with the prophet Samuel at Ramah (v. 18). When Saul sends messengers for David, they find Samuel leading a group of prophets; the messengers are seized by God's spirit and prophesy with them. When Saul comes himself, he too is seized by the spirit and is caught up in a prophetic state of possession, a repeat of the experience after Samuel had anointed

him (10:10–13). This time it is ironic when the people ask, *"Is Saul also among the prophets?"* (19:24). The spirit that empowered him in the beginning now prevents him from killing David, God's anointed in place of Saul.

20:1–42 The Friendship of David and Jonathan

20:1–11—This is one of the great stories of friendship, not only in the Bible, but in all literature. We have already seen that Jonathan loved David

my guilt? And what is my sin against your father that he is trying to take my life?" ²He said to him, "Far from it! You shall not die. My father does nothing either great or small without disclosing it to me; and why should my father hide this from me? Never!" ³But David also swore, "Your father knows well that you like me; and he thinks, 'Do not let Jonathan know this, or he will be grieved.' But truly, as the LORD lives and as you yourself live, there is but a step between me and death." ⁴Then Jonathan said to David, "Whatever you say, I will do for you." ⁵David said to Jonathan, "Tomorrow is the new moon, and I should not fail to sit with the king at the meal; but let me go, so that I may hide in the field until the third evening. ⁶If your father misses me at all, then say, 'David earnestly asked leave of me to run to Bethlehem his city; for there is a yearly sacrifice there for all the family.' ⁷If he says, 'Good!' it will be well with your servant; but if he is angry, then know that evil has been determined by him. ⁸Therefore deal kindly with your servant, for you have brought your servant into a sacred covenant*a* with you. But if there is guilt in me, kill me yourself; why should you bring me to your father?" ⁹Jonathan said, "Far be it from you! If I knew that it was decided by my father that evil should come upon you, would I not tell you?" ¹⁰Then David said to Jonathan, "Who will tell me if your father answers you harshly?" ¹¹Jonathan replied to David, "Come, let us go out into the field." So they both went out into the field.

12 Jonathan said to David, "By the LORD, the God of Israel! When I have sounded out my father, about this time tomorrow, or on the third day, if he is well disposed toward David, shall I not then send and disclose it to you? ¹³But if my father intends to do you harm, the LORD do so to Jonathan, and more also, if I do not disclose it to you, and send you away, so that you may go in safety. May the LORD be with you, as he has been with my father. ¹⁴If I am still alive, show me the faithful love of the LORD; but if I die,*b* ¹⁵never cut off your faithful love from my house, even if the LORD were to cut off every one of the enemies of David from the face of the earth." ¹⁶Thus Jonathan made a covenant with the house of David, saying, "May the LORD seek out the enemies of David." ¹⁷Jonathan made David swear again by his love for him; for he loved him as he loved his own life.

18 Jonathan said to him, "Tomorrow is the new moon; you will be missed, because your place will be empty. ¹⁹On the day after tomorrow, you shall go a long way down; go to the place where you hid yourself earlier, and remain beside the stone there.*b* ²⁰I will shoot three arrows to the side of it, as though I shot at a mark. ²¹Then I will send the boy, saying, 'Go, find the arrows.' If I say to the boy, 'Look, the arrows are on this side of you, collect them,' then you are to come, for, as the LORD lives, it is safe for you and there is no danger. ²²But if I say to the young man, 'Look, the arrows are beyond you,' then go; for the LORD has sent you away. ²³As for the matter about which you and I have spoken, the

a Heb *a covenant of the LORD*   *b* Meaning of Heb uncertain

from the beginning and made a covenant with him (18:1–5). Jonathan seems to recognize that God intends David, not him, for the throne. David is fearful of returning to the court because Saul has been trying to kill him. Jonathan is reluctant to believe that his father is serious in this but agrees to test his father's sentiments while David is absent. Jonathan will get word to David if his father's deadly threat is serious.

20:12–23—Turning aside into the field, David and Jonathan exchange moving pledges of loyalty and commitment to one another. Their mutual oath is dominated by a Hebrew word often associated with God's covenant with Israel, which means "steadfast love" or "loyal love." Jonathan asks for David's commitment of love toward his own descendants if he should die. David later carries out this commitment in care for Mephibosheth, the son of Jonathan (2 Sam. 9).

LORD is witness[a] between you and me forever."

24 So David hid himself in the field. When the new moon came, the king sat at the feast to eat. 25 The king sat upon his seat, as at other times, upon the seat by the wall. Jonathan stood, while Abner sat by Saul's side; but David's place was empty.

26 Saul did not say anything that day; for he thought, "Something has befallen him; he is not clean, surely he is not clean." 27 But on the second day, the day after the new moon, David's place was empty. And Saul said to his son Jonathan, "Why has the son of Jesse not come to the feast, either yesterday or today?" 28 Jonathan answered Saul, "David earnestly asked leave of me to go to Bethlehem; 29 he said, 'Let me go; for our family is holding a sacrifice in the city, and my brother has commanded me to be there. So now, if I have found favor in your sight, let me get away, and see my brothers.' For this reason he has not come to the king's table."

30 Then Saul's anger was kindled against Jonathan. He said to him, "You son of a perverse, rebellious woman! Do I not know that you have chosen the son of Jesse to your own shame, and to the shame of your mother's nakedness? 31 For as long as the son of Jesse lives upon the earth, neither you nor your kingdom shall be established. Now send and bring him to me, for he shall surely die." 32 Then Jonathan answered his father Saul, "Why should he be put to death? What has he done?" 33 But Saul threw his spear at him to strike him; so Jonathan knew that it was the deci-

sion of his father to put David to death. 34 Jonathan rose from the table in fierce anger and ate no food on the second day of the month, for he was grieved for David, and because his father had disgraced him.

35 In the morning Jonathan went out into the field to the appointment with David, and with him was a little boy. 36 He said to the boy, "Run and find the arrows that I shoot." As the boy ran, he shot an arrow beyond him. 37 When the boy came to the place where Jonathan's arrow had fallen, Jonathan called after the boy and said, "Is the arrow not beyond you?" 38 Jonathan called after the boy, "Hurry, be quick, do not linger." So Jonathan's boy gathered up the arrows and came to his master. 39 But the boy knew nothing; only Jonathan and David knew the arrangement. 40 Jonathan gave his weapons to the boy and said to him, "Go and carry them to the city." 41 As soon as the boy had gone, David rose from beside the stone heap[b] and prostrated himself with his face to the ground. He bowed three times, and they kissed each other, and wept with each other; David wept the more.[c] 42 Then Jonathan said to David, "Go in peace, since both of us have sworn in the name of the LORD, saying, 'The LORD shall be between me and you, and between my descendants and your descendants, forever.'" He got up and left; and Jonathan went into the city.[d]

David and the Holy Bread

21 [e] David came to Nob to the priest Ahimelech. Ahimelech came

---

[a] Gk: Heb lacks witness [b] Gk: Heb from beside the south [c] Vg: Meaning of Heb uncertain [d] This sentence is 21.1 in Heb [e] Ch 21.2 in Heb

---

20:24–30—Saul reveals his intent to kill David, and Jonathan defends him to no avail. Saul sees David as a threat to displace Jonathan from the throne, but this is of no concern to Jonathan, who leaves to warn David.

20:41–42—In a touching portrait of friendship and loyalty, Jonathan and David part, knowing they may never meet again. Their commitment is *in the name of the LORD* and for future genera-

tions as well. Jonathan cannot abandon his father in spite of Saul's madness; because of Saul's madness David must abandon him. Both have public responsibilities of leadership in Israel that will not allow them to make the personal choices they might wish.

21:1–9 David and the Priest at Nob

David seeks help to provision his men, and Ahimelech, the priest at Nob, gives him the ho

trembling to meet David, and said to him, "Why are you alone, and no one with you?" ²David said to the priest Ahimelech, "The king has charged me with a matter, and said to me, 'No one must know anything of the matter about which I send you, and with which I have charged you.' I have made an appointment*a* with the young men for such and such a place. ³Now then, what have you at hand? Give me five loaves of bread, or whatever is here." ⁴The priest answered David, "I have no ordinary bread at hand, only holy bread—provided that the young men have kept themselves from women." ⁵David answered the priest, "Indeed women have been kept from us as always when I go on an expedition; the vessels of the young men are holy even when it is a common journey; how much more today will their vessels be holy?" ⁶So the priest gave him the holy bread; for there was no bread there except the bread of the Presence, which is removed from before the LORD, to be replaced by hot bread on the day it is taken away.

7 Now a certain man of the servants of Saul was there that day, detained before the LORD; his name was Doeg the Edomite, the chief of Saul's shepherds.

8 David said to Ahimelech, "Is there no spear or sword here with you? I did not bring my sword or my weapons with me, because the king's business required haste." ⁹The priest said, "The sword of Goliath the Philistine, whom you killed in the valley of Elah, is here wrapped in a cloth behind the ephod; if you will take that, take it, for there is none here except that one." David said, "There is none like it; give it to me."

David Flees to Gath

10 David rose and fled that day from Saul; he went to King Achish of Gath. ¹¹The servants of Achish said to him, "Is this not David the king of the land? Did they not sing to one another of him in dances,

'Saul has killed his thousands,
   and David his ten thousands'?"
¹²David took these words to heart and was very much afraid of King Achish of Gath. ¹³So he changed his behavior before them; he pretended to be mad when in their presence.*b* He scratched marks on the doors of the gate, and let his spittle run down his beard. ¹⁴Achish said to his servants, "Look, you see the man is mad; why then have you brought him to me? ¹⁵Do I lack madmen, that you have brought this fellow to play the madman in my presence? Shall this fellow come into my house?"

David and His Followers at Adullam

22 David left there and escaped to the cave of Adullam; when his brothers and all his father's house heard of it, they went down there to him. ²Everyone who was in distress, and everyone who was in debt, and everyone who was discontented gathered to

a Q Ms Vg Compare Gk: Meaning of MT uncertain   *b* Heb *in their hands*

---

bread of the presence there. The normal boundaries between the sacred and the profane give way to the larger purposes God has for the future of the kingdom. The priest asks a minimum of respect for holy tradition (v. 4) but willingly gives holy bread to make a difference in a profane world where Saul is seeking to prevent the advent of God's kingdom in David. Jesus later cites this moment with approval as a precedent when he is confronted by the Pharisees with breaking the Sabbath by plucking grain (Matt. 12:1–8; Mark 2:23–28; Luke 6:1–5).

21:10–23:20 David on the Run

21:10–15—David must play the madman to escape a situation where the Philistines in Gath have recognized him. But in the process they acknowledge him as king of the land (v. 11). This is the latest in a growing list of those who recognize in David Israel's future king: even the Philistines, but not yet Saul, who seeks to kill him.

22:2—David gathers around him the marginalized and the misfits of Saul's kingdom. The anointed one of God finds his first loyal followers among those cast out by the respected people of Israel. One cannot help but draw a parallel to Jesus as God's anointed, associating with the outcasts of his time. These men become the core of a personal force loyal to David throughout his life.

him; and he became captain over them. Those who were with him numbered about four hundred.

3 David went from there to Mizpeh of Moab. He said to the king of Moab, "Please let my father and mother come*a* to you, until I know what God will do for me." **4** He left them with the king of Moab, and they stayed with him all the time that David was in the stronghold. **5** Then the prophet Gad said to David, "Do not remain in the stronghold; leave, and go into the land of Judah." So David left, and went into the forest of Hereth.

Saul Slaughters the Priests at Nob

6 Saul heard that David and those who were with him had been located. Saul was sitting at Gibeah, under the tamarisk tree on the height, with his spear in his hand, and all his servants were standing around him. **7** Saul said to his servants who stood around him, "Hear now, you Benjaminites; will the son of Jesse give every one of you fields and vineyards, will he make you all commanders of thousands and commanders of hundreds? **8** Is that why all of you have conspired against me? No one discloses to me when my son makes a league with the son of Jesse, none of you is sorry for me or discloses to me that my son has stirred up my servant against me, to lie in wait, as he is doing today." **9** Doeg the Edomite, who was in charge of Saul's servants, answered, "I saw the son of Jesse coming to Nob, to Ahimelech son of Ahitub; **10** he inquired of the LORD for him, gave him provisions, and gave him the sword of Goliath the Philistine."

11 The king sent for the priest Ahimelech son of Ahitub and for all his father's house, the priests who were at Nob; and all of them came to the king. **12** Saul said, "Listen now, son of Ahitub." He answered, "Here I am, my lord." **13** Saul said to him, "Why have you conspired against me, you and the son of Jesse, by giving him bread and a sword, and by inquiring of God for him, so that he has risen against me, to lie in wait, as he is doing today?"

14 Then Ahimelech answered the king, "Who among all your servants is so faithful as David? He is the king's son-in-law, and is quick*b* to do your bidding, and is honored in your house. **15** Is today the first time that I have inquired of God for him? By no means! Do not let the king impute anything to his servant or to any member of my father's house; for your servant has known nothing of all this, much or little." **16** The king said, "You shall surely die, Ahimelech, you and all your father's house." **17** The king said to the guard who stood around him, "Turn and kill the priests of the LORD, because their hand also is with David; they knew that he fled, and did not disclose it to me." But the servants of the king would not raise their hand to attack the priests of the LORD. **18** Then the king said to Doeg, "You, Doeg, turn and attack the priests." Doeg the Edomite turned and attacked the priests; on that day he killed eighty-five who wore the linen ephod. **19** Nob, the city of the priests, he put to the sword; men and women, children and infants, oxen, donkeys, and sheep, he put to the sword.

20 But one of the sons of Ahimelech

a Syr Vg: Heb *come out*   *b* Heb *and turns aside*

22:7–9—Saul turns on his own commanders, accusing them of loyalty to David. David is becoming his obsession, to the neglect of other royal duties. A foreigner, Doeg the Edomite, betrays the information that Ahimelech helped David.

22:10–19—Saul orders the slaughter of Ahimelech and the priests of Nob for their kindness to David, but his own men will not carry out the order. Doeg, the Edomite, carries out the massacre of priests and their families. Saul is losing the respect of his own troops.

22:20–23—Ahimelech's son, Abiathar, escapes and is welcomed by David. In a time when Saul is acting without responsibility, David says, *"I am responsible."* David refuses to wash his hands and attribute evil only to Saul. In choosing responsibility David positions himself to offer a new future, to Abiathar and to Israel.

son of Ahitub, named Abiathar, escaped and fled after David. **21** Abiathar told David that Saul had killed the priests of the LORD. **22** David said to Abiathar, "I knew on that day, when Doeg the Edomite was there, that he would surely tell Saul. I am responsible*a* for the lives of all your father's house. **23** Stay with me, and do not be afraid; for the one who seeks my life seeks your life; you will be safe with me."

David Saves the City of Keilah

23 Now they told David, "The Philistines are fighting against Keilah, and are robbing the threshing floors." **2** David inquired of the LORD, "Shall I go and attack these Philistines?" The LORD said to David, "Go and attack the Philistines and save Keilah." **3** But David's men said to him, "Look, we are afraid here in Judah; how much more then if we go to Keilah against the armies of the Philistines?" **4** Then David inquired of the LORD again. The LORD answered him, "Yes, go down to Keilah; for I will give the Philistines into your hand." **5** So David and his men went to Keilah, fought with the Philistines, brought away their livestock, and dealt them a heavy defeat. Thus David rescued the inhabitants of Keilah.

6 When Abiathar son of Ahimelech fled to David at Keilah, he came down with an ephod in his hand. **7** Now it was told Saul that David had come to Keilah. And Saul said, "God has given*b* him into my hand; for he has shut himself in by entering a town that has gates and bars." **8** Saul summoned all the people to war, to go down to Keilah, to besiege David and his men. **9** When David learned that Saul was plotting evil against him, he said to the priest Abiathar, "Bring the ephod here." **10** David said, "O LORD, the God of Israel, your servant has heard that Saul seeks to come to Keilah, to destroy the city on my account. **11** And now, will*c* Saul come down as your servant has heard? O LORD, the God of Israel, I beseech you, tell your servant." The LORD said, "He will come down." **12** Then David said, "Will the men of Keilah surrender me and my men into the hand of Saul?" The LORD said, "They will surrender you." **13** Then David and his men, who were about six hundred, set out and left Keilah; they wandered wherever they could go. When Saul was told that David had escaped from Keilah, he gave up the expedition. **14** David remained in the strongholds in the wilderness, in the hill country of the Wilderness of Ziph. Saul sought him every day, but the LORD*d* did not give him into his hand.

David Eludes Saul in the Wilderness

15 David was in the Wilderness of Ziph at Horesh when he learned that*e* Saul had come out to seek his life. **16** Saul's son Jonathan set out and came to David at Horesh; there he strengthened his hand through the LORD.*f* **17** He said to him, "Do not be afraid; for the hand of my father Saul shall not find you; you shall be king over Israel, and I shall be second to you; my father Saul also knows that this is so." **18** Then the two of them made a covenant before the LORD; David remained at Horesh, and Jonathan went home.

a Gk Vg: Meaning of Heb uncertain *b* Gk Tg: Heb *made a stranger of* *c* Q Ms Compare Gk: MT *Will the men of Keilah surrender me into his hand? Will* *d* Q Ms Gk: MT *God* *e* Or *saw that* *f* Compare Q Ms Gk: MT *God*

23:1–29—This chapter tells the stories of numerous escapes by David from the pursuit of Saul. God does not dramatically intervene to save David, yet we have a strong sense of divine providence operating in these events. These stories model the interconnection between resourceful human action and trust in divine providence that marks the books of Samuel. David is courageous, resourceful, quick in response, and wise in decision making, but he is also constantly in prayer (vv. 2, 4, 11, 18). His resources include a strong faith as well as a strong arm and a fleet foot. Trusting prayer and a discerning mind seem to go together for David. This suggests that prayer groups and missional response committees perhaps should not be as separate as they are in some congregations.

19 Then some Ziphites went up to Saul at Gibeah and said, "David is hiding among us in the strongholds of Horesh, on the hill of Hachilah, which is south of Jeshimon. 20 Now, O king, whenever you wish to come down, do so; and our part will be to surrender him into the king's hand." 21 Saul said, "May you be blessed by the LORD for showing me compassion! 22 Go and make sure once more; find out exactly where he is, and who has seen him there; for I am told that he is very cunning. 23 Look around and learn all the hiding places where he lurks, and come back to me with sure information. Then I will go with you; and if he is in the land, I will search him out among all the thousands of Judah." 24 So they set out and went to Ziph ahead of Saul.

David and his men were in the wilderness of Maon, in the Arabah to the south of Jeshimon. 25 Saul and his men went to search for him. When David was told, he went down to the rock and stayed in the wilderness of Maon. When Saul heard that, he pursued David into the wilderness of Maon. 26 Saul went on one side of the mountain, and David and his men on the other side of the mountain. David was hurrying to get away from Saul, while Saul and his men were closing in on David and his men to capture them. 27 Then a messenger came to Saul, saying, "Hurry and come; for the Philistines have made a raid on the land." 28 So Saul stopped pursuing David, and went against the Philistines; therefore that place was called the Rock of Escape. a 29b David then went up from

there, and lived in the strongholds of En-gedi.

David Spares Saul's Life

24 When Saul returned from following the Philistines, he was told, "David is in the wilderness of En-gedi." 2 Then Saul took three thousand chosen men out of all Israel, and went to look for David and his men in the direction of the Rocks of the Wild Goats. 3 He came to the sheepfolds beside the road, where there was a cave; and Saul went in to relieve himself.c Now David and his men were sitting in the innermost parts of the cave. 4 The men of David said to him, "Here is the day of which the LORD said to you, 'I will give your enemy into your hand, and you shall do to him as it seems good to you.'" Then David went and stealthily cut off a corner of Saul's cloak. 5 Afterward David was stricken to the heart because he had cut off a corner of Saul's cloak. 6 He said to his men, "The LORD forbid that I should do this thing to my lord, the LORD's anointed, to raise my hand against him; for he is the LORD's anointed." 7 So David scolded his men severely and did not permit them to attack Saul. Then Saul got up and left the cave, and went on his way.

8 Afterwards David also rose up and went out of the cave and called after Saul, "My lord the king!" When Saul looked behind him, David bowed with his face to the ground, and did obeisance. 9 David said to Saul, "Why do you listen to the words of those who say, 'David

a Or Rock of Division; meaning of Heb uncertain   b Ch 24.1 in Heb
c Heb to cover his feet

24:1–22 David Spares Saul
This is the first of three chapters (chaps. 24–26) establishing that David does not secure his kingdom by the use of violence. He came to the throne with no blood on his hands. Twice (chaps. 24 and 26) he has the life of Saul in his hand and does not kill him, out of respect for God's anointed. In chap. 25, the resourceful Abigail intervenes to keep David from violence.

24:4–7—When Saul is placed in a compromising position where David could easily kill him,

David refuses, simply because Saul is God's anointed. His men cannot understand this. Their way is the way of exercising power advantages. David chooses a path of mercy and respect, but he does cut a corner of Saul's cloak to use in confronting him.

24:8–15—Showing mercy does not mean avoiding political advantage, so David confronts Saul with the evidence of David's respect for Saul and his office, in contrast to the murderous intent of Saul toward David.

seeks to do you harm'? [10] This very day your eyes have seen how the LORD gave you into my hand in the cave; and some urged me to kill you, but I spared[a] you. I said, 'I will not raise my hand against my lord; for he is the LORD's anointed.' [11] See, my father, see the corner of your cloak in my hand; for by the fact that I cut off the corner of your cloak, and did not kill you, you may know for certain that there is no wrong or treason in my hands. I have not sinned against you, though you are hunting me to take my life. [12] May the LORD judge between me and you! May the LORD avenge me on you; but my hand shall not be against you. [13] As the ancient proverb says, 'Out of the wicked comes forth wickedness'; but my hand shall not be against you. [14] Against whom has the king of Israel come out? Whom do you pursue? A dead dog? A single flea? [15] May the LORD therefore be judge, and give sentence between me and you. May he see to it, and plead my cause, and vindicate me against you."

16 When David had finished speaking these words to Saul, Saul said, "Is this your voice, my son David?" Saul lifted up his voice and wept. [17] He said to David, "You are more righteous than I; for you have repaid me good, whereas I have repaid you evil. [18] Today you have explained how you have dealt well with me, in that you did not kill me when the LORD put me into your hands. [19] For who has ever found an enemy, and sent the enemy safely away? So may the LORD reward you with good for what you have done to me this day. [20] Now I know that you shall surely be king, and that the kingdom of Israel shall be established in your hand. [21] Swear to me therefore by the LORD that you will not cut off my descendants after me, and that you will not wipe out my name from my father's house." [22] So David swore this to Saul. Then Saul went home; but David and his men went up to the stronghold.

Death of Samuel

25 Now Samuel died; and all Israel assembled and mourned for him. They buried him at his home in Ramah.

Then David got up and went down to the wilderness of Paran.

David and the Wife of Nabal

2 There was a man in Maon, whose property was in Carmel. The man was very rich; he had three thousand sheep and a thousand goats. He was shearing his sheep in Carmel. [3] Now the name of the man was Nabal, and the name of his wife Abigail. The woman was clever and beautiful, but the man was surly and mean; he was a Calebite. [4] David heard in the wilderness that Nabal was shearing his sheep. [5] So David sent ten young men; and David said to the young men, "Go up to Carmel, and go to Nabal, and greet him in my name. [6] Thus you shall salute him: 'Peace be to you, and peace be to your house, and peace be to all that you have. [7] I hear that you have shearers; now your shepherds have been with us, and we did them no harm, and

[a] Gk Syr Tg Vg: Heb *it* (my eye) spared

24:16–22—David's mercy has an effect on Saul. He seems momentarily in possession of his better self and acknowledges David's graceful restraint. In fact, Saul himself becomes the last of a growing chorus of witnesses who acknowledge David as the future king of Israel. Saul now voices that conviction himself and asks David's mercy toward his name and his descendants (vv. 20–21), and David swears an oath to this end. One wonders if the execution of seven of Saul's grandsons in 2 Sam. 21 violates this oath.

25:1—The death of Samuel, the prophet, ends an era in Israel's life. He anointed both Saul and David, and although now gone from the scene, he returns to the stage once more in chap. 28.

25:2–44 David, Nabal, and Abigail

A resourceful woman named Abigail intervenes to keep David from incurring bloodguilt in the murder of her husband, Nabal.

25:2–3—Abigail is introduced as clever and beautiful and her husband, Nabal, is introduced as rich, surly, and mean. Indeed, his name, Nabal, is a word meaning "fool."

they missed nothing, all the time they were in Carmel. **8** Ask your young men, and they will tell you. Therefore let my young men find favor in your sight; for we have come on a feast day. Please give whatever you have at hand to your servants and to your son David.'"

9 When David's young men came, they said all this to Nabal in the name of David; and then they waited. **10** But Nabal answered David's servants, "Who is David? Who is the son of Jesse? There are many servants today who are breaking away from their masters. **11** Shall I take my bread and my water and the meat that I have butchered for my shearers, and give it to men who come from I do not know where?" **12** So David's young men turned away, and came back and told him all this. **13** David said to his men, "Every man strap on his sword!" And every one of them strapped on his sword; David also strapped on his sword; and about four hundred men went up after David, while two hundred remained with the baggage.

14 But one of the young men told Abigail, Nabal's wife, "David sent messengers out of the wilderness to salute our master; and he shouted insults at them. **15** Yet the men were very good to us, and we suffered no harm, and we never missed anything when we were in the fields, as long as we were with them; **16** they were a wall to us both by night and by day, all the while we were with them keeping the sheep. **17** Now

therefore know this and consider what you should do; for evil has been decided against our master and against all his house; he is so ill-natured that no one can speak to him."

18 Then Abigail hurried and took two hundred loaves, two skins of wine, five sheep ready dressed, five measures of parched grain, one hundred clusters of raisins, and two hundred cakes of figs. She loaded them on donkeys **19** and said to her young men, "Go on ahead of me; I am coming after you." But she did not tell her husband Nabal. **20** As she rode on the donkey and came down under cover of the mountain, David and his men came down toward her; and she met them. **21** Now David had said, "Surely it was in vain that I protected all that this fellow has in the wilderness, so that nothing was missed of all that belonged to him; but he has returned me evil for good. **22** God do so to David[a] and more also, if by morning I leave so much as one male of all who belong to him."

23 When Abigail saw David, she hurried and alighted from the donkey, and fell before David on her face, bowing to the ground. **24** She fell at his feet and said, "Upon me alone, my lord, be the guilt; please let your servant speak in your ears, and hear the words of your servant. **25** My lord, do not take seriously this ill-natured fellow, Nabal; for as his name is, so is he; Nabal[b] is his name,

---

[a] Gk Compare Syr: Heb *the enemies of David*   [b] That is *Fool*

25:9–13—David is in need of provisions for his growing force of men. He sends emissaries to Nabal asking for assistance in return for the protection his men have given to Nabal's shepherds and flocks who have been in the area of David's men. Nabal treats David with contempt, and David responds impulsively by preparing his men for battle and setting out for Nabal's home. It appears that David wishes both revenge and provisions.

25:18–22—Abigail hears a report of her husband's insulting behavior toward David's men and responds immediately. She sends a caravan of food and provisions and follows close behind to meet David.

25:23–31—Abigail shows herself to be a woman not only of bold action but of persuasive speech. She takes responsibility for her "fool" of a husband and makes an argument to David, not by pleading for mercy, but by declaring the interests of his kingdom. She argues persuasively that the Lord will secure David's kingdom and his house; therefore, he should not come to the throne with innocent or self-interested blood on his own hands. Her speech is eloquent, seems to know of David's history (e.g., reference to Goliath in v. 29), and reminds David that he is the Lord's servant.

and folly is with him; but I, your servant, did not see the young men of my lord, whom you sent.

26 "Now then, my lord, as the LORD lives, and as you yourself live, since the LORD has restrained you from bloodguilt and from taking vengeance with your own hand, now let your enemies and those who seek to do evil to my lord be like Nabal. 27 And now let this present that your servant has brought to my lord be given to the young men who follow my lord. 28 Please forgive the trespass of your servant; for the LORD will certainly make my lord a sure house, because my lord is fighting the battles of the LORD; and evil shall not be found in you so long as you live. 29 If anyone should rise up to pursue you and to seek your life, the life of my lord shall be bound in the bundle of the living under the care of the LORD your God; but the lives of your enemies he shall sling out as from the hollow of a sling. 30 When the LORD has done to my lord according to all the good that he has spoken concerning you, and has appointed you prince over Israel, 31 my lord shall have no cause of grief, or pangs of conscience, for having shed blood without cause or for having saved himself. And when the LORD has dealt well with my lord, then remember your servant."

32 David said to Abigail, "Blessed be the LORD, the God of Israel, who sent you to meet me today! 33 Blessed be your good sense, and blessed be you, who have kept me today from bloodguilt and from avenging myself by my own hand! 34 For as surely as the LORD the God of Israel lives, who has restrained me from hurting you, unless you had hurried and come to meet me, truly by morning there would not have been left to Nabal so much as one male." 35 Then David received from her hand what she had brought him; he said to her, "Go up to your house in peace; see, I have heeded your voice, and I have granted your petition."

36 Abigail came to Nabal; he was holding a feast in his house, like the feast of a king. Nabal's heart was merry within him, for he was very drunk; so she told him nothing at all until the morning light. 37 In the morning, when the wine had gone out of Nabal, his wife told him these things, and his heart died within him; he became like a stone. 38 About ten days later the LORD struck Nabal, and he died.

39 When David heard that Nabal was dead, he said, "Blessed be the LORD who has judged the case of Nabal's insult to me, and has kept back his servant from evil; the LORD has returned the evildoing of Nabal upon his own head." Then David sent and wooed Abigail, to make her his wife. 40 When David's servants came to Abigail at Carmel, they said to her, "David has sent us to you to take you to him as his wife." 41 She rose and bowed down, with her face to the ground, and said, "Your servant is a slave to wash the feet of the servants of my lord." 42 Abigail got up hurriedly and rode away on a donkey; her five maids attended her. She went after the messengers of David and became his wife.

43 David also married Ahinoam of Jezreel; both of them became his wives. 44 Saul had given his daughter Michal,

---

25:32–35—David instantly recognizes Abigail's wisdom. He admits that he was bent on blood vengeance—the destruction of Nabal's entire household. And he blesses the woman who has now deterred him from this ill-advised act and what would surely have been the negative reputation that would have come from it. He blesses her and sends her away in peace—the peace she herself has restored.

25:36–38—Nabal, drunk and indulgent, is told the fate he almost suffered; he sickens and dies, a death attributed to the Lord and not the hand of David. The position of this story also suggests that the Lord will deal with the fool Saul as well, so David need not kill him.

25:39–42—Hearing of the death of Nabal, David recognizes both the justice of God and the wisdom of Abigail. He sends for Abigail to make her his wife, and she accepts.

David's wife, to Palti son of Laish, who was from Gallim.

David Spares Saul's Life a Second Time

26 Then the Ziphites came to Saul at Gibeah, saying, "David is in hiding on the hill of Hachilah, which is opposite Jeshimon."*a* 2 So Saul rose and went down to the Wilderness of Ziph, with three thousand chosen men of Israel, to seek David in the Wilderness of Ziph. 3 Saul encamped on the hill of Hachilah, which is opposite Jeshimon*a* beside the road. But David remained in the wilderness. When he learned that Saul had come after him into the wilderness, 4 David sent out spies, and learned that Saul had indeed arrived. 5 Then David set out and came to the place where Saul had encamped; and David saw the place where Saul lay, with Abner son of Ner, the commander of his army. Saul was lying within the encampment, while the army was encamped around him.

6 Then David said to Ahimelech the Hittite, and to Joab's brother Abishai son of Zeruiah, "Who will go down with me into the camp to Saul?" Abishai said, "I will go down with you." 7 So David and Abishai went to the army by night; there Saul lay sleeping within the encampment, with his spear stuck in the ground at his head; and Abner and the army lay around him. 8 Abishai said to David, "God has given your enemy into your hand today; now therefore let me pin him to the ground with one stroke of the spear; I will not strike him twice." 9 But David said to Abishai, "Do not destroy him; for who can raise his hand against the LORD's anointed, and be guiltless?" 10 David said, "As the LORD lives, the LORD will strike him down; or his day will come to die; or he will go down into battle and perish. 11 The LORD forbid that I should raise my hand against the LORD's anointed; but now take the spear that is at his head, and the water jar, and let us go." 12 So David took the spear that was at Saul's head and the water jar, and they went away. No one saw it, or knew it, nor did anyone awake; for they were all asleep, because a deep sleep from the LORD had fallen upon them.

13 Then David went over to the other side, and stood on top of a hill far away, with a great distance between them. 14 David called to the army and to Abner son of Ner, saying, "Abner! Will you not answer?" Then Abner replied, "Who are you that calls to the king?" 15 David said to Abner, "Are you not a man? Who is like you in Israel? Why then have you not kept watch over your lord the king? For one of the people came in to destroy your lord the king. 16 This thing that you have done is not good. As the LORD lives, you deserve to die, because you have not kept watch over your lord, the LORD's anointed. See now, where is the king's spear, or the water jar that was at his head?"

17 Saul recognized David's voice, and said, "Is this your voice, my son David?" David said, "It is my voice, my lord, O king." 18 And he added, "Why does my lord pursue his servant? For what have I

a Or opposite the wasteland

26:1–25 David Again Spares Saul

This is a second story in which David spares the life of Saul. Some details are different: Abner has a role in the story as Saul's general. David has a companion, Abishai, who wants to take violence into his own hands, and David restrains him, even as Abigail restrained David. David still respects Saul as God's anointed and even more explicitly trusts in God to deal with Saul (v. 9). Saul's death is foreshadowed in v. 10.

26:17–25—The final interaction between David and Saul, the most remarkable element of this story, fittingly climaxes the three chapters in which David refuses or is kept from violence. David pleads his innocence before Saul (vv. 18–20), but it is Saul's speech that is striking. He confesses wrongdoing, pledges not to seek further harm to David, and calls himself a fool, evoking the image of Nabal in the preceding chapter (v. 21). David returns Saul's spear, perhaps the one Saul threw at David, and again states that he cannot harm God's anointed (vv. 23–24). Saul parts from David for the final time with the giving of a blessing.

done? What guilt is on my hands? [19] Now therefore let my lord the king hear the words of his servant. If it is the LORD who has stirred you up against me, may he accept an offering; but if it is mortals, may they be cursed before the LORD, for they have driven me out today from my share in the heritage of the LORD, saying, 'Go, serve other gods.' [20] Now therefore, do not let my blood fall to the ground, away from the presence of the LORD; for the king of Israel has come out to seek a single flea, like one who hunts a partridge in the mountains."

21 Then Saul said, "I have done wrong; come back, my son David, for I will never harm you again, because my life was precious in your sight today; I have been a fool, and have made a great mistake." [22] David replied, "Here is the spear, O king! Let one of the young men come over and get it. [23] The LORD rewards everyone for his righteousness and his faithfulness; for the LORD gave you into my hand today, but I would not raise my hand against the LORD's anointed. [24] As your life was precious today in my sight, so may my life be precious in the sight of the LORD, and may he rescue me from all tribulation." [25] Then Saul said to David, "Blessed be you, my son David! You will do many things and will succeed in them." So David went his way, and Saul returned to his place.

David Serves King Achish of Gath

27 David said in his heart, "I shall now perish one day by the hand of Saul; there is nothing better for me than to escape to the land of the Philis-

tines; then Saul will despair of seeking me any longer within the borders of Israel, and I shall escape out of his hand." [2] So David set out and went over, he and the six hundred men who were with him, to King Achish son of Maoch of Gath. [3] David stayed with Achish at Gath, he and his troops, every man with his household, and David with his two wives, Ahinoam of Jezreel, and Abigail of Carmel, Nabal's widow. [4] When Saul was told that David had fled to Gath, he no longer sought for him.

5 Then David said to Achish, "If I have found favor in your sight, let a place be given me in one of the country towns, so that I may live there; for why should your servant live in the royal city with you?" [6] So that day Achish gave him Ziklag; therefore Ziklag has belonged to the kings of Judah to this day. [7] The length of time that David lived in the country of the Philistines was one year and four months.

8 Now David and his men went up and made raids on the Geshurites, the Girzites, and the Amalekites; for these were the landed settlements from Telam[a] on the way to Shur and on to the land of Egypt. [9] David struck the land, leaving neither man nor woman alive, but took away the sheep, the oxen, the donkeys, the camels, and the clothing, and came back to Achish. [10] When Achish asked, "Against whom[b] have you made a raid today?" David would say, "Against the Negeb of Judah," or "Against the Negeb of the Jerahmeelites," or, "Against the Negeb of the Kenites." [11] David left

---

a Compare Gk 15.4: Heb *from of old*   *b* Q Ms Gk Vg: MT lacks *whom*

27:1–28:2 David with the Philistines

27:1–4—In spite of Saul's pledge to give up pursuit of David (26:21), David clearly does not intend to rely on that word, and he seeks refuge with one of the Philistine kings, Achish of Gath.

27:5–7—David and his six hundred men become a part of Achish's mercenary force, and David is given the territory of Ziklag to oversee. David is supposed to use Ziklag as a base to extend Philistine control and collect tribute.

27:8–28:2—David deceives Achish by raiding

and collecting tribute only from the traditional enemies of Judah, while reporting to Achish that he had done so to Judah and its kin. Achish then believes, mistakenly, that David has severed his ties to his own tribe of Judah. Achish feels secure enough in David's loyalty to make him and his men part of the Philistine army and Achish's own bodyguard. A battle against Saul is coming soon and Achish is beginning to muster his forces. This will pose a dilemma for David, since he will be expected to fight against Israelites.

neither man nor woman alive to be brought back to Gath, thinking, "They might tell about us, and say, 'David has done so and so.'" Such was his practice all the time he lived in the country of the Philistines. [12] Achish trusted David, thinking, "He has made himself utterly abhorrent to his people Israel; therefore he shall always be my servant."

28 In those days the Philistines gathered their forces for war, to fight against Israel. Achish said to David, "You know, of course, that you and your men are to go out with me in the army." [2] David said to Achish, "Very well, then you shall know what your servant can do." Achish said to David, "Very well, I will make you my bodyguard for life."

Saul Consults a Medium

3 Now Samuel had died, and all Israel had mourned for him and buried him in Ramah, his own city. Saul had expelled the mediums and the wizards from the land. [4] The Philistines assembled, and came and encamped at Shunem. Saul gathered all Israel, and they encamped at Gilboa. [5] When Saul saw the army of the Philistines, he was afraid, and his heart trembled greatly. [6] When Saul inquired of the LORD, the LORD did not answer him, not by dreams, or by Urim, or by prophets. [7] Then Saul said to his servants, "Seek out for me a woman who is a medium, so that I may go to her and inquire of her." His servants said to him, "There is a medium at Endor."

[8] So Saul disguised himself and put on other clothes and went there, he and two men with him. They came to the woman by night. And he said, "Consult a spirit for me, and bring up for me the one whom I name to you." [9] The woman said to him, "Surely you know what Saul has done, how he has cut off the mediums and the wizards from the land. Why then are you laying a snare for my life to bring about my death?" [10] But Saul swore to her by the LORD, "As the LORD lives, no punishment shall come upon you for this thing." [11] Then the woman said, "Whom shall I bring up for you?" He answered, "Bring up Samuel for me." [12] When the woman saw Samuel, she cried out with a loud voice; and the woman said to Saul, "Why have you deceived me? You are Saul!" [13] The king said to her, "Have no fear; what do you see?" The woman said to Saul, "I see a divine being[a] coming up out of the ground." [14] He said to her, "What is his appearance?" She said, "An old man is coming up; he is wrapped in a robe." So Saul knew that it was Samuel, and he bowed with his face to the ground, and did obeisance.

15 Then Samuel said to Saul, "Why have you disturbed me by bringing me up?" Saul answered, "I am in great distress, for the Philistines are warring against me, and God has turned away from me and answers me no more, either by prophets or by dreams; so I

[a] Or *a god; or gods*

28:3–25 Saul and a Medium at Endor
This is a story of great pathos and our last story of Saul before his death. A Philistine army has been mustered to put down the upstart kingdom of Saul, and Saul is rightly afraid. In his fear he desperately seeks out a medium to bring back the ghost of Samuel. Saul is still plagued by the rupture of relationship with the prophet. However, this enterprise does not turn out well for Saul.

28:3–7—Saul, himself, outlawed mediums and wizards, yet wishes to consult one when traditional means of seeking the will of the Lord fail him.

28:8–14—The woman at Endor is suspicious that she is being set up to do something illegal, and

she is terrified when she recognizes Saul. Saul betrays his identity by asking for the prophet Samuel to be summoned. Even at the end of his life Saul seems incapable of making clear decisions and seems to be seeking some sort of reconciliation with Samuel, who has died (25:1).

28:15–19—The spirit of Samuel is no more comforting to Saul than Samuel had been when he was alive. Samuel seems angered at being disturbed and only foretells the death of Saul and his son, while using the words of the rejection in 15:28 to say (28:17) that God *has torn the kingdom* from Saul and given it to a *neighbor*, a reference to David.

have summoned you to tell me what I should do." ¹⁶ Samuel said, "Why then do you ask me, since the LORD has turned from you and become your enemy? ¹⁷ The LORD has done to you just as he spoke by me; for the LORD has torn the kingdom out of your hand, and given it to your neighbor, David. ¹⁸ Because you did not obey the voice of the LORD, and did not carry out his fierce wrath against Amalek, therefore the LORD has done this thing to you today. ¹⁹ Moreover the LORD will give Israel along with you into the hands of the Philistines; and tomorrow you and your sons shall be with me; the LORD will also give the army of Israel into the hands of the Philistines."

20 Immediately Saul fell full length on the ground, filled with fear because of the words of Samuel; and there was no strength in him, for he had eaten nothing all day and all night. ²¹ The woman came to Saul, and when she saw that he was terrified, she said to him, "Your servant has listened to you; I have taken my life in my hand, and have listened to what you have said to me. ²² Now therefore, you also listen to your servant; let me set a morsel of bread before you. Eat, that you may have strength when you go on your way." ²³ He refused, and said, "I will not eat." But his servants, together with the woman, urged him; and he listened to their words. So he got up from the ground and sat on the bed. ²⁴ Now the woman had a fatted calf in the house. She quickly slaughtered it, and she took flour, kneaded it, and baked unleavened cakes. ²⁵ She put them before Saul and

his servants, and they ate. Then they rose and went away that night.

The Philistines Reject David

29 Now the Philistines gathered all their forces at Aphek, while the Israelites were encamped by the fountain that is in Jezreel. ² As the lords of the Philistines were passing on by hundreds and by thousands, and David and his men were passing on in the rear with Achish, ³ the commanders of the Philistines said, "What are these Hebrews doing here?" Achish said to the commanders of the Philistines, "Is this not David, the servant of King Saul of Israel, who has been with me now for days and years? Since he deserted to me I have found no fault in him to this day." ⁴ But the commanders of the Philistines were angry with him; and the commanders of the Philistines said to him, "Send the man back, so that he may return to the place that you have assigned to him; he shall not go down with us to battle, or else he may become an adversary to us in the battle. For how could this fellow reconcile himself to his lord? Would it not be with the heads of the men here? ⁵ Is this not David, of whom they sing to one another in dances,

'Saul has killed his thousands,
    and David his ten thousands'?"

6 Then Achish called David and said to him, "As the LORD lives, you have been honest, and to me it seems right that you should march out and in with me in the campaign; for I have found nothing wrong in you from the day of your coming to me until today. Nevertheless

---

28:20–25—In the end, the only comfort available to Saul is not from Samuel but from the hospitality of the woman at Endor. The woman takes pity on Saul, who is prostrate in fear, and feeds him, but Saul is sent away as a doomed and tragic figure. Saul has desperately tried to restore his past and escape his future, but there is no escape, and Saul has helped to create his bleak future.

29:1–11 David Leaves the Philistines
David and his men come with Achish to the gathering of the Philistine army to face Saul and

his sons, but the Philistine commanders do not approve of David's presence. They know his reputation as a warrior and are afraid he will turn on them in the battle. Achish argues for David as a loyal retainer, and David seems to wish to stay, although we as readers know he is less loyal than Achish knows. It is intriguing to wonder if, in battle, David will go to the aid of his friend Jonathan. David is sent reluctantly back to Ziklag. This story may be told in detail to make clear to readers that, although David served with the Philistines, he never lifted the sword against Israelites.

the lords do not approve of you. [7] So go back now; and go peaceably; do nothing to displease the lords of the Philistines." [8] David said to Achish, "But what have I done? What have you found in your servant from the day I entered your service until now, that I should not go and fight against the enemies of my lord the king?" [9] Achish replied to David, "I know that you are as blameless in my sight as an angel of God; nevertheless, the commanders of the Philistines have said, 'He shall not go up with us to the battle.' [10] Now then rise early in the morning, you and the servants of your lord who came with you, and go to the place that I appointed for you. As for the evil report, do not take it to heart, for you have done well before me.[a] Start early in the morning, and leave as soon as you have light." [11] So David set out with his men early in the morning, to return to the land of the Philistines. But the Philistines went up to Jezreel.

David Avenges the Destruction of Ziklag

30 Now when David and his men came to Ziklag on the third day, the Amalekites had made a raid on the Negeb and on Ziklag. They had attacked Ziklag, burned it down, [2] and taken captive the women and all[b] who were in it,

both small and great; they killed none of them, but carried them off, and went their way. [3] When David and his men came to the city, they found it burned down, and their wives and sons and daughters taken captive. [4] Then David and the people who were with him raised their voices and wept, until they had no more strength to weep. [5] David's two wives also had been taken captive, Ahinoam of Jezreel, and Abigail the widow of Nabal of Carmel. [6] David was in great danger; for the people spoke of stoning him, because all the people were bitter in spirit for their sons and daughters. But David strengthened himself in the LORD his God.

7 David said to the priest Abiathar son of Ahimelech, "Bring me the ephod." So Abiathar brought the ephod to David. [8] David inquired of the LORD, "Shall I pursue this band? Shall I overtake them?" He answered him, "Pursue; for you shall surely overtake and shall surely rescue." [9] So David set out, he and the six hundred men who were with him. They came to the Wadi Besor, where those stayed who were left behind. [10] But David went on with the pursuit, he and four hundred men; two hundred stayed behind, too exhausted to cross the Wadi Besor.

[a] Gk: Heb lacks *and go to the place . . . done well before me*   [b] Gk: Heb lacks *and all*

30:1–31 David Attacks the Amalekites
David returns to find Ziklag burned and looted by Amalekites, who have also carried off all the women and children. What follows could be regarded as just another battle story, with David taking revenge and recovering what was lost. Yet, even as Saul's kingship is ending, the story shows David acting in ways that demonstrate the qualities of a new kingdom about to emerge.

30:6—Before taking any action, still grieving his own loss, and facing rebellion among his men, David **strengthened himself in the LORD his God**. David's strength as a warrior, leader, and future king is grounded in spiritual strength. Abiathar, the priest, aids him in asking God's guidance, but this is no end in itself. David then makes wise and pragmatic decisions founded on this spiritual base.

30:7–31—Samuel had warned of a king who

would "take" from the people (8:11–18). David here models generosity instead. He is generous and compassionate to the Egyptian servant of the Amalekites (30:11–15), to the two hundred exhausted men left to guard the baggage (vv. 10, 21–25), to the elders of the cities of Judah (vv. 26–31). These are not just soft-hearted moments but part of a genuine alternative in seeking his own goals as a leader. For David such generosity is both genuine and pragmatic, and it models a different kind of power that is not simply self-serving. David is willing to make a new policy of economic distribution because it is just, but we can see the potential for greater solidarity and community. David had a right by ancient custom to keep the spoils of his battle for himself and his men, but he chose to share these goods with those he would soon govern. On the brink of becoming king, David shows himself again to be the man after God's own heart.

11 In the open country they found an Egyptian, and brought him to David. They gave him bread and he ate; they gave him water to drink; ¹² they also gave him a piece of fig cake and two clusters of raisins. When he had eaten, his spirit revived; for he had not eaten bread or drunk water for three days and three nights. ¹³ Then David said to him, "To whom do you belong? Where are you from?" He said, "I am a young man of Egypt, servant to an Amalekite. My master left me behind because I fell sick three days ago. ¹⁴ We had made a raid on the Negeb of the Cherethites and on that which belongs to Judah and on the Negeb of Caleb; and we burned Ziklag down." ¹⁵ David said to him, "Will you take me down to this raiding party?" He said, "Swear to me by God that you will not kill me, or hand me over to my master, and I will take you down to them."

16 When he had taken him down, they were spread out all over the ground, eating and drinking and dancing, because of the great amount of spoil they had taken from the land of the Philistines and from the land of Judah. ¹⁷ David attacked them from twilight until the evening of the next day. Not one of them escaped, except four hundred young men, who mounted camels and fled. ¹⁸ David recovered all that the Amalekites had taken; and David rescued his two wives. ¹⁹ Nothing was missing, whether small or great, sons or daughters, spoil or anything that had been taken; David brought back everything. ²⁰ David also captured all the flocks and herds, which were driven ahead of the other cattle; people said, "This is David's spoil."

21 Then David came to the two hundred men who had been too exhausted to follow David, and who had been left at the Wadi Besor. They went out to meet David and to meet the people who were with him. When David drew near to the people he saluted them. ²² Then all the corrupt and worthless fellows among the men who had gone with David said, "Because they did not go with us, we will not give them any of the spoil that we have recovered, except that each man may take his wife and children, and leave." ²³ But David said, "You shall not do so, my brothers, with what the LORD has given us; he has preserved us and handed over to us the raiding party that attacked us. ²⁴ Who would listen to you in this matter? For the share of the one who goes down into the battle shall be the same as the share of the one who stays by the baggage; they shall share alike." ²⁵ From that day forward he made it a statute and an ordinance for Israel; it continues to the present day.

26 When David came to Ziklag, he sent part of the spoil to his friends, the elders of Judah, saying, "Here is a present for you from the spoil of the enemies of the LORD"; ²⁷ it was for those in Bethel, in Ramoth of the Negeb, in Jattir, ²⁸ in Aroer, in Siphmoth, in Eshtemoa, ²⁹ in Racal, in the towns of the Jerahmeelites, in the towns of the Kenites, ³⁰ in Hormah, in Bor-ashan, in Athach, ³¹ in Hebron, all the places where David and his men had roamed.

The Death of Saul and His Sons

31 Now the Philistines fought against Israel; and the men of Israel fled before the Philistines, and many fell^a on Mount Gilboa. ² The Philistines overtook Saul and his sons; and the Philistines killed Jonathan and Abinadab and Malchishua, the sons of Saul.

^a Heb *and they fell slain*

31:1–7 The Death of Saul

Saul's end is narrated in economic brevity. There is a battle in which the Philistines overwhelm Israel's army. Saul's sons, including Jonathan, are killed. Not wishing to be captured, Saul asks his armor-bearer to kill him, but he cannot do it. So Saul falls on his own sword, dead by his own hand. The text treats this as an honorable death to avoid the humiliation and torture of capture. There is no hint here of moral reflection on suicide.

³ The battle pressed hard upon Saul; the archers found him, and he was badly wounded by them. ⁴ Then Saul said to his armor-bearer, "Draw your sword and thrust me through with it, so that these uncircumcised may not come and thrust me through, and make sport of me." But his armor-bearer was unwilling; for he was terrified. So Saul took his own sword and fell upon it. ⁵ When his armor-bearer saw that Saul was dead, he also fell upon his sword and died with him. ⁶ So Saul and his three sons and his armor-bearer and all his men died together on the same day. ⁷ When the men of Israel who were on the other side of the valley and those beyond the Jordan saw that the men of Israel had fled and that Saul and his sons were dead, they forsook their towns and fled; and the Philistines came and occupied them.

⁸ The next day, when the Philistines came to strip the dead, they found Saul and his three sons fallen on Mount Gilboa. ⁹ They cut off his head, stripped off his armor, and sent messengers throughout the land of the Philistines to carry the good news to the houses of their idols and to the people. ¹⁰ They put his armor in the temple of Astarte;[a] and they fastened his body to the wall of Beth-shan. ¹¹ But when the inhabitants of Jabesh-gilead heard what the Philistines had done to Saul, ¹² all the valiant men set out, traveled all night long, and took the body of Saul and the bodies of his sons from the wall of Beth-shan. They came to Jabesh and burned them there. ¹³ Then they took their bones and buried them under the tamarisk tree in Jabesh, and fasted seven days.

[a] Heb plural

31:8–13 The Burial of Saul

The Philistines subject Saul's body to display and abuse, but the men of Jabesh-gilead rescue Saul's body and those of his sons and give them a respectful burial. It is fitting that our final encounter with Saul evokes the memory of his heroic rescue of Jabesh-gilead (chap. 11). Saul was God's anointed and came to Israel's aid in a time of trouble. It is Saul's tragedy that his reign descended into jealousy, fear, and mental anguish, leading to this sad end to his life and service. Another account of his death appears at the beginning of 2 Samuel (1:1–16), as well as David's eulogy for Saul and Jonathan (1:17–27).

The Book of

2 SAMUEL

David Mourns for Saul and Jonathan

1 After the death of Saul, when David had returned from defeating the Amalekites, David remained two days in Ziklag. ² On the third day, a man came from Saul's camp, with his clothes torn and dirt on his head. When he came to David, he fell to the ground and did obeisance. ³ David said to him, "Where have you come from?" He said to him, "I have escaped from the camp of Israel." ⁴ David said to him, "How did things go? Tell me!" He answered, "The army fled from the battle, but also many of the army fell and died; and Saul and his son Jonathan also died." ⁵ Then David asked the young man who was reporting to him, "How do you know that Saul and his son Jonathan died?" ⁶ The young man reporting to him said, "I happened to be on Mount Gilboa; and there was Saul leaning on his spear, while the chariots and the horsemen drew close to him. ⁷ When he looked behind him, he saw me, and called to me. I answered, 'Here sir.' ⁸ And he said to me, 'Who are you?' I answered him, 'I am an Amalekite.' ⁹ He said to me, 'Come, stand over me and kill me; for convulsions have seized me, and yet my life still lingers.' ¹⁰ So I stood over him, and killed him, for I knew that he could not live after he had fallen. I took the crown that was on his head and the armlet that was on his arm, and I have brought them here to my lord."

11 Then David took hold of his clothes and tore them; and all the men who were with him did the same. ¹² They mourned and wept, and fasted until evening for Saul and for his son Jonathan, and for the army of the LORD and for the house of Israel, because they had fallen by the sword. ¹³ David said to the young man

---

1 Sam. 16:1–2 Sam. 5:10 The Rise of David

The first section of 2 Samuel completes the history of the rise of David that began with David's anointing (1 Sam. 16). The major theological theme of these chapters is that God was with David, a statement made numerous times throughout these chapters (see note at 1 Sam. 18:12–30), and emphasized in the concluding statement of 2 Sam. 5:10: *And David became greater and greater, for the LORD, the God of hosts, was with him.* In the opening chapters of 2 Samuel the emphasis is on legitimating David by clearing him of charges of bloodguilt in the political conflicts of the period and making clear that he bore no ongoing animosity toward the house of Saul or complicity in his death. Thus 2 Samuel opens with a second account of Saul's death (see 1 Sam. 31) and David's moving lament over the deaths of Saul and Jonathan.

1:1–10 Report of Saul's Death

This story of Saul's death is different in its details from that found in 1 Sam. 31:1–6. This has led some to suggest that the Amalekite is lying and simply engaging in an opportunity to gain David's favor by claiming to have killed a presumed enemy of David. There is, however, no suggestion of this in the text. We must simply reckon with two variant accounts of Saul's death, not uncommon even for contemporary dramatic events. In both accounts Saul is doomed to a more humiliating death at the hands of the Philistines.

1:11–16 David's Response

What is important in this story is David's response. He is immediately grief-stricken and he orders the death of the Amalekite for the taking of the life of God's anointed. This often shocks readers because the Amalekite seems little more than an opportunist wishing to ingratiate himself to David, and we live in a culture that often admires such opportunism. The story summons us to look beyond self-interest, represented by the Amalekite, to community loss and loyalty to God's anointed one, as seen in David's grief. David's response will still seem harsh to us, but we are nevertheless asked to examine our capacity for righteous anger in behalf of the violation of community or divine interests over against the elevation of self-interest.

who had reported to him, "Where do you come from?" He answered, "I am the son of a resident alien, an Amalekite." ¹⁴ David said to him, "Were you not afraid to lift your hand to destroy the LORD's anointed?" ¹⁵ Then David called one of the young men and said, "Come here and strike him down." So he struck him down and he died. ¹⁶ David said to him, "Your blood be on your head; for your own mouth has testified against you, saying, 'I have killed the LORD's anointed.'"

17 David intoned this lamentation over Saul and his son Jonathan. ¹⁸ (He ordered that The Song of the Bow*a* be taught to the people of Judah; it is written in the Book of Jashar.) He said:

¹⁹ Your glory, O Israel, lies slain upon
    your high places!
  How the mighty have fallen!
²⁰ Tell it not in Gath,
    proclaim it not in the streets of
      Ashkelon;
  or the daughters of the Philistines
      will rejoice,
    the daughters of the
      uncircumcised will exult.
²¹ You mountains of Gilboa,
    let there be no dew or rain upon
      you,
  nor bounteous fields!*b*

For there the shield of the mighty
    was defiled,
  the shield of Saul, anointed with
      oil no more.
²² From the blood of the slain,
    from the fat of the mighty,
  the bow of Jonathan did not turn
      back,
    nor the sword of Saul return
      empty.
²³ Saul and Jonathan, beloved and
    lovely!
  In life and in death they were not
      divided;
  they were swifter than eagles,
    they were stronger than lions.
²⁴ O daughters of Israel, weep over
    Saul,
  who clothed you with crimson, in
      luxury,
  who put ornaments of gold on
      your apparel.
²⁵ How the mighty have fallen
    in the midst of the battle!

Jonathan lies slain upon your high
    places.
²⁶ I am distressed for you, my brother
    Jonathan;

a Heb *that The Bow*   *b* Meaning of Heb uncertain

1:17–27 David's Lament

David sings eloquently and movingly of the loss of Saul and Jonathan. It is both a personal lament and at the same time an expression of community loss. In his song David teaches us the need for moments that transcend politics and business as usual. David will become king in place of Saul, and Jonathan will not inherit his father's throne, but there is no note of triumph in David's singing. Triumphant politics would only divide Israel at this point. David gives voice to the truth the church knows in the cross, that only after acknowledging the depth of our losses and sufferings, can we be open to the realities of God's future. David leads Israel in acknowledging Saul's death as the loss of a future that can no longer come. It remains for God to open a future with David as king, and that future will not come at once or without struggle. In his own grief David exposes the woundedness of Israel in the experience of Saul; such exposure of our wounds is the prerequisite to any healing that might be hoped for from God.

1:26—This verse speaks of the bonds of love and commitment between David and Jonathan. This loyalty goes beyond death, as we later see in David's kindness toward Jonathan's son (chap. 9). The statement that David's love for Jonathan surpassed the love of women is less an indication of a homosexual relationship than a comment on the status of women in the ancient world. In a world of arranged marriages, love was not the basis of men's relationships with women. Such relationships were focused on childbearing and householding in marriage and lust outside of marriage (1 Sam. 11). David's lament for Jonathan reflects a loyal, committed love (cf. 1 Sam. 20) between these two friends that would have been unlikely between a man and a woman. Whether that included a sexual relationship is not a matter of comment in the biblical text.

greatly beloved were you to me;
　your love to me was wonderful,
　　passing the love of women.

27 How the mighty have fallen,
　and the weapons of war perished!

David Anointed King of Judah

2 After this David inquired of the LORD, "Shall I go up into any of the cities of Judah?" The LORD said to him, "Go up." David said, "To which shall I go up?" He said, "To Hebron." ²So David went up there, along with his two wives, Ahinoam of Jezreel, and Abigail the widow of Nabal of Carmel. ³David brought up the men who were with him, every one with his household; and they settled in the towns of Hebron. ⁴Then the people of Judah came, and there they anointed David king over the house of Judah.

When they told David, "It was the people of Jabesh-gilead who buried Saul," ⁵David sent messengers to the people of Jabesh-gilead, and said to them, "May you be blessed by the LORD, because you showed this loyalty to Saul your lord, and buried him! ⁶Now may the LORD show steadfast love and faith-fulness to you! And I too will reward you because you have done this thing. ⁷Therefore let your hands be strong, and be valiant; for Saul your lord is dead, and the house of Judah has anointed me king over them."

Ishbaal King of Israel

8 But Abner son of Ner, commander of Saul's army, had taken Ishbaal*a* son of Saul, and brought him over to Maha-naim. ⁹He made him king over Gilead, the Ashurites, Jezreel, Ephraim, Benja-min, and over all Israel. ¹⁰Ishbaal,*a* Saul's son, was forty years old when he began to reign over Israel, and he reigned two years. But the house of Judah followed David. ¹¹The time that David was king in Hebron over the house of Judah was seven years and six months.

The Battle of Gibeon

12 Abner son of Ner, and the ser-vants of Ishbaal*a* son of Saul, went out from Mahanaim to Gibeon. ¹³Joab son of Zeruiah, and the servants of David, went out and met them at the pool of Gibeon. One group sat on one side of the pool, while the other sat on the

a Gk Compare 1 Chr 8.33; 9.39: Heb *Ish-bosheth*, "man of shame"

2:1–7 David Anointed King of Judah

2:1—It is noteworthy that David's first act after acknowledging the death of Saul is not an im-mediate political action. He prays to the Lord, and in response to God's guidance he goes to Hebron.

2:4–7—In Hebron the tribe of Judah, acting alone, anoints David as king. But even David's first act as king of Judah is to honor the people of Jabesh-gilead for their loyalty to the fallen king, Saul. They rescued Saul's body from humiliation by the Philistines (1 Sam. 31:11–13), and David invokes the blessing of God's love and faithful-ness on them for such loyalty to God's anointed. David will not allow his own self-interest to blind him to the larger importance of the office of God's anointed, which comes both as the gift of God and the affirmation of the people.

2:8–3:5 War between the Houses of Saul and David

2:8–11—Saul's general, Abner, tries to continue Saul's kingdom by supporting Ishbaal, a surviving son of Saul, probably a very young man. In con-trast to David, the verbs of this action are focused in the realities of power politics and self-interest. Abner takes, brings, and makes a king. There is no role for prayer, God, or people here. The lead-ership of God's kingdom must always be a shared partnership with God and community.

2:12–32—Tragically the kingdom of God's anointed one cannot come apart from a facing of the realities of violence and bloodshed that afflict David's world and our own. This story is one of petty conflicts between competing kingdoms, senseless loss of young lives, and cycles of vengeance that perpetuate the bloodshed. In the chapters ahead David must face these realities. The accounts are eager to emphasize that such violent events were not of David's making, but if God's kingdom is to be established through him he will have to deal with the Abners and Joabs and the harsh political realities they represent. Those who would serve the kingdom cannot remain aloof from the violent struggles of the world, but must find alternatives to such realities or paths to futures beyond them.

other side of the pool. **14** Abner said to Joab, "Let the young men come forward and have a contest before us." Joab said, "Let them come forward." **15** So they came forward and were counted as they passed by, twelve for Benjamin and Ishbaal*ᵃ* son of Saul, and twelve of the servants of David. **16** Each grasped his opponent by the head, and thrust his sword in his opponent's side; so they fell down together. Therefore that place was called Helkath-hazzurim,*ᵇ* which is at Gibeon. **17** The battle was very fierce that day; and Abner and the men of Israel were beaten by the servants of David.

18 The three sons of Zeruiah were there, Joab, Abishai, and Asahel. Now Asahel was as swift of foot as a wild gazelle. **19** Asahel pursued Abner, turning neither to the right nor to the left as he followed him. **20** Then Abner looked back and said, "Is it you, Asahel?" He answered, "Yes, it is." **21** Abner said to him, "Turn to your right or to your left, and seize one of the young men, and take his spoil." But Asahel would not turn away from following him. **22** Abner said again to Asahel, "Turn away from following me; why should I strike you to the ground? How then could I show my face to your brother Joab?" **23** But he refused to turn away. So Abner struck him in the stomach with the butt of his spear, so that the spear came out at his back. He fell there, and died where he lay. And all those who came to the place where Asahel had fallen and died, stood still.

24 But Joab and Abishai pursued Abner. As the sun was going down they came to the hill of Ammah, which lies before Giah on the way to the wilderness of Gibeon. **25** The Benjaminites rallied around Abner and formed a single band; they took their stand on the top of a hill. **26** Then Abner called to Joab, "Is

the sword to keep devouring forever? Do you not know that the end will be bitter? How long will it be before you order your people to turn from the pursuit of their kinsmen?" **27** Joab said, "As God lives, if you had not spoken, the people would have continued to pursue their kinsmen, not stopping until morning." **28** Joab sounded the trumpet and all the people stopped; they no longer pursued Israel or engaged in battle any further.

29 Abner and his men traveled all that night through the Arabah; they crossed the Jordan, and, marching the whole forenoon,*ᶜ* they came to Mahanaim. **30** Joab returned from the pursuit of Abner; and when he had gathered all the people together, there were missing of David's servants nineteen men besides Asahel. **31** But the servants of David had killed of Benjamin three hundred sixty of Abner's men. **32** They took up Asahel and buried him in the tomb of his father, which was at Bethlehem. Joab and his men marched all night, and the day broke upon them at Hebron.

Abner Defects to David

3 There was a long war between the house of Saul and the house of David; David grew stronger and stronger, while the house of Saul became weaker and weaker.

2 Sons were born to David at Hebron: his firstborn was Amnon, of Ahinoam of Jezreel; **3** his second, Chileab, of Abigail the widow of Nabal of Carmel; the third, Absalom son of Maacah, daughter of King Talmai of Geshur; **4** the fourth, Adonijah son of Haggith; the fifth, Shephatiah son of Abital; **5** and the sixth, Ithream, of David's wife Eglah. These were born to David in Hebron.

6 While there was war between the house of Saul and the house of David,

---

ᵃ Gk Compare 1 Chr 8.33; 9.39: Heb *Ish-bosheth*, "man of shame" *ᵇ* That is *Field of Sword-edges* *ᶜ* Meaning of Heb uncertain

---

3:6–30 Joab Murders Abner
The cycle of violence and vengeance begun in 2:12–32 continues with the senseless murder of

Abner by Joab just as Abner is about to present the opportunity for a unifying of the two Israelite kingdoms now in conflict for seven years (2:11).

Abner was making himself strong in the house of Saul. ⁷ Now Saul had a concubine whose name was Rizpah daughter of Aiah. And Ishbaal*a* said to Abner, "Why have you gone in to my father's concubine?" ⁸ The words of Ishbaal*b* made Abner very angry; he said, "Am I a dog's head for Judah? Today I keep showing loyalty to the house of your father Saul, to his brothers, and to his friends, and have not given you into the hand of David; and yet you charge me now with a crime concerning this woman. ⁹ So may God do to Abner and so may he add to it! For just what the LORD has sworn to David, that will I accomplish for him, ¹⁰ to transfer the kingdom from the house of Saul, and set up the throne of David over Israel and over Judah, from Dan to Beer-sheba." ¹¹ And Ishbaal*a* could not answer Abner another word, because he feared him.

12 Abner sent messengers to David at Hebron,*c* saying, "To whom does the land belong? Make your covenant with me, and I will give you my support to bring all Israel over to you." ¹³ He said, "Good; I will make a covenant with you. But one thing I require of you: you shall never appear in my presence unless you bring Saul's daughter Michal when you come to see me." ¹⁴ Then David sent messengers to Saul's son Ishbaal,*d* saying, "Give me my wife Michal, to whom I became engaged at the price of one hundred foreskins of the Philistines." ¹⁵ Ishbaal*d* sent and took her from her husband Paltiel the son of Laish. ¹⁶ But her husband went with her, weeping as he walked behind her all the way to Bahurim. Then Abner said to him, "Go back home!" So he went back.

17 Abner sent word to the elders of Israel, saying, "For some time past you have been seeking David as king over you. ¹⁸ Now then bring it about; for the LORD has promised David: Through my servant David I will save my people Israel from the hand of the Philistines, and from all their enemies." ¹⁹ Abner also spoke directly to the Benjaminites; then Abner went to tell David at Hebron all that Israel and the whole house of Benjamin were ready to do.

20 When Abner came with twenty men to David at Hebron, David made a feast for Abner and the men who were with him. ²¹ Abner said to David, "Let me go and rally all Israel to my lord the king, in order that they may make a covenant with you, and that you may reign over all that your heart desires." So David dismissed Abner, and he went away in peace.

Abner Is Killed by Joab

22 Just then the servants of David arrived with Joab from a raid, bringing much spoil with them. But Abner was not with David at Hebron, for David*e* had dismissed him, and he had gone away in peace. ²³ When Joab and all the army that was with him came, it was told Joab, "Abner son of Ner came to the king, and he has dismissed him, and he has gone away in peace." ²⁴ Then Joab went to the king and said, "What have you done? Abner came to you; why did you dismiss him, so that he got away? ²⁵ You know that Abner son of Ner came to deceive you, and to learn your comings and goings and to learn all that you are doing."

26 When Joab came out from David's

---

a Heb *And he* *b* Gk Compare 1 Chr 8.33; 9.39: Heb *Ish-bosheth,* "man of shame" *c* Gk: Heb *where he was* *d* Heb *Ish-bosheth* *e* Heb *he*

Personal agendas are allowed to override the needs of the community, and promising leaders are cut down when their gifts are most needed. In our own time, we have seen leaders literally assassinated in their prime (John and Robert Kennedy, Martin Luther King Jr.), but promising leaders are also often eliminated by ideological attack instead of physical weapons. The results are the same as in David's time. Community interests are ignored to give vent to personal vendettas of self-interest, and leadership is not allowed to develop. Joabs seem to appear in every generation and every cultural context.

presence, he sent messengers after Abner, and they brought him back from the cistern of Sirah; but David did not know about it. [27] When Abner returned to Hebron, Joab took him aside in the gateway to speak with him privately, and there he stabbed him in the stomach. So he died for shedding[a] the blood of Asahel, Joab's[b] brother. [28] Afterward, when David heard of it, he said, "I and my kingdom are forever guiltless before the LORD for the blood of Abner son of Ner. [29] May the guilt[c] fall on the head of Joab, and on all his father's house; and may the house of Joab never be without one who has a discharge, or who is leprous,[d] or who holds a spindle, or who falls by the sword, or who lacks food!" [30] So Joab and his brother Abishai murdered Abner because he had killed their brother Asahel in the battle at Gibeon.

31 Then David said to Joab and to all the people who were with him, "Tear your clothes, and put on sackcloth, and mourn over Abner." And King David followed the bier. [32] They buried Abner at Hebron. The king lifted up his voice and wept at the grave of Abner, and all the people wept. [33] The king lamented for Abner, saying,

"Should Abner die as a fool dies?
[34] Your hands were not bound,
      your feet were not fettered;
   as one falls before the wicked
      you have fallen."

And all the people wept over him again. [35] Then all the people came to persuade David to eat something while it was still day; but David swore, saying, "So may God do to me, and more, if I taste bread or anything else before the sun goes down!" [36] All the people took notice of it, and it pleased them; just as everything the king did pleased all the people. [37] So all the people and all Israel understood that day that the king had no part in the killing of Abner son of Ner. [38] And the king said to his servants, "Do you not know that a prince and a great man has fallen this day in Israel? [39] Today I am powerless, even though anointed king; these men, the sons of Zeruiah, are too violent for me. The LORD pay back the one who does wickedly in accordance with his wickedness!"

Ishbaal Assassinated

4 When Saul's son Ishbaal[e] heard that Abner had died at Hebron, his

[a] Heb lacks shedding   [b] Heb his   [c] Heb May it   [d] A term for several skin diseases; precise meaning uncertain   [e] Heb lacks Ishbaal

---

3:31–39 David's Response to Abner's Murder

Although David himself may be innocent of the violence done to Abner, his kingdom can no longer be innocent. As leader he must take responsibility for what has happened through his subordinates and deal with that reality. David does not ignore what has happened and hope it will pass by if he lies low. He holds Joab accountable (vv. 28–29); he names the offense in public acceptance of responsibility and personal remorse for what has happened, and he acknowledges his inability to control all events. Even the king must ultimately trust in the power of the Lord to render full judgment on the powers of violence and evil (v. 39).

4:1–12 David's Response to Ishbaal's Murder

David must face one more encounter with those who would hand him the kingdom by violence. The death of Abner has left Saul's son, Ishbaal, defenseless, and two opportunistic members of his own military kill him while he is at rest on his own bed. They bring his head to David expect-

ing reward, but David has them executed for their treachery against the innocent son of God's anointed king. This is consistent with his action against the Amalekite in 1:13–16. David knows he cannot legitimate God's kingdom by violence, even if it is not his own. Once again, though claiming innocence himself, David must face the reality of violence in the arenas of political power and deal with it. We cannot imagine that innocence allows the naive ignoring of political power. But this story cannot be cynically read as mere propaganda for a David manipulating events to his own advantage. Such a reading imagines manipulation, compromise, and self-interest as the necessary compromises for entry into the arenas of power. David's response to the combining of power and violence, here and earlier with Abner's death and the loss of Saul and Jonathan, is to mourn the losses, to respond to the perpetrators, and to trust that the Lord ultimately redeems our compromised kingdoms (4:9).

courage failed, and all Israel was dismayed. [2] Saul's son had two captains of raiding bands; the name of the one was Baanah, and the name of the other Rechab. They were sons of Rimmon a Benjaminite from Beeroth—for Beeroth is considered to belong to Benjamin. [3] (Now the people of Beeroth had fled to Gittaim and are there as resident aliens to this day).

[4] Saul's son Jonathan had a son who was crippled in his feet. He was five years old when the news about Saul and Jonathan came from Jezreel. His nurse picked him up and fled; and, in her haste to flee, it happened that he fell and became lame. His name was Mephibosheth.[a]

[5] Now the sons of Rimmon the Beerothite, Rechab and Baanah, set out, and about the heat of the day they came to the house of Ishbaal,[b] while he was taking his noonday rest. [6] They came inside the house as though to take wheat, and they struck him in the stomach; then Rechab and his brother Baanah escaped.[c] [7] Now they had come into the house while he was lying on his couch in his bedchamber; they attacked him, killed him, and beheaded him. Then they took his head and traveled by way of the Arabah all night long. [8] They brought the head of Ishbaal[b] to David at Hebron and said to the king, "Here is the head of Ishbaal,[b] son of Saul, your enemy, who sought your life; the Lord has avenged my lord the king this day on Saul and on his offspring."

[9] David answered Rechab and his brother Baanah, the sons of Rimmon the Beerothite, "As the Lord lives, who has redeemed my life out of every adversity, [10] when the one who told me, 'See, Saul is dead,' thought he was bringing good news, I seized him and killed him at Ziklag—this was the reward I gave him for his news. [11] How much more then, when wicked men have killed a righteous man on his bed in his own house! And now shall I not require his blood at your hand, and destroy you from the earth?" [12] So David commanded the young men, and they killed them; they cut off their hands and feet, and hung their bodies beside the pool at Hebron. But the head of Ishbaal[b] they took and buried in the tomb of Abner at Hebron.

David Anointed King of All Israel

5 Then all the tribes of Israel came to David at Hebron, and said, "Look, we are your bone and flesh. [2] For some time, while Saul was king over us, it was you who led out Israel and brought it in. The Lord said to you: It is you who shall be shepherd of my people Israel, you who shall be ruler over Israel." [3] So all the elders of Israel came to the king at Hebron; and King David made a covenant with them at Hebron before the Lord, and they anointed David king over Israel. [4] David was thirty years old when he began to reign, and he reigned forty years. [5] At Hebron he reigned over Judah seven years and six months; and at Jerusalem he reigned over all Israel and Judah thirty-three years.

Jerusalem Made Capital of the United Kingdom

[6] The king and his men marched to Jerusalem against the Jebusites, the inhabitants of the land, who said to

---

[a] In 1 Chr 8.34 and 9.40, *Merib-baal* [b] Heb *Ish-bosheth* [c] Meaning of Heb of verse 6 uncertain

---

4:4—This verse gives us the background for David's act of loyalty to his friendship with Jonathan in chap. 9.

5:1–5 David Anointed King of All Israel
After a long and difficult period David is now made king over Israel, the northern tribes, as well as the tribe of Judah. Forty years may not be an exact reckoning of the years of David's reign but often appears as the number to indicate a genera-

tion, although the more precise numbers of v. 5 may indicate actual dating.

5:6–10 David Makes Jerusalem His Capital
In an astute move to prevent his capital city from being located in either Israel or Judah David captures the Jebusite city of Jerusalem and makes it his royal city. It literally becomes *the city of David* (v. 9), rather than a city identified with any of the previous tribal territories. The reference to

David, "You will not come in here, even the blind and the lame will turn you back"—thinking, "David cannot come in here." [7] Nevertheless David took the stronghold of Zion, which is now the city of David. [8] David had said on that day, "Whoever would strike down the Jebusites, let him get up the water shaft to attack the lame and the blind, those whom David hates." [a] Therefore it is said, "The blind and the lame shall not come into the house." [9] David occupied the stronghold, and named it the city of David. David built the city all around from the Millo inward. [10] And David became greater and greater, for the LORD, the God of hosts, was with him.

11 King Hiram of Tyre sent messengers to David, along with cedar trees, and carpenters and masons who built David a house. [12] David then perceived that the LORD had established him king over Israel, and that he had exalted his kingdom for the sake of his people Israel.

13 In Jerusalem, after he came from Hebron, David took more concubines and wives; and more sons and daughters were born to David. [14] These are the names of those who were born to him in Jerusalem: Shammua, Shobab, Nathan, Solomon, [15] Ibhar, Elishua, Nepheg, Japhia, [16] Elishama, Eliada, and Eliphelet.

Philistine Attack Repulsed

17 When the Philistines heard that David had been anointed king over Israel, all the Philistines went up in search of David; but David heard about it and went down to the stronghold. [18] Now the Philistines had come and spread out in the valley of Rephaim. [19] David inquired of the LORD, "Shall I go up against the Philistines? Will you give them into my hand?" The LORD said to David, "Go up; for I will certainly give the Philistines into your hand." [20] So David came to Baal-perazim, and David defeated them there. He said, "The LORD has burst forth against [b] my enemies before me, like a bursting flood." Therefore that place is called Baal-perazim. [c] [21] The Philistines abandoned their idols there, and David and his men carried them away.

22 Once again the Philistines came up, and were spread out in the valley of Rephaim. [23] When David inquired of the LORD, he said, "You shall not go up; go around to their rear, and come upon them opposite the balsam trees. [24] When you hear the sound of marching in the tops of the balsam trees, then be on the alert; for then the LORD has gone out before you to strike down the army of the Philistines." [25] David did just as the LORD had commanded him; and he struck down the Philistines from Geba all the way to Gezer.

David Brings the Ark to Jerusalem

6 David again gathered all the chosen men of Israel, thirty thousand.

[a] Another reading is *those who hate David* [b] Heb *paraz* [c] That is *Lord of Bursting Forth*

---

the lame and the blind (v. 8) is obscure, with no agreed-upon meaning in this context. With this unpromising beginning in conquest and with references to exclusion in God's house begins a Jerusalem tradition that ends in quite a different place. Jerusalem becomes the place redeemed by God's holy dwelling there, and eventually is the prototype of the holy city, the New Jerusalem, which descends from the heavens to usher in God's kingdom of peace, justice, and inclusion of all (Rev. 21:2–4).

5:10—This verse concludes the history of the rise of David by restating its main theological theme: the Lord was with David.

5:11–10:19 The Reign of David

5:17–25 Victory over the Philistines

David finally wins the victories over the Philistines that restore all of Israel's territory and brings freedom from Philistine domination. These traditions do affirm the importance of David as a military leader in difficult times, but not without emphasis on his constant resort to prayer and communication with God as the necessary prelude to human action and the ultimate resource that brings deliverance (vv. 19, 23–24). The combination of human agency and divine providence is put forward as the essence of leadership for God's people.

6:1–19 The Ark in Jerusalem

The ark of the covenant, the symbol of God's

² David and all the people with him set out and went from Baale-judah, to bring up from there the ark of God, which is called by the name of the LORD of hosts who is enthroned on the cherubim. ³ They carried the ark of God on a new cart, and brought it out of the house of Abinadab, which was on the hill. Uzzah and Ahio,ᵃ the sons of Abinadab, were driving the new cart ⁴ with the ark of God;ᵇ and Ahioᵃ went in front of the ark. ⁵ David and all the house of Israel were dancing before the LORD with all their might, with songsᶜ and lyres and harps and tambourines and castanets and cymbals.

6 When they came to the threshing floor of Nacon, Uzzah reached out his hand to the ark of God and took hold of it, for the oxen shook it. ⁷ The anger of the LORD was kindled against Uzzah; and God struck him there because he reached out his hand to the ark;ᵈ and he died there beside the ark of God. ⁸ David was angry because the LORD had burst forth with an outburst upon Uzzah; so that place is called Perez-uzzah,ᵉ to this day. ⁹ David was afraid of the LORD that day; he said, "How can the ark of the LORD come into my care?" ¹⁰ So David was unwilling to take the ark of the LORD into his care in the city of David; instead David took it to the house of Obed-edom the Gittite. ¹¹ The ark of the LORD remained in the house of Obed-edom the Gittite three months; and the LORD blessed Obed-edom and all his household.

12 It was told King David, "The LORD has blessed the household of Obed-edom and all that belongs to him, because of the ark of God." So David went and brought up the ark of God from the house of Obed-edom to the city of David with rejoicing; ¹³ and when those who bore the ark of the LORD had gone six paces, he sacrificed an ox and a fatling. ¹⁴ David danced before the LORD with all his might; David was girded with a linen ephod. ¹⁵ So David and all the house of Israel brought up the ark of the LORD with shouting, and with the sound of the trumpet.

16 As the ark of the LORD came into the city of David, Michal daughter of Saul looked out of the window, and saw King David leaping and dancing before the LORD; and she despised him in her heart.

17 They brought in the ark of the LORD, and set it in its place, inside the tent that David had pitched for it; and David offered burnt offerings and offerings of well-being before the LORD. ¹⁸ When David had finished offering the burnt offerings and the offerings of well-being, he blessed the people in the name of the LORD of hosts, ¹⁹ and dis-

ᵃ Or and his brother　ᵇ Compare Gk: Heb and brought it out of the house of Abinadab, which was on the hill with the ark of God　ᶜ Q Ms Gk 1 Chr 13.8: Heb fir trees　ᵈ 1 Chr 13.10 Compare Q Ms: Meaning of Heb uncertain　ᵉ That is Bursting Out Against Uzzah

---

enthroned presence in the midst of Israel, has been lost since its capture by the Philistines (1 Sam. 4). David finds it (cf. Ps. 132) and brings it to Jerusalem, dancing before it in procession, and allying his kingdom with the older religious traditions of the tribal league. This story of David's transfer of the ark to Jerusalem is more than a story of David's personal devotion and praise to the Lord. It is an invitation to contemplate the thin line that separates public honoring of true power in God and the cynical manipulation of religious symbols to enhance political power. David's dancing before the ark has been interpreted in both ways, and both possibilities are present for us to contemplate in the text. This suggests that worship is a riskier business than we normally think. David took the risk of personal involvement and even royal humbling in his dancing as an honoring of the Lord, Israel's true king. But Michal saw only a manipulation of public sentiment for political advantage, because she knew her own return to David's household was not for love but for political gain (2 Sam. 6:20–23). This story confronts us with these two possibilities for understanding David's action, but challenges us to risk involvement in the encounter between religious symbol and public life. The dangers are real, but the possibilities of moral accountability in public life cannot be actualized apart from risking religious engagement in the arenas of public power. The death of Uzzah for laying hands on the ark (vv. 6–7) is disturbing but serves as a reminder that God's holiness is a dangerous thing and management of God's holiness is risky business.

tributed food among all the people, the whole multitude of Israel, both men and women, to each a cake of bread, a portion of meat,[a] and a cake of raisins. Then all the people went back to their homes.

20 David returned to bless his household. But Michal the daughter of Saul came out to meet David, and said, "How the king of Israel honored himself today, uncovering himself today before the eyes of his servants' maids, as any vulgar fellow might shamelessly uncover himself!" 21 David said to Michal, "It was before the LORD, who chose me in place of your father and all his household, to appoint me as prince over Israel, the people of the LORD, that I have danced before the LORD. 22 I will make myself yet more contemptible than this, and I will be abased in my own eyes; but by the maids of whom you have spoken, by them I shall be held in honor." 23 And Michal the daughter of Saul had no child to the day of her death.

God's Covenant with David

7 Now when the king was settled in his house, and the LORD had given him rest from all his enemies around

[a] Vg: Meaning of Heb uncertain

6:20–23 David and Michal

Michal, always identified here as the daughter of Saul, once loved David (1 Sam. 18:20), but we are never told that David loved Michal. She is given in marriage three times for political reasons (1 Sam. 18:27; 25:44; 2 Sam. 3:14–16). One can hardly blame her for being cynical and bitter now. She cannot see in David the glory of God's anointed king—only a man who needs her again for political purposes. That her story is included here reminds us that the books of Samuel know another reality than the one defined only by men's power. First Samuel opened with the story of God's regard for the childless Hannah (1 Sam. 1), and David's use of Michal for his own self-interest may foreshadow his lustful taking of Bathsheba (2 Sam. 11:2–5) and the judgment of God through the prophet Nathan that follows (12:7).

7:1–17 Nathan's Oracle of Promise

The prophet Nathan responds to David's desire to build a house for the Lord to equal the king's own house by the giving of a divine promise to build a house (dynasty) for David. David will not build the temple, but his son Solomon will (v. 13). This oracle of promise for an enduring dynasty of David (v. 16) is one of the cornerstones of a Davidic or royal theology that sees in the ongoing line of David a new evidence of God's saving grace in Israel. Some have seen here a covenant with David, extending and reshaping the covenant with Moses on Sinai. Others, however, have seen this chapter as crass political propaganda, seeking to absolutize the political power of Davidic rulers. There can be no doubt that this text has ideological interests seeking to legitimate Davidic rule. But this text is also a witness to a divine power beyond the power of kings—a divine power that nevertheless takes the risk of engagement with political and public realities. Even kings may be chastised (v. 14, and prophets regularly do so),

but God will insist on ongoing relationship to the arenas of power, lest religion become a disinterested and unengaged spiritual practice apart from the realities of the world.

The dynastic oracle of promise to David has had an important theological role in the history of the church. Particularly since the Protestant Reformation this text has been seen as the introduction of the reality of God's unconditional grace into the language of biblical faith. The covenant with Israel was conditional: "If you obey my voice and keep my covenant, then . . . you shall be my [people]" (Exod. 19:5). The "if" of moral demand is not removed here. Even kings may be judged and chastised (2 Sam. 7:14), but God's steadfast love will endure forever (v. 15). The "if" of moral demand is encompassed by a divine faithfulness that endures even in the face of disobedience from God's king or God's people. This allowed hope to endure even in times of crisis that might suggest divine abandonment, particularly the later crisis of Babylonian exile.

This leads to a second important theological strand in this text. In the events leading up to and through exile to Babylon in 587 BCE, God's enduring promise to David became the basis for the development of messianic hopes. Even when the line of Davidic kings seems to end in exile, God's promise provides the basis for the hope that an anointed one (Heb. *mashiach*) will yet come and establish God's righteous kingdom. The early Christian church saw Jesus in the light of this promise. In the annunciation to Mary in Luke 1:31–33 the angel Gabriel announces the coming birth of Jesus as the fulfillment of God's promise to David. In the church today, the text of Nathan's oracle of promise to David is a reading for the fourth Sunday of Advent in Cycle B of the Revised Common Lectionary. We are invited to consider the birth of Jesus in connection with God's engagement with the political issues of

him, [2] the king said to the prophet Nathan, "See now, I am living in a house of cedar, but the ark of God stays in a tent." [3] Nathan said to the king, "Go, do all that you have in mind; for the LORD is with you."

[4] But that same night the word of the LORD came to Nathan: [5] Go and tell my servant David: Thus says the LORD: Are you the one to build me a house to live in? [6] I have not lived in a house since the day I brought up the people of Israel from Egypt to this day, but I have been moving about in a tent and a tabernacle. [7] Wherever I have moved about among all the people of Israel, did I ever speak a word with any of the tribal leaders[a] of Israel, whom I commanded to shepherd my people Israel, saying, "Why have you not built me a house of cedar?" [8] Now therefore thus you shall say to my servant David: Thus says the LORD of hosts: I took you from the pasture, from following the sheep to be prince over my people Israel; [9] and I have been with you wherever you went, and have cut off all your enemies from before you; and I will make for you a great name, like the name of the great ones of the earth. [10] And I will appoint a place for my people Israel and will plant them, so that they may live in their own place, and be disturbed no more; and evildoers shall afflict them no more, as formerly, [11] from the time that I appointed judges over my people Israel; and I will give you rest from all your enemies. Moreover the LORD declares to you that the LORD will make you a house. [12] When your days are fulfilled and you lie down with your ancestors, I will raise up your offspring after you, who shall come forth from your body, and I will establish his kingdom. [13] He shall build a house for my name, and I will establish the throne of his kingdom forever. [14] I will be a father to him, and he shall be a son to me. When he commits iniquity, I will punish him with a rod such as mortals use, with blows inflicted by human beings. [15] But I will not take[b] my steadfast love from him, as I took it from Saul, whom I put away from before you. [16] Your house and your kingdom shall be made sure forever before me;[c] your throne shall be established forever. [17] In accordance with all these words and with all this vision, Nathan spoke to David.

David's Prayer

[18] Then King David went in and sat before the LORD, and said, "Who am I, O Lord GOD, and what is my house, that you have brought me thus far? [19] And yet this was a small thing in your eyes, O Lord GOD; you have spoken also of your

---

[a] Or any of the tribes [b] Gk Syr Vg 1 Chr 17.13: Heb shall not depart
[c] Gk Heb Mss: MT before you; Compare 2 Sam 7.26, 29

---

justice and power seen in the promise to David. If we see this connection, we should not be surprised to find Mary's song in the Magnificat of Luke 1:46–55 responding with the voiced hope of transformations of worldly power, similar to those Hannah's song in 1 Sam. 2:1–10 anticipated in God's raising up of David.

7:18–29 David's Prayer

David's prayer in response to God's promise through the prophet Nathan sounds audacious to our ears. David acknowledges the sovereignty of God, but at the same time he seems to demand that God remain faithful to the divine promises, both to Israel and to the house of David. Most of our religious traditions relate prayer to an attitude of humility before God, and we are unaccustomed to the boldness of David's prayer. Yet this is in keeping with Hebrew concepts of

prayer, which have something to teach us. In Hebrew prayer it is customary to lay all of life's concerns and passions before God, often in terms that seem blunt and straightforward to our ears. The psalms of lament are an often-cited example. David in his prayer seems concerned for ideological state interests, the stability of his kingdom, and the ongoing welfare of his people. But these are appropriate interests for a king, and David's prayer reminds us that even the ideological self-interests of a king may be submitted to God with an acknowledgment of God's ultimate sovereignty. To pray in ways that reveal our self-interests is, of course, dangerous prayer, but perhaps less dangerous than praying only "safe" prayers that fail to trust in God to judge the appropriateness of our expressed self-interests and to direct us beyond self-interest to the purposes of God's kingdom.

servant's house for a great while to come. May this be instruction for the people,[a] O Lord God! [20] And what more can David say to you? For you know your servant, O Lord God! [21] Because of your promise, and according to your own heart, you have wrought all this greatness, so that your servant may know it. [22] Therefore you are great, O Lord God; for there is no one like you, and there is no God besides you, according to all that we have heard with our ears. [23] Who is like your people, like Israel? Is there another[b] nation on earth whose God went to redeem it as a people, and to make a name for himself, doing great and awesome things for them,[c] by driving out[d] before his people nations and their gods?[e] [24] And you established your people Israel for yourself to be your people forever; and you, O Lord, became their God. [25] And now, O Lord God, as for the word that you have spoken concerning your servant and concerning his house, confirm it forever; do as you have promised. [26] Thus your name will be magnified forever in the saying, 'The Lord of hosts is God over Israel'; and the house of your servant David will be established before you. [27] For you, O Lord of hosts, the God of Israel, have made this revelation to your servant, saying, 'I will build you a house'; therefore your servant has found courage to pray this prayer to you. [28] And now, O Lord God, you are God, and your words are true, and you have promised this good thing to your servant; [29] now therefore may it please you to bless the house of your servant, so that it may continue forever before you; for you, O Lord God, have spoken, and with your

blessing shall the house of your servant be blessed forever."

David's Wars

8 Some time afterward, David attacked the Philistines and subdued them; David took Metheg-ammah out of the hand of the Philistines.

2 He also defeated the Moabites and, making them lie down on the ground, measured them off with a cord; he measured two lengths of cord for those who were to be put to death, and one length[f] for those who were to be spared. And the Moabites became servants to David and brought tribute.

3 David also struck down King Hadadezer son of Rehob of Zobah, as he went to restore his monument[g] at the river Euphrates. [4] David took from him one thousand seven hundred horsemen, and twenty thousand foot soldiers. David hamstrung all the chariot horses, but left enough for a hundred chariots. [5] When the Arameans of Damascus came to help King Hadadezer of Zobah, David killed twenty-two thousand men of the Arameans. [6] Then David put garrisons among the Arameans of Damascus; and the Arameans became servants to David and brought tribute. The Lord gave victory to David wherever he went. [7] David took the gold shields that were carried by the servants of Hadadezer, and brought them to Jerusalem. [8] From Betah and from Berothai, towns of Hadadezer, King David took a great amount of bronze.

9 When King Toi of Hamath heard

[a] Meaning of Heb uncertain   [b] Gk: Heb one   [c] Heb you   [d] Gk 1 Chr 17.21: Heb for your land   [e] Cn: Heb before your people, whom you redeemed for yourself from Egypt, nations and its gods   [f] Heb one full length   [g] Compare 1 Sam 15.12 and 2 Sam 18.18

8:1–14 David at War

In a series of brief reports we hear of David's victories over traditional enemies (Philistines, Moabites, Arameans, Edomites, Amalekites) and the recognition of his sovereignty by others (Toi of Hamath, v. 9). Twice we are told that the Lord gave David these victories (vv. 6 and 14), but absent are the notices of David's consultation with God in prayer before important military

encounters that we saw frequently in his early career. Further, we are told in v. 13 that David's motive for these victories is to **win a name for himself**. God is still present in David's reign, but a tension has arisen between David's own self-justifying authority and God's purposes. That clash of authority will reach a climax in David's self-interested behavior in chap. 11 and God's judgment on that in chap. 12.

that David had defeated the whole army of Hadadezer, **10** Toi sent his son Joram to King David, to greet him and to congratulate him because he had fought against Hadadezer and defeated him. Now Hadadezer had often been at war with Toi. Joram brought with him articles of silver, gold, and bronze; **11** these also King David dedicated to the LORD, together with the silver and gold that he dedicated from all the nations he subdued, **12** from Edom, Moab, the Ammonites, the Philistines, Amalek, and from the spoil of King Hadadezer son of Rehob of Zobah.

13 David won a name for himself. When he returned, he killed eighteen thousand Edomites[a] in the Valley of Salt. **14** He put garrisons in Edom; throughout all Edom he put garrisons, and all the Edomites became David's servants. And the LORD gave victory to David wherever he went.

David's Officers

15 So David reigned over all Israel; and David administered justice and equity to all his people. **16** Joab son of Zeruiah was over the army; Jehoshaphat son of Ahilud was recorder; **17** Zadok son of Ahitub and Ahimelech son of Abiathar were priests; Seraiah was secretary; **18** Benaiah son of Jehoiada was over[b] the Cherethites and the Pelethites; and David's sons were priests.

David's Kindness to Mephibosheth

9 David asked, "Is there still anyone left of the house of Saul to whom I may show kindness for Jonathan's sake?" **2** Now there was a servant of the

---

[a] Gk: Heb *returned from striking down eighteen thousand Arameans*
[b] Syr Tg Vg 20.23; 1 Chr 18.17: Heb lacks *was over*

8:15 David's Rule

Although there are some danger signs in David's behavior toward the nations, his reign is nevertheless characterized by justice and equity toward his people. Seldom can we characterize any exercise of political power as solely positive or negative. David is still God's king, chosen for this moment in Israel's life. In most ways he is worthy of this choice, but there will come a moment in his story when he loses sight of God's authority in the self-interested exercise of his own power (chap. 11). For the moment, the ideals of covenant obedience (*justice and equity*) stand side by side with the necessary organization of bureaucratic structures (vv. 16–18). This is the balance that all who labor in the arenas of public power must seek.

9:1–13 David and Mephibosheth

The word "kindness" (Heb. *hesed*), which appears in vv. 1, 3, and 7, is a reference back to the faithful love sworn between David and Jonathan (1 Sam. 20:8, 14, 15, 17) and between their descendants forever (1 Sam. 20:15, 42). Mephibosheth, the surviving son of Jonathan, was injured and permanently crippled in the retreat following the defeat and death of Saul and Jonathan (2 Sam. 4:4). His name is reported in 1 Chr. 8:34 and 9:40 as Merib-baal but the Deuteronomic Historian has probably substituted the word *bosheth* ("shame") for the word *baal* ("Lord," a title also used as the name of the Canaanite god Ba'al). It is significant that between accounts of David's growing power as king (chaps. 8 and 10) and prior to David's clear

abuse of that power (chap. 11) we are reminded of the qualities of love, compassion, and loyalty that make it understandable that he is the "man after God's own heart" (1 Sam. 13:14). This need not be seen as a cynical act by David to keep an eye on one of the descendants of Saul. Mephibosheth is no threat to David, and David's acts of kindness leave Jonathan's son much more empowered than he was previously. He is given land, servants (Ziba and his household, a former servant of Saul), and a place at the king's table like one of the king's sons (2 Sam. 9:11). Three additional times it is stressed that Mephibosheth is to eat at the king's table, and all of these use the term in Hebrew that means "eat continuously" (vv. 7, 10, 13). The only other time this phrase appears in the Hebrew Bible it is used to tell us that Jehoiachin, the king of Judah carried from Jerusalem into exile, "every day of his life dined regularly in the king's presence" in Babylon (2 Kgs. 25:29). Since the books of Samuel likely received final shape during this time of exile, it is intriguing to think of David's graciousness toward the remnant of Saul foreshadowing the graciousness shown to the remnant of David's house in exile. The full character of such graciousness is perhaps revealed in 2 Sam. 9:3 when David's kindness is characterized as *the kindness of God*. It is ultimately a divine sovereign who invites us to sit at the table and shows us the kindness that restores life. In medieval and Renaissance art, David and Mephibosheth were a frequent subject in painting, sculpture, and stained glass, and the food on the king's table was depicted as the bread and cup of the

house of Saul whose name was Ziba, and he was summoned to David. The king said to him, "Are you Ziba?" And he said, "At your service!" ³ The king said, "Is there anyone remaining of the house of Saul to whom I may show the kindness of God?" Ziba said to the king, "There remains a son of Jonathan; he is crippled in his feet." ⁴ The king said to him, "Where is he?" Ziba said to the king, "He is in the house of Machir son of Ammiel, at Lo-debar." ⁵ Then King David sent and brought him from the house of Machir son of Ammiel, at Lo-debar. ⁶ Mephibosheth*ᵃ* son of Jonathan son of Saul came to David, and fell on his face and did obeisance. David said, "Mephibosheth!"*ᵃ* He answered, "I am your servant." ⁷ David said to him, "Do not be afraid, for I will show you kindness for the sake of your father Jonathan; I will restore to you all the land of your grandfather Saul, and you yourself shall eat at my table always." ⁸ He did obeisance and said, "What is your servant, that you should look upon a dead dog such as I?"

9 Then the king summoned Saul's servant Ziba, and said to him, "All that belonged to Saul and to all his house I have given to your master's grandson. ¹⁰ You and your sons and your servants shall till the land for him, and shall bring in the produce, so that your master's grandson may have food to eat; but your master's grandson Mephibosheth*ᵃ* shall always eat at my table." Now Ziba had fifteen sons and twenty servants. ¹¹ Then Ziba said to the king, "According to all that my lord the king commands his ser-

vant, so your servant will do." Mephibosheth*ᵃ* ate at David's*ᵇ* table, like one of the king's sons. ¹² Mephibosheth*ᵃ* had a young son whose name was Mica. And all who lived in Ziba's house became Mephibosheth's*ᶜ* servants. ¹³ Mephibosheth*ᵃ* lived in Jerusalem, for he always ate at the king's table. Now he was lame in both his feet.

The Ammonites and Arameans Are Defeated

10 Some time afterward, the king of the Ammonites died, and his son Hanun succeeded him. ² David said, "I will deal loyally with Hanun son of Nahash, just as his father dealt loyally with me." So David sent envoys to console him concerning his father. When David's envoys came into the land of the Ammonites, ³ the princes of the Ammonites said to their lord Hanun, "Do you really think that David is honoring your father just because he has sent messengers with condolences to you? Has not David sent his envoys to you to search the city, to spy it out, and to overthrow it?" ⁴ So Hanun seized David's envoys, shaved off half the beard of each, cut off their garments in the middle at their hips, and sent them away. ⁵ When David was told, he sent to meet them, for the men were greatly ashamed. The king said, "Remain at Jericho until your beards have grown, and then return."

6 When the Ammonites saw that they had become odious to David, the Ammonites sent and hired the

ᵃ Or *Merib-baal:* See 4.4 note *ᵇ* Gk: Heb *my* *ᶜ* Or *Merib-baal's:* See 4.4 note

---

Eucharist. The kindness we show to one another is ultimately, as David recognizes, the kindness of God, and our hospitality to one another is an extension of the table of God at which we all may "continually eat."

10:1–19 War with the Ammonites and Arameans

10:2—It is notable that in a chapter devoted to the difficult affairs of state and military crises that confront David, it is still David's declared intention to **deal loyally** in matters of state. The

Hebrew word here is *hesed,* the same word used to describe David's personal kindness toward Mephibosheth in the previous chapter. The same loyal commitment that marks the covenant between God and Israel, that characterizes the friendship of David and Jonathan, that is shown in compassion to Mephibosheth, is the principle that David tries to employ in his actions as a sovereign king in the dealings of nations. One would hope for such integrity in the rulers of nations in all generations.

Arameans of Beth-rehob and the Arameans of Zobah, twenty thousand foot soldiers, as well as the king of Maacah, one thousand men, and the men of Tob, twelve thousand men. 7 When David heard of it, he sent Joab and all the army with the warriors. 8 The Ammonites came out and drew up in battle array at the entrance of the gate; but the Arameans of Zobah and of Rehob, and the men of Tob and Maacah, were by themselves in the open country.

9 When Joab saw that the battle was set against him both in front and in the rear, he chose some of the picked men of Israel, and arrayed them against the Arameans; 10 the rest of his men he put in the charge of his brother Abishai, and he arrayed them against the Ammonites. 11 He said, "If the Arameans are too strong for me, then you shall help me; but if the Ammonites are too strong for you, then I will come and help you. 12 Be strong, and let us be courageous for the sake of our people, and for the cities of our God; and may the LORD do what seems good to him." 13 So Joab and the people who were with him moved forward into battle against the Arameans; and they fled before him. 14 When the Ammonites saw that the Arameans fled, they likewise fled before Abishai,

and entered the city. Then Joab returned from fighting against the Ammonites, and came to Jerusalem.

15 But when the Arameans saw that they had been defeated by Israel, they gathered themselves together. 16 Hadadezer sent and brought out the Arameans who were beyond the Euphrates; and they came to Helam, with Shobach the commander of the army of Hadadezer at their head. 17 When it was told David, he gathered all Israel together, and crossed the Jordan, and came to Helam. The Arameans arrayed themselves against David and fought with him. 18 The Arameans fled before Israel; and David killed of the Arameans seven hundred chariot teams, and forty thousand horsemen,*a* and wounded Shobach the commander of their army, so that he died there. 19 When all the kings who were servants of Hadadezer saw that they had been defeated by Israel, they made peace with Israel, and became subject to them. So the Arameans were afraid to help the Ammonites any more.

David Commits Adultery with Bathsheba

11 In the spring of the year, the time when kings go out to battle,

a 1 Chr 19.18 and some Gk Mss read foot soldiers

10:12—Faced with a crisis in battle, it is David's commander, Joab, who voices an ultimate trust that events rest in the hands of God. Such a sentiment has often been expressed by David, and Joab is usually the pragmatic warrior, but here even David's servant recognizes that beyond the exercise of our own power we must acknowledge the providence of God. Our power will always and necessarily be tinged with self-interest, but the recognition that God's will is ultimately determinative is the corrective to the temptation to absolutize our own power. Unfortunately, David is about to learn of God's judgment when he forgets that even royal power is not absolute.

11:1–20:26 The Court History of David
11:1–12:31 David, Bathsheba, and Nathan
This is a story of the arrogant use of royal power to satisfy the personal lust of the king. It is a credit to the honesty of the tradition that such a negative portrait of David is included in his

story. Indeed, the book of 1 Chronicles omits this story and shows the process of idealizing David underway. It has been difficult for Jewish and Christian tradition to face this element of David's story directly. Theological and artistic interpreters have looked for ways to soften David's guilt. This has been achieved by various strategies: shifting the blame to Bathsheba as a seductress; suggesting that there were mitigating circumstances for David's action; romanticizing the narrative as a great love story. None of these is warranted by the text itself. Second Samuel 11:4 in the Hebrew states clearly that David "took" Bathsheba, and this is a direct fulfillment of Samuel's warning to the people about the dangers of kingship—kings "take" from the people (1 Sam. 8:11–18; the verb "take" is used 6x). Even this verb of coercion is softened in most translations by making the messengers and not David the subject and by saying they simply went *to get her*. David has no evident intention of an ongoing relationship, and

David sent Joab with his officers and all Israel with him; they ravaged the Ammonites, and besieged Rabbah. But David remained at Jerusalem.

2 It happened, late one afternoon, when David rose from his couch and was walking about on the roof of the king's house, that he saw from the roof a woman bathing; the woman was very beautiful. 3 David sent someone to inquire about the woman. It was reported, "This is Bathsheba daughter of Eliam, the wife of Uriah the Hittite." 4 So David sent messengers to get her, and she came to him, and he lay with her. (Now she was purifying herself after her period.) Then she returned to her house. 5 The woman conceived; and she sent and told David, "I am pregnant."

6 So David sent word to Joab, "Send me Uriah the Hittite." And Joab sent Uriah to David. 7 When Uriah came to him, David asked how Joab and the people fared, and how the war was going. 8 Then David said to Uriah, "Go down to your house, and wash your feet." Uriah went out of the king's house, and there followed him a present from the king. 9 But Uriah slept at the entrance of the king's house with all the servants of his lord, and did not go down to his house. 10 When they told David, "Uriah did not go down to his house," David said to Uriah, "You have just come from a journey. Why did you not go down to your house?" 11 Uriah said to David, "The ark and Israel and Judah remain in booths;[a] and my lord Joab and the servants of my lord are camping in the open field; shall I then go to my house, to eat and to drink, and to lie with my wife? As you live, and as your soul lives, I will not do such a thing." 12 Then David said to Uriah, "Remain here today also, and tomorrow I will send you back." So Uriah remained in Jerusalem that day. On the next day, 13 David invited him to eat and drink in his presence and made him drunk; and in the evening he went out to lie on his couch with the servants of his lord, but he did not go down to his house.

David Has Uriah Killed

14 In the morning David wrote a letter to Joab, and sent it by the hand of Uriah. 15 In the letter he wrote, "Set Uriah in the forefront of the hardest fighting, and then draw back from him, so that

a *Or at Succoth*

---

has further dealings with Bathsheba only because she becomes pregnant (11:5). Even then, David prefers a deception that will cause Bathsheba's husband Uriah to think he is the father.

11:6–13—The drama of David's self-serving lust takes a new turn when David tries to lie and cover up his action. The story becomes a reminder of how easily our efforts to escape accountability for a misdeed can lead into greater deceits and involve us in acts that deepen our complicity in self-interested actions that harm others. This section of the story recounts an elaborate effort to make Uriah think that the child conceived by Bathsheba is his own. The effort fails because Uriah is too loyal and refuses to go to the comfort of his own home while his fellow soldiers are still in the battlefield. Recent popular films of David's story have portrayed Uriah as a neglectful or even abusive husband, thus partially justifying David's later action. These portrayals are given no support in the biblical text.

11:14–27—David's sin now escalates to murder. To preserve the king's public reputation, David arranges for Uriah to die by having his general, Joab, send Uriah into heavy fighting and withdraw from around him (v. 15). He sends this order to Joab by Uriah's own hand. When David hears that Uriah is dead, he then marries Bathsheba and she gives birth to a son (v. 27). A noteworthy comment in the text is somewhat obscured by English translations. In v. 25 David sends word to comfort Joab over his complicity in Uriah's death. The phrase **Do not let this matter trouble you** literally reads in Hebrew "Do not let this be evil in your eyes." The last line of v. 27 then reports literally in Hebrew "the thing David had done was evil in the eyes of the LORD." To read David's story honestly is to face our own tendencies to excuse abuses of power—our own and those of others. We live in times when news reports frequently chronicle the misuse of authority by politicians, clergy, teachers, military officers, and corporate executives. To face David's sin directly is to face our own temptations to engage in such self-interested and harmful behavior or to overlook it in others.

he may be struck down and die." ¹⁶ As Joab was besieging the city, he assigned Uriah to the place where he knew there were valiant warriors. ¹⁷ The men of the city came out and fought with Joab; and some of the servants of David among the people fell. Uriah the Hittite was killed as well. ¹⁸ Then Joab sent and told David all the news about the fighting; ¹⁹ and he instructed the messenger, "When you have finished telling the king all the news about the fighting, ²⁰ then, if the king's anger rises, and if he says to you, 'Why did you go so near the city to fight? Did you not know that they would shoot from the wall? ²¹ Who killed Abimelech son of Jerubbaal?*a* Did not a woman throw an upper millstone on him from the wall, so that he died at Thebez? Why did you go so near the wall?' then you shall say, 'Your servant Uriah the Hittite is dead too.'"

22 So the messenger went, and came and told David all that Joab had sent him to tell. ²³ The messenger said to David, "The men gained an advantage over us, and came out against us in the field; but we drove them back to the entrance of the gate. ²⁴ Then the archers shot at your servants from the wall; some of the king's servants are dead; and your servant Uriah the Hittite is dead also." ²⁵ David said to the messenger, "Thus you shall say to Joab, 'Do not let this matter trouble you, for the sword devours now one and now another; press your attack on the city, and overthrow it.' And encourage him."

26 When the wife of Uriah heard that her husband was dead, she made lamentation for him. ²⁷ When the mourning was over, David sent and brought her to his house, and she became his wife, and bore him a son.

Nathan Condemns David

12 But the thing that David had done displeased the LORD, ¹ and the LORD sent Nathan to David. He came to him, and said to him, "There were two men in a certain city, the one rich and the other poor. ² The rich man had very many flocks and herds; ³ but the poor man had nothing but one little ewe lamb, which he had bought. He brought it up, and it grew up with him and with his children; it used to eat of his meager fare, and drink from his cup, and lie in his bosom, and it was like a daughter to him. ⁴ Now there came a traveler to the rich man, and he was loath to take one of his own flock or herd to prepare for the wayfarer who had come to him, but he took the poor man's lamb, and prepared that for the guest who had come to him." ⁵ Then David's anger was greatly kindled against the man. He said to Nathan, "As

a Gk Syr Judg 7.1: Heb *Jerubbesheth*

12:1–12—Nathan, the prophet, comes before David to speak the truth to power in the name of God's judgment. Even David, the king, can be held accountable. But it can be dangerous to speak truth to power, and we should note the subtlety of Nathan's speech. If Nathan approached him directly, David could simply refuse to hear. Instead, Nathan tells the parable and lures David into rendering his own judgment of death before he realizes it is the judgment of God he has pronounced on himself. Nathan's bold *"You are the man!"* (v. 7) is followed by an extended oracle of divine judgment on David for his adultery, deception, and murder. David's actions will carry consequences, particularly within his own family. Nathan's judgment oracle foreshadows the conflict and tragedy that will play out between David's children. Rape, murder, rebellion, and tragedy all lie ahead. Much of this results from self-interested and willful behavior on the part of David's children, much like the behavior he has himself modeled in the matter of Bathsheba and Uriah.

Note that both David and Nathan represent the community of faith in this story. They are both God's called agents, and we should read this story with an understanding that at times we have all played both roles. We cannot imagine ourselves to be solely either the utterly righteous speakers of the prophetic word or the unredeemedly guilty of sin. The church, as readers of this text, must understand its task to encompass both the proclamation of God's judging word and the reception of such judgment itself. We are called to both oppose and repent of that which makes for brokenness in the world.

the LORD lives, the man who has done this deserves to die; ⁶ he shall restore the lamb fourfold, because he did this thing, and because he had no pity."

7 Nathan said to David, "You are the man! Thus says the LORD, the God of Israel: I anointed you king over Israel, and I rescued you from the hand of Saul; ⁸ I gave you your master's house, and your master's wives into your bosom, and gave you the house of Israel and of Judah; and if that had been too little, I would have added as much more. ⁹ Why have you despised the word of the LORD, to do what is evil in his sight? You have struck down Uriah the Hittite with the sword, and have taken his wife to be your wife, and have killed him with the sword of the Ammonites. ¹⁰ Now therefore the sword shall never depart from your house, for you have despised me, and have taken the wife of Uriah the Hittite to be your wife. ¹¹ Thus says the LORD: I will raise up trouble against you from within your own house; and I will take your wives before your eyes, and give them to your neighbor, and he shall lie with your wives in the sight of this very sun. ¹² For you did it secretly; but

I will do this thing before all Israel, and before the sun." ¹³ David said to Nathan, "I have sinned against the LORD." Nathan said to David, "Now the LORD has put away your sin; you shall not die. ¹⁴ Nevertheless, because by this deed you have utterly scorned the LORD,ᵃ the child that is born to you shall die." ¹⁵ Then Nathan went to his house.

Bathsheba's Child Dies

The LORD struck the child that Uriah's wife bore to David, and it became very ill. ¹⁶ David therefore pleaded with God for the child; David fasted, and went in and lay all night on the ground. ¹⁷ The elders of his house stood beside him, urging him to rise from the ground; but he would not, nor did he eat food with them. ¹⁸ On the seventh day the child died. And the servants of David were afraid to tell him that the child was dead; for they said, "While the child was still alive, we spoke to him, and he did not listen to us; how then can we tell him the child is dead? He may do himself some harm." ¹⁹ But when David saw that his servants were whispering together,

ᵃ Ancient scribal tradition: Compare 1 Sam 25.22 note: Heb *scorned the enemies of the LORD*

12:13–14—David's immediate and forthright response of repentance is almost as startling as Nathan's accusation. Not all future kings in Israel will respond to prophetic confrontation in this way. The great prayer of repentance in Ps. 51 is associated in its superscription with this moment in David's story. David's repentance reminds us that the goal hoped for in speaking judgment is the transformation made possible by repentance, a concept in Hebrew associated with turning and moving in a new direction. Not to hope for and recognize repentance following on judgment is to settle for guilt as the goal of prophetic speech. David's repentance invokes from Nathan the immediate response that David will not die, the sentence unwittingly pronounced by David (2 Sam. 12:5) on himself. Nathan does go on, however, to make the troubling statement that the child born to David and Bathsheba will die.

12:15–23—We do not want to accept the notion that God might take the innocent life of a child as a punishment on the sins of its parents. But this text assumes that all events ultimately come from God and that all circumstances of our lives can

be used by God for God's purposes. The focus here is on David, who as king acted as if he was the controller of destinies and lives. Here David must learn that even a king stands humbled before the tragedies that sometimes come into human life and cannot be controlled by our own power or position. David must discover his own vulnerability and powerlessness, and his response as he does so has something to teach us. David's behavior seems to reverse the usual process of loss and grief in his culture. While the child was ill, David prayed, fasted, and grieved (v. 16). But when the child died, he washed, dressed, worshiped, and ate (vv. 19–20). David felt deeply about the loss of his son and hoped fervently that God's healing grace might come (v. 22), but when death came he refused to let death have the final word and instead reaffirmed his life and the future horizon of life in God through which he and his son might be someday reunited in death (v. 23). For Christians this is the reality of the resurrection of Christ, the reaffirming of life at the very moment that death seems to prevail.

he perceived that the child was dead; and David said to his servants, "Is the child dead?" They said, "He is dead."

20 Then David rose from the ground, washed, anointed himself, and changed his clothes. He went into the house of the LORD, and worshiped; he then went to his own house; and when he asked, they set food before him and he ate. **21** Then his servants said to him, "What is this thing that you have done? You fasted and wept for the child while it was alive; but when the child died, you rose and ate food." **22** He said, "While the child was still alive, I fasted and wept; for I said, 'Who knows? The LORD may be gracious to me, and the child may live.' **23** But now he is dead; why should I fast? Can I bring him back again? I shall go to him, but he will not return to me."

Solomon Is Born

24 Then David consoled his wife Bathsheba, and went to her, and lay with her; and she bore a son, and he named him Solomon. The LORD loved him, **25** and sent a message by the prophet Nathan; so he named him Jedidiah,*a* because of the LORD.

The Ammonites Crushed

26 Now Joab fought against Rabbah of the Ammonites, and took the royal city. **27** Joab sent messengers to David, and said, "I have fought against Rabbah; moreover, I have taken the water city. **28** Now, then, gather the rest of the people together, and encamp against the city, and take it; or I myself will take the city, and it will be called by my name." **29** So David gathered all the people together and went to Rabbah, and fought against it and took it. **30** He took the crown of Milcom*b* from his head; the weight of it was a talent of gold, and in it was a precious stone; and it was placed on David's head. He also brought forth the spoil of the city, a very great amount. **31** He brought out the people who were in it, and set them to work with saws and iron picks and iron axes, or sent them to the brickworks. Thus he did to all the cities of the Ammonites. Then David and all the people returned to Jerusalem.

Amnon and Tamar

13 Some time passed. David's son Absalom had a beautiful sister whose name was Tamar; and David's son Amnon fell in love with her. **2** Amnon was so tormented that he made himself ill because of his sister Tamar, for she was a virgin and it seemed impossible to Amnon to do anything to her. **3** But Amnon had a friend whose name was Jonadab, the son of David's brother Shimeah; and Jonadab was a very crafty man. **4** He said to him, "O son of the king, why are you so haggard morning after morning? Will you not tell me?" Amnon said to him, "I love Tamar, my brother Absalom's sister." **5** Jonadab said to him, "Lie down on your bed, and pretend to be ill; and when your father comes to see you, say to him, 'Let my sister Tamar come and give me something to eat, and prepare the food in my sight, so that I may see it and eat it from

a That is Beloved of the LORD b Gk See 1 Kings 11.5, 33: Heb their kings

---

12:24–25—Solomon will become the son who succeeds David on the throne (1 Kgs. 1–2), and his mother, along with the prophet Nathan, will play an important role in this.

13:1–19 The Rape of Tamar
The tragic consequences of David's sin and judgment begin to unfold in his family as Nathan's oracle had foreshadowed. This is a heartbreaking story of unbridled lust that led David's oldest son, Amnon, to lure his half sister Tamar under false pretenses into his bedchamber where he raped her and then heartlessly turned her out as a bro-

ken woman. We do not like to read such stories as part of our Scripture. But such a failure to read Tamar's story renders her invisible, just as many victims of violence in our own time are left invisible and unheard. Tamar is victimized, but even in her tragic story we can recognize her extraordinary compassion, even though that compassion was used to trick her into Amnon's chamber. We can also acknowledge her courage and resourcefulness in speaking to Amnon with persuasive alternatives, even though Amnon refuses them.

her hand.'" ⁶ So Amnon lay down, and pretended to be ill; and when the king came to see him, Amnon said to the king, "Please let my sister Tamar come and make a couple of cakes in my sight, so that I may eat from her hand."

7 Then David sent home to Tamar, saying, "Go to your brother Amnon's house, and prepare food for him." ⁸ So Tamar went to her brother Amnon's house, where he was lying down. She took dough, kneaded it, made cakes in his sight, and baked the cakes. ⁹ Then she took the pan and set them*a* out before him, but he refused to eat. Amnon said, "Send out everyone from me." So everyone went out from him. ¹⁰ Then Amnon said to Tamar, "Bring the food into the chamber, so that I may eat from your hand." So Tamar took the cakes she had made, and brought them into the chamber to Amnon her brother. ¹¹ But when she brought them near him to eat, he took hold of her, and said to her, "Come, lie with me, my sister." ¹² She answered him, "No, my brother, do not force me; for such a thing is not done in Israel; do not do anything so vile! ¹³ As for me, where could I carry my shame? And as for you, you would be as one of the scoundrels in Israel. Now therefore, I beg you, speak to the king; for he will not withhold me from you." ¹⁴ But he would not listen to her; and being stronger than she, he forced her and lay with her.

15 Then Amnon was seized with a very great loathing for her; indeed, his loathing was even greater than the lust he had felt for her. Amnon said to her, "Get out!" ¹⁶ But she said to him, "No, my brother;*b* for this wrong in sending me away is greater than the other that you did to me." But he would not listen to her. ¹⁷ He called the young man who served him and said, "Put this woman out of my presence, and bolt the door after her." ¹⁸ (Now she was wearing a long robe with sleeves; for this is how the virgin daughters of the king were clothed in earlier times.*c*) So his servant put her out, and bolted the door after her. ¹⁹ But Tamar put ashes on her head, and tore the long robe that she was wearing; she put her hand on her head, and went away, crying aloud as she went.

20 Her brother Absalom said to her, "Has Amnon your brother been with you? Be quiet for now, my sister; he is your brother; do not take this to heart." So Tamar remained, a desolate woman, in her brother Absalom's house. ²¹ When King David heard of all these things, he became very angry, but he would not punish his son Amnon, because he loved him, for he was his firstborn.*d* ²² But Absalom spoke to Amnon neither good nor bad; for Absalom hated Amnon, because he had raped his sister Tamar.

Absalom Avenges the Violation of His Sister

23 After two full years Absalom had

---

a Heb *and poured*   *b* Cn Compare Gk Vg: Meaning of Heb uncertain   *c* Cn: Heb *were clothed in robes*   *d* Q Ms Gk: MT lacks *but he would not punish . . . firstborn*

13:20–22 The Response of Absalom and David

Tamar's tragedy is compounded by the response of the men who should have taken up her case for justice. Absalom, her brother, quiets her and demeans her grief and pain (v. 20). We will see soon that he sees in this tragedy only the opportunity for a personal vengeance against his brother Amnon that results in his own elevated status as heir to the throne. David, Tamar's father, is angry but does nothing (v. 21). He refuses to punish Amnon and seems more concerned not to do injury to him than to act in response to the injury already suffered by Tamar. As we shall see, the cycle of violence, if it is not broken, leads only to further violence. David's sons are beginning to emulate his own willful and destructive behavior, and David refuses to stop it. Tamar is left desolate and without a future, for she is now considered unmarriageable.

13:23–39 The Murder of Amnon

The violence escalates. Absalom nurses his hatred of Amnon and after two years seizes an opportunity when Amnon is unsuspecting and defenseless to kill him (vv. 28–29). David, thinking all of his sons have been murdered by Absalom, is grief-stricken, but later learns only Amnon has died (vv. 32–33). Absalom flees into exile, where

sheepshearers at Baal-hazor, which is near Ephraim, and Absalom invited all the king's sons. 24 Absalom came to the king, and said, "Your servant has sheep-shearers; will the king and his servants please go with your servant?" 25 But the king said to Absalom, "No, my son, let us not all go, or else we will be burden-some to you." He pressed him, but he would not go but gave him his blessing. 26 Then Absalom said, "If not, please let my brother Amnon go with us." The king said to him, "Why should he go with you?" 27 But Absalom pressed him until he let Amnon and all the king's sons go with him. Absalom made a feast like a king's feast.a 28 Then Absalom commanded his servants, "Watch when Amnon's heart is merry with wine, and when I say to you, 'Strike Amnon,' then kill him. Do not be afraid; have I not myself commanded you? Be courageous and valiant." 29 So the servants of Absa-lom did to Amnon as Absalom had com-manded. Then all the king's sons rose, and each mounted his mule and fled.

30 While they were on the way, the report came to David that Absalom had killed all the king's sons, and not one of them was left. 31 The king rose, tore his garments, and lay on the ground; and all his servants who were standing by tore their garments. 32 But Jonadab, the son of David's brother Shimeah, said, "Let not my lord suppose that they have killed all the young men the king's sons; Amnon alone is dead. This has been determined by Absalom from the day Amnonb raped his sister Tamar. 33 Now therefore, do not let my lord the king take it to heart, as if all the king's sons were dead; for Amnon alone is dead."

34 But Absalom fled. When the young man who kept watch looked up, he saw many people coming from the Horo-naim roadc by the side of the mountain. 35 Jonadab said to the king, "See, the king's sons have come; as your servant said, so it has come about." 36 As soon as he had finished speaking, the king's sons arrived, and raised their voices and wept; and the king and all his servants also wept very bitterly.

37 But Absalom fled, and went to Tal-mai son of Ammihud, king of Geshur. David mourned for his son day after day. 38 Absalom, having fled to Geshur, stayed there three years. 39 And the heart ofd the king went out, yearning for Absalom; for he was now consoled over the death of Amnon.

Absalom Returns to Jerusalem

14 Now Joab son of Zeruiah per-ceived that the king's mind was on Absalom. 2 Joab sent to Tekoa and brought from there a wise woman. He

a Gk Compare Q Ms: MT lacks *Absalom made a feast like a king's feast*
b Heb *he*   c Cn Compare Gk: Heb *the road behind him*   d Q Ms Gk: MT *And David*

---

he remains for three years while David mourns now for the loss of Absalom's presence. Again David does nothing to assert justice and end the cycle of violence. Now the seeds of Absalom's revolt against David himself are being sown.

14:1–24 Absalom Returns to Jerusalem
Through the intervention of a wise woman from Tekoa (arranged by David's general, Joab) David has an opportunity to make a new beginning with his son Absalom. The woman's story is designed to confront David with his own situa-tion, and it is very much like the strategy used by the prophet Nathan in telling a parable through which the king renders judgment on himself. The purpose of the story told by the woman is not judgment but reconciliation (12:1–6). If David can decide to preserve the woman's relation-ship with her alienated son, why cannot the king reconcile with his alienated son, Absalom? David sees the hand of Joab behind the woman's story, but still he grants Joab's request to allow the return to Jerusalem of Absalom. This episode can-not help but recall Jesus' parable of the Prodigal Son (Luke 15:11–32), where a son's choices have separated him from the love of a father whose love endures and forgives. Readers of this chapter in David's story can rightly take hope that cycles of violence can be broken by the opportunity for love and reconciliation. But the chance for a new beginning can also be squandered, and we read ominously in 2 Sam. 14:24 that, although Absa-lom is allowed to return to Jerusalem, he is not allowed into David's presence. There are no open arms of a waiting and forgiving father here.

said to her, "Pretend to be a mourner; put on mourning garments, do not anoint yourself with oil, but behave like a woman who has been mourning many days for the dead. ³Go to the king and speak to him as follows." And Joab put the words into her mouth.

4 When the woman of Tekoa came to the king, she fell on her face to the ground and did obeisance, and said, "Help, O king!" ⁵The king asked her, "What is your trouble?" She answered, "Alas, I am a widow; my husband is dead. ⁶Your servant had two sons, and they fought with one another in the field; there was no one to part them, and one struck the other and killed him. ⁷Now the whole family has risen against your servant. They say, 'Give up the man who struck his brother, so that we may kill him for the life of his brother whom he murdered, even if we destroy the heir as well.' Thus they would quench my one remaining ember, and leave to my husband neither name nor remnant on the face of the earth."

8 Then the king said to the woman, "Go to your house, and I will give orders concerning you." ⁹The woman of Tekoa said to the king, "On me be the guilt, my lord the king, and on my father's house; let the king and his throne be guiltless." ¹⁰The king said, "If anyone says anything to you, bring him to me, and he shall never touch you again." ¹¹Then she said, "Please, may the king keep the LORD your God in mind, so that the avenger of blood may kill no more, and my son not be destroyed." He said, "As the LORD lives, not one hair of your son shall fall to the ground."

12 Then the woman said, "Please let your servant speak a word to my lord the king." He said, "Speak." ¹³The woman said, "Why then have you planned such a thing against the people of God? For in giving this decision the king convicts himself, inasmuch as the king does not bring his banished one home again. ¹⁴We must all die; we are like water spilled on the ground, which cannot be

gathered up. But God will not take away a life; he will devise plans so as not to keep an outcast banished forever from his presence.ᵃ ¹⁵Now I have come to say this to my lord the king because the people have made me afraid; your servant thought, 'I will speak to the king; it may be that the king will perform the request of his servant. ¹⁶For the king will hear, and deliver his servant from the hand of the man who would cut both me and my son off from the heritage of God.' ¹⁷Your servant thought, 'The word of my lord the king will set me at rest'; for my lord the king is like the angel of God, discerning good and evil. The LORD your God be with you!"

18 Then the king answered the woman, "Do not withhold from me anything I ask you." The woman said, "Let my lord the king speak." ¹⁹The king said, "Is the hand of Joab with you in all this?" The woman answered and said, "As surely as you live, my lord the king, one cannot turn right or left from anything that my lord the king has said. For it was your servant Joab who commanded me; it was he who put all these words into the mouth of your servant. ²⁰In order to change the course of affairs your servant Joab did this. But my lord has wisdom like the wisdom of the angel of God to know all things that are on the earth."

21 Then the king said to Joab, "Very well, I grant this; go, bring back the young man Absalom." ²²Joab prostrated himself with his face to the ground and did obeisance, and blessed the king; and Joab said, "Today your servant knows that I have found favor in your sight, my lord the king, in that the king has granted the request of his servant." ²³So Joab set off, went to Geshur, and brought Absalom to Jerusalem. ²⁴The king said, "Let him go to his own house; he is not to come into my presence." So Absalom went to his own house, and did not come into the king's presence.

ᵃ Meaning of Heb uncertain

David Forgives Absalom

25 Now in all Israel there was no one to be praised so much for his beauty as Absalom; from the sole of his foot to the crown of his head there was no blemish in him. 26 When he cut the hair of his head (for at the end of every year he used to cut it; when it was heavy on him, he cut it), he weighed the hair of his head, two hundred shekels by the king's weight. 27 There were born to Absalom three sons, and one daughter whose name was Tamar; she was a beautiful woman.

28 So Absalom lived two full years in Jerusalem, without coming into the king's presence. 29 Then Absalom sent for Joab to send him to the king; but Joab would not come to him. He sent a second time, but Joab would not come. 30 Then he said to his servants, "Look, Joab's field is next to mine, and he has barley there; go and set it on fire." So Absalom's servants set the field on fire. 31 Then Joab rose and went to Absalom at his house, and said to him, "Why have your servants set my field on fire?"

32 Absalom answered Joab, "Look, I sent word to you: Come here, that I may send you to the king with the question, 'Why have I come from Geshur? It would be better for me to be there still.' Now let me go into the king's presence; if there is guilt in me, let him kill me!" 33 Then Joab went to the king and told him; and he summoned Absalom. So he came to the king and prostrated himself with his face to the ground before the king; and the king kissed Absalom.

Absalom Usurps the Throne

15 After this Absalom got himself a chariot and horses, and fifty men to run ahead of him. 2 Absalom used to rise early and stand beside the road into the gate; and when anyone brought a suit before the king for judgment, Absalom would call out and say, "From what city are you?" When the person said, "Your servant is of such and such a tribe in Israel," 3 Absalom would say, "See, your claims are good and right; but there is no one deputed by the king to hear you." 4 Absalom said moreover, "If only I were judge in the land! Then all who had a suit

---

14:25–33 David Forgives Absalom Too Late

14:25–26—The note on Absalom's beauty, and especially his head of luxurious hair, foreshadows his ultimate fate (18:9).

14:28–33—It is tragic that two years have passed since Absalom's return to Jerusalem, and David still has not seen his son face to face. It takes a bold device on Absalom's part to force a meeting with Joab to send by him a request to meet with his father David. Only after being forced into such a meeting does David kiss his son returned from exile (v. 33). This kiss comes too late. The moment for reconciliation has long since passed. Unlike the prodigal son, Absalom does not return to find the father's love waiting to forgive and begin again. David's kiss comes grudgingly to a resentful Absalom, and the cycle of violence in David's family is not ended but renewed. The resentful Absalom begins to plot rebellion (chap. 15). When God's children, Israel, are in exile in Babylon, the prophet of the exile speaks in God's voice to announce that God has already forgiven and forgotten Israel's sins and has done so "for my own sake" (Isa. 43:25). David does not realize that forgiveness of Absalom is for the sake of his own future, not only Absalom's. In the end

David will be left with only loss, grief, and regret (2 Sam. 18:33). As persons of faith we can learn from David's missed opportunity the importance of modeling God's forgiveness in our own willingness to embrace the new futures that come through forgiveness and reconciliation.

15:1–12 Absalom's Rebellion

Absalom cunningly ingratiates himself to many of the common people in his father's kingdom by making himself more accessible and responsive to their grievances. He is actively sowing the seeds of a rebellion to seize the throne from his father David. His strategy is successful (v. 6), and as readers we are not surprised. David has not extended any effort to address the grievances in his own family, let alone the grievances of the people. David seems to have become a bystander in his own story, while events dominated by the violent ambitions and desires of his sons hold center stage. After four years of preparing his support (v. 7), Absalom travels to Hebron on a pretext and there declares himself king, openly in opposition to his father (v. 10). With him in the rebellion is an important counselor to David named Ahithophel, who will play a dramatic role in the later story (v. 12).

or cause might come to me, and I would give them justice." ⁵ Whenever people came near to do obeisance to him, he would put out his hand and take hold of them, and kiss them. ⁶ Thus Absalom did to every Israelite who came to the king for judgment; so Absalom stole the hearts of the people of Israel.

7 At the end of four[a] years Absalom said to the king, "Please let me go to Hebron and pay the vow that I have made to the LORD. ⁸ For your servant made a vow while I lived at Geshur in Aram: If the LORD will indeed bring me back to Jerusalem, then I will worship the LORD in Hebron."[b] ⁹ The king said to him, "Go in peace." So he got up, and went to Hebron. ¹⁰ But Absalom sent secret messengers throughout all the tribes of Israel, saying, "As soon as you hear the sound of the trumpet, then shout: Absalom has become king at Hebron!" ¹¹ Two hundred men from Jerusalem went with Absalom; they were invited guests, and they went in their innocence, knowing nothing of the matter. ¹² While Absalom was offering the sacrifices, he sent for[c] Ahithophel the Gilonite, David's counselor, from his city Giloh. The con-

spiracy grew in strength, and the people with Absalom kept increasing.

David Flees from Jerusalem

13 A messenger came to David, saying, "The hearts of the Israelites have gone after Absalom." ¹⁴ Then David said to all his officials who were with him at Jerusalem, "Get up! Let us flee, or there will be no escape for us from Absalom. Hurry, or he will soon overtake us, and bring disaster down upon us, and attack the city with the edge of the sword." ¹⁵ The king's officials said to the king, "Your servants are ready to do whatever our lord the king decides." ¹⁶ So the king left, followed by all his household, except ten concubines whom he left behind to look after the house. ¹⁷ The king left, followed by all the people; and they stopped at the last house. ¹⁸ All his officials passed by him; and all the Cherethites, and all the Pelethites, and all the six hundred Gittites who had followed him from Gath, passed on before the king.

19 Then the king said to Ittai the Gittite, "Why are you also coming with us?

---

[a] Gk Syr: Heb forty [b] Gk Mss: Heb lacks in Hebron [c] Or he sent

---

15:13–16:14 David's Flight from Jerusalem
David's retreat from Jerusalem can be read as a penitential journey. It is David the sinner, with all his flaws, who begins this journey, but in its course, through a series of remarkable encounters, we also rediscover elements of the David we knew earlier in the story. The journey becomes redemptive and renewing, in a way that does not make light of David's losses, pain, and failure, but that makes clear the power of God to renew from such crises. David's willingness to turn again to that God makes the difference in this journey.

15:13–14—When David hears of Absalom's rebellion, he declares an immediate retreat from Jerusalem so that he will not be trapped there. It seems clear that David is not surprised to hear that his son has captured the hearts of the people. He must have seen and heard reports of Absalom's activities, but once more he has done nothing to break the cycle of violence in his family. This moment when David seems to have lost everything may be the low point of his entire story. It is not only a crisis of external political

events, but the moment when, in this journey of loss, David must confront his own personal crisis.

15:19–22—A touch of David's generous spirit shows again in his response to Ittai, the Gittite. In the custom of small kingships of the time, David's military included mercenary forces recruited from non-Israelite peoples. Ittai commands six hundred men (v. 18) and these Gittites are in the retreat entourage leaving with David from Jerusalem. David, of course, can use all of the military strength he can get in his circumstances, but his response is instead the generous one of reminding Ittai that he need not risk himself or his men in this civil war between father and son. So David implores him to stay in Jerusalem, to forgo the hardships of the wilderness into which David is fleeing, and to do so with the blessing of the Lord's *steadfast love and faithfulness* (v. 20). This is more like the David we have seen earlier, generous and relying on the Lord in difficult circumstances. Ittai's loyal response that he will stay with David as his servant reminds us as well of the loyalty David often commanded among his men (v. 21).

Go back, and stay with the king; for you are a foreigner, and also an exile from your home. ²⁰ You came only yesterday, and shall I today make you wander about with us, while I go wherever I can? Go back, and take your kinsfolk with you; and may the LORD show*a* steadfast love and faithfulness to you." ²¹ But Ittai answered the king, "As the LORD lives, and as my lord the king lives, wherever my lord the king may be, whether for death or for life, there also your servant will be." ²² David said to Ittai, "Go then, march on." So Ittai the Gittite marched on, with all his men and all the little ones who were with him. ²³ The whole country wept aloud as all the people passed by; the king crossed the Wadi Kidron, and all the people moved on toward the wilderness.

24 Abiathar came up, and Zadok also, with all the Levites, carrying the ark of the covenant of God. They set down the ark of God, until the people had all passed out of the city. ²⁵ Then the king said to Zadok, "Carry the ark of God back into the city. If I find favor in the eyes of the LORD, he will bring me back and let me see both it and the place where it stays. ²⁶ But if he says, 'I take no pleasure in you,' here I am, let him do to me what seems good to him." ²⁷ The king also said to the priest Zadok, "Look,*b* go back to the city in peace, you and Abiathar,*c* with your two sons, Ahimaaz

your son, and Jonathan son of Abiathar. ²⁸ See, I will wait at the fords of the wilderness until word comes from you to inform me." ²⁹ So Zadok and Abiathar carried the ark of God back to Jerusalem, and they remained there.

30 But David went up the ascent of the Mount of Olives, weeping as he went, with his head covered and walking barefoot; and all the people who were with him covered their heads and went up, weeping as they went. ³¹ David was told that Ahithophel was among the conspirators with Absalom. And David said, "O LORD, I pray you, turn the counsel of Ahithophel into foolishness."

Hushai Becomes David's Spy

32 When David came to the summit, where God was worshiped, Hushai the Archite came to meet him with his coat torn and earth on his head. ³³ David said to him, "If you go on with me, you will be a burden to me. ³⁴ But if you return to the city and say to Absalom, 'I will be your servant, O king; as I have been your father's servant in time past, so now I will be your servant,' then you will defeat for me the counsel of Ahithophel. ³⁵ The priests Zadok and Abiathar will be with you there. So whatever you hear from the king's house, tell it to the priests Zadok and Abiathar. ³⁶ Their

a Gk Compare 2.6: Heb lacks *may the* LORD *show*   *b* Gk: Heb *Are you a seer or Do you see?*   *c* Cn: Heb lacks *and Abiathar*

15:24–28—When the priests Abiathar and Zadok come out to join David, bringing the ark of the covenant with them, David once more implores them to remain in Jerusalem and not to remove the ark from its dwelling place in Jerusalem (vv. 24–25a). While David wishes them to remain as his eyes and ears in Jerusalem (vv. 27–28), at the same time David makes an important statement of trust in God. In vv. 25b–26 David willingly casts his fate into the hands of God. He commits himself to the judgment of the Lord on his future, as a man and as a king. If he finds favor with God, then God will return him to Jerusalem; but if not, David is willing to accept that judgment as well. This is the first clear expression of David's reliance on the Lord in his story since his prayer in 2 Sam. 7:18–29.

15:30–31—David weeps, covers his head, and walks barefoot. The impression is strengthened that his retreat takes on the trappings of a penitential journey. When he hears that Ahithophel is with the conspirators, he prays to the Lord to confound Ahithophel's counsel. This is the David of prayer we often saw earlier in his story.

15:32–37—The David who prays is also the David who takes action. Thus, when another of his trusted advisers, Hushai, comes to join David's penitential retreat, David sends him back to Jerusalem to pretend loyalty to Absalom and counter the advice of Ahithophel. Through Hushai, Abiathar, and Zadok, David hopes to remain informed of Absalom's plans. Some translations read for v. 32 that on reaching the summit of the Mount of Olives, David "worshiped God."

two sons are with them there, Zadok's son Ahimaaz and Abiathar's son Jonathan; and by them you shall report to me everything you hear." [37] So Hushai, David's friend, came into the city, just as Absalom was entering Jerusalem.

David's Adversaries

16 When David had passed a little beyond the summit, Ziba the servant of Mephibosheth[a] met him, with a couple of donkeys saddled, carrying two hundred loaves of bread, one hundred bunches of raisins, one hundred of summer fruits, and one skin of wine. [2] The king said to Ziba, "Why have you brought these?" Ziba answered, "The donkeys are for the king's household to ride, the bread and summer fruit for the young men to eat, and the wine is for those to drink who faint in the wilderness." [3] The king said, "And where is your master's son?" Ziba said to the king, "He remains in Jerusalem; for he said, 'Today the house of Israel will give me back my grandfather's kingdom.'" [4] Then the king said to Ziba, "All that belonged to Mephibosheth[a] is now yours." Ziba said, "I do obeisance; let me find favor in your sight, my lord the king."

Shimei Curses David

[5] When King David came to Bahurim, a man of the family of the house of Saul came out whose name was Shimei son of Gera; he came out cursing. [6] He threw stones at David and at all the servants of King David; now all the people and all the warriors were on his right and on his left. [7] Shimei shouted while he cursed, "Out! Out! Murderer! Scoundrel! [8] The LORD has avenged on all of you the blood of the house of Saul, in whose place you have reigned; and the LORD has given the kingdom into the hand of your son Absalom. See, disaster has overtaken you; for you are a man of blood."

[9] Then Abishai son of Zeruiah said to the king, "Why should this dead dog curse my lord the king? Let me go over and take off his head." [10] But the king said, "What have I to do with you, you sons of Zeruiah? If he is cursing because the LORD has said to him, 'Curse David,' who then shall say, 'Why have you done so?'" [11] David said to Abishai and to all his servants, "My own son seeks my life; how much more now may this Benjaminite! Let him alone, and let him curse; for the LORD has bidden him. [12] It

[a] Or Merib-baal: See 4.4 note

16:1–4—David is met by Ziba, the servant of Saul assigned by David to administer lands for Mephibosheth, the son of Jonathan to whom David shows kindness (chap. 9). Ziba brings provisions for David and his men and accuses Mephibosheth of disloyalty to David, in the hope of recovering Saul's kingdom (16:3). David responds by impulsively giving all of Mephibosheth's property to Ziba. This drama is, however, not complete. Even on first impression it seems unlikely that Mephibosheth would hope to recover the Saulide throne when Absalom is obviously the alternative to David. Later, on his return to Jerusalem, David will meet Mephibosheth, who has another version of events to recount, and David will have a difficult decision to make (19:24–30).

16:5–14—The final person David meets on his retreat from Jerusalem is Shimei, a man related to the house of Saul. He curses David, throws stones, and accuses him of murder and treachery. He is the epitome of the person who relishes kicking someone who is down but probably lacked the courage to say such things when that

person was in power. Abishai, the brother of Joab and one of David's most trusted warriors, wants to kill Shimei for such vile treatment of the king (v. 9). David could have kept silence once again and allowed violence to unfold in the midst of this journey, but this penitential retreat from Jerusalem has seen the reappearance of a David unwilling to be a bystander to events. David restrains Abishai. Instead, he chooses to trust in what God is doing through these events. If his own son Absalom has taken arms against him, who is David to suggest that this Saulide has no right to curse him? David is willing to let the Lord decide whether or not he deserves the cursing of Shimei, and to let the Lord decide whether there is further good that yet can come to David (vv. 11–12). Violent responses to those who speak ill of us cannot be used as an alternative to faithfully addressing the issues that divide us from others. It is in the faithful facing of our genuine conflicts that we trust God will be present making a new future possible. Simply silencing opponents changes nothing.

may be that the LORD will look on my distress,[a] and the LORD will repay me with good for this cursing of me today." [13] So David and his men went on the road, while Shimei went along on the hillside opposite him and cursed as he went, throwing stones and flinging dust at him. [14] The king and all the people who were with him arrived weary at the Jordan;[b] and there he refreshed himself.

The Counsel of Ahithophel

[15] Now Absalom and all the Israelites[c] came to Jerusalem; Ahithophel was with him. [16] When Hushai the Archite, David's friend, came to Absalom, Hushai said to Absalom, "Long live the king! Long live the king!" [17] Absalom said to Hushai, "Is this your loyalty to your friend? Why did you not go with your friend?" [18] Hushai said to Absalom, "No; but the one whom the LORD and this people and all the Israelites have chosen, his I will be, and with him I will remain. [19] Moreover, whom should I serve? Should it not be his son? Just as I have served your father, so I will serve you."

[20] Then Absalom said to Ahithophel, "Give us your counsel; what shall we do?" [21] Ahithophel said to Absalom, "Go in to your father's concubines, the ones he has left to look after the house; and all Israel will hear that you have made yourself odious to your father, and the hands of all who are with you will be strengthened." [22] So they pitched a tent for Absalom upon the roof; and Absalom went in to his father's concubines in the sight of all Israel. [23] Now in those days the counsel that Ahithophel gave was as if one consulted the oracle[d] of God; so all the counsel of Ahithophel was esteemed, both by David and by Absalom.

17 Moreover Ahithophel said to Absalom, "Let me choose twelve thousand men, and I will set out and pursue David tonight. [2] I will come upon him while he is weary and discouraged, and throw him into a panic; and all the people who are with him will flee. I will strike down only the king, [3] and I will

[a] Gk Vg: Heb *iniquity*   [b] Gk: Heb lacks *at the Jordan*   [c] Gk: Heb *all the people, the men of Israel*   [d] Heb *word*

16:15–17:23 The Counsel of Ahithophel and Hushai

This detailed narrative gives us a full account of the opposing counsels of Ahithophel and Hushai. Absalom's choice of Hushai's plan is the turning point of the rebellion and leads to Absalom's death. Earlier English literature was fascinated by these two advisers, and although we are no longer as familiar with this story, the types represented are a staple in modern literature as well. Ahithophel is the epitome of the clever traitor whose loyalty is given in self-interested efforts to be on the winning side. His suicide (17:23) has been considered, like that of Judas, to be appropriate to his treachery. Hushai, on the other hand, represents loyalty willing to risk all for the sake of a commitment he believes to be right—the undercover patriot. The story of these two men might well reward a modern reading. We live in times prone to choose loyalties on the basis of what seems likely to be successful. We want to be on the successful side of issues, trends, and practices in public or private life. In this story, David's cause did not look like a winning prospect, but Hushai's loyalty was given because he believed David was in the right. For Christians, the following of a crucified one does

not often seem a success-oriented prospect. The key for the story of Ahithophel and Hushai, and the key for readers of their story today, is found in 17:14. It is the working of God's providence that makes the difference. Measured in human terms, much of what God is doing does not look likely to succeed. Like Hushai, we are called to make a faithful commitment to those loyalties that seem aligned with our best understanding of what God is doing in the world and trust that in so doing we might become channels for divine providence. Choosing loyalties on the basis of what looks likely of success with little risk may lead us to the tragic fate of Ahithophel.

16:20–23—Ahithophel's first advice to Absalom leads to the fulfillment of Nathan's oracle of judgment that God "will take your wives before your eyes, and give them to your neighbor, and he shall lie with your wives in the sight of this very sun. For you did it secretly; but I will do this thing before all Israel, and before the sun" (12:11b–12).

17:1–4—Ahithophel's advice to Absalom is to make a quick strike against David and his men while they are tired, discouraged, and disorganized. A key element in his plan is that Absalom would remain safe in Jerusalem, and Ahithophel would seek to kill only David.

bring all the people back to you as a bride comes home to her husband. You seek the life of only one man,[a] and all the people will be at peace." **4** The advice pleased Absalom and all the elders of Israel.

The Counsel of Hushai

5 Then Absalom said, "Call Hushai the Archite also, and let us hear too what he has to say." **6** When Hushai came to Absalom, Absalom said to him, "This is what Ahithophel has said; shall we do as he advises? If not, you tell us." **7** Then Hushai said to Absalom, "This time the counsel that Ahithophel has given is not good." **8** Hushai continued, "You know that your father and his men are warriors, and that they are enraged, like a bear robbed of her cubs in the field. Besides, your father is expert in war; he will not spend the night with the troops. **9** Even now he has hidden himself in one of the pits, or in some other place. And when some of our troops[b] fall at the first attack, whoever hears it will say, 'There has been a slaughter among the troops who follow Absalom.' **10** Then even the valiant warrior, whose heart is like the heart of a lion, will utterly melt with fear; for all Israel knows that your father is a warrior, and that those who are with him are valiant warriors. **11** But my counsel is that all Israel be gathered to you, from Dan to Beer-sheba, like the sand by the sea for multitude, and that you go

to battle in person. **12** So we shall come upon him in whatever place he may be found, and we shall light on him as the dew falls on the ground; and he will not survive, nor will any of those with him. **13** If he withdraws into a city, then all Israel will bring ropes to that city, and we shall drag it into the valley, until not even a pebble is to be found there." **14** Absalom and all the men of Israel said, "The counsel of Hushai the Archite is better than the counsel of Ahithophel." For the LORD had ordained to defeat the good counsel of Ahithophel, so that the LORD might bring ruin on Absalom.

Hushai Warns David to Escape

15 Then Hushai said to the priests Zadok and Abiathar, "Thus and so did Ahithophel counsel Absalom and the elders of Israel; and thus and so I have counseled. **16** Therefore send quickly and tell David, 'Do not lodge tonight at the fords of the wilderness, but by all means cross over; otherwise the king and all the people who are with him will be swallowed up.'" **17** Jonathan and Ahimaaz were waiting at En-rogel; a servant-girl used to go and tell them, and they would go and tell King David; for they could not risk being seen entering the city. **18** But a boy saw them, and told Absalom; so both of them went away quickly, and came to the house of a man at Bahurim, who had a well in his courtyard;

[a] Gk: Heb *like the return of the whole (is) the man whom you seek*   [b] Gk Mss: Heb *some of them*

17:5–14—Hushai's advice is to wait until Absalom can gather a large army and lead it personally into the field to ensure victory. His argument is a masterful playing on what all Israel knows about David's previous reputation as a warrior and the seasoned warriors who are still with him. David and his key commanders are by this time all old men, but Hushai plays on Absalom's fears as well as his ego. Why should Absalom not lead an undefeatable army himself and get the credit? Absalom and his supporters choose this more glorious alternative to the quick surgical strike of Ahithophel. But, of course, the text reports that God's providential hand is at work in this (v. 14b).

17:15–23—Hushai sends word to David to move across the Jordan to safety, lest Ahithophel's plan be implemented, and Jonathan and Ahimaaz (the sons of Abiathar and Zadok) avoid capture and reach David. David's entourage moves to safety, and the stage is set for the decisive battle, but not before David's troops can be rested and resupplied (vv. 27–28). Ahithophel, whose words had been considered as if one "consulted the oracle of God" (16:23), knows that Absalom's cause is now lost. He sets his affairs in order and takes his own life (17:23). Historically, commentators have regarded his suicide as an admission that his choice in support of Absalom was opportunistic and made in callous disregard of his relationship to David.

and they went down into it. ¹⁹ The man's wife took a covering, stretched it over the well's mouth, and spread out grain on it; and nothing was known of it. ²⁰ When Absalom's servants came to the woman at the house, they said, "Where are Ahimaaz and Jonathan?" The woman said to them, "They have crossed over the brook*ᵃ* of water." And when they had searched and could not find them, they returned to Jerusalem.

21 After they had gone, the men came up out of the well, and went and told King David. They said to David, "Go and cross the water quickly; for thus and so has Ahithophel counseled against you." ²² So David and all the people who were with him set out and crossed the Jordan; by daybreak not one was left who had not crossed the Jordan.

23 When Ahithophel saw that his counsel was not followed, he saddled his donkey and went off home to his own city. He set his house in order, and hanged himself; he died and was buried in the tomb of his father.

24 Then David came to Mahanaim, while Absalom crossed the Jordan with all the men of Israel. ²⁵ Now Absalom had set Amasa over the army in the place of Joab. Amasa was the son of a man named Ithra the Ishmaelite,*ᵇ* who had married Abigal daughter of Nahash, sister of Zeruiah, Joab's mother. ²⁶ The Israelites and Absalom encamped in the land of Gilead.

27 When David came to Mahanaim, Shobi son of Nahash from Rabbah of the Ammonites, and Machir son of Ammiel from Lo-debar, and Barzillai the Gileadite from Rogelim, ²⁸ brought beds, basins, and earthen vessels, wheat, barley, meal, parched grain, beans and lentils,*ᶜ* ²⁹ honey and curds, sheep, and cheese from the herd, for David and the people with him to eat; for they said, "The troops are hungry and weary and thirsty in the wilderness."

The Defeat and Death of Absalom

18 Then David mustered the men who were with him, and set over them commanders of thousands and commanders of hundreds. ² And David divided the army into three groups:*ᵈ* one third under the command of Joab, one third under the command of Abishai son of Zeruiah, Joab's brother, and one third under the command of Ittai the Gittite. The king said to the men, "I myself will also go out with you." ³ But the men said, "You shall not go out. For if we flee, they will not care about us. If half of us die, they will not care about us. But you are worth ten thousand of us;*ᵉ* therefore it is better that you send us help from the city." ⁴ The king said to them, "Whatever seems best to you I will do." So the king stood at the side of the gate, while all the army marched out by hundreds and by thousands. ⁵ The king ordered Joab and Abishai and Ittai, saying, "Deal gently for my sake with the young man Absalom." And all the people heard when the king gave orders to all the commanders concerning Absalom.

6 So the army went out into the field against Israel; and the battle was fought in the forest of Ephraim. ⁷ The men of Israel were defeated there by the servants of David, and the slaughter there was great on that day, twenty thousand men. ⁸ The battle spread over the face of all the country; and the forest claimed more victims that day than the sword.

ᵃ Meaning of Heb uncertain ᵇ 1 Chr 2.17: Heb Israelite ᶜ Heb and lentils and parched grain ᵈ Gk: Heb sent forth the army ᵉ Gk Vg Symmachus: Heb for now there are ten thousand such as we

18:1–19:8 The Defeat and Death of Absalom
18:5—David the king and warrior is once more evident in his organization of troops for battle (vv. 1–2a) and his own willingness to go to battle at their head (vv. 2b–4). Yet at the last it is David the father who issues the most urgent orders. He wants his commanders and troops to deal gently with his son Absalom. Absalom is not pictured as betrayer and usurper, but as son. David is caught in the tension between his public and private roles, an all-too-common dilemma for those in positions of public leadership.

9 Absalom happened to meet the servants of David. Absalom was riding on his mule, and the mule went under the thick branches of a great oak. His head caught fast in the oak, and he was left hanging[a] between heaven and earth, while the mule that was under him went on. 10 A man saw it, and told Joab, "I saw Absalom hanging in an oak." 11 Joab said to the man who told him, "What, you saw him! Why then did you not strike him there to the ground? I would have been glad to give you ten pieces of silver and a belt." 12 But the man said to Joab, "Even if I felt in my hand the weight of a thousand pieces of silver, I would not raise my hand against the king's son; for in our hearing the king commanded you and Abishai and Ittai, saying: For my sake protect the young man Absalom! 13 On the other hand, if I had dealt treacherously against his life[b] (and there is nothing hidden from the king), then you yourself would have stood aloof." 14 Joab said, "I will not waste time like this with you." He took three spears in his hand, and thrust them into the heart of Absalom, while he was still alive in the oak. 15 And ten young men, Joab's armor-bearers, surrounded Absalom and struck him, and killed him.

16 Then Joab sounded the trumpet, and the troops came back from pursuing Israel, for Joab restrained the troops. 17 They took Absalom, threw him into a great pit in the forest, and raised over him a very great heap of stones. Meanwhile all the Israelites fled to their homes. 18 Now Absalom in his lifetime had taken and set up for himself a pillar that is in the King's Valley, for he said, "I have no son to keep my name in remembrance"; he called the pillar by his own name. It is called Absalom's Monument to this day.

David Hears of Absalom's Death

19 Then Ahimaaz son of Zadok said, "Let me run, and carry tidings to the king

[a] Gk Syr Tg: Heb *was put*   [b] Another reading is *at the risk of my life*

18:9–15—Absalom, fleeing from the lost battle, is caught up in the branches of a tree by his hair, the very symbol of his vanity and beauty (14:26). Although hanging helplessly, Absalom's life is spared by those who first find him. They fear the anger of the king and only report the plight of Absalom to Joab. Joab, in spite of the king's direct order to spare Absalom, kills him (18:14). It is noteworthy that Joab played a role in trying to reconcile David and Absalom earlier (chap. 14), but neither David nor Absalom made the best of this possibility for reconciliation. Now Joab, ever the pragmatist in David's story, takes matters into his own hands. Absalom is a traitor who would have taken David's life, and Joab acts accordingly. The text seems to suggest that when times for reconciliation are allowed to pass, they may not easily be available again. Joab as family friend tried to effect reunion, but as David's general must act decisively in later circumstances.

18:19–33—These verses give an elaborate build-up to the final arrival of tragic news to David. The runners believe they are bringing the good news of victory over David's enemies, but they also bring the news of Absalom's death, and it is this news to which David reacts. No single text in all of literature more poignantly portrays a parent's grief over the loss of a child than v. 33. Every parent can identify with David's willingness to die in his son's place. Many can recognize in David's grief the particular pain that comes from being unable to turn a child from a self-destructive path. In David's grief we recognize the inability of great love to completely shield our children from harm.

Yet, David's grief is more complex than simple parental loss. David's weeping must be seen in part as weeping for himself. Absalom is yet one more son who has played out the self-centered grasping for power and privilege that David modeled in taking Bathsheba and killing Uriah. David's judgment is to see these same patterns played out in his sons, first Amnon (chap. 13) and now Absalom. And David has failed to break this pattern when he had the opportunity. He is torn between his roles as king and father, and often unwisely chooses the dominant role. When he could have welcomed Absalom back into the loving arms of a father, David was only the king (14:24–28). Now that Absalom is in full rebellion, the country is plunged into civil war, and David's own life is in danger, David needs to be warrior and king to save the nation and his throne. But he can become the father only now, when it is too late. For modern readers of this tragic story we might think of its meaning in social as well as familial terms. Too often we mourn the outbreaks of violence and rebellion in our communities and

that the LORD has delivered him from the power of his enemies." ²⁰ Joab said to him, "You are not to carry tidings today; you may carry tidings another day, but today you shall not do so, because the king's son is dead." ²¹ Then Joab said to a Cushite, "Go, tell the king what you have seen." The Cushite bowed before Joab, and ran. ²² Then Ahimaaz son of Zadok said again to Joab, "Come what may, let me also run after the Cushite." And Joab said, "Why will you run, my son, seeing that you have no reward*a* for the tidings?" ²³ "Come what may," he said, "I will run." So he said to him, "Run." Then Ahimaaz ran by the way of the Plain, and outran the Cushite.

24 Now David was sitting between the two gates. The sentinel went up to the roof of the gate by the wall, and when he looked up, he saw a man running alone. ²⁵ The sentinel shouted and told the king. The king said, "If he is alone, there are tidings in his mouth." He kept coming, and drew near. ²⁶ Then the sentinel saw another man running; and the sentinel called to the gatekeeper and said, "See, another man running alone!" The king said, "He also is bringing tidings." ²⁷ The sentinel said, "I think the running of the first one is like the running of Ahimaaz son of Zadok." The king said, "He is a good man, and comes with good tidings."

28 Then Ahimaaz cried out to the king, "All is well!" He prostrated himself before the king with his face to the ground, and said, "Blessed be the LORD your God, who has delivered up

the men who raised their hand against my lord the king." ²⁹ The king said, "Is it well with the young man Absalom?" Ahimaaz answered, "When Joab sent your servant,*b* I saw a great tumult, but I do not know what it was." ³⁰ The king said, "Turn aside, and stand here." So he turned aside, and stood still.

31 Then the Cushite came; and the Cushite said, "Good tidings for my lord the king! For the LORD has vindicated you this day, delivering you from the power of all who rose up against you." ³² The king said to the Cushite, "Is it well with the young man Absalom?" The Cushite answered, "May the enemies of my lord the king, and all who rise up to do you harm, be like that young man."

David Mourns for Absalom

33*c* The king was deeply moved, and went up to the chamber over the gate, and wept; and as he went, he said, "O my son Absalom, my son, my son Absalom! Would I had died instead of you, O Absalom, my son, my son!"

19 It was told Joab, "The king is weeping and mourning for Absalom." ² So the victory that day was turned into mourning for all the troops; for the troops heard that day, "The king is grieving for his son." ³ The troops stole into the city that day as soldiers steal in who are ashamed when they flee in battle. ⁴ The king covered his face, and the king cried with a loud voice, "O my son Absalom, O Absalom, my son, my son!"

---

a Meaning of Heb uncertain   *b* Heb *the king's servant, your servant*   *c* Ch 19.1 in Heb

---

our world when we have failed to give the earlier responses of love, reconciliation, and justice that might have forestalled such violence.

19:1–8—This conflict between the roles of king and father comes to a head for David in the reaction of the people to his grief. They perceive that David would have been happier if Absalom, the traitor and usurper, had been spared and all of those willing to give their lives for the king had been lost. David the father is still David the king. Again the pragmatic Joab reminds David of his role, and David reluctantly responds. As difficult

as it may seem, those who accept the responsibilities of leadership must keep the larger welfare of the community in view, even in difficult personal circumstances. The balance of public and private responsibilities is one of the most difficult challenges of leadership, and a resolution of this balance lopsidedly in either direction is a sure prescription for disaster. David's grief touches our hearts, but it can also remind us of the need to keep in view both private and public responsibilities, lest we come, like David, to a moment when our grief is too late.

⁵ Then Joab came into the house to the king, and said, "Today you have covered with shame the faces of all your officers who have saved your life today, and the lives of your sons and your daughters, and the lives of your wives and your concubines, ⁶ for love of those who hate you and for hatred of those who love you. You have made it clear today that commanders and officers are nothing to you; for I perceive that if Absalom were alive and all of us were dead today, then you would be pleased. ⁷ So go out at once and speak kindly to your servants; for I swear by the LORD, if you do not go, not a man will stay with you this night; and this will be worse for you than any disaster that has come upon you from your youth until now." ⁸ Then the king got up and took his seat in the gate. The troops were all told, "See, the king is sitting in the gate"; and all the troops came before the king.

David Recalled to Jerusalem

Meanwhile, all the Israelites had fled to their homes. ⁹ All the people were disputing throughout all the tribes of Israel, saying, "The king delivered us from the hand of our enemies, and saved us from the hand of the Philistines; and now he has fled out of the land because of Absa-

lom. ¹⁰ But Absalom, whom we anointed over us, is dead in battle. Now therefore why do you say nothing about bringing the king back?"

11 King David sent this message to the priests Zadok and Abiathar, "Say to the elders of Judah, 'Why should you be the last to bring the king back to his house? The talk of all Israel has come to the king.ᵃ ¹² You are my kin, you are my bone and my flesh; why then should you be the last to bring back the king?' ¹³ And say to Amasa, 'Are you not my bone and my flesh? So may God do to me, and more, if you are not the commander of my army from now on, in place of Joab.'" ¹⁴ Amasaᵇ swayed the hearts of all the people of Judah as one, and they sent word to the king, "Return, both you and all your servants." ¹⁵ So the king came back to the Jordan; and Judah came to Gilgal to meet the king and to bring him over the Jordan.

16 Shimei son of Gera, the Benjaminite, from Bahurim, hurried to come down with the people of Judah to meet King David; ¹⁷ with him were a thousand people from Benjamin. And Ziba, the servant of the house of Saul, with his fifteen sons and his twenty servants, rushed down to the Jordan ahead of the

ᵃ Gk: Heb to the king, to his house ᵇ Heb He

19:9–20:22 David's Return to Jerusalem and Securing of the Kingdom

Absalom's rebellion has failed, but David is left with ongoing political, social, and military issues that must be faced. He had wisely trusted his future to the providence of God (16:12); now he must face that future and its difficult realities. There is no explicit reference to God in the events of these chapters, but we must take them as the circumstances in which David's expressed trust must be maintained and lived out. David has been to the depths of personal and public loss, but he is still God's anointed king. He must live out his expressed trust in God's future in the face of complex and challenging circumstances. David's journey back to Jerusalem and the political situation immediately following his return face him with difficult issues of leadership. Each episode is different, but collectively we see that David reasserts himself as a discerning leader and models qualities to consider in our own roles

of leadership. We would do well to show compassion to those who have wronged us (Shimei, 19:16–23), wise mediation of complex situations where truth cannot be fully known to us (Ziba and Mephibosheth, 19:24–30), affirmation of those who have shown us loyalty and courage (Barzillai, 19:31–40), decisive action when some seek to take advantage of circumstances and create further division (the rebellion of Sheba, 20:1–13), and readiness to accept advice on wise alternatives (the wise woman of Abel, 20:14–22).

19:16–23—Shimei cursed David when he retreated from Jerusalem (16:5–14) and is now eager to ingratiate himself to the king he has reviled. Once again, some of David's men think he deserves to die, but David has had enough of death, and acts with compassion. Shimei is allowed to live. We must note, however, that David is not willing to entirely forget Shimei's treachery. He advises his son Solomon to deal with Shimei after David's death (1 Kgs. 2:8–9).

king, [18] while the crossing was taking place,[a] to bring over the king's household, and to do his pleasure.

David's Mercy to Shimei

Shimei son of Gera fell down before the king, as he was about to cross the Jordan, [19] and said to the king, "May my lord not hold me guilty or remember how your servant did wrong on the day my lord the king left Jerusalem; may the king not bear it in mind. [20] For your servant knows that I have sinned; therefore, see, I have come this day, the first of all the house of Joseph to come down to meet my lord the king." [21] Abishai son of Zeruiah answered, "Shall not Shimei be put to death for this, because he cursed the LORD's anointed?" [22] But David said, "What have I to do with you, you sons of Zeruiah, that you should today become an adversary to me? Shall anyone be put to death in Israel this day? For do I not know that I am this day king over Israel?" [23] The king said to Shimei, "You shall not die." And the king gave him his oath.

David and Mephibosheth Meet

24 Mephibosheth[b] grandson of Saul came down to meet the king; he had not taken care of his feet, or trimmed his beard, or washed his clothes, from the day the king left until the day he came back in safety. [25] When he came from Jerusalem to meet the king, the king said to him, "Why did you not go with me, Mephibosheth?"[b] [26] He answered, "My lord, O king, my servant deceived me; for your servant said to him, 'Saddle a donkey for me,[c] so that I may ride on it and go with the king.' For your servant is lame. [27] He has slandered your servant to my lord the king. But my lord the king is like the angel of God; do therefore what seems good to you. [28] For all my father's house were doomed to death before my lord the king; but you set your servant among those who eat at your table. What further right have I, then, to appeal to the king?" [29] The king said to him, "Why speak any more of your affairs? I have decided: you and Ziba shall divide the land." [30] Mephibosheth[b] said to the king, "Let him take it all, since my lord the king has arrived home safely."

David's Kindness to Barzillai

31 Now Barzillai the Gileadite had come down from Rogelim; he went on with the king to the Jordan, to escort him over the Jordan. [32] Barzillai was a very aged man, eighty years old. He had provided the king with food while he stayed at Mahanaim, for he was a very wealthy man. [33] The king said to Barzillai, "Come over with me, and I will provide for you in Jerusalem at my side." [34] But Barzillai said to the king, "How many years have I still to live, that I should go up with the king to Jerusalem? [35] Today I am eighty years old; can I discern what is pleasant and what is not? Can your servant taste what he eats or what he drinks? Can I still listen to the voice of singing men and singing women? Why then should

a Cn: Heb *the ford crossed*   *b* Or *Merib-baal;* See 4.4 note   *c* Gk Syr Vg: Heb *said, 'I will saddle a donkey for myself*

19:24–30—Mephibosheth meets David with a different story from that told by Ziba during David's retreat from Jerusalem (16:1–4). He claims that, being lame, he could not saddle a donkey to ride with David and Ziba left him behind. To back his claim, he has not washed or cared for himself since David left Jerusalem. Who is telling the truth? David, wisely seeing that there is no easy way to determine this, divides the land of Saul's estate between Ziba and Mephibosheth. Mephibosheth leaves a good impression with the reader when his final response is to say that Ziba can take it all. Mephibosheth is satisfied that the king is safe. It is a fitting final view of the loyalty between David and Jonathan and their descendants (cf. 9:1–13).

19:31–40—David returns kindness for loyalty. He tries to reward Barzillai for his loyal support by bringing him to the court in Jerusalem, but Barzillai is eighty years old and wants only to retire to his home and live out his years in peace. Instead he seeks a place in David's house for Chimham (vv. 37–38), who most believe is one of the sons of Barzillai commended to Solomon in 1 Kgs. 2:6.

your servant be an added burden to my lord the king? **36** Your servant will go a little way over the Jordan with the king. Why should the king recompense me with such a reward? **37** Please let your servant return, so that I may die in my own town, near the graves of my father and my mother. But here is your servant Chimham; let him go over with my lord the king; and do for him whatever seems good to you." **38** The king answered, "Chimham shall go over with me, and I will do for him whatever seems good to you; and all that you desire of me I will do for you." **39** Then all the people crossed over the Jordan, and the king crossed over; the king kissed Barzillai and blessed him, and he returned to his own home. **40** The king went on to Gilgal, and Chimham went on with him; all the people of Judah, and also half the people of Israel, brought the king on his way.

41 Then all the people of Israel came to the king, and said to him, "Why have our kindred the people of Judah stolen you away, and brought the king and his household over the Jordan, and all David's men with him?" **42** All the people of Judah answered the people of Israel, "Because the king is near of kin to us. Why then are you angry over this matter? Have we eaten at all at the king's expense? Or has he given us any gift?" **43** But the people of Israel answered the people of Judah, "We have ten shares in the king, and in David also we have more than you. Why then did you despise us? Were we not the first to speak of bring-ing back our king?" But the words of the people of Judah were fiercer than the words of the people of Israel.

The Rebellion of Sheba

20 Now a scoundrel named Sheba son of Bichri, a Benjaminite, happened to be there. He sounded the trumpet and cried out,

"We have no portion in David,
 no share in the son of Jesse!
Everyone to your tents, O Israel!"

2 So all the people of Israel withdrew from David and followed Sheba son of Bichri; but the people of Judah followed their king steadfastly from the Jordan to Jerusalem.

3 David came to his house at Jerusalem; and the king took the ten concubines whom he had left to look after the house, and put them in a house under guard, and provided for them, but did not go in to them. So they were shut up until the day of their death, living as if in widowhood.

4 Then the king said to Amasa, "Call the men of Judah together to me within three days, and be here yourself." **5** So Amasa went to summon Judah; but he delayed beyond the set time that had been appointed him. **6** David said to Abishai, "Now Sheba son of Bichri will do us more harm than Absalom; take your lord's servants and pursue him, or he will find fortified cities for himself, and escape from us." **7** Joab's men went out after him, along with the Chereth-ites, the Pelethites, and all the warriors;

19:41–20:2—These verses reflect ongoing ten-sions between Judah and the ten northern tribes of Israel. These tensions go back to the days before David's kingship, and he had become king separately over these two tribal territories (2 Sam. 2:4; 5:3). Now conflict over who has the greater claim on David provides the opening for Sheba, a Benjaminite (Saul's tribe), to declare a rebellion. The country is about to be plunged into a new civil war. Although this rebellion will not be successful, Sheba's cry (20:1) is echoed in the later separation of the northern tribes from Judah after Solomon's death (1 Kgs. 12:16). That divi-sion will be permanent.

20:4–13—Once again Joab, in carrying out David's orders, adds his own violent element to it. David seeks to send Amasa as head of an army to pursue Sheba, but when Amasa delays, Abishai and Joab (the sons of Zeruiah in David's inner circle) take up the chase. When Amasa arrives late, Joab treacherously kills him and continues the pursuit with Abishai. This was clearly not what David desired. Later, on his deathbed, David names Joab's murder of Abner (3:27) and Amasa as justification for Solomon to remove Joab as a possible threat to his own throne (1 Kgs. 2:5–6).

they went out from Jerusalem to pursue Sheba son of Bichri. ⁸ When they were at the large stone that is in Gibeon, Amasa came to meet them. Now Joab was wearing a soldier's garment and over it was a belt with a sword in its sheath fastened at his waist; as he went forward it fell out. ⁹ Joab said to Amasa, "Is it well with you, my brother?" And Joab took Amasa by the beard with his right hand to kiss him. ¹⁰ But Amasa did not notice the sword in Joab's hand; Joab struck him in the belly so that his entrails poured out on the ground, and he died. He did not strike a second blow.

Then Joab and his brother Abishai pursued Sheba son of Bichri. ¹¹ And one of Joab's men took his stand by Amasa, and said, "Whoever favors Joab, and whoever is for David, let him follow Joab." ¹² Amasa lay wallowing in his blood on the highway, and the man saw that all the people were stopping. Since he saw that all who came by him were stopping, he carried Amasa from the highway into a field, and threw a garment over him. ¹³ Once he was removed from the highway, all the people went on after Joab to pursue Sheba son of Bichri.

14 Sheba[a] passed through all the tribes of Israel to Abel of Beth-maacah;[b] and all the Bichrites[c] assembled, and followed him inside. ¹⁵ Joab's forces[d] came and besieged him in Abel of Beth-maacah; they threw up a siege ramp against the city, and it stood against the rampart. Joab's forces were battering the wall to break it down. ¹⁶ Then a wise woman called from the city, "Listen! Listen! Tell Joab, 'Come here, I want to speak to you.'" ¹⁷ He came near her; and

the woman said, "Are you Joab?" He answered, "I am." Then she said to him, "Listen to the words of your servant." He answered, "I am listening." ¹⁸ Then she said, "They used to say in the old days, 'Let them inquire at Abel'; and so they would settle a matter. ¹⁹ I am one of those who are peaceable and faithful in Israel; you seek to destroy a city that is a mother in Israel; why will you swallow up the heritage of the LORD?" ²⁰ Joab answered, "Far be it from me, far be it, that I should swallow up or destroy! ²¹ That is not the case! But a man of the hill country of Ephraim, called Sheba son of Bichri, has lifted up his hand against King David; give him up alone, and I will withdraw from the city." The woman said to Joab, "His head shall be thrown over the wall to you." ²² Then the woman went to all the people with her wise plan. And they cut off the head of Sheba son of Bichri, and threw it out to Joab. So he blew the trumpet, and they dispersed from the city, and all went to their homes, while Joab returned to Jerusalem to the king.

23 Now Joab was in command of all the army of Israel;[e] Benaiah son of Jehoiada was in command of the Cherethites and the Pelethites; ²⁴ Adoram was in charge of the forced labor; Jehoshaphat son of Ahilud was the recorder; ²⁵ Sheva was secretary; Zadok and Abiathar were priests; ²⁶ and Ira the Jairite was also David's priest.

David Avenges the Gibeonites

21 Now there was a famine in the days of David for three years, year after year; and David inquired of

[a] Heb *He* [b] Compare 20.15: Heb *and Beth-maacah* [c] Compare Gk Vg: Heb *Berites* [d] Heb *They* [e] Cn: Heb *Joab to all the army, Israel*

20:14–22—When the rebel Sheba takes refuge in the city of Abel, Joab prepares to conquer the city. A wise woman of Abel enters into negotiations with Joab and surrenders the head of Sheba rather than risk the destruction of the city.

21:1–24:25 Final Davidic Traditions

These chapters, often described as appendices to the books of Samuel, do not fit into the chronological sequence of David's story and interrupt

the connection to the narrative of David's death in 1 Kgs. 1–2. Recent interpreters, however, have not seen this arrangement as random. There seem to be both a pattern to these chapters and a purpose for their inclusion. The pattern is symmetrical, with two poetic songs in the center, each emphasizing God's relationship to David (22:1–51, focused on God's deliverance of David; 23:1–7, focused on God's promise to David). On either

the LORD. The LORD said, "There is bloodguilt on Saul and on his house, because he put the Gibeonites to death." ²So the king called the Gibeonites and spoke to them. (Now the Gibeonites were not of the people of Israel, but of the remnant of the Amorites; although the people of Israel had sworn to spare them, Saul had tried to wipe them out in his zeal for the people of Israel and Judah.) ³David said to the Gibeonites, "What shall I do for you? How shall I make expiation, that you may bless the heritage of the LORD?" ⁴The Gibeonites said to him, "It is not a matter of silver or gold between us and Saul or his house; neither is it for us to put anyone to death in Israel." He said, "What do you say that I should do for you?" ⁵They said to the king, "The man who consumed us and planned to destroy us, so that we should have no place in all the territory of Israel— ⁶let seven of his sons be handed over to us, and we will impale them before the LORD at Gibeon on the mountain of the LORD."[a] The king said, "I will hand them over."

7 But the king spared Mephibosheth,[b] the son of Saul's son Jonathan, because of the oath of the LORD that was between them, between David and Jonathan son of Saul. ⁸The king took the two sons of Rizpah daughter of Aiah, whom she bore to Saul, Armoni and Mephibosheth;[b] and the five sons of Merab[c] daughter of Saul, whom she bore to Adriel son of Barzillai the Meholathite; ⁹he gave them into the hands of the Gibeonites, and they impaled them on the mountain before the LORD. The seven of them perished together. They were put to death in the first days of harvest, at the beginning of barley harvest.

10 Then Rizpah the daughter of Aiah

[a] Cn Compare Gk and 21.9: Heb at Gibeah of Saul, the chosen of the LORD [b] Or Merib-baal: See 4.4 note [c] Two Heb Mss Syr Compare Gk: MT Michal

---

side of these songs stand lists of heroes with brief notices of their deeds (21:15–22; 23:8–39) and narratives on the expiation of royal guilt (of Saul in 21:1–14; of David in 24:1–25). The materials in these chapters relate to times early in David's reign and in some instances before he became king (e.g., 23:13–17). Collectively these chapters remind us that even kings can be declared guilty before the Lord, that David was not acting alone as the only hero in Israel during this time, and that David's success and the promise of his reign were dependent on his relationship with the Lord. These themes prevent a return to an ideology of absolute power focused on the king. David has been confronted and judged for the mistaken notion that his power was absolute (chap. 12). He has experienced the tragic consequences of this resort to grasping power in his kingdom and his family (chaps. 13–19). In chap. 20 David has been restored to power, and his general, Joab, has once again acted with violence that seems unnecessary in the situation. David's deathbed story in 1 Kgs. 1–2 will be marked by vengeance and bloodbaths. Lest there be an unremarked return to the violent use of royal power, the appendices of chaps. 21–24 remind us that David's true power lies with the Lord, who is the source of both blessing and judgment, even for kings. These chapters are a welcome corrective to the tendency of power in leadership to be become self-serving and self-justifying.

21:1–14 Avenging the Gibeonites

This story reflects a primitive notion of bloodguilt that we can no longer affirm. Because of an unknown atrocity committed by Saul against the Gibeonites, seven of Saul's descendants are handed over to the Gibeonites for execution. This is done in hopes of ending a famine in the land. We can no longer morally justify the notion of bloodguilt that carries over to subsequent generations, although the effects of sin and violence do continue to be felt beyond the lives of perpetrators and must be morally addressed. Some have commented that David's action seems self-serving because it eliminates all potential claimants to Saul's throne (Mephibosheth is the exception, v. 7; see chap. 9). We have no way to examine David's motives, but this story can remind us how easily political advantage can masquerade as pious duty. We can examine uses of religious justification in the political arenas of our own time. Use of religious language as motive for political action must be critically examined, and self-serving hypocrisy in such uses must be exposed. Use of religious appeals cannot result in an exclusion from public political scrutiny. Although we cannot examine David's motives, the ambiguity left in reading his story can urge us to examine our own.

21:10–14—Rizpah, the mother of two of the men executed by the Gibeonites, refuses to leave their bodies to the humiliation of no honorable burial.

took sackcloth, and spread it on a rock for herself, from the beginning of harvest until rain fell on them from the heavens; she did not allow the birds of the air to come on the bodies*a* by day, or the wild animals by night. ¹¹ When David was told what Rizpah daughter of Aiah, the concubine of Saul, had done, ¹² David went and took the bones of Saul and the bones of his son Jonathan from the people of Jabesh-gilead, who had stolen them from the public square of Beth-shan, where the Philistines had hung them up, on the day the Philistines killed Saul on Gilboa. ¹³ He brought up from there the bones of Saul and the bones of his son Jonathan; and they gathered the bones of those who had been impaled. ¹⁴ They buried the bones of Saul and of his son Jonathan in the land of Benjamin in Zela, in the tomb of his father Kish; they did all that the king commanded. After that, God heeded supplications for the land.

Exploits of David's Men

15 The Philistines went to war again with Israel, and David went down together with his servants. They fought against the Philistines, and David grew weary. ¹⁶ Ishbi-benob, one of the descendants of the giants, whose spear weighed three hundred shekels of bronze, and who was fitted out with new weapons,*b* said he would kill David. ¹⁷ But Abishai son of Zeruiah came to his aid, and attacked the Philistine and killed him. Then David's men swore to him, "You shall not go out with us to battle any longer, so that you do not quench the lamp of Israel."

18 After this a battle took place with the Philistines, at Gob; then Sibbecai the Hushathite killed Saph, who was one of the descendants of the giants. ¹⁹ Then there was another battle with the Philistines at Gob; and Elhanan son of Jaare-oregim, the Bethlehemite, killed Goliath the Gittite, the shaft of whose spear was like a weaver's beam. ²⁰ There was again war at Gath, where there was a man of great size, who had six fingers on each hand, and six toes on each foot, twenty-four in number; he too was descended from the giants. ²¹ When he taunted Israel, Jonathan son of David's brother Shimei, killed him. ²² These four were descended from the giants in Gath; they fell by the hands of David and his servants.

David's Song of Thanksgiving

22 David spoke to the LORD the words of this song on the day

---

a Heb *them*   *b* Heb *was belted anew*

Simple humanity would not leave the grandsons of Israel's king to become carrion for birds and wild beasts. Her vigil becomes a moral witness by a powerless mother in appeal to a powerful king. Rizpah's persistent action reminds us that political power can be effected by moral power. The power of rulers is not absolute; it is rooted only in human realities. Moral witness takes its stance on grounds that transcend human power. To David's credit he recognizes the moral power of Rizpah's witness, and in his song in chap. 22 understands the power beyond his own to rest in the Lord. Rizpah's persistence can encourage us to resist political power, when it acts unjustly, with the integrity of our own moral witness rooted in God's power.

21:15–22 Exploits of David's Warriors

These brief notices all report the exploits of David's warriors against the Philistines. Each involves the defeat of a giant Philistine warrior,

reminding us of David's defeat of Goliath (1 Sam. 17). Indeed, v. 19 reports the defeat by Elhanan, the Bethlehemite, of a Philistine named Goliath. This may be a variant tradition of the story in 1 Sam. 17. The effect of these notices, however, is to make clear that David was not alone in bringing Israel's new future, free from Philistine occupation. Leaders may be tempted to think that they alone make the difference, but leaders require communities of support with their own heroes. Especially since these notices include the exclusion of David from the field of battle (v. 17) the emphasis is on leadership as a corporate effort.

22:1–51 David's Song

This poetic song is a near duplicate of Ps. 18. The superscription of Ps. 18 is identical to v. 1 here, but the psalm opens with an additional line, "I love you, O LORD, my strength." The poem is a song of thanksgiving in the voice of the king.

when the LORD delivered him from the hand of all his enemies, and from the hand of Saul. ² He said:

The LORD is my rock, my fortress,
and my deliverer,
³ my God, my rock, in whom I take refuge,
my shield and the horn of my salvation,
my stronghold and my refuge,
my savior; you save me from violence.
⁴ I call upon the LORD, who is worthy to be praised,
and I am saved from my enemies.

⁵ For the waves of death encompassed me,
the torrents of perdition assailed me;
⁶ the cords of Sheol entangled me,
the snares of death confronted me.

⁷ In my distress I called upon the LORD;
to my God I called.
From his temple he heard my voice,
and my cry came to his ears.

⁸ Then the earth reeled and rocked;
the foundations of the heavens trembled
and quaked, because he was angry.
⁹ Smoke went up from his nostrils,
and devouring fire from his mouth;
glowing coals flamed forth from him.
¹⁰ He bowed the heavens, and came down;

thick darkness was under his feet.
¹¹ He rode on a cherub, and flew;
he was seen upon the wings of the wind.
¹² He made darkness around him a canopy,
thick clouds, a gathering of water.
¹³ Out of the brightness before him coals of fire flamed forth.
¹⁴ The LORD thundered from heaven;
the Most High uttered his voice.
¹⁵ He sent out arrows, and scattered them
—lightning, and routed them.
¹⁶ Then the channels of the sea were seen,
the foundations of the world were laid bare
at the rebuke of the LORD,
at the blast of the breath of his nostrils.
¹⁷ He reached from on high, he took me,
he drew me out of mighty waters.
¹⁸ He delivered me from my strong enemy,
from those who hated me;
for they were too mighty for me.
¹⁹ They came upon me in the day of my calamity,
but the LORD was my stay.
²⁰ He brought me out into a broad place;
he delivered me, because he delighted in me.

²¹ The LORD rewarded me according to my righteousness;

22:2–20—The first section of this song celebrates the power of God to deliver. The king appears as a supplicant for help (v. 7). Although deliverance may be experienced over against threatening enemies, the deliverance of the Lord is described as the more elemental power of God to overcome the threat of chaos and maintain the divinely created order. For David's generation and our own, the crises of personal and public life are challenges to the basic notion that God is sovereign over the powers of chaos. This song is an affirmation that we can rely on God for deliverance when our human capacities allow us only to cry for God's help.

22:21–28—This second section of David's song has been troubling to some, for it suggests that human obedience and righteousness can guarantee divine favor. Further, in the context of David's story, the assertion of blamelessness (v. 24) does not ring true after we have read of David's sin against Bathsheba and Uriah with its disastrous consequences. But this section cannot be read in isolation from sections that bracket it. God surely does desire our righteousness, but David's voice claiming to be blameless and righteous (vv. 24–25) can only be read ironically. We are grateful that we already know a God who delivers without regard to merit and is celebrated in

according to the cleanness of my
    hands he recompensed me.
22 For I have kept the ways of the
    LORD,
    and have not wickedly departed
        from my God.
23 For all his ordinances were before me,
    and from his statutes I did not
        turn aside.
24 I was blameless before him,
    and I kept myself from guilt.
25 Therefore the LORD has
    recompensed me according to
        my righteousness,
    according to my cleanness in his
        sight.

26 With the loyal you show yourself
    loyal;
    with the blameless you show
        yourself blameless;
27 with the pure you show yourself
    pure,
    and with the crooked you show
        yourself perverse.
28 You deliver a humble people,
    but your eyes are upon the
        haughty to bring them
        down.
29 Indeed, you are my lamp, O LORD,
    the LORD lightens my darkness.
30 By you I can crush a troop,
    and by my God I can leap over a
        wall.
31 This God—his way is perfect;
    the promise of the LORD proves
        true;

he is a shield for all who take
    refuge in him.
32 For who is God, but the LORD?
    And who is a rock, except our
        God?
33 The God who has girded me with
    strength[a]
    has opened wide my path.[b]
34 He made my[c] feet like the feet of
    deer,
    and set me secure on the heights.
35 He trains my hands for war,
    so that my arms can bend a bow of
        bronze.
36 You have given me the shield of your
    salvation,
    and your help[d] has made me great.
37 You have made me stride freely,
    and my feet do not slip;
38 I pursued my enemies and destroyed
    them,
    and did not turn back until they
        were consumed.
39 I consumed them; I struck them
        down, so that they did not rise;
    they fell under my feet.
40 For you girded me with strength for
    the battle;
    you made my assailants sink
        under me.
41 You made my enemies turn their
    backs to me,
    those who hated me, and I
        destroyed them.

[a] Q Ms Gk Syr Vg Compare Ps 18.32: MT *God is my strong refuge*
[b] Meaning of Heb uncertain   [c] Another reading is *his*   [d] Q Ms: MT *your answering*

---

vv. 2–20. The place for David's righteousness, and our own, is in a context where we all are known by our stories to fall short of what God desires, and we must rely on God's power to deliver us from chaos, even the chaos that comes of our own making.

22:29–50—It is only in the third section of this psalm that we see the combination of divine providence and human abilities that are so uniquely emphasized in the books of Samuel. God has chosen to act in, through, and even in spite of our human efforts. Over and over again in this section, David's voice asserts his own abilities ("I can . . .") but always with acknowledgment of the divine empowerment that makes this possible ("By you . . ."). **"By you I can crush a troop, and by my God I can leap over a wall"** (v. 30). This declaration and celebration of partnership between God's grace and our own human agency puts the first sections of this song in perspective. God alone has the power to deliver from chaos (vv. 2–20); our efforts to be blameless and righteous are looked upon favorably by God (vv. 21–28), but these efforts always fall short (as we know from David's story and our own). But God has chosen to enter a divine-human partnership in order to move the divine purposes forward, and even our greatest abilities are to be understood as enabled by God's grace (vv. 29–50).

⁴² They looked, but there was no one to
 save them;
  they cried to the LORD, but he did
   not answer them.
⁴³ I beat them fine like the dust of the
 earth,
  I crushed them and stamped them
   down like the mire of the
   streets.

⁴⁴ You delivered me from strife with
 the peoples;^a
  you kept me as the head of the
   nations;
  people whom I had not known
   served me.
⁴⁵ Foreigners came cringing to me;
  as soon as they heard of me, they
   obeyed me.
⁴⁶ Foreigners lost heart,
  and came trembling out of their
   strongholds.

⁴⁷ The LORD lives! Blessed be my
 rock,
  and exalted be my God, the rock of
   my salvation,
⁴⁸ the God who gave me vengeance
  and brought down peoples under
   me,
⁴⁹ who brought me out from my
 enemies;

you exalted me above my
 adversaries,
 you delivered me from the violent.
⁵⁰ For this I will extol you, O LORD,
  among the nations,
  and sing praises to your name.
⁵¹ He is a tower of salvation for his
 king,
  and shows steadfast love to his
   anointed,
  to David and his descendants
   forever.

The Last Words of David

23 Now these are the last words of
 David:
 The oracle of David, son of Jesse,
  the oracle of the man whom God
   exalted,^b
  the anointed of the God of Jacob,
   the favorite of the Strong One of
   Israel:
² The spirit of the LORD speaks
  through me,
  his word is upon my tongue.
³ The God of Israel has spoken,
  the Rock of Israel has said to me:
 One who rules over people justly,
  ruling in the fear of God,

^a Gk: Heb *from strife with my people* ^b Q Ms: MT *who was raised on high*

22:51—It is the declared and celebrated divine-human enterprise in David's song that becomes in the end the basis of trust in God's promise of salvation and steadfast love through God's king, God's anointed one. The promise of Nathan in chap. 7 is reaffirmed. The hope of Hannah at the beginning of the books of Samuel (1 Sam. 2:10b) is recalled at the end of the books of Samuel. And, for Christians, the coming of God's anointed one (messiah) in Jesus as the son of David is anticipated.

23:1–7 The Last Words of David

This song, *the last words of David*, reaffirms God's promise to the house of David as *an everlasting covenant* (v. 5, cf. 7:14–16). David announces God's word that a just and faithful ruler is *like the light of morning* sun (vv. 2–4). He then seems to break in exuberantly in his own voice to declare that his house is *like this* (v. 5a). As readers we might be incredulous. What of David's sin and the resulting chaos in his own family

and kingdom? The key is David's coupling of this claim with his recognition that the truth of this assertion lies not with what David has done, but with what God has done. David's house is *like this* only *with God* and by virtue of God's commitment to an *everlasting covenant* (v. 5a). It is God that causes our efforts for help or fulfillment *to prosper* (v. 5b). The *godless* (Heb. worthless) are lost because they do not recognize the source of salvation in God (vv. 6–7). This final song from David should not be understood as an outburst of royal hubris. It is the bold declaration that we are all saved finally by the reliability of God's promise. By our own efforts our "houses" can never be the source of light in the world. David's example here urges us boldly to claim God's promise as the basis for our own efforts to rule justly and bring light. Our own efforts by themselves will, as with David, fall short, but our bold claim on the trustworthiness of God's promise will give us hope beyond the realistic prospect of human possibilities.

4 is like the light of morning,
   like the sun rising on a cloudless
      morning,
   gleaming from the rain on the
      grassy land.

5 Is not my house like this with God?
   For he has made with me an
      everlasting covenant,
   ordered in all things and secure.
   Will he not cause to prosper
   all my help and my desire?
6 But the godless are *a* all like thorns
      that are thrown away;
   for they cannot be picked up with
      the hand;
7 to touch them one uses an iron
      bar
   or the shaft of a spear.
   And they are entirely consumed in
      fire on the spot.*b*

David's Mighty Men

8 These are the names of the warriors whom David had: Josheb-basshebeth a Tahchemonite; he was chief of the Three;*c* he wielded his spear*d* against eight hundred whom he killed at one time.

9 Next to him among the three warriors was Eleazar son of Dodo son of Ahohi. He was with David when they defied the Philistines who were gathered there for battle. The Israelites withdrew, 10 but he stood his ground. He struck down the Philistines until his arm grew weary, though his hand clung to the sword. The Lord brought about a great victory that day. Then the people came back to him—but only to strip the dead.

11 Next to him was Shammah son of Agee, the Hararite. The Philistines gathered together at Lehi, where there was a plot of ground full of lentils; and the army fled from the Philistines. 12 But he took his stand in the middle of the plot, defended it, and killed the Philistines; and the Lord brought about a great victory.

13 Towards the beginning of harvest three of the thirty*e* chiefs went down to join David at the cave of Adullam, while a band of Philistines was encamped in the valley of Rephaim. 14 David was then in the stronghold; and the garrison of the Philistines was then at Bethlehem. 15 David said longingly, "O that someone would give me water to drink from the well of Bethlehem that is by the gate!" 16 Then the three warriors broke through the camp of the Philistines, drew water from the well of Bethlehem that was by the gate, and brought it to David. But he would not drink of it; he poured it out to the Lord, 17 for he said, "The Lord forbid that I should do this. Can I drink the blood of the men who went at the risk of their lives?" Therefore he would not drink it. The three warriors did these things.

18 Now Abishai son of Zeruiah, the brother of Joab, was chief of the Thirty.*f* With his spear he fought against three hundred men and killed them, and won a name beside the Three. 19 He was the most renowned of the Thirty,*g* and became their commander; but he did not attain to the Three.

a Heb *But worthlessness* *b* Heb *in sitting* *c* Gk Vg Compare 1 Chr 11.11: Meaning of Heb uncertain *d* 1 Chr 11.11: Meaning of Heb uncertain *e* Heb adds *head* *f* Two Heb Mss Syr: MT *Three* *g* Syr Compare 1 Chr 11.25: Heb *Was he the most renowned of the Three?*

23:8–39 David's Warriors

Like 21:15–22, this section reminds us that David's leadership of Israel was supported by a remarkable community of able and committed followers. David was not the only doer of mighty deeds that brought the kingdom into God's new future. In a culture that tends to admire self-sufficient and self-promoting leadership, this passage provides a corrective that acknowledges the importance of leadership that enables the contributions of many. Particularly touching in this regard is David's pouring out of the water brought to him from the well at Bethlehem at great risk by his men (vv. 13–17). It is a liturgical act (*poured it out to the Lord*), sacrificing David's own self satisfaction (drinking the water) in a expression of solidarity and gratitude for those whose courage and commitment made his own leadership effective. It models for us a leadership not focused on the leader but on the community and the Lord who makes such community possible and meaningful.

20 Benaiah son of Jehoiada was a valiant warrior[a] from Kabzeel, a doer of great deeds; he struck down two sons of Ariel[b] of Moab. He also went down and killed a lion in a pit on a day when snow had fallen. 21 And he killed an Egyptian, a handsome man. The Egyptian had a spear in his hand; but Benaiah went against him with a staff, snatched the spear out of the Egyptian's hand, and killed him with his own spear. 22 Such were the things Benaiah son of Jehoiada did, and won a name beside the three warriors. 23 He was renowned among the Thirty, but he did not attain to the Three. And David put him in charge of his bodyguard.

24 Among the Thirty were Asahel brother of Joab; Elhanan son of Dodo of Bethlehem; 25 Shammah of Harod; Elika of Harod; 26 Helez the Paltite; Ira son of Ikkesh of Tekoa; 27 Abiezer of Anathoth; Mebunnai the Hushathite; 28 Zalmon the Ahohite; Maharai of Netophah; 29 Heleb son of Baanah of Netophah; Ittai son of Ribai of Gibeah of the Benjaminites; 30 Benaiah of Pirathon; Hiddai of the torrents of Gaash; 31 Abi-albon the Arbathite; Azmaveth of Bahurim; 32 Eliahba of Shaalbon; the sons of Jashen: Jonathan 33 son of[c] Shammah the Hararite; Ahiam son of Sharar the Hararite; 34 Eliphelet son of Ahasbai of Maacah; Eliam son of Ahithophel the Gilonite; 35 Hezro[d] of Carmel; Paarai the Arbite; 36 Igal son of Nathan of Zobah; Bani the Gadite; 37 Zelek the Ammonite; Naharai of Beeroth, the armor-bearer of Joab son of Zeruiah; 38 Ira the Ithrite; Gareb the Ithrite; 39 Uriah the Hittite—thirty-seven in all.

David's Census of Israel and Judah

24 Again the anger of the LORD was kindled against Israel, and he incited David against them, saying, "Go, count the people of Israel and Judah." 2 So the king said to Joab and the commanders of the army,[e] who were with him, "Go through all the tribes of Israel, from Dan to Beer-sheba, and take a census of the people, so that I may know how many there are." 3 But Joab said to the king, "May the LORD your God increase the number of the people a hundredfold, while the eyes of my lord the king can still see it! But why does my lord the king want to do this?" 4 But the king's word prevailed against Joab and the commanders of the army. So Joab and the commanders of the army went out from the presence of the king to take a census of the people of Israel. 5 They crossed the Jordan, and began from[f] Aroer and from the city that is in the middle of the valley, toward Gad and on to Jazer. 6 Then they came to Gilead, and to Kadesh in the land of the Hittites;[g] and they came to Dan, and from Dan[h] they went around to Sidon, 7 and came to the fortress of Tyre and to all the cities of the Hivites and Canaanites; and

---

a Another reading is *the son of Ish-hai*   *b* Gk: Heb lacks *sons of*   *c* Gk: Heb lacks *son of*   *d* Another reading is *Hezrai*   *e* 1 Chr 21.2 Gk: Heb *to Joab the commander of the army*   *f* Gk Mss: Heb *encamped in Aroer south of*   *g* Gk: Heb *to the land of Tahtim-hodshi*   *h* Cn Compare Gk: Heb *they came to Dan-jaan and*

24:1–25 David's Census
The books of Samuel end with the story of a census David authorizes, which displeases the Lord and results in a pestilence that kills many people. We would not make such a direct link between a natural disaster and the will of God. Indeed, even biblical writers were troubled by the notion that God incited David to this action out of anger (v. 1) and the historian of 1 Chr. 21:1 substitutes Satan for the anger of God as the inciter of David's action.

24:2–3—It is difficult for many readers to see why David's census should be regarded as a negative thing. To those comfortable with power and authority, such processes seem neutral. But as v. 9 shows, the purpose of such a census is probably to identify those who might be conscripted for military service or required to pay taxes. To those whose lives are lived on the margins, such processes are not neutral. Even today some officials estimate that as much as 25 percent of the U.S. population refused to be counted in the last census, for fear information would be used with taxation, immigration, or police authorities. Even Joab, David's pragmatic commander, questions the wisdom of David's decision (vv. 3–4).

they went out to the Negeb of Judah at Beer-sheba. **8** So when they had gone through all the land, they came back to Jerusalem at the end of nine months and twenty days. **9** Joab reported to the king the number of those who had been recorded: in Israel there were eight hundred thousand soldiers able to draw the sword, and those of Judah were five hundred thousand.

Judgment on David's Sin

10 But afterward, David was stricken to the heart because he had numbered the people. David said to the LORD, "I have sinned greatly in what I have done. But now, O LORD, I pray you, take away the guilt of your servant; for I have done very foolishly." **11** When David rose in the morning, the word of the LORD came to the prophet Gad, David's seer, saying, **12** "Go and say to David: Thus says the LORD: Three things I offer*a* you; choose one of them, and I will do it to you." **13** So Gad came to David and told him; he asked him, "Shall three*b* years of fam-

ine come to you on your land? Or will you flee three months before your foes while they pursue you? Or shall there be three days' pestilence in your land? Now consider, and decide what answer I shall return to the one who sent me." **14** Then David said to Gad, "I am in great distress; let us fall into the hand of the LORD, for his mercy is great; but let me not fall into human hands."

15 So the LORD sent a pestilence on Israel from that morning until the appointed time; and seventy thousand of the people died, from Dan to Beer-sheba. **16** But when the angel stretched out his hand toward Jerusalem to destroy it, the LORD relented concerning the evil, and said to the angel who was bringing destruction among the people, "It is enough; now stay your hand." The angel of the LORD was then by the threshing floor of Araunah the Jebusite. **17** When David saw the angel who was destroying the people, he said to the LORD, "I alone have sinned, and

a Or *hold over* · *b* 1 Chr 21.12 Gk: Heb *seven*

24:10—What makes this story remarkable is David's own recognition that he has acted out of the interests of bureaucratic power and not in the interests of the people. His response is one of confession and prayer (and willingness to accept responsibility as leader, v. 17). There are still consequences from David's action, but his own response opens new possibilities of trust in God's mercy. In our recognition of brokenness within the community, we often rush to reform of structures and processes without the first step of confession and prayer. In so doing, we risk missing the working of God's mercy in our midst and the new possibilities offered by God's grace.

24:11–16—Once again a prophet brings God's judgment to David; this time the prophet is not Nathan (chap. 12) but Gad (24:11). David refuses to choose a punishment but casts his fate on the mercy of the Lord (v. 14), and in the end God's mercy prevails (v. 16). Again, we are troubled that persons should die from pestilence because of David's sin. In the ancient world natural disasters were often considered as the outgrowth of personal or corrupt offense to the divine powers. The focus of this account, however, is on David's recognition and repentance from the self-serving use of his own power. That such self-serving actions have harmful consequences is still a proper

understanding, even if we would not see these played out in natural disasters.

24:17–25—It is fitting that our final view of David in the books of Samuel should be related to his own confession, his resort to prayer, his participation in an act of worship, and his well-founded reliance on the mercy of God. This is the David who was the man after God's own heart (1 Sam. 13:14). The books of Samuel begin with the prayerful petition of Hannah (1 Sam. 1) and end with David's prayerful petition. The context for Hannah and David is in worship, and their trustful petition is to the mercy of God. Eli and his sons corrupted the future of Israel (1 Sam. 2:11–17); David and his own sons jeopardized the future of Israel. Yet the message of the books of Samuel is that the providence of God is the true source of Israel's future. In the end, David has become known to us as flawed and sinful, yet he is the instrument through whom God has chosen to act. His prayerful confession and his worshipful reliance on God's grace show us again why David occupies a special place in the biblical story. We, like David, have no hope of leadership in God's community that does not reflect our own flawed lives as sinners. In the end, through prayer, confession, and worship we bring our best efforts at leadership into partnership with

I alone have done wickedly; but these sheep, what have they done? Let your hand, I pray, be against me and against my father's house."

David's Altar on the Threshing Floor

18 That day Gad came to David and said to him, "Go up and erect an altar to the LORD on the threshing floor of Araunah the Jebusite." 19 Following Gad's instructions, David went up, as the LORD had commanded. 20 When Araunah looked down, he saw the king and his servants coming toward him; and Araunah went out and prostrated himself before the king with his face to the ground. 21 Araunah said, "Why has my lord the king come to his servant?" David said, "To buy the threshing floor from you in order to build an altar to the LORD, so that the plague may be averted from the people." 22 Then Araunah said to David, "Let my lord the king take and offer up what seems good to him; here are the oxen for the burnt offering, and the threshing sledges and the yokes of the oxen for the wood. 23 All this, O king, Araunah gives to the king." And Araunah said to the king, "May the LORD your God respond favorably to you."

24 But the king said to Araunah, "No, but I will buy them from you for a price; I will not offer burnt offerings to the LORD my God that cost me nothing." So David bought the threshing floor and the oxen for fifty shekels of silver. 25 David built there an altar to the LORD, and offered burnt offerings and offerings of well-being. So the LORD answered his supplication for the land, and the plague was averted from Israel.

---

the providential working of God's mercy and the bringing to reality of God's future. The threshing floor of Araunah is said to have become the site of the main altar of the temple in Jerusalem (1 Chr. 21–22). Through our own prayer and worship, confession and reliance on God's mercy become the foundations for the actions that build faithful community.

Introduction to
1–2 KINGS

F irst–Second Kings recount the story of ancient Israel from Solomon's succession as king over Israel and Judah—thus securing a Davidic dynasty—through the division of Solomon's kingdom upon his death, and on to the destruction and exile of northern Israel at the hands of the Assyrians and of Judah and Jerusalem by the Babylonians. First–Second Kings bring to a conclusion an account of the ancient nation of Israel from its birth to its demise, which is presented in the books of Joshua (and even Deuteronomy) through 2 Kings—what some call the Deuteronomistic History. Indeed, 1–2 Kings brings to a close an even more extended accounting of Israel's story that begins with creation itself, an account that runs from Genesis through 2 Kings (compare the very different construction of that story in 1–2 Chronicles).

First–Second Kings, and the more extended accounts of which it may be a part, is broadly a history under judgment. Not simply a chronicle of events and persons, it is a careful selection of events and persons—drawn no doubt from a variety of sources—woven into an extended narrative that is shaped by and inculcates a particular theological set of values. Broadly the ideology or theology that shapes 1–2 Kings (and much that precedes it) is defined by the book of Deuteronomy. Central to Deuteronomy, and to most of the judgments and evaluations made in 1–2 Kings, is an emphasis on worship of the deity YHWH, and YHWH alone, in the proper forms in one central location, Jerusalem. Worship of YHWH elsewhere, especially in the so-called "high places," falls short of this ideal and calls for rebuke. Worship of other gods along with or in competition with YHWH is cause for scathing indictment. The latter is a temptation especially held out by remnants of "the Canaanites" who held the land before Israel and of those living in the lands surrounding Israel. Mixing with these peoples, especially through marriage, brings one into patterns of worship of gods that Deuteronomy and the narrator of 1–2 Kings judge as extreme apostasy and cause for severe judgment and rejection. This even casts a shadow back over the reign of Solomon, who constructed the temple in Jerusalem, otherwise so dear to the narrator of 1–2 Kings. Worship in high places calls forth from the narrator of 1–2 Kings milder rebukes of most Davidic kings who succeed Solomon (except Hezekiah and Josiah). Worship of Baal, Asherah, and other deities evokes even stronger rebukes of Jeroboam I, the first king of northern Israel, and of those who succeed him. Even more blatant rejections of YHWH, as the narrator sees it, promoted by Ahab and his house in the north and by Manasseh in Judah, provide grounds for YHWH's rejection of the kingdoms, their destruction by Assyria and then Babylon, and the exile of their peoples.

The story of the kings in their overlapping successions is interwoven with accounts of a succession of named and unnamed prophets. Sometimes the prophets support kings, but more often they stand in opposition to them. These prophetic episodes climax for the north in the extended series of stories dealing with Elijah and Elisha and in the south in several episodes involving Isaiah and King Hezekiah. The

prophetic announcements and judgments reinforce the evaluations provided by the narrator for the succession of kings in Israel and in Judah.

Some scholars have proposed that earlier editions of a Deuteronomistic History (and thus 1–2 Kings) once ended with the reign and reform of Hezekiah, while more have suggested an earlier form ending with Josiah's reforms and attempt to reinstate the kingdom of David under the Torah of Moses. Each edition was constructed to support reforming policies and actions by these two kings, who receive the most positive evaluations from the narrator for removing the high places and all traces of other gods. The form of 1–2 Kings we now have, however, ends with the devastation of destruction and exile, offering just the faintest hope for the future in the appointment in exile of Jehoiachin to the table of the king of Babylon—the house of David is still alive.

The notes that follow center on the form of 1–2 Kings we now have, rather than on proposed earlier editions. First–Second Kings begins with the glories of Solomon's reign (tempered by disquiet over his excessive wealth and women) and the temple he constructed. It ends with the destruction of Jerusalem and its temple, the land empty, and the last vestiges of old Israel in exile in Babylon or as fugitives in Egypt. This trajectory from glory to devastation is finally, in the narrator's view, YHWH's doing, a response to a people and their rulers who repeatedly abandoned YHWH and the Torah. This is why the states of Israel and Judah failed. This theological history of Israel under her kings finally suggests YHWH's judgments are righteous, even if they are severe at times. Essentially it looks back to explain a course of history ending in devastation. It may provide a glimmer of hope for a different future in its last brief glance at Jehoiachin in exile in Babylon.

The fundamental demand shaping this theological history is that YHWH's people acknowledge and submit to YHWH alone, as the God who shapes the destiny of these people. At times this entails adherence to certain ethical standards—especially as evidenced in the breach, for example, by Jezebel and Ahab as they abuse their royal power to rob Naboth of his land and life. But even more fundamentally, submission to YHWH demands absolute rejection of all other deities and appropriate worship in that place where above all others people meet with YHWH—the temple in Jerusalem. Yet in the end even this temple, and the nation for which it is the center, proves expendable. For YHWH is tied to no place, to no particular nation. YHWH is there to sustain those who submit, but does not guarantee to lift them out of the turmoil, danger, and suffering such submission may entail. While a few faithful kings are noted, again and again YHWH seems to side with those outside the official hierarchy of the state, those at the fringes of the social, economic, political and religious order—prophets, widows, the poor. More often than not, it is such figures who in 1–2 Kings provide models of the devotion and discipleship YHWH seeks.

—W. Lee Humphreys

The Book of
1 KINGS

The Struggle for the Succession

1 King David was old and advanced in years; and although they covered him with clothes, he could not get warm. ² So his servants said to him, "Let a young virgin be sought for my lord the king, and let her wait on the king, and be his attendant; let her lie in your bosom, so that my lord the king may be warm." ³ So they searched for a beautiful girl throughout all the territory of Israel, and found Abishag the Shunammite, and brought her to the king. ⁴ The girl was very beautiful. She became the king's attendant and served him, but the king did not know her sexually.

5 Now Adonijah son of Haggith exalted himself, saying, "I will be king"; he prepared for himself chariots and horsemen, and fifty men to run before him. ⁶ His father had never at any time displeased him by asking, "Why have you done thus and so?" He was also a very handsome man, and he was born next after Absalom. ⁷ He conferred with Joab son of Zeruiah and with the priest Abiathar, and they supported Adonijah. ⁸ But the priest Zadok, and Benaiah son of Jehoiada, and the prophet Nathan, and Shimei, and Rei, and David's own warriors did not side with Adonijah.

9 Adonijah sacrificed sheep, oxen, and fatted cattle by the stone Zoheleth, which is beside En-rogel, and he invited all his brothers, the king's sons, and all the royal officials of Judah, ¹⁰ but he did not invite the prophet Nathan or Benaiah or the warriors or his brother Solomon.

11 Then Nathan said to Bathsheba, Solomon's mother, "Have you not heard that Adonijah son of Haggith has become king and our lord David does not know it? ¹² Now therefore come, let me give you advice, so that you may

---

1:1–11:43 The Reign of Solomon

1:1–53 Solomon Succeeds David

Political intrigue marks David's final days as king and scars the succession of Solomon. The account, fulfilling God's unconditional promise to David in 2 Sam. 7:12, 16, bridges the story of David's reign in 2 Samuel and Solomon's in 1 Kgs. 2–11.

1:1–4—The aged David may be warmed by the young and beautiful Abishag, but her presence underscores his impotency, a striking image for his waning power over his family and court. All this merely underscores how frantic and feeble are his efforts to maintain power in the waning days of his rule.

1:3 *Shunammite*—Abishag is brought to David from her home in Shunem in the Valley of Jezreel.

1:5–6—*Adonijah* recalls Absalom in his striking appearance and quest for the throne. With Amnon (2 Sam. 13:28–29), Absalom (2 Sam. 18:14–15), and apparently Chileab dead, Adonijah is David's oldest surviving son. However, that

the house of David will establish a dynasty and his oldest son naturally succeed him is not yet established.

1:7–8—In David's last days, the discord and divisions that marked his family, court, and kingdom reach a climax. The priests are divided as *Abiathar* supports Adonijah in opposition to *Zadok.* The military splits, with *Joab* supporting Adonijah in opposition to *Benaiah* and David's own elite warriors. These divisions may reflect long-standing tensions, as those serving David the longest support Adonijah and those more recent to his court support Solomon.

1:11—God's promise to David does not preclude political power plays by those for whom the stakes are highest, especially *Nathan,* who approaches *Bathsheba,* who with her son stands to loose all, he suggests, if Adonijah is successful in claiming kingship. This suggests that those vested with institutional authority maintain a fine balance as they wield political power and serve as God's representatives to the nation as the people of God.

save your own life and the life of your son Solomon. ¹³ Go in at once to King David, and say to him, 'Did you not, my lord the king, swear to your servant, saying: Your son Solomon shall succeed me as king, and he shall sit on my throne? Why then is Adonijah king?' ¹⁴ Then while you are still there speaking with the king, I will come in after you and confirm your words."

15 So Bathsheba went to the king in his room. The king was very old; Abishag the Shunammite was attending the king. ¹⁶ Bathsheba bowed and did obeisance to the king, and the king said, "What do you wish?" ¹⁷ She said to him, "My lord, you swore to your servant by the LORD your God, saying: Your son Solomon shall succeed me as king, and he shall sit on my throne. ¹⁸ But now suddenly Adonijah has become king, though you, my lord the king, do not know it. ¹⁹ He has sacrificed oxen, fatted cattle, and sheep in abundance, and has invited all the children of the king, the priest Abiathar, and Joab the commander of the army; but your servant Solomon he has not invited. ²⁰ But you, my lord the king—the eyes of all Israel are on you to tell them who shall sit on the throne of my lord the king after him. ²¹ Otherwise it will come to pass, when my lord the king sleeps with his ancestors, that my son Solomon and I will be counted offenders."

22 While she was still speaking with the king, the prophet Nathan came in. ²³ The king was told, "Here is the prophet Nathan." When he came in before the king, he did obeisance to the king, with his face to the ground. ²⁴ Nathan said, "My lord the king, have you said, 'Adonijah shall succeed me as king, and he

shall sit on my throne'? ²⁵ For today he has gone down and has sacrificed oxen, fatted cattle, and sheep in abundance, and has invited all the king's children, Joab the commander*a* of the army, and the priest Abiathar, who are now eating and drinking before him, and saying, 'Long live King Adonijah!' ²⁶ But he did not invite me, your servant, and the priest Zadok, and Benaiah son of Jehoiada, and your servant Solomon. ²⁷ Has this thing been brought about by my lord the king and you have not let your servants know who should sit on the throne of my lord the king after him?"

The Accession of Solomon

28 King David answered, "Summon Bathsheba to me." So she came into the king's presence, and stood before the king. ²⁹ The king swore, saying, "As the LORD lives, who has saved my life from every adversity, ³⁰ as I swore to you by the LORD, the God of Israel, 'Your son Solomon shall succeed me as king, and he shall sit on my throne in my place,' so will I do this day." ³¹ Then Bathsheba bowed with her face to the ground, and did obeisance to the king, and said, "May my lord King David live forever!"

32 King David said, "Summon to me the priest Zadok, the prophet Nathan, and Benaiah son of Jehoiada." When they came before the king, ³³ the king said to them, "Take with you the servants of your lord, and have my son Solomon ride on my own mule, and bring him down to Gihon. ³⁴ There let the priest Zadok and the prophet Nathan anoint him king over Israel; then blow the trumpet, and say, 'Long live King Solomon!' ³⁵ You

a Gk: Heb *the commanders*

1:13—No record exists of such an oath by David.
1:15–21—The aged Bathsheba, perhaps with jealousy enflamed by the silent presence of Abishag, says all Nathan advises and more.
1:22–27—Nathan reinforces her words and presents the situation in the starkest of terms.

Solomon plays no active role in their adroit manipulation of David.
1:28–31—For David the oath becomes a reality he puts into effect.
1:31—Bathsheba's wish to David is ironic in light of the promise just made to her and his plans to make Solomon his coregent and successor.

shall go up following him. Let him enter and sit on my throne; he shall be king in my place; for I have appointed him to be ruler over Israel and over Judah." [36] Benaiah son of Jehoiada answered the king, "Amen! May the LORD, the God of my lord the king, so ordain. [37] As the LORD has been with my lord the king, so may he be with Solomon, and make his throne greater than the throne of my lord King David."

38 So the priest Zadok, the prophet Nathan, and Benaiah son of Jehoiada, and the Cherethites and the Pelethites, went down and had Solomon ride on King David's mule, and led him to Gihon. [39] There the priest Zadok took the horn of oil from the tent and anointed Solomon. Then they blew the trumpet, and all the people said, "Long live King Solomon!" [40] And all the people went up following him, playing on pipes and rejoicing with great joy, so that the earth quaked at their noise.

41 Adonijah and all the guests who were with him heard it as they finished feasting. When Joab heard the sound of the trumpet, he said, "Why is the city in an uproar?" [42] While he was still speaking, Jonathan son of the priest Abiathar arrived. Adonijah said, "Come in, for you are a worthy man and surely you bring good news." [43] Jonathan answered Adonijah, "No, for our lord King David has made Solomon king; [44] the king has sent with him the priest Zadok, the prophet Nathan, and Benaiah son of Jehoiada, and the Cherethites and the Pelethites; and they had him ride on the king's mule; [45] the priest Zadok and the prophet Nathan have anointed him king at Gihon; and they have gone up from there rejoicing, so that the city is in an uproar. This is the noise that you heard. [46] Solomon now sits on the royal throne. [47] Moreover the king's servants came to congratulate our lord King David, saying, 'May God make the name of Solomon more famous than yours, and make his throne greater than your throne.' The king bowed in worship on the bed [48] and went on to pray thus, 'Blessed be the LORD, the God of Israel, who today has granted one of my offspring[a] to sit on my throne and permitted me to witness it.' "

49 Then all the guests of Adonijah got up trembling and went their own ways. [50] Adonijah, fearing Solomon, got up and went to grasp the horns of the altar. [51] Solomon was informed, "Adonijah is afraid of King Solomon; see, he has laid hold of the horns of the altar, saying, 'Let King Solomon swear to me first that he will not kill his servant with the sword.' " [52] So Solomon responded, "If he proves to be a worthy man, not one of his hairs shall fall to the ground; but if wickedness is found in him, he shall die." [53] Then King Solomon sent to have him brought down from the altar. He came to do obeisance to King Solomon; and Solomon said to him, "Go home."

David's Instruction to Solomon

2 When David's time to die drew near, he charged his son Solomon, saying:

[a] Gk: Heb one

1:38—A *mule* was transport especially fit for one claiming kingship (2 Sam. 18:9; Zech. 9:9). Symbolic and real power lie with those supporting Solomon, as is made quite clear to Adonijah and his supporters.

1:41–49—David's arrangements for Solomon to be his successor, throwing Adonijah's carefully staged coronation into confusion, demonstrate that the waning king still commands his kingdom.

1:48—David's prayer as reported to Adonijah echoes YHWH's promise in 2 Sam. 7:12.

1:49–53—Solomon, for whom others acted to this point, is now designated *king* as he places Adonijah under constraints.

1:50—The *horns of the altar* jutted out from its four top corners, and seizing them constituted a claim of sanctuary only for those whose crime was unintended (Exod. 21:14).

2:1–9 David's Last Words

David, like other great Israelites before him (Jacob in Gen. 48–49; Moses in Deuteronomy; Joshua in Josh. 23–24; Samuel in 1 Sam. 12), mark their passing with final advice to the next generation. David's words are both broadly

² "I am about to go the way of all the earth. Be strong, be courageous, ³ and keep the charge of the LORD your God, walking in his ways and keeping his statutes, his commandments, his ordinances, and his testimonies, as it is written in the law of Moses, so that you may prosper in all that you do and wherever you turn. ⁴ Then the LORD will establish his word that he spoke concerning me: 'If your heirs take heed to their way, to walk before me in faithfulness with all their heart and with all their soul, there shall not fail you a successor on the throne of Israel.'

5 "Moreover you know also what Joab son of Zeruiah did to me, how he dealt with the two commanders of the armies of Israel, Abner son of Ner, and Amasa son of Jether, whom he murdered, retaliating in time of peace for blood that had been shed in war, and putting the blood of war on the belt around his waist, and on the sandals on his feet. ⁶ Act therefore according to your wisdom, but do not let his gray head go down to Sheol in peace. ⁷ Deal loyally, however, with the sons of Barzillai the Gileadite, and let them be among those who eat at your table; for with such loyalty they met me when I

fled from your brother Absalom. ⁸ There is also with you Shimei son of Gera, the Benjaminite from Bahurim, who cursed me with a terrible curse on the day when I went to Mahanaim; but when he came down to meet me at the Jordan, I swore to him by the LORD, 'I will not put you to death with the sword.' ⁹ Therefore do not hold him guiltless, for you are a wise man; you will know what you ought to do to him, and you must bring his gray head down with blood to Sheol."

Death of David

10 Then David slept with his ancestors, and was buried in the city of David. ¹¹ The time that David reigned over Israel was forty years; he reigned seven years in Hebron, and thirty-three years in Jerusalem. ¹² So Solomon sat on the throne of his father David; and his kingdom was firmly established.

Solomon Consolidates His Reign

13 Then Adonijah son of Haggith came to Bathsheba, Solomon's mother. She asked, "Do you come peaceably?" He said, "Peaceably." ¹⁴ Then he said, "May I have a word with you?" She said, "Go on." ¹⁵ He said, "You know that the

theological, in the mode of a Deuteronomic preacher (1 Kgs. 2:2–4), and bluntly pragmatic, like a Mafia don's advice to his successor (vv. 5–9). David's words reflect at once the ideal king in his submission to YHWH and the Torah (see Deut. 17) and the crassly pragmatic politician securing his son's position against all who might challenge it. The tension between these images of David leaves us wondering what place violence has in the divine plan for Israel.

2:2–4—The model is the king as depicted in Deut. 7:14–20, with emphasis on adherence to *the law of Moses* as the condition for an ongoing dynasty. This stands in marked tension with and may modify the unconditional promise in 2 Sam. 7:14–16.

2:5–9—David directs Solomon on how he is, in his *wisdom*, to deal with key figures in David's court. Joab killed *Abner* (2 Sam. 3:22–30) and *Amasa* (2 Sam. 17:25; 19:11–15) to secure both his own position and the throne of David. *Barzillai* provisioned David in his flight from Absalom (2 Sam. 17:27–29) and welcomed him

on his return to Jerusalem (2 Sam. 19:31–40). By contrast, *Shimei* cursed the fleeing David (2 Sam.16:5–13); his penance before the returning king earned him respite during David's reign (2 Sam. 19:16–23) but not that of Solomon.

2:10–11—Jerusalem, *the city of David*, was royal property. David reigned over Judah from *Hebron* and then over all *Israel* from Jerusalem for a nice round total of forty years.

2:13–46 Solomon Secures His Rule

2:13–26—Just what Adonijah intended by requesting *Abishag* as wife, and what *Bathsheba*, as the powerful queen mother, intended in conveying the request to her son, is not stated. While David "did not know her sexually" (1:4), Solomon assumes she is among his father's concubines, and reads Adonijah's request as a challenge to his rule (see 2 Sam. 3:6–7; 12:8; 16:21–22) and an excuse to have him executed. The text leaves it to us as readers to decide if this and other actions by Solomon at the outset of his reign to secure his throne are in line with keeping "the charge of the LORD your God" (1 Kgs. 2:2).

kingdom was mine, and that all Israel expected me to reign; however, the kingdom has turned about and become my brother's, for it was his from the LORD. ¹⁶ And now I have one request to make of you; do not refuse me." She said to him, "Go on." ¹⁷ He said, "Please ask King Solomon—he will not refuse you—to give me Abishag the Shunammite as my wife." ¹⁸ Bathsheba said, "Very well; I will speak to the king on your behalf."

¹⁹ So Bathsheba went to King Solomon, to speak to him on behalf of Adonijah. The king rose to meet her, and bowed down to her; then he sat on his throne, and had a throne brought for the king's mother, and she sat on his right. ²⁰ Then she said, "I have one small request to make of you; do not refuse me." And the king said to her, "Make your request, my mother; for I will not refuse you." ²¹ She said, "Let Abishag the Shunammite be given to your brother Adonijah as his wife." ²² King Solomon answered his mother, "And why do you ask Abishag the Shunammite for Adonijah? Ask for him the kingdom as well! For he is my elder brother; ask not only for him but also for the priest Abiathar and for Joab son of Zeruiah!" ²³ Then King Solomon swore by the LORD, "So may God do to me, and more also, for Adonijah has devised this scheme at the risk of his life! ²⁴ Now therefore as the LORD lives, who has established me and placed me on the throne of my father David, and who has made me a house as he promised, today Adonijah shall be put to death." ²⁵ So King Solomon sent Benaiah son of Jehoiada; he struck him down, and he died.

²⁶ The king said to the priest Abiathar, "Go to Anathoth, to your estate; for you deserve death. But I will not at this time put you to death, because you carried the ark of the Lord GOD before my father David, and because you shared in all the hardships my father endured." ²⁷ So Solomon banished Abiathar from being priest to the LORD, thus fulfilling the word of the LORD that he had spoken concerning the house of Eli in Shiloh.

²⁸ When the news came to Joab—for Joab had supported Adonijah though he had not supported Absalom—Joab fled to the tent of the LORD and grasped the horns of the altar. ²⁹ When it was told King Solomon, "Joab has fled to the tent of the LORD and now is beside the altar," Solomon sent Benaiah son of Jehoiada, saying, "Go, strike him down." ³⁰ So Benaiah came to the tent of the LORD and said to him, "The king commands, 'Come out.'" But he said, "No, I will die here." Then Benaiah brought the king word again, saying, "Thus said Joab, and thus he answered me." ³¹ The king replied to him, "Do as he has said, strike him down and bury him; and thus take away from me and from my father's house the guilt for the blood that Joab shed without cause. ³² The LORD will bring back his bloody deeds on his own head, because, without the knowledge of my father David, he attacked and killed with the sword two men more righteous and better than himself, Abner son of Ner, commander of the army of Israel, and Amasa son of Jether, commander of the army of Judah. ³³ So shall their blood come back on the head of Joab and on the head of his descendants forever; but to David, and to his descendants, and to his house, and to his throne, there shall be peace from the LORD forevermore." ³⁴ Then Benaiah son of Jehoiada went up and struck him down and killed him; and he was buried at his own house near

---

2:26–27—*Abiathar*, a supporter of Adonijah (1:7), is banished to *Anathoth*, just north of Jerusalem, but he is spared for his long service to David. On the judgment on *the house of Eli*, see 1 Sam. 2:22–36. Anathoth is some centuries later the birthplace of Jeremiah, a prophet whose words remind us how scathing prophetic condemnation of Israel's kings could be.

2:28–34—*Joab* realizes Solomon is removing all possible opponents to his rule and seeks sanctuary at *the altar*. Solomon declares Joab guilty of willful murder as he orders him struck down.

the wilderness. ³⁵ The king put Benaiah son of Jehoiada over the army in his place, and the king put the priest Zadok in the place of Abiathar.

36 Then the king sent and summoned Shimei, and said to him, "Build yourself a house in Jerusalem, and live there, and do not go out from there to any place whatever. ³⁷ For on the day you go out, and cross the Wadi Kidron, know for certain that you shall die; your blood shall be on your own head." ³⁸ And Shimei said to the king, "The sentence is fair; as my lord the king has said, so will your servant do." So Shimei lived in Jerusalem many days.

39 But it happened at the end of three years that two of Shimei's slaves ran away to King Achish son of Maacah of Gath. When it was told Shimei, "Your slaves are in Gath," ⁴⁰ Shimei arose and saddled a donkey, and went to Achish in Gath, to search for his slaves; Shimei went and brought his slaves from Gath. ⁴¹ When Solomon was told that Shimei had gone from Jerusalem to Gath and returned, ⁴² the king sent and summoned Shimei, and said to him, "Did I not make you swear by the LORD, and solemnly adjure you, saying, 'Know for certain that on the day you go out and go to any place whatever, you shall die'? And you said to me, 'The sentence

is fair; I accept.' ⁴³ Why then have you not kept your oath to the LORD and the commandment with which I charged you?" ⁴⁴ The king also said to Shimei, "You know in your own heart all the evil that you did to my father David; so the LORD will bring back your evil on your own head. ⁴⁵ But King Solomon shall be blessed, and the throne of David shall be established before the LORD forever." ⁴⁶ Then the king commanded Benaiah son of Jehoiada; and he went out and struck him down, and he died.

So the kingdom was established in the hand of Solomon.

Solomon's Prayer for Wisdom

3 Solomon made a marriage alliance with Pharaoh king of Egypt; he took Pharaoh's daughter and brought her into the city of David, until he had finished building his own house and the house of the LORD and the wall around Jerusalem. ² The people were sacrificing at the high places, however, because no house had yet been built for the name of the LORD.

3 Solomon loved the LORD, walking in the statutes of his father David; only, he sacrificed and offered incense at the high places. ⁴ The king went to Gibeon to sacrifice there, for that was the principal high place; Solomon used to offer a thousand burnt offerings on that altar. ⁵ At Gibeon the LORD appeared to

---

2:35—*Benaiah*, Solomon's hit man, assumes Joab's command of the army, and *Zadok* takes Abiathar's place as priest, an office he will fill in the temple about to be constructed in Jerusalem.

2:39–46—Altering his father's advice, Solomon first confines *Shimei* to Jerusalem, executing him only when Shimei breaks conditions he accepted.

2:46—See v. 12. Solomon's rule is *established*, but it commences with bloodshed that continues the violence marking much of David's reign. Again we wonder if violent means appropriately serve divinely sanctioned ends.

3:1–28 Solomon's Wisdom

3:1–15—Having dealt with dangerous legacies from the past, Solomon now turns to the future, especially in his prayer for wisdom to rule justly.

3:1—Solomon's marriage alliance with *Pharaoh*

king of Egypt indicates he was active at the highest levels of international politics. At the level of royal international diplomacy, marriage serves ends quite different from those within which we experience it today.

3:2–4—*High places* were open-air sanctuaries where Israel worshiped. Upon completion of the temple in Jerusalem this practice is condemned in 1–2 Kings as a lure to worship other deities along with or in place of YHWH. Even without overt condemnation, Solomon's enthusiastic activity, especially at *Gibeon*, seems a blot on his devotion to YHWH and otherwise unrecorded *statutes of David*.

3:5–10—*Dreams* serve, despite some disclaimers (Jer. 23:23–32), as a means of divine-human contact, revelation, and dialogue (Gen. 20:3–7; 28:12–16; 1 Sam. 3:1–15).

Solomon in a dream by night; and God said, "Ask what I should give you." ⁶ And Solomon said, "You have shown great and steadfast love to your servant my father David, because he walked before you in faithfulness, in righteousness, and in uprightness of heart toward you; and you have kept for him this great and steadfast love, and have given him a son to sit on his throne today. ⁷ And now, O LORD my God, you have made your servant king in place of my father David, although I am only a little child; I do not know how to go out or come in. ⁸ And your servant is in the midst of the people whom you have chosen, a great people, so numerous they cannot be numbered or counted. ⁹ Give your servant therefore an understanding mind to govern your people, able to discern between good and evil; for who can govern this your great people?"

10 It pleased the Lord that Solomon had asked this. ¹¹ God said to him, "Because you have asked this, and have not asked for yourself long life or riches, or for the life of your enemies, but have asked for yourself understanding to discern what is right, ¹² I now do according to your word. Indeed I give you a wise and discerning mind; no one like you has been before you and no one like you shall arise after you. ¹³ I give you also what you have not asked, both riches and honor all your life; no other king shall compare with you. ¹⁴ If you will walk in my ways, keeping my statutes and my commandments, as your father David walked, then I will lengthen your life."

15 Then Solomon awoke; it had been a dream. He came to Jerusalem where he stood before the ark of the covenant of the LORD. He offered up burnt offerings and offerings of well-being, and provided a feast for all his servants.

Solomon's Wisdom in Judgment

16 Later, two women who were prostitutes came to the king and stood before him. ¹⁷ The one woman said, "Please, my lord, this woman and I live in the same house; and I gave birth while she was in the house. ¹⁸ Then on the third day after I gave birth, this woman also gave birth. We were together; there was no one else with us in the house, only the two of us were in the house. ¹⁹ Then this woman's son died in the night, because she lay on him. ²⁰ She got up in the middle of the night and took my son from beside me while your servant slept. She laid him at her breast, and laid her dead son at my breast. ²¹ When I rose in the morning to nurse my son, I saw that he was dead; but when I looked at him closely in the morning, clearly it was not the son I had borne." ²² But the other woman said, "No, the living son is mine, and the dead son is yours." The first said, "No, the dead son is yours, and the living son is mine." So they argued before the king.

23 Then the king said, "The one says, 'This is my son that is alive, and your son is dead'; while the other says, 'Not so! Your son is dead, and my son is the

---

3:6—Reciprocal fidelity marks Solomon's description of the relation between YHWH and David, a glowing depiction that ignores the checkered story found in 1–2 Samuel and 1 Kings 1–2. The emphasis seems to be on David's unswerving allegiance to YHWH alone, a trend continued in 1–2 Chronicles.

3:7—Solomon's depiction of himself as *a little child* is hyperbolic humility and perhaps ironic in light of what surrounds it.

3:9—An *understanding mind* (a "hearing heart") is seen as essential to effective rule. Here Solomon is depicted at his Deuteronomic best as he

approximates the model for kingship in Deut. 17:14–20.

3:13–14—Solomon's wealth and fame are presented as YHWH's gift, granted because Solomon did not request them. Long life is contingent on obedience to YHWH's Torah.

3:16–28—The narrator immediately presents an example demonstrating Solomon's governing wisdom to *all Israel* (v. 28). Yet one wonders at Solomon's brutal threat and about what might have happened if the second woman (v. 26) remained silent or repeated what the first said.

living one.'" ²⁴ So the king said, "Bring me a sword," and they brought a sword before the king. ²⁵ The king said, "Divide the living boy in two; then give half to the one, and half to the other." ²⁶ But the woman whose son was alive said to the king—because compassion for her son burned within her—"Please, my lord, give her the living boy; certainly do not kill him!" The other said, "It shall be neither mine nor yours; divide it." ²⁷ Then the king responded: "Give the first woman the living boy; do not kill him. She is his mother." ²⁸ All Israel heard of the judgment that the king had rendered; and they stood in awe of the king, because they perceived that the wisdom of God was in him, to execute justice.

Solomon's Administrative Officers

4 King Solomon was king over all Israel, ² and these were his high officials: Azariah son of Zadok was the priest; ³ Elihoreph and Ahijah sons of Shisha were secretaries; Jehoshaphat son of Ahilud was recorder; ⁴ Benaiah son of Jehoiada was in command of the army; Zadok and Abiathar were priests; ⁵ Azariah son of Nathan was over the officials; Zabud son of Nathan was priest and king's friend; ⁶ Ahishar was in charge of the palace; and Adoniram son of Abda was in charge of the forced labor.

7 Solomon had twelve officials over all Israel, who provided food for the king and his household; each one had to make provision for one month in the year. ⁸ These were their names: Ben-hur, in the hill country of Ephraim; ⁹ Ben-deker, in Makaz, Shaalbim, Beth-shemesh, and Elon-beth-hanan; ¹⁰ Ben-hesed, in Arubboth (to him belonged Socoh and all the land of Hepher); ¹¹ Ben-abinadab, in all Naphath-dor (he had Taphath, Solomon's daughter, as his wife); ¹² Baana son of Ahilud, in Taanach, Megiddo, and all Beth-shean, which is beside Zarethan below Jezreel, and from Beth-shean to Abel-meholah, as far as the other side of Jokmeam; ¹³ Ben-geber, in Ramoth-gilead (he had the villages of Jair son of Manasseh, which are in Gilead, and he had the region of Argob, which is in Bashan, sixty great cities with walls and bronze bars); ¹⁴ Ahinadab son of Iddo, in Mahanaim; ¹⁵ Ahimaaz, in Naphtali (he had taken Basemath, Solomon's daughter, as his wife); ¹⁶ Baana son of Hushai, in Asher and Bealoth; ¹⁷ Jehoshaphat son of Paruah, in Issachar; ¹⁸ Shimei son of Ela, in Benjamin; ¹⁹ Geber son of Uri, in the land of Gilead, the country of King Sihon of the Amorites and of King Og of Bashan. And there was one official in the land of Judah.

Magnificence of Solomon's Rule

20 Judah and Israel were as numerous as the sand by the sea; they ate and drank and were happy. ²¹ᵃ Solomon was

ᵃ Ch 5.1 in Heb

4:1–34 Solomon's Establishment
Solomon's bureaucracy demonstrates how completely Israel and Judah have been transformed from the loose federation of tribes depicted in Judges to an extensive centralized monarchy.

4:2–6—See 2 Sam. 8:15–18 and 20:23–26 for shorter lists of David's officials. Some of Solomon's officials served David; others are sons of powerful figures in the prior reign. The *secretaries* and *recorder* had power beyond what their titles denote. *Priests* are members of the royal administration as the civil encompasses the sacral under Davidic rule. The *king's friend* was likely an adviser. *Adoniram, in charge of the forced labor,* represents a complex system of taxation in kind and labor. The complex royal administrative hierarchy and especially the imposed taxation and labor forced from the people represent a marked departure from images of an earlier Israel as strictly egalitarian, in which each man and his family stand directly as subject to YHWH and YHWH alone.

4:7–19—The districts listed do not correspond to the older tribal system, thereby reducing its significance. Several are administered by persons with ties to the court. Again older ideals are undone.

4:19—*Judah,* the tribe of David and Solomon, seems to stand outside the system of twelve districts, being thus excused from the monthly rotation for provisioning the court.

4:20–21—The expansion of all Israel under Solomon recalls God's promise to Abraham in Gen.

sovereign over all the kingdoms from the Euphrates to the land of the Philistines, even to the border of Egypt; they brought tribute and served Solomon all the days of his life.

22 Solomon's provision for one day was thirty cors of choice flour, and sixty cors of meal, [23] ten fat oxen, and twenty pasture-fed cattle, one hundred sheep, besides deer, gazelles, roebucks, and fatted fowl. [24] For he had dominion over all the region west of the Euphrates from Tiphsah to Gaza, over all the kings west of the Euphrates; and he had peace on all sides. [25] During Solomon's lifetime Judah and Israel lived in safety, from Dan even to Beer-sheba, all of them under their vines and fig trees. [26] Solomon also had forty thousand stalls of horses for his chariots, and twelve thousand horsemen. [27] Those officials supplied provisions for King Solomon and for all who came to King Solomon's table, each one in his month; they let nothing be lacking. [28] They also brought to the required place barley and straw for the horses and swift steeds, each according to his charge.

Fame of Solomon's Wisdom

29 God gave Solomon very great wisdom, discernment, and breadth of understanding as vast as the sand on the seashore, [30] so that Solomon's wisdom surpassed the wisdom of all the people of the east, and all the wisdom of Egypt. [31] He was wiser than anyone else, wiser than Ethan the Ezrahite, and Heman, Calcol, and Darda, children of Mahol; his fame spread throughout all the surrounding nations. [32] He composed three thousand proverbs, and his songs numbered a thousand and five. [33] He would speak of trees, from the cedar that is in the Lebanon to the hyssop that grows in the wall; he would speak of animals, and birds, and reptiles, and fish. [34] People came from all the nations to hear the wisdom of Solomon; they came from all the kings of the earth who had heard of his wisdom.

Preparations and Materials for the Temple

5 [a] Now King Hiram of Tyre sent his servants to Solomon, when he heard that they had anointed him king in place of his father; for Hiram had always been a friend to David. [2] Solomon sent word to Hiram, saying, [3] "You know that my father David could not build a house for the name of the LORD his God because of

[a] Ch 5.15 in Heb

15:18–19 (see Deut. 1:7–8), suggesting that in the court's eyes Solomon fulfilled what was pledged long ago. One wonders if there is a note of irony in the second half of v. 20, given what the court must have demanded of the people.

4:22–23—The size of Solomon's court, and its privileged position in relation to the rest of Israelite society, is mirrored in the measure of supplies it consumed. A *cor* is about fourteen bushels.

4:25—*Dan to Beer-sheba* represents the more traditional extent of Israel. One wonders if those who bore the burden of supporting the court would be in full agreement with this picture of peace and prosperity, for Solomon and his establishment seem most secure and sated. Did this outward power and security come at the cost of their covenantal soul as defined by the Deuteronomic perspective of the narrator of 1–2 Kings?

4:29–34—The range and depth of Solomon's *wisdom* is evidenced when what is said here is combined with 3:16–28. Solomon is presented as a patron of wisdom and founder of a tradition reflected in several books linked with him.

5:1–6:38 Solomon Builds YHWH's Temple

5:1–18—While Solomon is by now firmly established as David's successor, as promised by God in 2 Sam. 7:12–16, one is struck, when reading of Solomon's building activities and the toll they took on his people, by marked departures from the model of God's dutiful king set forth in Deut. 17:14–20. He seems to be taking on the pattern of the despot warned against 1 Sam. 8:10–18. In the Near East kings often built temple-palace complexes to mark the solidarity of king and deity as a new reign began. Yet one wonders if Solomon is serving himself or his God and God's kingdom.

5:1–6—*Hiram of Tyre*, a Phoenician ruler with links back to David (2 Sam. 5:11), could provide Solomon invaluable material, artisans, and expertise in building on a royal scale.

5:3—Solomon provided a reason for David's

the warfare with which his enemies surrounded him, until the LORD put them under the soles of his feet.*a* *4* But now the LORD my God has given me rest on every side; there is neither adversary nor misfortune. *5* So I intend to build a house for the name of the LORD my God, as the LORD said to my father David, 'Your son, whom I will set on your throne in your place, shall build the house for my name.' *6* Therefore command that cedars from the Lebanon be cut for me. My servants will join your servants, and I will give you whatever wages you set for your servants; for you know that there is no one among us who knows how to cut timber like the Sidonians."

7 When Hiram heard the words of Solomon, he rejoiced greatly, and said, "Blessed be the LORD today, who has given to David a wise son to be over this great people." *8* Hiram sent word to Solomon, "I have heard the message that you have sent to me; I will fulfill all your needs in the matter of cedar and cypress timber. *9* My servants shall bring it down to the sea from the Lebanon; I will make it into rafts to go by sea to the place you indicate. I will have them broken up there for you to take away. And you shall meet my needs by providing food for my household." *10* So Hiram supplied Solomon's every need for timber of cedar and cypress. *11* Solomon in turn gave Hiram twenty thousand cors of wheat as food for his household, and twenty cors of fine oil. Solomon gave this to Hiram year by year. *12* So the LORD gave Solomon wisdom, as he promised him. There was peace between Hiram and Solomon; and the two of them made a treaty.

13 King Solomon conscripted forced labor out of all Israel; the levy numbered thirty thousand men. *14* He sent them to the Lebanon, ten thousand a month in shifts; they would be a month in the Lebanon and two months at home; Adoniram was in charge of the forced labor. *15* Solomon also had seventy thousand laborers and eighty thousand stonecutters in the hill country, *16* besides Solomon's three thousand three hundred supervisors who were over the work, having charge of the people who did the work. *17* At the king's command, they quarried out great, costly stones in order to lay the foundation of the house with dressed stones. *18* So Solomon's builders and Hiram's builders and the Gebalites did the stonecutting and prepared the timber and the stone to build the house.

Solomon Builds the Temple

6 In the four hundred eightieth year after the Israelites came out of the land of Egypt, in the fourth year of Solomon's reign over Israel, in the month of Ziv, which is the second month, he began to build the house of the LORD. *2* The house that King Solomon built for

---

a Gk Tg Vg: Heb *my feet* or *his feet*

---

failure to **build a house** for his God, toning down God's rejection of the idea in 2 Sam. 7:5–7.

5:6—*Cedars from the Lebanon* were especially treasured for building. Solomon offers to send Israelites to work with *Sidonians* in cutting the timber and to pay the wages of the latter.

5:7–12—Hiram makes a counter offer to provide the labor and deliver the cut timber in return for Solomon's provisioning his court establishment. The amount of *wheat* and *fine [olive] oil* delivered annually makes one wonder about Solomon's wisdom (v. 12) in making a treaty on these terms.

5:13–18—Along with likely taxes to make payments to Hiram and the tax needed to enable each district to supply his court, Solomon must now establish the oppressive *levy* to conscript *labor* for his building projects. On *Adoniram,* see 4:6.

6:1–10—This description of the temple Solomon built is designed to impress readers and perhaps make them neglect questions about its cost to the Israelites.

6:1—The temple was built ten generations (of forty years each) after the exodus from Egypt. *Ziv* would be April–May.

6:2—A *cubit* is eighteen inches, making the temple 90′ × 30′ × 45′. The model seems to be Phoenician.

the LORD was sixty cubits long, twenty cubits wide, and thirty cubits high. ³ The vestibule in front of the nave of the house was twenty cubits wide, across the width of the house. Its depth was ten cubits in front of the house. ⁴ For the house he made windows with recessed frames.ᵃ ⁵ He also built a structure against the wall of the house, running around the walls of the house, both the nave and the inner sanctuary; and he made side chambers all around. ⁶ The lowest storyᵇ was five cubits wide, the middle one was six cubits wide, and the third was seven cubits wide; for around the outside of the house he made offsets on the wall in order that the supporting beams should not be inserted into the walls of the house.

7 The house was built with stone finished at the quarry, so that neither hammer nor ax nor any tool of iron was heard in the temple while it was being built.

8 The entrance for the middle story was on the south side of the house: one went up by winding stairs to the middle story, and from the middle story to the third. ⁹ So he built the house, and finished it; he roofed the house with beams and planks of cedar. ¹⁰ He built the structure against the whole house, each storyᶜ five cubits high, and it was joined to the house with timbers of cedar.

11 Now the word of the LORD came to Solomon, ¹² "Concerning this house that you are building, if you will walk in my statutes, obey my ordinances, and keep all my commandments by walking in them, then I will establish my promise with you, which I made to your father David. ¹³ I will dwell among the children of Israel, and will not forsake my people Israel."

14 So Solomon built the house, and finished it. ¹⁵ He lined the walls of the house on the inside with boards of cedar; from the floor of the house to the rafters of the ceiling, he covered them on the inside with wood; and he covered the floor of the house with boards of cypress. ¹⁶ He built twenty cubits of the rear of the house with boards of cedar from the floor to the rafters, and he built this within as an inner sanctuary, as the most holy place. ¹⁷ The house, that is, the nave in front of the inner sanctuary, was forty cubits long. ¹⁸ The cedar within the house had carvings of gourds and open flowers; all was cedar, no stone was seen. ¹⁹ The inner sanctuary he prepared in the innermost part of the house, to set there the ark of the covenant of the LORD. ²⁰ The interior of the inner sanctuary was twenty cubits long, twenty cubits wide, and twenty cubits high; he overlaid it with pure gold. He also overlaid the altar with cedar.ᵈ ²¹ Solomon

ᵃ Gk: Meaning of Heb uncertain ᵇ Gk: Heb structure ᶜ Heb lacks each story ᵈ Meaning of Heb uncertain

---

6:3–10—To the front of the central building was added a *vestibule* through which one entered the sanctuary and then the Holy of Holies. A support and storage structure of three stories surrounded the building on the remaining three sides.

6:11–13—Tempering the impression created by the description of the temple, an insertion has YHWH state that the promise to Solomon and supporting presence within Israel is conditioned by the king's obedience to the Torah (see 2:4). This stands in tension with the unconditional promise made to David about his dynasty's eternal relationship with YHWH and YHWH's everlasting presence in the temple (see Ps. 68:16). With notices like this, the narrator nuances any suggestion that YHWH's promise to David and his dynasty was unconditional and YHWH's presence assured in sustaining Jerusalem forever.

6:11–22—The material used in finishing the temple is even more impressive than its size.

6:19—*The ark of the covenant* can be traced back to Israel's time in the wilderness after the exodus from Egypt. It accompanied Israel in war (1 Sam. 4:4) and was seen by some as housing the tablets of the Torah (Exod. 25:16). David brought it to Jerusalem (2 Sam. 6), and when Solomon installed it in the temple as a throne for the invisible YHWH, he joined the old symbol of YHWH's presence (the ark) with the new symbol of YHWH's grandeur and grace (the temple).

6:20—The Holy of Holies is a cube of thirty feet on all sides.

6:21–22—The repetition of the word *gold* nicely captures the sumptuousness of the house Solomon built for his God.

overlaid the inside of the house with pure gold, then he drew chains of gold across, in front of the inner sanctuary, and overlaid it with gold. 22 Next he overlaid the whole house with gold, in order that the whole house might be perfect; even the whole altar that belonged to the inner sanctuary he overlaid with gold.

The Furnishings of the Temple

23 In the inner sanctuary he made two cherubim of olivewood, each ten cubits high. 24 Five cubits was the length of one wing of the cherub, and five cubits the length of the other wing of the cherub; it was ten cubits from the tip of one wing to the tip of the other. 25 The other cherub also measured ten cubits; both cherubim had the same measure and the same form. 26 The height of one cherub was ten cubits, and so was that of the other cherub. 27 He put the cherubim in the innermost part of the house; the wings of the cherubim were spread out so that a wing of one was touching the one wall, and a wing of the other cherub was touching the other wall; their other wings toward the center of the house were touching wing to wing. 28 He also overlaid the cherubim with gold.

29 He carved the walls of the house all around about with carved engravings of cherubim, palm trees, and open flowers, in the inner and outer rooms. 30 The floor of the house he overlaid with gold, in the inner and outer rooms.

31 For the entrance to the inner sanctuary he made doors of olivewood; the lintel and the doorposts were five-sided.*a*

32 He covered the two doors of olivewood with carvings of cherubim, palm trees, and open flowers; he overlaid them with gold, and spread gold on the cherubim and on the palm trees.

33 So also he made for the entrance to the nave doorposts of olivewood, four-sided each, 34 and two doors of cypress wood; the two leaves of the one door were folding, and the two leaves of the other door were folding. 35 He carved cherubim, palm trees, and open flowers, overlaying them with gold evenly applied upon the carved work. 36 He built the inner court with three courses of dressed stone to one course of cedar beams.

37 In the fourth year the foundation of the house of the LORD was laid, in the month of Ziv. 38 In the eleventh year, in the month of Bul, which is the eighth month, the house was finished in all its parts, and according to all its specifications. He was seven years in building it.

Solomon's Palace and Other Buildings

7 Solomon was building his own house thirteen years, and he finished his entire house.

2 He built the House of the Forest of the Lebanon one hundred cubits long, fifty cubits wide, and thirty cubits high, built on four rows of cedar pillars, with cedar beams on the pillars. 3 It was roofed with cedar on the forty-five rafters, fifteen in each row, which were on the pillars. 4 There were window frames in the three rows, facing each other in the three rows. 5 All the doorways and

a Meaning of Heb uncertain

6:23–36—The temple appointments are as lavish as the temple itself; the decorative motifs reflect an array of Near Eastern traditions. *Cherubim* were composite creatures who stood as guardians or throne supports, upon which God was also said to ride (2 Sam. 22:11; Ps. 18:10; Ezek. 1; 10).

6:37–38—*Seven years* devoted to building the temple seems extensive until one compares it with the thirteen years devoted to Solomon's own house (7:1).

7:1–51 Solomon's Palace and Temple Furnishings

The briefer notice about Solomon's palace (vv. 1–12) is bracketed by more extensive notices on the building (chap. 6) and furnishing of the temple (7:13–51)—the king's palace is enveloped by the sacred court of YHWH. Royal and divine establishments become effectively one. The course of history would show, however, that YHWH is not bound unconditionally to the Davidic throne, the temple, or the city of Jerusalem.

doorposts had four-sided frames, opposite, facing each other in the three rows.

6 He made the Hall of Pillars fifty cubits long and thirty cubits wide. There was a porch in front with pillars, and a canopy in front of them.

7 He made the Hall of the Throne where he was to pronounce judgment, the Hall of Justice, covered with cedar from floor to floor.

8 His own house where he would reside, in the other court back of the hall, was of the same construction. Solomon also made a house like this hall for Pharaoh's daughter, whom he had taken in marriage.

9 All these were made of costly stones, cut according to measure, sawed with saws, back and front, from the foundation to the coping, and from outside to the great court. 10 The foundation was of costly stones, huge stones, stones of eight and ten cubits. 11 There were costly stones above, cut to measure, and cedarwood. 12 The great court had three courses of dressed stone to one layer of cedar beams all around; so had the inner court of the house of the LORD, and the vestibule of the house.

Products of Hiram the Bronzeworker

13 Now King Solomon invited and received Hiram from Tyre. 14 He was the son of a widow of the tribe of Naphtali, whose father, a man of Tyre, had been an artisan in bronze; he was full of skill, intelligence, and knowledge in working bronze. He came to King Solomon, and did all his work.

15 He cast two pillars of bronze. Eighteen cubits was the height of the one, and a cord of twelve cubits would encircle it; the second pillar was the same.*a* 16 He also made two capitals of molten bronze, to set on the tops of the pillars; the height of the one capital was five cubits, and the height of the other capital was five cubits. 17 There were nets of checker work with wreaths of chain work for the capitals on the tops of the pillars; seven*b* for the one capital, and seven*b* for the other capital. 18 He made the columns with two rows around each latticework to cover the capitals that were above the pomegranates; he did the same with the other capital. 19 Now the capitals that were on the tops of the pillars in the vestibule were of lily-work, four cubits high. 20 The capitals were on the two pillars and also above the rounded projection that was beside the latticework; there were two hundred pomegranates in rows all around; and so with the other capital. 21 He set up the pillars at the vestibule of the temple; he set up the pillar on the south and called it Jachin; and he set up the pillar on the north and called it Boaz. 22 On the tops of the pillars was lily-work. Thus the work of the pillars was finished.

23 Then he made the molten sea; it was round, ten cubits from brim to brim, and five cubits high. A line of thirty cubits would encircle it completely. 24 Under its brim were panels all around it, each of ten cubits, surrounding the sea; there were two rows of panels, cast when it was cast. 25 It stood on twelve oxen, three facing north, three facing west, three facing south, and three facing east; the sea was set on them. The hindquarters of each

---

a Cn: Heb *and a cord of twelve cubits encircled the second pillar*; Compare Jer 52.21   *b* Heb: Gk *a net*

7:8—That one of Solomon's wives was the *daughter* of the Egyptian Pharaoh demonstrates both the extent of his significance and a reduced level of Egyptian sway over Syria-Palestine.

7:13–51—Like the temple, its furnishings were significantly the product of Phoenician craft, mirroring Phoenician themes and practice.

7:13—This *Hiram* is not the king of chap. 5, but a skilled metalworker.

7:15–22—The *pillars of bronze*, at the temple's entrance, served a symbolic function expressed by their names: *Jachin* = "He establishes"; *Boaz* = "In strength."

7:23–26—The function and symbolism of the huge *molten sea* (a *bath* equals about 5 1/2 gallons) is debated.

were toward the inside. **26** Its thickness was a handbreadth; its brim was made like the brim of a cup, like the flower of a lily; it held two thousand baths.*a*

27 He also made the ten stands of bronze; each stand was four cubits long, four cubits wide, and three cubits high. **28** This was the construction of the stands: they had borders; the borders were within the frames; **29** on the borders that were set in the frames were lions, oxen, and cherubim. On the frames, both above and below the lions and oxen, there were wreaths of beveled work. **30** Each stand had four bronze wheels and axles of bronze; at the four corners were supports for a basin. The supports were cast with wreaths at the side of each. **31** Its opening was within the crown whose height was one cubit; its opening was round, as a pedestal is made; it was a cubit and a half wide. At its opening there were carvings; its borders were four-sided, not round. **32** The four wheels were underneath the borders; the axles of the wheels were in the stands; and the height of a wheel was a cubit and a half. **33** The wheels were made like a chariot wheel; their axles, their rims, their spokes, and their hubs were all cast. **34** There were four supports at the four corners of each stand; the supports were of one piece with the stands. **35** On the top of the stand there was a round band half a cubit high; on the top of the stand, its stays and its borders were of one piece with it. **36** On the surfaces of its stays and on its borders he carved cherubim, lions, and palm trees, where each had space, with wreaths all around. **37** In this way he made the ten stands; all of them were cast alike, with the same size and the same form.

38 He made ten basins of bronze; each basin held forty baths,*a* each basin measured four cubits; there was a basin for each of the ten stands. **39** He set five of the stands on the south side of the house, and five on the north side of the house; he set the sea on the southeast corner of the house.

40 Hiram also made the pots, the shovels, and the basins. So Hiram finished all the work that he did for King Solomon on the house of the LORD: **41** the two pillars, the two bowls of the capitals that were on the tops of the pillars, the two latticeworks to cover the two bowls of the capitals that were on the tops of the pillars; **42** the four hundred pomegranates for the two latticeworks, two rows of pomegranates for each latticework, to cover the two bowls of the capitals that were on the pillars; **43** the ten stands, the ten basins on the stands; **44** the one sea, and the twelve oxen underneath the sea.

45 The pots, the shovels, and the basins, all these vessels that Hiram made for King Solomon for the house of the LORD were of burnished bronze. **46** In the plain of the Jordan the king cast them, in the clay ground between Succoth and Zarethan. **47** Solomon left all the vessels unweighed, because there were so many of them; the weight of the bronze was not determined.

48 So Solomon made all the vessels that were in the house of the LORD: the golden altar, the golden table for the bread of the Presence, **49** the lampstands of pure gold, five on the south side and five on the north, in front of the inner sanctuary; the flowers, the lamps, and the tongs, of gold; **50** the cups, snuffers, basins, dishes for incense, and firepans, of pure gold; the sockets for the doors of the innermost part of the house, the most holy place, and for the doors of the nave of the temple, of gold.

51 Thus all the work that King Solomon

a A Heb measure of volume

7:40–50—The vessels echo the description of the tabernacle found in the latter part of Exodus, although here they are made by a Phoenician.

Gold is the appropriate last word before the concluding summary in v. 51.

7:51—See 2 Sam. 8:9–12 and 1 Chr. 29:1–5.

did on the house of the LORD was finished. Solomon brought in the things that his father David had dedicated, the silver, the gold, and the vessels, and stored them in the treasuries of the house of the LORD.

Dedication of the Temple

8 Then Solomon assembled the elders of Israel and all the heads of the tribes, the leaders of the ancestral houses of the Israelites, before King Solomon in Jerusalem, to bring up the ark of the covenant of the LORD out of the city of David, which is Zion. ² All the people of Israel assembled to King Solomon at the festival in the month Ethanim, which is the seventh month. ³ And all the elders of Israel came, and the priests carried the ark. ⁴ So they brought up the ark of the LORD, the tent of meeting, and all the holy vessels that were in the tent; the priests and the Levites brought them up. ⁵ King Solomon and all the congregation of Israel, who had assembled before him, were with him before the ark, sacrificing so many sheep and oxen that they could not be counted or numbered. ⁶ Then the priests brought the ark of the covenant of the LORD to its place, in the inner sanctuary of the house, in the most holy place, underneath the wings of the cherubim. ⁷ For the cherubim spread out their wings over the place of the ark, so that the cherubim made a covering above the ark and its poles. ⁸ The poles were so long that the ends of the poles were seen from the holy place in front of the inner sanctuary; but they

could not be seen from outside; they are there to this day. ⁹ There was nothing in the ark except the two tablets of stone that Moses had placed there at Horeb, where the LORD made a covenant with the Israelites, when they came out of the land of Egypt. ¹⁰ And when the priests came out of the holy place, a cloud filled the house of the LORD, ¹¹ so that the priests could not stand to minister because of the cloud; for the glory of the LORD filled the house of the LORD.

12 Then Solomon said,
"The LORD has said that he would
  dwell in thick darkness.
¹³ I have built you an exalted house,
  a place for you to dwell in forever."

Solomon's Speech

14 Then the king turned around and blessed all the assembly of Israel, while all the assembly of Israel stood. ¹⁵ He said, "Blessed be the LORD, the God of Israel, who with his hand has fulfilled what he promised with his mouth to my father David, saying, ¹⁶ 'Since the day that I brought my people Israel out of Egypt, I have not chosen a city from any of the tribes of Israel in which to build a house, that my name might be there; but I chose David to be over my people Israel.' ¹⁷ My father David had it in mind to build a house for the name of the LORD, the God of Israel. ¹⁸ But the LORD said to my father David, 'You did well to consider building a house for my name; ¹⁹ nevertheless you shall not build the house, but your son who shall be born to you shall build the house for

8:1–66 Solomon Dedicates the Temple

8:1–9—With the installation of *the ark* (see 6:19) the old and new are brought together under the aegis of Solomon. The *elders* and *heads of the tribes* represent older traditional leadership. The event takes place in the fall almost a year after the temple is completed at what is probably the fall *festival* of Sukkoth, a time when the Torah of Moses was recalled (Exod. 23:16; 34:22; Deut. 16:13–17). The *cherubim* (see 6:23–36) spread their protective *wings* over the ark, here said to contain the *tablets* deposited by Moses that record YHWH's *covenant* with Israel at Sinai. The

sight of *the poles* used to carry the ark remind all that this ancient mobile symbol of YHWH's presence now resides in Solomon's temple. That *they are there to this day* suggests a narrative perspective before the destruction of the temple by the Babylonians in 587/86 BCE.

8:10–13—The *cloud* and YHWH's *glory* recall YHWH's presence at Sinai.

8:14–21—Solomon's opening speech recalls YHWH's unconditional promise made in 2 Sam. 7 and suggests he and his building project stand as fulfillment of what was promised to David.

my name.' ²⁰ Now the LORD has upheld the promise that he made; for I have risen in the place of my father David; I sit on the throne of Israel, as the LORD promised, and have built the house for the name of the LORD, the God of Israel. ²¹ There I have provided a place for the ark, in which is the covenant of the LORD that he made with our ancestors when he brought them out of the land of Egypt."

Solomon's Prayer of Dedication

22 Then Solomon stood before the altar of the LORD in the presence of all the assembly of Israel, and spread out his hands to heaven. ²³ He said, "O LORD, God of Israel, there is no God like you in heaven above or on earth beneath, keeping covenant and steadfast love for your servants who walk before you with all their heart, ²⁴ the covenant that you kept for your servant my father David as you declared to him; you promised with your mouth and have this day fulfilled with your hand. ²⁵ Therefore, O LORD, God of Israel, keep for your servant my father David that which you promised him, saying, 'There shall never fail you a successor before me to sit on the throne of Israel, if only your children look to their way, to walk before me as you have walked before me.' ²⁶ Therefore, O God of Israel, let your word be confirmed, which you promised to your servant my father David.

27 "But will God indeed dwell on the earth? Even heaven and the highest heaven cannot contain you, much less this house that I have built! ²⁸ Regard your servant's prayer and his plea, O LORD my God, heeding the cry and the prayer that your servant prays to you today; ²⁹ that your eyes may be open night and day toward this house, the place of which you said, 'My name shall be there,' that you may heed the prayer that your servant prays toward this place. ³⁰ Hear the plea of your servant and of your people Israel when they pray toward this place; O hear in heaven your dwelling place; heed and forgive.

31 "If someone sins against a neighbor and is given an oath to swear, and comes and swears before your altar in this house, ³² then hear in heaven, and act, and judge your servants, condemning the guilty by bringing their conduct on their own head, and vindicating the righteous by rewarding them according to their righteousness.

33 "When your people Israel, having sinned against you, are defeated before an enemy but turn again to you, confess your name, pray and plead with you in this house, ³⁴ then hear in heaven, forgive the sin of your people Israel, and bring them again to the land that you gave to their ancestors.

35 "When heaven is shut up and there is no rain because they have sinned against you, and then they pray toward this place, confess your name, and turn from their sin, because you punish[a] them, ³⁶ then hear in heaven, and forgive the sin of your servants, your people Israel, when you teach them the good way in which they should walk; and grant rain on your land, which you have given to your people as an inheritance.

37 "If there is famine in the land, if there

[a] Or when you answer

8:22–53—By contrast, Solomon's extended prayer seems a definitive statement of an overriding Deuteronomic perspective that governs most of 1–2 Kings: YHWH's support depends on Israel's continued faithfulness to YHWH's expectations of them.
8:22–26—God's covenant with David is recalled within the conditional framework underscored by the qualifying *if* of v. 25.

8:27–30—Tension between God's transcendence and immanence is mediated by noting that God cannot be contained by the **highest heaven**, but it is self-decreed that God's **name**, as representative of divine authority, be present in the temple.
8:31–51—Seven petitions are offered, and in all but the first the phrase **hear in heaven** stresses God's transcendent authority and willingness to forgive sins and reverse chastisements.

is plague, blight, mildew, locust, or caterpillar; if their enemy besieges them in any[a] of their cities; whatever plague, whatever sickness there is; ³⁸ whatever prayer, whatever plea there is from any individual or from all your people Israel, all knowing the afflictions of their own hearts so that they stretch out their hands toward this house; ³⁹ then hear in heaven your dwelling place, forgive, act, and render to all whose hearts you know—according to all their ways, for only you know what is in every human heart— ⁴⁰ so that they may fear you all the days that they live in the land that you gave to our ancestors.

41 "Likewise when a foreigner, who is not of your people Israel, comes from a distant land because of your name ⁴² —for they shall hear of your great name, your mighty hand, and your outstretched arm—when a foreigner comes and prays toward this house, ⁴³ then hear in heaven your dwelling place, and do according to all that the foreigner calls to you, so that all the peoples of the earth may know your name and fear you, as do your people Israel, and so that they may know that your name has been invoked on this house that I have built.

44 "If your people go out to battle against their enemy, by whatever way you shall send them, and they pray to the LORD toward the city that you have chosen and the house that I have built for your name, ⁴⁵ then hear in heaven their prayer and their plea, and maintain their cause.

46 "If they sin against you—for there is no one who does not sin—and you are angry with them and give them to an enemy, so that they are carried away captive to the land of the enemy, far off or near; ⁴⁷ yet if they come to their senses in the land to which they have been taken captive, and repent, and plead with you in the land of their captors, saying, 'We have sinned, and have done wrong; we have acted wickedly'; ⁴⁸ if they repent with all their heart and soul in the land of their enemies, who took them captive, and pray to you toward their land, which you gave to their ancestors, the city that you have chosen, and the house that I have built for your name; ⁴⁹ then hear in heaven your dwelling place their prayer and their plea, maintain their cause ⁵⁰ and forgive your people who have sinned against you, and all their transgressions that they have committed against you; and grant them compassion in the sight of their captors, so that they may have compassion on them ⁵¹ (for they are your people and heritage, which you brought out of Egypt, from the midst of the iron-smelter). ⁵² Let your eyes be open to the plea of your servant, and to the plea of your people Israel, listening to them whenever they call to you. ⁵³ For you have separated them from among all the peoples of the earth, to be your heritage, just as you promised through Moses, your servant, when you brought our ancestors out of Egypt, O Lord GOD."

Solomon Blesses the Assembly

54 Now when Solomon finished offering all this prayer and this plea to the LORD, he arose from facing the altar of the LORD, where he had knelt with hands outstretched toward heaven; ⁵⁵ he

[a] Gk Syr: Heb *in the land*

8:41–43—The temple will draw even *foreigners* to it in search of this God.

8:46–51—Even in exile the people's plea can be heard by God and their fate reversed, suggesting perhaps the circumstances of the audience to which 1–2 Kings was directed.

8:51–53—Solomon ends with a reminder of Israel's particular relation with God, looking back to God's relation with *Moses* rather than with

David. Ironically, he looks back to foundational traditions that will be used by prophets like Jeremiah to rebuke and condemn in God's name the very rule Solomon here seeks to secure.

8:54–61—Solomon blesses the people, a role usually assigned priests. He again looks to God's promises and expectations set through *Moses*, appearing as much successor to Moses as to David.

stood and blessed all the assembly of Israel with a loud voice:

56 "Blessed be the LORD, who has given rest to his people Israel according to all that he promised; not one word has failed of all his good promise, which he spoke through his servant Moses. 57 The LORD our God be with us, as he was with our ancestors; may he not leave us or abandon us, 58 but incline our hearts to him, to walk in all his ways, and to keep his commandments, his statutes, and his ordinances, which he commanded our ancestors. 59 Let these words of mine, with which I pleaded before the LORD, be near to the LORD our God day and night, and may he maintain the cause of his servant and the cause of his people Israel, as each day requires; 60 so that all the peoples of the earth may know that the LORD is God; there is no other. 61 Therefore devote yourselves completely to the LORD our God, walking in his statutes and keeping his commandments, as at this day."

Solomon Offers Sacrifices

62 Then the king, and all Israel with him, offered sacrifice before the LORD. 63 Solomon offered as sacrifices of well-being to the LORD twenty-two thousand oxen and one hundred twenty thousand sheep. So the king and all the people of Israel dedicated the house of the LORD. 64 The same day the king consecrated the middle of the court that was in front of the house of the LORD; for there he offered the burnt offerings and the grain offerings and the fat pieces of the sacrifices of well-being, because the bronze altar that was before the LORD was too small to receive the burnt offerings and the grain offerings and the fat pieces of the sacrifices of well-being.

65 So Solomon held the festival at that time, and all Israel with him—a great assembly, people from Lebo-hamath to the Wadi of Egypt—before the LORD our God, seven days.*a* 66 On the eighth day he sent the people away; and they blessed the king, and went to their tents, joyful and in good spirits because of all the goodness that the LORD had shown to his servant David and to his people Israel.

God Appears Again to Solomon

9 When Solomon had finished building the house of the LORD and the king's house and all that Solomon desired to build, 2 the LORD appeared to Solomon a second time, as he had appeared to him at Gibeon. 3 The LORD said to him, "I have heard your prayer and your plea, which you made before me; I have consecrated this house that you have built, and put my name there forever; my eyes and my heart will be there for all time. 4 As for you, if you will walk before me, as David your father walked, with integrity of heart and uprightness, doing according to all that I have commanded you, and keeping my statutes and my ordinances, 5 then I will establish your royal throne over Israel forever, as I promised your father David, saying, 'There shall not fail you a successor on the throne of Israel.'

6 "If you turn aside from following

a Compare Gk: Heb *seven days and seven days, fourteen days*

8:62–66—Solomon assumes priestly duties in offering the *sacrifices* that complete the dedication of the temple. The seven-day festival involved all Israel, from *Lebo-hamath* (somewhere in Syria) *to the Wadi of Egypt*, an expression of Israel's extent under Solomon.

9:1–9 YHWH's Response

YHWH's response to Solomon's prayer signals the overriding theological stance that will be used in evaluating Solomon and the kings who follow him. One is thus reminded that all institutions and structures, however strong their claim to divine legitimization, can come under God's judgment if they fail to submit to YHWH and the Torah.

9:3–5—YHWH's *name* is placed in the temple; indeed, even more, *my eyes and my heart will be there for all time*. The "for all time" and the *forever* that characterize YHWH's presence in the temple and Solomon's rule are qualified by the conditions set by YHWH.

9:6–9—YHWH next addresses Israel broadly and warns them of disaster if they forsake the

me, you or your children, and do not keep my commandments and my statutes that I have set before you, but go and serve other gods and worship them, [7] then I will cut Israel off from the land that I have given them; and the house that I have consecrated for my name I will cast out of my sight; and Israel will become a proverb and a taunt among all peoples. [8] This house will become a heap of ruins;[a] everyone passing by it will be astonished, and will hiss; and they will say, 'Why has the LORD done such a thing to this land and to this house?' [9] Then they will say, 'Because they have forsaken the LORD their God, who brought their ancestors out of the land of Egypt, and embraced other gods, worshiping them and serving them; therefore the LORD has brought this disaster upon them.' "

[10] At the end of twenty years, in which Solomon had built the two houses, the house of the LORD and the king's house, [11] King Hiram of Tyre having supplied Solomon with cedar and cypress timber and gold, as much as he desired, King Solomon gave to Hiram twenty cities in the land of Galilee. [12] But when Hiram came from Tyre to see the cities that Solomon had given him, they did not please him. [13] Therefore he said, "What kind of cities are these that you have given me, my brother?" So they are called the land of Cabul[b] to this day. [14] But Hiram had sent to the king one hundred twenty talents of gold.

Other Acts of Solomon

[15] This is the account of the forced labor that King Solomon conscripted to build the house of the LORD and his own house, the Millo and the wall of Jerusalem, Hazor, Megiddo, Gezer [16] (Pharaoh king of Egypt had gone up and captured Gezer and burned it down, had killed the Canaanites who lived in the city, and had given it as dowry to his daughter, Solomon's wife; [17] so Solomon rebuilt Gezer), Lower Beth-horon, [18] Baalath, Tamar in the wilderness, within the land, [19] as well as all of Solomon's storage cities, the cities for his chariots, the cities for his cavalry, and whatever Solomon desired to build, in Jerusalem, in Lebanon, and in all the land of his dominion. [20] All the people who were left of the Amorites, the Hittites, the Perizzites, the Hivites, and the Jebusites, who were not of the people of Israel— [21] their descendants who were still left in the land, whom the Israelites were unable to destroy completely—these Solomon conscripted for slave labor, and so they are to this day. [22] But of the Israelites Solomon made no slaves; they were the soldiers, they were his officials, his commanders, his captains, and the commanders of his chariotry and cavalry.

[23] These were the chief officers who were over Solomon's work: five hundred fifty, who had charge of the people who carried on the work.

[24] But Pharaoh's daughter went up from the city of David to her own house that Solomon had built for her; then he built the Millo.

[25] Three times a year Solomon used to offer up burnt offerings and sacrifices

---

[a] Syr Old Latin: Heb *will become high*   [b] Perhaps meaning *a land good for nothing*

---

commandments and **statutes**, in particular if they embrace and **serve other gods**. Being cut off from their homeland and a byword for disaster would have particularly strong resonance for those in exile.

9:10–28 Particulars of Solomon's Rule

9:10–14—Having already paid Hiram for the temple materials (5:9–11), the gift of these *cities* may reverse a negative flow of wealth that resulted from Solomon's building projects. Hiram is not impressed with the cities, but as they are in **Galilee** near **Tyre**, he completes the transaction.

9:15–28—Brief notices suggest the extent of Solomon's additional activities and the effort needed to maintain his establishment.

9:20–23—Remnants of earlier Canaanites in the land, whom Deuteronomy set for destruction (Deut. 7:1–6; 20:16–18), are conscripted into labor gangs. Verse 22 stands in contradiction to what was said in 1 Kgs. 5:13–18 (see 12:4).

9:24—See 3:1.

of well-being on the altar that he built for the LORD, offering incense[a] before the LORD. So he completed the house.

Solomon's Commercial Activity

26 King Solomon built a fleet of ships at Ezion-geber, which is near Eloth on the shore of the Red Sea,[b] in the land of Edom. 27 Hiram sent his servants with the fleet, sailors who were familiar with the sea, together with the servants of Solomon. 28 They went to Ophir, and imported from there four hundred twenty talents of gold, which they delivered to King Solomon.

Visit of the Queen of Sheba

10 When the queen of Sheba heard of the fame of Solomon (fame due to[c] the name of the LORD), she came to test him with hard questions. 2 She came to Jerusalem with a very great retinue, with camels bearing spices, and very much gold, and precious stones; and when she came to Solomon, she told him all that was on her mind. 3 Solomon answered all her questions; there was nothing hidden from the king that he could not explain to her. 4 When the queen of Sheba had observed all the wisdom of Solomon, the house that he had built, 5 the food of his table, the seating of his officials, and the attendance of his servants, their clothing, his valets, and his burnt offerings that he offered at the house of the LORD, there was no more spirit in her.

6 So she said to the king, "The report was true that I heard in my own land of your accomplishments and of your wisdom, 7 but I did not believe the reports until I came and my own eyes had seen it. Not even half had been told me; your wisdom and prosperity far surpass the report that I had heard. 8 Happy are your wives![d] Happy are these your servants, who continually attend you and hear your wisdom! 9 Blessed be the LORD your God, who has delighted in you and set you on the throne of Israel! Because the LORD loved Israel forever, he has made you king to execute justice and righteousness." 10 Then she gave the king one hundred twenty talents of gold, a great quantity of spices, and precious stones; never again did spices come in such quantity as that which the queen of Sheba gave to King Solomon.

11 Moreover, the fleet of Hiram, which carried gold from Ophir, brought from Ophir a great quantity of almug wood and precious stones. 12 From the almug wood the king made supports for the house of the LORD, and for the king's house, lyres also and harps for the singers; no such almug wood has come or been seen to this day.

13 Meanwhile King Solomon gave to the queen of Sheba every desire that she expressed, as well as what he gave her out of Solomon's royal bounty. Then she returned to her own land, with her servants.

[a] Gk: Heb offering incense with it that was [b] Or Sea of Reeds [c] Meaning of Heb uncertain [d] Gk Syr: Heb men

---

9:26–28—Solomon further expands his economic base, provisioning *a fleet of ships* sailing from *Ezion-geber* in the Gulf of Aqaba. A crew composed of Phoenicians and Israelites brings back a vast amount of *gold* (a *talent* = about 75 pounds) from the fabled *Ophir*. First Kings 10:11–12 suggest the seagoing ventures were under the direction of Hiram. First Kings 10:22 notes Solomon's own fleet of ships of Tarshish.

10:1–29 The Queen of Sheba Visits Solomon
Having impressed readers with Solomon's religious activities, we are now shown the secular side of his extended projects, wisdom, and wealth, first through the eyes of *the queen of Sheba*, from southwestern Arabia and a center for trade in *gold*, *precious stones*, and *spices*.

10:1—She tests Solomon's wisdom with *hard questions* (lit. "riddles") in a contest of the type Samson set for the Philistines (Judg. 14:12–18), mastery of which was a proverbial sign of wisdom (Prov. 1:6).

10:6–10—Her words of praise link Solomon's wealth and splendor to God's delight in him, and suggests God (see 3:1–15) gave him the wisdom that is their source.

10:13—Behind the exchange of gifts, favors, and praise may stand trade agreements designed to enrich Israel and Sheba.

14 The weight of gold that came to Solomon in one year was six hundred sixty-six talents of gold, ¹⁵ besides that which came from the traders and from the business of the merchants, and from all the kings of Arabia and the governors of the land. ¹⁶ King Solomon made two hundred large shields of beaten gold; six hundred shekels of gold went into each large shield. ¹⁷ He made three hundred shields of beaten gold; three minas of gold went into each shield; and the king put them in the House of the Forest of Lebanon. ¹⁸ The king also made a great ivory throne, and overlaid it with the finest gold. ¹⁹ The throne had six steps. The top of the throne was rounded in the back, and on each side of the seat were arm rests and two lions standing beside the arm rests, ²⁰ while twelve lions were standing, one on each end of a step on the six steps. Nothing like it was ever made in any kingdom. ²¹ All King Solomon's drinking vessels were of gold, and all the vessels of the House of the Forest of Lebanon were of pure gold; none were of silver—it was not considered as anything in the days of Solomon. ²² For the king had a fleet of ships of Tarshish at sea with the fleet of Hiram. Once every three years the fleet of ships of Tarshish used to come bringing gold, silver, ivory, apes, and peacocks.ᵃ

23 Thus King Solomon excelled all the kings of the earth in riches and in wisdom. ²⁴ The whole earth sought the presence of Solomon to hear his wisdom, which God had put into his mind. ²⁵ Every one of them brought a present, objects of silver and gold, garments, weaponry, spices, horses, and mules, so much year by year.

26 Solomon gathered together chariots and horses; he had fourteen hundred chariots and twelve thousand horses, which he stationed in the chariot cities and with the king in Jerusalem. ²⁷ The king made silver as common in Jerusalem as stones, and he made cedars as numerous as the sycamores of the Shephelah. ²⁸ Solomon's import of horses was from Egypt and Kue, and the king's traders received them from Kue at a price. ²⁹ A chariot could be imported from Egypt for six hundred shekels of silver, and a horse for one hundred fifty; so through the king's traders they were exported to all the kings of the Hittites and the kings of Aram.

Solomon's Errors

11 King Solomon loved many foreign women along with the daughter of Pharaoh: Moabite, Ammonite, Edomite, Sidonian, and Hittite women, ² from the nations concerning which the LORD had said to the Israelites, "You shall not enter into marriage with them, neither shall they with you; for they will surely incline your heart to follow their gods"; Solomon clung to these in love. ³ Among his wives were seven hundred princesses and three hundred concubines; and his wives

ᵃ Or baboons

10:14–25—Again the word *gold* rings repeatedly in this description of Solomon's own wealth and splendor, as in the description of what he constructed for his God (see 7:40–51).

10:26–29—Solomon is active in arms trading, joining *horses* and *chariots* brought *from Egypt and Kue* (in Anatolia) and trading them to *kings of the Hittites* and *Aram* in Syria. Such trade with Egypt contrasts with the image of the ideal king in Deut. 17:14–20. In spite of his renowned wealth and splendor, all is not right in Solomon's reign, in the eyes of those who constructed 1–2 Kings.

11:1–43 Judgment upon Solomon's Rule

11:1–13—What was hinted at in the reports of Solomon's grandeur now becomes explicit in a theological judgment on his reign. Other than his Egyptian wife (3:1; 9:24), no mention has been made of Solomon's wives or heirs. We now learn he had numerous wives from surrounding nations. This is read as a violation of God's command (11:2 and Deut. 7:1–6). These wives lead the now-aged king into the worship of other gods. Because of his divided loyalties YHWH tears Solomon's kingdom asunder, leaving the house of David only a part.

turned away his heart. ⁴ For when Solomon was old, his wives turned away his heart after other gods; and his heart was not true to the LORD his God, as was the heart of his father David. ⁵ For Solomon followed Astarte the goddess of the Sidonians, and Milcom the abomination of the Ammonites. ⁶ So Solomon did what was evil in the sight of the LORD, and did not completely follow the LORD, as his father David had done. ⁷ Then Solomon built a high place for Chemosh the abomination of Moab, and for Molech the abomination of the Ammonites, on the mountain east of Jerusalem. ⁸ He did the same for all his foreign wives, who offered incense and sacrificed to their gods.

9 Then the LORD was angry with Solomon, because his heart had turned away from the LORD, the God of Israel, who had appeared to him twice, ¹⁰ and had commanded him concerning this matter, that he should not follow other gods; but he did not observe what the LORD commanded. ¹¹ Therefore the LORD said to Solomon, "Since this has been your mind and you have not kept my covenant and my statutes that I have commanded you, I will surely tear the kingdom from you and give it to your servant. ¹² Yet for the sake of your father David I will not do it in your lifetime; I will tear it out of the hand of your son. ¹³ I will not, however, tear away the entire kingdom; I will give one tribe to your son, for the sake of my servant David and for the sake of Jerusalem, which I have chosen."

Adversaries of Solomon

14 Then the LORD raised up an adversary against Solomon, Hadad the Edomite; he was of the royal house in Edom. ¹⁵ For when David was in Edom, and Joab the commander of the army went up to bury the dead, he killed every male in Edom ¹⁶ (for Joab and all Israel remained there six months, until he had eliminated every male in Edom); ¹⁷ but Hadad fled to Egypt with some Edomites who were servants of his father. He was a young boy at that time. ¹⁸ They set out from Midian and came to Paran; they took people with them from Paran and came to Egypt, to Pharaoh king of Egypt, who gave him a house, assigned him an allowance of food, and gave him land. ¹⁹ Hadad found great favor in the sight of Pharaoh, so that he gave him his sister-in-law for a wife, the sister of Queen Tahpenes. ²⁰ The sister of Tahpenes gave birth by him to his son Genubath, whom Tahpenes weaned in Pharaoh's house; Genubath was in Pharaoh's house among the children of Pharaoh. ²¹ When Hadad heard in Egypt that David slept with his ancestors and that Joab the commander of the army was dead, Hadad said to Pharaoh, "Let me depart, that I may go to my own country." ²² But Pharaoh said to him, "What do you lack with me that you now seek to go to your own country?" And he said, "No, do let me go."

23 God raised up another adversary against Solomon,ᵃ Rezon son of Eliada, who had fled from his master, King Hadadezer of Zobah. ²⁴ He gathered followers around him and became leader of a marauding band, after the slaughter by David; they went to Damascus, settled there, and made him king in Damascus. ²⁵ He was an adversary of Israel all the days of Solomon, making

---

ᵃ Heb *him*

11:5—*Astarte*, a Canaanite goddess, was linked with Baal, the storm god who insured fertility. *Milcom* is a form of Baal.

11:7—*Chemosh* and *Molech* are presented as the national gods of *Moab* and Edom, nations east of Israel.

11:12–13—Only YHWH's favor for David prevents the dissolution of the empire and united monarchy in Solomon's lifetime, retaining for David's dynasty a remnant to rule from Jerusalem.

11:14–25—We now learn that Solomon's reign was marred by conflict with foreign adversaries, contrasting to the mutually beneficial relations with Hiram.

trouble as Hadad did; he despised Israel and reigned over Aram.

Jeroboam's Rebellion

26 Jeroboam son of Nebat, an Ephra-imite of Zeredah, a servant of Solomon, whose mother's name was Zeruah, a widow, rebelled against the king. ²⁷ The following was the reason he rebelled against the king. Solomon built the Millo, and closed up the gap in the wall*ᵃ* of the city of his father David. ²⁸ The man Jeroboam was very able, and when Solomon saw that the young man was industrious he gave him charge over all the forced labor of the house of Joseph. ²⁹ About that time, when Jeroboam was leaving Jerusalem, the prophet Ahijah the Shilonite found him on the road. Ahijah had clothed himself with a new garment. The two of them were alone in the open country ³⁰ when Ahijah laid hold of the new garment he was wear-ing and tore it into twelve pieces. ³¹ He then said to Jeroboam: Take for yourself ten pieces; for thus says the LORD, the God of Israel, "See, I am about to tear the kingdom from the hand of Solo-mon, and will give you ten tribes. ³² One tribe will remain his, for the sake of my servant David and for the sake of Jeru-salem, the city that I have chosen out of all the tribes of Israel. ³³ This is because he has*ᵇ* forsaken me, worshiped Astarte the goddess of the Sidonians, Chemosh the god of Moab, and Milcom the god of the Ammonites, and has*ᵇ* not walked in my ways, doing what is right in my sight and keeping my statutes and my ordinances, as his father David did. ³⁴ Nevertheless I will not take the whole kingdom away from him but will make him ruler all the days of his life, for the sake of my servant David whom I chose and who did keep my commandments and my statutes; ³⁵ but I will take the kingdom away from his son and give it to you—that is, the ten tribes. ³⁶ Yet to his son I will give one tribe, so that my servant David may always have a lamp before me in Jerusalem, the city where I have chosen to put my name. ³⁷ I will take you, and you shall reign over all that your soul desires; you shall be king over Israel. ³⁸ If you will listen to all that I command you, walk in my ways, and do what is right in my sight by keeping my statutes and my commandments, as David my servant did, I will be with you, and will build you an enduring house, as I built for David, and I will give Israel to you. ³⁹ For this reason I will punish the descendants of David, but not for-ever." ⁴⁰ Solomon sought therefore to kill Jeroboam; but Jeroboam promptly fled to Egypt, to King Shishak of Egypt, and remained in Egypt until the death of Solomon.

Death of Solomon

41 Now the rest of the acts of Solomon, all that he did as well as his wisdom, are they not written in the Book of the Acts of Solomon? ⁴² The time that Solomon

ᵃ Heb lacks *in the wall* *ᵇ* Gk Syr Vg: Heb *they have*

11:26–40—*The prophet Ahijah* from Shiloh proclaims the tearing of most of Solomon's kingdom from the house of David. *Jeroboam*, an official in Solomon's service, is enticed into rebellion against his king, and this leads to his flight from Solomon and refuge in Egypt. The math of *ten tribes* for Jeroboam and one for Solomon does not account for all twelve pieces of Ahijah's *garment* (v. 30), but presumably Benjamin was counted with Judah, as it bor-dered on Jerusalem to the north and remained in Davidic hands.

11:38—The promise to build an *enduring house* for Jeroboam like David's has an ironic ring

concluding an announcement of the rending of David's house.

11:40—*Shishak*, the Egyptian Pharaoh Shoshenq I (931–910 BCE), granted refuge to Jeroboam, suggesting relations between Solomon and Egypt have soured since Solomon wed Pharaoh's daughter.

11:41–43—This summary ends the account of Solomon's reign with reference to an otherwise unknown source from which material in this ac-count may have been drawn and to which read-ers might once have referred for more, lending an air of authority to the account even for readers unable to access this source.

reigned in Jerusalem over all Israel was forty years. [43] Solomon slept with his ancestors and was buried in the city of his father David; and his son Rehoboam succeeded him.

The Northern Tribes Secede

12 Rehoboam went to Shechem, for all Israel had come to Shechem to make him king. [2] When Jeroboam son of Nebat heard of it (for he was still in Egypt, where he had fled from King Solomon), then Jeroboam returned from[a] Egypt. [3] And they sent and called him; and Jeroboam and all the assembly of Israel came and said to Rehoboam, [4] "Your father made our yoke heavy. Now therefore lighten the hard service of your father and his heavy yoke that he placed on us, and we will serve you." [5] He said to them, "Go away for three days, then come again to me." So the people went away.

[6] Then King Rehoboam took counsel with the older men who had attended his father Solomon while he was still alive, saying, "How do you advise me to answer this people?" [7] They answered him, "If you will be a servant to this people today and serve them, and speak good words to them when you answer them, then they will be your servants forever." [8] But he disregarded the advice that the older men gave him, and consulted with the young men who had grown up with him and now attended him. [9] He said to them, "What do you advise that we answer this people who have said to me, 'Lighten the yoke that your father put on us'?" [10] The young men who had grown up with him said to him, "Thus you should say to this people who spoke to you, 'Your father made our yoke heavy, but you must lighten it for us'; thus you should say to them, 'My little finger is thicker than my father's loins. [11] Now, whereas my father laid on you a heavy yoke, I will add to your yoke. My father disciplined you with whips, but I will discipline you with scorpions.'"

[12] So Jeroboam and all the people came to Rehoboam the third day, as the king had said, "Come to me again the third day." [13] The king answered the people harshly. He disregarded the advice that the older men had given him [14] and spoke to them according to the advice of the young men, "My father made your yoke heavy, but I will add to your yoke; my father disciplined you with whips, but I will discipline you with scorpions." [15] So the king did not listen to the people, because it was a turn of affairs brought about by the LORD that he might fulfill his word, which the LORD had spoken by Ahijah the Shilonite to Jeroboam son of Nebat.

[16] When all Israel saw that the king

---

[a] Gk Vg Compare 2 Chr 10.2: Heb *lived in*

12:1–16:34 The Division of the Kingdom

12:1–20 Israel Breaks from the House of David

We discover now that what united all Israel under Davidic rule was common allegiance to the king, an allegiance threatened by the burden Solomon's building projects and court establishment placed on his people. Solomon's son **Rehoboam** and his cronies in court are insensitive to the threat these burdens pose. The result is the collapse of Davidic rule over a united Israel. Within one generation the house of David becomes an example of what can happen when leaders and their cronies become detached from the needs and desires of their people.

12:1—*Shechem* was a covenant site in early Israel (Deut. 27; Josh. 24). Rehoboam's seeking the allegiance of **all Israel** there could reflect some sensitivity to political and religious concerns of the northern tribes or remarkable insensitivity to possibilities for rebellion.

12:2—*Jeroboam* (see 11:26–40) now returns from asylum in *Egypt* to lead negotiations on behalf of those oppressed by Solomon's policies.

12:10—The response proposed by Rehoboam's younger men may contain an obscenity now masked by time, expressing their arrogance and contempt for those seeking release.

12:15—Rehoboam's rejection of the people's demands results not simply from his own obstinacy but also reflects YHWH's shaping of events as announced through Ahijah (vv. 29–39).

12:16—The people's response echoes northern words of rebelling against David (2 Sam. 20:1).

would not listen to them, the people answered the king,

"What share do we have in David?
We have no inheritance in the son of Jesse.
To your tents, O Israel!
Look now to your own house,
     O David."

So Israel went away to their tents. ¹⁷ But Rehoboam reigned over the Israelites who were living in the towns of Judah. ¹⁸ When King Rehoboam sent Adoram, who was taskmaster over the forced labor, all Israel stoned him to death. King Rehoboam then hurriedly mounted his chariot to flee to Jerusalem. ¹⁹ So Israel has been in rebellion against the house of David to this day.

First Dynasty: Jeroboam Reigns over Israel

20 When all Israel heard that Jeroboam had returned, they sent and called him to the assembly and made him king over all Israel. There was no one who followed the house of David, except the tribe of Judah alone.

21 When Rehoboam came to Jerusalem, he assembled all the house of Judah and the tribe of Benjamin, one hundred eighty thousand chosen troops to fight against the house of Israel, to restore the kingdom to Rehoboam son of Solomon. ²² But the word of God came to Shemaiah the man of God: ²³ Say to King Rehoboam of Judah, son of Solomon, and to all the house of Judah and Benjamin, and to the rest of the people, ²⁴ "Thus says the LORD, You shall not go up or fight against your kindred the people of Israel. Let everyone go home, for this thing is from me." So they heeded the word of the LORD and went home again, according to the word of the LORD.

Jeroboam's Golden Calves

25 Then Jeroboam built Shechem in the hill country of Ephraim, and resided there; he went out from there and built Penuel. ²⁶ Then Jeroboam said to himself, "Now the kingdom may well revert to the house of David. ²⁷ If this people continues to go up to offer sacrifices in the house of the LORD at Jerusalem, the heart of this people will turn again to their master, King Rehoboam of Judah; they will kill me and return to King Rehoboam of Judah." ²⁸ So the king took counsel, and made two calves of gold. He said to the people,ᵃ "You have gone up to Jerusalem long enough. Here are your gods, O Israel, who brought you up out of the land of Egypt." ²⁹ He set

ᵃ Gk: Heb to them

12:17–20—Stoning *Adoram* (see 4:6) and enthroning Jeroboam seals the rebellion of the northern tribes against the house of David, as even Rehoboam now acknowledges. First Kings now begins its interwoven accounts of the history of both Israel and Judah down through the destruction of the former in 722 BCE and the latter in 587/86 BCE. Detached and insensitive leaders invite schism and weakness.

12:20–33 Jeroboam Rules Israel

12:21–24—One final attempt by Rehoboam to *restore* the rebels to his rule is checked by God, when *Shemaiah* affirms the new situation as God's will.

12:25–32—A terse overview of Jeroboam's cultic actions presents him as violating the most fundamental of Deuteronomic prescriptions for proper worship. Jeroboam's fear that continued worship in Jerusalem will lead to the return of his people to Rehoboam's rule leads

him to construct images (Exod. 20:4–6; Deut. 4:15–19; 5:8–10) of gods (Deut. 5:7; 6:4) other than YHWH, establish cultic sites other than Jerusalem (Deut. 12:2–7), institute non-Levitical clergy (Deut. 18:1–8), and redesign the cultic calendar.

12:25—Dual capitals at *Shechem* and *Penuel* allowed Jeroboam to rule from centers west and east of the Jordan River long associated with early Israelite tradition, especially with the patriarch Jacob (Gen. 33:19–34:31; 32:22–32).

12:28—The *calves of gold* (see Exod. 32) are probably bull images linked with the Canaanite El and Baal and expressive of their life-giving powers of generative fertility. This could be blatant apostasy, or it could be a melding of Canaanite images with more traditional Israelite Yahwism.

12:29—*Bethel* and *Dan* represent the southern and northern extent of the northern kingdom.

one in Bethel, and the other he put in Dan. [30] And this thing became a sin, for the people went to worship before the one at Bethel and before the other as far as Dan.[a] [31] He also made houses[b] on high places, and appointed priests from among all the people, who were not Levites. [32] Jeroboam appointed a festival on the fifteenth day of the eighth month like the festival that was in Judah, and he offered sacrifices on the altar; so he did in Bethel, sacrificing to the calves that he had made. And he placed in Bethel the priests of the high places that he had made. [33] He went up to the altar that he had made in Bethel on the fifteenth day in the eighth month, in the month that he alone had devised; he appointed a festival for the people of Israel, and he went up to the altar to offer incense.

A Man of God from Judah

13 While Jeroboam was standing by the altar to offer incense, a man of God came out of Judah by the word of the LORD to Bethel [2] and proclaimed against the altar by the word of the LORD, and said, "O altar, altar, thus says the LORD: 'A son shall be born to the house of David, Josiah by name; and he shall sacrifice on you the priests of the high places who offer incense on you, and human bones shall be burned on you.'" [3] He gave a sign the same day, saying,

"This is the sign that the LORD has spoken: 'The altar shall be torn down, and the ashes that are on it shall be poured out.'" [4] When the king heard what the man of God cried out against the altar at Bethel, Jeroboam stretched out his hand from the altar, saying, "Seize him!" But the hand that he stretched out against him withered so that he could not draw it back to himself. [5] The altar also was torn down, and the ashes poured out from the altar, according to the sign that the man of God had given by the word of the LORD. [6] The king said to the man of God, "Entreat now the favor of the LORD your God, and pray for me, so that my hand may be restored to me." So the man of God entreated the LORD; and the king's hand was restored to him, and became as it was before. [7] Then the king said to the man of God, "Come home with me and dine, and I will give you a gift." [8] But the man of God said to the king, "If you give me half your kingdom, I will not go in with you; nor will I eat food or drink water in this place. [9] For thus I was commanded by the word of the LORD: You shall not eat food, or drink water, or return by the way that you came." [10] So he went another way, and did not return by the way that he had come to Bethel.

11 Now there lived an old prophet in

---

[a] Compare Gk: Heb *went to the one as far as Dan* [b] Gk Vg Compare 13.32: Heb *a house*

Bethel is especially linked with Jacob (Gen. 28:10–22; 35:1–15).

13:1–34 Early Prophets
As 1–2 Kings enters the period of divided Israel, episodes from the reigns of kings are interlaced with stories of prophetic "men of God" who often stand in opposition to the kings (see 12:22–24). Jeroboam is met by a *man of God* from Judah who speaks *the word of the LORD to Bethel against the altar* there (13:1–10). A disturbingly strange story follows about what happened to this man of God as he set out for home (vv. 11–32). In the eyes of the narrator of 1–2 Kings, YHWH's word was often with those found on the margins of society, even with figures who might be considered bizarre or insane.

13:2—Naming *Josiah* as the Davidic king to desecrate the altar at Bethel in this dramatic way

allows the narrative to loop far into the future and connect with events in 2 Kgs. 23:15–18, signaling at the outset the certainty of YHWH's judgment against Israel and its kings.

13:3–6—The dual signs affecting *the altar* and *the king* certify the truth of the oracle and the power of the prophet to afflict and to heal. Even the king is powerless before prophetic authority. We find that genuine authority does not always reside with those in power.

13:11–32—While this story demonstrates the power of the divine word and warns prophets to adhere to the letter of their instructions, it also leaves the reader with a sense of unfairness and even dread in the face of the fate of those caught up in delivering YHWH's word and marching to YHWH's orders.

13:11—The *old prophet* and *his sons* may

Bethel. One of his sons came and told him all that the man of God had done that day in Bethel; the words also that he had spoken to the king, they told to their father. ¹²Their father said to them, "Which way did he go?" And his sons showed him the way that the man of God who came from Judah had gone. ¹³Then he said to his sons, "Saddle a donkey for me." So they saddled a donkey for him, and he mounted it. ¹⁴He went after the man of God, and found him sitting under an oak tree. He said to him, "Are you the man of God who came from Judah?" He answered, "I am." ¹⁵Then he said to him, "Come home with me and eat some food." ¹⁶But he said, "I cannot return with you, or go in with you; nor will I eat food or drink water with you in this place; ¹⁷for it was said to me by the word of the LORD: You shall not eat food or drink water there, or return by the way that you came." ¹⁸Then the other*a* said to him, "I also am a prophet as you are, and an angel spoke to me by the word of the LORD: Bring him back with you into your house so that he may eat food and drink water." But he was deceiving him. ¹⁹Then the man of God*a* went back with him, and ate food and drank water in his house.

20 As they were sitting at the table, the word of the LORD came to the prophet who had brought him back; ²¹and he proclaimed to the man of God who came from Judah, "Thus says the LORD: Because you have disobeyed the word of the LORD, and have not kept the commandment that the LORD your God commanded you, ²²but have come back

and have eaten food and drunk water in the place of which he said to you, 'Eat no food, and drink no water,' your body shall not come to your ancestral tomb." ²³After the man of God*a* had eaten food and had drunk, they saddled for him a donkey belonging to the prophet who had brought him back. ²⁴Then as he went away, a lion met him on the road and killed him. His body was thrown in the road, and the donkey stood beside it; the lion also stood beside the body. ²⁵People passed by and saw the body thrown in the road, with the lion standing by the body. And they came and told it in the town where the old prophet lived.

26 When the prophet who had brought him back from the way heard of it, he said, "It is the man of God who disobeyed the word of the LORD; therefore the LORD has given him to the lion, which has torn him and killed him according to the word that the LORD spoke to him." ²⁷Then he said to his sons, "Saddle a donkey for me." So they saddled one, ²⁸and he went and found the body thrown in the road, with the donkey and the lion standing beside the body. The lion had not eaten the body or attacked the donkey. ²⁹The prophet took up the body of the man of God, laid it on the donkey, and brought it back to the city,*b* to mourn and to bury him. ³⁰He laid the body in his own grave; and they mourned over him, saying, "Alas, my brother!" ³¹After he had buried him, he said to his sons,

---

a Heb he *b* Gk: Heb *he came to the town of the old prophet*

---

represent a prophetic guild rather than a biological family.

13:18–19—The deceit of the old prophet is unmotivated, and it is striking in light of his later reverence for the prophet he deceives. In fact, his statement that he received his *word of the LORD* from *an angel* leaves readers wondering if the deceit is his or the deity's. At the least, YHWH allows this prophet to meet a terrible fate for what appears a minor unintended defection from instructions. Apparently one prophet can-

not determine the truth or falsehood of another prophet's statement.

13:28—The unusual behavior of *the lion* and *donkey* suggests a numinous quality in the event.

13:29–32—The burial of the prophet from Judah and the old prophet's plans for his own burial beside him underscore both the truth of the latter's condemnation of the former for failing to follow his instructions, and the latter's recognition that what the prophet from Judah said *against the altar in Bethel* would be fulfilled.

"When I die, bury me in the grave in which the man of God is buried; lay my bones beside his bones. ³²For the saying that he proclaimed by the word of the LORD against the altar in Bethel, and against all the houses of the high places that are in the cities of Samaria, shall surely come to pass."

33 Even after this event Jeroboam did not turn from his evil way, but made priests for the high places again from among all the people; any who wanted to be priests he consecrated for the high places. ³⁴This matter became sin to the house of Jeroboam, so as to cut it off and to destroy it from the face of the earth.

Judgment on the House of Jeroboam

14 At that time Abijah son of Jeroboam fell sick. ²Jeroboam said to his wife, "Go, disguise yourself, so that it will not be known that you are the wife of Jeroboam, and go to Shiloh; for the prophet Ahijah is there, who said of me that I should be king over this people. ³Take with you ten loaves, some cakes, and a jar of honey, and go to him; he will tell you what shall happen to the child."

4 Jeroboam's wife did so; she set out and went to Shiloh, and came to the house of Ahijah. Now Ahijah could not see, for his eyes were dim because of his age. ⁵But the LORD said to Ahijah, "The wife of Jeroboam is coming to inquire of you concerning her son; for he is sick. Thus and thus you shall say to her."

When she came, she pretended to be another woman. ⁶But when Ahijah heard the sound of her feet, as she came in at the door, he said, "Come in, wife of Jeroboam; why do you pretend to be another? For I am charged with heavy tidings for you. ⁷Go, tell Jeroboam, 'Thus says the LORD, the God of Israel: Because I exalted you from among the people, made you leader over my people Israel, ⁸and tore the kingdom away from the house of David to give it to you; yet you have not been like my servant David, who kept my commandments and followed me with all his heart, doing only that which was right in my sight, ⁹but you have done evil above all those who were before you and have gone and made for yourself other gods, and cast images, provoking me to anger, and have thrust me behind your back; ¹⁰therefore, I will bring evil upon the house of Jeroboam. I will cut off from Jeroboam every male, both bond and free in Israel, and will consume the house of Jeroboam, just as one burns up dung until it is all gone. ¹¹Anyone belonging to Jeroboam who dies in the city, the dogs shall eat; and anyone who dies in the open country, the birds of the air shall eat; for the LORD has spoken.' ¹²Therefore set out, go to your house. When your feet enter the city, the child shall die. ¹³All Israel shall mourn for him and bury him; for he alone of Jeroboam's family shall come to the grave, because in him there is found something pleasing to the LORD, the

---

13:33–34—In spite of his invitation to the prophet in v. 7, *Jeroboam* is set in his plans for his own official cultic establishments and thus set irrevocably against God and on a sure path to the destruction of his house.

14:1–20 Jeroboam's House Is Judged
Jeroboam's bitter confrontations with prophets and the God who sends them continues in this encounter between *his wife* and *Ahijah*.

14:2—There seems a sense of futility in the *disguise*, for a prophet who could state what would happen to the sick Abijah would surely know who was sick.

14:7–9—Like David (2 Sam. 7:8), Jeroboam is

presented as *leader* (possibly a technical term for the king designate). In YHWH's eyes it is presumably David's unflagging allegiance to the God who selected him, and not his failings as recounted in 2 Samuel that qualify him as God's *servant*. It is not clear who the *all those who were before you* were. What Jeroboam did is outlined in 12:26–34.

14:10–11—The fate pronounced on Jeroboam and his *house* is obscenely violent.

14:12–13—There is also a certain crassness in the announcement that the queen's son will die the moment she returns home, and that he alone, because in some way he pleased YHWH, will be regularly buried.

God of Israel, in the house of Jeroboam. [14] Moreover the LORD will raise up for himself a king over Israel, who shall cut off the house of Jeroboam today, even right now![a]

15 "The LORD will strike Israel, as a reed is shaken in the water; he will root up Israel out of this good land that he gave to their ancestors, and scatter them beyond the Euphrates, because they have made their sacred poles,[b] provoking the LORD to anger. [16] He will give Israel up because of the sins of Jeroboam, which he sinned and which he caused Israel to commit."

17 Then Jeroboam's wife got up and went away, and she came to Tirzah. As she came to the threshold of the house, the child died. [18] All Israel buried him and mourned for him, according to the word of the LORD, which he spoke by his servant the prophet Ahijah.

Death of Jeroboam

19 Now the rest of the acts of Jeroboam, how he warred and how he reigned, are written in the Book of the Annals of the Kings of Israel. [20] The time that Jeroboam reigned was twenty-two years; then he slept with his ancestors, and his son Nadab succeeded him.

Rehoboam Reigns over Judah

21 Now Rehoboam son of Solomon reigned in Judah. Rehoboam was forty-one years old when he began to reign, and he reigned seventeen years in Jerusalem, the city that the LORD had cho-sen out of all the tribes of Israel, to put his name there. His mother's name was Naamah the Ammonite. [22] Judah did what was evil in the sight of the LORD; they provoked him to jealousy with their sins that they committed, more than all that their ancestors had done. [23] For they also built for themselves high places, pillars, and sacred poles[b] on every high hill and under every green tree; [24] there were also male temple prostitutes in the land. They committed all the abominations of the nations that the LORD drove out before the people of Israel.

25 In the fifth year of King Rehoboam, King Shishak of Egypt came up against Jerusalem; [26] he took away the treasures of the house of the LORD and the treasures of the king's house; he took everything. He also took away all the shields of gold that Solomon had made; [27] so King Rehoboam made shields of bronze instead, and committed them to the hands of the officers of the guard, who kept the door of the king's house. [28] As often as the king went into the house of the LORD, the guard carried them and brought them back to the guardroom.

29 Now the rest of the acts of Rehoboam, and all that he did, are they not written in the Book of the Annals of the Kings of Judah? [30] There was war between Rehoboam and Jeroboam continually. [31] Rehoboam slept with his ancestors and was buried with his ancestors in the city of David. His mother's name was

a Meaning of Heb uncertain   b Heb Asherim

14:15–16—Jeroboam's crimes become a snare for his entire kingdom in an addendum to YHWH's pronouncement that looks to its destruction and exile (see 2 Kgs. 17). The *sacred poles* or *asherim* probably represents a flourishing green tree, an appropriate symbol for the goddess Asherah, a force for fertility linked with both the Canaanite El and Baal, and possibly with YHWH in popular Israelite tradition.

14:17–20—Summary statements announce the fulfillment of what was projected for their child and closes the reign of Jeroboam.

14:19—*The Book of the Annals of the Kings of Israel*, if not simply a device to add credence to the narrator's theological history, was likely a formal and official chronicle now lost.

14:21–31 Rehoboam Rules Judah

A general evaluation of Rehoboam's reign envelops a brief account of his defeat by *Shishak* (see 11:40). Rehoboam, in this respect his father's son, appears to have tolerated a range of religious practices and symbols, including temple prostitutes, linked with the Canaanites (14:15–16) and associated with the worship of Baal and promotion of fertility. *The Book of the Annals of the Kings of Judah*, like its northern counterpart (v. 19), no longer exists.

Naamah the Ammonite. His son Abijam succeeded him.

Abijam Reigns over Judah: Idolatry and War

15 Now in the eighteenth year of King Jeroboam son of Nebat, Abijam began to reign over Judah. ²He reigned for three years in Jerusalem. His mother's name was Maacah daughter of Abishalom. ³He committed all the sins that his father did before him; his heart was not true to the LORD his God, like the heart of his father David. ⁴Nevertheless for David's sake the LORD his God gave him a lamp in Jerusalem, setting up his son after him, and establishing Jerusalem; ⁵because David did what was right in the sight of the LORD, and did not turn aside from anything that he commanded him all the days of his life, except in the matter of Uriah the Hittite. ⁶The war begun between Rehoboam and Jeroboam continued all the days of his life. ⁷The rest of the acts of Abijam, and all that he did, are they not written in the Book of the Annals of the Kings of Judah? There was war between Abijam and Jeroboam. ⁸Abijam slept with his ancestors, and they buried him in the city of David. Then his son Asa succeeded him.

Asa Reigns over Judah

⁹In the twentieth year of King Jeroboam of Israel, Asa began to reign over Judah; ¹⁰he reigned forty-one years in Jerusalem. His mother's name was Maacah daughter of Abishalom. ¹¹Asa did what was right in the sight of the LORD, as his father David had done. ¹²He put away the male temple prostitutes out of the land, and removed all the idols that his ancestors had made.

¹³He also removed his mother Maacah from being queen mother, because she had made an abominable image for Asherah; Asa cut down her image and burned it at the Wadi Kidron. ¹⁴But the high places were not taken away. Nevertheless the heart of Asa was true to the LORD all his days. ¹⁵He brought into the house of the LORD the votive gifts of his father and his own votive gifts—silver, gold, and utensils.

Alliance with Aram against Israel

¹⁶There was war between Asa and King Baasha of Israel all their days. ¹⁷King Baasha of Israel went up against Judah, and built Ramah, to prevent anyone from going out or coming in to King Asa of Judah. ¹⁸Then Asa took all the silver and the gold that were left in the treasures of the house of the LORD and the treasures of the king's house, and gave them into the hands of his servants. King Asa sent them to King Benhadad son of Tabrimmon son of Hezion of Aram, who resided in Damascus, saying, ¹⁹"Let there be an alliance between me and you, like that between my father and your father: I am sending you a present of silver and gold; go, break your alliance with King Baasha of Israel, so that he may withdraw from me." ²⁰Benhadad listened to King Asa, and sent the commanders of his armies against the cities of Israel. He conquered Ijon, Dan, Abel-beth-maacah, and all Chinneroth, with all the land of Naphtali. ²¹When Baasha heard of it, he stopped building Ramah and lived in Tirzah. ²²Then King Asa made a proclamation to all Judah, none was exempt: they carried away the stones of Ramah and its timber, with

---

15:1–16:34 Kings of Israel and Judah

15:1–8—*Abijam*'s brief reign gains but summary condemnation when compared to David's. On David's arranged murder of Uriah, see 2 Sam. 11–12.

15:9–15—*Asa* receives a positive evaluation from the narrator for largely undoing the effects of the religious tolerance of his predecessors. *Maacah*

was also mother of Abijam (cf. 2 Chr. 13:2), making him and Asa brothers. She loses her powerful position under her second son.

15:16–24—Conflicts and shifting alliances involving Israel, Judah, and Aram in Syria mark much of the history of the divided states. *Ben-hadad* took significant territory from Baasha of Israel, shifting the tide of conflict with Judah.

which Baasha had been building; with them King Asa built Geba of Benjamin and Mizpah. ²³Now the rest of all the acts of Asa, all his power, all that he did, and the cities that he built, are they not written in the Book of the Annals of the Kings of Judah? But in his old age he was diseased in his feet. ²⁴Then Asa slept with his ancestors, and was buried with his ancestors in the city of his father David; his son Jehoshaphat succeeded him.

Nadab Reigns over Israel

25 Nadab son of Jeroboam began to reign over Israel in the second year of King Asa of Judah; he reigned over Israel two years. ²⁶He did what was evil in the sight of the LORD, walking in the way of his ancestor and in the sin that he caused Israel to commit.

27 Baasha son of Ahijah, of the house of Issachar, conspired against him; and Baasha struck him down at Gibbethon, which belonged to the Philistines; for Nadab and all Israel were laying siege to Gibbethon. ²⁸So Baasha killed Nadab*a* in the third year of King Asa of Judah, and succeeded him. ²⁹As soon as he was king, he killed all the house of Jeroboam; he left to the house of Jeroboam not one that breathed, until he had destroyed it, according to the word of the LORD that he spoke by his servant Ahijah the Shilonite— ³⁰because of the sins of Jeroboam that he committed and that he caused Israel to commit, and because of the anger to which he provoked the LORD, the God of Israel.

31 Now the rest of the acts of Nadab, and all that he did, are they not written in the Book of the Annals of the Kings of Israel? ³²There was war between Asa and King Baasha of Israel all their days.

Second Dynasty: Baasha Reigns over Israel

33 In the third year of King Asa of Judah, Baasha son of Ahijah began to reign over all Israel at Tirzah; he reigned twenty-four years. ³⁴He did what was evil in the sight of the LORD, walking in the way of Jeroboam and in the sin that he caused Israel to commit.

16 The word of the LORD came to Jehu son of Hanani against Baasha, saying, ²"Since I exalted you out of the dust and made you leader over my people Israel, and you have walked in the way of Jeroboam, and have caused my people Israel to sin, provoking me to anger with their sins, ³therefore, I will consume Baasha and his house, and I will make your house like the house of Jeroboam son of Nebat. ⁴Anyone belonging to Baasha who dies in the city the dogs shall eat; and anyone of his who dies in the field the birds of the air shall eat."

5 Now the rest of the acts of Baasha, what he did, and his power, are they not written in the Book of the Annals of the Kings of Israel? ⁶Baasha slept with his ancestors, and was buried at Tirzah; and his son Elah succeeded him. ⁷Moreover the word of the LORD came by the prophet Jehu son of Hanani against Baasha and his house, both because of all the evil that he did in the sight of the LORD, provoking him to anger with the work of his hands, in being like the house of Jeroboam, and also because he destroyed it.

Elah Reigns over Israel

8 In the twenty-sixth year of King Asa of Judah, Elah son of Baasha began to reign over Israel in Tirzah; he reigned

a Heb *him*

15:25–32—The assassination of *Nadab* is understood by the narrator as fulfillment of YHWH's words against the dynasty of Jeroboam delivered by Ahijah (14:7–14).

15:33–16:7—In the formal notice of his reign *Baasha* fares no better than Jeroboam, whose

dynasty he eliminated. Jeroboam becomes proverbial for northern sinfulness. YHWH condemns him through *Jehu son of Hanani*, echoing his words spoken through Ahijah of Shiloh against Jeroboam (cf. 16:4 and 14:11).

16:8–14—*Elah*'s brief reign ends as he is assas-

two years. [9] But his servant Zimri, commander of half his chariots, conspired against him. When he was at Tirzah, drinking himself drunk in the house of Arza, who was in charge of the palace at Tirzah, [10] Zimri came in and struck him down and killed him, in the twenty-seventh year of King Asa of Judah, and succeeded him.

11 When he began to reign, as soon as he had seated himself on his throne, he killed all the house of Baasha; he did not leave him a single male of his kindred or his friends. [12] Thus Zimri destroyed all the house of Baasha, according to the word of the LORD, which he spoke against Baasha by the prophet Jehu— [13] because of all the sins of Baasha and the sins of his son Elah that they committed, and that they caused Israel to commit, provoking the LORD God of Israel to anger with their idols. [14] Now the rest of the acts of Elah, and all that he did, are they not written in the Book of the Annals of the Kings of Israel?

Third Dynasty: Zimri
Reigns over Israel

15 In the twenty-seventh year of King Asa of Judah, Zimri reigned seven days in Tirzah. Now the troops were encamped against Gibbethon, which belonged to the Philistines, [16] and the troops who were encamped heard it said, "Zimri has conspired, and he has killed the king"; therefore all Israel made Omri, the commander of the army, king over Israel that day in the camp. [17] So Omri went up from Gibbethon, and all Israel with him, and they besieged Tirzah. [18] When Zimri saw that the city was taken, he went into the citadel of the king's house; he burned down the king's house over himself with fire, and died— [19] because of the sins that he committed, doing evil in the sight of the LORD, walking in the way of Jeroboam, and for the sin that he committed, causing Israel to sin. [20] Now the rest of the acts of Zimri, and the conspiracy that he made, are they not written in the Book of the Annals of the Kings of Israel?

Fourth Dynasty: Omri
Reigns over Israel

21 Then the people of Israel were divided into two parts; half of the people followed Tibni son of Ginath, to make him king, and half followed Omri. [22] But the people who followed Omri overcame the people who followed Tibni son of Ginath; so Tibni died, and Omri became king. [23] In the thirty-first year of King Asa of Judah, Omri began to reign over Israel; he reigned for twelve years, six of them in Tirzah.

Samaria the New Capital

24 He bought the hill of Samaria from Shemer for two talents of silver; he fortified the hill, and called the city that he built, Samaria, after the name of Shemer, the owner of the hill.

25 Omri did what was evil in the sight of the LORD; he did more evil than all who were before him. [26] For he walked in all the way of Jeroboam son of Nebat, and in the sins that he caused Israel to commit, provoking the LORD, the God of Israel, to anger by their idols. [27] Now the rest of the acts of Omri that he did, and the power that he showed, are they not written in the Book of the Annals of the Kings of Israel? [28] Omri slept with his

---

sinated while *drunk* by *Zimri*, an official in his army. This ends the dynasty of Baasha, as again prophecy is fulfilled.

16:15–20—Zimri's assassination of Elah sparks division in the ranks of the army as *Omri*, a commander at *Gibbethon*, is made king and attacks Zimri in *Tirzah*, leading to the latter's suicide. Zimri is judged like those before him, even though he had little time for sins like Jeroboam's in his seven-day reign.

16:21–28—The brief references to Omri's success over the followers of one *Tibni* and his creating a new capital at *Samaria*, along with the ritual condemnation of his reign, do not reflect his significance in the eyes of others in the ancient Near East, who referred to Israel as the "land of Omri" for generations.

ancestors, and was buried in Samaria; his son Ahab succeeded him.

Ahab Reigns over Israel

29 In the thirty-eighth year of King Asa of Judah, Ahab son of Omri began to reign over Israel; Ahab son of Omri reigned over Israel in Samaria twenty-two years. 30 Ahab son of Omri did evil in the sight of the LORD more than all who were before him.

Ahab Marries Jezebel and Worships Baal

31 And as if it had been a light thing for him to walk in the sins of Jeroboam son of Nebat, he took as his wife Jezebel daughter of King Ethbaal of the Sidonians, and went and served Baal, and worshiped him. 32 He erected an altar for Baal in the house of Baal, which he built in Samaria. 33 Ahab also made a sacred pole.*a* Ahab did more to provoke the anger of the LORD, the God of Israel, than had all the kings of Israel who were before him. 34 In his days Hiel of Bethel built Jericho; he laid its foundation at the cost of Abiram his firstborn, and set up its gates at the cost of his youngest son Segub, according to the word of the LORD, which he spoke by Joshua son of Nun.

Elijah Predicts a Drought

17 Now Elijah the Tishbite, of Tishbe*b* in Gilead, said to Ahab, "As the LORD the God of Israel lives, before whom I stand, there shall be neither dew nor rain these years, except by my word." 2 The word of the LORD came to him, saying, 3 "Go from here and turn eastward, and hide yourself by the Wadi Cherith, which is east of the Jordan. 4 You shall drink from the wadi, and I have commanded the ravens to feed you there." 5 So he went and did according to the word of the LORD; he went and lived by the Wadi Cherith, which is east of the Jordan. 6 The ravens brought him bread and meat in the morning, and bread and meat in the evening; and he drank from the wadi. 7 But after a while the wadi dried up, because there was no rain in the land.

The Widow of Zarephath

8 Then the word of the LORD came to him, saying, 9 "Go now to Zarephath, which belongs to Sidon, and live there; for I have commanded a widow there to feed you." 10 So he set out and went to Zarephath. When he came to the gate of the town, a widow was there gathering sticks; he called to her and said, "Bring me a little water in a vessel, so that I may drink." 11 As she was going to bring it, he called to her and said, "Bring me a morsel of bread in your hand." 12 But she said, "As the LORD your God lives, I have nothing baked, only a handful of

a Heb Asherah *b* Gk: Heb of the settlers

16:29–33—Omri's son *Ahab* is introduced as Israel's worst king yet. His marriage to *Jezebel, daughter of King Ethbaal of Sidon*, prompted him to introduce the temple and cult of the Canaanite storm and fertility deity *Baal* into the new Israelite capital.

16:34—See Josh. 6:29.

17:1–22:53 The Reign of Ahab and Jezebel

17:1–18:20 Elijah and Ahab of Israel

To this point in 1 Kings prophets have played a significant but reserved role in the narrative. Now, in the face of the apostasy of Ahab, prophets, especially Elijah, loom large. As prophets come to loom larger in the story, we become aware of how YHWH's authority resists institutionalization and how YHWH's word is often found with an array of figures from society's fringes.

17:1–7—Elijah's abrupt introduction mirrors an erratic quality to his appearances throughout. Suspension by *Elijah* of the annual cycle of rain and dryness presents a challenge to Baal on his own grounds as the Canaanite deity responsible for fertility in the land and therefore life for humans and their livestock. YHWH and Baal begin a sustained life-and-death struggle.

17:4–7—In the face of famine God sustains this prophet through the water of *the wadi* and food brought by *ravens*.

17:8–16—YHWH sends Elijah to *Zarephath* on the coast of *Sidon*—the heart of Baal's territory—to preserve him alive. Widows, with orphans and resident aliens, were among society's

meal in a jar, and a little oil in a jug; I am now gathering a couple of sticks, so that I may go home and prepare it for myself and my son, that we may eat it, and die." ¹³ Elijah said to her, "Do not be afraid; go and do as you have said; but first make me a little cake of it and bring it to me, and afterwards make something for yourself and your son. ¹⁴ For thus says the LORD the God of Israel: The jar of meal will not be emptied and the jug of oil will not fail until the day that the LORD sends rain on the earth." ¹⁵ She went and did as Elijah said, so that she as well as he and her household ate for many days. ¹⁶ The jar of meal was not emptied, neither did the jug of oil fail, according to the word of the LORD that he spoke by Elijah.

Elijah Revives the Widow's Son

17 After this the son of the woman, the mistress of the house, became ill; his illness was so severe that there was no breath left in him. ¹⁸ She then said to Elijah, "What have you against me, O man of God? You have come to me to bring my sin to remembrance, and to cause the death of my son!" ¹⁹ But he said to her, "Give me your son." He took him from her bosom, carried him up into the upper chamber where he was lodging, and laid him on his own bed. ²⁰ He cried out to the LORD, "O LORD my God, have you brought calamity even upon the widow with whom I am staying, by killing her son?" ²¹ Then he stretched himself upon the child three times, and cried out to the LORD, "O LORD my God, let this child's life come into him again." ²² The LORD listened to the voice of Elijah; the life of the child came into him again, and he revived. ²³ Elijah took

the child, brought him down from the upper chamber into the house, and gave him to his mother; then Elijah said, "See, your son is alive." ²⁴ So the woman said to Elijah, "Now I know that you are a man of God, and that the word of the LORD in your mouth is truth."

Elijah's Message to Ahab

18 After many days the word of the LORD came to Elijah, in the third year of the drought,ᵃ saying, "Go, present yourself to Ahab; I will send rain on the earth." ² So Elijah went to present himself to Ahab. The famine was severe in Samaria. ³ Ahab summoned Obadiah, who was in charge of the palace. (Now Obadiah revered the LORD greatly; ⁴ when Jezebel was killing off the prophets of the LORD, Obadiah took a hundred prophets, hid them fifty to a cave, and provided them with bread and water.) ⁵ Then Ahab said to Obadiah, "Go through the land to all the springs of water and to all the wadis; perhaps we may find grass to keep the horses and mules alive, and not lose some of the animals." ⁶ So they divided the land between them to pass through it; Ahab went in one direction by himself, and Obadiah went in another direction by himself.

7 As Obadiah was on the way, Elijah met him; Obadiah recognized him, fell on his face, and said, "Is it you, my lord Elijah?" ⁸ He answered him, "It is I. Go, tell your lord that Elijah is here." ⁹ And he said, "How have I sinned, that you would hand your servant over to Ahab, to kill me? ¹⁰ As the LORD your God lives, there is no nation or kingdom to which my lord has not sent to seek you; and when they would say, 'He is not here,' he

ᵃ Heb lacks of the drought

---

most vulnerable unless especially supported by the king and community (see Exod. 22:21–24; Deut. 14:28–29; 26:12–15).

17:17–24—YHWH and Elijah restore life in the face of death as the widowed mother of the revived son recognizes the true source of this life-giving power.

18:1–16—YHWH, who brought the drought through Elijah, will also, as announced through Elijah, end it by bringing *rain*, as the anti-Baalist emphasis in this series of stories moves to its climax. **Obadiah** ("Servant of YHWH"), a high official of Ahab and his Baalist queen Jezebel, is caught in YHWH's struggle with Baal as he serves his king and also secretly serves YHWH.

would require an oath of the kingdom or nation, that they had not found you. ¹¹ But now you say, 'Go, tell your lord that Elijah is here.' ¹² As soon as I have gone from you, the spirit of the LORD will carry you I know not where; so, when I come and tell Ahab and he cannot find you, he will kill me, although I your servant have revered the LORD from my youth. ¹³ Has it not been told my lord what I did when Jezebel killed the prophets of the LORD, how I hid a hundred of the LORD's prophets fifty to a cave, and provided them with bread and water? ¹⁴ Yet now you say, 'Go, tell your lord that Elijah is here'; he will surely kill me." ¹⁵ Elijah said, "As the LORD of hosts lives, before whom I stand, I will surely show myself to him today." ¹⁶ So Obadiah went to meet Ahab, and told him; and Ahab went to meet Elijah.

17 When Ahab saw Elijah, Ahab said to him, "Is it you, you troubler of Israel?" ¹⁸ He answered, "I have not troubled Israel; but you have, and your father's house, because you have forsaken the commandments of the LORD and followed the Baals. ¹⁹ Now therefore have all Israel assemble for me at Mount Carmel, with the four hundred fifty prophets of Baal and the four hundred prophets of Asherah, who eat at Jezebel's table."

Elijah's Triumph over the Priests of Baal

20 So Ahab sent to all the Israelites, and assembled the prophets at Mount Carmel. ²¹ Elijah then came near to all the people, and said, "How long will you go limping with two different opinions? If the LORD is God, follow him; but if Baal, then follow him." The people did not answer him a word. ²² Then Elijah said to the people, "I, even I only, am left a prophet of the LORD; but Baal's prophets number four hundred fifty. ²³ Let two bulls be given to us; let them choose one bull for themselves, cut it in pieces, and lay it on the wood, but put no fire to it; I will prepare the other bull and lay it on the wood, but put no fire to it. ²⁴ Then you call on the name of your god and I will call on the name of the LORD; the god who answers by fire is indeed God." All the people answered, "Well spoken!" ²⁵ Then Elijah said to the prophets of Baal, "Choose for yourselves one bull and prepare it first, for you are many; then call on the name of your god, but put no fire to it." ²⁶ So they took the bull that was given them, prepared it, and called on the name of Baal from morning until noon, crying, "O Baal, answer us!" But there was no voice, and no answer. They limped about the altar that they had made. ²⁷ At noon Elijah mocked them, saying, "Cry aloud! Surely he is a god; either he is meditating, or he has wandered away, or he is on a journey, or perhaps he is asleep and must be awakened." ²⁸ Then they cried aloud and, as was their custom, they cut themselves with swords and lances until

---

18:17–40—*Baals* in the plural reflects many local manifestations of this essential god of fertility within the Canaanite system. Ahab is rebuked and then vanishes from the story (as do the prophets of Asherah) after having the prophets of Baal assembled at *Mount Carmel* on the western edge of Israel. The people (vv. 21, 24, 30, 39) become the focus for Elijah's demonstration of YHWH's power.

18:20–46 Contest on Mount Carmel

This is YHWH's victorious climax in the contest with Baal. For Elijah, as God's prophet, the issue of allegiance is a stark choice, allowing no divided loyalties or middle ground that melds the traditions of Canaanite and Israelite. In a poly-

theistic world of multiple allegiances and fluid mixing of traditions, a demand such as Elijah makes is radical.

18:22—Elijah's perception of his position clashes with what Obadiah claims in v. 13.

18:24—*Fire* is associated with Baal in the lightning of the storm and often with appearances of YHWH as well (Gen. 15:18; Exod. 14:24; 19:18; Deut. 5:22–24).

18:27—Elijah's mockery is biting and even crude, suggesting Baal is distracted, relieving himself, or on his annual journey that takes him into the netherworld and the powers of death for the dry season.

18:28—Cutting the body is associated with

the blood gushed out over them. ²⁹ As midday passed, they raved on until the time of the offering of the oblation, but there was no voice, no answer, and no response.

30 Then Elijah said to all the people, "Come closer to me"; and all the people came closer to him. First he repaired the altar of the LORD that had been thrown down; ³¹ Elijah took twelve stones, according to the number of the tribes of the sons of Jacob, to whom the word of the LORD came, saying, "Israel shall be your name"; ³² with the stones he built an altar in the name of the LORD. Then he made a trench around the altar, large enough to contain two measures of seed. ³³ Next he put the wood in order, cut the bull in pieces, and laid it on the wood. He said, "Fill four jars with water and pour it on the burnt offering and on the wood." ³⁴ Then he said, "Do it a second time"; and they did it a second time. Again he said, "Do it a third time"; and they did it a third time, ³⁵ so that the water ran all around the altar, and filled the trench also with water.

36 At the time of the offering of the oblation, the prophet Elijah came near and said, "O LORD, God of Abraham, Isaac, and Israel, let it be known this day that you are God in Israel, that I am your servant, and that I have done all these things at your bidding. ³⁷ Answer me, O LORD, answer me, so that this people may know that you, O LORD, are God, and that you have turned their hearts back." ³⁸ Then the fire of the LORD fell and consumed the burnt offering, the wood, the stones, and the dust, and even licked up the water that was in the trench. ³⁹ When all the people saw it, they fell on their faces and said, "The LORD indeed is God; the LORD indeed is God." ⁴⁰ Elijah said to them, "Seize the prophets of Baal; do not let one of them escape." Then they seized them; and Elijah brought them down to the Wadi Kishon, and killed them there.

The Drought Ends

41 Elijah said to Ahab, "Go up, eat and drink; for there is a sound of rushing rain." ⁴² So Ahab went up to eat and to drink. Elijah went up to the top of Carmel; there he bowed himself down upon the earth and put his face between his knees. ⁴³ He said to his servant, "Go up now, look toward the sea." He went up and looked, and said, "There is nothing." Then he said, "Go again seven times." ⁴⁴ At the seventh time he said, "Look, a little cloud no bigger than a person's hand is rising out of the sea." Then he said, "Go say to Ahab, 'Harness your chariot and go down before the rain stops you.'" ⁴⁵ In a little while the heavens grew black with clouds and wind; there was a heavy rain. Ahab rode off and went to Jezreel. ⁴⁶ But the hand of the LORD was on Elijah; he girded up his loins and ran in front of Ahab to the entrance of Jezreel.

Elijah Flees from Jezebel

19 Ahab told Jezebel all that Elijah had done, and how he had

---

mourning and may reflect attempts to raise Baal from the realm of death.

18:29—*The offering of the oblation* was made in the early evening, suggesting the frantic but unsuccessful efforts of Baal's prophets lasted all day.

18:30–35—Elijah, by contrast, deliberately restores a destroyed *altar* to YHWH, prepares the sacrifice, and then sets conditions that will make victory all the more impressive. The *water* he poured on the offering was striking, considering the prolonged drought.

18:39–40—The people are won over to YHWH, and with Elijah execute Baal's prophets as demanded in Deut. 13:1–5.

18:41–46—Elijah, empowered by YHWH to stop the rain, now announces its coming to end the drought. Even Ahab seems convinced. Just how convinced, however, might be open to question, as the prophet drives home again and again YHWH's demand for complete submission to YHWH alone. A figure like Elijah leaves no room for half measures.

19:1–18—Elijah Flees

Jezebel, however, is not convinced. Hearing of the slaughter of the prophets of Baal, she vows to

killed all the prophets with the sword.
²Then Jezebel sent a messenger to Elijah, saying, "So may the gods do to me, and more also, if I do not make your life like the life of one of them by this time tomorrow." ³Then he was afraid; he got up and fled for his life, and came to Beer-sheba, which belongs to Judah; he left his servant there.

4 But he himself went a day's journey into the wilderness, and came and sat down under a solitary broom tree. He asked that he might die: "It is enough; now, O LORD, take away my life, for I am no better than my ancestors." ⁵Then he lay down under the broom tree and fell asleep. Suddenly an angel touched him and said to him, "Get up and eat." ⁶He looked, and there at his head was a cake baked on hot stones, and a jar of water. He ate and drank, and lay down again. ⁷The angel of the LORD came a second time, touched him, and said, "Get up and eat, otherwise the journey will be too much for you." ⁸He got up, and ate and drank; then he went in the strength of that food forty days and forty nights to Horeb the mount of God. ⁹At that place he came to a cave, and spent the night there.

Then the word of the LORD came to him, saying, "What are you doing here, Elijah?" ¹⁰He answered, "I have been very zealous for the LORD, the God of hosts; for the Israelites have forsaken your covenant, thrown down your altars, and killed your prophets with the sword. I alone am left, and they are seeking my life, to take it away."

Elijah Meets God at Horeb

11 He said, "Go out and stand on the mountain before the LORD, for the LORD is about to pass by." Now there was a great wind, so strong that it was splitting mountains and breaking rocks in pieces before the LORD, but the LORD was not in the wind; and after the wind an earthquake, but the LORD was not in the earthquake; ¹²and after the earthquake a fire, but the LORD was not in the fire; and after the fire a sound of sheer silence. ¹³When Elijah heard it, he wrapped his face in his mantle and went out and stood at the entrance of the cave. Then there came a voice to him that said, "What are you doing here, Elijah?" ¹⁴He answered, "I have been very zealous for the LORD, the God of hosts; for the Israelites have forsaken your covenant, thrown down your altars, and killed your prophets with the sword. I alone am left, and they are seeking my life, to take it away." ¹⁵Then the LORD said to him, "Go, return on your way to the wilderness of Damascus; when you arrive, you shall anoint Hazael as king over Aram. ¹⁶Also you shall anoint Jehu son of Nimshi as king over Israel; and you shall anoint Elisha son of Shaphat of

take Elijah's life. At the moment of apparent triumph, Elijah must flee Israel into the wilderness, where he seeks death. Without YHWH's sustaining challenge and support, even this boldest of prophets appears to falter in his task.

19:4–10—Echoes of Israel's forty years in *the wilderness* and Moses' forty days on *the mount of God* receiving the Torah (Exod. 24:27–28) recall the exodus story. The *cave* mirrors the cave where Moses was shielded from the direct sight of God (Exod. 33:17–23). Elijah's reluctance to accept God's challenge to him recalls Moses' reluctance (Exod. 3–4).

19:11–12—*Wind*, *earthquake*, and *fire* are linked to God's appearances elsewhere, but here they do not contain God. Just what *a sound of sheer silence* denotes is not clear, and perhaps is

not designed to be. It may suggest God's appearance is not confined to any particular concrete physical phenomenon, however magnificent or terrifying. The silence ends in God's *"What are you doing here, Elijah?"* Why is the prophet on the mountaintop and not in the midst of the contest between YHWH and Baal?

19:14—Elijah is not overwhelmed as he repeats his objection of v. 10. He exaggerates his perceived dilemma; he is not the only Yahwist left.

19:15–18—YHWH is ready to move back into the fray and use others to deal with all who rebel. Elijah is to designate those through whom YHWH will work. Elijah will actually designate only *Elisha*, and Elisha will designate the others. YHWH's final words suggest Elijah's reading of his situation is exaggerated.

Abel-meholah as prophet in your place.
¹⁷ Whoever escapes from the sword of
Hazael, Jehu shall kill; and whoever
escapes from the sword of Jehu, Elisha
shall kill. ¹⁸ Yet I will leave seven thousand in Israel, all the knees that have not
bowed to Baal, and every mouth that
has not kissed him."

Elisha Becomes Elijah's Disciple

19 So he set out from there, and found
Elisha son of Shaphat, who was plowing.
There were twelve yoke of oxen ahead
of him, and he was with the twelfth.
Elijah passed by him and threw his
mantle over him. ²⁰ He left the oxen, ran
after Elijah, and said, "Let me kiss my
father and my mother, and then I will
follow you." Then Elijahᵃ said to him,
"Go back again; for what have I done
to you?" ²¹ He returned from following
him, took the yoke of oxen, and slaughtered them; using the equipment from
the oxen, he boiled their flesh, and gave
it to the people, and they ate. Then he
set out and followed Elijah, and became
his servant.

Ahab's Wars with the Arameans

20 King Ben-hadad of Aram gathered all his army together; thirty-
two kings were with him, along with
horses and chariots. He marched against
Samaria, laid siege to it, and attacked it.
² Then he sent messengers into the city
to King Ahab of Israel, and said to him:
"Thus says Ben-hadad: ³ Your silver and
gold are mine; your fairest wives and
children also are mine." ⁴ The king of
Israel answered, "As you say, my lord,
O king, I am yours, and all that I have."
⁵ The messengers came again and said:

"Thus says Ben-hadad: I sent to you,
saying, 'Deliver to me your silver and
gold, your wives and children'; ⁶ nevertheless I will send my servants to you
tomorrow about this time, and they
shall search your house and the houses
of your servants, and lay hands on whatever pleases them,ᵇ and take it away."

7 Then the king of Israel called all the
elders of the land, and said, "Look now!
See how this man is seeking trouble; for
he sent to me for my wives, my children,
my silver, and my gold; and I did not
refuse him." ⁸ Then all the elders and all
the people said to him, "Do not listen or
consent." ⁹ So he said to the messengers
of Ben-hadad, "Tell my lord the king: All
that you first demanded of your servant
I will do; but this thing I cannot do." The
messengers left and brought him word
again. ¹⁰ Ben-hadad sent to him and said,
"The gods do so to me, and more also, if
the dust of Samaria will provide a handful for each of the people who follow
me." ¹¹ The king of Israel answered, "Tell
him: One who puts on armor should not
brag like one who takes it off." ¹² When
Ben-hadad heard this message—now he
had been drinking with the kings in the
booths—he said to his men, "Take your
positions!" And they took their positions against the city.

Prophetic Opposition to Ahab

13 Then a certain prophet came up to
King Ahab of Israel and said, "Thus says
the LORD, Have you seen all this great
multitude? Look, I will give it into your
hand today; and you shall know that I
am the LORD." ¹⁴ Ahab said, "By whom?"

ᵃ Heb *he* ᵇ Gk Syr Vg: Heb *you*

19:19–21 The Call of Elisha
Elisha is designated, if not strictly anointed, by
Elijah, who in demanding immediate obedience
seems to hold his *servant* to a higher standard
than he always exemplifies in relation to God.

20:1–43 Ahab's War with the Arameans

20:1–12—From Solomon's reign on, Aram (today
Syria) and Israel were occasional opponents
(11:23–25; 15:18–21). While David made Aram

his vassal (2 Sam. 8:5–12), *Ahab* appears willing
to be vassal to *Ben-hadad*.

20:11—Ahab cites a proverb in responding to
Ben-hadad's boast.

20:13–22—Ahab enjoys rare prophetic support
against Aram. His victory against larger forces
suggests YHWH also supports him. The dutiful
Ahab is contrasted to the drunken and barely
coherent Ben-hadad.

He said, "Thus says the LORD, By the young men who serve the district governors." Then he said, "Who shall begin the battle?" He answered, "You." [15] Then he mustered the young men who served the district governors, two hundred thirty-two; after them he mustered all the people of Israel, seven thousand.

16 They went out at noon, while Ben-hadad was drinking himself drunk in the booths, he and the thirty-two kings allied with him. [17] The young men who served the district governors went out first. Ben-hadad had sent out scouts,[a] and they reported to him, "Men have come out from Samaria." [18] He said, "If they have come out for peace, take them alive; if they have come out for war, take them alive."

19 But these had already come out of the city: the young men who served the district governors, and the army that followed them. [20] Each killed his man; the Arameans fled and Israel pursued them, but King Ben-hadad of Aram escaped on a horse with the cavalry. [21] The king of Israel went out, attacked the horses and chariots, and defeated the Arameans with a great slaughter.

22 Then the prophet approached the king of Israel and said to him, "Come, strengthen yourself, and consider well what you have to do; for in the spring the king of Aram will come up against you."

The Arameans Are Defeated

23 The servants of the king of Aram said to him, "Their gods are gods of the hills, and so they were stronger than we; but let us fight against them in the plain, and surely we shall be stronger than they. [24] Also do this: remove the kings, each from his post, and put commanders in place of them; [25] and muster an army like the army that you have lost, horse for horse, and chariot for chariot; then we will fight against them in the plain, and surely we shall be stronger than they." He heeded their voice, and did so.

26 In the spring Ben-hadad mustered the Arameans and went up to Aphek to fight against Israel. [27] After the Israelites had been mustered and provisioned, they went out to engage them; the people of Israel encamped opposite them like two little flocks of goats, while the Arameans filled the country. [28] A man of God approached and said to the king of Israel, "Thus says the LORD: Because the Arameans have said, 'The LORD is a god of the hills but he is not a god of the valleys,' therefore I will give all this great multitude into your hand, and you shall know that I am the LORD." [29] They encamped opposite one another seven days. Then on the seventh day the battle began; the Israelites killed one hundred thousand Aramean foot soldiers in one day. [30] The rest fled into the city of Aphek; and the wall fell on twenty-seven thousand men that were left.

Ben-hadad also fled, and entered the city to hide. [31] His servants said to him, "Look, we have heard that the kings of the house of Israel are merciful kings; let us put sackcloth around our waists and ropes on our heads, and go out to the king of Israel; perhaps he will spare your life." [32] So they tied sackcloth around their waists, put ropes on their heads, went to the king of Israel, and said, "Your servant Ben-hadad says, 'Please let me live.'" And he said, "Is he still alive? He is my brother." [33] Now the

---

a Heb lacks *scouts*

20:22—*Spring* is a traditional time for kings to wage war (2 Sam. 11:1).

20:23–30a—Ben-hadad's *servants* offer a limited reading of Israel's God (*gods*). YHWH can fight on any territory.

20:30b–34—*Sackcloth*, a coarse fabric made from camel or goat hair, originally used for sacks to store grain, was worn as a sign of mourning or submission. *Brother* is a diplomatic term to denote equal partners in a treaty. Unlike his rival, Ahab seeks peace without humiliating his opponent.

men were watching for an omen; they quickly took it up from him and said, "Yes, Ben-hadad is your brother." Then he said, "Go and bring him." So Ben-hadad came out to him; and he had him come up into the chariot. ³⁴ Ben-hadad*ᵃ* said to him, "I will restore the towns that my father took from your father; and you may establish bazaars for yourself in Damascus, as my father did in Samaria." The king of Israel responded,*ᵇ* "I will let you go on those terms." So he made a treaty with him and let him go.

A Prophet Condemns Ahab

35 At the command of the LORD a certain member of a company of proph-ets*ᶜ* said to another, "Strike me!" But the man refused to strike him. ³⁶ Then he said to him, "Because you have not obeyed the voice of the LORD, as soon as you have left me, a lion will kill you." And when he had left him, a lion met him and killed him. ³⁷ Then he found another man and said, "Strike me!" So the man hit him, striking and wounding him. ³⁸ Then the prophet departed, and waited for the king along the road, disguising himself with a bandage over his eyes. ³⁹ As the king passed by, he cried to the king and said, "Your servant went out into the thick of the battle; then a soldier turned and brought a man to me, and said, 'Guard this man; if he is missing, your life shall be given for his life, or else you shall pay a talent of silver.' ⁴⁰ While your servant was busy here and there, he was gone." The king of Israel

said to him, "So shall your judgment be; you yourself have decided it." ⁴¹ Then he quickly took the bandage away from his eyes. The king of Israel recognized him as one of the prophets. ⁴² Then he said to him, "Thus says the LORD, 'Because you have let the man go whom I had devoted to destruction, therefore your life shall be for his life, and your people for his people.'" ⁴³ The king of Israel set out toward home, resentful and sullen, and came to Samaria.

Naboth's Vineyard

21 Later the following events took place: Naboth the Jezreelite had a vineyard in Jezreel, beside the palace of King Ahab of Samaria. ² And Ahab said to Naboth, "Give me your vineyard, so that I may have it for a vegetable garden, because it is near my house; I will give you a better vineyard for it; or, if it seems good to you, I will give you its value in money." ³ But Naboth said to Ahab, "The LORD forbid that I should give you my ancestral inheritance." ⁴ Ahab went home resentful and sullen because of what Naboth the Jezreelite had said to him; for he had said, "I will not give you my ancestral inheritance." He lay down on his bed, turned away his face, and would not eat.

5 His wife Jezebel came to him and said, "Why are you so depressed that you will not eat?" ⁶ He said to her, "Because I spoke to Naboth the Jezreelite and said to him, 'Give me your vineyard

ᵃ Heb He *ᵇ* Heb lacks *The king of Israel responded* *ᶜ* Heb *of the sons of the prophets*

20:35–43—Any joy in victory over Ben-hadad and renewed peace is muted by an unnamed prophet's announcement that YHWH expected total annihilation of the enemy, as demanded in Deut. 20 and 1 Sam. 15. The prophet speaks with compelling force (1 Kgs. 20:36), with a wound (v. 37) and **bandage** (v. 38) hiding his identity and making him appear a combatant. His parable (vv. 39–40a) is designed, like Nathan's before David (2 Sam. 12), to trap his hearer into announcing his own guilt and punishment (1 Kgs. 20:40b–41).

21:1–29 Ahab and Naboth

21:1–16—Naboth's refusal (v. 3) to give up his land reflects ancient concerns to prevent property from passing out of family control. Sale was possible, but not in perpetuity (so Lev. 25:8–17). The dejected Ahab (see 1 Kgs. 20:43) neglects to give Naboth's reasons for refusal (21:6). Jezebel, reflecting a tradition where the king's requests could not be refused and in direct contrast to older Israelite tradition, arranges the judicial stoning of Naboth through the testimony of two false witnesses (Deut. 17:6–7; 19:15) who accuse him of cursing YHWH and the king (Exod. 22:28; Lev. 24:14–16).

for money; or else, if you prefer, I will give you another vineyard for it'; but he answered, 'I will not give you my vineyard.'" 7 His wife Jezebel said to him, "Do you now govern Israel? Get up, eat some food, and be cheerful; I will give you the vineyard of Naboth the Jezreelite."

8 So she wrote letters in Ahab's name and sealed them with his seal; she sent the letters to the elders and the nobles who lived with Naboth in his city. 9 She wrote in the letters, "Proclaim a fast, and seat Naboth at the head of the assembly; 10 seat two scoundrels opposite him, and have them bring a charge against him, saying, 'You have cursed God and the king.' Then take him out, and stone him to death." 11 The men of his city, the elders and the nobles who lived in his city, did as Jezebel had sent word to them. Just as it was written in the letters that she had sent to them, 12 they proclaimed a fast and seated Naboth at the head of the assembly. 13 The two scoundrels came in and sat opposite him; and the scoundrels brought a charge against Naboth, in the presence of the people, saying, "Naboth cursed God and the king." So they took him outside the city, and stoned him to death. 14 Then they sent to Jezebel, saying, "Naboth has been stoned; he is dead."

15 As soon as Jezebel heard that Naboth had been stoned and was dead, Jezebel said to Ahab, "Go, take possession of the vineyard of Naboth the Jezreelite, which he refused to give you for money; for Naboth is not alive, but dead." 16 As soon as Ahab heard that Naboth was dead, Ahab set out to go down to the vineyard of Naboth the Jezreelite, to take possession of it.

Elijah Pronounces God's Sentence

17 Then the word of the LORD came to Elijah the Tishbite, saying: 18 Go down to meet King Ahab of Israel, who rules*a* in Samaria; he is now in the vineyard of Naboth, where he has gone to take possession. 19 You shall say to him, "Thus says the LORD: Have you killed, and also taken possession?" You shall say to him, "Thus says the LORD: In the place where dogs licked up the blood of Naboth, dogs will also lick up your blood."

20 Ahab said to Elijah, "Have you found me, O my enemy?" He answered, "I have found you. Because you have sold yourself to do what is evil in the sight of the LORD, 21 I will bring disaster on you; I will consume you, and will cut off from Ahab every male, bond or free, in Israel; 22 and I will make your house like the house of Jeroboam son of Nebat, and like the house of Baasha son of Ahijah, because you have provoked me to anger and have caused Israel to sin. 23 Also concerning Jezebel the LORD said, 'The dogs shall eat Jezebel within the bounds of Jezreel.' 24 Anyone belonging to Ahab who dies in the city the dogs shall eat; and anyone of his who dies in the open country the birds of the air shall eat."

25 (Indeed, there was no one like Ahab, who sold himself to do what was evil in the sight of the LORD, urged on by his wife Jezebel. 26 He acted most abominably in going after idols, as the Amorites had done, whom the LORD drove out before the Israelites.)

27 When Ahab heard those words, he tore his clothes and put sackcloth over

a Heb *who is*

21:17–29—Elijah meets Ahab at the scene of his crime, with condemnations similar to those pronounced against Jeroboam (14:10–11) and Baasha (16:3–4). Ahab's immediate crime is abuse of royal power in taking Naboth's land, but his more extensive crime is failure to promote worship of YHWH alone (1 Kgs. 21:22, 26). Jezebel, who provoked both crimes, is condemned almost as an aside (v. 23), suggesting Ahab allowed his reign to be shaped by a foreign woman committed to alien gods.

21:25–26—An editorial aside makes clear that Ahab is judged the worst Israelite king to date.

21:27–29—Ahab's impressive show of penance and grief, and the reshaping of the judgment against him, stands in marked contrast to what the narrator just said (vv. 25–26). Judgment

his bare flesh; he fasted, lay in the sack-cloth, and went about dejectedly. ²⁸ Then the word of the LORD came to Elijah the Tishbite: ²⁹ "Have you seen how Ahab has humbled himself before me? Because he has humbled himself before me, I will not bring the disaster in his days; but in his son's days I will bring the disaster on his house."

Joint Campaign with Judah against Aram

22 For three years Aram and Israel continued without war. ² But in the third year King Jehoshaphat of Judah came down to the king of Israel. ³ The king of Israel said to his servants, "Do you know that Ramoth-gilead belongs to us, yet we are doing nothing to take it out of the hand of the king of Aram?" ⁴ He said to Jehoshaphat, "Will you go with me to battle at Ramoth-gilead?" Jehoshaphat replied to the king of Israel, "I am as you are; my people are your people, my horses are your horses."

5 But Jehoshaphat also said to the king of Israel, "Inquire first for the word of the LORD." ⁶ Then the king of Israel gathered the prophets together, about four hundred of them, and said to them, "Shall I go to battle against Ramoth-gilead, or shall I refrain?" They said, "Go up; for the LORD will give it into the hand of the king." ⁷ But Jehoshaphat said, "Is there no other prophet of the LORD here of whom we may inquire?" ⁸ The king of Israel said to Jehoshaphat, "There is still one other by whom we

may inquire of the LORD, Micaiah son of Imlah; but I hate him, for he never prophesies anything favorable about me, but only disaster." Jehoshaphat said, "Let the king not say such a thing." ⁹ Then the king of Israel summoned an officer and said, "Bring quickly Micaiah son of Imlah." ¹⁰ Now the king of Israel and King Jehoshaphat of Judah were sitting on their thrones, arrayed in their robes, at the threshing floor at the entrance of the gate of Samaria; and all the prophets were prophesying before them. ¹¹ Zedekiah son of Chenaanah made for himself horns of iron, and he said, "Thus says the LORD: With these you shall gore the Arameans until they are destroyed." ¹² All the prophets were prophesying the same and saying, "Go up to Ramoth-gilead and triumph; the LORD will give it into the hand of the king."

Micaiah Predicts Failure

13 The messenger who had gone to summon Micaiah said to him, "Look, the words of the prophets with one accord are favorable to the king; let your word be like the word of one of them, and speak favorably." ¹⁴ But Micaiah said, "As the LORD lives, whatever the LORD says to me, that I will speak."

15 When he had come to the king, the king said to him, "Micaiah, shall we go to Ramoth-gilead to battle, or shall we refrain?" He answered him, "Go up and triumph; the LORD will give it into the hand of the king." ¹⁶ But the king said to

---

against Ahab's dynasty (2 Kgs. 10:17) and Jezebel (2 Kgs. 9:30–37) comes in time, while disaster meets Ahab in the events next recounted.

22:1–53 Israel and Judah against Aram

22:1–12—The peace Ahab made with Aram (1 Kgs. 20) holds until Ahab considers breaking it with the aid of Jehoshaphat of Judah, who is apparently his vassal. As custom demands, prophets are consulted before the proposed attack. In spite of the favorable message by 400 prophets, and *Zedekiah*'s symbolic enactment of it, Jehoshaphat is not satisfied till the lone holdout is summoned.

22:13–18—*Micaiah*'s encounter with Ahab dem-

onstrates what can happen when different prophets speak at cross-purposes. In the conflict between Zedekiah and Micaiah, it should be noted that the former is deceived by *a lying spirit* (v. 22) sent by YHWH and knows not that his message is false. In such circumstances it is hard to know how the kings are to judge which prophet speaks YHWH's word—especially since YHWH is intent on destroying Ahab. Ahab's problem reflects a larger uncertainty as to whether a claim to speak YHWH's word is always to be accepted. Criteria for certainty in this matter are often lacking, and what evidence there is, is ambiguous.

him, "How many times must I make you swear to tell me nothing but the truth in the name of the LORD?" [17] Then Micaiah[a] said, "I saw all Israel scattered on the mountains, like sheep that have no shepherd; and the LORD said, 'These have no master; let each one go home in peace.'" [18] The king of Israel said to Jehoshaphat, "Did I not tell you that he would not prophesy anything favorable about me, but only disaster?"

[19] Then Micaiah[a] said, "Therefore hear the word of the LORD: I saw the LORD sitting on his throne, with all the host of heaven standing beside him to the right and to the left of him. [20] And the LORD said, 'Who will entice Ahab, so that he may go up and fall at Ramoth-gilead?' Then one said one thing, and another said another, [21] until a spirit came forward and stood before the LORD, saying, 'I will entice him.' [22] 'How?' the LORD asked him. He replied, 'I will go out and be a lying spirit in the mouth of all his prophets.' Then the LORD[a] said, 'You are to entice him, and you shall succeed; go out and do it.' [23] So you see, the LORD has put a lying spirit in the mouth of all these your prophets; the LORD has decreed disaster for you."

[24] Then Zedekiah son of Chenaanah came up to Micaiah, slapped him on the cheek, and said, "Which way did the spirit of the LORD pass from me to speak to you?" [25] Micaiah replied, "You will find out on that day when you go in to hide in an inner chamber." [26] The king of Israel then ordered, "Take Micaiah, and return him to Amon the governor of the city and to Joash the king's son, [27] and say, 'Thus says the king: Put this fellow in prison, and feed him on reduced rations of bread and water until I come in peace.'" [28] Micaiah said, "If you return in peace, the LORD has not

spoken by me." And he said, "Hear, you peoples, all of you!"

Defeat and Death of Ahab

[29] So the king of Israel and King Jehoshaphat of Judah went up to Ramoth-gilead. [30] The king of Israel said to Jehoshaphat, "I will disguise myself and go into battle, but you wear your robes." So the king of Israel disguised himself and went into battle. [31] Now the king of Aram had commanded the thirty-two captains of his chariots, "Fight with no one small or great, but only with the king of Israel." [32] When the captains of the chariots saw Jehoshaphat, they said, "It is surely the king of Israel." So they turned to fight against him; and Jehoshaphat cried out. [33] When the captains of the chariots saw that it was not the king of Israel, they turned back from pursuing him. [34] But a certain man drew his bow and unknowingly struck the king of Israel between the scale armor and the breastplate; so he said to the driver of his chariot, "Turn around, and carry me out of the battle, for I am wounded." [35] The battle grew hot that day, and the king was propped up in his chariot facing the Arameans, until at evening he died; the blood from the wound had flowed into the bottom of the chariot. [36] Then about sunset a shout went through the army, "Every man to his city, and every man to his country!"

[37] So the king died, and was brought to Samaria; they buried the king in Samaria. [38] They washed the chariot by the pool of Samaria; the dogs licked up his blood, and the prostitutes washed themselves in it,[b] according to the word of the LORD that he had spoken. [39] Now the rest of the acts of Ahab, and all that he did, and the ivory house that he built,

[a] Heb he   [b] Heb lacks in it

22:29–38—A chance arrow mortally wounds Ahab, and the grim details of his death and burial broadly fulfill (Ahab's blood is not spilled in Jezreel; *prostitutes* washing in it is new) what Elijah and Micaiah said about him.

22:39–40—The formal closure on Ahab's reign is strikingly without overt condemnation. *Ivory houses* were structures inlaid with ivory figurative designs.

and all the cities that he built, are they not written in the Book of the Annals of the Kings of Israel? **40** So Ahab slept with his ancestors; and his son Ahaziah succeeded him.

Jehoshaphat Reigns over Judah

41 Jehoshaphat son of Asa began to reign over Judah in the fourth year of King Ahab of Israel. **42** Jehoshaphat was thirty-five years old when he began to reign, and he reigned twenty-five years in Jerusalem. His mother's name was Azubah daughter of Shilhi. **43** He walked in all the way of his father Asa; he did not turn aside from it, doing what was right in the sight of the LORD; yet the high places were not taken away, and the people still sacrificed and offered incense on the high places. **44** Jehoshaphat also made peace with the king of Israel.

45 Now the rest of the acts of Jehoshaphat, and his power that he showed, and how he waged war, are they not written in the Book of the Annals of the Kings of Judah? **46** The remnant of the male temple prostitutes who were still in the land in the days of his father Asa, he exterminated.

47 There was no king in Edom; a deputy was king. **48** Jehoshaphat made ships of the Tarshish type to go to Ophir for gold; but they did not go, for the ships were wrecked at Ezion-geber. **49** Then Ahaziah son of Ahab said to Jehoshaphat, "Let my servants go with your servants in the ships," but Jehoshaphat was not willing. **50** Jehoshaphat slept with his ancestors and was buried with his ancestors in the city of his father David; his son Jehoram succeeded him.

Ahaziah Reigns over Israel

51 Ahaziah son of Ahab began to reign over Israel in Samaria in the seventeenth year of King Jehoshaphat of Judah; he reigned two years over Israel. **52** He did what was evil in the sight of the LORD, and walked in the way of his father and mother, and in the way of Jeroboam son of Nebat, who caused Israel to sin. **53** He served Baal and worshiped him; he provoked the LORD, the God of Israel, to anger, just as his father had done.

22:41–50—Jehoshaphat's long reign receives brief but generally positive notice. While not removing *the high places* and making *peace with Israel*, he removes *male temple prostitutes* (14:24). Unlike Solomon, he had no success in seagoing trade.

22:51–53—First Kings ends with a beginning—the standard opening to a new reign. Ahaziah in his two years earned total condemnation by the narrator.

2 KINGS

Elijah Denounces Ahaziah

1 After the death of Ahab, Moab rebelled against Israel.

2 Ahaziah had fallen through the lattice in his upper chamber in Samaria, and lay injured; so he sent messengers, telling them, "Go, inquire of Baal-zebub, the god of Ekron, whether I shall recover from this injury." ³ But the angel of the LORD said to Elijah the Tishbite, "Get up, go to meet the messengers of the king of Samaria, and say to them, 'Is it because there is no God in Israel that you are going to inquire of Baal-zebub, the god of Ekron?' ⁴ Now therefore thus says the LORD, 'You shall not leave the bed to which you have gone, but you shall surely die.' " So Elijah went.

5 The messengers returned to the king, who said to them, "Why have you returned?" ⁶ They answered him, "There came a man to meet us, who said to us, 'Go back to the king who sent you, and say to him: Thus says the LORD: Is it because there is no God in Israel that you are sending to inquire of Baal-zebub, the god of Ekron? Therefore you shall not leave the bed to which you have gone, but shall surely die.' " ⁷ He said to them, "What sort of man was he who came to meet you and told you these things?" ⁸ They answered him, "A hairy man, with a leather belt around his waist." He said, "It is Elijah the Tishbite."

9 Then the king sent to him a captain of fifty with his fifty men. He went up to Elijah, who was sitting on the top of a hill, and said to him, "O man of God, the king says, 'Come down.' " ¹⁰ But Elijah answered the captain of fifty, "If I am a man of God, let fire come down from heaven and consume you and your fifty." Then fire came down from heaven, and consumed him and his fifty.

11 Again the king sent to him another captain of fifty with his fifty. He went up*a* and said to him, "O man of God, this is the king's order: Come down quickly!" ¹² But Elijah answered them, "If I am a man of God, let fire come down from heaven and consume you and your fifty." Then the fire of God came down from heaven and consumed him and his fifty.

13 Again the king sent the captain of a third fifty with his fifty. So the third captain of fifty went up, and came and fell on his knees before Elijah, and entreated him, "O man of God, please let my life, and the life of these fifty servants of yours, be precious in your sight. ¹⁴ Look, fire came down from heaven and consumed the two former captains of fifty men with their fifties; but now let my life be precious in your sight." ¹⁵ Then the angel of the LORD said to Elijah, "Go down with him; do not be afraid of him." So he set out and went down with him to

---

a Gk Compare verses 9, 13: Heb *He answered*

1:1–8:15 Elijah and Elisha

1:1–2:18 Elijah's Last Days

1:1–18—The contest between YHWH and Baal continues, as YHWH's prophet again shows his power over the Canaanite deity and the Israelite king. Again we find YHWH's authority lodged with the marginal figure of the prophet over against the power of the king and his court.

1:1—See 3:4–27.

1:2—See 1 Kgs. 14:1–18. *Baal-zebub*, "Lord of the flies," is a polemical play on Baal-zebul, "Lord of princes." *Ekron*, west of Jerusalem, was in Philistine hands.

1:9–16—God protects Elijah, who speaks of and with his authority. See 1 Sam. 19:18–24 for a comparable threefold pattern.

1:10—Compare the *fire* sent by YHWH in 1 Kgs. 18:24.

the king, **16** and said to him, "Thus says the LORD: Because you have sent messengers to inquire of Baal-zebub, the god of Ekron,—is it because there is no God in Israel to inquire of his word?—therefore you shall not leave the bed to which you have gone, but you shall surely die."

Death of Ahaziah

17 So he died according to the word of the LORD that Elijah had spoken. His brother,*a* Jehoram succeeded him as king in the second year of King Jehoram son of Jehoshaphat of Judah, because Ahaziah had no son. **18** Now the rest of the acts of Ahaziah that he did, are they not written in the Book of the Annals of the Kings of Israel?

Elijah Ascends to Heaven

2 Now when the LORD was about to take Elijah up to heaven by a whirlwind, Elijah and Elisha were on their way from Gilgal. **2** Elijah said to Elisha, "Stay here; for the LORD has sent me as far as Bethel." But Elisha said, "As the LORD lives, and as you yourself live, I will not leave you." So they went down to Bethel. **3** The company of prophets*b* who were in Bethel came out to Elisha, and said to him, "Do you know that today the LORD will take your master away from you?" And he said, "Yes, I know; keep silent."

4 Elijah said to him, "Elisha, stay here; for the LORD has sent me to Jericho." But he said, "As the LORD lives, and as you yourself live, I will not leave you." So they came to Jericho. **5** The company of prophets*b* who were at Jericho drew near to Elisha, and said to him, "Do you know that today the LORD will take your master away from you?" And he answered, "Yes, I know; be silent."

6 Then Elijah said to him, "Stay here; for the LORD has sent me to the Jordan." But he said, "As the LORD lives, and as you yourself live, I will not leave you." So the two of them went on. **7** Fifty men of the company of prophets*b* also went, and stood at some distance from them, as they both were standing by the Jordan. **8** Then Elijah took his mantle and rolled it up, and struck the water; the water was parted to the one side and to the other, until the two of them crossed on dry ground.

9 When they had crossed, Elijah said to Elisha, "Tell me what I may do for you, before I am taken from you." Elisha said, "Please let me inherit a double share of your spirit." **10** He responded, "You have asked a hard thing; yet, if you see me as I am being taken from you, it will be granted you; if not, it will not." **11** As they continued walking and talking, a chariot of fire and horses of fire separated the two of them, and Elijah ascended in a whirlwind into heaven. **12** Elisha kept watching and crying out, "Father, father! The chariots of Israel and its horsemen!" But when he could no longer see him, he grasped his own clothes and tore them in two pieces.

Elisha Succeeds Elijah

13 He picked up the mantle of Elijah that had fallen from him, and went back

a Gk Syr: Heb lacks *His brother* *b* Heb *sons of the prophets*

1:17–18—The prophetic announcement of death is immediately confirmed. Ahaziah's brother Jehoram succeeds him, not to be confused with Jehoram king of Judah.

2:1–18—*The mantle of Elijah* dramatically passes to Elisha. In a threefold pattern of movement from *Gilgal* to *Bethel* to *Jericho* to the *Jordan River*, Elijah and Elisha roughly reverse the journeys of Joshua and the Israelites into the land of promise.

2:1—See Job 38:1; 40:6.

2:3—*The company ("sons") of prophets* was a guild under leadership of a "Father."

2:8—On Elijah's mantle as a symbol of authority, see 1 Kgs. 19:19. His parting the Jordan recalls the acts of Joshua (Josh. 4:7–17) and Moses (Exod. 14:21–22).

2:9—Elisha's request for *a double share* of Elijah's spirit is probably not for twice what he had but for the share granted an eldest son as stipulated in Deut. 21:15–17.

2:11–12—Fiery *chariot* and *horses* link Elijah with God's heavenly army.

2:13–15—Elisha parts the Jordan, demonstrating that Elijah's spirit has passed to him. The passing

and stood on the bank of the Jordan. [14] He took the mantle of Elijah that had fallen from him, and struck the water, saying, "Where is the LORD, the God of Elijah?" When he had struck the water, the water was parted to the one side and to the other, and Elisha went over.

15 When the company of prophets[a] who were at Jericho saw him at a distance, they declared, "The spirit of Elijah rests on Elisha." They came to meet him and bowed to the ground before him. [16] They said to him, "See now, we have fifty strong men among your servants; please let them go and seek your master; it may be that the spirit of the LORD has caught him up and thrown him down on some mountain or into some valley." He responded, "No, do not send them." [17] But when they urged him until he was ashamed, he said, "Send them." So they sent fifty men who searched for three days but did not find him. [18] When they came back to him (he had remained at Jericho), he said to them, "Did I not say to you, Do not go?"

Elisha Performs Miracles

19 Now the people of the city said to Elisha, "The location of this city is good, as my lord sees; but the water is bad, and the land is unfruitful." [20] He said, "Bring me a new bowl, and put salt in it." So they brought it to him. [21] Then he went to the spring of water and threw the salt into it, and said, "Thus says the LORD, I have made this water wholesome; from now on neither death nor miscarriage shall come from it." [22] So the water has been wholesome to this day, according to the word that Elisha spoke.

23 He went up from there to Bethel; and while he was going up on the way, some small boys came out of the city and jeered at him, saying, "Go away, baldhead! Go away, baldhead!" [24] When he turned around and saw them, he cursed them in the name of the LORD. Then two she-bears came out of the woods and mauled forty-two of the boys. [25] From there he went on to Mount Carmel, and then returned to Samaria.

Jehoram Reigns over Israel

3 In the eighteenth year of King Jehoshaphat of Judah, Jehoram son of Ahab became king over Israel in Samaria; he reigned twelve years. [2] He did what was evil in the sight of the LORD, though not like his father and mother, for he removed the pillar of Baal that his father had made. [3] Nevertheless he clung to the sin of Jeroboam son of Nebat, which he caused Israel to commit; he did not depart from it.

War with Moab

4 Now King Mesha of Moab was a sheep breeder, who used to deliver to the king of Israel one hundred thousand lambs, and the wool of one hundred thousand rams. [5] But when Ahab died, the king of Moab rebelled against the king of Israel. [6] So King Jehoram marched out of Samaria at that time and mustered all Israel. [7] As he went he sent word to King Jehoshaphat of Judah,

a Heb sons of the prophets

and possession of YHWH's spirit, rather than the right of birth or institutional designation, ensures continuity of YHWH's authority into the next generation.

2:19–25 Elisha's Power Demonstrated
Two brief stories further demonstrate that Elijah's authority has passed to Elisha.

2:19–22—Elisha recalls Moses' actions with the waters at Marah (Exod. 15:23–25), linking him, like his master, with his revered ancestor.

2:23–25—This episode suggests one does not trifle with God's prophets. The point is made with a brutality many readers may find troubling. *Baldhead* as a taunting cry may refer to a mark that identified certain individuals as part of prophetic guilds. Elisha passes to *Carmel* and then *Samaria*, where his master battled with Baal and Ahab's house.

3:1–27 Israel and Judah at War with Moab
Elisha next appears with the kings of Israel and Judah (and Edom) in war against Moab (cf. 1:1).

3:1–3—Jehoram of Israel is evil, but not like Ahab.

3:7—Jehoshaphat of Judah shows himself a loyal

"The king of Moab has rebelled against me; will you go with me to battle against Moab?" He answered, "I will; I am with you, my people are your people, my horses are your horses." 8 Then he asked, "By which way shall we march?" Jehoram answered, "By the way of the wilderness of Edom."

9 So the king of Israel, the king of Judah, and the king of Edom set out; and when they had made a roundabout march of seven days, there was no water for the army or for the animals that were with them. 10 Then the king of Israel said, "Alas! The LORD has summoned us, three kings, only to be handed over to Moab." 11 But Jehoshaphat said, "Is there no prophet of the LORD here, through whom we may inquire of the LORD?" Then one of the servants of the king of Israel answered, "Elisha son of Shaphat, who used to pour water on the hands of Elijah, is here." 12 Jehoshaphat said, "The word of the LORD is with him." So the king of Israel and Jehoshaphat and the king of Edom went down to him.

13 Elisha said to the king of Israel, "What have I to do with you? Go to your father's prophets or to your mother's." But the king of Israel said to him, "No; it is the LORD who has summoned us, three kings, only to be handed over to Moab." 14 Elisha said, "As the LORD of hosts lives, whom I serve, were it not that I have regard for King Jehoshaphat of Judah, I would give you neither a look nor a glance. 15 But get me a musician." And then, while the musician was playing, the power of the LORD came on him.

16 And he said, "Thus says the LORD, 'I will make this wadi full of pools.' 17 For thus says the LORD, 'You shall see neither wind nor rain, but the wadi shall be filled with water, so that you shall drink, you, your cattle, and your animals.' 18 This is only a trifle in the sight of the LORD, for he will also hand Moab over to you. 19 You shall conquer every fortified city and every choice city; every good tree you shall fell, all springs of water you shall stop up, and every good piece of land you shall ruin with stones." 20 The next day, about the time of the morning offering, suddenly water began to flow from the direction of Edom, until the country was filled with water.

21 When all the Moabites heard that the kings had come up to fight against them, all who were able to put on armor, from the youngest to the oldest, were called out and were drawn up at the frontier. 22 When they rose early in the morning, and the sun shone upon the water, the Moabites saw the water opposite them as red as blood. 23 They said, "This is blood; the kings must have fought together, and killed one another. Now then, Moab, to the spoil!" 24 But when they came to the camp of Israel, the Israelites rose up and attacked the Moabites, who fled before them; as they entered Moab they continued the attack.a 25 The cities they overturned, and on every good piece of land everyone threw a stone, until it was covered; every spring of water they stopped up, and every good tree they felled. Only at

a Compare Gk Syr: Meaning of Heb uncertain

---

vassal of Jehoram, supporting him when Moab withholds annual tribute.

3:9a—Edom is a vassal of Jehoshaphat (1 Kgs. 22:47 and 2 Kgs. 8:20).

3:9b–12—Jehoram's suggested march brings the kings against Moab from the south landing them in dire straits in the wilderness.

3:13–20—Elisha shows disdain for Jehoram and his parents and preference for Jehoshaphat, but declares that YHWH will aid both by providing water.

3:15—See 1 Sam. 10:5–6 for prophetic use of music to invoke YHWH's spirit.

3:17—A *wadi* generally ran with water only in the rainy season.

3:19—Elisha commands for YHWH a destruction of Moab that violates rules of war in Deut. 20:19–20.

3:20–27—Whether deceived by a miracle or a trick of nature, all the fighting men of Moab are drawn to defeat.

Kir-hareseth did the stone walls remain, until the slingers surrounded and attacked it. ²⁶ When the king of Moab saw that the battle was going against him, he took with him seven hundred swordsmen to break through, opposite the king of Edom; but they could not. ²⁷ Then he took his firstborn son who was to succeed him, and offered him as a burnt offering on the wall. And great wrath came upon Israel, so they withdrew from him and returned to their own land.

Elisha and the Widow's Oil

4 Now the wife of a member of the company of prophets*ᵃ* cried to Elisha, "Your servant my husband is dead; and you know that your servant feared the LORD, but a creditor has come to take my two children as slaves." ² Elisha said to her, "What shall I do for you? Tell me, what do you have in the house?" She answered, "Your servant has nothing in the house, except a jar of oil." ³ He said, "Go outside, borrow vessels from all your neighbors, empty vessels and not just a few. ⁴ Then go in, and shut the door behind you and your children, and start pouring into all these vessels; when each is full, set it aside." ⁵ So she left him and shut the door behind her and her children; they kept bringing vessels to her, and she kept pouring. ⁶ When the vessels were full, she said to her son, "Bring me another vessel." But he said

to her, "There are no more." Then the oil stopped flowing. ⁷ She came and told the man of God, and he said, "Go sell the oil and pay your debts, and you and your children can live on the rest."

Elisha Raises the Shunammite's Son

8 One day Elisha was passing through Shunem, where a wealthy woman lived, who urged him to have a meal. So whenever he passed that way, he would stop there for a meal. ⁹ She said to her husband, "Look, I am sure that this man who regularly passes our way is a holy man of God. ¹⁰ Let us make a small roof chamber with walls, and put there for him a bed, a table, a chair, and a lamp, so that he can stay there whenever he comes to us."

11 One day when he came there, he went up to the chamber and lay down there. ¹² He said to his servant Gehazi, "Call the Shunammite woman." When he had called her, she stood before him. ¹³ He said to him, "Say to her, Since you have taken all this trouble for us, what may be done for you? Would you have a word spoken on your behalf to the king or to the commander of the army?" She answered, "I live among my own people." ¹⁴ He said, "What then may be done for her?" Gehazi answered, "Well, she has no son, and her husband is old." ¹⁵ He said, "Call her." When he had called her, she stood at the door. ¹⁶ He said, "At this

ᵃ Heb *the sons of the prophets*

3:26–27—The king of Moab apparently snatches his life from sure defeat through the sacrifice of his son and heir. Just what or whose is the **wrath** that leads to Israel's withdrawal is not clear, as the episode ends on a mysterious and disturbing note. The unsettled feelings the reader experiences mirror the unsettled times being described in the story of Israel and Judah.

4:1–8:15 Elilsha and Israel

4:1–44—The narrator offers four stories in which the prophet Elisha grants or restores life. They serve to enhance his authority as leader of a company of prophets (see 2:3) and presumably the authority of his god YHWH, who is strikingly absent in this series of miracle stories. The prophet, as bearer of YHWH's authority,

is not bound by what we recognize as laws of nature.

4:1–7—Widows and orphans were especially vulnerable to oppression in a society where family members could be sold to pay debts (Exod. 21:7; Amos 2:6; 8:6). Compare Elijah's actions in 1 Kgs. 17:10–16.

4:8–37—Comparisons with Elijah's actions in 1 Kgs. 17:17–24 suggest Elisha is his heir.

4:11–16—While Elisha wishes to reward the barren woman and suggests his powers have considerable range, he deals with her indirectly through *his servant Gehazi* until his announcement that she will *embrace a son*, an announcement she is unable to believe.

season, in due time, you shall embrace a son." She replied, "No, my lord, O man of God; do not deceive your servant."

17 The woman conceived and bore a son at that season, in due time, as Elisha had declared to her.

18 When the child was older, he went out one day to his father among the reapers. ¹⁹ He complained to his father, "Oh, my head, my head!" The father said to his servant, "Carry him to his mother." ²⁰ He carried him and brought him to his mother; the child sat on her lap until noon, and he died. ²¹ She went up and laid him on the bed of the man of God, closed the door on him, and left. ²² Then she called to her husband, and said, "Send me one of the servants and one of the donkeys, so that I may quickly go to the man of God and come back again." ²³ He said, "Why go to him today? It is neither new moon nor sabbath." She said, "It will be all right." ²⁴ Then she saddled the donkey and said to her servant, "Urge the animal on; do not hold back for me unless I tell you." ²⁵ So she set out, and came to the man of God at Mount Carmel.

When the man of God saw her coming, he said to Gehazi his servant, "Look, there is the Shunammite woman; ²⁶ run at once to meet her, and say to her, Are you all right? Is your husband all right? Is the child all right?" She answered, "It is all right." ²⁷ When she came to the man of God at the mountain, she caught hold of his feet. Gehazi approached to push her away. But the man of God said, "Let her alone, for she is in bitter distress; the LORD has hidden it from me and has

not told me." ²⁸ Then she said, "Did I ask my lord for a son? Did I not say, Do not mislead me?" ²⁹ He said to Gehazi, "Gird up your loins, and take my staff in your hand, and go. If you meet anyone, give no greeting, and if anyone greets you, do not answer; and lay my staff on the face of the child." ³⁰ Then the mother of the child said, "As the LORD lives, and as you yourself live, I will not leave without you." So he rose up and followed her. ³¹ Gehazi went on ahead and laid the staff on the face of the child, but there was no sound or sign of life. He came back to meet him and told him, "The child has not awakened."

32 When Elisha came into the house, he saw the child lying dead on his bed. ³³ So he went in and closed the door on the two of them, and prayed to the LORD. ³⁴ Then he got up on the bed[a] and lay upon the child, putting his mouth upon his mouth, his eyes upon his eyes, and his hands upon his hands; and while he lay bent over him, the flesh of the child became warm. ³⁵ He got down, walked once to and fro in the room, then got up again and bent over him; the child sneezed seven times, and the child opened his eyes. ³⁶ Elisha[b] summoned Gehazi and said, "Call the Shunammite woman." So he called her. When she came to him, he said, "Take your son." ³⁷ She came and fell at his feet, bowing to the ground; then she took her son and left.

Elisha Purifies the Pot of Stew

38 When Elisha returned to Gilgal, there was a famine in the land. As the

---

[a] Heb lacks *on the bed*   [b] Heb *he*

4:17—The announcement of birth to a barren wife and old husband at a set time recalls especially the story of Sarah and Abraham (Gen. 18:1–15) and other examples of a common scene in biblical narrative (Gen. 30:1–24; Judg. 13:1–25; 1 Sam. 1:1–28).

4:18–25a—The Shunammite's son is given only to be apparently taken from her, by what may be sunstroke. She strikingly sees this as a matter between her and Elisha, leaving her husband out.

4:25b–31—This time (v. 26) she will not deal with Elisha through Gehazi. From her barely veiled rebuke in v. 28, the prophet recognizes what the problem is and dispatches his servant with instructions on solving it.

4:32–37—Gehazi's efforts fail, and Elisha, at the woman's urging and with some effort, becomes the channel for life for the dead child.

4:38–41—Elisha saves the guild of *prophets* from accidental death through poisoning.

company of prophets was[a] sitting before him, he said to his servant, "Put the large pot on, and make some stew for the company of prophets."[b] **39** One of them went out into the field to gather herbs; he found a wild vine and gathered from it a lapful of wild gourds, and came and cut them up into the pot of stew, not knowing what they were. **40** They served some for the men to eat. But while they were eating the stew, they cried out, "O man of God, there is death in the pot!" They could not eat it. **41** He said, "Then bring some flour." He threw it into the pot, and said, "Serve the people and let them eat." And there was nothing harmful in the pot.

Elisha Feeds One Hundred Men

42 A man came from Baal-shalishah, bringing food from the first fruits to the man of God: twenty loaves of barley and fresh ears of grain in his sack. Elisha said, "Give it to the people and let them eat." **43** But his servant said, "How can I set this before a hundred people?" So he repeated, "Give it to the people and let them eat, for thus says the LORD, 'They shall eat and have some left.'" **44** He set it before them, they ate, and had some left, according to the word of the LORD.

The Healing of Naaman

5 Naaman, commander of the army of the king of Aram, was a great man and in high favor with his master, because by him the LORD had given victory to Aram. The man, though a mighty warrior, suffered from leprosy.[c] **2** Now the Arameans on one of their raids had taken a young girl captive from the land of Israel, and she served Naaman's wife. **3** She said to her mistress, "If only my lord were with the prophet who is in Samaria! He would cure him of his leprosy."[c] **4** So Naaman[d] went in and told his lord just what the girl from the land of Israel had said. **5** And the king of Aram said, "Go then, and I will send along a letter to the king of Israel."

He went, taking with him ten talents of silver, six thousand shekels of gold, and ten sets of garments. **6** He brought the letter to the king of Israel, which read, "When this letter reaches you, know that I have sent to you my servant Naaman, that you may cure him of his leprosy."[c] **7** When the king of Israel read the letter, he tore his clothes and said, "Am I God, to give death or life, that this man sends word to me to cure a man of his leprosy?[c] Just look and see how he is trying to pick a quarrel with me."

8 But when Elisha the man of God heard that the king of Israel had torn his clothes, he sent a message to the king, "Why have you torn your clothes? Let him come to me, that he may learn that there is a prophet in Israel." **9** So Naaman came with his horses and chariots, and halted at the entrance of Elisha's house. **10** Elisha sent a messenger to him, saying, "Go, wash in the Jordan seven times, and your flesh shall be restored and you shall be clean." **11** But Naaman became angry and went away, saying, "I thought that for me he would surely come out, and stand and call on the name of the LORD his God, and would wave his hand over the spot, and cure the leprosy![c] **12** Are not Abana[e] and Pharpar, the rivers of Damascus, better than all

[a] Heb sons of the prophets were   [b] Heb sons of the prophets   [c] A term for several skin diseases; precise meaning uncertain   [d] Heb he   [e] Another reading is Amana

---

4:42–44—See similar stories about Jesus in Matt. 14:13–21; 15:32–38; Mark 8:1–10.

5:1–27—Elisha's reputation reaches to the highest levels of Aram as *Naaman*, a commander of the king's army who is successful due to YHWH, seeks a cure for some sort of skin disease conventionally translated as *leprosy*.

5:3b—The reward Naaman brought is huge.

5:6–7—Naaman assumes the prophet mentioned by the Israelite slave girl is in the employ of the king, a misunderstanding that leads the king to misunderstand the king of Aram's intentions.

5:10—Elisha first deals with Naaman through an intermediary.

the waters of Israel? Could I not wash in them, and be clean?" He turned and went away in a rage. [13] But his servants approached and said to him, "Father, if the prophet had commanded you to do something difficult, would you not have done it? How much more, when all he said to you was, 'Wash, and be clean'?" [14] So he went down and immersed himself seven times in the Jordan, according to the word of the man of God; his flesh was restored like the flesh of a young boy, and he was clean.

[15] Then he returned to the man of God, he and all his company; he came and stood before him and said, "Now I know that there is no God in all the earth except in Israel; please accept a present from your servant." [16] But he said, "As the LORD lives, whom I serve, I will accept nothing!" He urged him to accept, but he refused. [17] Then Naaman said, "If not, please let two mule-loads of earth be given to your servant; for your servant will no longer offer burnt offering or sacrifice to any god except the LORD. [18] But may the LORD pardon your servant on one count: when my master goes into the house of Rimmon to worship there, leaning on my arm, and I bow down in the house of Rimmon, when I do bow down in the house of Rimmon, may the LORD pardon your servant on this one count." [19] He said to him, "Go in peace."

Gehazi's Greed

But when Naaman had gone from him a short distance, [20] Gehazi, the servant of Elisha the man of God, thought, "My master has let that Aramean Naaman off too lightly by not accepting from him what he offered. As the LORD lives, I will run after him and get something out of him." [21] So Gehazi went after Naaman. When Naaman saw someone running after him, he jumped down from the chariot to meet him and said, "Is everything all right?" [22] He replied, "Yes, but my master has sent me to say, 'Two members of a company of prophets[a] have just come to me from the hill country of Ephraim; please give them a talent of silver and two changes of clothing.'" [23] Naaman said, "Please accept two talents." He urged him, and tied up two talents of silver in two bags, with two changes of clothing, and gave them to two of his servants, who carried them in front of Gehazi.[b] [24] When he came to the citadel, he took the bags[c] from them, and stored them inside; he dismissed the men, and they left.

[25] He went in and stood before his master; and Elisha said to him, "Where have you been, Gehazi?" He answered, "Your servant has not gone anywhere at all." [26] But he said to him, "Did I not go with you in spirit when someone left his chariot to meet you? Is this a time to accept money and to accept clothing, olive orchards and vineyards, sheep and oxen, and male and female slaves? [27] Therefore the leprosy[d] of Naaman shall cling to you, and to your descendants forever." So he left his presence leprous,[d] as white as snow.

[a] Heb sons of the prophets [b] Heb him [c] Heb lacks the bags [d] A term for several skin diseases; precise meaning uncertain

---

5:13–14—A *servant* steers Naaman onto the right course of action (compare the Israelite slave girl in 5:2–3).

5:15–19a—Naaman becomes a convinced and converted Yahwist, but believes this *God in all the earth* (v. 15) can be worshiped only on Israelite turf. Thus he takes Israelite soil home to set up a small plot of Israel in the heart of Aram. He also seeks pardon for going through the necessary official ceremony in bowing to *Rimmon* ("thunderer," the Syrian Hadad and Canaanite

Baal). Elisha surprisingly gives his assent, perhaps in recognition of how difficult it is—in a world of many gods and foci for allegiance—to submit totally to YHWH alone.

5:19b–27—Gehazi's greed contrasts with Elisha's refusal of any reward. His deceit is exposed through the prophet's spiritual insight. In a nice reversal Gehazi suffers the disease that afflicted Naaman, marking a contrast between foreign convert and Israelite Gehazi.

The Miracle of the Ax Head

6 Now the company of prophets[a] said to Elisha, "As you see, the place where we live under your charge is too small for us. ²Let us go to the Jordan, and let us collect logs there, one for each of us, and build a place there for us to live." He answered, "Do so." ³Then one of them said, "Please come with your servants." And he answered, "I will." ⁴So he went with them. When they came to the Jordan, they cut down trees. ⁵But as one was felling a log, his ax head fell into the water; he cried out, "Alas, master! It was borrowed." ⁶Then the man of God said, "Where did it fall?" When he showed him the place, he cut off a stick, and threw it in there, and made the iron float. ⁷He said, "Pick it up." So he reached out his hand and took it.

The Aramean Attack Is Thwarted

8 Once when the king of Aram was at war with Israel, he took counsel with his officers. He said, "At such and such a place shall be my camp." ⁹But the man of God sent word to the king of Israel, "Take care not to pass this place, because the Arameans are going down there." ¹⁰The king of Israel sent word to the place of which the man of God spoke. More than once or twice he warned such a place[b] so that it was on the alert.

11 The mind of the king of Aram was greatly perturbed because of this; he called his officers and said to them, "Now tell me who among us sides with the king of Israel?" ¹²Then one of his officers said, "No one, my lord king. It is Elisha, the prophet in Israel, who tells the king of Israel the words that you speak in your bedchamber." ¹³He said, "Go and find where he is; I will send and seize him." He was told, "He is in Dothan." ¹⁴So he sent horses and chariots there and a great army; they came by night, and surrounded the city.

15 When an attendant of the man of God rose early in the morning and went out, an army with horses and chariots was all around the city. His servant said, "Alas, master! What shall we do?" ¹⁶He replied, "Do not be afraid, for there are more with us than there are with them." ¹⁷Then Elisha prayed: "O LORD, please open his eyes that he may see." So the LORD opened the eyes of the servant, and he saw; the mountain was full of horses and chariots of fire all around Elisha. ¹⁸When the Arameans[c] came down against him, Elisha prayed to the LORD, and said, "Strike this people, please, with blindness." So he struck them with blindness as Elisha had asked. ¹⁹Elisha said to them, "This is not the way, and this is not the city; follow me, and I will bring you to the man whom you seek." And he led them to Samaria.

20 As soon as they entered Samaria, Elisha said, "O LORD, open the eyes of these men so that they may see." The LORD opened their eyes, and they saw that they were inside Samaria. ²¹When the king of Israel saw them he said to Elisha, "Father, shall I kill them? Shall I kill them?" ²²He answered, "No! Did you capture with your sword and your bow those whom you want to kill? Set food and water before them so that they may eat and drink; and let them go to their master." ²³So he prepared for them a great feast; after they ate and drank, he sent them on their way, and they went to their master. And the Arameans no longer came raiding into the land of Israel.

---

a Heb *sons of the prophets*   *b* Heb *warned it*   *c* Heb *they*

6:1–7—Elisha's ability to circumvent normal patterns of nature again enhances his power in a story with no direct mention of God.

6:8–23—Elisha's powers, especially to divine the secrets of others, save him and Israel from the Arameans.

6:17—See 2:11.

6:21—The king of Israel recognizes the power of Elisha, calling him **father**.

6:22–23—The combined demonstration of supernatural power and unexpected kindness transforms Aramean policy regarding Israel, at least for a time.

Ben-hadad's Siege of Samaria

24 Some time later King Ben-hadad of Aram mustered his entire army; he marched against Samaria and laid siege to it. **25** As the siege continued, famine in Samaria became so great that a donkey's head was sold for eighty shekels of silver, and one-fourth of a kab of dove's dung for five shekels of silver. **26** Now as the king of Israel was walking on the city wall, a woman cried out to him, "Help, my lord king!" **27** He said, "No! Let the LORD help you. How can I help you? From the threshing floor or from the wine press?" **28** But then the king asked her, "What is your complaint?" She answered, "This woman said to me, 'Give up your son; we will eat him today, and we will eat my son tomorrow.' **29** So we cooked my son and ate him. The next day I said to her, 'Give up your son and we will eat him.' But she has hidden her son." **30** When the king heard the words of the woman he tore his clothes—now since he was walking on the city wall, the people could see that he had sackcloth on his body underneath— **31** and he said, "So may God do to me, and more, if the head of Elisha son of Shaphat stays on his shoulders today." **32** So he dispatched a man from his presence.

Now Elisha was sitting in his house, and the elders were sitting with him. Before the messenger arrived, Elisha said to the elders, "Are you aware that this murderer has sent someone to take off my head? When the messenger comes, see that you shut the door and hold it closed against him. Is not the sound of his master's feet behind him?" **33** While he was still speaking with them, the king[a] came down to him and said, "This trouble is from the LORD! Why should I hope in the LORD any longer?" **7** **1** But Elisha said, "Hear the word of the LORD: thus says the LORD, Tomorrow about this time a measure of choice meal shall be sold for a shekel, and two measures of barley for a shekel, at the gate of Samaria." **2** Then the captain on whose hand the king leaned said to the man of God, "Even if the LORD were to make windows in the sky, could such a thing happen?" But he said, "You shall see it with your own eyes, but you shall not eat from it."

The Arameans Flee

3 Now there were four leprous[b] men outside the city gate, who said to one another, "Why should we sit here until we die? **4** If we say, 'Let us enter the city,' the famine is in the city, and we shall die there; but if we sit here, we shall also die. Therefore, let us desert to the Aramean camp; if they spare our lives, we shall live; and if they kill us, we shall but die." **5** So they arose at twilight to go to the Aramean camp; but when they came to the edge of the Aramean camp, there

[a] See 7.2: Heb *messenger*　[b] A term for several skin diseases; precise meaning uncertain

6:24–32a—Under King Ben-hadad Aramean policy changes again as Samaria comes under a dreadful *siege* and severe *famine*, a marked contrast to the "great feast" (v. 23) offered the captured Arameans in the previous episode.

6:25—Both the most unappealing food and dung for fuel to cook it are exorbitantly priced.

6:26–30—The king is helpless in the face of the famine (v. 27) and the cry for justice in a horrid situation. There is irony in his opening *"Let the LORD help you."*

6:31–32a—Other than Elisha's close links to YHWH's power and authority, no reason is given for blaming Elisha for Samaria's distress.

6:32b–7:2—The king sees the siege and famine as YHWH's doing, but sent for no reason, and therefore as reason to abandon hope in the God of Israel. Elisha states, in contrast, that YHWH will dramatically transform famine into lavish relief.

7:2—*The captain on whose hand the king leaned* is apparently a close adviser. He assumes that even with rain, new crops would take time.

7:3–15—Those who were *leprous* (see 5:1), were not allowed within the city (Lev. 13:11, 46; Num. 12:14–16). Their despair is turned into surprise and greed and then into remorse and an announcement of deliverance as they find the camp of the enemy deserted. The narrator makes it clear this is YHWH's marvelous doing.

was no one there at all. ⁶ For the Lord had caused the Aramean army to hear the sound of chariots, and of horses, the sound of a great army, so that they said to one another, "The king of Israel has hired the kings of the Hittites and the kings of Egypt to fight against us." ⁷ So they fled away in the twilight and abandoned their tents, their horses, and their donkeys leaving the camp just as it was, and fled for their lives. ⁸ When these leprous*ᵃ* men had come to the edge of the camp, they went into a tent, ate and drank, carried off silver, gold, and clothing, and went and hid them. Then they came back, entered another tent, carried off things from it, and went and hid them.

9 Then they said to one another, "What we are doing is wrong. This is a day of good news; if we are silent and wait until the morning light, we will be found guilty; therefore let us go and tell the king's household." ¹⁰ So they came and called to the gatekeepers of the city, and told them, "We went to the Aramean camp, but there was no one to be seen or heard there, nothing but the horses tied, the donkeys tied, and the tents as they were." ¹¹ Then the gatekeepers called out and proclaimed it to the king's household. ¹² The king got up in the night, and said to his servants, "I will tell you what the Arameans have prepared against us. They know that we are starving; so they have left the camp to hide themselves in the open country, thinking, 'When they come out of the city, we shall take them alive and get into the city.'" ¹³ One of his servants said, "Let some men take five of the remaining horses, since those left here will suffer the fate of the whole multitude of Israel that have perished already;*ᵇ* let us send and find out." ¹⁴ So

they took two mounted men, and the king sent them after the Aramean army, saying, "Go and find out." ¹⁵ So they went after them as far as the Jordan; the whole way was littered with garments and equipment that the Arameans had thrown away in their haste. So the messengers returned, and told the king.

16 Then the people went out, and plundered the camp of the Arameans. So a measure of choice meal was sold for a shekel, and two measures of barley for a shekel, according to the word of the LORD. ¹⁷ Now the king had appointed the captain on whose hand he leaned to have charge of the gate; the people trampled him to death in the gate, just as the man of God had said when the king came down to him. ¹⁸ For when the man of God had said to the king, "Two measures of barley shall be sold for a shekel, and a measure of choice meal for a shekel, about this time tomorrow in the gate of Samaria," ¹⁹ the captain had answered the man of God, "Even if the LORD were to make windows in the sky, could such a thing happen?" And he had answered, "You shall see it with your own eyes, but you shall not eat from it." ²⁰ It did indeed happen to him; the people trampled him to death in the gate.

The Shunammite Woman's Land Restored

8 Now Elisha had said to the woman whose son he had restored to life, "Get up and go with your household, and settle wherever you can; for the LORD has called for a famine, and it will come on the land for seven years." ² So the woman got up and did according to the word of the man of God; she went

---

ᵃ A term for several skin diseases; precise meaning uncertain   *ᵇ* Compare Gk Syr Vg: Meaning of Heb uncertain

---

7:11–15—The Israelite king suspects a trap, but is rescued from this by a courtier.

7:16–20—See vv. 1–2. The narrator seems to want to drive home an obvious point.

8:1–6—In this sequel to 4:8–37, Elisha again

restores life to the Shunammite woman and her son by warning of famine and having their lands and income restored.

8:1–2—Apparently unrelated to the famine recounted in chap. 7, this is of limited extent.

with her household and settled in the land of the Philistines seven years. ³ At the end of the seven years, when the woman returned from the land of the Philistines, she set out to appeal to the king for her house and her land. ⁴ Now the king was talking with Gehazi the servant of the man of God, saying, "Tell me all the great things that Elisha has done." ⁵ While he was telling the king how Elisha had restored a dead person to life, the woman whose son he had restored to life appealed to the king for her house and her land. Gehazi said, "My lord king, here is the woman, and here is her son whom Elisha restored to life." ⁶ When the king questioned the woman, she told him. So the king appointed an official for her, saying, "Restore all that was hers, together with all the revenue of the fields from the day that she left the land until now."

Death of Ben-hadad

7 Elisha went to Damascus while King Ben-hadad of Aram was ill. When it was told him, "The man of God has come here," ⁸ the king said to Hazael, "Take a present with you and go to meet the man of God. Inquire of the LORD through him, whether I shall recover from this illness." ⁹ So Hazael went to meet him, taking a present with him, all kinds of goods of Damascus, forty camel loads. When he entered and stood before him, he said, "Your son King Ben-hadad of Aram has sent me to you, saying, 'Shall I recover from this illness?'" ¹⁰ Elisha said

to him, "Go, say to him, 'You shall certainly recover'; but the LORD has shown me that he shall certainly die." ¹¹ He fixed his gaze and stared at him, until he was ashamed. Then the man of God wept. ¹² Hazael asked, "Why does my lord weep?" He answered, "Because I know the evil that you will do to the people of Israel; you will set their fortresses on fire, you will kill their young men with the sword, dash in pieces their little ones, and rip up their pregnant women." ¹³ Hazael said, "What is your servant, who is a mere dog, that he should do this great thing?" Elisha answered, "The LORD has shown me that you are to be king over Aram." ¹⁴ Then he left Elisha, and went to his master Ben-hadad,ᵃ who said to him, "What did Elisha say to you?" And he answered, "He told me that you would certainly recover." ¹⁵ But the next day he took the bed-cover and dipped it in water and spread it over the king's face, until he died. And Hazael succeeded him.

Jehoram Reigns over Judah

16 In the fifth year of King Joram son of Ahab of Israel,ᵇ Jehoram son of King Jehoshaphat of Judah began to reign. ¹⁷ He was thirty-two years old when he became king, and he reigned eight years in Jerusalem. ¹⁸ He walked in the way of the kings of Israel, as the house of Ahab had done, for the daughter of Ahab was his wife. He did what was evil in the sight of the LORD. ¹⁹ Yet the LORD would

---

ᵃ Heb lacks Ben-hadad   ᵇ Gk Syr: Heb adds Jehoshaphat being king of Judah,

---

8:4—In contrast to 6:31, the king reveres Elisha. In spite of 5:20–27, Gehazi still serves the prophet.

8:5–6—Elisha's reputation and the woman's past connections with him gain her a favorable ruling.

8:7–15—Ben-hadad's illness provides occasion for Elisha to intervene in the political affairs of Damascus, recalling YHWH's charge to Elijah in 1 Kgs. 19:15. While not anointing Hazael, he indirectly suggests a coup.

8:8–9—Elisha is now as welcome in Damascus as he is in Samaria, as revered by the king of Aram as the king of Israel.

8:10—Elisha suggests Hazael lie to Ben-hadad.

8:12–15—Elisha seems to dread what Hazael will do, but also plants the suggestion that leads Hazael to murder and overthrow Ben-hadad.

8:16–17:41 Kings of Judah and Israel

8:16–29 The Judean Kings Jehoram and Ahaziah
Both kings, closely linked with the Israelite house of Omri and its Canaanite connections, are roundly condemned.

8:16–24—Jehoram's marriage to Ahab's daughter Athaliah may well have sealed the treaty Jehoshaphat made with Ahab to be his vassal.

8:19—Only YHWH's promise to David spared Judah at this time.

not destroy Judah, for the sake of his servant David, since he had promised to give a lamp to him and to his descendants forever.

20 In his days Edom revolted against the rule of Judah, and set up a king of their own. ²¹ Then Joram crossed over to Zair with all his chariots. He set out by night and attacked the Edomites and their chariot commanders who had surrounded him;^a but his army fled home. ²² So Edom has been in revolt against the rule of Judah to this day. Libnah also revolted at the same time. ²³ Now the rest of the acts of Joram, and all that he did, are they not written in the Book of the Annals of the Kings of Judah? ²⁴ So Joram slept with his ancestors, and was buried with them in the city of David; his son Ahaziah succeeded him.

Ahaziah Reigns over Judah

25 In the twelfth year of King Joram son of Ahab of Israel, Ahaziah son of King Jehoram of Judah began to reign. ²⁶ Ahaziah was twenty-two years old when he began to reign; he reigned one year in Jerusalem. His mother's name was Athaliah, a granddaughter of King Omri of Israel. ²⁷ He also walked in the way of the house of Ahab, doing what was evil in the sight of the LORD, as the house of Ahab had done, for he was son-in-law to the house of Ahab.

28 He went with Joram son of Ahab to wage war against King Hazael of Aram at Ramoth-gilead, where the Arameans wounded Joram. ²⁹ King Joram returned to be healed in Jezreel of the wounds that the Arameans had inflicted on him at Ramah, when he fought against King Hazael of Aram. King Ahaziah son of Jehoram of Judah went down to see Joram son of Ahab in Jezreel, because he was wounded.

Anointing of Jehu

9 Then the prophet Elisha called a member of the company of prophets^b and said to him, "Gird up your loins; take this flask of oil in your hand, and go to Ramoth-gilead. ² When you arrive, look there for Jehu son of Jehoshaphat, son of Nimshi; go in and get him to leave his companions, and take him into an inner chamber. ³ Then take the flask of oil, pour it on his head, and say, 'Thus says the LORD: I anoint you king over Israel.' Then open the door and flee; do not linger."

4 So the young man, the young prophet, went to Ramoth-gilead. ⁵ He arrived while the commanders of the army were in council, and he announced, "I have a message for you, commander." "For which one of us?" asked Jehu. "For you, commander." ⁶ So Jehu^c got up and went inside; the young man poured the oil on his head, saying to him, "Thus says the LORD the God of Israel: I anoint you king over the people of the LORD, over Israel. ⁷ You shall strike down the house of your master Ahab, so that I may avenge on Jezebel the blood of my servants the prophets, and the blood of all the servants of the LORD. ⁸ For the whole house of Ahab shall perish; I will

---

^a Meaning of Heb uncertain ^b Heb *sons of the prophets* ^c Heb *he*

8:23–24—See 1 Kgs. 14:19.

8:25–27—Ahaziah, son of **Athaliah**, and thus grandson of Ahab, rules one year and is condemned as under his mother's influence.

8:28–29—*Hazael of Aram* begins to afflict Israel as Elisha foretold (v. 12), the encounter at *Ramoth-gilead* preparing for the fall of the house of Ahab.

9:1–10:36 Jehu Becomes King of Israel

Elisha indirectly sparks the coup staged by *Jehu*, a thorough and violent annihilation of the house

of Ahab and the Baalism it supported. He earns the broad approval of the narrator in spite of his brutality and his rhetoric. Violence begets violence, and readers may find they do not fully share the values and perspectives of the narrator, as they question whether such means are justified by the ends attained.

9:1–13—Elisha, through a member of his prophetic following, fulfills YHWH's charge to Elijah in 1 Kgs. 19:15–17.

9:6–10—Elisha's emissary expands in brutal ways the terse words given him for Jehu.

cut off from Ahab every male, bond or free, in Israel. ⁹ I will make the house of Ahab like the house of Jeroboam son of Nebat, and like the house of Baasha son of Ahijah. ¹⁰ The dogs shall eat Jezebel in the territory of Jezreel, and no one shall bury her." Then he opened the door and fled.

11 When Jehu came back to his master's officers, they said to him, "Is everything all right? Why did that madman come to you?" He answered them, "You know the sort and how they babble." ¹² They said, "Liar! Come on, tell us!" So he said, "This is just what he said to me: 'Thus says the LORD, I anoint you king over Israel.'" ¹³ Then hurriedly they all took their cloaks and spread them for him on the bare*a* steps; and they blew the trumpet, and proclaimed, "Jehu is king."

Joram of Israel Killed

14 Thus Jehu son of Jehoshaphat son of Nimshi conspired against Joram. Joram with all Israel had been on guard at Ramoth-gilead against King Hazael of Aram; ¹⁵ but King Joram had returned to be healed in Jezreel of the wounds that the Arameans had inflicted on him, when he fought against King Hazael of Aram. So Jehu said, "If this is your wish, then let no one slip out of the city to go and tell the news in Jezreel." ¹⁶ Then Jehu mounted his chariot and went to Jezreel, where Joram was lying ill. King Ahaziah of Judah had come down to visit Joram.

17 In Jezreel, the sentinel standing on the tower spied the company of Jehu arriving, and said, "I see a company."

Joram said, "Take a horseman; send him to meet them, and let him say, 'Is it peace?'" ¹⁸ So the horseman went to meet him; he said, "Thus says the king, 'Is it peace?'" Jehu responded, "What have you to do with peace? Fall in behind me." The sentinel reported, saying, "The messenger reached them, but he is not coming back." ¹⁹ Then he sent out a second horseman, who came to them and said, "Thus says the king, 'Is it peace?'" Jehu answered, "What have you to do with peace? Fall in behind me." ²⁰ Again the sentinel reported, "He reached them, but he is not coming back. It looks like the driving of Jehu son of Nimshi; for he drives like a maniac."

21 Joram said, "Get ready." And they got his chariot ready. Then King Joram of Israel and King Ahaziah of Judah set out, each in his chariot, and went to meet Jehu; they met him at the property of Naboth the Jezreelite. ²² When Joram saw Jehu, he said, "Is it peace, Jehu?" He answered, "What peace can there be, so long as the many whoredoms and sorceries of your mother Jezebel continue?" ²³ Then Joram reined about and fled, saying to Ahaziah, "Treason, Ahaziah!" ²⁴ Jehu drew his bow with all his strength, and shot Joram between the shoulders, so that the arrow pierced his heart; and he sank in his chariot. ²⁵ Jehu said to his aide Bidkar, "Lift him out, and throw him on the plot of ground belonging to Naboth the Jezreelite; for remember, when you and I rode side by side behind his father Ahab how the

a Meaning of Heb uncertain

9:11–13—While initially dismissed as a *madman*, the young man's words when repeated by Jehu are strikingly effective.

9:14–37—Elisha plays no further role as Jehu executes a thoroughly bloody coup. Words of Elijah are taken up by Jehu and expanded as justification for his violence.

9:14–16—See 8:28–29.

9:17—Joram appears to suspect at worst a setback in the war with Aram, not the fate to befall him.

9:20—Jehu's *driving* is broadly emblematic of his style of action.

9:21—The meeting of Jehu and the kings of Israel and Judah on the property of Naboth (1 Kgs. 21, esp. v. 19) suggests a divine design shaping the course of history. However, a divine design may be apparent only to the narrator and reader, and not to those involved within the world created by the text.

9:25–26—See 1 Kgs 21:19–22.

LORD uttered this oracle against him: [26] 'For the blood of Naboth and for the blood of his children that I saw yesterday, says the LORD, I swear I will repay you on this very plot of ground.' Now therefore lift him out and throw him on the plot of ground, in accordance with the word of the LORD."

Ahaziah of Judah Killed

27 When King Ahaziah of Judah saw this, he fled in the direction of Beth-haggan. Jehu pursued him, saying, "Shoot him also!" And they shot him[a] in the chariot at the ascent to Gur, which is by Ibleam. Then he fled to Megiddo, and died there. [28] His officers carried him in a chariot to Jerusalem, and buried him in his tomb with his ancestors in the city of David.

29 In the eleventh year of Joram son of Ahab, Ahaziah began to reign over Judah.

Jezebel's Violent Death

30 When Jehu came to Jezreel, Jezebel heard of it; she painted her eyes, and adorned her head, and looked out of the window. [31] As Jehu entered the gate, she said, "Is it peace, Zimri, murderer of your master?" [32] He looked up to the window and said, "Who is on my side? Who?" Two or three eunuchs looked out at him. [33] He said, "Throw her down." So they threw her down; some of her blood spattered on the wall and on the horses, which trampled on her. [34] Then he went in and ate and drank; he said, "See to that cursed woman and bury her; for she is a king's daughter." [35] But when they went to bury her, they found no more of her than the skull and the feet and the palms of her hands. [36] When they came back and told him, he said, "This is the word of the LORD, which he spoke by his servant Elijah the Tishbite, 'In the territory of Jezreel the dogs shall eat the flesh of Jezebel; [37] the corpse of Jezebel shall be like dung on the field in the territory of Jezreel, so that no one can say, This is Jezebel.'"

Massacre of Ahab's Descendants

10 Now Ahab had seventy sons in Samaria. So Jehu wrote letters and sent them to Samaria, to the rulers of Jezreel,[b] to the elders, and to the guardians of the sons of[c] Ahab, saying, [2] "Since your master's sons are with you and you have at your disposal chariots and horses, a fortified city, and weapons, [3] select the son of your master who is the best qualified, set him on his father's throne, and fight for your master's house." [4] But they were utterly terrified and said, "Look, two kings could not withstand him; how then can we stand?" [5] So the steward of the palace, and the governor of the city, along with the elders and the guardians, sent word to Jehu: "We are your ser-

[a] Syr Vg Compare Gk: Heb lacks *and they shot him*   [b] Or *of the city;* Vg Compare Gk   [c] Gk: Heb lacks *of the sons of*

9:27–29—*Ahaziah of Judah* is caught up in Jehu's purge as a vassal of Joram and therefore likely to support his dynasty and religious practices. Verse 29 seems a correction of 8:25.

9:30–37—Finally Jezebel, the narrator's real villain, meets a grisly end.

9:30–31—Her presence and taunt comparing Jehu to the murderous and short-lived *Zimri* (1 Kgs. 16:8–14) show her defiant to the last.

9:32–37—Her death is brutally obscene in its graphic detail and in Jehu's elaboration on Elijah's words (cf. 1 Kgs. 21:23). Jehu eats and mocks while she is eaten. This royal Canaanite woman was clearly a threat to and despised by devout Yahwists. In their eyes idolatry receives its just reward!

10:1–27—Having eliminated the principals, Jehu now slaughters members of the royal family, their followers, and all drawn to worship Baal. YHWH's triumph over Baal seems complete.

10:1–11—New rulers have destroyed potential opponents before (2 Sam. 3–4; 1 Kgs. 2; 1 Kgs. 15:28–30; 16:8–14), but Jehu excels them all in sweep and violence.

10:1—Compare Gideon's seventy sons as possible kings in Judg. 9:5.

10:2–6—Jehu mocks the old ruling family and its supporters with barbs tinged with irony in a letter playing on two possible meaning of *head*.

vants; we will do anything you say. We will not make anyone king; do whatever you think right." **6** Then he wrote them a second letter, saying, "If you are on my side, and if you are ready to obey me, take the heads of your master's sons and come to me at Jezreel tomorrow at this time." Now the king's sons, seventy persons, were with the leaders of the city, who were charged with their upbringing. **7** When the letter reached them, they took the king's sons and killed them, seventy persons; they put their heads in baskets and sent them to him at Jezreel. **8** When the messenger came and told him, "They have brought the heads of the king's sons," he said, "Lay them in two heaps at the entrance of the gate until the morning." **9** Then in the morning when he went out, he stood and said to all the people, "You are innocent. It was I who conspired against my master and killed him; but who struck down all these? **10** Know then that there shall fall to the earth nothing of the word of the LORD, which the LORD spoke concerning the house of Ahab; for the LORD has done what he said through his servant Elijah." **11** So Jehu killed all who were left of the house of Ahab in Jezreel, all his leaders, close friends, and priests, until he left him no survivor.

12 Then he set out and went to Samaria. On the way, when he was at Beth-eked of the Shepherds, **13** Jehu met relatives of King Ahaziah of Judah and said, "Who are you?" They answered, "We are kin of Ahaziah; we have come down to visit the royal princes and the sons of the queen mother." **14** He said, "Take them alive." They took them alive,

and slaughtered them at the pit of Beth-eked, forty-two in all; he spared none of them.

15 When he left there, he met Jehonadab son of Rechab coming to meet him; he greeted him, and said to him, "Is your heart as true to mine as mine is to yours?"*a* Jehonadab answered, "It is." Jehu said,*b* "If it is, give me your hand." So he gave him his hand. Jehu took him up with him into the chariot. **16** He said, "Come with me, and see my zeal for the LORD." So he*c* had him ride in his chariot. **17** When he came to Samaria, he killed all who were left to Ahab in Samaria, until he had wiped them out, according to the word of the LORD that he spoke to Elijah.

Slaughter of Worshipers of Baal

18 Then Jehu assembled all the people and said to them, "Ahab offered Baal small service; but Jehu will offer much more. **19** Now therefore summon to me all the prophets of Baal, all his worshipers, and all his priests; let none be missing, for I have a great sacrifice to offer to Baal; whoever is missing shall not live." But Jehu was acting with cunning in order to destroy the worshipers of Baal. **20** Jehu decreed, "Sanctify a solemn assembly for Baal." So they proclaimed it. **21** Jehu sent word throughout all Israel; all the worshipers of Baal came, so that there was no one left who did not come. They entered the temple of Baal, until the temple of Baal was filled from wall to wall. **22** He said to the keeper of the wardrobe, "Bring

a Gk: Heb *Is it right with your heart, as my heart is with your heart?*
b Gk: Heb lacks *Jehu said* *c* Gk Syr Tg: Heb *they*

10:7—The leaders, fearing for their own heads, take his command literally.

10:9–11—Jehu's play on words may allow him to claim innocence in the slaughter of the seventy, but he is quick to read it as fulfilling Elijah's prophecy (1 Kgs. 21:21–24).

10:12–14—Again links between Ahaziah of Judah and the house of Ahab spell death.

10:15–17—*Jehonadab*, like all Rechabites, was

fanatically devoted to YHWH, a devotion that was expressed in fierce opposition to all giving allegiance to other deities and to all practices associated with the Canaanites (cf. the Nazirites in Num. 6:1–21). His alliance with Jehu is apt.

10:18–27—The followers of the cult of Baal established by Jezebel and Ahab are slaughtered/sacrificed to their own deity, as Jehu again plays on words in vv. 18–19 to lure them to destruction and their temple to an obscene fate.

out the vestments for all the worshipers of Baal." So he brought out the vestments for them. ²³ Then Jehu entered the temple of Baal with Jehonadab son of Rechab; he said to the worshipers of Baal, "Search and see that there is no worshiper of the LORD here among you, but only worshipers of Baal." ²⁴ Then they proceeded to offer sacrifices and burnt offerings.

Now Jehu had stationed eighty men outside, saying, "Whoever allows any of those to escape whom I deliver into your hands shall forfeit his life." ²⁵ As soon as he had finished presenting the burnt offering, Jehu said to the guards and to the officers, "Come in and kill them; let no one escape." So they put them to the sword. The guards and the officers threw them out, and then went into the citadel of the temple of Baal. ²⁶ They brought out the pillar*a* that was in the temple of Baal, and burned it. ²⁷ Then they demolished the pillar of Baal, and destroyed the temple of Baal, and made it a latrine to this day.

²⁸ Thus Jehu wiped out Baal from Israel. ²⁹ But Jehu did not turn aside from the sins of Jeroboam son of Nebat, which he caused Israel to commit—the golden calves that were in Bethel and in Dan. ³⁰ The LORD said to Jehu, "Because you have done well in carrying out what I consider right, and in accordance with all that was in my heart have dealt with the house of Ahab, your sons of the fourth generation shall sit on the throne of Israel." ³¹ But Jehu was not careful to follow the law of the LORD the God of Israel with all his heart; he did not turn

from the sins of Jeroboam, which he caused Israel to commit.

Death of Jehu

32 In those days the LORD began to trim off parts of Israel. Hazael defeated them throughout the territory of Israel: ³³ from the Jordan eastward, all the land of Gilead, the Gadites, the Reubenites, and the Manassites, from Aroer, which is by the Wadi Arnon, that is, Gilead and Bashan. ³⁴ Now the rest of the acts of Jehu, all that he did, and all his power, are they not written in the Book of the Annals of the Kings of Israel? ³⁵ So Jehu slept with his ancestors, and they buried him in Samaria. His son Jehoahaz succeeded him. ³⁶ The time that Jehu reigned over Israel in Samaria was twenty-eight years.

Athaliah Reigns over Judah

11 Now when Athaliah, Ahaziah's mother, saw that her son was dead, she set about to destroy all the royal family. ² But Jehosheba, King Joram's daughter, Ahaziah's sister, took Joash son of Ahaziah, and stole him away from among the king's children who were about to be killed; she put*b* him and his nurse in a bedroom. Thus she*c* hid him from Athaliah, so that he was not killed; ³ he remained with her six years, hidden in the house of the LORD, while Athaliah reigned over the land.

Jehoiada Anoints the Child Joash

4 But in the seventh year Jehoiada summoned the captains of the Carites and

a Gk Vg Syr Tg: Heb *pillars*   *b* With 2 Chr 22.11: Heb lacks *she put*
c Gk Syr Vg Compare 2 Chr 22.11: Heb *they*

10:28–31—The narrator's positive evaluation of Jehu is tempered, not by qualms over his thoroughgoing violence, but by his failure to undo the work of Jeroboam (1 Kgs. 12:26–32). Jehu might have viewed the cults and **golden calves** of **Bethel** and **Dan** as legitimate worship of YHWH (1 Kgs. 12:28). God grants him a dynasty of four generations (see 2 Kgs. 15:12).

10:32–36—As Elisha announced (8:12), Hazael took from Israel the land east of the Jordan.

11:1–21 Athaliah Rules Judah

11:1–3—Jehu's slaying of Ahaziah disrupts affairs in Jerusalem, but it does not immediately eliminate the house of Ahab or the Baalism it supports. Athaliah, daughter of Ahab and the queen mother, seizes control, slaughtering the royal family, including presumably her own blood. **Joash** (Jehoash in v. 21), whom **Jehosheba** hides in the temple, is her grandson.

11:4–20—The account of Athaliah's overthrow suggests little sustained support for her, making her seven years in control all the more striking.

of the guards and had them come to him in the house of the LORD. He made a covenant with them and put them under oath in the house of the LORD; then he showed them the king's son. ⁵ He commanded them, "This is what you are to do: one-third of you, those who go off duty on the sabbath and guard the king's house ⁶ (another third being at the gate Sur and a third at the gate behind the guards), shall guard the palace; ⁷ and your two divisions that come on duty in force on the sabbath and guard the house of the LORD*a* ⁸ shall surround the king, each with weapons in hand; and whoever approaches the ranks is to be killed. Be with the king in his comings and goings."

9 The captains did according to all that the priest Jehoiada commanded; each brought his men who were to go off duty on the sabbath, with those who were to come on duty on the sabbath, and came to the priest Jehoiada. ¹⁰ The priest delivered to the captains the spears and shields that had been King David's, which were in the house of the LORD; ¹¹ the guards stood, every man with his weapons in his hand, from the south side of the house to the north side of the house, around the altar and the house, to guard the king on every side. ¹² Then he brought out the king's son, put the crown on him, and gave him the covenant;*b* they proclaimed him king, and anointed him; they clapped their hands and shouted, "Long live the king!"

Death of Athaliah

13 When Athaliah heard the noise of the guard and of the people, she went into the house of the LORD to the people; ¹⁴ when she looked, there was the king standing by the pillar, according to custom, with the captains and the trumpeters beside the king, and all the people of the land rejoicing and blowing trumpets. Athaliah tore her clothes and cried, "Treason! Treason!" ¹⁵ Then the priest Jehoiada commanded the captains who were set over the army, "Bring her out between the ranks, and kill with the sword anyone who follows her." For the priest said, "Let her not be killed in the house of the LORD." ¹⁶ So they laid hands on her; she went through the horses' entrance to the king's house, and there she was put to death.

17 Jehoiada made a covenant between the LORD and the king and people, that they should be the LORD's people; also between the king and the people. ¹⁸ Then all the people of the land went to the house of Baal, and tore it down; his altars and his images they broke in pieces, and they killed Mattan, the priest of Baal, before the altars. The priest posted guards over the house of the LORD. ¹⁹ He took the captains, the Carites, the guards, and all the people of the land; then they brought the king down from the house of the LORD, marching through the gate of the guards to the king's house. He took his seat on the throne of the kings. ²⁰ So all the people of the land rejoiced; and the city was quiet after Athaliah had been killed with the sword at the king's house.

21*c* Jehoash*d* was seven years old when he began to reign.

a Heb *the* LORD *to the king*   *b* Or *treaty* or *testimony;* Heb *eduth*   *c* Ch 12.1 in Heb   *d* Another spelling is *Joash;* see verse 19

11:4—*Jehoiada*, who leads the restoration, is said in 2 Chr. 22:11 to be Jehosheba's husband. The *Carites* are professional guards of the palace and temple; their support is key to the restoration of a Davidic king.

11:5–11—The coronation of the young son of King Ahaziah is carefully staged, even though some details are unclear.

11:13–14—From an inside view of the coronation

we move outside to Athaliah's experience. *The people of the land* seem to be landholders with power they use repeatedly to support Davidic succession (21:24; 23:30).

11:17–20—Jehoiada acts as covenant mediator, restoring relationships between YHWH, king, and people.

11:21—*Jehoash*'s age suggests that control lay with people like Jehoiada.

The Temple Repaired

12 In the seventh year of Jehu, Jehoash began to reign; he reigned forty years in Jerusalem. His mother's name was Zibiah of Beer-sheba. [2] Jehoash did what was right in the sight of the LORD all his days, because the priest Jehoiada instructed him. [3] Nevertheless the high places were not taken away; the people continued to sacrifice and make offerings on the high places.

[4] Jehoash said to the priests, "All the money offered as sacred donations that is brought into the house of the LORD, the money for which each person is assessed—the money from the assessment of persons—and the money from the voluntary offerings brought into the house of the LORD, [5] let the priests receive from each of the donors; and let them repair the house wherever any need of repairs is discovered." [6] But by the twenty-third year of King Jehoash the priests had made no repairs on the house. [7] Therefore King Jehoash summoned the priest Jehoiada with the other priests and said to them, "Why are you not repairing the house? Now therefore do not accept any more money from your donors but hand it over for the repair of the house." [8] So the priests agreed that they would neither accept more money from the people nor repair the house.

[9] Then the priest Jehoiada took a chest, made a hole in its lid, and set it beside the altar on the right side as one entered the house of the LORD; the priests who guarded the threshold put in it all the money that was brought into the house of the LORD. [10] Whenever they saw that there was a great deal of money in the chest, the king's secretary and the high priest went up, counted the money that was found in the house of the LORD, and tied it up in bags. [11] They would give the money that was weighed out into the hands of the workers who had the oversight of the house of the LORD; then they paid it out to the carpenters and the builders who worked on the house of the LORD, [12] to the masons and the stonecutters, as well as to buy timber and quarried stone for making repairs on the house of the LORD, as well as for any outlay for repairs of the house. [13] But for the house of the LORD no basins of silver, snuffers, bowls, trumpets, or any vessels of gold, or of silver, were made from the money that was brought into the house of the LORD, [14] for that was given to the workers who were repairing the house of the LORD with it. [15] They did not ask an accounting from those into whose hand they delivered the money to pay out to the workers, for they dealt honestly. [16] The money from the guilt offerings and the money from the sin offerings was not brought into the house of the LORD; it belonged to the priests.

Hazael Threatens Jerusalem

[17] At that time King Hazael of Aram went up, fought against Gath, and took it. But when Hazael set his face to go up against Jerusalem, [18] King Jehoash of Judah took all the votive gifts that Jehoshaphat, Jehoram, and Ahaziah, his ancestors, the kings of Judah, had dedi-

---

12:1–21 Jehoash and Temple Repairs
The length of Jehoash's rule and general approval of him stand in tension with the account of struggles to repair the temple and then the use of its wealth to buy off Hazael of Aram.

12:1–3—In spite of priestly instruction and broad approval of him, Jehoash, like Davidic kings before him (1 Kgs. 3:2 14:29), did not remove *the high places*.

12:4–8—Jehoash's plan for temple *repair* appar-

ently met with priestly inertia, resulting in a plan that essentially removed priests from sole control of the process.

12:9–16—The new arrangement offers clear lines of authority and specifically defined tasks. The priests still receive proceeds from *guilt and sin offerings* as their due.

12:17–18—Hazael is bought off by giving him *votive gifts* that earlier kings gave the temple as signs of devotion, along with the gold in YHWH's and the king's houses.

cated, as well as his own votive gifts, all the gold that was found in the treasuries of the house of the LORD and of the king's house, and sent these to King Hazael of Aram. Then Hazael withdrew from Jerusalem.

Death of Joash

19 Now the rest of the acts of Joash, and all that he did, are they not written in the Book of the Annals of the Kings of Judah? 20 His servants arose, devised a conspiracy, and killed Joash in the house of Millo, on the way that goes down to Silla. 21 It was Jozacar son of Shimeath and Jehozabad son of Shomer, his servants, who struck him down, so that he died. He was buried with his ancestors in the city of David; then his son Amaziah succeeded him.

Jehoahaz Reigns over Israel

13 In the twenty-third year of King Joash son of Ahaziah of Judah, Jehoahaz son of Jehu began to reign over Israel in Samaria; he reigned seventeen years. 2 He did what was evil in the sight of the LORD, and followed the sins of Jeroboam son of Nebat, which he caused Israel to sin; he did not depart from them. 3 The anger of the LORD was kindled against Israel, so that he gave them repeatedly into the hand of King Hazael of Aram, then into the hand of Ben-hadad son of Hazael. 4 But Jehoahaz entreated the LORD, and the LORD heeded him; for he saw the oppression of Israel, how the king of Aram oppressed them. 5 Therefore the LORD gave Israel a savior, so that they escaped from the hand of the Arameans; and the people of Israel lived in their homes as formerly. 6 Nevertheless they did not depart from the sins of the house of Jeroboam, which he caused Israel to sin, but walked[a] in them; the sacred pole[b] also remained in Samaria. 7 So Jehoahaz was left with an army of not more than fifty horsemen, ten chariots and ten thousand footmen; for the king of Aram had destroyed them and made them like the dust at threshing. 8 Now the rest of the acts of Jehoahaz and all that he did, including his might, are they not written in the Book of the Annals of the Kings of Israel? 9 So Jehoahaz slept with his ancestors, and they buried him in Samaria; then his son Joash succeeded him.

Jehoash Reigns over Israel

10 In the thirty-seventh year of King Joash of Judah, Jehoash son of Jehoahaz began to reign over Israel in Samaria; he reigned sixteen years. 11 He also did what was evil in the sight of the LORD; he did not depart from all the sins of Jeroboam son of Nebat, which he caused Israel to sin, but he walked in them. 12 Now the rest of the acts of Joash, and all that he did, as well as the might with which he fought against King Amaziah of Judah, are they not written in the Book of the Annals of the Kings of Israel? 13 So Joash slept with his ancestors, and Jeroboam sat upon his throne; Joash was buried in Samaria with the kings of Israel.

Death of Elisha

14 Now when Elisha had fallen sick with the illness of which he was to die,

[a] Gk Syr Tg Vg: Heb *he walked* [b] Heb *Asherah*

12:19–21—No motive is stated for the assassination of Joash (Jehoash). One wonders if it was related to his dealings with Hazael (cf. 2 Chr. 24:23–27).

13:1–16:20 Kings over Israel and Judah

13:1–9—The brief account of the reign of Jehoahaz of Israel echoes Judges, especially the notice that Israel's sin (v. 2) caused YHWH's anger (v. 3a) and punishment through affliction by a foreign ruler (v. 3b), the notice of *a savior* (unnamed in v. 5) when the afflicted seek relief (v. 4), and the renewed sin of Israel (v. 6). The result is a severe reduction of Israelite power.

13:10–13—*Jehoash* (Joash) of Israel, distinct from Jehoash (Joash) of Judah, is summarily noted and negatively evaluated.

13:14–21—Yet Joash appears genuinely distraught when confronted by Elisha's final illness after more than fifty years as a prophet (see 1 Kgs. 19:19–21). Joash's cry recalls Elisha's when Elijah vanished in the whirlwind (2 Kgs. 2:12).

King Joash of Israel went down to him, and wept before him, crying, "My father, my father! The chariots of Israel and its horsemen!" 15 Elisha said to him, "Take a bow and arrows"; so he took a bow and arrows. 16 Then he said to the king of Israel, "Draw the bow"; and he drew it. Elisha laid his hands on the king's hands. 17 Then he said, "Open the window eastward"; and he opened it. Elisha said, "Shoot"; and he shot. Then he said, "The LORD's arrow of victory, the arrow of victory over Aram! For you shall fight the Arameans in Aphek until you have made an end of them." 18 He continued, "Take the arrows"; and he took them. He said to the king of Israel, "Strike the ground with them"; he struck three times, and stopped. 19 Then the man of God was angry with him, and said, "You should have struck five or six times; then you would have struck down Aram until you had made an end of it, but now you will strike down Aram only three times."

20 So Elisha died, and they buried him. Now bands of Moabites used to invade the land in the spring of the year. 21 As a man was being buried, a marauding band was seen and the man was thrown into the grave of Elisha; as soon as the man touched the bones of Elisha, he came to life and stood on his feet.

Israel Recaptures Cities from Aram

22 Now King Hazael of Aram oppressed Israel all the days of Jehoahaz. 23 But the LORD was gracious to them and had compassion on them; he turned toward them, because of his covenant with Abraham, Isaac, and Jacob, and would not destroy them; nor has he banished them from his presence until now.

24 When King Hazael of Aram died, his son Ben-hadad succeeded him. 25 Then Jehoash son of Jehoahaz took again from Ben-hadad son of Hazael the towns that he had taken from his father Jehoahaz in war. Three times Joash defeated him and recovered the towns of Israel.

Amaziah Reigns over Judah

14 In the second year of King Joash son of Joahaz of Israel, King Amaziah son of Joash of Judah, began to reign. 2 He was twenty-five years old when he began to reign, and he reigned twenty-nine years in Jerusalem. His mother's name was Jehoaddin of Jerusalem. 3 He did what was right in the sight of the LORD, yet not like his ancestor David; in all things he did as his father Joash had done. 4 But the high places were not removed; the people still sacrificed and made offerings on the high places. 5 As soon as the royal power was firmly in his hand he killed his servants who had murdered his father the king. 6 But he did not put to death the children of the murderers; according to what is written in the book of the law of Moses, where the LORD commanded, "The parents shall not be put to death for the children, or the children be put to death for the parents; but all shall be put to death for their own sins."

7 He killed ten thousand Edomites in the Valley of Salt and took Sela by storm; he called it Jokthe-el, which is its name to this day.

13:15–19—Elisha's final act serves Israel against Aram, but in his eyes even this descendant of Jehu falls short in his execution of the symbolic action the prophet demands.

13:20–21—Even dead, Elisha can restore life when touched (see 4:32–35).

13:22–25—Elisha's words come true when Jehoash defeats Ben-hadad, son of Hazael, three times. This is attributed to YHWH's covenant with the patriarchs in Genesis. The effect is to place Elisha in a long line of deliverers, often unexpected and sometimes troubling bearers of YHWH's authority.

14:1–22—Amaziah receives a basically positive evaluation, yet the specifics for his reign move from military success against Edom to disaster when he challenges Israel. The temple and royal establishment again suffer severe losses.

14:5—See 12:19–21.

14:6—See Deut. 24:16. This is one of the rare quotations from a book of law.

8 Then Amaziah sent messengers to King Jehoash son of Jehoahaz, son of Jehu, of Israel, saying, "Come, let us look one another in the face." ⁹ King Jehoash of Israel sent word to King Amaziah of Judah, "A thornbush on Lebanon sent to a cedar on Lebanon, saying, 'Give your daughter to my son for a wife'; but a wild animal of Lebanon passed by and trampled down the thornbush. ¹⁰ You have indeed defeated Edom, and your heart has lifted you up. Be content with your glory, and stay at home; for why should you provoke trouble so that you fall, you and Judah with you?"

11 But Amaziah would not listen. So King Jehoash of Israel went up; he and King Amaziah of Judah faced one another in battle at Beth-shemesh, which belongs to Judah. ¹² Judah was defeated by Israel; everyone fled home. ¹³ King Jehoash of Israel captured King Amaziah of Judah son of Jehoash, son of Ahaziah, at Beth-shemesh; he came to Jerusalem, and broke down the wall of Jerusalem from the Ephraim Gate to the Corner Gate, a distance of four hundred cubits. ¹⁴ He seized all the gold and silver, and all the vessels that were found in the house of the LORD and in the treasuries of the king's house, as well as hostages; then he returned to Samaria.

15 Now the rest of the acts that Jehoash did, his might, and how he fought with King Amaziah of Judah, are they not written in the Book of the Annals of the Kings of Israel? ¹⁶ Jehoash slept with his ancestors, and was buried in Samaria with the kings of Israel; then his son Jeroboam succeeded him.

17 King Amaziah son of Joash of Judah lived fifteen years after the death of King Jehoash son of Jehoahaz of Israel. ¹⁸ Now the rest of the deeds of Amaziah, are they not written in the Book of the Annals of the Kings of Judah? ¹⁹ They made a conspiracy against him in Jerusalem, and he fled to Lachish. But they sent after him to Lachish, and killed him there. ²⁰ They brought him on horses; he was buried in Jerusalem with his ancestors in the city of David. ²¹ All the people of Judah took Azariah, who was sixteen years old, and made him king to succeed his father Amaziah. ²² He rebuilt Elath and restored it to Judah, after King Amaziah*a* slept with his ancestors.

Jeroboam II Reigns over Israel

23 In the fifteenth year of King Amaziah son of Joash of Judah, King Jeroboam son of Joash of Israel began to reign in Samaria; he reigned forty-one years. ²⁴ He did what was evil in the sight of the LORD; he did not depart from all the sins of Jeroboam son of Nebat, which he caused Israel to sin. ²⁵ He restored the border of Israel from Lebo-hamath as far as the Sea of the Arabah, according to the word of the LORD, the God of Israel, which he spoke by his servant Jonah son of Amittai, the prophet, who was from Gath-hepher. ²⁶ For the LORD saw that the distress of Israel was very bitter; there was no one left, bond

a Heb *the king*

14:8–10—Jehoash of Israel reads Amaziah's call for a meeting as hostile, a challenge to the vassal relationship Israel had over Judah. Jehoash responds with a fable (cf. Jotham in Judg. 9:7–15) in which a boastful but worthless *thornbush* is put in its place in relation to the majestic and valued *cedar*.

14:11–14—Amaziah ignores the warning, suffers a defeat, and is humiliated.

14:15–16—A repeat of 13:12–13.

14:17–22—Amaziah, like his father, is assassinated. Again no motive is given, but the defeat just recounted would provide cause. **The people of Judah** ensure his son Azariah succeeds him.

14:23–29—The forty-one-year reign of Jeroboam II receives the standard negative evaluation given Israelite kings, comparing him to his namesake, and his reign receives brief notice. Yet what is noted is strikingly positive, suggesting he restored Israel to its Solomonic dimensions, in fulfillment of the word of a prophet Jonah (otherwise known through the book of Jonah), who notes YHWH's remarkable mercy for those who broke from Davidic rule. Relationships with Damascus are reversed.

or free, and no one to help Israel. ²⁷ But the LORD had not said that he would blot out the name of Israel from under heaven, so he saved them by the hand of Jeroboam son of Joash.

28 Now the rest of the acts of Jeroboam, and all that he did, and his might, how he fought, and how he recovered for Israel Damascus and Hamath, which had belonged to Judah, are they not written in the Book of the Annals of the Kings of Israel? ²⁹ Jeroboam slept with his ancestors, the kings of Israel; his son Zechariah succeeded him.

Azariah Reigns over Judah

15 In the twenty-seventh year of King Jeroboam of Israel King Azariah son of Amaziah of Judah began to reign. ² He was sixteen years old when he began to reign, and he reigned fifty-two years in Jerusalem. His mother's name was Jecoliah of Jerusalem. ³ He did what was right in the sight of the LORD, just as his father Amaziah had done. ⁴ Nevertheless the high places were not taken away; the people still sacrificed and made offerings on the high places. ⁵ The LORD struck the king, so that he was leprous*a* to the day of his death, and lived in a separate house. Jotham the king's son was in charge of the palace, governing the people of the land. ⁶ Now the rest of the acts of Azariah, and all that he did, are they not written in the Book of the Annals of the Kings of Judah? ⁷ Azariah slept with his ancestors; they buried him with his ancestors in the city of David; his son Jotham succeeded him.

Zechariah Reigns over Israel

8 In the thirty-eighth year of King Azariah of Judah, Zechariah son of Jeroboam reigned over Israel in Samaria six months. ⁹ He did what was evil in the sight of the LORD, as his ancestors had done. He did not depart from the sins of Jeroboam son of Nebat, which he caused Israel to sin. ¹⁰ Shallum son of Jabesh conspired against him, and struck him down in public and killed him, and reigned in place of him. ¹¹ Now the rest of the deeds of Zechariah are written in the Book of the Annals of the Kings of Israel. ¹² This was the promise of the LORD that he gave to Jehu, "Your sons shall sit on the throne of Israel to the fourth generation." And so it happened.

Shallum Reigns over Israel

13 Shallum son of Jabesh began to reign in the thirty-ninth year of King Uzziah of Judah; he reigned one month in Samaria. ¹⁴ Then Menahem son of Gadi came up from Tirzah and came to Samaria; he struck down Shallum son of Jabesh in Samaria and killed him; he reigned in place of him. ¹⁵ Now the rest of the deeds of Shallum, including the conspiracy that he made, are written in the Book of the Annals of the Kings of Israel. ¹⁶ At that time Menahem sacked Tiphsah, all who were in it and its territory from Tirzah on; because they did not open it to him, he sacked it. He ripped open all the pregnant women in it.

a A term for several skin diseases; precise meaning uncertain

---

15:1–31—If Israel's fortunes reach a new high point under the second Jeroboam, his death marks the end. A series of assassinations, coups, and dynastic changes bring Israel under the control of the Assyrians of Mesopotamia as they move to shape an empire stretching across the Near East.

15:1–7—*Amaziah* (also called *Uzziah*) ruled Judah for fifty-two years, but other than the qualified positive evaluation of him, we are told only of his skin disease (see 5:1) and that his son

Jotham ruled with him for an extended period. Amaziah's long reign essentially serves as backdrop for successive kings of Israel.

15:8–12—*Zechariah* reigns but *six months* before he is assassinated. His brief reign gave the house of Jehu its four generations promised by God (10:30).

15:13–16—*Shallum*'s one-month reign does not even merit evaluation. *Menahem* killed him and took his place and is noted for a barbarity in warfare that is usually attributed to foreigners (8:12; Hos. 13:16; Amos 1:13).

Menahem Reigns over Israel

17 In the thirty-ninth year of King Azariah of Judah, Menahem son of Gadi began to reign over Israel; he reigned ten years in Samaria. 18 He did what was evil in the sight of the LORD; he did not depart all his days from any of the sins of Jeroboam son of Nebat, which he caused Israel to sin. 19 King Pul of Assyria came against the land; Menahem gave Pul a thousand talents of silver, so that he might help him confirm his hold on the royal power. 20 Menahem exacted the money from Israel, that is, from all the wealthy, fifty shekels of silver from each one, to give to the king of Assyria. So the king of Assyria turned back, and did not stay there in the land. 21 Now the rest of the deeds of Menahem, and all that he did, are they not written in the Book of the Annals of the Kings of Israel? 22 Menahem slept with his ancestors, and his son Pekahiah succeeded him.

Pekahiah Reigns over Israel

23 In the fiftieth year of King Azariah of Judah, Pekahiah son of Menahem began to reign over Israel in Samaria; he reigned two years. 24 He did what was evil in the sight of the LORD; he did not turn away from the sins of Jeroboam son of Nebat, which he caused Israel to sin. 25 Pekah son of Remaliah, his captain, conspired against him with fifty of the Gileadites, and attacked him in Samaria, in the citadel of the palace along with Argob and Arieh; he killed him, and reigned in place of him. 26 Now the rest of the deeds of Pekahiah, and all that he did, are written in the Book of the Annals of the Kings of Israel.

Pekah Reigns over Israel

27 In the fifty-second year of King Azariah of Judah, Pekah son of Remaliah began to reign over Israel in Samaria; he reigned twenty years. 28 He did what was evil in the sight of the LORD; he did not depart from the sins of Jeroboam son of Nebat, which he caused Israel to sin. 29 In the days of King Pekah of Israel, King Tiglath-pileser of Assyria came and captured Ijon, Abel-beth-maacah, Janoah, Kedesh, Hazor, Gilead, and Galilee, all the land of Naphtali; and he carried the people captive to Assyria. 30 Then Hoshea son of Elah made a conspiracy against Pekah son of Remaliah, attacked him, and killed him; he reigned in place of him, in the twentieth year of Jotham son of Uzziah. 31 Now the rest of the acts of Pekah, and all that he did, are written in the Book of the Annals of the Kings of Israel.

Jotham Reigns over Judah

32 In the second year of King Pekah son of Remaliah of Israel, King Jotham son of Uzziah of Judah began to reign. 33 He was twenty-five years old when he began to reign and reigned sixteen years in Jerusalem. His mother's name was Jerusha daughter of Zadok. 34 He did what was right in the sight of the LORD, just as his father Uzziah had done. 35 Nevertheless the high places were not removed; the people still sacrificed and made offerings on the high places. He built the upper gate of the house of the LORD. 36 Now the rest of the acts of Jotham, and all that he did, are they not written in the Book of the Annals of the Kings of Judah? 37 In those days the LORD began to send King Rezin of Aram and Pekah son of Remaliah against Judah.

15:17–22—For all his brutality, Menahem becomes vassal to the Assyrian *King Pul* (Tiglath-pileser III, 745–727 BCE), raising the money to buy his throne and stop Assyrian advances through a severe tax on *the wealthy* in Israel.

15:23–26—Menaham dies of natural causes, but his son *Pekahiah* is assassinated after a *two-year* reign.

15:27–31—*Pekah's twenty years* seem unduly long and received the standard negative evaluation. *Tiglath-pileser of Assyria* strips Israel of much northern and eastern territory. Pekah's assassination by *Hoshea* is the last of a series of coups.

15:32–38—The chapter ends as it began, with notice of a Judean king, *Jotham* (see v. 5), who receives qualified praise.

38 Jotham slept with his ancestors, and was buried with his ancestors in the city of David, his ancestor; his son Ahaz succeeded him.

Ahaz Reigns over Judah

16 In the seventeenth year of Pekah son of Remaliah, King Ahaz son of Jotham of Judah began to reign. 2 Ahaz was twenty years old when he began to reign; he reigned sixteen years in Jerusalem. He did not do what was right in the sight of the LORD his God, as his ancestor David had done, 3 but he walked in the way of the kings of Israel. He even made his son pass through fire, according to the abominable practices of the nations whom the LORD drove out before the people of Israel. 4 He sacrificed and made offerings on the high places, on the hills, and under every green tree.

5 Then King Rezin of Aram and King Pekah son of Remaliah of Israel came up to wage war on Jerusalem; they besieged Ahaz but could not conquer him. 6 At that time the king of Edom[a] recovered Elath for Edom,[b] and drove the Judeans from Elath; and the Edomites came to Elath, where they live to this day. 7 Ahaz sent messengers to King Tiglath-pileser of Assyria, saying, "I am your servant and your son. Come up, and rescue me from the hand of the king of Aram and from the hand of the king of Israel, who are attacking me." 8 Ahaz also took the silver and gold found in the house of the LORD and in the treasures of the king's house, and sent a present to the king of Assyria. 9 The king of Assyria listened to him; the king of Assyria marched up against Damascus, and took it, carrying its people captive to Kir; then he killed Rezin.

10 When King Ahaz went to Damascus to meet King Tiglath-pileser of Assyria, he saw the altar that was at Damascus. King Ahaz sent to the priest Uriah a model of the altar, and its pattern, exact in all its details. 11 The priest Uriah built the altar; in accordance with all that King Ahaz had sent from Damascus, just so did the priest Uriah build it, before King Ahaz arrived from Damascus. 12 When the king came from Damascus, the king viewed the altar. Then the king drew near to the altar, went up on it, 13 and offered his burnt offering and his grain offering, poured his drink offering, and dashed the blood of his offerings of well-being against the altar. 14 The bronze altar that was before the LORD he removed from the front of the house, from the place between his altar and the house of the LORD, and put it on the north side of his altar. 15 King Ahaz commanded the priest Uriah, saying, "Upon the great altar offer the morning burnt offering, and the evening grain offering, and the king's burnt offering, and his grain offering, with the burnt offering of all the people of the land, their grain offering, and their drink offering; then dash against it all the blood of the burnt offering, and all the blood of the sacrifice; but the bronze altar shall be for me to inquire by." 16 The priest Uriah did everything that King Ahaz commanded.

17 Then King Ahaz cut off the frames

a Cn: Heb King Rezin of Aram   b Cn: Heb Aram

16:1–14—*Ahaz* is one of few Davidic kings to receive a negative evaluation for cultic practices linked with Canaanites, including a form of child sacrifice (Deut. 18:9–14) and worship of forces for fertility. He is the first since Solomon to be linked with **high places** (1 Kgs. 2:3).

16:5–9—Ahaz became a vassal of Assyria. *Rezin* of Aram and Pekah of Israel sought to overthrow Ahaz, forcing Judah to join their pact to resist Assyria (see Isa. 7). Ahaz offered tribute to As-syria and sought their help. Assyria devastated Damascus and according to 15:29 stripped Israel of significant territory.

16:10–16—What attracted Ahaz to **the altar** in **Damascus** is not clear. His personal dedication of it recalls Solomon's dedication of the altar in his newly built temple (1 Kgs. 8:64) and Jeroboam's dedications in Dan and Bethel (1 Kgs. 12:32).

16:17–20—Ahaz's looting of the temple of central

of the stands, and removed the laver from them; he removed the sea from the bronze oxen that were under it, and put it on a pediment of stone. [18] The covered portal for use on the sabbath that had been built inside the palace, and the outer entrance for the king he removed from[a] the house of the LORD. He did this because of the king of Assyria. [19] Now the rest of the acts of Ahaz that he did, are they not written in the Book of the Annals of the Kings of Judah? [20] Ahaz slept with his ancestors, and was buried with his ancestors in the city of David; his son Hezekiah succeeded him.

Hoshea Reigns over Israel

17 In the twelfth year of King Ahaz of Judah, Hoshea son of Elah began to reign in Samaria over Israel; he reigned nine years. [2] He did what was evil in the sight of the LORD, yet not like the kings of Israel who were before him. [3] King Shalmaneser of Assyria came up against him; Hoshea became his vassal, and paid him tribute. [4] But the king of Assyria found treachery in Hoshea; for he had sent messengers to King So of Egypt, and offered no tribute to the king of Assyria, as he had done year by year; therefore the king of Assyria confined him and imprisoned him.

Israel Carried Captive to Assyria

5 Then the king of Assyria invaded all the land and came to Samaria; for three years he besieged it. [6] In the ninth year of Hoshea the king of Assyria captured Samaria; he carried the Israelites away to Assyria. He placed them in Halah, on the Habor, the river of Gozan, and in the cities of the Medes.

7 This occurred because the people of Israel had sinned against the LORD their God, who had brought them up out of the land of Egypt from under the hand of Pharaoh king of Egypt. They had worshiped other gods [8] and walked in the customs of the nations whom the LORD drove out before the people of Israel, and in the customs that the kings of Israel had introduced.[b] [9] The people of Israel secretly did things that were not right against the LORD their God. They built for themselves high places at all their towns, from watchtower to fortified city; [10] they set up for themselves pillars and sacred poles[c] on every high hill and under every green tree; [11] there they made offerings on all the high places, as the nations did whom the LORD carried away before them. They did wicked things, provoking the LORD

[a] Cn: Heb lacks *from*   [b] Meaning of Heb uncertain   [c] Heb *Asherim*

---

objects recalls Solomon's construction and dedication of these objects.

17:1–41 The Fall of Israel to Assyria

17:1–6—The end is briefly told. *Hoshea*, the last king, became a vassal of the Assyrian Shalmaneser (727–722 BCE), but seems to switch allegiance to Egypt (*King So* is not otherwise known). Assyria reacted, and after a three-year siege Samaria fell (in 722/721 BCE, to Sargon II, Shalmaneser's successor). As was Assyrian policy, Israelites were transplanted to locations in Mesopotamia.

17:2—Hoshea, Israel's last king, is judged with remarkable leniency and is not linked in the formula of walking in the ways of Jeroboam, Israel's first king.

17:7–23—The terse notice of the fall of Israel sets off a more extensive theological statement of why Israel fell and why YHWH was justified in causing it. To this point in 1–2 Kings, the kings of the northern state have been heavily criticized, but now the sins of the people themselves

are accented as the reason for destruction. The theological basis for this justification is rooted in Deuteronomy. Specific sins mentioned deal with practices prohibited in that book, and Deuteronomy defined a conditional covenant shaping the relationship between YHWH and Israel. Within this covenant YHWH supports and sustains the people only as they observe the stated stipulations. Should they fail to do so, YHWH may warn them through prophets, but if they do not heed the prophets, God will withdraw support and in time even destroy them as a nation. No nation state may assume that it stands under God's unconditional support regardless of its actions and allegiances.

17:7—Worship of other gods is the fundamental betrayal of YHWH and YHWH's covenant (Deut. 6:4–15; 7:1–6).

17:8–18—The several practices decried are said to result from Israel aping the Canaanite nations they were to displace.

to anger; [12] they served idols, of which the LORD had said to them, "You shall not do this." [13] Yet the LORD warned Israel and Judah by every prophet and every seer, saying, "Turn from your evil ways and keep my commandments and my statutes, in accordance with all the law that I commanded your ancestors and that I sent to you by my servants the prophets." [14] They would not listen but were stubborn, as their ancestors had been, who did not believe in the LORD their God. [15] They despised his statutes, and his covenant that he made with their ancestors, and the warnings that he gave them. They went after false idols and became false; they followed the nations that were around them, concerning whom the LORD had commanded them that they should not do as they did. [16] They rejected all the commandments of the LORD their God and made for themselves cast images of two calves; they made a sacred pole,[a] worshiped all the host of heaven, and served Baal. [17] They made their sons and their daughters pass through fire; they used divination and augury; and they sold themselves to do evil in the sight of the LORD, provoking him to anger. [18] Therefore the LORD was very angry with Israel and removed them out of his sight; none was left but the tribe of Judah alone.

19 Judah also did not keep the commandments of the LORD their God but walked in the customs that Israel had introduced. [20] The LORD rejected all the descendants of Israel; he punished them and gave them into the hand of plunder-

ers, until he had banished them from his presence.

21 When he had torn Israel from the house of David, they made Jeroboam son of Nebat king. Jeroboam drove Israel from following the LORD and made them commit great sin. [22] The people of Israel continued in all the sins that Jeroboam committed; they did not depart from them [23] until the LORD removed Israel out of his sight, as he had foretold through all his servants the prophets. So Israel was exiled from their own land to Assyria until this day.

Assyria Resettles Samaria

24 The king of Assyria brought people from Babylon, Cuthah, Avva, Hamath, and Sepharvaim, and placed them in the cities of Samaria in place of the people of Israel; they took possession of Samaria, and settled in its cities. [25] When they first settled there, they did not worship the LORD; therefore the LORD sent lions among them, which killed some of them. [26] So the king of Assyria was told, "The nations that you have carried away and placed in the cities of Samaria do not know the law of the god of the land; therefore he has sent lions among them; they are killing them, because they do not know the law of the god of the land." [27] Then the king of Assyria commanded, "Send there one of the priests whom you carried away from there; let him[b] go and live there, and teach them the law of the god of the land." [28] So one of the priests whom they had carried away from Samaria came and lived in Bethel;

[a] Heb Asherah [b] Syr Vg: Heb them

17:18–20—Judah was spared at this time, but was no better than Israel. Thus the narrator suggests it too is rejected by YHWH, reflecting an exilic perspective following the destruction of Judah and Jerusalem.

17:21–23—Only now is Jeroboam noted.

17:24–41—While the people are removed from the land YHWH gave them, the land remains YHWH's. Thus the narrator shows a marked interest in what happened within that land among

those settled there by the Assyrians from other parts of their empire rather than following the fate of those exiled. The choice of a priest from Bethel is unfortunate in light of the role that site played in Jeroboam I's religious policy (1 Kgs. 12:25–33; 13:1–4). The new inhabitants seek to worship YHWH appropriately, but do not understand the theology that pervades 1–2 Kings. Worship of YHWH is exclusive: One is to worship YHWH and YHWH alone.

he taught them how they should worship the LORD.

29 But every nation still made gods of its own and put them in the shrines of the high places that the people of Samaria had made, every nation in the cities in which they lived; 30 the people of Babylon made Succoth-benoth, the people of Cuth made Nergal, the people of Hamath made Ashima; 31 the Avvites made Nibhaz and Tartak; the Sepharvites burned their children in the fire to Adrammelech and Anammelech, the gods of Sepharvaim. 32 They also worshiped the LORD and appointed from among themselves all sorts of people as priests of the high places, who sacrificed for them in the shrines of the high places. 33 So they worshiped the LORD but also served their own gods, after the manner of the nations from among whom they had been carried away. 34 To this day they continue to practice their former customs.

They do not worship the LORD and they do not follow the statutes or the ordinances or the law or the commandment that the LORD commanded the children of Jacob, whom he named Israel. 35 The LORD had made a covenant with them and commanded them, "You shall not worship other gods or bow yourselves to them or serve them or sacrifice to them, 36 but you shall worship the LORD, who brought you out of the land of Egypt with great power and with an outstretched arm; you shall bow yourselves to him, and to him you shall sacrifice. 37 The statutes and the ordinances and the law and the commandment that he wrote for you, you shall always be careful to observe. You shall not worship other gods; 38 you shall not forget the covenant that I have made with you. You shall not worship other gods, 39 but you shall worship the LORD your God; he will deliver you out of the hand of all your enemies." 40 They would not listen, however, but they continued to practice their former custom.

41 So these nations worshiped the LORD, but also served their carved images; to this day their children and their children's children continue to do as their ancestors did.

Hezekiah's Reign over Judah

18 In the third year of King Hoshea son of Elah of Israel, Hezekiah son of King Ahaz of Judah began to reign. 2 He was twenty-five years old when he began to reign; he reigned twenty-nine years in Jerusalem. His mother's name was Abi daughter of Zechariah. 3 He did what was right in the sight of the LORD just as his ancestor David had done. 4 He removed the high places, broke down the pillars, and cut down the sacred pole.[a] He broke in pieces the bronze serpent that Moses had made, for until those days the people of Israel had made offerings to it; it was called Nehushtan. 5 He trusted in the LORD the God of Israel; so that there was no one like him among all the kings of Judah after him, or among those who were before him. 6 For he held fast to the LORD; he did not depart from following him but kept the commandments that the LORD commanded Moses. 7 The LORD was with him; wherever he went, he prospered. He rebelled against the king of Assyria and would not serve him. 8 He attacked the Philistines as far

[a] Heb Asherah

18:1–25:30 Kings of Judah

18:1–20:21 Hezekiah Rules Judah

In an extended account we see how YHWH was with Hezekiah, and Hezekiah with YHWH, when he is threatened both by Sennacherib of Assyria (705–681 BCE) and by illness.

18:1–8—Hezekiah receives the highest praise yet for doing as David did and removing sites and elements of Canaanite worship, as well as *the bronze serpent* linked to Moses in the wilderness (Num. 21:4–9), around which a cult had apparently formed. Hezekiah reestablishes control over Philistine territory once under Davidic rule. Such reciprocity of commitment between the nation and its God is exactly what is absent in the contrasting case of Israel, accounting for its fall (2 Kgs. 17:7–23).

as Gaza and its territory, from watch-tower to fortified city.

9 In the fourth year of King Hezekiah, which was the seventh year of King Hoshea son of Elah of Israel, King Shalmaneser of Assyria came up against Samaria, besieged it, ¹⁰ and at the end of three years, took it. In the sixth year of Hezekiah, which was the ninth year of King Hoshea of Israel, Samaria was taken. ¹¹ The king of Assyria carried the Israelites away to Assyria, settled them in Halah, on the Habor, the river of Gozan, and in the cities of the Medes, ¹² because they did not obey the voice of the LORD their God but transgressed his covenant—all that Moses the servant of the LORD had commanded; they neither listened nor obeyed.

Sennacherib Invades Judah

13 In the fourteenth year of King Hezekiah, King Sennacherib of Assyria came up against all the fortified cities of Judah and captured them. ¹⁴ King Hezekiah of Judah sent to the king of Assyria at Lachish, saying, "I have done wrong; withdraw from me; whatever you impose on me I will bear." The king of Assyria demanded of King Hezekiah of Judah three hundred talents of silver and thirty talents of gold. ¹⁵ Hezekiah gave him all the silver that was found in the house of the LORD and in the treasuries of the king's house. ¹⁶ At that time Hezekiah stripped the gold from the doors of the temple of the LORD, and from the doorposts that King Hezekiah of Judah had overlaid and gave it to the king of Assyria. ¹⁷ The king of Assyria sent the Tartan, the Rabsaris, and the Rabshakeh with a great army from Lachish to King Hezekiah at Jerusalem. They went up and came to Jerusalem. When they arrived, they came and stood by the conduit of the upper pool, which is on the highway to the Fuller's Field. ¹⁸ When they called for the king, there came out to them Eliakim son of Hilkiah, who was in charge of the palace, and Shebnah the secretary, and Joah son of Asaph, the recorder.

19 The Rabshakeh said to them, "Say to Hezekiah: Thus says the great king, the king of Assyria: On what do you base this confidence of yours? ²⁰ Do you think that mere words are strategy and power for war? On whom do you now rely, that you have rebelled against me? ²¹ See, you are relying now on Egypt, that broken reed of a staff, which will pierce the hand of anyone who leans on it. Such is Pharaoh king of Egypt to all who rely on him. ²² But if you say to me, 'We rely on the LORD our God,' is it not he whose high places and altars Hezekiah has removed, saying to Judah and to Jerusalem, 'You shall worship before this altar in Jerusalem'? ²³ Come now, make a wager with my master the king of Assyria: I will give you two thousand horses, if you are able on your part to set riders on them. ²⁴ How then can you repulse a single captain among the least of my master's servants, when you rely on Egypt for chariots and for horsemen? ²⁵ Moreover, is it without the LORD that I have come up against this place to destroy it? The LORD said to me, Go up against this land, and destroy it."

26 Then Eliakim son of Hilkiah, and

18:9–12—This precis of chap. 17 (see 17:5–8) underscores the contrast between Israel and Judah, their respective kings, and the fate of each.

18:13–19:37—See Isa. 36–39, which deals with the same events.

18:13–18—Hezekiah's first response to Sennacherib's attack is submission and a large tribute (a *talent* is seventy-five pounds) from the palace and temple sent to the Assyrian base in Judean *Lachish*. This does not deter Sennacherib, who seeks more than a vassal. He sends high officials to demand the full surrender of Jerusalem.

18:19–25—The *Rabshakeh*'s first address is a rhetorical tour de force, designed to undercut Judah's reliance on Egypt (with whom it has allied against Assyria) and YHWH. Indeed, he turns the narrator's own theology against Judah, claiming YHWH supports Sennacherib against Judah because Hezekiah removed YHWH's high places.

18:26–27—Hezekiah's officials ask the Rab-

Shebnah, and Joah said to the Rabshakeh, "Please speak to your servants in the Aramaic language, for we understand it; do not speak to us in the language of Judah within the hearing of the people who are on the wall." 27 But the Rabshakeh said to them, "Has my master sent me to speak these words to your master and to you, and not to the people sitting on the wall, who are doomed with you to eat their own dung and to drink their own urine?"

28 Then the Rabshakeh stood and called out in a loud voice in the language of Judah, "Hear the word of the great king, the king of Assyria! 29 Thus says the king: 'Do not let Hezekiah deceive you, for he will not be able to deliver you out of my hand. 30 Do not let Hezekiah make you rely on the LORD by saying, The LORD will surely deliver us, and this city will not be given into the hand of the king of Assyria.' 31 Do not listen to Hezekiah; for thus says the king of Assyria: 'Make your peace with me and come out to me; then every one of you will eat from your own vine and your own fig tree, and drink water from your own cistern, 32 until I come and take you away to a land like your own land, a land of grain and wine, a land of bread and vineyards, a land of olive oil and honey, that you may live and not die. Do not listen to Hezekiah when he misleads you by saying, The LORD will deliver us.' 33 Has any of the gods of the nations ever delivered its land out of the hand of the king of Assyria? 34 Where are the gods of Hamath and Arpad? Where are the gods of Sepharvaim, Hena, and Ivvah? Have they delivered Samaria out of my hand? 35 Who among all the gods of the countries have delivered their countries out of my hand, that the LORD should deliver Jerusalem out of my hand?'"

36 But the people were silent and answered him not a word, for the king's command was, "Do not answer him." 37 Then Eliakim son of Hilkiah, who was in charge of the palace, and Shebna the secretary, and Joah son of Asaph, the recorder, came to Hezekiah with their clothes torn and told him the words of the Rabshakeh.

Hezekiah Consults Isaiah

19 When King Hezekiah heard it, he tore his clothes, covered himself with sackcloth, and went into the house of the LORD. 2 And he sent Eliakim, who was in charge of the palace, and Shebna the secretary, and the senior priests, covered with sackcloth, to the prophet Isaiah son of Amoz. 3 They said to him, "Thus says Hezekiah, This day is a day of distress, of rebuke, and of disgrace; children have come to the birth, and there is no strength to bring them forth. 4 It may be that the LORD your God heard all the words of the Rabshakeh, whom his master the king of Assyria has sent to mock the living God, and will rebuke the words that the LORD your God has heard; therefore lift up your prayer for the remnant that is left." 5 When the servants of King Hezekiah came to Isaiah, 6 Isaiah said to them, "Say to your master, 'Thus says the LORD: Do not be afraid because of the words that you have heard, with which the servants of the king of Assyria have reviled me. 7 I myself will put a spirit

shakeh to speak in *Aramaic*, the international language of diplomacy and trade, not understood by most of Jerusalem's population.

18:28–35—The Rabshakeh responds by addressing just this population, changing theological directions. YHWH will not fulfill any promises to secure Davidic kings and Jerusalem. YHWH is as powerless as the gods of other cities captured by Sennacherib, including Samaria, yet also offers them exile to a land like theirs where they may thrive.

18:36–37—Tension is high as Jerusalem awaits Hezekiah's response.

19:1–7—Hezekiah shows himself a model Yahwist, mourning and seeking divine aid through a prophet. He also sets the issue as a contest between YHWH and Sennacherib. *Isaiah's* response assumes this construction of the situation, announcing YHWH's salvation. Even overwhelming military might such as that of Assyria crumbles before the God of Israel.

in him, so that he shall hear a rumor and return to his own land; I will cause him to fall by the sword in his own land.'"

Sennacherib's Threat

8 The Rabshakeh returned, and found the king of Assyria fighting against Libnah; for he had heard that the king had left Lachish. 9 When the king[a] heard concerning King Tirhakah of Ethiopia,[b] "See, he has set out to fight against you," he sent messengers again to Hezekiah, saying, 10 "Thus shall you speak to King Hezekiah of Judah: Do not let your God on whom you rely deceive you by promising that Jerusalem will not be given into the hand of the king of Assyria. 11 See, you have heard what the kings of Assyria have done to all lands, destroying them utterly. Shall you be delivered? 12 Have the gods of the nations delivered them, the nations that my predecessors destroyed, Gozan, Haran, Rezeph, and the people of Eden who were in Telassar? 13 Where is the king of Hamath, the king of Arpad, the king of the city of Sepharvaim, the king of Hena, or the king of Ivvah?"

Hezekiah's Prayer

14 Hezekiah received the letter from the hand of the messengers and read it; then Hezekiah went up to the house of the LORD and spread it before the LORD. 15 And Hezekiah prayed before the LORD, and said: "O LORD the God of Israel, who are enthroned above the cherubim, you are God, you alone, of all the kingdoms of the earth; you have made heaven and earth. 16 Incline your ear, O LORD, and hear; open your eyes, O LORD, and see; hear the words of Sennacherib, which he has sent to mock the living God. 17 Truly, O LORD, the kings of Assyria have laid waste the nations and their lands, 18 and have hurled their gods into the fire, though they were no gods but the work of human hands—wood and stone—and so they were destroyed. 19 So now, O LORD our God, save us, I pray you, from his hand, so that all the kingdoms of the earth may know that you, O LORD, are God alone."

20 Then Isaiah son of Amoz sent to Hezekiah, saying, "Thus says the LORD, the God of Israel: I have heard your prayer to me about King Sennacherib of Assyria. 21 This is the word that the LORD has spoken concerning him:

She despises you, she scorns you—
    virgin daughter Zion;
she tosses her head—behind your
    back,
    daughter Jerusalem.
22 "Whom have you mocked and
    reviled?
    Against whom have you raised
        your voice
and haughtily lifted your eyes?
    Against the Holy One of Israel!
23 By your messengers you have
    mocked the Lord,
    and you have said, 'With my many
        chariots
I have gone up the heights of the
    mountains,
    to the far recesses of Lebanon;
I felled its tallest cedars,
    its choicest cypresses;
I entered its farthest retreat,
    its densest forest.

a Heb *he* *b* Or *Nubia*; Heb *Cush*

19:8–13—Events seem to override the prophet's oracle of deliverance. *King Tirhakah of Ethiopia*, in time Pharaoh of Egypt, may have set out to aid Jerusalem, resulting in a new threat by Sennacherib that repeats what the Rabshakeh earlier said.

19:14–19—This new threat drives Hezekiah into the very presence of YHWH. Again Hezekiah sets the issue as between YHWH and Sennacherib, who mocks him.

19:20–28—Isaiah's response has Jerusalem—personified as a young woman—mock in return. He claims Assyria's success is simply part of his plan formed *from days of old*. Sennacherib's assumption that his accomplishments (vv. 23–24) result from his own efforts betrays an arrogance that will now result in his humiliating retreat home.

²⁴ I dug wells
    and drank foreign waters,
    I dried up with the sole of my foot
      all the streams of Egypt.'

²⁵ "Have you not heard
    that I determined it long ago?
    I planned from days of old
      what now I bring to pass,
    that you should make fortified cities
      crash into heaps of ruins,
²⁶ while their inhabitants, shorn of
      strength,
    are dismayed and confounded;
    they have become like plants of the
      field
    and like tender grass,
    like grass on the housetops,
      blighted before it is grown.

²⁷ "But I know your rising*ᵃ* and your
      sitting,
    your going out and coming in,
    and your raging against me.
²⁸ Because you have raged against me
    and your arrogance has come to
      my ears,
    I will put my hook in your nose
      and my bit in your mouth;
    I will turn you back on the way
      by which you came.

29 "And this shall be the sign for you: This year you shall eat what grows of itself, and in the second year what springs from that; then in the third year sow, reap, plant vineyards, and eat their fruit. ³⁰ The surviving remnant of the house of Judah shall again take root downward, and bear fruit upward; ³¹ for from Jerusalem a remnant shall go out, and from Mount Zion a band of survivors. The zeal of the LORD of hosts will do this.

32 "Therefore thus says the LORD concerning the king of Assyria: He shall not come into this city, shoot an arrow there, come before it with a shield, or cast up a siege ramp against it. ³³ By the way that he came, by the same he shall return; he shall not come into this city, says the LORD. ³⁴ For I will defend this city to save it, for my own sake and for the sake of my servant David."

Sennacherib's Defeat and Death

35 That very night the angel of the LORD set out and struck down one hundred eighty-five thousand in the camp of the Assyrians; when morning dawned, they were all dead bodies. ³⁶ Then King Sennacherib of Assyria left, went home, and lived at Nineveh. ³⁷ As he was worshiping in the house of his god Nisroch, his sons Adrammelech and Sharezer killed him with the sword, and they escaped into the land of Ararat. His son Esar-haddon succeeded him.

Hezekiah's Illness

20 In those days Hezekiah became sick and was at the point of death. The prophet Isaiah son of Amoz came to him, and said to him, "Thus says the LORD: Set your house in order, for you shall die; you shall not recover." ² Then Hezekiah turned his face to the wall and prayed to the LORD: ³ "Remember now, O LORD, I implore you, how I have walked before you in faithfulness with a whole heart, and have done what is good in your sight." Hezekiah wept bitterly. ⁴ Before Isaiah had gone out of the middle court, the word of the LORD came to him: ⁵ "Turn back, and say to Hezekiah prince of my people, Thus

ᵃ Gk Compare Isa 37.27 Q Ms: MT lacks *rising*

19:29–31—By contrast, Jerusalem and its surviving remnant shall—in time—flourish.

19:32–34—In more prosaic terms Isaiah makes clear YHWH will defend Jerusalem.

19:35–36—In tersely dramatic terms, Isaiah's prediction is fulfilled. Jerusalem is delivered, Sennacherib defeated and destroyed by his own sons, but Assyrian power remains in the hands of his successor **Esar-haddon** (681–669 BCE).

20:1–11—Compare Isa. 38:1–22. Verse 6 suggests Hezekiah's illness takes us back before Sennacherib's retreat. The account demonstrates the Judean king's piety and YHWH's recognition of it by reversing the first message.

says the LORD, the God of your ancestor David: I have heard your prayer, I have seen your tears; indeed, I will heal you; on the third day you shall go up to the house of the LORD. ⁶ I will add fifteen years to your life. I will deliver you and this city out of the hand of the king of Assyria; I will defend this city for my own sake and for my servant David's sake." ⁷ Then Isaiah said, "Bring a lump of figs. Let them take it and apply it to the boil, so that he may recover."

8 Hezekiah said to Isaiah, "What shall be the sign that the LORD will heal me, and that I shall go up to the house of the LORD on the third day?" ⁹ Isaiah said, "This is the sign to you from the LORD, that the LORD will do the thing that he has promised: the shadow has now advanced ten intervals; shall it retreat ten intervals?" ¹⁰ Hezekiah answered, "It is normal for the shadow to lengthen ten intervals; rather let the shadow retreat ten intervals." ¹¹ The prophet Isaiah cried to the LORD; and he brought the shadow back the ten intervals, by which the sunᵃ had declined on the dial of Ahaz.

Envoys from Babylon

12 At that time King Merodach-baladan son of Baladan of Babylon sent envoys with letters and a present to Hezekiah, for he had heard that Hezekiah had been sick. ¹³ Hezekiah welcomed them;ᵇ he showed them all his treasure house, the silver, the gold, the spices, the precious oil, his armory, all that was found in his storehouses; there was nothing in his house or in all his realm that Hezekiah did not show them. ¹⁴ Then the prophet Isaiah came to King Hezekiah, and said to him, "What did these men say? From where did they come to you?" Hezekiah answered, "They have come from a far country, from Babylon." ¹⁵ He said, "What have they seen in your house?" Hezekiah answered, "They have seen all that is in my house; there is nothing in my storehouses that I did not show them."

16 Then Isaiah said to Hezekiah, "Hear the word of the LORD: ¹⁷ Days are coming when all that is in your house, and that which your ancestors have stored up until this day, shall be carried to Babylon; nothing shall be left, says the LORD. ¹⁸ Some of your own sons who are born to you shall be taken away; they shall be eunuchs in the palace of the king of Babylon." ¹⁹ Then Hezekiah said to Isaiah, "The word of the LORD that you have spoken is good." For he thought, "Why not, if there will be peace and security in my days?"

Death of Hezekiah

20 The rest of the deeds of Hezekiah, all his power, how he made the pool and the conduit and brought water into the city, are they not written in the Book of the Annals of the Kings of Judah?

ᵃ Syr See Isa 38.8 and Tg: Heb it ᵇ Gk Vg Syr: Heb *When Hezekiah heard about them*

20:7—The prophet *Isaiah* appears not only as a messenger (cf. 1 Kgs. 14:1–18) but as a healer like Elijah and Elisha.

20:8–11—Hezekiah's request for a sign is presented, not as a sign of his doubts, but as certification of Isaiah's oracle. *The dial of Ahaz* measured time by the sun's movement.

20:12–19—*King Merodach-baladan* ruled Babylon 722–710 and 704–703 BCE, being then deposed by Sennacherib. Thus this account of his envoys to Hezekiah and their remarkably cordial reception by the Judean king also relates events before Jerusalem's deliverance. Any alliance between Judah and Babylon would be of concern to Assyrian rulers, who found Babylon a source of regular trouble.

20:14–18—Isaiah grills the king about this visit and then harshly denounces his reception of the Babylonians. His words look forward to events that conclude 1–2 Kings, marking also the first blot on the depiction of Hezekiah.

20:19—Hezekiah's response further damages his image.

20:20–21—The formulaic notice of Hezekiah's death notes specifically a remarkable water tunnel constructed to secure Jerusalem under siege; it is still there to be traversed by visitors to Jerusalem.

²¹ Hezekiah slept with his ancestors; and his son Manasseh succeeded him.

Manasseh Reigns over Judah

21 Manasseh was twelve years old when he began to reign; he reigned fifty-five years in Jerusalem. His mother's name was Hephzibah. ² He did what was evil in the sight of the Lord, following the abominable practices of the nations that the Lord drove out before the people of Israel. ³ For he rebuilt the high places that his father Hezekiah had destroyed; he erected altars for Baal, made a sacred pole,ᵃ as King Ahab of Israel had done, worshiped all the host of heaven, and served them. ⁴ He built altars in the house of the Lord, of which the Lord had said, "In Jerusalem I will put my name." ⁵ He built altars for all the host of heaven in the two courts of the house of the Lord. ⁶ He made his son pass through fire; he practiced soothsaying and augury, and dealt with mediums and with wizards. He did much evil in the sight of the Lord, provoking him to anger. ⁷ The carved image of Asherah that he had made he set in the house of which the Lord said to David and to his son Solomon, "In this house, and in Jerusalem, which I have chosen out of all the tribes of Israel, I will put my name forever; ⁸ I will not cause the feet of Israel to wander any more out of the land that I gave to their ancestors, if only they will be careful to do according to all that I have commanded them, and according to all the law that my servant Moses commanded them." ⁹ But they did not listen; Manasseh misled them to do more evil than the nations had done that the Lord destroyed before the people of Israel.

10 The Lord said by his servants the prophets, ¹¹ "Because King Manasseh of Judah has committed these abominations, has done things more wicked than all that the Amorites did, who were before him, and has caused Judah also to sin with his idols; ¹² therefore thus says the Lord, the God of Israel, I am bringing upon Jerusalem and Judah such evil that the ears of everyone who hears of it will tingle. ¹³ I will stretch over Jerusalem the measuring line for Samaria, and the plummet for the house of Ahab; I will wipe Jerusalem as one wipes a dish, wiping it and turning it upside down. ¹⁴ I will cast off the remnant of my heritage, and give them into the hand of their enemies; they shall become a prey and a spoil to all their enemies, ¹⁵ because they have done what is evil in my sight and have provoked me to anger, since the day their ancestors came out of Egypt, even to this day."

16 Moreover Manasseh shed very much innocent blood, until he had filled Jerusalem from one end to another, besides the sin that he caused Judah to sin so that they did what was evil in the sight of the Lord.

17 Now the rest of the acts of Manasseh, all that he did, and the sin that he committed, are they not written in the Book of the Annals of the Kings of Judah? ¹⁸ Manasseh slept with his ancestors, and was buried in the garden of his house, in

ᵃ Heb *Asherah*

21:1–9 Manasseh Rules Judah

If Hezekiah is a model Yahwist with a few blemishes, his son *Manasseh* is a model apostate with no redeeming features. The condemnation of him reads like a catalogue of evils prohibited in Deuteronomy. He undoes the work of his father and exceeds the work of his grandfather Ahaz, being compared to Ahab of Israel.

21:10–15—Unnamed prophets announce YHWH's judgment—destruction like that visited on Israel.

21:16—Civil crimes add to Manasseh's religious evils.

21:17–18—Manasseh's fifty-five-year reign (the longest of any of David's dynasty) and apparently peaceful death and burial stand in disturbing contrast to the depiction of him. At the very least, this suggests that the narrator of 1–2 Kings, and we as readers, cannot assume events always readily conform to our theological schema.

the garden of Uzza. His son Amon succeeded him.

Amon Reigns over Judah

19 Amon was twenty-two years old
when he began to reign; he reigned two
years in Jerusalem. His mother's name
was Meshullemeth daughter of Haruz
of Jotbah. 20 He did what was evil in the
sight of the LORD, as his father Manasseh
had done. 21 He walked in all the way in
which his father walked, served the idols
that his father served, and worshiped
them; 22 he abandoned the LORD, the
God of his ancestors, and did not walk
in the way of the LORD. 23 The servants of
Amon conspired against him, and killed
the king in his house. 24 But the people
of the land killed all those who had
conspired against King Amon, and the
people of the land made his son Josiah
king in place of him. 25 Now the rest of
the acts of Amon that he did, are they
not written in the Book of the Annals of
the Kings of Judah? 26 He was buried in
his tomb in the garden of Uzza; then his
son Josiah succeeded him.

Josiah Reigns over Judah

22 Josiah was eight years old when
he began to reign; he reigned
thirty-one years in Jerusalem. His mother's name was Jedidah daughter of
Adaiah of Bozkath. 2 He did what was
right in the sight of the LORD, and
walked in all the way of his father David;
he did not turn aside to the right or to
the left.

Hilkiah Finds the Book of the Law

3 In the eighteenth year of King Josiah,
the king sent Shaphan son of Azaliah,
son of Meshullam, the secretary, to the
house of the LORD, saying, 4 "Go up to
the high priest Hilkiah, and have him
count the entire sum of the money that
has been brought into the house of the
LORD, which the keepers of the threshold have collected from the people; 5 let
it be given into the hand of the workers
who have the oversight of the house of
the LORD; let them give it to the workers who are at the house of the LORD,
repairing the house, 6 that is, to the carpenters, to the builders, to the masons;
and let them use it to buy timber and
quarried stone to repair the house. 7 But
no accounting shall be asked from them
for the money that is delivered into their
hand, for they deal honestly."

8 The high priest Hilkiah said to
Shaphan the secretary, "I have found
the book of the law in the house of the
LORD." When Hilkiah gave the book to
Shaphan, he read it. 9 Then Shaphan the
secretary came to the king, and reported
to the king, "Your servants have emptied out the money that was found in
the house, and have delivered it into the
hand of the workers who have oversight
of the house of the LORD." 10 Shaphan the
secretary informed the king, "The priest
Hilkiah has given me a book." Shaphan
then read it aloud to the king.

11 When the king heard the words of
the book of the law, he tore his clothes.

21:19–26—*Amon*, Manasseh's son, follows his
father's ways and is assassinated. The **people of
the land** kill his killers, securing the Davidic line
(cf. 11:13–14).

22:1–23:30 Josiah's Reform

22:1–2—*Josiah* receives unqualified praise, setting him in the pattern not only of David, but of
Moses and Joshua as well. Of all Judean kings, he
is cast in the model provided in Deut. 17:14–
20—especially in his being guided by a **book of
the law** (vv. 8, 11)—and thereby the antithesis of
Solomon (and Manasseh) in critical ways.

22:3–10—Josiah is first active as he comes of

age, involved in apparent ongoing repairs to the
temple, like Jehoash in 12:4–16. Many believe
that the book of the law was some form of Deuteronomy, especially because Josiah's reforms
undertaken in light of it stress worship of YHWH
as the one God and in one place, celebration of
Passover, and covenant renewal.

22:11–20—The impact of the book on Josiah is
immediate, but he seeks validation from *Huldah*,
a **prophetess** otherwise unmentioned but apparently respected in Jerusalem. Her initial words
announce disaster for Jerusalem (cf. 21:10–15)
and recall Deut. 27–28. Josiah's attitude earns
him and his followers a reprieve (cf. 23:28–30).

¹²Then the king commanded the priest Hilkiah, Ahikam son of Shaphan, Achbor son of Micaiah, Shaphan the secretary, and the king's servant Asaiah, saying, ¹³"Go, inquire of the LORD for me, for the people, and for all Judah, concerning the words of this book that has been found; for great is the wrath of the LORD that is kindled against us, because our ancestors did not obey the words of this book, to do according to all that is written concerning us."

14 So the priest Hilkiah, Ahikam, Achbor, Shaphan, and Asaiah went to the prophetess Huldah the wife of Shallum son of Tikvah, son of Harhas, keeper of the wardrobe; she resided in Jerusalem in the Second Quarter, where they consulted her. ¹⁵She declared to them, "Thus says the LORD, the God of Israel: Tell the man who sent you to me, ¹⁶Thus says the LORD, I will indeed bring disaster on this place and on its inhabitants—all the words of the book that the king of Judah has read. ¹⁷Because they have abandoned me and have made offerings to other gods, so that they have provoked me to anger with all the work of their hands, therefore my wrath will be kindled against this place, and it will not be quenched. ¹⁸But as to the king of Judah, who sent you to inquire of the LORD, thus shall you say to him, Thus says the LORD, the God of Israel: Regarding the words that you have heard, ¹⁹because your heart was penitent, and you humbled yourself before the LORD, when you heard how I spoke against this place, and against its inhabitants, that they should become a desolation and a curse, and because you have torn your clothes and wept before me, I also have heard you, says the LORD. ²⁰Therefore, I will gather you to your ancestors, and you shall be gathered to your grave in peace; your eyes shall not see all the disaster that I will bring on this place." They took the message back to the king.

Josiah's Reformation

23 Then the king directed that all the elders of Judah and Jerusalem should be gathered to him. ²The king went up to the house of the LORD, and with him went all the people of Judah, all the inhabitants of Jerusalem, the priests, the prophets, and all the people, both small and great; he read in their hearing all the words of the book of the covenant that had been found in the house of the LORD. ³The king stood by the pillar and made a covenant before the LORD, to follow the LORD, keeping his commandments, his decrees, and his statutes, with all his heart and all his soul, to perform the words of this covenant that were written in this book. All the people joined in the covenant.

4 The king commanded the high priest Hilkiah, the priests of the second order, and the guardians of the threshold, to bring out of the temple of the LORD all the vessels made for Baal, for Asherah, and for all the host of heaven; he burned them outside Jerusalem in the fields of the Kidron, and carried their ashes to Bethel. ⁵He deposed the idolatrous priests whom the kings of Judah had ordained to make offerings in the high places at the cities of Judah and around Jerusalem; those also who made offerings to Baal, to the sun, the moon, the constellations, and all the host of the heavens. ⁶He brought out the image of[a] Asherah from the house of the LORD, outside Jerusalem, to the Wadi Kidron, burned it at the Wadi Kidron, beat it to dust and threw the dust of it upon the graves of the common people.

[a] Heb lacks *image of*

23:1–27—Josiah's reform is thorough, implementing key elements in Deuteronomy and also undoing what kings of both Judah (esp. Solomon, Ahaz, and Manasseh) and Israel (esp. Jeroboam I and Ahab) enacted.

23:1–3—In light of Huldah's announcement this covenant seems futile, but it suggests Josiah seeks to obey YHWH regardless of outcome.

23:4–7—The initial reforms destroy all traces of what is traditionally Canaanite religious practice.

7 He broke down the houses of the male temple prostitutes that were in the house of the LORD, where the women did weaving for Asherah. 8 He brought all the priests out of the towns of Judah, and defiled the high places where the priests had made offerings, from Geba to Beersheba; he broke down the high places of the gates that were at the entrance of the gate of Joshua the governor of the city, which were on the left at the gate of the city. 9 The priests of the high places, however, did not come up to the altar of the LORD in Jerusalem, but ate unleavened bread among their kindred. 10 He defiled Topheth, which is in the valley of Ben-hinnom, so that no one would make a son or a daughter pass through fire as an offering to Molech. 11 He removed the horses that the kings of Judah had dedicated to the sun, at the entrance to the house of the LORD, by the chamber of the eunuch Nathan-melech, which was in the precincts;a then he burned the chariots of the sun with fire. 12 The altars on the roof of the upper chamber of Ahaz, which the kings of Judah had made, and the altars that Manasseh had made in the two courts of the house of the LORD, he pulled down from there and broke in pieces, and threw the rubble into the Wadi Kidron. 13 The king defiled the high places that were east of Jerusalem, to the south of the Mount of Destruction, which King Solomon of Israel had built for Astarte the abomination of the Sidonians, for Chemosh the abomination of Moab, and for Milcom the abomination of the Ammonites. 14 He broke the pillars in pieces, cut down the sacred poles,b and covered the sites with human bones.

15 Moreover, the altar at Bethel, the high place erected by Jeroboam son of Nebat, who caused Israel to sin—he pulled down that altar along with the high place. He burned the high place, crushing it to dust; he also burned the sacred pole.c 16 As Josiah turned, he saw the tombs there on the mount; and he sent and took the bones out of the tombs, and burned them on the altar, and defiled it, according to the word of the LORD that the man of God proclaimed,d when Jeroboam stood by the altar at the festival; he turned and looked up at the tomb of the man of God who had predicted these things. 17 Then he said, "What is that monument that I see?" The people of the city told him, "It is the tomb of the man of God who came from Judah and predicted these things that you have done against the altar at Bethel." 18 He said, "Let him rest; let no one move his bones." So they let his bones alone, with the bones of the prophet who came out of Samaria. 19 Moreover, Josiah removed all the shrines of the high places that were in the towns of Samaria, which kings of Israel had made, provoking the LORD to anger; he did to them just as he had done at Bethel. 20 He slaughtered on the altars all the priests of the high places who were there, and burned human bones on them. Then he returned to Jerusalem.

The Passover Celebrated

21 The king commanded all the people, "Keep the passover to the LORD your God as prescribed in this book of

a Meaning of Heb uncertain b Heb Asherim c Heb Asherah d Gk: Heb proclaimed, who had predicted these things

---

23:8–9—The high places and priests were dedicated to YHWH, but done away with to centralize worship in Jerusalem (Deut. 12). Geba to Beer-sheba takes in all Judah. Priests of the high places do not claim the right granted in Deut. 18:6–8.

23:10–14—Installations and practices of prior kings are destroyed.

23:15–20—Josiah fulfills the prophecy against the altar at Bethel in 1 Kgs. 13. These actions take Josiah into what is technically a province of Assyria and may be read as rebellion against that now-weakening empire (see vv. 28–30) and assertion of Davidic rule over a once-united Israel, north and south.

23:21–23—Collective celebration of Passover (see Deut. 16:5–6), which has not occurred since the

the covenant." ²² No such passover had been kept since the days of the judges who judged Israel, even during all the days of the kings of Israel and of the kings of Judah; ²³ but in the eighteenth year of King Josiah this passover was kept to the LORD in Jerusalem.

24 Moreover Josiah put away the mediums, wizards, teraphim,ᵃ idols, and all the abominations that were seen in the land of Judah and in Jerusalem, so that he established the words of the law that were written in the book that the priest Hilkiah had found in the house of the LORD. ²⁵ Before him there was no king like him, who turned to the LORD with all his heart, with all his soul, and with all his might, according to all the law of Moses; nor did any like him arise after him.

26 Still the LORD did not turn from the fierceness of his great wrath, by which his anger was kindled against Judah, because of all the provocations with which Manasseh had provoked him. ²⁷ The LORD said, "I will remove Judah also out of my sight, as I have removed Israel; and I will reject this city that I have chosen, Jerusalem, and the house of which I said, My name shall be there."

Josiah Dies in Battle

28 Now the rest of the acts of Josiah, and all that he did, are they not written in the Book of the Annals of the Kings of Judah? ²⁹ In his days Pharaoh Neco king of Egypt went up to the king of Assyria to the river Euphrates. King Josiah went to meet him; but when Pharaoh Neco met him at Megiddo, he killed him. ³⁰ His servants carried him dead in a chariot from Megiddo, brought him to Jerusalem, and buried him in his own tomb. The people of the land took Jehoahaz son of Josiah, anointed him, and made him king in place of his father.

Reign and Captivity of Jehoahaz

31 Jehoahaz was twenty-three years old when he began to reign; he reigned three months in Jerusalem. His mother's name was Hamutal daughter of Jeremiah of Libnah. ³² He did what was evil in the sight of the LORD, just as his ancestors had done. ³³ Pharaoh Neco confined him at Riblah in the land of Hamath, so that he might not reign in Jerusalem, and imposed tribute on the land of one hundred talents of silver and a talent of gold. ³⁴ Pharaoh Neco made Eliakim son of Josiah king in place of his father Josiah, and changed his name to Jehoiakim. But he took Jehoahaz away; he came to Egypt, and died there. ³⁵ Jehoiakim gave the silver and the gold to Pharaoh, but he taxed the land in order to meet Pharaoh's demand for money. He exacted the silver and the gold from the

ᵃ Or household gods

---

days of Joshua (Josh. 5:10–11), links Josiah with Moses' successor.

23:24–25—The narrator's summary praise is unstinted, even linking Josiah with Moses. Josiah is a leader who fully conforms to the covenantal ideal of Deut. 17:14–20, one who built his leadership on God's will as revealed in the Torah.

23:26–27—In a jarring juxtaposition, readers are reminded of YHWH's wrath and the destruction awaiting Judah and Jerusalem announced by Huldah (22:16–17), prophets in Manasseh's time (21:10–15), and Isaiah (20:16–18).

23:28–30—Political implications of Josiah's reform become apparent in the stark announcement of his death. A weakened Assyria was now supported by Egypt against Babylon. Why Josiah met *Pharaoh Neco* and why Neco killed him are

not stated, but some suggest Josiah was seeking to prevent the Egyptian from aiding Assyria, against which Josiah had rebelled. The contrasts between the lives and deaths of Josiah and Manasseh are disturbing, especially in light of Huldah's announcement in 22:20. The apparently unjust suffering and death of the innocent and righteous are something familiar to sensitive readers in all ages and raise theological and pastoral questions that cannot be avoided, even as they are not easily resolved.

23:31–25:26 The Destruction of Judah and Exile

23:31–35—Again *the people of the land* ensure Davidic succession, but Neco replaces Josiah's son *Jehoahaz* with another son, *Jehoiakim (Eliakim)*, who was presumably more amenable to Egyptian interests.

people of the land, from all according to their assessment, to give it to Pharaoh Neco.

Jehoiakim Reigns over Judah

36 Jehoiakim was twenty-five years old when he began to reign; he reigned eleven years in Jerusalem. His mother's name was Zebidah daughter of Pedaiah of Rumah. 37 He did what was evil in the sight of the LORD, just as all his ancestors had done.

Judah Overrun by Enemies

24 In his days King Nebuchadnezzar of Babylon came up; Jehoiakim became his servant for three years; then he turned and rebelled against him. 2 The LORD sent against him bands of the Chaldeans, bands of the Arameans, bands of the Moabites, and bands of the Ammonites; he sent them against Judah to destroy it, according to the word of the LORD that he spoke by his servants the prophets. 3 Surely this came upon Judah at the command of the LORD, to remove them out of his sight, for the sins of Manasseh, for all that he had committed, 4 and also for the innocent blood that he had shed; for he filled Jerusalem with innocent blood, and the LORD was not willing to pardon. 5 Now the rest of the deeds of Jehoiakim, and all that he did, are they not written in the Book of the Annals of the Kings of Judah? 6 So Jehoiakim slept with his ancestors; then his son Jehoiachin succeeded him. 7 The king of Egypt did not come again out of his land, for the king of Babylon had taken over all that belonged to the king of Egypt from the Wadi of Egypt to the River Euphrates.

Reign and Captivity of Jehoiachin

8 Jehoiachin was eighteen years old when he began to reign; he reigned three months in Jerusalem. His mother's name was Nehushta daughter of Elnathan of Jerusalem. 9 He did what was evil in the sight of the LORD, just as his father had done.

10 At that time the servants of King Nebuchadnezzar of Babylon came up to Jerusalem, and the city was besieged. 11 King Nebuchadnezzar of Babylon came to the city, while his servants were besieging it; 12 King Jehoiachin of Judah gave himself up to the king of Babylon, himself, his mother, his servants, his officers, and his palace officials. The king of Babylon took him prisoner in the eighth year of his reign.

Capture of Jerusalem

13 He carried off all the treasures of the house of the LORD, and the treasures of the king's house; he cut in pieces all the vessels of gold in the temple of the LORD, which King Solomon of Israel had made, all this as the LORD had foretold. 14 He carried away all Jerusalem, all the officials, all the warriors, ten thousand captives, all the artisans and the smiths; no one remained, except the poorest people of the land. 15 He carried away Jehoiachin to Babylon; the king's mother, the king's wives, his officials, and the elite of the land, he took into captivity from Jerusalem to Babylon. 16 The king of Babylon brought captive to Babylon all the men of valor, seven thousand, the artisans and the smiths, one thousand, all of them strong and fit for war. 17 The king of Babylon made Mattaniah, Jehoiachin's uncle, king in his place, and changed his name to Zedekiah.

23:36–37—The narrator judges both sons negatively.

24:1–7—Jehoiakim's changing allegiances reflect desperate attempts to survive in the struggle between Babylon (*Chaldeans*) and Egypt. The narrator presents this theologically as YHWH's use of Babylon and other enemies to destroy Judah for *the sins of Manasseh*.

24:8–17—Jehoiakim dies in the midst of this, and his son Jehoiachin suffers defeat by Babylon. Jerusalem is captured in March 597 BCE and the king, royal family, and establishment are exiled to Babylon with thousands of Judeans. Only *the poorest people of the land* remain, ruled by the Babylonian appointed *Zedekiah (Mattaniah)*.

Zedekiah Reigns over Judah

18 Zedekiah was twenty-one years old when he began to reign; he reigned eleven years in Jerusalem. His mother's name was Hamutal daughter of Jeremiah of Libnah. [19] He did what was evil in the sight of the Lord, just as Jehoiakim had done. [20] Indeed, Jerusalem and Judah so angered the Lord that he expelled them from his presence.

The Fall and Captivity of Judah

Zedekiah rebelled against the king of Babylon. 25 [1] And in the ninth year of his reign, in the tenth month, on the tenth day of the month, King Nebuchadnezzar of Babylon came with all his army against Jerusalem, and laid siege to it; they built siegeworks against it all around. [2] So the city was besieged until the eleventh year of King Zedekiah. [3] On the ninth day of the fourth month the famine became so severe in the city that there was no food for the people of the land. [4] Then a breach was made in the city wall;[a] the king with all the soldiers fled[b] by night by the way of the gate between the two walls, by the king's garden, though the Chaldeans were all around the city. They went in the direction of the Arabah. [5] But the army of the Chaldeans pursued the king, and overtook him in the plains of Jericho; all his army was scattered, deserting him. [6] Then they captured the king and brought him up to the king of Babylon at Riblah, who passed sentence on him. [7] They slaughtered the sons of Zedekiah before his eyes, then put out the eyes of Zedekiah; they bound him in fetters and took him to Babylon.

8 In the fifth month, on the seventh day of the month—which was the nineteenth year of King Nebuchadnezzar, king of Babylon—Nebuzaradan, the captain of the bodyguard, a servant of the king of Babylon, came to Jerusalem. [9] He burned the house of the Lord, the king's house, and all the houses of Jerusalem; every great house he burned down. [10] All the army of the Chaldeans who were with the captain of the guard broke down the walls around Jerusalem. [11] Nebuzaradan the captain of the guard carried into exile the rest of the people who were left in the city and the deserters who had defected to the king of Babylon—all the rest of the population. [12] But the captain of the guard left some of the poorest people of the land to be vinedressers and tillers of the soil.

13 The bronze pillars that were in the house of the Lord, as well as the stands and the bronze sea that were in the house of the Lord, the Chaldeans broke in pieces, and carried the bronze to Babylon. [14] They took away the pots, the shovels, the snuffers, the dishes for incense, and all the bronze vessels used in the temple service, [15] as well as the firepans and the basins. What was made of gold the captain of the guard took away for the gold, and what was made of silver, for the silver. [16] As for the two pillars, the one sea, and the stands, which Solomon had made for the house of the Lord, the bronze of all these vessels was beyond weighing. [17] The height of the one pillar was eighteen cubits, and on it was a bronze capital; the height of the

[a] Heb lacks wall [b] Gk Compare Jer 39.4; 52.7: Heb lacks the king and lacks fled

---

24:18–25:21—Notice of Zedekiah's reign begins with a negative evaluation and YHWH's determination to *expel* Jerusalem and Judah *from his presence*. His struggles to survive in the turbulent international conflict are doomed in the narrator's eyes.

25:1–2—Nebuchadnezzar's eight-month siege began in January 587.

25:3–7—In July 586 BCE, Jerusalem's wall was breached, and Zedekiah and remnant of his

forces fled. Zedekiah was captured, forced to witness the execution of his sons, blinded, and taken bound to Babylon (see Jer. 52).

25:8–12—The temple was destroyed in August 586 BCE, and a second deportation of the people followed.

25:13–17—This brief account of the spoilage of the temple stands as a negative frame to the extensive account of its building at the beginning of 1–2 Kings (1 Kgs. 6–7).

capital was three cubits; latticework and pomegranates, all of bronze, were on the capital all around. The second pillar had the same, with the latticework.

18 The captain of the guard took the chief priest Seraiah, the second priest Zephaniah, and the three guardians of the threshold; [19] from the city he took an officer who had been in command of the soldiers, and five men of the king's council who were found in the city; the secretary who was the commander of the army who mustered the people of the land; and sixty men of the people of the land who were found in the city. [20] Nebuzaradan the captain of the guard took them, and brought them to the king of Babylon at Riblah. [21] The king of Babylon struck them down and put them to death at Riblah in the land of Hamath. So Judah went into exile out of its land.

Gedaliah Made Governor of Judah

22 He appointed Gedaliah son of Ahikam son of Shaphan as governor over the people who remained in the land of Judah, whom King Nebuchad-nezzar of Babylon had left. [23] Now when all the captains of the forces and their men heard that the king of Babylon had appointed Gedaliah as governor, they came with their men to Gedaliah at Mizpah, namely, Ish-mael son of Nethaniah, Johanan son of Kareah, Seraiah son of Tanhumeth the Netophathite, and Jaazaniah son of the Maacathite. [24] Gedaliah swore to them and their men, saying, "Do not be afraid because of the Chaldean offi-cials; live in the land, serve the king of Babylon, and it shall be well with you." [25] But in the seventh month, Ishmael son of Nethaniah son of Elishama, of the royal family, came with ten men; they struck down Gedaliah so that he died, along with the Judeans and Chal-deans who were with him at Mizpah. [26] Then all the people, high and low,[a] and the captains of the forces set out and went to Egypt; for they were afraid of the Chaldeans.

Jehoiachin Released from Prison

27 In the thirty-seventh year of the exile of King Jehoiachin of Judah, in the twelfth month, on the twenty-seventh day of the month, King Evil-merodach of Babylon, in the year that he began to reign, released King Jehoiachin of Judah from prison; [28] he spoke kindly to him, and gave him a seat above the other seats of the kings who were with him in Babylon. [29] So Jehoiachin put aside his prison clothes. Every day of his life he dined regularly in the king's presence. [30] For his allowance, a regular allowance was given him by the king, a portion every day, as long as he lived.

[a] Or young and old

25:18–21—Remaining religious, civil, and military leaders are executed.

25:22–26—In the confusion that results, the pro-Babylonian **Gedaliah**, from a powerful Judean family and appointed governor by Nebuchadnez-zar, is assassinated by one **Ishmael** from the royal family. The narrator suggests all remaining people flee to Egypt in a type of reverse exodus, as the land of promise is left empty.

25:27–30 Jehoiachin Is Released from Prison in Exile

In an afterword, we are taken to Babylon in the time of **Evil-merodach** (562–560 BCE). Jehoiachin is released from prison and made a pensioner of the Babylonian king—the house of David is in exile but not destroyed. First–Second Kings leaves readers with a challenge—a challenge both to Israel of old and to all who stand in its traditions—to forge in exile a mode of life in covenant with God. They will have to reside in, but not become too much a part of, a world that is not home. They will have to live with a hope and trust that God's kingdom will come to fruition in a future we can anticipate and live toward with the guidance of God and God's Torah.

1–2 CHRONICLES

The two books of Chronicles were originally one and should be read as a unity. Though they follow Ezra–Nehemiah at the end of the Hebrew canon, they appear among the historical books, between 2 Kings and Ezra–Nehemiah, in the Septuagint, Vulgate, and English versions.

Chronicles was written in Jerusalem, after the Babylonian exile, sometime in the fourth century BCE, by an anonymous author called "the chronicler." Similarities of style, language, and general outlook have suggested that this author also wrote Ezra–Nehemiah. This, however, has been challenged by a growing number of scholars, who point to different treatments of such key theological matters as the significance of the exodus, the nature of "Israel," intermarriage, prophecy, retributive justice, Levitical function, and the promise to David. Though the chronicler's primary source was 1 Sam. 31–2 Kgs. 25, material from the Pentateuch, Joshua, Judges, Ezra–Nehemiah, Psalms, Isaiah, Jeremiah, Lamentations, Ezekiel, Zechariah, and several ancient sources no longer extant also appears.

Chronicles begins with an extensive genealogical introduction (1 Chr. 1–9) that stresses the election and unity of "all Israel" while emphasizing continuity with the tribes of Judah, Levi, and Benjamin, the core of the chronicler's postexilic community. The reigns of David and Solomon are next presented as a united monarchy (1 Chr. 10–2 Chr. 9) in which the Davidic dynasty (1 Chr. 17:3–14) and the temple (2 Chr. 7:11–22) are established as divine institutions. The account of the divided monarchy that follows (2 Chr. 10–28) concentrates almost exclusively upon the kings of Judah as it evaluates their faithfulness to these institutions and holds them up as examples to follow or reject. An account of how Hezekiah, as a second David and Solomon, restores the monarchy and of the nation's tragic decline into exile (2 Chr. 29–36) concludes the work.

Within this literary construct three major theological themes repeatedly emerge. The first is a concern to demonstrate continuity between the postexilic community and the Israel of the past. Despite the horrors of exile, God had not abandoned Israel. The genealogies of the first nine chapters trace Israel from Adam (1 Chr. 1:1) to the chronicler's contemporary community (1 Chr. 9), linking them to their historical, geographical, and spiritual roots. The centrality of the temple, especially its connection to the wilderness tabernacle (2 Chr. 7:1–3), and the Levitical concern for proper worship would strengthen the community's sense of identity and relation to their forebears and their God.

The concept of "all Israel" is a second regularly occurring theological theme. Unlike Ezra–Nehemiah, which envisions an exclusive community comprised of those who had returned from exile, the chronicler's inclusive vision of Israel returns to the ancient ideal of twelve tribes as seen in the structure of the genealogies and in the acclamation of "all Israel" at major junctures in the narrative, especially at both

David's and Solomon's accession and Hezekiah's efforts to reunite the north and south.

The third theme is the theology of immediate retribution, which blesses obedience and punishes disobedience, often described as the chronicler's hallmark. While this does play an important role in 2 Chr. 10–36, the chronicler's usage is neither mechanical nor simplistic. Judgment is withheld following the repentant response to prophetic warnings (1 Chr. 21:15–19; 2 Chr. 12:5; 15:1–7; 36:15). This suggests that the chronicler is more concerned with restoration than retribution.

These major theological themes are supported by a number of other recurring motifs. (1) The twin concerns of king and cult, that is, the dynastic promise made to David (1 Chr. 17:4–14) and the promise of forgiveness given to Solomon at the dedication of the temple (2 Chr. 7:11–22), are especially significant. God's commitment to the line of David, repeatedly necessary in the following narrative, attests the inability of human sin and intransigence to overthrow God's purposes. Similarly, God promises to forgive and heal those who turn in prayer and repentance. (2) "Seeking God" not only sets a pattern for David's reign in contrast to Saul's faithlessness, but becomes the Chronicler's primary way of speaking about a life of faith that includes repentance and proper worship (1 Chr. 13–16). (3) The chronicler's underlying assumption of the sovereignty of God, itself an earthly manifestation of the kingdom of God, rarely surfaces in the narrative. The theme of God's dominion and rule does, however, explicitly appear in David's final prayer (1 Chr. 29:10–19).

The chronicler's purpose is simply to address the situation of the struggling postexilic community by retelling the familiar stories of Judah's kings in ways that emphasize situations of "exile" or "restoration." Exilic situations result from unfaithfulness, trusting in foreign alliances, or failing to "seek the Lord." Though literal deportation may not result, ruinous consequences and the loss of God's blessing inevitably follow. Repentance and claiming God's promise of forgiveness (2 Chr. 7:14) can bring about situations of reversal and restoration, marked by victory in war, large families, and successful building projects. The stories of Judah's kings become examples of God's ability to change the present situation, when prophetic warnings are heeded, and testimonies to the consequences of failing to do so.

—Mark A. Throntveit

From Adam to Abraham

1 Adam, Seth, Enosh; [2] Kenan, Mahalalel, Jared; [3] Enoch, Methuselah, Lamech; [4] Noah, Shem, Ham, and Japheth.

5 The descendants of Japheth: Gomer, Magog, Madai, Javan, Tubal, Meshech, and Tiras. [6] The descendants of Gomer: Ashkenaz, Diphath,[a] and Togarmah. [7] The descendants of Javan: Elishah, Tarshish, Kittim, and Rodanim.[b]

8 The descendants of Ham: Cush, Egypt, Put, and Canaan. [9] The descendants of Cush: Seba, Havilah, Sabta, Raama, and Sabteca. The descendants of Raamah: Sheba and Dedan. [10] Cush became the father of Nimrod; he was the first to be a mighty one on the earth.

11 Egypt became the father of Ludim, Anamim, Lehabim, Naphtuhim, [12] Pathrusim, Casluhim, and Caphtorim, from whom the Philistines come.[c]

13 Canaan became the father of Sidon his firstborn, and Heth, [14] and the Jebusites, the Amorites, the Girgashites, [15] the Hivites, the Arkites, the Sinites, [16] the Arvadites, the Zemarites, and the Hamathites.

17 The descendants of Shem: Elam, Asshur, Arpachshad, Lud, Aram, Uz, Hul, Gether, and Meshech.[d] [18] Arpachshad became the father of Shelah; and Shelah became the father of Eber. [19] To Eber were born two sons: the name of the one was Peleg (for in his days the earth was divided), and the name of his brother Joktan. [20] Joktan became the father of Almodad, Sheleph, Hazarmaveth, Jerah, [21] Hadoram, Uzal, Diklah, [22] Ebal, Abimael, Sheba, [23] Ophir, Havilah, and Jobab; all these were the descendants of Joktan.

24 Shem, Arpachshad, Shelah; [25] Eber, Peleg, Reu; [26] Serug, Nahor, Terah; [27] Abram, that is, Abraham.

From Abraham to Jacob

28 The sons of Abraham: Isaac and Ishmael. [29] These are their genealogies: the firstborn of Ishmael, Nebaioth; and Kedar, Adbeel, Mibsam, [30] Mishma, Dumah, Massa, Hadad, Tema, [31] Jetur, Naphish, and Kedemah. These are the sons of Ishmael. [32] The sons of Keturah, Abraham's concubine: she bore Zimran, Jokshan, Medan, Midian, Ishbak, and Shuah. The sons of Jokshan: Sheba and Dedan. [33] The sons of Midian: Ephah, Epher, Hanoch, Abida, and Eldaah. All these were the descendants of Keturah.

34 Abraham became the father of Isaac. The sons of Isaac: Esau and Israel. [35] The sons of Esau: Eliphaz, Reuel, Jeush, Jalam, and Korah. [36] The sons of Eliphaz: Teman, Omar, Zephi, Gatam, Kenaz, Timna, and Amalek. [37] The sons of Reuel: Nahath, Zerah, Shammah, and Mizzah.

38 The sons of Seir: Lotan, Shobal,

[a] Gen 10.3 *Ripath;* See Gk Vg   [b] Gen 10.4 *Dodanim;* See Syr Vg
[c] Heb *Casluhim, from which the Philistines come, Caphtorim;* See Am 9.7, Jer 47.4   [d] *Mash* in Gen 10.23

1:1–9:44 Genealogical Introduction
Chronicles begins with nine chapters of genealogies that trace Israel's ancestry back to Adam. The lists claim that God chose Israel from the very beginning and link historic Israel (chaps. 1–8) with the chronicler's own community (chap. 9).

1:1–2:2 Adam to Israel
Information from lists in Gen. 5; 10–11; 25;

35–36 is rearranged so that the line leading to Israel is presented last, stressing their election and position in the wider context of humanity.

1:28–34—*Abraham's* descendants are traced through their mothers with the primary line (*Isaac*) presented last.

Zibeon, Anah, Dishon, Ezer, and Dishan. **39** The sons of Lotan: Hori and Homam; and Lotan's sister was Timna. **40** The sons of Shobal: Alian, Manahath, Ebal, Shephi, and Onam. The sons of Zibeon: Aiah and Anah. **41** The sons of Anah: Dishon. The sons of Dishon: Hamran, Eshban, Ithran, and Cheran. **42** The sons of Ezer: Bilhan, Zaavan, and Jaakan.*a* The sons of Dishan:*b* Uz and Aran.

43 These are the kings who reigned in the land of Edom before any king reigned over the Israelites: Bela son of Beor, whose city was called Dinhabah. **44** When Bela died, Jobab son of Zerah of Bozrah succeeded him. **45** When Jobab died, Husham of the land of the Temanites succeeded him. **46** When Husham died, Hadad son of Bedad, who defeated Midian in the country of Moab, succeeded him; and the name of his city was Avith. **47** When Hadad died, Samlah of Masrekah succeeded him. **48** When Samlah died, Shaul*c* of Rehoboth on the Euphrates succeeded him. **49** When Shaul*c* died, Baal-hanan son of Achbor succeeded him. **50** When Baal-hanan died, Hadad succeeded him; the name of his city was Pai, and his wife's name Mehetabel daughter of Matred, daughter of Me-zahab. **51** And Hadad died.

The clans*d* of Edom were: clans*d* Timna, Aliah,*e* Jetheth, **52** Oholibamah, Elah, Pinon, **53** Kenaz, Teman, Mibzar, **54** Magdiel, and Iram; these are the clans*d* of Edom.

The Sons of Israel and the Descendants of Judah

2 These are the sons of Israel: Reuben, Simeon, Levi, Judah, Issachar, Zebulun, **2** Dan, Joseph, Benjamin, Naphtali, Gad, and Asher. **3** The sons of Judah: Er, Onan, and Shelah; these three the Canaanite woman Bath-shua bore to him. Now Er, Judah's firstborn, was wicked in the sight of the LORD, and he put him to death. **4** His daughter-in-law Tamar also bore him Perez and Zerah. Judah had five sons in all.

a Or and Akan; See Gen 36.27   *b* See 1.38: Heb Dishon   *c* Or Saul
d Or chiefs   *e* Or Alvah; See Gen 36.40

2:1–2 The sons of Israel—The chronicler always refers to Jacob as Israel (16:13, 17, are quotations of Ps. 105:6, 10). The inclusion of Levi, Joseph, and Benjamin results in a complete listing of Jacob's sons (Dinah is omitted) and points to the chronicler's concern for all Israel. From this point through 9:1, the tribes of Israel are concentrically arranged (i.e., in an A B C x C' B' A' pattern) to emphasize the tribes of Judah, Benjamin, and Levi, which had remained loyal to David at the time of the schism (922 BCE), and now formed the bulk of the postexilic community. **Judah** (2:3–4:23) comes first because *a ruler* (David, cf. 11:2; 17:7) *came from him* (5:2). Benjamin, ancestor of Saul, balances Judah's royal claims at the end (8:1–40), while the priestly tribe of Levi anchors the middle (6:1–81). The genealogies of the northern tribes east of Jordan (5:1–26) have been placed between Judah and Levi, to balance the northern tribes of the Jordan's western bank, placed between Levi and Benjamin (7:1–40). This arrangement gives prominence to the royal tribes of Judah and Benjamin and the priestly tribe of Levi and foreshadows the chronicler's primary concerns of king and cult. The inclusion of the northern tribes within this framework indicates concern for all Israel.

2:3–4:23 The Tribe of Judah

The preceding pattern of presenting secondary lines first is reversed with the **sons of Judah**. Although Judah is born fourth (2:1), his genealogy appears first. The following lists form a secondary concentric arrangement that falls into five parts. At the center is the crucial family of **Hezron**, David's clan (2:9–3:24). Framing this we find material concerning Judah's twin sons **Perez and Zerah** (2:5–8; 4:1–20). The presentation of **Shelah**'s descendants is split to enclose the whole (2:3–4; 4:21–24).

2:3–8 Judah to Hezron—Brief lists containing short, theological illustrations of God's involvement.

2:3–4—God's dealings with the line of Judah drawn from Gen. 38. Judah's first three sons were born to Judah's Canaanite wife, "the daughter of Shua" (not **Bath-shua** as in NRSV and most versions). **Er**, Judah's firstborn, so angered God that he was put to death. Judah's two other sons, **Perez and Zerah**, were the product of an incestuous relationship with his daughter-in-law, **Tamar**. Though God's judgment is seen in the swift dispatch of Er, God's grace appears in the working out of the promise through the ill-conceived line of Perez. David, and ultimately Jesus (Matt. 1:3), will be born to this line, suggesting that God can turn even evil human intent to good.

5 The sons of Perez: Hezron and Hamul. ⁶ The sons of Zerah: Zimri, Ethan, Heman, Calcol, and Dara,ᵃ five in all. ⁷ The sons of Carmi: Achar, the troubler of Israel, who transgressed in the matter of the devoted thing; ⁸ and Ethan's son was Azariah.

9 The sons of Hezron, who were born to him: Jerahmeel, Ram, and Chelubai. ¹⁰ Ram became the father of Amminadab, and Amminadab became the father of Nahshon, prince of the sons of Judah. ¹¹ Nahshon became the father of Salma, Salma of Boaz, ¹² Boaz of Obed, Obed of Jesse. ¹³ Jesse became the father of Eliab his firstborn, Abinadab the second, Shimea the third, ¹⁴ Nethanel the fourth, Raddai the fifth, ¹⁵ Ozem the sixth, David the seventh; ¹⁶ and their sisters were Zeruiah and Abigail. The sons of Zeruiah: Abishai, Joab, and Asahel, three. ¹⁷ Abigail bore Amasa, and the father of Amasa was Jether the Ishmaelite.

18 Caleb son of Hezron had children by his wife Azubah, and by Jerioth; these were her sons: Jesher, Shobab, and Ardon. ¹⁹ When Azubah died, Caleb married Ephrath, who bore him Hur. ²⁰ Hur became the father of Uri, and Uri became the father of Bezalel.

21 Afterward Hezron went in to the daughter of Machir father of Gilead, whom he married when he was sixty years old; and she bore him Segub; ²² and Segub became the father of Jair, who had twenty-three towns in the land of Gilead. ²³ But Geshur and Aram took from them Havvoth-jair, Kenath and its villages, sixty towns. All these were descendants of Machir, father of Gilead. ²⁴ After the death of Hezron, in Caleb-ephrathah, Abijah wife of Hezron bore him Ashhur, father of Tekoa.

25 The sons of Jerahmeel, the firstborn of Hezron: Ram his firstborn, Bunah, Oren, Ozem, and Ahijah. ²⁶ Jerahmeel

also had another wife, whose name was Atarah; she was the mother of Onam. ²⁷ The sons of Ram, the firstborn of Jerahmeel: Maaz, Jamin, and Eker. ²⁸ The sons of Onam: Shammai and Jada. The sons of Shammai: Nadab and Abishur. ²⁹ The name of Abishur's wife was Abihail, and she bore him Ahban and Molid. ³⁰ The sons of Nadab: Seled and Appaim; and Seled died childless. ³¹ The sonᵇ of Appaim: Ishi. The sonᵇ of Ishi: Sheshan. The sonᵇ of Sheshan: Ahlai. ³² The sons of Jada, Shammai's brother: Jether and Jonathan; and Jether died childless. ³³ The sons of Jonathan: Peleth and Zaza. These were the descendants of Jerahmeel. ³⁴ Now Sheshan had no sons, only daughters; but Sheshan had an Egyptian slave, whose name was Jarha. ³⁵ So Sheshan gave his daughter in marriage to his slave Jarha; and she bore him Attai. ³⁶ Attai became the father of Nathan, and Nathan of Zabad. ³⁷ Zabad became the father of Ephlal, and Ephlal of Obed. ³⁸ Obed became the father of Jehu, and Jehu of Azariah. ³⁹ Azariah became the father of Helez, and Helez of Eleasah. ⁴⁰ Eleasah became the father of Sismai, and Sismai of Shallum. ⁴¹ Shallum became the father of Jekamiah, and Jekamiah of Elishama.

42 The sons of Caleb brother of Jerahmeel: Meshaᶜ his firstborn, who was father of Ziph. The sons of Mareshah father of Hebron. ⁴³ The sons of Hebron: Korah, Tappuah, Rekem, and Shema. ⁴⁴ Shema became father of Raham, father of Jorkeam; and Rekem became the father of Shammai. ⁴⁵ The son of Shammai: Maon; and Maon was the father of Beth-zur. ⁴⁶ Ephah also, Caleb's concubine, bore Haran, Moza, and Gazez; and Haran became the father of Gazez. ⁴⁷ The sons of Jahdai: Regem, Jotham, Geshan, Pelet, Ephah, and Shaaph. ⁴⁸ Maacah,

ᵃ Or Darda; Compare Syr Tg some Gk Mss; See 1 Kings 4.31
ᵇ Heb sons ᶜ Gk reads Mareshah

2:7 *Achar, the troubler of Israel*—In Josh. 7, Achan was stoned to death for violating the stipulations of holy war. God also punished Israel by giving victory to Ai. Since Achar means "trouble," the misspelling may be a pun highlighting Achan's guilt.

Caleb's concubine, bore Sheber and Tirhanah. [49] She also bore Shaaph father of Madmannah, Sheva father of Machbenah and father of Gibea; and the daughter of Caleb was Achsah. [50] These were the descendants of Caleb.

The sons[a] of Hur the firstborn of Ephrathah: Shobal father of Kiriath-jearim, [51] Salma father of Bethlehem, and Hareph father of Beth-gader. [52] Shobal father of Kiriath-jearim had other sons: Haroeh, half of the Menuhoth. [53] And the families of Kiriath-jearim: the Ithrites, the Puthites, the Shumathites, and the Mishraites; from these came the Zorathites and the Eshtaolites. [54] The sons of Salma: Bethlehem, the Netophathites, Atroth-beth-joab, and half of the Manahathites, the Zorites. [55] The families also of the scribes that lived at Jabez: the Tirathites, the Shimeathites, and the Sucathites. These are the Kenites who came from Hammath, father of the house of Rechab.

Descendants of David and Solomon

3 These are the sons of David who were born to him in Hebron: the firstborn Amnon, by Ahinoam the Jezreelite; the second Daniel, by Abigail the Carmelite; [2] the third Absalom, son of Maacah, daughter of King Talmai of Geshur; the fourth Adonijah, son of Haggith; [3] the fifth Shephatiah, by Abital; the sixth Ithream, by his wife Eglah; [4] six were born to him in Hebron, where he reigned for seven years and six months. And he reigned thirty-three years in Jerusalem. [5] These were born to him in Jerusalem: Shimea, Shobab, Nathan, and Solomon, four by Bathshua, daughter of Ammiel; [6] then Ibhar, Elishama, Eliphelet, [7] Nogah, Nepheg, Japhia, [8] Elishama, Eliada, and Eliphelet, nine. [9] All these were David's sons, besides the sons of the concubines; and Tamar was their sister.

10 The descendants of Solomon: Rehoboam, Abijah his son, Asa his son, Jehoshaphat his son, [11] Joram his son, Ahaziah his son, Joash his son, [12] Amaziah his son, Azariah his son, Jotham his son, [13] Ahaz his son, Hezekiah his son, Manasseh his son, [14] Amon his son, Josiah his son. [15] The sons of Josiah: Johanan the firstborn, the second Jehoiakim, the third Zedekiah, the fourth Shallum. [16] The descendants of Jehoiakim: Jeconiah his son, Zedekiah his son; [17] and the sons of Jeconiah, the captive: Shealtiel his son, [18] Malchiram, Pedaiah, Shenazzar, Jekamiah, Hoshama, and Nedabiah; [19] The sons of Pedaiah: Zerubbabel and Shimei; and the sons of Zerubbabel: Meshullam and Hananiah, and Shelomith was their sister; [20] and Hashubah, Ohel, Berechiah, Hasadiah, and Jushab-hesed, five. [21] The sons of Hananiah: Pelatiah and Jeshaiah, his son[b] Rephaiah, his son[b] Arnan, his son[b] Obadiah, his son[b] Shecaniah. [22] The son[c] of Shecaniah: Shemaiah. And the sons of Shemaiah: Hattush, Igal, Bariah, Neariah, and Shaphat, six. [23] The sons of Neariah: Elioenai, Hizkiah, and Azrikam, three. [24] The sons of Elioenai:

[a] Gk Vg: Heb *son* [b] Gk Compare Syr Vg: Heb *sons of* [c] Heb *sons*

3:1–24—David's royal family dominates the center of the concentric arrangement of Judah's genealogy.

3:1–9—The fullest listing of David's immediate family.

3:5 *Bath-shua*—Alternate spelling of Bathsheba, not an attempt to disguise David's adultery (2 Sam. 11–12). Solomon's three brothers are found only here.

3:10–16 *Solomon . . . Zedekiah*—The omission of the northern kings allows this section to function as a listing of the Davidic dynasty down to the exile. Ahab's daughter, Athaliah, who had usurped the throne, is intentionally omitted.

3:17–24—Postexilic descendants of *Jeconiah* (the Jehoiakin of 2 Kgs. 24:8). Verses 19–24 are unique to Chronicles.

3:19 *Zerubbabel*—First governor of the Persian province of Yehud (Judah) after the exile. As a Davidic descendant (through Pedaiah, a younger son of Jehoiachin; Ezra 3:2 sees Jehoiachin's eldest son, Shealtiel, as the father), Zerubbabel establishes continuity with the postexilic community.

Hodaviah, Eliashib, Pelaiah, Akkub, Johanan, Delaiah, and Anani, seven.

Descendants of Judah

4 The sons of Judah: Perez, Hezron, Carmi, Hur, and Shobal. [2] Reaiah son of Shobal became the father of Jahath, and Jahath became the father of Ahumai and Lahad. These were the families of the Zorathites. [3] These were the sons[a] of Etam: Jezreel, Ishma, and Idbash; and the name of their sister was Hazzelelponi, [4] and Penuel was the father of Gedor, and Ezer the father of Hushah. These were the sons of Hur, the firstborn of Ephrathah, the father of Bethlehem. [5] Ashhur father of Tekoa had two wives, Helah and Naarah; [6] Naarah bore him Ahuzzam, Hepher, Temeni, and Haahashtari.[b] These were the sons of Naarah. [7] The sons of Helah: Zereth, Izhar,[c] and Ethnan. [8] Koz became the father of Anub, Zobebah, and the families of Aharhel son of Harum. [9] Jabez was honored more than his brothers; and his mother named him Jabez, saying, "Because I bore him in pain." [10] Jabez called on the God of Israel, saying, "Oh that you would bless me and enlarge my border, and that your hand might be with me, and that you would keep me from hurt and harm!" And God granted what he asked. [11] Chelub the brother of Shuhah became the father of Mehir, who was the father of Eshton. [12] Eshton became the father of Beth-rapha, Paseah, and Tehinnah the father of Ir-nahash. These are the men of Recah. [13] The sons of Kenaz: Othniel and Seraiah; and the sons of Othniel: Hathath and Meonothai.[d] [14] Meonothai became the father of Ophrah; and Seraiah became the father of Joab father of Ge-harashim,[e] so-called because they were artisans. [15] The sons of Caleb son of Jephunneh: Iru, Elah, and Naam; and the son[f] of Elah:

Kenaz. [16] The sons of Jehallelel: Ziph, Ziphah, Tiria, and Asarel. [17] The sons of Ezrah: Jether, Mered, Epher, and Jalon. These are the sons of Bithiah, daughter of Pharaoh, whom Mered married;[g] and she conceived and bore[h] Miriam, Shammai, and Ishbah father of Eshtemoa. [18] And his Judean wife bore Jered father of Gedor, Heber father of Soco, and Jekuthiel father of Zanoah. [19] The sons of the wife of Hodiah, the sister of Naham, were the fathers of Keilah the Garmite and Eshtemoa the Maacathite. [20] The sons of Shimon: Amnon, Rinnah, Ben-hanan, and Tilon. The sons of Ishi: Zoheth and Ben-zoheth. [21] The sons of Shelah son of Judah: Er father of Lecah, Laadah father of Mareshah, and the families of the guild of linen workers at Beth-ashbea; [22] and Jokim, and the men of Cozeba, and Joash, and Saraph, who married into Moab but returned to Lehem[i] (now the records[j] are ancient). [23] These were the potters and inhabitants of Netaim and Gederah; they lived there with the king in his service.

Descendants of Simeon

24 The sons of Simeon: Nemuel, Jamin, Jarib, Zerah, Shaul;[k] [25] Shallum was his son, Mibsam his son, Mishma his son. [26] The sons of Mishma: Hammuel his son, Zaccur his son, Shimei his son. [27] Shimei had sixteen sons and six daughters; but his brothers did not have many children, nor did all their family multiply like the Judeans. [28] They lived in Beer-sheba, Moladah, Hazar-shual, [29] Bilhah, Ezem, Tolad, [30] Bethuel, Hormah, Ziklag, [31] Beth-marcaboth, Hazar-susim, Beth-biri, and Shaaraim. These were their towns until David became king. [32] And their villages were Etam,

---

[a] Gk Compare Vg: Heb *the father*   [b] Or *Ahashtari*   [c] Another reading is *Zohar*   [d] Gk Vg: Heb lacks *and Meonothai*   [e] That is *Valley of artisans*   [f] Heb *sons*   [g] The clause: *These are . . . married* is transposed from verse 18   [h] Heb lacks *and bore*   [i] Vg Compare Gk: Heb *and Jashubi-lahem*   [j] Or *matters*   [k] Or *Saul*

4:1–23—Shorter genealogies, unparalleled in the Old Testament, gathered for a complete presentation of the tribe of Judah.

4:24–43 The Tribe of Simeon
A transition between Judah (2:3–4:23) and the northern tribes east of the Jordan (5:1–26).

Ain, Rimmon, Tochen, and Ashan, five towns, 33 along with all their villages that were around these towns as far as Baal. These were their settlements. And they kept a genealogical record.

34 Meshobab, Jamlech, Joshah son of Amaziah, 35 Joel, Jehu son of Joshibiah son of Seraiah son of Asiel, 36 Elioenai, Jaakobah, Jeshohaiah, Asaiah, Adiel, Jesimiel, Benaiah, 37 Ziza son of Shiphi son of Allon son of Jedaiah son of Shimri son of Shemaiah— 38 these mentioned by name were leaders in their families, and their clans increased greatly. 39 They journeyed to the entrance of Gedor, to the east side of the valley, to seek pasture for their flocks, 40 where they found rich, good pasture, and the land was very broad, quiet, and peaceful; for the former inhabitants there belonged to Ham. 41 These, registered by name, came in the days of King Hezekiah of Judah, and attacked their tents and the Meunim who were found there, and exterminated them to this day, and settled in their place, because there was pasture there for their flocks. 42 And some of them, five hundred men of the Simeonites, went to Mount Seir, having as their leaders Pelatiah, Neariah, Rephaiah, and Uzziel, sons of Ishi; 43 they destroyed the remnant of the Amalekites that had escaped, and they have lived there to this day.

Descendants of Reuben

5 The sons of Reuben the firstborn of Israel. (He was the firstborn, but because he defiled his father's bed his birthright was given to the sons of Joseph son of Israel, so that he is not enrolled in the genealogy according to the birthright; 2 though Judah became prominent among his brothers and a ruler came from him, yet the birthright belonged to Joseph.) 3 The sons of Reuben, the firstborn of Israel: Hanoch, Pallu, Hezron, and Carmi. 4 The sons of Joel: Shemaiah his son, Gog his son, Shimei his son, 5 Micah his son, Reaiah his son, Baal his son, 6 Beerah his son, whom King Tilgath-pilneser of Assyria carried away into exile; he was a chieftain of the Reubenites. 7 And his kindred by their families, when the genealogy of their generations was reckoned: the chief, Jeiel, and Zechariah, 8 and Bela son of Azaz, son of Shema, son of Joel, who lived in Aroer, as far as Nebo and Baal-meon. 9 He also lived to the east as far as the beginning of the desert this side of the Euphrates, because their cattle had multiplied in the land of Gilead. 10 And in the days of Saul they made war on the Hagrites, who fell by their hand; and they lived in their tents throughout all the region east of Gilead.

Descendants of Gad

11 The sons of Gad lived beside them in the land of Bashan as far as Salecah:

4:39–43—Traditional material concerned with geographical expansion. The first of these occurred in the days of Hezekiah and relates Simeon's expansion into Philistia (the Septuagint reads "Gerar" for *Gedor*) to the northwest (vv. 39–41). The second reminiscence reports the displacement of the *Amalekites* who lived in the hill country of Seir in Edom (vv. 42–43). The significance of these stories of faithfulness rewarded with land would not have been lost on the chronicler's postexilic community, esp. when contrasted with the experience of the northern tribes east of the Jordan that follows (5:1–26).

5:1–26 The Transjordanian Tribes

Reuben (vv. 1–10), *Gad* (vv. 11–22), and *the half-tribe of Manasseh* (vv. 23–26) are located on the eastern bank of the Jordan River and rep-

resent a significant portion of the northern tribes that eventually fell to Assyria. The chronicler sees them as one (cf. vv. 18, 26) and uses them, along with the remaining northern tribes on the west bank of the Jordan (chap. 7), to frame the presentation of Levi in chap. 6.

5:1–10—The tribe of Reuben.

5:1—Firstborn privilege was transferred to *the sons of Joseph* (Ephraim and Manasseh) because of Reuben's incest with Bilhah, Jacob's concubine (see Gen. 35:22; 49:3–4).

5:2 *Ruler*—David.

5:6 *Tiglath-pilneser*—Variant spelling of Tiglath-pileser III, the Assyrian king also known as Pul, who defeated Gilead ca. 733 BCE.

5:11–22—The tribes of Gad and Manasseh, to

¹²Joel the chief, Shapham the second, Janai, and Shaphat in Bashan. ¹³And their kindred according to their clans: Michael, Meshullam, Sheba, Jorai, Jacan, Zia, and Eber, seven. ¹⁴These were the sons of Abihail son of Huri, son of Jaroah, son of Gilead, son of Michael, son of Jeshishai, son of Jahdo, son of Buz; ¹⁵Ahi son of Abdiel, son of Guni, was chief in their clan; ¹⁶and they lived in Gilead, in Bashan and in its towns, and in all the pasture lands of Sharon to their limits. ¹⁷All of these were enrolled by genealogies in the days of King Jotham of Judah, and in the days of King Jeroboam of Israel.

18 The Reubenites, the Gadites, and the half-tribe of Manasseh had valiant warriors, who carried shield and sword, and drew the bow, expert in war, forty-four thousand seven hundred sixty, ready for service. ¹⁹They made war on the Hagrites, Jetur, Naphish, and Nodab; ²⁰and when they received help against them, the Hagrites and all who were with them were given into their hands, for they cried to God in the battle, and he granted their entreaty because they trusted in him. ²¹They captured their livestock: fifty thousand of their camels, two hundred fifty thousand sheep, two thousand donkeys, and one hundred thousand captives. ²²Many fell slain, because the war was of God. And they lived in their territory until the exile.

The Half-Tribe of Manasseh

23 The members of the half-tribe of Manasseh lived in the land; they were very numerous from Bashan to Baal-hermon, Senir, and Mount Hermon. ²⁴These were the heads of their clans: Epher,ᵃ Ishi, Eliel, Azriel, Jeremiah, Hodaviah, and Jahdiel, mighty warriors, famous men, heads of their clans. ²⁵But they transgressed against the God of their ancestors, and prostituted themselves to the gods of the peoples of the land, whom God had destroyed before them. ²⁶So the God of Israel stirred up the spirit of King Pul of Assyria, the spirit of King Tilgath-pilneser of Assyria, and he carried them away, namely, the Reubenites, the Gadites, and the half-tribe of Manasseh, and brought them to Halah, Habor, Hara, and the river Gozan, to this day.

Descendants of Levi

6ᵇ The sons of Levi: Gershom,ᶜ Kohath, and Merari. ²The sons of Kohath: Amram, Izhar, Hebron, and Uzziel. ³The children of Amram: Aaron, Moses, and Miriam. The sons of Aaron: Nadab, Abihu, Eleazar, and Ithamar. ⁴Eleazar became the father of Phinehas, Phinehas of Abishua, ⁵Abishua of Bukki, Bukki of Uzzi, ⁶Uzzi of Zerahiah, Zerahiah of Meraioth, ⁷Meraioth of Amariah, Amariah of Ahitub, ⁸Ahitub

ᵃ Gk Vg: Heb and Epher   ᵇCh 5.27 in Heb   ᶜHeb Gershon, variant of Gershom; See 6.16

---

the north of Reuben, were considered as one. The war stories (vv. 18–22) use exaggerated numbers to emphasize the greatness of God's people and portray the battle as a holy war in which God grants victory to those who demonstrate their trust through prayer. This belief in God's retributive justice is a major theme in Chronicles.

5:22 *Until the exile*—The Assyrian deportation of the northern tribes in 722 BCE.

5:25–26—In this negative instance of retributive justice, based upon 2 Kgs. 15:29, God's people are defeated in battle because they worshiped other gods.

6:1–81 The Tribe of Levi
The importance of the priestly tribe of Levi

dictates the length and location of this material within the concentric arrangement of the tribal listings.

6:1–15—Major omissions in this incomplete list of high priests include Eli (1 Sam. 2:27–36), Jehoiada (2 Chr. 22:11), Uriah (2 Kgs. 16:10–16), and at least two other Azariahs (2 Chr. 26:20; 31:10–13). The list legitimates the priesthood of the postexilic community through *Jehozadak*, the father of Joshua, first high priest of the return (v. 14; Ezra 3:2; Neh. 12:26; Hag. 1:1).

6:4 *Phinehas*—Priest whose religious zeal earned a covenant of eternal priesthood (Num. 25:1–13).

6:8 *Zadok*—David's main priest, who restored the high priesthood to the line of Phinehas.

of Zadok, Zadok of Ahimaaz, ⁹Ahimaaz of Azariah, Azariah of Johanan, ¹⁰and Johanan of Azariah (it was he who served as priest in the house that Solomon built in Jerusalem). ¹¹Azariah became the father of Amariah, Amariah of Ahitub, ¹²Ahitub of Zadok, Zadok of Shallum, ¹³Shallum of Hilkiah, Hilkiah of Azariah, ¹⁴Azariah of Seraiah, Seraiah of Jehozadak; ¹⁵and Jehozadak went into exile when the LORD sent Judah and Jerusalem into exile by the hand of Nebuchadnezzar.

16ᵃ The sons of Levi: Gershom, Kohath, and Merari. ¹⁷These are the names of the sons of Gershom: Libni and Shimei. ¹⁸The sons of Kohath: Amram, Izhar, Hebron, and Uzziel. ¹⁹The sons of Merari: Mahli and Mushi. These are the clans of the Levites according to their ancestry. ²⁰Of Gershom: Libni his son, Jahath his son, Zimmah his son, ²¹Joah his son, Iddo his son, Zerah his son, Jeatherai his son. ²²The sons of Kohath: Amminadab his son, Korah his son, Assir his son, ²³Elkanah his son, Ebiasaph his son, Assir his son, ²⁴Tahath his son, Uriel his son, Uzziah his son, and Shaul his son. ²⁵The sons of Elkanah: Amasai and Ahimoth, ²⁶Elkanah his son, Zophai his son, Nahath his son, ²⁷Eliab his son, Jeroham his son, Elkanah his son. ²⁸The sons of Samuel: Joelᵇ his firstborn, the second Abijah.ᶜ ²⁹The sons of Merari: Mahli, Libni his son, Shimei his son, Uzzah his son, ³⁰Shimea his son, Haggiah his son, and Asaiah his son.

Musicians Appointed by David

31 These are the men whom David put in charge of the service of song in the house of the LORD, after the ark came to rest there. ³²They ministered with song before the tabernacle of the tent of meeting, until Solomon had built the house of the LORD in Jerusalem; and they performed their service in due order. ³³These are the men who served; and their sons were: Of the Kohathites: Heman, the singer, son of Joel, son of Samuel, ³⁴son of Elkanah, son of Jeroham, son of Eliel, son of Toah, ³⁵son of Zuph, son of Elkanah, son of Mahath, son of Amasai, ³⁶son of Elkanah, son of Joel, son of Azariah, son of Zephaniah, ³⁷son of Tahath, son of Assir, son of Ebiasaph, son of Korah, ³⁸son of Izhar, son of Kohath, son of Levi, son of Israel; ³⁹and his brother Asaph, who stood on his right, namely, Asaph son of Berechiah, son of Shimea, ⁴⁰son of Michael, son of Baaseiah, son of Malchijah, ⁴¹son of Ethni, son of Zerah, son of Adaiah, ⁴²son of Ethan, son of Zimmah, son of Shimei, ⁴³son of Jahath, son of Gershom, son of Levi. ⁴⁴On the left were their kindred the sons of Merari: Ethan son of Kishi, son of Abdi, son of Malluch, ⁴⁵son of Hashabiah, son of Amaziah, son of Hilkiah, ⁴⁶son of Amzi, son of Bani, son of Shemer, ⁴⁷son of Mahli, son of Mushi, son of Merari, son of Levi; ⁴⁸and their kindred the Levites were appointed for all the service of the tabernacle of the house of God.

49 But Aaron and his sons made offerings on the altar of burnt offering and on the altar of incense, doing all the work of the most holy place, to make

ᵃCh 6.1 in Heb   ᵇGk Syr Compare verse 33 and 1 Sam 8.2: Heb lacks Joel   ᶜHeb reads Vashni, and Abijah for the second Abijah, taking the second as a proper name

---

6:13 *Hilkiah*—High priest who found the book of the law of the Lord in the temple, thereby precipitating Josiah's reform in 622 (2 Chr. 34:14–21).

6:16–30—The central genealogies of the Levites are traced through *Gershom* (vv. 17, 20–21), *Kohath* (vv. 18, 22–28), and *Merari* (vv. 19, 29–30). *Samuel* (v. 28) was an Ephraimite, not a Levite (1 Sam. 1:1).

6:31–48—Levitical musicians, listed in order of importance, follow a summary of David's institution of the singing of praise in the temple as the highest form of worship (vv. 31–32; cf. chaps. 15–16). David's contemporaries Heman, Asaph, and Ethan legitimate the claims of present cultic officials.

6:49–53 *Sons of Aaron*—The resumption of the priestly line echoes vv. 1–15. It also provides a priestly framework around the Levitical material of vv. 16–48, and distinguishes the duties of the

atonement for Israel, according to all that Moses the servant of God had commanded. [50] These are the sons of Aaron: Eleazar his son, Phinehas his son, Abishua his son, [51] Bukki his son, Uzzi his son, Zerahiah his son, [52] Meraioth his son, Amariah his son, Ahitub his son, [53] Zadok his son, Ahimaaz his son.

Settlements of the Levites

54 These are their dwelling places according to their settlements within their borders: to the sons of Aaron of the families of Kohathites—for the lot fell to them first— [55] to them they gave Hebron in the land of Judah and its surrounding pasture lands, [56] but the fields of the city and its villages they gave to Caleb son of Jephunneh. [57] To the sons of Aaron they gave the cities of refuge: Hebron, Libnah with its pasture lands, Jattir, Eshtemoa with its pasture lands, [58] Hilen[a] with its pasture lands, Debir with its pasture lands, [59] Ashan with its pasture lands, and Beth-shemesh with its pasture lands. [60] From the tribe of Benjamin, Geba with its pasture lands, Alemeth with its pasture lands, and Anathoth with its pasture lands. All their towns throughout their families were thirteen.

61 To the rest of the Kohathites were given by lot out of the family of the tribe, out of the half-tribe, the half of Manasseh, ten towns. [62] To the Gershomites according to their families were allotted thirteen towns out of the tribes of Issachar, Asher, Naphtali, and Manasseh in Bashan. [63] To the Merarites according to their families were allotted twelve towns out of the tribes of Reuben, Gad, and Zebulun. [64] So the people of Israel gave the Levites the towns with

their pasture lands. [65] They also gave them by lot out of the tribes of Judah, Simeon, and Benjamin these towns that are mentioned by name.

66 And some of the families of the sons of Kohath had towns of their territory out of the tribe of Ephraim. [67] They were given the cities of refuge: Shechem with its pasture lands in the hill country of Ephraim, Gezer with its pasture lands, [68] Jokmeam with its pasture lands, Beth-horon with its pasture lands, [69] Aijalon with its pasture lands, Gath-rimmon with its pasture lands; [70] and out of the half-tribe of Manasseh, Aner with its pasture lands, and Bileam with its pasture lands, for the rest of the families of the Kohathites.

71 To the Gershomites: out of the half-tribe of Manasseh: Golan in Bashan with its pasture lands and Ashtaroth with its pasture lands; [72] and out of the tribe of Issachar: Kedesh with its pasture lands, Daberath[b] with its pasture lands, [73] Ramoth with its pasture lands, and Anem with its pasture lands; [74] out of the tribe of Asher: Mashal with its pasture lands, Abdon with its pasture lands, [75] Hukok with its pasture lands, and Rehob with its pasture lands; [76] and out of the tribe of Naphtali: Kedesh in Galilee with its pasture lands, Hammon with its pasture lands, and Kiriathaim with its pasture lands. [77] To the rest of the Merarites out of the tribe of Zebulun: Rimmono with its pasture lands, Tabor with its pasture lands, [78] and across the Jordan from Jericho, on the east side of the Jordan, out of the tribe of Reuben: Bezer in the steppe with its pasture lands, Jahzah with its pasture lands,

---

[a] Other readings *Hilez, Holon;* See Josh 21.15   [b] Or *Dobrath*

Levites, which included leading in music and providing security in the cult (chaps. 25–26), teaching and administration among the people (9:26), and even prophesying (25:2–3), from those of the priests, who alone could *make offerings* (Exod. 27:1–8), burn *incense* (Exod. 30:1–10), and *make atonement* (Lev. 4:31; 16).

6:55–60—The cities allocated to the priests are

all located in the territories of Judah (vv. 55–59) and Benjamin (v. 60), the geographical heart of the chronicler's postexilic community.

6:61–81—The Levites received these cities instead of a tribal allotment (Num. 1:47–53). The importance of a Levitical presence throughout all Israel is stressed in the even distribution of these cities.

⁷⁹Kedemoth with its pasture lands, and Mephaath with its pasture lands; ⁸⁰and out of the tribe of Gad: Ramoth in Gilead with its pasture lands, Mahanaim with its pasture lands, ⁸¹Heshbon with its pasture lands, and Jazer with its pasture lands.

Descendants of Issachar

7 The sons[a] of Issachar: Tola, Puah, Jashub, and Shimron, four. ²The sons of Tola: Uzzi, Rephaiah, Jeriel, Jahmai, Ibsam, and Shemuel, heads of their ancestral houses, namely of Tola, mighty warriors of their generations, their number in the days of David being twenty-two thousand six hundred. ³The son[b] of Uzzi: Izrahiah. And the sons of Izrahiah: Michael, Obadiah, Joel, and Isshiah, five, all of them chiefs; ⁴and along with them, by their generations, according to their ancestral houses, were units of the fighting force, thirty-six thousand, for they had many wives and sons. ⁵Their kindred belonging to all the families of Issachar were in all eighty-seven thousand mighty warriors, enrolled by genealogy.

Descendants of Benjamin

6 The sons of Benjamin: Bela, Becher, and Jediael, three. ⁷The sons of Bela: Ezbon, Uzzi, Uzziel, Jerimoth, and Iri, five, heads of ancestral houses, mighty warriors; and their enrollment by genealogies was twenty-two thousand thirty-four. ⁸The sons of Becher: Zemirah, Joash, Eliezer, Elioenai, Omri, Jeremoth, Abijah, Anathoth, and Alemeth. All these were the sons of Becher; ⁹and their enrollment by genealogies, according to their generations, as heads of their ancestral houses, mighty war-

riors, was twenty thousand two hundred. ¹⁰The sons of Jediael: Bilhan. And the sons of Bilhan: Jeush, Benjamin, Ehud, Chenaanah, Zethan, Tarshish, and Ahishahar. ¹¹All these were the sons of Jediael according to the heads of their ancestral houses, mighty warriors, seventeen thousand two hundred, ready for service in war. ¹²And Shuppim and Huppim were the sons of Ir, Hushim the son[b] of Aher.

Descendants of Naphtali

13 The descendants of Naphtali: Jahziel, Guni, Jezer, and Shallum, the descendants of Bilhah.

Descendants of Manasseh

14 The sons of Manasseh: Asriel, whom his Aramean concubine bore; she bore Machir the father of Gilead. ¹⁵And Machir took a wife for Huppim and for Shuppim. The name of his sister was Maacah. And the name of the second was Zelophehad; and Zelophehad had daughters. ¹⁶Maacah the wife of Machir bore a son, and she named him Peresh; the name of his brother was Sheresh; and his sons were Ulam and Rekem. ¹⁷The son[b] of Ulam: Bedan. These were the sons of Gilead son of Machir, son of Manasseh. ¹⁸And his sister Hammolecheth bore Ishhod, Abiezer, and Mahlah. ¹⁹The sons of Shemida were Ahian, Shechem, Likhi, and Aniam.

Descendants of Ephraim

20 The sons of Ephraim: Shuthelah, and Bered his son, Tahath his son, Eleadah his son, Tahath his son, ²¹Zabad his son, Shuthelah his son, and Ezer and Elead. Now the people of Gath, who were born

---

[a] Syr Compare Vg: Heb *And to the sons*   [b] Heb *sons*

7:1–40 The Tribes of the West Jordan Drawn from military lists of David's time (cf. the numerical data in vv. 2, 4, 5, 7, 9, 11), these lists complete the tribal genealogies begun in 2:1. With the inexplicable exception of Benjamin, these northern tribes west of the Jordan balance and complement the northern tribes east of the Jordan in chapter 5. The unity of all the tribes of

Israel is an important theme in Chronicles, as seen in the united support for David's kingship (chap. 12) and the building of Solomon's temple (chap. 27). Later, Hezekiah will call for a united response in worship (2 Chr. 30). The chronicler's vision of the unity of all God's people can inform contemporary efforts to eliminate racial, ethnic, and religious tensions.

in the land, killed them, because they came down to raid their cattle. ²²And their father Ephraim mourned many days, and his brothers came to comfort him. ²³Ephraim[a] went in to his wife, and she conceived and bore a son; and he named him Beriah, because disaster[b] had befallen his house. ²⁴His daughter was Sheerah, who built both Lower and Upper Beth-horon, and Uzzen-sheerah. ²⁵Rephah was his son, Resheph his son, Telah his son, Tahan his son, ²⁶Ladan his son, Ammihud his son, Elishama his son, ²⁷Nun[c] his son, Joshua his son. ²⁸Their possessions and settlements were Bethel and its towns, and eastward Naaran, and westward Gezer and its towns, Shechem and its towns, as far as Ayyah and its towns; ²⁹also along the borders of the Manassites, Beth-shean and its towns, Taanach and its towns, Megiddo and its towns, Dor and its towns. In these lived the sons of Joseph son of Israel.

Descendants of Asher

30 The sons of Asher: Imnah, Ishvah, Ishvi, Beriah, and their sister Serah. ³¹The sons of Beriah: Heber and Malchiel, who was the father of Birzaith. ³²Heber became the father of Japhlet, Shomer, Hotham, and their sister Shua. ³³The sons of Japhlet: Pasach, Bimhal, and Ashvath. These are the sons of Japhlet. ³⁴The sons of Shemer: Ahi, Rohgah, Hubbah, and Aram. ³⁵The sons of Helem[d] his brother: Zophah, Imna, Shelesh, and Amal. ³⁶The sons of Zophah: Suah, Harnepher, Shual, Beri, Imrah, ³⁷Bezer, Hod, Shamma, Shilshah, Ithran, and Beera. ³⁸The sons of Jether: Jephunneh, Pispa, and Ara. ³⁹The sons of Ulla: Arah, Hanniel, and Rizia. ⁴⁰All of these were men of Asher, heads of ancestral houses, select mighty warriors, chief of the princes. Their number enrolled by genealogies, for service in war, was twenty-six thousand men.

Descendants of Benjamin

8 Benjamin became the father of Bela his firstborn, Ashbel the second, Aharah the third, ²Nohah the fourth, and Rapha the fifth. ³And Bela had sons: Addar, Gera, Abihud,[e] ⁴Abishua, Naaman, Ahoah, ⁵Gera, Shephuphan, and Huram. ⁶These are the sons of Ehud (they were heads of ancestral houses of the inhabitants of Geba, and they were carried into exile to Manahath): ⁷Naaman,[f] Ahijah, and Gera, that is, Heglam,[g] who became the father of Uzza and Ahihud. ⁸And Shaharaim had sons in the country of Moab after he had sent away his wives Hushim and Baara. ⁹He had sons by his wife Hodesh: Jobab, Zibia, Mesha, Malcam, ¹⁰Jeuz, Sachia, and Mirmah. These were his sons, heads of ancestral houses. ¹¹He also had sons by Hushim: Abitub and Elpaal. ¹²The sons of Elpaal: Eber, Misham, and Shemed, who built Ono and Lod with its towns, ¹³and Beriah and Shema (they were heads of ancestral houses of the inhabitants of Aijalon, who put to flight the inhabitants of Gath); ¹⁴and Ahio, Shashak, and Jeremoth. ¹⁵Zebadiah, Arad, Eder, ¹⁶Michael, Ishpah, and Joha were sons of Beriah. ¹⁷Zebadiah, Meshullam, Hizki, Heber, ¹⁸Ishmerai, Izliah, and Jobab were the sons of Elpaal. ¹⁹Jakim, Zichri, Zabdi, ²⁰Elienai, Zillethai, Eliel, ²¹Adaiah, Beraiah, and Shimrath were the sons of Shimei. ²²Ishpan, Eber, Eliel, ²³Abdon, Zichri, Hanan, ²⁴Hananiah, Elam, Anthothijah, ²⁵Iphdeiah, and Penuel were the sons of Shashak. ²⁶Shamsherai, Shehariah, Athaliah, ²⁷Jaareshiah, Elijah, and Zichri were the sons of Jeroham. ²⁸These were the heads of ancestral houses, according to their generations, chiefs. These lived in Jerusalem.

[a] Heb He [b] Heb beraah [c] Here spelled Non; see Ex 33.11 [d] Or Hotham; see 7.32 [e] Or father of Ehud; see 8.6 [f] Heb and Naaman [g] Or he carried them into exile

---

8:1–40 The Tribe of Benjamin
The genealogy conflicts with other Benjaminite genealogies (Gen. 46:21; Num. 26:38–40; 1 Chr. 7:6–11). Its importance lies in its presentation of the genealogy of *Saul*, Israel's first king (1 Chr. 8:33–40).

29 Jeiel[a] the father of Gibeon lived in Gibeon, and the name of his wife was Maacah. [30] His firstborn son: Abdon, then Zur, Kish, Baal,[b] Nadab, [31] Gedor, Ahio, Zecher, [32] and Mikloth, who became the father of Shimeah. Now these also lived opposite their kindred in Jerusalem, with their kindred. [33] Ner became the father of Kish, Kish of Saul,[c] Saul[c] of Jonathan, Malchishua, Abinadab, and Esh-baal; [34] and the son of Jonathan was Merib-baal; and Merib-baal became the father of Micah. [35] The sons of Micah: Pithon, Melech, Tarea, and Ahaz. [36] Ahaz became the father of Jehoaddah; and Jehoaddah became the father of Alemeth, Azmaveth, and Zimri; Zimri became the father of Moza. [37] Moza became the father of Binea; Raphah was his son, Eleasah his son, Azel his son. [38] Azel had six sons, and these are their names: Azrikam, Bocheru, Ishmael, Sheariah, Obadiah, and Hanan; all these were the sons of Azel. [39] The sons of his brother Eshek: Ulam his firstborn, Jeush the second, and Eliphelet the third. [40] The sons of Ulam were mighty warriors, archers, having many children and grandchildren, one hundred fifty. All these were Benjaminites.

9 So all Israel was enrolled by genealogies; and these are written in the Book of the Kings of Israel. And Judah was taken into exile in Babylon because of their unfaithfulness. [2] Now the first to live again in their possessions in their towns were Israelites, priests, Levites, and temple servants.

Inhabitants of Jerusalem after the Exile

3 And some of the people of Judah, Benjamin, Ephraim, and Manasseh lived in Jerusalem: [4] Uthai son of Ammihud, son of Omri, son of Imri, son of Bani, from the sons of Perez son of Judah. [5] And of the Shilonites: Asaiah the firstborn, and his sons. [6] Of the sons of Zerah: Jeuel and their kin, six hundred ninety. [7] Of the Benjaminites: Sallu son of Meshullam, son of Hodaviah, son of Hassenuah, [8] Ibneiah son of Jeroham, Elah son of Uzzi, son of Michri, and Meshullam son of Shephatiah, son of Reuel, son of Ibnijah; [9] and their kindred according to their generations, nine hundred fifty-six. All these were heads of families according to their ancestral houses.

Priestly Families

10 Of the priests: Jedaiah, Jehoiarib, Jachin, [11] and Azariah son of Hilkiah, son of Meshullam, son of Zadok, son of Meraioth, son of Ahitub, the chief officer of the house of God; [12] and Adaiah son of Jeroham, son of Pashhur, son of Malchijah, and Maasai son of Adiel, son of Jahzerah, son of Meshullam, son of Meshillemith, son of Immer; [13] besides their kindred, heads of their ancestral houses, one thousand seven hundred sixty, qualified for the work of the service of the house of God.

Levitical Families

14 Of the Levites: Shemaiah son of Hasshub, son of Azrikam, son of Hashabiah, of the sons of Merari; [15] and Bakbakkar, Heresh, Galal, and Mattaniah son of Mica, son of Zichri, son of Asaph; [16] and Obadiah son of Shemaiah, son of Galal, son of Jeduthun, and Berechiah son of Asa, son of Elkanah, who lived in the villages of the Netophathites.

[a] Compare 9.35: Heb lacks *Jeiel* [b] Gk Ms adds *Ner*; Compare 8.33 and 9.36 [c] Or *Shaul*

9:1 Conclusion of the Tribal List
This summary verse concludes the preexilic genealogy of chaps. 2–8. The unity of the people, the *exile* and its cause, the *unfaithfulness* of the people, will continue as major themes.

9:2–34 The People in Jerusalem
This list of those who returned from exile forges a crucial link between Israel's past and the chronicler's postexilic community.

9:2b—The following listing of the inhabitants of Jerusalem is structured in three classes: lay *Israelites* (vv. 3–9), *priests* (vv. 10–13), and, finally, *Levites* (vv. 14–34). Interestingly, the lay people are listed before the clergy.

17 The gatekeepers were: Shallum, Akkub, Talmon, Ahiman; and their kindred Shallum was the chief, 18 stationed previously in the king's gate on the east side. These were the gatekeepers of the camp of the Levites. 19 Shallum son of Kore, son of Ebiasaph, son of Korah, and his kindred of his ancestral house, the Korahites, were in charge of the work of the service, guardians of the thresholds of the tent, as their ancestors had been in charge of the camp of the LORD, guardians of the entrance. 20 And Phinehas son of Eleazar was chief over them in former times; the LORD was with him. 21 Zechariah son of Meshelemiah was gatekeeper at the entrance of the tent of meeting. 22 All these, who were chosen as gatekeepers at the thresholds, were two hundred twelve. They were enrolled by genealogies in their villages. David and the seer Samuel established them in their office of trust. 23 So they and their descendants were in charge of the gates of the house of the LORD, that is, the house of the tent, as guards. 24 The gatekeepers were on the four sides, east, west, north, and south; 25 and their kindred who were in their villages were obliged to come in every seven days, in turn, to be with them; 26 for the four chief gatekeepers, who were Levites, were in charge of the chambers and the treasures of the house of God. 27 And they would spend the night near the house of God; for on them lay the duty of watching, and they had charge of opening it every morning.

28 Some of them had charge of the utensils of service, for they were required to count them when they were brought in and taken out. 29 Others of them were appointed over the furniture, and over all the holy utensils, also over the choice flour, the wine, the oil, the incense, and the spices. 30 Others, of the sons of the priests, prepared the mixing of the spices,

31 and Mattithiah, one of the Levites, the firstborn of Shallum the Korahite, was in charge of making the flat cakes. 32 Also some of their kindred of the Kohathites had charge of the rows of bread, to prepare them for each sabbath.

33 Now these are the singers, the heads of ancestral houses of the Levites, living in the chambers of the temple free from other service, for they were on duty day and night. 34 These were heads of ancestral houses of the Levites, according to their generations; these leaders lived in Jerusalem.

The Family of King Saul

35 In Gibeon lived the father of Gibeon, Jeiel, and the name of his wife was Maacah. 36 His firstborn son was Abdon, then Zur, Kish, Baal, Ner, Nadab, 37 Gedor, Ahio, Zechariah, and Mikloth; 38 and Mikloth became the father of Shimeam; and these also lived opposite their kindred in Jerusalem, with their kindred. 39 Ner became the father of Kish, Kish of Saul, Saul of Jonathan, Malchishua, Abinadab, and Esh-baal; 40 and the son of Jonathan was Meribbaal; and Merib-baal became the father of Micah. 41 The sons of Micah: Pithon, Melech, Tahrea, and Ahaz;*a* 42 and Ahaz became the father of Jarah, and Jarah of Alemeth, Azmaveth, and Zimri; and Zimri became the father of Moza. 43 Moza became the father of Binea; and Rephaiah was his son, Eleasah his son, Azel his son. 44 Azel had six sons, and these are their names: Azrikam, Bocheru, Ishmael, Sheariah, Obadiah, and Hanan; these were the sons of Azel.

Death of Saul and His Sons

10 Now the Philistines fought against Israel; and the men of Israel fled before the Philistines, and fell

a Compare 8.35: Heb lacks *and Ahaz*

9:35–44 Saul's Family
The repetition of Saul's genealogy from 8:29–38 forms a transition to his tragic death.

1 Chr. 10:1–2 Chr. 9:31 The United Monarchy: The Kingdom of David and Solomon

In Samuel, the question was whether Israel's desire for a king would nullify God's kingship

slain on Mount Gilboa. ²The Philistines overtook Saul and his sons; and the Philistines killed Jonathan and Abinadab and Malchishua, sons of Saul. ³The battle pressed hard on Saul; and the archers found him, and he was wounded by the archers. ⁴Then Saul said to his armor-bearer, "Draw your sword, and thrust me through with it, so that these uncircumcised may not come and make sport of me." But his armor-bearer was unwilling, for he was terrified. So Saul took his own sword and fell on it. ⁵When his armor-bearer saw that Saul was dead, he also fell on his sword and died. ⁶Thus Saul died; he and his three sons and all his house died together. ⁷When all the men of Israel who were in the valley saw that the army*a* had fled and that Saul and his sons were dead, they abandoned their towns and fled; and the Philistines came and occupied them.

8 The next day when the Philistines came to strip the dead, they found Saul and his sons fallen on Mount Gilboa. ⁹They stripped him and took his head and his armor, and sent messengers throughout the land of the Philistines to carry the good news to their idols and to the people. ¹⁰They put his armor in the temple of their gods, and fastened his head in the temple of Dagon. ¹¹But when all Jabesh-gilead heard everything that the Philistines had done to Saul, ¹²all the valiant warriors got up and took away the body of Saul and the bodies of his sons, and brought them to Jabesh. Then they buried their bones under the oak in Jabesh, and fasted seven days.

13 So Saul died for his unfaithfulness; he was unfaithful to the LORD in that he did not keep the command of the LORD; moreover, he had consulted a medium, seeking guidance, ¹⁴and did not seek guidance from the LORD. Therefore the LORD*b* put him to death and turned the kingdom over to David son of Jesse.

David Anointed King of All Israel

11 Then all Israel gathered together to David at Hebron and said,

a Heb *they*   *b* Heb *he*

(1 Sam. 8). For the chronicler's postexilic community, the question has become, what does kingship mean in a land ruled by Persia? To answer that question, the chronicler presents the reigns of David and Solomon as a time in which God's will for Israel was realized in an especially clear way. Their rule is depicted in 1–2 Chronicles as a unity with individual stories that parallel and complement each other.

The story of David is related in six lengthy sections. Saul's death (10:1–14) introduces the period of the united monarchy. This is followed by the recognition of David's kingship by all Israel (11:1–12:40), David's transport of the ark to Jerusalem (13:1–16:43), God's promise of a Davidic dynasty (17:1–27), the consolidation of the empire (18:1–20:8), and David's acquisition of the temple site (21:1–22:1).

10:1–14 The Death of Saul
The chronicler is interested in Saul's death (1 Sam. 31), not his reign, as a negative example of "exile." The concluding theological evaluation that *the LORD put him to death and turned the kingdom over to David* as a direct consequence of Saul's *unfaithfulness* (1 Chr. 10:13–14), means that this is the end of Saul's line. Later, both the north and the south will similarly experience military defeat and exile due to their unfaithfulness

(5:25, "they transgressed"; 9:1; cf. 2 Chr. 36:14). Thus the united monarchy begins with a picture of Israel in exile, defeated by enemies because of the unfaithfulness of a king that embodied everything a king should not be.

11:1–12:40 All Israel Recognizes David as King
A concentric ordering of chronologically and geographically dissimilar lists demonstrates the immediate and unanimous recognition of David's kingship by a united Israel. An outer framework describing David's anointing at Hebron (11:1–3; 12:38–40) encloses lists of military personnel in attendance (11:10–47; 12:23–38), while an inner framework of David's forces stationed at Ziklag (12:1–7; 12:19–22) frames those who were at *the stronghold* (12:8–18). These chapters seek to portray David (and later, Solomon) as kings who faithfully seek God, in marked contrast to the failures of Saul just related.

11:1–47 The beginnings of David's reign—Disputes between the families of David and Saul (2 Sam. 1–4) are omitted, since all Saul's house perished in the battle with the Philistines (10:6).

11:1–3 King over Israel—David's anointing ignores the separate ceremonies performed by Judah (2 Sam. 2:4) and Israel (2 Sam. 5:3) and emphasizes his acceptance by all.

"See, we are your bone and flesh. ²For some time now, even while Saul was king, it was you who commanded the army of Israel. The LORD your God said to you: It is you who shall be shepherd of my people Israel, you who shall be ruler over my people Israel." ³So all the elders of Israel came to the king at Hebron, and David made a covenant with them at Hebron before the LORD. And they anointed David king over Israel, according to the word of the LORD by Samuel.

Jerusalem Captured

4 David and all Israel marched to Jerusalem, that is Jebus, where the Jebusites were, the inhabitants of the land. ⁵The inhabitants of Jebus said to David, "You will not come in here." Nevertheless David took the stronghold of Zion, now the city of David. ⁶David had said, "Whoever attacks the Jebusites first shall be chief and commander." And Joab son of Zeruiah went up first, so he became chief. ⁷David resided in the stronghold; therefore it was called the city of David. ⁸He built the city all around, from the Millo in complete circuit; and Joab repaired the rest of the city. ⁹And David became greater and greater, for the LORD of hosts was with him.

David's Mighty Men and Their Exploits

10 Now these are the chiefs of David's warriors, who gave him strong support in his kingdom, together with all Israel, to make him king, according to the word of the LORD concerning Israel. ¹¹This is an account of David's mighty warriors: Jashobeam, son of Hachmoni,ᵃ was chief of the Three;ᵇ he wielded his spear against three hundred whom he killed at one time.

12 And next to him among the three warriors was Eleazar son of Dodo, the Ahohite. ¹³He was with David at Pasdammim when the Philistines were gathered there for battle. There was a plot of ground full of barley. Now the people had fled from the Philistines, ¹⁴but he and David took their stand in the middle of the plot, defended it, and killed the Philistines; and the LORD saved them by a great victory.

15 Three of the thirty chiefs went down to the rock to David at the cave of Adullam, while the army of Philistines was encamped in the valley of Rephaim. ¹⁶David was then in the stronghold; and the garrison of the Philistines was then at Bethlehem. ¹⁷David said longingly, "O that someone would give me water to drink from the well of Bethlehem that is by the gate!" ¹⁸Then the Three broke through the camp of the Philistines, and drew water from the well of Bethlehem that was by the gate, and they brought it to David. But David would not drink of it; he poured it out to the LORD, ¹⁹and said, "My God forbid that I should do this. Can I drink the blood of these men? For at the risk of their lives they brought it." Therefore he would not drink it. The three warriors did these things.

20 Now Abishai,ᶜ the brother of Joab, was chief of the Thirty.ᵈ With his spear he fought against three hundred and killed them, and won a name beside the Three. ²¹He was the most renownedᵉ of the Thirty,ᵈ and became their commander; but he did not attain to the Three.

22 Benaiah son of Jehoiada was a

ᵃ Or a Hachmonite ᵇ Compare 2 Sam 23.8: Heb Thirty or captains
ᶜ Gk Vg Tg Compare 2 Sam 23.18: Heb Abishai ᵈ Syr: Heb Three
ᵉ Compare 2 Sam 23.19: Heb more renowned among the two

11:4–9—David and all Israel capture Jerusalem. The first task of a united Israel under David's command is to capture **Jebus**, a neutral city situated between Judah and Benjamin and later known as Jerusalem, David's political and religious center.

11:10–46—Lists of military heroes underline

David's widespread support. The strange story of David's pouring out the **water** retrieved **from Bethlehem** by **the three warriors** (vv. 15–19) is a testimony to David's recognition of the bravery of the warriors who had risked their lives for him. As such it praises the loyalty of the warriors as well as the reverent leadership of David.

valiant man[a] of Kabzeel, a doer of great deeds; he struck down two sons of[b] Ariel of Moab. He also went down and killed a lion in a pit on a day when snow had fallen. 23 And he killed an Egyptian, a man of great stature, five cubits tall. The Egyptian had in his hand a spear like a weaver's beam; but Benaiah went against him with a staff, snatched the spear out of the Egyptian's hand, and killed him with his own spear. 24 Such were the things Benaiah son of Jehoiada did, and he won a name beside the three warriors. 25 He was renowned among the Thirty, but he did not attain to the Three. And David put him in charge of his bodyguard.

26 The warriors of the armies were Asahel brother of Joab, Elhanan son of Dodo of Bethlehem, 27 Shammoth of Harod,[c] Helez the Pelonite, 28 Ira son of Ikkesh of Tekoa, Abiezer of Anathoth, 29 Sibbecai the Hushathite, Ilai the Ahohite, 30 Maharai of Netophah, Heled son of Baanah of Netophah, 31 Ithai son of Ribai of Gibeah of the Benjaminites, Benaiah of Pirathon, 32 Hurai of the wadis of Gaash, Abiel the Arbathite, 33 Azmaveth of Baharum, Eliahba of Shaalbon, 34 Hashem[d] the Gizonite, Jonathan son of Shagee the Hararite, 35 Ahiam son of Sachar the Hararite, Eliphal son of Ur, 36 Hepher the Mecherathite, Ahijah the Pelonite, 37 Hezro of Carmel, Naarai son of Ezbai, 38 Joel the brother of Nathan, Mibhar son of Hagri, 39 Zelek the Ammonite, Naharai of Beeroth, the armor-bearer of Joab son of Zeruiah, 40 Ira the Ithrite, Gareb the Ithrite, 41 Uriah the Hittite, Zabad son of Ahlai, 42 Adina son of Shiza the Reubenite, a leader of the Reubenites, and thirty with him, 43 Hanan son of Maacah, and Joshaphat the Mithnite, 44 Uzzia the Ashterathite, Shama and Jeiel sons of Hotham the Aroerite, 45 Jediael son of Shimri, and his brother Joha the Tizite, 46 Eliel the Mahavite, and Jeribai and Joshaviah sons of Elnaam, and Ithmah the Moabite, 47 Eliel, and Obed, and Jaasiel the Mezobaite.

David's Followers in the Wilderness

12 The following are those who came to David at Ziklag, while he could not move about freely because of Saul son of Kish; they were among the mighty warriors who helped him in war. 2 They were archers, and could shoot arrows and sling stones with either the right hand or the left; they were Benjaminites, Saul's kindred. 3 The chief was Ahiezer, then Joash, both sons of Shemaah of Gibeah; also Jeziel and Pelet sons of Azmaveth; Beracah, Jehu of Anathoth, 4 Ishmaiah of Gibeon, a warrior among the Thirty and a leader over the Thirty; Jeremiah,[e] Jahaziel, Johanan, Jozabad of Gederah, 5 Eluzai,[f] Jerimoth, Bealiah, Shemariah, Shephatiah the Haruphite; 6 Elkanah, Isshiah, Azarel, Joezer, and Jashobeam, the Korahites; 7 and Joelah and Zebadiah, sons of Jeroham of Gedor.

8 From the Gadites there went over to David at the stronghold in the wilderness mighty and experienced warriors, expert with shield and spear, whose faces were like the faces of lions, and who were swift as gazelles on the mountains: 9 Ezer the chief, Obadiah second, Eliab third, 10 Mishmannah fourth, Jeremiah fifth, 11 Attai sixth, Eliel seventh, 12 Johanan eighth, Elzabad ninth, 13 Jeremiah tenth,

---

[a] Syr: Heb the son of a valiant man   [b] See 2 Sam 23.20: Heb lacks sons of   [c] Compare 2 Sam 23.25: Heb the Harorite   [d] Compare Gk and 2 Sam 23.32: Heb the sons of Hashem   [e] Heb verse 5   [f] Heb verse 6

12:1–37—Flashbacks emphasize the main theme of these chapters: all Israel's early support of David.

12:1–7 *Ziklag*—David hid from Saul and set up a command center here for his alliance with the Philistines (1 Sam. 27). Therefore, *the mighty warriors* who join David from the tribes of *Ben-* jamin (1 Chr. 12:1–7) and *Manasseh* (vv. 19–22) do so before the ceremony at Hebron.

12:8–18—The story moves back in time again to David's mercenary days in the wilderness (1 Sam. 23–26), where warriors from the tribe of *Gad* join others from *Benjamin* and *Judah*.

Machbannai eleventh. ¹⁴ These Gadites were officers of the army, the least equal to a hundred and the greatest to a thousand. ¹⁵ These are the men who crossed the Jordan in the first month, when it was overflowing all its banks, and put to flight all those in the valleys, to the east and to the west.

16 Some Benjaminites and Judahites came to the stronghold to David. ¹⁷ David went out to meet them and said to them, "If you have come to me in friendship, to help me, then my heart will be knit to you; but if you have come to betray me to my adversaries, though my hands have done no wrong, then may the God of our ancestors see and give judgment." ¹⁸ Then the spirit came upon Amasai, chief of the Thirty, and he said,

"We are yours, O David;
    and with you, O son of Jesse!
Peace, peace to you,
    and peace to the one who helps you!
    For your God is the one who helps you."

Then David received them, and made them officers of his troops.

19 Some of the Manassites deserted to David when he came with the Philistines for the battle against Saul. (Yet he did not help them, for the rulers of the Philistines took counsel and sent him away, saying, "He will desert to his master Saul at the cost of our heads.") ²⁰ As he went to Ziklag these Manassites deserted to him: Adnah, Jozabad, Jediael, Michael, Jozabad, Elihu, and Zillethai, chiefs of the thousands in Manasseh. ²¹ They helped David against the band of raiders,ᵃ for they were all warriors and commanders in the army. ²² Indeed from day to day

people kept coming to David to help him, until there was a great army, like an army of God.

David's Army at Hebron

23 These are the numbers of the divisions of the armed troops who came to David in Hebron to turn the kingdom of Saul over to him, according to the word of the LORD. ²⁴ The people of Judah bearing shield and spear numbered six thousand eight hundred armed troops. ²⁵ Of the Simeonites, mighty warriors, seven thousand one hundred. ²⁶ Of the Levites four thousand six hundred. ²⁷ Jehoiada, leader of the house of Aaron, and with him three thousand seven hundred. ²⁸ Zadok, a young warrior, and twenty-two commanders from his own ancestral house. ²⁹ Of the Benjaminites, the kindred of Saul, three thousand, of whom the majority had continued to keep their allegiance to the house of Saul. ³⁰ Of the Ephraimites, twenty thousand eight hundred, mighty warriors, notables in their ancestral houses. ³¹ Of the half-tribe of Manasseh, eighteen thousand, who were expressly named to come and make David king. ³² Of Issachar, those who had understanding of the times, to know what Israel ought to do, two hundred chiefs, and all their kindred under their command. ³³ Of Zebulun, fifty thousand seasoned troops, equipped for battle with all the weapons of war, to help Davidᵇ with singleness of purpose. ³⁴ Of Naphtali, a thousand commanders, with whom there were thirty-seven thousand armed with shield and spear. ³⁵ Of the Danites, twenty-eight thousand six hundred equipped for battle. ³⁶ Of

---

ᵃ Or as officers of his troops   ᵇ Gk: Heb lacks David

12:18 *Peace*—The usual translation is inadequate. "Prosperity" and "success" are closer, but fall short of the emphasis on wholeness, coherence, and integrity that the Hebrew word connotes and that *Amasai* wishes for the people.

12:18 *The one who helps*—God is the true source of help (vv. 1, 17, 18, 19, 21, 22) that will bring David victory.

12:19–37—The huge numbers (340,822; cf. 2 Sam. 6:1, where Israel's army numbers 30,000) of northern troops that join the enthusiastic support of all Israel for David have been exaggerated to emphasize their similarity to a veritable *army of God* (v. 22).

Asher, forty thousand seasoned troops ready for battle. ³⁷ Of the Reubenites and Gadites and the half-tribe of Manasseh from beyond the Jordan, one hundred twenty thousand armed with all the weapons of war.

38 All these, warriors arrayed in battle order, came to Hebron with full intent to make David king over all Israel; likewise all the rest of Israel were of a single mind to make David king. ³⁹ They were there with David for three days, eating and drinking, for their kindred had provided for them. ⁴⁰ And also their neighbors, from as far away as Issachar and Zebulun and Naphtali, came bringing food on donkeys, camels, mules, and oxen— abundant provisions of meal, cakes of figs, clusters of raisins, wine, oil, oxen, and sheep, for there was joy in Israel.

The Ark Brought from Kiriath-jearim

13 David consulted with the commanders of the thousands and of the hundreds, with every leader. ² David said to the whole assembly of Israel, "If it seems good to you, and if it is the will of the LORD our God, let us send abroad to our kindred who remain in all the land of Israel, including the priests and Levites in the cities that have pasture lands, that they may come together to us. ³ Then let us bring again the ark of our God to us; for we did not turn to it in the days of Saul." ⁴ The whole assembly agreed to do so, for the thing pleased all the people.

5 So David assembled all Israel from the Shihor of Egypt to Lebo-hamath, to bring the ark of God from Kiriath-jearim. ⁶ And David and all Israel went up to Baalah, that is, to Kiriath-jearim, which belongs to Judah, to bring up from there the ark of God, the LORD, who is enthroned on the cherubim, which is called by his^a name. ⁷ They carried the ark of God on a new cart, from the house of Abinadab, and Uzzah and Ahio^b were driving the cart. ⁸ David and all Israel were dancing before God with all their might, with song and lyres and harps and tambourines and cymbals and trumpets.

9 When they came to the threshing floor of Chidon, Uzzah put out his hand to hold the ark, for the oxen shook it. ¹⁰ The anger of the LORD was kindled against Uzzah; he struck him down because he put out his hand to the ark; and he died there before God. ¹¹ David was angry because the LORD had burst out against Uzzah; so that place is called Perez-uzzah^c to this day. ¹² David was afraid of God that day; he said, "How can I bring the ark of God into my care?" ¹³ So David did not take the ark into his care into the city of David; he took it instead to the house of Obed-edom the Gittite. ¹⁴ The ark of God remained with the household of Obed-edom in his house three months, and the LORD blessed the household of Obed-edom and all that he had.

^a Heb lacks his   ^b Or and his brother   ^c That is Bursting Out Against Uzzah

---

12:38–40—David's unanimous recognition as king. The unity of purpose between God, David, and the people, in which God provides the focus for David and Israel's obedience, offers an abiding foundational model for all who seek to live together in community.

12:40 *Joy*—This term happily tags a number of significant religious events in Chronicles.

13:1–16:43 David Brings the Ark to Jerusalem

The description of David's two attempts to transfer the ark from Kiriath-jearim to Jerusalem also presents one of the chronicler's key themes: seeking God.

13:1–14—A failed first attempt. David's adher-

ence to Israel's cultic institutions contrasts sharply with Saul, who lost his life and his kingdom by neglecting the ark (v. 3). Saul's neglect of the ark was really a neglect of God that led to "exile." David represents the way to restoration: active concern for God and the religious duties that such concern requires.

13:9–14—Unfortunately, the unintentional transgression of cultic regulations by *Uzzah* ruins David's first attempt to transfer the ark. Uzzah's death, despite his good intentions, seems unfair to modern readers, but the chronicler intends to show God's sovereignty here, especially as regards the ark.

David Established at Jerusalem

14 King Hiram of Tyre sent messengers to David, along with cedar logs, and masons and carpenters to build a house for him. ² David then perceived that the LORD had established him as king over Israel, and that his kingdom was highly exalted for the sake of his people Israel.

3 David took more wives in Jerusalem, and David became the father of more sons and daughters. ⁴ These are the names of the children whom he had in Jerusalem: Shammua, Shobab, and Nathan; Solomon, ⁵ Ibhar, Elishua, and Elpelet; ⁶ Nogah, Nepheg, and Japhia; ⁷ Elishama, Beeliada, and Eliphelet.

Defeat of the Philistines

8 When the Philistines heard that David had been anointed king over all Israel, all the Philistines went up in search of David; and David heard of it and went out against them. ⁹ Now the Philistines had come and made a raid in the valley of Rephaim. ¹⁰ David inquired of God, "Shall I go up against the Philistines? Will you give them into my hand?" The LORD said to him, "Go up, and I will give them into your hand." ¹¹ So he went up to Baal-perazim, and David defeated them there. David said, "God has burst out*ª* against my enemies by my hand, like a bursting flood." Therefore that place is called Baal-perazim.*ᵇ* ¹² They abandoned their gods there, and at David's command they were burned.

13 Once again the Philistines made a raid in the valley. ¹⁴ When David again inquired of God, God said to him, "You shall not go up after them; go around and come on them opposite the balsam trees. ¹⁵ When you hear the sound of marching in the tops of the balsam trees, then go out to battle; for God has gone out before you to strike down the army of the Philistines." ¹⁶ David did as God had commanded him, and they struck down the Philistine army from Gibeon to Gezer. ¹⁷ The fame of David went out into all lands, and the LORD brought the fear of him on all nations.

The Ark Brought to Jerusalem

15 David*ᶜ* built houses for himself in the city of David, and he prepared a place for the ark of God and pitched a tent for it. ² Then David commanded that no one but the Levites

ª Heb *paraz*   *ᵇ* That is *Lord of Bursting Out*   *ᶜ* Heb *He*

14:1–17—God blesses David. David's success in Jerusalem is attributed to the Lord (vv. 2, 17). In Chronicles, fame, children, and military victory frequently indicate divine favor. Here they result from David's seeking of God as a counterpoint to Saul's bad example.

14:1–2 *King Hiram of Tyre*—Building materials to build the *house* (i.e., the royal palace) from a foreign power provide the first indication of blessing, suggesting the spread of David's international reputation. In 2 Chr. 2, Huram (as the name usually appears in Chronicles) will also provide materials for the temple. David's fame leads to the glorification of God rather than the self-aggrandizement that often besets those in leadership positions.

14:3–7—The thirteen *children* born to David in Jerusalem are a second indication of blessing.

14:8–17—David's defeat of *the Philistines* is a third indication of blessing. By placing David's prosperity after his care for the ark, the chronicler presents fame, children, and military victory as rewards for piety. This reverses the paradigm of

Israel "in exile," drawn in the portrait of Saul's demise (chap. 10): David's kingdom is established (14:2), Saul's has been taken away (10:14); David's house increased (14:3–7), Saul's was eliminated (10:6); David sought God (14:10, 14), Saul did not (10:13–14); David defeats the Philistines who defeated Saul and burns the gods before whom Saul's head was presented (14:16; 10:8–10).

15:1–16:3—A successful second attempt. Encouraged by his success, David again attempts to bring the ark to Jerusalem. This time he follows the guidelines prescribed by Moses. Not following these guidelines had cost Uzzah his life (13:6–10). Communities thrive when they are able to cultivate a sense of order and even ritual, based upon Scripture.

15:1 *Tent*—A new structure. The Mosaic tabernacle is still in Gibeon (16:39).

15:2 *Levites*—This time, a place is prepared (vv. 1, 3, 12), and only Levites bear the ark (vv. 2, 12–15), as Moses had commanded (v. 15; cf. Deut. 10:8).

were to carry the ark of God, for the LORD had chosen them to carry the ark of the LORD and to minister to him forever. ³David assembled all Israel in Jerusalem to bring up the ark of the LORD to its place, which he had prepared for it. ⁴Then David gathered together the descendants of Aaron and the Levites: ⁵of the sons of Kohath, Uriel the chief, with one hundred twenty of his kindred; ⁶of the sons of Merari, Asaiah the chief, with two hundred twenty of his kindred; ⁷of the sons of Gershom, Joel the chief, with one hundred thirty of his kindred; ⁸of the sons of Elizaphan, Shemaiah the chief, with two hundred of his kindred; ⁹of the sons of Hebron, Eliel the chief, with eighty of his kindred; ¹⁰of the sons of Uzziel, Amminadab the chief, with one hundred twelve of his kindred.

11 David summoned the priests Zadok and Abiathar, and the Levites Uriel, Asaiah, Joel, Shemaiah, Eliel, and Amminadab. ¹²He said to them, "You are the heads of families of the Levites; sanctify yourselves, you and your kindred, so that you may bring up the ark of the LORD, the God of Israel, to the place that I have prepared for it. ¹³Because you did not carry it the first time,ᵃ the LORD our God burst out against us, because we did not give it proper care." ¹⁴So the priests and the Levites sanctified themselves to bring up the ark of the LORD, the God of Israel. ¹⁵And the Levites carried the ark of God on their shoulders with the poles, as Moses had commanded according to the word of the LORD.

16 David also commanded the chiefs of the Levites to appoint their kindred as the singers to play on musical instruments, on harps and lyres and cymbals, to raise loud sounds of joy. ¹⁷So the Levites appointed Heman son of Joel;

and of his kindred Asaph son of Berechiah; and of the sons of Merari, their kindred, Ethan son of Kushaiah; ¹⁸and with them their kindred of the second order, Zechariah, Jaaziel, Shemiramoth, Jehiel, Unni, Eliab, Benaiah, Maaseiah, Mattithiah, Eliphelehu, and Mikneiah, and the gatekeepers Obed-edom and Jeiel. ¹⁹The singers Heman, Asaph, and Ethan were to sound bronze cymbals; ²⁰Zechariah, Aziel, Shemiramoth, Jehiel, Unni, Eliab, Maaseiah, and Benaiah were to play harps according to Alamoth; ²¹but Mattithiah, Eliphelehu, Mikneiah, Obed-edom, Jeiel, and Azaziah were to lead with lyres according to the Sheminith. ²²Chenaniah, leader of the Levites in music, was to direct the music, for he understood it. ²³Berechiah and Elkanah were to be gatekeepers for the ark. ²⁴Shebaniah, Joshaphat, Nethanel, Amasai, Zechariah, Benaiah, and Eliezer, the priests, were to blow the trumpets before the ark of God. Obed-edom and Jehiah also were to be gatekeepers for the ark.

25 So David and the elders of Israel, and the commanders of the thousands, went to bring up the ark of the covenant of the LORD from the house of Obed-edom with rejoicing. ²⁶And because God helped the Levites who were carrying the ark of the covenant of the LORD, they sacrificed seven bulls and seven rams. ²⁷David was clothed with a robe of fine linen, as also were all the Levites who were carrying the ark, and the singers, and Chenaniah the leader of the music of the singers; and David wore a linen ephod. ²⁸So all Israel brought up the ark of the covenant of the LORD with shouting, to the sound of the horn, trumpets, and cymbals, and made loud music on harps and lyres.

ᵃ Meaning of Heb uncertain

15:16–24—The ark is brought to Jerusalem in a liturgical procession, accompanied by the Levitical musicians and *singers* named in this list.

15:25–16:3—The description of the transfer of the ark to Jerusalem follows 2 Sam. 6:12b–19, with significant differences.

15:26 *Levites*—In 2 Sam. 6:13 David sacrifices an ox and a fatling. Here the Levites perform this task, and the number of sacrificial animals is increased to *seven bulls and seven rams*, as in later times.

29 As the ark of the covenant of the LORD came to the city of David, Michal daughter of Saul looked out of the window, and saw King David leaping and dancing; and she despised him in her heart.

The Ark Placed in the Tent

16 They brought in the ark of God, and set it inside the tent that David had pitched for it; and they offered burnt offerings and offerings of well-being before God. **²** When David had finished offering the burnt offerings and the offerings of well-being, he blessed the people in the name of the LORD; **³** and he distributed to every person in Israel—man and woman alike—to each a loaf of bread, a portion of meat,*a* and a cake of raisins.

4 He appointed certain of the Levites as ministers before the ark of the LORD, to invoke, to thank, and to praise the LORD, the God of Israel. **⁵** Asaph was the chief, and second to him Zechariah, Jeiel, Shemiramoth, Jehiel, Mattithiah, Eliab, Benaiah, Obed-edom, and Jeiel, with harps and lyres; Asaph was to sound the cymbals, **⁶** and the priests Benaiah and Jahaziel were to blow trumpets regularly, before the ark of the covenant of God.

David's Psalm of Thanksgiving

7 Then on that day David first appointed the singing of praises to the LORD by Asaph and his kindred.

8   O give thanks to the LORD, call on
     his name,
     make known his deeds among the
       peoples.
9   Sing to him, sing praises to him,
     tell of all his wonderful works.
10   Glory in his holy name;
     let the hearts of those who seek the
       LORD rejoice.
11   Seek the LORD and his strength,
     seek his presence continually.
12   Remember the wonderful works he
       has done,
     his miracles, and the judgments he
       uttered,
13   O offspring of his servant Israel,*b*
     children of Jacob, his chosen ones.

14   He is the LORD our God;
     his judgments are in all the earth.
15   Remember his covenant forever,
     the word that he commanded, for
       a thousand generations,
16   the covenant that he made with
       Abraham,
     his sworn promise to Isaac,
17   which he confirmed to Jacob as a
       statute,
     to Israel as an everlasting covenant,
18   saying, "To you I will give the land
       of Canaan
     as your portion for an inheritance."

19   When they were few in number,
     of little account, and strangers in
       the land,*c*
20   wandering from nation to nation,
     from one kingdom to another
       people,

a Compare Gk Syr Vg: Meaning of Heb uncertain   *b* Another reading is *Abraham* (compare Ps 105.6)   *c* Heb *in it*

15:29 *Michal daughter of Saul*—By despising David she recalls her father's failure to seek God through neglect of the ark (10:13–14). The chronicler omits her mocking of David (cf. 2 Sam. 6:16–23).

16:4–43—The ark narrative concludes with the institution of worship. The appointment of cultic personnel (vv. 4–6; 37–42) frames a hymn of thanksgiving that fuses Pss. 105:1–15 (vv. 8–22); 96:1b–13a (vv. 23–33); and 106:1, 47–48 (vv. 34–36).

16:4–7 *To invoke, to thank, and to praise*—The Levites were charged with these functions be-

cause sacrifice could take place only at Gibeon before the dedication of the temple.

16:8–22—See Ps. 105:1–15. The detailed recounting of God's deliverance, covenant faithfulness, and promise of land to the patriarchs is designed to encourage the postexilic community, recently returned to the land. The exhortation to *seek the LORD* (v. 11) continues this all-important theme and introduces the following recital of all that God had done for Israel in the past (vv. 15–18). The smallness of Israel's numbers requiring God's protection from hostile neighbors (vv. 19–22) strongly resonates with the vulnerable and dependent in society.

21 he allowed no one to oppress them;
  he rebuked kings on their account,
22 saying, "Do not touch my anointed
  ones;
  do my prophets no harm."

23 Sing to the LORD, all the earth.
  Tell of his salvation from day to day.
24 Declare his glory among the nations,
  his marvelous works among all the
  peoples.
25 For great is the LORD, and greatly to
  be praised;
  he is to be revered above all gods.
26 For all the gods of the peoples are
  idols,
  but the LORD made the heavens.
27 Honor and majesty are before him;
  strength and joy are in his place.

28 Ascribe to the LORD, O families of
  the peoples,
  ascribe to the LORD glory and
  strength.
29 Ascribe to the LORD the glory due
  his name;
  bring an offering, and come before
  him.
  Worship the LORD in holy splendor;
30   tremble before him, all the earth.
  The world is firmly established; it
  shall never be moved.
31 Let the heavens be glad, and let the
  earth rejoice,
  and let them say among the
  nations, "The LORD is king!"
32 Let the sea roar, and all that fills it;
  let the field exult, and everything
  in it.
33 Then shall the trees of the forest sing
  for joy
  before the LORD, for he comes to
  judge the earth.
34 O give thanks to the LORD, for he is
  good;

for his steadfast love endures
  forever.
35 Say also:
"Save us, O God of our salvation,
  and gather and rescue us from
  among the nations,
that we may give thanks to your holy
  name,
  and glory in your praise.
36 Blessed be the LORD, the God of
  Israel,
  from everlasting to everlasting."
Then all the people said "Amen!" and
praised the LORD.

Regular Worship Maintained

37 David left Asaph and his kinsfolk there before the ark of the covenant of the LORD to minister regularly before the ark as each day required, 38 and also Obed-edom and his*a* sixty-eight kinsfolk; while Obed-edom son of Jeduthun and Hosah were to be gatekeepers. 39 And he left the priest Zadok and his kindred the priests before the tabernacle of the LORD in the high place that was at Gibeon, 40 to offer burnt offerings to the LORD on the altar of burnt offering regularly, morning and evening, according to all that is written in the law of the LORD that he commanded Israel. 41 With them were Heman and Jeduthun, and the rest of those chosen and expressly named to render thanks to the LORD, for his steadfast love endures forever. 42 Heman and Jeduthun had with them trumpets and cymbals for the music, and instruments for sacred song. The sons of Jeduthun were appointed to the gate.

43 Then all the people departed to their homes, and David went home to bless his household.

a Gk Syr Vg: Heb *their*

16:23–33—See Ps. 96. The declaration of God's sovereignty over the gods of other nations would reassure a community under Persian rule that God is ultimately in control.

16:35—*Of our salvation* and *rescue us*. This reference, added to Ps. 106:47, makes a direct

application of the promises of the psalm to its hearers. The psalm's lament of Israel's sin and God's judgment are omitted.

16:37–43—David also provides for the Gibeon tabernacle (see note at vv. 4–7).

God's Covenant with David

17 Now when David settled in his house, David said to the prophet Nathan, "I am living in a house of cedar, but the ark of the covenant of the LORD is under a tent." ² Nathan said to David, "Do all that you have in mind, for God is with you."

3 But that same night the word of the LORD came to Nathan, saying: ⁴ Go and tell my servant David: Thus says the LORD: You shall not build me a house to live in. ⁵ For I have not lived in a house since the day I brought out Israel to this very day, but I have lived in a tent and a tabernacle.*a* ⁶ Wherever I have moved about among all Israel, did I ever speak a word with any of the judges of Israel, whom I commanded to shepherd my people, saying, Why have you not built me a house of cedar? ⁷ Now therefore thus you shall say to my servant David: Thus says the LORD of hosts: I took you from the pasture, from following the sheep, to be ruler over my people Israel; ⁸ and I have been with you wherever you went, and have cut off all your enemies before you; and I will make for you a name, like the name of the great ones of the earth. ⁹ I will appoint a place for my people Israel, and will plant them, so that they may live in their own place, and be disturbed no more; and evildoers shall wear them down no more, as they did formerly, ¹⁰ from the time that I appointed judges over my people Israel; and I will subdue all your enemies.

Moreover I declare to you that the LORD will build you a house. ¹¹ When your days are fulfilled to go to be with your ancestors, I will raise up your offspring after you, one of your own sons, and I will establish his kingdom. ¹² He shall build a house for me, and I will establish his throne forever. ¹³ I will be a father to him, and he shall be a son to me. I will not take my steadfast love from him, as I took it from him who was before you, ¹⁴ but I will confirm him in my house and in my kingdom forever, and his throne shall be established forever. ¹⁵ In accordance with all these words and all this vision, Nathan spoke to David.

David's Prayer

16 Then King David went in and sat before the LORD, and said, "Who am I, O LORD God, and what is my house, that

---

a Gk 2 Sam 7.6: Heb *but I have been from tent to tent and from tabernacle*

17:1–27 God's Promise of a Dynasty to David
David must learn that his task of defeating Israel's enemies is preparatory to the construction of the temple by Solomon.

17:1–2—David's desire to build a *house* (temple) for *the ark* omits "the LORD had given him rest" (2 Sam. 7:1) because of the reference to David's wars in v. 10 and chaps. 18–20.

17:3–15—Nathan's oracle follows a dream in which God corrected the prophet's earlier encouragement of David's hopes to build the temple. An extended pun on the word "house" in Hebrew, which can mean "palace" (v. 1); "the temple" (v. 4); or a "dynasty" (vv. 10b, 14), makes three points. Though David will not be permitted to build a house (temple) for God (v. 4), God will build a house (dynasty) for David (v. 10). One of that house (one of David's descendants) will build a house (the temple) for the Lord (v. 12a). Through his house (descendants) David's throne will be established forever (v. 12b).

17:10 *Subdue*—In 2 Sam. 7:11, YHWH, through Nathan, promises, "And I will give you rest" (cf. 2 Sam. 7:1). In Chronicles, Solomon is associated with rest, David with war. Both traditions assumed that proper worship was possible only after the Lord had given rest from their enemies (Deut. 12:10–11). They differed as to when the rest was received.

17:14 *My house and my kingdom*—Instead of "your house and your kingdom" (2 Sam. 7:16). In 2 Samuel "your house" means David's descendants; in 1 Chronicles *my house* means God's house, that is, the temple. It also stresses the chronicler's understanding that God in fact rules.

17:16–27—David shows that he has learned to accept the task he has been given, rather than the one he thought he should have had, by responding with a model prayer employing elements of thanksgiving, praise, and petition.

17:16–19—David thanks God for present help and the promise of an eternal dynasty.

17:16 *House*—The Davidic dynasty (see vv. 17, 23, 24, 27).

you have brought me thus far? [17] And even this was a small thing in your sight, O God; you have also spoken of your servant's house for a great while to come. You regard me as someone of high rank,[a] O Lord God! [18] And what more can David say to you for honoring your servant? You know your servant. [19] For your servant's sake, O Lord, and according to your own heart, you have done all these great deeds, making known all these great things. [20] There is no one like you, O Lord, and there is no God besides you, according to all that we have heard with our ears. [21] Who is like your people Israel, one nation on the earth whom God went to redeem to be his people, making for yourself a name for great and terrible things, in driving out nations before your people whom you redeemed from Egypt? [22] And you made your people Israel to be your people forever; and you, O Lord, became their God.

23 "And now, O Lord, as for the word that you have spoken concerning your servant and concerning his house, let it be established forever, and do as you have promised. [24] Thus your name will be established and magnified forever in the saying, 'The Lord of hosts, the God of Israel, is Israel's God'; and the house of your servant David will be established in your presence. [25] For you, my God, have revealed to your servant that you will build a house for him; there-fore your servant has found it possible to pray before you. [26] And now, O Lord, you are God, and you have promised this good thing to your servant; [27] therefore may it please you to bless the house of your servant, that it may continue for-ever before you. For you, O Lord, have blessed and are blessed[b] forever."

David's Kingdom Established and Extended

18 Some time afterward, David attacked the Philistines and sub-dued them; he took Gath and its villages from the Philistines.

2 He defeated Moab, and the Moabites became subject to David and brought tribute.

3 David also struck down King Had-adezer of Zobah, toward Hamath,[a] as he went to set up a monument at the river Euphrates. [4] David took from him one thousand chariots, seven thousand cav-alry, and twenty thousand foot soldiers. David hamstrung all the chariot horses, but left one hundred of them. [5] When the Arameans of Damascus came to help King Hadadezer of Zobah, David killed twenty-two thousand Arameans. [6] Then David put garrisons[c] in Aram of Damas-cus; and the Arameans became subject to David, and brought tribute. The Lord gave victory to David wherever he went.

[a] Meaning of Heb uncertain   [b] Or and it is blessed   [c] Gk Vg 2 Sam 8.6 Compare Syr: Heb lacks garrisons

---

17:20–22—David praises God for past mercies, especially the exodus. From now on, God's promise to David, not the exodus, will guarantee the covenant.

17:23–27—The prayer concludes with a peti-tion concerning the future of God's promise, the fulfillment of which the chronicler sees as already having begun (cf. 2 Sam. 7:29).

18:1–20:8 David's Empire Won through War Three chapters omit David's increasing inability to govern his personal and family affairs (2 Sam. 11–12: David's adultery with Bathsheba; 2 Sam. 13: the incest and murder of Amnon; and 2 Sam. 15–20: the rebellions of Absalom and Sheba). These omissions are not attempts to idealize David, as can be seen in the omission of several episodes that reflect favorably upon the king (2 Sam. 9: David's kindness to Saul's family; 2 Sam. 12:24–25: the birth of Solomon; and 2 Sam. 22; 23:1–7: David's psalms). The chroni-cler stresses David's empire building that links the dynastic promise (1 Chr. 17) with prepara-tions for building the temple (1 Chr. 21–29).

18:1–17—Subjugation of *the Philistines* (v. 1), *Moab* (v. 2), *Zobah* (vv. 3–4), *Damascus* (vv. 5–6), and *Edom* (vv. 12–13) fulfills a key element of the promise to "subdue all [David's] enemies" (17:10).

18:6 Garrisons—The garrisons consolidate the kingdom and set the stage for David's final prepa-rations. Ironically, these victories, sanctioned by God (v. 13b), prevent David from building the temple (see 22:8–9).

7 David took the gold shields that were carried by the servants of Hadadezer, and brought them to Jerusalem. 8 From Tibhath and from Cun, cities of Hadadezer, David took a vast quantity of bronze; with it Solomon made the bronze sea and the pillars and the vessels of bronze.

9 When King Tou of Hamath heard that David had defeated the whole army of King Hadadezer of Zobah, 10 he sent his son Hadoram to King David, to greet him and to congratulate him, because he had fought against Hadadezer and defeated him. Now Hadadezer had often been at war with Tou. He sent all sorts of articles of gold, of silver, and of bronze; 11 these also King David dedicated to the LORD, together with the silver and gold that he had carried off from all the nations, from Edom, Moab, the Ammonites, the Philistines, and Amalek.

12 Abishai son of Zeruiah killed eighteen thousand Edomites in the Valley of Salt. 13 He put garrisons in Edom; and all the Edomites became subject to David. And the LORD gave victory to David wherever he went.

David's Administration

14 So David reigned over all Israel; and he administered justice and equity to all his people. 15 Joab son of Zeruiah was over the army; Jehoshaphat son of Ahilud was recorder; 16 Zadok son of Ahitub and Ahimelech son of Abiathar were priests; Shavsha was secretary; 17 Benaiah son of Jehoiada was over the Cherethites and the Pelethites; and David's sons were the chief officials in the service of the king.

Defeat of the Ammonites and Arameans

19 Some time afterward, King Nahash of the Ammonites died, and his son succeeded him. 2 David said, "I will deal loyally with Hanun son of Nahash, for his father dealt loyally with me." So David sent messengers to console him concerning his father. When David's servants came to Hanun in the land of the Ammonites, to console him, 3 the officials of the Ammonites said to Hanun, "Do you think, because David has sent consolers to you, that he is honoring your father? Have not his servants come to you to search and to overthrow and to spy out the land?" 4 So Hanun seized David's servants, shaved them, cut off their garments in the middle at their hips, and sent them away; 5 and they departed. When David was told about the men, he sent messengers to them, for they felt greatly humiliated. The king said, "Remain at Jericho until your beards have grown, and then return."

6 When the Ammonites saw that they had made themselves odious to David, Hanun and the Ammonites sent a thousand talents of silver to hire chariots and cavalry from Mesopotamia, from Aram-maacah and from Zobah. 7 They hired thirty-two thousand chariots and the king of Maacah with his army, who came and camped before Medeba. And the Ammonites were mustered from their cities and came to battle. 8 When David heard of it, he sent Joab and all the army of the warriors. 9 The Ammonites came out and drew up in battle array at the entrance of the city, and the kings who had come were by themselves in the open country.

10 When Joab saw that the line of battle was set against him both in front and in the rear, he chose some of the picked men of Israel and arrayed them against the Arameans; 11 the rest of his troops he put in the charge of his brother

---

18:11—The spoils of war will be dedicated to the Lord, not destroyed as in the holy-war traditions. They will be used in the building of the temple and so anticipate that major theme of these books.

18:14–17—David's complex administration resembles the administrative organization of Egypt, as this roster of officials suggests, and provides one more indication that the kingdom will be secure and marked by justice.

19:1–20:3—This version of David's defeat of the *Ammonites* omits his adultery with Bathsheba (cf. 2 Sam. 10–12).

Abishai, and they were arrayed against the Ammonites. [12] He said, "If the Arameans are too strong for me, then you shall help me; but if the Ammonites are too strong for you, then I will help you. [13] Be strong, and let us be courageous for our people and for the cities of our God; and may the LORD do what seems good to him." [14] So Joab and the troops who were with him advanced toward the Arameans for battle; and they fled before him. [15] When the Ammonites saw that the Arameans fled, they likewise fled before Abishai, Joab's brother, and entered the city. Then Joab came to Jerusalem.

[16] But when the Arameans saw that they had been defeated by Israel, they sent messengers and brought out the Arameans who were beyond the Euphrates, with Shophach the commander of the army of Hadadezer at their head. [17] When David was informed, he gathered all Israel together, crossed the Jordan, came to them, and drew up his forces against them. When David set the battle in array against the Arameans, they fought with him. [18] The Arameans fled before Israel; and David killed seven thousand Aramean charioteers and forty thousand foot soldiers, and also killed Shophach the commander of their army. [19] When the servants of Hadadezer saw that they had been defeated by Israel, they made peace with David, and became subject to him. So the Arameans were not willing to help the Ammonites any more.

Siege and Capture of Rabbah

20 In the spring of the year, the time when kings go out to battle, Joab led out the army, ravaged the country of the Ammonites, and came and besieged Rabbah. But David remained at Jerusalem. Joab attacked Rabbah, and overthrew it. [2] David took the crown of Milcom[a] from his head; he found that it weighed a talent of gold, and in it was a precious stone; and it was placed on David's head. He also brought out the booty of the city, a very great amount. [3] He brought out the people who were in it, and set them to work[b] with saws and iron picks and axes.[c] Thus David did to all the cities of the Ammonites. Then David and all the people returned to Jerusalem.

Exploits against the Philistines

4 After this, war broke out with the Philistines at Gezer; then Sibbecai the Hushathite killed Sippai, who was one of the descendants of the giants; and the Philistines were subdued. [5] Again there was war with the Philistines; and Elhanan son of Jair killed Lahmi the brother of Goliath the Gittite, the shaft of whose spear was like a weaver's beam. [6] Again there was war at Gath, where there was a man of great size, who had six fingers on each hand, and six toes on each foot, twenty-four in number; he also was descended from the giants. [7] When he taunted Israel, Jonathan son of Shimea, David's brother, killed him. [8] These were descended from the giants in Gath; they fell by the hand of David and his servants.

The Census and Plague

21 Satan stood up against Israel, and incited David to count the

---

[a] Gk Vg See 1 Kings 11.5, 33: MT *of their king*   [b] Compare 2 Sam 12.31: Heb *and he sawed*   [c] Compare 2 Sam 12.31: Heb *saws*

21:1–22:1 The Temple Site

David's census of the people (2 Sam. 24) is transformed by the following alterations: Rather than "the anger of the LORD," (2 Sam. 24:1), it is *Satan* who incites David to count the people (1 Chr. 21:1). (This is the only time in the Hebrew Bible in which "Satan" is used as the proper name of an evil being. Elsewhere it is the title—"the Prosecutor"—of an officer of the heavenly court. See Zech. 3:1–2, Job 1–2.) Joab's accusation, *"Why should he [David] bring guilt on Israel?"* (1 Chr. 21:3b) and abhorrence (v. 6) have been added to the account in 2 Samuel to increase David's guilt. When God *struck Israel,* David is moved to repentance (v. 7); in 2 Sam. 24:10 "David was stricken to the heart." David's payment of six hundred shekels of gold is designated *for the site,* i.e., the temple (v. 25), instead of the fifty

people of Israel. ² So David said to Joab and the commanders of the army, "Go, number Israel, from Beer-sheba to Dan, and bring me a report, so that I may know their number." ³ But Joab said, "May the LORD increase the number of his people a hundredfold! Are they not, my lord the king, all of them my lord's servants? Why then should my lord require this? Why should he bring guilt on Israel?" ⁴ But the king's word prevailed against Joab. So Joab departed and went throughout all Israel, and came back to Jerusalem. ⁵ Joab gave the total count of the people to David. In all Israel there were one million one hundred thousand men who drew the sword, and in Judah four hundred seventy thousand who drew the sword. ⁶ But he did not include Levi and Benjamin in the numbering, for the king's command was abhorrent to Joab.

7 But God was displeased with this thing, and he struck Israel. ⁸ David said to God, "I have sinned greatly in that I have done this thing. But now, I pray you, take away the guilt of your servant; for I have done very foolishly." ⁹ The LORD spoke to Gad, David's seer, saying, ¹⁰ "Go and say to David, 'Thus says the LORD: Three things I offer you; choose one of them, so that I may do it to you.'" ¹¹ So Gad came to David and said to him, "Thus says the LORD, 'Take your choice: ¹² either three years of famine; or three months of devastation by your foes, while the sword of your enemies overtakes you; or three days of the sword of the LORD, pestilence on the land, and the angel of the LORD destroying throughout all the territory of Israel.' Now decide what answer I shall return to the one who sent me." ¹³ Then David said to Gad, "I am in great distress; let me fall into the hand of the LORD, for his mercy is very great; but let me not fall into human hands."

14 So the LORD sent a pestilence on Israel; and seventy thousand persons fell in Israel. ¹⁵ And God sent an angel to Jerusalem to destroy it; but when he was about to destroy it, the LORD took note and relented concerning the calamity; he said to the destroying angel, "Enough! Stay your hand." The angel of the LORD was then standing by the threshing floor of Ornan the Jebusite. ¹⁶ David looked up and saw the angel of the LORD standing between earth and heaven, and in his hand a drawn sword stretched out over Jerusalem. Then David and the elders, clothed in sackcloth, fell on their faces. ¹⁷ And David said to God, "Was it not I who gave the command to count the people? It is I who have sinned and done very wickedly. But these sheep, what have they done? Let your hand, I pray, O LORD my God, be against me and against my father's house; but do not let your people be plagued!"

David's Altar and Sacrifice

18 Then the angel of the LORD commanded Gad to tell David that he should go up and erect an altar to the LORD on the threshing floor of Ornan the Jebusite. ¹⁹ So David went up following Gad's instructions, which he had spoken in the name of the LORD. ²⁰ Ornan turned and saw the angel; and while his four sons who were with him hid themselves, Ornan continued to thresh wheat. ²¹ As David came to Ornan, Ornan looked and saw David; he went out from the threshing floor, and did obeisance to David with his face to the ground. ²² David said to Ornan, "Give me

---

shekels of silver paid to **Ornan** ("Araunah" in 2 Samuel) for "the threshing floor and the oxen," (2 Sam. 24:24). Finally, God confirms the temple's future site by sending **fire from heaven** (v. 26; cf. 2 Chr. 7:1; Lev. 9:24; Judg. 6:21; 1 Kgs. 18:38). These differences suggest the story has been reworked to emphasize David's repentance and God's forgiveness (1 Chr. 21:15–27), rather than David's sin and God's judgment (vv. 1–14). The new ending to the story (21:26b–22:1) reveals the primary purpose: the connection between this place of reconciliation and forgiveness and the site of the future temple. The connection between individual sin and social consequences is also important.

the site of the threshing floor that I may build on it an altar to the LORD—give it to me at its full price—so that the plague may be averted from the people." ²³ Then Ornan said to David, "Take it; and let my lord the king do what seems good to him; see, I present the oxen for burnt offerings, and the threshing sledges for the wood, and the wheat for a grain offering. I give it all." ²⁴ But King David said to Ornan, "No; I will buy them for the full price. I will not take for the LORD what is yours, nor offer burnt offerings that cost me nothing." ²⁵ So David paid Ornan six hundred shekels of gold by weight for the site. ²⁶ David built there an altar to the LORD and presented burnt offerings and offerings of well-being. He called upon the LORD, and he answered him with fire from heaven on the altar of burnt offering. ²⁷ Then the LORD commanded the angel, and he put his sword back into its sheath.

The Place Chosen for the Temple

28 At that time, when David saw that the LORD had answered him at the threshing floor of Ornan the Jebusite, he made his sacrifices there. ²⁹ For the tabernacle of the LORD, which Moses had made in the wilderness, and the altar of burnt offering were at that time in the high place at Gibeon; ³⁰ but David could not go before it to inquire of God, for he was afraid of the sword of the angel of the LORD. ¹ Then David said, "Here shall be the house of the LORD God and here the altar of burnt offering for Israel."

22

David Prepares to Build the Temple

2 David gave orders to gather together the aliens who were residing in the land of Israel, and he set stonecutters to prepare dressed stones for building the house of God. ³ David also provided great stores of iron for nails for the doors of the gates and for clamps, as well as bronze in quantities beyond weighing, ⁴ and cedar logs without number—for the Sidonians and Tyrians brought great quantities of cedar to David. ⁵ For David said, "My son Solomon is young and inexperienced, and the house that is to be built for the LORD must be exceedingly magnificent, famous and glorified throughout all lands; I will therefore make preparation for it." So David provided materials in great quantity before his death.

David's Charge to Solomon and the Leaders

6 Then he called for his son Solomon and charged him to build a house for the LORD, the God of Israel. ⁷ David said to Solomon, "My son, I had planned to build a house to the name of the LORD my God. ⁸ But the word of the LORD came to me, saying, 'You have shed much blood and have waged great wars; you shall not build a house to my name, because you have shed so much blood in my sight on the earth. ⁹ See, a son shall be born to you; he shall be a man of peace. I will give

---

22:2–29:30 Final Preparations for the Temple These chapters, unique to Chronicles, are filled with the chronicler's characteristic themes: David's final preparations for the construction and administration of the temple, the legitimacy of the priests and Levites, and the unity of the reigns of David and Solomon.

22:2–5—David's final preparations for the temple.

22:5—Solomon's youthful inexperience justifies David's elaborate preparations. God refused to let David build the temple, showing him the necessity of proper preparation. Here the complementary nature of the reigns is emphasized. If David

needs Solomon to build, Solomon needs David to plan. God gives different talents and different tasks to different people.

22:6–10—David explains God's promise of a temple and a dynasty (cf. 17:1–15). Since David's military campaigns had disqualified him from building the temple, **Solomon**, the "offspring" of 17:11, is now revealed as the designated temple builder who will fulfill the dynastic promise of chap. 17.

22:9 Peace—Deuteronomy provides the timetable for the temple's construction: first, God gives the people "rest" in the land; then the people gather in the central sanctuary (Deut. 12:8–14).

him peace from all his enemies on every side; for his name shall be Solomon,*a* and I will give peace*b* and quiet to Israel in his days. 10 He shall build a house for my name. He shall be a son to me, and I will be a father to him, and I will establish his royal throne in Israel forever." 11 Now, my son, the LORD be with you, so that you may succeed in building the house of the LORD your God, as he has spoken concerning you. 12 Only, may the LORD grant you discretion and understanding, so that when he gives you charge over Israel you may keep the law of the LORD your God. 13 Then you will prosper if you are careful to observe the statutes and the ordinances that the LORD commanded Moses for Israel. Be strong and of good courage. Do not be afraid or dismayed. 14 With great pains I have provided for the house of the LORD one hundred thousand talents of gold, one million talents of silver, and bronze and iron beyond weighing, for there is so much of it; timber and stone too I have provided. To these you must add more. 15 You have an abundance of workers: stonecutters, masons, carpenters, and all kinds of artisans without number, skilled in working 16 gold, silver, bronze, and iron. Now begin the work, and the LORD be with you."

17 David also commanded all the leaders of Israel to help his son Solomon, saying, 18 "Is not the LORD your God with you? Has he not given you peace on every side? For he has delivered the inhabitants of the land into my hand; and the land is subdued before the LORD and his people. 19 Now set your mind and heart to seek the LORD your God. Go and build the sanctuary of the LORD God so that the ark of the covenant of the LORD and the holy vessels of God may be brought into a house built for the name of the LORD."

Families of the Levites and Their Functions

23 When David was old and full of days, he made his son Solomon king over Israel.

2 David assembled all the leaders of Israel and the priests and the Levites. 3 The Levites, thirty years old and upward, were counted, and the total was thirty-eight thousand. 4 "Twenty-four thousand of these," David said, "shall have charge of the work in the house of the LORD, six thousand shall be officers and judges, 5 four thousand gatekeepers, and four thousand shall offer praises to the LORD with the instruments that I have made for praise." 6 And David

a Heb *Shelomoh* *b* Heb *shalom*

David cannot build the temple because of the bloodshed associated with his military campaigns (1 Chr. 22:8; cf. 28:3). Solomon fulfills God's promise of a son who will build the temple (17:11–14) following the necessary condition of God's gift of "rest" for the land. This is illustrated by deriving Solomon's name from "shalom" ("peace," 22:9b). Consequently, the phrases *man of peace* and *I will give him peace* (v. 9a, NRSV) should be translated "man of rest" and "I will give him rest."

22:11–16—David commissions Solomon for the task in language modeled upon Moses' commissioning of Joshua in Deut. 31 and Josh. 1. All of these include a promise of God's presence, a description of the task, and formulas of encouragement.

22:17–19—David privately solicits the support of Israel's leaders. The private conversation will be made public in 28:1–8.

22:18 *Peace*—Better, "rest" (see note at v. 9).

23:1–27:34—Varied lists portray the internal organization of the kingdom. David's devotion to the temple continues here in the concern for administration and worship. The narrative will resume in 28:1.

23:1—The orderly succession of kingship contrasts sharply with the machinations of 1 Kgs. 1–2. The formula *old and full of days* conveys veneration, not senility (cf. Abraham, Gen. 25:8; Isaac, Gen. 35:29; and Job, Job 42:17). David transfers to Solomon an organized administrative system as the climax of his reign.

23:2–32—The divisions of the Levites and their duties are listed to provide another link between David and the postexilic community.

23:3 *Thirty years old*—The initial age for Levitical service varies: It is thirty years here and in Num. 4:3, 23, 30; but twenty years in 1 Chr. 23:24, 27; 2 Chr. 31:17, and Ezra 3:8; and twenty-five in Num. 8:24.

organized them in divisions corresponding to the sons of Levi: Gershon,[a] Kohath, and Merari.

7 The sons of Gershon[b] were Ladan and Shimei. [8] The sons of Ladan: Jehiel the chief, Zetham, and Joel, three. [9] The sons of Shimei: Shelomoth, Haziel, and Haran, three. These were the heads of families of Ladan. [10] And the sons of Shimei: Jahath, Zina, Jeush, and Beriah. These four were the sons of Shimei. [11] Jahath was the chief, and Zizah the second; but Jeush and Beriah did not have many sons, so they were enrolled as a single family.

12 The sons of Kohath: Amram, Izhar, Hebron, and Uzziel, four. [13] The sons of Amram: Aaron and Moses. Aaron was set apart to consecrate the most holy things, so that he and his sons forever should make offerings before the LORD, and minister to him and pronounce blessings in his name forever; [14] but as for Moses the man of God, his sons were to be reckoned among the tribe of Levi. [15] The sons of Moses: Gershom and Eliezer. [16] The sons of Gershom: Shebuel the chief. [17] The sons of Eliezer: Rehabiah the chief; Eliezer had no other sons, but the sons of Rehabiah were very numerous. [18] The sons of Izhar: Shelomith the chief. [19] The sons of Hebron: Jeriah the chief, Amariah the second, Jahaziel the third, and Jekameam the fourth. [20] The sons of Uzziel: Micah the chief and Isshiah the second.

21 The sons of Merari: Mahli and Mushi. The sons of Mahli: Eleazar and Kish. [22] Eleazar died having no sons, but only daughters; their kindred, the sons of Kish, married them. [23] The sons of Mushi: Mahli, Eder, and Jeremoth, three.

24 These were the sons of Levi by their ancestral houses, the heads of families as they were enrolled according to the number of the names of the individuals from twenty years old and upward who were to do the work for the service of the house of the LORD. [25] For David said, "The LORD, the God of Israel, has given rest to his people; and he resides in Jerusalem forever. [26] And so the Levites no longer need to carry the tabernacle or any of the things for its service"— [27] for according to the last words of David these were the number of the Levites from twenty years old and upward— [28] "but their duty shall be to assist the descendants of Aaron for the service of the house of the LORD, having the care of the courts and the chambers, the cleansing of all that is holy, and any work for the service of the house of God; [29] to assist also with the rows of bread, the choice flour for the grain offering, the wafers of unleavened bread, the baked offering, the offering mixed with oil, and all measures of quantity or size. [30] And they shall stand every morning, thanking and praising the LORD, and likewise at evening, [31] and whenever burnt offerings are offered to the LORD on sabbaths, new moons, and appointed festivals, according to the number required of them, regularly before the LORD. [32] Thus they shall keep charge of the tent of meeting and the sanctuary, and shall attend the descendants of Aaron, their kindred, for the service of the house of the LORD."

Divisions of the Priests

24 The divisions of the descendants of Aaron were these. The sons

---

[a] Or Gershom; See 1 Chr 6.1, note, and 23.15　[b] Vg Compare Gk Syr: Heb to the Gershonite

---

23:29 *All measures*—Maintenance of standard weights and measures is a prerequisite of justice. When it is abused, God is angered (Lev. 19:35–36; Amos 8:5). Here this royal responsibility is given to the Levites.

24:1–19—After tracing the primary priestly families of Aaron's sons *Eleazar* and *Ithamar* (vv.

1–6a), these verses present David's division of the priesthood into twenty-four courses. That the divisions took place *by lot* (v. 5) should not trouble us. It is an indication of a principle of equality in that it seeks to prevent more prominent priestly families from gaining a monopoly and distributes the responsibility among all the priests.

of Aaron: Nadab, Abihu, Eleazar, and Ithamar. ² But Nadab and Abihu died before their father, and had no sons; so Eleazar and Ithamar became the priests. ³ Along with Zadok of the sons of Eleazar, and Ahimelech of the sons of Ithamar, David organized them according to the appointed duties in their service. ⁴ Since more chief men were found among the sons of Eleazar than among the sons of Ithamar, they organized them under sixteen heads of ancestral houses of the sons of Eleazar, and eight of the sons of Ithamar. ⁵ They organized them by lot, all alike, for there were officers of the sanctuary and officers of God among both the sons of Eleazar and the sons of Ithamar. ⁶ The scribe Shemaiah son of Nethanel, a Levite, recorded them in the presence of the king, and the officers, and Zadok the priest, and Ahimelech son of Abiathar, and the heads of ancestral houses of the priests and of the Levites; one ancestral house being chosen for Eleazar and one chosen for Ithamar.

7 The first lot fell to Jehoiarib, the second to Jedaiah, ⁸ the third to Harim, the fourth to Seorim, ⁹ the fifth to Malchijah, the sixth to Mijamin, ¹⁰ the seventh to Hakkoz, the eighth to Abijah, ¹¹ the ninth to Jeshua, the tenth to Shecaniah, ¹² the eleventh to Eliashib, the twelfth to Jakim, ¹³ the thirteenth to Huppah, the fourteenth to Jeshebeab, ¹⁴ the fifteenth to Bilgah, the sixteenth to Immer, ¹⁵ the seventeenth to Hezir, the eighteenth to Happizzez, ¹⁶ the nineteenth to Pethahiah, the twentieth to Jehezkel, ¹⁷ the twenty-first to Jachin, the twenty-second to Gamul, ¹⁸ the twenty-third to Delaiah, the twenty-fourth to Maaziah. ¹⁹ These had as their appointed duty in their service to enter the house of the LORD according to the procedure

established for them by their ancestor Aaron, as the LORD God of Israel had commanded him.

Other Levites

20 And of the rest of the sons of Levi: of the sons of Amram, Shubael; of the sons of Shubael, Jehdeiah. ²¹ Of Rehabiah: of the sons of Rehabiah, Isshiah the chief. ²² Of the Izharites, Shelomoth; of the sons of Shelomoth, Jahath. ²³ The sons of Hebron:ᵃ Jeriah the chief,ᵇ Amariah the second, Jahaziel the third, Jekameam the fourth. ²⁴ The sons of Uzziel, Micah; of the sons of Micah, Shamir. ²⁵ The brother of Micah, Isshiah; of the sons of Isshiah, Zechariah. ²⁶ The sons of Merari: Mahli and Mushi. The sons of Jaaziah: Beno.ᶜ ²⁷ The sons of Merari: of Jaaziah, Beno,ᶜ Shoham, Zaccur, and Ibri. ²⁸ Of Mahli: Eleazar, who had no sons. ²⁹ Of Kish, the sons of Kish: Jerahmeel. ³⁰ The sons of Mushi: Mahli, Eder, and Jerimoth. These were the sons of the Levites according to their ancestral houses. ³¹ These also cast lots corresponding to their kindred, the descendants of Aaron, in the presence of King David, Zadok, Ahimelech, and the heads of ancestral houses of the priests and of the Levites, the chief as well as the youngest brother.

The Temple Musicians

25 David and the officers of the army also set apart for the service the sons of Asaph, and of Heman, and of Jeduthun, who should prophesy with lyres, harps, and cymbals. The list of those who did the work and of their duties was: ² Of the sons of Asaph: Zaccur, Joseph, Nethaniah, and Asarelah, sons of Asaph, under the direction of Asaph, who prophesied under the direction

ᵃ See 23.19: Heb lacks *Hebron*   ᵇ See 23.19: Heb lacks *the chief*   ᶜ Or *his son*: Meaning of Heb uncertain

---

25:1–31—David divides the musicians into twenty-four courses of twelve musicians each. As in chaps. 15–16, the musicians are Levites from the three families of *Asaph* (four divisions, 25:2), *Jeduthun* (six divisions, v. 3), and *Heman* (fourteen divisions, vv. 4–5).

25:1–3 *Prophesy*—Several times the chronicler equates music with prophecy. By this linking the musicians to the early cultic functions of preexilic seers and prophets, the singers become proclaimers.

of the king. ³ Of Jeduthun, the sons of Jeduthun: Gedaliah, Zeri, Jeshaiah, Shimei,ᵃ Hashabiah, and Mattithiah, six, under the direction of their father Jeduthun, who prophesied with the lyre in thanksgiving and praise to the LORD. ⁴ Of Heman, the sons of Heman: Bukkiah, Mattaniah, Uzziel, Shebuel, and Jerimoth, Hananiah, Hanani, Eliathah, Giddalti, and Romamti-ezer, Joshbekashah, Mallothi, Hothir, Mahazioth. ⁵ All these were the sons of Heman the king's seer, according to the promise of God to exalt him; for God had given Heman fourteen sons and three daughters. ⁶ They were all under the direction of their father for the music in the house of the LORD with cymbals, harps, and lyres for the service of the house of God. Asaph, Jeduthun, and Heman were under the order of the king. ⁷ They and their kindred, who were trained in singing to the LORD, all of whom were skillful, numbered two hundred eighty-eight. ⁸ And they cast lots for their duties, small and great, teacher and pupil alike.

9 The first lot fell for Asaph to Joseph; the second to Gedaliah, to him and his brothers and his sons, twelve; ¹⁰ the third to Zaccur, his sons and his brothers, twelve; ¹¹ the fourth to Izri, his sons and his brothers, twelve; ¹² the fifth to Nethaniah, his sons and his brothers, twelve; ¹³ the sixth to Bukkiah, his sons and his brothers, twelve; ¹⁴ the seventh to Jesarelah,ᵇ his sons and his brothers, twelve; ¹⁵ the eighth to Jeshaiah, his sons and his brothers, twelve; ¹⁶ the ninth to Mattaniah, his sons and his brothers, twelve; ¹⁷ the tenth to Shimei, his sons and his brothers, twelve; ¹⁸ the eleventh to Azarel, his sons and his brothers, twelve; ¹⁹ the twelfth to Hashabiah, his sons and his brothers, twelve; ²⁰ to the thirteenth, Shubael, his sons and his brothers, twelve; ²¹ to the fourteenth, Mattithiah, his sons and his brothers,

twelve; ²² to the fifteenth, to Jeremoth, his sons and his brothers, twelve; ²³ to the sixteenth, to Hananiah, his sons and his brothers, twelve; ²⁴ to the seventeenth, to Joshbekashah, his sons and his brothers, twelve; ²⁵ to the eighteenth, to Hanani, his sons and his brothers, twelve; ²⁶ to the nineteenth, to Mallothi, his sons and his brothers, twelve; ²⁷ to the twentieth, to Eliathah, his sons and his brothers, twelve; ²⁸ to the twenty-first, to Hothir, his sons and his brothers, twelve; ²⁹ to the twenty-second, to Giddalti, his sons and his brothers, twelve; ³⁰ to the twenty-third, to Mahazioth, his sons and his brothers, twelve; ³¹ to the twenty-fourth, to Romamti-ezer, his sons and his brothers, twelve.

The Gatekeepers

26 As for the divisions of the gatekeepers: of the Korahites, Meshelemiah son of Kore, of the sons of Asaph. ² Meshelemiah had sons: Zechariah the firstborn, Jediael the second, Zebadiah the third, Jathniel the fourth, ³ Elam the fifth, Jehohanan the sixth, Eliehoenai the seventh. ⁴ Obed-edom had sons: Shemaiah the firstborn, Jehozabad the second, Joah the third, Sachar the fourth, Nethanel the fifth, ⁵ Ammiel the sixth, Issachar the seventh, Peullethai the eighth; for God blessed him. ⁶ Also to his son Shemaiah sons were born who exercised authority in their ancestral houses, for they were men of great ability. ⁷ The sons of Shemaiah: Othni, Rephael, Obed, and Elzabad, whose brothers were able men, Elihu and Semachiah. ⁸ All these, sons of Obed-edom with their sons and brothers, were able men qualified for the service; sixty-two of Obed-edom. ⁹ Meshelemiah had sons and brothers, able men, eighteen. ¹⁰ Hosah, of the sons of Merari, had sons: Shimri the chief

ᵃ One Ms: Gk: MT lacks *Shimei* ᵇ Or *Asarelah*; see 25.2

26:1–32—The list of *gatekeepers* (vv. 1–19) and other officials (vv. 20–32). The seemingly mundane considerations of stewardship and security are important indications of the intersection between sacred space and the secular workplace. Consistency is needed in both.

583 1 CHRONICLES 27:1

(for though he was not the firstborn, his father made him chief), **11** Hilkiah the second, Tebaliah the third, Zechariah the fourth: all the sons and brothers of Hosah totaled thirteen.

12 These divisions of the gatekeepers, corresponding to their leaders, had duties, just as their kindred did, ministering in the house of the LORD; **13** and they cast lots by ancestral houses, small and great alike, for their gates. **14** The lot for the east fell to Shelemiah. They cast lots also for his son Zechariah, a prudent counselor, and his lot came out for the north. **15** Obed-edom's came out for the south, and to his sons was allotted the storehouse. **16** For Shuppim and Hosah it came out for the west, at the gate of Shallecheth on the ascending road. Guard corresponded to guard. **17** On the east there were six Levites each day,*a* on the north four each day, on the south four each day, as well as two and two at the storehouse; **18** and for the colonnade*b* on the west there were four at the road and two at the colonnade.*b* **19** These were the divisions of the gatekeepers among the Korahites and the sons of Merari.

The Treasurers, Officers, and Judges

20 And of the Levites, Ahijah had charge of the treasuries of the house of God and the treasuries of the dedicated gifts. **21** The sons of Ladan, the sons of the Gershonites belonging to Ladan, the heads of families belonging to Ladan the Gershonite: Jehieli.*c* **22** The sons of Jehieli, Zetham and his brother Joel, were in charge of the treasuries of the house of the LORD. **23** Of the Amramites, the Izharites, the Hebronites, and the Uzzielites: **24** Shebuel son of Gershom, son of Moses, was chief officer in charge of the treasuries. **25** His brothers: from Eliezer were his son Rehabiah, his son Jeshaiah, his son

Joram, his son Zichri, and his son Shelomoth. **26** This Shelomoth and his brothers were in charge of all the treasuries of the dedicated gifts that King David, and the heads of families, and the officers of the thousands and the hundreds, and the commanders of the army, had dedicated. **27** From booty won in battles they dedicated gifts for the maintenance of the house of the LORD. **28** Also all that Samuel the seer, and Saul son of Kish, and Abner son of Ner, and Joab son of Zeruiah had dedicated—all dedicated gifts were in the care of Shelomoth*d* and his brothers.

29 Of the Izharites, Chenaniah and his sons were appointed to outside duties for Israel, as officers and judges. **30** Of the Hebronites, Hashabiah and his brothers, one thousand seven hundred men of ability, had the oversight of Israel west of the Jordan for all the work of the LORD and for the service of the king. **31** Of the Hebronites, Jerijah was chief of the Hebronites. (In the fortieth year of David's reign search was made, of whatever genealogy or family, and men of great ability among them were found at Jazer in Gilead.) **32** King David appointed him and his brothers, two thousand seven hundred men of ability, heads of families, to have the oversight of the Reubenites, the Gadites, and the half-tribe of the Manassites for everything pertaining to God and for the affairs of the king.

The Military Divisions

27 This is the list of the people of Israel, the heads of families, the commanders of the thousands and the hundreds, and their officers who served the king in all matters concerning the divisions that came and went,

a Gk: Heb lacks *each day* *b* Heb *parbar*: meaning uncertain *c* The Hebrew text of verse 21 is confused *d* Gk Compare 26.28: Heb *Shelomith*

27:1–34—Four lists of secular officials in David's administration, two national (vv. 1–15; 16–24), and two royal (vv. 25–31; 32–34). The first list follows the pattern of the earlier, more religious temple lists. This strengthens the impression that the temple is the center and basis for all of society and that God is concerned with civil matters as well as secular.

month after month throughout the year, each division numbering twenty-four thousand:

2 Jashobeam son of Zabdiel was in charge of the first division in the first month; in his division were twenty-four thousand. 3 He was a descendant of Perez, and was chief of all the commanders of the army for the first month. 4 Dodai the Ahohite was in charge of the division of the second month; Mikloth was the chief officer of his division. In his division were twenty-four thousand. 5 The third commander, for the third month, was Benaiah son of the priest Jehoiada, as chief; in his division were twenty-four thousand. 6 This is the Benaiah who was a mighty man of the Thirty and in command of the Thirty; his son Ammizabad was in charge of his division.a 7 Asahel brother of Joab was fourth, for the fourth month, and his son Zebadiah after him; in his division were twenty-four thousand. 8 The fifth commander, for the fifth month, was Shamhuth, the Izrahite; in his division were twenty-four thousand. 9 Sixth, for the sixth month, was Ira son of Ikkesh the Tekoite; in his division were twenty-four thousand. 10 Seventh, for the seventh month, was Helez the Pelonite, of the Ephraimites; in his division were twenty-four thousand. 11 Eighth, for the eighth month, was Sibbecai the Hushathite, of the Zerahites; in his division were twenty-four thousand. 12 Ninth, for the ninth month, was Abiezer of Anathoth, a Benjaminite; in his division were twenty-four thousand. 13 Tenth, for the tenth month, was Maharai of Netophah, of the Zerahites; in his division were twenty-four thousand. 14 Eleventh, for the eleventh month, was Benaiah of Pirathon, of the Ephraimites; in his division were twenty-four thousand. 15 Twelfth, for the twelfth month, was Heldai the Netophathite, of Othniel; in his division were twenty-four thousand.

Leaders of Tribes

16 Over the tribes of Israel, for the Reubenites, Eliezer son of Zichri was chief officer; for the Simeonites, Shephatiah son of Maacah; 17 for Levi, Hashabiah son of Kemuel; for Aaron, Zadok; 18 for Judah, Elihu, one of David's brothers; for Issachar, Omri son of Michael; 19 for Zebulun, Ishmaiah son of Obadiah; for Naphtali, Jerimoth son of Azriel; 20 for the Ephraimites, Hoshea son of Azaziah; for the half-tribe of Manasseh, Joel son of Pedaiah; 21 for the half-tribe of Manasseh in Gilead, Iddo son of Zechariah; for Benjamin, Jaasiel son of Abner; 22 for Dan, Azarel son of Jeroham. These were the leaders of the tribes of Israel. 23 David did not count those below twenty years of age, for the LORD had promised to make Israel as numerous as the stars of heaven. 24 Joab son of Zeruiah began to count them, but did not finish; yet wrath came upon Israel for this, and the number was not entered into the account of the Annals of King David.

Other Civic Officials

25 Over the king's treasuries was Azmaveth son of Adiel. Over the treasuries in the country, in the cities, in the villages and in the towers, was Jonathan son of Uzziah. 26 Over those who did the work of the field, tilling the soil, was Ezri son of Chelub. 27 Over the vineyards was Shimei the Ramathite. Over the produce of the vineyards for the wine cellars was Zabdi the Shiphmite. 28 Over the olive and sycamore trees in the Shephelah was Baal-hanan the Gederite. Over the stores of oil was Joash. 29 Over the herds that pastured in Sharon was Shitrai the Sharonite. Over the herds in the valleys was Shaphat son of Adlai. 30 Over the camels was Obil the Ishmaelite. Over the donkeys was Jehdeiah the Meronothite. Over the flocks was Jaziz the Hagrite. 31 All these were stewards of King David's property.

a Gk Vg: Heb Ammizabad was his division

32 Jonathan, David's uncle, was a counselor, being a man of understanding and a scribe; Jehiel son of Hachmoni attended the king's sons. ³³ Ahithophel was the king's counselor, and Hushai the Archite was the king's friend. ³⁴ After Ahithophel came Jehoiada son of Benaiah, and Abiathar. Joab was commander of the king's army.

Solomon Instructed to Build the Temple

28 David assembled at Jerusalem all the officials of Israel, the officials of the tribes, the officers of the divisions that served the king, the commanders of the thousands, the commanders of the hundreds, the stewards of all the property and cattle of the king and his sons, together with the palace officials, the mighty warriors, and all the warriors. ² Then King David rose to his feet and said: "Hear me, my brothers and my people. I had planned to build a house of rest for the ark of the covenant of the LORD, for the footstool of our God; and I made preparations for building. ³ But God said to me, 'You shall not build a house for my name, for you are a warrior and have shed blood.' ⁴ Yet the LORD God of Israel chose me from all my ancestral house to be king over Israel forever; for he chose Judah as leader, and in the house of Judah my father's house, and among my father's sons he took delight in making me king over all Israel. ⁵ And of all my sons, for the LORD has given me many, he has chosen my son Solomon to sit upon the throne of the kingdom of the LORD over Israel. ⁶ He said to me, 'It is your son Solomon who shall build my house and my courts, for I have chosen him to be a son to me, and I will be a father to him. ⁷ I will establish his kingdom forever if he continues resolute in keeping my commandments and my ordinances, as he is today.' ⁸ Now therefore in the sight of all Israel, the assembly of the LORD, and in the hearing of our God, observe and search out all the commandments of the LORD your God; that you may possess this good land, and leave it for an inheritance to your children after you forever.

9 "And you, my son Solomon, know the God of your father, and serve him with single mind and willing heart; for the LORD searches every mind, and understands every plan and thought. If you seek him, he will be found by you; but if you forsake him, he will abandon you forever. ¹⁰ Take heed now, for the LORD has chosen you to build a house as the sanctuary; be strong, and act."

11 Then David gave his son Solomon the plan of the vestibule of the temple, and of its houses, its treasuries, its upper rooms, and its inner chambers, and of

---

28:1–29:25 Solomon's enthronement—The description of Solomon's enthronement actually concerns the temple. Throughout this section political matters will be subordinated to worship, as several of the chronicler's favorite themes are gathered together.

28:2–10—David's speech addresses the leaders (vv. 2–8) before Solomon (vv. 9–10).

28:2–3—God rejects David's offer to build the *house* (the temple) because David was a warrior (cf. 22:7–9).

28:4–5—God's choice of Solomon begins a different *house*, i.e., the Davidic dynasty (cf. 22:9).

28:6—Solomon's election by God is unique to Chronicles (cf. v. 5; 10; 22:10) and adds to the impression that the reigns of David and Solomon are to be seen as a unity.

28:7 *As he is today*—The conditional nature of the promise (*if*) is an attainable goal.

28:8 *Observe and search out*—Israel's obedience is also called for, as these plural imperatives show.

28:11–21—The transfer of the temple plans to Solomon subordinates the transfer of political leadership to worship.

28:11–12—Moses (Exod. 25:9, 40; 26:30) and Ezekiel (Ezek. 40–48) serve as models for David and the temple. All three projects are divinely revealed, and the Hebrew word for *the plan* (1 Chr. 28:11, 12, 18, 19) is used of the tabernacle in Exod. 25:9, 40, as is a related Hebrew term in Ezek. 43:10.

the room for the mercy seat;*a* ¹²and the plan of all that he had in mind: for the courts of the house of the LORD, all the surrounding chambers, the treasuries of the house of God, and the treasuries for dedicated gifts; ¹³for the divisions of the priests and of the Levites, and all the work of the service in the house of the LORD; for all the vessels for the service in the house of the LORD, ¹⁴the weight of gold for all golden vessels for each service, the weight of silver vessels for each service, ¹⁵the weight of the golden lampstands and their lamps, the weight of gold for each lampstand and its lamps, the weight of silver for a lampstand and its lamps, according to the use of each in the service, ¹⁶the weight of gold for each table for the rows of bread, the silver for the silver tables, ¹⁷and pure gold for the forks, the basins, and the cups; for the golden bowls and the weight of each; for the silver bowls and the weight of each; ¹⁸for the altar of incense made of refined gold, and its weight; also his plan for the golden chariot of the cherubim that spread their wings and covered the ark of the covenant of the LORD.

19 "All this, in writing at the LORD's direction, he made clear to me—the plan of all the works."

20 David said further to his son Solomon, "Be strong and of good courage, and act. Do not be afraid or dismayed; for the LORD God, my God, is with you. He will not fail you or forsake you, until all the work for the service of the house of the LORD is finished. ²¹Here are the divi-sions of the priests and the Levites for all the service of the house of God; and with you in all the work will be every volunteer who has skill for any kind of service; also the officers and all the people will be wholly at your command."

Offerings for Building the Temple

29 King David said to the whole assembly, "My son Solomon, whom alone God has chosen, is young and inexperienced, and the work is great; for the temple*b* will not be for mortals but for the LORD God. ²So I have provided for the house of my God, so far as I was able, the gold for the things of gold, the silver for the things of silver, and the bronze for the things of bronze, the iron for the things of iron, and wood for the things of wood, besides great quantities of onyx and stones for setting, antimony, colored stones, all sorts of precious stones, and marble in abundance. ³Moreover, in addition to all that I have provided for the holy house, I have a treasure of my own of gold and silver, and because of my devotion to the house of my God I give it to the house of my God: ⁴three thousand talents of gold, of the gold of Ophir, and seven thousand talents of refined silver, for overlaying the walls of the house, ⁵and for all the work to be done by artisans, gold for the things of gold and silver for the things of silver. Who then will offer willingly, consecrating themselves today to the LORD?"

6 Then the leaders of ancestral houses

a Or the cover *b* Heb fortress

29:1–9—David's final speech continues to model David's temple preparations on Moses' preparations for the tabernacle (Exod. 25–31; 35–40).

29:2—David provides the same materials for the construction of temple that Moses used for the tabernacle (*iron*, unknown in Moses' time, is anachronistic).

29:3–4—Unlike Moses, David also generously contributes. The exaggerated figures—hundreds of tons—enhance the magnificence of the temple and the completeness of David's preparations.

29:5—Like Moses (Exod. 25:1–7; 35:4–9, 20–29), David seeks contributions from the people. This has the effect of allowing the people to participate in the preparations for the building of the temple and thereby witness to the glory of their God. *Consecrating themselves*—The exact meaning of this Priestly terminology, lit. "fill their hand," describes their response. It has to do with what happens at a newly ordained priest's first offer of sacrifice (Exod. 28:41). He, as well as the offering, is consecrated to God. By encouraging the people to offer their financial support, David gives them an opportunity to declare their commitment to God's mission.

29:6–9—Exaggerated figures demonstrate the

made their freewill offerings, as did also the leaders of the tribes, the commanders of the thousands and of the hundreds, and the officers over the king's work. ⁷ They gave for the service of the house of God five thousand talents and ten thousand darics of gold, ten thousand talents of silver, eighteen thousand talents of bronze, and one hundred thousand talents of iron. ⁸ Whoever had precious stones gave them to the treasury of the house of the LORD, into the care of Jehiel the Gershonite. ⁹ Then the people rejoiced because these had given willingly, for with single mind they had offered freely to the LORD; King David also rejoiced greatly.

David's Praise to God

10 Then David blessed the LORD in the presence of all the assembly; David said: "Blessed are you, O LORD, the God of our ancestor Israel, forever and ever. ¹¹ Yours, O LORD, are the greatness, the power, the glory, the victory, and the majesty; for all that is in the heavens and on the earth is yours; yours is the kingdom, O LORD, and you are exalted as head above all. ¹² Riches and honor come from you, and you rule over all. In your hand are power and might; and it is in your hand to make great and to give strength to all. ¹³ And now, our God, we give thanks to you and praise your glorious name.

14 "But who am I, and what is my people, that we should be able to make this freewill offering? For all things come from you, and of your own have we given you. ¹⁵ For we are aliens and transients before you, as were all our ancestors; our days on the earth are like a shadow, and there is no hope. ¹⁶ O

LORD our God, all this abundance that we have provided for building you a house for your holy name comes from your hand and is all your own. ¹⁷ I know, my God, that you search the heart, and take pleasure in uprightness; in the uprightness of my heart I have freely offered all these things, and now I have seen your people, who are present here, offering freely and joyously to you. ¹⁸ O LORD, the God of Abraham, Isaac, and Israel, our ancestors, keep forever such purposes and thoughts in the hearts of your people, and direct their hearts toward you. ¹⁹ Grant to my son Solomon that with single mind he may keep your commandments, your decrees, and your statutes, performing all of them, and that he may build the temple*a* for which I have made provision."

20 Then David said to the whole assembly, "Bless the LORD your God." And all the assembly blessed the LORD, the God of their ancestors, and bowed their heads and prostrated themselves before the LORD and the king. ²¹ On the next day they offered sacrifices and burnt offerings to the LORD, a thousand bulls, a thousand rams, and a thousand lambs, with their libations, and sacrifices in abundance for all Israel; ²² and they ate and drank before the LORD on that day with great joy.

Solomon Anointed King

They made David's son Solomon king a second time; they anointed him as the LORD's prince, and Zadok as priest. ²³ Then Solomon sat on the throne of the LORD, succeeding his father David as king; he prospered, and all Israel obeyed him.

a Heb *fortress*

---

obedience of those addressed in 28:8 and recall Moses' similar appeal for the tabernacle (Exod. 35:4–9).

29:10–19—David's temple preparations end as they began (17:16–27), with prayer employing the primary elements of worship: praise of God's sovereignty (29:10–12), thanksgiving for the people's freewill offering emphasizing that every-

thing comes from God (vv. 13–17), and petitions for God's continued presence (vv. 18–19).

29:20–25—Solomon's enthronement frames David's reign as a whole by repeating the themes of David's rise to power (10:1–12:40), especially the *all Israel* theme found in 29:21, 23, and 25 (cf. 11:1–3; 12:38–40).

24 All the leaders and the mighty warriors, and also all the sons of King David, pledged their allegiance to King Solomon. 25 The LORD highly exalted Solomon in the sight of all Israel, and bestowed upon him such royal majesty as had not been on any king before him in Israel.

Summary of David's Reign

26 Thus David son of Jesse reigned over all Israel. 27 The period that he reigned over Israel was forty years; he reigned seven years in Hebron, and thirty-three years in Jerusalem. 28 He died in a good old age, full of days, riches, and honor; and his son Solomon succeeded him. 29 Now the acts of King David, from first to last, are written in the records of the seer Samuel, and in the records of the prophet Nathan, and in the records of the seer Gad, 30 with accounts of all his rule and his might and of the events that befell him and Israel and all the kingdoms of the earth.

29:24—The all-Israel theme comes to a climax in this pointed contradiction of the account of the rebellion of David's son Adonijah against his half brother Solomon in 1 Kgs. 1–2.

29:26–30—The account of David's reign concludes with a glowing summary and death notice expanded from 1 Kgs. 2:10–12. Placing the account after Solomon's accession highlights the unity of the reigns of David and Solomon.

29:27 *Forty years*—Probably 1005–965 BCE.

The Book of
2 CHRONICLES

Solomon Requests Wisdom

1 Solomon son of David established himself in his kingdom; the LORD his God was with him and made him exceedingly great.

2 Solomon summoned all Israel, the commanders of the thousands and of the hundreds, the judges, and all the leaders of all Israel, the heads of families. ³ Then Solomon, and the whole assembly with him, went to the high place that was at Gibeon; for God's tent of meeting, which Moses the servant of the LORD had made in the wilderness, was there. ⁴ (But David had brought the ark of God up from Kiriath-jearim to the place that David had prepared for it; for he had pitched a tent for it in Jerusalem.) ⁵ Moreover the bronze altar that Bezalel son of Uri, son of Hur, had made, was there in front of the tabernacle of the LORD. And Solomon and the assembly inquired at it. ⁶ Solomon went up there to the bronze altar before the LORD, which was at the tent of meeting, and offered a thousand burnt offerings on it.

7 That night God appeared to Solomon, and said to him, "Ask what I should give you." ⁸ Solomon said to God, "You have shown great and steadfast love to my father David, and have made me succeed him as king. ⁹ O LORD God, let your promise to my father David now be fulfilled, for you have made me king over a people as numerous as the dust of the earth. ¹⁰ Give me now wisdom and knowledge to go out and come in before this people, for who can rule this great people of yours?" ¹¹ God answered Solomon, "Because this was in your heart, and you have not asked for possessions, wealth, honor, or the life of those who hate you, and have not even asked for long life, but have asked for wisdom and knowledge for yourself that you may rule my people over whom I have made you king, ¹² wisdom and knowledge are granted to you. I will also give you riches, possessions, and honor, such as none of the kings had who were before you, and none after you shall have the like." ¹³ So Solomon came from*a* the high place at Gibeon, from the tent of meeting, to Jerusalem. And he reigned over Israel.

Solomon's Military and Commercial Activity

14 Solomon gathered together chariots and horses; he had fourteen hundred

a Gk Vg: Heb to

1:1–9:31 The Reign of Solomon
The modern division of Chronicles into two books obscures the presentation of the reigns of David and Solomon as a unity. Solomon's reign is a detailed discussion of the construction of the temple that completes David's preparations. The actual construction (3:1–5:1) and dedication (5:2–7:22) of the temple are framed by Solomon's initial preparations (2:1–18) and finishing touches (8:1–16). Solomon's wisdom and wealth enclose the whole (1:1–17; 8:17–9:31).

1:1–17 Solomon's Worship, Wisdom, and Wealth

1:2–6—Solomon is introduced as a pious king leading all Israel in worship. The *tent of meeting* (cf. Lev. 17:8–9) made *Gibeon* the only legitimate site for sacrifice at this time.

1:7–13—Solomon's prayer for *wisdom* (v. 10; granted in v. 12) fulfills David's request (1 Chr. 22:12). Wisdom equips Solomon for temple construction, not prudence, administrative skill, or insight into the natural sciences. Solomon asked for what God wanted him to be. This is the true prayer, praying within God's will, rather than trying to get out of God as much as possible.

1:14–17—Placing Solomon's commercial activity

chariots and twelve thousand horses, which he stationed in the chariot cities and with the king in Jerusalem. ¹⁵ The king made silver and gold as common in Jerusalem as stone, and he made cedar as plentiful as the sycamore of the Shephelah. ¹⁶ Solomon's horses were imported from Egypt and Kue; the king's traders received them from Kue at the prevailing price. ¹⁷ They imported from Egypt, and then exported, a chariot for six hundred shekels of silver, and a horse for one hundred fifty; so through them these were exported to all the kings of the Hittites and the kings of Aram.

Preparations for Building the Temple

2 ᵃ Solomon decided to build a temple for the name of the LORD, and a royal palace for himself. ²ᵇ Solomon conscripted seventy thousand laborers and eighty thousand stonecutters in the hill country, with three thousand six hundred to oversee them.

Alliance with Huram of Tyre

3 Solomon sent word to King Huram of Tyre: "Once you dealt with my father David and sent him cedar to build himself a house to live in. ⁴ I am now about to build a house for the name of the LORD my God and dedicate it to him for offering fragrant incense before him, and for the regular offering of the rows of bread, and for burnt offerings morning and evening, on the sabbaths and the new moons and the appointed festivals of the LORD our God, as ordained forever for Israel. ⁵ The house that I am about to build will be great, for our God is greater than other gods. ⁶ But who is

able to build him a house, since heaven, even highest heaven, cannot contain him? Who am I to build a house for him, except as a place to make offerings before him? ⁷ So now send me an artisan skilled to work in gold, silver, bronze, and iron, and in purple, crimson, and blue fabrics, trained also in engraving, to join the skilled workers who are with me in Judah and Jerusalem, whom my father David provided. ⁸ Send me also cedar, cypress, and algum timber from Lebanon, for I know that your servants are skilled in cutting Lebanon timber. My servants will work with your servants ⁹ to prepare timber for me in abundance, for the house I am about to build will be great and wonderful. ¹⁰ I will provide for your servants, those who cut the timber, twenty thousand cors of crushed wheat, twenty thousand cors of barley, twenty thousand bathsᶜ of wine, and twenty thousand baths of oil."

11 Then King Huram of Tyre answered in a letter that he sent to Solomon, "Because the LORD loves his people he has made you king over them." ¹² Huram also said, "Blessed be the LORD God of Israel, who made heaven and earth, who has given King David a wise son, endowed with discretion and understanding, who will build a temple for the LORD, and a royal palace for himself.

13 "I have dispatched Huram-abi, a skilled artisan, endowed with understanding, ¹⁴ the son of one of the Danite women, his father a Tyrian. He is trained to work in gold, silver, bronze, iron, stone, and wood, and in purple, blue,

ᵃ Ch 1.18 in Heb   ᵇ Ch 2.1 in Heb   ᶜ A Hebrew measure of volume

---

before the construction of the temple, instead of at the end of his reign (1 Kgs. 10:26–29), fulfills God's promise (2 Chr. 1:12b) and gathers capital for the temple construction. Wealth functions positively in Chronicles (and generally in the Old Testament) as a symbol of God's favor. We would rather separate the spiritual from the material.

2:1–18 Preparations for Construction

Correspondence with *Huram*, king of Tyre ("Hiram" in 1 Kings). Solomon is in complete control.

2:3—Solomon, as the designated temple builder, not Huram, initiates the correspondence and sets the price for the timber (v. 10; cf. 1 Kgs. 5:1, 9).

2:4–6—The temple is a place of sacrificial worship, not God's dwelling (cf. 7:12).

2:13–14—The *artisan Huram-abi*'s skills here and in v. 7 are those of Bezalel and Oholiab, who built the wilderness tabernacle (Exod. 31:1–11; 35:30–35).

and crimson fabrics and fine linen, and to do all sorts of engraving and execute any design that may be assigned him, with your artisans, the artisans of my lord, your father David. ¹⁵ Now, as for the wheat, barley, oil, and wine, of which my lord has spoken, let him send them to his servants. ¹⁶ We will cut whatever timber you need from Lebanon, and bring it to you as rafts by sea to Joppa; you will take it up to Jerusalem."

17 Then Solomon took a census of all the aliens who were residing in the land of Israel, after the census that his father David had taken; and there were found to be one hundred fifty-three thousand six hundred. ¹⁸ Seventy thousand of them he assigned as laborers, eighty thousand as stonecutters in the hill country, and three thousand six hundred as overseers to make the people work.

Solomon Builds the Temple

3 Solomon began to build the house of the LORD in Jerusalem on Mount Moriah, where the LORD had appeared to his father David, at the place that David had designated, on the threshing floor of Ornan the Jebusite. ² He began to build on the second day of the second month of the fourth year of his reign. ³ These are Solomon's measurements*ᵃ* for building the house of God: the length, in cubits of the old standard, was sixty cubits, and the width twenty cubits. ⁴ The vestibule in front of the nave of the house was twenty cubits long, across the width of the house;*ᵇ* and its height was one hun-

dred twenty cubits. He overlaid it on the inside with pure gold. ⁵ The nave he lined with cypress, covered it with fine gold, and made palms and chains on it. ⁶ He adorned the house with settings of precious stones. The gold was gold from Parvaim. ⁷ So he lined the house with gold—its beams, its thresholds, its walls, and its doors; and he carved cherubim on the walls.

8 He made the most holy place; its length, corresponding to the width of the house, was twenty cubits, and its width was twenty cubits; he overlaid it with six hundred talents of fine gold. ⁹ The weight of the nails was fifty shekels of gold. He overlaid the upper chambers with gold.

10 In the most holy place he made two carved cherubim and overlaid*ᶜ* them with gold. ¹¹ The wings of the cherubim together extended twenty cubits: one wing of the one, five cubits long, touched the wall of the house, and its other wing, five cubits long, touched the wing of the other cherub; ¹² and of this cherub, one wing, five cubits long, touched the wall of the house, and the other wing, also five cubits long, was joined to the wing of the first cherub. ¹³ The wings of these cherubim extended twenty cubits; the cherubim*ᵈ* stood on their feet, facing the nave. ¹⁴ And Solomon*ᵉ* made the curtain of blue and purple and crimson fabrics and fine linen, and worked cherubim into it.

15 In front of the house he made two pillars thirty-five cubits high, with a

ᵃ Syr: Heb *foundations* *ᵇ* Compare 1 Kings 6.3: Meaning of Heb uncertain *ᶜ* Heb *they overlaid* *ᵈ* Heb *they* *ᵉ* Heb *he*

2:17 *Aliens*—No Israelites work on the temple, in accordance with Lev. 25:39–45. Solomon faithfully follows the law.

3:1–4:1 The Temple Is Built
By shortening 1 Kgs. 6–7, Chronicles stresses worship over architecture. God allows the temple to be built as a concrete symbol of divine presence. God is not fully contained in it, however.

3:1–2—First Kings 6:1 recalls the exodus, the beginning of the nation. The chronicler connects David's designation of the temple site (1 Chr. 22:1) with Mount Moriah, site of Abraham's obedience (cf. Gen. 22:2, 14). In Chroni-

cles the covenant with David is more important than the covenant with Moses.

3:3–17—Several parallels link temple and tabernacle. First, God enabled both Moses and Solomon to do their respective building projects (Exod. 35:31; 2 Chr. 2:3–7). Second, both make the bronze altar (Exod. 27:1–2; 2 Chr. 4:1) and the other furnishings for their respective sanctuaries (Exod. 31; 2 Chr. 4). Finally, **the nails** (v. 9, only here in Chronicles) serve as "hooks" in the tabernacle (e.g., Exod. 26:32) as does **the curtain** (v. 14, only here with reference to the temple) that normally appears in the tabernacle (Exod. 26:31–35; 36:35–36).

capital of five cubits on the top of each. ¹⁶ He made encircling*ᵃ* chains and put them on the tops of the pillars; and he made one hundred pomegranates, and put them on the chains. ¹⁷ He set up the pillars in front of the temple, one on the right, the other on the left; the one on the right he called Jachin, and the one on the left, Boaz.

Furnishings of the Temple

4 He made an altar of bronze, twenty cubits long, twenty cubits wide, and ten cubits high. ² Then he made the molten sea; it was round, ten cubits from rim to rim, and five cubits high. A line of thirty cubits would encircle it completely. ³ Under it were panels all around, each of ten cubits, surrounding the sea; there were two rows of panels, cast when it was cast. ⁴ It stood on twelve oxen, three facing north, three facing west, three facing south, and three facing east; the sea was set on them. The hindquarters of each were toward the inside. ⁵ Its thickness was a handbreadth; its rim was made like the rim of a cup, like the flower of a lily; it held three thousand baths.*ᵇ* ⁶ He also made ten basins in which to wash, and set five on the right side, and five on the left. In these they were to rinse what was used for the burnt offering. The sea was for the priests to wash in.

7 He made ten golden lampstands as prescribed, and set them in the temple, five on the south side and five on the north. ⁸ He also made ten tables and placed them in the temple, five on the right side and five on the left. And he made one hundred basins of gold. ⁹ He made the court of the priests, and the great court, and doors for the court; he overlaid their doors with bronze. ¹⁰ He set the sea at the southeast corner of the house.

11 And Huram made the pots, the shovels, and the basins. Thus Huram finished the work that he did for King Solomon on the house of God: ¹² the two pillars, the bowls, and the two capitals on the top of the pillars; and the two latticeworks to cover the two bowls of the capitals that were on the top of the pillars; ¹³ the four hundred pomegranates for the two latticeworks, two rows of pomegranates for each latticework, to cover the two bowls of the capitals that were on the pillars. ¹⁴ He made the stands, the basins on the stands, ¹⁵ the one sea, and the twelve oxen underneath it. ¹⁶ The pots, the shovels, the forks, and all the equipment for these Huram-abi made of burnished bronze for King Solomon for the house of the LORD. ¹⁷ In the plain of the Jordan the king cast them, in the clay ground between Succoth and Zeredah. ¹⁸ Solomon made all these things in great quantities, so that the weight of the bronze was not determined.

19 So Solomon made all the things that were in the house of God: the golden altar, the tables for the bread of the Presence, ²⁰ the lampstands and their lamps of pure gold to burn before the inner sanctuary, as prescribed; ²¹ the flowers, the lamps, and the tongs, of purest gold; ²² the snuffers, basins, ladles, and firepans, of pure gold. As for the entrance to the temple: the inner doors to the most holy place and the doors of the nave of the temple were of gold.

5 Thus all the work that Solomon did for the house of the LORD was finished. Solomon brought in the things that his father David had dedicated, and stored the silver, the gold, and all the vessels in the treasuries of the house of God.

The Ark Brought into the Temple

2 Then Solomon assembled the elders of Israel and all the heads of the tribes,

ᵃ Cn: Heb *in the inner sanctuary*   *ᵇ* A Hebrew measure of volume

---

4:1–5:1—Solomon Furnishes the Temple
5:2–7:22 The Dedication of the Temple

5:2–6:2—Installation of the ark in the sanctuary parallels David's transfer of the ark to Jerusalem (cf. 1 Chr. 13–16). Both occur at national as-

the leaders of the ancestral houses of the people of Israel, in Jerusalem, to bring up the ark of the covenant of the LORD out of the city of David, which is Zion. ³ And all the Israelites assembled before the king at the festival that is in the seventh month. ⁴ And all the elders of Israel came, and the Levites carried the ark. ⁵ So they brought up the ark, the tent of meeting, and all the holy vessels that were in the tent; the priests and the Levites brought them up. ⁶ King Solomon and all the congregation of Israel, who had assembled before him, were before the ark, sacrificing so many sheep and oxen that they could not be numbered or counted. ⁷ Then the priests brought the ark of the covenant of the LORD to its place, in the inner sanctuary of the house, in the most holy place, underneath the wings of the cherubim. ⁸ For the cherubim spread out their wings over the place of the ark, so that the cherubim made a covering above the ark and its poles. ⁹ The poles were so long that the ends of the poles were seen from the holy place in front of the inner sanctuary; but they could not be seen from outside; they are there to this day. ¹⁰ There was nothing in the ark except the two tablets that Moses put there at Horeb, where the LORD made a covenant*a* with the people of Israel after they came out of Egypt.

11 Now when the priests came out of the holy place (for all the priests who were present had sanctified themselves, without regard to their divisions), ¹² all the levitical singers, Asaph, Heman, and Jeduthun, their sons and kindred, arrayed in fine linen, with cymbals, harps, and lyres, stood east of the altar with one hundred twenty priests who were trumpeters. ¹³ It was the duty of the trumpeters and singers to make them-

selves heard in unison in praise and thanksgiving to the LORD, and when the song was raised, with trumpets and cymbals and other musical instruments, in praise to the LORD,

"For he is good,
    for his steadfast love endures
        forever,"

the house, the house of the LORD, was filled with a cloud, ¹⁴ so that the priests could not stand to minister because of the cloud; for the glory of the LORD filled the house of God.

Dedication of the Temple

6 Then Solomon said, "The LORD has said that he would reside in thick darkness. ² I have built you an exalted house, a place for you to reside in forever."

3 Then the king turned around and blessed all the assembly of Israel, while all the assembly of Israel stood. ⁴ And he said, "Blessed be the LORD, the God of Israel, who with his hand has fulfilled what he promised with his mouth to my father David, saying, ⁵ 'Since the day that I brought my people out of the land of Egypt, I have not chosen a city from any of the tribes of Israel in which to build a house, so that my name might be there, and I chose no one as ruler over my people Israel; ⁶ but I have chosen Jerusalem in order that my name may be there, and I have chosen David to be over my people Israel.' ⁷ My father David had it in mind to build a house for the name of the LORD, the God of Israel. ⁸ But the LORD said to my father David, 'You did well to consider building a house for my name; ⁹ nevertheless you shall not build the house, but your son who shall be born to you shall build the house for my name.' ¹⁰ Now the LORD has fulfilled his

a Heb lacks *a covenant*

---

semblies, with sacrifices during the procession and installation, musical accompaniment, and a royal blessing. In both, *the Levites* carry the ark and sing praise to the Lord. As at the tabernacle's dedication (Exod. 40:34–38), the temple is filled

with a *cloud* (2 Chr. 5:13–14) signifying God's presence and acceptance (6:1–2).

6:10—Solomon looks back to God's promises fulfilled when he became king and built the temple.

promise that he made; for I have succeeded my father David, and sit on the throne of Israel, as the LORD promised, and have built the house for the name of the LORD, the God of Israel. [11] There I have set the ark, in which is the covenant of the LORD that he made with the people of Israel."

Solomon's Prayer of Dedication

12 Then Solomon[a] stood before the altar of the LORD in the presence of the whole assembly of Israel, and spread out his hands. [13] Solomon had made a bronze platform five cubits long, five cubits wide, and three cubits high, and had set it in the court; and he stood on it. Then he knelt on his knees in the presence of the whole assembly of Israel, and spread out his hands toward heaven. [14] He said, "O LORD, God of Israel, there is no God like you, in heaven or on earth, keeping covenant in steadfast love with your servants who walk before you with all their heart— [15] you who have kept for your servant, my father David, what you promised to him. Indeed, you promised with your mouth and this day have fulfilled with your hand. [16] Therefore, O LORD, God of Israel, keep for your servant, my father David, that which you promised him, saying, 'There shall never fail you a successor before me to sit on the throne of Israel, if only your children keep to their way, to walk in my law as you have walked before me.' [17] Therefore, O LORD, God of Israel, let your word be confirmed, which you promised to your servant David.

18 "But will God indeed reside with mortals on earth? Even heaven and the highest heaven cannot contain you, how much less this house that I have built!

[19] Regard your servant's prayer and his plea, O LORD my God, heeding the cry and the prayer that your servant prays to you. [20] May your eyes be open day and night toward this house, the place where you promised to set your name, and may you heed the prayer that your servant prays toward this place. [21] And hear the plea of your servant and of your people Israel, when they pray toward this place; may you hear from heaven your dwelling place; hear and forgive.

22 "If someone sins against another and is required to take an oath and comes and swears before your altar in this house, [23] may you hear from heaven, and act, and judge your servants, repaying the guilty by bringing their conduct on their own head, and vindicating those who are in the right by rewarding them in accordance with their righteousness.

24 "When your people Israel, having sinned against you, are defeated before an enemy but turn again to you, confess your name, pray and plead with you in this house, [25] may you hear from heaven, and forgive the sin of your people Israel, and bring them again to the land that you gave to them and to their ancestors.

26 "When heaven is shut up and there is no rain because they have sinned against you, and then they pray toward this place, confess your name, and turn from their sin, because you punish them, [27] may you hear in heaven, forgive the sin of your servants, your people Israel, when you teach them the good way in which they should walk; and send down rain upon your land, which you have given to your people as an inheritance.

28 "If there is famine in the land, if there is plague, blight, mildew, locust, or

[a] Heb *he*

6:11 *With the people of Israel*—Omitting the exodus reference in 1 Kgs. 8:21. Chronicles usually plays down the exodus in favor of David.

6:14–17—With construction completed, Solomon asks God to fulfill the dynastic promise that God made to David in 1 Chr. 17:10–14 (see also 2 Sam. 7:16).

6:18–21—God is not confined to the temple; it is simply the place where petitions are offered.

6:24–39—Solomon lays the groundwork for the many prayers that will be offered in and toward the temple in chaps. 10–36.

caterpillar; if their enemies besiege them in any of the settlements of the lands; whatever suffering, whatever sickness there is; ²⁹ whatever prayer, whatever plea from any individual or from all your people Israel, all knowing their own suffering and their own sorrows so that they stretch out their hands toward this house; ³⁰ may you hear from heaven, your dwelling place, forgive, and render to all whose heart you know, according to all their ways, for only you know the human heart. ³¹ Thus may they fear you and walk in your ways all the days that they live in the land that you gave to our ancestors.

32 "Likewise when foreigners, who are not of your people Israel, come from a distant land because of your great name, and your mighty hand, and your outstretched arm, when they come and pray toward this house, ³³ may you hear from heaven your dwelling place, and do whatever the foreigners ask of you, in order that all the peoples of the earth may know your name and fear you, as do your people Israel, and that they may know that your name has been invoked on this house that I have built.

34 "If your people go out to battle against their enemies, by whatever way you shall send them, and they pray to you toward this city that you have chosen and the house that I have built for your name, ³⁵ then hear from heaven their prayer and their plea, and maintain their cause.

36 "If they sin against you—for there is no one who does not sin—and you are angry with them and give them to an enemy, so that they are carried away captive to a land far or near; ³⁷ then if they come to their senses in the land to which they have been taken captive,

and repent, and plead with you in the land of their captivity, saying, 'We have sinned, and have done wrong; we have acted wickedly'; ³⁸ if they repent with all their heart and soul in the land of their captivity, to which they were taken captive, and pray toward their land, which you gave to their ancestors, the city that you have chosen, and the house that I have built for your name, ³⁹ then hear from heaven your dwelling place their prayer and their pleas, maintain their cause and forgive your people who have sinned against you. ⁴⁰ Now, O my God, let your eyes be open and your ears attentive to prayer from this place.

⁴¹ "Now rise up, O Lord God, and go
    to your resting place,
    you and the ark of your might.
Let your priests, O Lord God, be
    clothed with salvation,
    and let your faithful rejoice in your
      goodness.
⁴² O Lord God, do not reject your
    anointed one.
    Remember your steadfast love for
      your servant David."

Solomon Dedicates the Temple

7 When Solomon had ended his prayer, fire came down from heaven and consumed the burnt offering and the sacrifices; and the glory of the Lord filled the temple. ² The priests could not enter the house of the Lord, because the glory of the Lord filled the Lord's house. ³ When all the people of Israel saw the fire come down and the glory of the Lord on the temple, they bowed down on the pavement with their faces to the ground, and worshiped and gave thanks to the Lord, saying,

"For he is good,
    for his steadfast love endures
      forever."

6:41–42—The prayer ends with David and the ark (Ps. 132:8–10), not Moses and the exodus (cf. 1 Kgs. 8:51–53).

7:1–3—God's confirmation of David's and Solomon's work underscores the continuity be-

tween the wilderness tabernacle and the temple. As in the wilderness sacrifices (Lev. 9:23–24) and the designation of the temple site (1 Chr. 21:26), there is *fire from heaven*. As in the installation of the ark (2 Chr. 5:13–14; Exod. 40:34–38) *the glory of the Lord* appears.

4 Then the king and all the people offered sacrifice before the LORD. ⁵ King Solomon offered as a sacrifice twenty-two thousand oxen and one hundred twenty thousand sheep. So the king and all the people dedicated the house of God. ⁶ The priests stood at their posts; the Levites also, with the instruments for music to the LORD that King David had made for giving thanks to the LORD—for his steadfast love endures forever—whenever David offered praises by their ministry. Opposite them the priests sounded trumpets; and all Israel stood.

7 Solomon consecrated the middle of the court that was in front of the house of the LORD; for there he offered the burnt offerings and the fat of the offerings of well-being because the bronze altar Solomon had made could not hold the burnt offering and the grain offering and the fat parts.

8 At that time Solomon held the festival for seven days, and all Israel with him, a very great congregation, from Lebo-hamath to the Wadi of Egypt. ⁹ On the eighth day they held a solemn assembly; for they had observed the dedication of the altar seven days and the festival seven days. ¹⁰ On the twenty-third day of the seventh month he sent the people away to their homes, joyful and in good spirits because of the goodness that the LORD had shown to David and to Solomon and to his people Israel.

11 Thus Solomon finished the house of the LORD and the king's house; all that Solomon had planned to do in the house of the LORD and in his own house he successfully accomplished.

God's Second Appearance to Solomon

12 Then the LORD appeared to Solomon in the night and said to him: "I have heard your prayer, and have chosen this place for myself as a house of sacrifice. ¹³ When I shut up the heavens so that there is no rain, or command the locust to devour the land, or send pestilence among my people, ¹⁴ if my people who are called by my name humble themselves, pray, seek my face, and turn from their wicked ways, then I will hear from heaven, and will forgive their sin and heal their land. ¹⁵ Now my eyes will be open and my ears attentive to the prayer that is made in this place. ¹⁶ For now I have chosen and consecrated this house so that my name may be there forever; my eyes and my heart will be there for all time. ¹⁷ As for you, if you walk before me, as your father David walked, doing according to all that I have commanded you and keeping my statutes and my ordinances, ¹⁸ then I will establish your royal throne, as I made covenant with your father David saying, 'You shall never lack a successor to rule over Israel.'

19 "But if you*ᵃ* turn aside and forsake my statutes and my commandments that I have set before you, and go and serve other gods and worship them, ²⁰ then I will pluck you*ᵇ* up from the land that I have given you;*ᵇ* and this house, which I have consecrated for my name, I will cast out of my sight, and will make it a proverb and a byword among all peoples. ²¹ And regarding this house, now exalted, everyone passing by will be astonished, and say, 'Why has the LORD done such a thing to this land and to this house?' ²² Then they will say, 'Because they abandoned the LORD the God of their ancestors who brought them out of the land of Egypt, and they adopted other gods, and worshiped them and

---

ᵃ The word *you* in this verse is plural *ᵇ* Heb *them*

7:6 *Instruments for music*—Music and sacrifice are combined for the first time.

7:9–10—The celebration lasts for two weeks (cf. Hezekiah's Passover, 30:23).

7:14 *Humble themselves, pray, seek my face, and turn from their wicked ways*—This vocabulary of repentance will temper the theme of retributive justice in the following narrative. This promise and the promise of the Davidic dynasty (1 Chr. 17) comprise the heart of the chronicler's message.

served them; therefore he has brought all this calamity upon them.'"

Various Activities of Solomon

8 At the end of twenty years, during which Solomon had built the house of the LORD and his own house, ² Solomon rebuilt the cities that Huram had given to him, and settled the people of Israel in them.

3 Solomon went to Hamath-zobah, and captured it. ⁴ He built Tadmor in the wilderness and all the storage towns that he built in Hamath. ⁵ He also built Upper Beth-horon and Lower Beth-horon, fortified cities, with walls, gates, and bars, ⁶ and Baalath, as well as all Solomon's storage towns, and all the towns for his chariots, the towns for his cavalry, and whatever Solomon desired to build, in Jerusalem, in Lebanon, and in all the land of his dominion. ⁷ All the people who were left of the Hittites, the Amorites, the Perizzites, the Hivites, and the Jebusites, who were not of Israel, ⁸ from their descendants who were still left in the land, whom the people of Israel had not destroyed—these Solomon conscripted for forced labor, as is still the case today. ⁹ But of the people of Israel Solomon made no slaves for his work; they were soldiers, and his officers, the commanders of his chariotry and cavalry. ¹⁰ These were the chief officers of King Solomon, two hundred fifty of them, who exercised authority over the people.

11 Solomon brought Pharaoh's daughter from the city of David to the house that he had built for her, for he said, "My wife shall not live in the house of King David of Israel, for the places to which the ark of the LORD has come are holy."

12 Then Solomon offered up burnt offerings to the LORD on the altar of the LORD that he had built in front of the vestibule, ¹³ as the duty of each day required, offering according to the commandment of Moses for the sabbaths, the new moons, and the three annual festivals—the festival of unleavened bread, the festival of weeks, and the festival of booths. ¹⁴ According to the ordinance of his father David, he appointed the divisions of the priests for their service, and the Levites for their offices of praise and ministry alongside the priests as the duty of each day required, and the gatekeepers in their divisions for the several gates; for so David the man of God had commanded. ¹⁵ They did not turn away from what the king had commanded the priests and Levites regarding anything at all, or regarding the treasuries.

16 Thus all the work of Solomon was accomplished from*ᵃ* the day the foundation of the house of the LORD was laid until the house of the LORD was finished completely.

17 Then Solomon went to Eziongeber and Eloth on the shore of the sea, in the land of Edom. ¹⁸ Huram sent him, in the care of his servants, ships and servants familiar with the sea. They went to Ophir, together with the servants of Solomon, and imported from there four hundred fifty talents of gold and brought it to King Solomon.

Visit of the Queen of Sheba

9 When the queen of Sheba heard of the fame of Solomon, she came to Jerusalem to test him with hard questions, having a very great retinue

ᵃ Gk Syr Vg: Heb *to*

8:1–16 Finishing Touches
Solomon's other achievements, especially building projects that typify blessing.

8:2—Huram's ceding of twenty cities to Solomon reverses 1 Kgs. 9:11 and glorifies Solomon.

8:3 *Captured it*—Solomon's only military campaign.

8:12–15 *Sabbaths, the new moons . . . Levites*— Additions demonstrating Solomon's compliance with the cultic organization of Moses (Num. 28–29) and David (1 Chr. 23–27).

8:17–9:31 Solomon's Wisdom, Wealth, and Fame

8:17–18 *Huram sent him*—Huram provides the ships and capital (cf. 1 Kgs. 9:26–28).

and camels bearing spices and very much gold and precious stones. When she came to Solomon, she discussed with him all that was on her mind. ²Solomon answered all her questions; there was nothing hidden from Solomon that he could not explain to her. ³When the queen of Sheba had observed the wisdom of Solomon, the house that he had built, ⁴the food of his table, the seating of his officials, and the attendance of his servants, and their clothing, his valets, and their clothing, and his burnt offerings*a* that he offered at the house of the LORD, there was no more spirit left in her.

5 So she said to the king, "The report was true that I heard in my own land of your accomplishments and of your wisdom, ⁶but I did not believe the*b* reports until I came and my own eyes saw it. Not even half of the greatness of your wisdom had been told to me; you far surpass the report that I had heard. ⁷Happy are your people! Happy are these your servants, who continually attend you and hear your wisdom! ⁸Blessed be the LORD your God, who has delighted in you and set you on his throne as king for the LORD your God. Because your God loved Israel and would establish them forever, he has made you king over them, that you may execute justice and righteousness." ⁹Then she gave the king one hundred twenty talents of gold, a very great quantity of spices, and precious stones: there were no spices such as those that the queen of Sheba gave to King Solomon.

10 Moreover the servants of Huram and the servants of Solomon who brought gold from Ophir brought algum wood and precious stones. ¹¹From the algum wood, the king made steps*c* for the house of the LORD and for the king's house, lyres also and harps for the singers; there never was seen the like of them before in the land of Judah.

12 Meanwhile King Solomon granted the queen of Sheba every desire that she expressed, well beyond what she had brought to the king. Then she returned to her own land, with her servants.

Solomon's Great Wealth

13 The weight of gold that came to Solomon in one year was six hundred sixty-six talents of gold, ¹⁴besides that which the traders and merchants brought; and all the kings of Arabia and the governors of the land brought gold and silver to Solomon. ¹⁵King Solomon made two hundred large shields of beaten gold; six hundred shekels of beaten gold went into each large shield. ¹⁶He made three hundred shields of beaten gold; three hundred shekels of gold went into each shield; and the king put them in the House of the Forest of Lebanon. ¹⁷The king also made a great ivory throne, and overlaid it with pure gold. ¹⁸The throne had six steps and a footstool of gold, which were attached to the throne, and on each side of the seat were arm rests and two lions standing beside the arm rests, ¹⁹while twelve lions were standing, one on each end of a step on the six steps. The like of it was never made in any kingdom. ²⁰All King Solomon's drinking vessels were of gold, and all the vessels of the House of the Forest of Lebanon were of pure gold; silver was not considered as anything in

a Gk Syr Vg 1 Kings 10:5: Heb *ascent*   *b* Heb *their*   *c* Gk Vg: Meaning of Heb uncertain

---

9:3–6—*The queen of Sheba* (modern Yemen) praises Solomon's wisdom, though Solomon's control of the trade routes made this tribute a political necessity.

9:8—God's rule, even without a king *on his [i.e., God's] throne* (cf. 1 Chr. 17:14; 28:5; 29:23; 2 Chr. 13:8) was especially important for the postexilic community.

9:9 *One hundred twenty talents*—Four and one-half tons.

9:13–21—Solomon's wealth.

9:13 *Six hundred sixty-six talents*—Twenty-five tons.

the days of Solomon. [21] For the king's ships went to Tarshish with the servants of Huram; once every three years the ships of Tarshish used to come bringing gold, silver, ivory, apes, and peacocks.[a]

22 Thus King Solomon excelled all the kings of the earth in riches and in wisdom. [23] All the kings of the earth sought the presence of Solomon to hear his wisdom, which God had put into his mind. [24] Every one of them brought a present, objects of silver and gold, garments, weaponry, spices, horses, and mules, so much year by year. [25] Solomon had four thousand stalls for horses and chariots, and twelve thousand horses, which he stationed in the chariot cities and with the king in Jerusalem. [26] He ruled over all the kings from the Euphrates to the land of the Philistines, and to the border of Egypt. [27] The king made silver as common in Jerusalem as stone, and cedar as plentiful as the sycamore of the Shephelah. [28] Horses were imported for Solomon from Egypt and from all lands.

Death of Solomon

29 Now the rest of the acts of Solomon, from first to last, are they not written in the history of the prophet Nathan, and in the prophecy of Ahijah the Shilonite, and in the visions of the seer Iddo concerning Jeroboam son of Nebat? [30] Solomon reigned in Jerusalem over all Israel forty years. [31] Solomon slept with his ancestors and was buried in the city of his father David; and his son Rehoboam succeeded him.

The Revolt against Rehoboam

10 Rehoboam went to Shechem, for all Israel had come to Shechem to make him king. [2] When Jeroboam son of Nebat heard of it (for he was in Egypt, where he had fled from King Solomon), then Jeroboam returned from Egypt. [3] They sent and called him; and Jeroboam and all Israel came and said to Rehoboam, [4] "Your father made our yoke heavy. Now therefore lighten the hard service of your father and his heavy yoke that he placed on us, and we will serve you." [5] He said to them, "Come to me again in three days." So the people went away.

6 Then King Rehoboam took counsel with the older men who had attended his father Solomon while he was still alive, saying, "How do you advise me to answer this people?" [7] They answered him, "If you will be kind to this people and please them, and speak good words to them, then they will be your servants forever." [8] But he rejected the advice that the older men gave him, and consulted the young men who had grown up with

[a] Or baboons

9:22–31—Solomon's fame brings tribute from *all the kings of the earth*.

9:26—Solomon's apostasy (1 Kgs. 11) is replaced with a statement of his dominance drawn from 1 Kgs. 4:21.

9:29–31—Solomon's death notice.

10:1–28:27 The Divided Monarchy

The focus upon Judah means references to the north are scattered. Kings are measured against David and Solomon (cf. 7:10; 11:17; 35:4). Obedient kings are blessed with wealth, military victory, "rest," building projects, and large families. Disobedient kings endure punishment, military defeat, and illness. A host of unknown prophets who point to these failures also hold out the possibility of repentance and forgiveness, in accordance with God's promise to Solomon (7:14).

10:1–12:16 Rehoboam

The chronicler has used the reign of Rehoboam, the first Judean king to follow the united reigns of David and Solomon, to establish three patterns that will govern the following narrative: sin brings failure (10:1–11:4), obedience brings success (11:5–23), and repentance brings deliverance (12:1–16).

10:1–11:4—The northern tribes reject Rehoboam's arrogance and establish the northern kingdom of Israel under Jeroboam. Solomon's imposition (10:4, 9–11, 14), Rehoboam's failure to take advice (vv. 6–8, 13), and Jeroboam's rebellion (v. 19) suggest that all three share responsibility for the split (though see v. 15, where God is held responsible).

him and now attended him. [9] He said to them, "What do you advise that we answer this people who have said to me, 'Lighten the yoke that your father put on us'?" [10] The young men who had grown up with him said to him, "Thus should you speak to the people who said to you, 'Your father made our yoke heavy, but you must lighten it for us'; tell them, 'My little finger is thicker than my father's loins. [11] Now, whereas my father laid on you a heavy yoke, I will add to your yoke. My father disciplined you with whips, but I will discipline you with scorpions.'"

12 So Jeroboam and all the people came to Rehoboam the third day, as the king had said, "Come to me again the third day." [13] The king answered them harshly. King Rehoboam rejected the advice of the older men; [14] he spoke to them in accordance with the advice of the young men, "My father made your yoke heavy, but I will add to it; my father disciplined you with whips, but I will discipline you with scorpions." [15] So the king did not listen to the people, because it was a turn of affairs brought about by God so that the LORD might fulfill his word, which he had spoken by Ahijah the Shilonite to Jeroboam son of Nebat.

16 When all Israel saw that the king would not listen to them, the people answered the king,

"What share do we have in David?
　We have no inheritance in the son
　　of Jesse.
Each of you to your tents, O Israel!
　Look now to your own house,
　　O David."

So all Israel departed to their tents. [17] But Rehoboam reigned over the people of Israel who were living in the cities of Judah. [18] When King Rehoboam sent Hadoram, who was taskmaster over the forced labor, the people of Israel stoned him to death. King Rehoboam hurriedly mounted his chariot to flee to Jerusalem. [19] So Israel has been in rebellion against the house of David to this day.

Judah and Benjamin Fortified

11 When Rehoboam came to Jerusalem, he assembled one hundred eighty thousand chosen troops of the house of Judah and Benjamin to fight against Israel, to restore the kingdom to Rehoboam. [2] But the word of the LORD came to Shemaiah the man of God: [3] Say to King Rehoboam of Judah, son of Solomon, and to all Israel in Judah and Benjamin, [4] "Thus says the LORD: You shall not go up or fight against your kindred. Let everyone return home, for this thing is from me." So they heeded the word of the LORD and turned back from the expedition against Jeroboam.

5 Rehoboam resided in Jerusalem, and he built cities for defense in Judah. [6] He built up Bethlehem, Etam, Tekoa, [7] Beth-zur, Soco, Adullam, [8] Gath, Mareshah, Ziph, [9] Adoraim, Lachish, Azekah, [10] Zorah, Aijalon, and Hebron, fortified cities that are in Judah and in Benjamin. [11] He made the fortresses strong, and put commanders in them, and stores of food, oil, and wine. [12] He also put large shields and spears in all the cities, and made them very strong. So he held Judah and Benjamin.

Priests and Levites Support Rehoboam

13 The priests and the Levites who were in all Israel presented themselves to him from all their territories. [14] The Levites had left their common lands and their holdings and had come to Judah and Jerusalem, because Jeroboam and his sons had prevented them from serving as priests of the LORD, [15] and had appointed his own

---

11:5–23—God rewards Rehoboam's faithful obedience with prosperity and blessing *for three years* (v. 17).

11:5–12—Rehoboam's fortifications are present-ed before Shishak's invasion (12:1–12) to portray Rehoboam as an obedient king who prospers.

11:13–17—*Priests* and *Levites* defecting to Jerusalem risked losing their land holdings.

priests for the high places, and for the goat-demons, and for the calves that he had made. [16] Those who had set their hearts to seek the LORD God of Israel came after them from all the tribes of Israel to Jerusalem to sacrifice to the LORD, the God of their ancestors. [17] They strengthened the kingdom of Judah, and for three years they made Rehoboam son of Solomon secure, for they walked for three years in the way of David and Solomon.

Rehoboam's Marriages

18 Rehoboam took as his wife Mahalath daughter of Jerimoth son of David, and of Abihail daughter of Eliab son of Jesse. [19] She bore him sons: Jeush, Shemariah, and Zaham. [20] After her he took Maacah daughter of Absalom, who bore him Abijah, Attai, Ziza, and Shelomith. [21] Rehoboam loved Maacah daughter of Absalom more than all his other wives and concubines (he took eighteen wives and sixty concubines, and became the father of twenty-eight sons and sixty daughters). [22] Rehoboam appointed Abijah son of Maacah as chief prince among his brothers, for he intended to make him king. [23] He dealt wisely, and distributed some of his sons through all the districts of Judah and Benjamin, in all the fortified cities; he gave them abundant provisions, and found many wives for them.

Egypt Attacks Judah

12 When the rule of Rehoboam was established and he grew strong, he abandoned the law of the LORD, he and all Israel with him. [2] In the fifth year of King Rehoboam, because they had been unfaithful to the LORD, King Shishak of Egypt came up against Jerusalem [3] with twelve hundred chariots and sixty thousand cavalry. A countless army came with him from Egypt—Libyans, Sukkiim, and Ethiopians.[a] [4] He took the fortified cities of Judah and came as far as Jerusalem. [5] Then the prophet Shemaiah came to Rehoboam and to the officers of Judah, who had gathered at Jerusalem because of Shishak, and said to them, "Thus says the LORD: You abandoned me, so I have abandoned you to the hand of Shishak." [6] Then the officers of Israel and the king humbled themselves and said, "The LORD is in the right." [7] When the LORD saw that they humbled themselves, the word of the LORD came to Shemaiah, saying: "They have humbled themselves; I will not destroy them, but I will grant them some deliverance, and my wrath shall not be poured out on Jerusalem by the hand of Shishak. [8] Nevertheless they shall be his servants, so that they may know the difference between serving me and serving the kingdoms of other lands."

9 So King Shishak of Egypt came up against Jerusalem; he took away the treasures of the house of the LORD and the treasures of the king's house; he took everything. He also took away the shields of gold that Solomon had made; [10] but King Rehoboam made in place of them shields of bronze, and committed them to the hands of the officers of the guard, who kept the door of the king's house. [11] Whenever the king went into the house of the LORD, the guard would come along bearing them, and would then bring them back to the guardroom. [12] Because he humbled himself the wrath of the LORD turned from him, so as not

[a] Or Nubians; Heb Cushites

11:18–23—Twenty-eight sons and sixty daughters is a third sign of blessing.

12:1–16—Repentance brings deliverance.

12:1 *He abandoned*—Rehoboam joins Judah's apostasy (1 Kgs. 14:22–24).

12:2 *Shishak of Egypt*—Shoshenq I, ca. 945–924 BCE.

12:6 *Humbled themselves*—In response to *Shemaiah*, Rehoboam and the leaders repent.

12:7—Judah is spared because they repented. This is the first fulfillment of God's promise to Solomon (7:14).

to destroy them completely; moreover, conditions were good in Judah.

Death of Rehoboam

13 So King Rehoboam established himself in Jerusalem and reigned. Rehoboam was forty-one years old when he began to reign; he reigned seventeen years in Jerusalem, the city that the LORD had chosen out of all the tribes of Israel to put his name there. His mother's name was Naamah the Ammonite. [14] He did evil, for he did not set his heart to seek the LORD.

15 Now the acts of Rehoboam, from first to last, are they not written in the records of the prophet Shemaiah and of the seer Iddo, recorded by genealogy? There were continual wars between Rehoboam and Jeroboam. [16] Rehoboam slept with his ancestors and was buried in the city of David; and his son Abijah succeeded him.

Abijah Reigns over Judah

13 In the eighteenth year of King Jeroboam, Abijah began to reign over Judah. [2] He reigned for three years in Jerusalem. His mother's name was Micaiah daughter of Uriel of Gibeah.

Now there was war between Abijah and Jeroboam. [3] Abijah engaged in battle, having an army of valiant warriors, four hundred thousand picked men; and Jeroboam drew up his line of battle against him with eight hundred thousand picked mighty warriors. [4] Then Abijah stood on the slope of Mount Zemaraim that is in the hill country of Ephraim, and said, "Listen to me, Jeroboam and all Israel! [5] Do you not know that the LORD God of Israel gave the kingship over Israel forever to David and his sons by a covenant of salt? [6] Yet Jeroboam son of Nebat, a servant of Solomon son of David, rose up and rebelled against his lord; [7] and certain worthless scoundrels gathered around him and defied Rehoboam son of Solomon, when Rehoboam was young and irresolute and could not withstand them.

8 "And now you think that you can withstand the kingdom of the LORD in the hand of the sons of David, because you are a great multitude and have with you the golden calves that Jeroboam made as gods for you. [9] Have you not driven out the priests of the LORD, the descendants of Aaron, and the Levites, and made priests for yourselves like the peoples of other lands? Whoever comes to be consecrated with a young bull or seven rams becomes a priest of what are no gods. [10] But as for us, the LORD is our God, and we have not abandoned him. We have priests ministering to the LORD who are descendants of Aaron, and Levites for their service. [11] They offer to the LORD every morning and every evening burnt offerings and fragrant incense, set out the rows of bread on the table of pure gold, and care for the golden lampstand so that its lamps may burn every evening; for we keep the charge of the LORD our God, but you have abandoned

---

13:1–14:1 Abijah
Reliance upon God links the reigns of Abijah and Asa (the use of the term "rely" is unusually frequent in the reports of these reigns. See 13:18; 14:11; 16:7 [twice], 16: 8). Earlier, 1 Kgs. 15:3–6 had condemned this eloquent defender of the faith.

13:3—The huge numbers and two-to-one odds against Judah indicate the divine source of Abijah's victory (see v. 15).

13:4–12—Abijah's speech presents three of the chronicler's central theological themes: the Davidic dynasty, the Jerusalem cult, and all Israel.

13:5 *Covenant of salt*—Salt's preservative qualities illustrate the eternal nature of God's covenant loyalty (cf. Lev. 2:13, and Num. 18:19).

13:6–7 *Young and irresolute*—Rationalizing Rehoboam's accountability for the division of the monarchy. He was actually forty-one (cf. 12:13).

13:8b–11—With a faithful Davidic king on the throne and proper worship in the temple, there is no reason for the north to continue in their rebellion. Abijah, therefore, invites the north to return to all Israel, restoring the unity lost in the schism of 922 BCE. Later, Hezekiah will offer a similar invitation, following the north's fall to Assyria in 722 BCE (30:6–9).

him. ¹²See, God is with us at our head, and his priests have their battle trumpets to sound the call to battle against you. O Israelites, do not fight against the LORD, the God of your ancestors; for you cannot succeed."

13 Jeroboam had sent an ambush around to come on them from behind; thus his troops*a* were in front of Judah, and the ambush was behind them. ¹⁴When Judah turned, the battle was in front of them and behind them. They cried out to the LORD, and the priests blew the trumpets. ¹⁵Then the people of Judah raised the battle shout. And when the people of Judah shouted, God defeated Jeroboam and all Israel before Abijah and Judah. ¹⁶The Israelites fled before Judah, and God gave them into their hands. ¹⁷Abijah and his army defeated them with great slaughter; five hundred thousand picked men of Israel fell slain. ¹⁸Thus the Israelites were subdued at that time, and the people of Judah prevailed, because they relied on the LORD, the God of their ancestors. ¹⁹Abijah pursued Jeroboam, and took cities from him: Bethel with its villages and Jeshanah with its villages and Ephron*b* with its villages. ²⁰Jeroboam did not recover his power in the days of Abijah; the LORD struck him down, and he died. ²¹But Abijah grew strong. He took

fourteen wives, and became the father of twenty-two sons and sixteen daughters. ²²The rest of the acts of Abijah, his behavior and his deeds, are written in the story of the prophet Iddo.

Asa Reigns

14 *c*So Abijah slept with his ancestors, and they buried him in the city of David. His son Asa succeeded him. In his days the land had rest for ten years. ²*d*Asa did what was good and right in the sight of the LORD his God. ³He took away the foreign altars and the high places, broke down the pillars, hewed down the sacred poles,*e* ⁴and commanded Judah to seek the LORD, the God of their ancestors, and to keep the law and the commandment. ⁵He also removed from all the cities of Judah the high places and the incense altars. And the kingdom had rest under him. ⁶He built fortified cities in Judah while the land had rest. He had no war in those years, for the LORD gave him peace. ⁷He said to Judah, "Let us build these cities, and surround them with walls and towers, gates and bars; the land is still ours because we have sought the LORD our God; we have sought him, and he has given us peace on every side." So they built and prospered. ⁸Asa had an army

---

a Heb *they*　*b* Another reading is *Ephrain*　*c* Ch 13.23 in Heb
d Ch 14.1 in Heb　*e* Heb *Asherim*

13:12—Fighting *against the LORD* is futile in holy war. Abijah pleads for the reunification of north and south under one God and one king. Abijah's "ecumenical" overtures, however, are made from an uncompromising theological stance.

13:13–14:1—The battle account expands the holy war imagery.

13:14–18—Reliance, seen in the people's prayer and the priests' trumpets, results in God's deliverance.

13:19–14:1—Added holdings (v. 19), many wives and children (v. 21), and *rest* (14:1, actually in Asa's reign) indicate divine favor.

14:2–16:14 Asa

Reliance upon God, introduced in Abijah's reign, continues with the emergence of another key element in the chronicler's theology. Two Hebrew words meaning "seek" appear nine times in these

chapters. Like Rehoboam's, Asa's reign divides into two periods, the first marked by the blessings of faithfulness (14:2–15:19) and the second marred by the results of apostasy (16:1–14). Asa is depicted as a good person who goes bad and serves to caution us about the dangers of not paying enough attention to our spiritual well-being.

14:2–15:19—The favorable report of Asa's cultic reforms (1 Kgs. 15:9–15) is expanded to accentuate blessing as the reward of faithfulness.

14:2–8—Asa prospers for *ten years* because of his obedience (see v. 1).

14:6a—Fortifications are another sign of blessing.

14:6b–7 *Peace . . . peace*—Better, "rest" (cf. Deut. 12:10). Verses 1b, 5, and 6a employ a different Hebrew term.

14:8 *Army*—580,000 warriors, a final indication of blessing.

of three hundred thousand from Judah, armed with large shields and spears, and two hundred eighty thousand troops from Benjamin who carried shields and drew bows; all these were mighty warriors.

Ethiopian Invasion Repulsed

9 Zerah the Ethiopian[a] came out against them with an army of a million men and three hundred chariots, and came as far as Mareshah. [10] Asa went out to meet him, and they drew up their lines of battle in the valley of Zephathah at Mareshah. [11] Asa cried to the LORD his God, "O LORD, there is no difference for you between helping the mighty and the weak. Help us, O LORD our God, for we rely on you, and in your name we have come against this multitude. O LORD, you are our God; let no mortal prevail against you." [12] So the LORD defeated the Ethiopians[b] before Asa and before Judah, and the Ethiopians[b] fled. [13] Asa and the army with him pursued them as far as Gerar, and the Ethiopians[b] fell until no one remained alive; for they were broken before the LORD and his army. The people of Judah[c] carried away a great quantity of booty. [14] They defeated all the cities around Gerar, for the fear of the LORD was on them. They plundered all the cities; for there was much plunder in them. [15] They also attacked the tents of those who had livestock,[d] and carried away sheep and goats in abundance, and camels. Then they returned to Jerusalem.

15 The spirit of God came upon Azariah son of Oded. [2] He went out to meet Asa and said to him, "Hear me, Asa, and all Judah and Benjamin: The LORD is with you, while you are with him. If you seek him, he will be found by you, but if you abandon him, he will abandon you. [3] For a long time Israel was without the true God, and without a teaching priest, and without law; [4] but when in their distress they turned to the LORD, the God of Israel, and sought him, he was found by them. [5] In those times it was not safe for anyone to go or come, for great disturbances afflicted all the inhabitants of the lands. [6] They were broken in pieces, nation against nation and city against city, for God troubled them with every sort of distress. [7] But you, take courage! Do not let your hands be weak, for your work shall be rewarded."

8 When Asa heard these words, the prophecy of Azariah son of Oded,[e] he took courage, and put away the abominable idols from all the land of Judah and Benjamin and from the towns

[a] Or Nubian; Heb Cushite [b] Or Nubians; Heb Cushites [c] Heb They
[d] Meaning of Heb uncertain [e] Compare Syr Vg: Heb the prophecy, the prophet Obed

---

14:9–15—Invasion by the otherwise unknown *Zerah the Ethiopian*.

14:9 *A million*—Asa is outnumbered two to one (cf. Abijah's similar predicament, 13:3).

14:11 *Rely*—Asa shows total reliance upon God in the second appearance of this key term (cf. note at 13:1–14:1).

14:12—God answers Asa's prayer as promised to Solomon (6:34–35).

15:1–19—Asa's further reforms.

15:1–7—One of several addresses composed by the chronicler to explicate the theology of retribution and repentance. Often delivered by otherwise unknown prophets, they do not follow the usual outlines of prophetic speech. The format of a doctrinal statement followed by an application and an exhortation suggests that they are sermons on biblical themes well established in the postexilic community.

15:2b—Azariah's address begins with a doctrinal statement that the Lord will be with them as long as they remain faithful.

15:3–6—The application recalls Israel's past (the time of the judges) to show the effects of faithful and unfaithful response.

15:7—The exhortation quotes Jer. 31:16 and Zeph. 3:16 and urges Asa to complete his cultic reform.

15:8–19—Asa responds to Azariah with a second round of reforms (cf. 14:1–8).

15:8–9 *Ephraim, Manasseh*—These northern tribes reflect the chronicler's inclusive concern for the unity of all Israel. Jehoshaphat, Hezekiah, and Josiah will also include the north in their reforms.

that he had taken in the hill country of Ephraim. He repaired the altar of the LORD that was in front of the vestibule of the house of the LORD.*a* *9* He gathered all Judah and Benjamin, and those from Ephraim, Manasseh, and Simeon who were residing as aliens with them, for great numbers had deserted to him from Israel when they saw that the LORD his God was with him. *10* They were gathered at Jerusalem in the third month of the fifteenth year of the reign of Asa. *11* They sacrificed to the LORD on that day, from the booty that they had brought, seven hundred oxen and seven thousand sheep. *12* They entered into a covenant to seek the LORD, the God of their ancestors, with all their heart and with all their soul. *13* Whoever would not seek the LORD, the God of Israel, should be put to death, whether young or old, man or woman. *14* They took an oath to the LORD with a loud voice, and with shouting, and with trumpets, and with horns. *15* All Judah rejoiced over the oath; for they had sworn with all their heart, and had sought him with their whole desire, and he was found by them, and the LORD gave them rest all around.

16 King Asa even removed his mother Maacah from being queen mother because she had made an abominable image for Asherah. Asa cut down her image, crushed it, and burned it at the Wadi Kidron. *17* But the high places were not taken out of Israel. Nevertheless the heart of Asa was true all his days. *18* He brought into the house of God the votive gifts of his father and his own votive gifts— silver, gold, and utensils. *19* And there was no more war until the thirty-fifth year of the reign of Asa.

Alliance with Aram Condemned

16 In the thirty-sixth year of the reign of Asa, King Baasha of Israel went up against Judah, and built Ramah, to prevent anyone from going out or coming into the territory of*b* King Asa of Judah. *2* Then Asa took silver and gold from the treasures of the house of the LORD and the king's house, and sent them to King Ben-hadad of Aram, who resided in Damascus, saying, *3* "Let there be an alliance between me and you, like that between my father and your father; I am sending to you silver and gold; go, break your alliance with King Baasha of Israel, so that he may withdraw from me." *4* Ben-hadad listened to King Asa, and sent the commanders of his armies against the cities of Israel. They conquered Ijon, Dan, Abel-maim, and all the store-cities of Naphtali. *5* When Baasha heard of it, he stopped building Ramah, and let his work cease. *6* Then King Asa brought all Judah, and they carried away the stones of Ramah and its timber, with which Baasha had been building, and with them he built up Geba and Mizpah.

7 At that time the seer Hanani came to King Asa of Judah, and said to him, "Because you relied on the king of Aram, and did not rely on the LORD your God, the army of the king of Aram has escaped you. *8* Were not the Ethiopians*c* and the Libyans a huge army with exceedingly many chariots and cavalry? Yet because you relied on the LORD, he gave them into your hand. *9* For the eyes of the LORD range throughout the entire earth, to strengthen those whose heart is true to him. You have done foolishly in this; for from now on you will have wars." *10* Then Asa was angry with the seer, and put him in the stocks, in prison, for he was in a rage with him because of this. And Asa inflicted cruelties on some of the people at the same time.

a Heb *the vestibule of the* LORD   *b* Heb lacks *the territory of*   *c* Or Nubians; Heb *Cushites*

15:11–15—Jehoiada (23:16), Hezekiah (29:10), and Josiah (34:31) also institute covenant renewals.

15:17 *Israel*—The northern kingdom.

16:1–14—Asa's negative period.

16:2–10—Asa now "relies" upon a foreign alliance with **Ben-hadad**, for which he is rebuked by an otherwise unknown seer.

Asa's Disease and Death

11 The acts of Asa, from first to last, are written in the Book of the Kings of Judah and Israel. [12] In the thirty-ninth year of his reign Asa was diseased in his feet, and his disease became severe; yet even in his disease he did not seek the LORD, but sought help from physicians. [13] Then Asa slept with his ancestors, dying in the forty-first year of his reign. [14] They buried him in the tomb that he had hewn out for himself in the city of David. They laid him on a bier that had been filled with various kinds of spices prepared by the perfumer's art; and they made a very great fire in his honor.

Jehoshaphat's Reign

17 His son Jehoshaphat succeeded him, and strengthened himself against Israel. [2] He placed forces in all the fortified cities of Judah, and set garrisons in the land of Judah, and in the cities of Ephraim that his father Asa had taken. [3] The LORD was with Jehoshaphat, because he walked in the earlier ways of his father;[a] he did not seek the Baals, [4] but sought the God of his father and walked in his commandments, and not according to the ways of Israel. [5] Therefore the LORD established the kingdom in his hand. All Judah brought tribute to Jehoshaphat, and he had great riches and honor. [6] His heart was courageous in the ways of the LORD; and furthermore he removed the high places and the sacred poles[b] from Judah.

7 In the third year of his reign he sent his officials, Ben-hail, Obadiah, Zechariah, Nethanel, and Micaiah, to teach in the cities of Judah. [8] With them were the Levites, Shemaiah, Nethaniah, Zebadiah, Asahel, Shemiramoth, Jehonathan, Adonijah, Tobijah, and Tob-adonijah; and with these Levites, the priests Elishama and Jehoram. [9] They taught in Judah, having the book of the law of the LORD with them; they went around through all the cities of Judah and taught among the people.

10 The fear of the LORD fell on all the kingdoms of the lands around Judah, and they did not make war against Jehoshaphat. [11] Some of the Philistines brought Jehoshaphat presents, and silver for tribute; and the Arabs also brought him seven thousand seven hundred rams and seven thousand seven hundred male goats. [12] Jehoshaphat grew steadily greater. He built fortresses and storage cities in Judah. [13] He carried out great works in the cities of Judah. He had soldiers, mighty warriors, in Jerusalem. [14] This was the muster of them by ancestral houses: Of Judah, the commanders of the thousands: Adnah the commander, with three hundred thousand mighty warriors, [15] and next to him Jehohanan the commander, with two hundred eighty thousand, [16] and next to him Amasiah son of Zichri, a volunteer for the service of the LORD, with two hundred thousand mighty warriors. [17] Of Benjamin: Eliada, a mighty warrior, with two hundred thousand armed with bow and shield, [18] and next to him Jehozabad with one hundred eighty thousand armed for war. [19] These were in the service of the king, besides those

---

a Another reading is *his father David*   *b* Heb *Asherim*

16:11–14 *Sought help from physicians*—Ironic for a king named "He (God) heals."

17:1–21:1 Jehoshaphat

Building projects, honor, wealth, rest, and victory in battle open and close this reign. Nevertheless, he experiences prophetic censure (19:1–3) and punishment (20:37) for his alliance with the northern kings Ahab and Ahaziah.

17:1–19—Jehoshaphat's reign opens positively.

17:2–6—The construction of extensive fortifications in Judah as well as those Ephraimite garrisons captured by Asa (v. 2), seeking God (v. 4), and removal of *the high places* (v. 6, contra 20:33) demonstrate Jehoshaphat's piety.

17:7–9—Sixteen princes, priests, and Levites form an itinerant teaching commission charged with instructing the people in *the book of the law* (the Pentateuch). See 19:4–11.

17:13–19—The huge garrison in Jerusalem similarly indicates divine favor.

whom the king had placed in the fortified cities throughout all Judah.

Micaiah Predicts Failure

18 Now Jehoshaphat had great riches and honor; and he made a marriage alliance with Ahab. ² After some years he went down to Ahab in Samaria. Ahab slaughtered an abundance of sheep and oxen for him and for the people who were with him, and induced him to go up against Ramoth-gilead. ³ King Ahab of Israel said to King Jehoshaphat of Judah, "Will you go with me to Ramoth-gilead?" He answered him, "I am with you, my people are your people. We will be with you in the war."

4 But Jehoshaphat also said to the king of Israel, "Inquire first for the word of the LORD." ⁵ Then the king of Israel gathered the prophets together, four hundred of them, and said to them, "Shall we go to battle against Ramoth-gilead, or shall I refrain?" They said, "Go up; for God will give it into the hand of the king." ⁶ But Jehoshaphat said, "Is there no other prophet of the LORD here of whom we may inquire?" ⁷ The king of Israel said to Jehoshaphat, "There is still one other by whom we may inquire of the LORD, Micaiah son of Imlah; but I hate him, for he never prophesies anything favorable about me, but only disaster." Jehoshaphat said, "Let the king not say such a thing." ⁸ Then the king of Israel summoned an officer and said, "Bring quickly Micaiah son of Imlah." ⁹ Now the king of Israel and King Jehoshaphat

of Judah were sitting on their thrones, arrayed in their robes; and they were sitting at the threshing floor at the entrance of the gate of Samaria; and all the prophets were prophesying before them. ¹⁰ Zedekiah son of Chenaanah made for himself horns of iron, and he said, "Thus says the LORD: With these you shall gore the Arameans until they are destroyed." ¹¹ All the prophets were prophesying the same and saying, "Go up to Ramoth-gilead and triumph; the LORD will give it into the hand of the king."

12 The messenger who had gone to summon Micaiah said to him, "Look, the words of the prophets with one accord are favorable to the king; let your word be like the word of one of them, and speak favorably." ¹³ But Micaiah said, "As the LORD lives, whatever my God says, that I will speak."

14 When he had come to the king, the king said to him, "Micaiah, shall we go to Ramoth-gilead to battle, or shall I refrain?" He answered, "Go up and triumph; they will be given into your hand." ¹⁵ But the king said to him, "How many times must I make you swear to tell me nothing but the truth in the name of the LORD?" ¹⁶ Then Micaiah[a] said, "I saw all Israel scattered on the mountains, like sheep without a shepherd; and the LORD said, 'These have no master; let each one go home in peace.'" ¹⁷ The king of Israel said to Jehoshaphat, "Did I not tell you

[a] Heb he

18:1–19:3 Alliance with Ahab—The story of Micaiah (1 Kgs. 22) warns against the dangers of foreign alliances with the addition of a new introduction (2 Chr. 18:1–2) and conclusion (19:1–3).

18:1–2—Kings often consolidate their position through marriage alliances. The marriage of Athaliah, the daughter of Ahab and Jezebel, to Jehoram, Jehoshaphat's son (2 Kgs. 8:18; 2 Chr. 21:6) was unnecessary (v. 1a) and had disastrous consequences: occupation of the Davidic throne by the northern Omride dynasty, the undoing of Jehoshaphat's reforms, the spread of Baal worship, and the near elimination of the Davidic line (22:10–12).

18:4–34—Jehoshaphat and Ahab of Israel join forces against Aram (Syria).

18:4–27 *Micaiah*—Jehoshaphat seeks guidance from this true prophet, who has stood in the heavenly council, or assembly of heavenly beings believed to assist God in governing the world and communicating with humanity (cf. Jer. 23:22), rather than the self-serving assurances of the four hundred court prophets. In spite of the advice he receives, however, Jehoshaphat goes to war (2 Chr. 18:28).

that he would not prophesy anything favorable about me, but only disaster?"

18 Then Micaiah[a] said, "Therefore hear the word of the Lord: I saw the Lord sitting on his throne, with all the host of heaven standing to the right and to the left of him. [19] And the Lord said, 'Who will entice King Ahab of Israel, so that he may go up and fall at Ramoth-gilead?' Then one said one thing, and another said another, [20] until a spirit came forward and stood before the Lord, saying, 'I will entice him.' The Lord asked him, 'How?' [21] He replied, 'I will go out and be a lying spirit in the mouth of all his prophets.' Then the Lord[a] said, 'You are to entice him, and you shall succeed; go out and do it.' [22] So you see, the Lord has put a lying spirit in the mouth of these your prophets; the Lord has decreed disaster for you."

23 Then Zedekiah son of Chenaanah came up to Micaiah, slapped him on the cheek, and said, "Which way did the spirit of the Lord pass from me to speak to you?" [24] Micaiah replied, "You will find out on that day when you go in to hide in an inner chamber." [25] The king of Israel then ordered, "Take Micaiah, and return him to Amon the governor of the city and to Joash the king's son; [26] and say, 'Thus says the king: Put this fellow in prison, and feed him on reduced rations of bread and water until I return in peace.'" [27] Micaiah said, "If you return in peace, the Lord has not spoken by me." And he said, "Hear, you peoples, all of you!"

Defeat and Death of Ahab

28 So the king of Israel and King Jehoshaphat of Judah went up to Ramoth-gilead. [29] The king of Israel said to Jehoshaphat, "I will disguise myself and go into battle, but you wear your robes." So the king of Israel disguised himself, and they went into battle. [30] Now the king of Aram had commanded the captains of his chariots, "Fight with no one small or great, but only with the king of Israel." [31] When the captains of the chariots saw Jehoshaphat, they said, "It is the king of Israel." So they turned to fight against him; and Jehoshaphat cried out, and the Lord helped him. God drew them away from him, [32] for when the captains of the chariots saw that it was not the king of Israel, they turned back from pursuing him. [33] But a certain man drew his bow and unknowingly struck the king of Israel between the scale armor and the breastplate; so he said to the driver of his chariot, "Turn around, and carry me out of the battle, for I am wounded." [34] The battle grew hot that day, and the king of Israel propped himself up in his chariot facing the Arameans until evening; then at sunset he died.

19 King Jehoshaphat of Judah returned in safety to his house in Jerusalem. [2] Jehu son of Hanani the seer went out to meet him and said to King Jehoshaphat, "Should you help the wicked and love those who hate the Lord? Because of this, wrath has gone out against you from the Lord. [3] Nevertheless, some good is found in you, for you destroyed the sacred poles[b] out of the land, and have set your heart to seek God."

The Reforms of Jehoshaphat

4 Jehoshaphat resided at Jerusalem; then he went out again among the people, from Beer-sheba to the hill country

---

a Heb he b Heb Asheroth

18:28–34—God diverts the Arameans and directs arrows to Ahab despite his disguise.

19:1–3 Jehu—Another prophet (see 1 Kgs. 16:1, 7) voices the chronicler's rebuke of Jehoshaphat's disregard of Micaiah's counsel (2 Chr. 18:28).

19:4–11—This judicial reform, appropriate to one whose name means "YHWH judges," appears

only here. The king responds to Jehu's warning (vv. 2–3) by creating a system of local Levitical judges under priestly oversight in Jerusalem. The system conforms with Deut. 16:18–17:13 (cf. David's institution, 1 Chr. 23:4; 26:29–32) except for the postexilic division into *matters of the Lord* and *the king's matters* (2 Chr. 19:11). Despite this separation into spiritual and secular

of Ephraim, and brought them back to the LORD, the God of their ancestors. ⁵ He appointed judges in the land in all the fortified cities of Judah, city by city, ⁶ and said to the judges, "Consider what you are doing, for you judge not on behalf of human beings but on the LORD's behalf; he is with you in giving judgment. ⁷ Now, let the fear of the LORD be upon you; take care what you do, for there is no perversion of justice with the LORD our God, or partiality, or taking of bribes."

8 Moreover in Jerusalem Jehoshaphat appointed certain Levites and priests and heads of families of Israel, to give judgment for the LORD and to decide disputed cases. They had their seat at Jerusalem. ⁹ He charged them: "This is how you shall act: in the fear of the LORD, in faithfulness, and with your whole heart; ¹⁰ whenever a case comes to you from your kindred who live in their cities, concerning bloodshed, law or commandment, statutes or ordinances, then you shall instruct them, so that they may not incur guilt before the LORD and wrath may not come on you and your kindred. Do so, and you will not incur guilt. ¹¹ See, Amariah the chief priest is over you in all matters of the LORD; and Zebadiah son of Ishmael, the governor of the house of Judah, in all the king's matters; and the Levites will serve you as officers. Deal courageously, and may the LORD be with the good!"

Invasion from the East

20 After this the Moabites and Ammonites, and with them some of the Meunites,ᵃ came against Jehoshaphat for battle. ²Messengersᵇ came and told Jehoshaphat, "A great multitude is coming against you from Edom,ᶜ from beyond the sea; already they are at Hazazon-tamar" (that is, En-gedi). ³Jehoshaphat was afraid; he set himself to seek the LORD, and proclaimed a fast throughout all Judah. ⁴ Judah assembled to seek help from the LORD; from all the towns of Judah they came to seek the LORD.

Jehoshaphat's Prayer and Victory

5 Jehoshaphat stood in the assembly of Judah and Jerusalem, in the house of the LORD, before the new court, ⁶ and said, "O LORD, God of our ancestors, are you not God in heaven? Do you not rule over all the kingdoms of the nations? In your hand are power and might, so that no one is able to withstand you. ⁷ Did you not, O our God, drive out the inhabitants of this land before your people Israel, and give it forever to the descendants of your friend Abraham? ⁸ They have lived in it, and in it have built you a sanctuary for your name, saying, ⁹ 'If disaster comes upon us, the sword, judgment,ᵈ or pestilence, or famine, we will stand before this house, and before you, for your name is in this house, and cry to you in our distress, and you will hear and save.' ¹⁰ See now, the people of Ammon, Moab, and Mount Seir, whom you would not let Israel invade when they came from the land of Egypt,

ᵃ Compare 26.7: Heb Ammonites ᵇ Heb They ᶜ One Ms: MT Aram
ᵈ Or the sword of judgment

---

areas, God's people are committed to social justice as a matter of faith.

20:1–30—The mention of a battle in 1 Kgs. 22:45 has been expanded to form the centerpiece of the account of the divided monarchy (2 Chr. 10–28). The primary theme is the effectiveness of faith, illustrated in three sections: Jehoshaphat's prayer (20:5–13), God's response (vv. 14–19), and the story of the battle itself (vv. 20–27). Verses 1–4 and 28–30 frame these accounts, contrasting Jehoshaphat's fear (*afraid*, v. 3) with **the fear of God** that overcame Israel's enemies (v. 29). Within this structure, "stand" functions as a co-

hesive element. The first and third sections begin with the phrase **Jehoshaphat stood** (vv. 5, 20b) and all three sections include a key statement with this word that recalls a significant moment from Israel's past. The story as a whole encourages those who are in the grip of despair to seek the Lord in prayer.

20:5–13—In Jehoshaphat's prayer, **we will stand before this house . . . and cry to you in our distress, and you will hear and save** (v. 9), recalls Solomon's prayer at the dedication of the temple (6:20, 28–30; cf. 7:13–15) and is a fine testimony to human dependence upon God.

and whom they avoided and did not destroy— ¹¹ they reward us by coming to drive us out of your possession that you have given us to inherit. ¹² O our God, will you not execute judgment upon them? For we are powerless against this great multitude that is coming against us. We do not know what to do, but our eyes are on you."

13 Meanwhile all Judah stood before the LORD, with their little ones, their wives, and their children. ¹⁴ Then the spirit of the LORD came upon Jahaziel son of Zechariah, son of Benaiah, son of Jeiel, son of Mattaniah, a Levite of the sons of Asaph, in the middle of the assembly. ¹⁵ He said, "Listen, all Judah and inhabitants of Jerusalem, and King Jehoshaphat: Thus says the LORD to you: 'Do not fear or be dismayed at this great multitude; for the battle is not yours but God's. ¹⁶ Tomorrow go down against them; they will come up by the ascent of Ziz; you will find them at the end of the valley, before the wilderness of Jeruel. ¹⁷ This battle is not for you to fight; take your position, stand still, and see the victory of the LORD on your behalf, O Judah and Jerusalem.' Do not fear or be dismayed; tomorrow go out against them, and the LORD will be with you."

18 Then Jehoshaphat bowed down with his face to the ground, and all Judah and the inhabitants of Jerusalem fell down before the LORD, worshiping the LORD. ¹⁹ And the Levites, of the Kohathites and the Korahites, stood up to praise the LORD, the God of Israel, with a very loud voice.

20 They rose early in the morning and went out into the wilderness of Tekoa;

and as they went out, Jehoshaphat stood and said, "Listen to me, O Judah and inhabitants of Jerusalem! Believe in the LORD your God and you will be established; believe his prophets." ²¹ When he had taken counsel with the people, he appointed those who were to sing to the LORD and praise him in holy splendor, as they went before the army, saying,

"Give thanks to the LORD,
 for his steadfast love endures
  forever."

²² As they began to sing and praise, the LORD set an ambush against the Ammonites, Moab, and Mount Seir, who had come against Judah, so that they were routed. ²³ For the Ammonites and Moab attacked the inhabitants of Mount Seir, destroying them utterly; and when they had made an end of the inhabitants of Seir, they all helped to destroy one another.

24 When Judah came to the watchtower of the wilderness, they looked toward the multitude; they were corpses lying on the ground; no one had escaped. ²⁵ When Jehoshaphat and his people came to take the booty from them, they found livestock[a] in great numbers, goods, clothing, and precious things, which they took for themselves until they could carry no more. They spent three days taking the booty, because of its abundance. ²⁶ On the fourth day they assembled in the Valley of Beracah, for there they blessed the LORD; therefore that place has been called the Valley of Beracah[b] to this day. ²⁷ Then all the people of Judah and Jerusalem, with Jehoshaphat at their head, returned to Jerusalem with

a Gk: Heb *among them*   *b* That is *Blessing*

20:14–19—The people are advised to *stand still and see the victory of the LORD* (v. 17). Compare Moses' instructions at the Red Sea (Exod. 14:13).

20:20–27—The confusion that caused the enemies to destroy each other when *the Ammonites and Moab attacked* (Heb. "stood against") *the inhabitants of Mount Seir* (v. 23) recalls a similar situation in Gideon's day (Judg. 7:15–23).

20:20 *Believe in the LORD your God and you*

will be established—The postexilic community, in conflict with the descendants of these same peoples (v. 1; cf. Neh. 2:19; 4:1–3, 7–9; 6:1–4; 13), would appreciate this positive reformulation of Isa. 7:9 that can serve as a terse summary of the message of 2 Chronicles. *Believe his prophets [and you will be successful]*—The bracketed conclusion is inexplicably omitted by NRSV and should be restored.

joy, for the LORD had enabled them to rejoice over their enemies. **28** They came to Jerusalem, with harps and lyres and trumpets, to the house of the LORD. **29** The fear of God came on all the kingdoms of the countries when they heard that the LORD had fought against the enemies of Israel. **30** And the realm of Jehoshaphat was quiet, for his God gave him rest all around.

The End of Jehoshaphat's Reign

31 So Jehoshaphat reigned over Judah. He was thirty-five years old when he began to reign; he reigned twenty-five years in Jerusalem. His mother's name was Azubah daughter of Shilhi. **32** He walked in the way of his father Asa and did not turn aside from it, doing what was right in the sight of the LORD. **33** Yet the high places were not removed; the people had not yet set their hearts upon the God of their ancestors.

34 Now the rest of the acts of Jehoshaphat, from first to last, are written in the Annals of Jehu son of Hanani, which are recorded in the Book of the Kings of Israel.

35 After this King Jehoshaphat of Judah joined with King Ahaziah of Israel, who did wickedly. **36** He joined him in building ships to go to Tarshish; they built the ships in Ezion-geber. **37** Then Eliezer son of Dodavahu of Mareshah prophesied against Jehoshaphat, saying, "Because you have joined with Ahaziah, the LORD will destroy what you have made." And the ships were wrecked and were not able to go to Tarshish.

Jehoram's Reign

21 Jehoshaphat slept with his ancestors and was buried with his ancestors in the city of David; his son Jehoram succeeded him. **2** He had brothers, the sons of Jehoshaphat: Azariah, Jehiel, Zechariah, Azariah, Michael, and Shephatiah; all these were the sons of King Jehoshaphat of Judah.*a* **3** Their father gave them many gifts, of silver, gold, and valuable possessions, together with fortified cities in Judah; but he gave the kingdom to Jehoram, because he was the firstborn. **4** When Jehoram had ascended the throne of his father and was established, he put all his brothers to the sword, and also some of the officials of Israel. **5** Jehoram was thirty-two years old when he began to reign; he reigned eight years in Jerusalem. **6** He walked in the way of the kings of Israel, as the house of Ahab had done; for the daughter of Ahab was his wife. He did what was evil in the sight of the LORD. **7** Yet the LORD would not destroy the house of David because of the covenant that he had made with David, and since he had promised to give a lamp to him and to his descendants forever.

Revolt of Edom

8 In his days Edom revolted against the rule of Judah and set up a king of

a Gk Syr: Heb *Israel*

20:31–21:1—Two summaries of Jehoshaphat's reign (20:31–34; 21:1) frame a final prophetic rebuke (20:35–37).

20:35–37 *Joined with*—Financial foreign alliances are as disastrous as Jehoshaphat's military alliances (see 18:1–2; 19:1–3).

21:2–22:1 Jehoram

The first king to receive a totally negative presentation. His reign is the first of three in which the Davidic dynasty is threatened with extinction. Jehoram jealously tried to preserve his own interests to the point of controlling, and taking, the lives of others. This affront to God's sovereignty also threatened the continuance of the dynasty.

Society needs to discern those places where the authoritarian use of power usurps the providence of God.

21:6–7, 18–19—The chronicler's prosaic judgment of Jehoram (vv. 6–7) contrasts sharply with God's gruesome judgment (vv. 18–19a) and the eerie judgment of the people who *made no fire in his honor*, thereby denying this wicked king the funerary rites of his ancestors (v. 19b). The only positive aspect of Jehoram's evil reign, his preservation of David's line (v. 17), points to God's promise regarding **the house of David** (v. 7; cf. 1 Chr. 17:12; not "Judah," as in 2 Kgs. 8:19).

21:8–11, 16–17—Retributive justice appears in

their own. **9** Then Jehoram crossed over with his commanders and all his chariots. He set out by night and attacked the Edomites, who had surrounded him and his chariot commanders. **10** So Edom has been in revolt against the rule of Judah to this day. At that time Libnah also revolted against his rule, because he had forsaken the LORD, the God of his ancestors.

Elijah's Letter

11 Moreover he made high places in the hill country of Judah, and led the inhabitants of Jerusalem into unfaithfulness, and made Judah go astray. **12** A letter came to him from the prophet Elijah, saying: "Thus says the LORD, the God of your father David: Because you have not walked in the ways of your father Jehoshaphat or in the ways of King Asa of Judah, **13** but have walked in the way of the kings of Israel, and have led Judah and the inhabitants of Jerusalem into unfaithfulness, as the house of Ahab led Israel into unfaithfulness, and because you also have killed your brothers, members of your father's house, who were better than yourself, **14** see, the LORD will bring a great plague on your people, your children, your wives, and all your possessions, **15** and you yourself will have a severe sickness with a disease of your bowels, until your bowels come out, day after day, because of the disease."

16 The LORD aroused against Jehoram the anger of the Philistines and of the Arabs who are near the Ethiopians.*a* **17** They came up against Judah, invaded it, and carried away all the possessions they found that belonged to the king's house, along with his sons and his wives,

so that no son was left to him except Jehoahaz, his youngest son.

Disease and Death of Jehoram

18 After all this the LORD struck him in his bowels with an incurable disease. **19** In course of time, at the end of two years, his bowels came out because of the disease, and he died in great agony. His people made no fire in his honor, like the fires made for his ancestors. **20** He was thirty-two years old when he began to reign; he reigned eight years in Jerusalem. He departed with no one's regret. They buried him in the city of David, but not in the tombs of the kings.

Ahaziah's Reign

22 The inhabitants of Jerusalem made his youngest son Ahaziah king as his successor; for the troops who came with the Arabs to the camp had killed all the older sons. So Ahaziah son of Jehoram reigned as king of Judah. **2** Ahaziah was forty-two years old when he began to reign; he reigned one year in Jerusalem. His mother's name was Athaliah, a granddaughter of Omri. **3** He also walked in the ways of the house of Ahab, for his mother was his counselor in doing wickedly. **4** He did what was evil in the sight of the LORD, as the house of Ahab had done; for after the death of his father they were his counselors, to his ruin. **5** He even followed their advice, and went with Jehoram son of King Ahab of Israel to make war against King Hazael of Aram at Ramoth-gilead. The Arameans wounded Joram, **6** and he returned to be healed in Jezreel of the wounds that he had received at Ramah,

a Or Nubians; Heb Cushites

---

these paired rebellions. The poetic justice of a reign that began with the murder of brothers (v. 4) and ended with the loss of sons and wives (v. 17; 22:1) is grisly.

21:12–15—Elijah's *letter*. This announcement of judgment functions as the theological touchstone for comparing the paired rebellions and appraisals that surround it.

22:2–9 Ahaziah

Though Ahaziah's family of origin was hardly a positive influence, he is judged for his own sin. Scripture embraces the principle that we are ultimately responsible for ourselves.

22:3–4—*Ahab*'s evil northern influence continues through Athaliah.

22:5–6—Ahaziah's northern entanglements surpassed those of Judah's other kings.

when he fought King Hazael of Aram. And Ahaziah son of King Jehoram of Judah went down to see Joram son of Ahab in Jezreel, because he was sick.

7 But it was ordained by God that the downfall of Ahaziah should come about through his going to visit Joram. For when he came there he went out with Jehoram to meet Jehu son of Nimshi, whom the LORD had anointed to destroy the house of Ahab. ⁸ When Jehu was executing judgment on the house of Ahab, he met the officials of Judah and the sons of Ahaziah's brothers, who attended Ahaziah, and he killed them. ⁹ He searched for Ahaziah, who was captured while hiding in Samaria and was brought to Jehu, and put to death. They buried him, for they said, "He is the grandson of Jehoshaphat, who sought the LORD with all his heart." And the house of Ahaziah had no one able to rule the kingdom.

Athaliah Seizes the Throne

10 Now when Athaliah, Ahaziah's mother, saw that her son was dead, she set about to destroy all the royal family of the house of Judah. ¹¹ But Jehoshabeath, the king's daughter, took Joash son of Ahaziah, and stole him away from among the king's children who were about to be killed; she put him and his nurse in a bedroom. Thus Jehoshabeath, daughter of King Jehoram and wife of the priest Jehoiada—because she was a sister of Ahaziah—hid him from Athaliah, so that she did not kill him; ¹² he remained with them six years, hidden in the house of God, while Athaliah reigned over the land.

23 But in the seventh year Jehoiada took courage, and entered into a compact with the commanders of the hundreds, Azariah son of Jeroham, Ishmael son of Jehohanan, Azariah son of Obed, Maaseiah son of Adaiah, and Elishaphat son of Zichri. ² They went around through Judah and gathered the Levites from all the towns of Judah, and the heads of families of Israel, and they came to Jerusalem. ³ Then the whole assembly made a covenant with the king in the house of God. Jehoiada*ᵃ* said to them, "Here is the king's son! Let him reign, as the LORD promised concerning the sons of David. ⁴ This is what you are to do: one-third of you, priests and Levites, who come on duty on the sabbath, shall be gatekeepers, ⁵ one-third shall be at the king's house, and one-third at the Gate of the Foundation; and all the people shall be in the courts of the house of the LORD. ⁶ Do not let anyone enter the house of the LORD except the priests and ministering Levites; they may enter, for they are holy, but all the other*ᵇ* people shall observe the instructions of the LORD. ⁷ The Levites shall surround the king, each with his weapons in his hand; and whoever enters the house shall be killed. Stay with the king in his comings and goings."

ᵃ Heb He   ᵇ Heb lacks other

22:7–9a—Ahaziah's death with the rest of the house of Ahab in Jehu's bloody coup (2 Kgs. 8:28–10:31) is attributed to God.

22:9b *No one able to rule*—God's promise of an eternal dynasty (1 Chr. 17:12) is threatened when Ahaziah dies without an heir. This is the low point of the Davidic dynasty.

22:10–23:21 Athaliah

Israel's only ruling queen is the only break in the Davidic dynasty and the final consequence of Jehoshaphat's alliance with Ahab. Omission of the standard royal formulas indicates that the chronicler considered her reign illegitimate, as does the book of Kings.

22:10–12 *Jehoshabeath*—Joash's deliverer, the wife of Jehoiada the priest, is a model of faithful courage. The duel between these two women, Athaliah and Jehoshabeath, contrasts calculating evil and opposition to God with a valiant attempt to protect the child who represents the promise. The hiding of Moses in the bulrushes and the whisking away of the infant Jesus to Egypt are other scriptural accounts of the deliverance of special children by their protectors.

23:1–15—Jehoiada dramatically presents seven-year-old Joash as the true king.

23:3—Recalling God's dynastic promise (1 Chr. 17:12).

Joash Crowned King

8 The Levites and all Judah did according to all that the priest Jehoiada commanded; each brought his men, who were to come on duty on the sabbath, with those who were to go off duty on the sabbath; for the priest Jehoiada did not dismiss the divisions. 9 The priest Jehoiada delivered to the captains the spears and the large and small shields that had been King David's, which were in the house of God; 10 and he set all the people as a guard for the king, everyone with weapon in hand, from the south side of the house to the north side of the house, around the altar and the house. 11 Then he brought out the king's son, put the crown on him, and gave him the covenant;a they proclaimed him king, and Jehoiada and his sons anointed him; and they shouted, "Long live the king!"

Athaliah Murdered

12 When Athaliah heard the noise of the people running and praising the king, she went into the house of the LORD to the people; 13 and when she looked, there was the king standing by his pillar at the entrance, and the captains and the trumpeters beside the king, and all the people of the land rejoicing and blowing trumpets, and the singers with their musical instruments leading in the celebration. Athaliah tore her clothes, and cried, "Treason! Treason!" 14 Then the priest Jehoiada brought out the captains who were set over the army, saying to them, "Bring her out between the ranks; anyone who follows her is to be put to the sword." For the priest said, "Do not put her to death in the house of the LORD." 15 So they laid hands on her;

she went into the entrance of the Horse Gate of the king's house, and there they put her to death.

16 Jehoiada made a covenant between himself and all the people and the king that they should be the LORD's people. 17 Then all the people went to the house of Baal, and tore it down; his altars and his images they broke in pieces, and they killed Mattan, the priest of Baal, in front of the altars. 18 Jehoiada assigned the care of the house of the LORD to the levitical priests whom David had organized to be in charge of the house of the LORD, to offer burnt offerings to the LORD, as it is written in the law of Moses, with rejoicing and with singing, according to the order of David. 19 He stationed the gatekeepers at the gates of the house of the LORD so that no one should enter who was in any way unclean. 20 And he took the captains, the nobles, the governors of the people, and all the people of the land, and they brought the king down from the house of the LORD, marching through the upper gate to the king's house. They set the king on the royal throne. 21 So all the people of the land rejoiced, and the city was quiet after Athaliah had been killed with the sword.

Joash Repairs the Temple

24 Joash was seven years old when he began to reign; he reigned forty years in Jerusalem; his mother's name was Zibiah of Beer-sheba. 2 Joash did what was right in the sight of the LORD all the days of the priest Jehoiada. 3 Jehoiada got two wives for him, and he became the father of sons and daughters.

a Or treaty, or testimony; Heb eduth

23:16–21—Restoring the exclusive worship of God (cf. 15:12).

23:16—Jehoiada's inclusion as a covenant partner reflects the expanded role of the high priest in the postexilic community. Only the people and God are covenant partners in 2 Kgs. 11:17.

24:1–27 Joash

The inconsistency between Joash's positive evalu-

ation in 2 Kgs. 12:2 and his violent death in 2 Kgs. 12:21–22 is explained by returning to the pattern of a period of success (2 Chr. 24:1–14) followed by a period of decline (vv. 17–27). The chronicler uses this to illustrate the importance of staying the course.

24:1–14—Joash repairs the temple. This is the faithful period of his reign.

4 Some time afterward Joash decided to restore the house of the LORD. 5 He assembled the priests and the Levites and said to them, "Go out to the cities of Judah and gather money from all Israel to repair the house of your God, year by year; and see that you act quickly." But the Levites did not act quickly. 6 So the king summoned Jehoiada the chief, and said to him, "Why have you not required the Levites to bring in from Judah and Jerusalem the tax levied by Moses, the servant of the LORD, on*a* the congregation of Israel for the tent of the covenant?"*b* 7 For the children of Athaliah, that wicked woman, had broken into the house of God, and had even used all the dedicated things of the house of the LORD for the Baals.

8 So the king gave command, and they made a chest, and set it outside the gate of the house of the LORD. 9 A proclamation was made throughout Judah and Jerusalem to bring in for the LORD the tax that Moses the servant of God laid on Israel in the wilderness. 10 All the leaders and all the people rejoiced and brought their tax and dropped it into the chest until it was full. 11 Whenever the chest was brought to the king's officers by the Levites, when they saw that there was a large amount of money in it, the king's secretary and the officer of the chief priest would come and empty the chest and take it and return it to its place. So they did day after day, and collected money in abundance.

12 The king and Jehoiada gave it to those who had charge of the work of the house of the LORD, and they hired masons and carpenters to restore the house of the LORD, and also workers in iron and bronze to repair the house of the LORD. 13 So those who were engaged in the work labored, and the repairing went forward at their hands, and they restored the house of God to its proper condition and strengthened it. 14 When they had finished, they brought the rest of the money to the king and Jehoiada, and with it were made utensils for the house of the LORD, utensils for the service and for the burnt offerings, and ladles, and vessels of gold and silver. They offered burnt offerings in the house of the LORD regularly all the days of Jehoiada.

Apostasy of Joash

15 But Jehoiada grew old and full of days, and died; he was one hundred thirty years old at his death. 16 And they buried him in the city of David among the kings, because he had done good in Israel, and for God and his house.

17 Now after the death of Jehoiada the officials of Judah came and did obeisance to the king; then the king listened to them. 18 They abandoned the house of the LORD, the God of their ancestors, and served the sacred poles*c* and the idols. And wrath came upon Judah and

a Compare Vg: Heb *and* *b* Or *treaty*, or *testimony*; Heb *eduth*
c Heb *Asherim*

24:4 *Restore*—Structural repair was needed after 130 years of use. Ritual cleansing corrected the abuses of Baal worship.

24:5–6—*The Levites* are slow in collecting a tax Moses instituted for the tabernacle (Exod. 30:12–16; 38:25–26), later used by David and Solomon for the construction of the temple (1 Chr. 29:1–9).

24:7 *Children of Athaliah*—Literally, "her sons," probably her officials.

24:10—The joyful generosity of the people recalls the people's response upon the completion of the tabernacle (Exod. 36:4–7) and that of David's subjects (1 Chr. 29:9).

24:15–16—Jehoiada's death. Not mentioned in Kings, his passing separates the two periods of Joash's reign. Jehoiada kept the young king faithful (vv. 1–14; cf. v. 2). Without his influence, however, the king repeats the sins of his ancestors (vv. 17–27). The priest's faithful service is rewarded with long life and burial in the royal tombs, an honor denied to Joash (v. 25).

24:17–27—Joash abandons the temple.

24:17–19 *Listened*—The Hebrew verb connotes "obedience" and means Joash condoned the idolatry.

Jerusalem for this guilt of theirs. ¹⁹Yet he sent prophets among them to bring them back to the LORD; they testified against them, but they would not listen.

20 Then the spirit of God took possession of*ᵃ* Zechariah son of the priest Jehoiada; he stood above the people and said to them, "Thus says God: Why do you transgress the commandments of the LORD, so that you cannot prosper? Because you have forsaken the LORD, he has also forsaken you." ²¹But they conspired against him, and by command of the king they stoned him to death in the court of the house of the LORD. ²²King Joash did not remember the kindness that Jehoiada, Zechariah's father, had shown him, but killed his son. As he was dying, he said, "May the LORD see and avenge!"

Death of Joash

23 At the end of the year the army of Aram came up against Joash. They came to Judah and Jerusalem, and destroyed all the officials of the people from among them, and sent all the booty they took to the king of Damascus. ²⁴Although the army of Aram had come with few men, the LORD delivered into their hand a very great army, because they had abandoned the LORD, the God of their ancestors. Thus they executed judgment on Joash.

25 When they had withdrawn, leaving him severely wounded, his servants conspired against him because of the blood of the son*ᵇ* of the priest Jehoiada, and they killed him on his bed. So he died; and they buried him in the city of David, but they did not bury him in the tombs of the kings. ²⁶Those who conspired against him were Zabad son of Shimeath the Ammonite, and Jehozabad son of Shimrith the Moabite. ²⁷Accounts of his sons, and of the many oracles against him, and of the rebuilding*ᶜ* of the house of God are written in the Commentary on the Book of the Kings. And his son Amaziah succeeded him.

Reign of Amaziah

25 Amaziah was twenty-five years old when he began to reign, and he reigned twenty-nine years in Jerusalem. His mother's name was Jehoaddan of Jerusalem. ²He did what was right in the sight of the LORD, yet not with a true heart. ³As soon as the royal power was firmly in his hand he killed his servants who had murdered his father the king. ⁴But he did not put their children to death, according to what is written in the law, in the book of Moses, where the LORD commanded, "The parents shall not be put to death for the children, or the children be put to death for the parents; but all shall be put to death for their own sins."

Slaughter of the Edomites

5 Amaziah assembled the people of Judah, and set them by ancestral houses

ᵃ Heb *clothed itself with*   *ᵇ* Gk Vg: Heb *sons*   *ᶜ* Heb *founding*

24:20—The beginning of Zechariah's rebuke recalls Moses' rebuke in the wilderness (Num. 14:41). The end fulfills Azariah's warning to Asa (2 Chr. 15:2b).

24:21–24—Zechariah's execution (v. 21) precipitates invasion by Aram (v. 23).

24:24 *The LORD*—Defeat of Judah's larger force indicates God's retributive justice.

24:25—Joash's assassination by *his servants* answers Zechariah's dying request for retributive justice, *May the LORD see and avenge!* (v. 22).

25:1–26:2 Amaziah
As in the account of Joash, the reign is divided into faithful (vv. 1–13) and unfaithful (vv. 14–28) periods.

25:1–13—Amaziah's faithful period.

25:2 *Yet not with a true heart*—This addition qualifies the evaluation that Amaziah *did what was right in the sight of the LORD*, as does the omission of "like his ancestor David" from 2 Kgs. 14:3. Amaziah's problem was compromise. Knowing what is right is necessary but not sufficient. One must carry through, unlike Amaziah's halfhearted attempts, which ultimately ended in apostasy.

25:4—Amaziah respects the law (see Deut. 24:16).

25:5–13—The battle with Edom.

under commanders of the thousands and of the hundreds for all Judah and Benjamin. He mustered those twenty years old and upward, and found that they were three hundred thousand picked troops fit for war, able to handle spear and shield. 6 He also hired one hundred thousand mighty warriors from Israel for one hundred talents of silver. 7 But a man of God came to him and said, "O king, do not let the army of Israel go with you, for the LORD is not with Israel—all these Ephraimites. 8 Rather, go by yourself and act; be strong in battle, or God will fling you down before the enemy; for God has power to help or to overthrow." 9 Amaziah said to the man of God, "But what shall we do about the hundred talents that I have given to the army of Israel?" The man of God answered, "The LORD is able to give you much more than this." 10 Then Amaziah discharged the army that had come to him from Ephraim, letting them go home again. But they became very angry with Judah, and returned home in fierce anger.

11 Amaziah took courage, and led out his people; he went to the Valley of Salt, and struck down ten thousand men of Seir. 12 The people of Judah captured another ten thousand alive, took them to the top of Sela, and threw them down from the top of Sela, so that all of them were dashed to pieces. 13 But the men of the army whom Amaziah sent back, not letting them go with him to battle, fell on the cities of Judah from Samaria to Beth-horon; they killed three thousand people in them, and took much booty.

14 Now after Amaziah came from the slaughter of the Edomites, he brought the gods of the people of Seir, set them up as his gods, and worshiped them, making offerings to them. 15 The LORD was angry with Amaziah and sent to him a prophet, who said to him, "Why have you resorted to a people's gods who could not deliver their own people from your hand?" 16 But as he was speaking the king[a] said to him, "Have we made you a royal counselor? Stop! Why should you be put to death?" So the prophet stopped, but said, "I know that God has determined to destroy you, because you have done this and have not listened to my advice."

Israel Defeats Judah

17 Then King Amaziah of Judah took counsel and sent to King Joash son of Jehoahaz son of Jehu of Israel, saying, "Come, let us look one another in the face." 18 King Joash of Israel sent word to King Amaziah of Judah, "A thornbush on Lebanon sent to a cedar on Lebanon, saying, 'Give your daughter to my son for a wife'; but a wild animal of Lebanon passed by and trampled down the thornbush. 19 You say, 'See, I have defeated Edom,' and your heart has lifted you up in boastfulness. Now stay at home; why should you provoke trouble so that you fall, you and Judah with you?"

20 But Amaziah would not listen—it was God's doing, in order to hand them over, because they had sought the gods of Edom. 21 So King Joash of Israel went up; he and King Amaziah of Judah faced one another in battle at Beth-shemesh, which belongs to Judah. 22 Judah was defeated by Israel; everyone fled home. 23 King Joash of Israel captured King Amaziah of Judah, son of Joash, son of Ahaziah, at Beth-shemesh; he brought

a Heb he

25:7–9—An unknown prophet announces the dangers of foreign alliance (cf. 13:4–12; 16:1–9; 19:1–13; 22:1–7).

25:10–13—Amaziah obediently dismisses the mercenaries.

25:14–28—War with the north contextualizes the faithless half of Amaziah's reign.

25:15–16—Another nameless prophet announces the certainty of divine retribution.

25:17–19—Joash, the northern king, tells Amaziah the fable of the **thornbush** and the **cedar**, indicating that arrogance leads to disaster.

25:20 *God's doing*—Amaziah's stubbornness came from God.

him to Jerusalem, and broke down the wall of Jerusalem from the Ephraim Gate to the Corner Gate, a distance of four hundred cubits. ²⁴ He seized all the gold and silver, and all the vessels that were found in the house of God, and Obed-edom with them; he seized also the treasuries of the king's house, also hostages; then he returned to Samaria.

Death of Amaziah

25 King Amaziah son of Joash of Judah, lived fifteen years after the death of King Joash son of Jehoahaz of Israel. ²⁶ Now the rest of the deeds of Amaziah, from first to last, are they not written in the Book of the Kings of Judah and Israel? ²⁷ From the time that Amaziah turned away from the LORD they made a conspiracy against him in Jerusalem, and he fled to Lachish. But they sent after him to Lachish, and killed him there. ²⁸ They brought him back on horses; he was buried with his ancestors in the city of David.

Reign of Uzziah

26 Then all the people of Judah took Uzziah, who was sixteen years old, and made him king to succeed his father Amaziah. ² He rebuilt Eloth and restored it to Judah, after the king slept with his ancestors. ³ Uzziah was sixteen years old when he began to reign, and he reigned fifty-two years in Jerusalem. His mother's name was Jecoliah of Jerusalem. ⁴ He did what was right in the sight of the LORD, just as his father Amaziah had done. ⁵ He set himself to seek God in the days of Zechariah, who instructed him in the fear of God; and as long as he sought the LORD, God made him prosper.

6 He went out and made war against the Philistines, and broke down the wall of Gath and the wall of Jabneh and the wall of Ashdod; he built cities in the territory of Ashdod and elsewhere among the Philistines. ⁷ God helped him against the Philistines, against the Arabs who lived in Gur-baal, and against the Meunites. ⁸ The Ammonites paid tribute to Uzziah, and his fame spread even to the border of Egypt, for he became very strong. ⁹ Moreover Uzziah built towers in Jerusalem at the Corner Gate, at the Valley Gate, and at the Angle, and fortified them. ¹⁰ He built towers in the wilderness and hewed out many cisterns, for he had large herds, both in the Shephelah and in the plain, and he had farmers and vinedressers in the hills and in the fertile lands, for he loved the soil. ¹¹ Moreover Uzziah had an army of soldiers, fit for war, in divisions according to the numbers in the muster made by the secretary Jeiel and the officer Maaseiah, under the direction of Hananiah, one of the king's commanders. ¹² The whole number of the heads of ancestral houses of mighty warriors was two thousand six hundred. ¹³ Under their command was an army of three hundred seven thousand five hundred, who could make war with mighty power, to help the king against the enemy. ¹⁴ Uzziah provided for all the army the shields, spears, helmets, coats of mail, bows, and stones for slinging. ¹⁵ In Jerusalem he set up machines, invented by skilled workers, on the towers and the corners for shooting arrows

---

25:27 *From the time that Amaziah turned away from the LORD*—Another addition attributes the conspiracy to Amaziah's idolatry, reported in vv. 14, 20. Amaziah's assassination fulfilled the prophecy of his death recorded in v. 16.

26:1–2—These last verses clearly conclude Amaziah's reign in 2 Kgs. 14:21–22. Here, they form a transition to the reign of Uzziah.

26:3–23 Uzziah (Azariah in Kings)
The account is again divided into two periods,

one with Uzziah engaged in worthwhile projects (vv. 4–15), and a second explaining the leprosy that struck the king later in life (2 Kgs. 15:5) as the result of unfaithfulness (2 Chr. 26:16–21). Discipleship is a lifelong process; the need for faithfulness continues past the first flush of response.

26:4–15—Uzziah's faithful first period.

26:6–15—Success in war and fame (vv. 6–8); building projects (vv. 9–10); and military might (vv. 11–15) are signs of blessing.

and large stones. And his fame spread far, for he was marvelously helped until he became strong.

Pride and Apostasy

16 But when he had become strong he grew proud, to his destruction. For he was false to the LORD his God, and entered the temple of the LORD to make offering on the altar of incense. 17 But the priest Azariah went in after him, with eighty priests of the LORD who were men of valor; 18 they withstood King Uzziah, and said to him, "It is not for you, Uzziah, to make offering to the LORD, but for the priests the descendants of Aaron, who are consecrated to make offering. Go out of the sanctuary; for you have done wrong, and it will bring you no honor from the LORD God." 19 Then Uzziah was angry. Now he had a censer in his hand to make offering, and when he became angry with the priests a leprous*a* disease broke out on his forehead, in the presence of the priests in the house of the LORD, by the altar of incense. 20 When the chief priest Azariah, and all the priests, looked at him, he was leprous*a* in his forehead. They hurried him out, and he himself hurried to get out, because the LORD had struck him. 21 King Uzziah was leprous*a* to the day of his death, and being leprous*a* lived in a separate house, for he was excluded from the house of the LORD. His son Jotham was in charge of the palace of the king, governing the people of the land.

22 Now the rest of the acts of Uzziah, from first to last, the prophet Isaiah son of Amoz wrote. 23 Uzziah slept with his ancestors; they buried him near his ancestors in the burial field that belonged to the kings, for they said, "He is leprous."*a* His son Jotham succeeded him.

Reign of Jotham

27 Jotham was twenty-five years old when he began to reign; he reigned sixteen years in Jerusalem. His mother's name was Jerushah daughter of Zadok. 2 He did what was right in the sight of the LORD just as his father Uzziah had done—only he did not invade the temple of the LORD. But the people still followed corrupt practices. 3 He built the upper gate of the house of the LORD, and did extensive building on the wall of Ophel. 4 Moreover he built cities in the hill country of Judah, and forts and towers on the wooded hills. 5 He fought with the king of the Ammonites and prevailed against them. The Ammonites gave him that year one hundred talents of silver, ten thousand cors of wheat and ten thousand of barley. The Ammonites paid him the same amount in the second and the third years. 6 So Jotham became strong because he ordered his ways before the LORD his God. 7 Now the rest of the acts of Jotham, and all his wars and his ways, are written in the Book of the Kings of Israel and Judah. 8 He was twenty-five years old when he began to

a A term for several skin diseases; precise meaning uncertain

---

26:16–21—Uzziah's faithless second period accounts for his leprosy by drawing parallels with Joash and Amaziah.

26:16 *Grew proud*—The source of Amaziah's downfall (25:19). *Incense*—Only priests are permitted to offer incense (Num. 16:40).

26:17–18 *Azariah*—A priest, functioning as a prophet, rebukes Uzziah.

26:20—Uzziah's leprosy, though not what we call leprosy, was a serious skin condition that rendered Uzziah ritually unclean and prevented him from ruling as well as from worship.

26:23—Uzziah's disease precluded burial in the royal cemetery.

27:1–9 Jotham

Jotham's brief account is the first untarnished report since Abijah. Through comparisons with Uzziah, his father, the chronicler shows that heredity is not a factor in proper behavior. Individuals and communities can choose to live justly. The same point will be made in relation to the next king, Ahaz, who is as bad as his father Jotham is good.

27:2 *He did not invade the temple*—Unlike his father (26:16–20).

27:3–4—Like Uzziah, Jotham engages in building projects.

27:6—Jotham's success derived from a consistent placing of God at the center of his life.

reign; he reigned sixteen years in Jerusalem. ⁹Jotham slept with his ancestors, and they buried him in the city of David; and his son Ahaz succeeded him.

Reign of Ahaz

28 Ahaz was twenty years old when he began to reign; he reigned sixteen years in Jerusalem. He did not do what was right in the sight of the LORD, as his ancestor David had done, ²but he walked in the ways of the kings of Israel. He even made cast images for the Baals; ³and he made offerings in the valley of the son of Hinnom, and made his sons pass through fire, according to the abominable practices of the nations whom the LORD drove out before the people of Israel. ⁴He sacrificed and made offerings on the high places, on the hills, and under every green tree.

Aram and Israel Defeat Judah

5 Therefore the LORD his God gave him into the hand of the king of Aram, who defeated him and took captive a great number of his people and brought them to Damascus. He was also given into the hand of the king of Israel, who defeated him with great slaughter. ⁶Pekah son of Remaliah killed one hundred twenty thousand in Judah in one day, all of them valiant warriors, because they had abandoned the LORD, the God of their ancestors. ⁷And Zichri, a mighty warrior of Ephraim, killed the king's son Maaseiah, Azrikam the commander of the palace, and Elkanah the next in authority to the king.

Intervention of Oded

8 The people of Israel took captive two hundred thousand of their kin, women, sons, and daughters; they also took much booty from them and brought the booty to Samaria. ⁹But a prophet of the LORD was there, whose name was Oded; he went out to meet the army that came to Samaria, and said to them, "Because the LORD, the God of your ancestors, was angry with Judah, he gave them into your hand, but you have killed them in a rage that has reached up to heaven. ¹⁰Now you intend to subjugate the people of Judah and Jerusalem, male and female, as your slaves. But what have you except sins against the LORD your God? ¹¹Now hear me, and send back the captives whom you have taken from your kindred, for the fierce wrath of the LORD is upon you." ¹²Moreover, certain chiefs of the Ephraimites, Azariah son of Johanan, Berechiah son of Meshillemoth, Jehizkiah son of Shallum, and Amasa son of Hadlai, stood up against those who were coming from the war, ¹³and said to them, "You shall not bring the captives in here, for you propose to bring on us guilt against the LORD in addition to our present sins and guilt. For our guilt is already great, and there

---

28:1–27 Ahaz

The divided monarchy (10:1–28:27) ends as it had begun (chaps. 10–13), in rebellion and apostasy. This time, however, it is Judah who sins. Abijah's programmatic speech (13:4–12) still sets the agenda, but it is Ahaz, not Jeroboam, who makes *cast images* and worships foreign gods (28:2, 10–16, 23; cf. 13:8–9), closes the temple doors (28:24), repudiates the consecrated bread (29:18), extinguishes the lamps, and stops the sacrifices (29:7). The reversal of Israel and Judah is similarly depicted. Israel was defeated in Abijah's day (13:18); now Judah suffers defeat (28:19). At the schism Judah heeded Shemaiah with regard to Israel (11:1–4); now Israel obeys *Oded* with regard to Judah (28:9). Judah under Ahaz has now fallen to the northern level of apostasy at the schism.

28:5–15—The Syro-Ephraimite War.

28:5–8—God defeats Ahaz, using both *Aram* (Syria) and Israel (*Ephraim*) in separate battles.

28:9–10 Oded—Another prophet urges the north to reunite with their *kindred* (v. 11, 15; cf. v. 8) in the south and stop their deplorable treatment of the captives. A hallmark of justice is its humanitarian concern for all people, friend and foe alike.

28:12–15 Chiefs—A better translation is "leaders," i.e., not the king. The demise of the northern kings makes possible the reunification of all Israel, the inclusive goal of the chronicler's message to his community. Their confession of guilt follows the accusations of Abijah's address (13:4–12). The northerners now appear in a better light than the favored but apostate Judeans.

is fierce wrath against Israel." [14] So the warriors left the captives and the booty before the officials and all the assembly. [15] Then those who were mentioned by name got up and took the captives, and with the booty they clothed all that were naked among them; they clothed them, gave them sandals, provided them with food and drink, and anointed them; and carrying all the feeble among them on donkeys, they brought them to their kindred at Jericho, the city of palm trees. Then they returned to Samaria.

Assyria Refuses to Help Judah

[16] At that time King Ahaz sent to the king[a] of Assyria for help. [17] For the Edomites had again invaded and defeated Judah, and carried away captives. [18] And the Philistines had made raids on the cities in the Shephelah and the Negeb of Judah, and had taken Beth-shemesh, Aijalon, Gederoth, Soco with its villages, Timnah with its villages, and Gimzo with its villages; and they settled there. [19] For the LORD brought Judah low because of King Ahaz of Israel, for he had behaved without restraint in Judah and had been faithless to the LORD. [20] So King Tilgath-pilneser of Assyria came against him, and oppressed him instead of strengthening him. [21] For Ahaz plundered the house of the LORD and the houses of the king and of the officials, and gave tribute to the king of Assyria; but it did not help him.

Apostasy and Death of Ahaz

[22] In the time of his distress he became yet more faithless to the LORD—this same King Ahaz. [23] For he sacrificed to the gods of Damascus, which had defeated him, and said, "Because the gods of the kings of Aram helped them, I will sacrifice to them so that they may help me." But they were the ruin of him, and of all Israel. [24] Ahaz gathered together the utensils of the house of God, and cut in pieces the utensils of the house of God. He shut up the doors of the house of the LORD and made himself altars in every corner of Jerusalem. [25] In every city of Judah he made high places to make offerings to other gods, provoking to anger the LORD, the God of his ancestors. [26] Now the rest of his acts and all his ways, from first to last, are written in the Book of the Kings of Judah and Israel. [27] Ahaz slept with his ancestors, and they buried him in the city, in Jerusalem; but they did not bring him into the tombs of the kings of Israel. His son Hezekiah succeeded him.

Reign of Hezekiah

29 Hezekiah began to reign when he was twenty-five years old; he reigned twenty-nine years in Jerusalem. His mother's name was Abijah daughter of Zechariah. [2] He did what was right in the sight of the LORD, just as his ancestor David had done.

The Temple Cleansed

[3] In the first year of his reign, in the first month, he opened the doors of the house of the LORD and repaired them. [4] He brought in the priests and the

---

[a] Gk Syr Vg Compare 2 Kings 16.7: Heb kings

28:24—Ahab's greatest offense was to prevent public access to the temple.

29:1–36:23 The Reunited Monarchy
The genealogical introduction (1 Chr. 1–9) and the united monarchy of David and Solomon (1 Chr. 10–2 Chr. 9) had presented all Israel as a people united under a Davidic king around the Jerusalem temple. The third section, however, had presented all Israel as a divided monarchy (2 Chr. 10–28). In this final section, the Assyrian defeat of the north (2 Chr. 30:6) and the apostasy of Ahaz (28:6, 24–25) completely reverse the

situation that prevailed at the start of the divided monarchy.

29:1–32:33 Hezekiah
Hezekiah is presented as a second David and Solomon, who repairs the temple, reestablishes proper worship, and invites the north to join in passover celebration, restoring the ideal situation that had been lost. Whereas Kings emphasizes his political activity, Chronicles stresses the reforms.

29:1–36—Hezekiah first restores the temple.

29:3—Hezekiah reverses the apostasy of Ahaz

Levites and assembled them in the square on the east. ⁵He said to them, "Listen to me, Levites! Sanctify yourselves, and sanctify the house of the LORD, the God of your ancestors, and carry out the filth from the holy place. ⁶For our ancestors have been unfaithful and have done what was evil in the sight of the LORD our God; they have forsaken him, and have turned away their faces from the dwelling of the LORD, and turned their backs. ⁷They also shut the doors of the vestibule and put out the lamps, and have not offered incense or made burnt offerings in the holy place to the God of Israel. ⁸Therefore the wrath of the LORD came upon Judah and Jerusalem, and he has made them an object of horror, of astonishment, and of hissing, as you see with your own eyes. ⁹Our fathers have fallen by the sword and our sons and our daughters and our wives are in captivity for this. ¹⁰Now it is in my heart to make a covenant with the LORD, the God of Israel, so that his fierce anger may turn away from us. ¹¹My sons, do not now be negligent, for the LORD has chosen you to stand in his presence to minister to him, and to be his ministers and make offerings to him."

12 Then the Levites arose, Mahath son of Amasai, and Joel son of Azariah, of the sons of the Kohathites; and of the sons of Merari, Kish son of Abdi, and Azariah son of Jehallelel; and of the Gershonites, Joah son of Zimmah, and Eden son of Joah; ¹³and of the sons of Elizaphan, Shimri and Jeuel; and of the sons of Asaph, Zechariah and Matta-

niah; ¹⁴and of the sons of Heman, Jehuel and Shimei; and of the sons of Jeduthun, Shemaiah and Uzziel. ¹⁵They gathered their brothers, sanctified themselves, and went in as the king had commanded, by the words of the LORD, to cleanse the house of the LORD. ¹⁶The priests went into the inner part of the house of the LORD to cleanse it, and they brought out all the unclean things that they found in the temple of the LORD into the court of the house of the LORD; and the Levites took them and carried them out to the Wadi Kidron. ¹⁷They began to sanctify on the first day of the first month, and on the eighth day of the month they came to the vestibule of the LORD; then for eight days they sanctified the house of the LORD, and on the sixteenth day of the first month they finished. ¹⁸Then they went inside to King Hezekiah and said, "We have cleansed all the house of the LORD, the altar of burnt offering and all its utensils, and the table for the rows of bread and all its utensils. ¹⁹All the utensils that King Ahaz repudiated during his reign when he was faithless, we have made ready and sanctified; see, they are in front of the altar of the LORD."

Temple Worship Restored

20 Then King Hezekiah rose early, assembled the officials of the city, and went up to the house of the LORD. ²¹They brought seven bulls, seven rams, seven lambs, and seven male goats for a sin offering for the kingdom and for the sanctuary and for Judah. He commanded the priests the descendants of Aaron to offer them on the altar of

---

who had "shut up the doors of the house of the LORD" (28:24). By unlocking the door of the temple, Hezekiah symbolically reestablishes access to God.

29:4–19—Hezekiah literally cleanses the temple.

29:4–11—Hezekiah's instructions to the Levites recall Abijah's similar address (13:4–12).

29:5 *Filth*—Usually found in ritual contexts, here the word refers to neglect, not idolatry, since the temple had been closed.

29:6–10—Hezekiah's theological rationale employs the chronicler's familiar vocabulary: *unfaithful, forsaken him* (v. 6), *covenant* (v. 10) to stress the neglect of God and the temple under Ahaz.

29:18–19 *Utensils*—Symbols of religious continuity after the exile.

29:20–30—Hezekiah rededicates the sanctuary and the altar.

the LORD. [22] So they slaughtered the bulls, and the priests received the blood and dashed it against the altar; they slaughtered the rams and their blood was dashed against the altar; they also slaughtered the lambs and their blood was dashed against the altar. [23] Then the male goats for the sin offering were brought to the king and the assembly; they laid their hands on them, [24] and the priests slaughtered them and made a sin offering with their blood at the altar, to make atonement for all Israel. For the king commanded that the burnt offering and the sin offering should be made for all Israel.

25 He stationed the Levites in the house of the LORD with cymbals, harps, and lyres, according to the commandment of David and of Gad the king's seer and of the prophet Nathan, for the commandment was from the LORD through his prophets. [26] The Levites stood with the instruments of David, and the priests with the trumpets. [27] Then Hezekiah commanded that the burnt offering be offered on the altar. When the burnt offering began, the song to the LORD began also, and the trumpets, accompanied by the instruments of King David of Israel. [28] The whole assembly worshiped, the singers sang, and the trumpeters sounded; all this continued until the burnt offering was finished. [29] When the offering was finished, the king and all who were present with him bowed down and worshiped. [30] King Hezekiah and the officials commanded the Levites to sing praises to the LORD with the words of David and of the seer Asaph. They sang praises with gladness, and they bowed down and worshiped.

31 Then Hezekiah said, "You have now consecrated yourselves to the LORD; come near, bring sacrifices and thank offerings to the house of the LORD." The assembly brought sacrifices and thank offerings; and all who were of a willing heart brought burnt offerings. [32] The number of the burnt offerings that the assembly brought was seventy bulls, one hundred rams, and two hundred lambs; all these were for a burnt offering to the LORD. [33] The consecrated offerings were six hundred bulls and three thousand sheep. [34] But the priests were too few and could not skin all the burnt offerings, so, until other priests had sanctified themselves, their kindred, the Levites, helped them until the work was finished—for the Levites were more conscientious[a] than the priests in sanctifying themselves. [35] Besides the great number of burnt offerings there was the fat of the offerings of well-being, and there were the drink offerings for the burnt offerings. Thus the service of the house of the LORD was restored. [36] And Hezekiah and all the people rejoiced because of what God had done for the people; for the thing had come about suddenly.

The Great Passover

30 Hezekiah sent word to all Israel and Judah, and wrote letters also to Ephraim and Manasseh, that they should come to the house of the LORD

[a] Heb upright in heart

29:24 *All Israel . . . all Israel*—The repetition highlights concern for the members of the north.

29:25–30—Hezekiah restores sacrifice and worship under the musical leadership of the Levites, recalling David's installation of the ark (1 Chr. 15:16) and Solomon's dedication of the temple (2 Chr. 7:6).

29:31–36—Hezekiah reintroduces regular worship.

29:31 *Burnt offerings*—Totally consumed on the altar, these offerings symbolize a complete self-giving of the people, who willingly exceed Hezekiah's request (cf. 1 Chr. 29:17–18).

29:36b *Suddenly*—The speedy completion of the task within three weeks (cf. vv. 3 and 17) is gratefully attributed to God.

30:1–31:1—Second stage of the reform: *Passover*. Traditionally a commemoration of Israel's deliverance from Egypt, celebrated in the home, Passover is used here to reunite the nation in worship at the recently restored temple.

30:1–12—Hezekiah invites *all Israel and Judah*

at Jerusalem, to keep the passover to the LORD the God of Israel. ²For the king and his officials and all the assembly in Jerusalem had taken counsel to keep the passover in the second month ³(for they could not keep it at its proper time because the priests had not sanctified themselves in sufficient number, nor had the people assembled in Jerusalem). ⁴The plan seemed right to the king and all the assembly. ⁵So they decreed to make a proclamation throughout all Israel, from Beer-sheba to Dan, that the people should come and keep the passover to the LORD the God of Israel, at Jerusalem; for they had not kept it in great numbers as prescribed. ⁶So couriers went throughout all Israel and Judah with letters from the king and his officials, as the king had commanded, saying, "O people of Israel, return to the LORD, the God of Abraham, Isaac, and Israel, so that he may turn again to the remnant of you who have escaped from the hand of the kings of Assyria. ⁷Do not be like your ancestors and your kindred, who were faithless to the LORD God of their ancestors, so that he made them a desolation, as you see. ⁸Do not now be stiff-necked as your ancestors were, but yield yourselves to the LORD and come to his sanctuary, which he has sanctified forever, and serve the LORD your God, so that his fierce anger may turn away from you. ⁹For as you return to the LORD, your kindred and your children

will find compassion with their captors, and return to this land. For the LORD your God is gracious and merciful, and will not turn away his face from you, if you return to him."

10 So the couriers went from city to city through the country of Ephraim and Manasseh, and as far as Zebulun; but they laughed them to scorn, and mocked them. ¹¹Only a few from Asher, Manasseh, and Zebulun humbled themselves and came to Jerusalem. ¹²The hand of God was also on Judah to give them one heart to do what the king and the officials commanded by the word of the LORD.

13 Many people came together in Jerusalem to keep the festival of unleavened bread in the second month, a very large assembly. ¹⁴They set to work and removed the altars that were in Jerusalem, and all the altars for offering incense they took away and threw into the Wadi Kidron. ¹⁵They slaughtered the passover lamb on the fourteenth day of the second month. The priests and the Levites were ashamed, and they sanctified themselves and brought burnt offerings into the house of the LORD. ¹⁶They took their accustomed posts according to the law of Moses the man of God; the priests dashed the blood that they received[a] from the hands of the Levites. ¹⁷For there were many in the assembly

---

[a] Heb lacks *that they received*

(v. 1) *from Beer-sheba to Dan* (v. 5), to celebrate Passover, thus framing the period of the divided monarchy with calls to repentance (see Abijah's speech at the time of the schism, 13:4–12), thereby refusing to exclude the north as unbelievers, but rather recognizing them as fellow believers worthy of being welcomed in the name of the Lord.

30:2 *Second month*—Passover falls in the first month. Hezekiah allows an exception for those who are unclean or absent (Num. 9:9–11) to apply to all.

30:6–9—Hezekiah calls for the reunification of the nation following the Assyrian destruction of the northern kings.

30:6 *All Israel and Judah*—Hezekiah summons all to repentance, not just the north.

30:9 *Return*—Note the threefold repetition of this verb, which also means "repent."

30:10–12 *Only a few*—The number of northerners who *humbled themselves* (v. 11; cf. 7:14) to reunite all Israel was small, but its significance was great.

30:13–31:1—With the people reunified, at least symbolically, the chronicler describes the Passover, here called *festival of unleavened bread* (v. 13).

30:13–14—The priests had purified the sanctuary (29:16); now the people purify the city.

30:17—To accommodate the northerners, who

who had not sanctified themselves; therefore the Levites had to slaughter the passover lamb for everyone who was not clean, to make it holy to the LORD. [18] For a multitude of the people, many of them from Ephraim, Manasseh, Issachar, and Zebulun, had not cleansed themselves, yet they ate the passover otherwise than as prescribed. But Hezekiah prayed for them, saying, "The good LORD pardon all [19] who set their hearts to seek God, the LORD the God of their ancestors, even though not in accordance with the sanctuary's rules of cleanness." [20] The LORD heard Hezekiah, and healed the people. [21] The people of Israel who were present at Jerusalem kept the festival of unleavened bread seven days with great gladness; and the Levites and the priests praised the LORD day by day, accompanied by loud instruments for the LORD. [22] Hezekiah spoke encouragingly to all the Levites who showed good skill in the service of the LORD. So the people ate the food of the festival for seven days, sacrificing offerings of well-being and giving thanks to the LORD the God of their ancestors.

[23] Then the whole assembly agreed together to keep the festival for another seven days; so they kept it for another seven days with gladness. [24] For King Hezekiah of Judah gave the assembly a thousand bulls and seven thousand sheep for offerings, and the officials gave the assembly a thousand bulls and ten thousand sheep. The priests sanctified themselves in great numbers. [25] The whole assembly of Judah, the priests and the Levites, and the whole assembly that came out of Israel, and the resident aliens who came out of the land of Israel, and the resident aliens who lived in Judah, rejoiced. [26] There was great joy in Jerusalem, for since the time of Solomon son of King David of Israel there had been nothing like this in Jerusalem. [27] Then the priests and the Levites stood up and blessed the people, and their voice was heard; their prayer came to his holy dwelling in heaven.

Pagan Shrines Destroyed

31 Now when all this was finished, all Israel who were present went out to the cities of Judah and broke down the pillars, hewed down the sacred poles,[a] and pulled down the high places and the altars throughout all Judah and Benjamin, and in Ephraim and Manasseh, until they had destroyed them all. Then all the people of Israel returned to their cities, all to their individual properties.

2 Hezekiah appointed the divisions of the priests and of the Levites, division by division, everyone according to his service, the priests and the Levites, for burnt offerings and offerings of well-being, to minister in the gates of the camp of the LORD and to give thanks and praise. [3] The contribution of the king from his own possessions was for the burnt offerings: the burnt offerings of morning and evening, and the burnt offerings for the sabbaths, the new moons, and the appointed festivals, as it is written in the law of the LORD. [4] He commanded the people who lived in Jerusalem to give the portion due

[a] Heb *Asherim*

---

apparently had not been able to purify themselves, *the Levites* prepared some *passover lambs*. Ordinarily, heads of households should slaughter the lambs (Exod. 12:6).

30:18–20—Recalling Solomon's prayer (cf. 7:14), Hezekiah reminds the people of God's forgiveness.

31:1 *Ephraim and Manasseh*—The purging of Ahaz's idolatry expands into the north.

31:2–21—In stage three, Hezekiah provides for regular worship. This passage displays the importance of stewardship. The greater burden always seems to fall on the people, then as now.

31:2–4—Appointment of priestly and Levitical divisions, provision of sacrificial animals, and arrangements for clergy stipends (cf. 1 Chr. 23–26; 29:3 for David, and 2 Chr. 8:12–16; 9:10–11; 7:5 for Solomon).

to the priests and the Levites, so that they might devote themselves to the law of the LORD. ⁵ As soon as the word spread, the people of Israel gave in abundance the first fruits of grain, wine, oil, honey, and of all the produce of the field; and they brought in abundantly the tithe of everything. ⁶ The people of Israel and Judah who lived in the cities of Judah also brought in the tithe of cattle and sheep, and the tithe of the dedicated things that had been consecrated to the LORD their God, and laid them in heaps. ⁷ In the third month they began to pile up the heaps, and finished them in the seventh month. ⁸ When Hezekiah and the officials came and saw the heaps, they blessed the LORD and his people Israel. ⁹ Hezekiah questioned the priests and the Levites about the heaps. ¹⁰ The chief priest Azariah, who was of the house of Zadok, answered him, "Since they began to bring the contributions into the house of the LORD, we have had enough to eat and have plenty to spare; for the LORD has blessed his people, so that we have this great supply left over."

Reorganization of Priests and Levites

11 Then Hezekiah commanded them to prepare store-chambers in the house of the LORD; and they prepared them. ¹² Faithfully they brought in the contributions, the tithes and the dedicated things. The chief officer in charge of them was Conaniah the Levite, with his brother Shimei as second; ¹³ while Jehiel, Azaziah, Nahath, Asahel, Jerimoth, Jozabad, Eliel, Ismachiah, Mahath, and Benaiah were overseers assisting Conaniah and his brother Shimei, by the appointment of King Hezekiah and of Azariah the chief officer of the house of God. ¹⁴ Kore son of Imnah the Levite, keeper of the east gate, was in charge of the freewill offerings to God, to apportion the contribution reserved for the LORD and the most holy offerings. ¹⁵ Eden, Miniamin, Jeshua, Shemaiah, Amariah, and Shecaniah were faithfully assisting him in the cities of the priests, to distribute the portions to their kindred, old and young alike, by divisions, ¹⁶ except those enrolled by genealogy, males from three years old and upwards, all who entered the house of the LORD as the duty of each day required, for their service according to their offices, by their divisions. ¹⁷ The enrollment of the priests was according to their ancestral houses; that of the Levites from twenty years old and upwards was according to their offices, by their divisions. ¹⁸ The priests were enrolled with all their little children, their wives, their sons, and their daughters, the whole multitude; for they were faithful in keeping themselves holy. ¹⁹ And for the descendants of Aaron, the priests, who were in the fields of common land belonging to their towns, town by town, the people designated by name were to distribute portions to every male among the priests and to everyone among the Levites who was enrolled.

20 Hezekiah did this throughout all Judah; he did what was good and right and faithful before the LORD his God. ²¹ And every work that he undertook in the service of the house of God, and in accordance with the law and the commandments, to seek his God, he did with all his heart; and he prospered.

Sennacherib's Invasion

32 After these things and these acts of faithfulness, King Sennacherib of Assyria came and invaded Judah

---

31:5–10—The generous response recalls contributions to the tabernacle (Exod. 36:2–7) and the temple (1 Chr. 29:1–9).

31:11–19—Arrangements for storing (vv. 11–13) and distributing (vv. 14–19) the contributions.

32:1–33—Hezekiah's political achievements.

Framing statements of success (31:20–21; 32:30) illustrate that blessing is the reward of faithfulness.

32:1–23—Hezekiah's trust in foreign alliances, surrender to Sennacherib, payment of tribute, and stripping of the temple (cf. 2 Kgs. 18–20; Isa.

and encamped against the fortified cities, thinking to win them for himself. [2] When Hezekiah saw that Sennacherib had come and intended to fight against Jerusalem, [3] he planned with his officers and his warriors to stop the flow of the springs that were outside the city; and they helped him. [4] A great many people were gathered, and they stopped all the springs and the wadi that flowed through the land, saying, "Why should the Assyrian kings come and find water in abundance?" [5] Hezekiah[a] set to work resolutely and built up the entire wall that was broken down, and raised towers on it,[b] and outside it he built another wall; he also strengthened the Millo in the city of David, and made weapons and shields in abundance. [6] He appointed combat commanders over the people, and gathered them together to him in the square at the gate of the city and spoke encouragingly to them, saying, [7] "Be strong and of good courage. Do not be afraid or dismayed before the king of Assyria and all the horde that is with him; for there is one greater with us than with him. [8] With him is an arm of flesh; but with us is the LORD our God, to help us and to fight our battles." The people were encouraged by the words of King Hezekiah of Judah.

[9] After this, while King Sennacherib of Assyria was at Lachish with all his forces, he sent his servants to Jerusalem to King Hezekiah of Judah and to all the people of Judah that were in Jerusalem, saying, [10] "Thus says King Sennacherib of Assyria: On what are you relying, that you undergo the siege of Jerusalem? [11] Is not Hezekiah misleading you, handing you over to die by famine and by thirst, when he tells you, 'The LORD our God will save us from the hand of the king of Assyria'? [12] Was it not this same Hezekiah who took away his high places and his altars and commanded Judah and Jerusalem, saying, 'Before one altar you shall worship, and upon it you shall make your offerings'? [13] Do you not know what I and my ancestors have done to all the peoples of other lands? Were the gods of the nations of those lands at all able to save their lands out of my hand? [14] Who among all the gods of those nations that my ancestors utterly destroyed was able to save his people from my hand, that your God should be able to save you from my hand? [15] Now therefore do not let Hezekiah deceive you or mislead you in this fashion, and do not believe him, for no god of any nation or kingdom has been able to save his people from my hand or from the hand of my ancestors. How much less will your God save you out of my hand!"

16 His servants said still more against the Lord GOD and against his servant Hezekiah. [17] He also wrote letters to throw contempt on the LORD the God of Israel and to speak against him, saying, "Just as the gods of the nations in other lands did not rescue their people from my hands, so the God of Hezekiah will not rescue his people from my hand." [18] They shouted it with a loud voice in the language of Judah to the people of Jerusalem who were on the wall, to frighten and terrify them, in order that they might take the city. [19] They spoke of the God of Jerusalem as if he were like the gods of the peoples of the earth, which are the work of human hands.

[a] Heb He　[b] Vg: Heb and raised on the towers

38–39) are omitted, leaving an emphasis on the effectiveness of prayer.

32:1 *Sennacherib*—King of Assyria (705–681 BCE) who invaded Judah in 701.

32:2–6—Building projects, fortifications, and the mustering of large armies prepare for battle and indicate divine favor.

32:7–8—Hezekiah expresses complete trust in God, as had David, Asa, and Jehoshaphat (1 Chr. 22:13; 2 Chr. 14:11; 19:5–7; 20:15–17, 20).

32:9–12—Sennacherib taunts the people.

32:12–15—Wrongly assuming that Hezekiah had destroyed God's sanctuaries, the Assyrian messenger insinuates that Hezekiah cannot be trusted and that God cannot deliver Judah.

Sennacherib's Defeat and Death

20 Then King Hezekiah and the prophet Isaiah son of Amoz prayed because of this and cried to heaven. 21 And the LORD sent an angel who cut off all the mighty warriors and commanders and officers in the camp of the king of Assyria. So he returned in disgrace to his own land. When he came into the house of his god, some of his own sons struck him down there with the sword. 22 So the LORD saved Hezekiah and the inhabitants of Jerusalem from the hand of King Sennacherib of Assyria and from the hand of all his enemies; he gave them rest*a* on every side. 23 Many brought gifts to the LORD in Jerusalem and precious things to King Hezekiah of Judah, so that he was exalted in the sight of all nations from that time onward.

Hezekiah's Sickness

24 In those days Hezekiah became sick and was at the point of death. He prayed to the LORD, and he answered him and gave him a sign. 25 But Hezekiah did not respond according to the benefit done to him, for his heart was proud. Therefore wrath came upon him and upon Judah and Jerusalem. 26 Then Hezekiah humbled himself for the pride of his heart, both he and the inhabitants of Jerusalem, so that the wrath of the LORD did not come upon them in the days of Hezekiah.

Hezekiah's Prosperity and Achievements

27 Hezekiah had very great riches and honor; and he made for himself trea-suries for silver, for gold, for precious stones, for spices, for shields, and for all kinds of costly objects; 28 storehouses also for the yield of grain, wine, and oil; and stalls for all kinds of cattle, and sheepfolds.*b* 29 He likewise provided cities for himself, and flocks and herds in abundance; for God had given him very great possessions. 30 This same Hezekiah closed the upper outlet of the waters of Gihon and directed them down to the west side of the city of David. Hezekiah prospered in all his works. 31 So also in the matter of the envoys of the officials of Babylon, who had been sent to him to inquire about the sign that had been done in the land, God left him to himself, in order to test him and to know all that was in his heart.

32 Now the rest of the acts of Hezekiah, and his good deeds, are written in the vision of the prophet Isaiah son of Amoz in the Book of the Kings of Judah and Israel. 33 Hezekiah slept with his ancestors, and they buried him on the ascent to the tombs of the descendants of David; and all Judah and the inhabitants of Jerusalem did him honor at his death. His son Manasseh succeeded him.

Reign of Manasseh

33 Manasseh was twelve years old when he began to reign; he reigned fifty-five years in Jerusalem. 2 He did what was evil in the sight of the LORD, according to the abominable

a Gk Vg: Heb *guided them*   *b* Gk Vg: Heb *flocks for folds*

32:20–23—Hezekiah and Isaiah pray together. Deliverance follows (cf. 7:13–15). Rest, tribute, and international regard portray Hezekiah as a second Solomon (1 Chr. 22:8–10; 2 Chr. 9:23–24).

32:24–26—Hezekiah's *pride* leads to divine *wrath*. Unlike Asa (16:12) and Uzziah (26:16–21), however, Hezekiah *humbled himself* (cf. God's promise to Solomon in 7:14) and experienced a reprieve.

32:27–33—This laudatory summary of Hezekiah includes the usual indicators of blessing: wealth, building projects, and prosperity.

33:1–20 Manasseh

Elsewhere, Manasseh is the worst of Judah's kings, totally unrepentant, and responsible for the Babylonian exile (2 Kgs. 21:11–16; cf. 24:3–4; Jer. 15:4). Chronicles, however, blames the exile on the unfaithfulness of Judah, not Manasseh (2 Chr. 36:14–17). Manasseh is portrayed as a paradigm of exile and restoration who suffered divine punishment (33:11) for his sins (vv. 2–9) but who repented, changed his ways, and received forgiveness (vv. 12–19). He is thus a very positive example of what can be accomplished through repentance.

practices of the nations whom the LORD drove out before the people of Israel. ³For he rebuilt the high places that his father Hezekiah had pulled down, and erected altars to the Baals, made sacred poles,ᵃ worshiped all the host of heaven, and served them. ⁴He built altars in the house of the LORD, of which the LORD had said, "In Jerusalem shall my name be forever." ⁵He built altars for all the host of heaven in the two courts of the house of the LORD. ⁶He made his son pass through fire in the valley of the son of Hinnom, practiced soothsaying and augury and sorcery, and dealt with mediums and with wizards. He did much evil in the sight of the LORD, provoking him to anger. ⁷The carved image of the idol that he had made he set in the house of God, of which God said to David and to his son Solomon, "In this house, and in Jerusalem, which I have chosen out of all the tribes of Israel, I will put my name forever; ⁸I will never again remove the feet of Israel from the land that I appointed for your ancestors, if only they will be careful to do all that I have commanded them, all the law, the statutes, and the ordinances given through Moses." ⁹Manasseh misled Judah and the inhabitants of Jerusalem, so that they did more evil than the nations whom the LORD had destroyed before the people of Israel.

Manasseh Restored after Repentance

10 The LORD spoke to Manasseh and to his people, but they gave no heed. ¹¹Therefore the LORD brought against them the commanders of the army of the king of Assyria, who took Manasseh captive in manacles, bound him with fetters, and brought him to Babylon. ¹²While he was in distress he entreated the favor of the LORD his God and humbled himself greatly before the God of his ancestors. ¹³He prayed to him, and God received his entreaty, heard his plea, and restored him again to Jerusalem and to his kingdom. Then Manasseh knew that the LORD indeed was God.

14 Afterward he built an outer wall for the city of David west of Gihon, in the valley, reaching the entrance at the Fish Gate; he carried it around Ophel, and raised it to a very great height. He also put commanders of the army in all the fortified cities in Judah. ¹⁵He took away the foreign gods and the idol from the house of the LORD, and all the altars that he had built on the mountain of the house of the LORD and in Jerusalem, and he threw them out of the city. ¹⁶He also restored the altar of the LORD and offered on it sacrifices of well-being and of thanksgiving; and he commanded Judah to serve the LORD the God of Israel. ¹⁷The people, however, still sacrificed at the high places, but only to the LORD their God.

Death of Manasseh

18 Now the rest of the acts of Manasseh, his prayer to his God, and the words of the seers who spoke to him in the name of the LORD God of Israel, these are in the Annals of the Kings of Israel. ¹⁹His prayer, and how God received his entreaty, all his sin and his

ᵃ Heb Asheroth

33:1—The extraordinary length of Manasseh's reign may account for the chronicler's positive portrayal. Nowhere else, however, is length of reign a sign of blessing.

33:3—Manasseh worshiped old Canaanite fertility deities (Asherah) and gods associated with the zodiac (Deut. 4:19; 17:3).

33:11—Manasseh's exile to *Babylon* by an Assyrian king foreshadows the later exile of the people.

33:12–13—Manasseh's unexpected repentance and restoration, perhaps the major theme of these books, confirms God's promise to Solomon (7:14).

33:14–17—Building programs are a frequent sign of blessing (11:5; 14:6–7; 17:12; 27:3–4; 34:10–13), as are strong armies (11:1; 14:8; 25:5; 26:10). In the reforms, Manasseh cancels his own cultic innovations and reestablishes proper worship, though he fails to completely undo the evil of 33:2–9.

faithlessness, the sites on which he built high places and set up the sacred poles[a] and the images, before he humbled himself, these are written in the records of the seers.[b] 20 So Manasseh slept with his ancestors, and they buried him in his house. His son Amon succeeded him.

Amon's Reign and Death

21 Amon was twenty-two years old when he began to reign; he reigned two years in Jerusalem. 22 He did what was evil in the sight of the LORD, as his father Manasseh had done. Amon sacrificed to all the images that his father Manasseh had made, and served them. 23 He did not humble himself before the LORD, as his father Manasseh had humbled himself, but this Amon incurred more and more guilt. 24 His servants conspired against him and killed him in his house. 25 But the people of the land killed all those who had conspired against King Amon; and the people of the land made his son Josiah king to succeed him.

Reign of Josiah

34 Josiah was eight years old when he began to reign; he reigned thirty-one years in Jerusalem. 2 He did what was right in the sight of the LORD, and walked in the ways of his ancestor David; he did not turn aside to the right or to the left. 3 For in the eighth year of his reign, while he was still a boy, he began to seek the God of his ancestor David, and in the twelfth year he began to purge Judah and Jerusalem of the high places, the sacred poles,[a] and the carved and the cast images. 4 In his presence they pulled down the altars of the Baals; he demolished the incense altars that stood above them. He broke down the sacred poles[a] and the carved and the cast images; he made dust of them and scattered it over the graves of those who had sacrificed to them. 5 He also burned the bones of the priests on their altars, and purged Judah and Jerusalem. 6 In the towns of Manasseh, Ephraim, and Simeon, and as far as Naphtali, in their ruins[c] all around, 7 he broke down the altars, beat the sacred poles[a] and the images into powder, and demolished all the incense altars throughout all the land of Israel. Then he returned to Jerusalem.

Discovery of the Book of the Law

8 In the eighteenth year of his reign, when he had purged the land and the house, he sent Shaphan son of Azaliah, Maaseiah the governor of the city, and Joah son of Joahaz, the recorder, to repair the house of the LORD his God. 9 They came to the high priest Hilkiah and delivered the money that had been brought into the house of God, which the Levites, the keepers of the threshold, had collected from Manasseh and Ephraim and from all the remnant of Israel and from all Judah and Benjamin and from the inhabitants of Jerusalem. 10 They

---

[a] Heb *Asherim* [b] One Ms Gk: MT *of Hozai* [c] Meaning of Heb uncertain

---

33:21–25 Amon
Amon's evil reverses the good of Manasseh's last years and sets the stage for Josiah's reforms.

34:1–36:1 Josiah
Josiah was one of Israel's most important kings. This portrayal is less glowing than that of Kings. The sequence of events is also different. Second Kings depicts the reforms and repair of the temple as a single response to the discovery of the book of the law in Josiah's eighteenth year. In 2 Chronicles, however, the reform begins with Josiah seeking God in the eighth year of his reign (34:3a) and continues through his twelfth (v. 3b) and eighteenth year (v. 8). The emphasis on religious reform is also reduced to highlight the Passover.

34:1–7—Early reforms. Josiah's youth (sixteen years old when he began his reforms) reminds the church that God uses faithful followers of all ages.

34:6 *Manasseh, Ephraim, Simeon, and Naphtali*—In a strong effort of inclusivity Josiah carries his reform to areas of the former northern kingdom reclaimed from Assyrian domination, re-uniting all Israel under a Davidic king. Even Hezekiah had only invited the north to participate.

34:8–33—Temple repair, discovery of the book of the law, and covenant renewal.

delivered it to the workers who had the oversight of the house of the LORD, and the workers who were working in the house of the LORD gave it for repairing and restoring the house. 11 They gave it to the carpenters and the builders to buy quarried stone, and timber for binders, and beams for the buildings that the kings of Judah had let go to ruin. 12 The people did the work faithfully. Over them were appointed the Levites Jahath and Obadiah, of the sons of Merari, along with Zechariah and Meshullam, of the sons of the Kohathites, to have oversight. Other Levites, all skillful with instruments of music, 13 were over the burden bearers and directed all who did work in every kind of service; and some of the Levites were scribes, and officials, and gatekeepers.

14 While they were bringing out the money that had been brought into the house of the LORD, the priest Hilkiah found the book of the law of the LORD given through Moses. 15 Hilkiah said to the secretary Shaphan, "I have found the book of the law in the house of the LORD"; and Hilkiah gave the book to Shaphan. 16 Shaphan brought the book to the king, and further reported to the king, "All that was committed to your servants they are doing. 17 They have emptied out the money that was found in the house of the LORD and have delivered it into the hand of the overseers and the workers." 18 The secretary Shaphan informed the king, "The priest Hilkiah has given me a book." Shaphan then read it aloud to the king.

19 When the king heard the words of the law he tore his clothes. 20 Then the king commanded Hilkiah, Ahikam son of Shaphan, Abdon son of Micah, the secretary Shaphan, and the king's servant Asaiah: 21 "Go, inquire of the LORD for me and for those who are left in Israel and in Judah, concerning the words of the book that has been found; for the wrath of the LORD that is poured out on us is great, because our ancestors did not keep the word of the LORD, to act in accordance with all that is written in this book."

The Prophet Huldah Consulted

22 So Hilkiah and those whom the king had sent went to the prophet Huldah, the wife of Shallum son of Tokhath son of Hasrah, keeper of the wardrobe (who lived in Jerusalem in the Second Quarter) and spoke to her to that effect. 23 She declared to them, "Thus says the LORD, the God of Israel: Tell the man who sent you to me, 24 Thus says the LORD: I will indeed bring disaster upon this place and upon its inhabitants, all the curses that are written in the book that was read before the king of Judah. 25 Because they have forsaken me and have made offerings to other gods, so that they have provoked me to anger with all the works of their hands, my wrath will be poured out on this place and will not be quenched. 26 But as to the king of Judah, who sent you to inquire of the LORD, thus shall you say to him: Thus says the LORD, the God of Israel: Regarding the words that you have heard, 27 because your heart was penitent and you humbled yourself before God when you heard his words against this place and its inhabitants, and you have humbled yourself before me, and have torn your clothes and wept before me, I also have heard you, says the

---

34:14—*The book of the law* Hilkiah found during the temple repairs (2 Kgs. 22:8) is possibly some form of the book of Deuteronomy.

34:21 *Inquire of the LORD*—Prophets often warn kings in Chronicles. Here Josiah actively seeks God's guidance. Discipleship is more than passively knowing, and the young king's active seeking is exemplary.

34:22–25—*Huldah* announces Jerusalem's destruction.

34:26–28 *In peace*—Josiah's tragic death (35:23–24) conflicts with this assurance. God's response to Josiah's repentance is another instance of the promise made to Solomon in 7:14.

Lord. ²⁸ I will gather you to your ancestors and you shall be gathered to your grave in peace; your eyes shall not see all the disaster that I will bring on this place and its inhabitants." They took the message back to the king.

The Covenant Renewed

29 Then the king sent word and gathered together all the elders of Judah and Jerusalem. ³⁰ The king went up to the house of the Lord, with all the people of Judah, the inhabitants of Jerusalem, the priests and the Levites, all the people both great and small; he read in their hearing all the words of the book of the covenant that had been found in the house of the Lord. ³¹ The king stood in his place and made a covenant before the Lord, to follow the Lord, keeping his commandments, his decrees, and his statutes, with all his heart and all his soul, to perform the words of the covenant that were written in this book. ³² Then he made all who were present in Jerusalem and in Benjamin pledge themselves to it. And the inhabitants of Jerusalem acted according to the covenant of God, the God of their ancestors. ³³ Josiah took away all the abominations from all the territory that belonged to the people of Israel, and made all who were in Israel worship the Lord their God. All his days they did not turn away from following the Lord the God of their ancestors.

Celebration of the Passover

35 Josiah kept a passover to the Lord in Jerusalem; they slaughtered the passover lamb on the fourteenth day of the first month. ² He appointed the priests to their offices and encouraged them in the service of the house of the Lord. ³ He said to the Levites who taught all Israel and who were holy to the Lord, "Put the holy ark in the house that Solomon son of David, king of Israel, built; you need no longer carry it on your shoulders. Now serve the Lord your God and his people Israel. ⁴ Make preparations by your ancestral houses by your divisions, following the written directions of King David of Israel and the written directions of his son Solomon. ⁵ Take position in the holy place according to the groupings of the ancestral houses of your kindred the people, and let there be Levites for each division of an ancestral house.^a ⁶ Slaughter the passover lamb, sanctify yourselves, and on behalf of your kindred make preparations, acting according to the word of the Lord by Moses."

7 Then Josiah contributed to the people, as passover offerings for all that were present, lambs and kids from the flock to the number of thirty thousand, and three thousand bulls; these were from the king's possessions. ⁸ His officials contributed willingly to the people, to the priests, and to the Levites. Hilkiah, Zechariah, and Jehiel, the chief officers of the house of God, gave to the priests for the passover offerings two thousand six hundred lambs and kids and three hundred bulls. ⁹ Conaniah also, and his brothers Shemaiah and Nethanel, and Hashabiah and Jeiel and Jozabad, the chiefs of the Levites, gave to the Levites for the passover offerings five thousand lambs and kids and five hundred bulls.

10 When the service had been prepared for, the priests stood in their

^a Meaning of Heb uncertain

34:29–32—Josiah renews *the covenant*. By placing the religious reforms in 2 Kgs. 23:1–3 before the discovery of the law book (see 2 Chr. 34:3–7 and summarized in v. 33), the covenant renewal now introduces a more detailed account of Josiah's Passover.

35:1–19—Josiah's *Passover*. Josiah's concern to bring the community back to their roots in worship reminds us that worship brings meaning and identity to lives that are often mundane.

35:3–4—The *Levites'* role increases to include teaching, bearing the ark, and the slaughter and preparation of sacrificial animals.

35:7 *King's possessions*—The size of Josiah's contribution recalls David's (1 Chr. 29:3–9).

place, and the Levites in their divisions according to the king's command. [11] They slaughtered the passover lamb, and the priests dashed the blood that they received[a] from them, while the Levites did the skinning. [12] They set aside the burnt offerings so that they might distribute them according to the groupings of the ancestral houses of the people, to offer to the LORD, as it is written in the book of Moses. And they did the same with the bulls. [13] They roasted the passover lamb with fire according to the ordinance; and they boiled the holy offerings in pots, in caldrons, and in pans, and carried them quickly to all the people. [14] Afterward they made preparations for themselves and for the priests, because the priests the descendants of Aaron were occupied in offering the burnt offerings and the fat parts until night; so the Levites made preparations for themselves and for the priests, the descendants of Aaron. [15] The singers, the descendants of Asaph, were in their place according to the command of David, and Asaph, and Heman, and the king's seer Jeduthun. The gatekeepers were at each gate; they did not need to interrupt their service, for their kindred the Levites made preparations for them.

16 So all the service of the LORD was prepared that day, to keep the passover and to offer burnt offerings on the altar of the LORD, according to the command of King Josiah. [17] The people of Israel who were present kept the passover at that time, and the festival of unleavened bread seven days. [18] No passover like it had been kept in Israel since the days of the prophet Samuel; none of the kings of Israel had kept such a passover as was kept by Josiah, by the priests and the Levites, by all Judah and Israel who were present, and by the inhabitants of Jerusalem. [19] In the eighteenth year of the reign of Josiah this passover was kept.

Defeat by Pharaoh Neco and Death of Josiah

20 After all this, when Josiah had set the temple in order, King Neco of Egypt went up to fight at Carchemish on the Euphrates, and Josiah went out against him. [21] But Neco[b] sent envoys to him, saying, "What have I to do with you, king of Judah? I am not coming against you today, but against the house with which I am at war; and God has commanded me to hurry. Cease opposing God, who is with me, so that he will not destroy you." [22] But Josiah would not turn away from him, but disguised himself in order to fight with him. He did not listen to the words of Neco from the mouth of God, but joined battle in the plain of Megiddo. [23] The archers shot King Josiah; and the king said to his servants, "Take me away, for I am badly wounded." [24] So his servants took him out of the chariot and carried him in his second chariot[c] and brought him to Jerusalem. There he died, and was buried in the tombs of his ancestors. All Judah and Jerusalem mourned for Josiah. [25] Jeremiah also uttered a lament for Josiah, and all the singing men and singing women have spoken of Josiah in their laments to this day. They made these a custom in Israel; they are recorded in the Laments. [26] Now the rest of the acts of Josiah and his faithful deeds in accordance with what is written in the law of the LORD, [27] and his acts, first and last, are written in the Book of the Kings of Israel and Judah.

---

a Heb lacks *that they received*   *b* Heb *he*   *c* Or *the chariot of his deputy*

35:17–18 *And Israel*—The presence of northerners shows an inclusive concern for all Israel.

35:20–36:1—Josiah's death. Josiah's tragic death, thirteen years later, is due to the king's failure to heed a "prophetic" word *from the mouth of God* (v. 22) couched in an Egyptian pharaoh's request for safe passage. Believers must be able to discern God's word, regardless of who speaks it. While 1 John 4:1 warns us about false prophets, this text encourages us to be open to God's activity in unexpected quarters.

Reign of Jehoahaz

36 The people of the land took Jehoahaz son of Josiah and made him king to succeed his father in Jerusalem. ² Jehoahaz was twenty-three years old when he began to reign; he reigned three months in Jerusalem. ³ Then the king of Egypt deposed him in Jerusalem and laid on the land a tribute of one hundred talents of silver and one talent of gold. ⁴ The king of Egypt made his brother Eliakim king over Judah and Jerusalem, and changed his name to Jehoiakim; but Neco took his brother Jehoahaz and carried him to Egypt.

Reign and Captivity of Jehoiakim

5 Jehoiakim was twenty-five years old when he began to reign; he reigned eleven years in Jerusalem. He did what was evil in the sight of the LORD his God. ⁶ Against him King Nebuchadnezzar of Babylon came up, and bound him with fetters to take him to Babylon. ⁷ Nebuchadnezzar also carried some of the vessels of the house of the LORD to Babylon and put them in his palace in Babylon. ⁸ Now the rest of the acts of Jehoiakim, and the abominations that he did, and what was found against him, are written in the Book of the Kings of Israel and Judah; and his son Jehoiachin succeeded him.

Reign and Captivity of Jehoiachin

9 Jehoiachin was eight years old when he began to reign; he reigned three months and ten days in Jerusalem. He did what was evil in the sight of the LORD. ¹⁰ In the spring of the year King Nebuchadnezzar sent and brought him to Babylon, along with the precious vessels of the house of the LORD, and made his brother Zedekiah king over Judah and Jerusalem.

Reign of Zedekiah

11 Zedekiah was twenty-one years old when he began to reign; he reigned eleven years in Jerusalem. ¹² He did what was evil in the sight of the LORD his God. He did not humble himself before the prophet Jeremiah who spoke from the mouth of the LORD. ¹³ He also rebelled against King Nebuchadnezzar, who had made him swear by God; he stiffened his neck and hardened his heart against turning to the LORD, the God of Israel. ¹⁴ All the leading priests and the people also were exceedingly unfaithful, following all the abominations of the nations; and they polluted the house of the LORD that he had consecrated in Jerusalem.

The Fall of Jerusalem

15 The LORD, the God of their ancestors, sent persistently to them by his

---

36:2–21 Judah's Last Kings
Judah's last four kings ruled during the power struggle that accompanied the waning of Assyria. The chronicler depicts a spiraling decline in which the fate of Israel is foreshadowed in the personal "exile" of each of these kings. Repeated references to doing *evil* (vv. 5, 9, 12), deportation (vv. 3, 4, 6, 10) and loss of temple *vessels* (vv. 7, 10, 18, 19) provide a theological rationale for the inevitability of the exile.

36:2–4—Jehoahaz.

36:4—Egyptian domination is implied in the change of name from *Eliakim* to *Jehoiakim*.

36:5–8—Jehoiakim. The themes of royal deportation and temple desecration again predominate to the exclusion of most of 2 Kgs. 23:34–24:6.

36:9–10—Jehoiakin. Only the themes of deportation and desecration remain, apart from the necessary details of accession.

36:9 *Eight years old*—Better, "eighteen" (2 Kgs. 24:13).

36:11–16—Zedekiah. The pattern of royal deportation and plunder of the temple vessels becomes a theological explanation of Judah's final destruction and exile.

36:12–13—Zedekiah's disobedience is blamed for the exile.

36:14 *Unfaithful*—The people share the guilt. Their faithlessness, seen in the genealogies (1 Chr. 5:25–26; 9:1), in Saul (1 Chr. 10:13), and regularly throughout Chronicles, brings this familiar theme to a climax.

36:15–16—Failure to repent caused the exile, not the accumulated guilt and sin of the people, as in 2 Kings.

messengers, because he had compassion on his people and on his dwelling place; [16] but they kept mocking the messengers of God, despising his words, and scoffing at his prophets, until the wrath of the LORD against his people became so great that there was no remedy.

17 Therefore he brought up against them the king of the Chaldeans, who killed their youths with the sword in the house of their sanctuary, and had no compassion on young man or young woman, the aged or the feeble; he gave them all into his hand. [18] All the vessels of the house of God, large and small, and the treasures of the house of the LORD, and the treasures of the king and of his officials, all these he brought to Babylon. [19] They burned the house of God, broke down the wall of Jerusalem, burned all its palaces with fire, and destroyed all its precious vessels. [20] He took into exile in Babylon those who had escaped from the sword, and they became servants to him and to his sons until the establishment of the kingdom of Persia, [21] to fulfill the word of the LORD by the mouth of Jeremiah, until the land had made up for its sabbaths. All the days that it lay desolate it kept sabbath, to fulfill seventy years.

Cyrus Proclaims Liberty for the Exiles

22 In the first year of King Cyrus of Persia, in fulfillment of the word of the LORD spoken by Jeremiah, the LORD stirred up the spirit of King Cyrus of Persia so that he sent a herald throughout all his kingdom and also declared in a written edict: [23] "Thus says King Cyrus of Persia: The LORD, the God of heaven, has given me all the kingdoms of the earth, and he has charged me to build him a house at Jerusalem, which is in Judah. Whoever is among you of all his people, may the LORD his God be with him! Let him go up."

36:17–21—The chronicler's theological explanation of the exile.

36:17–20 All—Five repetitions emphasize God's total destruction of the temple and the city and the complete elimination of the people from the land.

36:21—The exile is limited to seventy years (Jer. 25:11–12; 29:10), during which time the land will experience Sabbath rest to atone for 490 (7 × 70) years of neglect (Lev. 26:34–39).

36:22–23—A citation of Ezra 1:1–3a, itself a citation of the decree of Cyrus in 538 BCE, offers hope by reversing the exilic situation of 2 Chr. 17–21 and showing that exile need not be God's final word. God had previously used Nebuchadnezzar of Babylon to destroy the temple (36:17–19) and exile the survivors (v. 20). Now God uses another foreign ruler to rebuild the temple and bring the exiles home. God's invitation, delivered through Cyrus, affirms that the future is always open with God.

EZRA–NEHEMIAH

The books of Ezra and Nehemiah, separate works in English Bibles, appear as a single book in the earliest manuscripts, suggesting that they are best read and interpreted as a literary whole. The work was written in Judah, probably in Jerusalem, sometime during the Persian period (586–332 BCE), after the return from Babylon. Uncertain dates for Ezra and differing understandings of the compositional history of this material make precise dating impossible, though recent scholarship seems to favor a date somewhere in the first quarter of the fourth century. The traditional ordering holds that Ezra arrived in Jerusalem in 458, in the seventh year of King Artaxerxes (Ezra 7:7–8) and that Nehemiah followed him in 445, in the twentieth year of Artaxerxes (Neh. 1:1; 2:1; 5:14). There is some historical warrant for supposing that Nehemiah preceded Ezra historically, and many scholars have assumed this to be the case. If this is true, then the present shape of Ezra–Nehemiah is a theologically significant reordering of the material that places Ezra's religious and humanitarian work of reestablishing the community of those who had returned from Babylon under the provisions of the law before Nehemiah's more political work of seeing to the security of the community by rebuilding the walls of Jerusalem.

Similarities of style, language, and general outlook have suggested that whoever wrote Ezra–Nehemiah also wrote the two books of Chronicles. This, however, has been challenged by a growing number of scholars who point to different treatments of such key theological matters as the significance of the exodus, the nature of "Israel," intermarriage, prophecy, retributive justice, Levitical function, and the promise to David. The following notes assume that Ezra–Nehemiah is separate from the books of Chronicles.

A variety of sources have been utilized in Ezra–Nehemiah. Most important is the Nehemiah memoir, an autobiographical narrative that presents Nehemiah's own interpretation of the building of the Jerusalem wall (Neh. 1–7; 12:27–43; 13:4–31). A similar Ezra memoir forms the basis of Ezra 7–10 and Nehemiah 8–9. Much of the material in Aramaic, the diplomatic language of the Persian Empire (Ezra 4:7–6:18, and 7:12–26), may come from a collection of official correspondence between the Persian throne and Jerusalem. Other sources include various lists, especially the parallel lists of returnees found in Ezra 2:1–70 and Nehemiah 7:6–73.

Ezra–Nehemiah begins by seeing the decree of Cyrus that allowed the exiles to return as the fulfillment of God's promise in Jeremiah 29:10 (Ezra 1:1–4). Three similarly structured episodes follow: return and reconstruction of the temple under Zerubbabel (Ezra 1:5–6:22); return and reconstruction of the community under Ezra (Ezra 7–10); return and reconstruction of the walls under Nehemiah (Neh. 1:1–7:3a). In each, return and reconstruction authorized by the Persian crown meet with opposition that is eventually overcome with God's help. The purpose of this first major section is to demonstrate the postexilic community's continuity with the past. A second

major section (Neh. 7:4–12:43) turns to the renewal and reform necessary for the community's survival. It is significant that the joyous dedication of the final building project is delayed until the final verses of this section. The work closes with a coda (Neh. 12:44–13:31) in which Nehemiah, in a second term as governor, deals with the relapses that renewal and reform inevitably experience.

Though the situations we face are quite different from those encountered by the postexilic community, both Ezra and Nehemiah provide many examples of hard work coupled with prayer and an unshakable faith in God as a formula for successful problem solving that is as relevant today as it was then.

—**Mark A. Throntveit**

The Book of

EZRA

End of the Babylonian Captivity

1 In the first year of King Cyrus of Persia, in order that the word of the LORD by the mouth of Jeremiah might be accomplished, the LORD stirred up the spirit of King Cyrus of Persia so that he sent a herald throughout all his kingdom, and also in a written edict declared:

2 "Thus says King Cyrus of Persia: The LORD, the God of heaven, has given me all the kingdoms of the earth, and he has charged me to build him a house at Jerusalem in Judah. 3 Any of those among you who are of his people—may their God be with them!—are now permitted to go up to Jerusalem in Judah, and rebuild the house of the LORD, the God of Israel—he is the God who is in Jerusalem; 4 and let all survivors, in whatever place they reside, be assisted by the people of their place with silver and gold, with goods and with animals, besides freewill offerings for the house of God in Jerusalem."

5 The heads of the families of Judah and Benjamin, and the priests and the Levites—everyone whose spirit God had stirred—got ready to go up and rebuild the house of the LORD in Jerusalem. 6 All their neighbors aided them with silver vessels, with gold, with goods, with animals, and with valuable gifts, besides all that was freely offered. 7 King Cyrus himself brought out the vessels of the house of the LORD that Nebuchadnezzar had carried away from Jerusalem and placed in the house of his gods. 8 King Cyrus of Persia had them released into the charge of Mithredath the treasurer, who counted them out to Sheshbazzar the prince of Judah. 9 And this was the inventory: gold basins, thirty; silver basins, one thousand; knives,*a* twenty-nine; 10 gold bowls, thirty; other silver bowls, four hundred ten; other vessels, one thousand; 11 the total of the gold and silver vessels was five thousand four

a Vg: Meaning of Heb uncertain

1:1–6:22 Zerubbabel Returns and Rebuilds the Temple

Ezra does not appear in the first half of the book that bears his name. These chapters relate the experiences of the first to return from exile in Babylon. As they sought to forge a community, they faced opposition in the form of threats and political schemes from their neighbors and a twenty-year period of demoralization, only to rally in the end and overcome these obstacles to rebuild the temple and rejoice in their achievements.

1:1–4 Cyrus Orders the Exiles to Return from Babylon

Cyrus, the Persian king who conquered Babylon in 539 BCE, may have been politically motivated to release the Jews living in Babylon so that they might rebuild their temple. In contrast to the Assyrian and Babylonian rulers with their policy of destruction, Cyrus is known to have restored the temples of conquered peoples. The text, however, insists that the Lord is the moving force behind

these actions so that the prophecy of *Jeremiah,* who had announced both the exile and the return (Jer. 25:11–12; 29:10), might be fulfilled. The text of the decree of Cyrus then follows in Ezra 1:2–4 (cf. 2 Chr. 36:22–23; Ezra 6:2–5).

1:5–11 A Second Exodus

The return from Babylon recalls images from Israel's deliverance from Egypt (Exod. 1–15). It was in the exodus that God first formed the community that became Israel. Use of this imagery suggests that God is recreating the community.

1:6—The financial support of *their neighbors* recalls the exodus theme of despoiling the Egyptians (Exod. 3:21–22; 11:2; 12:35–36).

1:7–11—The return of the vessels recalls another exodus theme (Isa. 52:11–12).

1:8 *Sheshbazzar*—First governor of the Persian province of Yehud (Judah); see 5:14. The curious title *prince of Judah* can mean that Sheshbazzar was of the royal line of David, but it need not mean anything other than "ruler" or "official."

hundred. All these Sheshbazzar brought up, when the exiles were brought up from Babylonia to Jerusalem.

List of the Returned Exiles

2 Now these were the people of the province who came from those captive exiles whom King Nebuchadnezzar of Babylon had carried captive to Babylonia; they returned to Jerusalem and Judah, all to their own towns. [2] They came with Zerubbabel, Jeshua, Nehemiah, Seraiah, Reelaiah, Mordecai, Bilshan, Mispar, Bigvai, Rehum, and Baanah.

The number of the Israelite people: [3] the descendants of Parosh, two thousand one hundred seventy-two. [4] Of Shephatiah, three hundred seventy-two. [5] Of Arah, seven hundred seventy-five. [6] Of Pahath-moab, namely the descendants of Jeshua and Joab, two thousand eight hundred twelve. [7] Of Elam, one thousand two hundred fifty-four. [8] Of Zattu, nine hundred forty-five. [9] Of Zaccai, seven hundred sixty. [10] Of Bani, six hundred forty-two. [11] Of Bebai, six hundred twenty-three. [12] Of Azgad, one thousand two hundred twenty-two. [13] Of Adonikam, six hundred sixty-six. [14] Of Bigvai, two thousand fifty-six. [15] Of Adin, four hundred fifty-four. [16] Of Ater, namely of Hezekiah, ninety-eight. [17] Of Bezai, three hundred twenty-three. [18] Of Jorah, one hundred twelve. [19] Of Hashum, two hundred twenty-three. [20] Of Gibbar, ninety-five. [21] Of Bethlehem, one hundred twenty-three. [22] The people of Netophah, fifty-six. [23] Of Anathoth, one hundred twenty-eight. [24] The descendants of Azmaveth, forty-two. [25] Of Kiriatharim, Chephirah, and Beeroth, seven hundred forty-three. [26] Of Ramah and Geba, six hundred twenty-

one. [27] The people of Michmas, one hundred twenty-two. [28] Of Bethel and Ai, two hundred twenty-three. [29] The descendants of Nebo, fifty-two. [30] Of Magbish, one hundred fifty-six. [31] Of the other Elam, one thousand two hundred fifty-four. [32] Of Harim, three hundred twenty. [33] Of Lod, Hadid, and Ono, seven hundred twenty-five. [34] Of Jericho, three hundred forty-five. [35] Of Senaah, three thousand six hundred thirty.

36 The priests: the descendants of Jedaiah, of the house of Jeshua, nine hundred seventy-three. [37] Of Immer, one thousand fifty-two. [38] Of Pashhur, one thousand two hundred forty-seven. [39] Of Harim, one thousand seventeen.

40 The Levites: the descendants of Jeshua and Kadmiel, of the descendants of Hodaviah, seventy-four. [41] The singers: the descendants of Asaph, one hundred twenty-eight. [42] The descendants of the gatekeepers: of Shallum, of Ater, of Talmon, of Akkub, of Hatita, and of Shobai, in all one hundred thirty-nine.

43 The temple servants: the descendants of Ziha, Hasupha, Tabbaoth, [44] Keros, Siaha, Padon, [45] Lebanah, Hagabah, Akkub, [46] Hagab, Shamlai, Hanan, [47] Giddel, Gahar, Reaiah, [48] Rezin, Nekoda, Gazzam, [49] Uzza, Paseah, Besai, [50] Asnah, Meunim, Nephisim, [51] Bakbuk, Hakupha, Harhur, [52] Bazluth, Mehida, Harsha, [53] Barkos, Sisera, Temah, [54] Neziah, and Hatipha.

55 The descendants of Solomon's servants: Sotai, Hassophereth, Peruda, [56] Jaalah, Darkon, Giddel, [57] Shephatiah, Hattil, Pochereth-hazzebaim, and Ami.

58 All the temple servants and the descendants of Solomon's servants were three hundred ninety-two.

59 The following were those who came

2:1–70 The List of Returnees

Several groups are included: leaders (vv. 1–2), laity (vv. 3–35), priests (vv. 36–39), Levites (vv. 40–42), temple servants (vv. 43–58), and those of unconfirmed genealogy (vv. 59–63). The significance of the list lies in the sense of identity it provided for the returnees. They now represented

Israel of old. Restoring Nahamani to the list of leaders (cf. v. 2, Neh. 7:7) brings their number to twelve, recalling the twelve tribes. Lay and clergy alike have places in God's purpose. Their generous contributions would rebuild the temple.

2:59—Membership in the community required verifiable genealogy.

up from Tel-melah, Tel-harsha, Cherub, Addan, and Immer, though they could not prove their families or their descent, whether they belonged to Israel: ⁶⁰ the descendants of Delaiah, Tobiah, and Nekoda, six hundred fifty-two. ⁶¹ Also, of the descendants of the priests: the descendants of Habaiah, Hakkoz, and Barzillai (who had married one of the daughters of Barzillai the Gileadite, and was called by their name). ⁶² These looked for their entries in the genealogical records, but they were not found there, and so they were excluded from the priesthood as unclean; ⁶³ the governor told them that they were not to partake of the most holy food, until there should be a priest to consult Urim and Thummim.

64 The whole assembly together was forty-two thousand three hundred sixty, ⁶⁵ besides their male and female servants, of whom there were seven thousand three hundred thirty-seven; and they had two hundred male and female singers. ⁶⁶ They had seven hundred thirty-six horses, two hundred forty-five mules, ⁶⁷ four hundred thirty-five camels, and six thousand seven hundred twenty donkeys.

68 As soon as they came to the house of the LORD in Jerusalem, some of the heads of families made freewill offerings for the house of God, to erect it on its site. ⁶⁹ According to their resources they gave to the building fund sixty-one thousand darics of gold, five thousand minas of silver, and one hundred priestly robes.

70 The priests, the Levites, and some of the people lived in Jerusalem and its vicinity;ᵃ and the singers, the gatekeepers, and the temple servants lived in their towns, and all Israel in their towns.

Worship Restored at Jerusalem

3 When the seventh month came, and the Israelites were in the towns, the people gathered together in Jerusalem. ²Then Jeshua son of Jozadak, with his fellow priests, and Zerubbabel son of Shealtiel with his kin set out to build the altar of the God of Israel, to offer burnt offerings on it, as prescribed in the law of Moses the man of God. ³They set up the altar on its foundation, because they were in dread of the neighboring peoples, and they offered burnt offerings upon it to the LORD, morning and evening. ⁴And they kept the festival of booths,ᵇ as prescribed, and offered the daily burnt offerings by number accord-

---

ᵃ 1 Esdras 5.46: Heb lacks *lived in Jerusalem and its vicinity*
ᵇ Or *tabernacles*; Heb *succoth*

2:63 Urim and Thummim—Priestly instruments for discerning God's will (Exod. 28:30).

2:64 Forty-two thousand three hundred sixty—The group totals are some 12,000 less than the actual totals of the lists. The larger figure may have also included the women who returned.

2:69 darics . . . minas—The contribution was immense and must be taken metaphorically as an expression of enthusiastic support of the temple.

3:1–13 Worship Restored

This passage falls into two parts, the reconstruction of the altar (vv. 1–6) and the laying of the temple foundations (vv. 7–13). Here the theme of continuity with Israel of old is presented through the community's worship, that sacred element of a people's life that binds them together in response to God's grace.

3:1 Seventh month—September–October of the year they returned, 538 BCE. As the most important month of the liturgical year, this was an auspicious time to embark on these new ventures. The fact that **the people gathered together** is also an expression of their unity.

3:2 Law of Moses—Probably the Pentateuch, which **prescribed** unhewn (Heb. "whole") stone for the altar (Deut. 27:6–7). **Jeshua**—The high priest in Haggai. Listed first because of the religious context. **Zerubbabel**—Governor appointed by Darius, of Davidic descent.

3:3 Set . . . foundation—The foundation of the old altar provided continuity as did the reinstatement of worship. **Dread of the neighboring peoples** will prove to be justified.

3:4 Festival of booths—According to Lev. 23:42–43, this feast celebrated God's gracious deliverance of their ancestors from Egypt as well as God's provision in the wilderness. In the community's tenuous position the liturgy would help in the recognition of their dependence upon God's mercy.

ing to the ordinance, as required for each day, [5] and after that the regular burnt offerings, the offerings at the new moon and at all the sacred festivals of the LORD, and the offerings of everyone who made a freewill offering to the LORD. [6] From the first day of the seventh month they began to offer burnt offerings to the LORD. But the foundation of the temple of the LORD was not yet laid. [7] So they gave money to the masons and the carpenters, and food, drink, and oil to the Sidonians and the Tyrians to bring cedar trees from Lebanon to the sea, to Joppa, according to the grant that they had from King Cyrus of Persia.

Foundation Laid for the Temple

8 In the second year after their arrival at the house of God at Jerusalem, in the second month, Zerubbabel son of Shealtiel and Jeshua son of Jozadak made a beginning, together with the rest of their people, the priests and the Levites and all who had come to Jerusalem from the captivity. They appointed the Levites, from twenty years old and upward, to have the oversight of the work on the house of the LORD. [9] And Jeshua with his sons and his kin, and Kadmiel and his sons, Binnui and Hodaviah[a] along with the sons of Henadad, the Levites, their sons and kin, together took charge of the workers in the house of God.

10 When the builders laid the foundation of the temple of the LORD, the priests in their vestments were stationed to praise the LORD with trumpets, and the Levites, the sons of Asaph, with cymbals, according to the directions of King David of Israel; [11] and they sang responsively, praising and giving thanks to the LORD,

"For he is good,
    for his steadfast love endures forever
        toward Israel."

And all the people responded with a great shout when they praised the LORD, because the foundation of the house of the LORD was laid. [12] But many of the priests and Levites and heads of families, old people who had seen the first house on its foundations, wept with a loud voice when they saw this house, though many shouted aloud for joy, [13] so that the people could not distinguish the sound of the joyful shout from the sound of the people's weeping, for the people shouted so loudly that the sound was heard far away.

Resistance to Rebuilding the Temple

4 When the adversaries of Judah and Benjamin heard that the returned exiles were building a temple to the LORD, the God of Israel, [2] they approached Zerubbabel and the heads of families and said to them, "Let us build with you, for we worship your God as you do, and we have been sacrificing to him ever since the days of King Esar-haddon of Assyria who brought us here." [3] But Zerubbabel, Jeshua, and the

[a] Compare 2.40; Neh 7.43; 1 Esdras 5.58: Heb sons of Judah

3:12 *Many . . . wept*—Why some of the people wept is unknown. It may be merely an aspect of the ritual, not a mourning of the past.

4:1–24 Opposition
Opposition to the reconstruction of the temple in the time of Cyrus, Cambyses, and Darius, 538–520 (vv. 1–5), and to Jerusalem's walls during Artaxerxes' reign, 464–424 (vv. 7–23). Conflict between the community and their neighbors will continue through the end of Nehemiah. God will use this ever-present opposition to help the community grow and develop in conformity with the prescriptions of the law, in recognition of their dependence upon God.

4:2 *Esar-haddon*—King of Assyria (681–669) who replaced the Israelites deported from the northern kingdom in 721 with other deportees. These people, of mixed ethnic and religious character (see 2 Kgs. 17:24–41), are the *adversaries of Judah* in v. 1. Their offer of cooperation to help build the temple sounds genuine enough, but Zerubbabel is not fooled.

4:3 *We alone*—The returnees consider themselves the true people of God with exclusive rights from Cyrus. While harsh to our ears, Zerubbabel's curt reply is politically astute in that he recognizes the necessity for scrupulous adherence to the decree of Cyrus. Theologically, he is also maintaining the religious purity

rest of the heads of families in Israel said to them, "You shall have no part with us in building a house to our God; but we alone will build to the LORD, the God of Israel, as King Cyrus of Persia has commanded us."

4 Then the people of the land discouraged the people of Judah, and made them afraid to build, ⁵ and they bribed officials to frustrate their plan throughout the reign of King Cyrus of Persia and until the reign of King Darius of Persia.

Rebuilding of Jerusalem Opposed

6 In the reign of Ahasuerus, in his accession year, they wrote an accusation against the inhabitants of Judah and Jerusalem.

7 And in the days of Artaxerxes, Bishlam and Mithredath and Tabeel and the rest of their associates wrote to King Artaxerxes of Persia; the letter was written in Aramaic and translated.ᵃ ⁸ Rehum the royal deputy and Shimshai the scribe wrote a letter against Jerusalem to King Artaxerxes as follows ⁹ (then Rehum the royal deputy, Shimshai the scribe, and the rest of their associates, the judges, the envoys, the officials, the Persians, the people of Erech, the Babylonians, the people of Susa, that is, the Elamites, ¹⁰ and the rest of the nations whom the great and noble Osnappar deported and settled in the cities of Samaria and in the rest of the province Beyond the River wrote—and now ¹¹ this is a copy of the letter that they sent):

"To King Artaxerxes: Your servants, the people of the province Beyond the River, send greeting. And now ¹² may it be known to the king that the Jews who came up from you to us have gone to Jerusalem. They are rebuilding that rebellious and wicked city; they are finishing the walls and repairing the foundations. ¹³ Now may it be known to the king that, if this city is rebuilt and the walls finished, they will not pay tribute, custom, or toll, and the royal revenue will be reduced. ¹⁴ Now because we share the salt of the palace and it is not fitting for us to witness the king's dishonor, therefore we send and inform the king, ¹⁵ so that a search may be made in the annals of your ancestors. You will discover in the annals that this is a rebellious city, hurtful to kings and provinces, and that sedition was stirred up in it from long ago. On that account this city was laid waste. ¹⁶ We make known to the king that, if this city is rebuilt and its walls finished, you will then have no possession in the province Beyond the River."

17 The king sent an answer: "To Rehum the royal deputy and Shimshai the scribe and the rest of their associates who live in Samaria and in the rest of the province Beyond the River, greeting. And now ¹⁸ the letter that you sent to us has been read in translation before me. ¹⁹ So I made a decree, and someone searched and discovered that this city

---

ᵃ Heb adds *in Aramaic*, indicating that 4.8–6.18 is in Aramaic. Another interpretation is *The letter was written in the Aramaic script and set forth in the Aramaic language*

---

of the people so meticulously achieved through the genealogical screening of the list in chap. 2, where everyone had to prove their ancestry. The hard-won insight of the exile had been that God demanded exclusive worship. The adversaries of the people were a bad risk in this regard as they continued to worship other gods along with the Lord (see 2 Kgs. 17:33–34).

4:4–5 *People of the land*—Those who had not been exiled managed to *frustrate* the reconstruction for sixteen years by convincing Cyrus to reverse his edict.

4:11b–16—The letter insinuates that sedition will financially affect the empire and challenges the king to search the royal archives for evidence of Jerusalem's previous rebellion. There is some truth to this disparaging portrayal of Jerusalem as a *rebellious and wicked city*. The revolts of Jehoiakim and Zedekiah had ultimately precipitated the Babylonian exiles of 597 and 586 BCE. But the charges are trumped up by the adversaries.

4:13 *Tribute, custom, or toll*—Reduction of these "expected" gifts, taxes, and forced labor will result in reduction of *the royal revenue*.

4:14 *Share the salt of the palace*—The accusers are government officials (v. 8).

4:17–24—Artaxerxes' reply stops construction.

has risen against kings from long ago, and that rebellion and sedition have been made in it. [20] Jerusalem has had mighty kings who ruled over the whole province Beyond the River, to whom tribute, custom, and toll were paid. [21] Therefore issue an order that these people be made to cease, and that this city not be rebuilt, until I make a decree. [22] Moreover, take care not to be slack in this matter; why should damage grow to the hurt of the king?"

23 Then when the copy of King Artaxerxes' letter was read before Rehum and the scribe Shimshai and their associates, they hurried to the Jews in Jerusalem and by force and power made them cease. [24] At that time the work on the house of God in Jerusalem stopped and was discontinued until the second year of the reign of King Darius of Persia.

Restoration of the Temple Resumed

5 Now the prophets, Haggai[a] and Zechariah son of Iddo, prophesied to the Jews who were in Judah and Jerusalem, in the name of the God of Israel who was over them. [2] Then Zerubbabel son of Shealtiel and Jeshua son of Jozadak set out to rebuild the house of God in Jerusalem; and with them were the prophets of God, helping them.

3 At the same time Tattenai the governor of the province Beyond the River and Shethar-bozenai and their associates came to them and spoke to them thus, "Who gave you a decree to build this house and to finish this structure?" [4] They[b] also asked them this, "What are the names of the men who are building this building?" [5] But the eye of their God was upon the elders of the Jews, and they did not stop them until a report reached Darius and then answer was returned by letter in reply to it.

6 The copy of the letter that Tattenai the governor of the province Beyond the River and Shethar-bozenai and his associates the envoys who were in the province Beyond the River sent to King Darius; [7] they sent him a report, in which was written as follows: "To Darius the king, all peace! [8] May it be known to the king that we went to the province of Judah, to the house of the great God. It is being built of hewn stone, and timber is laid in the walls; this work is being done diligently and prospers in their hands. [9] Then we spoke to those elders and asked them, 'Who gave you a decree to build this house and to finish this structure?' [10] We also asked them their names, for your information, so that we might write down the names of the men at their head. [11] This was their reply to us: 'We are the servants of the God of

---

[a] Aram adds *the prophet*   [b] Gk Syr: Aram We

4:21 *Until I make a decree*—Later, Nehemiah secures permission to rebuild the walls (Neh. 2:4–8).

5:1–6:22 The Temple Reconstructed
After a long interruption, temple building is resumed (5:1–6:12), completed (6:13–15), and celebrated (6:16–22). These chapters continue a major theme of Ezra–Nehemiah, namely, to encourage the community to be the people of God within whatever political structures currently exist. The letters to the Persian officials that comprise most of these chapters will demonstrate that God has again graciously moved these political figures to favor the Jewish community, as had been the case in chap. 1.

5:1–2 *Haggai and Zechariah*—Canonical prophets urge the people to resume work on the temple in 520, the second year of Darius (Hag. 1:2),

5:3–17—Tattenai's inquiry leads to renewed permission to build.

5:3 *Tattenai*—Persian official appearing in Babylonian tablets as governor of *Beyond the River* (see 4:10).

5:5 *The eye of their God*—Not "the hand" as elsewhere in these books (7:6, 9, 28; 8:18, 22, 31; Neh. 2:8, 18) that connotes royal bounty (1 Kgs. 10:13; Esth. 1:7); rather, the divine protection is implied here. God's activity through these Persian officials had set these events in motion (Ezra 1:1). The people can count on God's protection and Persian support in the midst of their neighbor's attacks.

5:6–17—Tattenai's bureaucratic letter informs Darius of work on the temple and asks about proper authorization, reversing the opponents' letters of 4:7–16.

heaven and earth, and we are rebuilding the house that was built many years ago, which a great king of Israel built and finished. ¹² But because our ancestors had angered the God of heaven, he gave them into the hand of King Nebuchadnezzar of Babylon, the Chaldean, who destroyed this house and carried away the people to Babylonia. ¹³ However, King Cyrus of Babylon, in the first year of his reign, made a decree that this house of God should be rebuilt. ¹⁴ Moreover, the gold and silver vessels of the house of God, which Nebuchadnezzar had taken out of the temple in Jerusalem and had brought into the temple of Babylon, these King Cyrus took out of the temple of Babylon, and they were delivered to a man named Sheshbazzar, whom he had made governor. ¹⁵ He said to him, "Take these vessels; go and put them in the temple in Jerusalem, and let the house of God be rebuilt on its site." ¹⁶ Then this Sheshbazzar came and laid the foundations of the house of God in Jerusalem; and from that time until now it has been under construction, and it is not yet finished.' ¹⁷ And now, if it seems good to the king, have a search made in the royal archives there in Babylon, to see whether a decree was issued by King Cyrus for the rebuilding of this house of God in Jerusalem. Let the king send us his pleasure in this matter."

The Decree of Darius

6 Then King Darius made a decree, and they searched the archives where the documents were stored in Babylon. ² But it was in Ecbatana, the capital in the province of Media, that a scroll was found on which this was written: "A record. ³ In the first year of his reign, King Cyrus issued a decree: Concerning the house of God at Jerusalem, let the house be rebuilt, the place where sacrifices are offered and burnt offerings are brought;^a its height shall be sixty cubits and its width sixty cubits, ⁴ with three courses of hewn stones and one course of timber; let the cost be paid from the royal treasury. ⁵ Moreover, let the gold and silver vessels of the house of God, which Nebuchadnezzar took out of the temple in Jerusalem and brought to Babylon, be restored and brought back to the temple in Jerusalem, each to its place; you shall put them in the house of God."

⁶ "Now you, Tattenai, governor of the province Beyond the River, Shethar-bozenai, and you, their associates, the envoys in the province Beyond the River, keep away; ⁷ let the work on this house of God alone; let the governor of the Jews and the elders of the Jews rebuild this house of God on its site. ⁸ Moreover I make a decree regarding what you shall do for these elders of the Jews for the rebuilding of this house of God: the cost is to be paid to these people, in full and without delay, from the royal revenue, the tribute of the province Beyond the River. ⁹ Whatever is needed—young bulls, rams, or sheep for burnt offer-

^a Meaning of Aram uncertain

5:12 *Nebuchadnezzar*—Neo-Babylonian (Chaldean) ruler 605–562 BCE, who destroyed Solomon's temple and exiled the people to Babylon in 597 and 587.

5:17—The purpose of Tattenai's letter was to determine whether Cyrus had authorized the project and if Darius wished it to continue.

6:1–12—The decrees of Cyrus and Darius authorize the work to continue.

6:3 *Sixty cubits*—A cubit was roughly eighteen inches. Only the height and width of the temple are provided, but these suggest a much larger edifice than Solomon's temple (cf. 1 Kgs. 6:2). For example, if the length of Solomon's temple as reported in 1 Kgs. 6:2 is used here, the new temple would be six times larger in volume! As nothing is made of this in the text, we must assume that the figures are corrupt. It is probable that the new temple was to be no larger than Solomon's.

6:8–12—Darius implements Cyrus's earlier decree with financial support and provides for the *burnt offerings* (Lev. 1), grain offerings (Lev. 2:1–13), and drink offerings (Lev. 23:13), so that prayers for *the king [Darius] and his children* may be offered there. The decree ends with characteristic sanctions against those who would impede the project.

ings to the God of heaven, wheat, salt, wine, or oil, as the priests in Jerusalem require—let that be given to them day by day without fail, ¹⁰ so that they may offer pleasing sacrifices to the God of heaven, and pray for the life of the king and his children. ¹¹ Furthermore I decree that if anyone alters this edict, a beam shall be pulled out of the house of the perpetrator, who then shall be impaled on it. The house shall be made a dunghill. ¹² May the God who has established his name there overthrow any king or people that shall put forth a hand to alter this, or to destroy this house of God in Jerusalem. I, Darius, make a decree; let it be done with all diligence."

Completion and Dedication of the Temple

13 Then, according to the word sent by King Darius, Tattenai, the governor of the province Beyond the River, Shethar-bozenai, and their associates did with all diligence what King Darius had ordered. ¹⁴ So the elders of the Jews built and prospered, through the prophesying of the prophet Haggai and Zechariah son of Iddo. They finished their building by command of the God of Israel and by decree of Cyrus, Darius, and King Artaxerxes of Persia; ¹⁵ and this house was finished on the third day of the month of Adar, in the sixth year of the reign of King Darius.

16 The people of Israel, the priests and the Levites, and the rest of the returned exiles, celebrated the dedication of this house of God with joy. ¹⁷ They offered at the dedication of this house of God one hundred bulls, two hundred rams, four hundred lambs, and as a sin offering for all Israel, twelve male goats, according to the number of the tribes of Israel. ¹⁸ Then they set the priests in their divisions and the Levites in their courses for the service of God at Jerusalem, as it is written in the book of Moses.

The Passover Celebrated

19 On the fourteenth day of the first month the returned exiles kept the passover. ²⁰ For both the priests and the Levites had purified themselves; all of them were clean. So they killed the passover lamb for all the returned exiles, for their fellow priests, and for themselves. ²¹ It was eaten by the people of Israel who had returned from exile, and also by all who had joined them and separated themselves from the pollutions of the nations of the land to worship the LORD, the God of Israel. ²² With joy they celebrated the festival of unleavened bread seven days; for the LORD had made them joyful, and had turned the heart of the

---

6:13–15—The temple is completed. The brief description is inversely proportional to its significance.

6:14 *By command . . . by decree*—The different words for *command* are important. The temple was completed because the sovereign God of the universe had issued a command. The decrees of three of the world's most powerful potentates provide collateral support.

6:15 *Third day of . . . Adar . . . sixth year*—March 12, 515, a Sabbath, suggesting a parallel with God's completion of the creation of the world on the Sabbath (Gen. 2:2–3).

6:16–22—The completion of the temple is celebrated with a dedication service (vv. 16–18) reminiscent of Solomon's dedication in 2 Chr. 7:4–7, followed by the celebration of Passover and unleavened bread (Ezra 6:19–22).

6:17—The number of sacrifices is considerably fewer than at Solomon's dedication.

6:18—Moses established only the classes of priest and Levite. David divided them into their *courses* (1 Chr. 23–26).

6:19–22 *Passover . . . unleavened bread*—The celebration of these feasts makes an appropriate conclusion for a second exodus. The theme of redemption that permeates the Passover resonates with the freedom of God's deliverance from the long years of exile. Just as the people throw out the old leaven and prepare for the bounty of the new grain harvest as they celebrate the feast of unleavened bread, so at this turning point in the narrative, as the purified people of God at worship once again in the land of Israel at their newly restored and dedicated temple, the people throw out the old leaven of their past sinfulness and prepare to walk in the newness that lies ahead.

king of Assyria to them, so that he aided them in the work on the house of God, the God of Israel.

The Coming and Work of Ezra

7 After this, in the reign of King Artaxerxes of Persia, Ezra son of Seraiah, son of Azariah, son of Hilkiah, ²son of Shallum, son of Zadok, son of Ahitub, ³son of Amariah, son of Azariah, son of Meraioth, ⁴son of Zerahiah, son of Uzzi, son of Bukki, ⁵son of Abishua, son of Phinehas, son of Eleazar, son of the chief priest Aaron— ⁶this Ezra went up from Babylonia. He was a scribe skilled in the law of Moses that the LORD the God of Israel had given; and the king granted him all that he asked, for the hand of the LORD his God was upon him.

7 Some of the people of Israel, and some of the priests and Levites, the singers and gatekeepers, and the temple servants also went up to Jerusalem, in the seventh year of King Artaxerxes. ⁸They came to Jerusalem in the fifth month, which was in the seventh year of the king. ⁹On the first day of the first month the journey up from Babylon was begun, and on the first day of the fifth month he came to Jerusalem, for the gracious hand of his God was upon him. ¹⁰For Ezra had set his heart to study the law of the LORD, and to do it, and to teach the statutes and ordinances in Israel.

The Letter of Artaxerxes to Ezra

11 This is a copy of the letter that King Artaxerxes gave to the priest Ezra, the scribe, a scholar of the text of the commandments of the LORD and his statutes for Israel: ¹²"Artaxerxes, king of kings, to the priest Ezra, the scribe of the law of the God of heaven: Peace.ᵃ And now ¹³I decree that any of the people of Israel or their priests or Levites in my kingdom who freely offers to go to Jerusalem may go with you. ¹⁴For you are sent by the king and his seven counselors to make inquiries about Judah and Jerusalem according to the law of your God, which is in your hand, ¹⁵and also to convey the silver and gold that the king and his counselors have freely offered to the God of Israel, whose dwelling is in Jerusalem, ¹⁶with all the silver and gold that you shall find in the whole province of Babylonia, and with the freewill offerings of the people and the priests, given willingly for the house of their God in Jerusalem. ¹⁷With this money, then, you shall with all diligence buy bulls, rams, and lambs, and their grain offerings and their drink offerings, and you shall offer them on the altar of the house of your God in Jerusalem. ¹⁸Whatever seems good to you and your colleagues to do with the rest of the silver and gold, you may do, according to the will of your God. ¹⁹The vessels that have been given you for the service of the house of your God, you shall deliver before the God of Jerusalem. ²⁰And whatever else is required for the house of your God, which you are responsible for providing, you may provide out of the king's treasury.

21 "I, King Artaxerxes, decree to all the treasurers in the province Beyond the River: Whatever the priest Ezra, the scribe of the law of the God of heaven,

ᵃ Syr Vg 1 Esdras 8.9: Aram *Perfect*

7:1–10:44 Ezra Returns and Rebuilds the Community in 458 BCE

7:1–10 Introduction to Ezra

7:6—Ezra was a scholar with expertise in the Pentateuch. This was especially important since his task was to interpret the law for the people's new situation. In Jewish tradition he is regarded as a second lawgiver on a plane with Moses. *The hand of the LORD his God was upon him*—Variations on this refrain will echo through the rest of the book, assuring the reader that God is in charge of all that transpires. This divine empowerment allows Ezra to fulfill his mission to *study*, *do*, and *teach* the *law of the LORD* (v. 10).

7:11–27 Artaxerxes' Letter

This Aramaic letter commissions Ezra to lead a return to Jerusalem (v. 13), determine the level of compliance with Pentateuchal legislation (v. 14), manage various forms of financial support for the temple (vv. 15–20, a copy of this letter is included in vv. 21–24), and appoint *magistrates and judges* to teach the law (vv. 25–26).

requires of you, let it be done with all diligence, [22] up to one hundred talents of silver, one hundred cors of wheat, one hundred baths[a] of wine, one hundred baths[a] of oil, and unlimited salt. [23] Whatever is commanded by the God of heaven, let it be done with zeal for the house of the God of heaven, or wrath will come upon the realm of the king and his heirs. [24] We also notify you that it shall not be lawful to impose tribute, custom, or toll on any of the priests, the Levites, the singers, the doorkeepers, the temple servants, or other servants of this house of God.

25 "And you, Ezra, according to the God-given wisdom you possess, appoint magistrates and judges who may judge all the people in the province Beyond the River who know the laws of your God; and you shall teach those who do not know them. [26] All who will not obey the law of your God and the law of the king, let judgment be strictly executed on them, whether for death or for banishment or for confiscation of their goods or for imprisonment."

27 Blessed be the LORD, the God of our ancestors, who put such a thing as this into the heart of the king to glorify the house of the LORD in Jerusalem, [28] and who extended to me steadfast love before the king and his counselors, and before all the king's mighty officers. I took courage, for the hand of the LORD my God was upon me, and I gathered leaders from Israel to go up with me.

Heads of Families Who Returned with Ezra

8 These are their family heads, and this is the genealogy of those who went up with me from Babylonia, in the reign of King Artaxerxes: [2] Of the descendants of Phinehas, Gershom. Of Ithamar, Daniel. Of David, Hattush, [3] of the descendants of Shecaniah. Of Parosh, Zechariah, with whom were registered one hundred fifty males. [4] Of the descendants of Pahath-moab, Eliehoenai son of Zerahiah, and with him two hundred males. [5] Of the descendants of Zattu,[b] Shecaniah son of Jahaziel, and with him three hundred males. [6] Of the descendants of Adin, Ebed son of Jonathan, and with him fifty males. [7] Of the descendants of Elam, Jeshaiah son of Athaliah, and with him seventy males. [8] Of the descendants of Shephatiah, Zebadiah son of Michael, and with him eighty males. [9] Of the descendants of Joab, Obadiah son of Jehiel, and with him two hundred eighteen males. [10] Of the descendants of Bani,[c] Shelomith son of Josiphiah, and with him one hundred sixty males. [11] Of the descendants of Bebai, Zechariah son of Bebai, and with him twenty-eight males. [12] Of the descendants of Azgad, Johanan son of Hakkatan, and with him one hundred ten males. [13] Of the descendants of Adonikam, those who came later, their names being Eliphelet, Jeuel, and Shemaiah, and with them sixty males. [14] Of the descendants of Bigvai, Uthai and Zaccur, and with them seventy males.

Servants for the Temple

15 I gathered them by the river that runs to Ahava, and there we camped three days. As I reviewed the people and

[a] A Heb measure of volume   [b] Gk 1 Esdras 8.32: Heb lacks of Zattu
[c] Gk 1 Esdras 8.36: Heb lacks Bani

7:27–8:36 Ezra's Journey to Jerusalem
Once again the return is presented as a second exodus in the repetition of "to go up," the technical term for "exodus" (7:6, 7, 9, 28; 8:1): the beginning of the journey on the same day as the Passover (7:9; cf. Exod. 12:2); the theme of despoiling the Egyptians (7:15–17); and an unusual concentration on the number twelve throughout chap. 8. Three variations of *the hand of our God*

was upon us attribute the success of the journey to God (8:18, 22, 31).

8:1–14—A list of 1,500 *males* (6,000 people) returning to Jerusalem in twelve families symbolizes the twelve tribes.

8:15–20—The Levites may not have wished to return to inferior positions. Their presence, however, was required by Artaxerxes (7:13), and their absence mars the parallel with the original exodus.

the priests, I found there none of the descendants of Levi. ¹⁶ Then I sent for Eliezer, Ariel, Shemaiah, Elnathan, Jarib, Elnathan, Nathan, Zechariah, and Meshullam, who were leaders, and for Joiarib and Elnathan, who were wise, ¹⁷ and sent them to Iddo, the leader at the place called Casiphia, telling them what to say to Iddo and his colleagues the temple servants at Casiphia, namely, to send us ministers for the house of our God. ¹⁸ Since the gracious hand of our God was upon us, they brought us a man of discretion, of the descendants of Mahli son of Levi son of Israel, namely Sherebiah, with his sons and kin, eighteen; ¹⁹ also Hashabiah and with him Jeshaiah of the descendants of Merari, with his kin and their sons, twenty; ²⁰ besides two hundred twenty of the temple servants, whom David and his officials had set apart to attend the Levites. These were all mentioned by name.

Fasting and Prayer for Protection

21 Then I proclaimed a fast there, at the river Ahava, that we might deny ourselvesᵃ before our God, to seek from him a safe journey for ourselves, our children, and all our possessions. ²² For I was ashamed to ask the king for a band of soldiers and cavalry to protect us against the enemy on our way, since we had told the king that the hand of our God is gracious to all who seek him, but his power and his wrath are against all who forsake him. ²³ So we fasted and petitioned our God for this, and he listened to our entreaty.

Gifts for the Temple

24 Then I set apart twelve of the leading priests: Sherebiah, Hashabiah, and ten of their kin with them. ²⁵ And I weighed out to them the silver and the gold and the vessels, the offering for the house of our God that the king, his counselors, his lords, and all Israel there present had offered; ²⁶ I weighed out into their hand six hundred fifty talents of silver, and one hundred silver vessels worth . . . talents,ᵇ and one hundred talents of gold, ²⁷ twenty gold bowls worth a thousand darics, and two vessels of fine polished bronze as precious as gold. ²⁸ And I said to them, "You are holy to the LORD, and the vessels are holy; and the silver and the gold are a freewill offering to the LORD, the God of your ancestors. ²⁹ Guard them and keep them until you weigh them before the chief priests and the Levites and the heads of families in Israel at Jerusalem, within the chambers of the house of the LORD." ³⁰ So the priests and the Levites took over the silver, the gold, and the vessels as they were weighed out, to bring them to Jerusalem, to the house of our God.

The Return to Jerusalem

31 Then we left the river Ahava on the twelfth day of the first month, to go to Jerusalem; the hand of our God was upon us, and he delivered us from the hand of the enemy and from ambushes along the way. ³² We came to Jerusalem and remained there three days. ³³ On the fourth day, within the house of our God, the silver, the gold, and the vessels were weighed into the hands of the priest Meremoth son of Uriah, and with him was Eleazar son of Phinehas, and with them were the Levites, Jozabad son of Jeshua and Noadiah son of Binnui. ³⁴ The total was counted and weighed, and the weight of everything was recorded.

35 At that time those who had come from captivity, the returned exiles, offered burnt offerings to the God of Israel, twelve bulls for all Israel, ninety-

---

ᵃ Or *might fast*   ᵇ The number of talents is lacking

8:21–30—Spiritual preparations for the journey included fasting and prayer for God's (not the king's) protection (vv. 21–23). The loyalty of these leaders is not divided. God remains their constant source of hope.

8:31–36—Arrival. The group celebrates *a safe journey* (v. 21) with sacrifices in multiples of twelve that signify the group's continuity with Israel.

six rams, seventy-seven lambs, and as a sin offering twelve male goats; all this was a burnt offering to the LORD. **36** They also delivered the king's commissions to the king's satraps and to the governors of the province Beyond the River; and they supported the people and the house of God.

Denunciation of Mixed Marriages

9 After these things had been done, the officials approached me and said, "The people of Israel, the priests, and the Levites have not separated themselves from the peoples of the lands with their abominations, from the Canaanites, the Hittites, the Perizzites, the Jebusites, the Ammonites, the Moabites, the Egyptians, and the Amorites. **2** For they have taken some of their daughters as wives for themselves and for their sons. Thus the holy seed has mixed itself with the peoples of the lands, and in this faithlessness the officials and leaders have led the way." **3** When I heard this, I tore my garment and my mantle, and pulled hair from my head and beard, and sat appalled. **4** Then all who trembled at the words of the God of Israel, because of the faithlessness of the returned exiles, gathered around me while I sat appalled until the evening sacrifice.

Ezra's Prayer

5 At the evening sacrifice I got up from my fasting, with my garments and my mantle torn, and fell on my knees, spread out my hands to the LORD my God, **6** and said,

"O my God, I am too ashamed and embarrassed to lift my face to you, my God, for our iniquities have risen higher than our heads, and our guilt has mounted up to the heavens. **7** From the days of our ancestors to this day we have been deep in guilt, and for our iniquities we, our kings, and our priests have been handed over to the kings of the lands, to the sword, to captivity, to plundering, and to utter shame, as is now the case. **8** But now for a brief moment favor has been shown by the LORD our God, who has left us a remnant, and given us a stake in his holy place, in order that he*a* may brighten our eyes and grant us a little sustenance in our slavery. **9** For we are slaves; yet our God has not forsaken us in our slavery, but has extended to us his steadfast love before the kings of Persia, to give us new life to set up the house of our God, to repair its ruins, and to give us a wall in Judea and Jerusalem.

10 "And now, our God, what shall we say after this? For we have forsaken your commandments, **11** which you commanded by your servants the prophets, saying, 'The land that you are entering to possess is a land unclean with the pollutions of the peoples of the lands, with their abominations. They have filled it from end to end with their uncleanness. **12** Therefore do not give your daughters to their sons, neither take their daughters for your sons, and never seek their peace or prosperity, so

a Heb *our God*

9:1–10:44 Intermarriage Threatens the Community
Ezra's successful application of the Pentateuch's teaching to the present situation resulted in the community's realization that intermarriage with the inhabitants of Canaan was forbidden (Exod. 34:11–16; Deut. 7:3–6). He responds with mourning (9:3–5) and prayer (9:6–15).

9:1—Not only did the law forbid intermarriage with the peoples of the land, but it also required their destruction (Deut. 7:1–3). Notable instances of marriage to foreign wives include Joseph (Gen. 41:45), Moses (Exod. 2:1; Num. 12:1), David (2 Sam. 3:3), and Solomon (1 Kgs. 11:1; 14:21).

9:6–15—Functioning as a catechetical device to teach and admonish, Ezra's prayer confesses Israel's sin throughout its history, countered with God's gracious activity resulting in their return to the land. The people are overwhelmed by this demonstration of God's grace and are driven to repentance.

9:6—The use of first person plurals throughout witnesses to Ezra's identification with the people.

9:11–12 *By . . . the prophets*—Rather, the priestly legislation (Lev. 18:24–30) and Deuteronomy (Deut. 7:3–4), both of which fear that the foreign wives will be a source of religious corruption.

that you may be strong and eat the good of the land and leave it for an inheritance to your children forever.' [13] After all that has come upon us for our evil deeds and for our great guilt, seeing that you, our God, have punished us less than our iniquities deserved and have given us such a remnant as this, [14] shall we break your commandments again and intermarry with the peoples who practice these abominations? Would you not be angry with us until you destroy us without remnant or survivor? [15] O LORD, God of Israel, you are just, but we have escaped as a remnant, as is now the case. Here we are before you in our guilt, though no one can face you because of this."

The People's Response

10 While Ezra prayed and made confession, weeping and throwing himself down before the house of God, a very great assembly of men, women, and children gathered to him out of Israel; the people also wept bitterly. [2] Shecaniah son of Jehiel, of the descendants of Elam, addressed Ezra, saying, "We have broken faith with our God and have married foreign women from the peoples of the land, but even now there is hope for Israel in spite of this. [3] So now let us make a covenant with our God to send away all these wives and their children, according to the counsel of my lord and of those who tremble at the commandment of our God; and let it be done according to the law. [4] Take action, for it is your duty, and we are with you; be strong, and do it." [5] Then Ezra stood up and made the leading priests, the Levites,

and all Israel swear that they would do as had been said. So they swore.

Foreign Wives and Their Children Rejected

[6] Then Ezra withdrew from before the house of God, and went to the chamber of Jehohanan son of Eliashib, where he spent the night.[a] He did not eat bread or drink water, for he was mourning over the faithlessness of the exiles. [7] They made a proclamation throughout Judah and Jerusalem to all the returned exiles that they should assemble at Jerusalem, [8] and that if any did not come within three days, by order of the officials and the elders all their property should be forfeited, and they themselves banned from the congregation of the exiles.

[9] Then all the people of Judah and Benjamin assembled at Jerusalem within the three days; it was the ninth month, on the twentieth day of the month. All the people sat in the open square before the house of God, trembling because of this matter and because of the heavy rain. [10] Then Ezra the priest stood up and said to them, "You have trespassed and married foreign women, and so increased the guilt of Israel. [11] Now make confession to the LORD the God of your ancestors, and do his will; separate yourselves from the peoples of the land and from the foreign wives." [12] Then all the assembly answered with a loud voice, "It is so; we must do as you have said. [13] But the people are many, and it is a time of heavy rain; we cannot stand in the open. Nor is this a task for one day or for two, for many of us have transgressed in this

---

[a] 1 Esdras 9.2: Heb *where he went*

10:1–44—The crisis of intermarriage is resolved through public confession of guilt and a decision to oppose intermarriage.

10:2–3 *Shecaniah*—A prominent lay person, not Ezra, proposes to *send away* the foreign wives and their children as a solution. The term he uses for "married" is not used of marriage elsewhere and means "brought into (the house?)," suggesting that these were not really marriages after all. This is a major reinterpretation of Deut. 7:3–4,

which does not prescribe divorce. This drastic measure was deemed necessary to preserve as strong a sense of religious identity as possible in the struggling postexilic community. After all, it was this very lack of faithfulness on Israel's part that had resulted in exile. At Shittim (Num. 25:1–9) the problem of intermarriage was "resolved" by stoning husband, wives, and children to death.

matter. **14** Let our officials represent the whole assembly, and let all in our towns who have taken foreign wives come at appointed times, and with them the elders and judges of every town, until the fierce wrath of our God on this account is averted from us." **15** Only Jonathan son of Asahel and Jahzeiah son of Tikvah opposed this, and Meshullam and Shabbethai the Levites supported them.

16 Then the returned exiles did so. Ezra the priest selected men,*a* heads of families, according to their families, each of them designated by name. On the first day of the tenth month they sat down to examine the matter. **17** By the first day of the first month they had come to the end of all the men who had married foreign women.

18 There were found of the descendants of the priests who had married foreign women, of the descendants of Jeshua son of Jozadak and his brothers: Maaseiah, Eliezer, Jarib, and Gedaliah. **19** They pledged themselves to send away their wives, and their guilt offering was a ram of the flock for their guilt. **20** Of the descendants of Immer: Hanani and Zebadiah. **21** Of the descendants of Harim: Maaseiah, Elijah, Shemaiah, Jehiel, and Uzziah. **22** Of the descendants of Pashhur: Elioenai, Maaseiah, Ishmael, Nethanel, Jozabad, and Elasah.

23 Of the Levites: Jozabad, Shimei, Kelaiah (that is, Kelita), Pethahiah, Judah, and Eliezer. **24** Of the singers: Eliashib. Of the gatekeepers: Shallum, Telem, and Uri.

25 And of Israel: of the descendants of Parosh: Ramiah, Izziah, Malchijah, Mijamin, Eleazar, Hashabiah,*b* and Benaiah. **26** Of the descendants of Elam: Mattaniah, Zechariah, Jehiel, Abdi, Jeremoth, and Elijah. **27** Of the descendants of Zattu: Elioenai, Eliashib, Mattaniah, Jeremoth, Zabad, and Aziza. **28** Of the descendants of Bebai: Jehohanan, Hananiah, Zabbai, and Athlai. **29** Of the descendants of Bani: Meshullam, Malluch, Adaiah, Jashub, Sheal, and Jeremoth. **30** Of the descendants of Pahath-moab: Adna, Chelal, Benaiah, Maaseiah, Mattaniah, Bezalel, Binnui, and Manasseh. **31** Of the descendants of Harim: Eliezer, Isshijah, Malchijah, Shemaiah, Shimeon, **32** Benjamin, Malluch, and Shemariah. **33** Of the descendants of Hashum: Mattenai, Mattattah, Zabad, Eliphelet, Jeremai, Manasseh, and Shimei. **34** Of the descendants of Bani: Maadai, Amram, Uel, **35** Benaiah, Bedeiah, Cheluhi, **36** Vaniah, Meremoth, Eliashib, **37** Mattaniah, Mattenai, and Jaasu. **38** Of the descendants of Binnui:*c* Shimei, **39** Shelemiah, Nathan, Adaiah, **40** Machnadebai, Shashai, Sharai, **41** Azarel, Shelemiah, Shemariah, **42** Shallum, Amariah, and Joseph. **43** Of the descendants of Nebo: Jeiel, Mattithiah, Zabad, Zebina, Jaddai, Joel, and Benaiah. **44** All these had married foreign women, and they sent them away with their children.*d*

a 1 Esdras 9.16: Syr: Heb *And there were selected Ezra,*   *b* 1 Esdras 9.26 Gk: Heb *Malchijah*   *c* Gk: Heb *Bani, Binnui*   *d* 1 Esdras 9.36; meaning of Heb uncertain

---

10:18–44—Ezra concludes with a list of twenty-seven clergy and eighty-six Israelites who had intermarried. It is clear that the problem was relatively rare, less than 0.7 percent of the population, and that the actions of a few threatened the well-being of the whole community.

10:44 *They sent them away with their chil-*

dren—The text is very uncertain. NRSV reads with 1 Esd. 9:36. The Hebrew may say, "Some had wives with whom they had children." This is the most offensive aspect of this troubling text. At best, we do not know what provisions were made for the women and children of these unfortunate marriages.

The Book of
NEHEMIAH

Nehemiah Prays for His People

1 The words of Nehemiah son of Hacaliah. In the month of Chislev, in the twentieth year, while I was in Susa the capital, ² one of my brothers, Hanani, came with certain men from Judah; and I asked them about the Jews that survived, those who had escaped the captivity, and about Jerusalem. ³ They replied, "The survivors there in the province who escaped captivity are in great trouble and shame; the wall of Jerusalem is broken down, and its gates have been destroyed by fire."

4 When I heard these words I sat down and wept, and mourned for days, fasting and praying before the God of heaven. ⁵ I said, "O LORD God of heaven, the great and awesome God who keeps covenant and steadfast love with those who love him and keep his commandments; ⁶ let your ear be attentive and your eyes open to hear the prayer of your servant that I now pray before you day and night for your servants, the people of Israel, confessing the sins of the people of Israel, which we have sinned against you. Both I and my family have sinned. ⁷ We have offended you deeply, failing to keep the commandments, the statutes, and the ordinances that you commanded your servant Moses. ⁸ Remember the word that you commanded your servant Moses, 'If you are unfaithful, I will scatter you among the peoples; ⁹ but if you return to me and keep my commandments and do them, though your outcasts are under the farthest skies, I will gather them from there and bring them to the place at which I have chosen to establish my name.' ¹⁰ They are your servants and your people, whom you redeemed by your great power and your strong hand. ¹¹ O Lord, let your ear be attentive to the prayer of your servant, and to the prayer of your servants who delight in revering your name. Give success to your servant today, and grant him mercy in the sight of this man!"

At the time, I was cupbearer to the king.

Nehemiah Sent to Judah

2 In the month of Nisan, in the twentieth year of King Artaxerxes, when

---

1:1–7:73a Nehemiah Returns and Rebuilds the Walls of Jerusalem

This personal account from Nehemiah's memoirs relates his part in the building of Jerusalem's walls, increasing its population, and dealing with various social problems, opposition, and mixed marriages.

1:1–2:20 Nehemiah Returns to Jerusalem and Becomes Governor

1:1 *Nehemiah*—A trusted palace official of the Persian king, Artaxerxes I (465–424 BCE). *Chislev*—November–December 445 BCE. *Susa*—Winter palace of Persian kings, 200 miles east of Babylon.

1:3 *Wall of Jerusalem . . . fire*—The royal agent Rehum may have destroyed the city while carrying out Artaxerxes' order to stop the rebuilding

of Jerusalem (see Ezra 4:7–23). This is not the Babylonian destruction 140 years earlier.

1:4 *Mourned*—Nehemiah mourns Jerusalem as Ezra had mourned the exiles' sin (Ezra 10:6).

1:5–11—Nehemiah's prayer stresses God's faithfulness and asks God to respond to this crisis. While he acknowledges the people's sin, Nehemiah also affirms repentance can bring them back to God. References to the exodus recall God's mercy and deliverance and encourage Nehemiah to hold God to these promises.

1:6 *We*—Like Ezra (Ezra 9:7), Nehemiah includes himself in the confession.

1:11 *Cupbearer*—The one who tasted the king's wine for poison was necessarily a highly trusted confidant.

2:1–10—Artaxerxes commissions Nehemiah.

wine was served him, I carried the wine and gave it to the king. Now, I had never been sad in his presence before. 2 So the king said to me, "Why is your face sad, since you are not sick? This can only be sadness of the heart." Then I was very much afraid. 3 I said to the king, "May the king live forever! Why should my face not be sad, when the city, the place of my ancestors' graves, lies waste, and its gates have been destroyed by fire?" 4 Then the king said to me, "What do you request?" So I prayed to the God of heaven. 5 Then I said to the king, "If it pleases the king, and if your servant has found favor with you, I ask that you send me to Judah, to the city of my ancestors' graves, so that I may rebuild it." 6 The king said to me (the queen also was sitting beside him), "How long will you be gone, and when will you return?" So it pleased the king to send me, and I set him a date. 7 Then I said to the king, "If it pleases the king, let letters be given me to the governors of the province Beyond the River, that they may grant me passage until I arrive in Judah; 8 and a letter to Asaph, the keeper of the king's forest, directing him to give me timber to make beams for the gates of the temple fortress, and for the wall of the city, and for the house that I shall occupy." And the king granted me what I asked,

for the gracious hand of my God was upon me.

9 Then I came to the governors of the province Beyond the River, and gave them the king's letters. Now the king had sent officers of the army and cavalry with me. 10 When Sanballat the Horonite and Tobiah the Ammonite official heard this, it displeased them greatly that someone had come to seek the welfare of the people of Israel.

Nehemiah's Inspection of the Walls

11 So I came to Jerusalem and was there for three days. 12 Then I got up during the night, I and a few men with me; I told no one what my God had put into my heart to do for Jerusalem. The only animal I took was the animal I rode. 13 I went out by night by the Valley Gate past the Dragon's Spring and to the Dung Gate, and I inspected the walls of Jerusalem that had been broken down and its gates that had been destroyed by fire. 14 Then I went on to the Fountain Gate and to the King's Pool; but there was no place for the animal I was riding to continue. 15 So I went up by way of the valley by night and inspected the wall. Then I turned back and entered by the Valley Gate, and so returned. 16 The officials did not know where I had gone or what I was doing; I had not yet told the Jews, the priests, the nobles, the

---

Nehemiah demonstrates how politically astute he is as he carefully discusses the situation of Jerusalem with the king. Concern for justice is not enough. Political savvy and trust in God enabled Nehemiah to implement his convictions.

2:2 I was . . . afraid—The word translated *sad* in these verses is literally "evil." Nehemiah may fear that the king has misinterpreted the *sadness* (evil) in his *heart* as treason.

2:3 My ancestors' graves—Nehemiah tactfully avoids mentioning any political motives for rebuilding a city the king believed to be rebellious (Ezra 4:18–22).

2:8 Hand of . . . God—Nehemiah credits God for his success (cf. Ezra 7:9; 8:18, 22, 31; Neh. 2:18).

2:9–10—Artaxerxes provides Nehemiah with a military escort (contrast Ezra 8:22).

2:10 When . . . heard—Each stage of the reconstruction is met with opposition introduced by this formula (2:19; 4:7; 6:1, 16). *Sanballat* was governor of Samaria until 407. The names given for two of his sons in an Egyptian source may indicate he was Jewish. The same is true of *Tobiah*, possibly Sanballat's deputy. These two were *displeased* because the rebuilding of Jerusalem would lessen the influence of Samaria and Ammon in the region.

2:11–20—Evening inspection of the walls. Nehemiah continues to demonstrate his political acumen by secretly inspecting the walls by night in order to gather trustworthy information (vv. 11–16) and proposes a plan of reconstruction despite the opposition of Sanballat, Tobiah, and now *Geshem the Arab* (vv. 17–20). Throughout, Nehemiah acts decisively, leaving the outcome to God (vv. 18, 20).

officials, and the rest that were to do the work.

Decision to Restore the Walls

17 Then I said to them, "You see the trouble we are in, how Jerusalem lies in ruins with its gates burned. Come, let us rebuild the wall of Jerusalem, so that we may no longer suffer disgrace." 18 I told them that the hand of my God had been gracious upon me, and also the words that the king had spoken to me. Then they said, "Let us start building!" So they committed themselves to the common good. 19 But when Sanballat the Horonite and Tobiah the Ammonite official, and Geshem the Arab heard of it, they mocked and ridiculed us, saying, "What is this that you are doing? Are you rebelling against the king?" 20 Then I replied to them, "The God of heaven is the one who will give us success, and we his servants are going to start building; but you have no share or claim or historic right in Jerusalem."

Organization of the Work

3 Then the high priest Eliashib set to work with his fellow priests and rebuilt the Sheep Gate. They consecrated it and set up its doors; they consecrated it as far as the Tower of the Hundred and as far as the Tower of Hananel. 2 And the men of Jericho built next to him. And next to them[a] Zaccur son of Imri built.

3 The sons of Hassenaah built the Fish Gate; they laid its beams and set up its doors, its bolts, and its bars. 4 Next to them Meremoth son of Uriah son of Hakkoz made repairs. Next to them Meshullam son of Berechiah son of Meshezabel made repairs. Next to them Zadok son of Baana made repairs. 5 Next to them the Tekoites made repairs; but

their nobles would not put their shoulders to the work of their Lord.[b]

6 Joiada son of Paseah and Meshullam son of Besodeiah repaired the Old Gate; they laid its beams and set up its doors, its bolts, and its bars. 7 Next to them repairs were made by Melatiah the Gibeonite and Jadon the Meronothite—the men of Gibeon and of Mizpah—who were under the jurisdiction of[c] the governor of the province Beyond the River. 8 Next to them Uzziel son of Harhaiah, one of the goldsmiths, made repairs. Next to him Hananiah, one of the perfumers, made repairs; and they restored Jerusalem as far as the Broad Wall. 9 Next to them Rephaiah son of Hur, ruler of half the district of[d] Jerusalem, made repairs. 10 Next to them Jedaiah son of Harumaph made repairs opposite his house; and next to him Hattush son of Hashabneiah made repairs. 11 Malchijah son of Harim and Hasshub son of Pahath-moab repaired another section and the Tower of the Ovens. 12 Next to him Shallum son of Hallohesh, ruler of half the district of[d] Jerusalem, made repairs, he and his daughters.

13 Hanun and the inhabitants of Zanoah repaired the Valley Gate; they rebuilt it and set up its doors, its bolts, and its bars, and repaired a thousand cubits of the wall, as far as the Dung Gate.

14 Malchijah son of Rechab, ruler of the district of[e] Beth-haccherem, repaired the Dung Gate; he rebuilt it and set up its doors, its bolts, and its bars.

15 And Shallum son of Col-hozeh, ruler of the district of[e] Mizpah, repaired the Fountain Gate; he rebuilt it and covered it and set up its doors, its bolts, and

a Heb *him*   *b* Or *lords*   *c* Meaning of Heb uncertain   *d* Or *supervisor of half the portion assigned to*   *e* Or *supervisor of the portion assigned to*

3:1–32 List of Builders
A list of those who rebuilt the wall, beginning with the *Sheep Gate* (vv. 1, 32) in the northeastern corner of the city and continuing in a counterclockwise direction: north wall (vv. 1–5), west wall (vv. 6–14), and east wall (vv. 15–32). Only

repair was needed in the north and the west. The eastern wall, however required new construction. Nehemiah's considerable leadership and organizational skills contributed to the success of the project.

its bars; and he built the wall of the Pool of Shelah of the king's garden, as far as the stairs that go down from the City of David. **16** After him Nehemiah son of Azbuk, ruler of half the district of*a* Beth-zur, repaired from a point opposite the graves of David, as far as the artificial pool and the house of the warriors. **17** After him the Levites made repairs: Rehum son of Bani; next to him Hashabiah, ruler of half the district of*a* Keilah, made repairs for his district. **18** After him their kin made repairs: Binnui,*b* son of Henadad, ruler of half the district of*a* Keilah; **19** next to him Ezer son of Jeshua, ruler*c* of Mizpah, repaired another section opposite the ascent to the armory at the Angle. **20** After him Baruch son of Zabbai repaired another section from the Angle to the door of the house of the high priest Eliashib. **21** After him Meremoth son of Uriah son of Hakkoz repaired another section from the door of the house of Eliashib to the end of the house of Eliashib. **22** After him the priests, the men of the surrounding area, made repairs. **23** After them Benjamin and Hasshub made repairs opposite their house. After them Azariah son of Maaseiah son of Ananiah made repairs beside his own house. **24** After him Binnui son of Henadad repaired another section, from the house of Azariah to the Angle and to the corner. **25** Palal son of Uzai repaired opposite the Angle and the tower projecting from the upper house of the king at the court of the guard. After him Pedaiah son of Parosh **26** and the temple servants living*d* on Ophel made repairs up to a point opposite the Water Gate on the east and the projecting tower. **27** After him the Tekoites repaired another sec-

tion opposite the great projecting tower as far as the wall of Ophel.

28 Above the Horse Gate the priests made repairs, each one opposite his own house. **29** After them Zadok son of Immer made repairs opposite his own house. After him Shemaiah son of Shecaniah, the keeper of the East Gate, made repairs. **30** After him Hananiah son of Shelemiah and Hanun sixth son of Zalaph repaired another section. After him Meshullam son of Berechiah made repairs opposite his living quarters. **31** After him Malchijah, one of the goldsmiths, made repairs as far as the house of the temple servants and of the merchants, opposite the Muster Gate,*e* and to the upper room of the corner. **32** And between the upper room of the corner and the Sheep Gate the goldsmiths and the merchants made repairs.

Hostile Plots Thwarted

4[f] Now when Sanballat heard that we were building the wall, he was angry and greatly enraged, and he mocked the Jews. **2** He said in the presence of his associates and of the army of Samaria, "What are these feeble Jews doing? Will they restore things? Will they sacrifice? Will they finish it in a day? Will they revive the stones out of the heaps of rubbish—and burned ones at that?" **3** Tobiah the Ammonite was beside him, and he said, "That stone wall they are building—any fox going up on it would break it down!" **4** Hear, O our God, for we are despised; turn their taunt back on their own heads, and give them over as plunder in a land of captivity. **5** Do not

---

a Or *supervisor of half the portion assigned to* *b* Gk Syr Compare verse 24, 10.9: Heb *Bavvai* *c* Or *supervisor* *d* Cn: Heb *were living* *e* Or *Hammiphkad Gate* *f* Ch 3.33 in Heb

---

4:1–23 Opposition in the Form of Intimidation
Nehemiah responds with characteristic leadership and faith in God.

4:1–3—Sanballat's sarcasm attempts to demoralize the builders by questioning their ability, their dependence upon God, and the quality of the building materials.

4:4–5—When Sanballat insults the project, he

insults God. Nehemiah responds with prayer. The strong language is similar to psalmic imprecations (e.g., Pss. 58:6–9; 59:5; 109:6–19) that leave vindication to God. Jesus' advice that we love our enemies and pray for them (Matt. 5:44) should give us pause here. Nevertheless, these offensive words indicate the depth of Nehemiah's feelings. He realized that these threats were a direct attack upon God's plans for the community.

cover their guilt, and do not let their sin be blotted out from your sight; for they have hurled insults in the face of the builders.

6 So we rebuilt the wall, and all the wall was joined together to half its height; for the people had a mind to work.

7[a] But when Sanballat and Tobiah and the Arabs and the Ammonites and the Ashdodites heard that the repairing of the walls of Jerusalem was going forward and the gaps were beginning to be closed, they were very angry, 8 and all plotted together to come and fight against Jerusalem and to cause confusion in it. 9 So we prayed to our God, and set a guard as a protection against them day and night.

10 But Judah said, "The strength of the burden bearers is failing, and there is too much rubbish so that we are unable to work on the wall." 11 And our enemies said, "They will not know or see anything before we come upon them and kill them and stop the work." 12 When the Jews who lived near them came, they said to us ten times, "From all the places where they live[b] they will come up against us."[c] 13 So in the lowest parts of the space behind the wall, in open places, I stationed the people according to their families,[d] with their swords, their spears, and their bows. 14 After I looked these things over, I stood up and said to the nobles and the officials and the rest of the people, "Do not be afraid of them. Remember the LORD, who is great and awesome, and fight for your kin, your sons, your daughters, your wives, and your homes."

15 When our enemies heard that their plot was known to us, and that God had frustrated it, we all returned to the wall, each to his work. 16 From that day on, half of my servants worked on construction, and half held the spears, shields, bows, and body-armor; and the leaders posted themselves behind the whole house of Judah, 17 who were building the wall. The burden bearers carried their loads in such a way that each labored on the work with one hand and with the other held a weapon. 18 And each of the builders had his sword strapped at his side while he built. The man who sounded the trumpet was beside me. 19 And I said to the nobles, the officials, and the rest of the people, "The work is great and widely spread out, and we are separated far from one another on the wall. 20 Rally to us wherever you hear the sound of the trumpet. Our God will fight for us."

21 So we labored at the work, and half of them held the spears from break of dawn until the stars came out. 22 I also said to the people at that time, "Let every man and his servant pass the night inside Jerusalem, so that they may be a guard for us by night and may labor by day." 23 So neither I nor my brothers nor my servants nor the men of the guard who followed me ever took off our clothes; each kept his weapon in his right hand.[e]

Nehemiah Deals with Oppression

5 Now there was a great outcry of the people and of their wives against

[a] Ch 4.1 in Heb   [b] Cn: Heb *you return*   [c] Compare Gk Syr: Meaning of Heb uncertain   [d] Meaning of Heb uncertain   [e] Cn: Heb *each his weapon the water*

4:9 *Set a guard*—In addition to prayer, Nehemiah provides for defense. He perfectly balances spiritual and physical readiness by having some of the builders serve as guards (see v. 13). Prayer without action deprives God of vehicles through which deliverance may be won.

4:10–12—Internal collapse, as seen in a demoralizing lament (v. 10), the confidence of the enemies (v. 11), and the constant (*ten times* means "over and over") pleas of their neighbors to give up and return home (v. 12).

4:13–23—Nehemiah responds by rallying the workers with material from Israel's holy war traditions (vv. 14–15) and improving security. Again, Nehemiah augments faith in God with reassuring practical measures.

4:16 *My servants*—Nehemiah's personal bodyguard.

5:1–19 Economic Injustice Threatens the Community

The added pressures of the wall-building project

their Jewish kin. ²For there were those who said, "With our sons and our daughters, we are many; we must get grain, so that we may eat and stay alive." ³There were also those who said, "We are having to pledge our fields, our vineyards, and our houses in order to get grain during the famine." ⁴And there were those who said, "We are having to borrow money on our fields and vineyards to pay the king's tax. ⁵Now our flesh is the same as that of our kindred; our children are the same as their children; and yet we are forcing our sons and daughters to be slaves, and some of our daughters have been ravished; we are powerless, and our fields and vineyards now belong to others."

6 I was very angry when I heard their outcry and these complaints. ⁷After thinking it over, I brought charges against the nobles and the officials; I said to them, "You are all taking interest from your own people." And I called a great assembly to deal with them, ⁸and said to them, "As far as we were able, we have bought back our Jewish kindred who had been sold to other nations; but now you are selling your own kin, who must then be bought back by us!" They were silent, and could not find a word

to say. ⁹So I said, "The thing that you are doing is not good. Should you not walk in the fear of our God, to prevent the taunts of the nations our enemies? ¹⁰Moreover I and my brothers and my servants are lending them money and grain. Let us stop this taking of interest. ¹¹Restore to them, this very day, their fields, their vineyards, their olive orchards, and their houses, and the interest on money, grain, wine, and oil that you have been exacting from them." ¹²Then they said, "We will restore everything and demand nothing more from them. We will do as you say." And I called the priests, and made them take an oath to do as they had promised. ¹³I also shook out the fold of my garment and said, "So may God shake out everyone from house and from property who does not perform this promise. Thus may they be shaken out and emptied." And all the assembly said, "Amen," and praised the LORD. And the people did as they had promised.

The Generosity of Nehemiah

14 Moreover from the time that I was appointed to be their governor in the land of Judah, from the twentieth year to the thirty-second year of King

---

fostered an economic crisis when creditors began to foreclose on their neighbors.

5:2–4—Three separate complaints: from those who owned no land and had no food (v. 2), those who had to mortgage their land to obtain food (v. 3), and those who needed to mortgage their land to pay taxes to Persia (v. 4).

5:5 Our flesh . . . kindred—The creditors were foreclosing on members of their own community.

5:6–13—Nehemiah responds by convening a public assembly.

5:7 Taking interest—Charging interest was forbidden (Deut. 23:19–20); however, it was not the problem. The **nobles and officials** were foreclosing on pledges, which is legal, though limited (Exod. 22:25–27; Deut. 24:10). Taking advantage of kin was far more upsetting to Nehemiah, who took pledges (Neh. 5:10) but apparently did not foreclose on them.

5:8–11—Nehemiah reminds them that they have just **bought back** their kindred from debt slavery.

The community, above all, should realize the problems that this kind of injustice fosters. Then, appealing to their faith, **Should you not walk in the fear of our God?** as well as their pride, **to prevent the taunts of the nations our enemies?** he urges them to stop (vv. 9–11).

5:12–13—The priests administer an oath to solidify the transgressors' promise to comply and to rekindle the community's sense of unity, now that the division caused by the foreclosures had been removed.

5:14–19—While this account of Nehemiah's generosity comes from a later period, during his second term as governor, it nicely illustrates the principle of Nehemiah's leading by example.

5:14—Nehemiah's first term as governor lasted **twelve years** (445–433 BCE), after which he returned to Persia (13:6).

5:14–19—Unlike other governors, Nehemiah refused Persian provisions that came from taxes his people paid.

Artaxerxes, twelve years, neither I nor my brothers ate the food allowance of the governor. [15] The former governors who were before me laid heavy burdens on the people, and took food and wine from them, besides forty shekels of silver. Even their servants lorded it over the people. But I did not do so, because of the fear of God. [16] Indeed, I devoted myself to the work on this wall, and acquired no land; and all my servants were gathered there for the work. [17] Moreover there were at my table one hundred fifty people, Jews and officials, besides those who came to us from the nations around us. [18] Now that which was prepared for one day was one ox and six choice sheep; also fowls were prepared for me, and every ten days skins of wine in abundance; yet with all this I did not demand the food allowance of the governor, because of the heavy burden of labor on the people. [19] Remember for my good, O my God, all that I have done for this people.

Intrigues of Enemies Foiled

6 Now when it was reported to Sanballat and Tobiah and to Geshem the Arab and to the rest of our enemies that I had built the wall and that there was no gap left in it (though up to that time I had not set up the doors in the gates), [2] Sanballat and Geshem sent to me, saying, "Come and let us meet together in one of the villages in the plain of Ono." But they intended to do me harm. [3] So I sent messengers to them, saying, "I am doing a great work and I cannot come down. Why should the work stop while I leave it to come down to you?" [4] They sent to me four times in this way, and I answered them in the same manner. [5] In the same way Sanballat for the fifth time sent his servant to me with an open letter in his hand. [6] In it was written, "It is reported among the nations—and Geshem[a] also says it—that you and the Jews intend to rebel; that is why you are building the wall; and according to this report you wish to become their king. [7] You have also set up prophets to proclaim in Jerusalem concerning you, 'There is a king in Judah!' And now it will be reported to the king according to these words. So come, therefore, and let us confer together." [8] Then I sent to him, saying, "No such things as you say have been done; you are inventing them out of your own mind" [9]—for they all wanted to frighten us, thinking, "Their hands will drop from the work, and it will not be done." But now, O God, strengthen my hands.

10 One day when I went into the house of Shemaiah son of Delaiah son of Mehetabel, who was confined to his house, he said, "Let us meet together in the house of God, within the temple, and let us close the doors of the temple, for they are coming to kill you; indeed, tonight they are coming to kill you." [11] But I said, "Should a man like me run away? Would a man like me go into the temple to save his life? I will not go in!" [12] Then I perceived and saw that God had not sent him at all, but he had pronounced the prophecy against me because Tobiah and Sanballat had hired

[a] Heb Gashmu

5:19 Remember [me]—Similar prayers appear in 13:14, 22, 31 (cf. 6:14; 13:29). While it sounds somewhat self-righteous, an addition in 13:22, "according to the greatness of your steadfast love," makes it clear that God's grace lies behind Nehemiah's exemplary public service.

6:1–7:3 Nehemiah Completes the Wall

The opponents turn against Nehemiah with three episodes of intimidation, one involving each of the three relationships that mattered most to him: Artaxerxes, God, and the community.

6:1–9—After failing to lure Nehemiah to a secluded village to harm him (vv. 2–4), Sanballat threatens to blackmail him with charges of sedition (vv. 5–7) that would discredit him with Artaxerxes. Nehemiah resists, as always, by looking to God for help in prayer (v. 9).

6:10–14—In a second attempted intimidation Tobiah seeks to lure Nehemiah into the temple sanctuary, forbidden to laypersons (Num. 18:7) to discredit him with God. Again, Nehemiah resists through fervent prayer (Neh. 6:14).

him. ¹³He was hired for this purpose, to intimidate me and make me sin by acting in this way, and so they could give me a bad name, in order to taunt me. ¹⁴Remember Tobiah and Sanballat, O my God, according to these things that they did, and also the prophetess Noadiah and the rest of the prophets who wanted to make me afraid.

The Wall Completed

15 So the wall was finished on the twenty-fifth day of the month Elul, in fifty-two days. ¹⁶And when all our enemies heard of it, all the nations around us were afraid*a* and fell greatly in their own esteem; for they perceived that this work had been accomplished with the help of our God. ¹⁷Moreover in those days the nobles of Judah sent many letters to Tobiah, and Tobiah's letters came to them. ¹⁸For many in Judah were bound by oath to him, because he was the son-in-law of Shecaniah son of Arah: and his son Jehohanan had married the daughter of Meshullam son of Berechiah. ¹⁹Also they spoke of his good deeds in my presence, and reported my words to him. And Tobiah sent letters to intimidate me.

7 Now when the wall had been built and I had set up the doors, and the gatekeepers, the singers, and the Levites had been appointed, ²I gave my brother Hanani charge over Jerusalem, along with Hananiah the commander of the citadel—for he was a faithful man and feared God more than many. ³And I said to them, "The gates of Jerusalem are not to be opened until the sun is hot; while the gatekeepers*b* are still standing guard, let them shut and bar the doors. Appoint guards from among the inhabitants of Jerusalem, some at their watch posts, and others before their own houses." ⁴The city was wide and large, but the people within it were few and no houses had been built.

Lists of the Returned Exiles

5 Then my God put it into my mind to assemble the nobles and the officials and the people to be enrolled by genealogy. And I found the book of the genealogy of those who were the first to come back, and I found the following written in it:

6 These are the people of the province who came up out of the captivity of those exiles whom King Nebuchadnezzar of Babylon had carried into exile; they returned to Jerusalem and Judah, each to his town. ⁷They came with Zerubbabel, Jeshua, Nehemiah, Azariah, Raamiah, Nahamani, Mordecai, Bilshan, Mispereth, Bigvai, Nehum, Baanah.

The number of the Israelite people: ⁸the descendants of Parosh, two thousand one hundred seventy-two. ⁹Of Shephatiah, three hundred seventy-two. ¹⁰Of Arah, six hundred fifty-two. ¹¹Of Pahath-moab, namely the descendants of Jeshua and Joab, two thousand eight

*a*Another reading is *saw*   *b*Heb *while they*

6:15–16—The wall is completed in a remarkably short time. We can marvel at the efficient leadership of Nehemiah and credit him with the speedy completion of the project, but Nehemiah's enemies know the real reason: *the help of our God.*

6:17–19—In a third attempted intimidation *the nobles of Judah* seek to discredit Nehemiah with the people through correspondence with Tobiah.

7:1–3—Nehemiah secures the city and appoints his *brother Hanani*, who had first alerted him to the problem (1:2), in charge.

7:4–73a List of Returnees

This list of returnees repeats Ezra 2:1–70. The lists together frame the three episodes of return and reconstruction: Zerubbabel and the rebuilding of the temple (Ezra 1–6); Ezra and the rebuilding of the community (Ezra 7–10); and Nehemiah and the rebuilding of the walls of Jerusalem (Neh. 1:1–7:3). By repeating this list Nehemiah makes the important point that those who had returned from exile—only to meet problems of religious identity, economic injustice, physically taxing building projects, and emotionally draining opposition complete with slander and intimidation—had triumphed with the help of their God and solid leadership. They now take their place as the inheritors of the great tradition of Israel, ready to be unified in the hearing of God's word.

hundred eighteen. ¹²Of Elam, one thousand two hundred fifty-four. ¹³Of Zattu, eight hundred forty-five. ¹⁴Of Zaccai, seven hundred sixty. ¹⁵Of Binnui, six hundred forty-eight. ¹⁶Of Bebai, six hundred twenty-eight. ¹⁷Of Azgad, two thousand three hundred twenty-two. ¹⁸Of Adonikam, six hundred sixty-seven. ¹⁹Of Bigvai, two thousand sixty-seven. ²⁰Of Adin, six hundred fifty-five. ²¹Of Ater, namely of Hezekiah, ninety-eight. ²²Of Hashum, three hundred twenty-eight. ²³Of Bezai, three hundred twenty-four. ²⁴Of Hariph, one hundred twelve. ²⁵Of Gibeon, ninety-five. ²⁶The people of Bethlehem and Netophah, one hundred eighty-eight. ²⁷Of Anathoth, one hundred twenty-eight. ²⁸Of Beth-azmaveth, forty-two. ²⁹Of Kiriath-jearim, Chephirah, and Beeroth, seven hundred forty-three. ³⁰Of Ramah and Geba, six hundred twenty-one. ³¹Of Michmas, one hundred twenty-two. ³²Of Bethel and Ai, one hundred twenty-three. ³³Of the other Nebo, fifty-two. ³⁴The descendants of the other Elam, one thousand two hundred fifty-four. ³⁵Of Harim, three hundred twenty. ³⁶Of Jericho, three hundred forty-five. ³⁷Of Lod, Hadid, and Ono, seven hundred twenty-one. ³⁸Of Senaah, three thousand nine hundred thirty.

39 The priests: the descendants of Jedaiah, namely the house of Jeshua, nine hundred seventy-three. ⁴⁰Of Immer, one thousand fifty-two. ⁴¹Of Pashhur, one thousand two hundred forty-seven. ⁴²Of Harim, one thousand seventeen.

43 The Levites: the descendants of Jeshua, namely of Kadmiel of the descendants of Hodevah, seventy-four. ⁴⁴The singers: the descendants of Asaph, one hundred forty-eight. ⁴⁵The gatekeepers: the descendants of Shallum, of Ater, of Talmon, of Akkub, of Hatita, of Shobai, one hundred thirty-eight.

46 The temple servants: the descendants of Ziha, of Hasupha, of Tabbaoth, ⁴⁷of Keros, of Sia, of Padon, ⁴⁸of Lebana, of Hagaba, of Shalmai, ⁴⁹of Hanan, of

Giddel, of Gahar, ⁵⁰of Reaiah, of Rezin, of Nekoda, ⁵¹of Gazzam, of Uzza, of Paseah, ⁵²of Besai, of Meunim, of Nephushesim, ⁵³of Bakbuk, of Hakupha, of Harhur, ⁵⁴of Bazlith, of Mehida, of Harsha, ⁵⁵of Barkos, of Sisera, of Temah, ⁵⁶of Neziah, of Hatipha.

57 The descendants of Solomon's servants: of Sotai, of Sophereth, of Perida, ⁵⁸of Jaala, of Darkon, of Giddel, ⁵⁹of Shephatiah, of Hattil, of Pochereth-hazzebaim, of Amon.

60 All the temple servants and the descendants of Solomon's servants were three hundred ninety-two.

61 The following were those who came up from Tel-melah, Tel-harsha, Cherub, Addon, and Immer, but they could not prove their ancestral houses or their descent, whether they belonged to Israel: ⁶²the descendants of Delaiah, of Tobiah, of Nekoda, six hundred forty-two. ⁶³Also, of the priests: the descendants of Hobaiah, of Hakkoz, of Barzillai (who had married one of the daughters of Barzillai the Gileadite and was called by their name). ⁶⁴These sought their registration among those enrolled in the genealogies, but it was not found there, so they were excluded from the priesthood as unclean; ⁶⁵the governor told them that they were not to partake of the most holy food, until a priest with Urim and Thummim should come.

66 The whole assembly together was forty-two thousand three hundred sixty, ⁶⁷besides their male and female slaves, of whom there were seven thousand three hundred thirty-seven; and they had two hundred forty-five singers, male and female. ⁶⁸They had seven hundred thirty-six horses, two hundred forty-five mules,ᵃ ⁶⁹four hundred thirty-five camels, and six thousand seven hundred twenty donkeys.

70 Now some of the heads of ancestral houses contributed to the work. The governor gave to the treasury one thousand

ᵃ Ezra 2.66 and the margins of some Hebrew Mss: MT lacks *They had . . . forty-five mules*

darics of gold, fifty basins, and five hundred thirty priestly robes. ⁷¹ And some of the heads of ancestral houses gave into the building fund twenty thousand darics of gold and two thousand two hundred minas of silver. ⁷² And what the rest of the people gave was twenty thousand darics of gold, two thousand minas of silver, and sixty-seven priestly robes.

73 So the priests, the Levites, the gatekeepers, the singers, some of the people, the temple servants, and all Israel settled in their towns.

Ezra Summons the People to Obey the Law

When the seventh month came—the people of Israel being settled in their **8** towns— ¹ all the people gathered together into the square before the Water Gate. They told the scribe Ezra to bring the book of the law of Moses, which the LORD had given to Israel. ² Accordingly, the priest Ezra brought the law before the assembly, both men and women and all who could hear with understanding. This was on the first day of the seventh month. ³ He read from it facing the square before the Water Gate from early morning until midday, in the presence of the men and the women and those who could understand; and the ears of all the people were attentive to the book of the law. ⁴ The scribe Ezra stood on a wooden platform that had been made for the purpose; and beside him stood Mattithiah, Shema, Anaiah, Uriah, Hilkiah, and Maase-

iah on his right hand; and Pedaiah, Mishael, Malchijah, Hashum, Hashbaddanah, Zechariah, and Meshullam on his left hand. ⁵ And Ezra opened the book in the sight of all the people, for he was standing above all the people; and when he opened it, all the people stood up. ⁶ Then Ezra blessed the LORD, the great God, and all the people answered, "Amen, Amen," lifting up their hands. Then they bowed their heads and worshiped the LORD with their faces to the ground. ⁷ Also Jeshua, Bani, Sherebiah, Jamin, Akkub, Shabbethai, Hodiah, Maaseiah, Kelita, Azariah, Jozabad, Hanan, Pelaiah, the Levites,ᵃ helped the people to understand the law, while the people remained in their places. ⁸ So they read from the book, from the law of God, with interpretation. They gave the sense, so that the people understood the reading.

9 And Nehemiah, who was the governor, and Ezra the priest and scribe, and the Levites who taught the people said to all the people, "This day is holy to the LORD your God; do not mourn or weep." For all the people wept when they heard the words of the law. ¹⁰ Then he said to them, "Go your way, eat the fat and drink sweet wine and send portions of them to those for whom nothing is prepared, for this day is holy to our LORD; and do not be grieved, for the joy of the LORD is your strength." ¹¹ So the Levites stilled all the people, saying,

ᵃ 1 Esdras 9.48 Vg: Heb *and the Levites*

7:73b–10:39 Covenant Renewal

Ezra, the priest and scribe familiar from Ezra 7–10, now takes center stage to deal with matters of law, confession, and renewal. The joyful celebration of the Festival of Booths provides an appropriate backdrop for Israel's rejoicing when they hear the law read for the first time.

7:73b–8:12 Ezra Reads the Law

At their request, an early version of the Pentateuch, compiled during the exile, is presented to the people for the first time. Its message will change their lives.

7:73b *Seventh month*—September/October 444.

The altar and sacrificial worship had been reestablished also in the seventh month (Ezra 3:1). In later Judaism this day is New Year's Day.

8:3–8—Ezra read, in Hebrew, for six hours, from *a wooden platform* (lit. a "tower"), while the *Levites* interpreted, probably in Aramaic.

8:9–12—The people are chided for lamenting their failure to observe the law, possibly because this day (*the first day of the seventh month*, v. 2) was to be a day of rejoicing and sharing (Num. 29:1). Proper understanding of the biblical message, even the law, leads to joy in the Lord and compassionate concern for others.

"Be quiet, for this day is holy; do not be grieved." ¹² And all the people went their way to eat and drink and to send portions and to make great rejoicing, because they had understood the words that were declared to them.

The Festival of Booths Celebrated

13 On the second day the heads of ancestral houses of all the people, with the priests and the Levites, came together to the scribe Ezra in order to study the words of the law. ¹⁴ And they found it written in the law, which the LORD had commanded by Moses, that the people of Israel should live in booths*a* during the festival of the seventh month, ¹⁵ and that they should publish and proclaim in all their towns and in Jerusalem as follows, "Go out to the hills and bring branches of olive, wild olive, myrtle, palm, and other leafy trees to make booths,*a* as it is written." ¹⁶ So the people went out and brought them, and made booths*a* for themselves, each on the roofs of their houses, and in their courts and in the courts of the house of God, and in the square at the Water Gate and in the square at the Gate of Ephraim. ¹⁷ And all the assembly of those who had returned from the captivity made booths*a* and lived in them; for from the days of Jeshua son of Nun to that day the people of Israel had not done so. And there was very great rejoicing. ¹⁸ And day by day,

from the first day to the last day, he read from the book of the law of God. They kept the festival seven days; and on the eighth day there was a solemn assembly, according to the ordinance.

National Confession

9 Now on the twenty-fourth day of this month the people of Israel were assembled with fasting and in sackcloth, and with earth on their heads.*b* ² Then those of Israelite descent separated themselves from all foreigners, and stood and confessed their sins and the iniquities of their ancestors. ³ They stood up in their place and read from the book of the law of the LORD their God for a fourth part of the day, and for another fourth they made confession and worshiped the LORD their God. ⁴ Then Jeshua, Bani, Kadmiel, Shebaniah, Bunni, Sherebiah, Bani, and Chenani stood on the stairs of the Levites and cried out with a loud voice to the LORD their God. ⁵ Then the Levites, Jeshua, Kadmiel, Bani, Hashabneiah, Sherebiah, Hodiah, Shebaniah, and Pethahiah, said, "Stand up and bless the LORD your God from everlasting to everlasting. Blessed be your glorious name, which is exalted above all blessing and praise."

6 And Ezra said:*c* "You are the LORD, you alone; you have made heaven, the

a Or *tabernacles;* Heb *succoth*   *b* Heb *on them*   *c* Gk: Heb lacks *And Ezra said*

8:13–18 The Festival of Booths

Further study convinced the people to observe the Festival of Booths (Lev. 23:33–43), which had not been celebrated since the conquest of the land (Neh. 8:17). This conflicts with Ezra 3:4. Perhaps the text means that the festival had never before been celebrated with so much joy.

9:1–37 Confession of Sins

The people confess their sin and renew the covenant at a second liturgical assembly.

9:1–6a—Preparations include fasting and wearing sackcloth and ashes, signs of repentance usually associated with the Day of Atonement, usually observed on the tenth of the month (Lev. 23:26–32). Neither Ezra nor Nehemiah appears in this section so that the Levites lead the people's six-hour service of reading and confes-

sion and recite the following prayer (Heb. lacks *Ezra said*, Neh. 9:6a).

9:6b–37—The prayer, consisting of citations and allusions to Scripture, falls into five sections: Confession in the form of historical retrospect (vv. 6–31) and confession of present sin (vv. 33–35) frame the only petition (v. 32), while brief praise (v. 5b) and lament (vv. 36–37) open and close the prayer. After praising God's goodness and grace (vv. 6–11), evident even in the face of Israel's repeated rebellion (vv. 12–31), the community prays for mercy in their time (v. 32). The second round of confession indicates that the people now recognize themselves in the sins of their ancestors (vv. 33–35) and that their present situation is not due to any lack on God's part (vv. 35–37). The prayer reminds us that the

heaven of heavens, with all their host, the earth and all that is on it, the seas and all that is in them. To all of them you give life, and the host of heaven worships you. [7] You are the LORD, the God who chose Abram and brought him out of Ur of the Chaldeans and gave him the name Abraham; [8] and you found his heart faithful before you, and made with him a covenant to give to his descendants the land of the Canaanite, the Hittite, the Amorite, the Perizzite, the Jebusite, and the Girgashite; and you have fulfilled your promise, for you are righteous.

[9] "And you saw the distress of our ancestors in Egypt and heard their cry at the Red Sea.[a] [10] You performed signs and wonders against Pharaoh and all his servants and all the people of his land, for you knew that they acted insolently against our ancestors. You made a name for yourself, which remains to this day. [11] And you divided the sea before them, so that they passed through the sea on dry land, but you threw their pursuers into the depths, like a stone into mighty waters. [12] Moreover, you led them by day with a pillar of cloud, and by night with a pillar of fire, to give them light on the way in which they should go. [13] You came down also upon Mount Sinai, and spoke with them from heaven, and gave them right ordinances and true laws, good statutes and commandments, [14] and you made known your holy sabbath to them and gave them commandments and statutes and a law through your servant Moses. [15] For their hunger you gave them bread from heaven, and for their thirst you brought water for them out of the rock, and you told them to go in to possess the land that you swore to give them.

[16] "But they and our ancestors acted presumptuously and stiffened their necks and did not obey your command-ments; [17] they refused to obey, and were not mindful of the wonders that you performed among them; but they stiffened their necks and determined to return to their slavery in Egypt. But you are a God ready to forgive, gracious and merciful, slow to anger and abounding in steadfast love, and you did not forsake them. [18] Even when they had cast an image of a calf for themselves and said, 'This is your God who brought you up out of Egypt,' and had committed great blasphemies, [19] you in your great mercies did not forsake them in the wilderness; the pillar of cloud that led them in the way did not leave them by day, nor the pillar of fire by night that gave them light on the way by which they should go. [20] You gave your good spirit to instruct them, and did not withhold your manna from their mouths, and gave them water for their thirst. [21] Forty years you sustained them in the wilderness so that they lacked nothing; their clothes did not wear out and their feet did not swell. [22] And you gave them kingdoms and peoples, and allotted to them every corner,[b] so they took possession of the land of King Sihon of Heshbon and the land of King Og of Bashan. [23] You multiplied their descendants like the stars of heaven, and brought them into the land that you had told their ancestors to enter and possess. [24] So the descendants went in and possessed the land, and you subdued before them the inhabitants of the land, the Canaanites, and gave them into their hands, with their kings and the peoples of the land, to do with them as they pleased. [25] And they captured fortress cities and a rich land, and took possession of houses filled with all sorts of goods, hewn cisterns, vineyards, olive orchards, and fruit trees in abundance; so they ate, and were filled and became fat, and delighted themselves in your great goodness.

[a] Or Sea of Reeds   [b] Meaning of Heb uncertain

---

sins of the community, past and present, are as problematic as our individual shortcomings. It also promises the grace of God for instruction, encouragement, and forgiveness.

26 "Nevertheless they were disobedient and rebelled against you and cast your law behind their backs and killed your prophets, who had warned them in order to turn them back to you, and they committed great blasphemies. 27 Therefore you gave them into the hands of their enemies, who made them suffer. Then in the time of their suffering they cried out to you and you heard them from heaven, and according to your great mercies you gave them saviors who saved them from the hands of their enemies. 28 But after they had rest, they again did evil before you, and you abandoned them to the hands of their enemies, so that they had dominion over them; yet when they turned and cried to you, you heard from heaven, and many times you rescued them according to your mercies. 29 And you warned them in order to turn them back to your law. Yet they acted presumptuously and did not obey your commandments, but sinned against your ordinances, by the observance of which a person shall live. They turned a stubborn shoulder and stiffened their neck and would not obey. 30 Many years you were patient with them, and warned them by your spirit through your prophets; yet they would not listen. Therefore you handed them over to the peoples of the lands. 31 Nevertheless, in your great mercies you did not make an end of them or forsake them, for you are a gracious and merciful God.

32 "Now therefore, our God—the great and mighty and awesome God, keeping covenant and steadfast love— do not treat lightly all the hardship that has come upon us, upon our kings, our officials, our priests, our prophets, our ancestors, and all your people, since the time of the kings of Assyria until today. 33 You have been just in all that has come upon us, for you have dealt faithfully and we have acted wickedly; 34 our kings, our officials, our priests, and our ancestors have not kept your law or heeded the commandments and the warnings that you gave them. 35 Even in their own kingdom, and in the great goodness you bestowed on them, and in the large and rich land that you set before them, they did not serve you and did not turn from their wicked works. 36 Here we are, slaves to this day—slaves in the land that you gave to our ancestors to enjoy its fruit and its good gifts. 37 Its rich yield goes to the kings whom you have set over us because of our sins; they have power also over our bodies and over our livestock at their pleasure, and we are in great distress."

Those Who Signed the Covenant

38[a] Because of all this we make a firm agreement in writing, and on that sealed document are inscribed the names of our officials, our Levites, and our priests.

10[b] Upon the sealed document are the names of Nehemiah the governor, son of Hacaliah, and Zedekiah; 2 Seraiah, Azariah, Jeremiah, 3 Pashhur, Amariah, Malchijah, 4 Hattush, Shebaniah, Malluch, 5 Harim, Meremoth, Obadiah, 6 Daniel, Ginnethon, Baruch, 7 Meshullam, Abijah, Mijamin, 8 Maaziah, Bilgai, Shemaiah; these are the priests. 9 And the Levites: Jeshua son of Azaniah, Binnui of the sons of Henadad, Kadmiel; 10 and their associates, Shebaniah, Hodiah, Kelita, Pelaiah, Hanan, 11 Mica, Rehob, Hashabiah, 12 Zaccur,

a Ch 10.1 in Heb b Ch 10.2 in Heb

9:38–10:39 Covenant Renewal
The people decide to enter into a binding agreement with God to observe the law. It consists of two lists: those who signed the pledge (10:1–28) and the stipulations of the agreement (10:29–39). Taken together, these three Covenant Renewal chapters (7:73–10:39) provide a model for life together in community: Hearing God's word leads to self-reflection and confession, which in turn manifests itself in faithful service to others.

9:38 Firm agreement—A pledge initiated by the people, not the word for "covenant," that refers to divinely initiated promises in the postexilic period.

Sherebiah, Shebaniah, [13] Hodiah, Bani, Beninu. [14] The leaders of the people: Parosh, Pahath-moab, Elam, Zattu, Bani, [15] Bunni, Azgad, Bebai, [16] Adonijah, Bigvai, Adin, [17] Ater, Hezekiah, Azzur, [18] Hodiah, Hashum, Bezai, [19] Hariph, Anathoth, Nebai, [20] Magpiash, Meshullam, Hezir, [21] Meshezabel, Zadok, Jaddua, [22] Pelatiah, Hanan, Anaiah, [23] Hoshea, Hananiah, Hasshub, [24] Hallohesh, Pilha, Shobek, [25] Rehum, Hashabnah, Maaseiah, [26] Ahiah, Hanan, Anan, [27] Malluch, Harim, and Baanah.

Summary of the Covenant

28 The rest of the people, the priests, the Levites, the gatekeepers, the singers, the temple servants, and all who have separated themselves from the peoples of the lands to adhere to the law of God, their wives, their sons, their daughters, all who have knowledge and understanding, [29] join with their kin, their nobles, and enter into a curse and an oath to walk in God's law, which was given by Moses the servant of God, and to observe and do all the commandments of the LORD our Lord and his ordinances and his statutes. [30] We will not give our daughters to the peoples of the land or take their daughters for our sons; [31] and if the peoples of the land bring in merchandise or any grain on the sabbath day to sell, we will not buy it from them on the sabbath or on a holy day; and we will forego the crops of the seventh year and the exaction of every debt.

32 We also lay on ourselves the obligation to charge ourselves yearly one-third of a shekel for the service of the house of our God: [33] for the rows of bread, the regular grain offering, the regular burnt offering, the sabbaths, the new moons, the appointed festivals, the sacred donations, and the sin offerings to make atonement for Israel, and for all the work of the house of our God. [34] We have also cast lots among the priests, the Levites, and the people, for the wood offering, to bring it into the house of our God, by ancestral houses, at appointed times, year by year, to burn on the altar of the LORD our God, as it is written in the law. [35] We obligate ourselves to bring the first fruits of our soil and the first fruits of all fruit of every tree, year by year, to the house of the LORD; [36] also to bring to the house of our God, to the priests who minister in the house of our God, the firstborn of our sons and of our livestock, as it is written in the law, and the firstlings of our herds and of our flocks; [37] and to bring the first of our dough, and our contributions, the fruit of every tree, the wine and the oil, to the priests, to the chambers of the house of our God; and to bring to the Levites the tithes from our soil, for it is the Levites who collect the tithes in all our rural towns. [38] And the priest, the descendant of Aaron, shall be with the Levites when the Levites receive the tithes; and the Levites shall bring up a tithe of the tithes to the house of our God, to the chambers of the storehouse. [39] For the people of Israel and the sons of Levi shall bring the contribution of grain, wine, and oil to the storerooms where the vessels of the sanctuary are, and where the priests that minister, and the gatekeepers and the singers are. We will not neglect the house of our God.

Population of the City Increased

11 Now the leaders of the people lived in Jerusalem; and the rest of the people cast lots to bring one out of ten to live in the holy city Jerusalem,

---

11:1–12:26 Jerusalem Repopulated
These lists, compiled from different sources, return to where the narrative of 7:1–5a broke off, the problem of the reduced population of the city.

11:1–2—Nehemiah redistributed the population by bringing 10 percent of the outlying population back into the city—in effect, tithing God's people.

while nine-tenths remained in the other towns. ² And the people blessed all those who willingly offered to live in Jerusalem.

3 These are the leaders of the province who lived in Jerusalem; but in the towns of Judah all lived on their property in their towns: Israel, the priests, the Levites, the temple servants, and the descendants of Solomon's servants. ⁴ And in Jerusalem lived some of the Judahites and of the Benjaminites. Of the Judahites: Athaiah son of Uzziah son of Zechariah son of Amariah son of Shephatiah son of Mahalalel, of the descendants of Perez; ⁵ and Maaseiah son of Baruch son of Col-hozeh son of Hazaiah son of Adaiah son of Joiarib son of Zechariah son of the Shilonite. ⁶ All the descendants of Perez who lived in Jerusalem were four hundred sixty-eight valiant warriors.

7 And these are the Benjaminites: Sallu son of Meshullam son of Joed son of Pedaiah son of Kolaiah son of Maaseiah son of Ithiel son of Jeshaiah. ⁸ And his brothers*a* Gabbai, Sallai: nine hundred twenty-eight. ⁹ Joel son of Zichri was their overseer; and Judah son of Hassenuah was second in charge of the city.

10 Of the priests: Jedaiah son of Joiarib, Jachin, ¹¹ Seraiah son of Hilkiah son of Meshullam son of Zadok son of Meraioth son of Ahitub, officer of the house of God, ¹² and their associates who did the work of the house, eight hundred twenty-two; and Adaiah son of Jeroham son of Pelaliah son of Amzi son of Zechariah son of Pashhur son of Malchijah, ¹³ and his associates, heads of ancestral houses, two hundred forty-two; and Amashsai son of Azarel son of Ahzai son of Meshillemoth son of Immer, ¹⁴ and their associates, valiant warriors, one hundred twenty-eight; their overseer was Zabdiel son of Haggedolim.

15 And of the Levites: Shemaiah son of Hasshub son of Azrikam son of Hasha-

biah son of Bunni; ¹⁶ and Shabbethai and Jozabad, of the leaders of the Levites, who were over the outside work of the house of God; ¹⁷ and Mattaniah son of Mica son of Zabdi son of Asaph, who was the leader to begin the thanksgiving in prayer, and Bakbukiah, the second among his associates; and Abda son of Shammua son of Galal son of Jeduthun. ¹⁸ All the Levites in the holy city were two hundred eighty-four.

19 The gatekeepers, Akkub, Talmon and their associates, who kept watch at the gates, were one hundred seventy-two. ²⁰ And the rest of Israel, and of the priests and the Levites, were in all the towns of Judah, all of them in their inheritance. ²¹ But the temple servants lived on Ophel; and Ziha and Gishpa were over the temple servants.

22 The overseer of the Levites in Jerusalem was Uzzi son of Bani son of Hashabiah son of Mattaniah son of Mica, of the descendants of Asaph, the singers, in charge of the work of the house of God. ²³ For there was a command from the king concerning them, and a settled provision for the singers, as was required every day. ²⁴ And Pethahiah son of Meshezabel, of the descendants of Zerah son of Judah, was at the king's hand in all matters concerning the people.

Villages outside Jerusalem

25 And as for the villages, with their fields, some of the people of Judah lived in Kiriath-arba and its villages, and in Dibon and its villages, and in Jekabzeel and its villages, ²⁶ and in Jeshua and in Moladah and Beth-pelet, ²⁷ in Hazarshual, in Beer-sheba and its villages, ²⁸ in Ziklag, in Meconah and its villages, ²⁹ in En-rimmon, in Zorah, in Jarmuth, ³⁰ Zanoah, Adullam, and their villages, Lachish and its fields, and Azekah and its villages. So they camped from Beersheba to the valley of Hinnom. ³¹ The people of Benjamin also lived from

a Gk Mss: Heb *And after him*

Geba onward, at Michmash, Aija, Bethel and its villages, 32 Anathoth, Nob, Ananiah, 33 Hazor, Ramah, Gittaim, 34 Hadid, Zeboim, Neballat, 35 Lod, and Ono, the valley of artisans. 36 And certain divisions of the Levites in Judah were joined to Benjamin.

A List of Priests and Levites

12 These are the priests and the Levites who came up with Zerubbabel son of Shealtiel, and Jeshua: Seraiah, Jeremiah, Ezra, 2 Amariah, Malluch, Hattush, 3 Shecaniah, Rehum, Meremoth, 4 Iddo, Ginnethoi, Abijah, 5 Mijamin, Maadiah, Bilgah, 6 Shemaiah, Joiarib, Jedaiah, 7 Sallu, Amok, Hilkiah, Jedaiah. These were the leaders of the priests and of their associates in the days of Jeshua.

8 And the Levites: Jeshua, Binnui, Kadmiel, Sherebiah, Judah, and Mattaniah, who with his associates was in charge of the songs of thanksgiving. 9 And Bakbukiah and Unno their associates stood opposite them in the service. 10 Jeshua was the father of Joiakim, Joiakim the father of Eliashib, Eliashib the father of Joiada, 11 Joiada the father of Jonathan, and Jonathan the father of Jaddua.

12 In the days of Joiakim the priests, heads of ancestral houses, were: of Seraiah, Meraiah; of Jeremiah, Hananiah; 13 of Ezra, Meshullam; of Amariah, Jehohanan; 14 of Malluchi, Jonathan; of Shebaniah, Joseph; 15 of Harim, Adna; of Meraioth, Helkai; 16 of Iddo, Zechariah; of Ginnethon, Meshullam; 17 of Abijah, Zichri; of Miniamin, of Moadiah, Piltai; 18 of Bilgah, Shammua; of Shemaiah, Jehonathan; 19 of Joiarib, Mattenai; of Jedaiah, Uzzi; 20 of Sallai, Kallai; of Amok, Eber; 21 of Hilkiah, Hashabiah; of Jedaiah, Nethanel.

22 As for the Levites, in the days of Eliashib, Joiada, Johanan, and Jaddua, there were recorded the heads of ancestral houses; also the priests until the reign of Darius the Persian. 23 The Levites, heads of ancestral houses, were recorded in the Book of the Annals until the days of Johanan son of Eliashib. 24 And the leaders of the Levites: Hashabiah, Sherebiah, and Jeshua son of Kadmiel, with their associates over against them, to praise and to give thanks, according to the commandment of David the man of God, section opposite to section. 25 Mattaniah, Bakbukiah, Obadiah, Meshullam, Talmon, and Akkub were gatekeepers standing guard at the storehouses of the gates. 26 These were in the days of Joiakim son of Jeshua son of Jozadak, and in the days of the governor Nehemiah and of the priest Ezra, the scribe.

Dedication of the City Wall

27 Now at the dedication of the wall of Jerusalem they sought out the Levites in all their places, to bring them to Jerusalem to celebrate the dedication with rejoicing, with thanksgivings and with singing, with cymbals, harps, and lyres. 28 The companies of the singers gathered together from the circuit around Jerusalem and from the villages of the Netophathites; 29 also from Beth-gilgal and from the region of Geba and Azmaveth; for the singers had built for themselves villages around Jerusalem. 30 And the priests and the Levites purified themselves; and they purified the people and the gates and the wall.

12:27–43 Dedication of the Walls
Two symmetrical companies, one led by Ezra (v. 36), the other led by Nehemiah (v. 38), leave the city through the Valley Gate on the western wall and process in opposite directions around the city. Upon their arrival at the Guard's Gate (supposedly near the temple) the companies enter the city to join in a combined service of praise and thanksgiving in the temple. But more than walls

are being dedicated here. The community has arrived, been purified, been nurtured by appropriate application of God's word and law to their situation, and been endowed with the religious leadership it will need to survive as the reconstituted people of God. This text functions as a climax to Ezra–Nehemiah.

12:30 *Purified . . . the gates and the wall*—Purification takes place prior to the celebration.

31 Then I brought the leaders of Judah up onto the wall, and appointed two great companies that gave thanks and went in procession. One went to the right on the wall to the Dung Gate; 32 and after them went Hoshaiah and half the officials of Judah, 33 and Azariah, Ezra, Meshullam, 34 Judah, Benjamin, Shemaiah, and Jeremiah, 35 and some of the young priests with trumpets: Zechariah son of Jonathan son of Shemaiah son of Mattaniah son of Micaiah son of Zaccur son of Asaph; 36 and his kindred, Shemaiah, Azarel, Milalai, Gilalai, Maai, Nethanel, Judah, and Hanani, with the musical instruments of David the man of God; and the scribe Ezra went in front of them. 37 At the Fountain Gate, in front of them, they went straight up by the stairs of the city of David, at the ascent of the wall, above the house of David, to the Water Gate on the east.

38 The other company of those who gave thanks went to the left,[a] and I followed them with half of the people on the wall, above the Tower of the Ovens, to the Broad Wall, 39 and above the Gate of Ephraim, and by the Old Gate, and by the Fish Gate and the Tower of Hananel and the Tower of the Hundred, to the Sheep Gate; and they came to a halt at the Gate of the Guard. 40 So both companies of those who gave thanks stood in the house of God, and I and half of the officials with me; 41 and the priests Eliakim, Maaseiah, Miniamin, Micaiah, Elioenai, Zechariah, and Hananiah, with trumpets; 42 and Maaseiah, Shemaiah, Eleazar, Uzzi, Jehohanan, Malchijah, Elam, and Ezer. And the singers sang with Jezrahiah as their leader. 43 They offered great sacrifices that day and rejoiced, for God had made them rejoice with great joy; the women and children also rejoiced. The joy of Jerusalem was heard far away.

Temple Responsibilities

44 On that day men were appointed over the chambers for the stores, the contributions, the first fruits, and the tithes, to gather into them the portions required by the law for the priests and for the Levites from the fields belonging to the towns; for Judah rejoiced over the priests and the Levites who ministered. 45 They performed the service of their God and the service of purification, as did the singers and the gatekeepers, according to the command of David and his son Solomon. 46 For in the days of David and Asaph long ago there was a leader of the singers, and there were songs of praise and thanksgiving to God. 47 In the days of Zerubbabel and in the days of Nehemiah all Israel gave the daily portions for the singers and the gatekeepers. They set apart that which was for the Levites; and the Levites set apart that which was for the descendants of Aaron.

[a] Cn: Heb *opposite*

The purification of the priests and Levites may have included bathing, abstinence from sexual intercourse, washing clothes, fasting, and ritual sprinkling. The purification of the gates and the wall is unprecedented in the Bible. It may mean that Jerusalem is a holy city, or that it needs to be ritually cleansed of the defilement of its previously ruined state.

12:44–13:31 Coda: Nehemiah's Second Term as Governor

Following the climactic dedication of the walls the narrative concludes with several episodes from Nehemiah's second term as governor. Nehemiah leaves Jerusalem in the thirty-second year of Artaxerxes (433 BCE; 13:6, cf. 5:14), returning to Persia as he has promised (2:6). While he is gone, however, the community falls back into their old, sinful ways by failing to maintain the purity of the temple (vv. 4–14) and the sanctity of the Sabbath (vv. 15–22). In addition, despite Ezra's reforms (Ezra 9–10) intermarriage with the Ashdodites is again a problem. Nehemiah's violent attack upon all three situations needs to be seen as indicative of the seriousness of the threat of foreign influence upon this community at this time, not as a model of enlightened leadership. His very human reaction makes us all the more empathetic to his struggle to do God's will in a difficult situation. Rather than focus on his involvement in ethnic cleansing (Neh. 13:30), we would be better advised to look to his ceaseless prayer and trust in God's continuing grace.

Foreigners Separated from Israel

13 On that day they read from the book of Moses in the hearing of the people; and in it was found written that no Ammonite or Moabite should ever enter the assembly of God, [2] because they did not meet the Israelites with bread and water, but hired Balaam against them to curse them—yet our God turned the curse into a blessing. [3] When the people heard the law, they separated from Israel all those of foreign descent.

The Reforms of Nehemiah

[4] Now before this, the priest Eliashib, who was appointed over the chambers of the house of our God, and who was related to Tobiah, [5] prepared for Tobiah a large room where they had previously put the grain offering, the frankincense, the vessels, and the tithes of grain, wine, and oil, which were given by commandment to the Levites, singers, and gatekeepers, and the contributions for the priests. [6] While this was taking place I was not in Jerusalem, for in the thirty-second year of King Artaxerxes of Babylon I went to the king. After some time I asked leave of the king [7] and returned to Jerusalem. I then discovered the wrong that Eliashib had done on behalf of Tobiah, preparing a room for him in the courts of the house of God. [8] And I was very angry, and I threw all the household furniture of Tobiah out of the room. [9] Then I gave orders and they cleansed the chambers, and I brought back the vessels of the house of God, with the grain offering and the frankincense.

[10] I also found out that the portions of the Levites had not been given to them; so that the Levites and the singers, who had conducted the service, had gone back to their fields. [11] So I remonstrated with the officials and said, "Why is the house of God forsaken?" And I gathered them together and set them in their stations. [12] Then all Judah brought the tithe of the grain, wine, and oil into the storehouses.

[13] And I appointed as treasurers over the storehouses the priest Shelemiah, the scribe Zadok, and Pedaiah of the Levites, and as their assistant Hanan son of Zaccur son of Mattaniah, for they were considered faithful; and their duty was to distribute to their associates. [14] Remember me, O my God, concerning this, and do not wipe out my good deeds that I have done for the house of my God and for his service.

Sabbath Reforms Begun

[15] In those days I saw in Judah people treading wine presses on the sabbath, and bringing in heaps of grain and loading them on donkeys; and also wine, grapes, figs, and all kinds of burdens, which they brought into Jerusalem on the sabbath day; and I warned them at that time against selling food. [16] Tyrians also, who lived in the city, brought in fish and all kinds of merchandise and sold them on the sabbath to the people of Judah, and in Jerusalem. [17] Then I remonstrated with the nobles of Judah and said to them, "What is this evil thing that you are doing, profaning the sabbath day? [18] Did not your ancestors act in this way, and did not our God bring all this disaster on us and on this city? Yet you bring more wrath on Israel by profaning the sabbath."

[19] When it began to be dark at the gates of Jerusalem before the sabbath, I commanded that the doors should be shut and gave orders that they should not be opened until after the sabbath. And I set some of my servants over the gates, to prevent any burden from being brought in on the sabbath day. [20] Then the merchants and sellers of all kinds of merchandise spent the night outside Jerusalem once or twice. [21] But I warned them and said to them, "Why do you spend the night in front of the wall? If you do so again, I will lay hands on you." From that time on they did not come on the sabbath. [22] And I commanded the Levites that they should purify themselves and come and guard the gates, to

keep the sabbath day holy. Remember this also in my favor, O my God, and spare me according to the greatness of your steadfast love.

Mixed Marriages Condemned

23 In those days also I saw Jews who had married women of Ashdod, Ammon, and Moab; 24 and half of their children spoke the language of Ashdod, and they could not speak the language of Judah, but spoke the language of various peoples. 25 And I contended with them and cursed them and beat some of them and pulled out their hair; and I made them take an oath in the name of God, saying, "You shall not give your daughters to their sons, or take their daughters for your sons or for yourselves. 26 Did not King Solomon of Israel sin on account of such women? Among the many nations there was no king like him, and he was beloved by his God, and God made him king over all Israel; nevertheless, foreign women made even him to sin. 27 Shall we then listen to you and do all this great evil and act treacherously against our God by marrying foreign women?"

28 And one of the sons of Jehoiada, son of the high priest Eliashib, was the son-in-law of Sanballat the Horonite; I chased him away from me. 29 Remember them, O my God, because they have defiled the priesthood, the covenant of the priests and the Levites.

30 Thus I cleansed them from everything foreign, and I established the duties of the priests and Levites, each in his work; 31 and I provided for the wood offering, at appointed times, and for the first fruits. Remember me, O my God, for good.

The Book of
ESTHER

The story of Esther is often known as the biblical book that includes a beauty pageant. Yet far more than beauty, the primary character displays wisdom, loyalty, and political savvy. Esther grows up before our eyes, beginning as a young, passive girl and maturing into a strong and compassionate leader. The characters are well drawn. Ahasuerus is a lazy, fun-loving king who prefers to delegate legislation to others rather than to make it himself. Haman is excessively proud, a characteristic that causes him to attempt to exterminate an entire people when he feels that he has not been properly honored. Mordecai is an enigma, a representative Jew who achieves high political rank but whose motives remain inscrutable. This book, of course, is the basis for the holiday of Purim, a joyous remembrance of victory celebrated with good food, gift giving, costumes, and noise making.

The book is a literary masterpiece, an artfully crafted short story. The plot is suspenseful, keeping readers on the edges of their seats, wondering what will happen next. Who will be chosen as the new queen? What will happen when Esther finally reveals to the royal court that she is Jewish? Will Esther succeed in eliminating Haman's vendetta? The elements of the plot are carefully woven together with frequent repetition of words, phrases, and entire sentences. Many elements of the story are quite humorous. Despite its serious overall topic, surely we are to laugh at a king who needs numerous advisers to make up his mind, government officials who are unable to do anything without being well lubricated with drink, and a party that lasts half a year. Everything in this court environment is carried out by decrees, which characters choose to disobey as well as obey. There are also surprising reversals: an orphan who becomes queen, a man who is hung on the very gallows he built for someone else, a wife who switches her allegiance within a matter of hours, a man marked for death who becomes the kingdom's second in command.

The book is important for ethnic and gender concerns, a story about how people live with others who are unlike themselves. Ultimately it is a question of minority survival. How does one survive when threatened as a person of a minority group? The Jews are a foreign people within the Persian kingdom, an environment that is presented as generally hospitable to many different types of people. Yet how easily ethnic discrimination is allowed to persist, to the degree of the planned annihilation of an entire ethnic population. Esther and Mordecai show how persons of a minority culture can be loyal to and benefit the dominant culture. Esther, as a female Jew, is an individual who has to learn to live between two minority communities. The female characters (Vashti, Esther, Zeresh) are strong women who have to make their way in a man's world. They model different strategies for women who face patriarchal systems. Vashti is outspoken and forthright, whereas Esther chooses to be more diplomatic. The overall concern of the book is for liberation, a protest against injustice, and a struggle of a people's emancipation.

Though the story is set in the fifth century BCE in the Persian Empire, it was probably written later than that, in the fourth or third century BCE, and most likely outside of Palestine. It reflects the situation of the Diaspora, and certainly one reason it was produced was to address the needs of the Jewish community living outside of the homeland, wrestling with how to live in a new and different cultural environment. Though some of the elements reflect what is known about ancient Persia, many others do not, and therefore it is most certainly a fictional story.

Two aspects of the story often prove troubling to readers. First, though this story is part of the biblical canon, it does not once mention God. God does not bring about victory, but instead human beings (Esther and Mordecai) do. Yet this detail about the story is actually not a problem but a benefit, mirroring the ambiguity we often feel in our spiritual lives. It reflects the very human situation of looking back over a situation that has turned out well and asking, "Did God do that?" but never being able to know for certain. Second, the ending of the story is quite bloody, a concern that becomes more pressing as our United States culture is becoming more and more violent. We must realize, however, that this story is a farce, and the violence is not realistic but imagined. For communities that are themselves facing oppression, reading the story actually functions more as a safety valve for their own frustrations.

Standing at the present place in history, only a few decades after the Holocaust, we cannot but hear eerie echoes of Hitler's "final solution" to the "Jewish problem" in Haman's decree for genocide. Reading the book of Esther in a post-Holocaust world means that we cannot forget that its horrors have been personally experienced. It is not only a fiction, a tale of a long-ago time in a faraway place, but a warning of how easy it is for society to succumb to such evil against minority peoples and a call to action against anti-Semitism whenever we see it.

—Linda Day

King Ahasuerus Deposes Queen Vashti

1 This happened in the days of Ahasuerus, the same Ahasuerus who ruled over one hundred twenty-seven provinces from India to Ethiopia.[a] ² In those days when King Ahasuerus sat on his royal throne in the citadel of Susa, ³ in the third year of his reign, he gave a banquet for all his officials and ministers. The army of Persia and Media and the nobles and governors of the provinces were present, ⁴ while he displayed the great wealth of his kingdom and the splendor and pomp of his majesty for many days, one hundred eighty days in all.

5 When these days were completed, the king gave for all the people present in the citadel of Susa, both great and small, a banquet lasting for seven days, in the court of the garden of the king's palace. ⁶ There were white cotton curtains and blue hangings tied with cords of fine linen and purple to silver rings[b] and marble pillars. There were couches of gold and silver on a mosaic pavement of porphyry, marble,

a Or Nubia; Heb Cush   b Or rods

1:1–8 Two Royal Parties

1:4—The reason why King Ahasuerus wants to throw his parties is to show off his *great wealth*. His actions represent a blatant consumerism, an effort to "keep up with the Joneses."

1:5—The second party, for the general populace, is egalitarian, inviting subjects of *great and small* income levels.

1:6–7—The many rare objects give a sense of the beauty and luxury of the royal garden court, items the common people would not often see.

mother-of-pearl, and colored stones. [7] Drinks were served in golden goblets, goblets of different kinds, and the royal wine was lavished according to the bounty of the king. [8] Drinking was by flagons, without restraint; for the king had given orders to all the officials of his palace to do as each one desired. [9] Furthermore, Queen Vashti gave a banquet for the women in the palace of King Ahasuerus.

10 On the seventh day, when the king was merry with wine, he commanded Mehuman, Biztha, Harbona, Bigtha and Abagtha, Zethar and Carkas, the seven eunuchs who attended him, [11] to bring Queen Vashti before the king, wearing the royal crown, in order to show the peoples and the officials her beauty; for she was fair to behold. [12] But Queen Vashti refused to come at the king's command conveyed by the eunuchs. At this the king was enraged, and his anger burned within him.

13 Then the king consulted the sages who knew the laws[a] (for this was the king's procedure toward all who were versed in law and custom, [14] and those next to him were Carshena, Shethar, Admatha, Tarshish, Meres, Marsena, and Memucan, the seven officials of Persia and Media, who had access to the king, and sat first in the kingdom): [15] "According to the law, what is to be done to Queen Vashti because she has not performed the command of King Ahasuerus conveyed by the eunuchs?"

[16] Then Memucan said in the presence of the king and the officials, "Not only has Queen Vashti done wrong to the king, but also to all the officials and all the peoples who are in all the provinces of King Ahasuerus. [17] For this deed of the queen will be made known to all women, causing them to look with contempt on their husbands, since they will say, 'King Ahasuerus commanded Queen Vashti to be brought before him, and she did not come.' [18] This very day the noble ladies of Persia and Media who have heard of the queen's behavior will rebel against[b] the king's officials, and there will be no end of contempt and wrath! [19] If it pleases the king, let a royal order go out from him, and let it be written among the laws of the Persians and the Medes so that it may not be altered, that Vashti is never again to come before King Ahasuerus; and let the king give her royal position to another who is better than she. [20] So when the decree made by the king is proclaimed throughout all his kingdom, vast as it is, all women will give honor to their husbands, high and low alike."

21 This advice pleased the king and the officials, and the king did as Memucan proposed; [22] he sent letters to all the royal provinces, to every province in its own script and to every people in its own language, declaring that every man should be master in his own house.[c]

[a] Cn: Heb *times*   [b] Cn: Heb *will tell*   [c] Heb adds *and speak according to the language of his people*

1:8—The drinking *without restraint* would most likely lead to inebriation for at least some of the party guests. As at a college keg party, free-flowing alcohol surely would lead to a lively atmosphere.

1:9–2:4 Vashti Says No

1:9—Women are given their own party in a gender-segregated event.

1:10—In ancient cultures *eunuchs* often held important positions in government administration.

1:10, 12—Ahasuerus has great power and wealth, yet childishly throws a tantrum when faced with something he cannot have. The reason

why Vashti *refused to come* to his party is not explained, but it may be that she finds it degrading to be treated like the king's possession and be ogled by his party guests who, like the king, are most likely drunkenly *merry with wine*.

1:16–18—Memucan blows Vashti's action way out of proportion in suggesting that it will lead to mass rebellion and anarchy. He plays on the fears of men in a patriarchal culture that they will not be able to keep their places of power.

1:20, 22—The new law decrees that men must be the head of the household and women are to be subservient.

Esther Becomes Queen

2 After these things, when the anger of King Ahasuerus had abated, he remembered Vashti and what she had done and what had been decreed against her. ²Then the king's servants who attended him said, "Let beautiful young virgins be sought out for the king. ³And let the king appoint commissioners in all the provinces of his kingdom to gather all the beautiful young virgins to the harem in the citadel of Susa under custody of Hegai, the king's eunuch, who is in charge of the women; let their cosmetic treatments be given them. ⁴And let the girl who pleases the king be queen instead of Vashti." This pleased the king, and he did so.

5 Now there was a Jew in the citadel of Susa whose name was Mordecai son of Jair son of Shimei son of Kish, a Benjaminite. ⁶Kish[a] had been carried away from Jerusalem among the captives carried away with King Jeconiah of Judah, whom King Nebuchadnezzar of Babylon had carried away. ⁷Mordecai[b] had brought up Hadassah, that is Esther, his cousin, for she had neither father nor mother; the girl was fair and beautiful, and when her father and her mother died, Mordecai adopted her as his own daughter. ⁸So when the king's order and his edict were proclaimed, and when many young women were gathered in the citadel of Susa in custody of Hegai, Esther also was taken into the king's palace and put in custody of Hegai, who had charge of the women. ⁹The girl pleased him and won his favor, and he quickly provided her with her cosmetic treatments and her portion of food, and with seven chosen maids from the king's palace, and advanced her and her maids to the best place in the harem. ¹⁰Esther did not reveal her people or kindred, for Mordecai had charged her not to tell. ¹¹Every day Mordecai would walk around in front of the court of the harem, to learn how Esther was and how she fared.

12 The turn came for each girl to go in to King Ahasuerus, after being twelve months under the regulations for the women, since this was the regular period of their cosmetic treatment, six months with oil of myrrh and six months with perfumes and cosmetics for women. ¹³When the girl went in to the king she was given whatever she asked for to take with her from the harem to the king's palace. ¹⁴In the evening she went in; then in the morning she came back to the second harem in custody of Shaashgaz,

---

a Heb *a Benjaminite* *6who* *b* Heb *He*

2:1—Ahasuerus regrets what happened to Vashti. How easy it is to do something in *anger*, then later wish that we had acted more rationally.

2:2–4—The new plan will take teenage girls away from their families, who will be forced to deal with the mixed emotions of pride in having their daughters serve their country, yet worry for their offspring's well-being while they are far away from home.

2:5–20 The Choice of a New Queen

2:5—Mordecai and Esther are Jewish, therefore foreigners in the land of Persia.

2:7—Adoption was not a very common practice in ancient societies. As both an orphan and a girl, Esther holds an especially humble place in society. Mordecai shows how it is possible to love a child who is not one's own.

2:7—In the Bible numerous other characters are described as physically attractive (for example, Sarah, Rebekah, David, Bathsheba, Absalom). The designation of someone as *fair and beautiful* often indicates a person's larger importance in biblical history as well as personal beauty.

2:9—Esther begins to be noticed as someone of special talent and is thus treated well.

2:10, 20—Esther hides from the royal court the fact that she is Jewish. Her situation is not unlike others who feel that they must hide aspects of themselves (for instance, a physical handicap, sexual orientation, a mental illness) to be accepted by others.

2:12–14—The experience of spending the night with the king physically divides the young women. Their preparation surely would have included instruction on how to please a man as well as the lengthy beauty preparations. The young women are valued according to their physical and sexual attractiveness.

the king's eunuch, who was in charge of the concubines; she did not go in to the king again, unless the king delighted in her and she was summoned by name.

15 When the turn came for Esther daughter of Abihail the uncle of Mordecai, who had adopted her as his own daughter, to go in to the king, she asked for nothing except what Hegai the king's eunuch, who had charge of the women, advised. Now Esther was admired by all who saw her. 16 When Esther was taken to King Ahasuerus in his royal palace in the tenth month, which is the month of Tebeth, in the seventh year of his reign, 17 the king loved Esther more than all the other women; of all the virgins she won his favor and devotion, so that he set the royal crown on her head and made her queen instead of Vashti. 18 Then the king gave a great banquet to all his officials and ministers—"Esther's banquet." He also granted a holiday*a* to the provinces, and gave gifts with royal liberality.

Mordecai Discovers a Plot

19 When the virgins were being gathered together,*b* Mordecai was sitting at the king's gate. 20 Now Esther had not revealed her kindred or her people, as Mordecai had charged her; for Esther obeyed Mordecai just as when she was brought up by him. 21 In those days, while Mordecai was sitting at the king's gate, Bigthan and Teresh, two of the king's eunuchs, who guarded the threshold, became angry and conspired to assassi-

nate*c* King Ahasuerus. 22 But the matter came to the knowledge of Mordecai, and he told it to Queen Esther, and Esther told the king in the name of Mordecai. 23 When the affair was investigated and found to be so, both the men were hanged on the gallows. It was recorded in the book of the annals in the presence of the king.

Haman Undertakes to Destroy the Jews

3 After these things King Ahasuerus promoted Haman son of Hammedatha the Agagite, and advanced him and set his seat above all the officials who were with him. 2 And all the king's servants who were at the king's gate bowed down and did obeisance to Haman; for the king had so commanded concerning him. But Mordecai did not bow down or do obeisance. 3 Then the king's servants who were at the king's gate said to Mordecai, "Why do you disobey the king's command?" 4 When they spoke to him day after day and he would not listen to them, they told Haman, in order to see whether Mordecai's words would avail; for he had told them that he was a Jew. 5 When Haman saw that Mordecai did not bow down or do obeisance to him, Haman was infuriated. 6 But he thought it beneath him to lay hands on Mordecai alone. So, having been told who Mordecai's people were, Haman plotted to destroy all the Jews, the people of Mordecai, throughout the whole kingdom of Ahasuerus.

a Or *an amnesty* *b* Heb adds *a second time* *c* Heb *to lay hands on*

2:18—Ahasuerus celebrates Esther's enthronement with a tax **holiday** and **gifts**, showing generosity. Certainly getting a tax cut will help the citizens form a positive impression of the new queen.

2:21–3:15 A Decree Mandating Genocide

2:21–22—Mordecai's and Esther's allegiance to the crown becomes clear. In saving the king's life they show that Jews can be loyal subjects.

3:1—The fact that Haman is **the Agagite** is highly significant. During the time of Saul, Agag was the king of the Amalekites, who were Israel's ancient enemy (cf. 1 Sam. 15:1–33; Exod. 17:8–16;

Deut. 25:19). Like Esther, Haman is a foreigner in the Persian court. Like Saul, Mordecai is from the tribe of Benjamin (Esth. 2:5). The bad blood between Haman and Mordecai goes way back. It reflects how difficult it is for peoples to get past old rivalries.

3:2–5—There is no reason given why Mordecai will not **bow down**, as there is no prohibition against Jews bowing down to others (cf. Gen. 43:26–28; 2 Sam. 14:4; 1 Kgs. 1:16).

3:6—Instead of taking revenge upon only Mordecai for his actions, Haman vows to punish all of Mordecai's people in an act of ethnic cleansing.

7 In the first month, which is the month of Nisan, in the twelfth year of King Ahasuerus, they cast Pur—which means "the lot"—before Haman for the day and for the month, and the lot fell on the thirteenth day[a] of the twelfth month, which is the month of Adar. 8 Then Haman said to King Ahasuerus, "There is a certain people scattered and separated among the peoples in all the provinces of your kingdom; their laws are different from those of every other people, and they do not keep the king's laws, so that it is not appropriate for the king to tolerate them. 9 If it pleases the king, let a decree be issued for their destruction, and I will pay ten thousand talents of silver into the hands of those who have charge of the king's business, so that they may put it into the king's treasuries." 10 So the king took his signet ring from his hand and gave it to Haman son of Hammedatha the Agagite, the enemy of the Jews. 11 The king said to Haman, "The money is given to you, and the people as well, to do with them as it seems good to you."

12 Then the king's secretaries were summoned on the thirteenth day of the first month, and an edict, according to all that Haman commanded, was written to the king's satraps and to the governors over all the provinces and to the officials of all the peoples, to every province in its own script and every people in its own language; it was writ-

ten in the name of King Ahasuerus and sealed with the king's ring. 13 Letters were sent by couriers to all the king's provinces, giving orders to destroy, to kill, and to annihilate all Jews, young and old, women and children, in one day, the thirteenth day of the twelfth month, which is the month of Adar, and to plunder their goods. 14 A copy of the document was to be issued as a decree in every province by proclamation, calling on all the peoples to be ready for that day. 15 The couriers went quickly by order of the king, and the decree was issued in the citadel of Susa. The king and Haman sat down to drink; but the city of Susa was thrown into confusion.

Esther Agrees to Help the Jews

4 When Mordecai learned all that had been done, Mordecai tore his clothes and put on sackcloth and ashes, and went through the city, wailing with a loud and bitter cry; 2 he went up to the entrance of the king's gate, for no one might enter the king's gate clothed with sackcloth. 3 In every province, wherever the king's command and his decree came, there was great mourning among the Jews, with fasting and weeping and lamenting, and most of them lay in sackcloth and ashes.

4 When Esther's maids and her eunuchs came and told her, the queen was deeply distressed; she sent garments

---

a Cn Compare Gk and verse 13 below: Heb the twelfth month

3:7—*The lot* perhaps consisted of bowls and instruments similar to modern dice.

3:8–9—Haman's argument is wickedly masterful. He falsely presents the situation in "us against them" language, insinuating that the Jews are a threat to national security and depersonalizing them as an unnamed *certain people*. His desire for the Jews' demise is so great that he will pay *ten thousand talents*, which is two-thirds of the annual income of the entire Persian Empire.

3:12—The Persian Empire shows itself to be a multicultural environment, accommodating to *all the peoples* in their *own script* and their *own language*.

3:15—The juxtaposition of these two images is

shocking; the two men toasting the new edict in contrast to the *confusion* and despair in the streets below.

4:1–17 Esther's Moment of Decision

4:1–3—*Sackcloth and ashes* was a sign of mourning in Israel and other ancient cultures (cf. Isa. 58:5; Jer. 6:26; Jonah 3:6).

4:4—Esther exhibits an innate sympathy with her people as she becomes distressed along with them before even knowing why. She follows a typical response to a catastrophic situation, first mourning, then pulling herself together to take action. Esther tries to care for Mordecai by providing the proper clothing he will need to enter the palace compound, but he refuses her help.

to clothe Mordecai, so that he might take off his sackcloth; but he would not accept them. ⁵ Then Esther called for Hathach, one of the king's eunuchs, who had been appointed to attend her, and ordered him to go to Mordecai to learn what was happening and why. ⁶ Hathach went out to Mordecai in the open square of the city in front of the king's gate, ⁷ and Mordecai told him all that had happened to him, and the exact sum of money that Haman had promised to pay into the king's treasuries for the destruction of the Jews. ⁸ Mordecai also gave him a copy of the written decree issued in Susa for their destruction, that he might show it to Esther, explain it to her, and charge her to go to the king to make supplication to him and entreat him for her people.

⁹ Hathach went and told Esther what Mordecai had said. ¹⁰ Then Esther spoke to Hathach and gave him a message for Mordecai, saying, ¹¹ "All the king's servants and the people of the king's provinces know that if any man or woman goes to the king inside the inner court without being called, there is but one law—all alike are to be put to death. Only if the king holds out the golden scepter to someone, may that person live. I myself have not been called to come in to the king for thirty days." ¹² When they told Mordecai what Esther had said, ¹³ Mordecai told them to reply to Esther, "Do not think that in the king's palace you will escape any more than all the other Jews. ¹⁴ For if you keep silence at such a time as this, relief and deliverance will rise for the Jews from another quarter, but you and your father's family will perish. Who knows? Perhaps you have come to royal dignity for just such a time as this." ¹⁵ Then Esther said in reply to Mordecai, ¹⁶ "Go, gather all the Jews to be found in Susa, and hold a fast on my behalf, and neither eat nor drink for three days, night or day. I and my maids will also fast as you do. After that I will go to the king, though it is against the law; and if I perish, I perish." ¹⁷ Mordecai then went away and did everything as Esther had ordered him.

Esther's Banquet

5 On the third day Esther put on her royal robes and stood in the inner court of the king's palace, opposite the king's hall. The king was sitting on his royal throne inside the palace opposite the entrance to the palace. ² As soon as the king saw Queen Esther standing in the court, she won his favor and he held out to her the golden scepter that was in his hand. Then Esther approached and touched the top of the scepter. ³ The king said to her, "What is it, Queen Esther? What is your request? It shall be given you, even to the half of my kingdom." ⁴ Then Esther said, "If it pleases the king, let the king and Haman come today to a banquet that I have prepared for the king." ⁵ Then the king said, "Bring Haman quickly, so that we may do as Esther desires." So the king and

---

4:14—Some scholars see *from another quarter* as a veiled reference to God. Instead of God, though, Mordecai speaks in the language of fate as he asks, *"Who knows?"* He suggests that stepping up and taking action may be Esther's destiny. It is an eternal human question to ask, "What is my purpose for living?"

4:16—Esther expresses a willingness to be martyred, exhibiting tremendous courage in deciding to approach the king.

4:17—In a complete role reversal, Mordecai is now doing what Esther tells him (2:10, 20). Esther has grown up from her earlier appearance five years ago. Her conversation with Mordecai reflects the moment in all individuals' lives when they realize that it is time to take on adult responsibilities.

5:1–8 Esther Approaches and Hosts

5:1—Esther prepares carefully to present a powerful and queenly demeanor, which is now more important than her physical attractiveness. When we are faced with an important task, somehow we find the power within ourselves to carry it out.

5:4—Esther shows excellent strategy in inviting Ahasuerus to *a banquet*, for she knows how much he likes parties (1:3, 5; 2:18; 3:15).

Haman came to the banquet that Esther had prepared. ⁶ While they were drinking wine, the king said to Esther, "What is your petition? It shall be granted you. And what is your request? Even to the half of my kingdom, it shall be fulfilled." ⁷ Then Esther said, "This is my petition and request: ⁸ If I have won the king's favor, and if it pleases the king to grant my petition and fulfill my request, let the king and Haman come tomorrow to the banquet that I will prepare for them, and then I will do as the king has said."

Haman Plans to Have Mordecai Hanged

9 Haman went out that day happy and in good spirits. But when Haman saw Mordecai in the king's gate, and observed that he neither rose nor trembled before him, he was infuriated with Mordecai; ¹⁰ nevertheless Haman restrained himself and went home. Then he sent and called for his friends and his wife Zeresh, ¹¹ and Haman recounted to them the splendor of his riches, the number of his sons, all the promotions with which the king had honored him, and how he had advanced him above the officials and the ministers of the king. ¹² Haman added, "Even Queen Esther let no one but myself come with the king to the banquet that she prepared. Tomorrow also I am invited by her, together with the king. ¹³ Yet all this does me no

good so long as I see the Jew Mordecai sitting at the king's gate." ¹⁴ Then his wife Zeresh and all his friends said to him, "Let a gallows fifty cubits high be made, and in the morning tell the king to have Mordecai hanged on it; then go with the king to the banquet in good spirits." This advice pleased Haman, and he had the gallows made.

The King Honors Mordecai

6 On that night the king could not sleep, and he gave orders to bring the book of records, the annals, and they were read to the king. ² It was found written how Mordecai had told about Bigthana and Teresh, two of the king's eunuchs, who guarded the threshold, and who had conspired to assassinate[a] King Ahasuerus. ³ Then the king said, "What honor or distinction has been bestowed on Mordecai for this?" The king's servants who attended him said, "Nothing has been done for him." ⁴ The king said, "Who is in the court?" Now Haman had just entered the outer court of the king's palace to speak to the king about having Mordecai hanged on the gallows that he had prepared for him. ⁵ So the king's servants told him, "Haman is there, standing in the court." The king said, "Let him come in." ⁶ So Haman came in, and the king said to him, "What shall be done for the man whom

[a] Heb *to lay hands on*

5:6—The fact that he is *drinking wine* puts Ahasuerus in an expansive mood, and he generously promises Esther that she can have whatever she wants.

5:8—It is not clear why Esther proposes a second party the next day rather than telling the king her request immediately. Perhaps she wants to put her guests at ease, or perhaps she is using the suspense to heighten the king's curiosity, or perhaps she loses her nerve.

5:9–6:14 Haman's Pride Goes before His Fall

5:9—Haman's mood changes quickly from being *happy* to *infuriated*. The mere sight of Mordecai can make Haman angry all over again. Like a schoolyard bully, what he wants most is for Mordecai to show fear of him.

5:11–12—Haman's excessive pride is shown through his bragging to his friends and wife. What is most important to him are superficial things: his bank account, his good job, the important people he knows, and the number (not the quality) of his sons.

5:14—The *gallows* will be in a very public place, ensuring that Mordecai will be shamed in front of the entire city. Its great height, *fifty cubits high* (roughly eighty feet), is one of the exaggerated features of the story.

6:1–11—This entire scene is humorous, built upon coincidences and misunderstandings. It just happens that Ahasuerus experiences insomnia, that the passage about Mordecai is chosen, and that Haman is listening in the wings, thinking that he is the one to be honored.

the king wishes to honor?" Haman said to himself, "Whom would the king wish to honor more than me?" ⁷So Haman said to the king, "For the man whom the king wishes to honor, ⁸let royal robes be brought, which the king has worn, and a horse that the king has ridden, with a royal crown on its head. ⁹Let the robes and the horse be handed over to one of the king's most noble officials; let him*a* robe the man whom the king wishes to honor, and let him*a* conduct the man on horseback through the open square of the city, proclaiming before him: 'Thus shall it be done for the man whom the king wishes to honor.'" ¹⁰Then the king said to Haman, "Quickly, take the robes and the horse, as you have said, and do so to the Jew Mordecai who sits at the king's gate. Leave out nothing that you have mentioned." ¹¹So Haman took the robes and the horse and robed Mordecai and led him riding through the open square of the city, proclaiming, "Thus shall it be done for the man whom the king wishes to honor."

12 Then Mordecai returned to the king's gate, but Haman hurried to his house, mourning and with his head covered. ¹³When Haman told his wife Zeresh and all his friends everything that had happened to him, his advisers and his wife Zeresh said to him, "If Mordecai, before whom your downfall has begun, is of the Jewish people, you will not prevail against him, but will surely fall before him."

Haman's Downfall and Mordecai's Advancement

14 While they were still talking with him, the king's eunuchs arrived and hurried Haman off to the banquet that Esther had prepared. ¹So the king and Haman went in to feast with Queen Esther. ²On the second day, as they were drinking wine, the king again said to Esther, "What is your petition, Queen Esther? It shall be granted you. And what is your request? Even to the half of my kingdom, it shall be fulfilled." ³Then Queen Esther answered, "If I have won your favor, O king, and if it pleases the king, let my life be given me—that is my petition—and the lives of my people—that is my request. ⁴For we have been sold, I and my people, to be destroyed, to be killed, and to be annihilated. If we had been sold merely as slaves, men and women, I would have held my peace; but no enemy can compensate for this damage to the king."*b* ⁵Then King Ahasuerus said to Queen Esther, "Who is he, and where is he, who has presumed to do this?" ⁶Esther said, "A foe and enemy, this wicked Haman!" Then Haman was terrified before the king and the queen. ⁷The king rose from the feast in wrath and went into the palace garden, but Haman stayed to beg his life from Queen Esther, for he saw that the king had determined to destroy him. ⁸When the king returned from the palace garden to the banquet hall, Haman

a Heb *them*   *b* Meaning of Heb uncertain

6:7–9—The proud Haman chooses what he himself would most desire, to play dress-up as a king and to have everyone in the city see him publicly honored. It is a great irony that he instead has to carry it out for his greatest enemy.

6:13—Zeresh displays foresight, even women's intuition, as she predicts that her husband will not be successful against Mordecai. She is the first Gentile to side with the Jews (8:17; 9:3). Ironically, Zeresh disobeys the decree about wives giving proper honor to their husbands (1:20).

7:1–8:2 Esther Comes Out

7:2—With the same *wine* and line of question-

ing, this banquet begins just as did the previous one (5:6). What a surprise it will be to the male guests, therefore, that it ends so differently!

7:3–4—Esther again displays wisdom and rhetorical skill in her response. Up to this point Ahasuerus and Haman have not known that Esther is Jewish, nor has Ahasuerus known that the people to be destroyed are the Jews (3:8). *To be destroyed, to be killed, and to be annihilated* repeats exactly the language of Haman's decree (3:13).

7:8—Haman begs for mercy, but Ahasuerus misunderstands, thinking that he is sexually assaulting Esther. Though the death penalty is the

had thrown himself on the couch where Esther was reclining; and the king said, "Will he even assault the queen in my presence, in my own house?" As the words left the mouth of the king, they covered Haman's face. ⁹ Then Harbona, one of the eunuchs in attendance on the king, said, "Look, the very gallows that Haman has prepared for Mordecai, whose word saved the king, stands at Haman's house, fifty cubits high." And the king said, "Hang him on that." ¹⁰ So they hanged Haman on the gallows that he had prepared for Mordecai. Then the anger of the king abated.

Esther Saves the Jews

8 On that day King Ahasuerus gave to Queen Esther the house of Haman, the enemy of the Jews; and Mordecai came before the king, for Esther had told what he was to her. ² Then the king took off his signet ring, which he had taken from Haman, and gave it to Mordecai. So Esther set Mordecai over the house of Haman.

3 Then Esther spoke again to the king; she fell at his feet, weeping and pleading with him to avert the evil design of Haman the Agagite and the plot that he had devised against the Jews. ⁴ The king held out the golden scepter to Esther, ⁵ and Esther rose and stood before the king. She said, "If it pleases the king, and if I have won his favor, and if the thing seems right before the king, and I have his approval, let an order be written to revoke the letters devised by Haman son of Hammedatha the Agagite, which he wrote giving orders to destroy the Jews who are in all the provinces of the king. ⁶ For how can I bear to see the calamity that is coming on my people? Or how can I bear to see the destruction of my kindred?" ⁷ Then King Ahasuerus said to Queen Esther and to the Jew Mordecai, "See, I have given Esther the house of Haman, and they have hanged him on the gallows, because he plotted to lay hands on the Jews. ⁸ You may write as you please with regard to the Jews, in the name of the king, and seal it with the king's ring; for an edict written in the name of the king and sealed with the king's ring cannot be revoked."

9 The king's secretaries were summoned at that time, in the third month, which is the month of Sivan, on the twenty-third day; and an edict was written, according to all that Mordecai commanded, to the Jews and to the satraps and the governors and the officials of the provinces from India to Ethiopia,ᵃ one hundred twenty-seven provinces,

ᵃ Or Nubia; Heb Cush

---

punishment we might think he deserves, he receives it for a crime he does not actually commit.

7:9—It is fitting that Haman is the one shamed, in the very way he intended to shame Mordecai. As on an occasion when a KKK member's hood is removed, Haman's prejudice will now be revealed to everyone. How appropriate that he will be "hoist with his own petard."

8:1–2—Ahasuerus gives to Esther Haman's estate, over which she appoints Mordecai as a manager. His *house* indicates all of Haman's household possessions. Like many widows and orphans, however, Zeresh and her sons will be left without financial support after losing their husband and father.

8:3–17 Esther's Request, Mordecai's Decree

8:3—Though the Jews' enemy may be gone, his genocidal edict still remains. Esther therefore needs to go to the king again. This time she uses overt "feminine charm" to convince the king, by *weeping and pleading*. Ahasuerus is not the first, and will not be the last, man to melt at a pretty woman's tears.

8:6—Referring to them as *my people* and *my kindred*, Esther is here showing her full and undivided support for the Jews. Like many persons who fit into more than one social category, Esther has to negotiate between the two aspects of herself, Jewish and Persian.

8:8—Ahasuerus chooses to solve this problem in the same way he has solved problems previously, by letting others write and disseminate a decree under his name (1:21–22; 3:10–15).

8:9–14—The new edicts exactly parallels Haman's previous edict. Though the language is violent, the Jews are permitted to act only in self-defense, to protect themselves if someone attacks them.

to every province in its own script and to every people in its own language, and also to the Jews in their script and their language. ¹⁰ He wrote letters in the name of King Ahasuerus, sealed them with the king's ring, and sent them by mounted couriers riding on fast steeds bred from the royal herd.ᵃ ¹¹ By these letters the king allowed the Jews who were in every city to assemble and defend their lives, to destroy, to kill, and to annihilate any armed force of any people or province that might attack them, with their children and women, and to plunder their goods ¹² on a single day throughout all the provinces of King Ahasuerus, on the thirteenth day of the twelfth month, which is the month of Adar. ¹³ A copy of the writ was to be issued as a decree in every province and published to all peoples, and the Jews were to be ready on that day to take revenge on their enemies. ¹⁴ So the couriers, mounted on their swift royal steeds, hurried out, urged by the king's command. The decree was issued in the citadel of Susa.

15 Then Mordecai went out from the presence of the king, wearing royal robes of blue and white, with a great golden crown and a mantle of fine linen and purple, while the city of Susa shouted and rejoiced. ¹⁶ For the Jews there was light and gladness, joy and honor. ¹⁷ In every province and in every city, wherever the king's command and his edict came, there was gladness and joy among the Jews, a festival and a holiday. Further-more, many of the peoples of the country professed to be Jews, because the fear of the Jews had fallen upon them.

Destruction of the Enemies of the Jews

9 Now in the twelfth month, which is the month of Adar, on the thirteenth day, when the king's command and edict were about to be executed, on the very day when the enemies of the Jews hoped to gain power over them, but which had been changed to a day when the Jews would gain power over their foes, ² the Jews gathered in their cities throughout all the provinces of King Ahasuerus to lay hands on those who had sought their ruin; and no one could withstand them, because the fear of them had fallen upon all peoples. ³ All the officials of the provinces, the satraps and the governors, and the royal officials were supporting the Jews, because the fear of Mordecai had fallen upon them. ⁴ For Mordecai was powerful in the king's house, and his fame spread throughout all the provinces as the man Mordecai grew more and more powerful. ⁵ So the Jews struck down all their enemies with the sword, slaughtering, and destroying them, and did as they pleased to those who hated them. ⁶ In the citadel of Susa the Jews killed and destroyed five hundred people. ⁷ They killed Parshandatha, Dalphon, Aspatha, ⁸ Poratha, Adalia, Aridatha, ⁹ Parmashta, Arisai, Aridai, Vaizatha, ¹⁰ the ten sons of

ᵃ Meaning of Heb uncertain

8:15–16—Mordecai's fine clothing and the people's *joy* is a direct contrast to the sackcloth and despair after the previous edict (4:1–3). What a relief we feel when a bad situation is finally turned around after a long time of worry!

8:17—The indication that many people *professed to be Jews* most likely means that they took the Jewish side in the conflict. Peoples of different ethnic groups are joined together to resist the discrimination of Haman's edict.

9:1–19 Jewish Victory

9:4—Mordecai is now the one who is powerful, receiving the fame and the promotion that Haman cherished.

9:5—It is difficult to know how to understand the violence of the Jews' action. Even those whose views tend to the pacifist might be surprised at how they respond when placed in a position of having physically to defend themselves and their families.

9:7—Why Haman's sons are killed is not clear. Perhaps the people are afraid that they will follow in their father's evil footsteps; like father, like son.

9:10, 15, 16—It is emphasized that the Jews *did not touch the plunder*, which indicates that they do not want to receive any financial gain from the skirmish. Even in war they are very careful to act honorably.

Haman son of Hammedatha, the enemy of the Jews; but they did not touch the plunder.

11 That very day the number of those killed in the citadel of Susa was reported to the king. 12 The king said to Queen Esther, "In the citadel of Susa the Jews have killed five hundred people and also the ten sons of Haman. What have they done in the rest of the king's provinces? Now what is your petition? It shall be granted you. And what further is your request? It shall be fulfilled." 13 Esther said, "If it pleases the king, let the Jews who are in Susa be allowed tomorrow also to do according to this day's edict, and let the ten sons of Haman be hanged on the gallows." 14 So the king commanded this to be done; a decree was issued in Susa, and the ten sons of Haman were hanged. 15 The Jews who were in Susa gathered also on the fourteenth day of the month of Adar and they killed three hundred persons in Susa; but they did not touch the plunder.

16 Now the other Jews who were in the king's provinces also gathered to defend their lives, and gained relief from their enemies, and killed seventy-five thousand of those who hated them; but they laid no hands on the plunder. 17 This was on the thirteenth day of the month of Adar, and on the fourteenth day they rested and made that a day of feasting and gladness.

The Feast of Purim Inaugurated

18 But the Jews who were in Susa gathered on the thirteenth day and on the fourteenth, and rested on the fifteenth day, making that a day of feasting and gladness. 19 Therefore the Jews of the villages, who live in the open towns, hold the fourteenth day of the month of Adar as a day for gladness and feasting, a holiday on which they send gifts of food to one another.

20 Mordecai recorded these things, and sent letters to all the Jews who were in all the provinces of King Ahasuerus, both near and far, 21 enjoining them that they should keep the fourteenth day of the month Adar and also the fifteenth day of the same month, year by year, 22 as the days on which the Jews gained relief from their enemies, and as the month that had been turned for them from sorrow into gladness and from mourning into a holiday; that they should make them days of feasting and gladness, days for sending gifts of food to one another and presents to the poor. 23 So the Jews adopted as a custom what they had begun to do, as Mordecai had written to them.

24 Haman son of Hammedatha the Agagite, the enemy of all the Jews, had plotted against the Jews to destroy them, and had cast Pur—that is "the lot"—to crush and destroy them; 25 but when Esther came before the king, he gave orders in writing that the wicked

---

9:13—For the first time, Esther speaks forthrightly when telling Ahasuerus what she wants. She acts like a person who has reached a time in her life when she no longer has the patience or desire to beat around the bush. The addition of the second day of fighting probably reflects different traditions about the timing of events.

9:16—The death of *seventy-five thousand* is another of the exaggerated features of the story, as certainly the historical Persian population would not have been able to support such a drastic loss.

9:17–19—Urban and rural populations celebrate slightly differently, with the same *feasting and gladness* but on different days.

9:20–10:3 The New Holiday of Purim Is Established

9:22—During Purim, people are not only to focus on their own enjoyment but they are to be generous, giving *food* and *presents* to those less fortunate.

9:23—The celebration of this new holiday began with the common folk, as Mordecai only authorizes their practices. In current religious terminology we would say that the new practice was initiated by laypersons rather than by the clergy.

9:24–26—This summary of the events changes the details, emphasizing the role of Ahasuerus and explaining how the holiday obtained its name.

plot that he had devised against the Jews should come upon his own head, and that he and his sons should be hanged on the gallows. ²⁶ Therefore these days are called Purim, from the word Pur. Thus because of all that was written in this letter, and of what they had faced in this matter, and of what had happened to them, ²⁷ the Jews established and accepted as a custom for themselves and their descendants and all who joined them, that without fail they would continue to observe these two days every year, as it was written and at the time appointed. ²⁸ These days should be remembered and kept throughout every generation, in every family, province, and city; and these days of Purim should never fall into disuse among the Jews, nor should the commemoration of these days cease among their descendants.

29 Queen Esther daughter of Abihail, along with the Jew Mordecai, gave full written authority, confirming this second letter about Purim. ³⁰ Letters were sent wishing peace and security to all the Jews, to the one hundred twenty-seven provinces of the kingdom of Ahasuerus, ³¹ and giving orders that these days of Purim should be observed at their appointed seasons, as the Jew Mordecai and Queen Esther enjoined on the Jews, just as they had laid down for themselves and for their descendants regulations concerning their fasts and their lamentations. ³² The command of Queen Esther fixed these practices of Purim, and it was recorded in writing.

10 King Ahasuerus laid tribute on the land and on the islands of the sea. ² All the acts of his power and might, and the full account of the high honor of Mordecai, to which the king advanced him, are they not written in the annals of the kings of Media and Persia? ³ For Mordecai the Jew was next in rank to King Ahasuerus, and he was powerful among the Jews and popular with his many kindred, for he sought the good of his people and interceded for the welfare of all his descendants.

9:29–32—Esther's letter repeats much of the same information in Mordecai's letter. *Fasts* and *lamentations* show her realization that life is not all joy. Victory is grand and certainly should be celebrated, but people will also inevitably face hard times again.

10:1–3—The story ends with the hope that as long as Mordecai has a position in the political administration, things will be well for the Jews. Someone will be watching out for human rights violations, so that such a situation will not occur again.

The Book of JOB

N early every possible date has been offered for the origin of Job, from the early belief that Moses himself wrote it in the second millennium BCE to some scholars' convictions that it is one of the latest books in the Hebrew Bible, perhaps from the third century BCE. It was probably a production of the Babylonian exile of Israel (sixth century BCE) or soon thereafter. The theological issues raised would certainly have been prominent during that wrenching time in Israel's history. About possible authors we know nothing more than literary clues offered by the text itself. The author was clearly broadly educated, possessing a rich vocabulary, peppered with a seasoned wit based on vast metaphorical resources from farm and field, city and commerce.

Literary Type

Job has long been classed as one of the books of the wisdom tradition of Israel. However, that designation has often been used so broadly as to lose any specific meaning. Certainly the book of Job wrestles with questions that have long plagued thinkers and writers of the ancient Near East. Why is there suffering and evil? How do human beings survive in the midst of such evil? How do they respond to evil? What role does the divine world play in the production and implementation of such evil? How can human life have any significant or lasting meaning when the world throws up such horror, such tragedy?

Not only does the book work with these questions, among others; it does so in rich poetry and prose, using vocabularies designed to stimulate thought and discussion concerning these large issues. One does not end such a book with the certainty of easy answers; one closes the book with as many questions as one began with, or more. No bumper sticker truth can be gleaned from a struggle with Job! Such poetic theology is designed to tease a reader into active thought.

Three Traditional Basic Concerns of the Book

It is common to discuss the book of Job in terms of its philosophical/theological themes: (1) the question of theodicy: why do bad things happen to good people, when God is thought to be the author of good only? (2) the issue of the origin of evil: is God the creator both of good and of bad for humanity, and what does the adversary (the Satan) have to do with it? (3) the concern of the various ways human beings act in the midst of suffering and tragedy: should we accept quietly the inevitable agonies the world brings to us, or should we rail against the apparent injustice of it all? To these three issues others could be added, but an important observation needs to be made concerning these questions: they all tend to be addressed in the form of dispassionate discussion and debate. Job and his friends are often taken to be representatives of academic theologians who engage in argument—albeit often rather acrimonious argument—while they sit about a gentleman's club, tamping their pipes.

On the contrary, Job and his friends are real story characters, not merely ciphers or analogues of philosophical positions. They debate one another, to be sure, but the debate is genuine give-and-take, real confrontations over real-life pain and horror. To reduce their passionate discussion to intellectual chitchat is to trivialize the story, reducing it to a game of the mind.

An Often Forgotten Theme: Justice

The issues at stake are certainly philosophical in nature, but all such issues are rooted deeply in the actual affairs that make up human existence. More specifically, what Job and his friends, and ultimately God, are talking about is justice, the stark realities of the ways in which human beings and God do or do not manifest in their actions and words fair dealings with one another. This is no pleasant theological treatise on the possibility of believing this or not believing that; it is a very serious and very basic drama of the ways God and God's creations treat one another in a world of vast mystery and equally vast horror. Job's accusation that God is nothing more than a monster who "destroys both the blameless and the wicked" and "mocks at the calamity of the innocent" (9:22–23) is more than the ravings of a madman. It is an observation Job has made based on his own actual life and his actual experience of the wider world. The friends' continuous attempts to slander Job are likewise not general claims but quite specific charges that he has engaged in the most egregious injustices against his fellow human beings. In short, they accuse Job of acting in his world in the same ways that Job accuses God (and occasionally his friends as well) of acting in Job's world.

In addition, it is crucial that we understand that the debate is far more than a wispy, ethereal chat. All of these charges revolve around the distribution of the goods of society, and are not merely general claims of wickedness. Unless we get that clear, we will not be able to hear the sharpness of the debate and will reduce it to an otherworldly one. This great book, so concerned with the question of justice, cannot be disconnected from the central Old Testament concern that energized the prophets and stands as one of the great gifts the Hebrew Bible has to offer us in our time.

The basic charges by which the friends assault Job tend to revolve around issues of the poor and the origins of poverty. Of course, the friends completely reject Job's claims that he is innocent of any wrongdoing worthy of God's incredible attacks against him (see Job's claims at 9:21 and the friends' rejections of those claims at 8:4 [Bildad]; 11:4 [Zophar]; 15:5–6 [Eliphaz] among many others). But their most trenchant criticism concerns Job's denial of the rights of the poor. Listen to Zophar in chapter 20:

> [The rich] swallow down riches and vomit them up again; . . .
>> the tongue of a viper will kill them . . .
> They will give back the fruit of their toil,
>> and will not swallow it down;
> from the profit of their trading
>> they will get no enjoyment.
> For they have crushed and abandoned the poor,
>> they have seized a house that they did not build. (vv. 15a, 16b, 18–19)

Or Eliphaz in chapter 22:

> Is not your wickedness great?
>> There is no end to your iniquities.
> For you have exacted pledges from your family for no reason,
>> and stripped the naked of their clothing.
> You have given no water to the weary to drink,
>> and you have withheld bread from the hungry . . .
> You have sent widows away empty-handed,
>> and the arms of the orphans you have crushed. (vv. 5–7, 9)

Note the specificity of these charges; Job is nothing less than a poster boy for the unjust Israelite! He has not only "crushed and abandoned the poor," but has also regularly not concerned himself with them at all. He has offered them no water or bread, even neglecting the widow's cries for help. The prophets of Israel over and over admonished the people that nations are judged precisely on the ways the poor were treated. The litany of "widow, orphan, stranger, foreigner" was raised whenever the evils of Israel were enumerated. According to the friends of Job, he has denied these most basic demands for justice and has received from the hands of the righteous God exactly what he deserves.

Job's response? He denies it all in a remarkable oath of innocence in chapter 31.

> If I have withheld anything that the poor desired,
>> or have caused the eyes of the widow to fail,
> or have eaten my morsel alone,
>> and the orphan has not eaten from it— . . .
> if I have seen anyone perish for lack of clothing,
>> or a poor person without covering, . . .
> if I have raised my hand against the orphan,
>> because I saw I had supporters at the gate;
> then let my shoulder blade fall from my shoulder;
>> and let my arm be broken from its socket. (vv. 16–17, 19, 21–22)

Job simply tells the friends that they are wrong; he has not acted unjustly. Quite the contrary, he is a man of exemplary justice. The terrible things God has done to him do not have their origins in Job's supposed unjust actions. Hence the friends' accusations are themselves unjust and wrong.

The author of Job thus connects closely with the great prophets of Israel on the question of justice and its demands. However, there is one very important difference: the prophets insist that God will eventually right the wrongs in an unjust world; Job is terrified that injustice will never end. At least his observations of the world give him little hope. At 21:7–13 Job complains (as does Jeremiah at Jer. 12:1), "Why do the wicked live on, reach old age, and grow mighty in power?" Their lives are long, their children are happy and comfortable, their cattle breed without fail. All are deliriously happy until they die in complete peace. And at 24:1–4, Job grows even more pointed in his complaints:

> Why are times not kept by the Almighty,
>> and why do those who know him never see his days?

> The wicked remove landmarks;
>> they seize flocks and pasture them.
> They drive away the donkey of the orphan;
>> they take the widow's ox for a pledge.
> They thrust the needy off the road;
>> the poor of the earth all hide themselves.

Job has seen that the wicked rule the earth completely, and God does nothing at all to stop them. In fact, the source of the wealth of the wicked is nothing less than theft from the poor. This claim flies in the face of beliefs enshrined in the book of Proverbs, that the source of wealth is industry and hard work, and the source of poverty is laziness (see Prov. 6:6–11 and 24:30–33 among others).

This way of thinking about the origins of wealth and poverty is nothing less than a new/old way of viewing the world. Job has defined the "wicked" as those who take the goods of the poor; wealth, he says, is stolen. This radical vision echoes the harsh words of the prophets. In Amos 8, for example, two wealthy merchants sit in the back of the sanctuary waiting for the boring worship service to end so that they can get back to cheating their customers with dirt-filled wheat and dishonest scales (Amos 8:4–6)! Too often in our own time we have accused the poor of laziness and praised the wealthy for their industry. Job reminds us that the differences between the rich and the poor are not always differences between energy and sloth, or between cleverness and stupidity.

One more conclusion may be drawn from Job's concern for the poor. Because he is so adamant to reject the friends' claims concerning his treatment of the poor, Job connects those claims to innocence directly with his exemplary relationship to the poor. To act justly with the poor is to claim innocence. That fact is important in the light of the speeches of God at the book's end. God speaks to Job, the one who claimed right treatment of the poor, and not to the friends who accused Job of evil with respect to the poor. God does far more in the speeches than "shut Job up." God reveals to Job something of the divine world, a world filled with mystery and wonder and even terror (see Behemoth and Leviathan), yet a world where a divine order exists under the seeming chaos and randomness experienced by Job. Far from rebuking Job for his words, God says to Eliphaz, "You have not spoken of me what is right, as my servant Job has" (42:7). Job has spoken the harsh truths of a painful and tragic world, but his solidarity with the poor has brought him close to the call of Israel's prophets and close to the will and way of God.

This introduction has focused on issues of social justice because this theme has not often been seen as important in Job. Too often the individual concerns of personal right belief or personal right relationship to God have taken the lion's share of Joban commentary. Those issues are certainly important ones. However, as we read through Job, we need to keep our eyes open for themes of social justice; they are very important to this remarkable author and should remain important to us as we strive to apply the Bible's crucial teaching to our own movements toward discipleship in the twenty-first century.

Note: The language of the book is among the most difficult in the Hebrew Bible. It has been said that fully 10 percent of the Hebrew text is practically unreadable. In a brief series of notes to the book, only a hint of the difficulties can be suggested.

—**John C. Holbert**

Job and His Family

1 There was once a man in the land of Uz whose name was Job. That man was blameless and upright, one who feared God and turned away from evil. ² There were born to him seven sons and three daughters. ³ He had seven thousand sheep, three thousand camels, five hundred yoke of oxen, five hundred donkeys, and very many servants; so that this man was the greatest of all the people of the east. ⁴ His sons used to go and hold feasts in one another's houses in turn; and they would send and invite their three sisters to eat and drink with them. ⁵ And when the feast days had run their course, Job would send and sanctify them, and he would rise early in the morning and offer burnt offerings according to the number of them all; for Job said, "It may be that my children have sinned, and cursed God in their hearts." This is what Job always did.

Attack on Job's Character

6 One day the heavenly beings*a* came to present themselves before the LORD, and Satan*b* also came among them. ⁷ The LORD said to Satan,*b* "Where have you come from?" Satan*b* answered the LORD, "From going to and fro on the earth, and from walking up and down on it." ⁸ The LORD said to Satan,*b* "Have you considered my servant Job? There is no one like him on the earth, a blameless and upright man who fears God and turns away from evil." ⁹ Then Satan*b* answered the LORD, "Does Job fear God for nothing? ¹⁰ Have you not put a fence around him and his house and all that he has, on every side? You have blessed the work of his hands, and his possessions have increased in the land. ¹¹ But stretch out your hand now, and touch all that he has, and he will curse you to your face." ¹² The LORD said to Satan,*b* "Very well, all that he has is in your power; only do not stretch out your hand against him!" So Satan*b* went out from the presence of the LORD.

Job Loses Property and Children

13 One day when his sons and daughters were eating and drinking wine in

---

a Heb *sons of God*   *b* Or *the Accuser*; Heb *ha-satan*

1:1—The two adjectives used to describe Job are important: *blameless* and *upright*. A possible translation might be "absolutely innocent." Thus, at the very beginning of the story we are told that Job has done nothing that could possibly suggest that he deserves what he finally receives, namely an ash heap of the ruins of his once-prosperous life.

1:5—Job is said to be fantastically religious in a very traditional sense. After each one of the nearly continuous feasts of his ten children, Job goes immediately to the place of worship in order to offer up ten whole *burnt offerings* for each one of his children, merely on the off chance that one of them may have sinned and *cursed God in their hearts* (i.e., "to themselves"). These actions are not only very time-consuming, they are also extremely expensive—ten whole animals at least ten times per year! These actions certainly give the impression that Job is deeply fearful that the God he worships is anxious to pounce on the wrongdoings, whether verbal or physical, of God's people. This view of God will be evident in other places in the story.

1:6–12—These verses, nearly repeated in 2:1–6, have caused endless commentary. Just what sort

of God is this? Goaded into an assault on one of God's finest creatures by the blandishments of the *Satan*? It is at least clear that God is vitally interested in just how Job will respond to the attacks of the Satan. It should also be noted that the story here describes a "test" rather than a "wager," as commentators often say. Perhaps Gen. 22 is a helpful parallel.

1:9 *Satan*—The NRSV's translation of this word as a proper name is misleading. It is actually a title and should be read "the Satan." It means something like " the adversary" (cf. Zech. 3:1–2; 1 Chr. 21:1). Perhaps the modern "prosecuting attorney" is a helpful analogy. The Satan raises here one of the crucial themes of the book: the distribution of goods. The Satan believes that if Job is divested of all his many possessions, Job will in fact *curse* God. Surely in at least one sense the Satan is proven right: Job's astonishing claim at 9:22–24 that God kills righteous and wicked and laughs at the dying is by any light a curse of some sort! At least the kind of God Job claims to understand is cursed by Job's words. A God like that perhaps deserves a curse or two!

1:13–22—In four terrible blows Job loses everything: his livestock, his servants, and finally all

the eldest brother's house, [14] a messenger came to Job and said, "The oxen were plowing and the donkeys were feeding beside them, [15] and the Sabeans fell on them and carried them off, and killed the servants with the edge of the sword; I alone have escaped to tell you." [16] While he was still speaking, another came and said, "The fire of God fell from heaven and burned up the sheep and the servants, and consumed them; I alone have escaped to tell you." [17] While he was still speaking, another came and said, "The Chaldeans formed three columns, made a raid on the camels and carried them off, and killed the servants with the edge of the sword; I alone have escaped to tell you." [18] While he was still speaking, another came and said, "Your sons and daughters were eating and drinking wine in their eldest brother's house, [19] and suddenly a great wind came across the desert, struck the four corners of the house, and it fell on the young people, and they are dead; I alone have escaped to tell you."

[20] Then Job arose, tore his robe, shaved his head, and fell on the ground and worshiped. [21] He said, "Naked I came from my mother's womb, and naked shall I return there; the LORD gave, and the LORD has taken away; blessed be the name of the LORD."

[22] In all this Job did not sin or charge God with wrongdoing.

Attack on Job's Health

2 One day the heavenly beings[a] came to present themselves before the LORD, and Satan[b] also came among them to present himself before the LORD. [2] The LORD said to Satan,[b] "Where have you come from?" Satan[c] answered the LORD, "From going to and fro on the earth, and from walking up and down on it." [3] The LORD said to Satan,[b] "Have you considered my servant Job? There is no one like him on the earth, a blameless and upright man who fears God and turns away from evil. He still persists in his integrity, although you incited me against him, to destroy him for no reason." [4] Then Satan[b] answered the LORD, "Skin for skin! All that people have they will give to save their lives.[d] [5] But stretch out your hand now and touch his bone and his flesh, and he will curse you to your face." [6] The LORD said to Satan,[b] "Very well, he is in your power; only spare his life."

7 So Satan[b] went out from the presence of the LORD, and inflicted loathsome sores on Job from the sole of his foot to the crown of his head. [8] Job[e] took a potsherd with which to scrape himself, and sat among the ashes.

9 Then his wife said to him, "Do you still persist in your integrity? Curse[f] God, and die." [10] But he said to her, "You speak as any foolish woman would

---

a Heb sons of God   *b* Or the Accuser; Heb ha-satan   *c* Or The Accuser; Heb ha-satan   *d* Or All that the man has he will give for his life   *e* Heb He   *f* Heb Bless

---

ten of his children. The means of his losses are both human (by *Sabeans* and *Chaldeans*) and natural (by a divine *fire* and *a great wind*). In response to these massive tragedies Job states a powerful and simple religious belief (v. 21). The storyteller ends the scene with the comment that Job neither sinned nor charged God with any wrongdoing. The reader is left to ask: if Job is not at fault and if God has done no wrong, then why have all these things happened? The theological and human tension of the story grows.

2:9–10—Job's wife has been portrayed as a shrew, even as a tool of Satan in some readings. Nothing in the story suggests that. She is a woman horrified to witness the end of her life

and the unimaginable suffering of her husband. Perhaps she urges him to go on and curse this God who, by her own observations, has inexplicably turned against Job. In that way, his suffering will end. Now after the onset of his unspeakable disease, he asks a question of his anguished wife. That question need not be seen as merely rhetorical. *Shall we receive the good at the hand of God, and not receive the bad?* Job is now not so certain about his traditional beliefs. After Job's first response to his huge losses in chapter 1 (1:21), we were told that "Job did not . . . charge God with wrongdoing." His question to his wife raises the question if perhaps his earlier belief needs further testing.

speak. Shall we receive the good at the hand of God, and not receive the bad?" In all this Job did not sin with his lips.

Job's Three Friends

11 Now when Job's three friends heard of all these troubles that had come upon him, each of them set out from his home—Eliphaz the Temanite, Bildad the Shuhite, and Zophar the Naamathite. They met together to go and console and comfort him. ¹² When they saw him from a distance, they did not recognize him, and they raised their voices and wept aloud; they tore their robes and threw dust in the air upon their heads. ¹³ They sat with him on the ground seven days and seven nights, and no one spoke a word to him, for they saw that his suffering was very great.

Job Curses the Day He Was Born

3 After this Job opened his mouth and cursed the day of his birth. ² Job said:

³ "Let the day perish in which I was
        born,
    and the night that said,
        'A man-child is conceived.'
⁴ Let that day be darkness!
    May God above not seek it,
        or light shine on it.
⁵ Let gloom and deep darkness claim it.
    Let clouds settle upon it;
        let the blackness of the day terrify it.

⁶ That night—let thick darkness seize
        it!
    let it not rejoice among the days of
        the year;
    let it not come into the number of
        the months.
⁷ Yes, let that night be barren;
    let no joyful cry be heardᵃ in it.
⁸ Let those curse it who curse the
        Sea,ᵇ
    those who are skilled to rouse up
        Leviathan.
⁹ Let the stars of its dawn be dark;
    let it hope for light, but have none;
    may it not see the eyelids of the
        morning—
¹⁰ because it did not shut the doors of
        my mother's womb,
    and hide trouble from my eyes.

¹¹ "Why did I not die at birth,
    come forth from the womb and
        expire?
¹² Why were there knees to receive me,
    or breasts for me to suck?
¹³ Now I would be lying down and
        quiet;
    I would be asleep; then I would be
        at rest
¹⁴ with kings and counselors of the
        earth
    who rebuild ruins for themselves,
¹⁵ or with princes who have gold,

ᵃ Heb come   ᵇ Cn: Heb day

2:11–13—The three friends have often been said to be very empathetic with Job, since they sit in silence around his heap of affliction for an astonishing seven days and seven nights. This silence could be heard another way. They see his great agony from a distance, weep, tear their clothes (signs of typical mourning), but then throw *dust in the air upon their heads*. The only other time this strange action occurs in the Bible is when Moses "throws dust in the air" to initiate the sixth plague of Egypt (Exod. 9:8). The dust turns into boils on humans and animals. This action on the part of the friends, far from being an act of mourning or sympathy, could be a sign of their certainty that Job is the foulest of sinners, the object of some divine attack, like the Egyptians of old. The friends are thus trying to protect themselves from the sinner. That is why they stay far off; that is why they are silent. They are waiting for the sinner to die in agony, a fate he obviously deserves. Their later attacks on Job make this interpretation very plausible.

3:1–26—Job's loud assault against the day of his birth suggests that his patience has run out (cf. Jer. 20:14–18). That old saw, "the patience of Job," lasts but two chapters! His wish to be dead, never to have been born at all, or better never to have been thought of at all (!), leads him to the terrible imaginative insight that the day that saw his birth should drop out of the calendar, that it should be cursed by the terrible monster, Leviathan, risen from the sea to wreak vengeance on that day (Job 3:8). If the friends have hoped that Job would simply die in silence, due to the just punishment of God, they are now sadly disappointed.

who fill their houses with silver.

¹⁶ Or why was I not buried like a
stillborn child,
like an infant that never sees the
light?

¹⁷ There the wicked cease from
troubling,
and there the weary are at rest.

¹⁸ There the prisoners are at ease
together;
they do not hear the voice of the
taskmaster.

¹⁹ The small and the great are there,
and the slaves are free from their
masters.

²⁰ "Why is light given to one in misery,
and life to the bitter in soul,

²¹ who long for death, but it does not
come,
and dig for it more than for hidden
treasures;

²² who rejoice exceedingly,
and are glad when they find the
grave?

²³ Why is light given to one who
cannot see the way,
whom God has fenced in?

²⁴ For my sighing comes like*a* my bread,
and my groanings are poured out
like water.

²⁵ Truly the thing that I fear comes
upon me,
and what I dread befalls me.

²⁶ I am not at ease, nor am I quiet;
I have no rest; but trouble comes."

Eliphaz Speaks: Job Has Sinned

4 Then Eliphaz the Temanite answered:

² "If one ventures a word with you,
will you be offended?
But who can keep from speaking?

³ See, you have instructed many;
you have strengthened the weak
hands.

⁴ Your words have supported those
who were stumbling,
and you have made firm the feeble
knees.

⁵ But now it has come to you, and you
are impatient;
it touches you, and you are
dismayed.

⁶ Is not your fear of God your
confidence,
and the integrity of your ways your
hope?

⁷ "Think now, who that was innocent
ever perished?
Or where were the upright cut off?

⁸ As I have seen, those who plow
iniquity
and sow trouble reap the same.

⁹ By the breath of God they perish,
and by the blast of his anger they
are consumed.

¹⁰ The roar of the lion, the voice of the
fierce lion,
and the teeth of the young lions
are broken.

¹¹ The strong lion perishes for lack of
prey,
and the whelps of the lioness are
scattered.

¹² "Now a word came stealing to me,
my ear received the whisper of it.

a Heb *before*

4:1–9—*Eliphaz*'s opening speech has been seen
as a model of discretion and tact. That is not the
only way to hear it. He reminds Job that he has
been helpful to others in the past, but now that
trouble has come his way, he is **impatient**. *"Is
not your fear [worship] of God your confidence,
and the integrity of your ways your hope?"* In
other words, if Job really *were* a man of integrity,
he would not be where he is; only evil folk end
up on ash heaps with nothing. That is the way the
world of God works. *"Where were the upright
cut off?"* asks Eliphaz. Job was called "upright"

in the prologue three times (1:1, 8; 2:3). Eliphaz's
nasty jibe is empty, because the proof of the
falsehood of his belief sits before him on the ash
heap!

4:12–21—Eliphaz claims that his vast wisdom
about the world's ways comes straight from the
Almighty. He describes a vision where he is
visited by *a word*, *a spirit*, and *a form*. What he
learns is that no one is pure or righteous in the
sight of God, who does not trust even the angels,
let alone any human beings (vv. 17–19).

13 Amid thoughts from visions of the
       night,
    when deep sleep falls on mortals,
14 dread came upon me, and
       trembling,
    which made all my bones shake.
15 A spirit glided past my face;
    the hair of my flesh bristled.
16 It stood still,
    but I could not discern its
       appearance.
    A form was before my eyes;
    there was silence, then I heard a
       voice:
17 'Can mortals be righteous before[a]
       God?
    Can human beings be pure before[a]
       their Maker?
18 Even in his servants he puts no trust,
    and his angels he charges with
       error;
19 how much more those who live in
       houses of clay,
    whose foundation is in the dust,
    who are crushed like a moth.
20 Between morning and evening they
       are destroyed;
    they perish forever without any
       regarding it.
21 Their tent-cord is plucked up within
       them,
    and they die devoid of wisdom.'

Job Is Corrected by God

5 "Call now; is there anyone who will
       answer you?
    To which of the holy ones will you
       turn?
2 Surely vexation kills the fool,
    and jealousy slays the simple.
3 I have seen fools taking root,
    but suddenly I cursed their
       dwelling.
4 Their children are far from safety,
    they are crushed in the gate,

    and there is no one to deliver
       them.
5 The hungry eat their harvest,
    and they take it even out of the
       thorns;[b]
    and the thirsty[c] pant after their
       wealth.
6 For misery does not come from the
       earth,
    nor does trouble sprout from the
       ground;
7 but human beings are born to
       trouble
    just as sparks[d] fly upward.

8 "As for me, I would seek God,
    and to God I would commit my
       cause.
9 He does great things and
       unsearchable,
    marvelous things without number.
10 He gives rain on the earth
    and sends waters on the fields;
11 he sets on high those who are lowly,
    and those who mourn are lifted to
       safety.
12 He frustrates the devices of the
       crafty,
    so that their hands achieve no
       success.
13 He takes the wise in their own
       craftiness;
    and the schemes of the wily are
       brought to a quick end.
14 They meet with darkness in the
       daytime,
    and grope at noonday as in the
       night.
15 But he saves the needy from the
       sword of their mouth,
    from the hand of the mighty.
16 So the poor have hope,
    and injustice shuts its mouth.

[a] Or *more than*   [b] Meaning of Heb uncertain   [c] Aquila Symmachus Syr
Vg: Heb *snare*   [d] Or *birds;* Heb *sons of Resheph*

5:15–16—Eliphaz here affirms what the prophets of Israel so firmly believed: God saves *the
needy* ('ebyon) from *the mighty* ones who would
exploit them. Amos uses this word several times
to indicate those in Israel who were being abused
by the rich (Amos 2:6; 4:1; 5:12; 8:4, 6). As the
result of God's saving of the needy, *the poor
have hope, and injustice shuts its mouth.* Job
will reject this belief out of hand again and again.

17 "How happy is the one whom God
         reproves;
      therefore do not despise the
         discipline of the Almighty.*a*
18 For he wounds, but he binds up;
      he strikes, but his hands heal.
19 He will deliver you from six troubles;
      in seven no harm shall touch you.
20 In famine he will redeem you from
         death,
      and in war from the power of the
         sword.
21 You shall be hidden from the
         scourge of the tongue,
      and shall not fear destruction
         when it comes.
22 At destruction and famine you shall
         laugh,
      and shall not fear the wild animals
         of the earth.
23 For you shall be in league with the
         stones of the field,
      and the wild animals shall be at
         peace with you.
24 You shall know that your tent is safe,
      you shall inspect your fold and
         miss nothing.
25 You shall know that your
         descendants will be many,
      and your offspring like the grass of
         the earth.
26 You shall come to your grave in ripe
         old age,
      as a shock of grain comes up to the
         threshing floor in its season.
27 See, we have searched this out; it is
         true.
      Hear, and know it for yourself."

Job Replies: My Complaint Is Just

6 Then Job answered:
2 "O that my vexation were
         weighed,
      and all my calamity laid in the
         balances!

3 For then it would be heavier than
         the sand of the sea;
      therefore my words have been
         rash.
4 For the arrows of the Almighty*a* are
         in me;
      my spirit drinks their poison;
      the terrors of God are arrayed
         against me.
5 Does the wild ass bray over its grass,
      or the ox low over its fodder?
6 Can that which is tasteless be eaten
         without salt,
      or is there any flavor in the juice of
         mallows?*b*
7 My appetite refuses to touch them;
      they are like food that is loathsome
         to me.*b*
8 "O that I might have my request,
      and that God would grant my
         desire;
9 that it would please God to crush
         me,
      that he would let loose his hand
         and cut me off!
10 This would be my consolation;
      I would even exult*b* in unrelenting
         pain;
      for I have not denied the words of
         the Holy One.
11 What is my strength, that I should
         wait?
      And what is my end, that I should
         be patient?
12 Is my strength the strength of stones,
      or is my flesh bronze?
13 In truth I have no help in me,
      and any resource is driven from
         me.

14 "Those who withhold*c* kindness
         from a friend
      forsake the fear of the Almighty.*a*

a Traditional rendering of Heb *Shaddai*   *b* Meaning of Heb uncertain
c Syr Vg Compare Tg: Meaning of Heb uncertain

6:2–4—Job insists to the furious Eliphaz that he is
not crying out in his pain for no reason; God has
attacked him!

6:14—The phrase is difficult to translate, but
the NRSV appears generally correct: "To reject
devotion for a friend is to abandon the worship of
Shaddai" may be more literal. This reading nicely
introduces Job's anger at his friends in the next
verses (vv. 15–27).

15 My companions are treacherous like
     a torrent-bed,
   like freshets that pass away,
16 that run dark with ice,
     turbid with melting snow.
17 In time of heat they disappear;
     when it is hot, they vanish from
       their place.
18 The caravans turn aside from their
       course;
   they go up into the waste, and
       perish.
19 The caravans of Tema look,
     the travelers of Sheba hope.
20 They are disappointed because they
       were confident;
   they come there and are
       confounded.
21 Such you have now become to me;*a*
     you see my calamity, and are
       afraid.
22 Have I said, 'Make me a gift'?
     Or, 'From your wealth offer a bribe
       for me'?
23 Or, 'Save me from an opponent's
       hand'?
   Or, 'Ransom me from the hand of
       oppressors'?

24 "Teach me, and I will be silent;
     make me understand how I have
       gone wrong.
25 How forceful are honest words!
     But your reproof, what does it
       reprove?
26 Do you think that you can reprove
       words,
   as if the speech of the desperate
       were wind?
27 You would even cast lots over the
       orphan,
   and bargain over your friend.

28 "But now, be pleased to look at me;
     for I will not lie to your face.
29 Turn, I pray, let no wrong be
       done.

Turn now, my vindication is at
       stake.
30 Is there any wrong on my tongue?
     Cannot my taste discern calamity?

Job: My Suffering Is without End

7 "Do not human beings have a hard
       service on earth,
   and are not their days like the days
       of a laborer?
2 Like a slave who longs for the
       shadow,
   and like laborers who look for
       their wages,
3 so I am allotted months of emptiness,
     and nights of misery are
       apportioned to me.
4 When I lie down I say, 'When shall I
       rise?'
   But the night is long,
     and I am full of tossing until dawn.
5 My flesh is clothed with worms and
       dirt;
   my skin hardens, then breaks out
       again.
6 My days are swifter than a weaver's
       shuttle,
   and come to their end without
       hope.*b*

7 "Remember that my life is a breath;
     my eye will never again see good.
8 The eye that beholds me will see me
       no more;
   while your eyes are upon me, I
       shall be gone.
9 As the cloud fades and vanishes,
     so those who go down to Sheol do
       not come up;
10 they return no more to their houses,
     nor do their places know them any
       more.

11 "Therefore I will not restrain my
       mouth;

a Cn Compare Gk Syr: Meaning of Heb uncertain   *b* Or *as the thread runs out*

7:11–21—Job unleashes a direct assault on God. He, among other things, accuses God of confusing him with the great monster of the sea, Yam, of terrifying him **with dreams** (a reference to the dream of Eliphaz at 4:12–21), of watching him far too closely and for no apparent reason, parodying Ps. 8 (Ps. 8:17–18). Finally Job demands that God just get away from him long enough for

I will speak in the anguish of my
spirit;
I will complain in the bitterness of
my soul.

¹² Am I the Sea, or the Dragon,
that you set a guard over me?
¹³ When I say, 'My bed will
comfort me,
my couch will ease my
complaint,'
¹⁴ then you scare me with dreams
and terrify me with visions,
¹⁵ so that I would choose strangling
and death rather than this body.
¹⁶ I loathe my life; I would not live
forever.
Let me alone, for my days are a
breath.
¹⁷ What are human beings, that you
make so much of them,
that you set your mind on them,
¹⁸ visit them every morning,
test them every moment?
¹⁹ Will you not look away from me for
a while,
let me alone until I swallow my
spittle?
²⁰ If I sin, what do I do to you, you
watcher of humanity?
Why have you made me your
target?
Why have I become a burden to
you?
²¹ Why do you not pardon my
transgression
and take away my iniquity?
For now I shall lie in the earth;

you will seek me, but I shall
not be."

Bildad Speaks: Job Should Repent

8 Then Bildad the Shuhite answered:
² "How long will you say these
things,
and the words of your mouth be a
great wind?
³ Does God pervert justice?
Or does the Almighty*ᵃ* pervert the
right?
⁴ If your children sinned against him,
he delivered them into the power
of their transgression.
⁵ If you will seek God
and make supplication to the
Almighty,*ᵃ*
⁶ if you are pure and upright,
surely then he will rouse himself
for you
and restore to you your rightful
place.
⁷ Though your beginning was small,
your latter days will be very great.

⁸ "For inquire now of bygone
generations,
and consider what their ancestors
have found;
⁹ for we are but of yesterday, and we
know nothing,
for our days on earth are but a
shadow.
¹⁰ Will they not teach you and tell you
and utter words out of their
understanding?

ᵃ Traditional rendering of Heb Shaddai

---

him to swallow his spit (Job 7:19)! He ends this
astonishing speech by demanding that God just
pardon whatever sins Job supposedly has done,
because, if not, it may be too late. Job is about to
die, and God will look in vain for him, either to
pardon or to wreak destruction!

8:1–4—*Bildad* is appalled by Job's gross intem-
perance toward God, who can never **pervert justice** or **pervert the right**. Bildad, with incredible
cruelty, says that the death of Job's children in the
prologue was nothing less than they deserved
(v. 4)!

8:8–10—Eliphaz had claimed that God had
spoken to him directly in a miraculous vision

(4:12–21). When people say that God has spoken
to them in vision or dream, it is difficult to argue
with such statements. Bildad chooses a different
source for his wise knowledge: the tradition. Because our knowledge is limited to our tiny span
of days on earth, we must consult the **bygone
generations**, those whose experience is so much
greater than our own. We immediately want to
agree with Bildad's good advice; we do want to
remember and take seriously what those who
have preceded us in the faith have said. Unfortunately, however, Bildad seems to have learned
from his study of the past only that Job is a foul
sinner. A more complete reading of our tradition
offers broader wisdom than such narrow ideas.

11 "Can papyrus grow where there is no
    marsh?
    Can reeds flourish where there is
      no water?
12 While yet in flower and not cut
    down,
    they wither before any other plant.
13 Such are the paths of all who forget
    God;
    the hope of the godless shall
      perish.
14 Their confidence is gossamer,
    a spider's house their trust.
15 If one leans against its house, it will
    not stand;
    if one lays hold of it, it will not
      endure.
16 The wicked thrive[a] before the sun,
    and their shoots spread over the
      garden.
17 Their roots twine around the
    stoneheap;
    they live among the rocks.[b]
18 If they are destroyed from their
    place,
    then it will deny them, saying, 'I
      have never seen you.'
19 See, these are their happy ways,[c]
    and out of the earth still others
      will spring.

20 "See, God will not reject a blameless
    person,
    nor take the hand of evildoers.
21 He will yet fill your mouth with
    laughter,
    and your lips with shouts of joy.
22 Those who hate you will be clothed
    with shame,
    and the tent of the wicked will be
      no more."

Job Replies: There Is No Mediator

9 Then Job answered:
2 "Indeed I know that this is so;
    but how can a mortal be just
      before God?
3 If one wished to contend with him,
    one could not answer him once in
      a thousand.
4 He is wise in heart, and mighty in
    strength
    —who has resisted him, and
      succeeded?—
5 he who removes mountains, and
    they do not know it,
    when he overturns them in his
      anger;
6 who shakes the earth out of its place,
    and its pillars tremble;
7 who commands the sun, and it does
    not rise;
    who seals up the stars;
8 who alone stretched out the heavens
    and trampled the waves of the
      Sea;[d]
9 who made the Bear and Orion,
    the Pleiades and the chambers of
      the south;
10 who does great things beyond
    understanding,
    and marvelous things without
      number.
11 Look, he passes by me, and I do not
    see him;
    he moves on, but I do not perceive
      him.
12 He snatches away; who can stop
    him?
    Who will say to him, 'What are
      you doing?'

[a] Heb He thrives   [b] Gk Vg: Meaning of Heb uncertain   [c] Meaning of Heb uncertain   [d] Or trampled the back of the sea dragon

---

9:2–21—After admitting that he has heard such talk all of his life, namely, that evil acts cause bad things to happen (v. 2), Job quickly imagines a courtroom drama where he plays the role of attorney while God is forced to sit in the witness chair. He wants to know just how any mortal can be *just before God* (v. 2). (Remember that Eliphaz's vision had revealed to him that *no one* could be just before God, 4:17–19). Job's demands for justice become more insistent. In v.

3 the NRSV translates the Hebrew *rib* as *contend with*. This verb signals the scene of the court. Immediately Job despairs of ever having a fair hearing in this court, precisely because his accuser is a God who has vast power (vv. 3–10), but who also seems to be unaware or unconcerned with the effects of that power (vv. 17–18). Job says that God will not listen (v. 16) but instead *crushes* him with a storm/*tempest*.

13 "God will not turn back his anger;
     the helpers of Rahab bowed
         beneath him.

14 How then can I answer him,
     choosing my words with him?

15 Though I am innocent, I cannot
         answer him;
     I must appeal for mercy to my
         accuser.[a]

16 If I summoned him and he
         answered me,
     I do not believe that he would
         listen to my voice.

17 For he crushes me with a tempest,
     and multiplies my wounds without
         cause;

18 he will not let me get my breath,
     but fills me with bitterness.

19 If it is a contest of strength, he is the
         strong one!
     If it is a matter of justice, who can
         summon him?[b]

20 Though I am innocent, my own
         mouth would condemn me;
     though I am blameless, he would
         prove me perverse.

21 I am blameless; I do not know
         myself;
     I loathe my life.

22 It is all one; therefore I say,
     he destroys both the blameless and
         the wicked.

23 When disaster brings sudden
         death,
     he mocks at the calamity[c] of the
         innocent.

24 The earth is given into the hand of
         the wicked;
     he covers the eyes of its judges—
     if it is not he, who then is it?

25 "My days are swifter than a runner;
     they flee away, they see no good.

26 They go by like skiffs of reed,
     like an eagle swooping on the prey.

27 If I say, 'I will forget my complaint;
     I will put off my sad countenance
         and be of good cheer,'

28 I become afraid of all my suffering,
     for I know you will not hold me
         innocent.

29 I shall be condemned;
     why then do I labor in vain?

30 If I wash myself with soap
     and cleanse my hands with lye,

31 yet you will plunge me into filth,
     and my own clothes will abhor me.

32 For he is not a mortal, as I am, that I
         might answer him,
     that we should come to trial
         together.

33 There is no umpire[d] between us,
     who might lay his hand on us
         both.

34 If he would take his rod away from
         me,
     and not let dread of him terrify
         me,

35 then I would speak without fear of
         him,
     for I know I am not what I am
         thought to be.[e]

Job: I Loathe My Life

10 "I loathe my life;
     I will give free utterance to my
         complaint;
     I will speak in the bitterness of my
         soul.

[a] Or for my right   [b] Compare Gk: Heb me   [c] Meaning of Heb uncertain
[d] Another reading is Would that there were an umpire   [e] Cn: Heb for I am
not so in myself

9:22–24—Job caps a furious rejection of God's ways with him with these memorable lines. In sum, God is a monster, destroying all people, whether righteous or wicked, and laughing while they die. The earth is run by a sadist, as far as Job can see; if it is not God, then who in the world can it be? Job here agrees with the friends that God does all things (see also Isa. 45:7).

9:33–35—For the first time, but not the last, Job's imagination reaches toward the possibility that some third party may exist to help him against

this monstrous God. He here names an *umpire*, a mediator, who could *lay his hand on us both* in order to make the contest a more equal one. The NRSV's reading **there is no umpire** could also be read "if only there were an umpire." The latter translation better captures the profound hope for some helper for the despairing Job, but at the same time speaks to the longing hopelessness to which his life's horrors are leading him.

10:1–7—That tragic combination of hope and hopelessness finds evidence in chap. 10. Because

2 I will say to God, Do not
        condemn me;
    let me know why you contend
        against me.
3 Does it seem good to you to oppress,
        to despise the work of your hands
    and favor the schemes of the
        wicked?
4 Do you have eyes of flesh?
        Do you see as humans see?
5 Are your days like the days of
        mortals,
    or your years like human years,
6 that you seek out my iniquity
        and search for my sin,
7 although you know that I am not
        guilty,
    and there is no one to deliver out
        of your hand?
8 Your hands fashioned and made me;
        and now you turn and
        destroy me.*a*
9 Remember that you fashioned me
        like clay;
    and will you turn me to dust
        again?
10 Did you not pour me out like milk
        and curdle me like cheese?
11 You clothed me with skin and flesh,
        and knit me together with bones
        and sinews.
12 You have granted me life and
        steadfast love,
    and your care has preserved my
        spirit.
13 Yet these things you hid in your
        heart;

I know that this was your
        purpose.
14 If I sin, you watch me,
        and do not acquit me of my
        iniquity.
15 If I am wicked, woe to me!
    If I am righteous, I cannot lift up
        my head,
    for I am filled with disgrace
        and look upon my affliction.
16 Bold as a lion you hunt me;
        you repeat your exploits
        against me.
17 You renew your witnesses
        against me,
    and increase your vexation
        toward me;
    you bring fresh troops against me.*b*
18 "Why did you bring me forth from
        the womb?
    Would that I had died before any
        eye had seen me,
19 and were as though I had not been,
        carried from the womb to the
        grave.
20 Are not the days of my life few?*c*
    Let me alone, that I may find a
        little comfort*d*
21 before I go, never to return,
        to the land of gloom and deep
        darkness,
22 the land of gloom*e* and chaos,
        where light is like darkness."

a Cn Compare Gk Syr: Heb *made me together all around, and you destroy
me*   *b* Cn Compare Gk: Heb *toward me; changes and a troop are with me*
c Cn Compare Gk Syr: Heb *Are not my days few? Let him cease!*   *d* Heb *that
I may brighten up a little*   *e* Heb *gloom as darkness, deep darkness*

Job's life on the ash heap is so repulsive, he feels
free to say anything he wants (v. 1). He asks God
why Job has become the object of divine fury (v.
2). And then, astonishingly, Job wants to know
if God in fact enjoys hating God's own creation
while favoring the evil plans of the wicked (v. 3).
Plaintively, or sarcastically, Job wonders whether
God can understand what it is like to be human.
In fact, the only human trait God appears to
exhibit is seeking for Job's sins, scrutinizing him
for possible evil. God, thinks Job, acts just like
the friends!

10:8–12—Job now appeals to God's creative
acts. Why would God make Job, only to **turn**

around and **destroy** him? Has God forgotten how
carefully Job was **fashioned**, how gracefully God
gave him life and steadfast love, how God's care
preserved his very breath?

10:13–22—But all of those gifts, all of that careful
creation, were only a sham, a cruel trick! All
along, Job was created only in order that God
could attack him. Whether he is righteous or a
sinner makes no difference (v. 15); God simply
uses Job for target practice, and the inevitable
result will be Job's journey toward death. That
death is characterized by **darkness** and **gloom**, a
place where even the light is only darkness.

Zophar Speaks: Job's Guilt Deserves Punishment

11 Then Zophar the Naamathite answered:

2 "Should a multitude of words go
      unanswered,
   and should one full of talk be
      vindicated?
3 Should your babble put others to
      silence,
   and when you mock, shall no one
      shame you?
4 For you say, 'My conduct[a] is pure,
   and I am clean in God's[b] sight.'
5 But O that God would speak,
   and open his lips to you,
6 and that he would tell you the secrets
      of wisdom!
   For wisdom is many-sided.[c]
   Know then that God exacts of you
      less than your guilt deserves.

7 "Can you find out the deep things of
      God?
   Can you find out the limit of the
      Almighty?[d]
8 It is higher than heaven[e]—what can
      you do?
   Deeper than Sheol—what can you
      know?
9 Its measure is longer than the
      earth,
   and broader than the sea.
10 If he passes through, and
      imprisons,
   and assembles for judgment, who
      can hinder him?
11 For he knows those who are
      worthless;
   when he sees iniquity, will he not
      consider it?

12 But a stupid person will get
      understanding,
   when a wild ass is born human.[c]

13 "If you direct your heart rightly,
   you will stretch out your hands
      toward him.
14 If iniquity is in your hand, put it far
      away,
   and do not let wickedness reside in
      your tents.
15 Surely then you will lift up your face
      without blemish;
   you will be secure, and will not
      fear.
16 You will forget your misery;
   you will remember it as waters that
      have passed away.
17 And your life will be brighter than
      the noonday;
   its darkness will be like the
      morning.
18 And you will have confidence,
      because there is hope;
   you will be protected[f] and take
      your rest in safety.
19 You will lie down, and no one will
      make you afraid;
   many will entreat your favor.
20 But the eyes of the wicked will fail;
   all way of escape will be lost to
      them,
   and their hope is to breathe their
      last."

Job Replies: I Am a Laughingstock

12 Then Job answered:
2 "No doubt you are the people,
   and wisdom will die with you.

---

[a] Gk: Heb *teaching*   [b] Heb *your*   [c] Meaning of Heb uncertain   [d] Traditional rendering of Heb *Shaddai*   [e] Heb *The heights of heaven*   [f] Or *you will look around*

11:1–12—*Zophar's* first speech is among the angriest of the book, laced with sarcasm and ridicule. Job's claims for righteousness and purity are complete fiction (v. 4); in fact God has given Job *less* than he deserves (v. 6)! After telling Job that he can know nothing of this vast God's ways (vv. 7–11), he announces that *a stupid person will get understanding, when a wild ass is born human* (v. 12)! In other words—never! While Eliphaz claimed his wisdom came from his

personal vision, and Bildad announced that his knowledge was as a result of his reading of the tradition, Zophar refers to the deep wisdom of God as his source, a wisdom closed to the stupid person (e.g., Job), but apparently open to the wise person (e.g., Zophar).

12:2–25—In this chapter Job summarily dismisses the supposed great wisdom of the friends. Their certainty that God rewards righteous and punishes wicked, claimed by them to be proven

³ But I have understanding as well as
    you;
  I am not inferior to you.
  Who does not know such things as
    these?
⁴ I am a laughingstock to my friends;
  I, who called upon God and he
    answered me,
  a just and blameless man, I am a
    laughingstock.
⁵ Those at ease have contempt for
    misfortune,ᵃ
  but it is ready for those whose feet
    are unstable.
⁶ The tents of robbers are at peace,
  and those who provoke God are
    secure,
  who bring their god in their
    hands.ᵇ
⁷ "But ask the animals, and they will
    teach you;
  the birds of the air, and they will
    tell you;
⁸ ask the plants of the earth,ᶜ and they
    will teach you;
  and the fish of the sea will declare
    to you.
⁹ Who among all these does not know
    that the hand of the LORD has
    done this?
¹⁰ In his hand is the life of every living
    thing
  and the breath of every human
    being.
¹¹ Does not the ear test words
  as the palate tastes food?
¹² Is wisdom with the aged,
  and understanding in length of
    days?
¹³ "With Godᵈ are wisdom and
    strength;

he has counsel and understanding.
¹⁴ If he tears down, no one can rebuild;
  if he shuts someone in, no one can
    open up.
¹⁵ If he withholds the waters, they
    dry up;
  if he sends them out, they
    overwhelm the land.
¹⁶ With him are strength and wisdom;
  the deceived and the deceiver are
    his.
¹⁷ He leads counselors away stripped,
  and makes fools of judges.
¹⁸ He looses the sash of kings,
  and binds a waistcloth on their
    loins.
¹⁹ He leads priests away stripped,
  and overthrows the mighty.
²⁰ He deprives of speech those who are
    trusted,
  and takes away the discernment of
    the elders.
²¹ He pours contempt on princes,
  and looses the belt of the strong.
²² He uncovers the deeps out of
    darkness,
  and brings deep darkness to light.
²³ He makes nations great, then
    destroys them;
  he enlarges nations, then leads
    them away.
²⁴ He strips understanding from the
    leadersᵉ of the earth,
  and makes them wander in a
    pathless waste.
²⁵ They grope in the dark without light;
  he makes them stagger like a
    drunkard.

ᵃ Meaning of Heb uncertain ᵇ Or whom God brought forth by his hand;
Meaning of Heb uncertain ᶜ Or speak to the earth ᵈ Heb him ᵉ Heb adds
of the people

true in vision, tradition, and divine wisdom, Job
thoroughly rejects. His argument is simple; the
very structure of human and animal experience
gives the lie to the friends' absurd beliefs. **Ask
animals, birds** and **fish**; ask even **the plants**!
Everything in the universe knows that God does
all, and that so many of God's acts are dark and
mysterious—tearing down, shutting up, bringing drought, then bringing flood, making wise

counselors and judges fools, ripping the garments
off priests in public humiliation, overthrowing
even the mightiest of rulers. Great nations are destroyed; even nations that appear to be endlessly
expanding are soon sent to exile. Job's point is
that the simple mechanical world of the friends
clearly does not exist; God's world is far less neat
and tidy.

13 "Look, my eye has seen all this,
my ear has heard and
understood it.
2 What you know, I also know;
I am not inferior to you.
3 But I would speak to the Almighty,[a]
and I desire to argue my case with
God.
4 As for you, you whitewash with lies;
all of you are worthless physicians.
5 If you would only keep silent,
that would be your wisdom!
6 Hear now my reasoning,
and listen to the pleadings of my
lips.
7 Will you speak falsely for God,
and speak deceitfully for him?
8 Will you show partiality toward
him,
will you plead the case for God?
9 Will it be well with you when he
searches you out?
Or can you deceive him, as one
person deceives another?
10 He will surely rebuke you
if in secret you show partiality.
11 Will not his majesty terrify you,
and the dread of him fall upon
you?
12 Your maxims are proverbs of ashes,
your defenses are defenses of clay.

13 "Let me have silence, and I will
speak,
and let come on me what may.
14 I will take my flesh in my teeth,
and put my life in my hand.[b]
15 See, he will kill me; I have no hope;[c]
but I will defend my ways to his
face.
16 This will be my salvation,

that the godless shall not come
before him.
17 Listen carefully to my words,
and let my declaration be in your
ears.
18 I have indeed prepared my case;
I know that I shall be vindicated.
19 Who is there that will contend
with me?
For then I would be silent and die.

Job's Despondent Prayer

20 Only grant two things to me,
then I will not hide myself from
your face:
21 withdraw your hand far from me,
and do not let dread of you
terrify me.
22 Then call, and I will answer;
or let me speak, and you reply
to me.
23 How many are my iniquities and my
sins?
Make me know my transgression
and my sin.
24 Why do you hide your face,
and count me as your enemy?
25 Will you frighten a windblown leaf
and pursue dry chaff?
26 For you write bitter things
against me,
and make me reap[d] the iniquities
of my youth.
27 You put my feet in the stocks,
and watch all my paths;
you set a bound to the soles of my
feet.
28 One wastes away like a rotten thing,
like a garment that is moth-eaten.

a Traditional rendering of Heb *Shaddai*   b Gk: Heb *Why should I take . . .
in my hand?*   c Or *Though he kill me, yet I will trust in him*   d Heb *inherit*

13:1–28—Job himself has observed the world he
has just described. After all, his own wretched
life, a life now empty of family, goods, and any
real friends, is proof positive of the strange ways
of this apparently cruel God of power. Finally,
Job grows tired of debate with the friends and
proclaims that he is once again anxious to go
to court **with God** alone (v. 3). He first turns on
the friends and accuses them of whitewashing
the real truth of the world, of being **worthless**

physicians (quacks). They are, in short, no friends
at all! Their greatest wisdom would be their
silence (v. 5), warning them that if God would
really speak to them concerning their attempts
to defend God, God would not reveal nuggets
of wisdom, as they have claimed, but rebukes
for their ridiculous arguments (v. 10). It is well to
remember that the only sentence God utters to
any of the friends is precisely a rebuke for their
ridiculous arguments (42:7)!

14 ¹ "A mortal, born of woman, few
of days and full of trouble,
²   comes up like a flower and
withers,
flees like a shadow and does not
last.
³ Do you fix your eyes on such a one?
Do you bring me into judgment
with you?
⁴ Who can bring a clean thing out of
an unclean?
No one can.
⁵ Since their days are determined,
and the number of their months is
known to you,
and you have appointed the
bounds that they cannot pass,
⁶ look away from them, and desist,^a
that they may enjoy, like laborers,
their days.

⁷ "For there is hope for a tree,
if it is cut down, that it will sprout
again,
and that its shoots will not cease.
⁸ Though its root grows old in the
earth,
and its stump dies in the ground,
⁹ yet at the scent of water it will bud
and put forth branches like a
young plant.
¹⁰ But mortals die, and are laid low;
humans expire, and where are
they?
¹¹ As waters fail from a lake,
and a river wastes away and
dries up,
¹² so mortals lie down and do not rise
again;
until the heavens are no more,
they will not awake

or be roused out of their sleep.
¹³ O that you would hide me in
Sheol,
that you would conceal me until
your wrath is past,
that you would appoint me a set
time, and remember me!
¹⁴ If mortals die, will they live again?
All the days of my service I would
wait
until my release should come.
¹⁵ You would call, and I would answer
you;
you would long for the work of
your hands.
¹⁶ For then you would not^b number my
steps,
you would not keep watch over my
sin;
¹⁷ my transgression would be sealed up
in a bag,
and you would cover over my
iniquity.

¹⁸ "But the mountain falls and
crumbles away,
and the rock is removed from its
place;
¹⁹ the waters wear away the stones;
the torrents wash away the soil of
the earth;
so you destroy the hope of
mortals.
²⁰ You prevail forever against them,
and they pass away;
you change their countenance, and
send them away.
²¹ Their children come to honor, and
they do not know it;

^a Cn: Heb *that they may desist*   ^b Syr: Heb lacks *not*

14:1–22—Job closes the first cycle of speeches
with a superb poem on the transience of human
life and the finality of human death. Though
some have heard a glimmer of a belief in life after
death in Job's words—a belief evidenced clearly
in very few places of the Hebrew Bible (Dan.
12:2 is the most certain reference)—noting Job
14:13, the thrust of Job's words speak against it.
Verse 12 says directly that *mortals lie down and
do not rise again*, even after the heavens disappear. And the melancholy v. 19 says that just as

surely as *waters wear away the stones*, so God
wears away *the hope of mortals*. Unlike trees
(vv. 7–9), which can still be regrown with water
and patience, mortals die and nothing can bring
them back from death. Even Job's wild imaginative idea (v. 13) that perhaps God could hide him
in Sheol (the place of death for the Hebrews)
until God's anger cools off, and then remember
him (!), is no hope for afterlife, but an absurd
picture of an out-of-control God as portrayed by
a man grasping at straws.

they are brought low, and it goes
  unnoticed.

22 They feel only the pain of their own
  bodies,
    and mourn only for themselves."

Eliphaz Speaks: Job Undermines Religion

15 Then Eliphaz the Temanite answered:

2 "Should the wise answer with windy
  knowledge,
    and fill themselves with the east
      wind?

3 Should they argue in unprofitable
  talk,
    or in words with which they can
      do no good?

4 But you are doing away with the fear
  of God,
    and hindering meditation before
      God.

5 For your iniquity teaches your
  mouth,
    and you choose the tongue of the
      crafty.

6 Your own mouth condemns you,
  and not I;
    your own lips testify against
      you.

7 "Are you the firstborn of the human
  race?
    Were you brought forth before the
      hills?

8 Have you listened in the council of
  God?
    And do you limit wisdom to
      yourself?

9 What do you know that we do not
  know?
    What do you understand that is
      not clear to us?

10 The gray-haired and the aged are on
  our side,
    those older than your father.

11 Are the consolations of God too
  small for you,
    or the word that deals gently with
      you?

12 Why does your heart carry you away,
  and why do your eyes flash,[a]

13 so that you turn your spirit against
  God,
    and let such words go out of your
      mouth?

14 What are mortals, that they can be
  clean?
    Or those born of woman, that they
      can be righteous?

15 God puts no trust even in his holy
  ones,
    and the heavens are not clean in
      his sight;

16 how much less one who is
  abominable and corrupt,
    one who drinks iniquity like water!

17 "I will show you; listen to me;
  what I have seen I will declare—

18 what sages have told,
  and their ancestors have not
    hidden,

19 to whom alone the land was given,
  and no stranger passed among
    them.

20 The wicked writhe in pain all their
  days,
    through all the years that are laid
      up for the ruthless.

21 Terrifying sounds are in their ears;
  in prosperity the destroyer will
    come upon them.

22 They despair of returning from
  darkness,

[a] Meaning of Heb uncertain

15:1–6—*Eliphaz* begins the second cycle of
speeches with a furious attack on Job, whom
he is now certain is the foulest sinner in human
history. Eliphaz is indignant and frustrated at
Job's refusal to accept the truth of Eliphaz's clear
sermon concerning Job's guilt and his need for
repentance. His comment in v. 6 suggests that
Job's very words about God and God's world

have in fact condemned him; Eliphaz feels he has
no need to add anything to these blasphemous
words. Eliphaz includes in this his second speech
no suggestion that Job can in any way find a
new start with God; he will now receive what all
sinners deserve. Verses 17–35 provide a colorful
picture of Job's terrifying future.

and they are destined for the
     sword.
23 They wander abroad for bread,
     saying, 'Where is it?'
They know that a day of darkness
     is ready at hand;
24 distress and anguish terrify them;
     they prevail against them, like a
     king prepared for battle.
25 Because they stretched out their
     hands against God,
and bid defiance to the Almighty,[a]
26 running stubbornly against him
     with a thick-bossed shield;
27 because they have covered their
     faces with their fat,
and gathered fat upon their loins,
28 they will live in desolate cities,
     in houses that no one should
     inhabit,
houses destined to become heaps
     of ruins;
29 they will not be rich, and their
     wealth will not endure,
nor will they strike root in the
     earth;[b]
30 they will not escape from darkness;
     the flame will dry up their shoots,
and their blossom[c] will be swept
     away[d] by the wind.
31 Let them not trust in emptiness,
     deceiving themselves;
for emptiness will be their
     recompense.
32 It will be paid in full before their time,
     and their branch will not be green.
33 They will shake off their unripe
     grape, like the vine,
and cast off their blossoms, like
     the olive tree.
34 For the company of the godless is
     barren,
and fire consumes the tents of
     bribery.
35 They conceive mischief and bring
     forth evil
and their heart prepares deceit."

Job Reaffirms His Innocence

16 Then Job answered:
2 "I have heard many such
     things;
miserable comforters are you all.
3 Have windy words no limit?
     Or what provokes you that you
     keep on talking?
4 I also could talk as you do,
     if you were in my place;
I could join words together against
     you,
     and shake my head at you.
5 I could encourage you with my
     mouth,
and the solace of my lips would
     assuage your pain.

6 "If I speak, my pain is not assuaged,
     and if I forbear, how much of it
     leaves me?
7 Surely now God has worn me out;
     he has[e] made desolate all my
     company.
8 And he has[e] shriveled me up,
     which is a witness against me;
my leanness has risen up against me,
     and it testifies to my face.
9 He has torn me in his wrath, and
     hated me;
he has gnashed his teeth at me;
     my adversary sharpens his eyes
     against me.
10 They have gaped at me with their
     mouths;
they have struck me insolently on
     the cheek;
they mass themselves together
     against me.
11 God gives me up to the ungodly,
     and casts me into the hands of the
     wicked.
12 I was at ease, and he broke me in
     two;
he seized me by the neck and
     dashed me to pieces;

[a] Traditional rendering of Heb *Shaddai*   [b] Vg: Meaning of Heb uncertain   [c] Gk: Heb *mouth*   [d] Cn: Heb *will depart*   [e] Heb *you have*

16:2–5—Job reacts with furious words to the attack of Eliphaz, especially accusing him and his friends of being *miserable comforters* (v. 2). Most readers could only agree!

he set me up as his target;

13   his archers surround me.
He slashes open my kidneys, and
        shows no mercy;
    he pours out my gall on the
        ground.

14 He bursts upon me again and again;
    he rushes at me like a warrior.

15 I have sewed sackcloth upon my
        skin,
    and have laid my strength in the
        dust.

16 My face is red with weeping,
    and deep darkness is on my
        eyelids,

17 though there is no violence in my
        hands,
    and my prayer is pure.

18 "O earth, do not cover my blood;
    let my outcry find no resting place.

19 Even now, in fact, my witness is in
        heaven,
    and he that vouches for me is on
        high.

20 My friends scorn me;
    my eye pours out tears to God,

21 that he would maintain the right of a
        mortal with God,
    as^a one does for a neighbor.

22 For when a few years have come,
    I shall go the way from which I
        shall not return.

Job Prays for Relief

17 My spirit is broken, my days are
    extinct,
    the grave is ready for me.

2   Surely there are mockers around me,
    and my eye dwells on their
        provocation.

3   "Lay down a pledge for me with
        yourself;
    who is there that will give surety
        for me?

4   Since you have closed their minds to
        understanding,
    therefore you will not let them
        triumph.

5   Those who denounce friends for
        reward—
    the eyes of their children will fail.

6   "He has made me a byword of the
        peoples,
    and I am one before whom people
        spit.

7   My eye has grown dim from grief,
    and all my members are like a
        shadow.

8   The upright are appalled at this,
    and the innocent stir themselves
        up against the godless.

9   Yet the righteous hold to their way,
    and they that have clean hands
        grow stronger and stronger.

10 But you, come back now, all of you,
    and I shall not find a sensible
        person among you.

11 My days are past, my plans are
        broken off,
    the desires of my heart.

12 They make night into day;
    'The light,' they say, 'is near to the
        darkness.'^{b}

13 If I look for Sheol as my house,
    if I spread my couch in darkness,

14 if I say to the Pit, 'You are my father,'
    and to the worm, 'My mother,' or
        'My sister,'

15 where then is my hope?

^{a} Syr Vg Tg: Heb *and* ^{b} Meaning of Heb uncertain

16:18–22—Job returns to his imaginative belief that a third party may exist to help him against God. He first refers to the Cain and Abel story (Gen. 4) to remind all that innocent blood never is forgotten, but perpetually cries out from the ground for justice. He then affirms that his *witness* is in the sky. He claims that this witness is on his side, and is ready to vouch for his innocence, apparently even after his innocent death. Verse 20 is difficult in Hebrew, but the verse appears to read: "My witness is my friend to God; my eyes drip (tears?)." Then v. 21 makes it quite clear that the witness is not God, because the role of the witness is to *maintain the right of a mortal with God, as one does for a neighbor*. Job has in mind a heavenly attorney who is ready to take his case against an unjust God. But, as in chap. 10, Job turns to deep lament in chap. 17 after this burst of imaginative enthusiasm in chap. 16.

Who will see my hope?
16 Will it go down to the bars of Sheol?
   Shall we descend together into the
      dust?"

Bildad Speaks: God Punishes
the Wicked

18 Then Bildad the Shuhite answered:
2 "How long will you hunt for words?
   Consider, and then we shall
      speak.
3 Why are we counted as cattle?
   Why are we stupid in your sight?
4 You who tear yourself in your
      anger—
   shall the earth be forsaken because
      of you,
   or the rock be removed out of its
      place?

5 "Surely the light of the wicked is put
      out,
   and the flame of their fire does not
      shine.
6 The light is dark in their tent,
   and the lamp above them is put
      out.
7 Their strong steps are shortened,
   and their own schemes throw
      them down.
8 For they are thrust into a net by their
      own feet,
   and they walk into a pitfall.
9 A trap seizes them by the heel;
   a snare lays hold of them.
10 A rope is hid for them in the ground,
   a trap for them in the path.
11 Terrors frighten them on every side,
   and chase them at their heels.
12 Their strength is consumed by
      hunger,*a*
   and calamity is ready for their
      stumbling.
13 By disease their skin is consumed,*b*

the firstborn of Death consumes
   their limbs.
14 They are torn from the tent in which
      they trusted,
   and are brought to the king of
      terrors.
15 In their tents nothing remains;
   sulfur is scattered upon their
      habitations.
16 Their roots dry up beneath,
   and their branches wither above.
17 Their memory perishes from the
      earth,
   and they have no name in the
      street.
18 They are thrust from light into
      darkness,
   and driven out of the world.
19 They have no offspring or
      descendant among their
      people,
   and no survivor where they used
      to live.
20 They of the west are appalled at their
      fate,
   and horror seizes those of the east.
21 Surely such are the dwellings of the
      ungodly,
   such is the place of those who do
      not know God."

Job Replies: I Know That My
Redeemer Lives

19 Then Job answered:
2 "How long will you torment
   me,
   and break me in pieces with
      words?
3 These ten times you have cast
      reproach upon me;
   are you not ashamed to wrong me?
4 And even if it is true that I have
      erred,

---

a Or *Disaster is hungry for them*   *b* Cn: Heb *It consumes the limbs of his skin*

18:1–4—*Bildad* is enraged by Job's attacks on the friends in chap. 16, and responds with his own fury. He answers in two ways. He first demands to know why Job thinks they are stupid as cattle; they are obviously men of great wisdom and insight, as they have gone out of their way to share with Job. Second, he demands that Job realize that not a single stone of God's universe will be moved because of Job's obnoxious language and actions. In short, Bildad says that Job has a far greater opinion of his knowledge and his importance than he should.

my error remains with me.
5 If indeed you magnify yourselves
      against me,
   and make my humiliation an
      argument against me,
6 know then that God has put me in
      the wrong,
   and closed his net around me.
7 Even when I cry out, 'Violence!' I am
      not answered;
   I call aloud, but there is no justice.
8 He has walled up my way so that I
      cannot pass,
   and he has set darkness upon my
      paths.
9 He has stripped my glory from me,
   and taken the crown from my
      head.
10 He breaks me down on every side,
      and I am gone,
   he has uprooted my hope like a
      tree.
11 He has kindled his wrath against me,
   and counts me as his adversary.
12 His troops come on together;
   they have thrown up siegeworks[a]
      against me,
   and encamp around my tent.

13 "He has put my family far from me,
   and my acquaintances are wholly
      estranged from me.

14 My relatives and my close friends
      have failed me;
15   the guests in my house have
      forgotten me;
   my serving girls count me as a
      stranger;
   I have become an alien in their
      eyes.
16 I call to my servant, but he gives me
      no answer;
   I must myself plead with him.
17 My breath is repulsive to my wife;
   I am loathsome to my own family.
18 Even young children despise me;
   when I rise, they talk against me.
19 All my intimate friends abhor me,
   and those whom I loved have
      turned against me.
20 My bones cling to my skin and to my
      flesh,
   and I have escaped by the skin of
      my teeth.
21 Have pity on me, have pity on me,
      O you my friends,
   for the hand of God has touched
      me!
22 Why do you, like God, pursue me,
   never satisfied with my flesh?

23 "O that my words were written
      down!

_a_ Cn: Heb _their way_

19:7—Here is a summary of Job's intemperate attacks against God. *"I cry out, 'Violence!' I am not answered; I call aloud, but there is no justice."* God is regularly depicted in the Bible as the one who is the guarantor of justice, the one who responds to the cries of those who are oppressed. Job's cries have gone unheeded; he believes this to be so because the one who ought to be the bringer of justice has become the oppressor.

19:23–27—These may be the most famous lines in the book, made especially memorable by the soprano aria that begins Part III of Handel's oratorio, *Messiah*. Indeed, that lovely music has made it hard to hear these words in any other way than as a reference to the resurrection of Job after his untimely death. The KJV translation, whence Handel's text comes, makes the connection explicit. "Though worms destroy this body, yet in my flesh shall I see God" (v. 26). However, the Hebrew text of vv. 25–26 is extremely difficult to read and is subject to several possibilities. Perhaps the meaning of the word translated *Redeemer* is key. There are three possible meanings: (1) *Go'el* in Hebrew can mean "one who redeems," for example, a piece of property (see Ruth). (2) It can be used as a reference to God as the One who saves. See, for example, Isa. 41:14, where God is said to be the Redeemer of Israel. (3) In Num. 35:12, 16–21 the word may be translated "avenger." If an injustice is done by one tribe against another, a *go'el*, an avenger of blood, is chosen to right the wrong. What may Job have in mind at this point in the drama? Is the *go'el* another heavenly attorney, like the one in Job 16:21? Does Job have God in mind here, as the NRSV's capitalization of the word in v. 25 suggests? Or does Job want an avenger of blood, someone to kill God after God has killed Job, thus righting the injustice caused by the death of the innocent? As amazing as that third possibility may sound, Job's anguish and hopelessness may make that possibility more than an absurd one.

O that they were inscribed in a book!

24 O that with an iron pen and with lead
they were engraved on a rock forever!

25 For I know that my Redeemer[a] lives,
and that at the last he[b] will stand upon the earth;[c]

26 and after my skin has been thus destroyed,
then in[d] my flesh I shall see God,[e]

27 whom I shall see on my side,[f]
and my eyes shall behold, and not another.
My heart faints within me!

28 If you say, 'How we will persecute him!'
and, 'The root of the matter is found in him';

29 be afraid of the sword,
for wrath brings the punishment of the sword,
so that you may know there is a judgment.'"

Zophar Speaks: Wickedness Receives Just Retribution

20 Then Zophar the Naamathite answered:

2 "Pay attention! My thoughts urge me to answer,
because of the agitation within me.

3 I hear censure that insults me,
and a spirit beyond my understanding answers me.

4 Do you not know this from of old,
ever since mortals were placed on earth,

5 that the exulting of the wicked is short,
and the joy of the godless is but for a moment?

6 Even though they mount up high as the heavens,
and their head reaches to the clouds,

7 they will perish forever like their own dung;
those who have seen them will say, 'Where are they?'

8 They will fly away like a dream, and not be found;
they will be chased away like a vision of the night.

9 The eye that saw them will see them no more,
nor will their place behold them any longer.

10 Their children will seek the favor of the poor,
and their hands will give back their wealth.

11 Their bodies, once full of youth,
will lie down in the dust with them.

12 "Though wickedness is sweet in their mouth,
though they hide it under their tongues,

13 though they are loath to let it go,
and hold it in their mouths,

14 yet their food is turned in their stomachs;
it is the venom of asps within them.

15 They swallow down riches and vomit them up again;
God casts them out of their bellies.

16 They will suck the poison of asps;
the tongue of a viper will kill them.

17 They will not look on the rivers,
the streams flowing with honey and curds.

---

[a] Or *Vindicator* [b] Or *that he the Last* [c] Heb *dust* [d] Or *without* [e] Meaning of Heb of this verse uncertain [f] Or *for myself*

20:10—After Job's amazing fury at God, *Zophar*'s own fury is palpable. Here is one example of the way the friends of Job have made specific their conviction that Job is wicked. First, his intemperate attacks against God in chap. 19 announce to the friends that he is a blasphemer. And second, his belief that there is in fact no justice to be had in a monstrous universe says clearly that he is wicked. Wicked is as wicked says and does! The fate of all wicked—especially Job—is to return their wealth to the poor. Zophar believes that the wealth of the wicked has been taken from the poor but eventually will be returned to them; God will see to it (v. 23)!

¹⁸ They will give back the fruit of their
toil,
and will not swallow it down;
from the profit of their trading
they will get no enjoyment.
¹⁹ For they have crushed and
abandoned the poor,
they have seized a house that they
did not build.

²⁰ "They knew no quiet in their
bellies;
in their greed they let nothing
escape.
²¹ There was nothing left after they had
eaten;
therefore their prosperity will not
endure.
²² In full sufficiency they will be in
distress;
all the force of misery will come
upon them.
²³ To fill their belly to the full
Godᵃ will send his fierce anger
into them,
and rain it upon them as their
food.ᵇ
²⁴ They will flee from an iron weapon;
a bronze arrow will strike them
through.
²⁵ It is drawn forth and comes out of
their body,
and the glittering point comes out
of their gall;
terrors come upon them.
²⁶ Utter darkness is laid up for their
treasures;
a fire fanned by no one will devour
them;
what is left in their tent will be
consumed.
²⁷ The heavens will reveal their
iniquity,
and the earth will rise up against
them.
²⁸ The possessions of their house will
be carried away,

dragged off in the day of God'sᶜ
wrath.
²⁹ This is the portion of the wicked
from God,
the heritage decreed for them by
God."

Job Replies: The Wicked Often Go Unpunished

21 Then Job answered:
² "Listen carefully to my words,
and let this be your consolation.
³ Bear with me, and I will speak;
then after I have spoken, mock on.
⁴ As for me, is my complaint
addressed to mortals?
Why should I not be impatient?
⁵ Look at me, and be appalled,
and lay your hand upon your
mouth.
⁶ When I think of it I am dismayed,
and shuddering seizes my flesh.
⁷ Why do the wicked live on,
reach old age, and grow mighty in
power?
⁸ Their children are established in
their presence,
and their offspring before their
eyes.
⁹ Their houses are safe from fear,
and no rod of God is upon them.
¹⁰ Their bull breeds without fail;
their cow calves and never
miscarries.
¹¹ They send out their little ones like a
flock,
and their children dance around.
¹² They sing to the tambourine and the
lyre,
and rejoice to the sound of the pipe.
¹³ They spend their days in prosperity,
and in peace they go down to
Sheol.
¹⁴ They say to God, 'Leave us alone!
We do not desire to know your
ways.

ᵃ Heb *he* ᵇ Cn: Meaning of Heb uncertain ᶜ Heb *his*

21:7–13—Job agrees with Zophar that wicked people ought to receive a just punishment for their evil. The problem is that they do not. Quite the contrary! They prosper and remain prosperous until they die in peace.

15 What is the Almighty,*a* that we
    should serve him?
    And what profit do we get if we
      pray to him?'
16 Is not their prosperity indeed their
    own achievement?*b*
    The plans of the wicked are
      repugnant to me.
17 "How often is the lamp of the wicked
    put out?
    How often does calamity come
      upon them?
    How often does God*c* distribute
      pains in his anger?
18 How often are they like straw before
    the wind,
    and like chaff that the storm
      carries away?
19 You say, 'God stores up their iniquity
    for their children.'
    Let it be paid back to them, so that
      they may know it.
20 Let their own eyes see their
    destruction,
    and let them drink of the wrath of
      the Almighty.*a*
21 For what do they care for their
    household after them,
    when the number of their months
      is cut off?
22 Will any teach God knowledge,
    seeing that he judges those that are
      on high?
23 One dies in full prosperity,
    being wholly at ease and secure,
24 his loins full of milk
    and the marrow of his bones moist.
25 Another dies in bitterness of soul,
    never having tasted of good.
26 They lie down alike in the dust,
    and the worms cover them.

27 "Oh, I know your thoughts,
    and your schemes to wrong me.

28 For you say, 'Where is the house of
    the prince?
    Where is the tent in which the
      wicked lived?'
29 Have you not asked those who travel
    the roads,
    and do you not accept their
      testimony,
30 that the wicked are spared in the day
    of calamity,
    and are rescued in the day of
      wrath?
31 Who declares their way to their face,
    and who repays them for what
      they have done?
32 When they are carried to the grave,
    a watch is kept over their tomb.
33 The clods of the valley are sweet to
    them;
    everyone will follow after,
    and those who went before are
      innumerable.
34 How then will you comfort me with
    empty nothings?
    There is nothing left of your
      answers but falsehood."

**Eliphaz Speaks: Job's
Wickedness Is Great**

22 Then Eliphaz the Temanite answered:
2 "Can a mortal be of use to God?
    Can even the wisest be of service
      to him?
3 Is it any pleasure to the Almighty*a* if
    you are righteous,
    or is it gain to him if you make
      your ways blameless?
4 Is it for your piety that he reproves
    you,
    and enters into judgment with
      you?
5 Is not your wickedness great?

a Traditional rendering of Heb *Shaddai*   *b* Heb *in their hand*   *c* Heb *he*

22:4–11—*Eliphaz*, apparently weary of the attempted subtleties of his friends, boldly says what
he has long believed: Job is wicked! God is not
singling out Job for correction because of his
religious faith, but because **there is no end to
[his] iniquities**! And those iniquities all concern

justice for the poor. Job has either neglected
his responsibilities for justice or actively done
injustice. The list of his victims reads like that of
an eighth-century prophet: **naked, weary, hungry,
widows, orphans**.

There is no end to your iniquities.

6 For you have exacted pledges from
    your family for no reason,
    and stripped the naked of their
    clothing.

7 You have given no water to the
    weary to drink,
    and you have withheld bread from
    the hungry.

8 The powerful possess the land,
    and the favored live in it.

9 You have sent widows away
    empty-handed,
    and the arms of the orphans you
    have crushed.*a*

10 Therefore snares are around you,
    and sudden terror overwhelms
    you,

11 or darkness so that you cannot see;
    a flood of water covers you.

12 "Is not God high in the heavens?
    See the highest stars, how lofty
    they are!

13 Therefore you say, 'What does God
    know?
    Can he judge through the deep
    darkness?

14 Thick clouds enwrap him, so that he
    does not see,
    and he walks on the dome of
    heaven.'

15 Will you keep to the old way
    that the wicked have trod?

16 They were snatched away before
    their time;
    their foundation was washed away
    by a flood.

17 They said to God, 'Leave us alone,'
    and 'What can the Almighty*b* do
    to us?'*c*

18 Yet he filled their houses with good
    things—
    but the plans of the wicked are
    repugnant to me.

19 The righteous see it and are glad;
    the innocent laugh them to
    scorn,

20 saying, 'Surely our adversaries are
    cut off,

and what they left, the fire has
    consumed.'

21 "Agree with God,*d* and be at peace;
    in this way good will come to you.

22 Receive instruction from his mouth,
    and lay up his words in your
    heart.

23 If you return to the Almighty,*a* you
    will be restored,
    if you remove unrighteousness
    from your tents,

24 if you treat gold like dust,
    and gold of Ophir like the stones
    of the torrent-bed,

25 and if the Almighty*a* is your gold
    and your precious silver,

26 then you will delight yourself in the
    Almighty,*a*
    and lift up your face to God.

27 You will pray to him, and he will
    hear you,
    and you will pay your vows.

28 You will decide on a matter, and it
    will be established for you,
    and light will shine on your ways.

29 When others are humiliated, you say
    it is pride;
    for he saves the humble.

30 He will deliver even those who are
    guilty;
    they will escape because of the
    cleanness of your hands."*e*

Job Replies: My Complaint Is Bitter

23 Then Job answered:
    2 "Today also my complaint is
    bitter;*f*
    his*g* hand is heavy despite my
    groaning.

3 Oh, that I knew where I might find
    him,
    that I might come even to his
    dwelling!

4 I would lay my case before him,
    and fill my mouth with arguments.

5 I would learn what he would
    answer me,

---

a Gk Syr Tg Vg: Heb *were crushed* *b* Traditional rendering of Heb
Shaddai *c* Gk Syr: Heb *them* *d* Heb *him* *e* Meaning of Heb uncertain
f Syr Vg Tg: Heb *rebellious* *g* Gk Syr: Heb *my*

and understand what he would say
to me.
6 Would he contend with me in the
greatness of his power?
No; but he would give heed to me.
7 There an upright person could
reason with him,
and I should be acquitted forever
by my judge.

8 "If I go forward, he is not there;
or backward, I cannot perceive
him;
9 on the left he hides, and I cannot
behold him;
I turn*a* to the right, but I cannot
see him.
10 But he knows the way that I take;
when he has tested me, I shall
come out like gold.
11 My foot has held fast to his steps;
I have kept his way and have not
turned aside.
12 I have not departed from the
commandment of his lips;
I have treasured in*b* my bosom the
words of his mouth.
13 But he stands alone and who can
dissuade him?
What he desires, that he does.
14 For he will complete what he
appoints for me;
and many such things are in his
mind.
15 Therefore I am terrified at his
presence;
when I consider, I am in dread of
him.
16 God has made my heart faint;
the Almighty*c* has terrified me;
17 If only I could vanish in darkness,
and thick darkness would cover
my face!*d*

Job Complains of Violence on the Earth

24 "Why are times not kept by the
Almighty,*c*

and why do those who know him
never see his days?
2 The wicked*e* remove landmarks;
they seize flocks and pasture them.
3 They drive away the donkey of the
orphan;
they take the widow's ox for a
pledge.
4 They thrust the needy off the road;
the poor of the earth all hide
themselves.
5 Like wild asses in the desert
they go out to their toil,
scavenging in the wasteland
food for their young.
6 They reap in a field not their own
and they glean in the vineyard of
the wicked.
7 They lie all night naked, without
clothing,
and have no covering in the cold.
8 They are wet with the rain of the
mountains,
and cling to the rock for want of
shelter.

9 "There are those who snatch the
orphan child from the breast,
and take as a pledge the infant of
the poor.
10 They go about naked, without
clothing;
though hungry, they carry the
sheaves;
11 between their terraces*f* they press
out oil;
they tread the wine presses, but
suffer thirst.
12 From the city the dying groan,
and the throat of the wounded
cries for help;
yet God pays no attention to their
prayer.

a Syr Vg: Heb *he turns*   *b* Gk Vg: Heb *from*   *c* Traditional rendering of
Heb *Shaddai*   *d* Or *But I am not destroyed by the darkness; he has concealed
the thick darkness from me*   *e* Gk: Heb *they*   *f* Meaning of Heb uncertain

---

24:1–4—Again Job agrees that wicked people (he
certainly does not believe that he is one of them)
deserve condemnation and judgment from God.
But the facts say that it does not occur. Terrible
injustices do happen against those very people
named by Eliphaz: *orphan, widow, needy, poor.*
But there is no time of judgment from God.

13 "There are those who rebel against
    the light,
  who are not acquainted with its
    ways,
  and do not stay in its paths.
14 The murderer rises at dusk
  to kill the poor and needy,
  and in the night is like a thief.
15 The eye of the adulterer also waits
    for the twilight,
  saying, 'No eye will see me';
  and he disguises his face.
16 In the dark they dig through houses;
  by day they shut themselves up;
  they do not know the light.
17 For deep darkness is morning to all
    of them;
  for they are friends with the
    terrors of deep darkness.

18 "Swift are they on the face of the
    waters;
  their portion in the land is cursed;
  no treader turns toward their
    vineyards.
19 Drought and heat snatch away the
    snow waters;
  so does Sheol those who have
    sinned.
20 The womb forgets them;
  the worm finds them sweet;
 they are no longer remembered;
  so wickedness is broken like a
    tree.
21 "They harm[a] the childless woman,
  and do no good to the widow.
22 Yet God[b] prolongs the life of the
    mighty by his power;
  they rise up when they despair of
    life.
23 He gives them security, and they are
    supported;
  his eyes are upon their ways.
24 They are exalted a little while, and
    then are gone;

they wither and fade like the
    mallow;[c]
  they are cut off like the heads of
    grain.
25 If it is not so, who will prove me a
    liar,
  and show that there is nothing in
    what I say?"

Bildad Speaks: How Can a Mortal Be Righteous Before God?

25 Then Bildad the Shuhite an-
    swered:
2 "Dominion and fear are with God;[d]
  he makes peace in his high heaven.
3 Is there any number to his armies?
  Upon whom does his light not
    arise?
4 How then can a mortal be righteous
    before God?
  How can one born of woman be
    pure?
5 If even the moon is not bright
  and the stars are not pure in his
    sight,
6 how much less a mortal, who is a
    maggot,
  and a human being, who is a
    worm!"

Job Replies: God's Majesty Is Unsearchable

26 Then Job answered:
2 "How you have helped one
    who has no power!
  How you have assisted the arm
    that has no strength!
3 How you have counseled one who
    has no wisdom,
  and given much good advice!
4 With whose help have you uttered
    words,
  and whose spirit has come forth
    from you?

[a] Gk Tg: Heb *feed on* or *associate with*   [b] Heb *he*   [c] Gk: Heb *like all others*   [d] Heb *him*

25:1–6—Chapters 25–28 are much disputed. *Bildad*'s speech is only five verses long, ending in the notion that human beings are only *maggots* and *worms*. Could it be that this is the result of the theology that Bildad has espoused?

26:1–4—This chapter sounds rather more like a speech of a friend, but is found in the mouth of *Job*.

5 The shades below tremble,
  the waters and their inhabitants.
6 Sheol is naked before God,
  and Abaddon has no covering.
7 He stretches out Zaphon[a] over the void,
  and hangs the earth upon nothing.
8 He binds up the waters in his thick clouds,
  and the cloud is not torn open by them.
9 He covers the face of the full moon,
  and spreads over it his cloud.
10 He has described a circle on the face of the waters,
  at the boundary between light and darkness.
11 The pillars of heaven tremble,
  and are astounded at his rebuke.
12 By his power he stilled the Sea;
  by his understanding he struck down Rahab.
13 By his wind the heavens were made fair;
  his hand pierced the fleeing serpent.
14 These are indeed but the outskirts of his ways;
  and how small a whisper do we hear of him!
  But the thunder of his power who can understand?"

Job Maintains His Integrity

27 Job again took up his discourse and said:

2 "As God lives, who has taken away my right,
  and the Almighty,[b] who has made my soul bitter,
3 as long as my breath is in me
  and the spirit of God is in my nostrils,
4 my lips will not speak falsehood,
  and my tongue will not utter deceit.
5 Far be it from me to say that you are right;

until I die I will not put away my integrity from me.
6 I hold fast my righteousness, and will not let it go;
  my heart does not reproach me for any of my days.

7 "May my enemy be like the wicked,
  and may my opponent be like the unrighteous.
8 For what is the hope of the godless when God cuts them off,
  when God takes away their lives?
9 Will God hear their cry
  when trouble comes upon them?
10 Will they take delight in the Almighty?[b]
  Will they call upon God at all times?
11 I will teach you concerning the hand of God;
  that which is with the Almighty[b] I will not conceal.
12 All of you have seen it yourselves;
  why then have you become altogether vain?

13 "This is the portion of the wicked with God,
  and the heritage that oppressors receive from the Almighty:[b]
14 If their children are multiplied, it is for the sword;
  and their offspring have not enough to eat.
15 Those who survive them the pestilence buries,
  and their widows make no lamentation.
16 Though they heap up silver like dust,
  and pile up clothing like clay—
17 they may pile it up, but the just will wear it,
  and the innocent will divide the silver.
18 They build their houses like nests,
  like booths made by sentinels of the vineyard.

[a] Or the North   [b] Traditional rendering of Heb Shaddai

27:1–6—These verses present a defiant Job, but vv. 7–23 sound again more like the friends.

19 They go to bed with wealth, but will
      do so no more;
   they open their eyes, and it is gone.
20 Terrors overtake them like a flood;
   in the night a whirlwind carries
      them off.
21 The east wind lifts them up and they
      are gone;
   it sweeps them out of their place.
22 It[a] hurls at them without pity;
   they flee from its[b] power in
      headlong flight.
23 It[a] claps its[b] hands at them,
   and hisses at them from its[b] place.

Interlude: Where Wisdom Is Found

28 "Surely there is a mine for silver,
   and a place for gold to be
      refined.
2 Iron is taken out of the earth,
   and copper is smelted from ore.
3 Miners put[c] an end to darkness,
   and search out to the farthest
      bound
   the ore in gloom and deep
      darkness.
4 They open shafts in a valley away
      from human habitation;
   they are forgotten by travelers,
   they sway suspended, remote from
      people.
5 As for the earth, out of it comes
      bread;
   but underneath it is turned up as
      by fire.
6 Its stones are the place of sapphires,[d]
   and its dust contains gold.

7 "That path no bird of prey knows,
   and the falcon's eye has not
      seen it.
8 The proud wild animals have not
      trodden it;
   the lion has not passed over it.

9 "They put their hand to the flinty
      rock,

   and overturn mountains by the
      roots.
10 They cut out channels in the rocks,
   and their eyes see every precious
      thing.
11 The sources of the rivers they
      probe;[e]
   hidden things they bring to light.

12 "But where shall wisdom be found?
   And where is the place of
      understanding?
13 Mortals do not know the way to it,[f]
   and it is not found in the land of
      the living.
14 The deep says, 'It is not in me,'
   and the sea says, 'It is not with me.'
15 It cannot be gotten for gold,
   and silver cannot be weighed out
      as its price.
16 It cannot be valued in the gold of
      Ophir,
   in precious onyx or sapphire.[d]
17 Gold and glass cannot equal it,
   nor can it be exchanged for jewels
      of fine gold.
18 No mention shall be made of coral
      or of crystal;
   the price of wisdom is above
      pearls.
19 The chrysolite of Ethiopia[g] cannot
      compare with it,
   nor can it be valued in pure gold.

20 "Where then does wisdom come
      from?
   And where is the place of
      understanding?
21 It is hidden from the eyes of all
      living,
   and concealed from the birds of
      the air.
22 Abaddon and Death say,
   'We have heard a rumor of it with
      our ears.'

a Or He (that is God) b Or his c Heb He puts d Or lapis lazuli e Gk Vg:
Heb bind f Gk: Heb its price g Or Nubia; Heb Cush

28:1–28—This is a wonderful poem on the mysteries of wisdom, which are to be found only in
God. It is in the mouth of Job, but sounds more
like a comment on the entire poem to date; all
the talk must be subsumed under the traditional
belief that *the fear of the Lord, that is wisdom*
(v. 28). Perhaps a later reader of the story here
includes his own interpretation!

23 "God understands the way to it,
and he knows its place.
24 For he looks to the ends of the earth,
and sees everything under the
heavens.
25 When he gave to the wind its weight,
and apportioned out the waters by
measure;
26 when he made a decree for the rain,
and a way for the thunderbolt;
27 then he saw it and declared it;
he established it, and searched it
out.
28 And he said to humankind,
'Truly, the fear of the Lord, that is
wisdom;
and to depart from evil is
understanding.'"

Job Finishes His Defense

29 Job again took up his discourse
and said:
2 "O that I were as in the months of
old,
as in the days when God watched
over me;
3 when his lamp shone over my head,
and by his light I walked through
darkness;
4 when I was in my prime,
when the friendship of God was
upon my tent;
5 when the Almighty[a] was still with
me,
when my children were around
me;
6 when my steps were washed with
milk,
and the rock poured out for me
streams of oil!
7 When I went out to the gate of the
city,

when I took my seat in the square,
8 the young men saw me and
withdrew,
and the aged rose up and stood;
9 the nobles refrained from talking,
and laid their hands on their
mouths;
10 the voices of princes were hushed,
and their tongues stuck to the roof
of their mouths.
11 When the ear heard, it
commended me,
and when the eye saw, it approved;
12 because I delivered the poor who
cried,
and the orphan who had no
helper.
13 The blessing of the wretched came
upon me,
and I caused the widow's heart to
sing for joy.
14 I put on righteousness, and it
clothed me;
my justice was like a robe and a
turban.
15 I was eyes to the blind,
and feet to the lame.
16 I was a father to the needy,
and I championed the cause of the
stranger.
17 I broke the fangs of the unrighteous,
and made them drop their prey
from their teeth.
18 Then I thought, 'I shall die in my
nest,
and I shall multiply my days like
the phoenix;[b]
19 my roots spread out to the waters,
with the dew all night on my
branches;

[a] Traditional rendering of Heb *Shaddai*   [b] Or *like sand*

29:1–25—This entire chapter has been taken as a portrait of an ancient ethical ideal. Job remembers his early life to be one of wise leadership, coupled with exemplary behavior toward the poor and the marginalized. He rejects all that the friends have tried to accuse him of by these beautiful portraits of his life before the attacks of God and the friends.

29:12–16—Specifically, Job rejects the claims

of the friends that he has not acted justly. He *has delivered the poor* when they cried; he *has caused the widow's heart to sing for joy*; he *was eyes to the blind, and feet to the lame*; he *was father to the needy* and champion of the *stranger*. In short, Job was and is a paragon of just behavior. Far from deserving God's condemnation, he should be receiving the Nobel Peace Prize for his exemplary works!

20 my glory was fresh with me,
   and my bow ever new in my hand.'

21 "They listened to me, and waited,
   and kept silence for my counsel.
22 After I spoke they did not speak
   again,
   and my word dropped upon them
   like dew.*a*
23 They waited for me as for the rain;
   they opened their mouths as for
   the spring rain.
24 I smiled on them when they had no
   confidence;
   and the light of my countenance
   they did not extinguish.*b*
25 I chose their way, and sat as chief,
   and I lived like a king among his
   troops,
   like one who comforts mourners.

30 "But now they make sport
   of me,
   those who are younger than I,
   whose fathers I would have
   disdained
   to set with the dogs of my flock.
2 What could I gain from the strength
   of their hands?
   All their vigor is gone.
3 Through want and hard hunger
   they gnaw the dry and desolate
   ground,
4 they pick mallow and the leaves of
   bushes,
   and to warm themselves the roots
   of broom.
5 They are driven out from society;
   people shout after them as after a
   thief.
6 In the gullies of wadis they must live,
   in holes in the ground, and in the
   rocks.
7 Among the bushes they bray;
   under the nettles they huddle
   together.
8 A senseless, disreputable brood,
   they have been whipped out of the
   land.

9 "And now they mock me in song;
   I am a byword to them.
10 They abhor me, they keep aloof
   from me;
   they do not hesitate to spit at the
   sight of me.
11 Because God has loosed my
   bowstring and humbled me,
   they have cast off restraint in my
   presence.
12 On my right hand the rabble rise up;
   they send me sprawling,
   and build roads for my ruin.
13 They break up my path,
   they promote my calamity;
   no one restrains*c* them.
14 As through a wide breach they come;
   amid the crash they roll on.
15 Terrors are turned upon me;
   my honor is pursued as by the
   wind,
   and my prosperity has passed away
   like a cloud.

16 "And now my soul is poured out
   within me;
   days of affliction have taken hold
   of me.
17 The night racks my bones,
   and the pain that gnaws me takes
   no rest.
18 With violence he seizes my
   garment;*d*
   he grasps me by*e* the collar of my
   tunic.
19 He has cast me into the mire,
   and I have become like dust and
   ashes.
20 I cry to you and you do not
   answer me;
   I stand, and you merely look
   at me.
21 You have turned cruel to me;
   with the might of your hand you
   persecute me.
22 You lift me up on the wind, you
   make me ride on it,

a Heb lacks *like dew*   *b* Meaning of Heb uncertain   *c* Cn: Heb *helps*
d Gk: Heb *my garment is disfigured*   *e* Heb *like*

30:1–31—Job's life now has become horrible; he has fallen to the bottom of society's dregs.

and you toss me about in the roar
　　of the storm.
23 I know that you will bring me to
　　death,
　　and to the house appointed for all
　　　living.
24 "Surely one does not turn against the
　　needy,*a*
　　when in disaster they cry for help.*b*
25 Did I not weep for those whose day
　　was hard?
　　Was not my soul grieved for the
　　　poor?
26 But when I looked for good, evil
　　came;
　　and when I waited for light,
　　　darkness came.
27 My inward parts are in turmoil, and
　　are never still;
　　days of affliction come to meet me.
28 I go about in sunless gloom;
　　I stand up in the assembly and cry
　　　for help.
29 I am a brother of jackals,
　　and a companion of ostriches.
30 My skin turns black and falls from
　　me,
　　and my bones burn with heat.
31 My lyre is turned to mourning,
　　and my pipe to the voice of those
　　　who weep.

31 "I have made a covenant with
　　my eyes;
　　how then could I look upon a
　　　virgin?
2 What would be my portion from
　　God above,
　　and my heritage from the
　　　Almighty*c* on high?
3 Does not calamity befall the
　　unrighteous,
　　and disaster the workers of iniquity?
4 Does he not see my ways,
　　and number all my steps?

5 "If I have walked with falsehood,
　　and my foot has hurried to
　　　deceit—
6 let me be weighed in a just balance,
　　and let God know my integrity!—
7 if my step has turned aside from the
　　way,
　　and my heart has followed my
　　　eyes,
　　and if any spot has clung to my
　　　hands;
8 then let me sow, and another eat;
　　and let what grows for me be
　　　rooted out.
9 "If my heart has been enticed by a
　　woman,
　　and I have lain in wait at my
　　　neighbor's door;
10 then let my wife grind for another,
　　and let other men kneel over her.
11 For that would be a heinous
　　crime;
　　that would be a criminal offense;
12 for that would be a fire consuming
　　down to Abaddon,
　　and it would burn to the root all
　　　my harvest.
13 "If I have rejected the cause of my
　　male or female slaves,
　　when they brought a complaint
　　　against me;
14 what then shall I do when God
　　rises up?
　　When he makes inquiry, what
　　　shall I answer him?
15 Did not he who made me in the
　　womb make them?
　　And did not one fashion us in the
　　　womb?
16 "If I have withheld anything that the
　　poor desired,

a Heb ruin　　*b* Cn: Meaning of Heb uncertain　　*c* Traditional rendering of
Heb *Shaddai*

31:16—Job repeats his claims of superb just actions in the midst of a liturgical oath of clearance. Such an oath may take its model from suggestions of liturgical actions in certain psalms (cf. the movement from anguish to victory in Pss. 6:8–9; 13:4–5; 22:21–22, among others). He demands that terrible things happen to him if he ever *withheld anything that the poor desired, or ... caused ... the widow to fail.*

or have caused the eyes of the
widow to fail,

[17] or have eaten my morsel alone,
and the orphan has not eaten from
it—

[18] for from my youth I reared the
orphan[a] like a father,
and from my mother's womb I
guided the widow[b]—

[19] if I have seen anyone perish for lack
of clothing,
or a poor person without
covering,

[20] whose loins have not blessed me,
and who was not warmed with the
fleece of my sheep;

[21] if I have raised my hand against the
orphan,
because I saw I had supporters at
the gate;

[22] then let my shoulder blade fall from
my shoulder,
and let my arm be broken from its
socket.

[23] For I was in terror of calamity from
God,
and I could not have faced his
majesty.

[24] "If I have made gold my trust,
or called fine gold my
confidence;

[25] if I have rejoiced because my wealth
was great,
or because my hand had gotten
much;

[26] if I have looked at the sun[c] when it
shone,
or the moon moving in splendor,

[27] and my heart has been secretly
enticed,
and my mouth has kissed my
hand;

[28] this also would be an iniquity to be
punished by the judges,
for I should have been false to God
above.

[29] "If I have rejoiced at the ruin of
those who hated me,
or exulted when evil overtook
them—

[30] I have not let my mouth sin
by asking for their lives with a
curse—

[31] if those of my tent ever said,
'O that we might be sated with his
flesh!'[d]—

[32] the stranger has not lodged in the
street;
I have opened my doors to the
traveler—

[33] if I have concealed my transgressions
as others do,[e]
by hiding my iniquity in my
bosom,

[34] because I stood in great fear of the
multitude,
and the contempt of families
terrified me,
so that I kept silence, and did not
go out of doors—

[35] O that I had one to hear me!
(Here is my signature! Let the
Almighty[f] answer me!)
O that I had the indictment
written by my adversary!

[36] Surely I would carry it on my
shoulder;
I would bind it on me like a crown;

[37] I would give him an account of all
my steps;
like a prince I would approach
him.

[a] Heb *him*   [b] Heb *her*   [c] Heb *the light*   [d] Meaning of Heb uncertain
[e] Or *as Adam did*   [f] Traditional rendering of Heb *Shaddai*

31:17–23—Job offers his wonderful treatment of
orphans as a sign of his innocence and justice.
No orphan ever went hungry when Job had food,
nor was lonely when Job could act as father to
him, nor was ever physically abused by Job even
when other elders of the community affirmed that
physical punishment was called for (the apparent
meaning of v. 21).

31:35–37—Among the most defiant speeches
of Job in the book. Job directly challenges God
to come and join him in dispute. *"Let Shaddai
[NRSV the Almighty] answer me!"* The reader
expects God to appear and end the angry debate;
Job certainly seems to expect an appearance of
God.

38 "If my land has cried out against me,
and its furrows have wept together;
39 if I have eaten its yield without
payment,
and caused the death of its owners;
40 let thorns grow instead of wheat,
and foul weeds instead of barley."

The words of Job are ended.

Elihu Rebukes Job's Friends

32 So these three men ceased to
answer Job, because he was righteous in his own eyes. 2 Then Elihu son
of Barachel the Buzite, of the family of
Ram, became angry. He was angry at
Job because he justified himself rather
than God; 3 he was angry also at Job's
three friends because they had found no
answer, though they had declared Job to
be in the wrong.a 4 Now Elihu had waited
to speak to Job, because they were older
than he. 5 But when Elihu saw that there
was no answer in the mouths of these
three men, he became angry.

6 Elihu son of Barachel the Buzite
answered:
"I am young in years,
and you are aged;
therefore I was timid and afraid
to declare my opinion to you.
7 I said, 'Let days speak,
and many years teach wisdom.'
8 But truly it is the spirit in a mortal,
the breath of the Almighty,b that
makes for understanding.
9 It is not the oldc that are wise,
nor the aged that understand what
is right.
10 Therefore I say, 'Listen to me;
let me also declare my opinion.'
11 "See, I waited for your words,
I listened for your wise sayings,
while you searched out what to
say.
12 I gave you my attention,
but there was in fact no one that
confuted Job,
no one among you that answered
his words.
13 Yet do not say, 'We have found
wisdom;
God may vanquish him, not a
human.'
14 He has not directed his words
against me,
and I will not answer him with
your speeches.
15 "They are dismayed, they answer no
more;
they have not a word to say.
16 And am I to wait, because they do
not speak,
because they stand there, and
answer no more?
17 I also will give my answer;
I also will declare my opinion.
18 For I am full of words;
the spirit within me
constrains me.
19 My heart is indeed like wine that has
no vent;
like new wineskins, it is ready to
burst.
20 I must speak, so that I may find
relief;
I must open my lips and answer.
21 I will not show partiality to any
person
or use flattery toward anyone.
22 For I do not know how to flatter—
or my Maker would soon put an
end to me!

a Another ancient tradition reads answer, and had put God in the wrong
b Traditional rendering of Heb Shaddai c Gk Syr Vg: Heb many

32:1–22—Abruptly, a fourth friend is introduced.
His name is **Elihu** ("He is my God" in Hebrew).
He comes from nowhere and disappears after
chap. 37. It could be said, as a possible explanation of Elihu's appearance, that an impasse has
been reached in the debate. The friends say that
Job is getting what he deserves from a righteous
God who always punishes unrighteous, wicked
behavior. But Job proves from his own life that he
is far from wicked, and although he wishes God
would indeed punish those who are, he says that
in fact God does not do so. And through all this
God is insufferably silent. This fourth friend later
agrees with the other friends that God "does not
keep the wicked alive, but gives the afflicted their
right" (36:6).

Elihu Rebukes Job

33 ¹"But now, hear my speech,
O Job,
and listen to all my words.
² See, I open my mouth;
the tongue in my mouth speaks.
³ My words declare the uprightness of
my heart,
and what my lips know they speak
sincerely.
⁴ The spirit of God has made me,
and the breath of the Almighty[a]
gives me life.
⁵ Answer me, if you can;
set your words in order before me;
take your stand.
⁶ See, before God I am as you are;
I too was formed from a piece of
clay.
⁷ No fear of me need terrify you;
my pressure will not be heavy on
you.

⁸ "Surely, you have spoken in my
hearing,
and I have heard the sound of your
words.
⁹ You say, 'I am clean, without
transgression;
I am pure, and there is no iniquity
in me.
¹⁰ Look, he finds occasions
against me,
he counts me as his enemy;
¹¹ he puts my feet in the stocks,
and watches all my paths.'

¹² "But in this you are not right. I will
answer you:
God is greater than any mortal.
¹³ Why do you contend against him,
saying, 'He will answer none of
my[b] words'?
¹⁴ For God speaks in one way,
and in two, though people do not
perceive it.
¹⁵ In a dream, in a vision of the night,
when deep sleep falls on mortals,
while they slumber on their beds,
¹⁶ then he opens their ears,
and terrifies them with warnings,

¹⁷ that he may turn them aside from
their deeds,
and keep them from pride,
¹⁸ to spare their souls from the Pit,
their lives from traversing the
River.
¹⁹ They are also chastened with pain
upon their beds,
and with continual strife in their
bones,
²⁰ so that their lives loathe bread,
and their appetites dainty food.
²¹ Their flesh is so wasted away that it
cannot be seen;
and their bones, once invisible,
now stick out.
²² Their souls draw near the Pit,
and their lives to those who bring
death.
²³ Then, if there should be for one of
them an angel,
a mediator, one of a thousand,
one who declares a person upright,
²⁴ and he is gracious to that person,
and says,
'Deliver him from going down into
the Pit;
I have found a ransom;
²⁵ let his flesh become fresh with
youth;
let him return to the days of his
youthful vigor';
²⁶ then he prays to God, and is
accepted by him,
he comes into his presence with
joy,
and God[c] repays him for his
righteousness.
²⁷ That person sings to others and
says,
'I sinned, and perverted what was
right,
and it was not paid back to me.
²⁸ He has redeemed my soul from
going down to the Pit,
and my life shall see the light.'

²⁹ "God indeed does all these things,
twice, three times, with mortals,

---

a Traditional rendering of Heb *Shaddai*   *b* Compare Gk: Heb *his*   *c* Heb *he*

30 to bring back their souls from the
        Pit,
   so that they may see the light of
        life.*a*

31 Pay heed, Job, listen to me;
   be silent, and I will speak.
32 If you have anything to say, answer
       me;
   speak, for I desire to justify you.
33 If not, listen to me;
   be silent, and I will teach you
       wisdom."

Elihu Proclaims God's Justice

34 Then Elihu continued and said:
2 "Hear my words, you wise
       men,
   and give ear to me, you who know;
3 for the ear tests words
   as the palate tastes food.
4 Let us choose what is right;
   let us determine among ourselves
       what is good.
5 For Job has said, 'I am innocent,
   and God has taken away my right;
6 in spite of being right I am counted a
       liar;
   my wound is incurable, though I
       am without transgression.'
7 Who is there like Job,
   who drinks up scoffing like water,
8 who goes in company with evildoers
   and walks with the wicked?
9 For he has said, 'It profits one
       nothing
   to take delight in God.'

10 "Therefore, hear me, you who have
       sense,
   far be it from God that he should
       do wickedness,
   and from the Almighty*b* that he
       should do wrong.
11 For according to their deeds he will
       repay them,
   and according to their ways he will
       make it befall them.
12 Of a truth, God will not do wickedly,
   and the Almighty*b* will not pervert
       justice.

13 Who gave him charge over the earth
   and who laid on him*c* the whole
       world?
14 If he should take back his spirit*d* to
       himself,
   and gather to himself his breath,
15 all flesh would perish together,
   and all mortals return to dust.

16 "If you have understanding, hear
       this;
   listen to what I say.
17 Shall one who hates justice govern?
   Will you condemn one who is
       righteous and mighty,
18 who says to a king, 'You scoundrel!'
   and to princes, 'You wicked men!';
19 who shows no partiality to nobles,
   nor regards the rich more than the
       poor,
   for they are all the work of his
       hands?
20 In a moment they die;
   at midnight the people are shaken
       and pass away,
   and the mighty are taken away by
       no human hand.

21 "For his eyes are upon the ways of
       mortals,
   and he sees all their steps.
22 There is no gloom or deep darkness
   where evildoers may hide
       themselves.
23 For he has not appointed a time*e* for
       anyone
   to go before God in judgment.
24 He shatters the mighty without
       investigation,
   and sets others in their place.
25 Thus, knowing their works,
   he overturns them in the night,
       and they are crushed.
26 He strikes them for their wickedness
   while others look on,
27 because they turned aside from
       following him,
   and had no regard for any of his
       ways,

a Syr: Heb to be lighted with the light of life   *b* Traditional rendering of
Heb *Shaddai*   *c* Heb lacks on him   *d* Heb his heart his spirit   *e* Cn: Heb yet

28 so that they caused the cry of the
        poor to come to him,
    and he heard the cry of the
        afflicted—
29 When he is quiet, who can condemn?
    When he hides his face, who can
        behold him,
    whether it be a nation or an
        individual?—
30 so that the godless should not reign,
    or those who ensnare the people.

31 "For has anyone said to God,
    'I have endured punishment; I will
        not offend any more;
32 teach me what I do not see;
    if I have done iniquity, I will do it
        no more'?
33 Will he then pay back to suit you,
    because you reject it?
    For you must choose, and not I;
    therefore declare what you know.*a*
34 Those who have sense will say to me,
    and the wise who hear me will say,
35 'Job speaks without knowledge,
    his words are without insight.'
36 Would that Job were tried to the
        limit,
    because his answers are those of
        the wicked.
37 For he adds rebellion to his sin;
    he claps his hands among us,
    and multiplies his words against
        God."

Elihu Condemns Self-Righteousness

35 Elihu continued and said:
2 "Do you think this to be just?
    You say, 'I am in the right before
        God.'
3 If you ask, 'What advantage have I?
    How am I better off than if I had
        sinned?'
4 I will answer you
    and your friends with you.

5 Look at the heavens and see;
    observe the clouds, which are
        higher than you.
6 If you have sinned, what do you
        accomplish against him?
    And if your transgressions are
        multiplied, what do you do to
        him?
7 If you are righteous, what do you
        give to him;
    or what does he receive from your
        hand?
8 Your wickedness affects others like
        you,
    and your righteousness, other
        human beings.

9 "Because of the multitude of
        oppressions people cry out;
    they call for help because of the
        arm of the mighty.
10 But no one says, 'Where is God my
        Maker,
    who gives strength in the night,
11 who teaches us more than the
        animals of the earth,
    and makes us wiser than the birds
        of the air?'
12 There they cry out, but he does not
        answer,
    because of the pride of evildoers.
13 Surely God does not hear an empty
        cry,
    nor does the Almighty*b* regard it.
14 How much less when you say that
        you do not see him,
    that the case is before him, and
        you are waiting for him!
15 And now, because his anger does not
        punish,
    and he does not greatly heed
        transgression,*c*

a Meaning of Heb of verses 29-33 uncertain *b* Traditional rendering of Heb *Shaddai* *c* Theodotion Symmachus Compare Vg: Meaning of Heb uncertain

---

34:29—Elihu here offers his most important contribution to the discussion. It could be translated, "When God is silent, who will speak evil; when God's face is hidden, who can see it, whether nation or individual?" Elihu reminds Job that God's silence does not indicate God's evil or indifference. When God is hidden from us, we must neither speak evil of God nor expect to see precisely what God is doing. God is more mysterious, and more engaged with us, than we can know on our own. And, Elihu says, God will eventually speak. How right he is!

16 Job opens his mouth in empty talk,
    he multiplies words without
        knowledge."

Elihu Exalts God's Goodness

36 Elihu continued and said:
    2 "Bear with me a little, and I
        will show you,
    for I have yet something to say on
        God's behalf.
3 I will bring my knowledge from far
        away,
    and ascribe righteousness to my
        Maker.
4 For truly my words are not false;
    one who is perfect in knowledge is
        with you.

5 "Surely God is mighty and does not
        despise any;
    he is mighty in strength of
        understanding.
6 He does not keep the wicked alive,
    but gives the afflicted their right.
7 He does not withdraw his eyes from
        the righteous,
    but with kings on the throne
    he sets them forever, and they are
        exalted.
8 And if they are bound in fetters
    and caught in the cords of
        affliction,
9 then he declares to them their work
    and their transgressions, that they
        are behaving arrogantly.
10 He opens their ears to instruction,
    and commands that they return
        from iniquity.
11 If they listen, and serve him,
    they complete their days in
        prosperity,
    and their years in pleasantness.
12 But if they do not listen, they shall
        perish by the sword,
    and die without knowledge.

13 "The godless in heart cherish anger;
    they do not cry for help when he
        binds them.
14 They die in their youth,
    and their life ends in shame.*a*

15 He delivers the afflicted by their
        affliction,
    and opens their ear by adversity.
16 He also allured you out of distress
    into a broad place where there was
        no constraint,
    and what was set on your table was
        full of fatness.

17 "But you are obsessed with the case
        of the wicked;
    judgment and justice seize you.
18 Beware that wrath does not entice
        you into scoffing,
    and do not let the greatness of the
        ransom turn you aside.
19 Will your cry avail to keep you from
        distress,
    or will all the force of your
        strength?
20 Do not long for the night,
    when peoples are cut off in their
        place.
21 Beware! Do not turn to iniquity;
    because of that you have been
        tried by affliction.
22 See, God is exalted in his power;
    who is a teacher like him?
23 Who has prescribed for him his way,
    or who can say, 'You have done
        wrong'?

Elihu Proclaims God's Majesty

24 "Remember to extol his work,
    of which mortals have sung.
25 All people have looked on it;
    everyone watches it from far away.
26 Surely God is great, and we do not
        know him;
    the number of his years is
        unsearchable.
27 For he draws up the drops of water;
    he distills*b* his mist in rain,
28 which the skies pour down
    and drop upon mortals
        abundantly.
29 Can anyone understand the
        spreading of the clouds,
    the thunderings of his pavilion?

a Heb ends among the temple prostitutes   *b* Cn: Heb they distill

³⁰ See, he scatters his lightning around
    him
    and covers the roots of the sea.
³¹ For by these he governs peoples;
    he gives food in abundance.
³² He covers his hands with the
    lightning,
    and commands it to strike the
    mark.
³³ Its crashing*ᵃ* tells about him;
    he is jealous*ᵃ* with anger against
    iniquity.

37 ¹ "At this also my heart trembles,
        and leaps out of its place.
² Listen, listen to the thunder of his
    voice
    and the rumbling that comes from
    his mouth.
³ Under the whole heaven he lets it
    loose,
    and his lightning to the corners of
    the earth.
⁴ After it his voice roars;
    he thunders with his majestic voice
    and he does not restrain the
    lightnings*ᵇ* when his voice is
    heard.
⁵ God thunders wondrously with his
    voice;
    he does great things that we
    cannot comprehend.
⁶ For to the snow he says, 'Fall on the
    earth';
    and the shower of rain, his heavy
    shower of rain,
⁷ serves as a sign on everyone's hand,
    so that all whom he has made may
    know it.*ᶜ*
⁸ Then the animals go into their lairs
    and remain in their dens.
⁹ From its chamber comes the
    whirlwind,
    and cold from the scattering
    winds.
¹⁰ By the breath of God ice is given,
    and the broad waters are frozen
    fast.
¹¹ He loads the thick cloud with
    moisture;

    the clouds scatter his lightning.
¹² They turn round and round by his
    guidance,
    to accomplish all that he
    commands them
    on the face of the habitable
    world.
¹³ Whether for correction, or for his
    land,
    or for love, he causes it to happen.

¹⁴ "Hear this, O Job;
    stop and consider the wondrous
    works of God.
¹⁵ Do you know how God lays his
    command upon them,
    and causes the lightning of his
    cloud to shine?
¹⁶ Do you know the balancings of the
    clouds,
    the wondrous works of the one
    whose knowledge is perfect,
¹⁷ you whose garments are hot
    when the earth is still because of
    the south wind?
¹⁸ Can you, like him, spread out the
    skies,
    hard as a molten mirror?
¹⁹ Teach us what we shall say to him;
    we cannot draw up our case
    because of darkness.
²⁰ Should he be told that I want to
    speak?
    Did anyone ever wish to be
    swallowed up?
²¹ Now, no one can look on the light
    when it is bright in the skies,
    when the wind has passed and
    cleared them.
²² Out of the north comes golden
    splendor;
    around God is awesome majesty.
²³ The Almighty*ᵈ*—we cannot find
    him;
    he is great in power and justice,
    and abundant righteousness he
    will not violate.
²⁴ Therefore mortals fear him;

ᵃ Meaning of Heb uncertain *ᵇ* Heb them *ᶜ* Meaning of Heb of verse 7
uncertain *ᵈ* Traditional rendering of Heb Shaddai

he does not regard any who are
    wise in their own conceit."

The LORD Answers Job

38 Then the LORD answered Job out
of the whirlwind:

2 "Who is this that darkens counsel by
    words without knowledge?
3 Gird up your loins like a man,
    I will question you, and you shall
      declare to me.

4 "Where were you when I laid the
    foundation of the earth?
    Tell me, if you have understanding.
5 Who determined its
    measurements—surely you
    know!
    Or who stretched the line upon it?

6 On what were its bases sunk,
    or who laid its cornerstone
7 when the morning stars sang
    together
    and all the heavenly beings[a]
      shouted for joy?

8 "Or who shut in the sea with doors
    when it burst out from the womb?—
9 when I made the clouds its garment,
    and thick darkness its swaddling
      band,
10 and prescribed bounds for it,
    and set bars and doors,
11 and said, 'Thus far shall you come,
    and no farther,
    and here shall your proud waves
      be stopped'?

a Heb *sons of God*

38:1–42:17 The Speeches of God

Understanding the speeches of God is crucial for understanding the book of Job. The problem is that for every two commentators of the speeches, there are three understandings! The following two ideas may be derived from a reading of the two speeches of God.

1. The belief of Job and his four friends that the universe is based on a simple mechanical model of reward and punishment is rejected completely. In fact, nature is filled with all manner of creatures that have nothing to do with human behavior at all, whether righteous or wicked. Behemoth and Leviathan, stars of the second speech, are wild chaos monsters, creations of God, but massive beings who are the sources of earthquake and tidal wave and ocean storm. They are made by God "just as Job was made" (40:15) and are part of God's universe as much as Job and his friends are.

2. The universe of God is mysterious, holy, and not easily graspable by simple human minds. All the actors in the play imagined that they knew precisely what God was up to. For the friends, God was punishing the wicked Job for his massive injustices. For Job, God was either frustratingly silent in the face of his demands for justice or was monstrous in the absurd ways in which Job's righteous life had brought him to an ash heap. All of these observations are rendered false in the face of the God we hear in these speeches. The God of the speeches is creator and sustainer of the universe, but is not a rewarder of righteous behavior. This God struggles with a complex creation, filled with mystery, surprise, and wonder. It could be said that the very premises on which the debate of the book have been based are quite wrong. Because God does not reward or punish in an easily understood mechanical way, the God of the friends simply does not exist, but neither does the monstrous God conjured by Job.

Here is no bumper-sticker God, who can be captured in one brief sentence or one sole thought. All actors must think again after God speaks.

38:2–3—Like a bolt from the blue, God's voice thunders out of a storm! Any reader should immediately ask just what he or she expects and wants God to say. Job has again and again demanded to know why he has not received justice at the hands of the God who supposedly is in the business of dispensing justice to those in need. But instead of answering the question of justice, God goes on, at enormous length, about the structures of the meteorological and animal worlds. God says precisely nothing directly about justice or about Job's demands. The opening words of God might be paraphrased: "Who is this who obscures my design out of sheer ignorance?" Such an opening could be heard in many ways; two of them are: (1) How dare you, little man, question the ways I choose to run the universe that I made? (2) Your claims to justice for yourself amid the mysteries and wonders of my complex world may not be the right claims to present to me. Your first problem is that you have "obscured my design"; in other words you have argued from the wrong premises, both you and your friends.

38:4–21—God's first display of creation is its very bases—the foundations of all, the seas restrained, the morning light, the gates of death and darkness. If Job thinks he is so great as to understand all this, let him reveal the secrets of this vast creation!

¹² "Have you commanded the morning
          since your days began,
     and caused the dawn to know its
          place,
¹³ so that it might take hold of the
          skirts of the earth,
     and the wicked be shaken out
          of it?
¹⁴ It is changed like clay under the
          seal,
     and it is dyed*a* like a garment.
¹⁵ Light is withheld from the wicked,
     and their uplifted arm is broken.

¹⁶ "Have you entered into the springs
          of the sea,
     or walked in the recesses of the
          deep?
¹⁷ Have the gates of death been
          revealed to you,
     or have you seen the gates of deep
          darkness?
¹⁸ Have you comprehended the
          expanse of the earth?
     Declare, if you know all this.

¹⁹ "Where is the way to the dwelling of
          light,
     and where is the place of darkness,
²⁰ that you may take it to its territory
     and that you may discern the paths
          to its home?
²¹ Surely you know, for you were born
          then,
     and the number of your days is
          great!

²² "Have you entered the storehouses of
          the snow,
     or have you seen the storehouses
          of the hail,
²³ which I have reserved for the time of
          trouble,
     for the day of battle and war?
²⁴ What is the way to the place where
          the light is distributed,
     or where the east wind is scattered
          upon the earth?

²⁵ "Who has cut a channel for the
          torrents of rain,
     and a way for the thunderbolt,
²⁶ to bring rain on a land where no one
          lives,
     on the desert, which is empty of
          human life,
²⁷ to satisfy the waste and desolate
          land,
     and to make the ground put forth
          grass?

²⁸ "Has the rain a father,
     or who has begotten the drops of
          dew?
²⁹ From whose womb did the ice come
          forth,
     and who has given birth to the
          hoarfrost of heaven?
³⁰ The waters become hard like stone,
     and the face of the deep is frozen.

³¹ "Can you bind the chains of the
          Pleiades,
     or loose the cords of Orion?
³² Can you lead forth the Mazzaroth in
          their season,
     or can you guide the Bear with its
          children?
³³ Do you know the ordinances of the
          heavens?
     Can you establish their rule on the
          earth?

³⁴ "Can you lift up your voice to the
          clouds,
     so that a flood of waters may cover
          you?
³⁵ Can you send forth lightnings, so
          that they may go
     and say to you, 'Here we are'?
³⁶ Who has put wisdom in the inward
          parts,*b*
     or given understanding to the
          mind?*b*
³⁷ Who has the wisdom to number the
          clouds?

a Cn: Heb *and they stand forth*   *b* Meaning of Heb uncertain

38:22–38—God then turns to the forces of the weather: the snow, the hail, the rain, the lightning and thunder, the dew, the ice, the clouds. There is also talk of stars and constellations as a part of the great design of God's world.

Or who can tilt the waterskins of
    the heavens,
38 when the dust runs into a mass
    and the clods cling together?

39 "Can you hunt the prey for the lion,
    or satisfy the appetite of the young
      lions,
40 when they crouch in their dens,
    or lie in wait in their covert?
41 Who provides for the raven its
      prey,
    when its young ones cry to God,
    and wander about for lack of food?

39
"Do you know when the
    mountain goats give birth?
Do you observe the calving of the
    deer?
2 Can you number the months that
    they fulfill,
    and do you know the time when
    they give birth,
3 when they crouch to give birth to
    their offspring,
    and are delivered of their young?
4 Their young ones become strong,
    they grow up in the open;
    they go forth, and do not return to
    them.

5 "Who has let the wild ass go free?
    Who has loosed the bonds of the
    swift ass,
6 to which I have given the steppe for
    its home,
    the salt land for its dwelling place?
7 It scorns the tumult of the city;
    it does not hear the shouts of the
    driver.
8 It ranges the mountains as its
    pasture,

and it searches after every green
    thing.
9 "Is the wild ox willing to serve you?
    Will it spend the night at your
    crib?
10 Can you tie it in the furrow with
    ropes,
    or will it harrow the valleys after
    you?
11 Will you depend on it because its
    strength is great,
    and will you hand over your labor
    to it?
12 Do you have faith in it that it will
    return,
    and bring your grain to your
    threshing floor?[a]

13 "The ostrich's wings flap wildly,
    though its pinions lack plumage.[b]
14 For it leaves its eggs to the earth,
    and lets them be warmed on the
    ground,
15 forgetting that a foot may crush them,
    and that a wild animal may
    trample them.
16 It deals cruelly with its young, as if
    they were not its own;
    though its labor should be in vain,
    yet it has no fear;
17 because God has made it forget
    wisdom,
    and given it no share in
    understanding.
18 When it spreads its plumes aloft,[b]
    it laughs at the horse and its rider.

19 "Do you give the horse its might?
    Do you clothe its neck with mane?

[a] Heb your grain and your threshing floor   [b] Meaning of Heb uncertain

---

38:39–40:30—The animal kingdom is now portrayed, but the choice of animals is significant. Not one of them, save the great war horse of 39:19–25, has any relationship to human beings. The lion, the mountain goat, the wild ass, the wild ox, the hawk, and the eagle are all creatures living their lives apart from humanity. Even the war horse is nearly supernatural in its lack of fear and its fantastic fierceness. And the ostrich (39:13–18) is also a part of God's grand design. What a ridiculous creature it is! Caring nothing for its young (apparently not true, according to modern ornithologists!), flapping its useless little wings for no reason or effect, yet able to outrun even a swift horse, the ostrich is also one of God's own. In short, the lengthy speech seems to say to Job that God's grand world goes along in amazing complexity quite apart from little Job's demands for individual justice. Job needs to think more about God's ostriches; it might offer him a helpful context in the surprising world of God!

20 Do you make it leap like the locust?
   Its majestic snorting is terrible.
21 It paws*a* violently, exults mightily;
   it goes out to meet the weapons.
22 It laughs at fear, and is not dismayed;
   it does not turn back from the
      sword.
23 Upon it rattle the quiver,
   the flashing spear, and the javelin.
24 With fierceness and rage it swallows
      the ground;
   it cannot stand still at the sound of
      the trumpet.
25 When the trumpet sounds, it says
      'Aha!'
   From a distance it smells the
      battle,
   the thunder of the captains, and
      the shouting.

26 "Is it by your wisdom that the hawk
      soars,
   and spreads its wings toward the
      south?
27 Is it at your command that the eagle
      mounts up
   and makes its nest on high?
28 It lives on the rock and makes its
      home
   in the fastness of the rocky crag.
29 From there it spies the prey;
   its eyes see it from far away.
30 Its young ones suck up blood;
   and where the slain are, there it is."

40 And the LORD said to Job:
2 "Shall a faultfinder contend
   with the Almighty?*b*

Anyone who argues with God
   must respond."

Job's Response to God

3 Then Job answered the LORD:
4 "See, I am of small account; what
      shall I answer you?
   I lay my hand on my mouth.
5 I have spoken once, and I will not
      answer;
   twice, but will proceed no further."

God's Challenge to Job

6 Then the LORD answered Job out of
   the whirlwind:
7 "Gird up your loins like a man;
   I will question you, and you
      declare to me.
8 Will you even put me in the wrong?
   Will you condemn me that you
      may be justified?
9 Have you an arm like God,
   and can you thunder with a voice
      like his?

10 "Deck yourself with majesty and
      dignity;
   clothe yourself with glory and
      splendor.
11 Pour out the overflowings of your
      anger,
   and look on all who are proud, and
      abase them.
12 Look on all who are proud, and
      bring them low;
   tread down the wicked where they
      stand.

a Gk Syr Vg: Heb *they dig*   *b* Traditional rendering of Heb *Shaddai*

40:3–5—Job apparently does not get the point! "I am trivial," he says. "How can I answer you? *I lay my hand on my mouth*," an action mentioned in two other places in Job. At 21:5, Job demands that the friends "lay their hands on their mouths" (i.e., shut up!) as they gaze upon his wasted frame on the ash heap. And at 29:9, in Job's greater days, elders of the city would "lay their hands on their mouths" in hushed awe whenever the great Job would walk by. Job decides he has said enough in the face of the vastness of God. Verse 5 in this chapter makes the same point.

40:6–14—But God will have none of that! God does not care for Job's capitulation. God has

something else to say. Verse 8 says that God has in reality heard exactly what Job has been saying. Job has, in fact, said that God is in the wrong and that Job should thereby be justified. But are those two alternatives the only ones possible? Must Job be right and God wrong, or God right and Job wrong? Verses 9–14 may be read playfully. God bids Job act as he has been saying God should be acting! Stomp the evil ones! Smash them into the ground! I, says God, will stand over here and watch. The fact is that of course Job cannot do that, but the more important fact is that God *does* not do that. Job and his friends have that all wrong.

13 Hide them all in the dust together;
    bind their faces in the world
        below.ª
14 Then I will also acknowledge to you
    that your own right hand can give
        you victory.

15 "Look at Behemoth,
    which I made just as I made you;
    it eats grass like an ox.
16 Its strength is in its loins,
    and its power in the muscles of its
        belly.
17 It makes its tail stiff like a cedar;
    the sinews of its thighs are knit
        together.
18 Its bones are tubes of bronze,
    its limbs like bars of iron.

19 "It is the first of the great acts of
        God—
    only its Maker can approach it
        with the sword.
20 For the mountains yield food for it
    where all the wild animals play.
21 Under the lotus plants it lies,
    in the covert of the reeds and in
        the marsh.
22 The lotus trees cover it for shade;
    the willows of the wadi
        surround it.
23 Even if the river is turbulent, it is not
        frightened;
    it is confident though Jordan
        rushes against its mouth.
24 Can one take it with hooksᵇ
    or pierce its nose with a snare?

41 ᶜ "Can you draw out Leviathanᵈ
        with a fishhook,
    or press down its tongue with a
        cord?
2 Can you put a rope in its nose,

or pierce its jaw with a hook?
3 Will it make many supplications to
        you?
    Will it speak soft words to you?
4 Will it make a covenant with you
    to be taken as your servant
        forever?
5 Will you play with it as with a bird,
    or will you put it on leash for your
        girls?
6 Will traders bargain over it?
    Will they divide it up among the
        merchants?
7 Can you fill its skin with
        harpoons,
    or its head with fishing spears?
8 Lay hands on it;
    think of the battle; you will not do
        it again!
9ᵉ Any hope of capturing itᶠ will be
        disappointed;
    were not even the godsᵍ
        overwhelmed at the sight of it?
10 No one is so fierce as to dare to stir
        it up.
    Who can stand before it?ʰ
11 Who can confront itʰ and be safe?ⁱ
    —under the whole heaven, who?ʲ

12 "I will not keep silence concerning
        its limbs,
    or its mighty strength, or its
        splendid frame.
13 Who can strip off its outer garment?
    Who can penetrate its double coat
        of mail?ᵏ
14 Who can open the doors of its face?
    There is terror all around its teeth.
15 Its backˡ is made of shields in rows,

ª Heb *the hidden place* ᵇ Cn: Heb *in his eyes* ᶜ Ch 40.25 in Heb ᵈ Or *the crocodile* ᵉ Ch 41.1 in Heb ᶠ Heb *of it* ᵍ Compare Symmachus Syr: Heb *one is* ʰ Heb *me* ⁱ Gk: Heb *that I shall repay* ʲ Heb *to me* ᵏ Gk: Heb *bridle* ˡ Cn Compare Gk Vg: Heb *pride*

40:15–24—*Behemoth* is decidedly not a hippopotamus, despite what some older translations suggested. It is The Beast par excellence. It is a mythological creature, living under the ground, whose arched back would bring earthquakes to the land. Yet, says God, *"I made [it] just as I made you"* (v. 15). Behemoth, a dangerous and cosmic creature, is also a creature of God and a part of God's vast and wondrous design.

41:1–34—*Leviathan* is not a simple crocodile. It, like Behemoth, is a cosmic creature, one who swims in the great ocean, rising up for destruction (see 3:8), patrolling the vast dark waters of God's seas (Ps. 104:26). It too is one of God's creatures. Behemoth and Leviathan are signs that God's design is not to be reduced to mechanical simplicity. Add the ostrich, and you have a wild, wild world indeed!

shut up closely as with a seal.
16 One is so near to another
    that no air can come between
        them.
17 They are joined one to another;
    they clasp each other and cannot
        be separated.
18 Its sneezes flash forth light,
    and its eyes are like the eyelids of
        the dawn.
19 From its mouth go flaming torches;
    sparks of fire leap out.
20 Out of its nostrils comes smoke,
    as from a boiling pot and burning
        rushes.
21 Its breath kindles coals,
    and a flame comes out of its
        mouth.
22 In its neck abides strength,
    and terror dances before it.
23 The folds of its flesh cling together;
    it is firmly cast and immovable.
24 Its heart is as hard as stone,
    as hard as the lower millstone.
25 When it raises itself up the gods are
        afraid;
    at the crashing they are beside
        themselves.
26 Though the sword reaches it, it does
        not avail,
    nor does the spear, the dart, or the
        javelin.
27 It counts iron as straw,
    and bronze as rotten wood.
28 The arrow cannot make it flee;
    slingstones, for it, are turned to
        chaff.
29 Clubs are counted as chaff;
    it laughs at the rattle of javelins.

30 Its underparts are like sharp
        potsherds;
    it spreads itself like a threshing
        sledge on the mire.
31 It makes the deep boil like a pot;
    it makes the sea like a pot of
        ointment.
32 It leaves a shining wake behind it;
    one would think the deep to be
        white-haired.
33 On earth it has no equal,
    a creature without fear.
34 It surveys everything that is lofty;
    it is king over all that are proud.”

Job Is Humbled and Satisfied

42 Then Job answered the LORD:
2 “I know that you can do all
        things,
    and that no purpose of yours can
        be thwarted.
3 ‘Who is this that hides counsel
        without knowledge?’
Therefore I have uttered what I did
        not understand,
    things too wonderful for me,
        which I did not know.
4 ‘Hear, and I will speak;
    I will question you, and you
        declare to me.’
5 I had heard of you by the hearing of
        the ear,
    but now my eye sees you;
6 therefore I despise myself,
    and repent in dust and ashes.”

Job's Friends Are Humiliated

7 After the LORD had spoken these
words to Job, the LORD said to Eliphaz
the Temanite: “My wrath is kindled

42:2–6—Job does not “repent” in this speech; he does not recant any of his demands for justice. The word of v. 6 translated in the NRSV **repent** usually means “change one’s mind.” Job does not retract either his passion for justice or his sharp rejections of the cruel absurdities of the friends. He “changes his mind” about God, whom he now sees as completely different from the “monster of the skies” he thought he had known after his experiences on the ash heap. His last sentence suggests that he now rejects his lamentation and fury on the ash heap; he no longer

stands in the position of adversary over against God. He now sees God as one who struggles with the powers of the cosmos at the same time God offers wondrous care for Job and for that cosmos.

42:7—God affirms Job’s new understanding by turning to Eliphaz and saying, *“You have not spoken to [the usual meaning of the preposition] me . . . as my servant Job has.”* Job’s exemplary life of justice for the poor is here affirmed by God. When Job joined his own life’s work of justice with his sharp demands for justice for all

against you and against your two friends; for you have not spoken of me what is right, as my servant Job has. [8] Now therefore take seven bulls and seven rams, and go to my servant Job, and offer up for yourselves a burnt offering; and my servant Job shall pray for you, for I will accept his prayer not to deal with you according to your folly; for you have not spoken of me what is right, as my servant Job has done." [9] So Eliphaz the Temanite and Bildad the Shuhite and Zophar the Naamathite went and did what the LORD had told them; and the LORD accepted Job's prayer.

Job's Fortunes Are Restored Twofold

[10] And the LORD restored the fortunes of Job when he had prayed for his friends; and the LORD gave Job twice as much as he had before. [11] Then there came to him all his brothers and sisters and all who had known him before, and they ate bread with him in his house; they showed him sympathy and comforted him for all the evil that the LORD had brought upon him; and each of them gave him a piece of money[a] and a gold ring. [12] The LORD blessed the latter days of Job more than his beginning; and he had fourteen thousand sheep, six thousand camels, a thousand yoke of oxen, and a thousand donkeys. [13] He also had seven sons and three daughters. [14] He named the first Jemimah, the second Keziah, and the third Keren-happuch. [15] In all the land there were no women so beautiful as Job's daughters; and their father gave them an inheritance along with their brothers. [16] After this Job lived one hundred and forty years, and saw his children, and his children's children, four generations. [17] And Job died, old and full of days.

[a] Heb a qesitah

---

of the universe, he became the great model for all those who would be just in the sight of the God of ultimate justice.

42:10–17—This "epilogue" has often been seen as a pallid end to a story of such raging demands for new thinking and new ways of looking at God and the world. It appears to say that Job receives double what he lost *when he had prayed for his friends*. It is not necessary to read that sentence as if Job's gifts from God came only when he prayed, as *a result* of that prayer. There need be no direct cause-and-effect connection between the fact of Job's prayer and the gift of God. It can be heard as if the gifts of God to him were just that—gifts. The world of Job at the end of the story is in fact new. The community has been reformed; Job's fortune and family have been reconstituted. But, perhaps more importantly, in this new world of God, Job's daughters (not the sons) get names, and the daughters receive an inheritance in Job's estate, a new idea in Israel. Numbers 27:1–8 says that women can be heirs only when there are no male heirs. Not so in Job's and God's new world. Job's suffering, along with his astonishing conviction to tell the truth about his experience in the universe, has led to this new world, a world characterized by joy in a newly ordered community. It could be said that Job's unremitting calls for justice have been answered in the story after all.

THE PSALMS

Psalms 1–2 and the Shape of the Psalter

From its very beginning, the book of Psalms invites attention to God's will for justice, righteousness, and peace on a world-encompassing scale. Psalms 1–2, a paired introduction to the collection of 150 psalms, set the theological agenda for the book. Psalm 1 portrays blessedness or happiness as constant orientation to God's "instruction" (twice in 1:2; NRSV "law")—or God's will—which subsequent psalms explicitly define as justice and righteousness. This is especially the case in the so-called enthronement psalms (Pss. 29, 47, 93, 95–99), where God, the heavenly sovereign, is portrayed as "coming" into the world (96:13; 98:9) to "establish justice in the world with righteousness" (96:13; 98:9; NRSV "judge the world with righteousness"). Indeed, the focus on justice (sometimes translated "judgment"), righteousness, and/or peace, is often explicitly linked with God's sovereignty.

Whereas Psalm 1 features the will of the heavenly sovereign, Psalm 2 introduces God's "anointed" (v. 2; Heb. *mashiach*)—that is, the earthly sovereign who is entrusted with the mission of enacting on earth what the heavenly God wills: justice and righteousness. This is especially evident in Psalm 72:1–7, a prayer for a new king upon his coronation day perhaps, where justice, righteousness, and *shalom* (NRSV "prosperity" in v. 3 and "peace" in v. 7) are the essence of the king's vocation. Thus, even though Psalm 2 does not mention justice, righteousness, or peace, it bears a connection to these crucial concepts by featuring God's "anointed." Not surprisingly, Psalm 2 concludes by inviting submission to God's sovereignty: "Serve the LORD" (v. 11). The only time this invitation occurs again is in Psalm 100:2, immediately following the sustained portrayal of God's sovereignty in Psalms 93, 95–99.

Taken together as an introduction to the book, Psalms 1–2 invite the reader to be constantly attentive to the related matters of God's sovereign claim upon the world and God's will for the world—justice, righteousness, and peace. This invitation is reinforced by the fact that other psalms featuring the earthly king appear at crucial places in the book—Psalm 72 at the conclusion of Book II (Pss. 42–72) and Psalm 89 at the conclusion of Book III (Pss. 73–89)—giving the Psalter a messianic orientation. The nature of this messianic shaping is debated, because Psalm 89:38–51 suggests that God's covenant with the Davidic monarchy has failed. Hence, it makes good sense that Psalm 90 begins Book IV (Pss. 90–106) with the only psalm attributed to Moses, who led the people of God when their only king was God alone (see Exod. 15:18). Furthermore, Book IV seems to respond to the failure of the Davidic monarchy (which was destroyed along with Jerusalem and the temple in 587 BCE, the beginning of the Babylonian exile) by explicitly proclaiming God's kingship in Psalms 93, 95–99 (see above), which some scholars identify as the theological heart of the Psalms.

Even so, psalms featuring the earthly king continue to appear in Book V (Pss. 107–150)—Psalms 110, 132, 144. This may indicate an ongoing messianism in the form

of hopes for a restored Davidic monarchy, but not necessarily. In the postexilic era, the Davidic monarchy may have come to symbolize any desire for the earthly expression of God's will. Psalm 144, for instance, is a recasting of Psalm 18, an earlier psalm about David's "triumphs" (v. 50); but Psalm 144 assumes a desperate situation in which "aliens" prevail (v. 11), and it concludes with a prayer for "the people" (v. 15). Thus, it implies that the former vocation of the Davidic monarchy— to enact God's justice, righteousness, and peace on earth—has been transferred to the whole people. This impression is even stronger in Psalm 149, which assigns to "the faithful" (v. 5; see v. 9) the role that Psalm 2 had described for the "anointed"— the international enactment of God's will, which Psalm 149:9 explicitly calls "justice" (NRSV " judgment"; cf. 2:8–12). In any case, the messianic dimension of the Psalter invites attention to the claim of God's sovereignty, as well as to the importance of the earthly expression of God's will for justice, righteousness, and peace on a world-encompassing scale. It now remains to suggest how various types of psalms participate in the Psalter's fundamental orientation toward justice, righteousness, and peace.

Prayers for Help

Prayers for help are the dominant type of speech in the Psalter, especially in Books I and II. Often called laments or complaints, the prayers demonstrate sharply that God's sovereignty and God's will are regularly opposed, as Psalms 1–2 had already suggested (see "the wicked" in Ps. 1, as well as the "nations," "peoples," "kings," and "rulers" in Ps. 2). In short, God always has enemies, as do those entrusted with the earthly enactment of God's will for justice, righteousness, and *shalom*—the king and/or the people (see 3:1–2). This reality has extraordinary implications.

In terms of understanding God's sovereignty, for instance, it means that God simply does not unilaterally impose God's will on the world. God will only work incarnationally—that is, through earthly agents, such as the monarchy or God's people. This means, of course, that people (including God's people; see Pss. 32, 51, 130) are free to disobey God; and they regularly do. Indeed, this is what those who pray the psalms—"the righteous" (see 1:6 and frequently throughout the book)—regularly lament or complain about. As victims of injustice and unrighteousness, they look to God for help.

Again, the implications of this situation are crucial. Because it is *the righteous* who are suffering, suffering cannot be viewed as punishment from God. The doctrine of retribution is obliterated. Although the psalmists sometimes speak as if God is punishing them (see 38:1–4, 17–18), their prayers actually undermine the doctrine of retribution by way of the affirmation that God is on the side of suffering victims (see 38:19–22). This means that victims cannot be blamed or scapegoated—for instance, "the poor" (a regular synonym for "the righteous") cannot be blamed for being poor.

A doctrine of retribution also seems to be in view when the psalmists ask God to destroy their enemies and/or affirm that God will do so (see 3:7; 5:10; 6:10; 7:12–16; 9:5–6; 11:6; 12:3–4; and many other examples). But the wicked are always present; apparently God simply does *not* act unilaterally to destroy them. This suggests that the requests for vengeance are, in essence, prayers for justice by victims—in short, "your will be done" (Matt. 6:10). But God's justice cannot be understood retributively. Rather, the function of the requests for vengeance is to affirm that God "stands at the

right hand of the needy" (e.g., 109:31). To be sure, this conviction is meant to comfort the afflicted; but it is also meant to empower them, as well as to invite the comfortable into solidarity with the afflicted. Trusting that God is with them and on their side (see 22:24), the poor and afflicted are energized to pursue the justice, righteousness, and peace that God wills (see 22:25–31). Thus God's sovereignty, which may look like weakness, turns out to be real power; but it is the incarnational power of love rather than the unilateral power of sheer force.

The victims who pray the psalms never fail to trust God or praise God. With one exception (Ps. 88), the prayers end with (or include at some point) trust or praise. This means that the Psalter regularly holds together hurt and hope, pain and praise, at the same time that there are psalms devoted primarily to trust and praise.

Psalms of Trust

While the wicked deny God's existence or sovereign ability to help (see 3:1–2; 10:4, 6, 11, 13; 12:4; 14:1; 42:3, 10; 53:1; 64:5–6; 73:11; 79:10; 94:7; 115:2), the psalmists unfailingly trust God and entrust themselves to God. Expressions of trust are found within the prayers for help (see 3:8; 4:8; 7:1; and often); in fact, in certain psalms, profession of trust predominates (Pss. 11, 23, 46, 48, 62, 63). The function of such professions is to assert God's sovereignty in circumstances that seem to deny it. The effect again is to hold together hurt and hope as simultaneous realities in the life of faith. In a word, the psalmists find in God their "refuge" (5:11; 7:1; 11:1; 31:1, 19; 46:1; 62:7–8; and often), which is genuine happiness, as announced already in 2:12. As suggested above, it is this hope-filled assurance that motivates and energizes the psalmists to pursue God's purposes of justice, righteousness, and peace amid persistent and powerful opposition. For those who are inclined to trust themselves or their own resources (see 49:6; 52:7), the psalmists' trust is a call to self-examination and repentance.

Songs of Praise

For those whose lives are oriented completely to God's will and who know that their lives derive from and depend upon God, the natural response is praise or thanksgiving. Like trust, praise regularly occurs in the prayers for help (see 7:17; 13:6; 22:22–24; and often); but some psalms are primarily songs of praise that generally invite others to praise God and express reasons for praising God (see Pss. 29, 33, 95–100, 103–104, 107, 117–118, 145–150). Because praise is both the liturgy and the lifestyle of those who entrust themselves to God, the Psalter in Hebrew is aptly named "Praises."

The regular juxtaposition of pain and praise in the Psalter reinforces the portrayal of God's sovereignty as love rather than force; and it prevents praise from being simply the ideology of the prosperous, the privileged, and the powerful—that is, from being essentially self-congratulation. Praise is directed to God by those committed to God and to God's will. In short, praise has everything to do with justice and righteousness. In this regard, it is revealing that the centrally important enthronement collection (Pss. 29, 47, 93, 95–99) invites praise for a sovereign God whose will is portrayed precisely as justice and righteousness on a universe-encompassing scale. God's "coming" (96:13; 98:9) is hailed not just by all the peoples (96:7), but also by all creation (96:11–12; 98:7–8). Indeed, the Psalter regularly suggests that God will properly be

worshiped only when the congregation is universe-encompassing (66:1, 4; 67:1–5; 100:1; 117:1; 145:21; 148:1–12; 150:6). In short, all peoples and nations are partners with all creatures and creation in praising God. This ultimately is the justice, righteousness, and *shalom* that God wills. The social, political, economic, and ecological implications are nothing short of astounding!

The Psalms and the New Testament

To Christian readers of the Psalms, much will sound familiar. Not only do the passion narratives in the Gospels portray Jesus in the role of righteous sufferer (see esp. Pss. 22, 31, 69), but also Jesus' life and teaching cohere with the theological dynamics of the Psalms. The heart of Jesus' message involved God's sovereignty—"the kingdom of heaven" (Matt. 4:17; 5:3, 10, 19–20; 6:10, 33)—manifesting itself in a greater "righteousness" (Matt. 5:20; see 6:33). Jesus offered a happiness (Matt. 5:3–12) that results, as in Psalms 1–2 and throughout the Psalter, from the yielding of the self to God, and from unyielding attentiveness to God's will. It is happiness that flows from the hope-filled commitment to live for God in the midst of the powerful and persistent opposition that regularly seems to be evoked by faithfulness to God and God's will for world-encompassing justice, righteousness, and peace.

The Psalms and Discipleship: A Guide for Readers

In order to point the reader toward particular passages related to key psalmic themes that are of particular relevance for thoughtful discipleship, this final section offers a summary of the preceding, including extensive listings of passages related to each theme:

1. *God's Universal Sovereignty and God's Will for Justice, Righteousness, and Peace.* Proclamations of God's sovereignty or the address of God as sovereign ("King") pervade the Psalter. In particular, the enthronement psalms (Pss. 29, 47, 93, 95–99) connect God's sovereign claim on the world with God's will for universe-encompassing justice and righteousness (see note at 96:11–13), the result of which is *shalom*, "peace" (see note at 29:11). But beyond the enthronement psalms, God's will for justice, righteousness, and peace is also explicit, and is often expressed in conjunction with affirmations of God's sovereignty. See the following passages: 5:2, 8; 7:11; 9:7–8; 10:16–18; 11:7; 33:4–5; 36:5–6; 37:28; 48:9–11; 58:11; 67:4; 72:1–7; 75:2, 7; 76:8–9; 82:1–4, 8; 85:10–13; 89:14; 94:2, 15; 103:6; 106:3; 119:137–144; 122:5–8; 140:12; 145:17; 146:7–10; 149:9.

2. *The Psalter's Ecological Theology.* Because God's claim on the world really is *universe*-encompassing, the Psalter envisions a community of praise composed not only of persons, but also of all creatures and all creation. This resulting partnership between humans and the rest of creation provides a profound theological foundation for ecological awareness and action that is particularly evident in the following psalms: 8, 65, 96, 98, 104, 148, 150.

3. *The* Messiah *as God's Strategy for Doing on Earth What Is Willed in Heaven.* Beginning with Psalm 2, the importance of the earthly king or "anointed" (Heb. *mashiach*) is evident. Several other psalms feature the earthly monarch and his work (see Pss. 18, 20, 21, 45, 72, 89, 110, 132). Psalm 72 is especially important, because it suggests that the king's role amounted to doing on earth what the heavenly God wills—justice, righteousness, and *shalom* (see esp. 72:1–7, 12–14). Hence, the royal

or messianic references in the Psalter should be taken not as historical artifacts of an ancient era, but rather as expressions of God's desire and plan to implement on earth the justice, righteousness, and *shalom* that God wills. The recasting of Psalm 18 by Psalm 144 and the reconstrual of Psalm 2 by Psalm 149 suggest that the calling to implement God's will on earth was finally understood to be the responsibility of the whole people of God.

4. *God Sides with the Poor and Needy.* As Psalm 72:12–14 makes clear, the crucial criterion of justice and righteousness involves the well-being of the poor and needy. The king's role is to be an advocate for the poor and needy, and this reflects what God wills and where God "stands" (109:31). God regularly sides with the victimized, and this has crucial implications. For instance, suffering cannot be construed as divine punishment (and thus victims cannot be blamed). This, in turn, invites the prosperous to disavow self-congratulation in favor of solidarity with the poor and needy. God's stand with and for the victimized is implied in all the prayers for help, but it is especially evident in the following passages: 9:18; 10:14, 17–18; 12:5; 35:10; 40:17; 68:5–6; 72:1–7, 12–14; 76:9; 82:1–4; 102:17–22; 103:6; 107:39–41; 109:31; 113:7–9; 140:12; 146:7–9.

5. *Requests for Vengeance as Victims' Prayers for Justice.* As suggested above, the prayers for help should be heard as prayers of those who have been victimized by opponents of God and God's purposes. The frequent affirmations of or requests for divine vengeance against enemies should not be heard, therefore, as if the issue were simply personal revenge. Rather, the issue is the need for the establishment of God's justice in situations where it is desperately and painfully lacking. Thus, the request is essentially what Christians regularly pray for in the Lord's Prayer, "Your will be done, on earth as it is in heaven." The following passages involve either requests for or affirmations of divine vengeance: 3:7; 5:10; 6:10; 7:12–16; 9:5–6; 11:6; 12:3–4; 17:13–14; 31:17–18, 23; 34:21; 35:1–6; 37:1–2; 40:14; 41:11; 43:1; 52:5–7; 54:5; 55:9, 19, 23; 56:7; 57:3; 58:6–9; 59:5, 11–13; 62:12; 63:9–10; 64:7–8; 68:1–2; 69:22–28; 70:1–3; 71:13; 73:18–20; 74:22–23; 75:8; 76:5–6; 79:6, 10; 82:6–7; 83:9–18; 92:9; 94:1–3, 23; 97:7; 104:35; 109:29; 110:5–6; 125:5; 137:7–9; 140:10–11; 141:7, 10; 143:12; 145:20; 146:9.

6. *Taking Refuge in God.* Discipleship may be thought of essentially as a matter of trust. As the Psalms themselves point out, it is perfectly possible to trust something like wealth (see 49:6; 52:7). Furthermore, wickedness in the Psalms amounts fundamentally to autonomy—that is, trusting the self rather than trusting God (see the speech of the wicked in 3:1–2; 10:4, 6, 11, 13; 12:4). The faithful alternative is to trust God and entrust life to God, an alternative frequently articulated by the concept of "refuge." Amid powerful and persistent opposition and victimization, the faithful psalmists repeatedly affirm that their hope, security, and genuine happiness in life result from taking "refuge" in God. See the following passages: 2:12; 5:11; 11:1; 16:1; 17:7; 31:1, 2, 19; 34:8, 22; 36:7; 46:1; 52:7–8; 57:1; 61:3–4; 62:7–8; 64:10; 71:1, 3, 7; 73:28; 91:2, 4, 9; 118:8–9; 141:8; 142:5; 144:8.

7. *The Love of God.* To some ways of thinking, a sovereign God who has enemies seems like an anomaly. But God and God's purposes regularly meet opposition in the Psalms, suggesting that God's sovereignty or power is essentially love, not sheer force. Not surprisingly, therefore, references to God's "steadfast love" (Heb. *hesed*) pervade the Psalter, occurring in all types of psalms. The psalmists celebrate God's love in the

songs of praise (see 33:5; 36:5; 100:5); they appeal to God's love in the prayers for help (see 17:7; 109:26); and they often express their hope and trust in God's love (see 5:7; 13:5). References to God's "steadfast love" are often accompanied by the mention of God's faithfulness, compassion, grace, or mercy. See the following passages: 5:7; 13:5; 17:7; 23:6 (NRSV "mercy"); 25:6, 7, 10; 26:3; 31:7, 16, 21; 32:10; 33:5, 18, 22; 36:5, 7, 10; 41:10; 44:26; 48:9; 51:1; 57:3, 10; 59:10, 16, 17; 61:7; 62:12; 63:3; 66:20; 69:13, 16; 77:8; 85:10; 86:5, 15; 89:1, 2, 14, 24, 28, 33, 49; 90:14; 92:2; 98:3; 100:5; 101:1 (NRSV "loyalty"); 103:4, 8, 11, 17; 106:7, 45; 107:1, 8, 15, 21, 31, 43; 108:4; 109:21, 26; 117:2; 118:1–4, 29; 119:41, 64, 76, 88, 124, 149, 159; 130:7; 136:1–26; 138:2, 8; 143:8, 12; 145:8; 147:11. In a real sense, to be a disciple is to join the psalmists in celebrating God's love, in trusting God's love, in hoping in God's love, and in living in dependence upon the loving God.

—Clint McCann

BOOK I
(Psalms 1–41)

Psalm 1
The Two Ways

1 Happy are those
  who do not follow the advice of
    the wicked,
  or take the path that sinners tread,
  or sit in the seat of scoffers;
2 but their delight is in the law of the
  LORD,
  and on his law they meditate day
    and night.
3 They are like trees
  planted by streams of water,
  which yield their fruit in its
    season,

  and their leaves do not wither.
  In all that they do, they prosper.

4 The wicked are not so,
  but are like chaff that the wind
    drives away.
5 Therefore the wicked will not stand
  in the judgment,
  nor sinners in the congregation of
    the righteous;
6 for the LORD watches over the way of
  the righteous,
  but the way of the wicked will
    perish.

Psalm 2
God's Promise to His Anointed

1 Why do the nations conspire,
  and the peoples plot in vain?

Psalm 1

1:1 *Happy*—Happiness is first defined negatively, to emphasize two contrasting lifestyles; see 2:12.

1:2 *Law*—Hebrew *torah* is better translated "instruction" or "teaching." It can mean something as broad as God's will, which the Psalms will later define as justice, righteousness, and peace (see introduction, "Psalms 1–2 and the Shape of the Psalter"; 72:1–7; 96:11–13). Happiness is radically God-centered, undercutting the pervasive autonomy and individualism that characterize the contemporary world.

1:3 *Prosper*—It does not indicate material prosperity nor the absence of suffering, but rather deep rootedness in God. A tree with deep roots

can withstand all kinds of adversity. See 52:8–9; 92:12–15; Josh. 1:8; Jer. 17:7–8.

1:4 *The wicked*—Having no rootedness in God, they are easily swayed and destroyed by their own failure to attend to God. Wickedness is essentially self-centeredness and self-directedness.

1:5—Verse 5a could also be translated, "Therefore the wicked will not stand up for justice." Unlike *the righteous*, they do not attend to God's will.

1:6—The point is not that God directly punishes the wicked (see introduction, "Prayers for Help"). Rather, their failure to embody God's will means that they miss the point of genuine life and true prosperity.

2 The kings of the earth set
    themselves,
  and the rulers take counsel
      together,
  against the Lord and his anointed,
      saying,
3 "Let us burst their bonds asunder,
  and cast their cords from us."

4 He who sits in the heavens
    laughs;
  the Lord has them in derision.
5 Then he will speak to them in his
    wrath,
  and terrify them in his fury,
      saying,
6 "I have set my king on Zion, my holy
    hill."

7 I will tell of the decree of the Lord:
  He said to me, "You are my son;
    today I have begotten you.
8 Ask of me, and I will make the
    nations your heritage,
  and the ends of the earth your
    possession.
9 You shall break them with a rod of
    iron,
  and dash them in pieces like a
    potter's vessel."

10 Now therefore, O kings, be wise;
  be warned, O rulers of the earth.
11 Serve the Lord with fear,
  with trembling 12 kiss his feet,[a]

or he will be angry, and you will
    perish in the way;
  for his wrath is quickly kindled.

Happy are all who take refuge in him.

Psalm 3
Trust in God under Adversity

A Psalm of David, when he fled from his son
Absalom.

1 O Lord, how many are my foes!
  Many are rising against me;
2 many are saying to me,
  "There is no help for you[b] in God."
                                    Selah

3 But you, O Lord, are a shield
    around me,
  my glory, and the one who lifts up
    my head.
4 I cry aloud to the Lord,
  and he answers me from his holy
    hill.   *Selah*
5 I lie down and sleep;
  I wake again, for the Lord
    sustains me.
6 I am not afraid of ten thousands of
    people
  who have set themselves against
    me all around.

7 Rise up, O Lord!
  Deliver me, O my God!

[a] Cn: Meaning of Heb of verses 11b and 12a is uncertain [b] Syr: Heb *him*

Psalm 2

2:2 *Anointed*—The Heb. *mashiach* refers to the earthly king, who was entrusted with the enactment of God's justice and righteousness (see introduction, "Psalms 1–2 and the Shape of the Psalter"; 72:1–7).

2:4 *Laughs*—God is not threatened by opposition; see 37:13; 59:8.

2:6—Perhaps spoken originally by a prophetic or priestly representative at a royal coronation in the temple, which was located on Mount Zion.

2:7 *Son*—Kings were viewed as adopted sons of God (see 89:26–27; 2 Sam. 7:14; Mark 1:11).

2:8–9—The function of the imagery is to assert God's universal sovereignty (see 72:8–11; 149:6–9; Rev. 2:26–27).

2:11—The king's rule is aimed at the enactment

of God's universal reign. *Fear* connotes reverent obedience.

2:12 *Happy . . . him*—Recalling 1:1, happiness is defined in thoroughly God-centered terms. *Refuge*, a major theme of Books I–II, means to live in dependence upon God rather than self (see introduction, "Psalms of Trust").

Psalm 3

3 (Title) *Of David*—Seventy-three psalms are linked to David, but "of David" need not indicate authorship. Thirteen psalms mention episodes in David's life (Pss. 3, 7, 18, 34, 51, 52, 54, 56, 57, 59, 60, 63, 142). The information is not historical, but invites identification with David's life and struggles. The allusion here is to 2 Sam. 15–18.

3:7 *Deliver*—The same Hebrew word is translated "help" in v. 2. In contrast to the wicked, the psalmists always trust God and entrust

For you strike all my enemies on the
   cheek;
   you break the teeth of the wicked.

8 Deliverance belongs to the LORD;
   may your blessing be on your
   people!   *Selah*

Psalm 4
Confident Plea for Deliverance
from Enemies

*To the leader: with stringed instruments.
A Psalm of David.*

1 Answer me when I call, O God of
   my right!
   You gave me room when I was in
   distress.
   Be gracious to me, and hear my
   prayer.

2 How long, you people, shall my
   honor suffer shame?
   How long will you love vain words,
   and seek after lies?   *Selah*

3 But know that the LORD has set
   apart the faithful for himself;
   the LORD hears when I call to him.

4 When you are disturbed,*a* do not
   sin;
   ponder it on your beds, and be
   silent.
                                Selah

5 Offer right sacrifices,
   and put your trust in the LORD.

6 There are many who say, "O that we
   might see some good!

Let the light of your face shine on
   us, O LORD!"

7 You have put gladness in my heart
   more than when their grain and
   wine abound.

8 I will both lie down and sleep in
   peace;
   for you alone, O LORD, make me
   lie down in safety.

Psalm 5
Trust in God for Deliverance
from Enemies

*To the leader: for the flutes. A Psalm
of David.*

1 Give ear to my words, O LORD;
   give heed to my sighing.

2 Listen to the sound of my cry,
   my King and my God, for to you I
   pray.

3 O LORD, in the morning you hear
   my voice;
   in the morning I plead my case to
   you, and watch.

4 For you are not a God who delights
   in wickedness;
   evil will not sojourn with you.

5 The boastful will not stand before
   your eyes;
   you hate all evildoers.

6 You destroy those who speak lies;
   the LORD abhors the bloodthirsty
   and deceitful.

a Or *are angry*

---

themselves to God's help (see introduction,
"Psalms of Trust"). On the apparently retributive
activity of v. 7, see introduction, "Prayers for
Help."

Psalm 4

4:2–5—The psalmist speaks to others, probably
opponents in vv. 2–3 and others of *the faithful* in
vv. 4–5. The point, then and now, is to invite **trust
in the LORD** (see introduction, "Psalms of Trust").

4:6 *Light of your face*—Symbolizing God's presence, this is the source of true joy and peace (see
31:16; 67:1; Num. 6:25).

4:7—Genuine joy lies beyond material things
(see 52:7–8; Luke 12:15).

4:8 *Peace*—Linked elsewhere with justice and
righteousness (see introduction, "Psalms 1–2 and
the Shape of the Psalter"; 72:1–7; 96:11–13), *shalom* is the gift of God that offers genuine security
and life, even amid opposition (see vv. 1–2; John
14:27).

Psalm 5

5:2 *King*—The first mention of God's sovereignty
is made in the context of the competing claims of
the enemies described in vv. 4–5, suggesting that
God's power consists not of sheer force but of
love (see v. 7; introduction, "Prayers for Help").
As king, God wills justice and *righteousness* (v.
8; see introduction, "Psalms 1–2 and the Shape
of the Psalter"; 96:11–13).

7 But I, through the abundance of
        your steadfast love,
    will enter your house,
  I will bow down toward your holy
        temple
    in awe of you.
8 Lead me, O Lord, in your
        righteousness
    because of my enemies;
    make your way straight before me.

9 For there is no truth in their mouths;
    their hearts are destruction;
  their throats are open graves;
    they flatter with their tongues.
10 Make them bear their guilt, O God;
    let them fall by their own
        counsels;
  because of their many transgressions
        cast them out,
    for they have rebelled against you.

11 But let all who take refuge in you
        rejoice;
    let them ever sing for joy.
  Spread your protection over them,
    so that those who love your name
        may exult in you.
12 For you bless the righteous,
        O Lord;
    you cover them with favor as with
        a shield.

Psalm 6
Prayer for Recovery from Grave Illness

*To the leader: with stringed instruments;
according to The Sheminith. A Psalm
of David.*

1 O Lord, do not rebuke me in your
        anger,
    or discipline me in your wrath.
2 Be gracious to me, O Lord, for I am
        languishing;
    O Lord, heal me, for my bones are
        shaking with terror.
3 My soul also is struck with terror,
    while you, O Lord—how long?

4 Turn, O Lord, save my life;
    deliver me for the sake of your
        steadfast love.
5 For in death there is no
        remembrance of you;
    in Sheol who can give you praise?

6 I am weary with my moaning;
    every night I flood my bed with
        tears;
    I drench my couch with my
        weeping.
7 My eyes waste away because of grief;
    they grow weak because of all my
        foes.

8 Depart from me, all you workers of
        evil,

5:7 Steadfast love—A frequent and very important word in the Psalms and throughout the Old Testament, it describes God's essential character (see 23:6; 31:7, 16, 21; 32:10; 33:5, 18, 22; and many more; Exod. 34:6–7). God's love is the psalmist's guiding force, and the psalmist is at home in God's **house**, the **holy temple** (see 23:6).

5:10—The request for vengeance is essentially a prayer for God to set things right for the victimized psalmist—that is, a prayer for justice (see introduction, "Prayers for Help").

5:11 Refuge—The quintessential position of **the righteous** (see introduction, "Psalms of Trust"; 2:12).

5:12 Bless—Recalling the synonym "happy" in 1:1 and 2:12, the word in this context suggests that happiness or blessedness is not something experienced apart from opposition from those who oppose God's purposes.

Psalm 6

6:1—While the psalmist seems to uphold a retributional scheme, vv. 8–10 undercut it by claiming God's help for the one who is victimized by **workers of evil** (v. 8; see introduction, "Prayers for Help"). Although there is no mention of sin, Psalm 6 is one of the church's seven Penitential Psalms (see also Pss. 32, 38, 51, 102, 130, 143), apparently because it commends humble reliance on God's gracious love (see 6:4).

6:4—Moses asks God to **turn** in Exod. 32:12, an episode that culminates in the revealing of God's **steadfast love** (Exod. 34:6; see Ps. 5:7).

6:5 Sheol—The realm of the dead, a place to which even God ordinarily has no access (see, however, 22:29; 49:15; 139:8). The psalmist is sometimes understood to be bargaining with God, but 6:5 is better seen as an expression of the psalmist's love of life.

for the Lord has heard the sound
　　of my weeping.
9 The Lord has heard my
　　supplication;
　　the Lord accepts my prayer.
10 All my enemies shall be ashamed
　　and struck with terror;
　　they shall turn back, and in a
　　moment be put to shame.

Psalm 7

Plea for Help against Persecutors

*A Shiggaion of David, which he sang to the
Lord concerning Cush, a Benjaminite.*

1 O Lord my God, in you I take
　　refuge;
　　save me from all my pursuers, and
　　deliver me,
2 or like a lion they will tear me apart;
　　they will drag me away, with no
　　one to rescue.

3 O Lord my God, if I have done this,
　　if there is wrong in my hands,
4 if I have repaid my ally with harm
　　or plundered my foe without
　　cause,
5 then let the enemy pursue and
　　overtake me,
　　trample my life to the ground,
　　and lay my soul in the dust.　*Selah*

6 Rise up, O Lord, in your anger;
　　lift yourself up against the fury of
　　my enemies;
　　awake, O my God;*a* you have
　　appointed a judgment.
7 Let the assembly of the peoples be
　　gathered around you,

and over it take your seat*b* on high.
8 The Lord judges the peoples;
　　judge me, O Lord, according to
　　my righteousness
　　and according to the integrity that
　　is in me.

9 O let the evil of the wicked come to
　　an end,
　　but establish the righteous,
　　you who test the minds and hearts,
　　O righteous God.
10 God is my shield,
　　who saves the upright in heart.
11 God is a righteous judge,
　　and a God who has indignation
　　every day.

12 If one does not repent, God*c* will
　　whet his sword;
　　he has bent and strung his bow;
13 he has prepared his deadly weapons,
　　making his arrows fiery shafts.
14 See how they conceive evil,
　　and are pregnant with mischief,
　　and bring forth lies.
15 They make a pit, digging it out,
　　and fall into the hole that they
　　have made.
16 Their mischief returns upon their
　　own heads,
　　and on their own heads their
　　violence descends.

17 I will give to the Lord the thanks
　　due to his righteousness,
　　and sing praise to the name of the
　　Lord, the Most High.

a Or awake for me　*b* Cn: Heb return　*c* Heb he

Psalm 7

7 (Title)—See Ps. 3. No *Cush* appears in the
stories about David.

7:1 *Refuge*—See introduction, "Psalms of Trust."

7:3–5—The psalmist's oath of innocence does
not assert sinfulness in general, but rather right-
ness in a specific case. It is similar to Job 31,
where Job also entrusts his case to God (see also
Ps. 17:3–5).

7:6 *Appointed a judgment*—More literally, "ordained justice." The repetition of *judge* (or "establish justice") in vv. 8, 11, along with fivefold

occurrence of *righteous(ness)* (vv. 8, 9 [twice],
11, 17), suggests that God wills and works for the
establishment of justice, both in individual cases
of injustice and regularly on a cosmic scale (see
introduction, "Psalms 1–2 and the Shape of the
Psalter"; 96:11–13).

7:12–16—God is also portrayed as a warrior
for justice in 64:7; Deut. 32:41–42; Lam. 2:4;
but, in essence, it is the behavior of the wicked
that leads to their destruction (see introduction, "Prayers for Help";1:6; 9:16; 35:7–8; 57:6;
141:10; Prov. 26:27).

Psalm 8
Divine Majesty and Human Dignity

To the leader: according to The Gittith.
A Psalm of David.

1 O LORD, our Sovereign,
   how majestic is your name in all
      the earth!

You have set your glory above the
   heavens.
2   Out of the mouths of babes and
      infants
you have founded a bulwark because
   of your foes,
   to silence the enemy and the
      avenger.

3 When I look at your heavens, the
      work of your fingers,
   the moon and the stars that you
      have established;
4 what are human beings that you are
      mindful of them,
   mortals*a* that you care for them?

5 Yet you have made them a little
      lower than God,*b*
   and crowned them with glory and
      honor.
6 You have given them dominion over
      the works of your hands;
   you have put all things under their
      feet,
7 all sheep and oxen,

and also the beasts of the field,
8 the birds of the air, and the fish of
      the sea,
   whatever passes along the paths of
      the seas.

9 O LORD, our Sovereign,
   how majestic is your name in all
      the earth!

Psalm 9
God's Power and Justice

To the leader: according to Muth-labben.
A Psalm of David.

1 I will give thanks to the LORD with
      my whole heart;
   I will tell of all your wonderful
      deeds.
2 I will be glad and exult in you;
   I will sing praise to your name,
      O Most High.

3 When my enemies turned back,
   they stumbled and perished before
      you.
4 For you have maintained my just
      cause;
   you have sat on the throne giving
      righteous judgment.

5 You have rebuked the nations, you
      have destroyed the wicked;

---

a Heb ben adam, lit. son of man   *b* Or than the divine beings or angels: Heb elohim

---

Psalm 8

8:1 *Sovereign*—This word offers a clue that the psalm will involve an exploration of God's power (see also v. 9). The rest of v. 1, along with v. 2, communicates the strangeness of God's power; for God uses the most vulnerable of creatures—human *infants* (v. 2)—to establish strength.

8:4 *Human beings*—While the boundaries of the psalm focus on God's identity, this central verse raises the question of human identity. The two are inextricably related.

8:5—God's sovereign majesty is clear (vv. 1, 9); but the human being also has a remarkably exalted status, which is here described in terms of royalty—*crowned*, *glory*, and *honor*.

8:6 *Dominion*—This is the royal prerogative of the heavenly *Sovereign* (vv. 1, 9), God; but God shares God's power with humankind (see Gen. 1:26–31), to the extent of putting *all things under*

their feet. Thus, human beings are God's partners in the care and preservation of creation.

8:9 *All*—The repetition of v. 1 suggests that God's "all"-ness (see "all" in vv. 1, 6, 7, 9) is now inextricably bound up with the exercise of human *dominion* (v. 6). Ecology and theology are inseparable (see Ps. 104).

Psalm 9

9:1–3—It is likely that Pss. 9–10 were originally one psalm, so the celebration of deliverance here should be heard in the context of the description of the triumph of the wicked in 10:1–11.

9:4, 7–8—The vocabulary of justice is pervasive here (see also vv. 16, 19; 10:18). As elsewhere in the Psalms, the heavenly sovereign wills and works for justice and righteousness (see introduction, "Psalms 1–2 and the Shape of the Psalter"; 96:11–13).

you have blotted out their name
  forever and ever.
6 The enemies have vanished in
    everlasting ruins;
  their cities you have rooted out;
  the very memory of them has
    perished.

7 But the LORD sits enthroned forever,
  he has established his throne for
    judgment.
8 He judges the world with
    righteousness;
  he judges the peoples with equity.
9 The LORD is a stronghold for the
    oppressed,
  a stronghold in times of trouble.
10 And those who know your name put
    their trust in you,
  for you, O LORD, have not forsaken
    those who seek you.

11 Sing praises to the LORD, who dwells
    in Zion.
  Declare his deeds among the
    peoples.
12 For he who avenges blood is mindful
    of them;
  he does not forget the cry of the
    afflicted.

13 Be gracious to me, O LORD.
  See what I suffer from those who
    hate me;
  you are the one who lifts me up
    from the gates of death,
14 so that I may recount all your praises,
  and, in the gates of daughter Zion,
  rejoice in your deliverance.

15 The nations have sunk in the pit that
    they made;
  in the net that they hid has their
    own foot been caught.

16 The LORD has made himself known,
  he has executed judgment;
  the wicked are snared in the work
    of their own hands.
                    Higgaion. Selah

17 The wicked shall depart to Sheol,
  all the nations that forget God.

18 For the needy shall not always be
    forgotten,
  nor the hope of the poor perish
    forever.

19 Rise up, O LORD! Do not let mortals
    prevail;
  let the nations be judged before
    you.

20 Put them in fear, O LORD;
  let the nations know that they are
    only human.   *Selah*

Psalm 10
Prayer for Deliverance from Enemies
1 Why, O LORD, do you stand far off?
  Why do you hide yourself in times
    of trouble?
2 In arrogance the wicked persecute
    the poor—
  let them be caught in the schemes
    they have devised.

3 For the wicked boast of the desires
    of their heart,
  those greedy for gain curse and
    renounce the LORD.
4 In the pride of their countenance the
    wicked say, "God will not seek
    it out";
  all their thoughts are, "There is no
    God."
5 Their ways prosper at all times;
  your judgments are on high, out of
    their sight;

9:9 *The oppressed*—This is one of several synonyms for "the righteous." God's establishment of justice aims at liberation of the oppressed, *afflicted* (v. 12), *needy* (v. 18), and *poor* (v. 18; see introduction, "Prayers for Help").

Psalm 10
10:1–13—Although 9:16 suggests the demise of *the wicked*, they are very much alive and prospering (10:5), all the while persecuting *the poor* (vv. 2, 9). As in 3:2, the wicked are quoted (10:4, 6, 11, 13), and their words reveal their arrogant self-assertion (see 1:4).

as for their foes, they scoff at them.
[6] They think in their heart, "We shall
not be moved;
throughout all generations we
shall not meet adversity."

[7] Their mouths are filled with cursing
and deceit and oppression;
under their tongues are mischief
and iniquity.
[8] They sit in ambush in the villages;
in hiding places they murder the
innocent.

Their eyes stealthily watch for the
helpless;
[9] they lurk in secret like a lion in its
covert;
they lurk that they may seize the
poor;
they seize the poor and drag them
off in their net.

[10] They stoop, they crouch,
and the helpless fall by their
might.
[11] They think in their heart, "God has
forgotten,
he has hidden his face, he will
never see it."

[12] Rise up, O LORD; O God, lift up your
hand;
do not forget the oppressed.
[13] Why do the wicked renounce God,
and say in their hearts, "You will
not call us to account"?

[14] But you do see! Indeed you note
trouble and grief,
that you may take it into your
hands;

the helpless commit themselves to
you;
you have been the helper of the
orphan.
[15] Break the arm of the wicked and
evildoers;
seek out their wickedness until you
find none.
[16] The LORD is king forever and ever;
the nations shall perish from his
land.
[17] O LORD, you will hear the desire of
the meek;
you will strengthen their heart,
you will incline your ear
[18] to do justice for the orphan and the
oppressed,
so that those from earth may strike
terror no more.[a]

Psalm 11
Song of Trust in God
To the leader. Of David.

[1] In the LORD I take refuge; how can
you say to me,
"Flee like a bird to the mountains;[b]
[2] for look, the wicked bend the
bow,
they have fitted their arrow to the
string,
to shoot in the dark at the upright
in heart.
[3] If the foundations are destroyed,
what can the righteous do?"

[4] The LORD is in his holy temple;
the LORD's throne is in heaven.

---

[a] Meaning of Heb uncertain   [b] Gk Syr Jerome Tg: Heb *flee to your
mountain, O bird*

10:16 *The LORD is king*—As always, the psalmists
assert God's sovereignty in the midst of evil and
suffering, suggesting God's rule is exercised not
as force but as love (see introduction, "Psalms
1–2 and the Shape of the Psalter" and "Prayers
for Help").

10:17–18—Again, God's kingdom is about justice, the setting of things right for the needy. An
orphan (see also v. 14) was especially vulnerable
in a patriarchal society (see 68:5; 94:6; 146:9;
Exod. 22:22–23; Deut. 24:17–20).

Psalm 11

11:1 *Refuge*—For the reasons expressed in vv.
2–3, the psalmist has apparently been advised to
seek refuge other than in God (see introduction,
"Psalms of Trust").

11:4—Despite the chaos, the psalmist trusts
God's sovereignty, symbolized by God's earthly
presence *in his holy temple* (see 5:7) and God's
heavenly *throne*. The psalmist affirms what the
wicked deny in 10:11.

His eyes behold, his gaze examines
    humankind.
5 The LORD tests the righteous and the
    wicked,
    and his soul hates the lover of
      violence.
6 On the wicked he will rain coals of
    fire and sulfur;
    a scorching wind shall be the
      portion of their cup.
7 For the LORD is righteous;
he loves righteous deeds;
    the upright shall behold his
      face.

Psalm 12
Plea for Help in Evil Times

*To the leader: according to The Sheminith.
A Psalm of David.*

1 Help, O LORD, for there is no longer
    anyone who is godly;
    the faithful have disappeared from
      humankind.
2 They utter lies to each other;
    with flattering lips and a double
      heart they speak.

3 May the LORD cut off all flattering
    lips,
    the tongue that makes great
      boasts,
4 those who say, "With our tongues we
    will prevail;
    our lips are our own—who is our
      master?"

5 "Because the poor are despoiled,
    because the needy groan,

I will now rise up," says the LORD;
"I will place them in the safety for
    which they long."
6 The promises of the LORD are
    promises that are pure,
    silver refined in a furnace on the
      ground,
    purified seven times.

7 You, O LORD, will protect us;
    you will guard us from this
      generation forever.
8 On every side the wicked prowl,
    as vileness is exalted among
      humankind.

Psalm 13
Prayer for Deliverance from Enemies

To the leader. A Psalm of David.

1 How long, O LORD? Will you forget
    me forever?
    How long will you hide your face
      from me?
2 How long must I bear pain[a] in my
    soul,
    and have sorrow in my heart all
      day long?
    How long shall my enemy be exalted
      over me?

3 Consider and answer me, O LORD
    my God!
    Give light to my eyes, or I will
      sleep the sleep of death,
4 and my enemy will say, "I have
    prevailed";

a Syr: Heb *hold counsels*

11:5 *Tests*—A part of the process of setting things right or establishing justice.

11:6 *Coals of fire ... sulfur ... cup*—The first two images of judgment recall Gen. 19:24; on "cup," see 75:9; Isa. 51:17; Jer. 25:15.

11:7—As always, the sovereign God stands for justice and righteousness (see introduction, "Psalms 1–2 and the Shape of the Psalter"; 96:11–13). *Behold his face*—The phrase communicates that the psalmist renounces self-help, depending on God for life, for the strength to resist evil (vv. 2–3), and for the courage to do the *righteous deeds* that God wills (see 24:5–6).

Psalm 12

12:1—This prayer for help would be especially appropriate amid the chaos described in 11:2–3.

12:4 *Our lips are our own*—Literally, "our lips are with us," suggesting that the wicked trust themselves rather than God (see "lips" also in vv. 2–3). Their speech starkly reveals their arrogant self-centeredness, the very opposite of trusting God (see introduction, "Psalms of Trust"; 1:4–6).

12:5—Responding to arrogant speech, God speaks. As always, the God of justice and righteousness stands with the victimized—*the poor* and *the needy* (see introduction, "Prayers for Help").

my foes will rejoice because I am
  shaken.
5 But I trusted in your steadfast love;
  my heart shall rejoice in your
    salvation.
6 I will sing to the LORD,
  because he has dealt bountifully
    with me.

Psalm 14
Denunciation of Godlessness
To the leader. Of David.

1 Fools say in their hearts, "There is
    no God."
  They are corrupt, they do
    abominable deeds;
  there is no one who does good.

2 The LORD looks down from heaven
    on humankind
  to see if there are any who are
    wise,
  who seek after God.

3 They have all gone astray, they are
    all alike perverse;
  there is no one who does good,
    no, not one.

4 Have they no knowledge, all the
    evildoers
  who eat up my people as they eat
    bread,
  and do not call upon the LORD?

5 There they shall be in great terror,
  for God is with the company of the
    righteous.
6 You would confound the plans of the
    poor,
  but the LORD is their refuge.

7 O that deliverance for Israel would
    come from Zion!
  When the LORD restores the
    fortunes of his people,
  Jacob will rejoice; Israel will be
    glad.

Psalm 15
Who Shall Abide in God's Sanctuary?
A Psalm of David.

1 O LORD, who may abide in your
    tent?
  Who may dwell on your holy hill?
2 Those who walk blamelessly, and do
    what is right,

Psalm 13

13:5 *Trusted*—The present tense, "trust," is preferable. Characteristically, amid trouble and persecution, and the apparent absence of God (vv. 1–2), the psalmist trusts God (see introduction, "Psalms of Trust"), as he or she prays for help (vv. 3–4; see introduction, "Prayers for Help"). This suggests that the faithful life simultaneously involves hurt and hope, pain and praise, threat and trust. ***Steadfast love***—See note at 5:7. ***Your salvation***—The phrase indicates the gift of life received from God.

Psalm 14

14:1 *Fools*—A synonym for the wicked, "fools" indicates not an intellectual deficiency, but rather the failure to acknowledge God, as their speech indicates (see 3:2; 10:4; 12:4). In short, foolishness involves arrogant self-centeredness, which inevitably results in destructive behavior (see also v. 4; 1:4–6).

14:3—This seems to be hyperbole, since vv. 4–6 narrow the indictment to ***evildoers***. But there is some wisdom in acknowledging the universal perversity of humankind; see Rom. 3:1–8, where Paul cites 14:1, 3.

14:5–6—As always, God stands with the victimized, including ***the poor*** (see introduction, "Prayers for Help"). This constitutes their ***refuge*** (see introduction, "Psalms of Trust").

14:7 *When the LORD restores the fortunes*—The psalmists regularly trust God to do what the wicked say is impossible (v. 1; see 85:1).

Psalm 15

15:1 *Tent . . . holy hill*—Both refer to the temple (see 2:6; 3:4); and the questions indicate that the psalm may have been used as a liturgy for persons entering the temple (see Ps. 24). Because the temple symbolized God's presence, the psalm may be appropriated by later generations as a portrayal of a lifestyle shaped by God and God's values.

15:2 *Blamelessly*—The word connotes not sinlessness (see 14:1–3), but rather the wholeness that results from complete dependence upon God for life and security (see 19:13). Because God wills justice and righteousness (see introduction, "Psalms 1–2 and the Shape of the Psalter"; 96:11–13), those following God do ***what is right***.

and speak the truth from their
heart;
3 who do not slander with their
tongue,
and do no evil to their friends,
nor take up a reproach against
their neighbors;
4 in whose eyes the wicked are despised,
but who honor those who fear the
LORD;
who stand by their oath even to their
hurt;
5 who do not lend money at interest,
and do not take a bribe against the
innocent.

Those who do these things shall
never be moved.

Psalm 16
Song of Trust and Security in God
A Miktam of David.

1 Protect me, O God, for in you I take
refuge.
2 I say to the LORD, "You are my Lord;
I have no good apart from you."*a*

3 As for the holy ones in the land, they
are the noble,
in whom is all my delight.

4 Those who choose another god
multiply their sorrows;*b*
their drink offerings of blood I will
not pour out
or take their names upon my lips.

5 The LORD is my chosen portion and
my cup;

you hold my lot.
6 The boundary lines have fallen for
me in pleasant places;
I have a goodly heritage.

7 I bless the LORD who gives me
counsel;
in the night also my heart
instructs me.
8 I keep the LORD always before me;
because he is at my right hand, I
shall not be moved.

9 Therefore my heart is glad, and my
soul rejoices;
my body also rests secure.
10 For you do not give me up to Sheol,
or let your faithful one see the
Pit.

11 You show me the path of life.
In your presence there is fullness
of joy;
in your right hand are pleasures
forevermore.

Psalm 17
Prayer for Deliverance from Persecutors
A Prayer of David.

1 Hear a just cause, O LORD; attend to
my cry;
give ear to my prayer from lips free
of deceit.
2 From you let my vindication come;
let your eyes see the right.

3 If you try my heart, if you visit me
by night,

a Jerome Tg: Meaning of Heb uncertain   *b* Cn: Meaning of Heb uncertain

---

15:5—Not charging interest (Exod. 22:25; Lev. 25:36–37) benefits the poor, as God wills (see 9:18; 12:5); and not taking bribes is elsewhere associated with the establishment of justice (Exod. 23:8; Deut. 10:17–18; 16:19–20; 1 Sam. 8:3).

Psalm 16

16:1 *Refuge*—A key theme in Books I–II (see introduction, "Psalms of Trust").

16:2—In sharp contrast to the speech of the wicked (see 3:2; 10:4, 6, 11, 13; 12:4; 14:1), the psalmist articulates fundamental dependence upon God for life and livelihood (see also vv. 5,

7–8, 11), a lifestyle that means rejoicing in other people as well (v. 3).

16:10 *Sheol . . . Pit*—See 6:5; "Pit" is a synonym for Sheol.

Psalm 17

17:1–2 *Just cause . . . vindication*—The first word is usually translated "righteousness"; the appeal is to a God who wills justice and righteousness (see introduction, "Psalms 1–2 and the Shape of the Psalter"; 96:11–13). "Vindication" is more literally "justice."

17:3–5—An oath of innocence; see 7:3–5.

if you test me, you will find no
wickedness in me;
my mouth does not transgress.
4 As for what others do, by the word
of your lips
I have avoided the ways of the
violent.
5 My steps have held fast to your paths;
my feet have not slipped.

6 I call upon you, for you will answer
me, O God;
incline your ear to me, hear my
words.
7 Wondrously show your steadfast
love,
O savior of those who seek refuge
from their adversaries at your
right hand.

8 Guard me as the apple of the eye;
hide me in the shadow of your
wings,
9 from the wicked who despoil me,
my deadly enemies who
surround me.
10 They close their hearts to pity;
with their mouths they speak
arrogantly.
11 They track me down;*a* now they
surround me;
they set their eyes to cast me to the
ground.
12 They are like a lion eager to tear,
like a young lion lurking in
ambush.
13 Rise up, O Lord, confront them,
overthrow them!
By your sword deliver my life from
the wicked,
14 from mortals—by your hand,
O Lord—

from mortals whose portion in life
is in this world.
May their bellies be filled with what
you have stored up for them;
may their children have more than
enough;
may they leave something over to
their little ones.

15 As for me, I shall behold your face in
righteousness;
when I awake I shall be satisfied,
beholding your likeness.

Psalm 18
Royal Thanksgiving for Victory

*To the leader. A Psalm of David the servant
of the Lord, who addressed the words of
this song to the Lord on the day when the
Lord delivered him from the hand of all his
enemies, and from the hand of Saul. He said:*

1 I love you, O Lord, my strength.
2 The Lord is my rock, my fortress,
and my deliverer,
my God, my rock in whom I take
refuge,
my shield, and the horn of my
salvation, my stronghold.
3 I call upon the Lord, who is worthy
to be praised,
so I shall be saved from my
enemies.

4 The cords of death encompassed me;
the torrents of perdition
assailed me;
5 the cords of Sheol entangled me;
the snares of death confronted me.

6 In my distress I called upon the
Lord;

a One Ms Compare Syr: MT *Our steps*

17:7 *Steadfast love*—See note at 5:7.

17:8 *Shadow of your wings*—The image may
have arisen from the practice of seeking refuge
in the temple, where the symbolism of the ark
contained winged creatures; or it may portray
God as a mother bird protecting her young (see
36:7; 57:1; 63:7).

17:13–14—On requests for vengeance as prayers
for justice, see introduction, "Prayers for Help."

Psalm 18

18 (Title)—See 2 Sam. 22, which is virtually
identical.

18:1–6—As the prayer of a king, Ps. 18 recalls Ps.
2 (see *refuge* in 18:2, 30 and 2:12). Because the
king is the earthly agent of God's sovereignty, it is
telling that he is in *distress* (18:6; see introduction, "Psalms 1–2 and the Shape of the Psalter").

to my God I cried for help.
From his temple he heard my voice,
   and my cry to him reached his ears.

7 Then the earth reeled and rocked;
   the foundations also of the
      mountains trembled
   and quaked, because he was angry.
8 Smoke went up from his nostrils,
   and devouring fire from his
      mouth;
   glowing coals flamed forth from
      him.
9 He bowed the heavens, and came
      down;
   thick darkness was under his feet.
10 He rode on a cherub, and flew;
   he came swiftly upon the wings of
      the wind.
11 He made darkness his covering
      around him,
   his canopy thick clouds dark with
      water.
12 Out of the brightness before him
   there broke through his clouds
   hailstones and coals of fire.
13 The Lord also thundered in the
      heavens,
   and the Most High uttered his
      voice.*a*
14 And he sent out his arrows, and
      scattered them;
   he flashed forth lightnings, and
      routed them.
15 Then the channels of the sea were
      seen,
   and the foundations of the world
      were laid bare
   at your rebuke, O Lord,
   at the blast of the breath of your
      nostrils.

16 He reached down from on high, he
      took me;

he drew me out of mighty waters.
17 He delivered me from my strong
      enemy,
   and from those who hated me;
   for they were too mighty for me.
18 They confronted me in the day of
      my calamity;
   but the Lord was my support.
19 He brought me out into a broad
      place;
   he delivered me, because he
      delighted in me.

20 The Lord rewarded me according to
      my righteousness;
   according to the cleanness of my
      hands he recompensed me.
21 For I have kept the ways of the
      Lord,
   and have not wickedly departed
      from my God.
22 For all his ordinances were
      before me,
   and his statutes I did not put away
      from me.
23 I was blameless before him,
   and I kept myself from guilt.
24 Therefore the Lord has
      recompensed me according to
      my righteousness,
   according to the cleanness of my
      hands in his sight.

25 With the loyal you show yourself
      loyal;
   with the blameless you show
      yourself blameless;
26 with the pure you show yourself
      pure;
   and with the crooked you show
      yourself perverse.
27 For you deliver a humble people,
   but the haughty eyes you bring
      down.

a Gk See 2 Sam 22.14: Heb adds *hailstones and coals of fire*

18:7–19—God's response begins in the form of a theophany, an account of a divine appearance (vv. 7–15). Theophanies are often linked explicitly with God's cosmic sovereignty (see 29:3–9; 97:3–5; 99:1).
18:20–30—What sounds like the king's boasting intends to say that the king has conformed to God's will (as was his vocation), which involves *righteousness* (v. 20) and "deeds of justice" (v. 22; NRSV *ordinances*; see introduction, "Psalms 1–2 and the Shape of the Psalter"). As vv. 25–30 suggest, the credit belongs to God.

28 It is you who light my lamp;
    the LORD, my God, lights up my
      darkness.
29 By you I can crush a troop,
    and by my God I can leap over a
      wall.
30 This God—his way is perfect;
    the promise of the LORD proves
      true;
    he is a shield for all who take
      refuge in him.

31 For who is God except the LORD?
    And who is a rock besides our
      God?—
32 the God who girded me with strength,
    and made my way safe.
33 He made my feet like the feet of a
      deer,
    and set me secure on the heights.
34 He trains my hands for war,
    so that my arms can bend a bow of
      bronze.
35 You have given me the shield of your
      salvation,
    and your right hand has
      supported me;
    your help*a* has made me great.
36 You gave me a wide place for my
      steps under me,
    and my feet did not slip.
37 I pursued my enemies and overtook
      them;
    and did not turn back until they
      were consumed.
38 I struck them down, so that they
      were not able to rise;
    they fell under my feet.
39 For you girded me with strength for
      the battle;
    you made my assailants sink
      under me.
40 You made my enemies turn their
      backs to me,
    and those who hated me I
      destroyed.

41 They cried for help, but there was no
      one to save them;
    they cried to the LORD, but he did
      not answer them.
42 I beat them fine, like dust before the
      wind;
    I cast them out like the mire of the
      streets.

43 You delivered me from strife with
      the peoples;*b*
    you made me head of the nations;
    people whom I had not known
      served me.
44 As soon as they heard of me they
      obeyed me;
    foreigners came cringing to me.
45 Foreigners lost heart,
    and came trembling out of their
      strongholds.

46 The LORD lives! Blessed be my rock,
    and exalted be the God of my
      salvation,
47 the God who gave me vengeance
    and subdued peoples under me;
48 who delivered me from my enemies;
    indeed, you exalted me above my
      adversaries;
    you delivered me from the violent.

49 For this I will extol you, O LORD,
      among the nations,
    and sing praises to your name.
50 Great triumphs he gives to his king,
    and shows steadfast love to his
      anointed,
    to David and his descendants
      forever.

Psalm 19

God's Glory in Creation and the Law

To the leader. A Psalm of David.

1 The heavens are telling the glory of
      God;

a Or *gentleness*   *b* Gk Tg: Heb *people*

18:31–50—Appropriately, the king praises God.
The king must be trained *for war* (v. 34), because
God has enemies (see Ps. 2). But as other psalms
indicate, God wills and "fights" for world-
encompassing peace, grounded in justice and
righteousness.

Psalm 19

19:1–6—That all creation praises God is

and the firmament[a] proclaims his
handiwork.
2 Day to day pours forth speech,
and night to night declares
knowledge.
3 There is no speech, nor are there
words;
their voice is not heard;
4 yet their voice[b] goes out through all
the earth,
and their words to the end of the
world.

In the heavens[c] he has set a tent for
the sun,
5 which comes out like a bridegroom
from his wedding canopy,
and like a strong man runs its
course with joy.
6 Its rising is from the end of the
heavens,
and its circuit to the end of them;
and nothing is hid from its heat.

7 The law of the LORD is perfect,
reviving the soul;
the decrees of the LORD are sure,
making wise the simple;
8 the precepts of the LORD are right,
rejoicing the heart;
the commandment of the LORD is
clear,
enlightening the eyes;
9 the fear of the LORD is pure,
enduring forever;
the ordinances of the LORD are
true
and righteous altogether.
10 More to be desired are they than
gold,
even much fine gold;

sweeter also than honey,
and drippings of the honeycomb.

11 Moreover by them is your servant
warned;
in keeping them there is great
reward.
12 But who can detect their errors?
Clear me from hidden faults.
13 Keep back your servant also from
the insolent;[d]
do not let them have dominion
over me.
Then I shall be blameless,
and innocent of great
transgression.

14 Let the words of my mouth and the
meditation of my heart
be acceptable to you,
O LORD, my rock and my
redeemer.

Psalm 20
Prayer for Victory
To the leader. A Psalm of David.

1 The LORD answer you in the day of
trouble!
The name of the God of Jacob
protect you!
2 May he send you help from the
sanctuary,
and give you support from Zion.
3 May he remember all your
offerings,
and regard with favor your burnt
sacrifices.   *Selah*

4 May he grant you your heart's desire,
and fulfill all your plans.

[a] Or dome   [b] Gk Jerome Compare Syr: Heb line   [c] Heb In them   [d] Or from
proud thoughts

extraordinarily important, suggesting a community of praise that includes humans, nonhuman
creatures, and the creation itself (see introduction, "Songs of Praise"; Pss. 96, 98, 148, 150).

19:7–10—This is often viewed as the start of a
separate psalm, due to the focus on *law*. But
torah connotes God's "instruction" or will (see
1:2), which involves justice and righteousness
on a cosmic scale, so "law" and creation belong
together. The concept of justice is explicitly pres-

ent in v. 9, where **ordinances** is more literally
"justices" or "deeds of justice."

19:13 Blameless—As vv. 11–12 show, this communicates not sinlessness but forgiveness and
ongoing dependence upon God (see 15:2).

19:14 Words—The repetition recalls the speech
of the universe in vv. 1–4, so the psalmist stays
in tune with the cosmos by providing a grateful
witness to God and God's ways.

5 May we shout for joy over your
victory,
and in the name of our God set up
our banners.
May the LORD fulfill all your
petitions.

6 Now I know that the LORD will help
his anointed;
he will answer him from his holy
heaven
with mighty victories by his right
hand.
7 Some take pride in chariots, and
some in horses,
but our pride is in the name of the
LORD our God.
8 They will collapse and fall,
but we shall rise and stand
upright.

9 Give victory to the king, O LORD;
answer us when we call.[a]

Psalm 21

Thanksgiving for Victory

To the leader. A Psalm of David.

1 In your strength the king rejoices,
O LORD,
and in your help how greatly he
exults!
2 You have given him his heart's
desire,
and have not withheld the request
of his lips.   *Selah*
3 For you meet him with rich
blessings;
you set a crown of fine gold on his
head.

4 He asked you for life; you gave it to
him—
length of days forever and ever.
5 His glory is great through your help;
splendor and majesty you bestow
on him.
6 You bestow on him blessings forever;
you make him glad with the joy of
your presence.
7 For the king trusts in the LORD,
and through the steadfast love of
the Most High he shall not be
moved.

8 Your hand will find out all your
enemies;
your right hand will find out those
who hate you.
9 You will make them like a fiery
furnace
when you appear.
The LORD will swallow them up in
his wrath,
and fire will consume them.
10 You will destroy their offspring from
the earth,
and their children from among
humankind.
11 If they plan evil against you,
if they devise mischief, they will
not succeed.
12 For you will put them to flight;
you will aim at their faces with
your bows.

13 Be exalted, O LORD, in your
strength!
We will sing and praise your power.

[a] Gk: Heb *give victory, O LORD; let the King answer us when we call*

Psalm 20

20:5 *Victory*—The translation is unnecessarily
triumphalistic. The word (see also vv. 6, 9) means
"help" (see 21:1, 5) or "deliverance"; that is, God
has saved the king's life.

20:6 *Anointed*—Hebrew *mashiach*, a title for the
king (see 2:2). As in Ps. 2, the king has enemies.
So, the saving of his life may mean *victories*; but
the point is the preservation of the one entrusted
with the earthly enactment of God's justice and
righteousness (see introduction, "Psalms 1–2 and
the Shape of the Psalter"; 72:1–7).

Psalm 21

21:1, 5 *Help*—This represents the same word
translated "victory" or "victories" in 20:5, 6, 9.
Psalm 21:1–7 clearly indicates that the king is
gifted to be God's earthly agent (see 20:6).

21:7 *Trust*—The king, as he was supposed to
be, is a model of faithfulness (see 4:5; 9:10;
13:5; introduction, "Psalms of Trust"). ***Steadfast
love***—See 5:7; 13:5; 2 Sam. 7:15.

21:8–12—The function of this hyperbolic imagery
is to express God's universal sovereignty (see
2:8–9; 18:31–50).

Psalm 22
Plea for Deliverance from Suffering and Hostility

To the leader: according to The Deer of the Dawn. A Psalm of David.

1 My God, my God, why have you
    forsaken me?
  Why are you so far from helping
    me, from the words of my
    groaning?
2 O my God, I cry by day, but you do
    not answer;
  and by night, but find no rest.

3 Yet you are holy,
  enthroned on the praises of Israel.
4 In you our ancestors trusted;
  they trusted, and you delivered
    them.
5 To you they cried, and were saved;
  in you they trusted, and were not
    put to shame.

6 But I am a worm, and not human;
  scorned by others, and despised by
    the people.
7 All who see me mock at me;
  they make mouths at me, they
    shake their heads;
8 "Commit your cause to the LORD; let
    him deliver—
  let him rescue the one in whom he
    delights!"

9 Yet it was you who took me from the
    womb;
  you kept me safe on my mother's
    breast.
10 On you I was cast from my birth,
  and since my mother bore me you
    have been my God.
11 Do not be far from me,
  for trouble is near
  and there is no one to help.

12 Many bulls encircle me,
  strong bulls of Bashan surround
    me;
13 they open wide their mouths at me,
  like a ravening and roaring lion.

14 I am poured out like water,
  and all my bones are out of joint;
  my heart is like wax;
    it is melted within my breast;
15 my mouth[a] is dried up like a
    potsherd,
  and my tongue sticks to my jaws;
  you lay me in the dust of death.

16 For dogs are all around me;
  a company of evildoers
    encircles me.
  My hands and feet have shriveled;[b]
17 I can count all my bones.
  They stare and gloat over me;
18 they divide my clothes among
    themselves,
  and for my clothing they cast lots.

19 But you, O LORD, do not be far
    away!
  O my help, come quickly to my
    aid!
20 Deliver my soul from the sword,
  my life[c] from the power of the dog!
21   Save me from the mouth of the
    lion!

From the horns of the wild oxen you
    have rescued[d] me.
22 I will tell of your name to my
    brothers and sisters;[e]
  in the midst of the congregation I
    will praise you:
23 You who fear the LORD, praise him!
  All you offspring of Jacob, glorify
    him;

a Cn: Heb *strength*   *b* Meaning of Heb uncertain   *c* Heb *my only one*
d Heb *answered*   *e* Or *kindred*

Psalm 22

22:1—See Matt. 27:45; Mark 15:34. That Jesus is portrayed as praying this typical complaint or prayer for help casts Jesus in the role of the righteous one who suffers as a result of faithfully embodying God's will (see Pss. 31, 69). Verses 6–8, 18 of Ps. 22 also have resonances with the passion narratives (see introduction, "The Psalms and the New Testament").

22:21b Rescued me—The Hebrew "answered me" is better (see NRSV footnote), suggesting that God's "answer" comes in the midst of, rather than beyond, the affliction.

stand in awe of him, all you
   offspring of Israel!
24 For he did not despise or abhor
      the affliction of the afflicted;
   he did not hide his face from me,*a*
      but heard when I*b* cried to him.

25 From you comes my praise in the
      great congregation;
   my vows I will pay before those
      who fear him.
26 The poor*c* shall eat and be
      satisfied;
   those who seek him shall praise
      the LORD.
   May your hearts live forever!

27 All the ends of the earth shall
      remember
   and turn to the LORD;
   and all the families of the nations
      shall worship before him.*d*
28 For dominion belongs to the
      LORD,
   and he rules over the nations.

29 To him,*e* indeed, shall all who sleep
      in*f* the earth bow down;
   before him shall bow all who go
      down to the dust,
   and I shall live for him.*g*
30 Posterity will serve him;
   future generations will be told
      about the Lord,

31 and*h* proclaim his deliverance to a
      people yet unborn,
   saying that he has done it.

Psalm 23
The Divine Shepherd
A Psalm of David.

1 The LORD is my shepherd, I shall not
      want.
2   He makes me lie down in green
         pastures;
   he leads me beside still waters;*i*
3   he restores my soul.*j*
   He leads me in right paths*k*
      for his name's sake.

4   Even though I walk through the
         darkest valley,*l*
   I fear no evil;
   for you are with me;
      your rod and your staff—
      they comfort me.

5   You prepare a table before me
         in the presence of my
            enemies;
   you anoint my head with oil;
      my cup overflows.

a Heb him *b* Heb he *c* Or afflicted *d* Gk Syr Jerome: Heb you *e* Cn: Heb
They have eaten and *f* Cn: Heb all the fat ones *g* Compare Gk Syr Vg:
Heb and he who cannot keep himself alive *h* Compare Gk: Heb it will be
told about the Lord to the generation, *31* they will come and *i* Heb waters of
rest *j* Or life *k* Or paths of righteousness *l* Or the valley of the shadow of
death

22:26—Apparently energized by knowing that
God is on his or her side (see v. 24), and appropriately grateful, the psalmist sponsors a thanksgiving sacrificial meal for other afflicted ones.

22:27–31—The meal (v. 26) finally includes the
whole world, which God claims (v. 28). And according to the poet's expansive vision, even the
dead (v. 29) and those yet to be born (vv. 30–31)
will feast in God's household. At this point, Ps.
22 also anticipates the life and ministry of Jesus
as much as his suffering and death, especially
the justice and righteousness involved in Jesus'
scandalously inclusive table fellowship.

Psalm 23

23:1 *Shepherd*—The term can designate a king;
and as sovereigns were supposed to do, God
graciously provides what people need to live (see
Jer. 23:1–6; Ezek. 34:1–16, both of which connect God's shepherding with the establishment of
justice).

23:2 *Green pastures*—The provision of daily
food. *Still waters*—The provision of drinkable
water.

23:3 *Restores my soul*—Better translated, "keeps
me alive." *For his name's sake*—It is God's character graciously to provide the basic necessities
of life.

23:5–6—The metaphor shifts to gracious host,
who also provides food (*table*), drink (*cup*), and
hospitality (see 36:5–6). *Enemies* are present,
and it is they who usually pursue the psalmists.
But here it is God's *goodness* and "steadfast
love" (NRSV *mercy*; see 5:7) that "pursue"
(NRSV *follow*) the psalmist. This vision of feasting
peacefully in God's house recalls the end of Ps.
22, where the psalmist sponsors a world-encompassing thanksgiving meal. NRSV's *my whole life
long* suggests the aptness of this vision for this
life, not simply for a future life beyond the earthly
realm of existence.

6 Surely[a] goodness and mercy[b] shall
      follow me
   all the days of my life,
   and I shall dwell in the house of the
      LORD
   my whole life long.[c]

Psalm 24

Entrance into the Temple

Of David. A Psalm.

1 The earth is the LORD's and all that
      is in it,
   the world, and those who live in it;
2 for he has founded it on the seas,
   and established it on the rivers.

3 Who shall ascend the hill of the LORD?
   And who shall stand in his holy
      place?
4 Those who have clean hands and
      pure hearts,
   who do not lift up their souls to
      what is false,
   and do not swear deceitfully.
5 They will receive blessing from the
      LORD,
   and vindication from the God of
      their salvation.
6 Such is the company of those who
      seek him,
   who seek the face of the God of
      Jacob.[d]   *Selah*

7 Lift up your heads, O gates!
   and be lifted up, O ancient doors!
   that the King of glory may
      come in.
8 Who is the King of glory?
   The LORD, strong and mighty,
   the LORD, mighty in battle.
9 Lift up your heads, O gates!
   and be lifted up, O ancient doors!
   that the King of glory may
      come in.
10 Who is this King of glory?
   The LORD of hosts,
   he is the King of glory.   *Selah*

Psalm 25

Prayer for Guidance and for Deliverance

Of David.

1 To you, O LORD, I lift up my soul.
2 O my God, in you I trust;
   do not let me be put to shame;
   do not let my enemies exult
      over me.
3 Do not let those who wait for you be
      put to shame;
   let them be ashamed who are
      wantonly treacherous.

4 Make me to know your ways,
   O LORD;

*a Or Only b Or kindness c Heb for length of days d Gk Syr: Heb your face,
O Jacob*

Psalm 24

24:1–2—The cosmic sovereignty of God is affirmed (see also *King* in vv. 8–10). God's claim upon the whole world and all its peoples explains why God wills justice and righteousness on a universe-encompassing scale (see introduction, "Psalms 1–2 and the Shape of the Psalter"; 96:11–13). The *seas* and *rivers* represent the chaotic forces that God has ordered (see v. 8; 93:3–4).

24:3—Recalling 15:1, the questions may indicate that the psalm was originally used as people entered the temple.

24:4 *Lift up their souls*—Better translated, "offer their lives" (see 25:1). Worship involves the offering of one's whole life to God.

24:5 *Vindication*—The word is usually translated "righteousness." The point is not reward, but rather right relationship with God, which makes life truly rewarding (see Ps. 1).

24:6 *Seek the face*—The phrase suggests living in dependence upon God (see 11:7).

24:8 *Mighty in battle*—Creation in the ancient world was often viewed as a battle against chaos. Thus, v. 8 may recall v. 2, as well as the more general reality that God and God's purposes are regularly opposed (see Ps. 2). Psalm 24:7–10 may have been used in liturgical processions in which the ark, symbolizing God's earthly throne, entered the temple.

Psalm 25

25:1 *I lift up my soul*—See 24:4. To offer one's life to God is the essence of *trust* (25:2; see introduction, "Psalms of Trust").

25:4 *Your ways*—The noun recurs in vv. 9, 12; and the verb *lead(s)* is the same root (vv. 5, 9). Verse 9a is more literally, "He leads the humble into justice." As the Psalms make clear, God's "ways" are fundamentally justice and righteousness (see introduction, "Psalms 1–2 and the

teach me your paths.
⁵ Lead me in your truth, and
teach me,
for you are the God of my
salvation;
for you I wait all day long.

⁶ Be mindful of your mercy, O Lord,
and of your steadfast love,
for they have been from of old.
⁷ Do not remember the sins of my
youth or my transgressions;
according to your steadfast love
remember me,
for your goodness' sake, O Lord!

⁸ Good and upright is the Lord;
therefore he instructs sinners in
the way.
⁹ He leads the humble in what is right,
and teaches the humble his way.
¹⁰ All the paths of the Lord are
steadfast love and faithfulness,
for those who keep his covenant
and his decrees.

¹¹ For your name's sake, O Lord,
pardon my guilt, for it is great.
¹² Who are they that fear the Lord?
He will teach them the way that
they should choose.
¹³ They will abide in prosperity,
and their children shall possess the
land.
¹⁴ The friendship of the Lord is for
those who fear him,
and he makes his covenant known
to them.
¹⁵ My eyes are ever toward the Lord,
for he will pluck my feet out of the
net.

¹⁶ Turn to me and be gracious to me,
for I am lonely and afflicted.
¹⁷ Relieve the troubles of my heart,
and bring me[a] out of my distress.
¹⁸ Consider my affliction and my
trouble,
and forgive all my sins.
¹⁹ Consider how many are my foes,
and with what violent hatred they
hate me.
²⁰ O guard my life, and deliver me;
do not let me be put to shame, for
I take refuge in you.
²¹ May integrity and uprightness
preserve me,
for I wait for you.

²² Redeem Israel, O God,
out of all its troubles.

Psalm 26
Plea for Justice and Declaration of Righteousness
Of David.

¹ Vindicate me, O Lord,
for I have walked in my integrity,
and I have trusted in the Lord
without wavering.
² Prove me, O Lord, and try me;
test my heart and mind.
³ For your steadfast love is before my
eyes,
and I walk in faithfulness to you.[b]

⁴ I do not sit with the worthless,
nor do I consort with hypocrites;
⁵ I hate the company of evildoers,
and will not sit with the wicked.

---

[a] Or *The troubles of my heart are enlarged; bring me*   [b] Or *in your faithfulness*

Shape of the Psalter"; 96:11–13), which God pursues by way of **steadfast love** (25:6, 10; see 5:7).

25:13–21—A comparison of vv. 13–14 with vv. 17–21 indicates that prosperity and relatedness to God (*covenant* in v. 14) do not mean an untroubled life (see introduction, "Psalms of Trust"). To *wait for* God (vv. 3, 5, 21) means to entrust one's life to God (see vv. 1–2) amid these difficulties.

Psalm 26
26:1 *Vindicate me*—More literally, "Establish jus-

tice for me" (see 7:8; 17:1–2); "justice" is at the heart of God's will (see introduction, "Psalms 1–2 and the Shape of the Psalter"; 96:11–13). Psalm 26:1–7 is, like 7:3–5 and 17:4–5, an oath of innocence—claiming not sinlessness in general but innocence in a particular case.

26:3 *Steadfast love . . . faithfulness*—These are fundamental to God's character (see 5:7; Exod. 34:6–7). The psalmist's loyalty consists, in essence, of imitating God, the ultimate in trust (see Ps. 26:1; 112:2–5).

6 I wash my hands in innocence,
   and go around your altar, O Lord,
7 singing aloud a song of
      thanksgiving,
   and telling all your wondrous
      deeds.

8 O Lord, I love the house in which
      you dwell,
   and the place where your glory
      abides.
9 Do not sweep me away with sinners,
   nor my life with the bloodthirsty,
10 those in whose hands are evil
      devices,
   and whose right hands are full of
      bribes.

11 But as for me, I walk in my integrity;
   redeem me, and be gracious
      to me.
12 My foot stands on level ground;
   in the great congregation I will
      bless the Lord.

Psalm 27
Triumphant Song of Confidence
Of David.

1 The Lord is my light and my
      salvation;
   whom shall I fear?
   The Lord is the stronghold[a] of my
      life;
   of whom shall I be afraid?

2 When evildoers assail me
   to devour my flesh—
   my adversaries and foes—
   they shall stumble and fall.

3 Though an army encamp against me,
   my heart shall not fear;
   though war rise up against me,
   yet I will be confident.

4 One thing I asked of the Lord,
   that will I seek after:
   to live in the house of the Lord
   all the days of my life,
   to behold the beauty of the Lord,
   and to inquire in his temple.

5 For he will hide me in his shelter
   in the day of trouble;
   he will conceal me under the cover
      of his tent;
   he will set me high on a rock.

6 Now my head is lifted up
   above my enemies all around me,
   and I will offer in his tent
   sacrifices with shouts of joy;
   I will sing and make melody to the
      Lord.

7 Hear, O Lord, when I cry aloud,
   be gracious to me and answer me!
8 "Come," my heart says, "seek his
      face!"
   Your face, Lord, do I seek.
9   Do not hide your face from me.

   Do not turn your servant away in
      anger,
   you who have been my help.
   Do not cast me off, do not
      forsake me,
   O God of my salvation!
10 If my father and mother
      forsake me,
   the Lord will take me up.

11 Teach me your way, O Lord,
   and lead me on a level path
   because of my enemies.
12 Do not give me up to the will of my
      adversaries,
   for false witnesses have risen
      against me,

a Or refuge

26:11 *My integrity*—The psalmist's integrity is not just his or her own; it is grounded in trusting God (v. 2), imitating God (v. 3), abiding in God's place (v. 8), and living in community with God's people (v. 12).

Psalm 27

27:1 *My light*—"Light" anticipates the mention of God's "face," which appears as light or "shines" (see, for example, 4:6; 67:1; Num. 6:25). Psalm 27:1–6 is an eloquent expression of trust in God.

27:8 *Your face . . . I seek*—See 11:7; 24:6. The prayer for help in 27:7–12 indicates the simultaneity of trust and threat in the faithful life (see introduction, "Psalms of Trust").

and they are breathing out
　　violence.
13 I believe that I shall see the goodness
　　　of the Lord
　　in the land of the living.
14 Wait for the Lord;
　　be strong, and let your heart take
　　　courage;
　　wait for the Lord!

Psalm 28

Prayer for Help and Thanksgiving for It

Of David.

1 To you, O Lord, I call;
　　my rock, do not refuse to hear me,
　　for if you are silent to me,
　　I shall be like those who go down
　　　to the Pit.
2 Hear the voice of my supplication,
　　as I cry to you for help,
　　as I lift up my hands
　　toward your most holy sanctuary.[a]

3 Do not drag me away with the
　　　wicked,
　　with those who are workers of evil,
　　who speak peace with their
　　　neighbors,
　　while mischief is in their hearts.
4 Repay them according to their
　　　work,
　　and according to the evil of their
　　　deeds;
　　repay them according to the work of
　　　their hands;
　　render them their due reward.
5 Because they do not regard the
　　　works of the Lord,

or the work of his hands,
　　he will break them down and build
　　　them up no more.
6 Blessed be the Lord,
　　for he has heard the sound of my
　　　pleadings.
7 The Lord is my strength and my
　　　shield;
　　in him my heart trusts;
　　so I am helped, and my heart
　　　exults,
　　and with my song I give thanks to
　　　him.
8 The Lord is the strength of his
　　　people;
　　he is the saving refuge of his
　　　anointed.
9 O save your people, and bless your
　　　heritage;
　　be their shepherd, and carry them
　　　forever.

Psalm 29

The Voice of God in a Great Storm

A Psalm of David.

1 Ascribe to the Lord, O heavenly
　　　beings,[b]
　　ascribe to the Lord glory and
　　　strength.
2 Ascribe to the Lord the glory of his
　　　name;
　　worship the Lord in holy
　　　splendor.
3 The voice of the Lord is over the
　　　waters;

[a] Heb *your innermost sanctuary*　[b] Heb *sons of gods*

27:14 *Wait . . . wait*—Synonymous with trust (see 25:3, 5, 21).

Psalm 28

28:1 *Pit*—See 6:5; 16:10.

28:3–4—The prayer for vengeance against *the wicked* is, in essence, a prayer for justice by a victim of injustice (see introduction, "Prayers for Help").

28:7 *Trusts*—As always, amid threat, the psalmist "trusts" (see, for example, 4:5: 13:5; introduction, "Psalms of Trust").

28:9 *Shepherd*—See 23:1.

Psalm 29

29:1 *Heavenly beings*—Reflecting the ancient Near Eastern polytheistic context, Ps. 29 is often considered among the oldest of the psalms (see also Pss. 58, 82).

29:2 *Glory*—See v. 9, where the heavenly beings respond as invited here; that is, they recognize God's sovereignty.

29:3–9—This recognition comes after God's display of power. The repeated *voice* is meant to be thunder, as suggested by the description of a storm hitting the coast of Canaan.

the God of glory thunders,
the LORD, over mighty waters.
4 The voice of the LORD is powerful;
the voice of the LORD is full of
majesty.

5 The voice of the LORD breaks the
cedars;
the LORD breaks the cedars of
Lebanon.
6 He makes Lebanon skip like a calf,
and Sirion like a young wild ox.

7 The voice of the LORD flashes forth
flames of fire.
8 The voice of the LORD shakes the
wilderness;
the LORD shakes the wilderness of
Kadesh.

9 The voice of the LORD causes the
oaks to whirl,*a*
and strips the forest bare;
and in his temple all say,
"Glory!"

10 The LORD sits enthroned over the
flood;
the LORD sits enthroned as king
forever.
11 May the LORD give strength to his
people!
May the LORD bless his people
with peace!

Psalm 30
Thanksgiving for Recovery
from Grave Illness

*A Psalm. A Song at the dedication of the
temple. Of David.*

1 I will extol you, O LORD, for you
have drawn me up,
and did not let my foes rejoice
over me.
2 O LORD my God, I cried to you for
help,
and you have healed me.
3 O LORD, you brought up my soul
from Sheol,
restored me to life from among
those gone down to the Pit.*b*

4 Sing praises to the LORD, O you his
faithful ones,
and give thanks to his holy name.
5 For his anger is but for a moment;
his favor is for a lifetime.
Weeping may linger for the night,
but joy comes with the morning.

6 As for me, I said in my prosperity,
"I shall never be moved."
7 By your favor, O LORD,
you had established me as a strong
mountain;
you hid your face;
I was dismayed.

a Or causes the deer to calve b Or that I should not go down to the Pit

---

**29:10 *The LORD sits enthroned . . . as king for-
ever*—**In Canaanite religion, Baal was lord of the
storm; but here the Lord's sovereignty is explicitly
asserted.

29:11 *Peace*—As other enthronement psalms
suggest, the heavenly sovereign wills justice and
righteousness (see introduction, "Psalms 1–2 and
the Shape of the Psalter"; 96:11–13), the result
of which is *shalom*, "peace" (see 72:1–7). Peace
begins with the recognition of God's claim on
the world, not with our efforts or achievements.
To glorify God is thus the chief end not only
of humankind, but of all creation as well (see
19:1–6; 96:11–13). See Luke 2:13–14, where
heavenly beings also proclaim glory and peace,
Luke's way of affirming that the humble birth of
Jesus represented nothing short of a new display
of God's power in the world.

Psalm 30

30 (Title) *At the dedication of the temple*—
Jewish sources associate Ps. 30 with the Feast of
Dedication (Hanukkah), for which its celebratory
tone is appropriate.

30:1–3—The psalmist praises God for saving his
or her life. *Sheol* and *Pit* suggest a near-death
situation (see 6:5).

30:4–5—As witness to God's life-giving work, the
psalmist draws others into the praise.

30:6–12—In an apparent flashback, the psalmist
suggests that adversity dislodged a false confidence (vv. 6–7), making way for genuine praise
and thanksgiving that will last *forever* (v. 12),
presumably even amid future setbacks. That
the psalmist prays and praises simultaneously
suggests a new ability to hold together hurt and
hope, threat and trust (see introduction, "Psalms
of Trust").

8 To you, O Lord, I cried,
 and to the Lord I made
 supplication:
9 "What profit is there in my death,
 if I go down to the Pit?
 Will the dust praise you?
 Will it tell of your faithfulness?
10 Hear, O Lord, and be gracious to me!
 O Lord, be my helper!"

11 You have turned my mourning into
 dancing;
 you have taken off my sackcloth
 and clothed me with joy,
12 so that my soul*a* may praise you and
 not be silent.
 O Lord my God, I will give thanks
 to you forever.

Psalm 31
Prayer and Praise for Deliverance
from Enemies
To the leader. A Psalm of David.

1 In you, O Lord, I seek refuge;
 do not let me ever be put to shame;
 in your righteousness deliver me.
2 Incline your ear to me;
 rescue me speedily.
 Be a rock of refuge for me,
 a strong fortress to save me.

3 You are indeed my rock and my
 fortress;
 for your name's sake lead me and
 guide me,
4 take me out of the net that is hidden
 for me,
 for you are my refuge.
5 Into your hand I commit my spirit;
 you have redeemed me, O Lord,
 faithful God.

6 You hate*b* those who pay regard to
 worthless idols,
 but I trust in the Lord.
7 I will exult and rejoice in your
 steadfast love,
 because you have seen my
 affliction;
 you have taken heed of my
 adversities,
8 and have not delivered me into the
 hand of the enemy;
 you have set my feet in a broad
 place.

9 Be gracious to me, O Lord, for I am
 in distress;
 my eye wastes away from grief,
 my soul and body also.
10 For my life is spent with sorrow,
 and my years with sighing;
 my strength fails because of my
 misery,*c*
 and my bones waste away.
11 I am the scorn of all my adversaries,
 a horror*d* to my neighbors,
 an object of dread to my
 acquaintances;
 those who see me in the street flee
 from me.
12 I have passed out of mind like one
 who is dead;
 I have become like a broken vessel.
13 For I hear the whispering of many—
 terror all around!—
 as they scheme together against me,
 as they plot to take my life.

14 But I trust in you, O Lord;
 I say, "You are my God."

a Heb *that glory* *b* One Heb Ms Gk Syr Jerome: MT *I hate* *c* Gk Syr: Heb
my iniquity *d* Cn: Heb *exceedingly*

Psalm 31

31:1 *Refuge*—A key concept here and elsewhere
(see vv. 2, 19; introduction, "Psalms of Trust"),
it indicates trust in God (see vv. 6, 14), despite
adversity (vv. 4, 7, 9–13, 15, 17–18, 22).

31:5 *Into your hand . . . spirit*—The psalmist entrusts life fully to God. See the similar affirmation
in v. 15. According to Luke 23:46, Jesus quotes v.
5 from the cross, modeling faithfulness that trusts
amid suffering.

31:7 *Steadfast love*—The simultaneity of hurt
and hope suggests that God's sovereignty consists
essentially of steadfast love (see vv. 16, 21; 5:7;
introduction, "Prayers for Help").

31:13—See Jer. 20:3, 10. The prophets, as well
as Jesus, regularly suffered on account of their
faithful proclamation and embodiment of God's
will.

15 My times are in your hand;
　　deliver me from the hand of my
　　　enemies and persecutors.
16 Let your face shine upon your
　　　servant;
　　save me in your steadfast love.
17 Do not let me be put to shame,
　　O Lord,
　　for I call on you;
　　let the wicked be put to shame;
　　　let them go dumbfounded to
　　　　Sheol.
18 Let the lying lips be stilled
　　that speak insolently against the
　　　righteous
　　with pride and contempt.

19 O how abundant is your goodness
　　that you have laid up for those
　　　who fear you,
　　and accomplished for those who
　　　take refuge in you,
　　in the sight of everyone!
20 In the shelter of your presence you
　　　hide them
　　from human plots;
　　you hold them safe under your
　　　shelter
　　from contentious tongues.

21 Blessed be the Lord,
　　for he has wondrously shown his
　　　steadfast love to me
　　when I was beset as a city under
　　　siege.
22 I had said in my alarm,
　　"I am driven far*a* from your sight."
　　But you heard my supplications
　　　when I cried out to you for help.

23 Love the Lord, all you his saints.
　　The Lord preserves the faithful,
　　but abundantly repays the one who
　　　acts haughtily.

24 Be strong, and let your heart take
　　　courage,
　　all you who wait for the Lord.

Psalm 32
The Joy of Forgiveness
Of David. A Maskil.

1 Happy are those whose transgression
　　is forgiven,
　　whose sin is covered.
2 Happy are those to whom the Lord
　　imputes no iniquity,
　　and in whose spirit there is no
　　　deceit.

3 While I kept silence, my body
　　wasted away
　　through my groaning all day long.
4 For day and night your hand was
　　heavy upon me;
　　my strength was dried up*b* as by
　　　the heat of summer.　　*Selah*

5 Then I acknowledged my sin to you,
　　and I did not hide my iniquity;
　　I said, "I will confess my
　　　transgressions to the Lord,"
　　and you forgave the guilt of my
　　　sin.　　*Selah*

6 Therefore let all who are faithful
　　offer prayer to you;
　　at a time of distress,*c* the rush of
　　　mighty waters
　　shall not reach them.
7 You are a hiding place for me;
　　you preserve me from trouble;
　　you surround me with glad cries of
　　　deliverance.　　*Selah*

8 I will instruct you and teach you the
　　way you should go;

a Another reading is *cut off*　*b* Meaning of Heb uncertain　*c* Cn: Heb *at a time of finding only*

31:24—Trusting God's love makes *courage* possible; on *wait*, see 25:3, 5, 21; 27:14.
Psalm 32
32:1–2 *Happy*—Recalling 1:1, vv. 1–2 make clear that happiness or righteousness involves not merit but grace (see Rom. 4:7–8). Psalm 32 is one of the church's seven Penitential Psalms (see Ps. 6).

32:3–5—One does not have to adopt a mechanical doctrine of retribution in order to appreciate the reality that sin has consequences, even physical consequences (see introduction, "Prayers for Help").
32:8–9—As in 51:13–17, the forgiven sinner becomes a teacher.

I will counsel you with my eye
    upon you.
9 Do not be like a horse or a mule,
    without understanding,
    whose temper must be curbed
      with bit and bridle,
    else it will not stay near you.

10 Many are the torments of the
    wicked,
    but steadfast love surrounds those
      who trust in the LORD.
11 Be glad in the LORD and rejoice,
    O righteous,
    and shout for joy, all you upright
      in heart.

Psalm 33
The Greatness and Goodness of God

1 Rejoice in the LORD, O you
    righteous.
    Praise befits the upright.
2 Praise the LORD with the lyre;
    make melody to him with the harp
      of ten strings.
3 Sing to him a new song;
    play skillfully on the strings, with
      loud shouts.

4 For the word of the LORD is upright,
    and all his work is done in
      faithfulness.
5 He loves righteousness and justice;
    the earth is full of the steadfast
      love of the LORD.

6 By the word of the LORD the heavens
    were made,
    and all their host by the breath of
      his mouth.

7 He gathered the waters of the sea as
    in a bottle;
    he put the deeps in storehouses.

8 Let all the earth fear the LORD;
    let all the inhabitants of the world
      stand in awe of him.
9 For he spoke, and it came to be;
    he commanded, and it stood firm.

10 The LORD brings the counsel of the
    nations to nothing;
    he frustrates the plans of the
      peoples.
11 The counsel of the LORD stands
    forever,
    the thoughts of his heart to all
      generations.
12 Happy is the nation whose God is
    the LORD,
    the people whom he has chosen as
      his heritage.

13 The LORD looks down from heaven;
    he sees all humankind.
14 From where he sits enthroned he
    watches
    all the inhabitants of the earth—
15 he who fashions the hearts of them
    all,
    and observes all their deeds.
16 A king is not saved by his great
    army;
    a warrior is not delivered by his
      great strength.
17 The war horse is a vain hope for
    victory,
    and by its great might it cannot
      save.

32:10 *Steadfast love*—See 5:7; 31:7, 16, 21; God's love is the source and object of trust (see 13:5).

Psalm 33

33:1—This seems to suggest that Ps. 33 is a direct response to 32:11.

33:3 *New song*—Associated elsewhere with the celebration of God's reign, which is also in view here (see v. 14; 96:1; 98:1; 149:1). The original song may be the song of Moses and Miriam in Exod. 15:1–21.

33:5—The sovereign God wills *righteousness*

and justice (see introduction, "Psalms 1–2 and the Shape of the Psalter"; 96:11–13), which derive from God's *steadfast love* (see 5:7; 32:10). It is an extraordinarily important insight that justice begins with love (see also 33:18, 22; 36:5–6).

33:8 *All the earth*—The songs of praise (see introduction, "Songs of Praise") regularly advocate the world-encompassing worship and service of God. See *all* in vv. 13, 14, 15.

33:10–17—True life and security will not result from strategic national planning (v. 10) or military might (vv. 16–17).

18 Truly the eye of the LORD is on those
    who fear him,
  on those who hope in his steadfast
    love,
19 to deliver their soul from death,
  and to keep them alive in famine.

20 Our soul waits for the LORD;
  he is our help and shield.
21 Our heart is glad in him,
  because we trust in his holy name.
22 Let your steadfast love, O LORD, be
    upon us,
  even as we hope in you.

Psalm 34

Praise for Deliverance from Trouble

*Of David, when he feigned madness before
Abimelech, so that he drove him out, and he
went away.*

1 I will bless the LORD at all times;
  his praise shall continually be in
    my mouth.
2 My soul makes its boast in the
    LORD;
  let the humble hear and be glad.
3 O magnify the LORD with me,
  and let us exalt his name together.

4 I sought the LORD, and he answered
    me,
  and delivered me from all my
    fears.
5 Look to him, and be radiant;
  so your*a* faces shall never be
    ashamed.
6 This poor soul cried, and was heard
    by the LORD,
  and was saved from every trouble.
7 The angel of the LORD encamps

around those who fear him, and
    delivers them.
8 O taste and see that the LORD is
    good;
  happy are those who take refuge
    in him.
9 O fear the LORD, you his holy ones,
  for those who fear him have no
    want.
10 The young lions suffer want and
    hunger,
  but those who seek the LORD lack
    no good thing.

11 Come, O children, listen to me;
  I will teach you the fear of the
    LORD.
12 Which of you desires life,
  and covets many days to enjoy
    good?
13 Keep your tongue from evil,
  and your lips from speaking deceit.
14 Depart from evil, and do good;
  seek peace, and pursue it.

15 The eyes of the LORD are on the
    righteous,
  and his ears are open to their cry.
16 The face of the LORD is against
    evildoers,
  to cut off the remembrance of
    them from the earth.
17 When the righteous cry for help, the
    LORD hears,
  and rescues them from all their
    troubles.
18 The LORD is near to the
    brokenhearted,
  and saves the crushed in spirit.

a Gk Syr Jerome: Heb *their*

33:18–22—These verses bring together faith/*trust*
(v. 21), **hope** (vv. 18, 22), and love (vv. 18–22),
the essence of discipleship (see 1 Cor. 13:13).

Psalm 34

34 (Title)—See Ps. 3; 1 Sam. 21:13 (though the
king's name differs).

34:1 *Bless*—Originally meaning "to kneel," the
word indicates a recognition of God's sovereignty
and an intent to live in dependence upon God
(see v. 2)—in short, to find *refuge* in God (vv. 8,
22; introduction, "Psalms of Trust").

34:6 *Poor*—As always, God sides with victims—
the poor (introduction, "Prayers for Help"), as
well as *the brokenhearted* and *crushed in spirit*
(v. 18).

34:8 *Taste and see*—Perhaps the original setting
was a thanksgiving sacrificial meal (see 22:26).

34:11 *Fear of the LORD*—Not fright, but reverent
trust and obedience (see 2:11).

34:14 *Peace*—What God wills, the fruit of justice
and righteousness (see 29:11; 72:1–7).

¹⁹ Many are the afflictions of the
　　　righteous,
　　but the LORD rescues them from
　　　them all.
²⁰ He keeps all their bones;
　　not one of them will be broken.
²¹ Evil brings death to the wicked,
　　and those who hate the righteous
　　　will be condemned.
²² The LORD redeems the life of his
　　　servants;
　　none of those who take refuge in
　　　him will be condemned.

Psalm 35
Prayer for Deliverance from Enemies
Of David.

¹ Contend, O LORD, with those who
　　　contend with me;
　　fight against those who fight
　　　against me!
² Take hold of shield and buckler,
　　and rise up to help me!
³ Draw the spear and javelin
　　against my pursuers;
　　say to my soul,
　　"I am your salvation."

⁴ Let them be put to shame and
　　　dishonor
　　who seek after my life.
　　Let them be turned back and
　　　confounded
　　who devise evil against me.
⁵ Let them be like chaff before the
　　　wind,
　　with the angel of the LORD driving
　　　them on.
⁶ Let their way be dark and slippery,
　　with the angel of the LORD
　　　pursuing them.

⁷ For without cause they hid their net*a*
　　　for me;
　　without cause they dug a pit*b* for
　　　my life.
⁸ Let ruin come on them unawares.
　　And let the net that they hid ensnare
　　　them;
　　let them fall in it—to their ruin.

⁹ Then my soul shall rejoice in the
　　　LORD,
　　exulting in his deliverance.
¹⁰ All my bones shall say,
　　"O LORD, who is like you?
　You deliver the weak
　　from those too strong for them,
　　the weak and needy from those
　　　who despoil them."

¹¹ Malicious witnesses rise up;
　　they ask me about things I do not
　　　know.
¹² They repay me evil for good;
　　my soul is forlorn.
¹³ But as for me, when they were sick,
　　I wore sackcloth;
　　I afflicted myself with fasting.
　I prayed with head bowed*c* on my
　　　bosom,
¹⁴ 　　as though I grieved for a friend or
　　　a brother;
　I went about as one who laments for
　　　a mother,
　　bowed down and in mourning.
¹⁵ But at my stumbling they gathered
　　　in glee,
　　they gathered together against me;
　ruffians whom I did not know
　　tore at me without ceasing;

a Heb *a pit, their net* *b* The word *pit* is transposed from the preceding
line *c* Or *My prayer turned back*

34:19—Another indication that the life of faith
holds together hurt and hope, threat and trust
(see introduction, "Psalms of Trust").

Psalm 35

35:1 *Contend*—A legal term (it appears as *my
cause* in v. 23), it prepares for the mention of *justice* and *righteousness* in vv. 23–24, 27–28. The
request for vengeance against enemies in vv. 1–6
is a prayer for justice (see introduction, "Prayers
for Help").

35:10—It is characteristic of God to stand with
victims—*the weak and needy* (see introduction,
"Prayers for Help").

35:13–14—Unlike the opponents (vv. 11–12,
15–16), the psalmist shows solidarity with
victims. Furthermore, the psalmist renounces a
retributional lifestyle, and lives by grace.

16 they impiously mocked more and
          more,[a]
     gnashing at me with their teeth.

17 How long, O LORD, will you look
          on?
     Rescue me from their ravages,
          my life from the lions!

18 Then I will thank you in the great
          congregation;
     in the mighty throng I will praise
          you.

19 Do not let my treacherous enemies
          rejoice over me,
     or those who hate me without
          cause wink the eye.

20 For they do not speak peace,
     but they conceive deceitful words
          against those who are quiet in the
          land.

21 They open wide their mouths
          against me;
     they say, "Aha, Aha,
          our eyes have seen it."

22 You have seen, O LORD; do not be
          silent!
     O Lord, do not be far from me!

23 Wake up! Bestir yourself for my
          defense,
     for my cause, my God and my
          Lord!

24 Vindicate me, O LORD, my God,
     according to your righteousness,
     and do not let them rejoice over me.

25 Do not let them say to themselves,
     "Aha, we have our heart's desire."
     Do not let them say, "We have
          swallowed you[b] up."

26 Let all those who rejoice at my
          calamity

     be put to shame and confusion;
     let those who exalt themselves
          against me
     be clothed with shame and
          dishonor.

27 Let those who desire my vindication
          shout for joy and be glad,
     and say evermore,
     "Great is the LORD,
          who delights in the welfare of his
          servant."

28 Then my tongue shall tell of your
          righteousness
     and of your praise all day long.

Psalm 36
Human Wickedness and Divine Goodness

To the leader. Of David, the servant of the LORD.

1 Transgression speaks to the wicked
          deep in their hearts;
     there is no fear of God
          before their eyes.

2 For they flatter themselves in their
          own eyes
     that their iniquity cannot be found
          out and hated.

3 The words of their mouths are
          mischief and deceit;
     they have ceased to act wisely and
          do good.

4 They plot mischief while on their
          beds;
     they are set on a way that is not
          good;
     they do not reject evil.

5 Your steadfast love, O LORD, extends
          to the heavens,

---

[a] Cn Compare Gk: Heb *like the profanest of mockers of a cake*   [b] Heb *him*

35:20 *Peace*—*Shalom* is what God wills and works for (see *shalom* also in v. 27, NRSV *welfare*), but the opponents do not.

35:23–24 *My defense . . . Vindicate me*—More literally, "my justice" and "establish justice for me." Justice and *righteousness* (see also v. 28 and v. 27, NRSV *vindication*) produce the *shalom* God wills (see introduction, "Psalms 1–2 and the Shape of the Psalter"; 29:11).

Psalm 36

36:1–4, 11–12—The verses that frame the psalm acknowledge the reality of *the wicked* (vv. 1, 11); but in the midst of evil, the psalmist proclaims God's *steadfast love* (vv. 5, 7, 10). The wicked accept no accountability for their actions (v. 2; see also 10:11, 13).

36:5–6—*Steadfast love* and *faithfulness* are a summary of God's character (see Exod. 34:6–7),

your faithfulness to the clouds.
⁶ Your righteousness is like the mighty
     mountains,
   your judgments are like the great
     deep;
   you save humans and animals
     alike, O LORD.

⁷ How precious is your steadfast love,
     O God!
   All people may take refuge in the
     shadow of your wings.
⁸ They feast on the abundance of your
     house,
   and you give them drink from the
     river of your delights.
⁹ For with you is the fountain of life;
   in your light we see light.

¹⁰ O continue your steadfast love to
     those who know you,
   and your salvation to the upright
     of heart!
¹¹ Do not let the foot of the arrogant
     tread on me,
   or the hand of the wicked drive me
     away.
¹² There the evildoers lie prostrate;
   they are thrust down, unable to
     rise.

Psalm 37
Exhortation to Patience and Trust
Of David.

¹ Do not fret because of the wicked;
   do not be envious of wrongdoers,

² for they will soon fade like the
     grass,
   and wither like the green herb.
³ Trust in the LORD, and do good;
   so you will live in the land, and
     enjoy security.
⁴ Take delight in the LORD,
   and he will give you the desires of
     your heart.
⁵ Commit your way to the LORD;
   trust in him, and he will act.
⁶ He will make your vindication shine
     like the light,
   and the justice of your cause like
     the noonday.

⁷ Be still before the LORD, and wait
     patiently for him;
   do not fret over those who prosper
     in their way,
   over those who carry out evil
     devices.

⁸ Refrain from anger, and forsake
     wrath.
   Do not fret—it leads only to evil.
⁹ For the wicked shall be cut off,
   but those who wait for the LORD
     shall inherit the land.

¹⁰ Yet a little while, and the wicked will
     be no more;
   though you look diligently for
     their place, they will not be
     there.
¹¹ But the meek shall inherit the land,

---

while *righteousness* and justice (NRSV *judgments*) are a summary of God's will (see introduction, "Psalms 1–2 and the Shape of the Psalter"; 96:11–13). God's character and purposes fill the universe from top (*heavens*) to bottom (*deep*), embracing the human and nonhuman creation for the purpose of life (see 33:5; Col. 1:20).

36:7 *Refuge*—See introduction, "Psalms of Trust." God's love means that God wills life and protection for **all people**, although some may reject the offer (see vv. 1–2; introduction, "Songs of Praise"). *Shadow . . . wings*—See note at 17:8.

36:8—Perhaps indicating an original temple setting, the claim is that God's hospitality is for all (see 23:5–6).

36:9—God is the source of all *life*, and life is to

be received as a gift. On *light*, see 27:1. John 1:4 also links life and light.

Psalm 37

37:3, 5 *Trust*—This is the quintessential posture of discipleship (see 4:5; 13:5; introduction, "Psalms of Trust").

37:6 *Vindication . . . justice*—"Vindication" is more literally "righteousness"; and with "justice," it summarizes God's will for people and the world (see vv. 28, 30; introduction, "Psalms 1–2 and the Shape of the Psalter"; 36:5–6; 96:11–13). For the psalmist, the ascendancy of **the wicked** seems to call this into question.

37:11—See Matt. 5:5, where "the meek" also receive essentially the same promise. *Prosperity*

and delight themselves in
　　abundant prosperity.

12 The wicked plot against the
　　righteous,
　and gnash their teeth at them;
13 but the LORD laughs at the wicked,
　for he sees that their day is
　　coming.

14 The wicked draw the sword and
　　bend their bows
　to bring down the poor and
　　needy,
　to kill those who walk uprightly;
15 their sword shall enter their own
　　heart,
　and their bows shall be broken.

16 Better is a little that the righteous
　　person has
　than the abundance of many
　　wicked.
17 For the arms of the wicked shall be
　　broken,
　but the LORD upholds the
　　righteous.

18 The LORD knows the days of the
　　blameless,
　and their heritage will abide
　　forever;
19 they are not put to shame in evil
　　times,
　in the days of famine they have
　　abundance.

20 But the wicked perish,
　and the enemies of the LORD are
　　like the glory of the pastures;
　they vanish—like smoke they
　　vanish away.

21 The wicked borrow, and do not pay
　　back,
　but the righteous are generous and
　　keep giving;

22 for those blessed by the LORD shall
　　inherit the land,
　but those cursed by him shall be
　　cut off.

23 Our steps[a] are made firm by the
　　LORD,
　when he delights in our[b] way;
24 though we stumble,[c] we[d] shall not
　　fall headlong,
　for the LORD holds us[e] by the hand.

25 I have been young, and now am old,
　yet I have not seen the righteous
　　forsaken
　or their children begging bread.
26 They are ever giving liberally and
　　lending,
　and their children become a
　　blessing.

27 Depart from evil, and do good;
　so you shall abide forever.
28 For the LORD loves justice;
　he will not forsake his faithful
　　ones.

　The righteous shall be kept safe
　　forever,
　but the children of the wicked
　　shall be cut off.
29 The righteous shall inherit the land,
　and live in it forever.

30 The mouths of the righteous utter
　　wisdom,
　and their tongues speak justice.
31 The law of their God is in their
　　hearts;
　their steps do not slip.

32 The wicked watch for the righteous,
　and seek to kill them.
33 The LORD will not abandon them to
　　their power,

---

a Heb A man's steps　b Heb his　c Heb he stumbles　d Heb he　e Heb him

---

translates *shalom*, usually "peace" (see 29:11).
God promises peace, though it is "not . . . as the
world gives" (John 14:27).

37:13—God's laughter indicates God's sovereignty in the face of competing claims (see 2:4).

37:27–31—Despite the apparent success of the
wicked, the psalmist continues to counsel God-
like behavior (see vv. 21, 26). As God *loves justice* (v. 28), so God's people *speak justice* (v. 30),
which is the essence of God's "instruction" (v. 31,
NRSV *law*) or will (see introduction, "Psalms 1–2
and the Shape of the Psalter"; 96:11–13).

or let them be condemned when
they are brought to trial.

34 Wait for the LORD, and keep to his
way,
and he will exalt you to inherit the
land;
you will look on the destruction of
the wicked.

35 I have seen the wicked oppressing,
and towering like a cedar of
Lebanon.*a*

36 Again I*b* passed by, and they were no
more;
though I sought them, they could
not be found.

37 Mark the blameless, and behold the
upright,
for there is posterity for the
peaceable.

38 But transgressors shall be altogether
destroyed;
the posterity of the wicked shall be
cut off.

39 The salvation of the righteous is
from the LORD;
he is their refuge in the time of
trouble.

40 The LORD helps them and rescues
them;
he rescues them from the wicked,
and saves them,
because they take refuge in him.

Psalm 38

A Penitent Sufferer's Plea for Healing

A Psalm of David, for the memorial offering.

1 O LORD, do not rebuke me in your
anger,
or discipline me in your wrath.

2 For your arrows have sunk into me,

and your hand has come down
on me.

3 There is no soundness in my flesh
because of your indignation;
there is no health in my bones
because of my sin.

4 For my iniquities have gone over my
head;
they weigh like a burden too heavy
for me.

5 My wounds grow foul and fester
because of my foolishness;

6 I am utterly bowed down and
prostrate;
all day long I go around mourning.

7 For my loins are filled with burning,
and there is no soundness in my
flesh.

8 I am utterly spent and crushed;
I groan because of the tumult of
my heart.

9 O Lord, all my longing is known to
you;
my sighing is not hidden from
you.

10 My heart throbs, my strength fails
me;
as for the light of my eyes—it also
has gone from me.

11 My friends and companions stand
aloof from my affliction,
and my neighbors stand far off.

12 Those who seek my life lay their
snares;
those who seek to hurt me speak
of ruin,
and meditate treachery all day
long.

13 But I am like the deaf, I do not hear;
like the mute, who cannot speak.

a Gk: Meaning of Heb uncertain *b* Gk Syr Jerome: Heb *he*

37:37 The peaceable—Literally, "man of peace." Accepting the offer of God's peace is ultimately more rewarding and enduring than wickedness.

Psalm 38

38:1—Like Ps. 6, Ps. 38 is one of the church's seven Penitential Psalms.

38:11—Compare behavior of the *friends* to 35:13–14, where the psalmist refuses to blame victims, treating them graciously instead.

¹⁴ Truly, I am like one who does not
　　　hear,
　　　and in whose mouth is no retort.

¹⁵ But it is for you, O LORD, that I wait;
　　　it is you, O Lord my God, who will
　　　　answer.
¹⁶ For I pray, "Only do not let them
　　　rejoice over me,
　　　those who boast against me when
　　　　my foot slips."

¹⁷ For I am ready to fall,
　　　and my pain is ever with me.
¹⁸ I confess my iniquity;
　　　I am sorry for my sin.
¹⁹ Those who are my foes without
　　　cause*ᵃ* are mighty,
　　　and many are those who hate me
　　　　wrongfully.
²⁰ Those who render me evil for good
　　　are my adversaries because I
　　　　follow after good.

²¹ Do not forsake me, O LORD;
　　　O my God, do not be far from me;
²² make haste to help me,
　　　O Lord, my salvation.

Psalm 39
Prayer for Wisdom and Forgiveness
*To the leader: to Jeduthun. A Psalm
of David.*

¹ I said, "I will guard my ways
　　　that I may not sin with my tongue;
　　I will keep a muzzle on my mouth
　　　as long as the wicked are in my
　　　　presence."
² I was silent and still;
　　　I held my peace to no avail;
　　my distress grew worse,
³ 　　my heart became hot within me.

While I mused, the fire burned;
　　　then I spoke with my tongue:

⁴ "LORD, let me know my end,
　　　and what is the measure of my
　　　　days;
　　let me know how fleeting my
　　　　life is.
⁵ You have made my days a few
　　　handbreadths,
　　　and my lifetime is as nothing in
　　　　your sight.
　　Surely everyone stands as a mere
　　　　breath.　　　　　　　　*Selah*
⁶ 　　Surely everyone goes about like a
　　　　shadow.
　　Surely for nothing they are in
　　　　turmoil;
　　　they heap up, and do not know
　　　　who will gather.

⁷ "And now, O Lord, what do I wait
　　　for?
　　My hope is in you.
⁸ Deliver me from all my
　　　transgressions.
　　Do not make me the scorn of the
　　　　fool.
⁹ I am silent; I do not open my
　　　mouth,
　　　for it is you who have done it.
¹⁰ Remove your stroke from me;
　　　I am worn down by the blows*ᵇ* of
　　　　your hand.

¹¹ "You chastise mortals
　　　in punishment for sin,
　　consuming like a moth what is dear
　　　　to them;
　　surely everyone is a mere breath.
　　　　　　　　　　　　　　Selah

*ᵃ*Q Ms: MT *my living foes*　*ᵇ*Heb *hostility*

38:15 *Wait*—Connotes the entrusting of life to
God (see 25:3, 5, 21; 27:14).

38:18–20—Although the psalmist seems to
uphold a retributional scheme, he or she actually
undercuts this in v. 20, claiming God's life-giving
help (v. 22; see 22:19) for the victimized (see
introduction, "Prayers for Help").

Psalm 39

39:1–3—Although announcing silence, the

psalmist cannot help but speak, as he or she does
for the rest of the psalm.

39:4–6—The beginning of the speech acknowledges the transience of human life (see 90:9–10;
Eccl. 2:18–21).

39:7–11—Even so, there is *hope*, although the
psalmist seems to waver between hope (v. 7) and
despair (v. 9).

¹² "Hear my prayer, O LORD,
and give ear to my cry;
do not hold your peace at my
tears.
For I am your passing guest,
an alien, like all my forebears.
¹³ Turn your gaze away from me, that I
may smile again,
before I depart and am no more."

Psalm 40
Thanksgiving for Deliverance and Prayer for Help

To the leader. Of David. A Psalm.

¹ I waited patiently for the LORD;
he inclined to me and heard my
cry.
² He drew me up from the desolate
pit,^a
out of the miry bog,
and set my feet upon a rock,
making my steps secure.
³ He put a new song in my mouth,
a song of praise to our God.
Many will see and fear,
and put their trust in the LORD.

⁴ Happy are those who make
the LORD their trust,
who do not turn to the proud,
to those who go astray after false
gods.
⁵ You have multiplied, O LORD my
God,
your wondrous deeds and your
thoughts toward us;
none can compare with you.
Were I to proclaim and tell of them,
they would be more than can be
counted.

⁶ Sacrifice and offering you do not
desire,
but you have given me an open ear.^b
Burnt offering and sin offering
you have not required.
⁷ Then I said, "Here I am;
in the scroll of the book it is
written of me.^c
⁸ I delight to do your will, O my God;
your law is within my heart."

⁹ I have told the glad news of
deliverance
in the great congregation;
see, I have not restrained my lips,
as you know, O LORD.
¹⁰ I have not hidden your saving help
within my heart,
I have spoken of your faithfulness
and your salvation;
I have not concealed your steadfast
love and your faithfulness
from the great congregation.

¹¹ Do not, O LORD, withhold
your mercy from me;

^a Cn: Heb *pit of tumult*   ^b Heb *ears you have dug for me*   ^c Meaning of Heb uncertain

---

39:12–13—Although *passing guest* and *alien* seem negative, and although the psalmist seems to desire God's absence (v. 13), he or she has dared to speak rather openly to God for ten verses. This in itself is an affirmation of human dignity. The psalmist's wavering effectively communicates the paradox of human life—it is both maddeningly short and incredibly wonderful. Hurt and hope are inseparable (see introduction, "Psalms of Trust"). The claim of alien status may be an act of hope that rests solely in God, rather than human achievement (see Lev. 25:23; 1 Chr. 29:15; Heb. 11:13; 1 Pet. 2:11).

Psalm 40

40:3 *New song*—See note at 33:3.

40:4 *Happy*—See 1:1; 2:12. Happiness is a matter of trusting God and orienting life completely to God, including what God wills (40:6–10).

40:6—The psalmist turns to what God wills; see Isa. 1:12–17; Hos. 6:6; Amos 5:21–24.

40:7—The image of *the book* communicates belonging to God; see 56:8; 69:28; 139:16.

40:8–10—Recalling *delight* and *law* in 1:2, the psalmist affirms openness to God's "instruction" (NRSV *law*) and *will*, which is fundamentally justice and righteousness (see introduction, "Psalms 1–2 and the Shape of the Psalter"; 96:11–13). Appropriately, *glad news of deliverance* (v. 9) and *saving help* (v. 10) derive from the Hebrew root meaning "righteousness." God's will for setting things right in the world derives from God's *faithfulness* and *steadfast love*, which the psalmist also proclaims (see 5:7; 36:5–6).

40:11–16—The complaint and prayer for help indicate the regular opposition to God's will (see Ps. 2). Psalm 40:13–17 appears later as Ps. 70.

let your steadfast love and your
    faithfulness
  keep me safe forever.
12 For evils have encompassed me
    without number;
  my iniquities have overtaken me,
    until I cannot see;
  they are more than the hairs of my
    head,
    and my heart fails me.

13 Be pleased, O LORD, to deliver me;
  O LORD, make haste to help me.
14 Let all those be put to shame and
    confusion
  who seek to snatch away my life;
  let those be turned back and brought
    to dishonor
  who desire my hurt.
15 Let those be appalled because of
    their shame
  who say to me, "Aha, Aha!"

16 But may all who seek you
  rejoice and be glad in you;
  may those who love your salvation
  say continually, "Great is the LORD!"
17 As for me, I am poor and needy,
  but the Lord takes thought for me.
  You are my help and my deliverer;
  do not delay, O my God.

Psalm 41
Assurance of God's Help
and a Plea for Healing

To the leader. A Psalm of David.

1 Happy are those who consider the
    poor;[a]
  the LORD delivers them in the day
    of trouble.

2 The LORD protects them and keeps
    them alive;
  they are called happy in the land.
  You do not give them up to the
    will of their enemies.
3 The LORD sustains them on their
    sickbed;
  in their illness you heal all their
    infirmities.[b]

4 As for me, I said, "O LORD, be
    gracious to me;
  heal me, for I have sinned against
    you."
5 My enemies wonder in malice
  when I will die, and my name
    perish.
6 And when they come to see me, they
    utter empty words,
  while their hearts gather mischief;
  when they go out, they tell it
    abroad.
7 All who hate me whisper together
    about me;
  they imagine the worst for me.

8 They think that a deadly thing has
    fastened on me,
  that I will not rise again from
    where I lie.
9 Even my bosom friend in whom I
    trusted,
  who ate of my bread, has lifted the
    heel against me.
10 But you, O LORD, be gracious to me,
  and raise me up, that I may repay
    them.

11 By this I know that you are pleased
    with me;

a Or weak *b* Heb you change all his bed

40:17—As always, God's justice and righteousness take the form of siding with the *poor and needy* (see introduction, "Prayers for Help").

Psalm 41

41:1 *Happy . . . poor*—Recalling 1:1, "happy" (see also 41:2) forms an envelope structure for Book I. Psalm 1 calls "happy" those who orient themselves to God's "instruction" or will, which means considering "the poor" as God considers them (see 40:17). Taken together, 1:1 and 41:1 commend love of God and love of neighbor.

41:4–10—The protection promised in vv. 2–3 does not mean a life free of adversity. While v. 4 seems to suggest a retributional scheme, the rest of the psalm undercuts this, claiming God's presence with the sinner and victim (see introduction, "Prayers for Help"). Thus, it is not surprising that v. 9b is echoed in John 13:18 (see introduction, "The Psalms and the New Testament").

41:11 *Pleased with me*—This is the same word as "delight" in 1:2. The two verses together sug-

because my enemy has not
    triumphed over me.
12 But you have upheld me because of
    my integrity,
    and set me in your presence forever.
13 Blessed be the LORD, the God of
    Israel,
    from everlasting to everlasting.
        Amen and Amen.

BOOK II
(Psalms 42–72)

Psalm 42
Longing for God and His Help in Distress

To the leader. A Maskil of the Korahites.

1 As a deer longs for flowing streams,
    so my soul longs for you, O God.
2 My soul thirsts for God,
    for the living God.
When shall I come and behold
    the face of God?
3 My tears have been my food
    day and night,
while people say to me continually,
    "Where is your God?"

4 These things I remember,
    as I pour out my soul:
how I went with the throng,*a*
    and led them in procession to the
    house of God,
with glad shouts and songs of
    thanksgiving,
    a multitude keeping festival.
5 Why are you cast down, O my soul,
    and why are you disquieted within
    me?

Hope in God; for I shall again praise
    him,
    my help 6 and my God.

My soul is cast down within me;
    therefore I remember you
from the land of Jordan and of
    Hermon,
    from Mount Mizar.
7 Deep calls to deep
    at the thunder of your cataracts;
all your waves and your billows
    have gone over me.
8 By day the LORD commands his
    steadfast love,
    and at night his song is with me,
    a prayer to the God of my life.
9 I say to God, my rock,
    "Why have you forgotten me?
Why must I walk about mournfully
    because the enemy oppresses me?"
10 As with a deadly wound in my body,
    my adversaries taunt me,
while they say to me continually,
    "Where is your God?"

11 Why are you cast down, O my soul,
    and why are you disquieted within
    me?
Hope in God; for I shall again praise
    him,
    my help and my God.

Psalm 43
Prayer to God in Time of Trouble
1 Vindicate me, O God, and defend
    my cause
    against an ungodly people;

a Meaning of Heb uncertain

---

gest a mutuality of "delight" between God and the faithful.

41:13—The concluding doxology for Book I; see similar "book" conclusions in 72:18–19; 89:52; 106:48.

Psalm 42

42:3 *Where is your God?*—The suffering of the faithful frequently raises this question; see v. 10; 79:10; 115:2.

42:5—The refrain recurs in v. 11 and in 43:5 (Pss. 42–43 are a single poem). The faithful inevitably

have doubts and questions (see also 42:9; 43:2), but they never stop hoping in God or looking to God for help (see 3:2, 7–8).

42:8 *Steadfast love*—Regularly cited as the basis for trusting in God (see note at 5:7).

Psalm 43

43:1 *Vindicate me*—More literally, "Establish justice for me," further evidence that the psalmists never give up on God (see 26:1; 35:24), who wills justice and righteousness (see introduction, "Psalms 1–2 and the Shape of the Psalter"; 96:11–13).

from those who are deceitful and
 unjust
  deliver me!
2 For you are the God in whom I take
  refuge;
 why have you cast me off?
 Why must I walk about mournfully
  because of the oppression of the
  enemy?

3 O send out your light and your
  truth;
  let them lead me;
 let them bring me to your holy hill
  and to your dwelling.
4 Then I will go to the altar of God,
  to God my exceeding joy;
 and I will praise you with the harp,
  O God, my God.

5 Why are you cast down, O my
  soul,
 and why are you disquieted within
  me?
 Hope in God; for I shall again praise
  him,
  my help and my God.

Psalm 44
National Lament and Prayer for Help
To the leader. Of the Korahites. A Maskil.

1 We have heard with our ears, O God,
  our ancestors have told us,
 what deeds you performed in their
  days,
  in the days of old:
2 you with your own hand drove out
  the nations,
  but them you planted;
 you afflicted the peoples,
  but them you set free;

3 for not by their own sword did they
  win the land,
 nor did their own arm give them
  victory;
 but your right hand, and your arm,
  and the light of your countenance,
  for you delighted in them.

4 You are my King and my God;
 you command[a] victories for Jacob.
5 Through you we push down our
  foes;
 through your name we tread down
  our assailants.
6 For not in my bow do I trust,
  nor can my sword save me.
7 But you have saved us from our foes,
  and have put to confusion those
  who hate us.
8 In God we have boasted continually,
 and we will give thanks to your
  name forever.   *Selah*

9 Yet you have rejected us and abased
  us,
 and have not gone out with our
  armies.
10 You made us turn back from the foe,
 and our enemies have gotten spoil.
11 You have made us like sheep for
  slaughter,
 and have scattered us among the
  nations.
12 You have sold your people for a
  trifle,
 demanding no high price for
  them.
13 You have made us the taunt of our
  neighbors,

[a] Gk Syr: Heb *You are my King, O God; command*

43:3 *Holy hill*—See 2:6; 3:4. Originally perhaps a hope for returning to the temple, it functions to articulate any request for an experience of God's presence and power.

Psalm 44

44:4 *My King*—The sovereignty of God (see introduction, "Psalms 1–2 and the Shape of the Psalter") is affirmed in the context of remembrance (vv. 1–3, 7), *trust* (vv. 5–6), and celebration (v. 8).

44:9–22—Nothing in vv. 1–8 prepares for the abrupt shift at v. 9. The people are suffering; they claim innocence; and they blame God. The historical circumstances are unclear; but the similar vv. 11, 22 are reminiscent of Isa. 53:7. This kind of thinking, which probably grew out of the exile, opened the way for a new understanding of the suffering that seems an inevitable part of the vocation of serving God and doing God's will—that is, of participating in the *covenant* (Ps. 44:17; see Matt. 5:10–11; Rom. 8:35–36).

the derision and scorn of those
   around us.
14 You have made us a byword among
      the nations,
   a laughingstock*a* among the
      peoples.
15 All day long my disgrace is before
      me,
   and shame has covered my face
16 at the words of the taunters and
      revilers,
   at the sight of the enemy and the
      avenger.

17 All this has come upon us,
   yet we have not forgotten you,
   or been false to your covenant.
18 Our heart has not turned back,
   nor have our steps departed from
      your way,
19 yet you have broken us in the haunt
      of jackals,
   and covered us with deep
      darkness.

20 If we had forgotten the name of our
      God,
   or spread out our hands to a
      strange god,
21 would not God discover this?
   For he knows the secrets of the
      heart.
22 Because of you we are being killed
      all day long,
   and accounted as sheep for the
      slaughter.

23 Rouse yourself! Why do you sleep,
      O Lord?
   Awake, do not cast us off forever!
24 Why do you hide your face?
   Why do you forget our affliction
      and oppression?

25 For we sink down to the dust;
   our bodies cling to the ground.
26 Rise up, come to our help.
   Redeem us for the sake of your
      steadfast love.

Psalm 45
Ode for a Royal Wedding

*To the leader: according to Lilies. Of the
Korahites. A Maskil. A love song.*

1 My heart overflows with a goodly
      theme;
   I address my verses to the king;
   my tongue is like the pen of a
      ready scribe.

2 You are the most handsome of men;
   grace is poured upon your lips;
   therefore God has blessed you
      forever.
3 Gird your sword on your thigh,
      O mighty one,
   in your glory and majesty.

4 In your majesty ride on victoriously
   for the cause of truth and to
      defend*b* the right;
   let your right hand teach you
      dread deeds.
5 Your arrows are sharp
   in the heart of the king's enemies;
   the peoples fall under you.

6 Your throne, O God,*c* endures
      forever and ever.
   Your royal scepter is a scepter of
      equity;
7   you love righteousness and hate
      wickedness.
   Therefore God, your God, has
      anointed you

a Heb *a shaking of the head* *b* Cn: Heb *and the meekness of* *c* Or *Your throne
is a throne of God, it*

44:23–26—The people correctly affirm that God
cares about **affliction and oppression** (see introduction, "Prayers for Help"), because of God's
steadfast love (see 5:7).

Psalm 45

45 (Title) *A love song*—Unique in the Psalter, Ps.
45 perhaps was written for use in royal wedding
ceremonies (see *king* in v. 1 and *anointed you* in
v. 7; see 2:2).

**45:7 *You love righteousness*—A reminder that
the king's vocation was to enact the justice and
righteousness that God wills (see 72:1–7). The
relationship between God and king is so intimate
that the king even appears to be addressed *O
God* (45:6), rather than the more usual "son" of
God (2:7); but the text is uncertain.

with the oil of gladness beyond
　　your companions;
8　your robes are all fragrant with
　　myrrh and aloes and cassia.
From ivory palaces stringed
　　instruments make you glad;
9　daughters of kings are among your
　　ladies of honor;
at your right hand stands the
　　queen in gold of Ophir.

10　Hear, O daughter, consider and
　　incline your ear;
forget your people and your
　　father's house,
11　and the king will desire your
　　beauty.
Since he is your lord, bow to him;
12　the people[a] of Tyre will seek your
　　favor with gifts,
the richest of the people [13]with all
　　kinds of wealth.

The princess is decked in her
　　chamber with gold-woven
　　robes;[b]
14　in many-colored robes she is led to
　　the king;
behind her the virgins, her
　　companions, follow.
15　With joy and gladness they are led
　　along
as they enter the palace of the king.

16　In the place of ancestors you,
　　O king,[c] shall have sons;
you will make them princes in all
　　the earth.
17　I will cause your name to be
　　celebrated in all generations;
therefore the peoples will praise
　　you forever and ever.

Psalm 46
God's Defense of His City and People

*To the leader. Of the Korahites. According
to Alamoth. A Song.*

1　God is our refuge and strength,
　　a very present[d] help in trouble.
2　Therefore we will not fear, though
　　the earth should change,
though the mountains shake in the
　　heart of the sea;
3　though its waters roar and foam,
　　though the mountains tremble
　　with its tumult.　　*Selah*

4　There is a river whose streams make
　　glad the city of God,
the holy habitation of the Most
　　High.
5　God is in the midst of the city;[e] it
　　shall not be moved;
God will help it when the morning
　　dawns.
6　The nations are in an uproar, the
　　kingdoms totter;
he utters his voice, the earth
　　melts.
7　The LORD of hosts is with us;
　　the God of Jacob is our refuge.[f]
　　　　　　　　　　Selah

8　Come, behold the works of the
　　LORD;
see what desolations he has
　　brought on the earth.
9　He makes wars cease to the end of
　　the earth;
he breaks the bow, and shatters the
　　spear;
he burns the shields with fire.

a Heb *daughter*　b Or *people.*　13*All glorious is the princess within; gold
embroidery is her clothing*　c Heb lacks *O king*　d Or *well proved*　e Heb *of
it*　f Or *fortress*

45:10–15—The advice to and description of **the
queen** (v. 9) reflect the arrangements of a patriarchal culture.

Psalm 46

46:1–3—The ancients believed that the mountains held up the sky and held back the cosmic
waters. For the mountains to **shake** meant the
world was collapsing.

46:4 *The city of God*—Jerusalem is seen as a

stable anchor amid cosmic (vv. 1–3) and international chaos (v. 6). Its name contains the word
shalom, "peace"; and elsewhere it is the site for
God's establishment of worldwide justice and
peace (see 87:4–6; 122:5–8; Isa. 2:2–4; Mic.
4:1–3).

46:8–9—God's *desolations* actually involve the
destruction of the implements of war (v. 9).

10 "Be still, and know that I am God!
    I am exalted among the nations,
    I am exalted in the earth."
11 The LORD of hosts is with us;
    the God of Jacob is our refuge.*a*

Selah

Psalm 47
God's Rule over the Nations
To the leader. Of the Korahites. A Psalm.

1 Clap your hands, all you peoples;
    shout to God with loud songs of
    joy.
2 For the LORD, the Most High, is
    awesome,
    a great king over all the earth.
3 He subdued peoples under us,
    and nations under our feet.
4 He chose our heritage for us,
    the pride of Jacob whom he loves.

Selah

5 God has gone up with a shout,
    the LORD with the sound of a
    trumpet.
6 Sing praises to God, sing praises;
    sing praises to our King, sing
    praises.
7 For God is the king of all the
    earth;
    sing praises with a psalm.*b*

8 God is king over the nations;
    God sits on his holy throne.
9 The princes of the peoples gather

as the people of the God of
    Abraham.
For the shields of the earth belong to
    God;
    he is highly exalted.

Psalm 48
The Glory and Strength of Zion
A Song. A Psalm of the Korahites.

1 Great is the LORD and greatly to be
    praised
    in the city of our God.
His holy mountain, 2beautiful in
    elevation,
    is the joy of all the earth,
Mount Zion, in the far north,
    the city of the great King.
3 Within its citadels God
    has shown himself a sure defense.

4 Then the kings assembled,
    they came on together.
5 As soon as they saw it, they were
    astounded;
    they were in panic, they took to
    flight;
6 trembling took hold of them there,
    pains as of a woman in labor,
7 as when an east wind shatters
    the ships of Tarshish.
8 As we have heard, so have we seen
    in the city of the LORD of hosts,
in the city of our God,

a Or *fortress* *b* Heb *Maskil*

46:10 *Be still*—More accurately "Stop," or something like "Cease fire." The recognition of God's world-encompassing sovereignty is the basis for peace (see introduction, "Songs of Praise").

Psalm 47

47:2 *Great king*—The worldwide sovereignty of God implied in Ps. 46 is explicit in 47:1–4 (see also *our King* in v. 6, *king of all the earth* in v. 7, and *king over the nations* in v. 8). God's royal will for the world is justice, righteousness, and peace (see introduction, "Psalms 1–2 and the Shape of the Psalter"; 29:11; 96:11–13).

47:9—Although the usual words for defining God's will do not appear here, v. 9 portrays what world peace looks like—God gathers representatives of all nations as God's own people (see Gen. 12:1–3; Isa. 19:23–25). The logic is stun-

ningly simple—one God (who claims all nations), one worldwide family! As v. 9 suggests, to adopt this logic will mean a surrender of weapons to God and God's purposes—in essence, waging peace.

Psalm 48

48:1 *City of our God*—See v. 8; 46:4. Because God claims the whole world (see Ps. 47), God's city must have universal significance (see Pss. 46, 76, 87, 122).

48:2 *North*—Hebrew *zaphon*, it is the name of the mountain of the Canaanite pantheon. The claim for Zion expresses God's universal preeminence (see Ps. 82).

48:4–8—The hyperbole is palpable; the point is that all other kings yield to the *great King* (v. 2; see 47:2).

which God establishes forever.
Selah

9 We ponder your steadfast love, O God,
    in the midst of your temple.
10 Your name, O God, like your praise,
    reaches to the ends of the earth.
    Your right hand is filled with victory.
11   Let Mount Zion be glad,
    let the towns*a* of Judah rejoice
    because of your judgments.

12 Walk about Zion, go all around it,
    count its towers,
13 consider well its ramparts;
    go through its citadels,
    that you may tell the next generation
14   that this is God,
    our God forever and ever.
    He will be our guide forever.

Psalm 49
The Folly of Trust in Riches

To the leader. Of the Korahites. A Psalm.

1 Hear this, all you peoples;
    give ear, all inhabitants of the
        world,
2 both low and high,
    rich and poor together.
3 My mouth shall speak wisdom;
    the meditation of my heart shall be
        understanding.
4 I will incline my ear to a proverb;
    I will solve my riddle to the music
        of the harp.

5 Why should I fear in times of
        trouble,

when the iniquity of my
        persecutors surrounds me,
6 those who trust in their wealth
    and boast of the abundance of
        their riches?
7 Truly, no ransom avails for one's
        life,*b*
    there is no price one can give to
        God for it.
8 For the ransom of life is costly,
    and can never suffice,
9 that one should live on forever
    and never see the grave.*c*

10 When we look at the wise, they die;
    fool and dolt perish together
    and leave their wealth to others.
11 Their graves*d* are their homes
        forever,
    their dwelling places to all
        generations,
    though they named lands their own.
12 Mortals cannot abide in their pomp;
    they are like the animals that
        perish.

13 Such is the fate of the foolhardy,
    the end of those*e* who are pleased
        with their lot.   *Selah*
14 Like sheep they are appointed for
        Sheol;
    Death shall be their shepherd;
    straight to the grave they descend,*f*
    and their form shall waste away;

a Heb *daughters* *b* Another reading is *no one can ransom a brother*
c Heb *the pit* *d* Gk Syr Compare Tg: Heb *their inward* (thought)
e Tg: Heb *after them* *f* Cn: Heb *the upright shall have dominion over them in the morning*

48:9–11—This psalm was perhaps used as a pilgrimage psalm (see Ps. 122). The city itself puts visitors in touch with God's character—**steadfast love** (v. 9; see 5:7)—and God's will—"righteousness" (v. 10; NRSV **victory**) and "deeds of justice" (v. 11, NRSV **judgments**; see introduction, "Psalms 1–2 and the Shape of the Psalter"; 96:11–13).

48:12–14—A tour of God's city means an enduring experience of God (see vv. 9–11) that motivates the visitor to educate future generations about God and God's will.

Psalm 49

49:3 *Wisdom*—Vocabulary of the biblical Wisdom literature is prevalent in vv. 1–4.

49:6 *Trust*—A key issue in the Psalms is "trust" (see introduction, "Psalms of Trust"). Then, as now, people are inclined to trust wealth rather than God (see 52:7; Luke 12:13–21).

49:12—See v. 20. Death should be a reminder that wealth and worldly reputation (see v. 18) are illusory.

49:14–15 *Sheol*—See 6:5. Verse 15 seems to expand the usual understanding of Sheol as a place to which even God has no access (see 22:29; 73:24; 139:8).

Sheol shall be their home.*a*

15 But God will ransom my soul from
    the power of Sheol,
    for he will receive me.   *Selah*

16 Do not be afraid when some become
    rich,
    when the wealth of their houses
      increases.

17 For when they die they will carry
    nothing away;
    their wealth will not go down after
      them.

18 Though in their lifetime they count
    themselves happy
    —for you are praised when you do
      well for yourself—

19 they*b* will go to the company of their
    ancestors,
    who will never again see the light.

20 Mortals cannot abide in their
    pomp;
    they are like the animals that
      perish.

Psalm 50

The Acceptable Sacrifice

A Psalm of Asaph.

1 The mighty one, God the LORD,
    speaks and summons the earth
    from the rising of the sun to its
      setting.

2 Out of Zion, the perfection of
    beauty,
    God shines forth.

3 Our God comes and does not keep
    silence,
    before him is a devouring fire,
    and a mighty tempest all around
      him.

4 He calls to the heavens above

and to the earth, that he may judge
    his people:

5 "Gather to me my faithful ones,
    who made a covenant with me by
      sacrifice!"

6 The heavens declare his
    righteousness,
    for God himself is judge.   *Selah*

7 "Hear, O my people, and I will
    speak,
    O Israel, I will testify against you.
    I am God, your God.

8 Not for your sacrifices do I rebuke
    you;
    your burnt offerings are
      continually before me.

9 I will not accept a bull from your
    house,
    or goats from your folds.

10 For every wild animal of the forest is
    mine,
    the cattle on a thousand hills.

11 I know all the birds of the air,*c*
    and all that moves in the field is
      mine.

12 "If I were hungry, I would not tell
    you,
    for the world and all that is in it is
      mine.

13 Do I eat the flesh of bulls,
    or drink the blood of goats?

14 Offer to God a sacrifice of
    thanksgiving,*d*
    and pay your vows to the Most
      High.

15 Call on me in the day of trouble;
    I will deliver you, and you shall
      glorify me."

a Meaning of Heb uncertain   *b* Cn: Heb *you*   *c* Gk Syr Tg: Heb *mountains*
d Or *make thanksgiving your sacrifice to God*

Psalm 50

50:2 *Zion . . . beauty*—See 48:2. Psalm 50:2–3 is a theophany (see 18:7–19), the function of which is to portray God's sovereignty.

50:4 *Judge his people*—As always, the sovereign God wills justice and righteousness (see introduction, "Psalms 1–2 and the Shape of the Psalter"; 96:11–13). Because God's own people have gone astray (50:7–22), setting things right here means

judgment (see also *righteousness* and *judge* in v. 6).

50:5 *Covenant*—Recalls the covenant-making ceremony in Exod. 24:7–10, where the people pledge to do God's will.

50:7–15—Like the prophets, the Psalms call for a proper understanding of sacrifice—not rote ritual but practice grounded in gratitude (see 40:6–8; 51:16–19; Hos. 6:6; Amos 5:21–24).

16 But to the wicked God says:
   "What right have you to recite my
     statutes,
   or take my covenant on your lips?
17 For you hate discipline,
   and you cast my words behind you.
18 You make friends with a thief when
     you see one,
   and you keep company with
     adulterers.

19 "You give your mouth free rein for
     evil,
   and your tongue frames deceit.
20 You sit and speak against your kin;
   you slander your own mother's
     child.
21 These things you have done and I
     have been silent;
   you thought that I was one just
     like yourself.
   But now I rebuke you, and lay the
     charge before you.

22 "Mark this, then, you who forget God,
   or I will tear you apart, and there
     will be no one to deliver.
23 Those who bring thanksgiving as
     their sacrifice honor me;
   to those who go the right way[a]
   I will show the salvation of God."

Psalm 51
Prayer for Cleansing and Pardon

To the leader. A Psalm of David, when the prophet Nathan came to him, after he had gone in to Bathsheba.

1 Have mercy on me, O God,
   according to your steadfast love;
   according to your abundant mercy
     blot out my transgressions.
2 Wash me thoroughly from my
     iniquity,
   and cleanse me from my sin.

3 For I know my transgressions,
   and my sin is ever before me.
4 Against you, you alone, have I sinned,
   and done what is evil in your sight,
   so that you are justified in your
     sentence
   and blameless when you pass
     judgment.
5 Indeed, I was born guilty,
   a sinner when my mother
     conceived me.

6 You desire truth in the inward being;[b]
   therefore teach me wisdom in my
     secret heart.
7 Purge me with hyssop, and I shall be
     clean;
   wash me, and I shall be whiter
     than snow.
8 Let me hear joy and gladness;
   let the bones that you have
     crushed rejoice.
9 Hide your face from my sins,
   and blot out all my iniquities.

10 Create in me a clean heart, O God,
   and put a new and right[c] spirit
     within me.
11 Do not cast me away from your
     presence,

[a] Heb *who set a way*   [b] Meaning of Heb uncertain   [c] Or *steadfast*

50:16–21—Here *the wicked* are God's people, whose daily lives do not reflect covenant behavior any better than their worship does (see vv. 7–15).

50:23—See v. 14. Gratitude indicates a right relationship with God; see Rom. 12:1–2.

Psalm 51

51 (Title)—See Ps. 3; 2 Sam. 11:1–12:25. This is one of the church's seven Penitential Psalms.

51:1 *Mercy . . . steadfast love . . . mercy*—The confession of sin and prayer for forgiveness (vv. 1–12) focus first on God's character (see Exod. 34:6–7). On "steadfast love," see notes at 5:7;

36:5. The second "mercy" is related to a noun that means "womb," and could be translated "motherly compassion."

51:4 *Justified . . . judgment*—The two Hebrew words here are from roots that mean "righteousness" and "justice," the two roots that summarize God's will (see introduction, "Psalms 1–2 and the Shape of the Psalter"; 96:11–13). Thus, the psalmist finally suggests that God sets things right by way of forgiveness—in other words, God establishes justice by showing grace (see Rom. 3:4, where Paul quotes this verse).

51:10–12—Forgiveness offers the possibility of a new creation; see 2 Cor. 5:17–20.

and do not take your holy spirit
from me.
12 Restore to me the joy of your
salvation,
and sustain in me a willing*a* spirit.

13 Then I will teach transgressors your
ways,
and sinners will return to you.
14 Deliver me from bloodshed, O God,
O God of my salvation,
and my tongue will sing aloud of
your deliverance.

15 O Lord, open my lips,
and my mouth will declare your
praise.
16 For you have no delight in sacrifice;
if I were to give a burnt offering,
you would not be pleased.
17 The sacrifice acceptable to God*b* is a
broken spirit;
a broken and contrite heart,
O God, you will not despise.

18 Do good to Zion in your good
pleasure;
rebuild the walls of Jerusalem,
19 then you will delight in right
sacrifices,
in burnt offerings and whole burnt
offerings;
then bulls will be offered on your
altar.

Psalm 52
Judgment on the Deceitful

*To the leader. A Maskil of David, when Doeg
the Edomite came to Saul and said to him,
"David has come to the house of Ahimelech."*

1 Why do you boast, O mighty one,

of mischief done against the
godly?*c*
All day long 2 you are plotting
destruction.
Your tongue is like a sharp razor,
you worker of treachery.
3 You love evil more than good,
and lying more than speaking the
truth.   *Selah*
4 You love all words that devour,
O deceitful tongue.

5 But God will break you down
forever;
he will snatch and tear you from
your tent;
he will uproot you from the land
of the living.   *Selah*
6 The righteous will see, and
fear,
and will laugh at the evildoer,*d*
saying,
7 "See the one who would not take
refuge in God,
but trusted in abundant riches,
and sought refuge in wealth!"*e*

8 But I am like a green olive tree
in the house of God.
I trust in the steadfast love of God
forever and ever.
9 I will thank you forever,
because of what you have
done.
In the presence of the faithful
I will proclaim*f* your name, for it
is good.

a Or generous *b* Or My sacrifice, O God, *c* Cn Compare Syr: Heb *the
kindness of God* *d* Heb *him* *e* Syr Tg: Heb *in his destruction* *f* Cn: Heb
wait for

51:13–17—See 32:8–9 where the forgiven psalmist also becomes a teacher of God's ways.

Psalm 52

52 (Title)—See Ps. 3; 1 Sam. 21–22. The quote of
1 Sam. 22:9 identifies *Doeg* as **the mighty one**
(52:1) whose behavior is described in vv. 1–4;
however, the psalm is appropriate wherever and
whenever the faithful are threatened.

52:5–6—The attack on the wicked serves the
purpose of establishing justice in a situation of
oppression (see introduction, "Prayers for Help").

52:7 *Refuge*—See introduction, "Psalms of Trust."
A persistent temptation, then and now, is to trust
our own wealth and resources more than God
(see 49:6).

52:8–9—Recalling 1:3, the psalmist is like a
healthy tree, renouncing *refuge* (52:7) or trust
in things in favor of trusting God's *steadfast love*
(see 5:7; 13:5). This is true happiness (1:1; 2:12)
and prosperity (1:3), evidenced in gratitude (see
50:14, 23).

Psalm 53
Denunciation of Godlessness

To the leader: according to Mahalath.
A Maskil of David.

1 Fools say in their hearts, "There is
   no God."
   They are corrupt, they commit
   abominable acts;
   there is no one who does good.

2 God looks down from heaven on
   humankind
   to see if there are any who are
   wise,
   who seek after God.

3 They have all fallen away, they are all
   alike perverse;
   there is no one who does good,
   no, not one.

4 Have they no knowledge, those
   evildoers,
   who eat up my people as they eat
   bread,
   and do not call upon God?

5 There they shall be in great
   terror,
   in terror such as has not been.
   For God will scatter the bones of the
   ungodly;*a*
   they will be put to shame,*b* for God
   has rejected them.

6 O that deliverance for Israel would
   come from Zion!
   When God restores the fortunes of
   his people,

Jacob will rejoice; Israel will be
   glad.

Psalm 54
Prayer for Vindication

To the leader: with stringed instruments. A
Maskil of David, when the Ziphites went and
told Saul, "David is in hiding among us."

1 Save me, O God, by your name,
   and vindicate me by your might.

2 Hear my prayer, O God;
   give ear to the words of my mouth.

3 For the insolent have risen against
   me,
   the ruthless seek my life;
   they do not set God before them.
                                   Selah

4 But surely, God is my helper;
   the Lord is the upholder of*c* my
   life.

5 He will repay my enemies for their
   evil.
   In your faithfulness, put an end to
   them.

6 With a freewill offering I will
   sacrifice to you;
   I will give thanks to your name,
   O LORD, for it is good.

7 For he has delivered me from every
   trouble,
   and my eye has looked in triumph
   on my enemies.

*a*Cn Compare Gk Syr: Heb *him who encamps against you*   *b*Gk: Heb *you
have put* (them) *to shame*   *c*Gk Syr Jerome: Heb *is of those who uphold* or *is
with those who uphold*

Psalm 53

53:1–6—See Ps. 14, which is nearly identical,
with the exception that 53:5 focuses more on
God's action against the wicked (see 52:5–7) than
does 14:5–6.

Psalm 54

54 (Title)—See Ps. 3; 1 Sam. 23:13–15.

54:1 Save . . . vindicate me—The latter plea
could be translated "establish justice for me"
(see 26:1; 35:24). Justice and righteousness
are the essence of God's will (see introduction, "Psalms 1–2 and the Shape of the Psalter";
96:11–13), and the parallelism here makes it

clear that God's justice means life for the threatened and victimized (see 54:3).

54:4 God is my helper—Located at the center
of the psalm, this affirmation is also of central
importance theologically. Whether v. 7 narrates
an actual deliverance is unclear, but the threatened psalmists never stop trusting that God sides
with the victimized (see introduction, "Prayers
for Help"), and they never fail to express their
gratitude (v. 6; see 52:9).

54:5—In situations of victimization, a prayer for
vengeance is a plea for justice (see introduction,
"Prayers for Help").

Psalm 55

Complaint about a Friend's Treachery

To the leader: with stringed instruments.
A Maskil of David.

1 Give ear to my prayer, O God;
    do not hide yourself from my
      supplication.
2 Attend to me, and answer me;
    I am troubled in my complaint.
  I am distraught ³by the noise of the
      enemy,
    because of the clamor of the
      wicked.
  For they bring*ᵃ* trouble upon me,
    and in anger they cherish enmity
      against me.

4 My heart is in anguish within me,
    the terrors of death have fallen
      upon me.
5 Fear and trembling come upon me,
    and horror overwhelms me.
6 And I say, "O that I had wings like a
      dove!
    I would fly away and be at rest;
7 truly, I would flee far away;
    I would lodge in the wilderness;
                              Selah
8 I would hurry to find a shelter for
      myself
    from the raging wind and
      tempest."

9 Confuse, O Lord, confound their
      speech;
    for I see violence and strife in the
      city.
10 Day and night they go around it
    on its walls,
  and iniquity and trouble are
      within it;

11 ruin is in its midst;
  oppression and fraud
    do not depart from its
      marketplace.
12 It is not enemies who taunt me—
    I could bear that;
  it is not adversaries who deal
      insolently with me—
    I could hide from them.
13 But it is you, my equal,
    my companion, my familiar friend,
14 with whom I kept pleasant company;
    we walked in the house of God
      with the throng.
15 Let death come upon them;
    let them go down alive to Sheol;
  for evil is in their homes and in
      their hearts.
16 But I call upon God,
    and the Lord will save me.
17 Evening and morning and at noon
    I utter my complaint and moan,
    and he will hear my voice.
18 He will redeem me unharmed
    from the battle that I wage,
    for many are arrayed against me.
19 God, who is enthroned from of old,
                              Selah
  will hear, and will humble them—
  because they do not change,
    and do not fear God.

20 My companion laid hands on a
      friend
    and violated a covenant with me *ᵇ*
21 with speech smoother than butter,
    but with a heart set on war;
  with words that were softer than oil,
    but in fact were drawn swords.

ᵃ Cn Compare Gk: Heb *they cause to totter*   *ᵇ* Heb lacks *with me*

Psalm 55

55:1–8—See Jer. 9 for a similar description of oppressive conditions, from which even "the birds
. . . have fled" (Jer. 9:10; see Ps. 55:7–8; 11:1–3).

55:9—Not only does this verse recall Gen. 11:1–
9, but also Psalm 55:9–11 is a chillingly relevant
description of many contemporary cities.

55:12–14—General societal chaos, then and
now, is accompanied by skewed personal rela-

tionships (see also vv. 20–21; 31:11; 41:9; 88:8,
18; Jer. 9:4–6; Mic. 7:5–6).

55:16–19—Although no human can be trusted,
God can be (see v. 23). The word **unharmed**
(v. 18) is literally "in peace"; and peace is the
outcome of the justice and righteousness that
the sovereign God wills (see 29:11; 72:1–7). The
psalmist looks for help to the sovereign God (see
enthroned in 55:19).

22 Cast your burden[a] on the LORD,
   and he will sustain you;
he will never permit
   the righteous to be moved.

23 But you, O God, will cast them down
      into the lowest pit;
   the bloodthirsty and treacherous
      shall not live out half their days.
   But I will trust in you.

Psalm 56

Trust in God under Persecution

*To the leader: according to The Dove on Far-
off Terebinths. Of David. A Miktam, when
the Philistines seized him in Gath.*

1 Be gracious to me, O God, for
      people trample on me;
   all day long foes oppress me;
2 my enemies trample on me all day
      long,
   for many fight against me.
   O Most High, ³ when I am afraid,
   I put my trust in you.
4 In God, whose word I praise,
   in God I trust; I am not afraid;
   what can flesh do to me?

5 All day long they seek to injure my
      cause;
   all their thoughts are against me
      for evil.
6 They stir up strife, they lurk,
   they watch my steps.
   As they hoped to have my life,
7 so repay[b] them for their crime;
   in wrath cast down the peoples,
      O God!

8 You have kept count of my tossings;
   put my tears in your bottle.
   Are they not in your record?
9 Then my enemies will retreat
   in the day when I call.
   This I know, that[c] God is for me.
10 In God, whose word I praise,
   in the LORD, whose word I praise,
11 in God I trust; I am not afraid.
   What can a mere mortal do
      to me?

12 My vows to you I must perform,
      O God;
   I will render thank offerings to
      you.
13 For you have delivered my soul from
      death,
   and my feet from falling,
   so that I may walk before God
   in the light of life.

Psalm 57

Praise and Assurance under Persecution

*To the leader: Do Not Destroy. Of David. A
Miktam, when he fled from Saul, in the cave.*

1 Be merciful to me, O God, be
      merciful to me,
   for in you my soul takes refuge;
   in the shadow of your wings I will
      take refuge,
   until the destroying storms pass
      by.
2 I cry to God Most High,
   to God who fulfills his purpose
      for me.

[a] Or *Cast what he has given you*   [b] Cn: Heb *rescue*   [c] Or *because*

55:22—The psalmist's advice is a profession of trust that makes it clear that the faithful life inevitably involves hurt and hope, threat and **trust** (see v. 23), pain and praise (see introduction, "Prayers for Help").

Psalm 56

56 (Title)—See Ps. 3; 1 Sam. 21:10–14.

56:3–4 *Afraid . . . not afraid*—The movement from "afraid" to "not afraid" is a matter of **trust** (see also v. 11), always a crucial issue in the Psalms and in life (see introduction, "Psalms of Trust"; 4:5; 13:5; 52:7–8; 55:23).

56:7—The desire for vengeance is a plea for justice (see introduction, "Prayers for Help").

56:8—See 40:7 for a similar statement of God's recordkeeping.

56:9 *For me*—God always stands with the threatened and the victimized (see introduction, "Prayers for Help").

56:12–13—Gratitude characterizes the faithful life (see note at 54:4).

Psalm 57

57 (Title)—See Ps. 3; 1 Sam. 22:1; 24:3.

57:1 *Refuge*—A persistent theme in the Psalter, especially Books I–II (see introduction, "Psalms of Trust"). *Shadow of your wings*—An image of God's protecting presence (see 17:8).

³ He will send from heaven and
    save me,
  he will put to shame those who
    trample on me.   *Selah*
God will send forth his steadfast love
  and his faithfulness.

⁴ I lie down among lions
  that greedily devour*ᵃ* human prey;
their teeth are spears and arrows,
  their tongues sharp swords.
⁵ Be exalted, O God, above the
    heavens.
  Let your glory be over all the
    earth.

⁶ They set a net for my steps;
  my soul was bowed down.
They dug a pit in my path,
  but they have fallen into it
    themselves.   *Selah*
⁷ My heart is steadfast, O God,
  my heart is steadfast.
I will sing and make melody.
⁸   Awake, my soul!
Awake, O harp and lyre!
  I will awake the dawn.
⁹ I will give thanks to you, O Lord,
  among the peoples;
I will sing praises to you among
  the nations.
¹⁰ For your steadfast love is as high as
    the heavens;
  your faithfulness extends to the
    clouds.

¹¹ Be exalted, O God, above the
    heavens.

Let your glory be over all the
  earth.

Psalm 58
Prayer for Vengeance

To the leader: Do Not Destroy. Of David.
A Miktam.

¹ Do you indeed decree what is right,
  you gods?*ᵇ*
  Do you judge people fairly?
² No, in your hearts you devise
    wrongs;
  your hands deal out violence on
    earth.

³ The wicked go astray from the
    womb;
  they err from their birth, speaking
    lies.
⁴ They have venom like the venom of
    a serpent,
  like the deaf adder that stops its ear,
⁵ so that it does not hear the voice of
    charmers
  or of the cunning enchanter.

⁶ O God, break the teeth in their
    mouths;
  tear out the fangs of the young
    lions, O Lᴏʀᴅ!
⁷ Let them vanish like water that runs
    away;
  like grass let them be trodden
    down*ᶜ* and wither.
⁸ Let them be like the snail that
    dissolves into slime;

ᵃ Cn: Heb *are aflame for* *ᵇ* Or *mighty lords* *ᶜ* Cn: Meaning of Heb
uncertain

57:3 *Steadfast love and . . . faithfulness*—These
are fundamental attributes of God; see 5:7; 36:5;
Exod. 34:6–7. By the end of the psalm (57:10),
and despite the current turmoil (vv. 4, 6), the
psalmist envisions them filling the universe (see
33:5; 36:5–6).

57:5, 11—Like the similar vv. 3 and 10, this
refrain portrays God's presence pervading the
world. Thus, amid the present misery of life, the
psalmist can perceive the mysterious presence of
divine love. Psalm 57:7–10 recurs as 108:1–4.

Psalm 58

58:1 *Right*—This word, along with *judge*, sug-

gests that the psalm will explore the issue of
justice and righteousness, the fundamentals of
God's will (see introduction, "Psalms 1–2 and the
Shape of the Psalter"; 96:11–13). *You gods*—It is
not certain that other gods are being addressed
(see NRSV footnote), but it is likely, especially in
light of Ps. 82. In any case, the gods have their
followers, then and now—persons perfectly willing to assert themselves and their violent agendas
over against God's justice, righteousness, and
peace (see 58:3–5).

58:6–9—In view of the *violence* (v. 2) that already exists, the plea is for justice (see introduction, "Prayers for Help").

like the untimely birth that never
    sees the sun.
⁹ Sooner than your pots can feel the
    heat of thorns,
    whether green or ablaze, may he
    sweep them away!

¹⁰ The righteous will rejoice when they
    see vengeance done;
    they will bathe their feet in the
    blood of the wicked.
¹¹ People will say, "Surely there is a
    reward for the righteous;
    surely there is a God who judges
    on earth."

Psalm 59

Prayer for Deliverance from Enemies

*To the leader: Do Not Destroy. Of David. A
Miktam, when Saul ordered his house to be
watched in order to kill him.*

¹ Deliver me from my enemies, O my
    God;
    protect me from those who rise up
    against me.
² Deliver me from those who work
    evil;
    from the bloodthirsty save me.

³ Even now they lie in wait for my
    life;
    the mighty stir up strife
    against me.
For no transgression or sin of mine,
    O LORD,
⁴   for no fault of mine, they run and
    make ready.

Rouse yourself, come to my help and
    see!

⁵ You, LORD God of hosts, are God
    of Israel.
Awake to punish all the nations;
    spare none of those who
    treacherously plot evil.   *Selah*

⁶ Each evening they come back,
    howling like dogs
    and prowling about the city.
⁷ There they are, bellowing with their
    mouths,
    with sharp words*a* on their lips—
    for "Who," they think,*b* "will hear
    us?"

⁸ But you laugh at them, O LORD;
    you hold all the nations in
    derision.
⁹ O my strength, I will watch for
    you;
    for you, O God, are my fortress.
¹⁰ My God in his steadfast love will
    meet me;
    my God will let me look in
    triumph on my enemies.

¹¹ Do not kill them, or my people may
    forget;
    make them totter by your power,
    and bring them down,
    O Lord, our shield.
¹² For the sin of their mouths, the
    words of their lips,
    let them be trapped in their pride.
For the cursing and lies that they
    utter,
¹³   consume them in wrath;
    consume them until they are no
    more.

a Heb *with swords*   *b* Heb lacks *they think*

58:11 *A God who judges on earth*—Better, "a
God who establishes justice on earth." But in the
face of prevailing injustice, God must "fight" for
justice and peace.

Psalm 59

59 (Title)—See Ps. 3; 1 Sam. 19:11.

59:1–5—As is regularly the case, the psalmist is
opposed. The prayer for *help* (v. 4) and plea for
punishment of *the nations* (see also vv. 11–13)
constitute essentially a victim's prayer for justice
(see introduction, "Prayers for Help").

59:6, 14—The ancient imagery captures well

the violent, dog-eat-dog world that often passes
today for business as usual.

59:8—God's laughter affirms God's sovereignty
amid opposition (see 2:4).

59:9–10, 13b, 16–17—Amid the apparent preeminence of the wicked, the psalmist finds *refuge*
(v. 16; see introduction, "Psalms of Trust") and
strength in God and God's *steadfast love* (vv.
10, 16, 17; see 5:7; 36:5). The inseparability of
pain and praise (v. 17) is affirmed, as well as the
reality that God stands with the afflicted (see
introduction, "Prayers for Help").

Then it will be known to the ends of
the earth
that God rules over Jacob.   *Selah*

14 Each evening they come back,
howling like dogs
and prowling about the city.
15 They roam about for food,
and growl if they do not get their
fill.

16 But I will sing of your might;
I will sing aloud of your steadfast
love in the morning.
For you have been a fortress
for me
and a refuge in the day of my
distress.
17 O my strength, I will sing praises to
you,
for you, O God, are my
fortress,
the God who shows me steadfast
love.

Psalm 60
Prayer for National Victory after Defeat

*To the leader: according to the Lily of
the Covenant. A Miktam of David; for
instruction; when he struggled with Aram-
naharaim and with Aram-zobah, and when
Joab on his return killed twelve thousand
Edomites in the Valley of Salt.*

1 O God, you have rejected us, broken
our defenses;
you have been angry; now
restore us!
2 You have caused the land to quake;
you have torn it open;
repair the cracks in it, for it is
tottering.

3 You have made your people suffer
hard things;
you have given us wine to drink
that made us reel.

4 You have set up a banner for those
who fear you,
to rally to it out of bowshot.*a*
                                    Selah

5 Give victory with your right hand,
and answer us,*b*
so that those whom you love may
be rescued.

6 God has promised in his
sanctuary:*c*
"With exultation I will divide up
Shechem,
and portion out the Vale of
Succoth.
7 Gilead is mine, and Manasseh is
mine;
Ephraim is my helmet;
Judah is my scepter.
8 Moab is my washbasin;
on Edom I hurl my shoe;
over Philistia I shout in triumph."

9 Who will bring me to the fortified
city?
Who will lead me to Edom?
10 Have you not rejected us, O God?
You do not go out, O God, with
our armies.
11 O grant us help against the foe,
for human help is worthless.
12 With God we shall do valiantly;
it is he who will tread down our
foes.

a Gk Syr Jerome: Heb *because of the truth* *b* Another reading is *me* *c* Or *by his holiness*

Psalm 60

60 (Title)—See Ps. 3; 2 Sam. 8:13–14; 1 Chr.
18:12–13.

60:1–3—Although impossible to date with confidence, the psalm articulates the experience of
communal suffering.

60:5 *Give victory*—Better translated "Save (our
lives)," it begins the request for help, to which
God responds in vv. 6–8.

60:6–8—Both Israelite and non-Israelite places

are mentioned. The function is to assert God's
sovereignty over all.

60:9–12—Although Edom is implicated in v. 9
(see 137:7; Obadiah), the real problem is God
(vv. 1–3). But God is also the people's only hope
and *help* (vv. 11–12). Thus, they entrust themselves to the God whom the Psalms elsewhere
portray as the sovereign of all (see 47:8–9;
96:11–13) and the special friend of the victimized (see introduction, "Prayers for Help").

Psalm 61
Assurance of God's Protection

To the leader: with stringed instruments.
Of David.

1 Hear my cry, O God;
    listen to my prayer.
2 From the end of the earth I call to you,
    when my heart is faint.

Lead me to the rock
    that is higher than I;
3 for you are my refuge,
    a strong tower against the enemy.

4 Let me abide in your tent forever,
    find refuge under the shelter of
       your wings.   *Selah*
5 For you, O God, have heard my vows;
    you have given me the heritage of
       those who fear your name.

6 Prolong the life of the king;
    may his years endure to all
       generations!
7 May he be enthroned forever before
       God;
    appoint steadfast love and
       faithfulness to watch over him!

8 So I will always sing praises to your
       name,
    as I pay my vows day after day.

Psalm 62
Song of Trust in God Alone

To the leader: according to Jeduthun.
A Psalm of David.

1 For God alone my soul waits in
    silence;

    from him comes my salvation.
2 He alone is my rock and my
       salvation,
    my fortress; I shall never be
       shaken.

3 How long will you assail a person,
    will you batter your victim, all of
       you,
    as you would a leaning wall, a
       tottering fence?
4 Their only plan is to bring down a
       person of prominence.
    They take pleasure in falsehood;
they bless with their mouths,
    but inwardly they curse.   *Selah*

5 For God alone my soul waits in
       silence,
    for my hope is from him.
6 He alone is my rock and my
       salvation,
    my fortress; I shall not be shaken.
7 On God rests my deliverance and
       my honor;
    my mighty rock, my refuge is in
       God.

8 Trust in him at all times,
       O people;
    pour out your heart before him;
    God is a refuge for us.   *Selah*

9 Those of low estate are but a breath,
    those of high estate are a
       delusion;
in the balances they go up;
    they are together lighter than a
       breath.

Psalm 61

61:2b *The rock that is higher than I*—To the
threatened psalmist (vv. 1–2a), God promises to
be a presence and power beyond any resource
that a human being can muster.

61:3–4 *Refuge*—The refuge found in God (see
introduction, "Psalms of Trust") is not merely
personal. It apparently impels the psalmist into
the temple (*tent*, v. 4)—that is, into the company
of God's people. *Shelter of your wings*—See
note at 17:8.

61:7 *Steadfast love and faithfulness*—The
fundamental attributes of God (see 5:7; 36:5;

57:3, 10). They are what motivate God to pursue
justice and righteousness, the task with which the
earthly king was entrusted (see 72:1–7).

Psalm 62

62:1–2, 5–6—Verses 1 and 5 are nearly identical,
as are vv. 2 and 6. Thus, the beginning and center
of the psalm look to *God alone* as the source and
sustainer of life, amid persistent opposition (vv.
3–4).

62:7–8 *Refuge*—Synonymous with *rock* (see
61:1) and *fortress* (see introduction, "Psalms of
Trust").

62:8 *Trust*—In a word, the issue is, as often in

10 Put no confidence in extortion,
　　and set no vain hopes on robbery;
　　if riches increase, do not set your
　　　　heart on them.

11 Once God has spoken;
　　twice have I heard this:
　　that power belongs to God,
12 and steadfast love belongs to you,
　　O Lord.
　　For you repay to all
　　　according to their work.

Psalm 63
Comfort and Assurance in God's Presence

*A Psalm of David, when he was in the
Wilderness of Judah.*

1 O God, you are my God, I seek you,
　　my soul thirsts for you;
　　my flesh faints for you,
　　　as in a dry and weary land where
　　　　there is no water.
2 So I have looked upon you in the
　　　sanctuary,
　　beholding your power and glory.
3 Because your steadfast love is better
　　　than life,
　　my lips will praise you.
4 So I will bless you as long as I live;
　　I will lift up my hands and call on
　　　your name.

5 My soul is satisfied as with a rich
　　　feast,*a*
　　and my mouth praises you with
　　　joyful lips
6 when I think of you on my bed,
　　and meditate on you in the
　　　watches of the night;
7 for you have been my help,
　　and in the shadow of your wings I
　　　sing for joy.
8 My soul clings to you;
　　your right hand upholds me.

9 But those who seek to destroy my
　　　life
　　shall go down into the depths of
　　　the earth;
10 they shall be given over to the power
　　　of the sword,
　　they shall be prey for jackals.
11 But the king shall rejoice in God;
　　all who swear by him shall exult,
　　for the mouths of liars will be
　　　stopped.

Psalm 64
Prayer for Protection from Enemies

To the leader. A Psalm of David.

1 Hear my voice, O God, in my
　　　complaint;
　　preserve my life from the dread
　　　enemy.

a Heb with fat and fatness

---

the Psalms, trust. The word recurs in v. 10 (NRSV *Put . . . confidence*). While it is possible to trust one's own machinations and resources (see 49:6; 52:7)—a decidedly contemporary inclination—the psalmist trusts "God alone" (62:1, 5) and the *power* of God's *steadfast love* (vv. 11, 12; see 5:7; 33:5; 36:5), which is God's form of power and its own reward (see introduction, "Prayers for Help").

Psalm 63

63 (Title)—See Ps. 3; 1 Sam. 23:14; 24:2.

63:1, 5–6—The rhythmic necessities of life are in view—drinking (v. 1), eating (v. 5), sleeping (v. 6). That the psalm is about the true source of life is indicated by the repetition of *soul*, better translated "life," in vv. 1, 5 (see also v. 8 and *life* in v. 9).

63:2–4—What truly sustains life, the psalmist affirms, is God's presence and *power* (v. 2), which God exercises as *steadfast love* (see introduction,

"Prayers for Help"; 5:7; 33:5; 36:5). The appropriate response is *praise* (v. 3; see v. 5).

63:7 *Shadow of your wings*—See 17:8. The satisfaction and security found in God exists amid persecution and threat to life (vv. 9–10), which is typical for the psalmists and other biblical worthies (see, among others, 35:4; 38:12; 54:3; Exod. 4:19; 1 Sam. 20:1; Mark 11:18).

63:11 *The king*—Originally perhaps a prayer for or by the king, the psalm has functioned to express the faith of God's people in many times and places.

Psalm 64

64:1–6—The complaint and plea for help indicate the typical situation of *the righteous* (v. 10). The words of *the wicked* (v. 2) reveal their arrogant self-centeredness (vv. 5–6; see 3:2; 10:4, 6, 11, 13).

² Hide me from the secret plots of the
         wicked,
      from the scheming of evildoers,
³ who whet their tongues like swords,
      who aim bitter words like arrows,
⁴ shooting from ambush at the
         blameless;
      they shoot suddenly and without
         fear.
⁵ They hold fast to their evil purpose;
      they talk of laying snares secretly,
   thinking, "Who can see us?ᵃ
⁶ Who can search out our crimes?ᵇ
   We have thought out a cunningly
         conceived plot."
      For the human heart and mind are
         deep.

⁷ But God will shoot his arrow at
         them;
      they will be wounded suddenly.
⁸ Because of their tongue he will bring
         them to ruin;ᶜ
      all who see them will shake with
         horror.
⁹ Then everyone will fear;
      they will tell what God has
         brought about,
      and ponder what he has done.

¹⁰ Let the righteous rejoice in the LORD
         and take refuge in him.
   Let all the upright in heart glory.

Psalm 65
Thanksgiving for Earth's Bounty
To the leader. A Psalm of David. A Song.

¹ Praise is due to you,

   O God, in Zion;
   and to you shall vows be performed,
² O you who answer prayer!
   To you all flesh shall come.
³ When deeds of iniquity overwhelm
         us,
      you forgive our transgressions.
⁴ Happy are those whom you choose
         and bring near
      to live in your courts.
   We shall be satisfied with the
         goodness of your house,
      your holy temple.

⁵ By awesome deeds you answer us
         with deliverance,
      O God of our salvation;
   you are the hope of all the ends of
         the earth
      and of the farthest seas.
⁶ By yourᵈ strength you established
         the mountains;
      you are girded with might.
⁷ You silence the roaring of the seas,
      the roaring of their waves,
      the tumult of the peoples.
⁸ Those who live at earth's farthest
         bounds are awed by your
         signs;
   you make the gateways of the
         morning and the evening
         shout for joy.

⁹ You visit the earth and water it,
      you greatly enrich it;
   the river of God is full of water;
      you provide the people with grain,

ᵃ Syr: Heb *them*   ᵇ Cn: Heb *They search out crimes*   ᶜ Cn: Heb *They will bring him to ruin, their tongue being against them*   ᵈ Gk Jerome: Heb *his*

64:7–9—The description of God's response articulates the psalmist's confidence that God stands with the victimized (see introduction, "Prayers for Help") and wills justice and righteousness (see introduction, "Psalms 1–2 and the Shape of the Psalter").

64:10 *Refuge*—See introduction, "Psalms of Trust."

Psalm 65
65:1 *Zion*—See 48:1–2, where the specific place, Zion, has universal significance.

65:2 *All flesh*—The expansive perspective of the songs of *praise* (v. 1) is evident here. God wills

to *forgive* (v. 3) and to host all people in God's *house*, the temple on Mount Zion (v. 4; see 23:5–6; 36:7–9; 63:5).

65:5–8—The universality of God's claim is again clear—upon people (vv. 5, 8), but also upon *seas* (v. 5), *the mountains* (v. 6), and more (see introduction, "Songs of Praise"; Pss. 47, 96–99, 145, 150).

65:9–13—God is source of life for *the earth* (v. 9), as well as *the people* (v. 9); and the creation responds abundantly and joyfully (vv. 12–13; see 96:11–13; 98:7–8). The mutual dependence of humankind and creation upon

for so you have prepared it.
10 You water its furrows abundantly,
    settling its ridges,
softening it with showers,
    and blessing its growth.
11 You crown the year with your
    bounty;
    your wagon tracks overflow with
    richness.
12 The pastures of the wilderness
    overflow,
    the hills gird themselves with joy,
13 the meadows clothe themselves with
    flocks,
    the valleys deck themselves with
    grain,
    they shout and sing together for
    joy.

Psalm 66
Praise for God's Goodness to Israel

To the leader. A Song. A Psalm.

1 Make a joyful noise to God, all the
    earth;
2   sing the glory of his name;
    give to him glorious praise.
3 Say to God, "How awesome are your
    deeds!
    Because of your great power, your
    enemies cringe before you.
4 All the earth worships you;
    they sing praises to you,
    sing praises to your name."   *Selah*

5 Come and see what God has done:
    he is awesome in his deeds among
    mortals.
6 He turned the sea into dry land;
    they passed through the river on
    foot.
There we rejoiced in him,
7   who rules by his might forever,
    whose eyes keep watch on the
    nations—
    let the rebellious not exalt
    themselves.   *Selah*

8 Bless our God, O peoples,
    let the sound of his praise be
    heard,
9 who has kept us among the living,
    and has not let our feet slip.
10 For you, O God, have tested us;
    you have tried us as silver is
    tried.
11 You brought us into the net;
    you laid burdens on our backs;
12 you let people ride over our heads;
    we went through fire and through
    water;
    yet you have brought us out to a
    spacious place.[a]

13 I will come into your house with
    burnt offerings;
    I will pay you my vows,
14 those that my lips uttered

[a] Cn Compare Gk Syr Jerome Tg: Heb *to a saturation*

God has profound ecological implications (see Pss. 8, 104). The use of this psalm at Thanksgiving is highly appropriate, suggesting that gratitude begins with the humble recognition that God is the source and sustainer of all life. Such gratitude is also the theological foundation for ecological awareness and activity.

Psalm 66

66:1, 4 *All the earth*—The songs of praise regularly invite a world-encompassing congregation to praise God (see introduction, "Songs of Praise").

66:3 *Your great power*—God's sovereignty is affirmed (see also *rules* in v. 7), a "power" which the Psalter ultimately reveals to be love (see *steadfast love* in v. 20; note at 62:8; introduction, "Prayers for Help").

66:6—This is an allusion to the exodus, in which God was characteristically opposing oppressors, in accordance with God's will for justice and righteousness (see introduction, "Psalms 1–2 and the Shape of the Psalter"), and which was intended to have creation-wide effects (see Exod. 9:16).

66:8 *Bless*—An invitation to recognize God's sovereign claim on the world (see 34:1).

66:10—To be *tested* does not mean to be punished. Often, "tests" involve an examination for the purpose of vindication or setting things right (see 11:5; 17:3; 26:2).

66:13–20—The psalmist claims a sort of personal exodus analogous to the exodus (see v. 6). Payment of *vows* (v. 13; see 50:14, 23) is a way of showing gratitude for God's *steadfast love* (v. 20; see 5:7; 36:5–7).

and my mouth promised when I
 was in trouble.
15 I will offer to you burnt offerings of
 fatlings,
 with the smoke of the sacrifice of
  rams;
I will make an offering of bulls and
  goats.   *Selah*

16 Come and hear, all you who fear
  God,
 and I will tell what he has done
  for me.
17 I cried aloud to him,
 and he was extolled with my
  tongue.
18 If I had cherished iniquity in my
 heart,
 the Lord would not have
  listened.
19 But truly God has listened;
 he has given heed to the words of
  my prayer.
20 Blessed be God,
 because he has not rejected my
  prayer
 or removed his steadfast love
  from me.

Psalm 67
The Nations Called to Praise God
To the leader: with stringed instruments.
A Psalm. A Song.

1 May God be gracious to us and
 bless us
 and make his face to shine
  upon us,   *Selah*

2 that your way may be known upon
 earth,
 your saving power among all
  nations.
3 Let the peoples praise you, O God;
 let all the peoples praise you.

4 Let the nations be glad and sing for
 joy,
 for you judge the peoples with
  equity
 and guide the nations upon earth.
        Selah
5 Let the peoples praise you, O God;
 let all the peoples praise you.

6 The earth has yielded its increase;
 God, our God, has blessed us.
7 May God continue to bless us;
 let all the ends of the earth revere
  him.

Psalm 68
Praise and Thanksgiving
To the leader. Of David. A Psalm. A Song.

1 Let God rise up, let his enemies be
 scattered;
 let those who hate him flee before
  him.
2 As smoke is driven away, so drive
 them away;
 as wax melts before the fire,
 let the wicked perish before God.
3 But let the righteous be joyful;
 let them exult before God;
 let them be jubilant with joy.

4 Sing to God, sing praises to his
 name;

Psalm 67

67:1–3—Recalling Gen. 12:1–3, God's blessing of God's people is ultimately to affect the whole world (see *bless[ed]* in Ps. 67:6–7; introduction, "Songs of Praise").

67:4–5—Consequently, *the nations* and *the peoples* respond with *praise*. God works universally to "establish justice among peoples" (NRSV *judge the peoples*), one of the hallmarks of God's will and universal sovereignty (see introduction, "Psalms 1–2 and the Shape of the Psalter"; 96:11–13).

Psalm 68

68:1–6—The function of God's warlike activity here and elsewhere (see also vv. 11–14, 21–23, 28–31) is to establish justice and righteousness, which are the foundations of enduring peace, as vv. 5–6 suggest (see 29:11). In short, God sides with the poor, needy, and victimized (see introduction, "Prayers for Help"). Justice and righteousness are also the hallmarks of God's reign, which is depicted and celebrated in the rest of the psalm, culminating in vv. 24–27 (see introduction, "Psalms 1–2 and the Shape of the Psalter").

lift up a song to him who rides
    upon the clouds[a]—
his name is the LORD—
    be exultant before him.

5 Father of orphans and protector of
    widows
    is God in his holy habitation.
6 God gives the desolate a home to
    live in;
    he leads out the prisoners to
        prosperity,
    but the rebellious live in a parched
        land.

7 O God, when you went out before
    your people,
    when you marched through the
        wilderness,   *Selah*
8 the earth quaked, the heavens
    poured down rain
    at the presence of God, the God of
        Sinai,
    at the presence of God, the God of
        Israel.
9 Rain in abundance, O God, you
    showered abroad;
    you restored your heritage when it
        languished;
10 your flock found a dwelling in it;
    in your goodness, O God, you
        provided for the needy.

11 The Lord gives the command;
    great is the company of those[b] who
        bore the tidings:
12   "The kings of the armies, they flee,
    they flee!"
The women at home divide the spoil,
13   though they stay among the
        sheepfolds—
    the wings of a dove covered with
        silver,
    its pinions with green gold.
14 When the Almighty[c] scattered kings
    there,
    snow fell on Zalmon.

15 O mighty mountain, mountain of
    Bashan;
    O many-peaked mountain,
        mountain of Bashan!
16 Why do you look with envy,
    O many-peaked mountain,
    at the mount that God desired for
        his abode,
    where the LORD will reside forever?
17 With mighty chariotry, twice ten
    thousand,
    thousands upon thousands,
    the Lord came from Sinai into the
        holy place.[d]
18 You ascended the high mount,
    leading captives in your train
    and receiving gifts from people,
    even from those who rebel against
        the LORD God's abiding there.
19 Blessed be the Lord,
    who daily bears us up;
    God is our salvation.   *Selah*
20 Our God is a God of salvation,
    and to GOD, the Lord, belongs
        escape from death.

21 But God will shatter the heads of his
    enemies,
    the hairy crown of those who walk
        in their guilty ways.
22 The Lord said,
    "I will bring them back from
        Bashan,
I will bring them back from the
    depths of the sea,
23 so that you may bathe[e] your feet in
    blood,
    so that the tongues of your dogs
        may have their share from the
        foe."

24 Your solemn processions are seen,[f]
    O God,

[a] Or *cast up a highway for him who rides through the deserts* [b] Or *company of the women* [c] Traditional rendering of Heb *Shaddai* [d] Cn: Heb *The Lord among them Sinai in the holy* (place) [e] Gk Syr Tg: Heb *shatter* [f] Or *have been seen*

68:7–18—After a probable allusion to the exodus (vv. 1–3), God leads the people *through the wilderness* (v. 7; see *Sinai* in v. 8), bypassing other mountains (see *Bashan* in v. 15) to take up residence in Jerusalem, *the high mount* (v. 18; see v. 29; 48:1–2).

68:24 *My King*—God's sovereignty is the issue (see vv. 26, 32–35) and is elaborately celebrated

the processions of my God, my
King, into the sanctuary—
25 the singers in front, the musicians
last,
between them girls playing
tambourines:
26 "Bless God in the great congregation,
the LORD, O you who are of Israel's
fountain!"
27 There is Benjamin, the least of them,
in the lead,
the princes of Judah in a body,
the princes of Zebulun, the princes
of Naphtali.

28 Summon your might, O God;
show your strength, O God, as you
have done for us before.
29 Because of your temple at Jerusalem
kings bear gifts to you.
30 Rebuke the wild animals that live
among the reeds,
the herd of bulls with the calves of
the peoples.
Trample*a* under foot those who lust
after tribute;
scatter the peoples who delight in
war.*b*
31 Let bronze be brought from Egypt;
let Ethiopia*c* hasten to stretch out
its hands to God.

32 Sing to God, O kingdoms of the
earth;
sing praises to the Lord,   *Selah*
33 O rider in the heavens, the ancient
heavens;
listen, he sends out his voice, his
mighty voice.
34 Ascribe power to God,
whose majesty is over Israel;
and whose power is in the skies.
35 Awesome is God in his*d* sanctuary,
the God of Israel;

he gives power and strength to his
people.

Blessed be God!

Psalm 69
Prayer for Deliverance from Persecution
To the leader: according to Lilies. Of David.

1 Save me, O God,
for the waters have come up to my
neck.
2 I sink in deep mire,
where there is no foothold;
I have come into deep waters,
and the flood sweeps over me.
3 I am weary with my crying;
my throat is parched.
My eyes grow dim
with waiting for my God.

4 More in number than the hairs of
my head
are those who hate me without
cause;
many are those who would destroy
me,
my enemies who accuse me falsely.
What I did not steal
must I now restore?
5 O God, you know my folly;
the wrongs I have done are not
hidden from you.

6 Do not let those who hope in you be
put to shame because of me,
O Lord GOD of hosts;
do not let those who seek you be
dishonored because of me,
O God of Israel.
7 It is for your sake that I have borne
reproach,
that shame has covered my face.

a Cn: Heb *Trampling* *b* Meaning of Heb of verse 30 is uncertain
c Or *Nubia;* Heb *Cush* *d* Gk: Heb *from your*

(v. 25). The point is not simply triumphant celebration, but rather the enactment of God's will
in the world (see vv. 5–6).

68:26 *Bless*—Invites submission to God's claim
on the world (see 34:1).

Psalm 69
69:7—More explicitly than most of the prayers

for help (see introduction, "Prayers for Help"),
this one makes it clear that the **reproach** (v. 7)
is for God's sake (see also vv. 9–10). "Reproach"
(or "insult") becomes the key word (see vv. 9–10,
19–20).

8 I have become a stranger to my
　　kindred,
　　an alien to my mother's children.

9 It is zeal for your house that has
　　consumed me;
　　the insults of those who insult you
　　have fallen on me.
10 When I humbled my soul with
　　fasting,*a*
　　they insulted me for doing so.
11 When I made sackcloth my
　　clothing,
　　I became a byword to them.
12 I am the subject of gossip for those
　　who sit in the gate,
　　and the drunkards make songs
　　about me.

13 But as for me, my prayer is to you,
　　O LORD.
　　At an acceptable time, O God,
　　in the abundance of your steadfast
　　love, answer me.
　　With your faithful help 14 rescue me
　　from sinking in the mire;
　　let me be delivered from my enemies
　　and from the deep waters.
15 Do not let the flood sweep over me,
　　or the deep swallow me up,
　　or the Pit close its mouth over me.

16 Answer me, O LORD, for your
　　steadfast love is good;
　　according to your abundant mercy,
　　turn to me.
17 Do not hide your face from your
　　servant,
　　for I am in distress—make haste to
　　answer me.

18 Draw near to me, redeem me,
　　set me free because of my enemies.
19 You know the insults I receive,
　　and my shame and dishonor;
　　my foes are all known to you.
20 Insults have broken my heart,
　　so that I am in despair.
　　I looked for pity, but there was
　　none;
　　and for comforters, but I found
　　none.
21 They gave me poison for food,
　　and for my thirst they gave me
　　vinegar to drink.

22 Let their table be a trap for them,
　　a snare for their allies.
23 Let their eyes be darkened so that
　　they cannot see,
　　and make their loins tremble
　　continually.
24 Pour out your indignation upon
　　them,
　　and let your burning anger
　　overtake them.
25 May their camp be a desolation;
　　let no one live in their tents.
26 For they persecute those whom you
　　have struck down,
　　and those whom you have
　　wounded, they attack still
　　more.*b*
27 Add guilt to their guilt;
　　may they have no acquittal from
　　you.
28 Let them be blotted out of the book
　　of the living;

a Gk Syr: Heb *I wept, with fasting my soul*, or *I made my soul mourn with
fasting*   *b* Gk Syr: Heb *recount the pain of*

69:21—See Matt. 27:34; Mark 15:23; Luke
23:36; John 19:29–30. The use of the psalm in
the narratives of Jesus' passion (compare also v. 4
with John 15:25; v. 9 with John 2:17; vv. 22–23
with Rom. 11:9–10) suggests the Gospel writers'
conviction that Jesus is the ultimate example of
the one who suffers because of faithfulness to
God (see introduction, "The Psalms and the New
Testament").

69:22–29—Although the cause of the suffering
seems to be attributed to God (especially in v.
26) as well as to the oppressors, the psalmist un-

dercuts any simple retributive scheme by having
claimed God's *steadfast love* (vv. 13, 16; see 5:7)
and *mercy* (v. 16). The ultimate claim is that God
sides with the *lowly* and those *in pain* (v. 29),
the oppressed (v. 32) and *the needy* (v. 33; see
introduction, "Prayers for Help"), which is the essence of the good news that Jesus preached (see
Luke 4:16–21), as well as the claim validated by
Jesus' resurrection. The function of the extended
plea for revenge (Ps. 69:22–28) is to request God
to set things right for the victimized (see introduction, "Prayers for Help").

let them not be enrolled among
   the righteous.
29 But I am lowly and in pain;
   let your salvation, O God, protect
     me.

30 I will praise the name of God with a
     song;
   I will magnify him with
     thanksgiving.
31 This will please the LORD more than
     an ox
   or a bull with horns and hoofs.
32 Let the oppressed see it and be glad;
   you who seek God, let your hearts
     revive.
33 For the LORD hears the needy,
   and does not despise his own that
     are in bonds.

34 Let heaven and earth praise him,
   the seas and everything that moves
     in them.
35 For God will save Zion
   and rebuild the cities of Judah;
   and his servants shall live[a] there and
     possess it;
36   the children of his servants shall
     inherit it,
   and those who love his name shall
     live in it.

Psalm 70

Prayer for Deliverance from Enemies

*To the leader. Of David, for the memorial
offering.*

1 Be pleased, O God, to deliver me.
   O LORD, make haste to help me!
2 Let those be put to shame and
     confusion
   who seek my life.

Let those be turned back and
     brought to dishonor
   who desire to hurt me.
3 Let those who say, "Aha, Aha!"
   turn back because of their shame.

4 Let all who seek you
   rejoice and be glad in you.
   Let those who love your salvation
   say evermore, "God is great!"
5 But I am poor and needy;
   hasten to me, O God!
   You are my help and my deliverer;
   O LORD, do not delay!

Psalm 71

Prayer for Lifelong Protection and Help

1 In you, O LORD, I take refuge;
   let me never be put to shame.
2 In your righteousness deliver me and
     rescue me;
   incline your ear to me and save
     me.
3 Be to me a rock of refuge,
   a strong fortress,[b] to save me,
   for you are my rock and my
     fortress.

4 Rescue me, O my God, from the
     hand of the wicked,
   from the grasp of the unjust and
     cruel.
5 For you, O Lord, are my hope,
   my trust, O LORD, from my youth.
6 Upon you I have leaned from my
     birth;
   it was you who took me from my
     mother's womb.
   My praise is continually of you.

---

[a] Syr: Heb *and they shall live*   [b] Gk Compare 31.3: Heb *to come continually
you have commanded*

Psalm 70

70:1—See 40:13–17.

Psalm 71

71:1 *Refuge*—Repeated in vv. 3, 7, it indicates
the entrusting of life and future to God (see introduction, "Psalms of Trust").

71:2 *Righteousness*—This is the key word in the
psalm; see also vv. 15, 16, 19, 24. "Righteousness" and "justice" form the essence of God's

will (see introduction, "Psalms 1–2 and the Shape
of the Psalter"; 96:11–13), and they mean *help*
(v. 24) for the victimized.

71:3 *Rock*—A synonym for *refuge*; see 61:3.

71:5–6, 9 *Youth . . . birth . . . old age*—Despite
troubles (vv. 4, 7, 10–11), the psalmist is convinced that for the entirety of life, one belongs
to God; see also vv. 17–18. This affirms that God
sides with victims, and it undercuts a doctrine of
retribution (see introduction, "Prayers for Help").

7 I have been like a portent to many,
   but you are my strong refuge.
8 My mouth is filled with your praise,
   and with your glory all day long.
9 Do not cast me off in the time of old
     age;
   do not forsake me when my
     strength is spent.
10 For my enemies speak concerning
     me,
   and those who watch for my life
     consult together.
11 They say, "Pursue and seize that
     person
   whom God has forsaken,
   for there is no one to deliver."

12 O God, do not be far from me;
   O my God, make haste to help me!
13 Let my accusers be put to shame and
     consumed;
   let those who seek to hurt me
   be covered with scorn and disgrace.
14 But I will hope continually,
   and will praise you yet more and
     more.
15 My mouth will tell of your righteous
     acts,
   of your deeds of salvation all day
     long,
   though their number is past my
     knowledge.
16 I will come praising the mighty
     deeds of the Lord GOD,
   I will praise your righteousness,
     yours alone.
17 O God, from my youth you have
     taught me,
   and I still proclaim your wondrous
     deeds.

18 So even to old age and gray hairs,
   O God, do not forsake me,
until I proclaim your might
   to all the generations to come.*a*
Your power 19 and your
     righteousness, O God,
   reach the high heavens.

You who have done great things,
   O God, who is like you?
20 You who have made me see many
     troubles and calamities
   will revive me again;
from the depths of the earth
   you will bring me up again.
21 You will increase my honor,
   and comfort me once again.

22 I will also praise you with the harp
     for your faithfulness, O my God;
I will sing praises to you with the
     lyre,
   O Holy One of Israel.
23 My lips will shout for joy
     when I sing praises to you;
   my soul also, which you have
     rescued.
24 All day long my tongue will talk of
     your righteous help,
for those who tried to do me harm
   have been put to shame, and
     disgraced.

Psalm 72
Prayer for Guidance and Support for the King
Of Solomon.

1 Give the king your justice, O God,
   and your righteousness to a king's
     son.

a Gk Compare Syr: Heb *to a generation, to all that come*

71:13—The request for vengeance is a plea for God to set things right (see v. 2; introduction, "Prayers for Help").

Psalm 72

72 (Title) *Of Solomon*—One of only two psalms attributed to Solomon (see Ps. 127), its significance derives not only from its content, but also from its key placement at the end of Book II (see introduction, "Psalms 1–2 and the Shape of the Psalter").

72:1–7, 12–14—The king was entrusted with doing on earth the *justice* and *righteousness* that are the heavenly will of God (see introduction, "Psalms 1–2 and the Shape of the Psalter"; 96:11–13; Matt. 6:10). As Ps. 72:3, 7 suggest, the result is *shalom* (NRSV *prosperity* in v. 3 and *peace* in v. 7) on a cosmic scale. The fundamental criterion for measuring the existence of justice and righteousness involves the well-being of the *poor* (vv. 2, 4, 12) and *needy* (vv. 4, 12, 13).

2 May he judge your people with
    righteousness,
    and your poor with justice.
3 May the mountains yield prosperity
    for the people,
    and the hills, in righteousness.
4 May he defend the cause of the poor
    of the people,
    give deliverance to the needy,
    and crush the oppressor.
5 May he live*a* while the sun endures,
    and as long as the moon,
    throughout all generations.
6 May he be like rain that falls on the
    mown grass,
    like showers that water the earth.
7 In his days may righteousness
    flourish
    and peace abound, until the moon
    is no more.
8 May he have dominion from sea to
    sea,
    and from the River to the ends of
    the earth.
9 May his foes*b* bow down before him,
    and his enemies lick the dust.
10 May the kings of Tarshish and of the
    isles
    render him tribute,
    may the kings of Sheba and Seba
    bring gifts.
11 May all kings fall down before him,
    all nations give him service.
12 For he delivers the needy when they
    call,
    the poor and those who have no
    helper.
13 He has pity on the weak and the
    needy,

and saves the lives of the needy.
14 From oppression and violence he
    redeems their life;
    and precious is their blood in his
    sight.
15 Long may he live!
    May gold of Sheba be given to him.
May prayer be made for him
    continually,
    and blessings invoked for him all
    day long.
16 May there be abundance of grain in
    the land;
    may it wave on the tops of the
    mountains;
    may its fruit be like Lebanon;
    and may people blossom in the cities
    like the grass of the field.
17 May his name endure forever,
    his fame continue as long as the sun.
May all nations be blessed in him;*c*
    may they pronounce him happy.

18 Blessed be the LORD, the God of Israel,
    who alone does wondrous things.
19 Blessed be his glorious name forever;
    may his glory fill the whole earth.
    Amen and Amen.

20 The prayers of David son of Jesse are
    ended.

BOOK III
(Psalms 73–89)

Psalm 73
Plea for Relief from Oppressors
A Psalm of Asaph.

1 Truly God is good to the upright,*d*

a Gk: Heb *may they fear you*   *b* Cn: Heb *those who live in the wilderness*   *c* Or *bless themselves by him*   *d* Or *good to Israel*

Because God sides with the poor and needy (see introduction, "Prayers for Help"), so will the king, God's "son" (2:7).

72:8–11, 15–17—What prevents this from being simply nationalistic propaganda is the material in vv. 1–7, 12–14—that is, the king's universal reign is an embodiment of God's will, at the heart of which is opposition to **oppression** (vv. 4, 14). Verse 17 recalls Gen. 12:3, suggesting that God wills for the king to effect a worldwide blessing.

72:18–19—This is the concluding doxology for Book II; see 41:13.

72:20—This is perhaps the conclusion of the collection Pss. 51–72, or even Pss. 3–72, most of which are associated with David.

Psalm 73

73:1–3—*Prosperity* in v. 3 is *shalom,* which is problematic, because the establishment of God's peace is supposed to involve justice and

to those who are pure in heart.
2 But as for me, my feet had almost
     stumbled;
   my steps had nearly slipped.
3 For I was envious of the arrogant;
   I saw the prosperity of the
     wicked.
4 For they have no pain;
   their bodies are sound and sleek.
5 They are not in trouble as others
     are;
   they are not plagued like other
     people.
6 Therefore pride is their necklace;
   violence covers them like a
     garment.
7 Their eyes swell out with fatness;
   their hearts overflow with follies.
8 They scoff and speak with malice;
   loftily they threaten oppression.
9 They set their mouths against
     heaven,
   and their tongues range over the
     earth.
10 Therefore the people turn and praise
     them,*a*
   and find no fault in them.*b*
11 And they say, "How can God know?
   Is there knowledge in the Most
     High?"
12 Such are the wicked;
   always at ease, they increase in
     riches.
13 All in vain I have kept my heart
     clean
   and washed my hands in
     innocence.
14 For all day long I have been plagued,
   and am punished every morning.

15 If I had said, "I will talk on in this
     way,"
   I would have been untrue to the
     circle of your children.
16 But when I thought how to
     understand this,
   it seemed to me a wearisome task,
17 until I went into the sanctuary of
     God;
   then I perceived their end.
18 Truly you set them in slippery
     places;
   you make them fall to ruin.
19 How they are destroyed in a moment,
   swept away utterly by terrors!
20 They are*c* like a dream when one
     awakes;
   on awaking you despise their
     phantoms.

21 When my soul was embittered,
   when I was pricked in heart,
22 I was stupid and ignorant;
   I was like a brute beast toward you.
23 Nevertheless I am continually with
     you;
   you hold my right hand.
24 You guide me with your counsel,
   and afterward you will receive me
     with honor.*d*
25 Whom have I in heaven but you?
   And there is nothing on earth that
     I desire other than you.
26 My flesh and my heart may fail,
   but God is the strength*e* of my
     heart and my portion forever.

27 Indeed, those who are far from you
     will perish;

a Cn: Heb *his people return here*   *b* Cn: Heb *abundant waters are drained by them*   *c* Cn: Heb *Lord*   *d* Or *to glory*   *e* Heb *rock*

---

righteousness (see 72:1–7). But here, **the wicked** prosper (see 73:4–12; compare 1:3).

73:4–12—The description of the wicked's prosperity includes a quote (v. 11), indicating their arrogant self-assertion (see 3:2; 10:4, 6, 11, 13; introduction, "Psalms of Trust").

73:13–14—The psalmist apparently resents the reality that his or her faithfulness has not paid off materially (see vv. 21–22).

73:15–20—The realization of solidarity with the

people of God marks a turning point (v. 15), leading the psalmist to enter the temple (v. 17), where she or he apparently comes to an understanding that the peace of the wicked is not true peace (vv. 18–20; see v. 27; 1:3–6).

73:23–26—True prosperity or peace is communion with God, which the psalmist apparently envisions as enduring beyond death (v. 24; see 22:29; 49:15). This gives the psalmist a renewed *heart* (v. 26).

you put an end to those who are
    false to you.
28 But for me it is good to be near God;
    I have made the Lord GOD my
    refuge,
    to tell of all your works.

Psalm 74
Plea for Help in Time
of National Humiliation

A Maskil of Asaph.

1 O God, why do you cast us off
    forever?
    Why does your anger smoke
    against the sheep of your
    pasture?
2 Remember your congregation,
    which you acquired long ago,
    which you redeemed to be the
    tribe of your heritage.
    Remember Mount Zion, where
    you came to dwell.
3 Direct your steps to the perpetual
    ruins;
    the enemy has destroyed
    everything in the sanctuary.

4 Your foes have roared within your
    holy place;
    they set up their emblems there.
5 At the upper entrance they hacked
    the wooden trellis with axes.*a*
6 And then, with hatchets and
    hammers,
    they smashed all its carved work.
7 They set your sanctuary on fire;
    they desecrated the dwelling place
    of your name,
    bringing it to the ground.
8 They said to themselves, "We will
    utterly subdue them";

they burned all the meeting places
    of God in the land.
9 We do not see our emblems;
    there is no longer any prophet,
    and there is no one among us who
    knows how long.
10 How long, O God, is the foe to scoff?
    Is the enemy to revile your name
    forever?
11 Why do you hold back your hand;
    why do you keep your hand in*b*
    your bosom?

12 Yet God my King is from of old,
    working salvation in the earth.
13 You divided the sea by your might;
    you broke the heads of the dragons
    in the waters.
14 You crushed the heads of Leviathan;
    you gave him as food*c* for the
    creatures of the wilderness.
15 You cut openings for springs and
    torrents;
    you dried up ever-flowing streams.
16 Yours is the day, yours also the
    night;
    you established the luminaries*d*
    and the sun.
17 You have fixed all the bounds of the
    earth;
    you made summer and winter.

18 Remember this, O LORD, how the
    enemy scoffs,
    and an impious people reviles your
    name.
19 Do not deliver the soul of your dove
    to the wild animals;

a Cn Compare Gk Syr: Meaning of Heb uncertain   *b* Cn: Heb *do you consume your right hand from*   *c* Heb *food for the people*   *d* Or *moon;* Heb *light*

Psalm 74

74:1–11—A communal prayer for help, it seems to assume the destruction of the temple, emphasizing the place—*Mount Zion* (v. 2; see 48:1–2), *sanctuary* (vv. 3, 7), *holy place* (v. 4), *dwelling place* (v. 7).

74:12–17—Despite the catastrophe, the psalmist still asserts God's sovereignty—*my King* (v. 12; see introduction, "Psalms 1–2 and the Shape of the Psalter"). Especially in view of God's taming

of chaotic forces, represented by *the sea* and *dragons* (v. 13) and *Leviathan*, a mythic chaos monster (v. 14; see 104:26; Job 3:8; 41:1), God's order-creating power is needed again.

74:19–21—Like the prayers of individuals, this one affirms that God is located on the side of the *poor* (vv. 19, 21), *downtrodden* (v. 21), and *needy* (v. 21; see introduction, "Prayers for Help"). Indeed, such opposition to oppression lies at the heart of God's relationship or *covenant*

do not forget the life of your poor
  forever.

20 Have regard for your[a] covenant,
    for the dark places of the land are
      full of the haunts of violence.
21 Do not let the downtrodden be put
    to shame;
    let the poor and needy praise your
      name.
22 Rise up, O God, plead your cause;
    remember how the impious scoff
      at you all day long.
23 Do not forget the clamor of your
    foes,
    the uproar of your adversaries that
      goes up continually.

Psalm 75

Thanksgiving for God's Wondrous Deeds

*To the leader: Do Not Destroy. A Psalm
  of Asaph. A Song.*

1 We give thanks to you, O God;
    we give thanks; your name is near.
  People tell of your wondrous deeds.

2 At the set time that I appoint
    I will judge with equity.
3 When the earth totters, with all its
    inhabitants,
    it is I who keep its pillars steady.
                                              Selah

4 I say to the boastful, "Do not
    boast,"
    and to the wicked, "Do not lift up
      your horn;
5 do not lift up your horn on high,
    or speak with insolent neck."

6 For not from the east or from the
    west
    and not from the wilderness
      comes lifting up;
7 but it is God who executes judgment,
    putting down one and lifting up
      another.
8 For in the hand of the LORD there is
    a cup
    with foaming wine, well mixed;
  he will pour a draught from it,
    and all the wicked of the earth
    shall drain it down to the dregs.
9 But I will rejoice[b] forever;
    I will sing praises to the God of
      Jacob.

10 All the horns of the wicked I will cut
    off,
    but the horns of the righteous shall
      be exalted.

Psalm 76

Israel's God—Judge of All the Earth

*To the leader: with stringed instruments.
  A Psalm of Asaph. A Song.*

1 In Judah God is known,
    his name is great in Israel.
2 His abode has been established in
    Salem,
    his dwelling place in Zion.
3 There he broke the flashing arrows,
    the shield, the sword, and the
      weapons of war.   *Selah*

4 Glorious are you, more majestic
    than the everlasting mountains.[c]
5 The stouthearted were stripped of
    their spoil;

[a] Gk Syr: Heb *the*   [b] Gk: Heb *declare*   [c] Gk: Heb *the mountains of prey*

(v. 20) with Israel and the world. Simultaneously,
however, it means that the life of faith will inevitably involve suffering (see Ps. 44).

Psalm 75

75:2 *I will judge with equity*—Better, "I will
establish justice with equity" (see also v. 7, where
executes judgment is better translated "establishes justice"). Justice and righteousness are the
essence of God's will (see introduction, "Psalms
1–2 and the Shape of the Psalter"). Despite how
vv. 8–10 may sound, the point is not retribution,

but rather the opposition to oppression on behalf
of "the poor and needy" (74:21; see introduction,
"Prayers for Help").

75:8 *A cup*—See also 11:6, where the fate of the
wicked is contained in a cup.

Psalm 76

76:2 *Salem*—An element of the name "Jerusalem," it derives from *shalom*, "peace" (see
122:6–8). ***Zion***—See 48:1–2.

76:3—Peace requires the destruction of military
hardware.

they sank into sleep;
none of the troops
was able to lift a hand.

6 At your rebuke, O God of Jacob,
both rider and horse lay stunned.

7 But you indeed are awesome!
Who can stand before you
when once your anger is roused?

8 From the heavens you uttered
judgment;
the earth feared and was still

9 when God rose up to establish
judgment,
to save all the oppressed of the
earth.   *Selah*

10 Human wrath serves only to praise
you,
when you bind the last bit of your[a]
wrath around you.

11 Make vows to the LORD your God,
and perform them;
let all who are around him bring
gifts
to the one who is awesome,

12 who cuts off the spirit of princes,
who inspires fear in the kings of
the earth.

Psalm 77
God's Mighty Deeds Recalled

*To the leader: according to Jeduthun.
Of Asaph. A Psalm.*

1 I cry aloud to God,
aloud to God, that he may hear me.

2 In the day of my trouble I seek the
Lord;
in the night my hand is stretched
out without wearying;
my soul refuses to be comforted.

3 I think of God, and I moan;
I meditate, and my spirit faints.
Selah

4 You keep my eyelids from closing;
I am so troubled that I cannot
speak.

5 I consider the days of old,
and remember the years of long
ago.

6 I commune[b] with my heart in the
night;
I meditate and search my spirit:[c]

7 "Will the Lord spurn forever,
and never again be favorable?

8 Has his steadfast love ceased forever?
Are his promises at an end for all
time?

9 Has God forgotten to be gracious?
Has he in anger shut up his
compassion?"
Selah

10 And I say, "It is my grief
that the right hand of the Most
High has changed."

11 I will call to mind the deeds of the
LORD;
I will remember your wonders of
old.

a Heb lacks *your*   *b* Gk Syr: Heb *My music*   *c* Syr Jerome: Heb *my spirit
searches*

76:6—This is an allusion to the exodus (see Exod.
15:1, 21), the prototypical example of God's opposition to oppression.

76:8–10—When God "fights," it is to oppose
oppressors and thus *to save all the oppressed
of the earth* (v. 9; see introduction, "Prayers for
Help"). God's "wrath" thus serves "to establish
justice" (v. 9; NRSV *to establish judgment*; see
v. 8).

76:12—This is testimony to God's sovereignty,
with which justice and righteousness are frequently associated (see introduction, "Psalms 1–2
and the Shape of the Psalter").

Psalm 77

77:1–10—The psalmist seems on the brink of
total despair, unable to see any evidence of God's

character and purposes in the world, namely,
steadfast love (v. 8), grace, and *compassion*
(v. 9).

77:11–20—Suddenly, while continuing to *remember* and *meditate*, everything is different.
The shift is marked by the beginning of direct
address to God at v. 12, but the reason for the
transformation is unclear. It may involve the
recital of the exodus story (vv. 16–20), perhaps
a reminder of God's characteristic opposition to
deadly oppression (see 76:6, 8–10). That God's
footprints were unseen (v. 19) may testify to the
difficulty of seeing evidence of God's work in
the world. The juxtaposition of vv. 1–10 and vv.
11–20 penetratingly portrays the inevitability of
doubt in the life of the faithful.

¹² I will meditate on all your work,
   and muse on your mighty deeds.
¹³ Your way, O God, is holy.
   What god is so great as our God?
¹⁴ You are the God who works
      wonders;
   you have displayed your might
      among the peoples.
¹⁵ With your strong arm you redeemed
      your people,
   the descendants of Jacob and
      Joseph.   *Selah*

¹⁶ When the waters saw you, O God,
   when the waters saw you, they
      were afraid;
   the very deep trembled.
¹⁷ The clouds poured out water;
   the skies thundered;
   your arrows flashed on every side.
¹⁸ The crash of your thunder was in the
      whirlwind;
   your lightnings lit up the world;
   the earth trembled and shook.
¹⁹ Your way was through the sea,
   your path, through the mighty
      waters;
   yet your footprints were unseen.
²⁰ You led your people like a flock
   by the hand of Moses and Aaron.

Psalm 78

God's Goodness and Israel's Ingratitude

A Maskil of Asaph.

¹ Give ear, O my people, to my
      teaching;
   incline your ears to the words of
      my mouth.
² I will open my mouth in a parable;
   I will utter dark sayings from of
      old,
³ things that we have heard and
      known,

that our ancestors have told us.
⁴ We will not hide them from their
      children;
   we will tell to the coming
      generation
   the glorious deeds of the Lord, and
      his might,
   and the wonders that he has done.

⁵ He established a decree in Jacob,
   and appointed a law in Israel,
   which he commanded our ancestors
      to teach to their children;
⁶ that the next generation might know
      them,
   the children yet unborn,
   and rise up and tell them to their
      children,
⁷   so that they should set their hope
      in God,
   and not forget the works of God,
   but keep his commandments;
⁸ and that they should not be like their
      ancestors,
   a stubborn and rebellious
      generation,
   a generation whose heart was not
      steadfast,
   whose spirit was not faithful to
      God.

⁹ The Ephraimites, armed with^a the
      bow,
   turned back on the day of battle.
¹⁰ They did not keep God's covenant,
   but refused to walk according to
      his law.
¹¹ They forgot what he had done,
   and the miracles that he had
      shown them.
¹² In the sight of their ancestors he
      worked marvels

^a Heb *armed with shooting*

Psalm 78

78:1–8—A historical recital like Pss. 105, 106, 135, and 136, this psalm is designed to **teach** (vv. 1, 5). Teaching is not merely imparting information, but is also inspiring gratitude and obedience (vv. 7–8). Then and now, education has to begin with **children** (vv. 4, 5, 6).

78:9–16, 40–55—Both sections begin by citing the people's disobedience (vv. 9–11, 40–42), but the focus is on God's activity on their behalf in Egypt, in the wilderness, and in their new land.

in the land of Egypt, in the fields
of Zoan.
13 He divided the sea and let them pass
through it,
and made the waters stand like a
heap.
14 In the daytime he led them with a
cloud,
and all night long with a fiery
light.
15 He split rocks open in the
wilderness,
and gave them drink abundantly
as from the deep.
16 He made streams come out of the
rock,
and caused waters to flow down
like rivers.

17 Yet they sinned still more against
him,
rebelling against the Most High in
the desert.
18 They tested God in their heart
by demanding the food they
craved.
19 They spoke against God, saying,
"Can God spread a table in the
wilderness?
20 Even though he struck the rock so
that water gushed out
and torrents overflowed,
can he also give bread,
or provide meat for his people?"

21 Therefore, when the LORD heard, he
was full of rage;
a fire was kindled against Jacob,
his anger mounted against Israel,
22 because they had no faith in God,
and did not trust his saving power.
23 Yet he commanded the skies above,
and opened the doors of heaven;
24 he rained down on them manna to
eat,
and gave them the grain of heaven.

25 Mortals ate of the bread of angels;
he sent them food in abundance.
26 He caused the east wind to blow in
the heavens,
and by his power he led out the
south wind;
27 he rained flesh upon them like dust,
winged birds like the sand of the
seas;
28 he let them fall within their camp,
all around their dwellings.
29 And they ate and were well filled,
for he gave them what they craved.
30 But before they had satisfied their
craving,
while the food was still in their
mouths,
31 the anger of God rose against them
and he killed the strongest of
them,
and laid low the flower of Israel.

32 In spite of all this they still sinned;
they did not believe in his
wonders.
33 So he made their days vanish like a
breath,
and their years in terror.
34 When he killed them, they sought
for him;
they repented and sought God
earnestly.
35 They remembered that God was
their rock,
the Most High God their
redeemer.
36 But they flattered him with their
mouths;
they lied to him with their
tongues.
37 Their heart was not steadfast toward
him;
they were not true to his covenant.
38 Yet he, being compassionate,
forgave their iniquity,

78:17–20, 56–58—The people were not gratefully obedient; instead, they rebelled and failed
to trust.

78:21–32, 59–64—God's initial response involved
anger and punishment.

78:33–39, 65–72—But God, *being compassionate* (v. 38), would not let rejection be the final
word. Such grace invites grateful conformity to
God's purposes (vv. 7–8).

and did not destroy them;
often he restrained his anger,
    and did not stir up all his wrath.
39 He remembered that they were but
    flesh,
    a wind that passes and does not
    come again.
40 How often they rebelled against him
    in the wilderness
    and grieved him in the desert!
41 They tested God again and again,
    and provoked the Holy One of
    Israel.
42 They did not keep in mind his
    power,
    or the day when he redeemed
    them from the foe;
43 when he displayed his signs in
    Egypt,
    and his miracles in the fields of
    Zoan.
44 He turned their rivers to blood,
    so that they could not drink of
    their streams.
45 He sent among them swarms of flies,
    which devoured them,
    and frogs, which destroyed them.
46 He gave their crops to the caterpillar,
    and the fruit of their labor to the
    locust.
47 He destroyed their vines with hail,
    and their sycamores with frost.
48 He gave over their cattle to the hail,
    and their flocks to thunderbolts.
49 He let loose on them his fierce anger,
    wrath, indignation, and distress,
    a company of destroying angels.
50 He made a path for his anger;
    he did not spare them from death,
    but gave their lives over to the
    plague.
51 He struck all the firstborn in Egypt,
    the first issue of their strength in
    the tents of Ham.
52 Then he led out his people like
    sheep,
    and guided them in the wilderness
    like a flock.
53 He led them in safety, so that they
    were not afraid;

but the sea overwhelmed their
    enemies.
54 And he brought them to his holy
    hill,
    to the mountain that his right
    hand had won.
55 He drove out nations before them;
    he apportioned them for a
    possession
    and settled the tribes of Israel in
    their tents.

56 Yet they tested the Most High God,
    and rebelled against him.
    They did not observe his decrees,
57 but turned away and were faithless
    like their ancestors;
    they twisted like a treacherous
    bow.
58 For they provoked him to anger with
    their high places;
    they moved him to jealousy with
    their idols.
59 When God heard, he was full of
    wrath,
    and he utterly rejected Israel.
60 He abandoned his dwelling at
    Shiloh,
    the tent where he dwelt among
    mortals,
61 and delivered his power to captivity,
    his glory to the hand of the foe.
62 He gave his people to the sword,
    and vented his wrath on his
    heritage.
63 Fire devoured their young men,
    and their girls had no marriage
    song.
64 Their priests fell by the sword,
    and their widows made no
    lamentation.
65 Then the Lord awoke as from sleep,
    like a warrior shouting because of
    wine.
66 He put his adversaries to rout;
    he put them to everlasting
    disgrace.

67 He rejected the tent of Joseph,
    he did not choose the tribe of
    Ephraim;

68 but he chose the tribe of Judah,
　　Mount Zion, which he loves.
69 He built his sanctuary like the high
　　　heavens,
　　like the earth, which he has
　　　founded forever.
70 He chose his servant David,
　　and took him from the sheepfolds;
71 from tending the nursing ewes he
　　　brought him
　　to be the shepherd of his people
　　　Jacob,
　　of Israel, his inheritance.
72 With upright heart he tended them,
　　and guided them with skillful
　　　hand.

Psalm 79

Plea for Mercy for Jerusalem

A Psalm of Asaph.

1 O God, the nations have come into
　　your inheritance;
　　they have defiled your holy temple;
　　they have laid Jerusalem in ruins.
2 They have given the bodies of your
　　　servants
　　to the birds of the air for food,
　　the flesh of your faithful to the
　　　wild animals of the earth.
3 They have poured out their blood
　　　like water
　　all around Jerusalem,
　　and there was no one to bury
　　　them.
4 We have become a taunt to our
　　　neighbors,
　　mocked and derided by those
　　　around us.

5 How long, O LORD? Will you be
　　angry forever?
　　Will your jealous wrath burn like
　　　fire?

6 Pour out your anger on the nations
　　that do not know you,
　　and on the kingdoms
　　that do not call on your name.
7 For they have devoured Jacob
　　and laid waste his habitation.

8 Do not remember against us the
　　　iniquities of our ancestors;
　　let your compassion come speedily
　　　to meet us,
　　for we are brought very low.
9 Help us, O God of our salvation,
　　for the glory of your name;
　　deliver us, and forgive our sins,
　　for your name's sake.
10 Why should the nations say,
　　"Where is their God?"
　　Let the avenging of the outpoured
　　　blood of your servants
　　be known among the nations
　　　before our eyes.
11 Let the groans of the prisoners come
　　　before you;
　　according to your great power
　　　preserve those doomed to
　　　die.
12 Return sevenfold into the bosom of
　　　our neighbors
　　the taunts with which they taunted
　　　you, O Lord!
13 Then we your people, the flock of
　　　your pasture,
　　will give thanks to you forever;
　　from generation to generation we
　　　will recount your praise.

Psalm 80

Prayer for Israel's Restoration

To the leader: on Lilies, a Covenant.
Of Asaph. A Psalm.

1 Give ear, O Shepherd of Israel,
　　you who lead Joseph like a flock!

Psalm 79

79:1–4—The destruction of Jerusalem recalls 74:1–11.

79:5–10—The basis for the plea for vengeance (vv. 6–7, 10) is God's *compassion* (v. 8; see 78:38) for the victimized—the *low* (v. 8; see also v. 11; 74:19, 21; introduction, "Prayers for

Help"). On the question by the nations (79:10), see 42:3. 10.

Psalm 80

80:1 *Shepherd*—means "feeder," but, unlike the food in 23:1, the food is not nurturing (see 80:5). *Enthroned*—"Shepherd" also denotes a sovereign, the one responsible for the *life* (v. 18)

You who are enthroned upon the
  cherubim, shine forth
2   before Ephraim and Benjamin and
    Manasseh.
  Stir up your might,
    and come to save us!

3 Restore us, O God;
  let your face shine, that we may be
    saved.

4 O LORD God of hosts,
  how long will you be angry with
    your people's prayers?
5 You have fed them with the bread of
    tears,
  and given them tears to drink in
    full measure.
6 You make us the scorn[a] of our
    neighbors;
  our enemies laugh among
    themselves.

7 Restore us, O God of hosts;
  let your face shine, that we may be
    saved.

8 You brought a vine out of Egypt;
  you drove out the nations and
    planted it.
9 You cleared the ground for it;
  it took deep root and filled the
    land.
10 The mountains were covered with its
    shade,
  the mighty cedars with its
    branches;
11 it sent out its branches to the sea,
  and its shoots to the River.
12 Why then have you broken down its
    walls,

so that all who pass along the way
  pluck its fruit?
13 The boar from the forest ravages it,
  and all that move in the field feed
    on it.

14 Turn again, O God of hosts;
  look down from heaven, and see;
  have regard for this vine,
15   the stock that your right hand
    planted.[b]
16 They have burned it with fire, they
    have cut it down;[c]
  may they perish at the rebuke of
    your countenance.
17 But let your hand be upon the one at
    your right hand,
  the one whom you made strong
    for yourself.
18 Then we will never turn back from
    you;
  give us life, and we will call on
    your name.

19 Restore us, O LORD God of hosts;
  let your face shine, that we may be
    saved.

Psalm 81
God's Appeal to Stubborn Israel
*To the leader: according to The Gittith.
Of Asaph.*

1 Sing aloud to God our strength;
  shout for joy to the God of Jacob.
2 Raise a song, sound the tambourine,
  the sweet lyre with the harp.
3 Blow the trumpet at the new moon,
  at the full moon, on our festal day.

[a] Syr: Heb *strife*   [b] Heb adds from verse 17 *and upon the one whom you made strong for yourself*   [c] Cn: Heb *it is cut down*

---

of his or her people. Although the people are not experiencing life, they continue to assert God's sovereignty, an act of faith accompanied by the hopeful prayer that follows.

80:3, 7, 19—The refrain is essentially a prayer for life, which the people properly recognize depends on God's *face* or presence (see 4:6). There is a variation of the refrain in 80:14. The prayer is founded on the conviction that God sides with the victimized (see introduction, "Prayers for Help").

80:8–13—A brief rehearsal of Israel's history, it

alludes to the exodus (v. 8), entry into *the land* (v. 9), and growth of the nation (vv. 10–11), all of which seem to have come to nothing (vv. 12–13).

80:17 *The one at your right hand*—Possibly a reference to the king or future king, it more likely designates Israel itself.

Psalm 81

81:1–3—The psalm begins like a song of praise, a sort of call to worship, preceding what amounts to a sermon in vv. 6–16. Verse 3 accords with Lev. 23:23–24; Num. 29:1–6.

4 For it is a statute for Israel,
  an ordinance of the God of Jacob.
5 He made it a decree in Joseph,
  when he went out over[a] the land of
    Egypt.

  I hear a voice I had not known:
6 "I relieved your[b] shoulder of the
    burden;
  your[c] hands were freed from the
    basket.
7 In distress you called, and I rescued
    you;
  I answered you in the secret place
    of thunder;
  I tested you at the waters of
    Meribah.   *Selah*
8 Hear, O my people, while I
    admonish you;
  O Israel, if you would but listen
    to me!
9 There shall be no strange god among
    you;
  you shall not bow down to a
    foreign god.
10 I am the LORD your God,
  who brought you up out of the
    land of Egypt.
  Open your mouth wide and I will
    fill it.

11 "But my people did not listen to my
    voice;
  Israel would not submit to me.
12 So I gave them over to their
    stubborn hearts,
  to follow their own counsels.

13 O that my people would listen to me,
  that Israel would walk in my ways!
14 Then I would quickly subdue their
    enemies,
  and turn my hand against their
    foes.
15 Those who hate the LORD would
    cringe before him,
  and their doom would last forever.
16 I would feed you[d] with the finest of
    the wheat,
  and with honey from the rock I
    would satisfy you."

Psalm 82
A Plea for Justice
A Psalm of Asaph.

1 God has taken his place in the divine
    council;
  in the midst of the gods he holds
    judgment:
2 "How long will you judge unjustly
  and show partiality to the wicked?
                              Selah
3 Give justice to the weak and the
    orphan;
  maintain the right of the lowly and
    the destitute.
4 Rescue the weak and the needy;
  deliver them from the hand of the
    wicked."

5 They have neither knowledge nor
    understanding,

[a] Or *against* [b] Heb *his* [c] Heb *his* [d] Cn Compare verse 16b: Heb *he would feed him*

81:5c–10—The *voice* (v. 5c), whoever it was, speaks the word of God. Verses 6–7 recall the exodus and wilderness (see Exod. 17:1–7), and vv. 9–10 recall the beginning of the Decalogue (Exod. 20:1–3). The point is to call the people to *listen* (v. 8).

81:11–16—The key word, *listen*, recurs in vv. 11 and 13, as the people are invited, in effect, to "follow me" (v. 13b; see Mark 1:17). The point in vv. 14–16 is not mechanical retribution, but rather that life is lived to the fullest when lived in relationship to God and in conformity with God's will (see Ps. 1).

Psalm 82

82:1 *Divine council*—The psalm offers a poetic portrayal of God's entry into the Canaanite pantheon (see 58:1) in order to put *the gods* on trial. *Holds judgment*—The purpose is to establish "justice" (NRSV *judgment*).

82:2–4—The charge against the gods is that they have failed to establish justice. The admonition in v. 3 pairs (in verbal forms) the key terms, "justice" and "righteousness," which become the essential criteria for true divinity (see introduction, "Psalms 1–2 and the Shape of the Psalter"; 96:11–13), and which are measured in terms of the treatment of *the weak and the needy* (v. 4; see 72:1–7, 12–14).

82:5—The *foundations of the earth* are the mountains, which hold the cosmos together

they walk around in darkness;
  all the foundations of the earth are
    shaken.

⁶ I say, "You are gods,
  children of the Most High, all of
    you;
⁷ nevertheless, you shall die like
    mortals,
  and fall like any prince."ᵃ

⁸ Rise up, O God, judge the earth;
  for all the nations belong to you!

Psalm 83
Prayer for Judgment on Israel's Foes
A Song. A Psalm of Asaph.

¹ O God, do not keep silence;
  do not hold your peace or be still,
    O God!
² Even now your enemies are in
    tumult;
  those who hate you have raised
    their heads.
³ They lay crafty plans against your
    people;
  they consult together against those
    you protect.
⁴ They say, "Come, let us wipe them
    out as a nation;
  let the name of Israel be
    remembered no more."
⁵ They conspire with one accord;
  against you they make a
    covenant—
⁶ the tents of Edom and the
    Ishmaelites,
  Moab and the Hagrites,

⁷ Gebal and Ammon and Amalek,
  Philistia with the inhabitants of
    Tyre;
⁸ Assyria also has joined them;
  they are the strong arm of the
    children of Lot.   *Selah*

⁹ Do to them as you did to Midian,
  as to Sisera and Jabin at the Wadi
    Kishon,
¹⁰ who were destroyed at En-dor,
  who became dung for the
    ground.
¹¹ Make their nobles like Oreb and
    Zeeb,
  all their princes like Zebah and
    Zalmunna,
¹² who said, "Let us take the pastures of
    God
  for our own possession."

¹³ O my God, make them like whirling
    dust,ᵇ
  like chaff before the wind.
¹⁴ As fire consumes the forest,
  as the flame sets the mountains
    ablaze,
¹⁵ so pursue them with your tempest
  and terrify them with your
    hurricane.
¹⁶ Fill their faces with shame,
  so that they may seek your name,
    O Lord.
¹⁷ Let them be put to shame and
    dismayed forever;
  let them perish in disgrace.
¹⁸ Let them know that you alone,
  whose name is the Lord,

ᵃ *Or* fall as one man, O princes ᵇ *Or* a tumbleweed

(see 46:1–3). The crucial claim is that injustice destroys the world!

82:6–7—For their destructive and deadly work, the *gods* are sentenced to death.

82:8 *Judge the earth*—Better translated "establish justice on earth," this fourth occurrence of "justice" demonstrates that God's sovereign claim on **all the nations** is inextricably linked with God's will for justice and righteousness in the world. This is essentially an element of the prayer that Jesus taught: "Your will be done, on earth as it is in heaven" (Matt. 6:10).

Psalm 83

83:1–8—What turns out to be a rather violent prayer (vv. 9–18) is more understandable in the context of the threat to Israel's very life (see esp. v. 4). This is another reminder (see Ps. 82) that God's purposes and God's people never go unopposed.

83:9–12—See Judg. 4–8.

83:13–18—Amid the violent-sounding requests for vengeance, vv. 16 and 18 suggest that the ultimate purpose is not revenge, but rather the recognition of God's sovereignty and the setting of things right for those threatened with annihilation (see introduction, "Prayers for Help").

are the Most High over all the
earth.

Psalm 84
The Joy of Worship in the Temple

To the leader: according to The Gittith.
Of the Korahites. A Psalm.

¹ How lovely is your dwelling place,
  O Lord of hosts!
² My soul longs, indeed it faints
    for the courts of the Lord;
  my heart and my flesh sing for joy
    to the living God.

³ Even the sparrow finds a home,
    and the swallow a nest for
      herself,
  where she may lay her young,
    at your altars, O Lord of hosts,
    my King and my God.
⁴ Happy are those who live in your
      house,
    ever singing your praise.   *Selah*

⁵ Happy are those whose strength is in
      you,
    in whose heart are the highways to
      Zion.ᵃ
⁶ As they go through the valley of
      Baca
    they make it a place of springs;
    the early rain also covers it with
      pools.
⁷ They go from strength to strength;
    the God of gods will be seen in
      Zion.

⁸ O Lord God of hosts, hear my
      prayer;
    give ear, O God of Jacob!   *Selah*

⁹ Behold our shield, O God;
    look on the face of your anointed.

¹⁰ For a day in your courts is better
    than a thousand elsewhere.
  I would rather be a doorkeeper in
    the house of my God
  than live in the tents of
    wickedness.
¹¹ For the Lord God is a sun and
    shield;
  he bestows favor and honor.
  No good thing does the Lord
    withhold
  from those who walk uprightly.
¹² O Lord of hosts,
    happy is everyone who trusts in
      you.

Psalm 85
Prayer for the Restoration
of God's Favor

To the leader. Of the Korahites. A Psalm.

¹ Lord, you were favorable to your
      land;
    you restored the fortunes of
      Jacob.
² You forgave the iniquity of your
      people;
    you pardoned all their sin.   *Selah*
³ You withdrew all your wrath;
    you turned from your hot anger.

⁴ Restore us again, O God of our
      salvation,
    and put away your indignation
      toward us.
⁵ Will you be angry with us forever?

ᵃ Heb lacks *to Zion*

Psalm 84

84:1–2—God's *dwelling place* was understood to be the temple on Mount Zion (see v. 7) in Jerusalem (see Pss. 46, 48, 76, 87, 122).

84:3 *My King*—See 48:2. The temple contained the ark, which symbolized God's earthly throne.

84:4–5 *Happy*—Happiness is defined here, as in 1:1–2, completely in terms of God-centeredness. Verses 5–7 suggest the use of the psalms by pilgrims to Jerusalem (see 48:9–11; 122:1–2).

84:9 *Your anointed*—See 2:2. The pilgrim prays for the king, which would have been natural,

since the king's palace was adjacent to the temple.

84:10–12—An experience of God's place was meant to put pilgrims in touch with God, their true spiritual home (see 48:12–14). Faithfulness is always a matter of what or whom one *trusts* (see 4:6; 13:5; 52:7–8; introduction, "Psalms of Trust").

Psalm 85

85:4–7—God's help, given before (vv. 1–3), is needed again (see 80:4); and the appeal for renewed life is grounded in God's essential character, *steadfast love* (85:7; see 5:7).

Will you prolong your anger to all
    generations?
6 Will you not revive us again,
    so that your people may rejoice in
      you?
7 Show us your steadfast love, O LORD,
    and grant us your salvation.

8 Let me hear what God the LORD will
    speak,
    for he will speak peace to his
      people,
    to his faithful, to those who turn to
      him in their hearts.*a*
9 Surely his salvation is at hand for
    those who fear him,
    that his glory may dwell in our
      land.

10 Steadfast love and faithfulness will
    meet;
    righteousness and peace will kiss
      each other.
11 Faithfulness will spring up from the
    ground,
    and righteousness will look down
      from the sky.
12 The LORD will give what is good,
    and our land will yield its increase.
13 Righteousness will go before him,
    and will make a path for his steps.

Psalm 86
Supplication for Help against Enemies
A Prayer of David.

1 Incline your ear, O LORD, and
    answer me,
    for I am poor and needy.

2 Preserve my life, for I am devoted to
    you;
    save your servant who trusts in
      you.
    You are my God; 3 be gracious to me,
      O Lord,
    for to you do I cry all day long.
4 Gladden the soul of your servant,
    for to you, O Lord, I lift up my
      soul.
5 For you, O Lord, are good and
    forgiving,
    abounding in steadfast love to all
      who call on you.
6 Give ear, O LORD, to my prayer;
    listen to my cry of supplication.
7 In the day of my trouble I call on
    you,
    for you will answer me.

8 There is none like you among the
    gods, O Lord,
    nor are there any works like yours.
9 All the nations you have made shall
    come
    and bow down before you, O Lord,
    and shall glorify your name.
10 For you are great and do wondrous
    things;
    you alone are God.
11 Teach me your way, O LORD,
    that I may walk in your truth;
    give me an undivided heart to
      revere your name.
12 I give thanks to you, O Lord my
    God, with my whole heart,

a Gk: Heb *but let them not turn back to folly*

85:10–13—Verse 10 features four repeated terms. *Steadfast love* and *faithfulness* summarize God's character (see 36:5–6; 57:3; 86:15; Exod. 34:6–7), while *righteousness and peace* summarize God's will, often associated with God's sovereign claim on the world (see introduction, "Psalms 1–2 and the Shape of the Psalter"; 96:11–13). These divine gifts constitute true goodness and abundant life (85:12), the foundation of genuine joy (see v. 6).

Psalm 86

86:1 *Poor and needy*—The victimized are regularly the beneficiaries of God's saving work (see introduction, "Prayers for Help").

86:2 *Your servant*—See vv. 4, 16. The psalmist models submission to God amid *trouble* (v. 7) and opposition (vv. 14, 17), thus demonstrating the normal position of the faithful (see introduction, "Prayers for Help").

86:4 *I lift up my soul*—Better translated, "I offer my life" (see 25:1).

86:5—The psalmist's hope lies in God's character, a summary of which is *steadfast love* (see vv. 13, 15; 5:7; 85:10–13).

86:9–12—Praise (vv. 9–10), openness to God's teaching (v. 11; see 1:1–2), and gratitude (v. 12) go hand in hand.

and I will glorify your name
  forever.
¹³ For great is your steadfast love
    toward me;
  you have delivered my soul from
    the depths of Sheol.

¹⁴ O God, the insolent rise up against
    me;
  a band of ruffians seeks my life,
  and they do not set you before
    them.
¹⁵ But you, O Lord, are a God merciful
    and gracious,
  slow to anger and abounding in
    steadfast love and faithfulness.
¹⁶ Turn to me and be gracious to me;
  give your strength to your servant;
  save the child of your serving
    girl.
¹⁷ Show me a sign of your favor,
  so that those who hate me may see
    it and be put to shame,
  because you, LORD, have helped
    me and comforted me.

Psalm 87
The Joy of Living in Zion

Of the Korahites. A Psalm. A Song.

¹ On the holy mount stands the city
    he founded;
²   the LORD loves the gates of Zion
    more than all the dwellings of
    Jacob.

³ Glorious things are spoken of you,
    O city of God.   *Selah*

⁴ Among those who know me I
    mention Rahab and Babylon;
  Philistia too, and Tyre, with
    Ethiopia*ᵃ*—
  "This one was born there," they
    say.

⁵ And of Zion it shall be said,
  "This one and that one were born
    in it";
  for the Most High himself will
    establish it.
⁶ The LORD records, as he registers the
    peoples,
  "This one was born there."   *Selah*

⁷ Singers and dancers alike say,
  "All my springs are in you."

Psalm 88
Prayer for Help in Despondency

*A Song. A Psalm of the Korahites. To the
leader: according to Mahalath Leannoth.
A Maskil of Heman the Ezrahite.*

¹ O LORD, God of my salvation,
  when, at night, I cry out in your
    presence,
² let my prayer come before you;
  incline your ear to my cry.

³ For my soul is full of troubles,
  and my life draws near to Sheol.

ᵃ Or Nubia; Heb Cush

86:13 *Sheol*—See note at 6:5.

86:15—Recalling Exod. 34:6–7, the focus again is on God's character (see 103:8). Entrusting self to God, and thus empowered by God's *strength* (86:16), the psalmist can live hopefully (v. 17) amid opposition.

Psalm 87

87:1–3 *Holy mount . . . city . . . Zion*—See Ps. 48:1–2.

87:4—*Rahab* is a name for Egypt (see Isa. 30:7), which is listed with other nations who were bitter enemies of Israel, especially *Babylon* (see 137:8) and *Philistia* (see 60:8). But here, in a striking reversal, these enemies claim Zion as their spiritual home (see vv. 5–6).

87:5–6—Zion has universal significance, because

God claims *the peoples* (v. 6; see 48:1–2; 67:4–7; Gen. 12:1–3; Isa. 2:2–4; 19:23–25; introduction, "Songs of Praise"). The simple but strikingly important claim is that God considers all people to be God's children.

Psalm 88

88:1 *God of my salvation*—Despite the terror-filled complaint that follows and the fact that Ps. 88 is unique in containing no explicit expression of trust or praise (see introduction, "Prayers for Help"), the psalmist still speaks to God and looks to God as the source of help and life. *At night*—See the other time words in v. 9 (*every day*), v. 13 (*in the morning*), and v. 17 (*all day long*). The problem and the prayer are continuous.

88:3–4 *Sheol . . . Pit*—See 6:5; 16:10. In 88:3–7 the psalmist feels as good as dead.

4 I am counted among those who go
     down to the Pit;
   I am like those who have no help,
5 like those forsaken among the dead,
   like the slain that lie in the grave,
   like those whom you remember no
     more,
   for they are cut off from your
     hand.
6 You have put me in the depths of the
     Pit,
   in the regions dark and deep.
7 Your wrath lies heavy upon me,
   and you overwhelm me with all
     your waves.   *Selah*

8 You have caused my companions to
     shun me;
   you have made me a thing of
     horror to them.
   I am shut in so that I cannot escape;
9   my eye grows dim through
     sorrow.
   Every day I call on you, O LORD;
   I spread out my hands to you.
10 Do you work wonders for the dead?
   Do the shades rise up to praise
     you?   *Selah*
11 Is your steadfast love declared in the
     grave,
   or your faithfulness in Abaddon?
12 Are your wonders known in the
     darkness,
   or your saving help in the land of
     forgetfulness?

13 But I, O LORD, cry out to you;
   in the morning my prayer comes
     before you.
14 O LORD, why do you cast me off?
   Why do you hide your face from
     me?
15 Wretched and close to death from
     my youth up,
   I suffer your terrors; I am
     desperate.*a*
16 Your wrath has swept over me;
   your dread assaults destroy me.
17 They surround me like a flood all
     day long;
   from all sides they close in on me.
18 You have caused friend and neighbor
     to shun me;
   my companions are in darkness.

Psalm 89
God's Covenant with David
A Maskil of Ethan the Ezrahite.

1 I will sing of your steadfast love,
     O LORD,*b* forever;
   with my mouth I will proclaim
     your faithfulness to all
     generations.
2 I declare that your steadfast love is
     established forever;
   your faithfulness is as firm as the
     heavens.

3 You said, "I have made a covenant
     with my chosen one,

a Meaning of Heb uncertain   *b* Gk: Heb *the steadfast love of the* LORD

88:6 *Dark*—This becomes the key word, including the final word of the psalm (see vv. 12, 15).

88:8—The psalmists often complain of being isolated from their former friends (see v. 18; 31:11; 41:9; 55:12–14).

88:11 *Abaddon*—This is another name for Sheol (see v. 3; Job 26:6). The psalmist reflects the traditional view that even God has no access to the realm of the dead, and hence that God's *steadfast love* can have no effect (see 6:4–5; compare 139:8).

88:16 *Wrath*—See v. 7. The psalmist echoes a traditional view that suffering is punishment for sin, but simultaneously undercuts this view by clinging to God anyway (see 6:1; introduction, "Prayers for Help").

Psalm 89

89:1–2 *Steadfast love . . . faithfulness*—Both are key words in the psalm; see vv. 5, 8, 14, 24, 28, 33, 49. By v. 49, however, both are called into question (see 5:7; 36:5–6).

89:3 *Covenant with . . . David*—Compare 2 Sam. 7:1–17. The psalm rehearses all the elements of the Davidic covenant (Ps. 89:19–37) before suggesting that the covenant has failed (vv. 38–51, esp. v. 39). The key placement of Ps. 89 at the end of Book III suggests that, in some sense, the remainder of the Psalter responds to the crisis articulated here (see introduction, "Psalms 1–2 and the Shape of the Psalter").

I have sworn to my servant David:
4 'I will establish your descendants
    forever,
    and build your throne for all
    generations.' "   *Selah*

5 Let the heavens praise your wonders,
    O LORD,
    your faithfulness in the assembly
    of the holy ones.
6 For who in the skies can be
    compared to the LORD?
    Who among the heavenly beings is
    like the LORD,
7 a God feared in the council of the
    holy ones,
    great and awesome[a] above all that
    are around him?
8 O LORD God of hosts,
    who is as mighty as you, O LORD?
    Your faithfulness surrounds you.
9 You rule the raging of the sea;
    when its waves rise, you still
    them.
10 You crushed Rahab like a carcass;
    you scattered your enemies with
    your mighty arm.
11 The heavens are yours, the earth also
    is yours;
    the world and all that is in it—you
    have founded them.
12 The north and the south[b]—you
    created them;
    Tabor and Hermon joyously praise
    your name.
13 You have a mighty arm;
    strong is your hand, high your
    right hand.
14 Righteousness and justice are the
    foundation of your throne;
    steadfast love and faithfulness go
    before you.
15 Happy are the people who know the
    festal shout,

who walk, O LORD, in the light of
    your countenance;
16 they exult in your name all day long,
    and extol[c] your righteousness.
17 For you are the glory of their
    strength;
    by your favor our horn is exalted.
18 For our shield belongs to the LORD,
    our king to the Holy One of
    Israel.

19 Then you spoke in a vision to your
    faithful one, and said:
    "I have set the crown[d] on one who
    is mighty,
    I have exalted one chosen from the
    people.
20 I have found my servant David;
    with my holy oil I have anointed
    him;
21 my hand shall always remain with
    him;
    my arm also shall strengthen
    him.
22 The enemy shall not outwit him,
    the wicked shall not humble him.
23 I will crush his foes before him
    and strike down those who hate
    him.
24 My faithfulness and steadfast love
    shall be with him;
    and in my name his horn shall be
    exalted.
25 I will set his hand on the sea
    and his right hand on the rivers.
26 He shall cry to me, 'You are my
    Father,
    my God, and the Rock of my
    salvation!'
27 I will make him the firstborn,
    the highest of the kings of the
    earth.

a Gk Syr: Heb greatly awesome *b* Or Zaphon and Yamin *c* Cn: Heb are
exalted in *d* Cn: Heb help

89:4—See 2 Sam. 7:13.
89:5–18—The focus here is on God's sovereignty, manifest in God's creative power (vv.
9–12; *Rahab* in v. 10, unlike in 87:4, refers to a
mythical chaos monster, which God defeats, as
in 74:12–14). As often in the Psalter, righteous-

ness and justice are explicitly linked to God's
sovereignty (v. 14; see introduction, "Psalms 1–2
and the Shape of the Psalter").

89:19–37—God's sovereign claim is to be enacted on earth by the Davidic kings, God's *anointed*
(v. 20; see vv. 38, 51; 2:2).

28 Forever I will keep my steadfast love
      for him,
   and my covenant with him will
      stand firm.
29 I will establish his line forever,
   and his throne as long as the
      heavens endure.
30 If his children forsake my law
   and do not walk according to my
      ordinances,
31 if they violate my statutes
   and do not keep my
      commandments,
32 then I will punish their transgression
      with the rod
   and their iniquity with scourges;
33 but I will not remove from him my
      steadfast love,
   or be false to my faithfulness.
34 I will not violate my covenant,
   or alter the word that went forth
      from my lips.
35 Once and for all I have sworn by my
      holiness;
   I will not lie to David.
36 His line shall continue forever,
   and his throne endure before me
      like the sun.
37 It shall be established forever like the
      moon,
   an enduring witness in the skies."
                                    Selah

38 But now you have spurned and
      rejected him;
   you are full of wrath against your
      anointed.
39 You have renounced the covenant
      with your servant;
   you have defiled his crown in the
      dust.
40 You have broken through all his
      walls;
   you have laid his strongholds in
      ruins.
41 All who pass by plunder him;

he has become the scorn of his
      neighbors.
42 You have exalted the right hand of
      his foes;
   you have made all his enemies
      rejoice.
43 Moreover, you have turned back the
      edge of his sword,
   and you have not supported him
      in battle.
44 You have removed the scepter from
      his hand,[a]
   and hurled his throne to the
      ground.
45 You have cut short the days of his
      youth;
   you have covered him with shame.
                                    Selah

46 How long, O Lord? Will you hide
      yourself forever?
   How long will your wrath burn
      like fire?
47 Remember how short my time is—[b]
   for what vanity you have created
      all mortals!
48 Who can live and never see death?
   Who can escape the power of
      Sheol?   Selah

49 Lord, where is your steadfast love of
      old,
   which by your faithfulness you
      swore to David?
50 Remember, O Lord, how your
      servant is taunted;
   how I bear in my bosom the
      insults of the peoples,[c]
51 with which your enemies taunt,
      O Lord,
   with which they taunted the
      footsteps of your anointed.

52 Blessed be the Lord forever.
      Amen and Amen.

[a] Cn: Heb *removed his cleanness* [b] Meaning of Heb uncertain [c] Cn: Heb *bosom all of many peoples*

89:38–51—What vv. 1–37 suggest is impossible has happened—that is, the "anointed" has been *rejected* (v. 38), reflecting the events of 587 BCE and prompting the painful questions of vv. 46 and 48–49, with which Book III concludes and to which Book IV responds.

89:52—This is the concluding doxology for Book III; see 41:13.

BOOK IV
(Psalms 90–106)

Psalm 90
God's Eternity and Human Frailty
A Prayer of Moses, the man of God.

1   Lord, you have been our dwelling
        place[a]
    in all generations.
2   Before the mountains were brought
        forth,
        or ever you had formed the earth
            and the world,
        from everlasting to everlasting you
            are God.

3   You turn us[b] back to dust,
        and say, "Turn back, you mortals."
4   For a thousand years in your sight
        are like yesterday when it is past,
        or like a watch in the night.
5   You sweep them away; they are like a
            dream,
        like grass that is renewed in the
            morning;
6   in the morning it flourishes and is
            renewed;
        in the evening it fades and withers.

7   For we are consumed by your anger;
        by your wrath we are
            overwhelmed.
8   You have set our iniquities before
            you,
        our secret sins in the light of your
            countenance.

9   For all our days pass away under
            your wrath;
        our years come to an end[c] like a
            sigh.
10 The days of our life are seventy
            years,
        or perhaps eighty, if we are
            strong;
    even then their span[d] is only toil and
            trouble;
        they are soon gone, and we fly
            away.

11 Who considers the power of your
            anger?
        Your wrath is as great as the fear
            that is due you.
12 So teach us to count our days
        that we may gain a wise heart.

13 Turn, O LORD! How long?
        Have compassion on your
            servants!
14 Satisfy us in the morning with your
            steadfast love,
        so that we may rejoice and be glad
            all our days.
15 Make us glad as many days as you
            have afflicted us,
        and as many years as we have seen
            evil.
16 Let your work be manifest to your
            servants,
        and your glorious power to their
            children.

a Another reading is *our refuge* *b* Heb *humankind* *c* Syr: Heb *we bring our years to an end* *d* Cn Compare Gk Syr Jerome Tg: Heb *pride*

Psalm 90

90 (Title) *Moses*—The only psalm attributed to Moses, its placement here is particularly apt after the failure described in 89:38–51, since Moses led the people before there was a monarchy, a temple, or a settled existence in the land (see introduction, "Psalms 1–2 and the Shape of the Psalter").

90:1 *Dwelling place*—Synonymous with "refuge," it suggests that God alone is the people's genuine and enduring security (see introduction, "Psalms of Trust").

90:3–6—Words for time are prevalent, as the transience of human life is described (see 89:47–48; Gen. 3:19; Isa. 40:6–8).

90:7–11—*Anger* and *wrath* here indicate not so much punishment as the experience of human limitations that often tempt us either to despair or to denial.

90:12—The translation of v. 12a is familiar but not helpful. It may be paraphrased, "Teach us to live day by day in dependence upon you."

90:13–17—Time words recur, but now in a context of hope rather than lament. Trusting God's *compassion* (v. 13) and *steadfast love* (v. 14; see 5:7; 36:5; Exod. 34:6–7) makes possible hope, joy (vv. 14–15), and constructive *work* (v. 17).

17 Let the favor of the Lord our God be
upon us,
and prosper for us the work of our
hands—
O prosper the work of our hands!

Psalm 91

Assurance of God's Protection

1 You who live in the shelter of the
Most High,
who abide in the shadow of the
Almighty,a
2 will say to the LORD, "My refuge and
my fortress;
my God, in whom I trust."
3 For he will deliver you from the
snare of the fowler
and from the deadly pestilence;
4 he will cover you with his pinions,
and under his wings you will find
refuge;
his faithfulness is a shield and
buckler.
5 You will not fear the terror of the
night,
or the arrow that flies by day,
6 or the pestilence that stalks in
darkness,
or the destruction that wastes at
noonday.
7 A thousand may fall at your side,
ten thousand at your right
hand,
but it will not come near you.
8 You will only look with your eyes
and see the punishment of the
wicked.

9 Because you have made the LORD
your refuge,b
the Most High your dwelling
place,
10 no evil shall befall you,
no scourge come near your tent.
11 For he will command his angels
concerning you
to guard you in all your ways.
12 On their hands they will bear you up,
so that you will not dash your foot
against a stone.
13 You will tread on the lion and the
adder,
the young lion and the serpent you
will trample under foot.
14 Those who love me, I will deliver;
I will protect those who know my
name.
15 When they call to me, I will answer
them;
I will be with them in trouble,
I will rescue them and honor them.
16 With long life I will satisfy them,
and show them my salvation.

Psalm 92

Thanksgiving for Vindication

A Psalm. A Song for the Sabbath Day.

1 It is good to give thanks to the LORD,
to sing praises to your name,
O Most High;
2 to declare your steadfast love in the
morning,

a Traditional rendering of Heb *Shaddai* b Cn: Heb *Because you, LORD, are
my refuge; you have made*

Psalm 91

91:2—The trust implied in 90:13–17 is explicit
here (see 4:5; 13:5; introduction, "Psalms of
Trust"). See *refuge* also in vv. 4, 9; 2:12.

91:4 *Under his wings*—Synonymous with *refuge*
(see 17:8).

91:11–12—The danger of superstitious appropriation of the promise here is illustrated when Jesus
refuses to claim it for his own benefit (see Matt.
4:5–7; Luke 4:9–12).

91:14–16—These verses emphasize that the
promise is "refuge," not a life free of *trouble*
(v. 15) or turmoil.

Psalm 92

92 (Title)—Late Jewish sources identify a psalm
for use in the temple on every day of the week,
but this is the only one given such a designation
in the canonical psalter. While Ps. 92 may indeed have been used on the Sabbath, the second-
century-CE Jewish work the *Mishnah* suggests
that it points toward the world to come, when
the implementation of God's *works* (vv. 4–5) will
constitute a perpetual Sabbath.

92:2 *Steadfast love . . . and your faithfulness*—
See 5:7; 36:5–6; 89:1–2; 90:14.

and your faithfulness by night,
³ to the music of the lute and the
harp,
to the melody of the lyre.
⁴ For you, O LORD, have made me
glad by your work;
at the works of your hands I sing
for joy.

⁵ How great are your works,
O LORD!
Your thoughts are very deep!
⁶ The dullard cannot know,
the stupid cannot understand
this:
⁷ though the wicked sprout like grass
and all evildoers flourish,
they are doomed to destruction
forever,
⁸ but you, O LORD, are on high
forever.
⁹ For your enemies, O LORD,
for your enemies shall perish;
all evildoers shall be scattered.

¹⁰ But you have exalted my horn like
that of the wild ox;
you have poured over me^a fresh
oil.
¹¹ My eyes have seen the downfall of
my enemies;
my ears have heard the doom of
my evil assailants.
¹² The righteous flourish like the palm
tree,
and grow like a cedar in Lebanon.

¹³ They are planted in the house of the
LORD;
they flourish in the courts of our
God.
¹⁴ In old age they still produce fruit;
they are always green and full of
sap,
¹⁵ showing that the LORD is upright;
he is my rock, and there is no
unrighteousness in him.

Psalm 93
The Majesty of God's Rule

¹ The LORD is king, he is robed in
majesty;
the LORD is robed, he is girded
with strength.
He has established the world; it shall
never be moved;
² your throne is established from of
old;
you are from everlasting.

³ The floods have lifted up, O LORD,
the floods have lifted up their voice;
the floods lift up their roaring.
⁴ More majestic than the thunders of
mighty waters,
more majestic than the waves^b of
the sea,
majestic on high is the LORD!

⁵ Your decrees are very sure;
holiness befits your house,
O LORD, forevermore.

^{a} Syr: Meaning of Heb uncertain ^{b} Cn: Heb *majestic are the waves*

92:4–5—The repetition of *work(s)* focuses attention on God and God's purposes, which is where praise begins (see v. 1; introduction, "Songs of Praise").

92:6–8—Stupidity and wickedness are synonymous (see 1:3–6; 14:1); both mean the failure to acknowledge God's sovereignty, as the psalmist does in v. 8.

92:9, 11—On the perishing of the wicked, see 1:3–6; introduction, "Prayers for Help."

92:12–15—For similar use of the imagery of a fruitful tree, see 1:3; 52:8–9.

Psalm 93

93:1 *The LORD is king*—Psalm 93 is part of a collection usually called the enthronement psalms

(93, 95–99), all of which explicitly assert God's sovereignty. They form a prominent part of Book IV and its response to the crisis articulated in 89:38–51 (see introduction, "Psalms 1–2 and the Shape of the Psalter").

93:3—Symbolic of the forces of chaos and disorder, the *floods* now belong under God's rule (see 24:1–2, 8).

93:5—The movement from God's creative power to God's *decrees* is a natural one (see the movement from 19:1–6 to 19:7–14), since monarchs were entrusted with creating order among their people by their "decrees." Psalms 96–99 will explicitly describe God's will in terms of justice and righteousness; and 99:3, 5, 9 will return to the theme of holiness.

Psalm 94
God the Avenger of the Righteous

1 O LORD, you God of vengeance,
　　you God of vengeance, shine forth!
2 Rise up, O judge of the earth;
　　give to the proud what they
　　　deserve!
3 O LORD, how long shall the wicked,
　　how long shall the wicked exult?

4 They pour out their arrogant words;
　　all the evildoers boast.
5 They crush your people, O LORD,
　　and afflict your heritage.
6 They kill the widow and the
　　　stranger,
　　they murder the orphan,
7 and they say, "The LORD does not
　　　see;
　　the God of Jacob does not
　　　perceive."

8 Understand, O dullest of the people;
　　fools, when will you be wise?
9 He who planted the ear, does he not
　　　hear?
　　He who formed the eye, does he not
　　　see?
10 He who disciplines the nations,
　　he who teaches knowledge to
　　　humankind,
　　does he not chastise?
11 The LORD knows our thoughts,[a]
　　that they are but an empty breath.

12 Happy are those whom you
　　　discipline, O LORD,
　　and whom you teach out of your
　　　law,

13 giving them respite from days of
　　　trouble,
　　until a pit is dug for the wicked.
14 For the LORD will not forsake his
　　　people;
　　he will not abandon his heritage;
15 for justice will return to the
　　　righteous,
　　and all the upright in heart will
　　　follow it.

16 Who rises up for me against the
　　　wicked?
　　Who stands up for me against
　　　evildoers?
17 If the LORD had not been my help,
　　my soul would soon have lived in
　　　the land of silence.
18 When I thought, "My foot is
　　　slipping,"
　　your steadfast love, O LORD, held
　　　me up.
19 When the cares of my heart are
　　　many,
　　your consolations cheer my soul.
20 Can wicked rulers be allied with
　　　you,
　　those who contrive mischief by
　　　statute?
21 They band together against the life
　　　of the righteous,
　　and condemn the innocent to
　　　death.
22 But the LORD has become my
　　　stronghold,
　　and my God the rock of my
　　　refuge.

[a] Heb *the thoughts of humankind*

Psalm 94

94:1–2—As the juxtaposition of vv. 1 and 2 suggests, the purpose of God's *vengeance* is to establish "justice" (NRSV *judge*; see introduction, "Prayers for Help"). Although an apparent interruption to the enthronement psalms, the concern with justice in Ps. 94 (see also v. 15) links it to this collection.

94:3–7—The *arrogant* (v. 4) and violent (vv. 6, 21) self-assertion of *the wicked* (v. 3) means that God's establishment of justice must take the form of ending oppression (see 72:4, 14), in order to save victims like the *widow* and *orphan* (see

10:14, 18; 68:5; 146:9). On the speech of the wicked (v. 7), see introduction, "Psalms of Trust."

94:8—Foolishness is the failure to acknowledge God's claim on human life (see 92:6).

94:12—The association of happiness and *law* (better translated "instruction") recalls 1:1–2.

94:18 *Steadfast love*—As is often the case, God's help is motivated by God's love (see 5:7; 36:5–6; 92:2).

94:22 *Refuge*—Amid adversity, the psalmists regularly find refuge in God (see introduction, "Psalms of Trust").

23 He will repay them for their
      iniquity
   and wipe them out for their
      wickedness;
   the LORD our God will wipe them
      out.

Psalm 95
A Call to Worship and Obedience

1 O come, let us sing to the LORD;
   let us make a joyful noise to the
      rock of our salvation!
2 Let us come into his presence with
      thanksgiving;
   let us make a joyful noise to him
      with songs of praise!
3 For the LORD is a great God,
   and a great King above all gods.
4 In his hand are the depths of the
      earth;
   the heights of the mountains are
      his also.
5 The sea is his, for he made it,
   and the dry land, which his hands
      have formed.

6 O come, let us worship and bow
      down,
   let us kneel before the LORD, our
      Maker!
7 For he is our God,
   and we are the people of his
      pasture,
   and the sheep of his hand.

   O that today you would listen to his
      voice!
8   Do not harden your hearts, as at
      Meribah,

as on the day at Massah in the
      wilderness,
9 when your ancestors tested me,
   and put me to the proof, though
      they had seen my work.
10 For forty years I loathed that
      generation
   and said, "They are a people whose
      hearts go astray,
   and they do not regard my ways."
11 Therefore in my anger I swore,
   "They shall not enter my rest."

Psalm 96
Praise to God Who Comes in Judgment

1 O sing to the LORD a new song;
   sing to the LORD, all the earth.
2 Sing to the LORD, bless his name;
   tell of his salvation from day to
      day.
3 Declare his glory among the nations,
   his marvelous works among all the
      peoples.
4 For great is the LORD, and greatly to
      be praised;
   he is to be revered above all gods.
5 For all the gods of the peoples are
      idols,
   but the LORD made the heavens.
6 Honor and majesty are before him;
   strength and beauty are in his
      sanctuary.
7 Ascribe to the LORD, O families of
      the peoples,
   ascribe to the LORD glory and
      strength.
8 Ascribe to the LORD the glory due
      his name;

94:23—On God's repayment of the wicked, see 1:3–6; 92:9, 11; introduction, "Prayers for Help."

Psalm 95

95:3 *Great King*—The explicit recognition of God's sovereignty is characteristic of the enthronement collection (see 93:1).

95:5—God's sovereignty is world-encompassing, and includes the chaotic waters (see 24:1–2).

95:7 *The sheep of his hand*—The role of shepherd also suggests God's sovereignty; see 23:1; 100:3. *Listen*—Because the sovereign is responsible for establishing order and harmony among

the people, the people need to listen (see 81:8, 11, 13).

95:8 *Meribah . . . Massah*—See 81:7; Exod. 17:1–7.

95:10–11—See Num. 14:33–35. Genuine praise is inseparable from trust and obedience (see introduction, "Songs of Praise").

Psalm 96

96:1 *New song*—See 33:3; 98:1. The invitation to *all the earth* to join the song is typical (see introduction, "Songs of Praise"). The same expansive perspective is evident in vv. 3, 7, 9, 10–13.

bring an offering, and come into
　　his courts.
9 Worship the LORD in holy splendor;
　　tremble before him, all the earth.

10 Say among the nations, "The LORD is
　　　king!
　　The world is firmly established; it
　　　shall never be moved.
　　He will judge the peoples with
　　　equity."
11 Let the heavens be glad, and let the
　　　earth rejoice;
　　let the sea roar, and all that fills it;
12 　　let the field exult, and everything
　　　in it.
　　Then shall all the trees of the forest
　　　sing for joy
13 　　before the LORD; for he is coming,
　　　for he is coming to judge the earth.
　　He will judge the world with
　　　righteousness,
　　and the peoples with his truth.

Psalm 97
The Glory of God's Reign

1 The LORD is king! Let the earth
　　　rejoice;
　　let the many coastlands be glad!
2 Clouds and thick darkness are all
　　　around him;
　　righteousness and justice are the
　　　foundation of his throne.
3 Fire goes before him,

and consumes his adversaries on
　　every side.
4 His lightnings light up the world;
　　the earth sees and trembles.
5 The mountains melt like wax before
　　the LORD,
　　before the Lord of all the earth.
6 The heavens proclaim his
　　　righteousness;
　　and all the peoples behold his
　　　glory.
7 All worshipers of images are put to
　　　shame,
　　those who make their boast in
　　　worthless idols;
　　all gods bow down before him.
8 Zion hears and is glad,
　　and the towns[a] of Judah rejoice,
　　because of your judgments, O God.
9 For you, O LORD, are most high over
　　　all the earth;
　　you are exalted far above all gods.

10 The LORD loves those who hate[b] evil;
　　he guards the lives of his faithful;
　　he rescues them from the hand of
　　　the wicked.
11 Light dawns[c] for the righteous,
　　and joy for the upright in heart.
12 Rejoice in the LORD, O you
　　　righteous,
　　and give thanks to his holy name!

[a] Heb *daughters*　[b] Cn: Heb *You who love the LORD hate*　[c] Gk Syr Jerome: Heb *is sown*

96:10 *The LORD is king!*—Characteristic of the enthronement collection (see 93:1).

96:11–13—It is highly significant that God's kingship is hailed not only by *the nations* (v. 10), but also by the whole creation (vv. 11–12). This partnership of praise forms a community of the human, the nonhuman creatures, and creation itself (see the original biblical covenant in Gen. 9:8–17, where the parties include God, human-kind, "every living creature," and "the earth"). God's *coming* or presence in the world is marked by God's will "to establish justice" (NRSV *judge* in vv. 10, 13) and *righteousness* among "the peoples" (see introduction, "Psalms 1–2 and the Shape of the Psalter"). When God is worshiped, the appropriate congregation includes the whole world (see introduction, "Songs of Praise").

Psalm 97

97:1 *The LORD is king!*—The world-encompassing claim of God is again in view (see introduction, "Songs of Praise;" 93:1).

97:2 *Righteousness and justice*—The essence of God's will, these terms are frequently associated with God's sovereignty (see introduction, "Psalms 1–2 and the Shape of the Psalter"; 96:11–13).

97:3–5—The theophany here, as elsewhere, functions to support the claim of God's universal sovereignty; see 18:7–19.

97:6—The whole creation joins in praise and proclamation (see 19:1; 96:11–13).

97:7–9—Because God's sovereignty is universal, the claims of any other gods are relativized (see Ps. 82).

97:8 *Zion*—See 48:1–2.

Psalm 98
Praise the Judge of the World
A Psalm.

1 O sing to the LORD a new song,
    for he has done marvelous things.
His right hand and his holy arm
    have gotten him victory.
2 The LORD has made known his victory;
    he has revealed his vindication in
        the sight of the nations.
3 He has remembered his steadfast
        love and faithfulness
    to the house of Israel.
All the ends of the earth have seen
    the victory of our God.

4 Make a joyful noise to the LORD, all
        the earth;
    break forth into joyous song and
        sing praises.
5 Sing praises to the LORD with the lyre,
    with the lyre and the sound of
        melody.
6 With trumpets and the sound of the
        horn

make a joyful noise before the
    King, the LORD.
7 Let the sea roar, and all that fills it;
    the world and those who live in it.
8 Let the floods clap their hands;
    let the hills sing together for joy
9 at the presence of the LORD, for he is
        coming
    to judge the earth.
He will judge the world with
        righteousness,
    and the peoples with equity.

Psalm 99
Praise to God for His Holiness

1 The LORD is king; let the peoples
        tremble!
He sits enthroned upon the
        cherubim; let the earth
        quake!
2 The LORD is great in Zion;
    he is exalted over all the peoples.
3 Let them praise your great and
        awesome name.
Holy is he!

Psalm 98

98:1 *New song*—Elsewhere, as here, explicitly associated with the proclamation of God's reign (see 33:3; 96:1). *Victory*—The translation here and in vv. 2–3 is unnecessarily triumphalistic. The Hebrew word is usually translated "salvation" or "deliverance" and means the creation or restoration of conditions that make life possible as God intends. Against the forces of chaos and death, God has prevailed. The allusion could be to creation or exodus or both, since both involved the "defeat" of forces that represented disorder or death (see 24:8; 68:1–6; 74:12–14).

98:2 *Vindication*—Again, the translation is unnecessarily triumphalistic. The word is usually translated "righteousness." What is being celebrated is that God has set things right in the world (see v. 9).

98:3 *Steadfast love and faithfulness*—These fundamental attributes of God are frequently celebrated and appealed to in prayer (see 5:7; 36:5–6; 92:2).

98:4 *All the earth*—The creation-wide perspective is typical (see introduction, "Songs of Praise"; 96:1).

98:6 *The King*—The sovereignty of God is explicitly proclaimed in the enthronement collection (see 93:1).

98:7–9—See 96:11–13. The final word, "equity," in 98:9 differs from 96:13. God's claim on the whole earth, including all "the nations" (98:2), establishes a solidarity among the families of the earth, but also between humankind and the non-human creation.

Psalm 99

99:1 *The LORD is king*—Typical of the enthronement collection (see 93:1). *Upon the cherubim*—This is a reference to the ark, the symbol of God's earthly throne (see note at 17:8).

99:2 *Great in Zion*—See 48:1–2.

99:3 *Holy is he!*—See also vv. 5 and 9. Holiness ordinarily connotes separateness for purity's sake. But God's holiness is inevitably relational, because it involves *justice and righteousness* (v. 4) and thus is all bound up with humankind, including the failings of even great leaders like *Moses, Aaron*, and *Samuel* (v. 6). Instead of withdrawing or separating from sinners, God stays involved as *a forgiving God to them* (v. 8). This has profound implications for understanding God's sovereignty—that is, God exercises power as love rather than as sheer force (see introduction, "Prayers for Help").

⁴ Mighty King,*a* lover of justice,
   you have established equity;
you have executed justice
   and righteousness in Jacob.
⁵ Extol the LORD our God;
   worship at his footstool.
   Holy is he!

⁶ Moses and Aaron were among his
      priests,
   Samuel also was among those who
      called on his name.
   They cried to the LORD, and he
      answered them.
⁷ He spoke to them in the pillar of
      cloud;
   they kept his decrees,
   and the statutes that he gave
      them.

⁸ O LORD our God, you answered
      them;
   you were a forgiving God to them,
   but an avenger of their
      wrongdoings.
⁹ Extol the LORD our God,
   and worship at his holy
      mountain;
   for the LORD our God is holy.

Psalm 100
All Lands Summoned to Praise God
A Psalm of thanksgiving.

¹ Make a joyful noise to the LORD, all
      the earth.
²   Worship the LORD with gladness;
   come into his presence with singing.

³ Know that the LORD is God.
   It is he that made us, and we are
      his;*b*
   we are his people, and the sheep of
      his pasture.

⁴ Enter his gates with thanksgiving,
   and his courts with praise.
   Give thanks to him, bless his name.

⁵ For the LORD is good;
   his steadfast love endures forever,
   and his faithfulness to all
      generations.

Psalm 101
A Sovereign's Pledge of Integrity
and Justice
Of David. A Psalm.

¹ I will sing of loyalty and of justice;

a Cn: Heb *And a king's strength* *b* Another reading is *and not we ourselves*

99:4 *Justice . . . and righteousness*—The essence of God's will (see introduction, "Psalms 1–2 and the Shape of the Psalter"; 96:11–13).

99:5 *Footstool*—This refers to the ark (see v. 1).

99:7 *Decrees*—This word recalls the beginning of the enthronement collection (see 93:5).

99:9 *Holy mountain*—See 48:1–2.

Psalm 100

100:1 *All the earth*—Immediately following the enthronement collection, Ps. 100 maintains the universe-wide perspective (see introduction, "Songs of Praise").

100:2 *Worship*—The word fundamentally means "serve" (see RSV); that is, the invitation is to submit to the sovereignty of God in the service of God's purposes. So, it is fitting that this invitation immediately follows the enthronement collection (Pss. 29, 47, 93, 95–99).

100:3 *Know*—Although this invitation is explicitly instructional, all the songs of praise teach about God and God's purposes for the world (see introduction, "Songs of Praise"). *We are his*—Some manuscripts support the NRSV

footnote, "and not we ourselves." In either case, the affirmation is that we humans are not self-constituted or self-grounded. Rather, we belong to God. This simple-sounding affirmation is a radical challenge to the excessive individualism that characterizes contemporary North American society (see note at 1:2).

100:4 *Thanksgiving . . . praise*—The lives of those who honor God's claim and thus posture themselves as servants of God (v. 2) will be characterized by gratitude and praise (see the title of the psalm as well; see also 50:14, 23).

100:5 *Steadfast love . . . faithfulness*—See 5:7; 36:5–6; 92:2; 98:3; Exod. 34:6–7. The songs of praise regularly cite God's fundamental character as the reason for praising God (see 107:1; 117:1; 118:1, 29; 136:1–22, 26).

Psalm 101

101:1 *I*—The speaker seems to be a person of authority and responsibility, and is often considered to be the king, in which case Ps. 101 may have functioned as a royal oath of office (see Pss. 2, 18, 72). After the monarchy disappeared, it could have served to represent the values that

to you, O LORD, I will sing.
2 I will study the way that is
   blameless.
   When shall I attain it?

   I will walk with integrity of heart
   within my house;
3 I will not set before my eyes
   anything that is base.

   I hate the work of those who fall
   away;
   it shall not cling to me.
4 Perverseness of heart shall be far
   from me;
   I will know nothing of evil.

5 One who secretly slanders a
   neighbor
   I will destroy.
   A haughty look and an arrogant
   heart
   I will not tolerate.

6 I will look with favor on the faithful
   in the land,
   so that they may live with me;
   whoever walks in the way that is
   blameless
   shall minister to me.

7 No one who practices deceit
   shall remain in my house;
   no one who utters lies
   shall continue in my presence.

8 Morning by morning I will destroy
   all the wicked in the land,
   cutting off all evildoers
   from the city of the LORD.

Psalm 102
Prayer to the Eternal King for Help
*A prayer of one afflicted, when faint
and pleading before the LORD.*

1 Hear my prayer, O LORD;
   let my cry come to you.
2 Do not hide your face from me
   in the day of my distress.
   Incline your ear to me;
   answer me speedily in the day
   when I call.

3 For my days pass away like smoke,
   and my bones burn like a
   furnace.
4 My heart is stricken and withered
   like grass;
   I am too wasted to eat my bread.
5 Because of my loud groaning
   my bones cling to my skin.
6 I am like an owl of the wilderness,
   like a little owl of the waste
   places.
7 I lie awake;
   I am like a lonely bird on the
   housetop.
8 All day long my enemies taunt me;
   those who deride me use my name
   for a curse.
9 For I eat ashes like bread,
   and mingle tears with my drink,
10 because of your indignation and
   anger;
   for you have lifted me up and
   thrown me aside.
11 My days are like an evening shadow;
   I wither away like grass.

God wills for all people, persons in authority or
otherwise.

101:1 *Loyalty . . . justice*—These are precisely
what the king should sing about, since he was
especially entrusted with enacting God's will
on earth, and since "loyalty" (usually translated
"steadfast love"; see 5:7; 36:5–6) is a summary
of God's character, and "justice" is a summary of
God's will (see introduction, "Psalms 1–2 and the
Shape of the Psalter"; 96:11–13).

101:2 *Blameless . . . integrity*—These words
translate the same Hebrew root, which connotes
not sinlessness, but rather a life lived in loyalty

to and dependence upon God (see 18:23). See
also v. 6.

101:5–8—After proclaiming his own loyalty to
God, the king promises, in effect, to run an administration that also has integrity. Verse 8 should
be heard not so much as revenge, but as opposition to oppression that perpetuates injustice (see
72:4, 14).

Psalm 102

102 (Title)—This accurately describes all the
prayers for help in the Psalter. It is one of the
church's seven Penitential Psalms (see Ps. 6).

¹² But you, O LORD, are enthroned
     forever;
       your name endures to all
         generations.
¹³ You will rise up and have
       compassion on Zion,
       for it is time to favor it;
       the appointed time has come.
¹⁴ For your servants hold its stones
       dear,
       and have pity on its dust.
¹⁵ The nations will fear the name of the
     LORD,
       and all the kings of the earth your
         glory.
¹⁶ For the LORD will build up Zion;
       he will appear in his glory.
¹⁷ He will regard the prayer of the
       destitute,
       and will not despise their prayer.

¹⁸ Let this be recorded for a generation
       to come,
       so that a people yet unborn may
         praise the LORD:
¹⁹ that he looked down from his holy
       height,
       from heaven the LORD looked at
         the earth,
²⁰ to hear the groans of the
       prisoners,
       to set free those who were doomed
         to die;
²¹ so that the name of the LORD may be
       declared in Zion,
       and his praise in Jerusalem,
²² when peoples gather together,
       and kingdoms, to worship the
         LORD.

²³ He has broken my strength in
       midcourse;
       he has shortened my days.
²⁴ "O my God," I say, "do not take me
       away
       at the midpoint of my life,
     you whose years endure
       throughout all generations."

²⁵ Long ago you laid the foundation of
       the earth,
       and the heavens are the work of
         your hands.
²⁶ They will perish, but you endure;
       they will all wear out like a
         garment.
     You change them like clothing, and
       they pass away;
²⁷ but you are the same, and your
       years have no end.
²⁸ The children of your servants shall
       live secure;
       their offspring shall be established
         in your presence.

Psalm 103
Thanksgiving for God's Goodness
Of David.

¹ Bless the LORD, O my soul,
       and all that is within me,
       bless his holy name.
² Bless the LORD, O my soul,
       and do not forget all his
         benefits—
³ who forgives all your iniquity,
       who heals all your diseases,
⁴ who redeems your life from the Pit,
       who crowns you with steadfast
         love and mercy,

102:12 *Enthroned forever*—Despite the lengthy complaint and plea (vv. 1–11), the psalmist still asserts God's sovereignty (see 80:1).

102:13 *Zion*—See 48:1–2. Verses 13–17 seem to suggest that Jerusalem has been destroyed.

102:17 *He . . . destitute*—As usual, the psalmist affirms that God sides with the victimized (see vv. 1–11, 22; introduction, "Prayers for Help").

102:28—After another round of complaint and plea (vv. 23–27), the psalmist returns to hope, suggesting the inseparability of pain and praise,

hurt and hope, in the faithful life (see introduction, "Prayers for Help").

Psalm 103

103:1 *Bless . . . O my soul*—Blessing connotes submission to God (see 34:1). "Soul" connotes one's whole life and being.

103:4 *Steadfast love and mercy*—See 5:7; 36:5–6; Exod. 34:6–7. These words become thematic—see "steadfast love" in 103:8, 11, 17, and "mercy/merciful/compassion" (all the same Heb. root) in vv. 8, 13. The psalm is essentially an exposition upon and celebration of God's gracious love.

5 who satisfies you with good as long
     as you live[a]
   so that your youth is renewed like
     the eagle's.

6 The LORD works vindication
     and justice for all who are
     oppressed.
7 He made known his ways to Moses,
     his acts to the people of Israel.
8 The LORD is merciful and gracious,
     slow to anger and abounding in
     steadfast love.
9 He will not always accuse,
     nor will he keep his anger forever.
10 He does not deal with us according
     to our sins,
   nor repay us according to our
     iniquities.
11 For as the heavens are high above
     the earth,
   so great is his steadfast love toward
     those who fear him;
12 as far as the east is from the west,
   so far he removes our
     transgressions from us.
13 As a father has compassion for his
     children,
   so the LORD has compassion for
     those who fear him.
14 For he knows how we were made;
   he remembers that we are dust.

15 As for mortals, their days are like
     grass;

they flourish like a flower of the
     field;
16 for the wind passes over it, and it is
     gone,
   and its place knows it no more.
17 But the steadfast love of the LORD
     is from everlasting to
     everlasting
   on those who fear him,
   and his righteousness to children's
     children,
18 to those who keep his covenant
     and remember to do his
     commandments.
19 The LORD has established his throne
     in the heavens,
   and his kingdom rules over all.
20 Bless the LORD, O you his angels,
     you mighty ones who do his
     bidding,
   obedient to his spoken word.
21 Bless the LORD, all his hosts,
     his ministers that do his will.
22 Bless the LORD, all his works,
     in all places of his dominion.
   Bless the LORD, O my soul.

Psalm 104
God the Creator and Provider
1 Bless the LORD, O my soul.
   O LORD my God, you are very
     great.

[a] Meaning of Heb uncertain

103:6 *Vindication . . . justice*—Often separated
from vv. 3–5, as in NRSV, v. 6 is actually the
summarizing culmination of the series of God's
actions. They all amount to manifestations of
God's "righteousness" (NRSV "vindication") and
"justice," the two words that summarize God's
will (see introduction, "Psalms 1–2 and the Shape
of the Psalter"; 96:11–13). It is the *oppressed*
who especially need for God to set things right,
and it is they with whom God regularly sides (see
introduction, "Prayers for Help").

103:8—See 86:15; Exod. 34:6–7.

103:13—See v. 4. Although the image associates
compassion with a loving father, the word is
related to a noun that means "womb," and hence
suggests motherly compassion (see 131:2–3).

103:17–18—God's love seems to be limited to
those who deserve it (see also vv. 11, 13), but

this is the psalmist's way of affirming that grace
does not mean that God has no standards. God
fervently wills faithful obedience (see Ps. 101),
but graciously forgives sinners.

103:19–22—The sovereign God of *all* (v. 19) is
to be blessed by all beings and even all things
(v. 22; see introduction, "Songs of Praise";
96:11–13; 148:1–12; 150:6). By blessing God,
the psalmist professes his or her own loyalty, thus
putting the self in tune with the praises of the
universe.

Psalm 104

104:1 *Bless . . . O my soul*—See v. 35; 103:1, 22.
A companion to Ps. 103, Ps. 104 elaborates upon
the *works* (103:22) that serve to bless God.

104:1–4—The focus is on God and the heavens.
In the Canaanite view, Baal was the cloud rider

You are clothed with honor and
    majesty,
2   wrapped in light as with a
      garment.
You stretch out the heavens like a tent,
3   you set the beams of your*a*
      chambers on the waters,
you make the clouds your*a* chariot,
    you ride on the wings of the wind,
4 you make the winds your*a*
    messengers,
    fire and flame your*a* ministers.

5 You set the earth on its foundations,
    so that it shall never be shaken.
6 You cover it with the deep as with a
    garment;
    the waters stood above the
      mountains.
7 At your rebuke they flee;
    at the sound of your thunder they
      take to flight.
8 They rose up to the mountains, ran
    down to the valleys
    to the place that you appointed for
      them.
9 You set a boundary that they may
    not pass,
    so that they might not again cover
      the earth.

10 You make springs gush forth in the
    valleys;
    they flow between the hills,
11 giving drink to every wild animal;
    the wild asses quench their thirst.
12 By the streams*b* the birds of the air
    have their habitation;
    they sing among the branches.
13 From your lofty abode you water the
    mountains;

the earth is satisfied with the fruit
    of your work.

14 You cause the grass to grow for the
    cattle,
    and plants for people to use,*c*
    to bring forth food from the earth,
15   and wine to gladden the human
      heart,
    oil to make the face shine,
    and bread to strengthen the
      human heart.
16 The trees of the LORD are watered
    abundantly,
    the cedars of Lebanon that he
      planted.
17 In them the birds build their nests;
    the stork has its home in the fir
      trees.
18 The high mountains are for the wild
    goats;
    the rocks are a refuge for the
      coneys.
19 You have made the moon to mark
    the seasons;
    the sun knows its time for setting.
20 You make darkness, and it is night,
    when all the animals of the forest
      come creeping out.
21 The young lions roar for their prey,
    seeking their food from God.
22 When the sun rises, they withdraw
    and lie down in their dens.
23 People go out to their work
    and to their labor until the
      evening.

24 O LORD, how manifold are your
    works!

---

a Heb *his* *b* Heb *By them* *c* Or *to cultivate*

---

and god of the storm, but here Israel's God is the
God of all creation.
104:5–13—The focus is on God and the earth,
including *waters* (v. 6), which often symbolize chaotic forces. God has tamed them (v. 7)
and put them at the service of the earth and its
creatures.
104:14–23—The focus is on God and *people* (see
vv. 14, 23), but people as part of a vast and complex network of plants, animals, and heavenly
bodies.

104:24–30—Everything described in vv. 1–23
is God's *works* (v. 24). Because God has **made
them all**, all creatures are *your creatures* (v. 24).
Human creatures are important, to be sure, but
their place is among all (vv. 24, 27) the others
for whom God provides (vv. 27–28) and who
depend upon God for life (vv. 29–30). Even
Leviathan (v. 26), the chaos monster, has a place
(see 74:14). The ecological implications are
astounding. The earth belongs not to us, but to
God; and the integrity of the whole ecosystem is

In wisdom you have made them
all;
the earth is full of your creatures.
25 Yonder is the sea, great and wide,
creeping things innumerable are
there,
living things both small and great.
26 There go the ships,
and Leviathan that you formed to
sport in it.
27 These all look to you
to give them their food in due
season;
28 when you give to them, they gather
it up;
when you open your hand, they
are filled with good things.
29 When you hide your face, they are
dismayed;
when you take away their breath,
they die
and return to their dust.
30 When you send forth your spirit,[a]
they are created;
and you renew the face of the
ground.

31 May the glory of the LORD endure
forever;
may the LORD rejoice in his
works—
32 who looks on the earth and it
trembles,
who touches the mountains and
they smoke.
33 I will sing to the LORD as long as I
live;

I will sing praise to my God while
I have being.
34 May my meditation be pleasing to
him,
for I rejoice in the LORD.
35 Let sinners be consumed from the
earth,
and let the wicked be no more.
Bless the LORD, O my soul.
Praise the LORD!

Psalm 105
God's Faithfulness to Israel

1 O give thanks to the LORD, call on
his name,
make known his deeds among the
peoples.
2 Sing to him, sing praises to him;
tell of all his wonderful works.
3 Glory in his holy name;
let the hearts of those who seek the
LORD rejoice.
4 Seek the LORD and his strength;
seek his presence continually.
5 Remember the wonderful works he
has done,
his miracles, and the judgments he
has uttered,
6 O offspring of his servant Abraham,[b]
children of Jacob, his chosen
ones.

7 He is the LORD our God;
his judgments are in all the earth.
8 He is mindful of his covenant
forever,

[a] Or your breath [b] Another reading is Israel (compare 1 Chr 16.13)

a theological as well as an ecological issue (see
Ps. 8).

104:31–35—God is portrayed as rejoicing in
God's *works* (v. 31; see v. 24), and the psalmist
rejoices in God (v. 34), suggesting a rejoicing too
in the manifold majesty of creation. The desire
expressed in v. 35 is not for revenge, but rather a
wish that violators of the integrity of creation be
stopped. In the contemporary era, we humans
must seriously consider the possibility that we
regularly play the role of *the wicked*.

104:35 *Praise the LORD!*—Hebrew "Hallelujah,"
this is the first occurrence of this invitation in the
Psalter.

Psalm 105

105:1–2—Like Pss. 78, 106, 135, and 136, Ps.
105 is a rehearsal of God's *deeds* or *wonderful
works* (vv. 2, 5), intended to foster *thanks* and
praises (v. 2) that will issue in obedience (v. 45).
Its companion, Ps. 106, suggests that the people
do not cooperate very readily.

105:5 *Judgments*—Better "acts of justice" (see
also v. 7), it is a summary of God's will for the
world (see introduction, "Psalms 1–2 and the
Shape of the Psalter"; 96:11–13).

105:8–10 *Covenant*—God's *wonderful works*
(vv. 2, 5) grow out of the commitment God has
made to *Abraham* (who, in turn, is commissioned

of the word that he commanded,
    for a thousand generations,
9 the covenant that he made with
    Abraham,
    his sworn promise to Isaac,
10 which he confirmed to Jacob as a
    statute,
    to Israel as an everlasting
    covenant,
11 saying, "To you I will give the land
    of Canaan
    as your portion for an inheritance."

12 When they were few in number,
    of little account, and strangers in it,
13 wandering from nation to nation,
    from one kingdom to another
    people,
14 he allowed no one to oppress them;
    he rebuked kings on their account,
15 saying, "Do not touch my anointed
    ones;
    do my prophets no harm."

16 When he summoned famine against
    the land,
    and broke every staff of bread,
17 he had sent a man ahead of them,
    Joseph, who was sold as a slave.
18 His feet were hurt with fetters,
    his neck was put in a collar of iron;
19 until what he had said came to pass,
    the word of the LORD kept testing
    him.
20 The king sent and released him;
    the ruler of the peoples set him free.
21 He made him lord of his house,
    and ruler of all his possessions,
22 to instruct[a] his officials at his
    pleasure,
    and to teach his elders wisdom.

23 Then Israel came to Egypt;
    Jacob lived as an alien in the land
    of Ham.

24 And the LORD made his people very
    fruitful,
    and made them stronger than their
    foes,
25 whose hearts he then turned to hate
    his people,
    to deal craftily with his servants.

26 He sent his servant Moses,
    and Aaron whom he had chosen.
27 They performed his signs among
    them,
    and miracles in the land of Ham.
28 He sent darkness, and made the land
    dark;
    they rebelled[b] against his words.
29 He turned their waters into
    blood,
    and caused their fish to die.
30 Their land swarmed with frogs,
    even in the chambers of their
    kings.
31 He spoke, and there came swarms of
    flies,
    and gnats throughout their
    country.
32 He gave them hail for rain,
    and lightning that flashed through
    their land.
33 He struck their vines and fig trees,
    and shattered the trees of their
    country.
34 He spoke, and the locusts came,
    and young locusts without
    number;
35 they devoured all the vegetation in
    their land,
    and ate up the fruit of their
    ground.
36 He struck down all the firstborn in
    their land,
    the first issue of all their strength.

a Gk Syr Jerome: Heb *to bind*   b Cn Compare Gk Syr: Heb *they did not rebel*

---

to bless "all the families of the earth"; see Gen. 12:3), Isaac, and *Jacob*.

105:12–15—See Gen. 12–50, the stories of the patriarchs and matriarchs. By calling the ancestors *anointed ones* (v. 15), the psalm may suggest that the whole people of God, not just the mon-

archs, bear the responsibility of embodying God's will in the world (see introduction, "Psalms 1–2 and the Shape of the Psalter"; 149:7–9).

105:26–28—See Exod. 1–15, the exodus narrative.

³⁷ Then he brought Israel^a out with
    silver and gold,
     and there was no one among their
      tribes who stumbled.
³⁸ Egypt was glad when they departed,
     for dread of them had fallen
      upon it.
³⁹ He spread a cloud for a covering,
     and fire to give light by night.
⁴⁰ They asked, and he brought quails,
     and gave them food from heaven
      in abundance.
⁴¹ He opened the rock, and water
     gushed out;
     it flowed through the desert like a
      river.
⁴² For he remembered his holy
     promise,
     and Abraham, his servant.

⁴³ So he brought his people out with
     joy,
     his chosen ones with singing.
⁴⁴ He gave them the lands of the
     nations,
     and they took possession of the
      wealth of the peoples,
⁴⁵ that they might keep his statutes
     and observe his laws.
     Praise the LORD!

Psalm 106
A Confession of Israel's Sins

¹ Praise the LORD!
    O give thanks to the LORD, for he
     is good;
    for his steadfast love endures
     forever.
² Who can utter the mighty doings of
     the LORD,
     or declare all his praise?

³ Happy are those who observe justice,
     who do righteousness at all times.

⁴ Remember me, O LORD, when you
     show favor to your people;
    help me when you deliver them;
⁵ that I may see the prosperity of your
     chosen ones,
    that I may rejoice in the gladness
     of your nation,
    that I may glory in your heritage.

⁶ Both we and our ancestors have
     sinned;
    we have committed iniquity, have
     done wickedly.
⁷ Our ancestors, when they were in
     Egypt,
    did not consider your wonderful
     works;
    they did not remember the
     abundance of your steadfast
     love,
    but rebelled against the Most
     High^b at the Red Sea.^c
⁸ Yet he saved them for his name's
     sake,
    so that he might make known his
     mighty power.
⁹ He rebuked the Red Sea,^c and it
     became dry;
    he led them through the deep as
     through a desert.
¹⁰ So he saved them from the hand of
     the foe,
    and delivered them from the hand
     of the enemy.
¹¹ The waters covered their adversaries;
     not one of them was left.

^a Heb *them* ^b Cn Compare 78.17, 56: Heb *rebelled at the sea* ^c Or *Sea of Reeds*

105:39–44—The rest of the Pentateuch, along with the book of Joshua, narrates Israel's movement through the wilderness and into Canaan (vv. 11, 44). The psalm suggests that all this is God's gracious gift, to which the people are to respond with grateful obedience (vv. 1–6, 45).

Psalm 106

106:1—See 100:5; 105:1. A companion to Ps. 105, Ps. 106 also rehearses Israel's story. But the focus is not on God's "wonderful works" (105:2,

5), except in vv. 1–3. The rest of the psalm focuses on Israel's wickedness (see v. 6)

106:3—*Justice* and *righteousness* are a summary of God's will (see introduction, "Psalms 1–2 and the Shape of the Psalter"; 96:11–13), so the claim is that happiness derives from doing God's will (see 1:1; 2:12; 41:1).

106:7–33—These verses epitomize the long history of the rebellion of God's people, first recounted in Exod. 1 through Num. 25.

¹² Then they believed his words;
   they sang his praise.
¹³ But they soon forgot his works;
   they did not wait for his counsel.
¹⁴ But they had a wanton craving in the
      wilderness,
   and put God to the test in the
      desert;
¹⁵ he gave them what they asked,
   but sent a wasting disease among
      them.
¹⁶ They were jealous of Moses in the
      camp,
   and of Aaron, the holy one of the
      LORD.
¹⁷ The earth opened and swallowed up
      Dathan,
   and covered the faction of Abiram.
¹⁸ Fire also broke out in their company;
   the flame burned up the wicked.
¹⁹ They made a calf at Horeb
   and worshiped a cast image.
²⁰ They exchanged the glory of God[a]
   for the image of an ox that eats
      grass.
²¹ They forgot God, their Savior,
   who had done great things in
      Egypt,
²² wondrous works in the land of
      Ham,
   and awesome deeds by the Red
      Sea.[b]
²³ Therefore he said he would destroy
      them—
   had not Moses, his chosen one,
   stood in the breach before him,
   to turn away his wrath from
      destroying them.
²⁴ Then they despised the pleasant
      land,
   having no faith in his promise.
²⁵ They grumbled in their tents,
   and did not obey the voice of the
      LORD.
²⁶ Therefore he raised his hand and
      swore to them

that he would make them fall in
      the wilderness,
²⁷ and would disperse[c] their
      descendants among the
      nations,
   scattering them over the lands.
²⁸ Then they attached themselves to
      the Baal of Peor,
   and ate sacrifices offered to the
      dead;
²⁹ they provoked the LORD to anger
      with their deeds,
   and a plague broke out among
      them.
³⁰ Then Phinehas stood up and
      interceded,
   and the plague was stopped.
³¹ And that has been reckoned to him
      as righteousness
   from generation to generation
      forever.
³² They angered the LORD[d] at the
      waters of Meribah,
   and it went ill with Moses on their
      account;
³³ for they made his spirit bitter,
   and he spoke words that were
      rash.
³⁴ They did not destroy the peoples,
   as the LORD commanded them,
³⁵ but they mingled with the nations
   and learned to do as they did.
³⁶ They served their idols,
   which became a snare to them.
³⁷ They sacrificed their sons
   and their daughters to the
      demons;
³⁸ they poured out innocent blood,
   the blood of their sons and
      daughters,
   whom they sacrificed to the idols of
      Canaan;
   and the land was polluted with
      blood.

[a] Compare Gk Mss: Heb *exchanged their glory*   [b] Or *Sea of Reeds*
[c] Syr Compare Ezek 20.23: Heb *cause to fall*   [d] Heb *him*

106:34–39—See Num. 33:50–56; Deut. 7:1–6; 13:6–18; 17:2–7; 20:16–18; 32:15–18; Judg. 1:1–2:5.

³⁹ Thus they became unclean by their
acts,
  and prostituted themselves in their
  doings.
⁴⁰ Then the anger of the LORD was
kindled against his people,
  and he abhorred his heritage;
⁴¹ he gave them into the hand of the
nations,
  so that those who hated them
  ruled over them.
⁴² Their enemies oppressed them,
  and they were brought into
  subjection under their power.
⁴³ Many times he delivered them,
  but they were rebellious in their
  purposes,
  and were brought low through
  their iniquity.
⁴⁴ Nevertheless he regarded their
distress
  when he heard their cry.
⁴⁵ For their sake he remembered his
covenant,
  and showed compassion according
  to the abundance of his
  steadfast love.
⁴⁶ He caused them to be pitied
  by all who held them captive.

⁴⁷ Save us, O LORD our God,
  and gather us from among the
  nations,
  that we may give thanks to your holy
  name
  and glory in your praise.

⁴⁸ Blessed be the LORD, the God of
Israel,

from everlasting to everlasting.
And let all the people say, "Amen."
Praise the LORD!

BOOK V
(Psalms 107–150)

Psalm 107
Thanksgiving for Deliverance
from Many Troubles

¹ O give thanks to the LORD, for he is
good;
  for his steadfast love endures
  forever.
² Let the redeemed of the LORD say so,
  those he redeemed from trouble
³ and gathered in from the lands,
  from the east and from the west,
  from the north and from the
  south.^a

⁴ Some wandered in desert wastes,
  finding no way to an inhabited
  town;
⁵ hungry and thirsty,
  their soul fainted within them.
⁶ Then they cried to the LORD in their
trouble,
  and he delivered them from their
  distress;
⁷ he led them by a straight way,
  until they reached an inhabited
  town.
⁸ Let them thank the LORD for his
steadfast love,
  for his wonderful works to
  humankind.
⁹ For he satisfies the thirsty,

^a Cn: Heb sea

106:40–46—See the repeated pattern in the book
of Judges (Judg. 2:11–19), but the pattern really
characterizes the whole of Israel's story, emphasizing that God's fundamental character is to
show *compassion* and abundant *steadfast love*
(v. 45; see vv. 1, 7; 5:7; 36:5–6; 103:4, 8; Exod.
34:6–7).

106:47—This seems to be an exilic prayer,
reflecting the crisis to which the whole of Book
IV responds (see 89:38–51; introduction, "Psalms
1–2 and the Shape of the Psalter").

106:48—This is the concluding doxology for
Book IV; see 41:13.

Psalm 107

107:1—See 100:5; 106:1.

107:2–3—See 106:47, to which Ps. 107 seems to
respond with gratitude.

107:6—See vv. 13, 19, 28. The pattern within
the four deliverance scenarios (vv. 4–9, 10–16,
17–22, 23–32) suggests God's orientation to the
victimized (see vv. 39–40; introduction, "Prayers
for Help").

107:8—See vv. 15, 21, 31, 43. As v. 1 anticipates,
the psalm proceeds as a grateful celebration of
God's *steadfast love*, manifest in God's gracious

and the hungry he fills with good
    things.

10 Some sat in darkness and in gloom,
    prisoners in misery and in irons,
11 for they had rebelled against the
    words of God,
    and spurned the counsel of the
    Most High.
12 Their hearts were bowed down with
    hard labor;
    they fell down, with no one to
    help.
13 Then they cried to the LORD in their
    trouble,
    and he saved them from their
    distress;
14 he brought them out of darkness and
    gloom,
    and broke their bonds asunder.
15 Let them thank the LORD for his
    steadfast love,
    for his wonderful works to
    humankind.
16 For he shatters the doors of bronze,
    and cuts in two the bars of iron.

17 Some were sick[a] through their sinful
    ways,
    and because of their iniquities
    endured affliction;
18 they loathed any kind of food,
    and they drew near to the gates of
    death.
19 Then they cried to the LORD in their
    trouble,
    and he saved them from their
    distress;
20 he sent out his word and healed
    them,
    and delivered them from
    destruction.
21 Let them thank the LORD for his
    steadfast love,
    for his wonderful works to
    humankind.
22 And let them offer thanksgiving
    sacrifices,

and tell of his deeds with songs of
    joy.

23 Some went down to the sea in ships,
    doing business on the mighty
    waters;
24 they saw the deeds of the LORD,
    his wondrous works in the deep.
25 For he commanded and raised the
    stormy wind,
    which lifted up the waves of the
    sea.
26 They mounted up to heaven, they
    went down to the depths;
    their courage melted away in their
    calamity;
27 they reeled and staggered like
    drunkards,
    and were at their wits' end.
28 Then they cried to the LORD in their
    trouble,
    and he brought them out from
    their distress;
29 he made the storm be still,
    and the waves of the sea were
    hushed.
30 Then they were glad because they
    had quiet,
    and he brought them to their
    desired haven.
31 Let them thank the LORD for his
    steadfast love,
    for his wonderful works to
    humankind.
32 Let them extol him in the
    congregation of the people,
    and praise him in the assembly of
    the elders.

33 He turns rivers into a desert,
    springs of water into thirsty
    ground,
34 a fruitful land into a salty waste,
    because of the wickedness of its
    inhabitants.
35 He turns a desert into pools of water,

[a] Cn: Heb *fools*

---

activity on behalf of *the needy* (v. 41; see 9:18;
40:17; 109:31). As expressions of praise and
thanks regularly do, Ps. 107 puts no limitations
on God's *wonderful works*; they are for *humankind* (see introduction, "Songs of Praise").

a parched land into springs of
water.

³⁶ And there he lets the hungry live,
and they establish a town to live in;

³⁷ they sow fields, and plant vineyards,
and get a fruitful yield.

³⁸ By his blessing they multiply greatly,
and he does not let their cattle
decrease.

³⁹ When they are diminished and
brought low
through oppression, trouble, and
sorrow,

⁴⁰ he pours contempt on princes
and makes them wander in
trackless wastes;

⁴¹ but he raises up the needy out of
distress,
and makes their families like
flocks.

⁴² The upright see it and are glad;
and all wickedness stops its mouth.

⁴³ Let those who are wise give heed to
these things,
and consider the steadfast love of
the LORD.

Psalm 108

Praise and Prayer for Victory

A Song. A Psalm of David.

¹ My heart is steadfast, O God, my
heart is steadfast;ᵃ
I will sing and make melody.
Awake, my soul!ᵇ

² Awake, O harp and lyre!
I will awake the dawn.

³ I will give thanks to you, O LORD,
among the peoples,
and I will sing praises to you
among the nations.

⁴ For your steadfast love is higher than
the heavens,
and your faithfulness reaches to
the clouds.

⁵ Be exalted, O God, above the
heavens,
and let your glory be over all the
earth.

⁶ Give victory with your right hand,
and answer me,
so that those whom you love may
be rescued.

⁷ God has promised in his sanctuary:ᶜ
"With exultation I will divide up
Shechem,
and portion out the Vale of
Succoth.

⁸ Gilead is mine; Manasseh is mine;
Ephraim is my helmet;
Judah is my scepter.

⁹ Moab is my washbasin;
on Edom I hurl my shoe;
over Philistia I shout in triumph."

¹⁰ Who will bring me to the fortified
city?
Who will lead me to Edom?

¹¹ Have you not rejected us, O God?
You do not go out, O God, with
our armies.

¹² O grant us help against the foe,
for human help is worthless.

¹³ With God we shall do valiantly;
it is he who will tread down our
foes.

Psalm 109

Prayer for Vindication and Vengeance

To the leader. Of David. A Psalm.

¹ Do not be silent, O God of my
praise.

² For wicked and deceitful mouths are
opened against me,
speaking against me with lying
tongues.

³ They beset me with words of hate,

ᵃ Heb Mss Gk Syr: MT lacks *my heart is steadfast*   ᵇ Compare 57.8: Heb
also *my soul* ᶜOr *by his holiness*

Psalm 108

108:1–5—See 57:7–11.
108:6–13—See 60:5–12.

Psalm 109

109:1–5—The psalm begins and ends (vv. 20–31)
like a typical prayer for help. What distinguishes
it is the prolonged request for vengeance in vv.
6–19.

and attack me without cause.
⁴ In return for my love they accuse
    me,
    even while I make prayer for them.*a*
⁵ So they reward me evil for good,
    and hatred for my love.

⁶ They say,*b* "Appoint a wicked man
    against him;
    let an accuser stand on his right.
⁷ When he is tried, let him be found
    guilty;
    let his prayer be counted as sin.
⁸ May his days be few;
    may another seize his position.
⁹ May his children be orphans,
    and his wife a widow.
¹⁰ May his children wander about and
    beg;
    may they be driven out of*c* the
    ruins they inhabit.
¹¹ May the creditor seize all that he has;
    may strangers plunder the fruits of
    his toil.
¹² May there be no one to do him a
    kindness,
    nor anyone to pity his orphaned
    children.
¹³ May his posterity be cut off;
    may his name be blotted out in the
    second generation.
¹⁴ May the iniquity of his father*d* be
    remembered before the LORD,
    and do not let the sin of his
    mother be blotted out.
¹⁵ Let them be before the LORD
    continually,
    and may his*e* memory be cut off
    from the earth.
¹⁶ For he did not remember to show
    kindness,
    but pursued the poor and needy

and the brokenhearted to their
    death.
¹⁷ He loved to curse; let curses come on
    him.
    He did not like blessing; may it be
    far from him.
¹⁸ He clothed himself with cursing as
    his coat,
    may it soak into his body like
    water,
    like oil into his bones.
¹⁹ May it be like a garment that he
    wraps around himself,
    like a belt that he wears every day."

²⁰ May that be the reward of my
    accusers from the LORD,
    of those who speak evil against my
    life.
²¹ But you, O LORD my Lord,
    act on my behalf for your name's
    sake;
    because your steadfast love is
    good, deliver me.
²² For I am poor and needy,
    and my heart is pierced within me.
²³ I am gone like a shadow at evening;
    I am shaken off like a locust.
²⁴ My knees are weak through fasting;
    my body has become gaunt.
²⁵ I am an object of scorn to my
    accusers;
    when they see me, they shake their
    heads.

²⁶ Help me, O LORD my God!
    Save me according to your
    steadfast love.
²⁷ Let them know that this is your
    hand;
    you, O LORD, have done it.

a Syr: Heb *I prayer* *b* Heb lacks *They say* *c* Gk: Heb *and seek* *d* Cn: Heb
fathers *e* Gk: Heb *their*

109:6–19—*They say* in v. 6 has been supplied
by the NRSV, thus assigning the bitter request
for vengeance to the psalmist's enemies. Even if
this is correct, the psalmist apparently claims this
request in v. 20.

109:21, 26 *Steadfast love*—The basis for the
psalmist's appeal is God's character (see 5:7;
36:5–6; 100:5). It is God's steadfast love that
motivates God to set things right for the victim-

ized by standing *at the right hand of the needy*
(v. 31; see 9:18; 40:17; 140:12). This is precisely
what the psalmist's enemies did *not* do (see v. 16,
where "kindness" is the same word as "steadfast
love"). Thus, the psalmist's request for vengeance
is fundamentally a victim's request for justice
and righteousness (see introduction, "Prayers for
Help").

28 Let them curse, but you will bless.
    Let my assailants be put to shame;*a*
      may your servant be glad.
29 May my accusers be clothed with
      dishonor;
    may they be wrapped in their own
      shame as in a mantle.
30 With my mouth I will give great
      thanks to the LORD;
    I will praise him in the midst of
      the throng.
31 For he stands at the right hand of the
      needy,
    to save them from those who
      would condemn them to death.

Psalm 110
Assurance of Victory
for God's Priest-King

Of David. A Psalm.

1 The LORD says to my lord,
    "Sit at my right hand
  until I make your enemies your
      footstool."

2 The LORD sends out from Zion
      your mighty scepter.
    Rule in the midst of your foes.
3 Your people will offer themselves
      willingly
    on the day you lead your forces
    on the holy mountains.*b*
  From the womb of the morning,
    like dew, your youth*c* will come to
      you.

4 The LORD has sworn and will not
      change his mind,
    "You are a priest forever according
      to the order of Melchizedek."*d*

5 The Lord is at your right hand;
    he will shatter kings on the day of
      his wrath.
6 He will execute judgment among the
      nations,
    filling them with corpses;
  he will shatter heads
    over the wide earth.
7 He will drink from the stream by the
      path;
    therefore he will lift up his head.

Psalm 111
Praise for God's Wonderful Works

1 Praise the LORD!
  I will give thanks to the LORD with
      my whole heart,
    in the company of the upright, in
      the congregation.
2 Great are the works of the LORD,
    studied by all who delight in them.
3 Full of honor and majesty is his
      work,
    and his righteousness endures
      forever.
4 He has gained renown by his
      wonderful deeds;
    the LORD is gracious and merciful.

a Gk: Heb *They have risen up and have been put to shame*   *b* Another reading is *in holy splendor*   *c* Cn: Heb *the dew of your youth*   *d* Or *forever, a rightful king by my edict*

Psalm 110

110:1 *The LORD says to my lord*—God is speaking to the king. After the disappearance of the monarchy, the psalm served (and does serve) to proclaim God's sovereignty (see introduction, "Psalms 1–2 and the Shape of the Psalter"). *"Sit at my right hand . . ."*—Occupying the place of honor, the king was entrusted with enacting God's will on earth (see Pss. 2, 72). The early church applied this saying to Jesus, professing its faith that the life and ministry of Jesus was a full embodiment of God's character and purposes (see Matt. 26:64; Mark 14:62; Luke 22:69; Acts 2:34–35; and more). Like God in the Psalter (see introduction, "Prayers for Help"), Jesus stood constantly on the side of the poor and needy (see 109:31).

110:2 *Zion*—The temple, God's house, was on Mount Zion (see 48:1–2), and the king's palace was adjacent to it.

110:4—See Gen. 14:18. The kings presided at liturgical events (see 1 Kgs. 8).

110:5–7—The function of God's activity on behalf of the king is to "establish justice among the nations" (v. 6, NRSV *execute judgment among the nations*), which will mean opposing oppressors (see 2:8–9; 72:4, 8–11, 14; 149:6–9).

Psalm 111

111:3 *Righteousness*—Along with justice (see *just* in v. 7), this word summarizes God's will for the world (see introduction, "Psalms 1–2 and the Shape of the Psalter"; 96:11–13).

111:4 *Gracious and merciful*—Along with

⁵ He provides food for those who fear
him;
he is ever mindful of his covenant.
⁶ He has shown his people the power
of his works,
in giving them the heritage of the
nations.
⁷ The works of his hands are faithful
and just;
all his precepts are trustworthy.
⁸ They are established forever and
ever,
to be performed with faithfulness
and uprightness.
⁹ He sent redemption to his people;
he has commanded his covenant
forever.
Holy and awesome is his name.
¹⁰ The fear of the LORD is the
beginning of wisdom;
all those who practice it*a* have a
good understanding.
His praise endures forever.

Psalm 112
Blessings of the Righteous

¹ Praise the LORD!
Happy are those who fear the
LORD,
who greatly delight in his
commandments.
² Their descendants will be mighty in
the land;
the generation of the upright will
be blessed.
³ Wealth and riches are in their
houses,

and their righteousness endures
forever.
⁴ They rise in the darkness as a light
for the upright;
they are gracious, merciful, and
righteous.
⁵ It is well with those who deal
generously and lend,
who conduct their affairs with
justice.
⁶ For the righteous will never be
moved;
they will be remembered forever.
⁷ They are not afraid of evil tidings;
their hearts are firm, secure in the
LORD.
⁸ Their hearts are steady, they will not
be afraid;
in the end they will look in
triumph on their foes.
⁹ They have distributed freely, they
have given to the poor;
their righteousness endures
forever;
their horn is exalted in honor.
¹⁰ The wicked see it and are angry;
they gnash their teeth and melt
away;
the desire of the wicked comes to
nothing.

Psalm 113
God the Helper of the Needy

¹ Praise the LORD!
Praise, O servants of the LORD;
praise the name of the LORD.

a Gk Syr: Heb *them*

"faithful" (v. 7), these words summarize God's
character (see 112:4; Exod. 34:6).

111:9 *Holy*—God's holiness is essentially relational (see 99:3).

111:10 *Fear of the LORD*—"Fear" consists of reverent obedience (see 2:11; 34:11). Essentially this
same verse occurs also in Job 28:28; Prov. 1:7;
9:10. Psalm 112 will describe the life of those
who fear the LORD (112:1).

Psalm 112

112:1—See 111:10. The definition of happiness
is fully God-centered, recalling 1:1; 2:12; 41:1;
106:3.

112:2–5—The description of those who fear God
should not be understood in terms of a retributional scheme. Rather, their "reward" comes from
being like God (v. 3; compare 111:4) and doing
what God wills—*righteousness* (v. 3) and *justice*
(v. 5; compare 111:3, 7; see also introduction,
"Psalms 1–2 and the Shape of the Psalter";
72:1–7; 96:11–13), including solidarity with *the
poor* (v. 9; see 9:18; 40:17; 140:12; introduction,
"Prayers for Help").

Psalm 113

113:1–3—The occurrence of *name* in each verse
prepares the reader to listen for a portrayal of
God's reputation or character.

2 Blessed be the name of the LORD
   from this time on and
      forevermore.
3 From the rising of the sun to its
      setting
   the name of the LORD is to be
      praised.
4 The LORD is high above all nations,
   and his glory above the heavens.

5 Who is like the LORD our God,
   who is seated on high,
6 who looks far down
   on the heavens and the earth?
7 He raises the poor from the dust,
   and lifts the needy from the ash
      heap,
8 to make them sit with princes,
   with the princes of his people.
9 He gives the barren woman a
      home,
   making her the joyous mother of
      children.
Praise the LORD!

Psalm 114
God's Wonders at the Exodus

1 When Israel went out from Egypt,
   the house of Jacob from a people
      of strange language,
2 Judah became God's*a* sanctuary,
   Israel his dominion.

3 The sea looked and fled;
   Jordan turned back.
4 The mountains skipped like rams,
   the hills like lambs.

5 Why is it, O sea, that you flee?
   O Jordan, that you turn back?
6 O mountains, that you skip like
      rams?
   O hills, like lambs?

7 Tremble, O earth, at the presence of
      the LORD,
   at the presence of the God of
      Jacob,
8 who turns the rock into a pool of
      water,
   the flint into a spring of water.

Psalm 115
The Impotence of Idols and the
Greatness of God

1 Not to us, O LORD, not to us, but to
      your name give glory,
   for the sake of your steadfast love
      and your faithfulness.
2 Why should the nations say,
   "Where is their God?"

3 Our God is in the heavens;
   he does whatever he pleases.
4 Their idols are silver and gold,
   the work of human hands.
5 They have mouths, but do not speak;
   eyes, but do not see.
6 They have ears, but do not hear;
   noses, but do not smell.
7 They have hands, but do not feel;
   feet, but do not walk;
   they make no sound in their
      throats.

a Heb *his*

113:5–6—In keeping with vv. 1–3, the question of God's characteristic activity is posed. God is *high*, but God *looks far down* (v. 6).

113:7–9—Not only does God look far down, but God also reaches down to lift up those who have been put down, including *the poor* and *the needy* (v. 7). This is characteristic of God in the Psalter and throughout the Bible (see introduction, "Prayers for Help"). That is, the humble are exalted (see 1 Sam. 2:4–5, 7–8; Luke 1:51–53; 18:14; 1 Cor. 1:26–29). Psalm 113 initiates a collection, the Egyptian Hallel, that is used by Jews at Passover, recalling and reactualizing the exodus as a prime example of God's uplifting the poor and needy.

Psalm 114

114:1 *When . . . Egypt*—The psalm is essentially a poetic reflection on the exodus (see esp. Exod. 14–15), the prototypical example of the liberating work featured in 113:7–9.

Psalm 115

115:1 *Steadfast love and . . . faithfulness*—See 5:7; 36:5–6; 103:8.

115:2—The same question occurs in 42:3, 10; 79:10.

115:3–6—See Ps. 82 for a poetic portrayal of the death of the gods. The point of 115:3 is not that God is capricious, but rather that God is sovereign.

8 Those who make them are like them;
   so are all who trust in them.

9 O Israel, trust in the LORD!
   He is their help and their shield.
10 O house of Aaron, trust in the LORD!
    He is their help and their shield.
11 You who fear the LORD, trust in the
    LORD!
    He is their help and their shield.

12 The LORD has been mindful of us; he
    will bless us;
    he will bless the house of Israel;
    he will bless the house of Aaron;
13 he will bless those who fear the
    LORD,
    both small and great.

14 May the LORD give you increase,
    both you and your children.
15 May you be blessed by the LORD,
    who made heaven and earth.

16 The heavens are the LORD's heavens,
    but the earth he has given to
    human beings.
17 The dead do not praise the LORD,
    nor do any that go down into
    silence.
18 But we will bless the LORD
    from this time on and
    forevermore.
    Praise the LORD!

Psalm 116
Thanksgiving for Recovery from Illness
1 I love the LORD, because he has
   heard

my voice and my
   supplications.
2 Because he inclined his ear
   to me,
   therefore I will call on him as long
   as I live.
3 The snares of death encompassed
   me;
   the pangs of Sheol laid hold
   on me;
   I suffered distress and anguish.
4 Then I called on the name of the
   LORD:
   "O LORD, I pray, save my life!"

5 Gracious is the LORD, and
   righteous;
   our God is merciful.
6 The LORD protects the simple;
   when I was brought low, he
   saved me.
7 Return, O my soul, to your rest,
   for the LORD has dealt bountifully
   with you.

8 For you have delivered my soul from
   death,
   my eyes from tears,
   my feet from stumbling.
9 I walk before the LORD
   in the land of the living.
10 I kept my faith, even when I said,
    "I am greatly afflicted";
11 I said in my consternation,
    "Everyone is a liar."

12 What shall I return to the LORD
    for all his bounty to me?

115:9–11 *Trust*—Faithfulness is essentially a matter of whom or what one trusts (see 4:5; 13:5; 52:7–8; introduction, "Psalms of Trust").

115:12–15 *Bless*—Blessedness or happiness derives from complete orientation to God and God's purposes (see 1:1; 2:12; 106:3; 112:1). *Who made heaven and earth*—See 121:2.

115:17—The same perspective is present in 6:5.

115:18 *Bless*—To bless God means to submit the self to God and God's purposes (see 34:1; 103:1, 22; 104:1, 35).

Psalm 116

116:1 *I love the LORD*—The rest of the psalm

demonstrates the psalmist's loving faithfulness to God, as the psalmist testifies to God's character (vv. 5–6), expresses gratitude (vv. 12–14, 17–19), and puts the self at God's disposal (v. 16).

116:3 *Sheol*—The realm of the dead (see 6:5).

116:5–6—God's character—*gracious* and *merciful* (see 103:8; Exod. 34:6)—and God's will—*righteous* (see introduction, "Psalms 1–2 and the Shape of the Psalter"; 96:11–13)—are the subject of the psalmist's witness. God sets things right by siding with the needy (v. 6; see introduction, "Prayers for Help").

116:10 *Afflicted*—The righteous are regularly afflicted (see 34:19).

¹³ I will lift up the cup of salvation
     and call on the name of the LORD,
¹⁴ I will pay my vows to the LORD
     in the presence of all his people.
¹⁵ Precious in the sight of the LORD
     is the death of his faithful ones.
¹⁶ O LORD, I am your servant;
     I am your servant, the child of
        your serving girl.
     You have loosed my bonds.
¹⁷ I will offer to you a thanksgiving
        sacrifice
     and call on the name of the LORD.
¹⁸ I will pay my vows to the LORD
     in the presence of all his people,
¹⁹ in the courts of the house of the LORD,
     in your midst, O Jerusalem.
     Praise the LORD!

Psalm 117
Universal Call to Worship

¹ Praise the LORD, all you nations!
     Extol him, all you peoples!
² For great is his steadfast love
        toward us,
     and the faithfulness of the LORD
        endures forever.
     Praise the LORD!

Psalm 118
A Song of Victory

¹ O give thanks to the LORD, for he is
        good;
     his steadfast love endures forever!

² Let Israel say,
     "His steadfast love endures
        forever."
³ Let the house of Aaron say,
     "His steadfast love endures
        forever."
⁴ Let those who fear the LORD say,
     "His steadfast love endures
        forever."

⁵ Out of my distress I called on the
        LORD;
     the LORD answered me and set me
        in a broad place.
⁶ With the LORD on my side I do not
        fear.
     What can mortals do to me?
⁷ The LORD is on my side to help me;
     I shall look in triumph on those
        who hate me.
⁸ It is better to take refuge in the LORD
     than to put confidence in
        mortals.
⁹ It is better to take refuge in the
        LORD
     than to put confidence in princes.

¹⁰ All nations surrounded me;
     in the name of the LORD I cut
        them off!
¹¹ They surrounded me, surrounded
        me on every side;
     in the name of the LORD I cut
        them off!
¹² They surrounded me like bees;

116:13 *Cup of salvation*—Psalm 116 came to be used at Passover (see 113:7–9), which involves the lifting up and blessing of cups of wine. In this context, the deliverance celebrated is the exodus, the greatest demonstration of God saving the lowly (see v. 6).

116:14, 18—The payment of *vows* expresses gratitude (see 50:14, 23; 66:13).

116:15 *Precious*—The word is better translated "costly"—that is, the lives of God's *faithful ones* are highly valued by God, and it hurts God to lose them.

116:17—Like the payment of vows, the *thanksgiving sacrifice* expresses gratitude (see 22:26).

Psalm 117

117:1 *All*—The songs of praise regularly invite a worldwide congregation to worship God (see

introduction, "Songs of Praise"). Taking this seriously, the apostle Paul invited the *nations* (Gentiles) into the church (see Rom. 15:11, where Paul cites 117:1).

Psalm 118

118:1—See v. 29; 106:1; 107:1. The repetition of *steadfast love* in vv. 1–4 suggests that it is God's active love that effects the deliverance(s) celebrated in vv. 5–24.

118:6–7 *On my side*—As always, God is on the side of those in *distress* (v. 5; see introduction, "Prayers for Help").

118:8–9 *Refuge*—See introduction, "Psalms of Trust." NRSV's *put confidence in* is usually translated "trust." Refuge is a matter of trust, and the psalmist trusts God rather than his or her own or other human resources.

they blazed[a] like a fire of thorns;
   in the name of the LORD I cut
     them off!
13 I was pushed hard,[b] so that I was
   falling,
   but the LORD helped me.
14 The LORD is my strength and my
   might;
   he has become my salvation.

15 There are glad songs of victory in
   the tents of the righteous:
   "The right hand of the LORD does
   valiantly;
16 the right hand of the LORD is
   exalted;
   the right hand of the LORD does
   valiantly."
17 I shall not die, but I shall live,
   and recount the deeds of the LORD.
18 The LORD has punished me severely,
   but he did not give me over to
   death.

19 Open to me the gates of
   righteousness,
   that I may enter through them
   and give thanks to the LORD.

20 This is the gate of the LORD;
   the righteous shall enter through it.

21 I thank you that you have
   answered me
   and have become my salvation.
22 The stone that the builders rejected

has become the chief cornerstone.
23 This is the LORD's doing;
   it is marvelous in our eyes.
24 This is the day that the LORD has
   made;
   let us rejoice and be glad in it.[c]

25 Save us, we beseech you, O LORD!
   O LORD, we beseech you, give us
   success!

26 Blessed is the one who comes in the
   name of the LORD.[d]
   We bless you from the house of the
   LORD.
27 The LORD is God,
   and he has given us light.
Bind the festal procession with
   branches,
   up to the horns of the altar.[e]

28 You are my God, and I will give
   thanks to you;
   you are my God, I will extol you.

29 O give thanks to the LORD, for he is
   good,
   for his steadfast love endures
   forever.

Psalm 119
The Glories of God's Law

1 Happy are those whose way is
   blameless,

[a] Gk: Heb were extinguished [b] Gk Syr Jerome: Heb You pushed me hard
[c] Or in him [d] Or Blessed in the name of the LORD is the one who comes
[e] Meaning of Heb uncertain

118:14—This is a quote of Exod. 15:2, suggesting that the deliverance narrated is analogous to the exodus, an event in which God clearly sides with the distressed (see v. 6; 113:7–9).

118:15 Victory—The word is usually translated "salvation" or "deliverance." The point is that the psalmist's life has been saved (see v. 17), for which thanks is offered (vv. 19, 21).

118:22—See Matt. 21:42; Luke 20:17; Acts 4:11–12. The early church viewed Jesus as the distressed and rejected one whom God had delivered from death to life.

118:24 This . . . made—Better translated "This is the day on which the LORD has acted," it recalls the exodus (see v. 14), an analogous deliverance. Among Christians, it is often used as a greeting for the Lord's Day, a celebration of the resurrection.

118:25 Save us—Although deliverance is celebrated, it is still prayed for, suggesting the simultaneity of pain and praise in the life of the faithful, as well as the constant need for dependence upon God (see introduction, "Prayers for Help").

118:26—See Mark 11:9–10, further evidence that the early church saw Jesus' experience through the lens of Ps. 118 (see also Pss. 22, 31, 69, 110; introduction, "The Psalms and the New Testament").

Psalm 119

119:1—See 1:1–2. The Hebrew torah, "teaching" or "instruction" (NRSV law), will occur twenty-four more times, at least once in every eight-verse section, except vv. 9–16. In addition, seven synonyms for torah will occur regularly. The effect is a comprehensive expression of torah piety, a faith

who walk in the law of the LORD.

2 Happy are those who keep his
    decrees,
    who seek him with their whole
    heart,

3 who also do no wrong,
    but walk in his ways.

4 You have commanded your precepts
    to be kept diligently.

5 O that my ways may be steadfast
    in keeping your statutes!

6 Then I shall not be put to shame,
    having my eyes fixed on all your
    commandments.

7 I will praise you with an upright
    heart,
    when I learn your righteous
    ordinances.

8 I will observe your statutes;
    do not utterly forsake me.

9 How can young people keep their
    way pure?
    By guarding it according to your
    word.

10 With my whole heart I seek you;
    do not let me stray from your
    commandments.

11 I treasure your word in my heart,
    so that I may not sin against you.

12 Blessed are you, O LORD;
    teach me your statutes.

13 With my lips I declare
    all the ordinances of your mouth.

14 I delight in the way of your decrees
    as much as in all riches.

15 I will meditate on your precepts,
    and fix my eyes on your ways.

16 I will delight in your statutes;
    I will not forget your word.

17 Deal bountifully with your servant,
    so that I may live and observe your
    word.

18 Open my eyes, so that I may behold
    wondrous things out of your law.

19 I live as an alien in the land;
    do not hide your commandments
    from me.

20 My soul is consumed with longing
    for your ordinances at all times.

21 You rebuke the insolent, accursed
    ones,
    who wander from your
    commandments;

22 take away from me their scorn and
    contempt,
    for I have kept your decrees.

23 Even though princes sit plotting
    against me,
    your servant will meditate on your
    statutes.

24 Your decrees are my delight,
    they are my counselors.

25 My soul clings to the dust;
    revive me according to your word.

26 When I told of my ways, you
    answered me;
    teach me your statutes.

27 Make me understand the way of
    your precepts,
    and I will meditate on your
    wondrous works.

28 My soul melts away for sorrow;
    strengthen me according to your
    word.

29 Put false ways far from me;
    and graciously teach me your law.

30 I have chosen the way of
    faithfulness;
    I set your ordinances before me.

31 I cling to your decrees, O LORD;
    let me not be put to shame.

32 I run the way of your
    commandments,
    for you enlarge my understanding.

---

stance that looks constantly to God for life and to God's word or will for instruction on how to live. The first word in each line of vv. 1–8 begins with *aleph*, the first letter of the Hebrew alphabet; and the subsequent twenty-one letters of the alphabet function similarly in the remaining twenty-one sections of the psalm.

119:22–23—Often accused of being legalistic, the psalm clearly suggests that the psalmist is *not* materially rewarded for his or her faithfulness. Rather, she or he is scorned and persecuted here and in vv. 42, 51, 61, 69, and elsewhere. Sorrow and affliction are also articulated in vv. 28, 50, 71, and elsewhere. Thus this *servant* (v. 17) is a suffering servant.

33 Teach me, O Lord, the way of your
statutes,
and I will observe it to the end.
34 Give me understanding, that I may
keep your law
and observe it with my whole
heart.
35 Lead me in the path of your
commandments,
for I delight in it.
36 Turn my heart to your decrees,
and not to selfish gain.
37 Turn my eyes from looking at
vanities;
give me life in your ways.
38 Confirm to your servant your
promise,
which is for those who fear you.
39 Turn away the disgrace that I dread,
for your ordinances are good.
40 See, I have longed for your precepts;
in your righteousness give me life.

41 Let your steadfast love come to me,
O Lord,
your salvation according to your
promise.
42 Then I shall have an answer for
those who taunt me,
for I trust in your word.
43 Do not take the word of truth utterly
out of my mouth,
for my hope is in your ordinances.
44 I will keep your law continually,
forever and ever.
45 I shall walk at liberty,
for I have sought your precepts.
46 I will also speak of your decrees
before kings,
and shall not be put to shame;
47 I find my delight in your
commandments,
because I love them.
48 I revere your commandments, which
I love,
and I will meditate on your
statutes.

49 Remember your word to your
servant,
in which you have made me hope.
50 This is my comfort in my distress,
that your promise gives me life.
51 The arrogant utterly deride me,
but I do not turn away from your
law.
52 When I think of your ordinances
from of old,
I take comfort, O Lord.
53 Hot indignation seizes me because
of the wicked,
those who forsake your law.
54 Your statutes have been my songs
wherever I make my home.
55 I remember your name in the night,
O Lord,
and keep your law.
56 This blessing has fallen to me,
for I have kept your precepts.

57 The Lord is my portion;
I promise to keep your words.
58 I implore your favor with all my
heart;
be gracious to me according to
your promise.
59 When I think of your ways,
I turn my feet to your decrees;
60 I hurry and do not delay
to keep your commandments.
61 Though the cords of the wicked
ensnare me,
I do not forget your law.
62 At midnight I rise to praise you,
because of your righteous
ordinances.
63 I am a companion of all who fear
you,
of those who keep your precepts.
64 The earth, O Lord, is full of your
steadfast love;
teach me your statutes.

65 You have dealt well with your
servant,
O Lord, according to your word.

119:64 *Steadfast love* ——As in 33:5; 36:5–6,
the psalmist expresses the pervasive presence of
God's love. See "steadfast love" also in 119:41,
76, 88, 124, 149, 159.

66 Teach me good judgment and
    knowledge,
    for I believe in your
      commandments.
67 Before I was humbled I went astray,
    but now I keep your word.
68 You are good and do good;
    teach me your statutes.
69 The arrogant smear me with lies,
    but with my whole heart I keep
      your precepts.
70 Their hearts are fat and gross,
    but I delight in your law.
71 It is good for me that I was humbled,
    so that I might learn your statutes.
72 The law of your mouth is better
    to me
    than thousands of gold and silver
      pieces.

73 Your hands have made and
    fashioned me;
    give me understanding that I may
      learn your commandments.
74 Those who fear you shall see me and
    rejoice,
    because I have hoped in your
      word.
75 I know, O LORD, that your
    judgments are right,
    and that in faithfulness you have
      humbled me.
76 Let your steadfast love become my
    comfort
    according to your promise to your
      servant.
77 Let your mercy come to me, that I
    may live;
    for your law is my delight.
78 Let the arrogant be put to shame,
    because they have subverted me
      with guile;
    as for me, I will meditate on your
      precepts.
79 Let those who fear you turn to me,
    so that they may know your
      decrees.

80 May my heart be blameless in your
    statutes,
    so that I may not be put to shame.

81 My soul languishes for your
    salvation;
    I hope in your word.
82 My eyes fail with watching for your
    promise;
    I ask, "When will you comfort
      me?"
83 For I have become like a wineskin in
    the smoke,
    yet I have not forgotten your
      statutes.
84 How long must your servant endure?
    When will you judge those who
      persecute me?
85 The arrogant have dug pitfalls for
    me;
    they flout your law.
86 All your commandments are
    enduring;
    I am persecuted without cause;
      help me!
87 They have almost made an end of
    me on earth;
    but I have not forsaken your
      precepts.
88 In your steadfast love spare my life,
    so that I may keep the decrees of
      your mouth.

89 The LORD exists forever;
    your word is firmly fixed in
      heaven.
90 Your faithfulness endures to all
    generations;
    you have established the earth, and
      it stands fast.
91 By your appointment they stand
    today,
    for all things are your servants.
92 If your law had not been my delight,
    I would have perished in my
      misery.
93 I will never forget your precepts,
    for by them you have given me life.

119:77 *That I may live*—The psalmist does not
claim to be perfectly obedient (see also v. 176),
but rather asks God for *mercy* (see 103:13),
knowing that life is a gift of God's grace. The
repeated requests for life suggest a posture of
fundamental dependence upon God.

⁹⁴ I am yours; save me,
   for I have sought your precepts.
⁹⁵ The wicked lie in wait to destroy me,
   but I consider your decrees.
⁹⁶ I have seen a limit to all perfection,
   but your commandment is
      exceedingly broad.

⁹⁷ Oh, how I love your law!
   It is my meditation all day long.
⁹⁸ Your commandment makes me
      wiser than my enemies,
   for it is always with me.
⁹⁹ I have more understanding than all
      my teachers,
   for your decrees are my
      meditation.
¹⁰⁰ I understand more than the aged,
   for I keep your precepts.
¹⁰¹ I hold back my feet from every evil
      way,
   in order to keep your word.
¹⁰² I do not turn away from your
      ordinances,
   for you have taught me.
¹⁰³ How sweet are your words to my
      taste,
   sweeter than honey to my mouth!
¹⁰⁴ Through your precepts I get
      understanding;
   therefore I hate every false way.

¹⁰⁵ Your word is a lamp to my feet
   and a light to my path.
¹⁰⁶ I have sworn an oath and
      confirmed it,
   to observe your righteous
      ordinances.
¹⁰⁷ I am severely afflicted;
   give me life, O LORD, according to
      your word.
¹⁰⁸ Accept my offerings of praise,
      O LORD,
   and teach me your ordinances.
¹⁰⁹ I hold my life in my hand
      continually,
   but I do not forget your law.
¹¹⁰ The wicked have laid a snare for me,
   but I do not stray from your
      precepts.
¹¹¹ Your decrees are my heritage forever;

   they are the joy of my heart.
¹¹² I incline my heart to perform your
      statutes
   forever, to the end.

¹¹³ I hate the double-minded,
   but I love your law.
¹¹⁴ You are my hiding place and my
      shield;
   I hope in your word.
¹¹⁵ Go away from me, you evildoers,
   that I may keep the
      commandments of my God.
¹¹⁶ Uphold me according to your
      promise, that I may live,
   and let me not be put to shame in
      my hope.
¹¹⁷ Hold me up, that I may be safe
   and have regard for your statutes
      continually.
¹¹⁸ You spurn all who go astray from
      your statutes;
   for their cunning is in vain.
¹¹⁹ All the wicked of the earth you
      count as dross;
   therefore I love your decrees.
¹²⁰ My flesh trembles for fear of you,
   and I am afraid of your
      judgments.

¹²¹ I have done what is just and right;
   do not leave me to my
      oppressors.
¹²² Guarantee your servant's
      well-being;
   do not let the godless oppress me.
¹²³ My eyes fail from watching for your
      salvation,
   and for the fulfillment of your
      righteous promise.
¹²⁴ Deal with your servant according to
      your steadfast love,
   and teach me your statutes.
¹²⁵ I am your servant; give me
      understanding,
   so that I may know your decrees.
¹²⁶ It is time for the LORD to act,
   for your law has been broken.
¹²⁷ Truly I love your commandments
   more than gold, more than fine
      gold.

128 Truly I direct my steps by all your
    precepts;[a]
    I hate every false way.

129 Your decrees are wonderful;
    therefore my soul keeps them.
130 The unfolding of your words gives
    light;
    it imparts understanding to the
    simple.
131 With open mouth I pant,
    because I long for your
    commandments.
132 Turn to me and be gracious to me,
    as is your custom toward those
    who love your name.
133 Keep my steps steady according to
    your promise,
    and never let iniquity have
    dominion over me.
134 Redeem me from human oppression,
    that I may keep your precepts.
135 Make your face shine upon your
    servant,
    and teach me your statutes.
136 My eyes shed streams of tears
    because your law is not kept.

137 You are righteous, O Lord,
    and your judgments are right.
138 You have appointed your decrees in
    righteousness
    and in all faithfulness.
139 My zeal consumes me
    because my foes forget your
    words.
140 Your promise is well tried,
    and your servant loves it.
141 I am small and despised,
    yet I do not forget your precepts.
142 Your righteousness is an everlasting
    righteousness,
    and your law is the truth.
143 Trouble and anguish have come
    upon me,
    but your commandments are my
    delight.
144 Your decrees are righteous forever;
    give me understanding that I may
    live.

145 With my whole heart I cry; answer
    me, O Lord.
    I will keep your statutes.
146 I cry to you; save me,
    that I may observe your decrees.
147 I rise before dawn and cry for help;
    I put my hope in your words.
148 My eyes are awake before each watch
    of the night,
    that I may meditate on your
    promise.
149 In your steadfast love hear my voice;
    O Lord, in your justice preserve
    my life.
150 Those who persecute me with evil
    purpose draw near;
    they are far from your law.
151 Yet you are near, O Lord,
    and all your commandments are
    true.
152 Long ago I learned from your
    decrees
    that you have established them
    forever.

153 Look on my misery and rescue me,
    for I do not forget your law.
154 Plead my cause and redeem me;
    give me life according to your
    promise.
155 Salvation is far from the wicked,
    for they do not seek your statutes.
156 Great is your mercy, O Lord;
    give me life according to your
    justice.
157 Many are my persecutors and my
    adversaries,
    yet I do not swerve from your
    decrees.
158 I look at the faithless with disgust,
    because they do not keep your
    commands.
159 Consider how I love your precepts;
    preserve my life according to your
    steadfast love.
160 The sum of your word is truth;
    and every one of your righteous
    ordinances endures forever.

[a] Gk Jerome: Meaning of Heb uncertain

161 Princes persecute me without cause,
    but my heart stands in awe of your
        words.
162 I rejoice at your word
    like one who finds great spoil.
163 I hate and abhor falsehood,
    but I love your law.
164 Seven times a day I praise you
    for your righteous ordinances.
165 Great peace have those who love
        your law;
    nothing can make them stumble.
166 I hope for your salvation, O LORD,
    and I fulfill your commandments.
167 My soul keeps your decrees;
    I love them exceedingly.
168 I keep your precepts and decrees,
    for all my ways are before you.

169 Let my cry come before you,
        O LORD;
    give me understanding according
        to your word.
170 Let my supplication come before
        you;
    deliver me according to your
        promise.
171 My lips will pour forth praise,
    because you teach me your statutes.
172 My tongue will sing of your promise,
    for all your commandments are
        right.
173 Let your hand be ready to help me,
    for I have chosen your precepts.
174 I long for your salvation, O LORD,
    and your law is my delight.
175 Let me live that I may praise you,
    and let your ordinances help me.

176 I have gone astray like a lost sheep;
    seek out your servant,
    for I do not forget your
        commandments.

Psalm 120
Prayer for Deliverance
from Slanderers

A Song of Ascents.

1 In my distress I cry to the LORD,
    that he may answer me:
2 "Deliver me, O LORD,
    from lying lips,
    from a deceitful tongue."

3 What shall be given to you?
    And what more shall be done to
        you,
    you deceitful tongue?
4 A warrior's sharp arrows,
    with glowing coals of the broom
        tree!

5 Woe is me, that I am an alien in
        Meshech,
    that I must live among the tents of
        Kedar.
6 Too long have I had my dwelling
    among those who hate peace.
7 I am for peace;
    but when I speak,
    they are for war.

Psalm 121
Assurance of God's Protection

A Song of Ascents.

1 I lift up my eyes to the hills—
    from where will my help come?

Psalm 120

120 (Title) *A Song of Ascents*—This title is attached to Pss. 120–134, a collection that was probably used originally by pilgrims on their "ascent" to Jerusalem (see 122:4 where *go up* is the same root as "Ascents").

120:5—The locations of the places are unknown, but appropriately for a pilgrimage situation, the psalmist is outside of home territory.

120:6–7 *Peace*—What God wills, it is the fruit of justice and righteousness (see 29:11; 72:1–7; 96:11–13; introduction, "Psalms 1–2 and the Shape of the Psalter"). These verses anticipate

122:6–8 and serve as a contemporary reminder that it is precisely efforts for world-encompassing peace that often provoke hostility from those who stand to benefit from ongoing injustice and inequity.

Psalm 121

121:1–2—The constant affirmation of the psalmists is that *help* comes from God, despite what their opponents say (see 3:1–2). The astounding claim is that the cosmic sovereign—*who made heaven and earth* (see 115:5; 124:8; 134:3; and the Apostles' Creed)—is also my help.

² My help comes from the Lord,
    who made heaven and earth.

³ He will not let your foot be moved;
    he who keeps you will not
        slumber.
⁴ He who keeps Israel
    will neither slumber nor sleep.

⁵ The Lord is your keeper;
    the Lord is your shade at your
        right hand.
⁶ The sun shall not strike you by day,
    nor the moon by night.

⁷ The Lord will keep you from all evil;
    he will keep your life.
⁸ The Lord will keep
    your going out and your coming in
    from this time on and
        forevermore.

Psalm 122
Song of Praise and Prayer for Jerusalem

A Song of Ascents. Of David.

¹ I was glad when they said to me,
    "Let us go to the house of the
        Lord!"
² Our feet are standing
    within your gates, O Jerusalem.

³ Jerusalem—built as a city
    that is bound firmly together.

⁴ To it the tribes go up,
    the tribes of the Lord,
as was decreed for Israel,
    to give thanks to the name of the
        Lord.
⁵ For there the thrones for judgment
        were set up,
    the thrones of the house of David.

⁶ Pray for the peace of Jerusalem:
    "May they prosper who love you.
⁷ Peace be within your walls,
    and security within your towers."
⁸ For the sake of my relatives and
        friends
    I will say, "Peace be within you."
⁹ For the sake of the house of the
        Lord our God,
    I will seek your good.

Psalm 123
Supplication for Mercy

A Song of Ascents.

¹ To you I lift up my eyes,
    O you who are enthroned in the
        heavens!
² As the eyes of servants
    look to the hand of their master,
as the eyes of a maid
    to the hand of her mistress,
so our eyes look to the Lord our God,
    until he has mercy upon us.

121:3 *Keeps*—The key word, it occurs five more times (vv. 4, 5, 7, 7, 8).

121:6 *Sun . . . moon*—For a traveler (see Ps. 120 Title), the sun could be a problem, and the ancients also believed moonlight could be dangerous (see Matt. 17:15, in which the Greek word translated "epileptic" would literally be "moonstruck").

121:8—Especially appropriate for a pilgrim, the imagery can also be applied more generally to the journey of life.

Psalm 122

122:1 *The house of the Lord*—See v. 9. The destination of the pilgrim (see Ps. 120 Title) was the temple in Jerusalem (see vv. 2–3). See Pss. 46, 48, 76, 84, 87.

122:5 *Judgment*—Better translated "justice," it is a reminder that the Davidic monarchs were entrusted with the earthly enactment of God's will—"justice" and "righteousness" (see 72:1–7; 96:11–

13; introduction, "Psalms 1–2 and the Shape of the Psalter"), toward the goal of *peace* (vv. 6–8).

122:6–8 *Peace*—*Shalom*, "peace," forms part of the name "Jeru*salem*." *Jerusalem*, then and now, is to be both a symbol of and a stimulus toward the peace that God wills (see Luke 19:41–42), a peace founded on "justice" (see v. 5; 29:11).

Psalm 123

123:1 *Enthroned*—Despite *contempt* (vv. 3–4) and *scorn* (v. 4), the psalmist still addresses God as sovereign, suggesting a particular shape for divine power—that is, love rather than force (see introduction, "Prayers for Help").

123:2 *Servants*—Because God is sovereign, "servants" describes the appropriate posture of God's people. As the Psalter demonstrates (and Jesus as well), such servanthood involves suffering (see 44:9–22).

123:2–3 *Mercy*—The plea is grounded in the conviction that God sides not with the powerful

³ Have mercy upon us, O Lord, have
    mercy upon us,
    for we have had more than enough
      of contempt.
⁴ Our soul has had more than its
    fill
    of the scorn of those who are at
      ease,
    of the contempt of the proud.

Psalm 124

Thanksgiving for Israel's Deliverance

A Song of Ascents. Of David.

¹ If it had not been the Lord who was
    on our side
    —let Israel now say—
² if it had not been the Lord who was
    on our side,
    when our enemies attacked us,
³ then they would have swallowed us
    up alive,
    when their anger was kindled
      against us;
⁴ then the flood would have swept us
    away,
    the torrent would have gone
      over us;
⁵ then over us would have gone
    the raging waters.

⁶ Blessed be the Lord,
    who has not given us
    as prey to their teeth.
⁷ We have escaped like a bird
    from the snare of the
      fowlers;

the snare is broken,
    and we have escaped.
⁸ Our help is in the name of the Lord,
    who made heaven and earth.

Psalm 125

The Security of God's People

A Song of Ascents.

¹ Those who trust in the Lord are like
    Mount Zion,
    which cannot be moved, but
      abides forever.
² As the mountains surround
    Jerusalem,
    so the Lord surrounds his
      people,
    from this time on and
      forevermore.
³ For the scepter of wickedness shall
    not rest
    on the land allotted to the
      righteous,
    so that the righteous might not
      stretch out
    their hands to do wrong.
⁴ Do good, O Lord, to those who are
    good,
    and to those who are upright in
      their hearts.
⁵ But those who turn aside to their
    own crooked ways
    the Lord will lead away with
      evildoers.
    Peace be upon Israel!

---

and *proud* (v. 4), but with the lowly and despised
(see introduction, "Prayers for Help").

Psalm 124

124:1–2 *On our side*—Not a triumphalisitic assertion, it claims God's *help* (v. 8) amid apparently overwhelming opposition (vv. 3–5). Trusting
such help enabled Israel to adopt a suffering servant vocation in the postexilic era (see 44:9–22;
123:2), and trusting such help later empowered
Jesus and Paul to embody God's gracious and
loving purposes amid bitter attacks by their opponents (see Rom. 8:31).

124:8—This affirmation serves as a sort of refrain
in the Songs of Ascents (see 121:2; 134:3).

Psalm 125

125:1 *Trust*—See 4:5; 13:5; 52:8; introduction,
"Psalms of Trust." *Mount Zion*—See 48:1–2. The
affirmation in vv. 1–2 makes particular sense in
the pilgrimage context (see Ps. 120 Title).

125:5—The positing of retribution must be heard
in the context of the articulation of ongoing distress and threat, including the threat that evil will
lure *the righteous . . . to do wrong* (v. 3; see Pss.
123–24; introduction, "Prayers for Help"). The
peace (see 122:6–8) that God gives is not "as the
world gives" (John 14:27), but rather means an
unshakable happiness (see 1:1–2; 106:3; 112:1)
that derives from trusting God, entrusting the self
to God, and pursuing God's ways rather than
their own crooked ways.

Psalm 126
A Harvest of Joy
A Song of Ascents.

1 When the LORD restored the
    fortunes of Zion,*a*
  we were like those who dream.
2 Then our mouth was filled with
    laughter,
  and our tongue with shouts of joy;
  then it was said among the nations,
  "The LORD has done great things
    for them."
3 The LORD has done great things for
    us,
  and we rejoiced.

4 Restore our fortunes, O LORD,
  like the watercourses in the Negeb.
5 May those who sow in tears
  reap with shouts of joy.
6 Those who go out weeping,
  bearing the seed for sowing,
  shall come home with shouts of joy,
  carrying their sheaves.

Psalm 127
God's Blessings in the Home
A Song of Ascents. Of Solomon.

1 Unless the LORD builds the house,
  those who build it labor in vain.
  Unless the LORD guards the city,

  the guard keeps watch in vain.
2 It is in vain that you rise up early
  and go late to rest,
  eating the bread of anxious toil;
  for he gives sleep to his beloved.*b*

3 Sons are indeed a heritage from the
    LORD,
  the fruit of the womb a reward.
4 Like arrows in the hand of a warrior
  are the sons of one's youth.
5 Happy is the man who has
  his quiver full of them.
He shall not be put to shame
  when he speaks with his enemies
    in the gate.

Psalm 128
The Happy Home of the Faithful
A Song of Ascents.

1 Happy is everyone who fears the
    LORD,
  who walks in his ways.
2 You shall eat the fruit of the labor of
    your hands;
  you shall be happy, and it shall go
    well with you.

3 Your wife will be like a fruitful vine
  within your house;

a Or brought back those who returned to Zion   *b* Or for he provides for his beloved during sleep

---

Psalm 126

126:1 *Restored the fortunes*—Often refers to the return from exile, but it may more generally indicate deliverance (see 14:7; 85:1).

126:4–6—Whatever **great things** (vv. 2–3) God had done, the people again stand in need. The psalm moves from celebration to supplication, suggesting the regular simultaneity of pain and praise, hurt and hope, in the lives of the faithful, as well as the perpetual need to depend upon God. See the same movement from 85:1–3 to 85:4–7, and from 118:5–24 to 118:25 (see introduction, "Prayers for Help").

Psalm 127

127 (Title) *Of Solomon*—Solomon is credited with building God's house, the temple; and this may explain the attribution (see Ps. 72). Given that Solomon spent almost twice as much time building his own house, however, and given the split of the kingdom after Solomon, the reader

should probably hear the attribution ironically. That is, Solomon illustrates the vanity of not grounding his efforts in God's will.

127:1–2—Daily realities—domestic concerns, neighborhood security, job—are to be entrusted to God and guided by God's purposes, not simply by our own agendas (see Matt. 6:25–34).

127:3–5—There has perhaps been no other time in human history when it is more urgent to see children as gifts of God, rather than, for instance, as extensions of our own ambitions.

Psalm 128

128:1–2 *Happy*—As always in the Psalms, happiness is radically God-centered (see 1:1; 2:12; 106:3; 112:1).

128:3–4—The promise of fruitfulness and blessing should not be understood mechanistically (see 125:5). Rather, the psalm encourages readers to view family members as gifts of God (see 127:1–2).

your children will be like olive
    shoots
    around your table.
⁴ Thus shall the man be blessed
    who fears the LORD.

⁵ The LORD bless you from Zion.
    May you see the prosperity of
       Jerusalem
    all the days of your life.
⁶ May you see your children's children.
    Peace be upon Israel!

Psalm 129
Prayer for the Downfall
of Israel's Enemies

A Song of Ascents.

¹ "Often have they attacked me from
    my youth"
    —let Israel now say—
² "often have they attacked me from
    my youth,
    yet they have not prevailed against
      me.
³ The plowers plowed on my back;
    they made their furrows long."
⁴ The LORD is righteous;
    he has cut the cords of the wicked.
⁵ May all who hate Zion
    be put to shame and turned
      backward.
⁶ Let them be like the grass on the
    housetops

that withers before it grows up,
⁷ with which reapers do not fill their
    hands
    or binders of sheaves their arms,
⁸ while those who pass by do not
    say,
    "The blessing of the LORD be upon
      you!
    We bless you in the name of the
      LORD!"

Psalm 130
Waiting for Divine Redemption

A Song of Ascents.

¹ Out of the depths I cry to you,
    O LORD.
²   Lord, hear my voice!
    Let your ears be attentive
    to the voice of my supplications!

³ If you, O LORD, should mark
    iniquities,
    Lord, who could stand?
⁴ But there is forgiveness with you,
    so that you may be revered.

⁵ I wait for the LORD, my soul waits,
    and in his word I hope;
⁶ my soul waits for the Lord
    more than those who watch for the
      morning,
    more than those who watch for the
      morning.

128:5 *Zion*—As a pilgrimage collection, the Songs of Ascents features Zion, the goal of the journey (see 48:1–2; 125:1).

128:6 *Peace*—A central theme of the Songs of Ascents (see 122:6–8; 125:5).

Psalm 129

129:1–4—As in 124:1–7, the people of God are being *attacked* (vv. 1–2).

129:5–8—The desire for vengeance is essentially a plea for justice (see introduction, "Prayers for Help"). For things to be set right, God will need to oppose those who oppose God, God's place, and God's purposes, all of which are symbolized by *Zion* (see 48:1–2; 125:5). Lest there be a tendency to read Ps. 129 triumphalistically, see 130:3.

Psalm 130

130:1 *Out of the depths*—This phrase accurately

characterizes the location from which arise all the prayers for help (see introduction, "Prayers for Help"). "Depths" symbolizes the chaotic forces that threaten human life.

130:3—The psalmist admits that the chaos of her or his own life is at least partly due to her or his own failures; and appropriately, Ps. 130 is one of the church's seven Penitential Psalms (see Ps. 6). Following Ps. 129, Ps. 130 honestly points out that opposition to God can be internal as well as external.

130:4 *Forgiveness*—Forgiveness follows from God's *steadfast love* (v. 7; see 5:7; 36:5–6; 103:3, 8; Exod. 34:6–7).

130:5 *Wait . . . waits*—Waiting, trust, and *hope* are essentially synonymous, all deriving from a life lived in fundamental dependence upon God.

7 O Israel, hope in the LORD!
  For with the LORD there is
    steadfast love,
  and with him is great power to
    redeem.
8 It is he who will redeem Israel
  from all its iniquities.

Psalm 131
Song of Quiet Trust

A Song of Ascents. Of David.

1 O LORD, my heart is not lifted up,
  my eyes are not raised too high;
  I do not occupy myself with things
    too great and too marvelous for
    me.
2 But I have calmed and quieted my
    soul,
  like a weaned child with its
    mother;
  my soul is like the weaned child
    that is with me.*a*

3 O Israel, hope in the LORD
  from this time on and
    forevermore.

Psalm 132
The Eternal Dwelling of God in Zion

A Song of Ascents.

1 O LORD, remember in David's favor
  all the hardships he endured;
2 how he swore to the LORD

and vowed to the Mighty One of
    Jacob,
3 "I will not enter my house
  or get into my bed;
4 I will not give sleep to my eyes
  or slumber to my eyelids,
5 until I find a place for the LORD,
  a dwelling place for the Mighty
    One of Jacob."

6 We heard of it in Ephrathah;
  we found it in the fields of Jaar.
7 "Let us go to his dwelling place;
  let us worship at his footstool."

8 Rise up, O LORD, and go to your
    resting place,
  you and the ark of your might.
9 Let your priests be clothed with
    righteousness,
  and let your faithful shout for joy.
10 For your servant David's sake
  do not turn away the face of your
    anointed one.

11 The LORD swore to David a sure
    oath
  from which he will not turn back:
  "One of the sons of your body
  I will set on your throne.
12 If your sons keep my covenant
  and my decrees that I shall teach
    them,

a Or my soul within me is like a weaned child

Psalm 131

131:1 *Things too great and too marvelous*—These Hebrew words ordinarily refer to God's wondrous deeds. If these are what the psalmist avoids thinking about, then the obvious humility expressed here may result not only from choice, but also from role restrictions, perhaps due to gender (see v. 2).

131:2 *That is with me*—A *weaned child* normally runs back to its mother for comfort. The phrase, *with me*, thus suggests that the psalmist is a woman. This is not unlikely, especially in a collection that may have been used by families on the journey to Jerusalem (see Ps. 120 Title).

131:3—See 130:8. The *hope* invited here is based on the image in 131:2. Thus, Israel's hope resides in its liberating ability to turn—like a needy and perhaps wayward child (see Ps. 130)—to God, its compassionate mother (see 103:13). The psalm

commends the same childlike trust in God that was taught by Jesus (see Matt. 18:1–4; Mark 9:33–37; 10:13–16), a teaching that contains within it the revolutionary good news that the last and the least—be they children, women, or whoever—are first in the eyes of God.

Psalm 132

132:1 *Remember*—See 89:47, 50, where the rejected Davidic figure makes essentially the same plea. Psalm 132 seems to reflect the same crisis recounted in 89:38–51 (see esp. 132:10, 17, which seem to suggest the absence of a king).

132:2–5—David's vow seems to be a poetic rendering of 2 Sam. 7:1–2.

132:6–7—See 2 Sam. 6:1–19, especially vv. 6–7. The *footstool* is the ark (see v. 8), which David brought to Jerusalem.

132:11–12—See 2 Sam. 7:8–16; Ps. 89:3–4.

their sons also, forevermore,
shall sit on your throne."

13 For the LORD has chosen Zion;
he has desired it for his habitation:

14 "This is my resting place forever;
here I will reside, for I have
desired it.

15 I will abundantly bless its provisions;
I will satisfy its poor with bread.

16 Its priests I will clothe with
salvation,
and its faithful will shout for joy.

17 There I will cause a horn to sprout
up for David;
I have prepared a lamp for my
anointed one.

18 His enemies I will clothe with
disgrace,
but on him, his crown will gleam."

Psalm 133
The Blessedness of Unity
A Song of Ascents.

1 How very good and pleasant it is
when kindred live together in
unity!

2 It is like the precious oil on the
head,
running down upon the beard,
on the beard of Aaron,
running down over the collar of
his robes.

3 It is like the dew of Hermon,

which falls on the mountains of
Zion.
For there the LORD ordained his
blessing,
life forevermore.

Psalm 134
Praise in the Night
A Song of Ascents.

1 Come, bless the LORD, all you
servants of the LORD,
who stand by night in the house of
the LORD!

2 Lift up your hands to the holy place,
and bless the LORD.

3 May the LORD, maker of heaven and
earth,
bless you from Zion.

Psalm 135
Praise for God's Goodness and Might

1 Praise the LORD!
Praise the name of the LORD;
give praise, O servants of the
LORD,

2 you that stand in the house of the
LORD,
in the courts of the house of our
God.

3 Praise the LORD, for the LORD is
good;
sing to his name, for he is
gracious.

132:13–17—*Zion* is featured here, as in Pss. 46, 48, 76, 84, 87, 122.

132:18—In the postexilic era, this verse could have expressed hope for a restored Davidic monarchy, or it could be using the older symbols to express hope for Israel's participation in the fulfillment of God's purposes (see 149:6–9).

Psalm 133

133:1—This seems to be a proverbial saying that focuses on the importance of family harmony.

133:2–3—The two similes suggest abundance, but the mention of *Aaron* and *Zion* (see 48:1–2) begins to refocus the family imagery of 133:1. In the final sentence, *there* refers to Zion, suggesting that true family harmony will be experienced in the gathering of the family of God's people in Jerusalem. This sentiment makes particularly good sense toward the end of a pilgrimage col-

lection (see Ps. 120 Title). God's focus on the family is a remarkably expansive one, as was Jesus' (see Mark 3:31–35).

Psalm 134

134:1 *Bless*—See 34:1; 103:1. The gathering *by night* may mark the final evening before pilgrims to Jerusalem were to start home (see Ps. 120 Title).

134:3 *Maker of heaven and earth*—See 121:2; 124:8. Zion's universal significance is implied (see Pss. 46, 48), as is the people's trust that their lives depend on God's provision.

Psalm 135

135:2—See 134:1–2. The juxtaposition presents Ps. 135 as the praise invited in 134:1–2 (see also *bless* in 135:19–21). See also Pss. 78, 105, 106, 136, which contain historical recitals.

4 For the LORD has chosen Jacob for
     himself,
       Israel as his own possession.

5 For I know that the LORD is great;
     our Lord is above all gods.
6 Whatever the LORD pleases he does,
     in heaven and on earth,
       in the seas and all deeps.
7 He it is who makes the clouds rise at
     the end of the earth;
       he makes lightnings for the rain
         and brings out the wind from his
           storehouses.

8 He it was who struck down the
     firstborn of Egypt,
       both human beings and animals;
9 he sent signs and wonders
     into your midst, O Egypt,
       against Pharaoh and all his
         servants.
10 He struck down many nations
     and killed mighty kings—
11 Sihon, king of the Amorites,
     and Og, king of Bashan,
       and all the kingdoms of Canaan—
12 and gave their land as a heritage,
     a heritage to his people Israel.

13 Your name, O LORD, endures
     forever,
       your renown, O LORD, throughout
         all ages.
14 For the LORD will vindicate his
     people,
       and have compassion on his
         servants.

15 The idols of the nations are silver
     and gold,
       the work of human hands.
16 They have mouths, but they do not
     speak;
       they have eyes, but they do not see;
17 they have ears, but they do not hear,
     and there is no breath in their
       mouths.
18 Those who make them
     and all who trust them
       shall become like them.

19 O house of Israel, bless the LORD!
     O house of Aaron, bless the LORD!
20 O house of Levi, bless the LORD!
     You that fear the LORD, bless the
       LORD!
21 Blessed be the LORD from Zion,
     he who resides in Jerusalem.
   Praise the LORD!

Psalm 136
God's Work in Creation and in History

1 O give thanks to the LORD, for he is
     good,
       for his steadfast love endures
         forever.
2 O give thanks to the God of gods,
     for his steadfast love endures
       forever.
3 O give thanks to the Lord of lords,
     for his steadfast love endures
       forever;

4 who alone does great wonders,
     for his steadfast love endures
       forever;

135:5–6—God's universal sovereignty is affirmed, appropriately introduced (vv. 1–3) and followed (vv. 19–21) by praise, which is essentially a yielding of the self to God (see introduction, "Songs of Praise").

135:7–12—Illustrative of God's sovereignty is the movement from creation (v. 7) to exodus (vv. 8–9) to Israel's entry into the land (vv. 10–11; see Num. 21:21–35).

135:13—See Exod. 3:15; 9:16. God's activity on Israel's behalf has larger, world-encompassing consequences (see Gen. 12:1–3).

135:15–18—Since idolatry is a matter of *trust* (v. 18), the contemporary manifestation of idolatry may be the extent to which we trust ourselves

and *the work of human hands*, in the form, for instance, of consumer goods and technology.

135:19–21—Blessing God connotes submission to God and God's purposes (see 34:1; 103:1; 134:1).

Psalm 136

136:1–3—The invitation to praise recalls 106:1; 107:1; 118:1.

136:4–22 *For his steadfast love endures forever*—An expansion of Ps. 135 and its rehearsal from creation to entry into the land (see 135:7–12), Ps. 136 has an obvious difference—the refrain featuring God's steadfast love. The affirmation is that God's creation of the world and care

⁵ who by understanding made the
     heavens,
          for his steadfast love endures
               forever;
⁶ who spread out the earth on the
     waters,
          for his steadfast love endures
               forever;
⁷ who made the great lights,
          for his steadfast love endures
               forever;
⁸ the sun to rule over the day,
          for his steadfast love endures
               forever;
⁹ the moon and stars to rule over the
     night,
          for his steadfast love endures
               forever;
¹⁰ who struck Egypt through their
     firstborn,
          for his steadfast love endures
               forever;
¹¹ and brought Israel out from among
     them,
          for his steadfast love endures
               forever;
¹² with a strong hand and an
     outstretched arm,
          for his steadfast love endures
               forever;
¹³ who divided the Red Sea[a] in
     two,
          for his steadfast love endures
               forever;
¹⁴ and made Israel pass through the
     midst of it,
          for his steadfast love endures
               forever;
¹⁵ but overthrew Pharaoh and his army
     in the Red Sea,[a]
          for his steadfast love endures
               forever;

¹⁶ who led his people through the
     wilderness,
          for his steadfast love endures
               forever;
¹⁷ who struck down great kings,
          for his steadfast love endures
               forever;
¹⁸ and killed famous kings,
          for his steadfast love endures
               forever;
¹⁹ Sihon, king of the Amorites,
          for his steadfast love endures
               forever;
²⁰ and Og, king of Bashan,
          for his steadfast love endures
               forever;
²¹ and gave their land as a heritage,
          for his steadfast love endures
               forever;
²² a heritage to his servant Israel,
          for his steadfast love endures
               forever.

²³ It is he who remembered us in our
     low estate,
          for his steadfast love endures
               forever;
²⁴ and rescued us from our foes,
          for his steadfast love endures
               forever;
²⁵ who gives food to all flesh,
          for his steadfast love endures
               forever.

²⁶ O give thanks to the God of heaven,
          for his steadfast love endures
               forever.

Psalm 137
Lament over the Destruction
of Jerusalem

¹ By the rivers of Babylon—

[a] Or Sea of Reeds

for God's people are motivated by God's gracious
love (see "steadfast love" in 5:7; 13:5; 23:6;
25:6, 7, 10; 33:5; 36:5; 103:4, 8, 11, 17; Exod.
34:6–7).

136:23–25—The Psalter repeatedly affirms God's
attentiveness to the lowly (v. 23; see introduction,
"Prayers for Help"); but God's will to provide for
the life of humankind extends ultimately to *all*

flesh (v. 25). In short, God loves the whole world;
and it is not coincidental that the Psalter regularly
invites a universe-encompassing congregation to
worship God (see 96:11–13; 148:1–12; 150:6;
introduction, "Songs of Praise").

Psalm 137

137:1—The psalm is set in the exile, 587–539
BCE.

there we sat down and there we wept
when we remembered Zion.
² On the willows*ᵃ* there
we hung up our harps.
³ For there our captors
asked us for songs,
and our tormentors asked for mirth,
saying,
"Sing us one of the songs of Zion!"

⁴ How could we sing the LORD's song
in a foreign land?
⁵ If I forget you, O Jerusalem,
let my right hand wither!
⁶ Let my tongue cling to the roof of
my mouth,
if I do not remember you,
if I do not set Jerusalem
above my highest joy.

⁷ Remember, O LORD, against the
Edomites
the day of Jerusalem's fall,
how they said, "Tear it down! Tear it
down!
Down to its foundations!"
⁸ O daughter Babylon, you devastator!*ᵇ*
Happy shall they be who pay you
back
what you have done to us!
⁹ Happy shall they be who take your
little ones
and dash them against the rock!

Psalm 138
Thanksgiving and Praise
Of David.

¹ I give you thanks, O LORD, with my
whole heart;

before the gods I sing your praise;
² I bow down toward your holy temple
and give thanks to your name for
your steadfast love and your
faithfulness;
for you have exalted your name
and your word
above everything.*ᶜ*
³ On the day I called, you answered
me,
you increased my strength of soul.*ᵈ*

⁴ All the kings of the earth shall praise
you, O LORD,
for they have heard the words of
your mouth.
⁵ They shall sing of the ways of the
LORD,
for great is the glory of the LORD.
⁶ For though the LORD is high, he
regards the lowly;
but the haughty he perceives from
far away.

⁷ Though I walk in the midst of
trouble,
you preserve me against the wrath
of my enemies;
you stretch out your hand,
and your right hand delivers me.
⁸ The LORD will fulfill his purpose
for me;
your steadfast love, O LORD,
endures forever.
Do not forsake the work of your
hands.

ᵃ Or poplars ᵇ Or you who are devastated ᶜ Cn: Heb you have exalted your word above all your name ᵈ Syr Compare Gk Tg: Heb you made me arrogant in my soul with strength

---

137:3 *The songs of Zion*—See Pss. 46, 48, 76, 84, 87, 122. While the people could not *sing*, neither could they *forget* (v. 5) *Jerusalem*. Memory meant hope.

137:7—The *Edomites* were traditional enemies (see Ezek. 35:5–15; Obadiah; Lam. 1:20–22).

137:8–9—The request, though shocking, simply asks for what most contemporary people think is fair—namely, that the punishment fit the crime. It reflects the typical practice of ancient (and modern) warfare (see 2 Kgs. 8:12; Isa. 13:16; Hos. 10:14; Nah. 3:10). Such pleas for vengeance

should be heard as requests for justice by the victimized (see introduction, "Prayers for Help").

Psalm 138

138:2 *Holy temple*—God's earthly abode, the temple, is also associated with God's *steadfast love* in 5:7. *Steadfast love and . . . faithfulness*—See v. 8; 5:7; 36:5–6; Exod. 34:6–7.

138:6—The same downward movement of God is featured in 113:5–9.

138:7–8—The psalmist articulates the pervasive conviction that God stands with those in *trouble*,

Psalm 139
The Inescapable God
To the leader. Of David. A Psalm.

1 O LORD, you have searched me and
    known me.
2 You know when I sit down and when
        I rise up;
    you discern my thoughts from far
        away.
3 You search out my path and my
        lying down,
    and are acquainted with all my
        ways.
4 Even before a word is on my tongue,
    O LORD, you know it completely.
5 You hem me in, behind and before,
    and lay your hand upon me.
6 Such knowledge is too wonderful
        for me;
    it is so high that I cannot attain it.

7 Where can I go from your spirit?
    Or where can I flee from your
        presence?
8 If I ascend to heaven, you are there;
    if I make my bed in Sheol, you are
        there.
9 If I take the wings of the morning
    and settle at the farthest limits of
        the sea,
10 even there your hand shall lead me,
    and your right hand shall hold me
        fast.
11 If I say, "Surely the darkness shall
        cover me,
    and the light around me become
        night,"
12 even the darkness is not dark to you;
    the night is as bright as the day,
    for darkness is as light to you.

13 For it was you who formed my
        inward parts;
    you knit me together in my
        mother's womb.
14 I praise you, for I am fearfully and
        wonderfully made.
    Wonderful are your works;
    that I know very well.
15 My frame was not hidden from
        you,
    when I was being made in secret,
        intricately woven in the depths of
        the earth.
16 Your eyes beheld my unformed
        substance.
    In your book were written
        all the days that were formed
            for me,
    when none of them as yet existed.
17 How weighty to me are your
        thoughts, O God!
    How vast is the sum of them!
18 I try to count them—they are more
        than the sand;
    I come to the end[a]—I am still with
        you.

19 O that you would kill the wicked,
        O God,
    and that the bloodthirsty would
        depart from me—
20 those who speak of you maliciously,
    and lift themselves up against you
        for evil![b]
21 Do I not hate those who hate you,
        O LORD?
    And do I not loathe those who rise
        up against you?
22 I hate them with perfect hatred;

[a] Or I awake   [b] Cn: Meaning of Heb uncertain

and that God's purposes will be fulfilled, despite
appearances to the contrary (see introduction,
"Prayers for Help").

Psalm 139

139:1 *Known*—This becomes the key word (see
vv. 2, 4, 6, 14, 23), occurring seven times, suggesting perhaps that God fully knows the psalmist. The point is not knowledge in the abstract,
but relational knowledge.

139:8 *Sheol*—See 6:5. Rejecting the usual view

of Sheol, the psalmist affirms that God's presence extends even into the realm of the dead (see
22:29).

139:16—See 40:7. The poetic description in vv.
13–16 articulates the psalmist's conviction that
his or her life belongs fully to God (see 100:3).

139:19–22—The psalmist affirms loyalty to God
by opposing God's enemies. The request for
vengeance is a victim's prayer for justice (see
introduction, "Prayers for Help").

I count them my enemies.
23 Search me, O God, and know my
heart;
test me and know my thoughts.
24 See if there is any wicked[a] way in me,
and lead me in the way everlasting.[b]

Psalm 140
Prayer for Deliverance from Enemies
To the leader. A Psalm of David.

1 Deliver me, O LORD, from evildoers;
protect me from those who are
violent,
2 who plan evil things in their minds
and stir up wars continually.
3 They make their tongue sharp as a
snake's,
and under their lips is the venom
of vipers.   *Selah*

4 Guard me, O LORD, from the hands
of the wicked;
protect me from the violent
who have planned my downfall.
5 The arrogant have hidden a trap
for me,
and with cords they have spread a
net,[c]
along the road they have set snares
for me.   *Selah*

6 I say to the LORD, "You are my God;
give ear, O LORD, to the voice of
my supplications."
7 O LORD, my Lord, my strong
deliverer,
you have covered my head in the
day of battle.
8 Do not grant, O LORD, the desires of
the wicked;

do not further their evil plot.[d]
          Selah

9 Those who surround me lift up their
heads;[e]
let the mischief of their lips
overwhelm them!
10 Let burning coals fall on them!
Let them be flung into pits, no
more to rise!
11 Do not let the slanderer be
established in the land;
let evil speedily hunt down the
violent!

12 I know that the LORD maintains the
cause of the needy,
and executes justice for the poor.
13 Surely the righteous shall give
thanks to your name;
the upright shall live in your
presence.

Psalm 141
Prayer for Preservation from Evil
A Psalm of David.

1 I call upon you, O LORD; come
quickly to me;
give ear to my voice when I call to
you.
2 Let my prayer be counted as incense
before you,
and the lifting up of my hands as
an evening sacrifice.

3 Set a guard over my mouth, O LORD;
keep watch over the door of my
lips.

---

[a] Heb *hurtful*   [b] Or *the ancient way*. Compare Jer 6.16   [c] Or *they have spread cords as a net*   [d] Heb adds *they are exalted*   [e] Cn Compare Gk: Heb *those who surround me are uplifted in head*; Heb divides verses 8 and 9 differently

---

Psalm 140

140:1, 3, 11 *Violent*—This repeated word is an apt reminder that the psalmists' frequent requests for vengeance (see vv. 10–11) come in response to violence that already exists, and of which they are victims (see introduction, "Prayers for Help"). In short, the psalmists pray for *justice* (v. 12), the essence of God's will (see introduction, "Psalms 1–2 and the Shape of the Psalter;" 96:11–13). It is grounded in God's abiding concern for *the needy, and . . . the poor* (v. 12; see introduction, "Prayers for Help"; 9:18; 40:17; 109:31).

The psalm can be a contemporary reminder that many in our world need to pray quite literally, *protect me from those who are violent* (v. 1). Paul's citation of v. 3 in Rom. 3:13 suggests the reality that all people participate in and need deliverance from the violent propensities of our own selves and our world.

Psalm 141

141:2—The ancient posture of prayer was *hands* uplifted.

141:3–5—In essence, the psalmist prays, "lead us

⁴ Do not turn my heart to any evil,
    to busy myself with wicked deeds
in company with those who work
    iniquity;
    do not let me eat of their delicacies.

⁵ Let the righteous strike me;
    let the faithful correct me.
Never let the oil of the wicked anoint
    my head,ᵃ
    for my prayer is continuallyᵇ
    against their wicked deeds.
⁶ When they are given over to those
    who shall condemn them,
then they shall learn that my
    words were pleasant.
⁷ Like a rock that one breaks apart and
    shatters on the land,
so shall their bones be strewn at
    the mouth of Sheol.ᶜ

⁸ But my eyes are turned toward you,
    O God, my Lord;
in you I seek refuge; do not leave
    me defenseless.
⁹ Keep me from the trap that they
    have laid for me,
and from the snares of evildoers.
¹⁰ Let the wicked fall into their own nets,
    while I alone escape.

Psalm 142

Prayer for Deliverance from Persecutors

*A Maskil of David. When he was in the cave.
A Prayer.*

¹ With my voice I cry to the Lord;
    with my voice I make supplication
    to the Lord.

² I pour out my complaint before him;
    I tell my trouble before him.
³ When my spirit is faint,
    you know my way.

In the path where I walk
    they have hidden a trap for me.
⁴ Look on my right hand and see—
    there is no one who takes notice
    of me;
no refuge remains to me;
    no one cares for me.

⁵ I cry to you, O Lord;
    I say, "You are my refuge,
    my portion in the land of the
    living."
⁶ Give heed to my cry,
    for I am brought very low.

Save me from my persecutors,
    for they are too strong for me.
⁷ Bring me out of prison,
    so that I may give thanks to your
    name.
The righteous will surround me,
    for you will deal bountifully with me.

Psalm 143

Prayer for Deliverance from Enemies

A Psalm of David.

¹ Hear my prayer, O Lord;
    give ear to my supplications in
    your faithfulness;
    answer me in your righteousness.
² Do not enter into judgment with
    your servant,

ᵃ Gk: Meaning of Heb uncertain   ᵇ Cn: Heb *for continually and my prayer*
ᶜ Meaning of Heb of verses 5-7 is uncertain

---

not into temptation, but deliver us from evil" (see also vv. 8–9).

141:8 *Refuge*—The power to resist the enticements of evil and self-centeredness is found in trusting God, including complete orientation to God's way. This is what "refuge" communicates (see Pss. 1–2, esp. 2:12; introduction, "Psalms of Trust").

Psalm 142

142:2 *Complaint*—The prayers for help are often known as the **complaints**. As here, **trouble** is the norm; and the psalmists always take it to God in prayer.

142:4 *No one cares for me*—The psalmists are always convinced that even when no one else cares, God does (see vv. 5, 7). So, a **refuge** is always available for the lowly (vv. 5–6; see 2:12; 141:8; introduction, "Psalms of Trust"). For more privileged persons, this wrenching prayer can be a reminder that many persons in our world can accurately say, "No one cares for me." Thus the privileged are invited into solidarity with the suffering of others (see introduction, "Prayers for Help").

Psalm 143

143:2—In a strikingly unique request, the psalm-

for no one living is righteous
before you.

3 For the enemy has pursued me,
crushing my life to the ground,
making me sit in darkness like
those long dead.
4 Therefore my spirit faints within me;
my heart within me is appalled.

5 I remember the days of old,
I think about all your deeds,
I meditate on the works of your
hands.
6 I stretch out my hands to you;
my soul thirsts for you like a
parched land.   *Selah*

7 Answer me quickly, O LORD;
my spirit fails.
Do not hide your face from me,
or I shall be like those who go
down to the Pit.
8 Let me hear of your steadfast love in
the morning,
for in you I put my trust.
Teach me the way I should go,
for to you I lift up my soul.

9 Save me, O LORD, from my enemies;
I have fled to you for refuge.*a*
10 Teach me to do your will,
for you are my God.
Let your good spirit lead me
on a level path.

11 For your name's sake, O LORD,
preserve my life.
In your righteousness bring me
out of trouble.
12 In your steadfast love cut off my
enemies,
and destroy all my adversaries,
for I am your servant.

Psalm 144
Prayer for National Deliverance and Security
Of David.

1 Blessed be the LORD, my rock,
who trains my hands for war, and
my fingers for battle;
2 my rock*b* and my fortress,
my stronghold and my deliverer,
my shield, in whom I take refuge,
who subdues the peoples*c*
under me.

3 O LORD, what are human beings that
you regard them,
or mortals that you think of them?
4 They are like a breath;
their days are like a passing shadow.

5 Bow your heavens, O LORD, and
come down;
touch the mountains so that they
smoke.

a One Heb Ms Gk: MT *to you I have hidden*   *b* With 18.2 and 2 Sam 22.2: Heb *my steadfast love*   *c* Heb Mss Syr Aquila Jerome: MT *my people*

---

ist asks that God *not* establish "justice" (NRSV *judgment*) for him or her. This is apparently his or her way of confessing sinfulness, which is shared by all persons. The apostle Paul cites this verse in Rom. 3:20, and Ps. 143 is one of the church's seven Penitential Psalms (see Ps. 6).

143:7–8—Despite unworthiness, the psalmist dares to ask God for help (see also vv. 11–12). The basis for the request is not merit, but rather God's *steadfast love* (v. 8; see v. 12; 5:7; 36:5; 103:3, 8; Exod. 34:6–7). Because of his or her conviction that God is essentially gracious, the psalmist can say, unworthiness and all, "I offer you my life" (NRSV *I lift up my soul*; see 24:4; 25:1).

143:10 *Teach me*—The psalmist recognizes that grace is not cheap. The offer of his or her life (v. 8) means openness to God's will (see also Ps. 1).

143:11 *In your righteousness*—The psalmist reveals that God's righteousness or justice is not merely retributive. He or she is aware that God pursues God's will—righteousness and justice (see introduction, "Psalms 1–2 and the Shape of the Psalter"; 96:11–13)—by way of forgiving love, as the apostle Paul would later affirm (see note at v. 2).

Psalm 144

144:1–2—See 18:1–2, 34. Psalm 144 seems to be a postexilic recasting of Ps. 18. Psalm 144:12–14 particularly suggests a postexilic setting.

144:3–4—Compare 8:4–5, which asks the same question but gives a much more exalted answer (see also 89:47–48).

144:5–7—See 18:9, 14, 16, 44–45, which have been turned into petitions, reflecting apparently the crisis articulated in 89:38–51 (see introduc-

⁶ Make the lightning flash and scatter
    them;
    send out your arrows and rout
      them.
⁷ Stretch out your hand from on high;
    set me free and rescue me from
      the mighty waters,
    from the hand of aliens,
⁸ whose mouths speak lies,
    and whose right hands are false.

⁹ I will sing a new song to you, O God;
    upon a ten-stringed harp I will
      play to you,
¹⁰ the one who gives victory to kings,
    who rescues his servant David.
¹¹ Rescue me from the cruel sword,
    and deliver me from the hand of
      aliens,
    whose mouths speak lies,
    and whose right hands are false.

¹² May our sons in their youth
    be like plants full grown,
    our daughters like corner pillars,
    cut for the building of a palace.
¹³ May our barns be filled,
    with produce of every kind;
    may our sheep increase by
      thousands,
    by tens of thousands in our fields,
¹⁴   and may our cattle be heavy with
      young.
    May there be no breach in the walls,ᵃ
      no exile,
    and no cry of distress in our
      streets.

¹⁵ Happy are the people to whom such
    blessings fall;
    happy are the people whose God is
      the LORD.

Psalm 145
The Greatness and the Goodness of God

Praise. Of David.

¹ I will extol you, my God and King,
    and bless your name forever and
      ever.
² Every day I will bless you,
    and praise your name forever and
      ever.
³ Great is the LORD, and greatly to be
    praised;
    his greatness is unsearchable.

⁴ One generation shall laud your
    works to another,
    and shall declare your mighty
      acts.
⁵ On the glorious splendor of your
    majesty,
    and on your wondrous works, I
      will meditate.
⁶ The might of your awesome deeds
    shall be proclaimed,
    and I will declare your
      greatness.
⁷ They shall celebrate the fame of your
    abundant goodness,
    and shall sing aloud of your
      righteousness.

ᵃ Heb lacks *in the walls*

---

tion, "Psalms 1–2 and the Shape of the Psalter"). The *aliens*, who, according to 18:44–45 ("foreigners"), had been dealt with by God, are the problem here.

144:9 *A new song*—See 33:1; 96:1; 98:1. A new deliverance is anticipated, to which a new song will be the grateful response. The switch to second-person pronouns may suggest that the whole people of God has inherited the vocation of the Davidic monarch—that is, to enact God's will in the world (see 105:12–15; 149:5–9; introduction, "Psalms 1–2 and the Shape of the Psalter").

144:15 *Happy*—As in 1:1–2; 2:12, and throughout the Psalms, happiness is essentially God-centered.

Psalm 145

145:1 *My God and King*—See 5:2; 93:1; introduction, "Psalms 1–2 and the Shape of the Psalter." Not surprisingly, the concluding collection of songs of praise begins with an explicit assertion of God's sovereignty (see also 145:11–13; 146:10; 149:2).

145:7 *Your righteousness*—The sovereign God wills justice and righteousness (see introduction, "Psalms 1–2 and the Shape of the Psalter"; 96:11–13) on nothing less than a cosmic scale, as the repeated word *all/every* suggests in the remainder of the psalm.

8 The LORD is gracious and merciful,
   slow to anger and abounding in
      steadfast love.
9 The LORD is good to all,
   and his compassion is over all that
      he has made.

10 All your works shall give thanks to
      you, O LORD,
   and all your faithful shall bless
      you.
11 They shall speak of the glory of your
      kingdom,
   and tell of your power,
12 to make known to all people your[a]
      mighty deeds,
   and the glorious splendor of your[b]
      kingdom.
13 Your kingdom is an everlasting
      kingdom,
   and your dominion endures
      throughout all generations.

   The LORD is faithful in all his words,
      and gracious in all his deeds.[c]
14 The LORD upholds all who are
      falling,
   and raises up all who are bowed
      down.
15 The eyes of all look to you,
   and you give them their food in
      due season.
16 You open your hand,
   satisfying the desire of every living
      thing.
17 The LORD is just in all his ways,
   and kind in all his doings.
18 The LORD is near to all who call on
      him,

to all who call on him in truth.
19 He fulfills the desire of all who fear
      him;
   he also hears their cry, and saves
      them.
20 The LORD watches over all who love
      him,
   but all the wicked he will destroy.

21 My mouth will speak the praise of
      the LORD,
   and all flesh will bless his holy
      name forever and ever.

Psalm 146
Praise for God's Help

1 Praise the LORD!
   Praise the LORD, O my soul!
2 I will praise the LORD as long as I
      live;
   I will sing praises to my God all
      my life long.

3 Do not put your trust in princes,
   in mortals, in whom there is no
      help.
4 When their breath departs, they
      return to the earth;
   on that very day their plans
      perish.

5 Happy are those whose help is the
      God of Jacob,
   whose hope is in the LORD their
      God,
6 who made heaven and earth,
   the sea, and all that is in them;
   who keeps faith forever;

a Gk Jerome Syr: Heb *his*   b Heb *his*   c These two lines supplied by Q Ms
Gk Syr

145:8—The fundamentals of God's character
are also rehearsed in 86:15; 103:8 (see Exod.
34:6–7).

145:21 *All flesh*—As usual, praise in the Psalter
is expansive, suggesting that the sovereign of the
universe wills to gather a universe-encompassing
congregation (see 148:1–12; 150:6; introduction,
"Songs of Praise"). The apparent exception of *the
wicked* (145:20) is not so much a limitation of
God's will, but rather a recognition that God and
God's purposes are regularly opposed (see Pss.
1–2; introduction, "Prayers for Help").

Psalm 146

146:1 *O my soul!*—"Soul" connotes the psalmist's whole being (see 103:1).

146:3—Praise is essentially a matter of whom or
what we *trust* (see 4:5; 13:5; 52:7–8; introduction, "Psalms of Trust"). Praising God indicates
submission to God's sovereign claim (see v.
10), and thereby all other claims and sources of
help are relativized (see introduction, "Songs of
Praise").

146:5—Happiness in the Psalms is always God-
centered (see 1:1–2; 2:12).

7   who executes justice for the
        oppressed;
    who gives food to the hungry.

    The LORD sets the prisoners free;
8   the LORD opens the eyes of the
        blind.
    The LORD lifts up those who are
        bowed down;
    the LORD loves the righteous.
9   The LORD watches over the
        strangers;
    he upholds the orphan and the
        widow,
    but the way of the wicked he
        brings to ruin.

10 The LORD will reign forever,
    your God, O Zion, for all
        generations.
    Praise the LORD!

Psalm 147
Praise for God's Care for Jerusalem

1   Praise the LORD!
    How good it is to sing praises to our
        God;
    for he is gracious, and a song of
        praise is fitting.
2   The LORD builds up Jerusalem;
        he gathers the outcasts of Israel.
3   He heals the brokenhearted,
        and binds up their wounds.
4   He determines the number of the
        stars;
    he gives to all of them their names.
5   Great is our Lord, and abundant in
        power;

his understanding is beyond
    measure.
6   The LORD lifts up the downtrodden;
    he casts the wicked to the ground.

7   Sing to the LORD with thanksgiving;
    make melody to our God on the
        lyre.
8   He covers the heavens with clouds,
    prepares rain for the earth,
    makes grass grow on the hills.
9   He gives to the animals their food,
    and to the young ravens when they
        cry.
10 His delight is not in the strength of
        the horse,
    nor his pleasure in the speed of a
        runner;*a*
11 but the LORD takes pleasure in those
        who fear him,
    in those who hope in his steadfast
        love.

12 Praise the LORD, O Jerusalem!
    Praise your God, O Zion!
13 For he strengthens the bars of your
        gates;
    he blesses your children within
        you.
14 He grants peace*b* within your
        borders;
    he fills you with the finest of
        wheat.
15 He sends out his command to the
        earth;
    his word runs swiftly.

a Heb legs of a person   *b* Or prosperity

146:7 *Justice for the oppressed*—God's sovereign will involves justice and righteousness (see introduction, "Psalms 1–2 and the Shape of the Psalter"; 96:11–13), which mean particular concern for those victimized and *oppressed* (see 146:7–9; introduction, "Prayers for Help"), as well as opposition to oppressors (v. 9; see 145:20).

Psalm 147

147:2–3—God is portrayed regularly as siding with the victimized and oppressed (see v. 6a; 146:7–9; introduction, "Prayers for Help").

147:6b—Recalling 145:20–21 and 146:9, the message is that for God to liberate the oppressed, God must oppose oppressors.

147:8–9—See 104:14, 27, which make similar affirmations.

147:10–11—Echoing yet another psalm, 33:16–18, Ps. 147 seems to be a sort of anthology of several other psalms.

147:12–14—*Zion* is God's place (see 48:1–2), and it is elsewhere associated with God's will for *peace* (see 122:6–8).

147:15–20—The phrase *his word* occurs in vv. 15, 18, 19. God's word not only commands creation, but also is addressed *to Jacob* (v. 19), suggesting that the vocation of God's particular people is the fulfillment of God's creative purposes. Thus, the same God who *determines the*

16 He gives snow like wool;
      he scatters frost like ashes.
17 He hurls down hail like crumbs—
      who can stand before his cold?
18 He sends out his word, and melts
         them;
      he makes his wind blow, and the
         waters flow.
19 He declares his word to Jacob,
      his statutes and ordinances to Israel.
20 He has not dealt thus with any other
         nation;
      they do not know his ordinances.
   Praise the LORD!

Psalm 148

Praise for God's Universal Glory

1 Praise the LORD!
   Praise the LORD from the heavens;
      praise him in the heights!
2 Praise him, all his angels;
      praise him, all his host!

3 Praise him, sun and moon;
      praise him, all you shining stars!
4 Praise him, you highest heavens,
      and you waters above the heavens!

5 Let them praise the name of the
         LORD,
      for he commanded and they were
         created.
6 He established them forever and ever;
      he fixed their bounds, which
         cannot be passed.*a*

7 Praise the LORD from the earth,
      you sea monsters and all deeps,

8 fire and hail, snow and frost,
      stormy wind fulfilling his
         command!

9 Mountains and all hills,
      fruit trees and all cedars!
10 Wild animals and all cattle,
      creeping things and flying birds!

11 Kings of the earth and all peoples,
      princes and all rulers of the earth!
12 Young men and women alike,
      old and young together!

13 Let them praise the name of the
         LORD,
      for his name alone is exalted;
      his glory is above earth and
         heaven.
14 He has raised up a horn for his
         people,
      praise for all his faithful,
      for the people of Israel who are
         close to him.
   Praise the LORD!

Psalm 149

Praise for God's Goodness to Israel

1 Praise the LORD!
   Sing to the LORD a new song,
      his praise in the assembly of the
         faithful.
2 Let Israel be glad in its Maker;
      let the children of Zion rejoice in
         their King.
3 Let them praise his name with
         dancing,

a Or *he set a law that cannot pass away*

... *stars* (v. 4) also *lifts up the downtrodden*
(v. 6). The very universe is stacked in favor of
God's "acts of justice" (vv. 19–20; NRSV *ordinances*).

Psalm 148

148:1 *From the heavens*—Verses 1–6 invite
praise from the creatures and features of the
heavenly realm.

148:7 *From the earth*—Verses 7–12 invite praise
from the creatures and features of the earth,
including *all peoples* (v. 11).

148:13–14—The combined effect of vv. 1–6 and
vv. 7–12 is to invite a universe-encompassing
congregation to worship the cosmic sovereign.

Although *the people of Israel* may be *close
to him*, they are joined by *all peoples* and all
things as God's very own (see 67:4–5; 96:11–13;
145:21; 150:6; introduction, "Songs of Praise").
The ecumenical, interfaith, and ecological implications are profound and far-reaching.

Psalm 149

149:1 *New song*—As in 98:1, the new song is
associated with God's sovereignty (149:2).

149:2 *Zion*—See 48:1–2. *King*—See 145:1.
God's sovereignty is in view from the very beginning of the Psalter. Not coincidentally, Ps. 149
recalls Ps. 2 (see 149:7–9; introduction, "Psalms
1–2 and the Shape of the Psalter").

making melody to him with
  tambourine and lyre.
4 For the LORD takes pleasure in his
  people;
  he adorns the humble with victory.
5 Let the faithful exult in glory;
  let them sing for joy on their
  couches.
6 Let the high praises of God be in
  their throats
  and two-edged swords in their
  hands,
7 to execute vengeance on the nations
  and punishment on the peoples,
8 to bind their kings with fetters
  and their nobles with chains of
  iron,
9 to execute on them the judgment
  decreed.
  This is glory for all his faithful
  ones.
Praise the LORD!

Psalm 150

Praise for God's Surpassing Greatness

1 Praise the LORD!
  Praise God in his sanctuary;
  praise him in his mighty
  firmament!*a*
2 Praise him for his mighty deeds;
  praise him according to his
  surpassing greatness!
3 Praise him with trumpet sound;
  praise him with lute and harp!
4 Praise him with tambourine and
  dance;
  praise him with strings and pipe!
5 Praise him with clanging cymbals;
  praise him with loud clashing
  cymbals!
6 Let everything that breathes praise
  the LORD!
  Praise the LORD!

a Or dome

149:7–9—Recalling 2:2–3, 8–9, these verses seem to have transferred the role of the Davidic monarchy to *the faithful*, suggesting that responsibility for the earthly enactment of God's will now belongs to the whole people of God. Quite appropriately, this work is described as "justice" (149:9, NRSV *judgment*), one of the words that summarizes God's will for the world (see 72:1–7; 96:11–13; introduction, "Psalms 1–2 and the Shape of the Psalter"). That *justice* must sometimes take the form of *vengeance* (149:7) is to be explained by the reality that God and God's purposes are regularly opposed by self-seeking and self-assertive people who benefit from injustice and oppression. It is the *glory* of God's faithful, then and now, to stand with God for the poor and needy (see 9:18; 40:17; 109:31; 140:12; introduction, "Prayers for Help").

Psalm 150

150:1 *Sanctuary*—This may refer to the temple, the earthly center of God's sovereignty (see 5:7; 24:8). To invite praise in the temple, as well as in God's *mighty firmament*, is to duplicate the invitation of Ps. 148 to praise God *from the heavens* (v. 1) and *from the earth* (v. 7).

150:3–5—The Psalter culminates by inviting a crescendo of *praise* with full instrumentation.

150:6—Finally, no praise will be sufficient unless it comes from *everything that breathes*, corresponding to God's universe-encompassing sovereignty (see 67:4–5; 96:11–13; 145:21; 148:1–12; introduction, "Songs of Praise").

The Book of
PROVERBS

O nly about half of the book called Proverbs consists of the type of short, pithy sayings English speakers think of as proverbs. Three groups of relatively lengthy, advice-giving speeches phrased in coaxing or sermonic-type language (called Instructions) have been placed at the beginning, the middle and the end of the book. Sandwiched in between the Instructions are two collections of abbreviated one-sentence sayings that resemble what an English speaker means by the term "proverbs." The editorial heading "Proverbs of Solomon" is used to introduce both types of literature (1:1, 10:1, 25:1), and both types are paralleled in the Wisdom literature of other ancient Near Eastern cultures. The reference to Solomon reminds us of his reputation as a recipient of wisdom from God (1 Kgs. 4:29) but cannot imply authorship of the whole book, since various parts are also identified as the "words of the wise," using a plural noun meaning "wise ones" (22:17–24:34); "the words of Agur, son of Jakeh" (chap. 30); and the words of King Lemuel's mother (chap. 31).

In the Instructions, unnamed teachers urge their listeners to think and act in ways that are life-enhancing ("wise") and to avoid ways that are life-threatening ("foolish"). The instructors use a variety of literary forms in their attempts to persuade their pupils to follow their instructions. Wisdom, Folly and Temptation are frequently personified (made to speak as if they were persons with the power to address learners directly), and the concluding acrostic poem (31:10–31) pictures wisdom as an extraordinary woman who manages her household and family affairs in an extraordinary way.

The proverb-type sayings in the book have been gathered into two collections. The first collection (10:1–22:16) contains 375 sayings phrased in a highly stylized manner. All but one of these sayings consist of a single sentence made up of two parallel phrases (the sole exception is a three-part saying in 19:7). The 140 sayings included in the second collection (25:1–29:27) are less regular in form and sometimes repeat sayings found in chapters 10–22 (e.g., 26:22 = 18:8). The heading to this collection says these sayings were "copied" in the time of Hezekiah (25:1).

Unlike the Instructions, which advocate or condemn certain types of behavior, the sentence-type proverbs usually describe or comment upon types of human behavior that occur often enough to be familiar to both the speaker and the listener. Thus, sayings such as 14:20 and 19:4 make observations on human behavior that (unfortunately) may prove true in many human settings. But the sages do not encourage their listeners to behave in this way. When the wise do give advice, it is usually situation-specific (i.e., appropriate in some circumstances but not in others, as in 26:4–5).

The book of Proverbs consists entirely of human speech directed to a human audience. God is never said to speak in Proverbs, and the "mighty acts" of God in Israel's history are never mentioned. In many ways the wisdom sayings of Israel resemble those of Israel's neighbors in the ancient world. The humans who speak in these collections reflect the sociocultural conditions, opinions, and experiences of their own

particular locations in history. Modern users of biblical proverbs should be prepared to sift and to sort through the observations made by the wise in Israel and to decide which still seem "wise" today and which do not (see, e.g., 10:13; 26:3). Since proverbial observations are made by humans, not by God, the faithful need not feel obliged to "go and do likewise."

—Kathleen Farmer

1 The proverbs of Solomon son of David, king of Israel:

Prologue

2 For learning about wisdom and
   instruction,
   for understanding words of
      insight,
3 for gaining instruction in wise
      dealing,
   righteousness, justice, and
      equity;
4 to teach shrewdness to the simple,
   knowledge and prudence to the
      young—
5 let the wise also hear and gain in
      learning,
   and the discerning acquire skill,
6 to understand a proverb and a
      figure,
   the words of the wise and their
      riddles.

7 The fear of the LORD is the
      beginning of knowledge;
   fools despise wisdom and
      instruction.

Warnings against Evil Companions

8 Hear, my child, your father's
   instruction,
   and do not reject your mother's
      teaching;
9 for they are a fair garland for your
      head,
   and pendants for your neck.
10 My child, if sinners entice you,
   do not consent.
11 If they say, "Come with us, let us lie
      in wait for blood;
   let us wantonly ambush the
      innocent;
12 like Sheol let us swallow them alive
   and whole, like those who go
      down to the Pit.
13 We shall find all kinds of costly
      things;
   we shall fill our houses with
      booty.
14 Throw in your lot among us;
   we will all have one purse"—
15 my child, do not walk in their way,
   keep your foot from their paths;
16 for their feet run to evil,
   and they hurry to shed blood.
17 For in vain is the net baited
   while the bird is looking on;
18 yet they lie in wait—to kill
      themselves!
   and set an ambush—for their own
      lives!

1:1–9:18 Instructions: Advice to and from Wisdom's Students

1:2–6 The Prologue
Advises the wise to use what follows for their own enrichment as well as for instruction of the young.

1:7 Fear of the LORD—This term (meaning a deep and abiding respect for the Lord and for the Lord's intentions) is used six times in the first nine chapters (1:7, 29; 2:5; 3:7; 8:13; 9:10), establishing at the outset a strong connection between "wisdom" and the faithful worship of the Lord.

1:8–19 Violence Is a Trap
A wisdom teacher (or parent) speaks to a pupil who is called *child*, giving very modern-sounding advice: don't let yourself be lured into bad company (v. 10) and don't go along with those who commit violence, either for a lark (1:11) or for personal gain (vv. 13–14), because violence is a trap (v. 17) that ensnares those who indulge in it (v. 18).

1:8 Father's, mother's—Wisdom is handed down from generation to generation, and mothers as well as fathers participate in the teaching-learning process (see also 6:20; 31:1, 26).

19 Such is the end*a* of all who are
     greedy for gain;
     it takes away the life of its
     possessors.

The Call of Wisdom

20 Wisdom cries out in the street;
     in the squares she raises her voice.
21 At the busiest corner she cries out;
     at the entrance of the city gates she
     speaks:
22 "How long, O simple ones, will you
     love being simple?
     How long will scoffers delight in
     their scoffing
     and fools hate knowledge?
23 Give heed to my reproof;
     I will pour out my thoughts to you;
     I will make my words known to
     you.
24 Because I have called and you
     refused,
     have stretched out my hand and
     no one heeded,
25 and because you have ignored all my
     counsel
     and would have none of my reproof,
26 I also will laugh at your calamity;
     I will mock when panic strikes
     you,
27 when panic strikes you like a storm,
     and your calamity comes like a
     whirlwind,
     when distress and anguish come
     upon you.
28 Then they will call upon me, but I
     will not answer;
     they will seek me diligently, but
     will not find me.
29 Because they hated knowledge
     and did not choose the fear of the
     LORD,

30 would have none of my counsel,
     and despised all my reproof,
31 therefore they shall eat the fruit of
     their way
     and be sated with their own
     devices.
32 For waywardness kills the simple,
     and the complacency of fools
     destroys them;
33 but those who listen to me will be
     secure
     and will live at ease, without dread
     of disaster."

The Value of Wisdom

2 My child, if you accept my words
     and treasure up my
     commandments within you,
2 making your ear attentive to
     wisdom
     and inclining your heart to
     understanding;
3 if you indeed cry out for insight,
     and raise your voice for
     understanding;
4 if you seek it like silver,
     and search for it as for hidden
     treasures—
5 then you will understand the fear of
     the LORD
     and find the knowledge of God.
6 For the LORD gives wisdom;
     from his mouth come knowledge
     and understanding;
7 he stores up sound wisdom for the
     upright;
     he is a shield to those who walk
     blamelessly,
8 guarding the paths of justice
     and preserving the way of his
     faithful ones.

a Gk: Heb *are the ways*

1:20–33 Wisdom Speaks for Herself
The teacher personifies the abstract concept of
wisdom (which is a feminine noun in Hebrew),
making the concept of Wisdom speak as if she
were a woman. Like the prophets, Wisdom warns
her listeners of dire consequences for those who
deliberately reject her teachings.

1:29–33—Since *knowledge* and *the fear of the*

LORD are two sides of the same coin, turning away
from wisdom is like turning away from God.

2:1–22 Wisdom and Faith Are Related
Having wisdom in one's heart is closely tied to
being one of the Lord's faithful followers. An active pursuit of wisdom leads also to the knowledge of God, who is the source of all insight and
understanding.

9 Then you will understand
    righteousness and justice
    and equity, every good path;
10 for wisdom will come into your
    heart,
    and knowledge will be pleasant to
    your soul;
11 prudence will watch over you;
    and understanding will guard you.
12 It will save you from the way of evil,
    from those who speak perversely,
13 who forsake the paths of uprightness
    to walk in the ways of darkness,
14 who rejoice in doing evil
    and delight in the perverseness of
    evil;
15 those whose paths are crooked,
    and who are devious in their ways.

16 You will be saved from the loose[a]
    woman,
    from the adulteress with her
    smooth words,
17 who forsakes the partner of her
    youth
    and forgets her sacred covenant;
18 for her way[b] leads down to death,
    and her paths to the shades;
19 those who go to her never come
    back,
    nor do they regain the paths of life.

20 Therefore walk in the way of the
    good,
    and keep to the paths of the just.
21 For the upright will abide in the
    land,
    and the innocent will remain in it;
22 but the wicked will be cut off from
    the land,

and the treacherous will be rooted
    out of it.

Admonition to Trust and Honor God

3 My child, do not forget my
    teaching,
    but let your heart keep my
    commandments;
2 for length of days and years of life
    and abundant welfare they will
    give you.

3 Do not let loyalty and faithfulness
    forsake you;
    bind them around your neck,
    write them on the tablet of your
    heart.
4 So you will find favor and good
    repute
    in the sight of God and of people.

5 Trust in the LORD with all your
    heart,
    and do not rely on your own
    insight.
6 In all your ways acknowledge him,
    and he will make straight your
    paths.
7 Do not be wise in your own eyes;
    fear the LORD, and turn away from
    evil.
8 It will be a healing for your flesh
    and a refreshment for your body.

9 Honor the LORD with your substance
    and with the first fruits of all your
    produce;
10 then your barns will be filled with
    plenty,

[a] Heb strange   [b] Cn: Heb house

2:16–17 *Loose woman . . . adulteress*—In Hebrew these words refer to foreignness or otherness, meaning whatever stands in direct contrast to wisdom and the fear of the Lord. The *way of evil* (mentioned in vv. 12–15) is personified in vv. 16–19 as a seductive female whose lures would be fatally attractive to the unwary (and presumably male) wisdom pupil (see 5:3, 20; 6:24; 7:15). The choice the wisdom pupil has to make is not simply one of marital fidelity, but a choice between lifestyles personified. The right way (personified as Wisdom) leads to life, and the wrong way (personified as the Other Woman) leads down to death (2:18–19). See also 5:5 and 7:24–27.

3:1–35 Wisdom's "Covenant"
Taken together, the words *teaching* (lit. *torah*) and *commandments* (v. 1), *loyalty, faithfulness, bind* and *tablet* (v. 3); the promise of prosperity in return for tithing (vv. 9–10), *the LORD's curse* (v. 33) and the ethical commandments in vv. 27–31 remind the reader of the covenantal passages in Deuteronomy, suggesting that wisdom is a part of God's commitment to humankind.

and your vats will be bursting with
  wine.

11 My child, do not despise the LORD's
    discipline
  or be weary of his reproof,
12 for the LORD reproves the one he
    loves,
  as a father the son in whom he
    delights.

The True Wealth

13 Happy are those who find wisdom,
  and those who get understanding,
14 for her income is better than silver,
  and her revenue better than gold.
15 She is more precious than jewels,
  and nothing you desire can
    compare with her.
16 Long life is in her right hand;
  in her left hand are riches and
    honor.
17 Her ways are ways of pleasantness,
  and all her paths are peace.
18 She is a tree of life to those who lay
    hold of her;
  those who hold her fast are called
    happy.

God's Wisdom in Creation

19 The LORD by wisdom founded the
    earth;
  by understanding he established
    the heavens;
20 by his knowledge the deeps broke
    open,
  and the clouds drop down the dew.

The True Security

21 My child, do not let these escape
    from your sight:
  keep sound wisdom and prudence,
22 and they will be life for your soul
  and adornment for your neck.
23 Then you will walk on your way
    securely
  and your foot will not stumble.
24 If you sit down,a you will not be
    afraid;
  when you lie down, your sleep will
    be sweet.

25 Do not be afraid of sudden panic,
  or of the storm that strikes the
    wicked;
26 for the LORD will be your confidence
  and will keep your foot from being
    caught.

27 Do not withhold good from those to
    whom it is due,b
  when it is in your power to do it.
28 Do not say to your neighbor, "Go,
    and come again,
  tomorrow I will give it"—when
    you have it with you.
29 Do not plan harm against your
    neighbor
  who lives trustingly beside you.
30 Do not quarrel with anyone without
    cause,
  when no harm has been done to
    you.
31 Do not envy the violent
  and do not choose any of their
    ways;
32 for the perverse are an abomination
    to the LORD,
  but the upright are in his
    confidence.
33 The LORD's curse is on the house of
    the wicked,
  but he blesses the abode of the
    righteous.
34 Toward the scorners he is scornful,
  but to the humble he shows favor.
35 The wise will inherit honor,
  but stubborn fools, disgrace.

Parental Advice

4 Listen, children, to a father's
    instruction,
  and be attentive, that you may
    gainc insight;
2 for I give you good precepts:
  do not forsake my teaching.
3 When I was a son with my father,
  tender, and my mother's favorite,
4 he taught me, and said to me,
  "Let your heart hold fast my words;
  keep my commandments, and live.

a Gk: Heb lie down   b Heb from its owners   c Heb know

5 Get wisdom; get insight: do not
    forget, nor turn away
  from the words of my mouth.
6 Do not forsake her, and she will keep
    you;
  love her, and she will guard you.
7 The beginning of wisdom is this: Get
    wisdom,
  and whatever else you get, get
    insight.
8 Prize her highly, and she will exalt
    you;
  she will honor you if you embrace
    her.
9 She will place on your head a fair
    garland;
  she will bestow on you a beautiful
    crown."

Admonition to Keep to the Right Path

10 Hear, my child, and accept my
    words,
  that the years of your life may be
    many.
11 I have taught you the way of wisdom;
  I have led you in the paths of
    uprightness.
12 When you walk, your step will not
    be hampered;
  and if you run, you will not
    stumble.
13 Keep hold of instruction; do not let
    go;
  guard her, for she is your life.
14 Do not enter the path of the wicked,
  and do not walk in the way of
    evildoers.
15 Avoid it; do not go on it;
  turn away from it and pass on.
16 For they cannot sleep unless they
    have done wrong;
  they are robbed of sleep unless
    they have made someone
    stumble.

17 For they eat the bread of wickedness
  and drink the wine of violence.
18 But the path of the righteous is like
    the light of dawn,
  which shines brighter and brighter
    until full day.
19 The way of the wicked is like deep
    darkness;
  they do not know what they
    stumble over.
20 My child, be attentive to my words;
  incline your ear to my sayings.
21 Do not let them escape from your
    sight;
  keep them within your heart.
22 For they are life to those who find
    them,
  and healing to all their flesh.
23 Keep your heart with all vigilance,
  for from it flow the springs of life.
24 Put away from you crooked speech,
  and put devious talk far from you.
25 Let your eyes look directly forward,
  and your gaze be straight before
    you.
26 Keep straight the path of your feet,
  and all your ways will be sure.
27 Do not swerve to the right or to the
    left;
  turn your foot away from evil.

Warning against Impurity and Infidelity

5 My child, be attentive to my
    wisdom;
  incline your ear to my
    understanding,
2 so that you may hold on to
    prudence,
  and your lips may guard
    knowledge.
3 For the lips of a loose[a] woman drip
    honey,

a Heb strange

4:10–19 Keep to the Right Path
Evil ways must be completely avoided, because even a small taste of wickedness can be addictive.

5:1–23 Non-Wisdom Ways Can Be Fatally Attractive

5:3, 20 Loose woman, another woman, adulteress—All come from Hebrew words meaning foreign or alien (see note at 2:16–17). The same root words are translated *strangers* in 5:10, 17 and *an alien* in 5:10. While the warning speaks literally against liaisons with non-Israelite

and her speech is smoother than
 oil;
[4] but in the end she is bitter as
 wormwood,
  sharp as a two-edged sword.
[5] Her feet go down to death;
 her steps follow the path to Sheol.
[6] She does not keep straight to the
  path of life;
 her ways wander, and she does
  not know it.

[7] And now, my child,[a] listen to me,
 and do not depart from the words
  of my mouth.
[8] Keep your way far from her,
 and do not go near the door of her
  house;
[9] or you will give your honor to
  others,
 and your years to the merciless,
[10] and strangers will take their fill of
  your wealth,
 and your labors will go to the
  house of an alien;
[11] and at the end of your life you will
  groan,
 when your flesh and body are
  consumed,
[12] and you say, "Oh, how I hated
  discipline,
 and my heart despised reproof!
[13] I did not listen to the voice of my
  teachers
 or incline my ear to my
  instructors.
[14] Now I am at the point of utter ruin
 in the public assembly."

[15] Drink water from your own cistern,
 flowing water from your own well.
[16] Should your springs be scattered
  abroad,
 streams of water in the streets?
[17] Let them be for yourself alone,

and not for sharing with
 strangers.
[18] Let your fountain be blessed,
 and rejoice in the wife of your
  youth,
[19] a lovely deer, a graceful doe.
May her breasts satisfy you at all
  times;
 may you be intoxicated always by
  her love.
[20] Why should you be intoxicated, my
  son, by another woman
 and embrace the bosom of an
  adulteress?
[21] For human ways are under the eyes
  of the LORD,
 and he examines all their paths.
[22] The iniquities of the wicked ensnare
  them,
 and they are caught in the toils of
  their sin.
[23] They die for lack of discipline,
 and because of their great folly
  they are lost.

Practical Admonitions

6 My child, if you have given your
  pledge to your neighbor,
 if you have bound yourself to
  another,[b]
[2] you are snared by the utterance of
  your lips,[c]
 caught by the words of your
  mouth.
[3] So do this, my child, and save
  yourself,
 for you have come into your
  neighbor's power:
 go, hurry,[d] and plead with your
  neighbor.
[4] Give your eyes no sleep
 and your eyelids no slumber;

[a] Gk Vg: Heb children   [b] Or a stranger   [c] Cn Compare Gk Syr: Heb the words of your mouth   [d] Or humble yourself

---

women, its ultimate concern is with foreign (non-Wisdom) ways and ideas, which are here personified as seductively attractive figures who ultimately lead the unwary to death (vv. 5, 14, 23).

6:1–19 Examples of Unwise Behavior
Going into debt (vv. 1–5), laziness (vv. 6–11), and *crooked speech* (vv. 12–15) have negative consequences, but it is arrogance, deceit, *discord* and the shedding of *innocent blood* (vv. 16–19) that the Lord *hates*. See note at 24:30–34.

5 save yourself like a gazelle from the
hunter,*a*
like a bird from the hand of the
fowler.

6 Go to the ant, you lazybones;
consider its ways, and be wise.
7 Without having any chief
or officer or ruler,
8 it prepares its food in summer,
and gathers its sustenance in
harvest.
9 How long will you lie there,
O lazybones?
When will you rise from your
sleep?
10 A little sleep, a little slumber,
a little folding of the hands to rest,
11 and poverty will come upon you like
a robber,
and want, like an armed warrior.

12 A scoundrel and a villain
goes around with crooked speech,
13 winking the eyes, shuffling the feet,
pointing the fingers,
14 with perverted mind devising evil,
continually sowing discord;
15 on such a one calamity will descend
suddenly;
in a moment, damage beyond
repair.

16 There are six things that the LORD
hates,
seven that are an abomination to
him:
17 haughty eyes, a lying tongue,
and hands that shed innocent
blood,
18 a heart that devises wicked plans,
feet that hurry to run to evil,
19 a lying witness who testifies falsely,
and one who sows discord in a
family.

20 My child, keep your father's
commandment,
and do not forsake your mother's
teaching.
21 Bind them upon your heart
always;
tie them around your neck.
22 When you walk, they*b* will lead you;
when you lie down, they*b* will
watch over you;
and when you awake, they*b* will
talk with you.
23 For the commandment is a lamp and
the teaching a light,
and the reproofs of discipline are
the way of life,
24 to preserve you from the wife of
another,*c*
from the smooth tongue of the
adulteress.
25 Do not desire her beauty in your
heart,
and do not let her capture you
with her eyelashes;
26 for a prostitute's fee is only a loaf of
bread,*d*
but the wife of another stalks a
man's very life.
27 Can fire be carried in the bosom
without burning one's clothes?
28 Or can one walk on hot coals
without scorching the feet?
29 So is he who sleeps with his
neighbor's wife;
no one who touches her will go
unpunished.
30 Thieves are not despised who steal
only
to satisfy their appetite when they
are hungry.
31 Yet if they are caught, they will pay
sevenfold;

a Cn: Heb *from the hand*   *b* Heb *it*   *c* Gk: MT *the evil woman*
d Cn Compare Gk Syr Vg Tg: Heb *for because of a harlot to a piece of bread*

6:20–35 Different Types of Infidelity
Another warning against intercourse with
Foreignness personified (vv. 20–25) is closely
followed by a warning that adultery (in the literal
sense) is dangerous (vv. 26–35).

6:24 *Wife of another, adulteress*—Again the
Hebrew refers to Foreignness personified as the
Evil Woman, who can be avoided by keeping
Wisdom's commandments.

6:29 *Neighbor's wife*—A similar phrase is used
in Exod. 20:17.

they will forfeit all the goods of
their house.

³² But he who commits adultery has no
sense;
he who does it destroys himself.

³³ He will get wounds and dishonor,
and his disgrace will not be wiped
away.

³⁴ For jealousy arouses a husband's
fury,
and he shows no restraint when he
takes revenge.

³⁵ He will accept no compensation,
and refuses a bribe no matter how
great.

The False Attractions of Adultery

7 My child, keep my words
and store up my commandments
with you;

² keep my commandments and live,
keep my teachings as the apple of
your eye;

³ bind them on your fingers,
write them on the tablet of your
heart.

⁴ Say to wisdom, "You are my sister,"
and call insight your intimate
friend,

⁵ that they may keep you from the
loose[a] woman,
from the adulteress with her
smooth words.

⁶ For at the window of my house
I looked out through my lattice,

⁷ and I saw among the simple ones,
I observed among the youths,
a young man without sense,

⁸ passing along the street near her
corner,
taking the road to her house

⁹ in the twilight, in the evening,
at the time of night and darkness.

¹⁰ Then a woman comes toward him,
decked out like a prostitute, wily of
heart.[b]

¹¹ She is loud and wayward;
her feet do not stay at home;

¹² now in the street, now in the
squares,
and at every corner she lies in wait.

¹³ She seizes him and kisses him,
and with impudent face she says
to him:

¹⁴ "I had to offer sacrifices,
and today I have paid my vows;

¹⁵ so now I have come out to meet you,
to seek you eagerly, and I have
found you!

¹⁶ I have decked my couch with
coverings,
colored spreads of Egyptian linen;

¹⁷ I have perfumed my bed with
myrrh,
aloes, and cinnamon.

¹⁸ Come, let us take our fill of love
until morning;
let us delight ourselves with love.

¹⁹ For my husband is not at home;
he has gone on a long journey.

²⁰ He took a bag of money with him;
he will not come home until full
moon."

²¹ With much seductive speech she
persuades him;
with her smooth talk she compels
him.

²² Right away he follows her,
and goes like an ox to the
slaughter,
or bounds like a stag toward the
trap[c]

²³ until an arrow pierces its entrails.
He is like a bird rushing into a snare,

---

[a] Heb strange [b] Meaning of Heb uncertain [c] Cn Compare Gk: Meaning
of Heb uncertain

6:32 *Adultery*—Comes from a completely different root word than *adulteress* (v. 24) and refers
here literally to marital infidelity.

7:1–27 Non-Wisdom Ways Are Seductive
Once again, the temptation to ignore wisdom
teachings is personified as a *loose woman* and

an *adulteress* (v. 5) who lures the wisdom pupil
into danger (see notes at 2:16–17; 5:3, 20).

7:4 *Sister*—Being closely related to Wisdom
should protect the pupil from temptation (personified as the Other Woman) whose *way* leads
down to *death* (v. 27). See notes at 2:16–17 and
5:3–23.

not knowing that it will cost him
his life.

24 And now, my children, listen to me,
and be attentive to the words of
my mouth.

25 Do not let your hearts turn aside to
her ways;
do not stray into her paths.

26 For many are those she has laid low,
and numerous are her victims.

27 Her house is the way to Sheol,
going down to the chambers of
death.

The Gifts of Wisdom

8 Does not wisdom call,
and does not understanding raise
her voice?

2 On the heights, beside the way,
at the crossroads she takes her
stand;

3 beside the gates in front of the town,
at the entrance of the portals she
cries out:

4 "To you, O people, I call,
and my cry is to all that live.

5 O simple ones, learn prudence;
acquire intelligence, you who lack
it.

6 Hear, for I will speak noble things,
and from my lips will come what
is right;

7 for my mouth will utter truth;
wickedness is an abomination to
my lips.

8 All the words of my mouth are
righteous;
there is nothing twisted or crooked
in them.

9 They are all straight to one who
understands

and right to those who find
knowledge.

10 Take my instruction instead of silver,
and knowledge rather than choice
gold;

11 for wisdom is better than jewels,
and all that you may desire cannot
compare with her.

12 I, wisdom, live with prudence,[a]
and I attain knowledge and
discretion.

13 The fear of the LORD is hatred of
evil.
Pride and arrogance and the way of
evil
and perverted speech I hate.

14 I have good advice and sound
wisdom;
I have insight, I have strength.

15 By me kings reign,
and rulers decree what is just;

16 by me rulers rule,
and nobles, all who govern rightly.

17 I love those who love me,
and those who seek me diligently
find me.

18 Riches and honor are with me,
enduring wealth and prosperity.

19 My fruit is better than gold, even
fine gold,
and my yield than choice silver.

20 I walk in the way of righteousness,
along the paths of justice,

21 endowing with wealth those who
love me,
and filling their treasuries.

Wisdom's Part in Creation

22 The LORD created me at the
beginning[b] of his work,[c]

a Meaning of Heb uncertain b Or me as the beginning c Heb way

---

7:27 Sheol—The Hebrew name given to the place where all the dead end up. It is not a place for rewards or punishments but is merely synonymous with death or the grave.

8:4–21 Wisdom Hawks Her Wares
Personified Wisdom again takes a stand in the busiest parts of the city and calls out to all who pass by, advertising what she has to offer her disciples (see note at 1:20–21).

8:22–36 Wisdom Traces Her Origins Back to Creation
Personified Wisdom argues that she is well qualified to give advice, having been either present at or instrumental in the creative process.

8:22 Created me—The ambiguity of the Hebrew makes it difficult to tell whether Wisdom describes herself as a creature (the first of God's creative acts), as a possession of God, or as

the first of his acts of long ago.

23 Ages ago I was set up,
    at the first, before the beginning of
        the earth.
24 When there were no depths I was
        brought forth,
    when there were no springs
        abounding with water.
25 Before the mountains had been
        shaped,
    before the hills, I was brought
        forth—
26 when he had not yet made earth and
        fields,[a]
    or the world's first bits of soil.
27 When he established the heavens, I
        was there,
    when he drew a circle on the face
        of the deep,
28 when he made firm the skies above,
    when he established the fountains
        of the deep,
29 when he assigned to the sea its limit,
    so that the waters might not
        transgress his command,
    when he marked out the foundations
        of the earth,
30   then I was beside him, like a
        master worker;[b]
    and I was daily his[c] delight,
        rejoicing before him always,
31 rejoicing in his inhabited world
    and delighting in the human race.

32 "And now, my children, listen to me:
        happy are those who keep my
        ways.
33 Hear instruction and be wise,
    and do not neglect it.
34 Happy is the one who listens to me,
    watching daily at my gates,
    waiting beside my doors.
35 For whoever finds me finds life
    and obtains favor from the LORD;
36 but those who miss me injure
        themselves;
    all who hate me love death."

Wisdom's Feast

9 Wisdom has built her house,
    she has hewn her seven pillars.
2 She has slaughtered her animals, she
        has mixed her wine,
    she has also set her table.
3 She has sent out her servant-girls,
        she calls
    from the highest places in the
        town,
4 "You that are simple, turn in here!"
    To those without sense she says,
5 "Come, eat of my bread
    and drink of the wine I have
        mixed.
6 Lay aside immaturity,[d] and live,
    and walk in the way of insight."

[a] Meaning of Heb uncertain [b] Another reading is *little child* [c] Gk: Heb lacks *his* [d] Or *simpleness*

God's firstborn child. The Hebrew verb translated "created" might also mean "possess" as well as "beget/conceive." In 23:23 it is translated "buy." The translation "created" seems to give Wisdom a degree of independent existence apart from God. But if the word had been translated "possessed" (implying that Wisdom was a personification of one of God's attributes or qualities), this passage would convey the same thought as that in 3:19–20 (that God used God's own wisdom in the creation of the universe).

This text played an important part in early church debates about the nature of Christ. Paul equates the "wisdom of God" with Christ (1 Cor. 1:24). Other New Testament texts (e.g., John 1:1–3) use language that resembles Prov. 8:22 to talk about Christ. Thus one group of early Christians (called the Arians) used this passage in Proverbs to support their claim that Christ, like Wisdom, was "created." The Arians argued that

as a creature of God, Christ was subordinate to God and not of the same substance as God. But the more powerful majority of Christian thinkers understood the verb in Prov. 8:22 to mean "begot" me, meaning that Wisdom (and therefore Christ) was God's firstborn child. The Nicene Creed represents the opinion of the majority of those who debated the issue at the Council of Nicaea: Christ is "begotten" (not created), and thus is of the same substance and status as God.

9:1–12 Wisdom Invites Us In

Personified Wisdom is introduced once more in vv. 1–3 and speaks for herself again in vv. 4–12. In vv. 7–12 she quotes a series of sentence proverbs, including (in v. 10) a variation of the statement with which the Instructions began (1:7). Here the link between wisdom/insight and reverence for the Lord/knowledge of the Holy One is said to be reciprocal (either one leads to the other).

General Maxims

7 Whoever corrects a scoffer wins
      abuse;
  whoever rebukes the wicked gets
      hurt.
8 A scoffer who is rebuked will only
      hate you;
  the wise, when rebuked, will love
      you.
9 Give instruction*a* to the wise, and
      they will become wiser still;
  teach the righteous and they will
      gain in learning.
10 The fear of the LORD is the
      beginning of wisdom,
  and the knowledge of the Holy
      One is insight.
11 For by me your days will be
      multiplied,
  and years will be added to your
      life.
12 If you are wise, you are wise for
      yourself;
  if you scoff, you alone will bear it.

Folly's Invitation and Promise

13 The foolish woman is loud;
  she is ignorant and knows
      nothing.
14 She sits at the door of her house,
  on a seat at the high places of the
      town,
15 calling to those who pass by,

who are going straight on their
      way,
16 "You who are simple, turn in here!"
  And to those without sense she
      says,
17 "Stolen water is sweet,
  and bread eaten in secret is
      pleasant."
18 But they do not know that the dead*b*
      are there,
  that her guests are in the depths of
      Sheol.

Wise Sayings of Solomon

10 The proverbs of Solomon.

A wise child makes a glad father,
  but a foolish child is a mother's
      grief.
2 Treasures gained by wickedness do
      not profit,
  but righteousness delivers from
      death.
3 The LORD does not let the righteous
      go hungry,
  but he thwarts the craving of the
      wicked.
4 A slack hand causes poverty,
  but the hand of the diligent makes
      rich.
5 A child who gathers in summer is
      prudent,

a Heb lacks *instruction*   *b* Heb *shades*

9:13–18 Folly Also Invites Us In
The *foolish woman* is Folly personified, who
speaks much the same language as Wisdom, trying to lure the *simple* into her house. However,
the proverb Folly quotes in v. 17 represents the
wrong way, which leads to death (v. 18). Only
those without sense (v. 16) would believe what
she says.

**10:1–22:16 The First Collection of Proverbial
Sentences**
The next thirteen chapters contain 375 self-
contained sayings. While a connected train of
thought cannot be traced completely through any
chapter, some of the sayings are grouped by topic
(e.g., 26:13–16 and 17–26), and some adjacent
sayings seem to be related to each other (as in
10:15–16 and 14:20–21).

10:1 *Proverbs of Solomon*—A new heading

marks the transition between the preceding
instructional speeches and the sentence literature
that follows. The opening saying reminds the
wise that both parents have a stake in the results
of their educational efforts (see also 15:20; 17:25;
23:22–25).

10:2 *Wickedness, righteousness*—Legal and
prophetic texts use these same traditional terms
for right and wrong. The sentence sayings often
describe the fruits (consequences) of wickedness
and righteousness and seldom specify what kind
of behavior falls into which category (but see
12:10; 13:5; 14:21; 17:23; 21:4, 7, 26; 29:7).

10:4 *A slack hand . . . diligent*—There is a strong
work ethic in the sentence proverbs (see also
10:5, 26; 12:24, 27, etc.). If everyone has equal
access to the resources of the land, a lack of work
may *cause poverty*. However, 13:23 notes that
this is not always the case or the cause.

but a child who sleeps in harvest
    brings shame.
6 Blessings are on the head of the
    righteous,
  but the mouth of the wicked
    conceals violence.
7 The memory of the righteous is a
    blessing,
  but the name of the wicked will
    rot.
8 The wise of heart will heed
    commandments,
  but a babbling fool will come to
    ruin.
9 Whoever walks in integrity walks
    securely,
  but whoever follows perverse ways
    will be found out.
10 Whoever winks the eye causes
    trouble,
  but the one who rebukes boldly
    makes peace.[a]
11 The mouth of the righteous is a
    fountain of life,
  but the mouth of the wicked
    conceals violence.
12 Hatred stirs up strife,
  but love covers all offenses.
13 On the lips of one who has
    understanding wisdom is
    found,
  but a rod is for the back of one
    who lacks sense.
14 The wise lay up knowledge,
  but the babbling of a fool brings
    ruin near.
15 The wealth of the rich is their fortress;
  the poverty of the poor is their
    ruin.
16 The wage of the righteous leads to
    life,
  the gain of the wicked to sin.
17 Whoever heeds instruction is on the
    path to life,

but one who rejects a rebuke goes
    astray.
18 Lying lips conceal hatred,
  and whoever utters slander is a
    fool.
19 When words are many, transgression
    is not lacking,
  but the prudent are restrained in
    speech.
20 The tongue of the righteous is choice
    silver;
  the mind of the wicked is of little
    worth.
21 The lips of the righteous feed many,
  but fools die for lack of sense.
22 The blessing of the LORD makes
    rich,
  and he adds no sorrow with it.[b]
23 Doing wrong is like sport to a fool,
  but wise conduct is pleasure to a
    person of understanding.
24 What the wicked dread will come
    upon them,
  but the desire of the righteous will
    be granted.
25 When the tempest passes, the
    wicked are no more,
  but the righteous are established
    forever.
26 Like vinegar to the teeth, and smoke
    to the eyes,
  so are the lazy to their employers.
27 The fear of the LORD prolongs life,
  but the years of the wicked will be
    short.
28 The hope of the righteous ends in
    gladness,
  but the expectation of the wicked
    comes to nothing.
29 The way of the LORD is a stronghold
    for the upright,
  but destruction for evildoers.

[a] Gk: Heb but a babbling fool will come to ruin [b] Or and toil adds nothing
to it

10:6, 11, 32 *The mouth of the righteous, the
mouth of the wicked*—The majority of sayings in
this chapter reflect on ways human communication can be used for good or for evil.

10:15 *Wealth, poverty*—Just as the English proverb "Penny wise, pound foolish" does not advocate the behavior it describes, so also this saying
describes (but does not advocate) the attitudes
rich and poor people sometimes have toward
their wealth (or lack of it). See 11:4, 28.

10:27–30—Stark contrasts are drawn between the
consequences of right and wrong behavior.

30 The righteous will never be removed,
    but the wicked will not remain in
        the land.
31 The mouth of the righteous brings
        forth wisdom,
    but the perverse tongue will be cut
        off.
32 The lips of the righteous know what
        is acceptable,
    but the mouth of the wicked what
        is perverse.

11 A false balance is an
        abomination to the LORD,
    but an accurate weight is his
        delight.
2 When pride comes, then comes
        disgrace;
    but wisdom is with the humble.
3 The integrity of the upright guides
        them,
    but the crookedness of the
        treacherous destroys them.
4 Riches do not profit in the day of
        wrath,
    but righteousness delivers from
        death.
5 The righteousness of the blameless
        keeps their ways straight,
    but the wicked fall by their own
        wickedness.
6 The righteousness of the upright
        saves them,
    but the treacherous are taken
        captive by their schemes.
7 When the wicked die, their hope
        perishes,
    and the expectation of the godless
        comes to nothing.
8 The righteous are delivered from
        trouble,
    and the wicked get into it instead.
9 With their mouths the godless would
        destroy their neighbors,
    but by knowledge the righteous are
        delivered.

10 When it goes well with the
        righteous, the city rejoices;
    and when the wicked perish, there
        is jubilation.
11 By the blessing of the upright a city
        is exalted,
    but it is overthrown by the mouth
        of the wicked.
12 Whoever belittles another lacks
        sense,
    but an intelligent person remains
        silent.
13 A gossip goes about telling secrets,
    but one who is trustworthy in
        spirit keeps a confidence.
14 Where there is no guidance, a
        nation[a] falls,
    but in an abundance of counselors
        there is safety.
15 To guarantee loans for a stranger
        brings trouble,
    but there is safety in refusing to
        do so.
16 A gracious woman gets honor,
    but she who hates virtue is covered
        with shame.[b]
    The timid become destitute,[c]
    but the aggressive gain riches.
17 Those who are kind reward
        themselves,
    but the cruel do themselves harm.
18 The wicked earn no real gain,
    but those who sow righteousness
        get a true reward.
19 Whoever is steadfast in
        righteousness will live,
    but whoever pursues evil will die.
20 Crooked minds are an abomination
        to the LORD,
    but those of blameless ways are his
        delight.
21 Be assured, the wicked will not go
        unpunished,

[a] Or *an army* [b] Compare Gk Syr: Heb lacks *but she . . . shame* [c] Gk: Heb
lacks *The timid . . . destitute*

11:1 *False balance*—A way to cheat the cus-
tomer. The wise believe the Lord favors equity
and fairness in human commerce (see also 16:11;
20:10, 23).
11:2–4—Pitfalls on the path to righteousness

include *pride* (v. 2), treachery (v. 3), and *riches*
(v. 4).
11:4, 28—Wealth is not an ultimately dependable form of protection (see 18:11).

but those who are righteous will
    escape.

22 Like a gold ring in a pig's snout
    is a beautiful woman without good
      sense.

23 The desire of the righteous ends only
    in good;
    the expectation of the wicked in
      wrath.

24 Some give freely, yet grow all the
    richer;
    others withhold what is due, and
      only suffer want.

25 A generous person will be enriched,
    and one who gives water will get
      water.

26 The people curse those who hold
    back grain,
    but a blessing is on the head of
      those who sell it.

27 Whoever diligently seeks good seeks
    favor,
    but evil comes to the one who
      searches for it.

28 Those who trust in their riches will
    wither,[a]
    but the righteous will flourish like
      green leaves.

29 Those who trouble their households
    will inherit wind,
    and the fool will be servant to the
      wise.

30 The fruit of the righteous is a tree of
    life,
    but violence[b] takes lives away.

31 If the righteous are repaid on earth,
    how much more the wicked and
      the sinner!

12 Whoever loves discipline loves
    knowledge,
    but those who hate to be rebuked
      are stupid.

2 The good obtain favor from the
    LORD,

but those who devise evil he
    condemns.

3 No one finds security by
    wickedness,
    but the root of the righteous will
      never be moved.

4 A good wife is the crown of her
    husband,
    but she who brings shame is like
      rottenness in his bones.

5 The thoughts of the righteous are
    just;
    the advice of the wicked is
      treacherous.

6 The words of the wicked are a deadly
    ambush,
    but the speech of the upright
      delivers them.

7 The wicked are overthrown and are
    no more,
    but the house of the righteous will
      stand.

8 One is commended for good sense,
    but a perverse mind is despised.

9 Better to be despised and have a
    servant,
    than to be self-important and lack
      food.

10 The righteous know the needs of
    their animals,
    but the mercy of the wicked is
      cruel.

11 Those who till their land will have
    plenty of food,
    but those who follow worthless
      pursuits have no sense.

12 The wicked covet the proceeds of
    wickedness,[c]
    but the root of the righteous bears
      fruit.

13 The evil are ensnared by the
    transgression of their lips,

[a] Cn: Heb *fall*   [b] Cn Compare Gk Syr: Heb *a wise man*   [c] Or *covet the catch of the wicked*

11:31—The belief that human behavior is rewarded or punished permeates Proverbs (but is
questioned in Job and Ecclesiastes).

12:4 *Good wife*—The word translated "good"
usually means "strong" (see note at 31:10, where
the same word is translated "capable").

12:10 *The righteous know the needs of their
animals*—This is one of the few proverbial sayings that specify what kinds of actions fit into the
category of righteous behavior. See also 13:5,
21:26; 29:7

12:11—See note at 10:4.

but the righteous escape from
    trouble.

14 From the fruit of the mouth one is
    filled with good things,
  and manual labor has its reward.

15 Fools think their own way is right,
  but the wise listen to advice.

16 Fools show their anger at once,
  but the prudent ignore an insult.

17 Whoever speaks the truth gives
    honest evidence,
  but a false witness speaks
    deceitfully.

18 Rash words are like sword thrusts,
  but the tongue of the wise brings
    healing.

19 Truthful lips endure forever,
  but a lying tongue lasts only a
    moment.

20 Deceit is in the mind of those who
    plan evil,
  but those who counsel peace have
    joy.

21 No harm happens to the righteous,
  but the wicked are filled with
    trouble.

22 Lying lips are an abomination to the
    LORD,
  but those who act faithfully are his
    delight.

23 One who is clever conceals
    knowledge,
  but the mind of a fool*a* broadcasts
    folly.

24 The hand of the diligent will rule,
  while the lazy will be put to forced
    labor.

25 Anxiety weighs down the human
    heart,
  but a good word cheers it up.

26 The righteous gives good advice to
    friends,*b*
  but the way of the wicked leads
    astray.

27 The lazy do not roast*c* their game,

but the diligent obtain precious
  wealth.*c*

28 In the path of righteousness there is
    life,
  in walking its path there is no
    death.

13 A wise child loves discipline,*d*
  but a scoffer does not listen to
    rebuke.

2 From the fruit of their words good
    persons eat good things,
  but the desire of the treacherous is
    for wrongdoing.

3 Those who guard their mouths
    preserve their lives;
  those who open wide their lips
    come to ruin.

4 The appetite of the lazy craves, and
    gets nothing,
  while the appetite of the diligent is
    richly supplied.

5 The righteous hate falsehood,
  but the wicked act shamefully and
    disgracefully.

6 Righteousness guards one whose
    way is upright,
  but sin overthrows the wicked.

7 Some pretend to be rich, yet have
    nothing;
  others pretend to be poor, yet have
    great wealth.

8 Wealth is a ransom for a person's life,
  but the poor get no threats.

9 The light of the righteous rejoices,
  but the lamp of the wicked goes
    out.

10 By insolence the heedless make strife,
  but wisdom is with those who take
    advice.

11 Wealth hastily gotten*e* will dwindle,
  but those who gather little by little
    will increase it.

a Heb *the heart of fools* *b* Syr: Meaning of Heb uncertain *c* Meaning of Heb uncertain *d* Cn: Heb A *wise child the discipline of his father* *e* Gk Vg: Heb *from vanity*

12:17–22 *Honesty vs. Dishonesty*—Truth telling is good in courtroom situations (v. 17), more helpful when done with tact (v. 18), and outlasts falsehood (v. 19). Lies are at the heart of evil (vv. 20, 22).

13:9 *Light, lamp*—Usually understood as metaphors for the life of the individual. The truth of this saying is questioned in Job 21:17ff.

¹² Hope deferred makes the heart sick,
    but a desire fulfilled is a tree of life.
¹³ Those who despise the word bring
    destruction on themselves,
    but those who respect the
    commandment will be
    rewarded.
¹⁴ The teaching of the wise is a
    fountain of life,
    so that one may avoid the snares of
    death.
¹⁵ Good sense wins favor,
    but the way of the faithless is their
    ruin.ᵃ
¹⁶ The clever do all things intelligently,
    but the fool displays folly.
¹⁷ A bad messenger brings trouble,
    but a faithful envoy, healing.
¹⁸ Poverty and disgrace are for the one
    who ignores instruction,
    but one who heeds reproof is
    honored.
¹⁹ A desire realized is sweet to the
    soul,
    but to turn away from evil is an
    abomination to fools.
²⁰ Whoever walks with the wise
    becomes wise,
    but the companion of fools suffers
    harm.
²¹ Misfortune pursues sinners,
    but prosperity rewards the
    righteous.
²² The good leave an inheritance to
    their children's children,
    but the sinner's wealth is laid up
    for the righteous.
²³ The field of the poor may yield
    much food,
    but it is swept away through
    injustice.
²⁴ Those who spare the rod hate their
    children,
    but those who love them are
    diligent to discipline them.

²⁵ The righteous have enough to satisfy
    their appetite,
    but the belly of the wicked is
    empty.

14 The wise womanᵇ builds her
    house,
    but the foolish tears it down with
    her own hands.
² Those who walk uprightly fear the
    Lᴏʀᴅ,
    but one who is devious in conduct
    despises him.
³ The talk of fools is a rod for their
    backs,ᶜ
    but the lips of the wise preserve
    them.
⁴ Where there are no oxen, there is no
    grain;
    abundant crops come by the
    strength of the ox.
⁵ A faithful witness does not lie,
    but a false witness breathes out
    lies.
⁶ A scoffer seeks wisdom in vain,
    but knowledge is easy for one who
    understands.
⁷ Leave the presence of a fool,
    for there you do not find words of
    knowledge.
⁸ It is the wisdom of the clever to
    understand where they go,
    but the folly of fools misleads.
⁹ Fools mock at the guilt offering,ᵈ
    but the upright enjoy God's favor.
¹⁰ The heart knows its own bitterness,
    and no stranger shares its joy.
¹¹ The house of the wicked is
    destroyed,
    but the tent of the upright
    flourishes.
¹² There is a way that seems right to a
    person,
    but its end is the way to death.ᵉ

ᵃ Cn Compare Gk Syr Vg Tg: Heb *is enduring* ᵇ Heb *Wisdom of women*
ᶜ Cn: Heb *a rod of pride* ᵈ Meaning of Heb uncertain ᵉ Heb *ways of death*

13:14—Compare 14:27; 16:22.

13:23—Poverty is not always caused by indo-lence (as implied in 10:15): greed and *injustice* on the part of the powerful take away equality of opportunity.

14:8, 12 *A way that seems right*—Wisdom helps us discern what is right, but even the wise can be fooled.

13 Even in laughter the heart is sad,
    and the end of joy is grief.
14 The perverse get what their ways
       deserve,
    and the good, what their deeds
       deserve.*a*
15 The simple believe everything,
    but the clever consider their steps.
16 The wise are cautious and turn away
       from evil,
    but the fool throws off restraint
       and is careless.
17 One who is quick-tempered acts
       foolishly,
    and the schemer is hated.
18 The simple are adorned with*b* folly,
    but the clever are crowned with
       knowledge.
19 The evil bow down before the
       good,
    the wicked at the gates of the
       righteous.
20 The poor are disliked even by their
       neighbors,
    but the rich have many friends.
21 Those who despise their neighbors
       are sinners,
    but happy are those who are kind
       to the poor.
22 Do they not err that plan evil?
    Those who plan good find loyalty
       and faithfulness.
23 In all toil there is profit,
    but mere talk leads only to
       poverty.
24 The crown of the wise is their
       wisdom,*c*
    but folly is the garland*d* of fools.
25 A truthful witness saves lives,
    but one who utters lies is a
       betrayer.
26 In the fear of the LORD one has
       strong confidence,

    and one's children will have a
       refuge.
27 The fear of the LORD is a fountain of
       life,
    so that one may avoid the snares of
       death.
28 The glory of a king is a multitude of
       people;
    without people a prince is ruined.
29 Whoever is slow to anger has great
       understanding,
    but one who has a hasty temper
       exalts folly.
30 A tranquil mind gives life to the
       flesh,
    but passion makes the bones rot.
31 Those who oppress the poor insult
       their Maker,
    but those who are kind to the
       needy honor him.
32 The wicked are overthrown by their
       evildoing,
    but the righteous find a refuge in
       their integrity.*e*
33 Wisdom is at home in the mind of
       one who has understanding,
    but it is not*f* known in the heart of
       fools.
34 Righteousness exalts a nation,
    but sin is a reproach to any people.
35 A servant who deals wisely has the
       king's favor,
    but his wrath falls on one who acts
       shamefully.

15 A soft answer turns away wrath,
    but a harsh word stirs up anger.
2 The tongue of the wise dispenses
       knowledge,*g*
    but the mouths of fools pour out
       folly.

a Cn: Heb *from upon him*   *b* Or *inherit*   *c* Cn Compare Gk: Heb *riches*
d Cn: Heb *is the folly*   *e* Gk Syr: Heb *in their death*   *f* Gk Syr: Heb *lacks not*   *g* Cn: Heb *makes knowledge good*

14:20–21—*The poor are disliked* is an observation on human behavior that may (unfortunately) prove true in a number of settings. However, the proverb does not imply that this is admirable behavior! The saying that follows (v. 21) clearly indicates that the speaker does not approve of the behavior described in v. 20. See also v. 31, 19:4.

14:31—Since the poor are also made in the image of God, what you do to them you do also to God (see 17:5).

15:1–2, 4, 7, 14—Human speech, represented as *word* (v. 1), *tongue* (vv. 2, 4), *lips* (v. 7) and *mouths* (v. 14), is a powerful force both for good and for evil.

3 The eyes of the LORD are in every
    place,
  keeping watch on the evil and the
    good.
4 A gentle tongue is a tree of life,
  but perverseness in it breaks the
    spirit.
5 A fool despises a parent's
    instruction,
  but the one who heeds admonition
    is prudent.
6 In the house of the righteous there is
    much treasure,
  but trouble befalls the income of
    the wicked.
7 The lips of the wise spread
    knowledge;
  not so the minds of fools.
8 The sacrifice of the wicked is an
    abomination to the LORD,
  but the prayer of the upright is his
    delight.
9 The way of the wicked is an
    abomination to the LORD,
  but he loves the one who pursues
    righteousness.
10 There is severe discipline for one
    who forsakes the way,
  but one who hates a rebuke will
    die.
11 Sheol and Abaddon lie open before
    the LORD,
  how much more human hearts!
12 Scoffers do not like to be rebuked;
  they will not go to the wise.
13 A glad heart makes a cheerful
    countenance,
  but by sorrow of heart the spirit is
    broken.
14 The mind of one who has
    understanding seeks
    knowledge,
  but the mouths of fools feed on
    folly.

15 All the days of the poor are hard,
  but a cheerful heart has a
    continual feast.
16 Better is a little with the fear of the
    LORD
  than great treasure and trouble
    with it.
17 Better is a dinner of vegetables
    where love is
  than a fatted ox and hatred with it.
18 Those who are hot-tempered stir up
    strife,
  but those who are slow to anger
    calm contention.
19 The way of the lazy is overgrown
    with thorns,
  but the path of the upright is a
    level highway.
20 A wise child makes a glad father,
  but the foolish despise their
    mothers.
21 Folly is a joy to one who has no sense,
  but a person of understanding
    walks straight ahead.
22 Without counsel, plans go wrong,
  but with many advisers they
    succeed.
23 To make an apt answer is a joy to
    anyone,
  and a word in season, how good
    it is!
24 For the wise the path of life leads
    upward,
  in order to avoid Sheol below.
25 The LORD tears down the house of
    the proud,
  but maintains the widow's
    boundaries.
26 Evil plans are an abomination to the
    LORD,
  but gracious words are pure.
27 Those who are greedy for unjust
    gain make trouble for their
    households,

15:8–11—The Lord knows what intentions lie
beneath our actions.
15:11—*Sheol* (see note at 7:27) and *Abaddon*
are used in Wisdom literature as synonyms for
death or the grave.
15:16–17 *Better . . . than*—A select number of
sayings follow the pattern "A with B is better
than C with D." Each of these "better sayings" acknowledges that otherwise desirable things (e.g.,
treasures, a fatted ox) often come with undesirable conditions attached (e.g., trouble, hatred).
See also 12:9; 16:8, 19; 17:1; 19:1; 28:6.

but those who hate bribes will live.

28 The mind of the righteous ponders
        how to answer,
    but the mouth of the wicked pours
        out evil.

29 The LORD is far from the wicked,
    but he hears the prayer of the
        righteous.

30 The light of the eyes rejoices the
        heart,
    and good news refreshes the
        body.

31 The ear that heeds wholesome
        admonition
    will lodge among the wise.

32 Those who ignore instruction
        despise themselves,
    but those who heed admonition
        gain understanding.

33 The fear of the LORD is instruction
        in wisdom,
    and humility goes before honor.

16 The plans of the mind belong to
        mortals,
    but the answer of the tongue is
        from the LORD.

2 All one's ways may be pure in one's
        own eyes,
    but the LORD weighs the spirit.

3 Commit your work to the LORD,
    and your plans will be established.

4 The LORD has made everything for
        its purpose,
    even the wicked for the day of
        trouble.

5 All those who are arrogant are an
        abomination to the LORD;
    be assured, they will not go
        unpunished.

6 By loyalty and faithfulness iniquity is
        atoned for,
    and by the fear of the LORD one
        avoids evil.

7 When the ways of people please the
        LORD,
    he causes even their enemies to be
        at peace with them.

8 Better is a little with righteousness
    than large income with injustice.

9 The human mind plans the way,
    but the LORD directs the steps.

10 Inspired decisions are on the lips of
        a king;
    his mouth does not sin in
        judgment.

11 Honest balances and scales are the
        LORD's;
    all the weights in the bag are his
        work.

12 It is an abomination to kings to do
        evil,
    for the throne is established by
        righteousness.

13 Righteous lips are the delight of a
        king,
    and he loves those who speak what
        is right.

14 A king's wrath is a messenger of
        death,
    and whoever is wise will appease
        it.

15 In the light of a king's face there is
        life,
    and his favor is like the clouds that
        bring the spring rain.

16 How much better to get wisdom
        than gold!
    To get understanding is to be
        chosen rather than silver.

17 The highway of the upright avoids
        evil;
    those who guard their way
        preserve their lives.

18 Pride goes before destruction,
    and a haughty spirit before a fall.

19 It is better to be of a lowly spirit
        among the poor

16:1–33—The Lord is mentioned more frequently in chap. 16 than in any other chapter of Proverbs.

16:1–9, 33 God has ultimate control—God always has the last word (v. 1); God discerns human motives (v. 2); God's plans take precedence over human *plans* (vv. 3, 33, see also 19:21).

16:10, 12–15—There may be a hint of irony in these sayings about how to deal with the power of *kings*.

16:11—See note at 11:1. The sense seems to be that honest commerce is the Lord's business.

than to divide the spoil with the
    proud.
20 Those who are attentive to a matter
    will prosper,
  and happy are those who trust in
    the LORD.
21 The wise of heart is called
    perceptive,
  and pleasant speech increases
    persuasiveness.
22 Wisdom is a fountain of life to one
    who has it,
  but folly is the punishment of
    fools.
23 The mind of the wise makes their
    speech judicious,
  and adds persuasiveness to their
    lips.
24 Pleasant words are like a
    honeycomb,
  sweetness to the soul and health to
    the body.
25 Sometimes there is a way that seems
    to be right,
  but in the end it is the way to
    death.
26 The appetite of workers works for
    them;
  their hunger urges them on.
27 Scoundrels concoct evil,
  and their speech is like a scorching
    fire.
28 A perverse person spreads strife,
  and a whisperer separates close
    friends.
29 The violent entice their neighbors,
  and lead them in a way that is not
    good.
30 One who winks the eyes plans*a*
    perverse things;
  one who compresses the lips
    brings evil to pass.
31 Gray hair is a crown of glory;
  it is gained in a righteous life.

32 One who is slow to anger is better
    than the mighty,
  and one whose temper is
    controlled than one who
    captures a city.
33 The lot is cast into the lap,
  but the decision is the LORD's
    alone.

17 Better is a dry morsel with quiet
    than a house full of feasting
    with strife.
2 A slave who deals wisely will
    rule over a child who acts
    shamefully,
  and will share the inheritance as
    one of the family.
3 The crucible is for silver, and the
    furnace is for gold,
  but the LORD tests the heart.
4 An evildoer listens to wicked lips;
  and a liar gives heed to a
    mischievous tongue.
5 Those who mock the poor insult
    their Maker;
  those who are glad at calamity will
    not go unpunished.
6 Grandchildren are the crown of the
    aged,
  and the glory of children is their
    parents.
7 Fine speech is not becoming to a
    fool,
  still less is false speech to a ruler.*b*
8 A bribe is like a magic stone in the
    eyes of those who give it;
  wherever they turn they prosper.
9 One who forgives an affront fosters
    friendship,
  but one who dwells on disputes
    will alienate a friend.
10 A rebuke strikes deeper into a
    discerning person
  than a hundred blows into a fool.

a Gk Syr Vg Tg: Heb *to plan*   *b* Or *a noble person*

16:27–28—Sayings against malicious gossip.
17:1—A "better" proverb (see note at 15:16–17).
17:3—God can separate purities from impurities
in human hearts.

17:8, 23—Observations on the giving and taking
of bribes.
17:10 *Blows*—Reflects the sociocultural assumptions and practices of the speaker's time.

¹¹ Evil people seek only rebellion,
    but a cruel messenger will be sent
       against them.
¹² Better to meet a she-bear robbed of
       its cubs
    than to confront a fool immersed
       in folly.
¹³ Evil will not depart from the house
    of one who returns evil for good.
¹⁴ The beginning of strife is like letting
       out water;
    so stop before the quarrel breaks
       out.
¹⁵ One who justifies the wicked and
       one who condemns the
       righteous
    are both alike an abomination to
       the LORD.
¹⁶ Why should fools have a price in
       hand
    to buy wisdom, when they have no
       mind to learn?
¹⁷ A friend loves at all times,
    and kinsfolk are born to share
       adversity.
¹⁸ It is senseless to give a pledge,
    to become surety for a neighbor.
¹⁹ One who loves transgression loves
       strife;
    one who builds a high threshold
       invites broken bones.
²⁰ The crooked of mind do not prosper,
    and the perverse of tongue fall into
       calamity.
²¹ The one who begets a fool gets
       trouble;
    the parent of a fool has no joy.
²² A cheerful heart is a good medicine,
    but a downcast spirit dries up the
       bones.
²³ The wicked accept a concealed bribe
    to pervert the ways of justice.
²⁴ The discerning person looks to
       wisdom,
    but the eyes of a fool to the ends of
       the earth.

²⁵ Foolish children are a grief to their
       father
    and bitterness to her who bore
       them.
²⁶ To impose a fine on the innocent is
       not right,
    or to flog the noble for their
       integrity.
²⁷ One who spares words is
       knowledgeable;
    one who is cool in spirit has
       understanding.
²⁸ Even fools who keep silent are
       considered wise;
    when they close their lips, they are
       deemed intelligent.

18 The one who lives alone is
       self-indulgent,
    showing contempt for all who have
       sound judgment.^a
² A fool takes no pleasure in
       understanding,
    but only in expressing personal
       opinion.
³ When wickedness comes, contempt
       comes also;
    and with dishonor comes disgrace.
⁴ The words of the mouth are deep
       waters;
    the fountain of wisdom is a
       gushing stream.
⁵ It is not right to be partial to the
       guilty,
    or to subvert the innocent in
       judgment.
⁶ A fool's lips bring strife,
    and a fool's mouth invites a
       flogging.
⁷ The mouths of fools are their ruin,
    and their lips a snare to
       themselves.
⁸ The words of a whisperer are like
       delicious morsels;
    they go down into the inner parts
       of the body.

---

^a Meaning of Heb uncertain

17:23 *The wicked*—One of the few sayings to specify what kinds of actions fit into the general category of wicked behavior. Allowing a bribe to affect a judicial decision clearly fits into that category. See also 14:21; 21:4, 7, 26; 29:7.

18:8 *Whisperer*—One who spreads gossip.

9 One who is slack in work
    is close kin to a vandal.
10 The name of the LORD is a strong
        tower;
    the righteous run into it and are
        safe.
11 The wealth of the rich is their strong
        city;
    in their imagination it is like a
        high wall.
12 Before destruction one's heart is
        haughty,
    but humility goes before honor.
13 If one gives answer before hearing,
    it is folly and shame.
14 The human spirit will endure
        sickness;
    but a broken spirit—who can
        bear?
15 An intelligent mind acquires
        knowledge,
    and the ear of the wise seeks
        knowledge.
16 A gift opens doors;
    it gives access to the great.
17 The one who first states a case seems
        right,
    until the other comes and
        cross-examines.
18 Casting the lot puts an end to
        disputes
    and decides between powerful
        contenders.
19 An ally offended is stronger than a
        city;[a]
    such quarreling is like the bars of
        a castle.
20 From the fruit of the mouth one's
        stomach is satisfied;
    the yield of the lips brings
        satisfaction.
21 Death and life are in the power of
        the tongue,
    and those who love it will eat its
        fruits.

22 He who finds a wife finds a good
        thing,
    and obtains favor from the LORD.
23 The poor use entreaties,
    but the rich answer roughly.
24 Some[b] friends play at friendship[c]
    but a true friend sticks closer than
        one's nearest kin.

19 Better the poor walking in
        integrity
    than one perverse of speech who
        is a fool.
2 Desire without knowledge is not
        good,
    and one who moves too hurriedly
        misses the way.
3 One's own folly leads to ruin,
    yet the heart rages against the LORD.
4 Wealth brings many friends,
    but the poor are left friendless.
5 A false witness will not go
        unpunished,
    and a liar will not escape.
6 Many seek the favor of the generous,
    and everyone is a friend to a giver
        of gifts.
7 If the poor are hated even by their
        kin,
    how much more are they shunned
        by their friends!
    When they call after them, they are
        not there.[d]
8 To get wisdom is to love oneself;
    to keep understanding is to
        prosper.
9 A false witness will not go
        unpunished,
    and the liar will perish.
10 It is not fitting for a fool to live in
        luxury,
    much less for a slave to rule over
        princes.

[a] Gk Syr Vg Tg: Meaning of Heb uncertain [b] Syr Tg: Heb A man of
[c] Cn Compare Syr Vg Tg: Meaning of Heb uncertain [d] Meaning of Heb
uncertain

18:10–11—True safety comes from the Lord; the protection of wealth can't be trusted.

18:22—This positive view of *a wife* understood as a blessing from God counteracts subsequent negative sayings (see 19:13–14; 21:9, 19)

18:23—The sage describes but does not advocate this observable human behavior.

19:4 *Wealth brings many friends*—An ironic comment implying this is one of the *dis*advantages of being rich (see 14:20–21).

11 Those with good sense are slow to
    anger,
    and it is their glory to overlook an
      offense.
12 A king's anger is like the growling of
    a lion,
    but his favor is like dew on the
      grass.
13 A stupid child is ruin to a father,
    and a wife's quarreling is a
      continual dripping of rain.
14 House and wealth are inherited from
    parents,
    but a prudent wife is from the
      LORD.
15 Laziness brings on deep sleep;
    an idle person will suffer hunger.
16 Those who keep the commandment
    will live;
    those who are heedless of their
      ways will die.
17 Whoever is kind to the poor lends to
    the LORD,
    and will be repaid in full.
18 Discipline your children while there
    is hope;
    do not set your heart on their
      destruction.
19 A violent tempered person will pay
    the penalty;
    if you effect a rescue, you will only
      have to do it again.[a]
20 Listen to advice and accept
    instruction,
    that you may gain wisdom for the
      future.
21 The human mind may devise many
    plans,
    but it is the purpose of the LORD
      that will be established.
22 What is desirable in a person is
    loyalty,
    and it is better to be poor than a
      liar.
23 The fear of the LORD is life indeed;
    filled with it one rests secure
    and suffers no harm.

24 The lazy person buries a hand in the
    dish,
    and will not even bring it back to
      the mouth.
25 Strike a scoffer, and the simple will
    learn prudence;
    reprove the intelligent, and they
      will gain knowledge.
26 Those who do violence to their
    father and chase away their
    mother
    are children who cause shame and
      bring reproach.
27 Cease straying, my child, from the
    words of knowledge,
    in order that you may hear
      instruction.
28 A worthless witness mocks at justice,
    and the mouth of the wicked
      devours iniquity.
29 Condemnation is ready for scoffers,
    and flogging for the backs of fools.

20 Wine is a mocker, strong drink
    a brawler,
    and whoever is led astray by it is
      not wise.
2 The dread anger of a king is like the
    growling of a lion;
    anyone who provokes him to anger
      forfeits life itself.
3 It is honorable to refrain from strife,
    but every fool is quick to quarrel.
4 The lazy person does not plow in
    season;
    harvest comes, and there is
      nothing to be found.
5 The purposes in the human mind
    are like deep water,
    but the intelligent will draw them
      out.
6 Many proclaim themselves loyal,
    but who can find one worthy of
      trust?
7 The righteous walk in integrity—
    happy are the children who follow
      them!

a Meaning of Heb uncertain

19:13–14—These adjacent sayings seem to be in dialogue with each other (see notes at 18:22;
21:9, etc.).

8 A king who sits on the throne of
    judgment
    winnows all evil with his eyes.
9 Who can say, "I have made my heart
    clean;
    I am pure from my sin"?
10 Diverse weights and diverse
    measures
    are both alike an abomination to
    the LORD.
11 Even children make themselves
    known by their acts,
    by whether what they do is pure
    and right.
12 The hearing ear and the seeing eye—
    the LORD has made them both.
13 Do not love sleep, or else you will
    come to poverty;
    open your eyes, and you will have
    plenty of bread.
14 "Bad, bad," says the buyer,
    then goes away and boasts.
15 There is gold, and abundance of
    costly stones;
    but the lips informed by
    knowledge are a precious
    jewel.
16 Take the garment of one who has
    given surety for a stranger;
    seize the pledge given as surety for
    foreigners.
17 Bread gained by deceit is sweet,
    but afterward the mouth will be
    full of gravel.
18 Plans are established by taking
    advice;
    wage war by following wise
    guidance.
19 A gossip reveals secrets;
    therefore do not associate with a
    babbler.
20 If you curse father or mother,
    your lamp will go out in utter
    darkness.

21 An estate quickly acquired in the
    beginning
    will not be blessed in the end.
22 Do not say, "I will repay evil";
    wait for the LORD, and he will help
    you.
23 Differing weights are an
    abomination to the LORD,
    and false scales are not good.
24 All our steps are ordered by the LORD;
    how then can we understand our
    own ways?
25 It is a snare for one to say rashly, "It
    is holy,"
    and begin to reflect only after
    making a vow.
26 A wise king winnows the wicked,
    and drives the wheel over them.
27 The human spirit is the lamp of the
    LORD,
    searching every inmost part.
28 Loyalty and faithfulness preserve the
    king,
    and his throne is upheld by
    righteousness.*a*
29 The glory of youths is their strength,
    but the beauty of the aged is their
    gray hair.
30 Blows that wound cleanse away evil;
    beatings make clean the innermost
    parts.

21 The king's heart is a stream of
    water in the hand of the LORD;
    he turns it wherever he will.
2 All deeds are right in the sight of the
    doer,
    but the LORD weighs the heart.
3 To do righteousness and justice
    is more acceptable to the LORD
    than sacrifice.
4 Haughty eyes and a proud heart—
    the lamp of the wicked—are sin.

a Gk: Heb *loyalty*

20:10, 23—See note at 11:1.

20:14—An intentionally humorous picture of common bargaining practices.

20:16 *Stranger, foreigners*—This saying (= 27:13) advocates treating outsiders differently than the law for neighbors does in Deut. 24:10–13, but

the translators have failed to communicate the religious or cultic overtones of idolatry that these terms for outsiders usually connote in the Old Testament.

21:2–3—The Lord judges intentions (motives) as well as deeds. See also 15:11; 16:2; 17:3; 20:27.

5 The plans of the diligent lead surely
  to abundance,
  but everyone who is hasty comes
  only to want.
6 The getting of treasures by a lying
  tongue
  is a fleeting vapor and a snare[a] of
  death.
7 The violence of the wicked will
  sweep them away,
  because they refuse to do what is
  just.
8 The way of the guilty is crooked,
  but the conduct of the pure is right.
9 It is better to live in a corner of the
  housetop
  than in a house shared with a
  contentious wife.
10 The souls of the wicked desire evil;
   their neighbors find no mercy in
   their eyes.
11 When a scoffer is punished, the
   simple become wiser;
   when the wise are instructed, they
   increase in knowledge.
12 The Righteous One observes the
   house of the wicked;
   he casts the wicked down to ruin.
13 If you close your ear to the cry of the
   poor,
   you will cry out and not be heard.
14 A gift in secret averts anger;
   and a concealed bribe in the
   bosom, strong wrath.
15 When justice is done, it is a joy to
   the righteous,
   but dismay to evildoers.
16 Whoever wanders from the way of
   understanding
   will rest in the assembly of the
   dead.
17 Whoever loves pleasure will suffer
   want;
   whoever loves wine and oil will
   not be rich.
18 The wicked is a ransom for the
   righteous,

and the faithless for the upright.
19 It is better to live in a desert land
   than with a contentious and fretful
   wife.
20 Precious treasure remains[b] in the
   house of the wise,
   but the fool devours it.
21 Whoever pursues righteousness and
   kindness
   will find life[c] and honor.
22 One wise person went up against a
   city of warriors
   and brought down the stronghold
   in which they trusted.
23 To watch over mouth and tongue
   is to keep out of trouble.
24 The proud, haughty person, named
   "Scoffer,"
   acts with arrogant pride.
25 The craving of the lazy person is fatal,
   for lazy hands refuse to labor.
26 All day long the wicked covet,[d]
   but the righteous give and do not
   hold back.
27 The sacrifice of the wicked is an
   abomination;
   how much more when brought
   with evil intent.
28 A false witness will perish,
   but a good listener will testify
   successfully.
29 The wicked put on a bold face,
   but the upright give thought to[e]
   their ways.
30 No wisdom, no understanding, no
   counsel,
   can avail against the LORD.
31 The horse is made ready for the day
   of battle,
   but the victory belongs to the
   LORD.

22 A good name is to be chosen
   rather than great riches,
   and favor is better than silver or
   gold.

[a] Gk: Heb *seekers*   [b] Gk: Heb *and oil*   [c] Gk: Heb *life and righteousness*
[d] Gk: Heb *all day long one covets covetously*   [e] Another reading is *establish*

21:9, 19 Contentious wife—Several sentence
proverbs represent the point of view of a dis-
gruntled husband (see also 19:13; 25:24, 27:15),
but these are balanced in the whole collection by
positive statements in 18:22; 19:14.

2 The rich and the poor have this in
    common:
    the LORD is the maker of them
    all.
3 The clever see danger and hide;
    but the simple go on, and suffer
    for it.
4 The reward for humility and fear of
    the LORD
    is riches and honor and life.
5 Thorns and snares are in the way of
    the perverse;
    the cautious will keep far from
    them.
6 Train children in the right way,
    and when old, they will not stray.
7 The rich rule over the poor,
    and the borrower is the slave of the
    lender.
8 Whoever sows injustice will reap
    calamity,
    and the rod of anger will fail.
9 Those who are generous are blessed,
    for they share their bread with the
    poor.
10 Drive out a scoffer, and strife goes
    out;
    quarreling and abuse will cease.
11 Those who love a pure heart and are
    gracious in speech
    will have the king as a friend.
12 The eyes of the LORD keep watch
    over knowledge,
    but he overthrows the words of the
    faithless.
13 The lazy person says, "There is a lion
    outside!
    I shall be killed in the streets!"
14 The mouth of a loose^a woman is a
    deep pit;

he with whom the LORD is angry
    falls into it.
15 Folly is bound up in the heart of a
    boy,
    but the rod of discipline drives it
    far away.
16 Oppressing the poor in order to
    enrich oneself,
    and giving to the rich, will lead
    only to loss.

Sayings of the Wise

17   The words of the wise:

Incline your ear and hear my words,^b
    and apply your mind to my
    teaching;
18 for it will be pleasant if you keep
    them within you,
    if all of them are ready on your lips.
19 So that your trust may be in the
    LORD,
    I have made them known to you
    today— yes, to you.
20 Have I not written for you thirty
    sayings
    of admonition and knowledge,
21 to show you what is right and true,
    so that you may give a true answer
    to those who sent you?

22 Do not rob the poor because they
    are poor,
    or crush the afflicted at the gate;
23 for the LORD pleads their cause
    and despoils of life those who
    despoil them.
24 Make no friends with those given to
    anger,

a Heb strange b Cn Compare Gk: Heb Incline your ear, and hear the words
of the wise

22:7–8—The saying in v. 7 makes an observation,
not a recommendation. Verse 8 seems to comment on the injustice of the situation described
in v. 7.

22:17–24:34 The Words of the Wise
The first collection of sentence proverbs ends
abruptly in 22:16. A new heading appears in
22:17 marking the beginning of another collection, called *The words of the wise.*

22:20–24:22 Thirty Sayings
While the following sayings are not numbered
in the text, several closely resemble parts of an
Egyptian collection known as the Thirty Instructions of Amenemope.

22:22–23 *Poor, afflicted*—The same Hebrew
words are used to describe the weak and helpless
in prophetic texts such as Amos 2:7; 5:12; Isa.
10:2, etc.). *At the gate*—Refers to the custom of
deciding legal disputes in the specially designed
entryways to fortified cities.

and do not associate with
   hotheads,
25 or you may learn their ways
   and entangle yourself in a snare.
26 Do not be one of those who give
   pledges,
   who become surety for debts.
27 If you have nothing with which to
   pay,
   why should your bed be taken
   from under you?
28 Do not remove the ancient landmark
   that your ancestors set up.
29 Do you see those who are skillful in
   their work?
   They will serve kings;
   they will not serve common
   people.

23 When you sit down to eat with
   a ruler,
   observe carefully what[a] is before
   you,
2 and put a knife to your throat
   if you have a big appetite.
3 Do not desire the ruler's[b] delicacies,
   for they are deceptive food.
4 Do not wear yourself out to get rich;
   be wise enough to desist.
5 When your eyes light upon it, it is
   gone;
   for suddenly it takes wings to
   itself,
   flying like an eagle toward heaven.
6 Do not eat the bread of the stingy;
   do not desire their delicacies;
7 for like a hair in the throat, so are
   they.[c]
   "Eat and drink!" they say to you;
   but they do not mean it.
8 You will vomit up the little you have
   eaten,
   and you will waste your pleasant
   words.

9 Do not speak in the hearing of a
   fool,
   who will only despise the wisdom
   of your words.
10 Do not remove an ancient landmark
   or encroach on the fields of
   orphans,
11 for their redeemer is strong;
   he will plead their cause against
   you.
12 Apply your mind to instruction
   and your ear to words of
   knowledge.
13 Do not withhold discipline from
   your children;
   if you beat them with a rod, they
   will not die.
14 If you beat them with the rod,
   you will save their lives from
   Sheol.
15 My child, if your heart is wise,
   my heart too will be glad.
16 My soul will rejoice
   when your lips speak what is right.
17 Do not let your heart envy sinners,
   but always continue in the fear of
   the LORD.
18 Surely there is a future,
   and your hope will not be cut off.

19 Hear, my child, and be wise,
   and direct your mind in the way.
20 Do not be among winebibbers,
   or among gluttonous eaters of
   meat;
21 for the drunkard and the glutton will
   come to poverty,
   and drowsiness will clothe them
   with rags.
22 Listen to your father who begot you,
   and do not despise your mother
   when she is old.

[a] Or who [b] Heb his [c] Meaning of Heb uncertain

22:26–27—The Lord is the advocate of the poor, but the wise will try to avoid becoming one of those who have only a garment to give in pledge for a debt. See Exod. 22:26–27; Amos 2:6–8.

22:28—Also found in Amenemope; see Deut. 19:14; Prov. 23:10–11.

23:1–8—The sayings in this section advise the wise not to place much value on such luxuries as exotic foods.

23:13–14 *Beat them with a rod*—The speakers reflect the sociocultural assumptions and practices of their own world and time. These can *not* be equated with God's will.

²³ Buy truth, and do not sell it;
buy wisdom, instruction, and
understanding.
²⁴ The father of the righteous will
greatly rejoice;
he who begets a wise son will be
glad in him.
²⁵ Let your father and mother be glad;
let her who bore you rejoice.

²⁶ My child, give me your heart,
and let your eyes observe^a my
ways.
²⁷ For a prostitute is a deep pit;
an adulteress^b is a narrow well.
²⁸ She lies in wait like a robber
and increases the number of the
faithless.

²⁹ Who has woe? Who has sorrow?
Who has strife? Who has
complaining?
Who has wounds without cause?
Who has redness of eyes?
³⁰ Those who linger late over wine,
those who keep trying mixed
wines.
³¹ Do not look at wine when it is red,
when it sparkles in the cup
and goes down smoothly.
³² At the last it bites like a serpent,
and stings like an adder.
³³ Your eyes will see strange things,
and your mind utter perverse
things.
³⁴ You will be like one who lies down
in the midst of the sea,
like one who lies on the top of a
mast.^c
³⁵ "They struck me," you will say,^d "but
I was not hurt;
they beat me, but I did not feel it.
When shall I awake?
I will seek another drink."

24 Do not envy the wicked,
nor desire to be with them;
² for their minds devise violence,
and their lips talk of mischief.

³ By wisdom a house is built,
and by understanding it is
established;
⁴ by knowledge the rooms are filled
with all precious and pleasant
riches.
⁵ Wise warriors are mightier than
strong ones,^e
and those who have knowledge
than those who have
strength;
⁶ for by wise guidance you can wage
your war,
and in abundance of counselors
there is victory.
⁷ Wisdom is too high for fools;
in the gate they do not open their
mouths.

⁸ Whoever plans to do evil
will be called a mischief-maker.
⁹ The devising of folly is sin,
and the scoffer is an abomination
to all.

¹⁰ If you faint in the day of adversity,
your strength being small;
¹¹ if you hold back from rescuing those
taken away to death,
those who go staggering to the
slaughter;
¹² if you say, "Look, we did not know
this"—
does not he who weighs the heart
perceive it?
Does not he who keeps watch over
your soul know it?

^a Another reading is *delight in*   ^b Heb *an alien woman*   ^c Meaning of Heb
uncertain   ^d Gk Syr Vg Tg: Heb lacks *you will say*   ^e Gk Compare Syr Tg:
Heb *A wise man is strength*

23:27 *Prostitute, adulteress*—Once again the
translators have failed to communicate the religious or cultic overtones of idolatry that almost
always accompany these terms in the Old Testament (see notes at 2:16–17; 5:3, 20).

23:29–35 *Who has woe?*—A vivid word picture
of an alcoholic.

24:8–9—Evildoers need to be named as such,
and their sins should be branded as folly.

24:10–12—Neither timidity nor pretended ignorance excuses you from the call to rescue those
who are being slaughtered.

And will he not repay all according
    to their deeds?

13 My child, eat honey, for it is good,
    and the drippings of the
        honeycomb are sweet to your
        taste.
14 Know that wisdom is such to your
    soul;
    if you find it, you will find a
        future,
    and your hope will not be cut off.

15 Do not lie in wait like an outlaw
    against the home of the
        righteous;
    do no violence to the place where
        the righteous live;
16 for though they fall seven times, they
    will rise again;
    but the wicked are overthrown by
        calamity.

17 Do not rejoice when your enemies
    fall,
    and do not let your heart be glad
        when they stumble,
18 or else the LORD will see it and be
    displeased,
    and turn away his anger from
        them.

19 Do not fret because of evildoers.
    Do not envy the wicked;
20 for the evil have no future;
    the lamp of the wicked will go out.

21 My child, fear the LORD and the king,
    and do not disobey either of
        them;*a*
22 for disaster comes from them
    suddenly,
    and who knows the ruin that both
        can bring?

Further Sayings of the Wise

23   These also are sayings of the wise:

Partiality in judging is not good.
24 Whoever says to the wicked, "You
    are innocent,"
    will be cursed by peoples,
        abhorred by nations;
25 but those who rebuke the wicked
    will have delight,
    and a good blessing will come
        upon them.
26 One who gives an honest answer
    gives a kiss on the lips.

27 Prepare your work outside,
    get everything ready for you in the
        field;
    and after that build your house.

28 Do not be a witness against your
    neighbor without cause,
    and do not deceive with your lips.
29 Do not say, "I will do to others as
    they have done to me;
    I will pay them back for what they
        have done."

30 I passed by the field of one who was
    lazy,
    by the vineyard of a stupid person;
31 and see, it was all overgrown with
    thorns;
    the ground was covered with nettles,
    and its stone wall was broken down.
32 Then I saw and considered it;
    I looked and received instruction.
33 A little sleep, a little slumber,
    a little folding of the hands to rest,
34 and poverty will come upon you like
    a robber,
    and want, like an armed warrior.

a Gk: Heb *do not associate with those who change*

24:20—See note at 13:9.

24:23–34 Additional Words of the Wise

24:23 *These also*—A new heading marks the
beginning of another short collection of the
sayings of the wise. *Partiality*—Includes acquitting the guilty (v. 24), as well as giving false
testimony (v. 28) in order to punish those who
have harmed you.

24:28–29—A caution to us against using the
Golden Rule in reverse.

24:30–34—The sage describes the context
needed to make sense of the saying found here
(vv. 33–34) and in 6:10–11.

Further Wise Sayings of Solomon

25 These are other proverbs of Solomon that the officials of King Hezekiah of Judah copied.

2 It is the glory of God to conceal
    things,
        but the glory of kings is to search
            things out.
3 Like the heavens for height, like the
    earth for depth,
        so the mind of kings is
            unsearchable.
4 Take away the dross from the silver,
    and the smith has material for a
        vessel;
5 take away the wicked from the
    presence of the king,
        and his throne will be established
            in righteousness.
6 Do not put yourself forward in the
    king's presence
        or stand in the place of the great;
7 for it is better to be told, "Come up
    here,"
        than to be put lower in the
            presence of a noble.

What your eyes have seen
8   do not hastily bring into court;
for[a] what will you do in the end,
    when your neighbor puts you to
        shame?
9 Argue your case with your neighbor
    directly,
        and do not disclose another's
            secret;
10 or else someone who hears you will
    bring shame upon you,
        and your ill repute will have no
            end.
11 A word fitly spoken
    is like apples of gold in a setting of
        silver.

12 Like a gold ring or an ornament of
    gold
        is a wise rebuke to a listening ear.
13 Like the cold of snow in the time of
    harvest
        are faithful messengers to those
            who send them;
        they refresh the spirit of their
            masters.
14 Like clouds and wind without rain
    is one who boasts of a gift never
        given.
15 With patience a ruler may be
    persuaded,
        and a soft tongue can break
            bones.
16 If you have found honey, eat only
    enough for you,
        or else, having too much, you will
            vomit it.
17 Let your foot be seldom in your
    neighbor's house,
        otherwise the neighbor will
            become weary of you and hate
                you.
18 Like a war club, a sword, or a sharp
    arrow
        is one who bears false witness
            against a neighbor.
19 Like a bad tooth or a lame foot
    is trust in a faithless person in
        time of trouble.
20 Like vinegar on a wound[b]
    is one who sings songs to a heavy
        heart.
    Like a moth in clothing or a worm in
        wood,
            sorrow gnaws at the human heart.[c]
21 If your enemies are hungry, give
    them bread to eat;
        and if they are thirsty, give them
            water to drink;

---

[a] Cn: Heb or else   [b] Gk: Heb *Like one who takes off a garment on a cold day,
like vinegar on lye*   [c] Gk Syr Tg: Heb lacks *Like a moth . . . human heart*

25:1–29:27 More Sentence Literature

25:1 *Other proverbs*—A new heading marks the beginning of a collection of 140 sayings said to be from the time of Hezekiah. These sayings are less regular in form and sometimes repeat sayings found in chaps. 10–22.

25:6–7—See Luke 14:7–11.

25:21–22—Paul quotes v. 21 and half of v. 22 (Rom. 12:20), but Jesus asks his disciples to take a less self-centered approach to dealing with enemies (Matt. 5:43–46).

²² for you will heap coals of fire on
their heads,
and the LORD will reward you.
²³ The north wind produces rain,
and a backbiting tongue, angry
looks.
²⁴ It is better to live in a corner of the
housetop
than in a house shared with a
contentious wife.
²⁵ Like cold water to a thirsty soul,
so is good news from a far
country.
²⁶ Like a muddied spring or a polluted
fountain
are the righteous who give way
before the wicked.
²⁷ It is not good to eat much honey,
or to seek honor on top of honor.
²⁸ Like a city breached, without walls,
is one who lacks self-control.

26 Like snow in summer or rain in
harvest,
so honor is not fitting for a fool.
² Like a sparrow in its flitting, like a
swallow in its flying,
an undeserved curse goes
nowhere.
³ A whip for the horse, a bridle for the
donkey,
and a rod for the back of fools.
⁴ Do not answer fools according to
their folly,
or you will be a fool yourself.
⁵ Answer fools according to their folly,
or they will be wise in their own
eyes.
⁶ It is like cutting off one's foot and
drinking down violence,
to send a message by a fool.
⁷ The legs of a disabled person hang
limp;

so does a proverb in the mouth of
a fool.
⁸ It is like binding a stone in a sling
to give honor to a fool.
⁹ Like a thornbush brandished by the
hand of a drunkard
is a proverb in the mouth of a fool.
¹⁰ Like an archer who wounds
everybody
is one who hires a passing fool or
drunkard.ᵃ
¹¹ Like a dog that returns to its vomit
is a fool who reverts to his folly.
¹² Do you see persons wise in their
own eyes?
There is more hope for fools than
for them.
¹³ The lazy person says, "There is a lion
in the road!
There is a lion in the streets!"
¹⁴ As a door turns on its hinges,
so does a lazy person in bed.
¹⁵ The lazy person buries a hand in the
dish,
and is too tired to bring it back to
the mouth.
¹⁶ The lazy person is wiser in
self-esteem
than seven who can answer
discreetly.
¹⁷ Like somebody who takes a passing
dog by the ears
is one who meddles in the quarrel
of another.
¹⁸ Like a maniac who shoots deadly
firebrands and arrows,
¹⁹ so is one who deceives a neighbor
and says, "I am only joking!"
²⁰ For lack of wood the fire goes out,
and where there is no whisperer,
quarreling ceases.

ᵃ Meaning of Heb uncertain

25:24—See note at the duplicate saying in 21:9.

26:1, 2–12—*Fool/fools* (*kesil*). Eleven sayings
about fools and their folly.

26:4–5—Two adjacent sayings give completely
opposite bits of advice: there are times when
it is wise to respond to fools in terms they can
understand (v. 5) and times when it is wiser not
to do so (25:4).

26:7–9—A proverb is useless *in the mouth of a
fool.*

26:13–16—Four ironic observations about those
who are *lazy*. Verse 15 almost duplicates 19:24.

26:17–26—Another listing of ways in which the
power of speech can be misused (see chaps 10,
15).

21 As charcoal is to hot embers and
        wood to fire,
        so is a quarrelsome person for
        kindling strife.
22 The words of a whisperer are like
        delicious morsels;
        they go down into the inner parts
        of the body.
23 Like the glaze[a] covering an earthen
        vessel
        are smooth[b] lips with an evil
        heart.
24 An enemy dissembles in speaking
        while harboring deceit within;
25 when an enemy speaks graciously,
        do not believe it,
        for there are seven abominations
        concealed within;
26 though hatred is covered with guile,
        the enemy's wickedness will be
        exposed in the assembly.
27 Whoever digs a pit will fall into it,
        and a stone will come back on the
        one who starts it rolling.
28 A lying tongue hates its victims,
        and a flattering mouth works ruin.

27 Do not boast about tomorrow,
        for you do not know what a day
        may bring.
2 Let another praise you, and not your
        own mouth—
        a stranger, and not your own lips.
3 A stone is heavy, and sand is
        weighty,
        but a fool's provocation is heavier
        than both.
4 Wrath is cruel, anger is
        overwhelming,
        but who is able to stand before
        jealousy?
5 Better is open rebuke
        than hidden love.
6 Well meant are the wounds a friend
        inflicts,

but profuse are the kisses of an
        enemy.
7 The sated appetite spurns honey,
        but to a ravenous appetite even the
        bitter is sweet.
8 Like a bird that strays from its nest
        is one who strays from home.
9 Perfume and incense make the heart
        glad,
        but the soul is torn by trouble.[c]
10 Do not forsake your friend or the
        friend of your parent;
        do not go to the house of your
        kindred in the day of your
        calamity.
        Better is a neighbor who is nearby
        than kindred who are far away.
11 Be wise, my child, and make my
        heart glad,
        so that I may answer whoever
        reproaches me.
12 The clever see danger and hide;
        but the simple go on, and suffer
        for it.
13 Take the garment of one who has
        given surety for a stranger;
        seize the pledge given as surety for
        foreigners.[d]
14 Whoever blesses a neighbor with a
        loud voice,
        rising early in the morning,
        will be counted as cursing.
15 A continual dripping on a rainy day
        and a contentious wife are alike;
16 to restrain her is to restrain the
        wind
        or to grasp oil in the right hand.[e]
17 Iron sharpens iron,
        and one person sharpens the wits[f]
        of another.
18 Anyone who tends a fig tree will eat
        its fruit,

a Cn: Heb *silver of dross*   *b* Gk: Heb *burning*   *c* Gk: Heb *the sweetness of a friend is better than one's own counsel*   *d* Vg and 20.16: Heb *for a foreign woman*   *e* Meaning of Heb uncertain   *f* Heb *face*

26:22—See note at the duplicate in 18:8.

26:27—Evil intentions trap the intender (also found in the Egyptian Instructions of Amen-emope).

27:5–6 *Hidden love*—Might have been better

translated "pretended love," so that v. 5 makes the same point as v. 6 (i.e., open rebuke = the well-intended criticism of a friend, is better than hidden/pretended love = the kisses of an enemy).

27:13—See note at the duplicate in 20:16.

and anyone who takes care of a
   master will be honored.
19 Just as water reflects the face,
   so one human heart reflects
      another.
20 Sheol and Abaddon are never
      satisfied,
   and human eyes are never
      satisfied.
21 The crucible is for silver, and the
      furnace is for gold,
   so a person is tested[a] by being
      praised.
22 Crush a fool in a mortar with a
      pestle
   along with crushed grain,
   but the folly will not be driven out.

23 Know well the condition of your
      flocks,
   and give attention to your herds;
24 for riches do not last forever,
   nor a crown for all generations.
25 When the grass is gone, and new
      growth appears,
   and the herbage of the mountains
      is gathered,
26 the lambs will provide your
      clothing,
   and the goats the price of a field;
27 there will be enough goats' milk for
      your food,
   for the food of your household
   and nourishment for your
      servant-girls.

28 The wicked flee when no one
      pursues,
   but the righteous are as bold as a
      lion.
2 When a land rebels
   it has many rulers;
   but with an intelligent ruler
   there is lasting order.[b]
3 A ruler[c] who oppresses the poor
   is a beating rain that leaves no
      food.
4 Those who forsake the law praise the
      wicked,

but those who keep the law
   struggle against them.
5 The evil do not understand justice,
   but those who seek the LORD
      understand it completely.
6 Better to be poor and walk in
      integrity
   than to be crooked in one's ways
      even though rich.
7 Those who keep the law are wise
      children,
   but companions of gluttons shame
      their parents.
8 One who augments wealth by
      exorbitant interest
   gathers it for another who is kind
      to the poor.
9 When one will not listen to the law,
   even one's prayers are an
      abomination.
10 Those who mislead the upright into
      evil ways
   will fall into pits of their own
      making,
   but the blameless will have a
      goodly inheritance.
11 The rich is wise in self-esteem,
   but an intelligent poor person sees
      through the pose.
12 When the righteous triumph, there
      is great glory,
   but when the wicked prevail,
      people go into hiding.
13 No one who conceals transgressions
      will prosper,
   but one who confesses and
      forsakes them will obtain
      mercy.
14 Happy is the one who is never
      without fear,
   but one who is hard-hearted will
      fall into calamity.
15 Like a roaring lion or a charging
      bear
   is a wicked ruler over a poor
      people.

a Heb lacks is tested   b Meaning of Heb uncertain   c Cn: Heb A poor person

---

27:20 *Sheol and Abaddon*—See note at 15:11.
28:6, 8, 11, 19, 20, 22, 24, 27—All make observations related to the *poor* and/or the *rich*. Compare v. 19 with 13:23.

¹⁶ A ruler who lacks understanding is a
   cruel oppressor;
   but one who hates unjust gain will
   enjoy a long life.
¹⁷ If someone is burdened with the
   blood of another,
   let that killer be a fugitive until
   death;
   let no one offer assistance.
¹⁸ One who walks in integrity will be
   safe,
   but whoever follows crooked ways
   will fall into the Pit.ᵃ
¹⁹ Anyone who tills the land will have
   plenty of bread,
   but one who follows worthless
   pursuits will have plenty of
   poverty.
²⁰ The faithful will abound with
   blessings,
   but one who is in a hurry to be
   rich will not go unpunished.
²¹ To show partiality is not good—
   yet for a piece of bread a person
   may do wrong.
²² The miser is in a hurry to get rich
   and does not know that loss is sure
   to come.
²³ Whoever rebukes a person will
   afterward find more favor
   than one who flatters with the
   tongue.
²⁴ Anyone who robs father or mother
   and says, "That is no crime,"
   is partner to a thug.
²⁵ The greedy person stirs up strife,
   but whoever trusts in the LORD
   will be enriched.
²⁶ Those who trust in their own wits
   are fools;
   but those who walk in wisdom
   come through safely.
²⁷ Whoever gives to the poor will lack
   nothing,
   but one who turns a blind eye will
   get many a curse.
²⁸ When the wicked prevail, people go
   into hiding;

but when they perish, the
   righteous increase.

29 One who is often reproved, yet
   remains stubborn,
   will suddenly be broken beyond
   healing.
² When the righteous are in authority,
   the people rejoice;
   but when the wicked rule, the
   people groan.
³ A child who loves wisdom makes a
   parent glad,
   but to keep company with
   prostitutes is to squander one's
   substance.
⁴ By justice a king gives stability to the
   land,
   but one who makes heavy
   exactions ruins it.
⁵ Whoever flatters a neighbor
   is spreading a net for the
   neighbor's feet.
⁶ In the transgression of the evil there
   is a snare,
   but the righteous sing and rejoice.
⁷ The righteous know the rights of the
   poor;
   the wicked have no such
   understanding.
⁸ Scoffers set a city aflame,
   but the wise turn away wrath.
⁹ If the wise go to law with fools,
   there is ranting and ridicule
   without relief.
¹⁰ The bloodthirsty hate the blameless,
   and they seek the life of the upright.
¹¹ A fool gives full vent to anger,
   but the wise quietly holds it back.
¹² If a ruler listens to falsehood,
   all his officials will be wicked.
¹³ The poor and the oppressor have
   this in common:
   the LORD gives light to the eyes of
   both.
¹⁴ If a king judges the poor with equity,
   his throne will be established
   forever.

ᵃ Syr: Heb *fall all at once*

29:1–27—Many of the sayings in this chapter are repetitions or variations of sayings found elsewhere.

and anyone who takes care of a
    master will be honored.
19 Just as water reflects the face,
    so one human heart reflects
    another.
20 Sheol and Abaddon are never
    satisfied,
    and human eyes are never
    satisfied.
21 The crucible is for silver, and the
    furnace is for gold,
    so a person is tested[a] by being
    praised.
22 Crush a fool in a mortar with a
    pestle
    along with crushed grain,
    but the folly will not be driven out.

23 Know well the condition of your
    flocks,
    and give attention to your herds;
24 for riches do not last forever,
    nor a crown for all generations.
25 When the grass is gone, and new
    growth appears,
    and the herbage of the mountains
    is gathered,
26 the lambs will provide your
    clothing,
    and the goats the price of a field;
27 there will be enough goats' milk for
    your food,
    for the food of your household
    and nourishment for your
    servant-girls.

28 The wicked flee when no one
    pursues,
    but the righteous are as bold as a
    lion.
2 When a land rebels
    it has many rulers;
    but with an intelligent ruler
    there is lasting order.[b]
3 A ruler[c] who oppresses the poor
    is a beating rain that leaves no
    food.
4 Those who forsake the law praise the
    wicked,

    but those who keep the law
    struggle against them.
5 The evil do not understand justice,
    but those who seek the LORD
    understand it completely.
6 Better to be poor and walk in
    integrity
    than to be crooked in one's ways
    even though rich.
7 Those who keep the law are wise
    children,
    but companions of gluttons shame
    their parents.
8 One who augments wealth by
    exorbitant interest
    gathers it for another who is kind
    to the poor.
9 When one will not listen to the law,
    even one's prayers are an
    abomination.
10 Those who mislead the upright into
    evil ways
    will fall into pits of their own
    making,
    but the blameless will have a
    goodly inheritance.
11 The rich is wise in self-esteem,
    but an intelligent poor person sees
    through the pose.
12 When the righteous triumph, there
    is great glory,
    but when the wicked prevail,
    people go into hiding.
13 No one who conceals transgressions
    will prosper,
    but one who confesses and
    forsakes them will obtain
    mercy.
14 Happy is the one who is never
    without fear,
    but one who is hard-hearted will
    fall into calamity.
15 Like a roaring lion or a charging
    bear
    is a wicked ruler over a poor
    people.

[a] Heb lacks *is tested*   [b] Meaning of Heb uncertain   [c] Cn: Heb *A poor person*

27:20 *Sheol and Abaddon*—See note at 15:11.
28:6, 8, 11, 19, 20, 22, 24, 27—All make observations related to the *poor* and/or the *rich*. Compare v. 19 with 13:23.

16 A ruler who lacks understanding is a
     cruel oppressor;
     but one who hates unjust gain will
       enjoy a long life.
17 If someone is burdened with the
     blood of another,
     let that killer be a fugitive until
       death;
     let no one offer assistance.
18 One who walks in integrity will be
     safe,
     but whoever follows crooked ways
       will fall into the Pit.*a*
19 Anyone who tills the land will have
     plenty of bread,
     but one who follows worthless
       pursuits will have plenty of
       poverty.
20 The faithful will abound with
     blessings,
     but one who is in a hurry to be
       rich will not go unpunished.
21 To show partiality is not good—
     yet for a piece of bread a person
       may do wrong.
22 The miser is in a hurry to get rich
     and does not know that loss is sure
       to come.
23 Whoever rebukes a person will
     afterward find more favor
     than one who flatters with the
       tongue.
24 Anyone who robs father or mother
     and says, "That is no crime,"
     is partner to a thug.
25 The greedy person stirs up strife,
     but whoever trusts in the Lord
       will be enriched.
26 Those who trust in their own wits
     are fools;
     but those who walk in wisdom
       come through safely.
27 Whoever gives to the poor will lack
     nothing,
     but one who turns a blind eye will
       get many a curse.
28 When the wicked prevail, people go
     into hiding;

     but when they perish, the
       righteous increase.

29 One who is often reproved, yet
     remains stubborn,
     will suddenly be broken beyond
       healing.
2 When the righteous are in authority,
     the people rejoice;
     but when the wicked rule, the
       people groan.
3 A child who loves wisdom makes a
     parent glad,
     but to keep company with
       prostitutes is to squander one's
       substance.
4 By justice a king gives stability to the
     land,
     but one who makes heavy
       exactions ruins it.
5 Whoever flatters a neighbor
     is spreading a net for the
       neighbor's feet.
6 In the transgression of the evil there
     is a snare,
     but the righteous sing and rejoice.
7 The righteous know the rights of the
     poor;
     the wicked have no such
       understanding.
8 Scoffers set a city aflame,
     but the wise turn away wrath.
9 If the wise go to law with fools,
     there is ranting and ridicule
       without relief.
10 The bloodthirsty hate the blameless,
     and they seek the life of the upright.
11 A fool gives full vent to anger,
     but the wise quietly holds it back.
12 If a ruler listens to falsehood,
     all his officials will be wicked.
13 The poor and the oppressor have
     this in common:
     the Lord gives light to the eyes of
       both.
14 If a king judges the poor with equity,
     his throne will be established
       forever.

a Syr: Heb *fall all at once*

29:1–27—Many of the sayings in this chapter are repetitions or variations of sayings found elsewhere.

put your hand on your mouth.
³³ For as pressing milk produces curds,
    and pressing the nose produces
        blood,
    so pressing anger produces strife.

The Teaching of King Lemuel's Mother

31 The words of King Lemuel. An oracle that his mother taught him:

² No, my son! No, son of my womb!
    No, son of my vows!
³ Do not give your strength to women,
    your ways to those who destroy
        kings.
⁴ It is not for kings, O Lemuel,
    it is not for kings to drink wine,
    or for rulers to desire^a strong
        drink;
⁵ or else they will drink and forget
        what has been decreed,
    and will pervert the rights of all
        the afflicted.
⁶ Give strong drink to one who is
        perishing,
    and wine to those in bitter distress;
⁷ let them drink and forget their
        poverty,
    and remember their misery no
        more.
⁸ Speak out for those who cannot
        speak,
    for the rights of all the destitute.^b
⁹ Speak out, judge righteously,

defend the rights of the poor and
    needy.

Ode to a Capable Wife

¹⁰ A capable wife who can find?
    She is far more precious than
        jewels.
¹¹ The heart of her husband trusts in
        her,
    and he will have no lack of gain.
¹² She does him good, and not harm,
    all the days of her life.
¹³ She seeks wool and flax,
    and works with willing hands.
¹⁴ She is like the ships of the merchant,
    she brings her food from far away.
¹⁵ She rises while it is still night
    and provides food for her
        household
    and tasks for her servant-girls.
¹⁶ She considers a field and buys it;
    with the fruit of her hands she
        plants a vineyard.
¹⁷ She girds herself with strength,
    and makes her arms strong.
¹⁸ She perceives that her merchandise
        is profitable.
    Her lamp does not go out at night.
¹⁹ She puts her hands to the distaff,
    and her hands hold the spindle.
²⁰ She opens her hand to the poor,
    and reaches out her hands to the
        needy.

^a Cn: Heb *where*   ^b Heb *all children of passing away*

31:1–31 Words of King Lemuel's Mother

31:1 *King Lemuel. An oracle.* Since no Israelite king was named Lemuel, the word translated "oracle" should be understood as Massa' (see note at 30:1), labeling what follows as "the words of King Lemuel of Massa' that his mother taught him."

31:2–9 No, My Son!

The queen mother warns her son to stay away from various forms of self-indulgence (such as women and alcoholic beverages) that might distract him from his primary duty to defend the rights of those who are otherwise without power or voice in society (vv. 8–9).

31:10–31 A Poem in Praise of Power Personified

Each verse in this closing poem begins with a new letter of the Hebrew alphabet, in alphabeti-

cal order. The word translated *capable* in v. 10 is translated *strength* in v. 3. When this word is used elsewhere in the Old Testament, it almost always means "strength" or "power" (referring either to physical strength, strength of character, or will power). If the poem is understood as a continuation of the queen mother's speech, it seems to describe the sort of strong woman Lemuel's mother wants her son to marry. If it is a new unit (an appendix to the whole book, rather than a part of the queen mother's instruction), the Strong Woman becomes one more personification of Wisdom (as in 1:20–33; 4:6–9; 8:1–36), seen this time as a wife who skillfully manages all her household and family affairs.

31:20—The Strong Woman does not let household affairs distract her from reaching out to help the *poor* and *needy*.

21 She is not afraid for her household
  when it snows,
    for all her household are clothed in
    crimson.
22 She makes herself coverings;
  her clothing is fine linen and
    purple.
23 Her husband is known in the city
  gates,
    taking his seat among the elders of
    the land.
24 She makes linen garments and sells
  them;
    she supplies the merchant with
    sashes.
25 Strength and dignity are her
  clothing,
    and she laughs at the time to
    come.
26 She opens her mouth with wisdom,

and the teaching of kindness is on
  her tongue.
27 She looks well to the ways of her
  household,
    and does not eat the bread of
    idleness.
28 Her children rise up and call her
  happy;
    her husband too, and he praises
    her:
29 "Many women have done excellently,
  but you surpass them all."
30 Charm is deceitful, and beauty is
  vain,
    but a woman who fears the LORD
    is to be praised.
31 Give her a share in the fruit of her
  hands,
    and let her works praise her in the
    city gates.

31:23 *City gates*—Where the political and judicial activities of the community take place. Marrying the Strong Woman will give a man resources and leisure enough to engage in such activities.

31:30—The book that began with the assertion that the "fear of the LORD is the beginning of knowledge" (1:7) ends with a hymn of praise for one whose behavior illustrates what wisdom and the fear of the Lord can do for those who espouse them.

31:31—While the tasks undertaken by this

female figure represent the wide range of things a woman might do in an Israelite household, clearly she is not a typical Israelite woman. Her extraordinary (rather than ordinary) efforts deserve both material rewards and praise. However, nothing indicates that she should be held up as a model for all women everywhere to follow. Jesus tells his disciples that a very small child (not someone able to do massive amounts of work) makes a better model for Christians, since the love and salvation we receive from God is unmerited (not earned by our own efforts).

The Book of
ECCLESIASTES

Tradition has long said that Solomon wrote this enigmatic book. After all, 1:1 states that these are "the words of the Teacher (*Qoheleth* in Hebrew), the son of David, king in Jerusalem." That same tradition fondly remembers Solomon as a man of extraordinary wisdom: see, for example, the comment made after Solomon's judgment concerning the two women and the baby (1 Kgs. 3:28): "All Israel heard of the judgment that the king had rendered; and they stood in awe of the king, because they perceived that the wisdom of God was in him, to execute justice." Several reasons speak against Solomonic authorship of this book, not the least of which is the existence of certain Persian words in the book (for example *pardes*, "park," 2:5—a Persian word which comes into English as "paradise"); this language was not available widely in the Middle East until some four centuries after the time of Solomon's reign. The author is then an unknown wise figure.

The date is very difficult to determine. Due to Persian influence, the earliest possible date would be sometime in the fifth century BCE, but dates as late as the third century have been suggested.

The Possible Meanings of the Book

The meaning and intent of this challenging book have long been the subject of debate. From its very earliest rabbinic evaluations, arguments erupted concerning the reason for its inclusion in the canon of Scripture at all. Any book that begins and ends with the startling claim that "all is emptiness [NRSV 'vanity']" (1:2 and 12:8) would appear to stand at odds with many of the Bible's greatest claims for the purposes of human creation and for the will of God for that creation.

The book has been interpreted in two general and quite distinct ways. First, many read it as a gloomy meditation on the emptiness of life, the lack of care from a distant God, and the inevitability of death that makes all human action finally meaningless. This reading recognizes the fact that Qoheleth does urge his readers to enjoy the life given to them by that distant God (e.g., 2:24–26), but the certainty of death for all, whether human or animal, whether wicked or righteous, undercuts the hope of life's enjoyment.

The second reading is nearly the opposite of the first. Here the passages where Qoheleth urges all to enjoy life (2:24–26; 3:12–13; 3:22; 5:17–19; 8:14–15; 9:7–10; 11:9–10) are made the center of the book's meaning. In the face of the realities of a tenuous and transitory human existence and a mysterious and basically unknowable God, the call to "eat and drink and find enjoyment in work" is seen as a positive possibility to "get on with it." *Carpe diem!* Seize the day! Rather than brood on life's inevitable end, its painfully obvious injustices, its basic incomprehensibility, one should focus on enjoyment of what one has been given. This reading should not be reduced to the maxim "Eat, drink and be merry, for tomorrow we die!" It does not call

us to hedonism but to honesty with ourselves and our world. Look at what you have, look at the world around you, and be grateful for the things you have been given. And enjoy them!

It may be possible to combine the best of these two readings to provide a fuller and richer portrait of what Qoheleth has to offer. His brooding commentary on life and God contains many insights and reflections that are painfully true and need to be recognized as such. His clear-eyed observations about the poor and the oppressed, and the lack of those who would comfort them (4:1), are stark testimony to an appalling reality of his age and our own. Yet nowhere does Qoheleth then urge his readers, or himself, to act on behalf of those oppressed ones. It is crucial, he says, to "tell it like it is," not to gloss over life's inequities and cruelties. But is that all there is? Can we only gaze out of our barred and locked windows at the pain of human life and say, "Tut-tut, how dreadful life can be"? The prophets of Israel—beginning with Nathan's sharp rebuke of King David's disgusting behavior (2 Sam. 12), and continuing with Elijah's unyielding rejection of Ahab's arranged murder of Naboth (1 Kgs. 21), Amos's and Hosea's assaults on the injustices of Israel, and Micah's and Isaiah's attacks on an equally unjust Judah—spent the bulk of their energy naming injustice, deploring injustice, and demanding that justice be served. Qoheleth is less than helpful when it comes to the biblical call for justice.

However, we can learn from him that constant backbreaking and mind-numbing labor can be less than fruitful. "All work and no play makes Sue a dull girl" all right, but it also can make Sue bitter, angry, and finally useless. Joy is a crucial part of life, and Qoheleth urges us to joy even in the midst of life's uncertainties and difficulties. Thus an honest appraisal of life, coupled with a full-blooded enjoyment of life, are what Qoheleth suggests.

However, this generally positive two-pronged reading of Qoheleth leads to many questions. Any reading of this brief book still may offer little in the way of traditional comfort. In between the author's opening and closing conviction that all is emptiness and "a herding of the wind" (NRSV "chasing after wind"), we find salient attacks on some of the dearest held certainties of biblical faith. Most notably we find the following:

1. *Creation is no sign of a good and munificent God* (so Gen. 1; Pss. 104, 121; and a host of other texts). Observation of nature leads Qoheleth to the belief that it is devoid of lasting meaning and merely reinforces his conviction that "all things are wearisome" (Eccl. 1:8). The psalmist may gaze longingly at the hills and find there initial evidence of a God who always helps (Ps. 121), but Qoheleth looks at sun, wind, and water and finds eternal sameness, a deadening weariness (Eccl. 1:4–8). Creation may be of God, and Qoheleth says that it is, but it is no sign of a God for us.

2. *Death undercuts all activity.* All work is finally meaningless, because it is transitory and has no long-term value. The fictional Solomon experiences all of life's supposed goods—wine, women, song, fame, power, wealth—but concludes, "Yet I perceived that the same fate befalls all of them. Then I said to myself, 'What happens to the fool will happen to me also; why then have I been so very wise?'" (2:14–15). And he decides that "this also is vanity." If a person works to accumulate great wealth, and finds some satisfaction in that work and accumulation, both the work and the wealth are rendered meaningless by the certain death of the worker and the possible passing of the wealth accumulated to a fool (2:20–21). Thus are wealth and work made empty by death.

3. *God and life's true meaning are finally unknowable.* The Wisdom writings of the Hebrew Bible, represented primarily by Job, Proverbs, certain Psalms, and Qoheleth, struggled with the knowledge of God. For much of Proverbs, God could be known both by right actions and by appropriate "fear." "The fear of God is the beginning of wisdom" is a hallmark phrase for the Wisdom writers. Qoheleth stands this idea on its head. Not only can God finally not be known, he says; what we apparently think we know of God is often dangerous knowledge. In fact, God appears to act with malevolence toward the creatures God made. For example, Qoheleth claims that God tests men and women to teach them that they are merely beasts (3:18), no better than animals. And after that familiar and beautiful poem announcing that there is an appropriate time for everything (3:1–8), Qoheleth concludes the poem by suggesting that God conceals any helpful knowledge of life's meaning, thereby making it impossible for human beings to understand or enjoy the gifts that God has supposedly given (3:11).

4. *The world is a crooked place.* As noted above, Qoheleth is quite clear that the world is filled with injustice and violence. Verses 3:16; 4:1; 5:8; 8:14 are the primary places where Qoheleth says that injustice is rampant in life. The implication is that this is the way God has made things; Qoheleth never denies the full sovereignty of God. However, in two places he hedges his bets concerning the origin of evil and injustice. At 5:8 he warns us not to be astonished when we witness oppression and injustice against the poor, because "the high official is watched by a higher, and there are yet higher ones over them." The assumption seems to be that oppression has as much a systemic, human cause as a divine one. This assumption is made clearer at 7:29 where we are told "God made human beings straightforward (the same adjective used to describe the righteous Job), but they have devised many schemes." Here again Qoheleth ascribes to human choice at least some of the world's ills.

Still, the overriding conviction that the world is a fixed place (see 3:1–8), and that human beings can have little effect on that unchanging world, presents a world far different from that of much of the Hebrew Bible. As noted above, the call to actions of justice is the central claim of vast portions of the scriptural text. That call is based on the belief that God is working for justice in the world and calls all to follow in that work, and that the world can in fact be changed for the good. Qoheleth denies both central beliefs. Social oppression is a fact, but the world does not operate according to any so-called divine will for justice. Moreover, human beings are not able to act in ways that can either confront evil or defeat it. Hence, Qoheleth speaks for the unchanging status quo; the world is corrupt, will always be corrupt, and cannot ever find justice. The search for the rule of God is useless, because God is not interested in the creation beyond a malicious tyrannical control. All we can do is enjoy what we have for the brief time we have it. If one has been blessed with many gifts, this status quo can be a very pleasant thing. But if one is found at the bottom of the social and economic ladder, the status quo is surely "emptiness and a herding of the wind" (NRSV "vanity and a chasing after wind").

What Can Biblical Disciples Learn in Dialogue with Qoheleth?

1. How one understands God is crucial when reflecting on human actions for justice. If God is as Qoheleth assumes—distant and sometimes cruel—actions on behalf of others have no basis in the work of God. I cannot sustain a life of service unless I have the conviction that God both calls me to that service and acts in the world with

me and for me and for others. Qoheleth's further belief that God is finally unknowable is deadly for my individual actions for justice. Qoheleth thus warns me that I need to work constantly on my view of God who both creates and sustains the universe.

2. Qoheleth's call for the enjoyment of work that has been given is an important reminder that without the experience of joy in my work, that work cannot be sustained. Work without joy is drudgery, however worthy or important the work is. At the same time, Qoheleth's claims that all work is transitory, with no lasting meaning or value, is a dangerous idea that can itself call work into question.

3. Despite what Qoheleth affirms, we can in fact achieve some measure of justice in our world. Acts of justice are not meaningless or foolish; righteous behavior is called for by God. Qoheleth's deep cynicism must be resisted by those who would follow the biblical way. Jews, Christians, and Muslims who have heard the call of God to act justly can never fall into cynicism, because they believe that God is certainly alive and active in the world, redeeming it and sustaining it for God's good purpose. Most especially Christians, who affirm that God is the God who brings forth life from death, must live their lives on the sure foundation of God's will for justice for all of God's creatures.

—John C. Holbert

Reflections of a Royal Philosopher

1 The words of the Teacher,[a] the son of David, king in Jerusalem.

2 Vanity of vanities, says the Teacher,[a]
   vanity of vanities! All is vanity.

3 What do people gain from all the toil
   at which they toil under the sun?

4 A generation goes, and a generation comes,
   but the earth remains forever.

5 The sun rises and the sun goes down,
   and hurries to the place where it rises.

6 The wind blows to the south,
   and goes around to the north;
   round and round goes the wind,
   and on its circuits the wind returns.

7 All streams run to the sea,
   but the sea is not full;
   to the place where the streams flow,
   there they continue to flow.

8 All things[b] are wearisome;
   more than one can express;
   the eye is not satisfied with seeing,
   or the ear filled with hearing.

9 What has been is what will be,
   and what has been done is what will be done;
   there is nothing new under the sun.

10 Is there a thing of which it is said,
   "See, this is new"?
   It has already been,
   in the ages before us.

11 The people of long ago are not remembered,
   nor will there be any remembrance
   of people yet to come
   by those who come after them.

[a] Heb Qoheleth, traditionally rendered Preacher [b] Or words

1:1 Teacher—The Heb. word, Qoheleth, is a feminine participle from the word qahal, "assembly." The implication may be that "Qoheleth" is some sort of leader of an assembly, a teacher or preacher (so Martin Luther's translation). The noun "Ecclesiastes" from the Greek translation of the word, follows a similar line of reasoning.

1:2 Vanity of vanities—"The most empty thing" (Heb. superlative), says Qoheleth. "The most empty thing! All is empty!" A one-word translation of the word "hebel" (NRSV **vanity**) is difficult. Included in the word are implications of meaninglessness, emptiness, absurdity, both in terms of what is expected and in terms of absolute mystery and ephemerality. The translation "empty" encompasses most of these possible implications. Perhaps the latter meaning of ephemerality, of that which passes quickly, should be emphasized.

The Futility of Seeking Wisdom

12 I, the Teacher,[a] when king over Israel in Jerusalem, [13] applied my mind to seek and to search out by wisdom all that is done under heaven; it is an unhappy business that God has given to human beings to be busy with. [14] I saw all the deeds that are done under the sun; and see, all is vanity and a chasing after wind.[b]

[15] What is crooked cannot be made
    straight,
  and what is lacking cannot be
    counted.

[16] I said to myself, "I have acquired great wisdom, surpassing all who were over Jerusalem before me; and my mind has had great experience of wisdom and knowledge." [17] And I applied my mind to know wisdom and to know madness and folly. I perceived that this also is but a chasing after wind.[b]

[18] For in much wisdom is much
    vexation,
  and those who increase knowledge
    increase sorrow.

The Futility of Self-Indulgence

2 I said to myself, "Come now, I will make a test of pleasure; enjoy yourself." But again, this also was vanity. [2] I said of laughter, "It is mad," and of pleasure, "What use is it?" [3] I searched with my mind how to cheer my body with wine—my mind still guiding me with wisdom—and how to lay hold on folly, until I might see what was good for mortals to do under heaven during the few days of their life. [4] I made great works; I built houses and planted vineyards for myself; [5] I made myself gardens and parks, and planted in them all kinds of fruit trees. [6] I made myself pools from which to water the forest of growing trees. [7] I bought male and female slaves, and had slaves who were born in my house; I also had great possessions of herds and flocks, more than any who had been before me in Jerusalem. [8] I also gathered for myself silver and gold and the treasure of kings and of the provinces; I got singers, both men and women, and delights of the flesh, and many concubines.[c]

9 So I became great and surpassed all who were before me in Jerusalem; also my wisdom remained with me. [10] Whatever my eyes desired I did not keep from them; I kept my heart from no pleasure, for my heart found pleasure in all my toil, and this was my reward for all my toil. [11] Then I considered all that my hands had done and the toil I had spent in doing it, and again, all was vanity and a chasing after wind,[b] and there was nothing to be gained under the sun.

Wisdom and Joy Given to One Who Pleases God

12 So I turned to consider wisdom and madness and folly; for what can the one do who comes after the king? Only what has already been done. [13] Then I saw that wisdom excels folly as light excels darkness.

[14] The wise have eyes in their head,
  but fools walk in darkness.

Yet I perceived that the same fate befalls all of them. [15] Then I said to myself, "What happens to the fool will happen to me also; why then have I been so very wise?" And I said to myself

[a] Heb Qoheleth, traditionally rendered Preacher [b] Or a feeding on wind. See Hos 12.1 [c] Meaning of Heb uncertain

---

1:14 A chasing after wind—The usual translations of "pursuing the wind" or "feeding on the wind" are both possible. But Hos. 12:1 (12:2 Heb.) suggests convincingly that "herding the wind" is better. Life, says Qoheleth is empty and transient; it is just like trying to herd the wind. Such an activity is absurd, pointless, fruitless, impossible.

2:14–17—Here is the basis for Qoheleth's untrammeled cynicism. After experiments with pleasure (vv. 1–3), fame (vv. 4–8), and wisdom (vv. 12–14), he finds no lasting value in anything, because the same fate befalls all of them. Those who have access to pleasure, fame, and wisdom end their lives in the same way as those who are denied or care nothing for any of those things: all die. How can the wise die just like fools? So I hated life.

that this also is vanity. [16] For there is no enduring remembrance of the wise or of fools, seeing that in the days to come all will have been long forgotten. How can the wise die just like fools? [17] So I hated life, because what is done under the sun was grievous to me; for all is vanity and a chasing after wind. [a]

[18] I hated all my toil in which I had toiled under the sun, seeing that I must leave it to those who come after me [19]—and who knows whether they will be wise or foolish? Yet they will be master of all for which I toiled and used my wisdom under the sun. This also is vanity. [20] So I turned and gave my heart up to despair concerning all the toil of my labors under the sun, [21] because sometimes one who has toiled with wisdom and knowledge and skill must leave all to be enjoyed by another who did not toil for it. This also is vanity and a great evil. [22] What do mortals get from all the toil and strain with which they toil under the sun? [23] For all their days are full of pain, and their work is a vexation; even at night their minds do not rest. This also is vanity.

[24] There is nothing better for mortals than to eat and drink, and find enjoyment in their toil. This also, I saw, is from the hand of God; [25] for apart from him [b] who can eat or who can have enjoyment? [26] For to the one who pleases him God gives wisdom and knowledge and joy; but to the sinner he gives the work of gathering and heaping, only to give to one who pleases God. This also is vanity and a chasing after wind. [a]

Everything Has Its Time

3 For everything there is a season, and a time for every matter under heaven:

[2] a time to be born, and a time to die;
   a time to plant, and a time to pluck up what is planted;
[3] a time to kill, and a time to heal;
   a time to break down, and a time to build up;
[4] a time to weep, and a time to laugh;
   a time to mourn, and a time to dance;
[5] a time to throw away stones, and a time to gather stones together;
   a time to embrace, and a time to refrain from embracing;
[6] a time to seek, and a time to lose;
   a time to keep, and a time to throw away;
[7] a time to tear, and a time to sew;
   a time to keep silence, and a time to speak;
[8] a time to love, and a time to hate;
   a time for war, and a time for peace.

The God-Given Task

[9] What gain have the workers from their toil? [10] I have seen the business

---

[a] Or *a feeding on wind.* See Hos 12.1   [b] Gk Syr: Heb *apart from me*

2:24–26—In the face of life's intractability, and the certainty of death, *there is nothing better for mortals than to eat and drink, and find enjoyment in their toil.* Yet even this positive claim is quickly undercut by the sheer randomness of the ways God apportions wisdom and ease to some and hard toil to others, the latter working only for the former. Thus even the enjoyment of some in their work is no guarantee that others will have access to that enjoyment. Thus "this also is emptiness, and a herding of the wind" (NRSV . . . "vanity and a chasing after wind").

3:1–8—Easily the most famous lines in the book, made so by popular song and public reading, both sacred and secular. Yet their meaning is far from clear. In lovely and stately poetry Qoheleth says that life has a rhythm within which there is

an appropriate time to perform all human action. Whether one hears this as a calming claim that one can count on life's enduring certainties, or as a damning claim that life is inexorably fixed and unchanging, will depend on how one hears the overall tenor of Qoheleth's ideas. The dependability of life's patterns can be a source of great comfort. But the unchangeable fixedness of life's patterns, which regularly and without fail provide killing and hate and death and sadness and loss, can be the source of deep pain and sorrow and fear.

3:9–11—An important section that sharpens Qoheleth's view of a mysterious God and human futility, and provides a kind of commentary on the famous poem that precedes it. *Gain*/profit (*yitron*)—This word is unique to Qoheleth. It

that God has given to everyone to be busy with. ¹¹ He has made everything suitable for its time; moreover he has put a sense of past and future into their minds, yet they cannot find out what God has done from the beginning to the end. ¹² I know that there is nothing better for them than to be happy and enjoy themselves as long as they live; ¹³ moreover, it is God's gift that all should eat and drink and take pleasure in all their toil. ¹⁴ I know that whatever God does endures forever; nothing can be added to it, nor anything taken from it; God has done this, so that all should stand in awe before him. ¹⁵ That which is, already has been; that which is to be, already is; and God seeks out what has gone by.ᵃ

Judgment and the Future Belong to God

16 Moreover I saw under the sun that in the place of justice, wickedness was there, and in the place of righteousness,

wickedness was there as well. ¹⁷ I said in my heart, God will judge the righteous and the wicked, for he has appointed a time for every matter, and for every work. ¹⁸ I said in my heart with regard to human beings that God is testing them to show that they are but animals. ¹⁹ For the fate of humans and the fate of animals is the same; as one dies, so dies the other. They all have the same breath, and humans have no advantage over the animals; for all is vanity. ²⁰ All go to one place; all are from the dust, and all turn to dust again. ²¹ Who knows whether the human spirit goes upward and the spirit of animals goes downward to the earth? ²² So I saw that there is nothing better than that all should enjoy their work, for that is their lot; who can bring them to see what will be after them?

4 Again I saw all the oppressions that are practiced under the sun. Look, the tears of the oppressed—with no one

ᵃ Heb *what is pursued*

---

might also be translated "advantage." A more colloquial reading is, "What good is it?" Why work at all? asks v. 9. *Business*/task/occupation (*'anyon*), again only found in Qoheleth (1:13; 2:23, 26; 3:10; 4:8; 5:13; 8:16). An English colloquial reading gets closer to the meaning. "To give someone the business" is to mess around with them, to play with their mind. That is the force of this word for Qoheleth. God is giving humanity "the business" by giving toil with no meaning, work without fruit. Eternity/*past and future* (NRSV)—The word *'olam* is much debated. In other places in the Heb. Bible the word denotes a past or future lengthy duration of time, perhaps without limits. The NRSV's translation attempts to capture that meaning. However the word itself is to be precisely understood, the more important point for Qoheleth is that God has put this sense of time into the minds of human beings in such a way that they *cannot find out what God has done from the beginning to the end*. In short, God teases humanity with just enough insight about divine activity to make them know that they are essentially ignorant of all that God is up to. This view of God as tease flies in the face of so much of the Bible that insists that God is "merciful and gracious . . . and abounding in steadfast love" (e.g., Exod. 34:6) for humanity and is urgently interested in humanity knowing and doing the divine will.

3:16–19—Qoheleth, like Job, admits that there

is the expectation of justice in the world, but the facts speak otherwise. Job's friends insist that God always punishes the wicked and rewards the righteous; for them the very universe itself is built on that belief. However, Job has no evidence of it. In fact, all evidence is to the contrary (Job 21). Qoheleth agrees with Job, but unlike Job he merely notes the fact of injustice. He does not demand that justice be done by the power of God or human beings. As he reflects on the fact of injustice, he generates two thoughts. First, he thinks to himself that God will take care of this problem of righteous and wicked, because *God will judge the righteous and the wicked, for he has appointed a time for every matter*. That sounds traditionally pious, but his second thought is that the whole notion of the confusion of righteous and wicked is just another way God has of testing humanity, proving to them that they are no more than beasts. For all die, beasts and human, and the latter have no advantage over the former. And he concludes, as always, "all is emptiness" (NRSV *vanity*). His distant view of God and his certainty of the unchanging nature of human society lead him to these dreadful conclusions.

4:1–3—Again Qoheleth observes the fact of oppression, and this time, perhaps more personally, he notes the tears of the oppressed. And he further sees that all power is on the side of the oppressor, so that the oppressed have no comforter at all. But rather than being led to demand justice

to comfort them! On the side of their oppressors there was power—with no one to comfort them. ²And I thought the dead, who have already died, more fortunate than the living, who are still alive; ³but better than both is the one who has not yet been, and has not seen the evil deeds that are done under the sun.

4 Then I saw that all toil and all skill in work come from one person's envy of another. This also is vanity and a chasing after wind.*a*

5   Fools fold their hands
    and consume their own flesh.
6   Better is a handful with quiet
    than two handfuls with toil,
    and a chasing after wind.*a*

7 Again, I saw vanity under the sun: ⁸the case of solitary individuals, without sons or brothers; yet there is no end to all their toil, and their eyes are never satisfied with riches. "For whom am I toiling," they ask, "and depriving myself of pleasure?" This also is vanity and an unhappy business.

The Value of a Friend

9 Two are better than one, because they have a good reward for their toil. ¹⁰For if they fall, one will lift up the other; but woe to one who is alone and falls and does not have another to help. ¹¹Again, if two lie together, they keep warm; but how can one keep warm alone? ¹²And though one might prevail against another, two will withstand one. A threefold cord is not quickly broken.

13 Better is a poor but wise youth than an old but foolish king, who will no longer take advice. ¹⁴One can indeed come out of prison to reign, even though born poor in the kingdom. ¹⁵I saw all the living who, moving about under the sun, follow that*b* youth who replaced the king;*c* ¹⁶there was no end to all those people whom he led. Yet those who come later will not rejoice in him. Surely this also is vanity and a chasing after wind.*a*

Reverence, Humility, and Contentment

5*d* Guard your steps when you go to the house of God; to draw near to listen is better than the sacrifice offered by fools; for they do not know how to keep from doing evil.*e* ²*f*Never be rash with your mouth, nor let your heart be quick to utter a word before God, for God is in heaven, and you upon earth; therefore let your words be few.

3 For dreams come with many cares, and a fool's voice with many words.

4 When you make a vow to God, do not delay fulfilling it; for he has no pleasure in fools. Fulfill what you vow. ⁵It is better that you should not vow than that you should vow and not fulfill it. ⁶Do not let your mouth lead you into sin, and do not say before the messenger that it was a mistake; why should God be angry at your words, and destroy the work of your hands?

7 With many dreams come vanities and a multitude of words;*g* but fear God.

8 If you see in a province the oppres-

---

a Or *a feeding on wind.* See Hos 12.1   *b* Heb *the second*   *c* Heb *him* *d* Ch 4.17 in Heb   *e* Cn: Heb *they do not know how to do evil*   *f* Ch 5.1 in Heb   *g* Meaning of Heb uncertain

---

from the oppressors or to offer any comfort to the comfortless oppressed, he merely broods that the dead are better off than the living, and better off than both are those who are not yet born! Contrast this section with Jer. 8:18–9:1, where, in the face of the oppressions practiced by his fellow Israelites against their own people, Jeremiah himself weeps on their behalf, mingling his tears of rage and pain with their own. One has a very hard time imagining any tears from Qoheleth!

5:1–2—Qoheleth urges caution in the face of the power of God. Because God is so far away and

so powerful, do not speak rashly to God or use many words to God. How different this advice is from the rash words of Abraham (Gen. 18), Moses (Exod. 32–34), and the prophets (Amos, Hosea, Micah, etc.), all of whose demands for justice to God are long, loud, and unending!

5:8—Here Qoheleth suggests a human cause for the evil he sees. He warns the reader not to be surprised to find **oppression of the poor** and **violation of justice and right**. After all, he says, hierarchical systems regularly engender such atrocities. **High officials** (literally "ones high") are

sion of the poor and the violation of justice and right, do not be amazed at the matter; for the high official is watched by a higher, and there are yet higher ones over them. 9 But all things considered, this is an advantage for a land: a king for a plowed field.*a*

10 The lover of money will not be satisfied with money; nor the lover of wealth, with gain. This also is vanity.

11 When goods increase, those who eat them increase; and what gain has their owner but to see them with his eyes?

12 Sweet is the sleep of laborers, whether they eat little or much; but the surfeit of the rich will not let them sleep.

13 There is a grievous ill that I have seen under the sun: riches were kept by their owners to their hurt, 14 and those riches were lost in a bad venture; though they are parents of children, they have nothing in their hands. 15 As they came from their mother's womb, so they shall go again, naked as they came; they shall take nothing for their toil, which they may carry away with their hands. 16 This also is a grievous ill: just as they came, so shall they go; and what gain do they have from toiling for the wind? 17 Besides, all their days they eat in darkness, in much vexation and sickness and resentment.

18 This is what I have seen to be good: it is fitting to eat and drink and find enjoyment in all the toil with which one toils under the sun the few days of the life God gives us; for this is our lot. 19 Likewise all to whom God gives

wealth and possessions and whom he enables to enjoy them, and to accept their lot and find enjoyment in their toil—this is the gift of God. 20 For they will scarcely brood over the days of their lives, because God keeps them occupied with the joy of their hearts.

The Frustration of Desires

6 There is an evil that I have seen under the sun, and it lies heavy upon humankind: 2 those to whom God gives wealth, possessions, and honor, so that they lack nothing of all that they desire, yet God does not enable them to enjoy these things, but a stranger enjoys them. This is vanity; it is a grievous ill. 3 A man may beget a hundred children, and live many years; but however many are the days of his years, if he does not enjoy life's good things, or has no burial, I say that a stillborn child is better off than he. 4 For it comes into vanity and goes into darkness, and in darkness its name is covered; 5 moreover it has not seen the sun or known anything; yet it finds rest rather than he. 6 Even though he should live a thousand years twice over, yet enjoy no good—do not all go to one place?

7 All human toil is for the mouth, yet the appetite is not satisfied. 8 For what advantage have the wise over fools? And what do the poor have who know how to conduct themselves before the living? 9 Better is the sight of the eyes than the wandering of desire; this also is vanity and a chasing after wind.*b*

---

a Meaning of Heb uncertain   *b* Or *a feeding on wind*. See Hos 12.1

---

guarded by ones **higher** who are in turn watched by **higher ones**. If leaders are always at work under the demanding gaze of greater leaders on up to the greatest leaders or leader, followers often are abused by those leaders who are ever "on the make" for higher authority and greater power. Unfortunately, v. 9, an apparent illustration or conclusion for this observation about systems, is impossible to translate.

5:13–17—Qoheleth observes the sad story of those who had riches, but lost them *in a bad venture*, thus having nothing to give to their chil-

dren. So the children came forth **naked** and died naked with nothing. This is **a grievous ill**, he says, since these sad children **eat in darkness . . . and sickness and resentment**.

6:1–2—Qoheleth recounts another sad scenario. God gives to some wealth, possessions, and honor, but does not allow them to enjoy any of these things. **This is vanity; it is a grievous ill**. Without enjoyment, there can be no real meaning, and since all die, ultimate meaning is finally impossible.

10 Whatever has come to be has already been named, and it is known what human beings are, and that they are not able to dispute with those who are stronger. 11 The more words, the more vanity, so how is one the better? 12 For who knows what is good for mortals while they live the few days of their vain life, which they pass like a shadow? For who can tell them what will be after them under the sun?

A Disillusioned View of Life

7 A good name is better than
     precious ointment,
   and the day of death, than the day
     of birth.
2 It is better to go to the house of
     mourning
   than to go to the house of feasting;
   for this is the end of everyone,
     and the living will lay it to heart.
3 Sorrow is better than laughter,
     for by sadness of countenance the
     heart is made glad.
4 The heart of the wise is in the house
     of mourning;
   but the heart of fools is in the
     house of mirth.
5 It is better to hear the rebuke of the
     wise
   than to hear the song of fools.
6 For like the crackling of thorns
     under a pot,
   so is the laughter of fools;
     this also is vanity.
7 Surely oppression makes the wise
     foolish,
   and a bribe corrupts the heart.
8 Better is the end of a thing than its
     beginning;
   the patient in spirit are better than
     the proud in spirit.
9 Do not be quick to anger,

for anger lodges in the bosom of
     fools.
10 Do not say, "Why were the former
     days better than these?"
   For it is not from wisdom that you
     ask this.
11 Wisdom is as good as an inheritance,
     an advantage to those who see the
     sun.
12 For the protection of wisdom is like
     the protection of money,
   and the advantage of knowledge
     is that wisdom gives life to the
     one who possesses it.
13 Consider the work of God;
   who can make straight what he has
     made crooked?
14 In the day of prosperity be joyful, and in the day of adversity consider; God has made the one as well as the other, so that mortals may not find out anything that will come after them.

The Riddles of Life

15 In my vain life I have seen everything; there are righteous people who perish in their righteousness, and there are wicked people who prolong their life in their evildoing. 16 Do not be too righteous, and do not act too wise; why should you destroy yourself? 17 Do not be too wicked, and do not be a fool; why should you die before your time? 18 It is good that you should take hold of the one, without letting go of the other; for the one who fears God shall succeed with both.

19 Wisdom gives strength to the wise more than ten rulers that are in a city.

20 Surely there is no one on earth so righteous as to do good without ever sinning.

21 Do not give heed to everything that people say, or you may hear your servant

---

7:10—Qoheleth warns those who imagine that there were some "good old days," *former days better* than the current ones. When one thinks like that, he says, *it is not from wisdom*. Life has never been better or worse than now, says Qoheleth. It is just life. Nostalgia is not helpful, because it is based on a lie.

7:14—Be happy while things are going well, he advises, and when things are not well, be reflective. Life has its inevitable ups and downs; God has made it so but in such a way that one cannot predict what the future holds. Live in the present, says Qoheleth; to think only of what is coming is both unproductive and useless.

cursing you; [22] your heart knows that many times you have yourself cursed others.

23 All this I have tested by wisdom; I said, "I will be wise," but it was far from me. [24] That which is, is far off, and deep, very deep; who can find it out? [25] I turned my mind to know and to search out and to seek wisdom and the sum of things, and to know that wickedness is folly and that foolishness is madness. [26] I found more bitter than death the woman who is a trap, whose heart is snares and nets, whose hands are fetters; one who pleases God escapes her, but the sinner is taken by her. [27] See, this is what I found, says the Teacher,[a] adding one thing to another to find the sum, [28] which my mind has sought repeatedly, but I have not found. One man among a thousand I found, but a woman among all these I have not found. [29] See, this alone I found, that God made human beings straightforward, but they have devised many schemes.

Obey the King and Enjoy Yourself

8 Who is like the wise man?
And who knows the interpretation of a thing?
Wisdom makes one's face shine,
and the hardness of one's
countenance is changed.

2 Keep[b] the king's command because of your sacred oath. [3] Do not be terrified; go from his presence, do not delay when the matter is unpleasant, for he does whatever he pleases. [4] For the word of the king is powerful, and who can say

to him, "What are you doing?" [5] Whoever obeys a command will meet no harm, and the wise mind will know the time and way. [6] For every matter has its time and way, although the troubles of mortals lie heavy upon them. [7] Indeed, they do not know what is to be, for who can tell them how it will be? [8] No one has power over the wind[c] to restrain the wind,[c] or power over the day of death; there is no discharge from the battle, nor does wickedness deliver those who practice it. [9] All this I observed, applying my mind to all that is done under the sun, while one person exercises authority over another to the other's hurt.

God's Ways Are Inscrutable

10 Then I saw the wicked buried; they used to go in and out of the holy place, and were praised in the city where they had done such things.[d] This also is vanity. [11] Because sentence against an evil deed is not executed speedily, the human heart is fully set to do evil. [12] Though sinners do evil a hundred times and prolong their lives, yet I know that it will be well with those who fear God, because they stand in fear before him, [13] but it will not be well with the wicked, neither will they prolong their days like a shadow, because they do not stand in fear before God.

14 There is a vanity that takes place on earth, that there are righteous people who are treated according to the conduct of the wicked, and there are wicked

---

[a] Qoheleth, traditionally rendered Preacher   [b] Heb I keep   [c] Or breath
[d] Meaning of Heb uncertain

8:14–15—Here Qoheleth directly connects his observations of injustice with his call for enjoyment of the work that God has given them. He first names the fact of wicked people being treated as though righteous and righteous people being treated as though wicked as "emptiness" (NRSV *vanity*). The meaning of the term in this place moves toward "absurdity." To punctuate just how absurd this reality is, he repeats the word at the end of the verse. As a result of this absurdity, Qoheleth says, *"I commend enjoyment"* (v. 15). The word translated "commends" is used by Qoheleth at 4:2, where he "com-

mends" the dead as superior to the living, since the world is so full of weeping oppressed. Here too, in the face of injustice, Qoheleth turns away (in horror or disgust or indifference?) from the fact of oppression. It appears that he simply cannot look too long at the world that he finds so utterly distasteful. In chap. 4 he quickly waxes philosophical about the living and the dead, while in chap. 8 he moves just as quickly toward the joys of pleasure, of eating and drinking. This pleasure, he avows, will *go with them . . . all the days of life God gives them under the sun*.

people who are treated according to the conduct of the righteous. I said that this also is vanity. [15] So I commend enjoyment, for there is nothing better for people under the sun than to eat, and drink, and enjoy themselves, for this will go with them in their toil through the days of life that God gives them under the sun.

[16] When I applied my mind to know wisdom, and to see the business that is done on earth, how one's eyes see sleep neither day nor night, [17] then I saw all the work of God, that no one can find out what is happening under the sun. However much they may toil in seeking, they will not find it out; even though those who are wise claim to know, they cannot find it out.

Take Life as It Comes

9 All this I laid to heart, examining it all, how the righteous and the wise and their deeds are in the hand of God; whether it is love or hate one does not know. Everything that confronts them [2] is vanity,*a* since the same fate comes to all, to the righteous and the wicked, to the good and the evil,*b* to the clean and the unclean, to those who sacrifice and those who do not sacrifice. As are the good, so are the sinners; those who swear are like those who shun an oath. [3] This is an evil in all that happens under the sun, that the same fate comes to everyone. Moreover, the hearts of all are full of evil; madness is in their hearts while they live, and after that they go to the dead. [4] But whoever is joined with all the living has hope, for a living dog is better than a dead lion. [5] The living know that they will die, but the dead know nothing; they have no more reward, and even the memory of them is lost. [6] Their love and their hate and their envy have already perished; never again will they have any share in all that happens under the sun.

[7] Go, eat your bread with enjoyment, and drink your wine with a merry heart; for God has long ago approved what you do. [8] Let your garments always be white; do not let oil be lacking on your head. [9] Enjoy life with the wife whom you love, all the days of your vain life that are given you under the sun, because that is your portion in life and in your toil at which you toil under the sun. [10] Whatever your hand finds to do, do with your might; for there is no work or thought or knowledge or wisdom in Sheol, to which you are going.

[11] Again I saw that under the sun the race is not to the swift, nor the battle to the strong, nor bread to the wise, nor riches to the intelligent, nor favor to the skillful; but time and chance happen to them all. [12] For no one can anticipate the time of disaster. Like fish taken in a cruel net, and like birds caught in a snare, so mortals are snared at a time of calamity, when it suddenly falls upon them.

Wisdom Superior to Folly

[13] I have also seen this example of wisdom under the sun, and it seemed great to me. [14] There was a little city with few people in it. A great king came against it and besieged it, building great siegeworks against it. [15] Now there was found in it a poor wise man, and he by his wisdom delivered the city. Yet no one remembered that poor man. [16] So I said, "Wisdom is better than might; yet the poor man's wisdom is despised, and his words are not heeded."
[17] The quiet words of the wise are more to be heeded

a Syr Compare Gk: Heb *Everything that confronts them* [2] *is everything*
b Gk Syr Vg: Heb lacks *and the evil*

9:4–6—The famous phrase *a living dog is better than a dead lion* is a good summary of much of Qoheleth's thought. If you are alive, there is hope. Even though the living know that they will die, the dead, even though they may once have been living lions, know nothing. There is no more reward for them, and the memory of them is very likely lost. Life is thus to be cherished and enjoyed while it is possible. Here Qoheleth moves a bit beyond a terrible cynicism to a call to live and enjoy.

than the shouting of a ruler among
fools.

18 Wisdom is better than weapons of
war,
but one bungler destroys much
good.

Miscellaneous Observations

10 Dead flies make the perfumer's
ointment give off a foul odor;
so a little folly outweighs wisdom
and honor.

2 The heart of the wise inclines to the
right,
but the heart of a fool to the left.

3 Even when fools walk on the road,
they lack sense,
and show to everyone that they are
fools.

4 If the anger of the ruler rises against
you, do not leave your post,
for calmness will undo great
offenses.

5 There is an evil that I have seen
under the sun, as great an error as if it
proceeded from the ruler: 6 folly is set in
many high places, and the rich sit in a
low place. 7 I have seen slaves on horseback, and princes walking on foot like
slaves.

8 Whoever digs a pit will fall into it;
and whoever breaks through a wall
will be bitten by a snake.

9 Whoever quarries stones will be hurt
by them;
and whoever splits logs will be
endangered by them.

10 If the iron is blunt, and one does not
whet the edge,
then more strength must be
exerted;
but wisdom helps one to succeed.

11 If the snake bites before it is
charmed,
there is no advantage in a
charmer.

12 Words spoken by the wise bring
them favor,
but the lips of fools consume them.

13 The words of their mouths begin in
foolishness,
and their talk ends in wicked
madness;

14 yet fools talk on and on.
No one knows what is to
happen,
and who can tell anyone what the
future holds?

15 The toil of fools wears them out,
for they do not even know the way
to town.

16 Alas for you, O land, when your king
is a servant,[a]
and your princes feast in the
morning!

17 Happy are you, O land, when your
king is a nobleman,
and your princes feast at the
proper time—
for strength, and not for
drunkenness!

18 Through sloth the roof sinks in,
and through indolence the house
leaks.

19 Feasts are made for laughter;
wine gladdens life,
and money meets every need.

20 Do not curse the king, even in your
thoughts,
or curse the rich, even in your
bedroom;
for a bird of the air may carry your
voice,
or some winged creature tell the
matter.

The Value of Diligence

11 Send out your bread upon the
waters,
for after many days you will get it
back.

2 Divide your means seven ways, or
even eight,
for you do not know what disaster
may happen on earth.

3 When clouds are full,
they empty rain on the earth;

a Or a child

whether a tree falls to the south or to
the north,
in the place where the tree falls,
there it will lie.
4 Whoever observes the wind will not
sow;
and whoever regards the clouds
will not reap.

5 Just as you do not know how the
breath comes to the bones in the mother's womb, so you do not know the work
of God, who makes everything.

6 In the morning sow your seed, and
at evening do not let your hands be idle;
for you do not know which will prosper,
this or that, or whether both alike will
be good.

Youth and Old Age

7 Light is sweet, and it is pleasant for
the eyes to see the sun.

8 Even those who live many years
should rejoice in them all; yet let them
remember that the days of darkness will
be many. All that comes is vanity.

9 Rejoice, young man, while you are
young, and let your heart cheer you in the
days of your youth. Follow the inclination of your heart and the desire of your
eyes, but know that for all these things
God will bring you into judgment.

10 Banish anxiety from your mind,
and put away pain from your body; for
youth and the dawn of life are vanity.

12 Remember your creator in the
days of your youth, before the
days of trouble come, and the years
draw near when you will say, "I have no
pleasure in them"; 2 before the sun and
the light and the moon and the stars are
darkened and the clouds return with[a]
the rain; 3 in the day when the guards of
the house tremble, and the strong men
are bent, and the women who grind
cease working because they are few, and
those who look through the windows see
dimly; 4 when the doors on the street are
shut, and the sound of the grinding is low,
and one rises up at the sound of a bird,
and all the daughters of song are brought
low; 5 when one is afraid of heights, and
terrors are in the road; the almond tree
blossoms, the grasshopper drags itself
along[b] and desire fails; because all must
go to their eternal home, and the mourners will go about the streets; 6 before the
silver cord is snapped,[c] and the golden
bowl is broken, and the pitcher is broken
at the fountain, and the wheel broken at
the cistern, 7 and the dust returns to the
earth as it was, and the breath[d] returns
to God who gave it. 8 Vanity of vanities,
says the Teacher;[e] all is vanity.

Epilogue

9 Besides being wise, the Teacher[e] also
taught the people knowledge, weigh-

[a] Or after; Heb 'ahar [b] Or is a burden [c] Syr Vg Compare Gk: Heb
is removed [d] Or the spirit [e] Qoheleth, traditionally rendered Preacher

---

12:1–7—Qoheleth's long musings are brought to
a close with the remarkable series of metaphors
found in chap. 12. These verses have often been
called the allegory of old age, but, as often with
supposed allegories, agreement on just what
each part of the allegory means has proven difficult. Rather than try to fix the meaning of each
suggestive metaphor, it is better to conclude that
the section is Qoheleth's final meditation on the
end of all human lives, an ending that leads to
the unchanging chaos that characterizes that life
always. A helpful comparison is Jer. 4:23–26,
where the prophet envisions a terrible return of
the world to the chaos of its beginnings in Gen.
1, due to the injustice he has seen in Israel. However, Qoheleth hardly connects this persistent
chaos to injustice; for him injustice is itself part of
the chaos of life at all times and places. Qohe-

leth's metaphors of a darkened sun, moon, and
stars (the order of their creation in Gen.1:14–16),
strong men bent over in age, weak-eyed women
who can no longer see to work, closed doors,
silent birds, the end of desire, mourners filling
the streets, a snapped silver cord, a broken bowl,
and pitcher, and wheel, and finally dust returning to the earth as it was, with the breath going
back to God, all speak of an end in whimpering
silence, rather than the bang of loud apocalypse.
And after all these ruminations, Qoheleth can
only conclude with his theme song: "Completely
empty; all is empty!" (NRSV *vanity of vanities
. . . all is vanity*). And we can only imagine that
Qoheleth would include all he has said himself
under the rubric of emptiness too.

12:9–14—It has been nearly universally claimed
that these last verses are a late addition to

ing and studying and arranging many proverbs. [10] The Teacher[a] sought to find pleasing words, and he wrote words of truth plainly.

11 The sayings of the wise are like goads, and like nails firmly fixed are the collected sayings that are given by one shepherd.[b] [12] Of anything beyond these, my child, beware. Of making many books there is no end, and much study is a weariness of the flesh.

13 The end of the matter; all has been heard. Fear God, and keep his commandments; for that is the whole duty of everyone. [14] For God will bring every deed into judgment, including[c] every secret thing, whether good or evil.

[a] *Qoheleth*, traditionally rendered *Preacher*   [b] Meaning of Heb uncertain   [c] *Or into the judgment on*

Qoheleth's words, designed somehow to get the old boy into a more traditional place. We are surely shocked to be told that Qoheleth *sought to find pleasing (!) words*, though we can agree that *he wrote words of truth plainly*, at least truth as he saw it. When this pious commentator concludes *all has been heard. Fear God, and keep his commandments, for that is the whole duty of everyone* (v. 13), we can hear Qoheleth offstage chortling with sardonic glee. If *that* is what this writer has heard Qoheleth say, then he has not heard him at all. Or perhaps he desperately wants Qoheleth's readers to hear these pious phrases, lest they finally believe what the old blasphemer has in fact tried to say!

Still, it is important to recognize that Qoheleth is far from consistent in his ruminations about life. There is cynicism to be sure, but there are also calls to enjoy life and to treasure living while there is time. He turns a hard glare on the world he knows, and would have us do the same, but life is not in itself evil. It is just life. Live it while you can! We cannot build our lives on Qoheleth's thoughts alone, but we avoid his words to our great peril.

THE SONG OF SOLOMON

The Book of

This collection of love songs can be read as a series of dramatic dialogues. In Hebrew the reader can discern at least four voices speaking in the book: an unnamed woman's voice, an unnamed man's voice, and two (or more) group voices. The group voice in 5:9; 6:1; and 8:5 may be the "daughters of Jerusalem" to whom the woman speaks in 2:7; 3:5, 10, 11; 5:8, 16; 8:4, but the speakers in 6:13 and 8:8–9 seem to be male. Most readers assume that the characters remain consistent throughout the book. However, if there is a story line or "plot" that links the various dialogues together, it is a very loosely knitted one.

The Hebrew name for the book is Song of Songs, meaning the greatest of all songs. Calling it The Song of Solomon links it to someone who represents the epitome of wisdom, wealth, power, and sexuality. However, Solomon himself does not have a speaking part in the text and most scholars think the finished form of the book comes from the postexilic period (i.e., at least 400 years after the time of Solomon).

The songs assume a rural, pastoral economy and a social setting in which an unmarried woman belongs to her mother's household. On two occasions the woman dreams of bringing her beloved home to her mother's house (3:4; 8:2), and she refers to her brothers as "my mother's sons" (1:6). The word "mother" appears seven times in these eight chapters (1:6, 3:4, 11; 6:9; 8:1, 2, 5), but the word "father" is never used.

Traditional Jewish and Christian interpreters have tried to understand this collection of songs as an allegory of God's love for the people of God. Modern interpreters recognize the speakers' own preoccupation with human forms of love *before* concluding that human sexual love can have something to tell us about the nature of divine love. That which is visible (human love) takes its ideal character or shape from that which is invisible (divine love).

—**Kathleen Farmer**

1 The Song of Songs, which is Solomon's.

Colloquy of Bride and Friends

² Let him kiss me with the kisses of his
      mouth!
   For your love is better than wine,
³   your anointing oils are fragrant,
   your name is perfume poured out;
      therefore the maidens love you.
⁴ Draw me after you, let us make
      haste.
   The king has brought me into his
      chambers.
   We will exult and rejoice in you;

1:1 The Title of the Collection

1:2–6 The Opening Song

An unidentified woman is the central character, the chief speaker, and the initiator of most of the action in the book. Here she speaks *about* a man (vv. 2a and 4b); *to* a man (vv. 2b–4a, 7); *to* a group of women called the **daughters of Jerusalem** (v. 5), who may also be the **maidens** who **rightly** admire this man (vv. 3–4); and *to* a group of men (v. 6).

we will extol your love more than
    wine;
  rightly do they love you.
5 I am black and beautiful,
    O daughters of Jerusalem,
  like the tents of Kedar,
  like the curtains of Solomon.
6 Do not gaze at me because I am
    dark,
    because the sun has gazed
      on me.
  My mother's sons were angry
    with me;
    they made me keeper of the
      vineyards,
  but my own vineyard I have not
    kept!
7 Tell me, you whom my soul
    loves,
    where you pasture your
      flock,
  where you make it lie down at
    noon;
  for why should I be like one who is
    veiled
  beside the flocks of your
    companions?
8 If you do not know,
    O fairest among women,
  follow the tracks of the flock,
    and pasture your kids
  beside the shepherds' tents.

Colloquy of Bridegroom, Friends, and Bride

9 I compare you, my love,
    to a mare among Pharaoh's
      chariots.
10 Your cheeks are comely with
    ornaments,
    your neck with strings of jewels.
11 We will make you ornaments of gold,
    studded with silver.

12 While the king was on his couch,
    my nard gave forth its fragrance.
13 My beloved is to me a bag of myrrh
    that lies between my breasts.
14 My beloved is to me a cluster of
    henna blossoms
    in the vineyards of En-gedi.

15 Ah, you are beautiful, my love;
    ah, you are beautiful;
    your eyes are doves.
16 Ah, you are beautiful, my beloved,
    truly lovely.
  Our couch is green;
17   the beams of our house are cedar,
    our rafters[a] are pine.

2 I am a rose[b] of Sharon,
  a lily of the valleys.

2 As a lily among brambles,
  so is my love among maidens.

[a] Meaning of Heb uncertain [b] Heb crocus

1:5 Black and beautiful—She is proud (not apologetic) about her sun-darkened skin. Her skin tone reflects her independent spirit: she has not hidden herself away from the sun as her brothers wished her to do.

1:6 My own vineyard—Throughout the book, "vine," "vineyard," and "garden" are used in both the literal sense and as metaphors for sexual experience. This metaphorical usage is easiest to see in the passage that begins *A garden locked is my sister, my bride* (4:12). When the woman subsequently invites the man to *come to his garden, and eat of its choicest fruits* (4:16), it is clear that this statement has sexual overtones. Once this link between the garden and sexual activity is made clear, the woman's statement that her brothers put her to work as *keeper of the vineyards*, but *my own vineyard I have not kept* (1:6), sounds like a reference to the loss of her virginity.

1:7–2:2 A Dialogue (Duet?) between Lovers
The woman speaks in 1:7, 12–14, 16; 2:1, and the man answers in 1:8–11, 15; 2:2. However, 1:17 could be said by either or by both in unison. The vocabulary of love is more varied in the Hebrew text than in the English. In this translation, the woman will refer to the man as *my beloved* (Heb. *dodi*) (1:13–14) and the man will refer to her as *my love* (Heb. *ra'yati*) (1:9, 15; 2:2). The root of *dodi* seems to connote kinship ties, while *ra'yati* has overtones of friendship or companionship. In 1:2, 4 the noun "love" (meaning the emotion, not the person loved) is from the same root as *dodi*. However, the verb that is translated "love" in 1:3, 4, 7 and the noun that is translated "love" in 2:4, 5, 7 all come from the Heb. root *'ahab* (a generic term with as wide a range of meaning as the English word "love").

3 As an apple tree among the trees of
    the wood,
  so is my beloved among young
    men.
  With great delight I sat in his
    shadow,
  and his fruit was sweet to my taste.
4 He brought me to the banqueting
    house,
  and his intention toward me was
    love.
5 Sustain me with raisins,
  refresh me with apples;
  for I am faint with love.
6 O that his left hand were under my
    head,
  and that his right hand
    embraced me!
7 I adjure you, O daughters of
    Jerusalem,
  by the gazelles or the wild does:
  do not stir up or awaken love
    until it is ready!

Springtime Rhapsody

8 The voice of my beloved!
    Look, he comes,
  leaping upon the mountains,
    bounding over the hills.
9 My beloved is like a gazelle
    or a young stag.
  Look, there he stands
    behind our wall,
  gazing in at the windows,
    looking through the lattice.
10 My beloved speaks and says to me:
  "Arise, my love, my fair one,
    and come away;
11 for now the winter is past,
    the rain is over and gone.

12 The flowers appear on the earth;
    the time of singing has come,
  and the voice of the turtledove
    is heard in our land.
13 The fig tree puts forth its figs,
    and the vines are in blossom;
    they give forth fragrance.
  Arise, my love, my fair one,
    and come away.
14 O my dove, in the clefts of the rock,
    in the covert of the cliff,
  let me see your face,
    let me hear your voice;
  for your voice is sweet,
    and your face is lovely.
15 Catch us the foxes,
    the little foxes,
  that ruin the vineyards—
    for our vineyards are in blossom."

16 My beloved is mine and I am his;
    he pastures his flock among the
    lilies.
17 Until the day breathes
    and the shadows flee,
  turn, my beloved, be like a gazelle
    or a young stag on the cleft
    mountains.*a*

Love's Dream

3 Upon my bed at night
    I sought him whom my soul loves;
  I sought him, but found him not;
    I called him, but he gave no
    answer.*b*
2 "I will rise now and go about the
    city,
    in the streets and in the squares;

a Or *on the mountains of Bether*; meaning of Heb uncertain   *b* Gk: Heb
lacks this line

2:3–3:5 Love Longing for Fulfillment

The woman tells her female companions that loving and knowing she is loved (2:16a) generates a
yearning for continuing intimacy.

2:3–7—As she remembers a previous occasion
when they were together, the woman longs for
her absent lover. The pain of separation seems to
elicit the advice she gives to her companions not
to *stir up love* until it can be consummated (2:7,
repeated in 3:5 and 8:4).

2:8–15—In her lover's absence she imagines a

scene in which he comes calling on her (vv. 8–9),
and quotes what he would say if he were there,
urging her to *come away* with him (vv. 10–15).

2:16–3:5—While she confidently affirms the
mutuality of their love (2:16), she is plagued by
what modern people might call anxiety dreams
(3:1–5). She has searched in her sleep for her
missing lover, sometimes in vain (3:1–3) and
sometimes successfully (3:4). Such unfulfilled
yearning is painful, leading her to repeat in 3:5
the advice she gave in 2:7.

I will seek him whom my soul loves."
    I sought him, but found him not.
3 The sentinels found me,
    as they went about in the city.
"Have you seen him whom my soul
      loves?"
4 Scarcely had I passed them,
    when I found him whom my soul
      loves.
I held him, and would not let
      him go
until I brought him into my
      mother's house,
and into the chamber of her that
      conceived me.
5 I adjure you, O daughters of
      Jerusalem,
    by the gazelles or the wild does:
do not stir up or awaken love
    until it is ready!

The Groom and His Party Approach

6 What is that coming up from the
      wilderness,
    like a column of smoke,
perfumed with myrrh and
      frankincense,
    with all the fragrant powders of
      the merchant?
7 Look, it is the litter of Solomon!
Around it are sixty mighty men
    of the mighty men of Israel,
8 all equipped with swords
    and expert in war,
each with his sword at his thigh
    because of alarms by night.
9 King Solomon made himself a
      palanquin
    from the wood of Lebanon.
10 He made its posts of silver,
    its back of gold, its seat of purple;
its interior was inlaid with love.ᵃ

Daughters of Jerusalem,
11   come out.
Look, O daughters of Zion,
    at King Solomon,
at the crown with which his mother
      crowned him
on the day of his wedding,
on the day of the gladness of his
      heart.

The Bride's Beauty Extolled

4 How beautiful you are, my love,
    how very beautiful!
Your eyes are doves
    behind your veil.
Your hair is like a flock of goats,
    moving down the slopes of Gilead.
2 Your teeth are like a flock of shorn
      ewes
    that have come up from the
      washing,
all of which bear twins,
    and not one among them is
      bereaved.
3 Your lips are like a crimson thread,
    and your mouth is lovely.
Your cheeks are like halves of a
      pomegranate
    behind your veil.
4 Your neck is like the tower of David,
    built in courses;
on it hang a thousand bucklers,
    all of them shields of warriors.
5 Your two breasts are like two fawns,
    twins of a gazelle,
    that feed among the lilies.
6 Until the day breathes
    and the shadows flee,
I will hasten to the mountain of
      myrrh
    and the hill of frankincense.

ᵃ Meaning of Heb uncertain

3:6–11 A Wedding Fit for a King

An unidentifiable speaker or a group of speakers describes a wedding procession elaborate enough to have been Solomon's own.

4:1–5:1 The Man's Song of Praise

Except for the woman's brief response in 4:16, this entire section is the man's song *to* and *about* his loved one, whom he calls *my sister, my*

bride. "Sister," used in conjunction with "bride" (as in 4:9, 10, 12; 5:1, 2), should be understood as an endearment (a "pet name") not as a reference to their biological relationship. While the metaphors used to describe her beauty may seem strange to modern readers, there is no doubt they were meant to be highly complimentary. Several are used again in a different song (4:1 = 6:5; 4:2 = 6:6; 4:3 = 6:7; 4:5 = 7:3).

7 You are altogether beautiful, my
        love;
    there is no flaw in you.
8 Come with me from Lebanon, my
        bride;
    come with me from Lebanon.
    Depart*a* from the peak of Amana,
        from the peak of Senir and
            Hermon,
    from the dens of lions,
        from the mountains of leopards.

9 You have ravished my heart, my
        sister, my bride,
    you have ravished my heart with a
        glance of your eyes,
    with one jewel of your necklace.
10 How sweet is your love, my sister,
        my bride!
    how much better is your love than
        wine,
    and the fragrance of your oils than
        any spice!
11 Your lips distill nectar, my bride;
    honey and milk are under your
        tongue;
    the scent of your garments is like
        the scent of Lebanon.
12 A garden locked is my sister, my
        bride,
    a garden locked, a fountain sealed.
13 Your channel*b* is an orchard of
        pomegranates
    with all choicest fruits,
        henna with nard,
14 nard and saffron, calamus and
        cinnamon,
    with all trees of frankincense,
    myrrh and aloes,
        with all chief spices—

15 a garden fountain, a well of living
        water,
    and flowing streams from
        Lebanon.

16 Awake, O north wind,
    and come, O south wind!
    Blow upon my garden
        that its fragrance may be wafted
            abroad.
    Let my beloved come to his garden,
        and eat its choicest fruits.

5 I come to my garden, my sister, my
        bride;
    I gather my myrrh with my spice,
    I eat my honeycomb with my
        honey,
    I drink my wine with my milk.

    Eat, friends, drink,
        and be drunk with love.

Another Dream

2 I slept, but my heart was awake.
    Listen! my beloved is knocking.
    "Open to me, my sister, my love,
        my dove, my perfect one;
    for my head is wet with dew,
        my locks with the drops of the
            night."
3 I had put off my garment;
        how could I put it on again?
    I had bathed my feet;
        how could I soil them?
4 My beloved thrust his hand into the
        opening,
    and my inmost being yearned for
        him.
5 I arose to open to my beloved,

---

a Or *Look*   *b* Meaning of Heb uncertain

4:12–5:1 Garden—See note at 1:6. According
to the first garden story, the loving relationship
God had intended to exist between a man and
a woman went astray as a result of human sin
(Gen. 2–3). The garden in the Song of Solomon
offers an alternate model of human love and
sexual intimacy maintained as God originally
intended them to be.

5:2–7 An Erotic Dream
The woman describes how her yearning for
intimacy took on the dream form of a suggestive encounter with her lover (vv. 2–5), who
vanished (as dream lovers often do) into thin air
(v. 6). She then dreamt that she pursued him and
was stripped and beaten by the sentinels making
their rounds of the city walls (v. 7). Other biblical
texts recognize that a yearning for intimacy with
another human being is built into the reality of
the human condition (Gen. 2:21–24). But the
Song acknowledges that such intimacy is not easily achieved. Love often seems to be an elusive
dream and the pursuit of love is fraught with
anxiety.

and my hands dripped with myrrh,
my fingers with liquid myrrh,
  upon the handles of the bolt.
6 I opened to my beloved,
  but my beloved had turned and
     was gone.
My soul failed me when he spoke.
I sought him, but did not find him;
  I called him, but he gave no
     answer.
7 Making their rounds in the city
  the sentinels found me;
they beat me, they wounded me,
  they took away my mantle,
    those sentinels of the walls.
8 I adjure you, O daughters of
    Jerusalem,
  if you find my beloved,
tell him this:
  I am faint with love.

Colloquy of Friends and Bride

9 What is your beloved more than
    another beloved,
  O fairest among women?
What is your beloved more than
    another beloved,
  that you thus adjure us?

10 My beloved is all radiant and ruddy,
    distinguished among ten
     thousand.
11 His head is the finest gold;
  his locks are wavy,
    black as a raven.
12 His eyes are like doves
  beside springs of water,
bathed in milk,
  fitly set.a
13 His cheeks are like beds of spices,
  yielding fragrance.
His lips are lilies,
  distilling liquid myrrh.
14 His arms are rounded gold,

set with jewels.
His body is ivory work,a
  encrusted with sapphires.b
15 His legs are alabaster columns,
  set upon bases of gold.
His appearance is like Lebanon,
  choice as the cedars.
16 His speech is most sweet,
  and he is altogether desirable.
This is my beloved and this is my
    friend,
  O daughters of Jerusalem.

6 Where has your beloved gone,
  O fairest among women?
Which way has your beloved turned,
  that we may seek him with you?

2 My beloved has gone down to his
    garden,
  to the beds of spices,
to pasture his flock in the gardens,
  and to gather lilies.
3 I am my beloved's and my beloved is
    mine;
  he pastures his flock among the
    lilies.

The Bride's Matchless Beauty

4 You are beautiful as Tirzah, my love,
  comely as Jerusalem,
    terrible as an army with banners.
5 Turn away your eyes from me,
  for they overwhelm me!
Your hair is like a flock of goats,
  moving down the slopes of
    Gilead.
6 Your teeth are like a flock of ewes,
  that have come up from the
    washing;
all of them bear twins,
  and not one among them is
    bereaved.

a Meaning of Heb uncertain   b Heb lapis lazuli

5:8–6:3 The Woman and Her Friends

The woman asks her female companions to carry a message to her beloved (5:8); they ask her to describe how he is different from any other man (5:9) and where they should look for him (6:1). She describes him at some length (5:10–16) and directs their search in metaphorical terms (6:2–3).

6:4–10 She Is "Terribly Beautiful"

The man describes the overwhelming effect his loved one's beauty has on him (vv. 4–7) and claims that numerous **maidens**, **queens**, and **concubines** (whose identity is unknown to us) are similarly impressed (vv. 8–10) by her appearance.

7 Your cheeks are like halves of a
   pomegranate
   behind your veil.
8 There are sixty queens and eighty
   concubines,
   and maidens without number.
9 My dove, my perfect one, is the only
   one,
   the darling of her mother,
   flawless to her that bore her.
The maidens saw her and called her
   happy;
   the queens and concubines also,
   and they praised her.
10 "Who is this that looks forth like the
   dawn,
   fair as the moon, bright as the sun,
   terrible as an army with banners?"

11 I went down to the nut orchard,
   to look at the blossoms of the
   valley,
   to see whether the vines had budded,
   whether the pomegranates were in
   bloom.
12 Before I was aware, my fancy set me
   in a chariot beside my prince.[a]

13[b] Return, return, O Shulammite!
   Return, return, that we may look
   upon you.

Why should you look upon the
   Shulammite,
   as upon a dance before two
   armies?[c]

Expressions of Praise

7 How graceful are your feet in
   sandals,
   O queenly maiden!

Your rounded thighs are like jewels,
   the work of a master hand.
2 Your navel is a rounded bowl
   that never lacks mixed wine.
Your belly is a heap of wheat,
   encircled with lilies.
3 Your two breasts are like two fawns,
   twins of a gazelle.
4 Your neck is like an ivory tower.
Your eyes are pools in Heshbon,
   by the gate of Bath-rabbim.
Your nose is like a tower of Lebanon,
   overlooking Damascus.
5 Your head crowns you like Carmel,
   and your flowing locks are like
   purple;
   a king is held captive in the tresses.[a]

6 How fair and pleasant you are,
   O loved one, delectable maiden![d]
7 You are stately[e] as a palm tree,
   and your breasts are like its
   clusters.
8 I say I will climb the palm tree
   and lay hold of its branches.
O may your breasts be like clusters
   of the vine,
   and the scent of your breath like
   apples,
9 and your kisses[f] like the best wine
   that goes down[g] smoothly,
   gliding over lips and teeth.[h]

10 I am my beloved's,
   and his desire is for me.
11 Come, my beloved,
   let us go forth into the fields,

---

[a] Cn: Meaning of Heb uncertain   [b] Ch 7.1 in Heb   [c] Or dance of Mahanaim   [d] Syr: Heb in delights   [e] Heb This your stature is   [f] Heb palate   [g] Heb down for my lover   [h] Gk Syr Vg: Heb lips of sleepers

---

6:11–12 In the Orchard
The woman's springtime visit to check on the budding crops turns into an imagined chariot ride with her beloved.

6:13–7:9 Praise for the Loved One
The Heb. text counts 6:13 as the first verse in chap. 7. A group voice (perhaps the man's companions) calls for the woman's return from the orchards (6:13a). The man responds to them in a challenging manner (6:13b) and then proceeds to describe his loved one's charms in graphic and suggestive terms (7:1–9). **Shulammite** seems to

be used as a title rather than a proper name, but the meaning of the term is unknown. It might suggest she is a feminine version of Solomon (or Solomon-like in some way).

7:10–8:4 Wishful Thinking about Intimacy
The woman wishfully suggests ways and means to achieve intimacy with her beloved. **Lodge** (v. 11) would be better translated "spend the night." **Mandrakes** (v. 13) are a tuberous plant associated in antiquity with sexual potency (Gen. 30:14–16).

and lodge in the villages;
¹² let us go out early to the vineyards,
   and see whether the vines have
      budded,
   whether the grape blossoms have
      opened
   and the pomegranates are in
      bloom.
   There I will give you my love.
¹³ The mandrakes give forth fragrance,
   and over our doors are all choice
      fruits,
   new as well as old,
   which I have laid up for you, O my
      beloved.

8 O that you were like a brother
         to me,
   who nursed at my mother's breast!
   If I met you outside, I would kiss
      you,
   and no one would despise me.
² I would lead you and bring you
   into the house of my mother,
   and into the chamber of the one
      who bore me.ᵃ
   I would give you spiced wine to
      drink,
   the juice of my pomegranates.

³ O that his left hand were under my
      head,
   and that his right hand
      embraced me!
⁴ I adjure you, O daughters of
      Jerusalem,
   do not stir up or awaken love
   until it is ready!

Homecoming

⁵ Who is that coming up from the
      wilderness,
   leaning upon her beloved?

   Under the apple tree I awakened
      you.
   There your mother was in labor with
      you;
   there she who bore you was in
      labor.
⁶ Set me as a seal upon your heart,
   as a seal upon your arm;
   for love is strong as death,
   passion fierce as the grave.
   Its flashes are flashes of fire,
   a raging flame.
⁷ Many waters cannot quench love,
   neither can floods drown it.

ᵃ Gk Syr: Heb *my mother; she (or you) will teach me*

8:1–2 Brother—She wishes she could be as free in showing her affection to her lover in public as she could be with her biological brother (giving us a glimpse of the behavioral expectations that govern relationships between men and women in the culture from which the Song comes). Once again (as in 2:6–7) the wish for intimacy (8:3) leads her to warn her companions against stirring up longings that cannot be satisfied (v. 4). According to the creation texts in Genesis, God saw that it was not good for human beings to be alone (Gen. 2:18), without companionship and intimacy. Since sexuality is a part of the created nature of human kind (Gen. 1:26), we often find it difficult to describe intimate relationships in anything other than sexual terms. But it is really intimacy that most of us seek in our quest for loving relationships. Intimacy with others is essential in order for us to achieve and maintain physical health and spiritual wholeness.

8:5–14 The Grand Finale

All of the voices contribute to the closing song. A chorus draws attention to the unification of the lovers (v. 5a), and the woman makes statements about the nature of love which most readers take to be the theological heart of the book (vv. 5b–7). The woman's brothers try to reassert their control over her future (vv. 8–9), but she informs them that she plans to retain control over her own *vineyard* (vv. 10–12). Her beloved calls out to her in v. 13, and she has the final word in the final verse, urging him to hurry to her. It is clear that the love embodied in the Song of Solomon is not the kind of fleeting emotion that people fall in and out of on a regular basis. Rather, the Song claims that true love *is strong as death* or as *fierce as the grave* (v. 6). Thus the Song gives us a measuring stick with which to test the validity of what we call love: even the mythological powers of chaos represented by the concepts *many waters* and *floods* cannot overcome the power of love (v. 7). On the one hand, this seems to be a comment on the strength of the God-approved attraction between a man and a woman (Gen. 2:24). But if sexual intimacy between humans can be understood as a metaphor for relationships between human beings and God, then we might also conclude that nothing in all creation will be able to separate us from the love God has for us (Rom. 8:38–39).

If one offered for love
all the wealth of one's house,
it would be utterly scorned.

8 We have a little sister,
and she has no breasts.
What shall we do for our sister,
on the day when she is spoken
for?
9 If she is a wall,
we will build upon her a
battlement of silver;
but if she is a door,
we will enclose her with boards of
cedar.
10 I was a wall,
and my breasts were like towers;
then I was in his eyes
as one who brings*a* peace.
11 Solomon had a vineyard at
Baal-hamon;

he entrusted the vineyard to
keepers;
each one was to bring for its fruit a
thousand pieces of silver.
12 My vineyard, my very own, is for
myself;
you, O Solomon, may have the
thousand,
and the keepers of the fruit two
hundred!

13 O you who dwell in the gardens,
my companions are listening for
your voice;
let me hear it.

14 Make haste, my beloved,
and be like a gazelle
or a young stag
upon the mountains of spices!

a Or *finds*

The Book of
ISAIAH

The prophets were not disembodied characters given to uttering generalities. They spoke in concrete terms to real people at actual historical moments in the history of ancient Israel. So it was with Isaiah, indeed, with all of the Isaiahs.

Isaiah 1–39 (Isaiah of Jerusalem or First Isaiah)

Isaiah ben Amoz, the inspired spokesman for YHWH, started the tradition preserved in this longest prophetic book of the Old Testament. The superscription of the book of Isaiah specifies that the prophet carried out his prophetic ministry ("vision") in the southern kingdom of Judah between the years ca. 742 BCE (the death of King Uzziah; see 6:1; 2 Kgs. 15:2) and ca. 687 BCE (the death of King Hezekiah; see 2 Kgs. 18:2). We know nothing of Isaiah's father Amoz.

Here is what else we do know about this first Isaiah, however.

He lived in a time of considerable political turmoil, and his oracles respond to three major crises that confronted Judah in his time. (1) During the reign of King Ahaz, the Syro-Ephraimite War (735–732 BCE) pitted Aram/Syria and Ephraim/Israel against Judah, which sought the protection of Assyria. (2) There were uprisings among the small Levantine states during the time of the Assyrian king Sargon II (720–710 BCE) and concurrent stirrings against Assyria by the nascent southern Mesopotamian superpower, Babylon. Perhaps Isaiah 21:1–10 follows that latter conflict down to 689 BCE, near the end of Isaiah's ministry, when a failed revolt against Sennacherib, in which Babylon joined in coalition with Elam, perhaps Media, and various Arab allies, resulted in the total destruction of Babylon. (3) The revolt by the Judean king Hezekiah against the Assyrian king Sennacherib (705–701) reverberated clear down to 689/688.

We also know from chapter 6 that First Isaiah received a call so intense that he felt obliged to proclaim the words that came to him as divine revelation. There is no hint in the call or anywhere else that Isaiah was an ecstatic who spoke in an out-of-body state. Instead, he spoke, as our best modern prophets do, in a state of intense empathy with the will and plan of God, but he always remained fully aware and fully responsible for himself.

We also know that much of what he said was preserved by the community and his disciples. His message was directed above all to the holy city of Jerusalem. To it and to surrounding Judah he proclaimed memorable words of judgment and of hope. In using such words, he stood with the rest of the prophets of the Old Testament, whose message typically lifted up four powerful themes: a call for social justice; judgment on corrupt elites; a summons to pure worship of the Lord, uncorrupted by idolatry in any form; and a proclamation of hope. In Isaiah 1–39 these broad themes of judgment and hope are often couched in terms of one or another of the prophet's four incandescent passions: God is holy and sovereign (e.g., 6:1–4); Jerusalem, God's chosen city, is under God's special protection and is therefore inviolable (e.g., 31:4–5); the house of David is God's elect dynasty (e.g., 9:2–7, 11:1–9); and after the

inevitable purge that lies ahead, the continuation of God's people will be assured by a "remnant," whom God will preserve in the land (e.g., 4:2–6) or bring back from exile (e.g., 11:11–16).

In addition to these incandescent ideas, Isaiah also describes YHWH as a holy warrior (e.g., 13:4–5). The image of the divine warrior is difficult for modern readers to reconcile with other biblical pictures of God as a tender parent (Hos. 11:1–9), a universal deliverer (Isa. 66:22–23), and a crucified and risen Savior (Matt. 28:16–20). God the warrior can best be understood as an image of hope for the otherwise hopelessly oppressed people of the earth, as a warning that God's justice is real and serious, and as a way of making morally comprehensible the hard facts of history, such as the destruction of the kingdom of Israel in 721 BCE and the total destruction of Babylon by the Assyrians in 689 BCE. The power of God as warrior can meet and overcome even the most oppressive of earthly powers.

Running through the entire corpus of First Isaiah is a consistent prophetic social ethic (e.g., 1:16–17) that demands that injustice be recognized for what it is and rejects the perversion of values that characterizes the present age. The present propensity of corrupt leaders is to call "evil good and good evil . . . bitter for sweet and sweet for bitter" (5:20). Truth, health, light, justice will all be restored to their proper place when the new age comes, and faithful people can anticipate that happy day by practicing covenant virtues now.

Mention of the present age and the coming new age hints at the eschatological or futuristic vision that runs through all of Isaiah. The prophet's scenario of the future has three stages (see notes at 11:1–9): the present age of sin and tribulation ends with a crisis or turning point, the day of the Lord. Beyond that day lies the new age of peace and harmony.

The beauty and power of Isaiah's words attracted disciples (8:16), who preserved the master's incandescent ideas and passed them on. This success led to the growth of the prophetic book over time. That is why we can speak of several "Isaiahs"—prophets who confronted different situations at different times and yet in language and vision that stayed within what can rightly be called the school of Isaiah.

Isaiah 40–55 (Deutero-Isaiah or Second Isaiah)

This section of the book begins with something like a "call" to an unknown prophet to proclaim a message that is the other side of First Isaiah's coin of judgment, namely, a message of liberation and hope. It presupposes a Babylonian exile, which necessitates a date sometime between the first conquest of Judah by the Babylonian king Nebuchadnezzar in 597 BCE and the final overthrow of Babylon by the Persian king Cyrus the Great in 539 BCE. The date must be toward the end of the exile because of the unique role Cyrus plays throughout Deutero-Isaiah. The Lord identifies this worshiper of another god, this Elamite conqueror of Persia, Media, Lydia, Assyria, and finally Babylon, as YHWH's own agent to effect the liberation of the captive Judean exiles. This liberation in fact occurred when, in the year following his capture of Babylon, Cyrus issued his famous edict (see text in Ezra 1:2–4, elaborated in Ezra 6:3–5) permitting the exiles to return to Jerusalem and giving them the warrant and the means to rebuild the temple.

Literarily speaking, Second Isaiah is quite distinguishable from the first for its long, lyrical promise oracles, its theme of new exodus, and its heavy emphasis on the

beauty and justice of the new age that now seems to lie immediately ahead after the long years of exile that were understood to be punishment for sin.

One unique feature of the preaching of Isaiah of the exile is the Servant Songs: Isaiah 42:1–4 (or 1–9); 49:1–6; 50:4–11; 52:13–53:12. The grouping together of these texts is a work of modern critical scholarship; the basis of the identification is that all of them speak of a single or a collective individual (such as Israel or the remnant of Israel) who brings forth universal justice, does the will of the Lord, and suffers in the process. These texts, in particular 52:13–53:12, contribute significantly to early Christian understanding of who Jesus was. Nowhere in the corpus is the servant also an anointed king of the house of David (i.e., messiah); nowhere is he identified with the coming son of man of apocalyptic expectation (Dan. 7:13–14); nowhere is he the eternal wisdom (Prov. 8:22–31) or Word (John 1:1) from on high. All of those figures of Old Testament expectation are mingled in early Christian thinking about the person of Jesus. The result is that he is understood both as the messiah of the house of David, but also, unexpectedly, as a servant messiah who suffers vicariously.

Isaiah 56–66 (Trito-Isaiah or Third Isaiah)

In the concluding eleven chapters of the book of Isaiah, the ecstatic joy of chapters 40–55 is toned down considerably. Indeed, Israel is castigated for backsliding. The setting of the author now seems to be Jerusalem itself, but the temple is still in ruins (all of which suggests a date between the return in 538 BCE and 515 BCE, when the second temple was dedicated). The imagery of a new exodus disappears, replaced by a greater emphasis on a coming worldwide theocratic polity within which a universally recognized and worshiped YHWH rules over the other nations through a central Israel. To that future Israel flows the wealth of nations (60:11, 61:6).

Isaiah 24–27 (The Isaiah Apocalypse)

Many contemporary commentators argue that the language and ideas of these four chapters set them apart from eighth-century Isaiah of Jerusalem and link them instead with the beginnings of the more radical apocalyptic form of prophetic eschatology perhaps as much as three centuries later. This early protoapocalyptic literature can also be seen in Joel 2:28–3:21 and Zechariah 9–14; it reaches its fullest Old Testament expression in Daniel 7–12. The themes are simply more cosmic in scope than anything seen elsewhere in Isaiah. The coming day of judgment entails the destruction of the earth and the disturbance of the whole universe. The ensuing restoration even involves the resurrection of the dead.

Though the book of Isaiah grew over the years in this way, a canonical coherence also exists. The various parts of the book respond to one another. The permeating message of the justice of divine judgment upon God's own people for their sin would be an incomplete message—something less than the full gospel—without the promise of a new age of redemption, an age of peace and bountifulness that lies beyond the crisis of judgment.

The Foreground of Isaiah

One of the earliest postcanonical mentions of the book of Isaiah is in the book of Ecclesiasticus or Sirach (ca. 200 BCE). In Sirach 48:23–25, the author of this text refers to the incident of the sundial that went backward (see Isa. 38:5–8) and speaks

of the comfort Isaiah offered to the "mourners in Zion" (see Isa. 40:1). In other words, he had at least the major parts of the book before him in canonical form. This is confirmed by the presence of the entire Isaiah in the ancient Greek translation of the Old Testament, the Septuagint, completed by the turn of the Christian era. Other evidence that Isaiah had achieved its present canonical form in the first century BCE is provided by the great Isaiah scroll from the Dead Sea (1QIsa[a]) as well as its more fragmentary cousin (1QIsa[b]).

The book of Isaiah is cited in the New Testament some eighty-six times, with all parts of the prophetic work drawn upon. The early Christians obviously valued the book both for its own teaching and as a vital resource for helping them set forth who they understood Jesus to be. Only seven of the twenty-seven New Testament books fail to quote from or allude to Isaiah. Nor did christological interpretation of Isaiah stop there. One of the most powerful artistic renditions of the meaning of the Christ event, Georg Friedrich Handel's 1741 oratorio *Messiah,* contains solos and choruses of seventeen texts of Isaiah, more than of any other book of the Old or New Testament.

That Isaiah continues to have vital importance for the life of faith is attested by the devotional readings, lections, sermons, and citations of all kinds that spring from its passionate words into the minds and mouths of believers. It continues to bring the guidance of God to us when we ask the key question of social ethics: What ought we then to do?

—W. Sibley Towner

1 The vision of Isaiah son of Amoz, which he saw concerning Judah and Jerusalem in the days of Uzziah, Jotham, Ahaz, and Hezekiah, kings of Judah.

The Wickedness of Judah

2 Hear, O heavens, and listen, O earth;
    for the LORD has spoken:
I reared children and brought them up,
    but they have rebelled against me.
3 The ox knows its owner,
    and the donkey its master's crib;
but Israel does not know,
    my people do not understand.

4 Ah, sinful nation,
    people laden with iniquity,
offspring who do evil,
    children who deal corruptly,
who have forsaken the LORD,
    who have despised the Holy One
        of Israel,
    who are utterly estranged!

5 Why do you seek further beatings?
    Why do you continue to rebel?
The whole head is sick,
    and the whole heart faint.
6 From the sole of the foot even to the
        head,
    there is no soundness in it,
but bruises and sores
    and bleeding wounds;

1:1–12:6 Isaiah of Jerusalem. Part 1: Oracles against God's People

1:1–31 The Fate of Judah

1:1—The superscription locates Isaiah ben Amoz in Jerusalem, ca. 742–687 BCE (see introduction).

1:2–23—The summons of heavens and earth as witnesses introduces a lengthy indictment of *Israel* (v. 3). The term is used in its generic sense of people descended from Jacob of old. Usually the actual addressee in Isaiah is the southern

kingdom of Judah, centered on Zion/Jerusalem. The metaphor of a trial, in which YHWH is the plaintiff and Israel the defendant, underlies this chapter as well as many others.

1:2–3 *They have rebelled against me*—The apostasy has already taken place, and the Lord is confronted with a rebellious child. The law requires the death of such a child (Deut. 21:18–21), though elsewhere in the prophetic canon YHWH refuses to carry out this demand of the law (Hos. 11:8–9).

they have not been drained, or
     bound up,
  or softened with oil.

7 Your country lies desolate,
     your cities are burned with fire;
  in your very presence
     aliens devour your land;
     it is desolate, as overthrown by
        foreigners.
8 And daughter Zion is left
     like a booth in a vineyard,
  like a shelter in a cucumber field,
  like a besieged city.
9 If the LORD of hosts
     had not left us a few survivors,
  we would have been like Sodom,
  and become like Gomorrah.

10 Hear the word of the LORD,
     you rulers of Sodom!
  Listen to the teaching of our God,
     you people of Gomorrah!
11 What to me is the multitude of your
        sacrifices?
     says the LORD;
  I have had enough of burnt offerings
        of rams
     and the fat of fed beasts;
  I do not delight in the blood of bulls,
     or of lambs, or of goats.

12 When you come to appear before me,*a*
     who asked this from your hand?
  Trample my courts no more;
13 bringing offerings is futile;
     incense is an abomination to me.

New moon and sabbath and calling
     of convocation—
  I cannot endure solemn assemblies
     with iniquity.
14 Your new moons and your
        appointed festivals
     my soul hates;
  they have become a burden to me,
     I am weary of bearing them.
15 When you stretch out your hands,
     I will hide my eyes from you;
  even though you make many
        prayers,
     I will not listen;
  your hands are full of blood.
16 Wash yourselves; make yourselves
        clean;
     remove the evil of your doings
        from before my eyes;
  cease to do evil,
17   learn to do good;
  seek justice,
     rescue the oppressed,
  defend the orphan,
     plead for the widow.

18 Come now, let us argue it out,
     says the LORD:
  though your sins are like scarlet,
     they shall be like snow;
  though they are red like crimson,
     they shall become like wool.
19 If you are willing and obedient,
     you shall eat the good of the land;
20 but if you refuse and rebel,

a Or see my face

1:7–8 *Your country lies desolate*—This verse suggests that an invasion has taken place, although ***daughter Zion*** has been spared. Such a situation obtained in 701 BCE, when the Assyrian king Sennacherib conquered Judah and besieged Jerusalem (see 36:1–3 and introduction). A major theme of chaps. 1–39 is God's election of Zion to special protection and responsibility (see introduction).

1:9–10—No one except Lot and his two daughters survived when God punished ***Sodom*** and ***Gomorrah*** (Gen. 19:24–29). To liken the ***rulers*** and ***people*** of Jerusalem to these cities is threatening in the extreme.

1:11–15—Consistent with the preaching of his near contemporaries Amos and Micah, Isaiah represents the Lord as condemning the attempts by the leaders and people to manipulate God with their rituals and sacrifices carried out in ***my courts*** (i.e., the temple; cf. Amos 5:21–24; Mic. 6:6–8).

1:16–17 *Learn to do good . . . plead for the widow*—This exhortation shows that the way to safety is espousal of the cause of the vulnerable and disadvantaged. The heart of the prophetic social ethic is here displayed (see also Amos 5:14–15); it centers on God's preferential option for the poor.

1:18–20—In the tradition of the Mosaic covenant, the proffered offer of forgiveness and life is contingent upon obedience (e.g., Deut. 30:15–20).

you shall be devoured by the
   sword;
for the mouth of the LORD has
   spoken.

The Degenerate City

21 How the faithful city
      has become a whore!
   She that was full of justice,
   righteousness lodged in her—
      but now murderers!
22 Your silver has become dross,
      your wine is mixed with
         water.
23 Your princes are rebels
      and companions of thieves.
   Everyone loves a bribe
      and runs after gifts.
   They do not defend the orphan,
      and the widow's cause does not
         come before them.

24 Therefore says the Sovereign, the
      LORD of hosts, the Mighty One
      of Israel:
   Ah, I will pour out my wrath on my
      enemies,
   and avenge myself on my foes!
25 I will turn my hand against you;
   I will smelt away your dross as
      with lye
   and remove all your alloy.
26 And I will restore your judges as at
      the first,
   and your counselors as at the
      beginning.

Afterward you shall be called the
   city of righteousness,
   the faithful city.

27 Zion shall be redeemed by justice,
      and those in her who repent, by
         righteousness.
28 But rebels and sinners shall be
         destroyed together,
   and those who forsake the LORD
      shall be consumed.
29 For you shall be ashamed of the oaks
      in which you delighted;
   and you shall blush for the gardens
      that you have chosen.
30 For you shall be like an oak
      whose leaf withers,
   and like a garden without water.
31 The strong shall become like tinder,
      and their work[a] like a spark;
   they and their work shall burn
         together,
   with no one to quench them.

The Future House of God

2 The word that Isaiah son of Amoz
   saw concerning Judah and Jerusalem.

2 In days to come
      the mountain of the LORD's house
   shall be established as the highest of
         the mountains,
      and shall be raised above the hills;
   all the nations shall stream to it.
3   Many peoples shall come and say,

[a] Or its makers

1:23—*Princes* are singled out for special condemnation because they fail to wield their authority on behalf of the most vulnerable members
of society, the *orphan* and the *widow*.

1:24–25—Pivoting on *therefore*, the indictment
turns to judgment. Images of smelting and burning warn Judah of the wrath to come.

1:26—One word of hope brightens the prospect.
The reference to *judges* and *counselors* may
suggest a return to a national polity like that
which Israel had before the rise of kingship. In
any case, Jerusalem after the purge will merit
the titles *city of righteousness* and *the faithful
city*. Here sounds a great theme of chaps. 1–39,
God's irreversible election of Zion/Jerusalem and
God's consequent refusal to abandon her even

in the aftermath of her sin and punishment. See
introduction; Pss. 46:5, 132:13–16.

2:1–22 Promise and Indictment

2:2–5—This beloved promise oracle, which appears in nearly identical form in Mic. 4:1–3, introduces the theme of *Zion*'s elevation above all
other mountains (compare Pss. 48:1–2, 78:68–
69; Ezek. 40:2; Zech. 14:10). The Day of the Lord
is a day of destruction (Isa. 2:20; 3:18; see Amos
5:18–20). But it also introduces the third part
of the three-part eschatological scenario of the
prophets (see introduction; 11:1–9), the *days to
come* of restoration and peace, when the *God of
Jacob* will be universally recognized among *the
nations* as sovereign judge and peacemaker.

"Come, let us go up to the mountain
　　of the LORD,
　　to the house of the God of Jacob;
　　that he may teach us his ways
　　　and that we may walk in his
　　　　paths."
For out of Zion shall go forth
　　instruction,
　　and the word of the LORD from
　　　Jerusalem.
4 He shall judge between the nations,
　　and shall arbitrate for many
　　　peoples;
　they shall beat their swords into
　　plowshares,
　and their spears into pruning
　　hooks;
　nation shall not lift up sword against
　　nation,
　neither shall they learn war any
　　more.

Judgment Pronounced on Arrogance

5 O house of Jacob,
　　come, let us walk
　　in the light of the LORD!
6 For you have forsaken the ways of*a*
　　your people,
　　O house of Jacob.
Indeed they are full of diviners*b*
　　from the east
　and of soothsayers like the
　　Philistines,
　and they clasp hands with
　　foreigners.
7 Their land is filled with silver and
　　gold,
　and there is no end to their
　　treasures;
　their land is filled with horses,
　　and there is no end to their
　　chariots.
8 Their land is filled with idols;

they bow down to the work of
　　their hands,
　to what their own fingers have
　　made.
9 And so people are humbled,
　　and everyone is brought low—
　　do not forgive them!
10 Enter into the rock,
　　and hide in the dust
　from the terror of the LORD,
　　and from the glory of his majesty.
11 The haughty eyes of people shall be
　　brought low,
　and the pride of everyone shall be
　　humbled;
　and the LORD alone will be exalted
　　on that day.
12 For the LORD of hosts has a day
　　against all that is proud and lofty,
　　against all that is lifted up and
　　　high;*c*
13 against all the cedars of Lebanon,
　　lofty and lifted up;
　and against all the oaks of Bashan;
14 against all the high mountains,
　　and against all the lofty hills;
15 against every high tower,
　　and against every fortified wall;
16 against all the ships of Tarshish,
　　and against all the beautiful craft.*d*
17 The haughtiness of people shall be
　　humbled,
　and the pride of everyone shall be
　　brought low;
　and the LORD alone will be exalted
　　on that day.
18 The idols shall utterly pass away.
19 Enter the caves of the rocks
　　and the holes of the ground,
　from the terror of the LORD,
　　and from the glory of his majesty,

a Heb lacks *the ways of*　*b* Cn: Heb lacks *of diviners*　*c* Cn Compare Gk:
Heb *low*　*d* Compare Gk: Meaning of Heb uncertain

2:4 *Swords into plowshares . . . spears into
pruning hooks*—This "floating oracle" appears
in reverse order in the protoapocalyptic vision
of Joel 3:10. In the blessed future age envisioned
here, the scourges of the present age, including
war, are displaced by their opposite conditions.

2:6–22—Though Isaiah elsewhere uses *Jacob*
to refer to the northern kingdom, destroyed by

the Assyrians in 721 BCE (see 9:8–12), the sense
here seems to include Judah as well. Polluted by
their recourse to *soothsayers* and *idols* as well as
their *pride*, the people will cower in filthy caves
before the coming *terror of the LORD.* No earthly
enemy is needed; YHWH appears in person to
effect judgment.

when he rises to terrify the earth.

20 On that day people will throw away
      to the moles and to the bats
    their idols of silver and their idols of
      gold,
    which they made for themselves to
      worship,
21 to enter the caverns of the rocks
      and the clefts in the crags,
    from the terror of the LORD,
      and from the glory of his majesty,
      when he rises to terrify the earth.
22 Turn away from mortals,
      who have only breath in their
        nostrils,
      for of what account are they?

3 For now the Sovereign, the LORD of
      hosts,
    is taking away from Jerusalem and
      from Judah
  support and staff—
    all support of bread,
    and all support of water—
2 warrior and soldier,
    judge and prophet,
    diviner and elder,
3 captain of fifty
    and dignitary,
  counselor and skillful magician
    and expert enchanter.
4 And I will make boys their princes,
    and babes shall rule over them.
5 The people will be oppressed,
    everyone by another
    and everyone by a neighbor;
  the youth will be insolent to the
    elder,
    and the base to the honorable.

6 Someone will even seize a relative,
    a member of the clan, saying,
  "You have a cloak;
    you shall be our leader,
  and this heap of ruins
    shall be under your rule."

7 But the other will cry out on that
    day, saying,
  "I will not be a healer;
    in my house there is neither bread
      nor cloak;
  you shall not make me
    leader of the people."
8 For Jerusalem has stumbled
    and Judah has fallen,
  because their speech and their deeds
    are against the LORD,
    defying his glorious presence.

9 The look on their faces bears witness
    against them;
  they proclaim their sin like Sodom,
    they do not hide it.
  Woe to them!
    For they have brought evil on
      themselves.
10 Tell the innocent how fortunate they
    are,
  for they shall eat the fruit of their
    labors.
11 Woe to the guilty! How unfortunate
    they are,
  for what their hands have done
    shall be done to them.
12 My people—children are their
    oppressors,
    and women rule over them.
  O my people, your leaders mislead
    you,
    and confuse the course of your
      paths.
13 The LORD rises to argue his case;
    he stands to judge the peoples.
14 The LORD enters into judgment
    with the elders and princes of his
      people:
  It is you who have devoured the
    vineyard;
    the spoil of the poor is in your
      houses.

3:1–4:6 Judah Punished and Purified
3:1–15—This lengthy indictment of Jerusalem
and Judah centers on the corruption of their
leadership cadres (v. 14). In court (v. 13), the Lord
accuses them: They have *devoured* the Lord's
vineyard (v. 14; see 5:1–7), robbed, crushed and

ground *the face of the poor* (v. 15). This dysfunctional society is condemned to a reversal of
social roles. Instead of the usual recognized leaders (vv. 2–3), it will be ruled by *boys . . . babes* (v.
4) and *women* (v. 12).

15 What do you mean by crushing my

people,

by grinding the face of the poor?
says the Lord GOD of hosts.

16 The LORD said:
Because the daughters of Zion are
haughty
and walk with outstretched necks,
glancing wantonly with their eyes,
mincing along as they go,
tinkling with their feet;
17 the Lord will afflict with scabs
the heads of the daughters of Zion,
and the LORD will lay bare their
secret parts.

18 In that day the Lord will take away
the finery of the anklets, the headbands,
and the crescents; 19 the pendants, the
bracelets, and the scarfs; 20 the headdresses, the armlets, the sashes, the perfume boxes, and the amulets; 21 the signet
rings and nose rings; 22 the festal robes,
the mantles, the cloaks, and the hand-
bags; 23 the garments of gauze, the linen
garments, the turbans, and the veils.
24 Instead of perfume there will be a
stench;
and instead of a sash, a rope;
and instead of well-set hair,
baldness;
and instead of a rich robe, a
binding of sackcloth;
instead of beauty, shame.[a]

25 Your men shall fall by the sword
and your warriors in battle.

26 And her gates shall lament and
mourn;
ravaged, she shall sit upon the
ground.

4 Seven women shall take hold of one
man in that day, saying,
"We will eat our own bread and wear
our own clothes;
just let us be called by your name;
take away our disgrace."

The Future Glory
of the Survivors in Zion

2 On that day the branch of the LORD
shall be beautiful and glorious, and the
fruit of the land shall be the pride and
glory of the survivors of Israel. 3 Whoever is left in Zion and remains in Jerusalem will be called holy, everyone who
has been recorded for life in Jerusalem,
4 once the Lord has washed away the filth
of the daughters of Zion and cleansed
the bloodstains of Jerusalem from its
midst by a spirit of judgment and by a
spirit of burning. 5 Then the LORD will
create over the whole site of Mount
Zion and over its places of assembly a
cloud by day and smoke and the shining
of a flaming fire by night. Indeed over
all the glory there will be a canopy. 6 It
will serve as a pavilion, a shade by day

[a] Q Ms: MT lacks *shame*

3:16–4:1—The *daughters of Zion* come in
for special judgment in this oracle. The Lord
threatens punishments that deprive them of any
warrant for their pride, lust, and vanity: *scabs*
and nudity (v. 17), loss of their *finery* (vv. 18–22),
stench, *baldness*, and rags (v. 24). In vv. 25–26
the metaphor shifts from Zion's daughters to ravaged Jerusalem herself.

4:1 *Called by your name*—In the aftermath of
the decimation of the male population, women
beg the remaining men to marry them in order to
achieve some measure of dignity.

4:2–6—A promise oracle that reflects on the
threats against Jerusalem and the daughter of
Zion.

4:2 *On that day*—See note at 2:2–5. *The branch
of the LORD*—In 11:1 and elsewhere, the term

refers to an offspring of the Davidic house, i.e., a
messiah ("anointed") figure.

4:3 *Whoever . . . remains*—Isaiah of Jerusalem
teaches that a remnant of Judah will survive the
purge that is coming. God will use these survivors to build the better world that lies beyond the
purge (see introduction; 6:13, 10:20). *Recorded
for life in Jerusalem*—In the Bible, two heavenly
books determine the fate of individuals. One is
the eternal book of destiny (Ps. 139:16), and the
other is the record book of deeds remembered
(Ps. 69:28; Dan. 7:10, 12:1; Mal. 3:16; in Rev.
20:12 both books are opened at the Last Judgment).

4:5—The *cloud* and the *fire* that form a protective shelter for the restored *places of assembly*
on Zion are drawn from the tabernacle tradition
in the exodus account (Exod. 40:38).

from the heat, and a refuge and a shelter
from the storm and rain.

The Song of the Unfruitful Vineyard

5 Let me sing for my beloved
my love-song concerning his
vineyard:
My beloved had a vineyard
on a very fertile hill.
2 He dug it and cleared it of stones,
and planted it with choice vines;
he built a watchtower in the midst
of it,
and hewed out a wine vat in it;
he expected it to yield grapes,
but it yielded wild grapes.

3 And now, inhabitants of Jerusalem
and people of Judah,
judge between me
and my vineyard.
4 What more was there to do for my
vineyard
that I have not done in it?
When I expected it to yield
grapes,
why did it yield wild grapes?

5 And now I will tell you
what I will do to my vineyard.
I will remove its hedge,
and it shall be devoured;
I will break down its wall,
and it shall be trampled down.
6 I will make it a waste;
it shall not be pruned or hoed,
and it shall be overgrown with
briers and thorns;

I will also command the clouds
that they rain no rain upon it.

7 For the vineyard of the LORD of
hosts
is the house of Israel,
and the people of Judah
are his pleasant planting;
he expected justice,
but saw bloodshed;
righteousness,
but heard a cry!

Social Injustice Denounced

8 Ah, you who join house to house,
who add field to field,
until there is room for no one but
you,
and you are left to live alone
in the midst of the land!
9 The LORD of hosts has sworn in my
hearing:
Surely many houses shall be desolate,
large and beautiful houses, without
inhabitant.
10 For ten acres of vineyard shall yield
but one bath,
and a homer of seed shall yield a
mere ephah.[a]

11 Ah, you who rise early in the
morning
in pursuit of strong drink,
who linger in the evening
to be inflamed by wine,
12 whose feasts consist of lyre and harp,

a The Heb bath, homer, and ephah are measures of quantity

5:1–30 Unjust Israel Is Unfruitful

5:1–7—Isaiah's parable of the Vineyard functions at several levels. It is described in v. 1 as a *love-song*; indeed, *vineyard* means "lover" in the nuptial poem, the Song of Solomon (e.g., Song 1:6, 8:12). The vineyard is defined as *the house of Israel* and *the people of Judah* (Isa. 5:7). As the song of the disappointed lover, YHWH, the *parable also functions as an indictment* (vv. 1–4, 7) and *threat* (vv. 5–6).

5:7—The indictment of the vineyard Israel culminates in a famous Hebrew pun: instead of *justice* (*mishpat*), God got *bloodshed* (*mispah*); instead of *righteousness* (*tsedaqah*), God *heard a cry* (*tse'aqah*). In short, Isaiah's own era was char-

acterized by a negation of positive values. The parable serves as an abiding reminder that God expects the chosen and beloved people to yield the genuine fruits of covenant obedience—justice and righteousness—and is disappointed and angry when they do not.

5:8–24—A collection of judgment oracles, mostly introduced by the Hebrew interjection *hoy!* (*Ah!*) The prophetic indictments of social injustice and corruption stand out here. Condemned are relentless land acquisition (v. 8), drunkenness and revelry (vv. 11–12, 22), falsehood (v. 18), reversal of true values (v. 20), puffery (v. 21), and perversion of justice (v. 23).

tambourine and flute and wine,
but who do not regard the deeds of
    the LORD,
  or see the work of his hands!
13 Therefore my people go into exile
    without knowledge;
  their nobles are dying of hunger,
    and their multitude is parched
    with thirst.
14 Therefore Sheol has enlarged its
    appetite
  and opened its mouth beyond
    measure;
  the nobility of Jerusalem[a] and her
    multitude go down,
  her throng and all who exult in her.
15 People are bowed down, everyone is
    brought low,
  and the eyes of the haughty are
    humbled.
16 But the LORD of hosts is exalted by
    justice,
  and the Holy God shows himself
    holy by righteousness.
17 Then the lambs shall graze as in
    their pasture,
  fatlings and kids[b] shall feed among
    the ruins.

18 Ah, you who drag iniquity along
    with cords of falsehood,
  who drag sin along as with cart
    ropes,
19 who say, "Let him make haste,
    let him speed his work
  that we may see it;
  let the plan of the Holy One of Israel
    hasten to fulfillment,
  that we may know it!"
20 Ah, you who call evil good
    and good evil,
  who put darkness for light
    and light for darkness,
  who put bitter for sweet
    and sweet for bitter!
21 Ah, you who are wise in your own
    eyes,

and shrewd in your own sight!
22 Ah, you who are heroes in drinking
    wine
  and valiant at mixing drink,
23 who acquit the guilty for a bribe,
  and deprive the innocent of their
    rights!

Foreign Invasion Predicted

24 Therefore, as the tongue of fire
    devours the stubble,
  and as dry grass sinks down in the
    flame,
  so their root will become rotten,
    and their blossom go up like dust;
  for they have rejected the instruction
    of the LORD of hosts,
  and have despised the word of the
    Holy One of Israel.

25 Therefore the anger of the LORD was
    kindled against his people,
  and he stretched out his hand
    against them and struck them;
  the mountains quaked,
  and their corpses were like refuse
    in the streets.
  For all this his anger has not turned
    away,
  and his hand is stretched out still.

26 He will raise a signal for a nation far
    away,
  and whistle for a people at the
    ends of the earth;
  Here they come, swiftly, speedily!
27 None of them is weary, none
    stumbles,
  none slumbers or sleeps,
  not a loincloth is loose,
  not a sandal-thong broken;
28 their arrows are sharp,
    all their bows bent,
  their horses' hoofs seem like flint,
    and their wheels like the
    whirlwind.
29 Their roaring is like a lion,
  like young lions they roar;

---

a Heb *her nobility*   *b* Cn Compare Gk: Heb *aliens*

5:26 *Whistle for a people*—Isaiah daringly pictures Judah's enemy, Assyria, as God's agent of judgment on Judah (see also 7:18–20).

they growl and seize their prey,
 they carry it off, and no one can
  rescue.
30 They will roar over it on that day,
  like the roaring of the sea.
And if one look to the land—
 only darkness and distress;
and the light grows dark with clouds.

A Vision of God in the Temple

6 In the year that King Uzziah died,
I saw the Lord sitting on a throne,
high and lofty; and the hem of his
robe filled the temple. ²Seraphs were
in attendance above him; each had six
wings: with two they covered their faces,
and with two they covered their feet, and
with two they flew. ³And one called to
another and said:
 "Holy, holy, holy is the LORD of
  hosts;
 the whole earth is full of his glory."
⁴The pivots*a* on the thresholds shook at

the voices of those who called, and the
house filled with smoke. ⁵And I said:
"Woe is me! I am lost, for I am a man of
unclean lips, and I live among a people
of unclean lips; yet my eyes have seen
the King, the LORD of hosts!"

6 Then one of the seraphs flew to me,
holding a live coal that had been taken
from the altar with a pair of tongs. ⁷The
seraph*b* touched my mouth with it and
said: "Now that this has touched your
lips, your guilt has departed and your
sin is blotted out." ⁸Then I heard the
voice of the Lord saying, "Whom shall
I send, and who will go for us?" And
I said, "Here am I; send me!" ⁹And he
said, "Go and say to this people:
 'Keep listening, but do not
  comprehend;
 keep looking, but do not
  understand.'
10 Make the mind of this people dull,

a Meaning of Heb uncertain   *b* Heb *He*

6:1–13 Isaiah's Commissioning

This famous passage is usually taken to be
Isaiah's prophetic call. However, the facts that it
is not at the beginning of the book and that the
setting is the heavenly council have led some to
see this simply as God's bestowal of a special
commission upon the prophet. The elements
usually present in a call narrative are here: appearance of a divine being (theophany, vv. 1–4);
objection by the prophet (v. 5); purification or
sign (vv. 6–7); acceptance (v. 8); and commission
(vv. 9–13). Compare the calls of Moses (Exod.
3:1–4:17), Gideon (Judg. 6:11–40), Jeremiah (Jer.
1:4–10), Mary (Luke 1:26–45), to see the same
elements at play.

6:1 *The year that King Uzziah died*—About 742
BCE.

6:2 *Seraphs*—The name of these six-winged
heavenly beings is derived from the verb *saraf*,
"to burn." Although they are mentioned only in
vv. 2, 6, we learn from these verses that the seraphs served the Holy One as throne attendants,
singers, and intermediaries with the prophet who
cowered in fear before the divine presence.

6:3–7 *Holy, holy, holy*—The hymn Trisagion,
"thrice-holy," so beloved in Christian liturgical tradition, is simply "Holy, holy" in the great
Isaiah scroll found at Qumran by the Dead Sea.
That small variant would certainly make the
hymn hard to sing! Of major interest in these
verses is the powerful assertion of God's holi-

ness, an assertion echoed throughout the book
of Isaiah. Thirty times God is referred to as "the
Holy One of Israel." Everything that belongs to
God is holy, e.g., God's arm (52:10), God's name
(57:15), God's mountain and city (27:13, 48:2),
God's people (62:12). To be holy is to be wholly
other, set apart, and consecrated. The attitude
appropriate to a human being who draws near to
God is put clearly in 8:13: "But the LORD of hosts,
him you shall regard as holy; let him be your fear,
and let him be your dread." Exactly that posture
is taken by the prophet in this beloved passage.
His cry, *Woe is me!* (6:5) perfectly expresses his
sense of danger at bringing his own unworthiness
into the holy presence of God. The cleansing
ministry of the seraphs enables him to accept his
call to discipleship. His entire experience serves
as a model for all believers who, in spite of our
awareness of our own unworthiness and frailty,
come at last to accept the burden and joy of
service in God's cause.

6:8 *Here am I; send me!*—Presumably not in an
out-of-body state of ecstasy, but with full awareness of what his acceptance means, Isaiah agrees
to participate in God's project.

6:9–10—The difficult notion that God commands
the prophet to render the people unable to
respond and therefore subject to judgment may
mean simply that they are to be who they are,
namely, persistently stubborn.

and stop their ears,
  and shut their eyes,
so that they may not look with their
  eyes,
  and listen with their ears,
and comprehend with their minds,
  and turn and be healed."
11 Then I said, "How long, O Lord?"
  And he said:
"Until cities lie waste
  without inhabitant,
and houses without people,
  and the land is utterly desolate;
12 until the LORD sends everyone far
  away,
  and vast is the emptiness in the
    midst of the land.
13 Even if a tenth part remain in it,
  it will be burned again,
like a terebinth or an oak
  whose stump remains standing
    when it is felled."*a*
The holy seed is its stump.

Isaiah Reassures King Ahaz

7 In the days of Ahaz son of Jotham
son of Uzziah, king of Judah, King
Rezin of Aram and King Pekah son of
Remaliah of Israel went up to attack
Jerusalem, but could not mount an
attack against it. 2 When the house of
David heard that Aram had allied itself
with Ephraim, the heart of Ahaz*b* and
the heart of his people shook as the trees
of the forest shake before the wind.

3 Then the LORD said to Isaiah, Go
out to meet Ahaz, you and your son
Shear-jashub,*c* at the end of the conduit
of the upper pool on the highway to
the Fuller's Field, 4 and say to him, Take
heed, be quiet, do not fear, and do not
let your heart be faint because of these
two smoldering stumps of firebrands,
because of the fierce anger of Rezin and
Aram and the son of Remaliah. 5 Because
Aram—with Ephraim and the son of
Remaliah—has plotted evil against you,
saying, 6 Let us go up against Judah and
cut off Jerusalem*d* and conquer it for
ourselves and make the son of Tabeel
king in it; 7 therefore thus says the Lord
GOD:
  It shall not stand,
    and it shall not come to pass.
8 For the head of Aram is Damascus,
    and the head of Damascus is
      Rezin.
  (Within sixty-five years Ephraim will
be shattered, no longer a people.)
9 The head of Ephraim is Samaria,
    and the head of Samaria is the son
      of Remaliah.
  If you do not stand firm in faith,
    you shall not stand at all.

Isaiah Gives Ahaz the Sign of Immanuel

10 Again the LORD spoke to Ahaz,
saying, 11 Ask a sign of the LORD your
God; let it be deep as Sheol or high as
heaven. 12 But Ahaz said, I will not ask,
and I will not put the LORD to the test.
13 Then Isaiah*e* said: "Hear then, O house
of David! Is it too little for you to weary
mortals, that you weary my God also?
14 Therefore the Lord himself will give

a Meaning of Heb uncertain *b* Heb *his heart* *c* That is *A remnant shall return* *d* Heb *cut it off* *e* Heb *he*

6:13 The holy seed is its stump—Whatever else
this textually corrupt verse may mean, it seems
to suggest hope for a saving remnant. See note
at 4:2.

7:1–25 Signs
This entire largely prose narrative is set in the
historical context of the Syro-Ephraimite War
(735–732 BCE), described in detail in 2 Kgs.
15:29–16:20.

7:1—King *Ahaz* of Judah (735–715 BCE) is
threatened by an anti-Assyrian coalition of *Aram*
(Syria) and *Ephraim* (Israel). Their intention is to

topple the Davidic dynasty of Judah and install a
puppet king (v. 6).

7:3—On the significance of the name of Isaiah's
son, *Shear-jashub*, "a remnant shall return," see
note at 4:2.

7:14 Immanuel—This second child with the
name that means "God is with us" is the *sign* (see
8:18) that God wills to give Ahaz to reassure him.
The name encapsulates Isaiah's faith in God's
reliability. The pregnancy of the anonymous
young woman, perhaps Isaiah's wife, makes the
sign possible. The NRSV footnote shows that the

you a sign. Look, the young woman*a* is with child and shall bear a son, and shall name him Immanuel.*b* **15** He shall eat curds and honey by the time he knows how to refuse the evil and choose the good. **16** For before the child knows how to refuse the evil and choose the good, the land before whose two kings you are in dread will be deserted. **17** The LORD will bring on you and on your people and on your ancestral house such days as have not come since the day that Ephraim departed from Judah—the king of Assyria."

18 On that day the LORD will whistle for the fly that is at the sources of the streams of Egypt, and for the bee that is in the land of Assyria. **19** And they will all come and settle in the steep ravines, and in the clefts of the rocks, and on all the thornbushes, and on all the pastures.

20 On that day the Lord will shave with a razor hired beyond the River— with the king of Assyria—the head and the hair of the feet, and it will take off the beard as well.

21 On that day one will keep alive a young cow and two sheep, **22** and will eat curds because of the abundance of milk that they give; for everyone that is left in the land shall eat curds and honey.

23 On that day every place where there used to be a thousand vines, worth a thousand shekels of silver, will become briers and thorns. **24** With bow and arrows one will go there, for all the land will be briers and thorns; **25** and as

for all the hills that used to be hoed with a hoe, you will not go there for fear of briers and thorns; but they will become a place where cattle are let loose and where sheep tread.

Isaiah's Son a Sign of the Assyrian Invasion

8 Then the LORD said to me, Take a large tablet and write on it in common characters, "Belonging to Maher-shalal-hash-baz,"*c* **2** and have it attested*d* for me by reliable witnesses, the priest Uriah and Zechariah son of Jeberechiah. **3** And I went to the prophetess, and she conceived and bore a son. Then the LORD said to me, Name him Maher-shalal-hash-baz; **4** for before the child knows how to call "My father" or "My mother," the wealth of Damascus and the spoil of Samaria will be carried away by the king of Assyria.

5 The LORD spoke to me again: **6** Because this people has refused the waters of Shiloah that flow gently, and melt in fear before*e* Rezin and the son of Remaliah; **7** therefore, the Lord is bringing up against it the mighty flood waters of the River, the king of Assyria and all his glory; it will rise above all its channels and overflow all its banks; **8** it will sweep on into Judah as a flood, and, pouring over, it will reach up to the neck; and its outspread wings will fill the breadth of your land, O Immanuel.

a Gk *the virgin*　*b* That is *God is with us*　*c* That is *The spoil speeds, the prey hastens*　*d* Q Ms Gk Syr: MT *and I caused to be attested*　*e* Cn: Meaning of Heb uncertain

---

word "virgin" used in Matt. 1:23 is taken from the ancient Greek (Septuagint) translation and not from the original Hebrew itself.

7:16–25—*Curds and honey* (v. 22) are food for newly weaned infants. This child will be only a few months or years old when all threat from the coalition will have passed. Judah's rescue from Syria and Israel by Assyria (see 8:4) is not, however, a cause for rejoicing (7:17), though a remnant will survive (vv. 18–25).

8:1–22 A Sign of Impending Ruin

8:1–4—Yet another son of Isaiah (see 7:3, 14) is saddled with an unwieldy but significant name,

"The spoil speeds, the prey hastens." He is a *sign* (8:18) of the impending destruction of Israel/Ephraim and Syria/Aram (see 7:1).

8:5–10—The flood of the Assyrian horde that sweeps away the enemies scours Judah as well. Twice, however, the prophet invokes the powerful name, *Immanuel* (vv. 8, 10), *God is with us*, to reassert his unshaken conviction in the inviolability of Zion. Jews and Christians of later centuries know, of course, that Judah and Jerusalem, too, could and would be destroyed. The trust in God's steadfastness toward us remains, however. This faith helps account for the survival of the Jewish people and of the Christian faith alike.

9 Band together, you peoples, and be
     dismayed;
   listen, all you far countries;
   gird yourselves and be dismayed;
     gird yourselves and be dismayed!
10 Take counsel together, but it shall be
     brought to naught;
   speak a word, but it will not stand,
     for God is with us.[a]

11 For the LORD spoke thus to me
while his hand was strong upon me, and
warned me not to walk in the way of this
people, saying: 12 Do not call conspiracy
all that this people calls conspiracy, and
do not fear what it fears, or be in dread.
13 But the LORD of hosts, him you shall
regard as holy; let him be your fear, and
let him be your dread. 14 He will become
a sanctuary, a stone one strikes against;
for both houses of Israel he will become
a rock one stumbles over—a trap and a
snare for the inhabitants of Jerusalem.
15 And many among them shall stumble;
they shall fall and be broken; they shall
be snared and taken.

Disciples of Isaiah

16 Bind up the testimony, seal the
teaching among my disciples. 17 I will
wait for the LORD, who is hiding his
face from the house of Jacob, and I will

hope in him. 18 See, I and the children
whom the LORD has given me are signs
and portents in Israel from the LORD
of hosts, who dwells on Mount Zion.
19 Now if people say to you, "Consult the
ghosts and the familiar spirits that chirp
and mutter; should not a people consult
their gods, the dead on behalf of the living, 20 for teaching and for instruction?"
surely, those who speak like this will
have no dawn! 21 They will pass through
the land,[b] greatly distressed and hungry; when they are hungry, they will be
enraged and will curse[c] their king and
their gods. They will turn their faces
upward, 22 or they will look to the earth,
but will see only distress and darkness,
the gloom of anguish; and they will be
thrust into thick darkness.[d]

The Righteous Reign
of the Coming King

9[e] But there will be no gloom for those
   who were in anguish. In the former
time he brought into contempt the land
of Zebulun and the land of Naphtali, but
in the latter time he will make glorious
the way of the sea, the land beyond the
Jordan, Galilee of the nations.

[a] Heb immanu el   [b] Heb it   [c] Or curse by   [d] Meaning of Heb uncertain
[e] Ch 8.23 in Heb

8:16—We do not know who the *disciples* were
who are charged by the prophet to preserve and
transmit his message. Perhaps the anonymous
voices that speak in the later strata of the book
can be counted among them. In any case, we
know that they listened and obeyed, for we have
the prophet's oracles and sermons that were
no doubt given orally by him. True prophets,
whether biblical or modern ones, are not lone
voices crying in the wilderness, but speak on behalf of constituencies who treasure and preserve
their guiding words.

8:19–22—The contrast between the true bearer of
the word of God and the chirping necromancers
and other phony seers could hardly be better portrayed. The chapter ends in darkness and gloom.

9:1–21 The Prince of Peace

9:1–7—Few can read this beloved promise oracle
without hearing the great chorus, based on v. 6,
that concludes Part I of Handel's *Messiah*. (Also
see note at 53:4–6.) Scholars often suggest that
the poem celebrates the accession of a new king

(Hezekiah, perhaps, in 715 BCE) and his ritual
adoption as God's son (a ceremony that is common in the ancient Near East and seems to be
implied in 2 Sam. 7:14 and Ps. 2:7, though never
explicitly described in the Bible; also see Matt.
3:17 and parallels). Others tie the birth in Isa.
9:6 to the child named Immanuel in 7:14. Yet the
oracle reaches beyond such historical bounds. Its
own language is messianic (the *child* is entitled
Mighty God, among other exalted titles, and he
occupies *the throne of David*). It is also eschatological, that is, it looks to the Day of the Lord and
the new age of *justice and . . . righteousness* that
this *Prince of Peace* will establish *forevermore*.
It is no wonder, then, that Gospel writers found
in this passage the right words to describe their
experience with the risen Christ (Matt. 4:15–16;
Luke 1:32–33, 79). These words also offer guidance to believers today. Only God can bring in
the messianic age, but we know what we must
do in the meantime: give foretastes of that new
age in our own lives of justice and righteousness.

2a The people who walked in darkness
       have seen a great light;
    those who lived in a land of deep
       darkness—
       on them light has shined.
3 You have multiplied the nation,
       you have increased its joy;
    they rejoice before you
       as with joy at the harvest,
       as people exult when dividing
          plunder.
4 For the yoke of their burden,
    and the bar across their shoulders,
    the rod of their oppressor,
       you have broken as on the day of
          Midian.
5 For all the boots of the tramping
       warriors
    and all the garments rolled in blood
    shall be burned as fuel for the fire.
6 For a child has been born for us,
    a son given to us;
       authority rests upon his shoulders;
       and he is named
    Wonderful Counselor, Mighty God,
       Everlasting Father, Prince of Peace.
7 His authority shall grow continually,
    and there shall be endless peace
    for the throne of David and his
       kingdom.
    He will establish and uphold it
    with justice and with righteousness
       from this time onward and
          forevermore.
    The zeal of the LORD of hosts will do
       this.

Judgment on Arrogance and Oppression

8 The Lord sent a word against Jacob,

    and it fell on Israel;
9 and all the people knew it—
       Ephraim and the inhabitants of
          Samaria—
       but in pride and arrogance of heart
          they said:
10 "The bricks have fallen,
       but we will build with dressed
          stones;
    the sycamores have been cut down,
       but we will put cedars in their
          place."
11 So the LORD raised adversariesb
          against them,
    and stirred up their enemies,
12 the Arameans on the east and the
          Philistines on the west,
    and they devoured Israel with
          open mouth.
    For all this his anger has not turned
          away;
       his hand is stretched out still.
13 The people did not turn to him who
          struck them,
    or seek the LORD of hosts.
14 So the LORD cut off from Israel head
          and tail,
    palm branch and reed in one
          day—
15 elders and dignitaries are the head,
    and prophets who teach lies are
          the tail;
16 for those who led this people led
          them astray,
    and those who were led by them
          were left in confusion.
17 That is why the Lord did not have
          pity onc their young people,

a Ch 9.1 in Heb b Cn: Heb the adversaries of Rezin c Q Ms: MT rejoice over

---

9:8–21—In sharp contrast, now comes a oracle in three strophes, each concluding with the refrain, *For all this his anger has not turned away; his hand is stretched out still*. This accounts for the carnage in the northern kingdom during the Syro-Ephraimite War (735–732 BCE; see v. 21, also 7:1–2) as the work of the Lord. *Arrogance* (v. 9), corrupt leadership (vv. 15–16), consuming *wickedness* (v. 18) fan God's wrath to such heat that no one—not even the young, the orphans, and the widows, for whom God has a prefer-

ential option—is spared. No doubt this terrible picture reflects actual events in the decade before the final fall of Israel in 721 BCE. We might question whether God acted in the atrocities of the Arameans and the Philistines (v. 12) or whether those peoples were solely responsible. Either way, this kind of judgment oracle helped ancient Israel understand its tragic past in terms of the consequences unleashed by faithless, corrupt deeds.

or compassion on their orphans
and widows;
for everyone was godless and an
evildoer,
and every mouth spoke folly.
For all this his anger has not turned
away;
his hand is stretched out still.

18 For wickedness burned like a fire,
consuming briers and thorns;
it kindled the thickets of the
forest,
and they swirled upward in a
column of smoke.
19 Through the wrath of the LORD of
hosts
the land was burned,
and the people became like fuel for
the fire;
no one spared another.
20 They gorged on the right, but still
were hungry,
and they devoured on the left, but
were not satisfied;
they devoured the flesh of their own
kindred;a
21 Manasseh devoured Ephraim, and
Ephraim Manasseh,
and together they were against
Judah.
For all this his anger has not turned
away;
his hand is stretched out still.

10 Ah, you who make iniquitous
decrees,
who write oppressive statutes,
2 to turn aside the needy from justice
and to rob the poor of my people
of their right,
that widows may be your spoil,
and that you may make the
orphans your prey!
3 What will you do on the day of
punishment,
in the calamity that will come
from far away?
To whom will you flee for help,
and where will you leave your
wealth,
4 so as not to crouch among the
prisoners
or fall among the slain?
For all this his anger has not turned
away;
his hand is stretched out still.

Arrogant Assyria Also Judged

5 Ah, Assyria, the rod of my anger—
the club in their hands is my fury!
6 Against a godless nation I send him,
and against the people of my wrath
I command him,
to take spoil and seize plunder,
and to tread them down like the
mire of the streets.
7 But this is not what he intends,
nor does he have this in mind;

a Or arm

10:1–34 The Fate of the Arrogant

10:1–4—The refrain of 9:8–21 reappears and ties this threat to the judgment and sentence pronounced there. The social ethic of the prophets is stated here in pure form. Those who pervert law and justice in order to rob the needy will have nowhere to flee on *the day of punishment*. A policy of oppressive use of power by the rich in order to get richer ends in a catastrophic failure.

10:5–34—The remainder of this chapter consists of various understandings of the present role and ultimate fate of Assyria, the superpower of the eighth and seventh centuries BCE. A kind of narrative line ties the oracles together. Originally God called up Assyria as a scourge for disobedient Israel and Judah (vv. 5–6). But arrogant Assyria exceeded its mandate when it threatened to smash Jerusalem (vv. 7–11). God had indeed the strange *work* (v. 12) of smelting away the dross of Jerusalem (1:25), but Assyria, which thinks of itself as autonomously powerful (10:12–14), rather than the mere ax in the hand of the cutter of nations (v. 15), will also be destroyed (vv. 16–19). (The reference to the *wasting sickness* in v. 16 may anticipate the report in 37:36 of a plague in the Assyrian army, even as it laid siege to Jerusalem.) Two promises ensue: (1) the survival of a saving remnant in 10:20–23 (already noted in the introduction and 4:2 as a theme characteristic of chaps. 1–39 and underscored in the name of the prophet's son, 7:4; see also Paul's more tragic view of the remnant in Rom. 9:27–29), and (2) the removal of the *yoke* of imperial Assyrian oppression from the neck of Zion/Judah (10:24–27).

but it is in his heart to destroy,
and to cut off nations not a few.
8 For he says:
"Are not my commanders all kings?
9 Is not Calno like Carchemish?
Is not Hamath like Arpad?
Is not Samaria like Damascus?
10 As my hand has reached to the
kingdoms of the idols
whose images were greater than
those of Jerusalem and
Samaria,
11 shall I not do to Jerusalem and her
idols
what I have done to Samaria and
her images?"

12 When the Lord has finished all his
work on Mount Zion and on Jerusalem,
he*a* will punish the arrogant boasting
of the king of Assyria and his haughty
pride. 13 For he says:
"By the strength of my hand I have
done it,
and by my wisdom, for I have
understanding;
I have removed the boundaries of
peoples,
and have plundered their
treasures;
like a bull I have brought down
those who sat on thrones.
14 My hand has found, like a nest,
the wealth of the peoples;
and as one gathers eggs that have
been forsaken,
so I have gathered all the earth;
and there was none that moved a
wing,
or opened its mouth, or chirped."

15 Shall the ax vaunt itself over the one
who wields it,
or the saw magnify itself against
the one who handles it?
As if a rod should raise the one who
lifts it up,
or as if a staff should lift the one
who is not wood!
16 Therefore the Sovereign, the Lord
of hosts,

will send wasting sickness among
his stout warriors,
and under his glory a burning will
be kindled,
like the burning of fire.
17 The light of Israel will become a fire,
and his Holy One a flame;
and it will burn and devour
his thorns and briers in one day.
18 The glory of his forest and his
fruitful land
the Lord will destroy, both soul
and body,
and it will be as when an invalid
wastes away.
19 The remnant of the trees of his forest
will be so few
that a child can write them down.

The Repentant Remnant of Israel

20 On that day the remnant of Israel
and the survivors of the house of Jacob
will no more lean on the one who struck
them, but will lean on the Lord, the
Holy One of Israel, in truth. 21 A remnant will return, the remnant of Jacob,
to the mighty God. 22 For though your
people Israel were like the sand of the
sea, only a remnant of them will return.
Destruction is decreed, overflowing
with righteousness. 23 For the Lord God
of hosts will make a full end, as decreed,
in all the earth.*b*

24 Therefore thus says the Lord God
of hosts: O my people, who live in Zion,
do not be afraid of the Assyrians when
they beat you with a rod and lift up their
staff against you as the Egyptians did.
25 For in a very little while my indignation will come to an end, and my anger
will be directed to their destruction.
26 The Lord of hosts will wield a whip
against them, as when he struck Midian at the rock of Oreb; his staff will be
over the sea, and he will lift it as he did
in Egypt. 27 On that day his burden will
be removed from your shoulder, and his
yoke will be destroyed from your neck.

a Heb *I*   *b* Or *land*

He has gone up from Rimmon,[a]
28 he has come to Aiath;
he has passed through Migron,
   at Michmash he stores his baggage;
29 they have crossed over the pass,
   at Geba they lodge for the night;
Ramah trembles,
   Gibeah of Saul has fled.
30 Cry aloud, O daughter Gallim!
   Listen, O Laishah!
   Answer her, O Anathoth!
31 Madmenah is in flight,
   the inhabitants of Gebim flee for
      safety.
32 This very day he will halt at Nob,
   he will shake his fist
   at the mount of daughter Zion,
   the hill of Jerusalem.

33 Look, the Sovereign, the LORD of
      hosts,
   will lop the boughs with terrifying
      power;
   the tallest trees will be cut down,
      and the lofty will be brought low.
34 He will hack down the thickets of
      the forest with an ax,
   and Lebanon with its majestic
      trees[b] will fall.

The Peaceful Kingdom

11 A shoot shall come out from the
      stump of Jesse,

and a branch shall grow out of his
   roots.
2 The spirit of the LORD shall rest on
      him,
   the spirit of wisdom and
      understanding,
   the spirit of counsel and might,
   the spirit of knowledge and the
      fear of the LORD.
3 His delight shall be in the fear of the
      LORD.

He shall not judge by what his eyes
   see,
   or decide by what his ears hear;
4 but with righteousness he shall judge
      the poor,
   and decide with equity for the
      meek of the earth;
he shall strike the earth with the rod
   of his mouth,
   and with the breath of his lips he
      shall kill the wicked.
5 Righteousness shall be the belt
      around his waist,
   and faithfulness the belt around
      his loins.

6 The wolf shall live with the lamb,
   the leopard shall lie down with the
      kid,

[a] Cn: Heb *and his yoke from your neck, and a yoke will be destroyed because of fatness* [b] Cn Compare Gk Vg: Heb *with a majestic one*

11:1–16 The Peaceable Kingdom

The promise oracle of vv. 1–9 is one of the most beloved texts of Scripture, often taken by Christians as christological prophecy. Certainly it is a "messianic" one, in that it describes the reign of a royal descendant of the line of Jesse's son, David (consistent with Nathan's dynastic oracle to David in 2 Sam. 7:16). The passage falls into the three scenes that typically give structure to the futuristic texts of the Bible, be they the relatively realistic visions of the earlier prophets or the cosmic and catastrophic scenarios of the later apocalyptic texts (see introduction; 2:2–5).

11:1–3a Onset—The coming of a new age is heralded by the appearance of an extraordinary figure of the Davidic line, uniquely equipped with *wisdom* and *the fear of the LORD*.

11:3b–5 Crisis—The day of judgment (often called the Day of the Lord) is good news for the *poor* and *meek of the earth*, because the

anointed ruler is righteous and just. For the same reason, the appearance of this king is bad news for *the wicked*.

11:6–9 Paradise—The new age that the just ruler inaugurates is pictured as a peaceable kingdom, in which even predators cease their killing and snakes stop striking. Though such a world is very different from the "red in tooth and claw" world that we know now, it is still "realistic" in the sense that the creatures are familiar ones, and the *holy mountain*, Zion, abides. No fire has destroyed the old world; no apocalypse has been consummated. No wonder the Quaker utopian visionary, Edward Hicks (1780–1849), made direct application of these verses to the American attempts to create a holy commonwealth on these shores. Hicks painted this scene more than 100 times, placing in the background of Isaiah's placid beasts the figures of William Penn and Delaware Indians making a treaty of peace in 1682, under an elm tree at Shackamaxon (now

the calf and the lion and the fatling
together,
and a little child shall lead them.
7 The cow and the bear shall graze,
their young shall lie down together;
and the lion shall eat straw like
the ox.
8 The nursing child shall play over the
hole of the asp,
and the weaned child shall put its
hand on the adder's den.
9 They will not hurt or destroy
on all my holy mountain;
for the earth will be full of the
knowledge of the LORD
as the waters cover the sea.

Return of the Remnant of Israel and Judah

10 On that day the root of Jesse shall
stand as a signal to the peoples; the
nations shall inquire of him, and his
dwelling shall be glorious.

11 On that day the Lord will extend
his hand yet a second time to recover
the remnant that is left of his people,
from Assyria, from Egypt, from Pathros,
from Ethiopia,*a* from Elam, from Shinar, from Hamath, and from the coastlands of the sea.

12 He will raise a signal for the nations,
and will assemble the outcasts of
Israel,
and gather the dispersed of Judah
from the four corners of the earth.

13 The jealousy of Ephraim shall depart,
the hostility of Judah shall be cut
off;
Ephraim shall not be jealous of
Judah,
and Judah shall not be hostile
towards Ephraim.
14 But they shall swoop down on the
backs of the Philistines in the
west,
together they shall plunder the
people of the east.
They shall put forth their hand
against Edom and Moab,
and the Ammonites shall obey
them.
15 And the LORD will utterly destroy
the tongue of the sea of Egypt;
and will wave his hand over the River
with his scorching wind;
and will split it into seven channels,
and make a way to cross on foot;
16 so there shall be a highway from
Assyria
for the remnant that is left of his
people,
as there was for Israel
when they came up from the land
of Egypt.

Thanksgiving and Praise

12 You will say in that day:
I will give thanks to you,
O LORD,

a Or Nubia; Heb Cush

---

part of Philadelphia), Pennsylvania. Utopians aside, the picture of a coming world free of violence remains a powerful image for the guidance of believers into the unknown future.

11:10–16—The theme of the return to the homeland of the remnant of *Ephraim* (the northern kingdom of Israel) and *Judah* recurs (see 7:3; 10:20–21). Previously, the Lord stretched out a hand to judge and destroy God's people (5:25). This *second time*, the divine hand reverses the sentence. The return from various ancient places of exile is anything but "peaceable," as Israel plunders and destroys its perennially hostile neighbors. This oracle is not meant to portray events of our history, such as the establishment in 1948 of the modern state of Israel, but anticipates the defeat of the Assyrians in Isaiah's own time

(see 37:36) or perhaps the later return from Babylonian exile (538 BCE).

11:16—In an anticipation of a theme common in the poetry of Isaiah of the exile (chaps. 40–55), the return from exile is portrayed as a new exodus.

12:1–6 Eschatological Hymnody

The first section of Isaiah concludes with a psalm of thanksgiving and hymn of praise in two stanzas (vv. 1–3, 4–6, respectively). Each stanza begins with the formula *You will say in that day* expressed with the singular *you* in v. 1 and the plural in v. 4. In eschatological texts, the phrase "in that day" refers to the coming "Day of the Lord" or eschaton, on which God triumphs over evil, saves the dispersed people, and inaugurates

for though you were angry
    with me,
your anger turned away,
    and you comforted me.

2 Surely God is my salvation;
    I will trust, and will not be afraid,
for the Lord God[a] is my strength
    and my might;
he has become my salvation.

3 With joy you will draw water from
the wells of salvation. 4 And you will say
in that day:
    Give thanks to the Lord,
        call on his name;
    make known his deeds among the
        nations;
    proclaim that his name is exalted.

5 Sing praises to the Lord, for he has
    done gloriously;
    let this be known[b] in all the earth.
6 Shout aloud and sing for joy,
    O royal[c] Zion,
    for great in your midst is the Holy
        One of Israel.

Proclamation against Babylon

13 The oracle concerning Babylon
that Isaiah son of Amoz saw.

2 On a bare hill raise a signal,
    cry aloud to them;
wave the hand for them to enter
    the gates of the nobles.
3 I myself have commanded my
    consecrated ones,
    have summoned my warriors, my
        proudly exulting ones,
    to execute my anger.

4 Listen, a tumult on the mountains
    as of a great multitude!
Listen, an uproar of kingdoms,
    of nations gathering together!
The Lord of hosts is mustering
    an army for battle.
5 They come from a distant land,
    from the end of the heavens,
the Lord and the weapons of his
    indignation,
    to destroy the whole earth.

6 Wail, for the day of the Lord is near;
    it will come like destruction from
        the Almighty![d]
7 Therefore all hands will be feeble,
    and every human heart will melt,
8   and they will be dismayed.

*a Heb for Yah, the Lord   b Or this is made known   c Or O inhabitant of
d Traditional rendering of Heb Shaddai*

the new age of peace and plenty (e.g., 10:20;
11:10–11; Zech 14:4, 6, 8, 9). That full narrative is left unspoken here, but clearly the singer
means to celebrate YHWH's victorious *strength*
and *might* that affect *salvation* for God's people
(Isa. 12:2; cf. Ps. 118:14) and radiate glory and
greatness from the holy dwelling place in *Zion*
(Isa. 12:6). Such language is consistent with the
so-called "enthronement psalms" (e.g., Pss. 96–
99), thought by some scholars to emanate from
an annual new year's festival at which YHWH
was ritually enthroned as divine sovereign. The
renewal of life that accompanied the renewal of
the Lord's rule may be symbolized by the water
drawn *from the wells of salvation* (Isa. 12:3).

13:1–23:18 Isaiah of Jerusalem. Part 2: Oracles against the Nations

When he groups together oracles against ten surrounding nations, Isaiah (or his editors) adopts a
strategy used by four of the other classical prophets of the Old Testament. Compare Jer. 46–51,
Ezek. 25–32, Amos 1–2, Zeph. 1–2.

13:1–22 Future Desolation of Babylon

The final destruction of the Neo-Babylonian
Empire did not occur until 539 BCE, when the
city surrendered without a fight to Cyrus, king of
Persia. During the prophetic ministry of Isaiah of
Jerusalem (ca. 742–687 BCE; see 1:1), Assyria,
not Babylon, was the dominant superpower of
the Near East. Babylon was gathering strength,
however, and had to be subdued repeatedly during the years of Isaiah's ministry. These Assyrian
campaigns culminated in the leveling of the city
in 689 BCE.

13:4–5—The *Lord of Hosts*, the divine warrior,
commands a heavenly *army* (see Zech. 14:5). As
in Isa. 5:26–30, however, this army is made up
of human warriors from *a distant land*. For a way
of looking at the troubling imagery of God as a
furious warrior who causes the death of *infants*
(v. 16) and the utter destruction of great cities (v.
19), see introduction.

13:6–13 *The day of the Lord*—is the usual
prophetic term for the crisis of divine intervention that spells doom for evildoers and prepares
the way for the new age of peace (see note at

Pangs and agony will seize them;
　　they will be in anguish like a
　　　woman in labor.
They will look aghast at one another;
　　their faces will be aflame.
9 See, the day of the LORD comes,
　　cruel, with wrath and fierce anger,
to make the earth a desolation,
　　and to destroy its sinners from it.
10 For the stars of the heavens and their
　　　constellations
　　will not give their light;
the sun will be dark at its rising,
　　and the moon will not shed its
　　　light.
11 I will punish the world for its evil,
　　and the wicked for their iniquity;
I will put an end to the pride of the
　　　arrogant,
　　and lay low the insolence of
　　　tyrants.
12 I will make mortals more rare than
　　　fine gold,
　　and humans than the gold of
　　　Ophir.
13 Therefore I will make the heavens
　　　tremble,
　　and the earth will be shaken out of
　　　its place,
at the wrath of the LORD of hosts
　　in the day of his fierce anger.
14 Like a hunted gazelle,
　　or like sheep with no one to gather
　　　them,
all will turn to their own people,
　　and all will flee to their own lands.
15 Whoever is found will be thrust
　　　through,
　　and whoever is caught will fall by
　　　the sword.
16 Their infants will be dashed to
　　　pieces

before their eyes;
　　their houses will be plundered,
　　　and their wives ravished.
17 See, I am stirring up the Medes
　　　against them,
　　who have no regard for silver
　　　and do not delight in gold.
18 Their bows will slaughter the young
　　　men;
　　they will have no mercy on the
　　　fruit of the womb;
　　their eyes will not pity children.
19 And Babylon, the glory of kingdoms,
　　the splendor and pride of the
　　　Chaldeans,
will be like Sodom and Gomorrah
　　when God overthrew them.
20 It will never be inhabited
　　or lived in for all generations;
Arabs will not pitch their tents
　　　there,
　　shepherds will not make their
　　　flocks lie down there.
21 But wild animals will lie down
　　　there,
　　and its houses will be full of
　　　howling creatures;
there ostriches will live,
　　and there goat-demons will dance.
22 Hyenas will cry in its towers,
　　and jackals in the pleasant palaces;
its time is close at hand,
　　and its days will not be prolonged.

Restoration of Judah

14 But the LORD will have compassion on Jacob and will again choose Israel, and will set them in their own land; and aliens will join them and attach themselves to the house of Jacob. 2 And the nations will take them and bring them to their place, and the

---

11:3b–5). Isaiah 13:11 specifically identifies *the arrogant* and *tyrants* as recipients of divine wrath, an assurance that continues to encourage victims of tyranny to this day. In vv. 10, 13 the judgment against Babylon already takes on some of the cosmic dimensions that typify the judgment day in later apocalyptic texts.

14:1–32 Good News and Bad News
14:1–2—A brief prose oracle of promise interrupts the threat against Babylon. The good news is that Israel will be restored to their land. The bad news is that they will find themselves in the role of slavemasters and oppressors themselves. Only faithfulness to the covenant rules of justice and righteousness will save them from perpetuating tyranny.

house of Israel will possess the nations*a*
as male and female slaves in the LORD's
land; they will take captive those who
were their captors, and rule over those
who oppressed them.

Downfall of the King of Babylon

3 When the LORD has given you rest
from your pain and turmoil and the
hard service with which you were made
to serve, **4** you will take up this taunt
against the king of Babylon:

How the oppressor has ceased!
  How his insolence*b* has ceased!
5 The LORD has broken the staff of the
    wicked,
  the scepter of rulers,
6 that struck down the peoples in
    wrath
  with unceasing blows,
  that ruled the nations in anger
  with unrelenting persecution.
7 The whole earth is at rest and quiet;
  they break forth into singing.
8 The cypresses exult over you,
  the cedars of Lebanon, saying,
"Since you were laid low,
  no one comes to cut us down."
9 Sheol beneath is stirred up
  to meet you when you come;
it rouses the shades to greet you,
  all who were leaders of the earth;
it raises from their thrones
  all who were kings of the nations.
10 All of them will speak
  and say to you:
"You too have become as weak
    as we!
  You have become like us!"
11 Your pomp is brought down to
    Sheol,
  and the sound of your harps;
maggots are the bed beneath you,
  and worms are your covering.

12 How you are fallen from heaven,
    O Day Star, son of Dawn!
How you are cut down to the
    ground,
  you who laid the nations low!
13 You said in your heart,
  "I will ascend to heaven;
I will raise my throne
  above the stars of God;
I will sit on the mount of assembly
  on the heights of Zaphon;*c*
14 I will ascend to the tops of the
    clouds,
  I will make myself like the Most
    High."
15 But you are brought down to Sheol,
  to the depths of the Pit.
16 Those who see you will stare at you,
  and ponder over you:
"Is this the man who made the earth
    tremble,
  who shook kingdoms,
17 who made the world like a desert
  and overthrew its cities,
  who would not let his prisoners go
    home?"
18 All the kings of the nations lie in
    glory,
  each in his own tomb;
19 but you are cast out, away from your
    grave,
  like loathsome carrion,*d*
clothed with the dead, those pierced
    by the sword,
  who go down to the stones of the
    Pit,
  like a corpse trampled underfoot.
20 You will not be joined with them in
    burial,
  because you have destroyed your
    land,
  you have killed your people.

a Heb *them*   *b* Q Ms Compare Gk Syr Vg: Meaning of MT uncertain
c Or *assembly in the far north*   *d* Cn Compare Gk: Heb *like a loathed branch*

14:3–23—This mocking poem, written in the
Hebrew meter of a dirge, repeatedly contrasts the
arrogant self-glorification of the king of Babylon
with his ultimate fate of being cast into the Pit,
the underworld of *Sheol*. The use of Canaanite
divine titles, *Day Star, son of Dawn,* and the

king's aspiration to sit on the Canaanite Olympus,
Mount *Zaphon,* add heavy irony to his fate, a fate
worse than death, because it involves no decent
burial (vv. 18–20) and threatens the slaughter of
his descendants who would be his only real hope
for immortality (vv. 21–22).

May the descendants of evildoers
        nevermore be named!
21 Prepare slaughter for his sons
        because of the guilt of their father.*
    Let them never rise to possess the
            earth
        or cover the face of the world with
            cities.

22 I will rise up against them, says
the LORD of hosts, and will cut off from
Babylon name and remnant, offspring
and posterity, says the LORD. 23 And I
will make it a possession of the hedgehog, and pools of water, and I will sweep
it with the broom of destruction, says
the LORD of hosts.

An Oracle concerning Assyria

24 The LORD of hosts has sworn:
    As I have designed,
        so shall it be;
    and as I have planned,
        so shall it come to pass:
25 I will break the Assyrian in my land,
        and on my mountains trample him
            under foot;
    his yoke shall be removed from
            them,
        and his burden from their
            shoulders.
26 This is the plan that is planned
        concerning the whole earth;
    and this is the hand that is stretched
            out
        over all the nations.
27 For the LORD of hosts has planned,

and who will annul it?
    His hand is stretched out,
        and who will turn it back?

An Oracle concerning Philistia

28 In the year that King Ahaz died this
oracle came:

29 Do not rejoice, all you Philistines,
        that the rod that struck you is
            broken,
    for from the root of the snake will
            come forth an adder,
        and its fruit will be a flying fiery
            serpent.
30 The firstborn of the poor will graze,
        and the needy lie down in safety;
    but I will make your root die of
            famine,
        and your remnant I* will kill.
31 Wail, O gate; cry, O city;
        melt in fear, O Philistia, all of you!
    For smoke comes out of the north,
        and there is no straggler in its
            ranks.
32 What will one answer the
            messengers of the nation?
    "The LORD has founded Zion,
        and the needy among his people
            will find refuge in her."

An Oracle concerning Moab

15
An oracle concerning Moab.

    Because Ar is laid waste in a night,

a Syr Compare Gk: Heb *fathers*   *b* Q Ms Vg: MT *he*

14:24–27—Against Assyria the prophet announces
only that the Lord has a *plan* to defeat the empire
and that *his hand is stretched out*, a gesture of
terrible and irresistible power against an enemy
of God.

14:28–32—Lying behind this datable oracle
against Judah's neighbor to the southwest, Philistia, is its revolt in 714 BCE against Assyrian rule.
Isaiah knows their cause is hopeless. The enemy
from the **north**, the bad-luck direction from which
enemies typically come, cannot be resisted. To
emissaries from Philistia seeking an alliance with
Judah, his answer (v. 32) is the same as it is to
Ahaz (7:3–9) earlier and Hezekiah later (37:35):
trust the Lord to defend Zion, which God has
declared to be inviolable.

15:1–16:13 Moab Brought Down

This dirge against Moab, Judah's neighbor to the
east (today the central part of Jordan), pictures
awesome destruction, city by city. The oracle may
reflect one or another of the several Assyrian sub-
jugations of the little country, or even devastating
Arab raids. The tone is more horrified than vengeful;
indeed, 16:3–5 implores the king of Judah to grant
asylum to Moabite refugees and then anticipates a
happier day for Moab under the just rule of a Davidic ruler. That vision is consistent with God's early
covenant with Israel, through Abram, that "in you
all the families of the earth shall be blessed" (Gen.
12:3), as well as with the divine promise, frequently
repeated in the later parts of Isaiah, that Israel will
be "a light to the nations" (e.g., 42:6, 49:6).

Moab is undone;
because Kir is laid waste in a night,
Moab is undone.

2 Dibon*a* has gone up to the temple,
to the high places to weep;
over Nebo and over Medeba
Moab wails.
On every head is baldness,
every beard is shorn;

3 in the streets they bind on sackcloth;
on the housetops and in the
squares
everyone wails and melts in tears.

4 Heshbon and Elealeh cry out,
their voices are heard as far as
Jahaz;
therefore the loins of Moab quiver;*b*
his soul trembles.

5 My heart cries out for Moab;
his fugitives flee to Zoar,
to Eglath-shelishiyah.
For at the ascent of Luhith
they go up weeping;
on the road to Horonaim
they raise a cry of destruction;

6 the waters of Nimrim
are a desolation;
the grass is withered, the new
growth fails,
the verdure is no more.

7 Therefore the abundance they have
gained
and what they have laid up
they carry away
over the Wadi of the Willows.

8 For a cry has gone
around the land of Moab;
the wailing reaches to Eglaim,
the wailing reaches to Beer-elim.

9 For the waters of Dibon*c* are full of
blood;
yet I will bring upon Dibon*c* even
more—
a lion for those of Moab who escape,
for the remnant of the land.

16 Send lambs
to the ruler of the land,
from Sela, by way of the desert,
to the mount of daughter Zion.

2 Like fluttering birds,

like scattered nestlings,
so are the daughters of Moab
at the fords of the Arnon.

3 "Give counsel,
grant justice;
make your shade like night
at the height of noon;
hide the outcasts,
do not betray the fugitive;

4 let the outcasts of Moab
settle among you;
be a refuge to them
from the destroyer."

When the oppressor is no more,
and destruction has ceased,
and marauders have vanished from
the land,

5 then a throne shall be established in
steadfast love
in the tent of David,
and on it shall sit in faithfulness
a ruler who seeks justice
and is swift to do what is right.

6 We have heard of the pride of Moab
—how proud he is!—
of his arrogance, his pride, and his
insolence;
his boasts are false.

7 Therefore let Moab wail,
let everyone wail for Moab.
Mourn, utterly stricken,
for the raisin cakes of Kir-hareseth.

8 For the fields of Heshbon languish,
and the vines of Sibmah,
whose clusters once made drunk
the lords of the nations,
reached to Jazer
and strayed to the desert;
their shoots once spread abroad
and crossed over the sea.

9 Therefore I weep with the weeping
of Jazer
for the vines of Sibmah;
I drench you with my tears,
O Heshbon and Elealeh;
for the shout over your fruit harvest

---

a Cn: Heb *the house and Dibon*   *b* Cn Compare Gk Syr: Heb *the armed men
of Moab cry aloud*   *c* Q Ms Vg Compare Syr: MT *Dimon*

and your grain harvest has ceased.
¹⁰ Joy and gladness are taken away
    from the fruitful field;
and in the vineyards no songs are
    sung,
    no shouts are raised;
no treader treads out wine in the
    presses;
    the vintage-shout is hushed.ᵃ
¹¹ Therefore my heart throbs like a
    harp for Moab,
and my very soul for Kir-heres.

12 When Moab presents himself, when he wearies himself upon the high place, when he comes to his sanctuary to pray, he will not prevail.

13 This was the word that the LORD spoke concerning Moab in the past. ¹⁴ But now the LORD says, In three years, like the years of a hired worker, the glory of Moab will be brought into contempt, in spite of all its great multitude; and those who survive will be very few and feeble.

An Oracle concerning Damascus

17 An oracle concerning Damascus.

See, Damascus will cease to be a city,
    and will become a heap of ruins.
² Her towns will be deserted forever;ᵇ
    they will be places for flocks,
    which will lie down, and no one
      will make them afraid.
³ The fortress will disappear from
    Ephraim,
and the kingdom from Damascus;
and the remnant of Aram will be
    like the glory of the children of
    Israel,
        says the LORD of hosts.

⁴ On that day
    the glory of Jacob will be brought
    low,
    and the fat of his flesh will grow
    lean.
⁵ And it shall be as when reapers
    gather standing grain
    and their arms harvest the
    ears,
and as when one gleans the ears of
    grain
    in the Valley of Rephaim.
⁶ Gleanings will be left in it,
    as when an olive tree is beaten—
two or three berries
    in the top of the highest bough,
four or five
    on the branches of a fruit tree,
        says the LORD God of Israel.

7 On that day people will regard their Maker, and their eyes will look to the Holy One of Israel; ⁸ they will not have regard for the altars, the work of their hands, and they will not look to what their own fingers have made, either the sacred polesᶜ or the altars of incense.

9 On that day their strong cities will be like the deserted places of the Hivites and the Amorites,ᵈ which they deserted because of the children of Israel, and there will be desolation.

¹⁰ For you have forgotten the God of
    your salvation,
    and have not remembered the
    Rock of your refuge;
therefore, though you plant pleasant
    plants
    and set out slips of an alien god,

ᵃ Gk: Heb I have hushed ᵇ Cn Compare Gk: Heb the cities of Aroer are deserted ᶜ Heb Asherim ᵈ Cn Compare Gk: Heb places of the wood and the highest bough

---

17:1–14 Mixed Threats and Promises

17:1–3—Because this oracle against Damascus, the Aramean capital northeast of Israel, also includes a threat against Ephraim, the northern kingdom of Israel, it probably reflects their failed alliance against Judah in the Syro-Ephraimite War (735–732 BCE).

17:4–14—Four short oracles point to different outcomes of *that day* of divine judgment.

17:4–6—So complete is the purge of *Jacob* (Judah and Israel alike), that only gleanings (perhaps the saving remnant) remain.

17:7–9—A guarded promise ensues—the chastened people will abandon their idolatrous practices, including veneration of the *sacred poles* borrowed from the Canaanite cult of the goddess Asherah, who was sometimes regarded in popular religion as YHWH's consort.

11 though you make them grow on the
day that you plant them,
and make them blossom in the
morning that you sow;
yet the harvest will flee away
in a day of grief and incurable pain.

12 Ah, the thunder of many peoples,
they thunder like the thundering
of the sea!
Ah, the roar of nations,
they roar like the roaring of
mighty waters!
13 The nations roar like the roaring of
many waters,
but he will rebuke them, and they
will flee far away,
chased like chaff on the mountains
before the wind
and whirling dust before the storm.
14 At evening time, lo, terror!
Before morning, they are no more.
This is the fate of those who
despoil us,
and the lot of those who plunder us.

An Oracle concerning Ethiopia

18 Ah, land of whirring wings
beyond the rivers of Ethiopia,[a]
2 sending ambassadors by the Nile
in vessels of papyrus on the waters!
Go, you swift messengers,
to a nation tall and smooth,
to a people feared near and far,
a nation mighty and conquering,
whose land the rivers divide.

3 All you inhabitants of the world,
you who live on the earth,

when a signal is raised on the
mountains, look!
When a trumpet is blown, listen!
4 For thus the LORD said to me:
I will quietly look from my dwelling
like clear heat in sunshine,
like a cloud of dew in the heat of
harvest.
5 For before the harvest, when the
blossom is over
and the flower becomes a ripening
grape,
he will cut off the shoots with
pruning hooks,
and the spreading branches he will
hew away.
6 They shall all be left
to the birds of prey of the
mountains
and to the animals of the earth.
And the birds of prey will summer
on them,
and all the animals of the earth
will winter on them.

7 At that time gifts will be brought to
the LORD of hosts from[b] a people tall
and smooth, from a people feared near
and far, a nation mighty and conquering, whose land the rivers divide, to
Mount Zion, the place of the name of
the LORD of hosts.

An Oracle concerning Egypt

19 An oracle concerning Egypt.

See, the LORD is riding on a swift
cloud

[a] Or Nubia; Heb Cush [b] Q Ms Gk Vg: MT of

17:12–14—The series concludes with a stirring reminder that God is sovereign over the chaotic forces that sweep around Jerusalem and leads to the general rule that *those who despoil us* will be no more. Although people of faith today can hardly take this as assurance that particular politi-cal and military enemies will suffer defeat at di-vine or even human hands, we can draw strength from the conviction that justice and righteousness are on God's side and therefore will ultimately prevail.

18:1–7 Cush Will Fall
Directed at Cush, which we identify with the

upper reaches of the Nile from southern Egypt to modern Sudan and *Ethiopia*, this oracle against the *tall and smooth* (clean-shaven, v. 2) Nubian warriors of that region horrifies. In vv. 4–6, the Lord's quiet glance from heaven, described in springtime imagery, leaves the Cushites littered about as carrion to be fed upon by *birds of prey* (v. 6).

19:1–25 Egypt Will Submit to YHWH

19:1–15—In this lengthy poetic oracle against Egypt, the Lord first threatens them with civil war, vv. 1–3, then an oppressive ruler, v. 4 (both of which could describe conditions in the eighth

and comes to Egypt;
the idols of Egypt will tremble at his
    presence,
    and the heart of the Egyptians will
        melt within them.
2 I will stir up Egyptians against
    Egyptians,
    and they will fight, one against the
        other,
    neighbor against neighbor,
    city against city, kingdom against
        kingdom;
3 the spirit of the Egyptians within
    them will be emptied out,
    and I will confound their plans;
    they will consult the idols and the
        spirits of the dead
    and the ghosts and the familiar
        spirits;
4 I will deliver the Egyptians
    into the hand of a hard master;
    a fierce king will rule over them,
        says the Sovereign, the Lord of
        hosts.

5 The waters of the Nile will be dried
    up,
    and the river will be parched and
        dry;
6 its canals will become foul,
    and the branches of Egypt's Nile
        will diminish and dry up,
    reeds and rushes will rot away.
7 There will be bare places by the
    Nile,
    on the brink of the Nile;
    and all that is sown by the Nile will
        dry up,
    be driven away, and be no more.
8 Those who fish will mourn;
    all who cast hooks in the Nile will
        lament,

and those who spread nets on the
    water will languish.
9 The workers in flax will be in
    despair,
    and the carders and those at the
        loom will grow pale.
10 Its weavers will be dismayed,
    and all who work for wages will be
        grieved.

11 The princes of Zoan are utterly
    foolish;
    the wise counselors of Pharaoh
        give stupid counsel.
How can you say to Pharaoh,
    "I am one of the sages,
    a descendant of ancient kings"?
12 Where now are your sages?
    Let them tell you and make known
    what the Lord of hosts has
        planned against Egypt.
13 The princes of Zoan have become
    fools,
    and the princes of Memphis are
        deluded;
    those who are the cornerstones of its
        tribes
    have led Egypt astray.
14 The Lord has poured into them[a]
    a spirit of confusion;
    and they have made Egypt stagger in
        all its doings
    as a drunkard staggers around in
        vomit.
15 Neither head nor tail, palm branch
    or reed,
    will be able to do anything for
        Egypt.

16 On that day the Egyptians will be
like women, and tremble with fear before

[a] Gk Compare Tg: Heb *it*

century BCE). Drought, the absence of the annual *Nile* flood, and crop failure follow next (vv.
5–10). The oracle concludes with expressions
of contempt for *the princes of Zoan* (Tanis, in
the Delta) (v. 11) and *Memphis* (the holy city
and capital of lower Egypt) (v. 13), who fail to
give Pharaoh wise counsel. Instead of the "spirit
of God" bestowed on Joseph that set him apart
from all other counselors of his Pharaoh, the Lord

pours upon these poor staggering fools *a spirit of
confusion*. Good government and public policy
are thus portrayed as gifts of God, and not merely
secular good luck.

19:16–25—There follows one of the most remarkable of all prophetic oracles. Written in prose
yet given strophic structure by the refrain *on
that day*, the futuristic or eschatological oracle
focuses initially on impending Egyptian *fear* of

the hand that the Lord of hosts raises against them. ¹⁷ And the land of Judah will become a terror to the Egyptians; everyone to whom it is mentioned will fear because of the plan that the Lord of hosts is planning against them.

Egypt, Assyria, and Israel Blessed

18 On that day there will be five cities in the land of Egypt that speak the language of Canaan and swear allegiance to the Lord of hosts. One of these will be called the City of the Sun.

19 On that day there will be an altar to the Lord in the center of the land of Egypt, and a pillar to the Lord at its border. ²⁰ It will be a sign and a witness to the Lord of hosts in the land of Egypt; when they cry to the Lord because of oppressors, he will send them a savior, and will defend and deliver them. ²¹ The Lord will make himself known to the Egyptians; and the Egyptians will know the Lord on that day, and will worship with sacrifice and burnt offering, and they will make vows to the Lord and perform them. ²² The Lord will strike Egypt, striking and healing; they will return to the Lord, and he will listen to their supplications and heal them.

23 On that day there will be a highway from Egypt to Assyria, and the Assyrian will come into Egypt, and the Egyptian into Assyria, and the Egyptians will worship with the Assyrians.

24 On that day Israel will be the third with Egypt and Assyria, a blessing in the midst of the earth, ²⁵ whom the Lord of hosts has blessed, saying, "Blessed be Egypt my people, and Assyria the work of my hands, and Israel my heritage."

Isaiah Dramatizes the Conquest of Egypt and Ethiopia

20 In the year that the commander-in-chief, who was sent by King Sargon of Assyria, came to Ashdod and fought against it and took it— ²at that time the Lord had spoken to Isaiah son of Amoz, saying, "Go, and loose the sackcloth from your loins and take your sandals off your feet," and he had done so, walking naked and barefoot. ³ Then the Lord said, "Just as my servant Isaiah has walked naked and barefoot for three years as a sign and a portent against Egypt and Ethiopia,ᵃ ⁴ so shall the king of Assyria lead away the Egyptians as captives and the Ethiopiansᵇ as exiles, both the young and the old, naked and barefoot, with buttocks uncovered, to the shame of Egypt. ⁵ And they shall be dismayed and confounded because of Ethiopiaᵃ their hope and of Egypt their boast. ⁶ In that day the inhabitants of this coastland will say, 'See, this is what has happened to those in whom we hoped and to whom we fled for help and deliverance from the king of Assyria! And we, how shall we escape?'"

ᵃ Or Nubia; Heb Cush   ᵇ Or Nubians; Heb Cushites

YHWH, Judah's Lord (vv. 16–17). Fear leads first to **allegiance** (v. 18) and then to altars, burnt offerings, vows, and all the rituals of worship (vv. 19–22). The Lord is portrayed as **striking and healing** Egypt, an image of God not congenial to modern Christians (guided as we are by the simple teaching of 1 John 4:16, "God is love"), yet not foreign to faith in a God who is both just and merciful.

19:23–25—The prose oracle culminates in a sweeping vision of universal love for Israel's God by the great powers, Egypt and Assyria, and YHWH's loving designation of the erstwhile hated enemies as one with Israel as **my people, the work of my hands,** and **my heritage.** When political and cultural tensions, even acts of terror, tempt us to vilify and demonize whole peoples, vv. 23–25 offer us an alternative view even of our enemies. From an understanding that our own Egypts and Assyrias are God's peoples can spring an alternate future.

20:1–6 Isaiah's Naked Walk

By the sign-act of walking naked at the Lord's command, Isaiah dramatizes to the Philistine city of Ashdod the folly of its reliance on foreign help in its revolt in 711 BCE against the powerful Assyrian king Sargon II. The prophet warned his own leaders against trusting for protection by foreign allies as well (e.g., 30:1–7, 31:1–3), insisting that safety lay in trust in the Lord as protector of inviolable Jerusalem (31:4–5).

Oracles concerning Babylon, Edom, and Arabia

21 The oracle concerning the wilderness of the sea.

As whirlwinds in the Negeb
    sweep on,
  it comes from the desert,
  from a terrible land.
2 A stern vision is told to me;
    the betrayer betrays,
    and the destroyer destroys.
  Go up, O Elam,
    lay siege, O Media;
  all the sighing she has caused
    I bring to an end.
3 Therefore my loins are filled with
      anguish;
    pangs have seized me,
    like the pangs of a woman in labor;
  I am bowed down so that I cannot
      hear,
    I am dismayed so that I cannot see.
4 My mind reels, horror has appalled
      me;
    the twilight I longed for
    has been turned for me into
      trembling.
5 They prepare the table,
    they spread the rugs,
    they eat, they drink.
  Rise up, commanders,
    oil the shield!
6 For thus the Lord said to me:
  "Go, post a lookout,
    let him announce what he sees.
7 When he sees riders, horsemen in
      pairs,
    riders on donkeys, riders on
      camels,
  let him listen diligently,
    very diligently."
8 Then the watcher[a] called out:

"Upon a watchtower I stand, O Lord,
    continually by day,
  and at my post I am stationed
    throughout the night.
9 Look, there they come, riders,
    horsemen in pairs!"
  Then he responded,
    "Fallen, fallen is Babylon;
  and all the images of her gods
    lie shattered on the ground."
10 O my threshed and winnowed one,
    what I have heard from the LORD
      of hosts,
  the God of Israel, I announce to
    you.

11 The oracle concerning Dumah.

One is calling to me from Seir,
  "Sentinel, what of the night?
  Sentinel, what of the night?"
12 The sentinel says:
  "Morning comes, and also the night.
    If you will inquire, inquire;
    come back again."

13 The oracle concerning the desert plain.

In the scrub of the desert plain you
      will lodge,
    O caravans of Dedanites.
14 Bring water to the thirsty,
    meet the fugitive with bread,
  O inhabitants of the land of Tema.
15 For they have fled from the swords,
    from the drawn sword,
  from the bent bow,
    and from the stress of battle.

16 For thus the Lord said to me: Within a year, according to the years of a hired worker, all the glory of Kedar will come to an end; 17 and the remaining bows

a Q Ms: MT *a lion*

21:1–16 Fallen, Fallen Is Babylon

21:1–10—The meaning of this enigmatic oracle is explicated in v. 9b: *Fallen, fallen is Babylon*. Acting as watchman, the prophet conveys to Judah, which looked to Babylon for protection against the Assyrian king, Sennacherib, the horrifying news that Babylon would offer no "cover" (22:8; see introduction).

21:11–12—Dumah was a city-state in the northern Arabian desert, also plundered by Sennacherib. From it, the sentinel can raise no answer. There is only the silence of death and destruction.

21:13–17—Various other north Arabian tribes or regions are also threatened with defeat and destruction.

of Kedar's warriors will be few; for the LORD, the God of Israel, has spoken.

A Warning of Destruction of Jerusalem

22 The oracle concerning the valley of vision.

What do you mean that you have
  gone up,
  all of you, to the housetops,
[2] you that are full of shoutings,
    tumultuous city, exultant town?
  Your slain are not slain by the
    sword,
    nor are they dead in battle.
[3] Your rulers have all fled together;
    they were captured without the use
    of a bow.*a*
  All of you who were found were
    captured,
    though they had fled far away.*b*
[4] Therefore I said:
  Look away from me,
    let me weep bitter tears;
  do not try to comfort me
    for the destruction of my beloved
    people.

[5] For the Lord GOD of hosts has a
    day
    of tumult and trampling and
    confusion
  in the valley of vision,
  a battering down of walls
    and a cry for help to the
    mountains.
[6] Elam bore the quiver
    with chariots and cavalry,*c*
    and Kir uncovered the shield.

[7] Your choicest valleys were full of
    chariots,
    and the cavalry took their stand at
    the gates.
[8] He has taken away the covering of
    Judah.

On that day you looked to the weapons of the House of the Forest, [9] and you saw that there were many breaches in the city of David, and you collected the waters of the lower pool. [10] You counted the houses of Jerusalem, and you broke down the houses to fortify the wall. [11] You made a reservoir between the two walls for the water of the old pool. But you did not look to him who did it, or have regard for him who planned it long ago.

[12] In that day the Lord GOD of hosts
    called to weeping and
    mourning,
    to baldness and putting on
    sackcloth;
[13] but instead there was joy and
    festivity,
    killing oxen and slaughtering
    sheep,
    eating meat and drinking wine.
  "Let us eat and drink,
    for tomorrow we die."
[14] The LORD of hosts has revealed
    himself in my ears:
  Surely this iniquity will not be
    forgiven you until you die,
    says the Lord GOD of hosts.

a Or without their bows *b* Gk Syr Vg: Heb *fled from far away* *c* Meaning of Heb uncertain

---

22:1–25 Jerusalem, Too, Is in Jeopardy
The collection of oracles against the nations (chaps. 13–23) is interrupted by two threats against Jerusalem itself, occasioned by the fall of its protector, Babylon.

22:1–14—Extrapolating from the description in vv. 8b–11 of siege preparations made in Jerusalem, including a possible reference to the Siloam water tunnel constructed by Hezekiah (715–687 BCE; see 2 Kgs. 20:20), the occasion of this oracle may be the defeat of rebellious Babylon and its allies by Sennacherib in 703 BCE. The sense of urgency pervading the oracle is that

Judah, Babylon's ally, would be next (as indeed it was in 701 BCE). The Judean lament is summed up in v. 8: *He has taken away the covering of Judah.* The prophet's response condemns the people for their failure to acknowledge that the Lord, the one *who planned it long ago* (v. 11), is the true protector to whom contrition and supplication should be directed (v. 12). Isaiah has no patience with the self-sufficient and even daredevil attitude of those who celebrate their puny preparations for war with festivities and the hedonistic cry, *Let us eat and drink, for tomorrow we die* (v. 13).

Denunciation of Self-Seeking Officials

15 Thus says the Lord GOD of hosts: Come, go to this steward, to Shebna, who is master of the household, and say to him: ¹⁶ What right do you have here? Who are your relatives here, that you have cut out a tomb here for yourself, cutting a tomb on the height, and carving a habitation for yourself in the rock? ¹⁷ The LORD is about to hurl you away violently, my fellow. He will seize firm hold on you, ¹⁸ whirl you round and round, and throw you like a ball into a wide land; there you shall die, and there your splendid chariots shall lie, O you disgrace to your master's house! ¹⁹ I will thrust you from your office, and you will be pulled down from your post.

20 On that day I will call my servant Eliakim son of Hilkiah, ²¹ and will clothe him with your robe and bind your sash on him. I will commit your authority to his hand, and he shall be a father to the inhabitants of Jerusalem and to the house of Judah. ²² I will place on his shoulder the key of the house of David; he shall open, and no one shall shut; he shall shut, and no one shall open. ²³ I will fasten him like a peg in a secure place, and he will become a throne of honor to his ancestral house. ²⁴ And they will hang on him the whole weight of his ancestral house, the offspring and issue, every small vessel, from the cups to all the flagons. ²⁵ On that day, says the LORD of hosts, the peg that was fastened in a secure place will give way; it will be cut down and fall, and the load that was on it will perish, for the LORD has spoken.

An Oracle concerning Tyre

23

The oracle concerning Tyre.

Wail, O ships of Tarshish,
    for your fortress is destroyed.ᵃ
When they came in from Cyprus
    they learned of it.
² Be still, O inhabitants of the coast,
    O merchants of Sidon,
your messengers crossed over the
        seaᵇ
³   and were on the mighty waters;
your revenue was the grain of
        Shihor,
    the harvest of the Nile;
    you were the merchant of the
        nations.
⁴ Be ashamed, O Sidon, for the sea has
        spoken,
    the fortress of the sea, saying:
"I have neither labored nor given
        birth,
    I have neither reared young men
    nor brought up young women."
⁵ When the report comes to Egypt,
    they will be in anguish over the
        report about Tyre.
⁶ Cross over to Tarshish—
    wail, O inhabitants of the coast!
⁷ Is this your exultant city
    whose origin is from days of old,
whose feet carried her
    to settle far away?
⁸ Who has planned this
    against Tyre, the bestower of
        crowns,
    whose merchants were princes,

ᵃ Cn Compare verse 14: Heb for it is destroyed, without houses   ᵇ Q Ms: MT crossing over the sea, they replenished you

---

22:15–25—This prose oracle reveals that corruption and intrigue flourished in the Jerusalem court even in the face of crisis. Hezekiah's steward, *Shebna*, having overreached in preparing a personal tomb in the royal cemetery, must go in favor of *Eliakim son of Hilkiah* (who will himself prove to be a weak peg on which to hang authority, v. 25). In 2 Kgs. 18:18, both men are serving together in Hezekiah's court.

23:1–18 Proud Tyre Brought Down

As with the threat against Jerusalem in the pre-

ceding chapter (22:11b), the prophet identifies an impending humiliation of the rich Canaanite/Phoenician seaport of Tyre as YHWH's work. It is the Lord's plan *to defile the pride of all glory* (23:9; see also the charge of pride in Ezekiel's remarkable oracle against the king of Tyre, Ezek. 28:1–19). Modern readers may find it difficult to accept the military defeat of a nation, then or now, as direct divine retribution for pride, but the notion that human autonomy is far from absolute in a world created and ruled by a just God is fundamental to faith.

whose traders were the honored of
the earth?

9 The LORD of hosts has planned it—
to defile the pride of all glory,
to shame all the honored of the
earth.

10 Cross over to your own land,
O ships of*a* Tarshish;
this is a harbor*b* no more.

11 He has stretched out his hand over
the sea,
he has shaken the kingdoms;
the LORD has given command
concerning Canaan
to destroy its fortresses.

12 He said:
You will exult no longer,
O oppressed virgin daughter
Sidon;
rise, cross over to Cyprus—
even there you will have no rest.

13 Look at the land of the Chaldeans! This is the people; it was not
Assyria. They destined Tyre for wild animals. They erected their siege towers,
they tore down her palaces, they made
her a ruin.*c*

14 Wail, O ships of Tarshish,
for your fortress is destroyed.

15 From that day Tyre will be forgotten
for seventy years, the lifetime of one
king. At the end of seventy years, it will
happen to Tyre as in the song about the
prostitute:

16 Take a harp,
go about the city,
you forgotten prostitute!
Make sweet melody,
sing many songs,
that you may be remembered.

17 At the end of seventy years, the LORD
will visit Tyre, and she will return to her
trade, and will prostitute herself with all
the kingdoms of the world on the face

of the earth. 18 Her merchandise and her
wages will be dedicated to the LORD; her
profits*d* will not be stored or hoarded,
but her merchandise will supply abundant food and fine clothing for those
who live in the presence of the LORD.

Impending Judgment on the Earth

24 Now the LORD is about to lay
waste the earth and make it
desolate,
and he will twist its surface and
scatter its inhabitants.

2 And it shall be, as with the people,
so with the priest;
as with the slave, so with his
master;
as with the maid, so with her
mistress;
as with the buyer, so with the seller;
as with the lender, so with the
borrower;
as with the creditor, so with the
debtor.

3 The earth shall be utterly laid waste
and utterly despoiled;
for the LORD has spoken this word.

4 The earth dries up and withers,
the world languishes and withers;
the heavens languish together with
the earth.

5 The earth lies polluted
under its inhabitants;
for they have transgressed laws,
violated the statutes,
broken the everlasting covenant.

6 Therefore a curse devours the earth,
and its inhabitants suffer for their
guilt;
therefore the inhabitants of the earth
dwindled,
and few people are left.

a Cn Compare Gk: Heb *like the Nile, daughter*   *b* Cn: Heb *restraint*
c Meaning of Heb uncertain   *d* Heb *it*

23:15–18—After a symbolic span of seventy years
(cf. Jer. 25:11, 12; Dan. 9:2, 24), Tyre, like an
aging prostitute, would get back in business. The
passage ends on a note common in oracles about
other nations throughout the book of Isaiah,

namely, that in end times the wealth of nations
would flow to the Lord in Jerusalem (e.g., Isa.
18:7; 60:5).

24:1–27:13 The Isaiah Apocalypse
24:1–23 God Will Judge the Earth

7 The wine dries up,
   the vine languishes,
   all the merry-hearted sigh.
8 The mirth of the timbrels is stilled,
   the noise of the jubilant has
      ceased,
   the mirth of the lyre is stilled.
9 No longer do they drink wine with
      singing;
   strong drink is bitter to those who
      drink it.
10 The city of chaos is broken down,
   every house is shut up so that no
      one can enter.
11 There is an outcry in the streets for
      lack of wine;
   all joy has reached its eventide;
   the gladness of the earth is
      banished.
12 Desolation is left in the city,
   the gates are battered into ruins.
13 For thus it shall be on the earth
   and among the nations,
   as when an olive tree is beaten,
   as at the gleaning when the grape
      harvest is ended.

14 They lift up their voices, they sing
      for joy;
   they shout from the west over the
      majesty of the LORD.
15 Therefore in the east give glory to
      the LORD;
   in the coastlands of the sea glorify
      the name of the LORD, the God
      of Israel.
16 From the ends of the earth we hear
      songs of praise,

of glory to the Righteous One.
   But I say, I pine away,
   I pine away. Woe is me!
For the treacherous deal
      treacherously,
   the treacherous deal very
      treacherously.

17 Terror, and the pit, and the snare
   are upon you, O inhabitant of the
      earth!
18 Whoever flees at the sound of the
      terror
   shall fall into the pit;
and whoever climbs out of the pit
   shall be caught in the snare.
For the windows of heaven are
      opened,
   and the foundations of the earth
      tremble.
19 The earth is utterly broken,
   the earth is torn asunder,
   the earth is violently shaken.
20 The earth staggers like a drunkard,
   it sways like a hut;
its transgression lies heavy upon it,
   and it falls, and will not rise again.

21 On that day the LORD will punish
   the host of heaven in heaven,
   and on earth the kings of the
      earth.
22 They will be gathered together
   like prisoners in a pit;
they will be shut up in a prison,
   and after many days they will be
      punished.
23 Then the moon will be abashed,

24:16—The essential message of the first of the three parts (see introduction and notes on 11:1–9) of this frightening oracle about the Day of the Lord is summed up in v. 11b: *the gladness of the earth is banished*. In its place *terror* (v. 17) and *desolation* (v. 12) reach into every household (v. 2) and every part of the world (v. 3). Even though to the ends of the earth people sing praises of the Lord (vv. 14–16a), their worship cannot offset the treachery of the wicked (v. 16b) that deserves punishment.

24:17–20—The second part of the future scenario pictures the Day itself. It cannot be escaped (v. 18; see Amos 5:18–20); it is comparable to the

deluge of Noah, when *the windows of heaven are opened* (v. 18b; see Gen. 7:11) to allow the chaotic waters that God restrained at the time of creation to fall through the "dome" of the sky (Gen. 1:6–8).

24:21–22—The angelic *host* and *the kings of the earth* alike are cast into *a pit* (Sheol, the underworld). This theme is expanded upon in Rev. 20:1–3, where Satan himself is imprisoned for 1,000 years; and in Rev. 21:24, where the kings of the earth emerge from the pit into the New Jerusalem.

24:23—This chapter closes with a mere hint of

and the sun ashamed;
for the LORD of hosts will reign
on Mount Zion and in Jerusalem,
and before his elders he will manifest
his glory.

Praise for Deliverance from Oppression

25 O LORD, you are my God;
I will exalt you, I will praise
your name;
for you have done wonderful things,
plans formed of old, faithful and
sure.
2 For you have made the city a heap,
the fortified city a ruin;
the palace of aliens is a city no more,
it will never be rebuilt.
3 Therefore strong peoples will glorify
you;
cities of ruthless nations will fear
you.
4 For you have been a refuge to the
poor,
a refuge to the needy in their
distress,
a shelter from the rainstorm and a
shade from the heat.
When the blast of the ruthless was
like a winter rainstorm,
5 the noise of aliens like heat in a
dry place,
you subdued the heat with the shade
of clouds;
the song of the ruthless was stilled.

6 On this mountain the LORD of hosts
will make for all peoples

a feast of rich food, a feast of well-
aged wines,
of rich food filled with marrow, of
well-aged wines strained
clear.
7 And he will destroy on this
mountain
the shroud that is cast over all
peoples,
the sheet that is spread over all
nations;
8 he will swallow up death forever.
Then the Lord GOD will wipe away
the tears from all faces,
and the disgrace of his people he
will take away from all the
earth,
for the LORD has spoken.
9 It will be said on that day,
Lo, this is our God; we have waited
for him, so that he might
save us.
This is the LORD for whom we
have waited;
let us be glad and rejoice in his
salvation.
10 For the hand of the LORD will rest on
this mountain.

The Moabites shall be trodden down
in their place
as straw is trodden down in a
dung-pit.
11 Though they spread out their hands
in the midst of it,
as swimmers spread out their
hands to swim,

---

the new age that lies beyond the catastrophe. The Lord's radiance manifested from the holy mountain *Zion* is so great that it *abashes* the astral deities, *sun* and *moon*. None of this should be read by us as history written in advance; instead, it is an evocation of the certainty that God will at last overcome evil and restore the world to its Edenic perfection.

25:1–12 Thanksgiving of the Oppressed

25:1–5—The Isaiah Apocalypse continues with a psalm of thanksgiving to God, placed on the lips of one of the wretched of the earth for whom the prospect that *the song of the ruthless* will be *stilled* (v. 5b) comes as good news. The news that God has a preferential option for the *poor*

and *needy* (v. 4) continues to inspire oppressed people with hope, and accounts for the considerable interest in biblical eschatology in third-world contexts.

25:6–10—The motif of the eschatological banquet *on this mountain* of the Lord picks up memories of the Sinai event (Exod. 24:9–11) and Solomon's dedication of the first temple (1 Kgs. 8:62–66). It also recurs in texts that tell what it is like in the kingdom of heaven (Matt. 8:11, 22:1–4; Rev. 19:9, "the marriage supper of the Lamb"). It is preserved in the language of the invitation to the Christian Eucharist, which is itself perceived as a foretaste of sitting at table in the kingdom of God.

their pride will be laid low despite
    the struggle*a* of their hands.
12 The high fortifications of his walls
    will be brought down,
    laid low, cast to the ground, even
    to the dust.

Judah's Song of Victory

26 On that day this song will be
    sung in the land of Judah:
We have a strong city;
    he sets up victory
    like walls and bulwarks.
2 Open the gates,
    so that the righteous nation that
        keeps faith
    may enter in.
3 Those of steadfast mind you keep in
        peace—
    in peace because they trust in you.
4 Trust in the LORD forever,
    for in the LORD GOD*b*
    you have an everlasting rock.
5 For he has brought low
    the inhabitants of the height;
    the lofty city he lays low.
He lays it low to the ground,
    casts it to the dust.
6 The foot tramples it,
    the feet of the poor,
    the steps of the needy.
7 The way of the righteous is level;
    O Just One, you make smooth the
        path of the righteous.
8 In the path of your judgments,
    O LORD, we wait for you;
your name and your renown
    are the soul's desire.
9 My soul yearns for you in the night,
    my spirit within me earnestly
        seeks you.
For when your judgments are in the
        earth,
    the inhabitants of the world learn
        righteousness.
10 If favor is shown to the wicked,

they do not learn righteousness;
in the land of uprightness they deal
    perversely
    and do not see the majesty of the
        LORD.
11 O LORD, your hand is lifted up,
    but they do not see it.
Let them see your zeal for your
        people, and be ashamed.
Let the fire for your adversaries
        consume them.
12 O LORD, you will ordain peace
    for us,
    for indeed, all that we have done,
    you have done for us.
13 O LORD our God,
    other lords besides you have ruled
        over us,
    but we acknowledge your name
        alone.
14 The dead do not live;
    shades do not rise—
because you have punished and
        destroyed them,
    and wiped out all memory of
        them.
15 But you have increased the nation,
    O LORD,
    you have increased the nation; you
        are glorified;
    you have enlarged all the borders
        of the land.
16 O LORD, in distress they sought
    you,
    they poured out a prayer*a*
    when your chastening was on
        them.
17 Like a woman with child,
    who writhes and cries out in her
        pangs
    when she is near her time,
so were we because of you,
    O LORD;
18   we were with child, we writhed,
    but we gave birth only to wind.

a Meaning of Heb uncertain   *b* Heb *in Yah, the* LORD

26:1–21 Judah's Song of Victory
Another psalm of praise to the victorious YHWH
(vv. 1–6), evidently intended as a processional

hymn (**Open the gates**, v. 2), followed by a lament (vv. 7–21).

We have won no victories on earth,
    and no one is born to inhabit the
       world.
¹⁹ Your dead shall live, their corpses^a
    shall rise.
    O dwellers in the dust, awake and
       sing for joy!
For your dew is a radiant dew,
    and the earth will give birth to
       those long dead.^b

²⁰ Come, my people, enter your
       chambers,
    and shut your doors behind you;
hide yourselves for a little while
    until the wrath is past.
²¹ For the LORD comes out from his
       place
    to punish the inhabitants of the
       earth for their iniquity;
the earth will disclose the blood
       shed on it,
    and will no longer cover its slain.

Israel's Redemption

27 On that day the LORD with his cruel and great and strong sword will punish Leviathan the fleeing serpent, Leviathan the twisting serpent, and he will kill the dragon that is in the sea.

² On that day:
    A pleasant vineyard, sing about it!

³   I, the LORD, am its keeper;
    every moment I water it.
I guard it night and day
    so that no one can harm it;
⁴   I have no wrath.
If it gives me thorns and briers,
    I will march to battle against it.
    I will burn it up.
⁵ Or else let it cling to me for
       protection,
    let it make peace with me,
    let it make peace with me.

⁶ In days to come^c Jacob shall take
       root,
    Israel shall blossom and put forth
       shoots,
    and fill the whole world with
       fruit.

⁷ Has he struck them down as he
       struck down those who struck
       them?
    Or have they been killed as their
       killers were killed?
⁸ By expulsion,^d by exile you struggled
       against them;
    with his fierce blast he removed
       them in the day of the east wind.
⁹ Therefore by this the guilt of Jacob
       will be expiated,

---

^a Cn Compare Syr Tg: Heb *my corpse*   ^b Heb *to the shades*   ^c Heb *Those to come*   ^b Meaning of Heb uncertain

---

26:19—A voice speaks with an assurance only YHWH could give. The bold announcement, *Your dead shall live*, is the earlier of only two unambiguous Old Testament statements of belief in the resurrection of the dead and the very possibility of life after death. (The other reference, in Dan. 12:2–3, can quite confidently be dated to 164 BCE. It prophesies a double resurrection of the dead on the last day, some to "life" and some to "shame and everlasting contempt.") Faith in an afterlife is thus associated from the very beginning with end times. It is no wonder, then, that the New Testament scholars speak of the resurrection of Jesus as the first eschatological event.

27:1–13 The New Day Coming

27:1—This verse, which may well belong with the preceding oracle, adds another detail to the work of the Lord *on that day* of culmination and judgment. Borrowing from the mythic tradition of Canaan, the prophet teaches that YHWH

will kill **Leviathan**, the seven-headed monster of the salt water, and **the dragon**, the embodiments of the chaos that God had to overcome in order to create the world in the first place and that has always threatened to break out again. (Compare Ps. 74:13–14; Job 26:12, one of the texts in which Leviathan is called Rahab. In Rev. 12:1–9 the great red dragon with seven heads is identified with Satan. In Job 41 the totality of YHWH's sovereignty is demonstrated by the fact that Leviathan becomes a fierce but favorite pet of the Creator.)

27:2–13—This collection of fragmentary oracles about Israel's salvation *on that day* or *in days to come* culminates in the motif, familiar in futuristic texts, of the ingathering of the exiles of Israel (vv. 12–13; see notes at 11:10–16). The hope for return from Diaspora has, of course, continued to live in Jewish liturgy and life.

and this will be the full fruit of the
    removal of his sin:
when he makes all the stones of the
    altars
    like chalkstones crushed to
        pieces,
    no sacred poles[a] or incense altars
        will remain standing.
10 For the fortified city is solitary,
    a habitation deserted and forsaken,
        like the wilderness;
the calves graze there,
    there they lie down, and strip its
        branches.
11 When its boughs are dry, they are
    broken;
    women come and make a fire of
        them.
For this is a people without
    understanding;
    therefore he that made them will
        not have compassion on
        them,
    he that formed them will show
        them no favor.

12 On that day the LORD will thresh
from the channel of the Euphrates to the
Wadi of Egypt, and you will be gathered
one by one, O people of Israel. 13 And on
that day a great trumpet will be blown,
and those who were lost in the land of
Assyria and those who were driven out
to the land of Egypt will come and worship the LORD on the holy mountain at
Jerusalem.

Judgment on Corrupt Rulers, Priests, and Prophets

28 Ah, the proud garland of the
    drunkards of Ephraim,
and the fading flower of its
    glorious beauty,
which is on the head of those
    bloated with rich food, of
    those overcome with wine!
2 See, the Lord has one who is mighty
    and strong;
    like a storm of hail, a destroying
        tempest,
    like a storm of mighty, overflowing
        waters;
    with his hand he will hurl them
        down to the earth.
3 Trampled under foot will be
    the proud garland of the
        drunkards of Ephraim.
4 And the fading flower of its glorious
    beauty,
    which is on the head of those
        bloated with rich food,
will be like a first-ripe fig before the
    summer;
    whoever sees it, eats it up
        as soon as it comes to hand.

5 In that day the LORD of hosts will be
    a garland of glory,
    and a diadem of beauty, to the
        remnant of his people;
6 and a spirit of justice to the one who
    sits in judgment,

[a] Heb *Asherim*

27:13—At the blast of *a great trumpet* (ram's
horn or shofar) the people will return to *worship
the LORD on the holy mountain at Jerusalem*.
The motif of the trumpet summons on the last day
enjoyed continued life in eschatological texts. In
the "little apocalypse" of Matthew, the trumpet,
as here, calls the elect from the four winds (Matt.
24:31). In Paul's great futuristic vision in
1 Cor. 15:52, the trumpet awakens the dead:
"For the trumpet will sound, and the dead will be
raised imperishable" (so also in 1 Thess. 4:16).
In Michelangelo's great judgment day fresco in
the Sistine Chapel, four trumpeters blast away at
the earth from which the dead are rising, some
headed for heaven and some for hell.

**28:1–33:24 Isaiah of Jerusalem. Part 3: Oracles
about Israel (Ephraim) and Judah**

28:1–29 No One Is Righteous, Not One

28:1–6—This chapter of indictments and threats
against the leadership cadres of Israel and Judah
opens with a condemnation of *the drunkards of
Ephraim*. Perhaps originating in the period of the
Syro-Ephraimite War (735–732 BCE; see 7:1–6),
which pitted Israel and its allies against Judah,
the oracle ironically contrasts the fading *garland*
of the rich and proud Israelite gluttons of the
present with the *garland of glory* that the Lord
will be *to the remnant of his people* (28:5) that
remains after the purge. In the remainder of the
chapter, the prophet announces the Lord's judgment against Judah.

and strength to those who turn
    back the battle at the gate.

7 These also reel with wine
    and stagger with strong drink;
the priest and the prophet reel with
    strong drink,
    they are confused with wine,
    they stagger with strong drink;
they err in vision,
    they stumble in giving judgment.
8 All tables are covered with filthy
    vomit;
    no place is clean.

9 "Whom will he teach knowledge,
    and to whom will he explain the
    message?
Those who are weaned from
    milk,
    those taken from the breast?
10 For it is precept upon precept,
    precept upon precept,
    line upon line, line upon line,
    here a little, there a little."ᵃ

11 Truly, with stammering lip
    and with alien tongue
he will speak to this people,
12   to whom he has said,
    "This is rest;
    give rest to the weary;
and this is repose";
    yet they would not hear.
13 Therefore the word of the Lord will
    be to them,
    "Precept upon precept, precept
    upon precept,
    line upon line, line upon line,
    here a little, there a little;"ᵃ
in order that they may go, and fall
    backward,

and be broken, and snared, and
    taken.

14 Therefore hear the word of the
    Lord, you scoffers
    who rule this people in Jerusalem.
15 Because you have said, "We have
    made a covenant with death,
    and with Sheol we have an
    agreement;
when the overwhelming scourge
    passes through
    it will not come to us;
for we have made lies our refuge,
    and in falsehood we have taken
    shelter";
16 therefore thus says the Lord God,
See, I am laying in Zion a foundation
    stone,
    a tested stone,
a precious cornerstone, a sure
    foundation:
    "One who trusts will not panic."
17 And I will make justice the line,
    and righteousness the plummet;
hail will sweep away the refuge of
    lies,
    and waters will overwhelm the
    shelter.
18 Then your covenant with death will
    be annulled,
    and your agreement with Sheol
    will not stand;
when the overwhelming scourge
    passes through
    you will be beaten down by it.
19 As often as it passes through, it will
    take you;
    for morning by morning it will
    pass through,

ᵃ Meaning of Heb of this verse uncertain

28:7–13—When these false prophets and priests speak, they reproduce Isaiah's message as mocking gibberish. The Lord's response will be to speak to them in the *alien tongue* (v. 11) of the (Assyrian) conqueror.

28:14–22—Jerusalem's rulers trust their *covenant with death* (v. 15—perhaps their military alliance with Egypt against *the overwhelming scourge* of Assyria) to save them. The true basis for trust is the *precious cornerstone, a sure foundation* (v. 16)

of YHWH's presence in Zion and the justice and righteousness associated with it. This same stone is a stumbling block for the disobedient (8:14; see also Rom. 9:33). Here it provides the basis for YHWH's *strange* and *alien work* (28:21) of the impending destruction of Judah. These motifs—mistrust of self-serving foreign alliances and trust in YHWH's vindication of the righteous—permeate all of Isaiah's thought, and remain as wise counsel to us in this era of power politics.

by day and by night;
and it will be sheer terror to
understand the message.

20 For the bed is too short to stretch
oneself on it,
and the covering too narrow to
wrap oneself in it.

21 For the LORD will rise up as on
Mount Perazim,
he will rage as in the valley of
Gibeon
to do his deed—strange is his
deed!—
and to work his work—alien is his
work!

22 Now therefore do not scoff,
or your bonds will be made
stronger;
for I have heard a decree of
destruction
from the Lord GOD of hosts upon
the whole land.

23 Listen, and hear my voice;
Pay attention, and hear my speech.

24 Do those who plow for sowing plow
continually?
Do they continually open and
harrow their ground?

25 When they have leveled its surface,
do they not scatter dill, sow
cummin,
and plant wheat in rows
and barley in its proper place,
and spelt as the border?

26 For they are well instructed;
their God teaches them.

27 Dill is not threshed with a threshing
sledge,

nor is a cart wheel rolled over
cummin;
but dill is beaten out with a stick,
and cummin with a rod.

28 Grain is crushed for bread,
but one does not thresh it forever;
one drives the cart wheel and horses
over it,
but does not pulverize it.

29 This also comes from the LORD of
hosts;
he is wonderful in counsel,
and excellent in wisdom.

The Siege of Jerusalem

29 Ah, Ariel, Ariel,
the city where David encamped!
Add year to year;
let the festivals run their round.

2 Yet I will distress Ariel,
and there shall be moaning and
lamentation,
and Jerusalem*a* shall be to me like
an Ariel.*b*

3 And like David*c* I will encamp
against you;
I will besiege you with towers
and raise siegeworks against you.

4 Then deep from the earth you shall
speak,
from low in the dust your words
shall come;
your voice shall come from the
ground like the voice of a
ghost,
and your speech shall whisper out
of the dust.

a Heb *she*   *b* Probable meaning, *altar hearth*; compare Ezek 43.15
c Gk: Meaning of Heb uncertain

29:1–24 In the End, Reversal of Fortune

29:1–4—This lengthy chapter of threats and promises begins with a threat against *Ariel* (the word is translated "altar hearth" in Ezek. 43:16, and is used only here as a title of Jerusalem). YHWH vows to replicate David's conquest of the holy city (2 Sam. 5:6–9) with a siege that will leave Jerusalem able to speak only in the chirping voice of a dead spirit coming up *from the ground* (Isa. 29:4; see 8:19).

29:7—When the Lord intervenes, Judah's enemies vanish overnight *like a dream*. Perhaps this

is a reflection of the withdrawal of the Assyrian invader Sennacherib from before Jerusalem in 701 BCE, reported in 2 Kgs. 19:35 and Isa. 37:36–37.

29:9–12—Isaiah perceives the incompetence and blindness of the prophets and seers to be a punishment from the Lord. This difficult notion of a God-inflicted stupor and loss of vision is consistent with the initial commission given to Isaiah himself, to "make the mind of this people dull, and stop their ears, and shut their eyes" (6:10).

5 But the multitude of your foes[a] shall
      be like small dust,
   and the multitude of tyrants like
      flying chaff.
And in an instant, suddenly,
6   you will be visited by the LORD of
      hosts
   with thunder and earthquake and
      great noise,
      with whirlwind and tempest, and
         the flame of a devouring fire.
7 And the multitude of all the nations
      that fight against Ariel,
   all that fight against her and her
      stronghold, and who distress
      her,
   shall be like a dream, a vision of
      the night.
8 Just as when a hungry person
      dreams of eating
   and wakes up still hungry,
   or a thirsty person dreams of
      drinking
   and wakes up faint, still thirsty,
   so shall the multitude of all the
      nations be
   that fight against Mount Zion.

9 Stupefy yourselves and be in a
      stupor,
   blind yourselves and be blind!
   Be drunk, but not from wine;
      stagger, but not from strong
         drink!
10 For the LORD has poured out upon
      you
   a spirit of deep sleep;
   he has closed your eyes, you
      prophets,
   and covered your heads, you seers.
11 The vision of all this has become
for you like the words of a sealed document. If it is given to those who can
read, with the command, "Read this,"
they say, "We cannot, for it is sealed."
12 And if it is given to those who cannot
read, saying, "Read this," they say, "We
cannot read."

13   The Lord said:
   Because these people draw near with
      their mouths
   and honor me with their lips,
      while their hearts are far from me,
   and their worship of me is a human
      commandment learned by
         rote;
14 so I will again do
   amazing things with this people,
      shocking and amazing.
   The wisdom of their wise shall
      perish,
      and the discernment of the
         discerning shall be hidden.

15 Ha! You who hide a plan too deep
      for the LORD,
   whose deeds are in the dark,
      and who say, "Who sees us? Who
         knows us?"
16 You turn things upside down!
   Shall the potter be regarded as the
      clay?
   Shall the thing made say of its
      maker,
      "He did not make me";
   or the thing formed say of the one
      who formed it,
      "He has no understanding"?

Hope for the Future

17 Shall not Lebanon in a very little
      while
   become a fruitful field,
      and the fruitful field be regarded
         as a forest?
18 On that day the deaf shall hear
      the words of a scroll,
   and out of their gloom and
      darkness
   the eyes of the blind shall see.

a Cn: Heb strangers

29:17–24—The chapter closes with two lovely promise oracles. When *the tyrant shall be no more* (v. 20), then those persons whose limitations are excessive—*the deaf, the blind, the meek*, and the needy (vv. 18–19)—will experience a reversal of their fates. It is one of the many reversals of present perverted realities that Isaiah anticipates for the future, after the Day of the Lord.

¹⁹ The meek shall obtain fresh joy in
the LORD,
and the neediest people shall exult
in the Holy One of Israel.
²⁰ For the tyrant shall be no more,
and the scoffer shall cease to be;
all those alert to do evil shall be
cut off—
²¹ those who cause a person to lose a
lawsuit,
who set a trap for the arbiter in the
gate,
and without grounds deny justice
to the one in the right.

22 Therefore thus says the LORD, who
redeemed Abraham, concerning the
house of Jacob:
No longer shall Jacob be ashamed,
no longer shall his face grow pale.
²³ For when he sees his children,
the work of my hands, in his
midst,
they will sanctify my name;
they will sanctify the Holy One of
Jacob,
and will stand in awe of the God of
Israel.
²⁴ And those who err in spirit will
come to understanding,
and those who grumble will accept
instruction.

The Futility of Reliance on Egypt

30 Oh, rebellious children, says the
LORD,
who carry out a plan, but not
mine;
who make an alliance, but against
my will,
adding sin to sin;

² who set out to go down to Egypt
without asking for my counsel,
to take refuge in the protection of
Pharaoh,
and to seek shelter in the shadow
of Egypt;
³ Therefore the protection of Pharaoh
shall become your shame,
and the shelter in the shadow of
Egypt your humiliation.
⁴ For though his officials are at Zoan
and his envoys reach Hanes,
⁵ everyone comes to shame
through a people that cannot
profit them,
that brings neither help nor profit,
but shame and disgrace.

6 An oracle concerning the animals of
the Negeb.
Through a land of trouble and
distress,
of lioness and roaring^a lion,
of viper and flying serpent,
they carry their riches on the backs
of donkeys,
and their treasures on the humps
of camels,
to a people that cannot profit
them.
⁷ For Egypt's help is worthless and
empty,
therefore I have called her,
"Rahab who sits still."^b

A Rebellious People
⁸ Go now, write it before them on a
tablet,
and inscribe it in a book,

^a Cn: Heb *from them*   ^b Meaning of Heb uncertain

30:1–33 True Hope Lies with the Lord

30:1–5—Through Isaiah's mouth, YHWH condemns the negotiations for Egyptian military
protection (and, no doubt, suzerainty) that are
known to have taken place during Hezekiah's
revolt against Assyria, 703–701 BCE. The
true guardian and protector of Zion is not Egypt but
YHWH (see also 31:1–5).

30:6–7—The picture of caravan loads of tribute
headed through *the Negeb* desert to Egypt is

pitiful, because *Egypt's help is worthless and
empty* (v. 7).

30:8–17—The Lord's instruction is simple: *In
returning and rest you shall be saved* (v. 15). The
problem is that the *faithless children* of Judah
will not hear the instruction of the LORD (v.
9), and actually implore prophets like Isaiah to
speak to us smooth things (v. 10). Preachers and
teachers, take note! The task of mediating God's
word to the community demands more than just
stroking people and making them feel good.

so that it may be for the time to
    come
    as a witness forever.
9 For they are a rebellious people,
    faithless children,
    children who will not hear
    the instruction of the LORD;
10 who say to the seers, "Do not see";
    and to the prophets, "Do not
        prophesy to us what is right;
    speak to us smooth things,
    prophesy illusions,
11 leave the way, turn aside from the
    path,
    let us hear no more about the Holy
    One of Israel."
12 Therefore thus says the Holy One of
    Israel:
    Because you reject this word,
    and put your trust in oppression
        and deceit,
    and rely on them;
13 therefore this iniquity shall become
    for you
    like a break in a high wall, bulging
        out, and about to collapse,
    whose crash comes suddenly, in an
        instant;
14 its breaking is like that of a potter's
    vessel
    that is smashed so ruthlessly
    that among its fragments not a sherd
        is found
    for taking fire from the hearth,
    or dipping water out of the cistern.

15 For thus said the Lord GOD, the
    Holy One of Israel:
    In returning and rest you shall be
        saved;
    in quietness and in trust shall be
        your strength.

But you refused 16 and said,
    "No! We will flee upon horses"—
    therefore you shall flee!
    and, "We will ride upon swift
        steeds"—
    therefore your pursuers shall be
        swift!
17 A thousand shall flee at the threat of
    one,
    at the threat of five you shall flee,
    until you are left
    like a flagstaff on the top of a
        mountain,
    like a signal on a hill.

God's Promise to Zion

18 Therefore the LORD waits to be
        gracious to you;
    therefore he will rise up to show
        mercy to you.
    For the LORD is a God of justice;
    blessed are all those who wait for
        him.

19 Truly, O people in Zion, inhabitants
of Jerusalem, you shall weep no more.
He will surely be gracious to you at the
sound of your cry; when he hears it, he
will answer you. 20 Though the Lord may
give you the bread of adversity and the
water of affliction, yet your Teacher will
not hide himself any more, but your eyes
shall see your Teacher. 21 And when you
turn to the right or when you turn to the
left, your ears shall hear a word behind
you, saying, "This is the way; walk in
it." 22 Then you will defile your silver-
covered idols and your gold-plated images.
You will scatter them like filthy rags; you
will say to them, "Away with you!"

23 He will give rain for the seed with
which you sow the ground, and grain,
the produce of the ground, which will

Truthtelling is not always comforting speech,
though truth is always gospel.

30:18–26—The bad news is immediately followed by good news that God is a **God of justice**
and mercy. As has been his consistent way, the
prophet attributes the suffering of Judah to the
Lord: **The Lord may give you the bread of adversity and the water of affliction** (v. 20). Although
this serves to make meaningful suffering that

might otherwise seem absurd, it is a theological
notion difficult to accept for Christians, whose
image of God is of one who accepts our suffering personally. Nevertheless, the accompanying
promise is uplifting: A guiding word follows,
saying, **This is the way; walk in it** (v. 21), and
provision is made in the coming new age of
abundance of crops, animals, fresh water, and
healing (vv. 23–26).

be rich and plenteous. On that day your cattle will graze in broad pastures; [24] and the oxen and donkeys that till the ground will eat silage, which has been winnowed with shovel and fork. [25] On every lofty mountain and every high hill there will be brooks running with water—on a day of the great slaughter, when the towers fall. [26] Moreover the light of the moon will be like the light of the sun, and the light of the sun will be sevenfold, like the light of seven days, on the day when the LORD binds up the injuries of his people, and heals the wounds inflicted by his blow.

Judgment on Assyria

[27] See, the name of the LORD comes
     from far away,
   burning with his anger, and in
     thick rising smoke;[a]
his lips are full of indignation,
     and his tongue is like a devouring
       fire;
[28] his breath is like an overflowing
       stream
     that reaches up to the neck—
to sift the nations with the sieve of
       destruction,
     and to place on the jaws of the
       peoples a bridle that leads
       them astray.

29 You shall have a song as in the night when a holy festival is kept; and gladness of heart, as when one sets out to the sound of the flute to go to the mountain of the LORD, to the Rock of Israel. [30] And the LORD will cause his majestic voice to be heard and the descending blow of his arm to be seen, in furious anger and a flame of devouring fire, with a cloudburst and tempest and hailstones. [31] The Assyrian will be terror-stricken at the voice of the LORD, when he strikes with his rod. [32] And every stroke of the staff of punishment that the LORD lays upon him will be to the sound of timbrels and lyres; battling with brandished arm he will fight with him. [33] For his burning place[b] has long been prepared; truly it is made ready for the king,[c] its pyre made deep and wide, with fire and wood in abundance; the breath of the LORD, like a stream of sulfur, kindles it.

Alliance with Egypt Is Futile

31 Alas for those who go down to
       Egypt for help
   and who rely on horses,
who trust in chariots because they
     are many
   and in horsemen because they are
     very strong,
but do not look to the Holy One of
     Israel
   or consult the LORD!
[2] Yet he too is wise and brings
     disaster;
   he does not call back his words,
but will rise against the house of the
     evildoers,
   and against the helpers of those
     who work iniquity.
[3] The Egyptians are human, and not
     God;
   their horses are flesh, and not spirit.
When the LORD stretches out his hand,
   the helper will stumble, and the
     one helped will fall,
   and they will all perish together.

[4] For thus the LORD said to me,
   As a lion or a young lion growls over
     its prey,

---

[a] Meaning of Heb uncertain   [b] Or Topheth   [c] Or Molech

---

30:27–33—This promise is followed by one probably reflective of the events of 701 BCE, when the Assyrian horde under Sennacherib is said to have withdrawn from before Jerusalem (37:36–37). The Assyrians, "the rod of the Lord's anger" (10:5), who came at the Lord's behest to inflict judgment upon Judah, are now terrified *at the voice of the LORD* (30:31).

31:1–9 Egypt and Assyria Cannot Save

31:1–3—Under the Lord's outstretched hand, the hapless Egyptian "allies" will stumble and fall along with God's own people.

31:4–5—These verses constitute one of the most dramatic renditions of YHWH as holy warrior mobilized to protect Jerusalem. Together with the heavenly host, *the LORD . . . will come down*

and—when a band of shepherds is
   called out against it—
is not terrified by their shouting
   or daunted at their noise,
so the LORD of hosts will come down
   to fight upon Mount Zion and
   upon its hill.
5 Like birds hovering overhead, so the
   LORD of hosts
   will protect Jerusalem;
he will protect and deliver it,
   he will spare and rescue it.

6 Turn back to him whom you[a] have
deeply betrayed, O people of Israel. 7 For
on that day all of you shall throw away
your idols of silver and idols of gold,
which your hands have sinfully made
for you.
8 "Then the Assyrian shall fall by a
   sword, not of mortals;
   and a sword, not of humans, shall
   devour him;
he shall flee from the sword,
   and his young men shall be put to
   forced labor.
9 His rock shall pass away in terror,
   and his officers desert the standard
   in panic,"
says the LORD, whose fire is in Zion,
   and whose furnace is in Jerusalem.

Government with Justice Predicted

32 See, a king will reign in
   righteousness,
   and princes will rule with justice.
2 Each will be like a hiding place from
   the wind,

a covert from the tempest,
   like streams of water in a dry place,
   like the shade of a great rock in a
   weary land.
3 Then the eyes of those who have
   sight will not be closed,
   and the ears of those who have
   hearing will listen.
4 The minds of the rash will have good
   judgment,
   and the tongues of stammerers will
   speak readily and distinctly.
5 A fool will no longer be called noble,
   nor a villain said to be honorable.
6 For fools speak folly,
   and their minds plot iniquity:
to practice ungodliness,
   to utter error concerning the LORD,
to leave the craving of the hungry
   unsatisfied,
   and to deprive the thirsty of drink.
7 The villainies of villains are evil;
   they devise wicked devices
to ruin the poor with lying words,
   even when the plea of the needy is
   right.
8 But those who are noble plan noble
   things,
   and by noble things they stand.

Complacent Women Warned of Disaster

9 Rise up, you women who are at ease,
   hear my voice;
   you complacent daughters, listen
   to my speech.

a Heb they

---

to fight upon Mount Zion. God will hover
overhead to *protect and deliver* Jerusalem.
Was such faith justified? Isaiah's contemporary
Judean prophet Micah did not think so, when he
threatened the corrupt leadership of Judah with
these words: "Zion shall be plowed as a field;
Jerusalem shall become a heap of ruins" (Mic.
3:12). Micah's verse is quoted a century later by
Jeremiah (Jer. 26:18–19), much to the dismay of
his audience, who seemed to prefer the Isaianic
doctrine. Subsequent events certainly erased any
notion that Jerusalem or any other city is invulnerable. Surely a prudent government makes provision for national defense. Yet in line with Isaiah
we say, "In God we trust," and mean perhaps

something like what Isaiah intended—that God
will remain faithful and if God's people remain
so as well, we can see it through together.

32:1–20 Future Peace and Abundance

32:1–8—Isaiah does not identify the ideal king
who *will reign in righteousness* (v. 1), but this
king's era will be a time when the true values of
vision, good judgment, honor, and nobility will
dislodge their opposites, which are the perversions of the present age. Reversal of values is a
motif characteristic of Isaiah (see introduction).

32:9–20—Isaiah warns his women hearers
against complacency, for between now and the
new age of *righteousness* and *peace* (v. 17) must

¹⁰ In little more than a year
   you will shudder, you complacent
      ones;
for the vintage will fail,
   the fruit harvest will not come.
¹¹ Tremble, you women who are at
      ease,
   shudder, you complacent ones;
strip, and make yourselves bare,
   and put sackcloth on your loins.
¹² Beat your breasts for the pleasant
      fields,
   for the fruitful vine,
¹³ for the soil of my people
   growing up in thorns and briers;
yes, for all the joyous houses
   in the jubilant city.
¹⁴ For the palace will be forsaken,
   the populous city deserted;
the hill and the watchtower
   will become dens forever,
the joy of wild asses,
   a pasture for flocks;
¹⁵ until a spirit from on high is poured
      out on us,
   and the wilderness becomes a
      fruitful field,
   and the fruitful field is deemed a
      forest.

The Peace of God's Reign

¹⁶ Then justice will dwell in the
      wilderness,
   and righteousness abide in the
      fruitful field.
¹⁷ The effect of righteousness will be
      peace,
   and the result of righteousness,
      quietness and trust forever.

¹⁸ My people will abide in a peaceful
      habitation,
   in secure dwellings, and in quiet
      resting places.
¹⁹ The forest will disappear
      completely,ᵃ
   and the city will be utterly laid low.
²⁰ Happy will you be who sow beside
      every stream,
   who let the ox and the donkey
      range freely.

A Prophecy of Deliverance from Foes

33 Ah, you destroyer,
   who yourself have not been
      destroyed;
you treacherous one,
   with whom no one has dealt
      treacherously!
When you have ceased to destroy,
   you will be destroyed;
and when you have stopped dealing
      treacherously,
   you will be dealt with
      treacherously.

² O LORD, be gracious to us; we wait
      for you.
   Be our arm every morning,
   our salvation in the time of
      trouble.
³ At the sound of tumult, peoples fled;
   before your majesty, nations
      scattered.
⁴ Spoil was gathered as the caterpillar
      gathers;
   as locusts leap, they leapedᵇ
      upon it.

ᵃ Cn: Heb *And it will hail when the forest comes down*   ᵇ Meaning of Heb uncertain

---

come the judgment, described in terms of crop failure, abandonment and destruction of *the populous city* (v. 14). All desolation is reversed when the *spirit from on high is poured out on us* (see v. 15; Joel 2:28; Acts 2:14–21) and the final era of abundance and security commences.

33:1–24 Deliverance for Zion
Reflecting both the anger (v. 1) and anguish (vv. 7–9, 19) of a Judah threatened by Assyria, this prophetic prayer liturgy also exalts the saving Lord (vv. 2–6) and offers rich guidance for social ethical behavior. Premised on the teaching of the

sages that *the fear of the LORD is Zion's treasure* (v. 6; e.g., Job 28:28; Prov. 1:7), that guidance affirms that the future belongs to *those who walk righteously and speak uprightly and despise the gain of oppression* (v. 15). The illicit gain is, among other things, acceptance of *bribes*, a corruption that the covenant tradition often condemned (e.g., Exod. 23:8; Deut. 16:19; Isa. 1:23, 5:23; Amos 5:12; Mic. 3:11, 7:3), because it blinds the eyes of the officials to the just pleas of the needy. The wrong is not unknown among us today!

5 The LORD is exalted, he dwells on
high;
   he filled Zion with justice and
righteousness;
6 he will be the stability of your times,
   abundance of salvation, wisdom,
and knowledge;
   the fear of the LORD is Zion's
treasure.*a*

7 Listen! the valiant*b* cry in the streets;
   the envoys of peace weep bitterly.
8 The highways are deserted,
   travelers have quit the road.
The treaty is broken,
   its oaths*c* are despised,
   its obligation*d* is disregarded.
9 The land mourns and languishes;
   Lebanon is confounded and
withers away;
Sharon is like a desert;
   and Bashan and Carmel shake off
their leaves.

10 "Now I will arise," says the LORD,
   "now I will lift myself up;
   now I will be exalted.
11 You conceive chaff, you bring forth
stubble;
   your breath is a fire that will
consume you.
12 And the peoples will be as if burned
to lime,
   like thorns cut down, that are
burned in the fire."

13 Hear, you who are far away, what I
have done;
   and you who are near,
acknowledge my might.
14 The sinners in Zion are afraid;
   trembling has seized the godless:
"Who among us can live with the
devouring fire?
   Who among us can live with
everlasting flames?"
15 Those who walk righteously and
speak uprightly,

who despise the gain of
oppression,
who wave away a bribe instead of
accepting it,
who stop their ears from hearing
of bloodshed
and shut their eyes from looking
on evil,
16 they will live on the heights;
   their refuge will be the fortresses
of rocks;
   their food will be supplied, their
water assured.

The Land of the Majestic King

17 Your eyes will see the king in his
beauty;
   they will behold a land that
stretches far away.
18 Your mind will muse on the terror:
"Where is the one who counted?
Where is the one who weighed the
tribute?
Where is the one who counted the
towers?"
19 No longer will you see the insolent
people,
   the people of an obscure speech
that you cannot comprehend,
stammering in a language that you
cannot understand.
20 Look on Zion, the city of our
appointed festivals!
   Your eyes will see Jerusalem,
a quiet habitation, an immovable
tent,
whose stakes will never be pulled up,
   and none of whose ropes will be
broken.
21 But there the LORD in majesty will
be for us
a place of broad rivers and
streams,
where no galley with oars can go,
   nor stately ship can pass.

a Heb *his treasure*; meaning of Heb uncertain   *b* Meaning of Heb uncertain   *c* Q Ms: MT *cities*   *d* Or *everyone*

33:20–23—The restored Jerusalem of the future is portrayed first as a peaceful *tent* or tabernacle and then, borrowing Canaanite mythic motifs, as a city set on a veritable river of God (compare Ps. 46:4; Ezek. 47:1–12; Rev. 22:1–2), *broad* but unapproachable by enemy ships (Isa. 33:21b, 23).

22 For the LORD is our judge, the LORD
    is our ruler,
  the LORD is our king; he will
    save us.

23 Your rigging hangs loose;
  it cannot hold the mast firm in its
    place,
  or keep the sail spread out.

Then prey and spoil in abundance
    will be divided;
  even the lame will fall to
    plundering.
24 And no inhabitant will say, "I am
    sick";
  the people who live there will be
    forgiven their iniquity.

Judgment on the Nations

34 Draw near, O nations, to hear;
  O peoples, give heed!
Let the earth hear, and all that fills it;
  the world, and all that comes
    from it.
2 For the LORD is enraged against all
    the nations,
  and furious against all their
    hordes;
  he has doomed them, has given
    them over for slaughter.
3 Their slain shall be cast out,
  and the stench of their corpses
    shall rise;
  the mountains shall flow with their
    blood.
4 All the host of heaven shall rot away,
  and the skies roll up like a scroll.
All their host shall wither
  like a leaf withering on a vine,
  or fruit withering on a fig tree.

5 When my sword has drunk its fill in
    the heavens,

lo, it will descend upon Edom,
  upon the people I have doomed to
    judgment.
6 The LORD has a sword; it is sated
    with blood,
  it is gorged with fat,
  with the blood of lambs and goats,
  with the fat of the kidneys of rams.
For the LORD has a sacrifice in
    Bozrah,
  a great slaughter in the land of
    Edom.
7 Wild oxen shall fall with them,
  and young steers with the mighty
    bulls.
Their land shall be soaked with blood,
  and their soil made rich with fat.

8 For the LORD has a day of vengeance,
  a year of vindication by Zion's
    cause.*a*
9 And the streams of Edom*b* shall be
    turned into pitch,
  and her soil into sulfur;
  her land shall become burning
    pitch.
10 Night and day it shall not be
    quenched;
  its smoke shall go up forever.
From generation to generation it
    shall lie waste;
  no one shall pass through it
    forever and ever.
11 But the hawk*c* and the hedgehog*c*
    shall possess it;
  the owl*c* and the raven shall live
    in it.
He shall stretch the line of confusion
    over it,
  and the plummet of chaos over*d* its
    nobles.

a Or *of recompense by Zion's defender*   *b* Heb *her streams*   *c* Identification uncertain   *d* Heb lacks *over*

34:1–35:10 Isaiah of Jerusalem. Part 4: Two Oracles from the School of Isaiah

34:1–17 Judgment on the Nations
The protoapocalyptic language of v. 4 (compare 24:21) and the threat against *Edom* (vv. 5–6, perhaps 9) of terrible destruction that is the subject of the entire chapter both suggest that it comes

from a later period. Invective against Bozrah (v. 6) and Edom occurs again in 63:1–6, in a portion of the book thought to be postexilic in date. A motive for this hatred can be found in vv. 1–14 of the exilic prophetic book of Obadiah, an oracle against Edom driven by Edom's participation in the Babylonian destruction of Jerusalem in 587 BCE.

¹² They shall name it No Kingdom
    There,
  and all its princes shall be nothing.
¹³ Thorns shall grow over its
    strongholds,
  nettles and thistles in its fortresses.
  It shall be the haunt of jackals,
    an abode for ostriches.
¹⁴ Wildcats shall meet with hyenas,
    goat-demons shall call to each
      other;
  there too Lilith shall repose,
    and find a place to rest.
¹⁵ There shall the owl nest
    and lay and hatch and brood in its
      shadow;
  there too the buzzards shall gather,
    each one with its mate.
¹⁶ Seek and read from the book of the
    LORD:
  Not one of these shall be missing;
    none shall be without its mate.
  For the mouth of the LORD has
    commanded,
    and his spirit has gathered them.
¹⁷ He has cast the lot for them,
    his hand has portioned it out to
      them with the line;
  they shall possess it forever,
    from generation to generation they
      shall live in it.

The Return of the Redeemed to Zion

35 The wilderness and the dry land
      shall be glad,

the desert shall rejoice and
    blossom;
like the crocus ² it shall blossom
    abundantly,
  and rejoice with joy and singing.
The glory of Lebanon shall be given
    to it,
  the majesty of Carmel and
    Sharon.
They shall see the glory of the LORD,
  the majesty of our God.

³ Strengthen the weak hands,
  and make firm the feeble knees.
⁴ Say to those who are of a fearful
    heart,
  "Be strong, do not fear!
Here is your God.
  He will come with vengeance,
with terrible recompense.
  He will come and save you."
⁵ Then the eyes of the blind shall be
    opened,
  and the ears of the deaf
    unstopped;
⁶ then the lame shall leap like a deer,
  and the tongue of the speechless
    sing for joy.
For waters shall break forth in the
    wilderness,
  and streams in the desert;
⁷ the burning sand shall become a
    pool,
  and the thirsty ground springs of
    water;

34:13–17—The puzzling command to *seek and read from the book of the LORD* may reference an earlier passage in the book of Isaiah (13:19–22), in which ruined Babylon is infested by many of the same howling wild things that ruined Edom, including *jackals*, *ostriches*, *hyenas* and the rare *goat-demons*.

34:14—Among the many wild things that congregate in the overgrown ruins of Edom is *Lilith*. Although mentioned nowhere else in Scripture, this lady enjoyed much mention in ancient Jewish lore. Talmudic references understand her as a woman with wings whose children are demons. Incantation bowls and amulets used to ward off demons show her trying to seize children. Some midrashim even claim that she was Adam's second wife, by whom he fathered demons.

35:1–10 The New Exodus
The language of this lovely promise oracle suggests that it belongs with chaps. 40–55, the songs of Isaiah of the exile (Deutero-Isaiah). So does the evident fact that the climax of the passage is the return of exiles to Zion (35:10).

35:1–4 *The desert shall . . . blossom like the crocus*—This motif of the future abundance of the wastelands appears again in 41:18–19; 51:3.

35:5–7—The new age will be a time of reversals (see introduction and notes at 5:6, 20; 29:17–24; 32:1–8). Be it human or an aspect of the natural order, all that was handicapped and unfruitful will become whole and productive.

the haunt of jackals shall become a
    swamp,[a]
  the grass shall become reeds and
    rushes.

8 A highway shall be there,
    and it shall be called the Holy
      Way;
  the unclean shall not travel on it,[b]
    but it shall be for God's people;[c]
  no traveler, not even fools, shall go
    astray.
9 No lion shall be there,
    nor shall any ravenous beast come
      up on it;
  they shall not be found there,
    but the redeemed shall walk
      there.
10 And the ransomed of the LORD shall
    return,
    and come to Zion with singing;
  everlasting joy shall be upon their
      heads;
  they shall obtain joy and gladness,
  and sorrow and sighing shall flee
    away.

Sennacherib Threatens Jerusalem

36 In the fourteenth year of King Hezekiah, King Sennacherib of Assyria came up against all the fortified cities of Judah and captured them. [2] The king of Assyria sent the Rabshakeh from Lachish to King Hezekiah at Jerusalem, with a great army. He stood by the conduit of the upper pool on the highway to the Fuller's Field. [3] And there came out to him Eliakim son of Hilkiah, who was in charge of the palace, and Shebna the secretary, and Joah son of Asaph, the recorder.

4 The Rabshakeh said to them, "Say to Hezekiah: Thus says the great king, the king of Assyria: On what do you base this confidence of yours? [5] Do you think that mere words are strategy and power for war? On whom do you now rely, that you have rebelled against me? [6] See, you are relying on Egypt, that broken reed of a staff, which will pierce the hand of anyone who leans on it. Such is Pharaoh

[a] Cn: Heb *in the haunt of jackals is her resting place*   [b] Or *pass it by*
[c] Cn: Heb *for them*

35:8–10—The motif of the holy *highway* reappears in Deutero-Isaiah (e.g., 40:3–4; 42:16). Verse 10 is taken verbatim from 51:11. Reminiscent of cultic procession ways known from sites as diverse as Luxor-Karnak in Egypt, the sacred roads of Babylon, and the Mayan causeways of Yucatan, this divinely provided holy and safe route for a new exodus brings the exiles home with songs on their lips.

36:1–39:8 Isaiah of Jerusalem. Part 5: Historical Appendix

With the exception of the thanksgiving psalm in 38:9–20, these chapters are imported from 2 Kgs. 18:13, 17–20:19. That they are not the work of Isaiah of Jerusalem is confirmed by the facts (a) that they are not short poetic oracles typical of the prophet, and (b) that they are written in the style of the seventh–sixth-century BCE historians who gave us 1–2 Kings. For the material in these chapters we have external evidence in the annals of the Assyrian king Sennacherib and in many archaeological remains.

36:1–22 Assyria Bullies Jerusalem

36:1 Fourteenth year—According to the more reliable Assyrian annals, the siege of Jerusalem described in these chapters occurred in 701 BCE, which would put the beginning of the reign of

Hezekiah in 715. *Fortified cities*—The Assyrian annals record forty-six of them, including *Lachish*, where excavations show evidence of great destruction at this time and a mass burial of some 1,500 bodies, together with pig bones.

36:2 Rabshakeh—The Assyrian title, "chief steward."

36:3—Cf. 22:15–25.

36:5 Rebelled—This is the first explicit acknowledgment in the book of Isaiah of an actual rebellion against Assyria by Hezekiah. This rebellion, including a refusal to pay tribute and aggressive action by Hezekiah against uncooperative neighboring cities, is described in 2 Kgs. 18:7–8, where it is directly linked with religious reform. This presumably entailed the removal from the temple and other sanctuaries of Assyrian images and even sacred time-honored Israelite symbols (2 Kgs. 18:3–6). The Assyrian propaganda machine plays on popular resentment against the latter move by saying that it was the Lord's altars that were removed (v. 7).

36:6 Egypt, that broken reed—See 30:1–7; 31:1–3. The description is supported by the failure of Egypt to deliver any material assistance to the rebel states in 701 BCE.

king of Egypt to all who rely on him. [7] But if you say to me, 'We rely on the LORD our God,' is it not he whose high places and altars Hezekiah has removed, saying to Judah and to Jerusalem, 'You shall worship before this altar'? [8] Come now, make a wager with my master the king of Assyria: I will give you two thousand horses, if you are able on your part to set riders on them. [9] How then can you repulse a single captain among the least of my master's servants, when you rely on Egypt for chariots and for horsemen? [10] Moreover, is it without the LORD that I have come up against this land to destroy it? The LORD said to me, Go up against this land, and destroy it."

11 Then Eliakim, Shebna, and Joah said to the Rabshakeh, "Please speak to your servants in Aramaic, for we understand it; do not speak to us in the language of Judah within the hearing of the people who are on the wall." [12] But the Rabshakeh said, "Has my master sent me to speak these words to your master and to you, and not to the people sitting on the wall, who are doomed with you to eat their own dung and drink their own urine?"

13 Then the Rabshakeh stood and called out in a loud voice in the language of Judah, "Hear the words of the great king, the king of Assyria! [14] Thus says the king: 'Do not let Hezekiah deceive you, for he will not be able to deliver you. [15] Do not let Hezekiah make you rely on the LORD by saying, The LORD will surely deliver us; this city will not be given into the hand of the king of Assyria.' [16] Do not listen to Hezekiah; for thus says the king of Assyria: 'Make your peace with me and come out to me; then every one of you will eat from your own vine and your own fig tree and drink water from your own cistern, [17] until I come and take you away to a land like your own land, a land of grain and wine, a land of bread and vineyards. [18] Do not let Hezekiah mislead you by saying, The LORD will save us. Has any of the gods of the nations saved their land out of the hand of the king of Assyria? [19] Where are the gods of Hamath and Arpad? Where are the gods of Sepharvaim? Have they delivered Samaria out of my hand? [20] Who among all the gods of these countries have saved their countries out of my hand, that the LORD should save Jerusalem out of my hand?'"

21 But they were silent and answered him not a word, for the king's command was, "Do not answer him." [22] Then Eliakim son of Hilkiah, who was in charge of the palace, and Shebna the secretary, and Joah son of Asaph, the recorder, came to Hezekiah with their clothes torn, and told him the words of the Rabshakeh.

Hezekiah Consults Isaiah

37 When King Hezekiah heard it, he tore his clothes, covered himself with sackcloth, and went into the house of the LORD. [2] And he sent Eliakim, who was in charge of the palace, and Shebna the secretary, and the senior priests, covered with sackcloth, to the prophet Isaiah son of Amoz. [3] They said to him, "Thus says Hezekiah, This day is a day of distress, of rebuke, and of disgrace; children have come to the birth, and there

---

36:10—The Rabshakeh has the audacity to claim that Sennacherib is the one doing the work of the Lord.

36:11–22—In spite of pleas by Hezekiah's staff to the Assyrians to speak only in Aramaic, so that the crowds gathered on the walls might not understand their threats, the envoys persist in speaking Hebrew. They make fun of the inability of the gods of the other subdued peoples, including Samaria, to save their peoples.

37:1–38 King and Prophet

37:1–7—A terrified Hezekiah seeks Isaiah's counsel. The prophet remains firm in his insistence that the Lord will protect Jerusalem, save a *remnant* (v. 4) of the people, and bring Sennacherib to his grave. The latter outcome fits better with a conjectured later operation by Sennacherib against Jerusalem, ca. 688 BCE (see note at v. 36). The writer of 2 Kings would have known that Sennacherib was assassinated in 681 by his own sons in a struggle for succession.

is no strength to bring them forth. ⁴ It may be that the LORD your God heard the words of the Rabshakeh, whom his master the king of Assyria has sent to mock the living God, and will rebuke the words that the LORD your God has heard; therefore lift up your prayer for the remnant that is left."

5 When the servants of King Hezekiah came to Isaiah, ⁶ Isaiah said to them, "Say to your master, 'Thus says the LORD: Do not be afraid because of the words that you have heard, with which the servants of the king of Assyria have reviled me. ⁷ I myself will put a spirit in him, so that he shall hear a rumor, and return to his own land; I will cause him to fall by the sword in his own land.'"

8 The Rabshakeh returned, and found the king of Assyria fighting against Libnah; for he had heard that the king had left Lachish. ⁹ Now the king*a* heard concerning King Tirhakah of Ethiopia,*b* "He has set out to fight against you." When he heard it, he sent messengers to Hezekiah, saying, ¹⁰ "Thus shall you speak to King Hezekiah of Judah: Do not let your God on whom you rely deceive you by promising that Jerusalem will not be given into the hand of the king of Assyria. ¹¹ See, you have heard what the kings of Assyria have done to all lands, destroying them utterly. Shall you be delivered? ¹² Have the gods of the nations delivered them, the nations that my predecessors destroyed, Gozan, Haran, Rezeph, and the people of Eden who were in Telassar? ¹³ Where is the king of Hamath, the king of Arpad, the king of the city of Sepharvaim, the king of Hena, or the king of Ivvah?"

Hezekiah's Prayer

14 Hezekiah received the letter from the hand of the messengers and read it; then Hezekiah went up to the house of the LORD and spread it before the LORD. ¹⁵ And Hezekiah prayed to the LORD, saying: ¹⁶ "O LORD of hosts, God of Israel, who are enthroned above the cherubim, you are God, you alone, of all the kingdoms of the earth; you have made heaven and earth. ¹⁷ Incline your ear, O LORD, and hear; open your eyes, O LORD, and see; hear all the words of Sennacherib, which he has sent to mock the living God. ¹⁸ Truly, O LORD, the kings of Assyria have laid waste all the nations and their lands, ¹⁹ and have hurled their gods into the fire, though they were no gods, but the work of human hands—wood and stone—and so they were destroyed. ²⁰ So now, O LORD our God, save us from his hand, so that all the kingdoms of the earth may know that you alone are the LORD."

21 Then Isaiah son of Amoz sent to Hezekiah, saying: "Thus says the LORD, the God of Israel: Because you have prayed to me concerning King Sennacherib of Assyria, ²² this is the word that the LORD has spoken concerning him:

She despises you, she scorns you—
  virgin daughter Zion;
she tosses her head—behind your
    back,
  daughter Jerusalem.
²³ "Whom have you mocked and
    reviled?
  Against whom have you raised
    your voice
and haughtily lifted your eyes?
  Against the Holy One of Israel!
²⁴ By your servants you have mocked
    the Lord,
  and you have said, 'With my many
    chariots

a Heb *he*   *b* Or *Nubia;* Heb *Cush*

37:8–20—A second arrogant scoffing message from Assyria leads Hezekiah to offer an earnest prose prayer for deliverance (vv. 16–20).

37:21–29—Through Isaiah, Hezekiah receives the Lord's answer to his prayer, which is addressed to Sennacherib himself. His successes are attributed to the Lord's own plan and permission (v. 26), but now he will be dragged like an animal back to his own land (v. 29).

I have gone up the heights of the
  mountains,
  to the far recesses of Lebanon;
I felled its tallest cedars,
  its choicest cypresses;
I came to its remotest height,
  its densest forest.
25 I dug wells
  and drank waters,
I dried up with the sole of my foot
  all the streams of Egypt.'

26 "Have you not heard
  that I determined it long ago?
I planned from days of old
  what now I bring to pass,
that you should make fortified cities
  crash into heaps of ruins,
27 while their inhabitants, shorn of
  strength,
  are dismayed and confounded;
they have become like plants of the
  field
  and like tender grass,
like grass on the housetops,
  blighted*a* before it is grown.

28 "I know your rising up*b* and your
  sitting down,
  your going out and coming in,
  and your raging against me.
29 Because you have raged against me
  and your arrogance has come to
  my ears,
I will put my hook in your nose
  and my bit in your mouth;
I will turn you back on the way
  by which you came.

30 "And this shall be the sign for you:
This year eat what grows of itself, and in
the second year what springs from that;
then in the third year sow, reap, plant
vineyards, and eat their fruit. 31 The surviving remnant of the house of Judah
shall again take root downward, and
bear fruit upward; 32 for from Jerusalem
a remnant shall go out, and from Mount
Zion a band of survivors. The zeal of the
LORD of hosts will do this.

33 "Therefore thus says the LORD concerning the king of Assyria: He shall
not come into this city, shoot an arrow
there, come before it with a shield, or
cast up a siege ramp against it. 34 By the
way that he came, by the same he shall
return; he shall not come into this city,
says the LORD. 35 For I will defend this
city to save it, for my own sake and for
the sake of my servant David."

Sennacherib's Defeat and Death

36 Then the angel of the LORD set out
and struck down one hundred eighty-
five thousand in the camp of the Assyrians; when morning dawned, they were
all dead bodies. 37 Then King Sennacherib of Assyria left, went home, and lived
at Nineveh. 38 As he was worshiping in
the house of his god Nisroch, his sons
Adrammelech and Sharezer killed him
with the sword, and they escaped into
the land of Ararat. His son Esar-haddon
succeeded him.

Hezekiah's Illness

38 In those days Hezekiah became
sick and was at the point of death.
The prophet Isaiah son of Amoz came
to him, and said to him, "Thus says the

a With 2 Kings 19.26: Heb *field*   *b* Q Ms Gk: MT lacks *your rising up*

37:35—Given the exact parallel in 2 Kgs. 19:34,
it appears that Isaiah's familiar assurance of the
invulnerability of Zion under the Lord's protection was taken as dogma by later generations (see
note at 31:4–5).

37:36 *Struck down*—What happened? An angelic attack? An outbreak of bubonic or some other
plague in the Assyrian camp? A hasty summons
to come home? Whatever occurred, the failure or
decision of Sennacherib not to seize and destroy
the city doubtless gave great credibility to Isaiah's

promises of divine protection for Jerusalem.
Assyrian records indicate that in 701 Hezekiah
actually capitulated and was forced to pay heavy
tribute. A hypothetical 688 BCE campaign may
have ended without Jerusalem being taken (see
note at vv. 1–7).

38:1–22 Hezekiah's Illness and Recovery

38:1–8—Apparently after the 701 events, Hezekiah prays for healing from a deathly illness and is
promised fifteen more years.

LORD: Set your house in order, for you shall die; you shall not recover." ² Then Hezekiah turned his face to the wall, and prayed to the LORD: ³ "Remember now, O LORD, I implore you, how I have walked before you in faithfulness with a whole heart, and have done what is good in your sight." And Hezekiah wept bitterly.

4 Then the word of the LORD came to Isaiah: ⁵ "Go and say to Hezekiah, Thus says the LORD, the God of your ancestor David: I have heard your prayer, I have seen your tears; I will add fifteen years to your life. ⁶ I will deliver you and this city out of the hand of the king of Assyria, and defend this city.

7 "This is the sign to you from the LORD, that the LORD will do this thing that he has promised: ⁸ See, I will make the shadow cast by the declining sun on the dial of Ahaz turn back ten steps." So the sun turned back on the dial the ten steps by which it had declined.*a*

9 A writing of King Hezekiah of Judah, after he had been sick and had recovered from his sickness:

¹⁰ I said: In the noontide of my days
     I must depart;
I am consigned to the gates of Sheol
     for the rest of my years.
¹¹ I said, I shall not see the LORD
     in the land of the living;
I shall look upon mortals no more
     among the inhabitants of the
         world.
¹² My dwelling is plucked up and
         removed from me
     like a shepherd's tent;
like a weaver I have rolled up my
         life;
he cuts me off from the loom;
from day to night you bring me to
     an end;*a*

¹³ I cry for help*b* until morning;
like a lion he breaks all my bones;
     from day to night you bring me to
         an end.*a*

¹⁴ Like a swallow or a crane*a* I clamor,
     I moan like a dove.
My eyes are weary with looking
         upward.
     O Lord, I am oppressed; be my
         security!
¹⁵ But what can I say? For he has
         spoken to me,
     and he himself has done it.
All my sleep has fled*c*
     because of the bitterness of my
         soul.

¹⁶ O Lord, by these things people live,
     and in all these is the life of my
         spirit.*a*
     Oh, restore me to health and make
         me live!
¹⁷ Surely it was for my welfare
     that I had great bitterness;
but you have held back*d* my life
     from the pit of destruction,
for you have cast all my sins
     behind your back.
¹⁸ For Sheol cannot thank you,
     death cannot praise you;
those who go down to the Pit cannot
         hope
     for your faithfulness.
¹⁹ The living, the living, they thank
         you,
     as I do this day;
fathers make known to children
     your faithfulness.

²⁰ The LORD will save me,
     and we will sing to stringed
         instruments*e*

a Meaning of Heb uncertain   *b* Cn: Meaning of Heb uncertain   *c* Cn Compare Syr: Heb *I will walk slowly all my years*   *d* Cn Compare Gk Vg: Heb *loved*   *e* Heb *my stringed instruments*

38:7—The *sign* of the reliability of this promise is the turning back of the sundial *ten steps* (suggesting that the *dial* was in fact a staircase). Verses 21–22 should perhaps be placed after v. 6, as indeed they are in 2 Kgs. 20:7.

38:9–20—Hezekiah offers a classical psalm of thanksgiving for personal deliverance in which he reminds the Lord that those who die and descend to *Sheol*, the abode of the shades, cannot praise God, but that those who live, as he does, do praise God.

all the days of our lives,
  at the house of the LORD.

21 Now Isaiah had said, "Let them take a lump of figs, and apply it to the boil, so that he may recover." 22 Hezekiah also had said, "What is the sign that I shall go up to the house of the LORD?"

Envoys from Babylon Welcomed

39 At that time King Merodach-baladan son of Baladan of Babylon sent envoys with letters and a present to Hezekiah, for he heard that he had been sick and had recovered. 2 Hezekiah welcomed them; he showed them his treasure house, the silver, the gold, the spices, the precious oil, his whole armory, all that was found in his storehouses. There was nothing in his house or in all his realm that Hezekiah did not show them. 3 Then the prophet Isaiah came to King Hezekiah and said to him, "What did these men say? From where did they come to you?" Hezekiah answered, "They have come to me from a far country, from Babylon."

4 He said, "What have they seen in your house?" Hezekiah answered, "They have seen all that is in my house; there is nothing in my storehouses that I did not show them."

5 Then Isaiah said to Hezekiah, "Hear the word of the LORD of hosts: 6 Days are coming when all that is in your house, and that which your ancestors have stored up until this day, shall be carried to Babylon; nothing shall be left, says the LORD. 7 Some of your own sons who are born to you shall be taken away; they shall be eunuchs in the palace of the king of Babylon." 8 Then Hezekiah said to Isaiah, "The word of the LORD that you have spoken is good." For he thought, "There will be peace and security in my days."

God's People Are Comforted

40 Comfort, O comfort my people,
  says your God.
2 Speak tenderly to Jerusalem,
     and cry to her
   that she has served her term,

39:1–8 Hezekiah's Foolishness

39:1–8—The king mentioned here, known in Babylonian sources as Marduk-apal-iddina, was a Chaldean prince who came to prominence in a successful rebellion against the Assyrian Sargon II and continued to rule an independent Babylon until 702. The report of envoys from this rebel leader enlisting the help of Hezekiah against Assyria fits very well with the latter's own assertions of independence 703–701. For his foolishness in showing the Babylonians all the riches of the temple treasury, Hezekiah is informed by his prophetic adviser Isaiah that all of it will be carried away to Babylon, together with his own sons.

39:8 *Good*—Hezekiah's response—at least there will be *peace* in our time—seems remarkably shortsighted, and is worthy of comparison with other famous temporary political fixes and appeasements, such as that of Neville Chamberlain in 1938.

40:1–55:13 Isaiah of the Exile (Deutero-Isaiah)

These chapters are widely recognized to be from a hand different from nearly all that precedes them, and to reflect a setting in Babylonian exile and not Judea (see introduction). In the present canonical shaping of the book of Isaiah, however, they provide a logical and welcome

counter-theme to the themes of judgment and destruction that predominate in the preaching of Isaiah of Jerusalem. The other side of the coin of wrath and judgment is forgiveness and mercy. The good news of deliverance is the message of this anonymous but greatest and most lyrical of all biblical poets.

40:1–31 The Call of Deutero-Isaiah

40:1–8—The setting of these verses is evidently God's heavenly council. God speaks first and is overheard by the unknown prophet, who stood in the tradition of the "disciples" of Isaiah of Jerusalem, among whom his "testimony" was preserved (8:16). In stark contrast to the commission given the earlier prophet to dull the mind of the people so that they could not "turn and be healed" (6:10–13), the new task, spoken in 40:1–2 initially in the plural to the divine council, is to proclaim *comfort* to *my people*.

40:2—The notion of double restitution for sin is not new. Long before Deutero-Isaiah, the book of the covenant (Exod. 20:22–23:33) demanded double restitution from thieves (see esp. Exod. 22:1–9). One of the major contributions of the prophets was to make the suffering of Israel and Judah intelligible by understanding it as the consequence of their infidelity. So offensive were

that her penalty is paid,
that she has received from the
Lord's hand
double for all her sins.

3 A voice cries out:
"In the wilderness prepare the way
of the Lord,
make straight in the desert a
highway for our God.
4 Every valley shall be lifted up,
and every mountain and hill be
made low;
the uneven ground shall become
level,
and the rough places a plain.
5 Then the glory of the Lord shall be
revealed,
and all people shall see it together,
for the mouth of the Lord has
spoken."
6 A voice says, "Cry out!"
And I said, "What shall I cry?"
All people are grass,
their constancy is like the flower of
the field.
7 The grass withers, the flower fades,
when the breath of the Lord blows
upon it;
surely the people are grass.
8 The grass withers, the flower fades;
but the word of our God will stand
forever.
9 Get you up to a high mountain,

O Zion, herald of good tidings;*a*
lift up your voice with strength,
O Jerusalem, herald of good
tidings,*b*
lift it up, do not fear;
say to the cities of Judah,
"Here is your God!"
10 See, the Lord God comes with
might,
and his arm rules for him;
his reward is with him,
and his recompense before him.
11 He will feed his flock like a
shepherd;
he will gather the lambs in his
arms,
and carry them in his bosom,
and gently lead the mother sheep.

12 Who has measured the waters in the
hollow of his hand
and marked off the heavens with
a span,
enclosed the dust of the earth in a
measure,
and weighed the mountains in
scales
and the hills in a balance?
13 Who has directed the spirit of the
Lord,
or as his counselor has instructed
him?

a Or *O herald of good tidings to Zion* *b* Or *O herald of good tidings to Jerusalem*

---

their sins that evidently even "double" could be understood as proportional. But God who is just is also merciful and knows when to cry, "Enough!"

40:3–5—Another *voice* in the council orders the preparation of a sacred way through the *desert* upon which the Lord will return to Zion, the divine light (*glory*) fully manifest to the people (see note at 35:8–10) In the Gospels (Luke 3:4–6 and parallels), by starting the direct quote in v. 3 after *wilderness*, the passage is made to apply to the wilderness preaching of John the Baptist.

40:6–8—When another heavenly voice says, *Cry out!* the prophet, like his master, Isaiah, before him (6:5), raises an objection to his commission to comfort the people. His premise is spelled out in vv. 6b–7: *All people are grass . . . the grass withers.*

40:8—The answer comes back. God's word endures and thus is a reliable source of strength to those who commit themselves to God's cause (see also 55:10–11).

40:9–11—*Zion* itself is now commanded, whether by God directly or by the prophet, to *herald* God's return in the double royal role of mighty warrior and tender *shepherd* of his people.

40:12–31—The remainder of the luminous opening chapter of Deutero-Isaiah is devoted to evocation of the magnificence of the Creator of all things and the folly of comparing any other powers on earth (v. 17) or in heaven (vv. 25–26) to the Lord. Especially contemptible is the making of an *idol* (vv. 19–20), the impotency of which this poet will point out again and again.

¹⁴ Whom did he consult for his
    enlightenment,
  and who taught him the path of
    justice?
Who taught him knowledge,
  and showed him the way of
    understanding?
¹⁵ Even the nations are like a drop from
    a bucket,
  and are accounted as dust on the
    scales;
  see, he takes up the isles like fine
    dust.
¹⁶ Lebanon would not provide fuel
    enough,
  nor are its animals enough for a
    burnt offering.
¹⁷ All the nations are as nothing before
    him;
  they are accounted by him as less
    than nothing and emptiness.

¹⁸ To whom then will you liken God,
  or what likeness compare with
    him?
¹⁹ An idol?—A workman casts it,
  and a goldsmith overlays it with
    gold,
  and casts for it silver chains.
²⁰ As a gift one chooses mulberry
    wood[a]
  —wood that will not rot—
then seeks out a skilled artisan
  to set up an image that will not
    topple.

²¹ Have you not known? Have you not
    heard?
  Has it not been told you from the
    beginning?
  Have you not understood from the
    foundations of the earth?
²² It is he who sits above the circle of
    the earth,
  and its inhabitants are like
    grasshoppers;
who stretches out the heavens like a
    curtain,

and spreads them like a tent to
    live in;
²³ who brings princes to naught,
  and makes the rulers of the earth
    as nothing.

²⁴ Scarcely are they planted, scarcely
    sown,
  scarcely has their stem taken root
    in the earth,
when he blows upon them, and they
    wither,
  and the tempest carries them off
    like stubble.

²⁵ To whom then will you compare me,
  or who is my equal? says the Holy
    One.
²⁶ Lift up your eyes on high and see:
  Who created these?
He who brings out their host and
    numbers them,
  calling them all by name;
because he is great in strength,
  mighty in power,
  not one is missing.

²⁷ Why do you say, O Jacob,
  and speak, O Israel,
"My way is hidden from the LORD,
  and my right is disregarded by my
    God"?
²⁸ Have you not known? Have you not
    heard?
The LORD is the everlasting God,
  the Creator of the ends of the earth.
He does not faint or grow weary;
  his understanding is unsearchable.
²⁹ He gives power to the faint,
  and strengthens the powerless.
³⁰ Even youths will faint and be weary,
  and the young will fall exhausted;
³¹ but those who wait for the LORD
    shall renew their strength,
  they shall mount up with wings
    like eagles,
  they shall run and not be weary,
  they shall walk and not faint.

[a] Meaning of Heb uncertain

40:27–31—In contrast, God has the power to renew *those who wait for the LORD . . . They shall* *mount up with wings like eagles* (see Ps. 103:5).

Israel Assured of God's Help

41 Listen to me in silence,
    O coastlands;
let the peoples renew their
    strength;
let them approach, then let them
    speak;
let us together draw near for
    judgment.

2 Who has roused a victor from the
    east,
    summoned him to his service?
He delivers up nations to him,
    and tramples kings under foot;
he makes them like dust with his
    sword,
    like driven stubble with his bow.
3 He pursues them and passes on
    safely,
    scarcely touching the path with his
    feet.
4 Who has performed and done this,
    calling the generations from the
    beginning?
I, the LORD, am first,
    and will be with the last.
5 The coastlands have seen and are
    afraid,
    the ends of the earth tremble;
    they have drawn near and come.
6 Each one helps the other,
    saying to one another, "Take
    courage!"
7 The artisan encourages the
    goldsmith,
    and the one who smooths with the
    hammer encourages the one
    who strikes the anvil,

saying of the soldering, "It is good";
    and they fasten it with nails so that
    it cannot be moved.
8 But you, Israel, my servant,
    Jacob, whom I have chosen,
    the offspring of Abraham, my
    friend;
9 you whom I took from the ends of
    the earth,
    and called from its farthest
    corners,
saying to you, "You are my servant,
    I have chosen you and not cast you
    off";
10 do not fear, for I am with you,
    do not be afraid, for I am your
    God;
I will strengthen you, I will help you,
    I will uphold you with my
    victorious right hand.

11 Yes, all who are incensed against you
    shall be ashamed and disgraced;
those who strive against you
    shall be as nothing and shall
    perish.
12 You shall seek those who contend
    with you,
    but you shall not find them;
those who war against you
    shall be as nothing at all.
13 For I, the LORD your God,
    hold your right hand;
it is I who say to you, "Do not fear,
    I will help you."

14 Do not fear, you worm Jacob,
    you insect*a* Israel!
    I will help you, says the LORD;

a Syr: Heb *men of*

41:1–29 God Will Help Israel

41:1–7—An oracle in the form of a courtroom trial.

41:1—God asks the *coastlands* and *peoples* to offer testimony.

41:2—YHWH asks how Cyrus, king of Persia, could have arisen, *a victor from the east* over Babylon, unless God empowered him to do so (see introduction). In fact, the conviction that nothing in human history occurs apart from God's sovereign will is expressed throughout the book of Isaiah and indeed is shared by all of the

prophets. The social-ethical implications of this conviction are these: because God is both just and good, in the long arc of history both justice and mercy will be vindicated, and those who side with God will emerge as victors.

41:7—The frantic nations prepare for the onslaught of divine power by nailing down their gold-plated idols (see 40:19–20, and note at 41:21–29 below).

41:8–16—*Israel, my servant* is invited to cast fear aside.

your Redeemer is the Holy One of
Israel.

15 Now, I will make of you a threshing
sledge,
sharp, new, and having teeth;
you shall thresh the mountains and
crush them,
and you shall make the hills like
chaff.

16 You shall winnow them and the
wind shall carry them away,
and the tempest shall scatter them.
Then you shall rejoice in the LORD;
in the Holy One of Israel you shall
glory.

17 When the poor and needy seek
water,
and there is none,
and their tongue is parched with
thirst,
I the LORD will answer them,
I the God of Israel will not forsake
them.

18 I will open rivers on the bare
heights,*a*
and fountains in the midst of the
valleys;
I will make the wilderness a pool of
water,
and the dry land springs of water.

19 I will put in the wilderness the
cedar,
the acacia, the myrtle, and the
olive;
I will set in the desert the cypress,
the plane and the pine together,

20 so that all may see and know,
all may consider and understand,

that the hand of the LORD has done
this,
the Holy One of Israel has
created it.

The Futility of Idols

21 Set forth your case, says the LORD;
bring your proofs, says the King of
Jacob.

22 Let them bring them, and tell us
what is to happen.
Tell us the former things, what they
are,
so that we may consider them,
and that we may know their
outcome;
or declare to us the things to come.

23 Tell us what is to come hereafter,
that we may know that you are
gods;
do good, or do harm,
that we may be afraid and
terrified.

24 You, indeed, are nothing
and your work is nothing at all;
whoever chooses you is an
abomination.

25 I stirred up one from the north, and
he has come,
from the rising of the sun he was
summoned by name.*b*
He shall trample*c* on rulers as on
mortar,
as the potter treads clay.

26 Who declared it from the beginning,
so that we might know,

a Or *trails*   *b* Cn Compare Q Ms Gk: MT *and he shall call on my name*
c Cn: Heb *come*

41:17–20—In all of the exercise of power, the
Lord bears in mind the *thirst* of *the poor and
needy*. Before their astonished eyes opens a vista
of abundance where before there was only desert
wilderness. The Day of the Lord, so feared by Isaiah of Jerusalem, seems to be behind the sufferers
now, and the new age near at hand. The fruitful,
peaceful world ahead is not an altogether new
one, as an apocalypse would imagine it (e.g.,
Rev. 21:1), but is this world in its perfected form,
as prophetic eschatology like that of Isa. 40–55
imagines it (see also prior examples in 11:6–9;
35:1–10).

41:21–29—Deutero-Isaiah's first lengthy oracle
against idolatry, one of his major themes (see
40:19–20, 41:7, 44:9–20, 45:20–25, 46:1–13).
The false gods are hailed into court to testify.

41:22—The Lord is confident that, being the
mute and impotent gold-plated pieces of wood
that they are, they can neither *tell the former
things* nor *declare to us the things to come* (cf.
42:9). This language is characteristic of chaps.
40–55.

and beforehand, so that we might
　　say, "He is right"?
There was no one who declared it,
　　none who proclaimed,
　　none who heard your words.
27 I first have declared it to Zion,*a*
　　and I give to Jerusalem a herald of
　　　good tidings.
28 But when I look there is no one;
　　among these there is no counselor
　　who, when I ask, gives an answer.
29 No, they are all a delusion;
　　their works are nothing;
　　their images are empty wind.

The Servant, a Light to the Nations

42 Here is my servant, whom I
　　uphold,
my chosen, in whom my soul
　　delights;
I have put my spirit upon him;
　　he will bring forth justice to the
　　　nations.
2 He will not cry or lift up his voice,
　　or make it heard in the street;
3 a bruised reed he will not break,
　　and a dimly burning wick he will
　　　not quench;
　　he will faithfully bring forth justice.
4 He will not grow faint or be crushed
　　until he has established justice in
　　　the earth;
　　and the coastlands wait for his
　　　teaching.

5 Thus says God, the LORD,
　　who created the heavens and
　　　stretched them out,
　　who spread out the earth and what
　　　comes from it,
who gives breath to the people
　　upon it
　　and spirit to those who walk in it:
6 I am the LORD, I have called you in
　　righteousness,
　　I have taken you by the hand and
　　　kept you;
I have given you as a covenant to the
　　people,*b*
　　a light to the nations,
7 　to open the eyes that are blind,
to bring out the prisoners from the
　　dungeon,
　　from the prison those who sit in
　　　darkness.
8 I am the LORD, that is my name;
　　my glory I give to no other,
　　nor my praise to idols.
9 See, the former things have come to
　　pass,
　　and new things I now declare;
before they spring forth,
　　I tell you of them.

A Hymn of Praise

10 Sing to the LORD a new song,
　　his praise from the end of the
　　　earth!

a Cn: Heb *First to Zion—Behold, behold them*　*b* Meaning of Heb
uncertain

41:27—YHWH, in contrast, could declare to
Zion the **good tidings** that Cyrus, the **one from
the north** (v. 25; see 14:31; Jer. 6:22), was coming as their liberator.

41:29—The verdict is handed down. The idols
are found out: *they are all a delusion*.

42:1–25 The Servant of the Lord

42:1–9—This passage is the first of four texts in
Deutero-Isaiah that make up the collection of
the Servant Songs (see also 49:1–6; 50:4–11;
52:13–53:12; introduction).

42:2–4—Though not explicitly suffering, the
Servant's touch is gentle and his voice quiet. His
mission is universal—*justice in the earth*—and
the nations (*coastlands*) eagerly await his word.

42:6—*The LORD* addresses the Servant with the
masculine singular pronoun, *you* (though that

does not rule out an implied collective antecedent).

42:7—The commission of this Servant, be he an
unknown individual or the servant people, Israel,
is enlightenment and liberation. If this is the function of the elect people in the age of restoration,
then the moral and ethical duty of believers is
made clearer. We should anticipate God's great
future liberation of all who are in darkness and
repression by working now to set people free.

42:10–17—This hymn of praise depicts the Lord
as the holy warrior who, after a long time of
silence (v. 14)—a divine restraint criticized by
Job, psalmists, and prophets alike, with cries of
"How long, O Lord?" and "Why do you remain
silent?"—will reorganize the very earth itself and
prepare the road for a new exodus for the exiles
returning from Babylon (see 43:14–21, 51:9–11).

Let the sea roar[a] and all that fills it,
  the coastlands and their
    inhabitants.
11 Let the desert and its towns lift up
    their voice,
  the villages that Kedar inhabits;
let the inhabitants of Sela sing for
    joy,
  let them shout from the tops of the
    mountains.
12 Let them give glory to the LORD,
  and declare his praise in the
    coastlands.
13 The LORD goes forth like a soldier,
  like a warrior he stirs up his fury;
he cries out, he shouts aloud,
  he shows himself mighty against
    his foes.

14 For a long time I have held my
    peace,
  I have kept still and restrained
    myself;
now I will cry out like a woman in
    labor,
  I will gasp and pant.
15 I will lay waste mountains and hills,
  and dry up all their herbage;
I will turn the rivers into islands,
  and dry up the pools.
16 I will lead the blind
  by a road they do not know,
by paths they have not known
  I will guide them.
I will turn the darkness before them
    into light,
  the rough places into level ground.
These are the things I will do,
  and I will not forsake them.
17 They shall be turned back and
    utterly put to shame—
  those who trust in carved images,
who say to cast images,
  "You are our gods."

18 Listen, you that are deaf;
  and you that are blind, look up
    and see!

19 Who is blind but my servant,
  or deaf like my messenger whom
    I send?
Who is blind like my dedicated
    one,
  or blind like the servant of the
    LORD?
20 He sees many things, but does[b] not
    observe them;
  his ears are open, but he does not
    hear.

Israel's Disobedience

21 The LORD was pleased, for the sake
    of his righteousness,
  to magnify his teaching and make
    it glorious.
22 But this is a people robbed and
    plundered,
  all of them are trapped in holes
  and hidden in prisons;
they have become a prey with no one
    to rescue,
  a spoil with no one to say,
    "Restore!"
23 Who among you will give heed to
    this,
  who will attend and listen for the
    time to come?
24 Who gave up Jacob to the
    spoiler,
  and Israel to the robbers?
Was it not the LORD, against whom
    we have sinned,
  in whose ways they would not
    walk,
  and whose law they would not
    obey?
25 So he poured upon him the heat of
    his anger
  and the fury of war;
it set him on fire all around, but he
    did not understand;
  it burned him, but he did not take
    it to heart.

a Cn Compare Ps 96.11; 98.7: Heb *Those who go down to the sea*
b Heb *You see many things but do*

42:18–25—Here the prophet addresses his own people, asking them to recognize their impris- onment as legitimate divine punishment for covenant disobedience (v. 24).

Restoration and Protection Promised

43

But now thus says the LORD,
he who created you, O Jacob,
he who formed you, O Israel:
Do not fear, for I have redeemed
you;
  I have called you by name, you are
mine.
2 When you pass through the waters, I
will be with you;
  and through the rivers, they shall
not overwhelm you;
when you walk through fire you
shall not be burned,
  and the flame shall not consume
you.
3 For I am the LORD your God,
  the Holy One of Israel, your
Savior.
I give Egypt as your ransom,
  Ethiopia*a* and Seba in exchange for
you.
4 Because you are precious in my
sight,
  and honored, and I love you,
I give people in return for you,
  nations in exchange for your life.
5 Do not fear, for I am with you;
  I will bring your offspring from
the east,
  and from the west I will gather you;
6 I will say to the north, "Give
them up,"
  and to the south, "Do not
withhold;
bring my sons from far away
  and my daughters from the end of
the earth—
7 everyone who is called by my name,
  whom I created for my glory,
  whom I formed and made."

8 Bring forth the people who are
blind, yet have eyes,
who are deaf, yet have ears!
9 Let all the nations gather together,
  and let the peoples assemble.
Who among them declared this,
  and foretold to us the former
things?
Let them bring their witnesses to
justify them,
  and let them hear and say, "It is
true."
10 You are my witnesses, says the LORD,
  and my servant whom I have
chosen,
so that you may know and
believe me
  and understand that I am he.
Before me no god was formed,
  nor shall there be any after me.
11 I, I am the LORD,
  and besides me there is no savior.
12 I declared and saved and
proclaimed,
  when there was no strange god
among you;
  and you are my witnesses, says the
LORD.
13 I am God, and also henceforth I am
He;
  there is no one who can deliver
from my hand;
  I work and who can hinder it?

14 Thus says the LORD,
  your Redeemer, the Holy One of
Israel:
For your sake I will send to Babylon
  and break down all the bars,
  and the shouting of the Chaldeans
will be turned to lamentation.*b*

a Or Nubia; Heb Cush   b Meaning of Heb uncertain

43:1–28 Joyous Promises

43:1–7—Doing an about-face on the opening conjunction *but*, the Lord now promises redemption.

43:8–13—In another trial scene, the formerly blind and deaf people of Israel are to be witnesses to the other peoples, whose own gods could not declare the meaning of history (v. 9).

43:14–21—The imagery of a new exodus, so characteristic of chaps. 40–55, becomes very explicit here.

43:14—The new exodus presupposes Babylonian captivity. Those who argue that the entire book of Isaiah is by the eighth-century prophet of Jerusalem have as much difficulty with this verse as with the frequent mention of the Persian king, Cyrus.

¹⁵ I am the LORD, your Holy One,
   the Creator of Israel, your King.
¹⁶ Thus says the LORD,
   who makes a way in the sea,
   a path in the mighty waters,
¹⁷ who brings out chariot and horse,
   army and warrior;
   they lie down, they cannot rise,
   they are extinguished, quenched
      like a wick:
¹⁸ Do not remember the former
      things,
   or consider the things of old.
¹⁹ I am about to do a new thing;
   now it springs forth, do you not
      perceive it?
   I will make a way in the wilderness
   and rivers in the desert.
²⁰ The wild animals will honor me,
   the jackals and the ostriches;
   for I give water in the wilderness,
      rivers in the desert,
   to give drink to my chosen
      people,
²¹ the people whom I formed for
      myself
   so that they might declare my
      praise.
²² Yet you did not call upon me,
      O Jacob;
   but you have been weary of me,
      O Israel!

²³ You have not brought me your sheep
      for burnt offerings,
   or honored me with your
      sacrifices.
   I have not burdened you with
      offerings,
   or wearied you with
      frankincense.
²⁴ You have not bought me sweet cane
      with money,
   or satisfied me with the fat of your
      sacrifices.
   But you have burdened me with
      your sins;
   you have wearied me with your
      iniquities.
²⁵ I, I am He
   who blots out your transgressions
      for my own sake,
   and I will not remember your
      sins.
²⁶ Accuse me, let us go to trial;
   set forth your case, so that you
      may be proved right.
²⁷ Your first ancestor sinned,
   and your interpreters transgressed
      against me.
²⁸ Therefore I profaned the princes of
      the sanctuary,
   I delivered Jacob to utter
      destruction,
   and Israel to reviling.

43:16–17—These verses echo the song of the sea (Exod. 15).

43:18–19—The charge not to *remember the former things* because *I am about to do a new thing* introduces once again the *way in the wilderness* comparable to the way through Sinai along which the pillars of cloud and fire led Israel of old. (In practical terms, the route from Babylon back to Jerusalem was as long, arid, and life-threatening as the road from Baghdad to Jerusalem is today—though without the danger of machine-gun fire and rocket-propelled grenades!)

43:20—YHWH will provide *rivers in the desert*, even as he provided water from rock for Israel of old (Exod. 17:1–7; see also Isa. 48:21. In 1 Cor. 10:4 and in later Jewish midrash, the rock followed them!). These themes of liberation from old ways and the forward look to the new thing remain vital resources to people of faith today as they seek to build a better world.

43:22–28—In another trial scene, Israel is invited to set forth its case for why it should not have suffered so.

43:27—YHWH's case begins with Adam and includes *your interpreters*, the prophets and priests who *transgressed against me*.

43:28—This long history of disobedience explains the *utter destruction* that Jacob has experienced. The fact is that other petty Near Eastern nations suffered the same fate of destruction and deportation under the imperial policies of Assyria and Babylon and that Judah would probably have suffered the same retribution for rebellion in any case. However, this does not negate the value of confession and contrition for coming to terms with bitter experience and for seizing the opportunity for a new beginning.

God's Blessing on Israel

44 But now hear, O Jacob my
      servant,
    Israel whom I have chosen!

2 Thus says the LORD who made you,
    who formed you in the womb and
      will help you:
    Do not fear, O Jacob my servant,
    Jeshurun whom I have chosen.

3 For I will pour water on the thirsty
      land,
    and streams on the dry ground;
    I will pour my spirit upon your
      descendants,
    and my blessing on your
      offspring.

4 They shall spring up like a green
      tamarisk,
    like willows by flowing streams.

5 This one will say, "I am the LORD's,"
    another will be called by the name
      of Jacob,
    yet another will write on the hand,
      "The LORD's,"
    and adopt the name of Israel.

6 Thus says the LORD, the King of
      Israel,
    and his Redeemer, the LORD of
      hosts:
    I am the first and I am the last;
    besides me there is no god.

7 Who is like me? Let them
      proclaim it,
    let them declare and set it forth
      before me.

Who has announced from of old the
      things to come?[a]
    Let them tell us[b] what is yet to be.

8 Do not fear, or be afraid;
    have I not told you from of old and
      declared it?
    You are my witnesses!
    Is there any god besides me?
    There is no other rock; I know not
      one.

The Absurdity of Idol Worship

9 All who make idols are nothing, and the things they delight in do not profit; their witnesses neither see nor know. And so they will be put to shame. 10 Who would fashion a god or cast an image that can do no good? 11 Look, all its devotees shall be put to shame; the artisans too are merely human. Let them all assemble, let them stand up; they shall be terrified, they shall all be put to shame.

12 The ironsmith fashions it[c] and works it over the coals, shaping it with hammers, and forging it with his strong arm; he becomes hungry and his strength fails, he drinks no water and is faint. 13 The carpenter stretches a line, marks it out with a stylus, fashions it with planes, and marks it with a compass; he makes it in human form, with human beauty, to be set up in a shrine. 14 He cuts down cedars or chooses a holm tree or an oak

a Cn: Heb *from my placing an eternal people and things to come*   b Tg: Heb *them*   c Cn: Heb *an ax*

44:1–28 There Is No God but YHWH

44:1–2—*Jacob*, also known as *Jeshurun* (Deut. 32:15), is identified once again as *my servant*. Again introduced by the adversative conjunction *but* (see 43:1), the ensuing promise (44:3–5) is the assurance of an alternate future to the condemnation explained in the previous trial scene.

44:8 *Is there any god besides me?*—This rhetorical question (answer: No!) rejects the henotheism implicit even in the First Commandment (Exod. 20:3; Deut. 5:7) that allows that other people might have their own gods. Now, with yet another epithet used also by Isaiah of Jerusalem (17:10, 26:4, 30:29), YHWH claims absolute status: *There is no other rock*. Other peoples, too, imaged their god as a rock. The Arab tribe,

the Nabateans, before and during Roman times, flanked the entrance to their rose-red city, Petra, with "god rocks," cubic megaliths symbolic of their deity. We can also think of the sacred Ka'aba in Mecca, the central shrine of Islam, which is a large black rock—certainly not understood to be Allah, but rather a focal point of the presence of Allah in the world.

44:9–20—This prose passage is Deutero-Isaiah's most mocking condemnation of idolatry. It vividly depicts an artisan who uses part of a cedar tree as fuel for cooking and warming and then uses the remainder to make an *idol* and *prays to it* for salvation (v. 17). The whole business is a fraud (v. 20; see note at 41:21–29)!

and lets it grow strong among the trees of the forest. He plants a cedar and the rain nourishes it. ¹⁵ Then it can be used as fuel. Part of it he takes and warms himself; he kindles a fire and bakes bread. Then he makes a god and worships it, makes it a carved image and bows down before it. ¹⁶ Half of it he burns in the fire; over this half he roasts meat, eats it and is satisfied. He also warms himself and says, "Ah, I am warm, I can feel the fire!" ¹⁷ The rest of it he makes into a god, his idol, bows down to it and worships it; he prays to it and says, "Save me, for you are my god!"

18 They do not know, nor do they comprehend; for their eyes are shut, so that they cannot see, and their minds as well, so that they cannot understand. ¹⁹ No one considers, nor is there knowledge or discernment to say, "Half of it I burned in the fire; I also baked bread on its coals, I roasted meat and have eaten. Now shall I make the rest of it an abomination? Shall I fall down before a block of wood?" ²⁰ He feeds on ashes; a deluded mind has led him astray, and he cannot save himself or say, "Is not this thing in my right hand a fraud?"

Israel Is Not Forgotten

21 Remember these things, O Jacob,
   and Israel, for you are my servant;
I formed you, you are my servant;
   O Israel, you will not be forgotten
     by me.
22 I have swept away your
     transgressions like a cloud,
   and your sins like mist;
   return to me, for I have redeemed
     you.

23 Sing, O heavens, for the LORD has
     done it;
   shout, O depths of the earth;
break forth into singing,
     O mountains,
     O forest, and every tree in it!
For the LORD has redeemed Jacob,
   and will be glorified in Israel.

24 Thus says the LORD, your Redeemer,
   who formed you in the womb:
I am the LORD, who made all
     things,
   who alone stretched out the
     heavens,
   who by myself spread out the
     earth;
25 who frustrates the omens of liars,
   and makes fools of diviners;
who turns back the wise,
   and makes their knowledge
     foolish;
26 who confirms the word of his
     servant,
   and fulfills the prediction of his
     messengers;
who says of Jerusalem, "It shall be
     inhabited,"
   and of the cities of Judah, "They
     shall be rebuilt,
   and I will raise up their ruins";
27 who says to the deep, "Be dry—
   I will dry up your rivers";
28 who says of Cyrus, "He is my
     shepherd,
   and he shall carry out all my
     purpose";
and who says of Jerusalem, "It shall
     be rebuilt,"
   and of the temple, "Your
     foundation shall be laid."

44:21–28—It is hard to imagine the joy and perhaps the disbelief with which a community of displaced Judeans in Babylon would receive such promises, but there they are. God's protection and care is prenatal! To **Jacob**, God's **servant** (v. 21), formed **in the womb** (v. 24), is now given the promise of homeland reconstruction (v. 26).

44:28—**Cyrus**, king of Persia, is again embraced as YHWH's **shepherd**. Perhaps YHWH says of Jerusalem and temple alike, **"It shall be rebuilt,"**

but Cyrus said it as well and issued his edict to that end (see Ezra 1:2–4, 6:3–5). The surprisingly positive treatment of the foreign conqueror by Deutero-Isaiah encourages people of faith in our time to make common cause with secular authorities of goodwill and people of other faiths in seeking the positive ends of political and economic justice, the care of the environment, and the creation of structures for peace.

Cyrus, God's Instrument

45 Thus says the LORD to his
anointed, to Cyrus,
whose right hand I have grasped
to subdue nations before him
and strip kings of their robes,
to open doors before him—
and the gates shall not be closed:
2 I will go before you
and level the mountains,*a*
I will break in pieces the doors of
bronze
and cut through the bars of iron,
3 I will give you the treasures of
darkness
and riches hidden in secret
places,
so that you may know that it is I, the
LORD,
the God of Israel, who call you by
your name.
4 For the sake of my servant Jacob,
and Israel my chosen,
I call you by your name,
I surname you, though you do not
know me.
5 I am the LORD, and there is no other;
besides me there is no god.
I arm you, though you do not
know me,
6 so that they may know, from the
rising of the sun
and from the west, that there is no
one besides me;

I am the LORD, and there is no
other.
7 I form light and create darkness,
I make weal and create woe;
I the LORD do all these things.

8 Shower, O heavens, from above,
and let the skies rain down
righteousness;
let the earth open, that salvation may
spring up,*b*
and let it cause righteousness to
sprout up also;
I the LORD have created it.

9 Woe to you who strive with your
Maker,
earthen vessels with the potter!*c*
Does the clay say to the one who
fashions it, "What are you
making"?
or "Your work has no handles"?
10 Woe to anyone who says to a father,
"What are you begetting?"
or to a woman, "With what are you
in labor?"
11 Thus says the LORD,
the Holy One of Israel, and its
Maker:
Will you question me*d* about my
children,
or command me concerning the
work of my hands?

a Q Ms Gk: MT *the swellings*   *b* Q Ms: MT *that they may bring forth salvation*   *c* Cn: Heb *with the potsherds, or with the potters*   *d* Cn: Heb *Ask me of things to come*

45:1–25 The Lord Rules over All

45:1–8—The high calling of Cyrus.

45:1—Nowhere else does the Lord, through the prophet, go so far as to entitle Cyrus *his anointed* (Heb.: *mashiah*; Gk.: *christos*).

45:4–5—The Lord acknowledges that Cyrus does not know YHWH, though the Lord **surnames** him (presumably with the royal title "Anointed") and **arms** him.

45:7 *I make weal and create woe*—This is the closest that Scripture ever comes to suggesting that God might be the source of evil. The Hebrew word here that NRSV translates "woe" is *ra'*, "evil, distress, calamity" (KJV: "evil"). Its antonym in v. 7 is not *tob*, "good," but *shalom*. (In the oldest witness to the Isaiah text, however, the great Isaiah scroll from the Dead Sea com-

munity of Qumran, the antonym is *tob*.) Only Job approaches charging God with evildoing (Job 30:26). The sense of the word here is probably close to that of the Job narrator who, in the denouement of the story, remarks that, after his restoration, Job's relatives and friends "comforted him for all the evil that the LORD had brought upon him" (Job 42:11). Woe/evil in this sense is not a moral category but rather disaster and suffering experienced as punitive activity of God. So, even with Isa. 45:7 taken into account, we can fairly say that the God of Scripture is not a dyad (both good and bad), but a monad (a good God only, though just and powerful against wrongdoing). We human beings are the dyads, capable of making the moral choice of good or evil.

12 I made the earth,
   and created humankind upon it;
it was my hands that stretched out
      the heavens,
   and I commanded all their host.
13 I have aroused Cyrus*a* in
         righteousness,
   and I will make all his paths
         straight;
he shall build my city
   and set my exiles free,
not for price or reward,
   says the LORD of hosts.
14 Thus says the LORD:
The wealth of Egypt and the
      merchandise of Ethiopia,*b*
   and the Sabeans, tall of stature,
shall come over to you and be yours,
   they shall follow you;
   they shall come over in chains and
      bow down to you.
They will make supplication to you,
      saying,
   "God is with you alone, and there
      is no other;
   there is no god besides him."
15 Truly, you are a God who hides
      himself,
   O God of Israel, the Savior.
16 All of them are put to shame and
      confounded,
   the makers of idols go in
      confusion together.
17 But Israel is saved by the LORD
      with everlasting salvation;
you shall not be put to shame or
      confounded
   to all eternity.

18 For thus says the LORD,
who created the heavens
      (he is God!),
who formed the earth and made it
      (he established it;
he did not create it a chaos,
   he formed it to be inhabited!):

I am the LORD, and there is no
      other.
19 I did not speak in secret,
   in a land of darkness;
I did not say to the offspring of
      Jacob,
   "Seek me in chaos."
I the LORD speak the truth,
   I declare what is right.

Idols Cannot Save Babylon

20 Assemble yourselves and come
      together,
   draw near, you survivors of the
      nations!
They have no knowledge—
   those who carry about their
      wooden idols,
and keep on praying to a god
   that cannot save.
21 Declare and present your case;
   let them take counsel together!
Who told this long ago?
   Who declared it of old?
Was it not I, the LORD?
   There is no other god besides me,
a righteous God and a Savior;
   there is no one besides me.

22 Turn to me and be saved,
   all the ends of the earth!
For I am God, and there is no
      other.
23 By myself I have sworn,
   from my mouth has gone forth in
      righteousness
   a word that shall not return:
"To me every knee shall bow,
   every tongue shall swear."

24 Only in the LORD, it shall be said
      of me,
   are righteousness and strength;
all who were incensed against him
   shall come to him and be ashamed.

a Heb *him*   *b* Or *Nubia;* Heb *Cush*

45:23—YHWH's universal sovereignty will one
day be acknowledged by all people, a future
outcome applied by Paul to the life of that eschatological community, the church (Rom. 14:11).
In an early Christian hymn quoted by Paul in

Phil. 2, following verses depicting the preexis-
tent Christ as one who humbled himself into a
suffering servant (Phil. 2:6–8), Isaiah's language
is applied to the resurrected and exalted Christ
(Phil. 2:9–11).

25 In the Lord all the offspring of
   Israel
      shall triumph and glory.

46

Bel bows down, Nebo stoops,
their idols are on beasts and
   cattle;
these things you carry are loaded
   as burdens on weary animals.
2 They stoop, they bow down
      together;
   they cannot save the burden,
      but themselves go into captivity.

3 Listen to me, O house of Jacob,
   all the remnant of the house of
      Israel,
who have been borne by me from
   your birth,
      carried from the womb;
4 even to your old age I am he,
   even when you turn gray I will
      carry you.
I have made, and I will bear;
   I will carry and will save.

5 To whom will you liken me and
      make me equal,
   and compare me, as though we
      were alike?
6 Those who lavish gold from the
      purse,
   and weigh out silver in the
      scales—
they hire a goldsmith, who makes it
   into a god;
      then they fall down and worship!
7 They lift it to their shoulders, they
      carry it,

they set it in its place, and it stands
   there;
   it cannot move from its place.
If one cries out to it, it does not
   answer
   or save anyone from trouble.

8 Remember this and consider,[a]
   recall it to mind, you transgressors,
9 remember the former things of
      old;
   for I am God, and there is no other;
   I am God, and there is no one like
      me,
10 declaring the end from the
      beginning
   and from ancient times things not
      yet done,
saying, "My purpose shall stand,
   and I will fulfill my intention,"
11 calling a bird of prey from the east,
   the man for my purpose from a far
      country.
I have spoken, and I will bring it to
   pass;
   I have planned, and I will do it.

12 Listen to me, you stubborn of heart,
   you who are far from deliverance:
13 I bring near my deliverance, it is not
      far off,
   and my salvation will not tarry;
I will put salvation in Zion,
   for Israel my glory.

The Humiliation of Babylon

47

Come down and sit in the dust,
virgin daughter Babylon!

[a] Meaning of Heb uncertain

46:1–13 The Impotence of Idols

This entire chapter is devoted to drawing the
contrast between the impotent handmade idols
of Babylon (**Bel** =Baal, "Lord," a title of Marduk,
Babylon's chief god; **Nebo**=Nabu, son of Bel)
and the true God who alone creates the world
and its people, plans history, and brings it to pass.

46:1–4—The disparity between the false gods
and the true God is sharpened by the contrast
of idols being carried (evacuated, as Cyrus approached!) by beasts of burden with the Lord
who says to the **remnant** of Jacob, **I have made,
and I will bear** (v. 4).

47:1–15 No One Can Save Babylon

This mocking address to Babylon imagined as
a virgin princess of **Chaldea** (a synonym for
Babylon, derived from the Aramean clan that led
the Neo-Babylonian renaissance), has a story line
complete in itself. The delicate young noblewom-
an will be stripped naked and humiliated (vv.
1–4). She mistook YHWH's ceding of the chosen
people to her for the purposes of punishment as
something she had done (vv. 5–7). In fact, she
claimed autonomy and self-determination to the
point of speaking like a god: **"I am, and there is
no one besides me"** (vv. 8, 10). Now, however,
the truth is out. She who **felt secure in [her]**

Sit on the ground without a throne,
    daughter Chaldea!
For you shall no more be called
    tender and delicate.
2 Take the millstones and grind meal,
    remove your veil,
strip off your robe, uncover your
    legs,
    pass through the rivers.
3 Your nakedness shall be uncovered,
    and your shame shall be seen.
I will take vengeance,
    and I will spare no one.
4 Our Redeemer—the LORD of hosts is
    his name—
    is the Holy One of Israel.

5 Sit in silence, and go into darkness,
    daughter Chaldea!
For you shall no more be called
    the mistress of kingdoms.
6 I was angry with my people,
    I profaned my heritage;
I gave them into your hand,
    you showed them no mercy;
on the aged you made your yoke
    exceedingly heavy.
7 You said, "I shall be mistress
    forever,"
so that you did not lay these things
    to heart
    or remember their end.

8 Now therefore hear this, you lover of
    pleasures,
    who sit securely,
who say in your heart,
    "I am, and there is no one
      besides me;
I shall not sit as a widow
    or know the loss of children"—
9 both these things shall come upon
    you
    in a moment, in one day:
the loss of children and widowhood
    shall come upon you in full
      measure,
in spite of your many sorceries

and the great power of your
    enchantments.

10 You felt secure in your wickedness;
    you said, "No one sees me."
Your wisdom and your knowledge
    led you astray,
and you said in your heart,
    "I am, and there is no one besides
      me."
11 But evil shall come upon you,
    which you cannot charm away;
disaster shall fall upon you,
    which you will not be able to ward
      off;
and ruin shall come on you
      suddenly,
    of which you know nothing.

12 Stand fast in your enchantments
    and your many sorceries,
with which you have labored from
      your youth;
perhaps you may be able to succeed,
    perhaps you may inspire terror.
13 You are wearied with your many
      consultations;
    let those who study*a* the heavens
stand up and save you,
    those who gaze at the stars,
and at each new moon predict
    what*b* shall befall you.

14 See, they are like stubble,
    the fire consumes them;
they cannot deliver themselves
    from the power of the flame.
No coal for warming oneself is this,
    no fire to sit before!
15 Such to you are those with whom
      you have labored,
    who have trafficked with you from
      your youth;
they all wander about in their own
      paths;
    there is no one to save you.

a Meaning of Heb uncertain   *b* Gk Syr Compare Vg: Heb *from what*

---

wickedness (v. 10) is ruined (v. 11). All of the enchanters, sorcerers, astrologers, and stargazers for which Babylon was so renowned cannot save themselves (vv. 12–14), much less Babylon herself (v. 15).

God the Creator and Redeemer

48 Hear this, O house of Jacob,
who are called by the name of
Israel,
and who came forth from the
loins[a] of Judah;
who swear by the name of the
LORD,
and invoke the God of Israel,
but not in truth or right.
2 For they call themselves after the
holy city,
and lean on the God of Israel;
the LORD of hosts is his name.

3 The former things I declared long
ago,
they went out from my mouth and
I made them known;
then suddenly I did them and they
came to pass.
4 Because I know that you are
obstinate,
and your neck is an iron sinew
and your forehead brass,
5 I declared them to you from long
ago,
before they came to pass I
announced them to you,
so that you would not say, "My idol
did them,
my carved image and my cast
image commanded them."

6 You have heard; now see all this;
and will you not declare it?
From this time forward I make you
hear new things,
hidden things that you have not
known.
7 They are created now, not long ago;
before today you have never heard
of them,
so that you could not say, "I
already knew them."

8 You have never heard, you have
never known,
from of old your ear has not been
opened.
For I knew that you would deal very
treacherously,
and that from birth you were
called a rebel.

9 For my name's sake I defer my anger,
for the sake of my praise I restrain
it for you,
so that I may not cut you off.
10 See, I have refined you, but not like[b]
silver;
I have tested you in the furnace of
adversity.
11 For my own sake, for my own sake, I
do it,
for why should my name[c] be
profaned?
My glory I will not give to another.

12 Listen to me, O Jacob,
and Israel, whom I called:
I am He; I am the first,
and I am the last.
13 My hand laid the foundation of the
earth,
and my right hand spread out the
heavens;
when I summon them,
they stand at attention.

14 Assemble, all of you, and hear!
Who among them has declared
these things?
The LORD loves him;
he shall perform his purpose on
Babylon,

---

a Cn: Heb *waters*   *b* Cn: Heb *with*   *c* Gk Old Latin: Heb *for why should it*

48:1–22 The Lord Has the Power to Save

The Lord addresses Israel through this entire chapter except v. 16b. In much of it God complains of the obstinacy of the people and their propensity to attribute the truths they learn from God either to their idols (v. 5) or their own wisdom (v. 7b).

48:9–11—YHWH explains that the survival of any remnant at all is entirely due to God's desire that the divine *name* not *be profaned* and the divine glory not be tarnished because of the total destruction of the elect people. (This appeal to God to sanctify the holy name by sparing Israel, lest other nations deride God as incapable of saving the chosen ones, is spelled out elsewhere in many texts, e.g., Ps. 79:9–10; Jer. 14:7–9, 21; Ezek. 36:16–32.)

and his arm shall be against the
  Chaldeans.
15 I, even I, have spoken and called
    him,
  I have brought him, and he will
    prosper in his way.
16 Draw near to me, hear this!
  From the beginning I have not
    spoken in secret,
  from the time it came to be I have
    been there.
  And now the Lord God has sent me
    and his spirit.

17 Thus says the Lord,
  your Redeemer, the Holy One of
    Israel:
  I am the Lord your God,
  who teaches you for your own
    good,
  who leads you in the way you
    should go.
18 O that you had paid attention to my
    commandments!
  Then your prosperity would have
    been like a river,
  and your success like the waves of
    the sea;
19 your offspring would have been like
    the sand,
  and your descendants like its grains;
  their name would never be cut off
  or destroyed from before me.

20 Go out from Babylon, flee from
    Chaldea,

declare this with a shout of joy,
  proclaim it,
send it forth to the end of the earth;
  say, "The Lord has redeemed his
    servant Jacob!"
21 They did not thirst when he led
    them through the deserts;
  he made water flow for them from
    the rock;
  he split open the rock and the
    water gushed out.
22 "There is no peace," says the Lord,
    "for the wicked."

The Servant's Mission

49 Listen to me, O coastlands,
  pay attention, you peoples from
    far away!
  The Lord called me before I was
    born,
  while I was in my mother's womb
    he named me.
2 He made my mouth like a sharp
    sword,
  in the shadow of his hand he
    hid me;
  he made me a polished arrow,
  in his quiver he hid me away.
3 And he said to me, "You are my
    servant,
  Israel, in whom I will be
    glorified."
4 But I said, "I have labored in vain,
  I have spent my strength for
    nothing and vanity;

48:17–21—Turning from a lament over the prosperity and progeny that an obedient Israel might have (vv. 17–19), the Lord now commands that the good news of redemption be proclaimed (v. 20b).

48:21—See Exod. 17:1–7; note at Isa. 43:18–19.

48:22—This often-quoted aphorism (also found in 57:21) originated with neither Shakespeare nor Ben Franklin, but right here with Isaiah! Even in the context of national liberation set in 48:20–21, the wicked have the option to exclude themselves from the peace to come.

49:1–26 The Light to the Nations

49:1–6—This chapter begins with the second of the four Servant Songs (see note at 42:1–9).

49:1—Speaking in the first person singular, the

servant reaffirms his sense that his election was a prenatal event (see also 44:2, 24). The prophet Jeremiah had earlier testified to the same sense of inescapable prophetic appointment (Jer. 1:5). The Gospel writers Matthew and Luke understood Jesus' servant messiah status, too, as originating at conception (Matt. 1:20; Luke 1:31).

49:2—The imagery of the Servant as a weapon held in the Lord's reserve does not necessarily imply imperial militancy (see note at v. 23 below), but rather the effectiveness that comes from speaking the Lord's word.

49:3—In this instance only, among the four Servant Songs, the Servant is explicitly identified as *Israel*. (This word is missing in some Hebrew manuscripts.)

yet surely my cause is with the LORD,
   and my reward with my God."

5 And now the LORD says,
   who formed me in the womb to be
      his servant,
to bring Jacob back to him,
   and that Israel might be gathered
      to him,
for I am honored in the sight of the
      LORD,
   and my God has become my
      strength—
6 he says,
"It is too light a thing that you
      should be my servant
   to raise up the tribes of Jacob
   and to restore the survivors of
      Israel;
I will give you as a light to the nations,
   that my salvation may reach to the
      end of the earth."

7 Thus says the LORD,
   the Redeemer of Israel and his
      Holy One,
to one deeply despised, abhorred by
      the nations,
   the slave of rulers,
"Kings shall see and stand up,
   princes, and they shall prostrate
      themselves,
because of the LORD, who is faithful,
   the Holy One of Israel, who has
      chosen you."

Zion's Children to Be Brought Home

8 Thus says the LORD:
In a time of favor I have answered
      you,

on a day of salvation I have helped
      you;
I have kept you and given you
   as a covenant to the people,*a*
to establish the land,
   to apportion the desolate
      heritages;
9 saying to the prisoners, "Come out,"
   to those who are in darkness,
      "Show yourselves."
They shall feed along the ways,
   on all the bare heights*b* shall be
      their pasture;
10 they shall not hunger or thirst,
   neither scorching wind nor sun
      shall strike them down,
for he who has pity on them will
      lead them,
   and by springs of water will guide
      them.
11 And I will turn all my mountains
      into a road,
   and my highways shall be raised up.
12 Lo, these shall come from far away,
   and lo, these from the north and
      from the west,
   and these from the land of Syene.*c*

13 Sing for joy, O heavens, and exult,
      O earth;
   break forth, O mountains, into
      singing!
For the LORD has comforted his
      people,
   and will have compassion on his
      suffering ones.

14 But Zion said, "The LORD has
      forsaken me,

a Meaning of Heb uncertain *b* Or *the trails* *c* Q Ms: MT *Sinim*

49:5—However, the Servant is apparently not all of Israel, for he is *formed* in order *to bring Jacob back* to the Lord. Perhaps, then, this view of the Servant can be equated with the concept of the saving remnant so prominent in chaps. 1–39 but otherwise mentioned only once (and in a similar womb-election context) in Deutero-Isaiah (46:3).

49:6—The task of redeeming Israel alone is, however, too small a vision. The Lord charges the Servant to move beyond the salvation of his own people into a universal realm. Through the ages Jews and Christians who have identified them-

selves with the Servant have taken this promise to be a mandate to be out and about with the good news of salvation, and all else that constitutes *a light to the nations*: being models of justice, human rights, preferential treatment of the poor and the sick, liberation of the oppressed.

49:7—Though not considered part of the second Servant Song, this verse portrays God's chosen people as the same *slave of rulers* to whom, in the age to come, *kings* will *prostrate themselves*.

my Lord has forgotten me."
15 Can a woman forget her nursing
    child,
    or show no compassion for the
      child of her womb?
Even these may forget,
    yet I will not forget you.
16 See, I have inscribed you on the
    palms of my hands;
    your walls are continually before
      me.
17 Your builders outdo your
    destroyers,*a*
    and those who laid you waste go
      away from you.
18 Lift up your eyes all around and see;
    they all gather, they come to you.
As I live, says the Lord,
    you shall put all of them on like an
      ornament,
    and like a bride you shall bind
      them on.

19 Surely your waste and your desolate
    places
    and your devastated land—
surely now you will be too crowded
    for your inhabitants,
    and those who swallowed you up
      will be far away.
20 The children born in the time of
    your bereavement
    will yet say in your hearing:
"The place is too crowded for me;
    make room for me to settle."
21 Then you will say in your heart,
    "Who has borne me these?
I was bereaved and barren,
    exiled and put away—
    so who has reared these?

I was left all alone—
    where then have these come
      from?"

22 Thus says the Lord God:
I will soon lift up my hand to the
    nations,
    and raise my signal to the
      peoples;
and they shall bring your sons in
    their bosom,
    and your daughters shall be
      carried on their shoulders.
23 Kings shall be your foster fathers,
    and their queens your nursing
      mothers.
With their faces to the ground they
    shall bow down to you,
    and lick the dust of your feet.
Then you will know that I am the
    Lord;
    those who wait for me shall not be
      put to shame.

24 Can the prey be taken from the
    mighty,
    or the captives of a tyrant*b* be
      rescued?
25 But thus says the Lord:
Even the captives of the mighty shall
    be taken,
    and the prey of the tyrant be
      rescued;
for I will contend with those who
    contend with you,
    and I will save your children.
26 I will make your oppressors eat their
    own flesh,

a Or *Your children come swiftly; your destroyers*   *b* Q Ms Syr Vg: MT *of a righteous person*

49:23—The same triumphalistic note is sounded with the promise that kings will **lick the dust of your feet**. This vision of the coming reversal of fortunes that leaves Israel and her God as central to the whole world obviously has its inherent dangers. Such a polity could be construed as both imperial and theocratic. It is a theme enlarged upon in the final stratum of the book of Isaiah (chaps. 56–66; see note at 60:4–7, 16–20). Nevertheless, the note of triumph heard here is surely not intended to be an invitation to future arrogance of power, given that the prophet is above all loyal to the covenant traditions of justice and peace, but springs from the joy the prophet experiences in the prospect of liberation and from the conviction that victorious future events in history are revelatory of who the Lord really is. Borrowing a sentence used more than fifty times by his near contemporary, the prophet Ezekiel, he says that when the exile ends and Israel regains its rightful place among the nations, **then you will know that I am the Lord**. That knowledge is security in itself.

and they shall be drunk with their
        own blood as with wine.
Then all flesh shall know
    that I am the LORD your Savior,
    and your Redeemer, the Mighty
        One of Jacob.

50 Thus says the LORD:
    Where is your mother's bill of
        divorce
    with which I put her away?
Or which of my creditors is it
    to whom I have sold you?
No, because of your sins you were
        sold,
    and for your transgressions your
        mother was put away.
2 Why was no one there when I
        came?
    Why did no one answer when I
        called?
Is my hand shortened, that it cannot
        redeem?
    Or have I no power to deliver?
By my rebuke I dry up the sea,
    I make the rivers a desert;
their fish stink for lack of water,
    and die of thirst.*a*
3 I clothe the heavens with blackness,
    and make sackcloth their
        covering.

The Servant's Humiliation
and Vindication

4 The Lord GOD has given me
    the tongue of a teacher,*b*
that I may know how to sustain
    the weary with a word.
Morning by morning he wakens—
    wakens my ear
to listen as those who are taught.
5 The Lord GOD has opened my ear,
    and I was not rebellious,

I did not turn backward.
6 I gave my back to those who
        struck me,
    and my cheeks to those who pulled
        out the beard;
I did not hide my face
    from insult and spitting.

7 The Lord GOD helps me;
    therefore I have not been
        disgraced;
therefore I have set my face like
        flint,
    and I know that I shall not be put
        to shame;
8 he who vindicates me is near.
Who will contend with me?
    Let us stand up together.
Who are my adversaries?
    Let them confront me.
9 It is the Lord GOD who helps me;
    who will declare me guilty?
All of them will wear out like a
        garment;
    the moth will eat them up.

10 Who among you fears the LORD
    and obeys the voice of his
        servant,
who walks in darkness
    and has no light,
yet trusts in the name of the LORD
    and relies upon his God?
11 But all of you are kindlers of fire,
    lighters of firebrands.*c*
Walk in the flame of your fire,
    and among the brands that you
        have kindled!
This is what you shall have from my
        hand:
    you shall lie down in torment.

a Or *die on the thirsty ground*   *b* Cn: Heb *of those who are taught*   *c* Syr: Heb
you gird yourselves with firebrands

50:1–11 Teachings of the Servant
50:4–11—The third of the Servant Songs (see note
at 42:1–9).
50:6—Though he is faithful and able to encourage *the weary* (v. 4), very much like Isaiah
himself, the Servant truly suffers. He is physically
abused, insulted, and spat upon.

50:7—Who does these things we do not know,
but God is on the Servant's side.
50:10–11—The Servant *walks in darkness* yet
relies on God. Evildoers, in contrast, *walk in
the flame* of the fire that they themselves *have
kindled*.

Blessings in Store for God's People

51 Listen to me, you that pursue
righteousness,
    you that seek the LORD.
Look to the rock from which you
    were hewn,
    and to the quarry from which you
      were dug.
2 Look to Abraham your father
    and to Sarah who bore you;
for he was but one when I called
    him,
    but I blessed him and made him
      many.
3 For the LORD will comfort Zion;
    he will comfort all her waste
      places,
and will make her wilderness like
    Eden,
    her desert like the garden of the
      LORD;
joy and gladness will be found in
    her,
    thanksgiving and the voice of
      song.

4 Listen to me, my people,
    and give heed to me, my nation;
for a teaching will go out from me,
    and my justice for a light to the
      peoples.
5 I will bring near my deliverance
    swiftly,
    my salvation has gone out
    and my arms will rule the peoples;
the coastlands wait for me,
    and for my arm they hope.
6 Lift up your eyes to the heavens,
and look at the earth beneath;
for the heavens will vanish like
    smoke,
    the earth will wear out like a
      garment,
    and those who live on it will die
      like gnats;[a]
but my salvation will be forever,
    and my deliverance will never be
      ended.

7 Listen to me, you who know
    righteousness,
    you people who have my teaching
      in your hearts;
do not fear the reproach of others,
    and do not be dismayed when they
      revile you.
8 For the moth will eat them up like a
    garment,
    and the worm will eat them like
      wool;
but my deliverance will be forever,
    and my salvation to all
      generations.

9 Awake, awake, put on strength,
    O arm of the LORD!
Awake, as in days of old,
    the generations of long ago!
Was it not you who cut Rahab in
    pieces,
    who pierced the dragon?
10 Was it not you who dried up the sea,
    the waters of the great deep;
who made the depths of the sea a
    way
    for the redeemed to cross over?

[a] Or *in like manner*

51:1–23 The Desert Will Blossom
Running through this collection of prophetic and
divine words is the persistent promise of coming
deliverance and the repeated announcement
that the oppressors will in the end drink from the
same bitter cup of suffering as that from which
they have made Israel drink.

51:1–3—*Abraham* and *Sarah* are likened unto a
rock and a *quarry* from which Israel was taken.
The point of the simile is that *Zion*, like the
blessed ancestors (Gen. 12:1–3), will again experience the joy of divine favor. Remembrance of
God's past faithfulness is itself a source of hope.

51:4–7—The Lord addresses *my people* with
the news that *salvation* will encompass all the
peoples (v. 5). In a flourish almost apocalyptic
in character, the Lord promises deliverance more
enduring than the heavens and earth themselves.

51:9–11—The prophet rouses the Lord's mighty
arm for the new exodus from Babylon (v. 11) by
recalling the divine act at the Red Sea (v. 10; see
Exod. 15; Ps. 136:12–16). He links the historical
salvation wrought for the *redeemed* at the sea
with the mythic tradition of the Creator's victory
over the chaos monster *Rahab*/Leviathan (see
27:1; Job 26:12; Ps. 74:12–14).

11 So the ransomed of the LORD shall
      return,
   and come to Zion with singing;
   everlasting joy shall be upon their
      heads;
      they shall obtain joy and gladness,
      and sorrow and sighing shall flee
         away.

12 I, I am he who comforts you;
      why then are you afraid of a mere
         mortal who must die,
      a human being who fades like
         grass?

13 You have forgotten the LORD, your
      Maker,
      who stretched out the heavens
      and laid the foundations of the
         earth.
   You fear continually all day long
      because of the fury of the
         oppressor,
   who is bent on destruction.
      But where is the fury of the
         oppressor?

14 The oppressed shall speedily be
      released;
      they shall not die and go down to
         the Pit,
      nor shall they lack bread.

15 For I am the LORD your God,
      who stirs up the sea so that its
         waves roar—
      the LORD of hosts is his name.

16 I have put my words in your mouth,
      and hidden you in the shadow of
         my hand,
   stretching out[a] the heavens
      and laying the foundations of the
         earth,
      and saying to Zion, "You are my
         people."

17 Rouse yourself, rouse yourself!
      Stand up, O Jerusalem,
   you who have drunk at the hand of
      the LORD
      the cup of his wrath,

who have drunk to the dregs
      the bowl of staggering.

18 There is no one to guide her
      among all the children she has
         borne;
   there is no one to take her by the
      hand
      among all the children she has
         brought up.

19 These two things have befallen you
      —who will grieve with you?—
   devastation and destruction, famine
      and sword—
      who will comfort you?[b]

20 Your children have fainted,
      they lie at the head of every street
      like an antelope in a net;
   they are full of the wrath of the
      LORD,
      the rebuke of your God.

21 Therefore hear this, you who are
      wounded,[c]
      who are drunk, but not with wine:

22 Thus says your Sovereign, the LORD,
      your God who pleads the cause of
         his people:
   See, I have taken from your hand the
      cup of staggering;
   you shall drink no more
      from the bowl of my wrath.

23 And I will put it into the hand of
      your tormentors,
      who have said to you,
      "Bow down, that we may walk on
         you";
   and you have made your back like
      the ground
   and like the street for them to
      walk on.

Let Zion Rejoice

52 Awake, awake,
   put on your strength, O Zion!
   Put on your beautiful garments,
      O Jerusalem, the holy city;

a Syr: Heb planting b Q Ms Gk Syr Vg: MT how may I comfort you?
c Or humbled

52:1–12 Messages to Zion
Four short addresses by the prophet to holy *Zion*.

52:1–2—Captive Jerusalem's beauty will be
restored and the unclean kept out.

for the uncircumcised and the
      unclean
   shall enter you no more.
2 Shake yourself from the dust, rise up,
      O captive*a* Jerusalem;
   loose the bonds from your neck,
      O captive daughter Zion!

3 For thus says the Lord: You were sold
for nothing, and you shall be redeemed
without money. 4 For thus says the Lord
God: Long ago, my people went down
into Egypt to reside there as aliens;
the Assyrian, too, has oppressed them
without cause. 5 Now therefore what
am I doing here, says the Lord, seeing
that my people are taken away without
cause? Their rulers howl, says the Lord,
and continually, all day long, my name
is despised. 6 Therefore my people shall
know my name; therefore in that day
they shall know that it is I who speak;
here am I.

7 How beautiful upon the mountains
      are the feet of the messenger who
         announces peace,
   who brings good news,
      who announces salvation,
      who says to Zion, "Your God
         reigns."
8 Listen! Your sentinels lift up their
      voices,

together they sing for joy;
   for in plain sight they see
      the return of the Lord to Zion.
9 Break forth together into singing,
      you ruins of Jerusalem;
   for the Lord has comforted his
         people,
   he has redeemed Jerusalem.
10 The Lord has bared his holy arm
      before the eyes of all the nations;
   and all the ends of the earth shall
         see
      the salvation of our God.

11 Depart, depart, go out from there!
      Touch no unclean thing;
   go out from the midst of it, purify
         yourselves,
      you who carry the vessels of the
         Lord.
12 For you shall not go out in haste,
      and you shall not go in flight;
   for the Lord will go before you,
      and the God of Israel will be your
         rear guard.

The Suffering Servant
13 See, my servant shall prosper;
      he shall be exalted and lifted up,
      and shall be very high.
14 Just as there were many who were
      astonished at him*b*

a Cn: Heb *rise up, sit*   *b* Syr Tg: Heb *you*

52:3–6—The Lord will vindicate the divine *name* against Babylon as the Lord did in earlier times against Egypt and Assyria.

52:7–10—*The messenger who announces peace . . . salvation* (presumably the prophet himself) summons the very *ruins of Jerusalem* (v. 9) to celebrate the Lord's success in comforting and redeeming the people. This passage functions as a kind of reprise of the prologue and call of Deutero-Isaiah in chap. 40. Now the prophet and the people witness that the Lord has accomplished the divine plan.

52:11–12—Whether addressed to all exiles about to leave unclean Babylon (see 48:20) or in a more general way to those whose purity must be maintained because they *carry the vessels of the Lord*, the point of these verses seems to be sharpened in v. 12. The exit can be made with stately confidence, because, as was the case in the exodus from Egypt (Exod. 14:19–20), *the*

God of Israel will be your rear guard. Down to our own time, those who seek to walk in God's way draw confidence from the scriptural assurance that faithful God marches with us.

52:13–53:12 The Suffering Servant

The fourth, final, and most extensive Servant Song had the greatest impact on Christian interpretation of Jesus as Suffering Servant. (It is cited or alluded to at least nine times in the New Testament.) At the same time, it is fraught with interpretive difficulties. Of all the four songs, this one seems to refer most clearly to a single individual. But who the prophet had in mind eludes us.

52:13–15—These verses move from a celebration of the future exaltation of *my servant* through an acknowledgment of his present astonishingly disfigured appearance and back to a report of *nations* startled and *kings* dumbstruck by the advent of the servant.

—so marred was his appearance,
> beyond human semblance,
> and his form beyond that of
> mortals—

15 so he shall startle[a] many nations;
> kings shall shut their mouths
> because of him;
> for that which had not been told
> them they shall see,
> and that which they had not heard
> they shall contemplate.

53

Who has believed what we have heard?
> And to whom has the arm of the
> LORD been revealed?

2 For he grew up before him like a
> young plant,
> and like a root out of dry
> ground;
> he had no form or majesty that we
> should look at him,
> nothing in his appearance that we
> should desire him.

3 He was despised and rejected by
> others;

a man of suffering[b] and acquainted
> with infirmity;
> and as one from whom others hide
> their faces[c]
> he was despised, and we held him
> of no account.

4 Surely he has borne our infirmities
> and carried our diseases;
> yet we accounted him stricken,
> struck down by God, and afflicted.

5 But he was wounded for our
> transgressions,
> crushed for our iniquities;
> upon him was the punishment that
> made us whole,
> and by his bruises we are healed.

6 All we like sheep have gone astray;
> we have all turned to our own way,
> and the LORD has laid on him
> the iniquity of us all.

7 He was oppressed, and he was
> afflicted,

a Meaning of Heb uncertain   b Or a man of sorrows   c Or as one who hides his face from us

---

53:1—For the fourth time in three chapters, the *arm of the LORD*, that is, God's irresistible strength, is mentioned (see 51:5, 9; 52:10). This time, however, it is manifested not in mighty historical events but in the quiet, unexpected career of a broken man. Apparently not everyone sees and believes. Observing that not all believed in the new Servant, Jesus, either, John 12:37–41 reminds readers of the original commission given Isaiah of Jerusalem (Isa. 6:10) to harden the hearts of the people lest they "turn and be healed."

53:2–3—The prophet now turns to look at the servant's past. He was more than merely inconspicuous. He was *despised and rejected by others*.

53:4–6—In another one of the seventeen Isaiah passages enshrined in the immortal music of G. F. Handel's *Messiah* (see note at 9:6), the prophetic speaker identifies himself with his people, even as he teaches that the Servant's suffering was vicarious.

53:5—Like a sacrificial animal, *he was wounded for our transgressions, crushed for our iniquities*. By taking upon himself the bruises we deserved *we are healed,* a notion that early Christian writers found vital in understanding the ministry and death of Jesus (e.g., 1 Pet. 2:24–25). A wrong choice among the various meanings of the Hebrew word *shalom* renders v. 5b almost

unintelligible in the KJV, which reads, "The chastisement of our peace (*shalom*) was upon him." The NRSV *upon him was the punishment that made us whole* (*shalom*) is much clearer.

53:6—Priestly legislation for the Day of Atonement provided for a scapegoat. The high priest would lay hands on the head of the goat, confess the sins of the people, and then send it away into the wilderness (Lev. 16:20–22). The vicarious suffering of the Servant works similarly: *the LORD has laid on him the iniquity of us all.* The New Testament counterpart to this Isaianic prototype is the ministry and suffering of Jesus. Through the ages and into our own time men and women dedicated to social justice and peace have followed the Servant and Jesus in their own vicarious sacrifice of wealth, power, and even life, in order that others might be liberated from their misery. Within the last century are Albert Schweitzer, Dietrich Bonhoeffer, Martin Luther King Jr., Archbishop Oscar Romero, Corrie ten Boom, and Mother Teresa, to name a few.

53:7–9—The innocent Servant was hounded to death. If the disturbed text of v. 9a is correctly understood by the NRSV, he was buried both *with the wicked* and in a rich person's tomb. Manifestly, this Servant Song influenced the passion narratives of the Gospels and lies behind both the siting of the cross between the two thieves (see

yet he did not open his mouth;
like a lamb that is led to the
    slaughter,
    and like a sheep that before its
        shearers is silent,
    so he did not open his mouth.
8 By a perversion of justice he was
    taken away.
    Who could have imagined his
        future?
For he was cut off from the land of
    the living,
    stricken for the transgression of
        my people.
9 They made his grave with the
    wicked
    and his tomb*a* with the rich,*b*
although he had done no violence,
    and there was no deceit in his
        mouth.

10 Yet it was the will of the Lord to
    crush him with pain.*c*
When you make his life an offering
    for sin,*d*
    he shall see his offspring, and shall
        prolong his days;
through him the will of the Lord
    shall prosper.
11 Out of his anguish he shall see
    light;*e*
he shall find satisfaction through his
    knowledge.
    The righteous one,*f* my servant,
        shall make many righteous,
    and he shall bear their iniquities.
12 Therefore I will allot him a portion
    with the great,

and he shall divide the spoil with
    the strong;
because he poured out himself to
    death,
    and was numbered with the
        transgressors;
yet he bore the sin of many,
    and made intercession for the
        transgressors.

The Eternal Covenant of Peace

54 Sing, O barren one who did not
    bear;
    burst into song and shout,
    you who have not been in labor!
For the children of the desolate
    woman will be more
    than the children of her that is
        married, says the Lord.
2 Enlarge the site of your tent,
    and let the curtains of your
        habitations be stretched out;
do not hold back; lengthen your
    cords
    and strengthen your stakes.
3 For you will spread out to the right
    and to the left,
    and your descendants will possess
        the nations
    and will settle the desolate towns.

4 Do not fear, for you will not be
    ashamed;
    do not be discouraged, for you will
        not suffer disgrace;

a Q Ms: MT *and in his death* *b* Cn: Heb *with a rich person* *c* Or *by disease*;
meaning of Heb uncertain *d* Meaning of Heb uncertain *e* Q Mss: MT
lacks *light* *f* Or *and he shall find satisfaction. Through his knowledge, the
righteous one*

---

transgressors, v. 12; also Mark 15:27–28), and
the rock-hewn tomb of Joseph of Arimathea (see
Mark 15:42–47 and parallels). The Ethiopian eunuch asked to be baptized when he understood
this text (Acts 8:26–40).

53:10—The final section of the tragic fourth Servant Song opens with the difficult assertion that *it
was the will of the Lord to crush him with pain*.
This prophetic assertion can be compared with
Jesus' prayer in Gethsemane, "Father, if you are
willing, remove this cup from me; yet, not my
will but yours be done" (Luke 22:42 and parallels). In the latter, we need not understand that
the crushing pain of crucifixion is itself willed by

God, but rather that Jesus remain steadfast to the
bitter end. The suffering of the Servant in Isaiah is
more akin to the fate of a sacrificial beast slain as
an offering for sin. As typically occurs in a psalm
of lament, a turnabout occurs in v. 10b. Speaking
now in the future tense, the prophet announces
the servant's apparent escape from death.

53:11–12—The song has a happy ending; God
announces that because of the Servant's steadfastness *I will allot him a portion with the great*.

54:1–17 The Future Peace of Jerusalem
This entire chapter of glorious promises is addressed to Jerusalem, personified as a woman.

for you will forget the shame of your
youth,
and the disgrace of your
widowhood you will
remember no more.
5 For your Maker is your husband,
the LORD of hosts is his name;
the Holy One of Israel is your
Redeemer,
the God of the whole earth he is
called.
6 For the LORD has called you
like a wife forsaken and grieved in
spirit,
like the wife of a man's youth when
she is cast off,
says your God.
7 For a brief moment I abandoned you,
but with great compassion I will
gather you.
8 In overflowing wrath for a moment
I hid my face from you,
but with everlasting love I will have
compassion on you,
says the LORD, your Redeemer.

9 This is like the days of Noah to me:
Just as I swore that the waters of
Noah
would never again go over the
earth,
so I have sworn that I will not be
angry with you
and will not rebuke you.
10 For the mountains may depart
and the hills be removed,
but my steadfast love shall not
depart from you,
and my covenant of peace shall not
be removed,

says the LORD, who has
compassion on you.

11 O afflicted one, storm-tossed, and
not comforted,
I am about to set your stones in
antimony,
and lay your foundations with
sapphires.*a*
12 I will make your pinnacles of rubies,
your gates of jewels,
and all your wall of precious
stones.
13 All your children shall be taught by
the LORD,
and great shall be the prosperity of
your children.
14 In righteousness you shall be
established;
you shall be far from oppression,
for you shall not fear;
and from terror, for it shall not
come near you.
15 If anyone stirs up strife,
it is not from me;
whoever stirs up strife with you
shall fall because of you.
16 See it is I who have created the
smith
who blows the fire of coals,
and produces a weapon fit for its
purpose;
I have also created the ravager to
destroy.
17 No weapon that is fashioned
against you shall prosper,
and you shall confute every tongue
that rises against you in
judgment.

a Or *lapis lazuli*

54:5 *Husband*—The daring metaphor of Jerusalem as YHWH's wife echoes Hosea's much
earlier use of the same metaphor to describe the
relation of YHWH and Israel (e.g., Hos. 2:16–20).

54:7–8—The exile is compared to a separation
or a divorce, but now *everlasting love* replaces
wrath with *compassion*.

54:9–10—The Lord offers another analogy, this
one to the promise to *Noah* of no more deluges
(Gen. 9:11). The new promise is of no more
removals of *my steadfast love* and *my covenant*

of peace. Trust in God's abiding compassion and
love continues to sustain those who persist in extending compassion to other people and nations.

54:11–12—The Lord projects onto the horizon a
picture of Jerusalem lavishly restored. Such perfection in beauty never happened in real time, of
course (it is deferred to a new world altogether in
the apocalyptic vision of Rev. 21:10–21), but the
vision serves as a magnet to draw God's people
forward into a better future.

This is the heritage of the servants of
the LORD
and their vindication from me,
says the LORD.

An Invitation to Abundant Life

55 Ho, everyone who thirsts,
come to the waters;
and you that have no money,
come, buy and eat!
Come, buy wine and milk
without money and without
price.
2 Why do you spend your money for
that which is not bread,
and your labor for that which does
not satisfy?
Listen carefully to me, and eat what
is good,
and delight yourselves in rich
food.
3 Incline your ear, and come to me;
listen, so that you may live.
I will make with you an everlasting
covenant,
my steadfast, sure love for David.
4 See, I made him a witness to the
peoples,
a leader and commander for the
peoples.
5 See, you shall call nations that you
do not know,
and nations that do not know you
shall run to you,
because of the LORD your God, the
Holy One of Israel,
for he has glorified you.

6 Seek the LORD while he may be
found,

call upon him while he is near;
7 let the wicked forsake their way,
and the unrighteous their
thoughts;
let them return to the LORD, that he
may have mercy on them,
and to our God, for he will
abundantly pardon.
8 For my thoughts are not your
thoughts,
nor are your ways my ways, says
the LORD.
9 For as the heavens are higher than
the earth,
so are my ways higher than your
ways
and my thoughts than your
thoughts.

10 For as the rain and the snow come
down from heaven,
and do not return there until they
have watered the earth,
making it bring forth and sprout,
giving seed to the sower and bread
to the eater,
11 so shall my word be that goes out
from my mouth;
it shall not return to me empty,
but it shall accomplish that which I
purpose,
and succeed in the thing for which
I sent it.

12 For you shall go out in joy,
and be led back in peace;
the mountains and the hills before
you
shall burst into song,
and all the trees of the field shall
clap their hands.

55:1–13 The Conclusion of Second Isaiah
Isaiah of the exile concludes his message of joy
at redemption with this lyrical address by the
Lord to those about to be liberated.

55:1–2—The people are invited to be the Lord's
guests at a royal banquet (see note at 25:6–10).

55:3–5—If they will *listen* (i.e., obey), God
will extend to the whole people the *everlasting covenant* that God made with *David* and
his house (2 Sam. 7:16). Just as God's covenant
made David a *commander for the peoples*, so

will the restored, obedient remnant of Judah lead
other nations.

55:11—The *word* of God is personified as a
dynamic force that goes out and returns with its
mission accomplished. This echoes the theme of
God's enduring word sounded in 40:8.

55:12—All of nature joins in manifestations of
joy and renewal as the exiles wend their way
home. Fruitfulness in the place of aridity is the
memorial to God's amazing grace.

¹³ Instead of the thorn shall come up
  the cypress;
 instead of the brier shall come up
  the myrtle;
and it shall be to the LORD for a
  memorial,
 for an everlasting sign that shall
  not be cut off.

The Covenant Extended
to All Who Obey

56 Thus says the LORD:
Maintain justice, and do what is
 right,
for soon my salvation will come,
 and my deliverance be revealed.

² Happy is the mortal who does
  this,
 the one who holds it fast,
who keeps the sabbath, not
  profaning it,
 and refrains from doing any evil.

³ Do not let the foreigner joined to the
  LORD say,
 "The LORD will surely separate me
  from his people";
and do not let the eunuch say,
 "I am just a dry tree."
⁴ For thus says the LORD:
To the eunuchs who keep my
  sabbaths,
 who choose the things that
  please me
 and hold fast my covenant,
⁵ I will give, in my house and within
  my walls,
 a monument and a name
 better than sons and daughters;

I will give them an everlasting name
 that shall not be cut off.

⁶ And the foreigners who join
  themselves to the LORD,
 to minister to him, to love the
  name of the LORD,
 and to be his servants,
all who keep the sabbath, and do not
  profane it,
 and hold fast my covenant—
⁷ these I will bring to my holy
  mountain,
 and make them joyful in my house
  of prayer;
their burnt offerings and their
  sacrifices
 will be accepted on my altar;
for my house shall be called a house
  of prayer
 for all peoples.
⁸ Thus says the Lord GOD,
 who gathers the outcasts of Israel,
I will gather others to them
 besides those already gathered.^a

The Corruption of Israel's Rulers
⁹ All you wild animals,
 all you wild animals in the forest,
  come to devour!
¹⁰ Israel's^b sentinels are blind,
 they are all without knowledge;
they are all silent dogs
 that cannot bark;
dreaming, lying down,
 loving to slumber.
¹¹ The dogs have a mighty appetite;
 they never have enough.

^a Heb besides his gathered ones ^b Heb His

56:1–66:24 Trito-Isaiah or Third Isaiah
Scholars frequently regard this as the work of yet
another latter-day disciple of Isaiah, sometimes
called Third or Trito-Isaiah (see introduction).

56:1–12 Foreigners Welcomed

56:2—*Sabbath* keeping was emphasized in the
exile and afterward as a hallmark of the Jewish
community (58:13–14; see also Neh. 13:15–22;
Jer. 17:19–27).

56:3–8—*The foreigner* and *the eunuch* who
hold fast [to God's] covenant are coinheritors
of the promises God makes to Israel, including

an everlasting name (v. 5b) and acceptance of
offerings made on God's *altar* (v. 7). This respect
for the worth of the individual, native or foreign,
characterizes the covenant tradition from the
ancient book of the covenant onward (e.g., Exod.
22:21; Deut. 14:29; 24:17).

56:7b—Jesus angrily contrasts Isaiah's report of
YHWH's welcome to all people to worship God
in God's house with the crass hawking of cultic
wares that actually took place in the temple of
his day (see Matt. 21:12–17; Mark 11:15–19;
Luke 19:45–48).

The shepherds also have no
　understanding;
　they have all turned to their own
　　way,
　to their own gain, one and all.
12 "Come," they say, "let us[a] get wine;
　let us fill ourselves with strong
　　drink.
　And tomorrow will be like today,
　great beyond measure."

Israel's Futile Idolatry

57 The righteous perish,
　and no one takes it to heart;
the devout are taken away,
　while no one understands.
For the righteous are taken away
　　from calamity,
2　and they enter into peace;
　those who walk uprightly
　will rest on their couches.
3 But as for you, come here,
　you children of a sorceress,
　you offspring of an adulterer and a
　　whore.[b]
4 Whom are you mocking?
　Against whom do you open your
　　mouth wide
　and stick out your tongue?
　Are you not children of
　　transgression,
　the offspring of deceit—
5 you that burn with lust among the
　　oaks,
　under every green tree;
you that slaughter your children in
　　the valleys,
　under the clefts of the rocks?
6 Among the smooth stones of the
　　valley is your portion;

they, they, are your lot;
to them you have poured out a drink
　　offering,
　you have brought a grain offering.
　Shall I be appeased for these
　　things?
7 Upon a high and lofty mountain
　you have set your bed,
　and there you went up to offer
　　sacrifice.
8 Behind the door and the doorpost
　you have set up your symbol;
for, in deserting me,[c] you have
　　uncovered your bed,
　you have gone up to it,
　you have made it wide;
and you have made a bargain for
　　yourself with them,
　you have loved their bed,
　you have gazed on their
　　nakedness.[d]
9 You journeyed to Molech[e] with oil,
　and multiplied your perfumes;
you sent your envoys far away,
　and sent down even to Sheol.
10 You grew weary from your many
　　wanderings,
　but you did not say, "It is useless."
You found your desire rekindled,
　and so you did not weaken.

11 Whom did you dread and fear
　so that you lied,
and did not remember me
　or give me a thought?
Have I not kept silent and closed my
　　eyes,[f]
　and so you do not fear me?

[a] Q Ms Syr Vg Tg: MT *me*　[b] Heb *an adulterer and she plays the whore*
[c] Meaning of Heb uncertain　[d] Or *their phallus*; Heb *the hand*　[e] Or *the king*
[f] Gk Vg: Heb *silent even for a long time*

57:1–21 No Peace for the Wicked
57:1–13—Once again, YHWH speaks out against
idolatry, as was also the case in the earlier
strata of the book of Isaiah. That the Lord should
condemn the pagan practices alluded to here
comes as no surprise. After all, idolatry is a major
violation of the covenant tradition (see First and
Second Commandments in Exod. 20:3–6 and
Deut. 5:7–10; also Deut. 12:2–4). The surprise is
that even after the experience of destruction and
exile, the inhabitants of Judea are still at it.

57:5—Canaanite fertility rites in sacred groves
are condemned by many other prophets, but
especially Hosea, who describes Israel's unfaithfulness to YHWH as whoredom (e.g., Hos.
1:2; 4:12–14). Child sacrifice also apparently
continued to occur (see 2 Kgs. 21:6; Jer. 19:5), a
practice particularly associated with the Canaanite deity **Molech** (Isa. 57:9; see also Lev. 20:1–5;
2 Kgs. 23:10; Jer. 32:35). Social justice was and is
incompatible with idolatry.

12 I will concede your righteousness
        and your works,
    but they will not help you.
13 When you cry out, let your
        collection of idols deliver you!
    The wind will carry them off,
    a breath will take them away.
    But whoever takes refuge in me shall
        possess the land
    and inherit my holy mountain.

A Promise of Help and Healing

14 It shall be said,
    "Build up, build up, prepare the way,
    remove every obstruction from my
        people's way."
15 For thus says the high and lofty one
    who inhabits eternity, whose name
        is Holy:
    I dwell in the high and holy place,
    and also with those who are
        contrite and humble in spirit,
    to revive the spirit of the humble,
    and to revive the heart of the
        contrite.
16 For I will not continually accuse,
    nor will I always be angry;
    for then the spirits would grow faint
        before me,
    even the souls that I have made.
17 Because of their wicked
        covetousness I was angry;
    I struck them, I hid and was
        angry;
    but they kept turning back to their
        own ways.
18 I have seen their ways, but I will heal
        them;
    I will lead them and repay them
        with comfort,
    creating for their mourners the
        fruit of the lips.*a*

19 Peace, peace, to the far and the near,
        says the LORD;
    and I will heal them.
20 But the wicked are like the tossing
        sea
    that cannot keep still;
    its waters toss up mire and mud.
21 There is no peace, says my God, for
        the wicked.

False and True Worship

58
Shout out, do not hold back!
Lift up your voice like a
        trumpet!
Announce to my people their
        rebellion,
    to the house of Jacob their sins.
2 Yet day after day they seek me
    and delight to know my ways,
    as if they were a nation that
        practiced righteousness
    and did not forsake the ordinance
        of their God;
    they ask of me righteous judgments,
    they delight to draw near to God.
3 "Why do we fast, but you do not see?
    Why humble ourselves, but you do
        not notice?"
    Look, you serve your own interest
        on your fast day,
    and oppress all your workers.
4 Look, you fast only to quarrel and to
        fight
    and to strike with a wicked fist.
    Such fasting as you do today
    will not make your voice heard on
        high.
5 Is such the fast that I choose,
    a day to humble oneself?
    Is it to bow down the head like a
        bulrush,

a Meaning of Heb uncertain

57:14–21—YHWH will heal and bring peace to those who repent.

57:15—The Lord is the transcendent one *who inhabits eternity*. At the same time, however, the Lord is also the immanent one who dwells *with those who are contrite and humble in spirit*.

57:21—This prophet draws upon the older Isaianic tradition (48:22) to warn the persistently

wicked that they will forfeit the benefits of salvation.

58:1–14 False and True Worship

At the heart of this divine argument against hollow and hypocritical worship are two remarkable summaries of the "social gospel" of the Old Testament, the practice of which constitutes true worship.

and to lie in sackcloth and ashes?
Will you call this a fast,
    a day acceptable to the LORD?
⁶ Is not this the fast that I choose:
    to loose the bonds of injustice,
    to undo the thongs of the yoke,
to let the oppressed go free,
    and to break every yoke?
⁷ Is it not to share your bread with the
        hungry,
    and bring the homeless poor into
        your house;
when you see the naked, to cover
        them,
    and not to hide yourself from your
        own kin?
⁸ Then your light shall break forth like
        the dawn,
    and your healing shall spring up
        quickly;
    your vindicator*a* shall go before
        you,
    the glory of the LORD shall be your
        rear guard.
⁹ Then you shall call, and the LORD
        will answer;
    you shall cry for help, and he will
        say, Here I am.

If you remove the yoke from among
        you,
    the pointing of the finger, the
        speaking of evil,
¹⁰ if you offer your food to the hungry
    and satisfy the needs of the
        afflicted,

then your light shall rise in the
        darkness
    and your gloom be like the
        noonday.
¹¹ The LORD will guide you
        continually,
    and satisfy your needs in parched
        places,
    and make your bones strong;
and you shall be like a watered
        garden,
    like a spring of water,
    whose waters never fail.
¹² Your ancient ruins shall be rebuilt;
    you shall raise up the foundations
        of many generations;
you shall be called the repairer of the
        breach,
    the restorer of streets to live in.

¹³ If you refrain from trampling the
        sabbath,
    from pursuing your own interests
        on my holy day;
if you call the sabbath a delight
    and the holy day of the LORD
        honorable;
if you honor it, not going your own
        ways,
    serving your own interests, or
        pursuing your own affairs;*b*
¹⁴ then you shall take delight in the
        LORD,
    and I will make you ride upon the
        heights of the earth;

a Or *vindication*   *b* Heb *or speaking words*

58:6–9a—A true *fast* consists of liberation, breaking *every yoke*, feeding and clothing the poor. Egalitarian justice like this elicits for the obedient person healing and help from the Lord.

58:9b–12—Conditional *if . . . then* sentences once again link justice and compassion to promises: *you shall be like a watered garden* (v. 11); *your ancient ruins shall be rebuilt* (v. 12—one hint that the prophet's work preceded the completion of the rebuilding of the temple in 515 BCE [see 61:4; Ezra 6:15]).

58:13–14—*Sabbath* observance, too, forms part of the social gospel of Isaiah. Once again drawing upon the covenant tradition (see the Fourth Commandment, Exod. 20:8–11; Deut. 5:12–15; also, among others, Exod. 31:12–17;

Jer. 17:21–27), the Lord warns against *pursuing your own interests on my holy day*. Though the teaching looks like an invitation to a "works righteousness" approach to Sabbath observance (if you honor the Sabbath, the Lord *will make you ride upon the heights of the earth* [Isa. 58:14]), this conditional promise can also be viewed on the person-to-person scale. One who follows the wishes of another can expect to receive good things from that other. In any event, this teaching deserves attention in a culture that is rapidly losing its Sabbath. When one spends Sunday afternoon shopping at the mall, it would be well to remember the Lord's word given to those who keep the holiness of the Sabbath, *I will feed you with the heritage of your ancestor Jacob* (v. 14b).

I will feed you with the heritage of
  your ancestor Jacob,
for the mouth of the LORD has
  spoken.

Injustice and Oppression
to Be Punished

59 See, the LORD's hand is not too
  short to save,
  nor his ear too dull to hear.
2 Rather, your iniquities have been
  barriers
  between you and your God,
and your sins have hidden his face
  from you
  so that he does not hear.
3 For your hands are defiled with
  blood,
  and your fingers with iniquity;
your lips have spoken lies,
  your tongue mutters wickedness.
4 No one brings suit justly,
  no one goes to law honestly;
they rely on empty pleas, they speak
  lies,
  conceiving mischief and begetting
  iniquity.
5 They hatch adders' eggs,
  and weave the spider's web;
whoever eats their eggs dies,
  and the crushed egg hatches out a
  viper.
6 Their webs cannot serve as
  clothing;
  they cannot cover themselves with
  what they make.
Their works are works of iniquity,
  and deeds of violence are in their
  hands.
7 Their feet run to evil,
  and they rush to shed innocent
  blood;

their thoughts are thoughts of
  iniquity,
  desolation and destruction are in
  their highways.
8 The way of peace they do not know,
  and there is no justice in their
  paths.
Their roads they have made crooked;
  no one who walks in them knows
  peace.

9 Therefore justice is far from us,
  and righteousness does not reach
  us;
we wait for light, and lo! there is
  darkness;
  and for brightness, but we walk in
  gloom.
10 We grope like the blind along a wall,
  groping like those who have no
  eyes;
we stumble at noon as in the
  twilight,
  among the vigorous[a] as though we
  were dead.
11 We all growl like bears;
  like doves we moan mournfully.
We wait for justice, but there is
  none;
  for salvation, but it is far from us.
12 For our transgressions before you
  are many,
  and our sins testify against us.
Our transgressions indeed are with
  us,
  and we know our iniquities:
13 transgressing, and denying the
  LORD,
  and turning away from following
  our God,
  talking oppression and revolt,

[a] Meaning of Heb uncertain

59:1–22 The Demands of Covenant
This chapter is rich with words bespeaking true
discipleship as defined by the covenant tradition of Israel: *peace* (v. 8), *righteousness* (vv. 9,
14, 17), *salvation* (vv. 11, 17), *truth* (vv. 14, 15),
uprightness (v. 14). *Justice* is mentioned no less
than four times (vv. 8, 9, 11, 14). These are the
responsibilities given by the Lord to the people,
and not their opposites: *lies* (vv. 3, 4, 13), *wick-*

edness (v. 3), *iniquity* (vv. 4, 7, 12), *the rush to
shed innocent blood* (v. 7), *talking oppression
and revolt* (v. 13).

59:2—The prophet speaks well and truly when
he says, *Your iniquities have been barriers
between you and your God.* Doing social justice
sets the doer in motion on the path in tandem
with the Lord; injustice will get nowhere because
it cannot approach the Lord.

conceiving lying words and
    uttering them from the heart.
¹⁴ Justice is turned back,
    and righteousness stands at a
        distance;
for truth stumbles in the public
    square,
    and uprightness cannot enter.
¹⁵ Truth is lacking,
    and whoever turns from evil is
        despoiled.

The Lord saw it, and it displeased
    him
    that there was no justice.
¹⁶ He saw that there was no one,
    and was appalled that there was no
        one to intervene;
so his own arm brought him
    victory,
    and his righteousness upheld him.
¹⁷ He put on righteousness like a
    breastplate,
    and a helmet of salvation on his
        head;
he put on garments of vengeance for
    clothing,
    and wrapped himself in fury as in
    a mantle.
¹⁸ According to their deeds, so will he
    repay;
    wrath to his adversaries, requital
        to his enemies;
to the coastlands he will render
    requital.
¹⁹ So those in the west shall fear the
    name of the Lord,
    and those in the east, his glory;

for he will come like a pent-up
    stream
    that the wind of the Lord drives
    on.
²⁰ And he will come to Zion as
    Redeemer,
    to those in Jacob who turn from
        transgression, says the Lord.
²¹ And as for me, this is my covenant
with them, says the Lord: my spirit that
is upon you, and my words that I have
put in your mouth, shall not depart out
of your mouth, or out of the mouths of
your children, or out of the mouths of
your children's children, says the Lord,
from now on and forever.

The Ingathering of the Dispersed

60 Arise, shine; for your light has
    come,
    and the glory of the Lord has
    risen upon you.
² For darkness shall cover the earth,
    and thick darkness the peoples;
but the Lord will arise upon you,
    and his glory will appear over you.
³ Nations shall come to your light,
    and kings to the brightness of your
    dawn.

⁴ Lift up your eyes and look around;
    they all gather together, they come
    to you;
your sons shall come from far
    away,
    and your daughters shall be
    carried on their nurses' arms.
⁵ Then you shall see and be radiant;

59:17—The Lord's armor consists of *righteousness* and *salvation* (see 61:10; Eph. 6:14–17).

59:21—The entire oracle is summed up in the promise that the words of *my covenant* will never depart from Israel. The prose text represents this promise as a unilateral gift of God rather than a promise contingent upon Israel's prior *turn from transgression* (v. 20).

60:1–22 God's New World Order

In this remarkable vision of its triumphant, even imperial future, Israel emerges as the central people of the world and YHWH as the central focus of all human worship.

60:1–3—Instead of a rising sun (see vv. 19–20), the *glory*/light *of the Lord* will radiate on Zion, leaving the other nations in darkness.

60:4–7—In this chapter the future central position of Israel and its worldwide hegemony is based solely upon God's favor, not Israel's extraordinary righteousness. (In fact, righteousness appears to be one of the many gifts conferred on Israel by the Lord [v. 21].) Israel's centrality is summed up in the promise that *the wealth of nations shall come to you* (v. 5).

your heart shall thrill and rejoice,[a]
because the abundance of the sea
   shall be brought to you,
   the wealth of the nations shall
   come to you.
6 A multitude of camels shall cover
   you,
   the young camels of Midian and
   Ephah;
   all those from Sheba shall come.
They shall bring gold and
   frankincense,
   and shall proclaim the praise of
   the LORD.
7 All the flocks of Kedar shall be
   gathered to you,
   the rams of Nebaioth shall
   minister to you;
they shall be acceptable on my altar,
   and I will glorify my glorious
   house.

8 Who are these that fly like a cloud,
   and like doves to their windows?
9 For the coastlands shall wait for me,
   the ships of Tarshish first,
to bring your children from far away,
   their silver and gold with them,
for the name of the LORD your God,
   and for the Holy One of Israel,
   because he has glorified you.
10 Foreigners shall build up your walls,
   and their kings shall minister to
   you;
for in my wrath I struck you down,
   but in my favor I have had mercy
   on you.
11 Your gates shall always be open;
   day and night they shall not be
   shut,

so that nations shall bring you their
   wealth,
   with their kings led in procession.
12 For the nation and kingdom
   that will not serve you shall perish;
   those nations shall be utterly laid
   waste.
13 The glory of Lebanon shall come to
   you,
   the cypress, the plane, and the
   pine,
to beautify the place of my
   sanctuary;
   and I will glorify where my feet
   rest.
14 The descendants of those who
   oppressed you
   shall come bending low to you,
and all who despised you
   shall bow down at your feet;
they shall call you the City of the
   LORD,
   the Zion of the Holy One of Israel.
15 Whereas you have been forsaken
   and hated,
   with no one passing through,
I will make you majestic forever,
   a joy from age to age.
16 You shall suck the milk of nations,
   you shall suck the breasts of kings;
and you shall know that I, the LORD,
   am your Savior
   and your Redeemer, the Mighty
   One of Jacob.

17 Instead of bronze I will bring gold,
   instead of iron I will bring silver;
   instead of wood, bronze,

[a] Heb be enlarged

60:11—The prophet's vision of the future is transformed into an apocalyptic one in Rev. 21:24–26,
where the kings of the earth flock into the New
Jerusalem out of the lake of fire, bringing with
them their glory (see note at vv. 17–20).

60:16—The future of God's universal hegemony
manifested historically in a central Israel is never
more dramatically put than in this verse. Indeed,
these great events are ultimately revelatory,
because through them **you shall know that I, the
LORD, am your Savior**. Deutero-Isaiah already
anticipated the deep honor given to Israel by the

other nations, even treating them as if they would
be vassals (e.g., notes at 49:6, 23).

60:17–20—Apparently the restoration work
underway in the time of Trito-Isaiah looked rather
meager to some (see Hag. 2:3). This prophet
looks well beyond the present hard realities to
a future city overseen by **Peace** and **Righteousness** (v. 17), gates named **Salvation** and **Praise**,
illuminated by neither sun nor moon but by the
Lord's **glory** (vv. 18–19). This vision is open to the
heightened imagination of the Apocalypse, which
projected all such promises into a new world and

instead of stones, iron.
I will appoint Peace as your overseer
and Righteousness as your
taskmaster.
18 Violence shall no more be heard in
your land,
devastation or destruction within
your borders;
you shall call your walls Salvation,
and your gates Praise.

God the Glory of Zion

19 The sun shall no longer be
your light by day,
nor for brightness shall the moon
give light to you by night;[a]
but the LORD will be your everlasting
light,
and your God will be your glory.
20 Your sun shall no more go down,
or your moon withdraw itself;
for the LORD will be your everlasting
light,
and your days of mourning shall
be ended.
21 Your people shall all be righteous;
they shall possess the land forever.
They are the shoot that I planted, the
work of my hands,
so that I might be glorified.
22 The least of them shall become a
clan,
and the smallest one a mighty
nation;
I am the LORD;
in its time I will accomplish it
quickly.

The Good News of Deliverance

61 The spirit of the Lord GOD is
upon me,
because the LORD has
anointed me;
he has sent me to bring good news
to the oppressed,
to bind up the brokenhearted,
to proclaim liberty to the captives,
and release to the prisoners;
2 to proclaim the year of the LORD's
favor,
and the day of vengeance of our
God;
to comfort all who mourn;
3 to provide for those who mourn in
Zion—
to give them a garland instead of
ashes,
the oil of gladness instead of
mourning,
the mantle of praise instead of a
faint spirit.
They will be called oaks of
righteousness,
the planting of the LORD, to
display his glory.
4 They shall build up the ancient
ruins,
they shall raise up the former
devastations;
they shall repair the ruined cities,
the devastations of many
generations.

[a] Q Ms Gk Old Latin Tg: MT lacks *by night*

---

a New Jerusalem yet to descend from heaven (see Rev. 21:1). The application of this chapter to the notion of a worldwide theocratic polity centered on Israel could be abused in an era of power politics. However, it is quite proper to place the emphasis on the universal validity of Israel's covenant values, namely, peace, egalitarian justice, recognition of the worth of the individual, and God's love for all peoples. The hope contained in the chapter would center, then, on the worldwide recognition of these humane principles and on their Author.

61:1–11 The Good News of Deliverance

61:1–3—The good news of liberation of cap-

tives and comfort of mourners is proclaimed by the prophet as the Lord's *anointed* (or even "servant"; cf. 42:1–9). This is the text from Isaiah that Jesus read out in the synagogue at Nazareth in order to explain who he was (Luke 4:16–21). The preferential treatment Jesus showed toward the disadvantaged and vulnerable was consistent both with covenant expectations and with the prophetic call to servanthood.

61:4—One of the tasks of the revived and comforted Zion would be to *build up the ancient ruins*, perhaps a reference to the reconstruction of the temple (see note at 58:12).

5 Strangers shall stand and feed your
   flocks,
      foreigners shall till your land and
         dress your vines;
6 but you shall be called priests of the
      LORD,
   you shall be named ministers of
      our God;
   you shall enjoy the wealth of the
      nations,
      and in their riches you shall
         glory.
7 Because their*a* shame was double,
      and dishonor was proclaimed as
         their lot,
   therefore they shall possess a double
      portion;
      everlasting joy shall be theirs.

8 For I the LORD love justice,
      I hate robbery and wrongdoing;*b*
   I will faithfully give them their
      recompense,
      and I will make an everlasting
         covenant with them.
9 Their descendants shall be known
      among the nations,
      and their offspring among the
         peoples;
   all who see them shall acknowledge
      that they are a people whom the
         LORD has blessed.
10 I will greatly rejoice in the LORD,
      my whole being shall exult in my
         God;
   for he has clothed me with the
      garments of salvation,
      he has covered me with the robe of
         righteousness,

as a bridegroom decks himself with
   a garland,
   and as a bride adorns herself with
      her jewels.
11 For as the earth brings forth its
      shoots,
      and as a garden causes what is
         sown in it to spring up,
   so the Lord GOD will cause
      righteousness and praise
   to spring up before all the
      nations.

The Vindication and Salvation of Zion

62 For Zion's sake I will not keep
      silent,
      and for Jerusalem's sake I will not
         rest,
   until her vindication shines out like
      the dawn,
      and her salvation like a burning
         torch.
2 The nations shall see your
      vindication,
      and all the kings your glory;
   and you shall be called by a new
      name
      that the mouth of the LORD will
         give.
3 You shall be a crown of beauty in the
      hand of the LORD,
      and a royal diadem in the hand of
         your God.
4 You shall no more be termed
      Forsaken,*c*
      and your land shall no more be
         termed Desolate;*d*

a Heb your *b* Or robbery with a burnt offering *c* Heb Azubah
d Heb Shemamah

61:8–11—More important in this chapter than the obeisance of foreign kings is the *everlasting covenant* (v. 8) that the Lord promises to the Lord's people. Salvation is not their work; rather, it is a gift of God. Zion compares the garments of *salvation* and *righteousness* given her by God—YHWH's very garments of vengeance in 59:17—to the finery of a *bride* and groom.

62:1–12 Zion Not Forsaken

In this poem, addressed in its entirety to Zion, the Lord makes many promises. They include public *vindication* (vv. 1–2), royal status by the hand of

YHWH (v. 3), and the assignment of many significant new names and titles (vv. 4, 12), including Beulah. *Married.* The last title introduces a comparison of the special status enjoyed by Zion with God to a marriage (cf. 54:5–6). Another promise, that Israel and not another will enjoy the fruits of its labors (62:8–9, a promise reiterated in 65:21–22), amounts to a future reversal of the sanctions against sinners announced in the covenant tradition (e.g., Deut. 28:30, 33; also mentioned by Job in his oath of righteous innocence, Job 31:8).

but you shall be called My Delight Is
   in Her,*a*
   and your land Married;*b*
for the LORD delights in you,
   and your land shall be married.
5 For as a young man marries a young
      woman,
   so shall your builder*c* marry you,
and as the bridegroom rejoices over
      the bride,
   so shall your God rejoice over you.
6 Upon your walls, O Jerusalem,
   I have posted sentinels;
all day and all night
   they shall never be silent.
You who remind the LORD,
   take no rest,
7 and give him no rest
   until he establishes Jerusalem
   and makes it renowned
      throughout the earth.
8 The LORD has sworn by his right hand
   and by his mighty arm:
I will not again give your grain
   to be food for your enemies,
and foreigners shall not drink the
      wine
   for which you have labored;
9 but those who garner it shall eat it
   and praise the LORD,
and those who gather it shall drink it
   in my holy courts.

10 Go through, go through the gates,
   prepare the way for the people;
build up, build up the highway,
   clear it of stones,
   lift up an ensign over the peoples.
11 The LORD has proclaimed
   to the end of the earth:
Say to daughter Zion,
   "See, your salvation comes;
his reward is with him,
   and his recompense before him."

12 They shall be called, "The Holy People,
   The Redeemed of the LORD";
and you shall be called, "Sought Out,
   A City Not Forsaken."

Vengeance on Edom

63 "Who is this that comes from
      Edom,
   from Bozrah in garments stained
      crimson?
Who is this so splendidly robed,
   marching in his great might?"

"It is I, announcing vindication,
   mighty to save."

2 "Why are your robes red,
   and your garments like theirs who
      tread the wine press?"

3 "I have trodden the wine press alone,
   and from the peoples no one was
      with me;
I trod them in my anger
   and trampled them in my wrath;
their juice spattered on my garments,
   and stained all my robes.
4 For the day of vengeance was in my
      heart,
   and the year for my redeeming
      work had come.
5 I looked, but there was no helper;
   I stared, but there was no one to
      sustain me;
so my own arm brought me victory,
   and my wrath sustained me.
6 I trampled down peoples in my
      anger,
   I crushed them in my wrath,
   and I poured out their lifeblood on
      the earth."

God's Mercy Remembered

7 I will recount the gracious deeds of
      the LORD,

a Heb Hephzibah *b* Heb Beulah *c* Cn: Heb your sons

63:1–19 Punishment and Repentance
This dramatic picture of the blood-stained divine warrior taking revenge on Edom (perhaps a symbol of all enemies of Israel) lies behind some of the imagery of Julia Ward Howe's Civil War anthem "The Battle Hymn of the Republic." That particular "application" of vv. 1–6 should awaken caution in the minds of its singers when we are tempted to claim that the divine warrior is on our side.

63:7–19—This communal lament (extending through 64:12) implores God to save the people as God did at the exodus of old (63:11–14).

the praiseworthy acts of the LORD,
because of all that the LORD has
    done for us,
  and the great favor to the house of
    Israel
that he has shown them according to
    his mercy,
  according to the abundance of his
    steadfast love.
8 For he said, "Surely they are my
    people,
  children who will not deal falsely";
and he became their savior
9   in all their distress.
It was no messenger*a* or angel
  but his presence that saved them;*b*
in his love and in his pity he
    redeemed them;
  he lifted them up and carried them
    all the days of old.

10 But they rebelled
  and grieved his holy spirit;
therefore he became their enemy;
  he himself fought against them.
11 Then they*c* remembered the days of
    old,
  of Moses his servant.*d*
Where is the one who brought them
    up out of the sea
  with the shepherds of his flock?
Where is the one who put within
    them
  his holy spirit,
12 who caused his glorious arm
    to march at the right hand of
      Moses,
who divided the waters before them
    to make for himself an everlasting
      name,
13   who led them through the
    depths?
Like a horse in the desert,
  they did not stumble.

14 Like cattle that go down into the
    valley,
  the spirit of the LORD gave them
    rest.
Thus you led your people,
  to make for yourself a glorious
    name.

A Prayer of Penitence

15 Look down from heaven and see,
  from your holy and glorious
    habitation.
Where are your zeal and your might?
  The yearning of your heart and
    your compassion?
  They are withheld from me.
16 For you are our father,
  though Abraham does not know
    us
  and Israel does not acknowledge
    us;
you, O LORD, are our father;
  our Redeemer from of old is your
    name.
17 Why, O LORD, do you make us stray
    from your ways
  and harden our heart, so that we
    do not fear you?
Turn back for the sake of your
    servants,
  for the sake of the tribes that are
    your heritage.
18 Your holy people took possession for
    a little while;
  but now our adversaries have
    trampled down your
    sanctuary.
19 We have long been like those whom
    you do not rule,
  like those not called by your name.

64 O that you would tear open the
    heavens and come down,

a Gk: Heb anguish   *b* Or savior. *9 In all their distress he was distressed; the
angel of his presence saved them;*   *c* Heb he   *d* Cn: Heb his people*

63:17—The prophet charges Israel's very
backsliding against the Lord's account, and thus
indirectly makes YHWH responsible for their
punishment and alienation from him. The concept is familiar not only from the hardening of
Pharaoh's heart in the prelude to the exodus (e.g.,

Exod. 7:1–5), but more immediately in the original prophetic commission to Isaiah of Jerusalem
(see Isa. 6:10–13).

64:1–12 Lament Continues

Continuing the same lament, the prophet confesses the sin of the people, but continues to sug-

so that the mountains would
    quake at your presence—
² *a* as when fire kindles brushwood
    and the fire causes water to boil—
to make your name known to your
    adversaries,
    so that the nations might tremble
        at your presence!
³ When you did awesome deeds that
        we did not expect,·
    you came down, the mountains
        quaked at your presence.
⁴ From ages past no one has heard,
    no ear has perceived,
no eye has seen any God besides
    you,
    who works for those who wait for
        him.
⁵ You meet those who gladly do right,
    those who remember you in your
        ways.
But you were angry, and we sinned;
    because you hid yourself we
        transgressed.*b*
⁶ We have all become like one who is
        unclean,
    and all our righteous deeds are like
        a filthy cloth.
We all fade like a leaf,
    and our iniquities, like the wind,
        take us away.
⁷ There is no one who calls on your
        name,
    or attempts to take hold of you;
for you have hidden your face
        from us,
    and have delivered*c* us into the
        hand of our iniquity.
⁸ Yet, O Lord, you are our Father;

we are the clay, and you are our
        potter;
    we are all the work of your hand.
⁹ Do not be exceedingly angry,
        O Lord,
    and do not remember iniquity
        forever.
    Now consider, we are all your
        people.
¹⁰ Your holy cities have become a
        wilderness,
    Zion has become a wilderness,
    Jerusalem a desolation.
¹¹ Our holy and beautiful house,
    where our ancestors praised you,
has been burned by fire,
    and all our pleasant places have
        become ruins.
¹² After all this, will you restrain
        yourself, O Lord?
    Will you keep silent, and punish us
        so severely?

The Righteousness of God's Judgment

65 I was ready to be sought out by
    those who did not ask,
    to be found by those who did not
        seek me.
I said, "Here I am, here I am,"
    to a nation that did not call on my
        name.
² I held out my hands all day long
    to a rebellious people,
who walk in a way that is not good,
    following their own devices;
³ a people who provoke me
    to my face continually,

a Ch 64.1 in Heb   *b* Meaning of Heb uncertain   *c* Gk Syr Old Latin Tg:
Heb *melted*

---

gest that the Lord permitted it (v. 7). The resulting
punishment has been terrible (vv. 10–11). The
destruction and continued ruin of the temple
are specifically mentioned. The entire lament
is permeated with the question with which it
closes: *Will you keep silent, and punish us so
severely?* (v. 12). Attempts to explain contemporary tragedies such as the 9/11/01 disaster as
God's punishment for national sin ring hollow,
but such moments can and should occasion
renewed determination to reach out to the world
with initiatives in political justice, economic
equity, respect, and peace.

65:1–25 A Glorious Vision

65:1–16—God defends the judgment executed
on Israel, recalling the rebellious and provocative
practices of idolatry.

65:3–5, 11—The list of idolatrous practices
includes *sacrificing in gardens* (perhaps akin to
the fertility rites and sacred prostitution already
condemned in 57:1–13), sitting *inside tombs*
(a suggestion of necromancy, long prohibited in
the covenant tradition; see Deut. 18:11–12; also
Isa. 8:19, and the story of the witch of Endor in
1 Sam. 28), and eating *swine's flesh* (not only a

sacrificing in gardens
　　and offering incense on bricks;
4 who sit inside tombs,
　　and spend the night in secret
　　　　places;
who eat swine's flesh,
　　with broth of abominable things in
　　　　their vessels;
5 who say, "Keep to yourself,
　　do not come near me, for I am too
　　　　holy for you."
These are a smoke in my nostrils,
　　a fire that burns all day long.
6 See, it is written before me:
　　I will not keep silent, but I will
　　　　repay;
I will indeed repay into their laps
7 their[a] iniquities and their[a]
　　　　ancestors' iniquities together,
　　　　　　　　says the LORD;
because they offered incense on the
　　　　mountains
　　and reviled me on the hills,
I will measure into their laps
　　full payment for their actions.
8 Thus says the LORD:
As the wine is found in the cluster,
　　and they say, "Do not destroy it,
　　for there is a blessing in it,"
so I will do for my servants' sake,
　　and not destroy them all.
9 I will bring forth descendants[b] from
　　　　Jacob,
　　and from Judah inheritors[c] of my
　　　　mountains;
my chosen shall inherit it,
　　and my servants shall settle there.
10 Sharon shall become a pasture for
　　　　flocks,
　　and the Valley of Achor a place for
　　　　herds to lie down,
　　for my people who have
　　　　sought me.
11 But you who forsake the LORD,

who forget my holy mountain,
who set a table for Fortune
　　and fill cups of mixed wine for
　　　　Destiny;
12 I will destine you to the sword,
　　and all of you shall bow down to
　　　　the slaughter;
because, when I called, you did not
　　　　answer,
　　when I spoke, you did not listen,
but you did what was evil in my
　　　　sight,
　　and chose what I did not
　　　　delight in.
13 Therefore thus says the Lord GOD:
My servants shall eat,
　　but you shall be hungry;
my servants shall drink,
　　but you shall be thirsty;
my servants shall rejoice,
　　but you shall be put to shame;
14 my servants shall sing for gladness of
　　　　heart,
　　but you shall cry out for pain of
　　　　heart,
　　and shall wail for anguish of spirit.
15 You shall leave your name to my
　　　　chosen to use as a curse,
　　and the Lord GOD will put you to
　　　　death;
　　but to his servants he will give a
　　　　different name.
16 Then whoever invokes a blessing in
　　　　the land
　　shall bless by the God of
　　　　faithfulness,
and whoever takes an oath in the
　　　　land
　　shall swear by the God of
　　　　faithfulness;
because the former troubles are
　　　　forgotten
　　and are hidden from my sight.

a Gk Syr: Heb your b Or a descendant c Or an inheritor

---

blatant violation of the prohibition on pork, Deut.
14:8, but possibly evidence of participation in
the Canaanite sacrificial cultus in which the pig
was a sacred animal; see 1 Macc. 1:47). Apparently some participated in worship of the pagan
deities *Fortune* and *Destiny* (Isa. 65:11).

65:8–16—In every respect, *my servants*, the
remnant whom God saves, will prosper in inverse
proportion to the unhappy fate of those who
forsake the Lord.

The Glorious New Creation

17 For I am about to create new
　　heavens
　　and a new earth;
　the former things shall not be
　　remembered
　　or come to mind.
18 But be glad and rejoice forever
　　in what I am creating;
　for I am about to create Jerusalem as
　　a joy,
　　and its people as a delight.
19 I will rejoice in Jerusalem,
　　and delight in my people;
　no more shall the sound of weeping
　　be heard in it,
　　or the cry of distress.
20 No more shall there be in it
　　an infant that lives but a few days,
　　or an old person who does not live
　　　out a lifetime;
　for one who dies at a hundred years
　　will be considered a youth,
　and one who falls short of a
　　hundred will be considered
　　accursed.
21 They shall build houses and inhabit
　　them;
　they shall plant vineyards and eat
　　their fruit.
22 They shall not build and another
　　inhabit;
　they shall not plant and another
　　eat;
　for like the days of a tree shall the
　　days of my people be,

and my chosen shall long enjoy the
　work of their hands.
23 They shall not labor in vain,
　　or bear children for calamity;*a*
　for they shall be offspring blessed by
　　the LORD—
　and their descendants as well.
24 Before they call I will answer,
　　while they are yet speaking I will
　　hear.
25 The wolf and the lamb shall feed
　　together,
　the lion shall eat straw like the ox;
　but the serpent—its food shall be
　　dust!
　They shall not hurt or destroy
　　on all my holy mountain,
　　　　　　　　says the LORD.

The Worship God Demands

66 Thus says the LORD:
Heaven is my throne
　and the earth is my footstool;
what is the house that you would
　　build for me,
　and what is my resting place?
2 All these things my hand has
　　made,
　and so all these things are mine,*b*
　　　　　　　　says the LORD.
But this is the one to whom I will
　　look,
　to the humble and contrite in
　　spirit,
　who trembles at my word.

a Or sudden terror　*b* Gk Syr: Heb these things came to be

65:17–25—The latter half of chap. 65 stands as one of the most lyrical futuristic visions in the entire prophetic canon. Its vision of the new age ahead has power to draw Godfearers, as if by a magnet, toward a better world of peace and abundance, and to guide them in shaping their ethical practice accordingly.

65:17—The contrast of the *former things* and the *new heavens and a new earth* that the Lord is creating echoes language of Deutero-Isaiah.

65:19–23—One of the hallmarks of the new age ahead is longevity. To live 100 years will be a low norm (v. 20b). People will live to enjoy the harvest of their own gardens (vv. 21–22; see 62:8–9), a promise indubitably to be cherished

by a community that had experienced a great deal of expulsion and death.

65:25—This vision of "the peaceable kingdom" recalls 11:6–9. The only variation is the echo of the primeval curse of Gen. 3:14, according to which the serpent is doomed to a diet of dust.

66:1–24 The Conclusion of Isaiah

The book of Isaiah concludes with a collection of oracles that generally condemn hypocritical and false worship, be it worship of YHWH or worship of idols.

66:1–2—The true joy of the Lord is not a temple made by human hands, but a human heart *humble and contrite in spirit*.

3 Whoever slaughters an ox is like one
     who kills a human being;
     whoever sacrifices a lamb, like one
         who breaks a dog's neck;
     whoever presents a grain offering,
         like one who offers swine's
         blood;*a*
     whoever makes a memorial
         offering of frankincense, like
         one who blesses an idol.
     These have chosen their own ways,
         and in their abominations they
         take delight;
4 I also will choose to mock*b* them,
     and bring upon them what they
         fear;
     because, when I called, no one
         answered,
     when I spoke, they did not listen;
     but they did what was evil in my
         sight,
     and chose what did not please me.

The Lord Vindicates Zion

5 Hear the word of the Lord,
     you who tremble at his word:
     Your own people who hate you
     and reject you for my name's sake
     have said, "Let the Lord be
         glorified,
     so that we may see your joy";
     but it is they who shall be put to
         shame.

6 Listen, an uproar from the city!
     A voice from the temple!
     The voice of the Lord,
     dealing retribution to his enemies!

7 Before she was in labor
     she gave birth;
     before her pain came upon her
     she delivered a son.
8 Who has heard of such a thing?
     Who has seen such things?
     Shall a land be born in one day?

     Shall a nation be delivered in one
         moment?
     Yet as soon as Zion was in labor
         she delivered her children.
9 Shall I open the womb and not
         deliver?
     says the Lord;
     shall I, the one who delivers, shut the
         womb?
     says your God.

10 Rejoice with Jerusalem, and be glad
         for her,
     all you who love her;
     rejoice with her in joy,
     all you who mourn over her—
11 that you may nurse and be satisfied
     from her consoling breast;
     that you may drink deeply with
         delight
     from her glorious bosom.

12 For thus says the Lord:
     I will extend prosperity to her like a
         river,
     and the wealth of the nations like
         an overflowing stream;
     and you shall nurse and be carried
         on her arm,
     and dandled on her knees.
13 As a mother comforts her child,
     so I will comfort you;
     you shall be comforted in
         Jerusalem.

The Reign and Indignation of God

14 You shall see, and your heart shall
         rejoice;
     your bodies*c* shall flourish like the
         grass;
     and it shall be known that the
         hand of the Lord is with his
         servants,
     and his indignation is against his
         enemies.

a Meaning of Heb uncertain   *b* Or to punish   *c* Heb bones

---

66:3–5—Phony, outward shows of piety, whether in sacrifices or in words (v. 5b), *shall be put to shame*.

66:7–16—Jerusalem is portrayed as a nurturing mother, nursing her children *from her consoling breast* (v. 11). Her milk is *prosperity*, the *wealth of the nations* (v. 12; see 60:5, 16). Appearing to Jerusalem's children as a comforting *mother* (v. 13), YHWH also appears to the enemies of God as wrathful warrior (vv. 14c–16).

15 For the LORD will come in fire,
    and his chariots like the
        whirlwind,
to pay back his anger in fury,
    and his rebuke in flames of fire.
16 For by fire will the LORD execute
        judgment,
    and by his sword, on all flesh;
    and those slain by the LORD shall
        be many.

17 Those who sanctify and purify themselves to go into the gardens, following the one in the center, eating the flesh of pigs, vermin, and rodents, shall come to an end together, says the LORD.

18 For I know*a* their works and their thoughts, and I am*b* coming to gather all nations and tongues; and they shall come and shall see my glory, 19 and I will set a sign among them. From them I will send survivors to the nations, to Tarshish, Put,*c* and Lud—which draw the bow—to Tubal and Javan, to the coastlands far away that have not heard of my fame or seen my glory; and they shall declare my glory among the nations. 20 They shall bring all your kindred from all the nations as an offering to the LORD,

on horses, and in chariots, and in litters, and on mules, and on dromedaries, to my holy mountain Jerusalem, says the LORD, just as the Israelites bring a grain offering in a clean vessel to the house of the LORD. 21 And I will also take some of them as priests and as Levites, says the LORD.

22 For as the new heavens and the new
        earth,
    which I will make,
shall remain before me, says the
        LORD;
    so shall your descendants and your
        name remain.
23 From new moon to new moon,
    and from sabbath to sabbath,
all flesh shall come to worship
        before me,
    says the LORD.

24 And they shall go out and look at the dead bodies of the people who have rebelled against me; for their worm shall not die, their fire shall not be quenched, and they shall be an abhorrence to all flesh.

a Gk Syr: Heb lacks *know*   *b* Gk Syr Vg Tg: Heb *it is*   *c* Gk: Heb *Pul*

66:17—A final threat against followers of foreign cults (see 65:3–5).

66:18–24—God will put the nations to work in bringing the exiles of Israel back to the holy mountain of Zion, and the nations themselves will stay to worship the Lord (v. 23) and even serve *as priests and Levites* (v. 21). The carcasses of dead rebels, however, will serve as a smoking and no doubt stinking reminder of the futility of hostility to God (v. 24).

The Book of
JEREMIAH

This book recounts the role of the prophet Jeremiah during the tumultuous years leading up to and immediately following Babylon's capture of Judah in 587 BCE.

The book of Jeremiah seems to offer a historical account of Judah's conquest by Babylon and something of a biography of the prophet. The book's initial verses indicate a historical setting for Jeremiah encompassing the reigns of several Judean kings: Josiah (640–609), Jehoiakim (609–597); Jehoiachin (597, then exiled to Babylon); Zedekiah (597–587). The book recounts Jeremiah's encounters with several of these kings and his involvement with events surrounding the fall of Jerusalem in 587 BCE. Some historical background is helpful in reading the book of Jeremiah.

At the conclusion of King Solomon's reign, about 900 BCE, Israel split into two kingdoms, Israel in the north and Judah in the south. Assyria, which became the dominant power in the ancient Near East about 745 BCE, defeated the northern kingdom, Israel, in 722 BCE. While Judah survived, it had to pay tribute to Assyria for many decades. After dominating the ancient Near East for more than 100 years, Assyria was in decline when Josiah became Judah's king in 640 BCE. Josiah sought to revitalize Judah both politically and religiously. Tragically, Josiah was killed at Megiddo in a battle with Egypt in 609 BCE. He was succeeded by his son Jehoiakim, who initially had to pay tribute to Egypt but by 605 BCE was threatened by Babylon. After years of paying tribute to Babylon, Jehoiakim resisted. Babylon sent an army toward Judah, but before it arrived, Jehoiakim died and was succeeded by his son, Jehoiachin. When the Babylonians reached Jerusalem in 597 BCE, they took Jehoiachin and other leaders of Judah captive to Babylon (thus, this era is referred to as the exile) and appointed one of Josiah's sons, whom they named Zedekiah, as king of Judah. In time, Zedekiah also refused to pay tribute to Babylon, and in 587 BCE the Babylonians invaded Judah, destroyed Jerusalem, burned the temple, captured and tortured Zedekiah, and took further captives. The book of Jeremiah concludes sometime after 587 BCE, when the Judean governor appointed by Babylon, Gedaliah, was assassinated. Subsequently Jeremiah was taken against his will to Egypt by a group of Judeans seeking to escape Babylonian domination. Jeremiah likely died in Egypt.

Jeremiah is portrayed as a prophet who continually confronts Judah's kings and other political and religious officials with the ways they have forsaken God. Like Hosea in Israel, Jeremiah is primarily concerned with the apostasy of his nation, especially the ways Judah turned from YHWH to worship fertility deities. However, Jeremiah also sees other ways that Judah has rebelled against God. Jeremiah condemns social practices that are unjust and dishonest and that injure the most vulnerable members of society. He is also critical of Judah's foreign and military policies through which Judah seeks security apart from YHWH. As a consequence of Judah's broken relationship with God, Jeremiah announces that God is sending Babylon as an instrument of

judgment and argues that the most faithful course for Judah is surrender to Babylon. Though Jeremiah is God's spokesperson, his message is rejected. He is portrayed as suffering social ostracism and finally is accused of being a traitor, for which he is imprisoned. Even after the Babylonians have conquered Judah, Jeremiah urges an unpopular course, cooperation with them.

The impression that the book of Jeremiah provides a historical account is reinforced by a number of passages that seem to give insight into the personal struggles and suffering of the prophet who is commanded by God to announce a message that results in his rejection by family and friends (e.g., see 11:18–23; 12:1–6; 15:10–21; 20:7–18). Reading the book of Jeremiah gives one a sense of intimacy with the prophet that is unusual in Old Testament prophetic literature. Older commentaries even characterized Jeremiah as "the weeping prophet," whose spiritual and emotional struggles are laid bare in this book. More recently, however, many commentators have questioned if the book of Jeremiah should be understood primarily as a historical report about Babylon's defeat of Judah and as a biography of the prophet.

The exile was a traumatic event for the people of Judah. With Judah's defeat by Babylon, the tangible symbols of the relationship between God and God's people were lost. For example, the Jerusalem temple, the symbol of God's presence with Judah, was destroyed. The king, understood to be God's regent, was imprisoned in Babylon. The land of Judah, which represented God's commitment to promises made long ago to Israel's ancestors, was controlled by the Babylonians. For many persons in Judah, the exile suggested one of two terrible possibilities: either YHWH had been defeated by the more powerful Babylonian deities, or, inexplicably, God had chosen to abandon Judah. The exile, though a historical calamity, was much more. It was a theological crisis that called into question all that God's people believed.

The exile required that God's people think deeply about who God was, what it meant to be in relationship with God, and why the exile might have occurred. Scholars have identified the book of Jeremiah as among several Old Testament texts whose concern was to make theological sense of the exile. These scholars understand that the purpose of the book of Jeremiah is to offer a theological reflection about the exile. The book of Jeremiah may contain historical information about the events of the early sixth century BCE and about Jeremiah's life. However, the primary purpose of the book is not to offer a detailed and objective analysis of Jeremiah's life or the political, economic, and military factors that led to Judah's defeat, such as we would expect in a biography or history book of our time. Rather, those who shaped the book of Jeremiah were most interested in theology, in reflecting about how God was involved in Judah's defeat and what it could mean to be God's people during the exile.

One of the central claims of the book of Jeremiah is an affirmation of God's sovereignty. God is affirmed to be sovereign over the creation, over humankind, over the nations, over Judah, and over Jeremiah. Jeremiah is remembered as a prophet whom God appointed "over nations and kingdoms, to pluck up and to pull down, to destroy and to overthrow, to build and to plant" (1:10). The book is clear that Babylon's defeat of Judah was not a geopolitical accident, and certainly not an indication of either God's defeat by Babylonian deities or God's unwarranted desertion of Judah. Rather, the book of Jeremiah claims that the exile occurred as God's judgment of Judah. Through Babylon Judah was called to account for forsaking YHWH through both

religious practices and social policies. While those in power in Jerusalem assumed that God would guarantee Judah's security forever, Jeremiah announced on God's behalf that Judah, like all the nations, stood accountable before God in ways Judah's kings had not imagined. The way that the book of Jeremiah portrays the prophet's rejection reinforces how little regard Judah's ruling elite had for God's sovereign authority. As the book presents Jeremiah, the prophet discerned that in Babylon's menacing rise to power in the ancient Near Eastern world, God was at work. At the same time, the book asserts that in time God would call Babylon to account for its unwarranted pride. God is affirmed to be the cosmic sovereign who directs the course of history.

Yet while the book of Jeremiah affirms God's cosmic sovereignty, God is not portrayed as distant, cruel, or uncaring. Instead, the book claims that God suffers and anguishes over Judah. God does not delight in the judgment of Judah but is pained by it. God's suffering and pain are given voice by Jeremiah, though one must be alert to how this happens. Often in this book, Jeremiah is portrayed as suffering and in pain because God commands him to announce judgment and this results in his rejection by Judah. At another level, however, Judah's rejection of Jeremiah is also a rejection of God. Further, the complaints of Jeremiah, who is God's spokesperson, need to be heard as expressions of God's own anguish. Indeed, at many places in the book of Jeremiah, it is difficult to determine if the speaker is Jeremiah, or if Jeremiah is speaking not for himself but for God. In the book of Jeremiah, God is affirmed to be a sovereign judge, but a judge who is anguished by the judgment that must be made.

God's judgment of Judah is the dominant concern of the book of Jeremiah. God plucks up and tears down Judah as well as other nations (chaps. 25, 46–52). In the end, however, the claim of the book of Jeremiah is that judgment is not God's ultimate purpose. Instead, it asserts that God finally intends to "restore the fortunes" of Judah (chaps. 30–33) and the nations. Because Judah and the nations resist God's intentions, God must call them to account, pluck them up, and tear them down. What God intends for nations, however, is peace and well-being. While this is a subdued theme, the book of Jeremiah asserts that God's ultimate intention for the nations is their restoration after judgment—building and planting after plucking up and tearing down—so that they can experience the blessing God intends for the whole creation.

The book of Jeremiah has developed through a complex process. At the core of the book are oracles of the prophet Jeremiah. However, exactly what material in the book can be attributed to the prophet is disputed. Some of Jeremiah's oracles may have been written down during the lifetime of the prophet. Scholars have debated what role Jeremiah's scribe, Baruch, may have played in preserving the prophet's words and accounts of his life. In any case, many redactors have had a hand in shaping the book as we now have it. Among these redactors, the most prominent shared the theological perspectives that are found in the book of Deuteronomy. Because the book has been redacted by so many persons, it does not read smoothly or easily. Still, the book of Jeremiah preserves the witness of persons living in very difficult circumstances to the anguished sovereignty of God. Before this God these persons had experienced painful judgment. In their despair, they turned to this God in the hope of restoration.

The book of Jeremiah continues to invite our prayerful pondering about what it means to live as God's people in difficult times. Among the issues raised for people reading this ancient book in the twenty-first century are these:

◆ The book of Jeremiah insists that God was at work to bring judgment upon Judah and transform the way Judah was living as God's people. The book challenges us still to ask how God is at work in the church attempting to transform the ways we are living as God's people.

◆ The book of Jeremiah understands that all nations are accountable to God, Babylon as well as Judah, along with Egypt, Moab, and others. This book challenges us still to ask how God might be at work in the social and political processes of our world, plucking up and tearing down, building and planting toward the goal of justice and peace in all God's creation.

◆ The core indictment of Jeremiah is that Judah was guilty of idolatry, of seeking security in false gods or through political and military alliances cleverly negotiated. While reading this book, we are still challenged to ask to which idols Christians now turn seeking security. Jeremiah also compels us to examine how churches of which we are a part may be attempting to arrange cleverly for their own security instead of seeking to serve God faithfully.

◆ Jeremiah is concerned about social justice, about the ways that Judah, and particularly Judah's political and religious leaders, exploited the poor of society and disregarded their needs. The book of Jeremiah presses us still to ask how our society exploits the poor and how communities of faith support such exploitation by their complicity or silence.

◆ The book of Jeremiah portrays the political and religious leaders of Judah as being so confident that God would keep them secure that they could not hear Jeremiah's warnings about judgment or his call to repent. They finally rejected Jeremiah but embraced prophets with a more reassuring message. We need to ask how in our time and place we too are readily drawn in by voices that offer reassurance, while rejecting persons speaking harder words that call us to account. "Cheap grace" has always been more comfortable than "costly discipleship" (Bonhoeffer).

◆ In the book of Jeremiah, God is grieved over the rebellion of Judah. So we must wonder what we might be about in our churches or, more broadly, as God's human family that might still be causing God deep grief.

The early twentieth-century theologian Karl Barth urged that one read with the Bible in one hand and a newspaper in the other. When one heeds Barth's urging with the Bible open to the book of Jeremiah, a challenging dialogue is evoked.

—**John M. Bracke**

1 The words of Jeremiah son of Hilkiah, of the priests who were in Anathoth in the land of Benjamin, ²to whom the word of the LORD came in the days of King Josiah son of Amon of Judah, in the thirteenth year of his reign. ³It came also in the days of King Jehoiakim son of Josiah of Judah, and until the end of the eleventh year of King Zedekiah son of Josiah of Judah,

---

1:1–3 Introducing the Prophet Jeremiah

1:1 *Anathoth*—The home of the priest Abiathar who opposed Solomon's succession of David (1 Kgs. 2). Solomon banished Abiathar to Anathoth (1 Kgs. 2:26–27). Jeremiah's association with a priestly family from Anathoth signals this book's suspicion of the monarchy.

1:2 *To whom the word of the LORD came*—Jeremiah does not speak for himself but for God.

1:3 *The captivity of Jerusalem*—This book is centrally concerned to interpret theologically the events related to the Babylonian exile, to understand them as having to do with God's relationship with Judah and the nations.

until the captivity of Jerusalem in the fifth month.

Jeremiah's Call and Commission

4 Now the word of the LORD came to me saying,

5   "Before I formed you in the womb I
       knew you,
  and before you were born I
       consecrated you;
  I appointed you a prophet to the
       nations."

6 Then I said, "Ah, Lord GOD! Truly I do not know how to speak, for I am only a boy." 7 But the LORD said to me,

  "Do not say, 'I am only a boy';
  for you shall go to all to whom I
      send you,
  and you shall speak whatever I
      command you.
8 Do not be afraid of them,
  for I am with you to deliver you,
            says the LORD."

9 Then the LORD put out his hand and touched my mouth; and the LORD said to me,

  "Now I have put my words in your
      mouth.
10 See, today I appoint you over nations
      and over kingdoms,
  to pluck up and to pull down,
  to destroy and to overthrow,
  to build and to plant."

11 The word of the LORD came to me, saying, "Jeremiah, what do you see?" And I said, "I see a branch of an almond tree."[a] 12 Then the LORD said to me, "You have seen well, for I am watching[b] over my word to perform it." 13 The word of the LORD came to me a second time, saying, "What do you see?" And I said, "I see a boiling pot, tilted away from the north."

14 Then the LORD said to me: Out of the north disaster shall break out on all the inhabitants of the land. 15 For now I am calling all the tribes of the kingdoms of the north, says the LORD; and they shall come and all of them shall set their thrones at the entrance of the gates of Jerusalem, against all its surrounding walls and against all the cities of Judah. 16 And I will utter my judgments against them, for all their wickedness in forsaking me; they have made offerings to other gods, and worshiped the works of their own hands. 17 But you, gird up your loins; stand up and tell them everything that I command you. Do not break down before them, or I will break you before them. 18 And I for my part have made you today a fortified city, an iron pillar, and a bronze wall, against the whole land—against the kings of Judah, its princes, its priests, and the people of the land. 19 They will fight against you; but they shall not prevail against you, for I am with you, says the LORD, to deliver you.

a Heb *shaqed* *b* Heb *shoqed*

1:4–10 God Claims Jeremiah

Jeremiah's call is reminiscent of Moses' (Exod. 3–4). Both are sent to speak on God's behalf but doubt their ability to do so effectively. Their objections are countered by God's reassurance. Jeremiah's charge to be *a prophet to the nations* (vv. 5, 10) indicates the broad scope of God's sovereignty claimed in this book.

1:10—The six verbs used in this verse are repeated several times in the book (18:7–8; 24:6; 31:28; 42:10; 45:4). This verse expresses pervasive themes in the book—the threat of God's judgment of Judah and the nations (*pluck up, pull down, destroy, overthrow*) and the hope of God's eventual restoration of them (*build, plant*).

1:11–19 Jeremiah's Visions

Jeremiah's first vision (vv. 11–13) indicates that God's word will come to fruition. The second (vv. 14–19) suggests that the fulfillment of God's word will mean disaster for Judah.

1:13—The *boiling pot*, spilling toward the south, points to Babylon's role in God's judgment of Judah. In ancient Near Eastern cultures, *north* was identified as the direction from which evil arose. Even though Babylon was more east than north of Judah, in this book God is imagined as "bringing evil from the north" (e.g., 4:6; 6:1; 6:22).

1:17–19—Jerusalem, thought to be an impenetrable fortress (see note at 6:14), will fall. Jeremiah, however, will be protected like an impenetrable fortress against the attacks of Judah's leaders.

God Pleads with Israel to Repent

2 The word of the LORD came to me, saying: ²Go and proclaim in the hearing of Jerusalem, Thus says the LORD:

I remember the devotion of your
    youth,
  your love as a bride,
how you followed me in the
    wilderness,
  in a land not sown.
³ Israel was holy to the LORD,
  the first fruits of his harvest.
All who ate of it were held guilty;
  disaster came upon them,
                    says the LORD.

4 Hear the word of the LORD, O house of Jacob, and all the families of the house of Israel. ⁵Thus says the LORD:

What wrong did your ancestors find
    in me
  that they went far from me,
and went after worthless things, and
    became worthless themselves?
⁶ They did not say, "Where is the
    LORD
  who brought us up from the land
    of Egypt,
who led us in the wilderness,
  in a land of deserts and pits,
in a land of drought and deep
    darkness,

in a land that no one passes
    through,
  where no one lives?"
⁷ I brought you into a plentiful land
  to eat its fruits and its good things.
But when you entered you defiled
    my land,
  and made my heritage an
    abomination.
⁸ The priests did not say, "Where is
    the LORD?"
  Those who handle the law did not
    know me;
the rulers*ᵃ* transgressed against me;
  the prophets prophesied by Baal,
  and went after things that do not
    profit.

⁹ Therefore once more I accuse you,
                    says the LORD,
  and I accuse your children's
    children.
¹⁰ Cross to the coasts of Cyprus and
    look,
  send to Kedar and examine with
    care;
  see if there has ever been such a
    thing.
¹¹ Has a nation changed its gods,
  even though they are no gods?
But my people have changed their
    glory

ᵃ Heb *shepherds*

2:1–3 Israel, the Lord's Faithful Bride

2:2—Israel's wilderness experience is recounted using the image of an ancient Near Eastern wedding in which the bride followed her husband from her family dwelling to their new residence. **Devotion**—The Hebrew word *hesed* almost always is used to describe God's enduring loyalty to Israel. Its use here to describe Israel is unusual, since Israel is rarely remembered as unfailingly loyal to God.

2:3—The **first fruits** of a **harvest** belonged to God and were to be set apart, **holy to the LORD,** to be presented as an offering (Lev. 23:9–14; Deut. 26:2–10).

2:4–13 God's Lawsuit against Judah

God first develops accusations against Judah (vv. 4–8); then, with the word **therefore** in v. 9, God announces a verdict (vv. 9–13).

2:5 Worthless—The Heb. word is *habel,* a

wordplay on the name of the Canaanite fertility god Baal, *ha-baal,* who is worthless to Judah.

2:6 They did not say—Israel no longer remembers the story of God's exodus deliverance.

2:7 Plentiful land—The promised land, Canaan. God's deliverance is not just *from* oppression in Egypt but *for* new life in the plentiful land. **Abomination**—This word (frequently translated "abhorrent" in the NRSV) indicates anything that is unacceptable to YHWH. While often related to sexual impropriety, the word also refers to idolatry (Deut. 7:25–26; 12:29–32; 17:2–7) and unjust social dealings (Deut. 25:13–16).

2:8 Priests . . . rulers . . . prophets—The depth of Judah's apostasy is evident in that the leaders of Judah have forgotten the story of God's deliverance and encourage the worship of Baal.

2:10 Cyprus . . . Kedar—These locations suggest distances as far away as one can imagine.

for something that does not profit.

12 Be appalled, O heavens, at this,
    be shocked, be utterly desolate,
                        says the LORD,
13 for my people have committed two
        evils:
    they have forsaken me,
    the fountain of living water,
    and dug out cisterns for
        themselves,
    cracked cisterns
        that can hold no water.

14 Is Israel a slave? Is he a homeborn
        servant?
    Why then has he become plunder?
15 The lions have roared against him,
    they have roared loudly.
    They have made his land a waste;
        his cities are in ruins, without
        inhabitant.
16 Moreover, the people of Memphis
        and Tahpanhes
    have broken the crown of your
        head.
17 Have you not brought this upon
        yourself
    by forsaking the LORD your God,
        while he led you in the way?
18 What then do you gain by going to
        Egypt,
    to drink the waters of the Nile?
    Or what do you gain by going to
        Assyria,
    to drink the waters of the
        Euphrates?

19 Your wickedness will punish you,
    and your apostasies will convict
        you.
    Know and see that it is evil and
        bitter
    for you to forsake the LORD your
        God;
    the fear of me is not in you,
                says the Lord GOD of hosts.

20 For long ago you broke your yoke
    and burst your bonds,
    and you said, "I will not serve!"
    On every high hill
    and under every green tree
    you sprawled and played the
        whore.
21 Yet I planted you as a choice vine,
    from the purest stock.
    How then did you turn degenerate
    and become a wild vine?
22 Though you wash yourself with lye
    and use much soap,
    the stain of your guilt is still
        before me,
                says the Lord GOD.
23 How can you say, "I am not defiled,
    I have not gone after the Baals"?
    Look at your way in the valley;
    know what you have done—
    a restive young camel interlacing her
        tracks,
24   a wild ass at home in the
        wilderness,
    in her heat sniffing the wind!
    Who can restrain her lust?

2:12 *O heavens*—The heavens are the jury hearing God's case.

2:13—In an arid land, to choose a *cistern*, especially a cracked cistern, over a well, a *fountain of living water,* would be very unwise.

2:14–19 Apostasy

Judah is accused not only of seeking security by worshiping other gods, but of political apostasy, seeking security through political and military alliances with neighboring states.

2:15 *Lions*—The symbol of Assyria, which dominated Israel and Judah approximately 745–640 BCE. Assyria defeated Israel in 722 BCE, while Judah repeatedly had to pay tribute as a vassal state.

2:16 *Memphis and Tahpanhes*—Egyptian cities to which envoys from Judah seeking Egypt's help against Babylon (see 37:3–10) may have gone. Both cities are also remembered in the book of Jeremiah as places where enclaves of Judeans settled after the defeat of Judah in 587 BCE (see 43:8–9; 44:1).

2:20–37 Israel, the Lover of Baal

2:20 *Whore*—The image suggests Judah's participation in cult prostitution, which was part of Baal worship. It contrasts with Israel as a devoted bride (vv. 2–3). The coarse images in vv. 20–25 all describe ways that Judah turned from YHWH to other gods.

None who seek her need weary
    themselves;
  in her month they will find her.
25 Keep your feet from going unshod
    and your throat from thirst.
But you said, "It is hopeless,
  for I have loved strangers,
  and after them I will go."

26 As a thief is shamed when caught,
    so the house of Israel shall be
    shamed—
  they, their kings, their officials,
    their priests, and their prophets,
27 who say to a tree, "You are my
    father,"
  and to a stone, "You gave me
    birth."
For they have turned their backs
    to me,
  and not their faces.
But in the time of their trouble they
    say,
  "Come and save us!"
28 But where are your gods
  that you made for yourself?
Let them come, if they can save
    you,
  in your time of trouble;
for you have as many gods
  as you have towns, O Judah.

29 Why do you complain against me?
  You have all rebelled against me,
        says the LORD.
30 In vain I have struck down your
    children;
  they accepted no correction.
Your own sword devoured your
    prophets
  like a ravening lion.

31 And you, O generation, behold the
    word of the LORD!ᵃ
Have I been a wilderness to Israel,
  or a land of thick darkness?
Why then do my people say, "We are
    free,
  we will come to you no more"?
32 Can a girl forget her ornaments,
  or a bride her attire?
Yet my people have forgotten me,
  days without number.

33 How well you direct your course
  to seek lovers!
So that even to wicked women
  you have taught your ways.
34 Also on your skirts is found
    the lifeblood of the innocent
    poor,
though you did not catch them
    breaking in.
  Yet in spite of all these thingsᵃ
35 you say, "I am innocent;
  surely his anger has turned from
    me."
Now I am bringing you to
    judgment
  for saying, "I have not sinned."
36 How lightly you gad about,
  changing your ways!
You shall be put to shame by Egypt
  as you were put to shame by
    Assyria.
37 From there also you will come away
  with your hands on your head;
for the LORD has rejected those in
    whom you trust,
  and you will not prosper through
    them.

ᵃ Meaning of Heb uncertain

2:27 *Tree . . . stone*—Objects of worship in Canaanite fertility cults.

2:28 *Save you*—God's saving deeds—the exodus
deliverance and wilderness journey (vv. 6–7)—
were central to Israel's experience of YHWH.

2:31 *Have I been a wilderness*—On the contrary,
YHWH led Israel through the wilderness to the
promised land (vv. 6–7).

2:32–33 *A bride her attire*—The imagery recalls
v. 2. Judah, the once-devoted bride of YHWH,

now turns for security to other *lovers*—other gods
and neighboring states.

2:34 *Lifeblood of the innocent*—This phrase,
used frequently in this book, indicates social
exploitation (see 7:6; 22:3, 17; 26:15). God freed
Israel from Pharaoh's oppression, but ironically
Judah now exploits the socially vulnerable.

2:36 *By Egypt . . . by Assyria*—Nations to whom
Judah turned for security will be the agents of
God's judgment.

Unfaithful Israel

3 If[a] a man divorces his wife
   and she goes from him
and becomes another man's wife,
   will he return to her?
Would not such a land be greatly
   polluted?
You have played the whore with
   many lovers;
   and would you return to me?
         says the Lord.
2 Look up to the bare heights,[b] and
   see!
  Where have you not been lain
   with?
By the waysides you have sat waiting
   for lovers,
  like a nomad in the wilderness.
You have polluted the land
  with your whoring and
   wickedness.
3 Therefore the showers have been
   withheld,
  and the spring rain has not come;
yet you have the forehead of a
   whore,
  you refuse to be ashamed.
4 Have you not just now called to me,
  "My Father, you are the friend of
   my youth—
5 will he be angry forever,
  will he be indignant to the end?"
This is how you have spoken,
  but you have done all the evil that
   you could.

A Call to Repentance

6 The Lord said to me in the days of
King Josiah: Have you seen what she did,
that faithless one, Israel, how she went
up on every high hill and under every
green tree, and played the whore there?
7 And I thought, "After she has done all
this she will return to me"; but she did
not return, and her false sister Judah
saw it. 8 She[c] saw that for all the adulteries of that faithless one, Israel, I had
sent her away with a decree of divorce;
yet her false sister Judah did not fear,
but she too went and played the whore.
9 Because she took her whoredom so
lightly, she polluted the land, committing adultery with stone and tree. 10 Yet
for all this her false sister Judah did not
return to me with her whole heart, but
only in pretense, says the Lord.

11 Then the Lord said to me: Faithless Israel has shown herself less guilty
than false Judah. 12 Go, and proclaim
these words toward the north, and say:
  Return, faithless Israel,
          says the Lord.
I will not look on you in anger,
  for I am merciful,
          says the Lord;
I will not be angry forever.
13 Only acknowledge your
   guilt,
  that you have rebelled against the
   Lord your God,
and scattered your favors among
   strangers under every green
   tree,
  and have not obeyed my
   voice,
          says the Lord.

[a] Q Ms Gk Syr: MT *Saying, If* [b] *Or the trails* [c] Q Ms Gk Mss Syr: MT *I*

3:1–4:4 Return!

God pleads with Judah to *return*.

3:1—A reference to Deut. 24:1–4, which prohibits a man from remarrying a wife whom he
divorced if she subsequently remarried. Judah's
situation is worse, since Judah had not been
divorced by God but was unfaithful to God.

3:2–3—Judah's pursuit of many lovers pollutes
the land. The consequence of polluting the land
is a curse; rain is withheld (Deut. 28:23–24; Lev.
26:19). Ironically, the fertility gods were supposed to ensure rain and the land's fertility.

3:8 *A decree of divorce*—An allusion to Israel's
defeat by Assyria in 722 BCE.

3:11–14 *Return, faithless Israel*—YHWH extends
to Israel an offer to return to relationship with
God (also vv. 14, 22; 4:1). It is likely that this
oracle originally addressed only remnants of the
fallen northern kingdom, Israel. As used here
in the book of Jeremiah, compiled after the fall
of Judah in 587 BCE, this call for repentance
addresses the southern kingdom, Judah. It is
astonishing what God will do for the sake of a
restored relationship.

14 Return, O faithless children,
               says the LORD,
      for I am your master;
   I will take you, one from a city and
               two from a family,
      and I will bring you to Zion.

15 I will give you shepherds after my own heart, who will feed you with knowledge and understanding. 16 And when you have multiplied and increased in the land, in those days, says the LORD, they shall no longer say, "The ark of the covenant of the LORD." It shall not come to mind, or be remembered, or missed; nor shall another one be made. 17 At that time Jerusalem shall be called the throne of the LORD, and all nations shall gather to it, to the presence of the LORD in Jerusalem, and they shall no longer stubbornly follow their own evil will. 18 In those days the house of Judah shall join the house of Israel, and together they shall come from the land of the north to the land that I gave your ancestors for a heritage.

19 I thought
      how I would set you among my
               children,
      and give you a pleasant land,
         the most beautiful heritage of all
               the nations.
   And I thought you would call me,
               My Father,
         and would not turn from following
               me.
20 Instead, as a faithless wife leaves her
               husband,

so you have been faithless to me,
      O house of Israel,
               says the LORD.

21 A voice on the bare heights[a] is heard,
      the plaintive weeping of Israel's
               children,
   because they have perverted their
               way,
      they have forgotten the LORD their
               God:
22 Return, O faithless children,
      I will heal your faithlessness.

   "Here we come to you;
      for you are the LORD our God.
23 Truly the hills are[b] a delusion,
      the orgies on the mountains.
   Truly in the LORD our God
      is the salvation of Israel.

24 "But from our youth the shameful thing has devoured all for which our ancestors had labored, their flocks and their herds, their sons and their daughters. 25 Let us lie down in our shame, and let our dishonor cover us; for we have sinned against the LORD our God, we and our ancestors, from our youth even to this day; and we have not obeyed the voice of the LORD our God."

4 If you return, O Israel,
               says the LORD,
      if you return to me,
   if you remove your abominations
               from my presence,
      and do not waver,
2 and if you swear, "As the LORD
               lives!"

---

a Or the trails   b Gk Syr Vg: Heb Truly from the hills is

3:14 *I am your master*—The name of the fertility deity Baal means "master" or "husband." However, Judah's *baal* is YHWH.

3:15–18—In this vision of restored Israel, God will place a king (*shepherd*) over God's people who will be obedient to God. Further, Jerusalem itself will take the place of *the ark of the covenant* as the symbol of God's presence.

3:19–22a—God laments faithless Israel whom God hears weeping because *they have forgotten the LORD* (vv. 19–21). So God pleads for Israel to *return* (v. 22).

3:22b–25—God's plea leads to a confession by God's people. However, nothing that follows in the book suggests that this confession led to changes in Judah's behavior. Judah refuses God's offer to return.

4:1–4 *If you return*—God persists in seeking a restored relationship with Judah.

4:2 *Swear*—Failure to keep an oath sworn with YHWH as the guarantor violated the commandment against taking God's name in vain (Exod. 20:7). *Nations shall be blessed*—God intended that through Abraham the nations would be

in truth, in justice, and in
　　uprightness,
then nations shall be blessed*a* by
　　him,
　　and by him they shall boast.

3 For thus says the LORD to the people of Judah and to the inhabitants of
Jerusalem:
　　Break up your fallow ground,
　　　and do not sow among thorns.
4 　Circumcise yourselves to the LORD,
　　　remove the foreskin of your hearts,
　　O people of Judah and inhabitants
　　　of Jerusalem,
　　or else my wrath will go forth like
　　　fire,
　　and burn with no one to quench it,
　　because of the evil of your doings.

Invasion and Desolation
of Judah Threatened

5 Declare in Judah, and proclaim in
Jerusalem, and say:
　　Blow the trumpet through the land;
　　　shout aloud*b* and say,
　　"Gather together, and let us go
　　　into the fortified cities!"
6 　Raise a standard toward Zion,
　　　flee for safety, do not delay,
　　for I am bringing evil from the
　　　north,
　　　and a great destruction.
7 　A lion has gone up from its thicket,
　　　a destroyer of nations has set out;
　　he has gone out from his place
　　to make your land a waste;
　　　your cities will be ruins

without inhabitant.
8 　Because of this put on sackcloth,
　　　lament and wail:
　　"The fierce anger of the LORD
　　　has not turned away from us."

9 On that day, says the LORD, courage
shall fail the king and the officials; the
priests shall be appalled and the prophets astounded. 10 Then I said, "Ah, Lord
GOD, how utterly you have deceived this
people and Jerusalem, saying, 'It shall be
well with you,' even while the sword is at
the throat!"

11 At that time it will be said to this
people and to Jerusalem: A hot wind
comes from me out of the bare heights*c*
in the desert toward my poor people,
not to winnow or cleanse— 12 a wind too
strong for that. Now it is I who speak in
judgment against them.
13 　Look! He comes up like clouds,
　　　his chariots like the whirlwind;
　　his horses are swifter than eagles—
　　　woe to us, for we are ruined!
14 　O Jerusalem, wash your heart clean
　　　of wickedness
　　　so that you may be saved.
　　How long shall your evil schemes
　　　lodge within you?
15 　For a voice declares from Dan
　　　and proclaims disaster from
　　　　Mount Ephraim.
16 　Tell the nations, "Here they are!"
　　　Proclaim against Jerusalem,

*a Or shall bless themselves b Or shout, take your weapons: Heb shout, fill
(your hand) c Or the trails*

---

blessed (Gen. 12:1–3; 22:18). God offers Judah
the opportunity to fulfill Abraham's mission to be
a blessing to the nations.

4:4 *Circumcise*—Circumcision symbolized that
one belonged to God's people (Gen. 17:9–14).
Here the term is used metaphorically to call
Judah to renounce other gods and return to
YHWH. The *heart* is associated with human will
or volition.

4:5–6:30 The Foe from the North

This section of the book includes vivid images of
the invasion of Judah from the north (see note at
1:13) and the terror it brings. Though this foe is
Babylon, initially the foe is not explicitly named

and so is presented as an unknown, menacing
threat.

4:5–8 *Blow the trumpet*—A warning sounds as
an army approaches Jerusalem.

4:9–10—Judah's officials are confident of God's
protection and downplay the Babylonian threat.
Jeremiah accuses God of allowing this deception
to go unchallenged.

4:11–18—Meteorological images are used to
portray the advance of an enemy upon Judah.

4:14 *Heart*—Because Judah has a "heart" problem, they refuse to obey God (see note at v. 4;
also 17:1; 31:31–34).

"Besiegers come from a distant land;
   they shout against the cities of
      Judah.
17 They have closed in around her like
      watchers of a field,
   because she has rebelled
      against me,
                   says the LORD.
18 Your ways and your doings
   have brought this upon you.
   This is your doom; how bitter it is!
   It has reached your very heart."

Sorrow for a Doomed Nation

19 My anguish, my anguish! I writhe in
      pain!
   Oh, the walls of my heart!
   My heart is beating wildly;
   I cannot keep silent;
   for I*a* hear the sound of the trumpet,
      the alarm of war.
20 Disaster overtakes disaster,
      the whole land is laid waste.
   Suddenly my tents are destroyed,
      my curtains in a moment.
21 How long must I see the standard,
      and hear the sound of the
         trumpet?
22 "For my people are foolish,
      they do not know me;
   they are stupid children,
      they have no understanding.
   They are skilled in doing evil,
      but do not know how to do good."

23 I looked on the earth, and lo, it was
         waste and void;
      and to the heavens, and they had
         no light.

24 I looked on the mountains, and lo,
      they were quaking,
   and all the hills moved to and fro.
25 I looked, and lo, there was no one
      at all,
   and all the birds of the air had fled.
26 I looked, and lo, the fruitful land was
      a desert,
      and all its cities were laid in ruins
   before the LORD, before his fierce
      anger.

27 For thus says the LORD: The whole
land shall be a desolation; yet I will not
make a full end.
28 Because of this the earth shall mourn,
      and the heavens above grow black;
   for I have spoken, I have purposed;
      I have not relented nor will I turn
         back.

29 At the noise of horseman and archer
      every town takes to flight;
   they enter thickets; they climb
         among rocks;
      all the towns are forsaken,
      and no one lives in them.
30 And you, O desolate one,
   what do you mean that you dress in
         crimson,
      that you deck yourself with
         ornaments of gold,
      that you enlarge your eyes with
         paint?
   In vain you beautify yourself.
      Your lovers despise you;
      they seek your life.
31 For I heard a cry as of a woman in
      labor,

a Another reading is *for you, O my soul,*

4:19–23 *My anguish*—While the speaker may be Jeremiah expressing anguish over Judah, Jeremiah's words also express God's pain. The prophet shares the pathos of God over the destruction of Judah.

4:20 *My tents are destroyed, my curtains*—An allusion to the Jerusalem temple.

4:23–28—The images in vv. 23–28 connect human disobedience with God's judgment and the collapse of the creation into chaos. This poem is like the flood story (Gen. 6–9) in miniature and challenges us today to reflect upon social, political, economic, and environmental chaos as indications of God's judgment.

4:27 *Not make a full end*—God's purposes will not be complete with Judah's destruction, with plucking up and tearing down (1:10).

4:29–31—Judah is personified as a prostitute making herself appealing to *lovers*, nations with whom Judah seeks alliances. Yet these nations will participate in Judah's destruction.

4:31 *Cry as of a woman in labor*—This image points in two directions. First, labor is uncontrollable and irresistible, like the approach of the foe

anguish as of one bringing forth
her first child,
the cry of daughter Zion gasping for
breath,
stretching out her hands,
"Woe is me! I am fainting before
killers!"

The Utter Corruption of God's People

5 Run to and fro through the streets
of Jerusalem,
look around and take note!
Search its squares and see
if you can find one person
who acts justly
and seeks truth—
so that I may pardon Jerusalem.[a]
2 Although they say, "As the LORD
lives,"
yet they swear falsely.
3 O LORD, do your eyes not look for
truth?
You have struck them,
but they felt no anguish;
you have consumed them,
but they refused to take
correction.
They have made their faces harder
than rock;
they have refused to turn back.

4 Then I said, "These are only the
poor,
they have no sense;
for they do not know the way of the
LORD,
the law of their God.
5 Let me go to the rich[b]
and speak to them;
surely they know the way of the
LORD,
the law of their God."

But they all alike had broken the
yoke,
they had burst the bonds.
6 Therefore a lion from the forest shall
kill them,
a wolf from the desert shall
destroy them.
A leopard is watching against their
cities;
everyone who goes out of them
shall be torn in pieces—
because their transgressions are many,
their apostasies are great.

7 How can I pardon you?
Your children have forsaken me,
and have sworn by those who are
no gods.
When I fed them to the full,
they committed adultery
and trooped to the houses of
prostitutes.
8 They were well-fed lusty stallions,
each neighing for his neighbor's
wife.
9 Shall I not punish them for these
things?
says the LORD;
and shall I not bring retribution
on a nation such as this?

10 Go up through her vine-rows and
destroy,
but do not make a full end;
strip away her branches,
for they are not the LORD's.
11 For the house of Israel and the house
of Judah
have been utterly faithless to me,
says the LORD.

[a] Heb it [b] Or the great

from the north sent by God. Second, however,
labor results in new life, and there may be a hint
that God's judgment may lead to Judah's renewal.

5:1–9—The scene recalls Abraham's search for
righteous persons to save Sodom (Gen. 18:16–
33). These verses indicate the collapse of just
and honest social interactions in Judah. One
accusation is that persons *swear falsely* (v. 2),
a violation of the commandment not to take
God's name in vain (also see 4:2). To swear

falsely is an effort to manipulate God and so
secure oneself.

5:7–8 *Neighing for his neighbor's wife*—Apostasy is linked with social collapse, the violation
of the first commandment with violation of the
commandment prohibiting adultery. Relationships with God and neighbor are complementary.

5:10–19—Judah, God's vineyard, must be uprooted (cf. Isa. 5:1–7; John 15:1–17).

12 They have spoken falsely of the
  LORD,
    and have said, "He will do nothing.
  No evil will come upon us,
    and we shall not see sword or
    famine."
13 The prophets are nothing but wind,
    for the word is not in them.
  Thus shall it be done to them!

14 Therefore thus says the LORD, the
    God of hosts:
  Because they*a* have spoken this
    word,
  I am now making my words in your
    mouth a fire,
    and this people wood, and the fire
    shall devour them.
15 I am going to bring upon you
    a nation from far away, O house of
    Israel,
                        says the LORD.
  It is an enduring nation,
    it is an ancient nation,
  a nation whose language you do not
    know,
    nor can you understand what they
    say.
16 Their quiver is like an open tomb;
    all of them are mighty warriors.
17 They shall eat up your harvest and
    your food;
    they shall eat up your sons and
    your daughters;
    they shall eat up your flocks and
    your herds;
    they shall eat up your vines and
    your fig trees;
    they shall destroy with the sword
    your fortified cities in which you
    trust.

18 But even in those days, says the
  LORD, I will not make a full end of you.
19 And when your people say, "Why has
  the LORD our God done all these things
  to us?" you shall say to them, "As you
  have forsaken me and served foreign
  gods in your land, so you shall serve
  strangers in a land that is not yours."

20 Declare this in the house of Jacob,
    proclaim it in Judah:
21 Hear this, O foolish and senseless
    people,
    who have eyes, but do not see,
    who have ears, but do not hear.
22 Do you not fear me? says the
    LORD;
    Do you not tremble before me?
  I placed the sand as a boundary for
    the sea,
    a perpetual barrier that it cannot
    pass;
  though the waves toss, they cannot
    prevail,
    though they roar, they cannot pass
    over it.
23 But this people has a stubborn and
    rebellious heart;
    they have turned aside and gone
    away.
24 They do not say in their hearts,
    "Let us fear the LORD our God,
  who gives the rain in its season,
    the autumn rain and the spring
    rain,
  and keeps for us
    the weeks appointed for the
    harvest."
25 Your iniquities have turned these
    away,

a Heb you

5:12—Judah's prophets should have spoken like Jeremiah, to call for repentance and warn of God's coming judgment. Instead they gave false assurance that all is well (cf. 4:9–10). Discerning who speaks for God is difficult, and this book is aware of the propensity to identify God's messengers as those who speak comforting words.

5:17—Once God considered Israel "first fruit" and would hold guilty any who "ate," that is,

harmed them (2:3). Now God threatens to send a nation to *eat up*, or destroy Judah.

5:20–31 *Foolish and senseless people*—A series of accusations indicate the reasons for God's judgment of Judah as foolish and senseless people.

5:22–23—*The sea*, a symbol of chaos, submits to God's sovereignty, in contrast to Judah, which rebels.

and your sins have deprived you of
    good.
26 For scoundrels are found among my
    people;
    they take over the goods of others.
Like fowlers they set a trap;*a*
    they catch human beings.
27 Like a cage full of birds,
    their houses are full of treachery;
therefore they have become great
    and rich,
28   they have grown fat and sleek.
They know no limits in deeds of
    wickedness;
    they do not judge with justice
the cause of the orphan, to make it
    prosper,
    and they do not defend the rights
    of the needy.
29 Shall I not punish them for these
    things?
                says the LORD,
    and shall I not bring retribution
    on a nation such as this?

30 An appalling and horrible thing
    has happened in the land:
31 the prophets prophesy falsely,
    and the priests rule as the prophets
    direct;*b*
my people love to have it so,
    but what will you do when the end
    comes?

The Imminence and Horror of the Invasion

6 Flee for safety, O children of
    Benjamin,
    from the midst of Jerusalem!
Blow the trumpet in Tekoa,

and raise a signal on
    Beth-haccherem;
for evil looms out of the north,
    and great destruction.
2 I have likened daughter Zion
    to the loveliest pasture.*c*
3 Shepherds with their flocks shall
    come against her.
They shall pitch their tents around
    her;
    they shall pasture, all in their places.
4 "Prepare war against her;
    up, and let us attack at noon!"
"Woe to us, for the day declines,
    the shadows of evening lengthen!"
5 "Up, and let us attack by night,
    and destroy her palaces!"
6 For thus says the LORD of hosts:
Cut down her trees;
    cast up a siege ramp against
    Jerusalem.
This is the city that must be
    punished;*d*
    there is nothing but oppression
    within her.
7 As a well keeps its water fresh,
    so she keeps fresh her wickedness;
violence and destruction are heard
    within her;
    sickness and wounds are ever
    before me.
8 Take warning, O Jerusalem,
    or I shall turn from you in disgust,
and make you a desolation,
    an uninhabited land.

9 Thus says the LORD of hosts:
Glean*e* thoroughly as a vine

a Meaning of Heb uncertain *b* Or *rule by their own authority* *c* Or *I will destroy daughter Zion, the loveliest pasture* *d* Or *the city of license* *e* Cn: Heb *They shall glean*

5:26–28—Judah's sin is social treachery that allows some to become *fat*, that is, wealthy, even while the weak and vulnerable, *the orphan* and *the needy*, are denied justice (regarding justice, see note at 22:3–5).

5:30–31—Judah's prophets fail to condemn the social injustices that infect Judah's life, and the priests too are corrupt. Exposure and indictment of corrupt leadership is a primary task of the prophets.

6:1–15—Further images of Judah's invasion are

introduced as an alarm is sounded to warn towns south of Jerusalem of an approaching army. Interspersed among these battle images are accusations against Judah.

6:3 *Shepherds with their flocks*—That is, kings with their armies.

6:8 *Take warning*—The Hebrew means "correction" or "discipline" (see 2:30 and 5:8, where the same word is used). Judah is called upon to repent or else!

the remnant of Israel;
like a grape-gatherer, pass your hand
  again
  over its branches.

10 To whom shall I speak and give
  warning,
  that they may hear?
See, their ears are closed,[a]
  they cannot listen.
The word of the LORD is to them an
  object of scorn;
  they take no pleasure in it.
11 But I am full of the wrath of the
  LORD;
  I am weary of holding it in.

Pour it out on the children in the
  street,
and on the gatherings of young
  men as well;
both husband and wife shall be
  taken,
  the old folk and the very aged.
12 Their houses shall be turned over to
  others,
  their fields and wives together;
for I will stretch out my hand
  against the inhabitants of the land,
     says the LORD.

13 For from the least to the greatest of
  them,
  everyone is greedy for unjust gain;
and from prophet to priest,
  everyone deals falsely.
14 They have treated the wound of my
  people carelessly,
  saying, "Peace, peace,"
  when there is no peace.

15 They acted shamefully, they
  committed abomination;
  yet they were not ashamed,
  they did not know how to blush.
Therefore they shall fall among
  those who fall;
  at the time that I punish them,
  they shall be overthrown,
     says the LORD.
16 Thus says the LORD:
Stand at the crossroads, and look,
  and ask for the ancient paths,
where the good way lies; and walk
  in it,
  and find rest for your souls.
But they said, "We will not walk
  in it."
17 Also I raised up sentinels for you:
  "Give heed to the sound of the
  trumpet!"
But they said, "We will not give
  heed."
18 Therefore hear, O nations,
  and know, O congregation, what
  will happen to them.
19 Hear, O earth; I am going to bring
  disaster on this people,
  the fruit of their schemes,
because they have not given heed to
  my words;
  and as for my teaching, they have
  rejected it.
20 Of what use to me is frankincense
  that comes from Sheba,
  or sweet cane from a distant land?
Your burnt offerings are not
  acceptable,

---

[a] Heb *are uncircumcised*

6:14 *Peace, peace*—The prophet is chagrined that the people of Judah assume God will continue to provide them with peace and security despite the injustice that pervades the land (see v. 13, *greedy for unjust gain*). Judah's orthodox religious assumption was that God would secure the line of David and God's temple forever (e.g., 2 Sam. 7:13–16; Ps. 48; Isa. 31:4–5). Jeremiah challenges this facile assumption, that God will secure Judah forever, by linking Judah's continued well-being to the demand for social and economic justice.

6:15 *Abomination*—Here is related to economic injustices (v. 13) that are ignored by Judah's prophets (v. 14).

6:16–21 *The crossroads . . . the ancient paths*—Judah broke the Mosaic covenant and its laws, including those demanding justice for the poor (e.g., Exod. 22:21–24; 23:6–8).

6:17 *Sentinels*—God's prophets, to whom Judah would not listen (see v. 10).

6:20—It is not worship itself that is condemned, but worship that justifies the status quo and does not transform Judah's apostasy and social oppression.

nor are your sacrifices pleasing
to me.

21 Therefore thus says the LORD:
See, I am laying before this people
stumbling blocks against which
they shall stumble;
parents and children together,
neighbor and friend shall perish.

22 Thus says the LORD:
See, a people is coming from the
land of the north,
a great nation is stirring from the
farthest parts of the earth.

23 They grasp the bow and the javelin,
they are cruel and have no mercy,
their sound is like the roaring sea;
they ride on horses,
equipped like a warrior for battle,
against you, O daughter Zion!

24 "We have heard news of them,
our hands fall helpless;
anguish has taken hold of us,
pain as of a woman in labor.

25 Do not go out into the field,
or walk on the road;
for the enemy has a sword,
terror is on every side."

26 O my poor people, put on sackcloth,
and roll in ashes;
make mourning as for an only child,
most bitter lamentation:
for suddenly the destroyer
will come upon us.

27 I have made you a tester and a
refiner*a* among my people

so that you may know and test
their ways.

28 They are all stubbornly rebellious,
going about with slanders;
they are bronze and iron,
all of them act corruptly.

29 The bellows blow fiercely,
the lead is consumed by the
fire;
in vain the refining goes on,
for the wicked are not removed.

30 They are called "rejected silver,"
for the LORD has rejected them.

Jeremiah Proclaims God's Judgment on the Nation

7 The word that came to Jeremiah
from the LORD: 2 Stand in the gate
of the LORD's house, and proclaim there
this word, and say, Hear the word of the
LORD, all you people of Judah, you that
enter these gates to worship the LORD.
3 Thus says the LORD of hosts, the God
of Israel: Amend your ways and your
doings, and let me dwell with you*b* in
this place. 4 Do not trust in these deceptive words: "This is*c* the temple of the
LORD, the temple of the LORD, the temple of the LORD."

5 For if you truly amend your ways
and your doings, if you truly act justly
one with another, 6 if you do not oppress
the alien, the orphan, and the widow, or
shed innocent blood in this place, and if
you do not go after other gods to your
own hurt, 7 then I will dwell with you in

a Or *a fortress*   *b* Or *and I will let you dwell*   *c* Heb *They are*

6:21—Judah's refusal to walk in covenantal
obedience (v. 16) will be punished, though how
is not specified.

6:27–30—Silver is refined from lead by smelting.
God charges Jeremiah to refine Judah, but as the
preceding material suggests, God finds in Judah
only *rejected silver* (v. 30) and nothing of value.

7:1–15 The Temple Sermon

Addressed to those gathering for worship in
Jerusalem, this oracle is organized around two
admonitions: *Amend your ways* and *Do not trust
in deceptive words . . .* (vv. 1–4). Subsequently,
each admonition is elaborated ("amend your
ways" in vv. 5–7 and "do not trust in deceptive

words" in vv. 8–12). The oracle concludes with a
pronouncement of judgment (vv. 13–15).

7:3–7—Continuation in the land demanded repentance entailing both justice for persons on the
social margins and exclusive devotion to YHWH.
Judah's responsibility for the marginalized derived from their relationship with God, who had
delivered them from slavery in Egypt (see Exod.
22:21–24; Deut. 24:17–22).

7:4 *This is the temple of the LORD*—A liturgical chant that offered assurance that God would
defend Zion (e.g., as articulated in Isa. 31:4–5;
see note at 6:14). Jeremiah labels this assurance
deceptive, a false claim of security.

this place, in the land that I gave of old to your ancestors forever and ever.

8 Here you are, trusting in deceptive words to no avail. 9 Will you steal, murder, commit adultery, swear falsely, make offerings to Baal, and go after other gods that you have not known, 10 and then come and stand before me in this house, which is called by my name, and say, "We are safe!"—only to go on doing all these abominations? 11 Has this house, which is called by my name, become a den of robbers in your sight? You know, I too am watching, says the LORD. 12 Go now to my place that was in Shiloh, where I made my name dwell at first, and see what I did to it for the wickedness of my people Israel. 13 And now, because you have done all these things, says the LORD, and when I spoke to you persistently, you did not listen, and when I called you, you did not answer, 14 therefore I will do to the house that is called by my name, in which you trust, and to the place that I gave to you and to your ancestors, just what I did to Shiloh. 15 And I will cast you out of my sight, just as I cast out all your kinsfolk, all the offspring of Ephraim.

The People's Disobedience

16 As for you, do not pray for this people, do not raise a cry or prayer on their behalf, and do not intercede with me, for I will not hear you. 17 Do you not see what they are doing in the towns of Judah and in the streets of Jerusalem? 18 The children gather wood, the fathers kindle fire, and the women knead dough, to make cakes for the queen of heaven; and they pour out drink offerings to other gods, to provoke me to anger. 19 Is it I whom they provoke? says the LORD. Is it not themselves, to their own hurt? 20 Therefore thus says the Lord GOD: My anger and my wrath shall be poured out on this place, on human beings and animals, on the trees of the field and the fruit of the ground; it will burn and not be quenched.

21 Thus says the LORD of hosts, the God of Israel: Add your burnt offerings to your sacrifices, and eat the flesh. 22 For in the day that I brought your ancestors out of the land of Egypt, I did not speak to them or command them concerning burnt offerings and sacrifices. 23 But this command I gave them, "Obey my voice, and I will be your God, and you shall be my people; and walk only in the way that I command you, so that it may be well with you." 24 Yet they did not obey or incline their ear, but, in the stubbornness of their evil will, they walked in their own counsels, and looked backward rather than forward. 25 From the day that your ancestors came out of the land of Egypt until this day, I have persistently sent all my servants the prophets to them, day after day; 26 yet they did not listen to me, or pay attention, but they stiffened their necks. They did worse than their ancestors did.

27 So you shall speak all these words to them, but they will not listen to you. You shall call to them, but they will not answer you. 28 You shall say to them:

7:9—The Ten Commandments are cited in reverse order. Right relationship with neighbors is grounded in right relationship with God.

7:11 *Den of robbers*—Judah perverted the temple as a place of sanctuary. They imagined that they could flee to the temple, which would guarantee their security despite their lack of obedience (cf. Matt. 21:13).

7:14 *Shiloh*—Just as the Lord destroyed this, a worship center, during Israel's tribal league era (Josh. 21:1–2; 1 Sam. 1:3, 9), God could also allow Jerusalem to be destroyed.

7:16–20 Do Not Pray

Because of Judah's continued apostasy, it was too late for Jeremiah to intercede.

7:21–8:3 Sacrifice and Obedience

Sacrifices had become hollow rituals that did not transform Judah's relationship with God or neighbor (7:21–28). Worse, sacrifices became perversions of God's intentions for Israel (7:29–8:3).

7:24—In Hebrew, the same word means both listen and *obey*. The charge is made four times that Judah failed to listen to or obey God: vv. 24, 26, 27, 28.

This is the nation that did not obey the voice of the LORD their God, and did not accept discipline; truth has perished; it is cut off from their lips.

29 Cut off your hair and throw it away;
raise a lamentation on the bare
heights,ᵃ
for the LORD has rejected and
forsaken
the generation that provoked his
wrath.

30 For the people of Judah have done evil in my sight, says the LORD; they have set their abominations in the house that is called by my name, defiling it. 31 And they go on building the high placeᵇ of Topheth, which is in the valley of the son of Hinnom, to burn their sons and their daughters in the fire—which I did not command, nor did it come into my mind. 32 Therefore, the days are surely coming, says the LORD, when it will no more be called Topheth, or the valley of the son of Hinnom, but the valley of Slaughter: for they will bury in Topheth until there is no more room. 33 The corpses of this people will be food for the birds of the air, and for the animals of the earth; and no one will frighten them away. 34 And I will bring to an end the sound of mirth and gladness, the voice of the bride and bridegroom in the cities of Judah and in the streets of Jerusalem; for the land shall become a waste.

8 At that time, says the LORD, the bones of the kings of Judah, the bones of its officials, the bones of the priests, the bones of the prophets, and the bones of the inhabitants of Jerusalem shall be brought out of their tombs; 2 and they shall be spread before the sun and the moon and all the host of heaven, which they have loved and served, which they have followed, and which they have inquired of and worshiped; and they shall not be gathered or buried; they shall be like dung on the surface of the ground. 3 Death shall be preferred to life by all the remnant that remains of this evil family in all the places where I have driven them, says the LORD of hosts.

The Blind Perversity of the Whole Nation

4 You shall say to them, Thus says the
LORD:
When people fall, do they not get up
again?
If they go astray, do they not turn
back?
5 Why then has this peopleᶜ turned
away
in perpetual backsliding?
They have held fast to deceit,
they have refused to return.
6 I have given heed and listened,
but they do not speak honestly;
no one repents of wickedness,
saying, "What have I done!"
All of them turn to their own course,
like a horse plunging headlong
into battle.
7 Even the stork in the heavens
knows its times;
and the turtledove, swallow, and
craneᵈ
observe the time of their coming;

ᵃ Or the trails ᵇ Gk Tg: Heb high places ᶜ One Ms Gk: MT this people, Jerusalem, ᵈ Meaning of Heb uncertain

---

7:31—If child sacrifice actually did occur, it was likely because of a perversion of the law requiring that firstborn be given to God (Exod. 22:29–30). The Judean kings Ahaz and Manasseh are said to have made their sons "pass through the fire" (2 Kgs. 16:3; 21:6).

7:33—See Deut. 28:26, which indicates a curse for breaking God's covenant.

7:34—No weddings mean no children and, therefore, no future (also see 16:1–4).

8:1–2—Judah had offered sacrifices to the "queen of heaven" (7:18). Here the bodies of the inhabitants of Judah are strewn unburied before the astral gods.

8:4–13 Repent

In these verses, the Hebrew word *shub* ("turn, repent") occurs six times, translated into English variously: "go astray," "turn back," "turned away," "backsliding," "return," "turn."

8:7—The birds return to their proper places in a way that Judah refuses (cf. 5:22–23).

but my people do not know
   the ordinance of the LORD.

8 How can you say, "We are wise,
   and the law of the LORD is
      with us,"
when, in fact, the false pen of the
      scribes
   has made it into a lie?
9 The wise shall be put to shame,
   they shall be dismayed and taken;
since they have rejected the word of
      the LORD,
   what wisdom is in them?
10 Therefore I will give their wives to
      others
   and their fields to conquerors,
because from the least to the greatest
   everyone is greedy for unjust gain;
from prophet to priest
   everyone deals falsely.
11 They have treated the wound of my
      people carelessly,
   saying, "Peace, peace,"
   when there is no peace.
12 They acted shamefully, they
      committed abomination;
   yet they were not at all ashamed,
   they did not know how to blush.
Therefore they shall fall among
      those who fall;
   at the time when I punish them,
      they shall be overthrown,
                  says the LORD.
13 When I wanted to gather them, says
      the LORD,
   there are^a no grapes on the vine,
   nor figs on the fig tree;
even the leaves are withered,
   and what I gave them has passed
      away from them.^{b}

14 Why do we sit still?
Gather together, let us go into the
      fortified cities
   and perish there;
for the LORD our God has doomed
      us to perish,
   and has given us poisoned water to
      drink,
   because we have sinned against the
      LORD.
15 We look for peace, but find no
      good,
   for a time of healing, but there is
      terror instead.

16 The snorting of their horses is heard
      from Dan;
   at the sound of the neighing of
      their stallions
   the whole land quakes.
They come and devour the land and
   all that fills it,
   the city and those who live in it.
17 See, I am letting snakes loose among
      you,
   adders that cannot be charmed,
   and they shall bite you,
                  says the LORD.

The Prophet Mourns for the People
18 My joy is gone, grief is upon me,
   my heart is sick.
19 Hark, the cry of my poor people
   from far and wide in the land:
"Is the LORD not in Zion?
   Is her King not in her?"
("Why have they provoked me to
      anger with their images,
   with their foreign idols?")

^{a} Or I will make an end of them, says the LORD. There are ^{b} Meaning of
Heb uncertain

8:8–13—Judah's scribes claim to be wise and
know God's *law (torah)*. Jeremiah sees that
Judah's leaders, *greedy for unjust gain* (v. 10),
engage in economic practices that are incompatible with God's ways.

8:14–9:3 Judgment and Grief
While God must call Judah to account, the judg-
ment causes God to grieve. Jeremiah shares in
God's pathos.

8:14–15—God, the "fountain of living water"
(2:13), will poison the water and bring Judah to
an end.

8:16–17 *Horses . . . snakes*—God's judgment and
its terror are inescapable and will come one way
or another.

8:18–21 *My joy is gone*—A lament over Judah,
whose false sense of security is about to be
shattered. The speaker may be Jeremiah, but the
pathos expressed is God's.

20 "The harvest is past, the summer is
    ended,
        and we are not saved."
21 For the hurt of my poor people I am
    hurt,
        I mourn, and dismay has taken
            hold of me.
22 Is there no balm in Gilead?
        Is there no physician there?
    Why then has the health of my poor
        people
            not been restored?

9 *a* O that my head were a spring of
        water,
    and my eyes a fountain of tears,
        so that I might weep day and night
            for the slain of my poor people!
2b O that I had in the desert
        a traveler's lodging place,
    that I might leave my people
        and go away from them!
    For they are all adulterers,
        a band of traitors.
3 They bend their tongues like
        bows;
    they have grown strong in the
        land for falsehood, and not for
            truth;
    for they proceed from evil to evil,
        and they do not know me, says the
            LORD.

4 Beware of your neighbors,
        and put no trust in any of your
            kin;*c*
    for all your kin*d* are supplanters,
        and every neighbor goes around
            like a slanderer.
5 They all deceive their neighbors,
        and no one speaks the truth;
    they have taught their tongues to
        speak lies;

they commit iniquity and are too
    weary to repent.*e*
6 Oppression upon oppression, deceit*f*
        upon deceit!
    They refuse to know me, says the
        LORD.

7 Therefore thus says the LORD of hosts:
    I will now refine and test them,
        for what else can I do with my
            sinful people?*g*
8 Their tongue is a deadly arrow;
        it speaks deceit through the
            mouth.
    They all speak friendly words to
        their neighbors,
    but inwardly are planning to lay an
        ambush.
9 Shall I not punish them for these
        things? says the LORD;
    and shall I not bring retribution
        on a nation such as this?

10 Take up*h* weeping and wailing for
        the mountains,
    and a lamentation for the pastures
        of the wilderness,
    because they are laid waste so that
        no one passes through,
    and the lowing of cattle is not
        heard;
    both the birds of the air and the
        animals
    have fled and are gone.
11 I will make Jerusalem a heap of ruins,
        a lair of jackals;
    and I will make the towns of Judah a
        desolation,
            without inhabitant.

a Ch 8.23 in Heb *b* Ch 9.1 in Heb *c* Heb in a brother *d* Heb for every
brother *e* Cn Compare Gk: Heb they weary themselves with iniquity. *6* Your
dwelling *f* Cn: Heb Your dwelling in the midst of deceit *g* Or my poor people
h Gk Syr: Heb I will take up

8:22—*Gilead* was a region known for the balsam
tree, whose sap had healing qualities. God intended to heal Judah, but they refused.

9:1–3—Judah is accused of *falsehood* and *evil*
(v. 3) that encompass apostasy, social oppression, and a deceitful sense of security. God's
response to Judah expresses both grief (*weep day
and night*) and revulsion (*that I might leave my
people*).

9:4–22 Deceit, Judgment, and Chaos
Bearing false witness against neighbors (Exod.
20:16) breeds oppression and will bring God's
judgment, resulting in chaos. These verses carry
the collapse of order to its logical extreme, the
lapse of creation into chaos (see 4:23–28).

12 Who is wise enough to understand this? To whom has the mouth of the LORD spoken, so that they may declare it? Why is the land ruined and laid waste like a wilderness, so that no one passes through? 13 And the LORD says: Because they have forsaken my law that I set before them, and have not obeyed my voice, or walked in accordance with it, 14 but have stubbornly followed their own hearts and have gone after the Baals, as their ancestors taught them. 15 Therefore thus says the LORD of hosts, the God of Israel: I am feeding this people with wormwood, and giving them poisonous water to drink. 16 I will scatter them among nations that neither they nor their ancestors have known; and I will send the sword after them, until I have consumed them.

The People Mourn in Judgment

17 Thus says the LORD of hosts:
    Consider, and call for the mourning
        women to come;
        send for the skilled women to
            come;
18 let them quickly raise a dirge
        over us,
    so that our eyes may run down
        with tears,
    and our eyelids flow with water.
19 For a sound of wailing is heard from
        Zion:
    "How we are ruined!
    We are utterly shamed,
    because we have left the land,
        because they have cast down our
            dwellings."

20 Hear, O women, the word of the
        LORD,
    and let your ears receive the word
        of his mouth;
    teach to your daughters a dirge,
        and each to her neighbor a
            lament.
21 "Death has come up into our
        windows,
    it has entered our palaces,
    to cut off the children from the
        streets
    and the young men from the
        squares."
22 Speak! Thus says the LORD:
    "Human corpses shall fall
        like dung upon the open field,
    like sheaves behind the reaper,
        and no one shall gather
            them."

23 Thus says the LORD: Do not let the wise boast in their wisdom, do not let the mighty boast in their might, do not let the wealthy boast in their wealth; 24 but let those who boast boast in this, that they understand and know me, that I am the LORD; I act with steadfast love, justice, and righteousness in the earth, for in these things I delight, says the LORD.

25 The days are surely coming, says the LORD, when I will attend to all those who are circumcised only in the foreskin: 26 Egypt, Judah, Edom, the Ammonites, Moab, and all those with shaven temples who live in the desert. For all these nations are uncircumcised, and all the house of Israel is uncircumcised in heart.

9:16 *Scatter them among the nations*—A curse for disobedience (see Deut. 28:25, 36, 49, 64).

9:17–22—When death was imminent, professional mourning women were called to express grief. God's judgment will bring death to Judah.

9:21 *Death*—The personification is a likely reference to the Canaanite god of death, Mot.

9:22—A curse for disobedience found in Deut. 28:26.

9:23–25 Competing Values

These verses contrast two sets of values. Judah is portrayed as a community that values *wisdom*, *might*, and *wealth*, through which Judah attempts to secure itself. YHWH, the God of the exodus, values *steadfast love, justice,* and *righteousness* (cf. Exod. 34:6–7), which create a humane community inclusive of the poor and marginalized.

9:25—Circumcision is a sign of belonging to God (see note at 4:4). Judah is regarded here as no different from other nations.

Idolatry Has Brought Ruin on Israel

10 Hear the word that the LORD speaks to you, O house of Israel.
2 Thus says the LORD:

Do not learn the way of the nations,
> or be dismayed at the signs of the
> heavens;
>> for the nations are dismayed at
>> them.

3 For the customs of the peoples are
> false:
a tree from the forest is cut down,
> and worked with an ax by the
> hands of an artisan;

4 people deck it with silver and gold;
> they fasten it with hammer and
> nails
so that it cannot move.

5 Their idols[a] are like scarecrows in a
> cucumber field,
and they cannot speak;
they have to be carried,
> for they cannot walk.
Do not be afraid of them,
> for they cannot do evil,
> nor is it in them to do good.

6 There is none like you, O LORD;
> you are great, and your name is
> great in might.

7 Who would not fear you, O King of
> the nations?
For that is your due;
among all the wise ones of the
> nations
and in all their kingdoms
there is no one like you.

8 They are both stupid and foolish;
> the instruction given by idols
> is no better than wood![b]

9 Beaten silver is brought from
> Tarshish,
> and gold from Uphaz.
They are the work of the artisan and
> of the hands of the goldsmith;
> their clothing is blue and purple;

they are all the product of skilled
> workers.

10 But the LORD is the true God;
> he is the living God and the
> everlasting King.
At his wrath the earth quakes,
> and the nations cannot endure his
> indignation.

11 Thus shall you say to them: The gods who did not make the heavens and the earth shall perish from the earth and from under the heavens.[c]

12 It is he who made the earth by his
> power,
> who established the world by his
> wisdom,
> and by his understanding
> stretched out the heavens.

13 When he utters his voice, there
> is a tumult of waters in the
> heavens,
> and he makes the mist rise from
> the ends of the earth.
He makes lightnings for the rain,
> and he brings out the wind from
> his storehouses.

14 Everyone is stupid and without
> knowledge;
> goldsmiths are all put to shame by
> their idols;
for their images are false,
> and there is no breath in them.

15 They are worthless, a work of
> delusion;
> at the time of their punishment
> they shall perish.

16 Not like these is the LORD,[d] the
> portion of Jacob,
> for he is the one who formed all
> things,
and Israel is the tribe of his
> inheritance;
> the LORD of hosts is his name.

---

[a] Heb *They* [b] Meaning of Heb uncertain [c] This verse is in Aramaic
[d] Heb lacks *the* LORD

10:1–16 God, the Creator and Sovereign of the Nations

God is contrasted with idols that are incapable of action (see 4:27–28). A similar comparison is prominent in that portion of the book of Isaiah dated to the exilic era: Isa. 40:18–20; 41:1–10, 21–29; 44:9–20.

The Coming Exile

17 Gather up your bundle from the
    ground,
    O you who live under siege!
18 For thus says the LORD:
I am going to sling out the
      inhabitants of the land
    at this time,
and I will bring distress on them,
    so that they shall feel it.

19 Woe is me because of my hurt!
    My wound is severe.
But I said, "Truly this is my
      punishment,
    and I must bear it."
20 My tent is destroyed,
    and all my cords are broken;
my children have gone from me,
    and they are no more;
there is no one to spread my tent
      again,
    and to set up my curtains.
21 For the shepherds are stupid,
    and do not inquire of the LORD;
therefore they have not prospered,
    and all their flock is scattered.

22 Hear, a noise! Listen, it is
      coming—
a great commotion from the land
      of the north
to make the cities of Judah a
      desolation,
    a lair of jackals.

23 I know, O LORD, that the way of
      human beings is not in their
      control,
that mortals as they walk cannot
    direct their steps.
24 Correct me, O LORD, but in just
      measure;
not in your anger, or you will bring
    me to nothing.

25 Pour out your wrath on the nations
    that do not know you,
and on the peoples that do not call
    on your name;
for they have devoured Jacob;
they have devoured him and
      consumed him,
and have laid waste his habitation.

Israel and Judah Have Broken the Covenant

11 The word that came to Jeremiah from the LORD: 2 Hear the words of this covenant, and speak to the people of Judah and the inhabitants of Jerusalem. 3 You shall say to them, Thus says the LORD, the God of Israel: Cursed be anyone who does not heed the words of this covenant, 4 which I commanded your ancestors when I brought them out of the land of Egypt, from the iron-smelter, saying, Listen to my voice, and do all that I command you. So shall you be my people, and I will be your God, 5 that I may perform the oath that I swore to your ancestors, to give them a land flowing with milk and honey, as at this day. Then I answered, "So be it, LORD."

6 And the LORD said to me: Proclaim all these words in the cities of Judah, and in the streets of Jerusalem: Hear

---

10:17–22 Exile

Judah will be exiled from the land, and Jerusalem, personified as a woman, laments her lost *children* (v. 20).

10:20 *Tent . . . cords . . . curtains*—Allusions to the Jerusalem temple.

10:21 *Shepherds*—Judah's kings.

10:23–25 An Intercessory Prayer

Jeremiah prays on behalf of Judah (or perhaps it is the people themselves who pray). The prayer seeks merciful punishment for Judah and destruction of Judah's enemies.

10:25—A quotation of Ps. 79:6, a prayer for the deliverance of Jerusalem.

11:1–17 A Broken Covenant

The *covenant* between God and Israel at Sinai was predicated upon God's deliverance of Israel from Egypt (v. 7). Violation of the covenant would result in covenant curses (v. 8) as are found in Deut. 28 and Lev. 26.

11:2–5—A paraphrase Deut. 27:26, part of a worship ritual though which Israel acknowledged their covenant obligations and the curses that they would incur for violation of the covenant.

the words of this covenant and do them. [7] For I solemnly warned your ancestors when I brought them up out of the land of Egypt, warning them persistently, even to this day, saying, Obey my voice. [8] Yet they did not obey or incline their ear, but everyone walked in the stubbornness of an evil will. So I brought upon them all the words of this covenant, which I commanded them to do, but they did not.

9 And the LORD said to me: Conspiracy exists among the people of Judah and the inhabitants of Jerusalem. [10] They have turned back to the iniquities of their ancestors of old, who refused to heed my words; they have gone after other gods to serve them; the house of Israel and the house of Judah have broken the covenant that I made with their ancestors. [11] Therefore, thus says the LORD, assuredly I am going to bring disaster upon them that they cannot escape; though they cry out to me, I will not listen to them. [12] Then the cities of Judah and the inhabitants of Jerusalem will go and cry out to the gods to whom they make offerings, but they will never save them in the time of their trouble. [13] For your gods have become as many as your towns, O Judah; and as many as the streets of Jerusalem are the altars to shame you have set up, altars to make offerings to Baal.

14 As for you, do not pray for this people, or lift up a cry or prayer on their behalf, for I will not listen when they call to me in the time of their trouble. [15] What right has my beloved in my house, when she has done vile deeds? Can vows[a] and sacrificial flesh avert your doom? Can you then exult? [16] The LORD once called you, "A green olive tree, fair with goodly fruit"; but with the roar of a great tempest he will set fire to it, and its branches will be consumed. [17] The LORD of hosts, who planted you, has pronounced evil against you, because of the evil that the house of Israel and the house of Judah have done, provoking me to anger by making offerings to Baal.

Jeremiah's Life Threatened

[18] It was the LORD who made it known
        to me, and I knew;
      then you showed me their evil
        deeds.
[19] But I was like a gentle lamb
        led to the slaughter.
      And I did not know it was
        against me
      that they devised schemes, saying,
      "Let us destroy the tree with its fruit,
        let us cut him off from the land of
          the living,
        so that his name will no longer be
          remembered!"
[20] But you, O LORD of hosts, who judge
        righteously,
      who try the heart and the mind,
      let me see your retribution upon
        them,
        for to you I have committed my
          cause.

21 Therefore thus says the LORD concerning the people of Anathoth, who seek your life, and say, "You shall not prophesy in the name of the LORD, or you will die by our hand"— [22] therefore thus says the LORD of hosts: I am going to punish them; the young men shall die by the sword; their sons and their daughters shall die by famine; [23] and not even a remnant shall be left of them. For I will bring disaster upon the people of Anathoth, the year of their punishment.

[a] Gk: Heb Can many

11:18–23 The First Complaint of Jeremiah
This is the first of a series of seven complaints by the prophet in chaps. 11–20 (see also 12:1–6; 15:10–21; 17:14–18; 18:18–23; 20:7–13; 20:14–18). These complaints are similar to lament psalms (e.g., Pss. 3–7, 35, 44, 54).

11:18–20—Jeremiah complains that he is the victim of a conspiracy.

11:21–23—God responds to Jeremiah's complaint. The people of Jeremiah's home town, *Anathoth* (see 1:1), plot against him and in so doing reject God for whom Jeremiah speaks.

Jeremiah Complains to God

12 You will be in the right, O LORD,
    when I lay charges against you;
    but let me put my case to you.
Why does the way of the guilty
    prosper?
    Why do all who are treacherous
        thrive?
2 You plant them, and they take root;
    they grow and bring forth fruit;
you are near in their mouths
    yet far from their hearts.
3 But you, O LORD, know me;
    You see me and test me—my heart
        is with you.
Pull them out like sheep for the
    slaughter,
    and set them apart for the day of
        slaughter.
4 How long will the land mourn,
    and the grass of every field wither?
For the wickedness of those who live
    in it
    the animals and the birds are
        swept away,
    and because people said, "He is
        blind to our ways."*a*

God Replies to Jeremiah

5 If you have raced with foot-runners
    and they have wearied you,
    how will you compete with
        horses?
    And if in a safe land you fall down,
        how will you fare in the thickets of
            the Jordan?
6 For even your kinsfolk and your own
    family,
    even they have dealt treacherously
        with you;
    they are in full cry after you;
do not believe them,

though they speak friendly words
    to you.

7 I have forsaken my house,
    I have abandoned my heritage;
I have given the beloved of my heart
    into the hands of her enemies.
8 My heritage has become to me
    like a lion in the forest;
    she has lifted up her voice against
        me—
    therefore I hate her.
9 Is the hyena greedy*b* for my heritage
        at my command?
    Are the birds of prey all around her?
Go, assemble all the wild animals;
    bring them to devour her.
10 Many shepherds have destroyed my
        vineyard,
    they have trampled down my
        portion,
they have made my pleasant portion
    a desolate wilderness.
11 They have made it a desolation;
    desolate, it mourns to me.
The whole land is made desolate,
    but no one lays it to heart.
12 Upon all the bare heights*c* in the
        desert
    spoilers have come;
for the sword of the LORD devours
    from one end of the land to the
        other;
    no one shall be safe.
13 They have sown wheat and have
        reaped thorns,
    they have tired themselves out but
        profit nothing.
They shall be ashamed of their*d*
    harvests

a Gk: Heb *to our future*   *b* Cn: Heb *Is the hyena, the bird of prey*   *c* Or *the trails*   *d* Heb *your*

12:1–6 Jeremiah's Second Complaint
See note at 11:18–23. In vv. 1–4, Jeremiah accuses God of allowing the wicked to prosper. This prayer may also voice the sentiments of those who experienced the exile, that God allowed Babylon to prosper.

12:5–6—God's response warns Jeremiah that yet more intense persecution awaits him. The book

of Jeremiah asserts that Judah's rejection of God's prophet is a cause of the exile.

12:7–13 God's Complaint
God laments the destruction of Judah.

12:7 *House*—This may refer to Judah or to the Jerusalem temple.

12:10 *Shepherds*—The kings of the nations attacking Judah.

because of the fierce anger of the LORD.

14 Thus says the LORD concerning all my evil neighbors who touch the heritage that I have given my people Israel to inherit: I am about to pluck them up from their land, and I will pluck up the house of Judah from among them. ¹⁵ And after I have plucked them up, I will again have compassion on them, and I will bring them again to their heritage and to their land, every one of them. ¹⁶ And then, if they will diligently learn the ways of my people, to swear by my name, "As the LORD lives," as they taught my people to swear by Baal, then they shall be built up in the midst of my people. ¹⁷ But if any nation will not listen, then I will completely uproot it and destroy it, says the LORD.

The Linen Loincloth

13 Thus said the LORD to me, "Go and buy yourself a linen loincloth, and put it on your loins, but do not dip it in water." ² So I bought a loincloth according to the word of the LORD, and put it on my loins. ³ And the word of the LORD came to me a second time, saying, ⁴ "Take the loincloth that you bought and are wearing, and go now to the Euphrates,ᵃ and hide it there in a cleft of the rock." ⁵ So I went, and hid it by the Euphrates,ᵃ as the LORD commanded me. ⁶ And after many days the LORD said to me, "Go now to the Euphrates,ᵃ and take from there the loincloth that I commanded you to hide there." ⁷ Then I

went to the Euphrates,ᵃ and dug, and I took the loincloth from the place where I had hidden it. But now the loincloth was ruined; it was good for nothing.

8 Then the word of the LORD came to me: ⁹ Thus says the LORD: Just so I will ruin the pride of Judah and the great pride of Jerusalem. ¹⁰ This evil people, who refuse to hear my words, who stubbornly follow their own will and have gone after other gods to serve them and worship them, shall be like this loincloth, which is good for nothing. ¹¹ For as the loincloth clings to one's loins, so I made the whole house of Israel and the whole house of Judah cling to me, says the LORD, in order that they might be for me a people, a name, a praise, and a glory. But they would not listen.

Symbol of the Wine-Jars

12 You shall speak to them this word: Thus says the LORD, the God of Israel: Every wine-jar should be filled with wine. And they will say to you, "Do you think we do not know that every wine-jar should be filled with wine?" ¹³ Then you shall say to them: Thus says the LORD: I am about to fill all the inhabitants of this land—the kings who sit on David's throne, the priests, the prophets, and all the inhabitants of Jerusalem—with drunkenness. ¹⁴ And I will dash them one against another, parents and children together, says the LORD. I will not pity or spare or have compassion when I destroy them.

ᵃ Or to Parah; Heb perath

12:14–17 The Nations

These verses use language from 1:10 to assert God's sovereignty over the nations and announce God's intent to restore Judah after the exile.

13:1–11 A Linen Loincloth

Frequently Israel's prophets illustrated their message by performing a symbolic act. This incident is the first of several sign acts in the book of Jeremiah.

13:6—It is doubtful that Jeremiah journeyed to the *Euphrates* River in Babylon. The Hebrew, *perath,* may indicate a river just north of Jerusalem.

13:9–11—Two interpretations of the symbolic act are offered. The first (vv. 10–11) signals God's intention to *ruin* Judah for its apostasy. A second expresses hope that, just as a *loincloth* clings to one's body, so Judah might *cling to* God, that is obey. Verse 11 suggests that this hope was disappointed.

13:12–14 A Proverb

These verses build on the proverb in v. 12, but just what is implied is difficult to discern. The proverb may express either a truism (what else would one do with *wine-jars*!) or complacency (of course, God will always bless us).

Exile Threatened

15 Hear and give ear; do not be
        haughty,
    for the LORD has spoken.
16 Give glory to the LORD your God
        before he brings darkness,
    and before your feet stumble
        on the mountains at twilight;
    while you look for light,
        he turns it into gloom
        and makes it deep darkness.
17 But if you will not listen,
        my soul will weep in secret for
            your pride;
    my eyes will weep bitterly and run
            down with tears,
        because the LORD's flock has been
            taken captive.

18 Say to the king and the queen
            mother:
    "Take a lowly seat,
    for your beautiful crown
        has come down from your head."*a*
19 The towns of the Negeb are shut up
        with no one to open them;
    all Judah is taken into exile,
        wholly taken into exile.

20 Lift up your eyes and see
        those who come from the north.
    Where is the flock that was given
            you,
        your beautiful flock?
21 What will you say when they set as
            head over you
        those whom you have trained
            to be your allies?
    Will not pangs take hold of you,
        like those of a woman in labor?

22 And if you say in your heart,
    "Why have these things come
            upon me?"
    it is for the greatness of your
            iniquity
    that your skirts are lifted up,
        and you are violated.
23 Can Ethiopians*b* change their skin
        or leopards their spots?
    Then also you can do good
        who are accustomed to do evil.
24 I will scatter you*c* like chaff
        driven by the wind from the
            desert.
25 This is your lot,
        the portion I have measured out to
            you, says the LORD,
    because you have forgotten me
        and trusted in lies.
26 I myself will lift up your skirts over
            your face,
        and your shame will be seen.
27 I have seen your abominations,
        your adulteries and neighings,
            your shameless prostitutions
        on the hills of the countryside.
    Woe to you, O Jerusalem!
        How long will it be
        before you are made clean?

The Great Drought

14 The word of the LORD that came
    to Jeremiah concerning the
drought:
2 Judah mourns
        and her gates languish;
    they lie in gloom on the ground,
        and the cry of Jerusalem goes up.

a Gk Syr Vg: Meaning of Heb uncertain *b* Or *Nubians*; Heb *Cushites*
c Heb *them*

13:15–27 Exile Threatened

These verses include three oracles, all of which
threaten God's judgment through exile.

13:15–17—This call for Judah to repent concludes with a further expression of divine grief.
Verse 16 may reflect the curse for disobedience
in Deut. 28:29.

13:18–19 *Queen mother*—The mother of the
reigning king may have had considerable power
(see 1 Kgs. 2:19; 2 Kgs. 11:1–3).

13:20–27—The reference to *the north* introduces
the concern of these verses, Babylon's imminent
invasion (see note at 1:13)

13:26–27—The references to *prostitution* condemn Judah's participation in cult prostitution
associated with the worship of fertility deities.

14:1–6 Judgment

Judgment takes the form of a drought so severe
that even wealthy nobility are impacted. Drought
is one of the curses for disobedience in Deut.
28:23–24.

3 Her nobles send their servants for
          water;
     they come to the cisterns,
they find no water,
     they return with their vessels
          empty.
They are ashamed and dismayed
     and cover their heads,
4 because the ground is cracked.
     Because there has been no rain on
          the land
the farmers are dismayed;
     they cover their heads.
5 Even the doe in the field forsakes her
          newborn fawn
     because there is no grass.
6 The wild asses stand on the bare
          heights,ᵃ
     they pant for air like jackals;
their eyes fail
     because there is no herbage.

7 Although our iniquities testify
          against us,
     act, O LORD, for your name's sake;
our apostasies indeed are many,
     and we have sinned against you.
8 O hope of Israel,
     its savior in time of trouble,
why should you be like a stranger in
          the land,
     like a traveler turning aside for the
          night?
9 Why should you be like someone
          confused,
     like a mighty warrior who cannot
          give help?
Yet you, O LORD, are in the midst
          of us,
     and we are called by your name;
     do not forsake us!

10 Thus says the LORD concerning this
     people:

Truly they have loved to wander,
     they have not restrained their
          feet;
therefore the LORD does not accept
          them,
     now he will remember their
          iniquity
     and punish their sins.

11 The LORD said to me: Do not pray
for the welfare of this people. 12 Although
they fast, I do not hear their cry, and
although they offer burnt offering and
grain offering, I do not accept them; but
by the sword, by famine, and by pestilence I consume them.

Denunciation of Lying Prophets

13 Then I said: "Ah, Lord GOD! Here
are the prophets saying to them, 'You
shall not see the sword, nor shall you have
famine, but I will give you true peace in
this place.'" 14 And the LORD said to me:
The prophets are prophesying lies in my
name; I did not send them, nor did I
command them or speak to them. They
are prophesying to you a lying vision,
worthless divination, and the deceit of
their own minds. 15 Therefore thus says
the LORD concerning the prophets who
prophesy in my name though I did not
send them, and who say, "Sword and
famine shall not come on this land":
By sword and famine those prophets
shall be consumed. 16 And the people to
whom they prophesy shall be thrown
out into the streets of Jerusalem, victims
of famine and sword. There shall be no
one to bury them—themselves, their
wives, their sons, and their daughters.
For I will pour out their wickedness
upon them.

ᵃ Or the trails

14:7–10 Judah's Confession Rejected
Judah confesses and pleads for deliverance. The
questions in vv. 8–9 urge God to act by challenging God's character and integrity. God, however,
rejects Judah's pleas because rather than obeying
God, Judah *loved to wander*.

14:11–12—See note at 7:16–20.

14:13–16 Lying Prophets
Jeremiah repeatedly condemns prophets who
ignore Judah's apostasy and social oppression
and promise Judah a secure future.

14:16 *No one to bury them*—See the curses for
disobedience in Deut. 28:26.

17 You shall say to them this word:
　　Let my eyes run down with tears
　　　　night and day,
　　　and let them not cease,
　　for the virgin daughter—my
　　　　people—is struck down with a
　　　　crushing blow,
　　with a very grievous wound.
18 If I go out into the field,
　　look—those killed by the sword!
　And if I enter the city,
　　look—those sick with*a* famine!
　For both prophet and priest ply their
　　　trade throughout the land,
　　and have no knowledge.

The People Plead for Mercy

19 Have you completely rejected Judah?
　　Does your heart loathe Zion?
　Why have you struck us down
　　so that there is no healing for us?
　We look for peace, but find no good;
　　for a time of healing, but there is
　　　terror instead.
20 We acknowledge our wickedness,
　　O Lord,
　　the iniquity of our ancestors,
　　for we have sinned against you.
21 Do not spurn us, for your name's
　　　sake;
　　do not dishonor your glorious
　　　throne;
　　remember and do not break your
　　　covenant with us.
22 Can any idols of the nations bring
　　rain?

Or can the heavens give showers?
　Is it not you, O Lord our God?
　We set our hope on you,
　　for it is you who do all this.

Punishment Is Inevitable

15 Then the Lord said to me:
Though Moses and Samuel stood
before me, yet my heart would not turn
toward this people. Send them out of my
sight, and let them go! 2 And when they
say to you, "Where shall we go?" you
shall say to them: Thus says the Lord:
　Those destined for pestilence, to
　　　pestilence,
　and those destined for the sword,
　　to the sword;
　those destined for famine, to famine,
　　and those destined for captivity, to
　　　captivity.
3 And I will appoint over them four
kinds of destroyers, says the Lord: the
sword to kill, the dogs to drag away, and
the birds of the air and the wild animals
of the earth to devour and destroy. 4 I
will make them a horror to all the kingdoms of the earth because of what King
Manasseh son of Hezekiah of Judah did
in Jerusalem.

5 Who will have pity on you,
　　O Jerusalem,
　or who will bemoan you?
　Who will turn aside
　　to ask about your welfare?

a Heb look—the sicknesses of

14:17–18 God's Grief Again

While the speaker may be Jeremiah or God, in
either case we hear God's grief over Judah's judgment.

14:19–22 The People Pray

The people pray with multiple purposes: to
complain (v. 19), to confess (v. 20), to plead
for deliverance (v. 21), to assert confidence in
YHWH (v. 22).

14:21 *Your glorious throne*—A reference to
Jerusalem. While Judah pleads with God not to
break covenant, the book indicates that Judah
has repeatedly broken covenant through apostasy
and social injustice, so that God's remembrance
of covenant (v. 10) will bring judgment on Judah.

Like other Old Testament prophetic books, the
book of Jeremiah is certain of the moral coherence of God's world. Whether by God's direct
intervention or by the working out of the moral
order inherent in God's creation, this book is
confident that breaking relationship with God by
injustice and idolatry will result in disaster. The
apostle Paul summarizes this claim in a phrase:
"The wages of sin is death" (Rom. 6:23).

15:1–9 Punishment to Come

15:1–4—*Moses and Samuel* are recalled because
of their role as mediators between God and Israel. God rejects any effort by Jeremiah to intercede
on Judah's behalf. Judgment is inevitable.

15:4 *King Manasseh*—Condemned in 2 Kgs.
21:1–18 for allowing apostasy to flourish.

6 You have rejected me, says the LORD,
   you are going backward;
so I have stretched out my hand
      against you and destroyed
      you—
   I am weary of relenting.
7 I have winnowed them with a
      winnowing fork
   in the gates of the land;
I have bereaved them, I have
      destroyed my people;
   they did not turn from their ways.
8 Their widows became more
      numerous
   than the sand of the seas;
I have brought against the mothers
      of youths
   a destroyer at noonday;
I have made anguish and terror
   fall upon her suddenly.
9 She who bore seven has languished;
   she has swooned away;
her sun went down while it was yet
      day;
   she has been shamed and
      disgraced.
And the rest of them I will give to
      the sword
   before their enemies,
                  says the LORD.

Jeremiah Complains Again
and Is Reassured

10 Woe is me, my mother, that you
ever bore me, a man of strife and contention to the whole land! I have not
lent, nor have I borrowed, yet all of
them curse me. 11 The LORD said: Surely

I have intervened in your life*a* for good,
surely I have imposed enemies on you
in a time of trouble and in a time of distress.*b* 12 Can iron and bronze break iron
from the north?

13 Your wealth and your treasures I
will give as plunder, without price, for
all your sins, throughout all your territory. 14 I will make you serve your enemies in a land that you do not know, for
in my anger a fire is kindled that shall
burn forever.
15 O LORD, you know;
   remember me and visit me,
   and bring down retribution for me
      on my persecutors.
In your forbearance do not take me
      away;
   know that on your account I suffer
      insult.
16 Your words were found, and I ate
      them,
   and your words became to me a joy
   and the delight of my heart;
for I am called by your name,
   O LORD, God of hosts.
17 I did not sit in the company of
      merrymakers,
   nor did I rejoice;
under the weight of your hand I sat
      alone,
   for you had filled me with
      indignation.
18 Why is my pain unceasing,
   my wound incurable,
   refusing to be healed?

a Heb *intervened with you* *b* Meaning of Heb uncertain

15:6–8—A reference to Assyrian and Egyptian
military victories over Judah in the century prior
to Jeremiah.

15:9 *Bore seven*—In 1 Sam. 2:5 and Ruth 4:15,
"seven children" are an indication of God's blessing. Judah will lose such blessing.

15:10–21 Jeremiah's Third Complaint
See note at 11:18–23.

15:10—Jeremiah, called to God's service from
the womb (1:5), regrets his birth because his
prophetic vocation has led to severe conflict (also
see 20:14–18).

15:12—This assurance suggests that the trouble

Jeremiah has experienced will prepare him for
the Babylonian invasion (*iron from the north*, cf.
1:18–19).

15:15–18—Jeremiah laments that despite his
faithfulness he experiences social ostracism.

15:16—Compare Ezek. 3:1–3. The images suggest these prophets were so filled with—that
is, consumed by—God's word that they were
compelled to proclaim it.

15:18 *Deceitful brook*—Jeremiah counters God's
claim in 2:13 to be a "fountain of living water."
Scriptural texts like this one give us warrant to express hurt and anger to God in prayer and liturgy.

Truly, you are to me like a deceitful
    brook,
  like waters that fail.

¹⁹ Therefore thus says the LORD:
If you turn back, I will take you back,
  and you shall stand before me.
If you utter what is precious, and not
    what is worthless,
  you shall serve as my mouth.
It is they who will turn to you,
  not you who will turn to them.
²⁰ And I will make you to this people
    a fortified wall of bronze;
they will fight against you,
  but they shall not prevail over you,
for I am with you
  to save you and deliver you,
               says the LORD.
²¹ I will deliver you out of the hand of
    the wicked,
  and redeem you from the grasp of
    the ruthless.

Jeremiah's Celibacy and Message

16 The word of the LORD came to me: ² You shall not take a wife, nor shall you have sons or daughters in this place. ³ For thus says the LORD concerning the sons and daughters who are born in this place, and concerning the mothers who bear them and the fathers who beget them in this land: ⁴ They shall die of deadly diseases. They shall not be lamented, nor shall they be buried; they shall become like dung on the surface of the ground. They shall perish by the sword and by famine, and their dead bodies shall become food for the birds of the air and for the wild animals of the earth.

5 For thus says the LORD: Do not enter the house of mourning, or go to lament, or bemoan them; for I have taken away my peace from this people, says the LORD, my steadfast love and mercy. ⁶ Both great and small shall die in this land; they shall not be buried, and no one shall lament for them; there shall be no gashing, no shaving of the head for them. ⁷ No one shall break bread*ᵃ* for the mourner, to offer comfort for the dead; nor shall anyone give them the cup of consolation to drink for their fathers or their mothers. ⁸ You shall not go into the house of feasting to sit with them, to eat and drink. ⁹ For thus says the LORD of hosts, the God of Israel: I am going to banish from this place, in your days and before your eyes, the voice of mirth and the voice of gladness, the voice of the bridegroom and the voice of the bride.

10 And when you tell this people all these words, and they say to you, "Why has the LORD pronounced all this great evil against us? What is our iniquity? What is the sin that we have committed against the LORD our God?" ¹¹ then you shall say to them: It is because your ancestors have forsaken me, says the LORD, and have gone after other gods and have served and worshiped them, and have forsaken me and have not kept my law; ¹² and because you have behaved worse than your ancestors, for here you are, every one of you, following your stubborn evil will, refusing to listen to me. ¹³ Therefore I will hurl you out of this land into a land that neither you nor your ancestors have known, and there you shall serve other gods day and night, for I will show you no favor.

ᵃ Two Mss Gk: MT break for them

15:19–21—God's response suggests that through his complaint Jeremiah had abandoned his prophetic vocation, to which God calls him to return. **15:20–21** *Bronze*—Recalls 1:17–18 (also see v. 12 above). God promises to protect Jeremiah, not to end the conflict that surrounds him.

16:1–13 The End of Judah

16:1–4—By not marrying or having children, Jeremiah signals that Judah has no future (see 7:34).

16:4—Compare the curses for disobedience in Deut. 28:22, 26.

16:5—Refusal to participate in Judah's funeral rites is an indication of the disgrace of the deceased. *Steadfast love and mercy*—See Exod. 34:6–7. God's enduring loyalty had sustained the relationship with God's people but will no longer.

God Will Restore Israel

14 Therefore, the days are surely coming, says the LORD, when it shall no longer be said, "As the LORD lives who brought the people of Israel up out of the land of Egypt," 15 but "As the LORD lives who brought the people of Israel up out of the land of the north and out of all the lands where he had driven them." For I will bring them back to their own land that I gave to their ancestors.

16 I am now sending for many fishermen, says the LORD, and they shall catch them; and afterward I will send for many hunters, and they shall hunt them from every mountain and every hill, and out of the clefts of the rocks. 17 For my eyes are on all their ways; they are not hidden from my presence, nor is their iniquity concealed from my sight. 18 And[a] I will doubly repay their iniquity and their sin, because they have polluted my land with the carcasses of their detestable idols, and have filled my inheritance with their abominations.

19 O LORD, my strength and my
    stronghold,
  my refuge in the day of trouble,
to you shall the nations come
    from the ends of the earth and say:
Our ancestors have inherited
    nothing but lies,
  worthless things in which there is
    no profit.
20 Can mortals make for themselves
    gods?
  Such are no gods!

21 "Therefore I am surely going to teach them, this time I am going to teach them my power and my might, and they shall know that my name is the LORD."

Judah's Sin and Punishment

17 The sin of Judah is written with an iron pen; with a diamond point it is engraved on the tablet of their hearts, and on the horns of their altars, 2 while their children remember their altars and their sacred poles,[b] beside every green tree, and on the high hills, 3 on the mountains in the open country. Your wealth and all your treasures I will give for spoil as the price of your sin[c] throughout all your territory. 4 By your own act you shall lose the heritage that I gave you, and I will make you serve your enemies in a land that you do not know, for in my anger a fire is kindled[d] that shall burn forever.

5 Thus says the LORD:
Cursed are those who trust in mere
    mortals
  and make mere flesh their
    strength,
  whose hearts turn away from the
    LORD.
6 They shall be like a shrub in the
    desert,
  and shall not see when relief
    comes.
They shall live in the parched places
    of the wilderness,
  in an uninhabited salt land.

[a] Gk: Heb *And first*   [b] Heb *Asherim*   [c] Cn: Heb *spoil your high places for sin*
[d] Two Mss Theodotion: *you kindled*

16:14–21 Restoration after Judgment

16:14–15—After Judah's judgment, God promises a new deliverance that will supplant memory of the exodus.

16:16 *Fishermen . . . hunters*—The references are obscure. This may refer to the nations whom God will send to judge Judah. However, it is also possible that vv. 16–18 indicate God's judgment of the nations.

16:18 *Doubly repay their iniquity*—Cf. Isa. 40:2.

16:19–20—After Judah is restored, the nations will turn to God. Cf. Isa. 2:3; Mic. 4:2.

16:21 *Teach them*—That is, the nations. This likely continues v. 18.

17:1–11 Judah's Heart Problem

17:1–4 *Tablet of their hearts*—An allusion to Sinai, where God's commandments were carved in stone (Exod. 24:12; 31:18). Jeremiah asserts that there is a problem with Judah's heart (also see Jer. 4:4, 14). They do not will to obey God. In the future God will write *torah* on their hearts (31:23).

17:5–8—This poem is similar to Ps. 1. It is linked to the prior verses by the reference to *hearts* in v. 5.

7 Blessed are those who trust in the
  LORD,
    whose trust is the LORD.
8 They shall be like a tree planted by
  water,
    sending out its roots by the stream.
  It shall not fear when heat comes,
    and its leaves shall stay green;
  in the year of drought it is not
    anxious,
    and it does not cease to bear fruit.

9 The heart is devious above all else;
    it is perverse—
    who can understand it?
10 I the LORD test the mind
    and search the heart,
  to give to all according to their
    ways,
    according to the fruit of their
    doings.

11 Like the partridge hatching what it
    did not lay,
  so are all who amass wealth
    unjustly;
  in mid-life it will leave them,
    and at their end they will prove to
    be fools.

12 O glorious throne, exalted from the
    beginning,
    shrine of our sanctuary!
13 O hope of Israel! O LORD!
  All who forsake you shall be put to
    shame;

those who turn away from you[a]
    shall be recorded in the
    underworld,[b]
  for they have forsaken the fountain
    of living water, the LORD.

Jeremiah Prays for Vindication

14 Heal me, O LORD, and I shall be
    healed;
    save me, and I shall be saved;
    for you are my praise.
15 See how they say to me,
    "Where is the word of the LORD?
    Let it come!"
16 But I have not run away from being
    a shepherd[c] in your service,
    nor have I desired the fatal day.
  You know what came from my lips;
    it was before your face.
17 Do not become a terror to me;
    you are my refuge in the day of
    disaster;
18 Let my persecutors be shamed,
    but do not let me be shamed;
  let them be dismayed,
    but do not let me be dismayed;
  bring on them the day of disaster;
    destroy them with double
    destruction!

Hallow the Sabbath Day

19 Thus said the LORD to me: Go and
stand in the People's Gate, by which the
kings of Judah enter and by which they

a Heb me   b Or in the earth   c Meaning of Heb uncertain

17:8 *A tree planted by water*—Similar to the image of God as "a fountain of living water" in 2:13 (see 17:13 below).

17:9–11—Judah's defective *heart* perverts relationship not only with God but also with neighbors, who are exploited for economic gain (cf. 6:13; 7:5–7; 8:10; Isa. 10:1–4; Amos 8:4–6).

17:12–13 A Brief Hymn
The reference to *the fountain of living water* reflects 2:13 (also alluded to in vv. 7–8 above).

17:14–18 Jeremiah's Fourth Complaint
Jeremiah's prayer indicates he trusts God and expects God's protection from those who are persecuting him.

17:16—*Fatal day* (also see v. 18, *day of disaster*) refers to the Day of the Lord, when God would

establish sovereignty over the world. While popularly imagined as the time when Israel's enemies would be judged, the prophets interpreted the Day of the Lord as a time when God's people would be judged (see Amos 5:18; 8:9–14; Zeph. 1:14–18).

17:19–27 Sabbath
Observance of the Sabbath required the cessation of normal activities (see Exod. 20:8–11). After the exile of 587 BCE, observance of the Sabbath became an important way for Israel to retain their identity without the temple, land, or monarchy (see Neh. 13:15–22). For Jewish and Christian communities alike, Sabbath observance continues to be an important mark of distinction from the secular world.

go out, and in all the gates of Jerusalem, [20] and say to them: Hear the word of the LORD, you kings of Judah, and all Judah, and all the inhabitants of Jerusalem, who enter by these gates. [21] Thus says the LORD: For the sake of your lives, take care that you do not bear a burden on the sabbath day or bring it in by the gates of Jerusalem. [22] And do not carry a burden out of your houses on the sabbath or do any work, but keep the sabbath day holy, as I commanded your ancestors. [23] Yet they did not listen or incline their ear; they stiffened their necks and would not hear or receive instruction.

[24] But if you listen to me, says the LORD, and bring in no burden by the gates of this city on the sabbath day, but keep the sabbath day holy and do no work on it, [25] then there shall enter by the gates of this city kings[a] who sit on the throne of David, riding in chariots and on horses, they and their officials, the people of Judah and the inhabitants of Jerusalem; and this city shall be inhabited forever. [26] And people shall come from the towns of Judah and the places around Jerusalem, from the land of Benjamin, from the Shephelah, from the hill country, and from the Negeb, bringing burnt offerings and sacrifices, grain offerings and frankincense, and bringing thank offerings to the house of the LORD. [27] But if you do not listen to me, to keep the sabbath day holy, and to carry in no burden through the gates of Jerusalem on the sabbath day, then I will kindle a fire in its gates; it shall devour the palaces of Jerusalem and shall not be quenched.

The Potter and the Clay

18 The word that came to Jeremiah from the LORD: [2] "Come, go down to the potter's house, and there I will let you hear my words." [3] So I went down to the potter's house, and there he was working at his wheel. [4] The vessel he was making of clay was spoiled in the potter's hand, and he reworked it into another vessel, as seemed good to him.

[5] Then the word of the LORD came to me: [6] Can I not do with you, O house of Israel, just as this potter has done? says the LORD. Just like the clay in the potter's hand, so are you in my hand, O house of Israel. [7] At one moment I may declare concerning a nation or a kingdom, that I will pluck up and break down and destroy it, [8] but if that nation, concerning which I have spoken, turns from its evil, I will change my mind about the disaster that I intended to bring on it. [9] And at another moment I may declare concerning a nation or a kingdom that I will build and plant it, [10] but if it does evil in my sight, not listening to my voice, then I will change my mind about the good that I had intended to do to it. [11] Now, therefore, say to the people of Judah and the inhabitants of Jerusalem: Thus says the LORD: Look, I am a potter shaping evil against you and devising a plan against you. Turn now, all of you from your evil way, and amend your ways and your doings.

Israel's Stubborn Idolatry

[12] But they say, "It is no use! We will follow our own plans, and each of us will act according to the stubbornness of our evil will."

[13] Therefore thus says the LORD:
　　Ask among the nations:
　　Who has heard the like of this?

a Cn: Heb *kings and officials*

18:1–12 The Potter
The activity of a *potter* suggests God's sovereignty over the nations (1:5, 10). The incident holds out the possibility that Judah might yet repent.

18:7 *Pluck up and break down*—See 1:10. Through repentance, God's judgment can be averted.

18:9 *Build and plant*—Again, see 1:10. While God may purpose good for a nation, its failure to obey God will result in judgment.

18:11–12—Judah is afforded an opportunity to repent but will not.

18:13–17 Judah on Trial
These verses portray a trial in which God is both

The virgin Israel has done
  a most horrible thing.
14 Does the snow of Lebanon leave
    the crags of Sirion?[a]
  Do the mountain[b] waters run dry,[c]
    the cold flowing streams?
15 But my people have forgotten me,
    they burn offerings to a delusion;
  they have stumbled[d] in their ways,
    in the ancient roads,
  and have gone into bypaths,
    not the highway,
16 making their land a horror,
    a thing to be hissed at forever.
  All who pass by it are horrified
    and shake their heads.
17 Like the wind from the east,
    I will scatter them before the
      enemy.
  I will show them my back, not my
      face,
    in the day of their calamity.

A Plot against Jeremiah

18 Then they said, "Come, let us make plots against Jeremiah—for instruction shall not perish from the priest, nor counsel from the wise, nor the word from the prophet. Come, let us bring charges against him,[e] and let us not heed any of his words."

19 Give heed to me, O Lord,
    and listen to what my adversaries
      say!
20 Is evil a recompense for good?
    Yet they have dug a pit for my life.
  Remember how I stood before you
    to speak good for them,
    to turn away your wrath from them.

21 Therefore give their children over to
    famine;
  hurl them out to the power of the
    sword,
  let their wives become childless and
    widowed.
  May their men meet death by
    pestilence,
  their youths be slain by the sword
    in battle.
22 May a cry be heard from their
    houses,
  when you bring the marauder
    suddenly upon them!
  For they have dug a pit to catch me,
    and laid snares for my feet.
23 Yet you, O Lord, know
    all their plotting to kill me.
  Do not forgive their iniquity,
    do not blot out their sin from your
      sight.
  Let them be tripped up before you;
    deal with them while you are
      angry.

The Broken Earthenware Jug

19 Thus said the Lord: Go and buy a potter's earthenware jug. Take with you[f] some of the elders of the people and some of the senior priests, 2 and go out to the valley of the son of Hinnom at the entry of the Potsherd Gate, and proclaim there the words that I tell you. 3 You shall say: Hear the word of the Lord, O kings of Judah and inhabitants of Jerusalem. Thus says the Lord of hosts, the God of Israel: I am going to

---

[a] Cn: Heb of the field [b] Cn: Heb foreign [c] Cn: Heb Are . . . plucked up?
[d] Gk Syr Vg: Heb they made them stumble [e] Heb strike him with the tongue
[f] Syr Tg Compare Gk: Heb lacks take with you

---

the prosecutor who queries witnesses (v. 13), and the judge who reaches a verdict (vv. 15–16) and pronounces a judgment (v. 17).

18:14–15 Sirion—Another name for Mount Hermon. The mountain **streams** observe God's ways, but God's **people** do not (see similar comparisons in 5:22 and 8:7).

18:18–23 Jeremiah's Fifth Complaint

Here Jeremiah seeks vengeance against his enemies (see note at 11:18–23). Such petitions are common in lament psalms (e.g., Pss. 5:10;

17:13–14; 64:7–8). However, vengeance is not enacted by the petitioner but is left to God.

19:1–15 The Earthenware Jug

This sign act is set just outside Jerusalem, where garbage was dumped.

19:3–5 Ears . . . will tingle—In 1 Sam. 3:11, Samuel uses this phrase to pronounce judgment against the priesthood. Here, Jeremiah condemns priests whom he holds accountable for Judah's idolatry.

bring such disaster upon this place that the ears of everyone who hears of it will tingle. ⁴Because the people have forsaken me, and have profaned this place by making offerings in it to other gods whom neither they nor their ancestors nor the kings of Judah have known, and because they have filled this place with the blood of the innocent, ⁵and gone on building the high places of Baal to burn their children in the fire as burnt offerings to Baal, which I did not command or decree, nor did it enter my mind; ⁶therefore the days are surely coming, says the LORD, when this place shall no more be called Topheth, or the valley of the son of Hinnom, but the valley of Slaughter. ⁷And in this place I will make void the plans of Judah and Jerusalem, and will make them fall by the sword before their enemies, and by the hand of those who seek their life. I will give their dead bodies for food to the birds of the air and to the wild animals of the earth. ⁸And I will make this city a horror, a thing to be hissed at; everyone who passes by it will be horrified and will hiss because of all its disasters. ⁹And I will make them eat the flesh of their sons and the flesh of their daughters, and all shall eat the flesh of their neighbors in the siege, and in the distress with which their enemies and those who seek their life afflict them.

10 Then you shall break the jug in the sight of those who go with you, ¹¹and shall say to them: Thus says the LORD of hosts: So will I break this people and this city, as one breaks a potter's vessel, so that it can never be mended. In Topheth they shall bury until there is no more room to bury. ¹²Thus will I do to this place, says the LORD, and to its inhabitants, making this city like Topheth. ¹³And the houses of Jerusalem and the houses of the kings of Judah shall be defiled like the place of Topheth—all the houses upon whose roofs offerings have been made to the whole host of heaven, and libations have been poured out to other gods.

14 When Jeremiah came from Topheth, where the LORD had sent him to prophesy, he stood in the court of the LORD's house and said to all the people: ¹⁵Thus says the LORD of hosts, the God of Israel: I am now bringing upon this city and upon all its towns all the disaster that I have pronounced against it, because they have stiffened their necks, refusing to hear my words.

Jeremiah Persecuted by Pashhur

20 Now the priest Pashhur son of Immer, who was chief officer in the house of the LORD, heard Jeremiah prophesying these things. ²Then Pashhur struck the prophet Jeremiah, and put him in the stocks that were in the upper Benjamin Gate of the house of the LORD. ³The next morning when Pashhur released Jeremiah from the stocks, Jeremiah said to him, The LORD has named you not Pashhur but "Terror-all-around." ⁴For thus says the LORD: I am making you a terror to yourself and to all your friends; and they shall fall by the sword of their enemies while you look on. And I will give all Judah into the hand of the king of Babylon; he shall carry them captive to Babylon, and shall

---

19:6–9—The consequences of Judah's idolatry and social injustice reflect curses for disobedience: v. 7, see Deut. 28:26; v. 8, see Deut. 28:25, 37; v. 9, see Deut. 28:53–54.

19:10–13—By breaking *the jug*, Jeremiah announces God's imminent destruction of Judah. In Ps. 2:9 breaking pottery symbolizes the destruction of a people.

20:1–6 Pashhur

Pashhur, a priest, having grasped the implica-

tions of Jeremiah breaking of the earthenware jug (vv. 1–2), has the prophet placed *in stocks*. When released, Jeremiah harshly condemns Pashhur (vv. 3–6).

20:3 *Terror-all-around*—Cf. 6:25. Names suggested the character or destiny of persons (e.g., Gen. 25:26; 32:28). Also, the one giving a name claimed sovereignty (e.g., 2 Kgs. 24:17; Gen. 2:19–20). By renaming Pashhur, Jeremiah asserts God's sovereignty over him and indicates the judgment he and Judah will face.

kill them with the sword. [5] I will give all the wealth of this city, all its gains, all its prized belongings, and all the treasures of the kings of Judah into the hand of their enemies, who shall plunder them, and seize them, and carry them to Babylon. [6] And you, Pashhur, and all who live in your house, shall go into captivity, and to Babylon you shall go; there you shall die, and there you shall be buried, you and all your friends, to whom you have prophesied falsely.

Jeremiah Denounces His Persecutors

[7] O LORD, you have enticed me,
  and I was enticed;
  you have overpowered me,
    and you have prevailed.
  I have become a laughingstock all
    day long;
    everyone mocks me.
[8] For whenever I speak, I must cry
    out,
  I must shout, "Violence and
    destruction!"
  For the word of the LORD has
    become for me
  a reproach and derision all day
    long.
[9] If I say, "I will not mention him,
  or speak any more in his name,"
  then within me there is something
    like a burning fire
  shut up in my bones;
  I am weary with holding it in,
    and I cannot.
[10] For I hear many whispering:

"Terror is all around!
Denounce him! Let us denounce
    him!"
  All my close friends
  are watching for me to stumble.
"Perhaps he can be enticed,
  and we can prevail against him,
  and take our revenge on him."
[11] But the LORD is with me like a dread
    warrior;
  therefore my persecutors will
    stumble,
  and they will not prevail.
They will be greatly shamed,
  for they will not succeed.
Their eternal dishonor
  will never be forgotten.
[12] O LORD of hosts, you test the
    righteous,
  you see the heart and the mind;
  let me see your retribution upon
    them,
  for to you I have committed my
    cause.

[13] Sing to the LORD;
  praise the LORD!
For he has delivered the life of the
    needy
  from the hands of evildoers.

[14] Cursed be the day
  on which I was born!
The day when my mother bore me,
  let it not be blessed!
[15] Cursed be the man
  who brought the news to my
    father, saying,

20:7–13 Jeremiah's Sixth Complaint
Jeremiah brings harsh accusations against God (see notes at 11:18–23 and 15:18).

20:7—Entice may suggest simple deception (1 Kgs. 22:20–21; Prov. 16:29). However, the word can also imply seduction (Exod. 22:16–17) and even rape (Deut. 22:25–27; 2 Sam. 13:14).

20:10 Terror is all around!—Cf. v. 3. Because of the threats of judgment he announces, Jeremiah is the object of a whispering campaign. Jeremiah is **enticed** by both God and the people to whom he speaks God's word. His prophetic office places Jeremiah awkwardly between God and God's people.

20:11–13—Prayers of complaint frequently conclude with expressions of confidence in God's deliverance (e.g., Pss. 22:22–31; 54:4–7).

20:14–18 Jeremiah's Seventh Complaint
See note at 11:18–23.

20:14–15 Cursed be the day—Jeremiah, who announces curses because of Judah's disobedience, also sees his own life as cursed. While Jeremiah shares God's pathos (e.g., 8:18–21), he also shares in the suffering of the people to whom he announces God's judgment.

"A child is born to you, a son,"
 making him very glad.
16 Let that man be like the cities
  that the LORD overthrew without
   pity;
 let him hear a cry in the morning
  and an alarm at noon,
17 because he did not kill me in the
   womb;
 so my mother would have been my
   grave,
 and her womb forever great.
18 Why did I come forth from the womb
 to see toil and sorrow,
 and spend my days in shame?

Jerusalem Will Fall to Nebuchadrezzar

21 This is the word that came to Jeremiah from the LORD, when King Zedekiah sent to him Pashhur son of Malchiah and the priest Zephaniah son of Maaseiah, saying, 2 "Please inquire of the LORD on our behalf, for King Nebuchadrezzar of Babylon is making war against us; perhaps the LORD will perform a wonderful deed for us, as he has often done, and will make him withdraw from us."

3 Then Jeremiah said to them: 4 Thus you shall say to Zedekiah: Thus says the LORD, the God of Israel: I am going to turn back the weapons of war that are in your hands and with which you are fighting against the king of Babylon and against the Chaldeans who are besieging you outside the walls; and I will bring them together into the center of this city. 5 I myself will fight against you with outstretched hand and mighty arm, in anger, in fury, and in great wrath. 6 And I will strike down the inhabitants of this city, both human beings and animals; they shall die of a great pestilence. 7 Afterward, says the LORD, I will give King Zedekiah of Judah, and his servants, and the people in this city—those who survive the pestilence, sword, and famine—into the hands of King Nebuchadrezzar of Babylon, into the hands of their enemies, into the hands of those who seek their lives. He shall strike them down with the edge of the sword; he shall not pity them, or spare them, or have compassion.

8 And to this people you shall say: Thus says the LORD: See, I am setting before you the way of life and the way of death. 9 Those who stay in this city shall die by the sword, by famine, and by pestilence; but those who go out and surrender to the Chaldeans who are besieging you shall live and shall have their lives as a prize of war. 10 For I have set my face against this city for evil and not for good, says the LORD: it shall be given into the hands of the king of Babylon, and he shall burn it with fire.

Message to the House of David

11 To the house of the king of Judah say: Hear the word of the LORD, 12 O house of David! Thus says the LORD:

20:18—God's claim on Jeremiah's life *from the womb* (1:5) was costly. Indeed, God's servants through the ages have testified to the cost of discipleship, including Christians such as the German theologian Dietrich Bonhoeffer, who resisted Adolf Hitler at the cost of his own life.

21:1–10 No Reprieve

21:1 *King Zedekiah* sends persons to Jeremiah hoping that the prophet might announce the deliverance of Judah (vv. 1–2). Jeremiah, however, announces no reprieve. *Pashhur*—This is not the priest Pashhur from chap. 20.

21:2 *Wonderful deeds*—In the Old Testament, God's acts of deliverance, including the exodus, are called "wonders" (see Exod. 3:20; 15:11; Pss.

9:1; 26:7; 86:10). Zedekiah hopes that God will deliver Judah.

21:5 *Outstretched hand and mighty arm*—This phrase describes God's exodus deliverance (see Exod. 6:6; Deut. 4:34; 5:15; 7:19; Ps. 136:12). Here Jeremiah reverses the sense of this image to announce God's judgment.

21:8—Israel's relationships with God and neighbor were choices of *life* and *death* (see Deut. 30:15–20). Judah had chosen death.

21:11–14 Judah's Kings

The next three chapters condemn the kings of Judah, who were to be God's agents of justice to protect persons from oppressors (e.g., see Ps.

Execute justice in the morning,
  and deliver from the hand of the
    oppressor
anyone who has been robbed,
or else my wrath will go forth like
    fire,
  and burn, with no one to quench it,
  because of your evil doings.

13 See, I am against you, O inhabitant
    of the valley,
  O rock of the plain,
                    says the LORD;
you who say, "Who can come down
    against us,
  or who can enter our places of
    refuge?"
14 I will punish you according to the
    fruit of your doings,
                    says the LORD;
  I will kindle a fire in its forest,
  and it shall devour all that is
    around it.

Exhortation to Repent

22 Thus says the LORD: Go down to
the house of the king of Judah,
and speak there this word, 2 and say: Hear
the word of the LORD, O King of Judah
sitting on the throne of David—you,
and your servants, and your people who
enter these gates. 3 Thus says the LORD:
Act with justice and righteousness, and
deliver from the hand of the oppressor
anyone who has been robbed. And do
no wrong or violence to the alien, the
orphan, and the widow, or shed innocent blood in this place. 4 For if you will

indeed obey this word, then through
the gates of this house shall enter kings
who sit on the throne of David, riding in
chariots and on horses, they, and their
servants, and their people. 5 But if you
will not heed these words, I swear by
myself, says the LORD, that this house
shall become a desolation. 6 For thus
says the LORD concerning the house of
the king of Judah:
  You are like Gilead to me,
    like the summit of Lebanon;
  but I swear that I will make you a
    desert,
    an uninhabited city.*a*
7 I will prepare destroyers against
    you,
  all with their weapons;
they shall cut down your choicest
    cedars
  and cast them into the fire.

8 And many nations will pass by this
city, and all of them will say one to
another, "Why has the LORD dealt in
this way with that great city?" 9 And they
will answer, "Because they abandoned
the covenant of the LORD their God,
and worshiped other gods and served
them."

10 Do not weep for him who is dead,
    nor bemoan him;
  weep rather for him who goes
    away,
    for he shall return no more
    to see his native land.

---

a Cn: Heb *uninhabited cities*

72:1–4, 12–14). While Judah's kings assumed
God's enduring protection (v. 13; cf. 2 Sam.
7:11–16), Jeremiah warns that kings will be
judged for their failure to execute justice (see
note at 22:3–5). Scripture takes it to be a general
and abiding principle that political leadership entails responsibility for the maintenance of equity
in society.

22:1–9 Duties of Kings

Jeremiah articulates the duty of Judah's kings to
act with justice and righteousness (v. 3). This
speech indicates the consequences if kings obey
(v. 4) or disobey (vv. 5–9) God's demand.

22:3–5—Jeremiah insists that the future of the

monarchy depends upon kings ordering society
justly. Those most socially vulnerable—the widow, orphan, and alien—are to be given particular
attention even as God paid particular attention
to the Hebrew slaves in Egypt. For Israel, justice
is not the blind equality of Western judicial practice, but an eyes-wide-open attention to those in
need.

22:6–7 *Gilead . . . the summit of Lebanon*—
These heavily wooded areas are used here
as symbols for the royal palace that will be
destroyed.

22:10–12 End of the Monarchy

Message to the Sons of Josiah

11 For thus says the Lord concerning Shallum son of King Josiah of Judah, who succeeded his father Josiah, and who went away from this place: He shall return here no more, ¹²but in the place where they have carried him captive he shall die, and he shall never see this land again.

¹³ Woe to him who builds his house by
        unrighteousness,
    and his upper rooms by injustice;
    who makes his neighbors work for
        nothing,
    and does not give them their
        wages;
¹⁴ who says, "I will build myself a
        spacious house
    with large upper rooms,"
    and who cuts out windows for it,
        paneling it with cedar,
        and painting it with vermilion.
¹⁵ Are you a king
        because you compete in cedar?
    Did not your father eat and drink
        and do justice and righteousness?
        Then it was well with him.
¹⁶ He judged the cause of the poor and
        needy;
        then it was well.
    Is not this to know me?
        says the Lord.
¹⁷ But your eyes and heart
        are only on your dishonest gain,

    for shedding innocent blood,
        and for practicing oppression and
            violence.
¹⁸ Therefore thus says the Lord concerning King Jehoiakim son of Josiah of Judah:
    They shall not lament for him,
        saying,
        "Alas, my brother!" or "Alas,
            sister!"
    They shall not lament for him,
        saying,
        "Alas, lord!" or "Alas, his majesty!"
¹⁹ With the burial of a donkey he shall
        be buried—
    dragged off and thrown out
        beyond the gates of Jerusalem.

²⁰ Go up to Lebanon, and cry out,
    and lift up your voice in Bashan;
    cry out from Abarim,
        for all your lovers are crushed.
²¹ I spoke to you in your prosperity,
        but you said, "I will not listen."
    This has been your way from your
        youth,
        for you have not obeyed my voice.
²² The wind shall shepherd all your
        shepherds,
    and your lovers shall go into
        captivity;
    then you will be ashamed and
        dismayed
        because of all your wickedness.
²³ O inhabitant of Lebanon,
        nested among the cedars,

22:11—*Shallum* is the personal name for King Jehoahaz, who ruled Judah briefly in 609 before being deported by the Egyptians who had defeated his father, *Josiah*. In v. 10, Josiah is the king who is *dead*; Shallum the king who went away.

22:13–19 An Unjust King and His End

22:13—The king forced laborers to construct a royal palace without paying *their wages* (cf. vv. 3–4).

22:14—The palace is extravagant—two stories with large windows, expensive woods and wall coverings. The opulence of the palace makes the exploitation of the workers building it more appalling.

22:15–17—Judah's kings are agents of the God who delivered slaves from oppression in Egypt.

What makes a king is not the trappings of royalty but administration of justice for persons on the social margins, *the poor and needy*. Then and now, the wretched of the earth are the primary victims of corrupt government.

22:18–19—The exploitative king will not be mourned because he has not been a *brother* to the citizens of Judah. The disposal of the king's body in the city garbage heap is a curse for disobedience (Deut. 28:26) befitting his failure to obey God.

22:20–23 Judgment on Jerusalem

Jerusalem is personified as one deserted by her *lovers* (see 2:32–33).

22:23—God's judgment, like a woman's *labor*, is irresistible and unstoppable.

how you will groan*a* when pangs
　　come upon you,
　　pain as of a woman in labor!

Judgment on Coniah (Jehoiachin)

24 As I live, says the LORD, even if
King Coniah son of Jehoiakim of Judah
were the signet ring on my right hand,
even from there I would tear you off
25 and give you into the hands of those
who seek your life, into the hands of
those of whom you are afraid, even into
the hands of King Nebuchadrezzar of
Babylon and into the hands of the Chaldeans. 26 I will hurl you and the mother
who bore you into another country,
where you were not born, and there you
shall die. 27 But they shall not return to
the land to which they long to return.

28　Is this man Coniah a despised
　　　　broken pot,
　　a vessel no one wants?
　Why are he and his offspring hurled
　　　　out
　　　and cast away in a land that they
　　　　do not know?
29　O land, land, land,
　　hear the word of the LORD!
30　Thus says the LORD:
　　Record this man as childless,
　　　a man who shall not succeed in his
　　　　days;
　　for none of his offspring shall
　　　　succeed
　　in sitting on the throne of David,
　　and ruling again in Judah.

Restoration after Exile

23 Woe to the shepherds who
destroy and scatter the sheep of
my pasture! says the LORD. 2 Therefore

thus says the LORD, the God of Israel,
concerning the shepherds who shepherd
my people: It is you who have scattered
my flock, and have driven them away,
and you have not attended to them. So
I will attend to you for your evil doings,
says the LORD. 3 Then I myself will
gather the remnant of my flock out of
all the lands where I have driven them,
and I will bring them back to their fold,
and they shall be fruitful and multiply.
4 I will raise up shepherds over them
who will shepherd them, and they shall
not fear any longer, or be dismayed, nor
shall any be missing, says the LORD.

The Righteous Branch of David

5 The days are surely coming, says the
LORD, when I will raise up for David a
righteous Branch, and he shall reign as
king and deal wisely, and shall execute
justice and righteousness in the land.
6 In his days Judah will be saved and
Israel will live in safety. And this is the
name by which he will be called: "The
LORD is our righteousness."

7 Therefore, the days are surely coming, says the LORD, when it shall no
longer be said, "As the LORD lives who
brought the people of Israel up out of
the land of Egypt," 8 but "As the LORD
lives who brought out and led the offspring of the house of Israel out of the
land of the north and out of all the lands
where he*b* had driven them." Then they
shall live in their own land.

False Prophets of Hope Denounced

9 Concerning the prophets:
　My heart is crushed within me,

a Gk Vg Syr: Heb *will be pitied*　*b* Gk: Heb *I*

22:24–30 *King Coniah*—This is the throne name
for the exiled King Jehoiachin. This text claims
that he will *not return* from exile, nor will his
children ever rule Judah.

23:1–8 The Monarchy Restored

23:1 *Shepherds who destroy*—An indication
of the failure of Judah's kings (cf. Ezek. 34:1–10;
contrast Ezek. 34:11–31; John 10:1–18).

23:3—When restored, Judah will enjoy the bless-

ing God intended for humankind. Blessing is
expressed here in terms of childbirth drawn from
Gen. 1:28.

23:5–6—After the exile, God promises kings who
will establish *justice and righteousness*.

23:7–8—See note at 16:14–15.

23:9–40 Oracles against Prophets

23:9–12—This oracle condemns Judah's leaders,
both prophets and priests (v. 11).

all my bones shake;
I have become like a drunkard,
    like one overcome by wine,
because of the LORD
    and because of his holy words.
10 For the land is full of adulterers;
    because of the curse the land
        mourns,
    and the pastures of the wilderness
        are dried up.
Their course has been evil,
    and their might is not right.
11 Both prophet and priest are
        ungodly;
    even in my house I have found
        their wickedness,
                    says the LORD.
12 Therefore their way shall be to them
    like slippery paths in the darkness,
    into which they shall be driven
        and fall;
    for I will bring disaster upon them
    in the year of their punishment,
                    says the LORD.
13 In the prophets of Samaria
    I saw a disgusting thing:
they prophesied by Baal
    and led my people Israel astray.
14 But in the prophets of Jerusalem
    I have seen a more shocking thing:
they commit adultery and walk in
        lies;
    they strengthen the hands of
        evildoers,
    so that no one turns from
        wickedness;
all of them have become like Sodom
        to me,
    and its inhabitants like Gomorrah.
15 Therefore thus says the LORD of
        hosts concerning the prophets:

"I am going to make them eat
        wormwood,
    and give them poisoned water to
        drink;
for from the prophets of Jerusalem
    ungodliness has spread throughout
        the land."

16 Thus says the LORD of hosts: Do not listen to the words of the prophets who prophesy to you; they are deluding you. They speak visions of their own minds, not from the mouth of the LORD. 17 They keep saying to those who despise the word of the LORD, "It shall be well with you"; and to all who stubbornly follow their own stubborn hearts, they say, "No calamity shall come upon you."

18 For who has stood in the council of
        the LORD
    so as to see and to hear his word?
    Who has given heed to his word so
        as to proclaim it?
19 Look, the storm of the LORD!
    Wrath has gone forth,
a whirling tempest;
    it will burst upon the head of the
        wicked.
20 The anger of the LORD will not turn
        back
    until he has executed and
        accomplished
    the intents of his mind.
In the latter days you will
        understand it clearly.

21 I did not send the prophets,
    yet they ran;
I did not speak to them,
    yet they prophesied.
22 But if they had stood in my council,

23:10—In Gen. 6:13, the land is full of violent persons and the consequence is the flood—chaos. In this text, *adulterers* are those who have turned from YHWH to other gods, bringing *curses* for disobedience and the ruin of the land—chaos.

23:13–15—Unlike Jeremiah, Judah's other *prophets* encouraged apostasy. The result is that Judah will face judgment like *Sodom* and *Gomorrah* (Gen. 18:16–19:29).

23:16–22 *Visions of their own minds*—Jeremiah claims that prophets giving assurances to Judah were not authorized by God.

23:18 *Council of the LORD*—Also v. 22. This council, the divine council, is imagined as an assembly of divine beings over which YHWH presides and from which divine mandates come (cf. 1 Kgs. 22:19–23; Job 1–2; Ps. 82).

then they would have proclaimed
   my words to my people,
and they would have turned them
   from their evil way,
   and from the evil of their doings.

23 Am I a God near by, says the LORD, and not a God far off? 24 Who can hide in secret places so that I cannot see them? says the LORD. Do I not fill heaven and earth? says the LORD. 25 I have heard what the prophets have said who prophesy lies in my name, saying, "I have dreamed, I have dreamed!" 26 How long? Will the hearts of the prophets ever turn back—those who prophesy lies, and who prophesy the deceit of their own heart? 27 They plan to make my people forget my name by their dreams that they tell one another, just as their ancestors forgot my name for Baal. 28 Let the prophet who has a dream tell the dream, but let the one who has my word speak my word faithfully. What has straw in common with wheat? says the LORD. 29 Is not my word like fire, says the LORD, and like a hammer that breaks a rock in pieces? 30 See, therefore, I am against the prophets, says the LORD, who steal my words from one another. 31 See, I am against the prophets, says the LORD, who use their own tongues and say, "Says the LORD." 32 See, I am against those who prophesy lying dreams, says the LORD, and who tell them, and who lead my people astray by their lies and their recklessness, when I did not send them or appoint them; so they do not profit this people at all, says the LORD.

33 When this people, or a prophet, or a priest asks you, "What is the burden of the LORD?" you shall say to them, "You are the burden,[a] and I will cast you off, says the LORD." 34 And as for the prophet, priest, or the people who say, "The burden of the LORD," I will punish them and their households. 35 Thus shall you say to one another, among yourselves, "What has the LORD answered?" or "What has the LORD spoken?" 36 But "the burden of the LORD" you shall mention no more, for the burden is everyone's own word, and so you pervert the words of the living God, the LORD of hosts, our God. 37 Thus you shall ask the prophet, "What has the LORD answered you?" or "What has the LORD spoken?" 38 But if you say, "the burden of the LORD," thus says the LORD: Because you have said these words, "the burden of the LORD," when I sent to you, saying, You shall not say, "the burden of the LORD," 39 therefore, I will surely lift you up[b] and cast you away from my presence, you and the city that I gave to you and your ancestors. 40 And I will bring upon you everlasting disgrace and perpetual shame, which shall not be forgotten.

The Good and the Bad Figs

24 The LORD showed me two baskets of figs placed before the temple of the LORD. This was after King Nebuchadrezzar of Babylon had taken into exile from Jerusalem King Jeconiah son of Jehoiakim of Judah, together with the officials of Judah, the artisans, and the smiths, and had brought them to Babylon. 2 One basket had very good figs, like first-ripe figs, but the other basket

---

a Gk Vg: Heb *What burden*   *b* Heb Mss Gk Vg: MT *forget you*

23:23–32—Judah's prophets are misrepresenting God and leading Judah astray. They probably offered an optimistic message that contradicted Jeremiah's.

23:25 *I have dreamed*—Dreams were the medium through which prophets claimed a revelation from God.

23:33–40—This passage plays on various meanings of the word **burden**. The root meaning of the word is "lift up" (v. 39), but the word also means

something heavy one must bear. Finally "burden" is a technical term for a prophetic oracle.

24:1–10 The Good and Bad Figs

God shows Jeremiah *two baskets of figs* (vv. 1–2) that become the basis for a pronouncement about the future of those exiled to Babylon in 597 BCE (vv. 4–7) and those who remained in Jerusalem (vv. 8–10). *Jeconiah* is King Jehoiachin.

had very bad figs, so bad that they could not be eaten. ³ And the LORD said to me, "What do you see, Jeremiah?" I said, "Figs, the good figs very good, and the bad figs very bad, so bad that they cannot be eaten."

4 Then the word of the LORD came to me: ⁵ Thus says the LORD, the God of Israel: Like these good figs, so I will regard as good the exiles from Judah, whom I have sent away from this place to the land of the Chaldeans. ⁶ I will set my eyes upon them for good, and I will bring them back to this land. I will build them up, and not tear them down; I will plant them, and not pluck them up. ⁷ I will give them a heart to know that I am the LORD; and they shall be my people and I will be their God, for they shall return to me with their whole heart.

8 But thus says the LORD: Like the bad figs that are so bad they cannot be eaten, so will I treat King Zedekiah of Judah, his officials, the remnant of Jerusalem who remain in this land, and those who live in the land of Egypt. ⁹ I will make them a horror, an evil thing, to all the kingdoms of the earth— a disgrace, a byword, a taunt, and a curse in all the places where I shall drive them. ¹⁰ And I will send sword, famine, and pestilence upon them, until they are utterly destroyed from the land that I gave to them and their ancestors.

The Babylonian Captivity Foretold

25 The word that came to Jeremiah concerning all the people of Judah, in the fourth year of King Jehoiakim son of Josiah of Judah (that was the first year of King Nebuchadrezzar of Babylon), ² which the prophet Jeremiah spoke to all the people of Judah and all the inhabitants of Jerusalem: ³ For twenty-three years, from the thirteenth year of King Josiah son of Amon of Judah, to this day, the word of the LORD has come to me, and I have spoken persistently to you, but you have not listened. ⁴ And though the LORD persistently sent you all his servants the prophets, you have neither listened nor inclined your ears to hear ⁵ when they said, "Turn now, every one of you, from your evil way and wicked doings, and you will remain upon the land that the LORD has given to you and your ancestors from of old and forever; ⁶ do not go after other gods to serve and worship them, and do not provoke me to anger with the work of your hands. Then I will do you no harm." ⁷ Yet you did not listen to me, says the LORD, and so you have provoked me to anger with the work of your hands to your own harm.

8 Therefore thus says the LORD of hosts: Because you have not obeyed my words, ⁹ I am going to send for all the tribes of the north, says the LORD, even for King Nebuchadrezzar of Babylon, my servant, and I will bring them against this land and its inhabitants, and against all these nations around; I will utterly destroy them, and make them an object of horror and of hissing, and an everlasting disgrace.ᵃ ¹⁰ And I will banish from them the sound of mirth and the sound of gladness, the voice of the bridegroom and the voice of the bride, the sound of the millstones and the light

---

ᵃ Gk Compare Syr: Heb *and everlasting desolations*

24:6 *Build*—See 1:10. Ironically, those exiled and who appear to be judged by God are deemed "good," while those who remain in Judah are designated "bad." Judgment is necessary before there can be any hope of restoration.

24:7 *Heart*—God's judgment occurs because Judah's will ("heart") is set against God (see 4:4, 14; 17:1). When restored, God will transform Judah so they will be faithful to God (see 31:31–34).

24:8—*Zedekiah* is placed in power by Babylon after King Jehoiachin is exiled in 597 BCE. Those who remain in Judah after 597 imagine themselves to be favored by God since they seem to have escaped judgment, but this text claims that judgment is necessary before restoration is possible.

25:1–14 The Lord Sent Prophets

Judah's failure to heed God's prophets, including Jeremiah, is one reason for the exile.

of the lamp. ¹¹ This whole land shall become a ruin and a waste, and these nations shall serve the king of Babylon seventy years. ¹² Then after seventy years are completed, I will punish the king of Babylon and that nation, the land of the Chaldeans, for their iniquity, says the LORD, making the land an everlasting waste. ¹³ I will bring upon that land all the words that I have uttered against it, everything written in this book, which Jeremiah prophesied against all the nations. ¹⁴ For many nations and great kings shall make slaves of them also; and I will repay them according to their deeds and the work of their hands.

The Cup of God's Wrath

15 For thus the LORD, the God of Israel, said to me: Take from my hand this cup of the wine of wrath, and make all the nations to whom I send you drink it. ¹⁶ They shall drink and stagger and go out of their minds because of the sword that I am sending among them.

17 So I took the cup from the LORD's hand, and made all the nations to whom the LORD sent me drink it: ¹⁸ Jerusalem and the towns of Judah, its kings and officials, to make them a desolation and a waste, an object of hissing and of cursing, as they are today; ¹⁹ Pharaoh king of Egypt, his servants, his officials, and all his people; ²⁰ all the mixed people;[a] all the kings of the land of Uz; all the kings of the land of the Philistines—Ashkelon, Gaza, Ekron, and the remnant of Ash-

dod; ²¹ Edom, Moab, and the Ammonites; ²² all the kings of Tyre, all the kings of Sidon, and the kings of the coastland across the sea; ²³ Dedan, Tema, Buz, and all who have shaven temples; ²⁴ all the kings of Arabia and all the kings of the mixed peoples[a] that live in the desert; ²⁵ all the kings of Zimri, all the kings of Elam, and all the kings of Media; ²⁶ all the kings of the north, far and near, one after another, and all the kingdoms of the world that are on the face of the earth. And after them the king of Sheshach[b] shall drink.

27 Then you shall say to them, Thus says the LORD of hosts, the God of Israel: Drink, get drunk and vomit, fall and rise no more, because of the sword that I am sending among you.

28 And if they refuse to accept the cup from your hand to drink, then you shall say to them: Thus says the LORD of hosts: You must drink! ²⁹ See, I am beginning to bring disaster on the city that is called by my name, and how can you possibly avoid punishment? You shall not go unpunished, for I am summoning a sword against all the inhabitants of the earth, says the LORD of hosts.

30 You, therefore, shall prophesy against them all these words, and say to them:

The LORD will roar from on high,
    and from his holy habitation utter
        his voice;

---

[a] Meaning of Heb uncertain [b] Sheshach is a cryptogram for Babel, Babylon

---

25:12 *Seventy years*—The time of a normal life span (Ps. 90:10), so that those exiled would not live to return. This significant figure becomes a rich source of speculation for later generations as they struggle to make sense of their own experiences of oppression and exile (see, e.g., Dan. 9:2–27). Prophets more optimistic than Jeremiah indicated that the exile would be short (see 27:16; 28:3).

25:15–29 The Cup of God's Wrath
Another symbolic act that asserts God's sovereignty over the nations. In the Old Testament, a number of texts refer to a *cup of wrath* that God pours out on the wicked: Pss. 11:6; 75:8; Isa. 51:17; Lam. 4:21; Ezek. 23:31–34. This passage

anticipates Jer. 46–51, a series of oracles against nations. Christians inevitably will compare this cup to the eucharistic cup of blessing and life. It is likely that the church too deserves the cup of judgment from which the nations are forced to drink in this passage, but is offered another cup only because of God's graciousness.

25:26 *Sheshach*—The word is Babylon (Babel) spelled in reverse Hebrew alphabetized order. Babylon was so terrible that one needed to be careful about even speaking the name.

25:30–38 Judgment of the Nations
God's judgment of the nations (vv. 30–33) results in lamentation (vv. 34–38).

he will roar mightily against his fold,
   and shout, like those who tread
      grapes,
   against all the inhabitants of the
      earth.
31 The clamor will resound to the ends
      of the earth,
   for the LORD has an indictment
      against the nations;
   he is entering into judgment with all
      flesh,
   and the guilty he will put to the
      sword,
                says the LORD.

32 Thus says the LORD of hosts:
   See, disaster is spreading
      from nation to nation,
   and a great tempest is stirring
      from the farthest parts of the
      earth!
33 Those slain by the LORD on that day
shall extend from one end of the earth to
the other. They shall not be lamented, or
gathered, or buried; they shall become
dung on the surface of the ground.
34 Wail, you shepherds, and cry out;
   roll in ashes, you lords of the flock,
   for the days of your slaughter have
      come—and your dispersions,[a]
   and you shall fall like a choice
      vessel.
35 Flight shall fail the shepherds,
   and there shall be no escape for
      the lords of the flock.
36 Hark! the cry of the shepherds,
   and the wail of the lords of the
      flock!
   For the LORD is despoiling their
      pasture,
37 and the peaceful folds are
      devastated,
   because of the fierce anger of the
      LORD.

38 Like a lion he has left his covert;
   for their land has become a waste
   because of the cruel sword,
      and because of his fierce anger.

Jeremiah's Prophecies in the Temple

26 At the beginning of the reign of King Jehoiakim son of Josiah of Judah, this word came from the LORD: ² Thus says the LORD: Stand in the court of the LORD's house, and speak to all the cities of Judah that come to worship in the house of the LORD; speak to them all the words that I command you; do not hold back a word. ³ It may be that they will listen, all of them, and will turn from their evil way, that I may change my mind about the disaster that I intend to bring on them because of their evil doings. ⁴ You shall say to them: Thus says the LORD: If you will not listen to me, to walk in my law that I have set before you, ⁵ and to heed the words of my servants the prophets whom I send to you urgently—though you have not heeded— ⁶ then I will make this house like Shiloh, and I will make this city a curse for all the nations of the earth.

7 The priests and the prophets and all the people heard Jeremiah speaking these words in the house of the LORD. ⁸ And when Jeremiah had finished speaking all that the LORD had commanded him to speak to all the people, then the priests and the prophets and all the people laid hold of him, saying, "You shall die! ⁹ Why have you prophesied in the name of the LORD, saying, 'This house shall be like Shiloh, and this city shall be desolate, without inhabitant'?" And all the people gathered around Jeremiah in the house of the LORD.

10 When the officials of Judah heard

[a] Meaning of Heb uncertain

25:34 *Shepherds*—Kings of the nations.
26:1–24 Jeremiah on Trial
Jeremiah 26 recounts an occasion when Jeremiah spoke at the Jerusalem temple (vv. 1–6). It also recounts various reactions to this speech (vv. 7–24). Jeremiah 7 may reflect this same event,

emphasizing the words Jeremiah spoke. Here the emphasis is on the reactions to Jeremiah's speech.
26:7–11—The prophets and priests who hear Jeremiah accuse him of treason, for which the punishment is death (vv. 8, 11).

these things, they came up from the king's house to the house of the LORD and took their seat in the entry of the New Gate of the house of the LORD. ¹¹ Then the priests and the prophets said to the officials and to all the people, "This man deserves the sentence of death because he has prophesied against this city, as you have heard with your own ears."

12 Then Jeremiah spoke to all the officials and all the people, saying, "It is the LORD who sent me to prophesy against this house and this city all the words you have heard. ¹³ Now therefore amend your ways and your doings, and obey the voice of the LORD your God, and the LORD will change his mind about the disaster that he has pronounced against you. ¹⁴ But as for me, here I am in your hands. Do with me as seems good and right to you. ¹⁵ Only know for certain that if you put me to death, you will be bringing innocent blood upon yourselves and upon this city and its inhabitants, for in truth the LORD sent me to you to speak all these words in your ears."

16 Then the officials and all the people said to the priests and the prophets, "This man does not deserve the sentence of death, for he has spoken to us in the name of the LORD our God." ¹⁷ And some of the elders of the land arose and said to all the assembled people, ¹⁸ "Micah of Moresheth, who prophesied during the days of King Hezekiah of Judah, said to all the people of Judah: 'Thus says the LORD of hosts,

    Zion shall be plowed as a field;

    Jerusalem shall become a heap of
       ruins,
    and the mountain of the house a
       wooded height.'

¹⁹ Did King Hezekiah of Judah and all Judah actually put him to death? Did he not fear the LORD and entreat the favor of the LORD, and did not the LORD change his mind about the disaster that he had pronounced against them? But we are about to bring great disaster on ourselves!"

20 There was another man prophesying in the name of the LORD, Uriah son of Shemaiah from Kiriath-jearim. He prophesied against this city and against this land in words exactly like those of Jeremiah. ²¹ And when King Jehoiakim, with all his warriors and all the officials, heard his words, the king sought to put him to death; but when Uriah heard of it, he was afraid and fled and escaped to Egypt. ²² Then King Jehoiakim sentᵃ Elnathan son of Achbor and men with him to Egypt, ²³ and they took Uriah from Egypt and brought him to King Jehoiakim, who struck him down with the sword and threw his dead body into the burial place of the common people.

24 But the hand of Ahikam son of Shaphan was with Jeremiah so that he was not given over into the hands of the people to be put to death.

The Sign of the Yoke

27 In the beginning of the reign of King Zedekiahᵇ son of Josiah

ᵃ Heb adds *men* to Egypt   ᵇ Another reading is *Jehoiakim*

26:12–15—Jeremiah defends himself by appealing to an understanding of prophecy, articulated in Deut. 18:9–22, that asserts God will hold accountable any who fail to heed a prophet whom God has sent.

26:16–19—In exonerating Jeremiah, Judah's officials appeal to the precedent of the prophet Micah. When Micah announced the destruction of Jerusalem (v. 18 quotes Mic. 3:12), King Hezekiah (715–587 BCE; see 2 Kgs. 18–20) heeded his words. There is no biblical text that recounts the incident remembered here involving Micah and Hezekiah.

26:20–23—*King Jehoiakim* is contrasted negatively to King Hezekiah, on account of his brutal murder of the prophet *Uriah*.

26:24—*Ahikam*, the *son of Shaphan* who was King Josiah's secretary and supported Josiah's reform effort (2 Kgs. 22–23). Jeremiah is rescued by persons committed to reform in Judah.

27:1–22 The Yoke Bars

Through the symbolic act of placing *yoke* bars on his *neck*, Jeremiah urges that Judah submit to God by surrendering to Babylon. The occasion may be a summit organized by King Zedekiah

of Judah, this word came to Jeremiah from the LORD. ² Thus the LORD said to me: Make yourself a yoke of straps and bars, and put them on your neck. ³ Send word*ᵃ* to the king of Edom, the king of Moab, the king of the Ammonites, the king of Tyre, and the king of Sidon by the hand of the envoys who have come to Jerusalem to King Zedekiah of Judah. ⁴ Give them this charge for their masters: Thus says the LORD of hosts, the God of Israel: This is what you shall say to your masters: ⁵ It is I who by my great power and my outstretched arm have made the earth, with the people and animals that are on the earth, and I give it to whomever I please. ⁶ Now I have given all these lands into the hand of King Nebuchadnezzar of Babylon, my servant, and I have given him even the wild animals of the field to serve him. ⁷ All the nations shall serve him and his son and his grandson, until the time of his own land comes; then many nations and great kings shall make him their slave.

8 But if any nation or kingdom will not serve this king, Nebuchadnezzar of Babylon, and put its neck under the yoke of the king of Babylon, then I will punish that nation with the sword, with famine, and with pestilence, says the LORD, until I have completed its*ᵇ* destruction by his hand. ⁹ You, therefore, must not listen to your prophets, your diviners, your dreamers,*ᶜ* your soothsayers, or your sorcerers, who are saying to you, "You shall not serve the king of Babylon." ¹⁰ For they are prophesying a lie to you, with the result that you will be removed far from your land; I will drive you out, and you will perish. ¹¹ But any nation that will bring its neck under the yoke of the king of Babylon and serve him, I will

leave on its own land, says the LORD, to till it and live there.

12 I spoke to King Zedekiah of Judah in the same way: Bring your necks under the yoke of the king of Babylon, and serve him and his people, and live. ¹³ Why should you and your people die by the sword, by famine, and by pestilence, as the LORD has spoken concerning any nation that will not serve the king of Babylon? ¹⁴ Do not listen to the words of the prophets who are telling you not to serve the king of Babylon, for they are prophesying a lie to you. ¹⁵ I have not sent them, says the LORD, but they are prophesying falsely in my name, with the result that I will drive you out and you will perish, you and the prophets who are prophesying to you.

16 Then I spoke to the priests and to all this people, saying, Thus says the LORD: Do not listen to the words of your prophets who are prophesying to you, saying, "The vessels of the LORD's house will soon be brought back from Babylon," for they are prophesying a lie to you. ¹⁷ Do not listen to them; serve the king of Babylon and live. Why should this city become a desolation? ¹⁸ If indeed they are prophets, and if the word of the LORD is with them, then let them intercede with the LORD of hosts, that the vessels left in the house of the LORD, in the house of the king of Judah, and in Jerusalem may not go to Babylon. ¹⁹ For thus says the LORD of hosts concerning the pillars, the sea, the stands, and the rest of the vessels that are left in this city, ²⁰ which King Nebuchadnezzar of Babylon did not

ᵃ Cn: Heb *send them*   *ᵇ* Heb *their*   *ᶜ* Gk Syr Vg: Heb *dreams*

---

early in his reign to persuade neighboring states to resist Babylon.

27:2—Jeremiah understands Babylon as God's instrument of judgment.

27:10 *Prophesying a lie*—See 23:9–40.

27:16—The optimistic view of the false prophets contradicts the view of Jeremiah. The debate

becomes more personal and dangerous in the next two chapters.

27:20—This verse refers to 597 BCE, when Babylon invaded Jerusalem and exiled key leaders but did not destroy the city or the temple. Jeremiah imagines worse trouble with Babylon to come (v. 22).

take away when he took into exile from Jerusalem to Babylon King Jeconiah son of Jehoiakim of Judah, and all the nobles of Judah and Jerusalem— [21] thus says the LORD of hosts, the God of Israel, concerning the vessels left in the house of the LORD, in the house of the king of Judah, and in Jerusalem: [22] They shall be carried to Babylon, and there they shall stay, until the day when I give attention to them, says the LORD. Then I will bring them up and restore them to this place.

Hananiah Opposes Jeremiah and Dies

28 In that same year, at the beginning of the reign of King Zedekiah of Judah, in the fifth month of the fourth year, the prophet Hananiah son of Azzur, from Gibeon, spoke to me in the house of the LORD, in the presence of the priests and all the people, saying, [2] "Thus says the LORD of hosts, the God of Israel: I have broken the yoke of the king of Babylon. [3] Within two years I will bring back to this place all the vessels of the LORD's house, which King Nebuchadnezzar of Babylon took away from this place and carried to Babylon. [4] I will also bring back to this place King Jeconiah son of Jehoiakim of Judah, and all the exiles from Judah who went to Babylon, says the LORD, for I will break the yoke of the king of Babylon."

5 Then the prophet Jeremiah spoke to the prophet Hananiah in the presence of the priests and all the people who were standing in the house of the LORD; [6] and the prophet Jeremiah said, "Amen! May the LORD do so; may the LORD fulfill the words that you have prophesied, and bring back to this place from Babylon the vessels of the house of the LORD,

and all the exiles. [7] But listen now to this word that I speak in your hearing and in the hearing of all the people. [8] The prophets who preceded you and me from ancient times prophesied war, famine, and pestilence against many countries and great kingdoms. [9] As for the prophet who prophesies peace, when the word of that prophet comes true, then it will be known that the LORD has truly sent the prophet."

10 Then the prophet Hananiah took the yoke from the neck of the prophet Jeremiah, and broke it. [11] And Hananiah spoke in the presence of all the people, saying, "Thus says the LORD: This is how I will break the yoke of King Nebuchadnezzar of Babylon from the neck of all the nations within two years." At this, the prophet Jeremiah went his way.

12 Sometime after the prophet Hananiah had broken the yoke from the neck of the prophet Jeremiah, the word of the LORD came to Jeremiah: [13] Go, tell Hananiah, Thus says the LORD: You have broken wooden bars only to forge iron bars in place of them! [14] For thus says the LORD of hosts, the God of Israel: I have put an iron yoke on the neck of all these nations so that they may serve King Nebuchadnezzar of Babylon, and they shall indeed serve him; I have even given him the wild animals. [15] And the prophet Jeremiah said to the prophet Hananiah, "Listen, Hananiah, the LORD has not sent you, and you made this people trust in a lie. [16] Therefore thus says the LORD: I am going to send you off the face of the earth. Within this year you will be dead, because you have spoken rebellion against the LORD."

17 In that same year, in the seventh month, the prophet Hananiah died.

28:1–17 Jeremiah and Hananiah Hananiah contradicts the symbolic act of Jeremiah reported in chap. 27.

28:3 *Within two years*—Jeremiah foresaw a much longer exile (see 25:12).

28:5–9—While Jeremiah wishes that Hananiah's

optimistic prophecy might be true, he doubts it. Reflecting a view of prophecy articulated in Deut. 18:21–22, Jeremiah suggests that the test of optimistic prophecy is its fulfillment.

28:15–17—According to Deut. 18:20, the consequence for a prophet who "presumes to speak" for God is death.

Jeremiah's Letter to the Exiles in Babylon

29 These are the words of the letter that the prophet Jeremiah sent from Jerusalem to the remaining elders among the exiles, and to the priests, the prophets, and all the people, whom Nebuchadnezzar had taken into exile from Jerusalem to Babylon. ² This was after King Jeconiah, and the queen mother, the court officials, the leaders of Judah and Jerusalem, the artisans, and the smiths had departed from Jerusalem. ³ The letter was sent by the hand of Elasah son of Shaphan and Gemariah son of Hilkiah, whom King Zedekiah of Judah sent to Babylon to King Nebuchadnezzar of Babylon. It said: ⁴ Thus says the Lord of hosts, the God of Israel, to all the exiles whom I have sent into exile from Jerusalem to Babylon: ⁵ Build houses and live in them; plant gardens and eat what they produce. ⁶ Take wives and have sons and daughters; take wives for your sons, and give your daughters in marriage, that they may bear sons and daughters; multiply there, and do not decrease. ⁷ But seek the welfare of the city where I have sent you into exile, and pray to the Lord on its behalf, for in its welfare you will find your welfare. ⁸ For thus says the Lord of hosts, the God of Israel: Do not let the prophets and the diviners who are among you deceive you, and do not listen to the dreams that they dream,ᵃ ⁹ for it is a lie that they are prophesying to you in my name; I did not send them, says the Lord.

10 For thus says the Lord: Only when Babylon's seventy years are completed will I visit you, and I will fulfill to you my promise and bring you back to this place. ¹¹ For surely I know the plans I have for you, says the Lord, plans for your welfare and not for harm, to give you a future with hope. ¹² Then when you call upon me and come and pray to me, I will hear you. ¹³ When you search for me, you will find me; if you seek me with all your heart, ¹⁴ I will let you find me, says the Lord, and I will restore your fortunes and gather you from all the nations and all the places where I have driven you, says the Lord, and I will bring you back to the place from which I sent you into exile.

15 Because you have said, "The Lord has raised up prophets for us in Babylon,"— ¹⁶ Thus says the Lord concerning the king who sits on the throne of David, and concerning all the people who live in this city, your kinsfolk who did not go out with you into exile: ¹⁷ Thus says the Lord of hosts, I am going to let loose on them sword, famine, and pestilence, and I will make them like rotten figs that are so bad they cannot be eaten. ¹⁸ I will pursue them with the sword, with famine, and with pestilence, and will make them a horror to all the kingdoms of the earth, to be an object of cursing, and horror, and hissing, and a derision among all the nations where I have driven them, ¹⁹ because they did not heed my words, says the Lord, when I persistently sent to you my servants the prophets, but theyᵇ would not listen, says the Lord. ²⁰ But now, all you exiles whom I sent away from Jeru-

ᵃ Cn: Heb *your dreams that you cause to dream*   ᵇ Syr: Heb *you*

29:1–23 Jeremiah's Letter to the Exiles
This is a letter that Jeremiah, living in Jerusalem, sent to those taken captive to Babylon in 597 BCE.

29:5 Build . . . plant—A variation on 1:10. Those exiled to Babylon in 597 BCE are urged to settle in for a long stay. See 29:10 below.

29:7—Rather than seek just a resigned endurance of their captivity, the exiles are urged to seek Babylon's well-being. Paul too urged believers to respect the authority of the Roman government, which he described as "God's servant for your good" (Rom. 13:4). The notion of praying for the welfare of the enemy remains as controversial as ever, though the prophetic message here is clear: God intends well-being for all peoples.

29:15–23—Among those exiled in Babylon were *prophets*, identified as *Ahab* and *Zedekiah*, whose message was similar to Hananiah's (chap. 28). Jeremiah condemns these optimistic prophets (vv. 20–23).

salem to Babylon, hear the word of the LORD: ²¹ Thus says the LORD of hosts, the God of Israel, concerning Ahab son of Kolaiah and Zedekiah son of Maaseiah, who are prophesying a lie to you in my name: I am going to deliver them into the hand of King Nebuchadrezzar of Babylon, and he shall kill them before your eyes. ²² And on account of them this curse shall be used by all the exiles from Judah in Babylon: "The LORD make you like Zedekiah and Ahab, whom the king of Babylon roasted in the fire," ²³ because they have perpetrated outrage in Israel and have committed adultery with their neighbors' wives, and have spoken in my name lying words that I did not command them; I am the one who knows and bears witness, says the LORD.

The Letter of Shemaiah

24 To Shemaiah of Nehelam you shall say: ²⁵ Thus says the LORD of hosts, the God of Israel: In your own name you sent a letter to all the people who are in Jerusalem, and to the priest Zephaniah son of Maaseiah, and to all the priests, saying, ²⁶ The LORD himself has made you priest instead of the priest Jehoiada, so that there may be officers in the house of the LORD to control any madman who plays the prophet, to put him in the stocks and the collar. ²⁷ So now why have you not rebuked Jeremiah of Anathoth who plays the prophet for you? ²⁸ For he has actually sent to us in Babylon, saying, "It will be a long time; build houses and live in them, and plant gardens and eat what they produce."

29 The priest Zephaniah read this letter in the hearing of the prophet Jeremiah. ³⁰ Then the word of the LORD came to Jeremiah: ³¹ Send to all the exiles, saying, Thus says the LORD concerning Shemaiah of Nehelam: Because Shemaiah has prophesied to you, though I did not send him, and has led you to trust in a lie, ³² therefore thus says the LORD: I am going to punish Shemaiah of Nehelam and his descendants; he shall not have anyone living among this people to see[a] the good that I am going to do to my people, says the LORD, for he has spoken rebellion against the LORD.

Restoration Promised for Israel and Judah

30 The word that came to Jeremiah from the LORD: ² Thus says the LORD, the God of Israel: Write in a book all the words that I have spoken to you. ³ For the days are surely coming, says the LORD, when I will restore the fortunes of my people, Israel and Judah, says the LORD, and I will bring them back to the land that I gave to their ancestors and they shall take possession of it.

4 These are the words that the LORD spoke concerning Israel and Judah:
⁵ Thus says the LORD:
    We have heard a cry of panic,
      of terror, and no peace.
⁶ Ask now, and see,
    can a man bear a child?
  Why then do I see every man
    with his hands on his loins like a
      woman in labor?
    Why has every face turned pale?
⁷ Alas! that day is so great
    there is none like it;
  it is a time of distress for Jacob;
    yet he shall be rescued from it.
8 On that day, says the LORD of hosts,

---

[a] Gk: Heb *and he shall not see*

29:24–32 The Response to Jeremiah's Letter
In response to Jeremiah's letter to Babylon, one of those exiled, *Shemaiah*, writes to the high *priest* in Jerusalem urging him to have Jeremiah imprisoned. When Jeremiah hears of Shemaiah's letter, he accuses Shemaiah of being a lying prophet.

30:1–33:26 Judah's Eventual Restoration
The theme is *restore the fortunes* (30:3, 18;

31:23; 32:44; 33:11, 26), a phrase indicating that what was lost through God's judgment will be restored. However, Judah's restoration will not occur soon, so God's promises are to be written down (30:2), so as to be remembered for a long time.

30:4–11—This promise of restoration makes reference to the Day of the Lord (*that day*, vv. 7–8). See note at 17:16.

I will break the yoke from off his[a] neck,
and I will burst his[a] bonds, and strangers shall no more make a servant of him.
[9] But they shall serve the LORD their God
and David their king, whom I will raise
up for them.

[10] But as for you, have no fear, my
servant Jacob, says the LORD,
and do not be dismayed, O Israel;
for I am going to save you from far
away,
and your offspring from the land
of their captivity.
Jacob shall return and have quiet
and ease,
and no one shall make him afraid.
[11] For I am with you, says the LORD, to
save you;
I will make an end of all the nations
among which I scattered you,
but of you I will not make an end.
I will chastise you in just measure,
and I will by no means leave you
unpunished.

[12] For thus says the LORD:
Your hurt is incurable,
your wound is grievous.
[13] There is no one to uphold your
cause,
no medicine for your wound,
no healing for you.
[14] All your lovers have forgotten you;
they care nothing for you;
for I have dealt you the blow of an
enemy,
the punishment of a merciless foe,
because your guilt is great,
because your sins are so
numerous.
[15] Why do you cry out over your hurt?
Your pain is incurable.

Because your guilt is great,
because your sins are so numerous,
I have done these things to you.
[16] Therefore all who devour you shall
be devoured,
and all your foes, every one of
them, shall go into captivity;
those who plunder you shall be
plundered,
and all who prey on you I will
make a prey.
[17] For I will restore health to you,
and your wounds I will heal,
says the LORD,
because they have called you an
outcast:
"It is Zion; no one cares for her!"

[18] Thus says the LORD:
I am going to restore the fortunes of
the tents of Jacob,
and have compassion on his
dwellings;
the city shall be rebuilt upon its
mound,
and the citadel set on its rightful
site.
[19] Out of them shall come
thanksgiving,
and the sound of merrymakers.
I will make them many, and they
shall not be few;
I will make them honored, and
they shall not be disdained.
[20] Their children shall be as of old,
their congregation shall be
established before me;
and I will punish all who oppress
them.
[21] Their prince shall be one of their
own,

[a] Cn: Heb *your*

30:10—The exile will end, and Judah will be restored to the land (cf. Isa. 40:1–11).

30:12–17—Incurable hurt healed.

30:16 *Therefore*—While this word often introduces a judgment speech (see 2:9), here it introduces a promise of deliverance. The promise makes sense only in view of the final phrase of v. 17.

30:17—The Lord is motivated to restore Judah by the nations who charge that God does not care for Judah.

30:18–22—While restoration will include rebuilding Jerusalem (v. 18), the repopulation of the land (vv. 19–20), and a new leader for Judah (v. 21), God's ultimate goal is a renewed relationship with God's *people*.

their ruler shall come from their
  midst;
I will bring him near, and he shall
    approach me,
  for who would otherwise dare to
    approach me?
                    says the LORD.

²² And you shall be my people,
  and I will be your God.

²³ Look, the storm of the LORD!
  Wrath has gone forth,
  a whirling*a* tempest;
    it will burst upon the head of the
      wicked.
²⁴ The fierce anger of the LORD will not
    turn back
  until he has executed and
    accomplished
  the intents of his mind.
In the latter days you will
    understand this.

The Joyful Return of the Exiles

31 At that time, says the LORD, I will
be the God of all the families of
Israel, and they shall be my people.
² Thus says the LORD:
The people who survived the sword
    found grace in the wilderness;
  when Israel sought for rest,
³   the LORD appeared to him*b* from
        far away.*c*
  I have loved you with an everlasting
      love;
    therefore I have continued my
      faithfulness to you.
⁴ Again I will build you, and you shall
    be built,
  O virgin Israel!
  Again you shall take*d* your
      tambourines,
  and go forth in the dance of the
      merrymakers.

⁵ Again you shall plant vineyards
  on the mountains of Samaria;
the planters shall plant,
  and shall enjoy the fruit.
⁶ For there shall be a day when
      sentinels will call
  in the hill country of Ephraim:
"Come, let us go up to Zion,
  to the LORD our God."

⁷ For thus says the LORD:
Sing aloud with gladness for Jacob,
  and raise shouts for the chief of the
      nations;
proclaim, give praise, and say,
  "Save, O LORD, your people,
  the remnant of Israel."
⁸ See, I am going to bring them from
      the land of the north,
  and gather them from the farthest
      parts of the earth,
among them the blind and the lame,
  those with child and those in
      labor, together;
  a great company, they shall return
      here.
⁹ With weeping they shall come,
  and with consolations*e* I will lead
      them back,
  I will let them walk by brooks of
      water,
    in a straight path in which they
      shall not stumble;
for I have become a father to Israel,
  and Ephraim is my firstborn.

¹⁰ Hear the word of the LORD,
      O nations,
  and declare it in the coastlands far
      away;
  say, "He who scattered Israel will
      gather him,

a One Ms: Meaning of MT uncertain *b* Gk: Heb *me* *c* Or *to him long ago* *d* Or *adorn yourself with* *e* Gk Compare Vg Tg: Heb *supplications*

30:24–31:1—God's judgment makes restoration of relationship with Judah possible.

31:2–6—Judah's restoration depends upon God's graciousness, such as Israel experienced in the wilderness after the exodus.

31:6—This verse envisions the reunification of the north (Ephraim–Israel) and south (Zion–

Judah), which had split after the reign of Solomon. Political reunification was a goal of Judah's King Josiah (see introduction).

31:9—God's judgment occurred because Judah refused God's parental care (cf. 3:19).

31:10–14—The effects of judgment—drought, desolation, lamentation—are reversed.

and will keep him as a shepherd a
 flock."

¹¹ For the LORD has ransomed Jacob,
 and has redeemed him from hands
  too strong for him.

¹² They shall come and sing aloud on
  the height of Zion,
 and they shall be radiant over the
  goodness of the LORD,
over the grain, the wine, and the oil,
 and over the young of the flock
  and the herd;
their life shall become like a watered
 garden,
 and they shall never languish
  again.

¹³ Then shall the young women rejoice
  in the dance,
 and the young men and the old
  shall be merry.
I will turn their mourning into joy,
 I will comfort them, and give them
  gladness for sorrow.

¹⁴ I will give the priests their fill of
 fatness,
 and my people shall be satisfied
  with my bounty,
    says the LORD.

¹⁵ Thus says the LORD:
A voice is heard in Ramah,
 lamentation and bitter weeping.
Rachel is weeping for her children;
 she refuses to be comforted for her
  children,
 because they are no more.

¹⁶ Thus says the LORD:
Keep your voice from weeping,
 and your eyes from tears;
for there is a reward for your work,
    says the LORD:
they shall come back from the land
 of the enemy;

¹⁷ there is hope for your future,
    says the LORD:

your children shall come back to
 their own country.

¹⁸ Indeed I heard Ephraim pleading:
"You disciplined me, and I took the
 discipline;
 I was like a calf untrained.
Bring me back, let me come back,
 for you are the LORD my God.

¹⁹ For after I had turned away I
 repented;
 and after I was discovered, I struck
  my thigh;
I was ashamed, and I was dismayed
 because I bore the disgrace of my
  youth."

²⁰ Is Ephraim my dear son?
 Is he the child I delight in?
As often as I speak against him,
 I still remember him.
Therefore I am deeply moved for
 him;
 I will surely have mercy on him,
    says the LORD.

²¹ Set up road markers for yourself,
 make yourself signposts;
consider well the highway,
 the road by which you went.
Return, O virgin Israel,
 return to these your cities.

²² How long will you waver,
 O faithless daughter?
For the LORD has created a new
 thing on the earth:
 a woman encompasses*a* a man.

23 Thus says the LORD of hosts, the
God of Israel: Once more they shall use
these words in the land of Judah and in
its towns when I restore their fortunes:
"The LORD bless you, O abode of
 righteousness,
 O holy hill!"

²⁴ And Judah and all its towns shall live

a Meaning of Heb uncertain

31:15–22—This promise of restoration identifies those exiled as the children of *Rachel*, one of Jacob's wives.

31:21–22 *A woman encompasses a man*—One interpretation of this difficult phrase is that

the woman personifies Israel, who will have a son, that is, posterity and so a future (cf. 7:34; 16:1–4).

31:23–30—The new speech of restoration.

there together, and the farmers and those who wander[a] with their flocks.

25 I will satisfy the weary,
and all who are faint I will
replenish.

26 Thereupon I awoke and looked, and my sleep was pleasant to me.

Individual Retribution

27 The days are surely coming, says the LORD, when I will sow the house of Israel and the house of Judah with the seed of humans and the seed of animals. 28 And just as I have watched over them to pluck up and break down, to overthrow, destroy, and bring evil, so I will watch over them to build and to plant, says the LORD. 29 In those days they shall no longer say:

"The parents have eaten sour grapes,
and the children's teeth are set on
edge."

30 But all shall die for their own sins; the teeth of everyone who eats sour grapes shall be set on edge.

A New Covenant

31 The days are surely coming, says the LORD, when I will make a new covenant with the house of Israel and the house of Judah. 32 It will not be like the covenant that I made with their ancestors when I took them by the hand to bring them out of the land of Egypt—a covenant that they broke, though I was their husband,[b] says the LORD. 33 But this is the covenant that I will make with the house of Israel after those days, says the LORD: I will put my law within them, and I will write it on their hearts; and I will be their God, and they shall be my

people. 34 No longer shall they teach one another, or say to each other, "Know the LORD," for they shall all know me, from the least of them to the greatest, says the LORD; for I will forgive their iniquity, and remember their sin no more.

35 Thus says the LORD,
who gives the sun for light by day
and the fixed order of the moon
and the stars for light by
night,
who stirs up the sea so that its waves
roar—
the LORD of hosts is his name:
36 If this fixed order were ever to cease
from my presence, says the LORD,
then also the offspring of Israel
would cease
to be a nation before me forever.

37 Thus says the LORD:
If the heavens above can be
measured,
and the foundations of the earth
below can be explored,
then I will reject all the offspring of
Israel
because of all they have done,
says the LORD.

Jerusalem to Be Enlarged

38 The days are surely coming, says the LORD, when the city shall be rebuilt for the LORD from the tower of Hananel to the Corner Gate. 39 And the measuring line shall go out farther, straight to the hill Gareb, and shall then turn to Goah. 40 The whole valley of the dead bodies and the ashes, and all the fields as far as the Wadi Kidron, to the corner

[a] Cn Compare Syr Vg Tg: Heb *and they shall wander*   [b] Or *master*

31:26—This verse may be related to a vision of the prophet Zechariah (Zech. 4) or intended as the reversal of one of the curses for disobedience in Deut. 28:65–67.

31:29–30—When restored, God's people will no longer complain about God's unfair treatment of them (cf. Ezek. 18).

31:31–34 *A new covenant*—While this new covenant is understood by the church in relation to Christ (see 1 Cor. 11:25; 2 Cor. 3:5–14; Heb.

8:8–13; 10:16–17), this promise needs to be understood first in relation to Judah's restoration after exile.

31:33–34 *Write it on their hearts*—The defective "heart" of God's people was a cause of the exile (see 17:1; 4:4, 14). When they are restored, God will transform their heart so they will obey God (cf. Ezek. 36:26 and Deut. 30:1–10).

31:35–40—God's enduring commitment.

of the Horse Gate toward the east, shall be sacred to the LORD. It shall never again be uprooted or overthrown.

Jeremiah Buys a Field During the Siege

32 The word that came to Jeremiah from the LORD in the tenth year of King Zedekiah of Judah, which was the eighteenth year of Nebuchadrezzar. [2] At that time the army of the king of Babylon was besieging Jerusalem, and the prophet Jeremiah was confined in the court of the guard that was in the palace of the king of Judah, [3] where King Zedekiah of Judah had confined him. Zedekiah had said, "Why do you prophesy and say: Thus says the LORD: I am going to give this city into the hand of the king of Babylon, and he shall take it; [4] King Zedekiah of Judah shall not escape out of the hands of the Chaldeans, but shall surely be given into the hands of the king of Babylon, and shall speak with him face to face and see him eye to eye; [5] and he shall take Zedekiah to Babylon, and there he shall remain until I attend to him, says the LORD; though you fight against the Chaldeans, you shall not succeed?"

[6] Jeremiah said, The word of the LORD came to me: [7] Hanamel son of your uncle Shallum is going to come to you and say, "Buy my field that is at Anathoth, for the right of redemption by purchase is yours." [8] Then my cousin Hanamel came to me in the court of the guard, in accordance with the word of the LORD, and said to me, "Buy my field that is at Anathoth in the land of Benjamin, for the right of possession and redemption is yours; buy it for yourself." Then I knew that this was the word of the LORD.

[9] And I bought the field at Anathoth from my cousin Hanamel, and weighed out the money to him, seventeen shekels of silver. [10] I signed the deed, sealed it, got witnesses, and weighed the money on scales. [11] Then I took the sealed deed of purchase, containing the terms and conditions, and the open copy; [12] and I gave the deed of purchase to Baruch son of Neriah son of Mahseiah, in the presence of my cousin Hanamel, in the presence of the witnesses who signed the deed of purchase, and in the presence of all the Judeans who were sitting in the court of the guard. [13] In their presence I charged Baruch, saying, [14] Thus says the LORD of hosts, the God of Israel: Take these deeds, both this sealed deed of purchase and this open deed, and put them in an earthenware jar, in order that they may last for a long time. [15] For thus says the LORD of hosts, the God of Israel: Houses and fields and vineyards shall again be bought in this land.

Jeremiah Prays for Understanding

[16] After I had given the deed of purchase to Baruch son of Neriah, I prayed to the LORD, saying: [17] Ah Lord GOD! It is you who made the heavens and the earth by your great power and by your outstretched arm! Nothing is too hard for you. [18] You show steadfast love to the thousandth generation,[a] but repay the guilt of parents into the laps of their children after them, O great and mighty

[a] Or to thousands

32:1–16 *Redemption*—Jeremiah's redemption of a family field points to God's restoration of Judah. The setting is 588–587 BCE during Babylon's siege of Jerusalem, when Jeremiah is imprisoned for treason (see 37:11–21).

32:7 *Right of redemption*—Family land was considered a trust from God. When property was to be lost because of economic hardship, relatives had an obligation to purchase the land so it could be kept in the family (see Lev. 25:25–28). God commands Jeremiah to redeem his uncle's field, even though Babylon was besieging Jerusalem, an unlikely time to buy real estate!

32:9–14—Jeremiah's purchase is to be publicly witnessed and preserved, so his action can be remembered for a long time.

32:15—The purchase signals God's intention to restore Judah.

32:16–44—This prayer of Jeremiah (vv. 16–25) and God's response to it (vv. 26–44) reinforce the promise, signaled by Jeremiah's purchase of the field, that God will restore Judah.

God whose name is the LORD of hosts, [19] great in counsel and mighty in deed; whose eyes are open to all the ways of mortals, rewarding all according to their ways and according to the fruit of their doings. [20] You showed signs and wonders in the land of Egypt, and to this day in Israel and among all humankind, and have made yourself a name that continues to this very day. [21] You brought your people Israel out of the land of Egypt with signs and wonders, with a strong hand and outstretched arm, and with great terror; [22] and you gave them this land, which you swore to their ancestors to give them, a land flowing with milk and honey; [23] and they entered and took possession of it. But they did not obey your voice or follow your law; of all you commanded them to do, they did nothing. Therefore you have made all these disasters come upon them. [24] See, the siege ramps have been cast up against the city to take it, and the city, faced with sword, famine, and pestilence, has been given into the hands of the Chaldeans who are fighting against it. What you spoke has happened, as you yourself can see. [25] Yet you, O Lord GOD, have said to me, "Buy the field for money and get witnesses"—though the city has been given into the hands of the Chaldeans.

God's Assurance of the People's Return

26 The word of the LORD came to Jeremiah: [27] See, I am the LORD, the God of all flesh; is anything too hard for me? [28] Therefore, thus says the LORD: I am going to give this city into the hands of the Chaldeans and into the hand of King Nebuchadrezzar of Babylon, and he shall take it. [29] The Chaldeans who are fighting against this city shall come, set it on fire, and burn it, with the houses on whose roofs offerings have been made to Baal and libations have been poured out to other gods, to provoke me to anger. [30] For the people of Israel and the people of Judah have done nothing but evil in my sight from their youth; the people of Israel have done nothing but provoke me to anger by the work of their hands, says the LORD. [31] This city has aroused my anger and wrath, from the day it was built until this day, so that I will remove it from my sight [32] because of all the evil of the people of Israel and the people of Judah that they did to provoke me to anger—they, their kings and their officials, their priests and their prophets, the citizens of Judah and the inhabitants of Jerusalem. [33] They have turned their backs to me, not their faces; though I have taught them persistently, they would not listen and accept correction. [34] They set up their abominations in the house that bears my name, and defiled it. [35] They built the high places of Baal in the valley of the son of Hinnom, to offer up their sons and daughters to Molech, though I did not command them, nor did it enter my mind that they should do this abomination, causing Judah to sin.

36 Now therefore thus says the LORD, the God of Israel, concerning this city of which you say, "It is being given into the hand of the king of Babylon by the sword, by famine, and by pestilence": [37] See, I am going to gather them from all the lands to which I drove them in my anger and my wrath and in great indignation; I will bring them back to this place, and I will settle them in safety. [38] They shall be my people, and I will be their God. [39] I will give them one heart and one way, that they may fear me for all time, for their own good and the good of their children after them. [40] I will make an everlasting covenant with them, never to draw back from doing good to them; and I will put the fear of me in their hearts, so that they may not turn from me. [41] I will rejoice in doing good to them, and I will plant them in this land in faithfulness, with all my heart and all my soul.

42 For thus says the LORD: Just as I have brought all this great disaster upon this people, so I will bring upon

them all the good fortune that I now promise them. ⁴³ Fields shall be bought in this land of which you are saying, It is a desolation, without human beings or animals; it has been given into the hands of the Chaldeans. ⁴⁴ Fields shall be bought for money, and deeds shall be signed and sealed and witnessed, in the land of Benjamin, in the places around Jerusalem, and in the cities of Judah, of the hill country, of the Shephelah, and of the Negeb; for I will restore their fortunes, says the LORD.

Healing after Punishment

33 The word of the LORD came to Jeremiah a second time, while he was still confined in the court of the guard: ² Thus says the LORD who made the earth,ᵃ the LORD who formed it to establish it—the LORD is his name: ³ Call to me and I will answer you, and will tell you great and hidden things that you have not known. ⁴ For thus says the LORD, the God of Israel, concerning the houses of this city and the houses of the kings of Judah that were torn down to make a defense against the siege ramps and before the sword:ᵇ ⁵ The Chaldeans are coming in to fightᶜ and to fill them with the dead bodies of those whom I shall strike down in my anger and my wrath, for I have hidden my face from this city because of all their wickedness. ⁶ I am going to bring it recovery and healing; I will heal them and reveal to them abundanceᵇ of prosperity and security. ⁷ I will restore the fortunes of Judah and the fortunes of Israel, and rebuild them as they were at first. ⁸ I will cleanse them from all the guilt of their sin against me, and I will forgive all the guilt of their sin and rebellion against me. ⁹ And this cityᵉ shall be to me a name of joy, a praise and a glory before all the nations of the earth

who shall hear of all the good that I do for them; they shall fear and tremble because of all the good and all the prosperity I provide for it.

10 Thus says the LORD: In this place of which you say, "It is a waste without human beings or animals," in the towns of Judah and the streets of Jerusalem that are desolate, without inhabitants, human or animal, there shall once more be heard ¹¹ the voice of mirth and the voice of gladness, the voice of the bridegroom and the voice of the bride, the voices of those who sing, as they bring thank offerings to the house of the LORD:

"Give thanks to the LORD of hosts,
　　for the LORD is good,
　　for his steadfast love endures
　　　　forever!"

For I will restore the fortunes of the land as at first, says the LORD.

12 Thus says the LORD of hosts: In this place that is waste, without human beings or animals, and in all its towns there shall again be pasture for shepherds resting their flocks. ¹³ In the towns of the hill country, of the Shephelah, and of the Negeb, in the land of Benjamin, the places around Jerusalem, and in the towns of Judah, flocks shall again pass under the hands of the one who counts them, says the LORD.

The Righteous Branch and the Covenant with David

14 The days are surely coming, says the LORD, when I will fulfill the promise I made to the house of Israel and the house of Judah. ¹⁵ In those days and at that time I will cause a righteous Branch to spring up for David; and he shall execute justice and righteousness in the

---

ᵃ Gk: Heb *it*　ᵇ Meaning of Heb uncertain　ᶜ Cn: Heb *They are coming in to fight against the Chaldeans*　ᵈ Heb *And it*

33:1–26 Judah's Fortunes Are Restored

33:1–13—Jeremiah describes restoration.

33:1 *A second time*—The first time was in 32:1.

33:11—Psalm 136:1. When Judah is restored, people will again sing God's praise.

33:14–18—The book of Jeremiah holds Judah's kings particularly responsible for the exile (see 21:11–22:8). In restored Judah, the kings will be attentive to justice. The unending succession to the throne of David fulfills the promise of 2 Sam. 7:16.

land. **16** In those days Judah will be saved and Jerusalem will live in safety. And this is the name by which it will be called: "The LORD is our righteousness."

17 For thus says the LORD: David shall never lack a man to sit on the throne of the house of Israel, **18** and the levitical priests shall never lack a man in my presence to offer burnt offerings, to make grain offerings, and to make sacrifices for all time.

19 The word of the LORD came to Jeremiah: **20** Thus says the LORD: If any of you could break my covenant with the day and my covenant with the night, so that day and night would not come at their appointed time, **21** only then could my covenant with my servant David be broken, so that he would not have a son to reign on his throne, and my covenant with my ministers the Levites. **22** Just as the host of heaven cannot be numbered and the sands of the sea cannot be measured, so I will increase the offspring of my servant David, and the Levites who minister to me.

23 The word of the LORD came to Jeremiah: **24** Have you not observed how these people say, "The two families that the LORD chose have been rejected by him," and how they hold my people in such contempt that they no longer regard them as a nation? **25** Thus says the LORD: Only if I had not established my covenant with day and night and the ordinances of heaven and earth, **26** would I reject the offspring of Jacob and of my servant David and not choose any of his descendants as rulers over the offspring of Abraham, Isaac, and Jacob. For I will restore their fortunes, and will have mercy upon them.

Death in Captivity Predicted for Zedekiah

34 The word that came to Jeremiah from the LORD, when King Nebuchadrezzar of Babylon and all his army and all the kingdoms of the earth and all the peoples under his dominion were fighting against Jerusalem and all its cities: **2** Thus says the LORD, the God of Israel: Go and speak to King Zedekiah of Judah and say to him: Thus says the LORD: I am going to give this city into the hand of the king of Babylon, and he shall burn it with fire. **3** And you yourself shall not escape from his hand, but shall surely be captured and handed over to him; you shall see the king of Babylon eye to eye and speak with him face to face; and you shall go to Babylon. **4** Yet hear the word of the LORD, O King Zedekiah of Judah! Thus says the LORD concerning you: You shall not die by the sword; **5** you shall die in peace. And as spices were burned*a* for your ancestors, the earlier kings who preceded you, so they shall burn spices*b* for you and lament for you, saying, "Alas, lord!" For I have spoken the word, says the LORD.

6 Then the prophet Jeremiah spoke all these words to Zedekiah king of Judah, in Jerusalem, **7** when the army of the king of Babylon was fighting against Jerusalem and against all the cities of Judah that were left, Lachish and Azekah; for these were the only fortified cities of Judah that remained.

Treacherous Treatment of Slaves

8 The word that came to Jeremiah from the LORD, after King Zedekiah had made a covenant with all the people in Jerusalem to make a proclamation of liberty

a Heb *as there was burning*　*b* Heb *shall burn*

33:19–26—Jeremiah pictures an enduring restoration (cf. 31:35–40).

34:1–7 Under Siege
The Babylonian siege of Jerusalem is quite advanced. Judah's defeat is not a historical accident but is directed by God. Jeremiah's message to King Zedekiah is surprisingly tempered, as other texts remember much harsher threats (21:7). Zedekiah's actual fate is awful (39:5–9).

34:8–22 A Covenant Broken
King Zedekiah led Judah to enter a covenant through which they agreed to release their *slaves*. This action was consistent with provisions that are found in Deut. 15 (quoted in v. 14), which

to them— ⁹that all should set free their Hebrew slaves, male and female, so that no one should hold another Judean in slavery. ¹⁰And they obeyed, all the officials and all the people who had entered into the covenant that all would set free their slaves, male or female, so that they would not be enslaved again; they obeyed and set them free. ¹¹But afterward they turned around and took back the male and female slaves they had set free, and brought them again into subjection as slaves. ¹²The word of the LORD came to Jeremiah from the LORD: ¹³Thus says the LORD, the God of Israel: I myself made a covenant with your ancestors when I brought them out of the land of Egypt, out of the house of slavery, saying, ¹⁴"Every seventh year each of you must set free any Hebrews who have been sold to you and have served you six years; you must set them free from your service." But your ancestors did not listen to me or incline their ears to me. ¹⁵You yourselves recently repented and did what was right in my sight by proclaiming liberty to one another, and you made a covenant before me in the house that is called by my name; ¹⁶but then you turned around and profaned my name when each of you took back your male and female slaves, whom you had set free according to their desire, and you brought them again into subjection to be your slaves. ¹⁷Therefore, thus says the LORD: You have not obeyed me by granting a release to your neighbors and friends; I am going to grant a release to you, says the LORD—a release

to the sword, to pestilence, and to famine. I will make you a horror to all the kingdoms of the earth. ¹⁸And those who transgressed my covenant and did not keep the terms of the covenant that they made before me, I will make like*a* the calf when they cut it in two and passed between its parts: ¹⁹the officials of Judah, the officials of Jerusalem, the eunuchs, the priests, and all the people of the land who passed between the parts of the calf ²⁰shall be handed over to their enemies and to those who seek their lives. Their corpses shall become food for the birds of the air and the wild animals of the earth. ²¹And as for King Zedekiah of Judah and his officials, I will hand them over to their enemies and to those who seek their lives, to the army of the king of Babylon, which has withdrawn from you. ²²I am going to command, says the LORD, and will bring them back to this city; and they will fight against it, and take it, and burn it with fire. The towns of Judah I will make a desolation without inhabitant.

The Rechabites Commended

35 The word that came to Jeremiah from the LORD in the days of King Jehoiakim son of Josiah of Judah: ²Go to the house of the Rechabites, and speak with them, and bring them to the house of the LORD, into one of the chambers; then offer them wine to drink. ³So I took Jaazaniah son of Jeremiah son of Habazziniah, and his brothers, and all his sons, and the whole house of

a Cn: Heb lacks *like*

---

ground the periodic release of slaves in the memory that God had freed Israel from *slavery* in Egypt. However, Judah reneged on this agreement and resubjected their slaves. This violation of covenant is cited as a reason for God's judgment.

34:18 *I will make [them] like the calf*—Regarding the ritual by which a covenant was ratified, see Gen. 15:7–21.

35:1–19 The Rechabites
Unlike surrounding material, this chapter is set many years before the siege of Jerusalem. Its

placement here is to contrast the actions of *the Rechabites* with those of the Judeans in the prior chapter. This group originated at the time of King Jehu of Israel (842–815 BCE) and was named after their founder, *Jonadab, son of Rechab*. They supported King Jehu's effort to abolish the worship of fertility gods and refrained from drinking wine associated with the cultic rituals of these gods.

35:3–11—Jeremiah offers a group of Rechabites wine, but honoring the prohibition of their founder, they refuse.

the Rechabites. ⁴I brought them to the house of the LORD into the chamber of the sons of Hanan son of Igdaliah, the man of God, which was near the chamber of the officials, above the chamber of Maaseiah son of Shallum, keeper of the threshold. ⁵Then I set before the Rechabites pitchers full of wine, and cups; and I said to them, "Have some wine." ⁶But they answered, "We will drink no wine, for our ancestor Jonadab son of Rechab commanded us, 'You shall never drink wine, neither you nor your children; ⁷nor shall you ever build a house, or sow seed; nor shall you plant a vineyard, or even own one; but you shall live in tents all your days, that you may live many days in the land where you reside.' ⁸We have obeyed the charge of our ancestor Jonadab son of Rechab in all that he commanded us, to drink no wine all our days, ourselves, our wives, our sons, or our daughters, ⁹and not to build houses to live in. We have no vineyard or field or seed; ¹⁰but we have lived in tents, and have obeyed and done all that our ancestor Jonadab commanded us, ¹¹But when King Nebuchadrezzar of Babylon came up against the land, we said, 'Come, and let us go to Jerusalem for fear of the army of the Chaldeans and the army of the Arameans.' That is why we are living in Jerusalem."

12 Then the word of the LORD came to Jeremiah: ¹³Thus says the LORD of hosts, the God of Israel: Go and say to the people of Judah and the inhabitants of Jerusalem, Can you not learn a lesson and obey my words? says the LORD. ¹⁴The command has been carried out that Jonadab son of Rechab gave to his descendants to drink no wine; and they drink none to this day, for they have obeyed their ancestor's command. But I myself have spoken to you persistently, and you have not obeyed me. ¹⁵I have sent to you all my servants the prophets, sending them persistently, saying, "Turn now every one of you from your evil way, and amend your doings, and do not go after other gods to serve them, and then you shall live in the land that I gave to you and your ancestors." But you did not incline your ear or obey me. ¹⁶The descendants of Jonadab son of Rechab have carried out the command that their ancestor gave them, but this people has not obeyed me. ¹⁷Therefore, thus says the LORD, the God of hosts, the God of Israel: I am going to bring on Judah and on all the inhabitants of Jerusalem every disaster that I have pronounced against them; because I have spoken to them and they have not listened, I have called to them and they have not answered.

18 But to the house of the Rechabites Jeremiah said: Thus says the LORD of hosts, the God of Israel: Because you have obeyed the command of your ancestor Jonadab, and kept all his precepts, and done all that he commanded you, ¹⁹therefore thus says the LORD of hosts, the God of Israel: Jonadab son of Rechab shall not lack a descendant to stand before me for all time.

The Scroll Read in the Temple

36 In the fourth year of King Jehoiakim son of Josiah of Judah, this word came to Jeremiah from the LORD: ²Take a scroll and write on it all the words that I have spoken to you against Israel and Judah and all the nations, from the day I spoke to you, from the days of Josiah until today. ³It may be that

---

35:12–19—Jeremiah contrasts Judah with the Rechabites. While the Rechabites obeyed their ancestor, Judah failed to obey God's prophets who called them to repentance.

36:1–32 Jeremiah's Scrolls
This chapter recounts how Jeremiah, banned from the temple, dictates a scroll to his scribe,

Baruch. The scroll contained *all the words* (v. 2) that Jeremiah had spoken and was read by Baruch as people gather for worship. The content of the scroll is the announcement of judgment, intended to bring about repentance and a change of heart (vv. 3, 7). The remainder of the chapter recounts reactions to this scroll.

when the house of Judah hears of all the disasters that I intend to do to them, all of them may turn from their evil ways, so that I may forgive their iniquity and their sin.

4 Then Jeremiah called Baruch son of Neriah, and Baruch wrote on a scroll at Jeremiah's dictation all the words of the LORD that he had spoken to him. 5 And Jeremiah ordered Baruch, saying, "I am prevented from entering the house of the LORD; 6 so you go yourself, and on a fast day in the hearing of the people in the LORD's house you shall read the words of the LORD from the scroll that you have written at my dictation. You shall read them also in the hearing of all the people of Judah who come up from their towns. 7 It may be that their plea will come before the LORD, and that all of them will turn from their evil ways, for great is the anger and wrath that the LORD has pronounced against this people." 8 And Baruch son of Neriah did all that the prophet Jeremiah ordered him about reading from the scroll the words of the LORD in the LORD's house.

9 In the fifth year of King Jehoiakim son of Josiah of Judah, in the ninth month, all the people in Jerusalem and all the people who came from the towns of Judah to Jerusalem proclaimed a fast before the LORD. 10 Then, in the hearing of all the people, Baruch read the words of Jeremiah from the scroll, in the house of the LORD, in the chamber of Gemariah son of Shaphan the secretary, which was in the upper court, at the entry of the New Gate of the LORD's house.

The Scroll Read in the Palace

11 When Micaiah son of Gemariah son of Shaphan heard all the words of the LORD from the scroll, 12 he went down to the king's house, into the secretary's chamber; and all the officials were sitting there: Elishama the secretary, Delaiah son of Shemaiah, Elnathan son of Achbor, Gemariah son of Shaphan, Zedekiah son of Hananiah, and all the officials. 13 And Micaiah told them all the words that he had heard, when Baruch read the scroll in the hearing of the people. 14 Then all the officials sent Jehudi son of Nethaniah son of Shelemiah son of Cushi to say to Baruch, "Bring the scroll that you read in the hearing of the people, and come." So Baruch son of Neriah took the scroll in his hand and came to them. 15 And they said to him, "Sit down and read it to us." So Baruch read it to them. 16 When they heard all the words, they turned to one another in alarm, and said to Baruch, "We certainly must report all these words to the king." 17 Then they questioned Baruch, "Tell us now, how did you write all these words? Was it at his dictation?" 18 Baruch answered them, "He dictated all these words to me, and I wrote them with ink on the scroll." 19 Then the officials said to Baruch, "Go and hide, you and Jeremiah, and let no one know where you are."

Jehoiakim Burns the Scroll

20 Leaving the scroll in the chamber of Elishama the secretary, they went to the court of the king; and they reported all the words to the king. 21 Then the king

---

36:11–19—The emphasis of this material is on the response to the word of the Lord proclaimed by Jeremiah through Baruch. The royal officials are alarmed and decide they must report the incident to the king.

36:11—*Shaphan* was the royal secretary to whom Hilkiah, the high priest, brought the book of law that led to King Josiah's reform (2 Kgs. 22:8–10). His grandson now reports to the king's cabinet that a new book of divine direction is being made public.

36:12—In 26:20–23, *Elnathan* led the party that captured the prophet Uriah and brought him back to be executed by King Jehoiachim.

36:20–26—King Jehoiakim burns the scroll. Jehoiakim's rejection of God's word contrasts sharply with the reaction of his father, King Josiah, who, when presented with the scroll found in the temple (2 Kgs. 22:11), tore his clothes in contrition.

sent Jehudi to get the scroll, and he took it from the chamber of Elishama the secretary; and Jehudi read it to the king and all the officials who stood beside the king. ²² Now the king was sitting in his winter apartment (it was the ninth month), and there was a fire burning in the brazier before him. ²³ As Jehudi read three or four columns, the king*a* would cut them off with a penknife and throw them into the fire in the brazier, until the entire scroll was consumed in the fire that was in the brazier. ²⁴ Yet neither the king, nor any of his servants who heard all these words, was alarmed, nor did they tear their garments. ²⁵ Even when Elnathan and Delaiah and Gemariah urged the king not to burn the scroll, he would not listen to them. ²⁶ And the king commanded Jerahmeel the king's son and Seraiah son of Azriel and Shelemiah son of Abdeel to arrest the secretary Baruch and the prophet Jeremiah. But the LORD hid them.

Jeremiah Dictates Another

27 Now, after the king had burned the scroll with the words that Baruch wrote at Jeremiah's dictation, the word of the LORD came to Jeremiah: ²⁸ Take another scroll and write on it all the former words that were in the first scroll, which King Jehoiakim of Judah has burned. ²⁹ And concerning King Jehoiakim of Judah you shall say: Thus says the LORD, You have dared to burn this scroll, saying, Why have you written in it that the king of Babylon will certainly come and destroy this land, and will cut off from it human beings and animals? ³⁰ Therefore thus says the LORD concerning King Jehoiakim of Judah: He shall have no one to sit upon the throne of David, and his dead body shall be cast out to the heat by day and the frost by night. ³¹ And I will pun-

ish him and his offspring and his servants for their iniquity; I will bring on them, and on the inhabitants of Jerusalem, and on the people of Judah, all the disasters with which I have threatened them—but they would not listen.

32 Then Jeremiah took another scroll and gave it to the secretary Baruch son of Neriah, who wrote on it at Jeremiah's dictation all the words of the scroll that King Jehoiakim of Judah had burned in the fire; and many similar words were added to them.

Zedekiah's Vain Hope

37 Zedekiah son of Josiah, whom King Nebuchadrezzar of Babylon made king in the land of Judah, succeeded Coniah son of Jehoiakim. ² But neither he nor his servants nor the people of the land listened to the words of the LORD that he spoke through the prophet Jeremiah.

3 King Zedekiah sent Jehucal son of Shelemiah and the priest Zephaniah son of Maaseiah to the prophet Jeremiah saying, "Please pray for us to the LORD our God." ⁴ Now Jeremiah was still going in and out among the people, for he had not yet been put in prison. ⁵ Meanwhile, the army of Pharaoh had come out of Egypt; and when the Chaldeans who were besieging Jerusalem heard news of them, they withdrew from Jerusalem.

6 Then the word of the LORD came to the prophet Jeremiah: ⁷ Thus says the LORD, God of Israel: This is what the two of you shall say to the king of Judah, who sent you to me to inquire of me: Pharaoh's army, which set out to help you, is going to return to its own land, to Egypt. ⁸ And the Chaldeans shall return and fight against this city; they shall

a Heb *he*

36:27–32—After Jehoiakim burns the first scroll, Jeremiah dictates a second, which announces judgment upon Jehoiakim and Judah because of the king's rejection of God's word. Some believe that these verses provide clues about the development of the book of Jeremiah.

37:1–10 Pray for Us!

When the advance of an Egyptian army results in a temporary lifting of the Babylonian siege of Jerusalem, Zedekiah asks Jeremiah to *pray* for the deliverance of the city.

take it and burn it with fire. ⁹ Thus says the LORD: Do not deceive yourselves, saying, "The Chaldeans will surely go away from us," for they will not go away. ¹⁰ Even if you defeated the whole army of Chaldeans who are fighting against you, and there remained of them only wounded men in their tents, they would rise up and burn this city with fire.

Jeremiah Is Imprisoned

11 Now when the Chaldean army had withdrawn from Jerusalem at the approach of Pharaoh's army, ¹² Jeremiah set out from Jerusalem to go to the land of Benjamin to receive his share of property*a* among the people there. ¹³ When he reached the Benjamin Gate, a sentinel there named Irijah son of Shelemiah son of Hananiah arrested the prophet Jeremiah saying, "You are deserting to the Chaldeans." ¹⁴ And Jeremiah said, "That is a lie; I am not deserting to the Chaldeans." But Irijah would not listen to him, and arrested Jeremiah and brought him to the officials. ¹⁵ The officials were enraged at Jeremiah, and they beat him and imprisoned him in the house of the secretary Jonathan, for it had been made a prison. ¹⁶ Thus Jeremiah was put in the cistern house, in the cells, and remained there many days.

17 Then King Zedekiah sent for him, and received him. The king questioned him secretly in his house, and said, "Is there any word from the LORD?" Jeremiah said, "There is!" Then he said, "You shall be handed over to the king of Babylon." ¹⁸ Jeremiah also said to King Zedekiah, "What wrong have I done to you or your servants or this people, that you have put me in prison? ¹⁹ Where are your prophets who prophesied to you, saying, 'The king of Babylon will not come against you and against this land'? ²⁰ Now please hear me, my lord king: be good enough to listen to my plea, and do not send me back to the house of the secretary Jonathan to die there." ²¹ So King Zedekiah gave orders, and they committed Jeremiah to the court of the guard; and a loaf of bread was given him daily from the bakers' street, until all the bread of the city was gone. So Jeremiah remained in the court of the guard.

Jeremiah in the Cistern

38 Now Shephatiah son of Mattan, Gedaliah son of Pashhur, Jucal son of Shelemiah, and Pashhur son of Malchiah heard the words that Jeremiah was saying to all the people, ² Thus says the LORD, Those who stay in this city shall die by the sword, by famine, and by pestilence; but those who go out to the Chaldeans shall live; they shall have their lives as a prize of war, and live. ³ Thus says the LORD, This city shall surely be handed over to the army of the king of Babylon and be taken. ⁴ Then the officials said to the king, "This man ought to be put to death, because he is discouraging the soldiers who are left in this city, and all the people, by speaking such words to them. For this man is not seeking the welfare of this people, but

a Meaning of Heb uncertain

37:10—This pronouncement of Jerusalem's destruction is an ironic twist on the lore that Jerusalem could be defended by the blind and lame (2 Sam. 5:6).

37:11–21 Jeremiah, a Deserter?

When Jeremiah attempts to leave Jerusalem, he is accused of desertion (also see 39:14) and imprisoned.

37:17—Though Jeremiah is imprisoned for desertion, King Zedekiah meets him secretly in an attempt to elicit some hopeful word from him.

38:1–6 Was It Treason?

The dispute between Jeremiah and Judah's leaders is fundamentally theological, pitting one understanding of God against another. Judah's leaders were certain that God would protect the kingdom, and so sought Egypt's help to deal with Babylon. These leaders were enraged that Jeremiah, believing that God intended Judah's defeat, urged surrender to Babylon. They persuade Zedekiah to turn Jeremiah over to them with the intention of killing him.

their harm." ⁵King Zedekiah said, "Here he is; he is in your hands; for the king is powerless against you." ⁶So they took Jeremiah and threw him into the cistern of Malchiah, the king's son, which was in the court of the guard, letting Jeremiah down by ropes. Now there was no water in the cistern, but only mud, and Jeremiah sank in the mud.

Jeremiah Is Rescued by Ebed-melech

7 Ebed-melech the Ethiopian,ᵃ a eunuch in the king's house, heard that they had put Jeremiah into the cistern. The king happened to be sitting at the Benjamin Gate, ⁸So Ebed-melech left the king's house and spoke to the king, ⁹"My lord king, these men have acted wickedly in all they did to the prophet Jeremiah by throwing him into the cistern to die there of hunger, for there is no bread left in the city." ¹⁰Then the king commanded Ebed-melech the Ethiopian,ᵃ "Take three men with you from here, and pull the prophet Jeremiah up from the cistern before he dies." ¹¹So Ebed-melech took the men with him and went to the house of the king, to a wardrobe ofᵇ the storehouse, and took from there old rags and worn-out clothes, which he let down to Jeremiah in the cistern by ropes. ¹²Then Ebed-melech the Ethiopianᵃ said to Jeremiah, "Just put the rags and clothes between your armpits and the ropes." Jeremiah did so. ¹³Then they drew Jeremiah up by the ropes and pulled him out of the cistern. And Jeremiah remained in the court of the guard.

Zedekiah Consults Jeremiah Again

¹⁴King Zedekiah sent for the prophet Jeremiah and received him at the third entrance of the temple of the LORD. The king said to Jeremiah, "I have something to ask you; do not hide anything from me." ¹⁵Jeremiah said to Zedekiah, "If I tell you, you will put me to death, will you not? And if I give you advice, you will not listen to me." ¹⁶So King Zedekiah swore an oath in secret to Jeremiah, "As the LORD lives, who gave us our lives, I will not put you to death or hand you over to these men who seek your life."

17 Then Jeremiah said to Zedekiah, "Thus says the LORD, the God of hosts, the God of Israel, If you will only surrender to the officials of the king of Babylon, then your life shall be spared, and this city shall not be burned with fire, and you and your house shall live. ¹⁸But if you do not surrender to the officials of the king of Babylon, then this city shall be handed over to the Chaldeans, and they shall burn it with fire, and you yourself shall not escape from their hand." ¹⁹King Zedekiah said to Jeremiah, "I am afraid of the Judeans who have deserted to the Chaldeans, for I might be handed over to them and they would abuse me." ²⁰Jeremiah said, "That will not happen. Just obey the voice of the LORD in what I say to you, and it shall go well with you, and your life shall be spared. ²¹But if you are determined not to surrender, this is what the LORD has shown me— ²²a vision of all the women remaining in the house of the king of Judah being led out to the officials of the king of Babylon and saying,

'Your trusted friends have seduced you
and have overcome you;

ᵃOr Nubian; Heb Cushite   ᵇCn: Heb to under

38:5—Zedekiah wavers between Jeremiah and Judah's officials. He is powerless because he is confused politically, strategically, and, most of all, theologically, in his understanding of who God is and what God is about.

38:7–13 *Ebed-melech*—An Ethiopian who served in the Jerusalem court. Though an outsider to Judah, he raises concerns that persuade the vacillating king to spare Jeremiah's life. As an outsider who grasps the ethos of Judah, Ebed-melech is like Uriah the Hittite (Bathsheba's husband), who resisted King David's efforts to have him sleep with his wife while consecrated for holy war (see 2 Sam. 11:6–13).

38:17–23—Jeremiah understands that obedience of God demands surrender to Babylon.

Now that your feet are stuck in the mud,
> they desert you.'

23 All your wives and your children shall be led out to the Chaldeans, and you yourself shall not escape from their hand, but shall be seized by the king of Babylon; and this city shall be burned with fire."

24 Then Zedekiah said to Jeremiah, "Do not let anyone else know of this conversation, or you will die. 25 If the officials should hear that I have spoken with you, and they should come and say to you, 'Just tell us what you said to the king; do not conceal it from us, or we will put you to death. What did the king say to you?' 26 then you shall say to them, 'I was presenting my plea to the king not to send me back to the house of Jonathan to die there.'" 27 All the officials did come to Jeremiah and questioned him; and he answered them in the very words the king had commanded. So they stopped questioning him, for the conversation had not been overheard. 28 And Jeremiah remained in the court of the guard until the day that Jerusalem was taken.

The Fall of Jerusalem

39 In the ninth year of King Zedekiah of Judah, in the tenth month, King Nebuchadrezzar of Babylon and all his army came against Jerusalem and besieged it; 2 in the eleventh year of Zedekiah, in the fourth month, on the ninth day of the month, a breach was made in the city. 3 When Jerusalem was taken,ᵃ all the officials of the king of Babylon came and sat in the middle gate: Nergal-sharezer, Samgar-nebo, Sarsechim the Rabsaris, Nergal-sharezer the Rabmag, with all the rest of the officials of the king of Babylon. 4 When King Zedekiah of Judah and all the soldiers saw them, they fled, going out of the city at night by way of the king's garden through the gate between the two walls; and they went toward the Arabah. 5 But the army of the Chaldeans pursued them, and overtook Zedekiah in the plains of Jericho; and when they had taken him, they brought him up to King Nebuchadrezzar of Babylon, at Riblah, in the land of Hamath; and he passed sentence on him. 6 The king of Babylon slaughtered the sons of Zedekiah at Riblah before his eyes; also the king of Babylon slaughtered all the nobles of Judah. 7 He put out the eyes of Zedekiah, and bound him in fetters to take him to Babylon. 8 The Chaldeans burned the king's house and the houses of the people, and broke down the walls of Jerusalem. 9 Then Nebuzaradan the captain of the guard exiled to Babylon the rest of the people who were left in the city, those who had deserted to him, and the people who remained. 10 Nebuzaradan the captain of the guard left in the land of Judah some of the poor people who owned nothing, and gave them vineyards and fields at the same time.

Jeremiah, Set Free, Remembers Ebed-melech

11 King Nebuchadrezzar of Babylon gave command concerning Jeremiah through Nebuzaradan, the captain of

---

ᵃ This clause has been transposed from 38:28

38:24–28—Zedekiah's vacillation continues and he wants his consultation with Jeremiah held in secret (see 37:17).

39:1–18 The Fall of Jerusalem
These verses stress that the word of God's judgment announced by Jeremiah against Judah is fulfilled with the fall of Jerusalem.

39:3 Sat in the middle gate—Compare Jeremiah's threat in 1:15.

39:6—Compare Jeremiah's threats against Zedekiah in 34:3 and 38:23.

39:8 Burned—Jeremiah frequently threatened that Jerusalem would be burned: 21:10; 34:2, 22; 38:17–18.

39:11–14 So he stayed with his own people—The charge against Jeremiah was that he was a deserter (37:11–16). Ironically, it is Zedekiah and Judah's nobles who desert when the Babylonians invade Jerusalem.

the guard, saying, [12] "Take him, look after him well and do him no harm, but deal with him as he may ask you." [13] So Nebuzaradan the captain of the guard, Nebushazban the Rabsaris, Nergalsharezer the Rabmag, and all the chief officers of the king of Babylon sent [14] and took Jeremiah from the court of the guard. They entrusted him to Gedaliah son of Ahikam son of Shaphan to be brought home. So he stayed with his own people.

[15] The word of the LORD came to Jeremiah while he was confined in the court of the guard: [16] Go and say to Ebed-melech the Ethiopian:[a] Thus says the LORD of hosts, the God of Israel: I am going to fulfill my words against this city for evil and not for good, and they shall be accomplished in your presence on that day. [17] But I will save you on that day, says the LORD, and you shall not be handed over to those whom you dread. [18] For I will surely save you, and you shall not fall by the sword; but you shall have your life as a prize of war, because you have trusted in me, says the LORD.

Jeremiah with Gedaliah the Governor

40 The word that came to Jeremiah from the LORD after Nebuzaradan the captain of the guard had let him go from Ramah, when he took him bound in fetters along with all the captives of Jerusalem and Judah who were being exiled to Babylon. [2] The captain of the guard took Jeremiah and said to him, "The LORD your God threatened this place with this disaster; [3] and now the LORD has brought it about, and has done as he said, because all of you sinned against the LORD and did not obey his voice. Therefore this thing has come upon you. [4] Now look, I have just released you today from the fetters on your hands. If you wish to come with me to Babylon, come, and I will take good care of you; but if you do not wish to come with me to Babylon, you need not come. See, the whole land is before you; go wherever you think it good and right to go. [5] If you remain,[b] then return to Gedaliah son of Ahikam son of Shaphan, whom the king of Babylon appointed governor of the towns of Judah, and stay with him among the people; or go wherever you think it right to go." So the captain of the guard gave him an allowance of food and a present, and let him go. [6] Then Jeremiah went to Gedaliah son of Ahikam at Mizpah, and stayed with him among the people who were left in the land.

[7] When all the leaders of the forces in the open country and their troops heard that the king of Babylon had appointed Gedaliah son of Ahikam governor in the land, and had committed to him men, women, and children, those of the poorest of the land who had not been taken into exile to Babylon, [8] they went to Gedaliah at Mizpah—Ishmael son of Nethaniah, Johanan son of Kareah, Seraiah son of Tanhumeth, the sons of Ephai the Netophathite, Jezaniah son of the Maacathite, they and their troops. [9] Gedaliah son of Ahikam son of Shaphan swore to them and their troops, saying, "Do not be afraid to serve the Chaldeans. Stay in the land and serve the king of Babylon, and it shall go well with you. [10] As for me, I am staying at Mizpah to represent

a Or Nubian; Heb Cushite   *b* Syr: Meaning of Heb uncertain

39:15–18 *Ebed-melech*—An Ethiopian outsider is praised because he trusted God and is promised safety. Jeremiah's criticism of the Jerusalem establishment was that they trusted fertility gods or neighboring states—not God—to keep them secure.

40:1–41:18 Gedaliah
Gedaliah, appointed by the Babylonians to govern Judah after 587 BCE, comes from a family committed to reform. His grandfather, Shaphan, was King Josiah's secretary who brought the king the scroll found in the temple that became the basis of a reform (2 Kgs. 22:8–10). Gedaliah's father had rescued Jeremiah after he was arrested for speaking at the temple (26:24).

40:9—Gedaliah supports the pro-Babylonian policy that Jeremiah urged.

you before the Chaldeans who come to us; but as for you, gather wine and summer fruits and oil, and store them in your vessels, and live in the towns that you have taken over." [11] Likewise, when all the Judeans who were in Moab and among the Ammonites and in Edom and in other lands heard that the king of Babylon had left a remnant in Judah and had appointed Gedaliah son of Ahikam son of Shaphan as governor over them, [12] then all the Judeans returned from all the places to which they had been scattered and came to the land of Judah, to Gedaliah at Mizpah; and they gathered wine and summer fruits in great abundance.

13 Now Johanan son of Kareah and all the leaders of the forces in the open country came to Gedaliah at Mizpah [14] and said to him, "Are you at all aware that Baalis king of the Ammonites has sent Ishmael son of Nethaniah to take your life?" But Gedaliah son of Ahikam would not believe them. [15] Then Johanan son of Kareah spoke secretly to Gedaliah at Mizpah, "Please let me go and kill Ishmael son of Nethaniah, and no one else will know. Why should he take your life, so that all the Judeans who are gathered around you would be scattered, and the remnant of Judah would perish?" [16] But Gedaliah son of Ahikam said to Johanan son of Kareah, "Do not do such a thing, for you are telling a lie about Ishmael."

Insurrection against Gedaliah

41 In the seventh month, Ishmael son of Nethaniah son of Elishama, of the royal family, one of the chief officers of the king, came with ten men to Gedaliah son of Ahikam, at Mizpah. As they ate bread together there at Mizpah, [2] Ishmael son of Nethaniah and the ten men with him got up and struck down Gedaliah son of Ahikam son of Shaphan with the sword and killed him, because the king of Babylon had appointed him governor in the land. [3] Ishmael also killed all the Judeans who were with Gedaliah at Mizpah, and the Chaldean soldiers who happened to be there.

4 On the day after the murder of Gedaliah, before anyone knew of it, [5] eighty men arrived from Shechem and Shiloh and Samaria, with their beards shaved and their clothes torn, and their bodies gashed, bringing grain offerings and incense to present at the temple of the LORD. [6] And Ishmael son of Nethaniah came out from Mizpah to meet them, weeping as he came. As he met them, he said to them, "Come to Gedaliah son of Ahikam." [7] When they reached the middle of the city, Ishmael son of Nethaniah and the men with him slaughtered them, and threw them[a] into a cistern. [8] But there were ten men among them who said to Ishmael, "Do not kill us, for we have stores of wheat, barley, oil, and honey hidden in the fields." So he refrained, and did not kill them along with their companions.

9 Now the cistern into which Ishmael had thrown all the bodies of the men whom he had struck down was the large cistern[b] that King Asa had made for defense against King Baasha of Israel; Ishmael son of Nethaniah filled that cistern with those whom he had killed.

a Syr: Heb lacks *and threw them*; compare verse 9   *b* Gk: Heb *whom he had killed by the hand of Gedaliah*

40:13–16—A plot against Gedaliah is launched by the king of Ammon, a territory east of Judah. The plot suggests that the Ammonites feared Judah's cooperation with Babylon under Gedaliah. Why Gedaliah does not allow his followers to intercept the plot against him is unclear.

41:1 *Ishmael*—Gedaliah's assassin was a member of a Judean royal family. His cooperation with the Ammonites reflects a dispute between the Jerusalem establishment, which favored a pro-Egyptian policy, and Gedaliah and Jeremiah, with their pro-Babylonian policy.

41:5—These pilgrims are going to Jerusalem to mourn the destroyed temple.

41:6–8—While Ishmael's assassination of Gedaliah may have had political motives, his slaughter of the pilgrims is an inexplicable act of violence.

10 Then Ishmael took captive all the rest of the people who were in Mizpah, the king's daughters and all the people who were left at Mizpah, whom Nebuzaradan, the captain of the guard, had committed to Gedaliah son of Ahikam. Ishmael son of Nethaniah took them captive and set out to cross over to the Ammonites.

11 But when Johanan son of Kareah and all the leaders of the forces with him heard of all the crimes that Ishmael son of Nethaniah had done, 12 they took all their men and went to fight against Ishmael son of Nethaniah. They came upon him at the great pool that is in Gibeon. 13 And when all the people who were with Ishmael saw Johanan son of Kareah and all the leaders of the forces with him, they were glad. 14 So all the people whom Ishmael had carried away captive from Mizpah turned around and came back, and went to Johanan son of Kareah. 15 But Ishmael son of Nethaniah escaped from Johanan with eight men, and went to the Ammonites. 16 Then Johanan son of Kareah and all the leaders of the forces with him took all the rest of the people whom Ishmael son of Nethaniah had carried away captive[a] from Mizpah after he had slain Gedaliah son of Ahikam—soldiers, women, children, and eunuchs, whom Johanan brought back from Gibeon.[b] 17 And they set out, and stopped at Geruth Chimham near Bethlehem, intending to go to Egypt 18 because of the Chaldeans; for they were afraid of them, because Ishmael son of Nethaniah had killed Gedaliah son of Ahikam, whom the king of Babylon had made governor over the land.

Jeremiah Advises Survivors Not to Migrate

42 Then all the commanders of the forces, and Johanan son of Kareah and Azariah[c] son of Hoshaiah, and all the people from the least to the greatest, approached 2 the prophet Jeremiah and said, "Be good enough to listen to our plea, and pray to the LORD your God for us—for all this remnant. For there are only a few of us left out of many, as your eyes can see. 3 Let the LORD your God show us where we should go and what we should do." 4 The prophet Jeremiah said to them, "Very well: I am going to pray to the LORD your God as you request, and whatever the LORD answers you I will tell you; I will keep nothing back from you." 5 They in their turn said to Jeremiah, "May the LORD be a true and faithful witness against us if we do not act according to everything that the LORD your God sends us through you. 6 Whether it is good or bad, we will obey the voice of the LORD our God to whom we are sending you, in order that it may go well with us when we obey the voice of the LORD our God."

7 At the end of ten days the word of the LORD came to Jeremiah. 8 Then he summoned Johanan son of Kareah and all the commanders of the forces who were with him, and all the people from the least to the greatest, 9 and said to them, "Thus says the LORD, the God of Israel, to whom you sent me to present your plea before him: 10 If you will only remain in this land, then I will build you up and not pull you down; I will plant you, and not pluck you up; for I am sorry

---

[a] Cn: Heb *whom he recovered from Ishmael son of Nethaniah*   [b] Meaning of Heb uncertain   [c] Gk: Heb *Jezaniah*

41:11–18—*Johanan*, a Judean military officer who had been loyal to Gedaliah (see 40:13), pursues Ishmael. He rescues some hostages, but Ishmael escapes. Johanan and those with him then set off *to Egypt*, apparently fearful of Babylonian reprisals for Gedaliah's murder.

42:1–43:7 Flight to Egypt

Johanan and those with him seek Jeremiah's counsel about going to Egypt. They swear to obey whatever word from the Lord Jeremiah has for them (42:1–6).

42:7–22—Jeremiah conveys God's demand that those intending to go to Egypt *remain* in Judah. Jeremiah's response is consistent with the pro-Babylonian and anti-Egyptian policy that he understood to be God's intention for Judah.

for the disaster that I have brought upon you. **11** Do not be afraid of the king of Babylon, as you have been; do not be afraid of him, says the LORD, for I am with you, to save you and to rescue you from his hand. **12** I will grant you mercy, and he will have mercy on you and restore you to your native soil. **13** But if you continue to say, 'We will not stay in this land,' thus disobeying the voice of the LORD your God **14** and saying, 'No, we will go to the land of Egypt, where we shall not see war, or hear the sound of the trumpet, or be hungry for bread, and there we will stay,' **15** then hear the word of the LORD, O remnant of Judah. Thus says the LORD of hosts, the God of Israel: If you are determined to enter Egypt and go to settle there, **16** then the sword that you fear shall overtake you there, in the land of Egypt; and the famine that you dread shall follow close after you into Egypt; and there you shall die. **17** All the people who have determined to go to Egypt to settle there shall die by the sword, by famine, and by pestilence; they shall have no remnant or survivor from the disaster that I am bringing upon them.

18 "For thus says the LORD of hosts, the God of Israel: Just as my anger and my wrath were poured out on the inhabitants of Jerusalem, so my wrath will be poured out on you when you go to Egypt. You shall become an object of execration and horror, of cursing and ridicule. You shall see this place no more. **19** The LORD has said to you, O remnant of Judah, Do not go to Egypt. Be well aware that I have warned you today **20** that you have made a fatal mistake. For you yourselves sent me to the LORD your God, saying, 'Pray for us to the LORD our God, and whatever the LORD our God says, tell us and we will do it.' **21** So I have told you today, but you have not obeyed the voice of the LORD your God in anything that he sent me to tell you. **22** Be well aware, then, that you shall die by the sword, by famine, and by pestilence in the place where you desire to go and settle."

Taken to Egypt, Jeremiah Warns of Judgment

43 When Jeremiah finished speaking to all the people all these words of the LORD their God, with which the LORD their God had sent him to them, **2** Azariah son of Hoshaiah and Johanan son of Kareah and all the other insolent men said to Jeremiah, "You are telling a lie. The LORD our God did not send you to say, 'Do not go to Egypt to settle there'; **3** but Baruch son of Neriah is inciting you against us, to hand us over to the Chaldeans, in order that they may kill us or take us into exile in Babylon." **4** So Johanan son of Kareah and all the commanders of the forces and all the people did not obey the voice of the LORD, to stay in the land of Judah. **5** But Johanan son of Kareah and all the commanders of the forces took all the remnant of Judah who had returned to settle in the land of Judah from all the nations to which they had been driven— **6** the men, the women, the children, the princesses, and everyone whom Nebuzaradan the captain of the guard had left with Gedaliah son of Ahikam son of Shaphan; also the prophet Jeremiah and Baruch son of Neriah. **7** And they came into the land of Egypt, for they did not obey the voice of the LORD. And they arrived at Tahpanhes.

43:2–3—In consulting with Jeremiah, those intending to go to Egypt swore an oath to heed Jeremiah, no matter what word from the Lord he brought to them (see 42:5–6).

43:2—Jeremiah had charged Judah with engaging in various deceptions and lies: assuming security in the temple (7:3–4); prophets supporting deceptive social practices (8:8–12; 23:14);

imagining that the Babylonian threat would soon pass (27:10; 28:15; 29:21). Now the charge of lying is thrown back at Jeremiah. Similarly, the people level at Jeremiah the accusation he had made against other prophets, that God *did not send you* (see 23:18–22).

43:4 *Did not obey the voice of the LORD*—Even defeat failed to bring Judah to obedience.

8 Then the word of the LORD came to Jeremiah in Tahpanhes: 9 Take some large stones in your hands, and bury them in the clay pavement[a] that is at the entrance to Pharaoh's palace in Tahpanhes. Let the Judeans see you do it, 10 and say to them, Thus says the LORD of hosts, the God of Israel: I am going to send and take my servant King Nebuchadrezzar of Babylon, and he[b] will set his throne above these stones that I have buried, and he will spread his royal canopy over them. 11 He shall come and ravage the land of Egypt, giving

> those who are destined for
> > pestilence, to pestilence,
> and those who are destined for
> > captivity, to captivity,
> and those who are destined for the
> > sword, to the sword.

12 He[b] shall kindle a fire in the temples of the gods of Egypt; and he shall burn them and carry them away captive; and he shall pick clean the land of Egypt, as a shepherd picks his cloak clean of vermin; and he shall depart from there safely. 13 He shall break the obelisks of Heliopolis, which is in the land of Egypt; and the temples of the gods of Egypt he shall burn with fire.

Denunciation of Persistent Idolatry

44 The word that came to Jeremiah for all the Judeans living in the land of Egypt, at Migdol, at Tahpanhes, at Memphis, and in the land of Pathros, 2 Thus says the LORD of hosts, the God of Israel: You yourselves have seen all the disaster that I have brought on Jerusalem and on all the towns of Judah. Look at them; today they are a desolation, without an inhabitant in them, 3 because of the wickedness that they committed, provoking me to anger, in that they went to make offerings and serve other gods

that they had not known, neither they, nor you, nor your ancestors. 4 Yet I persistently sent to you all my servants the prophets, saying, "I beg you not to do this abominable thing that I hate!" 5 But they did not listen or incline their ear, to turn from their wickedness and make no offerings to other gods. 6 So my wrath and my anger were poured out and kindled in the towns of Judah and in the streets of Jerusalem; and they became a waste and a desolation, as they still are today. 7 And now thus says the LORD God of hosts, the God of Israel: Why are you doing such great harm to yourselves, to cut off man and woman, child and infant, from the midst of Judah, leaving yourselves without a remnant? 8 Why do you provoke me to anger with the works of your hands, making offerings to other gods in the land of Egypt where you have come to settle? Will you be cut off and become an object of cursing and ridicule among all the nations of the earth? 9 Have you forgotten the crimes of your ancestors, of the kings of Judah, of their[c] wives, your own crimes and those of your wives, which they committed in the land of Judah and in the streets of Jerusalem? 10 They have shown no contrition or fear to this day, nor have they walked in my law and my statutes that I set before you and before your ancestors.

11 Therefore thus says the LORD of hosts, the God of Israel: I am determined to bring disaster on you, to bring all Judah to an end. 12 I will take the remnant of Judah who are determined to come to the land of Egypt to settle, and they shall perish, everyone; in the land of Egypt they shall fall; by the sword and by famine they shall perish; from the least to the greatest, they shall die by

a Meaning of Heb uncertain　*b* Gk Syr: Heb I　*c* Heb *his*

43:8–44:30 Jeremiah in Egypt

43:8–13—A symbolic act that indicates Babylon's eventual defeat of Egypt. Even in Egypt, the Judeans will not escape Babylon. Historically, Babylon never conquered Egypt.

44:1–14—Jeremiah summarizes the reasons for Judah's destruction.

the sword and by famine; and they shall become an object of execration and horror, of cursing and ridicule. **13** I will punish those who live in the land of Egypt, as I have punished Jerusalem, with the sword, with famine, and with pestilence, **14** so that none of the remnant of Judah who have come to settle in the land of Egypt shall escape or survive or return to the land of Judah. Although they long to go back to live there, they shall not go back, except some fugitives.

15 Then all the men who were aware that their wives had been making offerings to other gods, and all the women who stood by, a great assembly, all the people who lived in Pathros in the land of Egypt, answered Jeremiah: **16** "As for the word that you have spoken to us in the name of the LORD, we are not going to listen to you. **17** Instead, we will do everything that we have vowed, make offerings to the queen of heaven and pour out libations to her, just as we and our ancestors, our kings and our officials, used to do in the towns of Judah and in the streets of Jerusalem. We used to have plenty of food, and prospered, and saw no misfortune. **18** But from the time we stopped making offerings to the queen of heaven and pouring out libations to her, we have lacked everything and have perished by the sword and by famine." **19** And the women said,*a* "Indeed we will go on making offerings to the queen of heaven and pouring out libations to her; do you think that we made cakes for her, marked with her image, and poured out libations to her without our husbands' being involved?"

20 Then Jeremiah said to all the people, men and women, all the people who were giving him this answer: **21** "As for the offerings that you made in the towns of Judah and in the streets of Jerusalem, you and your ancestors, your kings and

your officials, and the people of the land, did not the LORD remember them? Did it not come into his mind? **22** The LORD could no longer bear the sight of your evil doings, the abominations that you committed; therefore your land became a desolation and a waste and a curse, without inhabitant, as it is to this day. **23** It is because you burned offerings, and because you sinned against the LORD and did not obey the voice of the LORD or walk in his law and in his statutes and in his decrees, that this disaster has befallen you, as is still evident today."

24 Jeremiah said to all the people and all the women, "Hear the word of the LORD, all you Judeans who are in the land of Egypt, **25** Thus says the LORD of hosts, the God of Israel: You and your wives have accomplished in deeds what you declared in words, saying, 'We are determined to perform the vows that we have made, to make offerings to the queen of heaven and to pour out libations to her.' By all means, keep your vows and make your libations! **26** Therefore hear the word of the LORD, all you Judeans who live in the land of Egypt: Lo, I swear by my great name, says the LORD, that my name shall no longer be pronounced on the lips of any of the people of Judah in all the land of Egypt, saying, 'As the Lord GOD lives.' **27** I am going to watch over them for harm and not for good; all the people of Judah who are in the land of Egypt shall perish by the sword and by famine, until not one is left. **28** And those who escape the sword shall return from the land of Egypt to the land of Judah, few in number; and all the remnant of Judah, who have come to the land of Egypt to settle, shall know whose words will stand, mine or theirs! **29** This shall be the sign to you, says the LORD, that I am going to punish you in

a Compare Syr: Heb lacks *And the women said*

44:15–19—The response to Jeremiah is one of utter defiance. Those who flee to Egypt are convinced that the fertility deities whom they worship are reliable sources of blessing and security.

44:20–23—Jeremiah again gives the reason for the disaster.

this place, in order that you may know that my words against you will surely be carried out: [30] Thus says the LORD, I am going to give Pharaoh Hophra, king of Egypt, into the hands of his enemies, those who seek his life, just as I gave King Zedekiah of Judah into the hand of King Nebuchadrezzar of Babylon, his enemy who sought his life."

A Word of Comfort to Baruch

45 The word that the prophet Jeremiah spoke to Baruch son of Neriah, when he wrote these words in a scroll at the dictation of Jeremiah, in the fourth year of King Jehoiakim son of Josiah of Judah: [2] Thus says the LORD, the God of Israel, to you, O Baruch: [3] You said, "Woe is me! The LORD has added sorrow to my pain; I am weary with my groaning, and I find no rest." [4] Thus you shall say to him, "Thus says the LORD: I am going to break down what I have built, and pluck up what I have planted—that is, the whole land. [5] And you, do you seek great things for yourself? Do not seek them; for I am going to bring disaster upon all flesh, says the LORD; but I will give you your life as a prize of war in every place to which you may go."

Judgment on Egypt

46 The word of the LORD that came to the prophet Jeremiah concerning the nations.

[2] Concerning Egypt, about the army of Pharaoh Neco, king of Egypt, which was by the river Euphrates at Carchemish and which King Nebuchadrezzar of Babylon defeated in the fourth year of King Jehoiakim son of Josiah of Judah:

[3] Prepare buckler and shield,
     and advance for battle!
[4] Harness the horses;
     mount the steeds!
   Take your stations with your
        helmets,
     whet your lances,
     put on your coats of mail!
[5] Why do I see them terrified?
     They have fallen back;
   their warriors are beaten down,
     and have fled in haste.
   They do not look back—
     terror is all around!
                    says the LORD.
[6] The swift cannot flee away,
     nor can the warrior escape;
   in the north by the river Euphrates
     they have stumbled and fallen.

[7] Who is this, rising like the Nile,
     like rivers whose waters surge?
[8] Egypt rises like the Nile,
     like rivers whose waters surge.
   It said, Let me rise, let me cover the
        earth,
     let me destroy cities and their
        inhabitants.
[9] Advance, O horses,
     and dash madly, O chariots!

44:30—Jeremiah sees the assassination of Pharaoh Hophra (570 BCE) as a sign of God's inevitable judgment of the Judeans practicing apostasy in Egypt.

45:1–5 Baruch
Jeremiah's scribe voices complaints to God similar to those of the prophet (see note at 11:18–23).

45:3–5—God rebukes Baruch's desire for *rest* (v. 3) and *great things* (v. 5) as inappropriate. God's promise to Baruch, his *life*, is appropriately modest at a time when many in Judah would lose their lives in the conflict with Babylon.

46:1–28 Against Egypt
God appointed Jeremiah a prophet "to the na-

tions" (1:5, 10). Chapters 46–51 develop this theme more fully with oracles against several nations that surround Judah. Often in these chapters, judgment of the nations is linked to Judah's restoration. However, these chapters also envision God's restoration of the nations. Other prophetic books include similar material: Isa. 13–23; Ezek. 25–32; Amos 1–2.

46:2—*Pharaoh Neco* was defeated by *Nebuchadrezzar of Babylon* in 605 BCE. This Babylonian victory marked the beginning of Babylonian dominance in the region.

46:9 *Ethiopia and Put . . . the Ludim*—Peoples from northern Africa who battle with Egypt.

Let the warriors go forth:
   Ethiopia[a] and Put who carry the
      shield,
   the Ludim, who draw[b] the bow.
10 That day is the day of the Lord GOD
      of hosts,
   a day of retribution,
      to gain vindication from his foes.
   The sword shall devour and be
      sated,
   and drink its fill of their blood.
   For the Lord GOD of hosts holds a
      sacrifice
   in the land of the north by the
      river Euphrates.
11 Go up to Gilead, and take balm,
   O virgin daughter Egypt!
   In vain you have used many
      medicines;
   there is no healing for you.
12 The nations have heard of your
      shame,
   and the earth is full of your cry;
   for warrior has stumbled against
      warrior;
   both have fallen together.

Babylonia Will Strike Egypt

13 The word that the LORD spoke to
the prophet Jeremiah about the coming
of King Nebuchadrezzar of Babylon to
attack the land of Egypt:
14 Declare in Egypt, and proclaim in
      Migdol;
   proclaim in Memphis and
      Tahpanhes;
   Say, "Take your stations and be
      ready,
   for the sword shall devour those
      around you."
15 Why has Apis fled?[c]
   Why did your bull not stand?
   —because the LORD thrust him
      down.
16 Your multitude stumbled[d] and fell,
   and one said to another,[e]

"Come, let us go back to our own
      people
   and to the land of our birth,
   because of the destroying sword."
17 Give Pharaoh, king of Egypt, the
      name
   "Braggart who missed his chance."
18 As I live, says the King,
   whose name is the LORD of hosts,
   one is coming
   like Tabor among the mountains,
   and like Carmel by the sea.
19 Pack your bags for exile,
   sheltered daughter Egypt!
   For Memphis shall become a
      waste,
   a ruin, without inhabitant.
20 A beautiful heifer is Egypt—
   a gadfly from the north lights
      upon her.
21 Even her mercenaries in her midst
   are like fatted calves;
   they too have turned and fled
      together,
   they did not stand;
   for the day of their calamity has
      come upon them,
   the time of their punishment.
22 She makes a sound like a snake
      gliding away;
   for her enemies march in force,
   and come against her with axes,
   like those who fell trees.
23 They shall cut down her forest,
                     says the LORD,
   though it is impenetrable,
   because they are more numerous
      than locusts;
   they are without number.
24 Daughter Egypt shall be put to
      shame;

[a] Or Nubia; Heb Cush [b] Cn: Heb who grasp, who draw [c] Gk: Heb Why
was it swept away [d] Gk: Meaning of Heb uncertain [e] Gk: Heb and fell one
to another and they said

46:10 *Day of the Lord*—See note at 17:16.
46:11 *Gilead*—See note at 8:22.
46:13–26—See 43:8–13.

46:15 *Apis*—An Egyptian fertility god.
46:19 *Memphis*—This one-time capital of Egypt
will meet the same fate as Jerusalem and the cities of Judah.

she shall be handed over to a
  people from the north.

25 The LORD of hosts, the God of
Israel, said: See, I am bringing punishment upon Amon of Thebes, and Pharaoh, and Egypt and her gods and her
kings, upon Pharaoh and those who
trust in him. 26 I will hand them over to
those who seek their life, to King Nebuchadrezzar of Babylon and his officers.
Afterward Egypt shall be inhabited as in
the days of old, says the LORD.

God Will Save Israel

27 But as for you, have no fear, my
      servant Jacob,
  and do not be dismayed,
      O Israel;
  for I am going to save you from far
      away,
  and your offspring from the land
      of their captivity.
  Jacob shall return and have quiet
      and ease,
  and no one shall make him afraid.
28 As for you, have no fear, my servant
      Jacob,
                    says the LORD,
  for I am with you.
  I will make an end of all the nations
      among which I have banished you,
  but I will not make an end of you!
  I will chastise you in just measure,
  and I will by no means leave you
      unpunished.

Judgment on the Philistines

47 The word of the LORD that came
  to the prophet Jeremiah concerning the Philistines, before Pharaoh
attacked Gaza:
  2 Thus says the LORD:

See, waters are rising out of the
      north
  and shall become an overflowing
      torrent;
  they shall overflow the land and all
      that fills it,
  the city and those who live in it.
  People shall cry out,
  and all the inhabitants of the land
      shall wail.
3 At the noise of the stamping of the
      hoofs of his stallions,
  at the clatter of his chariots, at the
      rumbling of their wheels,
  parents do not turn back for
      children,
  so feeble are their hands,
4 because of the day that is coming
      to destroy all the Philistines,
  to cut off from Tyre and Sidon
      every helper that remains.
  For the LORD is destroying the
      Philistines,
  the remnant of the coastland of
      Caphtor.
5 Baldness has come upon Gaza,
      Ashkelon is silenced.
  O remnant of their power!ᵃ
  How long will you gash
      yourselves?
6 Ah, sword of the LORD!
  How long until you are quiet?
  Put yourself into your scabbard,
      rest and be still!
7 How can itᵇ be quiet,
  when the LORD has given it an
      order?
  Against Ashkelon and against the
      seashore—
  there he has appointed it.

a Gk: Heb *their valley*   *b* Gk Vg: Heb *you*

46:25 *Amon*—An Egyptian sun god whose cult
was located in the city of Thebes.

46:26—Like Judah, Egypt will eventually be
restored (see 1:10; chaps. 30–33)

46:27–28—God's judgment of Egypt is linked to
Judah's restoration.

47:1–7 Against the Philistines
While v. 1 suggests an Egyptian defeat of Gaza,

the reference in v. 2 to *waters . . . rising out the
north* suggests Babylon's invasion of the region in
605 BCE, when they destroyed several Philistine
cities.

47:4 *Tyre and Sidon*—These Phoenician cities
are portrayed as allies of the Philistines.

47:5 *Ashkelon*—Another Philistine city that the
Babylonians destroyed in 605 BCE.

Judgment on Moab

48 Concerning Moab.

Thus says the LORD of hosts, the God of Israel:

Alas for Nebo, it is laid waste!
　　Kiriathaim is put to shame, it is taken;
the fortress is put to shame and broken down;
2　　the renown of Moab is no more.
In Heshbon they planned evil against her:
　　"Come, let us cut her off from being a nation!"
You also, O Madmen, shall be brought to silence;[a]
　　the sword shall pursue you.

3　Hark! a cry from Horonaim,
　　"Desolation and great destruction!"
4　"Moab is destroyed!"
　　her little ones cry out.
5　For at the ascent of Luhith
　　they go[b] up weeping bitterly;
for at the descent of Horonaim
　　they have heard the distressing cry of anguish.
6　Flee! Save yourselves!
　　Be like a wild ass[c] in the desert!

7　Surely, because you trusted in your strongholds[d] and your treasures,
　　you also shall be taken;
Chemosh shall go out into exile,
　　with his priests and his attendants.
8　The destroyer shall come upon every town,
　　and no town shall escape;
the valley shall perish,
　　and the plain shall be destroyed,
　　as the LORD has spoken.

9　Set aside salt for Moab,
　　for she will surely fall;
her towns shall become a desolation,
　　with no inhabitant in them.

10 Accursed is the one who is slack in doing the work of the LORD; and accursed is the one who keeps back the sword from bloodshed.

11　Moab has been at ease from his youth,
　　settled like wine[e] on its dregs;
he has not been emptied from vessel to vessel,
　　nor has he gone into exile;
therefore his flavor has remained
　　and his aroma is unspoiled.

12 Therefore, the time is surely coming, says the LORD, when I shall send to him decanters to decant him, and empty his vessels, and break his[f] jars in pieces. 13 Then Moab shall be ashamed of Chemosh, as the house of Israel was ashamed of Bethel, their confidence.

14　How can you say, "We are heroes and mighty warriors"?
15　The destroyer of Moab and his towns has come up,
　　and the choicest of his young men have gone down to slaughter,
　　says the King, whose name is the LORD of hosts.
16　The calamity of Moab is near at hand
　　and his doom approaches swiftly.
17　Mourn over him, all you his neighbors,
　　and all who know his name;
say, "How the mighty scepter is broken,
　　the glorious staff!"

---

a The place-name *Madmen* sounds like the Hebrew verb *to be silent*
b Cn: Heb *he goes*　*c* Gk Aquila: Heb *like Aroer*　*d* Gk: Heb *works*
e Heb lacks *like wine*　*f* Gk Aquila: Heb *their*

48:1–47 Against Moab
Conflict between Judah and Moab was long-standing (Num. 21; Judg. 3; 11) and continued to Jeremiah's time (2 Kgs. 24:1–2). Material in this chapter is similar to oracles against Moab found in other prophetic books. A standard way of viewing Moab may have developed by the time the book of Jeremiah took its final form.

48:2—It is unclear which nation is imagined to have invaded Moab.

48:7 *Chemosh*—The Moabite deity.

48:11–13—Moab, which has escaped invasion and exile, is compared to a fine *wine* that has not been poured to allow its sediment (*dregs*) to settle out. However, Moab will soon be exiled.

¹⁸ Come down from glory,
  and sit on the parched ground,
  enthroned daughter Dibon!
For the destroyer of Moab has come
  up against you;
  he has destroyed your strongholds.
¹⁹ Stand by the road and watch,
  you inhabitant of Aroer!
Ask the man fleeing and the woman
  escaping;
  say, "What has happened?"
²⁰ Moab is put to shame, for it is
  broken down;
  wail and cry!
Tell it by the Arnon,
  that Moab is laid waste.

21 Judgment has come upon the tableland, upon Holon, and Jahzah, and Mephaath, ²²and Dibon, and Nebo, and Beth-diblathaim, ²³and Kiriathaim, and Beth-gamul, and Beth-meon, ²⁴and Kerioth, and Bozrah, and all the towns of the land of Moab, far and near. ²⁵The horn of Moab is cut off, and his arm is broken, says the LORD.

26 Make him drunk, because he magnified himself against the LORD; let Moab wallow in his vomit; he too shall become a laughingstock. ²⁷Israel was a laughingstock for you, though he was not caught among thieves; but whenever you spoke of him you shook your head!

²⁸ Leave the towns, and live on the rock,
  O inhabitants of Moab!
Be like the dove that nests
  on the sides of the mouth of a
  gorge.
²⁹ We have heard of the pride of
  Moab—
  he is very proud—
of his loftiness, his pride, and his
  arrogance,
  and the haughtiness of his heart.
³⁰ I myself know his insolence, says the
  LORD;

his boasts are false,
  his deeds are false.
³¹ Therefore I wail for Moab;
  I cry out for all Moab;
  for the people of Kir-heres I
  mourn.
³² More than for Jazer I weep for you,
  O vine of Sibmah!
Your branches crossed over the sea,
  reached as far as Jazer;ᵃ
upon your summer fruits and your
  vintage
  the destroyer has fallen.
³³ Gladness and joy have been taken
  away
  from the fruitful land of Moab;
I have stopped the wine from the
  wine presses;
  no one treads them with shouts
  of joy;
  the shouting is not the shout of joy.

34 Heshbon and Elealeh cry out;ᵇ as far as Jahaz they utter their voice, from Zoar to Horonaim and Eglath-shelishiyah. For even the waters of Nimrim have become desolate. ³⁵And I will bring to an end in Moab, says the LORD, those who offer sacrifice at a high place and make offerings to their gods. ³⁶Therefore my heart moans for Moab like a flute, and my heart moans like a flute for the people of Kir-heres; for the riches they gained have perished.

37 For every head is shaved and every beard cut off; on all the hands there are gashes, and on the loins sackcloth. ³⁸On all the housetops of Moab and in the squares there is nothing but lamentation; for I have broken Moab like a vessel that no one wants, says the LORD. ³⁹How it is broken! How they wail! How Moab has turned his back in shame! So Moab has become a derision and a horror to all his neighbors.

⁴⁰ For thus says the LORD:

ᵃ Two Mss and Isa 16.8: MT *the sea of Jazer* ᵇ Cn: Heb *From the cry of Heshbon to Elealeh*

48:25 *Horn . . . arm*—Symbols of Moab's power.

48:31—God weeps for Moab as God wept over Judah's destruction (4:19–22; 8:18–9:2).

Look, he shall swoop down like an
    eagle,
  and spread his wings against
      Moab;
41 the towns[a] shall be taken
  and the strongholds seized.
  The hearts of the warriors of Moab,
      on that day,
  shall be like the heart of a woman
      in labor.
42 Moab shall be destroyed as a people,
  because he magnified himself
      against the LORD.
43 Terror, pit, and trap
  are before you, O inhabitants of
      Moab!
                    says the LORD.
44 Everyone who flees from the terror
  shall fall into the pit,
and everyone who climbs out of
      the pit
  shall be caught in the trap.
For I will bring these things[b] upon
      Moab
  in the year of their punishment,
                    says the LORD.

45 In the shadow of Heshbon
  fugitives stop exhausted;
for a fire has gone out from
      Heshbon,
  a flame from the house of Sihon;
it has destroyed the forehead of
      Moab,
  the scalp of the people of tumult.[c]
46 Woe to you, O Moab!
  The people of Chemosh have
      perished,
for your sons have been taken captive,
  and your daughters into captivity.
47 Yet I will restore the fortunes of
      Moab
  in the latter days, says the LORD.
Thus far is the judgment on Moab.

Judgment on the Ammonites

49 Concerning the Ammonites.

Thus says the LORD:
  Has Israel no sons?
    Has he no heir?
  Why then has Milcom dispossessed
      Gad,
    and his people settled in its towns?
2 Therefore, the time is surely coming,
      says the LORD,
  when I will sound the battle alarm
      against Rabbah of the Ammonites;
  it shall become a desolate mound,
    and its villages shall be burned
        with fire;
  then Israel shall dispossess those
      who dispossessed him,
    says the LORD.
3 Wail, O Heshbon, for Ai is laid
      waste!
    Cry out, O daughters[d] of Rabbah!
  Put on sackcloth,
    lament, and slash yourselves with
        whips![e]
  For Milcom shall go into exile,
    with his priests and his attendants.
4 Why do you boast in your strength?
    Your strength is ebbing,
  O faithless daughter.
    You trusted in your treasures,
        saying,
    "Who will attack me?"
5 I am going to bring terror upon you,
      says the Lord GOD of hosts,
    from all your neighbors,
  and you will be scattered, each
        headlong,
    with no one to gather the fugitives.
6 But afterward I will restore the fortunes of the Ammonites, says the LORD.

[a] Or Kerioth   [b] Gk Syr: Heb bring upon it   [c] Or of Shaon   [d] Or villages
[e] Cn: Meaning of Heb uncertain

48:45–47—Almost identical to Num. 21:28–29.
God defeated Moab once and will do so again.

48:47 *Restore the fortunes*—The promise that
God had made to Judah (chaps. 30–33) is also
made to Moab.

49:1–6 Against the Ammonites

49:1 *Milcom*—The god of the Ammonites. *Gad*
was a region of Judah invaded by Ammon,
though the details of this event are unclear.

49:3 *Heshbon*—This city, mentioned in 48:45 as
part of Moab, at times may have been under the
control of neighboring Ammon.

Judgment on Edom

7 Concerning Edom.

Thus says the LORD of hosts:
Is there no longer wisdom in
 Teman?
  Has counsel perished from the
   prudent?
  Has their wisdom vanished?
8 Flee, turn back, get down low,
  inhabitants of Dedan!
For I will bring the calamity of Esau
  upon him,
  the time when I punish him.
9 If grape-gatherers came to you,
  would they not leave gleanings?
If thieves came by night,
  even they would pillage only what
   they wanted.
10 But as for me, I have stripped Esau
   bare,
  I have uncovered his hiding places,
  and he is not able to conceal
   himself.
  His offspring are destroyed, his
   kinsfolk
  and his neighbors; and he is no
   more.
11 Leave your orphans, I will keep them
   alive;
  and let your widows trust in me.

12 For thus says the LORD: If those
who do not deserve to drink the cup
still have to drink it, shall you be the
one to go unpunished? You shall not go
unpunished; you must drink it. 13 For by
myself I have sworn, says the LORD, that
Bozrah shall become an object of horror
and ridicule, a waste, and an object of
cursing; and all her towns shall be perpetual wastes.
14 I have heard tidings from the LORD,
  and a messenger has been sent
   among the nations:
 "Gather yourselves together and
   come against her,
  and rise up for battle!"

15 For I will make you least among the
   nations,
  despised by humankind.
16 The terror you inspire
  and the pride of your heart have
   deceived you,
you who live in the clefts of the
   rock,*a*
  who hold the height of the hill.
Although you make your nest as
   high as the eagle's,
  from there I will bring you down,
          says the LORD.

17 Edom shall become an object of
horror; everyone who passes by it will
be horrified and will hiss because of
all its disasters. 18 As when Sodom and
Gomorrah and their neighbors were
overthrown, says the LORD, no one shall
live there, nor shall anyone settle in it.
19 Like a lion coming up from the thickets of the Jordan against a perennial pasture, I will suddenly chase Edom*b* away
from it; and I will appoint over it whomever I choose.*c* For who is like me? Who
can summon me? Who is the shepherd
who can stand before me? 20 Therefore
hear the plan that the LORD has made
against Edom and the purposes that he
has formed against the inhabitants of
Teman: Surely the little ones of the flock
shall be dragged away; surely their fold
shall be appalled at their fate. 21 At the
sound of their fall the earth shall tremble; the sound of their cry shall be heard
at the Red Sea.*d* 22 Look, he shall mount
up and swoop down like an eagle, and
spread his wings against Bozrah, and
the heart of the warriors of Edom in that
day shall be like the heart of a woman
in labor.

Judgment on Damascus

23 Concerning Damascus.

a Or *of Sela* *b* Heb *him* *c* Or *and I will single out the choicest of his rams:
Meaning of Heb uncertain* *d* Or *Sea of Reeds*

49:7–22 Against Edom
East of Judah and south of Moab, it is associated
with *Esau*, Jacob's brother (Gen. 25:25, 30).

49:23–27 Against Damascus
It is surprising that oracles against *Damascus*
(Syria) are included, since this nation played no

Hamath and Arpad are confounded,
  for they have heard bad news;
they melt in fear, they are troubled
    like the sea[a]
  that cannot be quiet.
24 Damascus has become feeble, she
      turned to flee,
  and panic seized her;
anguish and sorrows have taken
      hold of her,
  as of a woman in labor.
25 How the famous city is forsaken,[b]
  the joyful town![c]
26 Therefore her young men shall fall
      in her squares,
  and all her soldiers shall be
      destroyed in that day,
        says the LORD of hosts.
27 And I will kindle a fire at the wall of
      Damascus,
  and it shall devour the strongholds
      of Ben-hadad.

Judgment on Kedar and Hazor

28 Concerning Kedar and the kingdoms of Hazor that King Nebuchadrezzar of Babylon defeated.

Thus says the LORD:
Rise up, advance against Kedar!
  Destroy the people of the east!
29 Take their tents and their flocks,
  their curtains and all their goods;
carry off their camels for yourselves,
  and a cry shall go up: "Terror is all
      around!"
30 Flee, wander far away, hide in deep
      places,
  O inhabitants of Hazor!
        says the LORD.
For King Nebuchadrezzar of
      Babylon
  has made a plan against you
  and formed a purpose against you.

31 Rise up, advance against a nation at
      ease,
  that lives secure,
        says the LORD,
that has no gates or bars,
  that lives alone.
32 Their camels shall become booty,
  their herds of cattle a spoil.
I will scatter to every wind
  those who have shaven temples,
and I will bring calamity
  against them from every side,
        says the LORD.
33 Hazor shall become a lair of jackals,
  an everlasting waste;
no one shall live there,
  nor shall anyone settle in it.

Judgment on Elam

34 The word of the LORD that came to
the prophet Jeremiah concerning Elam,
at the beginning of the reign of King
Zedekiah of Judah.

35 Thus says the LORD of hosts: I am
going to break the bow of Elam, the
mainstay of their might; 36 and I will
bring upon Elam the four winds from
the four quarters of heaven; and I will
scatter them to all these winds, and
there shall be no nation to which the
exiles from Elam shall not come. 37 I will
terrify Elam before their enemies, and
before those who seek their life; I will
bring disaster upon them, my fierce
anger, says the LORD. I will send the
sword after them, until I have consumed
them; 38 and I will set my throne in Elam,
and destroy their king and officials, says
the LORD.

39 But in the latter days I will restore
the fortunes of Elam, says the LORD.

a Cn: Heb *there is trouble in the sea*   *b* Vg: Heb *is not forsaken*   *c* Syr Vg Tg: Heb *the town of my joy*

significant role in the region after its defeat by
Assyria in 732 BCE.

49:28–33 Against Kedar and Hazor
These kingdoms, located in the Arabian desert,
had little contact with Judah. They may be included to indicate the scope of God's sovereignty
(cf. 2:10).

49:34–39 Against Elam
Elam had once cooperated with Assyria against
Judah (Isa. 11:11; 21:2; 22:6) though more than
100 years before the time of Jeremiah. It is unclear why Elam is included.

Judgment on Babylon

50 The word that the LORD spoke concerning Babylon, concerning the land of the Chaldeans, by the prophet Jeremiah:

2 Declare among the nations and
    proclaim,
  set up a banner and proclaim,
  do not conceal it, say:
Babylon is taken,
  Bel is put to shame,
  Merodach is dismayed.
Her images are put to shame,
  her idols are dismayed.

3 For out of the north a nation has come up against her; it shall make her land a desolation, and no one shall live in it; both human beings and animals shall flee away.

4 In those days and in that time, says the LORD, the people of Israel shall come, they and the people of Judah together; they shall come weeping as they seek the LORD their God. 5 They shall ask the way to Zion, with faces turned toward it, and they shall come and join*a* themselves to the LORD by an everlasting covenant that will never be forgotten.

6 My people have been lost sheep; their shepherds have led them astray, turning them away on the mountains; from mountain to hill they have gone, they have forgotten their fold. 7 All who found them have devoured them, and their enemies have said, "We are not guilty, because they have sinned against the LORD, the true pasture, the LORD, the hope of their ancestors."

8 Flee from Babylon, and go out of the land of the Chaldeans, and be like male goats leading the flock. 9 For I am going to stir up and bring against Babylon a company of great nations from the land of the north; and they shall array themselves against her; from there she shall be taken. Their arrows are like the arrows of a skilled warrior who does not return empty-handed. 10 Chaldea shall be plundered; all who plunder her shall be sated, says the LORD.

11 Though you rejoice, though you
    exult,
  O plunderers of my heritage,
though you frisk about like a heifer
    on the grass,
  and neigh like stallions,
12 your mother shall be utterly shamed,
  and she who bore you shall be
    disgraced.
Lo, she shall be the last of the
    nations,
  a wilderness, dry land, and a
    desert.
13 Because of the wrath of the LORD
    she shall not be inhabited,
  but shall be an utter desolation;
everyone who passes by Babylon
    shall be appalled
  and hiss because of all her wounds.
14 Take up your positions around
    Babylon,
  all you that bend the bow;
shoot at her, spare no arrows,
  for she has sinned against the
    LORD.
15 Raise a shout against her from all
    sides,
  "She has surrendered;
her bulwarks have fallen,
  her walls are thrown down."
For this is the vengeance of the
    LORD:
  take vengeance on her,
  do to her as she has done.
16 Cut off from Babylon the sower,
  and the wielder of the sickle in
    time of harvest;
because of the destroying sword

a Gk: Heb *toward it. Come! They shall join*

50:1–51:64 Against Babylon

50:3—God calls Persia *out of the north* to judge Babylon even as God called Babylon out of the north to judge Judah (see note at 1:13).

50:4 *In those days*—Babylon's defeat will bring Judah's restoration.

50:6 *Shepherds*—Judah's kings.

all of them shall return to their
    own people,
and all of them shall flee to their
    own land.

17 Israel is a hunted sheep driven away by lions. First the king of Assyria devoured it, and now at the end King Nebuchadrezzar of Babylon has gnawed its bones. [18] Therefore, thus says the LORD of hosts, the God of Israel: I am going to punish the king of Babylon and his land, as I punished the king of Assyria. [19] I will restore Israel to its pasture, and it shall feed on Carmel and in Bashan, and on the hills of Ephraim and in Gilead its hunger shall be satisfied. [20] In those days and at that time, says the LORD, the iniquity of Israel shall be sought, and there shall be none; and the sins of Judah, and none shall be found; for I will pardon the remnant that I have spared.

21 Go up to the land of Merathaim;[a]
    go up against her,
and attack the inhabitants of Pekod[b]
    and utterly destroy the last of
      them,[c]
            says the LORD;
    do all that I have commanded you.
22 The noise of battle is in the land,
    and great destruction!
23 How the hammer of the whole earth
    is cut down and broken!
How Babylon has become
    a horror among the nations!
24 You set a snare for yourself and you
      were caught, O Babylon,
    but you did not know it;
you were discovered and seized,
    because you challenged the LORD.
25 The LORD has opened his armory,

and brought out the weapons of
    his wrath,
for the Lord GOD of hosts has a task
    to do
    in the land of the Chaldeans.
26 Come against her from every quarter;
    open her granaries;
pile her up like heaps of grain, and
      destroy her utterly;
    let nothing be left of her.
27 Kill all her bulls,
    let them go down to the slaughter.
Alas for them, their day has come,
    the time of their punishment!

28 Listen! Fugitives and refugees from the land of Babylon are coming to declare in Zion the vengeance of the LORD our God, vengeance for his temple.

29 Summon archers against Babylon, all who bend the bow. Encamp all around her; let no one escape. Repay her according to her deeds; just as she has done, do to her—for she has arrogantly defied the LORD, the Holy One of Israel. [30] Therefore her young men shall fall in her squares, and all her soldiers shall be destroyed on that day, says the LORD.

31 I am against you, O arrogant one,
    says the Lord GOD of hosts;
for your day has come,
    the time when I will punish you.
32 The arrogant one shall stumble and
      fall,
    with no one to raise him up,
and I will kindle a fire in his cities,
    and it will devour everything
      around him.

33 Thus says the LORD of hosts: The people of Israel are oppressed, and so

---

a Or of Double Rebellion   *b* Or of Punishment   *c* Tg: Heb destroy after them

---

50:17 *Assyria*—Defeated Israel in 722 BCE and dominated Judah from 745 BCE until after 640 BCE.

50:21 *Merathaim*—in Hebrew the word means "double rebellion" but also sounds like a region in southern Babylon. *Pekod* means "punishment" but also sounds like another region in Babylon. These wordplays are used to pronounce Babylon

guilty of double rebellion, for which it will be punished.

50:33–34—Compare the way Pharaoh treated the Hebrew slaves (Exod. 1:18–22). *Redeemer*—See note at 32:7. In this text, God is affirmed to be Judah's redeemer. In Isa. 40–55, God is often affirmed to be the redeemer of those exiled (e.g., Isa. 43:1; 44:24; 49:7; 54:5).

too are the people of Judah; all their captors have held them fast and refuse to let them go. [34] Their Redeemer is strong; the LORD of hosts is his name. He will surely plead their cause, that he may give rest to the earth, but unrest to the inhabitants of Babylon.

[35] A sword against the Chaldeans, says
    the LORD,
  and against the inhabitants of
    Babylon,
  and against her officials and her
    sages!
[36] A sword against the diviners,
  so that they may become fools!
A sword against her warriors,
  so that they may be destroyed!
[37] A sword against her[a] horses and
    against her[a] chariots,
  and against all the foreign troops
    in her midst,
  so that they may become women!
A sword against all her treasures,
  that they may be plundered!
[38] A drought[b] against her waters,
  that they may be dried up!
For it is a land of images,
  and they go mad over idols.

[39] Therefore wild animals shall live with hyenas in Babylon,[c] and ostriches shall inhabit her; she shall never again be peopled, or inhabited for all generations. [40] As when God overthrew Sodom and Gomorrah and their neighbors, says the LORD, so no one shall live there, nor shall anyone settle in her.

[41] Look, a people is coming from the
    north;
  a mighty nation and many kings
    are stirring from the farthest parts
    of the earth.
[42] They wield bow and spear,
  they are cruel and have no mercy.
The sound of them is like the
    roaring sea;
  they ride upon horses,

set in array as a warrior for battle,
  against you, O daughter Babylon!

[43] The king of Babylon heard news of
    them,
  and his hands fell helpless;
anguish seized him,
  pain like that of a woman in labor.

[44] Like a lion coming up from the thickets of the Jordan against a perennial pasture, I will suddenly chase them away from her; and I will appoint over her whomever I choose.[d] For who is like me? Who can summon me? Who is the shepherd who can stand before me? [45] Therefore hear the plan that the LORD has made against Babylon, and the purposes that he has formed against the land of the Chaldeans: Surely the little ones of the flock shall be dragged away; surely their[e] fold shall be appalled at their fate. [46] At the sound of the capture of Babylon the earth shall tremble, and her cry shall be heard among the nations.

51 Thus says the LORD:
    I am going to stir up a
      destructive wind[f]
  against Babylon
  and against the inhabitants of
    Leb-qamai;[g]
[2] and I will send winnowers to Babylon,
  and they shall winnow her.
They shall empty her land
  when they come against her from
    every side
  on the day of trouble.
[3] Let not the archer bend his bow,
  and let him not array himself in
    his coat of mail.
Do not spare her young men;
  utterly destroy her entire army.
[4] They shall fall down slain in the land
    of the Chaldeans,

[a] Cn: Heb *his*   [b] Another reading is *A sword*   [c] Heb lacks *in Babylon*
[d] Or *and I will single out the choicest of her rams*: Meaning of Heb uncertain
[e] Syr Gk Tg Compare 49.20: Heb lacks *their*   [f] Or *stir up the spirit of a
destroyer*   [g] *Leb-qamai* is a cryptogram for *Kasdim*, Chaldea

---

50:35 *Sword*—A judgment against Judah (12:12; 14:12–18; 15:2–3; 21:7–9) is now threatened against Babylon.

and wounded in her streets.
5 Israel and Judah have not been
    forsaken
        by their God, the Lord of hosts,
    though their land is full of guilt
        before the Holy One of Israel.

6 Flee from the midst of Babylon,
        save your lives, each of you!
    Do not perish because of her guilt,
        for this is the time of the Lord's
            vengeance;
        he is repaying her what is due.
7 Babylon was a golden cup in the
        Lord's hand,
        making all the earth drunken;
    the nations drank of her wine,
        and so the nations went mad.
8 Suddenly Babylon has fallen and is
        shattered;
    wail for her!
        Bring balm for her wound;
        perhaps she may be healed.
9 We tried to heal Babylon,
        but she could not be healed.
    Forsake her, and let each of us go
        to our own country;
    for her judgment has reached up to
        heaven
        and has been lifted up even to the
            skies.
10 The Lord has brought forth our
        vindication;
    come, let us declare in Zion
        the work of the Lord our God.

11 Sharpen the arrows!
        Fill the quivers!
The Lord has stirred up the spirit of the
kings of the Medes, because his purpose
concerning Babylon is to destroy it, for
that is the vengeance of the Lord, vengeance for his temple.
12 Raise a standard against the walls of
        Babylon;
        make the watch strong;
    post sentinels;
        prepare the ambushes;

for the Lord has both planned and
    done
    what he spoke concerning the
        inhabitants of Babylon.
13 You who live by mighty waters,
        rich in treasures,
    your end has come,
        the thread of your life is cut.
14 The Lord of hosts has sworn by
        himself:
    Surely I will fill you with troops like
        a swarm of locusts,
        and they shall raise a shout of
            victory over you.

15 It is he who made the earth by his
        power,
        who established the world by his
            wisdom,
    and by his understanding stretched
        out the heavens.
16 When he utters his voice there
        is a tumult of waters in the
            heavens,
        and he makes the mist rise from
            the ends of the earth.
    He makes lightnings for the rain,
        and he brings out the wind from
            his storehouses.
17 Everyone is stupid and without
        knowledge;
        goldsmiths are all put to shame by
            their idols;
    for their images are false,
        and there is no breath in them.
18 They are worthless, a work of
        delusion;
        at the time of their punishment
            they shall perish.
19 Not like these is the Lord,ᵃ the
        portion of Jacob,
        for he is the one who formed all
            things,
    and Israel is the tribe of his
        inheritance;
        the Lord of hosts is his name.

a Heb lacks the Lord

51:11 *Medes*—The Persians' allies who defeated
Babylon in 538 BCE.

51:15–19—A repetition of 10:12–16, to assert
God's sovereignty over the nations.

Israel the Creator's Instrument

20 You are my war club, my weapon of
        battle:
    with you I smash nations;
    with you I destroy kingdoms;
21 with you I smash the horse and its
        rider;
    with you I smash the chariot and
        the charioteer;
22 with you I smash man and woman;
    with you I smash the old man and
        the boy;
    with you I smash the young man and
        the girl;
23   with you I smash shepherds and
        their flocks;
    with you I smash farmers and their
        teams;
    with you I smash governors and
        deputies.

The Doom of Babylon

24 I will repay Babylon and all the
inhabitants of Chaldea before your very
eyes for all the wrong that they have
done in Zion, says the LORD.

25 I am against you, O destroying
        mountain,
                        says the LORD,
    that destroys the whole earth;
    I will stretch out my hand against you,
    and roll you down from the crags,
    and make you a burned-out
        mountain.
26 No stone shall be taken from you for
        a corner
    and no stone for a foundation,
    but you shall be a perpetual waste,
    says the LORD.

27 Raise a standard in the land,
    blow the trumpet among the
        nations;
    prepare the nations for war against
        her,

summon against her the kingdoms,
    Ararat, Minni, and Ashkenaz;
appoint a marshal against her,
    bring up horses like bristling
        locusts.
28 Prepare the nations for war against
        her,
    the kings of the Medes, with their
        governors and deputies,
    and every land under their
        dominion.
29 The land trembles and writhes,
    for the LORD's purposes against
        Babylon stand,
to make the land of Babylon a
        desolation,
    without inhabitant.
30 The warriors of Babylon have given
        up fighting,
    they remain in their strongholds;
their strength has failed,
    they have become women;
her buildings are set on fire,
    her bars are broken.
31 One runner runs to meet another,
    and one messenger to meet
        another,
to tell the king of Babylon
    that his city is taken from end to
        end:
32 the fords have been seized,
    the marshes have been burned
        with fire,
    and the soldiers are in panic.
33 For thus says the LORD of hosts, the
        God of Israel:
Daughter Babylon is like a threshing
        floor
    at the time when it is trodden;
yet a little while
    and the time of her harvest will
        come.

34 "King Nebuchadrezzar of Babylon
        has devoured me,

51:20–23—*You* is probably Cyrus, the king of
Persia.

51:27–29—God summons nations to judge
Babylon, even as God once summoned Babylon
to judge Judah.

51:34 *Monster*—Babylon is accused of being the
chaos monster (Rahab) that must be subdued for
there to be order in the creation (see Pss. 87:4;
89:10; Isa. 51:9).

he has crushed me;
he has made me an empty vessel,
    he has swallowed me like a
        monster;
he has filled his belly with my
    delicacies,
he has spewed me out.
35 May my torn flesh be avenged on
        Babylon,"
    the inhabitants of Zion shall say.
"May my blood be avenged on the
        inhabitants of Chaldea,"
    Jerusalem shall say.
36 Therefore thus says the LORD:
I am going to defend your cause
    and take vengeance for you.
I will dry up her sea
    and make her fountain dry;
37 and Babylon shall become a heap of
        ruins,
    a den of jackals,
an object of horror and of hissing,
    without inhabitant.

38 Like lions they shall roar together;
    they shall growl like lions' whelps.
39 When they are inflamed, I will set
        out their drink
    and make them drunk, until they
        become merry
and then sleep a perpetual sleep
    and never wake, says the LORD.
40 I will bring them down like lambs to
        the slaughter,
    like rams and goats.

41 How Sheshach*a* is taken,
    the pride of the whole earth
        seized!
How Babylon has become
    an object of horror among the
        nations!
42 The sea has risen over Babylon;
    she has been covered by its
        tumultuous waves.
43 Her cities have become an object of
        horror,
    a land of drought and a desert,

a land in which no one lives,
    and through which no mortal
        passes.
44 I will punish Bel in Babylon,
    and make him disgorge what he
        has swallowed.
The nations shall no longer stream
    to him;
    the wall of Babylon has fallen.

45 Come out of her, my people!
    Save your lives, each of you,
    from the fierce anger of the
        LORD!
46 Do not be fainthearted or fearful
    at the rumors heard in the land—
one year one rumor comes,
    the next year another,
rumors of violence in the land
    and of ruler against ruler.

47 Assuredly, the days are coming
    when I will punish the images of
        Babylon;
her whole land shall be put to
        shame,
    and all her slain shall fall in her
        midst.
48 Then the heavens and the earth,
    and all that is in them,
shall shout for joy over Babylon;
    for the destroyers shall come
        against them out of the north,
            says the LORD.
49 Babylon must fall for the slain of
        Israel,
    as the slain of all the earth have
        fallen because of Babylon.

50 You survivors of the sword,
    go, do not linger!
Remember the LORD in a distant
    land,
    and let Jerusalem come into your
        mind:
51 We are put to shame, for we have
        heard insults;

---

a Sheshach is a cryptogram for *Babel*, Babylon

51:41 *Sheshach*—See note at 25:26.

51:42–44—*Babylon*, that acted like a chaos monster (v. 34), will be overwhelmed by chaos.

dishonor has covered our face,
for aliens have come
    into the holy places of the LORD's
        house.

52 Therefore the time is surely coming,
        says the LORD,
    when I will punish her idols,
and through all her land
    the wounded shall groan.
53 Though Babylon should mount up
        to heaven,
    and though she should fortify her
        strong height,
from me destroyers would come
        upon her,
    says the LORD.

54 Listen!—a cry from Babylon!
    A great crashing from the land of
        the Chaldeans!
55 For the LORD is laying Babylon
        waste,
    and stilling her loud clamor.
Their waves roar like mighty waters,
    the sound of their clamor
        resounds;
56 for a destroyer has come against her,
        against Babylon;
her warriors are taken,
    their bows are broken;
for the LORD is a God of
        recompense,
    he will repay in full.
57 I will make her officials and her
        sages drunk,
    also her governors, her deputies,
        and her warriors;
they shall sleep a perpetual sleep and
        never wake,
    says the King, whose name is the
        LORD of hosts.

58 Thus says the LORD of hosts:
    The broad wall of Babylon
        shall be leveled to the ground,
    and her high gates
        shall be burned with fire.
The peoples exhaust themselves for
        nothing,
    and the nations weary themselves
        only for fire.[a]

Jeremiah's Command to Seraiah

59 The word that the prophet Jeremiah
commanded Seraiah son of Neriah son
of Mahseiah, when he went with King
Zedekiah of Judah to Babylon, in the
fourth year of his reign. Seraiah was
the quartermaster. 60 Jeremiah wrote
in a[b] scroll all the disasters that would
come on Babylon, all these words that
are written concerning Babylon. 61 And
Jeremiah said to Seraiah: "When you
come to Babylon, see that you read all
these words, 62 and say, 'O LORD, you
yourself threatened to destroy this place
so that neither human beings nor animals shall live in it, and it shall be desolate forever.' 63 When you finish reading
this scroll, tie a stone to it, and throw it
into the middle of the Euphrates, 64 and
say, 'Thus shall Babylon sink, to rise no
more, because of the disasters that I am
bringing on her.'"[c]
    Thus far are the words of Jeremiah.

The Destruction of Jerusalem Reviewed

52 Zedekiah was twenty-one years
old when he began to reign; he
reigned eleven years in Jerusalem. His
mother's name was Hamutal daughter

---

[a] Gk Syr Compare Hab 2.13: Heb *and the nations for fire, and they are weary* [b] Or *one* [c] Gk: Heb *on her. And they shall weary themselves*

51:55—Jeremiah, like the prophets before him, is unequivocal in asserting the difficult theological claim that the author of a nation's destruction is ultimately the judging Lord. The teaching applies to Judah and to Babylon alike. The notion of secular history is foreign to him.

51:59 *Seraiah*—Baruch's brother. Baruch re-corded Jeremiah's oracles in which Babylon was God's agent of judgment against Judah. Baruch's

brother writes down Jeremiah's oracles against the nations, in which Babylon is called to ac-count by God. These brothers represent the two perspectives about Babylon in the book.

52:1–11 The King Did Evil

In this chapter, nearly identical to 2 Kgs. 24:18–25:30, God's judgment is enacted through the political and military events recounted in vv. 3–11.

of Jeremiah of Libnah. ²He did what was evil in the sight of the LORD, just as Jehoiakim had done. ³Indeed, Jerusalem and Judah so angered the LORD that he expelled them from his presence.

Zedekiah rebelled against the king of Babylon. ⁴And in the ninth year of his reign, in the tenth month, on the tenth day of the month, King Nebuchadrezzar of Babylon came with all his army against Jerusalem, and they laid siege to it; they built siegeworks against it all around. ⁵So the city was besieged until the eleventh year of King Zedekiah. ⁶On the ninth day of the fourth month the famine became so severe in the city that there was no food for the people of the land. ⁷Then a breach was made in the city wall;ᵃ and all the soldiers fled and went out from the city by night by the way of the gate between the two walls, by the king's garden, though the Chaldeans were all around the city. They went in the direction of the Arabah. ⁸But the army of the Chaldeans pursued the king, and overtook Zedekiah in the plains of Jericho; and all his army was scattered, deserting him. ⁹Then they captured the king, and brought him up to the king of Babylon at Riblah in the land of Hamath, and he passed sentence on him. ¹⁰The king of Babylon killed the sons of Zedekiah before his eyes, and also killed all the officers of Judah at Riblah. ¹¹He put out the eyes of Zedekiah, and bound him in fetters, and the king of Babylon took him to Babylon, and put him in prison until the day of his death.

12 In the fifth month, on the tenth day of the month—which was the nineteenth year of King Nebuchadrezzar, king of Babylon—Nebuzaradan the captain of the bodyguard who served the king of Babylon, entered Jerusalem. ¹³He burned the house of the LORD,

the king's house, and all the houses of Jerusalem; every great house he burned down. ¹⁴All the army of the Chaldeans, who were with the captain of the guard, broke down all the walls around Jerusalem. ¹⁵Nebuzaradan the captain of the guard carried into exile some of the poorest of the people and the rest of the people who were left in the city and the deserters who had defected to the king of Babylon, together with the rest of the artisans. ¹⁶But Nebuzaradan the captain of the guard left some of the poorest people of the land to be vinedressers and tillers of the soil.

17 The pillars of bronze that were in the house of the LORD, and the stands and the bronze sea that were in the house of the LORD, the Chaldeans broke in pieces, and carried all the bronze to Babylon. ¹⁸They took away the pots, the shovels, the snuffers, the basins, the ladles, and all the vessels of bronze used in the temple service. ¹⁹The captain of the guard took away the small bowls also, the firepans, the basins, the pots, the lampstands, the ladles, and the bowls for libation, both those of gold and those of silver. ²⁰As for the two pillars, the one sea, the twelve bronze bulls that were under the sea, and the stands,ᵇ which King Solomon had made for the house of the LORD, the bronze of all these vessels was beyond weighing. ²¹As for the pillars, the height of the one pillar was eighteen cubits, its circumference was twelve cubits; it was hollow and its thickness was four fingers. ²²Upon it was a capital of bronze; the height of the capital was five cubits; latticework and pomegranates, all of bronze, encircled the top of the capital. And the second pillar had the same, with pomegranates. ²³There were ninety-six pomegranates on the sides; all the pomegranates

ᵃ Heb lacks wall ᵃ Cn: Heb that were under the stands

52:12–30 The Exile: A Reprise
The book of Jeremiah begins by indicating concern for "the captivity of Jerusalem" (1:3). At the

book's conclusion readers are invited to recall this book's understandings of why **Judah went into exile out of its land** (v. 27).

encircling the latticework numbered one hundred.

24 The captain of the guard took the chief priest Seraiah, the second priest Zephaniah, and the three guardians of the threshold; 25 and from the city he took an officer who had been in command of the soldiers, and seven men of the king's council who were found in the city; the secretary of the commander of the army who mustered the people of the land; and sixty men of the people of the land who were found inside the city. 26 Then Nebuzaradan the captain of the guard took them, and brought them to the king of Babylon at Riblah. 27 And the king of Babylon struck them down, and put them to death at Riblah in the land of Hamath. So Judah went into exile out of its land.

28 This is the number of the people whom Nebuchadrezzar took into exile: in the seventh year, three thousand twenty-three Judeans; 29 in the eighteenth year of Nebuchadrezzar he took into exile from Jerusalem eight hundred thirty-two persons; 30 in the twenty-third year of Nebuchadrezzar, Nebuzaradan the captain of the guard took into exile of the Judeans seven hundred forty-five persons; all the persons were four thousand six hundred.

Jehoiachin Favored in Captivity

31 In the thirty-seventh year of the exile of King Jehoiachin of Judah, in the twelfth month, on the twenty-fifth day of the month, King Evil-merodach of Babylon, in the year he began to reign, showed favor to King Jehoiachin of Judah and brought him out of prison; 32 he spoke kindly to him, and gave him a seat above the seats of the other kings who were with him in Babylon. 33 So Jehoiachin put aside his prison clothes, and every day of his life he dined regularly at the king's table. 34 For his allowance, a regular daily allowance was given him by the king of Babylon, as long as he lived, up to the day of his death.

52:28–30—The significance of Judah's defeat is far greater than the number of persons exiled, which totaled only about 4,600. The exile raised profound questions about the relationship between God and God's people. Nevertheless, by giving the broken, exiled Jewish community a way to account for its disaster, the prophet helped that community to maintain its faith and identity, and thus to survive the ordeal.

52:31–34 Jehoiachin's Release

In the book's last verses there is a hint that God's promised restoration of Judah ("build and plant," 1:10) might yet be fulfilled, even as was God's threat that Judah would be judged ("plucked up and broken down," 1:10).

LAMENTATIONS

T he songs of Lamentations were composed in the aftermath of the siege and
destruction of Jerusalem in 587 BCE. The songs reflect a traditional mourning
context, characteristic across cultures and through history, including the ancient
Near East. Singers composed by drawing upon and modifying stock lyrics and genres
from the living oral tradition, improvising with thought, emotion, and inspiration to
create a new song addressed to the immediate context. In Lamentations, two lead
singers are in dialogue; one comforts the other, a mourner, but they also strikingly
modify traditional dirges and lament prayers in an intense interchange about suffering
and justice.

Since the Enlightenment, scholarly treatment of Lamentations has primarily used a
modern literary method in pursuit of the "author" of the book. The consensus, contrary to traditional claims, was that Jeremiah could not have been its author, because
certain perspectives and terms in the book are too unlike the prophet's to be his. Yet
recent recognition that the work emerged from an oral-traditional mourning context
reflecting multiple singers allows for a reconsideration of Jeremiah's role as one of the
book's voices. In fact, the prior severing of any connection of Jeremiah to Lamentations also diverted attention away from the book's internal debate about prophetic
and divine justice. It has long been documented by anthropologists that mourning
laments are typically sung by women across cultures and through history, and women
were also temple singers in ancient Israel. Yet the woman singer's voice has been
neglected in Lamentations study. That her voice goes beyond women's traditional
mourning to lead the dialogical debate about God's justice in the context is a striking innovation in the Hebrew Bible, its then-current theology, and acceptable gender
roles.

The concerns of Lamentations for justice are evident in the two genres that the
singers use to express their grief and grapple with what has happened: the communal
dirge (Lam. 1, 2, and 4) and the lament prayer to God (parts of Lam. 1, 2, 3, and all
of 5). The communal dirge is typically uttered by Hebrew prophets as a warning to a
community that both idolatry and social injustice shall lead to its social collapse, the
"death" of the nation. This genre opening Lamentations 1 reveals a prophetic point
of view describing disaster after the fact and is consistent with Jeremiah, inasmuch as
the individual artistry in this singer's songs closely parallels Jeremiah's poetry in the
book of Jeremiah. But Lamentations also reveals a movement in Jeremiah's perspective from the justice of prophetic judgment, to compassion for the suffering city, to
anger against God for unjust excessive punishment and not protecting the innocent.

A second lead singer, on behalf of the city, utters a lament prayer to God to look
upon "her" suffering. Following prophetic theology, she admits the devastation is punishment for sin, but transforms the complaint typical of a lament into an expanded
accusation against God for carrying out excessive violent punishment. Its tenor is in

the spirit of Moses' complaints and is matched in its severity only by the later complaints in Job. One role of a traditional dirge singer in the context of mourning can be to accuse by name the perpetrator, the one who killed the victim, as a call for "public justice" in the community. In Lamentations 1–2, Jeremiah and the woman lament singer seem to draw on this popular practice and with increasing anger complain of God's destructive actions, particularly for allowing the suffering and deaths of innocent children. Thus they implicitly begin to critique a strict theology of retributive justice, in which the wicked/unrighteous are punished and God hears, rescues, and rewards only the good/righteous. They also lay the groundwork for undermining a wider theological claim (also common in the ancient Near East) that the deity leads a war to defeat a nation. The book's struggle with theodicy foreshadows and likely influences such debate in Job and is relevant to post-Holocaust discussions of the presence/absence of God in historical human catastrophes.

There has been no consensus as to the purpose of the alphabetical (acrostic) structure of the poetry of Lamentations. However, the other acrostics in the Bible (Pss. 9–10, 33, 34, 37, 94, 111, 112, 119, 145; except Prov. 31:10–31) are each heavily invested in the idea of retributive justice and accordingly defend God as just; two are confessional psalms (25 and 38). These texts reveal a tradition of singers who composed psalms espousing retributive justice, a theological "order" hammered home by every letter (and line) of their acrostic form. Lamentations, however, presents dissident singers who in their rebelling against such a simplistic understanding with complaints against God, employ the acrostic structure to invert that order of justice. Indeed, they even invert letters of the alphabet in Lamentations 2, 3, and 4. This rhetorical, theological battle becomes apparent in Lamentations 3, when the first two singers are engaged by two new singers, one of whom sounds much like Job's friends, who defends God's ways and calls upon the lament singer to stop complaints and confess in silence.

The book closes with a communal lament to God that suggests a time after the frenzied catastrophe, when those remaining in the land attempt to carry on and survive war's deprivations. The text gives no divine answer to their lament.

—Nancy C. Lee

The Deserted City

1 How lonely sits the city
  that once was full of people!
How like a widow she has become,
  she that was great among the
    nations!
She that was a princess among the
    provinces
  has become a vassal.

² She weeps bitterly in the night,
  with tears on her cheeks;
among all her lovers
  she has no one to comfort her;
all her friends have dealt
    treacherously with her,
  they have become her enemies.

³ Judah has gone into exile with
    suffering

1:1–9b *How*—Or, "Alas!" Strange to modern ears, the poetic singer personifies the city herself as feeling pain and suffering injury, in this case, like a widow weeping, bereft and beleaguered; ancient Near Eastern poets often depicted their cities as female; the opening formulaic term signals the prophet's communal dirge.

1:1–2 *Full of people . . . great among the*

nations—The underlying Hebrew wordplay is used by Jeremiah in similar fashion in Jer. 51:13. Its imagery contrasts the glory of what once was, to the present defeat of the nation's capital as seen by the world, its shocking loss of privileged power and prestige. *She weeps bitterly in the night, with tears on her cheeks . . . she has no one to comfort her*—Besides describing the

and hard servitude;
　she lives now among the nations,
　　and finds no resting place;
　her pursuers have all overtaken her
　　in the midst of her distress.

4 The roads to Zion mourn,
　　for no one comes to the festivals;
　all her gates are desolate,
　　her priests groan;
　her young girls grieve,[a]
　　and her lot is bitter.

5 Her foes have become the masters,
　　her enemies prosper,
　because the LORD has made her
　　　suffer
　　for the multitude of her
　　　transgressions;
　her children have gone away,
　　captives before the foe.

6 From daughter Zion has departed
　　all her majesty.
　Her princes have become like stags
　　that find no pasture;
　they fled without strength
　　before the pursuer.

7 Jerusalem remembers,
　　in the days of her affliction and
　　　wandering,
　all the precious things
　　that were hers in days of old.
　When her people fell into the hand
　　　of the foe,
　　and there was no one to help her,
　the foe looked on mocking
　　over her downfall.

8 Jerusalem sinned grievously,
　　so she has become a mockery;
　all who honored her despise her,
　　for they have seen her nakedness;
　she herself groans,
　　and turns her face away.

9 Her uncleanness was in her skirts;
　　she took no thought of her future;
　her downfall was appalling,
　　with none to comfort her.
　"O LORD, look at my affliction,
　　for the enemy has triumphed!"

10 Enemies have stretched out their
　　　hands
　　over all her precious things;
　she has even seen the nations
　　invade her sanctuary,
　those whom you forbade
　　to enter your congregation.

11 All her people groan
　　as they search for bread;
　they trade their treasures for food
　　to revive their strength.
　Look, O LORD, and see
　　how worthless I have become.

12 Is it nothing to you,[a] all you who
　　　pass by?
　　Look and see
　if there is any sorrow like my
　　　sorrow,
　　which was brought upon me,
　which the LORD inflicted
　　on the day of his fierce anger.

[a] Meaning of Heb uncertain

national persona, Jeremiah or a Jeremianic voice simultaneously speaks on an interpersonal level as the "comforter" in this crisis situation, compassionately addressing the woman singer, herself a survivor, as their dialogue unfolds.

1:7–9c *Her affliction*—The term can mean suffering but also rape, as the following verses suggest. This metaphor depicting the violation of a city, including the invasion of its sanctuary, is also used by other ancient poets; Jeremiah at once conveys the national tragedy, consoles the woman singer (a victim of rape), and critiques the injustice of her treatment by enemies. His recurring refrain, **with none to comfort her**, evokes her response; her first utterance is a direct lament

to God: *O LORD, look at my affliction* (or "rape"; v. 9c).

1:10–11b *Whom you forbade to enter your congregation [and sanctuary]*—Jeremiah joins in, also addressing God, mentioning God's broken promise to protect her.

1:11c—The woman cries out again to God.

1:12–22—With no divine response, she shifts to third-person dirge descriptions and lament phrases, first admitting her transgressions, but also attributing God's excessive violent punishment to divine anger. As a mother concerned for her *children* (v. 16) and the city's inhabitants, again she directly appeals to God (vv. 20–22).

13 From on high he sent fire;
    it went deep into my bones;
he spread a net for my feet;
    he turned me back;
he has left me stunned,
    faint all day long.

14 My transgressions were bound[a] into
        a yoke;
    by his hand they were fastened
        together;
they weigh on my neck,
    sapping my strength;
the Lord handed me over
    to those whom I cannot withstand.

15 The LORD has rejected
    all my warriors in the midst of me;
he proclaimed a time against me
    to crush my young men;
the Lord has trodden as in a wine
        press
    the virgin daughter Judah.

16 For these things I weep;
    my eyes flow with tears;
for a comforter is far from me,
    one to revive my courage;
my children are desolate,
    for the enemy has prevailed.

17 Zion stretches out her hands,
    but there is no one to comfort her;
the LORD has commanded against
        Jacob
    that his neighbors should become
        his foes;
Jerusalem has become
    a filthy thing among them.

18 The LORD is in the right,
    for I have rebelled against his
        word;

but hear, all you peoples,
    and behold my suffering;
my young women and young men
    have gone into captivity.

19 I called to my lovers
    but they deceived me;
my priests and elders
    perished in the city
while seeking food
    to revive their strength.

20 See, O LORD, how distressed I am;
    my stomach churns,
my heart is wrung within me,
    because I have been very
        rebellious.
In the street the sword bereaves;
    in the house it is like death.

21 They heard how I was groaning,
    with no one to comfort me.
All my enemies heard of my trouble;
    they are glad that you have done it.
Bring on the day you have
        announced,
    and let them be as I am.

22 Let all their evil doing come before
        you;
    and deal with them
as you have dealt with me
    because of all my transgressions;
for my groans are many
    and my heart is faint.

God's Warnings Fulfilled

2 How the Lord in his anger
    has humiliated[a] daughter Zion!
He has thrown down from heaven to
        earth
    the splendor of Israel;

[a] Meaning of Heb uncertain

1:13 *He spread a net for my feet*—Ironically, in lament psalms this language usually describes one's human enemy, rarely God, as here.

1:17 *Jerusalem has become a filthy thing*—Jeremiah's interjection; not filthy, but defiled/unclean (as a matter of ritual impurity), due to being splattered with blood after *trodden as in a wine press* (v. 15c); see Num. 35:33; Lev. 21:1–4.

1:18–19 *The LORD is in the right*—"The LORD

is just" or "the LORD is innocent." Traditionally interpreted as the woman's confession, but see Jeremiah's sarcastic use of this same formula (Jer. 12:1) in accusing God of unjustly allowing the wicked to prosper and the innocent to suffer.

2:1–10 *How*—Chapter 2 opens exactly like chap. 1, with a communal dirge by Jeremiah; yet this one intensifies the litany of God's destroying fury, still using lament psalm terms normally reserved for the human enemy.

he has not remembered his footstool
    in the day of his anger.

2 The Lord has destroyed without
    mercy
    all the dwellings of Jacob;
in his wrath he has broken down
    the strongholds of daughter Judah;
he has brought down to the ground
    in dishonor
    the kingdom and its rulers.

3 He has cut down in fierce anger
    all the might of Israel;
he has withdrawn his right hand
    from them
    in the face of the enemy;
he has burned like a flaming fire in
    Jacob,
    consuming all around.

4 He has bent his bow like an enemy,
    with his right hand set like a foe;
he has killed all in whom we took
    pride
    in the tent of daughter Zion;
he has poured out his fury like fire.

5 The Lord has become like an enemy;
    he has destroyed Israel.
He has destroyed all its palaces,
    laid in ruins its strongholds,
and multiplied in daughter Judah
    mourning and lamentation.

6 He has broken down his booth like a
    garden,
    he has destroyed his tabernacle;
the Lord has abolished in Zion
    festival and sabbath,
and in his fierce indignation has
    spurned
    king and priest.

7 The Lord has scorned his altar,
    disowned his sanctuary;
he has delivered into the hand of the
    enemy
the walls of her palaces;
a clamor was raised in the house of
    the Lord
    as on a day of festival.

8 The Lord determined to lay in
    ruins
    the wall of daughter Zion;
he stretched the line;
    he did not withhold his hand from
    destroying;
he caused rampart and wall to
    lament;
    they languish together.

9 Her gates have sunk into the ground;
    he has ruined and broken her
    bars;
her king and princes are among the
    nations;
    guidance is no more,
and her prophets obtain
    no vision from the Lord.

10 The elders of daughter Zion
    sit on the ground in silence;
they have thrown dust on their
    heads
    and put on sackcloth;
the young girls of Jerusalem
    have bowed their heads to the
    ground.

11 My eyes are spent with weeping;
    my stomach churns;
my bile is poured out on the ground
    because of the destruction of my
    people,
because infants and babes faint
    in the streets of the city.

12 They cry to their mothers,
    "Where is bread and wine?"
as they faint like the wounded
    in the streets of the city,
as their life is poured out
    on their mothers' bosom.

2:8c *Rampart and wall . . . lament; they languish together*—Or "collapse." Prophetic and ancient Near Eastern poems personify ruined city structures as mourning, but only Jeremiah extends the striking imagery precisely this way in the Bible: walls, like persons grieving, collapse to the ground (Jer. 14:2).

2:11–12 *My eyes are spent with weeping*—Jeremiah emotionally breaks down while witnessing the suffering of the people and the infant babes.

¹³ What can I say for you, to what
      compare you,
  O daughter Jerusalem?
To what can I liken you, that I may
      comfort you,
  O virgin daughter Zion?
For vast as the sea is your ruin;
  who can heal you?

¹⁴ Your prophets have seen for you
  false and deceptive visions;
they have not exposed your iniquity
  to restore your fortunes,
but have seen oracles for you
  that are false and misleading.

¹⁵ All who pass along the way
  clap their hands at you;
they hiss and wag their heads
  at daughter Jerusalem;
"Is this the city that was called
  the perfection of beauty,
  the joy of all the earth?"

¹⁶ All your enemies
  open their mouths against you;
they hiss, they gnash their teeth,
  they cry: "We have devoured her!
Ah, this is the day we longed for;
  at last we have seen it!"

¹⁷ The LORD has done what he
      purposed,
  he has carried out his threat;
as he ordained long ago,
  he has demolished without pity;
he has made the enemy rejoice over
      you,
  and exalted the might of your
      foes.

¹⁸ Cry aloud^a to the Lord!
  O wall of daughter Zion!
Let tears stream down like a torrent
  day and night!

Give yourself no rest,
  your eyes no respite!

¹⁹ Arise, cry out in the night,
  at the beginning of the watches!
Pour out your heart like water
  before the presence of the Lord!
Lift your hands to him
  for the lives of your children,
who faint for hunger
  at the head of every street.

²⁰ Look, O LORD, and consider!
  To whom have you done this?
Should women eat their offspring,
  the children they have borne?
Should priest and prophet be killed
  in the sanctuary of the Lord?

²¹ The young and the old are lying
  on the ground in the streets;
my young women and my young men
  have fallen by the sword;
in the day of your anger you have
      killed them,
  slaughtering without mercy.

²² You invited my enemies from all
      around
  as if for a day of festival;
and on the day of the anger of the
      LORD
  no one escaped or survived;
those whom I bore and reared
  my enemy has destroyed.

God's Steadfast Love Endures

3 I am one who has seen affliction
  under the rod of God's^b wrath;
² he has driven and brought me
  into darkness without any light;
³ against me alone he turns his hand,
  again and again, all day long.

^aCn: Heb *Their heart cried* ^bHeb *his*

2:13–19 *That I may comfort you*—Jeremiah poignantly speaks directly to the woman singer for the first time, trying to console her and imploring her to lament to God for her children.

2:20–22—She laments to and angrily blames God for the deaths of her children.

3:1–24 *I am the one who has seen affliction*—A new voice (possibly a soldier) joins in and,

continuing the unprecedented lament, complains that God's actions are like the enemy's against him. He is the only singer who does not explicitly confess that sin is the cause of his suffering. The chapter includes four different voices, each in a different place emotionally in response to the traumatic disaster.

4 He has made my flesh and my skin
    waste away,
  and broken my bones;
5 he has besieged and enveloped me
    with bitterness and tribulation;
6 he has made me sit in darkness
    like the dead of long ago.

7 He has walled me about so that I
    cannot escape;
  he has put heavy chains on me;
8 though I call and cry for help,
    he shuts out my prayer;
9 he has blocked my ways with hewn
    stones,
  he has made my paths crooked.

10 He is a bear lying in wait for me,
    a lion in hiding;
11 he led me off my way and tore me to
    pieces;
  he has made me desolate;
12 he bent his bow and set me
    as a mark for his arrow.

13 He shot into my vitals
    the arrows of his quiver;
14 I have become the laughingstock of
    all my people,
  the object of their taunt-songs all
    day long.
15 He has filled me with bitterness,
    he has sated me with wormwood.

16 He has made my teeth grind on
    gravel,
  and made me cower in ashes;
17 my soul is bereft of peace;
    I have forgotten what happiness is;
18 so I say, "Gone is my glory,
    and all that I had hoped for from
    the Lord."

19 The thought of my affliction and my
    homelessness

is wormwood and gall!
20 My soul continually thinks of it
    and is bowed down within me.
21 But this I call to mind,
    and therefore I have hope:

22 The steadfast love of the Lord never
    ceases,[a]
  his mercies never come to an end;
23 they are new every morning;
    great is your faithfulness.
24 "The Lord is my portion," says my
    soul,
  "therefore I will hope in him."
25 The Lord is good to those who wait
    for him,
  to the soul that seeks him.
26 It is good that one should wait
    quietly
  for the salvation of the Lord.

27 It is good for one to bear
    the yoke in youth,
28 to sit alone in silence
    when the Lord has imposed it,
29 to put one's mouth to the dust
    (there may yet be hope),
30 to give one's cheek to the smiter,
    and be filled with insults.

31 For the Lord will not
    reject forever.
32 Although he causes grief, he will
    have compassion
  according to the abundance of his
    steadfast love;
33 for he does not willingly afflict
    or grieve anyone.

34 When all the prisoners of the land
    are crushed under foot,
35 when human rights are perverted
    in the presence of the Most High,

a Syr Tg: Heb Lord, we are not cut off

3:19–20—Having reached a hopeless state, the man does not say, *the thought of my affliction*, but rather appeals to God: "Remember my affliction!" (imperative form).

3:22–24—After his appeal, the man finds hope in the constancy of God's *steadfast love* and mercy, and finds his confidence in God renewed, the first such expression in the book.

3:25–41—A second new voice responds to the soldier, defends God, advocates not lament but silent confession and bearing God's punishment. This singer has found the explanation of divine retributive justice acceptable.

³⁶ when one's case is subverted
　　—does the Lord not see it?

³⁷ Who can command and have it
　　done,
　　if the Lord has not ordained it?
³⁸ Is it not from the mouth of the Most
　　High
　　that good and bad come?
³⁹ Why should any who draw breath
　　complain
　　about the punishment of their
　　sins?

⁴⁰ Let us test and examine our ways,
　　and return to the LORD.
⁴¹ Let us lift up our hearts as well as
　　our hands
　　to God in heaven.
⁴² We have transgressed and rebelled,
　　and you have not forgiven.

⁴³ You have wrapped yourself with
　　anger and pursued us,
　　killing without pity;
⁴⁴ you have wrapped yourself with a
　　cloud
　　so that no prayer can pass
　　through.
⁴⁵ You have made us filth and rubbish
　　among the peoples.

⁴⁶ All our enemies
　　have opened their mouths against
　　us;
⁴⁷ panic and pitfall have come upon us,
　　devastation and destruction.
⁴⁸ My eyes flow with rivers of tears
　　because of the destruction of my
　　people.

⁴⁹ My eyes will flow without ceasing,
　　without respite,
⁵⁰ until the LORD from heaven
　　looks down and sees.
⁵¹ My eyes cause me grief

at the fate of all the young women
　　in my city.

⁵² Those who were my enemies
　　without cause
　　have hunted me like a bird;
⁵³ they flung me alive into a pit
　　and hurled stones on me;
⁵⁴ water closed over my head;
　　I said, "I am lost."

⁵⁵ I called on your name, O LORD,
　　from the depths of the pit;
⁵⁶ you heard my plea, "Do not close
　　your ear
　　to my cry for help, but give me
　　relief!"
⁵⁷ You came near when I called on you;
　　you said, "Do not fear!"

⁵⁸ You have taken up my cause, O Lord,
　　you have redeemed my life.
⁵⁹ You have seen the wrong done to
　　me, O LORD;
　　judge my cause.
⁶⁰ You have seen all their malice,
　　all their plots against me.

⁶¹ You have heard their taunts, O LORD,
　　all their plots against me.
⁶² The whispers and murmurs of my
　　assailants
　　are against me all day long.
⁶³ Whether they sit or rise—see,
　　I am the object of their
　　taunt-songs.

⁶⁴ Pay them back for their deeds,
　　O LORD,
　　according to the work of their
　　hands!
⁶⁵ Give them anguish of heart;
　　your curse be on them!
⁶⁶ Pursue them in anger and destroy
　　them
　　from under the LORD's heavens.

3:42–45—The woman singer answers the previous speaker, admitting sin, but angrily accuses God of not forgiving, punishing out of anger, and refusing to hear or answer lament.

3:46–51 *Destruction of my people*—Jeremiah rejoins the exchange, including a term of endear-

ment he typically uses (e.g., Jer. 4:11; 6:26; 8:11–23; 9:1–6; 14:17; Lam. 2:11; 4:3, 6, 10); his grief is overwhelming.

3:52–66—The first singer of Lam. 3 finishes his interrupted lament, confident that God will vindicate him against his human enemies.

The Punishment of Zion

4 How the gold has grown dim,
how the pure gold is changed!
The sacred stones lie scattered
at the head of every street.

2 The precious children of Zion,
worth their weight in fine gold—
how they are reckoned as earthen
pots,
the work of a potter's hands!

3 Even the jackals offer the breast
and nurse their young,
but my people has become cruel,
like the ostriches in the wilderness.

4 The tongue of the infant sticks
to the roof of its mouth for thirst;
the children beg for food,
but no one gives them anything.

5 Those who feasted on delicacies
perish in the streets;
those who were brought up in purple
cling to ash heaps.

6 For the chastisement*a* of my people
has been greater
than the punishment*b* of Sodom,
which was overthrown in a moment,
though no hand was laid on it.*c*

7 Her princes were purer than snow,
whiter than milk;
their bodies were more ruddy than
coral,
their hair*c* like sapphire.*d*

8 Now their visage is blacker than
soot;
they are not recognized in the
streets.
Their skin has shriveled on their
bones;
it has become as dry as wood.

9 Happier were those pierced by the
sword
than those pierced by hunger,
whose life drains away, deprived
of the produce of the field.

10 The hands of compassionate women
have boiled their own children;
they became their food
in the destruction of my people.

11 The LORD gave full vent to his wrath;
he poured out his hot anger,
and kindled a fire in Zion
that consumed its foundations.

12 The kings of the earth did not
believe,
nor did any of the inhabitants of
the world,
that foe or enemy could enter
the gates of Jerusalem.

13 It was for the sins of her prophets
and the iniquities of her priests,
who shed the blood of the righteous
in the midst of her.

14 Blindly they wandered through the
streets,
so defiled with blood
that no one was able
to touch their garments.

15 "Away! Unclean!" people shouted at
them;
"Away! Away! Do not touch!"
So they became fugitives and
wanderers;
it was said among the nations,
"They shall stay here no longer."

16 The LORD himself has scattered
them,
he will regard them no more;

a Or *iniquity*   *b* Or *sin*   *c* Meaning of Heb uncertain   *d* Or *lapis lazuli*

4:1–16 *How*—"Alas!" With a third communal dirge, Jeremiah again conveys the contrast between what once was and the graphic horrors of present devastation and deprivation.

4:2 *Earthen pots*—The people are shattered by the *potter* (God) (see Jer. 18:11; 19:1; Isa. 45:9–11).

4:13–16 *Fugitives and wanderers*—A new element is introduced: Jeremiah blames Judah's leadership, (false) *prophets* and *priests*, for bringing about the shedding of *the blood of the righteous* among the people. The leaders wander like Cain, soon to be banished east of Jerusalem.

no honor was shown to the priests,
  no favor to the elders.
17 Our eyes failed, ever watching
    vainly for help;
  we were watching eagerly
    for a nation that could not save.
18 They dogged our steps
    so that we could not walk in our
      streets;
  our end drew near; our days were
    numbered;
    for our end had come.
19 Our pursuers were swifter
    than the eagles in the heavens;
  they chased us on the mountains,
    they lay in wait for us in the
      wilderness.
20 The LORD's anointed, the breath of
    our life,
  was taken in their pits—
  the one of whom we said, "Under his
    shadow
  we shall live among the nations."
21 Rejoice and be glad, O daughter
    Edom,
  you that live in the land of Uz;
  but to you also the cup shall pass;
    you shall become drunk and strip
      yourself bare.
22 The punishment of your iniquity,
    O daughter Zion, is
      accomplished,
  he will keep you in exile no longer;
  but your iniquity, O daughter Edom,
    he will punish,
  he will uncover your sins.

A Plea for Mercy

5 Remember, O LORD, what has
    befallen us;

look, and see our disgrace!
2 Our inheritance has been turned
    over to strangers,
  our homes to aliens.
3 We have become orphans, fatherless;
  our mothers are like widows.
4 We must pay for the water we drink;
  the wood we get must be bought.
5 With a yoke[a] on our necks we are
    hard driven;
  we are weary, we are given no rest.
6 We have made a pact with[b] Egypt
    and Assyria,
  to get enough bread.
7 Our ancestors sinned; they are no
    more,
  and we bear their iniquities.
8 Slaves rule over us;
  there is no one to deliver us from
    their hand.
9 We get our bread at the peril of our
    lives,
  because of the sword in the
    wilderness.
10 Our skin is black as an oven
  from the scorching heat of famine.
11 Women are raped in Zion,
  virgins in the towns of Judah.
12 Princes are hung up by their hands;
  no respect is shown to the elders.
13 Young men are compelled to grind,
  and boys stagger under loads of
    wood.
14 The old men have left the city gate,
  the young men their music.
15 The joy of our hearts has ceased;
  our dancing has been turned to
    mourning.
16 The crown has fallen from our
    head;
  woe to us, for we have sinned!

[a] Symmachus: Heb lacks *With a yoke*   [b] Heb *have given the hand to*

5:1–22—This is a final communal lament for the survivors remaining in the land, probably composed some time later than the first four chapters. Note v. 7, *our ancestors sinned; they are no more*, a reference to those who died or went into exile. Subtle clues in the song suggest a female singer's experience in traditional culture and in this difficult context (e.g., collecting *water*, v. 4; securing *bread*, vv. 6, 9; millstone grinding, v. 13; contrast of men's singing to "our" *dancing* and *mourning*, vv. 14–15; and the tragedy of *rape*, v. 11). The book ends with the people's appeal to God to restore them, yet with an expressed fear that God may have ultimately rejected them in anger. There is no answer from God.

17 Because of this our hearts are sick,
      because of these things our eyes
          have grown dim:
18 because of Mount Zion, which lies
          desolate;
      jackals prowl over it.

19 But you, O LORD, reign forever;
      your throne endures to all
          generations.

20 Why have you forgotten us
          completely?
      Why have you forsaken us these
          many days?
21 Restore us to yourself, O LORD, that
      we may be restored;
      renew our days as of old—
22 unless you have utterly rejected us,
      and are angry with us beyond
          measure.

The Book of

EZEKIEL

The book is attributed to the priest Ezekiel, writing from exile in Babylon (Chaldea) between 593 and 571 BCE. Recent scholarship tends to affirm that the greater part of the book derives from a single author and that the dates given in the book are fully credible. The prophet was apparently among the first (and more politically influential) group of exiles taken to Babylon in 597. The book is commonly divided as follows: chapters 1–24, oracles of destruction against Judah and Jerusalem; chapters 25–32, oracles against foreign nations; and chapters 33–48, promises and visions of restoration. The book centers on Nebuchadrezzar's 587/86 BCE destruction of the Jerusalem temple, an event reported at the end of the oracles of doom (chap. 24) and confirmed at the beginning of the oracles of hope (chap. 33).

The judgment, destruction, and restoration of Judah are marked by four visions of YHWH (in chaps. 1–3; chaps. 8–11; 37:1–14; and chaps. 40–48), first taking revenge against enemies (including the faithless people of Judah), and then reestablishing God's kingdom. The book opens with YHWH appearing to Ezekiel in Babylon, riding a heavenly chariot and announcing judgment against the people. In chapters 8–11, Ezekiel is transported in a vision to Jerusalem, where he first witnesses the abominations committed within the temple and then watches YHWH's departure, signaling God's ultimate rejection of the defiled sanctuary. In chapter 37, following the destruction of Jerusalem and the second deportation of the Judeans, Ezekiel sees the vision of dry bones restored to life, symbolizing the rebirth of the Judean people. Finally, in chapters 40–48 Ezekiel is called upon once again to tour YHWH's temple. After witnessing the new and undefiled structure, the prophet looks on as the divine chariot enters and YHWH takes the throne to reign eternally from the sanctuary.

Over one-third of the book is devoted to Ezekiel's visions. Not only do these visions convey the book's "plot"—YHWH first goes forth to destroy enemies, brings a despairing Israel back to life, and then returns to reign—but they also serve predominantly as a means of affirming divine power at a time when God's power had become all but invisible. Ezekiel wrote at a time when the Judean people and their leaders experienced extreme powerlessness. None of the traditional apparatus for affirming national or religious identity remained in place. Military action had become first (before 587) futile and then (after Jerusalem's destruction) impossible. Political action was likewise meaningless. Even religious ritual could not continue as usual after the destruction of the temple in 587/86. All the familiar structures of Israel's life had been destroyed . . . and God had done nothing to prevent that destruction. In this context of national powerlessness, Ezekiel's visions asserted, against all appearances, the power of Israel's God, present and active in the people's midst. Through the medium of visions, Ezekiel set forth a great but unseen drama unfolding in Israel's history: YHWH had rejected the people for their intolerable sinfulness; God had left the temple and, using Babylon as a tool, was now fighting against the elect people. After

the nation had been punished, however, YHWH would once again call a people, bring them into the promised land, and reign from a holy temple. The visions tell the "invisible story" of God's hand at work behind events in Israel and Babylon.

Ezekiel made programmatic use of visions; he was also a master of the extended metaphor. Literary figures such as the lion of Judah (Gen. 49:9) and Jerusalem and Samaria as "sister cities" (Jer. 3:6–11) are developed in Ezekiel into fables, invariably with an ironic twist. The lion becomes a man-eater and the sisters engage in twin infidelities. The point is clear: every facet of Judah's national identity has become degraded, and Ezekiel is called to witness YHWH's destruction of this ungovernable people. Like the earlier prophets, Ezekiel carried out several sign acts or symbolic actions, a kind of street theater in which God's word is dramatically enacted. Ezekiel typically enacted both the role of YHWH and that of the people; for example, setting his face in judgment against Jerusalem (as YHWH; 4:3) and then eating siege rations while quaking in fear (as the people; 4:9–12). Detailed visions, extended metaphors, and vivid symbolic actions combine to make the book exceptionally rich in symbolic imagery. In fact, Ezekiel's striking imagery at times borders on the bizarre, as, for example, when the prophet is tied up by God for over a year (3:24–26; 4:4–8) or YHWH actually kills the prophet's wife in order to make Ezekiel a symbol of mourning (24:15–18). In the desperate last days of the Judean monarchy Ezekiel employs the most intense images available to convey the urgency of his message: Judah is doomed, its destruction is at hand, even YHWH will suffer the loss of home and land. And yet, the prophet affirms, God is present in this maelstrom, still calling Israel to repentance. YHWH's rage is implacable and vengeance is inescapable, but beyond the horrors of the exile, YHWH will at last renew the covenant with a restored Israel.

Concerned as the book of Ezekiel is with the fate of the temple and the Judean people, it centers on a still deeper concern: the honor of God. In Ezekiel's world, war was understood as a fight between divine powers, carried out by their human supporters. The winning god was affirmed as the more powerful. In Judah's case, the Babylonian exile, and particularly YHWH's inability to save even the holy temple, served as evidence that YHWH had been beaten by the Babylonian god Marduk. Many among the Judeans, both at home and in exile, must have responded to YHWH's defeat by giving their allegiance to other gods who still seemed powerful or in whose realm they were living. This problem—YHWH's apparent humiliation at the hands of the Babylonians—forms the constant backdrop of the book of Ezekiel. From the beginning of the book, YHWH asserts continued presence and power. Appearing in Babylon, in the heart of Marduk's realm, God announces the punishment of the Judean people for their offenses. In punishing the people, however, YHWH contributes to the divine humiliation. Because YHWH will continue to use the Babylonians as the instrument to punish Judah, the Israelite God must also face the disgrace of having the land, the people, and even the temple taken by the Babylonians and their god. As stated in 36:20, anyone seeing the exiled Judeans will think YHWH has been beaten: "These are the people of the LORD, and yet they had to go out of his land." YHWH's need to avenge God's honor by punishing the people thus creates the corresponding need for revenge *against* the Babylonians. The problem of how to affirm YHWH's sovereignty in the face of Babylon's continued military triumph underlies the book's constant emphasis on the presence, potency, and supremacy of Israel's God. Some seventy times YHWH announces that after divine action the people will "know that I am

YHWH." The Judean people will know this when God has devastated them; the nations will know this when God punishes them for their delight in Judah's devastation. The point here is not that people will know *who* YHWH is, but that, seeing God's power, they will acknowledge the divine sovereignty.

The Babylonian exile was the catalyst for a great rethinking of Israel's identity. Israel as the people of the land of Israel, the people whose God dwelt in the great temple of Jerusalem, and whose Davidic rulers were the chosen sons of YHWH, had vanished. As a result, Ezekiel, along with other biblical authors, was faced with the task of redefining the nature of God's relationship to the people.

The writings of Ezekiel articulate a distinctive anthropology in addition to a distinctive theology. Ezekiel frankly despairs of the human capacity for good: human hearts are hearts of stone and must be replaced with hearts of flesh before they are capable of obedience. Humankind must be recreated and enabled—even forced—to obey YHWH. Alongside Ezekiel's apparent hopelessness over human nature, however, comes a passionate and recurring call to moral accountability. In the midst of the collapse of moral, cultural, and religious benchmarks, Ezekiel asserts the need for meaningful repentance and assures the people of YHWH's ardent response. Ezekiel counters the people's moral lassitude with the call for them to turn and live—to believe in the imperative of choosing right over wrong and to know that the blessing or judgment of God hangs in the balance.

The book of Ezekiel, while not the most widely read of the prophets, has left a powerful legacy in Western religious thought. Ezekiel's use of visions as a way of revealing God's role in the course of human political events, and his message that God would soon inaugurate a new and perfect reign on earth, paved the way for apocalyptic literature. Elements taken from Ezekiel's visions reappear in several later apocalypses, including the Revelation of John. Ezekiel's visions also stand at the beginning of a long line of mystical speculation extending from the angelic liturgies of Qumran to medieval Jewish mysticism. Theologically, the prophet is probably best known for arguing against transgenerational punishment and urging the efficacy of individual repentance (chap. 18). In recent decades his depiction of nature restored under God's life-giving control (47:1–12) has become a resource for ecological thinking. Finally, his visions of the wheels (chap. 1) and of the dry bones (chap. 37) have become part of the popular legacy of Western song and art.

In addition to its positive legacy, the book of Ezekiel has recently emerged as a paradigm of the "difficult text," a text that reflects values that are not commonly affirmed within modern Christianity or Judaism. Perhaps the book's most troubling aspect is the persona of God it conveys. Juxtaposed with the imagery of a God who will raise Israel from its grave of despair (37:1–14) and fill them with the divine spirit (39:29) is the God who swears that the restoration of the people will be through no concern for them, but from concern to vindicate the holy name. YHWH will bring the people back, not from love or from pity, but from self-interest: "It is not for your sake, O house of Israel, that I am about to act, but for the sake of my holy name" (36:22). YHWH's punishment of the people—to the point of luring them into child sacrifice in 20:25–26—seems extraordinarily harsh. Similarly, YHWH's insistence that Israel *will* be God's people, whether they wish it or not, seems contrary to the very notion of free obedience to God's will. Finally, Ezekiel's depiction of YHWH as the husband of Jerusalem has become a stumbling block for many modern readers. Images of

Jerusalem as a shameless woman who literally "spreads [her] legs" (NRSV "offering yourself"; 16:25) for every passerby are matched by images of the divine husband who hands her over to be attacked, stripped, and finally hacked to pieces in order to "satisfy" (16:42) and "assuage" anger (16:35–42). In its ancient context YHWH's "wife abuse" fits squarely within societal expectations: violated honor—whether a husband's or a god's—demands vindication. Many readers, however, reject such a definition of honor, whether divine or human, and find that the text raises profound questions about how to hear the word of God in passages depicting God's use of violence to satisfy a need for personal vengeance.

The troubling aspects of the book can best be understood in light of the extraordinary trauma the Judean people and Ezekiel himself had recently undergone. Not only had the community endured the horrors of war and deportation; in a way modern people find difficult to imagine, YHWH had been grossly humiliated—indeed, bested by another god. Controlling neither land, people, nor even a throne room, YHWH lacked the very attributes that defined divinity in the ancient world. The prophet Ezekiel faced an unprecedented challenge of re-asserting YHWH's power and authority in light of apparently overwhelming evidence of defeat. Perhaps more than any other prophet, Ezekiel had to reclaim the very possibility that YHWH was a god worthy of Israel's worship. Ezekiel's visionary affirmations of divine sovereignty defy Judah's very concrete experience that the people, land, and house of God had been mowed down by the enemy and their idols. Later in the exile, Deutero-Isaiah would announce YHWH's tenderness and compassion for the people; Ezekiel was called first to declare that YHWH was still God. The result is a text filled with passion—rage, grief, and ultimately the assurance of redemption.

—Julie Galambush

The Vision of the Chariot

1 In the thirtieth year, in the fourth month, on the fifth day of the month, as I was among the exiles by the river Chebar, the heavens were opened, and I saw visions of God. ²On the fifth day of the month (it was the fifth year of the exile of King Jehoiachin), ³the word of the LORD came to the priest Ezekiel son of Buzi, in the land of the Chaldeans by the river Chebar; and the hand of the LORD was on him there.

4 As I looked, a stormy wind came out of the north: a great cloud with

---

1:1–3:27 Ezekiel's First Vision and Call
Ezekiel sees a vision of YHWH, present and active in Babylon. Initially overwhelmed by his experience, Ezekiel is then empowered to deliver God's word of judgment to **the rebellious house** (3:27) of Judah. God's appearance, or theophany, is described in traditional language: YHWH arrives with **wind**, **cloud**, and **fire** (1:4; Pss. 77:17–18; 50:3), enthroned above the waters (Ps. 29:10), sending out his mighty voice (Ps. 68:33; cf. Ps. 29:3–9). The divine throne (the ark, above which YHWH was enthroned) is here depicted as both throne and chariot (an image familiar from Near Eastern art) and is borne by creatures identified in 10:15, 20 as cherubim (cf. Pss. 18:10; 80:1). The cherubim, guardians of YHWH's throne in Exod. 25:10–22; 1 Kgs. 6:23–28, are composite creatures. Their four faces—human,

lion, ox, and eagle (1:10)—were later associated with Matthew, Mark, Luke, and John respectively (and cf. Rev. 4:6–7). The ensemble's multiple faces, multidirectional wheels, and encircling eyes combine to suggest the omnipresence of YHWH, who is able to appear to the prophet in a foreign land.

1:2 The fifth year—The date corresponds to July 593 BCE.

1:3 The hand of the LORD—The power of YHWH (cf. 3:14, 22; 8:1; 33:22; 37:1; 40:1), especially associated with the prophet's visions. The name Ezekiel, "God strengthens" or "hardens," is appropriate for a prophet who will undergo great personal hardship as part of his witness to the suffering of the Judean people and the strengthening power of God.

brightness around it and fire flashing forth continually, and in the middle of the fire, something like gleaming amber. ⁵ In the middle of it was something like four living creatures. This was their appearance: they were of human form. ⁶ Each had four faces, and each of them had four wings. ⁷ Their legs were straight, and the soles of their feet were like the sole of a calf's foot; and they sparkled like burnished bronze. ⁸ Under their wings on their four sides they had human hands. And the four had their faces and their wings thus: ⁹ their wings touched one another; each of them moved straight ahead, without turning as they moved. ¹⁰ As for the appearance of their faces: the four had the face of a human being, the face of a lion on the right side, the face of an ox on the left side, and the face of an eagle; ¹¹ such were their faces. Their wings were spread out above; each creature had two wings, each of which touched the wing of another, while two covered their bodies. ¹² Each moved straight ahead; wherever the spirit would go, they went, without turning as they went. ¹³ In the middle of*a* the living creatures there was something that looked like burning coals of fire, like torches moving to and fro among the living creatures; the fire was bright, and lightning issued from the fire. ¹⁴ The living creatures darted to and fro, like a flash of lightning.

15 As I looked at the living creatures, I saw a wheel on the earth beside the living creatures, one for each of the four of them.*b* ¹⁶ As for the appearance of the wheels and their construction: their appearance was like the gleaming of beryl; and the four had the same form, their construction being something like a wheel within a wheel. ¹⁷ When they moved, they moved in any of the four directions without veering as they

moved. ¹⁸ Their rims were tall and awesome, for the rims of all four were full of eyes all around. ¹⁹ When the living creatures moved, the wheels moved beside them; and when the living creatures rose from the earth, the wheels rose. ²⁰ Wherever the spirit would go, they went, and the wheels rose along with them; for the spirit of the living creatures was in the wheels. ²¹ When they moved, the others moved; when they stopped, the others stopped; and when they rose from the earth, the wheels rose along with them; for the spirit of the living creatures was in the wheels.

22 Over the heads of the living creatures there was something like a dome, shining like crystal,*c* spread out above their heads. ²³ Under the dome their wings were stretched out straight, one toward another; and each of the creatures had two wings covering its body. ²⁴ When they moved, I heard the sound of their wings like the sound of mighty waters, like the thunder of the Almighty,*d* a sound of tumult like the sound of an army; when they stopped, they let down their wings. ²⁵ And there came a voice from above the dome over their heads; when they stopped, they let down their wings.

26 And above the dome over their heads there was something like a throne, in appearance like sapphire;*e* and seated above the likeness of a throne was something that seemed like a human form. ²⁷ Upward from what appeared like the loins I saw something like gleaming amber, something that looked like fire enclosed all around; and downward from what looked like the loins I saw something that looked like fire, and there was a splendor all around. ²⁸ Like

a Gk OL: Heb *And the appearance of*   *b* Heb *of their faces*   *c* Gk: Heb *like the awesome crystal*   *d* Traditional rendering of Heb *Shaddai*   *e* Or *lapis lazuli*

1:28—The dazzlingly bright figure (cf. Dan. 10:4–9) is not identified directly as YHWH; rather, Ezekiel claims only to have seen *the appearance of the likeness* of YHWH's *glory*. Even this indirect glimpse of the divine glory, however, is enough literally to knock the prophet off his feet.

the bow in a cloud on a rainy day, such was the appearance of the splendor all around. This was the appearance of the likeness of the glory of the LORD.

When I saw it, I fell on my face, and I heard the voice of someone speaking.

The Vision of the Scroll

2 He said to me: O mortal,[a] stand up on your feet, and I will speak with you. [2] And when he spoke to me, a spirit entered into me and set me on my feet; and I heard him speaking to me. [3] He said to me, Mortal, I am sending you to the people of Israel, to a nation[b] of rebels who have rebelled against me; they and their ancestors have transgressed against me to this very day. [4] The descendants are impudent and stubborn. I am sending you to them, and you shall say to them, "Thus says the Lord GOD." [5] Whether they hear or refuse to hear (for they are a rebellious house), they shall know that there has been a prophet among them. [6] And you, O mortal, do not be afraid of them, and do not be afraid of their words, though briers and thorns surround you and you live among scorpions; do not be afraid of their words, and do not be dismayed at their looks, for they are a rebellious house. [7] You shall speak my words to them, whether they hear or refuse to hear; for they are a rebellious house.

[8] But you, mortal, hear what I say to you; do not be rebellious like that rebellious house; open your mouth and eat what I give you. [9] I looked, and a hand was stretched out to me, and a written scroll was in it. [10] He spread it before me; it had writing on the front and on the back, and written on it were words of lamentation and mourning and woe.

3 He said to me, O mortal, eat what is offered to you; eat this scroll, and go, speak to the house of Israel. [2] So I opened my mouth, and he gave me the scroll to eat. [3] He said to me, Mortal, eat this scroll that I give you and fill your stomach with it. Then I ate it; and in my mouth it was as sweet as honey.

[4] He said to me: Mortal, go to the house of Israel and speak my very words to them. [5] For you are not sent to a people of obscure speech and difficult language, but to the house of Israel— [6] not to many peoples of obscure speech and difficult language, whose words you cannot understand. Surely, if I sent you to them, they would listen to you. [7] But the house of Israel will not listen to you, for they are not willing to listen to me; because all the house of Israel have a hard forehead and a stubborn heart. [8] See, I have made your face hard against their faces, and your forehead hard against their foreheads. [9] Like the hardest stone, harder than flint, I have made your forehead; do not fear them or be dismayed at their looks, for they are a rebellious house. [10] He said to me: Mortal, all my words that I shall speak to you receive in your heart and hear with your ears; [11] then go to the exiles, to your people, and speak to them. Say to them, "Thus says the Lord GOD"; whether they hear or refuse to hear.

Ezekiel at the River Chebar

[12] Then the spirit lifted me up, and as the glory of the LORD rose[c] from its place, I heard behind me the sound of loud rumbling; [13] it was the sound of the wings of the living creatures brushing

[a] Or son of man; Heb ben adam (and so throughout the book when Ezekiel is addressed)　[b] Syr: Heb to nations　[c] Cn: Heb and blessed be the glory of the LORD

2:1—Ezekiel is addressed throughout the book as "son of man" (NRSV *mortal*), a term with a complex later history, including uses in Daniel (7:13) and by Jesus (e.g., Mark 8:31). These later uses depart from the term's original meaning of "mere mortal" (cf. Ps. 8:4), a phrase emphasizing the distance between the divine and human realms.

Used in this sense in Ezekiel, the term serves constantly to remind the prophet of his lowly status before the King of kings whom he serves.

3:12–15 *Tel-abib*—Ezekiel is carried away by a divine spirit (cf. the experience of Elijah; 1 Kgs. 18:12; 2 Kgs. 2:16) and placed among the exiles at Tel-abib, a Jewish settlement in Babylon.

against one another, and the sound of the wheels beside them, that sounded like a loud rumbling. **¹⁴** The spirit lifted me up and bore me away; I went in bitterness in the heat of my spirit, the hand of the LORD being strong upon me. **¹⁵** I came to the exiles at Tel-abib, who lived by the river Chebar.*ᵃ* And I sat there among them, stunned, for seven days.

16 At the end of seven days, the word of the LORD came to me: **¹⁷** Mortal, I have made you a sentinel for the house of Israel; whenever you hear a word from my mouth, you shall give them warning from me. **¹⁸** If I say to the wicked, "You shall surely die," and you give them no warning, or speak to warn the wicked from their wicked way, in order to save their life, those wicked persons shall die for their iniquity; but their blood I will require at your hand. **¹⁹** But if you warn the wicked, and they do not turn from their wickedness, or from their wicked way, they shall die for their iniquity; but you will have saved your life. **²⁰** Again, if the righteous turn from their righteousness and commit iniquity, and I lay a stumbling block before them, they shall die; because you have not warned them, they shall die for their sin, and their righteous deeds that they have done shall not be remembered; but their blood I will require at your hand. **²¹** If, however, you warn the righteous not

to sin, and they do not sin, they shall surely live, because they took warning; and you will have saved your life.

Ezekiel Isolated and Silenced

22 Then the hand of the LORD was upon me there; and he said to me, Rise up, go out into the valley, and there I will speak with you. **²³** So I rose up and went out into the valley; and the glory of the LORD stood there, like the glory that I had seen by the river Chebar; and I fell on my face. **²⁴** The spirit entered into me, and set me on my feet; and he spoke with me and said to me: Go, shut yourself inside your house. **²⁵** As for you, mortal, cords shall be placed on you, and you shall be bound with them, so that you cannot go out among the people; **²⁶** and I will make your tongue cling to the roof of your mouth, so that you shall be speechless and unable to reprove them; for they are a rebellious house. **²⁷** But when I speak with you, I will open your mouth, and you shall say to them, "Thus says the Lord GOD"; let those who will hear, hear; and let those who refuse to hear, refuse; for they are a rebellious house.

The Siege of Jerusalem Portrayed

4 And you, O mortal, take a brick and set it before you. On it portray a city,

ᵃ Two Mss Syr: Heb *Chebar, and to where they lived.* Another reading is *Chebar, and I sat where they sat*

3:16–21—Ezekiel receives the first of two commissions as Israel's sentinel (cf. 33:1–9). The prophet serves as part of the people's defense against the wrath of God, standing as watchman to warn the people of YHWH's hostile approach. Even if they choose not to repent, the people cannot claim they were unprepared for YHWH's judgment against them.

3:22–27—The command for Ezekiel to shut himself indoors, where he will be bound and unable to speak (see also 4:4–8), is enigmatic at best. Ezekiel's silence (cf. 24:26–27; 33:21–22) may represent an inability to speak anything except YHWH's oracles (after all, he has been informed in v. 18 that he *must* speak, on peril of his life). His silence may also be a way of describing the fact that Ezekiel was a *writing* prophet—one who stayed indoors writing rather than speaking aloud

in public. On the unique nature of Ezekiel's symbolic actions, see the introduction.

4:1–24:24 Oracles of Doom against Judah

Most of the first half of the book comprises oracles warning Judah of God's judgment, culminating with the death of Ezekiel's wife, a sign that Jerusalem has fallen. The people and their leaders are accused of a wide range of sins, from unspecified "violence" to adultery, idolatry and abuse of the poor. As Judah's peril grows the prophet employs a broadening range of reprimands, pleas, and fables, attempting to command or cajole the people to repentance.

4:1–8—Ezekiel sets his face against a clay model of Jerusalem, acting out YHWH's determination to destroy the city. The command (vv. 4–6) for Ezekiel to lie, first **three hundred ninety days** on his left side and then **forty days** on his right, is

Jerusalem; ²and put siegeworks against it, and build a siege wall against it, and cast up a ramp against it; set camps also against it, and plant battering rams against it all around. ³Then take an iron plate and place it as an iron wall between you and the city; set your face toward it, and let it be in a state of siege, and press the siege against it. This is a sign for the house of Israel.

4 Then lie on your left side, and place the punishment of the house of Israel upon it; you shall bear their punishment for the number of the days that you lie there. ⁵For I assign to you a number of days, three hundred ninety days, equal to the number of the years of their punishment; and so you shall bear the punishment of the house of Israel. ⁶When you have completed these, you shall lie down a second time, but on your right side, and bear the punishment of the house of Judah; forty days I assign you, one day for each year. ⁷You shall set your face toward the siege of Jerusalem, and with your arm bared you shall prophesy against it. ⁸See, I am putting cords on you so that you cannot turn from one side to the other until you have completed the days of your siege.

9 And you, take wheat and barley, beans and lentils, millet and spelt; put them into one vessel, and make bread for yourself. During the number of days that you lie on your side, three hundred ninety days, you shall eat it. ¹⁰The food that you eat shall be twenty shekels a day by weight; at fixed times you shall eat it. ¹¹And you shall drink water by mea-sure, one-sixth of a hin; at fixed times you shall drink. ¹²You shall eat it as a barley-cake, baking it in their sight on human dung. ¹³The LORD said, "Thus shall the people of Israel eat their bread, unclean, among the nations to which I will drive them." ¹⁴Then I said, "Ah Lord GOD! I have never defiled myself; from my youth up until now I have never eaten what died of itself or was torn by animals, nor has carrion flesh come into my mouth." ¹⁵Then he said to me, "See, I will let you have cow's dung instead of human dung, on which you may prepare your bread."

16 Then he said to me, Mortal, I am going to break the staff of bread in Jeru-salem; they shall eat bread by weight and with fearfulness; and they shall drink water by measure and in dismay. ¹⁷Lack-ing bread and water, they will look at one another in dismay, and waste away under their punishment.

A Sword against Jerusalem

5 And you, O mortal, take a sharp sword; use it as a barber's razor and run it over your head and your beard; then take balances for weighing, and divide the hair. ²One third of the hair you shall burn in the fire inside the city, when the days of the siege are completed; one third you shall take and strike with the sword all around the city;ᵃ and one third you shall scatter to the wind, and I will unsheathe the sword after them. ³Then you shall take from these a small number, and bind

ᵃHeb it

---

enigmatic, except in foreseeing a longer punish-ment for the north than for the south.

4:9–17—Ezekiel is to eat small rations of coarse grains (*twenty shekels* equals approx. 8 oz.), drink little (1/6 hin equals approx. 2/3 qt.), and use human excrement rather than animal dung as cooking fuel, all indicating the scarcity of sup-plies during the predicted siege. Apparently the priest Ezekiel has thus far been able to maintain his ritual purity even in exile, and YHWH's command that he intentionally defile himself is deeply distressing. His prophetic role, however, requires him to abandon received definitions of holiness and to act solely on the basis of God's direct command.

5:1–17—Ezekiel's symbolic action in vv. 1–4 has a double meaning: he shaves his hair as a pris-oner of war is shaved (cf. Isa. 7:20) and then uses the hair itself to symbolize the people, subjected to sword, plague, and famine. In vv. 5–17 YHWH (and not Babylon) proves to be the one who will unsheathe the sword and subject the people to the traditional punishments of pestilence, fire, and sword (cf. Lev. 26:25–26; Deut. 32:23–25).

them in the skirts of your robe. **4** From these, again, you shall take some, throw them into the fire and burn them up; from there a fire will come out against all the house of Israel.

5 Thus says the Lord GOD: This is Jerusalem; I have set her in the center of the nations, with countries all around her. **6** But she has rebelled against my ordinances and my statutes, becoming more wicked than the nations and the countries all around her, rejecting my ordinances and not following my statutes. **7** Therefore thus says the Lord GOD: Because you are more turbulent than the nations that are all around you, and have not followed my statutes or kept my ordinances, but have acted according to the ordinances of the nations that are all around you; **8** therefore thus says the Lord GOD: I, I myself, am coming against you; I will execute judgments among you in the sight of the nations. **9** And because of all your abominations, I will do to you what I have never yet done, and the like of which I will never do again. **10** Surely, parents shall eat their children in your midst, and children shall eat their parents; I will execute judgments on you, and any of you who survive I will scatter to every wind. **11** Therefore, as I live, says the Lord GOD, surely, because you have defiled my sanctuary with all your detestable things and with all your abominations—therefore I will cut you down;*a* my eye will not spare, and I will have no pity. **12** One third of you shall die of pestilence or be consumed by famine among you; one third shall fall by the sword around you; and one third I will scatter to every wind and will unsheathe the sword after them.

13 My anger shall spend itself, and I will vent my fury on them and satisfy myself; and they shall know that I, the LORD, have spoken in my jealousy, when I spend my fury on them. **14** Moreover I will make you a desolation and an object of mocking among the nations around you, in the sight of all that pass by. **15** You shall be*b* a mockery and a taunt, a warning and a horror, to the nations around you, when I execute judgments on you in anger and fury, and with furious punishments—I, the LORD, have spoken— **16** when I loose against you*c* my deadly arrows of famine, arrows for destruction, which I will let loose to destroy you, and when I bring more and more famine upon you, and break your staff of bread. **17** I will send famine and wild animals against you, and they will rob you of your children; pestilence and bloodshed shall pass through you; and I will bring the sword upon you. I, the LORD, have spoken.

Judgment on Idolatrous Israel

6 The word of the LORD came to me: **2** O mortal, set your face toward the mountains of Israel, and prophesy against them, **3** and say, You mountains of Israel, hear the word of the Lord GOD! Thus says the Lord GOD to the mountains and the hills, to the ravines and the valleys: I, I myself will bring a sword upon you, and I will destroy your high places. **4** Your altars shall become desolate, and your incense stands shall be broken; and I will throw down your slain in front of your idols. **5** I will lay the corpses of the people of Israel in front of their idols; and I will scatter your bones around your altars. **6** Wherever you live, your towns shall be waste and your high places ruined, so that your altars will be waste and ruined,*d* your idols broken and destroyed, your

a Another reading is *I will withdraw* *b* Gk Syr Vg Tg: Heb *It shall be* *c* Heb *them* *d* Syr Vg Tg: Heb *and be made guilty*

5:11 *As I live*—On three occasions in Ezekiel (see chaps. 17 and 20) YHWH utters a self-imprecation. The vow is a striking expression of God's profound investment in human affairs.

6:1–14—This oracle, specifically directed against the mountains (cf. 35:1–15; 36:1–15), focuses on the idolatrous worship conducted at *high places* (v. 6; 2 Kgs. 23:8). Ezekiel holds the land itself liable for the sins of its inhabitants.

incense stands cut down, and your works wiped out. ⁷ The slain shall fall in your midst; then you shall know that I am the LORD.

8 But I will spare some. Some of you shall escape the sword among the nations and be scattered through the countries. ⁹ Those of you who escape shall remember me among the nations where they are carried captive, how I was crushed by their wanton heart that turned away from me, and their wanton eyes that turned after their idols. Then they will be loathsome in their own sight for the evils that they have committed, for all their abominations. ¹⁰ And they shall know that I am the LORD; I did not threaten in vain to bring this disaster upon them.

11 Thus says the Lord GOD: Clap your hands and stamp your foot, and say, Alas for all the vile abominations of the house of Israel! For they shall fall by the sword, by famine, and by pestilence. ¹² Those far off shall die of pestilence; those nearby shall fall by the sword; and any who are left and are spared shall die of famine. Thus I will spend my fury upon them. ¹³ And you shall know that I am the LORD, when their slain lie among their idols around their altars, on every high hill, on all the mountain tops, under every green tree, and under every leafy oak, wherever they offered pleasing odor to all their idols. ¹⁴ I will stretch out my hand against them, and make the land desolate and waste, throughout all their settlements, from the wilderness to Riblah.ᵃ Then they shall know that I am the LORD.

Impending Disaster

7 The word of the LORD came to me: ² You, O mortal, thus says the Lord GOD to the land of Israel:
An end! The end has come
upon the four corners of the land.
³ Now the end is upon you,
I will let loose my anger upon you;
I will judge you according to your
ways,
I will punish you for all your
abominations.
⁴ My eye will not spare you, I will have
no pity.
I will punish you for your ways,
while your abominations are
among you.
Then you shall know that I am the
LORD.

5 Thus says the Lord GOD:
Disaster after disaster! See, it comes.
⁶ An end has come, the end has
come.
It has awakened against you; see, it
comes!
⁷ Your doom ᵇ has come to you,
O inhabitant of the land.
The time has come, the day is near—
of tumult, not of reveling on the
mountains.
⁸ Soon now I will pour out my wrath
upon you;
I will spend my anger against you.
I will judge you according to your
ways,
and punish you for all your
abominations.
⁹ My eye will not spare; I will have no
pity.

ᵃ Another reading is *Diblah*   ᵇ Meaning of Heb uncertain

6:7 *You shall know that I am the* LORD—YHWH's goal, repeated throughout the book, is that not only Israel, but all nations should acknowledge God's sovereignty. The same goal predominates in the exodus narrative (Exod. 14:4): YHWH's actions will be witnessed by both the Israelites *and* the nations, who will then confess God's sovereignty (38:23; 39:21–24).

6:11 *Clap your hands*—An expression of anger (cf. 21:14, 17; 22:13).

7:1–19 The day of the LORD—The day of God's judgment is understood as a cosmic battle in which YHWH triumphs over all enemies. Here Ezekiel announces that the day of YHWH will mean *the end* (v. 2) for Judah (cf. Amos 8:2). Later, in chaps. 38–39, he envisions another day of YHWH in which Israel and Judah will be restored.

I will punish you according to
    your ways,
while your abominations are
    among you.
Then you shall know that it is I the LORD
who strike.
10 See, the day! See, it comes!
    Your doom[a] has gone out.
    The rod has blossomed, pride has
        budded.
11   Violence has grown into a rod of
        wickedness.
    None of them shall remain,
    not their abundance, not their
        wealth;
    no pre-eminence among them.[a]
12 The time has come, the day draws
        near;
    let not the buyer rejoice, nor the
        seller mourn,
    for wrath is upon all their
        multitude.
13 For the sellers shall not return to what
has been sold as long as they remain
alive. For the vision concerns all their
multitude; it shall not be revoked.
Because of their iniquity, they cannot
maintain their lives.[a]
14 They have blown the horn and made
    everything ready;
    but no one goes to battle,
    for my wrath is upon all their
        multitude.
15 The sword is outside, pestilence and
    famine are inside;
    those in the field die by the sword;
    those in the city—famine and
        pestilence devour them.
16 If any survivors escape,
    they shall be found on the
        mountains
    like doves of the valleys,
    all of them moaning over their
        iniquity.
17 All hands shall grow feeble,
    all knees turn to water.

18 They shall put on sackcloth,
    horror shall cover them.
    Shame shall be on all faces,
    baldness on all their heads.
19 They shall fling their silver into the
    streets,
    their gold shall be treated as
        unclean.
Their silver and gold cannot save them
on the day of the wrath of the LORD.
They shall not satisfy their hunger or
fill their stomachs with it. For it was the
stumbling block of their iniquity. 20 From
their[b] beautiful ornament, in which they
took pride, they made their abominable
images, their detestable things; therefore I will make of it an unclean thing
to them.
21 I will hand it over to strangers as
    booty,
    to the wicked of the earth as
        plunder;
    they shall profane it.
22 I will avert my face from them,
    so that they may profane my
        treasured[c] place;
    the violent shall enter it,
    they shall profane it.
23 Make a chain![a]
    For the land is full of bloody
        crimes;
    the city is full of violence.
24 I will bring the worst of the nations
    to take possession of their houses.
    I will put an end to the arrogance of
        the strong,
    and their holy places shall be
        profaned.
25 When anguish comes, they will seek
    peace,
    but there shall be none.
26 Disaster comes upon disaster,
    rumor follows rumor;
    they shall keep seeking a vision from
        the prophet;

[a] Meaning of Heb uncertain [b] Syr Symmachus: Heb its [c] Or secret

7:19 Unclean—Literally, "like a menstruant."
Menstrual blood was a powerful source of ritual
pollution (Lev. 15:19–30; see also note on Ezek.
36:17).

7:24 The worst of the nations—Babylon, who
will profane the Jerusalem temple (cf. 28:7).

instruction shall perish from the
   priest,
and counsel from the elders.
27 The king shall mourn,
   the prince shall be wrapped in
     despair,
   and the hands of the people of the
     land shall tremble.
According to their way I will deal
   with them;
   according to their own judgments
     I will judge them.
And they shall know that I am the
Lord.

Abominations in the Temple

8 In the sixth year, in the sixth month,
on the fifth day of the month, as I
sat in my house, with the elders of Judah
sitting before me, the hand of the Lord
God fell upon me there. ²I looked,
and there was a figure that looked like
a human being;*a* below what appeared
to be its loins it was fire, and above the
loins it was like the appearance of brightness, like gleaming amber. ³It stretched
out the form of a hand, and took me by
a lock of my head; and the spirit lifted
me up between earth and heaven, and
brought me in visions of God to Jerusalem, to the entrance of the gateway of
the inner court that faces north, to the
seat of the image of jealousy, which provokes to jealousy. ⁴And the glory of the
God of Israel was there, like the vision
that I had seen in the valley.

5 Then God*b* said to me, "O mortal,
lift up your eyes now in the direction of
the north." So I lifted up my eyes toward
the north, and there, north of the altar
gate, in the entrance, was this image of
jealousy. ⁶He said to me, "Mortal, do
you see what they are doing, the great
abominations that the house of Israel
are committing here, to drive me far
from my sanctuary? Yet you will see still
greater abominations."

7 And he brought me to the entrance of
the court; I looked, and there was a hole
in the wall. ⁸Then he said to me, "Mortal,
dig through the wall"; and when I dug
through the wall, there was an entrance.
⁹He said to me, "Go in, and see the vile
abominations that they are committing
here." ¹⁰So I went in and looked; there,
portrayed on the wall all around, were
all kinds of creeping things, and loathsome animals, and all the idols of the
house of Israel. ¹¹Before them stood seventy of the elders of the house of Israel,
with Jaazaniah son of Shaphan standing
among them. Each had his censer in his
hand, and the fragrant cloud of incense
was ascending. ¹²Then he said to me,
"Mortal, have you seen what the elders of
the house of Israel are doing in the dark,
each in his room of images? For they say,
'The Lord does not see us, the Lord has
forsaken the land.'" ¹³He said also to me,
"You will see still greater abominations
that they are committing."

14 Then he brought me to the entrance
of the north gate of the house of the

a Gk: Heb *like fire*   *b* Heb *he*

8:1–11:25 Ezekiel's Second Vision

As in chap. 2, here Ezekiel is transported by the
divine spirit (8:3; cf. Elijah in 1 Kgs. 18:12). He
is given a tour of the Jerusalem temple, focusing
on the extreme infidelity of the religious leaders.
The prophet's role is as a witness: the temple is
entirely defiled, and the people entirely faithless.
YHWH is therefore fully justified in abandoning
both the temple and the people.

8:1 *The sixth year*—September 592 BCE. *The
elders* continue to function as leaders of the exilic
community. Ezekiel, in turn, is respected as an
official spokesperson for YHWH (cf. 14:1; 20:1;
33:31; and cf. Elisha in 2 Kgs. 6:32).

8:3, 5 *This image of jealousy*—The image is
probably a representation of Asherah (cf. 2 Kgs.
21:7), the Canaanite mother goddess. The consort
of the Canaanite father god El, Asherah seems to
have been worshiped by some as the wife of the
Israelite YHWH. Asherah is mentioned together
with YHWH in ancient inscriptions, and 2 Kings
contains numerous mentions of Asherah poles set
up in the Jerusalem temple.

8:14 *Tammuz*—Also called Dumuzi, a Sumerian
god widely worshiped in the ancient Near East,
whose annual death and rebirth represented the
cycle of the agricultural year.

LORD; women were sitting there weeping for Tammuz. 15 Then he said to me, "Have you seen this, O mortal? You will see still greater abominations than these."

16 And he brought me into the inner court of the house of the LORD; there, at the entrance of the temple of the LORD, between the porch and the altar, were about twenty-five men, with their backs to the temple of the LORD, and their faces toward the east, prostrating themselves to the sun toward the east. 17 Then he said to me, "Have you seen this, O mortal? Is it not bad enough that the house of Judah commits the abominations done here? Must they fill the land with violence, and provoke my anger still further? See, they are putting the branch to their nose! 18 Therefore I will act in wrath; my eye will not spare, nor will I have pity; and though they cry in my hearing with a loud voice, I will not listen to them."

The Slaughter of the Idolaters

9 Then he cried in my hearing with a loud voice, saying, "Draw near, you executioners of the city, each with his destroying weapon in his hand." 2 And six men came from the direction of the upper gate, which faces north, each with his weapon for slaughter in his hand; among them was a man clothed in linen, with a writing case at his side. They went in and stood beside the bronze altar.

3 Now the glory of the God of Israel had gone up from the cherub on which it rested to the threshold of the house. The LORD called to the man clothed in linen, who had the writing case at his side; 4 and said to him, "Go through the city, through Jerusalem, and put a mark on the foreheads of those who sigh and groan over all the abominations that are committed in it." 5 To the others he said in my hearing, "Pass through the city after him, and kill; your eye shall not spare, and you shall show no pity. 6 Cut down old men, young men and young women, little children and women, but touch no one who has the mark. And begin at my sanctuary." So they began with the elders who were in front of the house. 7 Then he said to them, "Defile the house, and fill the courts with the slain. Go!" So they went out and killed in the city. 8 While they were killing, and I was left alone, I fell prostrate on my face and cried out, "Ah Lord GOD! will you destroy all who remain of Israel as you pour out your wrath upon Jerusalem?" 9 He said to me, "The guilt of the house of Israel and Judah is exceedingly great; the land is full of bloodshed and the city full of perversity; for they say, 'The LORD has forsaken the land, and the LORD does not see.' 10 As for me, my eye will not spare, nor will I have pity, but I will bring down their deeds upon their heads."

11 Then the man clothed in linen,

8:16—*Sun* worship formed part of both Egyptian and Babylonian religions and seems at times to have formed part of YHWH-worship as well (2 Kgs. 23:5, 11; Ps. 84:11).

8:17 *Putting the branch to their nose*—The standard Hebrew text reflects a scribal emendation of the original, "putting a branch to *my* [YHWH's] nose." This is one of several recorded cases in which early scribes chose to alter the text rather than report actions considered blasphemous. The holiness of God outweighed even the holiness of the text.

9:3 *The glory of the God of Israel*—The divine glory leaves the Holy of Holies and advances as far as the threshold of the temple. The glory of YHWH has dwelt among the people since the

wilderness period, and its departure marks a cataclysmic rift between God and Israel. Then as now, the deepest grief is often expressed as a separation from God. *The cherub on which it rested*—The cherub that formed part of the temple furniture, not the living being (see 1:4–28).

9:4–6 *Mark on the foreheads*—The scene is reminiscent of the exodus narrative, but here most of the Israelites are designated for destruction. Only those who grieve over the city's sinfulness are spared. The penitent are marked with the Hebrew letter *taw* (written "X") on their foreheads (cf. Gen. 4:15; Exod. 12:22–23; Rev. 7:3–4).

with the writing case at his side, brought back word, saying, "I have done as you commanded me."

God's Glory Leaves Jerusalem

10 Then I looked, and above the dome that was over the heads of the cherubim there appeared above them something like a sapphire,*a* in form resembling a throne. ²He said to the man clothed in linen, "Go within the wheelwork underneath the cherubim; fill your hands with burning coals from among the cherubim, and scatter them over the city." He went in as I looked on. ³Now the cherubim were standing on the south side of the house when the man went in; and a cloud filled the inner court. ⁴Then the glory of the LORD rose up from the cherub to the threshold of the house; the house was filled with the cloud, and the court was full of the brightness of the glory of the LORD. ⁵The sound of the wings of the cherubim was heard as far as the outer court, like the voice of God Almighty*a* when he speaks.

6 When he commanded the man clothed in linen, "Take fire from within the wheelwork, from among the cherubim," he went in and stood beside a wheel. ⁷And a cherub stretched out his hand from among the cherubim to the fire that was among the cherubim, took some of it and put it into the hands of the man clothed in linen, who took it and went out. ⁸The cherubim appeared to have the form of a human hand under their wings.

9 I looked, and there were four wheels beside the cherubim, one beside each cherub; and the appearance of the wheels was like gleaming beryl. ¹⁰And as for their appearance, the four looked alike, something like a wheel within

a wheel. ¹¹When they moved, they moved in any of the four directions without veering as they moved; but in whatever direction the front wheel faced, the others followed without veering as they moved. ¹²Their entire body, their rims, their spokes, their wings, and the wheels—the wheels of the four of them—were full of eyes all around. ¹³As for the wheels, they were called in my hearing "the wheelwork." ¹⁴Each one had four faces: the first face was that of the cherub, the second face was that of a human being, the third that of a lion, and the fourth that of an eagle.

15 The cherubim rose up. These were the living creatures that I saw by the river Chebar. ¹⁶When the cherubim moved, the wheels moved beside them; and when the cherubim lifted up their wings to rise up from the earth, the wheels at their side did not veer. ¹⁷When they stopped, the others stopped, and when they rose up, the others rose up with them; for the spirit of the living creatures was in them.

18 Then the glory of the LORD went out from the threshold of the house and stopped above the cherubim. ¹⁹The cherubim lifted up their wings and rose up from the earth in my sight as they went out with the wheels beside them. They stopped at the entrance of the east gate of the house of the LORD; and the glory of the God of Israel was above them.

20 These were the living creatures that I saw underneath the God of Israel by the river Chebar; and I knew that they were cherubim. ²¹Each had four faces, each four wings, and underneath their wings something like human hands. ²²As for what their faces were like, they

a Or *lapis lazuli* *b* Traditional rendering of Heb *El Shaddai*

10:18–19—The throne chariot advances *from the threshold* of the temple (*house*) *to the east gate* of the courtyard. The east gate was the main ceremonial gateway, through which the ark may have been carried in ritual processions (Pss. 24:7–10; 68:24–26; 118:20). The symbolism evokes traditions of YHWH going forth as a warrior against enemies. In this case, however, the enemy is Israel itself.

were the same faces whose appearance I had seen by the river Chebar. Each one moved straight ahead.

Judgment on Wicked Counselors

11 The spirit lifted me up and brought me to the east gate of the house of the LORD, which faces east. There, at the entrance of the gateway, were twenty-five men; among them I saw Jaazaniah son of Azzur, and Pelatiah son of Benaiah, officials of the people. ² He said to me, "Mortal, these are the men who devise iniquity and who give wicked counsel in this city; ³ they say, 'The time is not near to build houses; this city is the pot, and we are the meat.' ⁴ Therefore prophesy against them; prophesy, O mortal."

5 Then the spirit of the LORD fell upon me, and he said to me, "Say, Thus says the LORD: This is what you think, O house of Israel; I know the things that come into your mind. ⁶ You have killed many in this city, and have filled its streets with the slain. ⁷ Therefore thus says the Lord GOD: The slain whom you have placed within it are the meat, and this city is the pot; but you shall be taken out of it. ⁸ You have feared the sword; and I will bring the sword upon you, says the Lord GOD. ⁹ I will take you out of it and give you over to the hands of foreigners, and execute judgments upon you. ¹⁰ You shall fall by the sword; I will judge you at the border of Israel. And you shall know that I am the LORD. ¹¹ This city shall not be your pot, and you shall not be the meat inside it; I will judge you at

the border of Israel. ¹² Then you shall know that I am the LORD, whose statutes you have not followed, and whose ordinances you have not kept, but you have acted according to the ordinances of the nations that are around you."

13 Now, while I was prophesying, Pelatiah son of Benaiah died. Then I fell down on my face, cried with a loud voice, and said, "Ah Lord GOD! will you make a full end of the remnant of Israel?"

God Will Restore Israel

14 Then the word of the LORD came to me: ¹⁵ Mortal, your kinsfolk, your own kin, your fellow exiles,ᵃ the whole house of Israel, all of them, are those of whom the inhabitants of Jerusalem have said, "They have gone far from the LORD; to us this land is given for a possession." ¹⁶ Therefore say: Thus says the Lord GOD: Though I removed them far away among the nations, and though I scattered them among the countries, yet I have been a sanctuary to them for a little whileᵇ in the countries where they have gone. ¹⁷ Therefore say: Thus says the Lord GOD: I will gather you from the peoples, and assemble you out of the countries where you have been scattered, and I will give you the land of Israel. ¹⁸ When they come there, they will remove from it all its detestable things and all its abominations. ¹⁹ I will give them oneᶜ heart, and put a new spirit within them; I will remove the heart of stone from their

ᵃ Gk Syr: Heb *people of your kindred*   ᵇ Or *to some extent*   ᶜ Another reading is *a new*

11:1–4—The men in the gateway are apparently the same as those mentioned in 8:16. *Jaazaniah* and *Peletiah* are otherwise unknown, but their *wicked counsel* (v. 2) probably consisted of revolt against Nebuchadrezzar in favor of the Egyptian Psammeticus II (cf. Jer. 27:1–3). The rulers are held responsible for the widespread suffering their decisions will cause.

11:11 *The border of Israel*—When Zedekiah was blinded at Riblah in Syria (12:1–16), several officials including "men of the king's council" were put to death. This oracle may anticipate that judgment.

11:15—The Judeans left in the land conclude that the exiles *have gone far from the LORD*, but that God has given the land to them (see the similar argument in 33:24). This scenario—that God had punished the rich and powerful (the exiles) while favoring the lowly—could easily have been understood as fulfilling the prophecies of prophets like Amos. Ezekiel, however, like Jeremiah (chap. 24), sees the exiles as YHWH's chosen, for whom YHWH serves as *a sanctuary* (v. 16) in exile, and whom God will bring back to possess the land.

11:19 *One heart . . . a heart of flesh*—Whereas Jeremiah promises that YHWH will engrave the

flesh and give them a heart of flesh, [20] so that they may follow my statutes and keep my ordinances and obey them. Then they shall be my people, and I will be their God. [21] But as for those whose heart goes after their detestable things and their abominations,[a] I will bring their deeds upon their own heads, says the Lord God.

22 Then the cherubim lifted up their wings, with the wheels beside them; and the glory of the God of Israel was above them. [23] And the glory of the Lord ascended from the middle of the city, and stopped on the mountain east of the city. [24] The spirit lifted me up and brought me in a vision by the spirit of God into Chaldea, to the exiles. Then the vision that I had seen left me. [25] And I told the exiles all the things that the Lord had shown me.

Judah's Captivity Portrayed

12 The word of the Lord came to me: [2] Mortal, you are living in the midst of a rebellious house, who have eyes to see but do not see, who have ears to hear but do not hear; [3] for they are a rebellious house. Therefore, mortal, prepare for yourself an exile's baggage, and go into exile by day in their sight; you shall go like an exile from your place to another place in their sight. Perhaps they will understand, though they are a rebellious house. [4] You shall bring out your baggage by day in their sight, as baggage for exile; and you shall go out yourself at evening in their sight, as those do who go into exile. [5] Dig through

the wall in their sight, and carry the baggage through it. [6] In their sight you shall lift the baggage on your shoulder, and carry it out in the dark; you shall cover your face, so that you may not see the land; for I have made you a sign for the house of Israel.

7 I did just as I was commanded. I brought out my baggage by day, as baggage for exile, and in the evening I dug through the wall with my own hands; I brought it out in the dark, carrying it on my shoulder in their sight.

8 In the morning the word of the Lord came to me: [9] Mortal, has not the house of Israel, the rebellious house, said to you, "What are you doing?" [10] Say to them, "Thus says the Lord God: This oracle concerns the prince in Jerusalem and all the house of Israel in it." [11] Say, "I am a sign for you: as I have done, so shall it be done to them; they shall go into exile, into captivity." [12] And the prince who is among them shall lift his baggage on his shoulder in the dark, and shall go out; he[b] shall dig through the wall and carry it through; he shall cover his face, so that he may not see the land with his eyes. [13] I will spread my net over him, and he shall be caught in my snare; and I will bring him to Babylon, the land of the Chaldeans, yet he shall not see it; and he shall die there. [14] I will scatter to every wind all who are around him, his helpers and all his troops; and I will unsheathe the sword behind them. [15] And they shall know that I am the

---

[a] Cn: Heb *And to the heart of their detestable things and their abominations their heart goes*   [b] Gk Syr: Heb *they*

---

law on the people's hearts (31:33–34; cf. 32:39), Ezekiel concludes that such stony hearts must be discarded altogether and replaced with hearts willing to follow YHWH's laws (cf. 18:31; 36:26). The change represents Ezekiel's less optimistic anthropology, which sees humankind as incorrigible, short of virtual re-creation.

11:23 *The mountain east of the city*—The Mount of Olives.

12:1–28 Escape from the Doomed City

12:1–16—The oracle begins as a pantomime suggesting the Jerusalemites escaping from the

besieged city by night. As exiles they would no longer *see the land* (v. 6). But in vv. 10–16 the oracle is declared to refer specifically to Zedekiah (*the prince in Jerusalem*, v. 10). The Judean monarch did try to escape the besieged Jerusalem in 586 but was captured by Nebuchadrezzar and blinded at Riblah (Jer. 39:1–7; 52:6–11). Although the passage has been interpreted as prophecy-after-the-event, blinding was a common punishment for disloyal vassals, and the oracle's meaning would have been readily understood already in 592 BCE.

LORD, when I disperse them among the nations and scatter them through the countries. [16] But I will let a few of them escape from the sword, from famine and pestilence, so that they may tell of all their abominations among the nations where they go; then they shall know that I am the LORD.

Judgment Not Postponed

[17] The word of the LORD came to me: [18] Mortal, eat your bread with quaking, and drink your water with trembling and with fearfulness; [19] and say to the people of the land, Thus says the Lord GOD concerning the inhabitants of Jerusalem in the land of Israel: They shall eat their bread with fearfulness, and drink their water in dismay, because their land shall be stripped of all it contains, on account of the violence of all those who live in it. [20] The inhabited cities shall be laid waste, and the land shall become a desolation; and you shall know that I am the LORD.

[21] The word of the LORD came to me: [22] Mortal, what is this proverb of yours about the land of Israel, which says, "The days are prolonged, and every vision comes to nothing"? [23] Tell them therefore, "Thus says the Lord GOD: I will put an end to this proverb, and they shall use it no more as a proverb in Israel." But say to them, The days are near, and the fulfillment of every vision. [24] For there shall no longer be any false vision or flattering divination within the house of Israel. [25] But I the LORD will speak the word that I speak, and it will be fulfilled. It will no longer be delayed; but in your days, O rebellious house, I will speak the word and fulfill it, says the Lord GOD.

[26] The word of the LORD came to me: [27] Mortal, the house of Israel is saying, "The vision that he sees is for many years ahead; he prophesies for distant times." [28] Therefore say to them, Thus says the Lord GOD: None of my words will be delayed any longer, but the word that I speak will be fulfilled, says the Lord GOD.

False Prophets Condemned

13 The word of the LORD came to me: [2] Mortal, prophesy against the prophets of Israel who are prophesying; say to those who prophesy out of their own imagination: "Hear the word of the LORD!" [3] Thus says the Lord GOD, Alas for the senseless prophets who follow their own spirit, and have seen nothing! [4] Your prophets have been like jackals among ruins, O Israel. [5] You have not gone up into the breaches, or repaired a wall for the house of Israel, so that it might stand in battle on the day of the LORD. [6] They have envisioned falsehood and lying divination; they say, "Says the LORD," when the LORD has not sent them, and yet they wait for the

---

12:21–28—The people console themselves both by assuming an "expiration date" for long-unfulfilled prophecies (v. 22) and by claiming that recent prophecies pertain only to the distant future (v. 27). Ironically, this means that all prophecy can safely be ignored: either it is ancient history or it refers to a vague by-and-by.

13:1–23 Against the False Prophets, Male and Female
Ezekiel condemns the Jerusalem prophets who give false hope to the people (vv. 10, 16; cf. Jer. 6:14; 14:13–16). In contrast to Ezekiel, who has been appointed a sentinel to stand on the walls and give warning, the false prophets have neither repaired the city's walls nor stood in *the breaches* (v. 5); that is, they have not addressed the city's underlying problems of idolatry and social

injustice. Rather, they have merely *whitewashed* (v. 10) or plastered over the flimsy wall of the people's hopes that all will be well. The passage is one of Ezekiel's many attempts to shake the Judeans out of their passivity and into active moral responsibility (see 18:1–32). A group of female prophets is also condemned for false prophecy, especially for magical rituals (vv. 17–23). Magic and divination, though condemned in Lev. 19:26, 31, were widely practiced, even in some cases by "orthodox" Yahwists (cf. the Urim and Thummim of 1 Sam. 14:41–42). The cloth *bands* and *veils* (v. 18) mentioned here may either have served as magical protection or have been used in divination. The *pieces of bread* (v. 19) could be either payment for services (cf. 1 Sam. 9:7) or offerings (cf. Jer. 44:15–19).

fulfillment of their word! ⁷ Have you not seen a false vision or uttered a lying divination, when you have said, "Says the LORD," even though I did not speak?

8 Therefore thus says the Lord GOD: Because you have uttered falsehood and envisioned lies, I am against you, says the Lord GOD. ⁹ My hand will be against the prophets who see false visions and utter lying divinations; they shall not be in the council of my people, nor be enrolled in the register of the house of Israel, nor shall they enter the land of Israel; and you shall know that I am the Lord GOD. ¹⁰ Because, in truth, because they have misled my people, saying, "Peace," when there is no peace; and because, when the people build a wall, these prophets*ᵃ* smear whitewash on it. ¹¹ Say to those who smear whitewash on it that it shall fall. There will be a deluge of rain,*ᵇ* great hailstones will fall, and a stormy wind will break out. ¹² When the wall falls, will it not be said to you, "Where is the whitewash you smeared on it?" ¹³ Therefore thus says the Lord GOD: In my wrath I will make a stormy wind break out, and in my anger there shall be a deluge of rain, and hailstones in wrath to destroy it. ¹⁴ I will break down the wall that you have smeared with whitewash, and bring it to the ground, so that its foundation will be laid bare; when it falls, you shall perish within it; and you shall know that I am the LORD. ¹⁵ Thus I will spend my wrath upon the wall, and upon those who have smeared it with whitewash; and I will say to you, The wall is no more, nor those who smeared it— ¹⁶ the prophets of Israel who prophesied concerning Jerusalem and saw visions of peace for it, when there was no peace, says the Lord GOD.

17 As for you, mortal, set your face against the daughters of your people, who prophesy out of their own imagi-

nation; prophesy against them ¹⁸ and say, Thus says the Lord GOD: Woe to the women who sew bands on all wrists, and make veils for the heads of persons of every height, in the hunt for human lives! Will you hunt down lives among my people, and maintain your own lives? ¹⁹ You have profaned me among my people for handfuls of barley and for pieces of bread, putting to death persons who should not die and keeping alive persons who should not live, by your lies to my people, who listen to lies.

20 Therefore thus says the Lord GOD: I am against your bands with which you hunt lives;*ᶜ* I will tear them from your arms, and let the lives go free, the lives that you hunt down like birds. ²¹ I will tear off your veils, and save my people from your hands; they shall no longer be prey in your hands; and you shall know that I am the LORD. ²² Because you have disheartened the righteous falsely, although I have not disheartened them, and you have encouraged the wicked not to turn from their wicked way and save their lives; ²³ therefore you shall no longer see false visions or practice divination; I will save my people from your hand. Then you will know that I am the LORD.

God's Judgments Justified

14 Certain elders of Israel came to me and sat down before me. ² And the word of the LORD came to me: ³ Mortal, these men have taken their idols into their hearts, and placed their iniquity as a stumbling block before them; shall I let myself be consulted by them? ⁴ Therefore speak to them, and say to them, Thus says the Lord GOD: Any of those of the house of Israel who take their idols into their hearts and place their iniquity as a stumbling

---

ᵃ Heb *they*   *ᵇ* Heb *rain and you*   *ᶜ* Gk Syr: Heb *lives for birds*

14:1–11 Elders of Israel

As in 8:1 (and cf. 20:1) the *elders* come before Ezekiel, this time specifically to inquire of YHWH, that is, to bring questions with the hope

of receiving a response mediated by the prophet (cf. Judg. 18:5). Instead, YHWH uses the opportunity to call the elders away from their idolatry.

block before them, and yet come to the prophet—I the LORD will answer those who come with the multitude of their idols, ⁵in order that I may take hold of the hearts of the house of Israel, all of whom are estranged from me through their idols.

6 Therefore say to the house of Israel, Thus says the Lord GOD: Repent and turn away from your idols; and turn away your faces from all your abominations. ⁷For any of those of the house of Israel, or of the aliens who reside in Israel, who separate themselves from me, taking their idols into their hearts and placing their iniquity as a stumbling block before them, and yet come to a prophet to inquire of me by him, I the LORD will answer them myself. ⁸I will set my face against them; I will make them a sign and a byword and cut them off from the midst of my people; and you shall know that I am the LORD.

9 If a prophet is deceived and speaks a word, I, the LORD, have deceived that prophet, and I will stretch out my hand against him, and will destroy him from the midst of my people Israel. ¹⁰And they shall bear their punishment—the punishment of the inquirer and the punishment of the prophet shall be the same— ¹¹so that the house of Israel may no longer go astray from me, nor defile themselves any more with all their transgressions. Then they shall be my people, and I will be their God, says the Lord GOD.

12 The word of the LORD came to me: ¹³Mortal, when a land sins against me by acting faithlessly, and I stretch out my hand against it, and break its staff of bread and send famine upon it, and cut off from it human beings and animals, ¹⁴even if Noah, Daniel,[a] and Job, these three, were in it, they would save only their own lives by their righteousness, says the Lord GOD. ¹⁵If I send wild animals through the land to ravage it, so that it is made desolate, and no one may pass through because of the animals; ¹⁶even if these three men were in it, as I live, says the Lord GOD, they would save neither sons nor daughters; they alone would be saved, but the land would be desolate. ¹⁷Or if I bring a sword upon that land and say, "Let a sword pass through the land," and I cut off human beings and animals from it; ¹⁸though these three men were in it, as I live, says the Lord GOD, they would save neither sons nor daughters, but they alone would be saved. ¹⁹Or if I send a pestilence into that land, and pour out my wrath upon it with blood, to cut off humans and animals from it; ²⁰even if Noah, Daniel,[a] and Job were in it, as I live, says the Lord GOD, they would save neither son nor daughter; they would save only their own lives by their righteousness.

[a] Or, as otherwise read, *Danel*

14:9–11—Ezekiel introduces the possibility that a "false" prophet may not be one who fabricates his or her prophecy, but one who has been deliberately deceived by YHWH (cf. 1 Kgs. 22:19–23). Such a prophet, even though deceived by YHWH, will be destroyed, and those who follow the prophet punished. The notion of YHWH entrapping worshipers in this way is somewhat alarming. The prophet, however, puts responsibility squarely on the shoulders of the people, who must take on the moral authority to discern the false prophet and reject his or her message.

14:12–23 Noah, Daniel, and Job
The passage responds to an implicit question of whether the presumed righteousness of the exiles might suffice to save their erring children still in the land. Noah, after all, was allowed to save his children from the flood (and cf. the similar expectation of Abraham regarding Lot in Gen. 18:22–33). The righteousness of Job, from a modern perspective, proved fruitless for his children, though perhaps the reference is to his second group of children as those who benefited from their father's righteousness. The case of Daniel is more difficult, due to what is almost certainly a mistranslation. Here and in 28:3 Ezekiel refers, not to the biblical Daniel, but to Dan'el, a righteous king who appears in the Canaanite Epic of Aqhat, and who is granted a son by the god El. Plainly, if even these paragons of virtue would be unable to save their children, then neither will the current generation of exiles (whose virtue is a matter of some debate) be able to do so.

21 For thus says the Lord God: How much more when I send upon Jerusalem my four deadly acts of judgment, sword, famine, wild animals, and pestilence, to cut off humans and animals from it! ²² Yet, survivors shall be left in it, sons and daughters who will be brought out; they will come out to you. When you see their ways and their deeds, you will be consoled for the evil that I have brought upon Jerusalem, for all that I have brought upon it. ²³ They shall console you, when you see their ways and their deeds; and you shall know that it was not without cause that I did all that I have done in it, says the Lord God.

The Useless Vine

15 The word of the Lord came to me:
² O mortal, how does the wood of the
    vine surpass all other wood—
the vine branch that is among the
    trees of the forest?
³ Is wood taken from it to make
    anything?
Does one take a peg from it on
    which to hang any object?
⁴ It is put in the fire for fuel;

when the fire has consumed both
    ends of it
and the middle of it is charred,
    is it useful for anything?
⁵ When it was whole it was used for
    nothing;
how much less—when the fire has
    consumed it,
and it is charred—
can it ever be used for anything!

6 Therefore thus says the Lord God: Like the wood of the vine among the trees of the forest, which I have given to the fire for fuel, so I will give up the inhabitants of Jerusalem. ⁷ I will set my face against them; although they escape from the fire, the fire shall still consume them; and you shall know that I am the Lord, when I set my face against them. ⁸ And I will make the land desolate, because they have acted faithlessly, says the Lord God.

God's Faithless Bride

16 The word of the Lord came to me: ² Mortal, make known to Jerusalem her abominations, ³ and say, Thus says the Lord God to Jerusalem: Your origin and your birth were in the land of the Canaanites; your father was

---

14:23 *Console you*—Ironically, the patent unrighteousness of the survivors will reassure the exiles that YHWH's punishment of their children was justified.

15:1–8 Judah the Vine
Cf. similar images in chap. 17; Isa. 5:1–7; Jer. 2:21; Ps. 80:8–18. A series of extended metaphors in chaps. 15–20 (interrupted by chap. 18) plays on traditional symbols of Israel and Judah: the fruitful vine (chaps. 15, 17, and 19), the beloved wife (chap. 16), the lion (chap. 19) and the recipients of the exodus covenant (20:1–44). All these icons of national identity are ironically subverted into emblems, not of glory, but of shame.
   Instead of focusing on the fruitfulness of the vine, Ezekiel points out the uselessness of its wood, especially if it has already been charred, as Jerusalem was by Nebuchadrezzar in 597.

16:1–63 Jerusalem as YHWH's Wife
The metaphor of the capital city (either Jerusalem or Samaria) as YHWH's bride appears in the eighth-century prophets (Hos. 1–3; Isa. 1:21), as well as in Jeremiah (2:2, 23–25). Prophetic use

of this metaphor invariably focuses on the wife's unworthiness and infidelity. The metaphor powerfully conveys the pathos of a God wounded by human faithlessness. The image is, however, problematic for many readers, because its emotional power depends on a worldview in which the woman is inherently unclean, untrustworthy, and ultimately, deserving of her husband's violent reprisals. Contemporary interpretation of texts such as this must acknowledge the immense cultural gap between the biblical world and our own, even as we recognize that the themes of human faithlessness and divine judgment apply in every age.

16:3 *Canaanites . . . Amorite . . . Hittite*—Jerusalem was founded by Canaanites (Jebusites, according to Judg. 1:21). The specific connection between Jerusalem and the Amorites and Hittites is not known, but Canaanites, Hittites (residents of Palestine, not Anatolia), and Amorites frequently appear together in biblical listings of the indigenous people of southern Palestine (cf. Judg. 3:5; Josh. 12:8).

an Amorite, and your mother a Hittite. **4** As for your birth, on the day you were born your navel cord was not cut, nor were you washed with water to cleanse you, nor rubbed with salt, nor wrapped in cloths. **5** No eye pitied you, to do any of these things for you out of compassion for you; but you were thrown out in the open field, for you were abhorred on the day you were born.

6 I passed by you, and saw you flailing about in your blood. As you lay in your blood, I said to you, "Live! **7** and grow up*a* like a plant of the field." You grew up and became tall and arrived at full womanhood;*b* your breasts were formed, and your hair had grown; yet you were naked and bare.

8 I passed by you again and looked on you; you were at the age for love. I spread the edge of my cloak over you, and covered your nakedness: I pledged myself to you and entered into a covenant with you, says the Lord GOD, and you became mine. **9** Then I bathed you with water and washed off the blood from you, and anointed you with oil. **10** I clothed you with embroidered cloth and with sandals of fine leather; I bound you in fine linen and covered you with rich fabric.*c* **11** I adorned you with ornaments: I put bracelets on your arms, a chain on your neck, **12** a ring on your nose, earrings in your ears, and a beautiful crown upon your head. **13** You were

adorned with gold and silver, while your clothing was of fine linen, rich fabric,*c* and embroidered cloth. You had choice flour and honey and oil for food. You grew exceedingly beautiful, fit to be a queen. **14** Your fame spread among the nations on account of your beauty, for it was perfect because of my splendor that I had bestowed on you, says the Lord GOD.

15 But you trusted in your beauty, and played the whore because of your fame, and lavished your whorings on any passer-by.*d* **16** You took some of your garments, and made for yourself colorful shrines, and on them played the whore; nothing like this has ever been or ever shall be.*c* **17** You also took your beautiful jewels of my gold and my silver that I had given you, and made for yourself male images, and with them played the whore; **18** and you took your embroidered garments to cover them, and set my oil and my incense before them. **19** Also my bread that I gave you—I fed you with choice flour and oil and honey—you set it before them as a pleasing odor; and so it was, says the Lord GOD. **20** You took your sons and your daughters, whom you had borne to me, and these you sacrificed to them to be devoured. As if your whorings were not enough! **21** You slaughtered my children and delivered

a Gk Syr: Heb *Live! I made you a myriad* *b* Cn: Heb *ornament of ornaments* *c* Meaning of Heb uncertain *d* Heb adds *let it be his*

16:4—None of the traditional procedures intended to protect the baby's health were performed on the unwanted child.

16:5—Exposure of unwanted infants was practiced in the ancient Near East, as in other ancient cultures.

16:8 *Spread the edge of my cloak*—A symbol of protection and responsibility (and possibly betrothal; Ruth 3:9).

16:9–10—Images of *oil, linen, fine leather*, and *rich fabric*, together with mention of the covenant, all evoke Jerusalem's status as the home of the temple (a similar list describes the tabernacle furnishings in Exod. 25:3–7).

16:15–22—Jerusalem's idolatry is represented as her bestowal of YHWH's cultic possessions

(gold, silver, incense, and oil) onto illicit lovers.

16:15—The expression to *play the whore* denotes acts of sexual infidelity (rather than literal prostitution). Here the metaphor of sexual liaisons is used to represent the community's illicit religious and political liaisons. Scholarly attempts to link the metaphor with supposed Canaanite fertility rituals are unfounded. Rather, the metaphor is intended to shame male Israelites by identifying them with the debased woman.

16:20—Charges of child sacrifice in early sixth-century Jerusalem appear in both Jeremiah (7:31; 19:4–6) and Ezekiel (23:37). Here Ezekiel claims the children were offered to other gods, but in 20:26 he suggests that such forbidden sacrifices were made to YHWH.

them up as an offering to them. ²² And in all your abominations and your whorings you did not remember the days of your youth, when you were naked and bare, flailing about in your blood.

23 After all your wickedness (woe, woe to you! says the Lord GOD), ²⁴ you built yourself a platform and made yourself a lofty place in every square; ²⁵ at the head of every street you built your lofty place and prostituted your beauty, offering yourself to every passer-by, and multiplying your whoring. ²⁶ You played the whore with the Egyptians, your lustful neighbors, multiplying your whoring, to provoke me to anger. ²⁷ Therefore I stretched out my hand against you, reduced your rations, and gave you up to the will of your enemies, the daughters of the Philistines, who were ashamed of your lewd behavior. ²⁸ You played the whore with the Assyrians, because you were insatiable; you played the whore with them, and still you were not satisfied. ²⁹ You multiplied your whoring with Chaldea, the land of merchants; and even with this you were not satisfied.

30 How sick is your heart, says the Lord GOD, that you did all these things, the deeds of a brazen whore; ³¹ building your platform at the head of every street, and making your lofty place in every square! Yet you were not like a whore, because you scorned payment. ³² Adulterous wife, who receives strangers instead of her husband! ³³ Gifts are given to all whores; but you gave your gifts to all your lovers, bribing them to come to you from all around for your whorings. ³⁴ So you were different from other women in your whorings: no one solicited you to play the whore; and you gave payment, while no payment was given to you; you were different.

35 Therefore, O whore, hear the word of the LORD: ³⁶ Thus says the Lord GOD, Because your lust was poured out and your nakedness uncovered in your whoring with your lovers, and because of all your abominable idols, and because of the blood of your children that you gave to them, ³⁷ therefore, I will gather all your lovers, with whom you took pleasure, all those you loved and all those you hated; I will gather them against you from all around, and will uncover your nakedness to them, so that they may see all your nakedness. ³⁸ I will judge you as women who commit adultery and shed blood are judged, and bring blood upon you in wrath and jealousy. ³⁹ I will deliver you into their hands, and they shall throw down your platform and break down your lofty places; they shall strip you of your clothes and take your beautiful objects and leave you naked and bare. ⁴⁰ They shall bring up a mob against you, and they shall stone you and cut you to pieces with their swords. ⁴¹ They shall burn your houses and execute judgments on you in the sight of many women; I will stop you from playing the whore, and you shall also make no more payments. ⁴² So I will satisfy my fury on you, and my jealousy shall turn away from you; I will be calm, and will be angry no longer. ⁴³ Because you

---

16:23–34 *Egyptians . . . Assyrians . . . Chaldeans*— Here YHWH's competitors are not other deities but nations with which Judah entered treaties, offering them *payment* (i.e., tribute money) for her own services!

16:37 *Uncover your nakedness*—Public exposure and stoning were both prescribed as punishments for adultery in the ancient Near East. The role of Jerusalem's lovers in her punishment fits the historical situation (foreign nations destroyed Judah) but is out of place in the metaphor, because adulterous males were also subject to punishment (Lev. 20:10). The image of God as a husband who finds satisfaction in witnessing the torture and vivisection of his unfaithful wife is horrifying for modern readers. While the husband's response reflects the norms of ancient Near Eastern law, the very suggestion that God would engage in (and thereby validate) domestic violence remains one of the most difficult aspects of the book of Ezekiel.

16:43b–63 *The sister of your sisters*—Jerusalem is compared with two sister cities, *Samaria* and *Sodom* (cf. Jer. 3:6–11), both infamously evil.

have not remembered the days of your youth, but have enraged me with all these things; therefore, I have returned your deeds upon your head, says the Lord God.

Have you not committed lewdness beyond all your abominations? **44** See, everyone who uses proverbs will use this proverb about you, "Like mother, like daughter." **45** You are the daughter of your mother, who loathed her husband and her children; and you are the sister of your sisters, who loathed their husbands and their children. Your mother was a Hittite and your father an Amorite. **46** Your elder sister is Samaria, who lived with her daughters to the north of you; and your younger sister, who lived to the south of you, is Sodom with her daughters. **47** You not only followed their ways, and acted according to their abominations; within a very little time you were more corrupt than they in all your ways. **48** As I live, says the Lord God, your sister Sodom and her daughters have not done as you and your daughters have done. **49** This was the guilt of your sister Sodom: she and her daughters had pride, excess of food, and prosperous ease, but did not aid the poor and needy. **50** They were haughty, and did abominable things before me; therefore I removed them when I saw it. **51** Samaria has not committed half your sins; you have committed more abominations than they, and have made your sisters appear righteous by all the abominations that you have committed. **52** Bear your disgrace, you also, for you have brought about for your sisters a more favorable judgment; because of your sins in which you acted more abominably than they, they are more in the right

than you. So be ashamed, you also, and bear your disgrace, for you have made your sisters appear righteous.

53 I will restore their fortunes, the fortunes of Sodom and her daughters and the fortunes of Samaria and her daughters, and I will restore your own fortunes along with theirs, **54** in order that you may bear your disgrace and be ashamed of all that you have done, becoming a consolation to them. **55** As for your sisters, Sodom and her daughters shall return to their former state, Samaria and her daughters shall return to their former state, and you and your daughters shall return to your former state. **56** Was not your sister Sodom a byword in your mouth in the day of your pride, **57** before your wickedness was uncovered? Now you are a mockery to the daughters of Aram*a* and all her neighbors, and to the daughters of the Philistines, those all around who despise you. **58** You must bear the penalty of your lewdness and your abominations, says the Lord.

An Everlasting Covenant

59 Yes, thus says the Lord God: I will deal with you as you have done, you who have despised the oath, breaking the covenant; **60** yet I will remember my covenant with you in the days of your youth, and I will establish with you an everlasting covenant. **61** Then you will remember your ways, and be ashamed when I*b* take your sisters, both your elder and your younger, and give them to you as daughters, but not on account of my*c* covenant with you. **62** I will establish my covenant with you, and you shall know that I am the Lord, **63** in order that you may remember and be confounded, and never open your mouth again because

a Another reading is *Edom*   *b* Syr: Heb *you*   *c* Heb lacks *my*

Both had already been destroyed by Ezekiel's day, and so are used as object lessons for the wayward Jerusalem. This is the only place in Scripture where the sin of Sodom is specifically named: the wealthy Sodomites showed callous disregard for the plight of the poor (v. 49; cf. Isa. 1:10–17; Gen. 19).

16:60–63—A rare, pre-586 promise of restoration (cf. the covenant of peace in 34:25; 36:31–32; 37:26). The promise breaks out of the metaphor, in which Jerusalem has already been cut to pieces in v. 40.

of your shame, when I forgive you all that you have done, says the Lord GOD.

The Two Eagles and the Vine

17 The word of the LORD came to me: ²O mortal, propound a riddle, and speak an allegory to the house of Israel. ³Say: Thus says the Lord GOD:

A great eagle, with great wings and
    long pinions,
  rich in plumage of many colors,
    came to the Lebanon.
He took the top of the cedar,
⁴ broke off its topmost shoot;
he carried it to a land of trade,
  set it in a city of merchants.
⁵ Then he took a seed from the land,
  placed it in fertile soil;
a plant*a* by abundant waters,
  he set it like a willow twig.
⁶ It sprouted and became a vine
  spreading out, but low;
its branches turned toward him,
  its roots remained where it stood.
So it became a vine;
  it brought forth branches,
  put forth foliage.

⁷ There was another great eagle,
  with great wings and much
    plumage.
And see! This vine stretched out
  its roots toward him;
it shot out its branches toward him,
  so that he might water it.
From the bed where it was planted
⁸ it was transplanted
to good soil by abundant waters,
  so that it might produce branches
  and bear fruit
  and become a noble vine.
⁹Say: Thus says the Lord GOD:
  Will it prosper?

Will he not pull up its roots,
  cause its fruit to rot*a* and wither,
  its fresh sprouting leaves to fade?
No strong arm or mighty army will
  be needed
  to pull it from its roots.
¹⁰ When it is transplanted, will it
  thrive?
When the east wind strikes it,
  will it not utterly wither,
  wither on the bed where it grew?

¹¹ Then the word of the LORD came to me: ¹²Say now to the rebellious house: Do you not know what these things mean? Tell them: The king of Babylon came to Jerusalem, took its king and its officials, and brought them back with him to Babylon. ¹³He took one of the royal offspring and made a covenant with him, putting him under oath (he had taken away the chief men of the land), ¹⁴so that the kingdom might be humble and not lift itself up, and that by keeping his covenant it might stand. ¹⁵But he rebelled against him by sending ambassadors to Egypt, in order that they might give him horses and a large army. Will he succeed? Can one escape who does such things? Can he break the covenant and yet escape? ¹⁶As I live, says the Lord GOD, surely in the place where the king resides who made him king, whose oath he despised, and whose covenant with him he broke—in Babylon he shall die. ¹⁷Pharaoh with his mighty army and great company will not help him in war, when ramps are cast up and siege walls built to cut off many lives. ¹⁸Because he despised the oath and broke the covenant, because he gave his hand and yet did all these things, he shall not escape.

a Meaning of Heb uncertain

17:1–24 Two Eagles and a Vine

An allegory is set forth in vv. 3–10 and interpreted in vv. 11–21. The great eagle is Nebuchadrezzar, who came to **Lebanon** (that is, "to the west," in this case, to Jerusalem) and took king Jehoiachin (the **topmost shoot** of the cedar), and carried him to Babylonia (the first deportation, in 597 BCE). The eagle also took a **seed** (v. 5),

Zedekiah, and planted him (as king over Judah). The seed grew, but only into a lowly **vine** (cf. 15:1–8; Ps. 80:8–18). The vine, however, is lured away from Nebuchadrezzar by a second eagle, Psammeticus II of Egypt, and will consequently be uprooted by Babylon, desiccated by **the east wind** (v. 10).

[19] Therefore thus says the Lord GOD: As I live, I will surely return upon his head my oath that he despised, and my covenant that he broke. [20] I will spread my net over him, and he shall be caught in my snare; I will bring him to Babylon and enter into judgment with him there for the treason he has committed against me. [21] All the pick[a] of his troops shall fall by the sword, and the survivors shall be scattered to every wind; and you shall know that I, the LORD, have spoken.

Israel Exalted at Last

22 Thus says the Lord GOD:
I myself will take a sprig
　from the lofty top of a cedar;
　I will set it out.
I will break off a tender one
　from the topmost of its young
　　twigs;
I myself will plant it
　on a high and lofty mountain.
[23] On the mountain height of Israel
　I will plant it,
in order that it may produce boughs
　　and bear fruit,
　and become a noble cedar.

Under it every kind of bird will live;
　in the shade of its branches will
　　nest
　winged creatures of every kind.
[24] All the trees of the field shall
　　know
　that I am the LORD.
I bring low the high tree,
　I make high the low tree;
I dry up the green tree
　and make the dry tree flourish.
I the LORD have spoken;
　I will accomplish it.

Individual Retribution

18 The word of the LORD came to me: [2] What do you mean by repeating this proverb concerning the land of Israel, "The parents have eaten sour grapes, and the children's teeth are set on edge"? [3] As I live, says the Lord GOD, this proverb shall no more be used by you in Israel. [4] Know that all lives are mine; the life of the parent as well as the life of the child is mine: it is only the person who sins that shall die.

5 If a man is righteous and does what

[a] Another reading is *fugitives*

17:16, 19 *As I live*—In response to Zedekiah's oath-breaking defilement of YHWH's name and honor, YHWH, too, takes a solemn oath, namely, to destroy Zedekiah (cf. 20:3, 31, 33).

17:19—Remarkably, YHWH refers to Zedekiah's vassal treaty with Nebuchadrezzar as *my oath* and *my covenant*. According to 2 Chr. 36:13, the oath was sworn in YHWH's name. Judah's rebellion against Nebuchadrezzar thus constituted a trespass against the holiness of YHWH.

18:1–32 Individual Responsibility and Repentance

Ezekiel refutes the tradition that the sins of the parents would be visited upon the children (Exod. 20:5; 34:7), claiming instead that each individual is responsible for his or her choices and will be judged accordingly. This passage is the most developed of Ezekiel's ongoing attempts to call Judah out of fatalism and into moral accountability (see also 3:16–21; 14:12–20; 33:10–20). Ezekiel's insistence on individual responsibility is one of the foundations of the focus on the importance of personal moral choice in Judaism and Christianity.

18:2 *The parents have eaten sour grapes*—The

proverb was used both by the exiles and by those in Jerusalem (cf. Jer. 31:29–30). The premise is that the current generation, whether at home or in exile, are suffering for sins committed by their ancestors (so, e.g., 2 Kgs. 20:16–18; 21:11–15). The proverb expresses self-pity, resignation, and self-exoneration, all adding up to a deeply held belief that someone else is to blame for the exiles' troubles. Throughout this passage Ezekiel's hearers will raise theoretical objections that keep them from accepting his core message: that it is *their* actions, based on their own free choice, that will determine whether they live or die. Ezekiel's oracle is designed to move his hearers away from an argument about who is to blame and on to the question of whether they are willing to change.

18:5–18 *If a man is righteous*—A righteous father, an evil son, and a righteous grandson will each be judged for his deeds alone. Ezekiel carefully enumerates the sins committed by the evil son (a thoroughgoing villain) but avoided by the father and grandson. He takes great pains to explain why it is right for the individual to bear the consequences of his or her own actions. Although Israelite society clearly accepted the idea of communal responsibility, the notion of

is lawful and right— [6] if he does not eat upon the mountains or lift up his eyes to the idols of the house of Israel, does not defile his neighbor's wife or approach a woman during her menstrual period, [7] does not oppress anyone, but restores to the debtor his pledge, commits no robbery, gives his bread to the hungry and covers the naked with a garment, [8] does not take advance or accrued interest, withholds his hand from iniquity, executes true justice between contending parties, [9] follows my statutes, and is careful to observe my ordinances, acting faithfully—such a one is righteous; he shall surely live, says the Lord GOD.

[10] If he has a son who is violent, a shedder of blood, [11] who does any of these things (though his father[a] does none of them), who eats upon the mountains, defiles his neighbor's wife, [12] oppresses the poor and needy, commits robbery, does not restore the pledge, lifts up his eyes to the idols, commits abomination, [13] takes advance or accrued interest; shall he then live? He shall not. He has done all these abominable things; he shall surely die; his blood shall be upon himself.

[14] But if this man has a son who sees all the sins that his father has done, considers, and does not do likewise, [15] who does not eat upon the mountains or lift up his eyes to the idols of the house of Israel, does not defile his neighbor's wife, [16] does not wrong anyone, exacts no pledge, commits no robbery, but gives his bread to the hungry and covers the naked with a garment, [17] withholds his hand from iniquity,[b] takes no advance or accrued interest, observes my ordi-

nances, and follows my statutes; he shall not die for his father's iniquity; he shall surely live. [18] As for his father, because he practiced extortion, robbed his brother, and did what is not good among his people, he dies for his iniquity.

[19] Yet you say, "Why should not the son suffer for the iniquity of the father?" When the son has done what is lawful and right, and has been careful to observe all my statutes, he shall surely live. [20] The person who sins shall die. A child shall not suffer for the iniquity of a parent, nor a parent suffer for the iniquity of a child; the righteousness of the righteous shall be his own, and the wickedness of the wicked shall be his own.

[21] But if the wicked turn away from all their sins that they have committed and keep all my statutes and do what is lawful and right, they shall surely live; they shall not die. [22] None of the transgressions that they have committed shall be remembered against them; for the righteousness that they have done they shall live. [23] Have I any pleasure in the death of the wicked, says the Lord GOD, and not rather that they should turn from their ways and live? [24] But when the righteous turn away from their righteousness and commit iniquity and do the same abominable things that the wicked do, shall they live? None of the righteous deeds that they have done shall be remembered; for the treachery of which they are guilty and the sin they have committed, they shall die.

[25] Yet you say, "The way of the Lord is

---

[a] Heb he   [b] Gk: Heb the poor

---

individual responsibility was by no means new. The audience's resistance to Ezekiel's message apparently stems more from their habit of denying responsibility than from any belief in a competing theology.

18:6 *Eat on the mountains*—Presumably at an illicit shrine (cf. 6:13). For the origins of the other prohibitions listed here, see Exod. 22:26; Lev. 18:19–20; 19:13; 25:17, 36.

18:19 *Why should not the son suffer?*—Ezekiel's

audience objects to YHWH's system, possibly because it breaks with the tradition of transgenerational punishment, but also because YHWH holds them, rather than their ancestors, responsible for their current situation.

18:21 *If the wicked turn*—YHWH changes the subject from transgenerational responsibility to the effect of moral choices within a single lifetime.

18:25 *Unfair*—Lit. "failing to conform to the stan-

unfair." Hear now, O house of Israel: Is my way unfair? Is it not your ways that are unfair? ²⁶ When the righteous turn away from their righteousness and commit iniquity, they shall die for it; for the iniquity that they have committed they shall die. ²⁷ Again, when the wicked turn away from the wickedness they have committed and do what is lawful and right, they shall save their life. ²⁸ Because they considered and turned away from all the transgressions that they had committed, they shall surely live; they shall not die. ²⁹ Yet the house of Israel says, "The way of the Lord is unfair." O house of Israel, are my ways unfair? Is it not your ways that are unfair?

30 Therefore I will judge you, O house of Israel, all of you according to your ways, says the Lord GOD. Repent and turn from all your transgressions; otherwise iniquity will be your ruin.^a ³¹ Cast away from you all the transgressions that you have committed against me, and get yourselves a new heart and a new spirit! Why will you die, O house of Israel? ³² For I have no pleasure in the death of anyone, says the Lord GOD. Turn, then, and live.

Israel Degraded

19 As for you, raise up a lamentation for the princes of Israel, ² and say:

What a lioness was your mother
    among lions!

She lay down among young lions,
    rearing her cubs.
³ She raised up one of her cubs;
    he became a young lion,
and he learned to catch prey;
    he devoured humans.
⁴ The nations sounded an alarm
       against him;
    he was caught in their pit;
and they brought him with hooks
    to the land of Egypt.
⁵ When she saw that she was thwarted,
    that her hope was lost,
she took another of her cubs
    and made him a young lion.
⁶ He prowled among the lions;
    he became a young lion,
and he learned to catch prey;
    he devoured people.
⁷ And he ravaged their strongholds,^b
    and laid waste their towns;
the land was appalled, and all in it,
    at the sound of his roaring.
⁸ The nations set upon him
    from the provinces all around;
they spread their net over him;
    he was caught in their pit.
⁹ With hooks they put him in a cage,
    and brought him to the king of
       Babylon;
    they brought him into custody,
so that his voice should be heard no
       more
    on the mountains of Israel.

^a Or so that they shall not be a stumbling block of iniquity to you ^b Heb *his widows*

---

dard." The people complain that YHWH doesn't play by known rules; YHWH retorts that it is they who are "unfair," violating God's rules and so meriting punishment.

18:30–32 *I will judge you*—Here YHWH abandons theoretical discussion and makes the implicit force of the argument explicit: the exiles bear ongoing responsibility for their own actions. YHWH makes it clear, however, that the goal is not to justify punishing the people but to motivate their repentance. Indeed, to bring about a change of heart was the goal of prophetic preaching of judgment.

19:1–14 *Two Dirges over the Princes of Israel*

19:1 *A lamentation*—A distinctive meter was

used for Israelite lamentations, and the genre was used ironically in oracles of doom—lamenting in advance over the downfall of a hated enemy (cf. Amos 5:2).

19:2 *A lioness*—Judah is often depicted as a lion (Gen. 49:9). A symbol of power and nobility is here twisted into a symbol of unbridled rapacity. The identity of the cubs and their mother is disputed. The most likely possibilities are Hamutal, mother of Jehoahaz and Zedekiah, or, as in 16:21, the city of Jerusalem, personified as the mother of her people.

19:7 *Widows*—Conquered (and therefore bereaved) cities were sometimes personified as widows (textual note).

¹⁰ Your mother was like a vine in a
        vineyard*a*
    transplanted by the water,
    fruitful and full of branches
        from abundant water.
¹¹ Its strongest stem became
        a ruler's scepter;*b*
    it towered aloft
        among the thick boughs;
    it stood out in its height
        with its mass of branches.
¹² But it was plucked up in fury,
        cast down to the ground;
    the east wind dried it up;
    its fruit was stripped off,
    its strong stem was withered;
        the fire consumed it.
¹³ Now it is transplanted into the
        wilderness,
    into a dry and thirsty land.
¹⁴ And fire has gone out from its stem,
        has consumed its branches and
        fruit,
    so that there remains in it no strong
        stem,
    no scepter for ruling.

This is a lamentation, and it is used as
a lamentation.

Israel's Continuing Rebellion

20 In the seventh year, in the fifth
month, on the tenth day of the
month, certain elders of Israel came to
consult the LORD, and sat down before

me. ²And the word of the LORD came
to me: ³Mortal, speak to the elders of
Israel, and say to them: Thus says the
Lord GOD: Why are you coming? To
consult me? As I live, says the Lord
GOD, I will not be consulted by you.
⁴Will you judge them, mortal, will
you judge them? Then let them know
the abominations of their ancestors,
⁵and say to them: Thus says the Lord
GOD: On the day when I chose Israel,
I swore to the offspring of the house of
Jacob—making myself known to them
in the land of Egypt—I swore to them,
saying, I am the LORD your God. ⁶On
that day I swore to them that I would
bring them out of the land of Egypt into
a land that I had searched out for them,
a land flowing with milk and honey, the
most glorious of all lands. ⁷And I said
to them, Cast away the detestable things
your eyes feast on, every one of you, and
do not defile yourselves with the idols
of Egypt; I am the LORD your God. ⁸But
they rebelled against me and would not
listen to me; not one of them cast away
the detestable things their eyes feasted
on, nor did they forsake the idols of
Egypt.

Then I thought I would pour out my
wrath upon them and spend my anger
against them in the midst of the land of
Egypt. ⁹But I acted for the sake of my

a Cn: Heb *in your blood*   *b* Heb *Its strongest stems became rulers' scepters*

19:10 *A vine*—Another common metaphor for Judah (see note at 15:1–8). The image recalls both
the cedar (Jehoiachin) and the vine (Zedekiah) of
chap. 17. Probably an ironic "lament in advance," the oracle foretells Zedekiah's downfall.

20:1–44 The Exodus Revisited
The history of Israel is retold as a series of episodes in which: (a) YHWH gives laws or makes
a promise to the people; (b) the people rebel; (c)
YHWH decides to destroy them; (d) YHWH repents, not for the people's sake, but for **the sake
of my name** (vv. 9, 14, 22, 44), in order not to be
perceived as weak or unfaithful. The same logic
governs Exod. 32:1–10 and Num. 14:13–16, in
which Moses dissuades YHWH from destroying
Israel, asking roughly, "What would the neighbors say if you destroyed your own people?" The
account of the exodus here differs substantially

from the narrative in the Torah. First, Israel is
"chosen" in Egypt (cf. 23:3), with no mention of
a covenant with Abraham or Jacob. Second, the
people revert to idolatry even before the exodus.
Third, after the second generation continues in
its infidelity, YHWH entraps the people by giving
them bad laws, including the command to offer
their children as sacrifices (vv. 25–26). The story
of YHWH and Israel is transformed here from a
love story into a chilling tale of mutual alienation. Ezekiel's retelling of Israel's national epic is
consistent with his pattern of subverting symbols
of Judah's glory into degrading examples of its
perversity.

20:1 *The seventh year*—August 591 BCE.
Elders…came—As in 14:1 (cf. 8:1), Ezekiel is
recognized by the elders as a prophet.

name, that it should not be profaned in the sight of the nations among whom they lived, in whose sight I made myself known to them in bringing them out of the land of Egypt. ¹⁰ So I led them out of the land of Egypt and brought them into the wilderness. ¹¹ I gave them my statutes and showed them my ordinances, by whose observance everyone shall live. ¹² Moreover I gave them my sabbaths, as a sign between me and them, so that they might know that I the LORD sanctify them. ¹³ But the house of Israel rebelled against me in the wilderness; they did not observe my statutes but rejected my ordinances, by whose observance everyone shall live; and my sabbaths they greatly profaned.

Then I thought I would pour out my wrath upon them in the wilderness, to make an end of them. ¹⁴ But I acted for the sake of my name, so that it should not be profaned in the sight of the nations, in whose sight I had brought them out. ¹⁵ Moreover I swore to them in the wilderness that I would not bring them into the land that I had given them, a land flowing with milk and honey, the most glorious of all lands, ¹⁶ because they rejected my ordinances and did not observe my statutes, and profaned my sabbaths; for their heart went after their idols. ¹⁷ Nevertheless my eye spared them, and I did not destroy them or make an end of them in the wilderness.

18 I said to their children in the wilderness, Do not follow the statutes of your parents, nor observe their ordinances, nor defile yourselves with their idols. ¹⁹ I the LORD am your God; follow my statutes, and be careful to observe my ordinances, ²⁰ and hallow my sabbaths that they may be a sign between me and you, so that you may know that I the LORD am your God. ²¹ But the children rebelled against me; they did not follow my statutes, and were not careful to observe my ordinances, by whose observance everyone shall live; they profaned my sabbaths.

Then I thought I would pour out my wrath upon them and spend my anger against them in the wilderness. ²² But I withheld my hand, and acted for the sake of my name, so that it should not be profaned in the sight of the nations, in whose sight I had brought them out. ²³ Moreover I swore to them in the wilderness that I would scatter them among the nations and disperse them through the countries, ²⁴ because they had not executed my ordinances, but had rejected my statutes and profaned my sabbaths, and their eyes were set on their ancestors' idols. ²⁵ Moreover I gave them statutes that were not good and ordinances by which they could not live. ²⁶ I defiled them through their very gifts, in their offering up all their firstborn, in order that I might horrify them, so that they might know that I am the LORD.

27 Therefore, mortal, speak to the house of Israel and say to them, Thus says the Lord GOD: In this again your ancestors blasphemed me, by dealing treacherously with me. ²⁸ For when I had brought them into the land that I swore to give them, then wherever they saw any high hill or any leafy tree, there they offered their sacrifices and presented the provocation of their offering; there they sent up their pleasing odors, and there they poured out their drink offerings. ²⁹ (I said to them, What is the high place to which you go? So it is called Bamah[a] to this day.) ³⁰ Therefore say to the house of Israel, Thus says the Lord GOD: Will you defile yourselves after the manner of your ancestors and go astray after their detestable things? ³¹ When you offer your gifts and make your children pass through the fire, you defile yourselves with all your idols to this day. And shall I be consulted by you, O house of Israel? As I live, says the Lord GOD, I will not be consulted by you.

32 What is in your mind shall never happen—the thought, "Let us be like the

[a] That is High Place

nations, like the tribes of the countries, and worship wood and stone."

God Will Restore Israel

33 As I live, says the Lord GOD, surely with a mighty hand and an outstretched arm, and with wrath poured out, I will be king over you. **34** I will bring you out from the peoples and gather you out of the countries where you are scattered, with a mighty hand and an outstretched arm, and with wrath poured out; **35** and I will bring you into the wilderness of the peoples, and there I will enter into judgment with you face to face. **36** As I entered into judgment with your ancestors in the wilderness of the land of Egypt, so I will enter into judgment with you, says the Lord GOD. **37** I will make you pass under the staff, and will bring you within the bond of the covenant. **38** I will purge out the rebels among you, and those who transgress against me; I will bring them out of the land where they reside as aliens, but they shall not enter the land of Israel. Then you shall know that I am the LORD.

39 As for you, O house of Israel, thus says the Lord GOD: Go serve your idols, every one of you now and hereafter, if you will not listen to me; but my holy name you shall no more profane with your gifts and your idols.

40 For on my holy mountain, the mountain height of Israel, says the Lord GOD, there all the house of Israel, all of them, shall serve me in the land; there I will accept them, and there I will require your contributions and the choicest of your gifts, with all your sacred things. **41** As a pleasing odor I will accept you, when I bring you out from the peoples, and gather you out of the countries where you have been scattered; and I will manifest my holiness among you in the sight of the nations. **42** You shall know that I am the LORD, when I bring you into the land of Israel, the country that I swore to give to your ancestors. **43** There you shall remember your ways and all the deeds by which you have polluted yourselves; and you shall loathe yourselves for all the evils that you have committed. **44** And you shall know that I am the LORD, when I deal with you for my name's sake, not according to your evil ways, or corrupt deeds, O house of Israel, says the Lord GOD.

A Prophecy against the Negeb

45[a] The word of the LORD came to me: **46** Mortal, set your face toward the south, preach against the south, and prophesy against the forest land in the Negeb; **47** say to the forest of the Negeb, Hear the word of the LORD: Thus says the Lord GOD, I will kindle a fire in you, and it shall devour every green tree in you and every dry tree; the blazing flame shall not be quenched, and all faces from south to north shall be scorched by it. **48** All flesh shall see that I the LORD have kindled it; it shall not be quenched. **49** Then I said,

[a] Ch 21.1 in Heb

20:33 *As I live*—See note at 17:16, 19. YHWH takes a solemn oath, first, not to respond to the elders' inquiry, and, second, to reign over the people, whether they wish it or not. Ezekiel repeatedly emphasizes that God's authority stands regardless of human disobedience or even disinterest.

20:37 *Pass under the staff*—A pastoral image of the people as YHWH's flock, further developed in the good shepherd passage in chap. 34. NRSV's *bring you within the bond* is a conjectural translation of the Hebrew, "bring you in by number." The Hebrew phrase recalls Lev. 27:32, in which a shepherd counts out the sheep that will be designated holy.

20:40–44—After the harsh denunciations of vv. 1–39, YHWH paints a gracious picture of acceptable worship on the **mountain** of God (cf. Exod. 3:12; Isa. 2:2–4; Zech. 8:3).

20:45–48—Although in Babylon, Ezekiel is told to face **the south** (Heb. *Negeb*) of Palestine.

20:46 *Forest land*—Lit. "forests of the field," or "scrubby" forest, a description fitting the arid, brushy forests of southern Palestine prior to extensive desertification that began already in antiquity.

20:49 *A maker of allegories*—As in 33:31–32, Ezekiel's complaint is that people do not take his

"Ah Lord God! they are saying of me, 'Is he not a maker of allegories?'"

The Drawn Sword of God

21 [a] The word of the Lord came to me: [2] Mortal, set your face toward Jerusalem and preach against the sanctuaries; prophesy against the land of Israel [3] and say to the land of Israel, Thus says the Lord: I am coming against you, and will draw my sword out of its sheath, and will cut off from you both righteous and wicked. [4] Because I will cut off from you both righteous and wicked, therefore my sword shall go out of its sheath against all flesh from south to north; [5] and all flesh shall know that I the Lord have drawn my sword out of its sheath; it shall not be sheathed again. [6] Moan therefore, mortal; moan with breaking heart and bitter grief before their eyes. [7] And when they say to you, "Why do you moan?" you shall say, "Because of the news that has come. Every heart will melt and all hands will be feeble, every spirit will faint and all knees will turn to water. See, it comes and it will be fulfilled," says the Lord God.

[8] And the word of the Lord came to me: [9] Mortal, prophesy and say: Thus says the Lord; Say:

A sword, a sword is sharpened,
    it is also polished;
[10] it is sharpened for slaughter,
    honed to flash like lightning!
How can we make merry?
    You have despised the rod,
    and all discipline.[b]
[11] The sword[c] is given to be polished,
    to be grasped in the hand;
it is sharpened, the sword is
        polished,
    to be placed in the slayer's hand.
[12] Cry and wail, O mortal,
    for it is against my people;
it is against all Israel's princes;
    they are thrown to the sword,
    together with my people.
    Ah! Strike the thigh!
[13] For consider: What! If you despise the rod, will it not happen?[b] says the Lord God.
[14] And you, mortal, prophesy;
    strike hand to hand.
Let the sword fall twice, thrice;
    it is a sword for killing.
A sword for great slaughter—
    it surrounds them;
[15] therefore hearts melt
    and many stumble.
At all their gates I have set
    the point[b] of the sword.
Ah! It is made for flashing,
    it is polished[d] for slaughter.
[16] Attack to the right!
    Engage to the left!
    —wherever your edge is directed.
[17] I too will strike hand to hand,
    I will satisfy my fury;
    I the Lord have spoken.
[18] The word of the Lord came to me:
[19] Mortal, mark out two roads for the

---

[a] Ch 21.6 in Heb [b] Meaning of Heb uncertain [c] Heb It [d] Tg: Heb wrapped up

---

prophecy seriously. He is received as a literary artist but his message goes unheard.

21:1–32 The Sword of God

21:2—Ezekiel is directed to speak against both the sanctuaries and the land of Israel. The use of the plural suggests that Ezekiel here addresses both illicit sanctuaries and the Jerusalem temple. Here as elsewhere in Ezekiel (cf. 6:1–7), the land itself is held guilty as if complicit in the people's abominations.

21:3 Righteous and wicked—This is a startling reversal of the promise in chap. 18 to judge each person independently. Here, however, YHWH is described not as a righteous judge but as a war-

rior. In the cosmic battle, *all flesh* (v. 5) will be destroyed (cf. Gen. 6:13).

21:10, 13 The rod—The accepted mode of punishment for disobedient children (cf. Prov. 13:24).

21:12 Strike the thigh—An expression of grief or shame (cf. Jer. 31:19).

21:19–23—The *signpost* marks out Nebuchadrezzar's option to attack either the Ammonite capital, *Rabbah*, or *Jerusalem*. Nebuchadrezzar engages in three types of *divination*, all of which would have been familiar to Ezekiel's audience: The arrows were apparently labeled and drawn like lots. *Teraphim* (v. 21) are known from Gen. 31:19; 1 Sam. 19:13–16; Hos. 3:4, but the

sword of the king of Babylon to come; both of them shall issue from the same land. And make a signpost, make it for a fork in the road leading to a city; ²⁰ mark out the road for the sword to come to Rabbah of the Ammonites or to Judah and to*a* Jerusalem the fortified. ²¹ For the king of Babylon stands at the parting of the way, at the fork in the two roads, to use divination; he shakes the arrows, he consults the teraphim,*b* he inspects the liver. ²² Into his right hand comes the lot for Jerusalem, to set battering rams, to call out for slaughter, for raising the battle cry, to set battering rams against the gates, to cast up ramps, to build siege towers. ²³ But to them it will seem like a false divination; they have sworn solemn oaths; but he brings their guilt to remembrance, bringing about their capture.

24 Therefore thus says the Lord GOD: Because you have brought your guilt to remembrance, in that your transgressions are uncovered, so that in all your deeds your sins appear—because you have come to remembrance, you shall be taken in hand.*c*

²⁵ As for you, vile, wicked prince of
    Israel,
    you whose day has come,
    the time of final punishment,
²⁶ thus says the Lord GOD:
    Remove the turban, take off the
        crown;
    things shall not remain as they are.
    Exalt that which is low,
    abase that which is high.
²⁷ A ruin, a ruin, a ruin—
    I will make it!
    (Such has never occurred.)

Until he comes whose right it is;
    to him I will give it.

28 As for you, mortal, prophesy, and say, Thus says the Lord GOD concerning the Ammonites, and concerning their reproach; say:

    A sword, a sword! Drawn for
        slaughter,
    polished to consume,*d* to flash like
        lightning.
²⁹ Offering false visions for you,
    divining lies for you,
    they place you over the necks
    of the vile, wicked ones—
    those whose day has come,
    the time of final punishment.
³⁰ Return it to its sheath!
    In the place where you were created,
    in the land of your origin,
    I will judge you.
³¹ I will pour out my indignation upon
        you,
    with the fire of my wrath
    I will blow upon you.
    I will deliver you into brutish
        hands,
    those skillful to destroy.
³² You shall be fuel for the fire,
    your blood shall enter the earth;
    you shall be remembered no more,
    for I the LORD have spoken.

The Bloody City

22 The word of the LORD came to me: ² You, mortal, will you judge, will you judge the bloody city? Then declare to it all its abominable deeds. ³ You shall say, Thus says the Lord GOD: A city! Shedding blood within itself; its time has come; making its idols, defiling

a Gk Syr: Heb *Judah in*   *b* Or *the household gods*   *c* Or *be taken captive*
d Cn: Heb *to contain*

---

mechanics of their use is unknown. Hepatoscopy, divination by inspecting animal livers, was practiced widely in the ancient Near East. Although Nebuchadrezzar uses magical means, YHWH controls the outcome.

21:25 *Wicked prince*—Zedekiah.

21:28–32 *Concerning the Ammonites*—Cf. 25:1–7. Ammon, spared in vv. 18–24, is informed that its reprieve is temporary. *A sword*—In

somewhat veiled language (probably necessary in light of Ezekiel's Babylonian location), the oracle announces YHWH's coming judgment on Nebuchadrezzar.

22:1–31 Sins of Jerusalem

The city is accused of a full range of cultic, financial, sexual, and violent crimes, a list recalling the stereotypic evil individual of 18:10–13.

itself. ⁴You have become guilty by the blood that you have shed, and defiled by the idols that you have made; you have brought your day near, the appointed time of your years has come. Therefore I have made you a disgrace before the nations, and a mockery to all the countries. ⁵Those who are near and those who are far from you will mock you, you infamous one, full of tumult.

6 The princes of Israel in you, everyone according to his power, have been bent on shedding blood. ⁷Father and mother are treated with contempt in you; the alien residing within you suffers extortion; the orphan and the widow are wronged in you. ⁸You have despised my holy things, and profaned my sabbaths. ⁹In you are those who slander to shed blood, those in you who eat upon the mountains, who commit lewdness in your midst. ¹⁰In you they uncover their fathers' nakedness; in you they violate women in their menstrual periods. ¹¹One commits abomination with his neighbor's wife; another lewdly defiles his daughter-in-law; another in you defiles his sister, his father's daughter. ¹²In you, they take bribes to shed blood; you take both advance interest and accrued interest, and make gain of your neighbors by extortion; and you have forgotten me, says the Lord GOD.

13 See, I strike my hands together at the dishonest gain you have made, and at the blood that has been shed within you. ¹⁴Can your courage endure, or can your hands remain strong in the days when I shall deal with you? I the LORD have spoken, and I will do it. ¹⁵I will scatter you among the nations and disperse you through the countries, and I will purge your filthiness out of you. ¹⁶And I*a* shall be profaned through you

in the sight of the nations; and you shall know that I am the LORD.

17 The word of the LORD came to me: ¹⁸Mortal, the house of Israel has become dross to me; all of them, silver,*b* bronze, tin, iron, and lead. In the smelter they have become dross. ¹⁹Therefore thus says the Lord GOD: Because you have all become dross, I will gather you into the midst of Jerusalem. ²⁰As one gathers silver, bronze, iron, lead, and tin into a smelter, to blow the fire upon them in order to melt them; so I will gather you in my anger and in my wrath, and I will put you in and melt you. ²¹I will gather you and blow upon you with the fire of my wrath, and you shall be melted within it. ²²As silver is melted in a smelter, so you shall be melted in it; and you shall know that I the LORD have poured out my wrath upon you.

23 The word of the LORD came to me: ²⁴Mortal, say to it: You are a land that is not cleansed, not rained upon in the day of indignation. ²⁵Its princes*c* within it are like a roaring lion tearing the prey; they have devoured human lives; they have taken treasure and precious things; they have made many widows within it. ²⁶Its priests have done violence to my teaching and have profaned my holy things; they have made no distinction between the holy and the common, neither have they taught the difference between the unclean and the clean, and they have disregarded my sabbaths, so that I am profaned among them. ²⁷Its officials within it are like wolves tearing the prey, shedding blood, destroying lives to get dishonest gain. ²⁸Its prophets have smeared whitewash on their behalf, seeing false visions and divining lies for

---

a Gk Syr Vg: Heb *you*   *b* Transposed from the end of the verse; compare verse 20   *c* Gk: Heb *indignation.* 25 *A conspiracy of its prophets*

22:16—The destruction of the temple and exile of the people will defile even YHWH, at least temporarily. YHWH, however, chooses self-inflicted profanation (cf. 20:22; 36:19–21) rather than allowing Judah to go unpunished.

22:17–22 *Become dross*—The language of smelt-

ing is used to describe Jerusalem's upcoming purification by fire (cf. Isa. 1:22–26).

22:26—To distinguish *between the holy and the common* was a basic responsibility of the priests (44:23; Lev. 10:11). The failure to do so amounts to an inability to recognize anything as sacred.

them, saying, "Thus says the Lord GOD," when the LORD has not spoken. ²⁹ The people of the land have practiced extortion and committed robbery; they have oppressed the poor and needy, and have extorted from the alien without redress. ³⁰ And I sought for anyone among them who would repair the wall and stand in the breach before me on behalf of the land, so that I would not destroy it; but I found no one. ³¹ Therefore I have poured out my indignation upon them; I have consumed them with the fire of my wrath; I have returned their conduct upon their heads, says the Lord GOD.

Oholah and Oholibah

23 The word of the LORD came to me: ² Mortal, there were two women, the daughters of one mother; ³ they played the whore in Egypt; they played the whore in their youth; their breasts were caressed there, and their virgin bosoms were fondled. ⁴ Oholah was the name of the elder and Oholibah the name of her sister. They became mine, and they bore sons and daughters. As for their names, Oholah is Samaria, and Oholibah is Jerusalem.

5 Oholah played the whore while she was mine; she lusted after her lovers the Assyrians, warriors*a* ⁶ clothed in blue, governors and commanders, all of them handsome young men, mounted horsemen. ⁷ She bestowed her favors upon them, the choicest men of Assyria all of them; and she defiled herself with all the idols of everyone for whom she lusted.

⁸ She did not give up her whorings that she had practiced since Egypt; for in her youth men had lain with her and fondled her virgin bosom and poured out their lust upon her. ⁹ Therefore I delivered her into the hands of her lovers, into the hands of the Assyrians, for whom she lusted. ¹⁰ These uncovered her nakedness; they seized her sons and her daughters; and they killed her with the sword. Judgment was executed upon her, and she became a byword among women.

11 Her sister Oholibah saw this, yet she was more corrupt than she in her lusting and in her whorings, which were worse than those of her sister. ¹² She lusted after the Assyrians, governors and commanders, warriors*a* clothed in full armor, mounted horsemen, all of them handsome young men. ¹³ And I saw that she was defiled; they both took the same way. ¹⁴ But she carried her whorings further; she saw male figures carved on the wall, images of the Chaldeans portrayed in vermilion, ¹⁵ with belts around their waists, with flowing turbans on their heads, all of them looking like officers—a picture of Babylonians whose native land was Chaldea. ¹⁶ When she saw them she lusted after them, and sent messengers to them in Chaldea. ¹⁷ And the Babylonians came to her into the bed of love, and they defiled her with their lust; and after she defiled herself with them, she turned from them in disgust. ¹⁸ When she carried on her whorings so openly and flaunted

a Meaning of Heb uncertain

23:1–49 Oholah and Oholibah
As in chap. 16, Jerusalem is personified as YHWH's wife. Here her sister Samaria is depicted as a co-wife (cf. 16:44–63; Jer. 3:6–11) who preceded her in both her infidelity and her destruction. Marriage to two sisters is forbidden in Lev. 18:18, but practiced by Jacob in Gen. 31.

23:3 *Played the whore*—See note at 16:15. The sisters are described as spending their youth in Egypt, where they were "handled" sexually before their marriage to YHWH (cf. 20:5–7). Victims of early abuse, they are portrayed here (23:21) as addicted to illicit sexual activity.

23:4 *Oholah . . . Oholibah*—Lit. "she has a tent" and "my tent is in her," an allusion to the separate sanctuaries ("tents") of the northern and southern kingdoms.

23:5–10—As in chap. 16, foreign alliances are depicted as infidelity to YHWH. Here the emphasis is on political rather than cultic liaisons. Samaria (Oholah), having become a vassal to *Assyria* in 842, revolted in 725 on the basis of an alliance with *Egypt*. The Assyrians retaliated, destroying the northern capital in 722.

her nakedness, I turned in disgust from her, as I had turned from her sister. ¹⁹ Yet she increased her whorings, remembering the days of her youth, when she played the whore in the land of Egypt ²⁰ and lusted after her paramours there, whose members were like those of donkeys, and whose emission was like that of stallions. ²¹ Thus you longed for the lewdness of your youth, when the Egyptians*ᵃ* fondled your bosom and caressed*ᵇ* your young breasts.

22 Therefore, O Oholibah, thus says the Lord GOD: I will rouse against you your lovers from whom you turned in disgust, and I will bring them against you from every side: ²³ the Babylonians and all the Chaldeans, Pekod and Shoa and Koa, and all the Assyrians with them, handsome young men, governors and commanders all of them, officers and warriors,*ᶜ* all of them riding on horses. ²⁴ They shall come against you from the north*ᵈ* with chariots and wagons and a host of peoples; they shall set themselves against you on every side with buckler, shield, and helmet, and I will commit the judgment to them, and they shall judge you according to their ordinances. ²⁵ I will direct my indignation against you, in order that they may deal with you in fury. They shall cut off your nose and your ears, and your survivors shall fall by the sword. They shall seize your sons and your daughters, and your survivors shall be devoured by fire. ²⁶ They shall also strip you of your clothes and take away your fine jewels. ²⁷ So I will put an end to your lewdness and your whoring brought from the land of Egypt; you shall not long for them, or remember Egypt any more. ²⁸ For thus says the Lord GOD: I will deliver you into the hands of those whom you hate, into the hands of those from whom you turned in disgust;

²⁹ and they shall deal with you in hatred, and take away all the fruit of your labor, and leave you naked and bare, and the nakedness of your whorings shall be exposed. Your lewdness and your whorings ³⁰ have brought this upon you, because you played the whore with the nations, and polluted yourself with their idols. ³¹ You have gone the way of your sister; therefore I will give her cup into your hand. ³² Thus says the Lord GOD:

You shall drink your sister's cup,
    deep and wide;
you shall be scorned and derided,
    it holds so much.
³³   You shall be filled with drunkenness
        and sorrow.
A cup of horror and desolation
    is the cup of your sister Samaria;
³⁴   you shall drink it and drain it out,
        and gnaw its sherds,
        and tear out your breasts;

for I have spoken, says the Lord GOD. ³⁵ Therefore thus says the Lord GOD: Because you have forgotten me and cast me behind your back, therefore bear the consequences of your lewdness and whorings.

36 The LORD said to me: Mortal, will you judge Oholah and Oholibah? Then declare to them their abominable deeds. ³⁷ For they have committed adultery, and blood is on their hands; with their idols they have committed adultery; and they have even offered up to them for food the children whom they had borne to me. ³⁸ Moreover this they have done to me: they have defiled my sanctuary on the same day and profaned my sabbaths. ³⁹ For when they had slaughtered their children for their idols, on the same day they came into my sanctuary to profane it. This is what they did in my house.

ᵃ Two Mss: MT *from Egypt*   *ᵇ* Cn: Heb *for the sake of*   *ᶜ* Compare verses 6 and 12: Heb *officers and called ones*   *ᵈ* Gk: Meaning of Heb uncertain

---

23:36—The restoration of Oholah is surprising, given her death in v. 10. Ezekiel, however, consistently anticipates the restoration and reunification of the northern and southern kingdoms (37:15–23).

23:37–39—Those who offer *their children* as sacrifices are also participating in worship at the temple. This, together with 20:25–26, suggests that some Jerusalemites were practicing child sacrifice to YHWH.

40 They even sent for men to come from far away, to whom a messenger was sent, and they came. For them you bathed yourself, painted your eyes, and decked yourself with ornaments; 41 you sat on a stately couch, with a table spread before it on which you had placed my incense and my oil. 42 The sound of a raucous multitude was around her, with many of the rabble brought in drunken from the wilderness; and they put bracelets on the arms[a] of the women, and beautiful crowns upon their heads.

43 Then I said, Ah, she is worn out with adulteries, but they carry on their sexual acts with her. 44 For they have gone in to her, as one goes in to a whore. Thus they went in to Oholah and to Oholibah, wanton women. 45 But righteous judges shall declare them guilty of adultery and of bloodshed; because they are adulteresses and blood is on their hands.

46 For thus says the Lord GOD: Bring up an assembly against them, and make them an object of terror and of plunder. 47 The assembly shall stone them and with their swords they shall cut them down; they shall kill their sons and their daughters, and burn up their houses. 48 Thus will I put an end to lewdness in the land, so that all women may take warning and not commit lewdness as you have done. 49 They shall repay you for your lewdness, and you shall bear the penalty for your sinful idolatry; and you shall know that I am the Lord GOD.

The Boiling Pot

24 In the ninth year, in the tenth month, on the tenth day of the month, the word of the LORD came to me: 2 Mortal, write down the name of this day, this very day. The king of Babylon has laid siege to Jerusalem this very day. 3 And utter an allegory to the rebellious house and say to them, Thus says the Lord GOD:

Set on the pot, set it on,
　　pour in water also;
4 put in it the pieces,
　　all the good pieces, the thigh and
　　　　the shoulder;
　　fill it with choice bones.
5 Take the choicest one of the flock,
　　pile the logs[b] under it;
boil its pieces,[c]
　　seethe[d] also its bones in it.

6 Therefore thus says the Lord GOD:
Woe to the bloody city,
　　the pot whose rust is in it,
　　whose rust has not gone out of it!
Empty it piece by piece,
　　making no choice at all.[e]
7 For the blood she shed is inside it;
　　she placed it on a bare rock;
she did not pour it out on the
　　　　ground,
　　to cover it with earth.
8 To rouse my wrath, to take vengeance,
　　I have placed the blood she shed
　　on a bare rock,
　　so that it may not be covered.
9 Therefore thus says the Lord GOD:
Woe to the bloody city!
　　I will even make the pile great.
10 Heap up the logs, kindle the fire;
　　boil the meat well, mix in the
　　　　spices,
　　let the bones be burned.
11 Stand it empty upon the coals,
　　so that it may become hot, its
　　　　copper glow,
　　its filth melt in it, its rust be
　　　　consumed.
12 In vain I have wearied myself;[f]
　　its thick rust does not depart.

[a] Heb hands　[b] Compare verse 10: Heb the bones　[c] Two Mss: Heb its boilings　[d] Cn: Heb its bones seethe　[e] Heb piece, no lot has fallen on it　[f] Cn: Meaning of Heb uncertain

---

23:48 *All women*—Probably other cities rather than literal women (cf. 16:27, 46).

24:1–14 A Boiling Pot

24:1 *The ninth year*—January 588 BCE, the beginning of Nebuchadrezzar's siege of Jerusalem.

24:7 *Bare rock*—Blood, as described in Lev. 17, is understood to "contain" life. Inappropriate treatment of blood is therefore sinful, profaning a life that properly belongs to God.

To the fire with its rust![a]

[13] Yet, when I cleansed you in your
     filthy lewdness,
     you did not become clean from
         your filth;
you shall not again be cleansed
     until I have satisfied my fury upon
         you.

[14] I the LORD have spoken; the time is
coming, I will act. I will not refrain, I
will not spare, I will not relent. According to your ways and your doings I will
judge you, says the Lord GOD.

Ezekiel's Bereavement

[15] The word of the LORD came to me:
[16] Mortal, with one blow I am about to
take away from you the delight of your
eyes; yet you shall not mourn or weep,
nor shall your tears run down. [17] Sigh,
but not aloud; make no mourning for
the dead. Bind on your turban, and
put your sandals on your feet; do not
cover your upper lip or eat the bread of
mourners.[b] [18] So I spoke to the people
in the morning, and at evening my wife
died. And on the next morning I did as
I was commanded.

[19] Then the people said to me, "Will
you not tell us what these things mean
for us, that you are acting this way?"
[20] Then I said to them: The word of the
LORD came to me: [21] Say to the house of

Israel, Thus says the Lord GOD: I will
profane my sanctuary, the pride of your
power, the delight of your eyes, and
your heart's desire; and your sons and
your daughters whom you left behind
shall fall by the sword. [22] And you shall
do as I have done; you shall not cover
your upper lip or eat the bread of mourners.[b] [23] Your turbans shall be on your
heads and your sandals on your feet;
you shall not mourn or weep, but you
shall pine away in your iniquities and
groan to one another. [24] Thus Ezekiel
shall be a sign to you; you shall do just
as he has done. When this comes, then
you shall know that I am the Lord GOD.

[25] And you, mortal, on the day when
I take from them their stronghold, their
joy and glory, the delight of their eyes
and their heart's affection, and also[c] their
sons and their daughters, [26] on that day,
one who has escaped will come to you
to report to you the news. [27] On that day
your mouth shall be opened to the one
who has escaped, and you shall speak
and no longer be silent. So you shall be
a sign to them; and they shall know that
I am the LORD.

Proclamation against Ammon

25 The word of the LORD came to
me: [2] Mortal, set your face toward

[a] Meaning of Heb uncertain   [b] Vg Tg: Heb of men   [c] Heb lacks and also

---

24:15–27 The Death of Ezekiel's Wife
The death of Ezekiel's wife and his response comprise the prophet's final symbolic action before the
fall of the Jerusalem temple. Ezekiel is forbidden to
perform the rituals of mourning, instead wearing
his sandals (cf. Mic. 1:8) and turban, abstaining
from *the bread of mourners* (v. 17; Jer. 16:7),
and stifling his tears. The traumatic impact of this
symbolic action can hardly be overstated. Ezekiel's
wife represents the Jerusalem temple, YHWH's
"beloved" (as in chap. 16) and the *delight* (v. 21)
of the Judean people. Ezekiel acts out the loss
felt by both God and the nation, at the same time
suffering his own wife's death at God's hands. The
passage starkly reveals the anguish inherent in the
prophetic calling, in which the divine prerogative
overwhelms human perspectives.

24:27 On that day—Verses 25–27 mark the end
of the first section of the book, building up to
the temple's destruction, during which time the

prophet's mouth has been closed (3:24–27). Following the oracles against foreign nations (chaps.
25–32), the arrival of the fugitive (33:21–22) will
inaugurate a new stage in Ezekiel's prophecy.

25:1–32:32 Oracles against Foreign Nations
Like Isaiah, Jeremiah, and most of the minor
prophets, Ezekiel includes a section of oracles
announcing YHWH's judgment upon nations other than Israel. In Ezekiel, most are punished for
profiting from Judah's destruction. These oracles
serve to proclaim to all nations YHWH's sovereignty. It is YHWH's own land and people whom
the nations have despoiled, and YHWH will be
avenged upon them. Each oracle announces that,
having suffered YHWH's vengeance, the nation
will then *know that I am the LORD*, acknowledging YHWH as the supreme God.

25:1–14 Against Ammon (cf. 21:28–32), Moab,
and Edom (cf. chap. 35)

the Ammonites and prophesy against them. ³ Say to the Ammonites, Hear the word of the Lord GOD: Thus says the Lord GOD, Because you said, "Aha!" over my sanctuary when it was profaned, and over the land of Israel when it was made desolate, and over the house of Judah when it went into exile; ⁴ therefore I am handing you over to the people of the east for a possession. They shall set their encampments among you and pitch their tents in your midst; they shall eat your fruit, and they shall drink your milk. ⁵ I will make Rabbah a pasture for camels and Ammon a fold for flocks. Then you shall know that I am the LORD. ⁶ For thus says the Lord GOD: Because you have clapped your hands and stamped your feet and rejoiced with all the malice within you against the land of Israel, ⁷ therefore I have stretched out my hand against you, and will hand you over as plunder to the nations. I will cut you off from the peoples and will make you perish out of the countries; I will destroy you. Then you shall know that I am the LORD.

Proclamation against Moab

8 Thus says the Lord GOD: Because Moab*a* said, The house of Judah is like all the other nations, ⁹ therefore I will lay open the flank of Moab from the towns*b* on its frontier, the glory of the country, Beth-jeshimoth, Baal-meon, and Kiriathaim. ¹⁰ I will give it along with Ammon to the people of the east as a possession. Thus Ammon shall be remembered no

more among the nations, ¹¹ and I will execute judgments upon Moab. Then they shall know that I am the LORD.

Proclamation against Edom

12 Thus says the Lord GOD: Because Edom acted revengefully against the house of Judah and has grievously offended in taking vengeance upon them, ¹³ therefore thus says the Lord GOD, I will stretch out my hand against Edom, and cut off from it humans and animals, and I will make it desolate; from Teman even to Dedan they shall fall by the sword. ¹⁴ I will lay my vengeance upon Edom by the hand of my people Israel; and they shall act in Edom according to my anger and according to my wrath; and they shall know my vengeance, says the Lord GOD.

Proclamation against Philistia

15 Thus says the Lord GOD: Because with unending hostilities the Philistines acted in vengeance, and with malice of heart took revenge in destruction; ¹⁶ therefore thus says the Lord GOD, I will stretch out my hand against the Philistines, cut off the Cherethites, and destroy the rest of the seacoast. ¹⁷ I will execute great vengeance on them with wrathful punishments. Then they shall know that I am the LORD, when I lay my vengeance on them.

Proclamation against Tyre

26 In the eleventh year, on the first day of the month, the word of

a Gk Old Latin: Heb *Moab and Seir*   *b* Heb *towns from its towns*

These nations' malicious pleasure at Judah's exile and the temple's destruction will be avenged. The oracles are undated but presume conditions following 586 BCE. Edom seems first to have joined Judah in rebellion against Babylon (Jer. 27:3) and then reverted to Babylonian allegiance, perhaps even despoiling Judean territory. Edom is therefore handed over, not to the Babylonians, but to Israel (v. 14), whom they betrayed.

25:15–17 Against the Philistines

No evidence exists for Philistine rebellion against Babylon in this period, and Nebuchadrezzar may well have rewarded their loyalty with opportunities to take *revenge* against Judah.

25:16 *Cherethites*—Probably a reference to the Philistines' origins on Crete (cf. Zeph. 2:5).

26:1–28:19 Against Tyre

Tyre, a wealthy trading center, was located on a coastal island, and apparently invulnerable to attack. Nebuchadrezzar laid siege to the island fortress for thirteen years but failed to take it. Tyre is singled out for lengthy condemnation, possibly because, of all rebels against Babylon, Tyre alone continued to prosper.

26:1 *The eleventh year*—586 BCE.

the LORD came to me: [2] Mortal, because Tyre said concerning Jerusalem,

> "Aha, broken is the gateway of the
> peoples;
> it has swung open to me;
> I shall be replenished,
> now that it is wasted,"

[3] therefore, thus says the Lord GOD:

> See, I am against you, O Tyre!
> I will hurl many nations against
> you,
> as the sea hurls its waves.
> [4] They shall destroy the walls of
> Tyre
> and break down its towers.
> I will scrape its soil from it
> and make it a bare rock.
> [5] It shall become, in the midst of the
> sea,
> a place for spreading nets.
> I have spoken, says the Lord GOD.
> It shall become plunder for the
> nations,
> [6] and its daughter-towns in the
> country
> shall be killed by the sword.

Then they shall know that I am the LORD.

7 For thus says the Lord GOD: I will bring against Tyre from the north King Nebuchadrezzar of Babylon, king of kings, together with horses, chariots, cavalry, and a great and powerful army.

> [8] Your daughter-towns in the
> country
> he shall put to the sword.
> He shall set up a siege wall against
> you,
> cast up a ramp against you,
> and raise a roof of shields against
> you.

> [9] He shall direct the shock of his
> battering rams against your
> walls
> and break down your towers with
> his axes.
> [10] His horses shall be so many
> that their dust shall cover you.
> At the noise of cavalry, wheels, and
> chariots
> your very walls shall shake,
> when he enters your gates
> like those entering a breached city.
> [11] With the hoofs of his horses
> he shall trample all your streets.
> He shall put your people to the
> sword,
> and your strong pillars shall fall to
> the ground.
> [12] They will plunder your riches
> and loot your merchandise;
> they shall break down your walls
> and destroy your fine houses.
> Your stones and timber and soil
> they shall cast into the water.
> [13] I will silence the music of your
> songs;
> the sound of your lyres shall be
> heard no more.
> [14] I will make you a bare rock;
> you shall be a place for spreading
> nets.
> You shall never again be rebuilt,
> for I the LORD have spoken,
> says the Lord GOD.

15 Thus says the Lord GOD to Tyre: Shall not the coastlands shake at the sound of your fall, when the wounded groan, when slaughter goes on within you? [16] Then all the princes of the sea shall step down from their thrones; they shall remove their robes and strip

---

26:2 *Aha*—The merchant-city Tyre sees Jerusalem's destruction as simply creating a trade opportunity.

26:4 *Bare rock*—Here and in v. 14 the oracle plays on Tyre's location, a rocky coastal island, and its name, which sounds like "rock" in Hebrew.

26:7 *Nebuchadrezzar*—This oracle is remarkable in that it went unfulfilled: Nebuchadrezzar did

not, in fact, destroy Tyre. A later oracle promising Egypt to the Babylonian monarch (29:17–21) implicitly acknowledges the problem. Ezekiel's frank treatment of his unfulfilled prophecy suggests that he did not consider the authority of his message dependent on its absolute, literal accuracy.

26:16 *Princes of the sea*—This may refer to mythological beings, but may also allude to Tyre's maritime allies.

off their embroidered garments. They shall clothe themselves with trembling, and shall sit on the ground; they shall tremble every moment, and be appalled at you. [17] And they shall raise a lamentation over you, and say to you:

How you have vanished[a] from the
    seas,
  O city renowned,
once mighty on the sea,
  you and your inhabitants,[b]
who imposed your[c] terror
  on all the mainland![d]

[18] Now the coastlands tremble
    on the day of your fall;
  the coastlands by the sea
    are dismayed at your passing.

[19] For thus says the Lord GOD: When I make you a city laid waste, like cities that are not inhabited, when I bring up the deep over you, and the great waters cover you, [20] then I will thrust you down with those who descend into the Pit, to the people of long ago, and I will make you live in the world below, among primeval ruins, with those who go down to the Pit, so that you will not be inhabited or have a place[e] in the land of the living. [21] I will bring you to a dreadful end, and you shall be no more; though sought for, you will never be found again, says the Lord GOD.

Lamentation over Tyre

27 The word of the LORD came to me: [2] Now you, mortal, raise a lamentation over Tyre, [3] and say to Tyre, which sits at the entrance to the sea, merchant of the peoples on many coastlands, Thus says the Lord GOD:

O Tyre, you have said,
  "I am perfect in beauty."
[4] Your borders are in the heart of the
    seas;

your builders made perfect your
    beauty.
[5] They made all your planks
    of fir trees from Senir;
  they took a cedar from Lebanon
    to make a mast for you.
[6] From oaks of Bashan
    they made your oars;
  they made your deck of pines[f]
    from the coasts of Cyprus,
    inlaid with ivory.
[7] Of fine embroidered linen from Egypt
    was your sail,
    serving as your ensign;
  blue and purple from the coasts of
    Elishah
    was your awning.
[8] The inhabitants of Sidon and Arvad
    were your rowers;
  skilled men of Zemer[g] were within
    you,
    they were your pilots.
[9] The elders of Gebal and its artisans
    were within you,
    caulking your seams;
  all the ships of the sea with their
    mariners were within you,
    to barter for your wares.
[10] Paras[h] and Lud and Put
    were in your army,
    your mighty warriors;
  they hung shield and helmet in you;
    they gave you splendor.
[11] Men of Arvad and Helech[i]
    were on your walls all around;
  men of Gamad were at your
    towers.
  They hung their quivers all around
    your walls;
    they made perfect your beauty.
[12] Tarshish did business with you out

[a] Gk OL Aquila: Heb have vanished, O inhabited one, [b] Heb it and its inhabitants [c] Heb their [d] Cn: Heb its inhabitants [e] Gk: Heb I will give beauty [f] Or boxwood [g] Cn Compare Gen 10.18: Heb your skilled men, O Tyre [h] Or Persia [i] Or and your army

---

26:20 *The Pit*—Sheol, the realm of the dead, located below the sea (see note at 31:16).

27:1–36—Tyre is pictured as a lavishly outfitted ship, carrying goods and sailors gathered from throughout the known world. The great trading vessel will set out in glory, only to suffer

shipwreck in vv. 26–36. As in his oracles against Judah, in depicting Tyre Ezekiel turns symbols of national pride into emblems of disgrace and ruin.

27:12 *Tarshish*—A port in southern Spain, the proverbial end of the earth (cf. Jonah 1:3).

of the abundance of your great wealth; silver, iron, tin, and lead they exchanged for your wares. ¹³ Javan, Tubal, and Meshech traded with you; they exchanged human beings and vessels of bronze for your merchandise. ¹⁴ Beth-togarmah exchanged for your wares horses, war horses, and mules. ¹⁵ The Rhodians*a* traded with you; many coast-lands were your own special markets; they brought you in payment ivory tusks and ebony. ¹⁶ Edom*b* did business with you because of your abundant goods; they exchanged for your wares tur-quoise, purple, embroidered work, fine linen, coral, and rubies. ¹⁷ Judah and the land of Israel traded with you; they exchanged for your merchandise wheat from Minnith, millet,*c* honey, oil, and balm. ¹⁸ Damascus traded with you for your abundant goods—because of your great wealth of every kind—wine of Helbon, and white wool. ¹⁹ Vedan and Javan from Uzal*c* entered into trade for your wares; wrought iron, cassia, and sweet cane were bartered for your mer-chandise. ²⁰ Dedan traded with you in saddlecloths for riding. ²¹ Arabia and all the princes of Kedar were your favored dealers in lambs, rams, and goats; in these they did business with you. ²² The merchants of Sheba and Raamah traded with you; they exchanged for your wares the best of all kinds of spices, and all precious stones, and gold. ²³ Haran, Can-neh, Eden, the merchants of Sheba, Asshur, and Chilmad traded with you. ²⁴ These traded with you in choice gar-ments, in clothes of blue and embroi-dered work, and in carpets of colored material, bound with cords and made secure; in these they traded with you.*d* ²⁵ The ships of Tarshish traveled for you in your trade.

So you were filled and heavily laden
   in the heart of the seas.
²⁶ Your rowers have brought you
   into the high seas.
The east wind has wrecked you
   in the heart of the seas.

²⁷ Your riches, your wares, your
      merchandise,
   your mariners and your pilots,
your caulkers, your dealers in
      merchandise,
   and all your warriors within you,
with all the company
   that is with you,
sink into the heart of the seas
   on the day of your ruin.
²⁸ At the sound of the cry of your pilots
   the countryside shakes,
²⁹ and down from their ships
   come all that handle the oar.
The mariners and all the pilots of the
      sea
   stand on the shore
³⁰ and wail aloud over you,
   and cry bitterly.
They throw dust on their heads
   and wallow in ashes;
³¹ they make themselves bald for you,
   and put on sackcloth,
and they weep over you in bitterness
      of soul,
   with bitter mourning.
³² In their wailing they raise a
      lamentation for you,
   and lament over you:
"Who was ever destroyed*e* like Tyre
   in the midst of the sea?
³³ When your wares came from the
      seas,
   you satisfied many peoples;
with your abundant wealth and
      merchandise
   you enriched the kings of the
      earth.
³⁴ Now you are wrecked by the seas,
   in the depths of the waters;
your merchandise and all your crew
   have sunk with you.
³⁵ All the inhabitants of the coastlands
   are appalled at you;
and their kings are horribly afraid,
   their faces are convulsed.
³⁶ The merchants among the peoples
   hiss at you;

a Gk: Heb *The Dedanites* *b* Another reading is *Aram* *c* Meaning of Heb uncertain *d* Cn: Heb *in your market* *e* Tg Vg: Heb *like silence*

you have come to a dreadful end
and shall be no more forever."

Proclamation against the King of Tyre

28 The word of the LORD came to me: [2] Mortal, say to the prince of Tyre, Thus says the Lord GOD:

Because your heart is proud
and you have said, "I am a god;
I sit in the seat of the gods,
in the heart of the seas,"
yet you are but a mortal, and no god,
though you compare your mind
with the mind of a god.

[3] You are indeed wiser than Daniel;[a]
no secret is hidden from you;

[4] by your wisdom and your
understanding
you have amassed wealth for
yourself,
and have gathered gold and silver
into your treasuries.

[5] By your great wisdom in trade
you have increased your wealth,
and your heart has become proud
in your wealth.

[6] Therefore thus says the Lord GOD:
Because you compare your mind
with the mind of a god,

[7] therefore, I will bring strangers
against you,
the most terrible of the nations;
they shall draw their swords against
the beauty of your wisdom
and defile your splendor.

[8] They shall thrust you down to
the Pit,

and you shall die a violent death
in the heart of the seas.

[9] Will you still say, "I am a god,"
in the presence of those who kill
you,
though you are but a mortal, and no
god,
in the hands of those who wound
you?

[10] You shall die the death of the
uncircumcised
by the hand of foreigners;
for I have spoken, says the Lord
GOD.

Lamentation over the King of Tyre

11 Moreover the word of the LORD came to me: [12] Mortal, raise a lamentation over the king of Tyre, and say to him, Thus says the Lord GOD:

You were the signet of perfection,[b]
full of wisdom and perfect in
beauty.

[13] You were in Eden, the garden of God;
every precious stone was your
covering,
carnelian, chrysolite, and
moonstone,
beryl, onyx, and jasper,
sapphire,[c] turquoise, and emerald;
and worked in gold were your
settings
and your engravings.[b]
On the day that you were created
they were prepared.

[a] Or, as otherwise read, *Danel*   [b] Meaning of Heb uncertain   [c] Or *lapis lazuli*

28:1–19—Ezekiel continues with a proclamation against the ruler of Tyre.

28:3 Daniel—The Hebrew, as in chap.14, is not Daniel, but Dan'el (see note at 14:12–23). Ezekiel acknowledges the Tyrian ruler's wisdom, if only in the area of commerce (vv. 3–5).

28:7 Most terrible of the nations—Babylon (cf. 7:24).

28:8–9—The ruler's ignominious **death** will definitively prove his mortal status.

28:10—The Phoenicians practiced circumcision, and therefore **the death of the uncircumcised** would signify a disgraceful death.

28:11–19—The king of Tyre is depicted in imagery recalling both Adam in Gen. 2–3 and the Israelite high priest. Like Adam, he is **in Eden, the garden of God**, until he sins and is driven out. The standard Hebrew text calls *him* a guardian cherub; NRSV emends to say that he was **with** a guardian cherub (v. 14). Like the high priest, he inhabits **the holy mountain of God** and wears a covering of **precious stones** (cf. the ephod in Exod. 28:17–20). Despite many scholarly attempts, Ezekiel's tantalizing connection between Tyre, Eden, and priestly traditions remains enigmatic.

14 With an anointed cherub as
　　　guardian I placed you;*a*
　　you were on the holy mountain of
　　　　God;
　　you walked among the stones of
　　　　fire.
15 You were blameless in your ways
　　from the day that you were created,
　　until iniquity was found in you.
16 In the abundance of your trade
　　you were filled with violence, and
　　　you sinned;
　　so I cast you as a profane thing from
　　　　the mountain of God,
　　and the guardian cherub drove
　　　　you out
　　from among the stones of fire.
17 Your heart was proud because of
　　　your beauty;
　　you corrupted your wisdom for
　　　　the sake of your splendor.
　　I cast you to the ground;
　　　I exposed you before kings,
　　to feast their eyes on you.
18 By the multitude of your iniquities,
　　in the unrighteousness of your
　　　　trade,
　　you profaned your sanctuaries.
　　So I brought out fire from within you;
　　　it consumed you,
　　and I turned you to ashes on the
　　　　earth
　　in the sight of all who saw you.
19 All who know you among the
　　　peoples
　　are appalled at you;
　　you have come to a dreadful end
　　　and shall be no more forever.

Proclamation against Sidon

20 The word of the LORD came to me:

21 Mortal, set your face toward Sidon,
and prophesy against it, 22 and say, Thus
says the Lord GOD:
　　I am against you, O Sidon,
　　　and I will gain glory in your midst.
　　They shall know that I am the LORD
　　　when I execute judgments in it,
　　　and manifest my holiness in it;
23 for I will send pestilence into it,
　　　and bloodshed into its streets;
　　and the dead shall fall in its midst,
　　　by the sword that is against it on
　　　　every side.
　　And they shall know that I am the
　　　　LORD.

24 The house of Israel shall no longer
find a pricking brier or a piercing thorn
among all their neighbors who have
treated them with contempt. And they
shall know that I am the Lord GOD.

Future Blessing for Israel

25 Thus says the Lord GOD: When
I gather the house of Israel from the
peoples among whom they are scattered, and manifest my holiness in them
in the sight of the nations, then they
shall settle on their own soil that I gave
to my servant Jacob. 26 They shall live in
safety in it, and shall build houses and
plant vineyards. They shall live in safety,
when I execute judgments upon all their
neighbors who have treated them with
contempt. And they shall know that I
am the LORD their God.

Proclamation against Egypt

29 In the tenth year, in the tenth
month, on the twelfth day of the
month, the word of the LORD came to

a Meaning of Heb uncertain

28:20–23 Against Sidon
Although Sidon was among the nations rebelling
against Nebuchadrezzar (Jer. 27:3), Ezekiel brings
no specific accusations against the city.

28:24–26 Hope for Israel
Ezekiel's oracles against six neighboring powers
conclude with a brief word of hope to Israel and
yet another reminder that after Israel's restoration
both Israel and the nations will acknowledge
YHWH.

29:1–32:32 Oracles against Egypt
Judah rebelled against Babylon on the basis of
promises of Egyptian support. During Nebuchadrezzar's 588 siege of Jerusalem, however,
Hophra gave only limited assistance before
withdrawing. Egypt, as the catalyst behind
Judah's rebellion against Babylon, is singled out
for especially harsh treatment. Seven oracles are
directed against Pharaoh and Egypt.

29:1 *The tenth year*—January 587 BCE.

me: ²Mortal, set your face against Pharaoh king of Egypt, and prophesy against him and against all Egypt; ³speak, and say, Thus says the Lord GOD:

I am against you,
   Pharaoh king of Egypt,
the great dragon sprawling
   in the midst of its channels,
saying, "My Nile is my own;
   I made it for myself."
⁴ I will put hooks in your jaws,
   and make the fish of your channels
     stick to your scales.
I will draw you up from your
     channels,
   with all the fish of your channels
     sticking to your scales.
⁵ I will fling you into the wilderness,
   you and all the fish of your
     channels;
you shall fall in the open field,
   and not be gathered and buried.
To the animals of the earth and to
     the birds of the air
   I have given you as food.
⁶ Then all the inhabitants of Egypt
     shall know
   that I am the LORD
because you[a] were a staff of reed
   to the house of Israel;
⁷ when they grasped you with the
     hand, you broke,
   and tore all their shoulders;
and when they leaned on you, you
     broke,
   and made all their legs unsteady.[b]

8 Therefore, thus says the Lord GOD: I will bring a sword upon you, and will cut off from you human being and animal; ⁹and the land of Egypt shall be a desolation and a waste. Then they shall know that I am the LORD.

Because you[c] said, "The Nile is mine, and I made it," ¹⁰therefore, I am against you, and against your channels, and I will make the land of Egypt an utter waste and desolation, from Migdol to Syene, as far as the border of Ethiopia.[d] ¹¹No human foot shall pass through it, and no animal foot shall pass through it; it shall be uninhabited forty years. ¹²I will make the land of Egypt a desolation among desolated countries; and her cities shall be a desolation forty years among cities that are laid waste. I will scatter the Egyptians among the nations, and disperse them among the countries.

13 Further, thus says the Lord GOD: At the end of forty years I will gather the Egyptians from the peoples among whom they were scattered; ¹⁴and I will restore the fortunes of Egypt, and bring them back to the land of Pathros, the land of their origin; and there they shall be a lowly kingdom. ¹⁵It shall be the most lowly of the kingdoms, and never again exalt itself above the nations; and I will make them so small that they will never again rule over the nations. ¹⁶The Egyptians[e] shall never again be the reliance of the house of Israel; they will recall their iniquity, when they turned to them for aid. Then they shall know that I am the Lord GOD.

Babylonia Will Plunder Egypt

17 In the twenty-seventh year, in the first month, on the first day of the

---

[a] Gk Syr Vg: Heb *they* [b] Syr: Heb *stand* [c] Gk Syr Vg: Heb *he*
[d] Or *Nubia;* Heb *Cush* [e] Heb *It*

29:2 *Pharaoh king of Egypt*—Hophra (Apries), 594–588 BCE.

29:3 *Dragon*—Probably a crocodile, depicted as a creature of mythic proportions, similar to Leviathan in Isa. 27:1; Job 41.

29:6–7 *A staff of reed*—As in Isa. 36:6, Egypt is a deceptive support that injures those who lean upon it.

29:17–21 *The twenty-seventh year*—April 571. This, the latest-dated oracle in Ezekiel, includes

the prophet's candid acknowledgment that his earlier prophecy—that Nebuchadrezzar would capture Tyre (see note at 26:7)—had failed to materialize. YHWH will therefore give Egypt to the Babylonian monarch as compensation for his fruitless efforts against Tyre. Ezekiel's openness about his unfulfilled prophecy suggests that he understood prophecy as a qualitatively different activity from the mere prediction of the future (a task fulfilled in the ancient world by countless professional diviners). The images from chaps.

month, the word of the LORD came to me: ¹⁸ Mortal, King Nebuchadrezzar of Babylon made his army labor hard against Tyre; every head was made bald and every shoulder was rubbed bare; yet neither he nor his army got anything from Tyre to pay for the labor that he had expended against it. ¹⁹ Therefore thus says the Lord GOD: I will give the land of Egypt to King Nebuchadrezzar of Babylon; and he shall carry off its wealth and despoil it and plunder it; and it shall be the wages for his army. ²⁰ I have given him the land of Egypt as his payment for which he labored, because they worked for me, says the Lord GOD.

21 On that day I will cause a horn to sprout up for the house of Israel, and I will open your lips among them. Then they shall know that I am the LORD.

Lamentation for Egypt

30 The word of the LORD came to me: ² Mortal, prophesy, and say, Thus says the Lord GOD:
Wail, "Alas for the day!"
³   For a day is near,
        the day of the LORD is near;
    it will be a day of clouds,
        a time of doom*a* for the nations.
⁴ A sword shall come upon Egypt,
        and anguish shall be in Ethiopia,*b*
    when the slain fall in Egypt,
        and its wealth is carried away,
        and its foundations are torn down.
⁵ Ethiopia,*b* and Put, and Lud, and all Arabia, and Libya,*c* and the people of the allied land*d* shall fall with them by the sword.

⁶   Thus says the LORD:
    Those who support Egypt shall
        fall,

and its proud might shall come
        down;
    from Migdol to Syene
        they shall fall within it by the sword,
    says the Lord GOD.
⁷   They shall be desolated among other
        desolated countries,
        and their cities shall lie among
            cities laid waste.
⁸   Then they shall know that I am the
        LORD,
        when I have set fire to Egypt,
        and all who help it are broken.

9 On that day, messengers shall go out from me in ships to terrify the unsuspecting Ethiopians;*b* and anguish shall come upon them on the day of Egypt's doom;*e* for it is coming!

10 Thus says the Lord GOD:
    I will put an end to the hordes of
        Egypt,
        by the hand of King
            Nebuchadrezzar of Babylon.
¹¹   He and his people with him, the
        most terrible of the nations,
    shall be brought in to destroy the
        land;
    and they shall draw their swords
        against Egypt,
        and fill the land with the slain.
¹²   I will dry up the channels,
        and will sell the land into the hand
            of evildoers;
    I will bring desolation upon the land
        and everything in it
        by the hand of foreigners;
    I the LORD have spoken.

13 Thus says the Lord GOD:
    I will destroy the idols

a Heb lacks *of doom*   *b* Or Nubia; Heb *Cush*   *c* Compare Gk Syr Vg: Heb *Cub*   *d* Meaning of Heb uncertain   *e* Heb *the day of Egypt*

---

3 and 33 of the prophet as sentinel, together with Ezekiel's passionate exhortations to moral responsibility (18:1–32; 37:11–14), depict the prophet as divine-human mediator and as moral teacher, rather than as prognosticator. Leaders of church and synagogue are called to be prophetic in precisely these ways.

29:21 A horn—A symbol of power (Pss. 75:5, 10;

148:14), possibly referring (as in Ps. 132:17) to the Davidic dynasty. **Open your lips**—Possibly a reference to the opening of Ezekiel's lips in 33:22 (and see 24:27).

30:3 The day of the LORD—Earlier (see note at 7:1–19) YHWH had a day of judgment against Judah; now the nations will also feel God's wrath.

and put an end to the images in
  Memphis;
there shall no longer be a prince in
  the land of Egypt;
so I will put fear in the land of
  Egypt.
14 I will make Pathros a desolation,
  and will set fire to Zoan,
  and will execute acts of judgment
  on Thebes.
15 I will pour my wrath upon Pelusium,
  the stronghold of Egypt,
  and cut off the hordes of Thebes.
16 I will set fire to Egypt;
  Pelusium shall be in great agony;
Thebes shall be breached,
  and Memphis face adversaries by
  day.
17 The young men of On and of Pi-
  beseth shall fall by the sword;
  and the cities themselves[a] shall go
  into captivity.
18 At Tehaphnehes the day shall be
  dark,
  when I break there the dominion
  of Egypt,
and its proud might shall come to an
  end;
  the city[b] shall be covered by a
  cloud,
  and its daughter-towns shall go
  into captivity.
19 Thus I will execute acts of judgment
  on Egypt.
  Then they shall know that I am the
  LORD.

Proclamation against Pharaoh

20 In the eleventh year, in the first
month, on the seventh day of the
month, the word of the LORD came to
me: 21 Mortal, I have broken the arm of
Pharaoh king of Egypt; it has not been
bound up for healing or wrapped with
a bandage, so that it may become strong
to wield the sword. 22 Therefore thus
says the Lord GOD: I am against Pharaoh king of Egypt, and will break his
arms, both the strong arm and the one
that was broken; and I will make the
sword fall from his hand. 23 I will scatter
the Egyptians among the nations, and
disperse them throughout the lands. 24 I
will strengthen the arms of the king of
Babylon, and put my sword in his hand;
but I will break the arms of Pharaoh,
and he will groan before him with the
groans of one mortally wounded. 25 I
will strengthen the arms of the king of
Babylon, but the arms of Pharaoh shall
fall. And they shall know that I am the
LORD, when I put my sword into the
hand of the king of Babylon. He shall
stretch it out against the land of Egypt,
26 and I will scatter the Egyptians among
the nations and disperse them throughout the countries. Then they shall know
that I am the LORD.

The Lofty Cedar

31 In the eleventh year, in the third
month, on the first day of the
month, the word of the LORD came to
me: 2 Mortal, say to Pharaoh king of
Egypt and to his hordes:
  Whom are you like in your
    greatness?
3   Consider Assyria, a cedar of
    Lebanon,
  with fair branches and forest shade,
    and of great height,
    its top among the clouds.[c]
4 The waters nourished it,

[a] Heb *and they* [b] Heb *she* [c] Gk: Heb *thick boughs*

30:20 *The eleventh year*—April 587.

30:21–22—One of Hophra's titles was "Possessor
of a Strong Arm." YHWH, however, claims to
have broken one of Pharaoh's arms and is now
preparing to go after the other.

30:25 *My sword*—As in Isaiah (10:5) and Jeremiah (25:9), the foreign monarch is merely acting as
YHWH's agent.

31:1–18—The image of a tree stretching from the
underworld (note *the deep* in v. 4) to the heavens
occurs in many Near Eastern traditions.

31:1 *The eleventh year*—June 587.

31:3—Egypt is compared with *Assyria*, the
recently-great empire, which now lies devastated.

the deep made it grow tall,
making its rivers flow[a]
  around the place it was planted,
sending forth its streams
  to all the trees of the field.
5 So it towered high
  above all the trees of the field;
its boughs grew large
  and its branches long,
from abundant water in its shoots.
6 All the birds of the air
  made their nests in its boughs;
under its branches all the animals of
    the field
  gave birth to their young;
and in its shade
  all great nations lived.
7 It was beautiful in its greatness,
  in the length of its branches;
for its roots went down
  to abundant water.
8 The cedars in the garden of God
    could not rival it,
  nor the fir trees equal its boughs;
the plane trees were as nothing
  compared with its branches;
no tree in the garden of God
  was like it in beauty.
9 I made it beautiful
  with its mass of branches,
the envy of all the trees of Eden
  that were in the garden of God.

10 Therefore thus says the Lord GOD:
Because it[b] towered high and set its top
among the clouds,[c] and its heart was
proud of its height, 11 I gave it into the
hand of the prince of the nations; he has
dealt with it as its wickedness deserves.
I have cast it out. 12 Foreigners from the
most terrible of the nations have cut
it down and left it. On the mountains

and in all the valleys its branches have
fallen, and its boughs lie broken in all
the watercourses of the land; and all the
peoples of the earth went away from its
shade and left it.
13 On its fallen trunk settle
  all the birds of the air,
and among its boughs lodge
  all the wild animals.
14 All this is in order that no trees by the
waters may grow to lofty height or set
their tops among the clouds,[c] and that
no trees that drink water may reach up
to them in height.
For all of them are handed over to
    death,
  to the world below;
along with all mortals,
  with those who go down to the Pit.

15 Thus says the Lord GOD: On the day
it went down to Sheol I closed the deep
over it and covered it; I restrained its rivers, and its mighty waters were checked.
I clothed Lebanon in gloom for it, and
all the trees of the field fainted because
of it. 16 I made the nations quake at the
sound of its fall, when I cast it down to
Sheol with those who go down to the
Pit; and all the trees of Eden, the choice
and best of Lebanon, all that were well
watered, were consoled in the world
below. 17 They also went down to Sheol
with it, to those killed by the sword,
along with its allies,[d] those who lived in
its shade among the nations.

18 Which among the trees of Eden
was like you in glory and in greatness?
Now you shall be brought down with
the trees of Eden to the world below;

a Gk: Heb *rivers going*   b Syr Vg: Heb *you*   c Gk: Heb *thick boughs*
d Heb *its arms*

31:9—As in 28:13 (and of course in Gen. 2:9),
Eden is understood to be God's own **garden**;
hence its extraordinary trees. Pleasure gardens, a
luxury in the ancient Near East, were understood
to be the special domain of kings and gods.

31:16—*Sheol*, the realm of the dead, was located
below the sea (see note at Gen. 1:6). *All mor-*
tals, not only the wicked, go there after death (v.
14). Although generally unpleasant, Sheol is not
a place of punishment or suffering. In fact, the

shadowy world of the dead offered the prospect
of rest to those who suffered in this life (see Job
3:17–19). Images of divine reward and punishment in the afterlife seem to have developed, or
at least to have become widespread, in response
to the Seleucid persecutions of the second century BCE.

31:18—At least some Egyptians practiced
circumcision; to be buried *among the uncircum-*
cised would be a disgrace to the pharaoh.

you shall lie among the uncircumcised,
with those who are killed by the sword.
This is Pharaoh and all his horde, says
the Lord GOD.

Lamentation over Pharaoh and Egypt

32 In the twelfth year, in the twelfth
month, on the first day of the
month, the word of the LORD came to
me: ²Mortal, raise a lamentation over
Pharaoh king of Egypt, and say to him:
You consider yourself a lion among
    the nations,
  but you are like a dragon in the
    seas;
you thrash about in your streams,
  trouble the water with your feet,
  and foul your*a* streams.
³ Thus says the Lord GOD:
  In an assembly of many peoples
  I will throw my net over you;
  and I*b* will haul you up in my
    dragnet.
⁴ I will throw you on the ground,
  on the open field I will fling
    you,
and will cause all the birds of the air
  to settle on you,
  and I will let the wild animals
    of the whole earth gorge
    themselves with you.
⁵ I will strew your flesh on the
    mountains,
  and fill the valleys with your
    carcass.*c*
⁶ I will drench the land with your
    flowing blood
  up to the mountains,
  and the watercourses will be filled
    with you.
⁷ When I blot you out, I will cover the
    heavens,
  and make their stars dark;
I will cover the sun with a cloud,
  and the moon shall not give its
    light.
⁸ All the shining lights of the heavens
  I will darken above you,

and put darkness on your land,
        says the Lord GOD.
⁹ I will trouble the hearts of many
    peoples,
  as I carry you captive*d* among the
    nations,
  into countries you have not
    known.
¹⁰ I will make many peoples appalled at
    you;
  their kings shall shudder because
    of you.
When I brandish my sword before
    them,
  they shall tremble every moment
for their lives, each one of them,
  on the day of your downfall.
¹¹ For thus says the Lord GOD:
The sword of the king of Babylon
  shall come against you.
¹² I will cause your hordes to fall
  by the swords of mighty ones,
  all of them most terrible among
    the nations.
They shall bring to ruin the pride of
    Egypt,
  and all its hordes shall perish.
¹³ I will destroy all its livestock
  from beside abundant waters;
and no human foot shall trouble
    them any more,
  nor shall the hoofs of cattle trouble
    them.
¹⁴ Then I will make their waters clear,
  and cause their streams to run like
    oil, says the Lord GOD.
¹⁵ When I make the land of Egypt
    desolate
  and when the land is stripped of
    all that fills it,
when I strike down all who live in it,
  then they shall know that I am the
    LORD.
¹⁶ This is a lamentation; it shall be
    chanted.

a Heb *their* *b* Gk Vg: Heb *they* *c* Symmachus Syr Vg: Heb *your height*
d Gk: Heb *bring your destruction*

32:1–32—Dirges over Pharaoh and Egypt conclude the oracles against Egypt.

32:1 *The twelfth year*—Various manuscripts give
differing dates, usually March 586 or 585 BCE.

The women of the nations shall
   chant it.
Over Egypt and all its hordes they
   shall chant it,
   says the Lord GOD.

Dirge over Egypt

17 In the twelfth year, in the first
month,[a] on the fifteenth day of the
month, the word of the LORD came to
me:
18 Mortal, wail over the hordes of
      Egypt,
   and send them down,
with Egypt[b] and the daughters of
      majestic nations,
   to the world below,
   with those who go down to the
      Pit.
19 "Whom do you surpass in beauty?
   Go down! Be laid to rest with the
      uncircumcised!"
20 They shall fall among those who are
killed by the sword. Egypt[c] has been
handed over to the sword; carry away
both it and its hordes. 21 The mighty
chiefs shall speak of them, with their
helpers, out of the midst of Sheol: "They
have come down, they lie still, the uncircumcised, killed by the sword."

22 Assyria is there, and all its company, their graves all around it, all of
them killed, fallen by the sword. 23 Their
graves are set in the uttermost parts of
the Pit. Its company is all around its
grave, all of them killed, fallen by the
sword, who spread terror in the land of
the living.

24 Elam is there, and all its hordes
around its grave; all of them killed,
fallen by the sword, who went down
uncircumcised into the world below,
who spread terror in the land of the living. They bear their shame with those
who go down to the Pit. 25 They have

made Elam[b] a bed among the slain with
all its hordes, their graves all around it,
all of them uncircumcised, killed by the
sword; for terror of them was spread in
the land of the living, and they bear their
shame with those who go down to the
Pit; they are placed among the slain.

26 Meshech and Tubal are there, and
all their multitude, their graves all
around them, all of them uncircumcised, killed by the sword; for they
spread terror in the land of the living.
27 And they do not lie with the fallen
warriors of long ago[d] who went down to
Sheol with their weapons of war, whose
swords were laid under their heads, and
whose shields[e] are upon their bones; for
the terror of the warriors was in the land
of the living. 28 So you shall be broken
and lie among the uncircumcised, with
those who are killed by the sword.

29 Edom is there, its kings and all its
princes, who for all their might are laid
with those who are killed by the sword;
they lie with the uncircumcised, with
those who go down to the Pit.

30 The princes of the north are there,
all of them, and all the Sidonians, who
have gone down in shame with the
slain, for all the terror that they caused
by their might; they lie uncircumcised
with those who are killed by the sword,
and bear their shame with those who go
down to the Pit.

31 When Pharaoh sees them, he will
be consoled for all his hordes—Pharaoh
and all his army, killed by the sword,
says the Lord GOD. 32 For he[f] spread terror in the land of the living; therefore
he shall be laid to rest among the uncircumcised, with those who are slain by
the sword—Pharaoh and all his multitude, says the Lord GOD.

[a] Gk: Heb lacks *in the first month* [b] Heb *it* [c] Heb *It* [d] Gk Old Latin: Heb
of the uncircumcised [e] Cn: Heb *iniquities* [f] Cn: Heb *I*

32:17–32—Expanding on the image of Egypt's
descent into Sheol in 31:18, Ezekiel describes the
layout of *the Pit*. Sheol is divided into more and
less desirable sections; those who died shameful
deaths seem to be separated from those who died

honorably. Egypt will lie *among the uncircumcised*, presumably in an area of dishonor.
32:17 *The twelfth year*—The versions give differing dates. Sometime in 586–585 BCE is likely.

Ezekiel Israel's Sentry

33 The word of the LORD came to me: ² O Mortal, speak to your people and say to them, If I bring the sword upon a land, and the people of the land take one of their number as their sentinel; ³ and if the sentinel sees the sword coming upon the land and blows the trumpet and warns the people; ⁴ then if any who hear the sound of the trumpet do not take warning, and the sword comes and takes them away, their blood shall be upon their own heads. ⁵ They heard the sound of the trumpet and did not take warning; their blood shall be upon themselves. But if they had taken warning, they would have saved their lives. ⁶ But if the sentinel sees the sword coming and does not blow the trumpet, so that the people are not warned, and the sword comes and takes any of them, they are taken away in their iniquity, but their blood I will require at the sentinel's hand.

7 So you, mortal, I have made a sentinel for the house of Israel; whenever you hear a word from my mouth, you shall give them warning from me. ⁸ If I say to the wicked, "O wicked ones, you shall surely die," and you do not speak to warn the wicked to turn from their ways, the wicked shall die in their iniquity, but their blood I will require at your hand. ⁹ But if you warn the wicked to turn from their ways, and they do not turn from their ways, the wicked shall die in their iniquity, but you will have saved your life.

God's Justice and Mercy

10 Now you, mortal, say to the house of Israel, Thus you have said: "Our transgressions and our sins weigh upon

us, and we waste away because of them; how then can we live?" ¹¹ Say to them, As I live, says the Lord GOD, I have no pleasure in the death of the wicked, but that the wicked turn from their ways and live; turn back, turn back from your evil ways; for why will you die, O house of Israel? ¹² And you, mortal, say to your people, The righteousness of the righteous shall not save them when they transgress; and as for the wickedness of the wicked, it shall not make them stumble when they turn from their wickedness; and the righteous shall not be able to live by their righteousness*a* when they sin. ¹³ Though I say to the righteous that they shall surely live, yet if they trust in their righteousness and commit iniquity, none of their righteous deeds shall be remembered; but in the iniquity that they have committed they shall die. ¹⁴ Again, though I say to the wicked, "You shall surely die," yet if they turn from their sin and do what is lawful and right— ¹⁵ if the wicked restore the pledge, give back what they have taken by robbery, and walk in the statutes of life, committing no iniquity—they shall surely live, they shall not die. ¹⁶ None of the sins that they have committed shall be remembered against them; they have done what is lawful and right, they shall surely live.

17 Yet your people say, "The way of the Lord is not just," when it is their own way that is not just. ¹⁸ When the righteous turn from their righteousness, and commit iniquity, they shall die for it.*b* ¹⁹ And when the wicked turn from their wickedness, and do what is lawful and right, they shall live by it.*b* ²⁰ Yet you

a Heb *by it*   *b* Heb *them*

33:1–39:29 Promises and Visions of Restoration

33:1–20 Ezekiel as Sentinel

The image of the prophet as *sentinel* (v. 3), introduced in 3:16–21, is combined here with a debate on the efficacy of repentance, echoing 18:1–32. Even after the destruction of Jerusalem,

Ezekiel bears ongoing responsibility to warn the people of their sins. The people have accepted that they are suffering the consequence of their own sins but are now taking refuge in moral fatalism: *"Our sins weigh upon us . . . how then can we live?"* (v. 10). As in chap. 18, the prophet insists that repentance is not only possible but necessary and, ultimately, life-giving.

say, "The way of the Lord is not just." O house of Israel, I will judge all of you according to your ways!

The Fall of Jerusalem

21 In the twelfth year of our exile, in the tenth month, on the fifth day of the month, someone who had escaped from Jerusalem came to me and said, "The city has fallen." ²² Now the hand of the LORD had been upon me the evening before the fugitive came; but he had opened my mouth by the time the fugitive came to me in the morning; so my mouth was opened, and I was no longer unable to speak.

The Survivors in Judah

23 The word of the LORD came to me: ²⁴ Mortal, the inhabitants of these waste places in the land of Israel keep saying, "Abraham was only one man, yet he got possession of the land; but we are many; the land is surely given us to possess." ²⁵ Therefore say to them, Thus says the Lord GOD: You eat flesh with the blood, and lift up your eyes to your idols, and shed blood; shall you then possess the land? ²⁶ You depend on your swords, you commit abominations, and each of you defiles his neighbor's wife; shall you then possess the land? ²⁷ Say this to them, Thus says the Lord GOD: As I live, surely those who are in the waste places shall fall by the sword; and those who are in the open field I will give to the wild animals to be devoured; and those who are in strongholds and in caves shall die by pestilence. ²⁸ I will make the land a desolation and a waste, and its proud might shall come to an end; and the mountains of Israel shall be so desolate that no one will pass through. ²⁹ Then they shall know that I am the LORD, when I have made the land a desolation and a waste because of all their abominations that they have committed.

30 As for you, mortal, your people who talk together about you by the walls, and at the doors of the houses, say to one another, each to a neighbor, "Come and hear what the word is that comes from the LORD." ³¹ They come to you as people come, and they sit before you as my people, and they hear your words, but they will not obey them. For flattery is on their lips, but their heart is set on their gain. ³² To them you are like a singer of love songs,ᵃ one who has a beautiful voice and plays well on an instrument; they hear what you say, but they will not do it. ³³ When this comes— and come it will!—then they shall know that a prophet has been among them.

Israel's False Shepherds

34 The word of the LORD came to me: ²Mortal, prophesy against the shepherds of Israel: prophesy, and say to them—to the shepherds: Thus says the Lord GOD: Ah, you shepherds of Israel who have been feeding yourselves! Should not shepherds feed the

ᵃ Cn: Heb *like a love song*

33:21 *The twelfth year*—January 585 BCE. Babylonian couriers must have brought word of Jerusalem's fall earlier, but the *fugitive* of vv. 21–22 seems to be the first Judean to arrive. The opening of Ezekiel's mouth fulfills the prophecy of 24:27 (and see 3:26–27).

33:23–33 The Judean Remnant

33:24 *Abraham*—Those left in Judah were few and poor (2 Kgs. 25:12), but they cite Abraham as precedent that God can work great blessings from small beginnings. Ironically, as in 11:15, the homelanders believe that the exile marks God's intervention on behalf of the poor, but Ezekiel (vv. 25–29) identifies the Judean remnant with the quintessentially evil person of 18:10–13, and prophesies still further destruction against them.

33:30–33—The people are eager to hear Ezekiel's prophecy, but they enjoy it only for its entertainment value (see also 20:49). Unlike prophets who underwent persecution, Ezekiel is accepted but trivialized. YHWH's response suggests that the fulfillment of Ezekiel's prophecies will validate his role.

34:1–31 Bad and Good Shepherds

34:2 *Shepherds*—Rulers. The image of the king as shepherd was common in the ancient Near East. Here, the exile is blamed on bad shepherding by Israel's rulers (see also Jer. 23:1–4).

sheep? ³ You eat the fat, you clothe yourselves with the wool, you slaughter the
fatlings; but you do not feed the sheep.
⁴ You have not strengthened the weak,
you have not healed the sick, you have
not bound up the injured, you have not
brought back the strayed, you have not
sought the lost, but with force and harshness you have ruled them. ⁵ So they were
scattered, because there was no shepherd; and scattered, they became food
for all the wild animals. ⁶ My sheep were
scattered, they wandered over all the
mountains and on every high hill; my
sheep were scattered over all the face of
the earth, with no one to search or seek
for them.

7 Therefore, you shepherds, hear
the word of the LORD: ⁸ As I live, says
the Lord GOD, because my sheep have
become a prey, and my sheep have
become food for all the wild animals, since there was no shepherd;
and because my shepherds have not
searched for my sheep, but the shepherds have fed themselves, and have
not fed my sheep; ⁹ therefore, you
shepherds, hear the word of the LORD:
¹⁰ Thus says the Lord GOD, I am against
the shepherds; and I will demand my
sheep at their hand, and put a stop to
their feeding the sheep; no longer shall
the shepherds feed themselves. I will
rescue my sheep from their mouths, so
that they may not be food for them.

God, the True Shepherd

11 For thus says the Lord GOD: I
myself will search for my sheep, and will
seek them out. ¹² As shepherds seek out
their flocks when they are among their
scattered sheep, so I will seek out my
sheep. I will rescue them from all the
places to which they have been scattered
on a day of clouds and thick darkness.
¹³ I will bring them out from the peoples
and gather them from the countries,
and will bring them into their own land;
and I will feed them on the mountains
of Israel, by the watercourses, and in
all the inhabited parts of the land. ¹⁴ I
will feed them with good pasture, and
the mountain heights of Israel shall be
their pasture; there they shall lie down
in good grazing land, and they shall
feed on rich pasture on the mountains
of Israel. ¹⁵ I myself will be the shepherd of my sheep, and I will make them
lie down, says the Lord GOD. ¹⁶ I will
seek the lost, and I will bring back the
strayed, and I will bind up the injured,
and I will strengthen the weak, but the
fat and the strong I will destroy. I will
feed them with justice.

17 As for you, my flock, thus says the
Lord GOD: I shall judge between sheep
and sheep, between rams and goats: ¹⁸ Is
it not enough for you to feed on the
good pasture, but you must tread down
with your feet the rest of your pasture?
When you drink of clear water, must
you foul the rest with your feet? ¹⁹ And
must my sheep eat what you have trodden with your feet, and drink what you
have fouled with your feet?

20 Therefore, thus says the Lord GOD
to them: I myself will judge between the
fat sheep and the lean sheep. ²¹ Because
you pushed with flank and shoulder,
and butted at all the weak animals with
your horns until you scattered them far
and wide, ²² I will save my flock, and
they shall no longer be ravaged; and I
will judge between sheep and sheep.

34:3 *Eat the fat*—Here as elsewhere, Ezekiel
exploits the underside of a familiar image. Judah's
shepherds slaughter and eat the sheep instead of
guarding them.

34:11—In contrast to the abusive rulers of this
world, YHWH is the good shepherd. Similar
imagery appears in 20:37; Isa. 40:11; Jer. 23:3–4;
31:10; Ps. 23:1–4, and is further developed in the
New Testament.

34:20–31—The good shepherd judges not only
the bad shepherds (rulers), but the sheep as well.
While the rulers bear primary responsibility
for the abuse of the poor, it is clear that the *fat
sheep*—the more prosperous citizens—have contributed to the inequities of society, and they will
be judged along with the rulers. Ezekiel clearly
understood all forms of power to entail social
responsibility.

23 I will set up over them one shepherd, my servant David, and he shall feed them: he shall feed them and be their shepherd. **24** And I, the LORD, will be their God, and my servant David shall be prince among them; I, the LORD, have spoken.

25 I will make with them a covenant of peace and banish wild animals from the land, so that they may live in the wild and sleep in the woods securely. **26** I will make them and the region around my hill a blessing; and I will send down the showers in their season; they shall be showers of blessing. **27** The trees of the field shall yield their fruit, and the earth shall yield its increase. They shall be secure on their soil; and they shall know that I am the LORD, when I break the bars of their yoke, and save them from the hands of those who enslaved them. **28** They shall no more be plunder for the nations, nor shall the animals of the land devour them; they shall live in safety, and no one shall make them afraid. **29** I will provide for them a splendid vegetation so that they shall no more be consumed with hunger in the land, and no longer suffer the insults of the nations. **30** They shall know that I, the LORD their God, am with them, and that they, the house of Israel, are my people, says the Lord GOD. **31** You are my sheep, the sheep of my pasture*a* and I am your God, says the Lord GOD.

Judgment on Mount Seir

35 The word of the LORD came to me: **2** Mortal, set your face against Mount Seir, and prophesy against it, **3** and say to it, Thus says the Lord GOD:

I am against you, Mount Seir;
    I stretch out my hand against you

to make you a desolation and a waste.

4 I lay your towns in ruins;
    you shall become a desolation,
    and you shall know that I am the LORD.

5 Because you cherished an ancient enmity, and gave over the people of Israel to the power of the sword at the time of their calamity, at the time of their final punishment; **6** therefore, as I live, says the Lord GOD, I will prepare you for blood, and blood shall pursue you; since you did not hate bloodshed, bloodshed shall pursue you. **7** I will make Mount Seir a waste and a desolation; and I will cut off from it all who come and go. **8** I will fill its mountains with the slain; on your hills and in your valleys and in all your watercourses those killed with the sword shall fall. **9** I will make you a perpetual desolation, and your cities shall never be inhabited. Then you shall know that I am the LORD.

10 Because you said, "These two nations and these two countries shall be mine, and we will take possession of them,"—although the LORD was there— **11** therefore, as I live, says the Lord GOD, I will deal with you according to the anger and envy that you showed because of your hatred against them; and I will make myself known among you,*b* when I judge you. **12** You shall know that I, the LORD, have heard all the abusive speech that you uttered against the mountains of Israel, saying, "They are laid desolate, they are given us to devour." **13** And you magnified yourselves against me with your mouth, and multiplied your words against me; I heard it. **14** Thus

a Gk OL: Heb *pasture, you are people*   *b* Gk: Heb *them*

34:23 *David*—A descendant of David who will restore the monarchy (37:22–25; Jer. 23:4–6).

34:25 *Covenant of peace*—In Hos. 2:18 a covenant is made *with* the animals (see also Ezek. 37:26). Ezekiel's image is less ecologically inclusive: *wild animals* must be banished in order to protect domestic livestock.

34:26–30 *Showers of blessing*—The well-being of the land is both sign and result of YHWH's covenant blessing (as in Lev. 26:4–12).

35:1–15 Judgment against Mount Seir

35:2 *Mount Seir*—A plateau in the Edomite heartland, here representing the nation of Edom.

35:10 *Two nations*—Israel and Judah.

says the Lord God: As the whole earth rejoices, I will make you desolate. ¹⁵ As you rejoiced over the inheritance of the house of Israel, because it was desolate, so I will deal with you; you shall be desolate, Mount Seir, and all Edom, all of it. Then they shall know that I am the Lord.

Blessing on Israel

36 And you, mortal, prophesy to the mountains of Israel, and say: O mountains of Israel, hear the word of the Lord. ² Thus says the Lord God: Because the enemy said of you, "Aha!" and, "The ancient heights have become our possession," ³ therefore prophesy, and say: Thus says the Lord God: Because they made you desolate indeed, and crushed you from all sides, so that you became the possession of the rest of the nations, and you became an object of gossip and slander among the people; ⁴ therefore, O mountains of Israel, hear the word of the Lord God: Thus says the Lord God to the mountains and the hills, the watercourses and the valleys, the desolate wastes and the deserted towns, which have become a source of plunder and an object of derision to the rest of the nations all around; ⁵ therefore thus says the Lord God: I am speaking in my hot jealousy against the rest of the nations, and against all Edom, who, with wholehearted joy and utter contempt, took my land as their possession, because of its pasture, to plunder it. ⁶ Therefore prophesy concerning the land of Israel, and say to the mountains and hills, to the watercourses and valleys, Thus says the Lord God: I am speaking in my jealous wrath, because you have suffered the insults of the nations; ⁷ therefore thus says the Lord God: I swear that the nations that are all around you shall themselves suffer insults.

8 But you, O mountains of Israel, shall shoot out your branches, and yield your fruit to my people Israel; for they shall soon come home. ⁹ See now, I am for you; I will turn to you, and you shall be tilled and sown; ¹⁰ and I will multiply your population, the whole house of Israel, all of it; the towns shall be inhabited and the waste places rebuilt; ¹¹ and I will multiply human beings and animals upon you. They shall increase and be fruitful; and I will cause you to be inhabited as in your former times, and will do more good to you than ever before. Then you shall know that I am the Lord. ¹² I will lead people upon you—my people Israel—and they shall possess you, and you shall be their inheritance. No longer shall you bereave them of children.

13 Thus says the Lord God: Because they say to you, "You devour people, and you bereave your nation of children," ¹⁴ therefore you shall no longer devour people and no longer bereave your nation of children, says the Lord God; ¹⁵ and no longer will I let you hear the insults of the nations, no longer shall you bear the disgrace of the peoples; and no longer shall you cause your nation to stumble, says the Lord God.

The Renewal of Israel

16 The word of the Lord came to me:

36:1–15 Hope for the Mountains of Israel

36:12–15 *Bereave them of children*—Probably a reference to the child sacrifice described in 16:21; 20:25–26; 23:37–39.

36:16–38 The Restoration of Israel

YHWH promises to bring the people back from exile and to make the desolate land *like the garden of Eden* (v. 35). God's promise, however, is always qualified by the insistence that Israel will not be restored for its own sake, but in order to vindicate YHWH's *holy name* (v. 22). The exile had made YHWH appear either unfaithful or impotent in the eyes of the nations, without control of land, people, or even a temple. As announced in 22:16, YHWH had chosen to be profaned, rather than allow Israel to go unpunished. Now, however, YHWH must address the image problem created by Israel's exile: *Wherever [Israel] came . . . it was said of them, "These are the people of the Lord, and yet they had to go out of his land"* (v. 20). YHWH will now act to restore the people, but only out of regard for the divine reputation among the nations. After this

¹⁷ Mortal, when the house of Israel lived on their own soil, they defiled it with their ways and their deeds; their conduct in my sight was like the uncleanness of a woman in her menstrual period. ¹⁸ So I poured out my wrath upon them for the blood that they had shed upon the land, and for the idols with which they had defiled it. ¹⁹ I scattered them among the nations, and they were dispersed through the countries; in accordance with their conduct and their deeds I judged them. ²⁰ But when they came to the nations, wherever they came, they profaned my holy name, in that it was said of them, "These are the people of the LORD, and yet they had to go out of his land." ²¹ But I had concern for my holy name, which the house of Israel had profaned among the nations to which they came.

22 Therefore say to the house of Israel, Thus says the Lord GOD: It is not for your sake, O house of Israel, that I am about to act, but for the sake of my holy name, which you have profaned among the nations to which you came. ²³ I will sanctify my great name, which has been profaned among the nations, and which you have profaned among them; and the nations shall know that I am the LORD, says the Lord GOD, when through you I display my holiness before their eyes. ²⁴ I will take you from the nations, and gather you from all the countries, and bring you into your own land. ²⁵ I will sprinkle clean water upon you, and you shall be clean from all your uncleannesses, and from all your idols I will cleanse you. ²⁶ A new heart I will give you, and a new spirit I will put within you; and I will remove from your body the heart of stone and give you a heart of flesh. ²⁷ I will put my spirit within you, and make you follow my statutes and be careful to observe my ordinances. ²⁸ Then you shall live in the land that I gave to your ancestors; and you shall be my people, and I will be your God. ²⁹ I will save you from all your uncleannesses, and I will summon the grain and make it abundant and lay no famine upon you. ³⁰ I will make the fruit of the tree and the produce of the field abundant, so that you may never again suffer the disgrace of famine among the nations. ³¹ Then you shall remember your evil ways, and your dealings that were not good; and you shall loathe yourselves for your iniquities and your abominable deeds. ³² It is not for your sake that I will act, says the Lord GOD; let that be known to you. Be ashamed and dismayed for your ways, O house of Israel.

33 Thus says the Lord GOD: On the day that I cleanse you from all your iniquities, I will cause the towns to be inhabited, and the waste places shall be

---

demonstration of power, **then they shall know** that YHWH is God (v. 38).

YHWH's lack of tenderness for the people, plus the apparent insecurity about reputation, may strike modern readers as unworthy of the creator, sustainer, and redeemer of the world. Every era and every culture, however, brings its own requirements for what a god must be and do in order fully to be God. Ancient doubts about a God who allowed people and temple to be destroyed were as compelling as modern questions about a God who allows devastating evil to persist. Ezekiel is intent on vindicating God's sovereignty. Thus YHWH repeatedly contends that Israel will experience divine rule, and the nations *will* acknowledge the name of YHWH.

36:17—*The uncleanness* of *menstrual* fluid is a common image in Ezekiel for the bloody city (7:19; 16:6–9; 22:1–16; 24:6–13). The use of menstruation as a symbol of human sinfulness depends on a worldview in which men and a male God (YHWH is unquestionably male in Ezekiel) define purity and holiness; women (and goddesses) are seen as inherently "other" and potentially threatening.

36:26–27 *Heart of flesh . . . my spirit*—As in 11:19, the people are so thoroughly corrupt that their old hearts cannot simply be corrected, but must be replaced. YHWH's promise to give them hearts capable of obedience is not, however, depicted as an act of grace. Rather, the reconstituted Israel will be *incapable* of *disobedience*. YHWH's primary concern is not to bless Israel, but to create a people worthy of the holy name.

rebuilt. ³⁴ The land that was desolate shall be tilled, instead of being the desolation that it was in the sight of all who passed by. ³⁵ And they will say, "This land that was desolate has become like the garden of Eden; and the waste and desolate and ruined towns are now inhabited and fortified." ³⁶ Then the nations that are left all around you shall know that I, the LORD, have rebuilt the ruined places, and replanted that which was desolate; I, the LORD, have spoken, and I will do it.

37 Thus says the Lord GOD: I will also let the house of Israel ask me to do this for them: to increase their population like a flock. ³⁸ Like the flock for sacrifices,ᵃ like the flock at Jerusalem during her appointed festivals, so shall the ruined towns be filled with flocks of people. Then they shall know that I am the LORD.

The Valley of Dry Bones

37 The hand of the LORD came upon me, and he brought me out by the spirit of the LORD and set me down in the middle of a valley; it was full of bones. ² He led me all around them; there were very many lying in the valley, and they were very dry. ³ He said to me, "Mortal, can these bones live?"

I answered, "O Lord GOD, you know." ⁴ Then he said to me, "Prophesy to these bones, and say to them: O dry bones, hear the word of the LORD. ⁵ Thus says the Lord GOD to these bones: I will cause breathᵇ to enter you, and you shall live. ⁶ I will lay sinews on you, and will cause flesh to come upon you, and cover you with skin, and put breathᵇ in you, and you shall live; and you shall know that I am the LORD."

7 So I prophesied as I had been commanded; and as I prophesied, suddenly there was a noise, a rattling, and the bones came together, bone to its bone. ⁸ I looked, and there were sinews on them, and flesh had come upon them, and skin had covered them; but there was no breath in them. ⁹ Then he said to me, "Prophesy to the breath, prophesy, mortal, and say to the breath:ᶜ Thus says the Lord GOD: Come from the four winds, O breath,ᶜ and breathe upon these slain, that they may live." ¹⁰ I prophesied as he commanded me, and the breath came into them, and they lived, and stood on their feet, a vast multitude.

11 Then he said to me, "Mortal, these bones are the whole house of Israel. They say, 'Our bones are dried up, and our hope is lost; we are cut off com-

ᵃ Heb flock of holy things   ᵇ Or spirit   ᶜ Or wind or spirit

---

36:35–36—Israel's regeneration will demonstrate YHWH's power in the sight of the nations, who had previously doubted it.

37:1–14 The Vision of the Dry Bones
As in his initial vision (3:22), Ezekiel is taken out to a valley. Now, however, the valley is filled with bones. The bones bring to mind the people killed in the destruction of Jerusalem, but they also symbolize the remaining, living people of Judah, who say, *"Our bones are dried up, and our hope is lost"* (v. 11). The people's fatalism has been a recurring theme in Ezekiel, from the Jerusalemites who cavalierly blame their ancestors for their suffering (18:2) to those who accept their guilt but will not accept responsibility for changing their actions (33:10).

37:3 *You know*—A deferentially ambiguous answer, which could mean either "You know they cannot live" or "You alone know the answer."

37:5—The entire prophecy plays on the He-

brew *ruach*, which can mean "wind," "breath," or "spirit." Ezekiel prophesies to the wind (or *breath*, or spirit; v. 9), the *breath* enters the Israelites' bodies (v. 10), and YHWH promises to bestow the *spirit* (v. 14; and see 36:27; 39:29). Similar wordplay on the Greek *pneuma* appears in John 3:1–10.

37:11–14—Ezekiel views the bones of the *slain* (v. 9) but his prophecy concerns, not the dead, but living exiles, who have given up hope. The devastated survivors are the ones whose *bones are dried up*, whose *hope is lost*, and who will be lifted out of their graves of despair. This extraordinarily beautiful passage has been taken in both Jewish and Christian traditions as a prophecy of the resurrection of the dead. While the original prophecy refers to the spiritual and emotional healing of the living, it is inevitable and even appropriate that this powerful image of life from death should later be understood as prefiguring the resurrection.

pletely.' ¹²Therefore prophesy, and say to them, Thus says the Lord God: I am going to open your graves, and bring you up from your graves, O my people; and I will bring you back to the land of Israel. ¹³And you shall know that I am the Lord, when I open your graves, and bring you up from your graves, O my people. ¹⁴I will put my spirit within you, and you shall live, and I will place you on your own soil; then you shall know that I, the Lord, have spoken and will act, says the Lord."

The Two Sticks

15 The word of the Lord came to me: ¹⁶Mortal, take a stick and write on it, "For Judah, and the Israelites associated with it"; then take another stick and write on it, "For Joseph (the stick of Ephraim) and all the house of Israel associated with it"; ¹⁷and join them together into one stick, so that they may become one in your hand. ¹⁸And when your people say to you, "Will you not show us what you mean by these?" ¹⁹say to them, Thus says the Lord God: I am about to take the stick of Joseph (which is in the hand of Ephraim) and the tribes of Israel associated with it; and I will put the stick of Judah upon it,ᵃ and make them one stick, in order that they may be one in my hand. ²⁰When the sticks on which you write are in your hand before their eyes, ²¹then say to them, Thus says the Lord God: I will take the people of Israel from the nations among which they have gone, and will gather them from every quarter, and bring them to their own land. ²²I will make them one nation in the land, on the mountains of Israel; and one king shall be king over them all. Never again shall they be two nations, and never again shall they be divided into two kingdoms. ²³They shall never again defile themselves with their idols and their detestable things, or with any of their transgressions. I will save them from all the apostasies into which they have fallen,ᵇ and will cleanse them. Then they shall be my people, and I will be their God.

24 My servant David shall be king over them; and they shall all have one shepherd. They shall follow my ordinances and be careful to observe my statutes. ²⁵They shall live in the land that I gave to my servant Jacob, in which your ancestors lived; they and their children and their children's children shall live there forever; and my servant David shall be their prince forever. ²⁶I will make a covenant of peace with them; it shall be an everlasting covenant with them; and I will blessᶜ them and multiply them, and will set my sanctuary among them forevermore. ²⁷My dwelling place shall be with them; and I will be their God, and they shall be my people. ²⁸Then the nations shall know that I the Lord sanctify Israel, when my sanctuary is among them forevermore.

Invasion by Gog

38 The word of the Lord came to me: ²Mortal, set your face

ᵃ Heb *I will put them upon it* ᵇ Another reading is *from all the settlements in which they have sinned* ᶜ Tg: Heb *give*

37:15–28 The Restoration of Israel and Judah
Despite the nearly 150 years since the northern kingdom's destruction, YHWH promises to reunite the two kingdoms under a Davidic monarch (see also 34:23–24). The restoration of a divinely supported monarchy is understood as a sign of YHWH's renewed covenant with and rulership over the land and people of Israel. The presence of YHWH's *sanctuary* (v. 26) is an outward manifestation of God's presence and favor (see also 43:7; Exod. 25:8).

38:1–39:29 Gog of Magog
Chapters 38–39 describe YHWH's victory over the ultimate enemy, paving the way for the reenthronement in chap. 43. The identity of *Gog* (mentioned also in Rev. 20:7–10) is a matter of uncertainty. The most likely candidate is Nebuchadrezzar, whose influence extended into the Anatolian regions of *Meshech and Tubal* (38:2). Living as a captive in Babylon, the prophet would not have risked criticizing the Babylonian monarch by name. Ezekiel, however, following the examples of Isaiah (10:5–19) and Jeremiah

toward Gog, of the land of Magog, the chief prince of Meshech and Tubal. Prophesy against him [3] and say: Thus says the Lord God: I am against you, O Gog, chief prince of Meshech and Tubal; [4] I will turn you around and put hooks into your jaws, and I will lead you out with all your army, horses and horsemen, all of them clothed in full armor, a great company, all of them with shield and buckler, wielding swords. [5] Persia, Ethiopia,[a] and Put are with them, all of them with buckler and helmet; [6] Gomer and all its troops; Beth-togarmah from the remotest parts of the north with all its troops—many peoples are with you.

7 Be ready and keep ready, you and all the companies that are assembled around you, and hold yourselves in reserve for them. [8] After many days you shall be mustered; in the latter years you shall go against a land restored from war, a land where people were gathered from many nations on the mountains of Israel, which had long lain waste; its people were brought out from the nations and now are living in safety, all of them. [9] You shall advance, coming on like a storm; you shall be like a cloud covering the land, you and all your troops, and many peoples with you.

10 Thus says the Lord God: On that day thoughts will come into your mind, and you will devise an evil scheme. [11] You will say, "I will go up against the land of unwalled villages; I will fall upon the quiet people who live in safety, all of them living without walls, and having no bars or gates"; [12] to seize spoil and carry off plunder; to assail the waste places that are now inhabited, and the people who were gathered from the nations, who are acquiring cattle and goods, who live at the center[b] of the earth. [13] Sheba

and Dedan and the merchants of Tarshish and all its young warriors[c] will say to you, "Have you come to seize spoil? Have you assembled your horde to carry off plunder, to carry away silver and gold, to take away cattle and goods, to seize a great amount of booty?"

14 Therefore, mortal, prophesy, and say to Gog: Thus says the Lord God: On that day when my people Israel are living securely, you will rouse yourself[d] [15] and come from your place out of the remotest parts of the north, you and many peoples with you, all of them riding on horses, a great horde, a mighty army; [16] you will come up against my people Israel, like a cloud covering the earth. In the latter days I will bring you against my land, so that the nations may know me, when through you, O Gog, I display my holiness before their eyes.

Judgment on Gog

17 Thus says the Lord God: Are you he of whom I spoke in former days by my servants the prophets of Israel, who in those days prophesied for years that I would bring you against them? [18] On that day, when Gog comes against the land of Israel, says the Lord God, my wrath shall be aroused. [19] For in my jealousy and in my blazing wrath I declare: On that day there shall be a great shaking in the land of Israel; [20] the fish of the sea, and the birds of the air, and the animals of the field, and all creeping things that creep on the ground, and all human beings that are on the face of the earth, shall quake at my presence, and the mountains shall be thrown down, and the cliffs shall fall, and every wall shall tumble to the ground. [21] I will summon the sword against Gog[e] in[f] all my moun-

---

[a] Or Nubia; Heb Cush   [b] Heb navel   [c] Heb young lions   [d] Gk: Heb will you not know?   [e] Heb him   [f] Heb to or for

---

(30:25), announces that the foreign king who has served as a tool in YHWH's hand must ultimately fall before the sovereign God. Like the pharaoh in the exodus narrative (Exod. 4:21–23), Gog is enticed to attack Israel (Ezek. 38:16), in order to allow YHWH to demonstrate superior power.

With Gog's defeat, both Israel and the nations will **know that I am the Lord** (39:21–23; cf. Exod. 14:4). The rather harsh depiction of YHWH receiving glory by destroying enemy warriors is tempered here by God's final act of pouring out the divine spirit upon the people (Ezek. 39:29).

tains, says the Lord God; the swords of all will be against their comrades. ²² With pestilence and bloodshed I will enter into judgment with him; and I will pour down torrential rains and hailstones, fire and sulfur, upon him and his troops and the many peoples that are with him. ²³ So I will display my greatness and my holiness and make myself known in the eyes of many nations. Then they shall know that I am the Lord.

Gog's Armies Destroyed

39 And you, mortal, prophesy against Gog, and say: Thus says the Lord God: I am against you, O Gog, chief prince of Meshech and Tubal! ² I will turn you around and drive you forward, and bring you up from the remotest parts of the north, and lead you against the mountains of Israel. ³ I will strike your bow from your left hand, and will make your arrows drop out of your right hand. ⁴ You shall fall on the mountains of Israel, you and all your troops and the peoples that are with you; I will give you to birds of prey of every kind and to the wild animals to be devoured. ⁵ You shall fall in the open field; for I have spoken, says the Lord God. ⁶ I will send fire on Magog and on those who live securely in the coastlands; and they shall know that I am the Lord.

7 My holy name I will make known among my people Israel; and I will not let my holy name be profaned any more; and the nations shall know that I am the Lord, the Holy One in Israel. ⁸ It has come! It has happened, says the Lord God. This is the day of which I have spoken.

9 Then those who live in the towns of Israel will go out and make fires of the weapons and burn them—bucklers and shields, bows and arrows, handpikes and spears—and they will make fires of them for seven years. ¹⁰ They will not need to take wood out of the field or cut down any trees in the forests, for they will make their fires of the weapons; they will despoil those who despoiled them, and plunder those who plundered them, says the Lord God.

The Burial of Gog

11 On that day I will give to Gog a place for burial in Israel, the Valley of the Travelersᵃ east of the sea; it shall block the path of the travelers, for there Gog and all his horde will be buried; it shall be called the Valley of Hamon-gog.ᵇ ¹² Seven months the house of Israel shall spend burying them, in order to cleanse the land. ¹³ All the people of the land shall bury them; and it will bring them honor on the day that I show my glory, says the Lord God. ¹⁴ They will set apart men to pass through the land regularly and bury any invadersᶜ who remain on the face of the land, so as to cleanse it; for seven months they shall make their search. ¹⁵ As the searchersᶜ pass through the land, anyone who sees a human bone shall set up a sign by it, until the buriers have buried it in the Valley of Hamon-gog.ᵇ ¹⁶ (A city Hamonahᵈ is there also.) Thus they shall cleanse the land.

17 As for you, mortal, thus says the Lord God: Speak to the birds of every kind and to all the wild animals: Assemble and come, gather from all around to the sacrificial feast that I am preparing

---

ᵃ Or of the Abarim   ᵇ That is, the Horde of Gog   ᶜ Heb travelers   ᵈ That is The Horde

---

39:7 *My holy name*—YHWH will put a decisive end to Israel's defilement of the divine holiness, but also to the defamation YHWH has caused by allowing the elect people to be taken into exile (see note at 36:16–38).

39:9–10 *Seven years*—The time required to burn the weapons emphasizes the power of the defeated enemy. The prophet also notes that because the enemy's weapons will be "recycled"

as firewood, Israel's trees will enjoy an extended Sabbath in which they are spared from the ax (see also Lev. 19:23–25).

39:15–16 *The Valley of Hamon-gog*—Probably a pun on the Valley of Hinnom, south of Jerusalem, a site of child sacrifice (2 Chr. 28:3; Jer. 7:31). The city called *Hamonah*, "tumultuous," is probably Jerusalem (see 5:7).

for you, a great sacrificial feast on the mountains of Israel, and you shall eat flesh and drink blood. [18] You shall eat the flesh of the mighty, and drink the blood of the princes of the earth—of rams, of lambs, and of goats, of bulls, all of them fatlings of Bashan. [19] You shall eat fat until you are filled, and drink blood until you are drunk, at the sacrificial feast that I am preparing for you. [20] And you shall be filled at my table with horses and charioteers,[a] with warriors and all kinds of soldiers, says the Lord GOD.

Israel Restored to the Land

21 I will display my glory among the nations; and all the nations shall see my judgment that I have executed, and my hand that I have laid on them. [22] The house of Israel shall know that I am the LORD their God, from that day forward. [23] And the nations shall know that the house of Israel went into captivity for their iniquity, because they dealt treacherously with me. So I hid my face from them and gave them into the hand of their adversaries, and they all fell by the sword. [24] I dealt with them according to their uncleanness and their transgressions, and hid my face from them.

25 Therefore thus says the Lord GOD: Now I will restore the fortunes of Jacob, and have mercy on the whole house of Israel; and I will be jealous for my holy name. [26] They shall forget[b] their shame, and all the treachery they have practiced against me, when they live securely in their land with no one to make them afraid, [27] when I have brought them back from the peoples and gathered them from their enemies' lands, and through them have displayed my holiness in the sight of many nations. [28] Then they shall know that I am the LORD their God because I sent them into exile among the nations, and then gathered them into their own land. I will leave none of them behind; [29] and I will never again hide my face from them, when I pour out my spirit upon the house of Israel, says the Lord GOD.

The Vision of the New Temple

40 In the twenty-fifth year of our exile, at the beginning of the year, on the tenth day of the month, in the

---

a Heb *chariots*   b Another reading is *They shall bear*

39:26—Throughout Ezekiel, Judah experiences shame, not before, but *after* being forgiven by YHWH (6:9; 16:63; 20:41–43; 36:29–31). Israel's newly found capacity for shame seems to be a function of their new and morally responsive heart (36:26).

39:29 *Pour out my spirit*—The image appears frequently in postexilic literature (Isa. 44:3; Joel 2:28–29; Zech. 12:10), as well as in the New Testament. The people's obedience is a direct result of YHWH's indwelling spirit.

40:1–48:35 The New Temple
Ezekiel's final vision reveals the future temple, from which YHWH will reign eternally (see Rev. 21). The temple is idealized, but it is not celestial, that is, existing only in a heavenly realm. This new temple is to be located next to the holy city, staffed by Levitical priests, and visited by the Israelite people and their prince. Just as Ezekiel in chaps. 8–11 witnessed the corruption of the old temple, here he is called upon to witness the perfection of the new. The visionary tour constantly emphasizes the purity of the new sanctuary, as well as the obedience of the people. While

modern readers may not be especially moved by images of good, thick walls and well-built altars, the vision touches the very heart of Israelite identity. The combination of holy space and holy people is the requisite condition for God to dwell in the midst of Israel. The image hearkens back to the traditions of the wilderness tabernacle, where YHWH first chose to make a home among the Israelites. The vision is thus not primarily a promise of a new temple, but the assurance of a renewed covenant, an outward sign of God's presence on earth. This is the temple from which YHWH will reign eternally, never again to reject God's people Israel.

40:1–47 The Temple Area
40:1 *The twenty-fifth year*—Either April or October 573. The vision of YHWH's enthronement and the land's restoration takes place at the beginning of a jubilee year, as indicated by the dating of the new year from the tenth day of the month (Lev. 25:9–10), rather than the first. The dating at the jubilee adds to the sense that the vision represents the fullest possible experience of life under God's blessing.

fourteenth year after the city was struck down, on that very day, the hand of the LORD was upon me, and he brought me there. ²He brought me, in visions of God, to the land of Israel, and set me down upon a very high mountain, on which was a structure like a city to the south. ³When he brought me there, a man was there, whose appearance shone like bronze, with a linen cord and a measuring reed in his hand; and he was standing in the gateway. ⁴The man said to me, "Mortal, look closely and listen attentively, and set your mind upon all that I shall show you, for you were brought here in order that I might show it to you; declare all that you see to the house of Israel."

5 Now there was a wall all around the outside of the temple area. The length of the measuring reed in the man's hand was six long cubits, each being a cubit and a handbreadth in length; so he measured the thickness of the wall, one reed; and the height, one reed. ⁶Then he went into the gateway facing east, going up its steps, and measured the threshold of the gate, one reed deep.ᵃ There were ⁷recesses, and each recess was one reed wide and one reed deep; and the space between the recesses, five cubits; and the threshold of the gate by the vestibule of the gate at the inner end was one reed deep. ⁸Then he measured the inner vestibule of the gateway, one cubit. ⁹Then he measured the vestibule of the gateway, eight cubits; and its pilasters, two cubits; and the vestibule of the gate was at the inner end. ¹⁰There were three recesses on either side of the east gate; the three were of the same size; and the pilasters on either side were of the same size. ¹¹Then he measured the width of the opening of the gateway, ten cubits;

and the width of the gateway, thirteen cubits. ¹²There was a barrier before the recesses, one cubit on either side; and the recesses were six cubits on either side. ¹³Then he measured the gate from the backᵇ of the one recess to the backᵇ of the other, a width of twenty-five cubits, from wall to wall.ᶜ ¹⁴He measuredᵈ also the vestibule, twenty cubits; and the gate next to the pilaster on every side of the court.ᵉ ¹⁵From the front of the gate at the entrance to the end of the inner vestibule of the gate was fifty cubits. ¹⁶The recesses and their pilasters had windows, with shuttersᵉ on the inside of the gateway all around, and the vestibules also had windows on the inside all around; and on the pilasters were palm trees.

17 Then he brought me into the outer court; there were chambers there, and a pavement, all around the court; thirty chambers fronted on the pavement. ¹⁸The pavement ran along the side of the gates, corresponding to the length of the gates; this was the lower pavement. ¹⁹Then he measured the distance from the inner front ofᶠ the lower gate to the outer front of the inner court, one hundred cubits.ᵍ

20 Then he measured the gate of the outer court that faced north—its depth and width. ²¹Its recesses, three on either side, and its pilasters and its vestibule were of the same size as those of the first gate; its depth was fifty cubits, and its width twenty-five cubits. ²²Its windows, its vestibule, and its palm trees were of the same size as those of the gate that faced toward the east. Seven steps led up to it; and its vestibule was on the inside.ʰ

ᵃ Heb deep, and one threshold, one reed deep   ᵇ Gk: Heb roof   ᶜ Heb opening facing opening   ᵈ Heb made   ᵉ Meaning of Heb uncertain   ᶠ Compare Gk: Heb from before   ᵍ Heb adds the east and the north   ʰ Gk: Heb before them

---

40:2—Fulfilling the prophecies of Isa. 2:2 and Mic. 4:1 (and see 17:22; 20:40), the mountain of YHWH is transformed and lifted up into a high peak.

40:5—The *long cubit* is estimated at 20.5 inches. The measuring rod is thus approximately 10′4″.

40:6–16 *Gateway facing east*—Ezekiel's tour will move successively inward (as in chap. 8), to areas of increasing holiness.

23 Opposite the gate on the north, as on the east, was a gate to the inner court; he measured from gate to gate, one hundred cubits.

24 Then he led me toward the south, and there was a gate on the south; and he measured its pilasters and its vestibule; they had the same dimensions as the others. 25 There were windows all around in it and in its vestibule, like the windows of the others; its depth was fifty cubits, and its width twenty-five cubits. 26 There were seven steps leading up to it; its vestibule was on the inside.*a* It had palm trees on its pilasters, one on either side. 27 There was a gate on the south of the inner court; and he measured from gate to gate toward the south, one hundred cubits.

28 Then he brought me to the inner court by the south gate, and he measured the south gate; it was of the same dimensions as the others. 29 Its recesses, its pilasters, and its vestibule were of the same size as the others; and there were windows all around in it and in its vestibule; its depth was fifty cubits, and its width twenty-five cubits. 30 There were vestibules all around, twenty-five cubits deep and five cubits wide. 31 Its vestibule faced the outer court, and palm trees were on its pilasters, and its stairway had eight steps.

32 Then he brought me to the inner court on the east side, and he measured the gate; it was of the same size as the others. 33 Its recesses, its pilasters, and its vestibule were of the same dimensions as the others; and there were windows all around in it and in its vestibule; its depth was fifty cubits, and its width twenty-five cubits. 34 Its vestibule faced the outer court, and it had palm trees on its pilasters, on either side; and its stairway had eight steps.

35 Then he brought me to the north gate, and he measured it; it had the same dimensions as the others. 36 Its recesses, its pilasters, and its vestibule were of the same size as the others;*b* and it had

windows all around. Its depth was fifty cubits, and its width twenty-five cubits. 37 Its vestibule*c* faced the outer court, and it had palm trees on its pilasters, on either side; and its stairway had eight steps.

38 There was a chamber with its door in the vestibule of the gate,*d* where the burnt offering was to be washed. 39 And in the vestibule of the gate were two tables on either side, on which the burnt offering and the sin offering and the guilt offering were to be slaughtered. 40 On the outside of the vestibule*e* at the entrance of the north gate were two tables; and on the other side of the vestibule of the gate were two tables. 41 Four tables were on the inside, and four tables on the outside of the side of the gate, eight tables, on which the sacrifices were to be slaughtered. 42 There were also four tables of hewn stone for the burnt offering, a cubit and a half long, and one cubit and a half wide, and one cubit high, on which the instruments were to be laid with which the burnt offerings and the sacrifices were slaughtered. 43 There were pegs, one handbreadth long, fastened all around the inside. And on the tables the flesh of the offering was to be laid.

44 On the outside of the inner gateway there were chambers for the singers in the inner court, one*f* at the side of the north gate facing south, the other at the side of the east gate facing north. 45 He said to me, "This chamber that faces south is for the priests who have charge of the temple, 46 and the chamber that faces north is for the priests who have charge of the altar; these are the descendants of Zadok, who alone among the descendants of Levi may come near to the LORD to minister to him." 47 He measured the court, one hundred cubits deep, and one hundred cubits wide, a square; and the altar was in front of the temple.

a Gk: Heb *before them* *b* One Ms: Compare verses 29 and 33: MT lacks *were of the same size as the others* *c* Gk Vg Compare verses 26, 31, 34: Heb *pilasters* *d* Cn: Heb *at the pilasters of the gates* *e* Cn: Heb *to him who goes up* *f* Heb lacks *one*

The Temple

48 Then he brought me to the vestibule of the temple and measured the pilasters of the vestibule, five cubits on either side; and the width of the gate was fourteen cubits; and the sidewalls of the gate were three cubits[a] on either side. 49 The depth of the vestibule was twenty cubits, and the width twelve[b] cubits; ten steps led up[c] to it; and there were pillars beside the pilasters on either side.

41 Then he brought me to the nave, and measured the pilasters; on each side six cubits was the width of the pilasters.[d] 2 The width of the entrance was ten cubits; and the sidewalls of the entrance were five cubits on either side. He measured the length of the nave, forty cubits, and its width, twenty cubits. 3 Then he went into the inner room and measured the pilasters of the entrance, two cubits; and the width of the entrance, six cubits; and the sidewalls[e] of the entrance, seven cubits. 4 He measured the depth of the room, twenty cubits, and its width, twenty cubits, beyond the nave. And he said to me, This is the most holy place.

5 Then he measured the wall of the temple, six cubits thick; and the width of the side chambers, four cubits, all around the temple. 6 The side chambers were in three stories, one over another, thirty in each story. There were offsets[f] all around the wall of the temple to serve as supports for the side chambers, so that they should not be supported by the wall of the temple. 7 The passageway[g] of the side chambers widened from story to story; for the structure was supplied with a stairway all around the temple. For this reason the structure became wider from story to story. One ascended from the bottom story to the uppermost story by way of the middle one. 8 I saw also that the temple had a raised platform all around; the foundations of the side chambers measured a full reed of six long cubits. 9 The thickness of the outer wall of the side chambers was five cubits; and the free space between the side chambers of the temple 10 and the chambers of the court was a width of twenty cubits all around the temple on every side. 11 The side chambers opened onto the area left free, one door toward the north, and another door toward the south; and the width of the part that was left free was five cubits all around.

12 The building that was facing the temple yard on the west side was seventy cubits wide; and the wall of the building was five cubits thick all around, and its depth ninety cubits.

13 Then he measured the temple, one hundred cubits deep; and the yard and the building with its walls, one hundred cubits deep; 14 also the width of the east front of the temple and the yard, one hundred cubits.

15 Then he measured the depth of the building facing the yard at the west, together with its galleries[h] on either side, one hundred cubits.

The nave of the temple and the inner room and the outer[i] vestibule 16 were paneled,[j] and, all around, all three had windows with recessed[k] frames. Facing the threshold the temple was paneled with wood all around, from the floor up to the windows (now the windows were covered), 17 to the space above the door, even to the inner room, and on the

[a] Gk: Heb *and the width of the gate was three cubits* [b] Gk: Heb *eleven* [c] Gk: Heb *and by steps that went up* [d] Compare Gk: Heb *tent* [e] Gk: Heb *width* [f] Gk Compare 1 Kings 6.6: Heb *they entered* [g] Cn: Heb *it was surrounded* [h] Cn: Meaning of Heb uncertain [i] Gk: Heb *of the court* [j] Gk: Heb *the thresholds* [k] Cn Compare Gk 1 Kings 6.4: Meaning of Heb uncertain

---

40:48–42:20 The Temple
The temple building is located, like the first temple, inside a large courtyard containing both an altar and facilities for preparing and storing sacrifices. The temple building consists of a vestibule (34′ × 20′), a central room (the nave; 34′ × 68′), and the Holy of Holies, or inner sanctum (34′ × 34′). Like Solomon's temple (1 Kgs. 6:15–30), Ezekiel's is decorated with palm trees, cherubim, and wood paneling. The decorative cherubim are, of course, separate from the living "throne bearers" described in 1:4–28; 10:1–14.

outside. And on all the walls all around in the inner room and the nave there was a pattern.*a* **18** It was formed of cherubim and palm trees, a palm tree between cherub and cherub. Each cherub had two faces: **19** a human face turned toward the palm tree on the one side, and the face of a young lion turned toward the palm tree on the other side. They were carved on the whole temple all around; **20** from the floor to the area above the door, cherubim and palm trees were carved on the wall.*b*

21 The doorposts of the nave were square. In front of the holy place was something resembling **22** an altar of wood, three cubits high, two cubits long, and two cubits wide;*c* its corners, its base,*d* and its walls were of wood. He said to me, "This is the table that stands before the LORD." **23** The nave and the holy place had each a double door. **24** The doors had two leaves apiece, two swinging leaves for each door. **25** On the doors of the nave were carved cherubim and palm trees, such as were carved on the walls; and there was a canopy of wood in front of the vestibule outside. **26** And there were recessed windows and palm trees on either side, on the sidewalls of the vestibule.*e*

The Holy Chambers and the Outer Wall

42 Then he led me out into the outer court, toward the north, and he brought me to the chambers that were opposite the temple yard and opposite the building on the north. **2** The length of the building that was on the north side*f* was*g* one hundred cubits, and the width fifty cubits. **3** Across the twenty cubits that belonged to the inner court, and facing the pavement that belonged to the outer court, the chambers rose*h* gallery*i* by gallery*i* in three stories. **4** In front of the chambers was a passage on the inner side, ten cubits wide and one hundred cubits deep,*j* and its*k* entrances were on the north. **5** Now the upper chambers were narrower, for the galleries*i* took more away from them than from the lower and middle chambers in the building. **6** For they were in three stories, and they had no pillars like the pillars of the outer*l* court; for this reason the upper chambers were set back from the ground more than the lower and the middle ones. **7** There was a wall outside parallel to the chambers, toward the outer court, opposite the chambers, fifty cubits long. **8** For the chambers on the outer court were fifty cubits long, while those opposite the temple were one hundred cubits long. **9** At the foot of these chambers ran a passage that one entered from the east in order to enter them from the outer court. **10** The width of the passage*m* was fixed by the wall of the court.

On the south*n* also, opposite the vacant area and opposite the building, there were chambers **11** with a passage in front of them; they were similar to the chambers on the north, of the same length and width, with the same exits*o* and arrangements and doors. **12** So the entrances of the chambers to the south were entered through the entrance at the head of the corresponding passage, from the east, along the matching wall.*i*

13 Then he said to me, "The north chambers and the south chambers opposite the vacant area are the holy chambers, where the priests who approach the LORD shall eat the most holy offerings; there they shall deposit the most holy offerings—the grain offering, the sin offering, and the guilt offering—for the place is holy. **14** When the priests enter the holy place, they shall not go out of it into the outer court without laying there the vestments in which they minister, for these are holy; they shall put on

---

a Heb measures   *b* Cn Compare verse 25: Heb and the wall   *c* Gk: Heb lacks two cubits wide   *d* Gk: Heb length   *e* Cn: Heb vestibule. And the side chambers of the temple and the canopies   *f* Gk: Heb door   *g* Gk: Heb before the length   *h* Heb lacks the chambers rose   *i* Meaning of Heb uncertain   *j* Gk Syr: Heb a way of one cubit   *k* Heb their   *l* Heb lacks outer   *m* Heb lacks of the passage   *n* Gk: Heb east   *o* Heb and all their exits

other garments before they go near to the area open to the people."

15 When he had finished measuring the interior of the temple area, he led me out by the gate that faces east, and measured the temple area all around. 16 He measured the east side with the measuring reed, five hundred cubits by the measuring reed. 17 Then he turned and measured[a] the north side, five hundred cubits by the measuring reed. 18 Then he turned and measured[a] the south side, five hundred cubits by the measuring reed. 19 Then he turned to the west side and measured, five hundred cubits by the measuring reed. 20 He measured it on the four sides. It had a wall around it, five hundred cubits long and five hundred cubits wide, to make a separation between the holy and the common.

The Divine Glory Returns to the Temple

43 Then he brought me to the gate, the gate facing east. 2 And there, the glory of the God of Israel was coming from the east; the sound was like the sound of mighty waters; and the earth shone with his glory. 3 The[b] vision I saw was like the vision that I had seen when he came to destroy the city, and[c] like the vision that I had seen by the river Chebar; and I fell upon my face. 4 As the glory of the LORD entered the temple by the gate facing east, 5 the spirit lifted me up, and brought me into the inner court; and the glory of the LORD filled the temple.

6 While the man was standing beside me, I heard someone speaking to me out of the temple. 7 He said to me: Mortal, this is the place of my throne and the place for the soles of my feet, where I will reside among the people of Israel forever. The house of Israel shall no more defile my holy name, neither they nor their kings, by their whoring, and by the corpses of their kings at their death.[d] 8 When they placed their threshold by my threshold and their doorposts beside my doorposts, with only a wall between me and them, they were defiling my holy name by their abominations that they committed; therefore I have consumed them in my anger. 9 Now let them put away their idolatry and the corpses of their kings far from me, and I will reside among them forever.

10 As for you, mortal, describe the temple to the house of Israel, and let them measure the pattern; and let them be ashamed of their iniquities. 11 When they are ashamed of all that they have done, make known to them the plan of the temple, its arrangement, its exits and its entrances, and its whole form—all its ordinances and its entire plan and all its laws; and write it down in their sight, so that they may observe and follow the entire plan and all its ordinances. 12 This is the law of the temple: the whole territory on the top of the mountain all

---

a Gk: Heb *measuring reed all around. He measured* *b* Gk: Heb *Like the vision* *c* Syr: Heb *and the visions* *d* Or *on their high places*

42:20 *To make a separation*—The physical barrier represents the distinction between the realm of *the holy* and the realm of the merely clean, or *common*, outside the wall (see note at 22:26; see also Lev. 10:10–11).

43:1–12 The Return of the Divine Chariot
Ezekiel looks on while the glory of YHWH returns as it left—entering through *the east* gate and on into *the temple*. Just as it did in the wilderness tabernacle (Exod. 40:34–35) and in the first temple (1 Kgs. 8:11), *the glory of the LORD* fills the temple, signifying God's presence. (Note a second account of this in 44:4.) The ark of the covenant is sometimes depicted as YHWH's throne (1 Sam. 4:4; Pss. 80:2; 99:1), and at other

times as God's footstool (1 Chr. 28:2; Ps. 99:5). Here YHWH calls the temple both *the place of my throne* and *the place for the soles of my feet* (v. 7). Having fully purified both the temple and the people, YHWH promises to *reside among [the people of Israel] forever* (43:7, 9).

43:7–8—YHWH condemns the minimal separation previously maintained between the temple and the palace complex. The exact nature of the *abominations* previously committed is unclear; perhaps they sinned by locating a burial ground adjacent to the temple complex or by venerating deceased rulers as gods.

43:12 *The law of the temple*—Lit. the *torah* of the temple: a new teaching governing a new era

around shall be most holy. This is the law of the temple.

The Altar

13 These are the dimensions of the altar by cubits (the cubit being one cubit and a handbreadth): its base shall be one cubit high,[a] and one cubit wide, with a rim of one span around its edge. This shall be the height of the altar: [14] From the base on the ground to the lower ledge, two cubits, with a width of one cubit; and from the smaller ledge to the larger ledge, four cubits, with a width of one cubit; [15] and the altar hearth, four cubits; and from the altar hearth projecting upward, four horns. [16] The altar hearth shall be square, twelve cubits long by twelve wide. [17] The ledge also shall be square, fourteen cubits long by fourteen wide, with a rim around it half a cubit wide, and its surrounding base, one cubit. Its steps shall face east.

18 Then he said to me: Mortal, thus says the Lord GOD: These are the ordinances for the altar: On the day when it is erected for offering burnt offerings upon it and for dashing blood against it, [19] you shall give to the levitical priests of the family of Zadok, who draw near to me to minister to me, says the Lord GOD, a bull for a sin offering. [20] And you shall take some of its blood, and put it on the four horns of the altar, and on the four corners of the ledge, and upon the rim all around; thus you shall purify it and make atonement for it. [21] You shall also take the bull of the sin offering, and it shall be burnt in the appointed place belonging to the temple, outside the sacred area.

22 On the second day you shall offer a male goat without blemish for a sin offering; and the altar shall be purified, as it was purified with the bull. [23] When you have finished purifying it, you shall offer a bull without blemish and a ram from the flock without blemish. [24] You shall present them before the LORD, and the priests shall throw salt on them and offer them up as a burnt offering to the LORD. [25] For seven days you shall provide daily a goat for a sin offering; also a bull and a ram from the flock, without blemish, shall be provided. [26] Seven days shall they make atonement for the altar and cleanse it, and so consecrate it. [27] When these days are over, then from the eighth day onward the priests shall offer upon the altar your burnt offerings and your offerings of well-being; and I will accept you, says the Lord GOD.

The Closed Gate

44 Then he brought me back to the outer gate of the sanctuary, which faces east; and it was shut. [2] The LORD said to me: This gate shall remain shut; it shall not be opened, and no one shall enter by it; for the LORD, the God of Israel, has entered by it; therefore it shall remain shut. [3] Only the prince, because he is a prince, may sit in it to eat food before the LORD; he shall enter by way of the vestibule of the gate, and shall go out by the same way.

Admission to the Temple

4 Then he brought me by way of the north gate to the front of the temple; and I looked, and lo! the glory of the LORD filled the temple of the LORD; and I fell upon my face. [5] The LORD said to

[a] Gk: Heb lacks high

of holiness, centered on YHWH's throneroom, the temple.

44:1–31 Admission to the Temple

44:2—The eastern gate, formerly a processional gateway (see note at 10:18–19), will be sealed, presumably as a sign of YHWH's promise never again to depart from the temple (43:7).

44:3—YHWH refers to Israel's future ruler as *prince*, not king (34:24; 37:25). YHWH alone will be king. The prince will be privileged to *eat before the LORD*, but may do so only in *the vestibule of the gate*, an area of lesser holiness than that used by the priests. While Ezekiel foresees the restoration of Davidic rulership as an element of God's new reign, here he downplays the role played by the earthly ruler in order to emphasize the complete sovereignty of God.

me: Mortal, mark well, look closely, and listen attentively to all that I shall tell you concerning all the ordinances of the temple of the Lord and all its laws; and mark well those who may be admitted to*a* the temple and all those who are to be excluded from the sanctuary. 6 Say to the rebellious house,*b* to the house of Israel, Thus says the Lord God: O house of Israel, let there be an end to all your abominations 7 in admitting foreigners, uncircumcised in heart and flesh, to be in my sanctuary, profaning my temple when you offer to me my food, the fat and the blood. You*c* have broken my covenant with all your abominations. 8 And you have not kept charge of my sacred offerings; but you have appointed foreigners*d* to act for you in keeping my charge in my sanctuary.

9 Thus says the Lord God: No foreigner, uncircumcised in heart and flesh, of all the foreigners who are among the people of Israel, shall enter my sanctuary. 10 But the Levites who went far from me, going astray from me after their idols when Israel went astray, shall bear their punishment. 11 They shall be ministers in my sanctuary, having oversight at the gates of the temple, and serving in the temple; they shall slaughter the burnt offering and the sacrifice for the people, and they shall attend on them and serve them. 12 Because they ministered to them before their idols and made the house of Israel stumble into iniquity, therefore I have sworn concerning them, says the Lord God, that they shall bear their punishment. 13 They shall not come near to me, to serve me as priest, nor come near any of my sacred offerings, the things that are most sacred; but they shall bear their shame, and the consequences of the abominations that they have committed. 14 Yet I will appoint them to keep charge of the temple, to do all its chores, all that is to be done in it.

The Levitical Priests

15 But the levitical priests, the descendants of Zadok, who kept the charge of my sanctuary when the people of Israel went astray from me, shall come near to me to minister to me; and they shall attend me to offer me the fat and the blood, says the Lord God. 16 It is they who shall enter my sanctuary, it is they who shall approach my table, to minister to me, and they shall keep my charge. 17 When they enter the gates of the inner court, they shall wear linen vestments; they shall have nothing of wool on them, while they minister at the gates of the inner court, and within. 18 They shall have linen turbans on their heads, and linen undergarments on their loins; they shall not bind themselves with anything that causes sweat. 19 When they go out into the outer court to the people, they shall remove the vestments in which they have been ministering, and lay them in the holy chambers; and they shall put on other garments, so that they may not communicate holiness to the people with their vestments. 20 They shall not shave their heads or let their locks grow long; they shall only trim the hair of their heads. 21 No priest shall drink wine when he enters the inner court. 22 They shall not marry a widow, or a divorced woman, but only a virgin of the stock of the house of Israel, or a widow who is the widow of a priest. 23 They shall teach my people the difference between the holy and the common, and show them how to distinguish

a Cn: Heb *the entrance of* *b* Gk: Heb lacks *house* *c* Gk Syr Vg: Heb *They* *d* Heb lacks *foreigners*

44:19—The condition of ritual holiness, like ritual defilement or pollution, was communicable. Care therefore needed to be taken not to allow unclean or defiled objects or persons to come into contact with objects or areas designated holy (see the fate of Uzzah in 2 Sam. 6:6–7).

44:22 *A widow*—Ezekiel's regulations are more liberal than those in Lev. 21:7, 13–14, which allow priests to marry only virgins of priestly lineage.

44:23—As in 22:26 (see note), Ezekiel emphasizes the central duty of the priesthood. The strict

between the unclean and the clean. ²⁴ In a controversy they shall act as judges, and they shall decide it according to my judgments. They shall keep my laws and my statutes regarding all my appointed festivals, and they shall keep my sabbaths holy. ²⁵ They shall not defile themselves by going near to a dead person; for father or mother, however, and for son or daughter, and for brother or unmarried sister they may defile themselves. ²⁶ After he has become clean, they shall count seven days for him. ²⁷ On the day that he goes into the holy place, into the inner court, to minister in the holy place, he shall offer his sin offering, says the Lord God.

28 This shall be their inheritance: I am their inheritance; and you shall give them no holding in Israel; I am their holding. ²⁹ They shall eat the grain offering, the sin offering, and the guilt offering; and every devoted thing in Israel shall be theirs. ³⁰ The first of all the first fruits of all kinds, and every offering of all kinds from all your offerings, shall belong to the priests; you shall also give to the priests the first of your dough, in order that a blessing may rest on your house. ³¹ The priests shall not eat of anything, whether bird or animal, that died of itself or was torn by animals.

The Holy District

45 When you allot the land as an inheritance, you shall set aside for the Lord a portion of the land as a holy district, twenty-five thousand cubits long and twenty*a* thousand cubits wide; it shall be holy throughout its entire extent. ² Of this, a square plot of five hundred by five hundred cubits shall be for the sanctuary, with fifty cubits for an open space around it. ³ In the holy district you shall measure off a section twenty-five thousand cubits long and ten thousand wide, in which shall be the sanctuary, the most holy place. ⁴ It shall be a holy portion of the land; it shall be for the priests, who minister in the sanctuary and approach the Lord to minister to him; and it shall be both a place for their houses and a holy place for the sanctuary. ⁵ Another section, twenty-five thousand cubits long and ten thousand cubits wide, shall be for the Levites who minister at the temple, as their holding for cities to live in.*b*

6 Alongside the portion set apart as the holy district you shall assign as a holding for the city an area five thousand cubits wide, and twenty-five thousand cubits long; it shall belong to the whole house of Israel.

7 And to the prince shall belong the land on both sides of the holy district and the holding of the city, alongside the holy district and the holding of the city, on the west and on the east, corresponding in length to one of the tribal portions, and extending from the western to the eastern boundary ⁸ of the land. It is to be his property in Israel. And my princes shall no longer oppress my people; but they shall let the house of Israel have the land according to their tribes.

9 Thus says the Lord God: Enough, O princes of Israel! Put away violence and oppression, and do what is just and right. Cease your evictions of my people, says the Lord God.

Weights and Measures

10 You shall have honest balances, an honest ephah, and an honest bath.*c* ¹¹ The

---

a Gk: Heb *ten*   *b* Gk: Heb *as their holding, twenty chambers*   *c* A Heb measure of volume

---

separation between holy and "clean" underscores the momentous significance of YHWH's presence among the people.

45:1–9 The Holy District (see also 48:8–14)

A sacred area of approximately fifty square miles is designated, with one half surrounding the temple complex and housing the priests and the other half housing the Levites. South of the holy district is the city, with royal holdings lying to the east and west of the square formed by the temple and city holdings.

45:10–46:24 Miscellaneous Regulations

45:10–12—*Mishpat* and *tsedaqah*, justice and

ephah and the bath shall be of the same measure, the bath containing one-tenth of a homer, and the ephah one-tenth of a homer; the homer shall be the standard measure. [12] The shekel shall be twenty gerahs. Twenty shekels, twenty-five shekels, and fifteen shekels shall make a mina for you.

Offerings

[13] This is the offering that you shall make: one-sixth of an ephah from each homer of wheat, and one-sixth of an ephah from each homer of barley, [14] and as the fixed portion of oil,[a] one-tenth of a bath from each cor (the cor,[b] like the homer, contains ten baths); [15] and one sheep from every flock of two hundred, from the pastures of Israel. This is the offering for grain offerings, burnt offerings, and offerings of well-being, to make atonement for them, says the Lord GOD. [16] All the people of the land shall join with the prince in Israel in making this offering. [17] But this shall be the obligation of the prince regarding the burnt offerings, grain offerings, and drink offerings, at the festivals, the new moons, and the sabbaths, all the appointed festivals of the house of Israel: he shall provide the sin offerings, grain offerings, the burnt offerings, and the offerings of well-being, to make atonement for the house of Israel.

Festivals

[18] Thus says the Lord GOD: In the first month, on the first day of the month, you shall take a young bull without blemish, and purify the sanctuary. [19] The priest shall take some of the blood of the sin offering and put it on the doorposts of the temple, the four corners of the ledge of the altar, and the posts of the gate of the inner court. [20] You shall do the same on the seventh day of the month for anyone who has sinned through error or ignorance; so you shall make atonement for the temple.

[21] In the first month, on the fourteenth day of the month, you shall celebrate the festival of the passover, and for seven days unleavened bread shall be eaten. [22] On that day the prince shall provide for himself and all the people of the land a young bull for a sin offering. [23] And during the seven days of the festival he shall provide as a burnt offering to the LORD seven young bulls and seven rams without blemish, on each of the seven days; and a male goat daily for a sin offering. [24] He shall provide as a grain offering an ephah for each bull, an ephah for each ram, and a hin of oil to each ephah. [25] In the seventh month, on the fifteenth day of the month and for the seven days of the festival, he shall make the same provision for sin offerings, burnt offerings, and grain offerings, and for the oil.

Miscellaneous Regulations

46 Thus says the Lord GOD: The gate of the inner court that faces east shall remain closed on the six working days; but on the sabbath day it shall be opened and on the day of the new moon it shall be opened. [2] The prince shall enter by the vestibule of the gate from outside, and shall take his stand by the post of the gate. The priests shall offer his burnt offering and his offerings of well-being, and he shall bow down at the threshold of the gate. Then he shall go out, but the gate shall not be closed until evening. [3] The people of the land shall bow down at the entrance of that gate before the LORD on the sabbaths and on the new moons. [4] The burnt offering that the prince offers to the LORD on the sabbath day shall be six lambs without blemish and a ram without blemish; [5] and the grain offering with the ram shall be an ephah, and the grain offering with the lambs shall be as much as he wishes to give,

---

[a] Cn: Heb oil, the bath the oil   [b] Vg: Heb homer

---

righteousness, were understood as the responsibility of the king throughout the Near East. Here

the core of the king's justice consists in ensuring honest dealings in land tenure and in commerce.

together with a hin of oil to each ephah. [6] On the day of the new moon he shall offer a young bull without blemish, and six lambs and a ram, which shall be without blemish; [7] as a grain offering he shall provide an ephah with the bull and an ephah with the ram, and with the lambs as much as he wishes, together with a hin of oil to each ephah. [8] When the prince enters, he shall come in by the vestibule of the gate, and he shall go out by the same way.

[9] When the people of the land come before the Lord at the appointed festivals, whoever enters by the north gate to worship shall go out by the south gate; and whoever enters by the south gate shall go out by the north gate: they shall not return by way of the gate by which they entered, but shall go out straight ahead. [10] When they come in, the prince shall come in with them; and when they go out, he shall go out.

[11] At the festivals and the appointed seasons the grain offering with a young bull shall be an ephah, and with a ram an ephah, and with the lambs as much as one wishes to give, together with a hin of oil to an ephah. [12] When the prince provides a freewill offering, either a burnt offering or offerings of well-being as a freewill offering to the Lord, the gate facing east shall be opened for him; and he shall offer his burnt offering or his offerings of well-being as he does on the sabbath day. Then he shall go out, and after he has gone out the gate shall be closed.

[13] He shall provide a lamb, a yearling, without blemish, for a burnt offering to the Lord daily; morning by morning he shall provide it. [14] And he shall provide a grain offering with it morning by morning regularly, one-sixth of an ephah, and one-third of a hin of oil to moisten the choice flour, as a grain offering to the Lord; this is the ordinance for all time.

[15] Thus the lamb and the grain offering and the oil shall be provided, morning by morning, as a regular burnt offering.

[16] Thus says the Lord God: If the prince makes a gift to any of his sons out of his inheritance,[a] it shall belong to his sons, it is their holding by inheritance. [17] But if he makes a gift out of his inheritance to one of his servants, it shall be his to the year of liberty; then it shall revert to the prince; only his sons may keep a gift from his inheritance. [18] The prince shall not take any of the inheritance of the people, thrusting them out of their holding; he shall give his sons their inheritance out of his own holding, so that none of my people shall be dispossessed of their holding.

[19] Then he brought me through the entrance, which was at the side of the gate, to the north row of the holy chambers for the priests; and there I saw a place at the extreme western end of them. [20] He said to me, "This is the place where the priests shall boil the guilt offering and the sin offering, and where they shall bake the grain offering, in order not to bring them out into the outer court and so communicate holiness to the people."

[21] Then he brought me out to the outer court, and led me past the four corners of the court; and in each corner of the court there was a court— [22] in the four corners of the court were small[b] courts, forty cubits long and thirty wide; the four were of the same size. [23] On the inside, around each of the four courts[c] was a row of masonry, with hearths made at the bottom of the rows all around. [24] Then he said to me, "These are the kitchens where those who serve at the temple shall boil the sacrifices of the people."

[a] Gk: Heb *it is his inheritance*   [b] Gk Syr Vg: Meaning of Heb uncertain
[c] Heb *the four of them*

46:17 The year of liberty—The jubilee year (see Lev. 25). The royal district must always revert to royal possession. By the same token, however, the royal family may not expropriate the family holdings of the people.

Water Flowing from the Temple

47 Then he brought me back to the entrance of the temple; there, water was flowing from below the threshold of the temple toward the east (for the temple faced east); and the water was flowing down from below the south end of the threshold of the temple, south of the altar. ² Then he brought me out by way of the north gate, and led me around on the outside to the outer gate that faces toward the east;*a* and the water was coming out on the south side.

3 Going on eastward with a cord in his hand, the man measured one thousand cubits, and then led me through the water; and it was ankle-deep. ⁴ Again he measured one thousand, and led me through the water; and it was knee-deep. Again he measured one thousand, and led me through the water; and it was up to the waist. ⁵ Again he measured one thousand, and it was a river that I could not cross, for the water had risen; it was deep enough to swim in, a river that could not be crossed. ⁶ He said to me, "Mortal, have you seen this?"

Then he led me back along the bank of the river. ⁷ As I came back, I saw on the bank of the river a great many trees on the one side and on the other. ⁸ He said to me, "This water flows toward the eastern region and goes down into the Arabah; and when it enters the sea, the sea of stagnant waters, the water will become fresh. ⁹ Wherever the river goes,*b* every living creature that swarms will live, and there will be very many fish, once these waters reach there. It will become fresh; and everything will live where the river goes. ¹⁰ People will stand fishing beside the sea*c* from En-gedi to En-eglaim; it will be a place for the spreading of nets; its fish will be of a great many kinds, like the fish of the Great Sea. ¹¹ But its swamps and marshes will not become fresh; they are to be left for salt. ¹² On the banks, on both sides of the river, there will grow all kinds of trees for food. Their leaves will not wither nor their fruit fail, but they will bear fresh fruit every month, because the water for them flows from the sanctuary. Their fruit will be for food, and their leaves for healing."

The New Boundaries of the Land

13 Thus says the Lord GOD: These are the boundaries by which you shall divide the land for inheritance among the twelve tribes of Israel. Joseph shall have two portions. ¹⁴ You shall divide it equally; I swore to give it to your ancestors, and this land shall fall to you as your inheritance.

15 This shall be the boundary of the

a Meaning of Heb uncertain   *b* Gk Syr Vg Tg: Heb *the two rivers go*
c Heb *it*

47:1–12 The Life-Giving River
The motif of streams flowing outward from a mountaintop temple was widespread in ancient Near Eastern texts and art. The streams symbolize the life-giving power of the god, and the importance of the temple to the welfare of the land and people. Various biblical texts describe YHWH as "enthroned above the waters" (Ps. 29:3, 10), or refer to a stream that flows from God's temple, garden, or city (Joel 3:17–18; Zech. 14:8–11; Gen. 2:10–14; Ps. 46:4). The image also appears in the book of Revelation (22:1–2). The presence of YHWH is affirmed here as healing, renewing, and supporting the vitality of the natural world.

47:8 The Arabah—Here the Jordan Valley north of the Dead Sea. **Fresh**—The Hebrew word is "healed" (see also 2 Kgs. 2:19–22); the Dead Sea has become a freshwater lake.

47:10 The Great Sea—The Mediterranean.

47:11 Left for salt—Ezekiel's "ecological" vision of earth's renewal includes provision for human needs. While the Dead Sea will be miraculously "healed," its salt marshes will be left to allow for the production of salt.

47:13–48:35 Boundaries and Division of the Land

47:13 Twelve tribes—Ezekiel takes the restoration of the northern tribes for granted (see 37:15–28). Contrary to the boundaries specified in Josh. 13–19, the tribal allotments are now to be of equal size. The precise location of each holding cannot be determined, but the territory as a whole corresponds roughly to the maximum area claimed for Israel in the Bible (1 Kgs. 4:21; 2 Kgs. 14:25).

land: On the north side, from the Great Sea by way of Hethlon to Lebo-hamath, and on to Zedad,[a] [16]Berothah, Sibraim (which lies between the border of Damascus and the border of Hamath), as far as Hazer-hatticon, which is on the border of Hauran. [17]So the boundary shall run from the sea to Hazer-enon, which is north of the border of Damascus, with the border of Hamath to the north.[b] This shall be the north side.

[18]On the east side, between Hauran and Damascus; along the Jordan between Gilead and the land of Israel; to the eastern sea and as far as Tamar.[c] This shall be the east side.

[19]On the south side, it shall run from Tamar as far as the waters of Meribath-kadesh, from there along the Wadi of Egypt[d] to the Great Sea. This shall be the south side.

[20]On the west side, the Great Sea shall be the boundary to a point opposite Lebo-hamath. This shall be the west side.

[21]So you shall divide this land among you according to the tribes of Israel. [22]You shall allot it as an inheritance for yourselves and for the aliens who reside among you and have begotten children among you. They shall be to you as citizens of Israel; with you they shall be allotted an inheritance among the tribes of Israel. [23]In whatever tribe aliens reside, there you shall assign them their inheritance, says the Lord GOD.

The Tribal Portions

48 These are the names of the tribes: Beginning at the northern border, on the Hethlon road,[e] from Lebo-hamath, as far as Hazar-enon (which is on the border of Damascus, with Hamath to the north), and[f] extending from the east side to the west,[g] Dan, one portion. [2]Adjoining the territory of Dan, from the east side to the west, Asher, one portion. [3]Adjoining the territory of Asher, from the east side to the west, Naphtali, one portion. [4]Adjoining the territory of Naphtali, from the east side to the west, Manasseh, one portion. [5]Adjoining the territory of Manasseh, from the east side to the west, Ephraim, one portion. [6]Adjoining the territory of Ephraim, from the east side to the west, Reuben, one portion. [7]Adjoining the territory of Reuben, from the east side to the west, Judah, one portion.

[8]Adjoining the territory of Judah, from the east side to the west, shall be the portion that you shall set apart, twenty-five thousand cubits in width, and in length equal to one of the tribal portions, from the east side to the west, with the sanctuary in the middle of it. [9]The portion that you shall set apart for the LORD shall be twenty-five thousand cubits in length, and twenty[h] thousand in width. [10]These shall be the allotments of the holy portion: the priests shall have an allotment measuring twenty-five thousand cubits on the northern side, ten thousand cubits in width on the western side, ten thousand in width on the eastern side, and twenty-five thousand in length on the southern side, with the sanctuary of the LORD in the middle of it. [11]This shall be for the consecrated priests, the descendants[i] of Zadok, who kept my charge, who did not go astray when the people of Israel went astray, as the Levites did. [12]It shall belong to them as a special portion from the holy portion of the land, a most holy place,

[a] Gk: Heb Lebo-zedad, [16]Hamath   [b] Meaning of Heb uncertain   [c] Compare Syr: Heb you shall measure   [d] Heb lacks of Egypt   [e] Compare 47.15: Heb by the side of the way   [f] Cn: Heb and they shall be his   [g] Gk Compare verses 2-8: Heb the east side the west   [h] Compare 45.1: Heb ten   [i] One Ms Gk: Heb of the descendants

---

47:22–23 *Aliens*—Although Lev. 19:33–34 and other laws protect the rights of resident aliens, nowhere else are non-Israelites extended a share in the tribal land allotments. The vision is remarkably inclusive, contrary to the narrow exclusiveness often attributed to Ezekiel. The stipulation that the aliens *have begotten children among you* ensures that they are permanent residents. Elsewhere in Ezekiel the *ger*, or resident alien, is expected to participate fully in the religious life of the community (14:7).

adjoining the territory of the Levites. [13] Alongside the territory of the priests, the Levites shall have an allotment twenty-five thousand cubits in length and ten thousand in width. The whole length shall be twenty-five thousand cubits and the width twenty[a] thousand. [14] They shall not sell or exchange any of it; they shall not transfer this choice portion of the land, for it is holy to the LORD.

[15] The remainder, five thousand cubits in width and twenty-five thousand in length, shall be for ordinary use for the city, for dwellings and for open country. In the middle of it shall be the city; [16] and these shall be its dimensions: the north side four thousand five hundred cubits, the south side four thousand five hundred, the east side four thousand five hundred, and the west side four thousand five hundred. [17] The city shall have open land: on the north two hundred fifty cubits, on the south two hundred fifty, on the east two hundred fifty, on the west two hundred fifty. [18] The remainder of the length alongside the holy portion shall be ten thousand cubits to the east, and ten thousand to the west, and it shall be alongside the holy portion. Its produce shall be food for the workers of the city. [19] The workers of the city, from all the tribes of Israel, shall cultivate it. [20] The whole portion that you shall set apart shall be twenty-five thousand cubits square, that is, the holy portion together with the property of the city.

[21] What remains on both sides of the holy portion and of the property of the city shall belong to the prince. Extending from the twenty-five thousand cubits of the holy portion to the east border, and westward from the twenty-five thousand cubits to the west border, parallel to the tribal portions, it shall belong to the prince. The holy portion with the sanctuary of the temple in the middle of it, [22] and the property of the Levites and of the city, shall be in the middle of that which belongs to the prince. The portion of the prince shall lie between the territory of Judah and the territory of Benjamin.

23 As for the rest of the tribes: from the east side to the west, Benjamin, one portion. [24] Adjoining the territory of Benjamin, from the east side to the west, Simeon, one portion. [25] Adjoining the territory of Simeon, from the east side to the west, Issachar, one portion. [26] Adjoining the territory of Issachar, from the east side to the west, Zebulun, one portion. [27] Adjoining the territory of Zebulun, from the east side to the west, Gad, one portion. [28] And adjoining the territory of Gad to the south, the boundary shall run from Tamar to the waters of Meribath-kadesh, from there along the Wadi of Egypt[b] to the Great Sea. [29] This is the land that you shall allot as an inheritance among the tribes of Israel, and these are their portions, says the Lord GOD.

30 These shall be the exits of the city: On the north side, which is to be four thousand five hundred cubits by measure, [31] three gates, the gate of Reuben, the gate of Judah, and the gate of Levi, the gates of the city being named after the tribes of Israel. [32] On the east side, which is to be four thousand five hundred cubits, three gates, the gate of Joseph, the gate of Benjamin, and the gate of Dan. [33] On the south side, which is to be four thousand five hundred cubits by measure, three gates, the gate of Simeon, the gate of Issachar, and the gate of Zebulun. [34] On the west

[a] Gk: Heb *ten*   [b] Heb lacks *of Egypt*

48:30–35 The LORD *is there*—The city's twelve gates provide unusual access and imply that fortification is unnecessary. The new city, which is never called Jerusalem, is here named *"YHWH shammah,"* YHWH is There (v. 35). The naming of the city is Ezekiel's final affirmation that YHWH will both reclaim sovereignty and once again bless people by being eternally present at the heart of their common life.

side, which is to be four thousand five hundred cubits, three gates,[a] the gate of Gad, the gate of Asher, and the gate of Naphtali. 35 The circumference of the city shall be eighteen thousand cubits. And the name of the city from that time on shall be, The LORD is There.

[a] One Ms Gk Syr: MT *their gates three*

The Book of
DANIEL

I n order to understand the Book of Daniel, one should have a grasp of the historical context of either the postexilic period or the Hellenistic period. This is because
the book of Daniel claims to be from the postexilic (Persian) period, even though
significant data from etymology and the like indicate a Hellenistic provenance for the
book. Whether one dates the book in the early postexilic period or the Hellenistic
period, it is clear that the events of the Persian period set in motion an appreciation
of history that builds in the Hellenistic period. The fall of Jerusalem and the exile in
Babylon (587 BCE) set in motion a new understanding of salvation history. The rise of
the Persian Empire and the ascendancy of Cyrus II the Great (559–530) mark a political shift. With the edict of Cyrus (539 BCE), the period of punishment (587–539 BCE)
comes to an end, and the time of redemption begins. Nonetheless, redemption does
not mean that the political realities of colonial life have disappeared. Indeed, Judea
was firmly ruled for over two centuries by a series of six major Persian kings, interspersed by lesser rulers. In addition to Cyrus, these kings included Cambyses (530–
522), Darius I (522–486), Xerxes (486–465), Artaxerxes I (465–424), and Artaxerxes II
(405–359).

With the fall of the Persian Empire and the rise of the Hellenistic Empire under
Alexander the Great (336–323 BCE) the cultural terrain shifted noticeably. The Battle
of Issus (333 BCE) solidified the role of Alexander in the region. However, the stability that brought was short-lived. Alexander died some ten years later (323 BCE). The
resulting chaos gave rise to the rule of the *diadachoi*, the coterie of generals under
Alexander who divided the empire among themselves when no one of them could
establish himself as the ultimate power over the entire empire. Seleucus I (312–281)
became the ruler of Mesopotamia, Syria, and supposedly Palestine. Ptolemy I (323–
282) became the ruler of Egypt. He, however, took Palestine as his own. This turn of
events spawned the wars between Syria (Seleucids) and Egypt (Ptolemies) over the
region of Palestine and the city of Jerusalem.

The date of the book of Daniel generates a good deal of controversy. Some argue that the claim of the book itself to date from the Babylonian exile is definitive
evidence for a sixth-century date. Others argue that the presence of *vaticinium ex
eventu*, or prophecy after the fact, indicates a much later date, namely the Hellenistic period around the time of the Maccabean revolt in 167 BCE. All agree, however,
that the book of Daniel witnesses to the response of faithful Jews to the oppression of
the imperial system and its unrelenting attempt to mold people into the image of the
empire's customs and values.

The book of Daniel comes to us in two languages, Hebrew (Dan. 1:1–2:2a and
chaps. 8–12) and Aramaic (Dan. 2:4b–7:28). The bilingualism of the book marks an
anticolonial strategy in the book itself. This point can be illustrated by reference to
contemporary Latino American literature. By moving from Spanish to English and
back again, this literature decenters the privilege that English often usurps.

The book also has two major literary types: the wisdom tales in the early chapters (1–6) and vision reports in the later chapters (7–8, 10–12). Chapter 9 presents a prayer.

The narrative chapters suggest an ethic of resistance. The believers assert that even if God does not deliver them, they will choose death over idolatry (Dan. 3:16–18).

That the Daniel tradition was popular in the Greco-Roman era and more elaborate than our present book is shown by the existence of several apocryphal additions to the book of Daniel, as well as a *Prayer of Nabonidus* found among the Dead Sea Scrolls (see note at 4:25).

—Stephen Breck Reid

Four Young Israelites at the Babylonian Court

1 In the third year of the reign of King Jehoiakim of Judah, King Nebuchadnezzar of Babylon came to Jerusalem and besieged it. ² The Lord let King Jehoiakim of Judah fall into his power, as well as some of the vessels of the house of God. These he brought to the land of Shinar,*ª* and placed the vessels in the treasury of his gods.

3 Then the king commanded his palace master Ashpenaz to bring some of the Israelites of the royal family and of the nobility, ⁴ young men without physical defect and handsome, versed in every branch of wisdom, endowed with knowledge and insight, and competent to serve in the king's palace; they were to be taught the literature and language of the Chaldeans. ⁵ The king assigned them a daily portion of the royal rations of food and wine. They were to be educated for three years, so that at the end of that time they could be stationed in the king's court. ⁶ Among them were Daniel, Hananiah, Mishael, and Azariah, from the tribe of Judah. ⁷ The palace master gave them other names: Daniel he called Belteshazzar, Hananiah he called Shadrach, Mishael he called Meshach, and Azariah he called Abednego.

8 But Daniel resolved that he would

ª Gk Theodotion: Heb adds *to the house of his own gods*

1:1–21 The Context

This first story lays out the nature of the marginalization of the conquered Judeans that provides the context for the subsequent narratives.

1:1—This is the beginning of the problems with the chronology in this book. *The third year of . . . Jehoiakim* (2 Kgs. 24:1) would be 606 BCE (see 2 Chr. 36:5–7). *Nebuchadnezzar*, the Jewish form of the Babylonian name of Nebuchadrezzar (605–562 BCE), had yet to ascend to the throne of Babylonia. Jehoiakim died in 598 BCE. Jehoiachin, son of Jehoiakim, reigned from 598 to 587 BCE.

1:2 *Vessels of the house of God*—Cf. 2 Chr. 28:24; 36:18; Neh. 13:9. This foreshadows the conflict in Dan. 5. *Shinar* is another name for Babylon (e.g., Gen. 10:10; Zech. 5:11). The assimilation of the prominent members of the marginalized community sets a theme for the rest of the book. The phrase *The Lord let . . .* accents God's control of history. Likewise, it relativizes the power of the Babylonians.

1:3—The selection of elite young men was a strategy of cultural transformation. The selection criteria resemble the criteria for priests (Lev. 21:17–23) and sacrificial animals (Lev. 22:19–22), and the signs of political leadership (1 Sam. 9:2; 16:12).

1:4—*Chaldeans* can refer to an Aramaic-speaking Neo-Babylonian people dwelling in the lower Euphrates and Tigris River valley or to persons trained in divination (e.g., 4:7). Sometimes the writer intentionally confuses these terms.

1:6–7—The bilingualism of the book extends even to a second name for each of the youths. *Daniel* ("God is judge"), *Hananiah* ("The Lord shows grace"), *Mishael* ("Who is what God is?"), *Azariah* ("The Lord helps") are given names that contain elements of the names of Babylonian deities. Daniel is also named *Belteshazzar* (Bel—the high god of Babylon—protects him). Hananiah becomes *Shadrach*, Mishael becomes *Meshach*, and Azariah becomes *Abednego*.

1:8—*Not to defile himself* refers to dietary laws (see Lev. 11). Dietary observance was a hallmark of Jewish identity, as other texts from the Greco-

not defile himself with the royal rations of food and wine; so he asked the palace master to allow him not to defile himself. ⁹Now God allowed Daniel to receive favor and compassion from the palace master. ¹⁰The palace master said to Daniel, "I am afraid of my lord the king; he has appointed your food and your drink. If he should see you in poorer condition than the other young men of your own age, you would endanger my head with the king." ¹¹Then Daniel asked the guard whom the palace master had appointed over Daniel, Hananiah, Mishael, and Azariah: ¹²"Please test your servants for ten days. Let us be given vegetables to eat and water to drink. ¹³You can then compare our appearance with the appearance of the young men who eat the royal rations, and deal with your servants according to what you observe." ¹⁴So he agreed to this proposal and tested them for ten days. ¹⁵At the end of ten days it was observed that they appeared better and fatter than all the young men who had been eating the royal rations. ¹⁶So the guard continued to withdraw their royal rations and the wine they were to drink, and gave them vegetables. ¹⁷To these four young men God gave knowledge and skill in every aspect of literature and wisdom;

Daniel also had insight into all visions and dreams.

18 At the end of the time that the king had set for them to be brought in, the palace master brought them into the presence of Nebuchadnezzar, ¹⁹and the king spoke with them. And among them all, no one was found to compare with Daniel, Hananiah, Mishael, and Azariah; therefore they were stationed in the king's court. ²⁰In every matter of wisdom and understanding concerning which the king inquired of them, he found them ten times better than all the magicians and enchanters in his whole kingdom. ²¹And Daniel continued there until the first year of King Cyrus.

Nebuchadnezzar's Dream

2 In the second year of Nebuchadnezzar's reign, Nebuchadnezzar dreamed such dreams that his spirit was troubled and his sleep left him. ²So the king commanded that the magicians, the enchanters, the sorcerers, and the Chaldeans be summoned to tell the king his dreams. When they came in and stood before the king, ³he said to them, "I have had such a dream that my spirit is troubled by the desire to understand it." ⁴The Chaldeans said to the king (in Aramaic),ᵃ

ᵃ The text from this point to the end of chapter 7 is in Aramaic

---

Roman period indicate (see Esth. 14:17; Tob. 1:10–11; Jdt. 10:5; 12:1–4; 1 Macc. 1:62–63; 2 Macc. 6–7).

1:12—*Please test* is a literary element that accents the contest apologetic of the folktale. The depiction of a court official, such as Ashpenaz, as a sympathetic person also appears frequently in these folktales.

1:17—God, not their Babylonian training, is the source of the wisdom of Daniel and his friends.

1:20—The term *magician* also occurs in the depiction of Moses and Aaron in their contest with the pharaoh and the Egyptians (Exod. 8:3, 14, 15; 9:11). This indicates that Daniel and his friends are emissaries for God, just like Moses and Aaron before them. A new category of diviners appears here with the introduction of the term *enchanters*.

1:21 *First year of King Cyrus*—539 BCE.

2:1–49 Nebuchadnezzar's Dream

2:1 *The second year of Nebuchadnezzar*— Once again we have a chronological problem. The second year of Nebuchadnezzar is 603 BCE, which is prior to the capture of Jerusalem and of the young Daniel in 597. Dreams as portents occur elsewhere in the Bible (see Gen. 15:12; 20:3; 28:10–22; 37:5–9). The most famous of these is Pharaoh and Joseph, which is similar to the folktales in Daniel (Gen. 41:1–32).

2:2—To the list of diviners, magicians, Chaldeans, and enchanters (see notes at 1:4, 20), a new group, *sorcerers*, is added. Once again parallels to the contest between God and Pharaoh lurk in the background. The term "sorcerer" occurs also in that context (see Exod. 7:11).

2:4—The language shifts from Hebrew to Aramaic. *O king, live forever!* is a form of address to a royal figure (see also 3:9; 5:10; 6:7, 22).

"O king, live forever! Tell your servants the dream, and we will reveal the interpretation." ⁵ The king answered the Chaldeans, "This is a public decree: if you do not tell me both the dream and its interpretation, you shall be torn limb from limb, and your houses shall be laid in ruins. ⁶ But if you do tell me the dream and its interpretation, you shall receive from me gifts and rewards and great honor. Therefore tell me the dream and its interpretation." ⁷ They answered a second time, "Let the king first tell his servants the dream, then we can give its interpretation." ⁸ The king answered, "I know with certainty that you are trying to gain time, because you see I have firmly decreed: ⁹ if you do not tell me the dream, there is but one verdict for you. You have agreed to speak lying and misleading words to me until things take a turn. Therefore, tell me the dream, and I shall know that you can give me its interpretation." ¹⁰ The Chaldeans answered the king, "There is no one on earth who can reveal what the king demands! In fact no king, however great and powerful, has ever asked such a thing of any magician or enchanter or Chaldean. ¹¹ The thing that the king is asking is too difficult, and no one can reveal it to the king except the gods, whose dwelling is not with mortals."

12 Because of this the king flew into a violent rage and commanded that all the wise men of Babylon be destroyed. ¹³ The decree was issued, and the wise men were about to be executed; and they looked for Daniel and his companions, to execute them. ¹⁴ Then Daniel responded with prudence and discretion to Arioch, the king's chief executioner, who had gone out to execute the wise men of Babylon; ¹⁵ he asked Arioch, the royal official, "Why is the decree of the king so urgent?" Arioch then explained the matter to Daniel. ¹⁶ So Daniel went in and requested that the king give him time and he would tell the king the interpretation.

God Reveals Nebuchadnezzar's Dream

17 Then Daniel went to his home and informed his companions, Hananiah, Mishael, and Azariah, ¹⁸ and told them to seek mercy from the God of heaven concerning this mystery, so that Daniel and his companions with the rest of the wise men of Babylon might not perish. ¹⁹ Then the mystery was revealed to Daniel in a vision of the night, and Daniel blessed the God of heaven.

²⁰ Daniel said:

"Blessed be the name of God from
　　age to age,
　　for wisdom and power are his.
²¹ He changes times and seasons,
　　deposes kings and sets up kings;
he gives wisdom to the wise
　　and knowledge to those who have
　　understanding.
²² He reveals deep and hidden things;
　　he knows what is in the darkness,
　　and light dwells with him.
²³ To you, O God of my ancestors,
　　I give thanks and praise,
for you have given me wisdom and
　　power,
　　and have now revealed to me what
　　we asked of you,
　　for you have revealed to us what
　　the king ordered."

2:5—The writer undermines the colonial ideology by depicting the all-powerful monarch as unable to control his own destiny. **Decree** language marks the folktales and the Aramaic section of the book (2:8, 15; 4:28, 30; 5:15, 26; 6:13, 15; 7:28). **Your houses shall be laid in ruins** indicates the familial nature of guilt in the world of the writer. Collective guilt calls for collective punishment.

2:18—*Mystery* is a key term in apocalyptic literature, especially in this chapter of Daniel (vv. 27, 47). **God of heaven** is a common phrase in Persian and Hellenistic literature. (539–167 BCE; e.g., Ezra 5:11; 7:12, 21, 23; Dan. 2:37, 44).

2:19 *Vision of the night*—The literary type is unclear: Are they waking dreams? Is the closer parallel Joseph or prophets such as Amos?

2:20–23 Prayer of Blessing

Daniel Interprets the Dream

24 Therefore Daniel went to Arioch, whom the king had appointed to destroy the wise men of Babylon, and said to him, "Do not destroy the wise men of Babylon; bring me in before the king, and I will give the king the interpretation."

25 Then Arioch quickly brought Daniel before the king and said to him: "I have found among the exiles from Judah a man who can tell the king the interpretation." 26 The king said to Daniel, whose name was Belteshazzar, "Are you able to tell me the dream that I have seen and its interpretation?" 27 Daniel answered the king, "No wise men, enchanters, magicians, or diviners can show to the king the mystery that the king is asking, 28 but there is a God in heaven who reveals mysteries, and he has disclosed to King Nebuchadnezzar what will happen at the end of days. Your dream and the visions of your head as you lay in bed were these: 29 To you, O king, as you lay in bed, came thoughts of what would be hereafter, and the revealer of mysteries disclosed to you what is to be. 30 But as for me, this mystery has not been revealed to me because of any wisdom that I have more than any other living being, but in order that the interpretation may be known to the king and that you may understand the thoughts of your mind.

31 "You were looking, O king, and lo! there was a great statue. This statue was huge, its brilliance extraordinary; it was standing before you, and its appearance was frightening. 32 The head of that statue was of fine gold, its chest and arms of silver, its middle and thighs of bronze, 33 its legs of iron, its feet partly of iron and partly of clay. 34 As you looked on, a stone was cut out, not by human hands, and it struck the statue on its feet of iron and clay and broke them in pieces. 35 Then the iron, the clay, the bronze, the silver, and the gold, were all broken in pieces and became like the chaff of the summer threshing floors; and the wind carried them away, so that not a trace of them could be found. But the stone that struck the statue became a great mountain and filled the whole earth.

36 "This was the dream; now we will tell the king its interpretation. 37 You, O king, the king of kings—to whom the God of heaven has given the kingdom, the power, the might, and the glory, 38 into whose hand he has given human beings, wherever they live, the wild animals of the field, and the birds of the air, and whom he has established as ruler over them all—you are the head of gold. 39 After you shall arise another kingdom inferior to yours, and yet a third kingdom of bronze, which shall rule over the whole earth. 40 And there shall be a fourth kingdom, strong as iron; just as iron crushes and smashes everything,[a] it shall crush and shatter all these. 41 As you saw the feet and toes partly of potter's clay and partly of iron, it shall be a divided kingdom; but some of the strength of iron shall be in it, as you saw the iron mixed with the clay. 42 As the toes of the feet were part iron and part clay, so the kingdom shall be partly strong and partly brittle. 43 As you saw the iron mixed with

[a] Gk Theodotion Syr Vg: Aram adds *and like iron that crushes*

2:26 *Belteshazzar*—See also 1:7; 4:5, 6, 15, 16; 5:12; 10:1.

2:28 *End of days*—In Daniel, apparently more than simply an indefinite future time; specifically the end of the present age (cf. 10:14).

2:34—*A stone was cut out, not by human hands* refers to the divine sovereignty and delimits human agency.

2:41—The interpretation of Nebuchadnezzar's dream is an allegory of five kingdoms: Babylonia (gold), Media (silver), Persia (bronze), Greece (iron and clay), and the one to come. *It shall be divided* refers to the breakup of Alexander the Great's empire into fiefdoms including those of the Ptolemies and the Seleucids, who will control Egypt and Syria-Palestine respectively.

2:43 *In marriage*—Lit. "in human seed." The issue of marriage and inheritance continues to be a hot topic throughout the biblical period, especially in the postexilic period (see Neh. 13).

clay, so will they mix with one another in marriage,[a] but they will not hold together, just as iron does not mix with clay. [44] And in the days of those kings the God of heaven will set up a kingdom that shall never be destroyed, nor shall this kingdom be left to another people. It shall crush all these kingdoms and bring them to an end, and it shall stand forever; [45] just as you saw that a stone was cut from the mountain not by hands, and that it crushed the iron, the bronze, the clay, the silver, and the gold. The great God has informed the king what shall be hereafter. The dream is certain, and its interpretation trustworthy."

Daniel and His Friends Promoted

[46] Then King Nebuchadnezzar fell on his face, worshiped Daniel, and commanded that a grain offering and incense be offered to him. [47] The king said to Daniel, "Truly, your God is God of gods and Lord of kings and a revealer of mysteries, for you have been able to reveal this mystery!" [48] Then the king promoted Daniel, gave him many great gifts, and made him ruler over the whole province of Babylon and chief prefect over all the wise men of Babylon. [49] Daniel made a request of the king, and he appointed Shadrach, Meshach, and Abednego over the affairs of the province of Babylon. But Daniel remained at the king's court.

The Golden Image

3 King Nebuchadnezzar made a golden statue whose height was sixty cubits and whose width was six cubits; he set it up on the plain of Dura in the province of Babylon. [2] Then King Nebuchadnezzar sent for the satraps, the prefects, and the governors, the counselors, the treasurers, the justices, the magistrates, and all the officials of the provinces, to assemble and come to the dedication of the statue that King Nebuchadnezzar had set up. [3] So the satraps, the prefects, and the governors, the counselors, the treasurers, the justices, the magistrates, and all the officials of the provinces, assembled for the dedication of the statue that King Nebuchadnezzar had set up. When they were standing before the statue that Nebuchadnezzar had set up, [4] the herald proclaimed aloud, "You are commanded, O peoples, nations, and languages, [5] that when you hear the sound of the horn, pipe, lyre, trigon, harp, drum, and entire musical ensemble, you are to fall down and worship the golden statue that King Nebuchadnezzar has set up. [6] Whoever does not fall down and worship shall immediately be thrown into a furnace of blazing fire." [7] Therefore, as soon as all the peoples heard the sound of the horn, pipe, lyre, trigon, harp, drum, and entire musical ensemble, all the peoples, nations, and languages fell down and worshiped the golden statue that King Nebuchadnezzar had set up.

[8] Accordingly, at this time certain Chaldeans came forward and denounced

[a] Aram *by human seed*

2:46 *Nebuchadnezzar . . . worshiped Daniel*— The recognition of God as the one and only deity is a theme in biblical texts (see Josh. 4; Jonah). However, here Daniel, not God, is the object of the worship rendered by the foreign king. The narrator forgoes any judgment on the act.

3:1–30 Three Youths in the Fiery Furnace

3:1–7—Large *statues* of deities were commonplace in ancient western Asia (a geographical designation preferable to the Eurocentric "Near East"). Herodotus (fifth-century BCE) describes a large golden statue of Zeus in Babylon. The dimensions of the Daniel statue are *sixty cubits* by *six cubits* = 30 x 3 meters, about 98 x 9.8 feet.

Dura means "fortress"; a specific location cannot be determined.

3:5—The list of instruments recurs several times in this chapter. The *trigon* was a three-cornered, four-stringed musical instrument. A number of the instruments in this list are Greek loanwords.

3:6—*Thrown* links the fiery furnace and the lions' den stories (3:11; 6:8, 13). The fire suggests both capital punishment (Gen. 38:24; Josh. 7:15; Jer. 29:10; 2 Macc. 13:4–8) and testing and purifying (Deut. 4:20; Isa. 48:10). The furnace or oven of the period was probably a type of kiln with a smokestack opening and a door.

3:8—*Chaldeans* here represent an adversary.

the Jews. [9] They said to King Nebuchadnezzar, "O king, live forever! [10] You, O king, have made a decree, that everyone who hears the sound of the horn, pipe, lyre, trigon, harp, drum, and entire musical ensemble, shall fall down and worship the golden statue, [11] and whoever does not fall down and worship shall be thrown into a furnace of blazing fire. [12] There are certain Jews whom you have appointed over the affairs of the province of Babylon: Shadrach, Meshach, and Abednego. These pay no heed to you, O king. They do not serve your gods and they do not worship the golden statue that you have set up."

13 Then Nebuchadnezzar in furious rage commanded that Shadrach, Meshach, and Abednego be brought in; so they brought those men before the king. [14] Nebuchadnezzar said to them, "Is it true, O Shadrach, Meshach, and Abednego, that you do not serve my gods and you do not worship the golden statue that I have set up? [15] Now if you are ready when you hear the sound of the horn, pipe, lyre, trigon, harp, drum, and entire musical ensemble to fall down and worship the statue that I have made, well and good.[a] But if you do not worship, you shall immediately be thrown into a furnace of blazing fire, and who is the god that will deliver you out of my hands?"

16 Shadrach, Meshach, and Abednego answered the king, "O Nebuchadnezzar, we have no need to present a defense to you in this matter. [17] If our God whom we serve is able to deliver us from the furnace of blazing fire and out of your hand, O king, let him deliver us.[b] [18] But

if not, be it known to you, O king, that we will not serve your gods and we will not worship the golden statue that you have set up."

The Fiery Furnace

19 Then Nebuchadnezzar was so filled with rage against Shadrach, Meshach, and Abednego that his face was distorted. He ordered the furnace heated up seven times more than was customary, [20] and ordered some of the strongest guards in his army to bind Shadrach, Meshach, and Abednego and to throw them into the furnace of blazing fire. [21] So the men were bound, still wearing their tunics,[c] their trousers,[c] their hats, and their other garments, and they were thrown into the furnace of blazing fire. [22] Because the king's command was urgent and the furnace was so overheated, the raging flames killed the men who lifted Shadrach, Meshach, and Abednego. [23] But the three men, Shadrach, Meshach, and Abednego, fell down, bound, into the furnace of blazing fire.

24 Then King Nebuchadnezzar was astonished and rose up quickly. He said to his counselors, "Was it not three men that we threw bound into the fire?" They answered the king, "True, O king." [25] He replied, "But I see four men unbound, walking in the middle of the fire, and they are not hurt; and the fourth has the appearance of a god."[d] [26] Nebuchadnezzar then approached the door of the furnace of blazing fire and said, "Shadrach, Meshach, and Abed-

[a] Aram lacks *well and good* [b] Or *If our God whom we serve is able to deliver us, he will deliver us from the furnace of blazing fire and out of your hand, O king.* [c] Meaning of Aram word uncertain [d] Aram *a son of the gods*

Denounced, lit. "eating at the pieces," indicates the carnivorous element of the conflict.

3:16–18—Speech of resistance. Despite the fact that all these folktales have happy endings for the believers, this speech anticipates the martyrs to come in the Greco-Roman period (e.g., 1 Macc. 1:2–7).

3:19–23—The miracle. *Seven times* is an expression of maximum increase.

3:20—The layering of the clothing accents the miraculous nature of the deliverance.

3:23—The Septuagint, Eastern Orthodox, and Roman Catholic Bibles insert the Prayer of Azariah and the Song of the Three Jews at this point.

3:25—The reference to the fourth being with *the appearance of a god*, lit. "appearing as a son of god," implies an angelic figure of the presence of God.

nego, servants of the Most High God, come out! Come here!" So Shadrach, Meshach, and Abednego came out from the fire. ²⁷And the satraps, the prefects, the governors, and the king's counselors gathered together and saw that the fire had not had any power over the bodies of those men; the hair of their heads was not singed, their tunics*a* were not harmed, and not even the smell of fire came from them. ²⁸Nebuchadnezzar said, "Blessed be the God of Shadrach, Meshach, and Abednego, who has sent his angel and delivered his servants who trusted in him. They disobeyed the king's command and yielded up their bodies rather than serve and worship any god except their own God. ²⁹Therefore I make a decree: Any people, nation, or language that utters blasphemy against the God of Shadrach, Meshach, and Abednego shall be torn limb from limb, and their houses laid in ruins; for there is no other god who is able to deliver in this way." ³⁰Then the king promoted Shadrach, Meshach, and Abednego in the province of Babylon.

Nebuchadnezzar's Second Dream

4*b* King Nebuchadnezzar to all peoples, nations, and languages that live throughout the earth: May you have abundant prosperity! ²The signs and wonders that the Most High God has worked for me I am pleased to recount.
³ How great are his signs,
       how mighty his wonders!

His kingdom is an everlasting
     kingdom,
   and his sovereignty is from
       generation to generation.
⁴*c* I, Nebuchadnezzar, was living at ease in my home and prospering in my palace. ⁵I saw a dream that frightened me; my fantasies in bed and the visions of my head terrified me. ⁶So I made a decree that all the wise men of Babylon should be brought before me, in order that they might tell me the interpretation of the dream. ⁷Then the magicians, the enchanters, the Chaldeans, and the diviners came in, and I told them the dream, but they could not tell me its interpretation. ⁸At last Daniel came in before me—he who was named Belteshazzar after the name of my god, and who is endowed with a spirit of the holy gods*d*—and I told him the dream: ⁹"O Belteshazzar, chief of the magicians, I know that you are endowed with a spirit of the holy gods*d* and that no mystery is too difficult for you. Hear*e* the dream that I saw; tell me its interpretation.
¹⁰*f* Upon my bed this is what I saw;
     there was a tree at the center of the
         earth,
   and its height was great.
¹¹ The tree grew great and strong,
       its top reached to heaven,
   and it was visible to the ends of the
         whole earth.

a Meaning of Aram word uncertain *b* Ch 3.31 in Aram *c* Ch 4.1 in Aram
d Or *a holy, divine spirit* *e* Theodotion: Aram *The visions of* *f* Theodotion
Syr Compare Gk: Aram adds *The visions of my head*

3:28–30—The king's speech on the sovereignty of God.

4:1–3 Nebuchadnezzar's Doxology

Follows previous theological pronouncements of Nebuchadnezzar (see also 2:47; 3:28–29).

4:4–18 The King's Vision

4:4—The first person witness *I, Nebuchadnezzar* (see also vv. 1, 6, 15, 27, 31, 34) will occur later in Daniel's vision reports, which are first person accounts introduced by the phrase "I, Daniel" (e.g., 7:2, 15, 28).

4:7—Once again, the writer emphasizes Daniel's gift by recounting the failure of the other courtiers (see 2:2).

4:8—The gloss or parenthetical remark on the name *Belteshazzar* by the king seems odd, given the emphasis on the sovereignty of God. Could this be an interfaith apologetic, comparable to that reported in Acts 17:16–34?

4:10 *Upon my bed*—Not surprisingly, the bed is a typical location for the genre of night visions or dream visions (e.g., Zech. 1:8; 4:1) *A tree at the center of the earth* is a reference to a world tree, at the center of the earth disk, that provides a canopy for the earth beneath its leaves (see also Ezek. 31:3–14).

¹² Its foliage was beautiful,
  its fruit abundant,
  and it provided food for all.
The animals of the field found shade
    under it,
  the birds of the air nested in its
    branches,
  and from it all living beings were
    fed.

¹³ "I continued looking, in the visions
of my head as I lay in bed, and there
was a holy watcher, coming down from
heaven. ¹⁴ He cried aloud and said:
  'Cut down the tree and chop off its
    branches,
  strip off its foliage and scatter its
    fruit.
Let the animals flee from beneath it
  and the birds from its branches.
¹⁵ But leave its stump and roots in the
    ground,
  with a band of iron and bronze,
  in the tender grass of the field.
Let him be bathed with the dew of
    heaven,
  and let his lot be with the animals
    of the field
  in the grass of the earth.
¹⁶ Let his mind be changed from that
    of a human,
  and let the mind of an animal be
    given to him.
  And let seven times pass over
    him.
¹⁷ The sentence is rendered by decree
    of the watchers,
  the decision is given by order of
    the holy ones,
in order that all who live may know
  that the Most High is sovereign
    over the kingdom of mortals;
he gives it to whom he will

and sets over it the lowliest of
  human beings.'

¹⁸ "This is the dream that I, King
Nebuchadnezzar, saw. Now you, Belteshazzar, declare the interpretation, since
all the wise men of my kingdom are
unable to tell me the interpretation. You
are able, however, for you are endowed
with a spirit of the holy gods."ᵃ

Daniel Interprets the Second Dream

¹⁹ Then Daniel, who was called Belteshazzar, was severely distressed for
a while. His thoughts terrified him.
The king said, "Belteshazzar, do not
let the dream or the interpretation terrify you." Belteshazzar answered, "My
lord, may the dream be for those who
hate you, and its interpretation for your
enemies! ²⁰ The tree that you saw, which
grew great and strong, so that its top
reached to heaven and was visible to the
end of the whole earth, ²¹ whose foliage
was beautiful and its fruit abundant,
and which provided food for all, under
which animals of the field lived, and
in whose branches the birds of the air
had nests— ²² it is you, O king! You have
grown great and strong. Your greatness
has increased and reaches to heaven,
and your sovereignty to the ends of the
earth. ²³ And whereas the king saw a holy
watcher coming down from heaven and
saying, 'Cut down the tree and destroy
it, but leave its stump and roots in the
ground, with a band of iron and bronze,
in the grass of the field; and let him be
bathed with the dew of heaven, and let
his lot be with the animals of the field,
until seven times pass over him'— ²⁴ this
is the interpretation, O king, and it is a

ᵃ Or a holy, divine spirit

4:13, 17, 23—*A holy watcher* comes from the
verb meaning "to be awake, to wake up." This
designation was connected to angels as "vigilant
ones." The angel interpreter becomes now the
angel advocate (cf. 8:13).

4:14—The destruction of the *tree* echoes Ezek.
17:1–24.

4:16—*Seven times* probably refers to seven years.

4:19–27 Daniel's Second Dream Interpretation

4:22—*It is you* points to the way in which persons are described as trees (see Pss. 1:3; 37:35;
Jer. 17:8), just as nations are (Ezek. 17:1–24). In
this case we have a fusion of the tree as a person
and as a nation.

decree of the Most High that has come upon my lord the king: [25] You shall be driven away from human society, and your dwelling shall be with the wild animals. You shall be made to eat grass like oxen, you shall be bathed with the dew of heaven, and seven times shall pass over you, until you have learned that the Most High has sovereignty over the kingdom of mortals, and gives it to whom he will. [26] As it was commanded to leave the stump and roots of the tree, your kingdom shall be re-established for you from the time that you learn that Heaven is sovereign. [27] Therefore, O king, may my counsel be acceptable to you: atone for[a] your sins with righteousness, and your iniquities with mercy to the oppressed, so that your prosperity may be prolonged."

Nebuchadnezzar's Humiliation

[28] All this came upon King Nebuchadnezzar. [29] At the end of twelve months he was walking on the roof of the royal palace of Babylon, [30] and the king said, "Is this not magnificent Babylon, which I have built as a royal capital by my mighty power and for my glorious majesty?" [31] While the words were still in the king's mouth, a voice came from heaven: "O King Nebuchadnezzar, to you it is declared: The kingdom has departed from you! [32] You shall be driven away from human society, and your dwelling shall be with the animals of the field. You shall be made to eat grass like oxen, and seven times shall pass over you, until you have learned that the Most High has sovereignty over

the kingdom of mortals and gives it to whom he will." [33] Immediately the sentence was fulfilled against Nebuchadnezzar. He was driven away from human society, ate grass like oxen, and his body was bathed with the dew of heaven, until his hair grew as long as eagles' feathers and his nails became like birds' claws.

Nebuchadnezzar Praises God

[34] When that period was over, I, Nebuchadnezzar, lifted my eyes to heaven, and my reason returned to me.

I blessed the Most High,
and praised and honored the one who lives forever.
For his sovereignty is an everlasting sovereignty,
and his kingdom endures from generation to generation.

[35] All the inhabitants of the earth are accounted as nothing,
and he does what he wills with the host of heaven
and the inhabitants of the earth.
There is no one who can stay his hand
or say to him, "What are you doing?"

[36] At that time my reason returned to me; and my majesty and splendor were restored to me for the glory of my kingdom. My counselors and my lords sought me out, I was re-established over my kingdom, and still more greatness was added to me. [37] Now I, Nebuchadnezzar, praise and extol and honor the King of heaven,
for all his works are truth,

[a] Aram *break off*

4:25—The king is to succumb to *insania zoanthropia*, a psychosis in which human beings take on the characteristics of animals. Here we see political irony: the one who determines and defines what it means to be human loses that humanity and reverts to animal behavior. While there is no other reference to the disappearance of Nebuchadnezzar, we have numerous sources that indicate that the last king of Babylon, Nabonidus, withdrew from the city for several years to north Arabia. Also the Qumran text called the

Prayer of Nabonidus records that the king's illness of seven years is cured by a Jewish exorcist.

4:28–33 Nebuchadnezzar's Punishment and Restoration

4:28—During an expression of hubris or pride, the prophecy is fulfilled.

4:34–35—Second doxology.

4:37—Final doxology (see also 2:20–21; 6:26–27).

and his ways are justice;
   and he is able to bring low
      those who walk in pride.

Belshazzar's Feast

5 King Belshazzar made a great festival for a thousand of his lords, and he was drinking wine in the presence of the thousand.

2 Under the influence of the wine, Belshazzar commanded that they bring in the vessels of gold and silver that his father Nebuchadnezzar had taken out of the temple in Jerusalem, so that the king and his lords, his wives, and his concubines might drink from them. ³ So they brought in the vessels of gold and silver[a] that had been taken out of the temple, the house of God in Jerusalem, and the king and his lords, his wives, and his concubines drank from them. ⁴ They drank the wine and praised the gods of gold and silver, bronze, iron, wood, and stone.

The Writing on the Wall

5 Immediately the fingers of a human hand appeared and began writing on the plaster of the wall of the royal palace, next to the lampstand. The king was watching the hand as it wrote. ⁶ Then the king's face turned pale, and his thoughts terrified him. His limbs gave way, and his knees knocked together. ⁷ The king cried aloud to bring in the enchanters, the Chaldeans, and the diviners; and the king said to the wise men of Babylon, "Whoever can read this writing and tell me its interpretation shall be clothed in purple, have a chain of gold around his neck, and rank third in the kingdom." ⁸ Then all the king's wise men came in, but they could not read the writing or tell the king the interpretation. ⁹ Then King Belshazzar became greatly terrified and his face turned pale, and his lords were perplexed.

10 The queen, when she heard the discussion of the king and his lords, came into the banqueting hall. The queen said, "O king, live forever! Do not let your thoughts terrify you or your face grow pale. ¹¹ There is a man in your kingdom who is endowed with a spirit of the holy gods.[b] In the days of your father he was found to have enlightenment, understanding, and wisdom like the wisdom of the gods. Your father, King Nebuchadnezzar, made him chief of the magicians, enchanters, Chaldeans, and diviners,[c] ¹² because an excellent spirit, knowledge, and understanding to interpret dreams, explain riddles, and solve problems were found in this Daniel, whom the king named Belteshazzar. Now let Daniel be called, and he will give the interpretation."

The Writing on the Wall Interpreted

13 Then Daniel was brought in before the king. The king said to Daniel, "So you are Daniel, one of the exiles of Judah, whom my father the king brought from Judah? ¹⁴ I have heard of you that a spirit

[a] Theodotion Vg: Aram lacks *and silver*   [b] Or *a holy, divine spirit*   [c] Aram adds *the king your father*

5:1–9 The Handwriting on the Wall

5:1—*King Belshazzar* was actually the son of Nabonidus, not of Nebuchadnezzar. In the waning days of his kingdom, Nabonidus made this son ruler of Babylon and commander of much of his army. This is the Aramaic form of the name, which is itself a corruption of the Akkadian name meaning "O Bel, protect the king."

5:2—*Under the influence of the wine* provides an interesting rationalization for the impertinence of Belshazzar. *The vessels* refers to those taken in the sacking of the temple in 597 BCE (see 1:2; Ezra 1:7–11). The banquet is a standard context for contest literature such as this. Compare Esth. 5–7.

5:4—This is probably a reference to libation offerings that often accompanied drinking. However, for this writer this is an expression of sacrilegious debauchery.

5:10–12 The Queen's Intervention

Just as the previous chapters offer sympathetic portraits of Babylonians such as Ashpenaz (1:9) and Arioch (2:25), this chapter locates such a person in the royal household itself. The queen is the only female voice in the book.

5:13–31 Deciphering the Handwriting

of the gods*a* is in you, and that enlightenment, understanding, and excellent wisdom are found in you. ¹⁵ Now the wise men, the enchanters, have been brought in before me to read this writing and tell me its interpretation, but they were not able to give the interpretation of the matter. ¹⁶ But I have heard that you can give interpretations and solve problems. Now if you are able to read the writing and tell me its interpretation, you shall be clothed in purple, have a chain of gold around your neck, and rank third in the kingdom."

17 Then Daniel answered in the presence of the king, "Let your gifts be for yourself, or give your rewards to someone else! Nevertheless I will read the writing to the king and let him know the interpretation. ¹⁸ O king, the Most High God gave your father Nebuchadnezzar kingship, greatness, glory, and majesty. ¹⁹ And because of the greatness that he gave him, all peoples, nations, and languages trembled and feared before him. He killed those he wanted to kill, kept alive those he wanted to keep alive, honored those he wanted to honor, and degraded those he wanted to degrade. ²⁰ But when his heart was lifted up and his spirit was hardened so that he acted proudly, he was deposed from his kingly throne, and his glory was stripped from him. ²¹ He was driven from human society, and his mind was made like that of an animal. His dwelling was with the wild asses, he was fed grass like oxen, and his body was bathed with the dew

of heaven, until he learned that the Most High God has sovereignty over the kingdom of mortals, and sets over it whomever he will. ²² And you, Belshazzar his son, have not humbled your heart, even though you knew all this! ²³ You have exalted yourself against the Lord of heaven! The vessels of his temple have been brought in before you, and you and your lords, your wives and your concubines have been drinking wine from them. You have praised the gods of silver and gold, of bronze, iron, wood, and stone, which do not see or hear or know; but the God in whose power is your very breath, and to whom belong all your ways, you have not honored.

24 "So from his presence the hand was sent and this writing was inscribed. ²⁵ And this is the writing that was inscribed: MENE, MENE, TEKEL, and PARSIN. ²⁶ This is the interpretation of the matter: MENE, God has numbered the days of*b* your kingdom and brought it to an end; ²⁷ TEKEL, you have been weighed on the scales and found wanting; ²⁸ PERES,*c* your kingdom is divided and given to the Medes and Persians."

29 Then Belshazzar gave the command, and Daniel was clothed in purple, a chain of gold was put around his neck, and a proclamation was made concerning him that he should rank third in the kingdom.

30 That very night Belshazzar, the Chaldean king, was killed. ³¹*d* And Da-

---

a Or *a divine spirit*　*b* Aram lacks *the days of*　*c* The singular of *Parsin*
d Ch 6.1 in Aram

5:17—Daniel rebuffs wages as if rejecting the notion of profiting from the gift he has from God. This parallels the speech of the young men as they faced the furnace (3:16–18).

5:24–28—Interpretation of the handwriting. *MENE* is a large weight. *TEKEL* is another weight, perhaps one-sixtieth of a mene. A *PERES* (parsin) is two half-minas. These foreign weights can be reread as Aramaic verbs: "to number," "to weigh," and "to divide." If the weights and the verbs are read together as an assessment of the politics of the region, then the Babylonian king Nebuchadnezzar is succeeded by mina-weight kings Evil-merodach

and Neriglissar, but their short-lived successor Labashi-Marduk weighs in as a mere *shekel*. In turn, his successors Nabonidus and Belshazzar divide a mina between them (= one parsin). The writer combines metaphors of weight, money and political leaders to announce the demise of the Babylonian Empire to the Medo-Persians.

5:29–31—Despite Daniel's earlier protestations, he now receives the reward. There is no such person as Darius the Mede, but we can find three other Persian kings named Darius. Further, we should note that Cyrus, rather than any king named Darius, overthrew the Babylonians.

rius the Mede received the kingdom, being about sixty-two years old.

The Plot against Daniel

6 It pleased Darius to set over the kingdom one hundred twenty satraps, stationed throughout the whole kingdom, ² and over them three presidents, including Daniel; to these the satraps gave account, so that the king might suffer no loss. ³ Soon Daniel distinguished himself above all the other presidents and satraps because an excellent spirit was in him, and the king planned to appoint him over the whole kingdom. ⁴ So the presidents and the satraps tried to find grounds for complaint against Daniel in connection with the kingdom. But they could find no grounds for complaint or any corruption, because he was faithful, and no negligence or corruption could be found in him. ⁵ The men said, "We shall not find any ground for complaint against this Daniel unless we find it in connection with the law of his God."

6 So the presidents and satraps conspired and came to the king and said to him, "O King Darius, live forever! ⁷ All the presidents of the kingdom, the prefects and the satraps, the counselors and the governors are agreed that the king should establish an ordinance and enforce an interdict, that whoever prays to anyone, divine or human, for thirty days, except to you, O king, shall be thrown into a den of lions. ⁸ Now, O king, establish the interdict and sign the document, so that it cannot be changed, according to the law of the Medes and the Persians, which cannot be revoked." ⁹ Therefore King Darius signed the document and interdict.

Daniel in the Lions' Den

10 Although Daniel knew that the document had been signed, he continued to go to his house, which had windows in its upper room open toward Jerusalem, and to get down on his knees three times a day to pray to his God and praise him, just as he had done previously. ¹¹ The conspirators came and found Daniel praying and seeking mercy before his God. ¹² Then they approached the king and said concerning the interdict, "O king! Did you not sign an interdict, that anyone who prays to anyone, divine or human, within thirty days except to you, O king, shall be thrown into a den of lions?" The king answered, "The thing stands fast, according to the law of the Medes and Persians, which cannot be revoked." ¹³ Then they responded to

---

6:1–29 Daniel in the Lions' Den

6:1—Darius I set up the Persian system of satrapies, that is, provinces each governed by a *satrap*. However, he was not a Mede. One hundred twenty satraps is a number routinely used to describe the empire (see Esth. 8:9).

6:3—The stories of Joseph and Mordecai give earlier examples of this motif, the elevation of the Jewish hero to high position in the foreign court. The conflict between Daniel and the other courtiers connects the tone of this chapter with chap. 3.

6:5—This is the first mention of *the law* in the book of Daniel.

6:7—Underlying this text is the ancient western Asian notion that the king had divine characteristics. We see this in the status of the pharaoh in ancient Egypt. Also, certain Caesars were deified in the Roman Empire.

6:8—Behind this story is the idea of the irrevocable nature of the civil *law of the Medes and the Persians*. As in the book of Esther, the monarchs Ahasuerus and Darius become dupes of their own bureaucrats (see Esth. 1:19; 8:8). This story is unusual because other sources indicate that the Persians afforded a degree of religious toleration that exceeded what we see in this story.

6:10 *Windows . . . open*—Daniel did not change his behavior. It is counterproductive to speculate whether he was willfully flaunting his opposition to the edict or not. *Toward Jerusalem*—There is some indication that it was the practice to pray in the direction of Jerusalem (see 1 Kgs. 8:35, 44, 48; 1 Esd. 4:58). *On his knees*—We have examples of such prominent people as Solomon (2 Chr. 6:13) and Ezra (Ezra 9:5) in this prayer posture. *Three times a day* seems to be an early rabbinic (*M. Berakot* 4.1) and Christian (*Didache* 8) tradition.

6:13–14—Daniel's major crime is that he was not one of the other courtiers. The king now perceives that he was duped and attempts to save Daniel.

the king, "Daniel, one of the exiles from Judah, pays no attention to you, O king, or to the interdict you have signed, but he is saying his prayers three times a day."

14 When the king heard the charge, he was very much distressed. He was determined to save Daniel, and until the sun went down he made every effort to rescue him. 15 Then the conspirators came to the king and said to him, "Know, O king, that it is a law of the Medes and Persians that no interdict or ordinance that the king establishes can be changed."

16 Then the king gave the command, and Daniel was brought and thrown into the den of lions. The king said to Daniel, "May your God, whom you faithfully serve, deliver you!" 17 A stone was brought and laid on the mouth of the den, and the king sealed it with his own signet and with the signet of his lords, so that nothing might be changed concerning Daniel. 18 Then the king went to his palace and spent the night fasting; no food was brought to him, and sleep fled from him.

Daniel Saved from the Lions

19 Then, at break of day, the king got up and hurried to the den of lions. 20 When he came near the den where Daniel was, he cried out anxiously to Daniel, "O Daniel, servant of the living God, has your God whom you faithfully serve been able to deliver you from the lions?" 21 Daniel then said to the king, "O king, live forever! 22 My God sent his angel and shut the lions' mouths so

that they would not hurt me, because I was found blameless before him; and also before you, O king, I have done no wrong." 23 Then the king was exceedingly glad and commanded that Daniel be taken up out of the den. So Daniel was taken up out of the den, and no kind of harm was found on him, because he had trusted in his God. 24 The king gave a command, and those who had accused Daniel were brought and thrown into the den of lions—they, their children, and their wives. Before they reached the bottom of the den the lions overpowered them and broke all their bones in pieces.

25 Then King Darius wrote to all peoples and nations of every language throughout the whole world: "May you have abundant prosperity! 26 I make a decree, that in all my royal dominion people should tremble and fear before the God of Daniel:

For he is the living God,
  enduring forever.
His kingdom shall never be destroyed,
  and his dominion has no end.
27 He delivers and rescues,
  he works signs and wonders in
    heaven and on earth;
  for he has saved Daniel
    from the power of the lions."
28 So this Daniel prospered during the reign of Darius and the reign of Cyrus the Persian.

Visions of the Four Beasts

7 In the first year of King Belshazzar of Babylon, Daniel had a dream and visions of his head as he lay in bed.

6:22—*My God sent his angel* reminds us of the fourth person in the fiery furnace (3:25). *I was found blameless*—Over the years the lions' den has been consistently used as the trial by ordeal as well as capital punishment. Inasmuch as Daniel emerges unscathed from the ordeal, he must also be blameless.

6:24 *Those who had accused*—Those who were conspirators are punished with the same instruments that they meant for Daniel. Here again the story echoes Esther. *Their children, and their wives*—The ancient idea of honor and shame

played into the idea that guilt was a family affair (see note at 2:5; also Josh. 7:24–26; Bel 21).

6:25–27—The doxology of Darius. The letter and doxology resemble others in this book (e.g., 4:1–3, 34–37).

6:28—Cyrus the Persian, who pronounced the edict that allowed the exiles to return home to Judea in 539 BCE, ruled 559–530 BCE (see Ezra 1:1–4; 6:3–5; Isa. 44:28; 45:1; 48:14).

7:1–28 The Vision of the Four Beasts
The focus of the material now changes from

Then he wrote down the dream:*a* *2* I,*b* Daniel, saw in my vision by night the four winds of heaven stirring up the great sea, *3* and four great beasts came up out of the sea, different from one another. *4* The first was like a lion and had eagles' wings. Then, as I watched, its wings were plucked off, and it was lifted up from the ground and made to stand on two feet like a human being; and a human mind was given to it. *5* Another beast appeared, a second one, that looked like a bear. It was raised up on one side, had three tusks*c* in its mouth among its teeth and was told, "Arise, devour many bodies!" *6* After this, as I watched, another appeared, like a leopard. The beast had four wings of a bird on its back and four heads; and dominion was given to it. *7* After this I saw in the visions by night a fourth beast, terrifying and dreadful and exceedingly strong. It had great iron teeth and was devouring, breaking in pieces, and stamping what was left with its feet. It was different from all the beasts that preceded it, and it had ten horns. *8* I was considering the horns, when another horn appeared, a little one coming up among them; to make room for it, three of the earlier horns were plucked up by the roots. There were eyes like human eyes in this horn, and a mouth speaking arrogantly.

Judgment before the Ancient One

9 As I watched,
    thrones were set in place,

---

a Q Ms Theodotion: MT adds *the beginning of the words; he said*
b Theodotion: Aram *Daniel answered and said, I*   *c* Or *ribs*

---

folktales to vision reports, from personal stories to predictions of world and national history—in short, from wisdom to apocalyptic.

7:1—*In the first year*, i.e., 554 BCE. This is a third-person introduction. The location of the dream vision at night and on the bed involves a blending of literary types. When several pieces of literature share metaphors, vocabulary, literary structure or other major common features, that group is a literary type. For instance we have the wise courtier literary type (chaps. 1–6; Gen. 39–47). The types blended here are the dream report and the vision report.

7:2 *I, Daniel*—The formula here marks the shift from third-person description to first-person report. However, it occurs frequently in the book of Daniel (see note at 4:4). *Four winds of heaven* is a phrase used particularly in the postexilic period vision reports and calls to repentance. Typically, it portends judgment. (Cf. Jer. 49:36; Ezek. 37:9; Dan. 8:8; 11:4; Zech. 2:6; 6:5.) *The great sea* (Gen. 1:2) refers to the primordial symbol of chaos, inhabited by monsters and dragons (see Job 26:12; Isa. 27:1; 51:9–10; Rev. 13:1).

7:3—The sea of chaos with dragons and monsters gives up four beasts, symbolizing empires. (Cf. 7:17; Pss. 68:30; 74:13; 87:4; Isa. 27:1; Ezek. 29:3, 32.)

7:4—The use of simile ("like") dominates this vision report. In the Jewish context, the hybrid nature of these monsters means, a priori, that they are unclean (cf. Lev. 11). The lion is often a symbol of political power (e.g., Gen. 49:9; Pss. 7:3; 10:9; Jer. 2:30; Hos. 11:10; Mic. 5:7). The winged *lion* represents the Babylonian Empire.

7:5—The *bear* most likely represents the Medes (enemies of the Babylonians, cf. Jer. 51:11). *Three tusks* (ribs) are extraordinarily large, which sets them apart from regular teeth.

7:6—The *leopard* likely represents Persia.

7:7—The *fourth beast* stands for the Greek Empire of Alexander the Great and its heirs, the *diadachoi*, which was the name given to the coterie of generals who took control of Alexander's empire after his untimely death in 323 BCE. *Stamping* language is interesting in light of the use of elephants in warfare during this time (1 Macc. 1:17; 3:34; 6:28–47; 3 Macc. 5:45). *Ten horns* refers to the Seleucid kingdom in Syria set up by Seleucus I, one of Alexander's generals. The theme of devouring human flesh, this time with iron teeth instead of three tusks, occurs again in this description of the empire.

7:8—The little *horn* is probably a reference to Antiochus IV Epiphanes (175–164 BCE) and his hubris. *Three of the earlier horns were plucked up by the roots* suggests a history of court intrigue and murder, but scholars are unable to agree on which of the many murdered Seleucid rulers or pretenders were "plucked up" by Antiochus.

7:9—The vision now shifts to a throne room scene. (See 1 Kgs. 22:19; Isa. 6; Ezek. 1:26–28; 3:22–24; 10:1; 1 Enoch 14; Matt. 19:28; Rev. 4:2; 20:4.) *Ancient One* probably refers to the head of the pantheon. The anthropomorphic detail of this description is unusual for the Hebrew Bible. *White* clothing. See Matt. 28:3; Rev. 3:5. *Hair of his head like pure wool* indicates that the color of the hair is white, which indicates age. Also, it

and an Ancient One[a] took his
    throne,
his clothing was white as snow,
    and the hair of his head like pure
        wool;
his throne was fiery flames,
    and its wheels were burning fire.
10 A stream of fire issued
    and flowed out from his presence.
A thousand thousands served him,
    and ten thousand times ten
        thousand stood attending him.
The court sat in judgment,
    and the books were opened.
11 I watched then because of the noise
of the arrogant words that the horn was
speaking. And as I watched, the beast
was put to death, and its body destroyed
and given over to be burned with fire.
12 As for the rest of the beasts, their
dominion was taken away, but their lives
were prolonged for a season and a time.
13 As I watched in the night visions,
    I saw one like a human being[b]
        coming with the clouds of heaven.
    And he came to the Ancient One[c]
        and was presented before him.
14 To him was given dominion
    and glory and kingship,
    that all peoples, nations, and
        languages

should serve him.
His dominion is an everlasting
    dominion
    that shall not pass away,
and his kingship is one
    that shall never be destroyed.

Daniel's Visions Interpreted

15 As for me, Daniel, my spirit was
troubled within me,[d] and the visions of
my head terrified me. 16 I approached
one of the attendants to ask him the
truth concerning all this. So he said that
he would disclose to me the interpretation of the matter: 17 "As for these four
great beasts, four kings shall arise out
of the earth. 18 But the holy ones of the
Most High shall receive the kingdom
and possess the kingdom forever—forever and ever."

19 Then I desired to know the truth
concerning the fourth beast, which was
different from all the rest, exceedingly
terrifying, with its teeth of iron and
claws of bronze, and which devoured
and broke in pieces, and stamped what
was left with its feet; 20 and concerning
the ten horns that were on its head, and
concerning the other horn, which came
up and to make room for which three

[a] Aram *an Ancient of Days* [b] Aram *one like a son of man* [c] Aram *the Ancient of Days* [d] Aram *troubled in its sheath*

---

suggests that the author places this metaphor in
an Afro-Asiatic context where coarse, curly hair
is the norm. The *fiery flames* and *wheels* of the
throne resonate with Ezekiel's vision in Ezek. 1:4,
15–21; 10:2.

7:10—The *books* may refer to the record kept in
heaven of human deeds (Ps. 56:9; Isa. 65:6; Mal.
3:16; 1 Enoch 90:20). The image of the opened
books is picked up again in the New Testament
(Rev. 20:12).

7:11—The first three empires simply lose power,
but the Greek Empire is singled out for destruction.

7:13—*One like a human being*, lit. "one like a
son of man," indicates that this is not a human
being, but only resembles one. However, over
history this figure has been interpreted as referring to human beings such as Judas Maccabeus
and Daniel himself. More likely suggestions
include guardian angels Michael (10:13, 21;
see also Rev. 12) and Gabriel (Dan. 9:21). The

messianic tone has led many to graft this passage
onto the "son of man" traditions. Early Jewish
apocalyptic works such as 1 Enoch connect this
metaphor with the messianic age. Canonical
Christian Gospels understand this passage as
the context for the self-designation "son of man"
used by Jesus.

7:15—*My spirit was troubled within me* seems
to accompany revelation (2:1; 4:1; 8:27; Gen.
41:8).

7:16—Here the writer employs an angel interpreter. (See also Zech. 1:9, 13, 14; 2:3; 4:4; 5:5,
10; 6:4.)

7:17—*Four great beasts* refer to Babylon, Media,
Persia, and Greece.

7:18—*The holy ones* are members of the heavenly court (Deut. 33:2; Job 5:1; 15:5; Ps. 89:5, 7;
Zech. 14:5; Dan. 8:13). It is unclear whether this
also refers to the members of the believing community who have been faithful.

of them fell out—the horn that had eyes and a mouth that spoke arrogantly, and that seemed greater than the others. ²¹ As I looked, this horn made war with the holy ones and was prevailing over them, ²² until the Ancient One*a* came; then judgment was given for the holy ones of the Most High, and the time arrived when the holy ones gained possession of the kingdom.

23 This is what he said: "As for the fourth beast,

    there shall be a fourth kingdom on earth
      that shall be different from all the other kingdoms;
    it shall devour the whole earth,
      and trample it down, and break it to pieces.
²⁴ As for the ten horns,
    out of this kingdom ten kings shall arise,
    and another shall arise after them.
    This one shall be different from the former ones,
      and shall put down three kings.
²⁵ He shall speak words against the Most High,
    shall wear out the holy ones of the Most High,
    and shall attempt to change the sacred seasons and the law;
    and they shall be given into his power
      for a time, two times,*b* and half a time.

²⁶ Then the court shall sit in judgment,
    and his dominion shall be taken away,
      to be consumed and totally destroyed.
²⁷ The kingship and dominion
    and the greatness of the kingdoms under the whole heaven
    shall be given to the people of the holy ones of the Most High;
    their kingdom shall be an everlasting kingdom,
    and all dominions shall serve and obey them."

28 Here the account ends. As for me, Daniel, my thoughts greatly terrified me, and my face turned pale; but I kept the matter in my mind.

Vision of a Ram and a Goat

8 In the third year of the reign of King Belshazzar a vision appeared to me, Daniel, after the one that had appeared to me at first. ² In the vision I was looking and saw myself in Susa the capital, in the province of Elam,*c* and I was by the river Ulai. *d* ³ I looked up and saw a ram standing beside the river.*e* It had two horns. Both horns were long, but one was longer than the other, and the longer one came up second. ⁴ I saw the ram charging westward and northward and southward. All beasts were powerless to withstand it, and no one could rescue

---

a Aram *the Ancient of Days*   *b* Aram *a time, times*   *c* Gk Theodotion: MT Q Ms repeat *in the vision I was looking*   *d* Or *the Ulai Gate*   *e* Or *gate*

7:25–28—A catalog of the offenses of Antiochus IV Epiphanes against the faith. *Words against the Most High* refers to the acts of Antiochus IV Epiphanes, the first Hellenistic king to use divine self-designation on the coins of the realm. *Wear out the holy ones of the Most High* probably refers to religious persecution during his reign (summed up in horrific detail in 1 Macc. 1:54–61). *Change the sacred seasons and the law* refers to the sweeping changes he instituted as part of his process of hellenization. The phrase *a time, two times, and half a time* indicates three and one-half years (cf. 8:14; 9:27; 12:7, 11, 12). The report that Daniel kept all of his visionary learnings in his mind coheres with a characteristic of apocalyptic literature that the revelation is

secret until the appropriate time. It provides a fictional setting for what is in fact mostly *vaticinium ex eventu* (prophecy after the fact).

8:1–27 The Vision of the Ram and the Male Goat

8:1—This chapter returns to Hebrew. *In the third year*—552 BCE.

8:2—*Susa* was the winter capital of Persian Empire during the reign of Darius. (See also Neh. 1:1; Esth. 1:2.) *Elam* is a region east of the Tigris River. Like Ezekiel's at the River Chebar (Ezek. 1:1), Daniel's vision occurs at a river, the Ulai.

8:3—*Ram* could refer to an astrological symbol. *Two horns* represent Media and Persia (cf. v. 20).

from its power; it did as it pleased and became strong.

5 As I was watching, a male goat appeared from the west, coming across the face of the whole earth without touching the ground. The goat had a horn[a] between its eyes. [6] It came toward the ram with the two horns that I had seen standing beside the river,[b] and it ran at it with savage force. [7] I saw it approaching the ram. It was enraged against it and struck the ram, breaking its two horns. The ram did not have power to withstand it; it threw the ram down to the ground and trampled upon it, and there was no one who could rescue the ram from its power. [8] Then the male goat grew exceedingly great; but at the height of its power, the great horn was broken, and in its place there came up four prominent horns toward the four winds of heaven.

9 Out of one of them came another[c] horn, a little one, which grew exceedingly great toward the south, toward the east, and toward the beautiful land. [10] It grew as high as the host of heaven.

It threw down to the earth some of the host and some of the stars, and trampled on them. [11] Even against the prince of the host it acted arrogantly; it took the regular burnt offering away from him and overthrew the place of his sanctuary. [12] Because of wickedness, the host was given over to it together with the regular burnt offering;[d] it cast truth to the ground, and kept prospering in what it did. [13] Then I heard a holy one speaking, and another holy one said to the one that spoke, "For how long is this vision concerning the regular burnt offering, the transgression that makes desolate, and the giving over of the sanctuary and host to be trampled?"[d] [14] And he answered him,[e] "For two thousand three hundred evenings and mornings; then the sanctuary shall be restored to its rightful state."

Gabriel Interprets the Vision

15 When I, Daniel, had seen the vision, I tried to understand it. Then someone

---

[a] Theodotion: Gk one horn; Heb a horn of vision [b] Or gate [c] Cn Compare 7.8: Heb one [d] Meaning of Heb uncertain [e] Gk Theodotion Syr Vg: Heb me

---

8:5—*Male goat* is also a sign of the zodiac. The directions may refer to Alexander's eastern campaign.

8:8—*The great horn* describes the rise and fall of Alexander the Great. *Four prominent horns* refer to the *diadachoi*, the four generals (Cassander, Lysimachus, Seleucus, and Ptolemy) who divided the empire after Alexander's death in 323 BCE.

8:9—A little *horn* is probably a reference to Antiochus IV Epiphanes (as in 7:8). *The beautiful land* refers to Judea in general and Jerusalem in particular (11:16, 41; Jer. 3:19; Ezek. 20:6, 15).

8:10—*Host of heaven* refers to heavenly beings, here associated with the stars. In the background of the depiction of Babylon here is the Canaanite myth of Helel and Shahar (Morning Star and Dawn), who fall to earth as result of a rebellion. In Christianity, this will be adapted into the story of the fall of Lucifer and his attendant angels.

8:11—Even though "prince" is used elsewhere in Daniel to refer to angels (10:13, 20–21), here *prince of the host* refers to God. *Took . . . away . . . and overthrew* calls attention to the replacement of Jewish sacrificial traditions with sacrifices to Zeus (1 Macc. 1:45, 59; 2 Macc. 5:5)

in 167 BCE by the Seleucid ruler Antiochus IV Epiphanes.

8:13 *How long*—A typical phrase in the Hebrew laments. (See Pss. 6:3; 13:1–2; 79:5; 80:4; 90:13; 94:3.) On occasion, the prophets would also use this literary and musical tradition (e.g., Isa. 6:11; Jer. 4:14, 21; 12:4; 23:26; 31:22; 47:5; Zech. 1:12). *The transgression that makes desolate* probably refers to an image erected in the temple by Antiochus IV. The Hebrew term *shiqquts shomem* sets up a wordplay on the expression *Baal Shamen* or "lord of heaven," which is a Greco-Syrian epithet of Zeus.

8:14—*Two thousand three hundred evenings and mornings* equals 1,150 days. The use of the language of evening and morning indicates the relationship of this prophecy to the ritual practice of evening and morning sacrifices. The sanctuary was restored on 25th Chislev (December 14), 164 BCE.

8:15–16—In Gabriel's interpretation (vv. 15–27), the references to *appearance of a man* and *human voice* indicate that this is an angel who typically provides information to human beings by taking on human form (see 7:13). The name *Gabriel* means either "warrior of God" or "God

appeared standing before me, having the appearance of a man, [16] and I heard a human voice by the Ulai, calling, "Gabriel, help this man understand the vision." [17] So he came near where I stood; and when he came, I became frightened and fell prostrate. But he said to me, "Understand, O mortal,[a] that the vision is for the time of the end."

18 As he was speaking to me, I fell into a trance, face to the ground; then he touched me and set me on my feet. [19] He said, "Listen, and I will tell you what will take place later in the period of wrath; for it refers to the appointed time of the end. [20] As for the ram that you saw with the two horns, these are the kings of Media and Persia. [21] The male goat[b] is the king of Greece, and the great horn between its eyes is the first king. [22] As for the horn that was broken, in place of which four others arose, four kingdoms shall arise from his[c] nation, but not with his power.

[23] At the end of their rule,
    when the transgressions have
        reached their full measure,
    a king of bold countenance shall arise,
        skilled in intrigue.
[24] He shall grow strong in power,[d]
        shall cause fearful destruction,
        and shall succeed in what he
            does.
    He shall destroy the powerful
        and the people of the holy ones.
[25] By his cunning
    he shall make deceit prosper under
        his hand,
    and in his own mind he shall be
        great.
    Without warning he shall destroy
        many
    and shall even rise up against the
        Prince of princes.
    But he shall be broken, and not by
        human hands.
[26] The vision of the evenings and the mornings that has been told is true. As for you, seal up the vision, for it refers to many days from now."

27 So I, Daniel, was overcome and lay sick for some days; then I arose and went about the king's business. But I

---

[a] Heb son of man   [b] Or shaggy male goat   [c] Gk Theodotion Vg: Heb the
[d] Theodotion and one Gk Ms: Heb repeats (from 8.22) but not with his power

---

is my warrior." This bifocal reading of the name Gabriel is in keeping with the bilingual (that is, double-voiced) tone of the book (see also note at 1:6–7). Gabriel appears again in the vision reports of Daniel (9:21) and is the divine messenger in the annunciation (Luke 1:19, 26). Gabriel has the status of archangel, that is, one of the top four angels in the hierarchy. These angels could function as messengers, intercessors, or destroyers. (See also 1 Enoch 9:1, 9–10; 40:6.)

8:17—End is a hallmark of eschatological (apocalyptic) writings such as the vision reports of Daniel (v. 19; 11:27, 35, 40; 12:4, 6, 9). "Eschatological" comes from the Greek terms eschaton, "last" or "end," and logos, "word" or "study of." We see it clearly in exilic prophecy (e.g., Ezek. 7:6; 21:30, 34; 35:5).

8:18—Trance is a state of deep sleep or unconsciousness. It is a state without human volition or agency. Adam was in this state during the creation of the woman (Gen. 2:21). The touch of an angel conveys power and commissioning (Dan. 9:21; 10:10, 16, 18; Isa. 6:7; Jer. 1:9).

8:23—The idea of transgressions needing to reach a critical mass before they were ready for appropriate retribution begins early, but finds fertile soil in the Greco-Roman era (see Gen. 15:16; 2 Macc. 6:14; 2 Esd. 4:36–37).

8:25—Without warning may be a reference to the surprise attack on Jerusalem by Antiochus IV Epiphanes (1 Macc. 1:29–30). Prince of princes, like its parallel prince of the host in v. 11, is a reference to God. In a supreme act of hubris and idolatry, Antiochus IV has assumed divine status. Not by human hands means that the sole responsibility for the end of the Seleucid oppression rests with God. This nod to pacifism contrasts sharply with the activism of some of the Maccabean followers (see also 2:34). A pacifistic framework for this passage is interesting, for in fact Antiochus IV may have been killed in battle (164 BCE) by the human hands not of Jews but of Persians. (Other accounts of Antiochus's death may be found in 11:40–45; 1 Macc. 6:1–17; 2 Macc. 1:13–17; 9:1–29.)

8:26—The instruction seal up the vision once again points to the element in prior revelations of secrecy, which is characteristic of apocalyptic literature and vaticinium ex eventu (prophecy after the fact; see 7:28).

was dismayed by the vision and did not understand it.

Daniel's Prayer for the People

9 In the first year of Darius son of Ahasuerus, by birth a Mede, who became king over the realm of the Chaldeans— ²in the first year of his reign, I, Daniel, perceived in the books the number of years that, according to the word of the LORD to the prophet Jeremiah, must be fulfilled for the devastation of Jerusalem, namely, seventy years.

3 Then I turned to the Lord God, to seek an answer by prayer and supplication with fasting and sackcloth and ashes. ⁴I prayed to the LORD my God and made confession, saying,

"Ah, Lord, great and awesome God, keeping covenant and steadfast love with those who love you and keep your commandments, ⁵we have sinned and done wrong, acted wickedly and rebelled, turning aside from your commandments and ordinances. ⁶We have not listened to your servants the prophets, who spoke in your name to our kings, our princes, and our ancestors, and to all the people of the land.

7 "Righteousness is on your side, O Lord, but open shame, as at this day, falls on us, the people of Judah, the inhabitants of Jerusalem, and all Israel, those who are near and those who are far away, in all the lands to which you have driven them, because of the treachery that they have committed against you. ⁸Open shame, O LORD, falls on us, our kings, our officials, and our ancestors, because we have sinned against you. ⁹To the Lord our God belong mercy and forgiveness, for we have rebelled against him, ¹⁰and have not obeyed the voice of the LORD our God by following his laws, which he set before us by his servants the prophets.

11 "All Israel has transgressed your law and turned aside, refusing to obey your voice. So the curse and the oath written in the law of Moses, the servant of God, have been poured out upon us, because we have sinned against you. ¹²He has confirmed his words, which he spoke against us and against our rulers, by bringing upon us a calamity so great that what has been done against Jerusalem has never before been done under the whole heaven. ¹³Just as it is written in the law of Moses, all this calamity has come upon us. We did not entreat the favor of the LORD our God, turning from our iniquities and reflecting on his*a* fidelity. ¹⁴So the LORD kept watch over this calamity until he brought it upon us. Indeed, the LORD our God is right in all that he has done; for we have disobeyed his voice.

15 "And now, O Lord our God, who brought your people out of the land of Egypt with a mighty hand and made your name renowned even to

a Heb *your*

9:1–27 Prophecy of the Seventy Weeks

9:1—*Ahasuerus* is the equivalent of Xerxes, a fictitious parent for a fictitious Darius.

9:2 *Jeremiah*—The explicit reference to another biblical book is unusual but reflects the intertextuality of the biblical literature of the Greco-Roman period. The passage referred to here predicts the *devastation of Jerusalem* in 587 BCE. The restoration after *seventy years* also alludes to the same biblical sources (see Jer. 25:11–12; 29:10–14).

9:3—*Fasting and sackcloth and ashes* were traditional signs of mourning (see Ezra 8:21–23; Esth. 4:1–4; Jer. 49:28–33; Joel 2:5; 1 Macc. 3:44–46; 2 Macc. 13:12). Sackcloth was gener-

ally dark-colored material of goat or camel hair. It was uncomfortable to wear and therefore appropriate as a sign of distress. Fasting could also be used to prepare for a special religious experience (e.g., Exod. 34:28; 1 Kgs. 19:8).

9:4—Communal *confession* was a staple of piety in the biblical period. (See 1 Kgs. 8:47; 2 Chr. 6:37; Ps. 106:6.) The postexilic community especially used this act of piety. (Cf. Neh. 1 and 9.)

9:11 *The curse and the oath*—An implicit reference to earlier legal tradition (see Deut. 28:15–45; Neh. 10:29).

9:13—*Written in the law of Moses* is another cross-reference to the Pentateuch (see Lev. 26:14–22; Deut. 30:1).

this day—we have sinned, we have done wickedly. [16] O Lord, in view of all your righteous acts, let your anger and wrath, we pray, turn away from your city Jerusalem, your holy mountain; because of our sins and the iniquities of our ancestors, Jerusalem and your people have become a disgrace among all our neighbors. [17] Now therefore, O our God, listen to the prayer of your servant and to his supplication, and for your own sake, Lord,[a] let your face shine upon your desolated sanctuary. [18] Incline your ear, O my God, and hear. Open your eyes and look at our desolation and the city that bears your name. We do not present our supplication before you on the ground of our righteousness, but on the ground of your great mercies. [19] O Lord, hear; O Lord, forgive; O Lord, listen and act and do not delay! For your own sake, O my God, because your city and your people bear your name!"

The Seventy Weeks

20 While I was speaking, and was praying and confessing my sin and the sin of my people Israel, and presenting my supplication before the LORD my God on behalf of the holy mountain of my God— [21] while I was speaking in prayer, the man Gabriel, whom I had seen before in a vision, came to me in swift flight at the time of the evening sacrifice. [22] He came[b] and said to me, "Daniel, I have now come out to give you wisdom and understanding. [23] At the beginning of your supplications a word went out, and I have come to declare it, for you are greatly beloved. So consider the word and understand the vision:

24 "Seventy weeks are decreed for your people and your holy city: to finish the transgression, to put an end to sin, and to atone for iniquity, to bring in everlasting righteousness, to seal both vision and prophet, and to anoint a most holy place.[c] [25] Know therefore and understand: from the time that the word went out to restore and rebuild Jerusalem until the time of an anointed prince, there shall be seven weeks; and for sixty-two weeks it shall be built again with streets and moat, but in a troubled time. [26] After the sixty-two weeks, an anointed one shall be cut off and shall have nothing, and the troops of the prince who is to come shall destroy the city and the sanctuary. Its[d] end shall come with a flood, and to the end there shall be war. Desolations are decreed. [27] He shall make a strong covenant with many for one week, and for half of the week he shall make sacrifice and offering cease; and in their place[e] shall be an abomination that desolates, until the decreed end is poured out upon the desolator."

[a] Theodotion Vg Compare Syr: Heb *for the Lord's sake*   [b] Gk Syr: Heb *He made to understand*   [c] Or *thing* or *one*   [d] Or *His*   [e] Cn: Meaning of Heb uncertain

---

9:16—Despite Daniel's location in exile, the focal point for restoration remains *Jerusalem*.

9:17—*Desolated sanctuary* describes the temple following the atrocities of Antiochus IV.

9:21—See note at 8:15–16.

9:24—Gabriel tells Daniel that the period of *seventy weeks*, derived from Jeremiah's prophecy, is interpreted as meaning seventy weeks of years (70 × 7). Such a reading would produce a figure of 490 years, which is a full jubilee cycle (see Lev. 25). The prediction echoes the earlier vision in Dan. 7:26–27.

9:25—*The word went out* refers to the edict of Cyrus (539 BCE) that allowed the exiles to return to Judea. *Seven weeks*—Forty-nine years. *Sixty-two weeks*—434 years. *An anointed prince* could be either Zerubbabel or Joshua. (See Zech. 4:14; also Ezra 2:2; 3:2; Hag. 1:1–14.)

9:26—The deposed *anointed* probably refers to Onias III (see 2 Macc. 4:23–28), who was murdered 171 BCE. The *prince . . . to come* surely refers to Antiochus IV, who will incite the war.

9:27—Antiochus IV made *a strong covenant* with Jason and others among the priestly families (1 Macc. 1:11). *One week*—Seven years. *Half of the week*—Three and one-half years (cf. note at 7:25–28).

Conflict of Nations
and Heavenly Powers

10 In the third year of King Cyrus of Persia a word was revealed to Daniel, who was named Belteshazzar. The word was true, and it concerned a great conflict. He understood the word, having received understanding in the vision.

2 At that time I, Daniel, had been mourning for three weeks. ³I had eaten no rich food, no meat or wine had entered my mouth, and I had not anointed myself at all, for the full three weeks. ⁴On the twenty-fourth day of the first month, as I was standing on the bank of the great river (that is, the Tigris), ⁵I looked up and saw a man clothed in linen, with a belt of gold from Uphaz around his waist. ⁶His body was like beryl, his face like lightning, his eyes like flaming torches, his arms and legs like the gleam of burnished bronze, and the sound of his words like the roar of a multitude. ⁷I, Daniel, alone saw the vision; the people who were with me did not see the vision, though a great trembling fell upon them, and they fled and hid themselves. ⁸So I was left alone to see this great vision. My strength left me, and my complexion grew deathly pale, and I retained no strength. ⁹Then I

heard the sound of his words; and when I heard the sound of his words, I fell into a trance, face to the ground.

10 But then a hand touched me and roused me to my hands and knees. ¹¹He said to me, "Daniel, greatly beloved, pay attention to the words that I am going to speak to you. Stand on your feet, for I have now been sent to you." So while he was speaking this word to me, I stood up trembling. ¹²He said to me, "Do not fear, Daniel, for from the first day that you set your mind to gain understanding and to humble yourself before your God, your words have been heard, and I have come because of your words. ¹³But the prince of the kingdom of Persia opposed me twenty-one days. So Michael, one of the chief princes, came to help me, and I left him there with the prince of the kingdom of Persia,ᵃ ¹⁴and have come to help you understand what is to happen to your people at the end of days. For there is a further vision for those days."

15 While he was speaking these words to me, I turned my face toward the ground and was speechless. ¹⁶Then one in human form touched my lips, and I opened my mouth to speak, and said to the one who stood before me, "My lord,

ᵃ Gk Theodotion: Heb I was left there with the kings of Persia

---

10:1–12:13 Daniel's Vision
The last three chapters of Daniel are a vision of Daniel concerning the future.

10:1—*Third year of King Cyrus* is 536 BCE. The cross-reference between the two names Daniel and Belteshazzar connects the folktales and the vision reports (see 1:7; 5:12).

10:4 *On the bank of the great river*—Typically this is the designation for the Euphrates (Gen. 31:21; Exod. 23:21; Num. 20:5). Sometimes there is even a gloss or parenthetical comment designating the river as the Euphrates (e.g., Gen. 15:18; Deut. 1:7; Josh. 1:4). However, here there is an unusual gloss (*that is, the Tigris*). It could have arisen because at one time in the transmission of the passage the location of the vision was assumed to be Babylon, which is on the Euphrates. At another time, probably later, the editor thought that the vision of chap. 10 occurred at the same place as the one recounted in chap. 8,

namely near Susa. This prompted the editor to place Daniel on the banks of the Tigris, which would be closer to Susa.

10:5–6—*Clothed in linen* indicates temple priesthood (cf. Ezek. 9:2–7). *Beryl* is a precious stone, sea green in color. It has two types: emerald and aquamarine. (Cf. Exod. 28:20; 39:13; Ezek. 1:16; 10:9; 28:13; Rev. 21:20.)

10:10–21 Gabriel's Encouragement

10:10 *Touched*—See note at 8:18.

10:13—*Prince of the kingdom of Persia* is clearly a reference to the patron angel of Persia. Here we see that patron or guardian angels engage in heavenly conflicts that match earthly ones. *Michael* was another patron angel of Israel (see 10:21; 12:1; Jude 9; Rev. 12:7).

10:16 *Touched my lips*—Reminiscent of prophetic call (commissioning) visions (Isa. 6:7; Jer. 1:9).

because of the vision such pains have come upon me that I retain no strength. [17] How can my lord's servant talk with my lord? For I am shaking,[a] no strength remains in me, and no breath is left in me."

18 Again one in human form touched me and strengthened me. [19] He said, "Do not fear, greatly beloved, you are safe. Be strong and courageous!" When he spoke to me, I was strengthened and said, "Let my lord speak, for you have strengthened me." [20] Then he said, "Do you know why I have come to you? Now I must return to fight against the prince of Persia, and when I am through with him, the prince of Greece will come. [21] But I am to tell you what is inscribed in the book of truth. There is no one with me who contends against these princes except

11 Michael, your prince. [1] As for me, in the first year of Darius the Mede, I stood up to support and strengthen him.

2 "Now I will announce the truth to you. Three more kings shall arise in Persia. The fourth shall be far richer than all of them, and when he has become strong through his riches, he shall stir up all against the kingdom of Greece. [3] Then a warrior king shall arise, who shall rule with great dominion and take action as he pleases. [4] And while

still rising in power, his kingdom shall be broken and divided toward the four winds of heaven, but not to his posterity, nor according to the dominion with which he ruled; for his kingdom shall be uprooted and go to others besides these.

5 "Then the king of the south shall grow strong, but one of his officers shall grow stronger than he and shall rule a realm greater than his own realm. [6] After some years they shall make an alliance, and the daughter of the king of the south shall come to the king of the north to ratify the agreement. But she shall not retain her power, and his offspring shall not endure. She shall be given up, she and her attendants and her child and the one who supported her.

"In those times [7] a branch from her roots shall rise up in his place. He shall come against the army and enter the fortress of the king of the north, and he shall take action against them and prevail. [8] Even their gods, with their idols and with their precious vessels of silver and gold, he shall carry off to Egypt as spoils of war. For some years he shall refrain from attacking the king of the north; [9] then the latter shall invade the realm of the king of the south, but will return to his own land.

[a] Gk: Heb *from now*

11:1–45 Daniel's Vision Continues: History Is a Tragic Record of Oppression

11:2—*Three more* Persian *kings* probably are Cambyses (530–522), Darius I (522–486), and Xerxes I (486–465). **The fourth** is probably either Darius III (336–330), a particularly weak king who would not match the description of the verse, or Artaxerxes I (465–424), who was sufficiently strong to match the description.

11:3—*Warrior king* almost surely refers to Alexander the Great (336–323 BCE).

11:4—*Divided toward the four winds* refers to the four generals, (Cassander, Lysimachus, Seleucus, and Ptolemy) who were not heirs (*posterity*) to Alexander, but who eventually ruled the divided empire. The Ptolemies and Seleucids struggled for control of Palestine.

11:5—*King of the south* refers to the house of

Ptolemy I Soter of Egypt (satrap 323–305; king 305–282). The *officer* was probably Seleucus I Nicanor (305–281), the first Seleucid, who ruled Mesopotamia and Syria.

11:6—A marriage alliance between *the king of the south* (Ptolemy II Philadelphus 285–246) and *the king of the north* (Antiochus II Theos 261–246) was forged with the marriage of Ptolemy's daughter Berenice to Antiochus in 252 BCE. The alliance failed when Berenice, her child, and attendants were murdered in an incident of court intrigue.

11:7–8—*A branch from her roots* probably refers to her brother Ptolemy III Euergetes (246–221), who successfully looted the Seleucid regions.

11:9—Reference to the ill-fated attack on Egypt (242–240) by Seleucus II Callinicius (246–225).

10 "His sons shall wage war and assemble a multitude of great forces, which shall advance like a flood and pass through, and again shall carry the war as far as his fortress. **11** Moved with rage, the king of the south shall go out and do battle against the king of the north, who shall muster a great multitude, which shall, however, be defeated by his enemy. **12** When the multitude has been carried off, his heart shall be exalted, and he shall overthrow tens of thousands, but he shall not prevail. **13** For the king of the north shall again raise a multitude, larger than the former, and after some years*a* he shall advance with a great army and abundant supplies.

14 "In those times many shall rise against the king of the south. The lawless among your own people shall lift themselves up in order to fulfill the vision, but they shall fail. **15** Then the king of the north shall come and throw up siegeworks, and take a well-fortified city. And the forces of the south shall not stand, not even his picked troops, for there shall be no strength to resist. **16** But he who comes against him shall take the actions he pleases, and no one shall withstand him. He shall take a position in the beautiful land, and all of it shall be in his power. **17** He shall set

his mind to come with the strength of his whole kingdom, and he shall bring terms of peace*b* and perform them. In order to destroy the kingdom,*c* he shall give him a woman in marriage; but it shall not succeed or be to his advantage. **18** Afterward he shall turn to the coastlands, and shall capture many. But a commander shall put an end to his insolence; indeed,*d* he shall turn his insolence back upon him. **19** Then he shall turn back toward the fortresses of his own land, but he shall stumble and fall, and shall not be found.

20 "Then shall arise in his place one who shall send an official for the glory of the kingdom; but within a few days he shall be broken, though not in anger or in battle. **21** In his place shall arise a contemptible person on whom royal majesty had not been conferred; he shall come in without warning and obtain the kingdom through intrigue. **22** Armies shall be utterly swept away and broken before him, and the prince of the covenant as well. **23** And after an alliance is made with him, he shall act deceitfully and become strong with a small party. **24** Without warning he shall come into the richest parts*e* of the province and

a Heb *and at the end of the times years* *b* Gk: Heb *kingdom, and upright ones with him* *c* Heb *it* *d* Meaning of Heb uncertain *e* Or *among the richest men*

11:10—*His sons* were Seleucus III (225–223) and Antiochus III (223–187).

11:11—Refers to the defeat of Antiochus' III by Ptolemy IV (221–204) at the battle of Raphia (217).

11:13—Despite defeat at the battle of Raphia, Antiochus III waged successful campaigns (212–205).

11:14—Reference to the unsuccessful insurrection against the child king Ptolemy V (204–180). *The lawless* may refer to the conflict between noble Judean families, the Tobiads and the Oniads, for control of the Jerusalem priesthood.

11:15–16—*A well-fortified city* refers possibly to Sidon. Once again, *the beautiful land* refers to Judea.

11:17—*Terms of peace* refers to another marriage alliance between the Ptolemies and the Seleucids (see note at 11:6). In 197 BCE, Antiochus III betrothed his daughter, Cleopatra I, to Ptolemy V Epiphanes.

11:18–19—Antiochus's adventures led to defeats in Greece at Thermopylae (191) and Magnesia (190) at the hands of the Romans, which left him with substantial tribute debt. Antiochus III was killed at Elymais (187) while he was robbing its temple of Bel in order to pay his tribute to Rome.

11:20—Seleucus IV Philopater (187–175), who succeeded Antiochus III, sought to pay the Roman indemnity by sacking the temple in Jerusalem. He sent an official, Heliodorus, as tribute collector. Heliodorus failed and died ingloriously (2 Macc. 3:1–40).

11:21—Antiochus IV Epiphanes (175–164) was the *contemptible person*.

11:22–23—*Prince of the covenant* refers to the deposed high priest Onias III, who was replaced by his assimilationist brother Jason. *A small party* indicates a tension between the supporters of Hellenism and the anti-Seleucid majority.

do what none of his predecessors had ever done, lavishing plunder, spoil, and wealth on them. He shall devise plans against strongholds, but only for a time. ²⁵ He shall stir up his power and determination against the king of the south with a great army, and the king of the south shall wage war with a much greater and stronger army. But he shall not succeed, for plots shall be devised against him ²⁶ by those who eat of the royal rations. They shall break him, his army shall be swept away, and many shall fall slain. ²⁷ The two kings, their minds bent on evil, shall sit at one table and exchange lies. But it shall not succeed, for there remains an end at the time appointed. ²⁸ He shall return to his land with great wealth, but his heart shall be set against the holy covenant. He shall work his will, and return to his own land.

29 "At the time appointed he shall return and come into the south, but this time it shall not be as it was before. ³⁰ For ships of Kittim shall come against him, and he shall lose heart and withdraw. He shall be enraged and take action against the holy covenant. He shall turn back and pay heed to those who forsake the holy covenant. ³¹ Forces sent by him shall occupy and profane the temple and fortress. They shall abolish the regular burnt offering and set up the abomination that makes desolate. ³² He shall seduce with intrigue those who violate the covenant; but the people who are loyal to their God shall stand firm and take action. ³³ The wise among the people shall give understanding to many; for some days, however, they shall fall by sword and flame, and suffer captivity and plunder. ³⁴ When they fall victim, they shall receive a little help, and many shall join them insincerely. ³⁵ Some of the wise shall fall, so that they may be refined, purified, and cleansed,ᵃ until the time of the end, for there is still an interval until the time appointed.

36 "The king shall act as he pleases. He shall exalt himself and consider himself greater than any god, and shall speak horrendous things against the God of gods. He shall prosper until the period of wrath is completed, for what is determined shall be done. ³⁷ He shall pay no respect to the gods of his ancestors, or to the one beloved by women; he shall pay no respect to any other god, for he shall consider himself greater than all. ³⁸ He shall honor the god of fortresses instead

ᵃ Heb *made them white*

11:25–28—Reflects the invasion of Egypt (169) by Antiochus IV, in which he captured Ptolemy VI. He quickly retreated and returned to Syria, his own land.

11:30—The second campaign to Egypt gets some problems from an unexpected source, the *Kittim,* that is, Rome (the name comes from Citium, Cyprus). Antiochus IV used the wrong group (*those who forsake the holy covenant*) of Jews to assess the climate there.

11:31—*The abomination that makes desolate* probably refers to a heathen altar erected by the Seleucid occupiers in the Holy of Holies in the temple in Jerusalem.

11:33–35—*The wise* (Heb. the *maskilim,* perhaps the very circles that wrote the book of Daniel) will provide insight but fall by sword and flame (1 Macc. 1:62–63). *A little help* may refer to the activity of the Maccabees, Matthias and his son Judas Maccabeus. However, the writer distinguishes between the wise and those who offer the "little help." Martyrdom as a process by which one can be *refined, purified, and cleansed* seems to be emerging in this passage. (See also Ps. 17:3; Jer. 6:29; 9:6; Zech. 13:9; Sir. 2:5.)

11:37—The hubris of Antiochus was so great that he would *pay no respect to the gods of his ancestors, or to the one beloved by women,* namely, Tammuz/Adonis (the Mesopotamian cult of this fertility god is referred to in Ezek. 8:14).

11:38–39—*The god of fortresses* is likely a reference to Zeus Olympios, the ancient Greek deity with whom the Greco-Syrian Seleucids identified their indigenous god, Baal Shamen. *The strongest fortress* mentioned is probably the citadel in Jerusalem known as the Akra, which housed occupying troops. The phrase *for a price* notes that this is an unusual exchange (2 Sam. 24:24; 1 Kgs. 10:28; 2 Chr. 1:16; Lam. 5:4; Mic. 3:11). The actions of God, both redemptive and retributive, are without price (see Isa. 45:13; Jer. 15:13).

of these; a god whom his ancestors did not know he shall honor with gold and silver, with precious stones and costly gifts. ³⁹ He shall deal with the strongest fortresses by the help of a foreign god. Those who acknowledge him he shall make more wealthy, and shall appoint them as rulers over many, and shall distribute the land for a price.

The Time of the End

40 "At the time of the end the king of the south shall attack him. But the king of the north shall rush upon him like a whirlwind, with chariots and horsemen, and with many ships. He shall advance against countries and pass through like a flood. ⁴¹ He shall come into the beautiful land, and tens of thousands shall fall victim, but Edom and Moab and the main part of the Ammonites shall escape from his power. ⁴² He shall stretch out his hand against the countries, and the land of Egypt shall not escape. ⁴³ He shall become ruler of the treasures of gold and of silver, and all the riches of Egypt; and the Libyans and the Ethiopians*a* shall follow in his train. ⁴⁴ But reports from the east and the north shall alarm him, and he shall go out with great fury to bring ruin and complete destruction to many. ⁴⁵ He shall pitch his palatial tents between the sea and the beautiful holy mountain.

Yet he shall come to his end, with no one to help him.

The Resurrection of the Dead

12 "At that time Michael, the great prince, the protector of your people, shall arise. There shall be a time of anguish, such as has never occurred since nations first came into existence. But at that time your people shall be delivered, everyone who is found written in the book. ² Many of those who sleep in the dust of the earth*b* shall awake, some to everlasting life, and some to shame and everlasting contempt. ³ Those who are wise shall shine like the brightness of the sky,*c* and those who lead many to righteousness, like the stars forever and ever. ⁴ But you, Daniel, keep the words secret and the book sealed until the time of the end. Many shall be running back and forth, and evil*d* shall increase."

5 Then I, Daniel, looked, and two others appeared, one standing on this bank of the stream and one on the other. ⁶ One of them said to the man clothed in linen, who was upstream, "How long shall it be until the end of these wonders?" ⁷ The man clothed in linen, who was upstream, raised his right hand and his left hand toward heaven. And I heard him swear by the one who lives forever

a Or Nubians; Heb Cushites   *b* Or the land of dust   *c* Or dome
d Cn Compare Gk: Heb knowledge

11:40—*The time of the end* moves from *vaticinium ex eventu* (prophecy after the fact) to speculation on the future. The predicted attack by *the king of the south,* Ptolemy, never actually materialized.

11:41–43—*Edom and Moab* and Ammon were traditional enemies of Israel.

11:45—*The beautiful holy mountain* is a reference to Zion.

12:1–13 Consummation

12:1 *Michael*—See note at 10:13. *Book*—See note at 7:9; also Ps. 69:28; Isa. 4:3; Mal. 3:16–18; Rev. 20:12, 15; 21:27.

12:2—*Sleep* is a euphemism for death. This is the first clear and explicit reference in the Bible to resurrection, with the commensurate accounting of reward or punishment. Isaiah 26:19 is the only

other text that seems to anticipate the revival of the dead, but it speaks of no accounting. Ezekiel 37:1–14 and Hos. 6:2 prophesy the temporal revival of suffering Israel; Job 19:26 apparently anticipates Job's personal renewal.

12:4—Apocalyptic typically works with esoteric information; therefore, Daniel's instruction to *keep the words secret and the book sealed* fits well into the tradition.

12:5–7—The reference to the *bank* probably alludes to the beginning of the vision report (10:4). *The man clothed in linen* could indicate a fusion of priest and angel, because priests traditionally wore linen (see note at 10:5). The question *"How long?"* echoes the angel's question in the second vision report (8:13). The response to the answer echoes the first vision report: *a time, two times and half a time* (7:25).

that it would be for a time, two times, and half a time,[a] and that when the shattering of the power of the holy people comes to an end, all these things would be accomplished. [8] I heard but could not understand; so I said, "My lord, what shall be the outcome of these things?" [9] He said, "Go your way, Daniel, for the words are to remain secret and sealed until the time of the end. [10] Many shall be purified, cleansed, and refined, but the wicked shall continue to act wickedly.

None of the wicked shall understand, but those who are wise shall understand. [11] From the time that the regular burnt offering is taken away and the abomination that desolates is set up, there shall be one thousand two hundred ninety days. [12] Happy are those who persevere and attain the thousand three hundred thirty-five days. [13] But you, go your way,[b] and rest; you shall rise for your reward at the end of the days."

[a] Heb *a time, times, and a half* [b] Gk Theodotion: Heb adds *to the end*

12:11–12—The figures *one thousand two hundred ninety days* and *thousand three hundred* thirty-five days appear to be later time adjustments.

The Book of

HOSEA

The prophetic book of Hosea opens a section of Scripture called at times the Minor Prophets or the Book of the Twelve. Both Hosea and Amos prophesied during the eighth century BCE, and both prophesied in the northern kingdom, but Hosea holds the distinction of being the only northern-born prophet for whom we have a prophetic book. Hosea was Amos's contemporary, but his style differs greatly, due to his emphasis upon God's unfailing love and the chaotic political context in which he preached.

Hosea's prophecy is tied up with family metaphors, understanding the relationship to God in terms of husband-wife (chaps. 1–3), children to father (chaps. 1–2), and father to son (chap. 11). Hosea employs such family metaphors against the religious backdrop of Syro-Canaanite Baalism, which understood God as fertility: human, vegetative, and animal. Baalism was essentially worship of the life process, identifying God with nature and its powers. By participating in certain rites, worshipers guaranteed productivity and security. Hosea in his prophecy uses some of the Baal language to speak of the creator God, who is separate from nature and yet involved relationally with people and the world. Hosea articulates one of the clearest statements of God's transcendence, that God is not one power among many, but above all powers, and yet related to us. The term that Hosea employs to speak of God's relationship to the world is "covenant." Hosea uses this term five times to indicate that the creator God is involved in the world, but not through human, animal, or vegetative life processes. Hosea's God relates to the world in justice, righteousness, steadfast love, and mercy (2:16–20). Hosea's prophecy is relevant to current discipleship concerns, particularly in Western society, where people worship/strive after material wealth, success, and productivity, essentially participating in Baalism by another name. Hosea's favorite term for those who ignore God and pursue Baal is harlotry or whoring. Because Hosea employs family metaphors, the key to understanding infidelity to God is rooted in family infidelity. Israel plays the whore with Baal, much as we would today play the whore with materialistic, success-driven society.

Hosea's use of the family metaphor causes some to cast suspicion on him, charging him with sexism, with an abusive understanding of God, and with a denigration of women. Yet ironically Hosea is trying to cast a vision of the biblical God that is separate from gender and from life process but is doing so by using Baalistic categories, which by definition are gendered and involved with life process. Hosea helps us to understand that the God of the Bible is personal and is related to creation, but not in a gendered, sexual way. Hosea's God is holy and involved and exhibits unfailing love.

Finally, Hosea lays the foundation for the New Testament crucifixion, in that it is God who turns away and absorbs the punishment that Israel deserves (chap. 11), and it is God who enables the repentance of people, not waiting for them to return, but turning to find the lost (chap. 14).

—Jefferson H. McCrory Jr.

1

The word of the LORD that came to Hosea son of Beeri, in the days of Kings Uzziah, Jotham, Ahaz, and Hezekiah of Judah, and in the days of King Jeroboam son of Joash of Israel.

The Family of Hosea

2 When the LORD first spoke through Hosea, the LORD said to Hosea, "Go, take for yourself a wife of whoredom and have children of whoredom, for the land commits great whoredom by forsaking the LORD." ³ So he went and took Gomer daughter of Diblaim, and she conceived and bore him a son.

4 And the LORD said to him, "Name him Jezreel;[a] for in a little while I will punish the house of Jehu for the blood of Jezreel, and I will put an end to the kingdom of the house of Israel. ⁵ On that day I will break the bow of Israel in the valley of Jezreel."

6 She conceived again and bore a daughter. Then the LORD said to him, "Name her Lo-ruhamah,[b] for I will no longer have pity on the house of Israel or forgive them. ⁷ But I will have pity on the house of Judah, and I will save them by the LORD their God; I will not save them by bow, or by sword, or by war, or by horses, or by horsemen."

8 When she had weaned Lo-ruhamah, she conceived and bore a son. ⁹ Then the LORD said, "Name him Lo-ammi,[c] for you are not my people and I am not your God."[d]

The Restoration of Israel

10[e] Yet the number of the people of Israel shall be like the sand of the sea, which can be neither measured nor numbered; and in the place where it was said to them, "You are not my people," it shall be said to them, "Children of the living God." ¹¹ The people of Judah and the people of Israel shall be gathered together, and they shall appoint for themselves one head; and they shall take possession of[f] the land, for great shall be the day of Jezreel.

2

[g] Say to your brother,[h] Ammi,[i] and to your sister,[j] Ruhamah.[k]

Israel's Infidelity, Punishment, and Redemption

² Plead with your mother, plead—
  for she is not my wife,
    and I am not her husband—
that she put away her whoring from
  her face,
    and her adultery from between her
    breasts,
³ or I will strip her naked

---

[a] That is God sows [b] That is Not pitied [c] That is Not my people [d] Heb I am not yours [e] Ch 2.1 in Heb [f] Heb rise up from [g] Ch 2.3 in Heb [h] Gk: Heb brothers [i] That is My people [j] Gk Vg: Heb sisters [k] That is Pitied

---

1:1 In the days of Kings—We know little about Hosea, except that unlike his contemporary Amos he was a professional prophet and that he spoke into a very confused, decaying societal context. After Jeroboam II died, there were six kings in twenty-two years, and by 721 BCE Israel was destroyed. The message of God's unfailing love speaks to those who are in the middle of difficult times.

1:2–9—Hosea's message from God comes through his troubled family. In order to symbolize Israel's infidelity to God, Hosea marries a prostitute and has children—who knows whether they were really his—who carry symbolic names. The names, **Jezreel, Lo-ruhamah** (no pity), and **Lo-ammi** (not my people) point to the political and social relationships that the northern kingdom of Israel had with God. A contemporary parallel would be for someone to name their children after the Holocaust or with a name such

as "No grace any more." The way God reached Hosea and Israel, working through Hosea's family, is applicable to the way we know God today. We learn about God mostly through those who are close to us, through our relationships. And although no person is God, it is through struggle and joy brought about by our family members that we learn something of God's presence.

2:1–16 "My husband," and no longer . . . "My Baal"—Hosea's central message to Israel is that the biblical God is not Baal. Baal is deified life process. Through Baal worship, Israel played the whore, that is, went off with a partner who was inappropriate to deserve the name God. By doing so, Israel had become enslaved to the powers in creation instead of serving the God of creation. We too can confuse our blessings with God and begin to worship that which God gives rather than the God who gives.

and expose her as in the day she
    was born,
and make her like a wilderness,
    and turn her into a parched land,
    and kill her with thirst.
4 Upon her children also I will have
    no pity,
    because they are children of
        whoredom.
5 For their mother has played the
    whore;
    she who conceived them has acted
        shamefully.
For she said, "I will go after my
    lovers;
    they give me my bread and my
        water,
    my wool and my flax, my oil and
        my drink."
6 Therefore I will hedge up her*a* way
    with thorns;
    and I will build a wall against her,
    so that she cannot find her paths.
7 She shall pursue her lovers,
    but not overtake them;
and she shall seek them,
    but shall not find them.
Then she shall say, "I will go
    and return to my first husband,
    for it was better with me then than
        now."
8 She did not know
    that it was I who gave her the
        grain,
    the wine, and the oil,
and who lavished upon her silver
    and gold that they used for Baal.
9 Therefore I will take back
    my grain in its time,
    and my wine in its season;
and I will take away my wool and my
    flax,
    which were to cover her
        nakedness.
10 Now I will uncover her shame
    in the sight of her lovers,

and no one shall rescue her out of
    my hand.
11 I will put an end to all her mirth,
    her festivals, her new moons, her
        sabbaths,
    and all her appointed festivals.
12 I will lay waste her vines and her fig
        trees,
    of which she said,
"These are my pay,
    which my lovers have given me."
I will make them a forest,
    and the wild animals shall devour
        them.
13 I will punish her for the festival days
        of the Baals,
    when she offered incense to them
and decked herself with her ring and
        jewelry,
    and went after her lovers,
    and forgot me, says the LORD.

14 Therefore, I will now allure her,
    and bring her into the wilderness,
    and speak tenderly to her.
15 From there I will give her her
        vineyards,
    and make the Valley of Achor a
        door of hope.
There she shall respond as in the
        days of her youth,
    as at the time when she came out
        of the land of Egypt.
16 On that day, says the LORD, you will
call me, "My husband," and no longer
will you call me, "My Baal."*b* 17 For I will
remove the names of the Baals from her
mouth, and they shall be mentioned by
name no more. 18 I will make for you*c*
a covenant on that day with the wild
animals, the birds of the air, and the
creeping things of the ground; and I will
abolish*d* the bow, the sword, and war
from the land; and I will make you lie
down in safety. 19 And I will take you for

a Gk Syr: Heb *your*   *b* That is, *"My master"*   *c* Heb *them*   *d* Heb *break*

2:18–23 Covenant—In place of an understanding
of God as life process, Hosea offers a God of the
covenant (v. 18) who integrates all of the cosmos
through *righteousness, justice, steadfast love,*
and mercy (v. 19). It is only when we worship the
God of creation and not the creation itself that
the pieces of our lives and of the cosmos come
together with integrity (vv. 21–23).

my wife forever; I will take you for my wife in righteousness and in justice, in steadfast love, and in mercy. **20** I will take you for my wife in faithfulness; and you shall know the LORD.

21 On that day I will answer, says the
LORD,
    I will answer the heavens
    and they shall answer the earth;
22 and the earth shall answer the grain,
        the wine, and the oil,
    and they shall answer Jezreel;*a*
23 and I will sow him*b* for myself in
        the land.
    And I will have pity on
        Lo-ruhamah,*c*
    and I will say to Lo-ammi,*d* "You
        are my people";
    and he shall say, "You are my God."

Further Assurances of God's Redeeming Love

3 The LORD said to me again, "Go, love a woman who has a lover and is an adulteress, just as the LORD loves the people of Israel, though they turn to other gods and love raisin cakes." **2** So I bought her for fifteen shekels of silver and a homer of barley and a measure of wine.*e* **3** And I said to her, "You must remain as mine for many days; you shall not play the whore, you shall not have intercourse with a man, nor I with you." **4** For the Israelites shall remain many days without king or prince, without sacrifice or pillar, without ephod or teraphim. **5** Afterward the Israelites shall return and seek the LORD their God, and David their king; they shall come in

awe to the LORD and to his goodness in the latter days.

God Accuses Israel

4 Hear the word of the LORD,
        O people of Israel;
    for the LORD has an indictment
        against the inhabitants of the
        land.
    There is no faithfulness or loyalty,
        and no knowledge of God in the
        land.
2 Swearing, lying, and murder,
        and stealing and adultery break
        out;
    bloodshed follows bloodshed.
3 Therefore the land mourns,
        and all who live in it languish;
    together with the wild animals
        and the birds of the air,
    even the fish of the sea are
        perishing.

4 Yet let no one contend,
        and let none accuse,
    for with you is my contention,
        O priest.*f*
5 You shall stumble by day;
        the prophet also shall stumble with
        you by night,
    and I will destroy your mother.
6 My people are destroyed for lack of
        knowledge;
    because you have rejected
        knowledge,
    I reject you from being a priest
        to me.

a That is *God sows* *b* Cn: Heb *her* *c* That is *Not pitied* *d* That is *Not my people* *e* Gk: Heb *a homer of barley and a lethech of barley* *f* Cn: Meaning of Heb uncertain

---

3:1–5 *Go, love a woman*—Hosea has to buy Gomer for a price. In the same way, God buys back his people for a price. This is true in both Old and New Testaments. The New Testament Scriptures speak of God paying the price through Jesus the Messiah in order to have a relationship with people (1 Cor. 6:20). Biblically it is always God who takes the initiative to restore us.

4:1–3 *No knowledge of God in the land*—Hosea indicates that knowledge of God is not esoteric Bible trivia but practical wisdom on how to live in society. When knowledge of God is absent,

relationships break down, crime breaks out, and there is environmental disaster. Our relationship with God affects the way we relate to spouses and children, to the local police department, and to the air we breathe, the animals we tend, and the plants we cultivate.

4:4 *O priest*—Hosea blames much of Israel's societal problems on the leaders: priest, prophet, and king (5:1). Leaders in any social context are to guide and lead people according to the law of God (v. 7), rather than greedily seek their own advantage (v. 8).

And since you have forgotten the law
of your God,
I also will forget your children.

7 The more they increased,
the more they sinned against me;
they changed[a] their glory into
shame.

8 They feed on the sin of my people;
they are greedy for their iniquity.

9 And it shall be like people, like
priest;
I will punish them for their ways,
and repay them for their deeds.

10 They shall eat, but not be satisfied;
they shall play the whore, but not
multiply;
because they have forsaken the LORD
to devote themselves to
11whoredom.

The Idolatry of Israel

Wine and new wine
take away the understanding.

12 My people consult a piece of wood,
and their divining rod gives them
oracles.
For a spirit of whoredom has led
them astray,
and they have played the whore,
forsaking their God.

13 They sacrifice on the tops of the
mountains,
and make offerings upon the hills,
under oak, poplar, and terebinth,
because their shade is good.

Therefore your daughters play the
whore,
and your daughters-in-law commit
adultery.

14 I will not punish your daughters
when they play the whore,
nor your daughters-in-law when
they commit adultery;
for the men themselves go aside with
whores,

and sacrifice with temple
prostitutes;
thus a people without understanding
comes to ruin.

15 Though you play the whore, O Israel,
do not let Judah become guilty.
Do not enter into Gilgal,
or go up to Beth-aven,
and do not swear, "As the LORD
lives."

16 Like a stubborn heifer,
Israel is stubborn;
can the LORD now feed them
like a lamb in a broad pasture?

17 Ephraim is joined to idols—
let him alone.

18 When their drinking is ended, they
indulge in sexual orgies;
they love lewdness more than their
glory.[b]

19 A wind has wrapped them[c] in its
wings,
and they shall be ashamed because
of their altars.[d]

Impending Judgment
on Israel and Judah

5 Hear this, O priests!
Give heed, O house of Israel!
Listen, O house of the king!
For the judgment pertains to
you;
for you have been a snare at
Mizpah,
and a net spread upon Tabor,

2 and a pit dug deep in Shittim;[e]
but I will punish all of them.

3 I know Ephraim,
and Israel is not hidden from me;
for now, O Ephraim, you have played
the whore;
Israel is defiled.

[a] Ancient Heb tradition: MT *I will change*   [b] Cn Compare Gk: Meaning
of Heb uncertain   [c] Heb *her*   [d] Gk Syr: Heb *sacrifices*   [e] Cn: Meaning of
Heb uncertain

4:15 Do not enter into Gilgal . . . Beth-aven—
These towns were sanctuary sites where Israel's
worship had become polluted with Baalistic
practices. Hosea in sarcasm has changed Bethel
("house of God") to Beth-aven ("house of evil"),
to signify that worship is the locus of the evil
that has spread throughout the land. We become
what we worship.

4 Their deeds do not permit them
    to return to their God.
  For the spirit of whoredom is within
      them,
  and they do not know the LORD.

5 Israel's pride testifies against him;
    Ephraim[a] stumbles in his guilt;
    Judah also stumbles with them.
6 With their flocks and herds they
      shall go
    to seek the LORD,
  but they will not find him;
    he has withdrawn from them.
7 They have dealt faithlessly with the
      LORD;
    for they have borne illegitimate
      children.
    Now the new moon shall devour
      them along with their fields.

8 Blow the horn in Gibeah,
    the trumpet in Ramah.
  Sound the alarm at Beth-aven;
    look behind you, Benjamin!
9 Ephraim shall become a desolation
    in the day of punishment;
  among the tribes of Israel
    I declare what is sure.
10 The princes of Judah have become
    like those who remove the
      landmark;
  on them I will pour out
    my wrath like water.
11 Ephraim is oppressed, crushed in
      judgment,
    because he was determined to go
      after vanity.[b]
12 Therefore I am like maggots to
    Ephraim,

and like rottenness to the house of
    Judah.
13 When Ephraim saw his sickness,
    and Judah his wound,
  then Ephraim went to Assyria,
    and sent to the great king.[c]
  But he is not able to cure you
    or heal your wound.
14 For I will be like a lion to Ephraim,
    and like a young lion to the house
      of Judah.
  I myself will tear and go away;
    I will carry off, and no one shall
      rescue.
15 I will return again to my place
    until they acknowledge their guilt
      and seek my face.
  In their distress they will beg my
      favor:

A Call to Repentance

6 "Come, let us return to the LORD;
    for it is he who has torn, and he
      will heal us;
  he has struck down, and he will
      bind us up.
2 After two days he will revive us;
    on the third day he will raise us up,
    that we may live before him.
3 Let us know, let us press on to know
      the LORD;
  his appearing is as sure as the dawn;
  he will come to us like the showers,
    like the spring rains that water the
      earth."

Impenitence of Israel and Judah

4 What shall I do with you,
    O Ephraim?

[a] Heb *Israel and Ephraim*   [b] Gk: Meaning of Heb uncertain   [c] Cn: Heb *to a king who will contend*

5:4 *Their deeds do not permit them to return—*
If obedience is the opener of eyes, rebellion and
disobedience blinds people to the truth. This is a
major theme of both Old and New Testaments.
Isaiah (Isa. 6:10) and Jesus (Mark 8:18) confront
a people whose eyes have been blinded and
whose ears have been stopped by their sin. When
people through repentance take a step toward
God, their eyes are opened and they hear once
again.

5:12 *I am like maggots to Ephraim—*God's
steadfast love for Israel (Ephraim) at times comes

to them in wrath. Distress and disaster can be the
other side of God's love for us. But conversely,
one cannot say that disaster or distress means
that God is angry with us. Hosea's overriding
understanding of God is of one who is committed
to loving people (3:1).

6:1 *Come, let us return to the LORD—*The purpose of disaster for Israel is return. The wrath of
God always is for restoration, to know the Lord,
so that people may experience healing, likened
to the coming of *the spring rains* (v. 3).

What shall I do with you, O Judah?
Your love is like a morning cloud,
    like the dew that goes away early.
5 Therefore I have hewn them by the
    prophets,
  I have killed them by the words of
    my mouth,
  and my*a* judgment goes forth as
    the light.
6 For I desire steadfast love and not
    sacrifice,
  the knowledge of God rather than
    burnt offerings.

7 But at*b* Adam they transgressed the
    covenant;
  there they dealt faithlessly with
    me.
8 Gilead is a city of evildoers,
    tracked with blood.
9 As robbers lie in wait*c* for someone,
  so the priests are banded
    together;*d*
  they murder on the road to
    Shechem,
  they commit a monstrous crime.
10 In the house of Israel I have seen a
    horrible thing;
  Ephraim's whoredom is there,
    Israel is defiled.

11 For you also, O Judah, a harvest is
    appointed.

When I would restore the fortunes
    of my people,
7 1 when I would heal Israel,
  the corruption of Ephraim is
    revealed,
  and the wicked deeds of Samaria;
  for they deal falsely,
    the thief breaks in,
    and the bandits raid outside.

2 But they do not consider
  that I remember all their
    wickedness.
Now their deeds surround them,
  they are before my face.
3 By their wickedness they make the
    king glad,
  and the officials by their treachery.
4 They are all adulterers;
  they are like a heated oven,
whose baker does not need to stir
    the fire,
  from the kneading of the dough
    until it is leavened.
5 On the day of our king the officials
  became sick with the heat of
    wine;
  he stretched out his hand with
    mockers.
6 For they are kindled*e* like an oven,
    their heart burns within them;
  all night their anger smolders;
  in the morning it blazes like a
    flaming fire.
7 All of them are hot as an oven,
    and they devour their rulers.
All their kings have fallen;
  none of them calls upon me.

8 Ephraim mixes himself with the
    peoples;
  Ephraim is a cake not turned.
9 Foreigners devour his strength,
    but he does not know it;
gray hairs are sprinkled upon him,
    but he does not know it.
10 Israel's pride testifies against*f* him;
  yet they do not return to the LORD
    their God,
  or seek him, for all this.

a Gk Syr: Heb *your* *b* Cn: Heb *like* *c* Cn: Meaning of Heb uncertain
d Syr: Heb *are a company* *e* Gk Syr: Heb *brought near* *f* Or *humbles*

6:6 *Steadfast love and not sacrifice*—Israel's sacrificial system was not an end in itself. By giving to God, Israel came into a closer love relationship with her God. This is central to Hosea's understanding of God. The purpose of all biblical religion is to draw us into a closer relationship with the creator God. Worship is about communing with the living God.

7:7 *All of them are hot as an oven*—Hosea employs graphic household language to describe the agitation people feel in the midst of their rebellion. People as well as leaders *devour* each other because they have not sought a solution to their problem in the Lord (v. 10). Hosea reminds us that life presents us with the context to seek the Lord. As Augustine once said, "Our hearts are restless until they find rest in you."

Futile Reliance on the Nations

11 Ephraim has become like a dove,
     silly and without sense;
     they call upon Egypt, they go to
          Assyria.
12 As they go, I will cast my net over
          them;
     I will bring them down like birds
          of the air;
     I will discipline them according
          to the report made to their
          assembly.*a*
13 Woe to them, for they have strayed
          from me!
     Destruction to them, for they have
          rebelled against me!
     I would redeem them,
          but they speak lies against me.

14 They do not cry to me from the heart,
          but they wail upon their beds;
     they gash themselves for grain and
          wine;
          they rebel against me.
15 It was I who trained and
          strengthened their arms,
     yet they plot evil against me.
16 They turn to that which does not
          profit;*a*
     they have become like a defective
          bow;
     their officials shall fall by the sword
          because of the rage of their tongue.
     So much for their babbling in the
          land of Egypt.

Israel's Apostasy

8 Set the trumpet to your lips!
     One like a vulture*a* is over the
          house of the LORD,

because they have broken my
          covenant,
     and transgressed my law.
2 Israel cries to me,
     "My God, we—Israel—know you!"
3 Israel has spurned the good;
     the enemy shall pursue him.

4 They made kings, but not through
          me;
     they set up princes, but without
          my knowledge.
     With their silver and gold they made
          idols
     for their own destruction.
5 Your calf is rejected, O Samaria.
     My anger burns against them.
     How long will they be incapable of
          innocence?
6 For it is from Israel,
     an artisan made it;
     it is not God.
     The calf of Samaria
     shall be broken to pieces.*b*

7 For they sow the wind,
     and they shall reap the whirlwind.
     The standing grain has no heads,
     it shall yield no meal;
     if it were to yield,
     foreigners would devour it.
8 Israel is swallowed up;
     now they are among the nations
     as a useless vessel.
9 For they have gone up to Assyria,
     a wild ass wandering alone;
     Ephraim has bargained for lovers.
10 Though they bargain with the
          nations,

a Meaning of Heb uncertain   *b* Or *shall go up in flames*

7:11 They call upon Egypt—People seek relief from their agitation, turning to powers that compound their misery rather than returning *to the LORD*, who heals the heart (v. 14).

8:1 Broken my covenant, and transgressed my law—Hosea understands the relationship of Israel to the Lord in terms of covenant (2:18–23), but a covenant that is defined with reference to law. Many have misinterpreted biblical law as destructive, having little to do with warm relationships. But biblical law is meant to provide good boundaries for maintaining the best in relation-

ships. God establishes a relationship with Israel coming out of Egypt (Exod. 1–15), then provides stipulations to enhance life (Exod. 19–Num. 10:10). God's good law provides the boundaries within which life can flourish.

8:7 They sow the wind—Hosea sets the stage for New Testament teaching regarding law, that persons reap what they sow (Gal. 6:7). God has established a world in justice and righteousness (Jer. 9:23–24), and when a person runs against the grain, he or she experiences the hardness of God's grace.

I will now gather them up.
They shall soon writhe
   under the burden of kings and
    princes.

11 When Ephraim multiplied altars to
    expiate sin,
   they became to him altars for
    sinning.
12 Though I write for him the
    multitude of my instructions,
   they are regarded as a strange
    thing.
13 Though they offer choice sacrifices,[a]
   though they eat flesh,
    the LORD does not accept them.
Now he will remember their
    iniquity,
   and punish their sins;
   they shall return to Egypt.
14 Israel has forgotten his Maker,
   and built palaces;
and Judah has multiplied fortified
    cities;
   but I will send a fire upon his cities,
   and it shall devour his strongholds.

Punishment for Israel's Sin

9 Do not rejoice, O Israel!
   Do not exult[b] as other nations do;
for you have played the whore,
    departing from your God.
   You have loved a prostitute's pay
   on all threshing floors.
2 Threshing floor and wine vat shall
    not feed them,
   and the new wine shall fail them.
3 They shall not remain in the land of
    the LORD;
   but Ephraim shall return to Egypt,
   and in Assyria they shall eat
    unclean food.
4 They shall not pour drink offerings
    of wine to the LORD,
   and their sacrifices shall not please
    him.

Such sacrifices shall be like
    mourners' bread;
   all who eat of it shall be defiled;
for their bread shall be for their
    hunger only;
   it shall not come to the house of
    the LORD.

5 What will you do on the day of
    appointed festival,
   and on the day of the festival of
    the LORD?
6 For even if they escape destruction,
   Egypt shall gather them,
   Memphis shall bury them.
Nettles shall possess their precious
    things of silver;[c]
   thorns shall be in their tents.

7 The days of punishment have come,
   the days of recompense have come;
   Israel cries,[d]
"The prophet is a fool,
   the man of the spirit is mad!"
Because of your great iniquity,
   your hostility is great.
8 The prophet is a sentinel for my God
    over Ephraim,
yet a fowler's snare is on all his ways,
   and hostility in the house of his
    God.
9 They have deeply corrupted
    themselves
   as in the days of Gibeah;
he will remember their iniquity,
   he will punish their sins.

10 Like grapes in the wilderness,
   I found Israel.
Like the first fruit on the fig tree,
   in its first season,
   I saw your ancestors.
But they came to Baal-peor,
   and consecrated themselves to a
    thing of shame,

a Cn: Meaning of Heb uncertain   b Gk: Heb To exultation   c Meaning of
Heb uncertain   d Cn Compare Gk: Heb shall know

9:8 The prophet is a sentinel—Hosea refers to
the task of a prophet to watch society for the sake
of the Lord (Ezek. 33:6; Hab. 2:1). Yet people do
not like prophets, because they point out sin.

People will never like prophets, because we do
not like to admit our addiction to sin, nor do we
turn toward health.

and became detestable like the
   thing they loved.
11 Ephraim's glory shall fly away like a
   bird—
   no birth, no pregnancy, no
      conception!
12 Even if they bring up children,
   I will bereave them until no one is
      left.
Woe to them indeed
   when I depart from them!
13 Once I saw Ephraim as a young
   palm planted in a lovely
      meadow,*a*
but now Ephraim must lead out
   his children for slaughter.
14 Give them, O Lord—
   what will you give?
Give them a miscarrying womb
   and dry breasts.

15 Every evil of theirs began at Gilgal;
   there I came to hate them.
Because of the wickedness of their
      deeds
I will drive them out of my house.
I will love them no more;
   all their officials are rebels.
16 Ephraim is stricken,
   their root is dried up,
   they shall bear no fruit.
Even though they give birth,
   I will kill the cherished offspring
      of their womb.
17 Because they have not listened to
      him,
   my God will reject them;
they shall become wanderers
   among the nations.

Israel's Sin and Captivity

10 Israel is a luxuriant vine
   that yields its fruit.
The more his fruit increased

the more altars he built;
as his country improved,
   he improved his pillars.
2 Their heart is false;
   now they must bear their guilt.
The Lord*b* will break down their
      altars,
   and destroy their pillars.

3 For now they will say:
   "We have no king,
for we do not fear the Lord,
   and a king—what could he do
      for us?"
4 They utter mere words;
   with empty oaths they make
      covenants;
so litigation springs up like
      poisonous weeds
in the furrows of the field.
5 The inhabitants of Samaria
      tremble
   for the calf*c* of Beth-aven.
Its people shall mourn for it,
   and its idolatrous priests shall
      wail*d* over it,
   over its glory that has departed
      from it.
6 The thing itself shall be carried to
      Assyria
   as tribute to the great king.*e*
Ephraim shall be put to shame,
   and Israel shall be ashamed of his
      idol.*f*

7 Samaria's king shall perish
   like a chip on the face of the
      waters.
8 The high places of Aven, the sin of
      Israel,
   shall be destroyed.
Thorn and thistle shall grow up
   on their altars.

a Meaning of Heb uncertain   *b* Heb *he*   *c* Gk Syr: Heb *calves*   *d* Cn: Heb
exult   *e* Cn: Heb *to a king who will contend*   *f* Cn: Heb *counsel*

9:15 *Every evil of theirs began at Gilgal*—How
would we like it if someone addressed us, "Every
evil begins at church, or at the synagogue"? Yet
Hosea realizes that our fundamental values are
rehearsed and worked out in worship.

10:1 *The more his fruit increased, the more*

***altars he built*—**As Israel increased in wealth, she
increased in idolatry. Success and the fruits of it
are the seedbed for idolatry. Idolatry at root is the
deification of human desire. And the more we
multiply objects of desire, the more we are prone
to idolatry.

They shall say to the mountains,
  Cover us,
  and to the hills, Fall on us.

9 Since the days of Gibeah you have
    sinned, O Israel;
  there they have continued.
  Shall not war overtake them in
    Gibeah?
10 I will come*a* against the wayward
    people to punish them;
  and nations shall be gathered
    against them
  when they are punished*b* for their
    double iniquity.

11 Ephraim was a trained heifer
    that loved to thresh,
  and I spared her fair neck;
  but I will make Ephraim break the
    ground;
  Judah must plow;
  Jacob must harrow for himself.
12 Sow for yourselves righteousness;
    reap steadfast love;
  break up your fallow ground;
  for it is time to seek the LORD,
    that he may come and rain
    righteousness upon you.

13 You have plowed wickedness,
    you have reaped injustice,
  you have eaten the fruit of lies.
  Because you have trusted in your
    power
  and in the multitude of your
    warriors,
14 therefore the tumult of war shall rise
    against your people,
  and all your fortresses shall be
    destroyed,
  as Shalman destroyed Beth-arbel on
    the day of battle

when mothers were dashed in
    pieces with their children.
15 Thus it shall be done to you,
    O Bethel,
  because of your great wickedness.
  At dawn the king of Israel
    shall be utterly cut off.

God's Compassion Despite Israel's Ingratitude

11 When Israel was a child, I loved
    him,
  and out of Egypt I called my son.
2 The more I*c* called them,
    the more they went from me;*d*
  they kept sacrificing to the Baals,
    and offering incense to idols.

3 Yet it was I who taught Ephraim to
    walk,
  I took them up in my*e* arms;
  but they did not know that I
    healed them.
4 I led them with cords of human
    kindness,
    with bands of love.
  I was to them like those
    who lift infants to their cheeks.*f*
  I bent down to them and fed them.

5 They shall return to the land of
    Egypt,
  and Assyria shall be their king,
    because they have refused to
    return to me.
6 The sword rages in their cities,
    it consumes their oracle-priests,
    and devours because of their
    schemes.
7 My people are bent on turning away
    from me.

a Cn Compare Gk: Heb *In my desire* *b* Gk: Heb *bound* *c* Gk: Heb *they*
d Gk: Heb *them* *e* Gk Syr Vg: Heb *his* *f* Or *who ease the yoke on their jaws*

10:12 Sow for yourselves righteousness—Israel has sown fruit toward evil (v. 1) and is now encouraged to sow the seeds of the covenant-keeping God. It is God's desire that all experience righteousness, that is, healthy relationships. This begins when one seeks the Lord, whose relationship lies at the center of all human societal structures. When we seek God, we find restorative relationships.

11:1 When Israel was a child—Hosea again uses the metaphor of family to describe Israel's relationship to God. This story is reminiscent of Jesus' parable of the Prodigal Son (Luke 15:11–32), describing a God who will not let judgment triumph over love.

To the Most High they call,
  but he does not raise them up at
    all.[a]
8 How can I give you up, Ephraim?
  How can I hand you over, O Israel?
How can I make you like Admah?
  How can I treat you like Zeboiim?
My heart recoils within me;
  my compassion grows warm and
    tender.
9 I will not execute my fierce anger;
  I will not again destroy Ephraim;
for I am God and no mortal,
  the Holy One in your midst,
  and I will not come in wrath.[a]

10 They shall go after the LORD,
  who roars like a lion;
when he roars,
  his children shall come trembling
    from the west.
11 They shall come trembling like birds
    from Egypt,
  and like doves from the land of
    Assyria;
  and I will return them to their
    homes, says the LORD.

12[b] Ephraim has surrounded me with
    lies,
  and the house of Israel with deceit;
but Judah still walks[c] with God,
  and is faithful to the Holy One.

12 Ephraim herds the wind,
  and pursues the east wind all
    day long;
they multiply falsehood and
    violence;
  they make a treaty with Assyria,
  and oil is carried to Egypt.

The Long History of Rebellion

2 The LORD has an indictment against
    Judah,
  and will punish Jacob according to
    his ways,
  and repay him according to his
    deeds.
3 In the womb he tried to supplant his
    brother,
  and in his manhood he strove with
    God.
4 He strove with the angel and
    prevailed,
  he wept and sought his favor;
he met him at Bethel,
  and there he spoke with him.[d]
5 The LORD the God of hosts,
  the LORD is his name!
6 But as for you, return to your God,
  hold fast to love and justice,
  and wait continually for your God.

7 A trader, in whose hands are false
    balances,
  he loves to oppress.
8 Ephraim has said, "Ah, I am rich,
  I have gained wealth for myself;
in all of my gain
  no offense has been found in me
    that would be sin."[a]
9 I am the LORD your God
  from the land of Egypt;
I will make you live in tents again,
  as in the days of the appointed
    festival.

10 I spoke to the prophets;
  it was I who multiplied visions,

[a] Meaning of Heb uncertain [b] Ch 12.1 in Heb [c] Heb *roams* or *rules*
[d] Gk Syr: Heb *us*

11:9 For I am God . . . the Holy One in your midst—In one of the highpoints of biblical teaching, Hosea identifies God as one who is present in our midst in holiness with a steadfast love that overcomes **wrath** by absorbing it into the depths of God's being (v. 8). The phrase "Holy One in your midst" is similar to Isaiah's favorite term for God, "Holy One of Israel" (Isa. 5:19). Hosea lifts up here the central biblical notion that God is not human but holy, and is present with us in love, even to the point of self-sacrifice. Hosea's teaching finds resonance with New Testament

teaching about Jesus, through whom the world is reconciled to God (2 Cor. 5:19).

12:3 In the womb he tried to supplant his brother—The story of Jacob and Esau becomes for biblical people their own story. We strive with God and with one another seeking to find our way, which forever lies in returning to God (v. 6).

12:10 I spoke to the prophets—Although society no longer has professional prophets, it is the task of God's people to attend to the teaching and preaching of God's ways.

and through the prophets I will
bring destruction.
11 In Gilead[a] there is iniquity,
they shall surely come to nothing.
In Gilgal they sacrifice bulls,
so their altars shall be like stone
heaps
on the furrows of the field.
12 Jacob fled to the land of Aram,
there Israel served for a wife,
and for a wife he guarded sheep.[b]
13 By a prophet the LORD brought
Israel up from Egypt,
and by a prophet he was guarded.
14 Ephraim has given bitter offense,
so his Lord will bring his crimes
down on him
and pay him back for his insults.

Relentless Judgment on Israel

13 When Ephraim spoke, there was
trembling;
he was exalted in Israel;
but he incurred guilt through Baal
and died.
2 And now they keep on sinning
and make a cast image for
themselves,
idols of silver made according to
their understanding,
all of them the work of artisans.
"Sacrifice to these," they say.[c]
People are kissing calves!
3 Therefore they shall be like the
morning mist
or like the dew that goes away
early,
like chaff that swirls from the
threshing floor
or like smoke from a window.

4 Yet I have been the LORD your God
ever since the land of Egypt;
you know no God but me,

and besides me there is no savior.
5 It was I who fed[d] you in the
wilderness,
in the land of drought.
6 When I fed[e] them, they were
satisfied;
they were satisfied, and their heart
was proud;
therefore they forgot me.
7 So I will become like a lion to
them,
like a leopard I will lurk beside the
way.
8 I will fall upon them like a bear
robbed of her cubs,
and will tear open the covering of
their heart;
there I will devour them like a lion,
as a wild animal would mangle
them.
9 I will destroy you, O Israel;
who can help you?[f]
10 Where now is[g] your king, that he
may save you?
Where in all your cities are your
rulers,
of whom you said,
"Give me a king and rulers"?
11 I gave you a king in my anger,
and I took him away in my
wrath.
12 Ephraim's iniquity is bound up;
his sin is kept in store.
13 The pangs of childbirth come for
him,
but he is an unwise son;
for at the proper time he does not
present himself
at the mouth of the womb.

[a] Compare Syr: Heb Gilead   [b] Heb lacks sheep   [c] Cn Compare Gk: Heb To these they say sacrifices of people   [d] Gk Syr: Heb knew   [e] Cn: Heb according to their pasture   [f] Gk Syr: Heb for in me is your help   [g] Gk Syr Vg: Heb I will be

---

13:4 Yet I have been the LORD your God ever since the land of Egypt—The Bible teaches that Israel met the Lord in the events of the exodus from Egypt. The encounter with God in the desert set in motion all thinking about prior encounters with God, whether through creation (Gen. 1–11) or through gods of other names (Gen. 12–40).

When we meet God for the first time, it sends us scurrying through our past looking for evidences of the God we now know but previously might have missed. Also, the encounter with God opens our eyes to the presence of God in the creation (see Ps. 19, which links the law and the exodus experience with the creation).

14 Shall I ransom them from the power
     of Sheol?
   Shall I redeem them from Death?
   O Death, where are[a] your plagues?
   O Sheol, where is[a] your
       destruction?
   Compassion is hidden from my
       eyes.

15 Although he may flourish among
     rushes,[b]
   the east wind shall come, a blast
     from the LORD,
   rising from the wilderness;
  and his fountain shall dry up,
   his spring shall be parched.
  It shall strip his treasury
   of every precious thing.
16[c] Samaria shall bear her guilt,
   because she has rebelled against
     her God;
  they shall fall by the sword,
   their little ones shall be dashed in
     pieces,
  and their pregnant women ripped
     open.

A Plea for Repentance

14 Return, O Israel, to the LORD
     your God,
   for you have stumbled because of
     your iniquity.
2 Take words with you
   and return to the LORD;
  say to him,
  "Take away all guilt;
  accept that which is good,
   and we will offer
   the fruit[d] of our lips.
3 Assyria shall not save us;
   we will not ride upon horses;

we will say no more, 'Our God,'
   to the work of our hands.
  In you the orphan finds mercy."

Assurance of Forgiveness

4 I will heal their disloyalty;
   I will love them freely,
   for my anger has turned from
     them.
5 I will be like the dew to Israel;
   he shall blossom like the lily,
   he shall strike root like the forests
     of Lebanon.[e]
6 His shoots shall spread out;
   his beauty shall be like the olive
     tree,
   and his fragrance like that of
     Lebanon.
7 They shall again live beneath my[f]
     shadow,
   they shall flourish as a garden;[g]
  they shall blossom like the vine,
   their fragrance shall be like the
     wine of Lebanon.
8 O Ephraim, what have I[h] to do with
     idols?
   It is I who answer and look after
     you.[i]
  I am like an evergreen cypress;
   your faithfulness[j] comes from me.
9 Those who are wise understand
     these things;
   those who are discerning know
     them.
  For the ways of the LORD are right,
   and the upright walk in them,
   but transgressors stumble in them.

[a] Gk Syr: Heb *I will be*   [b] Or *among brothers*   [c] Ch 14.1 in Heb   [d] Gk Syr: Heb *bulls*   [e] Cn: Heb *like Lebanon*   [f] Heb *his*   [g] Cn: Heb *they shall grow grain*   [h] Or *What more has Ephraim*   [i] Heb *him*   [j] Heb *your fruit*

13:14 *O Death, where are your plagues?*—Hosea hints at an understanding of God that will be developed only in the New Testament teaching regarding the resurrection (1 Cor. 15:55). Here Samaria will bear punishment, will experience death. But ultimately God's desire is for restoration.

14:4 *I will heal their disloyalty*—Many commentators do not like the fact that some biblical

prophetic books end with restoration and return (e.g., Amos 9:11–15). Yet it is always God's desire for people to return and be restored. Both Old Testament and New Testament, when weighed together, teach that God loves the world (John 3:16) and intends to bless all the families of the earth (Gen. 12:3). Thus the prophecy of Hosea ends on the major chord of God's desire for repentance and restoration.

The Book of
JOEL

This prophetic book is as enigmatic in its historical background as it is evocative in its poetry. Following a lament that vividly portrays a locust plague, characterized as a rampaging army (1:1–12), the prophet issues an impassioned call to repentance (1:13–2:17), delivers a consoling response from God (2:18–27), and concludes with an apocalyptic profile of the restored community (2:28–32) and a judgment against the nations (3:1–21). Among the minor prophets, Joel's messages are some of the most dramatic.

The book's rhetorical power, however, effectively hides its historical background. Joel's name ("The Lord is [my] God") is common enough, but his family identity ("son of Pethuel") occurs nowhere else in biblical tradition. Even if one should regard the locust plague as symbolic of an invading army, not much progress is made in identifying the book's historical context. The prophet describes the invaders as "northern" (2:20), which could point to any powerful nation or superpower (with the exception of Egypt) that at one time or another asserted control over Israel, particularly from the eighth to fourth centuries BCE. Moreover, Joel's language draws more from the realm of nature than from the arena of history. The breadth of the prophet's vision is cosmically expansive rather than historically specific. Many scholars propose that the strong apocalyptic elements featured in the second half of the book suggest a late rather than early dating. It appears that Joel was greatly influenced by the prophecies of Amos, the work of an eighth-century prophet who challenged Israel's powerful aristocracy and exposed their oppressive practices (cf., e.g., Joel 2:1–2 with Amos 5:18 and Joel 2:14 with Amos 5:15).

The theological center of Joel is found in the motif "the day of the Lord," repeated five times (1:15; 2:1, 11, 31; 3:14). It is a day of judgment and salvation, destruction and restoration, all occasioned by God's formidable approach toward Zion. In Joel, such a day marks both a new age of restoration and the convulsive demise of the old (cf. Amos 5:18–20). Distinctive of Joel is the positive emphasis upon public worship and religious ritual. Unlike the eighth-century prophets Amos, Micah, Hosea, and Isaiah, who criticized Israel's worship practices, Joel lodges Israel's repentance in the face of judgment *within* the ritual context of temple worship. Indeed, Joel's vision of the worshiping community is thoroughly egalitarian: both young and old, male and female are to have an equal share in God's spirit (2:28–29), a vision that provides scriptural warrant to the Pentecost event told in Acts 2:17–21.

Joel's message, in short, dramatically moves from repentance to the explosive possibilities of new life and worship. "Return to God," the prophet's clarion call to his people, sets the stage for the powerful witness of God's spirit creating new things.

—William P. Brown

1

The word of the LORD that came to Joel son of Pethuel:

Lament over the Ruin of the Country

2 Hear this, O elders,
    give ear, all inhabitants of the land!
Has such a thing happened in your
    days,
    or in the days of your ancestors?
3 Tell your children of it,
    and let your children tell their
        children,
    and their children another
        generation.

4 What the cutting locust left,
    the swarming locust has eaten.
What the swarming locust left,
    the hopping locust has eaten,
and what the hopping locust left,
    the destroying locust has eaten.

5 Wake up, you drunkards, and weep;
    and wail, all you wine-drinkers,
over the sweet wine,
    for it is cut off from your mouth.
6 For a nation has invaded my land,
    powerful and innumerable;
its teeth are lions' teeth,
    and it has the fangs of a lioness.
7 It has laid waste my vines,
    and splintered my fig trees;
it has stripped off their bark and
        thrown it down;
    their branches have turned white.

8 Lament like a virgin dressed in
        sackcloth
    for the husband of her youth.
9 The grain offering and the drink
        offering are cut off
    from the house of the LORD.
The priests mourn,

1:1 Word of the LORD—The prophet is a messenger of God. Not his own invention or the product of poetic imagination, the prophet's words convey God's message to the people (cf. Hos. 1:1; Mic. 1:1; Zeph. 1:1; Hag. 1:1; Zech. 1:1). The specified recipients are the *elders* and *inhabitants of the land* (Joel 1:2, 14). God's word is a word on target, one that confronts the political realities of the day and, specifically, those responsible for shaping those realities. **Joel son of Pethuel**—The name appears nowhere else in Scripture. The ancient Greek translation uses the patronym Bethuel, which occurs also in Gen. 22:23; 24:15, 24, 47.

1:2—Joel's oracle opens with an explosive call to attention, a verbal trumpet blast (2:1, 15; cf. Isa. 1:2; Hos. 5:1; Amos 3:1; Mic. 1:2; 6:1). The forcefulness of this opening "Now hear this!" cannot be underestimated in light of the infinite array of media-generated "hooks" designed to capture our attention and compliance. When sounded through the prophet Joel, God's call consigns all others to the trash bin.

1:3—Instructing *children* is of paramount concern in the Old Testament, for it preserves the faith community's identity from one generation to the next, shaped by the past for the sake of posterity (e.g., Exod. 12:26–27; Deut. 6:20–25; Prov. 1:4, 8–19). To teach our children what really matters in life before God is the highest calling.

1:4—*Locust* plagues were not uncommon in Palestine (see Judg. 6:5; 7:12; Ps. 105:34–35), as is still the case. The locusts are described in four different ways, perhaps corresponding to the insect's different stages of growth. See 2:25.

1:5 Wake up—So begins the prophet's call to lament (vv. 5–14). *Drunkards* and *wine-drinkers* may be more metaphorical than literal designations of those in authority who are oblivious to the enormity of the environmental catastrophe, the destruction of the fruit of the *vine* (v. 7). They deny the reality of destruction around them because they consider themselves immune or removed from dire threat and deprivation. By contrast, the poor and those who directly work the land are the hardest hit. Those with greater means, however, think they have the resources to protect themselves. Joel's message, however, levels the playing field: *all* face judgment.

1:6—The locusts are now described as an invading nation; their weapons are likened to the devouring mouths of lions (cf. 2:4–9; Rev. 9:7–8). God, however, does not gloat over such destruction. The land is identified as *God's* land, indicating that God's remorse underlies the judgment.

1:8—*Sackcloth* is an apparel signifying mourning (see also v. 13). Such pathos is likened to a bride bereft of her fiancé.

1:9a Grain offering—See Lev. 2. Given the land's decimated state, offerings of agricultural produce are no longer possible. While sacrificial worship is interrupted, severing thereby a crucial point of contact between God and Israel, Joel calls for a ritual of repentance.

1:9b–14—The whole community, from priests to farmers is called to lament, *fast*, and worship. An integral part of the community, the land, too, mourns over the drought that afflicts it (v. 12).

the ministers of the LORD.

¹⁰ The fields are devastated,
    the ground mourns;
for the grain is destroyed,
    the wine dries up,
    the oil fails.

¹¹ Be dismayed, you farmers,
    wail, you vinedressers,
over the wheat and the barley;
    for the crops of the field are
        ruined.

¹² The vine withers,
    the fig tree droops.
Pomegranate, palm, and apple—
    all the trees of the field are dried up;
surely, joy withers away
    among the people.

A Call to Repentance and Prayer

¹³ Put on sackcloth and lament, you
        priests;
    wail, you ministers of the altar.
Come, pass the night in sackcloth,
    you ministers of my God!
Grain offering and drink offering
    are withheld from the house of
        your God.

¹⁴ Sanctify a fast,
    call a solemn assembly.
Gather the elders
    and all the inhabitants of the land
to the house of the LORD your God,
    and cry out to the LORD.

¹⁵ Alas for the day!
For the day of the LORD is near,
    and as destruction from the
        Almighty[a] it comes.

¹⁶ Is not the food cut off
    before our eyes,
joy and gladness
    from the house of our God?

¹⁷ The seed shrivels under the clods,[b]
    the storehouses are desolate;
the granaries are ruined
    because the grain has failed.

¹⁸ How the animals groan!
    The herds of cattle wander about
because there is no pasture for them;
    even the flocks of sheep are dazed.[c]

¹⁹ To you, O LORD, I cry.
For fire has devoured
    the pastures of the wilderness,
and flames have burned
    all the trees of the field.

²⁰ Even the wild animals cry to you
    because the watercourses are
        dried up,
and fire has devoured
    the pastures of the wilderness.

2 Blow the trumpet in Zion;
    sound the alarm on my holy
        mountain!
Let all the inhabitants of the land
    tremble,

[a] Traditional rendering of Heb *Shaddai*   [b] Meaning of Heb uncertain
[c] Compare Gk Syr Vg: Meaning of Heb uncertain

These verses highlight the interconnectedness of the land and its people: the fate of the land determines the fate of its people, and the judgment brought about by the people's conduct is also experienced by the land. The land deeply suffers the moral negligence of its people (cf. Hos. 4:1–3).

1:15 *The day of the LORD*—The leading motif of the book (see also 2:1, 11, 31; 3:14). The earliest reference in Scripture is found in Amos 5:18, which suggests that the expression originally denoted God's victory over Israel's enemies, a cause for celebration. However, Amos, like Joel, deems it a day of darkness in light of the people's sins. For Joel, it is a day of devastation for both people and livestock (see also 2:2; Zeph. 1:14–16). For woe or for weal, this is the day of God's decisive action. Christians celebrate the Lord's Day in light of the resurrection, a day of victory that also

portends the imminent defeat of the principalities and powers that dehumanize and wield death.

1:19—To *cry* to God is to pray for all one's worth before God, who is ultimately worthy of prayer and praise (cf. Pss. 3:4; 5:2; 17:1; 22:1–2; 34:15; 61:1; 77:1). As the climax of the people's prayerful lament, the prophet joins the people's lament and acknowledges that *even the wild animals* pray to God for relief (Joel 1:20). Animals, too, have voice, if not standing, before God (see Jonah 4:11).

2:1—A *trumpet* or shofar is an instrument used to announce the commencement of special worship (see v. 15), as well as impending military engagement. Here it announces God's formidable approach in military strength to Zion, God's dwelling place among God's people, the temple-city Jerusalem (see vv. 2b, 4–8; 3:21; cf. Jer. 4:5). *The day of the LORD*—See note at 1:15.

for the day of the LORD is coming,
     it is near—
2 a day of darkness and gloom,
     a day of clouds and thick darkness!
Like blackness spread upon the
     mountains
     a great and powerful army comes;
their like has never been from of old,
     nor will be again after them
     in ages to come.

3 Fire devours in front of them,
     and behind them a flame burns.
Before them the land is like the
     garden of Eden,
but after them a desolate wilderness,
     and nothing escapes them.

4 They have the appearance of horses,
     and like war-horses they charge.
5 As with the rumbling of chariots,
     they leap on the tops of the
     mountains,
like the crackling of a flame of fire
     devouring the stubble,
like a powerful army
     drawn up for battle.

6 Before them peoples are in anguish,
     all faces grow pale.[a]
7 Like warriors they charge,
     like soldiers they scale the wall.
Each keeps to its own course,

they do not swerve from[b] their
     paths.
8 They do not jostle one another,
     each keeps to its own track;
they burst through the weapons
     and are not halted.
9 They leap upon the city,
     they run upon the walls;
they climb up into the houses,
     they enter through the windows
     like a thief.

10 The earth quakes before them,
     the heavens tremble.
The sun and the moon are darkened,
     and the stars withdraw their
     shining.
11 The LORD utters his voice
     at the head of his army;
how vast is his host!
     Numberless are those who obey
     his command.
Truly the day of the LORD is great;
     terrible indeed—who can endure it?

12 Yet even now, says the LORD,
     return to me with all your heart,
with fasting, with weeping, and with
     mourning;
13   rend your hearts and not your
     clothing.

_a_ Meaning of Heb uncertain   _b_ Gk Syr Vg: Heb _they do not take a pledge along_

2:2 Day of darkness—See 1:15; Amos 5:18. The plague of locusts is described as an army of foreign invaders (e.g., Assyrian or Babylonian). In any case, v. 11 reveals that God is in charge of the invasion.

2:3 Garden of Eden—Cf. Gen. 2:8–17. For the reverse sequence of the army's scorched-earth policy described in Joel, see Isa. 51:3, which describes God's fructified-land plan. As God's people can embody the harmony of the garden by receiving and sharing God's blessing, so the garden can be destroyed by their sin and its punishing consequences. The story of the garden describes an ever repeatable event.

2:10—Accompanying this invasion are the cataclysmic events that mark a divine theophany or approach (cf. Nah. 1:5). The darkening of the cosmos is also described in Joel 2:30–31; 3:15.

2:11 The day of the LORD—See note at 1:15.

2:12—Although continuing the note of lamen-

tation, here is an abrupt transition from harsh judgment to a gentle, even poignant, call to repentance (**return**). Acts of lamentation in the face of judgment lead to Israel's repentance and, in turn, God's change of heart toward grace and restoration (see 1:18–20).

2:13 Rend your hearts—The prophet contrasts inward reorientation ("hearts") with the external show of ritual acts (torn **clothing**). The former, Joel makes clear, is the mark of true repentance (see the language of inward appropriation in Jer. 31:31–34). **Return**—Or repent. "Return" is Joel's clarion call to a wayward people that has forgotten its roots. Israel's return to God will be met by God's turn from judgment toward blessing, in accordance with God's gracious forbearance. The rhythm of faith oscillates between the return for worship and dispersal for service in the world. One depends upon the other. **Gracious and merciful . . .**—These and the following words recall

Return to the LORD, your God,
　for he is gracious and merciful,
slow to anger, and abounding in
　steadfast love,
and relents from punishing.
14 Who knows whether he will not turn
　and relent,
and leave a blessing behind him,
a grain offering and a drink offering
　for the LORD, your God?

15 Blow the trumpet in Zion;
　sanctify a fast;
call a solemn assembly;
16 　gather the people.
Sanctify the congregation;
　assemble the aged;
gather the children,
　even infants at the breast.
Let the bridegroom leave his room,
　and the bride her canopy.

17 Between the vestibule and the
　altar
　let the priests, the ministers of the
　　LORD, weep.
Let them say, "Spare your people,
　O LORD,

and do not make your heritage a
　mockery,
a byword among the nations.
Why should it be said among the
　peoples,
'Where is their God?'"

God's Response and Promise

18 Then the LORD became jealous for
　his land,
and had pity on his people.
19 In response to his people the LORD
　said:
I am sending you
　grain, wine, and oil,
　and you will be satisfied;
and I will no more make you
　a mockery among the nations.

20 I will remove the northern army far
　from you,
　and drive it into a parched and
　　desolate land,
its front into the eastern sea,
　and its rear into the western sea;
its stench and foul smell will
　rise up.
Surely he has done great things!

God's solemn self-confession in Exod. 34:6–7, which takes place during the renewal of the covenant at Sinai. This series of divine qualities appears in variant forms elsewhere in Scripture (e.g., Num. 14:18; Neh. 9:17; Pss. 86:15; 103:8–9; 145:8; Jer. 32:18; Jonah 4:2; Nah. 1:3). With these words, God's very nature is revealed—God is constant in compassion and thus ready to rescind punishment without glossing over offense and sin. Paradoxically put, it is God's very constancy that perennially leaves open the opportunity for God's change of heart toward compassion. Out of compassion, God will search for any excuse to rescind judgment.

2:14 *Who knows*—On the one hand, if God proves willing to rescind judgment, such a reversal stems from God's sovereign freedom, not human manipulation (see also Amos 5:15b). On the other hand, God's response is not oblivious to the people's conduct, the prophet affirms. God's action is *in response to* the people (Joel 2:19a). Thus, human conduct, while it does not control God's will, is instrumental in divine action. With restored prosperity, the agricultural offerings, interrupted by God's judgment, will be reinstated.

2:15—The *trumpet* or shofar blast announces

the summons for all to worship God in penance *in Zion*. Even weddings are to be interrupted (v. 16b). The call to worship takes precedence over any other call, demand, or invitation to activity.

2:17—Israel is God's *heritage* or treasured possession (cf. Exod. 19:5). The priests appeal both to God's favor toward Israel and to God's reputation among the nations (cf. Exod. 32:11–14). The question *"Where is their God?"* strikes at the heart of God's solidarity with a particular people (see Pss. 42:4, 11; 79:10; Mic. 7:10; Mal. 2:17). In the eyes of outsiders, God has all but abandoned Israel. What *the nations* think is acknowledged as a legitimate source of concern and even complaint, for God's activity is not provincially bound.

2:18 *Jealous*—God's "jealousy" or zeal for Israel holds together the complementary qualities of gracious forbearance and punishing judgment (cf. Exod. 20:5). God's passion for Israel effects the turn from judgment to salvation.

2:19—*Grain, wine, and oil* are the emblematic products of agricultural fertility. For a more vivid description, see Hos. 2:21–23.

21 Do not fear, O soil;
     be glad and rejoice,
       for the LORD has done great
          things!
22 Do not fear, you animals of the field,
     for the pastures of the wilderness
          are green;
   the tree bears its fruit,
     the fig tree and vine give their full
          yield.

23 O children of Zion, be glad
     and rejoice in the LORD your God;
   for he has given the early rain[a] for
          your vindication,
   he has poured down for you
          abundant rain,
   the early and the later rain, as
          before.
24 The threshing floors shall be full of
          grain,
     the vats shall overflow with wine
          and oil.

25 I will repay you for the years
     that the swarming locust has eaten,
   the hopper, the destroyer, and the
          cutter,
     my great army, which I sent
          against you.

26 You shall eat in plenty and be
          satisfied,
     and praise the name of the LORD
          your God,
   who has dealt wondrously with you.
   And my people shall never again be
          put to shame.

27 You shall know that I am in the
          midst of Israel,
     and that I, the LORD, am your God
          and there is no other.
   And my people shall never again be
          put to shame.

God's Spirit Poured Out

28[b] Then afterward
     I will pour out my spirit on all
          flesh;
   your sons and your daughters shall
          prophesy,
     your old men shall dream dreams,
     and your young men shall see
          visions.
29 Even on the male and female slaves,
     in those days, I will pour out my
          spirit.

30 I will show portents in the heavens and on the earth, blood and fire and columns of smoke. 31 The sun shall be turned to darkness, and the moon to blood, before the great and terrible day of the LORD comes. 32 Then everyone who calls on the name of the LORD shall be saved; for in Mount Zion and in Jerusalem there shall be those who escape, as the LORD has said, and among the survivors shall be those whom the LORD calls.

3 [c] For then, in those days and at that time, when I restore the fortunes of Judah and Jerusalem, 2 I will gather all the nations and bring them down

[a] Meaning of Heb uncertain [b] Ch 3.1 in Heb [c] Ch 4.1 in Heb

---

2:21–22—"Do not fear" is the most common command in Scripture. Distinctive of Joel is the divine address to soil (v. 21) and wild animals (v. 22; cf. 1:10). Not only are God's people restored (v. 23) but also nature's potency, indicated in the renewal of the land. Joel's prophetic message, one that conveys both judgment and restoration, bears a distinctly ecological thrust. For comparative poetry, see Isa. 55:10–11; Ps. 147:15–20.

2:25—Cf. 1:4–7.

2:27 You shall know—The prophet reveals the purpose of God's turn from judgment to salvation (cf. Isa. 45:5–6; Ezek. 36:11; 39:28).

2:28–32—Israel's restoration is marked by an outpouring of God's spirit that breaks down barriers of class, age, and gender. The working of God's spirit is powerfully inclusive, if not egalitarian, in scope: young and old, women and men, slaves and free are equal recipients of God's spirit. Joel's prophecy serves as the central text of Peter's Pentecost sermon (Acts 2:17–21). The prophet's vision also features the imagery of cosmic convulsion and darkness, indicating the apocalyptic arrival of the Lord's great and terrible day (see Joel 2:2). On Mount Zion, however, deliverance awaits those who worship God.

3:2 The valley of Jehoshaphat—Lit. "the Lord judges." The place is also designated in v. 14 as the valley of decision (see also v. 12; Jer. 25:31). Although later tradition identifies the location

to the valley of Jehoshaphat, and I will enter into judgment with them there, on account of my people and my heritage Israel, because they have scattered them among the nations. They have divided my land, 3 and cast lots for my people, and traded boys for prostitutes, and sold girls for wine, and drunk it down.

4 What are you to me, O Tyre and Sidon, and all the regions of Philistia? Are you paying me back for something? If you are paying me back, I will turn your deeds back upon your own heads swiftly and speedily. 5 For you have taken my silver and my gold, and have carried my rich treasures into your temples.*a* 6 You have sold the people of Judah and Jerusalem to the Greeks, removing them far from their own border. 7 But now I will rouse them to leave the places to which you have sold them, and I will turn your deeds back upon your own heads. 8 I will sell your sons and your daughters into the hand of the people of Judah, and they will sell them to the Sabeans, to a nation far away; for the LORD has spoken.

Judgment in the Valley of Jehoshaphat

9 Proclaim this among the nations:
　Prepare war,*b*
　　stir up the warriors.
　Let all the soldiers draw near,
　　let them come up.
10 Beat your plowshares into swords,
　　and your pruning hooks into spears;
　let the weakling say, "I am a
　　warrior."

11 Come quickly,*c*
　all you nations all around,
　　gather yourselves there.
Bring down your warriors, O LORD.
12 Let the nations rouse themselves,
　and come up to the valley of
　　Jehoshaphat;
for there I will sit to judge
　all the neighboring nations.

13 Put in the sickle,
　for the harvest is ripe.
Go in, tread,
　for the wine press is full.
The vats overflow,
　for their wickedness is great.

14 Multitudes, multitudes,
　in the valley of decision!
For the day of the LORD is near
　in the valley of decision.
15 The sun and the moon are darkened,
　and the stars withdraw their
　　shining.

16 The LORD roars from Zion,
　and utters his voice from
　　Jerusalem,
　and the heavens and the earth
　　shake.
But the LORD is a refuge for his
　　people,
　a stronghold for the people of
　　Israel.

The Glorious Future of Judah

17 So you shall know that I, the LORD
　your God,

---

a Or palaces　*b* Heb sanctify war　*c* Meaning of Heb uncertain

---

with the Kidron valley (see 2 Chr. 29:16), the eastern valley of Jerusalem into which the Gihon spring flows, its precise location is still uncertain. There, judgment is reserved for the nations that have victimized Israel. As Israel's advocate and judge, God judges the nations.

3:4—Tyre and Sidon are coastal cities of Phoenicia, which along with Philistia, were Israel's neighbors to the west and northwest.

3:8 Sabeans—Traders from southwest Arabia.

3:10 Beat your plowshares—The imagery reverses the peaceful message found in Isa. 2:4 and Mic. 4:3, in which weapons of war are trans-

formed into agricultural implements. Joel's message, however, is directed not to Israel but to the nations. The command to forge weapons is part of a divine "dare, " a taunt to provoke the nations into conflict with the now fully restored Israel, an invitation to judgment (Joel 3:12). The nations thus are judged by their own standards of violence.

3:12 Valley of Jehoshaphat—See note at 3:2.

3:16 Roars from Zion—God's judgment threatens even the cosmos (cf. Jer. 25:30; Amos 1:2). Yet, amid judgment, God is **refuge** for Israel (see, e.g., Pss. 2:11; 7:1; 11:1; 18:1–2; 46:1, 7, 11).

3:17—See 2:27.

dwell in Zion, my holy mountain.
And Jerusalem shall be holy,
and strangers shall never again
pass through it.

¹⁸ In that day
the mountains shall drip sweet wine,
the hills shall flow with milk,
and all the stream beds of Judah
shall flow with water;
a fountain shall come forth from the
house of the LORD
and water the Wadi Shittim.

¹⁹ Egypt shall become a desolation
and Edom a desolate wilderness,
because of the violence done to the
people of Judah,
in whose land they have shed
innocent blood.
²⁰ But Judah shall be inhabited forever,
and Jerusalem to all generations.
²¹ I will avenge their blood, and I will
not clear the guilty,ᵃ
for the LORD dwells in Zion.

ᵃ Gk Syr: Heb *I will hold innocent their blood that I have not held innocent*

3:18 *In that day*—The future horizon of "the day of the LORD" will bring unparalleled fertility, matched perhaps only by Eden (cf. 2:3; Amos 9:13). Various biblical traditions develop the evocative image of a subterranean stream issuing forth from the temple: Ps. 46:4; Isa. 33.21; Ezek. 47:1–12; Zech. 14:8; Rev. 22:1–2. Dry washes will become perennial streams, giving life to all (cf. Ps. 42:1).

3:19—*Edom* was Israel's southern neighbor, despised for having betrayed Israel during the Babylonian siege (see Ps. 137:7; Obad. 11). The shedding of innocent blood is considered the most heinous crime of the nations.

3:21 *Not clear the guilty*—The counterpart to God's forbearance described in 2:13b (see Exod. 20:5–6; 34:6–7).

The Book of
AMOS

The prophetic book of Amos is a part of a larger collection of Old Testament prophets at times called Minor Prophets or the Book of the Twelve (Hosea–Malachi). Amos falls third place in this collection, coming after Hosea and Joel, largely due to the dating of his prophecy and the literary-theological connection with the prophet Joel (Joel 3:16 = Amos 1:2).

The prophecy of Amos is a compilation of oracles whose editor links the prophecy to the reigns of Uzziah of Judah (783–742 BCE) and Jeroboam II of Israel (786–746 BCE). Amos is distinctive among Old Testament prophets in that he is the earliest and first prophet to have a book named after him, and in that he sets the prophetic tone for the rest of the canonical prophets. Amos's prophecy fits best in a society where there is inequity between rich and poor, where exploitation is happening at a time of great prosperity. Amos arrives on the scene at Bethel in the northern kingdom not to comfort but to disturb the oppressive complacency of those who are at ease in Zion. We will always hear Amos best in such a context.

Amos's life had a great impact on his prophecy. He was a southerner by birth, who left Tekoa (1:1), a small town fifteen miles southeast from Jerusalem, to go north. Many have argued over his occupation, which he names as "herdsman" (7:14), a term referring to either one who watches over flocks (1:1) or one whom we might call a rancher, a landowner who manages herds. One thing is certain, though; Amos was not a professional prophet (7:14). Amos's lack of professional status lends credibility to so-called lay ministry. God's call to ministry goes out to all kinds of people in all kinds of professions, enabling them to follow the Lord in contexts outside religious institutions.

Amos's prophecy sets the tone for later prophets in several ways. His use of rhetoric establishes patterns that many of his successors use: vision reports (chaps. 7–9), funeral dirge (5:1–2), rhetorical questions (3:3–8), woe sayings (5:18–6:14), numerical sayings (chaps. 1–2), proverbs (3:3–6), hymns (4:13; 5:8–9; 9:5–6), irony (4:4), hyperbole (9:13), and puns and onomatopoeia (8:1). The variety with which Amos spoke teaches that God can use the many and varied gifts of numerous people to accomplish the divine will. There is no one way to follow the Lord. Finally, Amos clearly sets out the twin themes of justice and righteousness as central to understanding the presence of the Lord in society (1:3–2:16; 4:1–3; 5:6–7, 24). Wherever God's people go, they will find God where people are living in just situations and in right relationships within their given societal structures.

—Jefferson H. McCrory Jr.

1 The words of Amos, who was among the shepherds of Tekoa, which he saw concerning Israel in the days of King Uzziah of Judah and in the days of King Jeroboam son of Joash of Israel, two years[a] before the earthquake.

Judgment on Israel's Neighbors

2 And he said:
The LORD roars from Zion,
　　and utters his voice from
　　　　Jerusalem;
　　the pastures of the shepherds wither,
　　　　and the top of Carmel dries up.

3 Thus says the LORD:
For three transgressions of
　　　　Damascus,
　　and for four, I will not revoke the
　　　　punishment;[b]
because they have threshed Gilead
　　with threshing sledges of iron.
4 So I will send a fire on the house of
　　　　Hazael,
　　and it shall devour the strongholds
　　　　of Ben-hadad.
5 I will break the gate bars of
　　　　Damascus,
　　and cut off the inhabitants from
　　　　the Valley of Aven,
　　and the one who holds the scepter
　　　　from Beth-eden;
　　and the people of Aram shall go
　　　　into exile to Kir,
　　　　　　says the LORD.

6 Thus says the LORD:
For three transgressions of Gaza,
　　and for four, I will not revoke the
　　　　punishment;[b]
because they carried into exile entire
　　communities,
　　to hand them over to Edom.
7 So I will send a fire on the wall of
　　　　Gaza,
　　fire that shall devour its
　　　　strongholds.
8 I will cut off the inhabitants from
　　　　Ashdod,
　　and the one who holds the scepter
　　　　from Ashkelon;
I will turn my hand against Ekron,
　　and the remnant of the Philistines
　　　　shall perish,
　　　　　　says the Lord GOD.

9 Thus says the LORD:
For three transgressions of Tyre,
　　and for four, I will not revoke the
　　　　punishment;[b]
because they delivered entire
　　　　communities over to Edom,
　　and did not remember the
　　　　covenant of kinship.
10 So I will send a fire on the wall of
　　　　Tyre,
　　fire that shall devour its
　　　　strongholds.

11 Thus says the LORD:
For three transgressions of Edom,
　　and for four, I will not revoke the
　　　　punishment;[b]
because he pursued his brother with
　　　　the sword
　　and cast off all pity;
he maintained his anger perpetually,[c]
　　and kept his wrath[d] forever.

[a] Or *during two years*　[b] Heb *cause it to return*　[c] Syr Vg: Heb *and his anger tore perpetually*　[d] Gk Syr Vg: Heb *and his wrath kept*

1:1 *King Uzziah*—Amos goes north to prophesy during the greatest period of expansion for both Judah and Israel. He delivers his word in a time of unprecedented prosperity. This period of success gave rise to injustice and greed as well as flourishing religion (4:4; 5:5, 21–23). Amos's prophecy is particularly relevant in thriving societies, where economic greed pushes issues of justice and righteousness to the side.

1:2 *From Zion*—Amos is a southerner who has come north to preach for a short period at a rival sanctuary in Bethel (7:10). He brings a southern-Zion theology of YHWH as a roaring lion to bear upon northern indulgence, which has all the trappings of success but none of the heart of true religion (5:24–25).

1:3 *For three transgressions of Damascus*—In what must have been one of Amos's greatest sermons, the prophet shows his rhetorical style by circling about Israel touching upon some of the northern kingdom's rivals, e.g., Damascus. In this indictment Amos shows that God is concerned with more than those who name God's name.

¹² So I will send a fire on Teman,
  and it shall devour the strongholds
    of Bozrah.

¹³ Thus says the LORD:
For three transgressions of the
    Ammonites,
  and for four, I will not revoke the
    punishment;ᵃ
because they have ripped open
    pregnant women in Gilead
  in order to enlarge their territory.
¹⁴ So I will kindle a fire against the wall
    of Rabbah,
  fire that shall devour its
    strongholds,
with shouting on the day of battle,
  with a storm on the day of the
    whirlwind;
¹⁵ then their king shall go into exile,
  he and his officials together,
                    says the LORD.

2 Thus says the LORD:
  For three transgressions of Moab,
    and for four, I will not revoke the
      punishment;ᵃ
  because he burned to lime
    the bones of the king of Edom.
² So I will send a fire on Moab,
  and it shall devour the strongholds
    of Kerioth,
and Moab shall die amid uproar,
  amid shouting and the sound of
    the trumpet;
³ I will cut off the ruler from its midst,
  and will kill all its officials with
    him,
                    says the LORD.

Judgment on Judah

⁴ Thus says the LORD:
For three transgressions of Judah,

and for four, I will not revoke the
    punishment;ᵃ
because they have rejected the law of
    the LORD,
  and have not kept his statutes,
but they have been led astray by the
    same lies
  after which their ancestors walked.
⁵ So I will send a fire on Judah,
  and it shall devour the strongholds
    of Jerusalem.

Judgment on Israel

⁶ Thus says the LORD:
For three transgressions of Israel,
  and for four, I will not revoke the
    punishment;ᵃ
because they sell the righteous for
    silver,
  and the needy for a pair of
    sandals—
⁷ they who trample the head of the
    poor into the dust of the earth,
  and push the afflicted out of the
    way;
father and son go in to the same girl,
  so that my holy name is profaned;
⁸ they lay themselves down beside
    every altar
  on garments taken in pledge;
and in the house of their God they
    drink
  wine bought with fines they
    imposed.

⁹ Yet I destroyed the Amorite before
    them,
  whose height was like the height of
    cedars,
and who was as strong as oaks;
I destroyed his fruit above,

ᵃ Heb *cause it to return*

**2:6 *For three transgressions of Israel*—By the
time the prophet reaches his target of Israel,
he has his congregation so whipped up that
they don't realize they have begun to chant
against themselves. As one reads this text, one is
reminded of the eloquence of African American
preaching that leads a congregation to point a
finger at their own sin, which overtly they would
never do.

2:7 *They . . . trample the head of the poor*—
Amos targets Israel for exploiting economic
success upon the backs of the poor. The list of
practices in this chapter could be easily updated
to fit any period when the rich get richer and the
poor get poorer. A society is always judged, not
by how well the economy is going, but how the
least in the society are faring.

and his roots beneath.

10 Also I brought you up out of the
        land of Egypt,
    and led you forty years in the
        wilderness,
    to possess the land of the Amorite.
11 And I raised up some of your
        children to be prophets
    and some of your youths to be
        nazirites. *a*
    Is it not indeed so, O people of
        Israel?
                        says the LORD.

12 But you made the nazirites *a* drink
        wine,
    and commanded the prophets,
        saying, "You shall not prophesy."

13 So, I will press you down in your
        place,
    just as a cart presses down
    when it is full of sheaves. *b*
14 Flight shall perish from the swift,
    and the strong shall not retain
        their strength,
    nor shall the mighty save their
        lives;
15 those who handle the bow shall not
        stand,
    and those who are swift of foot
        shall not save themselves,
    nor shall those who ride horses
        save their lives;
16 and those who are stout of heart
        among the mighty
    shall flee away naked in that day,
                        says the LORD.

Israel's Guilt and Punishment

3 Hear this word that the LORD has
    spoken against you, O people of
Israel, against the whole family that I
brought up out of the land of Egypt:
2 You only have I known
    of all the families of the earth;

therefore I will punish you
    for all your iniquities.

3 Do two walk together
    unless they have made an
        appointment?
4 Does a lion roar in the forest,
    when it has no prey?
    Does a young lion cry out from its
        den,
    if it has caught nothing?
5 Does a bird fall into a snare on the
        earth,
    when there is no trap for it?
    Does a snare spring up from the
        ground,
    when it has taken nothing?
6 Is a trumpet blown in a city,
    and the people are not afraid?
    Does disaster befall a city,
    unless the LORD has done it?
7 Surely the Lord GOD does nothing,
    without revealing his secret
    to his servants the prophets.
8 The lion has roared;
    who will not fear?
    The Lord GOD has spoken;
    who can but prophesy?

9 Proclaim to the strongholds in
        Ashdod,
    and to the strongholds in the land
        of Egypt,
    and say, "Assemble yourselves on
        Mount *c* Samaria,
    and see what great tumults are
        within it,
    and what oppressions are in its
        midst."
10 They do not know how to do right,
        says the LORD,
    those who store up violence and
        robbery in their strongholds.

a That is, *those separated* or *those consecrated*   *b* Meaning of Heb uncertain
c Gk Syr: Heb *the mountains of*

3:1 *Against the whole family*—Amos, unlike
previous prophets in Israel and Judah, e.g., Elijah,
levels his charges against the whole nation.
Amos's word addresses those who think that
the covenant with God in both Old and New
Testaments is a covenant of privilege. In contrast, Amos tells us that our relationship to God
demands responsibility to God's intentions. Amos
thus hits a biblical theme that has roots in the call
to Abram to be a blessing to all the families of the
earth (Gen. 12:3) and not to line our own pockets
with God's blessing.

11 Therefore thus says the Lord GOD:
An adversary shall surround the
land,
and strip you of your defense;
and your strongholds shall be
plundered.

12 Thus says the LORD: As the shepherd rescues from the mouth of the lion two legs, or a piece of an ear, so shall the people of Israel who live in Samaria be rescued, with the corner of a couch and part*a* of a bed.

13 Hear, and testify against the house of
Jacob,
says the Lord GOD, the God of
hosts:
14 On the day I punish Israel for its
transgressions,
I will punish the altars of Bethel,
and the horns of the altar shall be
cut off
and fall to the ground.
15 I will tear down the winter house as
well as the summer house;
and the houses of ivory shall perish,
and the great houses*b* shall come to
an end,
says the LORD.

4 Hear this word, you cows of Bashan
who are on Mount Samaria,
who oppress the poor, who crush the
needy,
who say to their husbands, "Bring
something to drink!"
2 The Lord GOD has sworn by his
holiness:
The time is surely coming upon
you,

when they shall take you away with
hooks,
even the last of you with
fishhooks.
3 Through breaches in the wall you
shall leave,
each one straight ahead;
and you shall be flung out into
Harmon,*a*
says the LORD.
4 Come to Bethel—and transgress;
to Gilgal—and multiply
transgression;
bring your sacrifices every
morning,
your tithes every three days;
5 bring a thank offering of leavened
bread,
and proclaim freewill offerings,
publish them;
for so you love to do, O people of
Israel!
says the Lord GOD.

Israel Rejects Correction
6 I gave you cleanness of teeth in all
your cities,
and lack of bread in all your
places,
yet you did not return to me,
says the LORD.
7 And I also withheld the rain from
you
when there were still three months
to the harvest;
I would send rain on one city,
and send no rain on another city;
one field would be rained upon,

a Meaning of Heb uncertain　*b* Or *many houses*

3:15 *Houses of ivory*—The reference to houses of ivory shows the opulence of Israel in time when the gap between the rich and the poor was growing. There is no trickle-down prosperity, only greed, which demands the best in spite of poverty next door.

4:1 *Cows of Bashan*—Amos uses a rather crude but effective volley leveled at the women of Samaria. Cows of Bashan were cattle raised in the richest and most fertile area of Israel. The problem here is that the women are getting fat at the expense of the working poor, those who sweep

their houses and do their laundry. Amos would not have made friends with such a metaphor.

4:4 *Come to Bethel—and transgress*—Religion as well as economics flourished in Israel. The sanctuaries were full of people thanking the Lord for their success. But these same people did little to enact the presence of the Lord in society. Worship in ancient Israel as well as in modern churches is supposed to bring people into contact with the God who intends to bless all, not just a few. Amos says much the same as does Jesus: "You will know them by their fruits" (Matt. 7:16, 20).

and the field on which it did not
rain withered;
8 so two or three towns wandered to
one town
to drink water, and were not
satisfied;
yet you did not return to me,
says the LORD.

9 I struck you with blight and mildew;
I laid waste*a* your gardens and
your vineyards;
the locust devoured your fig trees
and your olive trees;
yet you did not return to me,
says the LORD.

10 I sent among you a pestilence after
the manner of Egypt;
I killed your young men with the
sword;
I carried away your horses;*b*
and I made the stench of your
camp go up into your nostrils;
yet you did not return to me,
says the LORD.

11 I overthrew some of you,
as when God overthrew Sodom
and Gomorrah,
and you were like a brand
snatched from the fire;
yet you did not return to me,
says the LORD.

12 Therefore thus I will do to you,
O Israel;
because I will do this to you,
prepare to meet your God,
O Israel!

13 For lo, the one who forms the
mountains, creates the wind,
reveals his thoughts to mortals,
makes the morning darkness,
and treads on the heights of the
earth—
the LORD, the God of hosts, is his
name!

A Lament for Israel's Sin

5 Hear this word that I take up over
you in lamentation, O house of
Israel:
2 Fallen, no more to rise,
is maiden Israel;
forsaken on her land,
with no one to raise her up.

3 For thus says the Lord GOD:
The city that marched out a
thousand
shall have a hundred left,
and that which marched out a
hundred
shall have ten left.*c*

4 For thus says the LORD to the house
of Israel:
Seek me and live;
5 but do not seek Bethel,
and do not enter into Gilgal
or cross over to Beer-sheba;
for Gilgal shall surely go into exile,
and Bethel shall come to nothing.

6 Seek the LORD and live,
or he will break out against the
house of Joseph like fire,
and it will devour Bethel, with no
one to quench it.
7 Ah, you that turn justice to
wormwood,
and bring righteousness to the
ground!

8 The one who made the Pleiades and
Orion,
and turns deep darkness into the
morning,
and darkens the day into night,
who calls for the waters of the sea,
and pours them out on the surface
of the earth,
the LORD is his name,
9 who makes destruction flash out
against the strong,

a Cn: Heb *the multitude of*   *b* Heb *with the captivity of your horses*   *c* Heb adds
to the house of Israel

5:1–2 *Lamentation*—Amos here employs language from funerary tradition in irony to speak about Israel as a dead maiden, even though she has yet to die. The effect of this would be similar to listening to one's own funeral, at which people complained about how greedy the person was.

so that destruction comes upon
  the fortress.

10 They hate the one who reproves in
  the gate,
    and they abhor the one who
      speaks the truth.
11 Therefore because you trample on
  the poor
    and take from them levies of
      grain,
  you have built houses of hewn stone,
    but you shall not live in them;
  you have planted pleasant vineyards,
    but you shall not drink their wine.
12 For I know how many are your
  transgressions,
    and how great are your sins—
  you who afflict the righteous, who
    take a bribe,
    and push aside the needy in the
      gate.
13 Therefore the prudent will keep
    silent in such a time;
    for it is an evil time.

14 Seek good and not evil,
    that you may live;
  and so the LORD, the God of hosts,
      will be with you,
    just as you have said.
15 Hate evil and love good,
    and establish justice in the gate;
  it may be that the LORD, the God of
    hosts,
    will be gracious to the remnant of
      Joseph.

16 Therefore thus says the LORD, the
    God of hosts, the Lord:

In all the squares there shall be
    wailing;
  and in all the streets they shall say,
    "Alas! alas!"
They shall call the farmers to
    mourning,
  and those skilled in lamentation,
    to wailing;
17 in all the vineyards there shall be
    wailing,
  for I will pass through the midst
      of you,
                    says the LORD.

The Day of the LORD a Dark Day

18 Alas for you who desire the day of
    the LORD!
  Why do you want the day of the
    LORD?
It is darkness, not light;
19   as if someone fled from a lion,
    and was met by a bear;
  or went into the house and rested a
      hand against the wall,
    and was bitten by a snake.
20 Is not the day of the LORD darkness,
    not light,
  and gloom with no brightness
    in it?

21 I hate, I despise your festivals,
    and I take no delight in your
      solemn assemblies.
22 Even though you offer me your
      burnt offerings and grain
        offerings,
    I will not accept them;
  and the offerings of well-being of
    your fatted animals

5:18 *The day of the LORD*—Amos takes what many have identified as holy war traditions and reverses the expectation usually associated with them. By the time Amos prophesied, Israel had taken the day of the Lord traditions to mean that the Lord would fight for Israel regardless of her behavior. Amos reverses this expectation, saying in essence that the Lord fights for justice and righteousness. Western society has taken its success as a sign of God's blessing, that is, that the Lord is on our side. Amos's words militate against our identification of economic success with the presence of God.

5:21–24 *Let justice roll down*—Amos links the behavior of people to their worship. In a compartmentalized society, people can change behaviors to fit a new context. Amos castigates those who praise God on Sunday and cheat people on Monday. Thus God hates worship, not because worship is performed poorly, but because worship is supposed to rehearse an identity that works all week long. These famous words of Amos sum up the prophet's message to ancient Israel as well as any other society.

I will not look upon.

23 Take away from me the noise of your
   songs;
   I will not listen to the melody of
   your harps.

24 But let justice roll down like waters,
   and righteousness like an ever-
   flowing stream.

25 Did you bring to me sacrifices and
offerings the forty years in the wilderness, O house of Israel? 26 You shall take
up Sakkuth your king, and Kaiwan your
star-god, your images,*a* which you made
for yourselves; 27 therefore I will take you
into exile beyond Damascus, says the
LORD, whose name is the God of hosts.

Complacent Self-Indulgence
Will Be Punished

6 Alas for those who are at ease in
   Zion,
   and for those who feel secure on
   Mount Samaria,
   the notables of the first of the
   nations,
   to whom the house of Israel
   resorts!

2 Cross over to Calneh, and see;
   from there go to Hamath the
   great;
   then go down to Gath of the
   Philistines.
   Are you better*b* than these
   kingdoms?
   Or is your*c* territory greater than
   their*d* territory,

3 O you that put far away the evil day,
   and bring near a reign of violence?

4 Alas for those who lie on beds of
   ivory,
   and lounge on their couches,
   and eat lambs from the flock,
   and calves from the stall;

5 who sing idle songs to the sound of
   the harp,

and like David improvise on
   instruments of music;

6 who drink wine from bowls,
   and anoint themselves with the
   finest oils,
   but are not grieved over the ruin
   of Joseph!

7 Therefore they shall now be the first
   to go into exile,
   and the revelry of the loungers
   shall pass away.

8 The Lord GOD has sworn by
   himself
   (says the LORD, the God of hosts):
   I abhor the pride of Jacob
   and hate his strongholds;
   and I will deliver up the city and
   all that is in it.

9 If ten people remain in one house,
they shall die. 10 And if a relative, one
who burns the dead,*e* shall take up the
body to bring it out of the house, and
shall say to someone in the innermost
parts of the house, "Is anyone else with
you?" the answer will come, "No." Then
the relative*f* shall say, "Hush! We must
not mention the name of the LORD."

11 See, the LORD commands,
   and the great house shall be
   shattered to bits,
   and the little house to pieces.

12 Do horses run on rocks?
   Does one plow the sea with
   oxen?*g*
But you have turned justice into
   poison
   and the fruit of righteousness into
   wormwood—

13 you who rejoice in Lo-debar,*h*
   who say, "Have we not by our own
   strength
   taken Karnaim*i* for ourselves?"

---

a Heb your images, your star-god   *b* Or Are they better   *c* Heb their
d Heb your   *e* Or who makes a burning for him   *f* Heb he   *g* Does one plow
them with oxen   *h* Or in a thing of nothingness   *i* Or horns

---

6:1–7 *At ease . . . on beds of ivory*—Setting the
stage for Jesus' pronouncement in the New Testament that the first shall be last and the last first
(Matt. 19:30), Amos says that those who are first

in indulgence will be first into the punishment.
God judges us not just for active persecution of
others, but also for inactive indifference.

¹⁴ Indeed, I am raising up against you a
nation,
  O house of Israel, says the LORD,
    the God of hosts,
and they shall oppress you from
    Lebo-hamath
  to the Wadi Arabah.

Locusts, Fire, and a Plumb Line

7 This is what the Lord GOD showed
me: he was forming locusts at the
time the latter growth began to sprout
(it was the latter growth after the king's
mowings). ²When they had finished eating the grass of the land, I said,
  "O Lord GOD, forgive, I beg you!
    How can Jacob stand?
    He is so small!"
³ The LORD relented concerning this;
  "It shall not be," said the LORD.

⁴ This is what the Lord GOD showed
me: the Lord GOD was calling for a
shower of fire,ᵃ and it devoured the
great deep and was eating up the land.
⁵ Then I said,
  "O Lord GOD, cease, I beg you!
    How can Jacob stand?
    He is so small!"
⁶ The LORD relented concerning this;
  "This also shall not be," said the
    Lord GOD.

⁷ This is what he showed me: the Lord
was standing beside a wall built with
a plumb line, with a plumb line in his
hand. ⁸ And the LORD said to me, "Amos,
what do you see?" And I said, "A plumb
line." Then the Lord said,
  "See, I am setting a plumb line

in the midst of my people
    Israel;
  I will never again pass them by;
⁹ the high places of Isaac shall be
    made desolate,
  and the sanctuaries of Israel shall
    be laid waste,
  and I will rise against the house of
    Jeroboam with the sword."

Amaziah Complains to the King

10 Then Amaziah, the priest of Bethel,
sent to King Jeroboam of Israel, saying,
"Amos has conspired against you in the
very center of the house of Israel; the
land is not able to bear all his words.
¹¹ For thus Amos has said,
  'Jeroboam shall die by the sword,
    and Israel must go into exile
      away from his land.' "
¹² And Amaziah said to Amos, "O seer,
go, flee away to the land of Judah, earn
your bread there, and prophesy there;
¹³ but never again prophesy at Bethel,
for it is the king's sanctuary, and it is a
temple of the kingdom."

14 Then Amos answered Amaziah,
"I amᵇ no prophet, nor a prophet's son;
but I amᵇ a herdsman, and a dresser of
sycamore trees, ¹⁵ and the LORD took me
from following the flock, and the LORD
said to me, 'Go, prophesy to my people
Israel.'
¹⁶ "Now therefore hear the word of the
    LORD.
  You say, 'Do not prophesy against
    Israel,

ᵃ Or for a judgment by fire ᵇ Or was

7:1 This is what the Lord GOD showed me—
Amos's first two visions highlight the intercessory
role of the prophet. Amos sees something and
then asks the Lord God to relent. The amazing
thing is that God responds to Amos's plea. God
listens to our prayers and responds. We do not
live with a mechanistic God, but with one who
engages us in accomplishing God's will.

7:7 With a plumb line in his hand—By the third
vision Amos has stopped interceding. He now
sees that the justice of God demands that something be done in the society. Amos has accepted
that judgment must come. There are times in our

lives when we see that the only way forward is
through the fire, which cleanses and prepares for
new life.

7:14 I am no prophet—Amos was not a professional prophet, yet he heard the call of God. The
Bible does not reserve the call of God for the
professional clergy. God calls every person to
respond in a unique way to bring about the coming kingdom. Thus every profession or position in
life can become the context for living out the call
of God. In responding to the call of God, though,
there is risk, as even Amos experienced in the
confrontation with Amaziah.

and do not preach against the
house of Isaac.'
17 Therefore thus says the LORD:
'Your wife shall become a prostitute
in the city,
and your sons and your daughters
shall fall by the sword,
and your land shall be parceled out
by line;
you yourself shall die in an unclean
land,
and Israel shall surely go into exile
away from its land.' "

The Basket of Fruit

8 This is what the Lord GOD showed
me—a basket of summer fruit.[a] 2 He
said, "Amos, what do you see?" And I
said, "A basket of summer fruit."[a] Then
the LORD said to me,
"The end[b] has come upon my people
Israel;
I will never again pass them by.
3   The songs of the temple[c] shall
become wailings in that day,"
says the Lord GOD;
"the dead bodies shall be many,
cast out in every place. Be silent!"

4 Hear this, you that trample on the
needy,
and bring to ruin the poor of the
land,
5 saying, "When will the new moon be
over
so that we may sell grain;
and the sabbath,
so that we may offer wheat for
sale?
We will make the ephah small and
the shekel great,
and practice deceit with false
balances,
6 buying the poor for silver

and the needy for a pair of sandals,
and selling the sweepings of the
wheat."

7 The LORD has sworn by the pride of
Jacob:
Surely I will never forget any of their
deeds.
8 Shall not the land tremble on this
account,
and everyone mourn who lives
in it,
and all of it rise like the Nile,
and be tossed about and sink
again, like the Nile of Egypt?

9 On that day, says the Lord GOD,
I will make the sun go down at
noon,
and darken the earth in broad
daylight.
10 I will turn your feasts into
mourning,
and all your songs into
lamentation;
I will bring sackcloth on all loins,
and baldness on every head;
I will make it like the mourning for
an only son,
and the end of it like a bitter day.

11 The time is surely coming, says the
Lord GOD,
when I will send a famine on the
land;
not a famine of bread, or a thirst for
water,
but of hearing the words of the
LORD.
12 They shall wander from sea to sea,
and from north to east;
they shall run to and fro, seeking the
word of the LORD,
but they shall not find it.

_a_ Heb _qayits_   _b_ Heb _qets_   _c_ Or _palace_

8:2 The end has come—Amos is popularly
known as a prophet of doom for statements such
as these. There comes a time when God has to
start over with a group of people. We always
think that God will give us another chance. Yet at
times God must act, if the justice of God must be
maintained.

**8:9 On that day . . . I will make the sun go down
at noon**—Amos once again hearkens back to the
Day of the Lord expectation, a day when people
thought God would arrive to reward them. To
their surprise God does arrive, but to punish
those who have identified themselves with other
than God through their actions.

¹³ In that day the beautiful young
       women and the young men
     shall faint for thirst.
¹⁴ Those who swear by Ashimah of
       Samaria,
     and say, "As your god lives, O Dan,"
     and, "As the way of Beer-sheba
       lives"—
     they shall fall, and never rise
       again.

The Destruction of Israel

9 I saw the LORD standing beside*ᵃ* the
   altar, and he said:
Strike the capitals until the
     thresholds shake,
   and shatter them on the heads of
     all the people;*ᵇ*
and those who are left I will kill with
     the sword;
   not one of them shall flee away,
   not one of them shall escape.

² Though they dig into Sheol,
     from there shall my hand take
       them;
   though they climb up to heaven,
     from there I will bring them down.
³ Though they hide themselves on the
     top of Carmel,
     from there I will search out and
       take them;
   and though they hide from my sight
     at the bottom of the sea,
     there I will command the sea-
       serpent, and it shall bite them.
⁴ And though they go into captivity in
     front of their enemies,
     there I will command the sword,
       and it shall kill them;
   and I will fix my eyes on them
     for harm and not for good.

⁵ The Lord, GOD of hosts,
   he who touches the earth and it
     melts,
   and all who live in it mourn,
   and all of it rises like the Nile,
     and sinks again, like the Nile of
       Egypt;
⁶ who builds his upper chambers in
     the heavens,
   and founds his vault upon the
     earth;
who calls for the waters of the sea,
   and pours them out upon the
     surface of the earth—
the LORD is his name.

⁷ Are you not like the Ethiopians*ᶜ*
     to me,
   O people of Israel? says the LORD.
Did I not bring Israel up from the
     land of Egypt,
   and the Philistines from
     Caphtor and the Arameans
     from Kir?
⁸ The eyes of the Lord GOD are upon
     the sinful kingdom,
   and I will destroy it from the face
     of the earth
   —except that I will not utterly
     destroy the house of Jacob,
          says the LORD.

⁹ For lo, I will command,
   and shake the house of Israel
     among all the nations
   as one shakes with a sieve,
     but no pebble shall fall to the
       ground.
¹⁰ All the sinners of my people shall die
     by the sword,
   who say, "Evil shall not overtake or
     meet us."

The Restoration of David's Kingdom

¹¹ On that day I will raise up
     the booth of David that is fallen,
   and repair its*ᵈ* breaches,

---

*ᵃ*Or *on*   *ᵇ*Heb *all of them*   *ᶜ*Or *Nubians;* Heb *Cushites*   *ᵈ*Gk: Heb *their*

9:7 Are you not like the Ethiopians to me—
Amos knows that the Lord is not a local deity but
the God of the universe, who has dealings with
all peoples. This view of God helps in pluralistic
discussions regarding other religions and the
presence of God.

**9:11 On that day I will raise up the booth of
David**—Amos's prophecy ends on a note of hope,
which has led some to discount it as not the real
Amos, since much of his word is harsh, expecting
an end for Israel with no acquittal. Regardless of
one's assessment of the real Amos, the prophe-

and raise up its[a] ruins,
and rebuild it as in the days of old;

12 in order that they may possess the
remnant of Edom
and all the nations who are called
by my name,
says the LORD who does this.

13 The time is surely coming, says the
LORD,
when the one who plows shall
overtake the one who reaps,
and the treader of grapes the one
who sows the seed;
the mountains shall drip sweet wine,
and all the hills shall flow with it.

14 I will restore the fortunes of my
people Israel,
and they shall rebuild the ruined
cities and inhabit them;
they shall plant vineyards and drink
their wine,
and they shall make gardens and
eat their fruit.

15 I will plant them upon their land,
and they shall never again be
plucked up
out of the land that I have given
them,
says the LORD your God.

a Gk: Heb *his*

---

cies in this book always leave room for the grace
of God, an expectation that reverberates with
the New Testament assertion of God's unfailing
grace.

The Book of
OBADIAH

The shortest book of the Old Testament, Obadiah dares to speak about an unspeakable crime of international significance. All twenty-one verses respond to a traumatic set of events in Israel's history, namely, Judah's exile to Babylon in the early sixth century BCE. However, the brunt of the prophet's wrath targets *not* the Babylonians but a neighboring nation, Edom, located in southern Palestine and east of the Arabah. Why? Because Edom was in some sense a brother. Neighbors of comparable political power, Judah and Edom suffered a love/hate relationship throughout their turbulent histories. Indeed, the book of Genesis traces the tension back to Isaac's wife, Rebekah, in whose womb two brothers are found already struggling to gain supremacy over the other, presaging "two nations . . . divided" (Gen. 25:23). While Jacob came to be known as Israel (Gen. 32:28), favored by God (Mal. 1:2), Esau became the eponymous founder of Edom. Historically, the sibling rivalry between Edom and his brother Judah (Obad. 12) reached its culmination at the time of Israel's defeat at the hands of the Babylonians (2 Kgs. 25:1–21). The prophet accuses Edom of betrayal and injury "on the day of [Judah's] misfortune [NRSV *distress*]" (Obad. 14). In short, Edom and Judah were blood brothers.

The book of Obadiah is divided neatly into two parts: verses 1–14 deal specifically with judgment against Edom; verses 15–21 envision Israel's restoration in the wake of divine judgment against the nations. Such judgment is nothing new among the Old Testament prophets; in fact, it is a common feature even among those books that speak of Israel's own judgment from God (e.g., Isa. 13–21; Jer. 46–51; Ezek. 26–32). In Obadiah's case, God's judgment against the nations, specifically one nation, is pronounced in the face of Israel's own victimization at their hands.

It is in light of this horrifying memory of Edom's atrocity against God's people that Obadiah issues his harsh judgment (cf. Ps. 137:7). Although historically specific, the book broaches larger issues of divine judgment and salvation, culminating in a grand vision of Israel's restoration as a nation. Central to the prophet's vision is the message of retribution: "As you have done, it shall be done to you" (v. 15), which establishes the moral basis for God's judgment against Edom. This serves as a warning to any people caught up in the fervor of nationalistic pride, which invariably balkanizes peoples and lands. A nation's jingoistic excesses lead only to self-defeat, the prophet claims. This small book levels a damning judgment on all forms of national hubris and offers a bold theological witness to the God who stands above all national aspirations, however lofty, only to let such aspirations fall. Obadiah's message is intended not add salt to Judah's wounds or to stir up vengeance against an oppressive neighbor, but to let God execute justice for a people whose past cannot be forgotten, yet can be vindicated. Read positively, Obadiah is about throwing a community's moral outrage upon God's shoulders instead of taking matters into its own hands.

—**William P. Brown**

Proud Edom Will Be Brought Low

1 The vision of Obadiah.

Thus says the Lord GOD concerning
    Edom:
We have heard a report from the
    LORD,
    and a messenger has been sent
        among the nations:
"Rise up! Let us rise against it for
        battle!"
² I will surely make you least among
        the nations;
    you shall be utterly despised.
³ Your proud heart has deceived you,
    you that live in the clefts of the
        rock,ᵃ
    whose dwelling is in the heights.
You say in your heart,
    "Who will bring me down to the
        ground?"
⁴ Though you soar aloft like the eagle,
    though your nest is set among the
        stars,
    from there I will bring you down,
            says the LORD.

Pillage and Slaughter Will Repay Edom's Cruelty

⁵ If thieves came to you,
    if plunderers by night
    —how you have been destroyed!—
    would they not steal only what
        they wanted?
If grape-gatherers came to you,
    would they not leave gleanings?
⁶ How Esau has been pillaged,
    his treasures searched out!
⁷ All your allies have deceived you,
    they have driven you to the border;
your confederates have prevailed
        against you;
    those who ateᵇ your bread have set
        a trap for you—
    there is no understanding of it.
⁸ On that day, says the LORD,
    I will destroy the wise out of Edom,
    and understanding out of Mount
        Esau.
⁹ Your warriors shall be shattered,
    O Teman,
    so that everyone from Mount Esau
        will be cut off.

Edom Mistreated His Brother

¹⁰ For the slaughter and violence done
    to your brother Jacob,
    shame shall cover you,
    and you shall be cut off forever.
¹¹ On the day that you stood aside,
    on the day that strangers carried
        off his wealth,

ᵃ Or *clefts of Sela* ᵇ Cn: Heb lacks *those who ate*

1—Though emphasis falls upon what the prophet *sees*, the vision includes what the prophet *hears* from God (vv. 1b, 4b). Visions are not uncommon among the prophets (2 Chr. 32:32; Isa. 1:1; Nah. 1:1; cf. Mic. 1:1). *Obadiah*—Nothing is known about the prophet himself. His name bears the meaning "servant of the LORD," an appropriate name for a prophet of God and a common one for an Israelite, designating twelve different persons in the Old Testament. *Edom*—Judah's southeastern neighbor. See introduction. Obadiah's judgment is not against the superpower Babylon but against a brother who has betrayed Israel.

3 *Proud heart*—Soaring national hubris is the flaw that brings down many a nation, a jingoistic pride that compels a nation to conduct its foreign policy with impunity and without regard for the well-being of other nations, Judah included. God stands alone as the nations rise and fall, along with their imperial aspirations. *Clefts of the rock*—Or clefts of Sela, an Edomite fortress also called Teman (v. 9), possibly located within the

later city of Petra, in what is now Jordan. Edom considered itself invulnerable, thereby deluding itself.

4—The prophet contrasts the heights of Edom's defenses (and hubris!) with the abject humbling of the nation in the wake of impending judgment.

7 *All your allies*—Lit. "men of your covenant" or treaty partners.

8—Edom was renowned for its wisdom (Jer. 49:7), which makes Edom's crime all the more alarming. The collected wisdom of a nation, when propped up by jingoistic pride, becomes self-delusional.

9 *Teman*—The capital of Edom.

10–14—The prophet describes in repetitive fashion, building in intensity, the heinous crimes Edom committed against Judah during and after the Babylonian invasion, from aloofness and boasting to looting and betrayal. The slide into outright violence, against a brother no less, begins with Edom having *stood aside* (v. 11) during

and foreigners entered his gates
and cast lots for Jerusalem,
you too were like one of them.
12 But you should not have gloated[a]
over[b] your brother
on the day of his misfortune;
you should not have rejoiced over
the people of Judah
on the day of their ruin;
you should not have boasted
on the day of distress.
13 You should not have entered the gate
of my people
on the day of their calamity;
you should not have joined in the
gloating over Judah's[c] disaster
on the day of his calamity;
you should not have looted his goods
on the day of his calamity.
14 You should not have stood at the
crossings
to cut off his fugitives;
you should not have handed over his
survivors
on the day of distress.

15 For the day of the LORD is near
against all the nations.
As you have done, it shall be done to
you;
your deeds shall return on your
own head.
16 For as you have drunk on my holy
mountain,
all the nations around you shall
drink;
they shall drink and gulp down,[d]
and shall be as though they had
never been.

Israel's Final Triumph

17 But on Mount Zion there shall be
those that escape,
and it shall be holy;
and the house of Jacob shall take
possession of those who
dispossessed them.
18 The house of Jacob shall be a fire,
the house of Joseph a flame,
and the house of Esau stubble;
they shall burn them and consume
them,
and there shall be no survivor of
the house of Esau;
for the LORD has spoken.
19 Those of the Negeb shall possess
Mount Esau,
and those of the Shephelah the
land of the Philistines;
they shall possess the land of
Ephraim and the land of
Samaria,
and Benjamin shall possess Gilead.
20 The exiles of the Israelites who are in
Halah[e]
shall possess[f] Phoenicia as far as
Zarephath;
and the exiles of Jerusalem who are
in Sepharad
shall possess the towns of the
Negeb.
21 Those who have been saved[g] shall go
up to Mount Zion
to rule Mount Esau;
and the kingdom shall be the
LORD's.

a Heb *But do not gloat (and similarly through verse 14)*   *b* Heb *on the day of*   *c* Heb *his*   *d* Meaning of Heb uncertain   *e* Cn: Heb *in this army*   *f* Cn: Meaning of Heb uncertain   *g* Or *Saviors*

Judah's decimation. Refusing to act in the face of another's aggression, the prophet implies, is tantamount to committing aggression.

15 *The day of the LORD*—A day of retribution against the nations. See Joel 2:1; Amos 5:18. The day is the Lord's: it is the Lord's prerogative to execute judgment, not Israel's.

16—The cup of judgment (see Ps. 75:8; Isa. 51:17–23; Jer. 25:15–17) from which Edom has drunk is now for *the nations*, including Babylonia, to drink as they suffer their own destruction because of their crime against God's people.

17 *Mount Zion*—The place of escape and refuge for Israel (see also v. 21).

19 *Negeb*—Southern Judah. ***Shephelah*—**The western foothills.

20 *Halah*—In northern Mesopotamia (2 Kgs. 17:6). ***Zarephath*—**A town in southern Phoenicia (1 Kgs. 17:9). ***Sepharad*—**perhaps a town in Asia Minor.

21—God's kingdom relativizes all earthly powers, and any nation that denies God's sovereign reign succumbs to nationalistic self-delusion.

The Book of

JONAH

Jonah is often called the reluctant prophet. We unfortunately know little to nothing about the figure of Jonah. This story is probably a tale that developed around the obscure prophet briefly mentioned in 2 Kings 14:25. The book divides neatly into two parallel scenes, chapters 1–2 and chapters 3–4, each having a similar plot and theme. Humorous and unlikely, larger-than-life elements permeate this little story, as do concerns of ecology. Natural elements (wind, sea, fish, bush, worm) play a necessary role in the events. Both God and the world of nature are presented as working together to bring about understanding and redemption to the human characters.

The city of Nineveh was the capital of the ancient Assyrian Empire. At other places in the Bible Nineveh is represented as a wicked, violent place and as an enemy of Israel (cf. Nah. 3; Zeph. 2:13). This is therefore a story of "insiders" (Jonah the Israelite) and foreigners or "outsiders" (the sailors and the Ninevites). It is notable that the foreigners act more faithfully to Israel's God than does Jonah. The fact that the foreigners never convert to the worship of YHWH or declare the Israelite God as the only god leads readers to reconsider their own attitudes to persons holding religious beliefs different from their own. The story ultimately portrays the extensive nature of God's compassion and presents God's concern for large, urban populations. As Jonah's problem is not really with Nineveh but with God, it draws into relief human perceptions of justice versus divine perceptions of mercy and justice.

It is difficult to determine with much certainty when and where this book was composed. Unlike other prophetic works, it includes no time indicator. Most likely, however, the book of Jonah was written during the postexilic period, during the fifth or fourth century BCE. The figure of Jonah would have served as a negative example to the Jewish exiles, highlighting God's character as a universal God who was calling them to care for the Babylonian and Persian people with whom they now lived.

—Linda Day

Jonah Tries to Run Away from God

1 Now the word of the LORD came to Jonah son of Amittai, saying, ²"Go at once to Nineveh, that great city, and cry out against it; for their wickedness has come up before me." ³But Jonah set out to flee to Tarshish from the presence of the LORD. He went down to Joppa and found a ship going to Tarshish; so he paid his fare and went on board, to go with them to Tarshish, away from the presence of the LORD.

1:1–16 Jonah's Response to God

1:1–3—God's request represents a prophetic call. Most biblical prophets protest when called by God (cf. Isa. 6:5; Jer. 1:6; Exod. 4:10–13). Jonah, however, says nothing; he just runs away. Jonah's action is a typical human response. When we are faced with the enormity of need in the world and the enormity of what God seems to be asking

us to do about it, our first reaction is often sheer panic. Jonah sets out to the east, the opposite direction from Nineveh. *Joppa* is a seaport on the Mediterranean Sea, and *Tarshish* is most likely in southern Spain. Jonah must be a person of some wealth, to be able to spare the great amount *his fare* would cost for such a lengthy voyage.

4 But the LORD hurled a great wind upon the sea, and such a mighty storm came upon the sea that the ship threatened to break up. 5 Then the mariners were afraid, and each cried to his god. They threw the cargo that was in the ship into the sea, to lighten it for them. Jonah, meanwhile, had gone down into the hold of the ship and had lain down, and was fast asleep. 6 The captain came and said to him, "What are you doing sound asleep? Get up, call on your god! Perhaps the god will spare us a thought so that we do not perish."

7 The sailors*a* said to one another, "Come, let us cast lots, so that we may know on whose account this calamity has come upon us." So they cast lots, and the lot fell on Jonah. 8 Then they said to him, "Tell us why this calamity has come upon us. What is your occupation? Where do you come from? What is your country? And of what people are you?" 9 "I am a Hebrew," he replied. "I worship the LORD, the God of heaven, who made the sea and the dry land." 10 Then the men were even more afraid, and said to him, "What is this that you have done!" For the men knew that he was fleeing from the presence of the LORD, because he had told them so.

11 Then they said to him, "What shall we do to you, that the sea may quiet down for us?" For the sea was growing more and more tempestuous. 12 He said to them, "Pick me up and throw me into the sea; then the sea will quiet down for

you; for I know it is because of me that this great storm has come upon you." 13 Nevertheless the men rowed hard to bring the ship back to land, but they could not, for the sea grew more and more stormy against them. 14 Then they cried out to the LORD, "Please, O LORD, we pray, do not let us perish on account of this man's life. Do not make us guilty of innocent blood; for you, O LORD, have done as it pleased you." 15 So they picked Jonah up and threw him into the sea; and the sea ceased from its raging. 16 Then the men feared the LORD even more, and they offered a sacrifice to the LORD and made vows.

17*b* But the LORD provided a large fish to swallow up Jonah; and Jonah was in the belly of the fish three days and three nights.

A Psalm of Thanksgiving

2 Then Jonah prayed to the LORD his God from the belly of the fish, 2 saying,

"I called to the LORD out of my
  distress,
    and he answered me;
out of the belly of Sheol I cried,
    and you heard my voice.
3 You cast me into the deep,
    into the heart of the seas,
    and the flood surrounded me;
all your waves and your billows
    passed over me.
4 Then I said, 'I am driven away

a Heb *They*   *b* Ch 2.1 in Heb

1:4—Reacting against the disobedience of a single human being, God places many others in danger.

1:6–14—The foreign sailors are more pious than Jonah. The captain chides Jonah for not praying, and the sailors are unwilling to let him die. They more fully comprehend God's ways and exhibit a proper balance between prayer and action. Jonah, on the other hand, acts self-servingly. He shows a great lack of concern for the danger in which he has placed his fellow seafarers.

1:12—Jonah's request to be thrown overboard *into the sea* is his only fully unselfish action throughout the story.

1:16—The sailors' initial fear of the storm (v. 5) has turned into faith, now a fear of the God who brought about the storm.

1:17–2:10 Jonah in the Fish

1:17—The story's most outlandish element is *the fish*—not a whale!—who swallows Jonah. Even animals can be agents of God's purpose (see 2:10).

2:1—It is only when Jonah is in the depths of despair that he finally decides to turn and respond to God. His prayer is actually a psalm that is much like other biblical psalms of thanksgiving.

2:3—Instead of engaging in self-examination, Jonah blames God for his present predicament.

from your sight;
how[a] shall I look again
  upon your holy temple?'
5 The waters closed in over me;
  the deep surrounded me;
weeds were wrapped around my
  head
6 at the roots of the mountains.
I went down to the land
  whose bars closed upon me
  forever;
yet you brought up my life from the
  Pit,
O LORD my God.
7 As my life was ebbing away,
  I remembered the LORD;
and my prayer came to you,
  into your holy temple.
8 Those who worship vain idols
  forsake their true loyalty.
9 But I with the voice of thanksgiving
  will sacrifice to you;
what I have vowed I will pay.
  Deliverance belongs to the LORD!"
10 Then the LORD spoke to the fish, and
it spewed Jonah out upon the dry land.

Conversion of Nineveh

3 The word of the LORD came to Jonah
a second time, saying, 2 "Get up, go
to Nineveh, that great city, and proclaim to it the message that I tell you."
3 So Jonah set out and went to Nineveh,
according to the word of the LORD. Now
Nineveh was an exceedingly large city,
a three days' walk across. 4 Jonah began
to go into the city, going a day's walk.
And he cried out, "Forty days more, and
Nineveh shall be overthrown!" 5 And the
people of Nineveh believed God; they
proclaimed a fast, and everyone, great
and small, put on sackcloth.

6 When the news reached the king
of Nineveh, he rose from his throne,
removed his robe, covered himself with
sackcloth, and sat in ashes. 7 Then he had
a proclamation made in Nineveh: "By
the decree of the king and his nobles:
No human being or animal, no herd or
flock, shall taste anything. They shall
not feed, nor shall they drink water.
8 Human beings and animals shall be
covered with sackcloth, and they shall
cry mightily to God. All shall turn from
their evil ways and from the violence
that is in their hands. 9 Who knows?
God may relent and change his mind; he
may turn from his fierce anger, so that
we do not perish."

10 When God saw what they did, how
they turned from their evil ways, God
changed his mind about the calamity
that he had said he would bring upon
them; and he did not do it.

Jonah's Anger

4 But this was very displeasing to
Jonah, and he became angry. 2 He

[a] Theodotion: Heb *surely*

2:5–6—Jonah is now in the absolute pits. The series of descending motions (1:3, 5, 15; 2:3) has concluded in *the Pit*, or Sheol (2:2), the nether-world. The imagery is visually dark and physically constrictive.

3:1–10 Jonah's Response to God, Take 2

3:1–3—This scene begins almost exactly like 1:1–2, although this *second time* Jonah decides to go to Nineveh as God requests.

3:4–5—Jonah experiences remarkable success. Not only a mental acquiescence, the Ninevites physically act upon their new faith with fasting and wearing *sackcloth*. The *small* would include the children and other persons whom society considers of less importance. Now, though, everyone is treated equally, all acting alike before God.

3:6—*The king* is the last to know of the people's actions. Often religious movements begin with the common folk, the general populace, and only secondarily are recognized by the authorities.

3:7–8—Despite the humorous image of *animals . . . covered with sackcloth*, the king's decree treats animals with the same importance as the human inhabitants of the city. The ill effects of sin fall not only upon the human realm but also upon the animal realm. All of creation must work together for God's compassion and toward holistic well-being.

3:10—The Ninevites' repentance is matched by God's repentance.

4:1–11 Jonah's Resentment

4:1–2—Jonah is unwilling for God to forgive others, for it offends his sense of justice. We

prayed to the LORD and said, "O LORD! Is not this what I said while I was still in my own country? That is why I fled to Tarshish at the beginning; for I knew that you are a gracious God and merciful, slow to anger, and abounding in steadfast love, and ready to relent from punishing. ³And now, O LORD, please take my life from me, for it is better for me to die than to live." ⁴And the LORD said, "Is it right for you to be angry?" ⁵Then Jonah went out of the city and sat down east of the city, and made a booth for himself there. He sat under it in the shade, waiting to see what would become of the city.

6 The LORD God appointed a bush,ᵃ and made it come up over Jonah, to give shade over his head, to save him from his discomfort; so Jonah was very happy about the bush. ⁷But when dawn came up the next day, God appointed a worm that attacked the bush, so that it withered. ⁸When the sun rose, God prepared a sultry east wind, and the sun beat down on the head of Jonah so that he was faint and asked that he might die. He said, "It is better for me to die than to live."

Jonah Is Reproved

9 But God said to Jonah, "Is it right for you to be angry about the bush?" And he said, "Yes, angry enough to die." ¹⁰Then the LORD said, "You are concerned about the bush, for which you did not labor and which you did not grow; it came into being in a night and perished in a night. ¹¹And should I not be concerned about Nineveh, that great city, in which there are more than a hundred and twenty thousand persons who do not know their right hand from their left, and also many animals?"

ᵃ Heb qiqayon, possibly the castor bean plant

---

humans have a tendency to resent it when blessing appears to come to someone who, in our minds, does not deserve it.

4:3, 8, 9—Jonah's suicide wishes are another aspect of his selfish nature. Death would be the ultimate way to run away from God's requirements and God's troubling actions.

4:9–10—Though *the bush* is not unimportant in God's eyes, it reflects Jonah's misplaced priorities.

4:11—The people's ignorance elicits divine compassion. And the very urban nature of Nineveh, *more than a hundred and twenty thousand persons*, influences God to act. This final rhetorical question is directed ultimately to the readers. Should we not allow God's love to encompass all the Ninevehs of our present world?

The Book of
MICAH

Micah—along with Isaiah, Hosea, and Amos—is one of the eighth-century BCE prophets best known for a passion for social justice. What we are best acquainted with from this prophet is his response to the question, "What does the LORD require of you?" Micah's answer, "To do justice, and to love kindness, and to walk humbly with your God" (6:8), situates him squarely in that tradition of social justice.

Authorship. Most scholars view the book of Micah as a product of redactional growth. They attribute chapters 1–3 to Micah, rural prophet and younger contemporary of Isaiah. The rest of the book, chapters 4–7, may have originated in the exilic and postexilic periods when Micah's words were revised and applied to the new situations.

Micah hails from Moresheth (1:1), probably a shortened form of Moresheth-gath in 1:14, located twenty-five miles southwest of Jerusalem. His name, Micah, is an abbreviated form of Micaiah, meaning "Who is like YHWH?" His name is mentioned in Jeremiah 26:18, in the context of the elders' defense of Jeremiah on account of his temple sermon.

Historical Setting. Micah's prophetic ministry, according to the superscription in 1:1, spans the reigns of three Judean kings: Jotham (742–735 BCE), Ahaz (735–715 BCE), and Hezekiah (715–687 BCE). Within the reigns of these kings, it is not possible to ascertain how long his ministry was. Micah may have had a relatively short career in the months immediately before Sennacherib's invasion in 701 BCE. Most scholars, however, believe that Micah's ministry began before the destruction of Samaria in 722 BCE.

Theology. There are several theological issues to which the reader needs to pay attention.

1. *Micah gives a multidimensional view of God.* The wrath of God is clearly displayed in the book of Micah. However, Micah also shows that God is reasonable: God makes a reasonable case against Samaria. Clearly God is angry, but God is willing to reason with humans. Moreover, God also shows the willingness to forgive and to start anew. God is not only the prosecutor of sinners but also the judge who is compassionate and who is willing to offer a second chance. We do an injustice to God and disservice to our fellow human beings if we view God one-dimensionally according to our need of the moment.

2. *The role of a prophet is not singular either.* Micah denounces social evils of his time; he condemns the leaders for their crimes against the defenseless, women, and children. But criticizing what is wrong with the world or pointing a finger at those who are oppressing and exploiting the most vulnerable members of society is not the only role of a prophet. A prophet must also offer hope and promise to the people. A prophet must empower the people to do what is right, rather than beat them to

submission with guilt. The oppressors do not have the last word; injustice is not permanent. Micah offers hope by showing and believing in God's vision of the world in which peace reigns supreme.

3. *Micah directs us above all to listen to what God expects of us.* We often want God to behave according to our needs. God's expectation shows what it means to be a godly person, a person after God's own heart. Outward symbols of piety are meaningless without the inward character of doing justice, loving kindness, and walking humbly with God. In other words, God is more interested in how we live our everyday lives than how we perform our religious practices.

4. *Micah has a vision of a religiously pluralistic world.* This is the most challenging theological issue in the book of Micah. In Micah there is no demonizing of other deities, but rather the recognition that other peoples will keep their gods while living in peace and harmony. Peace and harmony do not require that all people think, act, and believe alike. What they do require of everybody is mutual respect and the pursuit of the common good. Do we dare to work toward such a vision?

—**Jeffrey Kuan**

1 The word of the LORD that came to Micah of Moresheth in the days of Kings Jotham, Ahaz, and Hezekiah of Judah, which he saw concerning Samaria and Jerusalem.

Judgment Pronounced against Samaria

2 Hear, you peoples, all of you;
   listen, O earth, and all that is in it;
and let the Lord GOD be a witness against you,
   the Lord from his holy temple.
3 For lo, the LORD is coming out of his place,
   and will come down and tread upon the high places of the earth.
4 Then the mountains will melt under him
   and the valleys will burst open,
like wax near the fire,
   like waters poured down a steep place.
5 All this is for the transgression of Jacob
   and for the sins of the house of Israel.
What is the transgression of Jacob?
   Is it not Samaria?
And what is the high place[a] of Judah?
   Is it not Jerusalem?
6 Therefore I will make Samaria a heap in the open country,
   a place for planting vineyards.
I will pour down her stones into the valley,
   and uncover her foundations.
7 All her images shall be beaten to pieces,
   all her wages shall be burned with fire,

[a] Heb *what are the high places*

1:1 Superscription

The subjects of Micah's prophetic pronouncements are *Samaria and Jerusalem*, the capital cities of the northern kingdom of Israel and southern kingdom of Judah respectively.

1:2–7 God's Case against Samaria

In the language of a court of law, all nations are summoned to witness to God's testimony against Samaria. In this judicial proceeding, as well as in many others, God is both the prosecutor and the judge. The prophet describes God's appearance as awesome and frightening to the whole creation. Samaria is being accused of violating its exclusive worship of YHWH. Micah uses the language of prostitution as an image of Samaria's religious apostasy. The use of such an image is indicative of a patriarchal society that deprecates women, especially "uncontrolled" women. Readers must be careful about perpetuating such theological images that do harm to women.

and all her idols I will lay waste;
  for as the wages of a prostitute she
    gathered them,
  and as the wages of a prostitute
    they shall again be used.

The Doom of the Cities of Judah

8 For this I will lament and wail;
  I will go barefoot and naked;
  I will make lamentation like the
    jackals,
  and mourning like the ostriches.
9 For her wound*a* is incurable.
  It has come to Judah;
  it has reached to the gate of my
    people,
  to Jerusalem.

10 Tell it not in Gath,
  weep not at all;
  in Beth-leaphrah
  roll yourselves in the dust.
11 Pass on your way,
  inhabitants of Shaphir,
  in nakedness and shame;
  the inhabitants of Zaanan
  do not come forth;
  Beth-ezel is wailing
  and shall remove its support
    from you.
12 For the inhabitants of Maroth
  wait anxiously for good,
  yet disaster has come down from
    the LORD
  to the gate of Jerusalem.

13 Harness the steeds to the chariots,
  inhabitants of Lachish;
  it was the beginning of sin
    to daughter Zion,
  for in you were found
    the transgressions of Israel.
14 Therefore you shall give parting gifts
    to Moresheth-gath;
  the houses of Achzib shall be a
    deception
  to the kings of Israel.
15 I will again bring a conqueror upon
    you,
  inhabitants of Mareshah;
  the glory of Israel
  shall come to Adullam.
16 Make yourselves bald and cut off
    your hair
  for your pampered children;
  make yourselves as bald as the eagle,
  for they have gone from you into
    exile.

Social Evils Denounced

2 Alas for those who devise
    wickedness
  and evil deeds*b* on their beds!
When the morning dawns, they
    perform it,
  because it is in their power.
2 They covet fields, and seize them;
  houses, and take them away;
  they oppress householder and house,
  people and their inheritance.

a Gk Syr Vg: Heb *wounds* *b* Cn: Heb *work evil*

1:8–16 Micah's Lament

As a southerner, Micah does not rejoice in the impending punishment of Samaria. He is acutely aware that similar fate will befall his own people. Thus he engages in a symbolic action, common among prophets (see, e.g., Jer. 27:2), of lamenting and wailing as if destruction has already happened in Judah. Micah invites the people to join him in the mourning rites (Mic.1:16). He is aware that sin is contagious and, if not dealt with, has irreparable consequences.

2:1–13 Denunciation of Social Evils

Micah turns his attention to addressing the societal ills, crimes perpetrated by the wealthy against the defenseless, women, and children. He accuses the rich of seizing homes and inherited land from those who could not defend them-

selves, a violation of the covenant between God and Israel that seeks to guarantee that the inherited land remains within the family structure. The women and children, the most vulnerable in the society, are subjected to unjust treatment by being evicted from their homes. Micah promises the oppressors that their inheritance will be taken from them and parceled out to others (v. 4) and that they themselves will be evicted (v. 10). The situation Micah denounces exists today, not only in the so-called third world, where land is increasingly under the control of the powerful few, but also in the capitalist West, where large corporations are always taking over smaller ones in mergers that impact the livelihood of hundreds of thousands of people. Women and children continue to suffer the most under such exploitative conditions.

³ Therefore thus says the LORD:
Now, I am devising against this
family an evil
from which you cannot remove
your necks;
and you shall not walk haughtily,
for it will be an evil time.
⁴ On that day they shall take up a
taunt song against you,
and wail with bitter lamentation,
and say, "We are utterly ruined;
the LORDᵃ alters the inheritance of
my people;
how he removes it from me!
Among our captorsᵇ he parcels out
our fields."
⁵ Therefore you will have no one to
cast the line by lot
in the assembly of the LORD.

⁶ "Do not preach"—thus they
preach—
"one should not preach of such
things;
disgrace will not overtake us."
⁷ Should this be said, O house of
Jacob?
Is the LORD's patience exhausted?
Are these his doings?
Do not my words do good
to one who walks uprightly?
⁸ But you rise up against my peopleᶜ
as an enemy;
you strip the robe from the
peaceful,ᵈ
from those who pass by trustingly
with no thought of war.
⁹ The women of my people you drive
out
from their pleasant houses;
from their young children you take
away
my glory forever.
¹⁰ Arise and go;

for this is no place to rest,
because of uncleanness that destroys
with a grievous destruction.ᵉ
¹¹ If someone were to go about uttering
empty falsehoods,
saying, "I will preach to you of
wine and strong drink,"
such a one would be the preacher
for this people!

A Promise for the Remnant of Israel

¹² I will surely gather all of you,
O Jacob,
I will gather the survivors of Israel;
I will set them together
like sheep in a fold,
like a flock in its pasture;
it will resound with people.
¹³ The one who breaks out will go up
before them;
they will break through and pass
the gate,
going out by it.
Their king will pass on before them,
the LORD at their head.

Wicked Rulers and Prophets

3 And I said:
Listen, you heads of Jacob
and rulers of the house of Israel!
Should you not know justice?—
² you who hate the good and love
the evil,
who tear the skin off my people,ᶠ
and the flesh off their bones;
³ who eat the flesh of my people,
flay their skin off them,
break their bones in pieces,
and chop them up like meatᵍ in a
kettle,
like flesh in a caldron.

ᵃ Heb *he* ᵇ Cn: Heb *the rebellious* ᶜ Cn: Heb *But yesterday my people rose*
ᵈ Cn: Heb *from before a garment* ᵉ Meaning of Heb uncertain ᶠ Heb *from
them* ᵍ Gk: Heb *as*

**3:1–12 Judgment against Political
and Religious Leadership**

3:1–4—The prophetic tradition holds the leadership of the society accountable for the welfare of the people. The first group of people that come under Micah's indictment are the political and judicial leaders. These are the ones who are

supposed to uphold justice, but instead *hate the good and love the evil*. Micah likens their abuse of the less fortunate to cannibalism. As a punishment they will get a taste their own medicine; because they did not hear the cry of the needy, God will not answer their cry for help.

5

[a] Now you are walled around with a wall;[b]
  siege is laid against us;
with a rod they strike the ruler of Israel
  upon the cheek.

The Ruler from Bethlehem

[2c] But you, O Bethlehem of Ephrathah,
  who are one of the little clans of Judah,
from you shall come forth for me
  one who is to rule in Israel,
whose origin is from of old,
  from ancient days.
3 Therefore he shall give them up until the time
  when she who is in labor has brought forth;
then the rest of his kindred shall return
  to the people of Israel.
4 And he shall stand and feed his flock in the strength of the LORD,
  in the majesty of the name of the LORD his God.
And they shall live secure, for now he shall be great
  to the ends of the earth;
5 and he shall be the one of peace.

If the Assyrians come into our land
  and tread upon our soil, [d]
we will raise against them seven shepherds
  and eight installed as rulers.
6 They shall rule the land of Assyria with the sword,
  and the land of Nimrod with the drawn sword;[e]

they [f] shall rescue us from the Assyrians
  if they come into our land
  or tread within our border.

The Future Role of the Remnant

7 Then the remnant of Jacob,
  surrounded by many peoples,
shall be like dew from the LORD,
  like showers on the grass,
which do not depend upon people
  or wait for any mortal.
8 And among the nations the remnant of Jacob,
  surrounded by many peoples,
shall be like a lion among the animals of the forest,
  like a young lion among the flocks of sheep,
which, when it goes through, treads down
  and tears in pieces, with no one to deliver.
9 Your hand shall be lifted up over your adversaries,
  and all your enemies shall be cut off.

10 In that day, says the LORD,
  I will cut off your horses from among you
  and will destroy your chariots;
11 and I will cut off the cities of your land
  and throw down all your strongholds;
12 and I will cut off sorceries from your hand,
  and you shall have no more soothsayers;

[a] Ch 4.14 in Heb   [b] Cn Compare Gk: Meaning of Heb uncertain
[c] Ch 5.1 in Heb   [d] Gk: Heb *in our palaces*   [e] Cn: Heb *in its entrances*
[f] Heb *he*

5:1–15 The Future Ruler from Bethlehem
Continuing the theme of restoration comes the promise of a new ruler from Bethlehem. The text is best read against the backdrop of the siege of Jerusalem that Assyria, under Sennacherib, laid in 701 BCE. The **ruler of Israel** in v. 1, therefore, is Hezekiah. In the midst of the enormous threat to Jerusalem and its king, Micah delivers a message of hope, a hope of the continuity of the Davidic dynasty. This future Davidic king will ensure that peace will reign supreme. In that secured future, Israel's enemies will be cut off and Israel will take its place of prominence among the nations (vv. 7–9). In addition, God will remove from Israel objects that have led Israel away from her undivided devotion and trust in God: military armament, sorcery, and idolatrous paraphernalia (vv. 10–15).

13 and I will cut off your images
    and your pillars from among you,
and you shall bow down no more
    to the work of your hands;
14 and I will uproot your sacred poles*a*
    from among you
    and destroy your towns.
15 And in anger and wrath I will
    execute vengeance
    on the nations that did not obey.

God Challenges Israel

6 Hear what the LORD says:
   Rise, plead your case before the
    mountains,
    and let the hills hear your
    voice.
2 Hear, you mountains, the
    controversy of the LORD,
    and you enduring foundations of
    the earth;
for the LORD has a controversy with
    his people,
    and he will contend with Israel.

3 "O my people, what have I done to
    you?
In what have I wearied you?
    Answer me!
4 For I brought you up from the land
    of Egypt,
    and redeemed you from the house
    of slavery;
and I sent before you Moses,
    Aaron, and Miriam.

5 O my people, remember now what
    King Balak of Moab devised,
    what Balaam son of Beor answered
    him,
and what happened from Shittim to
    Gilgal,
    that you may know the saving acts
    of the LORD."

What God Requires

6 "With what shall I come before the
    LORD,
    and bow myself before God on high?
Shall I come before him with burnt
    offerings,
    with calves a year old?
7 Will the LORD be pleased with
    thousands of rams,
    with ten thousands of rivers of oil?
Shall I give my firstborn for my
    transgression,
    the fruit of my body for the sin of
    my soul?"
8 He has told you, O mortal, what is
    good;
    and what does the LORD require
    of you
but to do justice, and to love
    kindness,
    and to walk humbly with your God?

Cheating and Violence to Be Punished

9 The voice of the LORD cries to the
    city

a Heb Asherim

6:1–16 God's Case against Israel

6:1–5—Having painted a picture of a future of peace and security for Israel, led by a future Davidic king, Micah turns his attention back to the present situation of Israel. Using again the courtroom setting, God summons Israel to defend her case. As a prosecuting attorney, God reviews for Israel what God has done for her, from the exodus out of Egypt to the wanderings in the wilderness, where they had to be rescued from the evil devices of King Balak of Moab (Num. 22–24), to the crossing of the Jordan. In spite of these salvific experiences, Israel has not been faithful in living out her covenantal responsibilities.

6:6–8—Summoned to defend herself, Israel responds by asking God what God expects of her in the context of worship in order that her relationship with God might be restored. God's response strikes at the heart of what it means to be a godly person. Outward symbols of piety are meaningless without the inward character of doing justice, loving kindness, and walking humbly with God. In other words, God is more interested in how we live our everyday lives than how well we perform our religious practices. Doing justice is an active pursuit, not idle wishing. Loving kindness suggests a lifelong quest of right relationships with our fellow human beings. Walking humbly with God means living in the reality of God's grace and mercy. Such is a life of faith worthy to be brought before God.

6:9–16—Having been told what God expects of them, the people are now told that their behavior is a contradiction of God's expectation: unjust business dealings, violence, lies.

(it is sound wisdom to fear your
    name):
Hear, O tribe and assembly of the
    city![a]
10 Can I forget[b] the treasures of
    wickedness in the house of the
    wicked,
    and the scant measure that is
      accursed?
11 Can I tolerate wicked scales
    and a bag of dishonest weights?
12 Your[c] wealthy are full of violence;
    your[c] inhabitants speak lies,
    with tongues of deceit in their
      mouths.
13 Therefore I have begun[d] to strike
    you down,
    making you desolate because of
      your sins.
14 You shall eat, but not be satisfied,
    and there shall be a gnawing
      hunger within you;
    you shall put away, but not save,
    and what you save, I will hand
      over to the sword.
15 You shall sow, but not reap;
    you shall tread olives, but not
      anoint yourselves with oil;
    you shall tread grapes, but not
      drink wine.
16 For you have kept the statutes of
    Omri[e]
    and all the works of the house of
      Ahab,
    and you have followed their
      counsels.
    Therefore I will make you a
      desolation, and your[f]
      inhabitants an object of
      hissing;
    so you shall bear the scorn of my
      people.

The Total Corruption of the People

7 Woe is me! For I have become like
    one who,
    after the summer fruit has been
      gathered,

    after the vintage has been gleaned,
finds no cluster to eat;
    there is no first-ripe fig for which
      I hunger.
2 The faithful have disappeared from
    the land,
    and there is no one left who is
      upright;
they all lie in wait for blood,
    and they hunt each other with
      nets.
3 Their hands are skilled to do evil;
    the official and the judge ask for a
      bribe,
    and the powerful dictate what they
      desire;
    thus they pervert justice.[g]
4 The best of them is like a brier,
    the most upright of them a thorn
      hedge.
The day of their[h] sentinels, of their[h]
    punishment, has come;
    now their confusion is at
      hand.
5 Put no trust in a friend,
    have no confidence in a loved
      one;
guard the doors of your mouth
    from her who lies in your
      embrace;
6 for the son treats the father with
    contempt,
    the daughter rises up against her
      mother,
the daughter-in-law against her
    mother-in-law;
    your enemies are members of your
      own household.
7 But as for me, I will look to the
    LORD,
I will wait for the God of my
    salvation;
    my God will hear me.

[a] Cn Compare Gk: Heb *tribe, and who has appointed it yet?*   [b] Cn: Meaning
of Heb uncertain   [c] Heb *Whose*   [d] Gk Syr Vg: Heb *have made sick*
[e] Gk Syr Vg Tg: Heb *the statutes of Omri are kept*   [f] Heb *its*   [g] Cn: Heb *they
weave it*   [h] Heb *your*

7:1–7 Micah's Lament
The prophet laments the tragic state of the Judean
society, both in the public arena (vv. 1–4) and in
the privacy of home and relationships (vv. 5–6).

Penitence and Trust in God

8 Do not rejoice over me, O my
enemy;
   when I fall, I shall rise;
when I sit in darkness,
   the LORD will be a light to me.
9 I must bear the indignation of the
   LORD,
   because I have sinned against him,
until he takes my side
   and executes judgment for me.
He will bring me out to the light;
   I shall see his vindication.
10 Then my enemy will see,
   and shame will cover her who said
      to me,
   "Where is the LORD your God?"
My eyes will see her downfall;[a]
   now she will be trodden down
   like the mire of the streets.

A Prophecy of Restoration

11 A day for the building of your walls!
   In that day the boundary shall be
      far extended.
12 In that day they will come to you
   from Assyria to[b] Egypt,
and from Egypt to the River,
   from sea to sea and from
      mountain to mountain.
13 But the earth will be desolate
   because of its inhabitants,
   for the fruit of their doings.

14 Shepherd your people with your
   staff,
   the flock that belongs to you,
which lives alone in a forest
   in the midst of a garden land;
let them feed in Bashan and Gilead
   as in the days of old.

15 As in the days when you came out of
   the land of Egypt,
   show us[c] marvelous things.
16 The nations shall see and be
   ashamed
   of all their might;
they shall lay their hands on their
   mouths;
   their ears shall be deaf;
17 they shall lick dust like a snake,
   like the crawling things of the
      earth;
they shall come trembling out of
   their fortresses;
   they shall turn in dread to the
      LORD our God,
   and they shall stand in fear of you.

God's Compassion and Steadfast Love

18 Who is a God like you, pardoning
   iniquity
   and passing over the transgression
   of the remnant of your[d]
      possession?
He does not retain his anger forever,
   because he delights in showing
      clemency.
19 He will again have compassion
   upon us;
   he will tread our iniquities under
      foot.
You will cast all our[e] sins
   into the depths of the sea.
20 You will show faithfulness to Jacob
   and unswerving loyalty to
      Abraham,
as you have sworn to our ancestors
   from the days of old.

a Heb lacks downfall b One Ms: MT Assyria and cities of c Cn: Heb I will
show him d Heb his e Gk Syr Vg Tg: Heb their

7:8–20 Psalm of Hope
Micah's prophecies end with a note of hope.

The Book of

NAHUM

Nahum is a seventh-century BCE prophet whose prophecies are focused on Nineveh, the capital of Assyria. In Nahum, we encounter the theme of God's anger and vengeance on behalf of God's people.

Authorship. There is little agreement on the authorship of this small book. Some scholars view it as a single piece by one author, presumably Nahum, but with no agreement on how and why the document came to be written. One holds that the book comes from a cultic prophet and was a piece of political propaganda against Nineveh, modeled upon the cultic myth of YHWH's victory over foes. Another sees it as a letter, from a northern Israelite whose ancestors had been exiled by the Assyrians after the fall of Samaria, to encourage the Judeans during the height of Assyrian domination. Yet others view the book as a product of redaction, with the original prophecies coming before the fall of Nineveh in 612 BCE, and subsequent material added, some even as late as the postexilic period.

Little is known about the man Nahum. His name means "comfort," but the book hardly fits his name.

Historical Setting. The date of Nahum's prophetic activity is generally assigned to a time between the destruction of Thebes in 663 BCE (presupposed in 3:8) and the fall of Nineveh in 612 BCE. Given the prophet's expectation of the impending fall of Nineveh, most scholars suggest a date following the ascent of Nabopolassar, the king of the Marshland, to the Babylonian throne in 626 BCE.

Theology. The theological perspective that dominates this book has to do with the vengeance God exacts on God's enemies. Nahum portrays God as the divine warrior who is bent on taking vengeance on the hated Assyrians, who have oppressed the Judeans for over a century. In the book of Nahum there is an understanding of justice as "doing unto others as they have done unto us." Of course, no one has the right to ask the Judeans who suffered so much at the hands of the Assyrians to forgive them, but we must ask what some of the ramifications are when Assyrian oppression is redressed by violence, the same form of oppression the Assyrians used against them. The enemy is demonized. Is there no redeeming quality in the enemy? Nineveh with thousands of inhabitants is destroyed indiscriminately. Are there no righteous in Nineveh? Is God only on our side? In the name of retributive justice, is Nahum's theology not perpetuating the cycle of violence that God wants us to break out of? We humans do not have the right to ask the oppressed to forgive the oppressor, but God might be asking this question. Do we dare to forgive our enemies? Do we dare to aspire to "overcome evil with good" (Rom. 12:21)?

—Jeffrey Kuan

1 An oracle concerning Nineveh. The book of the vision of Nahum of Elkosh.

The Consuming Wrath of God

2 A jealous and avenging God is the LORD,
  the LORD is avenging and wrathful;
the LORD takes vengeance on his adversaries
  and rages against his enemies.
3 The LORD is slow to anger but great in power,
  and the LORD will by no means clear the guilty.

His way is in whirlwind and storm,
  and the clouds are the dust of his feet.
4 He rebukes the sea and makes it dry,
  and he dries up all the rivers;
Bashan and Carmel wither,
  and the bloom of Lebanon fades.
5 The mountains quake before him,
  and the hills melt;
the earth heaves before him,
  the world and all who live in it.

6 Who can stand before his indignation?
  Who can endure the heat of his anger?
His wrath is poured out like fire,
  and by him the rocks are broken in pieces.
7 The LORD is good,
  a stronghold in a day of trouble;
he protects those who take refuge in him,
8   even in a rushing flood.
He will make a full end of his adversaries,[a]
  and will pursue his enemies into darkness.
9 Why do you plot against the LORD?
  He will make an end;
  no adversary will rise up twice.
10 Like thorns they are entangled,
  like drunkards they are drunk;
  they are consumed like dry straw.
11 From you one has gone out
  who plots evil against the LORD,
  one who counsels wickedness.

Good News for Judah

12 Thus says the LORD,
"Though they are at full strength and many,[b]
  they will be cut off and pass away.
Though I have afflicted you,
  I will afflict you no more.
13 And now I will break off his yoke from you
  and snap the bonds that bind you."

a Gk: Heb *of her place*   *b* Meaning of Heb uncertain

1:1 Superscription

The superscription or title identifies *Nineveh*, the capital of Assyria, as the subject of the oracle by the prophet *Nahum*. No further information about Nahum is given, except his hometown, *Elkosh*, whose exact location is uncertain.

1:2–8 The Vengeful God

The section begins with a series of descriptors for God: *jealous and avenging*, *takes vengeance*, *wrathful*, *rages*. It goes on to juxtapose God's anger with God's incomparable power, manifested in the storm, the drought, and the earthquake. Because of God's awesome power, no one—particularly God's enemies, including Nineveh—can withstand God's anger. This image of a vengeful God must be set in the context of the warring ancient Near East, of ancient Judah's struggle under the oppressive superpower Assyria. It is a nationalistic hope that God would finally set things right for Judah. Taken out of context, there is the ever-present danger that people of faith can misappropriate this image of God, decide who God's enemy is, and thereby demonize their fellow human beings.

1:9–15 The Deliverance of Judah

The section is addressed to both Judah and Assyria—deliverance for the former and doom for the latter. Judah's deliverance will be secured through the destruction of Assyria. Addressing Judah's adversaries, Nahum sees the oppression of God's people as *evil against the LORD* (vv. 9–11). But, the affliction is now over; deliverance is at hand. God will *break* the *yoke* and *snap the bonds that bind* them (vv. 12–13); God will put an end to the might of Assyria (v. 14); the one who brings *good tidings* and *peace* has arrived (v. 15). People of faith should understand this as a nationalistic text and be cautious about claiming God on our side over against our adversaries without paying attention to the destructive nature of such claims.

¹⁴ The LORD has commanded
        concerning you:
  "Your name shall be perpetuated
        no longer;
  from the house of your gods I will
        cut off
    the carved image and the cast
        image.
  I will make your grave, for you are
        worthless."

¹⁵ᵃ Look! On the mountains the feet of
        one
  who brings good tidings,
      who proclaims peace!
  Celebrate your festivals, O Judah,
      fulfill your vows,
  for never again shall the wicked
        invade you;
      they are utterly cut off.

The Destruction of the Wicked City

2 A shattererᵇ has come up against
        you.
  Guard the ramparts;
  watch the road;
gird your loins;
  collect all your strength.

² (For the LORD is restoring the
        majesty of Jacob,
    as well as the majesty of Israel,
  though ravagers have ravaged them
      and ruined their branches.)

³ The shields of his warriors are red;
      his soldiers are clothed in
        crimson.
  The metal on the chariots flashes
      on the day when he musters them;
    the chargersᶜ prance.
⁴ The chariots race madly through the
        streets,

they rush to and fro through the
        squares;
  their appearance is like torches,
      they dart like lightning.
⁵ He calls his officers;
    they stumble as they come
        forward;
  they hasten to the wall,
      and the manteletᵈ is set up.
⁶ The river gates are opened,
      the palace trembles.
⁷ It is decreedᵈ that the cityᵉ be exiled,
      its slave women led away,
  moaning like doves
      and beating their breasts.
⁸ Nineveh is like a pool
      whose watersᶠ run away.
  "Halt! Halt!"—
      but no one turns back.
⁹ "Plunder the silver,
      plunder the gold!
  There is no end of treasure!
      An abundance of every precious
        thing!"

¹⁰ Devastation, desolation, and
        destruction!
    Hearts faint and knees tremble,
  all loins quake,
      all faces grow pale!
¹¹ What became of the lions' den,
      the caveᵍ of the young lions,
  where the lion goes,
      and the lion's cubs, with no one to
        disturb them?
¹² The lion has torn enough for his
        whelps
      and strangled prey for his
        lionesses;

ᵃCh 2.1 in Heb   ᵇCn: Heb *scatterer*   ᶜCn Compare Gk Syr: Heb
cypresses   ᵈMeaning of Heb uncertain   ᵉHeb *it*   ᶠCn Compare Gk:
Heb *a pool, from the days that she has become, and they*   ᵍCn: Heb *pasture*

2:1–13 The Fall of Nineveh
Nineveh is summoned to prepare for a military onslaught, and the one who will carry out the attack is none other than **the LORD of hosts** (v. 13), the divine warrior. Israel's understanding of their God as a divine warrior is rooted in the ancient Near Eastern myth of a battle between deities. By using the image of God as the divine warrior, biblical writers are making a theological claim that Israel's military battles were also the battles of Israel's God with other deities. The destruction of Nineveh will lead to the restoration of Israel. Nahum is aware that because of its relative military strength Judah is not in a position to defeat Assyria. Thus God's army can take a shape that is beyond Judah's military forces. This text should remind us of the gruesome nature of war, whether ancient or contemporary, on our soil or elsewhere.

he has filled his caves with prey
and his dens with torn flesh.

13 See, I am against you, says the LORD of hosts, and I will burn your[a] chariots in smoke, and the sword shall devour your young lions; I will cut off your prey from the earth, and the voice of your messengers shall be heard no more.

Ruin Imminent and Inevitable

3 Ah! City of bloodshed,
   utterly deceitful, full of booty—
     no end to the plunder!
2 The crack of whip and rumble of
     wheel,
   galloping horse and bounding
     chariot!
3 Horsemen charging,
   flashing sword and glittering
     spear,
   piles of dead,
     heaps of corpses,
   dead bodies without end—
     they stumble over the bodies!
4 Because of the countless
     debaucheries of the prostitute,
   gracefully alluring, mistress of
     sorcery,
   who enslaves[b] nations through her
     debaucheries,
   and peoples through her sorcery,
5 I am against you,
   says the LORD of hosts,
   and will lift up your skirts over
     your face;
   and I will let nations look on your
     nakedness
   and kingdoms on your shame.
6 I will throw filth at you
   and treat you with contempt,
   and make you a spectacle.
7 Then all who see you will shrink
     from you and say,

"Nineveh is devastated; who will
     bemoan her?"
   Where shall I seek comforters for
     you?
8 Are you better than Thebes[c]
   that sat by the Nile,
with water around her,
   her rampart a sea, water her wall?
9 Ethiopia[d] was her strength,
   Egypt too, and that without limit;
   Put and the Libyans were here[e]
     helpers.
10 Yet she became an exile,
   she went into captivity;
even her infants were dashed in
     pieces
   at the head of every street;
lots were cast for her nobles,
   all her dignitaries were bound in
     fetters.
11 You also will be drunken,
   you will go into hiding;[f]
you will seek
   a refuge from the enemy.
12 All your fortresses are like fig trees
   with first-ripe figs—
if shaken they fall
   into the mouth of the eater.
13 Look at your troops:
   they are women in your midst.
The gates of your land
   are wide open to your foes;
   fire has devoured the bars of your
     gates.

14 Draw water for the siege,
   strengthen your forts;
trample the clay,
   tread the mortar,
   take hold of the brick mold!

---

[a] Heb her   [b] Heb sells   [c] Heb No-amon   [d] Or Nubia; Heb Cush   [e] Gk: Heb your   [f] Meaning of Heb uncertain

---

3:1–19 Oracle against Nineveh
Nahum piles up image upon image to describe the horrible violence that happens to a city under siege. The heat of the battle almost always guarantees that there will be **piles of dead** and **heaps of corpses** (v. 3). Nahum likens Nineveh to a seductive **prostitute** (v. 4), whom God will publicly shame. A product of a patriarchal culture, the description of a city as a prostitute is a corollary of the often denigrating image of women in the Bible (cf. Ezek. 16 and 21). Careful reading of this text can help people of faith to call into question such unhelpful images of God humiliating a woman.

15 There the fire will devour you,
     the sword will cut you off.
   It will devour you like the locust.

   Multiply yourselves like the locust,
     multiply like the grasshopper!
16 You increased your merchants
     more than the stars of the heavens.
   The locust sheds its skin and flies
     away.
17 Your guards are like grasshoppers,
     your scribes like swarms*a* of
       locusts
   settling on the fences
     on a cold day—
   when the sun rises, they fly away;

no one knows where they have
  gone.
18 Your shepherds are asleep,
     O king of Assyria;
   your nobles slumber.
   Your people are scattered on the
     mountains
     with no one to gather them.
19 There is no assuaging your hurt,
     your wound is mortal.
   All who hear the news about you
     clap their hands over you.
   For who has ever escaped
     your endless cruelty?

a Meaning of Heb uncertain

The Book of
HABAKKUK

A prophet of the late seventh and early sixth centuries BCE, Habakkuk is best known for his saying in 2:4b, "the righteous live by their faith," from which the Christian doctrine of justification by faith developed. In Habakkuk too we find the example, not unlike Job, of a person of faith who is not afraid to question God about God's justice in the world.

Authorship. There is little disagreement among scholars that chapters 1–2 come from the prophet Habakkuk and reflect his theological interpretation of the events of the battle of Carchemish in 605 BCE and the first sacking of Jerusalem in 597 BCE. Chapter 3, however, has generated much discussion and debate. Many earlier scholars argued that the chapter was composed as a supplement to Habakkuk's earlier prophecies and added during the postexilic period. More recent scholars, however, have argued against that perspective, suggesting that this prayer was composed by Habakkuk himself, to express his trust in God in the midst of the disaster surrounding the invasion of Jerusalem.

Of this prophet, only his name is given. Scholars suggest that his name is related to a type of plant. Because of the liturgical nature of his oracles, some scholars have surmised that Habakkuk may have been a prophet employed by the temple.

Historical Setting. Habakkuk's prophetic ministry is generally assigned to the Babylonian period, a time between Babylonia's defeat of Assyria in 609 BCE and the first invasion of Jerusalem by Nebuchadnezzar and the Babylonian army in 597 BCE.

Theology. Habakkuk's theological reflections center on the issue of theodicy: the belief in God's justice, which often conflicts with apparent injustice in the world. How do we continue to trust in God's justice when the world seems so unjust? How do we remain faithful to God's vision of a just world when the world seems to go around according to human ambition? We can do what Habakkuk does—cry out for justice and accuse God of indifference—that is, engage in an honest dialogue with God. God responds by directing Habakkuk to the politico-historical events that will result in the punishment of those who perpetuate injustice in Jerusalem. But Habakkuk is not satisfied with this "solution," because Babylon, the superpower that is being used to punish Jerusalem, is unpunished. We are familiar with Habakkuk's complaint: we see the "little guys" get punished for their wrongdoings but often the rich and powerful individuals and nations go unpunished for their wrongdoing. "The righteous live by their faith" may mean that we do not need to see the absence of punishment on the "sinners" as the absence of justice. Our desire to see justice according to our understanding may conflict with God's justice. The righteous are called to work for justice, seeking God's vision rather than human ambition.

—Jeffrey Kuan

1

The oracle that the prophet Habakkuk saw.

The Prophet's Complaint

² O LORD, how long shall I cry for help,
    and you will not listen?
Or cry to you "Violence!"
    and you will not save?
³ Why do you make me see
      wrongdoing
    and look at trouble?
Destruction and violence are
      before me;
    strife and contention arise.
⁴ So the law becomes slack
    and justice never prevails.
The wicked surround the
      righteous—
    therefore judgment comes forth
      perverted.

⁵ Look at the nations, and see!
    Be astonished! Be astounded!
For a work is being done in your
      days
    that you would not believe if you
      were told.
⁶ For I am rousing the Chaldeans,
    that fierce and impetuous nation,
who march through the breadth of
      the earth
    to seize dwellings not their own.
⁷ Dread and fearsome are they;
    their justice and dignity proceed
      from themselves.

⁸ Their horses are swifter than
      leopards,
    more menacing than wolves at
      dusk;
    their horses charge.
Their horsemen come from far
      away;
    they fly like an eagle swift to
      devour.
⁹ They all come for violence,
    with faces pressing[a] forward;
    they gather captives like sand.
¹⁰ At kings they scoff,
    and of rulers they make sport.
They laugh at every fortress,
    and heap up earth to take it.
¹¹ Then they sweep by like the wind;
    they transgress and become guilty;
    their own might is their god!

¹² Are you not from of old,
    O LORD my God, my Holy One?
You[b] shall not die.
O LORD, you have marked them for
      judgment;
    and you, O Rock, have established
      them for punishment.
¹³ Your eyes are too pure to behold evil,
    and you cannot look on
      wrongdoing;
why do you look on the treacherous,
    and are silent when the wicked
      swallow

[a] Meaning of Heb uncertain   [b] Ancient Heb tradition: MT *We*

1:1 Superscription

Only the name of the prophet, *Habakkuk*, is
given in the superscription.

1:2–2:4 Habakkuk's Dialogue with God

The section consists of a series of intense exchanges between the prophet and God. In the
midst of uncertain times, the prophet is not afraid
to engage God in an honest conversation, taking
his complaints, even accusations, to God.

1:2–4—Habakkuk accuses God of being indifferent to the violence and injustice that prevail
in the society. Following the prophetic tradition,
Habakkuk exemplifies a strong commitment to
social justice. Habakkuk also appeals to tradition
and rebukes God for not responding to the cry of
the oppressed (cf. Exod. 2:23; Job 19:7; Isa. 5:7).

1:5–11—God responds by asking Habakkuk to
see what is happening in the international scene
and by announcing that God will use the Neo-
Babylonians (*Chaldeans*) as God's instrument of
judgment against the people for their injustices.
Here, the prophet shows great familiarity with the
terror of warfare mounted by the superpower.

1:12–17—These verses reveal Habakkuk's honest
struggle with theological thinking. Prophets like
Isaiah and Jeremiah had found little problem with
talking about foreign nations and superpowers
as God's instruments to carry out God's justice.
Habakkuk, however, raises the question: How
can God tolerate a superpower that is so evil and
use it to bring about justice in the world? It is a
question that challenges the justice of retributive
theology when the evil of the superpower seems
to go unpunished.

those more righteous than they?

14 You have made people like the fish
    of the sea,
  like crawling things that have no
    ruler.

15 The enemy[a] brings all of them up
    with a hook;
  he drags them out with his net,
  he gathers them in his seine;
    so he rejoices and exults.

16 Therefore he sacrifices to his net
    and makes offerings to his seine;
  for by them his portion is lavish,
    and his food is rich.

17 Is he then to keep on emptying
    his net,
  and destroying nations without
    mercy?

God's Reply to the Prophet's Complaint

2 I will stand at my watchpost,
  and station myself on the rampart;
  I will keep watch to see what he will
    say to me,
  and what he[b] will answer
    concerning my complaint.

2 Then the LORD answered me and
    said:
  Write the vision;
    make it plain on tablets,
  so that a runner may read it.

3 For there is still a vision for the
    appointed time;
  it speaks of the end, and does
    not lie.
  If it seems to tarry, wait for it;

it will surely come, it will not
    delay.

4 Look at the proud!
  Their spirit is not right in them,
  but the righteous live by their
    faith.[c]

5 Moreover, wealth[d] is treacherous;
  the arrogant do not endure.
They open their throats wide as
    Sheol;
  like Death they never have
    enough.
They gather all nations for
    themselves,
  and collect all peoples as their
    own.

The Woes of the Wicked

6 Shall not everyone taunt such people and, with mocking riddles, say about
them,
  "Alas for you who heap up what is
    not your own!"
  How long will you load
    yourselves with goods taken in
    pledge?

7 Will not your own creditors
    suddenly rise,
  and those who make you tremble
    wake up?
  Then you will be booty for them.

8 Because you have plundered many
    nations,
  all that survive of the peoples shall
    plunder you—

---

[a] Heb He [b] Syr: Heb I [c] Or faithfulness [d] Other Heb Mss read wine

---

2:1–4—God's second response does not provide
Habakkuk with a direct answer to his question.
Here we find the most famous verse in Habakkuk, *The righteous live by their faith*. The righteous, those who seek and work for justice in the
world, may not always find affirmation in their
work. Through their faithfulness and a broader
vision of how things should be, they will find
the strength to go on. Though the vision tarries,
promises the prophet, *Wait for it; it will surely
come* (v. 3).

2:5–20 Indictment of Babylonia

Using the speech of oppressed nations, Habakkuk indicts the imperial power for the way it has
carried out its colonial policies; the descriptors

are many and heart wrenching, from economic
exploitation to bloodshed. Habakkuk warns that
such ruthlessness on the part of the imperial
power will lead to its self-destruction. As citizens
of the remaining superpower, Americans need to
be alert for our own neocolonialism in the global
economy.

Another issue this text raises is idolatry. It is
possible for readers to deflect the issue by thinking of idolatry simply in socioeconomic terms.
We need to be aware, however, of Christianity's
tattered history of denigrating as idolatry other
religious traditions in its missionary enterprise.
Because of misperception and misrepresentation
of these traditions, demonizing of the religions
and their adherents has resulted.

because of human bloodshed, and
    violence to the earth,
  to cities and all who live in them.

9 "Alas for you who get evil gain for
    your house,
  setting your nest on high
  to be safe from the reach of harm!"
10 You have devised shame for your
    house
  by cutting off many peoples;
  you have forfeited your life.
11 The very stones will cry out from the
    wall,
  and the plaster*a* will respond from
    the woodwork.

12 "Alas for you who build a town by
    bloodshed,
  and found a city on iniquity!"
13 Is it not from the LORD of hosts
  that peoples labor only to feed the
    flames,
  and nations weary themselves for
    nothing?
14 But the earth will be filled
  with the knowledge of the glory of
    the LORD,
  as the waters cover the sea.

15 "Alas for you who make your
    neighbors drink,
  pouring out your wrath*b* until they
    are drunk,
  in order to gaze on their nakedness!"
16 You will be sated with contempt
    instead of glory.
  Drink, you yourself, and stagger!*c*
  The cup in the LORD's right hand
  will come around to you,
  and shame will come upon your
    glory!
17 For the violence done to Lebanon
    will overwhelm you;
  the destruction of the animals will
    terrify you—*d*

because of human bloodshed and
    violence to the earth,
  to cities and all who live in them.

18 What use is an idol
  once its maker has shaped it—
  a cast image, a teacher of lies?
  For its maker trusts in what has been
    made,
  though the product is only an idol
    that cannot speak!
19 Alas for you who say to the wood,
    "Wake up!"
  to silent stone, "Rouse yourself!"
  Can it teach?
  See, it is gold and silver plated,
  and there is no breath in it at all.

20 But the LORD is in his holy
    temple;
  let all the earth keep silence before
    him!

3 A prayer of the prophet Habakkuk
according to Shigionoth.

The Prophet's Prayer

2 O LORD, I have heard of your
    renown,
  and I stand in awe, O LORD, of
    your work.
  In our own time revive it;
  in our own time make it known;
  in wrath may you remember
    mercy.
3 God came from Teman,
  the Holy One from Mount Paran.
                                    Selah

  His glory covered the heavens,
  and the earth was full of his praise.
4 The brightness was like the sun;
  rays came forth from his hand,
  where his power lay hidden.
5 Before him went pestilence,

a Or beam *b* Or poison *c* Q Ms Gk: MT *be uncircumcised* *d* Gk Syr:
Meaning of Heb uncertain

3:1–19 Habakkuk's Prayer
The chapter, cast as a liturgical prayer, consists of a vision of God (vv. 3–15) framed by
Habakkuk's prayerful expression of trust in God
(vv. 2; 16–19a). The vision praises God for God's
actions in history, particularly the exodus event.

In this, God is depicted as the divine warrior, a
theological image that can lead to the glorification of warfare unless the reader pays attention to
the suffering that warfare inevitably brings to the
innocent.

and plague followed close behind.

6 He stopped and shook the earth;
  he looked and made the nations
  tremble.
The eternal mountains were
  shattered;
  along his ancient pathways
  the everlasting hills sank low.

7 I saw the tents of Cushan under
  affliction;
  the tent-curtains of the land of
  Midian trembled.

8 Was your wrath against the rivers,*a*
  O LORD?
  Or your anger against the rivers,*a*
  or your rage against the sea,*b*
when you drove your horses,
  your chariots to victory?

9 You brandished your naked bow,
  sated*c* were the arrows at your
  command.*d*   Selah
  You split the earth with rivers.

10 The mountains saw you, and
  writhed;
  a torrent of water swept by;
the deep gave forth its voice.
  The sun*e* raised high its hands;

11 the moon*f* stood still in its exalted
  place,
  at the light of your arrows
  speeding by,
  at the gleam of your flashing spear.

12 In fury you trod the earth,
  in anger you trampled nations.

13 You came forth to save your people,
  to save your anointed.
You crushed the head of the wicked
  house,
  laying it bare from foundation to
  roof.*d*   Selah

14 You pierced with their*g* own arrows
  the head*h* of his warriors,*i*
who came like a whirlwind to
  scatter us,*j*
  gloating as if ready to devour the
  poor who were in hiding.

15 You trampled the sea with your
  horses,
  churning the mighty waters.

16 I hear, and I tremble within;
  my lips quiver at the sound.
Rottenness enters into my bones,
  and my steps tremble*k* beneath me.
I wait quietly for the day of calamity
  to come upon the people who
  attack us.

Trust and Joy in the Midst of Trouble

17 Though the fig tree does not blossom,
  and no fruit is on the vines;
though the produce of the olive fails,
  and the fields yield no food;
though the flock is cut off from the
  fold,
  and there is no herd in the stalls,

18 yet I will rejoice in the LORD;
  I will exult in the God of my
  salvation.

19 GOD, the Lord, is my strength;
  he makes my feet like the feet of a
  deer,
  and makes me tread upon the
  heights.*l*

To the leader: with stringed*m*
  instruments.

a Or *against River* *b* Or *against Sea* *c* Cn: Heb *oaths* *d* Meaning of Heb
uncertain *e* Heb *It* *f* Heb *sun, moon* *g* Heb *his* *h* Or *leader*
i Vg Compare Gk Syr: Meaning of Heb uncertain *j* Heb *me*
k Cn Compare Gk: Meaning of Heb uncertain *l* Heb *my heights*
m Heb *my stringed*

The Book of
ZEPHANIAH

Zephaniah is a seventh-century BCE prophet of Judah, rooted firmly in the tradition of the great eighth-century prophets who exhibited tremendous concern for social justice. Zephaniah's harsh words of judgment are tempered with words of grace, forgiveness, and restoration.

Authorship. A broad consensus among critical scholars holds that the present form of the book reflects a layer of genuine, late preexilic oracles attributed to the prophet Zephaniah, to which has been attached a layer of postexilic material (3:9–14 and 2:7, 8, 9a, 10–11). However, other scholars have cautioned against characterizing all oracles of promise as secondary or postexilic.

Our knowledge of Zephaniah comes from the superscription in 1:1. He is given a patronym extending back four generations, perhaps to emphasize his royal descent from King Hezekiah (715–687 BCE). His prophetic ministry occurred sometime during the reign of Josiah, king of Judah (640–609 BCE). His name literally means "YHWH protects."

Historical Setting. The superscription locates the prophetic ministry of Zephaniah in the reign of Josiah, who was king over Judah 640–609 BCE. Josiah instituted a major socioreligious reform in the year 622 BCE. Since there is hardly any mention of the reform in Zephaniah's prophecies, it is likely that his ministry predated the reform. On the other hand, Josiah's reform dealt with many of the themes touched on by Zephaniah, to the extent that Zephaniah's message may have had an impact on the reform.

Theology. Zephaniah turns the traditional theology of "the day of the Lord" on its head to bring an indictment against the Jerusalemites. According to the tradition, "the day of the Lord" refers to the day of judgment on the enemies and of salvation to the Israelites. After all, people often assume that it is the others who need to face the day of reckoning, whereas they are victims in need of deliverance. However, Zephaniah's use of the day of the Lord as the day of reckoning for the Jerusalemites reminds us that we too must examine our role in maintaining and perpetuating injustice in our own society. Are we ready to examine honestly our role in the injustice and economic exploitation that we are so quick to point out in others? Zephaniah makes it clear that God is not indifferent to justice; rather, God is exasperated by continual violations against the covenant and wants to give up on this world and start anew. Nonetheless, Zephaniah issues a call to repentance, even with the dawning of the day of the Lord. We are not to wait for all to change and to commit themselves to God and the cause of justice. Instead, we are to seek first the Lord, righteousness, and humility, trusting that God can transform a society with the faithful few.

—Jeffrey Kuan

1

The word of the LORD that came to Zephaniah son of Cushi son of Gedaliah son of Amariah son of Hezekiah, in the days of King Josiah son of Amon of Judah.

The Coming Judgment on Judah

2 I will utterly sweep away everything
    from the face of the earth, says the
    LORD.
3 I will sweep away humans and
    animals;
  I will sweep away the birds of the
    air
  and the fish of the sea.
  I will make the wicked stumble.[a]
  I will cut off humanity
  from the face of the earth, says the
    LORD.
4 I will stretch out my hand against
    Judah,
  and against all the inhabitants of
    Jerusalem;
  and I will cut off from this place
    every remnant of Baal
  and the name of the idolatrous
    priests;[b]
5 those who bow down on the roofs
    to the host of the heavens;
  those who bow down and swear to
    the LORD,
  but also swear by Milcom;[c]

6 those who have turned back from
    following the LORD,
  who have not sought the LORD or
    inquired of him.

7 Be silent before the Lord GOD!
    For the day of the LORD is at hand;
  the LORD has prepared a sacrifice,
    he has consecrated his guests.
8 And on the day of the LORD's
    sacrifice
  I will punish the officials and the
    king's sons
  and all who dress themselves in
    foreign attire.
9 On that day I will punish
    all who leap over the threshold,
  who fill their master's house
    with violence and fraud.

10 On that day, says the LORD,
    a cry will be heard from the Fish
      Gate,
  a wail from the Second Quarter,
    a loud crash from the hills.
11 The inhabitants of the Mortar wail,
    for all the traders have perished;
  all who weigh out silver are cut off.
12 At that time I will search Jerusalem
    with lamps,

a Cn: Heb *sea, and those who cause the wicked to stumble*   b Compare Gk: Heb *the idolatrous priests with the priests*   c Gk Mss Syr Vg: Heb *Malcam* (or, *their king*)

1:1 Superscription
See introduction.

1:2–2:3 Oracles against Judah and Jerusalem
The section consists of oracles addressed particularly to Judah and Jerusalem. In it is also introduced the concept of *the day of the LORD*, the crisis moment when God's judgment will be meted out against those who have perverted God's justice.

1:2–3—The first oracle begins with a divine pronouncement of universal destruction of the whole earth. Readers will see the parallel of this pronouncement to the flood story of Gen. 6–8.

1:4–6—The reason for such severe judgment is the unfaithfulness of Judah and Jerusalem. The covenantal relationship between God and the Israelites required that the people worship YHWH alone (cf. Josh. 24:14–15). Multiple allegiances to other deities like *Baal*, the god of the Canaanites, and *Milcom*, the god of the Ammonites, violate

the covenant. There is, moreover, an emphasis in Israelite theology of a corporate responsibility. For Zephaniah, the Judeans bear the responsibility for making God desire to destroy the earth and start anew.

1:7–18—The second oracle introduces the traditional idea of *the day of the LORD*, but with a twist. According to the tradition, the day of the Lord refers to the day that God would appear to destroy Israel's enemies and deliver the Israelites. However, Zephaniah, adopting the prophetic stance taken by Amos a century before him (see Amos 5:18–20), announces that the day of the Lord will be turned against God's people. The leaders and the affluent will be special targets on account of their injustices and economic exploitation. Those whose complacency and arrogance have led them to reason that God is indifferent to justice after all (v. 12) will discover that it is not so.

and I will punish the people
who rest complacently[a] on their
   dregs,
those who say in their hearts,
"The LORD will not do good,
   nor will he do harm."
13 Their wealth shall be plundered,
   and their houses laid waste.
Though they build houses,
   they shall not inhabit them;
though they plant vineyards,
   they shall not drink wine from
   them.

The Great Day of the LORD

14 The great day of the LORD is near,
   near and hastening fast;
the sound of the day of the LORD is
   bitter,
the warrior cries aloud there.
15 That day will be a day of wrath,
   a day of distress and anguish,
a day of ruin and devastation,
   a day of darkness and gloom,
a day of clouds and thick darkness,
16   a day of trumpet blast and battle
   cry
against the fortified cities
   and against the lofty battlements.

17 I will bring such distress upon
   people
   that they shall walk like the
   blind;

because they have sinned against
   the LORD,
their blood shall be poured out like
   dust,
   and their flesh like dung.
18 Neither their silver nor their gold
   will be able to save them
   on the day of the LORD's wrath;
in the fire of his passion
   the whole earth shall be consumed;
for a full, a terrible end
   he will make of all the inhabitants
   of the earth.

Judgment on Israel's Enemies

2 Gather together, gather,
  O shameless nation,
2 before you are driven away
   like the drifting chaff,[b]
before there comes upon you
   the fierce anger of the LORD,
before there comes upon you
   the day of the LORD's wrath.
3 Seek the LORD, all you humble of the
   land,
   who do his commands;
seek righteousness, seek humility;
   perhaps you may be hidden
   on the day of the LORD's wrath.
4 For Gaza shall be deserted,
   and Ashkelon shall become a
   desolation;

[a] Heb *who thicken* [b] Cn Compare Gk Syr: Heb *before a decree is born; like chaff a day has passed away*

2:1–3—For Zephaniah, even with the dawning of the day of the Lord, all is not lost. He issues a call to repentance. *Those who have turned back from following the LORD* (1:6), are now urged to *seek* three things: *the LORD*, *righteousness*, and *humility*. This call resonates with Micah's famous saying: "What does the Lord require of you, but to do justice, and to love kindness, and to walk humbly with your God?" (Mic. 6:8). To seek God is to return to God and live under God's ethical demands. To seek righteousness is to turn back from the exploitative conduct that offends God. To seek humility is to repudiate one's arrogant behavior that had sought to live a life of indifference to God.

2:4–15 Oracles against the Nations

Such oracles belong to a particular form of prophetic speech found also in Isa. 13–23; Jer. 46–51; and Amos 1–2. These oracles relate to

the day of the Lord tradition and tie back to Zeph. 1:2–6, concerning God's intention to bring about destruction of the entire earth. The prophet begins with the indictment of Judah's immediate neighbors, *the Philistines* on the coast (2:5–7) and *Moab* and Ammon over in the Transjordan (vv. 8–11), before turning attention to the superpowers of the ancient Near East, *Ethiopia*/Egypt (v. 12) and *Assyria* (vv. 13–15). The oracles against the nations are founded on the perspective that all peoples belong to the family of nations and can be held responsible by God for what is right and wrong. In our time, the nations of the world are trying to live out the implication of holding one another accountable for what is right and wrong through the work of the United Nations. However, such work is never easy and is complicated by the self-determination of the sovereign state and the policies of the superpower.

Ashdod's people shall be driven out
    at noon,
and Ekron shall be uprooted.

5 Ah, inhabitants of the seacoast,
    you nation of the Cherethites!
The word of the Lord is against you,
    O Canaan, land of the Philistines;
and I will destroy you until no
    inhabitant is left.
6 And you, O seacoast, shall be
    pastures,
    meadows for shepherds
    and folds for flocks.
7 The seacoast shall become the
    possession
    of the remnant of the house of
      Judah,
    on which they shall pasture,
and in the houses of Ashkelon
    they shall lie down at evening.
For the Lord their God will be
    mindful of them
    and restore their fortunes.

8 I have heard the taunts of Moab
    and the revilings of the
      Ammonites,
how they have taunted my people
    and made boasts against their
      territory.
9 Therefore, as I live, says the Lord of
    hosts,
    the God of Israel,
Moab shall become like Sodom
    and the Ammonites like
      Gomorrah,
a land possessed by nettles and salt
    pits,
    and a waste forever.
The remnant of my people shall
    plunder them,
    and the survivors of my nation
      shall possess them.

10 This shall be their lot in return for
    their pride,
    because they scoffed and boasted
    against the people of the Lord of
      hosts.
11 The Lord will be terrible against
    them;
    he will shrivel all the gods of the
      earth,
and to him shall bow down,
    each in its place,
    all the coasts and islands of the
      nations.

12 You also, O Ethiopians,[a]
    shall be killed by my sword.

13 And he will stretch out his hand
    against the north,
    and destroy Assyria;
and he will make Nineveh a
    desolation,
    a dry waste like the desert.
14 Herds shall lie down in it,
    every wild animal;[b]
the desert owl[c] and the screech owl[c]
    shall lodge on its capitals;
the owl[d] shall hoot at the window,
    the raven[e] croak on the threshold;
    for its cedar work will be laid bare.
15 Is this the exultant city
    that lived secure,
that said to itself,
    "I am, and there is no one else"?
What a desolation it has become,
    a lair for wild animals!
Everyone who passes by it
    hisses and shakes the fist.

The Wickedness of Jerusalem

3 Ah, soiled, defiled,
    oppressing city!
2 It has listened to no voice;

---

a Or *Nubians;* Heb *Cushites* *b* Tg Compare Gk: Heb *nation* *c* Meaning of Heb uncertain *d* Cn: Heb *a voice* *e* Gk Vg: Heb *desolation*

3:1–13 Indictment of Jerusalem
The oracles against the nations culminate in the indictment of Jerusalem, God's own dwelling place (v. 5). Jerusalem is censured for rejecting its God, and its entire leadership—officials, judges, prophets, and priests—is rebuked for failing to live up to their responsibilities. In contrast to the leadership, God continues to dwell within Jerusalem, doing what the leadership is supposed to do, namely, upholding righteousness and executing fair judgment (v. 5). The city is encouraged to look at what is happening around it, at its destruction, and to learn from these things. But to God's chagrin, the city is determined to continue

it has accepted no correction.
It has not trusted in the LORD;
    it has not drawn near to its God.

3 The officials within it
    are roaring lions;
its judges are evening wolves
    that leave nothing until the
        morning.
4 Its prophets are reckless,
    faithless persons;
its priests have profaned what is
        sacred,
    they have done violence to the law.
5 The LORD within it is righteous;
    he does no wrong.
Every morning he renders his
        judgment,
    each dawn without fail;
    but the unjust knows no shame.

6 I have cut off nations;
    their battlements are in ruins;
I have laid waste their streets
    so that no one walks in them;
their cities have been made desolate,
    without people, without
        inhabitants.
7 I said, "Surely the city*a* will fear me,
    it will accept correction;
it will not lose sight*b*
    of all that I have brought upon it."
But they were the more eager
    to make all their deeds corrupt.

Punishment and Conversion of the Nations

8 Therefore wait for me, says the
        LORD,
    for the day when I arise as a
        witness.
For my decision is to gather nations,
    to assemble kingdoms,

to pour out upon them my
        indignation,
    all the heat of my anger;
for in the fire of my passion
    all the earth shall be consumed.

9 At that time I will change the speech
        of the peoples
    to a pure speech,
that all of them may call on the
        name of the LORD
    and serve him with one accord.
10 From beyond the rivers of Ethiopia*c*
    my suppliants, my scattered ones,
    shall bring my offering.

11 On that day you shall not be put to
        shame
    because of all the deeds by which
        you have rebelled against me;
for then I will remove from your
        midst
    your proudly exultant ones,
and you shall no longer be haughty
    in my holy mountain.
12 For I will leave in the midst of you
    a people humble and lowly.
They shall seek refuge in the name
        of the LORD—
13   the remnant of Israel;
they shall do no wrong
    and utter no lies,
nor shall a deceitful tongue
    be found in their mouths.
Then they will pasture and lie down,
    and no one shall make them
        afraid.

A Song of Joy

14 Sing aloud, O daughter Zion;
    shout, O Israel!

a Heb it   *b* Gk Syr: Heb *its dwelling will not be cut off*   *c* Or Nubia;
Heb *Cush*

its corrupt practices. Since Jerusalem is God's
dwelling place, God will seek to bring about
transformation from within by removing the
proud and the haughty and preserving a **remnant**
(v. 13), the faithful few. Societal transformation
can come from the faithful few who are committed to God and the cause of justice.

3:14–20 Song of Joy
Zephaniah's prophecies end with a song of joy

for the reversal of God's judgment on Jerusalem,
referred to as **daughter Zion** and **daughter Jerusalem**. This has come about through God's own
initiative to search out the faithful few, **a people
humble and lowly** (v. 12), to create transformation for the entire city. For the prophet, then, this
is about changed attitude and relationships with
God and with others.

Rejoice and exult with all your heart,
O daughter Jerusalem!
15 The LORD has taken away the
judgments against you,
he has turned away your enemies.
The king of Israel, the LORD, is in
your midst;
you shall fear disaster no more.
16 On that day it shall be said to
Jerusalem:
Do not fear, O Zion;
do not let your hands grow weak.
17 The LORD, your God, is in your
midst,
a warrior who gives victory;
he will rejoice over you with
gladness,
he will renew you[a] in his love;
he will exult over you with loud
singing

18 as on a day of festival.[b]
I will remove disaster from you,[c]
so that you will not bear reproach
for it.
19 I will deal with all your oppressors
at that time.
And I will save the lame
and gather the outcast,
and I will change their shame into
praise
and renown in all the earth.
20 At that time I will bring you home,
at the time when I gather you;
for I will make you renowned and
praised
among all the peoples of the earth,
when I restore your fortunes
before your eyes, says the LORD.

[a] Gk Syr: Heb *he will be silent* [b] Gk Syr: Meaning of Heb uncertain
[c] Cn: Heb *I will remove from you; they were*

The Book of
HAGGAI

This small, unassuming book conveys a powerful call to community action coupled with a grand theocratic vision. It offers a message of active resistance against paralyzing social indifference and communal pessimism. Seeing his people languish in despair, Haggai issues nothing short of a wake-up call.

The book attributed to Haggai covers a narrow slice of history, the few months between August and December 520 BCE. Yet this time marked a turning point in Israel's history after the exile. Since 539 BCE, after Babylon's defeat, Persia reigned as the superpower of the Fertile Crescent. One year later, the Persian emperor Cyrus released the Jewish exiles and expatriates of other conquered lands. They began to trickle back to Palestine, only to find their homeland devastated. Through the leadership of Sheshbazzar, appointed by Cyrus to return the holy vessels of the temple, work on the temple began immediately (Ezra 5:14–16). However, owing to limited resources and spirited opposition, restoration of the temple never got off the ground. In 520 BCE, the Persian king Darius I ascended the throne, sparking widespread insurrections throughout the empire. During this time of international turmoil, Haggai and his colleague Zechariah (Ezra 5:1; 6:14) began to prophesy. The temple was completed five years later (515 BCE). Whether the prophet lived to witness this, we do not know.

Nothing is known about the prophet himself; his message takes center stage while his personality remains shrouded in mystery. Nevertheless, his name suggests some connection to his message. Haggai is derived from a Hebrew verb that means "to make a pilgrimage" or "to hold a festival," an appropriate connection to worship in the temple.

Arranged chronologically, Haggai's message is divided into five major sections: 1:1–11; 1:12–15a; 1:15b–2:9; 2:10–19; 2:20–33. Haggai's declarations chronicle the temple's progress, from ruins to reconstruction, in a way that also charts the restoration of a community's values and commitments. Haggai specifically called for resumption of the temple construction as the way to restore the fledgling community. The forcefulness of his rhetoric indicates something of what the prophet was up against—the abject lack of the social wherewithal and communal resolve required to restart temple building and, thereby, to solidify the community. The prophet's "edifice complex" is matched only by his inordinate concern for the communal good. Haggai thus cannot be used as justification for expensive buildings and furnishings. The temple was no white elephant. Rather, for him the temple's reconstruction was the key to restoring the community's well-being. In other words, Haggai's "habitat for divinity" program was a way to restart a "habitat for humanity." The prophet vigorously argued the case that without the temple the community would only languish, bereft of identity and support.

—**William P. Brown**

The Command to Rebuild the Temple

1 In the second year of King Darius, in the sixth month, on the first day of the month, the word of the LORD came by the prophet Haggai to Zerubbabel son of Shealtiel, governor of Judah, and to Joshua son of Jehozadak, the high priest: ²Thus says the LORD of hosts: These people say the time has not yet come to rebuild the LORD's house. ³Then the word of the LORD came by the prophet Haggai, saying: ⁴Is it a time for you yourselves to live in your paneled houses, while this house lies in ruins? ⁵Now therefore thus says the LORD of hosts: Consider how you have fared. ⁶You have sown much, and harvested little; you eat, but you never have enough; you drink, but you never have your fill; you clothe yourselves, but no one is warm; and you that earn wages earn wages to put them into a bag with holes.

7 Thus says the LORD of hosts: Consider how you have fared. ⁸Go up to the hills and bring wood and build the house, so that I may take pleasure in it and be honored, says the LORD. ⁹You have looked for much, and, lo, it came to little; and when you brought it home, I blew it away. Why? says the LORD of hosts. Because my house lies in ruins, while all of you hurry off to your own houses. ¹⁰Therefore the heavens above you have withheld the dew, and the earth has withheld its produce. ¹¹And I have called for a drought on the land and the hills, on the grain, the new wine, the oil, on what the soil produces, on human beings and animals, and on all their labors.

12 Then Zerubbabel son of Shealtiel,

1:1–11 A Ruined Temple and a Command to Rebuild

1:1 *In the second year*—Haggai's first prophetic message is dated August 29, 520 BCE. Unlike the superscriptions of earlier prophetical books, Haggai's prophetic career is dated with respect to a *foreign* king, Darius I (the Great) of Persia. Although limited in its scope and audience, Haggai's prophetic message is given a distinctly global context.

1:2–4—God notes the people's lack of enthusiasm to rebuild the temple and counters their procrastination with a scathing rhetorical question that exposes their hypocrisy. While the people (no doubt only some) live in fortified housing, the temple remains *in ruins* (see also v. 9). Individual prosperity in the midst of impoverishment, thus, is no sign of God's blessing, but merely a symptom of a dysfunctional, dying community.

1:4—The verse refers to interior paneling, such as what the temple once had (1 Kgs. 7), evidence of well-furnished homes. The accusation is thick with irony: paneling that was perhaps intended for the temple is now being used to furnish homes (cf. 2 Sam. 7:2). Call it "temple blight." In any case, while individual homes prosper, the temple—the community's source and center—languishes, reflecting a scandalous level of self-serving indifference to the community's well-being (see v. 9).

1:6—God, through the prophet, makes clear that the state of the temple reflects the state of the community; both lie in ruins, despite isolated signs of individual prosperity in the community. Without a solidifying center (i.e., the temple, for Haggai), the community can exert all the effort it wants, but to no avail. In a culture of self-serving shallowness, material goods, from food to clothing, will not suffice.

1:8—The command is given to rebuild the temple. Only by restoring the temple can the community survive and flourish.

1:9—God accuses the people of indifference toward anything that reaches beyond mere selfish concern for individual security and prosperity. Retreating to one's domicile (*hurry off*), moreover, cuts off all opportunity to rebuild community and temple, which for the prophet are bound together. Like isolated enclaves, households have become barriers that prevent the flourishing of communal life. While the community decays, the walls of hearth and home have become cloistered. Concern only for individual enrichment drains a community's social capital, the intangible reservoir of human trust, coordination, cooperation, and mutual benefit that preserves and enhances a community. Inordinate self-interest comes at the expense of communal (and ecological) well-being.

1:12–15a Rebuilding Starts

In only three weeks after Haggai's prophetic utterances, the community is *stirred up* to take action on September 21, led by the governor and high priest, who spearhead a coordinated faith-based effort to restore the temple. And so begins the people's "habitat for divinity."

and Joshua son of Jehozadak, the high priest, with all the remnant of the people, obeyed the voice of the LORD their God, and the words of the prophet Haggai, as the LORD their God had sent him; and the people feared the LORD. ¹³ Then Haggai, the messenger of the LORD, spoke to the people with the LORD's message, saying, I am with you, says the LORD. ¹⁴ And the LORD stirred up the spirit of Zerubbabel son of Shealtiel, governor of Judah, and the spirit of Joshua son of Jehozadak, the high priest, and the spirit of all the remnant of the people; and they came and worked on the house of the LORD of hosts, their God, ¹⁵ on the twenty-fourth day of the month, in the sixth month.

The Future Glory of the Temple

2 In the second year of King Darius, ¹ in the seventh month, on the twenty-first day of the month, the word of the LORD came by the prophet Haggai, saying: ² Speak now to Zerubbabel son of Shealtiel, governor of Judah, and to Joshua son of Jehozadak, the high priest, and to the remnant of the people,

and say, ³ Who is left among you that saw this house in its former glory? How does it look to you now? Is it not in your sight as nothing? ⁴ Yet now take courage, O Zerubbabel, says the LORD; take courage, O Joshua, son of Jehozadak, the high priest; take courage, all you people of the land, says the LORD; work, for I am with you, says the LORD of hosts, ⁵ according to the promise that I made you when you came out of Egypt. My spirit abides among you; do not fear. ⁶ For thus says the LORD of hosts: Once again, in a little while, I will shake the heavens and the earth and the sea and the dry land; ⁷ and I will shake all the nations, so that the treasure of all nations shall come, and I will fill this house with splendor, says the LORD of hosts. ⁸ The silver is mine, and the gold is mine, says the LORD of hosts. ⁹ The latter splendor of this house shall be greater than the former, says the LORD of hosts; and in this place I will give prosperity, says the LORD of hosts.

A Rebuke and a Promise

10 On the twenty-fourth day of the ninth month, in the second year of

---

1:13 *I am with you*—In response to the people's fear (v. 12), the promise is given of God's solidarity with the community (cf. Ps. 23:4; Isa. 7:14). God thus enters into a building partnership with the people, inspiring them to action.

1:15b–2:9 I Am with You

Even after a month of great effort, no significant progress has been made, readily evident to those who participated in the Feast of Booths or Succoth, a fall pilgrimage festival in Jerusalem (Lev. 23:33–36). Amid disappointment, Haggai delivers a second message from God to the civil and religious authorities. Rather than issuing an indictment, the prophet imparts a message of encouragement based on God's promise of solidarity recalled from the exodus.

2:4 Take courage—Haggai encourages the people in the face of seemingly insurmountable fatigue, dwindling resources, and indifference. God's solidarity with the people (*"I am with you"*) not only casts out fear but musters the community to take action.

2:5 *Do not fear*—The most common command in Scripture.

2:6–9—God, the creator, will support the peo-

ple's efforts to construct a temple that will exceed the glory of the first temple, built by Solomon but destroyed by the Babylonians in 587/86 BCE. The restored temple will, in turn, become the source of prosperity for the community.

2:8—*The LORD of hosts* is the true owner of all wealth; the people are only the stewards.

2:10–19 God's Rebuke and Promise

2:10–14—Haggai's third prophetic address comes on the day the foundation of the temple is laid (v. 18), December 18, 520 BCE, two months after his second address (1:15b). The prophet delivers two questions to the priests for their ruling. In ancient Israel, it was the priest's vocation to preserve the boundaries between the holy and the profane (Lev. 10:10–11). Meat consecrated for sacrifice does not infect other meat with holiness, whereas impurity received through contact with a corpse is considered contagious. By analogy, the people remain in a state of impurity because their worship brings them into unavoidable contact with the ruins of a once-glorious edifice dedicated to honor God. The temple, like a dismembered corpse, remains a site of desecration rather than holiness, a ritual reminder of the urgency to complete its construction.

Darius, the word of the LORD came by the prophet Haggai, saying: ¹¹ Thus says the LORD of hosts: Ask the priests for a ruling: ¹² If one carries consecrated meat in the fold of one's garment, and with the fold touches bread, or stew, or wine, or oil, or any kind of food, does it become holy? The priests answered, "No." ¹³ Then Haggai said, "If one who is unclean by contact with a dead body touches any of these, does it become unclean?" The priests answered, "Yes, it becomes unclean." ¹⁴ Haggai then said, So is it with this people, and with this nation before me, says the LORD; and so with every work of their hands; and what they offer there is unclean. ¹⁵ But now, consider what will come to pass from this day on. Before a stone was placed upon a stone in the LORD's temple, ¹⁶ how did you fare?ª When one came to a heap of twenty measures, there were but ten; when one came to the wine vat to draw fifty measures, there were but twenty. ¹⁷ I struck you and all the products of your toil with blight and mildew and hail; yet you did not return to me, says the LORD.

¹⁸ Consider from this day on, from the twenty-fourth day of the ninth month. Since the day that the foundation of the LORD's temple was laid, consider: ¹⁹ Is there any seed left in the barn? Do the vine, the fig tree, the pomegranate, and the olive tree still yield nothing? From this day on I will bless you.

God's Promise to Zerubbabel

20 The word of the LORD came a second time to Haggai on the twenty-fourth day of the month: ²¹ Speak to Zerubbabel, governor of Judah, saying, I am about to shake the heavens and the earth, ²² and to overthrow the throne of kingdoms; I am about to destroy the strength of the kingdoms of the nations, and overthrow the chariots and their riders; and the horses and their riders shall fall, every one by the sword of a comrade. ²³ On that day, says the LORD of hosts, I will take you, O Zerubbabel my servant, son of Shealtiel, says the LORD, and make you like a signet ring; for I have chosen you, says the LORD of hosts.

ª Gk: Heb *since they were*

2:15–19—With the temple's foundations completed, there is no going back to a time of judgment and misery. Henceforth God resolves to bless the community, signaling a turning point from former judgment to future grace, from subsistence to shalom. Such blessing is communal in scope, in contrast to the prosperity pursued and grasped by individual households referred to in Haggai's first message (1:4).

2:20–23 A Final Promise

Haggai's final address occurs on the same day as his previous pronouncement. Addressed to Zerubbabel, the prophet conveys God's cosmic blessing for Israel at the expense of the nations'

powers. The language is reminiscent of the exodus, in which the horse and rider of Pharaoh's army were vanquished (Exod. 15:1–10). As the superpowers become incapacitated, Zerubbabel will ascend to power.

2:23—As the sign of power, the *signet ring* confers royal status to the governor (cf. Jer. 22:24). We do not know the historical fate of Zerubbabel. It is telling, however, that the book of Haggai, which began with reference to the reign of a foreign ruler, now ends with the promise of a new kingdom that will triumph over the principalities and powers of the world.

The Book of
ZECHARIAH

Like the book of Haggai, Zechariah is about resilient hope in the face of communal despair and apathy (see introduction to Haggai). As the most obscure book of the Minor Prophets, Zechariah is a composite work that divides itself into two parts, chapters 1–8 and 9–14, sometimes designated by scholars as First and Second Zechariah.

The historical setting of the first eight chapters of Zechariah overlaps with that of the previous prophetic book. Zechariah and Haggai were prophetic colleagues during the final decades of the sixth century BCE, a most tumultuous time. Darius I of Persia ascended the throne of the Persian Empire in 522 BCE, sparking widespread revolts and dissension throughout the empire, as well as igniting prophetic fervor to renew efforts toward reconstructing the temple (see also Haggai). Zechariah's prophecies during this time cover roughly two and a half years, from August 20, 520, to December 7, 518 BCE. These chapters comprise mostly visions (eight total) and speeches that, like the oracles of Haggai, stress the importance of rebuilding the temple for inaugurating a new era of communal blessing and order. Like Haggai, Zechariah links the vigor and well-being of the community to the state of the temple. "Habitat for humanity" rests entirely upon "habitat for divinity," that is, the Lord's house. But whereas Haggai addressed the immediacy of the situation, Zechariah places his message within the larger, sweeping history of God's saving grace and judgment.

Not much is known about the prophet. His name means "The Lord has remembered," which may suggest hope and promise for a people dispersed by exile in Babylonia. Zechariah is mentioned in Nehemiah 12:16 as having come from a priestly family. According to Ezra—in contradiction to what is said in Zechariah 1:1, 7—the prophet was the *son*, rather than grandson, of Iddo (see Ezra 5:1; 6:14). In addition, Matthew 23:35 makes mention of Zechariah's martyrdom, though this may be the result of a confusion with an entirely different Zechariah mentioned in 2 Chronicles 24:20–22. In short, all that can be said for certain is that the prophet came from a priestly family.

Chapters 9–14 of the book, however, are cut from a different cloth. Lacking the characteristic vision accounts of the first half of the book, this part is a patchwork of speeches uttered by various prophetic voices and brought together in convoluted fashion. (Matthew 27:9–10 attributes authorship of Zech. 11:12–13 to Jeremiah!) The overarching concern in these chapters is the end times, matched by an increasing disillusionment with the direction the faith community has taken. The tone of these chapters is quite strident, if not vitriolic, perhaps reflecting the work of authors who have been marginalized in Israel. Some scholars have placed these chapters a century later than the prophet Zechariah of the sixth century. In any case, while their historical background remains shrouded in mystery, these chapters helped to shape the gospel accounts of Jesus' ministry and death, as well as provided one of the most powerful portrayals of the coming age of peace in all of biblical literature (see 14:6–21).

—**William P. Brown**

Israel Urged to Repent

1 In the eighth month, in the second year of Darius, the word of the LORD came to the prophet Zechariah son of Berechiah son of Iddo, saying: ² The LORD was very angry with your ancestors. ³ Therefore say to them, Thus says the LORD of hosts: Return to me, says the LORD of hosts, and I will return to you, says the LORD of hosts. ⁴ Do not be like your ancestors, to whom the former prophets proclaimed, "Thus says the LORD of hosts, Return from your evil ways and from your evil deeds." But they did not hear or heed me, says the LORD. ⁵ Your ancestors, where are they? And the prophets, do they live forever? ⁶ But my words and my statutes, which I commanded my servants the prophets, did they not overtake your ancestors? So they repented and said, "The LORD of hosts has dealt with us according to our ways and deeds, just as he planned to do."

First Vision: The Horsemen

7 On the twenty-fourth day of the eleventh month, the month of Shebat, in the second year of Darius, the word of the LORD came to the prophet Zechariah son of Berechiah son of Iddo; and Zechariah*ᵃ* said, ⁸ In the night I saw a man riding on a red horse! He was standing among the myrtle trees in the glen; and behind him were red, sorrel, and white horses. ⁹ Then I said, "What are these, my lord?" The angel who talked with me said to me, "I will show you what they are." ¹⁰ So the man who was standing among the myrtle trees answered, "They are those whom the LORD has sent to patrol the earth." ¹¹ Then they spoke to the angel of the LORD who was standing among the myrtle trees, "We have patrolled the earth, and lo, the whole earth remains at peace." ¹² Then the angel of the LORD said, "O LORD of hosts, how long will you withhold mercy from Jerusalem and the cities of Judah, with which you have been angry these seventy years?" ¹³ Then the LORD replied with gracious and comforting words to the angel who talked with me. ¹⁴ So the angel who talked with me said to me, Proclaim this message: Thus says the LORD of hosts;

ᵃ Heb *and he*

1:1–8:23 *Visions of Zechariah*

1:1–6 A History of Prophecy: From Anger to Repentance

1:1 *Eighth month*—Mid-October to mid-November 520 BCE. *Zechariah*—Apropos of his name, the prophet recalls for his audience the history of the prophetic word with the previous generations of his people (vv. 4–6).

1:3–4 *Return*—God's change of heart toward the community is dependent upon the people's repentance. Zechariah encourages this generation not to repeat the mistakes of their history. Repentance rests upon the community's remembrance of its identity as constituted by God.

1:5–6—Even though the prophets and lawgivers are dead, both law (*statutes*) and prophecy (*words*), Zechariah acknowledges, remain valid, sustaining as well as convicting a people (cf. Isa. 40:8b).

1:7–17—Zechariah's First Vision: Complacency and Compassion

1:7 *Twenty-fourth day*—Mid-February 519 BCE.

1:8–9—The prophet begins the first of his eight vision reports that constitute the material of

1:8–6:15. Each vision reflects a standard pattern: (a) vision, (b) question, (c) answer. Zechariah's visions are highly symbolic and require interpretation, provided by an *angel*, or heavenly messenger.

1:11—In this context, *peace* refers simply to lack of conflict and nothing more, a complacent *ease* that casts a blind eye toward Judah's misery (v. 15)—in short, an unjust peace. In the angel's objection that follows (v. 12), this superficial peace is exposed as the maintenance of an oppressive status quo. True and lasting peace, by contrast, is founded upon justice and equity.

1:12—The angel complains of God *withhold[ing] mercy* at the expense of God's people. God can no more permanently suspend mercy than a person can hold his or her breath indefinitely. *Seventy*—A round number that refers to the time from Jerusalem's destruction in 587/86 to 519 BCE.

1:14—God's jealousy for Judah is more than an emotional state; it is a matter of singleminded resolve that translates directly into action in behalf of God's people. To attain true and lasting peace (v. 11), God's compassion cannot avoid

I am very jealous for Jerusalem and for Zion. [15] And I am extremely angry with the nations that are at ease; for while I was only a little angry, they made the disaster worse. [16] Therefore, thus says the LORD, I have returned to Jerusalem with compassion; my house shall be built in it, says the LORD of hosts, and the measuring line shall be stretched out over Jerusalem. [17] Proclaim further: Thus says the LORD of hosts: My cities shall again overflow with prosperity; the LORD will again comfort Zion and again choose Jerusalem.

Second Vision: The Horns and the Smiths

[18][a] And I looked up and saw four horns. [19] I asked the angel who talked with me, "What are these?" And he answered me, "These are the horns that have scattered Judah, Israel, and Jerusalem." [20] Then the LORD showed me four blacksmiths. [21] And I asked, "What are they coming to do?" He answered, "These are the horns that scattered Judah, so that no head could

be raised; but these have come to terrify them, to strike down the horns of the nations that lifted up their horns against the land of Judah to scatter its people."[b]

Third Vision: The Man with a Measuring Line

2[c] I looked up and saw a man with a measuring line in his hand. [2] Then I asked, "Where are you going?" He answered me, "To measure Jerusalem, to see what is its width and what is its length." [3] Then the angel who talked with me came forward, and another angel came forward to meet him, [4] and said to him, "Run, say to that young man: Jerusalem shall be inhabited like villages without walls, because of the multitude of people and animals in it. [5] For I will be a wall of fire all around it, says the LORD, and I will be the glory within it."

Interlude: An Appeal to the Exiles

6 Up, up! Flee from the land of the north, says the LORD; for I have spread

[a] Ch 2.1 in Heb   [b] Heb *it*   [c] Ch 2.5 in Heb

---

disturbing the world's complacency, whether it is leading slaves out of Egypt at the expense of Pharaoh's army or rendering judgment against the nations that have victimized Israel. While God used the nations to chasten Israel, the nations are culpable for having exceeded their role by making matters worse. Such is the political danger of enlisting the nations for divine purposes (a perennial liability!), for all too often the nations see themselves as gods to wreak havoc against other nations as they see fit. (See Isa. 10:5–19 in regard to Assyria's ambiguous role.)

1:16 *My house*—Zechariah considers the rebuilding of the temple to be a sign of God's reconciliation with Judah, of God's comfort and election of Zion (cf. Deut. 12:5, 11; Isa. 40:1). A renewal of urban prosperity will accompany the temple's completion (v. 17).

1:18–21 Zechariah's Second Vision: The Four Horns

1:18—Symbolic of political power, the *four horns* represent those superpowers that have, in effect, gored Israel in the past (Assyria, Egypt, and especially Babylon may be included). As with the points of a compass, the number four may simply convey a sense of global totality.

1:20—The *four blacksmiths* represent divine

agents poised to break the horns (i.e., the nations) that have decimated and dispersed God's people.

2:1–5 Zechariah's Third Vision: The Wall of Fire

2:3–5—This vision unveils an unprecedented urban plan: a city without walls! Jerusalem's population will not be contained by such structures any more than God can be contained within the temple. Nevertheless, the city will not remain defenseless: a *wall of fire* will be established around the metropolis (cf. Exod. 14:19–20). As a holy sanctuary for God's indwelling presence, the city will be impregnable from without and glorious from within (cf. Ezek. 43:1–5). God is shown to have a special love for cities, not just for green meadows and still waters (see Ps. 46:4–5). Indeed, the image of the restored city offers the most powerful and salutary model for human community (see Zech. 8:3–8; Jer. 29:7).

2:6–13 The People's Response: Homeward Bound

2:6–10—The prophet urges the people to come home, that is, to escape from the land of bondage, *Babylon*, and return to *Zion*, God's refuge. Zion serves as both God's home and the people's home. Jerusalem is where the community is at home with itself and with God.

you abroad like the four winds of heaven, says the LORD. ⁷ Up! Escape to Zion, you that live with daughter Babylon. ⁸ For thus said the LORD of hosts (after his glory*a* sent me) regarding the nations that plundered you: Truly, one who touches you touches the apple of my eye.*b* ⁹ See now, I am going to raise*c* my hand against them, and they shall become plunder for their own slaves. Then you will know that the LORD of hosts has sent me. ¹⁰ Sing and rejoice, O daughter Zion! For lo, I will come and dwell in your midst, says the LORD. ¹¹ Many nations shall join themselves to the LORD on that day, and shall be my people; and I will dwell in your midst. And you shall know that the LORD of hosts has sent me to you. ¹² The LORD will inherit Judah as his portion in the holy land, and will again choose Jerusalem.

13 Be silent, all people, before the LORD; for he has roused himself from his holy dwelling.

Fourth Vision: Joshua and Satan

3 Then he showed me the high priest Joshua standing before the angel of the LORD, and Satan*d* standing at his right hand to accuse him. ² And the LORD said to Satan,*d* "The LORD rebuke you, O Satan!*d* The LORD who has chosen Jerusalem rebuke you! Is not this man a brand plucked from the fire?" ³ Now Joshua was dressed with filthy clothes as he stood before the angel. ⁴ The angel said to those who were standing before him, "Take off his filthy clothes." And to him he said, "See, I have taken your guilt away from you, and I will clothe you with festal apparel." ⁵ And I said, "Let them put a clean turban on his head." So they put a clean turban on his head and clothed him with the apparel; and the angel of the LORD was standing by.

6 Then the angel of the LORD assured Joshua, saying ⁷ "Thus says the LORD of

a Cn: Heb *after glory he* *b* Heb *his eye* *c* Or *wave* *d* Or *the Accuser*; Heb *the Adversary*

2:8—*The apple of my eye* is a term of endearment that expresses God's protective intimacy with Judah (see also Deut. 32:10; Ps. 17:8). Judah is as close to God as is, figuratively speaking, the pupil of God's eye, one of the most sensitive parts of the body. Any violation of Judah causes personal injury to God that demands decisive and forceful retribution. God suffers when God's people suffer. Even a light "touch" against Judah warrants the imposition of God's hand, poised to strike back with full force (v. 9).

2:10—As Judah dwells in God as the eye's apple, so God will *dwell in [Israel's] midst* on Zion, God's holy habitation.

2:11—The prophet is no xenophobe, and biblical Israel is no fortified enclave set against the world. Zechariah's appeal is universal in acknowledging that even the heathen nations shall be joined to God and declared God's people.

2:12—It is rare that the Bible speaks of *God* inheriting a people; more widely attested is reference to a people inheriting God's gift of land (Exod. 23:30; 32:13; but cf. Exod. 19:5; Deut. 32:8–9; Ps. 82:8; Joel 2:17). Never again will God's claim upon Israel be challenged, much less annulled.

2:13—Silence is an appropriate response to God's presence on the move. Internationally, it means the silencing of saber rattling and battle cries in order to pave the way for peace and justice.

3:1–10 Zechariah's Fourth Vision: The High Priest Joshua

3:1 *Satan*—Lit. "the adversary," who accuses Joshua the high priest in the heavenly court of some undefined offense (cf. Job 1:6–8). Far from the demonic persona of later tradition, this accuser is evidently a member of the divine assembly in heaven who has the task of assaying the character of mortals. Although God readily "rebukes" Joshua's accuser, finding "the satan's" case against the high priest groundless, spiritual warfare between Satan and God is not be found here. God's rebuttal affirms Joshua's innocence of some alleged crime or calamity.

3:2—Joshua is likened to a burned piece of wood yanked *from the fire*, suggesting rescue from some ordeal. The same image is found in Amos 4:11, in which the firebrand signifies the aftermath of judgment. Joshua is delivered by God in the nick of time from some calamity and given a second chance at leadership.

3:3–4—The priestly vestments were considered sacred; hence dirt signifies the desecration of the priestly office. In his filthy apparel, Joshua remains in a state of ritual uncleanness. Through a change of clothes, the high priest is purified and can resume his duties on behalf of the people.

3:7—Joshua is given responsibilities traditionally reserved for the king (*rule*), reflecting a new theocratic order of the community. But such leader-

hosts: If you will walk in my ways and keep my requirements, then you shall rule my house and have charge of my courts, and I will give you the right of access among those who are standing here. **8** Now listen, Joshua, high priest, you and your colleagues who sit before you! For they are an omen of things to come: I am going to bring my servant the Branch. **9** For on the stone that I have set before Joshua, on a single stone with seven facets, I will engrave its inscription, says the LORD of hosts, and I will remove the guilt of this land in a single day. **10** On that day, says the LORD of hosts, you shall invite each other to come under your vine and fig tree."

Fifth Vision: The Lampstand and Olive Trees

4 The angel who talked with me came again, and wakened me, as one is wakened from sleep. **2** He said to me, "What do you see?" And I said, "I see a lampstand all of gold, with a bowl on the top of it; there are seven lamps on it, with seven lips on each of the lamps that are on the top of it. **3** And by it there are two olive trees, one on the right of the bowl and the other on its left." **4** I said to the angel who talked with me, "What are these, my lord?" **5** Then the angel who talked with me answered me, "Do you not know what these are?" I said, "No, my lord." **6** He said to me, "This is the word of the LORD to Zerubbabel: Not by might, nor by power, but by my spirit, says the LORD of hosts. **7** What are you, O great mountain? Before Zerubbabel you shall become a plain; and he shall bring out the top stone amid shouts of 'Grace, grace to it!'"

8 Moreover the word of the LORD came to me, saying, **9** "The hands of Zerubbabel have laid the foundation of this house; his hands shall also complete it. Then you will know that the LORD of hosts has sent me to you. **10** For whoever has despised the day of small things

---

ship, powerful as it may be, is entirely contingent upon the office holder's integrity and obedience to God (*walk* and *keep*). As a result, Joshua will be granted right of access to the heavenly realm so that he can intercede directly to God on behalf of the community.

3:8—*Branch* is the symbol of a Davidic ruler who is to share power with the high priest. The metaphor of plant growth traditionally (and aptly) represents a beneficent monarch who is to usher in the messianic age (Isa. 11:1; Jer. 23:5).

3:9—*The stone* is probably a veiled reference to the golden rosette that is to be fastened on the front of the chief priest's turban with the engraving "Holy to the Lord," spelled in Hebrew with seven letters or "facets" (Exod. 28:36). The engraving is to be done not by human hands but by God. Moreover, in conjunction with the high priest's renewed commission, God (and only God) will remove the people's guilt.

3:10—The *vine* and the *fig tree* are symbols of security. Once the land is cleansed (see v. 9), prosperity and peace will flourish, not just for a few but for all (see Mic. 4:4).

4:1–14 Zechariah's Fifth Vision: The Lampstand and Olive Trees

4:6–7—The introduction of *Zerubbabel* marks an abrupt shift from the lampstand imagery detailed above. The governor of Judah and messianic figure (see Hag. 1:1, 12; 2:23) is given a ringing endorsement by the angel: Zerubbabel's status is divinely ordained. The constructive work of God's spirit distinguishes itself from human power and might, yet proves itself to be more effective! Before Zerubbabel the massive ruins of the temple mount (*great mountain*) are leveled and cleared for rebuilding to take place (cf. Isa. 40:4). The vision affirms that what Zerubbabel is about to do, no human can do alone without divine help. God makes possible where human capacity fails.

4:7—The *top stone* is perhaps the cornerstone of the former temple, used as the first stone for the new temple, establishing continuity with the past. The placement of the stone was traditionally accompanied by great ceremony. Like most things of lasting value, the new must be built upon the old. Authentic innovation—be it political, social, or theological—must draw from tradition.

4:10—*The day of small things* describes the present situation, when everyone selfishly hoards resources and cannot think or act beyond their own needs and desires and, thus, cannot accomplish much of anything (cf. 1:4–6). By contrast, the building of the temple inaugurates a time of *great* things.

The plummet was a piece of precious metal deposited in the walls of the completed new structure. To witness the plummet in Zerubbabel's hand is to witness the completion of the temple.

shall rejoice, and shall see the plummet in the hand of Zerubbabel.

"These seven are the eyes of the LORD, which range through the whole earth." ¹¹ Then I said to him, "What are these two olive trees on the right and the left of the lampstand?" ¹² And a second time I said to him, "What are these two branches of the olive trees, which pour out the oil*a* through the two golden pipes?" ¹³ He said to me, "Do you not know what these are?" I said, "No, my lord." ¹⁴ Then he said, "These are the two anointed ones who stand by the Lord of the whole earth."

Sixth Vision: The Flying Scroll

5 Again I looked up and saw a flying scroll. ² And he said to me, "What do you see?" I answered, "I see a flying scroll; its length is twenty cubits, and its width ten cubits." ³ Then he said to me, "This is the curse that goes out over the face of the whole land; for everyone who steals shall be cut off according to the writing on one side, and everyone who swears falsely*b* shall be cut off according to the writing on the other side. ⁴ I have sent it out, says the LORD of hosts, and it shall enter the house of the thief, and the house of anyone who swears falsely by my name; and it shall abide in that house and consume it, both timber and stones."

Seventh Vision: The Woman in a Basket

5 Then the angel who talked with me came forward and said to me, "Look up and see what this is that is coming out." ⁶ I said, "What is it?" He said, "This is a basket*c* coming out." And he said, "This is their iniquity*d* in all the land." ⁷ Then a leaden cover was lifted, and there was a woman sitting in the basket! *c* ⁸ And he said, "This is Wickedness." So he thrust her back into the basket,*c* and pressed the leaden weight down on its mouth.

a Cn: Heb *gold*   *b* The word *falsely* added from verse 4   *c* Heb *ephah*
d Gk Compare Syr: Heb *their eye*

The top stone (v. 7) and the plummet represent, in effect, the alpha and omega of temple construction. Zechariah's prophecy conveys the hope for a new temple and, consequently, a fully restored community.

The *seven* lamps are likened to the seven *eyes of the LORD*, which range throughout the earth (cf. 1:11). God's all-knowing gaze denotes divine beneficence as well as judgment (see 2 Chr. 16:9; Ezra 5:5; Job 36:7; Ps. 34:15).

4:14—*The two anointed ones*, lit. "sons of oil," are Joshua and Zerubbabel, who are represented by the two branches of golden conduits that pour oil from the olive trees to the lamps. The kind of oil mentioned here refers to fresh, unprocessed oil, symbolizing new beginnings. The imagery connotes a new configuration of leadership for the community. Equal in relationship, these two figures stand by God's side in a doubled form of messiahship. In place of the old order of royal dominance over the priesthood, a new model of governance has emerged: royal and priestly figures are set on the same footing in interdependent relationship. By itself, oil does nothing: the lamps need the oil from the olive trees in order to provide light. It is God, thus, who empowers and sustains both priest and prince and, by extension, the community. The prophet's vision of the new community is characterized by a balancing of authority, implemented through a polity of *shared* leadership that weaves together the sacred and the secular.

5:1–4 Zechariah's Sixth Vision: The Flying Scroll

5:1—What modern readers refer to as the "long arm of the law," the prophet envisions as a *flying scroll* of immense proportions (ca. 30′ × 15′) that roams throughout the land, searching out and punishing those who steal and utter false oaths (v. 3).

5:3 *Steals . . . swears falsely*—Two violations of the covenant (see Exod. 20:7, 15–16). Theft threatens the very fabric of society. False swearing or lying under oath constitutes a flagrant violation of due process. The prophet's vision ensures that the new community remains subject to the normative traditions of God's covenant, which in turn enables the community to flourish in peace and justice.

5:5–11 Zechariah's Seventh Vision: A Basket for Babylon

5:6—Iniquity is symbolically contained in the *basket*. In the fourth vision, God promised to remove the community's guilt from the land (3:9). In this seventh vision, the act is accomplished.

5:8—Symbolizing *Wickedness*, this female figure is unabashedly misogynistic and is probably the basis for the mythic whore of Babylon in Rev. 17:1–18. The purpose of the vision, however, is

⁹Then I looked up and saw two women coming forward. The wind was in their wings; they had wings like the wings of a stork, and they lifted up the basket[a] between earth and sky. ¹⁰Then I said to the angel who talked with me, "Where are they taking the basket?"[a] ¹¹He said to me, "To the land of Shinar, to build a house for it; and when this is prepared, they will set the basket[a] down there on its base."

Eighth Vision: Four Chariots

6 And again I looked up and saw four chariots coming out from between two mountains—mountains of bronze. ²The first chariot had red horses, the second chariot black horses, ³the third chariot white horses, and the fourth chariot dappled gray[b] horses. ⁴Then I said to the angel who talked with me, "What are these, my lord?" ⁵The angel answered me, "These are the four winds[c] of heaven going out, after presenting themselves before the LORD of all the earth. ⁶The chariot with the black horses goes toward the north country, the white ones go toward the west country,[d] and

the dappled ones go toward the south country." ⁷When the steeds came out, they were impatient to get off and patrol the earth. And he said, "Go, patrol the earth." So they patrolled the earth. ⁸Then he cried out to me, "Lo, those who go toward the north country have set my spirit at rest in the north country."

The Coronation of the Branch

9 The word of the LORD came to me: ¹⁰Collect silver and gold[e] from the exiles—from Heldai, Tobijah, and Jedaiah—who have arrived from Babylon; and go the same day to the house of Josiah son of Zephaniah. ¹¹Take the silver and gold and make a crown,[f] and set it on the head of the high priest Joshua son of Jehozadak; ¹²say to him: Thus says the LORD of hosts: Here is a man whose name is Branch: for he shall branch out in his place, and he shall build the temple of the LORD. ¹³It is he that shall build the temple of the LORD; he shall bear royal honor, and shall sit upon his throne and rule. There shall be

---

[a] Heb *ephah*   [b] Compare Gk: Meaning of Heb uncertain   [c] Or *spirits*
[d] Cn: Heb *go after them*   [e] Cn Compare verse 11: Heb lacks *silver and gold*
[f] Gk Mss Syr Tg: Heb *crowns*

---

indicated in the destination to which the basket is carried by *two women* (v. 9), angelic beings. The feminine casting of these characters in the prophet's vision reflects the patriarchal spirit of antiquity: woman is seen as quintessentially other, both cursed and elevated, whore and angel.

5:11—*Shinar* is another name for Mesopotamia, specifically Babylon (Gen. 10:10; 11:2; Isa. 11:11). Wickedness sent to Babylon completes the removal of iniquity that began with the renewal of Joshua's priestly office in the fourth vision (3:1–10).

Babylon's *house* is the antithesis of the house of the Lord. Israel's purification, culminating in the establishment of a new temple and priesthood, will in turn bring about Babylon's contamination, which, absurdly enough, will be venerated by its own people. Zechariah's vision vividly illustrates how easy it is to fall into worshiping "iniquity" or, more broadly, the will to power, from military might to personal ambition.

6:1–8 Zechariah's Eighth Vision: The Four Chariots

6:8—*The north country* is traditionally the area

of Israel's enemies, including the land of Shinar (see 5:11). Of the *four chariots* (6:1) or *winds* (v. 5), identical to "spirits," it is the second chariot (with *black horses* [v. 6]) that gains the prophet's attention because of its northbound mission, that is, toward Babylon (see 2:6).

God's *spirit* will not rest until the warring nations, including the superpower Babylon, are subdued and at peace (cf. 1:11, 15). As God's spirit rested at the climax of creation (see Gen. 1:2; 2:1–3), so divine rest renders Israel free from the warring conflicts and injustices the nations have wrought.

6:9–15 The Coronation of Joshua

6:11—Joshua the high priest is crowned as king.

6:12 Branch—See 3:8. This passage comes from a later historical context in which Zerubbabel, whose name means "shoot (or branch) of Babylon," is no longer on the scene and the office of high priest has incorporated the royal office, along with the appointment of another priest (see 6:13). Most significantly, it is now Joshua who is appointed builder of the temple, in contrast to 4:9, which designates Zerubbabel temple builder.

a priest by his throne, with peaceful understanding between the two of them. ¹⁴ And the crown*a* shall be in the care of Heldai,*b* Tobijah, Jedaiah, and Josiah*c* son of Zephaniah, as a memorial in the temple of the LORD.

15 Those who are far off shall come and help to build the temple of the LORD; and you shall know that the LORD of hosts has sent me to you. This will happen if you diligently obey the voice of the LORD your God.

Hypocritical Fasting Condemned

7 In the fourth year of King Darius, the word of the LORD came to Zechariah on the fourth day of the ninth month, which is Chislev. ² Now the people of Bethel had sent Sharezer and Regem-melech and their men, to entreat the favor of the LORD, ³ and to ask the priests of the house of the LORD of hosts and the prophets, "Should I mourn and practice abstinence in the fifth month, as I have done for so many years?" ⁴ Then the word of the LORD of hosts came to

me: ⁵ Say to all the people of the land and the priests: When you fasted and lamented in the fifth month and in the seventh, for these seventy years, was it for me that you fasted? ⁶ And when you eat and when you drink, do you not eat and drink only for yourselves? ⁷ Were not these the words that the LORD proclaimed by the former prophets, when Jerusalem was inhabited and in prosperity, along with the towns around it, and when the Negeb and the Shephelah were inhabited?

Punishment for Rejecting God's Demands

8 The word of the LORD came to Zechariah, saying: ⁹ Thus says the LORD of hosts: Render true judgments, show kindness and mercy to one another; ¹⁰ do not oppress the widow, the orphan, the alien, or the poor; and do not devise evil in your hearts against one another. ¹¹ But they refused to listen, and turned

a Gk Syr: Heb *crowns* *b* Syr Compare verse 10: Heb *Helem* *c* Syr Compare verse 10: Heb *Hen*

6:15—Temple reconstruction requires the cooperation and effort of the whole community, including those who remain dispersed in foreign lands. Compare Exod. 35–36, which describes the inclusive effort of the community in the building of the tabernacle. The variegated nature of the tabernacle reflects the diversity of the community's contributions to its construction.

7:1–7 To Fast or to Feast: An Inquiry from the Priests

7:1 *Fourth year*—Zechariah's *word of the LORD* comes on December 7, 518 BCE.

7:3 *Fifth month*—A delegation from Bethel seeks guidance on whether to maintain a rite of lamentation in the month of Ab, the traditional time to commemorate the temple's destruction in August 587 BCE, when Nebuchadrezzar's troops conquered Jerusalem. The question marks the beginning of the end of mourning, the end of commemorating the interminable period of suffering and the beginning of a new time of grace and restoration.

7:5—Zechariah questions the very purpose of fasting. It is not for God's benefit that fasting has been practiced during the years of exile to the present. Fasting was frequently practiced as a way of petitioning God during times of lamentation (2 Sam. 12:15–32; Jer. 14:12). However, Zecha-

riah strips away all theological import associated with this rite without denying its human significance. Communal fasting can actually *sustain* a people in crisis, but it cannot sway God to act one way or another (for a different view of fasting, see Joel 2:12–13). In short, the prophet relativizes ritual.

7:8–14 The Message of the Former Prophets: Justice

7:9–10—Zechariah conveys a message from God that effectively summarizes the normative practices of the covenant community: justice. Defending the rights of the *widow, orphan,* sojourner (NRSV *alien*), and the *poor*—those most vulnerable in society—constitutes the yardstick by which any society is to be measured. The neglect of society's most vulnerable is more than an oversight; it is in God's eyes an abomination! (See Deut. 14:29; 24:19–21; Prov. 22:22–23; 23:10–11; Isa. 1:16–17; Jer. 22:3; 7:5–6; Amos 5:14–15, 21–24.)

7:11–14—Israel's history, according to Zechariah, is marred by the consistent refusal on the part of God's people to put into practice justice through obedience to God's *law*, thereby warranting divine punishment. Devastation and exile are the result. Injustice ruins a *pleasant land* (v. 14). The description of judgment, however, sets the stage for the following word of hope (8:1–8).

a stubborn shoulder, and stopped their ears in order not to hear. ¹²They made their hearts adamant in order not to hear the law and the words that the LORD of hosts had sent by his spirit through the former prophets. Therefore great wrath came from the LORD of hosts. ¹³Just as, when I*a* called, they would not hear, so, when they called, I would not hear, says the LORD of hosts, ¹⁴and I scattered them with a whirlwind among all the nations that they had not known. Thus the land they left was desolate, so that no one went to and fro, and a pleasant land was made desolate.

God's Promises to Zion

8 The word of the LORD of hosts came to me, saying: ²Thus says the LORD of hosts: I am jealous for Zion with great jealousy, and I am jealous for her with great wrath. ³Thus says the LORD: I will return to Zion, and will dwell in the midst of Jerusalem; Jerusalem shall be called the faithful city, and the mountain of the LORD of hosts shall be called the holy mountain. ⁴Thus says the LORD of hosts: Old men and old women shall again sit in the streets of Jerusalem, each with staff in hand because of their great age. ⁵And the streets of the city shall be full of boys and girls playing in its streets. ⁶Thus says the LORD of hosts: Even though it seems impossible to the remnant of this people in these

days, should it also seem impossible to me, says the LORD of hosts? ⁷Thus says the LORD of hosts: I will save my people from the east country and from the west country; ⁸and I will bring them to live in Jerusalem. They shall be my people and I will be their God, in faithfulness and in righteousness.

9 Thus says the LORD of hosts: Let your hands be strong—you that have recently been hearing these words from the mouths of the prophets who were present when the foundation was laid for the rebuilding of the temple, the house of the LORD of hosts. ¹⁰For before those days there were no wages for people or for animals, nor was there any safety from the foe for those who went out or came in, and I set them all against one another. ¹¹But now I will not deal with the remnant of this people as in the former days, says the LORD of hosts. ¹²For there shall be a sowing of peace; the vine shall yield its fruit, the ground shall give its produce, and the skies shall give their dew; and I will cause the remnant of this people to possess all these things. ¹³Just as you have been a cursing among the nations, O house of Judah and house of Israel, so I will save you and you shall be a blessing. Do not be afraid, but let your hands be strong.

14 For thus says the LORD of hosts: Just as I purposed to bring disaster upon

a Heb *he*

8:1–8 Zion's Restoration

8:3—Rooted in passionate concern, God's zeal for Israel is demonstrated in Zion's restoration (see also vv. 14–15). Divine jealousy yearns for a *return*, a reunion by which God will once again *dwell in . . . Jerusalem* (see 1:16). Even in wrath, God proves gracious. Divine anger is not senseless rage. There is reason behind the wrath: God's anger is a "temple tantrum" aimed at restoring Jerusalem physically and morally! (Cf. Matt. 2:12–13; Mark 11:15–19; Luke 19:45–48.)

8:4–6—One of the most evocative profiles of the restored city, filled with people of all ages, from the elderly to children, enjoying life in the streets in utter security and leisure. The devastated city will become a veritable playground! Justice in

the city ensures playgrounds, as well as equitable treatment and due process.

8:8—The last sentence is the sum and substance of God's covenantal relationship with Israel (see Jer. 7:23; 24:7; 31:33; 32:38).

8:9–17 Exhortation for Restoration

8:12—The evocative phrase *sowing of peace* conveys the intimate relationship between peace and prosperity. Peace is not only a blessing from God; it is also a goal realized through hard *work*. Hence, the prophet repeats his exhortation: *"Let your hands be strong"* (vv. 9 and 13).

8:13—Israel shall again be *a blessing* for the nations (cf. Gen. 12:2–3), not just for itself. To be blessed by God is also to share blessing with others.

you, when your ancestors provoked me to wrath, and I did not relent, says the LORD of hosts, 15 so again I have purposed in these days to do good to Jerusalem and to the house of Judah; do not be afraid. 16 These are the things that you shall do: Speak the truth to one another, render in your gates judgments that are true and make for peace, 17 do not devise evil in your hearts against one another, and love no false oath; for all these are things that I hate, says the LORD.

Joyful Fasting

18 The word of the LORD of hosts came to me, saying: 19 Thus says the LORD of hosts: The fast of the fourth month, and the fast of the fifth, and the fast of the seventh, and the fast of the tenth, shall be seasons of joy and gladness, and cheerful festivals for the house of Judah: therefore love truth and peace.

Many Peoples Drawn to Jerusalem

20 Thus says the LORD of hosts: Peoples shall yet come, the inhabitants of many cities; 21 the inhabitants of one city shall go to another, saying, "Come, let us go to entreat the favor of the LORD, and to seek the LORD of hosts; I myself am going." 22 Many peoples and strong nations shall come to seek the LORD of hosts in Jerusalem, and to entreat the favor of the LORD. 23 Thus says the LORD of hosts: In those days ten men from nations of every language shall take hold of a Jew, grasping his garment and saying, "Let us go with you, for we have heard that God is with you."

Judgment on Israel's Enemies

9 An Oracle.

The word of the LORD is against the land of Hadrach
　and will rest upon Damascus.
For to the LORD belongs the capital[a]
　of Aram,[b]
　as do all the tribes of Israel;
2 Hamath also, which borders on it,
　Tyre and Sidon, though they are
　very wise.
3 Tyre has built itself a rampart,
　and heaped up silver like dust,
　and gold like the dirt of the streets.
4 But now, the Lord will strip it of its
　possessions
　and hurl its wealth into the sea,
　and it shall be devoured by fire.

a Heb eye　b Cn: Heb of Adam (or of humankind)

8:16–17—The conditions for peace: speaking the truth, implementing justice, refraining from evil, and giving true testimony (see also 5:3–4).

8:18–23 The Seasons of Joy

8:18–19—By God's blessing of restoration, the appointed times of mourning and fasting give way to festivals of *joy and gladness* (cf. 7:3–7). Liturgy reflects reality.

8:22–23—The prophet paints a great pilgrimage to Jerusalem. By God's blessing, Jerusalem will become an international melting pot, a cosmopolis that embodies a universal peaceable kingdom (see Isa. 2:2–4; 11:6–9; 60:1–3; 66:18–21; Mic. 4:3). In addition, precedent can be found in God's gift to Abraham to be a blessing for "all the families of the earth" (Gen. 12:2–3). Even Gentiles (non-Jews) can proclaim, "I was glad when they said to me, 'Let us go to the house of the LORD!'" (Ps. 122:1). Zechariah concludes his prophecies with a vision of the shared journey, one in which people of different nationalities, ethnic backgrounds, and native languages share life together. Such is the journey of faith, a journey *shared*.

9:1–14:21 Post-Zecharian Prophecies

A new series of prophecies quite different from those given by Zechariah in chaps. 1–8 (see introduction).

9:1–8 The Divine Warrior Approaches Jerusalem

9:1—Here, *the word of the LORD*, lit. "oracle," conveys judgment against cities located in Syria (*Aram*), Phoenicia, and Philistia, frequent enemies of Israel. God's word is by no means confined to Israel; it has international scope, for even the foreign nations belong to God (v. 1). Approaching from the north, along the coast from Syria to Phoenicia to Philistia, God comes to restore justice throughout the land and encamp at the now completed temple, *my house* (v. 8), in order to protect Israel (see 2:12).

9:3–4—Wealth is no defense against God's resolve to execute justice. Because *Tyre's* wealth came from sea commerce, so its wealth will be hurled back into the sea.

5 Ashkelon shall see it and be afraid;
  Gaza too, and shall writhe in
    anguish;
  Ekron also, because its hopes are
    withered.
The king shall perish from Gaza;
  Ashkelon shall be uninhabited;
6 a mongrel people shall settle in
    Ashdod,
  and I will make an end of the pride
    of Philistia.
7 I will take away its blood from its
    mouth,
  and its abominations from
    between its teeth;
it too shall be a remnant for our
    God;
  it shall be like a clan in Judah,
  and Ekron shall be like the
    Jebusites.
8 Then I will encamp at my house as a
    guard,
  so that no one shall march to and
    fro;
no oppressor shall again overrun
    them,
  for now I have seen with my own
    eyes.

The Coming Ruler of God's People

9 Rejoice greatly, O daughter Zion!
  Shout aloud, O daughter
    Jerusalem!

Lo, your king comes to you;
  triumphant and victorious is he,
humble and riding on a donkey,
  on a colt, the foal of a donkey.
10 He[a] will cut off the chariot from
    Ephraim
  and the war-horse from Jerusalem;
and the battle bow shall be cut off,
  and he shall command peace to
    the nations;
his dominion shall be from sea to
    sea,
  and from the River to the ends of
    the earth.

11 As for you also, because of the blood
    of my covenant with you,
  I will set your prisoners free from
    the waterless pit.
12 Return to your stronghold,
    O prisoners of hope;
  today I declare that I will restore to
    you double.
13 For I have bent Judah as my bow;
    I have made Ephraim its arrow.
  I will arouse your sons, O Zion,
    against your sons, O Greece,
  and wield you like a warrior's
    sword.

14 Then the LORD will appear over them,
  and his arrow go forth like
    lightning;

a Gk: Heb I

9:9–13 God's Reign of Peace

9:9—*Daughter Zion* is a term of endearment used frequently in the context of deliverance (2:10; Isa. 12:6; 52:2; Mic. 4:8; Zeph. 3:14–15). Like Miriam at the banks of the Red Sea (Exod. 15:20–21), daughter Zion responds with praise and thanksgiving, celebrating God's victory.

Zion's king, the Lord, returns to Jerusalem in triumph, not in a chariot or on a war horse, but on a young *donkey*. The gospel writers draw from this text to describe Jesus' entry into Jerusalem (Matt. 21:5; John 12:14), commemorated on Palm Sunday. (Only one donkey is intended in Zech. 9:9. The picture in Matt. 21:7 of Jesus seated on two steeds at once is needlessly awkward!) The power of weakness proves more powerful than the power of power, for in powerlessness God will destroy all instruments of war (v. 10; cf. Ps. 46:8–9; Isa. 57:19). The nations are demilita-

rized by the divine warrior; they will "study war no more" (Isa. 2:4; Mic. 4:3). God's reign is a reign of peace, spreading from the inside out to include all the earth.

9:11a—*The blood of my covenant* ratified the formal relationship between God and the people established on Mount Sinai (Exod. 24:8).

9:11b–12—The ***prisoners*** are in exile or captivity who will be released to return to Jerusalem. God's peace cannot be realized without the release of prisoners. God's kingdom supersedes all others.

9:13—The community is God's weapon and means for executing justice.

9:14–17 The Day of the LORD

9:14—God's theophany or appearance will rout all enemies. God, who fights to protect God's own, wages the battle.

the Lord God will sound the
　　trumpet
　　and march forth in the whirlwinds
　　　　of the south.
15 The Lord of hosts will protect them,
　　and they shall devour and tread
　　　　down the slingers;*a*
they shall drink their blood*b* like
　　wine,
　　and be full like a bowl,
　　drenched like the corners of the
　　　　altar.

16 On that day the Lord their God will
　　save them
　　for they are the flock of his people;
for like the jewels of a crown
　　they shall shine on his land.
17 For what goodness and beauty are
　　his!
　　Grain shall make the young men
　　　　flourish,
　　and new wine the young women.

Restoration of Judah and Israel

10 Ask rain from the Lord
　　in the season of the spring rain,
from the Lord who makes the storm
　　clouds,
　　who gives showers of rain to you,*c*
　　the vegetation in the field to
　　　　everyone.
2 For the teraphim*d* utter nonsense,
　　and the diviners see lies;
the dreamers tell false dreams,
　　and give empty consolation.
Therefore the people wander like
　　sheep;
　　they suffer for lack of a shepherd.

3 My anger is hot against the
　　shepherds,
　　and I will punish the leaders;*e*
for the Lord of hosts cares for his
　　flock, the house of Judah,
　　and will make them like his proud
　　　　war-horse.
4 Out of them shall come the
　　cornerstone,
　　out of them the tent peg,
out of them the battle bow,
　　out of them every commander.
5 Together they shall be like warriors
　　in battle,
　　trampling the foe in the mud of
　　　　the streets;
they shall fight, for the Lord is with
　　them,
　　and they shall put to shame the
　　　　riders on horses.

6 I will strengthen the house of Judah,
　　and I will save the house of
　　　　Joseph.
I will bring them back because I
　　have compassion on them,
　　and they shall be as though I had
　　　　not rejected them;
　　for I am the Lord their God and I
　　　　will answer them.
7 Then the people of Ephraim shall
　　become like warriors,
　　and their hearts shall be glad as
　　　　with wine.
Their children shall see it and
　　rejoice,

a Cn: Heb *the slingstones*　*b* Gk: Heb *shall drink*　*c* Heb *them*
d Or *household gods*　*e* Or *male goats*

10:1–12 The Lord as Provider, Shepherd, and Redeemer

10:1—Here, God is no warrior deity (contrast 9:1–12), but an agricultural provider who makes possible the earth's fertile abundance.

10:2—All manner of divination, from dream analysis to examining sheep entrails, proves delusional. The authors of Scripture found particularly abhorrent any attempt to discern God's will other than through prayer, worship, and the study of God's word (see Ps. 1). Divination is no guide.

10:3–5—As *shepherd*, God empowers Israel. God's people are not only frail sheep but empowered people for whatever challenge they will face from the principalities and powers that dominate the world.

10:6a—*Judah* and *Joseph*, the two *houses*, represent the former southern and northern kingdoms. Their juxtaposition signals a reunified Israel. The reconstitution of both houses attests the strength in unity.

10:6b–12—God's resolve to *gather* and *bring . . . home* the dispersed is not without political consequences: the superpowers *Assyria* and *Egypt* will be laid low.

their hearts shall exult in the
    LORD.

8 I will signal for them and gather
    them in,
    for I have redeemed them,
  and they shall be as numerous as
    they were before.
9 Though I scattered them among the
    nations,
  yet in far countries they shall
    remember me,
  and they shall rear their children
    and return.
10 I will bring them home from the
    land of Egypt,
  and gather them from Assyria;
I will bring them to the land of
    Gilead and to Lebanon,
  until there is no room for them.
11 They*a* shall pass through the sea of
    distress,
  and the waves of the sea shall be
    struck down,
  and all the depths of the Nile
    dried up.
The pride of Assyria shall be laid low,
  and the scepter of Egypt shall
    depart.
12 I will make them strong in the LORD,
  and they shall walk in his name,
         says the LORD.

11 Open your doors, O Lebanon,
    so that fire may devour your
    cedars!

2 Wail, O cypress, for the cedar has
    fallen,
  for the glorious trees are ruined!
Wail, oaks of Bashan,
  for the thick forest has been felled!
3 Listen, the wail of the shepherds,
  for their glory is despoiled!
Listen, the roar of the lions,
  for the thickets of the Jordan are
    destroyed!

Two Kinds of Shepherds

4 Thus said the LORD my God: Be a
shepherd of the flock doomed to slaughter. 5 Those who buy them kill them and
go unpunished; and those who sell them
say, "Blessed be the LORD, for I have
become rich"; and their own shepherds
have no pity on them. 6 For I will no longer have pity on the inhabitants of the
earth, says the LORD. I will cause them,
every one, to fall each into the hand of a
neighbor, and each into the hand of the
king; and they shall devastate the earth,
and I will deliver no one from their
hand.

7 So, on behalf of the sheep merchants, I became the shepherd of the
flock doomed to slaughter. I took two
staffs; one I named Favor, the other I
named Unity, and I tended the sheep.
8 In one month I disposed of the three
shepherds, for I had become impatient
with them, and they also detested me.

a Gk: Heb *He*

10:11—The language echoes the exodus account
(e.g., Exod. 14:21, 29; 15:8; Ps. 78:13).

11:1–3 The Razing of Lebanon

11:2—The land is called upon to lament the
destruction of its vast forest in order to make it
sustainable for habitation. Various trees, as well
as shepherds and lions, are commanded to voice
their laments in the face of imminent ecological
destruction by an increasing population. To be
sure, environmental destruction from overpopu-
lation is not critiqued by the ancient text. Rather,
the leveling of forests is seen as the unfortunate
but necessary consequence of the reestablishment of Israel's population after a long history of
depletion and exile. Nonetheless, the passage
gives voice to both plant and animal life. For
modern readers, the text invites shared lamenta-

tion over the rampant destruction of rain forests
and wildlife habitations.

11:4–17 Two Kinds of Shepherds

Owing to its vague language, this is one of the
most enigmatic passages in the entire Bible. It
may be a parable, allegory, or historical account.
In general, the prophet is appointed as leader
of the people, a *flock doomed*, but the mission
fails. God, in turn, punitively raises up a leader
that the people deserve—one who does not care
(v. 12).

11:5—The figure of *the shepherd* denotes a position of prophetic leadership among other leaders
(cf. 10:3).

11:7—The identity of the *sheep merchants*
remains obscure (temple priests?).

⁹ So I said, "I will not be your shepherd. What is to die, let it die; what is to be destroyed, let it be destroyed; and let those that are left devour the flesh of one another!" ¹⁰ I took my staff Favor and broke it, annulling the covenant that I had made with all the peoples. ¹¹ So it was annulled on that day, and the sheep merchants, who were watching me, knew that it was the word of the LORD. ¹² I then said to them, "If it seems right to you, give me my wages; but if not, keep them." So they weighed out as my wages thirty shekels of silver. ¹³ Then the LORD said to me, "Throw it into the treasury"*a*—this lordly price at which I was valued by them. So I took the thirty shekels of silver and threw them into the treasury*a* in the house of the LORD. ¹⁴ Then I broke my second staff Unity, annulling the family ties between Judah and Israel.

15 Then the LORD said to me: Take once more the implements of a worthless shepherd. ¹⁶ For I am now raising up in the land a shepherd who does not care for the perishing, or seek the wandering,*b* or heal the maimed, or nourish the healthy,*c* but devours the flesh of the fat ones, tearing off even their hoofs.

¹⁷   Oh, my worthless shepherd,
    who deserts the flock!
  May the sword strike his arm
    and his right eye!
  Let his arm be completely
    withered,
      his right eye utterly blinded!

Jerusalem's Victory

12   An Oracle.

The word of the LORD concerning Israel: Thus says the LORD, who stretched out the heavens and founded the earth and formed the human spirit within: ² See, I am about to make Jerusalem a cup of reeling for all the surrounding peoples; it will be against Judah also in the siege against Jerusalem. ³ On that day I will make Jerusalem a heavy stone for all the peoples; all who lift it shall grievously hurt themselves. And all the nations of the earth shall come together against it. ⁴ On that day, says the LORD, I will strike every horse with panic, and its rider with madness. But on the house of Judah I will keep a watchful eye, when I strike every horse of the peoples with blindness. ⁵ Then the clans of Judah shall say to themselves, "The inhabitants of Jerusalem have strength through the LORD of hosts, their God."

6 On that day I will make the clans of Judah like a blazing pot on a pile of wood, like a flaming torch among sheaves; and they shall devour to the right and to the left all the surrounding peoples, while Jerusalem shall again be inhabited in its place, in Jerusalem.

7 And the LORD will give victory to the tents of Judah first, that the glory of the house of David and the glory of the inhabitants of Jerusalem may not

---

a Syr: Heb *it to the potter*   *b* Syr Compare Gk Vg: Heb *the youth*   *c* Meaning of Heb uncertain

---

11:12—*Thirty shekels of silver* are paid by the sheep merchants for services rendered. Such a sum of money is identical to what was due a slave owner when an ox gored a slave (Exod. 21:32). It is not an inconsequential sum. However, the prophet is disdainful of being paid. He is instructed by God to deposit (?) the money into the temple treasury, perhaps to show that corruption has struck even the temple, the heart of Israel's religious life (see Matt. 26:14–16; 27:3–10).

11:16—*A shepherd who does not care* is a leader bent on destroying, rather than protecting, the flock. Though negative in tone, the passage

vividly outlines the duties of political leadership: to care for the most vulnerable and sick, and to *nourish the healthy*.

12:1–9 The Empowerment of Jerusalem

12:1—As creator of *the heavens*, *the earth*, and *the human spirit*, God has the power to protect Jerusalem from any attack.

12:2—The *cup of reeling* denotes divine judgment against the nations (cf. Ps. 75:8; Isa. 51:17–23; Jer. 25:15–28). Other literary figures employed in this passage to illustrate Jerusalem's vindication against its attackers are boulder (v. 3), *blazing pot* (v. 6), and flaming torch (v. 6).

be exalted over that of Judah. **8** On that day the LORD will shield the inhabitants of Jerusalem so that the feeblest among them on that day shall be like David, and the house of David shall be like God, like the angel of the LORD, at their head. **9** And on that day I will seek to destroy all the nations that come against Jerusalem.

Mourning for the Pierced One

10 And I will pour out a spirit of compassion and supplication on the house of David and the inhabitants of Jerusalem, so that, when they look on the one*a* whom they have pierced, they shall mourn for him, as one mourns for an only child, and weep bitterly over him, as one weeps over a firstborn. **11** On that day the mourning in Jerusalem will be as great as the mourning for Hadad-rimmon in the plain of Megiddo. **12** The land shall mourn, each family by itself; the family of the house of David by itself, and their wives by themselves; the family of the house of Nathan by itself, and their wives by themselves; **13** the family of the house of Levi by itself, and

their wives by themselves; the family of the Shimeites by itself, and their wives by themselves; **14** and all the families that are left, each by itself, and their wives by themselves.

13 On that day a fountain shall be opened for the house of David and the inhabitants of Jerusalem, to cleanse them from sin and impurity.

Idolatry Cut Off

2 On that day, says the LORD of hosts, I will cut off the names of the idols from the land, so that they shall be remembered no more; and also I will remove from the land the prophets and the unclean spirit. **3** And if any prophets appear again, their fathers and mothers who bore them will say to them, "You shall not live, for you speak lies in the name of the LORD"; and their fathers and their mothers who bore them shall pierce them through when they prophesy. **4** On that day the prophets will be ashamed, every one, of their visions when they prophesy; they will not put on a hairy mantle in order to deceive,

a Heb *on me*

12:8—Just as David was the youngest in the family of Jesse, yet became king of Israel (1 Sam. 16), so the weakest of Jerusalem's inhabitants will become the strongest. In God's providence, the least shall become the first.

12:10–14 A Day of Mourning

12:10—The day of vindication and victory is also a day of *compassion* and remorse. *One whom they have pierced*—The historical identity of this victim of violence remains unclear. Perhaps he was a prophet who had a hand in writing some of these passages (see 13:3) or was a member of the Davidic line. Israel's history was frequently marked by deep-seated conflicts between prophets and kings (Matt. 23:37). The prophets Elijah, Jeremiah, Micah of Moresheth (Jer. 26:18), and Uriah ben Shemaiah (Jer. 26:20–23) all suffered persecution for their unpopular or subversive messages. In the same vein, the New Testament writers identified this enigmatic figure with Jesus (John 19:37; Rev. 1:7). Regardless of specific of identity, the victim of violence is no longer faceless. By recognizing our own and God's face in the face of the victim, the cycle of violence is broken and restoration begins.

12:11 *Hadad-rimmon*—Although originally

the name of a fertility god of Canaan (a.k.a. Baal), the name came to be associated with a site of mourning for the good king Josiah, who was killed in conflict with Pharaoh Neco near Megiddo in 609 BCE (2 Kgs. 23:28–30; 2 Chr. 35:24–27).

13:1–6 Purging of Jerusalem and the End of Prophecy

13:1—The image of the *fountain* opens a vivid depiction of Jerusalem's purgation and restoration (see also 14:8). The fountain or river both cleanses and sustains life (cf. Ps. 46:4; Ezek. 47:1–12; Joel 3:18; John 4:13–14; 7:37–38; Rev. 22:1–2).

13:2—Along with the city's restoration is also a purging of (false) prophecy. Here, *prophets* are associated with an *unclean spirit*, and their removal from the land is compared with the destruction of idols. By the time of Second Zechariah (see introduction), prophecy had become associated with deception and apostasy (cf. Deut. 18:20–22; Jer. 28; 1 Kgs. 22:13–28; Ezek. 13:2–3).

13:4 *Hairy mantle*—The trademark of the prophetic guild (1 Kgs. 19:13, 19; 2 Kgs. 2:8, 13; Matt. 3:4).

5 but each of them will say, "I am no prophet, I am a tiller of the soil; for the land has been my possession[a] since my youth." 6 And if anyone asks them, "What are these wounds on your chest?"[b] the answer will be "The wounds I received in the house of my friends."

The Shepherd Struck, the Flock Scattered

7 "Awake, O sword, against my shepherd,
    against the man who is my
        associate,"
            says the LORD of hosts.
Strike the shepherd, that the sheep
    may be scattered;
    I will turn my hand against the
        little ones.
8 In the whole land, says the LORD,
    two-thirds shall be cut off and
        perish,
    and one-third shall be left alive.
9 And I will put this third into the fire,
    refine them as one refines silver,
    and test them as gold is tested.
They will call on my name,
    and I will answer them.
I will say, "They are my people";
    and they will say, "The LORD is our
        God."

Future Warfare and Final Victory

14 See, a day is coming for the LORD, when the plunder taken from you will be divided in your midst. 2 For I will gather all the nations against Jerusalem to battle, and the city shall be taken and the houses looted and the women raped; half the city shall go into exile, but the rest of the people shall not be cut off from the city. 3 Then the LORD will go forth and fight against those nations as when he fights on a day of battle. 4 On that day his feet shall stand on the Mount of Olives, which lies before Jerusalem on the east; and the Mount of Olives shall be split in two from east to west by a very wide valley; so that one half of the Mount shall withdraw northward, and the other half southward. 5 And you shall flee by the valley of the LORD's mountain,[c] for the valley between the mountains shall reach to Azal;[d] and you shall flee as you fled from the earthquake in the days of King Uzziah of Judah. Then the LORD my God will come, and all the holy ones with him.

6 On that day there shall not be[e] either

---

a Cn: Heb for humankind has caused me to possess   b Heb wounds between your hands   c Heb my mountains   d Meaning of Heb uncertain   e Cn: Heb there shall not be light

---

13:5—The prophets are compelled to renounce their profession (see Amos 7:14a).

13:7–9 Sword against Shepherd

13:7—God summons the *sword* to mortally wound *my shepherd* and *associate*, a ruler who has betrayed God and the people (cf. 11:15–17; Mark 14:27).

13:9 *This third*—The refined remnant of God's people who will embody the intimate, covenantal relationship with God (Exod. 6:7; Deut. 26:17–18). The dissolution of the leaderless flock will open the way to a new order and covenant with God.

14:1–5 The Final Battle

14:1—A vivid description of the day of the Lord (cf. Joel 1:15; Amos 5:18–20; Zeph. 1:14–18), in which the golden rays of restoration are preceded by the storm clouds of destruction. With the city conquered and plundered, God will fight on Jerusalem's behalf (Zech. 14:3), suggesting that only by defeat is true victory won. God's battle is to end all battles (see v. 11).

14:4 *Mount of Olives*—A ridge situated east of the city and separated from Jerusalem by the Kidron Valley, which forms the city's eastern boundary (see 2 Sam. 15:32). Ezekiel has the mountain in mind when he describes God's "glory" resting east of the city (Ezek. 11:23). It is evidently the location of Gethsemane, a grove on the west side of the mount where Jesus prayed before his trial and crucifixion (Matt. 26:30–46).

14:5 *Azal*—An unknown location. The rift in the mountains caused by the crushing weight of God's *feet* (v. 4; see Amos 4:13; Mic. 1:2–4) allows the people to escape from the city.

14:6–11 Restoration of the Land

14:6–7—The primal division between light and darkness, set at creation (Gen. 1:1–5), will be overcome *on that day*, a new creation in which both *night* and *cold* are dispelled by uninterrupted light. See Rev. 22:5, which identifies this everlasting light with the Lord God (cf. Ps. 104:1–2).

cold or frost.*a* *7* And there shall be continuous day (it is known to the LORD), not day and not night, for at evening time there shall be light.

8 On that day living waters shall flow out from Jerusalem, half of them to the eastern sea and half of them to the western sea; it shall continue in summer as in winter.

9 And the LORD will become king over all the earth; on that day the LORD will be one and his name one.

10 The whole land shall be turned into a plain from Geba to Rimmon south of Jerusalem. But Jerusalem shall remain aloft on its site from the Gate of Benjamin to the place of the former gate, to the Corner Gate, and from the Tower of Hananel to the king's wine presses. *11* And it shall be inhabited, for never again shall it be doomed to destruction; Jerusalem shall abide in security.

12 This shall be the plague with which the LORD will strike all the peoples that wage war against Jerusalem: their flesh shall rot while they are still on their feet; their eyes shall rot in their sockets, and their tongues shall rot in their mouths. *13* On that day a great panic from the LORD shall fall on them, so that each will seize the hand of a neighbor, and the hand of the one will be raised against the hand of the other; *14* even Judah will fight at Jerusalem. And the wealth of all the surrounding nations shall be collected—gold, silver, and garments in great abundance. *15* And a plague like this plague shall fall on the horses, the mules, the camels, the donkeys, and whatever animals may be in those camps.

16 Then all who survive of the nations that have come against Jerusalem shall go up year after year to worship the King, the LORD of hosts, and to keep the

a Compare Gk Syr Vg Tg: Meaning of Heb uncertain

14:8—Accompanying perpetual light are the perennial streams issuing from **Jerusalem** or Zion. Fertility, blessing, purity, and life all figure in this evocative image of abundant water flowing from the city of God (see 13:1; Gen. 2:10; Ezek. 47:1–12; John 4:7–15).

14:9—The Lord asserts divine sovereignty over the land and **will be one**. The language echoes the famous Shema: "Hear, O Israel: The LORD is our God, the LORD alone" (or "is one"; Deut. 6:4). The issue is not so much God's unity, which is assumed, as the undivided allegiance and respect to be afforded God on the day of victory and restoration. God will become the one and only object of the world's adoration and praise.

14:10 *Geba, Rimmon*—The town of Geba lies just north of Jerusalem; Rimmon's location is not certain but presumably lies south of Jerusalem. Together, they represent the full extent of Jerusalem's environs. The hill country in which Jerusalem is situated will be leveled, with the exception of the city itself. The Mount of Olives, earlier divided in half (v. 4), will also be rendered a plain. Unmatched in height and security, the city will stand in sharp relief, overlooking the land (see Isa. 2:2; Mic. 4:1). *Hananel*—Lit. "God is gracious." Situated somewhere in the northwest area of the Temple Mount (Neh. 3:1; 12:39; Jer. 31:38).

14:12–15 The Plague

14:12—This section picks up the events described in vv. 3–5. As a prelude to the city's restoration, Jerusalem's enemies will suffer a pandemic whose outcome is as swift as it is irrevocable against both humans and animals. The ancient Hebrews understood the outbreak of pestilence as divine punishment, as some quite erroneously do today regarding AIDS, for example. The character of Job, who himself suffered severely from illness but nonetheless retained his integrity and God's favor, counters such an assumption (Job 2:7–9; 27:1–6). In Zechariah, the *plague* serves as an instrument of punishment against the nations that have victimized Jerusalem.

14:16–19 The Global Remnant

14:16—As the nations would come up against Jerusalem to attack the city, so they will come to join the city's inhabitants in worship of God. In worship, reconciliation reigns, and hated enemies become friends (cf. Ps. 23:5–6). *Festival of booths*—One of three pilgrimage feasts (see also v. 18). Sometimes called the Festival of Ingathering or Tabernacles, this event occurred during the fall harvest period, traditionally five days after the Day of Atonement or Yom Kippur (Exod. 23:16; 34:22; Lev. 23:33–36; Deut. 16:13–15; 31:9–31). It is associated with the wilderness wanderings described in Exodus and Numbers. The booths themselves represent the temporary dwellings or lean-tos in which the Israelites lived during this time of transition. For the prophet, this festival becomes all-inclusive.

festival of booths.*a* *17* If any of the families of the earth do not go up to Jerusalem to worship the King, the LORD of hosts, there will be no rain upon them. *18* And if the family of Egypt do not go up and present themselves, then on them shall*b* come the plague that the LORD inflicts on the nations that do not go up to keep the festival of booths.*a* *19* Such shall be the punishment of Egypt and the punishment of all the nations that do not go up to keep the festival of booths.*a*

20 On that day there shall be inscribed

on the bells of the horses, "Holy to the LORD." And the cooking pots in the house of the LORD shall be as holy as*c* the bowls in front of the altar; *21* and every cooking pot in Jerusalem and Judah shall be sacred to the LORD of hosts, so that all who sacrifice may come and use them to boil the flesh of the sacrifice. And there shall no longer be traders*d* in the house of the LORD of hosts on that day.

a Or tabernacles; Heb succoth *b* Gk Syr: Heb shall not *c* Heb shall be like *d* Or Canaanites

14:20–21 Sanctification of the Ordinary

14:20—As the crowning mark of restoration, even the most mundane things will achieve consecrated, holy status, comparable to the holy furnishings of the temple. No longer will sacrifice be conducted within the precincts of the temple; now it can be conducted anywhere and everywhere. From *cooking pots* to horse *bells*, the realm of the holy has become all-inclusive. Holiness infuses the mundane (cf. Matt. 27:51).

14:21—*Traders* is the word for Canaanites in Hebrew. While the boundary between the holy and the profane is removed, the demands of holiness are by no means compromised. The prophet of Second Zechariah found reprehensible the practice of conducting business within the *house of the LORD*. (Cf. Christ's ejection of the money changers in Matt. 21:12–16; Mark 11:14–17; Luke 19:45–46; John 2:13–17.) More broadly, the prophet envisions a time in which holiness and justice become inextricably wedded.

The Book of
MALACHI

As the last book in the collection known as the Twelve Prophets in the Hebrew canon, Malachi is also the final book in the Old Testament Christian canon. The name Malachi means "my messenger," although it is not clear whether this is the author's proper name or merely a title taken from 3:1. The author's life is shrouded in obscurity except for what can be inferred from his message. The matters with which Malachi was primarily concerned place him somewhere in the first half of the fifth century BCE.

Whoever Malachi was historically, the book attributed to him suggests that he was a whistleblower of sorts. His words condemn the abuse of priestly power and corrupt worship. Given the book's dominant themes of sin, judgment, repentance, and the day of the Lord, Malachi has traditionally been considered a prophet. In light of his strong interests in the priesthood and sacrificial system, however, it is equally plausible to consider Malachi a priest. Moreover, the dividing line between these offices is not clear; he may very well have been a priestly prophet like Joel or a prophetic priest like Ezekiel. Whether as prophet or as priest or as something in between, Malachi is a boundary crosser. Moreover, he aligned himself with a particular priestly circle—the Levitical priesthood (2:4–6)—over and against a rival priesthood that had gained control over the temple after its completion about 515 BCE (Ezek. 40:45–45; 44:9–31).

This priestly prophet, however, does not limit his in-house address to members of the priesthood; he speaks to a general audience of disheartened people who question both the love and the justice of God (1:2; 2:17). He accuses his community of committing worship offenses, entering into mixed marriages, divorcing, and failing to tithe, and discerns behind these offenses a paralyzing ennui or apathy on the part of God's people (1:13). By calling both his priestly colleagues and the larger community to renewed fidelity to God's covenant, Malachi shows himself to be a reformer. Malachi's message thus extends far beyond his own historical situation. Though specifically addressing the bitter conflicts of his day, Malachi broaches larger issues of faith and justice, including the challenge of living out one's convictions amid the perennial temptation to compromise. When it comes to living the faith in the face of corrupting influences that seek to trivialize certain beliefs and practices, Malachi boldly states, "Here I stand!"

—**William P. Brown**

1
An oracle. The word of the LORD to Israel by Malachi.*a*

Israel Preferred to Edom

2 I have loved you, says the LORD. But you say, "How have you loved us?" Is not Esau Jacob's brother? says the LORD. Yet I have loved Jacob ³ but I have hated Esau; I have made his hill country a desolation and his heritage a desert for jackals. ⁴ If Edom says, "We are shattered but we will rebuild the ruins," the LORD of hosts says: They may build, but I will tear down, until they are called the wicked country, the people with whom the LORD is angry forever. ⁵ Your own eyes shall see this, and you shall say, "Great is the LORD beyond the borders of Israel!"

Corruption of the Priesthood

6 A son honors his father, and servants their master. If then I am a father, where is the honor due me? And if I am a master, where is the respect due me? says the LORD of hosts to you, O priests, who despise my name. You say, "How have we despised your name?" ⁷ By offering polluted food on my altar. And you say, "How have we polluted it?"*b* By thinking that the LORD's table may be despised. ⁸ When you offer blind animals in sacrifice, is that not wrong? And when you offer those that are lame or sick, is that not wrong? Try presenting that to your governor; will he be pleased with you or show you favor? says the LORD of hosts. ⁹ And now implore the favor of God, that he may be gracious to us. The fault is yours. Will he show favor to any of you? says the LORD of hosts. ¹⁰ Oh, that someone among you would shut the temple*c* doors, so that you would not kindle fire

a Or *by my messenger*   *b* Gk: Heb *you*   *c* Heb lacks *temple*

1:1 Superscription

1:1 *Oracle*—Lit. "burden" in Hebrew. This term signifies a prophetic message of a judgmental nature (cf. Nah. 1:1; Zech. 9:1; Isa. 13:1; Jer. 23:33–38). Malachi's audience is all of Israel.

1:2–5 God's Preferential Love for Israel

1:2—*Esau* is the father figure of Edom, Israel's neighbor and "twin brother." Unlike Hosea, who employs the language of the exodus to illustrate God's compassion for Israel (Hos. 11:1), Malachi draws from the so-called patriarchal tradition concerning Isaac's two sons (Gen. 25:19–34; 27:1–45; 32:1–33:20; 36:1–43). *Jacob*, the younger of the two, was chosen by God over Esau. The family story of Jacob's reception of his father's blessing to the exclusion of Esau points to the historical establishment of Israel over and against its neighbors, in particular Edom. Located southeast of Palestine, Edom was a constant source of conflict throughout Israel's turbulent history (see Obad. 11–14, in contrast to the fraternal reconciliation depicted in Gen. 33:1–17).

1:3—Malachi employs the language of love and hatred to set in sharp relief God's preferential kindness toward Israel. God's yes to Israel involves a no to Edom. To modern readers, this sounds scandalously unfair: God is playing favorites. The scandal of the divine no is matched by the mystery of the God's gratuitous yes. Without the no, the yes loses all force. It is also worth noting that Malachi is not entering into a dispute with Edom over who is God's favorite; the prophet's assertion of God's exclusive love for Israel is set within an *internal* dispute between the prophet and those who question whether God loves *at all*. Malachi's contention is *not* with the Edomites, but with his own people. In the face of widespread disillusionment, the prophet reminds his people of who they are, the object of God's love.

1:5—God is not just the God of Israel, but also the Lord of the nations.

1:6–14 Priestly Misconduct

1:6—Malachi now addresses the *priests* who conduct temple sacrifices. What follows is an indictment that leads to judgment in chap. 2. In connection with worship, the *name* of the Lord is a manifestation of divine presence (Deut. 12:5; 26:15; 1 Kgs. 8:27–30, 43, 48–49). To despise the name, hence, is to violate the integrity of worship by profaning God's holiness (Lev. 18:21).

1:7—Malachi indicts his colleague priests for compromising their office by offering animals that are *blind*, *lame*, *sick*, and blemished, in violation of the sacrificial code (Lev. 22:20–22). Offering unfit animals marked a violation of sacred space and an affront to God's holiness. Not offering to God one's best bespeaks a lack of conviction over God's self-investment in a people.

1:8—Malachi suggests that by carelessly offering *polluted food* at the Lord's table (or *altar*) the priests show greater deference to their *governor*, a provincial administrator of a foreign empire (Persia), than to the Lord! The priests, unwittingly,

on my altar in vain! I have no pleasure in you, says the LORD of hosts, and I will not accept an offering from your hands. [11] For from the rising of the sun to its setting my name is great among the nations, and in every place incense is offered to my name, and a pure offering; for my name is great among the nations, says the LORD of hosts. [12] But you profane it when you say that the Lord's table is polluted, and the food for it[a] may be despised. [13] "What a weariness this is," you say, and you sniff at me,[b] says the LORD of hosts. You bring what has been taken by violence or is lame or sick, and this you bring as your offering! Shall I accept that from your hand? says the LORD. [14] Cursed be the cheat who has a male in the flock and vows to give it, and yet sacrifices to the Lord what is blemished; for I am a great King, says the LORD of hosts, and my name is reverenced among the nations.

2 And now, O priests, this command is for you. [2] If you will not listen, if you will not lay it to heart to give glory to my name, says the LORD of hosts, then I will send the curse on you and I will curse your blessings; indeed I have already cursed them,[c] because you do not lay it to heart. [3] I will rebuke your offspring, and spread dung on your faces, the dung of your offerings, and I will put you out of my presence.[d]

[4] Know, then, that I have sent this command to you, that my covenant with Levi may hold, says the LORD of hosts. [5] My covenant with him was a covenant of life and well-being, which I gave him; this called for reverence, and he revered me and stood in awe of my name. [6] True instruction was in his mouth, and no wrong was found on his lips. He walked with me in integrity and uprightness, and he turned many from iniquity. [7] For the lips of a priest should guard knowledge, and people should seek instruction from his mouth, for he is the messenger of the LORD of hosts. [8] But you have turned aside from the way; you have caused many to stumble by your instruction; you have corrupted the covenant of Levi, says the LORD of hosts, [9] and so I make you despised and abased before all the people, inasmuch as you have not kept my ways but have shown partiality in your instruction.

The Covenant Profaned by Judah

10 Have we not all one father? Has not one God created us? Why then are

---

[a] Compare Syr Tg: Heb *its fruit, its food*   [b] Another reading is *at it*   [c] Heb *it*
[d] Cn Compare Gk Syr: Heb *and he shall bear you to it*

---

have allowed the state to compromise the exercise of their priestly office.

1:13—The priests complain of the tiresome chores of worship. Afflicted with boredom, they denigrate the priestly office by their lack of interest in their sacred responsibilities. They simply go through the motions and *sniff* at God in indignation. To Malachi, this "why bother?" attitude is more than laziness; it is an abomination.

1:14—The height of irony: God's name is reverently honored *among the nations* while profaned at home.

2:1–9 The Failure of the Priesthood

2:4—The third son of Jacob (Gen. 29:34), Levi became the tribe that was never allocated territory because it was singularly chosen to serve God as priests (Josh. 18:7). The *covenant with Levi* (see also v. 8) represents God's promise of an enduring priestly house (Num. 25:12; Jer. 34:21–22). By tradition, the Levites were renowned for their zeal for God, having aligned

themselves with Moses against even their kin after the golden calf episode (Exod. 32:25–29; Deut. 33:8–11). It is such zeal that Malachi finds entirely lacking among his priestly colleagues.

2:7–9—See Deut. 33:9b–10 and Hos. 4:4–6, which describe the priesthood as the repository of the knowledge of God. The priests are teachers as well as worship leaders. In addition to the abuse of sacrifice, Malachi accuses his colleagues of imparting false instructions, in particular of showing partiality, in strict violation of covenantal practice (see Lev. 10:11; Deut. 21:5). The prophet considers teaching to be a vocation of grave responsibility.

2:10–16 Unity in Marriage and God

2:10 *One father*—God (see also Deut. 32:6). Malachi appeals to *all* Israelites by highlighting their common theological heritage. To acknowledge God as creator is also to recognize the unity of community, grounded in God. The oneness of God is acknowledged by the oneness

we faithless to one another, profaning the covenant of our ancestors? [11] Judah has been faithless, and abomination has been committed in Israel and in Jerusalem; for Judah has profaned the sanctuary of the LORD, which he loves, and has married the daughter of a foreign god. [12] May the LORD cut off from the tents of Jacob anyone who does this—any to witness[a] or answer, or to bring an offering to the LORD of hosts.

13 And this you do as well: You cover the LORD's altar with tears, with weeping and groaning because he no longer regards the offering or accepts it with favor at your hand. [14] You ask, "Why does he not?" Because the LORD was a witness between you and the wife of your youth, to whom you have been faithless, though she is your companion and your wife by covenant. [15] Did not one God make her?[b] Both flesh and spirit are his.[c] And what does the one God[d] desire? Godly off-

spring. So look to yourselves, and do not let anyone be faithless to the wife of his youth. [16] For I hate[e] divorce, says the LORD, the God of Israel, and covering one's garment with violence, says the LORD of hosts. So take heed to yourselves and do not be faithless.

17 You have wearied the LORD with your words. Yet you say, "How have we wearied him?" By saying, "All who do evil are good in the sight of the LORD, and he delights in them." Or by asking, "Where is the God of justice?"

The Coming Messenger

3 See, I am sending my messenger to prepare the way before me, and the Lord whom you seek will suddenly come to his temple. The messenger of the covenant in whom you delight— indeed, he is coming, says the LORD of hosts. [2] But who can endure the day of

[a] Cn Compare Gk: Heb *arouse*   [b] Or *Has he not made one?*   [c] Cn: Heb *and a remnant of spirit was his*   [d] Heb *he*   [e] Cn: Heb *he hates*

---

of community. Dissension and faithlessness, in effect, renounce God's oneness. Malachi moves from this general perspective to the unity of marriage (vv. 14–16).

2:11—*Daughter of a foreign god* refers to a foreign woman. To sever the bond of marriage not only violates the marriage covenant (v. 14b; cf. Gen. 2:24; Prov. 2:17), but also profanes *the* covenant, the bond between God and Israel, thereby fracturing the unity of Israel's identity uniquely grounded in the Creator. To acknowledge God's unity is to work for comm*un*ity, whose most intimate and basic form is marriage.

2:14 *Wife of your youth*—Malachi accuses his people of divorcing their spouses *by covenant* in order to marry foreigners for political or economic gain.

2:16 *Violence*—To highlight the gravity of the situation, Malachi sets *divorce* and violence side by side. His appeal is based on both humane and theological grounds. Faithlessness to one's spouse constitutes nothing less than a violation of God's solidarity with humankind, a breach that inevitably finds its way to the altar (v. 13).

2:17–3:5 "Where Is the God of Justice?"

2:17—The people are accused of taxing God with their complaints (not doubts!) concerning the lack of divine justice in the world. Although questions about God's justice in the face of evil and suffering (questions of theodicy) have their

place in biblical faith (e.g., Job 21:7–16; Jer. 12:1; Hab. 1:2, 4, 13), Malachi regards them as insincere, for they serve to cover or rationalize the people's offenses. Malachi's previous indictments against the priests and people nowhere imply that they themselves are suffering. To the contrary, they are profiting from new sexual liaisons, lax priestly standards, and showing partiality in judgment. To complain of injustice on the part of God, thus, is the height of hypocrisy.

3:1—In response to the questions posed in 2:17, Malachi heralds the Lord's coming. The messenger (see introduction and 1:1), whose identity is not divulged (cf. 4:5), is to prepare the way for the Lord's coming into the *temple* (cf. Isa. 6).

3:2—*Refiner's fire* and *fullers' soap* are powerful images in Malachi's pronouncement of judgment. A fuller bleaches and dyes cloth by first washing it with lye and cleansing it by stamping. Equal in severity to the fuller's actions, the refiner uses a blast oven to melt the metal into a liquid stage before removing the dross. Analogously, such extreme measures on the part of God or God's messenger are intended to purify the priestly class of Levi, transforming the very character of the one who makes an offering to the Lord. For Malachi, the integrity of worship begins with the character of the worshiping community, made whole by God. God's judgment thus is meant to cleanse and transform the community, not destroy it.

his coming, and who can stand when he appears?

For he is like a refiner's fire and like fullers' soap; [3] he will sit as a refiner and purifier of silver, and he will purify the descendants of Levi and refine them like gold and silver, until they present offerings to the Lord in righteousness.[a] [4] Then the offering of Judah and Jerusalem will be pleasing to the Lord as in the days of old and as in former years.

5 Then I will draw near to you for judgment; I will be swift to bear witness against the sorcerers, against the adulterers, against those who swear falsely, against those who oppress the hired workers in their wages, the widow and the orphan, against those who thrust aside the alien, and do not fear me, says the Lord of hosts.

6 For I the Lord do not change; therefore you, O children of Jacob, have not perished. [7] Ever since the days of your ancestors you have turned aside from my statutes and have not kept them. Return to me, and I will return to you, says the Lord of hosts. But you say, "How shall we return?"

Do Not Rob God

8 Will anyone rob God? Yet you are robbing me! But you say, "How are we robbing you?" In your tithes and offerings! [9] You are cursed with a curse, for you are robbing me—the whole nation of you! [10] Bring the full tithe into the storehouse, so that there may be food in my house, and thus put me to the test, says the Lord of hosts; see if I will not open the windows of heaven for you and pour down for you an overflowing blessing. [11] I will rebuke the locust[b] for you, so that it will not destroy the produce of your soil; and your vine in the field shall not be barren, says the Lord of hosts. [12] Then all nations will count you happy, for you will be a land of delight, says the Lord of hosts.

13 You have spoken harsh words against me, says the Lord. Yet you say, "How have we spoken against you?" [14] You have said, "It is vain to serve God. What do we profit by keeping his command or by going about as mourners before the Lord of hosts? [15] Now we count the arrogant happy; evildoers not only prosper, but when they put God to the test they escape."

[a] Or right offerings to the Lord [b] Heb devourer

3:5—God's judgment includes all of society. The effects of insincere and false worship against which Malachi railed in 1:7–14 have spread over the entire community. Like his prophetic predecessors, Malachi considers worship and justice, particularly in behalf of the most vulnerable in society, to be inseparably related. Worship is inauthentic—indeed, offensive to God—unless it seeks justice for the *widow*, *orphan*, and *alien* (see also 1:23; Jer. 7:5–10; Ezek. 22:7–13; Amos 5:21–24; Zech. 7:9–10). As the community gathers for worship, so it must also disperse to serve the world and call for justice.

3:6–12 The Blessings of Obedience

3:6—Malachi is not interested in philosophical speculation about divine immutability. God's unchangeableness for the prophet is tied directly to God's reliability and unwavering justice (see 2:17). The corollary is Israel's perpetual preservation.

3:8—Withholding tithes and offerings from the temple amounts to "robbing" God. As creator, God's ownership of all is acknowledged in the giving of tithes and offerings (see Ps. 50:12). As

in 1:7, Malachi demands that the people offer their best to the God who has given them life and identity.

3:10—The *tithe* is a tenth of all agricultural produce dedicated for sacral purposes (Lev. 27:30–33; Num. 18:21–24; Deut. 14:28–29). Israel is challenged to *test* the Lord to determine the extent to which God is able to provide for their well-being. Depending on the people's response, God promises to bring about the fertility of the land (Hag. 1:9–11; 2:15–19). Offering the tithe thus sets the occasion for abundant blessing, for greater giving on God's part. On giving a mere portion of one's livelihood rests the livelihood of the whole community.

3:13–4:3 The Book of Remembrance

3:14—Why serve God if one does not gain anything in doing so? What's the point of serving God? Such questions strike at the heart and source of human recalcitrance. Malachi finds them dangerous and absurd, for they reduce ethics, which according to the prophet should be God-centered, to the level of self-interest.

The Reward of the Faithful

16 Then those who revered the LORD spoke with one another. The LORD took note and listened, and a book of remembrance was written before him of those who revered the LORD and thought on his name. ¹⁷They shall be mine, says the LORD of hosts, my special possession on the day when I act, and I will spare them as parents spare their children who serve them. ¹⁸Then once more you shall see the difference between the righteous and the wicked, between one who serves God and one who does not serve him.

The Great Day of the LORD

4 ᵃSee, the day is coming, burning like an oven, when all the arrogant and all evildoers will be stubble; the day that comes shall burn them up, says the LORD of hosts, so that it will leave them neither root nor branch. ²But for you who revere my name the sun of righteousness shall rise, with healing in its wings. You shall go out leaping like calves from the stall. ³And you shall tread down the wicked, for they will be ashes under the soles of your feet, on the day when I act, says the LORD of hosts.

4 Remember the teaching of my servant Moses, the statutes and ordinances that I commanded him at Horeb for all Israel.

5 Lo, I will send you the prophet Elijah before the great and terrible day of the LORD comes. ⁶He will turn the hearts of parents to their children and the hearts of children to their parents, so that I will not come and strike the land with a curse.ᵇ

ᵃCh 4.1-6 are Ch 3.19-24 in Heb   ᵇOr a ban of utter destruction

---

3:16—God listens in on the discourse of the faithful and records their names on a heavenly scroll, the *book of remembrance* (see Exod. 32:32–33; Pss. 69:28; 87:6; Isa. 4:3; Dan. 12:1; Rev. 20:12, 15). Those in the book constitute God's *special possession* (Exod. 19:5; Deut. 7:6; 14:23; 26:18; Ps. 135:4). The book is kept on the shelf, as it were, until it is opened on the day when God decides to act, thereby preserving the distinction between those who serve God and those who refuse to do so.

4:2—The image of the winged sun-disk was a common motif in ancient Near East pictures from Egypt to Mesopotamia. As much as God's day is one of searing judgment for the wicked, it is a day of healing warmth for the righteous. The rising of the sun ushers in vindication for the righteous and a reestablishment of justice that is nothing short of cosmic in scope (Job 38:12–13; Ps. 46:5).

4:4–6 The Past as Key to the Future: Two Appendices

4:4—*Horeb* is also known as Sinai, where Moses received the laws that constitute covenantal *teaching* or *torah* (Deut. 5:1–5). This verse serves as a conclusion to the entire collection of prophetic writings (Former Prophets and Latter Prophets), whose beginning is found in Josh. 1:1–2.

4:5—This second postscript (vv. 5–6) identifies *Elijah* as the messenger referred to in 3:1. Since Elijah, according to tradition, was taken up to heaven by a chariot of fire with no mention of his death (2 Kgs. 2:10–12), Elijah could return to earth to usher in a new age (see Matt. 11:7–15; 17:10–13; Mark 6:14–16; Luke 1:17). With a focus on the family, Malachi concludes on a hopeful, harmonious note. The wounds within family and community are bound up. Reconciled are the warring factions both at home and throughout the land. As the Old Testament began with a dysfunctional family (Gen. 3–4), so it concludes (in the Protestant canon) with the promise of reconciliation and healing within the family.

APOCRYPHA

THE APOCRYPHAL/DEUTEROCANONICAL
BOOKS OF THE OLD TESTAMENT

New Revised Standard Version

The Book of
TOBIT

The book of Tobit is a delightful tale that combines a compelling plot and light-hearted moments with a serious message that centers on fidelity to God's teachings in the face of life's troubles. Like the book of Job, the story takes place in the Diaspora, that is, outside of Israel, and the plot focuses on the classic problem of the suffering of the righteous. Tobit is a model faithful Israelite (1:3), who does God's will by feeding the hungry, clothing the naked, and risking his life to bury the dead in defiance of an unjust edict (1:17–19; 2:8). Tobit is punished for following God's law when the ruler confiscates all of his possessions (1:20). Left with nothing, Tobit sends his son Tobias on a dangerous journey to retrieve money in a faraway land (6:2–11:6). Tobit becomes blind (2:9–10), his future daughter-in-law Sarah's seven husbands are murdered by a jealous demon (3:7–8), and it is feared that Tobias will not return home (5:18; 6:15; 10:7).

The tale has much to say about discipleship. As Deuteronomy 8:5–6 enjoins, Tobit instructs Tobias in how to be a faithful Israelite (4:3–19; 14:8–11), imparting wisdom that has parallels in Old Testament Wisdom literature (Proverbs and Sirach) and in Jesus' instructions to his disciples in the New Testament. Tobias receives further wisdom instructions from his traveling companion Azariah, the angel Raphael in disguise, whom God has sent to help bring about the return of Tobit and the restoration of Sarah to well-being. The story presents discipleship as devotion to God's law and maintaining group identity within Israel (family, clan, tribe) in the face of adversity, particularly the threat of assimilation into Gentile culture. The strong social value placed on the group is affirmed in the story by the recurrence of kinship language (e.g., "brother," "sister") and by the strong ethical admonitions rooted in the Torah, particularly in the book of Deuteronomy. Thus Tobit reminds Tobias of his duty to honor his parents in life and with proper burial; to marry a kinswoman from within the group (endogamy); and to perform deeds of social justice, alert to the needs of fellow covenant members. Ultimately obedience to the law is rewarded in accordance with the law.

The book of Tobit was probably written in Aramaic. Five fragmentary copies of the book were discovered in the mid-twentieth century among the Dead Sea Scrolls of Qumran, four in Aramaic and one in Hebrew. The work was composed anonymously in the Diaspora around the fourth or third century BCE. The oldest complete forms of the book are in Greek. There are three main Greek recensions: a short form (GI), found in Codices Vaticanus and Alexandrinus (translated in the RSV); a long recension (GII), represented by Codex Sinaiticus; and an intermediate form of the story (GIII) that is a composite of the other two. The long recension, translated here in the NRSV, is considered the earliest Greek form of the story; it corresponds substantially to the Qumran fragments. This long form of Tobit has two gaps (4:7–19 and 13:8–10) that are filled primarily through the Old Latin and other Greek witnesses.

Much loved in Christian history, the story takes on yet another form in Jerome's

free Latin rendering that adds, among other insertions, three nights of prayer and abstinence to Tobias and Sarah's wedding night. (Douay-Rheims contains a translation of this Vulgate form of the story.) There are also medieval Aramaic and Hebrew versions that provide additional variants and attest to the appreciation of this tale throughout much of Jewish history.

—Vincent Skemp

1 This book tells the story of Tobit son of Tobiel son of Hananiel son of Aduel son of Gabael son of Raphael son of Raguel of the descendants[a] of Asiel, of the tribe of Naphtali, ²who in the days of King Shalmaneser[b] of the Assyrians was taken into captivity from Thisbe, which is to the south of Kedesh Naphtali in Upper Galilee, above Asher toward the west, and north of Phogor.

Tobit's Youth and Virtuous Life

3 I, Tobit, walked in the ways of truth and righteousness all the days of my life. I performed many acts of charity for my kindred and my people who had gone with me in exile to Nineveh in the land of the Assyrians. ⁴When I was in my own country, in the land of Israel, while I was still a young man, the whole tribe of my ancestor Naphtali deserted the house of David and Jerusalem. This city had been chosen from among all the tribes of Israel, where all the tribes of Israel should offer sacrifice and where the temple, the dwelling of God, had been consecrated and established for all generations forever.

5 All my kindred and our ancestral house of Naphtali sacrificed to the calf[c]

that King Jeroboam of Israel had erected in Dan and on all the mountains of Galilee. ⁶But I alone went often to Jerusalem for the festivals, as it is prescribed for all Israel by an everlasting decree. I would hurry off to Jerusalem with the first fruits of the crops and the firstlings of the flock, the tithes of the cattle, and the first shearings of the sheep. ⁷I would give these to the priests, the sons of Aaron, at the altar; likewise the tenth of the grain, wine, olive oil, pomegranates, figs, and the rest of the fruits to the sons of Levi who ministered at Jerusalem. Also for six years I would save up a second tenth in money and go and distribute it in Jerusalem. ⁸A third tenth[d] I would give to the orphans and widows and to the converts who had attached themselves to Israel. I would bring it and give it to them in the third year, and we would eat it according to the ordinance decreed concerning it in the law of Moses and according to the instructions of Deborah, the mother of my father Tobiel,[e] for my father had died and left me an orphan. ⁹When I became a man I mar-

a Other ancient authorities lack of Raphael son of Raguel of the descendants   b Gk Enemessaros   c Other ancient authorities read heifer   d A third tenth added from other ancient authorities   e Lat: Gk Hananiel

---

1:1—The book opens with a genealogy to establish Tobit's family honor.

1:2 *Shalmaneser*—Shalmaneser V was king of the Assyrians (727–722 BCE), the superpower of the ancient Near East at that time. According to 2 Kgs. 15:29 it was Shalmaneser's father, Tiglath-pileser III (745–727) who first conquered much of the northern kingdom, deporting many of the people to Assyria around 732. Further deportations occurred when Shalmaneser led another conquest of northern Israel (2 Kgs. 17:3–23), which was continued by his successor Sargon II (722–705).

1:3 *Truth and righteousness . . . acts of char-*

ity—The description of Tobit's conduct forms a literary bracket with 14:9.

1:6 *Everlasting decree*—To worship the God of Israel in *Jerusalem* (Deut. 12:4–7, 11–14). The faithful Tobit would make the journey to the pilgrim festivals in Jerusalem (Deut. 16:16–17) rather than worship at the cultic sites set up by Jeroboam in Dan and Bethel in the northern kingdom (1 Kgs. 12:26–33).

1:9 *A member of our own family*—Like the patriarchs (Gen. 24:7, 37–38; 28:1–9; 29:19), Tobit practices endogamy, i.e., intratribal marriage (cf. Num. 36:3–9; Jdt. 8:2), and teaches Tobias to do likewise (Tob. 4:12–13).

ried a woman,[a] a member of our own family, and by her I became the father of a son whom I named Tobias.

Taken Captive to Nineveh

10 After I was carried away captive to Assyria and came as a captive to Nineveh, everyone of my kindred and my people ate the food of the Gentiles, [11] but I kept myself from eating the food of the Gentiles. [12] Because I was mindful of God with all my heart, [13] the Most High gave me favor and good standing with Shalmaneser,[b] and I used to buy everything he needed. [14] Until his death I used to go into Media, and buy for him there. While in the country of Media I left bags of silver worth ten talents in trust with Gabael, the brother of Gabri. [15] But when Shalmaneser[b] died, and his son Sennacherib reigned in his place, the highways into Media became unsafe and I could no longer go there.

Courage in Burying the Dead

16 In the days of Shalmaneser[b] I performed many acts of charity to my kindred, those of my tribe. [17] I would give my food to the hungry and my clothing to the naked; and if I saw the dead body of any of my people thrown out behind the wall of Nineveh, I would bury it. [18] I also buried any whom King Sennacherib put to death when he came fleeing from Judea in those days of judgment that the king of heaven executed upon him because of his blasphemies. For in his anger he put to death many Israelites; but I would secretly remove the bodies and bury them. So when Sennacherib looked for them he could not find them. [19] Then one of the Ninevites went and informed the king about me, that I was burying them; so I hid myself. But when I realized that the king knew about me and that I was being searched for to be put to death, I was afraid and ran away. [20] Then all my property was confiscated; nothing was left to me that was not taken into the royal treasury except my wife Anna and my son Tobias.

21 But not forty[c] days passed before two of Sennacherib's[d] sons killed him, and they fled to the mountains of Ararat, and his son Esar-haddon[e] reigned after him. He appointed Ahikar, the son of my brother Hanael[f] over all the accounts of his kingdom, and he had authority over the entire administration. [22] Ahikar interceded for me, and I returned to Nineveh. Now Ahikar was chief cupbearer, keeper of the signet, and in charge of administration of the accounts under King Sennacherib of Assyria; so Esar-haddon[e] reappointed him. He was my nephew and so a close relative.

[a] Other ancient authorities add *Anna* [b] Gk *Enemessaros* [c] Other ancient authorities read either *forty-five* or *fifty* [d] Gk *his* [e] Gk *Sacherdonos* [f] Other authorities read *Hananael*

1:10—*Nineveh* was the capital of the Assyrian Empire.

1:11 *Food of the Gentiles*—Tobit's special concern to follow Torah dietary teachings, despite the difficulties of doing so in a Gentile setting, is a value shared by Daniel and his companions (Dan. 1:8–16), Judith (Jdt. 10:5; 12:1–3), Esther (Esth. 14:17), and many early Jewish Christians (Acts 10:13–14; 15:20–21, 29; 21:25; cf. Matt. 15:10–20; Rom. 14:14–20; 1 Cor. 8:1–13; 10:23–33; 1 Tim. 4:2–4; Rev. 2:20).

1:14 *Media*—In the northwest area of modern Iran. At the time of the Tobit story, Media was part of the Assyrian Empire and the location of an Israelite settlement (2 Kgs. 17:6). *Bags of silver*—The money Tobit leaves in trust to his kinsman Gabael drives the story's plot: Tobit will send Tobias to retrieve the money; on the journey Tobias will acquire the fish entrails that will cure his father's blindness (2:10) and dispel the demon afflicting Sarah so that he can marry her (e.g., 3:7–9).

1:17—Tobit's acts of righteousness, giving *food to the hungry* and *clothing to the naked*, are covenant values found in Deut. 10:18; Isa. 58:7; Ezek. 18:7,16; and Matt. 25:35. Proper burial of the dead is a major motif in the story (Tob. 2:3–8; 4:3–4; 6:15; 8:12; 14:10–13). Corpse exposure would have been seen as indicating the utter depravity of the governing authorities in their hostility toward the legal and moral necessity of honorable burial (Gen. 23:4–20; Deut. 21:23; *b. Megillah* 3b). Remaining unburied was among the curses for covenant disobedience (Deut. 28:26) and is the shameful end of God's enemies in 1 QM 11:1 and Rev. 19:17–21.

2 Then during the reign of Esar-haddon[a] I returned home, and my wife Anna and my son Tobias were restored to me. At our festival of Pentecost, which is the sacred festival of weeks, a good dinner was prepared for me and I reclined to eat. [2] When the table was set for me and an abundance of food placed before me, I said to my son Tobias, "Go, my child, and bring whatever poor person you may find of our people among the exiles in Nineveh, who is wholeheartedly mindful of God,[b] and he shall eat together with me. I will wait for you, until you come back." [3] So Tobias went to look for some poor person of our people. When he had returned he said, "Father!" And I replied, "Here I am, my child." Then he went on to say, "Look, father, one of our own people has been murdered and thrown into the market place, and now he lies there strangled." [4] Then I sprang up, left the dinner before even tasting it, and removed the body[c] from the square[d] and laid it[c] in one of the rooms until sunset when I might bury it.[c] [5] When I returned, I washed myself and ate my food in sorrow. [6] Then I remembered the prophecy of Amos, how he said against Bethel,[e]

> "Your festivals shall be turned into mourning,
> and all your songs into lamentation."

And I wept.

Tobit Becomes Blind

[7] When the sun had set, I went and dug a grave and buried him. [8] And my neighbors laughed and said, "Is he still not afraid? He has already been hunted down to be put to death for doing this, and he ran away; yet here he is again burying the dead!" [9] That same night I washed myself and went into my courtyard and slept by the wall of the courtyard; and my face was uncovered because of the heat. [10] I did not know that there were sparrows on the wall; their fresh droppings fell into my eyes and produced white films. I went to physicians to be healed, but the more they treated me with ointments the more my vision was obscured by the white films, until I became completely blind. For four years I remained unable to see. All my kindred were sorry for me, and Ahikar took care of me for two years before he went to Elymais.

Tobit's Wife Earns Their Livelihood

[11] At that time, also, my wife Anna earned money at women's work. [12] She used to send what she made to the owners and they would pay wages to her. One day, the seventh of Dystrus, when she cut off a piece she had woven and sent it to the owners, they paid her full wages and also gave her a young goat for a meal. [13] When she returned to me, the goat began to bleat. So I called her and said, "Where did you get this goat? It is surely not stolen, is it? Return it to the owners; for we have no right to eat anything stolen." [14] But she said to me, "It was given to me as a gift in addition to my wages." But I did not believe her, and told her to return it to the owners. I became flushed with anger against her over this. Then she replied to me, "Where are your acts of charity? Where are your righteous deeds? These things are known about you!"[f]

Tobit's Prayer

3 Then with much grief and anguish of heart I wept, and with groaning began to pray:
[2] "You are righteous, O Lord,
  and all your deeds are just;
 all your ways are mercy and truth;
  you judge the world.[g]
[3] And now, O Lord, remember me

[a] Gk *Sacherdonos* [b] Lat: Gk *wholeheartedly mindful* [c] Gk *him* [d] Other ancient authorities lack *from the square* [e] Other ancient authorities read *against Bethlehem* [f] Or *to you;* Gk *with you* [g] Other ancient authorities read *you render true and righteous judgment forever*

2:2 *Whatever poor person*—Concern for the poor, particularly via almsgiving, is a major motif of the story (1:3, 8; 4:7–11, 16–17; 12:8–9; 14:8–11).

and look favorably upon me.
Do not punish me for my sins
and for my unwitting offenses
and those that my ancestors
committed before you.
They sinned against you,
4 and disobeyed your commandments.
So you gave us over to plunder, exile,
and death,
to become the talk, the byword,
and an object of reproach
among all the nations among
whom you have dispersed us.
5 And now your many judgments are
true
in exacting penalty from me for
my sins.
For we have not kept your
commandments
and have not walked in accordance
with truth before you.
6 So now deal with me as you will;
command my spirit to be taken
from me,
so that I may be released from the
face of the earth and become
dust.
For it is better for me to die than to
live,
because I have had to listen to
undeserved insults,
and great is the sorrow within me.
Command, O Lord, that I be
released from this distress;
release me to go to the eternal
home,
and do not, O Lord, turn your face
away from me.
For it is better for me to die
than to see so much distress in my
life
and to listen to insults."

Sarah Falsely Accused

7 On the same day, at Ecbatana in
Media, it also happened that Sarah, the
daughter of Raguel, was reproached by
one of her father's maids. 8 For she had
been married to seven husbands, and
the wicked demon Asmodeus had killed

each of them before they had been
with her as is customary for wives. So
the maid said to her, "You are the one
who kills*a* your husbands! See, you have
already been married to seven husbands
and have not borne the name of*b* a single one of them. 9 Why do you beat us?
Because your husbands are dead? Go
with them! May we never see a son or
daughter of yours!"

Sarah's Prayer for Death

10 On that day she was grieved in
spirit and wept. When she had gone up
to her father's upper room, she intended
to hang herself. But she thought it over
and said, "Never shall they reproach my
father, saying to him, 'You had only one
beloved daughter but she hanged herself
because of her distress.' And I shall bring
my father in his old age down in sorrow
to Hades. It is better for me not to hang
myself, but to pray the Lord that I may
die and not listen to these reproaches
anymore." 11 At that same time, with
hands outstretched toward the window,
she prayed and said,

"Blessed are you, merciful God!
Blessed is your name forever;
let all your works praise you
forever.
12 And now, Lord,*c* I turn my face to
you,
and raise my eyes toward you.
13 Command that I be released from
the earth
and not listen to such reproaches
any more.
14 You know, O Master, that I am
innocent
of any defilement with a man,
15 and that I have not disgraced my
name
or the name of my father in the
land of my exile.
I am my father's only child;
he has no other child to be his
heir;

---

a Other ancient authorities read *strangles*   *b* Other ancient authorities read
have had no benefit from   *c* Other ancient authorities lack *Lord*

and he has no close relative or other
kindred
for whom I should keep myself as
wife.
Already seven husbands of mine
have died.
Why should I still live?
But if it is not pleasing to you,
O Lord, to take my life,
hear me in my disgrace."

An Answer to Prayer

16 At that very moment, the prayers of both of them were heard in the glorious presence of God. [17] So Raphael was sent to heal both of them: Tobit, by removing the white films from his eyes, so that he might see God's light with his eyes; and Sarah, daughter of Raguel, by giving her in marriage to Tobias son of Tobit, and by setting her free from the wicked demon Asmodeus. For Tobias was entitled to have her before all others who had desired to marry her. At the same time that Tobit returned from the courtyard into his house, Sarah daughter of Raguel came down from her upper room.

Tobit Gives Instructions to His Son

4 That same day Tobit remembered the money that he had left in trust with Gabael at Rages in Media, [2] and he said to himself, "Now I have asked for death. Why do I not call my son Tobias and explain to him about the money

before I die?" [3] Then he called his son Tobias, and when he came to him he said, "My son, when I die,[a] give me a proper burial. Honor your mother and do not abandon her all the days of her life. Do whatever pleases her, and do not grieve her in anything. [4] Remember her, my son, because she faced many dangers for you while you were in her womb. And when she dies, bury her beside me in the same grave.

5 "Revere the Lord all your days, my son, and refuse to sin or to transgress his commandments. Live uprightly all the days of your life, and do not walk in the ways of wrongdoing; [6] for those who act in accordance with truth will prosper in all their activities. To all those who practice righteousness[b] [7] give alms from your possessions, and do not let your eye begrudge the gift when you make it. Do not turn your face away from anyone who is poor, and the face of God will not be turned away from you. [8] If you have many possessions, make your gift from them in proportion; if few, do not be afraid to give according to the little you have. [9] So you will be laying up a good treasure for yourself against the day of necessity. [10] For almsgiving delivers from death and keeps you from going into the

[a] Lat [b] The text of codex Sinaiticus goes directly from verse 6 to verse 19, reading *To those who practice righteousness* [19]*the Lord will give good counsel.* In order to fill the lacuna verses 7 to 18 are derived from other ancient authorities

---

3:17—The angel *Raphael*, whose name means "God heals," is sent from heaven to protect Tobias and to heal Tobit and Sarah. There is likely also reference to a guardian angel in Acts 12:15 (cf. Matt. 18:10; 26:53; Ps. 91:11). *Entitled to have her*—Tobias is Sarah's closest eligible relative (6:12).

4:1–19—In anticipation of his own death, Tobit offers his son a testament of instruction that is a veritable social gospel in its rehearsal of ethical and moral values.

4:7 *Do not let your eye begrudge*—This saying (also v. 16) concerns the "evil eye," a cultural reference to a selfish and envious disposition toward others, particularly in the use of possessions. This saying and its parallel in Matt. 6:22–23 concern a proper disposition when giving alms (cf. 2 Cor. 9:7).

4:8 *Possessions*—Giving alms in proportion to one's ability and station in life is encouraged in Sir. 35:9–10 and 2 Cor. 8:12–14.

4:9 *Laying up a good treasure*—The effectiveness of almsgiving expressed through the idiom of laying up or storing treasure is found in Sir. 29:11–12; 1 Tim. 6:19; and Matt. 19:21 (// Mark 10:21; Luke 18:22).

4:10 *Delivers from death*—Death here likely refers to an untimely death. That almsgiving rescues from death and keeps one from *going into the Darkness* derives from Prov. 10:2; 11:4, and may echo in Matt. 25:35 and Luke 16:19–31. The book affirms the effectiveness of good deeds (cf. Sir. 3:30); it does not contain a notion of an afterlife.

Darkness. ¹¹ Indeed, almsgiving, for all who practice it, is an excellent offering in the presence of the Most High.

12 "Beware, my son, of every kind of fornication. First of all, marry a woman from among the descendants of your ancestors; do not marry a foreign woman, who is not of your father's tribe; for we are the descendants of the prophets. Remember, my son, that Noah, Abraham, Isaac, and Jacob, our ancestors of old, all took wives from among their kindred. They were blessed in their children, and their posterity will inherit the land. ¹³ So now, my son, love your kindred, and in your heart do not disdain your kindred, the sons and daughters of your people, by refusing to take a wife for yourself from among them. For in pride there is ruin and great confusion. And in idleness there is loss and dire poverty, because idleness is the mother of famine.

14 "Do not keep over until the next day the wages of those who work for you, but pay them at once. If you serve God you will receive payment. Watch yourself, my son, in everything you do, and discipline yourself in all your conduct. ¹⁵ And what you hate, do not do to anyone. Do not

drink wine to excess or let drunkenness go with you on your way. ¹⁶ Give some of your food to the hungry, and some of your clothing to the naked. Give all your surplus as alms, and do not let your eye begrudge your giving of alms. ¹⁷ Place your bread on the grave of the righteous, but give none to sinners. ¹⁸ Seek advice from every wise person and do not despise any useful counsel. ¹⁹ At all times bless the Lord God, and ask him that your ways may be made straight and that all your paths and plans may prosper. For none of the nations has understanding, but the Lord himself will give them good counsel; but if he chooses otherwise, he casts down to deepest Hades. So now, my child, remember these commandments, and do not let them be erased from your heart.

Money Left in Trust with Gabael

20 "And now, my son, let me explain to you that I left ten talents of silver in trust with Gabael son of Gabrias, at Rages in Media. ²¹ Do not be afraid, my son, because we have become poor. You have great wealth if you fear God and flee from every sin and do what is good in the sight of the Lord your God."

4:11 *An excellent offering*—Almsgiving is as effective as the observance of temple ritual so important to Tobit (1:4–8). As in Sir. 35:1–13, the effectiveness of Torah piety does not mean that the sacrificial system is unimportant or ineffective. These books affirm that pious Jews who are unable to partake in temple rites while in the Diaspora please the Most High by their good deeds.

4:12 *Fornication*—Tobit instructs Tobias to have an honorable and holy marriage and to avoid sexual immorality. Similar instructions are found in 1 Cor. 7:2; Gal. 5:19; 1 Thess. 4:3–5. *Do not marry a foreign woman*—The prohibition on marrying foreign women (Gen. 28:1–2; Exod. 34:16; Deut. 7:3–4; Ezra 9:2, 12; Neh. 10:30; 13:25; Mal. 2:11) is an important teaching in Tobit (1:9; 3:17; 6:12–16; 7:10–11). Tobit advocates endogamy, the custom that he practiced (1:9), which is also in imitation of the patriarchs (Gen. 11:29; 24:3–4; 27:46–28:2; cf. Jubilees 4:33). The book of Tobit thus stands within the tradition regarding marriage found in Ezra 9–10 and Neh. 10:28–30, but in contrast to the views on this

matter expressed in the book of Ruth and *Joseph and Aseneth*. The apostle Paul gives his views on mixed marriages and the resulting children in 1 Cor. 7:12–14.

4:14 *Wages*—This teaching, based on Lev. 19:13 and Deut. 24:15, is also found in Jas. 5:4 in the New Testament.

4:15 *What you hate, do not do*—The Golden Rule in negative form is also found in Acts 15:29 (Codex D) and *Did.* 1:2. The positive form occurs in Matt. 7:12; Luke 6:31.

4:17 *Place your bread on the grave*—This phrase may refer to an ancient practice also mentioned in Augustine's *Confessions* VI ii (2) (cf. *Wisdom of Ahiqar* 2:10). *Give none to sinners*—Restricting charity to the righteous (cf. 2:2) echoes the New Testament admonition to give alms to the household of faith (Gal. 6:10).

4:21—The contrast of spiritual wealth and material poverty also occurs in 2 Cor. 6:10 and Jas. 2:5.

The Angel Raphael

5 Then Tobias answered his father Tobit, "I will do everything that you have commanded me, father; ²but how can I obtain the money*a* from him, since he does not know me and I do not know him? What evidence*b* am I to give him so that he will recognize and trust me, and give me the money? Also, I do not know the roads to Media, or how to get there." ³Then Tobit answered his son Tobias, "He gave me his bond and I gave him my bond. I*c* divided his in two; we each took one part, and I put one with the money. And now twenty years have passed since I left this money in trust. So now, my son, find yourself a trustworthy man to go with you, and we will pay him wages until you return. But get back the money from Gabael."*d*

4 So Tobias went out to look for a man to go with him to Media, someone who was acquainted with the way. He went out and found the angel Raphael standing in front of him; but he did not perceive that he was an angel of God. ⁵Tobias*e* said to him, "Where do you come from, young man?" "From your kindred, the Israelites," he replied, "and I have come here to work." Then Tobias*f* said to him, "Do you know the way to go to Media?" ⁶"Yes," he replied, "I have been there many times; I am acquainted with it and know all the roads. I have often traveled to Media, and would stay with our kinsman Gabael who lives in Rages of Media. It is a journey of two days from Ecbatana to Rages; for it lies in a mountainous area, while Ecbatana is in the middle of the plain." ⁷Then Tobias said to him, "Wait for me, young man, until I go in and tell my father; for I do need you to travel with me, and I will pay you your wages." ⁸He replied,

"All right, I will wait; but do not take too long."

9 So Tobias*f* went in to tell his father Tobit and said to him, "I have just found a man who is one of our own Israelite kindred!" He replied, "Call the man in, my son, so that I may learn about his family and to what tribe he belongs, and whether he is trustworthy enough to go with you."

10 Then Tobias went out and called him, and said, "Young man, my father is calling for you." So he went in to him, and Tobit greeted him first. He replied, "Joyous greetings to you!" But Tobit retorted, "What joy is left for me any more? I am a man without eyesight; I cannot see the light of heaven, but I lie in darkness like the dead who no longer see the light. Although still alive, I am among the dead. I hear people but I cannot see them." But the young man*f* said, "Take courage; the time is near for God to heal you; take courage." Then Tobit said to him, "My son Tobias wishes to go to Media. Can you accompany him and guide him? I will pay your wages, brother." He answered, "I can go with him and I know all the roads, for I have often gone to Media and have crossed all its plains, and I am familiar with its mountains and all of its roads."

11 Then Tobit*f* said to him, "Brother, of what family are you and from what tribe? Tell me, brother." ¹²He replied, "Why do you need to know my tribe?" But Tobit*f* said, "I want to be sure, brother, whose son you are and what your name is." ¹³He replied, "I am Azariah, the son of the great Hananiah, one of your relatives." ¹⁴Then Tobit said to him, "Welcome! God save you, brother.

a Gk it *b* Gk sign *c* Other authorities read He *d* Gk from him *e* Gk He *f* Gk he

---

5:1—Tobias's response affirms his desire to follow his father's Torah instructions and echoes the covenant affirmations of Exod. 19:8; 24:3; and Josh. 1:16.

5:11—The recurrence of the fictive kinship term *brother* (vv. 12, 14, 17; 6:7, 11, 13, 14, 16; 7:1, 3;

also *sister*, 8:4) reflects the social value placed on kinship in that culture. As in the New Testament, the term often is an insider term that refers to the group rather than literal kinship (e.g., Mark 3:33–35; Acts 7:2; 11:1; 1 Thess. 1:4).

Do not feel bitter toward me, brother, because I wanted to be sure about your ancestry. It turns out that you are a kinsman, and of good and noble lineage. For I knew Hananiah and Nathan,[a] the two sons of Shemeliah,[b] and they used to go with me to Jerusalem and worshiped with me there, and were not led astray. Your kindred are good people; you come of good stock. Hearty welcome!"

15 Then he added, "I will pay you a drachma a day as wages, as well as expenses for yourself and my son. So go with my son, 16 and[c] I will add something to your wages." Raphael[d] answered, "I will go with him; so do not fear. We shall leave in good health and return to you in good health, because the way is safe." 17 So Tobit[e] said to him, "Blessings be upon you, brother."

Then he called his son and said to him, "Son, prepare supplies for the journey and set out with your brother. May God in heaven bring you safely there and return you in good health to me; and may his angel, my son, accompany you both for your safety."

Before he went out to start his journey, he kissed his father and mother. Tobit then said to him, "Have a safe journey."

18 But his mother[f] began to weep, and said to Tobit, "Why is it that you have sent my child away? Is he not the staff of our hand as he goes in and out before us? 19 Do not heap money upon money, but let it be a ransom for our child. 20 For the life that is given to us by the Lord is enough for us." 21 Tobit[d] said to her, "Do not worry; our child will leave in good health and return to us in good health. Your eyes will see him on the day when he returns to you in good health. Say no more! Do not fear for them, my sister. 22 For a good angel will accompany him;

his journey will be successful, and he
6 will come back in good health." 1 So she stopped weeping.

Journey to Rages

The young man went out and the angel went with him; 2 and the dog came out with him and went along with them. So they both journeyed along, and when the first night overtook them they camped by the Tigris river. 3 Then the young man went down to wash his feet in the Tigris river. Suddenly a large fish leaped up from the water and tried to swallow the young man's foot, and he cried out. 4 But the angel said to the young man, "Catch hold of the fish and hang on to it!" So the young man grasped the fish and drew it up on the land. 5 Then the angel said to him, "Cut open the fish and take out its gall, heart, and liver. Keep them with you, but throw away the intestines. For its gall, heart, and liver are useful as medicine." 6 So after cutting open the fish the young man gathered together the gall, heart, and liver; then he roasted and ate some of the fish, and kept some to be salted.

The two continued on their way together until they were near Media.[g] 7 Then the young man questioned the angel and said to him, "Brother Azariah, what medicinal value is there in the fish's heart and liver, and in the gall?" 8 He replied, "As for the fish's heart and liver, you must burn them to make a smoke in the presence of a man or woman afflicted by a demon or evil spirit, and every affliction will flee away and never remain with that person any longer. 9 And as for the gall, anoint a person's

a Other ancient authorities read *Jathan* or *Nathaniah*   b Other ancient authorities read *Shemaiah*   c Other ancient authorities add *when you return safely*   d Gk *He*   e Gk *he*   f Other ancient authorities add *Anna*   g Other ancient authorities read *Ecbatana*

6:2—*The dog* appears in the GI version at 5:17, but first here in most other forms of the story. That a dog accompanies Tobias and Azariah on their dangerous journey (see also 11:4) is a feature unique to Jewish literature: dogs are among the unclean animals of Lev. 11:27. Associated with

Gentiles in later Jewish literature (*m. Nedarim* 4:3) and in the New Testament (Mark 7:27 // Matt. 15:26), the dog may serve as a metaphor for foreign influences ever present in the Diaspora. The dog gets removed from the medieval Aramaic and Hebrew forms of the story.

eyes where white films have appeared on them; blow upon them, upon the white films, and the eyes*a* will be healed."

Raphael's Instructions

10 When he entered Media and already was approaching Ecbatana,*b* 11 Raphael said to the young man, "Brother Tobias." "Here I am," he answered. Then Raphael*c* said to him, "We must stay this night in the home of Raguel. He is your relative, and he has a daughter named Sarah. 12 He has no male heir and no daughter except Sarah only, and you, as next of kin to her, have before all other men a hereditary claim on her. Also it is right for you to inherit her father's possessions. Moreover, the girl is sensible, brave, and very beautiful, and her father is a good man." 13 He continued, "You have every right to take her in marriage. So listen to me, brother; tonight I will speak to her father about the girl, so that we may take her to be your bride. When we return from Rages we will celebrate her marriage. For I know that Raguel can by no means keep her from you or promise her to another man without incurring the penalty of death according to the decree of the book of Moses. Indeed he knows that you, rather than any other man, are entitled to marry his daughter. So now listen to me, brother, and tonight we shall speak concerning the girl and arrange her engagement to you. And when we return from Rages we will take her and bring her back with us to your house."

14 Then Tobias said in answer to Raphael, "Brother Azariah, I have heard that she already has been married to seven husbands and that they died in the bridal chamber. On the night when they went in to her, they would die. I have heard people saying that it was a demon that killed them. 15 It does not harm her, but it kills anyone who desires to approach her. So now, since I am the only son my father has, I am afraid that I may die and bring my father's and

mother's life down to their grave, grieving for me—and they have no other son to bury them."

16 But Raphael*c* said to him, "Do you not remember your father's orders when he commanded you to take a wife from your father's house? Now listen to me, brother, and say no more about this demon. Take her. I know that this very night she will be given to you in marriage. 17 When you enter the bridal chamber, take some of the fish's liver and heart, and put them on the embers of the incense. An odor will be given off; 18 the demon will smell it and flee, and will never be seen near her any more. Now when you are about to go to bed with her, both of you must first stand up and pray, imploring the Lord of heaven that mercy and safety may be granted to you. Do not be afraid, for she was set apart for you before the world was made. You will save her, and she will go with you. I presume that you will have children by her, and they will be as brothers to you. Now say no more!" When Tobias heard the words of Raphael and learned that she was his kinswoman,*d* related through his father's lineage, he loved her very much, and his heart was drawn to her.

Arrival at Home of Raguel

7 Now when they*e* entered Ecbatana, Tobias*c* said to him, "Brother Azariah, take me straight to our brother Raguel." So he took him to Raguel's house, where they found him sitting beside the courtyard door. They greeted him first, and he replied, "Joyous greetings, brothers; welcome and good health!" Then he brought them into his house. 2 He said to his wife Edna, "How much the young man resembles my kinsman Tobit!" 3 Then Edna questioned them, saying, "Where are you from, brothers?" They answered, "We belong to the descendants of Naphtali

a Gk they *b* Other ancient authorities read *Rages* *c* Gk he *d* Gk *sister*
e Other ancient authorities read *he*

who are exiles in Nineveh." [4] She said to them, "Do you know our kinsman Tobit?" And they replied, "Yes, we know him." Then she asked them, "Is he[a] in good health?" [5] They replied, "He is alive and in good health." And Tobias added, "He is my father!" [6] At that Raguel jumped up and kissed him and wept. [7] He also spoke to him as follows, "Blessings on you, my child, son of a good and noble father![b] O most miserable of calamities that such an upright and beneficent man has become blind!" He then embraced his kinsman Tobias and wept. [8] His wife Edna also wept for him, and their daughter Sarah likewise wept. [9] Then Raguel[c] slaughtered a ram from the flock and received them very warmly.

Marriage of Tobias and Sarah

When they had bathed and washed themselves and had reclined to dine, Tobias said to Raphael, "Brother Azariah, ask Raguel to give me my kinswoman[d] Sarah." [10] But Raguel overheard it and said to the lad, "Eat and drink, and be merry tonight. For no one except you, brother, has the right to marry my daughter Sarah. Likewise I am not at liberty to give her to any other man than yourself, because you are my nearest relative. But let me explain to you the true situation more fully, my child. [11] I have given her to seven men of our kinsmen, and all died on the night when they went in to her. But now, my child, eat and drink, and the Lord will act on behalf of you both." But Tobias said, "I will neither eat nor drink anything until you settle the things that pertain to me." So Raguel said, "I will do so. She is given to you in accordance with the decree in the book of Moses, and it has been decreed from heaven that she be given to you. Take your kinswoman;[d] from now on you are her brother and she is your sister. She is given to you from today and for-

ever. May the Lord of heaven, my child, guide and prosper you both this night and grant you mercy and peace." [12] Then Raguel summoned his daughter Sarah. When she came to him he took her by the hand and gave her to Tobias,[e] saying, "Take her to be your wife in accordance with the law and decree written in the book of Moses. Take her and bring her safely to your father. And may the God of heaven prosper your journey with his peace." [13] Then he called her mother and told her to bring writing material; and he wrote out a copy of a marriage contract, to the effect that he gave her to him as wife according to the decree of the law of Moses. [14] Then they began to eat and drink.

15 Raguel called his wife Edna and said to her, "Sister, get the other room ready, and take her there." [16] So she went and made the bed in the room as he had told her, and brought Sarah[f] there. She wept for her daughter.[f] Then, wiping away the tears,[g] she said to her, "Take courage, my daughter; the Lord of heaven grant you joy[h] in place of your sorrow. Take courage, my daughter." Then she went out.

Tobias Routs the Demon

8 When they had finished eating and drinking they wanted to retire; so they took the young man and brought him into the bedroom. [2] Then Tobias remembered the words of Raphael, and he took the fish's liver and heart out of the bag where he had them and put them on the embers of the incense. [3] The odor of the fish so repelled the demon that he fled to the remotest parts[i] of Egypt. But Raphael followed him, and at once bound him there hand and foot.

4 When the parents[j] had gone out and

---

[a] Other ancient authorities add *alive and*   [b] Other ancient authorities add *When he heard that Tobit had lost his sight, he was stricken with grief and wept. Then he said,*   [c] Gk *he*   [d] Gk *sister*   [e] Gk *him*   [f] Gk *her*   [g] Other ancient authorities read *the tears of her daughter*   [h] Other ancient authorities read *favor*   [i] Or *fled through the air to the parts*   [j] Gk *they*

8:3—The desert as the dwelling place of **demons** is a common motif (Isa. 13:21; Matt. 4:1; 12:43; Luke 11:24; Rev. 18:2), as is the binding of a demon (Rev. 20:2; 1 Enoch 10:4, 10–12).

shut the door of the room, Tobias got out of bed and said to Sarah,[a] "Sister, get up, and let us pray and implore our Lord that he grant us mercy and safety." [5] So she got up, and they began to pray and implore that they might be kept safe. Tobias[b] began by saying,

> "Blessed are you, O God of our
>> ancestors,
>> and blessed is your name in all
>> generations forever.
> Let the heavens and the whole
>> creation bless you forever.
[6] You made Adam, and for him you
>> made his wife Eve
>> as a helper and support.
> From the two of them the human
>> race has sprung.
> You said, 'It is not good that the man
>> should be alone;
>> let us make a helper for him like
>> himself.'
[7] I now am taking this kinswoman of
>> mine,
>> not because of lust,
>> but with sincerity.
> Grant that she and I may find
>> mercy
>> and that we may grow old
>> together."

[8] And they both said, "Amen, Amen." [9] Then they went to sleep for the night.

But Raguel arose and called his servants to him, and they went and dug a grave, [10] for he said, "It is possible that he will die and we will become an object of ridicule and derision." [11] When they had finished digging the grave, Raguel went into his house and called his wife, [12] saying, "Send one of the maids and have her go in to see if he is alive. But if he is dead, let us bury him without anyone knowing it." [13] So they sent the maid, lit a lamp, and opened the door; and she went in and found them sound asleep together. [14] Then the maid came out and informed them that he was alive and that nothing was wrong. [15] So they blessed the God of heaven, and Raguel[c] said,

> "Blessed are you, O God, with every
>> pure blessing;
>> let all your chosen ones bless you.[d]
> Let them bless you forever.
[16] Blessed are you because you have
>> made me glad.
> It has not turned out as I expected,
>> but you have dealt with us
>> according to your great mercy.
[17] Blessed are you because you had
>> compassion
>> on two only children.
> Be merciful to them, O Master, and
>> keep them safe;
>> bring their lives to fulfillment
>> in happiness and mercy."

[18] Then he ordered his servants to fill in the grave before daybreak.

Wedding Feast

[19] After this he asked his wife to bake many loaves of bread; and he went out to the herd and brought two steers and four rams and ordered them to be slaughtered. So they began to make preparations. [20] Then he called for Tobias and swore on oath to him in these words:[e] "You shall not leave here for fourteen days, but shall stay here eating and drinking with me; and you shall cheer up my daughter, who has been depressed. [21] Take at once half of what I own and return in safety to your father; the other half will be yours when my wife and I die. Take courage, my child. I am your father and Edna is your mother, and we belong to you as well as to your wife[f] now and forever. Take courage, my child."

The Money Recovered

9 Then Tobias called Raphael and said to him, [2] "Brother Azariah, take four servants and two camels with you and travel to Rages. Go to the home of Gabael, give him the bond, get the money, and then bring him with you to the wedding celebration. [4] For you

---

[a] Gk her   [b] Gk He   [c] Gk they   [d] Other ancient authorities lack this line   [e] Other ancient authorities read *Tobias and said to him*   [f] Gk sister

know that my father must be counting the days, and if I delay even one day I will upset him very much. ³ You are witness to the oath Raguel has sworn, and I cannot violate his oath."*a* ⁵ So Raphael with the four servants and two camels went to Rages in Media and stayed with Gabael. Raphael*b* gave him the bond and informed him that Tobit's son Tobias had married and was inviting him to the wedding celebration. So Gabael*c* got up and counted out to him the money bags, with their seals intact; then they loaded them on the camels.*d* ⁶ In the morning they both got up early and went to the wedding celebration. When they came into Raguel's house they found Tobias reclining at table. He sprang up and greeted Gabael,*e* who wept and blessed him with the words, "Good and noble son of a father good and noble, upright and generous! May the Lord grant the blessing of heaven to you and your wife, and to your wife's father and mother. Blessed be God, for I see in Tobias the very image of my cousin Tobit."

Anxiety of the Parents

10 Now, day by day, Tobit kept counting how many days Tobias*c* would need for going and for returning. And when the days had passed and his son did not appear, ² he said, "Is it possible that he has been detained? Or that Gabael has died, and there is no one to give him the money?" ³ And he began to worry. ⁴ His wife Anna said, "My child has perished and is no longer among the living." And she began to weep and mourn for her son, saying, ⁵ "Woe to me, my child, the light of my eyes, that I let you make the journey." ⁶ But Tobit kept saying to her, "Be quiet and stop worrying, my dear;*f* he is all right. Probably something unexpected has happened there. The man who went with him is trustworthy and is one of our own kin. Do not grieve for him, my dear;*f* he will soon be here." ⁷ She answered him, "Be quiet yourself! Stop trying to deceive

me! My child has perished." She would rush out every day and watch the road her son had taken, and would heed no one.*g* When the sun had set she would go in and mourn and weep all night long, getting no sleep at all.

Tobias and Sarah Start for Home

Now when the fourteen days of the wedding celebration had ended that Raguel had sworn to observe for his daughter, Tobias came to him and said, "Send me back, for I know that my father and mother do not believe that they will see me again. So I beg of you, father, to let me go so that I may return to my own father. I have already explained to you how I left him." ⁸ But Raguel said to Tobias, "Stay, my child, stay with me; I will send messengers to your father Tobit and they will inform him about you." ⁹ But he said, "No! I beg you to send me back to my father." ¹⁰ So Raguel promptly gave Tobias his wife Sarah, as well as half of all his property: male and female slaves, oxen and sheep, donkeys and camels, clothing, money, and household goods. ¹¹ Then he saw them safely off; he embraced Tobias*e* and said, "Farewell, my child; have a safe journey. The Lord of heaven prosper you and your wife Sarah, and may I see children of yours before I die." ¹² Then he kissed his daughter Sarah and said to her, "My daughter, honor your father-in-law and your mother-in-law,*h* since from now on they are as much your parents as those who gave you birth. Go in peace, daughter, and may I hear a good report about you as long as I live." Then he bade them farewell and let them go. Then Edna said to Tobias, "My child and dear brother, the Lord of heaven bring you back safely, and may I live long enough to see children of you and of my daughter Sarah before I die. In the sight of the Lord I entrust my daughter to you;

a In other ancient authorities verse 3 precedes verse 4 *b* Gk He *c* Gk he
d Other ancient authorities lack *on the camels* *e* Gk him *f* Gk sister
g Other ancient authorities read *and she would eat nothing* *h* Other ancient authorities lack parts of *Then . . . mother-in-law*

do nothing to grieve her all the days of your life. Go in peace, my child. From now on I am your mother and Sarah is your beloved wife.*a* May we all prosper together all the days of our lives." Then she kissed them both and saw them safely off. [13] Tobias parted from Raguel with happiness and joy, praising the Lord of heaven and earth, King over all, because he had made his journey a success. Finally, he blessed Raguel and his wife Edna, and said, "I have been commanded by the Lord to honor you all the days of my life."*b*

Homeward Journey

11 When they came near to Kaserin, which is opposite Nineveh, Raphael said, [2] "You are aware of how we left your father. [3] Let us run ahead of your wife and prepare the house while they are still on the way." [4] As they went on together Raphael*c* said to him, "Have the gall ready." And the dog*d* went along behind them.

[5] Meanwhile Anna sat looking intently down the road by which her son would come. [6] When she caught sight of him coming, she said to his father, "Look, your son is coming, and the man who went with him!"

Tobit's Sight Restored

[7] Raphael said to Tobias, before he had approached his father, "I know that his eyes will be opened. [8] Smear the gall of the fish on his eyes; the medicine will make the white films shrink and peel off from his eyes, and your father will regain his sight and see the light." [9] Then Anna ran up to her son and threw her arms around him, saying, "Now that I have seen you, my child, I am ready to die." And she wept. [10] Then Tobit got up and came stumbling out through the courtyard door. Tobias went up to him, [11] with the gall of the fish in his hand, and holding him firmly, he blew into his eyes, saying, "Take courage, father." With this he applied the medicine on his eyes, [12] and it made them smart.*a* [13] Next, with both his hands he peeled off the white films from the corners of his eyes. Then Tobit*c* saw his son and*e* threw his arms around him, [14] and he wept and said to him, "I see you, my son, the light of my eyes!" Then he said,

"Blessed be God,
 and blessed be his great name,
 and blessed be all his holy angels.
May his holy name be blessed*f*
 throughout all the ages.
[15] Though he afflicted me,
 he has had mercy upon me.*g*
 Now I see my son Tobias!"

So Tobit went in rejoicing and praising God at the top of his voice. Tobias reported to his father that his journey had been successful, that he had brought the money, that he had married Raguel's daughter Sarah, and that she was, indeed, on her way there, very near to the gate of Nineveh.

[16] Then Tobit, rejoicing and praising God, went out to meet his daughter-in-law at the gate of Nineveh. When the people of Nineveh saw him coming, walking along in full vigor and with no one leading him, they were amazed. [17] Before them all, Tobit acknowledged that God had been merciful to him and had restored his sight. When Tobit met Sarah the wife of his son Tobias, he blessed her saying, "Come in, my daughter, and welcome. Blessed be your God who has brought you to us, my daughter. Blessed be your father and your mother, blessed be my son Tobias, and blessed be you, my daughter. Come in now to your home, and welcome, with blessing and joy. Come in, my daughter." So on that day there was rejoicing among all the Jews who were in Nineveh. [18] Ahikar and his nephew Nadab were also present to share Tobit's joy. With merriment they celebrated Tobias's wedding feast

a Gk *sister* *b* Lat: Meaning of Gk uncertain *c* Gk *he* *d* Codex Sinaiticus reads *And the Lord* *e* Other ancient authorities lack *saw his son and* *f* Codex Sinaiticus reads *May his great name be upon us and blessed be all the angels* *g* Lat: Gk lacks this line

for seven days, and many gifts were given to him.[a]

Raphael's Wages

12 When the wedding celebration was ended, Tobit called his son Tobias and said to him, "My child, see to paying the wages of the man who went with you, and give him a bonus as well." [2] He replied, "Father, how much shall I pay him? It would do no harm to give him half of the possessions brought back with me. [3] For he has led me back to you safely, he cured my wife, he brought the money back with me, and he healed you. How much extra shall I give him as a bonus?" [4] Tobit said, "He deserves, my child, to receive half of all that he brought back." [5] So Tobias[b] called him and said, "Take for your wages half of all that you brought back, and farewell."

Raphael's Exhortation

[6] Then Raphael[b] called the two of them privately and said to them, "Bless God and acknowledge him in the presence of all the living for the good things he has done for you. Bless and sing praise to his name. With fitting honor declare to all people the deeds[c] of God. Do not be slow to acknowledge him. [7] It is good to conceal the secret of a king, but to acknowledge and reveal the works of God, and with fitting honor to acknowledge him. Do good and evil will not overtake you. [8] Prayer with fasting[d] is good, but better than both is almsgiving with righteousness. A little with righteousness is better than wealth with wrongdoing.[e] It is better to give alms than to lay up gold. [9] For almsgiving saves from death and purges away every sin. Those who give alms will enjoy a full life, [10] but those who commit sin and do wrong are their own worst enemies.

Raphael Discloses His Identity

[11] "I will now declare the whole truth to you and will conceal nothing from you. Already I have declared it to you when I said, 'It is good to conceal the secret of a king, but to reveal with due honor the works of God.' [12] So now when you and Sarah prayed, it was I who brought and read[f] the record of your prayer before the glory of the Lord, and likewise whenever you would bury the dead. [13] And that time when you did not hesitate to get up and leave your dinner to go and bury the dead, [14] I was sent to you to test you. And at the same time God sent me to heal you and Sarah your daughter-in-law. [15] I am Raphael, one of the seven angels who stand ready and enter before the glory of the Lord."

[16] The two of them were shaken; they fell face down, for they were afraid. [17] But he said to them, "Do not be afraid; peace be with you. Bless God forevermore. [18] As for me, when I was with you, I was not acting on my own will, but by the will of God. Bless him each and every day; sing his praises. [19] Although you were watching me, I really did not eat or drink anything—but what you saw was a vision. [20] So now get up from the ground,[g] and acknowledge God. See, I am ascending to him who sent me. Write down all these things that have happened to you." And he ascended. [21] Then they stood up, and could see him no more. [22] They kept blessing God and singing his praises, and they acknowledged God for these marvelous deeds of his, when an angel of God had appeared to them.

Tobit's Thanksgiving to God

13 Then Tobit[b] said:
"Blessed be God who lives forever,

[a] Other ancient authorities lack parts of this sentence [b] Gk he [c] Gk words; other ancient authorities read words of the deeds [d] Codex Sinaiticus with sincerity [e] Lat [f] Lat: Gk lacks and read [g] Other ancient authorities read now bless the Lord on earth

---

12:8—These pillars of righteous conduct, i.e., **prayer**, **fasting**, and **almsgiving**, occur together as a threesome only here (more explicitly in GI and the Old Latin) in the Old Testament and in Matt. 6:2–18.

13:1 *Kingdom*—Praising God's kingdom recalls Matt. 6:10 and Luke 11:2. There are several striking parallels between Tobit 13 and the New Testament Sermon on the Mount and Sermon on

because his kingdom[a] lasts
throughout all ages.
2 For he afflicts, and he shows mercy;
he leads down to Hades in the
lowest regions of the earth,
and he brings up from the great
abyss,[b]
and there is nothing that can
escape his hand.
3 Acknowledge him before the
nations, O children of Israel;
for he has scattered you among
them.
4 He has shown you his greatness
even there.
Exalt him in the presence of every
living being,
because he is our Lord and he is
our God;
he is our Father and he is God
forever.
5 He will afflict[c] you for your
iniquities,
but he will again show mercy on
all of you.
He will gather you from all the
nations
among whom you have been
scattered.
6 If you turn to him with all your
heart and with all your soul,
to do what is true before him,
then he will turn to you
and will no longer hide his face
from you.
So now see what he has done for
you;
acknowledge him at the top of
your voice.
Bless the Lord of righteousness,
and exalt the King of the ages.[d]
In the land of my exile I
acknowledge him,

and show his power and majesty to
a nation of sinners:
'Turn back, you sinners, and do what
is right before him;
perhaps he may look with favor
upon you and show you
mercy.'
7 As for me, I exalt my God,
and my soul rejoices in the King of
heaven.
8 Let all people speak of his majesty,
and acknowledge him in
Jerusalem.
9 O Jerusalem, the holy city,
he afflicted[e] you for the deeds of
your hands,[f]
but will again have mercy on the
children of the righteous.
10 Acknowledge the Lord, for he is
good,[g]
and bless the King of the ages,
so that his tent[h] may be rebuilt in
you in joy.
May he cheer all those within you
who are captives,
and love all those within you who
are distressed,
to all generations forever.
11 A bright light will shine to all the
ends of the earth;
many nations will come to you
from far away,
the inhabitants of the remotest parts
of the earth to your holy
name,
bearing gifts in their hands for the
King of heaven.
Generation after generation will give
joyful praise in you;

a Other ancient authorities read *forever, and his kingdom*   b Gk *from destruction*   c Other ancient authorities read *He afflicted*   d The lacuna in codex Sinaiticus, verses 6b to 10a, is filled in from other ancient authorities   e Other ancient authorities read *will afflict*   f Other ancient authorities read *your children*   g Other ancient authorities read *Lord worthily*   h Or *tabernacle*

the Plain: the reference to *our Father* in v. 4 and invoking God's *holy name* in v. 17 echo Matt. 6:9 and Luke 11:2. God is called Father more frequently in Second Temple Jewish literature (Wis. 14:4; Sir. 23:1; 51:10; 3 Macc. 5:7; 6:3, 8). The beatitudes in Tob. 13:14–16 (*happy are*) find a close parallel in Matt. 5:3–6 and Luke 6:20–22.

13:5 *Gather you from all the nations*—The end-time gathering of the scattered tribes of Israel (here and in v. 13; 14:7) is a common motif in postexilic literature (Sir. 36:11; Bar. 4:21–5:9), including the New Testament (Matt. 19:28; Rom. 11:12; Rev. 21:12).

the name of the chosen city will
    endure forever.
12 Cursed are all who speak a harsh
    word against you;
  cursed are all who conquer you
    and pull down your walls,
all who overthrow your towers
  and set your homes on fire.
But blessed forever will be all who
  revere you.*a*
13 Go, then, and rejoice over the
    children of the righteous,
  for they will be gathered together
  and will praise the Lord of the
    ages.
14 Happy are those who love you,
  and happy are those who rejoice in
    your prosperity.
Happy also are all people who grieve
  with you
  because of your afflictions;
for they will rejoice with you
  and witness all your glory forever.
15 My soul blesses*b* the Lord, the great
  King!
16 For Jerusalem will be built*c* as his
  house for all ages.
How happy I will be if a remnant
  of my descendants should
  survive
to see your glory and acknowledge
  the King of heaven.
The gates of Jerusalem will be built
  with sapphire and emerald,
and all your walls with precious
  stones.
The towers of Jerusalem will be built
  with gold,
and their battlements with pure
  gold.
The streets of Jerusalem will be
  paved
with ruby and with stones of Ophir.
17 The gates of Jerusalem will sing
  hymns of joy,

and all her houses will cry,
  'Hallelujah!
Blessed be the God of Israel!'
  and the blessed will bless the holy
  name forever and ever."

Tobit's Final Counsel

14 So ended Tobit's words of praise. 2 Tobit*d* died in peace when he was one hundred twelve years old, and was buried with great honor in Nineveh. He was sixty-two*e* years old when he lost his eyesight, and after regaining it he lived in prosperity, giving alms and continually blessing God and acknowledging God's majesty.

3 When he was about to die, he called his son Tobias and the seven sons of Tobias*f* and gave this command: "My son, take your children 4 and hurry off to Media, for I believe the word of God that Nahum spoke about Nineveh, that all these things will take place and overtake Assyria and Nineveh. Indeed, everything that was spoken by the prophets of Israel, whom God sent, will occur. None of all their words will fail, but all will come true at their appointed times. So it will be safer in Media than in Assyria and Babylon. For I know and believe that whatever God has said will be fulfilled and will come true; not a single word of the prophecies will fail. All of our kindred, inhabitants of the land of Israel, will be scattered and taken as captives from the good land; and the whole land of Israel will be desolate, even Samaria and Jerusalem will be desolate. And the temple of God in it will be burned to the ground, and it will be desolate for a while.*g*

a Other ancient authorities read *who build you up*   *b* Or *O my soul, bless*   *c* Other ancient authorities add *for a city*   *d* Gk He   *e* Other ancient authorities read *fifty-eight*   *f* Lat: Gk lacks *and the seven sons of Tobias*   *g* Lat: Other ancient authorities read *of God will be in distress and will be burned for a while*

13:16–17 *Jerusalem*—The description of the eschatological Jerusalem is indebted to Isa. 54:11–14 and Ezek. 40–48. Other New Jerusalem texts include some references in the Dead Sea Scrolls (5QNJ [5Q15]; 11Q18) and Rev. 21:9–27.

14:6–7 *The nations*—The universalism expressed here, that all humanity will become God's people at the end time when the Gentiles worship the God of Israel, is derived particularly from Isaiah (Isa. 19:25; 25:6; 56:7; cf. Ps. 57:8–9; Rev. 21:3).

5 "But God will again have mercy on them, and God will bring them back into the land of Israel; and they will rebuild the temple of God, but not like the first one until the period when the times of fulfillment shall come. After this they all will return from their exile and will rebuild Jerusalem in splendor; and in it the temple of God will be rebuilt, just as the prophets of Israel have said concerning it. ⁶ Then the nations in the whole world will all be converted and worship God in truth. They will all abandon their idols, which deceitfully have led them into their error; ⁷ and in righteousness they will praise the eternal God. All the Israelites who are saved in those days and are truly mindful of God will be gathered together; they will go to Jerusalem and live in safety forever in the land of Abraham, and it will be given over to them. Those who sincerely love God will rejoice, but those who commit sin and injustice will vanish from all the earth. ⁸,⁹ So now, my children, I command you, serve God faithfully and do what is pleasing in his sight. Your children are also to be commanded to do what is right and to give alms, and to be mindful of God and to bless his name at all times with sincerity and with all their strength. So now, my son, leave Nineveh; do not remain here. ¹⁰ On whatever day you bury your mother beside me, do not stay overnight within the confines of the city. For I see that there is much wickedness within it, and that much deceit is practiced within it, while the people are without shame. See, my son, what Nadab did to Ahikar

who had reared him. Was he not, while still alive, brought down into the earth? For God repaid him to his face for this shameful treatment. Ahikar came out into the light, but Nadab went into the eternal darkness, because he tried to kill Ahikar. Because he gave alms, Ahikar[a] escaped the fatal trap that Nadab had set for him, but Nadab fell into it himself, and was destroyed. ¹¹ So now, my children, see what almsgiving accomplishes, and what injustice does—it brings death! But now my breath fails me."

Death of Tobit and Anna

Then they laid him on his bed, and he died; and he received an honorable funeral. ¹² When Tobias's mother died, he buried her beside his father. Then he and his wife and children[b] returned to Media and settled in Ecbatana with Raguel his father-in-law. ¹³ He treated his parents-in-law[c] with great respect in their old age, and buried them in Ecbatana of Media. He inherited both the property of Raguel and that of his father Tobit. ¹⁴ He died highly respected at the age of one hundred seventeen[d] years. ¹⁵ Before he died he heard[e] of the destruction of Nineveh, and he saw its prisoners being led into Media, those whom King Cyaxares[f] of Media had taken captive. Tobias[g] praised God for all he had done to the people of Nineveh and Assyria; before he died he rejoiced over Nineveh, and he blessed the Lord God forever and ever. Amen.[h]

---

[a] Gk *he*; other ancient authorities read *Manasses*　[b] Codex Sinaiticus lacks *and children*　[c] Gk *them*　[d] Other authorities read other numbers　[e] Codex Sinaiticus reads *saw and heard*　[f] Cn: Codex Sinaiticus *Ahikar*; other ancient authorities read *Nebuchadnezzar and Ahasuerus*　[g] Gk *He*　[h] Other ancient authorities lack *Amen*

The Book of

JUDITH

One of only four biblical books named for a woman (the others are Ruth, Esther, and Susanna), Judith has captivated through the centuries artists, writers, and composers with its story of a pious Jewish widow who seduces and beheads the powerful enemy general Holofernes in order to save her people. Diverse and contradictory interpretations of Judith—as *femme fatale*, female warrior, lying murderer, feminist heroine, virtue personified, and androgyne who transcends male and female categories—reveal more about the times and concerns of her interpreters than about Judith herself. Judith's courage was highlighted when the early church was threatened by persecutions. In support of a celibate priesthood, her chastity was praised, and she was seen as a type foreshadowing the Virgin Mary. During the Renaissance, when virtues were codified in icons, Judith was both the Good and Bad Woman, a favorite in portraiture as well as expensive erotica in bedrooms and bathrooms. During the Reformation, Judith symbolized Protestant rebellion against the Catholic Church. Judith was identified with queens in the sixteenth century, e.g., Elizabeth I and the queen of hearts in French playing cards. Judith became a pornographic focus of protest against Victorian conformity in the nineteenth century. In the twentieth century, Judith was used to reinforce gender boundaries blurred by world wars. These diverse interpretations suggest that the complex character of Judith challenges assumptions and stereotypes about gender and sex in her culture and our own.

Structure and Style

Judith unfolds in two balanced sections (chaps. 1–7 and 8–16), each with three parts that repeat their narrative elements in reverse order. This inverted structure is called a chiasm, from the Greek letter chi or X. Section one focuses upon men, war, and fear generated by King Nebuchadnezzar and his general Holofernes as they seek revenge against defiant subject nations. The chiasm (indicated in bold type) moves from (A) Holofernes' military campaign and the **surrender of nations**, to (B) a terrified Israel's **preparation for war**, to (C) Holofernes' conversation with **Achior** and his expulsion from the Assyrian camp. The chiasm moves in the opposite direction when (C′) **Achior** is taken into Bethulia and talks with the people, (B′) Holofernes **prepares for war**, and (A′) Holofernes campaigns against Bethulia whose people urge **surrender**.

Section one contrasts with and sets the stage for Judith's actions in section two, which focuses upon women, beauty, and courage. Judith finally enters the story in chapter 8, when the people are "in great misery" (7:32), ready to surrender. Judith (A) is **introduced** by a genealogy and declarations about her character. Judith (B) admonishes the town elders for putting God to the test, **announces her plan** to save Israel, and dresses to seduce Holofernes. Judith and her maid (C) **leave Bethulia** and are taken into the Assyrian camp where she (D) **cuts off the head** of a drunken Holofernes. Judith (C′) **returns to Bethulia** with Holofernes' head, (B′) **announces her plan** to

destroy Israel's enemy, and offers a hymn of praise. In a **concluding** note, Judith (A')
returns to her estate. Holofernes' beheading stands at the center of the chiasm, enveloped by the courage of Judith.

Irony, double meanings, repetition, suspense, chiasm, and contrast saturate the
book of Judith and unite its two sections. The pairs men/women, war/beauty, fear/
courage, pagan/Jew are presented in a way that calls into question the traditional
binary oppositions of gender, politics, and religion, both then and now. In section
one, Israelite men remain behind the security of their town walls, while in section
two, Judith and her maid leave that security in order to meet the enemy, while the
men watch (10:10). Holofernes' many military victories in section one are overshadowed by Judith's solitary act in section two. Judith cuts off Holofernes' head (13:8),
but Achior faints when he sees it (14:6). The pagan Achior converts to Judaism and
serves as the mirror image of Judith the believer, rather than her opposite. Both testify
to the superiority of the Jewish God and Jewish beliefs in the pagan Greco-Roman
world that threatened Jewish identity. Their witness challenges Christians today to examine both their commitment and witness to God amidst our secular and pluralistic
world and its encroachments on Christian identity.

Many argue that Judith is a Jewish novel, similar to Greek and Roman novels popular in the period between 200 BCE and 100 CE, when increased upper-class literacy
and the rise of a class of merchants and bureaucrats created an audience that read for
entertainment. Judith typifies the Jewish novel, with its fictionalized history and
female central character who experiences the threats to her people on a personal level. Judith helped Israel to deal with its uncertain situation in the Greco-Roman world
by affirming traditional Israelite covenant theology and identity; she prays (9:2–14;
12:8; 13:4–5, 7; 16:1–17), keeps kosher (12:2, 9), affirms the centrality of the temple
(8:21) and of sacrifice (16:18–20), and testifies to God's role as deliverer (8:12–17;
9:11–14; 11:16; 13:14; 16:5, 17). The author of Judith may have used the stories of
Esther, Deborah and Jael (Judg. 4–5), and Miriam (Exod. 15:21) as models for Judith.

Date

Judith is apocryphal (set aside from full canonical status, but useful for reading
and instruction) for Protestants, deuterocanonical (second canon, added later but
equally authoritative) for Catholics and Orthodox, and noncanonical for Jews. The
early Christian church knew Judith through the Greek of the Septuagint; no copies of
the probable Hebrew original have been found. Because *1 Clement* mentions Judith
in the first century CE, it had to be written before that time, probably in Palestine,
though when is debated: Persian period, Hellenistic period, or late Hasmonean period. Deliberate historical inaccuracies (1:1, 7, 11; 2:1, 4; 4:1) complicate the question of date. These inaccuracies would easily have been recognized by the audience
as signs of a fictional account.

—Denise Dombkowski Hopkins

Arphaxad Fortifies Ecbatana

1 It was the twelfth year of the reign of Nebuchadnezzar, who ruled over the Assyrians in the great city of Nineveh. In those days Arphaxad ruled over the Medes in Ecbatana. ²He built walls around Ecbatana with hewn stones three cubits thick and six cubits long; he made the walls seventy cubits high and fifty cubits wide. ³At its gates he raised towers one hundred cubits high and sixty cubits wide at the foundations. ⁴He made its gates seventy cubits high and forty cubits wide to allow his armies to march out in force and his infantry to form their ranks. ⁵Then King Nebuchadnezzar made war against King Arphaxad in the great plain that is on the borders of Ragau. ⁶There rallied to him all the people of the hill country and all those who lived along the Euphrates, the Tigris, and the Hydaspes, and, on the plain, Arioch, king of the Elymeans. Thus, many nations joined the forces of the Chaldeans.ᵃ

Nebuchadnezzar Issues Ultimatum

7 Then Nebuchadnezzar, king of the Assyrians, sent messengers to all who lived in Persia and to all who lived in the west, those who lived in Cilicia and Damascus, Lebanon and Antilebanon, and all who lived along the seacoast, ⁸and those among the nations of Carmel and Gilead, and Upper Galilee and the great plain of Esdraelon, ⁹and all who were in

Samaria and its towns, and beyond the Jordan as far as Jerusalem and Bethany and Chelous and Kadesh and the river of Egypt, and Tahpanhes and Raamses and the whole land of Goshen, ¹⁰even beyond Tanis and Memphis, and all who lived in Egypt as far as the borders of Ethiopia. ¹¹But all who lived in the whole region disregarded the summons of Nebuchadnezzar, king of the Assyrians, and refused to join him in the war; for they were not afraid of him, but regarded him as only one man.ᵇ So they sent back his messengers empty-handed and in disgrace.

12 Then Nebuchadnezzar became very angry with this whole region, and swore by his throne and kingdom that he would take revenge on the whole territory of Cilicia and Damascus and Syria, that he would kill with his sword also all the inhabitants of the land of Moab, and the people of Ammon, and all Judea, and every one in Egypt, as far as the coasts of the two seas.

Arphaxad Is Defeated

13 In the seventeenth year he led his forces against King Arphaxad and defeated him in battle, overthrowing the whole army of Arphaxad and all his cavalry and all his chariots. ¹⁴Thus he took possession of his towns and came to Ecbatana, captured its towers, plundered

ᵃSyr: Gk *Cheleoudites*   ᵇOr *a man*

1:1–16 Nebuchadnezzar's Campaign against Arphaxad

The opening section sounds the themes of war, fear, and men and anticipates the second half of the book with its emphasis upon beauty, courage, and women.

1:1—A deliberately erroneous dating formula opens the book (contra the historical books 1 Kgs. 15:1; 16:15; 2 Kgs. 12:1; 13:1) as a signal to the audience that this is not a historical work. Nebuchadnezzar (605–562 BCE) ruled over Babylonia, not Nineveh, the capital of the Assyrians destroyed in 612 BCE (before Nebuchadnezzar became king). Nebuchadnezzaar destroyed Jerusalem in 587 BCE. King Arphaxad is unknown to history.

1:2–4—*Ecbatana*, the summer capital of Persia, and later capital of the Medes, was known to Diaspora Jews (see Tob. 3:7; Ezra 6:2). The size of its defenses is exaggerated to underscore the power of Nebuchadnezzar in conquering it and to increase suspense. Similarly today, nations inflate the threat from other nations to rally support for waging war.

1:11–16—Nebuchadnezzar's shame and anger over nations who snubbed his summons fuel his declaration of revenge. Similarly, modern diplomacy too often suffers from the posturing of nations over their perceived status in the world.

its markets, and turned its glory into disgrace. [15] He captured Arphaxad in the mountains of Ragau and struck him down with his spears, thus destroying him once and for all. [16] Then he returned to Nineveh, he and all his combined forces, a vast body of troops; and there he and his forces rested and feasted for one hundred twenty days.

The Expedition against the West

2 In the eighteenth year, on the twenty-second day of the first month, there was talk in the palace of Nebuchadnezzar, king of the Assyrians, about carrying out his revenge on the whole region, just as he had said. [2] He summoned all his ministers and all his nobles and set before them his secret plan and recounted fully, with his own lips, all the wickedness of the region.[a] [3] They decided that every one who had not obeyed his command should be destroyed.

[4] When he had completed his plan, Nebuchadnezzar, king of the Assyrians, called Holofernes, the chief general of his army, second only to himself, and said to him, [5] "Thus says the Great King, the lord of the whole earth: Leave my presence and take with you men confident in their strength, one hundred twenty thousand foot soldiers and twelve thousand cavalry. [6] March out against all the land to the west, because they disobeyed my orders. [7] Tell them to prepare earth and water, for I am coming against them in my anger, and will cover the whole face of the earth with the feet of my troops, to whom I will hand them over to be plundered. [8] Their wounded shall fill their ravines and gullies, and the swelling river shall be filled with their dead. [9] I will lead them away captive to the ends of the whole earth. [10] You shall go and seize all their territory for me in advance. They must yield themselves to you, and you shall hold them for me until the day of their punishment. [11] But to those who resist show no mercy, but hand them over to slaughter and plunder throughout your whole region. [12] For as I live, and by the power of my kingdom, what I have spoken I will accomplish by my own hand. [13] And you—take care not to transgress any of your lord's commands, but carry them out exactly as I have ordered you; do it without delay."

Campaign of Holofernes

[14] So Holofernes left the presence of his lord, and summoned all the commanders, generals, and officers of the

[a] Meaning of Gk uncertain

2:1–28 Nebuchadnezzar Takes Revenge

The western nations from Persia to Egypt (*the whole region*) are targeted, under the command of the general Holofernes.

2:2—Nebuchadnezzar shares his *secret plan* while Judith does not (8:34), one of many ironic contrasts uniting the two sections of the book. The contrast challenges our stereotypes about weak women who can't keep secrets; here it is the powerful king who cannot keep a secret.

2:4 *Second only to himself*—The relationship between Nebuchadnezzar and Holofernes mirrors that between God and Judith (16:2, 5).

2:5–13—Nebuchadnezzar's speech. Exaggerated and graphic language (also vv. 19–20, 25, 27) contributes to the reader's perception of Nebuchadnezzar as savage villain. This technique cautions us to analyze how our national and ethnic biases shape political rhetoric about our opponents. Also, this hyperbolic language provokes our sympathy towards the non-Israelite cities threatened by Holofernes, and reminds us of America's missed opportunity for solidarity with the oppressed in the world after 9/11.

2:5 *The lord of the whole earth*—Nebuchadnezzar's grand claim introduces a succession of ironic double meanings centered on the word "lord" (Gk. *kyrios*) as God or as an earthly superior (king, master, husband). Judith's victory over Holofernes will prove that her God, not Nebuchadnezzar, is the true lord. This contrast between the arrogant ruler and God challenges us to assess our allegiances and pretensions on both the national and personal levels.

2:12 *By my own hand*—Nebuchadnezzar's boast creates an ironic contrast with Judith's declaration "by my hand" in 8:33; 12:4. Male military might is no match for "the hand of a woman" (16:5), suggesting that God can act through what society considers to be the weakest of instruments.

Assyrian army. **15** He mustered the picked troops by divisions as his lord had ordered him to do, one hundred twenty thousand of them, together with twelve thousand archers on horseback, **16** and he organized them as a great army is marshaled for a campaign. **17** He took along a vast number of camels and donkeys and mules for transport, and innumerable sheep and oxen and goats for food; **18** also ample rations for everyone, and a huge amount of gold and silver from the royal palace.

19 Then he set out with his whole army, to go ahead of King Nebuchadnezzar and to cover the whole face of the earth to the west with their chariots and cavalry and picked foot soldiers. **20** Along with them went a mixed crowd like a swarm of locusts, like the dust*a* of the earth—a multitude that could not be counted.

21 They marched for three days from Nineveh to the plain of Bectileth, and camped opposite Bectileth near the mountain that is to the north of Upper Cilicia. **22** From there Holofernes*b* took his whole army, the infantry, cavalry, and chariots, and went up into the hill country. **23** He ravaged Put and Lud, and plundered all the Rassisites and the Ishmaelites on the border of the desert, south of the country of the Chelleans. **24** Then he followed*c* the Euphrates and passed through Mesopotamia and destroyed all the fortified towns along the brook Abron, as far as the sea. **25** He also seized the territory of Cilicia, and killed everyone who resisted him. Then he came to the southern borders of Japheth, facing Arabia. **26** He surrounded

all the Midianites, and burned their tents and plundered their sheepfolds. **27** Then he went down into the plain of Damascus during the wheat harvest, and burned all their fields and destroyed their flocks and herds and sacked their towns and ravaged their lands and put all their young men to the sword.

28 So fear and dread of him fell upon all the people who lived along the seacoast, at Sidon and Tyre, and those who lived in Sur and Ocina and all who lived in Jamnia. Those who lived in Azotus and Ascalon feared him greatly.

Entreaties for Peace

3 They therefore sent messengers to him to sue for peace in these words: **2** "We, the servants of Nebuchadnezzar, the Great King, lie prostrate before you. Do with us whatever you will. **3** See, our buildings and all our land and all our wheat fields and our flocks and herds and all our encampments*d* lie before you; do with them as you please. **4** Our towns and their inhabitants are also your slaves; come and deal with them as you see fit."

5 The men came to Holofernes and told him all this. **6** Then he went down to the seacoast with his army and stationed garrisons in the fortified towns and took picked men from them as auxiliaries. **7** These people and all in the countryside welcomed him with garlands and dances and tambourines. **8** Yet he demolished all their shrines*e* and cut down their sacred groves; for he had been commissioned to destroy all

a Gk sand *b* Gk he *c* Or crossed *d* Gk all the sheepfolds of our tents
e Syr: Gk borders

2:15–18—Compare this huge army and their provisions with the successful guerilla bands of the Maccabean Revolt (1 Macc. 1:28; 3:16; 4:1, 6) and Judith's single act in 13:8. Might does not necessarily make right.

2:19–20 *Locusts*—The exaggerated description of Holofernes' army is propaganda meant to promote fear and to magnify Judith's victory. This technique raises questions about modern war propaganda that feeds our fears in order to

generate support for unpopular or risky military actions.

3:1–10 The Phoenician Coastal Cities Surrender

3:7—*Garlands and dances* foreshadow Israel's victory celebration (15:12–13).

3:8—Holofernes demolishes their **shrines** (a fate that awaits the Jerusalem temple, 8:21), so that they must **worship** only **Nebuchadnezzar** (cf. Dan. 3:6, and ironically, the Maccabees, 1 Macc.

the gods of the land, so that all nations should worship Nebuchadnezzar alone, and that all their dialects and tribes should call upon him as a god.

9 Then he came toward Esdraelon, near Dothan, facing the great ridge of Judea; ¹⁰ he camped between Geba and Scythopolis, and remained for a whole month in order to collect all the supplies for his army.

Judea on the Alert

4 When the Israelites living in Judea heard of everything that Holofernes, the general of Nebuchadnezzar, the king of the Assyrians, had done to the nations, and how he had plundered and destroyed all their temples, ² they were therefore greatly terrified at his approach; they were alarmed both for Jerusalem and for the temple of the Lord their God. ³ For they had only recently returned from exile, and all the people of Judea had just now gathered together, and the sacred vessels and the altar and the temple had been consecrated after their profanation. ⁴ So they sent word to every district of Samaria, and to Kona,

Beth-horon, Belmain, and Jericho, and to Choba and Aesora, and the valley of Salem. ⁵ They immediately seized all the high hilltops and fortified the villages on them and stored up food in preparation for war— since their fields had recently been harvested.

6 The high priest, Joakim, who was in Jerusalem at the time, wrote to the people of Bethulia and Betomesthaim, which faces Esdraelon opposite the plain near Dothan, ⁷ ordering them to seize the mountain passes, since by them Judea could be invaded; and it would be easy to stop any who tried to enter, for the approach was narrow, wide enough for only two at a time to pass.

Prayer and Penance

8 So the Israelites did as they had been ordered by the high priest Joakim and the senate of the whole people of Israel, in session at Jerusalem. ⁹ And every man of Israel cried out to God with great fervor, and they humbled themselves with much fasting. ¹⁰ They and their wives and their children and their cattle and every resident alien and hired laborer

---

2:45). Holofernes equates earthly with divine power, a mistake often made by modern governments.

3:10—A pause in the action contributes to the suspense.

4:1–15 A Terrified Judea Prepares for War
Protection of the Jerusalem temple is the central concern (vv. 3, 12).

4:3 *Only recently returned from exile*—A deliberately inaccurate reference to 539 BCE (cf. 2:1, "the eighteenth year," 587 BCE). Also *consecrated after their profanation* more likely refers to the rededication of the temple (Hanukkah) during the Maccabean revolt (1 Macc. 4:36–61; 2 Macc. 10:1–8). The book's message does not depend on historical accuracy.

4:6—The *high priest, Joakim*, functions with military and religious power like the Hasmonean rulers Jonathan (1 Macc. 10:18–21) and Simon (1 Macc. 14:41–43, 47), 152–104 BCE. Despite the separation of church and state in America, political leaders often use religious rhetoric to support their political and military agendas.

The name *Bethulia* is related to the Hebrew word for virgin, *betulah*. The exact location of

Bethulia is unknown, but it is within Samaritan territory; Samaria is the name of the capital and province of the northern kingdom, Israel. Traditional Samaritan/Jewish friction (Ezra 4; Neh. 4) is subsumed under a memory of a united Israel under David and Solomon. Similarly, our national memory smooths over disagreements and paints an uncritical picture of U.S. history, which ignores justice issues such as the taking of Native American lands and slave holding by the Founding Fathers.

4:9–15 *Cried out to God*—All of Israel publicly fasts and prays together (also 7:29; cf. Esth. 4:16). With our privatistic inclinations, American Christians do not seem very comfortable with communal lament, except as a rubber-stamp for imperialism and an "us versus them" mindset. Communal laments can promote national healing and raise political questions about the consequences of empire building (war, exploitation, refugees).

4:10—*Sackcloth* (a dark cloth woven from goat and camel hair) is a traditional sign of distress, mourning, penitence, and petition (cf. Esth. 4:1–2; 2 Macc. 3:19; Dan. 9:3; Neh. 1:4). The unrestrained use of sackcloth (even children,

and purchased slave—they all put sackcloth around their waists. ¹¹ And all the Israelite men, women, and children living at Jerusalem prostrated themselves before the temple and put ashes on their heads and spread out their sackcloth before the Lord. ¹² They even draped the altar with sackcloth and cried out in unison, praying fervently to the God of Israel not to allow their infants to be carried off and their wives to be taken as booty, and the towns they had inherited to be destroyed, and the sanctuary to be profaned and desecrated to the malicious joy of the Gentiles.

13 The Lord heard their prayers and had regard for their distress; for the people fasted many days throughout Judea and in Jerusalem before the sanctuary of the Lord Almighty. ¹⁴ The high priest Joakim and all the priests who stood before the Lord and ministered to the Lord, with sackcloth around their loins, offered the daily burnt offerings, the votive offerings, and freewill offerings of the people. ¹⁵ With ashes on their turbans, they cried out to the Lord with all their might to look with favor on the whole house of Israel.

Council against the Israelites

5 It was reported to Holofernes, the general of the Assyrian army, that the people of Israel had prepared for war and had closed the mountain passes and fortified all the high hilltops and set up barricades in the plains. ² In great anger he called together all the princes of Moab and the commanders of Ammon and all the governors of the coastland, ³ and said to them, "Tell me, you Canaanites, what people is this that lives in the hill country? What towns do they inhabit? How large is their army, and in what does their power and strength consist? Who rules over them as king and leads their army? ⁴ And why have they alone, of all who live in the west, refused to come out and meet me?"

Achior's Report

5 Then Achior, the leader of all the Ammonites, said to him, "May my lord

---

cattle, and the altar wear it) is probably meant to be humorous (cf. Jonah 3:8). Fasting and sackcloth are part of a postexilic penitential theology. Except perhaps for flying the American flag at half staff, Christians today embrace few public expressions of mourning, and even fewer that are distinctly Christian.

4:12—*Wives to be taken as booty* acknowledges the vulnerability of women and children in war, as Jael (Judg. 4:17–22), Rahab (Josh. 2; 6:24–25), and Sisera's mother knew (Judg. 5:28–30). This practice continues in warfare today, e.g., ethnic cleansing in Bosnia, Rwanda, and Darfur.

4:13—*The Lord heard their prayers* contradicts the people's complaint in 7:23–28. This assertion anticipates Judith's saving act and links her with the judges (Judg. 3:9; 6:7–8), whom God raises up in answer to the people's cries.

5:1–6:13 Holofernes Expels Achior from the Assyrian Camp

5:2—*Moab* and *Ammon* in the Transjordan are traditional enemies of Israel (Deut. 23:3–6) who were originally threatened by Holofernes (1:12) but who are now on his side. Rather than band together with other small nations, they bow to superior power for survival, a pattern often repeated in world politics today.

5:3–5—Holofernes' questions are ironic. He is concerned about earthly kings, but Israel knows that the only true king is God (Judg. 8:22–23; 1 Sam. 8:7). This tension prompts us to ponder what it means for America to be "one nation under God."

5:5–21—Achior responds to Holofernes' questions by recounting the history of Israel from Abraham to the exile (Deut. 26:5–10). This history is told from a Deuteronomic, act/consequence point of view: obedience to the covenant means God's blessing and protection for Israel (Deut. 30). God Bless America bumper stickers express this idea that we have earned God's blessing so that God is on our side. Such thinking can shield national policy from criticism and pit "us" against "them" in a kind of holy war.

5:5 *No falsehood shall come from your servant's mouth*—Another ironic contrast. Judith uses the same words to Holofernes, but she is lying (11:5). Achior's courage before Holofernes matches Judith's; he is the masculine, pagan version of the feminine, Jewish Judith. Achior does not tell Holofernes what he wants to hear, but rather the "truth" (packaged from Israel's point of view). His action reminds us of the dangers both of national policies protected from criticism and of propaganda that takes on a life of its own.

please listen to a report from the mouth of your servant, and I will tell you the truth about this people that lives in the mountain district near you. No falsehood shall come from your servant's mouth. ⁶ These people are descended from the Chaldeans. ⁷ At one time they lived in Mesopotamia, because they did not wish to follow the gods of their ancestors who were in Chaldea. ⁸ Since they had abandoned the ways of their ancestors, and worshiped the God of heaven, the God they had come to know, their ancestors*ᵃ* drove them out from the presence of their gods. So they fled to Mesopotamia, and lived there for a long time. ⁹ Then their God commanded them to leave the place where they were living and go to the land of Canaan. There they settled, and grew very prosperous in gold and silver and very much livestock. ¹⁰ When a famine spread over the land of Canaan they went down to Egypt and lived there as long as they had food. There they became so great a multitude that their race could not be counted. ¹¹ So the king of Egypt became hostile to them; he exploited them and forced them to make bricks. ¹² They cried out to their God, and he afflicted the whole land of Egypt with incurable plagues. So the Egyptians drove them out of their sight. ¹³ Then God dried up the Red Sea before them, ¹⁴ and he led them by the way of Sinai and Kadesh-barnea. They drove out all the people of the desert, ¹⁵ and took up residence in the land of the Amorites, and by their might destroyed all the inhabitants of Heshbon; and crossing over the Jordan they took possession of all the hill country. ¹⁶ They drove out before them the Canaanites, the Perizzites, the Jebusites, the Shechemites, and all the Gergesites, and lived there a long time.

¹⁷ "As long as they did not sin against their God they prospered, for the God who hates iniquity is with them. ¹⁸ But when they departed from the way he had prescribed for them, they were utterly defeated in many battles and were led away captive to a foreign land. The temple of their God was razed to the ground, and their towns were occupied by their enemies. ¹⁹ But now they have returned to their God, and have come back from the places where they were scattered, and have occupied Jerusalem, where their sanctuary is, and have settled in the hill country, because it was uninhabited.

20 "So now, my master and lord, if there is any oversight in this people and they sin against their God and we find out their offense, then we can go up and defeat them. ²¹ But if they are not a guilty nation, then let my lord pass them by; for their Lord and God will defend them, and we shall become the laughingstock of the whole world."

22 When Achior had finished saying these things, all the people standing around the tent began to complain; Holofernes' officers and all the inhabitants of the seacoast and Moab insisted that he should be cut to pieces. ²³ They said, "We are not afraid of the Israelites; they are a people with no strength or power for making war. ²⁴ Therefore let us go ahead, Lord Holofernes, and your vast army will swallow them up."

Achior Handed over to the Israelites

6 When the disturbance made by the people outside the council had died down, Holofernes, the commander of the Assyrian army, said to Achior*ᵇ* in the presence of all the foreign contingents: 2 "Who are you, Achior and you mer-

---

ᵃ Gk they ᵇ Other ancient authorities add *and to all the Moabites*

6:2 Who are you?—Holofernes' angry question anticipates Judith's challenge to Bethulia's elders in 8:12. These questions underscore the author's concern for clarity about Jewish identity in a Greco-Roman world which threatens that

identity. Many today would argue that Christian identity is threatened by our pluralistic, secular context. Holofernes' question challenges us to be clear about who and whose we are in our modern context. *What God is there except*

cenaries of Ephraim, to prophesy among us as you have done today and tell us not to make war against the people of Israel because their God will defend them? What god is there except Nebuchadnezzar? He will send his forces and destroy them from the face of the earth. Their God will not save them; [3] we the king's[a] servants will destroy them as one man. They cannot resist the might of our cavalry. [4] We will overwhelm them;[b] their mountains will be drunk with their blood, and their fields will be full of their dead. Not even their footprints will survive our attack; they will utterly perish. So says King Nebuchadnezzar, lord of the whole earth. For he has spoken; none of his words shall be in vain.

5 "As for you, Achior, you Ammonite mercenary, you have said these words in a moment of perversity; you shall not see my face again from this day until I take revenge on this race that came out of Egypt. [6] Then at my return the sword of my army and the spear[c] of my servants shall pierce your sides, and you shall fall among their wounded. [7] Now my slaves are going to take you back into the hill country and put you in one of the towns beside the passes. [8] You will not die until you perish along with them. [9] If you really hope in your heart that they will not be taken, then do not look downcast! I have spoken, and none of my words shall fail to come true."

10 Then Holofernes ordered his slaves, who waited on him in his tent, to seize Achior and take him away to Bethulia and hand him over to the Israelites. [11] So the slaves took him and led him out of the camp into the plain, and from the plain they went up into the hill country and came to the springs below Bethulia. [12] When the men of the town saw them,[d] they seized their weapons and ran out of the town to the top of the hill, and all the slingers kept them from coming up by throwing stones at them. [13] So having taken shelter below the hill, they bound Achior and left him lying at the foot of the hill, and returned to their master.

14 Then the Israelites came down from their town and found him; they untied him and brought him into Bethulia and placed him before the magistrates of their town, [15] who in those days were Uzziah son of Micah, of the tribe of Simeon, and Chabris son of Gothoniel, and Charmis son of Melchiel. [16] They called together all the elders of the town, and all their young men and women ran to the assembly. They set Achior in the midst of all their people, and Uzziah questioned him about what had happened. [17] He answered and told them what had taken place at the council of Holofernes, and all that he had said in the presence of the Assyrian leaders, and all that Holofernes had boasted he would do against the house of Israel.

[a] Gk his   [b] Other ancient authorities add with it   [c] Lat Syr: Gk people
[d] Other ancient authorities add on the top of the hill

Nebuchadnezzar?—Holofernes' question voices the book's central conflict: between military power and the power of God (see also 9:7, 14; 16:2, 5, 13, 17). His question undergirds the religious persecution of those he conquers (3:8) and recalls the persecutions of the Seleucid Antiochus IV Epiphanes that sparked the Maccabean revolt in 167 BCE, as well as the forced conversions (Idumea) and persecutions (Samaritans) under the Hasmonean John Hyrcanus. Liberators can too easily become conquerors when they forget their history, a sobering challenge to international politics today (Exod. 22:21).

6:4—Holofernes' description of impending destruction echoes that of the ban (herem) practiced by Israel in holy war (Deut. 20:16–18;

Josh. 10:40), another irony. Israel does not admit that its own policy may be as horrific as that of its enemies. Governments might take heed of this disconnect.

6:5 You shall not see my face again—Anticipates the reversal of 14:6, when Achior sees Holofernes' severed head.

6:14–21 Achior Is Taken into Bethulia from Holofernes' Camp

This is a foil or mirror image for Judith leaving Bethulia to enter Holofernes' camp (10:10). Achior converses with Uzziah, the town magistrate, in a reversal of his conversation with Holofernes. Achior betrays Holofernes, just as Judith pretends to betray Israel (11:11–15).

18 Then the people fell down and worshiped God, and cried out:

19 "O Lord God of heaven, see their arrogance, and have pity on our people in their humiliation, and look kindly today on the faces of those who are consecrated to you."

20 Then they reassured Achior, and praised him highly. 21 Uzziah took him from the assembly to his own house and gave a banquet for the elders; and all that night they called on the God of Israel for help.

The Campaign against Bethulia

7 The next day Holofernes ordered his whole army, and all the allies who had joined him, to break camp and move against Bethulia, and to seize the passes up into the hill country and make war on the Israelites. 2 So all their warriors marched off that day; their fighting forces numbered one hundred seventy thousand infantry and twelve thousand cavalry, not counting the baggage and the foot soldiers handling it, a very great multitude. 3 They encamped in the valley near Bethulia, beside the spring, and they spread out in breadth over Dothan as far as Balbaim and in length from Bethulia to Cyamon, which faces Esdraelon.

4 When the Israelites saw their vast numbers, they were greatly terrified and said to one another, "They will now strip clean the whole land; neither the high mountains nor the valleys nor the hills will bear their weight." 5 Yet they all seized their weapons, and when they had kindled fires on their towers, they remained on guard all that night.

6 On the second day Holofernes led out all his cavalry in full view of the Israelites in Bethulia. 7 He reconnoitered the approaches to their town, and visited the springs that supplied their water; he seized them and set guards of soldiers over them, and then returned to his army.

8 Then all the chieftains of the Edomites and all the leaders of the Moabites and the commanders of the coastland came to him and said, 9 "Listen to what we have to say, my lord, and your army will suffer no losses. 10 This people, the Israelites, do not rely on their spears but on the height of the mountains where they live, for it is not easy to reach the tops of their mountains. 11 Therefore, my lord, do not fight against them in regular formation, and not a man of your army will fall. 12 Remain in your camp, and keep all the men in your forces with you; let your servants take possession of the spring of water that flows from the foot of the mountain, 13 for this is where all the people of Bethulia get their water. So thirst will destroy them, and they will surrender their town. Meanwhile, we and our people will go up to the tops of the nearby mountains and camp there to keep watch to see that no one gets out of the town. 14 They and their wives and children will waste away with famine, and before the sword reaches them they will be strewn about in the streets where they live. 15 Thus you will pay them back with evil, because they rebelled and did not receive you peaceably."

16 These words pleased Holofernes and all his attendants, and he gave orders to do as they had said. 17 So the army of the Ammonites moved forward, together with five thousand Assyrians, and they encamped in the valley and seized the water supply and the springs of the Isra-

---

7:1–18 Bethulia under Siege

7:14 *Waste away*—The leaders of Israel's enemies show no compassion for the trapped wives and children of Bethulia who will die of famine. They are simply the pawns of war, payback for Bethulia's rebellion. We ought to be shocked by this, but ironically, modern warfare acknowledges "collateral damage" as inevitable. We are challenged to recognize the humanity of the weakest victims of war. Yet because this story is told from Israel's point of view, we are also reminded that Israel may be demonizing its enemies as unfeeling killers and that we may be guilty of the same distortion in our warfare.

elites. [18] And the Edomites and Ammonites went up and encamped in the hill country opposite Dothan; and they sent some of their men toward the south and the east, toward Egrebeh, which is near Chusi beside the Wadi Mochmur. The rest of the Assyrian army encamped in the plain, and covered the whole face of the land. Their tents and supply trains spread out in great number, and they formed a vast multitude.

The Distress of the Israelites

[19] The Israelites then cried out to the Lord their God, for their courage failed, because all their enemies had surrounded them, and there was no way of escape from them. [20] The whole Assyrian army, their infantry, chariots, and cavalry, surrounded them for thirty-four days, until all the water containers of every inhabitant of Bethulia were empty; [21] their cisterns were going dry, and on no day did they have enough water to drink, for their drinking water was rationed. [22] Their children were listless, and the women and young men fainted from thirst and were collapsing in the streets of the town and in the gateways; they no longer had any strength.

[23] Then all the people, the young men, the women, and the children, gathered around Uzziah and the rulers of the town and cried out with a loud voice, and said before all the elders, [24] "Let God judge between you and us! You have done us a great injury in not making peace with the Assyrians. [25] For now we have no one to help us; God has sold us into their hands, to be strewn before them in thirst and exhaustion. [26] Now summon them and surrender the whole town as booty to the army of Holofernes and to all his forces. [27] For it would be better for us to be captured by them.[a] We shall indeed become slaves, but our lives will be spared, and we shall not witness our little ones dying before our eyes, and our wives and children drawing their last breath. [28] We call to witness against you heaven and earth and our God, the Lord of our ancestors, who punishes us for our sins and the sins of our ancestors; do today the things that we have described!"

[29] Then great and general lamentation arose throughout the assembly, and they cried out to the Lord God with a loud voice. [30] But Uzziah said to them, "Courage, my brothers and sisters![b] Let us hold out for five days more; by that time the Lord our God will turn his mercy to us again, for he will not forsake

---

[a] Other ancient authorities add *than to die of thirst*   [b] Gk *Courage, brothers*

7:19–32 Bethulia's Distress
The emotional description is common in Greek and Jewish novels.

7:20—The siege lasts thirty-four days, a mirror of section two, in which Judith spends four days in the Assyrian camp (12:10) and the Israelites plunder the Assyrian camp for thirty days (15:11).

7:25 *God has sold us*—The people complain to their rulers that God has abandoned them (cf. Ps. 44:12; Judg. 2:14; 1 Sam. 12:9; Esth. 7:4) and urge surrender (v. 26). Like the Israelites in the wilderness who complain to Moses (Exod. 17:1–7, in which lack of water and the testing motif similarly play a part), they do not embrace the assurance of Jdt. 4:13 that God has heard their prayers (cf. Exod. 3:7). The people honestly express their experience of God's absence, seen as a just result of their sin (Jdt. 7:28), in line with the theory of act/consequence, or you get what you deserve (a theme of the wisdom tradition,

Prov. 10:3, Job 4:7–8; and the prophets, Mic. 2:1–5). Like the people of Bethulia, contemporary believers often believe we have done something to deserve our punishment. If we are not careful, we can victimize the victim and ignore the real causes of suffering.

7:28 *Who punishes us for our sins*—The people accept their guilt, which Judith will later deny (8:18–20, 25). Their sense of sin pushes them to surrender; they see no other way out. Sometimes guilt can overwhelm us, so that we give up too soon. Churches that do not hold God's grace in tension with God's judgment run the risk of either paralyzing us or letting us off the hook too easily.

7:30—*Uzziah* means "my strength is the Lord," an ironic twist, since his compromise leaves open the possibility that God will abandon them and provides a negative foil for Judith's courage rooted in faith.

us utterly. ³¹But if these days pass by, and no help comes for us, I will do as you say."

32 Then he dismissed the people to their various posts, and they went up on the walls and towers of their town. The women and children he sent home. In the town they were in great misery.

The Character of Judith

8 Now in those days Judith heard about these things: she was the daughter of Merari son of Ox son of Joseph son of Oziel son of Elkiah son of Ananias son of Gideon son of Raphain son of Ahitub son of Elijah son of Hilkiah son of Eliab son of Nathanael son of Salamiel son of Sarasadai son of Israel. ²Her husband Manasseh, who belonged to her tribe and family, had died during the barley harvest. ³For as he stood overseeing those who were binding sheaves in the field, he was overcome by the burning heat, and took to his bed and died in his town Bethulia.

So they buried him with his ancestors in the field between Dothan and Balamon. ⁴Judith remained as a widow for three years and four months ⁵at home where she set up a tent for herself on the roof of her house. She put sackcloth around her waist and dressed in widow's clothing. ⁶She fasted all the days of her widowhood, except the day before the sabbath and the sabbath itself, the day before the new moon and the day of the new moon, and the festivals and days of rejoicing of the house of Israel. ⁷She was beautiful in appearance, and was very lovely to behold. Her husband Manasseh had left her gold and silver, men and women slaves, livestock, and fields; and she maintained this estate. ⁸No one spoke ill of her, for she feared God with great devotion.

Judith and the Elders

9 When Judith heard the harsh words spoken by the people against the ruler, because they were faint for lack of water,

---

7:32 Great misery—Bethulia's dire situation sets the stage for Judith's entrance.

8:1–8 Section Two Begins; Judith Is Introduced
She enters the story abruptly, like many of the judges (Judg. 3:9, 15); **these things** summarizes the first seven chapters.

8:1—**Judith** has her own genealogy (usually reserved for men) to legitimate her: fourteen generations of male relatives, back to Jacob/**Israel** (lest there be any doubt about her Jewishness, since Bethulia is in Samaritan territory). Judith's tie to Jacob, the liar and trickster, suggests Judith's own deception of Holofernes. The name Judith (Heb. *yehudit*), a feminine form of the masculine name Judah or Judas (the Maccabean liberator), means "Jewess." Thus she metaphorically represents the Jewish nation and all women. In the Bible, the community is often represented positively and negatively by female figures such as a virgin (Amos 5:2; 2 Kgs. 19:21; Jer. 14:17; Lam. 1:15), a bride (Jer. 2:2–3; Hos. 2:15), a whore (Ezek.16; Jer.13:21–27), and a widow (Lam. 1:1; Isa. 54:4–8). We are cautioned against allowing negative metaphors to incite violence against women.

8:2–3 Manasseh—Judith's dead husband shares his name with the evil king who precipitated the Babylonian exile (2 Kgs. 21:12–15; 23:26–27; 24:3–4). Manasseh died when the heat "came

upon his head" (Gk.; NRSV **overcome by the burning heat**) during the barley harvest, anticipating Judith's sword severing the head of Holofernes (13:8; cf. Judg. 5:26; 9:50–54).

8:4—Judith mourns **for three years and four months**, or forty months, which suggests the forty years of Israelite wandering in the wilderness.

8:7–8—Though she wears sackcloth like them, the childless widow Judith is distanced from the other women of Bethulia by her exceptional beauty, piety, wealth, and reputation (**no one spoke ill of her**). These all enable her autonomy and bold action in ways not possible for most women of her time, who were defined by their husbands and children and the honor/shame culture. Her piety and chastity make her a model for later Christian asceticism (1 Cor. 7; 1 Tim. 5:14). She is also distanced from the men of the town by her courage; her only worthy partner is God. Judith is the idealized woman, above it all, on her roof. We are prompted to identify the ways in which American culture both idealizes and denigrates strong women.

8:9–36 Judith Rebukes the Leaders
Judith's faithful zeal is condemned by some who consider her too harsh or pushy and lauded by others as courageous. Where one stands in relation to power shapes one's assessment of her behavior. As a woman in patriarchal society,

and when she heard all that Uzziah said to them, and how he promised them under oath to surrender the town to the Assyrians after five days, [10] she sent her maid, who was in charge of all she possessed, to summon Uzziah and[a] Chabris and Charmis, the elders of her town. [11] They came to her, and she said to them:

"Listen to me, rulers of the people of Bethulia! What you have said to the people today is not right; you have even sworn and pronounced this oath between God and you, promising to surrender the town to our enemies unless the Lord turns and helps us within so many days. [12] Who are you to put God to the test today, and to set yourselves up in the place of[b] God in human affairs? [13] You are putting the Lord Almighty to the test, but you will never learn anything! [14] You cannot plumb the depths of the human heart or understand the workings of the human mind; how do you expect to search out God, who made all these things, and find out his mind or comprehend his thought? No, my brothers, do not anger the Lord our God. [15] For if he does not choose to help us within these five days, he has power to protect us within any time he pleases, or even to destroy us in the presence of our enemies. [16] Do not try to bind the purposes of the Lord our God; for God is not like a human being, to be threatened, or like a mere mortal, to be won over by pleading. [17] Therefore, while we wait for his deliverance, let us call upon him to help us, and he will hear our voice, if it pleases him.

[18] "For never in our generation, nor in these present days, has there been any tribe or family or people or town of ours that worships gods made with hands, as was done in days gone by. [19] That was why our ancestors were handed over to the sword and to pillage, and so they suffered a great catastrophe before our enemies. [20] But we know no other god but him, and so we hope that he will not disdain us or any of our nation. [21] For if we are captured, all Judea will be captured and our sanctuary will be plundered; and he will make us pay for its desecration with our blood. [22] The slaughter of our kindred and the captivity of the land and the desolation of our inheritance—all this he will bring on our heads among the Gentiles, wherever we serve as slaves; and we shall be an offense and a disgrace in the eyes of those who acquire us. [23] For our slavery will not bring us into favor, but the Lord our God will turn it to dishonor.

[24] "Therefore, my brothers, let us set an example for our kindred, for their lives depend upon us, and the sanctuary—

[a] Other ancient authorities lack *Uzziah and* (see verses 28 and 35)
[b] Or *above*

Judith rocks the boat. Often those on the margins are invisible and must push to be heard and taken seriously.

8:10—Judith boldly sends *her maid to summon the elders* to her, challenging traditional gender boundaries.

8:11 *"Listen to me"*—Like the personified woman Wisdom of Proverbs, Judith speaks with authority, using the formula that introduces instruction (Prov. 1:8, 20–21, 23; 5:1; 8:6, 32, 34). Ironically, Judith speaks as Lady Wisdom to claim power that the wisdom tradition upholds as the status quo of the male elite. We are invited to contemplate the ways in which American women claim power in today's culture.

8:12—*Who are you to put God to the test?* echoes Holofernes' question to Achior in 6:2 (cf.

Deut. 6:16), but in a woman's mouth it is a much bolder question. Time limits test God.

8:16—God cannot be *threatened* (by the Assyrians) or pleaded with (by the people, 7:23ff.). This contradicts the assertion in 4:13 that God heard the people's prayers; the ground of all laments is that God hears and can be moved to action. Such a contradiction prompts us to consider what we believe about the nature of prayer and about the God to whom we pray.

8:18–26—The people are innocent (no idol worship); God is testing them as God tested Abraham, Isaac, and Jacob. Judith challenges thinking that moves from suffering back to some sinful cause, which can disempower and paralyze the victim.

both the temple and the altar—rests upon us. ²⁵ In spite of everything let us give thanks to the Lord our God, who is putting us to the test as he did our ancestors. ²⁶ Remember what he did with Abraham, and how he tested Isaac, and what happened to Jacob in Syrian Mesopotamia, while he was tending the sheep of Laban, his mother's brother. ²⁷ For he has not tried us with fire, as he did them, to search their hearts, nor has he taken vengeance on us; but the Lord scourges those who are close to him in order to admonish them."

28 Then Uzziah said to her, "All that you have said was spoken out of a true heart, and there is no one who can deny your words. ²⁹ Today is not the first time your wisdom has been shown, but from the beginning of your life all the people have recognized your understanding, for your heart's disposition is right. ³⁰ But the people were so thirsty that they compelled us to do for them what we have promised, and made us take an oath that we cannot break. ³¹ Now since you are a God-fearing woman, pray for us, so that the Lord may send us rain to fill our cisterns. Then we will no longer feel faint from thirst."

32 Then Judith said to them, "Listen to me. I am about to do something that will go down through all generations of our descendants. ³³ Stand at the town gate tonight so that I may go out with my maid; and within the days after which you have promised to surrender the town to our enemies, the Lord will deliver Israel by my hand. ³⁴ Only, do not try to find out what I am doing; for I will not tell you until I have finished what I am about to do."

35 Uzziah and the rulers said to her, "Go in peace, and may the Lord God go before you, to take vengeance on our enemies." ³⁶ So they returned from the tent and went to their posts.

The Prayer of Judith

9 Then Judith prostrated herself, put ashes on her head, and uncovered the sackcloth she was wearing. At the very time when the evening incense was being offered in the house of God in Jerusalem, Judith cried out to the Lord with a loud voice, and said,

2 "O Lord God of my ancestor Simeon, to whom you gave a sword to take revenge on those strangers who had torn off a virgin's clothing[a] to defile her, and exposed her thighs to put her to shame, and polluted her womb to disgrace her; for you said, 'It shall not be done'—yet they did it; ³ so you gave up their rulers to be killed, and their bed, which was ashamed of the deceit they had practiced, was stained with blood, and you struck down slaves along with princes, and princes on their thrones. ⁴ You gave

[a] Cn: Gk loosed her womb

8:27—Judith comes dangerously close to proclaiming that suffering is good for you (cf. Job's friends, Job 5:17; Prov. 3:12); testing is akin to teaching and discipline. Not everyone can be as strong as the idealized Judith. The idea of testing can be a way for those in power to protect the status quo, minimize injustice, and block attempts at reform.

8:28–31—Uzziah praises Judith's wisdom but dismisses her rebuke by directing her to pray for rain, a traditional woman's role. We are pushed to consider the ways in which we dismiss critique from those on the margins in order to protect our power.

8:32–36 *"By my hand"*—Judith persists, and announces that the Lord will deliver Israel by her (cf. 2:2).

9:1–14 Judith's Prayer

Judith's prayer coincides with the *incense* offering in the Jerusalem temple, reinforcing her piety. She prays to the God of her *ancestor Simeon*, who avenged the rape of Dinah (Gen. 34). Judith simply refers to Dinah as a *virgin* without naming her, which suggests that she identifies with Simeon's role as protector-avenger or go'el ("redeemer," Num. 35:19; Deut. 19:6), rather than with Dinah's role as victim. According to cultural stereotypes, this is not what we would expect from a woman. Has Judith been co-opted by male power?

9:4—Judith simply accepts the male idea that women are *booty to be divided* among the winners (cf. Judg. 5:30) and shows no empathy for them, illustrating that shared gender is no guar-

up their wives for booty and their daughters to captivity, and all their booty to be divided among your beloved children who burned with zeal for you and abhorred the pollution of their blood and called on you for help. O God, my God, hear me also, a widow.

5 "For you have done these things and those that went before and those that followed. You have designed the things that are now, and those that are to come. What you had in mind has happened; 6 the things you decided on presented themselves and said, 'Here we are!' For all your ways are prepared in advance, and your judgment is with foreknowledge.

7 "Here now are the Assyrians, a greatly increased force, priding themselves in their horses and riders, boasting in the strength of their foot soldiers, and trusting in shield and spear, in bow and sling. They do not know that you are the Lord who crushes wars; the Lord is your name. 8 Break their strength by your might, and bring down their power in your anger; for they intend to defile your sanctuary, and to pollute the tabernacle where your glorious name resides, and to break off the horns[a] of your altar with the sword. 9 Look at their pride, and send your wrath upon their heads. Give to me, a widow, the strong hand to do what I plan. 10 By the deceit of my lips strike down the slave with the prince and the prince with his servant; crush their arrogance by the hand of a woman.

11 "For your strength does not depend on numbers, nor your might on the powerful. But you are the God of the lowly, helper of the oppressed, upholder of the weak, protector of the forsaken, savior of those without hope. 12 Please, please, God of my father, God of the heritage of Israel, Lord of heaven and earth, Creator of the waters, King of all your creation, hear my prayer! 13 Make my deceitful words bring wound and bruise on those who have planned cruel things against your covenant, and against your sacred house, and against Mount Zion, and against the house your children possess. 14 Let your whole nation and every tribe know and understand that you are God, the God of all power and might, and that there is no other who protects the people of Israel but you alone!"

Judith Prepares to Go to Holofernes

10 When Judith[b] had stopped crying out to the God of Israel, and had ended all these words, 2 she rose from where she lay prostrate. She called her maid and went down into the house where she lived on sabbaths and on her festal days. 3 She removed the sackcloth she had been wearing, took off her widow's garments, bathed her body with water, and anointed herself with precious ointment. She combed her hair, put on a tiara, and dressed herself in the festive attire that she used to wear while her husband Manasseh was living. 4 She put sandals on her feet, and put on her

[a] Syr: Gk *horn*   [b] Gk *she*

---

antee of solidarity. Yet despite her distancing from other women, Judith invokes her widowhood twice as a warrant for the God of the lowly, oppressed, and weak (Jdt. 9:4,10) to hear her prayer. She deliberately aligns herself with the traditional understanding of widows as weak and vulnerable in order to claim God's support. Judith's doublemindedness invites us to contemplate the often untenable position of women in a man's world.

9:10, 13—Twice Judith prays that God will sanction her deceit so that Holofernes can be defeated.

9:10 *By the hand of a woman*—A shameful

end recalling strong women in Judg. 5:26 and 9:50–54 and celebrated in Judg. 16:5.

10:1–8 Judith Prepares for Holofernes

After penitential prayer, Judith bathes (while the town faints from thirst), anoints herself, and dresses to kill, transforming herself from widow to seductress, like a male hero putting on armor for battle. This transition is similar to a rite of passage. This portrayal of beauty and deceit to evoke men's fear in a sexual context has been called "an anti-woman ideology."

10:4—Her beauty *entices* all (8:7; 10:7, 14, 19,

anklets, bracelets, rings, earrings, and all her other jewelry. Thus she made herself very beautiful, to entice the eyes of all the men who might see her. [5]She gave her maid a skin of wine and a flask of oil, and filled a bag with roasted grain, dried fig cakes, and fine bread;[a] then she wrapped up all her dishes and gave them to her to carry.

6 Then they went out to the town gate of Bethulia and found Uzziah standing there with the elders of the town, Chabris and Charmis. [7]When they saw her transformed in appearance and dressed differently, they were very greatly astounded at her beauty and said to her, [8]"May the God of our ancestors grant you favor and fulfill your plans, so that the people of Israel may glory and Jerusalem may be exalted." She bowed down to God.

9 Then she said to them, "Order the gate of the town to be opened for me so that I may go out and accomplish the things you have just said to me." So they ordered the young men to open the gate for her, as she requested. [10]When they had done this, Judith went out, accompanied by her maid. The men of the town watched her until she had gone down the mountain and passed through the valley, where they lost sight of her.

Judith Is Captured

11 As the women[b] were going straight on through the valley, an Assyrian patrol met her [12]and took her into custody. They asked her, "To what people do you belong, and where are you coming from, and where are you going?" She replied, "I am a daughter of the Hebrews, but I am fleeing from them, for they are about to be handed over to you to be devoured. [13]I am on my way to see Holofernes the commander of your army, to give him a true report; I will show him a way by which he can go and capture all the hill country without losing one of his men, captured or slain."

14 When the men heard her words, and observed her face—she was in their eyes marvelously beautiful—they said to her, [15]"You have saved your life by hurrying down to see our lord. Go at once to his tent; some of us will escort you and hand you over to him. [16]When you stand before him, have no fear in your heart, but tell him what you have just said, and he will treat you well."

17 They chose from their number a hundred men to accompany her and her maid, and they brought them to the tent of Holofernes. [18]There was great excitement in the whole camp, for her arrival was reported from tent to tent. They came and gathered around her as she stood outside the tent of Holofernes, waiting until they told him about her. [19]They marveled at her beauty and admired the Israelites, judging them by

[a]Other ancient authorities add *and cheese* [b]Gk *they*

23; 11:21, 23; 12:13), a regular motif in Greek novels; cf. Esther and Aseneth. We can consider how beauty and sex function in our culture.

10:8—The elders bless Judith before she leaves. It is comforting yet dangerous to believe that God is exclusively on one's own side.

10:9–10 Judith Leaves Bethulia

Like the mythological hero, Judith moves through the town gates into a dangerous, liminal (Latin: threshold) space (the Assyrian camp) in which she does what she does not normally do: lie, seduce, and kill. The danger is that we become comfortable with our liminal behaviors so that they become normative on a national and personal level, e.g., when civil liberties are curtailed in the name of security from terrorism.

10:11–23 Judith Is Captured

10:12–13—Judith's first words are lies. Condemned as morally weak for her lies and no better than Holofernes (who lies in 11:1, 23), she is also defended as doing what is necessary for the survival of underdog Israel; she is a trickster (cf. Rebekah, Gen. 27–28; Tamar, Gen. 38; the women around Moses, Exod. 1–2; Rahab, Josh. 2). These assessments push us to reflect upon whether or not the end (in this case, that all may *know . . . that you are God*, 9:14) justifies the means.

10:15—Irony and double meaning of the word "lord" (see 2:5).

10:19 *Women like this*—Such affirmations of ethnic superiority and fear too often fuel discrimination and war.

her. They said to one another, "Who can despise these people, who have women like this among them? It is not wise to leave one of their men alive, for if we let them go they will be able to beguile the whole world!"

Judith Is Brought before Holofernes

20 Then the guards of Holofernes and all his servants came out and led her into the tent. ²¹ Holofernes was resting on his bed under a canopy that was woven with purple and gold, emeralds and other precious stones. ²² When they told him of her, he came to the front of the tent, with silver lamps carried before him. ²³ When Judith came into the presence of Holofernes*a* and his servants, they all marveled at the beauty of her face. She prostrated herself and did obeisance to him, but his slaves raised her up.

11 Then Holofernes said to her, "Take courage, woman, and do not be afraid in your heart, for I have never hurt anyone who chose to serve Nebuchadnezzar, king of all the earth. ² Even now, if your people who live in the hill country had not slighted me, I would never have lifted my spear against them. They have brought this on themselves. ³ But now tell me why you have fled from them and have come over to us. In any event, you have come to safety. Take courage! You will live tonight and ever after. ⁴ No one will hurt you. Rather, all will treat you well, as they do the servants of my lord King Nebuchadnezzar."

Judith Explains Her Presence

5 Judith answered him, "Accept the words of your slave, and let your servant speak in your presence. I will say nothing false to my lord this night. ⁶ If you follow out the words of your servant, God will accomplish something through you, and my lord will not fail to achieve his purposes. ⁷ By the life of Nebuchadnezzar, king of the whole earth, and by the power of him who has sent you to direct every living being! Not only do human beings serve him because of you, but also the animals of the field and the cattle and the birds of the air will live, because of your power, under Nebuchadnezzar and all his house. ⁸ For we have heard of your wisdom and skill, and it is reported throughout the whole world that you alone are the best in the whole kingdom, the most informed and the most astounding in military strategy.

9 "Now as for Achior's speech in your council, we have heard his words, for the people of Bethulia spared him and he told them all he had said to you. ¹⁰ Therefore, lord and master, do not disregard what he said, but keep it in your mind, for it is true. Indeed our nation cannot be punished, nor can the sword prevail against them, unless they sin against their God.

11 "But now, in order that my lord may not be defeated and his purpose frustrated, death will fall upon them, for a sin has overtaken them by which they are about to provoke their God to anger when they do what is wrong. ¹² Since their food supply is exhausted and their water has almost given out, they have planned to kill their livestock and have determined to use all that God by his laws has forbidden them to eat. ¹³ They have decided to consume the first fruits of the grain and the tithes of the wine and oil, which they had consecrated and set aside for the priests who

a Gk *him*

10:20–12:9 Judith and Holofernes Their conversation is laced with lies and double meanings. Holofernes lies in 11:1, 23, contradicting 3:2, 8. Judith lies to Holofernes in 11:5, contradicting her argument to the Bethulians in 8:18–20; she lies again in 11:17–19. Her flattery in 11:7–8 is a form of lie.

11:3 *You have come to safety*— Or rescue. Holofernes' ironic remark unknowingly suggests Judith's role as a judge who will deliver her people (cf. Judg. 3:9, 15).

11:5, 6—Double meaning of *my lord*: Holofernes or God?

minister in the presence of our God in Jerusalem—things it is not lawful for any of the people even to touch with their hands. [14] Since even the people in Jerusalem have been doing this, they have sent messengers there in order to bring back permission from the council of the elders. [15] When the response reaches them and they act upon it, on that very day they will be handed over to you to be destroyed.

16 "So when I, your slave, learned all this, I fled from them. God has sent me to accomplish with you things that will astonish the whole world wherever people shall hear about them. [17] Your servant is indeed God-fearing and serves the God of heaven night and day. So, my lord, I will remain with you; but every night your servant will go out into the valley and pray to God. He will tell me when they have committed their sins. [18] Then I will come and tell you, so that you may go out with your whole army, and not one of them will be able to withstand you. [19] Then I will lead you through Judea, until you come to Jerusalem; there I will set your throne.[a] You will drive them like sheep that have no shepherd, and no dog will so much as growl at you. For this was told me to give me foreknowledge; it was announced to me, and I was sent to tell you."

20 Her words pleased Holofernes and all his servants. They marveled at her wisdom and said, [21] "No other woman from one end of the earth to the other looks so beautiful or speaks so wisely!" [22] Then Holofernes said to her, "God has done well to send you ahead of the people, to strengthen our hands and bring destruction on those who have despised

my lord. [23] You are not only beautiful in appearance, but wise in speech. If you do as you have said, your God shall be my God, and you shall live in the palace of King Nebuchadnezzar and be renowned throughout the whole world."

Judith as a Guest of Holofernes

12 Then he commanded them to bring her in where his silver dinnerware was kept, and ordered them to set a table for her with some of his own delicacies, and with some of his own wine to drink. [2] But Judith said, "I cannot partake of them, or it will be an offense; but I will have enough with the things I brought with me." [3] Holofernes said to her, "If your supply runs out, where can we get you more of the same? For none of your people are here with us." [4] Judith replied, "As surely as you live, my lord, your servant will not use up the supplies I have with me before the Lord carries out by my hand what he has determined."

5 Then the servants of Holofernes brought her into the tent, and she slept until midnight. Toward the morning watch she got up [6] and sent this message to Holofernes: "Let my lord now give orders to allow your servant to go out and pray." [7] So Holofernes commanded his guards not to hinder her. She remained in the camp three days. She went out each night to the valley of Bethulia, and bathed at the spring in the camp.[b] [8] After bathing, she prayed the Lord God of Israel to direct her way for the triumph of his[c] people. [9] Then she returned purified and stayed in the tent until she ate her food toward evening.

[a] Or chariot   [b] Other ancient authorities lack in the camp   [c] Other ancient authorities read her

---

11:23—Holofernes notes Judith's beauty and wisdom, which challenges the stereotype that beauty and brains do not mix. He appears foolish, which feeds Israel's sense of ethnic superiority. We are called to identify the ways in which we as Americans claim superiority over other nations.

12:1–4—Judith's kosher diet as a mark of Jewish identity is common in this period; cf. Dan.

1:8–16; Tob. 1:10–11; 2 Macc. 5:27. We are prompted to search for marks of Christian identity in secular American culture.

12:7–9—Judith establishes the pattern that will make her escape possible. She prays and ritually purifies herself by bathing (cf. 10:3). Her concern to discourage even the suggestion of impropriety seems out of place in our permissive society.

Judith Attends Holofernes' Banquet

10 On the fourth day Holofernes held a banquet for his personal attendants only, and did not invite any of his officers. ¹¹ He said to Bagoas, the eunuch who had charge of his personal affairs, "Go and persuade the Hebrew woman who is in your care to join us and to eat and drink with us. ¹² For it would be a disgrace if we let such a woman go without having intercourse with her. If we do not seduce her, she will laugh at us."

13 So Bagoas left the presence of Holofernes, and approached her and said, "Let this pretty girl not hesitate to come to my lord to be honored in his presence, and to enjoy drinking wine with us, and to become today like one of the Assyrian women who serve in the palace of Nebuchadnezzar." ¹⁴ Judith replied, "Who am I to refuse my lord? Whatever pleases him I will do at once, and it will be a joy to me until the day of my death." ¹⁵ So she proceeded to dress herself in all her woman's finery. Her maid went ahead and spread for her on the ground before Holofernes the lambskins she had received from Bagoas for her daily use in reclining.

16 Then Judith came in and lay down. Holofernes' heart was ravished with her and his passion was aroused, for he had been waiting for an opportunity to seduce her from the day he first saw her.

¹⁷ So Holofernes said to her, "Have a drink and be merry with us!" ¹⁸ Judith said, "I will gladly drink, my lord, because today is the greatest day in my whole life." ¹⁹ Then she took what her maid had prepared and ate and drank before him. ²⁰ Holofernes was greatly pleased with her, and drank a great quantity of wine, much more than he had ever drunk in any one day since he was born.

Judith Beheads Holofernes

13 When evening came, his slaves quickly withdrew. Bagoas closed the tent from outside and shut out the attendants from his master's presence. They went to bed, for they all were weary because the banquet had lasted so long. ² But Judith was left alone in the tent, with Holofernes stretched out on his bed, for he was dead drunk.

3 Now Judith had told her maid to stand outside the bedchamber and to wait for her to come out, as she did on the other days; for she said she would be going out for her prayers. She had said the same thing to Bagoas. ⁴ So everyone went out, and no one, either small or great, was left in the bedchamber. Then Judith, standing beside his bed, said in her heart, "O Lord God of all might, look in this hour on the work of my hands for the exaltation of Jerusalem. ⁵ Now indeed is the time to help your

---

12:10–20 The Banquet

12:12 *She will laugh at us*—If Holofernes does not seduce Judith, he will lose face before his army. His conquest of this "national beauty" is expected to mirror his army's conquest of Bethulia. Sex and power are intertwined, as we can see in current controversies over women in the American military, female prisoners of war, and ethnic cleansing.

12:14 *Who am I?*—Judith knows exactly who she is. Judith tricks Holofernes into false security, much like Jael (Judg. 5:25).

13:1–10a Judith Alone with Holofernes
The whole scene is laden with sexual imagery.

13:2 *Dead drunk*—The powerful foreigner who lusts for Judith passes out. Drinking led to the demise of Sisera (Judg. 4:19; 5:25) and Queen

Salome Alexandra's husband (Josephus, *Antiq.* 15:5). Israel ridicules Holofernes' vanity and masculinity. Caricatures of one's enemies can lead to feelings of national superiority and uncritical support of policies toward other nations.

13:4–8—Judith prays twice for success and cuts off Holofernes' head; cf. David and Goliath (1 Sam. 17), Jael and Sisera (Judg. 5). Judith becomes a female warrior, taking on male traits, which can be viewed as either liberating, threatening, or supportive of patriarchy. Some argue that Judith acts too much like a man and thereby diminishes women. Viewed as either assassin or national savior, Judith can support both terrorism and the status quo.

13:5 *My design*—God becomes the accessory to Judith's plan. Some would consider this

heritage and to carry out my design to destroy the enemies who have risen up against us."

6 She went up to the bedpost near Holofernes' head, and took down his sword that hung there. 7 She came close to his bed, took hold of the hair of his head, and said, "Give me strength today, O Lord God of Israel!" 8 Then she struck his neck twice with all her might, and cut off his head. 9 Next she rolled his body off the bed and pulled down the canopy from the posts. Soon afterward she went out and gave Holofernes' head to her maid, 10 who placed it in her food bag.

Judith Returns to Bethulia

Then the two of them went out together, as they were accustomed to do for prayer. They passed through the camp, circled around the valley, and went up the mountain to Bethulia, and came to its gates. 11 From a distance Judith called out to the sentries at the gates, "Open, open the gate! God, our God, is with us, still showing his power in Israel and his strength against our enemies, as he has done today!"

12 When the people of her town heard her voice, they hurried down to the town gate and summoned the elders of the town. 13 They all ran together, both small and great, for it seemed unbelievable that she had returned. They opened the gate and welcomed them. Then they lit a fire to give light, and gathered around them. 14 Then she said to them with a loud voice, "Praise God, O praise him! Praise God, who has not withdrawn his mercy from the house of Israel, but has destroyed our enemies by my hand this very night!"

15 Then she pulled the head out of the bag and showed it to them, and said, "See here, the head of Holofernes, the commander of the Assyrian army, and here is the canopy beneath which he lay in his drunken stupor. The Lord has struck him down by the hand of a woman. 16 As the Lord lives, who has protected me in the way I went, I swear that it was my face that seduced him to his destruction, and that he committed no sin with me, to defile and shame me."

17 All the people were greatly astonished. They bowed down and worshiped God, and said with one accord, "Blessed are you our God, who have this day humiliated the enemies of your people."

18 Then Uzziah said to her, "O daughter, you are blessed by the Most High God above all other women on earth; and blessed be the Lord God, who created the heavens and the earth, who has guided you to cut off the head of the leader of our enemies. 19 Your praise[a] will never depart from the hearts of those who remember the power of God. 20 May God grant this to be a perpetual honor to you, and may he reward you with blessings, because you risked your own life when our nation was brought low, and you averted our ruin, walking in the straight path before our God." And all the people said, "Amen. Amen."

Judith's Counsel

14 Then Judith said to them, "Listen to me, my friends. Take this

[a] Other ancient authorities read *hope*

---

blasphemy. Judith's claim invites us to consider the relationship between divine action and human agency.

13:10a—The food bag becomes a trophy bag for Holofernes' head.

13:10b–20 Judith Returns to Bethulia

13:11—*God is with us*, in contrast to the doubts of 7:25. Her command to open the gates parallels her departure from Bethulia in 10:9, and echoes Ps. 24.7.

13:18—Uzziah blesses Judith this time; cf. the blessings of Jael (Judg. 5:24), Mary (Luke 1:42), and Abram (Gen. 14:19–20).

14:1–10 Judith Gives Orders

Judith gives orders to defeat the Assyrians.

14:1 *"Listen to me"*—Judith again speaks with authority; cf. 8:11, 32.

head and hang it upon the parapet of your wall. ² As soon as day breaks and the sun rises on the earth, each of you take up your weapons, and let every able-bodied man go out of the town; set a captain over them, as if you were going down to the plain against the Assyrian outpost; only do not go down. ³ Then they will seize their arms and go into the camp and rouse the officers of the Assyrian army. They will rush into the tent of Holofernes and will not find him. Then panic will come over them, and they will flee before you. ⁴ Then you and all who live within the borders of Israel will pursue them and cut them down in their tracks. ⁵ But before you do all this, bring Achior the Ammonite to me so that he may see and recognize the man who despised the house of Israel and sent him to us as if to his death."

6 So they summoned Achior from the house of Uzziah. When he came and saw the head of Holofernes in the hand of one of the men in the assembly of the people, he fell down on his face in a faint. ⁷ When they raised him up he threw himself at Judith's feet, and did obeisance to her, and said, "Blessed are you in every tent of Judah! In every nation those who hear your name will be alarmed. ⁸ Now tell me what you have done during these days."

So Judith told him in the presence of the people all that she had done, from the day she left until the moment she began speaking to them. ⁹ When she had finished, the people raised a great shout and made a joyful noise in their town. ¹⁰ When Achior saw all that the God of Israel had done, he believed firmly in God. So he was circumcised, and joined the house of Israel, remaining so to this day.

Holofernes' Death Is Discovered

11 As soon as it was dawn they hung the head of Holofernes on the wall. Then they all took their weapons, and they went out in companies to the mountain passes. ¹² When the Assyrians saw them they sent word to their commanders, who then went to the generals and the captains and to all their other officers. ¹³ They came to Holofernes' tent and said to the steward in charge of all his personal affairs, "Wake up our lord, for the slaves have been so bold as to come down against us to give battle, to their utter destruction."

14 So Bagoas went in and knocked at the entry of the tent, for he supposed that he was sleeping with Judith. ¹⁵ But when no one answered, he opened it and went into the bedchamber and found him sprawled on the floor dead, with his head missing. ¹⁶ He cried out with a loud voice and wept and groaned and shouted, and tore his clothes. ¹⁷ Then he went to the tent where Judith had stayed, and when he did not find her, he rushed out to the people and shouted, ¹⁸ "The slaves have tricked us! One Hebrew woman has brought disgrace on the

---

14:6—In humorous contrast to brave Judith, who cut it off, Achior faints at the sight of Holofernes' head; cf. 6:5.

14:10—*He believed firmly in God*; cf. Abraham (Gen. 15:6); Abraham functions as a model for both Achior and Judith. Achior converts by believing in God and being circumcised (contra Deut. 23:3), a ritual seen as a mark of Jewish identity in the Greco-Roman world. We are prompted to identify the marks of Christian identity in American culture and what we believe about God. Achior serves as foil for Holofernes: the righteous Gentile in contrast to the wicked pagan. Judith presents us with only two ways to view foreigners: as enemies or converts, and

nothing in between, a dangerous us/them view in our pluralistic world.

14:11–15:7 The Assyrians Panic
The Assyrians panic over their headless general (cf. Israel in 4:1–2). The enemy is made to look ridiculous.

14:11—Holofernes' head is hung *on the wall* of Bethulia; cf. 1 Sam. 17:54; 31:9–10; 2 Kgs. 10:7–8; Matt. 14:8, and especially Nicanor's head severed by Judas Maccabeus, 1 Macc. 7:47; 2 Macc. 15:35.

14:14–18—Bagoas's comical discovery of Holofernes' headless body echoes Judg. 3:12–25.

house of King Nebuchadnezzar. Look, Holofernes is lying on the ground, and his head is missing!"

19 When the leaders of the Assyrian army heard this, they tore their tunics and were greatly dismayed, and their loud cries and shouts rose up throughout the camp.

The Assyrians Flee in Panic

15 When the men in the tents heard it, they were amazed at what had happened. ²Overcome with fear and trembling, they did not wait for one another, but with one impulse all rushed out and fled by every path across the plain and through the hill country. ³Those who had camped in the hills around Bethulia also took to flight. Then the Israelites, everyone that was a soldier, rushed out upon them. ⁴Uzziah sent men to Betomasthaim*a* and Choba and Kola, and to all the frontiers of Israel, to tell what had taken place and to urge all to rush out upon the enemy to destroy them. ⁵When the Israelites heard it, with one accord they fell upon the enemy,*b* and cut them down as far as Choba. Those in Jerusalem and all the hill country also came, for they were told what had happened in the camp of the enemy. The men in Gilead and in Galilee outflanked them with great slaughter, even beyond Damascus and its borders. ⁶The rest of the people of Bethulia fell upon the Assyrian camp and plundered it, acquiring great riches. ⁷And the Israelites, when they returned from the slaughter, took possession of what remained. Even the villages and towns in the hill country and in the plain got a great amount of booty, since there was a vast quantity of it.

The Israelites Celebrate Their Victory

8 Then the high priest Joakim and the elders of the Israelites who lived in Jerusalem came to witness the good things that the Lord had done for Israel, and to see Judith and to wish her well. ⁹When they met her, they all blessed her with one accord and said to her, "You are the glory of Jerusalem, you are the great boast of Israel, you are the great pride of our nation! ¹⁰You have done all this with your own hand; you have done great good to Israel, and God is well pleased with it. May the Almighty Lord bless you forever!" And all the people said, "Amen."

11 All the people plundered the camp for thirty days. They gave Judith the tent of Holofernes and all his silver dinnerware, his beds, his bowls, and all his furniture. She took them and loaded her mules and hitched up her carts and piled the things on them.

12 All the women of Israel gathered to see her, and blessed her, and some of them performed a dance in her honor. She took ivy-wreathed wands in her hands and distributed them to the women who were with her; ¹³and she and those who were with her crowned themselves with olive wreaths. She went before all the people in the dance, leading all the women, while all the men of Israel followed, bearing their arms and wearing garlands and singing hymns.

Judith Offers Her Hymn of Praise

14 Judith began this thanksgiving before all Israel, and all the people loudly

a Other ancient authorities add *and Bebai* *b* Gk *them*

15:6–7—Israel takes plunder as revenge (cf. Esth. 9; 1 Macc. 7:44–47) and carries out **great slaughter,** an echo of the ban (*herem*) of holy war. The line between justice and revenge is often blurred in foreign policy.

15:8–13 The Israelites Celebrate

15:8–10—Through the blessing of the high priest Joakim, God endorses what Judith has done. It is comforting and yet dangerous to believe that

God approves of our national policies. We are cautioned to be wary of the ways in which the religious establishment can rubber-stamp political and military action.

15:12–13—Like Miriam (Exod. 15:20), Judith leads the women in *dance* (also 1 Sam. 18:6), while the men follow behind. *Olive wreaths* are a Greek custom.

16 sang this song of praise. [1] And Judith said,

Begin a song to my God with
    tambourines,
  sing to my Lord with cymbals.
Raise to him a new psalm;[a]
  exalt him, and call upon his name.
[2] For the Lord is a God who crushes
    wars;
  he sets up his camp among his
    people;
  he delivered me from the hands of
    my pursuers.
[3] The Assyrian came down from the
    mountains of the north;
  he came with myriads of his
    warriors;
their numbers blocked up the wadis,
  and their cavalry covered the hills.
[4] He boasted that he would burn up
    my territory,
  and kill my young men with the
    sword,
and dash my infants to the ground,
  and seize my children as booty,
  and take my virgins as spoil.

[5] But the Lord Almighty has foiled
    them
  by the hand of a woman.[b]
[6] For their mighty one did not fall by
    the hands of the young men,
  nor did the sons of the Titans
    strike him down,
  nor did tall giants set upon him;
but Judith daughter of Merari
  with the beauty of her
    countenance undid him.

[7] For she put away her widow's
    clothing
  to exalt the oppressed in Israel.
She anointed her face with perfume;
[8]   she fastened her hair with a tiara

and put on a linen gown to beguile
    him.
[9] Her sandal ravished his eyes,
  her beauty captivated his mind,
  and the sword severed his neck!
[10] The Persians trembled at her
    boldness,
  the Medes were daunted at her
    daring.

[11] Then my oppressed people shouted;
  my weak people cried out,[c] and the
    enemy[d] trembled;
  they lifted up their voices, and the
    enemy[d] were turned back.
[12] Sons of slave-girls pierced them
    through
  and wounded them like the
    children of fugitives;
  they perished before the army of
    my Lord.

[13] I will sing to my God a new song:
O Lord, you are great and
    glorious,
  wonderful in strength, invincible.
[14] Let all your creatures serve you,
  for you spoke, and they were
    made.
You sent forth your spirit,[e] and it
    formed them;[f]
  there is none that can resist your
    voice.
[15] For the mountains shall be shaken
    to their foundations with the
    waters;
  before your glance the rocks shall
    melt like wax.
But to those who fear you
  you show mercy.

[a] Other ancient authorities read *a psalm and praise*   [b] Other ancient authorities add *he has confounded them*   [c] Other ancient authorities read *feared*   [d] Gk *they*   [e] Or *breath*   [f] Other ancient authorities read *they were created*

16:1–17 Judith's Hymn of Praise
May be modeled on the Song of Moses (Exod. 15) or the Song of Deborah (Judg. 5).

16:5—By the hand of a woman (cf. 8:33; 9:9–10; 13:4, 15) shames the Assyrians (also v. 13).

16:6—Judith emphasizes how unusual her murderous act was.

16:11—God is a God of reversals, a belief comforting to the **oppressed** but threatening to the oppressors.

16:13 A new song—Echoes the enthronement psalms, with motifs of judgment and shaking mountains (e.g., Pss. 96; 98).

16 For every sacrifice as a fragrant
offering is a small thing,
and the fat of all whole burnt
offerings to you is a very little
thing;
but whoever fears the Lord is great
forever.

17 Woe to the nations that rise up
against my people!
The Lord Almighty will take
vengeance on them in the day
of judgment;
he will send fire and worms into
their flesh;
they shall weep in pain forever.

18 When they arrived at Jerusalem, they worshiped God. As soon as the people were purified, they offered their burnt offerings, their freewill offerings, and their gifts. 19 Judith also dedicated to God all the possessions of Holofernes, which the people had given her; and the canopy that she had taken for herself from his bedchamber she gave as a votive offering. 20 For three months the people continued feasting in Jerusalem before the sanctuary, and Judith remained with them.

The Renown and Death of Judith

21 After this they all returned home to their own inheritances. Judith went to Bethulia, and remained on her estate. For the rest of her life she was honored throughout the whole country. 22 Many desired to marry her, but she gave herself to no man all the days of her life after her husband Manasseh died and was gathered to his people. 23 She became more and more famous, and grew old in her husband's house, reaching the age of one hundred five. She set her maid free. She died in Bethulia, and they buried her in the cave of her husband Manasseh; 24 and the house of Israel mourned her for seven days. Before she died she distributed her property to all those who were next of kin to her husband Manasseh, and to her own nearest kindred. 25 No one ever again spread terror among the Israelites during the lifetime of Judith, or for a long time after her death.

16:18–20 Judith Dedicates the Spoils
Judith gives up her tokens of public leadership, the spoils of war.

16:21–25 Conclusion
Judith returns to her estate but not to her ascetic lifestyle, frees her maid, and dies famous. Some argue that Judith is "domesticated" because she returns to her traditional role as widow and is buried with her husband when she dies. Only her fame remains in the public sphere (v. 23). She challenges us to examine our expectations of gender roles and the ways in which we idealize our heroes.

ESTHER

(The Greek Version Containing the Additional Chapters)

The story of Esther is found not only in its more common Hebrew version but also in a Greek version. The Greek version is a fairly literal translation of the Hebrew text, but with six blocks of additional material, which are often called the Additions. The most significant change in the story is the introduction of God, who is mentioned more than fifty times. The focus of the story is no longer human instrumentality, but God's action that brings the Jewish people to final victory. The additional portions include a prophetic dream that Mordecai has before all the events, and then its fulfillment at the end. The verbatim content of Haman's and Mordecai's decrees is provided. Esther and Mordecai are given lengthy prayers, and Esther's approach before the king is considerably different. The broad outline of the Greek version is the same as the Hebrew version, but the Greek version provides a different presentation of the events. Esther and Mordecai are characterized as pious individuals who take care to act in holy ways and see themselves as God's instruments. Whereas Esther's emotions are more vividly portrayed, she also appears more timid. Mordecai's role in the story is considerably expanded, and the focus shifts from Esther to him. Haman's enmity against the Jews is enhanced into a cosmic battle. The Persian king, who is here called Artaxerxes, is contrasted with the heavenly king, who influences the actions of Artaxerxes as well as the actions of the Jews.

As they reflect different original contexts, the additional pieces were most likely not all added to the story at the same time. The texts of the two decrees appear to have been composed in Greek, but the rest of the added material seems to have been written in either Hebrew or Aramaic and then translated into Greek. The translation was made for Greek-speaking Jews outside of Palestine, probably in the second century or even the first century BCE. The fact that new material was being produced, then translated, for the Esther story reveals how important the story must have been to ancient Jewish communities. To complicate matters even further, there exists a second Greek version of the Esther story that is considerably different from this one. All of this compositional activity demonstrates how Esther was perceived as a vibrant story and relevant to the needs of the community. Its complicated textual history provides an example of how contemporary faith communities can wrestle with the biblical text, interpreting it and reinterpreting it for their needs and to reflect their experiences of God.

The following textual notes will concentrate on the places where the Greek version of the book differs from the more familiar Hebrew version.

—Linda Day

NOTE. The deuterocanonical portions of the Book of Esther are several additional passages found in the Greek translation of the Hebrew Book of Esther, a translation that differs also in other respects from the Hebrew text (the latter is translated in the NRSV Old Testament). The disordered chapter numbers come from the displacement of the additions to the end of the canonical Book of Esther by Jerome in his Latin translation and from the subsequent division of the Bible into chapters by Stephen Langton, who numbered the additions consecutively as though they formed a direct continuation of the Hebrew text. So that the additions may be read in their proper context, the whole of the Greek version is here translated, though certain familiar names are given according to their Hebrew rather than their Greek form; for example, Mordecai

and Vashti instead of Mardocheus and Astin. The order followed is that of the Greek text, but the chapter and verse numbers conform to those of the King James or Authorized Version. The additions, conveniently indicated by the letters A—F, are located as follows: A, before 1.1; B after 3.13; C and D, after 4.17; E, after 8.12; F, after 10.3.

ADDITION A

Mordecai's Dream

11[a] [2] In the second year of the reign of Artaxerxes the Great, on the first day of Nisan, Mordecai son of Jair son of Shimei[b] son of Kish, of the tribe of Benjamin, had a dream. [3] He was a Jew living in the city of Susa, a great man, serving in the court of the king. [4] He was one of the captives whom King Nebuchadnezzar of Babylon had brought from Jerusalem with King Jeconiah of Judea. And this was his dream: [5] Noises[c] and confusion, thunders and earthquake, tumult on the earth! [6] Then two great dragons came forward, both ready to fight, and they roared terribly. [7] At their roaring every nation prepared for war, to fight against the righteous nation. [8] It was a day of darkness and gloom, of tribulation and distress, affliction and great tumult on the earth! [9] And the whole righteous nation was troubled; they feared the evils that threatened them,[d] and were ready to perish. [10] Then they cried out to God; and at their outcry, as though from a tiny spring, there came a great river, with

abundant water; [11] light came, and the sun rose, and the lowly were exalted and devoured those held in honor.

[12] Mordecai saw in this dream what God had determined to do, and after he awoke he had it on his mind, seeking all day to understand it in every detail.

A Plot against the King

12 Now Mordecai took his rest in the courtyard with Gabatha and Tharra, the two eunuchs of the king who kept watch in the courtyard. [2] He overheard their conversation and inquired into their purposes, and learned that they were preparing to lay hands on King Artaxerxes; and he informed the king concerning them. [3] Then the king examined the two eunuchs, and after they had confessed it, they were led away to execution. [4] The king made a permanent record of these things, and Mordecai wrote an account of them. [5] And the king ordered Mordecai to serve in the court, and rewarded him for these things. [6] But Haman son of Hammeda-

[a] Chapters 11.2—12.6 correspond to chapter A 1-17 in some translations. [b] Gk Semeios [c] Or Voices [d] Gk their own evils

---

11:2–12 Mordecai's Apocalyptic Dream

11:2–4—From the very beginning of the story Mordecai is described as an exile, part of the Diaspora. The fact that he is also *a great man* demonstrates that a minority person can do well in a dominant culture.

11:7—*The righteous nation* is the Jewish people. The entire Gentile population, *every nation*, is perceived to be a danger to the Jews. The conflict between Haman and Mordecai is placed on a vastly higher plane.

11:10—God acts as a liberator of the needy, just as God heard the cries of the Hebrew slaves in Egypt (Exod. 2:23–25). The *tiny spring* turning to *a great river* refers to Esther (cf. 10:6) and anticipates her growing maturity and authority throughout the story.

12:1–6 Mordecai Thwarts an Assassination Attempt

This is clearly a different version of an incident that is reported later (2:21–23). That it is included twice is an odd feature in the Greek version of Esther, making this passage seem out of place. Its repetition enhances Mordecai's importance and emphasizes his loyalty.

12:5—Mordecai is *rewarded* instantly with a promotion *to serve in the court* rather than having to wait several years (6:1–12).

12:6—It is not clear why Haman is upset, but the most logical possibility is that he must have been involved in the eunuchs' plot. If so, he is guilty not only of plotting against the Jews, but of treason.

tha, a Bougean, who was in great honor with the king, determined to injure Mordecai and his people because of the two eunuchs of the king.

END OF ADDITION A

Artaxerxes' Banquet

1 It was after this that the following things happened in the days of Artaxerxes, the same Artaxerxes who ruled over one hundred twenty-seven provinces from India to Ethiopia.[a] 2 In those days, when King Artaxerxes was enthroned in the city of Susa, 3 in the third year of his reign, he gave a banquet for his Friends and other persons of various nations, the Persians and Median nobles, and the governors of the provinces. 4 After this, when he had displayed to them the riches of his kingdom and the splendor of his bountiful celebration during the course of one hundred eighty days, 5 at the end of the festivity[b] the king gave a drinking party for the people of various nations who lived in the city. This was held for six days in the courtyard of the royal palace, 6 which was adorned with curtains of fine linen and cotton, held by cords of purple linen attached to gold and silver blocks on pillars of marble and other stones. Gold and silver couches were placed on a mosaic floor of emerald, mother-of-pearl, and marble. There were coverings of gauze, embroidered in various colors, with roses arranged around them. 7 The cups were of gold and silver, and a miniature cup was displayed, made of ruby, worth thirty thousand talents. There was abundant sweet wine, such as the king himself drank. 8 The drinking was not according to a fixed rule; but the king wished to have it so, and he commanded his stewards to comply with his pleasure and with that of the guests.

9 Meanwhile, Queen Vashti[c] gave a drinking party for the women in the palace where King Artaxerxes was.

Dismissal of Queen Vashti

10 On the seventh day, when the king was in good humor, he told Haman, Bazan, Tharra, Boraze, Zatholtha, Abataza, and Tharaba, the seven eunuchs who served King Artaxerxes, 11 to escort the queen to him in order to proclaim her as queen and to place the diadem on her head, and to have her display her beauty to all the governors and the people of various nations, for she was indeed a beautiful woman. 12 But Queen Vashti[c] refused to obey him and would not come with the eunuchs. This offended the king and he became furious. 13 He said to his Friends, "This is how Vashti[c] has answered me.[d] Give therefore your ruling and judgment on this matter." 14 Arkesaeus, Sarsathaeus, and Malesear, then the governors of the Persians and Medes who were closest to the king—Arkesaeus, Sarsathaeus, and Malesear, who sat beside him in the chief seats—came to him 15 and told him what must be done to Queen Vashti[c] for not obeying the order that the king had sent her by the eunuchs. 16 Then Muchaeus said to the king and the governors, "Queen Vashti[c] has insulted not only the king but also all the king's governors and officials" 17 (for he had reported to them what the queen had said and how she had defied the king). "And just as she defied King Artaxerxes, 18 so now the other ladies who are wives of the Persian and Median governors, on hearing what she has said to the king, will likewise dare to insult their husbands. 19 If therefore it pleases the king, let him issue a royal decree, inscribed in accordance with the laws of the Medes and Persians so that it may not be altered, that the queen may no longer come into his presence; but let the king give her royal rank to a woman better than she. 20 Let whatever law the

a Other ancient authorities lack to Ethiopia b Gk marriage feast c Gk Astin
d Gk Astin has said thus and so

---

king enacts be proclaimed in his kingdom, and thus all women will give honor
to their husbands, rich and poor alike."
²¹ This speech pleased the king and the
governors, and the kind did as Muchaeus
had recommended. ²² The king sent the
decree into all his kingdom, to every
province in its own language, so that in
every house respect would be shown to
every husband.

Esther Becomes Queen

2 After these things, the king's anger
abated, and he no longer was concerned about Vashti ᵃ or remembered
what he had said and how he had condemned her. ² Then the king's servants
said, "Let beautiful and virtuous girls be
sought out for the king. ³ The king shall
appoint officers in all the provinces of
his kingdom, and they shall select beautiful young virgins to be brought to the
harem in Susa, the capital. Let them be
entrusted to the king's eunuch who is in
charge of the women, and let ointments
and whatever else they need be given
them. ⁴ And the woman who pleases the
king shall be queen instead of Vashti." ᵃ
This pleased the king, and he did so.

5 Now there was a Jew in Susa the
capital whose name was Mordecai son
of Jair son of Shimei ᵇ son of Kish, of the
tribe of Benjamin; ⁶ he had been taken
captive from Jerusalem among those
whom King Nebuchadnezzar of Babylon had captured. ⁷ And he had a foster
child, the daughter of his father's brother,
Aminadab, and her name was Esther.
When her parents died, he brought her
up to womanhood as his own. The girl
was beautiful in appearance. ⁸ So, when
the decree of the king was proclaimed,
and many girls were gathered in Susa the
capital in custody of Gai, Esther also was
brought to Gai, who had custody of the
women. ⁹ The girl pleased him and won

his favor, and he quickly provided her
with ointments and her portion of food, ᶜ
as well as seven maids chosen from the
palace; he treated her and her maids with
special favor in the harem. ¹⁰ Now Esther
had not disclosed her people or country,
for Mordecai had commanded her not to
make it known. ¹¹ And every day Mordecai walked in the courtyard of the harem,
to see what would happen to Esther.

12 Now the period after which a girl
was to go to the king was twelve months.
During this time the days of beautifica-
tion are completed—six months while
they are anointing themselves with oil of
myrrh, and six months with spices and
ointments for women. ¹³ Then she goes
in to the king; she is handed to the person appointed, and goes with him from
the harem to the king's palace. ¹⁴ In the
evening she enters and in the morning
she departs to the second harem, where
Gai the king's eunuch is in charge of the
women; and she does not go in to the
king again unless she is summoned by
name.

15 When the time was fulfilled for
Esther daughter of Aminadab, the
brother of Mordecai's father, to go in
to the king, she neglected none of the
things that Gai, the eunuch in charge
of the women, had commanded. Now
Esther found favor in the eyes of all
who saw her. ¹⁶ So Esther went in to
King Artaxerxes in the twelfth month,
which is Adar, in the seventh year of his
reign. ¹⁷ And the king loved Esther and
she found favor beyond all the other
virgins, so he put on her the queen's
diadem. ¹⁸ Then the king gave a banquet
lasting seven days for all his Friends and
the officers to celebrate his marriage to
Esther; and he granted a remission of
taxes to those who were under his rule.

ᵃ Gk Astin ᵇ Gk Semeios ᶜ Gk lacks of food

2:5–20 The Choice of a New Queen

2:10, 20—Esther's instructions are not only to
keep secret her ethnic identity as a Jew but also
to fear God and keep his laws. As a Jew who can

"pass" in Persian society, surely maintaining her
religious practices will be harder than avoiding
mention of her Jewish ancestry.

The Plot Discovered

19 Meanwhile Mordecai was serving in the courtyard. 20 Esther had not disclosed her country—such were the instructions of Mordecai; but she was to fear God and keep his laws, just as she had done when she was with him. So Esther did not change her mode of life.

21 Now the king's eunuchs, who were chief bodyguards, were angry because of Mordecai's advancement, and they plotted to kill King Artaxerxes. 22 The matter became known to Mordecai, and he warned Esther, who in turn revealed the plot to the king. 23 He investigated the two eunuchs and hanged them. Then the king ordered a memorandum to be deposited in the royal library in praise of the goodwill shown by Mordecai.

Mordecai Refuses to Do Obeisance

3 After these events King Artaxerxes promoted Haman son of Hammedatha, a Bougean, advancing him and granting him precedence over all the king's*a* Friends. 2 So all who were at court used to do obeisance to Haman,*b* for so the king had commanded to be done. Mordecai, however, did not do obeisance. 3 Then the king's courtiers said to Mordecai, "Mordecai, why do you disobey the king's command?" 4 Day after day they spoke to him, but he would not listen to them. Then they informed Haman that Mordecai was resisting the king's command. Mordecai had told them that he was a Jew. 5 So when Haman learned that Mordecai was not doing obeisance to him, he became furiously angry, 6 and plotted to destroy all the Jews under Artaxerxes' rule.

7 In the twelfth year of King Artaxerxes Haman*c* came to a decision by casting lots, taking the days and the months one by one, to fix on one day to destroy the whole race of Mordecai. The lot fell on the fourteenth*d* day of the month of Adar.

Decree against the Jews

8 Then Haman*c* said to King Artaxerxes, "There is a certain nation scattered among the other nations in all your kingdom; their laws are different from those of every other nation, and they do not keep the laws of the king. It is not expedient for the king to tolerate them. 9 If it pleases the king, let it be decreed that they are to be destroyed, and I will pay ten thousand talents of silver into the king's treasury." 10 So the king took off his signet ring and gave it to Haman to seal the decree*e* that was to be written against the Jews. 11 The king told Haman, "Keep the money, and do whatever you want with that nation."

12 So on the thirteenth day of the first month the king's secretaries were summoned, and in accordance with Haman's instructions they wrote in the name of King Artaxerxes to the magistrates and the governors in every province from India to Ethiopia. There were one hundred twenty-seven provinces in all, and the governors were addressed each in his own language. 13 Instructions were sent by couriers throughout all the empire of Artaxerxes to destroy the Jewish people on a given day of the twelfth month, which is Adar, and to plunder their goods.

ADDITION B

The King's Letter

13 *f* This is a copy of the letter: "The Great King, Artaxerxes, writes the following to the governors of the hundred twenty-seven provinces from India to Ethiopia and to the officials under them:

2 "Having become ruler of many nations and master of the whole world

a Gk *all his*   *b* Gk *him*   *c* Gk *he*   *d* Other ancient witnesses read *thirteenth*; see 8.12   *e* Gk lacks *the decree*   *f* Chapter 13.1-7 corresponds to chapter B 1-7 in some translations.

2:21–3:13 A Decree Mandating Genocide
13:1–7 The Text of Haman's Decree

13:2—Artaxerxes is presented as a generous and open-minded monarch, working for the well-being of his subjects.

(not elated with presumption of authority but always acting reasonably and with kindness), I have determined to settle the lives of my subjects in lasting tranquility and, in order to make my kingdom peaceable and open to travel throughout all its extent, to restore the peace desired by all people.

3 "When I asked my counselors how this might be accomplished, Haman— who excels among us in sound judgment, and is distinguished for his unchanging goodwill and steadfast fidelity, and has attained the second place in the kingdom— ⁴ pointed out to us that among all the nations in the world there is scattered a certain hostile people, who have laws contrary to those of every nation and continually disregard the ordinances of kings, so that the unifying of the kingdom that we honorably intend cannot be brought about. ⁵ We understand that this people, and it alone, stands constantly in opposition to every nation, perversely following a strange manner of life and laws, and is ill-disposed to our government, doing all the harm they can so that our kingdom may not attain stability.

6 "Therefore we have decreed that those indicated to you in the letters written by Haman, who is in charge of affairs and is our second father, shall all—wives and children included—be utterly destroyed by the swords of their enemies, without pity or restraint, on the fourteenth day of the twelfth month, Adar, of this present year, ⁷ so that those who have long been hostile and remain so may in a single day go down in violence to Hades, and leave our government completely secure and untroubled hereafter."

END OF ADDITION B

3 ¹⁴ Copies of the document were posted in every province, and all the nations were ordered to be prepared for that day. ¹⁵ The matter was expedited also in Susa. And while the king and Haman caroused together, the city of Susa*ᵃ* was thrown into confusion.

Mordecai Seeks Esther's Aid

4 When Mordecai learned of all that had been done, he tore his clothes, put on sackcloth, and sprinkled himself with ashes; then he rushed through the street of the city, shouting loudly: "An innocent nation is being destroyed!" ² He got as far as the king's gate, and there he stopped, because no one was allowed to enter the courtyard clothed in sackcloth and ashes. ³ And in every province where the king's proclamation had been posted there was a loud cry of mourning and lamentation among the Jews, and they put on sackcloth and ashes. ⁴ When the queen's*ᵇ* maids and eunuchs came and told her, she was deeply troubled by what she heard had happened, and sent some clothes to Mordecai to put on instead of sackcloth; but he would not consent. ⁵ Then Esther summoned Hachratheus, the eunuch who attended her, and ordered him to get accurate information for her from Mordecai.*ᶜ*

7 So Mordecai told him what had happened and how Haman had promised to

ᵃ Gk the city *ᵇ* Gk When her *ᶜ* Other ancient witnesses add ⁶ So Hachratheus went out to Mordecai in the street of the city opposite the city gate.

13:3—As he is the one actually writing the decree, the depiction of Haman is exceptionally self-serving (cf. 3:12).

13:4–5—The language against the Jews is much harsher than Haman couched it earlier to Artaxerxes, and therefore even less accurate (3:8). He now accuses them not only of disobedience but of being outrightly *hostile* to others and *doing all the harm they can*.

13:7—The eradication of the Jews is promised to leave the kingdom *completely secure and untroubled.* Racist propaganda often (falsely) presents all of society's problems as the fault of one minority population.

3:14–15 A Royal Toast, a City's Confusion
4:1–17 Esther's Moment of Decision

pay ten thousand talents into the royal treasury to bring about the destruction of the Jews. [8] He also gave him a copy of what had been posted in Susa for their destruction, to show to Esther; and he told him to charge her to go in to the king and plead for his favor in behalf of the people. "Remember," he said, "the days when you were an ordinary person, being brought up under my care—for Haman, who stands next to the king, has spoken against us and demands our death. Call upon the Lord; then speak to the king in our behalf, and save us from death."

[9] Hachratheus went in and told Esther all these things. [10] And she said to him, "Go to Mordecai and say, [11] 'All nations of the empire know that if any man or woman goes to the king inside the inner court without being called, there is no escape for that person. Only the one to whom the king stretches out the golden scepter is safe—and it is now thirty days since I was called to go to the king.'"

[12] When Hachratheus delivered her entire message to Mordecai, [13] Mordecai told him to go back and say to her, "Esther, do not say to yourself that you alone among all the Jews will escape alive. [14] For if you keep quiet at such a time as this, help and protection will come to the Jews from another quarter, but you and your father's family will perish. Yet, who knows whether it was not for such a time as this that you were made queen?" [15] Then Esther gave the messenger this answer to take back to Mordecai: [16] "Go and gather all the Jews who are in Susa and fast on my behalf; for three days and nights do not eat or drink, and my maids and I will also go without food. After that I will go to the king, contrary to the law, even if I must die." [17] So Mordecai went away and did what Esther had told him to do.

Addition C

Mordecai's Prayer

13 [8a] Then Mordecai[b] prayed to the Lord, calling to remembrance all the works of the Lord.

[9] He said, "O Lord, Lord, you rule as King over all things, for the universe is in your power and there is no one who can oppose you when it is your will to save Israel, [10] for you have made heaven and earth and every wonderful thing under heaven. [11] You are Lord of all, and there is no one who can resist you, the Lord. [12] You know all things; you know, O Lord, that it was not in insolence or pride or for any love of glory that I did this, and refused to bow down to this proud Haman; [13] for I would have been willing to kiss the soles of his feet to save Israel! [14] But I did this so that I might not set human glory above the glory of God, and I will not bow down to anyone but you, who are my Lord; and I will not do these things in pride. [15] And now, O Lord God and King, God of Abraham, spare your people; for the eyes of our foes are upon us[c] to annihilate us, and they desire to destroy the inheritance that has been yours from the beginning. [16] Do not neglect your portion, which you redeemed for yourself out of the land of Egypt. [17] Hear my prayer, and have mercy upon your inheritance; turn our mourning into feasting that we

[a] Chapters 13.8—15.16 correspond to chapters C 1-30 and D 1-16 in some translations. [b] Gk he [c] Gk for they are eying us

---

4:8—Mordecai encourages Esther to pray, soliciting God's help for her endeavor, before approaching the king.

13:8–18 Mordecai's Prayer
The prayer stresses that only God can bring victory to Israel. It uses typical biblical language and imagery about God.

13:12—God is one who can look into the human heart and see its innermost intentions.

13:14—Mordecai explains why he did not bow before Haman, a significant detail not provided in the Hebrew version. He does not want to be guilty of idolatry. Unlike **proud Haman** (13:12), Mordecai is careful to avoid acting **in pride**. Sometimes an action that is very commonly acceptable can still take us away from properly honoring God.

may live and sing praise to your name, O Lord; do not destroy the lips[a] of those who praise you."

18 And all Israel cried out mightily, for their death was before their eyes.

Esther's Prayer

14 Then Queen Esther, seized with deadly anxiety, fled to the Lord. ² She took off her splendid apparel and put on the garments of distress and mourning, and instead of costly perfumes she covered her head with ashes and dung, and she utterly humbled her body; every part that she loved to adorn she covered with her tangled hair. ³ She prayed to the Lord God of Israel, and said: "O my Lord, you only are our king; help me, who am alone and have no helper but you, ⁴ for my danger is in my hand. ⁵ Ever since I was born I have heard in the tribe of my family that you, O Lord, took Israel out of all the nations, and our ancestors from among all their forebears, for an everlasting inheritance, and that you did for them all that you promised. ⁶ And now we have sinned before you, and you have handed us over to our enemies ⁷ because we glorified their gods. You are righteous, O Lord! ⁸ And now they are not satisfied that we are in bitter slavery, but they have covenanted with their idols ⁹ to abolish what your mouth has ordained, and to destroy your inheritance, to stop the mouths of those who praise you and to quench your altar and the glory of your house,

¹⁰ to open the mouths of the nations for the praise of vain idols, and to magnify forever a mortal king.

11 "O Lord, do not surrender your scepter to what has no being; and do not let them laugh at our downfall; but turn their plan against them, and make an example of him who began this against us. ¹² Remember, O Lord; make yourself known in this time of our affliction, and give me courage, O King of the gods and Master of all dominion! ¹³ Put eloquent speech in my mouth before the lion, and turn his heart to hate the man who is fighting against us, so that there may be an end of him and those who agree with him. ¹⁴ But save us by your hand, and help me, who am alone and have no helper but you, O Lord. ¹⁵ You have knowledge of all things, and you know that I hate the splendor of the wicked and abhor the bed of the uncircumcised and of any alien. ¹⁶ You know my necessity—that I abhor the sign of my proud position, which is upon my head on days when I appear in public. I abhor it like a filthy rag, and I do not wear it on the days when I am at leisure. ¹⁷ And your servant has not eaten at Haman's table, and I have not honored the king's feast or drunk the wine of libations. ¹⁸ Your servant has had no joy since the day that I was brought here until now, except in you, O Lord God of Abraham. ¹⁹ O God, whose might is over all, hear the voice of the despairing, and save us from the

[a] Gk mouth

13:18—The prayer is not the words of an individual but a communal prayer, as *all Israel* has been listening to Mordecai's words and cries out in agreement.

14:1–19 Esther's Prayer

14:2—*Garments of distress and mourning* are often used for penitential prayer.

14:3—Esther counts on God to hear her cries.

14:3–19—Esther's prayer is more passionate than Mordecai's prayer, and she refers to God in more personal terms. Her frequent requests for God to help her relate specifically to the fact that the Jews' salvation rests upon her own shoulders.

14:5–10—Esther has learned well her people's history. As women became more literate during Hellenistic times, perhaps Esther was well educated.

14:13—Esther's plan will be based upon *eloquent speech*, her rhetorical ability to persuade Artaxerxes.

14:15–18—Esther reveals how she dislikes being queen and has *no joy* in the role. Like Mordecai, she also defends her piety as she emphasizes that she has kept kosher all these years. To survive in a male-oriented environment, women often have to pretend to the outside world that they like something they actually dislike.

hands of evildoers. And save me from my fear!"

END OF ADDITION C

ADDITION D

Esther Is Received by the King

15 On the third day, when she ended her prayer, she took off the garments in which she had worshiped, and arrayed herself in splendid attire. ² Then, majestically adorned, after invoking the aid of the all-seeing God and Savior, she took two maids with her; ³ on one she leaned gently for support, ⁴ while the other followed, carrying her train. ⁵ She was radiant with perfect beauty, and she looked happy, as if beloved, but her heart was frozen with fear. ⁶ When she had gone through all the doors, she stood before the king. He was seated on his royal throne, clothed in the full array of his majesty, all covered with gold and precious stones. He was most terrifying.

7 Lifting his face, flushed with splendor, he looked at her in fierce anger. The queen faltered, and turned pale and faint, and collapsed on the head of the maid who went in front of her. ⁸ Then God changed the spirit of the king to gentleness, and in alarm he sprang from his throne and took her in his arms until she came to herself. He comforted her with soothing words, and said to her, ⁹ "What is it, Esther? I am your husband.ᵃ

Take courage; ¹⁰ You shall not die, for our law applies only to our subjects.ᵇ Come near."

11 Then he raised the golden scepter and touched her neck with it; ¹² he embraced her, and said, "Speak to me." ¹³ She said to him, "I saw you, my lord, like an angel of God, and my heart was shaken with fear at your glory. ¹⁴ For you are wonderful, my lord, and your countenance is full of grace." ¹⁵ And while she was speaking, she fainted and fell. ¹⁶ Then the king was agitated, and all his servants tried to comfort her.

END OF ADDITION D

5ᶜ ³ The king said to her, "What do you wish, Esther? What is your request? It shall be given you, even to half of my kingdom." ⁴ And Esther said, "Today is a special day for me. If it pleases the king, let him and Haman come to the dinner that I shall prepare today." ⁵ Then the king said, "Bring Haman quickly, so that we may do as Esther desires." So they both came to the dinner that Esther had spoken about. ⁶ While they were drinking wine, the king said to Esther, "What is it, Queen Esther? It shall be granted you." ⁷ She said, "My petition and request is: ⁸ if I have found favor in the sight of the king, let the king and Haman come to the dinner that I shall prepare them,

ᵃ Gk brother   ᵇ Meaning of Gk uncertain   ᶜ In Greek, Chapter D replaces verses 1 and 2 in Hebrew.

15:1–16 Esther Approaches Artaxerxes
This section replaces a much briefer depiction of the events in the Hebrew version (5:1–2). The suspense is greatly increased, and the overall picture of the approach is significantly altered. The sense of danger is more tangible, and Esther is less able to handle it with aplomb.

15:2–4—The *two maids* provide a sense of female solidarity, physically and emotionally helping Esther face her difficult task.

15:5—That Esther *looked happy* despite her great despair (14:15–18) shows what an accomplished actor she must be. Though afraid, Esther still carries on with her mission. When we know that others are counting on us, we often

feel more obligated to fulfill our responsibilities despite the difficulty.

15:7—Weak from fear and from hunger after her three-day fast, Esther *turned pale and faint, and collapsed*.

15:8—In this version, unlike the Hebrew version, what changes Artaxerxes' mind is ultimately God's action, not Esther's skills of persuasion.

15:13–15—In light of how she really feels about the king (14:15), Esther's calling him an *angel of God* is flattery. Her second fainting spell may also be part of her planned strategy, for it certainly achieves a beneficial result in igniting the king's compassion.

5:3–8 Esther Hosts

and tomorrow I will do as I have done today."

Haman's Plot against Mordecai

9 So Haman went out from the king joyful and glad of heart. But when he saw Mordecai the Jew in the courtyard, he was filled with anger. [10] Nevertheless, he went home and summoned his friends and his wife Zosara. [11] And he told them about his riches and the honor that the king had bestowed on him, and how he had advanced him to be the first in the kingdom. [12] And Haman said, "The queen did not invite anyone to the dinner with the king except me; and I am invited again tomorrow. [13] But these things give me no pleasure as long as I see Mordecai the Jew in the courtyard." [14] His wife Zosara and his friends said to him, "Let a gallows be made, fifty cubits high, and in the morning tell the king to have Mordecai hanged on it. Then, go merrily with the king to the dinner." This advice pleased Haman, and so the gallows was prepared.

Mordecai's Reward from the King

6 That night the Lord took sleep from the king, so he gave orders to his secretary to bring the book of daily records, and to read to him. [2] He found the words written about Mordecai, how he had told the king about the two royal eunuchs who were on guard and sought to lay hands on King Artaxerxes. [3] The king said, "What honor or dignity did we bestow on Mordecai?" The king's servants said, "You have not done anything for him." [4] While the king was inquiring about the goodwill shown by Mordecai, Haman was in the courtyard. The king asked, "Who is in the courtyard?" Now Haman had come to speak to the king about hanging Mordecai on the gallows that he had prepared. [5] The servants of the king answered, "Haman is standing in the courtyard." And the king said, "Summon him." [6] Then the king said to Haman, "What shall I do for the person whom I wish to honor?" And Haman said to himself, "Whom would the king wish to honor more than me?" [7] So he said to the king, "For a person whom the king wishes to honor, [8] let the king's servants bring out the fine linen robe that the king has worn, and the horse on which the king rides, [9] and let both be given to one of the king's honored Friends, and let him robe the person whom the king loves and mount him on the horse, and let it be proclaimed through the open square of the city, saying, 'Thus shall it be done to everyone whom the king honors.'" [10] Then the king said to Haman, "You have made an excellent suggestion! Do just as you have said for Mordecai the Jew, who is on duty in the courtyard. And let nothing be omitted from what you have proposed." [11] So Haman got the robe and the horse; he put the robe on Mordecai and made him ride through the open square of the city, proclaiming, "Thus shall it be done to everyone whom the king wishes to honor." [12] Then Mordecai returned to the courtyard, and Haman hurried back to his house, mourning and with his head covered. [13] Haman told his wife Zosara and his friends what had befallen him. His friends and his wife said to him, "If Mordecai is of the Jewish people, and you have begun to be humiliated before him, you will surely fall. You will not be able to defend yourself, because the living God is with him."

Haman at Esther's Banquet

14 While they were still talking, the eunuchs arrived and hurriedly brought Haman to the banquet that Esther had

---

5:9–6:14 Haman's Pride Goes before His Fall

6:1—It is not coincidence, as in the Hebrew version, but *the Lord* who causes the subsequent events to proceed as they do.

6:13—Haman's wife credits the perseverance of the Jewish race specifically to divine activity. Though Gentile, she also recognizes God's power.

7 prepared. [1]So the king and Haman went in to drink with the queen. [2]And the second day, as they were drinking wine, the king said, "What is it, Queen Esther? What is your petition and what is your request? It shall be granted to you, even to half of my kingdom." [3]She answered and said, "If I have found favor with the king, let my life be granted me at my petition, and my people at my request. [4]For we have been sold, I and my people, to be destroyed, plundered, and made slaves—we and our children—male and female slaves. This has come to my knowledge. Our antagonist brings shame on[a] the king's court." [5]Then the king said, "Who is the person that would dare to do this thing?" [6]Esther said, "Our enemy is this evil man Haman!" At this, Haman was terrified in the presence of the king and queen.

Punishment of Haman

[7]The king rose from the banquet and went into the garden, and Haman began to beg for his life from the queen, for he saw that he was in serious trouble. [8]When the king returned from the garden, Haman had thrown himself on the couch, pleading with the queen. The king said, "Will he dare even assault my wife in my own house?" Haman, when he heard, turned away his face. [9]Then Bugathan, one of the eunuchs, said to the king, "Look, Haman has even prepared a gallows for Mordecai, who gave information of concern to the king; it is standing at Haman's house, a gallows fifty cubits high." So the king said, "Let Haman be hanged on that." [10]So Haman was hanged on the gallows he had prepared for Mordecai. With that the anger of the king abated.

Royal Favor Shown the Jews

8 On that very day King Artaxerxes granted to Esther all the property of the persecutor[b] Haman. Mordecai was summoned by the king, for Esther had told the king[c] that he was related to her. [2]The king took the ring that had been taken from Haman, and gave it to Mordecai; and Esther set Mordecai over everything that had been Haman's.

[3]Then she spoke once again to the king and, falling at his feet, she asked him to avert all the evil that Haman had planned against the Jews. [4]The king extended his golden scepter to Esther, and she rose and stood before the king. [5]Esther said, "If it pleases you, and if I have found favor, let an order be sent rescinding the letters that Haman wrote and sent to destroy the Jews in your kingdom. [6]How can I look on the ruin of my people? How can I be safe if my ancestral nation[d] is destroyed?" [7]The king said to Esther, "Now that I[e] have granted all of Haman's property to you and have hanged him on a tree because he acted against the Jews, what else do you request? [8]Write in my name what you think best and seal it with my ring; for whatever is written at the king's command and sealed with my ring cannot be contravened."

[9]The secretaries were summoned on the twenty-third day of the first month, that is, Nisan, in the same year; and all that he commanded with respect to the Jews was given in writing to the administrators and governors of the provinces from India to Ethiopia, one hundred twenty-seven provinces, to each province in its own language. [10]The edict was written[f] with the king's authority and sealed with his ring, and sent out by couriers. [11]He ordered the Jews in every city to observe their own laws, to defend themselves, and to act as they wished against their opponents and enemies [12]on a certain day, the thirteenth of the twelfth month, which is Adar, throughout all the kingdom of Artaxerxes.

a Gk is not worthy of   *b* Gk slanderer   *c* Gk him   *d* Gk country   *e* Gk If I
f Gk It was written

ADDITION E

The Decree of Artaxerxes

16 [a] The following is a copy of this letter:

"The Great King, Artaxerxes, to the governors of the provinces from India to Ethiopia, one hundred twenty-seven provinces, and to those who are loyal to our government, greetings.

2 "Many people, the more they are honored with the most generous kindness of their benefactors, the more proud do they become, ³ and not only seek to injure our subjects, but in their inability to stand prosperity, they even undertake to scheme against their own benefactors. ⁴ They not only take away thankfulness from others, but, carried away by the boasts of those who know nothing of goodness, they even assume that they will escape the evil-hating justice of God, who always sees everything. ⁵ And often many of those who are set in places of authority have been made in part responsible for the shedding of innocent blood, and have been involved in irremediable calamities, by the persuasion of friends who have been entrusted with the administration of public affairs, ⁶ when these persons by the false trickery of their evil natures beguile the sincere goodwill of their sovereigns.

7 "What has been wickedly accomplished through the pestilent behavior of those who exercise authority unworthily can be seen, not so much from the more ancient records that we hand on, as from investigation of matters close at hand.[b] ⁸ In the future we will take care to render our kingdom quiet and peaceable for all, ⁹ by changing our methods and always judging what comes before our eyes with more equitable consideration. ¹⁰ For Haman son of Hammedatha, a Macedonian (really an alien to the Persian blood, and quite devoid of our kindliness), having become our guest, ¹¹ enjoyed so fully the goodwill that we have for every nation that he was called our father and was continually bowed down to by all as the person second to the royal throne. ¹² But, unable to restrain his arrogance, he undertook to deprive us of our kingdom and our life,[c] ¹³ and with intricate craft and deceit asked for the destruction of Mordecai, our savior and perpetual benefactor, and of Esther, the blameless partner of our kingdom, together with their whole nation. ¹⁴ He thought that by these methods he would catch us undefended and would transfer the kingdom of the Persians to the Macedonians.

15 "But we find that the Jews, who were consigned to annihilation by this thrice-accursed man, are not evildoers, but are governed by most righteous laws ¹⁶ and are children of the living God, most high, most mighty,[d] who has directed the kingdom both for us and for our ancestors in the most excellent order.

17 "You will therefore do well not to put in execution the letters sent by Haman son of Hammedatha, ¹⁸ since he, the one who did these things, has been

---

[a] Chapter 16.1-24 corresponds to chapter E 1-24 in some translations.
[b] Gk matters beside (your) feet   [c] Gk our spirit   [d] Gk greatest

---

16:1–24 The Text of Artaxerxes' Decree

16:2–6—Artaxerxes stresses the corrupting influence of power if it is not tempered with humility.

16:5–7—Leaders who are in *places of authority* bear extra responsibility to guard against injustice (cf. Ps. 72).

16:10—As Macedonians were enemies of Persians, this statement represents a racial slur. Persons belonging to one minority must avoid the all-too-frequent temptation to try to raise themselves up by putting down another minority group.

16:15—The minority population, the Jews, has proven beneficial to the larger society.

16:17–18—This statement displays discrepancies with the rest of the story by saying that the decree might not be *put in execution* (cf. 9:2–16) and that *his household* has already been hanged (cf. 9:14).

hanged at the gate of Susa with all his household—for God, who rules over all things, has speedily inflicted on him the punishment that he deserved.

19 "Therefore post a copy of this letter publicly in every place, and permit the Jews to live under their own laws. 20 And give them reinforcements, so that on the thirteenth day of the twelfth month, Adar, on that very day, they may defend themselves against those who attack them at the time of oppression. 21 For God, who rules over all things, has made this day to be a joy for his chosen people instead of a day of destruction for them.

22 "Therefore you shall observe this with all good cheer as a notable day among your commemorative festivals, 23 so that both now and hereafter it may represent deliverance for you[a] and the loyal Persians, but that it may be a reminder of destruction for those who plot against us.

24 "Every city and country, without exception, that does not act accordingly shall be destroyed in wrath with spear and fire. It shall be made not only impassable for human beings, but also most hateful to wild animals and birds for all time."

END OF ADDITION E

---

8 13 "Let copies of the decree be posted conspicuously in all the kingdom, and let all the Jews be ready on that day to fight against their enemies."

14 So the messengers on horseback set out with all speed to perform what the king had commanded; and the decree was published also in Susa. 15 Mordecai went out dressed in the royal robe and wearing a gold crown and a turban of purple linen. The people in Susa rejoiced on seeing him. 16 And the Jews had light and gladness 17 in every city and province wherever the decree was published; wherever the proclamation was made, the Jews had joy and gladness, a banquet and a holiday. And many of the Gentiles were circumcised and became Jews out of fear of the Jews.

Victory of the Jews

9 Now on the thirteenth day of the twelfth month, which is Adar, the decree written by the king arrived. 2 On that same day the enemies of the Jews perished; no one resisted, because they feared them. 3 The chief provincial governors, the princes, and the royal secretaries were paying honor to the Jews, because fear of Mordecai weighed upon them. 4 The king's decree required that Mordecai's name be held in honor throughout the kingdom.[b] 6 Now in the city of Susa the Jews killed five hundred people, 7 including Pharsannestain, Delphon, Phasga, 8 Pharadatha, Barea, Sarbacha, 9 Marmasima, Aruphaeus, Arsaeus, Zabutheus, 10 the ten sons of Haman son of Hammedatha, the Bougean, the enemy of the Jews—and they indulged[c] themselves in plunder.

11 That very day the number of those killed in Susa was reported to the king. 12 The king said to Esther, "In Susa, the capital, the Jews have destroyed five hundred people. What do you suppose they have done in the surrounding countryside? Whatever more you ask will be done for you." 13 And Esther said to the king, "Let the Jews be allowed to do the same tomorrow. Also, hang up

---

a Other ancient authorities read *for us*   b Meaning of Gk uncertain. Some ancient authorities add verse 5, *So the Jews struck down all their enemies with the sword, killing and destroying them, and they did as they pleased to those who hated them.*   c Other ancient authorities read *did not indulge*

16:19—The Persian culture does not adhere to a melting-pot ideology for its various peoples, but minority cultures are allowed to maintain *their own laws* and customs.

16:20–22—The Gentiles are to help the Jews defend themselves and to join in the Purim celebrations with the Jews. *God, who rules over all things*, is pleased by different ethnic groups joining in solidarity.

8:13–17 The Jews Rejoice

9:1–19 Jewish Victory

the bodies of Haman's ten sons." ¹⁴ So he permitted this to be done, and handed over to the Jews of the city the bodies of Haman's sons to hang up. ¹⁵ The Jews who were in Susa gathered on the fourteenth and killed three hundred people, but took no plunder.

16 Now the other Jews in the kingdom gathered to defend themselves, and got relief from their enemies. They destroyed fifteen thousand of them, but did not engage in plunder. ¹⁷ On the fourteenth day they rested and made that same day a day of rest, celebrating it with joy and gladness. ¹⁸ The Jews who were in Susa, the capital, came together also on the fourteenth, but did not rest. They celebrated the fifteenth with joy and gladness. ¹⁹ On this account then the Jews who are scattered around the country outside Susa keep the fourteenth of Adar as a joyful holiday, and send presents of food to one another, while those who live in the large cities keep the fifteenth day of Adar as their joyful holiday, also sending presents to one another.

The Festival of Purim

20 Mordecai recorded these things in a book, and sent it to the Jews in the kingdom of Artaxerxes both near and far, ²¹ telling them that they should keep the fourteenth and fifteenth days of Adar, ²² for on these days the Jews got relief from their enemies. The whole month (namely, Adar), in which their condition had been changed from sorrow into gladness and from a time of distress to a holiday, was to be celebrated as a time for feasting*a* and gladness and for sending presents of food to their friends and to the poor.

23 So the Jews accepted what Mordecai had written to them ²⁴—how Haman son of Hammedatha, the Macedonian,*b* fought against them, how he made a decree and cast lots*c* to destroy them, ²⁵ and how he went in to the king, tell-

ing him to hang Mordecai; but the wicked plot he had devised against the Jews came back upon himself, and he and his sons were hanged. ²⁶ Therefore these days were called "Purim," because of the lots (for in their language this is the word that means "lots"). And so, because of what was written in this letter, and because of what they had experienced in this affair and what had befallen them, Mordecai established this festival,*d* ²⁷ and the Jews took upon themselves, upon their descendants, and upon all who would join them, to observe it without fail.*e* These days of Purim should be a memorial and kept from generation to generation, in every city, family, and country. ²⁸ These days of Purim were to be observed for all time, and the commemoration of them was never to cease among their descendants.

29 Then Queen Esther daughter of Aminadab along with Mordecai the Jew wrote down what they had done, and gave full authority to the letter about Purim.*f* ³¹ And Mordecai and Queen Esther established this decision on their own responsibility, pledging their own well-being to the plan.*e* ³² Esther established it by a decree forever, and it was written for a memorial.

10 The king levied a tax upon his kingdom both by land and sea. ² And as for his power and bravery, and the wealth and glory of his kingdom, they were recorded in the annals of the kings of the Persians and the Medes. ³ Mordecai acted with authority on behalf of King Artaxerxes and was great in the kingdom, as well as honored by the Jews. His way of life was such as to make him beloved to his whole nation.

a Gk of weddings   *b* Other ancient witnesses read the Bougean   *c* Gk a lot
d Gk he established (it)   *e* Meaning of Gk uncertain   *f* Verse 30 in Heb is lacking in Gk: Letters were sent to all the Jews, to the one hundred twenty-seven provinces of the kingdom of Ahasuerus, in words of peace and truth.

9:20–10:3 The New Holiday of Purim Is Established

ADDITION F

Mordecai's Dream Fulfilled

4[a] And Mordecai said, "These things have come from God; [5] for I remember the dream that I had concerning these matters, and none of them has failed to be fulfilled. [6] There was the little spring that became a river, and there was light and sun and abundant water—the river is Esther, whom the king married and made queen. [7] The two dragons are Haman and myself. [8] The nations are those that gathered to destroy the name of the Jews. [9] And my nation, this is Israel, who cried out to God and was saved. The Lord has saved his people; the Lord has rescued us from all these evils; God has done great signs and wonders, wonders that have never happened among the nations. [10] For this purpose he made two lots, one for the people of God and one for all the nations, [11] and these two lots came to the hour and moment and day of decision before God and among all the nations. [12] And God remembered his people and vindicated his inheritance. [13] So they will observe these days in the month of Adar, on the fourteenth and fifteenth[b] of that month, with an assembly and joy and gladness before God, from generation to generation forever among his people Israel."

Postscript

11 [1] In the fourth year of the reign of Ptolemy and Cleopatra, Dositheus, who said that he was a priest and a Levite,[c] and his son Ptolemy brought to Egypt[d] the preceding Letter about Purim, which they said was authentic and had been translated by Lysimachus son of Ptolemy, one of the residents of Jerusalem.

END OF ADDITION F

---

[a] Chapter 10.4-13 and 11.1 correspond to chapter F 1-11 in some translations.   [b] Other ancient authorities lack *and fifteenth*   [c] Or *priest, and Levitas*   [d] Cn: Gk *brought in*

10:4–11:1 The Interpretation of Mordecai's Dream

10:4–13—Now, after all these years, Mordecai finally can understand his *dream*. It reinterprets all of the events on a cosmic, rather than a human, level. The details of the dream do not line up neatly with the details of the story.

10:4—The expression *these things have come from God* sums up well the essence of the Greek version of Esther. God is credited with everything that has occurred.

10:8—*The name* indicates the Jews' reputation. The Gentiles are interpreted as wanting *to destroy* them totally, so that their reputation is no longer known.

10:10—As *lots* represent chance, God is in control even of chance (cf. 3:7).

10:12–13—As *God remembered* the Jews, they are to remember down through the generations what God did for them when they celebrate Purim.

The Book of

WISDOM OF SOLOMON

The Wisdom of Solomon is at home in the Wisdom literature of the Bible, sharing insights into the meaning and nature of human existence and the importance of faithful discipleship for abundant living. The book of Wisdom, as it is known in the Latin Vulgate, is a literary fruit of Hellenistic Judaism but owes its preservation to the Christian community. It is found in the Septuagint, the Greek Old Testament, but because it was a product of Diaspora Judaism, it was not included in the official Jewish canon formed at Jamnia around 90 CE. It lost whatever official standing it may have had in the worship of the synagogue.

The author of the Wisdom of Solomon used the Septuagint version of the Law, Prophets, and Writings of the Hebrew Bible. Therefore it must have been written after the second century BCE. Because it is alluded to at various points in the New Testament, it must have been written prior to the second half of the first century CE. The Wisdom of Solomon does not seem to know the writings of Philo, so a date late in the first century BCE seems to be a good dating of the book.

The Wisdom of Solomon is not found as a Hebrew text, and its smooth Greek, including wordplay (paronomasia) in Greek, makes it most likely that the book was composed in Greek by a Hellenistic Jew of Alexandria, Egypt. The writer selects the persona of Solomon because the ancient Israelite king is the father of wisdom and the author wishes to have such an authority stand behind his words. He does, after all, place himself in the same tradition as Proverbs and Ecclesiastes.

Like the books of Daniel and Maccabees, Wisdom can be understood as an attempt to help an oppressed people endure persecution. The author of Wisdom, however, was challenged by more than the need to strengthen a persecuted people. His community of faith was threatened by the less malignant but more powerful pull of culture. Hellenistic culture was very attractive to Diaspora Jews. They were caught up in the sophisticated intelligence of Greek philosophy, the great advances of Greek science, and the commanding power of civil religion. The author's community was in danger of disappearing into the dominant culture by assimilation; his people would lose their Jewish distinctiveness by becoming like everyone else. Nevertheless, wisdom does not answer the threat with a wholesale rejection of and withdrawal from Hellenism. Instead, the author demonstrates that his faith is compatible with the best of Hellenistic culture and that it offers something even better.

The author of Wisdom demonstrates a certain type of acculturation of the Old Testament to Hellenism in his visualization of creation as bringing order to the chaos of formless matter (11:17) and in his use of a Greek philosopher to explain the origin of idols (14:16–21). The author includes the four cardinal virtues taught by Plato and popular among Stoic philosophers (self-control, prudence, justice, and courage) in the

teaching of Wisdom (8:7). The persona of Solomon expresses a great appreciation of Greek science as a gift from God (7:17–22). Even the description of Wisdom herself is expressed in terms reminiscent of Plato (7:24–26).

The major contribution of Wisdom's thought, which, with modifications, is a development of Hellenistic thought, is the concept of incorruption or immortality expressed in chapters 1–3. The fact that disciples can hope for eternal life (immortality) is new in biblical thought. Wisdom does not simply adopt the Greek idea of immortality of the human soul, however, but adapts it to Hebrew thought. The human being is indeed mortal, but through a relationship with God based upon righteousness, is granted immortality. God sustains the life of the faithful because God "made us in the image of his own eternity" (2:23). It is God's activity, not humanity's inherent nature, that grants incorruption to the human being (including the body) and therefore makes a person immortal, always understood in relationship with God.

The author of Wisdom also demonstrates a critical attitude toward Hellenism. He condemns and ridicules idolatry as fully as any Old Testament prophet or New Testament writer (13:1–15:17). In fact, the idol and the idol worshiper are equally condemned (14:8). Perhaps the harshest criticism of Hellenistic culture, however, lies in the extended comparison or contrast of the Egyptians and Israelites (11:5–19:22). While other peoples are included in this section (Canaanites, 12:3–11; Sodomites, 19:13–17), it is certainly the Egyptians who receive the most attention. Such emphasis not only owes itself to the historical realities of Israel, but indicates the geographical origin of Wisdom, namely, the Jewish community of Alexandria.

Often the teachings of Wisdom anticipate the thought of such New Testament writers as Paul, John, and the author of Hebrews. Certainly the Wisdom of Solomon can serve as a word from God to encourage the disciple to stand firm in the midst of oppression. It also enables the disciple to remain faithful to God and the community of faith when tempted to give in to the secularism and materialism of contemporary culture. Perhaps to the ears of some within the community of faith in a postmodern society, Wisdom will sound naively positive. However, if the disciple will remember its context, the teachings of Wisdom will be convincing once again in proclaiming that "righteousness is immortal."

—Gary Light

Exhortation to Uprightness

1 Love righteousness, you rulers of
    the earth,
think of the Lord in goodness
and seek him with sincerity of
    heart;

2 because he is found by those who do
    not put him to the test,
and manifests himself to those who
    do not distrust him.
3 For perverse thoughts separate
    people from God,

1:1 *Love righteousness [or justice]*—The book opens with an exhortation to align both thought and deed to what is right according to the instruction of God (Torah). Loving righteousness is putting it into practice in one's life. Solomon recognized that God loves uprightness of the heart (1 Chr. 29:17) and the psalmist makes loving righteousness a royal virtue (Ps. 45:7). *Rulers of the earth*—The admonition is directed to the

kings and those who hold the power of state, declaring that they are not free to make their own rules. Rulers are warned and oppressed believers encouraged: if the powerful do not practice righteousness, they will be held accountable.

The real audience, however, is the Jewish community of Alexandria. There are many who themselves want to feel powerful and see conforming to Hellenistic culture as the way to

and when his power is tested, it
    exposes the foolish;

4 because wisdom will not enter a
        deceitful soul,
    or dwell in a body enslaved to sin.

5 For a holy and disciplined spirit will
        flee from deceit,
    and will leave foolish thoughts
        behind,
    and will be ashamed at the approach
        of unrighteousness.

6 For wisdom is a kindly spirit,
    but will not free blasphemers from
        the guilt of their words;
    because God is witness of their
        inmost feelings,
    and a true observer of their hearts,
        and a hearer of their tongues.

7 Because the spirit of the Lord has
        filled the world,
    and that which holds all things
        together knows what is said,

8 therefore those who utter
        unrighteous things will not
        escape notice,
    and justice, when it punishes, will
        not pass them by.

9 For inquiry will be made into the
        counsels of the ungodly,
    and a report of their words will
        come to the Lord,
    to convict them of their lawless
        deeds;

10 because a jealous ear hears all things,

and the sound of grumbling does
    not go unheard.

11 Beware then of useless grumbling,
    and keep your tongue from slander;
    because no secret word is without
        result,[a]
    and a lying mouth destroys the soul.

12 Do not invite death by the error of
        your life,
    or bring on destruction by the works
        of your hands;

13 because God did not make death,
    and he does not delight in the death
        of the living.

14 For he created all things so that they
        might exist;
    the generative forces[b] of the world
        are wholesome,
    and there is no destructive poison in
        them,
    and the dominion[c] of Hades is not
        on earth.

15 For righteousness is immortal.

Life as the Ungodly See It

16 But the ungodly by their words and
        deeds summoned death;[d]
    considering him a friend, they pined
        away
    and made a covenant with him,
    because they are fit to belong to his
        company.

2 For they reasoned unsoundly,
        saying to themselves,

[a] Or will go unpunished   [b] Or the creatures   [c] Or palace   [d] Gk him

---

power. Here "ruler" speaks to every member of
the community of faith. Wisdom echoes the idea
that all humanity shares the image of God and
the royal characteristic of dominion (Gen. 1). The
command also is reminiscent of the prophet's
declaration, "He has told you, O mortal, what is
good; . . . to do justice, and to love kindness . . ."
(Mic. 6:8). Faithful living is the way of power for
the disciple.

1:13 God did not make death—The creative
purpose of God was life that finds its source in a
relationship with God. Reflecting an understanding of Gen. 3 as the fall, Wisdom teaches that
it was disobedience that invited death into the
world, not God's loving intention for humanity.
Death is experienced through the rupture of one's
obedient relationship with God. The theme is

repeated in Wis. 1:16 and 2:24, and Paul writes
from the same perspective in Rom. 5.

**1:14–15 For he created all things so that they
might exist . . . righteousness is immortal**—Wisdom, like Greek philosophy, teaches that humanity is immortal, but with an essential difference.
In contrast to Greek philosophy, Wisdom does
not teach that the human being possesses an
immortal soul. Instead, humanity owes its immortality to the grace of God as believers live in
relationship with God. God's creative purpose
was for life. All that God sets in motion is **wholesome**. And God does not allow a right relationship to perish.

2:1–5 Short and sorrowful is our life—Because
the ungodly do not have wisdom (1:3–4), they do

"Short and sorrowful is our life,
and there is no remedy when a life
comes to its end,
and no one has been known to
return from Hades.
2 For we were born by mere chance,
and hereafter we shall be as though
we had never been,
for the breath in our nostrils is
smoke,
and reason is a spark kindled by the
beating of our hearts;
3 when it is extinguished, the body
will turn to ashes,
and the spirit will dissolve like
empty air.
4 Our name will be forgotten in time,
and no one will remember our
works;
our life will pass away like the traces
of a cloud,
and be scattered like mist
that is chased by the rays of the sun
and overcome by its heat.
5 For our allotted time is the passing
of a shadow,
and there is no return from our
death,
because it is sealed up and no one
turns back.
6 "Come, therefore, let us enjoy the
good things that exist,
and make use of the creation to the
full as in youth.
7 Let us take our fill of costly wine and
perfumes,

and let no flower of spring pass
us by.
8 Let us crown ourselves with
rosebuds before they wither.
9 Let none of us fail to share in our
revelry;
everywhere let us leave signs of
enjoyment,
because this is our portion, and this
our lot.
10 Let us oppress the righteous poor
man;
let us not spare the widow
or regard the gray hairs of the aged.
11 But let our might be our law of
right,
for what is weak proves itself to be
useless.

12 "Let us lie in wait for the righteous
man,
because he is inconvenient to us and
opposes our actions;
he reproaches us for sins against the
law,
and accuses us of sins against our
training.
13 He professes to have knowledge of
God,
and calls himself a child[a] of the
Lord.
14 He became to us a reproof of our
thoughts;
15 the very sight of him is a burden
to us,

[a] Or servant

---

not know about immortality (2:5). Their life has
no purpose (v. 2), no permanence (vv. 2–3), and
no meaning (v. 4).

**2:6–11 Let us enjoy the good things that exist
. . . what is weak proves itself to be useless**—
The ungodly are unwise. They seek fulfillment
in pleasure (vv. 6–7) and literally take as their
theme: "Gather we rosebuds while we may" (v.
8). There is no restraint or regard for ethics in a
world where might makes right (vv. 10–11).

**2:12–20 Let us lie in wait for the righteous
man**—The true disciple suffers persecution because the ungodly see the righteous as a threat;
he is inconvenient because of the constant
reminders of God's instruction. The very presence

of the righteous person can become a **burden** on
the conscience of the ungodly because one way
of life contrasts sharply with the other (v. 15).

The disciple, however, should pause to ponder
the possibility that the witness of righteousness
may degenerate to the condescension of self-
righteousness (v. 16).

The life of the true disciple becomes a challenge to the ungodly, and persecution becomes
a way of testing the truth of the disciple's witness
(vv. 17, 19). Since the disciple claims that *God
is his father* and that the life of the disciple is
ultimately *happy* (v. 16), God will protect the
disciple from *a shameful death* if the benefits of
faith are a reality (v. 20).

because his manner of life is unlike
    that of others,
and his ways are strange.

16 We are considered by him as
    something base,
and he avoids our ways as unclean;
he calls the last end of the righteous
    happy,
and boasts that God is his father.

17 Let us see if his words are true,
and let us test what will happen at
    the end of his life;

18 for if the righteous man is God's
    child, he will help him,
and will deliver him from the hand
    of his adversaries.

19 Let us test him with insult and
    torture,
so that we may find out how gentle
    he is,
and make trial of his forbearance.

20 Let us condemn him to a shameful
    death,
for, according to what he says, he
    will be protected."

Error of the Wicked

21 Thus they reasoned, but they were
    led astray,
for their wickedness blinded them,

22 and they did not know the secret
    purposes of God,

nor hoped for the wages of holiness,
nor discerned the prize for blameless
    souls;

23 for God created us for
    incorruption,
and made us in the image of his own
    eternity,[a]

24 but through the devil's envy death
    entered the world,
and those who belong to his
    company experience it.

The Destiny of the Righteous

3 But the souls of the righteous are in
    the hand of God,
and no torment will ever touch
    them.

2 In the eyes of the foolish they
    seemed to have died,
and their departure was thought to
    be a disaster,

3 and their going from us to be their
    destruction;
but they are at peace.

4 For though in the sight of others
    they were punished,
their hope is full of immortality.

5 Having been disciplined a little, they
    will receive great good,
because God tested them and found
    them worthy of himself;

[a] Other ancient authorities read *nature*

2:21–24 They did not know the secret purposes of God—Wisdom advances the theological reflection of the Hebrew Bible with this explanation of God's purpose of granting immortality to the faithful even through earthly oppression. The unrighteous do not have the wisdom to know, discern, or even hope for the reward that God has in store for the righteous: **incorruption**. This incorruption is not the Greek idea of the immortality of the soul, but God's faithfulness to God's purpose in creation. Because humanity shares the image of the eternal God, God maintains the living relationship experienced by the faithful for eternity, even beyond the barrier of death. Paul speaks from this very perspective as he explains the meaning of the resurrection in 1 Cor. 15:42–49.

    Those who break this vital, faithful relationship with God, like the devil himself, will experience **death** in the very death of this relationship. They do not conceive of the **wages of holiness,**

immortality (Wis. 2:22), but receive instead the wages of sin (Rom. 6:23), death.

3:1–9 The righteous are in the hand of God—The concept of incorruption or **immortality** (v. 4) offers Wisdom a new perspective from which to explain the death, even a premature death, of the righteous: what is seen is not all that exists, and even visible events are not always as they seem. Wisdom takes a giant step away from the Old Testament idea of Sheol as the shadowy existence of all who are dead and toward the concept of heaven found in the New Testament. For the righteous there is life after death; through discipline and testing God has **found them worthy of himself** (v. 5). The Old Testament idea of eternal life, being remembered by one's descendants from generation to generation, gives way to an understanding of receiving **peace** (v. 3; wholeness/completeness) in a relationship that continues beyond death by the **love, grace,** and **mercy** of God (v. 9).

6 like gold in the furnace he tried them,
and like a sacrificial burnt offering
he accepted them.
7 In the time of their visitation they
will shine forth,
and will run like sparks through the
stubble.
8 They will govern nations and rule
over peoples,
and the Lord will reign over them
forever.
9 Those who trust in him will
understand truth,
and the faithful will abide with him
in love,
because grace and mercy are upon
his holy ones,
and he watches over his elect.*a*

The Destiny of the Ungodly

10 But the ungodly will be punished as
their reasoning deserves,
those who disregarded the
righteous*b*
and rebelled against the Lord;
11 for those who despise wisdom and
instruction are miserable.
Their hope is vain, their labors are
unprofitable,
and their works are useless.
12 Their wives are foolish, and their
children evil;
13 their offspring are accursed.

On Childlessness

For blessed is the barren woman
who is undefiled,
who has not entered into a sinful
union;
she will have fruit when God
examines souls.

14 Blessed also is the eunuch whose
hands have done no lawless
deed,
and who has not devised wicked
things against the Lord;
for special favor will be shown him
for his faithfulness,
and a place of great delight in the
temple of the Lord.
15 For the fruit of good labors is
renowned,
and the root of understanding does
not fail.
16 But children of adulterers will not
come to maturity,
and the offspring of an unlawful
union will perish.
17 Even if they live long they will be
held of no account,
and finally their old age will be
without honor.
18 If they die young, they will have no
hope
and no consolation on the day of
judgment.
19 For the end of an unrighteous
generation is grievous.

4 Better than this is childlessness
with virtue,
for in the memory of virtue*c* is
immortality,
because it is known both by God and
by mortals.
2 When it is present, people
imitate*d* it,
and they long for it when it has gone;
throughout all time it marches,
crowned in triumph,

---

a Text of this line uncertain; omitted by some ancient authorities. Compare
4.15   *b* Or *what is right*   *c* Gk *it*   *d* Other ancient authorities read *honor*

3:14 *Blessed also is the eunuch*—Isaiah 56:4–5
offers the eunuch a place among the people of
God. Wisdom echoes the prophet, declaring
even those thought to be unable to have a full
relationship with God, the *barren woman* (Wis.
3:13) and the eunuch, have far deeper, satisfying
relationships with God than the unrighteous can
hope to experience.

3:16–19 *The end of an unrighteous generation
is grievous*—Even if the unrighteous should obtain everything considered in the Old Testament
to be signs of God's favor (long life, wife, and
children), they bring no more assurance of God's
presence than dying young (v. 18). See 4:3–6.

4:1–2 *In the memory of virtue is immortality*—
The virtuous person has a more lasting memorial
than a person who has many children. While
alive, the example of virtue is imitated; when
dead, it is missed. Because virtue is permanent,
the virtuous is immortal.

victor in the contest for prizes that
    are undefiled.
3 But the prolific brood of the ungodly
        will be of no use,
    and none of their illegitimate
        seedlings will strike a deep root
    or take a firm hold.
4 For even if they put forth boughs for
        a while,
    standing insecurely they will be
        shaken by the wind,
    and by the violence of the winds
        they will be uprooted.
5 The branches will be broken off
        before they come to maturity,
    and their fruit will be useless,
    not ripe enough to eat, and good for
        nothing.
6 For children born of unlawful
        unions
    are witnesses of evil against their
        parents when God examines
        them.*a*
7 But the righteous, though they die
        early, will be at rest.
8 For old age is not honored for length
        of time,
    or measured by number of years;
9 but understanding is gray hair for
        anyone,
    and a blameless life is ripe old age.

10 There were some who pleased God
        and were loved by him,

and while living among sinners were
        taken up.
11 They were caught up so that evil
        might not change their
        understanding
    or guile deceive their souls.
12 For the fascination of wickedness
        obscures what is good,
    and roving desire perverts the
        innocent mind.
13 Being perfected in a short time, they
        fulfilled long years;
14 for their souls were pleasing to the
        Lord,
    therefore he took them quickly from
        the midst of wickedness.
15 Yet the peoples saw and did not
        understand,
    or take such a thing to heart,
    that God's grace and mercy are with
        his elect,
    and that he watches over his holy
        ones.

The Triumph of the Righteous

16 The righteous who have died will
        condemn the ungodly who are
        living,
    and youth that is quickly perfected*b*
        will condemn the prolonged
        old age of the unrighteous.
17 For they will see the end of the
        wise,

a Gk *at their examination*   *b* Or *ended*

4:7–9 *For old age is not honored for length of time*—Wisdom redefines *gray hair* and old age. They no longer are the results of a literal passing of time but synonyms for signs of wisdom: understanding and a life lived in harmony with God's will. Even the righteous who die young *rest* because they have achieved these things by obtaining wisdom.

4:10–15 *So that evil might not change their understanding*—Verse 10 alludes to Enoch, Gen. 5:21–24. Enoch died young (compare 365 years to the other life spans in the chapter!) and was righteous ("walked with God" describes Enoch's manner of living, not his manner of departing this world). Just as God took Enoch, the righteous who die young are *taken up* (a divine passive). Nevertheless, Wisdom's reasoning raises as many questions as it answers. God takes these young disciples whom he loves so that they will not

later fall into evil ways (Wis. 4:11, 14). Does God not trust them? What about the rest of those who struggle to live faithfully? Does God not love them as much? Is it really comforting to tell those mourning for loved ones prematurely lost, "God took them so they would not suffer later on," or "God needed them more than we did"?

4:16–19 *The Lord will laugh them to scorn*—The death of the young faithful does not call God's care or power into question for Wisdom. Instead, these deaths call the living ungodly into judgment. The ungodly misinterpret these deaths because they cannot *see the end of the wise* (their experience of incorruption) and contemptuously think that their lives have been wasted. God, however, knows the lives of the ungodly are ultimately *dry and barren* and that they will *perish* (v. 19) rather than receive immortality.

and will not understand what the
　　Lord purposed for them,
　and for what he kept them safe.

18 The unrighteous*a* will see, and will
　　have contempt for them,
　but the Lord will laugh them to
　　scorn.
　After this they will become
　　dishonored corpses,
　and an outrage among the dead
　　forever;

19 because he will dash them speechless
　　to the ground,
　and shake them from the
　　foundations;
　they will be left utterly dry and
　　barren,
　and they will suffer anguish,
　and the memory of them will
　　perish.

The Final Judgment

20 They will come with dread when
　　their sins are reckoned up,
　and their lawless deeds will convict
　　them to their face.

5 Then the righteous will stand with
　　great confidence
　in the presence of those who have
　　oppressed them
　and those who make light of their
　　labors.

2 When the unrighteous*a* see them,
　　they will be shaken with
　　dreadful fear,
　and they will be amazed at the
　　unexpected salvation of the
　　righteous.

3 They will speak to one another in
　　repentance,
　and in anguish of spirit they will
　　groan, and say,

4 "These are persons whom we once
　　held in derision
　and made a byword of reproach—
　　fools that we were!
　We thought that their lives were
　　madness
　and that their end was without
　　honor.

5 Why have they been numbered
　　among the children of God?
　And why is their lot among the
　　saints?

6 So it was we who strayed from the
　　way of truth,
　and the light of righteousness did
　　not shine on us,
　and the sun did not rise upon us.

7 We took our fill of the paths of
　　lawlessness and destruction,
　and we journeyed through trackless
　　deserts,
　but the way of the Lord we have not
　　known.

8 What has our arrogance
　　profited us?
　And what good has our boasted
　　wealth brought us?

9 "All those things have vanished like a
　　shadow,
　and like a rumor that passes by;

10 like a ship that sails through the
　　billowy water,
　and when it has passed no trace can
　　be found,
　no track of its keel in the waves;

11 or as, when a bird flies through the
　　air,
　no evidence of its passage is found;
　the light air, lashed by the beat of its
　　pinions

a Gk *They*

4:20–5:8 When the unrighteous see them—
Wisdom pictures a great recognition scene that
will occur on judgment day. Both the righteous
and the unrighteous will be present, and the very
presence of the righteous whom the ungodly had
dismissed will be enough to make the ungodly
recognize their error and pronounce their own
condemnation.

5:9–14 No evidence of its passage is found—
The ungodly offer some similes for the meaning
of their own lives: shadows, rumors, the disappearing wake of a ship, and the lack of a trail in
the air after birds or arrows have flown by. Without virtue, the hope of the wicked disappears like
seeds scattered by the wind, frost washed away
by the rain, smoke dispersed by the wind, or the
brief memory of a one-day visit of a guest.

and pierced by the force of its
rushing flight,
is traversed by the movement of its
wings,
and afterward no sign of its coming
is found there;

12 or as, when an arrow is shot at a
target,
the air, thus divided, comes together
at once,
so that no one knows its pathway.

13 So we also, as soon as we were born,
ceased to be,
and we had no sign of virtue to
show,
but were consumed in our
wickedness."

14 Because the hope of the ungodly is
like thistledown*a* carried by
the wind,
and like a light frost*b* driven away by
a storm;
it is dispersed like smoke before the
wind,
and it passes like the remembrance
of a guest who stays but a day.

The Reward of the Righteous

15 But the righteous live forever,
and their reward is with the Lord;
the Most High takes care of them.

16 Therefore they will receive a glorious
crown
and a beautiful diadem from the
hand of the Lord,
because with his right hand he will
cover them,
and with his arm he will shield them.

17 The Lord*c* will take his zeal as his
whole armor,

and will arm all creation to repel*d* his
enemies;

18 he will put on righteousness as a
breastplate,
and wear impartial justice as a
helmet;

19 he will take holiness as an invincible
shield,

20 and sharpen stern wrath for a sword,
and creation will join with him to
fight against his frenzied foes.

21 Shafts of lightning will fly with true
aim,
and will leap from the clouds to the
target, as from a well-drawn
bow,

22 and hailstones full of wrath will be
hurled as from a catapult;
the water of the sea will rage against
them,
and rivers will relentlessly
overwhelm them;

23 a mighty wind will rise against
them,
and like a tempest it will winnow
them away.
Lawlessness will lay waste the whole
earth,
and evildoing will overturn the
thrones of rulers.

Kings Should Seek Wisdom

6 Listen therefore, O kings, and
understand;
learn, O judges of the ends of the
earth.

2 Give ear, you that rule over
multitudes,
and boast of many nations.

a Other ancient authorities read *dust*   *b* Other ancient authorities read
spider's web   *c* Gk He   *d* Or *punish*

**5:15–23 But the righteous live forever, and their
reward is with the Lord**—The result of judgment
day for the righteous is presented quite briefly.
Their reward is that **the Most High takes care
of them** (v. 15); God gives them a crown. The
attention then turns to the Lord. The Lord protects
the righteous by becoming the divine warrior in
full armor defeating the forces of evil. The picture
is similar to Isa. 59:16–19 and Eph. 6:14–17.
Here the description includes the divine warrior's
ammunition, which is creation itself. Verse 23,

however, seems to say that sin and evil are
themselves responsible for the destruction of the
unrighteous on judgment day.

6:1—Severe judgment falls on those in high
places. Without using the name, the author of
Wisdom assumes the persona of Solomon. The
wisest king in history speaks to all kings about
power. It comes from God, and if misused, will
be judged by God. Only wisdom will help rulers
to rule justly.

3 For your dominion was given you
     from the Lord,
   and your sovereignty from the Most
     High;
   he will search out your works and
     inquire into your plans.
4 Because as servants of his kingdom
     you did not rule rightly,
   or keep the law,
   or walk according to the purpose of
     God,
5 he will come upon you terribly and
     swiftly,
   because severe judgment falls on
     those in high places.
6 For the lowliest may be pardoned in
     mercy,
   but the mighty will be mightily
     tested.
7 For the Lord of all will not stand in
     awe of anyone,
   or show deference to greatness;
   because he himself made both small
     and great,
   and he takes thought for all alike.
8 But a strict inquiry is in store for the
     mighty.
9 To you then, O monarchs, my words
     are directed,
   so that you may learn wisdom and
     not transgress.
10 For they will be made holy who
     observe holy things in holiness,
   and those who have been taught
     them will find a defense.
11 Therefore set your desire on my
     words;
   long for them, and you will be
     instructed.

Description of Wisdom

12 Wisdom is radiant and unfading,
   and she is easily discerned by those
     who love her,
   and is found by those who seek her.
13 She hastens to make herself known
     to those who desire her.
14 One who rises early to seek her will
     have no difficulty,
   for she will be found sitting at the
     gate.
15 To fix one's thought on her is perfect
     understanding,
   and one who is vigilant on her
     account will soon be free from
     care,
16 because she goes about seeking those
     worthy of her,
   and she graciously appears to them
     in their paths,
   and meets them in every thought.

17 The beginning of wisdom[a] is
     the most sincere desire for
     instruction,
   and concern for instruction is love
     of her,
18 and love of her is the keeping of her
     laws,
   and giving heed to her laws is
     assurance of immortality,
19 and immortality brings one near to
     God;
20 so the desire for wisdom leads to a
     kingdom.

21 Therefore if you delight in thrones
     and scepters, O monarchs over
     the peoples,

[a] Gk Her beginning

6:12–16 Wisdom . . . is easily discerned by those who love her—Considering the extraordinary efforts many rulers undertake to gain power, control, and wealth, it is amazing that wisdom, which is more precious than any of these, is so easily acquired! Wisdom *hastens to make herself known . . . . she graciously appears*. A prolonged personification of wisdom as a beautiful and desirable woman begins here (v. 20), and continues through 11:1 (compare Prov. 8:22–31; 9:1–6; Sir. 14:20–27; 24:1–12).

6:17–21 The desire for wisdom leads to a kingdom—Similar to Stoic philosophers, the author employs a logical step-by-step progression (a sorites) to show the great value of seeking wisdom. *Desire for instruction* leads to *love* of wisdom, which leads to *keeping of her laws*, which brings *immortality*, which is *being near to God*. To be near to God is to be within the kingdom of God. Therefore, every disciple can find a significant, meaningful place in an eternal kingdom, but in this kingdom, power is significantly redefined.

honor wisdom, so that you may
    reign forever.
22 I will tell you what wisdom is and
    how she came to be,
and I will hide no secrets from you,
but I will trace her course from the
    beginning of creation,
and make knowledge of her clear,
and I will not pass by the truth;
23 nor will I travel in the company of
    sickly envy,
for envy[a] does not associate with
    wisdom.
24 The multitude of the wise is the
    salvation of the world,
and a sensible king is the stability of
    any people.
25 Therefore be instructed by my
    words, and you will profit.

Solomon Like Other Mortals

7 I also am mortal, like everyone
    else,
a descendant of the first-formed
    child of earth;
and in the womb of a mother I was
    molded into flesh,
2 within the period of ten months,
    compacted with blood,
from the seed of a man and the
    pleasure of marriage.
3 And when I was born, I began to
    breathe the common air,
and fell upon the kindred earth;
my first sound was a cry, as is true
    of all.
4 I was nursed with care in swaddling
    cloths.
5 For no king has had a different
    beginning of existence;

6 there is for all one entrance into life,
    and one way out.

Solomon's Respect for Wisdom

7 Therefore I prayed, and
    understanding was given me;
I called on God, and the spirit of
    wisdom came to me.
8 I preferred her to scepters and
    thrones,
and I accounted wealth as nothing in
    comparison with her.
9 Neither did I liken to her any
    priceless gem,
because all gold is but a little sand in
    her sight,
and silver will be accounted as clay
    before her.
10 I loved her more than health and
    beauty,
and I chose to have her rather than
    light,
because her radiance never ceases.
11 All good things came to me along
    with her,
and in her hands uncounted wealth.
12 I rejoiced in them all, because
    wisdom leads them;
but I did not know that she was their
    mother.
13 I learned without guile and I impart
    without grudging;
I do not hide her wealth,
14 for it is an unfailing treasure for
    mortals;
those who get it obtain friendship
    with God,
commended for the gifts that come
    from instruction.

[a] Gk this

6:22–25 The multitude of the wise is the salvation of the world (v. 24)—The power of wisdom is nothing to be kept secret or hoarded. The persona of Solomon offers to reveal everything freely to others because the power of wisdom is at its greatest when shared.

7:1–6 I also am mortal—Solomon's story begins like any other person's. He is no different from any other king, and kings are no different from any other person. Solomon puts on his pants one leg at a time.

7:7–14 Therefore I prayed—What made Solomon special was his prayer before assuming the throne (1 Kgs. 3:5–14; 2 Chr. 1:7–13). Instead of riches, power, the lives of enemies, or even long life, Solomon prayed for wisdom. Then Solomon discovered the wonder of Wisdom: **All good things came to me along with her** (v. 11). Greater than any treasure, however, was that through Wisdom he would **obtain friendship with God** (v. 14).

Solomon Prays for Wisdom

15 May God grant me to speak with
     judgment,
   and to have thoughts worthy of what
     I have received;
   for he is the guide even of wisdom
   and the corrector of the wise.
16 For both we and our words are in his
     hand,
   as are all understanding and skill in
     crafts.
17 For it is he who gave me unerring
     knowledge of what exists,
   to know the structure of the
     world and the activity of the
     elements;
18 the beginning and end and middle
     of times,
   the alternations of the solstices and
     the changes of the seasons,
19 the cycles of the year and the
     constellations of the stars,
20 the natures of animals and the
     tempers of wild animals,
   the powers of spirits[a] and the
     thoughts of human beings,
   the varieties of plants and the virtues
     of roots;
21 I learned both what is secret and
     what is manifest,
22 for wisdom, the fashioner of all
     things, taught me.

The Nature of Wisdom

There is in her a spirit that is
     intelligent, holy,
unique, manifold, subtle,
mobile, clear, unpolluted,
distinct, invulnerable, loving the
     good, keen,
irresistible, 23 beneficent, humane,

steadfast, sure, free from anxiety,
all-powerful, overseeing all,
and penetrating through all spirits
that are intelligent, pure, and
     altogether subtle.
24 For wisdom is more mobile than any
     motion;
   because of her pureness she pervades
     and penetrates all things.
25 For she is a breath of the power of
     God,
   and a pure emanation of the glory of
     the Almighty;
   therefore nothing defiled gains
     entrance into her.
26 For she is a reflection of eternal
     light,
   a spotless mirror of the working of
     God,
   and an image of his goodness.
27 Although she is but one, she can do
     all things,
   and while remaining in herself, she
     renews all things;
   in every generation she passes into
     holy souls
   and makes them friends of God, and
     prophets;
28 for God loves nothing so much as
     the person who lives with
     wisdom.
29 She is more beautiful than the sun,
   and excels every constellation of the
     stars.
   Compared with the light she is
     found to be superior,
30 for it is succeeded by the night,
   but against wisdom evil does not
     prevail.

a Or *winds*

7:17–22a *It is he who gave me unerring knowl-edge of what exists*—The author of Wisdom celebrates the achievement of Greek science as the gift of God. If the Wisdom of God is *the fashioner all things* (v. 22) and Wisdom guides our quest, why should there be any fear of knowledge or scientific investigation?

7:22b–8:1 *Compared with the light she is found to be superior* (v. 29)—Wisdom is described fully with twenty-one attributes (3 × 7; three

is the divine number, and seven is the perfect number), reminiscent of Jas. 3:17–18. Wisdom's relation to God is described using Platonic terms. A series of paradoxes further describes Wisdom, whose greatest work is to make her disciples *friends of God* (Wis. 7:27). The spiritual nature of Wisdom allows her to be everywhere and be the order found in all things. Her beauty is beyond compare with anything else in creation, and evil holds no power over her.

8

She reaches mightily from one end
of the earth to the other,
and she orders all things well.

Solomon's Love for Wisdom

2 I loved her and sought her from my
youth;
I desired to take her for my bride,
and became enamored of her beauty.
3 She glorifies her noble birth by
living with God,
and the Lord of all loves her.
4 For she is an initiate in the
knowledge of God,
and an associate in his works.
5 If riches are a desirable possession in
life,
what is richer than wisdom, the
active cause of all things?
6 And if understanding is effective,
who more than she is fashioner of
what exists?
7 And if anyone loves righteousness,
her labors are virtues;
for she teaches self-control and
prudence,
justice and courage;
nothing in life is more profitable for
mortals than these.
8 And if anyone longs for wide
experience,
she knows the things of old, and
infers the things to come;
she understands turns of speech and
the solutions of riddles;
she has foreknowledge of signs and
wonders
and of the outcome of seasons and
times.

Wisdom Indispensible to Rulers

9 Therefore I determined to take her
to live with me,
knowing that she would give me
good counsel
and encouragement in cares and
grief.
10 Because of her I shall have glory
among the multitudes
and honor in the presence of the
elders, though I am young.
11 I shall be found keen in judgment,
and in the sight of rulers I shall be
admired.
12 When I am silent they will wait
for me,
and when I speak they will give
heed;
if I speak at greater length,
they will put their hands on their
mouths.
13 Because of her I shall have
immortality,
and leave an everlasting
remembrance to those who
come after me.
14 I shall govern peoples,
and nations will be subject to me;
15 dread monarchs will be afraid of me
when they hear of me;
among the people I shall show
myself capable, and
courageous in war.
16 When I enter my house, I shall find
rest with her;
for companionship with her has no
bitterness,
and life with her has no pain, but
gladness and joy.

**8:2–8 *I loved her and sought her from my
youth***—Solomon loved Wisdom from the beginning and wanted to have as intimate a relationship with her as with a wife. Whatever one
desires in life, Wisdom can provide. Wisdom is
even the source of the four cardinal virtues of the
Greeks: *self-control and prudence, justice and
courage* (v. 7). Wisdom understands all things
past and present and can help decipher the mysteries of human speech.

**8:9–21 *Therefore I determined to take her to
live with me***—Solomon knows how Wisdom

will increase his standing among the rulers of the
world. He also knows the personal satisfaction
and spiritual benefits that Wisdom can give (vv.
16–18). Solomon had great advantages in his
attempt to gain Wisdom: he was a gifted child.
Using Platonic terms, he declares his soul, *being
good*, was born in an *undefiled body* (v. 20).
He had every advantage—intelligence, physical
strength, and spiritual power—but none of these
would enable him to obtain Wisdom on his own.
Wisdom comes only as a gift from God; therefore, Solomon prays.

17 When I considered these things
     inwardly,
and pondered in my heart
that in kinship with wisdom there is
     immortality,
18 and in friendship with her, pure
     delight,
and in the labors of her hands,
     unfailing wealth,
and in the experience of her
     company, understanding,
and renown in sharing her words,
I went about seeking how to get her
     for myself.
19 As a child I was naturally gifted,
and a good soul fell to my lot;
20 or rather, being good, I entered an
     undefiled body.
21 But I perceived that I would not
     possess wisdom unless God
     gave her to me—
and it was a mark of insight to know
     whose gift she was—
so I appealed to the Lord and
     implored him,
and with my whole heart I said:

Solomon's Prayer for Wisdom

9 "O God of my ancestors and Lord
     of mercy,
who have made all things by your
     word,
2 and by your wisdom have formed
     humankind
to have dominion over the creatures
     you have made,
3 and rule the world in holiness and
     righteousness,
and pronounce judgment in
     uprightness of soul,
4 give me the wisdom that sits by your
     throne,
and do not reject me from among
     your servants.

5 For I am your servant[a] the son of
     your serving girl,
a man who is weak and short-lived,
with little understanding of
     judgment and laws;
6 for even one who is perfect among
     human beings
will be regarded as nothing without
     the wisdom that comes from
     you.
7 You have chosen me to be king of
     your people
and to be judge over your sons and
     daughters.
8 You have given command to build a
     temple on your holy mountain,
and an altar in the city of your
     habitation,
a copy of the holy tent that you
     prepared from the beginning.
9 With you is wisdom, she who knows
     your works
and was present when you made the
     world;
she understands what is pleasing in
     your sight
and what is right according to your
     commandments.
10 Send her forth from the holy
     heavens,
and from the throne of your glory
     send her,
that she may labor at my side,
and that I may learn what is pleasing
     to you.
11 For she knows and understands all
     things,
and she will guide me wisely in my
     actions
and guard me with her glory.
12 Then my works will be acceptable,
and I shall judge your people justly,

a Gk slave

9:1–18 *I am your servant* (v. 5)—Servanthood is the key to true leadership. Of Solomon's predecessors, Saul and David, only David was called God's servant. Solomon's prayer is directed toward the God who created the world through word/wisdom (cf. John 1:1–4), who still holds dominion, rules, and judges that creation.

Solomon makes his request based upon what God has chosen to do with Solomon and his own inadequacy for the task. Only Wisdom can help, and Wisdom comes only from God. *Wisdom* is parallel to God's *holy spirit* in Wis. 9:17, and this relationship explains how Solomon can say that *people were taught* and *saved by wisdom*.

and shall be worthy of the throne[a] of my father.

13 For who can learn the counsel of God? Or who can discern what the Lord wills?

14 For the reasoning of mortals is worthless, and our designs are likely to fail;

15 for a perishable body weighs down the soul, and this earthy tent burdens the thoughtful[b] mind.

16 We can hardly guess at what is on earth, and what is at hand we find with labor; but who has traced out what is in the heavens?

17 Who has learned your counsel, unless you have given wisdom and sent your holy spirit from on high?

18 And thus the paths of those on earth were set right, and people were taught what pleases you, and were saved by wisdom."

The Work of Wisdom from Adam to Moses

10 Wisdom[c] protected the first-formed father of the world, when he alone had been created; she delivered him from his transgression,

2 and gave him strength to rule all things.

3 But when an unrighteous man departed from her in his anger, he perished because in rage he killed his brother.

4 When the earth was flooded because of him, wisdom again saved it, steering the righteous man by a paltry piece of wood.

5 Wisdom[c] also, when the nations in wicked agreement had been put to confusion, recognized the righteous man and preserved him blameless before God, and kept him strong in the face of his compassion for his child.

6 Wisdom[c] rescued a righteous man when the ungodly were perishing; he escaped the fire that descended on the Five Cities.[d]

7 Evidence of their wickedness still remains: a continually smoking wasteland, plants bearing fruit that does not ripen, and a pillar of salt standing as a monument to an unbelieving soul.

8 For because they passed wisdom by, they not only were hindered from recognizing the good,

---

[a] Gk thrones   [b] Or anxious   [c] Gk She   [d] Or on Pentapolis

---

10:1–14 From Adam to Joseph—The author recounts how Wisdom benefited Adam, Noah, Abraham, Lot, Jacob, and Joseph in a roll call reminiscent of Heb. 11. The author also notes two failures, those of Cain and of Lot's wife. The greatest surprise is that Wisdom *delivered* Adam *from his transgression* (v. 1). This deliverance is in direct contrast to Cain's murderous departure from Wisdom, which resulted in Abel's death. How was Adam delivered? Was Cain's sin worse than Adam's? Indeed, Cain's sin seems to be the reason for the flood (v. 4)! Perhaps the difference between Adam and Cain is that Cain's sin resulted in the complete rupture of human relationship, and Wisdom always has to do with human community.

Wisdom's concern for human community may also be seen in the account of the *Five Cities* (v. 6; Sodom, Gomorrah, Admah, Zeboiim, and Zoar, of which only the latter survived; see Gen. 19:24–26; Deut. 29:23; Hos. 11:8). The destruction of the cities and the loss of Lot's wife are left as unfailing *reminders* to *humankind* of the price of forsaking Wisdom (Wis. 10:8).

Wisdom's deliverance does not mean the absence of any suffering; Abel dies, Jacob is oppressed, and Joseph goes to *the dungeon* (v. 13), but Wisdom does not abandon her disciples. Rather God transforms their situation through the divine attribute of Wisdom.

but also left for humankind a
reminder of their folly,
so that their failures could never go
unnoticed.

9 Wisdom rescued from troubles those
who served her.
10 When a righteous man fled from his
brother's wrath,
she guided him on straight paths;
she showed him the kingdom of
God,
and gave him knowledge of holy
things;
she prospered him in his labors,
and increased the fruit of his toil.
11 When his oppressors were covetous,
she stood by him and made him
rich.
12 She protected him from his enemies,
and kept him safe from those who
lay in wait for him;
in his arduous contest she gave him
the victory,
so that he might learn that godliness
is more powerful than
anything else.
13 When a righteous man was sold,
wisdom*a* did not desert him,
but delivered him from sin.
She descended with him into the
dungeon,
14 and when he was in prison she did
not leave him,
until she brought him the scepter of
a kingdom
and authority over his masters.
Those who accused him she showed
to be false,
and she gave him everlasting honor.

Wisdom Led the Israelites out of Egypt

15 A holy people and blameless race
wisdom delivered from a nation of
oppressors.
16 She entered the soul of a servant of
the Lord,
and withstood dread kings with
wonders and signs.
17 She gave to holy people the reward
of their labors;
she guided them along a marvelous
way,
and became a shelter to them by day,
and a starry flame through the night.
18 She brought them over the Red Sea,
and led them through deep waters;
19 but she drowned their enemies,
and cast them up from the depth of
the sea.
20 Therefore the righteous plundered
the ungodly;
they sang hymns, O Lord, to your
holy name,
and praised with one accord your
defending hand;
21 for wisdom opened the mouths of
those who were mute,
and made the tongues of infants
speak clearly.

Wisdom Led the Israelites through the Desert

11 Wisdom*b* prospered their works
by the hand of a holy prophet.
2 They journeyed through an
uninhabited wilderness,
and pitched their tents in untrodden
places.
3 They withstood their enemies and
fought off their foes.

a Gk *she*   *b* Gk *She*

10:15–21 Moses and the people of Israel—Wisdom's presence with Moses is linked to the fate of the people of Israel (again, similar to Heb. 11). Once more the concept of servanthood is tied to wise leadership (Wis. 10:16). The writer offers a new interpretation for the pillar of cloud that led the people by day (Exod. 13:21): it is not only Wisdom's provision of God's guidance; it also provides a protective shade (Wis. 10:17)!

11:1–5 A strange prosperity—Under the wise leadership of Moses, the *holy prophet*, the people wandered *through an uninhabited wilderness*, fought, and suffered thirst quenched by water obtained *out of flinty rock*. That may not sound like much, but compared to what their enemies suffered, their life was a miracle. The miracle was a result of God's activity, and God's activity is in the context of a personal relationship. Note the use of the pronoun *you* in reference to God beginning at v. 4!

4 When they were thirsty, they called
        upon you,
    and water was given them out of
        flinty rock,
    and from hard stone a remedy for
        their thirst.
5 For through the very things by
        which their enemies were
        punished,
    they themselves received benefit in
        their need.
6 Instead of the fountain of an ever-
        flowing river,
    stirred up and defiled with blood
7 in rebuke for the decree to kill the
        infants,
    you gave them abundant water
        unexpectedly,
8 showing by their thirst at that time
    how you punished their enemies.
9 For when they were tried, though
        they were being disciplined in
        mercy,
    they learned how the ungodly were
        tormented when judged in
        wrath.
10 For you tested them as a parent[a]
        does in warning,
    but you examined the ungodly[b]
        as a stern king does in
        condemnation.
11 Whether absent or present, they
        were equally distressed,
12 for a twofold grief possessed them,
    and a groaning at the memory of
        what had occurred.
13 For when they heard that through
        their own punishments
    the righteous[c] had received benefit,
        they perceived it was the
        Lord's doing.

14 For though they had mockingly
        rejected him who long before
        had been cast out and
        exposed,
    at the end of the events they
        marveled at him,
    when they felt thirst in a different
        way from the righteous.

Punishment of the Wicked

15 In return for their foolish and
        wicked thoughts,
    which led them astray to worship
        irrational serpents and
        worthless animals,
    you sent upon them a multitude of
        irrational creatures to punish
        them,
16 so that they might learn that one is
        punished by the very things by
        which one sins.
17 For your all-powerful hand,
    which created the world out of
        formless matter,
    did not lack the means to send upon
        them a multitude of bears, or
        bold lions,
18 or newly-created unknown beasts
        full of rage,
    or such as breathe out fiery breath,
    or belch forth a thick pall of smoke,
    or flash terrible sparks from their
        eyes;
19 not only could the harm they did
        destroy people,[d]
    but the mere sight of them could kill
        by fright.
20 Even apart from these, people[c] could
        fall at a single breath
    when pursued by justice

a Gk *a father* *b* Gk *those* *c* Gk *they* *d* Gk *them*

11:15–12:11 *One is punished by the very things by which one sins* (v. 16)—Wisdom argues that God's judgment is just. The punishment God gives fits the crime: since the Egyptians worshiped reptiles (*serpents*, 11:15), then they were punished with reptiles (frogs). Things could have been worse. God could have sent more ferocious animals, invented creatures of destruction, or even destroyed the people without any creature at all. Judgment, in fact, is only God's penulti- mate word; mercy is God's final word (11:23). Like all Wisdom literature, Wisdom demonstrates a more universal view of God's love than some other genres. The purpose of the plagues against Egypt was not to destroy the Egyptians, nor was the conquest to completely destroy the Canaanites. These trials were to lead them step by step to *put their trust* in God (12:2). True discipleship is faithfully learning by means of difficult discipline (Rom. 5:3–5).

and scattered by the breath of your
power.
But you have arranged all things
by measure and number and
weight.

God Is Powerful and Merciful

21 For it is always in your power to
show great strength,
and who can withstand the might of
your arm?
22 Because the whole world before you
is like a speck that tips the
scales,
and like a drop of morning dew that
falls on the ground.
23 But you are merciful to all, for you
can do all things,
and you overlook people's sins, so
that they may repent.
24 For you love all things that exist,
and detest none of the things that
you have made,
for you would not have made
anything if you had hated it.
25 How would anything have endured
if you had not willed it?
Or how would anything not called
forth by you have been
preserved?
26 You spare all things, for they are
yours, O Lord, you who love
the living.

12 For your immortal spirit is in all
things.
2 Therefore you correct little by little
those who trespass,
and you remind and warn them of
the things through which they
sin,
so that they may be freed from
wickedness and put their trust
in you, O Lord.

The Sins of the Canaanites

3 Those who lived long ago in your
holy land

4 you hated for their detestable
practices,
their works of sorcery and unholy
rites,
5 their merciless slaughter*a* of children,
and their sacrificial feasting on
human flesh and blood.
These initiates from the midst of a
heathen cult,*b*
6 these parents who murder helpless
lives,
you willed to destroy by the hands of
our ancestors,
7 so that the land most precious of all
to you
might receive a worthy colony of the
servants*c* of God.
8 But even these you spared, since
they were but mortals,
and sent wasps*d* as forerunners of
your army
to destroy them little by little,
9 though you were not unable to give
the ungodly into the hands of
the righteous in battle,
or to destroy them at one blow by
dread wild animals or your
stern word.
10 But judging them little by little you
gave them an opportunity to
repent,
though you were not unaware that
their origin*e* was evil
and their wickedness inborn,
and that their way of thinking would
never change.
11 For they were an accursed race from
the beginning,
and it was not through fear of
anyone that you left them
unpunished for their sins.

God Is Sovereign

12 For who will say, "What have you
done?"

a Gk *slaughterers*   *b* Meaning of Gk uncertain   *c* Or *children*   *d* Or *hornets*
e Or *nature*

12:12–18 *For who will say, "What have you
done?"*—Wisdom demonstrates confidence that
no one would dare accuse God of unjust judg-

ment. But what about the Holocaust? What about
AIDS? What about an accumulation of natural
disasters? What about ethnic cleansing, chemical

or will resist your judgment?
Who will accuse you for the
      destruction of nations that you
      made?
Or who will come before you to
      plead as an advocate for the
      unrighteous?

13 For neither is there any god besides
      you, whose care is for all
      people,*a*
to whom you should prove that you
      have not judged unjustly;
14 nor can any king or monarch
      confront you about those
      whom you have punished.
15 You are righteous and you rule all
      things righteously,
deeming it alien to your power
to condemn anyone who does not
      deserve to be punished.
16 For your strength is the source of
      righteousness,
and your sovereignty over all causes
      you to spare all.
17 For you show your strength when
      people doubt the completeness
      of your power,
and you rebuke any insolence among
      those who know it.*b*
18 Although you are sovereign in
      strength, you judge with
      mildness,
and with great forbearance you
      govern us;
for you have power to act whenever
      you choose.

God's Lessons for Israel
19 Through such works you have
      taught your people
that the righteous must be kind,
and you have filled your children
      with good hope,

because you give repentance for
      sins.
20 For if you punished with such great
      care and indulgence*c*
the enemies of your servants*d* and
      those deserving of death,
granting them time and opportunity
      to give up their wickedness,
21 with what strictness you have judged
      your children,
to whose ancestors you gave oaths
      and covenants full of good
      promises!
22 So while chastening us you scourge
      our enemies ten thousand
      times more,
so that, when we judge, we may
      meditate upon your goodness,
and when we are judged, we may
      expect mercy.

The Punishment of the Egyptians
23 Therefore those who lived
      unrighteously, in a life of folly,
you tormented through their own
      abominations.
24 For they went far astray on the paths
      of error,
accepting as gods those animals that
      even their enemies*e* despised;
they were deceived like foolish
      infants.
25 Therefore, as though to children
      who cannot reason,
you sent your judgment to mock
      them.
26 But those who have not heeded the
      warning of mild rebukes
will experience the deserved
      judgment of God.
27 For when in their suffering they
      became incensed

a Or *all things*   *b* Meaning of Gk uncertain   *c* Other ancient authorities lack
and indulgence; others read *and entreaty*   *d* Or *children*   *e* Gk *they*

---

warfare, environmental negligence, and global
terrorism? Can we accuse God of too harsh a
judgment? Will God be able to answer?

12:19–22 *Through such works you have taught
your people that the righteous must be kind—*
Wisdom points to even the judgment of God as
an aid to learning to be a disciple. Becoming

aware of the differences in punishments given to
the ungodly and the righteous should help the
faithful recognize more fully their responsibilities,
and it should make them become more merciful
themselves. How often has it done just the opposite, and caused the community of faith to be
self-righteous?

at those creatures that they had
   thought to be gods, being
   punished by means of them,
they saw and recognized as the true
   God the one whom they had
   before refused to know.
Therefore the utmost condemnation
   came upon them.

The Foolishness of Nature Worship

13 For all people who were
   ignorant of God were foolish
   by nature;
and they were unable from the good
   things that are seen to know
   the one who exists,
nor did they recognize the artisan
   while paying heed to his works;
2 but they supposed that either fire or
   wind or swift air,
or the circle of the stars, or turbulent
   water,
or the luminaries of heaven were the
   gods that rule the world.
3 If through delight in the beauty of
   these things people assumed
   them to be gods,
let them know how much better
   than these is their Lord,
for the author of beauty created
   them.
4 And if people*a* were amazed at their
   power and working,
let them perceive from them
how much more powerful is the one
   who formed them.
5 For from the greatness and beauty of
   created things

comes a corresponding perception
   of their Creator.
6 Yet these people are little to be
   blamed,
for perhaps they go astray
while seeking God and desiring to
   find him.
7 For while they live among his works,
   they keep searching,
and they trust in what they see,
   because the things that are
   seen are beautiful.
8 Yet again, not even they are to be
   excused;
9 for if they had the power to know so
   much
that they could investigate the world,
how did they fail to find sooner the
   Lord of these things?

The Foolishness of Idolatry

10 But miserable, with their hopes set
   on dead things, are those
who give the name "gods" to the
   works of human hands,
gold and silver fashioned with skill,
and likenesses of animals,
or a useless stone, the work of an
   ancient hand.
11 A skilled woodcutter may saw down
   a tree easy to handle
and skillfully strip off all its bark,
and then with pleasing workmanship
make a useful vessel that serves life's
   needs,
12 and burn the cast-off pieces of his
   work

a Gk *they*

13:1–9 Nature religion and natural revelation—
The author of Wisdom is well aware that many
worship the forces of nature, and their actions
are even understandable. Some see the goodness
and grandeur of nature but lack the wisdom to
see beyond them to the Creator. Wisdom offers
a prayer for such people (vv. 3–4) and declares
that nature itself can reveal God (v. 5). Nature
worship is the most understandable of all types of
false worship (vv. 6–7), but it is still inexcusable
(vv. 8–9). Compare this passage to Rom. 1:18–25.

13:10–19 *But miserable . . . are those who*
give the name "gods" to the works of human
hands—Wisdom offers a harsher judgment upon

idolaters. Like Isa. 44:9–20, Wisdom presents a
parody of the woodcutter making useful things
from the best wood and from the shavings making a fire to cook his food. Finally, with a stick
unfit for either, the woodcutter fashions an idol,
taking care to hide the blemishes in the wood.
The foolishness of idol worship is evident in Wis.
13:16–19. Few people today would be so foolish,
right? How much confidence do modern people
place in what they have constructed? What are
the perceived sources of security, happiness, and
fulfillment for many? Is idolatry alive and well in
our consumer society?

to prepare his food, and eat his fill.

13 But a cast-off piece from among
　　them, useful for nothing,
a stick crooked and full of knots,
he takes and carves with care in his
　　leisure,
and shapes it with skill gained in
　　idleness;[a]
he forms it in the likeness of a
　　human being,

14 or makes it like some worthless
　　animal,
giving it a coat of red paint and
　　coloring its surface red
and covering every blemish in it
　　with paint;

15 then he makes a suitable niche for it,
and sets it in the wall, and fastens it
　　there with iron.

16 He takes thought for it, so that it
　　may not fall,
because he knows that it cannot help
　　itself,
for it is only an image and has need
　　of help.

17 When he prays about possessions
　　and his marriage and children,
he is not ashamed to address a
　　lifeless thing.

18 For health he appeals to a thing that
　　is weak;
for life he prays to a thing that is
　　dead;
for aid he entreats a thing that is
　　utterly inexperienced;
for a prosperous journey, a thing
　　that cannot take a step;

19 for money-making and work and
　　success with his hands
he asks strength of a thing whose
　　hands have no strength.

Folly of a Navigator Praying to an Idol

14 Again, one preparing to sail and
about to voyage over raging
waves
calls upon a piece of wood more
　　fragile than the ship that
　　carries him.

2 For it was desire for gain that
　　planned that vessel,
and wisdom was the artisan who
　　built it;

3 but it is your providence, O Father,
　　that steers its course,
because you have given it a path in
　　the sea,
and a safe way through the waves,

4 showing that you can save from
　　every danger,
so that even a person who lacks skill
　　may put to sea.

5 It is your will that works of your
　　wisdom should not be without
　　effect;
therefore people trust their lives
　　even to the smallest piece of
　　wood,
and passing through the billows on a
　　raft they come safely to land.

6 For even in the beginning, when
　　arrogant giants were perishing,
the hope of the world took refuge on
　　a raft,
and guided by your hand left to
　　the world the seed of a new
　　generation.

7 For blessed is the wood by which
　　righteousness comes.

8 But the idol made with hands is
　　accursed, and so is the one
　　who made it—

[a] Other ancient authorities read *with intelligent skill*

14:1–7 Blessed is the wood by which the righteous comes (v. 7)—God can provide through wood what a wooden god cannot. There is nothing wrong with human desire for travel and commerce. Wisdom provides the art and technology for these things to be accomplished. But God (note the relatively rare pre-Jesus use of **Father** [v. 3] for God) carefully provides a path and guidance for the ship of trade. A wooden idol more

fragile than the boat cannot protect the passengers, but God, who has already saved humanity with Noah's ark, certainly can.

14:8–11 Equally hateful to God are the ungodly and their ungodliness (v. 9)—Some Christians are fond of saying, "God hates the sin, but loves the sinner." Is that what Wisdom says?

he for having made it, and the
perishable thing because it was
named a god.
9 For equally hateful to God are the
ungodly and their ungodliness;
10 for what was done will be punished
together with the one who
did it.
11 Therefore there will be a visitation
also upon the heathen idols,
because, though part of what God
created, they became an
abomination,
snares for human souls
and a trap for the feet of the foolish.

The Origin and Evils of Idolatry
12 For the idea of making idols was the
beginning of fornication,
and the invention of them was the
corruption of life;
13 for they did not exist from the
beginning,
nor will they last forever.
14 For through human vanity they
entered the world,
and therefore their speedy end has
been planned.

15 For a father, consumed with grief at
an untimely bereavement,
made an image of his child, who had
been suddenly taken from him;
he now honored as a god what was
once a dead human being,
and handed on to his dependents
secret rites and initiations.
16 Then the ungodly custom, grown
strong with time, was kept as a
law,
and at the command of monarchs
carved images were worshiped.

17 When people could not honor
monarchs[a] in their presence,
since they lived at a distance,
they imagined their appearance far
away,
and made a visible image of the king
whom they honored,
so that by their zeal they might
flatter the absent one as
though present.

18 Then the ambition of the artisan
impelled
even those who did not know the
king to intensify their worship.
19 For he, perhaps wishing to please his
ruler,
skillfully forced the likeness to take
more beautiful form,
20 and the multitude, attracted by the
charm of his work,
now regarded as an object of
worship the one whom shortly
before they had honored as a
human being.
21 And this became a hidden trap for
humankind,
because people, in bondage to
misfortune or to royal
authority,
bestowed on objects of stone or
wood the name that ought not
to be shared.

22 Then it was not enough for them
to err about the knowledge of
God,
but though living in great strife due
to ignorance,
they call such great evils peace.

[a] Gk them

14:12–21 *Idols . . . did not exist from the beginning* (v. 13)—Rather than express pure condemnation, Wisdom demonstrates remarkable understanding in offering some reasons for the beginning of idolatry. These reasons stem from the disappointments and limitations of human beings: the inconsolable loss of a child, the difficulty of being subject to a distant or absent ruler, and the marvelous power of art.

14:22–31 *The worship of idols . . . is the*

beginning and cause and end of every evil (v. 27)—Nevertheless, Wisdom is aware of the terrible consequences of idolatry. When one trusts in lifeless things, human life descends into confusion, unfaithfulness, violence, and perversion (vv. 22–27). Even if done out of ignorance, idolatry alienates one from a living relationship with God and leads to contempt for God's ways. Therefore, the punishment idolaters bring upon themselves is justified and inevitable.

23 For whether they kill children in
     their initiations, or celebrate
     secret mysteries,
   or hold frenzied revels with strange
     customs,
24 they no longer keep either their lives
     or their marriages pure,
   but they either treacherously kill one
     another, or grieve one another
     by adultery,
25 and all is a raging riot of blood
     and murder, theft and deceit,
     corruption, faithlessness,
     tumult, perjury,
26 confusion over what is good,
     forgetfulness of favors,
   defiling of souls, sexual perversion,
     disorder in marriages, adultery, and
     debauchery.
27 For the worship of idols not to be
     named
   is the beginning and cause and end
     of every evil.
28 For their worshipers*a* either rave in
     exultation,
   or prophesy lies, or live
     unrighteously, or readily
     commit perjury;
29 for because they trust in lifeless idols
   they swear wicked oaths and expect
     to suffer no harm.
30 But just penalties will overtake them
     on two counts:
   because they thought wrongly about
     God in devoting themselves to
     idols,
   and because in deceit they swore
     unrighteously through
     contempt for holiness.

31 For it is not the power of the things
     by which people swear,*b*
   but the just penalty for those who sin,
   that always pursues the transgression
     of the unrighteous.

Benefits of Worshiping the True God

15 But you, our God, are kind and
     true,
   patient, and ruling all things*c* in
     mercy.
2 For even if we sin we are yours,
     knowing your power;
   but we will not sin, because we know
     that you acknowledge us as
     yours.
3 For to know you is complete
     righteousness,
   and to know your power is the root
     of immortality.
4 For neither has the evil intent of
     human art misled us,
   nor the fruitless toil of painters,
   a figure stained with varied colors,
5 whose appearance arouses yearning
     in fools,
   so that they desire*d* the lifeless form
     of a dead image.
6 Lovers of evil things and fit for such
     objects of hope*e*
   are those who either make or desire
     or worship them.

The Foolishness of Worshiping
Clay Idols

7 A potter kneads the soft earth
   and laboriously molds each vessel
     for our service,

a Gk they *b* Or of the oaths people swear *c* Or ruling the universe *d* Gk and
he desires *e* Gk such hopes

15:1–6 True disciples are not perfect; their God
is merciful—Wisdom offers praise to God, who
is kind, true, patient, and merciful. It is not the
perfection of the disciple that results in immortality, but the knowledge of God, i.e., a relationship
with God (cf. v. 3 with John 17:3). This relationship with the living God helps the disciple avoid
seeking what is lifeless. Anyone who makes,
desires, or worships an idol becomes as lifeless
as the thing itself. What is at the center of one's
desire shapes the person that one becomes.
15:7–13 Life: a festival for profit—At the heart

of idol making is the conviction that *one must
get money however one can* (v. 12), regardless of what it does to others. Wisdom uses the
example of potters (themselves made of clay, like
all human beings) using clay to make different
vessels. Some objects are quite useful; others
are idolatrous. These workers do not think of
mortality or eternity, good or evil, or the potential
uses of their products. They think only in terms of
profits. They, *more than all others, know they sin*
(v. 13). Certainly this word applies to more than
idol makers, drug dealers, and gun runners.

fashioning out of the same clay
both the vessels that serve clean uses
and those for contrary uses, making
    all alike;
but which shall be the use of each of
    them
the worker in clay decides.

8 With misspent toil, these workers
        form a futile god from the
        same clay—
these mortals who were made of
        earth a short time before
and after a little while go to the earth
        from which all mortals are
        taken,
when the time comes to return the
        souls that were borrowed.

9 But the workers are not concerned
        that mortals are destined to die
or that their life is brief,
but they compete with workers in
        gold and silver,
and imitate workers in copper;
and they count it a glorious thing to
        mold counterfeit gods.

10 Their heart is ashes, their hope is
        cheaper than dirt,
and their lives are of less worth than
        clay,

11 because they failed to know the one
        who formed them
and inspired them with active souls
and breathed a living spirit into
        them.

12 But they considered our existence an
        idle game,
and life a festival held for profit,
for they say one must get money
        however one can, even by base
        means.

13 For these persons, more than all
        others, know that they sin
when they make from earthy matter
        fragile vessels and carved
        images.

14 But most foolish, and more
        miserable than an infant,
are all the enemies who oppressed
        your people.

15 For they thought that all their
        heathen idols were gods,
though these have neither the use of
        their eyes to see with,
nor nostrils with which to draw breath,
nor ears with which to hear,
nor fingers to feel with,
and their feet are of no use for walking.

16 For a human being made them,
and one whose spirit is borrowed
        formed them;
for none can form gods that are like
        themselves.

17 People are mortal, and what they
        make with lawless hands is
        dead;
for they are better than the objects
        they worship,
since*a* they have life, but the idols*b*
        never had.

Serpents in the Desert

18 Moreover, they worship even the
        most hateful animals,
which are worse than all others
        when judged by their lack of
        intelligence;

19 and even as animals they are not so
        beautiful in appearance that
        one would desire them,

a Other ancient authorities read *of which*   *b* Gk *but they*

15:14–17 *Most foolish . . . are all the enemies who oppressed your people*—The greatest condemnation is reserved for those who oppose the God and God's people based on a faith in a false god. What they do not understand is that their own life (*spirit*) *is borrowed* (v. 16) from God, and that they, being alive, are already better than the gods they make! They are the most foolish because they put their lives into the hands of something dead to oppose the very One who gave them life!

15:18–16:4 Contrast between Egypt and Israel—Returning to the theme of 11:15–16, Wisdom contrasts the experience of the Egyptians with animals and that of Israel. The Egyptians worshiped reptiles (snakes), so in a plague, God sent them reptiles (frogs). The creatures were so repugnant that the Egyptians lost their appetites (16:3). The Israelites, Wisdom points out, also suffered hunger for a short while, but God sent them *quails to eat* (16:2). Their brief punishment taught them how their *enemies* were *tormented* (16:4).

but they have escaped both the
praise of God and his blessing.

16 Therefore those people*a* were
deservedly punished through
such creatures,
and were tormented by a multitude
of animals.

2 Instead of this punishment you
showed kindness to your
people,
and you prepared quails to eat,
a delicacy to satisfy the desire of
appetite;

3 in order that those people, when
they desired food,
might lose the least remnant of
appetite*b*
because of the odious creatures sent
to them,
while your people,*a* after suffering
want a short time,
might partake of delicacies.

4 For it was necessary that upon those
oppressors inescapable want
should come,
while to these others it was merely
shown how their enemies were
being tormented.

5 For when the terrible rage of wild
animals came upon your
people*c*
and they were being destroyed by
the bites of writhing
serpents,
your wrath did not continue to the
end;

6 they were troubled for a little while
as a warning,
and received a symbol of deliverance
to remind them of your law's
command.

7 For the one who turned toward it
was saved, not by the thing
that was beheld,
but by you, the Savior of all.

8 And by this also you convinced our
enemies
that it is you who deliver from every
evil.

9 For they were killed by the bites of
locusts and flies,
and no healing was found for
them,
because they deserved to be
punished by such things.

10 But your children were not
conquered even by the fangs of
venomous serpents,
for your mercy came to their help
and healed them.

11 To remind them of your oracles they
were bitten,
and then were quickly delivered,
so that they would not fall into deep
forgetfulness
and become unresponsive*d* to your
kindness.

12 For neither herb nor poultice cured
them,
but it was your word, O Lord, that
heals all people.

13 For you have power over life and
death;
you lead mortals down to the gates
of Hades and back again.

14 A person in wickedness kills
another,
but cannot bring back the departed
spirit,
or set free the imprisoned soul.

a Gk they *b* Gk loathed the necessary appetite *c* Gk them *d* Meaning of Gk
uncertain

16:5–14 Other plagues that contrast the Egyptians and the Israelites—Wisdom combines the accounts of several plagues and a little exaggeration to show that Egyptians, in their opposition to God, died from **the bites** of pesky gnats, **flies**, and **locusts**. The Israelites suffered bites from **venomous** snakes, but they survived! They did not live because they were better than the Egyptians or because their bronze serpent was better than the idols of the Egyptians. Their lives were preserved by God alone. There is no room in the life of the disciple for trust in one's own superiority. Disciples must trust in God even when their problems seem greater than those of others.

16:13–14 A warning—It is easy to kill and destroy, but only God can restore **life**.

Disastrous Storms Strike Egypt

15 To escape from your hand is
impossible;
16 for the ungodly, refusing to know
you,
were flogged by the strength of your
arm,
pursued by unusual rains and hail
and relentless storms,
and utterly consumed by fire.
17 For—most incredible of all—in
water, which quenches all
things,
the fire had still greater effect,
for the universe defends the
righteous.
18 At one time the flame was
restrained,
so that it might not consume the
creatures sent against the
ungodly,
but that seeing this they might know
that they were being pursued by the
judgment of God;
19 and at another time even in the
midst of water it burned more
intensely than fire,
to destroy the crops of the
unrighteous land.

The Israelites Receive Manna

20 Instead of these things you gave your
people food of angels,
and without their toil you supplied
them from heaven with bread
ready to eat,
providing every pleasure and suited
to every taste.
21 For your sustenance manifested
your sweetness toward your
children;
and the bread, ministering[a] to the
desire of the one who took it,

was changed to suit everyone's
liking.
22 Snow and ice withstood fire without
melting,
so that they might know that the
crops of their enemies
were being destroyed by the fire that
blazed in the hail
and flashed in the showers of rain;
23 whereas the fire,[b] in order that the
righteous might be fed,
even forgot its native power.

24 For creation, serving you who
made it,
exerts itself to punish the
unrighteous,
and in kindness relaxes on behalf of
those who trust in you.
25 Therefore at that time also, changed
into all forms,
it served your all-nourishing bounty,
according to the desire of those who
had need,[c]
26 so that your children, whom you
loved, O Lord, might learn
that it is not the production of crops
that feeds humankind
but that your word sustains those
who trust in you.
27 For what was not destroyed by fire
was melted when simply warmed by
a fleeting ray of the sun,
28 to make it known that one must
rise before the sun to give you
thanks,
and must pray to you at the dawning
of the light;
29 for the hope of an ungrateful person
will melt like wintry frost,
and flow away like waste water.

a Gk and it, ministering b Gk this c Or who made supplication

16:15–29—Wisdom declares that creation serves God, punishing the ungodly and yielding good things to the righteous (v. 24). Is this true? The passage is poetic; snow and ice serve as metaphors for manna, for example. The disciple should not expect a literal fulfillment of these words any more than Jesus accepted Satan's attempt to force a literal application of

Ps. 91:11–12 (Matt. 4:5–7). What remains certain is that creation does demonstrate God's *all-nourishing bounty* (Wis. 16:25) and, therefore, it is not the production of crops that feeds humankind, but God's *word* (v. 26). Thus Wisdom advises that each day should begin with thanksgiving and prayer (v. 28).

Terror Strikes the Egyptians at Night

17 Great are your judgments and
hard to describe;
therefore uninstructed souls have
gone astray.

2 For when lawless people supposed
that they held the holy nation
in their power,
they themselves lay as captives of
darkness and prisoners of long
night,
shut in under their roofs, exiles from
eternal providence.

3 For thinking that in their secret sins
they were unobserved
behind a dark curtain of
forgetfulness,
they were scattered, terribly*a*
alarmed,
and appalled by specters.

4 For not even the inner chamber that
held them protected them
from fear,
but terrifying sounds rang out
around them,
and dismal phantoms with gloomy
faces appeared.

5 And no power of fire was able to
give light,
nor did the brilliant flames of the
stars
avail to illumine that hateful night.

6 Nothing was shining through to them
except a dreadful, self-kindled fire,
and in terror they deemed the things
that they saw
to be worse than that unseen
appearance.

7 The delusions of their magic art lay
humbled,
and their boasted wisdom was
scornfully rebuked.

8 For those who promised to drive off
the fears and disorders of a
sick soul
were sick themselves with ridiculous
fear.

9 For even if nothing disturbing
frightened them,
yet, scared by the passing of wild
animals and the hissing of
snakes

10 they perished in trembling fear,
refusing to look even at the air,
though it nowhere could be
avoided.

11 For wickedness is a cowardly
thing, condemned by its own
testimony;*b*
distressed by conscience, it has
always exaggerated*c* the
difficulties.

12 For fear is nothing but a giving up
of the helps that come from
reason;

13 and hope, defeated by this inward
weakness,
prefers ignorance of what causes the
torment.

14 But throughout the night, which was
really powerless
and which came upon them from
the recesses of powerless
Hades,

a Other ancient authorities read *unobserved, they were darkened behind a
dark curtain of forgetfulness, terribly*   *b* Meaning of Gk uncertain   *c* Other
ancient authorities read *anticipated*

17:1–18:4 *Still heavier than darkness were they
to themselves* (17:21)—Wisdom offers a meditation on darkness and light based upon the plague
of darkness (Exod. 10:21–27) and the pillar of fire
(Exod. 13:21). The ungodly may feel that darkness
provides security by hiding their wrongdoing, but
even that thought is part of their own captivity in
a greater darkness. Theirs is a darkness filled with
hate, doubt, and fear that does not permit any of
God's light (*fire*, Wis. 17:5) to enter that might
guide them. Instead, they seek to illumine their
own ways with their own healers incapable of
healing even themselves. Having refused Wisdom
and the ways of reason, they fear everything and
have no hope. From all walks of life they are the
same, and both the beauty and the power of nature *paralyze them with terror* (17:19). The rest
of creation lives in God's light and that makes
the darkness of the ungodly feel even worse. The
Israelites (*holy ones*, 18:1) give witness to the
light, but only enough to provide a sense of relief
that the Israelites did not also act out of the darkness of the hate that had been directed towards
them. To refuse the *light of the law* is to refuse
the light that illumines the world (18:4; cf. John
1:4–5; 8:12).

they all slept the same sleep,

15 and now were driven by monstrous
     specters,
and now were paralyzed by their
     souls' surrender;
for sudden and unexpected fear
     overwhelmed them.

16 And whoever was there fell down,
and thus was kept shut up in a
     prison not made of iron;

17 for whether they were farmers or
     shepherds
or workers who toiled in the
     wilderness,
they were seized, and endured the
     inescapable fate;
for with one chain of darkness they
     all were bound.

18 Whether there came a whistling
     wind,
or a melodious sound of birds in
     wide-spreading branches,
or the rhythm of violently rushing
     water,

19 or the harsh crash of rocks hurled
     down,
or the unseen running of leaping
     animals,
or the sound of the most savage
     roaring beasts,
or an echo thrown back from a
     hollow of the mountains,
it paralyzed them with terror.

20 For the whole world was illumined
     with brilliant light,
and went about its work
     unhindered,

21 while over those people alone heavy
     night was spread,

an image of the darkness that was
     destined to receive them;
but still heavier than darkness were
     they to themselves.

Light Shines on the Israelites

18 But for your holy ones there was
     very great light.
Their enemies[a] heard their voices
     but did not see their forms,
and counted them happy for not
     having suffered,

2 and were thankful that your holy
     ones,[b] though previously
     wronged, were doing them no
     injury;
and they begged their pardon for
     having been at variance with
     them.[b]

3 Therefore you provided a flaming
     pillar of fire
as a guide for your people's[c]
     unknown journey,
and a harmless sun for their glorious
     wandering.

4 For their enemies[d] deserved to
     be deprived of light and
     imprisoned in darkness,
those who had kept your children
     imprisoned,
through whom the imperishable
     light of the law was to be given
     to the world.

The Death of the Egyptian Firstborn

5 When they had resolved to kill the
     infants of your holy ones,
and one child had been abandoned
     and rescued,

---

a Gk *They*   *b* Meaning of Gk uncertain   *c* Gk *their*   *d* Gk *those persons*

18:5–25 Destruction and deliverance—Wisdom recounts Pharaoh's decree to kill all Hebrew males and Moses' deliverance in order to show God's punishment of the Egyptian firstborn was both deserved and just. The justness of God's judgment is seen through the recognition of God's righteousness by the ungodly (v. 13): they do not perish **without knowing why they suffered** (v. 19). The image of God dispensing cosmic justice as a divine warrior is reminiscent of the judgment passages in Amos and Revelation. It is just because it is applied equally to **commoner**

and **king** (v. 11). Even more, God's judgment is just because it serves to strengthen the faith of those who believe (vv. 6–7).

Next, Wisdom illustrates the justness of God's judgment by recalling that God punished Israel as well as Egypt (v. 8). The community of faith is not saved from its sin by its strength or by force, but by its words of confession and praise. The community of faith survives only when its leaders demonstrate their relationship with God through servanthood.

you in punishment took away a
multitude of their children;
and you destroyed them all together
by a mighty flood.

6 That night was made known
beforehand to our ancestors,
so that they might rejoice in sure
knowledge of the oaths in
which they trusted.

7 The deliverance of the righteous
and the destruction of their
enemies
were expected by your people.

8 For by the same means by which you
punished our enemies
you called us to yourself and
glorified us.

9 For in secret the holy children of
good people offered sacrifices,
and with one accord agreed to the
divine law,
so that the saints would share alike
the same things,
both blessings and dangers;
and already they were singing the
praises of the ancestors.[a]

10 But the discordant cry of their
enemies echoed back,
and their piteous lament for their
children was spread abroad.

11 The slave was punished with the
same penalty as the master,
and the commoner suffered the
same loss as the king;

12 and they all together, by the one
form[b] of death,
had corpses too many to count.
For the living were not sufficient
even to bury them,
since in one instant their most
valued children had been
destroyed.

13 For though they had disbelieved
everything because of their
magic arts,
yet, when their firstborn were
destroyed, they acknowledged
your people to be God's child.

14 For while gentle silence enveloped
all things,

and night in its swift course was now
half gone,

15 your all-powerful word leaped from
heaven, from the royal throne,
into the midst of the land that was
doomed,
a stern warrior

16 carrying the sharp sword of your
authentic command,
and stood and filled all things with
death,
and touched heaven while standing
on the earth.

17 Then at once apparitions in dreadful
dreams greatly troubled them,
and unexpected fears assailed them;

18 and one here and another there,
hurled down half dead,
made known why they were dying;

19 for the dreams that disturbed them
forewarned them of this,
so that they might not perish
without knowing why they
suffered.

Threat of Annihilation in the Desert

20 The experience of death touched
also the righteous,
and a plague came upon the
multitude in the desert,
but the wrath did not long continue.

21 For a blameless man was quick to act
as their champion;
he brought forward the shield of his
ministry,
prayer and propitiation by incense;
he withstood the anger and put an
end to the disaster,
showing that he was your servant.

22 He conquered the wrath[c] not by
strength of body,
not by force of arms,
but by his word he subdued the
avenger,
appealing to the oaths and covenants
given to our ancestors.

23 For when the dead had already fallen
on one another in heaps,

a Other ancient authorities read dangers, the ancestors already leading the
songs of praise   b Gk name   c Cn: Gk multitude

he intervened and held back the
  wrath,
and cut off its way to the living.
24 For on his long robe the whole world
  was depicted,
and the glories of the ancestors were
  engraved on the four rows of
  stones,
and your majesty was on the diadem
  upon his head.
25 To these the destroyer yielded, these
  he[a] feared;
for merely to test the wrath was
  enough.

The Red Sea

19 But the ungodly were assailed to
  the end by pitiless anger,
for God[b] knew in advance even their
  future actions:
2 how, though they themselves had
  permitted[c] your people to
  depart
and hastily sent them out,
they would change their minds and
  pursue them.
3 For while they were still engaged in
  mourning,
and were lamenting at the graves of
  their dead,
they reached another foolish
  decision,
and pursued as fugitives those
  whom they had begged and
  compelled to leave.
4 For the fate they deserved drew
  them on to this end,
and made them forget what had
  happened,

in order that they might fill up
  the punishment that their
  torments still lacked,
5 and that your people might
  experience[d] an incredible
  journey,
but they themselves might meet a
  strange death.

God Guides and Protects His People

6 For the whole creation in its nature
  was fashioned anew,
complying with your commands,
so that your children[e] might be kept
  unharmed.
7 The cloud was seen overshadowing
  the camp,
and dry land emerging where water
  had stood before,
an unhindered way out of the Red
  Sea,
and a grassy plain out of the raging
  waves,
8 where those protected by your
  hand passed through as one
  nation,
after gazing on marvelous wonders.
9 For they ranged like horses,
and leaped like lambs,
praising you, O Lord, who delivered
  them.
10 For they still recalled the events of
  their sojourn,
how instead of producing animals
  the earth brought forth gnats,
and instead of fish the river spewed

---

a Other ancient authorities read *they*   *b* Gk *he*   *c* Other ancient authorities read *had changed their minds to permit*   *d* Other ancient authorities read *accomplish*   *e* Or *servants*

19:1–21 The foolishness of the ungodly continues—The Egyptians did not acquire wisdom when they experienced God's judgment. Even as they buried their firstborn and let the Israelites go free, Pharaoh reconsidered and sent his army in pursuit of the former slaves. Their **strange death** (v. 5) at the Red Sea was just, in light of all the oppression the Egyptians had inflicted upon the Israelites. It was a revelation of the righteousness of God that put an end to the sin of Egypt and also launched Israel on **an incredible journey** (v. 5).

All creation was a witness and participant in this event. No one could accuse God of acting too rashly or too harshly because there was plenty of warning before each judgment event. These judgments were also deserved because the Egyptians had treated the Hebrews more harshly than any other people had done. They had at first welcomed them and received help from them, but then they enslaved the Israelites. Nature bears witness to the miraculous use of fire for guidance, of men and cattle crossing through the sea, and of manna sustaining a people in the wilderness.

out vast numbers of frogs.

11 Afterward they saw also a new kind[a]
of birds,
when desire led them to ask for
luxurious food;

12 for, to give them relief, quails came
up from the sea.

The Punishment of the Egyptians

13 The punishments did not come
upon the sinners
without prior signs in the violence of
thunder,
for they justly suffered because of
their wicked acts;
for they practiced a more bitter
hatred of strangers.

14 Others had refused to receive
strangers when they came to
them,
but these made slaves of guests who
were their benefactors.

15 And not only so—but, while
punishment of some sort will
come upon the former
for having received strangers with
hostility,

16 the latter, having first received them
with festal celebrations,
afterward afflicted with terrible
sufferings
those who had already shared the
same rights.

17 They were stricken also with loss of
sight—
just as were those at the door of the
righteous man—
when, surrounded by yawning
darkness,
all of them tried to find the way
through their own doors.

A New Harmony in Nature

18 For the elements changed[b] places
with one another,
as on a harp the notes vary the
nature of the rhythm,
while each note remains the same.[c]
This may be clearly inferred from
the sight of what took place.

19 For land animals were transformed
into water creatures,
and creatures that swim moved over
to the land.

20 Fire even in water retained its
normal power,
and water forgot its fire-quenching
nature.

21 Flames, on the contrary, failed to
consume
the flesh of perishable creatures that
walked among them,
nor did they melt[d] the crystalline,
quick-melting kind of
heavenly food.

Conclusion

22 For in everything, O Lord, you have
exalted and glorified your
people,
and you have not neglected to help
them at all times and in all
places.

a Or production   b Gk changing   c Meaning of Gk uncertain   d Cn: Gk nor
could be melted

19:22—Wisdom leads the reader in a benediction declaring God's faithfulness to the community of faith *in all times and in all places*. Such a declaration might be open to challenge if the disciple takes one moment of the journey of faith as the only measure of the truth. Nevertheless, Wisdom encourages the disciple to take a long view, a realistic view, and to find encouragement precisely in moments of trial or oppression, because the reality of faith is not to be found in an isolated event or a particular moment. The reality of God's faithfulness and providence is to be seen when one looks upon the whole of the incredible journey with God, which includes life on earth and eternal life.

Ecclesiasticus, or the Wisdom of Jesus Son of
SIRACH

S irach, part of the group of works called the Apocrypha, goes by several names, depending on the manuscript and language tradition. The Hebrew name, the Wisdom of Joshua ben (son of) Sira, comes from the name of the book's author, Joshua ben Eleazar ben Sira (50:27). The Greek name is the Wisdom of Jesus son of Sirach, often simply Sirach for short. In the Latin Vulgate the book is entitled Ecclesiasticus, or "the church's book." Even though Sirach was not included in the Jewish canon, early Christians retained it as part of their scriptural tradition. Protestants eliminated Sirach from their Bible, as they did the remainder of the Apocrypha, because it was not included in the Hebrew canon. Roman Catholicism places Sirach among the Old Testament Wisdom books.

Ben Sira wrote in Hebrew sometime in the early second century BCE, most likely before 180. According to the prologue to the Greek version, his grandson translated the book sometime after 132 BCE. It survived in a wide variety of languages, including Greek, Latin, Syriac, Coptic, and Armenian. Late in the 1890s, Hebrew medieval fragments of the book were discovered in a Cairo synagogue, and in the 1960s a large portion in Hebrew came to light at Masada, as did small fragments among the Dead Sea Scrolls.

The book contains much traditional practical wisdom aimed at enabling individuals to lead a life that is both good and pleasing to God. It also contains a number of examples of what has been called existential wisdom—knowledge about the workings of the physical universe and the place of wisdom in the cosmos.

Several important and recurring themes deserve comment.

A. *The nature of practical wisdom.* Sirach treats many topics found traditionally in ancient Wisdom literature, among them speech, business, wealth, friends, women, and children. In each case the author offers advice on how one should approach real-life problems connected with these topics, for example, how to tell a true friend from a false one. An interesting feature of practical wisdom is that it does not take the form of comment on Jewish law. In fact, although Sirach mentions the law on a number of occasions, specific citation or allusion to particular laws is almost completely lacking.

B. *Deuteronomic theology.* Sirach's outlook is heavily indebted to that of Deuteronomy—righteousness brings prosperity and success; wickedness leads to destruction. Ben Sira does not engage the observable fact that the world often fails to work this way. While other biblical books like Job and Ecclesiastes seem to recognize this problem and attempt to deal with it, Sirach does not.

C. *Honor and shame.* Sirach's wisdom reveals a heightened concern for personal honor and shame. In ancient Mediterranean society, a man's (in the ancient world *men* were the focus) reputation or honor determined his social status. Honor depended largely on his ability to control crucial aspects of personal identity in the face of the challenges of others to subvert that control. Many of these factors coincide

with the traditional wisdom topics listed above. Thus virtually all of the practical wisdom in the book somehow fits into this concern for, even obsession with, honor and shame. This system in some ways makes the book difficult reading in a contemporary society where honor and shame, which reinforce a conformity to generally agreed-upon social and cultural norms, have given way to an emphasis on individual rights and choices. So, for example, Sirach's infamous negative attitude toward women can really be understood only as stemming from an obsessive fixation on how women, despite not being able to accrue honor for themselves, can have a crucial impact on the honor or shame of their father or husband. Much of Sirach's transparent anxiety about women reflects his sense that their behavior, uncontrolled, has the potential to destroy a man's reputation and hence his place in society.

D. *One's name and immortality*. Sirach teaches the traditional Israelite view of death. The book does not recognize any afterlife of rewards and punishments, simply a shadelike existence in the place of the dead, Sheol (Hades in Greek). What lives on after a person is his or her name, especially as it is embodied in one's children. Sirach's overwhelming concern about honor and shame also has postmortem consequences. One's honorable name lives on in righteous children, and one's honored memory persists in the community. Achieving an honorable name means real immortality. For Sirach, leaving no memory at all is preferable to a disgraced name and the shame of leaving behind ungodly children.

E. *Wisdom as woman*. Sirach often portrays wisdom, a feminine noun in both Hebrew and Greek, as a woman, often a sexually seductive one. This personification is common in Wisdom literature. Wisdom has a universal character about her—that is, anyone who seeks her and submits to her discipline will find her—but Sirach makes another move and localizes this universal wisdom in the temple in Jerusalem and in the law (chap. 24).

The importance of these notions for the contemporary reader lies at least partially in the questions that they raise about biblical interpretation. Although in many ways life in antiquity had many continuities with the modern world, in most respects the ancient Jewish worldview and its social structures were very different from ours. How then does one make the interpretative transfer into contemporary situations of a scriptural text written in a world that was long ago and far away? How does the contemporary reader of Sirach regard social practices and attitudes that differ dramatically from those of the modern world? How one answers questions like these is at the heart of the process of interpreting Jewish Wisdom literature.

—**Benjamin G. Wright III**

The Prologue

Many great teachings have been given to us through the Law and the Prophets and the others*a* that followed them, and for these we should praise Israel for instruction and wisdom. Now, those who read the scriptures must not only themselves understand them, but must also as lovers of learning be able through the spoken and written word to help the outsiders. So my grandfather Jesus, who had devoted himself especially to the reading of the Law and the Prophets and the other books of our ancestors, and had acquired considerable proficiency in them, was himself also led to write something pertaining to instruction and wisdom, so that by becoming familiar also with his book*b* those who love learning might make even greater progress in living according to the law.

a Or other books *b* Gk with these things

You are invited therefore to read it with goodwill and attention, and to be indulgent in cases where, despite our diligent labor in translating, we may seem to have rendered some phrases imperfectly. For what was originally expressed in Hebrew does not have exactly the same sense when translated into another language. Not only this book, but even the Law itself, the Prophecies, and the rest of the books differ not a little when read in the original.

When I came to Egypt in the thirty-eighth year of the reign of Euergetes and stayed for some time, I found opportunity for no little instruction.[a] It seemed highly necessary that I should myself devote some diligence and labor to the translation of this book. During that time I have applied my skill day and night to complete and publish the book for those living abroad who wished to gain learning and are disposed to live according to the law.

In Praise of Wisdom

1 All wisdom is from the Lord,
    and with him it remains forever.
2 The sand of the sea, the drops of rain,
    and the days of eternity—who can
       count them?
3 The height of heaven, the breadth of
       the earth,
    the abyss, and wisdom[b]—who can
       search them out?
4 Wisdom was created before all other
       things,
    and prudent understanding from
       eternity.[c]

6 The root of wisdom—to whom has it
       been revealed?
    Her subtleties—who knows
       them?[d]
8 There is but one who is wise, greatly
       to be feared,
    seated upon his throne—the Lord.
9 It is he who created her;
    he saw her and took her measure;
    he poured her out upon all his
       works,
10 upon all the living according to his
       gift;
    he lavished her upon those who
       love him.[e]

Fear of the Lord Is True Wisdom

11 The fear of the Lord is glory and
       exultation,
    and gladness and a crown of
       rejoicing.
12 The fear of the Lord delights the
       heart,
    and gives gladness and joy and
       long life.[f]
13 Those who fear the Lord will have a
       happy end;
    on the day of their death they will
       be blessed.

14 To fear the Lord is the beginning of
       wisdom;

a Other ancient authorities read *I found a copy affording no little instruction*
b Other ancient authorities read *the depth of the abyss*   c Other ancient authorities add as verse 5, *The source of wisdom is God's word in the highest heaven, and her ways are the eternal commandments.*   d Other ancient authorities add as verse 7, *The knowledge of wisdom—to whom was it manifested? And her abundant experience—who has understood it?*   e Other ancient authorities add *Love of the Lord is glorious wisdom; to those to whom he appears he apportions her, that they may see him.*   f Other ancient authorities add *The fear of the Lord is a gift from the Lord; also for love he makes firm paths.*

1:1—*Wisdom* can be understood as God's primary contact with human beings. Acquired through the study of the Scriptures and attention to the sages, wisdom functioned as the mechanism by which people understood how to keep the covenant with God properly and to live a good and fulfilling life that pleased God. On wisdom pictured as a woman, see the introduction. Wisdom is intimately connected with fear of the Lord throughout Sirach (cf. vv. 11–13).

1:4—The idea that wisdom's origins precede creation has biblical roots (cf. Prov. 8:22–31). Wisdom knows the answers to the questions

of vv. 2–3. On human inability to answer such questions, cf. Job 38–40.

1:11–13—*Fear of the Lord* is a major theme in Sirach and should be understood in the English sense of awe. Contrary to what one might expect from English usage, rather than some grim and unhappy existence, fear of the Lord brings gladness and joy (cf. 34:14–20).

1:14–20—These verses emphasize the intimate connection between *fear of the Lord* and *wisdom*. Here is essentially a synopsis of Sirach's teaching. Fear is the beginning, fullness, crown

she is created with the faithful in
the womb.

15 She made[a] among human beings an
eternal foundation,
and among their descendants she
will abide faithfully.

16 To fear the Lord is fullness of wisdom;
she inebriates mortals with her
fruits;

17 she fills their[b] whole house with
desirable goods,
and their[b] storehouses with her
produce.

18 The fear of the Lord is the crown of
wisdom,
making peace and perfect health
to flourish.[c]

19 She rained down knowledge and
discerning comprehension,
and she heightened the glory of
those who held her fast.

20 To fear the Lord is the root of
wisdom,
and her branches are long life.[d]

22 Unjust anger cannot be justified,
for anger tips the scale to one's
ruin.

23 Those who are patient stay calm
until the right moment,
and then cheerfulness comes back
to them.

24 They hold back their words until the
right moment;
then the lips of many tell of their
good sense.

25 In the treasuries of wisdom are wise
sayings,
but godliness is an abomination to
a sinner.

26 If you desire wisdom, keep the
commandments,
and the Lord will lavish her upon
you.

27 For the fear of the Lord is wisdom
and discipline,
fidelity and humility are his
delight.

28 Do not disobey the fear of the Lord;
do not approach him with a
divided mind.

29 Do not be a hypocrite before others,
and keep watch over your lips.

30 Do not exalt yourself, or you may
fall
and bring dishonor upon yourself.
The Lord will reveal your secrets
and overthrow you before the
whole congregation,

[a] Gk made as a nest [b] Other ancient authorities read her [c] Other ancient
authorities add Both are gifts of God for peace; glory opens out for those who
love him. He saw her and took her measure. [d] Other ancient authorities add
as verse 21, The fear of the Lord drives away sins; and where it abides, it will
turn away all anger.

and root of wisdom. A series of images communicates the benefits of wisdom: she makes her
nest among humans; she delights just like wine;
she brings material benefit and long life; she
produces **peace** and **health**, **knowledge**, **glory**
and **long life**. Quite a motivation for seeking her
in the Scriptures and the words of the sages!

1:22—Much of Sirach's wisdom is practical and
life-oriented. Most of these practical topics occur
frequently in ancient Wisdom literature. **Anger**
is a common topic (cf. Prov. 12:16; 15:1; 19:12).
It poses a danger because it (1) creates internal
agitation in a person and (2) disrupts social
relationships and leads to sin; it can even lead to
violence (cf. Sir. 28:8–11).

1:23 *Right moment*—Anger and speech, the
topics here, have their proper moments. Words
and emotion expressed at the right time have the
desired effect. Actions taken at the wrong time
have no effect or, even worse, lead to personal
embarrassment and unintended consequences.

1:24—Speech can be good or bad. Part of the
value of speech depends on whether it occurs
at the proper moment or not. In the NT, see Jas.
3:1–12.

1:26—Keeping God's **commandments** is the
third component of a triad with wisdom and fear
of the Lord.

1:28 *Divided mind*—Lit. "a double heart." Holding back from God is equal to disobedience.

1:29–30—Ben Sira lived in an honor/shame society, and protection of one's reputation (or honor)
maintained social status (see introduction).
Honor was equated with virtue. Sirach cautions
against exposure to shame by being a *hypocrite*
or by exalting oneself. One may be able to deceive other people, but God will make the deceit
plain. The only possible result is *dishonor* and
shame, and God will bring that about.

because you did not come in the fear
    of the Lord,
  and your heart was full of deceit.

Duties toward God

2 My child, when you come to serve
    the Lord,
  prepare yourself for testing.[a]
2 Set your heart right and be steadfast,
  and do not be impetuous in time
    of calamity.
3 Cling to him and do not depart,
  so that your last days may be
    prosperous.
4 Accept whatever befalls you,
  and in times of humiliation be
    patient.
5 For gold is tested in the fire,
  and those found acceptable, in the
    furnace of humiliation.[b]
6 Trust in him, and he will help you;
  make your ways straight, and hope
    in him.

7 You who fear the Lord, wait for his
    mercy;
  do not stray, or else you may fall.
8 You who fear the Lord, trust in him,
  and your reward will not be lost.
9 You who fear the Lord, hope for
    good things,
  for lasting joy and mercy.[c]
10 Consider the generations of old and
    see:
  has anyone trusted in the Lord and
    been disappointed?
  Or has anyone persevered in the
    fear of the Lord[d] and been
    forsaken?
  Or has anyone called upon him
    and been neglected?

11 For the Lord is compassionate and
    merciful;
  he forgives sins and saves in time
    of distress.
12 Woe to timid hearts and to slack
    hands,
  and to the sinner who walks a
    double path!
13 Woe to the fainthearted who have no
    trust!
  Therefore they will have no
    shelter.
14 Woe to you who have lost your
    nerve!
  What will you do when the Lord's
    reckoning comes?

15 Those who fear the Lord do not
    disobey his words,
  and those who love him keep his
    ways.
16 Those who fear the Lord seek to
    please him,
  and those who love him are filled
    with his law.
17 Those who fear the Lord prepare
    their hearts,
  and humble themselves before
    him.
18 Let us fall into the hands of the Lord,
  but not into the hands of mortals;
  for equal to his majesty is his mercy,
  and equal to his name are his
    works.[e]

Duties toward Parents

3 Listen to me your father,
    O children;

[a] Or trials   [b] Other ancient authorities add *in sickness and poverty put your trust in him*   [c] Other ancient authorities add *For his reward is an everlasting gift with joy.*   [d] Gk *of him*   [e] Syr: Gk lacks this line

---

2:1–6—*Testing* is a frequent topic in Sirach. God does not abandon someone in such times. Just as gold is purified by melting, trials serve to purify one who follows the Lord.

2:7–11—Steadfastness characterizes fear of the Lord. Sirach encourages the reader to look to the past; none who have depended on God have been rejected (cf. chaps. 44–50).

2:12–14—These characteristics contrast with the ones enumerated in vv. 7–11.

2:14 *Reckoning*—Sirach has no concept of postmortem judgment where the righteous and sinners receive reward and punishment. They happen in this life (see introduction). In such a worldview, the importance of one's actions in this life becomes magnified, especially in light of the immediacy of God's response to them.

3:1–16—A poem highlighting the importance of honoring one's *parents*. God has established a hierarchy in the family, with parents having

act accordingly, that you may be kept in safety.

2 For the Lord honors a father above his children,
and he confirms a mother's right over her children.

3 Those who honor their father atone for sins,

4 and those who respect their mother are like those who lay up treasure.

5 Those who honor their father will have joy in their own children,
and when they pray they will be heard.

6 Those who respect their father will have long life,
and those who honor*a* their mother obey the Lord;

7 they will serve their parents as their masters.*b*

8 Honor your father by word and deed,
that his blessing may come upon you.

9 For a father's blessing strengthens the houses of the children,
but a mother's curse uproots their foundations.

10 Do not glorify yourself by dishonoring your father,
for your father's dishonor is no glory to you.

11 The glory of one's father is one's own glory,
and it is a disgrace for children not to respect their mother.

12 My child, help your father in his old age,
and do not grieve him as long as he lives;

13 even if his mind fails, be patient with him;
because you have all your faculties do not despise him.

14 For kindness to a father will not be forgotten,
and will be credited to you against your sins;

15 in the day of your distress it will be remembered in your favor;
like frost in fair weather, your sins will melt away.

16 Whoever forsakes a father is like a blasphemer,
and whoever angers a mother is cursed by the Lord.

Humility

17 My child, perform your tasks with humility;*c*
then you will be loved by those whom God accepts.

18 The greater you are, the more you must humble yourself;
so you will find favor in the sight of the Lord.*d*

20 For great is the might of the Lord;
but by the humble he is glorified.

21 Neither seek what is too difficult for you,
nor investigate what is beyond your power.

22 Reflect upon what you have been commanded,
for what is hidden is not your concern.

23 Do not meddle in matters that are beyond you,

a Heb: Other ancient authorities read *comfort* *b* In other ancient authorities this line is preceded by *Those who fear the Lord honor their father,* *c* Heb: Gk *meekness* *d* Other ancient authorities add as verse 19, *Many are lofty and renowned, but to the humble he reveals his secrets.*

authority over their children. Honoring parents brings atonement for sins, joy in one's own children, and parental blessing. Care for aging parents is an important filial responsibility. God will not tolerate one who abandons or angers his or her parents. Verse 16 makes honoring one's parents a religious duty. For examples of blessing children in the Bible, see Gen. 27:27–29; 48:15–20; 49:8–12.

3:17–18—*Humility*, the opposite of pride, brings a good reputation before others and before God (cf. Prov. 11:2; 15:33).

3:21–24—The desire to reach further than one's grasp is the equivalent of conceit and impaired judgment.

for more than you can understand
has been shown you.
24 For their conceit has led many
astray,
and wrong opinion has impaired
their judgment.
25 Without eyes there is no light;
without knowledge there is no
wisdom.[a]
26 A stubborn mind will fare badly at
the end,
and whoever loves danger will
perish in it.
27 A stubborn mind will be burdened
by troubles,
and the sinner adds sin to sins.
28 When calamity befalls the proud,
there is no healing,
for an evil plant has taken root in
him.
29 The mind of the intelligent
appreciates proverbs,
and an attentive ear is the desire of
the wise.

Alms for the Poor
30 As water extinguishes a blazing fire,
so almsgiving atones for sin.
31 Those who repay favors give thought
to the future;
when they fall they will find
support.

Duties toward the Poor
and the Oppressed
4 My child, do not cheat the poor of
their living,
and do not keep needy eyes
waiting.

2 Do not grieve the hungry,
or anger one in need.
3 Do not add to the troubles of the
desperate,
or delay giving to the needy.
4 Do not reject a suppliant in distress,
or turn your face away from the
poor.
5 Do not avert your eye from the
needy,
and give no one reason to curse
you;
6 for if in bitterness of soul some
should curse you,
their Creator will hear their
prayer.
7 Endear yourself to the congregation;
bow your head low to the great.
8 Give a hearing to the poor,
and return their greeting politely.
9 Rescue the oppressed from the
oppressor;
and do not be hesitant in giving a
verdict.
10 Be a father to orphans,
and be like a husband to their
mother;
you will then be like a son of the
Most High,
and he will love you more than
does your mother.

The Rewards of Wisdom
11 Wisdom teaches[b] her children
and gives help to those who seek
her.
12 Whoever loves her loves life,

[a] Heb: Other ancient authorities lack verse 25   [b] Heb Syr: Gk exalts

---

3:30—Care of the poor is an indispensable ethical value because it is a central feature of the covenant God made with Israel (see Deut. 15:7–11).

3:31—If one supports others, then they will return that support when it becomes necessary.

4:1–10—Attending to the needs of *the poor*, widows, and orphans is a barometer of social and personal piety (cf. Exod. 22:21–23; Deut. 10:17–18, 15:7–11). Lack of concern for these people is a frequent basis for prophetic critique (cf. Amos 2:6–7, 5:10–15).

4:6—God hears the prayers of those poor who have become bitter from mistreatment.

4:10—Widows and orphans were particularly vulnerable in their societies. For those who attend to the poor and marginalized, God's love exceeds even that of their mothers.

4:11–16—Faithfulness to God leads to the acquisition of *wisdom*. Whoever acquires wisdom obtains the foundation for living a truly happy and successful life.

and those who seek her from early
    morning are filled with joy.
13 Whoever holds her fast inherits
    glory,
    and the Lord blesses the place she*a*
    enters.
14 Those who serve her minister to the
    Holy One;
    the Lord loves those who love her.
15 Those who obey her will judge the
    nations,
    and all who listen to her will live
    secure.
16 If they remain faithful, they will
    inherit her;
    their descendants will also obtain
    her.
17 For at first she will walk with them
    on tortuous paths;
    she will bring fear and dread upon
    them,
    and will torment them by her
    discipline
    until she trusts them,*b*
    and she will test them with her
    ordinances.
18 Then she will come straight back to
    them again and gladden them,
    and will reveal her secrets to them.
19 If they go astray she will forsake
    them,
    and hand them over to their ruin.

20 Watch for the opportune time, and
    beware of evil,
    and do not be ashamed to be
    yourself.
21 For there is a shame that leads to sin,
    and there is a shame that is glory
    and favor.

22 Do not show partiality, to your own
    harm,
    or deference, to your downfall.
23 Do not refrain from speaking at the
    proper moment,*c*
    and do not hide your wisdom.*d*
24 For wisdom becomes known
    through speech,
    and education through the words
    of the tongue.
25 Never speak against the truth,
    but be ashamed of your ignorance.
26 Do not be ashamed to confess your
    sins,
    and do not try to stop the current
    of a river.
27 Do not subject yourself to a fool,
    or show partiality to a ruler.
28 Fight to the death for truth,
    and the Lord God will fight for you.

29 Do not be reckless in your speech,
    or sluggish and remiss in your
    deeds.
30 Do not be like a lion in your home,
    or suspicious of your servants.
31 Do not let your hand be stretched
    out to receive
    and closed when it is time to give.

Precepts for Everyday Living

5 Do not rely on your wealth,
    or say, "I have enough."
2 Do not follow your inclination and
    strength
    in pursuing the desires of your
    heart.

a Or he *b* Or until they remain faithful in their heart *c* Heb: Gk at a time of
salvation *d* So some Gk Mss and Heb Syr Lat: Other Gk Mss lack and do
not hide your wisdom

4:17–18—Too often people expect to have success and happiness without expending any effort.
These goals cannot be achieved without hard
work.

4:20–28—A section on appropriate and inappropriate **shame** that includes speech. Problems of
the tongue are important components of Sirach's
honor/shame code. This passage highlights again
the importance of knowing what to say and when
to say it. Speech as the primary mechanism of
human communication has enormous potential
for beneficial or destructive use.

5:1–8—Lack of circumspection about forgiveness
leads to further sin. Whoever presumes that God
will be forgiving and merciful will be in for a big
surprise. God's judgment can come at any time,
and postponing repentance poses a dangerous
risk. Pride makes people think that they can do
whatever they desire and God will still forgive.
Yet even in those times when it does not seem
that God has noticed, God sees human actions
and takes account of them.

3 Do not say, "Who can have power
　　over me?"
　　for the Lord will surely punish
　　　　you.

4 Do not say, "I sinned, yet what has
　　happened to me?"
　　for the Lord is slow to anger.

5 Do not be so confident of
　　forgiveness[a]
　　that you add sin to sin.

6 Do not say, "His mercy is great,
　　he will forgive[b] the multitude of
　　　　my sins,"
　　for both mercy and wrath are with
　　　　him,
　　and his anger will rest on sinners.

7 Do not delay to turn back to the
　　Lord,
　　and do not postpone it from day
　　　　to day;
　　for suddenly the wrath of the Lord
　　　　will come upon you,
　　and at the time of punishment you
　　　　will perish.

8 Do not depend on dishonest
　　wealth,
　　for it will not benefit you on the
　　　　day of calamity.

9 Do not winnow in every wind,
　　or follow every path.[c]

10 Stand firm for what you know,
　　and let your speech be consistent.

11 Be quick to hear,
　　but deliberate in answering.

12 If you know what to say, answer your
　　neighbor;
　　but if not, put your hand over your
　　　　mouth.

13 Honor and dishonor come from
　　speaking,

and the tongue of mortals may be
　　their downfall.

14 Do not be called double-tongued[d]
　　and do not lay traps with your
　　　　tongue;
　　for shame comes to the thief,
　　and severe condemnation to the
　　　　double-tongued.

15 In great and small matters cause no
　　harm,[e]

6 1 and do not become an enemy
　　instead of a friend;
　　for a bad name incurs shame and
　　　　reproach;
　　so it is with the double-tongued
　　　　sinner.

2 Do not fall into the grip of passion,[f]
　　or you may be torn apart as by a
　　　　bull.[g]

3 Your leaves will be devoured and
　　your fruit destroyed,
　　and you will be left like a withered
　　　　tree.

4 Evil passion destroys those who
　　have it,
　　and makes them the laughingstock
　　　　of their enemies.

Friendship, False and True

5 Pleasant speech multiplies friends,
　　and a gracious tongue multiplies
　　　　courtesies.

6 Let those who are friendly with you
　　be many,
　　but let your advisers be one in a
　　　　thousand.

7 When you gain friends, gain them
　　through testing,

a Heb: Gk atonement b Heb: Gk he (or it) will atone for c Gk adds so it is
with the double-tongued sinner (see 6.1) d Heb: Gk a slanderer e Heb Syr:
Gk be ignorant f Heb: Meaning of Gk uncertain g Meaning of Gk
uncertain

5:13–14—See 4:20–28. People who are **double-
tongued** (i.e., they use deceitful or slanderous
speech) ultimately cannot be trusted, and they
will have a difficult time rehabilitating their
ruined reputations.

6:1—The **name** is a symbolic stand-in for one's
reputation (see introduction).

6:2–4—Allowing oneself to be controlled by **passion** leads to dissipation.

6:5–17—There are many different sorts of
friends, and one must not trust too quickly. Testing reveals a friend's nature. Too many are fair-
weather friends who turn easily into foes. A true
friend is a rarity beyond price. One's behavior as
a friend influences the behavior of one's neighbor
(cf. Lev. 19:18).

and do not trust them hastily.

⁸ For there are friends who are such
    when it suits them,
    but they will not stand by you in
      time of trouble.

⁹ And there are friends who change
    into enemies,
    and tell of the quarrel to your
      disgrace.

¹⁰ And there are friends who sit at your
    table,
    but they will not stand by you in
      time of trouble.

¹¹ When you are prosperous, they
    become your second self,
    and lord it over your servants;

¹² but if you are brought low, they turn
    against you,
    and hide themselves from you.

¹³ Keep away from your enemies,
    and be on guard with your
      friends.

¹⁴ Faithful friends are a sturdy shelter:
    whoever finds one has found a
      treasure.

¹⁵ Faithful friends are beyond price;
    no amount can balance their
      worth.

¹⁶ Faithful friends are life-saving
    medicine;
    and those who fear the Lord will
      find them.

¹⁷ Those who fear the Lord direct their
    friendship aright,
    for as they are, so are their
      neighbors also.

Blessings of Wisdom

¹⁸ My child, from your youth choose
    discipline,
    and when you have gray hair you
      will still find wisdom.

¹⁹ Come to her like one who plows and
    sows,
    and wait for her good harvest.

For when you cultivate her you will
    toil but little,
    and soon you will eat of her
      produce.

²⁰ She seems very harsh to the
    undisciplined;
    fools cannot remain with her.

²¹ She will be like a heavy stone to test
    them,
    and they will not delay in casting
      her aside.

²² For wisdom is like her name;
    she is not readily perceived by
      many.

²³ Listen, my child, and accept my
    judgment;
    do not reject my counsel.

²⁴ Put your feet into her fetters,
    and your neck into her collar.

²⁵ Bend your shoulders and carry her,
    and do not fret under her bonds.

²⁶ Come to her with all your soul,
    and keep her ways with all your
      might.

²⁷ Search out and seek, and she will
    become known to you;
    and when you get hold of her, do
      not let her go.

²⁸ For at last you will find the rest she
    gives,
    and she will be changed into joy
      for you.

²⁹ Then her fetters will become for you
    a strong defense,
    and her collar a glorious robe.

³⁰ Her yoke*a* is a golden ornament,
    and her bonds a purple cord.

³¹ You will wear her like a glorious
    robe,
    and put her on like a splendid
      crown.*b*

³² If you are willing, my child, you can
    be disciplined,

---

a Heb: Gk *Upon her*   *b* Heb: Gk *crown of gladness*

6:18—The work and experience necessary to become wise make acquiring wisdom a lifelong enterprise.

6:23–30—Education begins by enduring Wisdom's **fetters** and **bonds** (vv. 24–25), but effort and endurance changes those bonds into priestly garments (vv. 29–31). Verse 26, cf. Deut. 6:5.

and if you apply yourself you will become clever.

33 If you love to listen you will gain knowledge,
and if you pay attention you will become wise.

34 Stand in the company of the elders.
Who is wise? Attach yourself to such a one.

35 Be ready to listen to every godly discourse,
and let no wise proverbs escape you.

36 If you see an intelligent person, rise early to visit him;
let your foot wear out his doorstep.

37 Reflect on the statutes of the Lord,
and meditate at all times on his commandments.
It is he who will give insight to[a] your mind,
and your desire for wisdom will be granted.

Miscellaneous Advice

7 Do no evil, and evil will never overtake you.

2 Stay away from wrong, and it will turn away from you.

3 Do[b] not sow in the furrows of injustice,
and you will not reap a sevenfold crop.

4 Do not seek from the Lord high office,
or the seat of honor from the king.

5 Do not assert your righteousness before the Lord,
or display your wisdom before the king.

6 Do not seek to become a judge,
or you may be unable to root out injustice;
you may be partial to the powerful,
and so mar your integrity.

7 Commit no offense against the public,
and do not disgrace yourself among the people.

8 Do not commit a sin twice;
not even for one will you go unpunished.

9 Do not say, "He will consider the great number of my gifts,
and when I make an offering to the Most High God, he will accept it."

10 Do not grow weary when you pray;
do not neglect to give alms.

11 Do not ridicule a person who is embittered in spirit,
for there is One who humbles and exalts.

12 Do not devise[c] a lie against your brother,
or do the same to a friend.

13 Refuse to utter any lie,
for it is a habit that results in no good.

14 Do not babble in the assembly of the elders,
and do not repeat yourself when you pray.

15 Do not hate hard labor
or farm work, which was created by the Most High.

[a] Heb: Gk will confirm   [b] Gk My child, do   [c] Heb: Gk plow

---

6:34–37—Wisdom begets wisdom. Where is wisdom found? In those who are wise and in the study of the Scriptures. Persons seeking wisdom need to put themselves in the right position to learn it (cf. Ps. 1:2).

7:1–26—The sequence of *do not*'s in these verses offers practical behaviors to avoid and represents a standard formula for articulating ethical norms (cf. Prov. 22:22–28). Most of the advice has everyday applicability and is intended to keep the hearer from shame or harm.

7:6—One who decides cases needs to have the highest ethical standards. Otherwise he or she might be predisposed in favor of the rich and socially powerful.

7:9—God will not overlook one's sins even in the face of bounteous offerings.

7:11—Looking down on those less fortunate ignores the fact that God determines one's place in life.

7:12–13—Lying to one's fellows becomes habitual.

7:15—One should not shun hard work, because God created it at the beginning and it is woven into all of life (cf. Gen. 2:15).

16 Do not enroll in the ranks of sinners;
     remember that retribution does
         not delay.
17 Humble yourself to the utmost,
     for the punishment of the ungodly
         is fire and worms.[a]

Relations with Others

18 Do not exchange a friend for money,
     or a real brother for the gold of
         Ophir.
19 Do not dismiss[b] a wise and good
         wife,
     for her charm is worth more than
         gold.
20 Do not abuse slaves who work
         faithfully,
     or hired laborers who devote
         themselves to their task.
21 Let your soul love intelligent slaves;[c]
     do not withhold from them their
         freedom.
22 Do you have cattle? Look after them;
     if they are profitable to you, keep
         them.
23 Do you have children? Discipline
         them,
     and make them obedient[d] from
         their youth.
24 Do you have daughters? Be
         concerned for their chastity,[e]
     and do not show yourself too
         indulgent with them.

25 Give a daughter in marriage, and
     you complete a great task;
     but give her to a sensible man.
26 Do you have a wife who pleases
     you?[f] Do not divorce her;
     but do not trust yourself to one
         whom you detest.
27 With all your heart honor your father,
     and do not forget the birth pangs
         of your mother.
28 Remember that it was of your
         parents[g] you were born;
     how can you repay what they have
         given to you?
29 With all your soul fear the Lord,
     and revere his priests.
30 With all your might love your Maker,
     and do not neglect his ministers.
31 Fear the Lord and honor the priest,
     and give him his portion, as you
         have been commanded:
     the first fruits, the guilt offering, the
         gift of the shoulders,
         the sacrifice of sanctification,
             and the first fruits of the holy
             things.
32 Stretch out your hand to the poor,
     so that your blessing may be
         complete.

[a] Heb for the expectation of mortals is worms [b] Heb: Gk deprive yourself
of [c] Heb Love a wise slave as yourself [d] Gk bend their necks [e] Gk body
[f] Heb Syr lack who pleases you [g] Gk them

7:16–17—Without a notion of a postmortem system of punishments and rewards, the emphasis is on God's ability to punish without delay. Retribution happens in this life, and thus people's actions and attitudes have significance in the here and now of daily life, not in some far-off time.

7:20–21—Sirach, like the Hebrew Bible generally, shows no evidence of any moral difficulty with the institution of slavery. He encourages good treatment of faithful *slaves*. Masters at death would sometimes release slaves (v. 21).

7:22–26—The subjects of these verses—*cattle, children,* and *wives*—were considered the man's household, and he must manage them wisely. The social values and roles described here highlight how much our contemporary world differs from Ben Sira's.

7:23—While obedience is the responsibility of

children, a father's obligation is to **discipline** his child.

7:24–25—*Daughters* highlight the honor/shame values that Sirach constantly keeps in view. A daughter's behavior has critical potential to affect the reputation of her father or husband (see 42:9–14 and introduction).

7:26—*Divorce* was an acceptable legal option in ancient Jewish life. Sirach discourages divorce of a good wife.

7:27–30 *With all your heart, with all your soul, with all your might*—See Deut. 6:5. These phrases allude to one of the most important verses in Jewish liturgy to encourage respect and honor for parents, priest and God.

7:28—Respect for *parents* is grounded in the realization that they gave life to their child.

7:32–36—Whoever acts in solidarity with those

33 Give graciously to all the living;
　　do not withhold kindness even
　　　　from the dead.
34 Do not avoid those who weep,
　　but mourn with those who mourn.
35 Do not hesitate to visit the sick,
　　because for such deeds you will be
　　　　loved.
36 In all you do, remember the end of
　　your life,
　　and then you will never sin.

Prudence and Common Sense

8 Do not contend with the powerful,
　　or you may fall into their hands.
2 Do not quarrel with the rich,
　　in case their resources outweigh
　　　　yours;
　　for gold has ruined many,
　　　　and has perverted the minds of
　　　　　　kings.
3 Do not argue with the loud of
　　mouth,
　　and do not heap wood on their
　　　　fire.
4 Do not make fun of one who is
　　ill-bred,
　　or your ancestors may be insulted.
5 Do not reproach one who is turning
　　away from sin;
　　remember that we all deserve
　　　　punishment.
6 Do not disdain one who is old,
　　for some of us are also growing
　　　　old.
7 Do not rejoice over anyone's death;
　　remember that we must all die.

8 Do not slight the discourse of the
　　sages,
　　but busy yourself with their
　　　　maxims;

because from them you will learn
　　discipline
　　and how to serve princes.
9 Do not ignore the discourse of the
　　aged,
　　for they themselves learned from
　　　　their parents;[a]
　　from them you learn how to
　　　　understand
　　and to give an answer when the
　　　　need arises.
10 Do not kindle the coals of sinners,
　　or you may be burned in their
　　　　flaming fire.
11 Do not let the insolent bring you to
　　your feet,
　　or they may lie in ambush against
　　　　your words.
12 Do not lend to one who is stronger
　　than you;
　　but if you do lend anything, count
　　　　it as a loss.
13 Do not give surety beyond your
　　means;
　　but if you give surety, be prepared
　　　　to pay.
14 Do not go to law against a judge,
　　for the decision will favor him
　　　　because of his standing.
15 Do not go traveling with the
　　reckless,
　　or they will be burdensome to you;
　　for they will act as they please,
　　　　and through their folly you will
　　　　　　perish with them.
16 Do not pick a fight with the
　　quick-tempered,
　　and do not journey with them
　　　　through lonely country,

a Or ancestors

---

who are distressed—*the poor, those who mourn, the sick*—receives *blessing* from God and the love of others.

8:1–7—One ought to exercise caution in certain social relationships (an important theme of Sirach) because one's actions have repercussions in one's own life. In cases like disdaining old age or rejoicing over death, we all share the same fate and need to be circumspect.

8:8–9—One should listen carefully to elders, since age confers a practical life wisdom that gets passed down through the generations.

8:10–19—These verses caution against relationships with people whom, for reasons of self-preservation, one ought to avoid.

because bloodshed means nothing
    to them,
and where no help is at hand, they
    will strike you down.
17 Do not consult with fools,
    for they cannot keep a secret.
18 In the presence of strangers do
    nothing that is to be kept secret,
    for you do not know what they
    will divulge.*a*
19 Do not reveal your thoughts to
    anyone,
    or you may drive away your
    happiness.*b*

Advice concerning Women

9 Do not be jealous of the wife of
    your bosom,
    or you will teach her an evil lesson
    to your own hurt.
2 Do not give yourself to a woman
    and let her trample down your
    strength.
3 Do not go near a loose woman,
    or you will fall into her snares.
4 Do not dally with a singing girl,
    or you will be caught by her tricks.
5 Do not look intently at a virgin,
    or you may stumble and incur
    penalties for her.
6 Do not give yourself to prostitutes,
    or you may lose your inheritance.
7 Do not look around in the streets of
    a city,
    or wander about in its deserted
    sections.
8 Turn away your eyes from a shapely
    woman,
    and do not gaze at beauty
    belonging to another;

many have been seduced by a
    woman's beauty,
    and by it passion is kindled like a
    fire.
9 Never dine with another man's
    wife,
    or revel with her at wine;
    or your heart may turn aside to her,
    and in blood*c* you may be plunged
    into destruction.

Choice of Friends
10 Do not abandon old friends,
    for new ones cannot equal them.
A new friend is like new wine;
    when it has aged, you can drink it
    with pleasure.

11 Do not envy the success of sinners,
    for you do not know what their
    end will be like.
12 Do not delight in what pleases the
    ungodly;
    remember that they will not be
    held guiltless all their lives.

13 Keep far from those who have power
    to kill,
    and you will not be haunted by the
    fear of death.
But if you approach them, make no
    misstep,
    or they may rob you of your life.
Know that you are stepping among
    snares,
    and that you are walking on the
    city battlements.

14 As much as you can, aim to know
    your neighbors,

a Or it will bring forth   *b* Heb: Gk and let him not return a favor to you   *c* Heb: Gk by your spirit

---

9:1–9—A list of women and situations that one should avoid. Like other practical matters, such as finances, friendship, and poverty, women are a frequent topic in Sirach and in Wisdom literature generally (cf. Prov. 5:18–20; 12:4; 31). Ben Sira's negative attitude toward women is well known (see introduction), and a verse like v. 2 displays it. Yet the broader notion of avoiding potentially compromising situations would still appear to be good advice in the contemporary world.

9:3 Loose woman—Lit. "strange woman"

(*'ishah zarah*). See Prov. 2:16–19; 5:3–6; 7:5–27; 9:13–18.

9:5 Penalties—For defiling a virgin, cf. Exod. 22:16.

9:9—A possible reference to the death penalty for adultery (Lev. 20:10; Deut. 22:22).

9:11–12—Although the wicked might prosper, realization of what awaits them should temper one's *envy* of them.

9:14–16—These verses form the positive antith-

and consult with the wise.

15 Let your conversation be with
  intelligent people,
    and let all your discussion be
      about the law of the Most
      High.
16 Let the righteous be your dinner
  companions,
    and let your glory be in the fear of
      the Lord.

Concerning Rulers

17 A work is praised for the skill of the
  artisan;
    so a people's leader is proved wise
      by his words.
18 The loud of mouth are feared in
  their city,
    and the one who is reckless in
      speech is hated.

10 A wise magistrate educates his
      people,
    and the rule of an intelligent
      person is well ordered.
2 As the people's judge is, so are his
  officials;
    as the ruler of the city is, so are all
      its inhabitants.
3 An undisciplined king ruins his
  people,
    but a city becomes fit to live in
      through the understanding of
      its rulers.
4 The government of the earth is in
  the hand of the Lord,
    and over it he will raise up the
      right leader for the time.
5 Human success is in the hand of the
  Lord,
    and it is he who confers honor
      upon the lawgiver.[a]

The Sin of Pride

6 Do not get angry with your neighbor
  for every injury,
    and do not resort to acts of
      insolence.
7 Arrogance is hateful to the Lord and
  to mortals,
    and injustice is outrageous to both.
8 Sovereignty passes from nation to
  nation
    on account of injustice and
      insolence and wealth.[b]
9 How can dust and ashes be proud?
    Even in life the human body
      decays.[c]
10 A long illness baffles the physician;[d]
    the king of today will die
      tomorrow.
11 For when one is dead
    he inherits maggots and vermin[e]
      and worms.
12 The beginning of human pride is to
  forsake the Lord;
    the heart has withdrawn from its
      Maker.
13 For the beginning of pride is sin,
    and the one who clings to it pours
      out abominations.
  Therefore the Lord brings upon
      them unheard-of calamities,
    and destroys them completely.
14 The Lord overthrows the thrones of
  rulers,
    and enthrones the lowly in their
      place.
15 The Lord plucks up the roots of the
  nations,[f]

---

a Heb: Gk *scribe*   *b* Other ancient authorities add here or after verse 9a,
*Nothing is more wicked than one who loves money, for such a person puts his
own soul up for sale.*   *c* Heb: Meaning of Gk uncertain   *d* Heb Lat: Meaning
of Gk uncertain   *e* Heb: Gk *wild animals*   *f* Other ancient authorities read
proud nations

---

esis of all that has preceded them. One should
know the character of one's *neighbors* and associate only with *the wise* and *righteous*.

9:17–10:5—A good *ruler* improves the lot of his
people, while a poor ruler invites ruin. The ideal
ruler governs according to wisdom. The governed
reflect the character of the one who governs (v. 2).

10:8—International strife often has *injustice*, arrogance, and money as root causes.

10:9—Although vv. 6–18 apply primarily to
rulers, the realization of human mortality should
temper every person's pride. *Dust and ashes*—Cf.
Gen. 18:27; Job 30:19.

10:14–16—God displaces the proud and installs
the humble in their stead. *Overthrow . . . pluck
up . . . destroy*—Cf. Jer. 1:10.

and plants the humble in their
place.

16 The Lord lays waste the lands of the
nations,
and destroys them to the
foundations of the earth.

17 He removes some of them and
destroys them,
and erases the memory of them
from the earth.

18 Pride was not created for human
beings,
or violent anger for those born of
women.

Persons Deserving Honor

19 Whose offspring are worthy of
honor?
Human offspring.
Whose offspring are worthy of
honor?
Those who fear the Lord.
Whose offspring are unworthy of
honor?
Human offspring.
Whose offspring are unworthy of
honor?
Those who break the
commandments.

20 Among family members their leader
is worthy of honor,
but those who fear the Lord are
worthy of honor in his eyes.*a*

22 The rich, and the eminent, and the
poor—
their glory is the fear of the Lord.

23 It is not right to despise one who is
intelligent but poor,
and it is not proper to honor one
who is sinful.

24 The prince and the judge and the
ruler are honored,
but none of them is greater than
the one who fears the Lord.

25 Free citizens will serve a wise servant,
and an intelligent person will not
complain.

Concerning Humility

26 Do not make a display of your
wisdom when you do your
work,
and do not boast when you are in
need.

27 Better is the worker who has goods
in plenty
than the boaster who lacks bread.

28 My child, honor yourself with
humility,
and give yourself the esteem you
deserve.

29 Who will acquit those who
condemn*b* themselves?
And who will honor those who
dishonor themselves?*c*

30 The poor are honored for their
knowledge,
while the rich are honored for
their wealth.

31 One who is honored in poverty, how
much more in wealth!
And one dishonored in wealth,
how much more in poverty!

The Deceptiveness of Appearances

11 The wisdom of the humble lifts
their heads high,

a Other ancient authorities add as verse 21, *The fear of the Lord is the
beginning of acceptance; obduracy and pride are the beginning of rejection.*
b Heb: Gk *sin against* *c* Heb Lat: Gk *their own life*

10:18—God did not intend *pride* or *anger* for
humanity.

10:19—The rhetorical questions reveal Ben Sira's
fundamental values for the individual (*honor/*
dishonor) and how they are acquired. Fear of
the Lord is the only meaningful determinant of
honor.

10:23–25—True honor is not necessarily concomitant with visible social rank and status. Fear
of the Lord trumps social status. While judges
and rulers may acquire honor because of their

social position, the *intelligent poor* and the wise
slave achieve honor for their fear of the Lord.

10:28–31—The problematic nature of wealth.
People magnify the wealthy because of their
riches. But *knowledge*/wisdom also confers
honor. So the pauper with knowledge, if he
becomes wealthy, acquires additional honor. The
dishonorable rich person upon losing his wealth
is dishonored even more.

11:1–6—One cannot judge by *appearance*. *Wisdom*, not social rank, exalts individuals.

and seats them among the great.

2 Do not praise individuals for their
good looks,
or loathe anyone because of
appearance alone.

3 The bee is small among flying
creatures,
but what it produces is the best of
sweet things.

4 Do not boast about wearing fine
clothes,
and do not exalt yourself when
you are honored;
for the works of the Lord are
wonderful,
and his works are concealed from
humankind.

5 Many kings have had to sit on the
ground,
but one who was never thought of
has worn a crown.

6 Many rulers have been utterly
disgraced,
and the honored have been
handed over to others.

Deliberation and Caution

7 Do not find fault before you
investigate;
examine first, and then criticize.

8 Do not answer before you listen,
and do not interrupt when another
is speaking.

9 Do not argue about a matter that
does not concern you,
and do not sit with sinners when
they judge a case.

10 My child, do not busy yourself with
many matters;
if you multiply activities, you will
not be held blameless.
If you pursue, you will not overtake,

and by fleeing you will not escape.

11 There are those who work and
struggle and hurry,
but are so much the more in want.

12 There are others who are slow and
need help,
who lack strength and abound in
poverty;
but the eyes of the Lord look kindly
upon them;
he lifts them out of their lowly
condition

13 and raises up their heads
to the amazement of the many.

14 Good things and bad, life and death,
poverty and wealth, come from the
Lord.*a*

17 The Lord's gift remains with the
devout,
and his favor brings lasting
success.

18 One becomes rich through diligence
and self-denial,
and the reward allotted to him is
this:

19 when he says, "I have found rest,
and now I shall feast on my
goods!"
he does not know how long it will be
until he leaves them to others and
dies.

20 Stand by your agreement and attend
to it,
and grow old in your work.

21 Do not wonder at the works of a
sinner,
but trust in the Lord and keep at
your job;

*a Other ancient authorities add as verses 15 and 16, 15Wisdom,
understanding, and knowledge of the law come from the Lord; affection and the
ways of good works come from him. 16Error and darkness were created with
sinners; evil grows old with those who take pride in malice.*

11:7–9—One should not act hastily, but careful
deliberation should precede acting or speaking.

11:11–13—A caution about the obsessive drive to
acquire things. Material wealth does not of itself
bring security. God, in mercy, can lift up the poor
to the amazement of the many, that is, contrary
to common expectation.

11:14—Sirach articulates an all-encompassing

monotheism in which everything, no matter
if it is good or bad, comes from God (cf. Isa.
45:7).

11:18–19—Riches constitute their own reward
that one may not live to enjoy (cf. Eccl. 2:20–21;
Luke 12:16–21).

11:21–22—The age-old question of why sinners
seem to prosper. Sirach's response is that God

for it is easy in the sight of the Lord
  to make the poor rich suddenly, in
    an instant.
22 The blessing of the Lord is[a] the
    reward of the pious,
  and quickly God causes his
    blessing to flourish.
23 Do not say, "What do I need,
  and what further benefit can be
    mine?"
24 Do not say, "I have enough,
  and what harm can come to me
    now?"
25 In the day of prosperity, adversity is
    forgotten,
  and in the day of adversity,
    prosperity is not remembered.
26 For it is easy for the Lord on the day
    of death
  to reward individuals according to
    their conduct.
27 An hour's misery makes one forget
    past delights,
  and at the close of one's life one's
    deeds are revealed.
28 Call no one happy before his death;
  by how he ends, a person becomes
    known.[b]

Care in Choosing Friends

29 Do not invite everyone into your
    home,

for many are the tricks of the
    crafty.
30 Like a decoy partridge in a cage, so
    is the mind of the proud,
  and like spies they observe your
    weakness;[c]
31 for they lie in wait, turning good
    into evil,
  and to worthy actions they attach
    blame.
32 From a spark many coals are
    kindled,
  and a sinner lies in wait to shed
    blood.
33 Beware of scoundrels, for they devise
    evil,
  and they may ruin your reputation
    forever.
34 Receive strangers into your home
  and they will stir up trouble
    for you,
  and will make you a stranger to
    your own family.

12 If you do good, know to whom
  you do it,
  and you will be thanked for your
    good deeds.
2 Do good to the devout, and you will
    be repaid—

[a] Heb: Gk is in [b] Heb: Gk and through his children a person becomes known
[c] Heb: Gk downfall

---

can at any moment rectify matters. The reward
from God, the divine *blessing*, comes in this life,
not in an afterlife.

11:23–28—People have short memories. Prosperity erases the memory of adversity and vice versa.
Yet the culmination of all life is in death. In life,
God may reward honor and reveal shame, but
since Sirach does not recognize any postmortem
rewards or punishments, the true reward is in
one's memory and name that lives on after death
(see introduction).

11:29–34—One must exercise caution in all human relationships. The *home* is the ultimate place
of safety and security, and to invite someone in is
to risk danger to one's honor, one's person, and
one's family relationships. Such caution, while
self-preserving, makes hospitality to *strangers*,
itself an important value in ancient society, difficult or even impossible. For a different approach
to hospitality to strangers, see Heb. 13:2.

12:1–7—Ben Sira operates with a deep ethic of

caution. He advocates giving and doing good
only *to the devout, not to the ungodly* (vv. 2, 4,
5, 7) whom God already hates and who deserve
punishment (v. 6). Why should one do good
to those who reject God and who intend to do
harm? Ben Sira's approach, however, reveals the
difficult choices that confront people as they
think about how to help others. For Ben Sira the
major concern is over social honor and dishonor,
but the questions that such an ethic raises are important in the contemporary world. For example,
how much should people expose themselves and
their families to potential social (and perhaps
even physical) dangers in order to relieve suffering? Ben Sira negotiates this quandary by extolling almsgiving, while at the same time caution-
ing against allowing strangers into one's home.
The New Testament Gospels, on the other hand,
attribute to Jesus a much more self-sacrificial and
vulnerable approach to helping others.

12:2—Doing good will always be *repaid* by God,

if not by them, certainly by the
   Most High.
3 No good comes to one who persists
   in evil
   or to one who does not give alms.
4 Give to the devout, but do not help
   the sinner.
5   Do good to the humble, but do not
   give to the ungodly;
   hold back their bread, and do not
   give it to them,
   for by means of it they might
   subdue you;
   then you will receive twice as much
   evil
   for all the good you have done to
   them.
6 For the Most High also hates sinners
   and will inflict punishment on the
   ungodly.[a]
7 Give to the one who is good, but do
   not help the sinner.
8 A friend is not known[b] in prosperity,
   nor is an enemy hidden in
   adversity.
9 One's enemies are friendly[c] when
   one prospers,
   but in adversity even one's friend
   disappears.
10 Never trust your enemy,
   for like corrosion in copper, so is
   his wickedness.
11 Even if he humbles himself and
   walks bowed down,
   take care to be on your guard
   against him.
   Be to him like one who polishes a
   mirror,
   to be sure it does not become
   completely tarnished.
12 Do not put him next to you,

or he may overthrow you and take
   your place.
Do not let him sit at your right hand,
   or else he may try to take your
   own seat,
and at last you will realize the truth
   of my words,
   and be stung by what I have said.
13 Who pities a snake charmer when he
   is bitten,
   or all those who go near wild
   animals?
14 So no one pities a person who
   associates with a sinner
   and becomes involved in the
   other's sins.
15 He stands by you for a while,
   but if you falter, he will not be
   there.
16 An enemy speaks sweetly with his
   lips,
   but in his heart he plans to throw
   you into a pit;
an enemy may have tears in his eyes,
   but if he finds an opportunity he
   will never have enough of your
   blood.
17 If evil comes upon you, you will find
   him there ahead of you;
   pretending to help, he will trip
   you up.
18 Then he will shake his head, and
   clap his hands,
   and whisper much, and show his
   true face.

Caution Regarding Associates

13 Whoever touches pitch gets
   dirty,

[a] Other ancient authorities add *and he is keeping them for the day of their punishment*   [b] Other ancient authorities read *punished*   [c] Heb: Gk *grieved*

---

even if not by other people. Pleasing God is more important than pleasing others.

12:10—While this verse does not say explicitly, "Hate one's enemies," it certainly warns against trusting them.

12:11—The image is of someone constantly polishing a copper mirror to keep it from tarnishing. Such constant vigilance is necessary when dealing with enemies (cf. v. 10).

12:13–18—If one associates with one's enemies and gets **bitten**, no one will feel sympathy. Enemies play the role of friend, but all the while they plot one's undoing. When it happens, they mock and rub it in.

13:1–7—The advice of this section assumes a highly stratified social structure—hence the metaphor of **the clay pot** and **the iron kettle** in v. 2. One should be cautious about associating

and whoever associates with a
  proud person becomes like him.
2 Do not lift a weight too heavy for you,
    or associate with one mightier and
      richer than you.
  How can the clay pot associate with
    the iron kettle?
  The pot will strike against it and
    be smashed.
3 A rich person does wrong, and even
    adds insults;
  a poor person suffers wrong, and
    must add apologies.
4 A rich person[a] will exploit you if you
    can be of use to him,
  but if you are in need he will
    abandon you.
5 If you own something, he will live
    with you;
  he will drain your resources
    without a qualm.
6 When he needs you he will deceive
    you,
  and will smile at you and
    encourage you;
  he will speak to you kindly and
    say, "What do you need?"
7 He will embarrass you with his
    delicacies,
  until he has drained you two or
    three times,
  and finally he will laugh at you.
  Should he see you afterwards, he will
    pass you by
  and shake his head at you.

8 Take care not to be led astray
    and humiliated when you are
      enjoying yourself.[b]

9 When an influential person invites
    you, be reserved,
  and he will invite you more
    insistently.
10 Do not be forward, or you may be
    rebuffed;
  do not stand aloof, or you will be
    forgotten.
11 Do not try to treat him as an equal,
    or trust his lengthy conversations;
  for he will test you by prolonged
    talk,
  and while he smiles he will be
    examining you.
12 Cruel are those who do not keep
    your secrets;
  they will not spare you harm or
    imprisonment.
13 Be on your guard and very careful,
    for you are walking about with
      your own downfall.[c]

15 Every creature loves its like,
    and every person the neighbor.
16 All living beings associate with their
    own kind,
  and people stick close to those like
    themselves.
17 What does a wolf have in common
    with a lamb?
  No more has a sinner with the
    devout.
18 What peace is there between a hyena
    and a dog?
  And what peace between the rich
    and the poor?

[a] Gk He [b] Other ancient authorities read *in your folly* [c] Other ancient
authorities add as verse 14, *When you hear these things in your sleep, wake
up! During all your life love the Lord, and call on him for your salvation.*

---

with people more powerful than oneself, because
such contact opens the possibility of exploitation
due to social inequality. The rich and powerful
associate with those lower than they on the social ladder for what they can get out of them, not
from any genuine desire for social intercourse.

13:8–13—Whoever deals with *influential* people
walks a thin line between success and failure.
These verses lay out a practical mode of cautious
behavior.

13:15–23—The problems of the relationship
between *the rich* and *the poor*. People mirror
the animal kingdom where like prefers like. The

natural order—sheep/*wolf*, *hyena*/*dog*, *wild
ass*/*lion*—illustrates the problems of different
social classes associating with one another.
Furthermore, the rich often get treated differently
from the poor. People justify the behavior of the
rich and denigrate the poor regardless of what
they do. Perhaps surprisingly, these verses do not
criticize wealth or prefer poverty per se. They
contend that wealth is good when it is free of
sin, and poverty is bad only to the impious. This
conclusion originates in the conviction that all
things come from God, even economic circumstance (cf. 11:14).

19 Wild asses in the wilderness are the
        prey of lions;
    likewise the poor are feeding
        grounds for the rich.
20 Humility is an abomination to the
        proud;
    likewise the poor are an
        abomination to the rich.
21 When the rich person totters, he is
        supported by friends,
    but when the humble*a* falls, he is
        pushed away even by friends.
22 If the rich person slips, many come
        to the rescue;
    he speaks unseemly words, but
        they justify him.
    If the humble person slips, they even
        criticize him;
    he talks sense, but is not given a
        hearing.
23 The rich person speaks and all are
        silent;
    they extol to the clouds what he
        says.
    The poor person speaks and they
        say, "Who is this fellow?"
    And should he stumble, they even
        push him down.
24 Riches are good if they are free from
        sin;
    poverty is evil only in the opinion
        of the ungodly.
25 The heart changes the countenance,
        either for good or for evil.*b*
26 The sign of a happy heart is a
        cheerful face,
    but to devise proverbs requires
        painful thinking.

14 Happy are those who do not
        blunder with their lips,
    and need not suffer remorse for
        sin.
2 Happy are those whose hearts do not
        condemn them,
    and who have not given up their
        hope.

Responsible Use of Wealth

3 Riches are inappropriate for a small-
        minded person;
    and of what use is wealth to a
        miser?
4 What he denies himself he collects
        for others;
    and others will live in luxury on
        his goods.
5 If one is mean to himself, to whom
        will he be generous?
    He will not enjoy his own riches.
6 No one is worse than one who is
        grudging to himself;
    this is the punishment for his
        meanness.
7 If ever he does good, it is by mistake;
    and in the end he reveals his
        meanness.
8 The miser is an evil person;
    he turns away and disregards
        people.
9 The eye of the greedy person is not
        satisfied with his share;
    greedy injustice withers the soul.
10 A miser begrudges bread,
    and it is lacking at his table.

11 My child, treat yourself well,
        according to your means,

a Other ancient authorities read *poor* *b* Other ancient authorities add *and a glad heart makes a cheerful countenance*

14:1–2—Happiness is the product of a clear conscience.

14:3–10—Wealth ought to be used; it is useless to whoever hoards it. Wealth is truly appreciated in generosity, and so the miser cannot enjoy it. In addition, the greedy cannot seem to be satisfied with what they have.

14:11–19—Since death is the fate of all, one should give generously to God and treat oneself well. Wealth should be used both for one's

own good and for that of others. The text even encourages indulging oneself. The rationale for such behavior is that death leaves one's wealth to others to divide up, and in the afterlife no one can seek luxury. Human productivity passes away, and people disappear along with their creations. These verses anticipate the proverb "You can't take it with you." For a similar outlook, see Ecclesiastes.

and present worthy offerings to
the Lord.

12 Remember that death does not tarry,
and the decree[a] of Hades has not
been shown to you.

13 Do good to friends before you die,
and reach out and give to them as
much as you can.

14 Do not deprive yourself of a day's
enjoyment;
do not let your share of desired
good pass by you.

15 Will you not leave the fruit of your
labors to another,
and what you acquired by toil to
be divided by lot?

16 Give, and take, and indulge yourself,
because in Hades one cannot look
for luxury.

17 All living beings become old like a
garment,
for the decree[b] from of old is, "You
must die!"

18 Like abundant leaves on a spreading
tree
that sheds some and puts forth
others,
so are the generations of flesh and
blood:
one dies and another is born.

19 Every work decays and ceases to exist,
and the one who made it will pass
away with it.

The Happiness of Seeking Wisdom

20 Happy is the person who meditates
on[c] wisdom
and reasons intelligently,

21 who[d] reflects in his heart on her
ways

and ponders her secrets,

22 pursuing her like a hunter,
and lying in wait on her paths;

23 who peers through her windows
and listens at her doors;

24 who camps near her house
and fastens his tent peg to her
walls;

25 who pitches his tent near her,
and so occupies an excellent
lodging place;

26 who places his children under her
shelter,
and lodges under her boughs;

27 who is sheltered by her from the
heat,
and dwells in the midst of her
glory.

15 Whoever fears the Lord will do
this,
and whoever holds to the law will
obtain wisdom.[e]

2 She will come to meet him like a
mother,
and like a young bride she will
welcome him.

3 She will feed him with the bread of
learning,
and give him the water of wisdom
to drink.

4 He will lean on her and not fall,
and he will rely on her and not be
put to shame.

5 She will exalt him above his
neighbors,
and will open his mouth in the
midst of the assembly.

[a] Heb Syr: Gk *covenant*   [b] Heb: Gk *covenant*   [c] Other ancient authorities
read *dies in*   [d] The structure adopted in verses 21–27 follows the Heb
[e] Gk *her*

14:20–27—Happiness comes to one who pursues *wisdom* intently. Various images communicate the intensity and goal of the pursuit: the hunter and prey; voyeurism; getting as close as possible by fastening a *tent peg to her walls*; living next door to her; bringing one's family *under her boughs*. On the image of wisdom as a tree of life, see 1:20, 24:13–17; Prov. 3:18. Inasmuch as the goals of pursuing wisdom are to please God and to live well, this same pursuit seems beneficial in today's world.

15:1—One who *fears the Lord* will seek wisdom in the ways described in 14:20–27.

15:2–6—The nurturing and sexual metaphors of *mother* and *bride* indicate Wisdom's attractiveness. Wisdom provides metaphorical *bread* and *water* (cf. Prov. 9:2, 5) and exalts whoever seeks her; the seeker obtains *an everlasting name*—immortality (see introduction).

6 He will find gladness and a crown of
    rejoicing,
    and will inherit an everlasting
    name.
7 The foolish will not obtain her,
    and sinners will not see her.
8 She is far from arrogance,
    and liars will never think of her.
9 Praise is unseemly on the lips of a
    sinner,
    for it has not been sent from the
    Lord.
10 For in wisdom must praise be
    uttered,
    and the Lord will make it prosper.

Freedom of Choice

11 Do not say, "It was the Lord's doing
    that I fell away";
    for he does not do[a] what he hates.
12 Do not say, "It was he who led me
    astray";
    for he has no need of the sinful.
13 The Lord hates all abominations;
    such things are not loved by those
    who fear him.
14 It was he who created humankind in
    the beginning,
    and he left them in the power of
    their own free choice.
15 If you choose, you can keep the
    commandments,
    and to act faithfully is a matter of
    your own choice.
16 He has placed before you fire and
    water;

stretch out your hand for
    whichever you choose.
17 Before each person are life and
    death,
    and whichever one chooses will be
    given.
18 For great is the wisdom of the Lord;
    he is mighty in power and sees
    everything;
19 his eyes are on those who fear him,
    and he knows every human action.
20 He has not commanded anyone to
    be wicked,
    and he has not given anyone
    permission to sin.

God's Punishment of Sinners

16 Do not desire a multitude of
    worthless[b] children,
    and do not rejoice in ungodly
    offspring.
2 If they multiply, do not rejoice in
    them,
    unless the fear of the Lord is in
    them.
3 Do not trust in their survival,
    or rely on their numbers;[c]
for one can be better than a
    thousand,
    and to die childless is better than
    to have ungodly children.
4 For through one intelligent person a
    city can be filled with people,

---

[a] Heb: Gk you ought not to do   [b] Heb: Gk unprofitable   [c] Other ancient
authorities add For you will groan in untimely mourning, and will know of
their sudden end.

15:7–9—Wisdom literature often contrasts the
fool with the true seeker of wisdom.

15:11–15—God cannot be blamed for human
sinfulness. God created human beings with the
capacity to choose good or evil. The Hebrew
word translated **choice** (v. 14) often designates
the propensity of human beings for both good
and evil (cf. Gen. 6:5; 8:21). Ultimately, people
choose righteousness or wickedness and are held
responsible for the choices that they make.

15:16–17—God places choices before mortals;
they receive what they desire. **Fire and water**
symbolize death and life.

15:18–20—Although God sees all human actions,
he has not given license to sin. Thus, he cannot
be held responsible for sinful decisions. Such a

perspective encourages a sense that all people
are accountable for the decisions that they make.

16:1–4—Children were viewed as signs of
blessing and as a source of eternal life, since
one's name lived on in them (see introduction).
Sirach counters that only righteous children are
blessings. That one should desire only children
who fear the Lord comes dramatically in the
claim that **to die childless is better than to have
ungodly children**. One should give up hope of
the eternal life that children can bring if they are
sinful. While in the contemporary world children
are not considered the locus of immortality, these
verses indirectly underscore the importance of
parental guidance in raising children who fear
the Lord.

but through a clan of outlaws it
becomes desolate.

5 Many such things my eye has seen,
and my ear has heard things more
striking than these.
6 In an assembly of sinners a fire is
kindled,
and in a disobedient nation wrath
blazes up.
7 He did not forgive the ancient
giants
who revolted in their might.
8 He did not spare the neighbors of
Lot,
whom he loathed on account of
their arrogance.
9 He showed no pity on the doomed
nation,
on those dispossessed because of
their sins;*a*
10 or on the six hundred thousand foot
soldiers
who assembled in their
stubbornness.*b*
11 Even if there were only one stiff-
necked person,
it would be a wonder if he
remained unpunished.
For mercy and wrath are with the
Lord;*c*
he is mighty to forgive—but he
also pours out wrath.
12 Great as is his mercy, so also is his
chastisement;
he judges a person according to his
or her deeds.
13 The sinner will not escape with
plunder,
and the patience of the godly will
not be frustrated.
14 He makes room for every act of
mercy;

everyone receives in accordance
with his or her deeds.*d*

17 Do not say, "I am hidden from the
Lord,
and who from on high has me in
mind?
Among so many people I am
unknown,
for what am I in a boundless
creation?
18 Lo, heaven and the highest heaven,
the abyss and the earth, tremble at
his visitation!*e*
19 The very mountains and the
foundations of the earth
quiver and quake when he looks
upon them.
20 But no human mind can grasp
this,
and who can comprehend his
ways?
21 Like a tempest that no one can see,
so most of his works are
concealed.*f*
22 Who is to announce his acts of
justice?
Or who can await them? For his
decree*g* is far off."*h*
23 Such are the thoughts of one devoid
of understanding;
a senseless and misguided person
thinks foolishly.

a Other ancient authorities add *All these things he did to the hard-hearted
nations, and by the multitude of his holy ones he was not appeased.* *b* Other
ancient authorities add *Chastising, showing mercy, striking, healing, the Lord
persisted in mercy and discipline.* *c* Gk *him* *d* Other ancient authorities
add *15The Lord hardened Pharaoh so that he did not recognize him, in
order that his works might be known under heaven. 16His mercy is manifest
to the whole of creation, and he divided his light and darkness with a plumb
line.* *e* Other ancient authorities add *The whole world past and present is
in his will.* *f* Meaning of Gk uncertain: Heb Syr *If I sin, no eye can see me,
and if I am disloyal all in secret, who is to know?* *g* Heb *the decree:* Gk *the
covenant* *h* Other ancient authorities add *and a scrutiny for all comes at
the end*

16:5–10—This list of biblical sinners provides
paradigmatic examples of things God does not
overlook or forgive: Korah, Dathan, and Abiram
(Num. 16; see Sir. 45:18–19), the *giants* (Gen.
6:1–4), Sodom (Gen. 19:1–11), probably the
Canaanites (cf. Deut. 7:1–2; 18:9–14), the male
Israelites who left Egypt (Exod. 12:37; see Sir.
46:8).

16:12–14—Both God's mercy and punishment
are great. God judges people *according to [their]
deeds*.

16:17–23—God may be the great ruler of all the
cosmos and be beyond human comprehension,
but only fools think that they are so small that
God will not notice them or that judgment happens way off in the future.

God's Wisdom Seen in Creation

24 Listen to me, my child, and acquire
  knowledge,
  and pay close attention to my
   words.
25 I will impart discipline precisely*a*
  and declare knowledge accurately.

26 When the Lord created*b* his works
  from the beginning,
  and, in making them, determined
   their boundaries,
27 he arranged his works in an eternal
  order,
  and their dominion*c* for all
   generations.
  They neither hunger nor grow
   weary,
  and they do not abandon their
   tasks.
28 They do not crowd one another,
  and they never disobey his word.
29 Then the Lord looked upon the
  earth,
  and filled it with his good things.
30 With all kinds of living beings he
  covered its surface,
  and into it they must return.

17 The Lord created human beings
  out of earth,
  and makes them return to it again.
2 He gave them a fixed number of
  days,
  but granted them authority over
   everything on the earth.*d*
3 He endowed them with strength like
  his own,*e*
  and made them in his own image.

4 He put the fear of them*f* in all living
  beings,
  and gave them dominion over
   beasts and birds.*g*
6 Discretion and tongue and eyes,
  ears and a mind for thinking he
   gave them.
7 He filled them with knowledge and
  understanding,
  and showed them good and evil.
8 He put the fear of him into*h* their
  hearts
  to show them the majesty of his
   works.*i*
10 And they will praise his holy name,
9 to proclaim the grandeur of his
   works.
11 He bestowed knowledge upon them,
  and allotted to them the law of
   life.*j*
12 He established with them an eternal
  covenant,
  and revealed to them his decrees.
13 Their eyes saw his glorious majesty,
  and their ears heard the glory of
   his voice.
14 He said to them, "Beware of all evil."
  And he gave commandment to
   each of them concerning the
   neighbor.
15 Their ways are always known to
  him;

a Gk by weight *b* Heb: Gk judged *c* Or elements *d* Lat: Gk it *e* Lat: Gk
proper to them *f* Syr: Gk him *g* Other ancient authorities add as verse 5,
*They obtained the use of the five faculties of the Lord; as sixth he distributed to
them the gift of mind, and as seventh, reason, the interpreter of one's faculties.*
h Other ancient authorities read *He set his eye upon* *i* Other ancient
authorities add *and he gave them to boast of his marvels forever* *j* Other
ancient authorities add *so that they may know that they who are alive now
are mortal*

16:26–30—When God created, order was
imposed on the cosmos. All things occupy the
places they were meant to, and all fulfill their
assigned roles. Thus, one can view every part
of creation as having a significance and value
imparted by God.

16:29—The phrase *good things* affirms the goodness of creation (cf. Gen. 1:4, 10, 18, 21, 25, 31).

16:30—God made all living things from dust and
to it all things *return* (cf. 17:1; Gen. 2:7; 3:19).

17:1–7—An interpretation of Gen. 1–3.

17:2–6—Human beings have limited life spans,

yet they share God's *image*. They are distinct
from the animals and stand higher in the created
order than they do.

17:7—Sirach attributes human knowledge of
good and evil to God, even though Genesis
suggests that human action resulted in such
knowledge (Gen. 3:4–7).

17:14—Commandments concerning neighbors
appear in the Decalogue (Exod. 20:13–17; Deut.
5:17–21) and in the commandment to love one's
neighbor as oneself (Lev. 19:18).

they will not be hid from his eyes.[a]

17 He appointed a ruler for every
    nation,
    but Israel is the Lord's own
        portion.[b]

19 All their works are as clear as the sun
        before him,
    and his eyes are ever upon their
        ways.

20 Their iniquities are not hidden from
        him,
    and all their sins are before the
        Lord.[c]

22 One's almsgiving is like a signet ring
        with the Lord,[d]
    and he will keep a person's
        kindness like the apple of his
        eye.[e]

23 Afterward he will rise up and repay
        them,
    and he will bring their recompense
        on their heads.

24 Yet to those who repent he grants a
        return,
    and he encourages those who are
        losing hope.

A Call to Repentance

25 Turn back to the Lord and forsake
        your sins;
    pray in his presence and lessen
        your offense.

26 Return to the Most High and turn
        away from iniquity,[f]
    and hate intensely what he
        abhors.

27 Who will sing praises to the Most
        High in Hades
    in place of the living who give
        thanks?

28 From the dead, as from one who
        does not exist, thanksgiving
        has ceased;
    those who are alive and well sing
        the Lord's praises.

29 How great is the mercy of the Lord,
    and his forgiveness for those who
        return to him!

30 For not everything is within human
        capability,
    since human beings are not
        immortal.

31 What is brighter than the sun? Yet it
        can be eclipsed.
    So flesh and blood devise evil.

32 He marshals the host of the height of
        heaven;
    but all human beings are dust and
        ashes.

The Majesty of God

18 He who lives forever created the
        whole universe;
2   the Lord alone is just.[g]
4 To none has he given power to
        proclaim his works;
    and who can search out his mighty
        deeds?
5 Who can measure his majestic power?
    And who can fully recount his
        mercies?

[a] Other ancient authorities add [16]*Their ways from youth tend toward evil, and they are unable to make for themselves hearts of flesh in place of their stony hearts.* [17]*For in the division of the nations of the whole earth, he appointed* [b] Other ancient authorities add as verse 18, *whom, being his firstborn, he brings up with discipline, and allotting to him the light of his love, he does not neglect him.* [c] Other ancient authorities add as verse 21, *But the Lord, who is gracious and knows how they are formed, has neither left them nor abandoned them, but has spared them.* [d] Gk *him* [e] Other ancient authorities add *apportioning repentance to his sons and daughters* [f] Other ancient authorities add *for he will lead you out of darkness to the light of health.* [g] Other ancient authorities add *and there is no other beside him;* [3]*he steers the world with the span of his hand, and all things obey his will; for he is king of all things by his power, separating among them the holy things from the profane.*

17:22—*Almsgiving* and *kindness* especially endear one to God.

17:25–32—God not only allows repentance (vv. 23–24), God encourages it. Since human beings are mortal and receive no postmortem reward, one must repent in this life in order to experience God's mercy (see introduction). In Sirach, the reality of the silent world of the dead encourages repentance and return to God in the here and now; there is no later in which to do it. Regardless of one's view of immortality, repenting now

restores one's ability to experience God's great mercy and to praise God.

18:1–12—Unlike humans, God *lives forever*, and God's works are beyond human ken (cf. Job 38–41). By contrast, human beings are small in the scope of things, and they have a short life span (cf. Job 14:1, 10–12; Ps. 39:4–6). Because humans are frail, have short life spans and end miserably, God is patient and merciful with them. The contrast between God's majesty and human frailty emphasizes the depth of God's

⁶ It is not possible to diminish or
        increase them,
    nor is it possible to fathom the
        wonders of the Lord.
⁷ When human beings have finished,
        they are just beginning,
    and when they stop, they are still
        perplexed.
⁸ What are human beings, and of what
        use are they?
    What is good in them, and what is
        evil?
⁹ The number of days in their life
        is great if they reach one
        hundred years.ᵃ
¹⁰ Like a drop of water from the sea
        and a grain of sand,
    so are a few years among the days
        of eternity.
¹¹ That is why the Lord is patient with
        them
    and pours out his mercy upon
        them.
¹² He sees and recognizes that their
        end is miserable;
    therefore he grants them
        forgiveness all the more.
¹³ The compassion of human beings is
        for their neighbors,
    but the compassion of the Lord is
        for every living thing.
    He rebukes and trains and teaches
        them,
    and turns them back, as a
        shepherd his flock.
¹⁴ He has compassion on those who
        accept his discipline
    and who are eager for his
        precepts.

The Right Spirit in Giving Alms
¹⁵ My child, do not mix reproach with
        your good deeds,
    or spoil your gift by harsh words.

¹⁶ Does not the dew give relief from
        the scorching heat?
    So a word is better than a gift.
¹⁷ Indeed, does not a word surpass a
        good gift?
    Both are to be found in a gracious
        person.
¹⁸ A fool is ungracious and abusive,
    and the gift of a grudging giver
        makes the eyes dim.

The Need of Reflection and Self-control
¹⁹ Before you speak, learn;
    and before you fall ill, take care of
        your health.
²⁰ Before judgment comes, examine
        yourself;
    and at the time of scrutiny you will
        find forgiveness.
²¹ Before falling ill, humble yourself;
    and when you have sinned, repent.
²² Let nothing hinder you from paying
        a vow promptly,
    and do not wait until death to be
        released from it.
²³ Before making a vow, prepare yourself;
    do not be like one who puts the
        Lord to the test.
²⁴ Think of his wrath on the day of
        death,
    and of the moment of vengeance
        when he turns away his face.
²⁵ In the time of plenty think of the
        time of hunger;
    in days of wealth think of poverty
        and need.
²⁶ From morning to evening conditions
        change;
    all things move swiftly before the
        Lord.
²⁷ One who is wise is cautious in
        everything;

ᵃ Other ancient authorities add *but the death of each one is beyond the calculation of all*

---

compassion (Sir. 17:29) and should temper human pride.

18:15–18—One's *gift*, probably almsgiving, should be accompanied by gracious *words*. The grudging giver compromises the value of the giving.

18:19–26—One needs to prepare with foresight before acting, because situations change rapidly. There may be no time to prepare later.

18:27—The wise person exercises caution and keeps away from sinning.

when sin is all around, one guards
    against wrongdoing.
28 Every intelligent person knows
    wisdom,
    and praises the one who finds her.
29 Those who are skilled in words
    become wise themselves,
    and pour forth apt proverbs.a

SELF-CONTROLb

30 Do not follow your base desires,
    but restrain your appetites.
31 If you allow your soul to take
    pleasure in base desire,
    it will make you the laughingstock
    of your enemies.
32 Do not revel in great luxury,
    or you may become impoverished
    by its expense.
33 Do not become a beggar by feasting
    with borrowed money,
    when you have nothing in your
    purse. c

19 The one who does thisd will not
    become rich;
    one who despises small things will
    fail little by little.
2 Wine and women lead intelligent
    men astray,
    and the man who consorts with
    prostitutes is reckless.
3 Decay and worms will take
    possession of him,
    and the reckless person will be
    snatched away.

Against Loose Talk

4 One who trusts others too quickly
    has a shallow mind,

and one who sins does wrong to
    himself.
5 One who rejoices in wickednesse will
    be condemned,f
6   but one who hates gossip has less
    evil.
7 Never repeat a conversation,
    and you will lose nothing at all.
8 With friend or foe do not report it,
    and unless it would be a sin for
    you, do not reveal it;
9 for someone may have heard you
    and watched you,
    and in time will hate you.
10 Have you heard something? Let it
    die with you.
    Be brave, it will not make you
    burst!
11 Having heard something, the fool
    suffers birth pangs
    like a woman in labor with a
    child.
12 Like an arrow stuck in a person's
    thigh,
    so is gossip inside a fool.
13 Question a friend; perhaps he did
    not do it;
    or if he did, so that he may not do
    it again.
14 Question a neighbor; perhaps he did
    not say it;
    or if he said it, so that he may not
    repeat it.

a Other ancient authorities add *Better is confidence in the one Lord than clinging with a dead heart to a dead one.*   b This heading is included in the Gk text.   c Other ancient authorities add *for you will be plotting against your own life*   d Heb: Gk A *worker who is a drunkard*   e Other ancient authorities read *heart*   f Other ancient authorities add *but one who withstands pleasures crowns his life.* 6 *One who controls the tongue will live without strife,*

18:30–33—Giving in to one's desires will provide enemies with the opportunity to bring shame, and whoever indulges too much becomes *impoverished*.

19:1—Wealth does not come to someone who acts in the ways described in 18:30–33. There is no criticism of wealth per se. More important than the drive to get wealth is that it is accumulated justly and used to good ends (see also notes at 11:11–13; 13:15–23; 14:3–10).

19:4—Sinful actions hurt not only others, but oneself as well.

19:7–12—As a rule, one should exercise discre-

tion in matters of speech, especially when it comes to gossip. The consequences of indiscreetly repeating what one hears are almost entirely bad. Gossip creates the obsessive impulse to repeat it, but keeping it quiet will not make one explode.

19:13–17—Find out the facts before accusing or threatening. In this way one overcomes the destructive consequences of believing rumors or unsubstantiated accusations. Even if the reports are true, this approach may enable friends or neighbors to change their behavior.

15 Question a friend, for often it is
      slander;
   so do not believe everything you
      hear.
16 A person may make a slip without
      intending it.
   Who has not sinned with his tongue?
17 Question your neighbor before you
      threaten him;
   and let the law of the Most High
      take its course.*a*

True and False Wisdom

20 The whole of wisdom is fear of the
      Lord,
   and in all wisdom there is the
      fulfillment of the law.*b*
22 The knowledge of wickedness is not
      wisdom,
   nor is there prudence in the
      counsel of sinners.
23 There is a cleverness that is detestable,
   and there is a fool who merely
      lacks wisdom.
24 Better are the God-fearing who lack
      understanding
   than the highly intelligent who
      transgress the law.
25 There is a cleverness that is exact but
      unjust,
   and there are people who abuse
      favors to gain a verdict.
26 There is the villain bowed down in
      mourning,
   but inwardly he is full of deceit.
27 He hides his face and pretends not to
      hear,
   but when no one notices, he will
      take advantage of you.
28 Even if lack of strength keeps him
      from sinning,
   he will nevertheless do evil when
      he finds the opportunity.

29 A person is known by his
      appearance,
   and a sensible person is known
      when first met, face to face.
30 A person's attire and hearty laughter,
   and the way he walks, show what
      he is.

Silence and Speech

20 There is a rebuke that is
      untimely,
   and there is the person who is wise
      enough to keep silent.
2 How much better it is to rebuke than
      to fume!
3 And the one who admits his fault
      will be kept from failure.
4 Like a eunuch lusting to violate a
      girl
   is the person who does right under
      compulsion.
5 Some people keep silent and are
      thought to be wise,
   while others are detested for being
      talkative.
6 Some people keep silent because
      they have nothing to say,
   while others keep silent because
      they know when to speak.
7 The wise remain silent until the
      right moment,
   but a boasting fool misses the right
      moment.
8 Whoever talks too much is detested,
   and whoever pretends to authority
      is hated.*c*

*a Other ancient authorities add and do not be angry. 18The fear of the Lord
is the beginning of acceptance, and wisdom obtains his love. 19The knowledge
of the Lord's commandments is life-giving discipline; and those who do what
is pleasing to him enjoy the fruit of the tree of immortality. b Other ancient
authorities add and the knowledge of his omnipotence. 21When a slave says to
his master, "I will not act as you wish," even if later he does it, he angers the one
who supports him. c Other ancient authorities add How good it is to show
repentance when you are reproved, for so you will escape deliberate sin!*

19:24–25—Real wisdom differs from mere human intelligence. Fear of the Lord is a higher
value than human cleverness, which often perpetuates injustice and transgression.

19:26–30—People's appearance and outward
actions oftentimes hide their true motives. They
appear to act one way and then act another. At
the same time, the appearance can be revealing.

One recognizes sensible people by their appearance—first impressions may reveal much.

20:1–8—Speech and silence each have their right
time. Silence generally is more highly valued
than talking. The wise know when to be *silent*
and *when to speak*; the foolish do not know the
value of silence.

Paradoxes

9 There may be good fortune for a
　　person in adversity,
　　and a windfall may result in a loss.
10 There is the gift that profits you
　　nothing,
　　and the gift to be paid back double.
11 There are losses for the sake of glory,
　　and there are some who have
　　　　raised their heads from
　　　　humble circumstances.
12 Some buy much for little,
　　but pay for it seven times over.
13 The wise make themselves beloved
　　by only few words,*a*
　　but the courtesies of fools are
　　　　wasted.
14 A fool's gift will profit you nothing,*b*
　　for he looks for recompense
　　　　sevenfold.*c*
15 He gives little and upbraids much;
　　he opens his mouth like a town
　　　　crier.
　　Today he lends and tomorrow he
　　　　asks it back;
　　such a one is hateful to God and
　　　　humans.*d*
16 The fool says, "I have no friends,
　　and I get no thanks for my good
　　　　deeds.
　　Those who eat my bread are
　　　　evil-tongued."
17 How many will ridicule him, and
　　how often!*e*

Inappropriate Speech

18 A slip on the pavement is better than
　　a slip of the tongue;
　　the downfall of the wicked will
　　　　occur just as speedily.
19 A coarse person is like an
　　　　inappropriate story,
　　continually on the lips of the
　　　　ignorant.

20 A proverb from a fool's lips will be
　　　　rejected,
　　for he does not tell it at the proper
　　　　time.
21 One may be prevented from sinning
　　by poverty;
　　so when he rests he feels no
　　　　remorse.
22 One may lose his life through shame,
　　or lose it because of human
　　　　respect.*f*
23 Another out of shame makes
　　　　promises to a friend,
　　and so makes an enemy for
　　　　nothing.

Lying

24 A lie is an ugly blot on a person;
　　it is continually on the lips of the
　　　　ignorant.
25 A thief is preferable to a habitual
　　　　liar,
　　but the lot of both is ruin.
26 A liar's way leads to disgrace,
　　and his shame is ever with him.

Proverbial Sayings *g*

27 The wise person advances himself by
　　his words,
　　and one who is sensible pleases the
　　　　great.
28 Those who cultivate the soil heap up
　　　　their harvest,
　　and those who please the great
　　　　atone for injustice.
29 Favors and gifts blind the eyes of the
　　　　wise;
　　like a muzzle on the mouth they
　　　　stop reproofs.

a Heb: Gk by words　*b* Other ancient authorities add *so it is with the envious
who give under compulsion*　*c* Syr: Gk *he has many eyes instead of one*
d Other ancient authorities lack *to God and humans*　*e* Other ancient
authorities add *for he has not honestly received what he has, and what he does
not have is unimportant to him*　*f* Other ancient authorities read *his foolish
look*　*g* This heading is included in the Gk text.

20:9—Circumstances may not be as they seem—
a tough situation can result in success and a good
one can turn bad.

20:18–20—It is better to risk physical injury than
to fall by means of the tongue. The harm brought
by the tongue is worse.

20:22–23—*Shame* may motivate one to make
promises to friends that cannot be kept, thereby
turning them into enemies.

20:29—Even the wise can be compromised by
gifts, because they may keep them from speaking
the truth.

30 Hidden wisdom and unseen
　　　treasure,
　　of what value is either?
31 Better are those who hide their folly
　　than those who hide their
　　wisdom. *a*

Various Sins

21 Have you sinned, my child? Do
　　　so no more,
　　but ask forgiveness for your past
　　sins.
2 Flee from sin as from a snake;
　　for if you approach sin, it will bite
　　you.
　Its teeth are lion's teeth,
　　and can destroy human lives.
3 All lawlessness is like a two-edged
　　sword;
　　there is no healing for the wound
　　it inflicts.
4 Panic and insolence will waste away
　　riches;
　　thus the house of the proud will be
　　laid waste. *b*
5 The prayer of the poor goes from
　　their lips to the ears of God, *c*
　　and his judgment comes speedily.
6 Those who hate reproof walk in the
　　sinner's steps,
　　but those who fear the Lord repent
　　in their heart.
7 The mighty in speech are widely
　　known;
　　when they slip, the sensible person
　　knows it.

8 Whoever builds his house with other
　　people's money
　　is like one who gathers stones for
　　his burial mound. *d*
9 An assembly of the wicked is like a
　　bundle of tow,
　　and their end is a blazing fire.
10 The way of sinners is paved with
　　smooth stones,
　　but at its end is the pit of Hades.

Wisdom and Foolishness

11 Whoever keeps the law controls his
　　thoughts,
　　and the fulfillment of the fear of
　　the Lord is wisdom.
12 The one who is not clever cannot be
　　taught,
　　but there is a cleverness that
　　increases bitterness.
13 The knowledge of the wise will
　　increase like a flood,
　　and their counsel like a life-giving
　　spring.
14 The mind *e* of a fool is like a broken
　　jar;
　　it can hold no knowledge.
15 When an intelligent person hears a
　　wise saying,
　　he praises it and adds to it;
　　when a fool *f* hears it, he laughs
　　at *g* it
　　and throws it behind his back.

a Other ancient authorities add *32Unwearied endurance in seeking the
Lord is better than a masterless charioteer of one's own life.* *b* Other ancient
authorities read *uprooted* *c* Gk *his ears* *d* Other ancient authorities read *for
the winter* *e* Syr Lat: Gk *entrails* *f* Syr: Gk *reveler* *g* Syr: Gk *dislikes*

21:1–3—*Sin* is subtle and dangerous, as the images here indicate. A two-pronged approach is recommended for sins. First, one must cease sinning; second, *ask forgiveness* for sins committed.

21:5—God hears *the prayer of the poor*. God's *judgment* vindicates the oppressed poor against their oppressors.

21:8–10—Ill-gotten wealth is unjust and leads to sin and judgment (cf. 13:24; 27:1–3; 31:5). These verses connect ill-gotten wealth with the *wicked* and *sinners*. For the idea that the way of sin is easy or smooth, see Matt. 7:13. The reference to *fire* (v. 9) refers to judgment in this world. On *Hades*, see introduction.

21:12—The word translated *clever* also has the connotation of "cunning" or "smart." Here it has a negative connotation, since some kinds of cleverness damage relationships.

21:13–14—Wisdom is *life-giving* water, and the fool's *broken jar* of a *mind* cannot hold any of it. It continually leaks out.

21:15–28—In these verses, which contrast the wise and the foolish, we see the practical aspects of wisdom. The topics of speech, knowledge/wisdom, social behavior, and manners are more oriented toward proper behavior in social relationships and situations than in fulfilling specific religious laws. Living a successful and good life is the goal of these admonitions.

16 A fool's chatter is like a burden on a
     journey,
   but delight is found in the speech
     of the intelligent.
17 The utterance of a sensible person is
     sought in the assembly,
   and they ponder his words in their
     minds.

18 Like a house in ruins is wisdom to a
     fool,
   and to the ignorant, knowledge is
     talk that has no meaning.
19 To a senseless person education is
     fetters on his feet,
   and like manacles on his right
     hand.
20 A fool raises his voice when he
     laughs,
   but the wise[a] smile quietly.
21 To the sensible person education is
     like a golden ornament,
   and like a bracelet on the right
     arm.
22 The foot of a fool rushes into a
     house,
   but an experienced person waits
     respectfully outside.
23 A boor peers into the house from
     the door,
   but a cultivated person remains
     outside.
24 It is ill-mannered for a person to
     listen at a door;
   the discreet would be grieved by
     the disgrace.

25 The lips of babblers speak of what is
     not their concern,[b]
   but the words of the prudent are
     weighed in the balance.

26 The mind of fools is in their mouth,
   but the mouth of the wise is in[c]
     their mind.
27 When an ungodly person curses an
     adversary,[d]
   he curses himself.
28 A whisperer degrades himself
   and is hated in his neighborhood.

The Idler

22 The idler is like a filthy stone,
   and every one hisses at his
     disgrace.
2 The idler is like the filth of
     dunghills;
   anyone that picks it up will shake
     it off his hand.

Degenerate Children

3 It is a disgrace to be the father of an
     undisciplined son,
   and the birth of a daughter is a
     loss.
4 A sensible daughter obtains a
     husband of her own,
   but one who acts shamefully is a
     grief to her father.
5 An impudent daughter disgraces
     father and husband,
   and is despised by both.
6 Like music in time of mourning is
     ill-timed conversation,
   but a thrashing and discipline are
     at all times wisdom.[e]

Wisdom and Folly

9 Whoever teaches a fool is like one
     who glues potsherds together,

[a] Syr Lat: Gk *clever*   [b] Other ancient authorities read *of strangers speak of
these things*   [c] Other ancient authorities omit *in*   [d] Or *curses Satan*   [e] Other
ancient authorities add [7]*Children who are brought up in a good life, conceal
the lowly birth of their parents.* [8]*Children who are disdainfully and boorishly
haughty stain the nobility of their kindred.*

22:3–6—This section on children demonstrates
again the importance of reputation and honor.
Well-behaved children bring honor to parents;
ill-behaved progeny bring shame. Daughters
were a greater potential liability than sons (since
in general, women were a potential source of
shame; see introduction). Ben Sira, like most ancient wisdom teachers, advocated corporal punishment to compel proper behavior (Prov. 13:24;
23:13–14). In cases like these we see some of the

fundamental differences between Sirach's social
assumptions and ours.

22:9—Cf. 21:14. Since the fool's mind can hold
no knowledge, teaching it is like trying to repair
the broken pot. The category of the *fool* is the foil
to the wise. As the wise become so by actively
pursuing learning, fools are such because they
reject wisdom. Before people can learn, they
have to be willing to be taught.

or who rouses a sleeper from deep slumber.

10 Whoever tells a story to a fool tells it to a drowsy man;
and at the end he will say, "What is it?"

11 Weep for the dead, for he has left the light behind;
and weep for the fool, for he has left intelligence behind.
Weep less bitterly for the dead, for he is at rest;
but the life of the fool is worse than death.

12 Mourning for the dead lasts seven days,
but for the foolish or the ungodly it lasts all the days of their lives.

13 Do not talk much with a senseless person
or visit an unintelligent person.[a]
Stay clear of him, or you may have trouble,
and be spattered when he shakes himself off.
Avoid him and you will find rest,
and you will never be wearied by his lack of sense.

14 What is heavier than lead?
And what is its name except "Fool"?

15 Sand, salt, and a piece of iron
are easier to bear than a stupid person.

16 A wooden beam firmly bonded into a building
is not loosened by an earthquake;
so the mind firmly resolved after due reflection
will not be afraid in a crisis.

17 A mind settled on an intelligent thought
is like stucco decoration that makes a wall smooth.

18 Fences[b] set on a high place
will not stand firm against the wind;
so a timid mind with a fool's resolve
will not stand firm against any fear.

The Preservation of Friendship

19 One who pricks the eye brings tears,
and one who pricks the heart makes clear its feelings.

20 One who throws a stone at birds scares them away,
and one who reviles a friend destroys a friendship.

21 Even if you draw your sword against a friend,
do not despair, for there is a way back.

22 If you open your mouth against your friend,
do not worry, for reconciliation is possible.
But as for reviling, arrogance, disclosure of secrets, or a treacherous blow—
in these cases any friend will take to flight.

23 Gain the trust of your neighbor in his poverty,
so that you may rejoice with him in his prosperity.
Stand by him in time of distress,
so that you may share with him in his inheritance.[c]

24 The vapor and smoke of the furnace precede the fire;
so insults precede bloodshed.

[a] Other ancient authorities add *For being without sense he will despise everything about you* [b] Other ancient authorities read *Pebbles* [c] Other ancient authorities add *For one should not always despise restricted circumstances, or admire a rich person who is stupid.*

22:12—*Seven days* (*shiva*) is the traditional period of *mourning* in Judaism. Mourning for the dead has an end, but one never ceases mourning over a fool or *the ungodly*.

22:16–18—In contrast to the broken and changeable mind of the fool, the mind of the wise is firm like sturdy construction that withstands even earthquakes.

22:20–26—Even *friends* can hurt each other. With true friends, *reconciliation* is almost always possible and enables preservation of the relationship. A real friend stays true in all circumstances.

25 I am not ashamed to shelter a friend,
　　and I will not hide from him.
26 But if harm should come to me
　　because of him,
　　whoever hears of it will beware of
　　him.

A Prayer for Help against Sinning

27 Who will set a guard over my
　　mouth,
　　and an effective seal upon my lips,
　so that I may not fall because of
　　them,
　　and my tongue may not destroy
　　me?

23 O Lord, Father and Master of
　　my life,
　do not abandon me to their
　　designs,
　and do not let me fall because of
　　them!
2 Who will set whips over my
　　thoughts,
　　and the discipline of wisdom over
　　my mind,
　so as not to spare me in my errors,
　and not overlook my*a* sins?
3 Otherwise my mistakes may be
　　multiplied,
　　and my sins may abound,
　and I may fall before my adversaries,
　and my enemy may rejoice
　　over me.*b*
4 O Lord, Father and God of my life,
　do not give me haughty eyes,
5 　and remove evil desire from me.
6 Let neither gluttony nor lust
　　overcome me,
　and do not give me over to
　　shameless passion.

Discipline of the Tongue*c*

7 Listen, my children, to instruction
　　concerning the mouth;

the one who observes it will never
　　be caught.
8 Sinners are overtaken through their
　　lips;
　by them the reviler and the
　　arrogant are tripped up.
9 Do not accustom your mouth to
　　oaths,
　nor habitually utter the name of
　　the Holy One;
10 for as a servant who is constantly
　　under scrutiny
　　will not lack bruises,
　so also the person who always
　　swears and utters the Name
　　will never be cleansed*d* from
　　sin.
11 The one who swears many oaths is
　　full of iniquity,
　　and the scourge will not leave his
　　house.
　If he swears in error, his sin remains
　　on him,
　　and if he disregards it, he sins
　　doubly;
　if he swears a false oath, he will not
　　be justified,
　　for his house will be filled with
　　calamities.

Foul Language

12 There is a manner of speaking
　　comparable to death;*e*
　may it never be found in the
　　inheritance of Jacob!
　Such conduct will be far from the
　　godly,
　　and they will not wallow in sins.
13 Do not accustom your mouth to
　　coarse, foul language,
　　for it involves sinful speech.

a Gk *their*　*b* Other ancient authorities add *From them the hope of your
mercy is remote*　*c* This heading is included in the Gk text.　*d* Syr *be free*
e Other ancient authorities read *clothed about with death*

22:27–23:6—A prayer of petition is in the mode
of a number of psalms (cf. Pss. 39, 141). It has a
purpose: (1) to keep the petitioner from sinning
by loss of control over speech and thoughts, and
(2) not to give enemies opportunity to rejoice
over the sin and bring shame.

23:9–10—Warnings against taking *oaths* and

using God's *name*. The use of the name of God,
presumably the four-letter name YHWH, creates
the potential for blasphemy (see Exod. 20:7; Lev.
24:11–16).

23:11—Swearing *many oaths* opens the possibility that they will not be kept, either intentionally
or unintentionally.

14 Remember your father and mother
    when you sit among the great,
  or you may forget yourself in their
    presence,
  and behave like a fool through bad
    habit;
  then you will wish that you had
    never been born,
  and you will curse the day of your
    birth.
15 Those who are accustomed to using
    abusive language
  will never become disciplined as
    long as they live.

Concerning Sexual Sins

16 Two kinds of individuals multiply
    sins,
  and a third incurs wrath.
  Hot passion that blazes like a fire
  will not be quenched until it burns
    itself out;
  one who commits fornication with
    his near of kin
  will never cease until the fire
    burns him up.
17 To a fornicator all bread is sweet;
  he will never weary until he dies.
18 The one who sins against his
    marriage bed
  says to himself, "Who can
    see me?
  Darkness surrounds me, the walls
    hide me,

and no one sees me. Why should I
    worry?
  The Most High will not remember
    sins."
19 His fear is confined to human eyes
  and he does not realize that the
    eyes of the Lord
  are ten thousand times brighter
    than the sun;
  they look upon every aspect of
    human behavior
  and see into hidden corners.
20 Before the universe was created, it
    was known to him,
  and so it is since its completion.
21 This man will be punished in the
    streets of the city,
  and where he least suspects it, he
    will be seized.
22 So it is with a woman who leaves her
    husband
  and presents him with an heir by
    another man.
23 For first of all, she has disobeyed the
    law of the Most High;
  second, she has committed an
    offense against her husband;
  and third, through her fornication
    she has committed adultery
  and brought forth children by
    another man.
24 She herself will be brought before
    the assembly,

23:14—The injunction to *remember* one's parents provides motivation for proper public behavior; foolish behavior will bring shame.

23:16–27—The text singles out three kinds of sexual sin: incest (v. 16), illicit sex (v. 17), adultery of husband (vv. 18–21) or wife (vv. 22–27). Despite the clear misogyny of the book, the underlying concern is for social and family stability, and sexual sin has the potential to disrupt family relationships perhaps more than any other sin.

23:18–19—Sexual sin takes place in private, and one might be tempted to think that privacy means none will know. God's *eyes*, however, see into the darkest corners of human existence. Whoever thinks God does not know is self-deceived.

23:21—The punishment for the man's adultery is public. The Hebrew Bible stipulates death (Lev. 20:10; Deut. 22:22–24), but the punishment is

not explicit here. Perhaps it is the shame and embarrassment of being found out.

23:22–23—The woman's adultery is revealed by the resultant pregnancy. Her offence is threefold: (1) disobeying God, (2) shaming her husband, and (3) creating social instability through bearing another man's children. Note that v. 22 calls the offspring of the union an *heir*. Inheritance was an important mechanism of family continuity and stability in ancient Jewish society; illicit offspring created confusion as to which children belonged to the husband and who would inherit his property. Although today the mechanisms for preserving social stability might differ from ancient ones, the concern is probably just as real.

23:24—Her *punishment* is public, just like the man's. Although *children* are not singled out for punishment in the Hebrew Bible, they are in

and her punishment will extend to
    her children.
25 Her children will not take root,
    and her branches will not bear
        fruit.
26 She will leave behind an accursed
        memory
    and her disgrace will never be
        blotted out.
27 Those who survive her will
        recognize
    that nothing is better than the fear
        of the Lord,
and nothing sweeter than to heed
    the commandments of the
    Lord.*a*

THE PRAISE OF WISDOM*b*

24 Wisdom praises herself,
and tells of her glory in the
    midst of her people.
2 In the assembly of the Most High
    she opens her mouth,
    and in the presence of his hosts
    she tells of her glory:
3 "I came forth from the mouth of the
    Most High,
    and covered the earth like a mist.
4 I dwelt in the highest heavens,
    and my throne was in a pillar of
        cloud.
5 Alone I compassed the vault of
    heaven

and traversed the depths of the
    abyss.
6 Over waves of the sea, over all the
    earth,
    and over every people and nation I
    have held sway.*c*
7 Among all these I sought a resting
    place;
    in whose territory should I abide?
8 "Then the Creator of all things gave
    me a command,
    and my Creator chose the place for
    my tent.
He said, 'Make your dwelling in
    Jacob,
    and in Israel receive your
    inheritance.'
9 Before the ages, in the beginning, he
    created me,
    and for all the ages I shall not
    cease to be.
10 In the holy tent I ministered before
    him,
    and so I was established in Zion.
11 Thus in the beloved city he gave me
    a resting place,
    and in Jerusalem was my domain.
12 I took root in an honored people,
    in the portion of the Lord, his
    heritage.

---

a Other ancient authorities add as verse 28, *It is a great honor to follow God, and to be received by him is long life.*   *b* This heading is included in the Gk text.   *c* Other ancient authorities read *I have acquired a possession*

Sirach (vv. 24–25). See Wis. 3:16–4:6, which expects that the offspring of such unions will perish (Wis. 3:16). Sirach's view reflects that of Deuteronomy, in which the sins of parents devolve onto their children (see introduction).

23:27—A reprise of the connection between *fear of the Lord* and keeping *the commandments*.

24:1–34—This chapter is one of the most important in Sirach. In vv. 1–22 wisdom is personified as a woman and speaks in the first person. Parts of the chapter reflect Prov. 8:22–31 and Job 28. The text recounts Wisdom's origins and cosmic scope. Sirach brings Wisdom into close relationship, even identity, with the Mosaic Torah. In a world where God could seem remote, the mythic account of Wisdom's descent from God emphasizes the presence of God with people. Even though God dwells remote from human beings, God has sent a representative, so to speak, who

beckons and instructs human beings through the Scriptures and the sages. So studying the Scriptures becomes a primary mechanism for knowing God.

24:1—Though cosmic in scope, Wisdom makes her speech *in the midst of her people*.

24:3–7—Wisdom speaks in language that recalls various passages in the Hebrew Bible: creation (Gen. 1; Prov. 8:22–31); the exodus from Egypt (Exod. 13:21); wisdom in creation (Job 28:20–27).

24:8–12—God dispatches Wisdom to take up residence in Jerusalem, among God's people. She dwells in the temple, the central place of worship. Verse 12 uses an agricultural metaphor to suggest that God plants Wisdom where she can take *root*—among people who are *honored*.

13 "I grew tall like a cedar in
          Lebanon,
    and like a cypress on the heights of
          Hermon.
14 I grew tall like a palm tree in
          En-gedi,^{a}
    and like rosebushes in Jericho;
    like a fair olive tree in the field,
          and like a plane tree beside water ^{b}
          I grew tall.
15 Like cassia and camel's thorn I gave
          forth perfume,
    and like choice myrrh I spread my
          fragrance,
    like galbanum, onycha, and stacte,
          and like the odor of incense in the
          tent.
16 Like a terebinth I spread out my
          branches,
    and my branches are glorious and
          graceful.
17 Like the vine I bud forth delights,
    and my blossoms become glorious
          and abundant fruit. ^{c}

19 "Come to me, you who desire me,
    and eat your fill of my fruits.
20 For the memory of me is sweeter
          than honey,
    and the possession of me sweeter
          than the honeycomb.
21 Those who eat of me will hunger for
          more,
    and those who drink of me will
          thirst for more.
22 Whoever obeys me will not be put to
          shame,
    and those who work with me will
          not sin."

Wisdom and the Law

23 All this is the book of the covenant
          of the Most High God,
    the law that Moses commanded us
          as an inheritance for the
          congregations of Jacob.^{d}
25 It overflows, like the Pishon, with
          wisdom,
    and like the Tigris at the time of
          the first fruits.
26 It runs over, like the Euphrates, with
          understanding,
    and like the Jordan at harvest time.
27 It pours forth instruction like the
          Nile,^{e}
    like the Gihon at the time of
          vintage.
28 The first man did not know wisdom^f
          fully,
    nor will the last one fathom her.
29 For her thoughts are more abundant
          than the sea,
    and her counsel deeper than the
          great abyss.

30 As for me, I was like a canal from a
          river,
    like a water channel into a garden.
31 I said, "I will water my garden
    and drench my flower-beds."
    And lo, my canal became a river,
    and my river a sea.
32 I will again make instruction shine
          forth like the dawn,

^{a} Other ancient authorities read *on the beaches* ^{b} Other ancient authorities omit *beside water* ^{c} Other ancient authorities add as verse 18, *I am the mother of beautiful love, of fear, of knowledge, and of holy hope; being eternal, I am given to all my children, to those who are named by him.* ^{d} Other ancient authorities add as verse 24, "Do not cease to be strong in the Lord, cling to him so that he may strengthen you; the Lord Almighty alone is God, and besides him there is no savior." ^{e} Syr: Gk It makes instruction shine forth like light ^{f} Gk her

---

24:13–22—Wisdom is likened to beneficial plants, and her aroma is as sweet as the substances used for *incense* (v. 15). Her fruit is abundant and luscious; she is sweet as *honey* (v. 20). Wisdom invites her devotee to a feast where she is the meal (v. 21). Obtaining wisdom produces the desire for more.

24:23—One finds wisdom in God's law, the Scriptures. God is revealed through wisdom embodied in the scriptural tradition. For *book of the covenant*, see Exod. 24:7; for *law that Moses commanded*, see Deut. 4:1–8.

24:28—Wisdom will never be exhausted.

24:30–34—The overflowing water metaphor of vv. 25–27 is reprised in these verses to describe Ben Sira's own teaching, thus connecting it, like the Mosaic Torah, with Wisdom. Notice the progression from small to large in *canal-river-sea* (v. 31). Whereas studying the Scriptures constitutes one way of knowing God, the teacher is another. Teachers have engaged in the pursuit of wisdom, and they transmit their knowledge, accumulated through study and experience, to those willing to learn.

and I will make it clear from far
   away.

³³ I will again pour out teaching like
   prophecy,
   and leave it to all future
   generations.

³⁴ Observe that I have not labored for
   myself alone,
   but for all who seek wisdom.*a*

Those Who Are Worthy of Praise

25 I take pleasure in three things,
   and they are beautiful in the
   sight of God and of mortals:*b*
agreement among brothers and
   sisters, friendship among
   neighbors,
   and a wife and a husband who live
   in harmony.

² I hate three kinds of people,
   and I loathe their manner of life:
a pauper who boasts, a rich person
   who lies,
   and an old fool who commits
   adultery.

³ If you gathered nothing in your
   youth,
   how can you find anything in your
   old age?

⁴ How attractive is sound judgment in
   the gray-haired,
   and for the aged to possess good
   counsel!

⁵ How attractive is wisdom in the
   aged,
   and understanding and counsel in
   the venerable!

⁶ Rich experience is the crown of the
   aged,
   and their boast is the fear of the
   Lord.

⁷ I can think of nine whom I would
   call blessed,
   and a tenth my tongue
   proclaims:
a man who can rejoice in his
   children;
   a man who lives to see the
   downfall of his foes.

⁸ Happy the man who lives with a
   sensible wife,
   and the one who does not plow
   with ox and ass together.*c*
Happy is the one who does not sin
   with the tongue,
   and the one who has not served an
   inferior.

⁹ Happy is the one who finds a
   friend,*d*
   and the one who speaks to
   attentive listeners.

¹⁰ How great is the one who finds
   wisdom!
   But none is superior to the one
   who fears the Lord.

¹¹ Fear of the Lord surpasses
   everything;
   to whom can we compare the one
   who has it?*e*

Some Extreme Forms of Evil

¹³ Any wound, but not a wound of the
   heart!
   Any wickedness, but not the
   wickedness of a woman!

¹⁴ Any suffering, but not suffering
   from those who hate!
   And any vengeance, but not the
   vengeance of enemies!

a Gk her   *b* Syr Lat: Gk *In three things I was beautiful and I stood in beauty
before the Lord and mortals.*   *c* Heb Syr: Gk *lacks and the one who does not
plow with ox and ass together*   *d* Lat Syr: Gk *good sense*   *e* Other ancient
authorities add as verse 12, *The fear of the Lord is the beginning of love for
him, and faith is the beginning of clinging to him.*

25:3–6—One prepares for *old age* in *youth*,
especially in acquiring wisdom. The mature
judgment and counsel of the aged is *attractive*
because of the experience that age confers.

25:10–11—*Fear of the Lord surpasses* all other
values.

25:13–26—These verses treat wicked women
generally and wicked wives specifically. Ben
Sira has frequently been called misogynistic, and

verses like these seem to warrant such a description, even in the light of a social world in which
women do not have the same value as men. He
is not terribly specific about what a woman's
wickedness is, but it extends to garrulousness (v.
20), perhaps economic *support* of *her husband*
(v. 22, which at the least brings shame), not making her husband happy (v. 23) and not listening to
her husband (v. 26). See introduction.

15 There is no venom[a] worse than a
    snake's venom,[a]
and no anger worse than a
    woman's[b] wrath.

The Evil of a Wicked Woman

16 I would rather live with a lion and a
    dragon
than live with an evil woman.
17 A woman's wickedness changes her
    appearance,
and darkens her face like that of a
    bear.
18 Her husband sits[c] among the
    neighbors,
and he cannot help sighing[d] bitterly.
19 Any iniquity is small compared to a
    woman's iniquity;
may a sinner's lot befall her!
20 A sandy ascent for the feet of the
    aged—
such is a garrulous wife to a quiet
    husband.
21 Do not be ensnared by a woman's
    beauty,
and do not desire a woman for her
    possessions.[e]
22 There is wrath and impudence and
    great disgrace
when a wife supports her husband.
23 Dejected mind, gloomy face,
    and wounded heart come from an
    evil wife.
Drooping hands and weak knees
    come from the wife who does not
    make her husband happy.
24 From a woman sin had its beginning,
and because of her we all die.
25 Allow no outlet to water,
    and no boldness of speech to an
    evil wife.
26 If she does not go as you direct,
    separate her from yourself.

The Joy of a Good Wife

26 Happy is the husband of a good
    wife;
the number of his days will be
    doubled.
2 A loyal wife brings joy to her
    husband,
and he will complete his years in
    peace.
3 A good wife is a great blessing;
she will be granted among the
    blessings of the man who fears
    the Lord.
4 Whether rich or poor, his heart is
    content,
and at all times his face is cheerful.

The Worst of Evils: A Wicked Wife

5 Of three things my heart is
    frightened,
and of a fourth I am in great fear:[f]
Slander in the city, the gathering of
    a mob,
and false accusation—all these are
    worse than death.
6 But it is heartache and sorrow when
    a wife is jealous of a rival,
and a tongue-lashing makes it
    known to all.
7 A bad wife is a chafing yoke;
taking hold of her is like grasping
    a scorpion.
8 A drunken wife arouses great anger;
she cannot hide her shame.
9 The haughty stare betrays an
    unchaste wife;
her eyelids give her away.
10 Keep strict watch over a headstrong
    daughter,

a Syr: Gk *head* b Other ancient authorities read *an enemy's* c Heb Syr:
Gk *loses heart* d Other ancient authorities read *and listening he sighs*
e Heb Syr: Other Gk authorities read *for her beauty* f Syr: Meaning of Gk
uncertain

25:24—Ben Sira adduces an interpretation of
Gen. 3 that has reached even into the contemporary world, in which Eve is blamed for the
misfortune that befell the first couple and thus all
human beings. Contemporary feminist readings
of Genesis indicate, however, that this interpretation is not the only possible reading or the necessary reading of the text.

26:1–4—In an honor/shame society *a good wife*
brings benefit to her husband (cf. Prov. 31).

26:10–12—The difficulty of raising a *daughter* (cf. 42:9–14; see introduction). The sexual
symbolism of sitting *in front of [a] tent peg* or
opening a *quiver* to an arrow is transparent.

or else, when she finds liberty, she
    will make use of it.
11 Be on guard against her impudent
    eye,
    and do not be surprised if she sins
      against you.
12 As a thirsty traveler opens his
    mouth
    and drinks from any water near
      him,
    so she will sit in front of every tent
      peg
    and open her quiver to the arrow.

The Blessing of a Good Wife

13 A wife's charm delights her husband,
    and her skill puts flesh on his
      bones.
14 A silent wife is a gift from the Lord,
    and nothing is so precious as her
      self-discipline.
15 A modest wife adds charm to charm,
    and no scales can weigh the value
      of her chastity.
16 Like the sun rising in the heights of
    the Lord,
    so is the beauty of a good wife in
      her well-ordered home.
17 Like the shining lamp on the holy
    lampstand,
    so is a beautiful face on a stately
      figure.
18 Like golden pillars on silver bases,
    so are shapely legs and steadfast
      feet.

Other ancient authorities add
verses 19–27:

19 *My child, keep sound the bloom of*
    your youth,
    and do not give your strength to
      strangers.
20 *Seek a fertile field within the whole*
    plain,

and sow it with your own seed,
    trusting in your fine stock.
21 *So your offspring will prosper,*
    and, having confidence in their
      good descent, will grow great.
22 *A prostitute is regarded as spittle,*
    and a married woman as a tower of
      death to her lovers.
23 *A godless wife is given as a portion to*
    a lawless man,
    but a pious wife is given to the man
      who fears the Lord.
24 *A shameless woman constantly acts*
    disgracefully,
    but a modest daughter will even
      be embarrassed before her
      husband.
25 *A headstrong wife is regarded as a*
    dog,
    but one who has a sense of shame
      will fear the Lord.
26 *A wife honoring her husband will*
    seem wise to all,
    but if she dishonors him in her
      pride she will be known to all
      as ungodly.
    Happy is the husband of a good
      wife;
    for the number of his years will be
      doubled.
27 *A loud-voiced and garrulous wife is*
    like a trumpet sounding the
      charge,
    and every person like this lives in
      the anarchy of war.

Three Depressing Things

28 At two things my heart is grieved,
    and because of a third anger comes
      over me:
    a warrior in want through
      poverty,
    intelligent men who are treated
      contemptuously,

26:13–18—Ben Sira's description of a good wife comes primarily from the view of a male-oriented worldview. In that world a wife should be charming, quiet, **modest**, a good housekeeper, and **beautiful** to look at.

26:17 Holy lampstand—The menorah in the temple.

and a man who turns back from
   righteousness to sin—
   the Lord will prepare him for the
      sword!

The Temptations of Commerce

29 A merchant can hardly keep from
      wrongdoing,
   nor is a tradesman innocent of sin.

27 Many have committed sin for
      gain,[a]
   and those who seek to get rich will
      avert their eyes.
2 As a stake is driven firmly into a
      fissure between stones,
   so sin is wedged in between selling
      and buying.
3 If a person is not steadfast in the fear
      of the Lord,
   his house will be quickly
      overthrown.

Tests in Life

4 When a sieve is shaken, the refuse
      appears;
   so do a person's faults when he
      speaks.
5 The kiln tests the potter's vessels;
   so the test of a person is in his
      conversation.
6 Its fruit discloses the cultivation of a
      tree;
   so a person's speech discloses the
      cultivation of his mind.
7 Do not praise anyone before he
      speaks,
   for this is the way people are tested.

Reward and Retribution

8 If you pursue justice, you will
      attain it

and wear it like a glorious robe.
9 Birds roost with their own kind,
   so honesty comes home to those
      who practice it.
10 A lion lies in wait for prey;
   so does sin for evildoers.

Varieties of Speech

11 The conversation of the godly is
      always wise,
   but the fool changes like the moon.
12 Among stupid people limit your
      time,
   but among thoughtful people
      linger on.
13 The talk of fools is offensive,
   and their laughter is wantonly
      sinful.
14 Their cursing and swearing make
      one's hair stand on end,
   and their quarrels make others
      stop their ears.
15 The strife of the proud leads to
      bloodshed,
   and their abuse is grievous to hear.

Betraying Secrets

16 Whoever betrays secrets destroys
      confidence,
   and will never find a congenial
      friend.
17 Love your friend and keep faith with
      him;
   but if you betray his secrets, do not
      follow after him.
18 For as a person destroys his enemy,
   so you have destroyed the
      friendship of your neighbor.
19 And as you allow a bird to escape
      from your hand,

[a] Other ancient authorities read a trifle

26:29—Commercial activity presents many opportunities for dishonesty, and it is very difficult in the pursuit of economic gain to maintain honesty and integrity.

27:1—The drive to be **rich** will often compromise one's values.

27:2—Sin is endemic in the **buying-selling** exchange (cf. 26:29).

27:4–7—Speech reveals the inner parts of a person and acts as a test of character.

27:9—The honest person will receive **honesty** in return.

27:11–15—One should avoid the **talk** of the foolish, **stupid** and **proud** because it causes embarrassment and shame. **Strife** (v. 15) probably refers to arguments that end up in physical violence.

27:16–21—Keeping **secrets** is a test of friendship. The fastest way to lose a friend for good is to betray a confidence.

so you have let your neighbor go,
  and will not catch him again.
20 Do not go after him, for he is too far
    off,
  and has escaped like a gazelle from
    a snare.
21 For a wound may be bandaged,
  and there is reconciliation after
    abuse,
  but whoever has betrayed secrets
    is without hope.

Hypocrisy and Retribution

22 Whoever winks the eye plots
    mischief,
  and those who know him will keep
    their distance.
23 In your presence his mouth is all
    sweetness,
  and he admires your words;
  but later he will twist his speech
    and with your own words he will
    trip you up.
24 I have hated many things, but him
    above all;
  even the Lord hates him.
25 Whoever throws a stone straight up
    throws it on his own head,
  and a treacherous blow opens up
    many wounds.
26 Whoever digs a pit will fall into it,
  and whoever sets a snare will be
    caught in it.
27 If a person does evil, it will roll back
    upon him,
  and he will not know where it
    came from.
28 Mockery and abuse issue from the
    proud,
  but vengeance lies in wait for them
    like a lion.

29 Those who rejoice in the fall of the
    godly will be caught in a snare,
  and pain will consume them
    before their death.

Anger and Vengeance

30 Anger and wrath, these also are
    abominations,
  yet a sinner holds on to them.

28 The vengeful will face the Lord's
    vengeance,
  for he keeps a strict account of[a]
    their sins.
2 Forgive your neighbor the wrong he
    has done,
  and then your sins will be
    pardoned when you pray.
3 Does anyone harbor anger against
    another,
  and expect healing from the Lord?
4 If one has no mercy toward another
    like himself,
  can he then seek pardon for his
    own sins?
5 If a mere mortal harbors wrath,
  who will make an atoning sacrifice
    for his sins?
6 Remember the end of your life, and
    set enmity aside;
  remember corruption and
    death, and be true to the
    commandments.
7 Remember the commandments,
    and do not be angry with your
    neighbor;
  remember the covenant of the
    Most High, and overlook faults.
8 Refrain from strife, and your sins
    will be fewer;

[a] Other ancient authorities read *for he firmly establishes*

27:23—Be careful to whom you speak; your
words may be used later against you.

27:26–27—The person who devises evil may well
be the victim of his or her own designs.

27:28–29—*Those who rejoice* in others' misfortune risk the vengeance of God. Notice the use of
the image of the *lion* waiting for prey. Sin is like
a lion in v. 10; here the lion is God who avenges
the godly.

28:1—God not only keeps track of sins but also

visits **vengeance** on the sinner for them (5:3–8;
11:26; 16:17; 35:24).

28:2–4—Cf. Matt. 6:14–15; Mark 11:25.

28:6—The appeal to be mindful of **death** and
physical **corruption** provides motivation for
performing the **commandments** and removing
hatred from one's life.

28:8–11—*Strife*, quarreling, and hatred produce
sin and anger, even leading to bloodshed.

for the hot-tempered kindle strife,

9 and the sinner disrupts friendships
and sows discord among those
who are at peace.

10 In proportion to the fuel, so will the
fire burn,
and in proportion to the obstinacy,
so will strife increase;[a]
in proportion to a person's strength
will be his anger,
and in proportion to his wealth he
will increase his wrath.

11 A hasty quarrel kindles a fire,
and a hasty dispute sheds blood.

The Evil Tongue

12 If you blow on a spark, it will glow;
if you spit on it, it will be put out;
yet both come out of your mouth.

13 Curse the gossips and the
double-tongued,
for they destroy the peace of many.

14 Slander[b] has shaken many,
and scattered them from nation to
nation;
it has destroyed strong cities,
and overturned the houses of the
great.

15 Slander[b] has driven virtuous women
from their homes,
and deprived them of the fruit of
their toil.

16 Those who pay heed to slander[c] will
not find rest,
nor will they settle down in
peace.

17 The blow of a whip raises a welt,
but a blow of the tongue crushes
the bones.

18 Many have fallen by the edge of the
sword,
but not as many as have fallen
because of the tongue.

19 Happy is the one who is protected
from it,
who has not been exposed to its
anger,
who has not borne its yoke,
and has not been bound with its
fetters.

20 For its yoke is a yoke of iron,
and its fetters are fetters of bronze;

21 its death is an evil death,
and Hades is preferable to it.

22 It has no power over the godly;
they will not be burned in its
flame.

23 Those who forsake the Lord will fall
into its power;
it will burn among them and will
not be put out.
It will be sent out against them like
a lion;
like a leopard it will mangle them.

24a As you fence in your property with
thorns,

25b so make a door and a bolt for your
mouth.

24b As you lock up your silver and gold,

25a so make balances and scales for
your words.

26 Take care not to err with your tongue,[d]
and fall victim to one lying in wait.

On Lending and Borrowing

29 The merciful lend to their
neighbors;
by holding out a helping hand they
keep the commandments.

2 Lend to your neighbor in his time of
need;

---

a Other ancient authorities read *burn*   *b* Gk A third tongue   *c* Gk it
d Gk with it

28:13–16—Gossip and slander destroy people's
lives and create social unrest and instability.
The tongue, if not controlled, can be a powerful
weapon that causes tremendous destruction, for
the speaker as well as for those against whom he
or she speaks.

28:18—The human *tongue* has destroyed more
people than *the sword* has killed.

28:19–21—The use of *yokes* and *fetters* conjures

up images of slavery and captivity. The tongue
has the capacity to enslave the one it masters.
Even *death* is *preferable* to enslavement by one's
tongue.

29:1—The word *merciful* connects lending to a
needy *neighbor* with almsgiving.

29:2—Biblical law requires loans to poor Israelites to be interest-free or otherwise profit-free
(Exod. 22:25; Lev. 25:35–37).

repay your neighbor when a loan
  falls due.
³ Keep your promise and be honest
    with him,
  and on every occasion you will
    find what you need.
⁴ Many regard a loan as a windfall,
  and cause trouble to those who
    help them.
⁵ One kisses another's hands until he
    gets a loan,
  and is deferential in speaking of
    his neighbor's money;
  but at the time for repayment he
    delays,
  and pays back with empty
    promises,
  and finds fault with the time.
⁶ If he can pay, his creditor*a* will
    hardly get back half,
  and will regard that as a windfall.
  If he cannot pay, the borrower*a* has
    robbed the other of his money,
  and he has needlessly made him
    an enemy;
  he will repay him with curses and
    reproaches,
  and instead of glory will repay him
    with dishonor.
⁷ Many refuse to lend, not because of
    meanness,
  but from fear*b* of being defrauded
    needlessly.

⁸ Nevertheless, be patient with
    someone in humble
    circumstances,

and do not keep him waiting for
    your alms.
⁹ Help the poor for the
    commandment's sake,
  and in their need do not send
    them away empty-handed.
¹⁰ Lose your silver for the sake of a
    brother or a friend,
  and do not let it rust under a stone
    and be lost.
¹¹ Lay up your treasure according to
    the commandments of the
    Most High,
  and it will profit you more than
    gold.
¹² Store up almsgiving in your treasury,
  and it will rescue you from every
    disaster;
¹³ better than a stout shield and a
    sturdy spear,
  it will fight for you against the
    enemy.

On Guaranteeing Debts

¹⁴ A good person will be surety for his
    neighbor,
  but the one who has lost all sense
    of shame will fail him.
¹⁵ Do not forget the kindness of your
    guarantor,
  for he has given his life for you.
¹⁶ A sinner wastes the property of his
    guarantor,
¹⁷   and the ungrateful person
    abandons his rescuer.

a Gk he   *b* Other ancient authorities read *many refuse to lend, therefore, because of such meanness; they are afraid*

29:3—Honesty is the best policy, in part because it ultimately gets repaid (cf. 27:9).

29:1–20 On lending and borrowing—Absent a system of banking, lending or providing surety for a loan were individual acts that assisted someone less well off. Potential dangers accompanied these individual acts of kindness (cf. Prov. 6:1–5; 11:15; 17:18; 22:26–27). Lenders often failed to get back what they lent, and those providing surety could easily lose the resources they offered. For this reason, lending can be compared to almsgiving. Particularly apt is the sentiment of Sir. 29:7 that many people **refuse to lend** out of concern about **being defrauded** and not out of stinginess or lack of concern. One solution to

the dilemma is that of v. 20: lend, but not to the point of imperiling oneself. Although the emphasis of this passage is on the dangers to the lender, a great moral responsibility falls on the borrower to repay the loan and not to endanger the welfare of the one who was willing to help.

29:8–9—Cf. 3:30–4:6. Helping the poor fulfills the obligations of the covenant (cf. Lev. 25:35; Deut. 15:7–11).

29:11–12 *Lay up your treasure*—Cf. Matt. 6:19–21. *Almsgiving* not only helps the poor, it may *rescue* the giver. Since one's fortunes can change quickly, the giver could find himself or herself impoverished and dependent on almsgiving.

18 Being surety has ruined many who
    were prosperous,
  and has tossed them about like
    waves of the sea;
  it has driven the influential into
    exile,
  and they have wandered among
    foreign nations.
19 The sinner comes to grief through
    surety;
  his pursuit of gain involves him in
    lawsuits.
20 Assist your neighbor to the best of
    your ability,
  but be careful not to fall yourself.

Home and Hospitality

21 The necessities of life are water,
    bread, and clothing,
  and also a house to assure
    privacy.
22 Better is the life of the poor under
    their own crude roof
  than sumptuous food in the house
    of others.
23 Be content with little or much,
  and you will hear no reproach for
    being a guest.ᵃ
24 It is a miserable life to go from house
    to house;
  as a guest you should not open
    your mouth;
25 you will play the host and provide
    drink without being thanked,
  and besides this you will hear rude
    words like these:
26 "Come here, stranger, prepare the
    table;
  let me eat what you have there."

27 "Be off, stranger, for an honored
    guest is here;
  my brother has come for a visit,
    and I need the guest-room."
28 It is hard for a sensible person to
    bear
  scolding about lodgingᵇ and the
    insults of the moneylender.

Concerning Childrenᶜ

30 He who loves his son will whip
    him often,
  so that he may rejoice at the way
    he turns out.
2 He who disciplines his son will
    profit by him,
  and will boast of him among
    acquaintances.
3 He who teaches his son will make
    his enemies envious,
  and will glory in him among his
    friends.
4 When the father dies he will not
    seem to be dead,
  for he has left behind him one like
    himself,
5 whom in his life he looked upon
    with joy
  and at death, without grief.
6 He has left behind him an avenger
    against his enemies,
  and one to repay the kindness of
    his friends.

7 Whoever spoils his son will bind up
    his wounds,
  and will suffer heartache at every
    cry.

ᵃ Lat: Gk reproach from your family; other ancient authorities lack this line
ᵇ Or scolding from the household   ᶜ This heading is included in the Gk text.

29:21–22—Having basic *necessities* enables the poor person to live without being indebted to others.

29:23–28—These verses demonstrate what happens when one is not *content* with what one has. The result is *a miserable life*. Ironically, one may even be made a table servant who has to wait on others.

30:1—Corporal punishment was the norm in antiquity (cf. 22:6; Prov. 13:24; 23:13–14).

30:4–6—Survival after death in ancient Israelite and Jewish conceptions was the continuation of

one's name in one's progeny (see introduction). A well-disciplined son is the image of the wise father, and his behavior will enhance his father's reputation. Furthermore the son will act in his stead to avenge him or to fulfill his obligations, thereby maintaining his honor.

30:7–13—In antiquity, one of a father's major roles was disciplinarian. The father needed to put strict limits on his son because, as with wives and daughters, the son's behavior brings him shame or honor.

8 An unbroken horse turns out
    stubborn,
    and an unchecked son turns out
      headstrong.
9 Pamper a child, and he will terrorize
    you;
    play with him, and he will grieve
      you.
10 Do not laugh with him, or you will
    have sorrow with him,
    and in the end you will gnash your
      teeth.
11 Give him no freedom in his youth,
    and do not ignore his errors.
12 Bow down his neck in his youth, *a*
    and beat his sides while he is
      young,
  or else he will become stubborn and
      disobey you,
    and you will have sorrow of soul
      from him.*b*
13 Discipline your son and make his
    yoke heavy,*c*
    so that you may not be offended
      by his shamelessness.

14 Better off poor, healthy, and fit
    than rich and afflicted in body.
15 Health and fitness are better than
    any gold,
    and a robust body than countless
      riches.
16 There is no wealth better than health
    of body,
    and no gladness above joy of
      heart.
17 Death is better than a life of misery,
    and eternal sleep*d* than chronic
      sickness.

Concerning Foods*e*

18 Good things poured out upon a
    mouth that is closed

are like offerings of food placed
    upon a grave.
19 Of what use to an idol is a sacrifice?
    For it can neither eat nor smell.
    So is the one punished by the Lord;
20 he sees with his eyes and groans
    as a eunuch groans when
      embracing a girl.*f*

21 Do not give yourself over to sorrow,
    and do not distress yourself
      deliberately.
22 A joyful heart is life itself,
    and rejoicing lengthens one's life
      span.
23 Indulge yourself*g* and take comfort,
    and remove sorrow far from
      you,
  for sorrow has destroyed many,
    and no advantage ever comes
      from it.
24 Jealousy and anger shorten life,
    and anxiety brings on premature
      old age.
25 Those who are cheerful and merry at
    table
    will benefit from their food.

Right Attitude toward Riches

31 Wakefulness over wealth wastes
    away one's flesh,
    and anxiety about it drives away
      sleep.
2 Wakeful anxiety prevents slumber,
    and a severe illness carries off
      sleep.*h*
3 The rich person toils to amass a
    fortune,

a Other ancient authorities lack this line and the preceding line   *b* Other ancient authorities lack this line   *c* Heb: Gk *take pains with him*   *d* Other ancient authorities lack *eternal sleep*   *e* This heading is included in the Gk text; other ancient authorities place the heading before verse 16   *f* Other ancient authorities add *So is the person who does right under compulsion*   *g* Other ancient authorities read *Beguile yourself*   *h* Other ancient authorities read *sleep carries off a severe illness*

30:14–17—Since illness can bring such misery, a *healthy body* is considered better than any kind of material wealth.

30:18–20—*Good things* are life's pleasures. Those who do not enjoy life can be compared with (1) senseless *idols* (reflecting a widespread Jewish criticism of idols in this period), (2) the dead, and (3) *eunuchs*.

30:22–25—One ought to enjoy the good things of life since joy lengthens life while *sorrow*, *jealousy*, and *anger* shorten it.

31:1–2—Preoccupation with wealth can be all-consuming. Such preoccupation even invades one's sleep.

and when he rests he fills himself
with his dainties.

4 The poor person toils to make a
meager living,
and if ever he rests he becomes
needy.

5 One who loves gold will not be
justified;
one who pursues money will be
led astray^a by it.

6 Many have come to ruin because of
gold,
and their destruction has met
them face to face.

7 It is a stumbling block to those who
are avid for it,
and every fool will be taken
captive by it.

8 Blessed is the rich person who is
found blameless,
and who does not go after gold.

9 Who is he, that we may praise
him?
For he has done wonders among
his people.

10 Who has been tested by it and been
found perfect?
Let it be for him a ground for
boasting.
Who has had the power to transgress
and did not transgress,
and to do evil and did not do it?

11 His prosperity will be established,^b
and the assembly will proclaim his
acts of charity.

Table Etiquette

12 Are you seated at the table of the
great?^c
Do not be greedy at it,
and do not say, "How much food
there is here!"

13 Remember that a greedy eye is a bad
thing.
What has been created more
greedy than the eye?
Therefore it sheds tears for any
reason.

14 Do not reach out your hand for
everything you see,
and do not crowd your neighbor^d
at the dish.

15 Judge your neighbor's feelings by
your own,
and in every matter be
thoughtful.

16 Eat what is set before you like a well
brought-up person,^e
and do not chew greedily, or you
will give offense.

17 Be the first to stop, as befits good
manners,
and do not be insatiable, or you
will give offense.

18 If you are seated among many
persons,
do not help yourself^f before
they do.

19 How ample a little is for a well-
disciplined person!
He does not breathe heavily when
in bed.

20 Healthy sleep depends on moderate
eating;
he rises early, and feels fit.
The distress of sleeplessness and of
nausea
and colic are with the glutton.

21 If you are overstuffed with food,
get up to vomit, and you will have
relief.

^a Heb Syr: Gk pursues destruction will be filled   ^b Other ancient authorities
add because of this   ^c Heb Syr: Gk at a great table   ^d Gk him   ^e Heb: Gk like
a human being   ^f Gk reach out your hand

31:5–7—Avarice and pursuit of wealth have more
potential to destroy one than to justify one before
God.

31:8–11—Although one could be *rich* and
blameless, the questions here are rhetorical, and
they imply that few can be both.

31:12–18—The meal is described in the manner of a dinner with subsequent symposium.

The basic advice for such social events is not to
be greedy and to have good manners. Verse 15
sums up the section in a way consistent with the
Golden Rule.

31:13—The eye is the primary organ of perception of the world—people want what they
see—and so the *greedy* eye makes a good metaphor for desire.

22 Listen to me, my child, and do not
disregard me,
and in the end you will appreciate
my words.
In everything you do be moderate,[a]
and no sickness will overtake you.
23 People bless the one who is liberal
with food,
and their testimony to his
generosity is trustworthy.
24 The city complains of the one who is
stingy with food,
and their testimony to his
stinginess is accurate.

Temperance in Drinking Wine

25 Do not try to prove your strength by
wine-drinking,
for wine has destroyed many.
26 As the furnace tests the work of the
smith,[b]
so wine tests hearts when the
insolent quarrel.
27 Wine is very life to human beings
if taken in moderation.
What is life to one who is without
wine?
It has been created to make people
happy.
28 Wine drunk at the proper time and
in moderation
is rejoicing of heart and gladness
of soul.
29 Wine drunk to excess leads to
bitterness of spirit,
to quarrels and stumbling.
30 Drunkenness increases the anger of
a fool to his own hurt,
reducing his strength and adding
wounds.

31 Do not reprove your neighbor at a
banquet of wine,
and do not despise him in his
merrymaking;
speak no word of reproach to him,
and do not distress him by making
demands of him.

Etiquette at a Banquet

32 If they make you master of the
feast, do not exalt yourself;
be among them as one of their
number.
Take care of them first and then sit
down;
2 when you have fulfilled all your
duties, take your place,
so that you may be merry along with
them
and receive a wreath for your
excellent leadership.
3 Speak, you who are older, for it is
your right,
but with accurate knowledge, and
do not interrupt the music.
4 Where there is entertainment, do
not pour out talk;
do not display your cleverness at
the wrong time.
5 A ruby seal in a setting of gold
is a concert of music at a banquet
of wine.
6 A seal of emerald in a rich setting of
gold
is the melody of music with good
wine.
7 Speak, you who are young, if you are
obliged to,

[a] Heb Syr: Gk *industrious* [b] Heb: Gk *tests the hardening of steel by dipping*

31:25–27—Excessive drinking, like pursuit of
riches, has ruined many (cf. v. 6). Sirach probably
refers to the drinking contests that accompanied
the symposium. In moderation, however, *wine*
is equated with *life* itself, a creation of God for
human happiness. This assessment fits into one
of the book's larger themes, that all creation is
purposeful, that what God made is good (Gen.
1). Misuse of the good things in creation has
detrimental results.

31:29–30—The negative consequences of drink-

ing too much wine have not changed much over
the centuries.

32:1–2—The *master of the feast* was responsible
for all the arrangements, and he was obliged
to take care of everyone else first. Only when
people fulfill all their social obligations can real
enjoyment be possible.

32:3–6—Ancient Near Eastern rules of etiquette
recognized elders first, but even those who have
the right to speak needed to do so at the proper
time.

but no more than twice, and only
if asked.

8 Be brief; say much in few words;
be as one who knows and can still
hold his tongue.

9 Among the great do not act as their
equal;
and when another is speaking, do
not babble.

10 Lightning travels ahead of the
thunder,
and approval goes before one who
is modest.

11 Leave in good time and do not be
the last;
go home quickly and do not linger.

12 Amuse yourself there to your heart's
content,
but do not sin through proud
speech.

13 But above all bless your Maker,
who fills you with his good gifts.

The Providence of God

14 The one who seeks God*a* will accept
his discipline,
and those who rise early to seek
him*b* will find favor.

15 The one who seeks the law will be
filled with it,
but the hypocrite will stumble
at it.

16 Those who fear the Lord will form
true judgments,
and they will kindle righteous
deeds like a light.

17 The sinner will shun reproof,
and will find a decision according
to his liking.

18 A sensible person will not overlook a
thoughtful suggestion;
an insolent*c* and proud person will
not be deterred by fear.*d*

19 Do nothing without deliberation,
but when you have acted, do not
regret it.

20 Do not go on a path full of hazards,
and do not stumble at an obstacle
twice.*e*

21 Do not be overconfident on a
smooth*f* road,

22 and give good heed to your paths.*g*

23 Guard*h* yourself in every act,
for this is the keeping of the
commandments.

24 The one who keeps the law preserves
himself,*i*
and the one who trusts the Lord
will not suffer loss.

33 No evil will befall the one who
fears the Lord,
but in trials such a one will be
rescued again and again.

2 The wise will not hate the law,
but the one who is hypocritical
about it is like a boat in a
storm.

3 The sensible person will trust in the
law;
for such a one the law is as
dependable as a divine oracle.

4 Prepare what to say, and then you
will be listened to;

a Heb: Gk *who fears the Lord* *b* Other ancient authorities lack *to seek him*
c Heb: Gk *alien* *d* Meaning of Gk uncertain. Other ancient authorities
add *and after acting, with him, without deliberation* *e* Heb: Gk *stumble
on stony ground* *f* Or *an unexplored* *g* Heb Syr: Gk *and beware of your
children* *h* Heb Syr: Gk *Trust* *i* Heb: Gk *who believes the law heeds the
commandments*

32:7–9—If the young speak out of turn and unnecessarily, they risk causing offense. Part of the
issue is being presumptuous. Speaking out of turn
or not knowing one's place brings shame.

32:10–13—By contrast, modesty requires good
manners and proper etiquette. These behaviors
bring honor and social approval.

32:16–17—The underlying stress is on integrity.
True judgments may not coincide with people's
desires, but fools simply look for what pleases
them.

32:18–33:3—This section encourages *deliberation* (32:19), caution, and self-preservation
as pious acts that fulfill the law. Central are
32:24–33:1, which rely on a Deuteronomistic
view of the world, that the one who is faithful to
God prospers (see introduction). The faithful will
not suffer evil and will be rescued out of their
trials. It was and still is difficult to maintain such
a view in the face of the realities of life, but Ben
Sira manages to try.

draw upon your training, and give
your answer.

5 The heart of a fool is like a cart
wheel,
and his thoughts like a turning
axle.

6 A mocking friend is like a stallion
that neighs no matter who the
rider is.

Differences in Nature
and in Humankind

7 Why is one day more important than
another,
when all the daylight in the year is
from the sun?

8 By the Lord's wisdom they were
distinguished,
and he appointed the different
seasons and festivals.

9 Some days he exalted and hallowed,
and some he made ordinary days.

10 All human beings come from the
ground,
and humankind*a* was created out
of the dust.

11 In the fullness of his knowledge the
Lord distinguished them
and appointed their different ways.

12 Some he blessed and exalted,
and some he made holy and
brought near to himself;
but some he cursed and brought
low,
and turned them out of their place.

13 Like clay in the hand of the potter,
to be molded as he pleases,
so all are in the hand of their Maker,
to be given whatever he decides.

14 Good is the opposite of evil,
and life the opposite of death;

so the sinner is the opposite of the
godly.

15 Look at all the works of the Most
High;
they come in pairs, one the
opposite of the other.

16 Now I was the last to keep vigil;
I was like a gleaner following the
grape-pickers;

17 by the blessing of the Lord I arrived
first,
and like a grape-picker I filled my
wine press.

18 Consider that I have not labored for
myself alone,
but for all who seek instruction.

19 Hear me, you who are great among
the people,
and you leaders of the
congregation, pay heed!

The Advantage of Independence

20 To son or wife, to brother or friend,
do not give power over yourself, as
long as you live;
and do not give your property to
another,
in case you change your mind and
must ask for it.

21 While you are still alive and have
breath in you,
do not let anyone take your place.

22 For it is better that your children
should ask from you
than that you should look to the
hand of your children.

23 Excel in all that you do;
bring no stain upon your honor.

24 At the time when you end the days
of your life,

---

a Heb: Gk *Adam*

33:7–15—These verses set out the doctrine
of syzygies, or ordered pairs of opposites in
creation, from festival days and ordinary days
(vv. 7–9; cf. Gen. 1:14) to righteous people and
sinners (vv. 10–13). These pairs demonstrate the
orderliness and meaningfulness of creation. See
42:24.

33:10—See Gen. 2–3.

33:13—For the image of God as *potter*, see Isa.
29:16; 45:9; 64:8; Jer. 18:1–12; Wis. 15:7–8.

33:16–19—The *grape-pickers* are probably the
great figures of Scripture after whom Ben Sira
comes to "glean."

33:20–24—Control of one's property means independence and an *inheritance* to pass on. Having
an inheritance to hand down assures the material
security of one's children.

in the hour of death, distribute
    your inheritance.

The Treatment of Slaves

25 Fodder and a stick and burdens for a
    donkey;
    bread and discipline and work for
      a slave.
26 Set your slave to work, and you will
    find rest;
    leave his hands idle, and he will
      seek liberty.
27 Yoke and thong will bow the neck,
    and for a wicked slave there are
      racks and tortures.
28 Put him to work, in order that he
    may not be idle,
29   for idleness teaches much evil.
30 Set him to work, as is fitting for him,
    and if he does not obey, make his
      fetters heavy.
Do not be overbearing toward anyone,
    and do nothing unjust.

31 If you have but one slave, treat him
    like yourself,
    because you have bought him with
      blood.
If you have but one slave, treat him
    like a brother,
    for you will need him as you need
      your life.
32 If you ill-treat him, and he leaves
    you and runs away,
33   which way will you go to seek
    him?

Dreams Mean Nothing

34 The senseless have vain and
    false hopes,
  and dreams give wings to fools.
2 As one who catches at a shadow and
    pursues the wind,
    so is anyone who believes in[a]
      dreams.
3 What is seen in dreams is but a
    reflection,
    the likeness of a face looking at
      itself.
4 From an unclean thing what can be
    clean?
    And from something false what
      can be true?
5 Divinations and omens and dreams
    are unreal,
    and like a woman in labor, the
      mind has fantasies.
6 Unless they are sent by intervention
    from the Most High,
    pay no attention to them.
7 For dreams have deceived many,
    and those who put their hope in
      them have perished.
8 Without such deceptions the law will
    be fulfilled,
    and wisdom is complete in the
      mouth of the faithful.

Experience as a Teacher

9 An educated[b] person knows many
    things,

a Syr: Gk *pays heed to*   *b* Other ancient authorities read *A traveled*

33:25–34—This passage provides insight into the disjunction between our contemporary world and that of the ancient Mediterranean. Slave holding was a fact of life in the ancient world. Without sophisticated machines to do the work, ancient Mediterranean societies and economies depended on slave labor to function. So, in contrast to our contemporary values, slavery was not considered a moral evil. For biblical laws governing slaves, see Exod. 21:2–6, 20–21, 26–27; Lev. 25:46; Deut. 15:12–18.

33:27–30—Slaves must be set to work; otherwise they will seek freedom. Sirach enjoins harsh punishment for *wicked slaves*.

33:31–33—Even though slaves may be necessary, good treatment of them is encouraged. The ill-treated slave will run away and be lost for good.

34:1–8—*Dreams* and visions are not real. They are *fantasies* (v. 5) and simply reflect what one wants to see. In a world where dreams were often thought to be vehicles of divine communication, this assessment looks very modern. Dreams are classified in v. 5 with *divination and omens*, which are forbidden in Israel (Deut. 18:9–13). Allowance is made for dreams *sent* by God, probably since many biblical figures receive them; see, for example, Joseph in Gen. 37. Unfortunately the text does not give any indication how one can tell the two types apart. Attention to the law and pursuit of the sages' wisdom makes dreams irrelevant.

34:9–11—One gains valuable life experience and wisdom through travel.

and one with much experience
     knows what he is talking
     about.
10 An inexperienced person knows few
     things,
11   but he that has traveled acquires
          much cleverness.
12 I have seen many things in my
     travels,
     and I understand more than I can
          express.
13 I have often been in danger of death,
     but have escaped because of these
          experiences.

Fear the Lord

14 The spirit of those who fear the Lord
     will live,
15   for their hope is in him who saves
          them.
16 Those who fear the Lord will not be
     timid,
     or play the coward, for he is their
          hope.
17 Happy is the soul that fears the Lord!
18   To whom does he look? And who
          is his support?
19 The eyes of the Lord are on those
     who love him,
     a mighty shield and strong support,
     a shelter from scorching wind and a
          shade from noonday sun,
     a guard against stumbling and a
          help against falling.
20 He lifts up the soul and makes the
     eyes sparkle;
     he gives health and life and
          blessing.

Offering Sacrifices

21 If one sacrifices ill-gotten goods, the
     offering is blemished;^a
22   the gifts^b of the lawless are not
          acceptable.
23 The Most High is not pleased with
     the offerings of the ungodly,
     nor for a multitude of sacrifices
          does he forgive sins.
24 Like one who kills a son before his
     father's eyes
     is the person who offers a sacrifice
          from the property of the poor.
25 The bread of the needy is the life of
     the poor;
     whoever deprives them of it is a
          murderer.
26 To take away a neighbor's living is to
     commit murder;
27   to deprive an employee of wages is
          to shed blood.
28 When one builds and another tears
     down,
     what do they gain but hard work?
29 When one prays and another curses,
     to whose voice will the Lord listen?
30 If one washes after touching a
     corpse, and touches it again,
     what has been gained by washing?
31 So if one fasts for his sins,
     and goes again and does the same
          things,
     who will listen to his prayer?
     And what has he gained by
          humbling himself?

^aOther ancient authorities read *is made in mockery* ^bOther ancient authorities read *mockery*

34:14–20—Fear of the Lord equals love of God. Note again the Deuteronomistic formula where fear of the Lord brings *health and life and blessing* (v. 20; see introduction). The basic message here is that in all circumstances those who love God will receive God's support and protection.

34:21–23—"Blemish" probably alludes to the quality of sacrificial victims, which must be "unblemished" (Lev. 22:21). God will not be bribed by gifts into overlooking a person's transgressions. The passage effectively combines ethical behavior with efficacy of sacrifices (cf. 35:5, 8–9). That is, one cannot simply go through the motions of public piety and expect God to respond. True

piety is found in the godly behavior, in this case care of the poor, that undergirds those public acts of piety.

34:24–27—To take *the property of the poor*, which robs them of their means of survival, is the same as committing murder.

34:30–31—*Touching a corpse* renders one ritually impure and in need of purification (Num. 19:11). Repentance needs to be linked with real change that eliminates the sinful behavior. People who repent superficially and then do the same thing again cannot expect that God will listen to them when they return in repentance.

The Law and Sacrifices

35 The one who keeps the law
makes many offerings;
2   one who heeds the
commandments makes an
offering of well-being.
3 The one who returns a kindness
offers choice flour,
4 and one who gives alms sacrifices
a thank offering.
5 To keep from wickedness is pleasing
to the Lord,
and to forsake unrighteousness is
an atonement.
6 Do not appear before the Lord
empty-handed,
7 for all that you offer is
in fulfillment of the
commandment.
8 The offering of the righteous
enriches the altar,
and its pleasing odor rises before
the Most High.
9 The sacrifice of the righteous is
acceptable,
and it will never be forgotten.
10 Be generous when you worship the
Lord,
and do not stint the first fruits of
your hands.
11 With every gift show a cheerful face,
and dedicate your tithe with
gladness.
12 Give to the Most High as he has
given to you,

and as generously as you can
afford.
13 For the Lord is the one who repays,
and he will repay you sevenfold.

Divine Justice

14 Do not offer him a bribe, for he will
not accept it;
15 and do not rely on a dishonest
sacrifice;
for the Lord is the judge,
and with him there is no partiality.
16 He will not show partiality to the poor;
but he will listen to the prayer of
one who is wronged.
17 He will not ignore the supplication
of the orphan,
or the widow when she pours out
her complaint.
18 Do not the tears of the widow run
down her cheek
19 as she cries out against the one
who causes them to fall?
20 The one whose service is pleasing to
the Lord will be accepted,
and his prayer will reach to the
clouds.
21 The prayer of the humble pierces the
clouds,
and it will not rest until it reaches
its goal;
it will not desist until the Most High
responds
22 and does justice for the righteous,
and executes judgment.

35:1–9—Here Ben Sira works to make both ethical behavior and public ritual meaningful in relation to each other. Proper ethical behavior goes hand in hand with participation in public religious life. Ethical behavior gives communal religious ritual content and meaning, and public ritual activity provides the necessary framework for ethical actions.

35:10–13—Offerings to God should be made generously and cheerfully. Proper consideration of the Lord and the law will ultimately benefit the doer (cf. 11:22; 12:2; 32:24). The cheerfulness of giving to God originates in the realization that all human beings have come from God to begin with. Offering gifts to God is a form of praise.

35:16–21—God does not give blanket partiality to the marginalized but God does hear the cries

of the oppressed—*the widow*, *the orphan*, *the poor*. God judges for them (cf. Deut. 10:17–18), and Israel was obligated to care for them (see Sir. 4:1–10 and notes). *Service* in 35:20 emphasizes the importance of action on behalf of the marginalized. Care for the poor and oppressed would later be central to Jesus' message. One of the main thrusts of such a position is that a society's values and commitment to God are reflected in the extent to which it cares for the poor and oppressed in its midst. Ben Sira's attitude here does, however, contrast somewhat with contemporary liberation theology, which takes as a given that God stands on the side of the poor and oppressed in all circumstances.

35:22—God hears the prayer of the marginalized, and God will execute justice on their behalf.

Indeed, the Lord will not delay,
and like a warrior[a] will not be
patient
until he crushes the loins of the
unmerciful
23   and repays vengeance on the
nations;
until he destroys the multitude of
the insolent,
and breaks the scepters of the
unrighteous;
24   until he repays mortals according to
their deeds,
and the works of all according to
their thoughts;
25   until he judges the case of his people
and makes them rejoice in his
mercy.
26   His mercy is as welcome in time of
distress
as clouds of rain in time of
drought.

A Prayer for God's People

36 Have mercy upon us, O God[b]
of all,
2   and put all the nations in fear of
you.
3   Lift up your hand against foreign
nations
and let them see your might.
4   As you have used us to show your
holiness to them,
so use them to show your glory to
us.
5   Then they will know,[c] as we have
known,
that there is no God but you,
O Lord.

6   Give new signs, and work other
wonders;
7   make your hand and right arm
glorious.
8   Rouse your anger and pour out your
wrath;
9   destroy the adversary and wipe out
the enemy.
10   Hasten the day, and remember the
appointed time,[d]
and let people recount your
mighty deeds.
11   Let survivors be consumed in the
fiery wrath,
and may those who harm your
people meet destruction.
12   Crush the heads of hostile rulers
who say, "There is no one but
ourselves."
13   Gather all the tribes of Jacob,[e]
16   and give them their inheritance, as
at the beginning.
17   Have mercy, O Lord, on the people
called by your name,
on Israel, whom you have named[f]
your firstborn,
18   Have pity on the city of your
sanctuary,[g]
Jerusalem, the place of your
dwelling.[h]
19   Fill Zion with your majesty,[i]
and your temple[j] with your glory.
20   Bear witness to those whom you
created in the beginning,

[a] Heb: Gk *and with them*   [b] Heb: Gk *O Master, the God*   [c] Heb: Gk *And
let them know you*   [d] Other ancient authorities read *remember your oath*
[e] Owing to a dislocation in the Greek Mss of Sirach, the verse numbers
14 and 15 are not used in chapter 36, though no text is missing.   [f] Other
ancient authorities read *you have likened to*   [g] Or *on your holy city*
[h] Heb: Gk *your rest*   [i] Heb Syr: Gk *the celebration of your wondrous deeds*
[j] Heb Syr: Gk Lat *people*

35:22–26—This section, which is a transition to
the prayer in 36:1–22, grounds the deliverance
of the oppressed and marginalized in God's
own character. God is a God who delivers from
oppression and has mercy on the oppressed;
those who worship God should have the same
character.

36:1–22—A prayer for deliverance and release
from foreign oppression. The eschatological character of this prayer makes it unexpected in Sirach,
since such expectation is found only here. Even
though it is grounded in the specific historical

context of Jerusalem in the early second century
BCE, the prayer reflects the desires of people
under the rule of others for freedom and peace.

36:6–7—*Signs* and *wonders* refer to the exodus
(Exod. 7:3).

36:10–16—The use of language of hastening time
combined with the plea to **gather all the tribes
of Jacob** shows a kind of nationalistic ideology
in which God will both defeat the nations and
restore Israel.

36:20–21—Sirach is referring to the Israelite

and fulfill the prophecies spoken
in your name.
21 Reward those who wait for you
and let your prophets be found
trustworthy.
22 Hear, O Lord, the prayer of your
servants, according to your
goodwill toward*a* your people,
and all who are on the earth will
know
that you are the Lord, the God of
the ages.

Concerning Discrimination

23 The stomach will take any food,
yet one food is better than another.
24 As the palate tastes the kinds of
game,
so an intelligent mind detects
false words.
25 A perverse mind will cause grief,
but a person with experience will
pay him back.
26 A woman will accept any man as a
husband,
but one girl is preferable to another.
27 A woman's beauty lights up a man's
face,
and there is nothing he desires
more.
28 If kindness and humility mark her
speech,
her husband is more fortunate
than other men.
29 He who acquires a wife gets his best
possession,*b*
a helper fit for him and a pillar of
support.*c*

30 Where there is no fence, the
property will be plundered;
and where there is no wife, a man
will become a fugitive and a
wanderer.*d*
31 For who will trust a nimble
robber
that skips from city to city?
So who will trust a man that has no
nest,
but lodges wherever night
overtakes him?

False Friends

37 Every friend says, "I too am a
friend";
but some friends are friends only
in name.
2 Is it not a sorrow like that for death
itself
when a dear friend turns into an
enemy?
3 O inclination to evil, why were you
formed
to cover the land with deceit?
4 Some companions rejoice in the
happiness of a friend,
but in time of trouble they are
against him.
5 Some companions help a friend for
their stomachs' sake,
yet in battle they will carry his
shield.
6 Do not forget a friend during the
battle,*e*

a Heb and two Gk witnesses: Lat and most Gk witnesses read *according to
the blessing of Aaron for*   *b* Heb: Gk *enters upon a possession*   *c* Heb: Gk *rest*
d Heb: Gk *wander about and sigh*   *e* Heb: Gk *in your heart*

---

prophets here. The claim that the biblical prophets' oracles had not been fulfilled in their own
time, but that they would come to pass in a later
period, is a very old one.

36:26—Perhaps an allusion to the fact that
women had no choice of a husband, but a man
was supposed to choose a wife carefully.

36:28—A good wife is beyond beauty. Qualities
in a wife such as *kindness and humility* make a
husband fortunate.

36:29—As part of a man's household, a *wife* was
regarded as one of a man's *possessions*. Sirach's
use of *helper*, which comes from Gen. 2:18, is

consistent with the interpretation of the creation
story that sees women as inferior to men. Many
contemporary interpreters reject such an interpretation and argue that the creation story in Gen.
2:4b–3:24 cannot be used to sustain such a view.

37:1—Sometimes it is difficult to know true
friends from false ones (cf. 6:7–13).

37:3 *Inclination to evil*—One of two opposing
impulses created by God within human beings
(cf. 15:11–15 and note).

37:5–6—Sometimes even superficial friends
prove themselves in adversity. Such a friend
should not be forgotten in prosperity.

and do not be unmindful of him
  when you distribute your
  spoils.[a]

Caution in Taking Advice

7 All counselors praise the counsel
    they give,
  but some give counsel in their own
    interest.
8 Be wary of a counselor,
    and learn first what is his interest,
    for he will take thought for himself.
  He may cast the lot against you
9   and tell you, "Your way is good,"
    and then stand aside to see what
      happens to you.
10 Do not consult the one who regards
    you with suspicion;
  hide your intentions from those
    who are jealous of you.
11 Do not consult with a woman about
    her rival
  or with a coward about war,
  with a merchant about business
  or with a buyer about selling,
  with a miser about generosity[b]
  or with the merciless about
    kindness,
  with an idler about any work
  or with a seasonal laborer about
    completing his work,
  with a lazy servant about a big
    task—
  pay no attention to any advice they
    give.
12 But associate with a godly person
    whom you know to be a keeper of
      the commandments,
  who is like-minded with yourself,
  and who will grieve with you if
    you fail.
13 And heed[c] the counsel of your own
    heart,

for no one is more faithful to you
  than it is.
14 For our own mind sometimes keeps
    us better informed
  than seven sentinels sitting high
    on a watchtower.
15 But above all pray to the Most High
    that he may direct your way in
      truth.

True and False Wisdom

16 Discussion is the beginning of every
    work,
  and counsel precedes every
    undertaking.
17 The mind is the root of all conduct;
18   it sprouts four branches,[d]
  good and evil, life and death;
    and it is the tongue that
      continually rules them.
19 Some people may be clever enough
    to teach many,
  and yet be useless to themselves.
20 A skillful speaker may be hated;
  he will be destitute of all food,
21 for the Lord has withheld the gift of
    charm,
  since he is lacking in all wisdom.
22 If a person is wise to his own
    advantage,
  the fruits of his good sense will be
    praiseworthy.[e]
23 A wise person instructs his own
    people,
  and the fruits of his good sense
    will endure.
24 A wise person will have praise
    heaped upon him,
  and all who see him will call him
    happy.

[a] Heb: Gk _him in your wealth_   [b] Heb: Gk _gratitude_   [c] Heb: Gk _establish_
[d] Heb: Gk _As a clue to changes of heart four kinds of destiny appear_   [e] Other
ancient witnesses read _trustworthy_

37:7–11—One needs to learn about anyone offering advice and to avoid counselors who act in their own self-interest. Verse 11 provides a list of topics to avoid with certain people.

37:12–15—While there are many potential sources of advice and many ready to give it, the best places to find it are from (1) **godly** people, (2) one's **own heart** and **mind** (deliberation and

instincts), and (3) God, _the_ most dependable counselor, who is available through prayer.

37:19–26—One's skill and talents must be used properly. Wisdom benefits the wise person who will be praised and honored in the community. (On immortality through the survival of one's name, see introduction.)

25 The days of a person's life are
numbered,
but the days of Israel are without
number.
26 One who is wise among his people
will inherit honor,*a*
and his name will live forever.

Concerning Moderation

27 My child, test yourself while you
live;
see what is bad for you and do not
give in to it.
28 For not everything is good for
everyone,
and no one enjoys everything.
29 Do not be greedy for every delicacy,
and do not eat without restraint;
30 for overeating brings sickness,
and gluttony leads to nausea.
31 Many have died of gluttony,
but the one who guards against it
prolongs his life.

Concerning Physicians and Health

38 Honor physicians for their
services,
for the Lord created them;
2 for their gift of healing comes from
the Most High,
and they are rewarded by the king.
3 The skill of physicians makes them
distinguished,
and in the presence of the great
they are admired.
4 The Lord created medicines out of
the earth,
and the sensible will not despise
them.
5 Was not water made sweet with a
tree
in order that its*b* power might be
known?
6 And he gave skill to human beings

that he*c* might be glorified in his
marvelous works.
7 By them the physician*d* heals and
takes away pain;
8 the pharmacist makes a mixture
from them.
God's*e* works will never be finished;
and from him health*f* spreads over
all the earth.

9 My child, when you are ill, do not
delay,
but pray to the Lord, and he will
heal you.
10 Give up your faults and direct your
hands rightly,
and cleanse your heart from all sin.
11 Offer a sweet-smelling sacrifice, and
a memorial portion of choice
flour,
and pour oil on your offering, as
much as you can afford.*g*
12 Then give the physician his place, for
the Lord created him;
do not let him leave you, for you
need him.
13 There may come a time when
recovery lies in the hands of
physicians,*h*
14 for they too pray to the Lord
that he grant them success in
diagnosis*i*
and in healing, for the sake of
preserving life.
15 He who sins against his Maker,
will be defiant toward the
physician.*j*

On Mourning for the Dead

16 My child, let your tears fall for the
dead,

a Other ancient authorities read *confidence* *b* Or *his* *c* Or *they* *d* Heb:
Gk *he* *e* Gk *His* *f* Or *peace* *g* Heb: Lat lacks *as much as you can afford*;
Meaning of Gk uncertain *h* Gk *in their hands* *i* Heb: Gk *rest* *j* Heb: Gk
may he fall into the hands of the physician

37:27–31—The importance of discrimination and
moderation. Not everything is good; restraint and
temperance help to prolong one's life.

38:1–15—This passage represents an attempt to
bring together the traditional view that sin causes
illness (see especially Job) and the "contemporary" Hellenistic position that illness has physical

causes, which the physician can cure. God has
given physicians their skill and their medicines.
They are part of the *works* of God (vv. 6, 8) and
ultimately their healing art comes from God.

38:16–23—The dead require proper mourning
and burial. *One day, or two* (v. 17) is less than
the traditional seven; cf. 22:12. Loss through

and as one in great pain begin the
lament.
Lay out the body with due ceremony,
and do not neglect the burial.
17 Let your weeping be bitter and your
wailing fervent;
make your mourning worthy of
the departed,
for one day, or two, to avoid
criticism;
then be comforted for your grief.
18 For grief may result in death,
and a sorrowful heart saps one's
strength.
19 When a person is taken away, sorrow
is over;
but the life of the poor weighs
down the heart.
20 Do not give your heart to grief;
drive it away, and remember your
own end.
21 Do not forget, there is no coming
back;
you do the dead*a* no good, and you
injure yourself.
22 Remember his*b* fate, for yours is
like it;
yesterday it was his,*c* and today it
is yours.
23 When the dead is at rest, let his
remembrance rest too,
and be comforted for him when
his spirit has departed.

Trades and Crafts
24 The wisdom of the scribe depends
on the opportunity of leisure;
only the one who has little
business can become wise.
25 How can one become wise who
handles the plow,
and who glories in the shaft of a
goad,

who drives oxen and is occupied
with their work,
and whose talk is about bulls?
26 He sets his heart on plowing
furrows,
and he is careful about fodder for
the heifers.
27 So it is with every artisan and master
artisan
who labors by night as well as by
day;
those who cut the signets of seals,
each is diligent in making a great
variety;
they set their heart on painting a
lifelike image,
and they are careful to finish their
work.
28 So it is with the smith, sitting by the
anvil,
intent on his iron-work;
the breath of the fire melts his flesh,
and he struggles with the heat of
the furnace;
the sound of the hammer deafens his
ears,*d*
and his eyes are on the pattern of
the object.
He sets his heart on finishing his
handiwork,
and he is careful to complete its
decoration.
29 So it is with the potter sitting at his
work
and turning the wheel with his
feet;
he is always deeply concerned over
his products,
and he produces them in quantity.
30 He molds the clay with his arm
and makes it pliable with his feet;

a Gk him   *b* Heb: Gk my   *c* Heb: Gk mine   *d* Cn: Gk renews his ear

---

death is painful, and mourning is the right place
to channel the tears of grief. Yet grief is productive only in its proper place and for the proper
time. Prolonged *grief* causes harm; it can even
cause *death* (v. 18). The advice that one who
mourns excessively does not do the dead any
good and is being potentially self-injurious is
both poignant and realistic.

38:24–30—The acquisition of wisdom depends
on the time to pursue it, which the farmer, *artisan*, *smith*, and *potter* do not have. Each of these
must be so concerned about their labor and its
product that they cannot spend the time necessary to pursue wisdom.

he sets his heart to finish the glazing,
    and he takes care in firing*a* the kiln.

31 All these rely on their hands,
    and all are skillful in their own
        work.
32 Without them no city can be
        inhabited,
    and wherever they live, they will
        not go hungry.*b*
Yet they are not sought out for the
    council of the people,*c*
33   nor do they attain eminence in the
    public assembly.
They do not sit in the judge's seat,
    nor do they understand the
        decisions of the courts;
they cannot expound discipline or
    judgment,
    and they are not found among the
        rulers.*d*
34 But they maintain the fabric of the
    world,
    and their concern is for*e* the
        exercise of their trade.

The Activity of the Scribe

How different the one who devotes
    himself
    to the study of the law of the Most
        High!

39

He seeks out the wisdom of all
    the ancients,
    and is concerned with prophecies;
2 he preserves the sayings of the
        famous
    and penetrates the subtleties of
        parables;

3 he seeks out the hidden meanings of
        proverbs
    and is at home with the obscurities
        of parables.
4 He serves among the great
    and appears before rulers;
he travels in foreign lands
    and learns what is good and evil in
        the human lot.
5 He sets his heart to rise early
    to seek the Lord who made him,
    and to petition the Most High;
he opens his mouth in prayer
    and asks pardon for his sins.

6 If the great Lord is willing,
    he will be filled with the spirit of
        understanding;
he will pour forth words of wisdom
    of his own
    and give thanks to the Lord in
        prayer.
7 The Lord*f* will direct his counsel and
    knowledge,
    as he meditates on his mysteries.
8 He will show the wisdom of what he
    has learned,
    and will glory in the law of the
        Lord's covenant.
9 Many will praise his understanding;
    it will never be blotted out.
His memory will not disappear,
    and his name will live through all
        generations.
10 Nations will speak of his wisdom,

a Cn: Gk *cleaning* *b* Syr: Gk *and people can neither live nor walk there* *c* Most ancient authorities lack this line *d* Cn: Gk *among parables* *e* Syr: Gk *prayer is in* *f* Gk *He himself*

38:31–34a—These working folk make possible the kind of urbane life that the city dweller experiences. They can feed themselves, but they will not be chosen for courts, political positions, etc. Verse 34a literally reads, "But they are the foundation of the world" (NRSV **they maintain the fabric of the world**). In the contemporary world, where everyday persons are not often the cultural and media heroes, it helps to be reminded that without these people, life as we know it and live it would be impossible.

39:1–3—In Sirach wisdom comes from studying the law and devoting oneself to the sayings of the sages. In these verses the wise person is able

to penetrate the obscurities of prophecies and parables. This passage emphasizes the intellectual focus of the wise person.

39:5—The sage, even though he studies, understands that seeking God through **prayer** is a prerequisite to receiving understanding.

39:6–11—The other aspect of getting wisdom is divine revelation. God will fill the sage with **wisdom** and **understanding**, the divine origin of which the sage acknowledges. Because of his wisdom, the sage will receive praise and honor. Subsequent generations will honor his memory/name.

and the congregation will proclaim
his praise.

11 If he lives long, he will leave a name
greater than a thousand,
and if he goes to rest, it is enough[a]
for him.

A Hymn of Praise to God

12 I have more on my mind to express;
I am full like the full moon.

13 Listen to me, my faithful children,
and blossom
like a rose growing by a stream of
water.

14 Send out fragrance like incense,
and put forth blossoms like a lily.
Scatter the fragrance, and sing a
hymn of praise;
bless the Lord for all his works.

15 Ascribe majesty to his name
and give thanks to him with praise,
with songs on your lips, and with
harps;
this is what you shall say in
thanksgiving:

16 "All the works of the Lord are very
good,
and whatever he commands will
be done at the appointed time.

17 No one can say, 'What is this?' or
'Why is that?'—
for at the appointed time all such
questions will be answered.
At his word the waters stood in a
heap,
and the reservoirs of water at the
word of his mouth.

18 When he commands, his every
purpose is fulfilled,

and none can limit his saving
power.

19 The works of all are before him,
and nothing can be hidden from
his eyes.

20 From the beginning to the end of
time he can see everything,
and nothing is too marvelous for
him.

21 No one can say, 'What is this?' or
'Why is that?'—
for everything has been created for
its own purpose.

22 "His blessing covers the dry land like
a river,
and drenches it like a flood.

23 But his wrath drives out the nations,
as when he turned a watered land
into salt.

24 To the faithful his ways are straight,
but full of pitfalls for the wicked.

25 From the beginning good things
were created for the good,
but for sinners good things and
bad.[b]

26 The basic necessities of human life
are water and fire and iron and salt
and wheat flour and milk and honey,
the blood of the grape and oil and
clothing.

27 All these are good for the godly,
but for sinners they turn into evils.

28 "There are winds created for
vengeance,
and in their anger they can
dislodge mountains;[c]

[a] Cn: Meaning of Gk uncertain   [b] Heb Lat: Gk *sinners bad things*
[c] Heb Syr: Gk *can scourge mightily*

39:12–15—The exuberance of being filled with
wisdom can result only in praise of God.

39:16–35—These verses comprise a long hymn of
praise that is enjoined by the author in v. 15. The
hymn is characterized by the ideas that everything God has made is good (cf. Gen. 1) and that
God is in control of all things, which respond to
God's commands.

39:16—*Very good* is an allusion to Gen. 1.
Appointed time (vv. 17, 31, 34) indicates that
nothing happens randomly in creation. It all takes
place according to God's command.

39:20—All of time stands within God's purview.

39:22–27—Even creation works differently for
the righteous and the wicked. Identical elements
in the creation are good for the righteous but
become evil for the wicked. Rather than see
these elements in creation as themselves conveying good or bad, we can see that what results
in good or bad stems from the attitudes that the
righteous and wicked have toward these things
and the use to which they put them.

on the day of reckoning they will
    pour out their strength
  and calm the anger of their Maker.
²⁹ Fire and hail and famine and
    pestilence,
  all these have been created for
    vengeance;
³⁰ the fangs of wild animals and
    scorpions and vipers,
  and the sword that punishes the
    ungodly with destruction.
³¹ They take delight in doing his
    bidding,
  always ready for his service on
    earth;
  and when their time comes they
    never disobey his command."

³² So from the beginning I have been
    convinced of all this
  and have thought it out and left it
    in writing:
³³ All the works of the Lord are good,
  and he will supply every need in
    its time.
³⁴ No one can say, "This is not as good
    as that,"
  for everything proves good in its
    appointed time.
³⁵ So now sing praise with all your
    heart and voice,
  and bless the name of the Lord.

Human Wretchedness

40 Hard work was created for
    everyone,
  and a heavy yoke is laid on the
    children of Adam,
from the day they come forth from
    their mother's womb
  until the day they return toᵃ the
    mother of all the living.ᵇ

² Perplexities and fear of heart are
    theirs,
  and anxious thought of the day of
    their death.
³ From the one who sits on a splendid
    throne
  to the one who grovels in dust and
    ashes,
⁴ from the one who wears purple and
    a crown
  to the one who is clothed in
    burlap,
⁵ there is anger and envy and trouble
    and unrest,
  and fear of death, and fury and
    strife.
And when one rests upon his bed,
  his sleep at night confuses his mind.
⁶ He gets little or no rest;
  he struggles in his sleep as he did
    by day.ᶜ
He is troubled by the visions of his
    mind
  like one who has escaped from the
    battlefield.
⁷ At the moment he reaches safety he
    wakes up,
  astonished that his fears were
    groundless.
⁸ To all creatures, human and animal,
  but to sinners seven times more,
⁹ come death and bloodshed and strife
    and sword,
  calamities and famine and ruin
    and plague.
¹⁰ All these were created for the wicked,
  and on their account the flood
    came.
¹¹ All that is of earth returns to earth,

ᵃ Other Gk and Lat authorities read *are buried in* ᵇ Heb: Gk *of all* ᶜ Arm: Meaning of Gk uncertain

---

39:34—From a limited human perspective no one can really say if something is better or worse than anything else. Everything turns out to be good at its proper time.

40:1—*Hard work* is woven into the fabric of human existence from cradle to grave. It was sanctioned in the beginning (cf. Gen. 3:17–19). *Mother of all the living* is a metaphor for the earth (cf. Gen. 3:19–20).

40:3–5—All people, regardless of status, share the same human condition.

40:8—A reprise of the Deuteronomistic theology, found throughout the book, that claims sinners ultimately do not fare as well as the righteous.

40:11—That which is *above* is the breath that God breathes into every person (cf. Gen. 2:7). The verse is not evidence for a belief in an immortal soul.

and what is from above returns
above.[a]

Injustice Will Not Prosper

12 All bribery and injustice will be
blotted out,
but good faith will last forever.
13 The wealth of the unjust will dry up
like a river,
and crash like a loud clap of
thunder in a storm.
14 As a generous person has cause to
rejoice,
so lawbreakers will utterly fail.
15 The children of the ungodly put out
few branches;
they are unhealthy roots on sheer
rock.
16 The reeds by any water or river bank
are plucked up before any grass;
17 but kindness is like a garden of
blessings,
and almsgiving endures forever.

The Joys of Life

18 Wealth and wages make life sweet,[b]
but better than either is finding a
treasure.
19 Children and the building of a city
establish one's name,
but better than either is the one
who finds wisdom.
Cattle and orchards make one
prosperous;[c]
but a blameless wife is accounted
better than either.
20 Wine and music gladden the heart,
but the love of friends[d] is better
than either.
21 The flute and the harp make sweet
melody,

but a pleasant voice is better than
either.
22 The eye desires grace and beauty,
but the green shoots of grain more
than either.
23 A friend or companion is always
welcome,
but a sensible wife[e] is better than
either.
24 Kindred and helpers are for a time of
trouble,
but almsgiving rescues better than
either.
25 Gold and silver make one stand
firm,
but good counsel is esteemed more
than either.
26 Riches and strength build up
confidence,
but the fear of the Lord is better
than either.
There is no want in the fear of the
Lord,
and with it there is no need to seek
for help.
27 The fear of the Lord is like a garden
of blessing,
and covers a person better than
any glory.

The Disgrace of Begging

28 My child, do not lead the life of a
beggar;
it is better to die than to beg.
29 When one looks to the table of
another,
one's way of life cannot be
considered a life.

[a] Heb Syr: Gk Lat *from the waters returns to the sea* [b] Heb: Gk *Life is
sweet for the self-reliant worker* [c] Heb Syr: Gk lacks *but better . . . prosperous*
[d] Heb: Gk *wisdom* [e] Heb Compare Syr: Gk *wife with her husband*

40:12–17—*Injustice* will eventually fail and *the
unjust* will be dishonored both in this life and in
their children.

40:22–27—This list of the good things in life
recalls other places in the book that encourage
enjoyment of life. Wealth, children, wine, music,
beauty, good friends, and family all make life
good. At the end of the list, however, stands *fear
of the Lord*, which is better than all the above
and provides the context in which to enjoy them.
So, for example, the one who fears the Lord

knows that wealth is good only if it is acquired
justly and used with generosity.

40:28–30—While the poor may have some
resources (cf. 29:21–23), begging constitutes a
kind of social death. Physical death is preferable to the shameful life of begging, because the
beggar has no *self-respect* and is dependent on
others for everything. Yet by not alleviating their
condition, society at large keeps beggars in that
circumstance.

One loses self-respect with another
person's food,
but one who is intelligent and well
instructed guards against that.
30 In the mouth of the shameless
begging is sweet,
but it kindles a fire inside him.

Concerning Death

41 O death, how bitter is the
thought of you
to the one at peace among
possessions,
who has nothing to worry about and
is prosperous in everything,
and still is vigorous enough to
enjoy food!
2 O death, how welcome is your
sentence
to one who is needy and failing in
strength,
worn down by age and anxious
about everything;
to one who is contrary, and has
lost all patience!
3 Do not fear death's decree for you;
remember those who went before
you and those who will come
after.
4 This is the Lord's decree for all
flesh;
why then should you reject the will
of the Most High?
Whether life lasts for ten years or a
hundred or a thousand,
there are no questions asked in
Hades.

The Fate of the Wicked

5 The children of sinners are
abominable children,
and they frequent the haunts of
the ungodly.
6 The inheritance of the children of
sinners will perish,
and on their offspring will be a
perpetual disgrace.
7 Children will blame an ungodly
father,
for they suffer disgrace because of
him.
8 Woe to you, the ungodly,
who have forsaken the law of the
Most High God!
9 If you have children, calamity will be
theirs;
you will beget them only for
groaning.
When you stumble, there is lasting
joy;*a*
and when you die, a curse is your
lot.
10 Whatever comes from earth returns
to earth;
so the ungodly go from curse to
destruction.
11 The human body is a fleeting
thing,
but a virtuous name will never be
blotted out.*b*
12 Have regard for your name, since it
will outlive you

a Heb: Meaning of Gk uncertain   *b* Heb: Gk *People grieve over the death of
the body, but the bad name of sinners will be blotted out*

41:1–2—For the person who has material comforts, the thought of death is a bitter blow, but
to one who is weighed down by poverty, age or
illness death may be seen as a welcome relief.
These verses provide a good illustration of how
Sirach's proverbs often describe life as it is, rather
than offer a vision for how it could be. The challenge for any time is not to be satisfied with a
description of the way things are, but to work for
how things might be.

41:3–4—One need *not fear death*, since it is the
common lot of all people, and it is God's will
for all. *Hades* is the place of the dead (cf. 14:16;
17:27; 21:10, see introduction).

41:5–10—Sinners not only reap what they sow in

this life, but the *disgrace* of the ungodly lives on
after them and affects their children. One's name
outlasts one's life, and children suffer for their
parents' shame. The consequences of sin become
a curse to succeeding generations (cf. Deut.
5:9–10; see introduction). People are sometimes
misled into thinking that their actions have only
a limited and present effect rather than a lasting
one.

41:11–13—Since physical life is short, but a
name lives on, one ought to be zealous to
guard it. This passage is the quintessential statement of the book's theology of immortality (see
introduction).

longer than a thousand hoards of
gold.

¹³ The days of a good life are
numbered,
but a good name lasts forever.

¹⁴ My children, be true to your training
and be at peace;
hidden wisdom and unseen
treasure—
of what value is either?

A Series of Contrasts

¹⁵ Better are those who hide their folly
than those who hide their
wisdom.

¹⁶ Therefore show respect for my
words;
for it is not good to feel shame in
every circumstance,
nor is every kind of abashment to
be approved.ᵃ

¹⁷ Be ashamed of sexual immorality,
before your father or mother;
and of a lie, before a prince or a
ruler;

¹⁸ of a crime, before a judge or
magistrate;
and of a breach of the law, before
the congregation and the
people;
of unjust dealing, before your
partner or your friend;

¹⁹ and of theft, in the place where
you live.
Be ashamed of breaking an oath or
agreement,ᵇ
and of leaning on your elbow at
meals;
of surliness in receiving or giving,

²⁰ and of silence, before those who
greet you;
of looking at a prostitute,

²¹ and of rejecting the appeal of a
relative;
of taking away someone's portion or
gift,
and of gazing at another man's
wife;

²² of meddling with his servant-girl—
and do not approach her bed;
of abusive words, before friends—
and do not be insulting after
making a gift.

42 Be ashamed of repeating what
you hear,
and of betraying secrets.
Then you will show proper shame,
and will find favor with everyone.

Of the following things do not be
ashamed,
and do not sin to save face:

² Do not be ashamed of the law of the
Most High and his covenant,
and of rendering judgment to
acquit the ungodly;

³ of keeping accounts with a partner
or with traveling companions,
and of dividing the inheritance of
friends;

⁴ of accuracy with scales and
weights,
and of acquiring much or little;

⁵ of profit from dealing with
merchants,
and of frequent disciplining of
children,
and of drawing blood from the
back of a wicked slave.

⁶ Where there is an untrustworthy
wife, a seal is a good thing;
and where there are many hands,
lock things up.

ᵃ Heb: Gk *and not everything is confidently esteemed by everyone*   ᵇ Heb: Gk
before the truth of God and the covenant

41:17–42:1a—This list of shameful behaviors
and the one that follows on behavior that is not
shameful highlight the importance of practical
wisdom as a guide to correct action and the
centrality of honor and shame as defining aspects
of identity (see introduction). Note that several
recurring topics in the book appear in this list:
sexuality, speech, manners, and business.

42:1e–8—Sometimes people are *ashamed* of
doing or saying things for which they should not
feel shame. This list contrasts with the one before
it and treats some of the same topics, including
following the law, rendering fair judgment, practicing honest business, controlling one's household, correcting sexual misbehavior.

7 When you make a deposit, be sure it
        is counted and weighed,
    and when you give or receive, put
        it all in writing.
8 Do not be ashamed to correct the
        stupid or foolish
    or the aged who are guilty of
        sexual immorality.
    Then you will show your sound
        training,
    and will be approved by all.

Daughters and Fathers

9 A daughter is a secret anxiety to her
        father,
    and worry over her robs him of
        sleep;
    when she is young, for fear she may
        not marry,
    or if married, for fear she may be
        disliked;
10 while a virgin, for fear she may be
        seduced
    and become pregnant in her
        father's house;
    or having a husband, for fear she
        may go astray,
    or, though married, for fear she
        may be barren.
11 Keep strict watch over a headstrong
        daughter,
    or she may make you a
        laughingstock to your
        enemies,
    a byword in the city and the
        assembly of*a* the people,
    and put you to shame in public
        gatherings.*b*
    See that there is no lattice in her
        room,

no spot that overlooks the
        approaches to the house.*c*
12 Do not let her parade her beauty
        before any man,
    or spend her time among married
        women;*a*
13 for from garments comes the moth,
    and from a woman comes woman's
        wickedness.
14 Better is the wickedness of a man
        than a woman who does good;
    it is woman who brings shame and
        disgrace.

The Works of God in Nature

15 I will now call to mind the works of
        the Lord,
    and will declare what I have seen.
    By the word of the Lord his works
        are made;
    and all his creatures do his will.*d*
16 The sun looks down on everything
        with its light,
    and the work of the Lord is full of
        his glory.
17 The Lord has not empowered even
        his holy ones
    to recount all his marvelous
        works,
    which the Lord the Almighty has
        established
    so that the universe may stand
        firm in his glory.
18 He searches out the abyss and the
        human heart;
    he understands their innermost
        secrets.

a Heb: Meaning of Gk uncertain   *b* Heb: Gk *to shame before the great
multitude*   *c* Heb: Gk lacks *See . . . house*   *d* Syr Compare Heb: most Gk
witnesses lack *and all . . . will*

42:9–14—Many aspects of this section reflect
traditional views about women in the ancient
world and the system of honor and shame that
determined a man's social status (see introduction). Proper marriage and bearing children were
the primary goals for women in Jewish society.
Shame comes in the form of public disgrace, just
as honor is found in public acclamation. The
negative attitude toward women of vv. 13–14
is unique to this book, however, and does not
represent a traditional assessment of women's behavior. Issues in Sirach like the status of women

do bring into relief the question of how contemporary biblical interpretation should regard
ancient social attitudes and practices that are not
shared by the modern world.

42:15—This verse is the beginning of a hymn
that runs through 43:33 praising God and God's
creation. For *word of the Lord*, see Gen. 1.

42:18–20—God's knowledge is all-encompassing. It extends to the deepest parts of the universe
(*the abyss*), to the innermost reaches of the human person (*the heart*), to past and future events.

For the Most High knows all that
　　may be known;
　　he sees from of old the things that
　　　are to come.*a*

19 He discloses what has been and what
　　is to be,
　　and he reveals the traces of hidden
　　things.

20 No thought escapes him,
　　and nothing is hidden from him.

21 He has set in order the splendors of
　　his wisdom;
　　he is from all eternity one and the
　　same.
　　Nothing can be added or taken away,
　　and he needs no one to be his
　　counselor.

22 How desirable are all his works,
　　and how sparkling they are to
　　see!*b*

23 All these things live and remain
　　forever;
　　each creature is preserved to meet
　　a particular need.*c*

24 All things come in pairs, one
　　opposite the other,
　　and he has made nothing
　　incomplete.

25 Each supplements the virtues of the
　　other,
　　Who could ever tire of seeing his
　　glory?

The Splendor of the Sun

43 The pride of the higher realms
　　is the clear vault of the sky,
　　as glorious to behold as the sight
　　of the heavens.

2 The sun, when it appears, proclaims
　　as it rises

what a marvelous instrument it is,
　　the work of the Most High.

3 At noon it parches the land,
　　and who can withstand its burning
　　heat?

4 A man tending*d* a furnace works in
　　burning heat,
　　but three times as hot is the sun
　　scorching the mountains;
　　it breathes out fiery vapors,
　　and its bright rays blind the eyes.

5 Great is the Lord who made it;
　　at his orders it hurries on its
　　course.

The Splendor of the Moon

6 It is the moon that marks the
　　changing seasons,*e*
　　governing the times, their
　　everlasting sign.

7 From the moon comes the sign for
　　festal days,
　　a light that wanes when it
　　completes its course.

8 The new moon, as its name suggests,
　　renews itself;*f*
　　how marvelous it is in this change,
　　a beacon to the hosts on high,
　　shining in the vault of the
　　heavens!

The Glory of the Stars
and the Rainbow

9 The glory of the stars is the beauty of
　　heaven,
　　a glittering array in the heights of
　　the Lord.

a Heb: Gk *he sees the sign(s) of the age* *b* Meaning of Gk uncertain *c* Heb:
Gk *forever for every need, and all are obedient* *d* Other ancient authorities
read *blowing upon* *e* Heb: Meaning of Gk uncertain *f* Heb: Gk *The month
is named after the moon*

42:21—The phrase *set in order* combines with
the second half of the verse to claim that creation
is complete and ordered.

42:23—All of creation is purposeful (cf. 16:26–
30; 39:16–21).

42:24—God's creation is complete and without
defect (33:15). The repeated emphasis in Sirach
on the completeness of God's creation fosters a
view that human beings make up one part of the
larger whole. They do not stand above or outside
of the created order.

43:1–26—The description of various aspects
of creation is offered as evidence of its completeness (see Ps. 104). The passage repeatedly
emphasizes that all things function according to
God's *orders* (Sir. 43:5, 10, 13, 16). God's word
holds everything together (v. 26).

43:1–5—*The sun* is singled out for its heat.

43:6–8—*The moon*, by contrast, is important for
its role in calendar reckoning.

¹⁰ On the orders of the Holy One
        they stand in their appointed
        places;
        they never relax in their watches.
¹¹ Look at the rainbow, and praise him
        who made it;
        it is exceedingly beautiful in its
        brightness.
¹² It encircles the sky with its glorious
        arc;
        the hands of the Most High have
        stretched it out.

The Marvels of Nature

¹³ By his command he sends the
        driving snow
        and speeds the lightnings of his
        judgment.
¹⁴ Therefore the storehouses are opened,
        and the clouds fly out like birds.
¹⁵ In his majesty he gives the clouds
        their strength,
        and the hailstones are broken in
        pieces.
¹⁷ᵃ The voice of his thunder rebukes the
        earth;
¹⁶ when he appears, the mountains
        shake.
    At his will the south wind blows;
¹⁷ᵇ   so do the storm from the north
        and the whirlwind.
    He scatters the snow like birds flying
        down,
        and its descent is like locusts
        alighting.
¹⁸ The eye is dazzled by the beauty of
        its whiteness,
        and the mind is amazed as it falls.
¹⁹ He pours frost over the earth like
        salt,

and icicles form like pointed
        thorns.
²⁰ The cold north wind blows,
        and ice freezes on the water;
    it settles on every pool of water,
        and the water puts it on like a
        breastplate.
²¹ He consumes the mountains and
        burns up the wilderness,
        and withers the tender grass like
        fire.
²² A mist quickly heals all things;
        the falling dew gives refreshment
        from the heat.
²³ By his plan he stilled the deep
        and planted islands in it.
²⁴ Those who sail the sea tell of its
        dangers,
        and we marvel at what we hear.
²⁵ In it are strange and marvelous
        creatures,
        all kinds of living things, and huge
        sea-monsters.
²⁶ Because of him each of his
        messengers succeeds,
        and by his word all things hold
        together.
²⁷ We could say more but could never
        say enough;
        let the final word be: "He is the
        all."
²⁸ Where can we find the strength to
        praise him?
        For he is greater than all his works.
²⁹ Awesome is the Lord and very great,
        and marvelous is his power.
³⁰ Glorify the Lord and exalt him as
        much as you can,
        for he surpasses even that.

43:14—*Storehouses* refers to heavenly places from which come the various weather phenomena.

43:23 *Stilled the deep*—Cf. Ps. 104:6–7; Isa. 51:9–10.

43:26—Sirach may be drawing on the Stoic idea of the *logos* (*word*), the principle that holds the universe together. This notion would seem to be natural for interpreting the creation account in Gen. 1, where God creates by God's word. Later Jewish and Christian authors like Philo of Alexan-

dria and the Gospel of John find this notion very productive.

43:27—*He is the all* should not be understood as pantheism, but in the sense that God made and sustains all things (cf. vv. 28, 33).

43:30—No human praise or exaltation can come close to the reality of God's greatness. God exists outside of the cosmos and is responsible for it. Human beings as part of that cosmos cannot know everything about what God has made, let alone about God's nature.

When you exalt him, summon all
   your strength,
and do not grow weary, for you
   cannot praise him enough.
³¹ Who has seen him and can describe
   him?
   Or who can extol him as he is?
³² Many things greater than these lie
   hidden,
   for I*a* have seen but few of his
   works.
³³ For the Lord has made all things,
   and to the godly he has given
   wisdom.

Hymn in Honor of Our Ancestors*b*

44 Let us now sing the praises of
   famous men,
   our ancestors in their generations.
² The Lord apportioned to them*c* great
   glory,
   his majesty from the beginning.
³ There were those who ruled in their
   kingdoms,
   and made a name for themselves
   by their valor;
   those who gave counsel because they
   were intelligent;
   those who spoke in prophetic
   oracles;
⁴ those who led the people by their
   counsels
   and by their knowledge of the
   people's lore;
   they were wise in their words of
   instruction;
⁵ those who composed musical tunes,
   or put verses in writing;

⁶ rich men endowed with resources,
   living peacefully in their homes—
⁷ all these were honored in their
   generations,
   and were the pride of their times.
⁸ Some of them have left behind a
   name,
   so that others declare their praise.
⁹ But of others there is no memory;
   they have perished as though they
   had never existed;
   they have become as though they
   had never been born,
   they and their children after
   them.
¹⁰ But these also were godly men,
   whose righteous deeds have not
   been forgotten;
¹¹ their wealth will remain with their
   descendants,
   and their inheritance with their
   children's children.*d*
¹² Their descendants stand by the
   covenants;
   their children also, for their sake.
¹³ Their offspring will continue forever,
   and their glory will never be
   blotted out.
¹⁴ Their bodies are buried in peace,
   but their name lives on generation
   after generation.
¹⁵ The assembly declares*e* their
   wisdom,
   and the congregation proclaims
   their praise.

a Heb: Gk *we*   *b* This title is included in the Gk text.   *c* Heb: Gk *created*
d Heb Compare Lat Syr: Meaning of Gk uncertain   *e* Heb: Gk *Peoples
declare*

44:1–50:24—The book essentially concludes
with a long hymn that praises the great figures
of Israelite history. The same God whose word
brought all things into being and holds all things
together has acted in the history of the people
down to the time of the author. The hymn culminates in an extended praise of the high priest
Simon II, who was probably high priest during
the life of the author. From this point on, the
practical wisdom so characteristic of the rest of
the book disappears. The connection between
practical wisdom and the figures that the author
praises may be that they embody the ideals found
elsewhere in the book, a concern for piety, keep-

ing of the law, and the welfare of their people.
These figures have received eternal life in the
persistence and memory of the honorable reputation attached to their names.

44:1–11—People leave many things behind when
they die: achievements, children, a memory.
In a way, these verses exemplify the adage that
one might be dead, but not really gone. All the
people mentioned in vv. 3–6 received honor in
their own times. Some persons and their progeny
have left no lasting memory, however. These
appear to be righteous people whose names did
not last until the author's time, even though their
deeds did.

Enoch

16 Enoch pleased the Lord and was
   taken up,
   an example of repentance to all
   generations.

Noah

17 Noah was found perfect and
   righteous;
   in the time of wrath he kept the
   race alive;*a*
   therefore a remnant was left on the
   earth
   when the flood came.
18 Everlasting covenants were made
   with him
   that all flesh should never again be
   blotted out by a flood.

Abraham

19 Abraham was the great father of a
   multitude of nations,
   and no one has been found like
   him in glory.
20 He kept the law of the Most High,
   and entered into a covenant with
   him;
   he certified the covenant in his flesh,
   and when he was tested he proved
   faithful.
21 Therefore the Lord*b* assured him
   with an oath
   that the nations would be blessed
   through his offspring;
   that he would make him as
   numerous as the dust of the
   earth,
   and exalt his offspring like the
   stars,

and give them an inheritance from
   sea to sea
   and from the Euphrates*c* to the
   ends of the earth.

Isaac and Jacob

22 To Isaac also he gave the same
   assurance
   for the sake of his father Abraham.
   The blessing of all people and the
   covenant
23 he made to rest on the head of
   Jacob;
   he acknowledged him with his
   blessings,
   and gave him his inheritance;
   he divided his portions,
   and distributed them among
   twelve tribes.

Moses

From his descendants the Lord*b*
   brought forth a godly man,
   who found favor in the sight of all

45 1 and was beloved by God and
   people,
   Moses, whose memory is blessed.
2 He made him equal in glory to the
   holy ones,
   and made him great, to the terror
   of his enemies.
3 By his words he performed swift
   miracles;*d*
   the Lord*b* glorified him in the
   presence of kings.
   He gave him commandments for his
   people,

a Heb: Gk *was taken in exchange* *b* Gk *he* *c* Syr: Heb Gk *River* *d* Heb: Gk
caused signs to cease

44:16—This verse and 49:14 form a kind of
inclusio for this hymn. Speculation about Enoch
flourished in Second Temple Judaism.

44:17 *Perfect and righteous*—Cf. Gen. 6:9.

44:19—Cf. Gen. 17:5.

44:20—Abraham fulfilled the law before Moses
received it. He is the first person to be circumcised as a sign of the covenant (cf. Gen.
17:10–14, 23–27; 26:5). *Tested* refers to the story
in Gen. 22.

44:21—See Gen. 15:5; 22:17.

44:22a—See Gen. 26:3–5.

44:22b–23e—See Gen. 28:3–4. The *inheritance*
is the land, which was divided up among Jacob's
twelve sons, the eponymous ancestors of the
twelve tribes.

45:2—*Holy ones* is probably a reference to
angels. Moses' *glory* is perhaps a reference to his
shining face in Exod. 34:29, 34–35.

45:3—*Miracles* recalls the "signs and wonders"
visited on the Egyptians (Exod. 7–11). **Commandments** probably refers to the Decalogue
(Exod. 20:1–17; Deut. 5:6–21).

and revealed to him his glory.
4 For his faithfulness and meekness he
consecrated him,
choosing him out of all humankind.
5 He allowed him to hear his voice,
and led him into the dark cloud,
and gave him the commandments
face to face,
the law of life and knowledge,
so that he might teach Jacob the
covenant,
and Israel his decrees.

Aaron

6 He exalted Aaron, a holy man like
Moses[a]
who was his brother, of the tribe
of Levi.
7 He made an everlasting covenant
with him,
and gave him the priesthood of the
people.
He blessed him with stateliness,
and put a glorious robe on him.
8 He clothed him in perfect splendor,
and strengthened him with the
symbols of authority,
the linen undergarments, the long
robe, and the ephod.
9 And he encircled him with
pomegranates,
with many golden bells all around,
to send forth a sound as he walked,
to make their ringing heard in the
temple
as a reminder to his people;
10 with the sacred vestment, of gold
and violet
and purple, the work of an
embroiderer;
with the oracle of judgment, Urim
and Thummim;
11 with twisted crimson, the work of
an artisan;
with precious stones engraved like
seals,
in a setting of gold, the work of a
jeweler,
to commemorate in engraved letters
each of the tribes of Israel;
12 with a gold crown upon his turban,
inscribed like a seal with
"Holiness,"
a distinction to be prized, the work
of an expert,
a delight to the eyes, richly
adorned.
13 Before him such beautiful things did
not exist.
No outsider ever put them on,
but only his sons
and his descendants in perpetuity.
14 His sacrifices shall be wholly burned
twice every day continually.
15 Moses ordained him,
and anointed him with holy oil;
it was an everlasting covenant for
him
and for his descendants as long as
the heavens endure,
to minister to the Lord[a] and serve as
priest
and bless his people in his name.
16 He chose him out of all the living
to offer sacrifice to the Lord,
incense and a pleasing odor as a
memorial portion,
to make atonement for the[b]
people.
17 In his commandments he gave him
authority and statutes and[c]
judgments,

[a] Gk him   [b] Other ancient authorities read his or your   [c] Heb: Gk authority
in covenants of

45:5—For the *dark cloud*, see Exod. 20:21;
24:18.

45:6–22—The section on Moses' brother, *Aaron*,
is the longest in the praise of the ancestors,
except for that on the high priest Simon II (chap.
50). Aaron is the ancestor of priests. Sirach
draws many of the details from the description
of Aaron's vestments and priestly accoutrements

from Exod. 28–29. The eternal character of the
covenant of *priesthood* with Aaron's progeny is
repeatedly emphasized (Sir. 45:7, 13, 15, 25).

45:15—On the perpetual character of the *covenant* with Aaron, see Exod. 28:43.

45:17—Aaron, and by extension his descendants,
also have the authority to teach (cf. Lev. 10:11;
Deut. 33:10).

to teach Jacob the testimonies,
and to enlighten Israel with his law.
¹⁸ Outsiders conspired against him,
and envied him in the wilderness,
Dathan and Abiram and their
followers
and the company of Korah, in
wrath and anger.
¹⁹ The Lord saw it and was not pleased,
and in the heat of his anger they
were destroyed;
he performed wonders against them
to consume them in flaming fire.
²⁰ He added glory to Aaron
and gave him a heritage;
he allotted to him the best of the first
fruits,
and prepared bread of first fruits
in abundance;
²¹ for they eat the sacrifices of the Lord,
which he gave to him and his
descendants.
²² But in the land of the people he has
no inheritance,
and he has no portion among the
people;
for the Lord*ᵃ* himself is his*ᵇ*
portion and inheritance.

Phinehas

²³ Phinehas son of Eleazar ranks third
in glory
for being zealous in the fear of the
Lord,
and standing firm, when the people
turned away,
in the noble courage of his soul;
and he made atonement for Israel.
²⁴ Therefore a covenant of friendship
was established with him,
that he should be leader of the
sanctuary and of his people,
that he and his descendants should
have

the dignity of the priesthood
forever.
²⁵ Just as a covenant was established
with David
son of Jesse of the tribe of Judah,
that the king's heritage passes only
from son to son,
so the heritage of Aaron is for his
descendants alone.

²⁶ And now bless the Lord
who has crowned you with glory.*ᶜ*
May the Lord*ᵃ* grant you wisdom of
mind
to judge his people with justice,
so that their prosperity may not
vanish,
and that their glory may endure
through all their generations.

Joshua and Caleb

46 Joshua son of Nun was mighty
in war,
and was the successor of Moses in
the prophetic office.
He became, as his name implies,
a great savior of God's*ᵈ* elect,
to take vengeance on the enemies
that rose against them,
so that he might give Israel its
inheritance.
² How glorious he was when he lifted
his hands
and brandished his sword against
the cities!
³ Who before him ever stood so firm?
For he waged the wars of the Lord.
⁴ Was it not through him that the sun
stood still
and one day became as long as
two?
⁵ He called upon the Most High, the
Mighty One,

ᵃ Gk he *ᵇ* Other ancient authorities read *your* *ᶜ* Heb: Gk lacks *And . . .
glory* *ᵈ* Gk *his*

45:18–19—See Num. 16.
45:23–24—See Num. 25.
45:25—In a time when both political and
religious leadership were contested, Ben Sira
emphasizes the eternal and dynastic character of
both priesthood and kingship.

46:1—See Josh. 1:1–2, 5. Moses was considered
a prophet in Jewish tradition. The name *Joshua*
comes from a Hebrew verb meaning "to save."
46:4—Josh. 10:12–14.
46:5—Josh. 10:11.

when enemies pressed him on
    every side,
and the great Lord answered him
    with hailstones of mighty power.
⁶ He overwhelmed that nation in battle,
    and on the slope he destroyed his
        opponents,
    so that the nations might know his
        armament,
    that he was fighting in the sight of
        the Lord;
    for he was a devoted follower of
        the Mighty One.
⁷ And in the days of Moses he proved
    his loyalty,
    he and Caleb son of Jephunneh:
    they opposed the congregation,ᵃ
    restrained the people from sin,
    and stilled their wicked grumbling.
⁸ And these two alone were spared
    out of six hundred thousand
        infantry,
    to lead the peopleᵇ into their
        inheritance,
    the land flowing with milk and
        honey.
⁹ The Lord gave Caleb strength,
    which remained with him in his
        old age,
    so that he went up to the hill country,
    and his children obtained it for an
        inheritance,
¹⁰ so that all the Israelites might see
    how good it is to follow the Lord.

The Judges

¹¹ The judges also, with their respective
    names,
    whose hearts did not fall into
        idolatry
    and who did not turn away from the
        Lord—

may their memory be blessed!
¹² May their bones send forth new life
    from where they lie,
    and may the names of those who
        have been honored
    live again in their children!

¹³ Samuel was beloved by his Lord;
    a prophet of the Lord, he
        established the kingdom
    and anointed rulers over his
        people.
¹⁴ By the law of the Lord he judged the
    congregation,
    and the Lord watched over Jacob.
¹⁵ By his faithfulness he was proved to
    be a prophet,
    and by his words he became
        known as a trustworthy seer.
¹⁶ He called upon the Lord, the Mighty
    One,
    when his enemies pressed him on
        every side,
    and he offered in sacrifice a
        suckling lamb.
¹⁷ Then the Lord thundered from
    heaven,
    and made his voice heard with a
        mighty sound;
¹⁸ he subdued the leaders of the enemyᶜ
    and all the rulers of the Philistines.
¹⁹ Before the time of his eternal sleep,
    Samuelᵈ bore witness before the
        Lord and his anointed:
    "No property, not so much as a pair
        of shoes,
    have I taken from anyone!"
    And no one accused him.
²⁰ Even after he had fallen asleep, he
    prophesied

ᵃ Other ancient authorities read *the enemy*   ᵇ Gk *them*   ᶜ Heb: Gk *leaders of
the people of Tyre*   ᵈ Gk *he*

46:7—Num. 14:5–25.

46:8—See Num. 11:21; 14:38; and Num. 26:65.

46:9—Josh. 14:6–15.

46:12—Perhaps to be understood in light of
the story of the burial place of Elisha in 2 Kgs.
13:20–21.

46:13—*Samuel anointed* both Saul and David
(1 Sam. 10:1; 16:13).

46:15—The test of a true *prophet* is that his
words come true (Deut. 18:19–22).

46:16–18—See 1 Sam. 7:7–11. Note the exact
parallel in Sir. 46:16 to Joshua (v. 5).

46:19—See 1 Sam. 12:1–5.

46:20—See 1 Sam. 28:3–25.

and made known to the king his
  death,
and lifted up his voice from the
  ground
in prophecy, to blot out the
  wickedness of the people.

Nathan

47 After him Nathan rose up
  to prophesy in the days of David.

David

2 As the fat is set apart from the
  offering of well-being,
  so David was set apart from the
  Israelites.
3 He played with lions as though they
  were young goats,
  and with bears as though they
  were lambs of the flock.
4 In his youth did he not kill a giant,
  and take away the people's
  disgrace,
  when he whirled the stone in the
  sling
  and struck down the boasting
  Goliath?
5 For he called on the Lord, the Most
  High,
  and he gave strength to his right
  arm
  to strike down a mighty warrior,
  and to exalt the power[a] of his
  people.
6 So they glorified him for the tens of
  thousands he conquered,
  and praised him for the blessings
  bestowed by the Lord,
  when the glorious diadem was
  given to him.
7 For he wiped out his enemies on
  every side,

and annihilated his adversaries the
  Philistines;
  he crushed their power[a] to our
  own day.
8 In all that he did he gave thanks
  to the Holy One, the Most High,
  proclaiming his glory;
  he sang praise with all his heart,
  and he loved his Maker.
9 He placed singers before the altar,
  to make sweet melody with their
  voices.[b]
10 He gave beauty to the festivals,
  and arranged their times
  throughout the year,[c]
  while they praised God's[d] holy name,
  and the sanctuary resounded from
  early morning.
11 The Lord took away his sins,
  and exalted his power[a] forever;
  he gave him a covenant of kingship
  and a glorious throne in Israel.

Solomon

12 After him a wise son rose up
  who because of him lived in
  security:[e]
13 Solomon reigned in an age of peace,
  because God made all his borders
  tranquil,
  so that he might build a house in his
  name
  and provide a sanctuary to stand
  forever.
14 How wise you were when you were
  young!
  You overflowed like the Nile[f] with
  understanding.
15 Your influence spread throughout
  the earth,

[a] Gk horn [b] Other ancient authorities add *and daily they sing his praises*
[c] Gk *to completion* [d] Gk *his* [e] Heb: Gk *in a broad place* [f] Heb: Gk *a river*

47:1—Nathan prophesies only during David's reign (cf. 2 Sam. 7 and 12).
47:3—See 1 Sam. 17:33–36.
47:4–5—See 1 Sam. 17.
47:6—Cf. 1 Sam. 18:7.
47:8–10—For David as the originator of temple worship and the planner of the temple itself, see 1 Chr. 16–17; 22:2–19; chap. 23.

47:11—A reference to the adulterous episode with Bathsheba (2 Sam. 11–12). On kingship, see especially 2 Sam. 7:12–16.
47:13— According to 1 Kgs. 5:3–5 and 1 Chr. 22:6–10, since David was a man of war he could not build a temple for God.

and you filled it with proverbs
　　having deep meaning.
16 Your fame reached to far-off islands,
　　and you were loved for your
　　　peaceful reign.
17 Your songs, proverbs, and parables,
　　and the answers you gave
　　　astounded the nations.
18 In the name of the Lord God,
　　who is called the God of Israel,
　you gathered gold like tin
　and amassed silver like lead.
19 But you brought in women to lie at
　　your side,
　　and through your body you were
　　　brought into subjection.
20 You stained your honor,
　　and defiled your family line,
　so that you brought wrath upon your
　　　children,
　　and they were grieved*a* at your folly,
21 because the sovereignty was divided
　　and a rebel kingdom arose out of
　　　Ephraim.
22 But the Lord will never give up his
　　mercy,
　　or cause any of his works to perish;
　he will never blot out the
　　　descendants of his chosen one,
　　or destroy the family line of him
　　　who loved him.
　So he gave a remnant to Jacob,
　　and to David a root from his own
　　　family.

Rehoboam and Jeroboam
23 Solomon rested with his ancestors,
　　and left behind him one of his sons,

broad in*b* folly and lacking in sense,
　　Rehoboam, whose policy drove
　　　the people to revolt.
　Then Jeroboam son of Nebat led
　　　Israel into sin
　　and started Ephraim on its sinful
　　　ways.
24 Their sins increased more and
　　　more,
　　until they were exiled from their
　　　land.
25 For they sought out every kind of
　　wickedness,
　　until vengeance came upon them.

Elijah
48 Then Elijah arose, a prophet like
　　fire,
　　and his word burned like a torch.
2 He brought a famine upon them,
　　and by his zeal he made them few
　　　in number.
3 By the word of the Lord he shut up
　　　the heavens,
　　and also three times brought down
　　　fire.
4 How glorious you were, Elijah, in
　　your wondrous deeds!
　　Whose glory is equal to yours?
5 You raised a corpse from death
　　and from Hades, by the word of
　　　the Most High.
6 You sent kings down to destruction,
　　and famous men, from their
　　　sickbeds.
7 You heard rebuke at Sinai

a Other ancient authorities read *I was grieved*　*b* Heb (with a play on the name Rehoboam) Syr: Gk *the people's*

47:17—Several biblical and nonbiblical Wisdom books have been traditionally attributed to Solomon: Proverbs, Song of Solomon, Ecclesiastes, Wisdom of Solomon, *Psalms of Solomon* and *Odes of Solomon.*

47:19—A reference to Solomon's foreign wives (1 Kgs. 11:1–8).

47:20–21—Solomon's kingdom *was divided* into two after his death.

47:22—See 2 Sam. 7:15–16. The *remnant* are the few righteous and faithful who always exist in Israel and because of whom God maintains faithfulness to Israel.

47:23–25—*Rehoboam*, Solomon's son, was responsible for the division of the kingdom (1 Kgs. 12:1–20). *Jeroboam*, who led the secession against Rehoboam, set up altars in Bethel and Dan, which the biblical writers deplore (1 Kgs. 12:25–33).

48:3—See 1 Kgs. 18:38; 2 Kgs. 1:9–12.

48:5—See 1 Kgs. 17:17–24.

48:6—See 1 Kgs. 21:20–22. *Sickbeds*—Cf. 1 Kgs. 21:4.

48:7–8—See 1 Kgs. 19:9b–18.

and judgments of vengeance at
   Horeb.
⁸ You anointed kings to inflict
   retribution,
   and prophets to succeed you.ᵃ
⁹ You were taken up by a whirlwind of
   fire,
   in a chariot with horses of fire.
¹⁰ At the appointed time, it is written,
   you are destinedᵇ
   to calm the wrath of God before it
   breaks out in fury,
   to turn the hearts of parents to their
   children,
   and to restore the tribes of Jacob.
¹¹ Happy are those who saw you
   and were adornedᶜ with your love!
   For we also shall surely live.ᵈ

Elisha

¹² When Elijah was enveloped in the
   whirlwind,
   Elisha was filled with his spirit.
   He performed twice as many signs,
   and marvels with every utterance
   of his mouth.ᵉ
   Never in his lifetime did he tremble
   before any ruler,
   nor could anyone intimidate him
   at all.
¹³ Nothing was too hard for him,
   and when he was dead, his body
   prophesied.
¹⁴ In his life he did wonders,
   and in death his deeds were
   marvelous.

¹⁵ Despite all this the people did not
   repent,
   nor did they forsake their sins,
   until they were carried off as plunder
   from their land,
   and were scattered over all the
   earth.
   The people were left very few in
   number,

but with a ruler from the house of
   David.
¹⁶ Some of them did what was right,
   but others sinned more and
   more.

Hezekiah

¹⁷ Hezekiah fortified his city,
   and brought water into its midst;
   he tunneled the rock with iron
   tools,
   and built cisterns for the water.
¹⁸ In his days Sennacherib invaded the
   country;
   he sent his commanderᶠ and
   departed;
   he shook his fist against Zion,
   and made great boasts in his
   arrogance.
¹⁹ Then their hearts were shaken and
   their hands trembled,
   and they were in anguish, like
   women in labor.
²⁰ But they called upon the Lord who is
   merciful,
   spreading out their hands toward
   him.
   The Holy One quickly heard them
   from heaven,
   and delivered them through
   Isaiah.
²¹ The Lordᵍ struck down the camp of
   the Assyrians,
   and his angel wiped them out.
²² For Hezekiah did what was pleasing
   to the Lord,
   and he kept firmly to the ways of
   his ancestor David,
   as he was commanded by the
   prophet Isaiah,
   who was great and trustworthy in
   his visions.

ᵃ Heb: Gk him ᵇ Heb: Gk are for reproofs ᶜ Other ancient authorities
read and have died ᵈ Text and meaning of Gk uncertain ᵉ Heb: Gk lacks
He performed . . . mouth ᶠ Other ancient authorities add from Lachish
ᵍ Gk He

48:9—See 2 Kgs. 2:11–12.
48:10—Cf. Mal. 4:5–6.
48:12—See 2 Kgs. 2:9–12.
48:13—See 2 Kgs. 13:20–21.

48:17 *Brought water into its midst*—See 2 Kgs.
20:20.
48:18–21—See 2 Kgs. 18:13–19:37.
48:22—See 2 Kgs. 18:3–8.

Isaiah

23 In Isaiah's[a] days the sun went
backward,
and he prolonged the life of the
king.
24 By his dauntless spirit he saw the
future,
and comforted the mourners in
Zion.
25 He revealed what was to occur to the
end of time,
and the hidden things before they
happened.

Josiah and Other Worthies

49 The name[b] of Josiah is like
blended incense
prepared by the skill of the
perfumer;
his memory[c] is as sweet as honey to
every mouth,
and like music at a banquet of
wine.
2 He did what was right by reforming
the people,
and removing the wicked
abominations.
3 He kept his heart fixed on the Lord;
in lawless times he made godliness
prevail.

4 Except for David and Hezekiah and
Josiah,
all of them were great sinners,
for they abandoned the law of the
Most High;
the kings of Judah came to an end.
5 They[d] gave their power to others,
and their glory to a foreign nation,
6 who set fire to the chosen city of the
sanctuary,

and made its streets desolate,
as Jeremiah had foretold.[e]
7 For they had mistreated him,
who even in the womb had been
consecrated a prophet,
to pluck up and ruin and destroy,
and likewise to build and to
plant.
8 It was Ezekiel who saw the vision of
glory,
which God[f] showed him above the
chariot of the cherubim.
9 For God[g] also mentioned Job
who held fast to all the ways of
justice.[h]
10 May the bones of the Twelve
Prophets
send forth new life from where
they lie,
for they comforted the people of
Jacob
and delivered them with confident
hope.

11 How shall we magnify Zerubbabel?
He was like a signet ring on the
right hand,
12 and so was Jeshua son of
Jozadak;
in their days they built the house
and raised a temple[i] holy to the
Lord,
destined for everlasting glory.
13 The memory of Nehemiah also is
lasting;
he raised our fallen walls,
and set up gates and bars,
and rebuilt our ruined houses.

[a] Gk his   [b] Heb: Gk memory   [c] Heb: Gk it   [d] Heb He   [e] Gk by the hand of
Jeremiah   [f] Gk He   [g] Gk he   [h] Heb Compare Syr: Meaning of Gk uncertain
[i] Other ancient authorities read people

48:23—See 2 Kgs. 20:9–11.

48:24—Cf. Isa. 40:1.

49:2 Wicked abominations—See 2 Kgs.
23:4–20.

49:6—A reference to the destruction of Jerusalem
by the Babylonians. Cf. 2 Kgs. 25.

49:7—Jer. 1:5, 10.

49:8—Ezek. 1.

49:9—Ezek. 14:19–20.

49:10—Cf. 46:12. Mention of *the Twelve* shows
that the books of the so-called Minor Prophets
were probably one corpus by Ben Sira's time.

49:11 Zerubbabel—A postexilic governor of
Judea (Ezra 3:2; Zech. 4:6–10). **Signet ring**—Hag.
2:23.

49:12—*Jeshua* was high priest at the time of
Zerubbabel. Ezra 3:2; Hag. 1:1; 2:2; Zech. 3:1.

49:13—Neh. 6:15–7:4.

Retrospect

14 Few have[a] ever been created on
    earth like Enoch,
    for he was taken up from the
    earth.
15 Nor was anyone ever born like
    Joseph;[b]
    even his bones were cared for.
16 Shem and Seth and Enosh were
    honored,[c]
    but above every other created
    living being was Adam.

Simon Son of Onias

50 The leader of his brothers and
    the pride of his people[d]
  was the high priest, Simon son of
    Onias,
  who in his life repaired the house,
    and in his time fortified the
    temple.
2 He laid the foundations for the high
    double walls,
    the high retaining walls for the
    temple enclosure.
3 In his days a water cistern was dug,[e]
    a reservoir like the sea in
    circumference.
4 He considered how to save his
    people from ruin,
    and fortified the city against
    siege.
5 How glorious he was, surrounded by
    the people,
    as he came out of the house of the
    curtain.
6 Like the morning star among the
    clouds,
    like the full moon at the festal
    season;[e]
7 like the sun shining on the temple of
    the Most High,

like the rainbow gleaming in
    splendid clouds;
8 like roses in the days of first fruits,
    like lilies by a spring of water,
    like a green shoot on Lebanon on a
    summer day;
9 like fire and incense in the censer,
    like a vessel of hammered gold
    studded with all kinds of precious
    stones;
10 like an olive tree laden with fruit,
    and like a cypress towering in the
    clouds.
11 When he put on his glorious robe
    and clothed himself in perfect
    splendor,
    when he went up to the holy altar,
    he made the court of the sanctuary
    glorious.
12 When he received the portions from
    the hands of the priests,
    as he stood by the hearth of the
    altar
    with a garland of brothers around
    him,
    he was like a young cedar on
    Lebanon
    surrounded by the trunks of palm
    trees.
13 All the sons of Aaron in their
    splendor
    held the Lord's offering in their
    hands
    before the whole congregation of
    Israel.
14 Finishing the service at the altars,[f]
    and arranging the offering to the
    Most High, the Almighty,

a Heb Syr: Gk No one has   b Heb Syr: Gk adds the leader of his brothers,
the support of the people   c Heb: Gk Shem and Seth were honored by
people   d Heb Syr: Gk lacks this line. Compare 49.15   e Heb: Meaning of
Gk uncertain   f Other ancient authorities read altar

49:14—Cf. 44:16; Gen. 5:24.
49:15—Gen. 50:25–26.
49:16—Gen. 5:3, 6, 32.
50:1—Simon II, high priest between 219 and
196 BCE, repaired the temple in the wake of
battles between Antiochus III and Ptolemy IV
Philopater and his son, Ptolemy V Epiphanes.
The praise of Simon II recalls some of the earlier

praise of Aaron (45:6–22) as well as the praise of
Wisdom (chap. 24).
50:5—House of the curtain is the temple.
50:10—Cf. 24:13–14.
50:11—Cf. 45:8.
50:12—Cf. 24:13–14.
50:13—Sons of Aaron are the priests (cf. 45:15).

15 he held out his hand for the cup
    and poured a drink offering of the
        blood of the grape;
    he poured it out at the foot of the altar,
    a pleasing odor to the Most High,
        the king of all.
16 Then the sons of Aaron shouted;
    they blew their trumpets of
        hammered metal;
    they sounded a mighty fanfare
    as a reminder before the Most High.
17 Then all the people together quickly
    fell to the ground on their faces
    to worship their Lord,
        the Almighty, God Most High.

18 Then the singers praised him with
        their voices
    in sweet and full-toned melody.*a*
19 And the people of the Lord Most
        High offered
    their prayers before the Merciful
        One,
    until the order of worship of the
        Lord was ended,
    and they completed his ritual.
20 Then Simon*b* came down and raised
        his hands
    over the whole congregation of
        Israelites,
    to pronounce the blessing of the
        Lord with his lips,
    and to glory in his name;
21 and they bowed down in worship a
        second time,
    to receive the blessing from the
        Most High.

A Benediction

22 And now bless the God of all,
    who everywhere works great
        wonders,

who fosters our growth from birth,
    and deals with us according to his
        mercy.
23 May he give us*c* gladness of heart,
    and may there be peace in our*d*
        days
    in Israel, as in the days of old.
24 May he entrust to us his mercy,
    and may he deliver us in our*e* days!

Epilogue

25 Two nations my soul detests,
    and the third is not even a people:
26 Those who live in Seir,*f* and the
        Philistines,
    and the foolish people that live in
        Shechem.

27 Instruction in understanding and
        knowledge
    I have written in this book,
    Jesus son of Eleazar son of Sirach*g* of
        Jerusalem,
    whose mind poured forth
        wisdom.
28 Happy are those who concern
        themselves with these things,
    and those who lay them to heart
        will become wise.
29 For if they put them into practice,
        they will be equal to anything,
    for the fear*h* of the Lord is their
        path.

PRAYER OF JESUS SON OF SIRACH*i*

51

I give you thanks, O Lord and
    King,
    and praise you, O God my Savior.
    I give thanks to your name,

a Other ancient authorities read *in sweet melody throughout the house*
b Gk *he*   *c* Other ancient authorities read *you*   *d* Other ancient authorities
read *your*   *e* Other ancient authorities read *his*   *f* Heb Compare Lat: Gk *on
the mountain of Samaria*   *g* Heb: Meaning of Gk uncertain   *h* Heb: Other
ancient authorities read *light*   *i* This title is included in the Gk text.

50:15—A libation of wine; cf. Num. 28:7–8.
50:16—Cf. Num. 10:1–10.
50:20—Likely the priestly *blessing* of Num.
6:24–27.
50:25–26—The Idumeans (*Seir*), Samaritans
(*Shechem*), and *Philistines* are ancient enemies
of Judah.
50:29—The purpose of learning the wisdom

in this book is to put it *into practice*. Wisdom
cannot be effective if people do not act on it. Acquiring wisdom requires active pursuit and hard
work; benefiting from acquired wisdom necessitates putting it into action.
51:1–12—A psalm of thanksgiving for deliverance from enemies reminiscent of biblical psalms
(cf., e.g., Pss. 17, 31, 35, 59).

² for you have been my protector
   and helper
and have delivered me from
   destruction
and from the trap laid by a
   slanderous tongue,
from lips that fabricate lies.
In the face of my adversaries
   you have been my helper ³and
   delivered me,
in the greatness of your mercy and
   of your name,
from grinding teeth about to
   devour me,
from the hand of those seeking my
   life,
from the many troubles I endured,
⁴ from choking fire on every side,
   and from the midst of fire that I
   had not kindled,
⁵ from the deep belly of Hades,
   from an unclean tongue and lying
   words—
⁶ the slander of an unrighteous
   tongue to the king.
My soul drew near to death,
   and my life was on the brink of
   Hades below.
⁷ They surrounded me on every side,
   and there was no one to help me;
I looked for human assistance,
   and there was none.
⁸ Then I remembered your mercy,
   O Lord,
and your kindness*ᵃ* from of old,
for you rescue those who wait for you
   and save them from the hand of
   their enemies.
⁹ And I sent up my prayer from the
   earth,
   and begged for rescue from death.
¹⁰ I cried out, "Lord, you are my
   Father;*ᵇ*
   do not forsake me in the days of
   trouble,
   when there is no help against the
   proud.
¹¹ I will praise your name continually,
   and will sing hymns of
   thanksgiving."

My prayer was heard,
¹² for you saved me from destruction
   and rescued me in time of
   trouble.
For this reason I thank you and
   praise you,
   and I bless the name of the Lord.

Heb adds:

*Give thanks to the LORD, for he is
   good,
   for his steadfast love endures
   forever;*

*Give thanks to the God of praises,
   for his steadfast love endures
   forever;*

*Give thanks to the guardian of Israel,
   for his steadfast love endures
   forever;*

*Give thanks to him who formed all
   things,
   for his steadfast love endures
   forever;*

*Give thanks to the redeemer of Israel,
   for his steadfast love endures
   forever;*

*Give thanks to him who gathers the
   dispersed of Israel,
   for his steadfast love endures
   forever;*

*Give thanks to him who rebuilt his
   city and his sanctuary,
   for his steadfast love endures
   forever;*

*Give thanks to him who makes a
   horn to sprout for the house of
   David,
   for his steadfast love endures
   forever;*

*Give thanks to him who has chosen
   the sons of Zadok to be priests,
   for his steadfast love endures
   forever;*

ᵃ Other ancient authorities read *work*   *ᵇ* Heb: Gk *the Father of my lord*

Give thanks to the shield of Abraham,
for his steadfast love endures
forever;

Give thanks to the rock of Isaac,
for his steadfast love endures
forever;

Give thanks to the mighty one of
Jacob,
for his steadfast love endures
forever;

Give thanks to him who has chosen
Zion,
for his steadfast love endures
forever;

Give thanks to the King of the kings of
kings,
for his steadfast love endures
forever;

He has raised up a horn for his
people,
praise for all his loyal ones.

For the children of Israel, the people
close to him.
Praise the LORD!

Autobiographical Poem on Wisdom

13 While I was still young, before I
went on my travels,
I sought wisdom openly in my
prayer.

14 Before the temple I asked for her,
and I will search for her until the
end.

15 From the first blossom to the
ripening grape
my heart delighted in her;
my foot walked on the straight path;
from my youth I followed her
steps.

16 I inclined my ear a little and received
her,
and I found for myself much
instruction.

17 I made progress in her;
to him who gives wisdom I will
give glory.

18 For I resolved to live according to
wisdom,*a*
and I was zealous for the good,
and I shall never be disappointed.

19 My soul grappled with wisdom,*a*
and in my conduct I was strict;*b*

I spread out my hands to the
heavens,
and lamented my ignorance of
her.

20 I directed my soul to her,
and in purity I found her.

With her I gained understanding
from the first;
therefore I will never be forsaken.

21 My heart was stirred to seek her;
therefore I have gained a prize
possession.

22 The Lord gave me my tongue as a
reward,
and I will praise him with it.

23 Draw near to me, you who are
uneducated,
and lodge in the house of
instruction.

24 Why do you say you are lacking in
these things,*c*
and why do you endure such great
thirst?

25 I opened my mouth and said,
Acquire wisdom*d* for yourselves
without money.

a Gk *her*   *b* Meaning of Gk uncertain   *c* Cn Compare Heb Syr: Meaning of Gk uncertain   *d* Heb: Gk lacks *wisdom*

51:13–30—An acrostic poem on Ben Sira's search for Wisdom that has erotic overtones. Some of the language (vv. 15 and 26, for example) is reminiscent of earlier passages in the book about pursuing Wisdom. This passage functions as an example of how the single-minded search for wisdom pays off. As a result of his endeavor, he became filled with wisdom and was able to pass on that wisdom.

51:19—To **spread out hands** is to assume a posture of prayer, which was said standing up.

51:23—**House of instruction** likely indicates a formal pedagogical setting for Ben Sira's teaching.

26 Put your neck under her*a* yoke,
　　and let your souls receive instruction;
　　it is to be found close by.

27 See with your own eyes that I have
　　　labored but little
　　and found for myself much
　　　serenity.

28 Hear but a little of my instruction,
　　and through me you will acquire
　　　silver and gold.*b*

29 May your soul rejoice in God's*c*
　　　mercy,
　　and may you never be ashamed to
　　　praise him.

30 Do your work in good time,
　　and in his own time God*d* will give
　　　you your reward.

a Heb: other ancient authorities read the *b* Syr Compare Heb: Gk
*Get instruction with a large sum of silver, and you will gain by it much
gold.* *c* Gk his *d* Gk he

51:26—*Under her yoke* evokes servitude to
Wisdom (cf. 6:23–31).

51:28—Learning wisdom brings economic
reward.

The Book of
BARUCH

The unthinkable happened to ancient Israel when Nebuchadnezzar, the king of Babylon, captured the city of Jerusalem, destroyed the temple, and carried off not only the royal family, but priests, prophets, and its other leaders and first families. What did those events mean for the faith and worship of the exiles and for Israelites who remained in Palestine? Had God abandoned them? What could they do to gain restoration? Such are the questions addressed in the book of Baruch. It consists of two halves roughly equal in length—the first (1:1–3:8) in prose, the second (3:9–5:9) in poetry. Each half also consists of two parts. The prose first half contains an introduction and narrative about the writing and subsequent reading of the book in Jerusalem (1:1–14) and a prayer of confession the community in Jerusalem is to offer (1:15–3:8). The poetic second half contains a salute to wisdom (3:9–4:4) and a series of admonitions (4:5–5:9).

The opening verses claim that the book was written by "Baruch, the son of Neraiah, the secretary of Jeremiah the prophet" (cf. Jer. 36:4) five years after the destruction of Jerusalem. That claim probably accounts for its placement in the Septuagint between Jeremiah and Lamentations, sometimes with the Letter of Jeremiah attached as a sixth chapter. (It was not included in the oldest copies of the Vulgate, but long has been part of the Roman Catholic canon.) The claim probably is incorrect, since Jeremiah 43:6–7 says Baruch accompanied Jeremiah to Egypt. It is probable that the book is a compilation of the work of several authors, one of whom penned Bar. 1:1–14 in the name of Baruch. The date of the book is uncertain, but it knows and uses the wisdom poem from Job 28 and the equation of Torah and wisdom known elsewhere first in Sirach 24:23. This last mentioned text points to a date for Baruch no earlier than 200 BCE, and a date as late as 100 CE is possible.

The ascription of the book to the scribe Baruch in Babylon does, however, suggest a plausible place and community for its origin. It is obviously an edited compilation of shorter pieces, and scribes were the people who performed those services. Furthermore, the book takes the point of view of someone outside of Palestine—in Babylon, to be specific. It makes the bold claim that Baruch was there and that he, not Sheshbazzar (see Ezra 1:8), returned the silver vessels taken by Nebuchadnezzar from the temple to their rightful place. Who else besides a group of pious scribes living in Babylon would nurse the tradition that Baruch went there and returned the temple vessels to their rightful place?

The book often quotes or alludes to Old Testament texts. In doing so from the perspective of Jeremiah's secretary, a respected scribe, it attempts to direct relevant portions of Scripture to life in the Diaspora (and Jerusalem too). It calls its readers to the service of God by advocating typical Hebrew piety (e.g., prayer, fasting, giving to support the temple). It blames the people rather than God for their problems, and equates wisdom with the Torah. It motivates service to God with its promise that the

righteous will prevail, while their persecutors will become wretched. It also calls the people to the service of Nebuchadnezzar as a duty commanded by God. Of course, these themes are also important for discipleship today. It remains important to serve God through Bible study, prayer, sacrificial giving, participating in the spiritual and material well-being of other people, and Christian citizenship.

—Paul L. Redditt

Baruch and the Jews in Babylon

1 These are the words of the book that Baruch son of Neriah son of Mahseiah son of Zedekiah son of Hasadiah son of Hilkiah wrote in Babylon, ²in the fifth year, on the seventh day of the month, at the time when the Chaldeans took Jerusalem and burned it with fire.

3 Baruch read the words of this book to Jeconiah son of Jehoiakim, king of Judah, and to all the people who came to hear the book, ⁴and to the nobles and the princes, and to the elders, and to all the people, small and great, all who lived in Babylon by the river Sud.

5 Then they wept, and fasted, and prayed before the Lord; ⁶they collected as much money as each could give, ⁷and sent it to Jerusalem to the high priest[a] Jehoiakim son of Hilkiah son of Shallum, and to the priests, and to all the people who were present with him in Jerusalem. ⁸At the same time, on the tenth day of Sivan, Baruch[b] took the vessels of the house of the Lord, which had been carried away from the temple, to return them to the land of Judah—the silver vessels that Zedekiah son of Josiah, king of Judah, had made, ⁹after King Nebuchadnezzar of Babylon had carried away from Jerusalem Jeconiah

[a] Gk the priest   [b] Gk he

1:1–14 Part One: Historical Background

1:1 *Baruch*—Jeremiah's secretary (Jer. 32:12).

1:2 *Fifth year . . . seventh day*—Possibly the fifth anniversary of the destruction of Jerusalem (see Jer. 51:12). *Chaldeans*—Babylonians. *Took Jerusalem*—In response to Judean revolts, the Babylonians under Nebuchadnezzar besieged Jerusalem at least twice, taking up to 10,000 people into exile in 597 BCE (2 Kgs. 24:14) and another 832 in 586 (Jer. 52:29), at which time he also robbed the city and burned it. The fall of Jerusalem to a pagan power must have created confusion and anger on the part of its citizens. Baruch exonerates God of all blame (Bar. 1:15; 2:6) and argues that the people themselves were at fault. This argument has implications for today. Christians have often participated in unfair structures of society, in acts of personal greed, and in individual behaviors that bring moral and even political chaos upon them.

1:3 *Jeconiah*—Called Jehoiachin in 2 Kgs. 24:6. He was taken to Babylon in 597.

1:4 *All the people, small and great*—The Babylonians exiled the king, his family, *nobles, princes, elders*, and others of means or skills valuable to the Babylonians. All of them, however, lived under the obligation to hear and practice the word of God, even in Babylon. The recognition of this obligation presupposes the theological break-

through that God's domain was not limited to the land of Israel but was worldwide. Discipleship knows no borders or boundaries. People living or only doing business abroad can serve God by caring for people they encounter and treating them fairly and justly. *River Sud*—Site unknown.

1:5 *Wept, and fasted, and prayed*—Typical acts for persons in mourning, here over the destruction of Jerusalem and over their part in its fall. Contrition and repentance are keys to discipleship. Without them, worship could become empty ritual.

1:6 *Collected . . . money*—Cf. Ezra 1:4. The verse emphasizes the sacrificial nature of the contributions. Their contrition led to an effort to help rebuild the temple. Unmotivated giving usually falls short in effort, and benefits the giver little as well.

1:8 *Vessels*—In addition to money raised from the exiles, they also returned the vessels of the temple taken by Nebuchadnezzar in 586. Ezra 1:7 says the Persian king Cyrus the Great gave the vessels to the Judeans, and Bar. 1:8 may assume that too, but makes Baruch the hero. These vessels, like the future temple to which they were returned, represent continuity with the past. While people need not be slaves to them, their traditions will help nurture people through challenging times.

and the princes and the prisoners and the nobles and the people of the land, and brought them to Babylon.

A Letter to Jerusalem

10 They said: Here we send you money; so buy with the money burnt offerings and sin offerings and incense, and prepare a grain offering, and offer them on the altar of the Lord our God; 11 and pray for the life of King Nebuchadnezzar of Babylon, and for the life of his son Belshazzar, so that their days on earth may be like the days of heaven. 12 The Lord will give us strength, and light to our eyes; we shall live under the protection*a* of King Nebuchadnez-

zar of Babylon, and under the protection of his son Belshazzar, and we shall serve them many days and find favor in their sight. 13 Pray also for us to the Lord our God, for we have sinned against the Lord our God, and to this day the anger of the Lord and his wrath have not turned away from us. 14 And you shall read aloud this scroll that we are sending you, to make your confession in the house of the Lord on the days of the festivals and at appointed seasons.

Confession of Sins

15 And you shall say: The Lord our God is in the right, but there is open

a Gk in the shadow

1:10—The money also was to pay for sacrifices. *Burnt offerings* were the primary means of expressing contrition for deliberate sins and of seeking atonement with God (see Lev. 1:1–17). *Sin offerings* atoned for inadvertent sins (see Lev. 4:1–5:13). *Incense* offerings were a mixture of spices burned in connection with sacrifices or alone on an incense altar in front of the Holy of Holies. *Grain offerings* were offered along with animal sacrifices (see Lev. 2:1–3). The exiles used a variety of sacrifices to express their contrition for the full range of sin they had confessed. Demonstrating one's contrition aids in moving beyond moral failures.

1:11 *Pray for . . . Nebuchadnezzar*—The exiles want Jews in Jerusalem to offer prayers of intercession for the conqueror Nebuchadnezzar and for his *son Belshazzar*, who desecrated the temple vessels (Dan. 5:3). (Actually, Belshazzar was the son of Nabonidus, not Nebuchadnezzar.) King Darius made a similar request that the people of Judah pray for the Persian king and his family (Ezra 6:10). Prayer for a nation's leaders is sometimes not easy, but it opens disciples to the possibility that they can serve God (and not just their own interests) through political action and government service.

1:12—The prayers were to ensure the prosperity of the Jewish community in *Babylon* and probably to show their loyalty to their sovereign. The difficulty was that Jews in Babylon lived in two worlds. The first was Jewish, with requirements for the exclusive worship of God, Sabbath observance, diet, and circumcision. The second was Babylonian, with requirements for political allegiance. Their political requirements could conflict with their religious requirements (cf. Dan. 1, 3, 4, 6). The view of the author of Baruch was that such conflicts could be avoided if his

readers used their religious requirements (e.g., to pray for the king) to help fulfill their political obligations. Today too, such requirements, e.g., to be honest, can lead to fulfilling political obligations such as paying one's full taxes or supporting equitable laws.

1:13—Sin is a violation of God's will. Since it threatened the relationship between them and God (their protector), it also threatened their existence. *The anger of the Lord*—God's punishment. The people of Israel had sinned by worshiping other gods, both Canaanite and Mesopotamian. The people confessed they had done the same and had experienced God's punishment. Hence, they requested intercessory prayer on their behalf by those in Jerusalem. Proper discipleship for them also included giving money for the upkeep of the temple (v. 6) and for sacrifices on their behalf (v. 10). Today it could include contributing financial and other resources to churches and other organizations that work to aid people and the environment.

1:14 *Festivals*—The feasts of Passover, Weeks, and Tabernacles. *Seasons*—Regularly scheduled times for festivals or other events. Residents of Jerusalem were to pray for forgiveness for their own sins as well.

1:15–3:8 Part Two: Prayer of Confession by Those in Jerusalem

1:15 *The Lord our God is in the right*—Cf. 2:6. The destruction of Jerusalem was not God's fault; rather, the failures of the people (1:13) led to the fall of Jerusalem and exile of many of its inhabitants. Some exiles blamed God for their situation, arguing that God was not interested in their plight (cf. Isa. 40:27) or that God was powerless before the gods of Babylon (Isa. 46). Both groups were mistaken. God was just and powerful. The

shame on us today, on the people of Judah, on the inhabitants of Jerusalem, [16] and on our kings, our rulers, our priests, our prophets, and our ancestors, [17] because we have sinned before the Lord. [18] We have disobeyed him, and have not heeded the voice of the Lord our God, to walk in the statutes of the Lord that he set before us. [19] From the time when the Lord brought our ancestors out of the land of Egypt until today, we have been disobedient to the Lord our God, and we have been negligent, in not heeding his voice. [20] So to this day there have clung to us the calamities and the curse that the Lord declared through his servant Moses at the time when he brought our ancestors out of the land of Egypt to give to us a land flowing with milk and honey. [21] We did not listen to the voice of the Lord our God in all the words of the prophets whom he sent to us, [22] but all of us followed the intent of our own wicked hearts by serving other gods and doing what is evil in the sight of the Lord our God.

2 So the Lord carried out the threat he spoke against us: against our judges who ruled Israel, and against our kings and our rulers and the people of Israel and Judah. [2] Under the whole heaven there has not been done the like of what he has done in Jerusalem, in accordance with the threats that were[a] written in the law of Moses. [3] Some of us ate the flesh of their sons and others the flesh of their daughters. [4] He made them subject to all

the kingdoms around us, to be an object of scorn and a desolation among all the surrounding peoples, where the Lord has scattered them. [5] They were brought down and not raised up, because our nation[b] sinned against the Lord our God, in not heeding his voice.

6 The Lord our God is in the right, but there is open shame on us and our ancestors this very day. [7] All those calamities with which the Lord threatened us have come upon us. [8] Yet we have not entreated the favor of the Lord by turning away, each of us, from the thoughts of our wicked hearts. [9] And the Lord has kept the calamities ready, and the Lord has brought them upon us, for the Lord is just in all the works that he has commanded us to do. [10] Yet we have not obeyed his voice, to walk in the statutes of the Lord that he set before us.

Prayer for Deliverance

11 And now, O Lord God of Israel, who brought your people out of the land of Egypt with a mighty hand and with signs and wonders and with great power and outstretched arm, and made yourself a name that continues to this day, [12] we have sinned, we have been ungodly, we have done wrong, O Lord our God, against all your ordinances. [13] Let your anger turn away from us, for we are left, few in number, among the nations where you have scattered us. [14] Hear, O Lord, our prayer and our supplication,

[a] Gk in accordance with what is [b] Gk because we

---

fault, therefore, had to lie with the people. The prayer that begins here traces the sinfulness of the people from the exodus to the exile, demonstrating that the destruction of Jerusalem and the relocation of the exiles to Babylon was justified. God had not, however, abandoned Israel. God does not abandon us to our own desires us either, even when we deserve it. See note at 1:2, "took Jerusalem."

1:18–19 *Disobeyed*—The penitent exiles did not plead ignorance of God's law, but confessed their disobedience and negligence (v. 19), as well as their idolatry (v. 22). Cf. 2:12.

2:3 *Ate the flesh*—See Jer. 19:9; Lam. 4:10. The

Judeans committed cannibalism during the Babylonian siege, demonstrating just how desperate even God's people can become when things do not go right.

2:8 *Thoughts of our wicked hearts*—Cf. Gen. 6:5. The heart was considered the seat of thinking. Unlike Greeks, who often conceived of people in terms of a sinful body and a pure soul or mind, Hebrews generally thought of people as unified beings. Sin, therefore, includes the whole being.

2:14 *For your own sake deliver us*—There was nothing in Israel's past or the people's character that obliged God to forgive. Forgiveness would

and for your own sake deliver us, and grant us favor in the sight of those who have carried us into exile; ¹⁵ so that all the earth may know that you are the Lord our God, for Israel and his descendants are called by your name.

16 O Lord, look down from your holy dwelling, and consider us. Incline your ear, O Lord, and hear; ¹⁷ open your eyes, O Lord, and see, for the dead who are in Hades, whose spirit has been taken from their bodies, will not ascribe glory or justice to the Lord; ¹⁸ but the person who is deeply grieved, who walks bowed and feeble, with failing eyes and famished soul, will declare your glory and righteousness, O Lord.

19 For it is not because of any righteous deeds of our ancestors or our kings that we bring before you our prayer for mercy, O Lord our God. ²⁰ For you have sent your anger and your wrath upon us, as you declared by your servants the prophets, saying: ²¹ Thus says the Lord: Bend your shoulders and serve the king of Babylon, and you will remain in the land that I gave to your ancestors. ²² But if you will not obey the voice of the Lord and will not serve the king of Babylon, ²³ I will make to cease from the towns of Judah and from the region around Jerusalem the voice of mirth and the voice of gladness, the voice of the bridegroom and the voice of the bride, and the whole land will be a desolation without inhabitants.

24 But we did not obey your voice, to serve the king of Babylon; and you have carried out your threats, which you spoke by your servants the prophets, that the bones of our kings and the bones of our ancestors would be brought out of their resting place; ²⁵ and indeed they have been thrown out to the heat of day and the frost of night. They perished in great misery, by famine and sword and pestilence. ²⁶ And the house that is called by your name you have made as it is today, because of the wickedness of the house of Israel and the house of Judah.

God's Promise Recalled

27 Yet you have dealt with us, O Lord our God, in all your kindness and in all your great compassion, ²⁸ as you spoke by your servant Moses on the day when you commanded him to write your law in the presence of the people of Israel, saying, ²⁹ "If you will not obey my voice, this very great multitude will surely turn into a small number among the nations, where I will scatter them. ³⁰ For I know that they will not obey me, for they are a stiff-necked people. But in the land of their exile they will come to themselves ³¹ and know that I am the Lord their

---

arise out of God's own character, particularly God's fidelity to God's covenant and people. Cf. v. 27. They could send money to Jerusalem and pray, but forgiveness ultimately came from God's love.

2:17 *Dead . . . in Hades*—Hades, like the Old Testament term sheol, is not hell, but the abode of all dead. Cf. 3:10–11, 19. *Whose spirit has been taken from their bodies*—"Spirit" here means "life," not "soul." The phrase simply refers to people who have died. They have no opportunity to repent, but those alive in Babylon do—and should (2:18). So should disciples today.

2:19 *Ancestors . . . kings*—They could not appeal to the merits of righteous ancestors (e.g., Abraham) or kings (e.g., David) as a basis for God's forgiveness.

2:22—Baruch agreed with Jeremiah (Jer. 27:11–12) that it was God's will for Judeans to serve Nebuchadnezzar.

2:24—The failure of preexilic Judah to heed God's command to serve Nebuchadnezzar should serve as a lesson to the exiles not to make the same mistake. Respectful service to the king was not sinful per se, but it was part of God's plan for Judeans living under foreign domination. Likewise, respectful submission to government today is incumbent on disciples, though not necessarily obedience to all laws. Civil-rights advocates have shown that it is possible to submit to governments and still refuse to obey unjust laws.

2:31 *A heart that obeys and ears that hear*—Cf. Ezek. 38:26. God would transform the human personality. Then God's laws could be internalized so that obedience would be possible. That same obedience is possible today through God's forgiveness of sins.

God. I will give them a heart that obeys and ears that hear; [32] they will praise me in the land of their exile, and will remember my name [33] and turn from their stubbornness and their wicked deeds; for they will remember the ways of their ancestors, who sinned before the Lord. [34] I will bring them again into the land that I swore to give to their ancestors, to Abraham, Isaac, and Jacob, and they will rule over it; and I will increase them, and they will not be diminished. [35] I will make an everlasting covenant with them to be their God and they shall be my people; and I will never again remove my people Israel from the land that I have given them."

3 O Lord Almighty, God of Israel, the soul in anguish and the wearied spirit cry out to you. [2] Hear, O Lord, and have mercy, for we have sinned before you. [3] For you are enthroned forever, and we are perishing forever. [4] O Lord Almighty, God of Israel, hear now the prayer of the people[a] of Israel, the children of those who sinned before you, who did not heed the voice of the Lord their God, so that calamities have clung to us. [5] Do not remember the iniquities of our ancestors, but in this crisis remember your power and your name. [6] For you are the Lord our God, and it is you, O Lord, whom we will praise. [7] For you have put the fear of you in our hearts so that we would call upon your name; and we will praise you in our exile, for we have put away from our hearts all the iniquity of our ancestors who sinned against you. [8] See, we are today in our exile where you have scattered us, to be reproached and cursed and punished for all the iniquities of our ancestors, who forsook the Lord our God.

In Praise of Wisdom

[9] Hear the commandments of life,
       O Israel;
        give ear, and learn wisdom!
[10] Why is it, O Israel, why is it that you
          are in the land of your enemies,
       that you are growing old in a
          foreign country,
       that you are defiled with the dead,
[11]   that you are counted among those
          in Hades?
[12] You have forsaken the fountain of
       wisdom.
[13] If you had walked in the way of God,
          you would be living in peace
          forever.
[14] Learn where there is wisdom,
          where there is strength,
          where there is understanding,
       so that you may at the same time
          discern
          where there is length of days, and
          life,
          where there is light for the eyes,
          and peace.
[15] Who has found her place?
       And who has entered her
          storehouses?
[16] Where are the rulers of the nations,

[a] Gk dead

2:35 *Everlasting covenant*—The term is used with regard to a covenant with all humanity (cf. Gen. 8:16), with Abraham (cf. Gen. 17:7, 13) and with David (cf. 2 Sam. 23:5). In the past all covenants had been broken by the human parties. Here God promised to return the people to their land and never again remove them from it, just as God had promised Noah God would never again destroy all flesh. Especially to those in the exile, the promise would function to inspire hope for a better future. God's past promises offer hope for struggling disciples today too.

3:7 *Fear of you*—To fear God is to revere God so much one obeys God.

3:9–4:4 Part Three: Salute to Wisdom

3:9—*Wisdom* was conceived of as obedience to *the commandments*. In other words, Torah provided all the guidance the exilic community would ever need. Their task was to learn from it.

3:16–19 *Rulers . . . and those who lorded it over animals; those who horded gold and schemed to get silver*—These rulers had died and been replaced by others. Their abusive power and ill-gotten wealth had benefited them nothing in the long run. Discipleship still involves caring for the world and sharing with other people.

and those who lorded it over the
    animals on earth;
17 those who made sport of the birds of
    the air,
    and who hoarded up silver and
      gold
in which people trust,
    and there is no end to their
      getting;
18 those who schemed to get silver, and
    were anxious,
    but there is no trace of their
      works?
19 They have vanished and gone down
    to Hades,
    and others have arisen in their
      place.

20 Later generations have seen the light
    of day,
    and have lived upon the earth;
but they have not learned the way to
    knowledge,
    nor understood her paths,
    nor laid hold of her.
21 Their descendants have strayed far
    from her[a] way.
22 She has not been heard of in Canaan,
    or seen in Teman;
23 the descendants of Hagar, who seek
    for understanding on the
    earth,
    the merchants of Merran and
      Teman,
    the story-tellers and the seekers for
      understanding,
have not learned the way to wisdom,
    or given thought to her paths.

24 O Israel, how great is the house of
    God,
    how vast the territory that he
      possesses!
25 It is great and has no bounds;
    it is high and immeasurable.
26 The giants were born there, who
    were famous of old,
    great in stature, expert in war.

27 God did not choose them,
    or give them the way to
      knowledge;
28 so they perished because they had
    no wisdom,
    they perished through their folly.

29 Who has gone up into heaven, and
    taken her,
    and brought her down from the
      clouds?
30 Who has gone over the sea, and
    found her,
    and will buy her for pure gold?
31 No one knows the way to her,
    or is concerned about the path to
      her.
32 But the one who knows all things
    knows her,
    he found her by his understanding.
The one who prepared the earth for
    all time
    filled it with four-footed creatures;
33 the one who sends forth the light,
    and it goes;
    he called it, and it obeyed him,
      trembling;
34 the stars shone in their watches, and
    were glad;
    he called them, and they said,
      "Here we are!"
    They shone with gladness for him
      who made them.
35 This is our God;
    no other can be compared to him.
36 He found the whole way to
    knowledge,
    and gave her to his servant Jacob
    and to Israel, whom he loved.
37 Afterward she appeared on earth
    and lived with humankind.

4 She is the book of the
    commandments of God,
    the law that endures forever.
    All who hold her fast will live,

[a] Other ancient authorities read *their*

4:1—Wisdom is found in the revealed *commandments of God*, not through unaided
reason. Cf. Sir. 24:23. Baruch teaches that the
Bible offers disciples the principles upon which
to grow in godly wisdom.

and those who forsake her will die.
2 Turn, O Jacob, and take her;
    walk toward the shining of her
       light.
3 Do not give your glory to another,
    or your advantages to an alien
       people.
4 Happy are we, O Israel,
    for we know what is pleasing to
       God.

Encouragement for Israel

5 Take courage, my people,
    who perpetuate Israel's name!
6 It was not for destruction
    that you were sold to the nations,
  but you were handed over to your
      enemies
    because you angered God.
7 For you provoked the one who made
      you
    by sacrificing to demons and not
      to God.
8 You forgot the everlasting God, who
      brought you up,
  and you grieved Jerusalem, who
      reared you.
9 For she saw the wrath that came
      upon you from God,
  and she said:
Listen, you neighbors of Zion,
    God has brought great sorrow
      upon me;
10 for I have seen the exile of my sons
      and daughters,
  which the Everlasting brought
      upon them.
11 With joy I nurtured them,
    but I sent them away with weeping
      and sorrow.
12 Let no one rejoice over me, a widow
    and bereaved of many;

I was left desolate because of the sins
    of my children,
  because they turned away from the
      law of God.
13 They had no regard for his statutes;
    they did not walk in the ways of
      God's commandments,
  or tread the paths his
      righteousness showed them.
14 Let the neighbors of Zion come;
    remember the capture of my sons
      and daughters,
  which the Everlasting brought
      upon them.
15 For he brought a distant nation
      against them,
  a nation ruthless and of a strange
      language,
  which had no respect for the aged
    and no pity for a child.
16 They led away the widow's beloved
      sons,
  and bereaved the lonely woman of
      her daughters.

17 But I, how can I help you?
18 For he who brought these calamities
      upon you
  will deliver you from the hand of
      your enemies.
19 Go, my children, go;
    for I have been left desolate.
20 I have taken off the robe of peace
    and put on sackcloth for my
      supplication;
  I will cry to the Everlasting all my
      days.

21 Take courage, my children, cry to
      God,
  and he will deliver you from the
      power and hand of the enemy.

4:2–4—Exhortation to Israel to repent, to turn from sin, to follow God and not give away their inheritance to someone else. Discipleship does not always pay materially, but in this case it would.

4:5–5:9 Part Four: Exhortations to Take Courage

4:5–9a—"Mother" Jerusalem addresses her "children," her former inhabitants.

4:5 *Take courage*—Exhortation to keep hope alive because God would rescue the exiles and punish their captors. They should cry to God for deliverance. Cf. vv. 21, 27, 30. In the midst of great trials, contemporary disciples must similarly struggle in and with faith to keep hope alive.

4:13–16—Their idolatry manifested itself in wholesale disobedience. Alienation from God manifests itself in all kinds of sins.

22 For I have put my hope in the
　　Everlasting to save you,
　and joy has come to me from the
　　Holy One,
　because of the mercy that will soon
　　come to you
　from your everlasting savior.[a]
23 For I sent you out with sorrow and
　　weeping,
　but God will give you back to me
　　with joy and gladness
　　forever.
24 For as the neighbors of Zion have
　　now seen your capture,
　so they soon will see your
　　salvation by God,
　which will come to you with great
　　glory
　and with the splendor of the
　　Everlasting.
25 My children, endure with patience
　　the wrath that has come upon
　　you from God.
　Your enemy has overtaken you,
　　but you will soon see their
　　destruction
　and will tread upon their necks.
26 My pampered children have traveled
　　rough roads;
　they were taken away like a flock
　　carried off by the enemy.
27 Take courage, my children, and cry
　　to God,
　for you will be remembered by the
　　one who brought this upon
　　you.
28 For just as you were disposed to go
　　astray from God,
　return with tenfold zeal to seek
　　him.
29 For the one who brought these
　　calamities upon you
　will bring you everlasting joy with
　　your salvation.

Jerusalem Is Assured of Help

30 Take courage, O Jerusalem,
　for the one who named you will
　　comfort you.
31 Wretched will be those who
　　mistreated you
　and who rejoiced at your fall.
32 Wretched will be the cities that your
　　children served as slaves;
　wretched will be the city that
　　received your offspring.
33 For just as she rejoiced at your
　　fall
　and was glad for your ruin,
　so she will be grieved at her own
　　desolation.
34 I will take away her pride in her
　　great population,
　and her insolence will be turned to
　　grief.
35 For fire will come upon her from
　　the Everlasting for many
　　days,
　and for a long time she will be
　　inhabited by demons.
36 Look toward the east, O Jerusalem,
　and see the joy that is coming to
　　you from God.
37 Look, your children are coming,
　　whom you sent away;
　they are coming, gathered from
　　east and west,
　at the word of the Holy One,
　　rejoicing in the glory of God.

5 Take off the garment of your
　　sorrow and affliction,
　　O Jerusalem,
　and put on forever the beauty of
　　the glory from God.
2 Put on the robe of the righteousness
　　that comes from God;
　put on your head the diadem of
　　the glory of the Everlasting;

[a] Or from the Everlasting, your savior

4:27–29—"Mother" Jerusalem exhorts her *children* to *cry to God* for help and turn to God with renewed zeal; then God would grant their request and save them. Disciples should learn from this verse never to give up on God's grace.

5:1–4—Jerusalem should remove her mourning clothes and put on *the beauty of the glory from God*. Her new garment would be *righteousness*, that is, fidelity to God's covenant.

3 for God will show your splendor
　　everywhere under heaven.
4 For God will give you evermore the
　　name,
　　"Righteous Peace, Godly Glory."

5 Arise, O Jerusalem, stand upon the
　　height;
　　look toward the east,
and see your children gathered from
　　west and east
　　at the word of the Holy One,
　　rejoicing that God has
　　remembered them.
6 For they went out from you on foot,
　　led away by their enemies;
but God will bring them back to you,
carried in glory, as on a royal
　　throne.
7 For God has ordered that every high
　　mountain and the everlasting
　　hills be made low
and the valleys filled up, to make
　　level ground,
so that Israel may walk safely in
　　the glory of God.
8 The woods and every fragrant tree
　　have shaded Israel at God's
　　command.
9 For God will lead Israel with joy,
　　in the light of his glory,
with the mercy and righteousness
　　that come from him.

The Letter of
JEREMIAH

The Letter of Jeremiah concentrates on the theme of resistance to idol worship. It purports to be a letter written by Jeremiah and given to the exiles who were being carried away into exile by the Babylonians (v. 1). The form is not that of a letter, however, but of a series of exhortations. This text is given as preparation for the impressive sights and sounds of a foreign land. The text urges those going into exile to look beyond the glitzy and beautiful "skin" of the idols that the Babylonians adore and to see what is really there, a block of wood (vv. 4, 8, 11, 20, 30, 39, 45, 50, 55, 57, 71)! Israel's God can send fire down to consume wood (v. 63), which is the core of these great gods. Do not fear these flashy idols!

In Latin translations of the Bible, this text is attached to the longer letter of Baruch; hence the text begins at chapter 6. However, in the earlier Greek translations, it is separate and placed immediately following the book of Lamentations. It appears that it was not written by Jeremiah but was assigned to him because of his presence in Jerusalem during the three deportations and his role as a prophet who speaks for God.

—Beth L. Tanner

6^a A copy of a letter that Jeremiah sent to those who were to be taken to Babylon as exiles by the king of the Babylonians, to give them the message that God had commanded him.

The People Face a Long Captivity

2 Because of the sins that you have committed before God, you will be taken to Babylon as exiles by Nebuchadnezzar, king of the Babylonians. ³ Therefore when you have come to Babylon you will remain there for many years, for a long time, up to seven generations; after that I will bring you away from there in peace. ⁴ Now in Babylon you will see gods made of silver and gold and wood, which people carry on their shoulders, and which cause the heathen to fear. ⁵ So beware of becoming at all like the foreigners or of letting fear for these gods^b possess you ⁶ when you see the multitude before and behind them worshiping them. But say in your heart, "It is you, O Lord, whom we must worship." ⁷ For my angel is with you, and he is watching over your lives.

The Helplessness of Idols

8 Their tongues are smoothed by the carpenter, and they themselves are overlaid with gold and silver; but they are false and cannot speak. ⁹ People^c take gold and make crowns for the heads of their gods, as they might for a girl who loves ornaments. ¹⁰ Sometimes the priests secretly take gold and silver from

^a The King James Version (like the Latin Vulgate) prints The Letter of Jeremiah as Chapter 6 of the Book of Baruch, and the chapter and verse numbers are here retained. In the Greek Septuagint, the Letter is separated from Baruch by the Book of Lamentations. ^b Gk for them ^c Gk They

---

6:1–7—This section serves as orientation to the exhortations. The gods are *made of silver, gold, and wood* (v. 4). They are not alive. As an antidote to fearful conformity, the assurance *For my angel is with you* (v. 7) offers God's presence to the departing exiles.

6:8–16—The Babylonian gods may be dressed in finery but they are helpless. A refrain emerges: *Do not fear them* (v. 16; see vv. 23, 29, 65, 69).

their gods and spend it on themselves, [11] or even give some of it to the prostitutes on the terrace. They deck their gods[a] out with garments like human beings—these gods of silver and gold and wood [12] that cannot save themselves from rust and corrosion. When they have been dressed in purple robes, [13] their faces are wiped because of the dust from the temple, which is thick upon them. [14] One of them holds a scepter, like a district judge, but is unable to destroy anyone who offends it. [15] Another has a dagger in its right hand, and an ax, but cannot defend itself from war and robbers. [16] From this it is evident that they are not gods; so do not fear them.

[17] For just as someone's dish is useless when it is broken, [18] so are their gods when they have been set up in the temples. Their eyes are full of the dust raised by the feet of those who enter. And just as the gates are shut on every side against anyone who has offended a king, as though under sentence of death, so the priests make their temples secure with doors and locks and bars, in order that they may not be plundered by robbers. [19] They light more lamps for them than they light for themselves, though their gods[b] can see none of them. [20] They are[c] just like a beam of the temple, but their hearts, it is said, are eaten away when crawling creatures from the earth devour them and their robes. They do not notice [21] when their faces have been blackened by the smoke of the temple. [22] Bats, swallows, and birds alight on their bodies and heads; and so do cats. [23] From this you will know that they are not gods; so do not fear them.

[24] As for the gold that they wear for beauty— it[d] will not shine unless someone wipes off the tarnish; for even when they were being cast, they did not feel it. [25] They are bought without regard to cost, but there is no breath in them. [26] Having no feet, they are carried on the shoulders of others, revealing to humankind their worthlessness. And those who serve them are put to shame [27] because, if any of these gods falls[e] to the ground, they themselves must pick it up. If anyone sets it upright, it cannot move itself; and if it is tipped over, it cannot straighten itself. Gifts are placed before them just as before the dead. [28] The priests sell the sacrifices that are offered to these gods[f] and use the money themselves. Likewise their wives preserve some of the meat[g] with salt, but give none to the poor or helpless. [29] Sacrifices to them may even be touched by women in their periods or at childbirth. Since you know by these things that they are not gods, do not fear them.

[30] For how can they be called gods? Women serve meals for gods of silver and gold and wood; [31] and in their temples the priests sit with their clothes torn, their heads and beards shaved, and their heads uncovered. [32] They howl and shout before their gods as some do at a funeral banquet. [33] The priests take some of the clothing of their gods[h] to clothe their wives and children. [34] Whether one does evil to them or good, they will not be able to repay it. They cannot set up a king or depose one. [35] Likewise they are not able to give either wealth or money; if one makes a vow to them and does not keep it, they will not require it. [36] They cannot save anyone from death or rescue the weak from the strong. [37] They

a Gk them *b* Gk they *c* Gk It is *d* Lat Syr: Gk they *e* Gk if they fall
f Gk to them *g* Gk of them *h* Gk some of their clothing

6:17–23—These gods cannot move and cannot even shoo away the *birds, bats,* and *cats* that land on them.

6:24–29—These gods can not prevent their own shame, i.e., "falling down" (v. 27), or being touched by those whom the Israelites consider unclean (v. 29; see Lev. 12; 15:19–30).

6:30–40—These gods can do nothing for human beings. They cannot *save, rescue,* or *restore* anyone (v. 36). Another refrain emerges: *Why . . . call them gods?* (v. 40; see vv. 44, 56).

cannot restore sight to the blind; they cannot rescue one who is in distress. ³⁸ They cannot take pity on a widow or do good to an orphan. ³⁹ These things that are made of wood and overlaid with gold and silver are like stones from the mountain, and those who serve them will be put to shame. ⁴⁰ Why then must anyone think that they are gods, or call them gods?

The Foolishness of Worshiping Idols

Besides, even the Chaldeans themselves dishonor them; for when they see someone who cannot speak, they bring Bel and pray that the mute may speak, as though Bel*a* were able to understand! ⁴¹ Yet they themselves cannot perceive this and abandon them, for they have no sense. ⁴² And the women, with cords around them, sit along the passageways, burning bran for incense. ⁴³ When one of them is led off by one of the passers-by and is taken to bed by him, she derides the woman next to her, because she was not as attractive as herself and her cord was not broken. ⁴⁴ Whatever is done for these idols*b* is false. Why then must anyone think that they are gods, or call them gods?

45 They are made by carpenters and goldsmiths; they can be nothing but what the artisans wish them to be. ⁴⁶ Those who make them will certainly not live very long themselves; ⁴⁷ how then can the things that are made by them be gods? They have left only lies and reproach for those who come after. ⁴⁸ For when war or calamity comes upon them, the priests consult together as to where they can hide themselves and their gods.*b* ⁴⁹ How then can one fail to see that these are not gods, for they cannot save themselves from war or calamity? ⁵⁰ Since they are made of wood and overlaid with gold and silver, it will afterward be known that they are false. ⁵¹ It will be manifest to all the nations and kings that they are not gods but the work of human hands, and that there is no work of God in them. ⁵² Who then can fail to know that they are not gods?*c*

53 For they cannot set up a king over a country or give rain to people. ⁵⁴ They cannot judge their own cause or deliver one who is wronged, for they have no power; ⁵⁵ they are like crows between heaven and earth. When fire breaks out in a temple of wooden gods overlaid with gold or silver, their priests will flee and escape, but the gods*d* will be burned up like timbers. ⁵⁶ Besides, they can offer no resistance to king or enemy. Why then must anyone admit or think that they are gods?

57 Gods made of wood and overlaid with silver and gold are unable to save themselves from thieves or robbers. ⁵⁸ Anyone who can will strip them of their gold and silver and of the robes they wear, and go off with this booty, and they will not be able to help themselves. ⁵⁹ So it is better to be a king who shows his courage, or a household utensil that serves its owner's need, than to be these false gods; better even the door of a house that protects its contents, than these false gods; better also a wooden pillar in a palace, than these false gods.

60 For sun and moon and stars are bright, and when sent to do a service, they are obedient. ⁶¹ So also the lightning, when it flashes, is widely seen; and the wind likewise blows in every land. ⁶² When God commands the clouds to go over the whole world, they carry

---

a Gk *he*   *b* Gk *them*   *c* Meaning of Gk uncertain   *d* Gk *they*

6:40b–44—The *Chaldeans* (Babylonians) are stupid for believing in these ineffective gods.

6:45–52—They are made by human beings and cannot even protect themselves in war.

6:53–56—These gods cannot even save themselves in a fire; they will burn.

6:57–65—These gods cannot stop *thieves* from stealing their clothes and silver. But your God controls the creation: *Sun and moon and stars . . . the wind . . . the clouds . . . and fire* (vv. 60–63).

out his command. [63] And the fire sent from above to consume mountains and woods does what it is ordered. But these idols[a] are not to be compared with them in appearance or power. [64] Therefore one must not think that they are gods, nor call them gods, for they are not able either to decide a case or to do good to anyone. [65] Since you know then that they are not gods, do not fear them.

66 They can neither curse nor bless kings; [67] they cannot show signs in the heavens for the nations, or shine like the sun or give light like the moon. [68] The wild animals are better than they are, for they can flee to shelter and help themselves. [69] So we have no evidence whatever that they are gods; therefore do not fear them.

70 Like a scarecrow in a cucumber bed, which guards nothing, so are their gods of wood, overlaid with gold and silver. [71] In the same way, their gods of wood, overlaid with gold and silver, are like a thornbush in a garden on which every bird perches; or like a corpse thrown out in the darkness. [72] From the purple and linen[b] that rot upon them you will know that they are not gods; and they will finally be consumed themselves, and be a reproach in the land. [73] Better, therefore, is someone upright who has no idols; such a person will be far above reproach.

[a] Gk these things [b] Cn: Gk marble, Syr silk

6:66–69—The Babylonian gods can neither bless nor curse. They have no power over creation.

6:70–72—The gods are nothing more than perches for birds and will be destroyed.

6:73—This final verse returns its focus to the exiles and reminds them that to be *upright*, one must have *no idols*.

Additions to Daniel

PRAYER of AZARIAH
and the SONG
of the THREE JEWS

*G*eneral Introduction. The additions to the book of Daniel exist largely in Greek or later languages. The themes of the poetic additions are lament and confession (Prayer of Azariah) and praise (Song of the Three Jews). The theme of the prose additions (Susanna and Bel and the Dragon) is wisdom. The additions allow Daniel to display the vast horizon of his powers. The wise one now becomes the sleuth who proves who is the living God.

Like the rest of the book of Daniel, the additions exist in two ancient Greek versions, the Septuagint (LXX) and Theodotion-Daniel. Even though the former was the earlier and more generally accepted Greek translation for the whole of the Hebrew Bible, in the case of Daniel and its apocryphal additions, Theodotion-Daniel has displaced the LXX in all extant and complete ancient manuscripts except one.

Prayer of Azariah and the Song of the Three Jews. The manuscript witnesses to the Prayer of Azariah and the Song of the Three Jews place the text between Daniel 3:23 and 3:24. In contrast to the surrounding canonical text, which uses the Babylonian names Shadrach, Meshach, and Abednego given in Daniel 1:7, these poetic additions use the Hebrew names as they were pronounced in Greek: Ananias, Azarias, and Misael (v. 66, as well as v. 1 in the Septuagint).

The structure of the passage begins with the poetic prayer (vv. 1–22), followed by a short prose report on the welfare of the three Jews in the furnace (vv. 23–27) and the song of the three Jews (vv. 28–68).

—**Stephen Breck Reid**

The Prayer of Azariah in the Furnace

1 They[a] walked around in the midst of the flames, singing hymns to God and blessing the Lord. 2 Then Azariah stood still in the fire and prayed aloud:
3 "Blessed are you, O Lord, God of
    our ancestors, and worthy of
    praise;
  and glorious is your name
    forever!

4 For you are just in all you have done;
    all your works are true and your
    ways right,
  and all your judgments are true.
5 You have executed true judgments in
    all you have brought upon us
  and upon Jerusalem, the holy city
    of our ancestors;

[a] That is, Hananiah, Mishael, and Azariah (Dan 2.17), the original names of Shadrach, Meshach, and Abednego (Dan 1.6-7)

1–22 The Prayer of Azariah

1—*They* refers to the three men mentioned in Dan. 1:6–7; 3:22–23.

3—See comparable formulas of blessing in 1 Chr. 29:10, 20.

4—Similar expressions of praise of God's justice are found in Neh. 9:33; Rev. 16:7; 19:2.

by a true judgment you have
brought all this upon us
because of our sins.
6 For we have sinned and broken your
law in turning away from you;
in all matters we have sinned
grievously.
7 We have not obeyed your
commandments,
we have not kept them or done
what you have commanded us
for our own good.
8 So all that you have brought upon us,
and all that you have done to us,
you have done by a true judgment.
9 You have handed us over to our
enemies, lawless and hateful
rebels,
and to an unjust king, the most
wicked in all the world.
10 And now we cannot open our mouths;
we, your servants who worship
you, have become a shame and
a reproach.
11 For your name's sake do not give us
up forever,
and do not annul your covenant.
12 Do not withdraw your mercy
from us,
for the sake of Abraham your beloved
and for the sake of your servant
Isaac
and Israel your holy one,
13 to whom you promised
to multiply their descendants like
the stars of heaven
and like the sand on the shore of
the sea.
14 For we, O Lord, have become fewer
than any other nation,
and are brought low this day in all
the world because of our sins.

15 In our day we have no ruler, or
prophet, or leader,
no burnt offering, or sacrifice, or
oblation, or incense,
no place to make an offering
before you and to find mercy.
16 Yet with a contrite heart and a
humble spirit may we be
accepted,
17 as though it were with burnt
offerings of rams and bulls,
or with tens of thousands of fat
lambs;
such may our sacrifice be in your
sight today,
and may we unreservedly follow
you,[a]
for no shame will come to those
who trust in you.
18 And now with all our heart we
follow you;
we fear you and seek your presence.
19 Do not put us to shame,
but deal with us in your patience
and in your abundant mercy.
20 Deliver us in accordance with your
marvelous works,
and bring glory to your name,
O Lord.
21 Let all who do harm to your servants
be put to shame;
let them be disgraced and deprived
of all power,
and let their strength be broken.
22 Let them know that you alone are
the Lord God,
glorious over the whole world."

The Song of the Three Jews

23 Now the king's servants who threw
them in kept stoking the furnace with

[a] Meaning of Gk uncertain

6–7—Postexilic texts made clear that the trauma of the exile was a result of the sin of the community (see, e.g., Isa. 59:12–13; Dan. 9:5–8; Bar. 1:17–18).

11–12—The invocation of someone close to the divine is a typical expression of petition. See 2 Chr. 6:32; Jer. 14:21; Dan. 3:34.

23–27—Stoking the furnace

Narrative report of the *stoking* of the fire by the king's servants. The scene is almost humorous—the great heat of the furnace incinerates Babylonian bystanders, but, thanks to the descent of the *angel of the Lord*, the three Jewish lads are quite comfortable. *Naphtha*—Petroleum, a word of Persian origin.

naphtha, pitch, tow, and brushwood.
²⁴ And the flames poured out above the furnace forty-nine cubits, ²⁵ and spread out and burned those Chaldeans who were caught near the furnace. ²⁶ But the angel of the Lord came down into the furnace to be with Azariah and his companions, and drove the fiery flame out of the furnace, ²⁷ and made the inside of the furnace as though a moist wind were whistling through it. The fire did not touch them at all and caused them no pain or distress.

28 Then the three with one voice praised and glorified and blessed God in the furnace:

²⁹ "Blessed are you, O Lord, God of our ancestors,
   and to be praised and highly exalted forever;
³⁰ And blessed is your glorious, holy name,
   and to be highly praised and highly exalted forever.
³¹ Blessed are you in the temple of your holy glory,
   and to be extolled and highly glorified forever.
³² Blessed are you who look into the depths from your throne on the cherubim,
   and to be praised and highly exalted forever.
³³ Blessed are you on the throne of your kingdom,
   and to be extolled and highly exalted forever.
³⁴ Blessed are you in the firmament of heaven,
   and to be sung and glorified forever.

³⁵ "Bless the Lord, all you works of the Lord;
   sing praise to him and highly exalt him forever.
³⁶ Bless the Lord, you heavens;
   sing praise to him and highly exalt him forever.
³⁷ Bless the Lord, you angels of the Lord;
   sing praise to him and highly exalt him forever.
³⁸ Bless the Lord, all you waters above the heavens;
   sing praise to him and highly exalt him forever.
³⁹ Bless the Lord, all you powers of the Lord;
   sing praise to him and highly exalt him forever.
⁴⁰ Bless the Lord, sun and moon;
   sing praise to him and highly exalt him forever.
⁴¹ Bless the Lord, stars of heaven;
   sing praise to him and highly exalt him forever.

⁴² "Bless the Lord, all rain and dew;
   sing praise to him and highly exalt him forever.
⁴³ Bless the Lord, all you winds;
   sing praise to him and highly exalt him forever.
⁴⁴ Bless the Lord, fire and heat;
   sing praise to him and highly exalt him forever.
⁴⁵ Bless the Lord, winter cold and summer heat;
   sing praise to him and highly exalt him forever.
⁴⁶ Bless the Lord, dews and falling snow;
   sing praise to him and highly exalt him forever.
⁴⁷ Bless the Lord, nights and days;

28–68 Song of the Three Jews

28—Narrative transition.

29–34—The song begins with eulogy to God. This language occurs elsewhere in the Septuagint, especially in the prayers of praise and lament (see Pss. 17:47; 27:6; 30:22; 40:14; 65:20; 67:19f, 36; 71:18; 88:53; 105:48; 118:12; 123:6; 134:21; 143:1). The section accents the sovereignty of God through connections to the past (i.e., ancestors and creation) as well as to the temple. The *kingdom* language indicates a political dimension of the reign of God.

35–51—The blessing moves from an adjectival form to a verb imperative. God is blessed, and now the entire universe must participate in that recognition (see also Pss. 147, 148, and 150).

sing praise to him and highly exalt him forever.

48 Bless the Lord, light and darkness;
sing praise to him and highly exalt him forever.

49 Bless the Lord, ice and cold;
sing praise to him and highly exalt him forever.

50 Bless the Lord, frosts and snows;
sing praise to him and highly exalt him forever.

51 Bless the Lord, lightnings and clouds;
sing praise to him and highly exalt him forever.

52 "Let the earth bless the Lord;
let it sing praise to him and highly exalt him forever.

53 Bless the Lord, mountains and hills;
sing praise to him and highly exalt him forever.

54 Bless the Lord, all that grows in the ground;
sing praise to him and highly exalt him forever.

55 Bless the Lord, seas and rivers;
sing praise to him and highly exalt him forever.

56 Bless the Lord, you springs;
sing praise to him and highly exalt him forever.

57 Bless the Lord, you whales and all that swim in the waters;
sing praise to him and highly exalt him forever.

58 Bless the Lord, all birds of the air;
sing praise to him and highly exalt him forever.

59 Bless the Lord, all wild animals and cattle;
sing praise to him and highly exalt him forever.

60 "Bless the Lord, all people on earth;
sing praise to him and highly exalt him forever.

61 Bless the Lord, O Israel;
sing praise to him and highly exalt him forever.

62 Bless the Lord, you priests of the Lord;
sing praise to him and highly exalt him forever.

63 Bless the Lord, you servants of the Lord;
sing praise to him and highly exalt him forever.

64 Bless the Lord, spirits and souls of the righteous;
sing praise to him and highly exalt him forever.

65 Bless the Lord, you who are holy and humble in heart;
sing praise to him and highly exalt him forever.

66 "Bless the Lord, Hananiah, Azariah, and Mishael;
sing praise to him and highly exalt him forever.
For he has rescued us from Hades and saved us from the power[a] of death,
and delivered us from the midst of the burning fiery furnace;
from the midst of the fire he has delivered us.

67 Give thanks to the Lord, for he is good,
for his mercy endures forever.

68 All who worship the Lord, bless the God of gods,
sing praise to him and give thanks to him,
for his mercy endures forever."

a Gk hand

52–65—The next stanza brings to animals and humans alike this call to bless the Lord. Thus does the song culminate in an ecotheology that recognizes it to be the vocation and responsibility of the entire universe, not merely the human community, to honor and praise the Creator.

Additions to Daniel

SUSANNA

A lthough the two Greek versions of Susanna share a common story, there is little verbatim similarity. The standard Theodotion account tells the story of two wicked elders who falsely accuse a virtuous lovely young woman, Susanna. The young and wise Daniel rescues her from her fate as a stigmatized woman. The point of the story is to celebrate not only virtuous women, but also youth.

Narrative differences in the two Greek versions may be schematized as follows:

Theodotion	Septuagint
Specific names	General titles
Trial in Susanna's home	Trial in the synagogue
God inspires the youth	An angel inspires the youth

In Theodotion, this folktale is placed at the beginning of the Daniel story, perhaps because Daniel is described as "a young lad" (v. 45). In the Septuagint, this story appears near the end of the book of Daniel, as chapter 13, just before the story of Bel and the Dragon. The location of the story after the vision reports changes the literary context of the vision reports substantially.

There is some debate whether this book was originally composed in Hebrew or Greek. The presence of Greek puns (vv. 54–55 and vv. 58–59) indicates an original Greek version. The presence of Semiticisms, on the other hand, suggests some sort of Hebrew background, if not a Hebrew original. The date of the composition could well be the second century BCE.

—**Stephen Breck Reid**

Susanna's Beauty Attracts Two Elders

1 There was a man living in Babylon whose name was Joakim. ²He married the daughter of Hilkiah, named Susanna, a very beautiful woman and one who feared the Lord. ³Her parents were righteous, and had trained their daughter according to the law of Moses. ⁴Joakim was very rich, and had a fine garden adjoining his house; the Jews used to come to him because he was the most honored of them all.

1–4 Introduction
The exile in Babylon is the supposed context for this story. The setting is idyllic and the characters are moral. Their names indicate the inner goodness of the protagonists. *Joakim* means "the Lord will establish." *Susanna* means "lily." *Hilkiah* means "the Lord is my portion." *Very beautiful woman* echoes the allegory of the unfaithful wife (Ezek. 16:13), which itself plays on earlier tradition (see 2 Sam. 5:6–10). The comments about

Susanna's beauty are buttressed by comparable comments about her fear of the Lord. Perhaps the good woman–bad woman dichotomy of the Hebrew wisdom tradition (cf. Prov. 9) lurks in the background here. The ideals of the writer can be summed up this way: beauty and piety for women, wealth and honor for men. Like other tales from the Daniel tradition, this one indicates that exile was not a barrier to wealth.

5 That year two elders from the people were appointed as judges. Concerning them the Lord had said: "Wickedness came forth from Babylon, from elders who were judges, who were supposed to govern the people." 6 These men were frequently at Joakim's house, and all who had a case to be tried came to them there.

7 When the people left at noon, Susanna would go into her husband's garden to walk. 8 Every day the two elders used to see her, going in and walking about, and they began to lust for her. 9 They suppressed their consciences and turned away their eyes from looking to Heaven or remembering their duty to administer justice. 10 Both were overwhelmed with passion for her, but they did not tell each other of their distress, 11 for they were ashamed to disclose their lustful desire to seduce her. 12 Day after day they watched eagerly to see her.

13 One day they said to each other, "Let us go home, for it is time for lunch." So they both left and parted from each other. 14 But turning back, they met again; and when each pressed the other for the reason, they confessed their lust. Then together they arranged for a time when they could find her alone.

The Elders Attempt to Seduce Susanna

15 Once, while they were watching for an opportune day, she went in as before with only two maids, and wished to bathe in the garden, for it was a hot day. 16 No one was there except the two elders, who had hidden themselves and were watching her. 17 She said to her maids, "Bring me olive oil and oint-

ments, and shut the garden doors so that I can bathe." 18 They did as she told them: they shut the doors of the garden and went out by the side doors to bring what they had been commanded; they did not see the elders, because they were hiding.

19 When the maids had gone out, the two elders got up and ran to her. 20 They said, "Look, the garden doors are shut, and no one can see us. We are burning with desire for you; so give your consent, and lie with us. 21 If you refuse, we will testify against you that a young man was with you, and this was why you sent your maids away."

22 Susanna groaned and said, "I am completely trapped. For if I do this, it will mean death for me; if I do not, I cannot escape your hands. 23 I choose not to do it; I will fall into your hands, rather than sin in the sight of the Lord."

24 Then Susanna cried out with a loud voice, and the two elders shouted against her. 25 And one of them ran and opened the garden doors. 26 When the people in the house heard the shouting in the garden, they rushed in at the side door to see what had happened to her. 27 And when the elders told their story, the servants felt very much ashamed, for nothing like this had ever been said about Susanna.

The Elders Testify against Susanna

28 The next day, when the people gathered at the house of her husband Joakim, the two elders came, full of their wicked plot to have Susanna put to death. In the presence of the people they said, 29 "Send for Susanna daughter

---

5–21 Confrontation by the Lustful Elders
We should note the contrasts highlighted in this section. The elders, who were present in Joakim's garden every day, were persistent in their lust. Susanna, on the other hand, was vulnerable only for the moment when her maidservants left.

17—*Oil* and perfumed *ointments* were typical after-bath toiletries for wealthy women of the time.

22–27 Susanna's Response
Susanna describes her situation as caught between two disastrous choices. Either she yields to the advances of the elders, or she is framed by them. Either way, Mosaic law stipulates death as the punishment of female marital infidelity (Lev. 20:10; Deut. 22:22).

23—Susanna's refusal to defile herself parallels Joseph's (Gen. 39:9).

28–43 Susanna's Trial

of Hilkiah, the wife of Joakim." ³⁰ So they sent for her. And she came with her parents, her children, and all her relatives.

31 Now Susanna was a woman of great refinement and beautiful in appearance. ³² As she was veiled, the scoundrels ordered her to be unveiled, so that they might feast their eyes on her beauty. ³³ Those who were with her and all who saw her were weeping.

34 Then the two elders stood up before the people and laid their hands on her head. ³⁵ Through her tears she looked up toward Heaven, for her heart trusted in the Lord. ³⁶ The elders said, "While we were walking in the garden alone, this woman came in with two maids, shut the garden doors, and dismissed the maids. ³⁷ Then a young man, who was hiding there, came to her and lay with her. ³⁸ We were in a corner of the garden, and when we saw this wickedness we ran to them. ³⁹ Although we saw them embracing, we could not hold the man, because he was stronger than we, and he opened the doors and got away. ⁴⁰ We did, however, seize this woman and asked who the young man was, ⁴¹ but she would not tell us. These things we testify."

Because they were elders of the people and judges, the assembly believed them and condemned her to death.

42 Then Susanna cried out with a loud voice, and said, "O eternal God, you know what is secret and are aware of all things before they come to be; ⁴³ you know that these men have given false evidence against me. And now I am

to die, though I have done none of the wicked things that they have charged against me!"

44 The Lord heard her cry. ⁴⁵ Just as she was being led off to execution, God stirred up the holy spirit of a young lad named Daniel, ⁴⁶ and he shouted with a loud voice, "I want no part in shedding this woman's blood!"

Daniel Rescues Susanna

47 All the people turned to him and asked, "What is this you are saying?" ⁴⁸ Taking his stand among them he said, "Are you such fools, O Israelites, as to condemn a daughter of Israel without examination and without learning the facts? ⁴⁹ Return to court, for these men have given false evidence against her."

50 So all the people hurried back. And the rest of the*ᵃ* elders said to him, "Come, sit among us and inform us, for God has given you the standing of an elder." ⁵¹ Daniel said to them, "Separate them far from each other, and I will examine them."

52 When they were separated from each other, he summoned one of them and said to him, "You old relic of wicked days, your sins have now come home, which you have committed in the past, ⁵³ pronouncing unjust judgments, condemning the innocent and acquitting the guilty, though the Lord said, 'You shall not put an innocent and righteous person to death.' ⁵⁴ Now then, if you really saw this woman, tell me this: Under what tree did you see them

ᵃ Gk lacks *rest of the*

34—Placing the hands on the head designates a person as guilty of blasphemy (Lev. 24:14).

35—The contrast persists. Susanna looks up to *Heaven*. The term is probably a metonym, a word associated with another word and used in its place, in this case, God (see 1 Macc. 3:18 and Luke 15:18). Whereas the lustful elders had averted "their eyes from looking to Heaven" (Sus. 9), Susanna looks up to Heaven, underscoring again the contrast between them. Also, this represents appeal to a higher authority (vv. 42–43).

44–59 Divine Interventions through Daniel

50—Here *the elders* refers to the ruling authorities, not the two accusers.

51—Daniel is a youth (v. 45) who is also an elder by office, so he can make such a request for a new trial and examination of witnesses. This strategy of separating witnesses typifies investigative procedure in modern crime novels. We see it here in an early short story.

53—Mosaic law expressly condemns subversion of the legal process (Exod. 23:7–8).

54–59—The Greek homophonic wordplay (see NRSV notes a and b) can be conveyed in English

being intimate with each other?" He answered, "Under a mastic tree."*a* [55] And Daniel said, "Very well! This lie has cost you your head, for the angel of God has received the sentence from God and will immediately cut*a* you in two."

56 Then, putting him to one side, he ordered them to bring the other. And he said to him, "You offspring of Canaan and not of Judah, beauty has beguiled you and lust has perverted your heart. [57] This is how you have been treating the daughters of Israel, and they were intimate with you through fear; but a daughter of Judah would not tolerate your wickedness. [58] Now then, tell me: Under what tree did you catch them being intimate with each other?" He answered, "Under an evergreen oak."*b* [59] Daniel said to him, "Very well! This lie has cost you also your head, for the angel of God is waiting with his sword to split*b* you in two, so as to destroy you both."

60 Then the whole assembly raised a great shout and blessed God, who saves those who hope in him. [61] And they took action against the two elders, because out of their own mouths Daniel had convicted them of bearing false witness; they did to them as they had wickedly planned to do to their neighbor. [62] Acting in accordance with the law of Moses, they put them to death. Thus innocent blood was spared that day.

63 Hilkiah and his wife praised God for their daughter Susanna, and so did her husband Joakim and all her relatives, because she was found innocent of a shameful deed. [64] And from that day onward Daniel had a great reputation among the people.

---

a The Greek words for *mastic tree* and *cut* are similar, thus forming an ironic wordplay   *b* The Greek words for *evergreen oak* and *split* are similar, thus forming an ironic wordplay

---

paraphrase "Under the *clove* tree . . . the angel will *cleave* you"; "under the *yew* tree . . . the angel will *hew* you asunder."

60–62 The Lustful Elders Are Condemned to Death

62—Mosaic law makes clear the punishment for false testimony (Deut. 19:16–21).

BEL and the DRAGON

The Septuagint and Theodotion versions cohere quite well in this text, which appears as Daniel 13 in the former and Daniel 14 in the latter. After a brief introduction (vv. 1–2), the story unfolds in three scenes. The story of the idol, Bel, turns on the issue of eating. The priests eat the food set out for Bel (vv. 3–15). The second scene opens as Daniel exposes Bel as an idol without efficacy (vv. 16–22). The third scene comes back to the lions' den story from earlier Daniel traditions. Here we have seven hungry lions that refuse to eat Daniel and a hungry Daniel who is fed miraculously. This story is a blend of the wise person in the court of the foreign king, court conflict, and parody on idolatry. The central theological question is, Who is the living God? Disaster falls on those who have answered the question improperly. The loser of this contest dies (v. 22). We see the same phenomenon in Esther, Susanna, and the early narratives of Daniel. Life in the colonial court was a zero-sum game.

—Stephen Breck Reid

Daniel and the Priests of Bel

1 When King Astyages was laid to rest with his ancestors, Cyrus the Persian succeeded to his kingdom. 2 Daniel was a companion of the king, and was the most honored of all his Friends.

3 Now the Babylonians had an idol called Bel, and every day they provided for it twelve bushels of choice flour and forty sheep and six measures*a* of wine. 4 The king revered it and went every day to worship it. But Daniel worshiped his own God.

So the king said to him, "Why do you not worship Bel?" 5 He answered, "Because I do not revere idols made with hands, but the living God, who created heaven and earth and has dominion over all living creatures."

6 The king said to him, "Do you not think that Bel is a living god? Do you not see how much he eats and drinks every day?" 7 And Daniel laughed, and said, "Do not be deceived, O king, for this thing is only clay inside and bronze outside, and it never ate or drank anything."

8 Then the king was angry and called the priests of Bel*b* and said to them, "If you do not tell me who is eating these provisions, you shall die. 9 But if you prove that Bel is eating them, Daniel shall die, because he has spoken blasphemy against Bel." Daniel said to the king, "Let it be done as you have said."

10 Now there were seventy priests of Bel, besides their wives and children. So the king went with Daniel into the temple of Bel. 11 The priests of Bel said,

a A little more than fifty gallons *b* Gk *his priests*

1–2 Introduction

1—The Median king *Astyages* opposed the upcoming Persian ruler, *Cyrus*, who conquered Babylon in 539 BCE.

3–22 The Story of Bel and the Fraudulent Priest

3—*Bel* is short for Bel-Marduk (cf. Jer. 50:2), but sound affinities also suggest a connection with the Canaanite god, Baal. Bel was the leading god of Babylon (Isa. 46:1). The writer is poking fun at the ineffective Babylonian god for the benefit of the new Persian monarch.

7—Daniel very cogently argues that inanimate objects do not eat (Sir. 30:19).

11—*Signet* rings sealed texts and, in this case,

"See, we are now going outside; you yourself, O king, set out the food and prepare the wine, and shut the door and seal it with your signet. [12] When you return in the morning, if you do not find that Bel has eaten it all, we will die; otherwise Daniel will, who is telling lies about us." [13] They were unconcerned, for beneath the table they had made a hidden entrance, through which they used to go in regularly and consume the provisions. [14] After they had gone out, the king set out the food for Bel. Then Daniel ordered his servants to bring ashes, and they scattered them throughout the whole temple in the presence of the king alone. Then they went out, shut the door and sealed it with the king's signet, and departed. [15] During the night the priests came as usual, with their wives and children, and they ate and drank everything.

16 Early in the morning the king rose and came, and Daniel with him. [17] The king said, "Are the seals unbroken, Daniel?" He answered, "They are unbroken, O king." [18] As soon as the doors were opened, the king looked at the table, and shouted in a loud voice, "You are great, O Bel, and in you there is no deceit at all!"

19 But Daniel laughed and restrained the king from going in. "Look at the floor," he said, "and notice whose footprints these are." [20] The king said, "I see the footprints of men and women and children."

21 Then the king was enraged, and he arrested the priests and their wives and children. They showed him the secret doors through which they used to enter to consume what was on the table. [22] Therefore the king put them to death, and gave Bel over to Daniel, who destroyed it and its temple.

Daniel Kills the Dragon

23 Now in that place[a] there was a great dragon, which the Babylonians revered. [24] The king said to Daniel, "You cannot deny that this is a living god; so worship him." [25] Daniel said, "I worship the Lord my God, for he is the living God. [26] But give me permission, O king, and I will kill the dragon without sword or club." The king said, "I give you permission."

27 Then Daniel took pitch, fat, and hair, and boiled them together and made cakes, which he fed to the dragon. The dragon ate them, and burst open. Then Daniel said, "See what you have been worshiping!"

28 When the Babylonians heard about it, they were very indignant and conspired against the king, saying, "The king has become a Jew; he has destroyed Bel, and killed the dragon, and slaughtered the priests." [29] Going to the king, they said, "Hand Daniel over to us, or else we will kill you and your household." [30] The king saw that they were pressing him hard, and under compulsion he handed Daniel over to them.

Daniel in the Lions' Den

31 They threw Daniel into the lions' den, and he was there for six days. [32] There were seven lions in the den, and every day they had been given two human bodies and two sheep; but now they were given nothing, so that they would devour Daniel.

33 Now the prophet Habakkuk was

[a] Other ancient authorities lack *in that place*

---

a space where the food was stored. Archaeologists have found numerous signet rings from the Babylonian period.

16–21—Cf. Dan. 2:12; 6:24.

22—Ancient sources claim that Xerxes destroyed the temple of Bel.

23–42 Story of the Dragon

23 *Great dragon*—Often associated with a living giant serpent worshiped as a god (Num. 21:8–9; 2 Kgs. 18:4).

31–32—Once again, pressure on the monarch from the people subjects Daniel to the *lions' den* (Dan. 6:16–24).

33–39—*Habakkuk*, whom we identify with the Book of the Twelve Prophets, models a prophetic service to those undergoing persecution.

in Judea; he had made a stew and had broken bread into a bowl, and was going into the field to take it to the reapers. **34** But the angel of the Lord said to Habakkuk, "Take the food that you have to Babylon, to Daniel, in the lions' den." **35** Habakkuk said, "Sir, I have never seen Babylon, and I know nothing about the den." **36** Then the angel of the Lord took him by the crown of his head and carried him by his hair; with the speed of the wind*a* he set him down in Babylon, right over the den.

37 Then Habakkuk shouted, "Daniel, Daniel! Take the food that God has sent you." **38** Daniel said, "You have remembered me, O God, and have not forsaken those who love you." **39** So Daniel got up and ate. And the angel of God immediately returned Habakkuk to his own place.

40 On the seventh day the king came to mourn for Daniel. When he came to the den he looked in, and there sat Daniel! **41** The king shouted with a loud voice, "You are great, O Lord, the God of Daniel, and there is no other besides you!" **42** Then he pulled Daniel*b* out, and threw into the den those who had attempted his destruction, and they were instantly eaten before his eyes.

a Or by the power of his spirit   *b* Gk him

Habakkuk's support of Daniel is possible only because of the intercession of the angel. The notion that one prophet would serve another prophet provides an interesting trope in the Greco-Roman period and even today.

36 *Carried him by his hair*—Ecstatic prophecy uses this metaphor to describe being pulled by the Spirit (Ezek. 8:3).

39—The *angel* (deliverer) returns Habakkuk to his home in Judea.

40–42—Daniel's Liberation

41—Cf. Dan. 6:26–27.

1 MACCABEES

Most Christians are not very familiar with the story of the revolt that stands at the center of 1 Maccabees. Led by the priest Mattathias, his five sons, and his grandson, the Maccabean revolt marked a turning point in Jewish history, resulting in Jewish religious and political independence and the institution of the religious festival of Hanukkah. Our understanding of 1 Maccabees is also complicated by its place in the canon. It is deuterocanon (second canon, added later but equally authoritative) for Catholics and Orthodox, apocryphal (set aside from full canonical status, but useful for reading and instruction) for Protestants, and noncanonical for Jews. Also, 1 Maccabees may be too militaristic and self-serving for some readers, since it focuses upon battles, destruction of cities, and the legitimation of the Maccabean leadership. Yet 1 Maccabees deserves our attention because it (along with 2 Maccabees) helps us to understand a period that gave rise to apocalyptic thinking and literature (Dan. 7–12, for example), acts of martyrdom that became models for the later church and for the early Zionist movement, belief in the resurrection of the dead, and varied and conflicting responses to the challenge of maintaining religious and cultural identity within a hostile culture, a challenge that many Christians face today.

Historical Setting

Foreign domination, which the Jews had experienced ever since Babylonian exile in 587 BCE, sets the stage for 1 Maccabees. When Persia defeated Babylon, Cyrus the Great allowed the Jews to return to Judea (a term for Jewish territory around Jerusalem under the Persians, which comes to include all of Palestine in the Maccabean period) in 539 BCE. His successors bankrolled the rebuilding of the Second Temple in 520–515 BCE. They supported the leadership of Nehemiah (445 BCE) and Ezra (398 BCE), who demanded separation from foreigners for the sake of Jewish identity and survival. When Alexander the Great burst upon the scene in 333, he toppled the Persians and created a vast empire. When Alexander died in 323 BCE, his generals fought for years for control of his kingdom. Eventually, the Seleucids came to rule over the northern part of Alexander's empire (Asia Minor, northern Syria) and the Ptolemies over the southern part (Egypt, Judea). In 198 BCE, the Seleucid Antiochus III won control over Judea from the Ptolemies; Judea remained under Seleucid control until the Maccabean revolt in 167 BCE.

Alexander and his successors promoted Hellenism, a fusion of Greek culture with the culture of the conquered, primarily by building new cities and restructuring old ones as centers of the Greek way of life (e.g., Alexandria in Egypt). For the most part, the Seleucids continued the Persian practice of allowing the Jews to live according to their ancestral laws while paying taxes to support the government. Existence under the Seleucids was generally peaceful, but friction among the rival wealthy families of Jerusalem increased as they struggled to balance Jewish identity with economic and

social advancement under the Seleucids. During this time the power of Rome grew as it took control of Greece and Egypt.

When Antiochus IV Epiphanes (Greek for "God manifest") came to the Seleucid throne in 175 BCE, the situation changed drastically. An arrogant Antiochus plundered the Jerusalem temple, set up a military garrison in Jerusalem (the Akra) (1:29ff.), and then issued a decree for the whole kingdom "that all should be one people" (1:41) and give up their particular customs. For the Jews this meant no Sabbath, circumcision, Torah scrolls, or temple sacrifices; they were forced to forget Mosaic law and sacrifice to idols or die. The Jerusalem temple was profaned by erecting a "desolating sacrilege" on the altar of burnt offering (1:54) and an altar was erected to the Greek god Zeus Olympias.

In the ancient world, practices, actions, and customs rather than theology and creeds determined the boundary between Jews and pagans and also boundaries within the Jewish community, so the decree of Antiochus struck at the heart of Jewish identity. Being Jewish became a matter of life and death; this situation is reflected in the apocalyptic visions of Daniel 7–12. Antiochus was supported by Jewish Hellenizers, mainly priests and members of the upper class led by Jason (note his Greek name; his Hebrew name was Joshua), brother of the high priest, Onias III. Jason purchased the high priesthood from Antiochus, meeting little Jewish resistance. Up until this time, the high priesthood had been an hereditary office (from the line of Zadok, established by Solomon in Jerusalem) and an internal Jewish affair. Antiochus violated Jewish custom by selling the high priesthood to the highest bidder but acted in line with Greek practice; wealthy Greeks could pay to be a priest for a year.

Led by Jason, Hellenizing Jews, called "renegades" (1:11) built a gymnasium (a center for Greek culture that trained young men physically and mentally to assume Greek citizenship through schooling, sports, political clubs, and social and cultural events) in Jerusalem. Scholars argue that the Hellenizers probably had a positive image of themselves as reformers of Judaism who sought to make it less distinctive in the Hellenistic environment in order to gain financial and political advantages under the Seleucids. This question about how a Jew should live in Gentile society and the variety of responses it generated can guide contemporary reflection on Christian identity amid secularism and religious pluralism.

Structure and Style

The sweep of history from Alexander to Antiochus IV is packed into chapter 1 of 1 Maccabees. In chapter 2, we are introduced to the priest Mattathias and his five sons, who have moved away from Jerusalem to escape persecution for following Jewish customs. Active resistance seems to have originated in the small towns of Judea and not in Jerusalem, where many of the elite were Hellenizers. The king's troops attack on the Sabbath, and the pious Jews, who refuse to fight and profane the Sabbath, are slaughtered. Beginning in 167 BCE, Mattathias and his sons wage guerilla warfare against the Seleucids from their base in the hills. With limited support from fellow Jews, they eventually retake and rededicate the temple (4:36) in 164 BCE and establish religious and political independence, as described in 1 Maccabees 4–16.

The introduction is followed by three major sections, each focusing upon one of the Maccabee brothers and his military exploits: Judas in 3:1–9:22; Jonathan in 9:23–12:53; and Simon and his son John Hyrcanus in chapters 13–16. Chapters 3–16 cover

the period from 175 to 135 BCE, from Antiochus IV to the death of Simon and the declaration that his son, John Hyrcanus, "became high priest after his father" (16:24). A concluding reference is made to the annals of John's high priesthood, but these annals are lost to us. Though not treated in 1 Maccabees, the Hasmonean dynasty continues until 63 BCE, when the Roman general Pompey marches into Jerusalem to settle the dispute between the two feuding sons of the last Hasmonean ruler, Queen Salome Alexandra. (The Maccabean family assumed the name "Hasmonean" when it took power.) This marks the end of Judean independence.

Judas rededicates the temple and institutes Hanukkah, the festival of lights. The Talmud (rabbinic commentary on Hebrew Bible) claims that during the rededication, one jar of oil miraculously kept the lamps lighted for eight days instead of one. Following Judas, Jonathan was named high priest and leader of the Jews in 152 BCE by the Seleucids. This move sparked Jewish opposition and may have prompted the establishment of the Qumran community on the shores of the Dead Sea as a sectarian protest against the Hasmoneans, who had usurped the high priesthood. Simon was confirmed by Demetrius II as high priest, commander, and chief of the Jews in 142 BCE.

First Maccabees intentionally imitates the biblical style to show that these Hasmoneans stand in the biblical tradition of earlier savior figures raised up by God (see the deathbed speech of Mattathias in 2:49–59), giving the Hasmonean dynasty the divine stamp of approval. The Maccabees are "the family of those men through whom deliverance was given to Israel" (5:62). First Maccabees also echoes holy war as described in the book of Joshua. Judas puts whole towns under the ban, destroying them completely (5:28, 35, 44).

Date, Sources

First Maccabees is the most extensive source of information for the years 175–135 BCE, down to the reign of Simon. Only the Greek text of 1 Maccabees survives (in the Septuagint), though it was originally written in Hebrew, probably in Judea. Since Josephus, a Jewish historian, paraphrases the Greek version, it was probably translated by the end of the first century CE. Scholars argue that the Hebrew text was written either during the reign of John Hyrcanus (135–104 BCE) as a pro-Hasmonean propaganda piece or after his death as a criticism of his assimilation of non-Jews by forced circumcision and the increasing wealth of the Hasmonean rulers. Perhaps 1 Maccabees did not make it into the Jewish canon because the rabbis post-70 CE did not agree with its antiresurrection stance and because revolt was not a safe topic after two unsuccessful Jewish revolts against Rome in 66 and 132 CE. For a comparison of 1 and 2 Maccabees, which differ greatly in motivation and style, see the introduction to 2 Maccabees.

—Denise Dombkowski Hopkins

Alexander the Great

1 After Alexander son of Philip, the Macedonian, who came from the land of Kittim, had defeated[a] King Darius of the Persians and the Medes, he succeeded him as king. (He had previously become king of Greece.) [2] He fought many battles, conquered strongholds, and put to death the kings of the earth. [3] He advanced to the ends of the earth, and plundered many nations. When the earth became quiet before him, he was exalted, and his heart was lifted up. [4] He gathered a very strong army and ruled over countries, nations, and princes, and they became tributary to him.

5 After this he fell sick and perceived that he was dying. [6] So he summoned his most honored officers, who had been brought up with him from youth, and divided his kingdom among them while he was still alive. [7] And after Alexander had reigned twelve years, he died.

8 Then his officers began to rule, each in his own place. [9] They all put on crowns after his death, and so did their descendants after them for many years; and they caused many evils on the earth.

Antiochus Epiphanes and Renegade Jews

10 From them came forth a sinful root, Antiochus Epiphanes, son of King Antiochus; he had been a hostage in Rome. He began to reign in the one hundred thirty-seventh year of the kingdom of the Greeks.[b]

11 In those days certain renegades came out from Israel and misled many, saying, "Let us go and make a covenant with the Gentiles around us, for since we separated from them many disasters have come upon us." [12] This proposal pleased them, [13] and some of the people eagerly went to the king, who authorized them to observe the ordinances of the Gentiles. [14] So they built a gymnasium in Jerusalem, according to Gentile custom, [15] and removed the marks of circumcision, and abandoned the holy covenant. They joined with the Gentiles and sold themselves to do evil.

[a] Gk adds *and he defeated*   [b] 175 B.C.

1:1–10 Historical Overview: Alexander the Great to Antiochus Epiphanes

Alexander "came out of" (Gk. *exalthen;* NRSV *came from*) **the land of the Kittim**, probably Macedonia, north of Greece (in later texts, Rome; always an oppressive power), to defeat Darius of Persia in 333 BCE and create a vast empire. Antiochus also "came out" (from among Alexander's generals). Their arrogance (vv. 3, 24) sets the stage for Maccabean revolt.

1:7 *And after Alexander had reigned twelve years, he died*—Alexander's sudden, unexplained death in 323 BCE can be seen as divine judgment, like the death of Antiochus in 6:8–9. Israel's God is the God of all nations (cf. Isa. 45:1).

1:9 *And they caused many evils on the earth*—After his death, Alexander's generals fight for years against one another, disrupting the lives of the people. Finally, the Seleucids win control of Judea from the Ptolemies in 198 BCE.

1:10 *A sinful root*—An offshoot of the Seleucid dynasty, Antiochus becomes king in 175 BCE, and troubles grow. The mention of Rome draws a bigger historical picture and anticipates Judas's alliance with Rome in chap. 8.

1:11–15 Jewish Hellenizers

1:11 *Certain renegades*—This term refers in Deut. 13:13 to those who lead people to worship other gods (apostasy). It refers here negatively to Jews, led by Jason, brother of the high priest (see introduction). The judgmental, emotional language used here to describe the opponents of the Hasmoneans calls into question the way in which we deal today with our "enemies," both foreign and domestic. Such language too easily distances opponents from us as "other."

1:14 *Gymnasium*—Center for literary, civil, and physical education in Greek cities to prepare young men to assume Greek citizenship.

1:15 *Removed the marks of circumcision*—So as to participate in the Greek games in the nude. Circumcision was a sign of covenant (Gen. 17:10), and marked the boundary between Jew and Gentile. Abandoning the practice is viewed negatively: They *sold themselves to do evil* (2 Kgs. 17:17; 21:20, 25). Reversing circumcision raises questions today about what distinguishes Christians from other people and the kinds of compromises Christians make with secular culture that may erode Christian identity.

Antiochus in Egypt

16 When Antiochus saw that his kingdom was established, he determined to become king of the land of Egypt, in order that he might reign over both kingdoms. 17 So he invaded Egypt with a strong force, with chariots and elephants and cavalry and with a large fleet. 18 He engaged King Ptolemy of Egypt in battle, and Ptolemy turned and fled before him, and many were wounded and fell. 19 They captured the fortified cities in the land of Egypt, and he plundered the land of Egypt.

Persecution of the Jews

20 After subduing Egypt, Antiochus returned in the one hundred forty-third year.*a* He went up against Israel and came to Jerusalem with a strong force. 21 He arrogantly entered the sanctuary and took the golden altar, the lampstand for the light, and all its utensils. 22 He took also the table for the bread of the Presence, the cups for drink offerings, the bowls, the golden censers, the curtain, the crowns, and the gold decoration on the front of the temple; he stripped it all off. 23 He took the silver and the gold, and the costly vessels; he took also the hidden treasures that he found. 24 Taking them all, he went into his own land.

He shed much blood,
   and spoke with great arrogance.
25 Israel mourned deeply in every
      community,
26   rulers and elders groaned,
   young women and young men
         became faint,
   the beauty of the women faded.
27 Every bridegroom took up the lament;

she who sat in the bridal chamber
      was mourning.
28 Even the land trembled for its
      inhabitants,
   and all the house of Jacob was
      clothed with shame.

The Occupation of Jerusalem

29 Two years later the king sent to the cities of Judah a chief collector of tribute, and he came to Jerusalem with a large force. 30 Deceitfully he spoke peaceable words to them, and they believed him; but he suddenly fell upon the city, dealt it a severe blow, and destroyed many people of Israel. 31 He plundered the city, burned it with fire, and tore down its houses and its surrounding walls. 32 They took captive the women and children, and seized the livestock. 33 Then they fortified the city of David with a great strong wall and strong towers, and it became their citadel. 34 They stationed there a sinful people, men who were renegades. These strengthened their position; 35 they stored up arms and food, and collecting the spoils of Jerusalem they stored them there, and became a great menace,

36 for the citadel*b* became an ambush
         against the sanctuary,
   an evil adversary of Israel at all
         times.
37 On every side of the sanctuary they
         shed innocent blood;
   they even defiled the sanctuary.
38 Because of them the residents of
         Jerusalem fled;
   she became a dwelling of strangers;
   she became strange to her offspring,
      and her children forsook her.

a 169 B.C.   *b* Gk *it*

1:16–62 The Oppression of Antiochus

1:16–24—Antiochus arrogantly overcomes the threat from the Ptolemies in Egypt in 170 BCE and in 169 BCE (vv. 21, 24) loots the Jerusalem temple, probably to raise money for his military campaigns.

1:29–40—Antiochus has been humiliated by his expulsion from Egypt by Rome in 168 BCE and

again seeks tribute from Jerusalem. See 2 Macc. 5:1–21. This time he attacks violently: slaughtering, burning, looting, taking women and children captives. Women and children were particularly vulnerable in war, because they represent the future of a people. Women are still spoils of war today, for example, in ethnic cleansing in the former Yugoslavia, Rwanda, Burundi, and Darfur.

³⁹ Her sanctuary became desolate like a
        desert;
    her feasts were turned into
        mourning,
    her sabbaths into a reproach,
        her honor into contempt.
⁴⁰ Her dishonor now grew as great as
        her glory;
    her exaltation was turned into
        mourning.

Installation of Gentile Cults

⁴¹ Then the king wrote to his whole
kingdom that all should be one people,
⁴² and that all should give up their particular customs. ⁴³ All the Gentiles accepted
the command of the king. Many even
from Israel gladly adopted his religion;
they sacrificed to idols and profaned the
sabbath. ⁴⁴ And the king sent letters by
messengers to Jerusalem and the towns
of Judah; he directed them to follow
customs strange to the land, ⁴⁵ to forbid
burnt offerings and sacrifices and drink
offerings in the sanctuary, to profane
sabbaths and festivals, ⁴⁶ to defile the
sanctuary and the priests, ⁴⁷ to build
altars and sacred precincts and shrines
for idols, to sacrifice swine and other
unclean animals, ⁴⁸ and to leave their
sons uncircumcised. They were to make
themselves abominable by everything
unclean and profane, ⁴⁹ so that they
would forget the law and change all the
ordinances. ⁵⁰ He added,ᵃ "And whoever
does not obey the command of the king
shall die."

⁵¹ In such words he wrote to his whole
kingdom. He appointed inspectors over
all the people and commanded the
towns of Judah to offer sacrifice, town
by town. ⁵² Many of the people, everyone
who forsook the law, joined them, and
they did evil in the land; ⁵³ they drove
Israel into hiding in every place of refuge they had.

⁵⁴ Now on the fifteenth day of Chislev,
in the one hundred forty-fifth year,ᵇ
they erected a desolating sacrilege on
the altar of burnt offering. They also
built altars in the surrounding towns
of Judah, ⁵⁵ and offered incense at the
doors of the houses and in the streets.
⁵⁶ The books of the law that they found
they tore to pieces and burned with fire.
⁵⁷ Anyone found possessing the book of
the covenant, or anyone who adhered
to the law, was condemned to death by
decree of the king. ⁵⁸ They kept using
violence against Israel, against those
who were found month after month in
the towns. ⁵⁹ On the twenty-fifth day of
the month they offered sacrifice on the
altar that was on top of the altar of burnt
offering. ⁶⁰ According to the decree, they
put to death the women who had their
children circumcised, ⁶¹ and their families and those who circumcised them;
and they hung the infants from their
mothers' necks.

⁶² But many in Israel stood firm and
were resolved in their hearts not to eat
unclean food. ⁶³ They chose to die rather
than to be defiled by food or to profane

ᵃ Gk lacks He added   ᵇ 167 B.C.

1:41–53—The decree of Antiochus outlaws Jewish religious practices (circumcision, Sabbath,
sacrifices) upon pain of death. He also commands the building of shrines and the offering of
sacrifices to various gods and goddesses, challenging the prohibition against idolatry in Exod.
20:4–6; Deut. 5:8–10. Jewish minority rights are
trampled, raising questions about the relationship
between minorities and dominant cultures today.
Calls for unity (*that all should be one people*,
v. 41) can mask a suppression of diversity for
purposes of control.

1:54–59—A *desolating sacrilege* (*shiggutz
meshomem*; see Dan. 11:31), perhaps a Hebrew
pun on the name Lord of heaven (Ba'al Shamen),
is erected on the altar on the fifteenth day of the
Jewish month Kislev, in mid-December 167 BCE.

1:60–64—Many Jews do what Antiochus commands, but those who resist, e.g., women who
circumcise their sons or those people who keep
kosher (obey dietary laws by not eating unclean
food; see Dan. 1:8–16), are killed. The text suggests that these martyrs bring *very great wrath*
upon Israel, v. 64. Jews are faced with life-and-
death choices about their identity, which many of
us today with religious freedom do not understand.

the holy covenant; and they did die. **64** Very great wrath came upon Israel.

Mattathias and His Sons

2 In those days Mattathias son of John son of Simeon, a priest of the family of Joarib, moved from Jerusalem and settled in Modein. **2** He had five sons, John surnamed Gaddi, **3** Simon called Thassi, **4** Judas called Maccabeus, **5** Eleazar called Avaran, and Jonathan called Apphus. **6** He saw the blasphemies being committed in Judah and Jerusalem, **7** and said,

"Alas! Why was I born to see this,
   the ruin of my people, the ruin of
      the holy city,
   and to live there when it was given
      over to the enemy,
   the sanctuary given over to aliens?
8 Her temple has become like a person
      without honor;*a*
9   her glorious vessels have been
      carried into exile.
   Her infants have been killed in her
      streets,
      her youths by the sword of the foe.
10 What nation has not inherited her
      palaces*b*
   and has not seized her spoils?
11 All her adornment has been taken
      away;
   no longer free, she has become a
      slave.
12 And see, our holy place, our
      beauty,
   and our glory have been laid
      waste;
   the Gentiles have profaned them.
13   Why should we live any longer?"

14 Then Mattathias and his sons tore their clothes, put on sackcloth, and mourned greatly.

Pagan Worship Refused

15 The king's officers who were enforcing the apostasy came to the town of Modein to make them offer sacrifice. **16** Many from Israel came to them; and Mattathias and his sons were assembled. **17** Then the king's officers spoke to Mattathias as follows: "You are a leader, honored and great in this town, and supported by sons and brothers. **18** Now be the first to come and do what the king commands, as all the Gentiles and the people of Judah and those that are left in Jerusalem have done. Then you and your sons will be numbered among the Friends of the king, and you and your sons will be honored with silver and gold and many gifts."

19 But Mattathias answered and said in a loud voice: "Even if all the nations that live under the rule of the king obey him, and have chosen to obey his commandments, every one of them abandoning the religion of their ancestors, **20** I and my sons and my brothers will continue to live by the covenant of our ancestors. **21** Far be it from us to desert the law and the ordinances. **22** We will not obey the king's words by turning aside from our religion to the right hand or to the left."

23 When he had finished speaking these words, a Jew came forward in the sight of all to offer sacrifice on the altar in Modein, according to the king's command. **24** When Mattathias saw it, he burned with zeal and his heart was stirred. He gave vent to righteous anger; he ran and killed him on the altar. **25** At the same time he killed the king's officer who was forcing them to sacrifice, and he tore down the altar. **26** Thus he burned

a Meaning of Gk uncertain   *b* Other ancient authorities read *has not had a part in her kingdom*

2:1–14 Mattathias and His Sons

2:2–4—This priestly family lived in *Modein*, seventeen miles northwest of Jerusalem. The military nickname for Judas, *Maccabeus* (Greek for "the hammerer"), was applied to the whole family. The Maccabees were also known as the Hasmoneans, a name perhaps derived from

Mattathias's father Simeon, also called Asamoneus by Josephus.

2:14—Torn *clothes* and *sackcloth* are traditional ritual acts of mourning (Gen. 37:34).

2:15–48 Hasmonean Defiance

2:26 *He burned with zeal for the law*—Mattathias

with zeal for the law, just as Phinehas did against Zimri son of Salu.

27 Then Mattathias cried out in the town with a loud voice, saying: "Let every one who is zealous for the law and supports the covenant come out with me!" 28 Then he and his sons fled to the hills and left all that they had in the town.

29 At that time many who were seeking righteousness and justice went down to the wilderness to live there, 30 they, their sons, their wives, and their livestock, because troubles pressed heavily upon them. 31 And it was reported to the king's officers, and to the troops in Jerusalem the city of David, that those who had rejected the king's command had gone down to the hiding places in the wilderness. 32 Many pursued them, and overtook them; they encamped opposite them and prepared for battle against them on the sabbath day. 33 They said to them, "Enough of this! Come out and do what the king commands, and you will live." 34 But they said, "We will not come out, nor will we do what the king commands and so profane the sabbath day." 35 Then the enemy*a* quickly attacked them. 36 But they did not answer them or hurl a stone at them or block up their hiding places, 37 for they said, "Let us all die in our innocence; heaven and earth testify for us that you are killing us unjustly." 38 So they attacked them on the sabbath, and they died, with their wives and children and livestock, to the number of a thousand persons.

39 When Mattathias and his friends learned of it, they mourned for them deeply. 40 And all said to their neighbors: "If we all do as our kindred have done and refuse to fight with the Gentiles for our lives and for our ordinances, they will quickly destroy us from the earth." 41 So they made this decision that day: "Let us fight against anyone who comes to attack us on the sabbath day; let us not all die as our kindred died in their hiding places."

Counter-Attack

42 Then there united with them a company of Hasideans, mighty warriors of Israel, all who offered themselves willingly for the law. 43 And all who became fugitives to escape their troubles joined them and reinforced them. 44 They organized an army, and struck down sinners in their anger and renegades in their wrath; the survivors fled to the Gentiles for safety. 45 And Mattathias and his friends went around and tore down the altars; 46 they forcibly circumcised all the uncircumcised boys that they found within the borders of Israel. 47 They hunted down the arrogant, and the work

a Gk they

---

places himself in line with biblical heroes of old like Phineas, whose zeal turned aside God's wrath against Israel because of worship of other gods and won for himself an eternal priestly covenant (Num. 25). The Maccabean zeal for Judaism will turn aside God's "very great wrath" (1 Macc. 64) and earn their credentials to lead the people.

2:40 They will quickly destroy us from the earth—Mattathias fears that Jewish martyrdom would lead to the elimination of the Jews altogether, so he suspends the Sabbath regulations in the Torah (the first five books of the Hebrew Bible, or Pentateuch; *torah* means "instruction"). The martyrs raise questions about the validity of pacifism and nonviolence in conflict. First Maccabees views pacifism negatively because it interferes with the Hasmonean political agenda.

2:42 Hasideans—From the Hebrew *hasidim*, "covenant loyalists" or "pious ones" (see Pss. 79:2–3; 149:1). A distinct group of Jews, probably associated with the scribes (1 Macc. 7:12–13) and possibly forerunners of the Pharisees. Hasideans join with Mattathias to attack Gentiles and renegade (v. 44) Jews and *forcibly circumcise all the uncircumcised [Jewish] boys* in Israel (v. 46), reinforcing the boundary between Jew and Gentile, "us" and "them," since circumcision was a distinctive mark of Judaism. Questions about treatment of civilians in war arise in connection with forced circumcision. This language also fuels the polarizing idea that only the self-determined righteous "get it" and are true adherents of a faith.

prospered in their hands. **48** They rescued the law out of the hands of the Gentiles and kings, and they never let the sinner gain the upper hand.

The Last Words of Mattathias

49 Now the days drew near for Mattathias to die, and he said to his sons: "Arrogance and scorn have now become strong; it is a time of ruin and furious anger. **50** Now, my children, show zeal for the law, and give your lives for the covenant of our ancestors.

51 "Remember the deeds of the ancestors, which they did in their generations; and you will receive great honor and an everlasting name. **52** Was not Abraham found faithful when tested, and it was reckoned to him as righteousness? **53** Joseph in the time of his distress kept the commandment, and became lord of Egypt. **54** Phinehas our ancestor, because he was deeply zealous, received the covenant of everlasting priesthood. **55** Joshua, because he fulfilled the command, became a judge in Israel. **56** Caleb, because he testified in the assembly, received an inheritance in the land. **57** David, because he was merciful, inherited the throne of the kingdom forever. **58** Elijah, because of great zeal for the law, was taken up into heaven. **59** Hananiah, Azariah, and Mishael believed and were saved from the flame. **60** Daniel, because of his innocence, was delivered from the mouth of the lions.

61 "And so observe, from generation to generation, that none of those who put their trust in him will lack strength.

62 Do not fear the words of sinners, for their splendor will turn into dung and worms. **63** Today they will be exalted, but tomorrow they will not be found, because they will have returned to the dust, and their plans will have perished. **64** My children, be courageous and grow strong in the law, for by it you will gain honor.

65 "Here is your brother Simeon who, I know, is wise in counsel; always listen to him; he shall be your father. **66** Judas Maccabeus has been a mighty warrior from his youth; he shall command the army for you and fight the battle against the peoples.*a* **67** You shall rally around you all who observe the law, and avenge the wrong done to your people. **68** Pay back the Gentiles in full, and obey the commands of the law."

69 Then he blessed them, and was gathered to his ancestors. **70** He died in the one hundred forty-sixth year*b* and was buried in the tomb of his ancestors at Modein. And all Israel mourned for him with great lamentation.

The Early Victories of Judas

3 Then his son Judas, who was called Maccabeus, took command in his place. **2** All his brothers and all who had joined his father helped him; they gladly fought for Israel.

3 He extended the glory of his people.
Like a giant he put on his
breastplate;
he bound on his armor of war and
waged battles,

a Or of the people *b* 166 B.C.

2:49–70 The Deathbed Words of Mattathias
Mattathias delivers a deathbed speech or testament, just as Jacob had done in Gen. 49. He passes the mantle of military leadership to Judas, just as Moses had done with Joshua (Deut. 31:7–23; Josh. 1:6–9). He lifts up the deeds and rewards of biblical heroes like *Abraham*, *Phinehas*, and *Daniel*. These carefully selected heroes suggest that the Hasmoneans stand in the line of biblical tradition. Just like Abraham, Mattathias is ready to sacrifice his sons. Just like Daniel, the Hasmoneans will win against heavy odds. This

rhetoric can inspire, but it can also discourage legitimate questions about a course of political action.

3:1–9:22 Judas Maccabeus

3:1–4:35—Violence is glorified as the victories of this outnumbered heroic warrior are described. In a spiral of violence the Seleucids counterattack, leading to a consideration of how nations today, particularly in the Middle East, might break the cycle of escalating retaliation to achieve peace.

protecting the camp by his sword.
4 He was like a lion in his deeds,
    like a lion's cub roaring for prey.
5 He searched out and pursued those
        who broke the law;
    he burned those who troubled his
        people.
6 Lawbreakers shrank back for fear of
        him;
    all the evildoers were confounded;
    and deliverance prospered by his
        hand.
7 He embittered many kings,
    but he made Jacob glad by his
        deeds,
    and his memory is blessed forever.
8 He went through the cities of Judah;
    he destroyed the ungodly out of
        the land;[a]
    thus he turned away wrath from
        Israel.
9 He was renowned to the ends of the
        earth;
    he gathered in those who were
        perishing.

10 Apollonius now gathered together Gentiles and a large force from Samaria to fight against Israel. 11 When Judas learned of it, he went out to meet him, and he defeated and killed him. Many were wounded and fell, and the rest fled. 12 Then they seized their spoils; and Judas took the sword of Apollonius, and used it in battle the rest of his life.

13 When Seron, the commander of the Syrian army, heard that Judas had gathered a large company, including a body of faithful soldiers who stayed with him and went out to battle, 14 he said, "I will make a name for myself and win honor in the kingdom. I will make war on Judas and his companions, who scorn the king's command." 15 Once again a strong army of godless men went up with him to help him, to take vengeance on the Israelites.

16 When he approached the ascent of Beth-horon, Judas went out to meet him with a small company. 17 But when they saw the army coming to meet them, they said to Judas, "How can we, few as we are, fight against so great and so strong a multitude? And we are faint, for we have eaten nothing today." 18 Judas replied, "It is easy for many to be hemmed in by few, for in the sight of Heaven there is no difference between saving by many or by few. 19 It is not on the size of the army that victory in battle depends, but strength comes from Heaven. 20 They come against us in great insolence and lawlessness to destroy us and our wives and our children, and to despoil us; 21 but we fight for our lives and our laws. 22 He himself will crush them before us; as for you, do not be afraid of them."

23 When he finished speaking, he rushed suddenly against Seron and his army, and they were crushed before him. 24 They pursued them[b] down the descent of Beth-horon to the plain; eight hundred of them fell, and the rest fled into the land of the Philistines. 25 Then Judas and his brothers began to be feared, and terror fell on the Gentiles all around them. 26 His fame reached the king, and the Gentiles talked of the battles of Judas.

The Policy of Antiochus

27 When King Antiochus heard these reports, he was greatly angered; and he sent and gathered all the forces of his kingdom, a very strong army. 28 He opened his coffers and gave a year's pay to his forces, and ordered them to be ready for any need. 29 Then he saw that the money in the treasury was exhausted, and that the revenues from the country were small because of the dissension and disaster that he had caused in the land by abolishing the laws that had existed from the earliest days. 30 He feared that he might not have such funds as he had before for his expenses and for the gifts that he used to give more lavishly than preceding kings. 31 He was greatly perplexed in mind; then he determined to go to Persia and collect the revenues

[a] Gk it [b] Other ancient authorities read him

from those regions and raise a large fund.

32 He left Lysias, a distinguished man of royal lineage, in charge of the king's affairs from the river Euphrates to the borders of Egypt. 33 Lysias was also to take care of his son Antiochus until he returned. 34 And he turned over to Lysias[a] half of his forces and the elephants, and gave him orders about all that he wanted done. As for the residents of Judea and Jerusalem, 35 Lysias was to send a force against them to wipe out and destroy the strength of Israel and the remnant of Jerusalem; he was to banish the memory of them from the place, 36 settle aliens in all their territory, and distribute their land by lot. 37 Then the king took the remaining half of his forces and left Antioch his capital in the one hundred and forty-seventh year.[b] He crossed the Euphrates river and went through the upper provinces.

Preparations for Battle

38 Lysias chose Ptolemy son of Dorymenes, and Nicanor and Gorgias, able men among the Friends of the king, 39 and sent with them forty thousand infantry and seven thousand cavalry to go into the land of Judah and destroy it, as the king had commanded. 40 So they set out with their entire force, and when they arrived they encamped near Emmaus in the plain. 41 When the traders of the region heard what was said to them, they took silver and gold in immense amounts, and fetters,[c] and went to the camp to get the Israelites for slaves. And forces from Syria and the land of the Philistines joined with them.

42 Now Judas and his brothers saw that misfortunes had increased and that the forces were encamped in their territory. They also learned what the king had commanded to do to the people to cause their final destruction. 43 But they said to one another, "Let us restore the ruins of our people, and fight for our people and the sanctuary." 44 So the con-

gregation assembled to be ready for battle, and to pray and ask for mercy and compassion.
45 Jerusalem was uninhabited like a
      wilderness;
   not one of her children went in or
      out.
   The sanctuary was trampled down,
      and aliens held the citadel;
   it was a lodging place for the
      Gentiles.
   Joy was taken from Jacob;
      the flute and the harp ceased to
      play.

46 Then they gathered together and went to Mizpah, opposite Jerusalem, because Israel formerly had a place of prayer in Mizpah. 47 They fasted that day, put on sackcloth and sprinkled ashes on their heads, and tore their clothes. 48 And they opened the book of the law to inquire into those matters about which the Gentiles consulted the likenesses of their gods. 49 They also brought the vestments of the priesthood and the first fruits and the tithes, and they stirred up the nazirites[d] who had completed their days; 50 and they cried aloud to Heaven, saying,

   "What shall we do with these?
      Where shall we take them?
51 Your sanctuary is trampled down
         and profaned,
      and your priests mourn in
         humiliation.
52 Here the Gentiles are assembled
         against us to destroy us;
      you know what they plot against
         us.
53 How will we be able to withstand
         them,
      if you do not help us?"

54 Then they sounded the trumpets and gave a loud shout. 55 After this Judas appointed leaders of the people, in charge of thousands and hundreds and fifties and tens. 56 Those who were building houses, or were about to be

---

[a] Gk him [b] 165 B.C. [c] Syr: Gk Mss, Vg slaves [d] That is those separated or those consecrated

married, or were planting a vineyard, or were fainthearted, he told to go home again, according to the law. ⁵⁷ Then the army marched out and encamped to the south of Emmaus.

⁵⁸ And Judas said, "Arm yourselves and be courageous. Be ready early in the morning to fight with these Gentiles who have assembled against us to destroy us and our sanctuary. ⁵⁹ It is better for us to die in battle than to see the misfortunes of our nation and of the sanctuary. ⁶⁰ But as his will in heaven may be, so shall he do."

The Battle at Emmaus

4 Now Gorgias took five thousand infantry and one thousand picked cavalry, and this division moved out by night ² to fall upon the camp of the Jews and attack them suddenly. Men from the citadel were his guides. ³ But Judas heard of it, and he and his warriors moved out to attack the king's force in Emmaus ⁴ while the division was still absent from the camp. ⁵ When Gorgias entered the camp of Judas by night, he found no one there, so he looked for them in the hills, because he said, "These men are running away from us."

⁶ At daybreak Judas appeared in the plain with three thousand men, but they did not have armor and swords such as they desired. ⁷ And they saw the camp of the Gentiles, strong and fortified, with cavalry all around it; and these men were trained in war. ⁸ But Judas said to those who were with him, "Do not fear their numbers or be afraid when they charge. ⁹ Remember how our ancestors were saved at the Red Sea, when Pharaoh with his forces pursued them. ¹⁰ And now, let us cry to Heaven, to see whether he will favor us and remember his covenant with our ancestors and crush this army before us today. ¹¹ Then all the Gentiles will

know that there is one who redeems and saves Israel."

¹² When the foreigners looked up and saw them coming against them, ¹³ they went out from their camp to battle. Then the men with Judas blew their trumpets ¹⁴ and engaged in battle. The Gentiles were crushed, and fled into the plain, ¹⁵ and all those in the rear fell by the sword. They pursued them to Gazara, and to the plains of Idumea, and to Azotus and Jamnia; and three thousand of them fell. ¹⁶ Then Judas and his force turned back from pursuing them, ¹⁷ and he said to the people, "Do not be greedy for plunder, for there is a battle before us; ¹⁸ Gorgias and his force are near us in the hills. But stand now against our enemies and fight them, and afterward seize the plunder boldly."

¹⁹ Just as Judas was finishing this speech, a detachment appeared, coming out of the hills. ²⁰ They saw that their army*ᵃ* had been put to flight, and that the Jews*ᵃ* were burning the camp, for the smoke that was seen showed what had happened. ²¹ When they perceived this, they were greatly frightened, and when they also saw the army of Judas drawn up in the plain for battle, ²² they all fled into the land of the Philistines. ²³ Then Judas returned to plunder the camp, and they seized a great amount of gold and silver, and cloth dyed blue and sea purple, and great riches. ²⁴ On their return they sang hymns and praises to Heaven— "For he is good, for his mercy endures forever." ²⁵ Thus Israel had a great deliverance that day.

First Campaign of Lysias

²⁶ Those of the foreigners who escaped went and reported to Lysias all that had happened. ²⁷ When he heard it, he was perplexed and discouraged, for things had not happened to Israel as he

ᵃ Gk they

4:8–11, 30–33—Judas prays before battle, evoking the exodus and David, implicitly legitimizing his own actions. Similarly, our nation lays hold of historical memories and uses history to justify present policy, sometimes in inappropriate ways.

had intended, nor had they turned out as the king had ordered. ²⁸ But the next year he mustered sixty thousand picked infantry and five thousand cavalry to subdue them. ²⁹ They came into Idumea and encamped at Beth-zur, and Judas met them with ten thousand men.

30 When he saw that their army was strong, he prayed, saying, "Blessed are you, O Savior of Israel, who crushed the attack of the mighty warrior by the hand of your servant David, and gave the camp of the Philistines into the hands of Jonathan son of Saul, and of the man who carried his armor. ³¹ Hem in this army by the hand of your people Israel, and let them be ashamed of their troops and their cavalry. ³² Fill them with cowardice; melt the boldness of their strength; let them tremble in their destruction. ³³ Strike them down with the sword of those who love you, and let all who know your name praise you with hymns."

34 Then both sides attacked, and there fell of the army of Lysias five thousand men; they fell in action.ᵃ ³⁵ When Lysias saw the rout of his troops and observed the boldness that inspired those of Judas, and how ready they were either to live or to die nobly, he withdrew to Antioch and enlisted mercenaries in order to invade Judea again with an even larger army.

Cleansing and Dedication of the Temple

36 Then Judas and his brothers said, "See, our enemies are crushed; let us go up to cleanse the sanctuary and dedicate it." ³⁷ So all the army assembled and went up to Mount Zion. ³⁸ There they saw the sanctuary desolate, the altar profaned, and the gates burned. In the courts they saw bushes sprung up as in a thicket, or as on one of the mountains. They

saw also the chambers of the priests in ruins. ³⁹ Then they tore their clothes and mourned with great lamentation; they sprinkled themselves with ashes ⁴⁰ and fell face down on the ground. And when the signal was given with the trumpets, they cried out to Heaven.

41 Then Judas detailed men to fight against those in the citadel until he had cleansed the sanctuary. ⁴² He chose blameless priests devoted to the law, ⁴³ and they cleansed the sanctuary and removed the defiled stones to an unclean place. ⁴⁴ They deliberated what to do about the altar of burnt offering, which had been profaned. ⁴⁵ And they thought it best to tear it down, so that it would not be a lasting shame to them that the Gentiles had defiled it. So they tore down the altar, ⁴⁶ and stored the stones in a convenient place on the temple hill until a prophet should come to tell what to do with them. ⁴⁷ Then they took unhewnᵇ stones, as the law directs, and built a new altar like the former one. ⁴⁸ They also rebuilt the sanctuary and the interior of the temple, and consecrated the courts. ⁴⁹ They made new holy vessels, and brought the lampstand, the altar of incense, and the table into the temple. ⁵⁰ Then they offered incense on the altar and lit the lamps on the lampstand, and these gave light in the temple. ⁵¹ They placed the bread on the table and hung up the curtains. Thus they finished all the work they had undertaken.

52 Early in the morning on the twenty-fifth day of the ninth month, which is the month of Chislev, in the one hundred forty-eighth year,ᶜ ⁵³ they rose and offered sacrifice, as the law directs, on the new altar of burnt offering that they had built. ⁵⁴ At the very season and on the very day that the Gentiles had

ᵃ Or and some fell on the opposite side ᵇ Gk whole ᶜ 164 B.C.

4:36–61—In December of 164 BCE, Judas purifies the temple, where God is present with the people and from which blessing radiates. We often lack this same sense of divine presence in our church buildings today. The dedication of the

temple is celebrated for eight days, which becomes the regularly observed festival of Hanukkah (v. 59), from the Hebrew word for "dedicate" (used in Solomon's temple dedication, 1 Kgs. 8:63; 2 Chr. 7:5).

profaned it, it was dedicated with songs and harps and lutes and cymbals. ⁵⁵ All the people fell on their faces and worshiped and blessed Heaven, who had prospered them. ⁵⁶ So they celebrated the dedication of the altar for eight days, and joyfully offered burnt offerings; they offered a sacrifice of well-being and a thanksgiving offering. ⁵⁷ They decorated the front of the temple with golden crowns and small shields; they restored the gates and the chambers for the priests, and fitted them with doors. ⁵⁸ There was very great joy among the people, and the disgrace brought by the Gentiles was removed.

59 Then Judas and his brothers and all the assembly of Israel determined that every year at that season the days of dedication of the altar should be observed with joy and gladness for eight days, beginning with the twenty-fifth day of the month of Chislev.

60 At that time they fortified Mount Zion with high walls and strong towers all around, to keep the Gentiles from coming and trampling them down as they had done before. ⁶¹ Judas*a* stationed a garrison there to guard it; he also fortified Beth-zur to guard it, so that the people might have a stronghold that faced Idumea.

Wars with Neighboring Peoples

5 When the Gentiles all around heard that the altar had been rebuilt and the sanctuary dedicated as it was before, they became very angry, ² and they determined to destroy the descendants of Jacob who lived among them. So they began to kill and destroy among the people. ³ But Judas made war on the descendants of Esau in Idumea, at Akrabattene, because they kept lying in wait

for Israel. He dealt them a heavy blow and humbled them and despoiled them. ⁴ He also remembered the wickedness of the sons of Baean, who were a trap and a snare to the people and ambushed them on the highways. ⁵ They were shut up by him in their*b* towers; and he encamped against them, vowed their complete destruction, and burned with fire their towers and all who were in them. ⁶ Then he crossed over to attack the Ammonites, where he found a strong band and many people, with Timothy as their leader. ⁷ He engaged in many battles with them, and they were crushed before him; he struck them down. ⁸ He also took Jazer and its villages; then he returned to Judea.

Liberation of Galilean Jews

9 Now the Gentiles in Gilead gathered together against the Israelites who lived in their territory, and planned to destroy them. But they fled to the stronghold of Dathema, ¹⁰ and sent to Judas and his brothers a letter that said, "The Gentiles around us have gathered together to destroy us. ¹¹ They are preparing to come and capture the stronghold to which we have fled, and Timothy is leading their forces. ¹² Now then, come and rescue us from their hands, for many of us have fallen, ¹³ and all our kindred who were in the land of Tob have been killed; the enemy*c* have captured their wives and children and goods, and have destroyed about a thousand persons there."

14 While the letter was still being read, other messengers, with their garments torn, came from Galilee and made a similar report; ¹⁵ they said that the people of Ptolemais and Tyre and Sidon, and all

a Gk He *b* Gk her *c* Gk they

5:1–68—In wars against surrounding hostile peoples, Judas puts whole towns under the ban, that is, destroys them and their inhabitants (v. 28; cf. vv. 35, 44, 51), just as cities were destroyed in holy war in the book of Joshua (so Jericho, 6:24, and Ai, 8:28). Viewed from the perspective of these exterminated peoples, the God who

sanctions such action is not the liberating God of the exodus, but God the conqueror. This God has become embedded in American consciousness and ideology, as in the slogan "God Bless America," which implies that God does not bless any other nation.

Galilee of the Gentiles,[a] had gathered together against them "to annihilate us." [16] When Judas and the people heard these messages, a great assembly was called to determine what they should do for their kindred who were in distress and were being attacked by enemies.[b] [17] Then Judas said to his brother Simon, "Choose your men and go and rescue your kindred in Galilee; Jonathan my brother and I will go to Gilead." [18] But he left Joseph, son of Zechariah, and Azariah, a leader of the people, with the rest of the forces, in Judea to guard it; [19] and he gave them this command, "Take charge of this people, but do not engage in battle with the Gentiles until we return." [20] Then three thousand men were assigned to Simon to go to Galilee, and eight thousand to Judas for Gilead.

21 So Simon went to Galilee and fought many battles against the Gentiles, and the Gentiles were crushed before him. [22] He pursued them to the gate of Ptolemais; as many as three thousand of the Gentiles fell, and he despoiled them. [23] Then he took the Jews[c] of Galilee and Arbatta, with their wives and children, and all they possessed, and led them to Judea with great rejoicing.

Judas and Jonathan in Gilead

24 Judas Maccabeus and his brother Jonathan crossed the Jordan and made three days' journey into the wilderness. [25] They encountered the Nabateans, who met them peaceably and told them all that had happened to their kindred in Gilead: [26] "Many of them have been shut up in Bozrah and Bosor, in Alema and Chaspho, Maked and Carnaim"—all these towns were strong and large— [27] "and some have been shut up in the other towns of Gilead; the enemy[d] are getting ready to attack the strongholds tomorrow and capture and destroy all these people in a single day."

28 Then Judas and his army quickly turned back by the wilderness road to Bozrah; and he took the town, and killed every male by the edge of the sword; then he seized all its spoils and burned it with fire. [29] He left the place at night, and they went all the way to the stronghold of Dathema.[e] [30] At dawn they looked out and saw a large company, which could not be counted, carrying ladders and engines of war to capture the stronghold, and attacking the Jews within.[f] [31] So Judas saw that the battle had begun and that the cry of the town went up to Heaven, with trumpets and loud shouts, [32] and he said to the men of his forces, "Fight today for your kindred!" [33] Then he came up behind them in three companies, who sounded their trumpets and cried aloud in prayer. [34] And when the army of Timothy realized that it was Maccabeus, they fled before him, and he dealt them a heavy blow. As many as eight thousand of them fell that day.

35 Next he turned aside to Maapha,[g] and fought against it and took it; and he killed every male in it, plundered it, and burned it with fire. [36] From there he marched on and took Chaspho, Maked, and Bosor, and the other towns of Gilead.

37 After these things Timothy gathered another army and encamped opposite Raphon, on the other side of the stream. [38] Judas sent men to spy out the camp, and they reported to him, "All the Gentiles around us have gathered to him; it is a very large force. [39] They also have hired Arabs to help them, and they are encamped across the stream, ready to come and fight against you." And Judas went to meet them.

40 Now as Judas and his army drew near to the stream of water, Timothy said to the officers of his forces, "If he crosses over to us first, we will not be able to resist him, for he will surely defeat us. [41] But if he shows fear and camps on the other side of the river, we will cross over to him and defeat him." [42] When

---

[a] Gk aliens [b] Gk them [c] Gk those [d] Gk they [e] Gk lacks of Dathema. See verse 9 [f] Gk and they were attacking them [g] Other ancient authorities read Alema

Judas approached the stream of water, he stationed the officers[a] of the army at the stream and gave them this command, "Permit no one to encamp, but make them all enter the battle." [43] Then he crossed over against them first, and the whole army followed him. All the Gentiles were defeated before him, and they threw away their arms and fled into the sacred precincts at Carnaim. [44] But he took the town and burned the sacred precincts with fire, together with all who were in them. Thus Carnaim was conquered; they could stand before Judas no longer.

The Return to Jerusalem

[45] Then Judas gathered together all the Israelites in Gilead, the small and the great, with their wives and children and goods, a very large company, to go to the land of Judah. [46] So they came to Ephron. This was a large and very strong town on the road, and they could not go around it to the right or to the left; they had to go through it. [47] But the people of the town shut them out and blocked up the gates with stones.

[48] Judas sent them this friendly message, "Let us pass through your land to get to our land. No one will do you harm; we will simply pass by on foot." But they refused to open to him. [49] Then Judas ordered proclamation to be made to the army that all should encamp where they were. [50] So the men of the forces encamped, and he fought against the town all that day and all the night, and the town was delivered into his hands. [51] He destroyed every male by the edge of the sword, and razed and plundered the town. Then he passed through the town over the bodies of the dead.

[52] Then they crossed the Jordan into the large plain before Beth-shan. [53] Judas kept rallying the laggards and encouraging the people all the way until he came to the land of Judah. [54] So they went up to Mount Zion with joy and gladness, and offered burnt offerings, because they had returned in safety; not one of them had fallen.

Joseph and Azariah Defeated

[55] Now while Judas and Jonathan were in Gilead and their[b] brother Simon was in Galilee before Ptolemais, [56] Joseph son of Zechariah, and Azariah, the commanders of the forces, heard of their brave deeds and of the heroic war they had fought. [57] So they said, "Let us also make a name for ourselves; let us go and make war on the Gentiles around us." [58] So they issued orders to the men of the forces that were with them and marched against Jamnia. [59] Gorgias and his men came out of the town to meet them in battle. [60] Then Joseph and Azariah were routed, and were pursued to the borders of Judea; as many as two thousand of the people of Israel fell that day. [61] Thus the people suffered a great rout because, thinking to do a brave deed, they did not listen to Judas and his brothers. [62] But they did not belong to the family of those men through whom deliverance was given to Israel.

[63] The man Judas and his brothers were greatly honored in all Israel and among all the Gentiles, wherever their name was heard. [64] People gathered to them and praised them.

Success at Hebron and Philistia

[65] Then Judas and his brothers went out and fought the descendants of Esau in the land to the south. He struck Hebron and its villages and tore down its strongholds and burned its towers on all sides. [66] Then he marched off to go into the land of the Philistines, and passed through Marisa.[c] [67] On that day some priests, who wished to do a brave deed, fell in battle, for they went out to battle unwisely. [68] But Judas turned aside to Azotus in the land of the Philistines; he tore down their altars, and the carved images of their gods he burned with fire; he plundered the towns and returned to the land of Judah.

[a] Or scribes　[b] Gk his　[c] Other ancient authorities read Samaria

The Last Days of Antiochus Epiphanes

6 King Antiochus was going through the upper provinces when he heard that Elymais in Persia was a city famed for its wealth in silver and gold. ² Its temple was very rich, containing golden shields, breastplates, and weapons left there by Alexander son of Philip, the Macedonian king who first reigned over the Greeks. ³ So he came and tried to take the city and plunder it, but he could not because his plan had become known to the citizens ⁴ and they withstood him in battle. So he fled and in great disappointment left there to return to Babylon.

5 Then someone came to him in Persia and reported that the armies that had gone into the land of Judah had been routed; ⁶ that Lysias had gone first with a strong force, but had turned and fled before the Jews;*a* that the Jews*b* had grown strong from the arms, supplies, and abundant spoils that they had taken from the armies they had cut down; ⁷ that they had torn down the abomination that he had erected on the altar in Jerusalem; and that they had surrounded the sanctuary with high walls as before, and also Beth-zur, his town.

8 When the king heard this news, he was astounded and badly shaken. He took to his bed and became sick from disappointment, because things had not turned out for him as he had planned. ⁹ He lay there for many days, because deep disappointment continually gripped him, and he realized that he was dying. ¹⁰ So he called all his Friends and said to them, "Sleep has departed from my eyes and I am downhearted with worry. ¹¹ I said to myself, 'To what distress I have come! And into what a great flood I now am plunged! For I was kind and beloved in my power.'

¹² But now I remember the wrong I did in Jerusalem. I seized all its vessels of silver and gold, and I sent to destroy the inhabitants of Judah without good reason. ¹³ I know that it is because of this that these misfortunes have come upon me; here I am, perishing of bitter disappointment in a strange land."

14 Then he called for Philip, one of his Friends, and made him ruler over all his kingdom. ¹⁵ He gave him the crown and his robe and the signet, so that he might guide his son Antiochus and bring him up to be king. ¹⁶ Thus King Antiochus died there in the one hundred forty-ninth year.*c* ¹⁷ When Lysias learned that the king was dead, he set up Antiochus the king's*d* son to reign. Lysias*e* had brought him up from boyhood; he named him Eupator.

Renewed Attacks from Syria

18 Meanwhile the garrison in the citadel kept hemming Israel in around the sanctuary. They were trying in every way to harm them and strengthen the Gentiles. ¹⁹ Judas therefore resolved to destroy them, and assembled all the people to besiege them. ²⁰ They gathered together and besieged the citadel*f* in the one hundred fiftieth year;*g* and he built siege towers and other engines of war. ²¹ But some of the garrison escaped from the siege and some of the ungodly Israelites joined them. ²² They went to the king and said, "How long will you fail to do justice and to avenge our kindred? ²³ We were happy to serve your father, to live by what he said, and to follow his commands. ²⁴ For this reason the sons of our people besieged the citadel*h* and became hostile to us; moreover, they have put to death as many of us as they have caught,

a Gk them   *b* Gk they   *c* 163 B.C.   *d* Gk his   *e* Gk He   *f* Gk it   *g* 162 B.C.
h Meaning of Gk uncertain

6:1–17—A bitter Antiochus IV dies in 164 BCE repenting of his treatment of the Jews.

6:18–9:22—Judas defeats the general Nicanor (7:39–50). Battles continue during the confusing period after the death of Antiochus IV. Judas

enters an alliance with the Romans, who are described idealistically in 8:1–16, raising questions about how governments overlook questionable national behavior when it suits them.

and they have seized our inheritances.
²⁵ It is not against us alone that they have
stretched out their hands; they have also
attacked all the lands on their borders.
²⁶ And see, today they have encamped
against the citadel in Jerusalem to take
it; they have fortified both the sanctuary and Beth-zur; ²⁷ unless you quickly
prevent them, they will do still greater
things, and you will not be able to stop
them."

28 The king was enraged when he
heard this. He assembled all his Friends,
the commanders of his forces and those
in authority.ᵃ ²⁹ Mercenary forces also
came to him from other kingdoms and
from islands of the seas. ³⁰ The number
of his forces was one hundred thousand
foot soldiers, twenty thousand horsemen, and thirty-two elephants accustomed to war. ³¹ They came through
Idumea and encamped against Beth-zur,
and for many days they fought and built
engines of war; but the Jewsᵇ sallied out
and burned these with fire, and fought
courageously.

The Battle at Beth-zechariah

32 Then Judas marched away from the
citadel and encamped at Beth-zechariah, opposite the camp of the king.
³³ Early in the morning the king set out
and took his army by a forced march
along the road to Beth-zechariah, and
his troops made ready for battle and
sounded their trumpets. ³⁴ They offered
the elephants the juice of grapes and
mulberries, to arouse them for battle.
³⁵ They distributed the animals among
the phalanxes; with each elephant they
stationed a thousand men armed with
coats of mail, and with brass helmets
on their heads; and five hundred picked
horsemen were assigned to each beast.
³⁶ These took their position beforehand
wherever the animal was; wherever it
went, they went with it, and they never
left it. ³⁷ On the elephantsᶜ were wooden
towers, strong and covered; they were
fastened on each animal by special har-

ness, and on each were fourᵈ armed
men who fought from there, and also its
Indian driver. ³⁸ The rest of the cavalry
were stationed on either side, on the two
flanks of the army, to harass the enemy
while being themselves protected by the
phalanxes. ³⁹ When the sun shone on
the shields of gold and brass, the hills
were ablaze with them and gleamed like
flaming torches.

40 Now a part of the king's army was
spread out on the high hills, and some
troops were on the plain, and they
advanced steadily and in good order.
⁴¹ All who heard the noise made by their
multitude, by the marching of the multitude and the clanking of their arms,
trembled, for the army was very large
and strong. ⁴² But Judas and his army
advanced to the battle, and six hundred
of the king's army fell. ⁴³ Now Eleazar,
called Avaran, saw that one of the animals was equipped with royal armor.
It was taller than all the others, and he
supposed that the king was on it. ⁴⁴ So
he gave his life to save his people and
to win for himself an everlasting name.
⁴⁵ He courageously ran into the midst of
the phalanx to reach it; he killed men
right and left, and they parted before
him on both sides. ⁴⁶ He got under the
elephant, stabbed it from beneath, and
killed it; but it fell to the ground upon
him and he died. ⁴⁷ When the Jewsᵇ saw
the royal might and the fierce attack of
the forces, they turned away in flight.

The Siege of the Temple

48 The soldiers of the king's army went
up to Jerusalem against them, and the
king encamped in Judea and at Mount
Zion. ⁴⁹ He made peace with the people
of Beth-zur, and they evacuated the town
because they had no provisions there to
withstand a siege, since it was a sabbatical year for the land. ⁵⁰ So the king took
Beth-zur and stationed a guard there to
hold it. ⁵¹ Then he encamped before the

ᵃ Gk those over the reins ᵇ Gk they ᶜ Gk them ᵈ Cn: Some authorities read
thirty; others thirty-two

sanctuary for many days. He set up siege towers, engines of war to throw fire and stones, machines to shoot arrows, and catapults. [52] The Jews[a] also made engines of war to match theirs, and fought for many days. [53] But they had no food in storage,[b] because it was the seventh year; those who had found safety in Judea from the Gentiles had consumed the last of the stores. [54] Only a few men were left in the sanctuary; the rest scattered to their own homes, for the famine proved too much for them.

Syria Offers Terms

55 Then Lysias heard that Philip, whom King Antiochus while still living had appointed to bring up his son Antiochus to be king, [56] had returned from Persia and Media with the forces that had gone with the king, and that he was trying to seize control of the government. [57] So he quickly gave orders to withdraw, and said to the king, to the commanders of the forces, and to the troops, "Daily we grow weaker, our food supply is scant, the place against which we are fighting is strong, and the affairs of the kingdom press urgently on us. [58] Now then let us come to terms with these people, and make peace with them and with all their nation. [59] Let us agree to let them live by their laws as they did before; for it was on account of their laws that we abolished that they became angry and did all these things."

60 The speech pleased the king and the commanders, and he sent to the Jews[c] an offer of peace, and they accepted it. [61] So the king and the commanders gave them their oath. On these conditions the Jews[a] evacuated the stronghold. [62] But when the king entered Mount Zion and saw what a strong fortress the place was, he broke the oath he had sworn and gave orders to tear down the wall all around. [63] Then he set off in haste and returned to Antioch. He found Philip in control of the city, but he fought against him, and took the city by force.

Expedition of Bacchides and Alcimus

7 In the one hundred fifty-first year[d] Demetrius son of Seleucus set out from Rome, sailed with a few men to a town by the sea, and there began to reign. [2] As he was entering the royal palace of his ancestors, the army seized Antiochus and Lysias to bring them to him. [3] But when this act became known to him, he said, "Do not let me see their faces!" [4] So the army killed them, and Demetrius took his seat on the throne of his kingdom.

5 Then there came to him all the renegade and godless men of Israel; they were led by Alcimus, who wanted to be high priest. [6] They brought to the king this accusation against the people: "Judas and his brothers have destroyed all your Friends, and have driven us out of our land. [7] Now then send a man whom you trust; let him go and see all the ruin that Judas[e] has brought on us and on the land of the king, and let him punish them and all who help them."

8 So the king chose Bacchides, one of the king's Friends, governor of the province Beyond the River; he was a great man in the kingdom and was faithful to the king. [9] He sent him, and with him he sent the ungodly Alcimus, whom he made high priest; and he commanded him to take vengeance on the Israelites. [10] So they marched away and came with a large force into the land of Judah; and he sent messengers to Judas and his brothers with peaceable but treacherous words. [11] But they paid no attention to their words, for they saw that they had come with a large force.

12 Then a group of scribes appeared in a body before Alcimus and Bacchides to ask for just terms. [13] The Hasideans were first among the Israelites to seek peace from them, [14] for they said, "A priest of the line of Aaron has come with the army, and he will not harm us." [15] Alcimus[f] spoke peaceable words

[a]Gk they [b]Other ancient authorities read *in the sanctuary* [c]Gk them
[d]161 B.C. [e]Gk he [f]Gk He

to them and swore this oath to them, "We will not seek to injure you or your friends." [16] So they trusted him; but he seized sixty of them and killed them in one day, in accordance with the word that was written,

[17] "The flesh of your faithful ones and
         their blood
     they poured out all around
         Jerusalem,
     and there was no one to bury
         them."

[18] Then the fear and dread of them fell on all the people, for they said, "There is no truth or justice in them, for they have violated the agreement and the oath that they swore."

[19] Then Bacchides withdrew from Jerusalem and encamped in Beth-zaith. And he sent and seized many of the men who had deserted to him,[a] and some of the people, and killed them and threw them into a great pit. [20] He placed Alcimus in charge of the country and left with him a force to help him; then Bacchides went back to the king.

[21] Alcimus struggled to maintain his high priesthood, [22] and all who were troubling their people joined him. They gained control of the land of Judah and did great damage in Israel. [23] And Judas saw all the wrongs that Alcimus and those with him had done among the Israelites; it was more than the Gentiles had done. [24] So Judas[b] went out into all the surrounding parts of Judea, taking vengeance on those who had deserted and preventing those in the city[c] from going out into the country. [25] When Alcimus saw that Judas and those with him had grown strong, and realized that he could not withstand them, he returned to the king and brought malicious charges against them.

Nicanor in Judea

[26] Then the king sent Nicanor, one of his honored princes, who hated and detested Israel, and he commanded him to destroy the people. [27] So Nicanor came to Jerusalem with a large force, and treacherously sent to Judas and his brothers this peaceable message, [28] "Let there be no fighting between you and me; I shall come with a few men to see you face to face in peace."

[29] So he came to Judas, and they greeted one another peaceably; but the enemy were preparing to kidnap Judas. [30] It became known to Judas that Nicanor[b] had come to him with treacherous intent, and he was afraid of him and would not meet him again. [31] When Nicanor learned that his plan had been disclosed, he went out to meet Judas in battle near Caphar-salama. [32] About five hundred of the army of Nicanor fell, and the rest[d] fled into the city of David.

Nicanor Threatens the Temple

[33] After these events Nicanor went up to Mount Zion. Some of the priests from the sanctuary and some of the elders of the people came out to greet him peaceably and to show him the burnt offering that was being offered for the king. [34] But he mocked them and derided them and defiled them and spoke arrogantly, [35] and in anger he swore this oath, "Unless Judas and his army are delivered into my hands this time, then if I return safely I will burn up this house." And he went out in great anger. [36] At this the priests went in and stood before the altar and the temple; they wept and said,

[37] "You chose this house to be called by
         your name,
     and to be for your people a house
         of prayer and supplication.
[38] Take vengeance on this man and on
         his army,
     and let them fall by the sword;
     remember their blasphemies,
     and let them live no longer."

The Death of Nicanor

[39] Now Nicanor went out from Jerusalem and encamped in Beth-horon, and

[a] Or many of his men who had deserted [b] Gk he [c] Gk and they were prevented [d] Gk they

the Syrian army joined him. ⁴⁰ Judas encamped in Adasa with three thousand men. Then Judas prayed and said, ⁴¹ "When the messengers from the king spoke blasphemy, your angel went out and struck down one hundred eighty-five thousand of the Assyrians.ᵃ ⁴² So also crush this army before us today; let the rest learn that Nicanorᵇ has spoken wickedly against the sanctuary, and judge him according to this wickedness."

43 So the armies met in battle on the thirteenth day of the month of Adar. The army of Nicanor was crushed, and he himself was the first to fall in the battle. ⁴⁴ When his army saw that Nicanor had fallen, they threw down their arms and fled. ⁴⁵ The Jewsᶜ pursued them a day's journey, from Adasa as far as Gazara, and as they followed they kept sounding the battle call on the trumpets. ⁴⁶ People came out of all the surrounding villages of Judea, and they outflanked the enemyᵈ and drove them back to their pursuers,ᵉ so that they all fell by the sword; not even one of them was left. ⁴⁷ Then the Jewsᶜ seized the spoils and the plunder; they cut off Nicanor's head and the right hand that he had so arrogantly stretched out, and brought them and displayed them just outside Jerusalem. ⁴⁸ The people rejoiced greatly and celebrated that day as a day of great gladness. ⁴⁹ They decreed that this day should be celebrated each year on the thirteenth day of Adar. ⁵⁰ So the land of Judah had rest for a few days.

A Eulogy of the Romans

8 Now Judas heard of the fame of the Romans, that they were very strong and were well-disposed toward all who made an alliance with them, that they pledged friendship to those who came to them, ² and that they were very strong. He had been told of their wars and of the brave deeds that they were doing among the Gauls, how they had defeated them and forced them to pay tribute, ³ and what they had done in the land of Spain to get control of the silver and gold mines there, ⁴ and how they had gained control of the whole region by their planning and patience, even though the place was far distant from them. They also subdued the kings who came against them from the ends of the earth, until they crushed them and inflicted great disaster on them; the rest paid them tribute every year. ⁵ They had crushed in battle and conquered Philip, and King Perseus of the Macedonians,ᶠ and the others who rose up against them. ⁶ They also had defeated Antiochus the Great, king of Asia, who went to fight against them with one hundred twenty elephants and with cavalry and chariots and a very large army. He was crushed by them; ⁷ they took him alive and decreed that he and those who would reign after him should pay a heavy tribute and give hostages and surrender some of their best provinces, ⁸ the countries of India, Media, and Lydia. These they took from him and gave to King Eumenes. ⁹ The Greeks planned to come and destroy them, ¹⁰ but this became known to them, and they sent a general against the Greeksᵈ and attacked them. Many of them were wounded and fell, and the Romansᶜ took captive their wives and children; they plundered them, conquered the land, tore down their strongholds, and enslaved them to this day. ¹¹ The remaining kingdoms and islands, as many as ever opposed them, they destroyed and enslaved; ¹² but with their friends and those who rely on them they have kept friendship. They have subdued kings far and near, and as many as have heard of their fame have feared them. ¹³ Those whom they wish to help and to make kings, they make kings, and those whom they wish they depose; and they have been greatly exalted. ¹⁴ Yet for all this not one of them has put on a crown or worn purple as a mark of pride, ¹⁵ but they have built for

---

ᵃ Gk of them   ᵇ Gk he   ᶜ Gk they   ᵈ Gk them   ᵉ Gk these   ᶠ Or Kittim

themselves a senate chamber, and every day three hundred twenty senators constantly deliberate concerning the people, to govern them well. [16] They trust one man each year to rule over them and to control all their land; they all heed the one man, and there is no envy or jealousy among them.

An Alliance with Rome

[17] So Judas chose Eupolemus son of John son of Accos, and Jason son of Eleazar, and sent them to Rome to establish friendship and alliance, [18] and to free themselves from the yoke; for they saw that the kingdom of the Greeks was enslaving Israel completely. [19] They went to Rome, a very long journey; and they entered the senate chamber and spoke as follows: [20] "Judas, who is also called Maccabeus, and his brothers and the people of the Jews have sent us to you to establish alliance and peace with you, so that we may be enrolled as your allies and friends." [21] The proposal pleased them, [22] and this is a copy of the letter that they wrote in reply, on bronze tablets, and sent to Jerusalem to remain with them there as a memorial of peace and alliance:

[23] "May all go well with the Romans and with the nation of the Jews at sea and on land forever, and may sword and enemy be far from them. [24] If war comes first to Rome or to any of their allies in all their dominion, [25] the nation of the Jews shall act as their allies wholeheartedly, as the occasion may indicate to them. [26] To the enemy that makes war they shall not give or supply grain, arms, money, or ships, just as Rome has decided; and they shall keep their obligations without receiving any return. [27] In the same way, if war comes first to the nation of the Jews, the Romans shall willingly act as their allies, as the occasion may indicate to them. [28] And to their enemies there shall not be given grain, arms, money, or ships, just as Rome has decided; and they shall keep these obligations and do

so without deceit. [29] Thus on these terms the Romans make a treaty with the Jewish people. [30] If after these terms are in effect both parties shall determine to add or delete anything, they shall do so at their discretion, and any addition or deletion that they may make shall be valid.

[31] "Concerning the wrongs that King Demetrius is doing to them, we have written to him as follows, 'Why have you made your yoke heavy on our friends and allies the Jews? [32] If now they appeal again for help against you, we will defend their rights and fight you on sea and on land.'"

Bacchides Returns to Judea

9 When Demetrius heard that Nicanor and his army had fallen in battle, he sent Bacchides and Alcimus into the land of Judah a second time, and with them the right wing of the army. [2] They went by the road that leads to Gilgal and encamped against Mesaloth in Arbela, and they took it and killed many people. [3] In the first month of the one hundred fifty-second year[a] they encamped against Jerusalem; [4] then they marched off and went to Berea with twenty thousand foot soldiers and two thousand cavalry.

5 Now Judas was encamped in Elasa, and with him were three thousand picked men. [6] When they saw the huge number of the enemy forces, they were greatly frightened, and many slipped away from the camp, until no more than eight hundred of them were left.

7 When Judas saw that his army had slipped away and the battle was imminent, he was crushed in spirit, for he had no time to assemble them. [8] He became faint, but he said to those who were left, "Let us get up and go against our enemies. We may have the strength to fight them." [9] But they tried to dissuade him, saying, "We do not have the strength. Let us rather save our own

[a] 160 B.C.

lives now, and let us come back with our kindred and fight them; we are too few." [10] But Judas said, "Far be it from us to do such a thing as to flee from them. If our time has come, let us die bravely for our kindred, and leave no cause to question our honor."

The Last Battle of Judas

[11] Then the army of Bacchides[a] marched out from the camp and took its stand for the encounter. The cavalry was divided into two companies, and the slingers and the archers went ahead of the army, as did all the chief warriors. [12] Bacchides was on the right wing. Flanked by the two companies, the phalanx advanced to the sound of the trumpets; and the men with Judas also blew their trumpets. [13] The earth was shaken by the noise of the armies, and the battle raged from morning until evening.

[14] Judas saw that Bacchides and the strength of his army were on the right; then all the stouthearted men went with him, [15] and they crushed the right wing, and he pursued them as far as Mount Azotus. [16] When those on the left wing saw that the right wing was crushed, they turned and followed close behind Judas and his men. [17] The battle became desperate, and many on both sides were wounded and fell. [18] Judas also fell, and the rest fled.

[19] Then Jonathan and Simon took their brother Judas and buried him in the tomb of their ancestors at Modein, [20] and wept for him. All Israel made great lamentation for him; they mourned many days and said,

[21] "How is the mighty fallen,
the savior of Israel!"

[22] Now the rest of the acts of Judas, and his wars and the brave deeds that he did, and his greatness, have not been recorded, but they were very many.

Jonathan Succeeds Judas

[23] After the death of Judas, the renegades emerged in all parts of Israel; all the wrongdoers reappeared. [24] In those days a very great famine occurred, and the country went over to their side. [25] Bacchides chose the godless and put them in charge of the country. [26] They made inquiry and searched for the friends of Judas, and brought them to Bacchides, who took vengeance on them and made sport of them. [27] So there was great distress in Israel, such as had not been since the time that prophets ceased to appear among them.

[28] Then all the friends of Judas assembled and said to Jonathan, [29] "Since the death of your brother Judas there has been no one like him to go against our enemies and Bacchides, and to deal with those of our nation who hate us. [30] Now therefore we have chosen you today to take his place as our ruler and leader, to fight our battle." [31] So Jonathan accepted the leadership at that time in place of his brother Judas.

The Campaigns of Jonathan

[32] When Bacchides learned of this, he tried to kill him. [33] But Jonathan and his brother Simon and all who were with him heard of it, and they fled into the wilderness of Tekoa and camped by the water of the pool of Asphar. [34] Bacchides found this out on the sabbath day, and he with all his army crossed the Jordan.

[35] So Jonathan[b] sent his brother as leader of the multitude and begged the Nabateans, who were his friends, for permission to store with them the great

[a] Gk lacks of Bacchides   [b] Gk he

9:23–12:53 Jonathan

9:23–27—Jonathan comes to power *after the death of Judas* in a time of *great distress*. This intentionally ties him to the book of Judges, which unfolds in repeated cycles of apostasy, oppression, repentance, and deliverance (e.g., Judg.

3:7–11). Like Judas, Jonathan stands in a long line of biblical deliverers. Political leaders often use religious associations and rhetoric to validate their power.

9:30—Jonathan is elected *ruler and leader* and battles the Seleucid governor *Bacchides*.

amount of baggage that they had. **36** But the family of Jambri from Medeba came out and seized John and all that he had, and left with it.

37 After these things it was reported to Jonathan and his brother Simon, "The family of Jambri are celebrating a great wedding, and are conducting the bride, a daughter of one of the great nobles of Canaan, from Nadabath with a large escort." **38** Remembering how their brother John had been killed, they went up and hid under cover of the mountain. **39** They looked out and saw a tumultuous procession with a great amount of baggage; and the bridegroom came out with his friends and his brothers to meet them with tambourines and musicians and many weapons. **40** Then they rushed on them from the ambush and began killing them. Many were wounded and fell, and the rest fled to the mountain; and the Jews*a* took all their goods. **41** So the wedding was turned into mourning and the voice of their musicians into a funeral dirge. **42** After they had fully avenged the blood of their brother, they returned to the marshes of the Jordan.

43 When Bacchides heard of this, he came with a large force on the sabbath day to the banks of the Jordan. **44** And Jonathan said to those with him, "Let us get up now and fight for our lives, for today things are not as they were before. **45** For look! the battle is in front of us and behind us; the water of the Jordan is on this side and on that, with marsh and thicket; there is no place to turn. **46** Cry out now to Heaven that you may be delivered from the hands of our enemies." **47** So the battle began, and Jonathan stretched out his hand to strike Bacchides, but he eluded him and went to the rear. **48** Then Jonathan and the men with him leaped into the Jordan and swam across to the other side, and the enemy*a* did not cross the Jordan to attack them. **49** And about one thousand of Bacchides' men fell that day.

Bacchides Builds Fortifications

50 Then Bacchides*b* returned to Jerusalem and built strong cities in Judea: the fortress in Jericho, and Emmaus, and Beth-horon, and Bethel, and Timnath, and*c* Pharathon, and Tephon, with high walls and gates and bars. **51** And he placed garrisons in them to harass Israel. **52** He also fortified the town of Beth-zur, and Gazara, and the citadel, and in them he put troops and stores of food. **53** And he took the sons of the leading men of the land as hostages and put them under guard in the citadel at Jerusalem.

54 In the one hundred and fifty-third year,*d* in the second month, Alcimus gave orders to tear down the wall of the inner court of the sanctuary. He tore down the work of the prophets! **55** But he only began to tear it down, for at that time Alcimus was stricken and his work was hindered; his mouth was stopped and he was paralyzed, so that he could no longer say a word or give commands concerning his house. **56** And Alcimus died at that time in great agony. **57** When Bacchides saw that Alcimus was dead, he returned to the king, and the land of Judah had rest for two years.

The End of the War

58 Then all the lawless plotted and said, "See! Jonathan and his men are living in quiet and confidence. So now let us bring Bacchides back, and he will capture them all in one night." **59** And they went and consulted with him. **60** He started to come with a large force, and secretly sent letters to all his allies in Judea, telling them to seize Jonathan and his men; but they were unable to

a Gk they *b* Gk he *c* Some authorities omit *and* *d* 159 B.C.

9:54–57—*Alcimus*, high priest appointed by Demetrius I and leader of the renegade Jews, dies a painful death. The Maccabees see this as divine punishment that justifies their rule. Bacchides leaves and the resulting peace gives Jonathan a chance to regroup. It is comforting and yet dangerous to believe that God is exclusively on one's own side.

do it, because their plan became known. [61] And Jonathan's men[a] seized about fifty of the men of the country who were leaders in this treachery, and killed them.

62 Then Jonathan with his men, and Simon, withdrew to Bethbasi in the wilderness; he rebuilt the parts of it that had been demolished, and they fortified it. [63] When Bacchides learned of this, he assembled all his forces, and sent orders to the men of Judea. [64] Then he came and encamped against Bethbasi; he fought against it for many days and made machines of war.

65 But Jonathan left his brother Simon in the town, while he went out into the country; and he went with only a few men. [66] He struck down Odomera and his kindred and the people of Phasiron in their tents. [67] Then he[b] began to attack and went into battle with his forces; and Simon and his men sallied out from the town and set fire to the machines of war. [68] They fought with Bacchides, and he was crushed by them. They pressed him very hard, for his plan and his expedition had been in vain. [69] So he was very angry at the renegades who had counseled him to come into the country, and he killed many of them. Then he decided to go back to his own land.

70 When Jonathan learned of this, he sent ambassadors to him to make peace with him and obtain release of the captives. [71] He agreed, and did as he said; and he swore to Jonathan[c] that he would not try to harm him as long as he lived. [72] He restored to him the captives whom he had taken previously from the land of Judah; then he turned and went back to his own land, and did not come again into their territory. [73] Thus the sword ceased from Israel. Jonathan settled in Michmash and began to judge the people; and he destroyed the godless out of Israel.

Revolt of Alexander Epiphanes

10 In the one hundred sixtieth year[d] Alexander Epiphanes, son of Antiochus, landed and occupied Ptolemais. They welcomed him, and there he began to reign. [2] When King Demetrius heard of it, he assembled a very large army and marched out to meet him in battle. [3] Demetrius sent Jonathan a letter in peaceable words to honor him; [4] for he said to himself, "Let us act first to make peace with him[e] before he makes peace with Alexander against us, [5] for he will remember all the wrongs that we did to him and to his brothers and his nation." [6] So Demetrius[f] gave him authority to recruit troops, to equip them with arms, and to become his ally; and he commanded that the hostages in the citadel should be released to him.

7 Then Jonathan came to Jerusalem and read the letter in the hearing of all the people and of those in the citadel. [8] They were greatly alarmed when they heard that the king had given him authority to recruit troops. [9] But those in the citadel released the hostages to Jonathan, and he returned them to their parents.

10 And Jonathan took up residence in Jerusalem and began to rebuild and restore the city. [11] He directed those who were doing the work to build the walls and encircle Mount Zion with squared stones, for better fortification; and they did so.

12 Then the foreigners who were in the strongholds that Bacchides had built fled; [13] all of them left their places and went back to their own lands. [14] Only in Beth-zur did some remain who had forsaken the law and the commandments, for it served as a place of refuge.

15 Now King Alexander heard of all the promises that Demetrius had sent to Jonathan, and he heard of the battles that Jonathan[f] and his brothers had fought, of the brave deeds that they had done, and of the troubles that they had endured. [16] So he said, "Shall we find another such man? Come now, we will

a Gk they   *b* Other ancient authorities read *they*   *c* Gk *him*   *d* 152 B.C.
e Gk *them*   *f* Gk *he*

make him our friend and ally." ¹⁷ And he wrote a letter and sent it to him, in the following words:

Jonathan Becomes High Priest

18 "King Alexander to his brother Jonathan, greetings. ¹⁹ We have heard about you, that you are a mighty warrior and worthy to be our friend. ²⁰ And so we have appointed you today to be the high priest of your nation; you are to be called the king's Friend and you are to take our side and keep friendship with us." He also sent him a purple robe and a golden crown.

21 So Jonathan put on the sacred vestments in the seventh month of the one hundred sixtieth year,ᵃ at the festival of booths,ᵇ and he recruited troops and equipped them with arms in abundance. ²² When Demetrius heard of these things he was distressed and said, ²³ "What is this that we have done? Alexander has gotten ahead of us in forming a friendship with the Jews to strengthen himself. ²⁴ I also will write them words of encouragement and promise them honor and gifts, so that I may have their help." ²⁵ So he sent a message to them in the following words:

A Letter from Demetrius to Jonathan

"King Demetrius to the nation of the Jews, greetings. ²⁶ Since you have kept your agreement with us and have continued your friendship with us, and have not sided with our enemies, we have heard of it and rejoiced. ²⁷ Now continue still to keep faith with us, and we will repay you with good for what you do for us. ²⁸ We will grant you many immunities and give you gifts.

29 "I now free you and exempt all the Jews from payment of tribute and salt tax and crown levies, ³⁰ and instead of collecting the third of the grain and the half of the fruit of the trees that I should receive, I release them from this day and henceforth. I will not collect them from the land of Judah or from the three districts added to it from Samaria and Galilee, from this day and for all time. ³¹ Jerusalem and its environs, its tithes and its revenues, shall be holy and free from tax. ³² I release also my control of the citadel in Jerusalem and give it to the high priest, so that he may station in it men of his own choice to guard it. ³³ And everyone of the Jews taken as a captive from the land of Judah into any part of my kingdom, I set free without payment; and let all officials cancel also the taxes on their livestock.

34 "All the festivals and sabbaths and new moons and appointed days, and the three days before a festival and the three after a festival—let them all be days of immunity and release for all the Jews who are in my kingdom. ³⁵ No one shall have authority to exact anything from them or annoy any of them about any matter.

36 "Let Jews be enrolled in the king's forces to the number of thirty thousand men, and let the maintenance be given them that is due to all the forces of the king. ³⁷ Let some of them be stationed in the great strongholds of the king, and let some of them be put in positions of trust in the kingdom. Let their officers and leaders be of their own number, and let them live by their own laws, just as the king has commanded in the land of Judah.

38 "As for the three districts that have been added to Judea from the country of Samaria, let them be annexed to Judea so that they may be considered to be under

ᵃ 152 B.C. ᵇ Or tabernacles

10:20—Jonathan benefits from the rivalry between Demetrius I and Alexander Balas for the Seleucid throne; in 152 BCE he is named high priest (though not of the high-priestly line) by the latter in exchange for his support. Smaller nations have played one side against the other for their own survival throughout history, which is sometimes difficult for powerful nations to understand.

10:25–45—Letter from Demetrius I to Jonathan, with promises of tax exemption, religious freedom, and a subsidy for Jerusalem.

one ruler and obey no other authority than the high priest. ³⁹ Ptolemais and the land adjoining it I have given as a gift to the sanctuary in Jerusalem, to meet the necessary expenses of the sanctuary. ⁴⁰ I also grant fifteen thousand shekels of silver yearly out of the king's revenues from appropriate places. ⁴¹ And all the additional funds that the government officials have not paid as they did in the first years,ᵃ they shall give from now on for the service of the temple.ᵇ ⁴² Moreover, the five thousand shekels of silver that my officialsᶜ have received every year from the income of the services of the temple, this too is canceled, because it belongs to the priests who minister there. ⁴³ And all who take refuge at the temple in Jerusalem, or in any of its precincts, because they owe money to the king or are in debt, let them be released and receive back all their property in my kingdom.

44 "Let the cost of rebuilding and restoring the structures of the sanctuary be paid from the revenues of the king. ⁴⁵ And let the cost of rebuilding the walls of Jerusalem and fortifying it all around, and the cost of rebuilding the walls in Judea, also be paid from the revenues of the king."

Death of Demetrius

46 When Jonathan and the people heard these words, they did not believe or accept them, because they remembered the great wrongs that Demetriusᵈ had done in Israel and how much he had oppressed them. ⁴⁷ They favored Alexander, because he had been the first to speak peaceable words to them, and they remained his allies all his days. ⁴⁸ Now King Alexander assembled large forces and encamped opposite Demetrius. ⁴⁹ The two kings met in battle, and the army of Demetrius fled, and Alexanderᵉ pursued him and defeated them. ⁵⁰ He pressed the battle strongly

until the sun set, and on that day Demetrius fell.

Treaty of Ptolemy and Alexander

51 Then Alexander sent ambassadors to Ptolemy king of Egypt with the following message: ⁵² "Since I have returned to my kingdom and have taken my seat on the throne of my ancestors, and established my rule—for I crushed Demetrius and gained control of our country; ⁵³ I met him in battle, and he and his army were crushed by us, and we have taken our seat on the throne of his kingdom— ⁵⁴ now therefore let us establish friendship with one another; give me now your daughter as my wife, and I will become your son-in-law, and will make gifts to you and to her in keeping with your position."

55 Ptolemy the king replied and said, "Happy was the day on which you returned to the land of your ancestors and took your seat on the throne of their kingdom. ⁵⁶ And now I will do for you as you wrote, but meet me at Ptolemais, so that we may see one another, and I will become your father-in-law, as you have said."

57 So Ptolemy set out from Egypt, he and his daughter Cleopatra, and came to Ptolemais in the one hundred sixty-second year.ᶠ ⁵⁸ King Alexander met him, and Ptolemyᵃ gave him his daughter Cleopatra in marriage, and celebrated her wedding at Ptolemais with great pomp, as kings do.

59 Then King Alexander wrote to Jonathan to come and meet him. ⁶⁰ So he went with pomp to Ptolemais and met the two kings; he gave them and their Friends silver and gold and many gifts, and found favor with them. ⁶¹ A group of malcontents from Israel, renegades, gathered together against him to accuse him; but the king paid no attention to them. ⁶² The king gave orders to take off

ᵃ Meaning of Gk uncertain ᵇ Gk house ᶜ Gk they ᵈ Gk he ᵉ Other ancient authorities read *Alexander fled, and Demetrius* ᶠ 150 B.C.

10:46–11:74—Jonathan's victories. His power grows after Demetrius I dies.

Jonathan's garments and to clothe him in purple, and they did so. ⁶³ The king also seated him at his side; and he said to his officers, "Go out with him into the middle of the city and proclaim that no one is to bring charges against him about any matter, and let no one annoy him for any reason." ⁶⁴ When his accusers saw the honor that was paid him, in accord with the proclamation, and saw him clothed in purple, they all fled. ⁶⁵ Thus the king honored him and enrolled him among his chief*a* Friends, and made him general and governor of the province. ⁶⁶ And Jonathan returned to Jerusalem in peace and gladness.

Apollonius Is Defeated by Jonathan

⁶⁷ In the one hundred sixty-fifth year*b* Demetrius son of Demetrius came from Crete to the land of his ancestors. ⁶⁸ When King Alexander heard of it, he was greatly distressed and returned to Antioch. ⁶⁹ And Demetrius appointed Apollonius the governor of Coelesyria, and he assembled a large force and encamped against Jamnia. Then he sent the following message to the high priest Jonathan:

⁷⁰ "You are the only one to rise up against us, and I have fallen into ridicule and disgrace because of you. Why do you assume authority against us in the hill country? ⁷¹ If you now have confidence in your forces, come down to the plain to meet us, and let us match strength with each other there, for I have with me the power of the cities. ⁷² Ask and learn who I am and who the others are that are helping us. People will tell you that you cannot stand before us, for your ancestors were twice put to flight in their own land. ⁷³ And now you will not be able to withstand my cavalry and such an army in the plain, where there is no stone or pebble, or place to flee."

⁷⁴ When Jonathan heard the words of Apollonius, his spirit was aroused. He chose ten thousand men and set out from Jerusalem, and his brother Simon met

him to help him. ⁷⁵ He encamped before Joppa, but the people of the city closed its gates, for Apollonius had a garrison in Joppa. ⁷⁶ So they fought against it, and the people of the city became afraid and opened the gates, and Jonathan gained possession of Joppa.

⁷⁷ When Apollonius heard of it, he mustered three thousand cavalry and a large army, and went to Azotus as though he were going farther. At the same time he advanced into the plain, for he had a large troop of cavalry and put confidence in it. ⁷⁸ Jonathan*c* pursued him to Azotus, and the armies engaged in battle. ⁷⁹ Now Apollonius had secretly left a thousand cavalry behind them. ⁸⁰ Jonathan learned that there was an ambush behind him, for they surrounded his army and shot arrows at his men from early morning until late afternoon. ⁸¹ But his men stood fast, as Jonathan had commanded, and the enemy's*d* horses grew tired.

⁸² Then Simon brought forward his force and engaged the phalanx in battle (for the cavalry was exhausted); they were overwhelmed by him and fled, ⁸³ and the cavalry was dispersed in the plain. They fled to Azotus and entered Beth-dagon, the temple of their idol, for safety. ⁸⁴ But Jonathan burned Azotus and the surrounding towns and plundered them; and the temple of Dagon, and those who had taken refuge in it, he burned with fire. ⁸⁵ The number of those who fell by the sword, with those burned alive, came to eight thousand.

⁸⁶ Then Jonathan left there and encamped against Askalon, and the people of the city came out to meet him with great pomp.

⁸⁷ He and those with him then returned to Jerusalem with a large amount of booty. ⁸⁸ When King Alexander heard of these things, he honored Jonathan still more; ⁸⁹ and he sent to him a golden buckle, such as it is the custom to give to the King's Kinsmen. He also

a Gk first *b* 147 B.C. *c* Gk he *d* Gk their

gave him Ekron and all its environs as his possession.

Ptolemy Invades Syria

11 Then the king of Egypt gathered great forces, like the sand by the seashore, and many ships; and he tried to get possession of Alexander's kingdom by trickery and add it to his own kingdom. ² He set out for Syria with peaceable words, and the people of the towns opened their gates to him and went to meet him, for King Alexander had commanded them to meet him, since he was Alexander's*ᵃ* father-in-law. ³ But when Ptolemy entered the towns he stationed forces as a garrison in each town.

4 When he*ᵇ* approached Azotus, they showed him the burnt-out temple of Dagon, and Azotus and its suburbs destroyed, and the corpses lying about, and the charred bodies of those whom Jonathan*ᶜ* had burned in the war, for they had piled them in heaps along his route. ⁵ They also told the king what Jonathan had done, to throw blame on him; but the king kept silent. ⁶ Jonathan met the king at Joppa with pomp, and they greeted one another and spent the night there. ⁷ And Jonathan went with the king as far as the river called Eleutherus; then he returned to Jerusalem.

8 So King Ptolemy gained control of the coastal cities as far as Seleucia by the sea, and he kept devising wicked designs against Alexander. ⁹ He sent envoys to King Demetrius, saying, "Come, let us make a covenant with each other, and I will give you in marriage my daughter who was Alexander's wife, and you shall reign over your father's kingdom. ¹⁰ I now regret that I gave him my daughter, for he has tried to kill me." ¹¹ He threw blame on Alexander*ᵈ* because he coveted his kingdom. ¹² So he took his daughter away from him and gave her to Demetrius. He was estranged from Alexander, and their enmity became manifest.

13 Then Ptolemy entered Antioch and put on the crown of Asia. Thus he put two crowns on his head, the crown of Egypt and that of Asia. ¹⁴ Now King Alexander was in Cilicia at that time, because the people of that region were in revolt. ¹⁵ When Alexander heard of it, he came against him in battle. Ptolemy marched out and met him with a strong force, and put him to flight. ¹⁶ So Alexander fled into Arabia to find protection there, and King Ptolemy was triumphant. ¹⁷ Zabdiel the Arab cut off the head of Alexander and sent it to Ptolemy. ¹⁸ But King Ptolemy died three days later, and his troops in the strongholds were killed by the inhabitants of the strongholds. ¹⁹ So Demetrius became king in the one hundred sixty-seventh year.*ᵉ*

Jonathan's Diplomacy

20 In those days Jonathan assembled the Judeans to attack the citadel in Jerusalem, and he built many engines of war to use against it. ²¹ But certain renegades who hated their nation went to the king and reported to him that Jonathan was besieging the citadel. ²² When he heard this he was angry, and as soon as he heard it he set out and came to Ptolemais; and he wrote Jonathan not to continue the siege, but to meet him for a conference at Ptolemais as quickly as possible.

23 When Jonathan heard this, he gave orders to continue the siege. He chose some of the elders of Israel and some of the priests, and put himself in danger, ²⁴ for he went to the king at Ptolemais, taking silver and gold and clothing and numerous other gifts. And he won his favor. ²⁵ Although certain renegades of his nation kept making complaints against him, ²⁶ the king treated him as his predecessors had treated him; he exalted him in the presence of all his Friends. ²⁷ He confirmed him in the high priesthood and in as many other honors as he had formerly had, and caused him to be reckoned among his chief*ᶠ*

ᵃ Gk *his*   *ᵇ* Other ancient authorities read *they*   *ᶜ* Gk *he*   *ᵈ* Gk *him*
ᵉ 145 B.C.   *ᶠ* Gk *first*

Friends. ²⁸ Then Jonathan asked the king to free Judea and the three districts of Samaria*a* from tribute, and promised him three hundred talents. ²⁹ The king consented, and wrote a letter to Jonathan about all these things; its contents were as follows:

³⁰ "King Demetrius to his brother Jonathan and to the nation of the Jews, greetings. ³¹ This copy of the letter that we wrote concerning you to our kinsman Lasthenes we have written to you also, so that you may know what it says. ³² 'King Demetrius to his father Lasthenes, greetings. ³³ We have determined to do good to the nation of the Jews, who are our friends and fulfill their obligations to us, because of the goodwill they show toward us. ³⁴ We have confirmed as their possession both the territory of Judea and the three districts of Aphairema and Lydda and Rathamin; the latter, with all the region bordering them, were added to Judea from Samaria. To all those who offer sacrifice in Jerusalem we have granted release from*b* the royal taxes that the king formerly received from them each year, from the crops of the land and the fruit of the trees. ³⁵ And the other payments henceforth due to us of the tithes, and the taxes due to us, and the salt pits and the crown taxes due to us—from all these we shall grant them release. ³⁶ And not one of these grants shall be canceled from this time on forever. ³⁷ Now therefore take care to make a copy of this, and let it be given to Jonathan and put up in a conspicuous place on the holy mountain.' "

The Intrigue of Trypho

³⁸ When King Demetrius saw that the land was quiet before him and that there was no opposition to him, he dismissed all his troops, all of them to their own homes, except the foreign troops that he had recruited from the islands of the nations. So all the troops who had served under his predecessors hated him. ³⁹ A certain Trypho had formerly been one of Alexander's supporters; he saw that all the troops were grumbling against Demetrius. So he went to Imalkue the Arab, who was bringing up Antiochus, the young son of Alexander, ⁴⁰ and insistently urged him to hand Antiochus*c* over to him, to become king in place of his father. He also reported to Imalkue*c* what Demetrius had done and told of the hatred that the troops of Demetrius*d* had for him; and he stayed there many days.

41 Now Jonathan sent to King Demetrius the request that he remove the troops of the citadel from Jerusalem, and the troops in the strongholds; for they kept fighting against Israel. ⁴² And Demetrius sent this message back to Jonathan: "Not only will I do these things for you and your nation, but I will confer great honor on you and your nation, if I find an opportunity. ⁴³ Now then you will do well to send me men who will help me, for all my troops have revolted." ⁴⁴ So Jonathan sent three thousand stalwart men to him at Antioch, and when they came to the king, the king rejoiced at their arrival.

45 Then the people of the city assembled within the city, to the number of a hundred and twenty thousand, and they wanted to kill the king. ⁴⁶ But the king fled into the palace. Then the people of the city seized the main streets of the city and began to fight. ⁴⁷ So the king called the Jews to his aid, and they all rallied around him and then spread

a Cn: Gk the three districts and Samaria   *b* Or Samaria, for all those who offer sacrifice in Jerusalem, in place of   *c* Gk him   *d* Gk his troops

---

11:41–53—Jonathan's alliance with Demetrius II results in the Jewish slaughter of thousands of civilians in Antioch who had legitimate grievances against Demetrius. The acquisition of "booty" (NRSV *spoil*, vv. 48, 51; cf. 10:87–89) does not justify their actions. Jonathan has been co-opted by the Seleucid bureaucracy. Shifting alliances are often necessary for a nation's survival in our present global context, but often at too high a cost.

out through the city; and they killed on that day about one hundred thousand. [48] They set fire to the city and seized a large amount of spoil on that day, and saved the king. [49] When the people of the city saw that the Jews had gained control of the city as they pleased, their courage failed and they cried out to the king with this entreaty: [50] "Grant us peace, and make the Jews stop fighting against us and our city." [51] And they threw down their arms and made peace. So the Jews gained glory in the sight of the king and of all the people in his kingdom, and they returned to Jerusalem with a large amount of spoil.

[52] So King Demetrius sat on the throne of his kingdom, and the land was quiet before him. [53] But he broke his word about all that he had promised; he became estranged from Jonathan and did not repay the favors that Jonathan[a] had done him, but treated him very harshly.

Trypho Seizes Power

[54] After this Trypho returned, and with him the young boy Antiochus who began to reign and put on the crown. [55] All the troops that Demetrius had discharged gathered around him; they fought against Demetrius,[b] and he fled and was routed. [56] Trypho captured the elephants[c] and gained control of Antioch. [57] Then the young Antiochus wrote to Jonathan, saying, "I confirm you in the high priesthood and set you over the four districts and make you one of the king's Friends." [58] He also sent him gold plates and a table service, and granted him the right to drink from gold cups and dress in purple and wear a gold buckle. [59] He appointed Jonathan's[d] brother Simon governor from the Ladder of Tyre to the borders of Egypt.

Campaigns of Jonathan and Simon

[60] Then Jonathan set out and traveled beyond the river and among the towns, and all the army of Syria gathered to him as allies. When he came to Askalon, the people of the city met him and paid him honor. [61] From there he went to Gaza, but the people of Gaza shut him out. So he besieged it and burned its suburbs with fire and plundered them. [62] Then the people of Gaza pleaded with Jonathan, and he made peace with them, and took the sons of their rulers as hostages and sent them to Jerusalem. And he passed through the country as far as Damascus.

[63] Then Jonathan heard that the officers of Demetrius had come to Kadesh in Galilee with a large army, intending to remove him from office. [64] He went to meet them, but left his brother Simon in the country. [65] Simon encamped before Beth-zur and fought against it for many days and hemmed it in. [66] Then they asked him to grant them terms of peace, and he did so. He removed them from there, took possession of the town, and set a garrison over it.

[67] Jonathan and his army encamped by the waters of Gennesaret. Early in the morning they marched to the plain of Hazor, [68] and there in the plain the army of the foreigners met him; they had set an ambush against him in the mountains, but they themselves met him face to face. [69] Then the men in ambush emerged from their places and joined battle. [70] All the men with Jonathan fled; not one of them was left except Mattathias son of Absalom and Judas son of Chalphi, commanders of the forces of the army. [71] Jonathan tore his clothes, put dust on his head, and prayed. [72] Then he turned back to the battle against the enemy[e] and routed them, and they fled. [73] When his men who were fleeing saw this, they returned to him and joined him in the pursuit as far as Kadesh, to their camp, and there they encamped. [74] As many as three thousand of the foreigners fell that day. And Jonathan returned to Jerusalem.

[a] Gk he   [b] Gk him   [c] Gk animals   [d] Gk his   [e] Gk them

Alliances with Rome and Sparta

12 Now when Jonathan saw that the time was favorable for him, he chose men and sent them to Rome to confirm and renew the friendship with them. [2] He also sent letters to the same effect to the Spartans and to other places. [3] So they went to Rome and entered the senate chamber and said, "The high priest Jonathan and the Jewish nation have sent us to renew the former friendship and alliance with them." [4] And the Romans[a] gave them letters to the people in every place, asking them to provide for the envoys[b] safe conduct to the land of Judah.

5 This is a copy of the letter that Jonathan wrote to the Spartans: [6] "The high priest Jonathan, the senate of the nation, the priests, and the rest of the Jewish people to their brothers the Spartans, greetings. [7] Already in time past a letter was sent to the high priest Onias from Arius,[c] who was king among you, stating that you are our brothers, as the appended copy shows. [8] Onias welcomed the envoy with honor, and received the letter, which contained a clear declaration of alliance and friendship. [9] Therefore, though we have no need of these things, since we have as encouragement the holy books that are in our hands, [10] we have undertaken to send to renew our family ties and friendship with you, so that we may not become estranged from you, for considerable time has passed since you sent your letter to us. [11] We therefore remember you constantly on every occasion, both at our festivals and on other appropriate days, at the sacrifices that we offer and in our prayers, as it is right and proper to remember brothers. [12] And we rejoice in your glory. [13] But as for ourselves, many trials and many wars have encircled us; the kings around us have waged war against us. [14] We were unwilling to annoy you and our other allies and friends with these wars, [15] for we have the help that comes from Heaven for our aid, and so we were delivered from our enemies, and our enemies were humbled. [16] We therefore have chosen Numenius son of Antiochus and Antipater son of Jason, and have sent them to Rome to renew our former friendship and alliance with them. [17] We have commanded them to go also to you and greet you and deliver to you this letter from us concerning the renewal of our family ties. [18] And now please send us a reply to this."

19 This is a copy of the letter that they sent to Onias: [20] "King Arius of the Spartans, to the high priest Onias, greetings. [21] It has been found in writing concerning the Spartans and the Jews that they are brothers and are of the family of Abraham. [22] And now that we have learned this, please write us concerning your welfare; [23] we on our part write to you that your livestock and your property belong to us, and ours belong to you. We therefore command that our envoys[a] report to you accordingly."

Further Campaigns of Jonathan and Simon

24 Now Jonathan heard that the commanders of Demetrius had returned, with a larger force than before, to wage war against him. [25] So he marched away from Jerusalem and met them in the region of Hamath, for he gave them no opportunity to invade his own country. [26] He sent spies to their camp, and they returned and reported to him that the enemy[a] were being drawn up in formation to attack the Jews[b] by night. [27] So when the sun had set, Jonathan commanded his troops to be alert and to keep their arms at hand so as to be ready all night for battle, and he stationed outposts around the camp. [28] When

a Gk they b Gk them c Vg Compare verse 20: Gk Darius

12:1–53—With his increased prestige, Jonathan engages in diplomacy with the Romans and Spartans. The shrewd Jonathan extends Judea's borders and organizes a powerful army. We are reminded that diplomacy can keep war at bay.

the enemy heard that Jonathan and his troops were prepared for battle, they were afraid and were terrified at heart; so they kindled fires in their camp and withdrew.[a] 29 But Jonathan and his troops did not know it until morning, for they saw the fires burning. 30 Then Jonathan pursued them, but he did not overtake them, for they had crossed the Eleutherus river. 31 So Jonathan turned aside against the Arabs who are called Zabadeans, and he crushed them and plundered them. 32 Then he broke camp and went to Damascus, and marched through all that region.

33 Simon also went out and marched through the country as far as Askalon and the neighboring strongholds. He turned aside to Joppa and took it by surprise, 34 for he had heard that they were ready to hand over the stronghold to those whom Demetrius had sent. And he stationed a garrison there to guard it.

35 When Jonathan returned he convened the elders of the people and planned with them to build strongholds in Judea, 36 to build the walls of Jerusalem still higher, and to erect a high barrier between the citadel and the city to separate it from the city, in order to isolate it so that its garrison[b] could neither buy nor sell. 37 So they gathered together to rebuild the city; part of the wall on the valley to the east had fallen, and he repaired the section called Chaphenatha. 38 Simon also built Adida in the Shephelah; he fortified it and installed gates with bolts.

Trypho Captures Jonathan

39 Then Trypho attempted to become king in Asia and put on the crown, and to raise his hand against King Antiochus. 40 He feared that Jonathan might not permit him to do so, but might make war on him, so he kept seeking to seize and kill him, and he marched out and came to Beth-shan. 41 Jonathan went out to meet him with forty thousand picked warriors, and he came to Beth-shan. 42 When Trypho saw that he had come with a large army, he was afraid to raise his hand against him. 43 So he received him with honor and commended him to all his Friends, and he gave him gifts and commanded his Friends and his troops to obey him as they would himself. 44 Then he said to Jonathan, "Why have you put all these people to so much trouble when we are not at war? 45 Dismiss them now to their homes and choose for yourself a few men to stay with you, and come with me to Ptolemais. I will hand it over to you as well as the other strongholds and the remaining troops and all the officials, and will turn around and go home. For that is why I am here."

46 Jonathan[c] trusted him and did as he said; he sent away the troops, and they returned to the land of Judah. 47 He kept with himself three thousand men, two thousand of whom he left in Galilee, while one thousand accompanied him. 48 But when Jonathan entered Ptolemais, the people of Ptolemais closed the gates and seized him, and they killed with the sword all who had entered with him.

49 Then Trypho sent troops and cavalry into Galilee and the Great Plain to destroy all Jonathan's soldiers. 50 But they realized that Jonathan had been seized and had perished along with his men, and they encouraged one another and kept marching in close formation, ready for battle. 51 When their pursuers saw that they would fight for their lives, they turned back. 52 So they all reached the land of Judah safely, and they mourned for Jonathan and his companions and were in great fear; and all

---

[a] Other ancient authorities omit *and withdrew* [b] Gk *they* [c] Gk *he*

12:39–53—Jonathan is captured by a deceptive Trypho. In his effort to survive, we must ask what Jonathan sacrificed in the process and whether his compromises were morally acceptable. Politics and ambition can overshadow religious faith.

Israel mourned deeply. [53] All the nations around them tried to destroy them, for they said, "They have no leader or helper. Now therefore let us make war on them and blot out the memory of them from humankind."

Simon Takes Command

13 Simon heard that Trypho had assembled a large army to invade the land of Judah and destroy it, [2] and he saw that the people were trembling with fear. So he went up to Jerusalem, and gathering the people together [3] he encouraged them, saying to them, "You yourselves know what great things my brothers and I and the house of my father have done for the laws and the sanctuary; you know also the wars and the difficulties that my brothers and I have seen. [4] By reason of this all my brothers have perished for the sake of Israel, and I alone am left. [5] And now, far be it from me to spare my life in any time of distress, for I am not better than my brothers. [6] But I will avenge my nation and the sanctuary and your wives and children, for all the nations have gathered together out of hatred to destroy us."

[7] The spirit of the people was rekindled when they heard these words, [8] and they answered in a loud voice, "You are our leader in place of Judas and your brother Jonathan. [9] Fight our battles, and all that you say to us we will do." [10] So he assembled all the warriors and hurried to complete the walls of Jerusalem, and he fortified it on every side. [11] He sent Jonathan son of Absalom to Joppa, and with him a considerable army; he drove out its occupants and remained there.

Deceit and Treachery of Trypho

[12] Then Trypho left Ptolemais with a large army to invade the land of Judah, and Jonathan was with him under guard. [13] Simon encamped in Adida, facing the plain. [14] Trypho learned that Simon had risen up in place of his brother Jonathan, and that he was about to join battle with him, so he sent envoys to him and said, [15] "It is for the money that your brother Jonathan owed the royal treasury, in connection with the offices he held, that we are detaining him. [16] Send now one hundred talents of silver and two of his sons as hostages, so that when released he will not revolt against us, and we will release him."

[17] Simon knew that they were speaking deceitfully to him, but he sent to get the money and the sons, so that he would not arouse great hostility among the people, who might say, [18] "It was because Simon[a] did not send him the money and the sons, that Jonathan[b] perished." [19] So he sent the sons and the hundred talents, but Trypho[b] broke his word and did not release Jonathan.

[20] After this Trypho came to invade the country and destroy it, and he circled around by the way to Adora. But Simon and his army kept marching along opposite him to every place he went. [21] Now the men in the citadel kept sending envoys to Trypho urging him to come to them by way of the wilderness and to send them food. [22] So Trypho got all his cavalry ready to go, but that night a very heavy snow fell, and he did not go because of the snow. He marched off and went into the land of Gilead. [23] When he approached Baskama, he killed Jonathan, and he was buried there. [24] Then Trypho turned and went back to his own land.

Jonathan's Tomb

[25] Simon sent and took the bones of his brother Jonathan, and buried him in

[a] Gk I [b] Gk he

13:1–16:24 Simon and John Hyrcanus

13:7–10—In gratitude for his service, the people and Jewish leaders proclaim Simon leader and high priest (later confirmed by Demetrius II) in 142 BCE (14:41). Though not in the line of Zadok or David, the Hasmoneans wield the power of king and high priest.

Modein, the city of his ancestors. ²⁶ All Israel bewailed him with great lamentation, and mourned for him many days. ²⁷ And Simon built a monument over the tomb of his father and his brothers; he made it high so that it might be seen, with polished stone at the front and back. ²⁸ He also erected seven pyramids, opposite one another, for his father and mother and four brothers. ²⁹ For the pyramids*a* he devised an elaborate setting, erecting about them great columns, and on the columns he put suits of armor for a permanent memorial, and beside the suits of armor he carved ships, so that they could be seen by all who sail the sea. ³⁰ This is the tomb that he built in Modein; it remains to this day.

Judea Gains Independence

31 Trypho dealt treacherously with the young King Antiochus; he killed him ³² and became king in his place, putting on the crown of Asia; and he brought great calamity on the land. ³³ But Simon built up the strongholds of Judea and walled them all around, with high towers and great walls and gates and bolts, and he stored food in the strongholds. ³⁴ Simon also chose emissaries and sent them to King Demetrius with a request to grant relief to the country, for all that Trypho did was to plunder. ³⁵ King Demetrius sent him a favorable reply to this request, and wrote him a letter as follows, ³⁶ "King Demetrius to Simon, the high priest and friend of kings, and to the elders and nation of the Jews, greetings. ³⁷ We have received the gold crown and the palm branch that you*b* sent, and we are ready to make a general peace with you and to write to our officials to grant you release from tribute. ³⁸ All the grants that we have made to you remain valid, and let the strongholds that you have built be your possession. ³⁹ We pardon any errors and offenses committed to this day, and cancel the crown tax

that you owe; and whatever other tax has been collected in Jerusalem shall be collected no longer. ⁴⁰ And if any of you are qualified to be enrolled in our bodyguard,*c* let them be enrolled, and let there be peace between us."

41 In the one hundred seventieth year*d* the yoke of the Gentiles was removed from Israel, ⁴² and the people began to write in their documents and contracts, "In the first year of Simon the great high priest and commander and leader of the Jews."

The Capture of Gazara by Simon

43 In those days Simon*e* encamped against Gazara*f* and surrounded it with troops. He made a siege engine, brought it up to the city, and battered and captured one tower. ⁴⁴ The men in the siege engine leaped out into the city, and a great tumult arose in the city. ⁴⁵ The men in the city, with their wives and children, went up on the wall with their clothes torn, and they cried out with a loud voice, asking Simon to make peace with them; ⁴⁶ they said, "Do not treat us according to our wicked acts but according to your mercy." ⁴⁷ So Simon reached an agreement with them and stopped fighting against them. But he expelled them from the city and cleansed the houses in which the idols were located, and then entered it with hymns and praise. ⁴⁸ He removed all uncleanness from it, and settled in it those who observed the law. He also strengthened its fortifications and built in it a house for himself.

Simon Regains the Citadel at Jerusalem

49 Those who were in the citadel at Jerusalem were prevented from going in and out to buy and sell in the country. So they were very hungry, and many of them perished from famine. ⁵⁰ Then

a Gk For these *b* The word you in verses 37-40 is plural *c* Or court *d* 142 B.C. *e* Gk he *f* Cn: Gk Gaza

---

13:49–52—Simon finally expels foreign troops from the Akra (*citadel*); the Maccabean victory is now complete.

they cried to Simon to make peace with them, and he did so. But he expelled them from there and cleansed the citadel from its pollutions. ⁵¹ On the twenty-third day of the second month, in the one hundred seventy-first year,ᵃ the Jewsᵇ entered it with praise and palm branches, and with harps and cymbals and stringed instruments, and with hymns and songs, because a great enemy had been crushed and removed from Israel. ⁵² Simonᶜ decreed that every year they should celebrate this day with rejoicing. He strengthened the fortifications of the temple hill alongside the citadel, and he and his men lived there. ⁵³ Simon saw that his son John had reached manhood, and so he made him commander of all the forces; and he lived at Gazara.

Capture of Demetrius

14 In the one hundred seventy-second yearᵈ King Demetrius assembled his forces and marched into Media to obtain help, so that he could make war against Trypho. ² When King Arsaces of Persia and Media heard that Demetrius had invaded his territory, he sent one of his generals to take him alive. ³ The generalᶜ went and defeated the army of Demetrius, and seized him and took him to Arsaces, who put him under guard.

Eulogy of Simon

⁴ The landᵉ had rest all the days of Simon.
He sought the good of his nation;
his rule was pleasing to them,
as was the honor shown him, all his days.
⁵ To crown all his honors he took Joppa for a harbor,
and opened a way to the isles of the sea.
⁶ He extended the borders of his nation,

and gained full control of the country.
⁷ He gathered a host of captives;
he ruled over Gazara and Beth-zur and the citadel,
and he removed its uncleanness from it;
and there was none to oppose him.
⁸ They tilled their land in peace;
the ground gave its increase,
and the trees of the plains their fruit.
⁹ Old men sat in the streets;
they all talked together of good things,
and the youths put on splendid military attire.
¹⁰ He supplied the towns with food,
and furnished them with the means of defense,
until his renown spread to the ends of the earth.
¹¹ He established peace in the land,
and Israel rejoiced with great joy.
¹² All the people sat under their own vines and fig trees,
and there was none to make them afraid.
¹³ No one was left in the land to fight them,
and the kings were crushed in those days.
¹⁴ He gave help to all the humble among his people;
he sought out the law,
and did away with all the renegades and outlaws.
¹⁵ He made the sanctuary glorious,
and added to the vessels of the sanctuary.

Diplomacy with Rome and Sparta

16 It was heard in Rome, and as far away as Sparta, that Jonathan had died, and they were deeply grieved. ¹⁷ When

ᵃ141 B.C. ᵇGk they ᶜGk He ᵈ140 B.C. ᵉOther ancient authorities add of Judah

---

14:4–15—Simon's rule is eulogized idealistically with biblical language. It is difficult to recognize the mistakes of the past when it is idealized.

they heard that his brother Simon had become high priest in his stead, and that he was ruling over the country and the towns in it, [18] they wrote to him on bronze tablets to renew with him the friendship and alliance that they had established with his brothers Judas and Jonathan. [19] And these were read before the assembly in Jerusalem.

[20] This is a copy of the letter that the Spartans sent:

"The rulers and the city of the Spartans to the high priest Simon and to the elders and the priests and the rest of the Jewish people, our brothers, greetings. [21] The envoys who were sent to our people have told us about your glory and honor, and we rejoiced at their coming. [22] We have recorded what they said in our public decrees, as follows, 'Numenius son of Antiochus and Antipater son of Jason, envoys of the Jews, have come to us to renew their friendship with us. [23] It has pleased our people to receive these men with honor and to put a copy of their words in the public archives, so that the people of the Spartans may have a record of them. And they have sent a copy of this to the high priest Simon.'"

[24] After this Simon sent Numenius to Rome with a large gold shield weighing one thousand minas, to confirm the alliance with the Romans.[a]

Official Honors for Simon

[25] When the people heard these things they said, "How shall we thank Simon and his sons? [26] For he and his brothers and the house of his father have stood firm; they have fought and repulsed Israel's enemies and established its freedom." [27] So they made a record on bronze tablets and put it on pillars on Mount Zion.

This is a copy of what they wrote: "On the eighteenth day of Elul, in the one hundred seventy-second year,[b] which is the third year of the great high priest Simon, [28] in Asaramel,[c] in the great assembly of the priests and the people

and the rulers of the nation and the elders of the country, the following was proclaimed to us:

[29] "Since wars often occurred in the country, Simon son of Mattathias, a priest of the sons[d] of Joarib, and his brothers, exposed themselves to danger and resisted the enemies of their nation, in order that their sanctuary and the law might be preserved; and they brought great glory to their nation. [30] Jonathan rallied the[e] nation, became their high priest, and was gathered to his people. [31] When their enemies decided to invade their country and lay hands on their sanctuary, [32] then Simon rose up and fought for his nation. He spent great sums of his own money; he armed the soldiers of his nation and paid them wages. [33] He fortified the towns of Judea, and Beth-zur on the borders of Judea, where formerly the arms of the enemy had been stored, and he placed there a garrison of Jews. [34] He also fortified Joppa, which is by the sea, and Gazara, which is on the borders of Azotus, where the enemy formerly lived. He settled Jews there, and provided in those towns[a] whatever was necessary for their restoration.

[35] "The people saw Simon's faithfulness[f] and the glory that he had resolved to win for his nation, and they made him their leader and high priest, because he had done all these things and because of the justice and loyalty that he had maintained toward his nation. He sought in every way to exalt his people. [36] In his days things prospered in his hands, so that the Gentiles were put out of the[e] country, as were also those in the city of David in Jerusalem, who had built themselves a citadel from which they used to sally forth and defile the environs of the sanctuary, doing great damage to its purity. [37] He settled Jews in it and fortified it for the safety of the country and

---

*a Gk them   b 140 B.C.   cThis word resembles the Hebrew words for *the court of the people of God* or *the prince of the people of God*   d Meaning of Gk uncertain   eGk their   fOther ancient authorities read *conduct**

of the city, and built the walls of Jerusalem higher.

38 "In view of these things King Demetrius confirmed him in the high priesthood, [39] made him one of his Friends, and paid him high honors. [40] For he had heard that the Jews were addressed by the Romans as friends and allies and brothers, and that the Romans[a] had received the envoys of Simon with honor.

41 "The Jews and their priests have resolved that Simon should be their leader and high priest forever, until a trustworthy prophet should arise, [42] and that he should be governor over them and that he should take charge of the sanctuary and appoint officials over its tasks and over the country and the weapons and the strongholds, and that he should take charge of the sanctuary, [43] and that he should be obeyed by all, and that all contracts in the country should be written in his name, and that he should be clothed in purple and wear gold.

44 "None of the people or priests shall be permitted to nullify any of these decisions or to oppose what he says, or to convene an assembly in the country without his permission, or to be clothed in purple or put on a gold buckle. [45] Whoever acts contrary to these decisions or rejects any of them shall be liable to punishment."

46 All the people agreed to grant Simon the right to act in accordance with these decisions. [47] So Simon accepted and agreed to be high priest, to be commander and ethnarch of the Jews and priests, and to be protector of them all.[b] [48] And they gave orders to inscribe this decree on bronze tablets, to put them up in a conspicuous place in the precincts of the sanctuary, [49] and to deposit copies of them in the treasury, so that Simon and his sons might have them.

Letter of Antiochus VII

15 Antiochus, son of King Demetrius, sent a letter from the islands of the sea to Simon, the priest and ethnarch of the Jews, and to all the nation; [2] its contents were as follows: "King Antiochus to Simon the high priest and ethnarch and to the nation of the Jews, greetings. [3] Whereas certain scoundrels have gained control of the kingdom of our ancestors, and I intend to lay claim to the kingdom so that I may restore it as it formerly was, and have recruited a host of mercenary troops and have equipped warships, [4] and intend to make a landing in the country so that I may proceed against those who have destroyed our country and those who have devastated many cities in my kingdom, [5] now therefore I confirm to you all the tax remissions that the kings before me have granted you, and a release from all the other payments from which they have released you. [6] I permit you to mint your own coinage as money for your country, [7] and I grant freedom to Jerusalem and the sanctuary. All the weapons that you have prepared and the strongholds that you have built and now hold shall remain yours. [8] Every debt you owe to the royal treasury and any such future debts shall be canceled for you from henceforth and for all time. [9] When we gain control of our kingdom, we will bestow great honor on you and your nation and the temple, so that your glory will become manifest in all the earth."

10 In the one hundred seventy-fourth year[c] Antiochus set out and invaded the land of his ancestors. All the troops rallied to him, so that there were only a few with Trypho. [11] Antiochus pursued him, and Trypho[d] came in his flight to Dor, which is by the sea; [12] for he knew that troubles had converged on him, and his troops had deserted him. [13] So Antiochus encamped against Dor, and with him were one hundred twenty thousand warriors and eight thousand cavalry. [14] He surrounded the town, and the ships joined battle from the sea; he pressed

a Gk they   b Or to preside over them all   c 138 B.C.   d Gk he

the town hard from land and sea, and permitted no one to leave or enter it.

Rome Supports the Jews

15 Then Numenius and his companions arrived from Rome, with letters to the kings and countries, in which the following was written: [16] "Lucius, consul of the Romans, to King Ptolemy, greetings. [17] The envoys of the Jews have come to us as our friends and allies to renew our ancient friendship and alliance. They had been sent by the high priest Simon and by the Jewish people [18] and have brought a gold shield weighing one thousand minas. [19] We therefore have decided to write to the kings and countries that they should not seek their harm or make war against them and their cities and their country, or make alliance with those who war against them. [20] And it has seemed good to us to accept the shield from them. [21] Therefore if any scoundrels have fled to you from their country, hand them over to the high priest Simon, so that he may punish them according to their law."

22 The consul[a] wrote the same thing to King Demetrius and to Attalus and Ariarathes and Arsaces, [23] and to all the countries, and to Sampsames,[b] and to the Spartans, and to Delos, and to Myndos, and to Sicyon, and to Caria, and to Samos, and to Pamphylia, and to Lycia, and to Halicarnassus, and to Rhodes, and to Phaselis, and to Cos, and to Side, and to Aradus and Gortyna and Cnidus and Cyprus and Cyrene. [24] They also sent a copy of these things to the high priest Simon.

Antiochus VII Threatens Simon

25 King Antiochus besieged Dor for the second time, continually throwing his forces against it and making engines of war; and he shut Trypho up and kept him from going out or in. [26] And Simon sent to Antiochus[c] two thousand picked troops, to fight for him, and silver and gold and a large amount of military equipment. [27] But he refused to receive them, and broke all the agreements he formerly had made with Simon, and became estranged from him. [28] He sent to him Athenobius, one of his Friends, to confer with him, saying, "You hold control of Joppa and Gazara and the citadel in Jerusalem; they are cities of my kingdom. [29] You have devastated their territory, you have done great damage in the land, and you have taken possession of many places in my kingdom. [30] Now then, hand over the cities that you have seized and the tribute money of the places that you have conquered outside the borders of Judea; [31] or else pay me five hundred talents of silver for the destruction that you have caused and five hundred talents more for the tribute money of the cities. Otherwise we will come and make war on you."

32 So Athenobius, the king's Friend, came to Jerusalem, and when he saw the splendor of Simon, and the sideboard with its gold and silver plate, and his great magnificence, he was amazed. When he reported to him the king's message, [33] Simon said to him in reply: "We have neither taken foreign land nor seized foreign property, but only the inheritance of our ancestors, which at one time had been unjustly taken by our enemies. [34] Now that we have the opportunity, we are firmly holding the inheritance of our ancestors. [35] As for Joppa and Gazara, which you demand, they were causing great damage among the people and to our land; for them we will give you one hundred talents."

Athenobius[a] did not answer him a word, [36] but returned in wrath to the king and reported to him these words, and also the splendor of Simon and all that he had seen. And the king was very angry.

Victory over Cendebeus

37 Meanwhile Trypho embarked on a ship and escaped to Orthosia. [38] Then

---

[a] Gk He   [b] The name is uncertain   [c] Gk him

the king made Cendebeus commander-in-chief of the coastal country, and gave him troops of infantry and cavalry. **39** He commanded him to encamp against Judea, to build up Kedron and fortify its gates, and to make war on the people; but the king pursued Trypho. **40** So Cendebeus came to Jamnia and began to provoke the people and invade Judea and take the people captive and kill them. **41** He built up Kedron and stationed horsemen and troops there, so that they might go out and make raids along the highways of Judea, as the king had ordered him.

16 John went up from Gazara and reported to his father Simon what Cendebeus had done. **2** And Simon called in his two eldest sons Judas and John, and said to them: "My brothers and I and my father's house have fought the wars of Israel from our youth until this day, and things have prospered in our hands so that we have delivered Israel many times. **3** But now I have grown old, and you by Heaven's*a* mercy are mature in years. Take my place and my brother's, and go out and fight for our nation, and may the help that comes from Heaven be with you."

4 So John*b* chose out of the country twenty thousand warriors and cavalry, and they marched against Cendebeus and camped for the night in Modein. **5** Early in the morning they started out and marched into the plain, where a large force of infantry and cavalry was coming to meet them; and a stream lay between them. **6** Then he and his army lined up against them. He saw that the soldiers were afraid to cross the stream, so he crossed over first; and when his troops saw him, they crossed over after him. **7** Then he divided the army and placed the cavalry in the center of the infantry,

for the cavalry of the enemy were very numerous. **8** They sounded the trumpets, and Cendebeus and his army were put to flight; many of them fell wounded and the rest fled into the stronghold. **9** At that time Judas the brother of John was wounded, but John pursued them until Cendebeus*c* reached Kedron, which he had built. **10** They also fled into the towers that were in the fields of Azotus, and John*c* burned it with fire, and about two thousand of them fell. He then returned to Judea safely.

Murder of Simon and His Sons

11 Now Ptolemy son of Abubus had been appointed governor over the plain of Jericho; he had a large store of silver and gold, **12** for he was son-in-law of the high priest. **13** His heart was lifted up; he determined to get control of the country, and made treacherous plans against Simon and his sons, to do away with them. **14** Now Simon was visiting the towns of the country and attending to their needs, and he went down to Jericho with his sons Mattathias and Judas, in the one hundred seventy-seventh year,*d* in the eleventh month, which is the month of Shebat. **15** The son of Abubus received them treacherously in the little stronghold called Dok, which he had built; he gave them a great banquet, and hid men there. **16** When Simon and his sons were drunk, Ptolemy and his men rose up, took their weapons, rushed in against Simon in the banquet hall and killed him and his two sons, as well as some of his servants. **17** So he committed an act of great treachery and returned evil for good.

John Succeeds Simon

18 Then Ptolemy wrote a report about these things and sent it to the king, ask-

a Gk *his*　*b* Other ancient authorities read *he*　*c* Gk *he*　*d* 134 b.c.

16:3—Leadership passes to Simon's son, John Hyrcanus, who rules 135–104 BCE. Josephus reports that John Hyrcanus and his successors forcibly converted Gentiles under their control (e.g., the Idumeans; Herod the Great's family became Jewish in this way), probably as the Hasmoneans became increasingly dependent upon converted Gentiles to support their illegitimate rule. Power is maintained at any price.

ing him to send troops to aid him and to turn over to him the towns and the country. ¹⁹ He sent other troops to Gazara to do away with John; he sent letters to the captains asking them to come to him so that he might give them silver and gold and gifts; ²⁰ and he sent other troops to take possession of Jerusalem and the temple hill. ²¹ But someone ran ahead and reported to John at Gazara that his father and brothers had perished, and that "he has sent men to kill you also." ²² When he heard this, he was greatly shocked; he seized the men who came to destroy him and killed them, for he had found out that they were seeking to destroy him.

23 The rest of the acts of John and his wars and the brave deeds that he did, and the building of the walls that he completed, and his achievements, ²⁴ are written in the annals of his high priesthood, from the time that he became high priest after his father.

16:23–24—John Hyrcanus inherits the high priesthood. We are left wondering at the end of 1 Maccabees about the irony of the growing Hellenization of the Hasmoneans, with their Greek names, wealth, and Greek mercenaries; those who had originally fought Hellenizers become Hellenizers themselves. Questions about their rule lead to civil war under Alexander Jannaeus, son of John Hyrcanus, in 88 BCE; this conflict paves the way for Roman rule. Compromises for the sake of power at the expense of one's identity can lead to disaster.

The Book of
2 MACCABEES

ing him to send troops to ... When he heard this he was
to turn over to him the town ... and he vexed the men who
country ... ra to do ...
to the capital ...
him so that he might give them silver ... 23 The rest of the acts of John and his
and gold and gifts, and he sent other wars and the brave deeds that he did,
troo ...
and ...

B oth 1 and 2 Maccabees present a history of the Maccabean revolt, but they offer independent and opposing views of it. Whereas in 1 Maccabees the holy warriors Judas Maccabeus and his brothers are celebrated for lifting the Seleucid oppression, in 2 Maccabees praise centers on the holy martyrs who make military success over the Seleucids possible. Second Maccabees pays more detailed attention to the events leading up to the revolt, beginning with the high priesthood of Onias III and the reign of Seleucus IV Philopator (187–175 BCE). It ends with the Jewish defeat of the Syrian general Nicanor in 161 BCE, leaving out the story of the brothers who followed Judas Maccabeus, probably as a silent criticism of their becoming high priests when they were not of the high-priestly line. The two books show us that history is not just "facts," but an interpretation of events from a particular point of view and place in society—just as today "terrorists" and "freedom fighters" are often the same people viewed through different lenses.

The Jerusalem temple occupies a central place in 2 Maccabees. Attacks on the temple organize the book into three major sections: (1) by Heliodorus, agent of Seleucus IV, who tries to rob the temple treasury (3:1–40); (2) by Antiochus IV Epiphanes, whose defeat leads to the purification of the temple by Judas Maccabeus (4:1–10:9); and (3) by Nicanor, general of Demetrius I, whose death means religious freedom for the Jews (10:10–15:36). The prologue (2:19–32) and epilogue (15:37–39) describe the kind of history found in 2 Maccabees, which is said to be a condensation (epitome) of a five-volume work by Jason of Cyrene (2:23), now lost to us. The author of 2 Maccabees, known as the epitomist, attempts to make this history pleasing, memorable, and profitable for his readers (2:25; 15:39). Chapter 1 contains two letters from the Jews in Jerusalem to Egyptian Jews (1:1–9; 1:10–2:18), inviting them to celebrate the festival of the purification of the temple (Hanukkah), which the letters connect with the eight-day Festival of Booths or Tabernacles (see 10:6). Perhaps the epitome was written in 124 BCE to accompany the first letter; the authenticity of the second letter is questioned. For more historical information about this period, see the introduction to 1 Maccabees.

Unlike 1 Maccabees, 2 Maccabees reports several miracles (3:13–40; 9:1–29; 10:24–38). Human initiative stands at the center of 1 Maccabees, whereas divine action dominates in 2 Maccabees; victory comes from the Lord "who works wonders" (3:30; 15:21). The emphasis upon miracles in 2 Maccabees challenges our modern sense of self-sufficiency and power, which leaves little room for the miraculous.

Whereas 1 Maccabees suggests that the obedient martyrs who keep the dietary laws and refuse to profane the Sabbath by fighting have brought God's wrath upon Israel (1 Macc. 1:62–64), 2 Maccabees makes it clear that it is the people's disobedience that has earned God's punishment: "we are suffering because of our own sins" (2 Macc. 7:32; see also 3:1; 4:13–16). Divine punishment in the form of Seleucid oppression was God's "discipline" of the people for their sins (6:12–17; 7:33), for "the adoption of

foreign ways" (4:13). God's discipline shows that actions have consequences, a theme that runs throughout the entire Bible—Wisdom literature (Proverbs, Job), the preexilic prophets, the Deuteronomistic History (Deuteronomy–2 Kings), the Gospel parables, and apocalyptic literature (Daniel, Revelation). Similarly, Judas and his group are successful because they observe the Sabbath (2 Macc. 8:27; 12:38), help widows and orphans (8:28; see Deut. 26:12–13), keep the festivals (12:31–32; 15:36) and the dietary laws (5:27), and pray to God for help (8:18; 10:4, 25–27, 41–42; 13:10–12; 15:8).

In contrast to militaristic 1 Maccabees, in 2 Maccabees martyrdom overshadows military might. The martyrdoms of the aged scribe Eleazar (6:18–31) and of the mother and her seven sons (7:1–42) and the suicide of the elder Razis (14:37–46) are graphically presented, in line with Greco-Roman "pathetic" histories of the day that played on the emotions. The martyrs in 2 Maccabees offer their deaths as atonement for Jewish sins and God's wrath (7:37–38), thereby taking their place among other sacrificial heroes in Greco-Roman traditions about noble death.

Second Maccabees was written in Greek; where (Antioch, elsewhere in the Diaspora, or Judea) and when (124 BCE, in conjunction with the first letter, or later) is disputed. The early church embraced the martyrs of 2 Maccabees as models for Christian martyrdom; their anniversary is celebrated on August 1. The church fathers Origen, Chrysostom, and Augustine incorporated them into their calendars of martyrs; a feast of the Maccabean martyrs was celebrated in Antioch. We may too easily dismiss these martyrs as naive and passively resigned to oppression. The Holocaust and Palestinian and Iraqi suicide bombers may contribute to negative thinking about martyrdom. But 2 Maccabees paints a very positive picture of martyrs as heroes who died a noble death and showed the world that earthly powers are subordinate to God's power.

—Denise Dombkowski Hopkins

A Letter to the Jews in Egypt

1 The Jews in Jerusalem and those in the land of Judea,
To their Jewish kindred in Egypt,
Greetings and true peace.

2 May God do good to you, and may he remember his covenant with Abraham and Isaac and Jacob, his faithful servants. ³ May he give you all a heart to worship him and to do his will with a strong heart and a willing spirit. ⁴ May he open your heart to his law and his commandments, and may he bring peace. ⁵ May he hear your prayers and be reconciled to you, and may he not forsake you in time of evil. ⁶ We are now praying for you here.

7 In the reign of Demetrius, in the one hundred sixty-ninth year,[a] we Jews wrote to you, in the critical distress that came upon us in those years after Jason and his company revolted from the holy land and the kingdom ⁸ and burned the gate and shed innocent blood. We prayed to the Lord and were heard, and we offered sacrifice and grain offering, and we lit the lamps and set out the loaves. ⁹ And now see that you keep the festival of booths in the month of Chislev, in the one hundred eighty-eighth year.[b]

A Letter to Aristobulus

10 The people of Jerusalem and of Judea and the senate and Judas,

[a] 143 B.C.   [b] 124 B.C.

1:1–2:18 Two Letters, 1:1–9 and 1:10–2:18
The Jews in Judea invite the Jews in Egypt to celebrate Hanukkah, i.e., temple purification by the Maccabees, connecting this festival in Chislev (December), to the Feast of Booths, also an eight-day festival. Memory embedded in liturgical celebration can foster community, identity, and solidarity.

To Aristobulus, who is of the family of the anointed priests, teacher of King Ptolemy, and to the Jews in Egypt,

Greetings and good health.

11 Having been saved by God out of grave dangers we thank him greatly for taking our side against the king,[a] 12 for he drove out those who fought against the holy city. 13 When the leader reached Persia with a force that seemed irresistible, they were cut to pieces in the temple of Nanea by a deception employed by the priests of the goddess[b] Nanea. 14 On the pretext of intending to marry her, Antiochus came to the place together with his Friends, to secure most of its treasures as a dowry. 15 When the priests of the temple of Nanea had set out the treasures and Antiochus had come with a few men inside the wall of the sacred precinct, they closed the temple as soon as he entered it. 16 Opening a secret door in the ceiling, they threw stones and struck down the leader and his men; they dismembered them and cut off their heads and threw them to the people outside. 17 Blessed in every way be our God, who has brought judgment on those who have behaved impiously.

Fire Consumes Nehemiah's Sacrifice

18 Since on the twenty-fifth day of Chislev we shall celebrate the purification of the temple, we thought it necessary to notify you, in order that you also may celebrate the festival of booths and the festival of the fire given when Nehemiah, who built the temple and the altar, offered sacrifices.

19 For when our ancestors were being led captive to Persia, the pious priests of that time took some of the fire of the altar and secretly hid it in the hollow of a dry cistern, where they took such precautions that the place was unknown to anyone. 20 But after many years had passed, when it pleased God, Nehemiah, having been commissioned by the king of Persia, sent the descendants of the priests who had hidden the fire to get it.

And when they reported to us that they had not found fire but only a thick liquid, he ordered them to dip it out and bring it. 21 When the materials for the sacrifices were presented, Nehemiah ordered the priests to sprinkle the liquid on the wood and on the things laid upon it. 22 When this had been done and some time had passed, and when the sun, which had been clouded over, shone out, a great fire blazed up, so that all marveled. 23 And while the sacrifice was being consumed, the priests offered prayer—the priests and everyone. Jonathan led, and the rest responded, as did Nehemiah. 24 The prayer was to this effect:

"O Lord, Lord God, Creator of all things, you are awe-inspiring and strong and just and merciful, you alone are king and are kind, 25 you alone are bountiful, you alone are just and almighty and eternal. You rescue Israel from every evil; you chose the ancestors and consecrated them. 26 Accept this sacrifice on behalf of all your people Israel and preserve your portion and make it holy. 27 Gather together our scattered people, set free those who are slaves among the Gentiles, look on those who are rejected and despised, and let the Gentiles know that you are our God. 28 Punish those who oppress and are insolent with pride. 29 Plant your people in your holy place, as Moses promised."

30 Then the priests sang the hymns. 31 After the materials of the sacrifice had been consumed, Nehemiah ordered that the liquid that was left should be poured on large stones. 32 When this was done, a flame blazed up; but when the light from the altar shone back, it went out. 33 When this matter became known, and it was reported to the king of the Persians that, in the place where the exiled priests had hidden the fire, the liquid had appeared with which Nehemiah and his associates had burned the materials of the sacrifice, 34 the king investigated

a Cn: Gk *as those who array themselves against a king*   *b* Gk lacks *the goddess*

the matter, and enclosed the place and made it sacred. [35] And with those persons whom the king favored he exchanged many excellent gifts. [36] Nehemiah and his associates called this "nephthar," which means purification, but by most people it is called naphtha.[a]

Jeremiah Hides the Tent, Ark, and Altar

2 One finds in the records that the prophet Jeremiah ordered those who were being deported to take some of the fire, as has been mentioned, [2] and that the prophet, after giving them the law, instructed those who were being deported not to forget the commandments of the Lord, or to be led astray in their thoughts on seeing the gold and silver statues and their adornment. [3] And with other similar words he exhorted them that the law should not depart from their hearts.

[4] It was also in the same document that the prophet, having received an oracle, ordered that the tent and the ark should follow with him, and that he went out to the mountain where Moses had gone up and had seen the inheritance of God. [5] Jeremiah came and found a cave-dwelling, and he brought there the tent and the ark and the altar of incense; then he sealed up the entrance. [6] Some of those who followed him came up intending to mark the way, but could not find it. [7] When Jeremiah learned of it, he rebuked them and declared: "The place shall remain unknown until God gathers his people together again and shows his mercy. [8] Then the Lord will disclose these things, and the glory of the Lord and the cloud will appear, as they were shown in the case of Moses, and as Solomon asked that the place should be specially consecrated."

[9] It was also made clear that being possessed of wisdom Solomon[b] offered sacrifice for the dedication and completion of the temple. [10] Just as Moses prayed to the Lord, and fire came down from heaven and consumed the sacrifices, so also Solomon prayed, and the fire came down and consumed the whole burnt offerings. [11] And Moses said, "They were consumed because the sin offering had not been eaten." [12] Likewise Solomon also kept the eight days.

[13] The same things are reported in the records and in the memoirs of Nehemiah, and also that he founded a library and collected the books about the kings and prophets, and the writings of David, and letters of kings about votive offerings. [14] In the same way Judas also collected all the books that had been lost on account of the war that had come upon us, and they are in our possession. [15] So if you have need of them, send people to get them for you.

[16] Since, therefore, we are about to celebrate the purification, we write to you. Will you therefore please keep the days? [17] It is God who has saved all his people, and has returned the inheritance to all, and the kingship and the priesthood and the consecration, [18] as he promised through the law. We have hope in God that he will soon have mercy on us and will gather us from everywhere under heaven into his holy place, for he has rescued us from great evils and has purified the place.

The Compiler's Preface

[19] The story of Judas Maccabeus and his brothers, and the purification of the great temple, and the dedication of the altar, [20] and further the wars against Antiochus Epiphanes and his son Eupator, [21] and the appearances that

[a] Gk nephthai [b] Gk he

2:19–32 The Epitomist's Preface
2:21–22 Appearances—(Gk. epiphaneia). God's saving appearance is a theme that runs throughout the book. Greco-Roman literature of the time also contained epiphany stories about gods and goddesses defending their temples, and soteria (deliverance) feasts were regularly celebrated.

came from heaven to those who fought bravely for Judaism, so that though few in number they seized the whole land and pursued the barbarian hordes, [22] and regained possession of the temple famous throughout the world, and liberated the city, and re-established the laws that were about to be abolished, while the Lord with great kindness became gracious to them—[23] all this, which has been set forth by Jason of Cyrene in five volumes, we shall attempt to condense into a single book. [24] For considering the flood of statistics involved and the difficulty there is for those who wish to enter upon the narratives of history because of the mass of material, [25] we have aimed to please those who wish to read, to make it easy for those who are inclined to memorize, and to profit all readers. [26] For us who have undertaken the toil of abbreviating, it is no light matter but calls for sweat and loss of sleep, [27] just as it is not easy for one who prepares a banquet and seeks the benefit of others. Nevertheless, to secure the gratitude of many we will gladly endure the uncomfortable toil, [28] leaving the responsibility for exact details to the compiler, while devoting our effort to arriving at the outlines of the condensation. [29] For as the master builder of a new house must be concerned with the whole construction, while the one who undertakes its painting and decoration has to consider only what is suitable for its adornment, such in my judgment is the case with us. [30] It is the duty of the original historian to occupy the ground, to discuss matters from every side, and to take trouble with details, [31] but the one who recasts the narrative should be allowed to strive for brevity of expression and to forego exhaustive treatment. [32] At this point therefore let us begin our narrative, without adding any more to what has already been said; for it would be foolish to lengthen the preface while cutting short the history itself.

Arrival of Heliodorus in Jerusalem

3 While the holy city was inhabited in unbroken peace and the laws were strictly observed because of the piety of the high priest Onias and his hatred of wickedness, [2] it came about that the kings themselves honored the place and glorified the temple with the finest presents, [3] even to the extent that King Seleucus of Asia defrayed from his own revenues all the expenses connected with the service of the sacrifices.

4 But a man named Simon, of the tribe of Benjamin, who had been made captain of the temple, had a disagreement with the high priest about the administration of the city market. [5] Since he could not prevail over Onias, he went to Apollonius of Tarsus,[a] who at that time was governor of Coelesyria and Phoenicia, [6] and reported to him that the treasury in Jerusalem was full of untold sums of money, so that the amount of the funds could not be reckoned, and that they did not belong to the account of the sacrifices, but that it was possible for them to fall under the control of the king. [7] When Apollonius met the king, he told him of the money about which he had been informed. The king[b] chose Heliodorus, who was in charge of his

---

[a] Gk Apollonius son of Tharseas   [b] Gk He

3:1–40 The First Attack on the Temple

3:1—Onias III was the legitimate high priest until 175 BCE, when his brother Jason purchased the office from the king. Under Onias, the situation in Jerusalem is viewed idealistically in contrast to the chaotic situation under the illegitimate high priests who follow him: the "ungodly" Jason (4:13–17), the "scoundrel" Menelaus (13:3–4); and the "defiled" Alcimus (14:3–10). This indictment of the corrupt Jewish leadership

for causing the people's suffering can remind us of our responsibility to call our own political and religious leaders to account for injustices at home and abroad.

3:6 The treasury in Jerusalem was full of untold sums of money—The temple functioned as a national bank for the Jews, holding private deposits as well as charity funds for the poor in society, a practice common throughout the ancient world.

affairs, and sent him with commands to effect the removal of the reported wealth. [8] Heliodorus at once set out on his journey, ostensibly to make a tour of inspection of the cities of Coelesyria and Phoenicia, but in fact to carry out the king's purpose.

9 When he had arrived at Jerusalem and had been kindly welcomed by the high priest of[a] the city, he told about the disclosure that had been made and stated why he had come, and he inquired whether this really was the situation. [10] The high priest explained that there were some deposits belonging to widows and orphans, [11] and also some money of Hyrcanus son of Tobias, a man of very prominent position, and that it totaled in all four hundred talents of silver and two hundred of gold. To such an extent the impious Simon had misrepresented the facts. [12] And he said that it was utterly impossible that wrong should be done to those people who had trusted in the holiness of the place and in the sanctity and inviolability of the temple that is honored throughout the whole world.

Heliodorus Plans to Rob the Temple

13 But Heliodorus, because of the orders he had from the king, said that this money must in any case be confiscated for the king's treasury. [14] So he set a day and went in to direct the inspection of these funds.

There was no little distress throughout the whole city. [15] The priests prostrated themselves before the altar in their priestly vestments and called toward heaven upon him who had given the law about deposits, that he should keep them safe for those who had deposited them. [16] To see the appearance of the high priest was to be wounded at heart, for his face and the change in his color disclosed the anguish of his soul. [17] For terror and bodily trembling had come over the man, which plainly showed to those who looked at him the pain lodged in his heart. [18] People also hurried out of their houses in crowds to make a general supplication because the holy place was about to be brought into dishonor. [19] Women, girded with sackcloth under their breasts, thronged the streets. Some of the young women who were kept indoors ran together to the gates, and some to the walls, while others peered out of the windows. [20] And holding up their hands to heaven, they all made supplication. [21] There was something pitiable in the prostration of the whole populace and the anxiety of the high priest in his great anguish.

The Lord Protects His Temple

22 While they were calling upon the Almighty Lord that he would keep what had been entrusted safe and secure for those who had entrusted it, [23] Heliodorus went on with what had been decided. [24] But when he arrived at the treasury with his bodyguard, then and there the Sovereign of spirits and of all authority caused so great a manifestation that all who had been so bold as to accompany him were astounded by the power of God, and became faint with terror. [25] For there appeared to them a magnificently caparisoned horse, with a rider of frightening mien; it rushed furiously at Heliodorus and struck at him with its front hoofs. Its rider was seen to have armor and weapons of gold. [26] Two young men also appeared to him, remarkably strong, gloriously beautiful and splendidly dressed, who stood

[a] Other ancient authorities read and

3:13–21—The distressed people resist Heliodorus through prayer, not armed conflict. The author endorses nonviolence as a faithful response to crisis, which challenges those today who would assert that violence is the only way to achieve peace.

3:22–40—God appears through angelic beings (see 5:2–3; 10:29; and 11:8) to defend the Jerusalem temple from being plundered by the king's agent, Heliodorus.

on either side of him and flogged him continuously, inflicting many blows on him. 27 When he suddenly fell to the ground and deep darkness came over him, his men took him up, put him on a stretcher, 28 and carried him away—this man who had just entered the aforesaid treasury with a great retinue and all his bodyguard but was now unable to help himself. They recognized clearly the sovereign power of God.

Onias Prays for Heliodorus

29 While he lay prostrate, speechless because of the divine intervention and deprived of any hope of recovery, 30 they praised the Lord who had acted marvelously for his own place. And the temple, which a little while before was full of fear and disturbance, was filled with joy and gladness, now that the Almighty Lord had appeared.

31 Some of Heliodorus's friends quickly begged Onias to call upon the Most High to grant life to one who was lying quite at his last breath. 32 So the high priest, fearing that the king might get the notion that some foul play had been perpetrated by the Jews with regard to Heliodorus, offered sacrifice for the man's recovery. 33 While the high priest was making an atonement, the same young men appeared again to Heliodorus dressed in the same clothing, and they stood and said, "Be very grateful to the high priest Onias, since for his sake the Lord has granted you your life. 34 And see that you, who have been flogged by heaven, report to all people the majestic power of God." Having said this they vanished.

The Conversion of Heliodorus

35 Then Heliodorus offered sacrifice to the Lord and made very great vows to the Savior of his life, and having bidden Onias farewell, he marched off with his forces to the king. 36 He bore testimony to all concerning the deeds of the supreme God, which he had seen with his own eyes. 37 When the king asked Heliodorus what sort of person would be suitable to send on another mission to Jerusalem, he replied, 38 "If you have any enemy or plotter against your government, send him there, for you will get him back thoroughly flogged, if he survives at all; for there is certainly some power of God about the place. 39 For he who has his dwelling in heaven watches over that place himself and brings it aid, and he strikes and destroys those who come to do it injury." 40 This was the outcome of the episode of Heliodorus and the protection of the treasury.

Simon Accuses Onias

4 The previously mentioned Simon, who had informed about the money against[a] his own country, slandered Onias, saying that it was he who had incited Heliodorus and had been the real cause of the misfortune. 2 He dared to designate as a plotter against the government the man who was the benefactor of the city, the protector of his compatriots, and a zealot for the laws. 3 When his hatred progressed to such a degree that even murders were committed by one of Simon's approved agents, 4 Onias recognized that the rivalry was serious and that Apollonius son of Menestheus,[b] and governor of Coelesyria and Phoenicia, was intensifying the malice of Simon. 5 So he appealed to the king, not accusing his compatriots but having in view the welfare, both public and private, of all the people. 6 For he saw that without the king's attention public affairs could not again reach a

a Gk and   *b* Vg Compare verse 21: Meaning of Gk uncertain

3:36—The healed Heliodorus comes to acknowledge *the supreme God*. He does not convert but shows that Jews and Gentiles can live with respect for one another, a model for religious interaction in our pluralistic world.

4:1–10:9 The Second Attack on the Temple

4:1–6—The rivalry among the ruling elite, represented by Onias III and Simon, captain of the temple, grows.

peaceful settlement, and that Simon would not stop his folly.

Jason's Reforms

7 When Seleucus died and Antiochus, who was called Epiphanes, succeeded to the kingdom, Jason the brother of Onias obtained the high priesthood by corruption, [8] promising the king at an interview[a] three hundred sixty talents of silver, and from another source of revenue eighty talents. [9] In addition to this he promised to pay one hundred fifty more if permission were given to establish by his authority a gymnasium and a body of youth for it, and to enroll the people of Jerusalem as citizens of Antioch. [10] When the king assented and Jason[b] came to office, he at once shifted his compatriots over to the Greek way of life.

11 He set aside the existing royal concessions to the Jews, secured through John the father of Eupolemus, who went on the mission to establish friendship and alliance with the Romans; and he destroyed the lawful ways of living and introduced new customs contrary to the law. [12] He took delight in establishing a gymnasium right under the citadel, and he induced the noblest of the young men to wear the Greek hat. [13] There was such an extreme of Hellenization and increase in the adoption of foreign ways because of the surpassing wickedness of Jason, who was ungodly and no true[c] high priest, [14] that the priests were no longer intent upon their service at the altar. Despising the sanctuary and neglecting the sacrifices, they hurried to take part in the unlawful proceedings in the wrestling arena after the signal for the discus-throwing, [15] disdaining the honors prized by their ancestors and putting the highest value upon Greek forms of prestige. [16] For this reason heavy disaster overtook them, and those whose ways of living they admired and wished to imitate completely became their enemies and punished them. [17] It is no light thing to show irreverence to the divine laws—a fact that later events will make clear.

Jason Introduces Greek Customs

18 When the quadrennial games were being held at Tyre and the king was present, [19] the vile Jason sent envoys, chosen as being Antiochian citizens from Jerusalem, to carry three hundred silver drachmas for the sacrifice to Hercules. Those who carried the money, however, thought best not to use it for sacrifice, because that was inappropriate, but to expend it for another purpose. [20] So this money was intended by the sender for the sacrifice to Hercules, but by the decision of its carriers it was applied to the construction of triremes.

21 When Apollonius son of Menestheus was sent to Egypt for the coronation[d] of Philometor as king, Antiochus learned that Philometor[b] had become hostile to his government, and he took

[a] Or by a petition   [b] Gk he   [c] Gk lacks true   [d] Meaning of Gk uncertain

---

4:7–22—Jason buys the high priesthood from the new king, Antiochus IV Epiphanes, builds a *gymnasium* (center for Greek culture), and gives Jerusalem a Greek name, *Antioch*; cf. 1 Macc. 1:41–61. Jewish identity is compromised. We may ponder how Christians today compromise their identity in the pursuit of power, recognition, and influence.

4:12 *The Greek hat*—A broad-brimmed hat to shade athletes from the sun, similar to the hat of Hermes, god of athletes.

4:13 *The surpassing wickedness of Jason, who was ungodly*—Jason leads the people to *extreme Hellenization*, the fusion of Greek with indigenous Jewish culture. The author views this fusion as the opposite of Judaism (see v. 38). The issue of Jewish identity under the Seleucids leads to struggles between Hellenizers, who want to reform or update Judaism, and the traditionalists, who refuse to change. Christians in secular culture today also struggle with this question of self-definition and the boundaries that mark Christian identity.

4:16–17—According to the theory of act/consequence, the author argues that people suffer Seleucid oppression because of Jason's leadership. We are cautioned to explore other probable causes than those that support one's own agenda.

measures for his own security. Therefore upon arriving at Joppa he proceeded to Jerusalem. ²² He was welcomed magnificently by Jason and the city, and ushered in with a blaze of torches and with shouts. Then he marched his army into Phoenicia.

Menelaus Becomes High Priest

23 After a period of three years Jason sent Menelaus, the brother of the previously mentioned Simon, to carry the money to the king and to complete the records of essential business. ²⁴ But he, when presented to the king, extolled him with an air of authority, and secured the high priesthood for himself, outbidding Jason by three hundred talents of silver. ²⁵ After receiving the king's orders he returned, possessing no qualification for the high priesthood, but having the hot temper of a cruel tyrant and the rage of a savage wild beast. ²⁶ So Jason, who after supplanting his own brother was supplanted by another man, was driven as a fugitive into the land of Ammon. ²⁷ Although Menelaus continued to hold the office, he did not pay regularly any of the money promised to the king. ²⁸ When Sostratus the captain of the citadel kept requesting payment—for the collection of the revenue was his responsibility—the two of them were summoned by the king on account of this issue. ²⁹ Menelaus left his own brother Lysimachus as deputy in the high priesthood, while Sostratus left Crates, the commander of the Cyprian troops.

The Murder of Onias

30 While such was the state of affairs, it happened that the people of Tarsus and of Mallus revolted because their cities had been given as a present to Antiochis, the king's concubine. ³¹ So the king went hurriedly to settle the trouble, leaving Andronicus, a man of high rank, to act as his deputy. ³² But Menelaus, thinking he had obtained a suitable opportunity, stole some of the gold vessels of the temple and gave them to Andronicus; other vessels, as it happened, he had sold to Tyre and the neighboring cities. ³³ When Onias became fully aware of these acts, he publicly exposed them, having first withdrawn to a place of sanctuary at Daphne near Antioch. ³⁴ Therefore Menelaus, taking Andronicus aside, urged him to kill Onias. Andronicus^a came to Onias, and resorting to treachery, offered him sworn pledges and gave him his right hand; he persuaded him, though still suspicious, to come out from the place of sanctuary; then, with no regard for justice, he immediately put him out of the way.

Andronicus Is Punished

35 For this reason not only Jews, but many also of other nations, were grieved and displeased at the unjust murder of the man. ³⁶ When the king returned from the region of Cilicia, the Jews in the city^b appealed to him with regard to the unreasonable murder of Onias, and the Greeks shared their hatred of the crime. ³⁷ Therefore Antiochus was grieved at heart and filled with pity, and wept because of the moderation and good conduct of the deceased. ³⁸ Inflamed with anger, he immediately stripped off the purple robe from Andronicus, tore off his clothes, and led him around the whole city to that

^a Gk He ^b Or in each city

4:23–50—Menelaus outbids Jason for the high priesthood and has Andronicus, agent of Antiochus, murder Onias. Antiochus IV needed money to pay heavy reparations to Rome, which was growing in power. Menelaus, who is not of the high-priestly family, is demonized as having *the rage of a savage wild beast* (v. 25), alerting us to analyze the ways in which we demonize our opponents today so that no dialogue is possible.

4:32—Menelaus steals golden vessels from the temple, showing us that personal gain at the expense of community welfare is not a new problem.

4:35–38—Andronicus is justly punished by a *grieved* and angry Antiochus, who is protecting his own kingship.

very place where he had committed the outrage against Onias, and there he dispatched the bloodthirsty fellow. The Lord thus repaid him with the punishment he deserved.

Unpopularity of Lysimachus and Menelaus

39 When many acts of sacrilege had been committed in the city by Lysimachus with the connivance of Menelaus, and when report of them had spread abroad, the populace gathered against Lysimachus, because many of the gold vessels had already been stolen. **40** Since the crowds were becoming aroused and filled with anger, Lysimachus armed about three thousand men and launched an unjust attack, under the leadership of a certain Auranus, a man advanced in years and no less advanced in folly. **41** But when the Jews[a] became aware that Lysimachus was attacking them, some picked up stones, some blocks of wood, and others took handfuls of the ashes that were lying around, and threw them in wild confusion at Lysimachus and his men. **42** As a result, they wounded many of them, and killed some, and put all the rest to flight; the temple robber himself they killed close by the treasury.

43 Charges were brought against Menelaus about this incident. **44** When the king came to Tyre, three men sent by the senate presented the case before him. **45** But Menelaus, already as good as beaten, promised a substantial bribe to Ptolemy son of Dorymenes to win over the king. **46** Therefore Ptolemy, tak-

ing the king aside into a colonnade as if for refreshment, induced the king to change his mind. **47** Menelaus, the cause of all the trouble, he acquitted of the charges against him, while he sentenced to death those unfortunate men, who would have been freed uncondemned if they had pleaded even before Scythians. **48** And so those who had spoken for the city and the villages[b] and the holy vessels quickly suffered the unjust penalty. **49** Therefore even the Tyrians, showing their hatred of the crime, provided magnificently for their funeral. **50** But Menelaus, because of the greed of those in power, remained in office, growing in wickedness, having become the chief plotter against his compatriots.

Jason Tries to Regain Control

5 About this time Antiochus made his second invasion of Egypt. **2** And it happened that, for almost forty days, there appeared over all the city golden-clad cavalry charging through the air, in companies fully armed with lances and drawn swords— **3** troops of cavalry drawn up, attacks and counterattacks made on this side and on that, brandishing of shields, massing of spears, hurling of missiles, the flash of golden trappings, and armor of all kinds. **4** Therefore everyone prayed that the apparition might prove to have been a good omen.

5 When a false rumor arose that Antiochus was dead, Jason took no fewer than a thousand men and suddenly made an assault on the city. When the

---

[a] Gk *they*   [b] Other ancient authorities read *the people*

4:39–50—The people revolt against Lysimachus, brother of Menelaus, for stealing the temple vessels and kill him at the site of his robbery (v. 42), though they are later executed for doing so. The outraged people of Tyre provide a funeral for those executed; in contrast to 1 Maccabees, the author notes that Jews can have beneficial relationships with Gentiles as long as Jewish law is observed. The line between "us" and "them" need not be so exclusively drawn.

5:1–27 Raging inwardly—Antiochus IV massacres the populace and attacks the temple in response

to a coup by Jason, who slaughters his compatriots and fittingly dies a disgraceful death as a fugitive without a proper burial. This absolutist view of justice leaves no room for mercy or grace.

5:1–4—Signs or portents create dramatic tension and point toward a significant event about to happen, a technique common to Jewish and non-Jewish literature of the time. Many Christians today too hastily dismiss as fanatics those who speak of tangible signs of God's activity in the world.

troops on the wall had been forced back and at last the city was being taken, Menelaus took refuge in the citadel. [6] But Jason kept relentlessly slaughtering his compatriots, not realizing that success at the cost of one's kindred is the greatest misfortune, but imagining that he was setting up trophies of victory over enemies and not over compatriots. [7] He did not, however, gain control of the government; in the end he got only disgrace from his conspiracy, and fled again into the country of the Ammonites. [8] Finally he met a miserable end. Accused[a] before Aretas the ruler of the Arabs, fleeing from city to city, pursued by everyone, hated as a rebel against the laws, and abhorred as the executioner of his country and his compatriots, he was cast ashore in Egypt. [9] There he who had driven many from their own country into exile died in exile, having embarked to go to the Lacedaemonians in hope of finding protection because of their kinship. [10] He who had cast out many to lie unburied had no one to mourn for him; he had no funeral of any sort and no place in the tomb of his ancestors.

11 When news of what had happened reached the king, he took it to mean that Judea was in revolt. So, raging inwardly, he left Egypt and took the city by storm. [12] He commanded his soldiers to cut down relentlessly everyone they met and to kill those who went into their houses. [13] Then there was massacre of young and old, destruction of boys, women, and children, and slaughter of young girls and infants. [14] Within the total of three days eighty thousand were destroyed, forty thousand in hand-to-hand fighting, and as many were sold into slavery as were killed.

Pillage of the Temple

15 Not content with this, Antiochus[b] dared to enter the most holy temple in all the world, guided by Menelaus, who had become a traitor both to the laws and to his country. [16] He took the holy vessels with his polluted hands, and swept away with profane hands the votive offerings that other kings had made to enhance the glory and honor of the place. [17] Antiochus was elated in spirit, and did not perceive that the Lord was angered for a little while because of the sins of those who lived in the city, and that this was the reason he was disregarding the holy place. [18] But if it had not happened that they were involved in many sins, this man would have been flogged and turned back from his rash act as soon as he came forward, just as Heliodorus had been, whom King Seleucus sent to inspect the treasury. [19] But the Lord did not choose the nation for the sake of the holy place, but the place for the sake of the nation. [20] Therefore the place itself shared in the misfortunes that befell the nation and afterward participated in its benefits; and what was forsaken in the wrath of the Almighty was restored again in all its glory when the great Lord became reconciled.

21 So Antiochus carried off eighteen hundred talents from the temple, and hurried away to Antioch, thinking in his arrogance that he could sail on the land and walk on the sea, because his mind was elated. [22] He left governors to oppress the people: at Jerusalem, Philip, by birth a Phrygian and in character more barbarous than the man who appointed him; [23] and at Gerizim, Andronicus; and besides these Menelaus, who lorded it over his compatriots worse than the others did. In his malice toward the Jewish citizens,[c] [24] Antiochus[b] sent Apollonius, the captain of the Mysians, with an army of twenty-two thousand, and commanded him to

[a] Cn: Gk Imprisoned [b] Gk he [c] Or worse than the others did in his malice toward the Jewish citizens

---

5:17–20—Antiochus can profane the temple only because God is using him as an instrument to punish the people for their sins (Deut. 30:15–20).

Once *reconciled*, God will restore the temple (see Solomon's prayer at the dedication of the temple, 1 Kgs. 8:46–53).

kill all the grown men and to sell the women and boys as slaves. 25 When this man arrived in Jerusalem, he pretended to be peaceably disposed and waited until the holy sabbath day; then, finding the Jews not at work, he ordered his troops to parade under arms. 26 He put to the sword all those who came out to see them, then rushed into the city with his armed warriors and killed great numbers of people.

27 But Judas Maccabeus, with about nine others, got away to the wilderness, and kept himself and his companions alive in the mountains as wild animals do; they continued to live on what grew wild, so that they might not share in the defilement.

The Suppression of Judaism

6 Not long after this, the king sent an Athenian[a] senator[b] to compel the Jews to forsake the laws of their ancestors and no longer to live by the laws of God; 2 also to pollute the temple in Jerusalem and to call it the temple of Olympian Zeus, and to call the one in Gerizim the temple of Zeus-the-Friend-of-Strangers, as did the people who lived in that place.

3 Harsh and utterly grievous was the onslaught of evil. 4 For the temple was filled with debauchery and reveling by the Gentiles, who dallied with prostitutes and had intercourse with women within the sacred precincts, and besides brought in things for sacrifice that were unfit. 5 The altar was covered with abominable offerings that were forbidden by the laws. 6 People could neither keep the sabbath, nor observe the festi-

vals of their ancestors, nor so much as confess themselves to be Jews.

7 On the monthly celebration of the king's birthday, the Jews[c] were taken, under bitter constraint, to partake of the sacrifices; and when a festival of Dionysus was celebrated, they were compelled to wear wreaths of ivy and to walk in the procession in honor of Dionysus. 8 At the suggestion of the people of Ptolemais[d] a decree was issued to the neighboring Greek cities that they should adopt the same policy toward the Jews and make them partake of the sacrifices, 9 and should kill those who did not choose to change over to Greek customs. One could see, therefore, the misery that had come upon them. 10 For example, two women were brought in for having circumcised their children. They publicly paraded them around the city, with their babies hanging at their breasts, and then hurled them down headlong from the wall. 11 Others who had assembled in the caves nearby, in order to observe the seventh day secretly, were betrayed to Philip and were all burned together, because their piety kept them from defending themselves, in view of their regard for that most holy day.

Providential Significance of the Persecution

12 Now I urge those who read this book not to be depressed by such calamities, but to recognize that these punishments were designed not to destroy but to discipline our people. 13 In fact, it is a sign of great kindness not to let the impious

---

a Other ancient authorities read *Antiochian* b Or *Geron an Athenian*
c Gk *they* d Cn: Gk *suggestion of the Ptolemies* (or *of Ptolemy*)

5:27 *Wilderness*—Judas Maccabeus escapes to the wilderness, away from the dietary and cultural defilements of the Hellenized city. The wilderness is traditionally a place of refuge in the Bible: see Moses (Exod. 3:1); David (1 Sam. 23:14); and Elijah (1 Kgs. 19:1–9). We too can experience wilderness as a positive place of refuge in which we can renew identity and acknowledge dependence upon God.

6:1–11—The Jews of Jerusalem are forced to

forsake Judaism and participate in pagan festivals or die. See 1 Macc. 1:60–61; 2:31–38. Seldom in our culture is being Christian a matter of life or death.

6:12–17—Seleucid oppression is short-term *discipline* for Jewish sin; the other nations build up sins over time for greater punishment. The danger in this thinking is that one community or nation sees itself as better than anyone else; positively, there can be solidarity in shared imperfections.

alone for long, but to punish them immediately. **14** For in the case of the other nations the Lord waits patiently to punish them until they have reached the full measure of their sins; but he does not deal in this way with us, **15** in order that he may not take vengeance on us afterward when our sins have reached their height. **16** Therefore he never withdraws his mercy from us. Although he disciplines us with calamities, he does not forsake his own people. **17** Let what we have said serve as a reminder; we must go on briefly with the story.

The Martyrdom of Eleazar

18 Eleazar, one of the scribes in high position, a man now advanced in age and of noble presence, was being forced to open his mouth to eat swine's flesh. **19** But he, welcoming death with honor rather than life with pollution, went up to the rack of his own accord, spitting out the flesh, **20** as all ought to go who have the courage to refuse things that it is not right to taste, even for the natural love of life.

21 Those who were in charge of that unlawful sacrifice took the man aside because of their long acquaintance with him, and privately urged him to bring meat of his own providing, proper for him to use, and to pretend that he was eating the flesh of the sacrificial meal that had been commanded by the king, **22** so that by doing this he might be saved from death, and be treated kindly on account of his old friendship with them. **23** But making a high resolve, worthy of his years and the dignity of his old age and the gray hairs that he had reached with distinction and his excellent life even from childhood, and moreover according to the holy God-given law, he declared himself quickly, telling them to send him to Hades.

24 "Such pretense is not worthy of our time of life," he said, "for many of the young might suppose that Eleazar in his ninetieth year had gone over to an alien religion, **25** and through my pretense, for the sake of living a brief moment longer, they would be led astray because of me, while I defile and disgrace my old age. **26** Even if for the present I would avoid the punishment of mortals, yet whether I live or die I will not escape the hands of the Almighty. **27** Therefore, by bravely giving up my life now, I will show myself worthy of my old age **28** and leave to the young a noble example of how to die a good death willingly and nobly for the revered and holy laws."

When he had said this, he went*a* at once to the rack. **29** Those who a little before had acted toward him with goodwill now changed to ill will, because the words he had uttered were in their opinion sheer madness.*b* **30** When he was about to die under the blows, he groaned aloud and said: "It is clear to the Lord in his holy knowledge that, though I might have been saved from death, I am enduring terrible sufferings in my body under this beating, but in my soul I am glad to suffer these things because I fear him."

31 So in this way he died, leaving in his death an example of nobility and a memorial of courage, not only to the young but to the great body of his nation.

The Martyrdom of Seven Brothers

7 It happened also that seven brothers and their mother were arrested

---

a Other ancient authorities read *was dragged* *b* Meaning of Gk uncertain

---

6:18–7:42—This section reflects on martyrdom as a response to persecution.

6:18–31—Eleazar, an aged and noble scribe (official), refuses to eat pork (forbidden in Lev. 11:7–8; Deut. 14:8) and willingly undergoes torture on the rack in order to leave a *noble example* for the young (2 Macc. 6:28, 31). He does not expect any reward, but resigns himself

to *Hades* (v. 23; Sheol, the abode of the dead). Our society today seems to lack prominent positive role models. All too often, "what's in it for me?" thinking dictates behavior. A popular bumper sticker sums up this attitude: "Whoever dies with the most toys, wins."

7:1–42—The martyrdom of the mother and her seven sons, a favorite topic in Jewish and Greek

and were being compelled by the king, under torture with whips and thongs, to partake of unlawful swine's flesh. ² One of them, acting as their spokesman, said, "What do you intend to ask and learn from us? For we are ready to die rather than transgress the laws of our ancestors."

3 The king fell into a rage, and gave orders to have pans and caldrons heated. ⁴ These were heated immediately, and he commanded that the tongue of their spokesman be cut out and that they scalp him and cut off his hands and feet, while the rest of the brothers and the mother looked on. ⁵ When he was utterly helpless, the king*a* ordered them to take him to the fire, still breathing, and to fry him in a pan. The smoke from the pan spread widely, but the brothers*b* and their mother encouraged one another to die nobly, saying, ⁶ "The Lord God is watching over us and in truth has compassion on us, as Moses declared in his song that bore witness against the people to their faces, when he said, 'And he will have compassion on his servants.' "*c*

7 After the first brother had died in this way, they brought forward the second for their sport. They tore off the skin of his head with the hair, and asked him, "Will you eat rather than have your body punished limb by limb?" ⁸ He replied in the language of his ancestors and said to them, "No." Therefore he in turn underwent tortures as the first brother had done. ⁹ And when he was at his last breath, he said, "You accursed wretch, you dismiss us from this present life, but the King of the universe will raise us up to an everlasting renewal of life, because we have died for his laws."

10 After him, the third was the victim of their sport. When it was demanded,

he quickly put out his tongue and courageously stretched forth his hands, ¹¹ and said nobly, "I got these from Heaven, and because of his laws I disdain them, and from him I hope to get them back again." ¹² As a result the king himself and those with him were astonished at the young man's spirit, for he regarded his sufferings as nothing.

13 After he too had died, they maltreated and tortured the fourth in the same way. ¹⁴ When he was near death, he said, "One cannot but choose to die at the hands of mortals and to cherish the hope God gives of being raised again by him. But for you there will be no resurrection to life!"

15 Next they brought forward the fifth and maltreated him. ¹⁶ But he looked at the king,*d* and said, "Because you have authority among mortals, though you also are mortal, you do what you please. But do not think that God has forsaken our people. ¹⁷ Keep on, and see how his mighty power will torture you and your descendants!"

18 After him they brought forward the sixth. And when he was about to die, he said, "Do not deceive yourself in vain. For we are suffering these things on our own account, because of our sins against our own God. Therefore*e* astounding things have happened. ¹⁹ But do not think that you will go unpunished for having tried to fight against God!"

20 The mother was especially admirable and worthy of honorable memory. Although she saw her seven sons perish within a single day, she bore it with good courage because of her hope in the Lord. ²¹ She encouraged each of them in the language of their ancestors. Filled

a Gk he *b* Gk they *c* Gk slaves *d* Gk at him *e* Lat: Other ancient authorities lack *Therefore*

---

literature. Tortures build in intensity to an emotional peak, with the seventh son who gives the longest speech explaining his action. The martyrs remain calm as the king rages (vv. 3, 39). It is too easy to dismiss one's enemies as raving lunatics. Such caricatures block any attempt at dialogue.

7:21, 27—The martyrs speak Hebrew to trick Antiochus and encourage one another. The marginalized often use trickery as a last resort against the powerful.

with a noble spirit, she reinforced her woman's reasoning with a man's courage, and said to them, ²²"I do not know how you came into being in my womb. It was not I who gave you life and breath, nor I who set in order the elements within each of you. ²³Therefore the Creator of the world, who shaped the beginning of humankind and devised the origin of all things, will in his mercy give life and breath back to you again, since you now forget yourselves for the sake of his laws."

24 Antiochus felt that he was being treated with contempt, and he was suspicious of her reproachful tone. The youngest brother being still alive, Antiochus*ᵃ* not only appealed to him in words, but promised with oaths that he would make him rich and enviable if he would turn from the ways of his ancestors, and that he would take him for his Friend and entrust him with public affairs. ²⁵Since the young man would not listen to him at all, the king called the mother to him and urged her to advise the youth to save himself. ²⁶After much urging on his part, she undertook to persuade her son. ²⁷But, leaning close to him, she spoke in their native language as follows, deriding the cruel tyrant: "My son, have pity on me. I carried you nine months in my womb, and nursed you for three years, and have reared you and brought you up to this point in your life, and have taken care of you.*ᵇ* ²⁸I beg you, my child, to look at the heaven and the earth and see everything that is in them, and recognize that God did not make them out of things that existed.*ᶜ* And in the same way the

human race came into being. ²⁹Do not fear this butcher, but prove worthy of your brothers. Accept death, so that in God's mercy I may get you back again along with your brothers."

30 While she was still speaking, the young man said, "What are you*ᵈ* waiting for? I will not obey the king's command, but I obey the command of the law that was given to our ancestors through Moses. ³¹But you,*ᵉ* who have contrived all sorts of evil against the Hebrews, will certainly not escape the hands of God. ³²For we are suffering because of our own sins. ³³And if our living Lord is angry for a little while, to rebuke and discipline us, he will again be reconciled with his own servants.*ᶠ* ³⁴But you, unholy wretch, you most defiled of all mortals, do not be elated in vain and puffed up by uncertain hopes, when you raise your hand against the children of heaven. ³⁵You have not yet escaped the judgment of the almighty, all-seeing God. ³⁶For our brothers after enduring a brief suffering have drunk*ᵍ* of everflowing life, under God's covenant; but you, by the judgment of God, will receive just punishment for your arrogance. ³⁷I, like my brothers, give up body and life for the laws of our ancestors, appealing to God to show mercy soon to our nation and by trials and plagues to make you confess that he alone is God, ³⁸and through me and my brothers to bring to an end the wrath of the Almighty that has justly fallen on our whole nation."

39 The king fell into a rage, and han-

---

*ᵃ*Gk he *ᵇ*Or have borne the burden of your education *ᶜ*Or God made them out of things that did not exist *ᵈ*The Gk here for you is plural *ᵉ*The Gk here for you is singular *ᶠ*Gk slaves *ᵍ*Cn: Gk fallen

---

7:28–29—The mother encourages her son's death by speaking of God who creates out of nothing (*creatio ex nihilo*) and who therefore must have the power to create their mutilated martyrs' bodies again from nothing (*I may get you back again*; cf. 14:46). This may simply be a declaration about the reanimation of the body that says nothing about the immortality of the soul (the latter is a prominent theme in 4 Maccabees, a later work).

7:36 *Under God's covenant*—Recognition of the special nature of the Jewish people. The son's martyr speech has a political motive—to cement Jewish identity under Seleucid oppression. The martyrs represent the Jewish people in a hostile environment. Christians need to examine what sets us apart and how our behavior expresses our identity in our secular culture today.

dled him worse than the others, being exasperated at his scorn. **40** So he died in his integrity, putting his whole trust in the Lord.

41 Last of all, the mother died, after her sons.

42 Let this be enough, then, about the eating of sacrifices and the extreme tortures.

The Revolt of Judas Maccabeus

8 Meanwhile Judas, who was also called Maccabeus, and his companions secretly entered the villages and summoned their kindred and enlisted those who had continued in the Jewish faith, and so they gathered about six thousand. **2** They implored the Lord to look upon the people who were oppressed by all; and to have pity on the temple that had been profaned by the godless; **3** to have mercy on the city that was being destroyed and about to be leveled to the ground; to hearken to the blood that cried out to him; **4** to remember also the lawless destruction of the innocent babies and the blasphemies committed against his name; and to show his hatred of evil.

5 As soon as Maccabeus got his army organized, the Gentiles could not withstand him, for the wrath of the Lord had turned to mercy. **6** Coming without warning, he would set fire to towns and villages. He captured strategic positions and put to flight not a few of the enemy. **7** He found the nights most advantageous for such attacks. And talk of his valor spread everywhere.

8 When Philip saw that the man was gaining ground little by little, and that he was pushing ahead with more frequent successes, he wrote to Ptolemy, the governor of Coelesyria and Phoenicia, to come to the aid of the king's government.

9 Then Ptolemy*a* promptly appointed Nicanor son of Patroclus, one of the king's chief*b* Friends, and sent him, in command of no fewer than twenty thousand Gentiles of all nations, to wipe out the whole race of Judea. He associated with him Gorgias, a general and a man of experience in military service. **10** Nicanor determined to make up for the king the tribute due to the Romans, two thousand talents, by selling the captured Jews into slavery. **11** So he immediately sent to the towns on the seacoast, inviting them to buy Jewish slaves and promising to hand over ninety slaves for a talent, not expecting the judgment from the Almighty that was about to overtake him.

Preparation for Battle

12 Word came to Judas concerning Nicanor's invasion; and when he told his companions of the arrival of the army, **13** those who were cowardly and distrustful of God's justice ran off and got away. **14** Others sold all their remaining property, and at the same time implored the Lord to rescue those who had been sold by the ungodly Nicanor before he ever met them, **15** if not for their own sake, then for the sake of the covenants made with their ancestors, and because he had called them by his holy and glorious name. **16** But Maccabeus gathered his forces together, to the number six thousand, and exhorted them not to be frightened by the enemy and not to fear the great multitude of Gentiles who were wickedly coming against them, but to fight nobly, **17** keeping before their eyes the lawless outrage that the Gentiles*c* had committed against the holy place, and the torture of the derided city, and besides, the overthrow of their ancestral way of life. **18** "For they trust to arms and

a Gk he *b* Gk one of the first *c* Gk they

8:1–36—Judas fights an increasingly successful guerilla war and defeats Nicanor with God's help (vv. 11, 18, 24).

8:18—A contrast between those who trust in armies and those who trust in God, which func-

tions to highlight the courage of Judas. We need to look at how we as a nation express our trust in God, especially in terms of our military and foreign policy, which often leaves no room for God to act apart from our own terms.

acts of daring," he said, "but we trust in the Almighty God, who is able with a single nod to strike down those who are coming against us, and even, if necessary, the whole world."

19 Moreover, he told them of the occasions when help came to their ancestors; how, in the time of Sennacherib, when one hundred eighty-five thousand perished, 20 and the time of the battle against the Galatians that took place in Babylonia, when eight thousand Jews[a] fought along with four thousand Macedonians; yet when the Macedonians were hard pressed, the eight thousand, by the help that came to them from heaven, destroyed one hundred twenty thousand Galatians[b] and took a great amount of booty.

Judas Defeats Nicanor

21 With these words he filled them with courage and made them ready to die for their laws and their country; then he divided his army into four parts. 22 He appointed his brothers also, Simon and Joseph and Jonathan, each to command a division, putting fifteen hundred men under each. 23 Besides, he appointed Eleazar to read aloud[c] from the holy book, and gave the watchword, "The help of God"; then, leading the first division himself, he joined battle with Nicanor.

24 With the Almighty as their ally, they killed more than nine thousand of the enemy, and wounded and disabled most of Nicanor's army, and forced them all to flee. 25 They captured the money of those who had come to buy them as slaves. After pursuing them for some distance, they were obliged to return because the hour was late. 26 It was the day before the sabbath, and for that reason they did not continue their pursuit. 27 When they had collected the arms of the enemy and stripped them of their spoils, they kept the sabbath, giving great praise and thanks to the Lord, who had preserved them for that day

and allotted it to them as the beginning of mercy. 28 After the sabbath they gave some of the spoils to those who had been tortured and to the widows and orphans, and distributed the rest among themselves and their children. 29 When they had done this, they made common supplication and implored the merciful Lord to be wholly reconciled with his servants.[d]

Judas Defeats Timothy and Bacchides

30 In encounters with the forces of Timothy and Bacchides they killed more than twenty thousand of them and got possession of some exceedingly high strongholds, and they divided a very large amount of plunder, giving to those who had been tortured and to the orphans and widows, and also to the aged, shares equal to their own. 31 They collected the arms of the enemy,[e] and carefully stored all of them in strategic places; the rest of the spoils they carried to Jerusalem. 32 They killed the commander of Timothy's forces, a most wicked man, and one who had greatly troubled the Jews. 33 While they were celebrating the victory in the city of their ancestors, they burned those who had set fire to the sacred gates, Callisthenes and some others, who had fled into one little house; so these received the proper reward for their impiety.[c]

34 The thrice-accursed Nicanor, who had brought the thousand merchants to buy the Jews, 35 having been humbled with the help of the Lord by opponents whom he regarded as of the least account, took off his splendid uniform and made his way alone like a runaway slave across the country until he reached Antioch, having succeeded chiefly in the destruction of his own army! 36 So he who had undertaken to secure tribute for the Romans by the capture of the people of Jerusalem proclaimed that the Jews had a Defender, and that therefore

---

[a] Gk lacks *Jews* [b] Gk lacks *Galatians* [c] Meaning of Gk uncertain [d] Gk *slaves* [e] Gk *their arms*

the Jews were invulnerable, because they followed the laws ordained by him.

The Last Campaign of Antiochus Epiphanes

9 About that time, as it happened, Antiochus had retreated in disorder from the region of Persia. ² He had entered the city called Persepolis and attempted to rob the temples and control the city. Therefore the people rushed to the rescue with arms, and Antiochus and his army were defeated,ᵃ with the result that Antiochus was put to flight by the inhabitants and beat a shameful retreat. ³ While he was in Ecbatana, news came to him of what had happened to Nicanor and the forces of Timothy. ⁴ Transported with rage, he conceived the idea of turning upon the Jews the injury done by those who had put him to flight; so he ordered his charioteer to drive without stopping until he completed the journey. But the judgment of heaven rode with him! For in his arrogance he said, "When I get there I will make Jerusalem a cemetery of Jews."

5 But the all-seeing Lord, the God of Israel, struck him with an incurable and invisible blow. As soon as he stopped speaking he was seized with a pain in his bowels, for which there was no relief, and with sharp internal tortures— ⁶ and that very justly, for he had tortured the bowels of others with many and strange inflictions. ⁷ Yet he did not in any way stop his insolence, but was even more filled with arrogance, breathing fire in his rage against the Jews, and giving orders to drive even faster. And so it came about that he fell out of his chariot as it was rushing along, and the fall was so hard as to torture every limb of his body. ⁸ Thus he who only a little while before had thought in his superhuman arrogance that he could command the waves of the sea, and had imagined that he could weigh the high mountains in a balance, was brought down to earth and carried in a litter, making the power of God manifest to all. ⁹ And so the ungodly man's body swarmed with worms, and while he was still living in anguish and pain, his flesh rotted away, and because of the stench the whole army felt revulsion at his decay. ¹⁰ Because of his intolerable stench no one was able to carry the man who a little while before had thought that he could touch the stars of heaven. ¹¹ Then it was that, broken in spirit, he began to lose much of his arrogance and to come to his senses under the scourge of God, for he was tortured with pain every moment. ¹² And when he could not endure his own stench, he uttered these words, "It is right to be subject to God; mortals should not think that they are equal to God."ᵇ

Antiochus Makes a Promise to God

13 Then the abominable fellow made a vow to the Lord, who would no longer have mercy on him, stating ¹⁴ that the holy city, which he was hurrying to level to the ground and to make a cemetery, he was now declaring to be free; ¹⁵ and the Jews, whom he had not considered worth burying but had planned to throw out with their children for the wild animals and for the birds to eat, he would make, all of them, equal to citizens of Athens; ¹⁶ and the holy sanctuary, which he had formerly plundered, he would adorn with the finest offerings; and all the holy vessels he would give back,

ᵃ Gk *they were defeated*   ᵇ Or *not think thoughts proper only to God*

9:1–29—God appears again to afflict an arrogant and enraged Antiochus Epiphanes, who dies fittingly in Persia after making repentant promises to God and the Jews. God presides over a system of rewards and punishments.

9:12 *Mortals should not think that they are equal to God*—Antiochus learns a hard lesson.

We need to analyze the ways in which our arrogance in relation to God is expressed today, on both the personal and national levels. "God Bless America" bumper stickers can be seen by the rest of the world as an expression of American arrogance.

many times over; and the expenses incurred for the sacrifices he would provide from his own revenues; [17] and in addition to all this he also would become a Jew and would visit every inhabited place to proclaim the power of God. [18] But when his sufferings did not in any way abate, for the judgment of God had justly come upon him, he gave up all hope for himself and wrote to the Jews the following letter, in the form of a supplication. This was its content:

Antiochus's Letter and Death

[19] "To his worthy Jewish citizens, Antiochus their king and general sends hearty greetings and good wishes for their health and prosperity. [20] If you and your children are well and your affairs are as you wish, I am glad. As my hope is in heaven, [21] I remember with affection your esteem and goodwill. On my way back from the region of Persia I suffered an annoying illness, and I have deemed it necessary to take thought for the general security of all. [22] I do not despair of my condition, for I have good hope of recovering from my illness, [23] but I observed that my father, on the occasions when he made expeditions into the upper country, appointed his successor, [24] so that, if anything unexpected happened or any unwelcome news came, the people throughout the realm would not be troubled, for they would know to whom the government was left. [25] Moreover, I understand how the princes along the borders and the neighbors of my kingdom keep watching for opportunities and waiting to see what will happen. So I have appointed my son Antiochus to be king, whom I have often entrusted and commended to most of you when I hurried off to the upper provinces; and I have written to him what is written here. [26] I therefore urge and beg you to remember the public and private services rendered to you and to maintain your present goodwill, each of you, toward me and my son. [27] For I am sure that he will follow my policy and will treat you with moderation and kindness."

[28] So the murderer and blasphemer, having endured the more intense suffering, such as he had inflicted on others, came to the end of his life by a most pitiable fate, among the mountains in a strange land. [29] And Philip, one of his courtiers, took his body home; then, fearing the son of Antiochus, he withdrew to Ptolemy Philometor in Egypt.

Purification of the Temple

10 Now Maccabeus and his followers, the Lord leading them on, recovered the temple and the city; [2] they tore down the altars that had been built in the public square by the foreigners, and also destroyed the sacred precincts. [3] They purified the sanctuary, and made another altar of sacrifice; then, striking fire out of flint, they offered sacrifices, after a lapse of two years, and they offered incense and lighted lamps and set out the bread of the Presence. [4] When they had done this, they fell prostrate and implored the Lord that they might never again fall into such misfortunes, but that, if they should ever sin, they might be disciplined by him with forbearance and not be handed over to blasphemous and barbarous nations. [5] It happened that on the same day on which the sanctuary had been profaned by the foreigners, the purification of the sanctuary took place, that is, on the twenty-fifth day of the same month, which was Chislev. [6] They celebrated it for eight days with rejoicing, in the manner of the festival of booths, remembering how not long before, during the festival of booths, they had been wandering in the mountains and caves like wild animals. [7] Therefore, carrying ivy-wreathed wands and beautiful

---

10:1–9—Judas purifies the temple; cf. 1 Macc. 4:36–59. The deaths of the martyrs enable Judas to reassert Jewish national and religious identity.

branches and also fronds of palm, they offered hymns of thanksgiving to him who had given success to the purifying of his own holy place. [8] They decreed by public edict, ratified by vote, that the whole nation of the Jews should observe these days every year.

9 Such then was the end of Antiochus, who was called Epiphanes.

Accession of Antiochus Eupator

10 Now we will tell what took place under Antiochus Eupator, who was the son of that ungodly man, and will give a brief summary of the principal calamities of the wars. [11] This man, when he succeeded to the kingdom, appointed one Lysias to have charge of the government and to be chief governor of Coelesyria and Phoenicia. [12] Ptolemy, who was called Macron, took the lead in showing justice to the Jews because of the wrong that had been done to them, and attempted to maintain peaceful relations with them. [13] As a result he was accused before Eupator by the king's Friends. He heard himself called a traitor at every turn, because he had abandoned Cyprus, which Philometor had entrusted to him, and had gone over to Antiochus Epiphanes. Unable to command the respect due his office,[a] he took poison and ended his life.

Campaign in Idumea

14 When Gorgias became governor of the region, he maintained a force of mercenaries, and at every turn kept attacking the Jews. [15] Besides this, the Idumeans, who had control of important strongholds, were harassing the Jews; they received those who were banished from Jerusalem, and endeavored to keep up the war. [16] But Maccabeus and his forces, after making solemn supplication and imploring God to fight on their side, rushed to the strongholds of the Idumeans. [17] Attacking them vigorously, they gained possession of the places, and beat off all who fought upon the wall, and slaughtered those whom they encountered, killing no fewer than twenty thousand.

18 When at least nine thousand took refuge in two very strong towers well equipped to withstand a siege, [19] Maccabeus left Simon and Joseph, and also Zacchaeus and his troops, a force sufficient to besiege them; and he himself set off for places where he was more urgently needed. [20] But those with Simon, who were money-hungry, were bribed by some of those who were in the towers, and on receiving seventy thousand drachmas let some of them slip away. [21] When word of what had happened came to Maccabeus, he gathered the leaders of the people, and accused these men of having sold their kindred for money by setting their enemies free to fight against them. [22] Then he killed these men who had turned traitor, and immediately captured the two towers. [23] Having success at arms in everything he undertook, he destroyed more than twenty thousand in the two strongholds.

Judas Defeats Timothy

24 Now Timothy, who had been defeated by the Jews before, gathered a tremendous force of mercenaries and collected the cavalry from Asia in no small number. He came on, intending to take Judea by storm. [25] As he drew near, Maccabeus and his men sprinkled dust on their heads and girded their loins with sackcloth, in supplication to God. [26] Falling upon the steps before

[a] Cn: Meaning of Gk uncertain

10:10–15:36 The Third Attack on the Temple

10:14–38—Judas defeats local governors Gorgias and Timothy, who were harassing the Jews, and he kills Jewish traitors. One is either for Judas or against him, though he does not go looking

for trouble. An analysis of U.S. political rhetoric reveals a similar attitude. We draw sharp lines in the sand to distinguish our allies from our enemies, and we curtail civil rights in the name of security.

the altar, they implored him to be gracious to them and to be an enemy to their enemies and an adversary to their adversaries, as the law declares. **27** And rising from their prayer they took up their arms and advanced a considerable distance from the city; and when they came near the enemy they halted. **28** Just as dawn was breaking, the two armies joined battle, the one having as pledge of success and victory not only their valor but also their reliance on the Lord, while the other made rage their leader in the fight.

29 When the battle became fierce, there appeared to the enemy from heaven five resplendent men on horses with golden bridles, and they were leading the Jews. **30** Two of them took Maccabeus between them, and shielding him with their own armor and weapons, they kept him from being wounded. They showered arrows and thunderbolts on the enemy, so that, confused and blinded, they were thrown into disorder and cut to pieces. **31** Twenty thousand five hundred were slaughtered, besides six hundred cavalry.

32 Timothy himself fled to a stronghold called Gazara, especially well garrisoned, where Chaereas was commander. **33** Then Maccabeus and his men were glad, and they besieged the fort for four days. **34** The men within, relying on the strength of the place, kept blaspheming terribly and uttering wicked words. **35** But at dawn of the fifth day, twenty young men in the army of Maccabeus, fired with anger because of the blasphemies, bravely stormed the wall and with savage fury cut down everyone they met. **36** Others who came up in the same way wheeled around against the defenders and set fire to the towers; they kindled fires and burned the blasphemers alive. Others broke open the gates and let in the rest of the force, and they occupied the city. **37** They killed Timothy, who was hiding in a cistern, and his brother Chaereas, and Apollophanes. **38** When they had accomplished these things, with hymns and thanksgivings they blessed the Lord who shows great kindness to Israel and gives them the victory.

Lysias Besieges Beth-zur

11 Very soon after this, Lysias, the king's guardian and kinsman, who was in charge of the government, being vexed at what had happened, **2** gathered about eighty thousand infantry and all his cavalry and came against the Jews. He intended to make the city a home for Greeks, **3** and to levy tribute on the temple as he did on the sacred places of the other nations, and to put up the high priesthood for sale every year. **4** He took no account whatever of the power of God, but was elated with his ten thousands of infantry, and his thousands of cavalry, and his eighty elephants. **5** Invading Judea, he approached Beth-zur, which was a fortified place about five stadia*a* from Jerusalem, and pressed it hard.

6 When Maccabeus and his men got word that Lysias*b* was besieging the strongholds, they and all the people, with lamentations and tears, prayed the Lord to send a good angel to save Israel. **7** Maccabeus himself was the first to take up arms, and he urged the others to risk their lives with him to aid their kindred. Then they eagerly rushed off together. **8** And there, while they were still near Jerusalem, a horseman appeared at their head, clothed in white and brandishing weapons of gold. **9** And together they all praised the merciful God, and were

a Meaning of Gk uncertain   *b* Gk he

11:1–38—Lysias, guardian of the young Antiochus V, makes peace with the Jews after disgraceful defeat, acknowledging that *the Hebrews were invincible because the mighty God fought on their side* (v. 13). Modern conflicts can become a kind of holy war when we believe that God chooses our side. By embracing a God who rubber-stamps national policy, we often silence honest critique of that policy, which results in a narrowly defined patriotism.

strengthened in heart, ready to assail not only humans but the wildest animals or walls of iron. [10] They advanced in battle order, having their heavenly ally, for the Lord had mercy on them. [11] They hurled themselves like lions against the enemy, and laid low eleven thousand of them and sixteen hundred cavalry, and forced all the rest to flee. [12] Most of them got away stripped and wounded, and Lysias himself escaped by disgraceful flight.

Lysias Makes Peace with the Jews

13 As he was not without intelligence, he pondered over the defeat that had befallen him, and realized that the Hebrews were invincible because the mighty God fought on their side. So he sent to them [14] and persuaded them to settle everything on just terms, promising that he would persuade the king, constraining him to be their friend.[a] [15] Maccabeus, having regard for the common good, agreed to all that Lysias urged. For the king granted every request in behalf of the Jews which Maccabeus delivered to Lysias in writing.

16 The letter written to the Jews by Lysias was to this effect:

"Lysias to the people of the Jews, greetings. [17] John and Absalom, who were sent by you, have delivered your signed communication and have asked about the matters indicated in it. [18] I have informed the king of everything that needed to be brought before him, and he has agreed to what was possible. [19] If you will maintain your goodwill toward the government, I will endeavor in the future to help promote your welfare. [20] And concerning such matters and their details, I have ordered these men and my representatives to confer with you. [21] Farewell. The one hundred forty-eighth year,[b] Dioscorinthius twenty-fourth."

22 The king's letter ran thus:

"King Antiochus to his brother Lysias, greetings. [23] Now that our father has gone on to the gods, we desire that the subjects of the kingdom be undisturbed in caring for their own affairs. [24] We have heard that the Jews do not consent to our father's change to Greek customs, but prefer their own way of living and ask that their own customs be allowed them. [25] Accordingly, since we choose that this nation also should be free from disturbance, our decision is that their temple be restored to them and that they shall live according to the customs of their ancestors. [26] You will do well, therefore, to send word to them and give them pledges of friendship, so that they may know our policy and be of good cheer and go on happily in the conduct of their own affairs."

27 To the nation the king's letter was as follows:

"King Antiochus to the senate of the Jews and to the other Jews, greetings. [28] If you are well, it is as we desire. We also are in good health. [29] Menelaus has informed us that you wish to return home and look after your own affairs. [30] Therefore those who go home by the thirtieth of Xanthicus will have our pledge of friendship and full permission [31] for the Jews to enjoy their own food and laws, just as formerly, and none of them shall be molested in any way for what may have been done in ignorance. [32] And I have also sent Menelaus to encourage you. [33] Farewell. The one hundred forty-eighth year,[b] Xanthicus fifteenth."

34 The Romans also sent them a letter, which read thus:

"Quintus Memmius and Titus Manius, envoys of the Romans, to the people of the Jews, greetings. [35] With regard to what Lysias the kinsman of the king has granted you, we also give consent. [36] But as to the matters that he decided are to be referred to the king, as soon as you have considered them, send some one promptly so that we may make proposals appropriate for you. For we are on

---

[a] Meaning of Gk uncertain   [b] 164 B.C

our way to Antioch. ³⁷ Therefore make haste and send messengers so that we may have your judgment. ³⁸ Farewell. The one hundred forty-eighth year,ᵃ Xanthicus fifteenth."

Incidents at Joppa and Jamnia

12 When this agreement had been reached, Lysias returned to the king, and the Jews went about their farming.

2 But some of the governors in various places, Timothy and Apollonius son of Gennaeus, as well as Hieronymus and Demophon, and in addition to these Nicanor the governor of Cyprus, would not let them live quietly and in peace. ³ And the people of Joppa did so ungodly a deed as this: they invited the Jews who lived among them to embark, with their wives and children, on boats that they had provided, as though there were no ill will to the Jews;ᵇ ⁴ and this was done by public vote of the city. When they accepted, because they wished to live peaceably and suspected nothing, the people of Joppaᶜ took them out to sea and drowned them, at least two hundred. ⁵ When Judas heard of the cruelty visited on his compatriots, he gave orders to his men ⁶ and, calling upon God, the righteous judge, attacked the murderers of his kindred. He set fire to the harbor by night, burned the boats, and massacred those who had taken refuge there. ⁷ Then, because the city's gates were closed, he withdrew, intending to come again and root out the whole community of Joppa. ⁸ But learning that the people in Jamnia meant in the same way to wipe out the Jews who were living among them, ⁹ he attacked the Jamnites by night and set fire to the harbor and the fleet, so that the glow of the light was seen in Jerusalem, thirty milesᵈ distant.

The Campaign in Gilead

10 When they had gone more than a mileᵉ from there, on their march against Timothy, at least five thousand Arabs with five hundred cavalry attacked them. ¹¹ After a hard fight, Judas and his companions, with God's help, were victorious. The defeated nomads begged Judas to grant them pledges of friendship, promising to give him livestock and to help his peopleᶠ in all other ways. ¹² Judas, realizing that they might indeed be useful in many ways, agreed to make peace with them; and after receiving his pledges they went back to their tents.

13 He also attacked a certain town that was strongly fortified with earthworksᵍ and walls, and inhabited by all sorts of Gentiles. Its name was Caspin. ¹⁴ Those who were within, relying on the strength of the walls and on their supply of provisions, behaved most insolently toward Judas and his men, railing at them and even blaspheming and saying unholy things. ¹⁵ But Judas and his men, calling upon the great Sovereign of the world, who without battering rams or engines of war overthrew Jericho in the days of Joshua, rushed furiously upon the walls. ¹⁶ They took the town by the will of God, and slaughtered untold numbers, so that the adjoining lake, a quarter of a mileʰ wide, appeared to be running over with blood.

Judas Defeats Timothy's Army

17 When they had gone ninety-five milesⁱ from there, they came to Charax, to the Jews who are called Toubiani. ¹⁸ They did not find Timothy in that region, for he had by then left there without accomplishing anything, though in one place he had left a very strong garrison. ¹⁹ Dositheus and Sosipater, who were captains under Maccabeus, marched out and destroyed those whom Timothy had left in the strong-

ᵃ 164 B.C. ᵇ Gk to them ᶜ Gk they ᵈ Gk two hundred forty stadia ᵉ Gk nine stadia ᶠ Gk them ᵍ Meaning of Gk uncertain ʰ Gk two stadia ⁱ Gk seven hundred fifty stadia

12:1–13:26—Local hostilities continue, but Judas is victorious because he trusts God and prays (12:38–42).

hold, more than ten thousand men. [20] But Maccabeus arranged his army in divisions, set men[a] in command of the divisions, and hurried after Timothy, who had with him one hundred twenty thousand infantry and two thousand five hundred cavalry. [21] When Timothy learned of the approach of Judas, he sent off the women and the children and also the baggage to a place called Carnaim; for that place was hard to besiege and difficult of access because of the narrowness of all the approaches. [22] But when Judas's first division appeared, terror and fear came over the enemy at the manifestation to them of him who sees all things. In their flight they rushed headlong in every direction, so that often they were injured by their own men and pierced by the points of their own swords. [23] Judas pressed the pursuit with the utmost vigor, putting the sinners to the sword, and destroyed as many as thirty thousand.

24 Timothy himself fell into the hands of Dositheus and Sosipater and their men. With great guile he begged them to let him go in safety, because he held the parents of most of them, and the brothers of some, to whom no consideration would be shown. [25] And when with many words he had confirmed his solemn promise to restore them unharmed, they let him go, for the sake of saving their kindred.

Judas Wins Other Victories

26 Then Judas[b] marched against Carnaim and the temple of Atargatis, and slaughtered twenty-five thousand people. [27] After the rout and destruction of these, he marched also against Ephron, a fortified town where Lysias lived with multitudes of people of all nationalities.[c] Stalwart young men took their stand before the walls and made a vigorous defense; and great stores of war engines and missiles were there. [28] But the Jews[d]

called upon the Sovereign who with power shatters the might of his enemies, and they got the town into their hands, and killed as many as twenty-five thousand of those who were in it.

29 Setting out from there, they hastened to Scythopolis, which is seventy-five miles[e] from Jerusalem. [30] But when the Jews who lived there bore witness to the goodwill that the people of Scythopolis had shown them and their kind treatment of them in times of misfortune, [31] they thanked them and exhorted them to be well disposed to their race in the future also. Then they went up to Jerusalem, as the festival of weeks was close at hand.

Judas Defeats Gorgias

32 After the festival called Pentecost, they hurried against Gorgias, the governor of Idumea, [33] who came out with three thousand infantry and four hundred cavalry. [34] When they joined battle, it happened that a few of the Jews fell. [35] But a certain Dositheus, one of Bacenor's men, who was on horseback and was a strong man, caught hold of Gorgias, and grasping his cloak was dragging him off by main strength, wishing to take the accursed man alive, when one of the Thracian cavalry bore down on him and cut off his arm; so Gorgias escaped and reached Marisa.

36 As Esdris and his men had been fighting for a long time and were weary, Judas called upon the Lord to show himself their ally and leader in the battle. [37] In the language of their ancestors he raised the battle cry, with hymns; then he charged against Gorgias's troops when they were not expecting it, and put them to flight.

Prayers for Those Killed in Battle

38 Then Judas assembled his army and went to the city of Adullam. As the

[a] Gk them   [b] Gk he   [c] Meaning of Gk uncertain   [d] Gk they   [e] Gk six hundred stadia

---

12:38–45—Judas collects a sin offering to atone for dead soldiers who have died because of their idolatry (act/consequence), motivated by his belief in resurrection; cf. 1 Macc. 2:39–41.

seventh day was coming on, they puri-fied themselves according to the cus-tom, and kept the sabbath there.

39 On the next day, as had now become necessary, Judas and his men went to take up the bodies of the fallen and to bring them back to lie with their kindred in the sepulchres of their ances-tors. 40 Then under the tunic of each one of the dead they found sacred tokens of the idols of Jamnia, which the law for-bids the Jews to wear. And it became clear to all that this was the reason these men had fallen. 41 So they all blessed the ways of the Lord, the righteous judge, who reveals the things that are hidden; 42 and they turned to supplication, pray-ing that the sin that had been commit-ted might be wholly blotted out. The noble Judas exhorted the people to keep themselves free from sin, for they had seen with their own eyes what had hap-pened as the result of the sin of those who had fallen. 43 He also took up a col-lection, man by man, to the amount of two thousand drachmas of silver, and sent it to Jerusalem to provide for a sin offering. In doing this he acted very well and honorably, taking account of the resurrection. 44 For if he were not expect-ing that those who had fallen would rise again, it would have been superfluous and foolish to pray for the dead. 45 But if he was looking to the splendid reward that is laid up for those who fall asleep in godliness, it was a holy and pious thought. Therefore he made atonement for the dead, so that they might be deliv-ered from their sin.

Menelaus Is Put to Death

13 In the one hundred forty-ninth year[a] word came to Judas and his men that Antiochus Eupator was com-ing with a great army against Judea, 2 and with him Lysias, his guardian, who had charge of the government. Each of them had a Greek force of one hundred ten thousand infantry, five thousand three hundred cavalry, twenty-two elephants,

and three hundred chariots armed with scythes.

3 Menelaus also joined them and with utter hypocrisy urged Antiochus on, not for the sake of his country's welfare, but because he thought that he would be established in office. 4 But the King of kings aroused the anger of Antio-chus against the scoundrel; and when Lysias informed him that this man was to blame for all the trouble, he ordered them to take him to Beroea and to put him to death by the method that is customary in that place. 5 For there is a tower there, fifty cubits high, full of ashes, and it has a rim running around it that on all sides inclines precipitously into the ashes. 6 There they all push to destruction anyone guilty of sacrilege or notorious for other crimes. 7 By such a fate it came about that Menelaus the lawbreaker died, without even burial in the earth. 8 And this was eminently just; because he had committed many sins against the altar whose fire and ashes were holy, he met his death in ashes.

A Battle Near the City of Modein

9 The king with barbarous arrogance was coming to show the Jews things far worse than those that had been done[b] in his father's time. 10 But when Judas heard of this, he ordered the people to call upon the Lord day and night, now if ever to help those who were on the point of being deprived of the law and their country and the holy temple, 11 and not to let the people who had just begun to revive fall into the hands of the blasphemous Gentiles. 12 When they had all joined in the same petition and had implored the merciful Lord with weeping and fasting and lying prostrate for three days without ceasing, Judas exhorted them and ordered them to stand ready.

13 After consulting privately with the elders, he determined to march out and decide the matter by the help of God

[a] 163 B.C.   [b] Or the worst of the things that had been done

before the king's army could enter Judea and get possession of the city. **14** So, committing the decision to the Creator of the world and exhorting his troops to fight bravely to the death for the laws, temple, city, country, and commonwealth, he pitched his camp near Modein. **15** He gave his troops the watchword, "God's victory," and with a picked force of the bravest young men, he attacked the king's pavilion at night and killed as many as two thousand men in the camp. He stabbed[a] the leading elephant and its rider. **16** In the end they filled the camp with terror and confusion and withdrew in triumph. **17** This happened, just as day was dawning, because the Lord's help protected him.

Antiochus Makes a Treaty with the Jews

18 The king, having had a taste of the daring of the Jews, tried strategy in attacking their positions. **19** He advanced against Beth-zur, a strong fortress of the Jews, was turned back, attacked again,[b] and was defeated. **20** Judas sent in to the garrison whatever was necessary. **21** But Rhodocus, a man from the ranks of the Jews, gave secret information to the enemy; he was sought for, caught, and put in prison. **22** The king negotiated a second time with the people in Beth-zur, gave pledges, received theirs, withdrew, attacked Judas and his men, was defeated; **23** he got word that Philip, who had been left in charge of the government, had revolted in Antioch; he was dismayed, called in the Jews, yielded and swore to observe all their rights, settled with them and offered sacrifice, honored the sanctuary and showed generosity to the holy place. **24** He received Maccabeus, left Hegemonides as governor from Ptolemais to Gerar, **25** and went to Ptolemais. The people of Ptolemais were indignant over the treaty; in fact they were so angry that they wanted to annul its terms.[a] **26** Lysias took the public platform, made the best possible defense, convinced them, appeased them, gained

their goodwill, and set out for Antioch. This is how the king's attack and withdrawal turned out.

Alcimus Speaks against Judas

14 Three years later, word came to Judas and his men that Demetrius son of Seleucus had sailed into the harbor of Tripolis with a strong army and a fleet, **2** and had taken possession of the country, having made away with Antiochus and his guardian Lysias.

3 Now a certain Alcimus, who had formerly been high priest but had willfully defiled himself in the times of separation,[c] realized that there was no way for him to be safe or to have access again to the holy altar, **4** and went to King Demetrius in about the one hundred fifty-first year,[d] presenting to him a crown of gold and a palm, and besides these some of the customary olive branches from the temple. During that day he kept quiet. **5** But he found an opportunity that furthered his mad purpose when he was invited by Demetrius to a meeting of the council and was asked about the attitude and intentions of the Jews. He answered:

6 "Those of the Jews who are called Hasideans, whose leader is Judas Maccabeus, are keeping up war and stirring up sedition, and will not let the kingdom attain tranquility. **7** Therefore I have laid aside my ancestral glory—I mean the high priesthood—and have now come here, **8** first because I am genuinely concerned for the interests of the king, and second because I have regard also for my compatriots. For through the folly of those whom I have mentioned our whole nation is now in no small misfortune. **9** Since you are acquainted, O king, with the details of this matter, may it please you to take thought for our country and our hard-pressed nation with the gracious kindness that you show to all. **10** For as long as Judas lives, it is

---

[a] Meaning of Gk uncertain   [b] Or faltered   [c] Other ancient authorities read of mixing   [d] 161 B.C.

impossible for the government to find peace." [11] When he had said this, the rest of the king's Friends,[a] who were hostile to Judas, quickly inflamed Demetrius still more. [12] He immediately chose Nicanor, who had been in command of the elephants, appointed him governor of Judea, and sent him off [13] with orders to kill Judas and scatter his troops, and to install Alcimus as high priest of the great[b] temple. [14] And the Gentiles throughout Judea, who had fled before[c] Judas, flocked to join Nicanor, thinking that the misfortunes and calamities of the Jews would mean prosperity for themselves.

Nicanor Makes Friends with Judas

15 When the Jews[d] heard of Nicanor's coming and the gathering of the Gentiles, they sprinkled dust on their heads and prayed to him who established his own people forever and always upholds his own heritage by manifesting himself. [16] At the command of the leader, they[e] set out from there immediately and engaged them in battle at a village called Dessau.[c] [17] Simon, the brother of Judas, had encountered Nicanor, but had been temporarily[f] checked because of the sudden consternation created by the enemy.

18 Nevertheless Nicanor, hearing of the valor of Judas and his troops and their courage in battle for their country, shrank from deciding the issue by bloodshed. [19] Therefore he sent Posidonius, Theodotus, and Mattathias to give and receive pledges of friendship. [20] When the terms had been fully considered, and the leader had informed the people, and it had appeared that they were of one mind, they agreed to the covenant. [21] The leaders[g] set a day on which to meet by themselves. A chariot came forward from each army; seats of honor were set in place; [22] Judas posted armed men in readiness at key places to prevent sudden treachery on the part of the enemy; so they duly held the consultation.

23 Nicanor stayed on in Jerusalem and did nothing out of the way, but dismissed the flocks of people that had gathered. [24] And he kept Judas always in his presence; he was warmly attached to the man. [25] He urged him to marry and have children; so Judas[e] married, settled down, and shared the common life.

Nicanor Turns against Judas

26 But when Alcimus noticed their goodwill for one another, he took the covenant that had been made and went to Demetrius. He told him that Nicanor was disloyal to the government, since he had appointed that conspirator against the kingdom, Judas, to be his successor. [27] The king became excited and, provoked by the false accusations of that depraved man, wrote to Nicanor, stating that he was displeased with the covenant and commanding him to send Maccabeus to Antioch as a prisoner without delay.

28 When this message came to Nicanor, he was troubled and grieved that he had to annul their agreement when the man had done no wrong. [29] Since it was not possible to oppose the king, he watched for an opportunity to accomplish this by a stratagem. [30] But Maccabeus, noticing that Nicanor was more austere in his dealings with him and was meeting him more rudely than had been

---

[a] Gk of the Friends [b] Gk greatest [c] Meaning of Gk uncertain [d] Gk they [e] Gk he [f] Other ancient authorities read slowly [g] Gk they

---

14:15–25—Unlike 1 Maccabees, which does not trust the Seleucids, 2 Maccabees reports that Nicanor admired Judas and made friends with him, allowing Judas to marry and settle into civilian life. In 2 Maccabees, war is not assumed to be the only way to deal with conflict.

14:26–36—Nicanor turns against Judas because of the false accusations of the high priest Alcimus. Following an unjust order from the king to take Judas prisoner, Nicanor's whole attitude changes, pushing us to recognize the ways in which our actions are distorted when we ignore our conscience.

his custom, concluded that this austerity did not spring from the best motives. So he gathered not a few of his men, and went into hiding from Nicanor. ³¹ When the latter became aware that he had been cleverly outwitted by the man, he went to the greatᵃ and holy temple while the priests were offering the customary sacrifices, and commanded them to hand the man over. ³² When they declared on oath that they did not know where the man was whom he wanted, ³³ he stretched out his right hand toward the sanctuary, and swore this oath: "If you do not hand Judas over to me as a prisoner, I will level this shrine of God to the ground and tear down the altar, and build here a splendid temple to Dionysus."

34 Having said this, he went away. Then the priests stretched out their hands toward heaven and called upon the constant Defender of our nation, in these words: ³⁵ "O Lord of all, though you have need of nothing, you were pleased that there should be a temple for your habitation among us; ³⁶ so now, O holy One, Lord of all holiness, keep undefiled forever this house that has been so recently purified."

Razis Dies for His Country

37 A certain Razis, one of the elders of Jerusalem, was denounced to Nicanor as a man who loved his compatriots and was very well thought of and for his goodwill was called father of the Jews. ³⁸ In former times, when there was no mingling with the Gentiles, he had been accused of Judaism, and he had most zealously risked body and life

for Judaism. ³⁹ Nicanor, wishing to exhibit the enmity that he had for the Jews, sent more than five hundred soldiers to arrest him; ⁴⁰ for he thought that by arrestingᵇ him he would do them an injury. ⁴¹ When the troops were about to capture the tower and were forcing the door of the courtyard, they ordered that fire be brought and the doors burned. Being surrounded, Razisᶜ fell upon his own sword, ⁴² preferring to die nobly rather than to fall into the hands of sinners and suffer outrages unworthy of his noble birth. ⁴³ But in the heat of the struggle he did not hit exactly, and the crowd was now rushing in through the doors. He courageously ran up on the wall, and bravely threw himself down into the crowd. ⁴⁴ But as they quickly drew back, a space opened and he fell in the middle of the empty space. ⁴⁵ Still alive and aflame with anger, he rose, and though his blood gushed forth and his wounds were severe he ran through the crowd; and standing upon a steep rock, ⁴⁶ with his blood now completely drained from him, he tore out his entrails, took them in both hands and hurled them at the crowd, calling upon the Lord of life and spirit to give them back to him again. This was the manner of his death.

Nicanor's Arrogance

15 When Nicanor heard that Judas and his troops were in the region of Samaria, he made plans to attack them with complete safety on the day of rest. ² When the Jews who were compelled to follow him said, "Do not destroy so

ᵃ Gk greatest ᵇ Meaning of Gk uncertain ᶜ Gk he

14:37–46—Nicanor tries to make the elder Razis an example of his hatred for the Jews by arresting him, but Razis commits suicide. He does not volunteer to kill himself; the situation is forced upon him. When Razis calls upon God to return to him the innards he has flung at the crowd, he testifies to God's power and his own faith and courage. His drawn out, graphic suicide is presented as a noble death, which challenges the stigma surrounding suicide today, and the notion that it is

an act of weakness and never acceptable. Razis pushes us to reconsider many related issues in medical ethics, including euthanasia.

15:1–37—Bolstered by fervent prayer, the outnumbered army of Judas defeats and kills Nicanor, winning religious freedom for the Jews. God has again saved God's temple (v. 34), prompting us to contemplate the ways in which God is at work in the world today.

savagely and barbarously, but show respect for the day that he who sees all things has honored and hallowed above other days," ³the thrice-accursed wretch asked if there were a sovereign in heaven who had commanded the keeping of the sabbath day. ⁴When they declared, "It is the living Lord himself, the Sovereign in heaven, who ordered us to observe the seventh day," ⁵he replied, "But I am a sovereign also, on earth, and I command you to take up arms and finish the king's business." Nevertheless, he did not succeed in carrying out his abominable design.

Judas Prepares the Jews for Battle

6 This Nicanor in his utter boastfulness and arrogance had determined to erect a public monument of victory over Judas and his forces. ⁷But Maccabeus did not cease to trust with all confidence that he would get help from the Lord. ⁸He exhorted his troops not to fear the attack of the Gentiles, but to keep in mind the former times when help had come to them from heaven, and so to look for the victory that the Almighty would give them. ⁹Encouraging them from the law and the prophets, and reminding them also of the struggles they had won, he made them the more eager. ¹⁰When he had aroused their courage, he issued his orders, at the same time pointing out the perfidy of the Gentiles and their violation of oaths. ¹¹He armed each of them not so much with confidence in shields and spears as with the inspiration of brave words, and he cheered them all by relating a dream, a sort of vision,ᵃ which was worthy of belief.

12 What he saw was this: Onias, who had been high priest, a noble and good man, of modest bearing and gentle manner, one who spoke fittingly and had been trained from childhood in all that belongs to excellence, was praying with outstretched hands for the whole body of the Jews. ¹³Then in the same fashion another appeared, distinguished by his gray hair and dignity, and of marvelous majesty and authority. ¹⁴And Onias spoke, saying, "This is a man who loves the family of Israel and prays much for the people and the holy city—Jeremiah, the prophet of God." ¹⁵Jeremiah stretched out his right hand and gave to Judas a golden sword, and as he gave it he addressed him thus: ¹⁶"Take this holy sword, a gift from God, with which you will strike down your adversaries."

17 Encouraged by the words of Judas, so noble and so effective in arousing valor and awaking courage in the souls of the young, they determined not to carry on a campaignᵇ but to attack bravely, and to decide the matter by fighting hand to hand with all courage, because the city and the sanctuary and the temple were in danger. ¹⁸Their concern for wives and children, and also for brothers and sistersᶜ and relatives, lay upon them less heavily; their greatest and first fear was for the consecrated sanctuary. ¹⁹And those who had to remain in the city were in no little distress, being anxious over the encounter in the open country.

The Defeat and Death of Nicanor

20 When all were now looking forward to the coming issue, and the enemy was already close at hand with their army drawn up for battle, the elephantsᵈ strategically stationed and the cavalry deployed on the flanks, ²¹Maccabeus, observing the masses that were in front of him and the varied supply of arms and the savagery of the elephants, stretched out his hands toward heaven and called upon the Lord who works wonders; for he knew that it is not by arms, but as the Lordᵉ decides, that he gains the victory for those who deserve it. ²²He called upon him in these words: "O Lord, you sent your angel in the time of King Hezekiah of Judea, and he killed fully one hundred eighty-five

ᵃ Meaning of Gk uncertain ᵇ Or to remain in camp ᶜ Gk for brothers
ᵈ Gk animals ᵉ Gk he

thousand in the camp of Sennacherib. ²³ So now, O Sovereign of the heavens, send a good angel to spread terror and trembling before us. ²⁴ By the might of your arm may these blasphemers who come against your holy people be struck down." With these words he ended his prayer.

25 Nicanor and his troops advanced with trumpets and battle songs, ²⁶ but Judas and his troops met the enemy in battle with invocations to God and prayers. ²⁷ So, fighting with their hands and praying to God in their hearts, they laid low at least thirty-five thousand, and were greatly gladdened by God's manifestation.

28 When the action was over and they were returning with joy, they recognized Nicanor, lying dead, in full armor. ²⁹ Then there was shouting and tumult, and they blessed the Sovereign Lord in the language of their ancestors. ³⁰ Then the man who was ever in body and soul the defender of his people, the man who maintained his youthful goodwill toward his compatriots, ordered them to cut off Nicanor's head and arm and carry them to Jerusalem. ³¹ When he arrived there and had called his compatriots together and stationed the priests before the altar, he sent for those who were in the citadel. ³² He showed them the vile Nicanor's head and that profane man's arm, which had been boastfully stretched out against the holy house of the Almighty. ³³ He cut out the tongue of the ungodly Nicanor and said that he would feed it piecemeal to the birds and would hang up these rewards of his folly opposite the sanctuary. ³⁴ And they all, looking to heaven, blessed the Lord who had manifested himself, saying, "Blessed is he who has kept his own place undefiled!" ³⁵ Judas[a] hung Nicanor's head from the citadel, a clear and conspicuous sign to everyone of the help of the Lord. ³⁶ And they all decreed by public vote never to let this day go unobserved, but to celebrate the thirteenth day of the twelfth month—which is called Adar in the Aramaic language—the day before Mordecai's day.

37 This, then, is how matters turned out with Nicanor, and from that time the city has been in the possession of the Hebrews. So I will here end my story.

The Compiler's Epilogue

38 If it is well told and to the point, that is what I myself desired; if it is poorly done and mediocre, that was the best I could do. ³⁹ For just as it is harmful to drink wine alone, or, again, to drink water alone, while wine mixed with water is sweet and delicious and enhances one's enjoyment, so also the style of the story delights the ears of those who read the work. And here will be the end.

[a] Gk He

15:32 Boastfully stretched out—Nicanor gets what he deserves: his arm and head are cut off (see also 4:38; 10:5–6; 13:8). Act/consequence thinking may be satisfying, but it can also be dangerous, not only on the personal, but on the social and global levels as well. When we work backwards from the consequence to the group or nation ("them") as a confirmation of their inferiority and subordination (to "us"), we run the risk of bullying and social control; this can block our investigation of the cause of the action and any life-enhancing transformation of the situation.

15:38–39—The Epitomist's Epilogue

The Book of
1 ESDRAS

I t is not easy to be faithful to God when one's world is falling apart or when powerful and unscrupulous people take advantage of others. First Esdras (called Third
Esdras in the Vulgate and many Latin manuscripts, and Second Esdras in Russian
Bibles) addresses that problem by selecting episodes from the books of 2 Chronicles,
Ezra, and Nehemiah that show the ruin and restitution of the religious establishment
in Jerusalem and of the hopes of people separated physically from that restitution. It
begins with the people of Israel observing the Passover at the temple (the true center
of Israelite faith) during the reign of the king Josiah (2 Chr. 35:1–27). Next it narrates the rebuilding of the temple under the auspices of the Persian government (Ezra
1–6). It continues with the career of Ezra (as recounted in Ezra 7–10) and ends with
Ezra's promulgating the Law once more in the temple precincts (Neh. 7:73–8:12). It
changes the order of the Hebrew Bible by moving the account of opposition given in
Ezra 4:7–23 to a position before the return of Zerubbabel (1 Esd. 2:16–30), adding a
lengthy narrative about Zerubbabel (1 Esd. 3:1–5:6), skipping Ezra 4:6, and omitting
all references to Nehemiah. The narrative about Zerubbabel probably was included to
introduce and magnify Zerubbabel, a hero of the author and someone who plays an
important role in rebuilding the temple. It is not, however, the key to the whole book
of 1 Esdras. The key is the centrality of the temple and the Law.

The relationship of 1 Esdras to the books of 2 Chronicles, Ezra, and Nehemiah
requires further discussion. Since the overlap between 1 Esdras and the three canonical books is too extensive to be accidental, scholars have offered three possible basic
explanations. (1) The account in the Hebrew Bible derived from an earlier version of
1 Esdras; (2) 1 Esdras was a later modification of the account in the Hebrew Bible;
and (3) both came from a common source. Since 1 Esdras seems to be a composite
from various sources, the first option seems to be the least likely. The second option
may be better than the third.

The book begins with Israel observing the Passover at the temple, which has been
purified by the actions of Josiah; it closes with Israel observing the Passover according
to the Law, with the people standing before the temple to hear the Law. The Law and
the temple were closely related. The Law commanded the people to sacrifice to God
at the temple. Those sacrifices expressed contrition for sins (Lev. 1:1–17; 4:1–5:13),
communion with God (Lev. 3:1–17), and a desire to make restitution to people
they had wronged (Lev. 5:14–6:7). In the postexilic situation, keeping the Law also
involved limiting one's marriage partner to members of the community. The scene of
men divorcing their wives (1 Esd. 8:91–9:36) may seem ill-advised and even cruel today, but it shows the lengths to which some members of the community were willing
to go to follow the Law.

The book takes its name from its primary but by no means only hero, Ezra, a priest
and scribe and the hero of Ezra 7–10 and Nehemiah 8:1–9:37. Ezra was not the

author, though he speaks in the first person singular in 8:28–9:90 (cf. Ezra 7:28–9:15). One reason for drawing this conclusion is the book's confusion over the order of Persian kings. It takes them in the following sequence: Cyrus (reigned 539–530 in 2:1, Artaxerxes I (r. 465–424) or Artaxerxes II (r. 404–358) in 2:16, and Darius I (r. 522–486) in 3:1. The man Ezra, whose career probably began in 458 (the seventh year of Artaxerxes I) or perhaps in 397 (the seventh year of Artaxerxes II), can hardly have been so confused about the sequence of kings in Persia during his own life. If the author was not Ezra, who was it? He seems to have been a Jew, perhaps living in Alexandria, Egypt, some time after 150 BCE. This date is suggested because of the similarity of the narrative in 3:1–5:6 to the *Letter of Aristeas*, a book that was probably produced in Alexandria. First Esdras was known to Josephus, who died some time after 100 CE, so it cannot be later than that.

The value of this book to modern disciples is that it urges them to persevere in service to God and others despite opposition from other people. It teaches disciples, among other lessons, to share what they have freely with others, to protect the environment as a God-given trust, to commit their ultimate loyalty to the truth so far as they know it, to accept assistance even from unlikely sources in their service to God, and to accept all classes of peoples.

—**Paul L. Redditt**

Josiah Celebrates the Passover

1 Josiah kept the passover to his Lord in Jerusalem; he killed the passover lamb on the fourteenth day of the first month, ² having placed the priests according to their divisions, arrayed in their vestments, in the temple of the Lord. ³ He told the Levites, the temple servants of Israel, that they should sanctify themselves to the Lord and put the holy ark of the Lord in the house that King Solomon, son of David, had built; ⁴ and he said, "You need no longer carry it on your shoulders. Now worship the Lord your God and serve his people Israel; prepare yourselves by your families and kindred, ⁵ in accordance with the directions of King David of Israel and the magnificence of his son Solomon. Stand in order in the temple according to the groupings of the ancestral houses of you Levites, who minister before your kindred the people of Israel, ⁶ and kill the passover lamb and prepare the sacrifices for your kindred, and keep the passover according to the commandment of the Lord that was given to Moses."

7 To the people who were present

1:1–22 Josiah's Passover (cf. 2 Chr. 35:1–19)

1:1 *Josiah*—King of Judah from 640 to 609, who instituted a sweeping reform of Israelite worship (cf. 2 Kgs. 22:1–23:35; 2 Chr. 34:1–35:19). His reform, as reform often does, involved a return to vital traditions and practices from the past. Contemporary disciples, too, need to change in ways that allow them to remain true to their central teachings and calling. *Passover*—Springtime sacrifice and communal meal, observed in March/April on the **fourteenth day of the first month** during the Feast of Unleavened Bread. It commemorated the liberation of the Israelites from slavery in Egypt (Exod. 11:4–8). Contemporary liberation theologies often point to the exodus as evidence that God liberates the oppressed from their oppressors.

1:3 *Sanctify*—To separate for use in the service of God. Such separation involved dedication to God, not withdrawal from the world. Here the word also means to purify from sins by means of sacrifices, so sanctification had a material cost as well. *Ark*—The ark of the covenant from the time of Moses.

1:4 *Worship . . . serve*—The worship of God should always result in service to other people. Here the service in view is officiating during the sacrificial worship, but Jeremiah (cf. 7:5–7) reminded his contemporaries that offering sacrifice was insufficient without a commitment to justice for the poor. See note at 1:23.

1:7–9—The generosity of the king toward the *people* receives emphasis here. Since Passover

Josiah gave thirty thousand lambs and kids, and three thousand calves; these were given from the king's possessions, as he promised, to the people and the priests and Levites. **8** Hilkiah, Zechariah, and Jehiel,*a* the chief officers of the temple, gave to the priests for the passover two thousand six hundred sheep and three hundred calves. **9** And Jeconiah and Shemaiah and his brother Nethanel, and Hashabiah and Ochiel and Joram, captains over thousands, gave the Levites for the passover five thousand sheep and seven hundred calves.

10 This is what took place. The priests and the Levites, having the unleavened bread, stood in proper order according to kindred **11** and the grouping of the ancestral houses, before the people, to make the offering to the Lord as it is written in the book of Moses; this they did in the morning. **12** They roasted the passover lamb with fire, as required; and they boiled the sacrifices in bronze pots and caldrons, with a pleasing odor, **13** and carried them to all the people. Afterward they prepared the passover for themselves and for their kindred the priests, the sons of Aaron, **14** because the priests were offering the fat until nightfall; so the Levites prepared it for themselves and for their kindred the priests, the sons of Aaron. **15** The temple singers, the sons of Asaph, were in their place according to the arrangement made by David, and also Asaph, Zechariah, and Eddinus, who represented the king. **16** The gatekeepers were at each gate; no one needed to interrupt his daily duties, for their kindred the Levites prepared the passover for them.

17 So the things that had to do with the sacrifices to the Lord were accomplished that day: the passover was kept **18** and the sacrifices were offered on the altar of the Lord, according to the command of King Josiah. **19** And the people of Israel who were present at that time kept the passover and the festival of unleavened bread seven days. **20** No passover like it had been kept in Israel since the times of the prophet Samuel; **21** none of the kings of Israel had kept such a passover as was kept by Josiah and the priests and Levites and the people of Judah and all of Israel who were living in Jerusalem. **22** In the eighteenth year of the reign of Josiah this passover was kept.

The End of Josiah's Reign

23 And the deeds of Josiah were upright in the sight of the Lord, for his heart was full of godliness. **24** In ancient times the events of his reign have been recorded—concerning those who sinned and acted wickedly toward the Lord beyond any other people or kingdom, and how they grieved the Lord*b* deeply, so that the words of the Lord fell upon Israel.

25 After all these acts of Josiah, it happened that Pharaoh, king of Egypt, went to make war at Carchemish on the Euphrates, and Josiah went out against him. **26** And the king of Egypt sent word to him saying, "What have we to do with each other, O king of Judea? **27** I was not

a Gk *Esyelus* *b* Gk *him*

---

lambs were eaten by the families and not shared with the *priests* and *Levites*, they would need their own animals. Generosity toward others is a virtue of disciples and a necessity in rectifying social inequities.

1:23–33 The Death of Josiah

1:23 *Deeds of Josiah*—Josiah instituted reforms that included both ritual and moral issues. He abolished images of and temples to other gods, provided for the Levites, and eliminated cultic prostitution in the temple (2 Kgs. 23:5–15). He also made sure the poor in his land received

justice (Jer. 22:15b–16). True spirituality involves proper attention to both worship and morality.

1:24 *Those who sinned*—Not even Josiah's godliness could atone for the sinfulness of the people of Israel. Faithfulness implies individual responsibility and accountability.

1:25 *Pharaoh*—Neco II, who ruled Egypt 610–593. In 609 Neco set out for Mesopotamia to bolster the sagging Assyrian Empire, passing through Israel in the plain of Megiddo.

1:26–27—According to 2 Chr. 35:21, Neco appealed to Josiah in the name of God to let him

sent against you by the Lord God, for my war is at the Euphrates. And now the Lord is with me! The Lord is with me, urging me on! Stand aside, and do not oppose the Lord."

28 Josiah, however, did not turn back to his chariot, but tried to fight with him, and did not heed the words of the prophet Jeremiah from the mouth of the Lord. 29 He joined battle with him in the plain of Megiddo, and the commanders came down against King Josiah. 30 The king said to his servants, "Take me away from the battle, for I am very weak." And immediately his servants took him out of the line of battle. 31 He got into his second chariot; and after he was brought back to Jerusalem he died, and was buried in the tomb of his ancestors.

32 In all Judea they mourned for Josiah. The prophet Jeremiah lamented for Josiah, and the principal men, with the women,*a* have made lamentation for him to this day; it was ordained that this should always be done throughout the whole nation of Israel. 33 These things are written in the book of the histories of the kings of Judea; and every one of the acts of Josiah, and his splendor, and his understanding of the law of the Lord, and the things that he had done before, and these that are now told, are recorded in the book of the kings of Israel and Judah.

The Last Kings of Judah

34 The men of the nation took Jeconiah*b* son of Josiah, who was twenty-three years old, and made him king in succes-sion to his father Josiah. 35 He reigned three months in Judah and Jerusalem. Then the king of Egypt deposed him from reigning in Jerusalem, 36 and fined the nation one hundred talents of silver and one talent of gold. 37 The king of Egypt made his brother Jehoiakim king of Judea and Jerusalem. 38 Jehoiakim put the nobles in prison, and seized his brother Zarius and brought him back from Egypt.

39 Jehoiakim was twenty-five years old when he began to reign in Judea and Jerusalem; he did what was evil in the sight of the Lord. 40 King Nebuchadnezzar of Babylon came up against him; he bound him with a chain of bronze and took him away to Babylon. 41 Nebuchadnezzar also took some holy vessels of the Lord, and carried them away, and stored them in his temple in Babylon. 42 But the things that are reported about Jehoiakim,*c* and his uncleanness and impiety, are written in the annals of the kings.

43 His son Jehoiachin*d* became king in his place; when he was made king he was eighteen years old, 44 and he reigned three months and ten days in Jerusalem. He did what was evil in the sight of the Lord. 45 A year later Nebuchadnezzar sent and removed him to Babylon, with the holy vessels of the Lord, 46 and made Zedekiah king of Judea and Jerusalem.

The Fall of Jerusalem

Zedekiah was twenty-one years old, and he reigned eleven years. 47 He also

a Or *their wives* *b* 2 Kings 23.30; 2 Chr 36.1 *Jehoahaz* *c* Gk *him* *d* Gk *Jehoiakim*

---

pass through Israel. Josiah refused and lost his life in the ensuing battle. First Esdras 1:28 adds that God had warned Josiah through the prophet Jeremiah (who flourished during and after Josiah's reign). Second Kings portrayed Josiah as heroic, but these three verses offer an explanation for why God allowed godly king Josiah to die at the hands of a pagan king: he ignored the warning of God's great prophet. If such a great man failed by not heeding the prophets, how much more should the readers of 1 Esdras—including moderns—heed their words.

1:34–58 The Fall of Judah and Jerusalem (cf. 2 Chr. 36:1–21)

The years following the death of Josiah saw three of his sons and one of his grandsons rule Judah: *Jeconiah* (609), *Jehoiakim* (609–598), *Jehoiachin* (598–597), and *Zedekiah* (597–586).

1:46—Zedekiah withheld tribute from Nebuchadnezzar in 588, even after taking an oath in God's name that he would pay. His political failure was at least partly moral. His fate serves as an object lesson against breaking one's oath.

did what was evil in the sight of the Lord, and did not heed the words that were spoken by the prophet Jeremiah from the mouth of the Lord. **48** Although King Nebuchadnezzar had made him swear by the name of the Lord, he broke his oath and rebelled; he stiffened his neck and hardened his heart and transgressed the laws of the Lord, the God of Israel. **49** Even the leaders of the people and of the priests committed many acts of sacrilege and lawlessness beyond all the unclean deeds of all the nations, and polluted the temple of the Lord in Jerusalem—the temple that God had made holy. **50** The God of their ancestors sent his messenger to call them back, because he would have spared them and his dwelling place. **51** But they mocked his messengers, and whenever the Lord spoke, they scoffed at his prophets, **52** until in his anger against his people because of their ungodly acts he gave command to bring against them the kings of the Chaldeans. **53** These killed their young men with the sword around their holy temple, and did not spare young man or young woman,*a* old man or child, for he gave them all into their hands. **54** They took all the holy vessels of the Lord, great and small, the treasure chests of the Lord, and the royal stores, and carried them away to Babylon. **55** They burned the house of the Lord, broke down the walls of Jerusalem, burned their towers with fire, **56** and utterly destroyed all its glorious things.

The survivors he led away to Babylon with the sword, **57** and they were servants to him and to his sons until the Persians began to reign, in fulfillment of the word of the Lord by the mouth of Jeremiah, **58** saying, "Until the land has enjoyed its sabbaths, it shall keep sabbath all the time of its desolation until the completion of seventy years."

Cyrus Permits the Exiles to Return

2 In the first year of Cyrus as king of the Persians, so that the word of the Lord by the mouth of Jeremiah might be accomplished— **2** the Lord stirred up the spirit of King Cyrus of the Persians, and he made a proclamation throughout all his kingdom and also put it in writing:

3 "Thus says Cyrus king of the Persians: The Lord of Israel, the Lord Most High, has made me king of the world, **4** and he has commanded me to build him a house at Jerusalem, which is in Judea. **5** If any of you, therefore, are of his people, may your Lord be with you; go up to Jerusalem, which is in Judea, and build the house of the Lord of Israel— he is the Lord who dwells in Jerusalem— **6** and let each of you, wherever you may live, be helped by the people of your place with gold and silver, **7** with gifts and with horses and cattle, besides the other things added as votive offerings for the temple of the Lord that is in Jerusalem."

8 Then arose the heads of families of the tribes of Judah and Benjamin,

a Gk *virgin*

1:58 *Sabbaths*—According to Lev. 26:1–7, farmland was to lie fallow every seventh year. The people of Judah had failed to keep the Sabbath years, so the exile would last ten Sabbaths or seventy years (see Jer. 29:10). Modern disciples too need to recognize the need to protect the environment as a God-given trust.

2:1–15 Cyrus Authorizes Return (cf. 2 Chr. 36:22–23; Ezra 1:1–11)

2:1—Cyrus became the king of Persia in 550 BCE and captured Babylon in 539.

2:3—Cyrus acknowledges that the *Lord of Israel* had made him king, an ironic twist since Israel's own kings often did not acknowledge God's

leadership in their lives. Cyrus's characterization demonstrates that responsiveness to God is more important than membership in a particular community.

2:4–7—The so-called edict of Cyrus, a proclamation allowing Jews to return to Jerusalem and rebuild the temple. God used this foreign king to accomplish God's purpose. Christians today likewise may work with non-Christian entities in pursuit of goals that would be pleasing to God.

2:7 *Votive*—Offerings for rebuilding the temple fulfilled a vow. Believers should keep their promises to God.

and the priests and the Levites, and all whose spirit the Lord had stirred to go up to build the house in Jerusalem for the Lord; [9] their neighbors helped them with everything, with silver and gold, with horses and cattle, and with a very great number of votive offerings from many whose hearts were stirred.

[10] King Cyrus also brought out the holy vessels of the Lord that Nebuchadnezzar had carried away from Jerusalem and stored in his temple of idols. [11] When King Cyrus of the Persians brought these out, he gave them to Mithridates, his treasurer, [12] and by him they were given to Sheshbazzar,[a] the governor of Judea. [13] The number of these was: one thousand gold cups, one thousand silver cups, twenty-nine silver censers, thirty gold bowls, two thousand four hundred ten silver bowls, and one thousand other vessels. [14] All the vessels were handed over, gold and silver, five thousand four hundred sixty-nine, [15] and they were carried back by Sheshbazzar with the returning exiles from Babylon to Jerusalem.

Opposition to Rebuilding Jerusalem

[16] In the time of King Artaxerxes of the Persians, Bishlam, Mithridates, Tabeel, Rehum, Beltethmus, the scribe Shimshai, and the rest of their associates, living in Samaria and other places, wrote him the following letter, against those who were living in Judea and Jerusalem:

[17] "To King Artaxerxes our lord, your servants the recorder Rehum and the scribe Shimshai and the other members of their council, and the judges in Coelesyria and Phoenicia: [18] Let it now be known to our lord the king that the Jews who came up from you to us have gone to Jerusalem and are building that rebellious and wicked city, repairing its market places and walls and laying the foundations for a temple. [19] Now if this city is built and the walls finished, they will not only refuse to pay tribute but will even resist kings. [20] Since the building of the temple is now going on, we think it best not to neglect such a matter, [21] but to speak to our lord the king, in order that, if it seems good to you, search may be made in the records of your ancestors. [22] You will find in the annals what has been written about them, and will learn that this city was rebellious, troubling both kings and other cities, [23] and that the Jews were rebels and kept setting up blockades in it from of old. That is why this city was laid waste. [24] Therefore we now make known to you, O lord and king, that if this city is built and its walls finished, you will no longer have access to Coelesyria and Phoenicia."

[25] Then the king, in reply to the recorder Rehum, Beltethmus, the scribe Shimshai, and the others associated with them and living in Samaria and Syria and Phoenicia, wrote as follows:

[26] "I have read the letter that you sent me. So I ordered search to be made, and it has been found that this city from of old has fought against kings, [27] that the people in it were given to rebellion and war, and that mighty and cruel kings ruled in Jerusalem and exacted tribute

[a] Gk Sanabassaros

2:10—Cyrus returned the vessels taken by Nebuchadnezzar, apparently as an act of piety and kindness, two virtues necessary for any disciple.

2:12, 15 Sheshbazzar—The Israelite leader of the first group to return to Jerusalem (probably in 538) authorized to rebuild the temple (cf. Ezra 1:8, 11; 5:14, 16).

2:16–30 Opposition to Rebuilding the City and the Temple (cf. Ezra 4:7–24)

2:16 Artaxerxes—Probably Artaxerxes I (r.

465–424). Since the letter was addressed to Artaxerxes, it was apparently from the time of Ezra, and its appearance here is an anachronism that nevertheless ties the two time frames together.

2:18—The letter complains that the people were rebuilding marketplaces and walls, not just the temple.

2:27 Mighty and cruel kings—The referents are unclear, but the connection between power and cruelty is clear.

from Coelesyria and Phoenicia. [28] Therefore I have now issued orders to prevent these people from building the city and to take care that nothing more be done [29] and that such wicked proceedings go no further to the annoyance of kings."

30 Then, when the letter from King Artaxerxes was read, Rehum and the scribe Shimshai and their associates went quickly to Jerusalem, with cavalry and a large number of armed troops, and began to hinder the builders. And the building of the temple in Jerusalem stopped until the second year of the reign of King Darius of the Persians.

The Debate of the Three Bodyguards

3 Now King Darius gave a great banquet for all that were under him, all that were born in his house, and all the nobles of Media and Persia, [2] and all the satraps and generals and governors that were under him in the hundred twenty-seven satrapies from India to Ethiopia. [3] They ate and drank, and when they were satisfied they went away, and King Darius went to his bedroom; he went to sleep, but woke up again.

4 Then the three young men of the bodyguard, who kept guard over the person of the king, said to one another, [5] "Let each of us state what one thing is strongest; and to the one whose statement seems wisest, King Darius will give rich gifts and great honors of vic-

tory. [6] He shall be clothed in purple, and drink from gold cups, and sleep on a gold bed,[a] and have a chariot with gold bridles, and a turban of fine linen, and a necklace around his neck; [7] and because of his wisdom he shall sit next to Darius and shall be called Kinsman of Darius."

8 Then each wrote his own statement, and they sealed them and put them under the pillow of King Darius, [9] and said, "When the king wakes, they will give him the writing; and to the one whose statement the king and the three nobles of Persia judge to be wisest the victory shall be given according to what is written." [10] The first wrote, "Wine is strongest." [11] The second wrote, "The king is strongest." [12] The third wrote, "Women are strongest, but above all things truth is victor."[b]

13 When the king awoke, they took the writing and gave it to him, and he read it. [14] Then he sent and summoned all the nobles of Persia and Media and the satraps and generals and governors and prefects, [15] and he took his seat in the council chamber, and the writing was read in their presence. [16] He said, "Call the young men, and they shall explain their statements." So they were summoned, and came in. [17] They said to them, "Explain to us what you have written."

[a] Gk on gold [b] Or but truth is victor over all things

2:30—Work halted in Jerusalem. Sometimes even service to God encounters obstacles. Ultimately in this case the faithful triumphed. Such is not always the case, but discipleship can be its own reward.

3:1–17a The Beginning of the Contest of the Three Bodyguards in Cyrus's Court

Variations on this court narrative appear elsewhere in the ancient Middle East. It was "Judaized" by identifying the third bodyguard with Zerubbabel, the descendant of David (through King Jehoiachin) who eventually succeeded in rebuilding the temple. Zerubbabel, along with Jeshua, the newly nominated high priest, led a group of repatriates from Babylon to Judah in 521. The prophets Haggai and Zechariah urged the people to help Zerubbabel build the temple.

First Esdras 3:1–5:6 fills in background "information" about him.

3:1 Great banquet—Presumably held in Susa, the capital. Cf. Dan. 5:1–31 and Esth. 1:1–9.

3:2 Satrapies—Administrative divisions of the Persian Empire.

3:4–12—Three bodyguards proposed a question for competition among the palace guards (what is the strongest thing in the world?) and wrote out their answers.

3:13–17a—Members of the court assembled.

3:17b–24 The Strength of Wine

The first guard extolled the strength of wine, which can make people happy, but also can make them forget social differences and respon-

The Speech about Wine

Then the first, who had spoken of the strength of wine, began and said: [18]"Gentlemen, how is wine the strongest? It leads astray the minds of all who drink it. [19]It makes equal the mind of the king and the orphan, of the slave and the free, of the poor and the rich. [20]It turns every thought to feasting and mirth, and forgets all sorrow and debt. [21]It makes all hearts feel rich, forgets kings and satraps, and makes everyone talk in millions.[a] [22]When people drink they forget to be friendly with friends and kindred, and before long they draw their swords. [23]And when they recover from the wine, they do not remember what they have done. [24]Gentlemen, is not wine the strongest, since it forces people to do these things?" When he had said this, he stopped speaking.

The Speech about the King

4 Then the second, who had spoken of the strength of the king, began to speak: [2]"Gentlemen, are not men strongest, who rule over land and sea and all that is in them? [3]But the king is stronger; he is their lord and master, and whatever he says to them they obey. [4]If he tells them to make war on one another, they do it; and if he sends them out against the enemy, they go, and conquer mountains, walls, and towers. [5]They kill and are killed, and do not disobey the king's command; if they win the victory, they bring everything to the king—whatever spoil they take and everything else. [6]Likewise those who do not serve in the army or make war but till the soil; whenever they sow and reap, they bring some to the king; and they compel one another to pay taxes to the king. [7]And yet he is only one man! If he tells them to kill, they kill; if he tells them to release, they release; [8]if he tells them to attack, they attack; if he tells them to lay waste, they lay waste; if he tells them to build, they build; [9]if he tells them to cut down, they cut down; if he tells them to plant, they plant. [10]All his people and his armies obey him. Furthermore, he reclines, he eats and drinks and sleeps, [11]but they keep watch around him, and no one may go away to attend to his own affairs, nor do they disobey him. [12]Gentlemen, why is not the king the strongest, since he is to be obeyed in this fashion?" And he stopped speaking.

The Speech about Women

13 Then the third, who had spoken of women and truth (and this was Zerubbabel), began to speak: [14]"Gentlemen, is not the king great, and are not men many, and is not wine strong? Who is it, then, that rules them, or has the mastery over them? Is it not women? [15]Women gave birth to the king and to every people that rules over sea and land. [16]From women they came; and women brought up the very men who plant the vineyards from which comes wine. [17]Women make men's clothes; they bring men glory; men cannot exist without women. [18]If men gather gold and silver or any other beautiful thing, and then see a woman lovely in appearance and beauty, [19]they let all those things go, and gape at her, and with open mouths stare at her, and all prefer her to gold or silver or any other beautiful thing. [20]A man leaves his own father, who brought him up, and his own country, and clings to his wife.

[a] Gk talents

---

sibilities and lead people to fight. Pleasure alone does not make people happy.

4:1–12 The Strength of Kings

The second guard suggested the strength of kings, who can force his subjects to obey. Political power too has its place, but is not ultimately satisfying.

4:13–32 The Strength of Women

Zerubbabel first said women are stronger than kings or other men, because they give them birth and rear them, lead them from their fathers' homes, receive booty from their warfare and other endeavors, and drive men mad!

21 With his wife he ends his days, with no thought of his father or his mother or his country. 22 Therefore you must realize that women rule over you!

"Do you not labor and toil, and bring everything and give it to women? 23 A man takes his sword, and goes out to travel and rob and steal and to sail the sea and rivers; 24 he faces lions, and he walks in darkness, and when he steals and robs and plunders, he brings it back to the woman he loves. 25 A man loves his wife more than his father or his mother. 26 Many men have lost their minds because of women, and have become slaves because of them. 27 Many have perished, or stumbled, or sinned because of women. 28 And now do you not believe me?

"Is not the king great in his power? Do not all lands fear to touch him? 29 Yet I have seen him with Apame, the king's concubine, the daughter of the illustrious Bartacus; she would sit at the king's right hand 30 and take the crown from the king's head and put it on her own, and slap the king with her left hand. 31 At this the king would gaze at her with mouth agape. If she smiles at him, he laughs; if she loses her temper with him, he flatters her, so that she may be reconciled to him. 32 Gentlemen, why are not women strong, since they do such things?"

The Speech about Truth

33 Then the king and the nobles looked at one another; and he began to speak about truth: 34 "Gentlemen, are not women strong? The earth is vast, and heaven is high, and the sun is swift in its course, for it makes the circuit of the heavens and returns to its place in one day. 35 Is not the one who does these things great? But truth is great, and stronger than all things. 36 The whole earth calls upon truth, and heaven blesses it. All God's works[a] quake and tremble, and with him there is nothing unrighteous. 37 Wine is unrighteous, the king is unrighteous, women are unrighteous, all human beings are unrighteous, all their works are unrighteous, and all such things. There is no truth in them and in their unrighteousness they will perish. 38 But truth endures and is strong forever, and lives and prevails forever and ever. 39 With it there is no partiality or preference, but it does what is righteous instead of anything that is unrighteous or wicked. Everyone approves its deeds, 40 and there is nothing unrighteous in its judgment. To it belongs the strength and the kingship and the power and the majesty of all the ages. Blessed be the God of truth!" 41 When he stopped speaking, all the people shouted and said, "Great is truth, and strongest of all!"

Zerubbabel's Reward

42 Then the king said to him, "Ask what you wish, even beyond what is written, and we will give it to you, for you have been found to be the wisest. You shall sit next to me, and be called my Kinsman." 43 Then he said to the king, "Remember the vow that you made on the day when you became king, to build Jerusalem, 44 and to send back all the vessels that were taken from Jerusalem, which Cyrus set apart when he began[b] to destroy Babylon, and vowed to send them back there. 45 You also vowed to build the temple, which the Edomites burned when Judea was laid waste by the Chaldeans. 46 And now, O lord the king, this is what I ask and request of you, and this befits your greatness. I pray therefore that you fulfill the vow whose fulfillment you vowed to the King of heaven with your own lips."

[a] Gk All the works   [b] Cn: Gk vowed

4:33–41 The Strength of Truth
Truth is stronger even than women, because wine, the king, and all humans, even women, are unrighteous, while the truth is righteous and endures forever. Today too, disciples must commit their ultimate loyalty to the truth.

4:42–57 Zerubbabel's Reward

47 Then King Darius got up and kissed him, and wrote letters for him to all the treasurers and governors and generals and satraps, that they should give safe conduct to him and to all who were going up with him to build Jerusalem. **48** And he wrote letters to all the governors in Coelesyria and Phoenicia and to those in Lebanon, to bring cedar timber from Lebanon to Jerusalem, and to help him build the city. **49** He wrote in behalf of all the Jews who were going up from his kingdom to Judea, in the interest of their freedom, that no officer or satrap or governor or treasurer should forcibly enter their doors; **50** that all the country that they would occupy should be theirs without tribute; that the Idumeans should give up the villages of the Jews that they held; **51** that twenty talents a year should be given for the building of the temple until it was completed, **52** and an additional ten talents a year for burnt offerings to be offered on the altar every day, in accordance with the commandment to make seventeen offerings; **53** and that all who came from Babylonia to build the city should have their freedom, they and their children and all the priests who came. **54** He wrote also concerning their support and the priests' vestments in which[a] they were to minister. **55** He wrote that the support for the Levites should be provided until the day when the temple would be finished and Jerusalem built. **56** He wrote that land and wages should be provided for all who guarded the city. **57** And he sent back from Babylon all the vessels that Cyrus had set apart; everything that Cyrus had ordered to be done, he also commanded to be done and to be sent to Jerusalem.

Zerubbabel's Prayer

58 When the young man went out, he lifted up his face to heaven toward Jerusalem, and praised the King of heaven, saying, **59** "From you comes the victory; from you comes wisdom, and yours is the glory. I am your servant. **60** Blessed are you, who have given me wisdom; I give you thanks, O Lord of our ancestors."

61 So he took the letters, and went to Babylon and told this to all his kindred. **62** And they praised the God of their ancestors, because he had given them release and permission **63** to go up and build Jerusalem and the temple that is called by his name; and they feasted, with music and rejoicing, for seven days.

List of the Returning Exiles

5 After this the heads of ancestral houses were chosen to go up, according to their tribes, with their wives and sons and daughters, and their male and female servants, and their livestock. **2** And Darius sent with them a thousand cavalry to take them back to Jerusalem in safety, with the music of drums and flutes; **3** all their kindred were making merry. And he made them go up with them.

4 These are the names of the men who went up, according to their ancestral houses in the tribes, over their groups: **5** the priests, the descendants of Phinehas son of Aaron; Jeshua son of Jozadak son of Seraiah and Joakim son of Zerubbabel son of Shealtiel, of the house of David, of the lineage of Phares, of the tribe of Judah, **6** who spoke wise words before King Darius of the Persians, in the second year of his reign, in the month of Nisan, the first month.

[a] Gk *in what priestly vestments*

4:47–57 Darius provides for the temple—Under the moral suasion of Zerubbabel, Darius agrees to rebuild Jerusalem and return the vessels taken by Nebuchadnezzar. The lesson for the exiles was that foreign powers would not necessarily hinder God. Disciples today may also receive help from unlikely sources in their service of God.

5:1–6 Introduction to the List of Returning Exiles

5:2 *Thousand cavalry*—An escort for the repatriates on their journey to Palestine, another benefit from loyalty to the Persians. Disciples need not reject the protection due them as citizens of a state.

7 These are the Judeans who came up out of their sojourn in exile, whom King Nebuchadnezzar of Babylon had carried away to Babylon 8 and who returned to Jerusalem and the rest of Judea, each to his own town. They came with Zerubbabel and Jeshua, Nehemiah, Seraiah, Resaiah, Eneneus, Mordecai, Beelsarus, Aspharasus, Reeliah, Rehum, and Baanah, their leaders.

9 The number of those of the nation and their leaders: the descendants of Parosh, two thousand one hundred seventy-two. The descendants of Shephatiah, four hundred seventy-two. 10 The descendants of Arah, seven hundred fifty-six. 11 The descendants of Pahath-moab, of the descendants of Jeshua and Joab, two thousand eight hundred twelve. 12 The descendants of Elam, one thousand two hundred fifty-four. The descendants of Zattu, nine hundred forty-five. The descendants of Chorbe, seven hundred five. The descendants of Bani, six hundred forty-eight. 13 The descendants of Bebai, six hundred twenty-three. The descendants of Azgad, one thousand three hundred twenty-two. 14 The descendants of Adonikam, six hundred sixty-seven. The descendants of Bigvai, two thousand sixty-six. The descendants of Adin, four hundred fifty-four. 15 The descendants of Ater, namely of Hezekiah, ninety-two. The descendants of Kilan and Azetas, sixty-seven. The descendants of Azaru, four hundred thirty-two. 16 The descendants of Annias, one hundred one. The descendants of Arom. The descendants of Bezai, three hundred twenty-three. The descendants of Arsiphurith, one hundred twelve. 17 The descendants of Baiterus, three thousand five. The descendants of Bethlomon, one hundred twenty-three. 18 Those from Netophah, fifty-five. Those from Anathoth, one hundred fifty-eight.

Those from Bethasmoth, forty-two. 19 Those from Kiriatharim, twenty-five. Those from Chephirah and Beeroth, seven hundred forty-three. 20 The Chadiasans and Ammidians, four hundred twenty-two. Those from Kirama and Geba, six hundred twenty-one. 21 Those from Macalon, one hundred twenty-two. Those from Betolio, fifty-two. The descendants of Niphish, one hundred fifty-six. 22 The descendants of the other Calamolalus and Ono, seven hundred twenty-five. The descendants of Jerechus, three hundred forty-five. 23 The descendants of Senaah, three thousand three hundred thirty.

24 The priests: the descendants of Jedaiah son of Jeshua, of the descendants of Anasib, nine hundred seventy-two. The descendants of Immer, one thousand and fifty-two. 25 The descendants of Pashhur, one thousand two hundred forty-seven. The descendants of Charme, one thousand seventeen.

26 The Levites: the descendants of Jeshua and Kadmiel and Bannas and Sudias, seventy-four. 27 The temple singers: the descendants of Asaph, one hundred twenty-eight. 28 The gatekeepers: the descendants of Shallum, the descendants of Ater, the descendants of Talmon, the descendants of Akkub, the descendants of Hatita, the descendants of Shobai, in all one hundred thirty-nine.

29 The temple servants: the descendants of Esau, the descendants of Hasupha, the descendants of Tabbaoth, the descendants of Keros, the descendants of Sua, the descendants of Padon, the descendants of Lebanah, the descendants of Hagabah, 30 the descendants of Akkub, the descendants of Uthai, the descendants of Ketab, the descendants of Hagab, the descendants of Subai, the descendants of Hana, the descendants

---

5:7–46 List of Returning Exiles (cf. Ezra 2:1–70; Neh. 7:6–73a)

All repatriates were important to the mission, from the leaders Zerubbabel and Jeshua to the servants. There is room in the service of God for all classes of people.

of Cathua, the descendants of Geddur, [31] the descendants of Jairus, the descendants of Daisan, the descendants of Noeba, the descendants of Chezib, the descendants of Gazera, the descendants of Uzza, the descendants of Phinoe, the descendants of Hasrah, the descendants of Basthai, the descendants of Asnah, the descendants of Maani, the descendants of Nephisim, the descendants of Acuph,[a] the descendants of Hakupha, the descendants of Asur, the descendants of Pharakim, the descendants of Bazluth, [32] the descendants of Mehida, the descendants of Cutha, the descendants of Charea, the descendants of Barkos, the descendants of Serar, the descendants of Temah, the descendants of Neziah, the descendants of Hatipha.

33 The descendants of Solomon's servants: the descendants of Assaphioth, the descendants of Peruda, the descendants of Jaalah, the descendants of Lozon, the descendants of Isdael, the descendants of Shephatiah, [34] the descendants of Agia, the descendants of Pochereth-hazzebaim, the descendants of Sarothie, the descendants of Masiah, the descendants of Gas, the descendants of Addus, the descendants of Subas, the descendants of Apherra, the descendants of Barodis, the descendants of Shaphat, the descendants of Allon.

35 All the temple servants and the descendants of Solomon's servants were three hundred seventy-two.

36 The following are those who came up from Tel-melah and Tel-harsha, under the leadership of Cherub, Addan, and Immer, [37] though they could not prove by their ancestral houses or lineage that they belonged to Israel: the descendants of Delaiah son of Tobiah, and the descendants of Nekoda, six hundred fifty-two.

38 Of the priests the following had assumed the priesthood but were not found registered: the descendants of Habaiah, the descendants of Hakkoz, and the descendants of Jaddus who had married Agia, one of the daughters of Barzillai, and was called by his name. [39] When a search was made in the register and the genealogy of these men was not found, they were excluded from serving as priests. [40] And Nehemiah and Attharias[b] told them not to share in the holy things until a high priest should appear wearing Urim and Thummim.[c]

41 All those of Israel, twelve or more years of age, besides male and female servants, were forty-two thousand three hundred sixty; [42] their male and female servants were seven thousand three hundred thirty-seven; there were two hundred forty-five musicians and singers. [43] There were four hundred thirty-five camels, and seven thousand thirty-six horses, two hundred forty-five mules, and five thousand five hundred twenty-five donkeys.

44 Some of the heads of families, when they came to the temple of God that is in Jerusalem, vowed that, to the best of their ability, they would erect the house on its site, [45] and that they would give to the sacred treasury for the work a thousand minas of gold, five thousand minas of silver, and one hundred priests' vestments.

46 The priests, the Levites, and some of the people[d] settled in Jerusalem and its vicinity; and the temple singers, the gatekeepers, and all Israel in their towns.

Worship Begins Again

47 When the seventh month came, and the Israelites were all in their own homes, they gathered with a single

[a] Other ancient authorities read Acub or Acum   [b] Or the governor
[c] Gk Manifestation and Truth   [d] Or those who were of the people

---

5:47–73 Temple Work Begun and Interrupted (cf. Ezra 3:1–4:5)

5:47 Their own homes—The first order of business was to build and settle in their own homes. Disciples have obligations to their own families too.

purpose in the square before the first gate toward the east. **48** Then Jeshua son of Jozadak, with his fellow priests, and Zerubbabel son of Shealtiel, with his kinsmen, took their places and prepared the altar of the God of Israel, **49** to offer burnt offerings upon it, in accordance with the directions in the book of Moses the man of God. **50** And some joined them from the other peoples of the land. And they erected the altar in its place, for all the peoples of the land were hostile to them and were stronger than they; and they offered sacrifices at the proper times and burnt offerings to the Lord morning and evening. **51** They kept the festival of booths, as it is commanded in the law, and offered the proper sacrifices every day, **52** and thereafter the regular offerings and sacrifices on sabbaths and at new moons and at all the consecrated feasts. **53** And all who had made any vow to God began to offer sacrifices to God, from the new moon of the seventh month, though the temple of God was not yet built. **54** They gave money to the masons and the carpenters, and food and drink **55** and carts*a* to the Sidonians and the Tyrians, to bring cedar logs from Lebanon and convey them in rafts to the harbor of Joppa, according to the decree that they had in writing from King Cyrus of the Persians.

The Foundations of the Temple Laid

56 In the second year after their coming to the temple of God in Jerusalem, in the second month, Zerubbabel son of Shealtiel and Jeshua son of Jozadak made a beginning, together with their kindred and the levitical priests and all who had come back to Jerusalem from exile; **57** and they laid the foundation of the temple of God on the new moon of the second month in the second year after they came to Judea and Jerusalem. **58** They appointed the Levites who were twenty or more years of age to have charge of the work of the Lord. And Jeshua arose, and his sons and kindred and his brother Kadmiel and the sons of Jeshua Emadabun and the sons of Joda son of Iliadun, with their sons and kindred, all the Levites, pressing forward the work on the house of God with a single purpose.

So the builders built the temple of the Lord. **59** And the priests stood arrayed in their vestments, with musical instruments and trumpets, and the Levites, the sons of Asaph, with cymbals, **60** praising the Lord and blessing him, according to the directions of King David of Israel; **61** they sang hymns, giving thanks to the Lord, "For his goodness and his glory are forever upon all Israel." **62** And all the people sounded trumpets and shouted with a great shout, praising the Lord for the erection of the house of the Lord. **63** Some of the levitical priests and heads of ancestral houses, old men who had seen the former house, came to the building of this one with outcries and loud weeping, **64** while many came with trumpets and a joyful noise, **65** so that the people could not hear the trumpets because of the weeping of the people.

For the multitude sounded the trumpets loudly, so that the sound was heard far away; **66** and when the enemies of the tribe of Judah and Benjamin heard it, they came to find out what the sound of the trumpets meant. **67** They learned that

a Meaning of Gk uncertain

5:50 *Other peoples of the land*—People left in the land, who had not gone into exile. Many opposed the work on the temple. Opposition, like help, can come from unlikely sources. Disciples should guard against being discouraged in the face of such "friendly-fire" opposition.

5:51 *Festival of booths*—The autumnal thanksgiving festival.

5:54—Repatriates made gifts above and beyond the required offerings to help pay for the restoration (cf. v. 44). Sacrifice is typically a component of discipleship.

5:58—Opposition continued, as it often does when people try to serve God.

those who had returned from exile were building the temple for the Lord God of Israel. **68** So they approached Zerubbabel and Jeshua and the heads of the ancestral houses and said to them, "We will build with you. **69** For we obey your Lord just as you do and we have been sacrificing to him ever since the days of King Esar-haddon*a* of the Assyrians, who brought us here." **70** But Zerubbabel and Jeshua and the heads of the ancestral houses in Israel said to them, "You have nothing to do with us in building the house for the Lord our God, **71** for we alone will build it for the Lord of Israel, as Cyrus, the king of the Persians, has commanded us." **72** But the peoples of the land pressed hard*b* upon those in Judea, cut off their supplies, and hindered their building; **73** and by plots and demagoguery and uprisings they prevented the completion of the building as long as King Cyrus lived. They were kept from building for two years, until the reign of Darius.

Work on the Temple Begins Again

6 Now in the second year of the reign of Darius, the prophets Haggai and Zechariah son of Iddo prophesied to the Jews who were in Judea and Jerusalem; they prophesied to them in the name of the Lord God of Israel. **2** Then Zerubbabel son of Shealtiel and Jeshua son of Jozadak began to build the house of the Lord that is in Jerusalem, with the help of the prophets of the Lord who were with them.

3 At the same time Sisinnes the governor of Syria and Phoenicia and Sathrabuzanes and their associates came to them and said, **4** "By whose order are you building this house and this roof and finishing all the other things? And who are the builders that are finishing these things?" **5** Yet the elders of the Jews were dealt with kindly, for the providence of the Lord was over the captives; **6** they were not prevented from building until word could be sent to Darius concerning them and a report made.

7 A copy of the letter that Sisinnes the governor of Syria and Phoenicia, and Sathrabuzanes, and their associates the local rulers in Syria and Phoenicia, wrote and sent to Darius:

8 "To King Darius, greetings. Let it be fully known to our lord the king that, when we went to the country of Judea and entered the city of Jerusalem, we found the elders of the Jews, who had been in exile, **9** building in the city of Jerusalem a great new house for the Lord, of hewn stone, with costly timber laid in the walls. **10** These operations are going on rapidly, and the work is prospering in their hands and being completed with all splendor and care. **11** Then we asked these elders, 'At whose command are you building this house and laying the foundations of this structure?' **12** In order that we might inform you in writing who the leaders are, we questioned them and asked them for a list of the names of those who are at

a Gk *Asbasareth*   *b* Meaning of Gk uncertain

5:68–71—Some residents who were not repatriates came offering to help, but Zerubbabel and Jeshua refused, since Darius had not included them in his instructions to rebuild.

5:72—Rebuffed by Zerubbabel and Jeshua, they intercepted supplies for the project. Whether Zerubbabel and Jeshua could have handled the situation more diplomatically and engendered less resistance must remain open. Disciples should be careful not to create difficulties by their treatment of other people.

6:1–7:15 Temple Work Completed (cf. Ezra 4:24–6:22)

6:1 *Haggai and Zechariah*—Prophets at whose urging construction on the temple resumed.

6:3—Governmental officials *Sisinnes* (Tattenai in Ezra 5:3) and *Sathrabuzanes* (Shethar-bozenai in Ezra 5:3) came from Samaria to investigate the work.

6:5–6—In God's providence, they allowed work to continue on the temple until Darius could be consulted. Often service to God and nation go together.

6:8–22—Letter to Darius inquiring about permission to rebuild the temple.

their head. ¹³ They answered us, "We are the servants of the Lord who created the heaven and the earth. ¹⁴ The house was built many years ago by a king of Israel who was great and strong, and it was finished. ¹⁵ But when our ancestors sinned against the Lord of Israel who is in heaven, and provoked him, he gave them over into the hands of King Nebuchadnezzar of Babylon, king of the Chaldeans; ¹⁶ and they pulled down the house, and burned it, and carried the people away captive to Babylon. ¹⁷ But in the first year that Cyrus reigned over the country of Babylonia, King Cyrus wrote that this house should be rebuilt. ¹⁸ And the holy vessels of gold and of silver, which Nebuchadnezzar had taken out of the house in Jerusalem and stored in his own temple, these King Cyrus took out again from the temple in Babylon, and they were delivered to Zerubbabel and Sheshbazzarᵃ the governor ¹⁹ with the command that he should take all these vessels back and put them in the temple at Jerusalem, and that this temple of the Lord should be rebuilt on its site. ²⁰ Then this Sheshbazzar, after coming here, laid the foundations of the house of the Lord that is in Jerusalem. Although it has been in process of construction from that time until now, it has not yet reached completion.' ²¹ Now therefore, O king, if it seems wise to do so, let search be made in the royal archives of our lordᵇ the king that are in Babylon; ²² if it is found that the building of the house of the Lord in Jerusalem was done with the consent of King Cyrus, and if it is approved by our lord the king, let him send us directions concerning these things."

Official Permission Granted

23 Then Darius commanded that search be made in the royal archives that were deposited in Babylon. And in Ecbatana, the fortress that is in the country of Media, a scrollᶜ was found in which this was recorded: ²⁴ "In the first year of the reign of King Cyrus, he ordered the building of the house of the Lord in Jerusalem, where they sacrifice with perpetual fire; ²⁵ its height to be sixty cubits and its width sixty cubits, with three courses of hewn stone and one course of new native timber; the cost to be paid from the treasury of King Cyrus; ²⁶ and that the holy vessels of the house of the Lord, both of gold and of silver, which Nebuchadnezzar took out of the house in Jerusalem and carried away to Babylon, should be restored to the house in Jerusalem, to be placed where they had been."

27 So Dariusᵈ commanded Sisinnes the governor of Syria and Phoenicia, and Sathrabuzanes, and their associates, and those who were appointed as local rulers in Syria and Phoenicia, to keep away from the place, and to permit Zerubbabel, the servant of the Lord and governor of Judea, and the elders of the Jews to build this house of the Lord on its site. ²⁸ "And I command that it be built completely, and that full effort be made to help those who have returned from the exile of Judea, until the house of the Lord is finished; ²⁹ and that out of the tribute of Coelesyria and Phoenicia a portion be scrupulously given to these men, that is, to Zerubbabel the governor, for sacrifices to the Lord, for bulls and rams and lambs, ³⁰ and likewise wheat and salt and wine and oil, regularly every year, without quibbling, for daily use as the priests in Jerusalem may indicate, ³¹ in order that libations may be made to the Most High God for the king and his children, and prayers be offered for their lives."

ᵃ Gk *Sanabassarus* ᵇ Other ancient authorities read *of Cyrus* ᶜ Other authorities read *passage* ᵈ Gk *he*

6:14 *King of Israel*—Solomon.

6:18—Both *Zerubbabel and Sheshbazzar* are mentioned here, though only Sheshbazzar was named in Ezra 5:4. Adding the name of Zerubba-bel was an attempt to make the letter fit the time of Zerubbabel and Darius.

6:23–34—Permission for the work to continue.

32 He commanded that if anyone should transgress or nullify any of the things herein written,*a* a beam should be taken out of the house of the perpetrator, who then should be impaled upon it, and all property forfeited to the king.

33 "Therefore may the Lord, whose name is there called upon, destroy every king and nation that shall stretch out their hands to hinder or damage that house of the Lord in Jerusalem.

34 "I, King Darius, have decreed that it be done with all diligence as here prescribed."

The Temple Is Dedicated

7 Then Sisinnes the governor of Coelesyria and Phoenicia, and Sathrabuzanes, and their associates, following the orders of King Darius, ²supervised the holy work with very great care, assisting the elders of the Jews and the chief officers of the temple. ³The holy work prospered, while the prophets Haggai and Zechariah prophesied; ⁴and they completed it by the command of the Lord God of Israel. So with the consent of Cyrus and Darius and Artaxerxes, kings of the Persians, ⁵the holy house

was finished by the twenty-third day of the month of Adar, in the sixth year of King Darius. ⁶And the people of Israel, the priests, the Levites, and the rest of those who returned from exile who joined them, did according to what was written in the book of Moses. ⁷They offered at the dedication of the temple of the Lord one hundred bulls, two hundred rams, four hundred lambs, ⁸and twelve male goats for the sin of all Israel, according to the number of the twelve leaders of the tribes of Israel; ⁹and the priests and the Levites stood arrayed in their vestments, according to kindred, for the services of the Lord God of Israel in accordance with the book of Moses; and the gatekeepers were at each gate.

The Passover

10 The people of Israel who came from exile kept the passover on the fourteenth day of the first month, after the priests and the Levites were purified together. ¹¹Not all of the returned captives were purified, but the Levites were all purified together,*b* ¹²and they sacrificed the

---

a Other authorities read *stated above* or *added in writing*   *b* Meaning of Gk uncertain

---

7:1–9—The temple completed and dedicated.

7:2—The Persian governor assisted with the completion of the temple, with no protests from Zerubbabel, Jeshua, Haggai, or Zechariah. The contrast with their reaction to some of the "peoples of the land" (5:72) suggests that all four were sympathetic towards the Persian overlords and/or were powerless to object.

7:4 *Cyrus and Darius and Artaxerxes*—Cf. Ezra 6:4. Since the temple was finished in 515 (see 1 Esd. 7:5) and Artaxerxes I ruled 465–424, both 1 Esdras and Ezra are in error that Artaxerxes helped with rebuilding the temple. He did permit the rebuilding of the wall around Jerusalem.

7:5 *Twenty-third day of the month of Adar*—Roughly February/March of Israel's lunar calendar. *The sixth year*—515 BCE.

7:6 *The rest of those who returned from exile who joined them*—Not all the inhabitants of Judah participated in the rebuilding of the temple. Were they too opposed to foreign rule to join in a movement led by Persian appointees? If so, did they allow partisanship or nationalism to interfere

with their service to God? *The book of Moses*—Exodus 29 and Lev. 8 describe the ordination and some of the duties of priests, while Num. 3–4 and 8 do the same for the Levites. Numbers 8:26 distinguishes sharply between the two groups.

7:10 *Passover*—First Esdras begins with the Passover in Jerusalem under Josiah, and reaches a first climax here with the celebration of Passover in Jerusalem again. The second climax would come at the Feast of Booths after the work of Ezra.

7:11 *Not all of the returned captives were purified*—The author gives no indication why this was so. He emphasizes instead that the Levites had been. Here purification was obtained by sacrifice, but for Christians today it comes through repentance.

7:12—The Levites *sacrificed the passover lamb*. At this first Passover back in Judah, the Passover was observed in the temple. At various times in ancient Israel it was observed in homes, as it is today. The Passover reminded Israelites that God had delivered them from slavery in Egypt. Disciples may take hope in the power and will of God to fulfill God's intentions.

passover lamb for all the returned captives and for their kindred the priests and for themselves. [13] The people of Israel who had returned from exile ate it, all those who had separated themselves from the abominations of the peoples of the land and sought the Lord. [14] They also kept the festival of unleavened bread seven days, rejoicing before the Lord, [15] because he had changed the will of the king of the Assyrians concerning them, to strengthen their hands for the service of the Lord God of Israel.

Ezra Arrives in Jerusalem

8 After these things, when Artaxerxes, the king of the Persians, was reigning, Ezra came, the son of Seraiah, son of Azariah, son of Hilkiah, son of Shallum, [2] son of Zadok, son of Ahitub, son of Amariah, son of Uzzi, son of Bukki, son of Abishua, son of Phineas, son of Eleazar, son of Aaron the high[a] priest. [3] This Ezra came up from Babylon as a scribe skilled in the law of Moses, which was given by the God of Israel; [4] and the king showed him honor, for he found favor before the king[b] in all his requests. [5] There came up with him to Jerusalem some of the people of Israel and some of the priests and Levites and temple singers and gatekeepers and temple servants, [6] in the seventh year of the reign of Artaxerxes, in the fifth month (this was the king's seventh year); for they left Babylon on the new moon of the first month and arrived in Jerusalem on the new moon of the fifth month, by the prosperous journey that the Lord gave them.[c] [7] For Ezra possessed great knowledge, so that he omitted nothing from the law of the Lord or the commandments, but taught all Israel all the ordinances and judgments.

The King's Mandate

8 The following is a copy of the written commission from King Artaxerxes that was delivered to Ezra the priest and reader of the law of the Lord:

9 "King Artaxerxes to Ezra the priest and reader of the law of the Lord, greeting. [10] In accordance with my gracious decision, I have given orders that those of the Jewish nation and of the priests and Levites and others in our realm, those who freely choose to do so, may go with you to Jerusalem. [11] Let as many as are so disposed, therefore, leave with you, just as I and the seven Friends who are my counselors have decided, [12] in order to look into matters in Judea and Jerusalem, in accordance with what is in the law of the Lord, [13] and to carry to

a Gk *the first*   b Gk *him*   c Other authorities add *for him* or *upon him*

7:13 *All those who had separated themselves*— While some of the repatriates participated in the meal, others did not. The latter group associated with *peoples of the land*, people who had not participated in the exile.

7:15 *King of the Assyrians*—King Darius of Persia.

8:1–67 Ezra Leads Exiles to Judah (cf. Ezra 7:1–8:36)

8:1 *Artaxerxes*—Probably Artaxerxes I, who ruled 465–424. The narrative moved ahead from 515 to 458 (see v. 6), skipping the reign of Xerxes (485–465) in the process. *Ezra*—Namesake of the book, he appears for the first time. He was a priest.

8:3 *Scribe*—Scribes were educated people who could read and write and made their living doing so. They kept records of government, business, and private transactions. They might teach other people to read and write and perform their jobs. Some scribes also collected, copied, edited, and even canonized literature. Ezra made a living at the king's court, but in 1 Esdras he functioned as a preserver and perhaps even canonizer of the Law of Moses.

8:5—Ezra brought with him another group of repatriates to Judah. It included more priests, Levites, and temple personnel, but no thousand guards like those accompanying Zerubbabel (cf. 5:2).

8:8–24—Ezra had a letter from Artaxerxes authorizing him to lead a party of repatriates to Jerusalem, to teach the Law, to take gifts from Artaxerxes (including temple vessels), to exempt priests and other temple officials from paying taxes, and to appoint judges and justices to enforce the law. The letter is similar to previous letters reported in 1 Esdras, except for the instructions about taxes and the law.

Jerusalem the gifts for the Lord of Israel that I and my Friends have vowed, and to collect for the Lord in Jerusalem all the gold and silver that may be found in the country of Babylonia, [14] together with what is given by the nation for the temple of their Lord that is in Jerusalem, both gold and silver for bulls and rams and lambs and what goes with them, [15] so as to offer sacrifices on the altar of their Lord that is in Jerusalem. [16] Whatever you and your kindred are minded to do with the gold and silver, perform it in accordance with the will of your God; [17] deliver the holy vessels of the Lord that are given you for the use of the temple of your God that is in Jerusalem. [18] And whatever else occurs to you as necessary for the temple of your God, you may provide out of the royal treasury.

[19] "I, King Artaxerxes, have commanded the treasurers of Syria and Phoenicia that whatever Ezra the priest and reader of the law of the Most High God sends for, they shall take care to give him, [20] up to a hundred talents of silver, and likewise up to a hundred cors of wheat, a hundred baths of wine, and salt in abundance. [21] Let all things prescribed in the law of God be scrupulously fulfilled for the Most High God, so that wrath may not come upon the kingdom of the king and his sons. [22] You are also informed that no tribute or any other tax is to be laid on any of the priests or Levites or temple singers or gatekeepers or temple servants or persons employed in this temple, and that no one has authority to impose any tax on them.

[23] "And you, Ezra, according to the wisdom of God, appoint judges and justices to judge all those who know the law of your God, throughout all Syria and Phoenicia; and you shall teach it to those who do not know it. [24] All who transgress the law of your God or the law of the kingdom shall be strictly punished, whether by death or some other punishment, either fine or imprisonment."

Ezra Praises God

[25] Then Ezra the scribe said,[a] "Blessed be the Lord alone, who put this into the heart of the king, to glorify his house that is in Jerusalem, [26] and who honored me in the sight of the king and his counselors and all his Friends and nobles. [27] I was encouraged by the help of the Lord my God, and I gathered men from Israel to go up with me."

The Leaders Who Returned

[28] These are the leaders, according to their ancestral houses and their groups, who went up with me from Babylon, in the reign of King Artaxerxes: [29] Of the descendants of Phineas, Gershom. Of the descendants of Ithamar, Gamael. Of the descendants of David, Hattush son of Shecaniah. [30] Of the descendants of Parosh, Zechariah, and with him a hundred fifty men enrolled. [31] Of the descendants of Pahath-moab, Eliehoenai son of Zerahiah, and with him two hundred men. [32] Of the descendants of Zattu, Shecaniah son of Jahaziel, and with him three hundred men. Of the descendants of Adin, Obed son of Jonathan, and with him two hundred fifty men. [33] Of the descendants of Elam, Jeshaiah son of Gotholiah, and with him seventy men. [34] Of the descendants of Shephatiah, Zeraiah son of Michael, and with him seventy men. [35] Of the descendants of Joab, Obadiah son of Jehiel, and with him two hundred twelve men. [36] Of the descendants of Bani, Shelomith son of Josiphiah, and with him a hundred sixty men. [37] Of the descendants of Bebai, Zechariah son of Bebai, and with him twenty-eight men. [38] Of the descendants of Azgad, Johanan son of Hakkatan, and with him a hundred ten men. [39] Of the descendants of Adonikam, the last ones, their names being Eliphelet, Jeuel, and Shemaiah, and with them seventy men. [40] Of the descendants of Bigvai, Uthai son of Istalcurus, and with him seventy men.

[a] Other ancient authorities lack *Then Ezra the scribe said*

41 I assembled them at the river called Theras, and we encamped there three days, and I inspected them. ⁴²When I found there none of the descendants of the priests or of the Levites, ⁴³I sent word to Eliezar, Iduel, Maasmas, ⁴⁴Elnathan, Shemaiah, Jarib, Nathan, Elnathan, Zechariah, and Meshullam, who were leaders and men of understanding; ⁴⁵I told them to go to Iddo, who was the leading man at the place of the treasury, ⁴⁶and ordered them to tell Iddo and his kindred and the treasurers at that place to send us men to serve as priests in the house of our Lord. ⁴⁷And by the mighty hand of our Lord they brought us competent men of the descendants of Mahli son of Levi, son of Israel, namely Sherebiah[a] with his descendants and kinsmen, eighteen; ⁴⁸also Hashabiah and Annunus and his brother Jeshaiah, of the descendants of Hananiah, and their descendants, twenty men; ⁴⁹and of the temple servants, whom David and the leaders had given for the service of the Levites, two hundred twenty temple servants; the list of all their names was reported.

Ezra Proclaims a Fast

50 There I proclaimed a fast for the young men before our Lord, to seek from him a prosperous journey for ourselves and for our children and the livestock that were with us. ⁵¹For I was ashamed to ask the king for foot soldiers and cavalry and an escort to keep us safe from our adversaries; ⁵²for we had said to the king, "The power of our Lord will be with those who seek him, and will support them in every way." ⁵³And again we prayed to our Lord about these things, and we found him very merciful.

The Gifts for the Temple

54 Then I set apart twelve of the leaders of the priests, Sherebiah and Hashabiah, and ten of their kinsmen with them; ⁵⁵and I weighed out to them the silver and the gold and the holy vessels of the house of our Lord, which the king himself and his counselors and the nobles and all Israel had given. ⁵⁶I weighed and gave to them six hundred fifty talents of silver, and silver vessels worth a hundred talents, and a hundred talents of gold, ⁵⁷and twenty golden bowls, and twelve bronze vessels of fine bronze that glittered like gold. ⁵⁸And I said to them, "You are holy to the Lord, and the vessels are holy, and the silver and the gold are vowed to the Lord, the Lord of our ancestors. ⁵⁹Be watchful and on guard until you deliver them to the leaders of the priests and the Levites, and to the heads of the ancestral houses of Israel, in Jerusalem, in the chambers of the house of our Lord." ⁶⁰So the priests and the Levites who took the silver and the gold and the vessels that had been in Jerusalem carried them to the temple of the Lord.

The Return to Jerusalem

61 We left the river Theras on the twelfth day of the first month; and we arrived in Jerusalem by the mighty hand of our Lord, which was upon us; he delivered us from every enemy on the way, and so we came to Jerusalem. ⁶²When we had been there three days, the silver and the gold were weighed and delivered in the house of our Lord to the priest Meremoth son of Uriah; ⁶³with him was Eleazar son of Phinehas, and with them were Jozabad son of

[a] Gk Asbebias

8:41 *River . . . Theras*—Probably a tributary of the Euphrates.

8:42—Since the volunteers included no Levites, Ezra drafted forty (to officiate at the altar), plus 220 temple servants. While religious bodies can exist without professional ministers, such people can give invaluable assistance.

8:54–60—*Holy* objects and people were those set aside for special service to God. The emphasis on the potential danger of the trip (cf. v. 61) suggests that these were people Ezra could trust in the midst of difficulty. Disciples need to be dependable.

Jeshua and Moeth son of Binnui,[a] the Levites. ⁶⁴ The whole was counted and weighed, and the weight of everything was recorded at that very time. ⁶⁵ And those who had returned from exile offered sacrifices to the Lord, the God of Israel, twelve bulls for all Israel, ninety-six rams, ⁶⁶ seventy-two lambs, and as a thank offering twelve male goats—all as a sacrifice to the Lord. ⁶⁷ They delivered the king's orders to the royal stewards and to the governors of Coelesyria and Phoenicia; and these officials[b] honored the people and the temple of the Lord.

Ezra's Prayer

68 After these things had been done, the leaders came to me and said, ⁶⁹ "The people of Israel and the rulers and the priests and the Levites have not put away from themselves the alien peoples of the land and their pollutions, the Canaanites, the Hittites, the Perizzites, the Jebusites, the Moabites, the Egyptians, and the Edomites. ⁷⁰ For they and their descendants have married the daughters of these people,[c] and the holy race has been mixed with the alien peoples of the land; and from the beginning of this matter the leaders and the nobles have been sharing in this iniquity."

71 As soon as I heard these things I tore my garments and my holy mantle, and pulled out hair from my head and beard,

and sat down in anxiety and grief. ⁷² And all who were ever moved at[d] the word of the Lord of Israel gathered around me, as I mourned over this iniquity, and I sat grief-stricken until the evening sacrifice. ⁷³ Then I rose from my fast, with my garments and my holy mantle torn, and kneeling down and stretching out my hands to the Lord ⁷⁴ I said,

"O Lord, I am ashamed and confused before your face. ⁷⁵ For our sins have risen higher than our heads, and our mistakes have mounted up to heaven ⁷⁶ from the times of our ancestors, and we are in great sin to this day. ⁷⁷ Because of our sins and the sins of our ancestors, we with our kindred and our kings and our priests were given over to the kings of the earth, to the sword and exile and plundering, in shame until this day. ⁷⁸ And now in some measure mercy has come to us from you, O Lord, to leave to us a root and a name in your holy place, ⁷⁹ and to uncover a light for us in the house of the Lord our God, and to give us food in the time of our servitude. ⁸⁰ Even in our bondage we were not forsaken by our Lord, but he brought us into favor with the kings of the Persians, so that they have given us food ⁸¹ and glorified the temple of our Lord, and raised Zion from desolation, to give us a stronghold in Judea and Jerusalem.

---

a Gk *Sabannus*   *b* Gk *they*   *c* Gk *their daughters*   *d* Or *zealous for*

8:68–9:36 Mixed Marriages among Priests and Levites (cf. Ezra 9:1–10:44)

8:68–70—Ezra learns about mixed marriages. *After these things*—Indications of the passage of time are sketchy, but 9:5 indicates that this meeting occurred on the twentieth day of the ninth month, i.e., in December. Unspecified "leaders" (from Ezra's group?) charged *the people of Israel and the rulers and the priests and Levites* with marrying the *alien peoples of the land*. Perhaps repatriates from the time of Sheshbazzar and Zerubbabel had married people who had never been exiled or people who had moved to Judah during the exile. Regardless, these leaders appealed to old laws forbidding Israel to have contact with the inhabitants of Canaan or of intermarrying with them (cf. Deut. 7:1–4) as the basis for objecting to those marriages. Despite

the language of 1 Esd. 8:70, such laws were not racially motivated, since everyone in the area would have belonged to the same race. Instead, they were based on religious exclusivism and resulted in forcing people to divorce. Possibly Mal. 2:13–16 was a protest against those divorces. It is the only passage in the Old Testament that opposes divorce.

8:71–90—Ezra responds to the information with expressions of grief (tearing his clothing, pulling his hair), by fasting until evening, and by offering a prayer of contrition. In that prayer he blames Israel, not God, for its problems. In particular, he blames the earlier generations for violating Deut. 7:1–4, the commandment against intermarrying, which he paraphrases. Finally, he blames some of his contemporaries for breaking the same commandment.

82 "And now, O Lord, what shall we say, when we have these things? For we have transgressed your commandments, which you gave by your servants the prophets, saying, 83 'The land that you are entering to take possession of is a land polluted with the pollution of the aliens of the land, and they have filled it with their uncleanness. 84 Therefore do not give your daughters in marriage to their descendants, and do not take their daughters for your descendants; 85 do not seek ever to have peace with them, so that you may be strong and eat the good things of the land and leave it for an inheritance to your children forever.' 86 And all that has happened to us has come about because of our evil deeds and our great sins. For you, O Lord, lifted the burden of our sins 87 and gave us such a root as this; but we turned back again to transgress your law by mixing with the uncleanness of the peoples of the land. 88 Were you not angry enough with us to destroy us without leaving a root or seed or name? 89 O Lord of Israel, you are faithful; for we are left as a root to this day. 90 See, we are now before you in our iniquities; for we can no longer stand in your presence because of these things."

The Plan for Ending Mixed Marriages

91 While Ezra was praying and making his confession, weeping and lying on the ground before the temple, there gathered around him a very great crowd of men and women and youths from Jerusalem; for there was great weeping among the multitude. 92 Then Shecaniah son of Jehiel, one of the men of Israel, called out, and said to Ezra, "We have sinned against the Lord, and have married foreign women from the peoples of the land; but even now there is hope for Israel. 93 Let us take an oath to the Lord about this, that we will put away all our foreign wives, with their children, 94 as seems good to you and to all who obey the law of the Lord. 95 Rise up[a] and take action, for it is your task, and we are with you to take strong measures." 96 Then Ezra rose up and made the leaders of the priests and Levites of all Israel swear that they would do this. And they swore to it.

The Expulsion of Foreign Wives

9 Then Ezra set out and went from the court of the temple to the chamber of Jehohanan son of Eliashib, 2 and spent the night there; and he did not eat bread or drink water, for he was mourning over the great iniquities of the multitude. 3 And a proclamation was made throughout Judea and Jerusalem to all who had returned from exile that they should assemble at Jerusalem, 4 and that if any did not meet there within two or three days, in accordance with the decision of the ruling elders, their livestock would be seized for sacrifice and the men themselves[b] expelled from the multitude of those who had returned from the captivity.

5 Then the men of the tribe of Judah and Benjamin assembled at Jerusalem within three days; this was the ninth month, on the twentieth day of the month. 6 All the multitude sat in the open square before the temple, shivering because of the bad weather that prevailed. 7 Then Ezra stood up and said to them, "You have broken the law and married foreign women, and so have increased the sin of Israel. 8 Now then make confession and give glory to the Lord the God of our ancestors, 9 and do his will; separate yourselves from the peoples of the land and from your foreign wives."

10 Then all the multitude shouted and

---

[a] Other ancient authorities read *as seems good to you." And all who obeyed the law of the Lord rose and said to Ezra,* 95"Rise up   [b] Gk *he himself*

9:5–9—Ezra commands repatriates with non-Jewish wives to divorce them. By contrast, the New Testament counsels Christians not to divorce unbelieving partners, but to seek their salvation (1 Cor. 7:12–16).

said with a loud voice, "We will do as you have said. [11] But the multitude is great and it is winter, and we are not able to stand in the open air. This is not a work we can do in one day or two, for we have sinned too much in these things. [12] So let the leaders of the multitude stay, and let all those in our settlements who have foreign wives come at the time appointed, [13] with the elders and judges of each place, until we are freed from the wrath of the Lord over this matter."

[14] Jonathan son of Asahel and Jahzeiah son of Tikvah[a] undertook the matter on these terms, and Meshullam and Levi and Shabbethai served with them as judges. [15] And those who had returned from exile acted in accordance with all this.

[16] Ezra the priest chose for himself the leading men of their ancestral houses, all of them by name; and on the new moon of the tenth month they began their sessions to investigate the matter. [17] And the cases of the men who had foreign wives were brought to an end by the new moon of the first month.

[18] Of the priests, those who were brought in and found to have foreign wives were: [19] of the descendants of Jeshua son of Jozadak and his kindred, Maaseiah, Eliezar, Jarib, and Jodan. [20] They pledged themselves to put away their wives, and to offer rams in expiation of their error. [21] Of the descendants of Immer: Hanani and Zebadiah and Maaseiah and Shemaiah and Jehiel and Azariah. [22] Of the descendants of Pashhur: Elioenai, Maaseiah, Ishmael, and Nathanael, and Gedaliah, and Salthas.

[23] And of the Levites: Jozabad and Shimei and Kelaiah, who was Kelita, and Pethahiah and Judah and Jonah. [24] Of the temple singers: Eliashib and Zaccur.[b] [25] Of the gatekeepers: Shallum and Telem.[c]

[26] Of Israel: of the descendants of Parosh: Ramiah, Izziah, Malchijah, Mijamin, and Eleazar, and Asibias, and Benaiah. [27] Of the descendants of Elam: Mattaniah and Zechariah, Jezrielus and Abdi, and Jeremoth and Elijah. [28] Of the descendants of Zamoth: Eliadas, Eliashib, Othoniah, Jeremoth, and Zabad and Zerdaiah. [29] Of the descendants of Bebai: Jehohanan and Hananiah and Zabbai and Emathis. [30] Of the descendants of Mani: Olamus, Mamuchus, Adaiah, Jashub, and Sheal and Jeremoth. [31] Of the descendants of Addi: Naathus and Moossias, Laccunus and Naidus, and Bescaspasmys and Sesthel, and Belnuus and Manasseas. [32] Of the descendants of Annan, Elionas and Asaias and Melchias and Sabbaias and Simon Chosamaeus. [33] Of the descendants of Hashum: Mattenai and Mattattah and Zabad and Eliphelet and Manasseh and Shimei. [34] Of the descendants of Bani: Jeremai, Momdius, Maerus, Joel, Mamdai and Bedeiah and Vaniah, Carabasion and Eliashib and Mamitanemus, Eliasis, Binnui, Elialis, Shimei, Shelemiah, Nethaniah. Of the descendants of Ezora: Shashai, Azarel, Azael, Samatus, Zambris, Joseph. [35] Of the descendants of Nooma: Mazitias, Zabad, Iddo, Joel, Benaiah. [36] All these had married foreign women, and they put them away together with their children.

Ezra Reads the Law to the People

[37] The priests and the Levites and the Israelites settled in Jerusalem and in the

[a] Gk Thocanos [b] Gk Bacchurus [c] Gk Tolbanes

9:37–55 Ezra's Reading of the Law (cf. Neh. 7:73–8:12)

The culmination of 1 Esdras is the reading of the Law by Ezra on the first day of the seventh month, i.e., two months before the event just narrated. The "law" in question is usually understood to have been the Torah or some portion of it that could be read aloud in a day. He read from a prepared podium in front of the east gate of the temple. Verse 48 indicates that thirteen Levites interpreted the meaning of the text. Probably they translated the Hebrew text into Aramaic while Ezra was reading.

country. On the new moon of the seventh month, when the people of Israel were in their settlements, [38] the whole multitude gathered with one accord in the open square before the east gate of the temple; [39] they told Ezra the chief priest and reader to bring the law of Moses that had been given by the Lord God of Israel. [40] So Ezra the chief priest brought the law, for all the multitude, men and women, and all the priests to hear the law, on the new moon of the seventh month. [41] He read aloud in the open square before the gate of the temple from early morning until midday, in the presence of both men and women; and all the multitude gave attention to the law. [42] Ezra the priest and reader of the law stood on the wooden platform that had been prepared; [43] and beside him stood Mattathiah, Shema, Ananias, Azariah, Uriah, Hezekiah, and Baalsamus on his right, [44] and on his left Pedaiah, Mishael, Malchijah, Lothasubus, Nabariah, and Zechariah. [45] Then Ezra took up the book of the law in the sight of the multitude, for he had the place of honor in the presence of all. [46] When he opened the law, they all stood erect. And Ezra blessed the Lord God Most High, the God of hosts, the Almighty, [47] and the multitude answered, "Amen." They lifted up their hands, and fell to the ground and worshiped the Lord. [48] Jeshua and Anniuth and Sherebiah, Jadinus, Akkub, Shabbethai, Hodiah, Maiannas and Kelita, Azariah and Jozabad, Hanan, Pelaiah, the Levites, taught the law of the Lord,[a] at the same time explaining what was read.

[49] Then Attharates[b] said to Ezra the chief priest and reader, and to the Levites who were teaching the multitude, and to all, [50] "This day is holy to the Lord"—now they were all weeping as they heard the law— [51] "so go your way, eat the fat and drink the sweet, and send portions to those who have none; [52] for the day is holy to the Lord; and do not be sorrowful, for the Lord will exalt you." [53] The Levites commanded all the people, saying, "This day is holy; do not be sorrowful." [54] Then they all went their way, to eat and drink and enjoy themselves, and to give portions to those who had none, and to make great rejoicing; [55] because they were inspired by the words which they had been taught. And they came together.[c]

[a] Other ancient authorities add *and read the law of the Lord to the multitude*
[b] Or *the governor*   [c] The Greek text ends abruptly: compare Neh 8.13

9:55 *And they came together*—The reading of the Law constituted the second climax of the book. The denouement is so brief as to be unsatisfactory to some scholars, who suggest that originally the book must have included at least the account of the Feast of Booths that follows in Neh. 8:13–18. It appears instead, however, that 1 Esdras was interested in the Law and the temple, and ended with the reestablishment of the Law in the time of Ezra.

The Prayer of
MANASSEH

Manasseh, king of Judah (687–642 BCE), was the very worst of Judah's monarchs, according to 2 Kings 21:9–18. Indeed, he is blamed for Jerusalem's eventual downfall in 587 BCE (2 Kgs. 21:12). This portrait sets up Manasseh as a candidate for a dramatic repentance, which is precisely what is recorded in 2 Chronicles 33:10–13. He is taken by the Assyrians to Babylon, and "while he was in distress he entreated the favor of the LORD his God and humbled himself greatly before the God of his ancestors" (2 Chr. 33:12). Manasseh's prayer is heard; he is restored to his reign in Jerusalem; and he proceeds to initiate several reform measures. Manasseh's prayer is not included in 2 Chronicles 13. The Prayer of Manasseh supposedly supplies his missing words, but most scholars date its origin to the first century CE, approximately seven hundred years after Manasseh's reign. If this is correct, the work perhaps was intended to offer hope to first-century Jews following the destruction of Jerusalem and the second temple by the Romans in 70 CE.

Regardless of the circumstances of its origin, the Prayer of Manasseh, like the book of Psalms, portrays God as a cosmic sovereign (vv. 2–4) who, because God wills righteousness (see vv. 1, 8), holds sinners accountable (vv. 5, 10). Yet, in the final analysis, because God is "very merciful" (v. 7; see vv. 6, 11, 14), God also forgives and rehabilitates sinners (see vv. 6–8, 13–15). In short, the Prayer of Manasseh, like the book of Psalms and indeed the whole Bible, portrays a God who ultimately pursues justice and righteousness by grace (see Exod. 32–34, esp. 34:6–7; Pss. 32, 51, 103, 130; Luke 5:29–32; Rom. 3–4).

—Clint McCann

Ascription of Praise

1 O Lord Almighty,
 God of our ancestors,
 of Abraham and Isaac and Jacob
 and of their righteous offspring;
2 you who made heaven and earth
 with all their order;
3 who shackled the sea by your word
 of command,

who confined the deep
and sealed it with your terrible and
 glorious name;
4 at whom all things shudder,
 and tremble before your power,
5 for your glorious splendor cannot be
 borne,
and the wrath of your threat to
 sinners is unendurable;

---

1 *God of our ancestors*—See the similar phrase in 2 Chr. 33:12 (see introduction).

2 *Who made heaven and earth*—See Pss. 115:15; 121:2; 124:8; 134:3; and the Apostles' Creed.

3—See Gen. 1:1–2; Job 38:8–11; Pss. 24:1–2; 74:13; 104:3, 6–7. The *sea* and *deep* represent chaos, out of which God brings *order* (Pr. Man. 2).

4—This is the language of theophany, an account of God's appearing, the function of which is to assert God's sovereignty (see Pss. 18:7–15; 50:3–4; 97:3–5).

5–6—As fervent as God is for *order* (v. 2), accounting for God's *threat to sinners* (v. 5), so God also shows *immeasurable . . . mercy* (v. 6). This means that God will finally tolerate the disorder that sinners inevitably create.

6 yet immeasurable and unsearchable
is your promised mercy,
7 for you are the Lord Most High,
of great compassion, long-suffering,
and very merciful,
and you relent at human suffering.
O Lord, according to your great
goodness
you have promised repentance and
forgiveness
to those who have sinned against
you,
and in the multitude of your mercies
you have appointed repentance for
sinners,
so that they may be saved.*a*
8 Therefore you, O Lord, God of the
righteous,
have not appointed repentance for
the righteous,
for Abraham and Isaac and Jacob,
who did not sin against you,
but you have appointed repentance
for me, who am a sinner.

Confession of Sins

9 For the sins I have committed are
more in number than the sand
of the sea;
my transgressions are multiplied,
O Lord, they are multiplied!
I am not worthy to look up and see
the height of heaven
because of the multitude of my
iniquities.
10 I am weighted down with many an
iron fetter,

so that I am rejected*b* because of my
sins,
and I have no relief;
for I have provoked your wrath
and have done what is evil in your
sight,
setting up abominations and
multiplying offenses.

Supplication for Pardon

11 And now I bend the knee of my
heart,
imploring you for your kindness.
12 I have sinned, O Lord, I have sinned,
and I acknowledge my
transgressions.
13 I earnestly implore you,
forgive me, O Lord, forgive me!
Do not destroy me with my
transgressions!
Do not be angry with me forever or
store up evil for me;
do not condemn me to the depths of
the earth.
For you, O Lord, are the God of
those who repent,
14 and in me you will manifest your
goodness;
for, unworthy as I am, you will save
me according to your great
mercy,
15 and I will praise you continually all
the days of my life.
For all the host of heaven sings your
praise,
and yours is the glory forever. Amen.

a Other ancient authorities lack *O Lord, according… be saved*   *b* Other
ancient authorities read *so that I cannot lift up my head*

7—The several synonyms for mercy recall Exod.
32–34, where God relented or "changed his
mind" (Exod. 32:14) about punishing the people
for making the golden calf, and where God revealed the divine self to Moses as "merciful and
gracious, . . . abounding in steadfast love and
faithfulness . . . forgiving iniquity and transgression and sin, yet by no means clearing the guilty"
(Exod. 34:6–7). The same vocabulary dominates
the beginning of Ps. 51, preceding a request for
forgiveness that the editors of the Psalter attribute

to David. The Prayer of Manasseh starts to parallel Ps. 51 at this point.

8—See Luke 5:32.

11 *Kindness*—See vv. 6–7; Ps. 51:1.

12—See Ps. 51:3–4.

13—See Pss. 32:5; 51:2.

14—See vv. 6–7.

15—See Ps. 51:15–17.

PSALM 151

salm 151 purports to be David's own testimony concerning his youth, the events leading up to his anointing by Samuel, and his defeat of the Philistine warrior Goliath. A few scholars date the composition as early as the sixth century BCE but it is probably much later. Nothing certain is known concerning date, author, or circumstances of origin; but the creation and transmission of the work almost certainly involves the same motivation that led editors of the book of Psalms to associate seventy-three psalms with David, including thirteen that are introduced with descriptions of specific events in David's life; see note at Psalm 3 (Title).

The late attachment of Psalm 151 to the book of Psalms in some manuscript traditions reinforces the "messianic" orientation of the collection—that is, it features psalms about the king, God's "anointed" (Heb. *mashiach*), at key places (see Pss. 2, 72, 89, 144). Even so, there is evidence that the vocation of the "anointed one"—to enact on earth God's justice and righteousness (see Ps. 72:1–7)—was transferred to the whole people (see note at Ps. 149:7–9). Hence, references to David and the Davidic monarchy would have served to express hope in God and God's purposes, especially amid the generally discouraging circumstances of the postexilic era. From this perspective, it is revealing perhaps that David's culminating act in Psalm 151 is to remove "disgrace from the people of Israel."

—Clint McCann

This psalm is ascribed to David as his own composition (though it is outside the number[a]), after he had fought in single combat with Goliath.

1 I was small among my brothers,
   and the youngest in my father's house;
   I tended my father's sheep.

2 My hands made a harp;
   my fingers fashioned a lyre.

3 And who will tell my Lord?
   The Lord himself; it is he who hears.[b]

4 It was he who sent his messenger[c]
   and took me from my father's sheep,
   and anointed me with his anointing oil.

5 My brothers were handsome and tall,
   but the Lord was not pleased with them.

6 I went out to meet the Philistine,[d]
   and he cursed me by his idols.

7 But I drew his own sword;
   I beheaded him, and took away disgrace from the people of Israel.

a Other ancient authorities add *of the one hundred fifty* (psalms)   *b* Other ancient authorities add *everything*; others add *me*; others read *who will hear me*   *c* Or *angel*   *d* Or *foreigner*

1—See 1 Sam. 16:11.

2—See 1 Sam. 16:23; 18:10.

3–5—See 1 Sam. 16:6–10, which suggests that David was chosen despite his being the youngest and the least impressive of the sons of Jesse in stature and looks. This actually accords well with the book of Psalms, where God shows a decided preference for the least and the lowly (see Pss. 40:17; 140:12).

6—See 1 Sam. 17:43.

7—See 1 Sam. 17:51.

3 MACCABEES

Third Maccabees really has little to do with the Maccabees; it receives its name because it is found after 1 and 2 Maccabees in some manuscripts. The action in 3 Maccabees takes place much earlier than the revolt in 1 Maccabees, during the reign of Ptolemy IV Philopator in Egypt (221–204 BCE) and Antiochus III, king of Syria (223–187 BCE). No testimonies about bodily resurrection and immortality are given as in 2 and 4 Maccabees, and no martyrs are lifted up as heroes. Some scenes from 2 Maccabees are echoed in 3 Maccabees, but the book seems to be more clearly connected to Esther and Daniel 1–6 in terms of dealing with Jewish identity in the Diaspora before the advent of Antiochus IV Epiphanes. Third Maccabees is found in only some manuscripts of the Septuagint, is excluded from the Latin Vulgate and the Protestant Apocrypha, and is only considered deuteroncanon (second canon) by the Eastern Orthodox churches. It nonetheless offers meaningful testimony about the efficacy of prayer and the struggle to maintain one's identity amid the pressures of the dominant culture. Christians today can be strengthened by such testimony.

Scholars agree on little about 3 Maccabees except that it was written in Greek by a Jew in Alexandria, Egypt. Dates for the work range from 100 BCE to 70 CE, based upon the specific political/historical crisis thought to be addressed. Yet 3 Maccabees does not reflect the mood of crisis. It is an optimistic book that does not waver in its belief that God answers prayer and works miraculously to deliver God's people (2:21–24; 5:28; 6:18) and punish the oppressors, in line with good Deuteronomic covenant theology (2:3; 7:6, 9). Perhaps 3 Maccabees was written, as its opening suggests, during the Ptolemaic period and not the Roman period, close to the time of the letter in 2 Maccabees 1:1–9 (124 BCE) sent to Egyptian Jews by Palestinian Jews about celebrating Hanukkah (see the introduction to 2 Maccabees). Its purpose may be to defend Egyptian Jews before Palestinian Jews who hold a low opinion of their piety and Torah observance; it also emphasizes the corporate unity of Israel. This intrafaith emphasis suggests that we look at tensions among and within denominations today and their challenge to the idea of Christian unity.

Third Maccabees is divided into three parts: (1) 1:1–7—an apostate Jew named Dosethius saves Ptolemy from assassination; (2) 1:8–2:24—Ptolemy attempts to enter the Jerusalem temple but is repulsed; and (3) 2:25–7:23—Ptolemy persecutes Egyptian Jews. Third Maccabees offers an example of "pathetic history," a telling of events designed to involve the emotions. It is viewed as a historical novel, embellishing history to make a religious point. It is meant to inspire rather than give a historical account.

—Denise Dombkowski Hopkins

The Battle of Raphia

1 When Philopator learned from those who returned that the regions that he had controlled had been seized by Antiochus, he gave orders to all his forces, both infantry and cavalry, took with him his sister Arsinoë, and marched out to the region near Raphia, where the army of Antiochus was encamped. [2] But a certain Theodotus, determined to carry out the plot he had devised, took with him the best of the Ptolemaic arms that had been previously issued to him,[a] and crossed over by night to the tent of Ptolemy, intending single-handed to kill him and thereby end the war. [3] But Dositheus, known as the son of Drimylus, a Jew by birth who later changed his religion and apostatized from the ancestral traditions, had led the king away and arranged that a certain insignificant man should sleep in the tent; and so it turned out that this man incurred the vengeance meant for the king.[b] [4] When a bitter fight resulted, and matters were turning out rather in favor of Antiochus, Arsinoë went to the troops with wailing and tears, her locks all disheveled, and exhorted them to defend themselves and their children and wives bravely, promising to give them each two minas of gold if they won the battle. [5] And so it came about that the enemy was routed in the action, and many captives also were taken. [6] Now that he had foiled the plot, Ptolemy[c] decided to visit the neighboring cities and encourage them. [7] By doing this, and by endowing their sacred enclosures with gifts, he strengthened the morale of his subjects.

Philopator Attempts to Enter the Temple

[8] Since the Jews had sent some of their council and elders to greet him, to bring him gifts of welcome, and to congratulate him on what had happened, he was all the more eager to visit them as soon as possible. [9] After he had arrived in Jerusalem, he offered sacrifice to the supreme God[d] and made thank offerings and did what was fitting for the holy place.[e] Then, upon entering the place and being impressed by its excellence and its beauty, [10] he marveled at the good order of the temple, and conceived a desire to enter the sanctuary. [11] When they said that this was not permitted, because not even members of their own nation were allowed to enter, not even all of the priests, but only the high priest who was pre-eminent over all—and he only once a year—the king was by no means persuaded. [12] Even after the law had been read to him, he did not cease to maintain that he ought to enter, saying, "Even if those men are deprived of this honor, I ought not to be." [13] And he inquired why, when he entered every other temple,[f] no one there had stopped him. [14] And someone answered thoughtlessly that it was wrong to take that as a portent.[g] [15] "But since this has happened," the king[c] said, "why should not I at least enter, whether they wish it or not?"

Jewish Resistance to Ptolemy

[16] Then the priests in all their vestments prostrated themselves and

---

[a] Or the best of the Ptolemaic soldiers previously put under his command
[b] Gk that one   [c] Gk he   [d] Gk the greatest God   [e] Gk the place   [f] Or entered the temple precincts   [g] Or to boast of this

---

1:1–7 Ptolemy Saved from Assassination
This happened during the battle of Raphia (217 BCE), a town near Gaza and the Egyptian border. This battle is described in Polybius's *The Histories* 5:79–86.

1:3 *Dositheus*—An apostate or renegade Jew who saves King Ptolemy IV Philapator (221–204 BCE), echoing the deeds of Mordecai, Esther's cousin, a closet Jew who uncovered a plot against King Ahasuerus (Esth. 2:19–23).

1:8–2:24 Philopater Attempts to Enter the Jerusalem Temple
Heliodorus had tried to do this in 2 Macc. 3.

1:11—Only the high priest could enter the Holy of Holies; see Exod. 30:10; Lev. 16:2, 11–12, 15, 34; Heb. 9:7. This sense of holiness can help us to recapture the distinctiveness of sacred and profane space in our churches today.

1:16–29—The Jews react with alarm and fervent

entreated the supreme God[a] to aid in the present situation and to avert the violence of this evil design, and they filled the temple with cries and tears; [17] those who remained behind in the city were agitated and hurried out, supposing that something mysterious was occurring. [18] Young women who had been secluded in their chambers rushed out with their mothers, sprinkled their hair with dust,[b] and filled the streets with groans and lamentations. [19] Those women who had recently been arrayed for marriage abandoned the bridal chambers[c] prepared for wedded union, and, neglecting proper modesty, in a disorderly rush flocked together in the city. [20] Mothers and nurses abandoned even newborn children here and there, some in houses and some in the streets, and without a backward look they crowded together at the most high temple. [21] Various were the supplications of those gathered there because of what the king was profanely plotting. [22] In addition, the bolder of the citizens would not tolerate the completion of his plans or the fulfillment of his intended purpose. [23] They shouted to their compatriots to take arms and die courageously for the ancestral law, and created a considerable disturbance in the holy place;[d] and being barely restrained by the old men and the elders,[e] they resorted to the same posture of supplication as the others. [24] Meanwhile the crowd, as before, was engaged in prayer, [25] while the elders near the king tried in various ways to change his arrogant mind from the plan that he had conceived. [26] But he, in his arrogance, took heed of nothing, and began now to approach, determined to bring the aforesaid plan to a conclusion. [27] When those who were around him observed this, they turned, together with our people, to call upon him who has all power to defend them in the present trouble and not to overlook this unlawful and haughty deed. [28] The continuous, vehement, and concerted cry of the crowds[f] resulted in an immense uproar; [29] for it seemed that not only the people but also the walls and the whole earth around echoed, because indeed all at that time[g] preferred death to the profanation of the place.

The Prayer of the High Priest Simon

2 Then the high priest Simon, facing the sanctuary, bending his knees and extending his hands with calm dignity, prayed as follows:[h] [2] "Lord, Lord, king of the heavens, and sovereign of all creation, holy among the holy ones, the only ruler, almighty, give attention to us who are suffering grievously from an impious and profane man, puffed up in his audacity and power. [3] For you, the creator of all things and the governor of all, are a just Ruler, and you judge those who have done anything in insolence and arrogance. [4] You destroyed those who in the past committed injustice, among whom were even giants who trusted in their strength and boldness, whom you destroyed by bringing on them a boundless flood. [5] You con-

---

[a] Gk the greatest God [b] Other ancient authorities add and ashes [c] Or the canopies [d] Gk the place [e] Other ancient authorities read priests [f] Other ancient authorities read vehement cry of the assembled crowds [g] Other ancient authorities lack at that time [h] Other ancient authorities lack verse 1

---

prayer, echoing the emotional language of 2 Macc. 3:15–22, over the actions of Heliodorus. Their emotion reminds people of faith that prayer need not be only quiet meditation, but can reflect the intensity of human experience in all its dimensions.

2:1–20—The prayer of Simon the high priest rehearses Israel's sacred history. God's acts of deliverance on Israel's behalf (see similar prayers in Ezra 9; Neh. 9; Dan. 9; Bar. 1:15–3:8) are cited in accordance with God's role as creator and judge. His prayer reminds us to look in our own lives for God's acts of deliverance, which we are often too busy to acknowledge. Simon is eulogized in Sir. 50 as one of Israel's heroes. Contemporary hype over sports figures and movie stars, as well as sex scandals rocking the church, often make it difficult for us to think of our religious leaders as heroes.

2:5 *Sodom*—See Gen. 19.

sumed with fire and sulfur the people of Sodom who acted arrogantly, who were notorious for their vices;[a] and you made them an example to those who should come afterward. [6] You made known your mighty power by inflicting many and varied punishments on the audacious Pharaoh who had enslaved your holy people Israel. [7] And when he pursued them with chariots and a mass of troops, you overwhelmed him in the depths of the sea, but carried through safely those who had put their confidence in you, the Ruler over the whole creation. [8] And when they had seen works of your hands, they praised you, the Almighty. [9] You, O King, when you had created the boundless and immeasurable earth, chose this city and sanctified this place for your name, though you have no need of anything; and when you had glorified it by your magnificent manifestation,[b] you made it a firm foundation for the glory of your great and honored name. [10] And because you love the house of Israel, you promised that if we should have reverses and tribulation should overtake us, you would listen to our petition when we come to this place and pray. [11] And indeed you are faithful and true. [12] And because oftentimes when our fathers were oppressed you helped them in their humiliation, and rescued them from great evils, [13] see now, O holy King, that because of our many and great sins we are crushed with suffering, subjected to our enemies, and over-

taken by helplessness. [14] In our downfall this audacious and profane man undertakes to violate the holy place on earth dedicated to your glorious name. [15] For your dwelling is the heaven of heavens, unapproachable by human beings. [16] But because you graciously bestowed your glory on your people Israel, you sanctified this place. [17] Do not punish us for the defilement committed by these men, or call us to account for this profanation, otherwise the transgressors will boast in their wrath and exult in the arrogance of their tongue, saying, [18] 'We have trampled down the house of the sanctuary as the houses of the abominations are trampled down.' [19] Wipe away our sins and disperse our errors, and reveal your mercy at this hour. [20] Speedily let your mercies overtake us, and put praises in the mouth of those who are downcast and broken in spirit, and give us peace."

God's Punishment of Ptolemy

21 Thereupon God, who oversees all things, the first Father of all, holy among the holy ones, having heard the lawful supplication, scourged him who had exalted himself in insolence and audacity. [22] He shook him on this side and that as a reed is shaken by the wind, so that he lay helpless on the ground and, besides being paralyzed in his limbs, was unable even to speak, since he was smitten[c] by a righteous judgment. [23] Then

---

[a] Other ancient authorities read *secret in their vices* [b] Or *epiphany* [c] Other ancient authorities read *pierced*

2:6 *Pharaoh*—See Exod. 7–12.

2:10—Prayers are especially heard in the Jerusalem temple; see 1 Kgs. 8:29. Contemporary worship has lost this ancient sense of the place of worship as a place in which God is especially present and the holy and the profane intersect. In our contemporary culture of hype, worship risks being just another point on the continuum of secular entertainment.

2:13—Confession of sin as a motivation for God to grant Simon's petitions on behalf of the people, based upon the theory of act/consequence, you get what you deserve. Confession is very difficult for a people or nation, as evidenced by the angry

reaction of many to 9/11. Rather than search for underlying causes and the larger global picture, anger fueled calls for revenge and the creation of scapegoats.

2:21–24—God miraculously punishes Ptolemy by afflicting his body, as God punished Heliodorus (2 Macc. 3:26) and Antiochus Epiphanes (2 Macc. 9:5). God presides over a just system of act/consequence. This gives hope and validation to those who are suffering unjustly. Yet the language describing the punishment also suggests a kind of triumphant revenge, which can be dangerous.

both friends and bodyguards, seeing the severe punishment that had overtaken him, and fearing that he would lose his life, quickly dragged him out, panic-stricken in their exceedingly great fear. [24] After a while he recovered, and though he had been punished, he by no means repented, but went away uttering bitter threats.

Hostile Measures against the Jews

25 When he arrived in Egypt, he increased in his deeds of malice, abetted by the previously mentioned drinking companions and comrades, who were strangers to everything just. [26] He was not content with his uncounted licentious deeds, but even continued with such audacity that he framed evil reports in the various localities; and many of his friends, intently observing the king's purpose, themselves also followed his will. [27] He proposed to inflict public disgrace on the Jewish community,[a] and he set up a stone[b] on the tower in the courtyard with this inscription: [28] "None of those who do not sacrifice shall enter their sanctuaries, and all Jews shall be subjected to a registration involving poll tax and to the status of slaves. Those who object to this are to be taken by force and put to death; [29] those who are registered are also to be branded on their bodies by fire with the ivy-leaf symbol of Dionysus, and they shall also be reduced to their former limited status." [30] In order that he might not appear to

be an enemy of all, he inscribed below: "But if any of them prefer to join those who have been initiated into the mysteries, they shall have equal citizenship with the Alexandrians."

31 Now some, however, with an obvious abhorrence of the price to be exacted for maintaining the religion of their city,[c] readily gave themselves up, since they expected to enhance their reputation by their future association with the king. [32] But the majority acted firmly with a courageous spirit and did not abandon their religion; and by paying money in exchange for life they confidently attempted to save themselves from the registration. [33] They remained resolutely hopeful of obtaining help, and they abhorred those who separated themselves from them, considering them to be enemies of the Jewish nation,[a] and depriving them of companionship and mutual help.

The Jews and Their Neighbors

3 When the impious king comprehended this situation, he became so infuriated that not only was he enraged against those Jews who lived in Alexandria, but was still more bitterly hostile toward those in the countryside; and he ordered that all should promptly be gathered into one place, and put to death by the most cruel means. [2] While these matters were being arranged, a hostile rumor was circulated against the

a Gk the nation *b* Gk stele *c* Meaning of Gk uncertain

2:25–7:23 Ptolemy Persecutes the Jews in Egypt

2:28 *Poll tax*—Perhaps introduced by Augustus in 24 BCE.

2:29 *Dionysus*—God of wine and revelry (see 2 Macc. 6:7). Branding or tattooing was associated with the worship of Dionysus, but the author may have confused this custom with the branding of slaves (see 1 Macc. 3:41).

2:30—The king offers Greek citizenship to the Jews of Alexandria if they participate in pagan religious acts; cf. 1 Macc. 2:18. We are often willing to give up varying degrees of our Christian identity for social and economic advantage.

2:31–33—Some renegade or apostate Jews (see

1 Macc. 1:52) were willing to give up their Jewish practices to become Greek, while the majority stood firm as Jews and "abhorred" the apostates. The split over Jewish identity created hard feelings. Christians today often judge other Christians harshly on the basis of their lifestyle, sexual orientation, or politics. The emotional intensity and rhetoric surrounding these disagreements fracture the sense of community.

3:1–10—Hostile rumors are spread about the Jews because they refuse to be registered for the poll tax. This lack of solidarity among minorities struggling in a dominant culture succeeds in strengthening the control of those in power.

Jewish nation by some who conspired to do them ill, a pretext being given by a report that they hindered others[a] from the observance of their customs. [3] The Jews, however, continued to maintain goodwill and unswerving loyalty toward the dynasty; [4] but because they worshiped God and conducted themselves by his law, they kept their separateness with respect to foods. For this reason they appeared hateful to some; [5] but since they adorned their style of life with the good deeds of upright people, they were established in good repute with everyone. [6] Nevertheless those of other races paid no heed to their good service to their nation, which was common talk among all; [7] instead they gossiped about the differences in worship and foods, alleging that these people were loyal neither to the king nor to his authorities, but were hostile and greatly opposed to his government. So they attached no ordinary reproach to them.

[8] The Greeks in the city, though wronged in no way, when they saw an unexpected tumult around these people and the crowds that suddenly were forming, were not strong enough to help them, for they lived under tyranny. They did try to console them, being grieved at the situation, and expected that matters would change; [9] for such a great community ought not be left to its fate when it had committed no offense. [10] And already some of their neighbors and friends and business associates had taken some of them aside privately and were pledging to protect them and to exert more earnest efforts for their assistance.

Ptolemy's Decree That All Jews Be Arrested

[11] Then the king, boastful of his present good fortune, and not considering the might of the supreme God,[b] but assuming that he would persevere constantly in his same purpose, wrote this letter against them:

[12] "King Ptolemy Philopator to his generals and soldiers in Egypt and all its districts, greetings and good health:

[13] "I myself and our government are faring well. [14] When our expedition took place in Asia, as you yourselves know, it was brought to conclusion, according to plan, by the gods' deliberate alliance with us in battle, [15] and we considered that we should not rule the nations inhabiting Coelesyria and Phoenicia by the power of the spear, but should cherish them with clemency and great benevolence, gladly treating them well. [16] And when we had granted very great revenues to the temples in the cities, we came on to Jerusalem also, and went up to honor the temple of those wicked people, who never cease from their folly. [17] They accepted our presence by word, but insincerely by deed, because when we proposed to enter their inner temple and honor it with magnificent and most beautiful offerings, [18] they were carried away by their traditional arrogance, and excluded us from entering; but they were spared the exercise of our power because of the benevolence that we have toward all. [19] By maintaining their manifest ill-will toward us, they become the only people among all nations who hold their heads high in defiance of kings and their own benefactors, and are unwilling to regard any action as sincere.

[20] "But we, when we arrived in Egypt victorious, accommodated ourselves to their folly and did as was proper, since we treat all nations with benevolence. [21] Among other things, we made known to all our amnesty toward their

[a] Gk them   [b] Gk the greatest God

3:8 *The Greeks in the city*—Not all Greeks are hostile to the Jews. Whole groups are often stigmatized by the actions of a few. The war on terrorism, for example, has led some to believe that all Muslims are terrorists.

3:11–30—The decree of Ptolemy orders the round up of all Jews in the provinces because the Alexandrian Jews spurned Greek citizenship and because the Jerusalem Jews barred Ptolemy from entering the temple. Cf. Esth. 3:13.

compatriots here, both because of their alliance with us and the myriad affairs liberally entrusted to them from the beginning; and we ventured to make a change, by deciding both to deem them worthy of Alexandrian citizenship and to make them participants in our regular religious rites.[a] 22 But in their innate malice they took this in a contrary spirit, and disdained what is good. Since they incline constantly to evil, 23 they not only spurn the priceless citizenship, but also both by speech and by silence they abominate those few among them who are sincerely disposed toward us; in every situation, in accordance with their infamous way of life, they secretly suspect that we may soon alter our policy. 24 Therefore, fully convinced by these indications that they are ill-disposed toward us in every way, we have taken precautions so that, if a sudden disorder later arises against us, we shall not have these impious people behind our backs as traitors and barbarous enemies. 25 Therefore we have given orders that, as soon as this letter arrives, you are to send to us those who live among you, together with their wives and children, with insulting and harsh treatment, and bound securely with iron fetters, to suffer the sure and shameful death that befits enemies. 26 For when all of these have been punished, we are sure that for the remaining time the government will be established for ourselves in good order and in the best state. 27 But those who shelter any of the Jews, whether old people or children or even infants, will be tortured to death with the most hateful torments, together with their families. 28 Any who are willing to give information will receive the property of those who incur the punishment, and also two thousand drachmas from the royal treasury, and will be awarded their freedom.[b] 29 Every place detected sheltering a Jew is to be made unapproachable and burned with fire, and shall become useless for all time to any mortal creature." 30 The letter was written in the above form.

The Jews Deported to Alexandria

4 In every place, then, where this decree arrived, a feast at public expense was arranged for the Gentiles with shouts and gladness, for the inveterate enmity that had long ago been in their minds was now made evident and outspoken. 2 But among the Jews there was incessant mourning, lamentation, and tearful cries; everywhere their hearts were burning, and they groaned because of the unexpected destruction that had suddenly been decreed for them. 3 What district or city, or what habitable place at all, or what streets were not filled with mourning and wailing for them? 4 For with such a harsh and ruthless spirit were they being sent off, all together, by the generals in the several cities, that at the sight of their unusual punishments, even some of their enemies, perceiving the common object of pity before their eyes, reflected on the uncertainty of life and shed tears at the most miserable expulsion of these people. 5 For a multitude of gray-headed old men, sluggish and bent with age, was being led away, forced to march at a swift pace by the violence with which they were driven in such a shameful manner. 6 And young women who had just entered the bridal chamber[c] to share married life exchanged joy for wailing, their myrrh-perfumed hair sprinkled with ashes, and were carried away unveiled, all together raising

---

[a] Other ancient authorities read partners of our regular priests [b] Gk crowned with freedom [c] Or the canopy

---

4:1–10—An emotional description of the imprisonment of the Jews (cf. Esth. 4:23 and Greek historiography of the time) intended to inspire and garner sympathy as "pathetic" history. Our emotional involvement can spur us into action on behalf of the oppressed, but the danger is that only those who hook our attention in this way will win our support. We often do not notice those who have no voice.

a lament instead of a wedding song, as they were torn by the harsh treatment of the heathen.[a] [7] In bonds and in public view they were violently dragged along as far as the place of embarkation. [8] Their husbands, in the prime of youth, their necks encircled with ropes instead of garlands, spent the remaining days of their marriage festival in lamentations instead of good cheer and youthful revelry, seeing death immediately before them.[b] [9] They were brought on board like wild animals, driven under the constraint of iron bonds; some were fastened by the neck to the benches of the boats, others had their feet secured by unbreakable fetters, [10] and in addition they were confined under a solid deck, so that, with their eyes in total darkness, they would undergo treatment befitting traitors during the whole voyage.

The Jews Imprisoned at Schedia

[11] When these people had been brought to the place called Schedia, and the voyage was concluded as the king had decreed, he commanded that they should be enclosed in the hippodrome that had been built with a monstrous perimeter wall in front of the city, and that was well suited to make them an obvious spectacle to all coming back into the city and to those from the city[c] going out into the country, so that they could neither communicate with the king's forces nor in any way claim to be inside the circuit of the city.[d] [12] And when this had happened, the king, hearing that the Jews' compatriots from the city frequently went out in secret to lament bitterly the ignoble misfortune of their kindred, [13] ordered in his rage that these people be dealt with in precisely the same fashion as the others, not omitting any detail of their punishment.

[14] The entire race was to be registered individually, not for the hard labor that has been briefly mentioned before, but to be tortured with the outrages that he had ordered, and at the end to be destroyed in the space of a single day. [15] The registration of these people was therefore conducted with bitter haste and zealous intensity from the rising of the sun until its setting, coming to an end after forty days but still uncompleted.

[16] The king was greatly and continually filled with joy, organizing feasts in honor of all his idols, with a mind alienated from truth and with a profane mouth, praising speechless things that are not able even to communicate or to come to one's help, and uttering improper words against the supreme God.[e] [17] But after the previously mentioned interval of time the scribes declared to the king that they were no longer able to take the census of the Jews because of their immense number, [18] though most of them were still in the country, some still residing in their homes, and some at the place;[f] the task was impossible for all the generals in Egypt. [19] After he had threatened them severely, charging that they had been bribed to contrive a means of escape, he was clearly convinced about the matter [20] when they said and proved that both the paper[g] and the pens they used for writing had already given out. [21] But this was an act of the invincible providence of him who was aiding the Jews from heaven.

Execution of the Jews Is Twice Thwarted

5 Then the king, completely inflexible, was filled with overpowering anger

---

[a] Other ancient authorities read *as though torn by heathen whelps* [b] Gk *seeing Hades already lying at their feet* [c] Gk *those of them* [d] Or *claim protection of the walls*; meaning of Gk uncertain [e] Gk *the greatest God* [f] Other ancient authorities read *on the way* [g] Or *paper factory*

4:11–21—The scribes are unable to complete the census of the Jews because they are so numerous; cf. 1 Kgs. 3:8. The author attributes this failure to God's *invincible providence* (v. 21). We do not often notice the ways in which God is at work behind the scenes in our lives today

because we tend to restrict God's activity to our pious moments or to our time in church. We are reminded to look for God's presence in every part of our lives.

5:1–51—The king's plans to have the Jews

and wrath; so he summoned Hermon, keeper of the elephants, [2] and ordered him on the following day to drug all the elephants—five hundred in number—with large handfuls of frankincense and plenty of unmixed wine, and to drive them in, maddened by the lavish abundance of drink, so that the Jews might meet their doom. [3] When he had given these orders he returned to his feasting, together with those of his Friends and of the army who were especially hostile toward the Jews. [4] And Hermon, keeper of the elephants, proceeded faithfully to carry out the orders. [5] The servants in charge of the Jews[a] went out in the evening and bound the hands of the wretched people and arranged for their continued custody through the night, convinced that the whole nation would experience its final destruction. [6] For to the Gentiles it appeared that the Jews were left without any aid, [7] because in their bonds they were forcibly confined on every side. But with tears and a voice hard to silence they all called upon the Almighty Lord and Ruler of all power, their merciful God and Father, praying [8] that he avert with vengeance the evil plot against them and in a glorious manifestation rescue them from the fate now prepared for them. [9] So their entreaty ascended fervently to heaven.

10 Hermon, however, when he had drugged the pitiless elephants until they had been filled with a great abundance of wine and satiated with frankincense, presented himself at the courtyard early in the morning to report to the king about these preparations. [11] But the Lord[b] sent upon the king a portion of sleep, that beneficence that from the beginning, night and day, is bestowed by him who grants it to whomever he wishes. [12] And by the action of the Lord he was overcome by so pleasant and deep a sleep[c] that he quite failed in his lawless purpose and was completely frustrated in his inflexible plan. [13] Then the Jews, since they had escaped the appointed hour, praised their holy God and again implored him who is easily reconciled to show the might of his all-powerful hand to the arrogant Gentiles.

14 But now, since it was nearly the middle of the tenth hour, the person who was in charge of the invitations, seeing that the guests were assembled, approached the king and nudged him. [15] And when he had with difficulty roused him, he pointed out that the hour of the banquet was already slipping by, and he gave him an account of the situation. [16] The king, after considering this, returned to his drinking, and ordered those present for the banquet to recline opposite him. [17] When this was done he urged them to give themselves over to revelry and to make the present[d] portion of the banquet joyful by celebrating all the more. [18] After the party had been going on for some time, the king summoned Hermon and with sharp threats demanded to know why the Jews had been allowed to remain alive through the present day. [19] But when he, with the corroboration of the king's[e] Friends, pointed out that while it was still night he had carried out completely the order given him, [20] the king,[f] possessed by a

---

[a] Gk them   [b] Gk he   [c] Other ancient authorities add *from evening until the ninth hour*   [d] Other ancient authorities read *delayed* (Gk *untimely*)   [e] Gk his   [f] Gk he

---

trampled by drugged elephants are defeated by God. A popular legend about drunken elephants was in circulation in the Greco-Roman world at the time.

5:4—*Hermon, keeper of the elephants*, corresponds with Haman, the king's agent who accuses the Jews (Esth. 3:1–8:1).

5:7–13—The Jews pray for deliverance, and God answers their prayer.

5:20 *Phalaris*—Sixth-century BCE tyrant of Agrigentum known for roasting people alive (also v. 42). Ptolemy is demonized as having *savagery* worse than Phalaris. We demonize our opponents in similar ways on the personal and national level, which blocks any attempt at reconciliation.

savagery worse than that of Phalaris, said that the Jews[a] were benefited by today's sleep, "but," he added, "tomorrow without delay prepare the elephants in the same way for the destruction of the lawless Jews!" 21 When the king had spoken, all those present readily and joyfully with one accord gave their approval, and all went to their own homes. 22 But they did not so much employ the duration of the night in sleep as in devising all sorts of insults for those they thought to be doomed.

23 Then, as soon as the cock had crowed in the early morning, Hermon, having equipped[b] the animals, began to move them along in the great colonnade. 24 The crowds of the city had been assembled for this most pitiful spectacle and they were eagerly waiting for daybreak. 25 But the Jews, at their last gasp—since the time had run out—stretched their hands toward heaven and with most tearful supplication and mournful dirges implored the supreme God[c] to help them again at once. 26 The rays of the sun were not yet shed abroad, and while the king was receiving his Friends, Hermon arrived and invited him to come out, indicating that what the king desired was ready for action. 27 But he, on receiving the report and being struck by the unusual invitation to come out—since he had been completely overcome by incomprehension—inquired what the matter was for which this had been so zealously completed for him. 28 This was the act of God who rules over all things, for he had implanted in the king's mind a forgetfulness of the things he had previously devised. 29 Then Hermon and all the king's Friends[d] pointed out that the animals and the armed forces were ready, "O king, according to your eager purpose."[e] 30 But at these words he was filled with an overpowering wrath, because by the providence of God his whole mind had been deranged concerning these matters; and with a threatening look he said, 31 "If your parents or children were present, I would have prepared them to be a rich feast for the savage animals instead of the Jews, who give me no ground for complaint and have exhibited to an extraordinary degree a full and firm loyalty to my ancestors. 32 In fact you would have been deprived of life instead of these, if it were not for an affection arising from our nurture in common and your usefulness." 33 So Hermon suffered an unexpected and dangerous threat, and his eyes wavered and his face fell. 34 The king's Friends one by one sullenly slipped away and dismissed[f] the assembled people to their own occupations. 35 Then the Jews, on hearing what the king had said, praised the manifest Lord God, King of kings, since this also was his aid that they had received.

36 The king, however, reconvened the party in the same manner and urged the guests to return to their celebrating. 37 After summoning Hermon he said in a threatening tone, "How many times, you poor wretch, must I give you orders about these things? 38 Equip[g] the elephants now once more for the destruction of the Jews tomorrow!" 39 But the officials who were at table with him, wondering at his instability of mind, remonstrated as follows: 40 "O king, how long will you put us to the test, as though we are idiots, ordering now for a third time that they be destroyed, and again revoking your decree in the matter?[h]

a Gk *they*   *b* Or *armed*   *c* Gk *the greatest God*   *d* Gk *all the Friends*   *e* Other ancient authorities read *pointed to the beasts and the armed forces, saying, "They are ready, O king, according to your eager purpose."*   *f* Other ancient authorities read *he dismissed*   *g* Or *Arm*   *h* Other ancient authorities read *when the matter is in hand*

5:28 *This was the act of God who rules over all things*—The king repeatedly changes his mind about the fate of the Jews because of forgetfulness sent by God; so 5:11–12, 30, 35 (cf. the hardening of Pharaoh's heart in Exod. 10:20).

5:33—Hermon experiences a reversal of fortune like Haman (Esth. 7:10). God keeps order by punishing the wicked according to the theory of act/consequence.

41 As a result the city is in a tumult because of its expectation; it is crowded with masses of people, and also in constant danger of being plundered."

42 At this the king, a Phalaris in everything and filled with madness, took no account of the changes of mind that had come about within him for the protection of the Jews, and he firmly swore an irrevocable oath that he would send them to death[a] without delay, mangled by the knees and feet of the animals, 43 and would also march against Judea and rapidly level it to the ground with fire and spear, and by burning to the ground the temple inaccessible to him[b] would quickly render it forever empty of those who offered sacrifices there. 44 Then the Friends and officers departed with great joy, and they confidently posted the armed forces at the places in the city most favorable for keeping guard.

45 Now when the animals had been brought virtually to a state of madness, so to speak, by the very fragrant draughts of wine mixed with frankincense and had been equipped with frightful devices, the elephant keeper 46 entered at about dawn into the courtyard—the city now being filled with countless masses of people crowding their way into the hippodrome—and urged the king on to the matter at hand. 47 So he, when he had filled his impious mind with a deep rage, rushed out in full force along with the animals, wishing to witness, with invulnerable heart and with his own eyes, the grievous and pitiful destruction of the aforementioned people.

48 When the Jews saw the dust raised by the elephants going out at the gate and by the following armed forces, as well as by the trampling of the crowd, and heard the loud and tumultuous noise, 49 they thought that this was their last moment of life, the end of their most miserable suspense, and giving way to lamentation and groans they kissed each other, embracing relatives and falling into one another's arms[c]—parents and children, mothers and daughters, and others with babies at their breasts who were drawing their last milk. 50 Not only this, but when they considered the help that they had received before from heaven, they prostrated themselves with one accord on the ground, removing the babies from their breasts, 51 and cried out in a very loud voice, imploring the Ruler over every power to manifest himself and be merciful to them, as they stood now at the gates of death.[d]

The Prayer of Eleazar

6 Then a certain Eleazar, famous among the priests of the country, who had attained a ripe old age and throughout his life had been adorned with every virtue, directed the elders around him to stop calling upon the holy God, and he prayed as follows: 2 "King of great power, Almighty God Most High, governing all creation with mercy, 3 look upon the descendants of Abraham, O Father, upon the children of the sainted Jacob, a people of your consecrated portion who are perishing as foreigners in a foreign land. 4 Pharaoh with his abundance of chariots, the former ruler of this Egypt, exalted with lawless insolence and boastful tongue, you destroyed together with his arrogant army by drowning them in the sea, manifesting the light of your mercy on the nation of Israel. 5 Sennacherib exulting in his countless forces, oppressive king of the Assyrians, who had already gained control of the whole world by the spear and was lifted up against your holy city, speaking grievous words with boasting and insolence, you, O Lord,

a Gk Hades b Gk us c Gk falling upon their necks d Gk Hades

6:1–15—The prayer of *Eleazar* (the name of the martyr in 2 Macc. 6:18–31 and 4 Macc. 5–7, and of the high priest in the *Letter of Aristeas* 41) celebrating God's saving history with Israel; this prayer balances the prayer of Simon in 3 Macc. 2. Exodus is again cited, as well as the unsuccessful siege of Jerusalem under Sennacherib (2 Kgs. 18–19) and Dan. 3 and 6.

broke in pieces, showing your power to many nations. **6** The three companions in Babylon who had voluntarily surrendered their lives to the flames so as not to serve vain things, you rescued unharmed, even to a hair, moistening the fiery furnace with dew and turning the flame against all their enemies. **7** Daniel, who through envious slanders was thrown down into the ground to lions as food for wild animals, you brought up to the light unharmed. **8** And Jonah, wasting away in the belly of a huge, seaborn monster, you, Father, watched over and restored[a] unharmed to all his family. **9** And now, you who hate insolence, all-merciful and protector of all, reveal yourself quickly to those of the nation of Israel[b]—who are being outrageously treated by the abominable and lawless Gentiles.

10 "Even if our lives have become entangled in impieties in our exile, rescue us from the hand of the enemy, and destroy us, Lord, by whatever fate you choose. **11** Let not the vain-minded praise their vanities[c] at the destruction of your beloved people, saying," Not even their god has rescued them.' **12** But you, O Eternal One, who have all might and all power, watch over us now and have mercy on us who by the senseless insolence of the lawless are being deprived of life in the manner of traitors. **13** And let the Gentiles cower today in fear of your invincible might, O honored One, who have power to save the nation of Jacob. **14** The whole throng of infants and their parents entreat you with tears. **15** Let it be shown to all the Gentiles that you are with us, O Lord, and have not turned your face from us; but just as you

have said, 'Not even when they were in the land of their enemies did I neglect them,' so accomplish it, O Lord."

Two Angels Rescue the Jews

16 Just as Eleazar was ending his prayer, the king arrived at the hippodrome with the animals and all the arrogance of his forces. **17** And when the Jews observed this they raised great cries to heaven so that even the nearby valleys resounded with them and brought an uncontrollable terror upon the army. **18** Then the most glorious, almighty, and true God revealed his holy face and opened the heavenly gates, from which two glorious angels of fearful aspect descended, visible to all but the Jews. **19** They opposed the forces of the enemy and filled them with confusion and terror, binding them with immovable shackles. **20** Even the king began to shudder bodily, and he forgot his sullen insolence. **21** The animals turned back upon the armed forces following them and began trampling and destroying them.

22 Then the king's anger was turned to pity and tears because of the things that he had devised beforehand. **23** For when he heard the shouting and saw them all fallen headlong to destruction, he wept and angrily threatened his Friends, saying, **24** "You are committing treason and surpassing tyrants in cruelty; and even me, your benefactor, you are now attempting to deprive of dominion and life by secretly devising acts of no advantage to the kingdom. **25** Who has driven from their homes those who faithfully kept our country's fortresses, and foolishly

---

[a] Other ancient authorities read *rescued and restored*; others, *mercifully restored* [b] Other ancient authorities read *to the saints of Israel* [c] Or *bless their vain gods*

6:11 *Not even their God has rescued them*—A motivation for God's granting the petition. God's honor and reputation are on the line if those who call on God are not answered; enemies will gloat. Though some may see this as bullying God to grant a desired outcome, this motivation witnesses to the belief that the people praying matter to God. This can be empowering and sustaining in crisis.

6:16–21—God's miraculous deliverance of the people by means of two angels (cf. 2 Macc. 3:26).

6:22–29 *The king's anger was turned to pity*—The king reverses his position.

6:25—The Jews kept the fortress at Elephantine in the fifth century BCE.

gathered every one of them here? [26] Who is it that has so lawlessly encompassed with outrageous treatment those who from the beginning differed from[a] all nations in their goodwill toward us and often have accepted willingly the worst of human dangers? [27] Loose and untie their unjust bonds! Send them back to their homes in peace, begging pardon for your former actions![b] [28] Release the children of the almighty and living God of heaven, who from the time of our ancestors until now has granted an unimpeded and notable stability to our government." [29] These then were the things he said; and the Jews, immediately released, praised their holy God and Savior, since they now had escaped death.

The Jews Celebrate Their Deliverance

30 Then the king, when he had returned to the city, summoned the official in charge of the revenues and ordered him to provide to the Jews both wines and everything else needed for a festival of seven days, deciding that they should celebrate their rescue with all joyfulness in that same place in which they had expected to meet their destruction. [31] Accordingly those disgracefully treated and near to death,[c] or rather, who stood at its gates, arranged for a banquet of deliverance instead of a bitter and lamentable death, and full of joy they apportioned to celebrants the place that had been prepared for their destruction and burial. [32] They stopped their chanting of dirges and took up the song of their ancestors, praising God, their Savior and worker of wonders.[d] Putting an end to all mourning and wailing, they formed choruses[e] as a sign of peaceful joy. [33] Likewise also the king, after convening a great banquet to celebrate these events, gave thanks to heaven unceasingly and lavishly for the unex-

pected rescue that he[f] had experienced. [34] Those who had previously believed that the Jews would be destroyed and become food for birds, and had joyfully registered them, groaned as they themselves were overcome by disgrace, and their fire-breathing boldness was ignominiously[g] quenched.

35 The Jews, as we have said before, arranged the aforementioned choral group[h] and passed the time in feasting to the accompaniment of joyous thanksgiving and psalms. [36] And when they had ordained a public rite for these things in their whole community and for their descendants, they instituted the observance of the aforesaid days as a festival, not for drinking and gluttony, but because of the deliverance that had come to them through God. [37] Then they petitioned the king, asking for dismissal to their homes. [38] So their registration was carried out from the twenty-fifth of Pachon to the fourth of Epeiph,[i] for forty days; and their destruction was set for the fifth to the seventh of Epeiph,[j] the three days [39] on which the Lord of all most gloriously revealed his mercy and rescued them all together and unharmed. [40] Then they feasted, being provided with everything by the king, until the fourteenth day,[k] on which also they made the petition for their dismissal. [41] The king granted their request at once and wrote the following letter for them to the generals in the cities, magnanimously expressing his concern:

Ptolemy's Letter on Behalf of the Jews

7 "King Ptolemy Philopator to the generals in Egypt and all in author-

---

[a] Or excelled above [b] Other ancient authorities read revoking your former commands [c] Gk Hades [d] Other ancient authorities read praising Israel and the wonder-working God; or praising Israel's Savior, the wonder-working God [e] Or dances [f] Other ancient authorities read they [g] Other ancient authorities read completely [h] Or dance [i] July 7—August 15 [j] August 16—18 [k] August 25

6:30–41—The Jews celebrate a festival of deliverance at public expense. Cf. Purim in Esth. 9.

6:31 A banquet of deliverance instead of a bitter and lamentable death—A reversal of fortune; cf. Ps. 30:11–12. Such reversals give us

the opportunity to witness to God's saving acts on our behalf (3 Macc. 6:32). They also can keep us open to newness and transformation.

7:1–9—Ptolemy's letter blames certain friends for inciting him against the Jews.

ity in his government, greetings and good health:

2 "We ourselves and our children are faring well, the great God guiding our affairs according to our desire. ³ Certain of our friends, frequently urging us with malicious intent, persuaded us to gather together the Jews of the kingdom in a body and to punish them with barbarous penalties as traitors; ⁴ for they declared that our government would never be firmly established until this was accomplished, because of the ill-will that these people had toward all nations. ⁵ They also led them out with harsh treatment as slaves, or rather as traitors, and, girding themselves with a cruelty more savage than that of Scythian custom, they tried without any inquiry or examination to put them to death. ⁶ But we very severely threatened them for these acts, and in accordance with the clemency that we have toward all people we barely spared their lives. Since we have come to realize that the God of heaven surely defends the Jews, always taking their part as a father does for his children, ⁷ and since we have taken into account the friendly and firm goodwill that they had toward us and our ancestors, we justly have acquitted them of every charge of whatever kind. ⁸ We also have ordered all people to return to their own homes, with no one in any place^a doing them harm at all or reproaching them for the irrational things that have happened. ⁹ For you should know that if we devise any evil against them or cause them any grief at all, we always shall have not a mortal but the Ruler over every power, the Most High God, in everything and inescapably as an antagonist to avenge such acts. Farewell."

The Jews Return Home with Joy

10 On receiving this letter the Jews^b did not immediately hurry to make their departure, but they requested of the king that at their own hands those of the Jewish nation who had willfully transgressed against the holy God and the law of God should receive the punishment they deserved. ¹¹ They declared that those who for the belly's sake had transgressed the divine commandments would never be favorably disposed toward the king's government. ¹² The king^c then, admitting and approving the truth of what they said, granted them a general license so that freely, and without royal authority or supervision, they might destroy those everywhere in his kingdom who had transgressed the law of God. ¹³ When they had applauded him in fitting manner, their priests and the whole multitude shouted the Hallelujah and joyfully departed. ¹⁴ And so on their way they punished and put to a public and shameful death any whom they met of their compatriots who had become defiled. ¹⁵ In that day they put to death more than three hundred men; and they kept the day as a joyful festival, since they had destroyed the profaners. ¹⁶ But those who had held fast to God even to death and had received the full enjoyment of deliverance began their departure from the city, crowned with all sorts of very fragrant flowers, joyfully and loudly giving thanks to the one God of their ancestors, the eternal Savior^d of Israel, in words of praise and all kinds of melodious songs.

17 When they had arrived at Ptolemais, called "rose-bearing" because of

---

^a Other ancient authorities read *way*   ^b Gk *they*   ^c Gk *He*   ^d Other ancient authorities read *the holy Savior*; others, *the holy one*

7:6 The God of heaven surely defends the Jews—Ptolemy acknowledges that God protects the Jews and punishes their enemies (v. 9). The kings in Dan. 2:47; 4:2, 37; 6:26; 2 Macc. 9:12, 13 make a similar declaration.

7:10–16—The Jews slaughter apostate Jews; cf. Esth. 8:11–13; 9:1–17, where Jews slaughter

Gentile enemies. Conflict within the Jewish community erupts into violence, just as conflicts over Christian identity have become violent throughout history, prompting us to think about other ways in which we might resolve our Christian differences.

7:17–23—The Jews return to their homes, and in

a characteristic of the place, the fleet waited for them, in accordance with the common desire, for seven days. [18] There they celebrated their deliverance,[a] for the king had generously provided all things to them for their journey until all of them arrived at their own houses. [19] And when they had all landed in peace with appropriate thanksgiving, there too in like manner they decided to observe these days as a joyous festival during the time of their stay. [20] Then, after inscribing them as holy on a pillar and dedicating a place of prayer at the site of the festival, they departed unharmed, free, and overjoyed, since at the king's command they had all of them been brought safely by land and sea and river to their own homes. [21] They also possessed greater prestige among their enemies, being held in honor and awe; and they were not subject at all to confiscation of their belongings by anyone. [22] Besides, they all recovered all of their property, in accordance with the registration, so that those who held any of it restored it to them with extreme fear.[b] So the supreme God perfectly performed great deeds for their deliverance. [23] Blessed be the Deliverer of Israel through all times! Amen.

[a] Gk they made a cup of deliverance   [b] Other ancient authorities read with a very large supplement

---

an ironic twist, recover all of their possessions because of the very census they resisted. God works through even the negative acts of human beings for good (cf. the Joseph story in Genesis).

The Book of
2 ESDRAS

Who are the true believers? What is wrong with humans that we behave as we do? Why do bad things happen to people? How long will evil prevail? Is God just? What will God or the Messiah do about evil in the world? What will be the final destiny of humans? These are some of the questions that 2 Esdras asks and attempts to answer. In doing so, it offered hope to its readers left reeling by the destruction of the temple by the Roman Empire in 70 CE.

The book is named after the biblical character Ezra, mentioned in 1:1 and 3:1 (where the name Salathiel is also given). He is mentioned also in 14:1, where God calls to him by name. Even so, the book was not written by Ezra. The author adopted as his pseudonym the name of the great lawgiver after the exile. In this work, Ezra receives from God the entire Hebrew Bible and seventy additional books as well. The Armenian version of the book calls it Third Ezra, and most Latin manuscripts call it Fourth Ezra, but the Geneva Bible, the King James Version, and the Revised Standard Version, old and New) call it Second Esdras. It was originally written in Hebrew or Aramaic (scholars still debate which), but it was lost. It seems first to have been translated into Greek, which was occasionally quoted by early church fathers. It was then translated into Latin, Syriac, Coptic, Ethiopic, Arabic, Armenian, and Georgian and survives only in translation.

Second Esdras is a composite of three works. The core of the book (chaps. 3–14, also known as 4 Ezra) was composed near the end of the first century CE. It seems to presuppose the fall of the temple in Jerusalem in 70 CE. Moreover, chapters 11–12 report a vision of an eagle, which scholars recognize as the Roman Empire. Toward the end of the vision, the eagle grows three heads, which are interpreted (12:23) as three kings. These heads most likely represent the Roman emperors Vespasian (reigned 69–79), Titus (r. 79–81), and Domitian (r. 81–96 CE). The vision concludes with the overthrow of the Roman Empire, which did not, of course, follow the death of Domitian. It seems likely, therefore, that 2 Esdras 3–14 was written late in the reign of Domitian or shortly after his death. The introductory chapters (sometimes referred to as 5 Ezra) perhaps appeared during the next century, and the last two (sometimes called 6 Ezra) during the third century CE (cf. note at 15:28–30).

Second Esdras 3–14 constitutes an apocalypse. An apocalypse is a literary genre in the form of a narrative (often a dream or vision) that reveals supernatural powers or forces at work in human and cosmic affairs. It will typically report a tour through cosmic regions or give a reading of history from the time of the putative seer to the time of the author. That reading is cast in the form of prophecy. Second Esdras does the latter. Often, the apocalyptic seer will not understand what he sees and must have an interpreter, sometimes an angel like Uriel in 2 Esdras 3–10 or God, as in 2 Esdras 11–14. The eschatology of apocalypses anticipates the imminent inbreak of God into history, which it deems to have gone awry. That inbreaking may be accompanied by

celestial signs and terrestrial warfare. It may include a messiah, as in 2 Esdras. The essence of that inbreaking, however, is that God will right wrongs. Oppressors will fall, and their victims will triumph. These images and predictions serve to remind the reader of who is in charge of the cosmos and to urge fidelity on the part of true believers. The role(s) those believers may play varies from apocalypse to apocalypse, but in 2 Esdras they are to do the following things: (1) They are to keep God's law, because it is binding upon all humans (7:21, 94). The righteous, those who keep the faith and observe the law, will receive a reward for doing so (7:98). (2) They are to pray for themselves, confessing their sins and asking for God's mercy (8:19–36), because after they died no one else could intercede for them (7:102–105). (3) They are to read this book and others like it to make themselves wise so they could keep up their courage (12:46–49). (4) They are to avoid the concerns of the world (16:35–52).

The two most important themes of 2 Esdras are theodicy and messianism. The term "theodicy" designates the quest for understanding how evil could exist in a moral universe created by a good God. Messianism designates either a future blessed kingdom ruled directly by God (cf. Isa. 24–27) or a kingdom ruled by God's messiah, as in 2 Esdras. Here the messiah will return to earth at the end of the present age to reprove the Roman emperors and reign over his people for four hundred years, after which the new age would commence. These two themes are also important for contemporary disciples. They too may wonder why bad things happen to good people, and they too may need encouragement that God has worked and will work through the messiah to overcome evil in the world.

—Paul L. Redditt

The Genealogy of Ezra

1 The book[a] of the prophet Ezra son of Seraiah, son of Azariah, son of Hilkiah, son of Shallum, son of Zadok, son of Ahitub, [2] son of Ahijah, son of Phinehas, son of Eli, son of Amariah, son of Azariah, son of Meraimoth, son of Arna, son of Uzzi, son of Borith, son of Abishua, son of Phinehas, son of Eleazar, [3] son of Aaron, of the tribe of Levi, who was a captive in the country of the Medes in the reign of Artaxerxes, king of the Persians.[b]

Ezra's Prophetic Call

[4] The word of the Lord came to me, saying, [5] "Go, declare to my people their evil deeds, and to their children the iniquities that they have committed against me, so that they may tell[c] their children's children [6] that the sins of their parents have increased in them, for they have forgotten me and have offered sac-

[a] Other ancient authorities read *The second book* [b] Other ancient authorities, which place chapters 1 and 2 after 16.78, lack verses 1–3 and begin the chapter: *The word of the Lord that came to Ezra son of Chusi in the days of King Nebuchadnezzar, saying, "Go,* [c] Other ancient authorities read *nourish*

1:1–2:48 Fifth Ezra

A Christian was responsible for these chapters as they stand. Ezra's address in 1:24–40 constitutes a rejection of Jews in favor of Christians, and 2:10–11 clearly distinguishes God's people from Israel and gives Jerusalem and God's glory to the new people.

1:1–3 Superscription and Ezra's Genealogy

These verses introduce Ezra the priest with a genealogy giving some of his more important priestly ancestors. Family can play as significant role in guiding one's spiritual development.

1:3 *Artaxerxes*—Probably Artaxerxes I, king of Persia from 465 to 424, though some scholars think of Artaxerxes II, king from 404 to 358.

1:4–2:9 Ezra's Call and Review of Israel's History

1:4–23—Ezra receives a prophetic message emphasizing God's mighty acts during the exodus and Israel's subsequent rebellion. Verses 5 and 8 command him to deliver the message. Obedience to God is fundamental to discipleship.

rifices to strange gods. [7] Was it not I who brought them out of the land of Egypt, out of the house of bondage? But they have angered me and despised my counsels. [8] Now you, pull out the hair of your head and hurl[a] all evils upon them, for they have not obeyed my law—they are a rebellious people. [9] How long shall I endure them, on whom I have bestowed such great benefits? [10] For their sake I have overthrown many kings; I struck down Pharaoh with his servants and all his army. [11] I destroyed all nations before them, and scattered in the east the peoples of two provinces,[b] Tyre and Sidon; I killed all their enemies.

God's Mercies to Israel

[12] "But speak to them and say, Thus says the Lord: [13] Surely it was I who brought you through the sea, and made safe highways for you where there was no road; I gave you Moses as leader and Aaron as priest; [14] I provided light for you from a pillar of fire, and did great wonders among you. Yet you have forgotten me, says the Lord.

[15] "Thus says the Lord Almighty:[c] The quails were a sign to you; I gave you camps for your protection, and in them you complained. [16] You have not exulted in my name at the destruction of your enemies, but to this day you still complain.[d] [17] Where are the benefits that I bestowed on you? When you were hungry and thirsty in the wilderness, did you not cry out to me, [18] saying, 'Why have you led us into this wilderness to kill us? It would have been better for us to serve the Egyptians than to die in this wilderness.' [19] I pitied your groanings and gave you manna for food; you ate the bread of angels. [20] When you were thirsty, did I not split the rock so that waters flowed in abundance? Because

of the heat I clothed you with the leaves of trees.[e] [21] I divided fertile lands among you; I drove out the Canaanites, the Perizzites, and the Philistines[f] before you. What more can I do for you? says the Lord. [22] Thus says the Lord Almighty:[c] When you were in the wilderness, at the bitter stream, thirsty and blaspheming my name, [23] I did not send fire on you for your blasphemies, but threw a tree into the water and made the stream sweet.

Israel's Disobedience and Rejection

[24] "What shall I do to you, O Jacob? You, Judah, would not obey me. I will turn to other nations and will give them my name, so that they may keep my statutes. [25] Because you have forsaken me, I also will forsake you. When you beg mercy of me, I will show you no mercy. [26] When you call to me, I will not listen to you; for you have defiled your hands with blood, and your feet are swift to commit murder. [27] It is not as though you had forsaken me; you have forsaken yourselves, says the Lord.

[28] "Thus says the Lord Almighty: Have I not entreated you as a father entreats his sons or a mother her daughters or a nurse her children, [29] so that you should be my people and I should be your God, and that you should be my children and I should be your father? [30] I gathered you as a hen gathers her chicks under her wings. But now, what shall I do to you? I will cast you out from my presence. [31] When you offer oblations to me, I will turn my face from you; for I have rejected your[g] festal days, and new

[a] Other ancient authorities read *and shake out*   [b] Other ancient authorities read *Did I not destroy the city of Bethsaida because of you, and to the south burn two cities…?*   [c] Other ancient authorities lack *Almighty*   [d] Other ancient authorities read verse 16, *Your pursuer with his army I sank in the sea, but still the people complain also concerning their own destruction.*   [e] Other ancient authorities read *I made for you trees with leaves*   [f] Other ancient authorities read *Perizzites and their children*   [g] Other ancient authorities read *I have not commanded for you*

1:24—This verse breaks the recitation of history with a threat directed toward the author's contemporaries. It is still true that a proper spiritual heritage does not guarantee proper discipleship.
1:31—In Isa. 1:14 and Hos. 2:11, God threatens

to put an end to the celebrations of new moons and festivals. It would be unusual for a Jew to say that God had rejected circumcision, but not for a Christian. The point here is that worship is no substitute for moral behavior.

moons, and circumcisions of the flesh.*a* *32* I sent you my servants the prophets, but you have taken and killed them and torn their bodies*b* in pieces; I will require their blood of you, says the Lord.*c*

33 "Thus says the Lord Almighty: Your house is desolate; I will drive you out as the wind drives straw; *34* and your sons will have no children, because with you*d* they have neglected my commandment and have done what is evil in my sight. *35* I will give your houses to a people that will come, who without having heard me will believe. Those to whom I have shown no signs will do what I have commanded. *36* They have seen no prophets, yet will recall their former state.*e* *37* I call to witness the gratitude of the people that is to come, whose children rejoice with gladness;*f* though they do not see me with bodily eyes, yet with the spirit they will believe the things I have said.

38 "And now, father,*g* look with pride and see the people coming from the east; *39* to them I will give as leaders Abraham, Isaac, and Jacob, and Hosea and Amos and Micah and Joel and Obadiah and Jonah *40* and Nahum and Habakkuk, Zephaniah, Haggai, Zechariah and Malachi, who is also called the messenger of the Lord.*h*

God's Judgment on Israel

2 "Thus says the Lord: I brought this people out of bondage, and I gave them commandments through my servants the prophets; but they would not

listen to them, and made my counsels void. *2* The mother who bore them*i* says to them, 'Go, my children, because I am a widow and forsaken. *3* I brought you up with gladness; but with mourning and sorrow I have lost you, because you have sinned before the Lord God and have done what is evil in my sight.*j* *4* But now what can I do for you? For I am a widow and forsaken. Go, my children, and ask for mercy from the Lord.' *5* Now I call upon you, father, as a witness in addition to the mother of the children, because they would not keep my covenant, *6* so that you may bring confusion on them and bring their mother to ruin, so that they may have no offspring. *7* Let them be scattered among the nations; let their names be blotted out from the earth, because they have despised my covenant.

8 "Woe to you, Assyria, who conceal the unrighteous within you! O wicked nation, remember what I did to Sodom

a Other ancient authorities lack *of the flesh*   *b* Other ancient authorities read *the bodies of the apostles*   *c* Other ancient authorities add *Thus says the Lord Almighty: Recently you also laid hands on me, crying out before the judge's seat for him to deliver me to you. You took me as a sinner, not as a father who freed you from slavery, and you delivered me to death by hanging me on the tree; these are the things you have done. Therefore, says the Lord, let my Father and his angels return and judge between you and me; if I have not kept the commandment of the Father, if I have not nourished you, if I have not done the things my Father commanded, I will contend in judgment with you, says the Lord.*   *d* Other ancient authorities lack *with you*   *e* Other ancient authorities read *their iniquities*   *f* Other ancient authorities read *The apostles bear witness to the coming people with joy*   *g* Other ancient authorities read *brother*   *h* Other ancient authorities read *and Jacob, Elijah and Enoch, Zechariah and Hosea, Amos, Joel, Micah, Obadiah, Zephaniah,* *40* *Nahum, Jonah, Mattia (or Mattathias), Habakkuk, and twelve angels with flowers*   *i* Other ancient authorities read *They begat for themselves a mother who*   *j* Other ancient authorities read *in his sight*

1:35—This verse seems to reverse God's command to Isaiah to preach even though the people would not see or hear (Isa. 6:9–10). The new people would hear gladly what Israel had refused to hear. Either way, discipleship requires persistence.

1:38 *Father*—God addresses Ezra as "father" (cf. 2:5), though some texts read "brother." Either would speak of Ezra's relationship to God's people. He is told to look with pride on the new Israel (Christians).

2:2 *Mother*—Probably Jerusalem (cf. 10:7). In this chapter Jerusalem is far more than a city; it is the community of those committed to God.

2:5–7—Old Testament law required two witnesses to convict a person of a crime (Deut. 17:6; 19:15), so God calls on Ezra to join Jerusalem as a witness against sinful Israel. Bringing the mother to ruin is probably an allusion to the destruction of the temple in 70 CE. That event was a stark reminder that worship without obedience is a sham.

2:8 *Assyria*—Israel's ancient oppressor, used as a symbol for Rome. ***Sodom and Gomorrah***—Ancient cites destroyed for their extreme sinfulness (Gen. 18:6–19:25).

and Gomorrah, [9] whose land lies in lumps of pitch and heaps of ashes.[a] That is what I will do to those who have not listened to me, says the Lord Almighty."

[10] Thus says the Lord to Ezra: "Tell my people that I will give them the kingdom of Jerusalem, which I was going to give to Israel. [11] Moreover, I will take back to myself their glory, and will give to these others the everlasting habitations, which I had prepared for Israel.[b] [12] The tree of life shall give them fragrant perfume, and they shall neither toil nor become weary. [13] Go[c] and you will receive; pray that your days may be few, that they may be shortened. The kingdom is already prepared for you; be on the watch! [14] Call, O call heaven and earth to witness: I set aside evil and created good; for I am the Living One, says the Lord.

Exhortation to Good Works

[15] "Mother, embrace your children; bring them up with gladness, as does a dove; strengthen their feet, because I have chosen you, says the Lord. [16] And I will raise up the dead from their places, and bring them out from their tombs, because I recognize my name in them. [17] Do not fear, mother of children, for I have chosen you, says the Lord. [18] I will send you help, my servants Isaiah and Jeremiah. According to their counsel I have consecrated and prepared for you twelve trees loaded with various fruits, [19] and the same number of springs flowing with milk and honey, and seven mighty mountains on which roses and lilies grow; by these I will fill your children with joy.

[20] "Guard the rights of the widow, secure justice for the ward, give to the needy, defend the orphan, clothe the naked, [21] care for the injured and the weak, do not ridicule the lame, protect the maimed, and let the blind have a vision of my splendor. [22] Protect the old and the young within your walls. [23] When you find any who are dead, commit them to the grave and mark it,[d] and I will give you the first place in my resurrection. [24] Pause and be quiet, my people, because your rest will come.

[25] "Good nurse, nourish your children; strengthen their feet. [26] Not one of the servants[e] whom I have given you will perish, for I will require them from among your number. [27] Do not be anxious, for when the day of tribulation and anguish comes, others shall weep and be sorrowful, but you shall rejoice and have abundance. [28] The nations shall envy you, but they shall not be able to do anything against you, says the Lord. [29] My power will protect[f] you, so that your children may not see hell.[g]

[30] "Rejoice, O mother, with your children, because I will deliver you, says the Lord. [31] Remember your children that

---

[a] Other ancient authorities read *Gomorrah, whose land descends to hell* [b] Lat *for those* [c] Other ancient authorities read *Seek* [d] Or *seal it; or mark them and commit them to the grave* [e] Or *slaves* [f] Lat *hands will cover* [g] Lat *Gehenna*

2:10–48 Visions Concerning the New Israel

2:10 *My people*—Christians, who would receive Jerusalem, which God had intended to return to Israel along with God's *glory*, i.e., God's presence (v. 11). Christian disciples share the hope for the future with the patriarchs and prophets of the Old Testament.

2:12 *Tree of life*—After Adam and Eve sinned, God drove them from the garden of Eden, lest they eat from the tree of life and acquire immortality (Gen. 3:22). Here God promises God's new people eternal life in the *everlasting habitations* (2:11), the new Jerusalem.

2:14—God calls *heaven and earth* as witnesses to God's creative power (cf. Isa. 1:2). God created good, but not evil. Trials and difficulties may be part of God's creative activity, but evil is not. Even toil and weariness would disappear in the new Jerusalem (2 Esd. 2:12). Such rewards are part of the promise to faithful disciples.

2:20–22—The mark of a just society for Isaiah (Isa. 1:17) and Jeremiah (Jer. 7:6; 22:3) was its care for the widow, the orphan, the resident alien—indeed, all the poor. Similarly, Jesus commanded his followers to clothe the naked (Matt. 25:31–46) and care for the wounded (Luke 10:29–37). Justice and compassion remain two primary marks of discipleship.

2:31 *Sleep*—Christians who have died.

sleep, because I will bring them out of the hiding places of the earth, and will show mercy to them; for I am merciful, says the Lord Almighty. **32** Embrace your children until I come, and proclaim mercy to them; because my springs run over, and my grace will not fail."

Ezra on Mount Horeb

33 I, Ezra, received a command from the Lord on Mount Horeb to go to Israel. When I came to them they rejected me and refused the Lord's commandment. **34** Therefore I say to you, O nations that hear and understand, "Wait for your shepherd; he will give you everlasting rest, because he who will come at the end of the age is close at hand. **35** Be ready for the rewards of the kingdom, because perpetual light will shine on you forevermore. **36** Flee from the shadow of this age, receive the joy of your glory; I publicly call on my savior to witness.*a* **37** Receive what the Lord has entrusted to you and be joyful, giving thanks to him who has called you to the celestial kingdoms. **38** Rise, stand erect and see the number of those who have been sealed at the feast of the Lord. **39** Those who have departed from the shadow of this age have received glorious garments from the Lord. **40** Take again your full number, O Zion, and close the list of your people who are clothed in white, who have fulfilled the law of the Lord. **41** The number of your children, whom you desired, is now complete; implore the Lord's authority that your people, who

have been called from the beginning, may be made holy."

Ezra Sees the Son of God

42 I, Ezra, saw on Mount Zion a great multitude that I could not number, and they all were praising the Lord with songs. **43** In their midst was a young man of great stature, taller than any of the others, and on the head of each of them he placed a crown, but he was more exalted than they. And I was held spellbound. **44** Then I asked an angel, "Who are these, my lord?" **45** He answered and said to me, "These are they who have put off mortal clothing and have put on the immortal, and have confessed the name of God. Now they are being crowned, and receive palms." **46** Then I said to the angel, "Who is that young man who is placing crowns on them and putting palms in their hands?" **47** He answered and said to me, "He is the Son of God, whom they confessed in the world." So I began to praise those who had stood valiantly for the name of the Lord.*b* **48** Then the angel said to me, "Go, tell my people how great and how many are the wonders of the Lord God that you have seen."

Ezra's Prayer of Complaint

3 In the thirtieth year after the destruction of the city, I was in Babylon—I, Salathiel, who am also called

a Other ancient authorities read *I testify that my savior has been commissioned by the Lord*   *b* Other ancient authorities read *to praise and glorify the Lord*

2:33–41—God commanded Ezra to go first to the people of Israel. When they rejected Ezra, God sent him to the new Israel. Disciples inherit the Old Testament and its witness to God's will for God's people and God's grace to aid them in following that will.

2:33 *Mount Horeb*—Another name for Mount Sinai, where God gave Moses the first law. As Israel of old rejected Moses (Exod. 32:1–6), so Israel of Ezra's day rejected Ezra. In response, he anticipated a new people of God, which comes into being through faith in Jesus.

2:34 *Shepherd*—Jesus, who would soon return for God's new people.

2:42–48—In a vision Ezra sees the new Israel beginning eternal life in the new Jerusalem. The tall *young man* is Jesus, the son of God. At the end of the vision (v. 48), God commissions Ezra to tell God's new people what he had seen.

3:1–14:48 Fourth Ezra

Following directly upon the vision with which 5 Ezra ended comes 4 Ezra, a Jewish apocalypse in seven visions.

Ezra. I was troubled as I lay on my bed, and my thoughts welled up in my heart, ² because I saw the desolation of Zion and the wealth of those who lived in Babylon. ³ My spirit was greatly agitated, and I began to speak anxious words to the Most High, and said, ⁴ "O sovereign Lord, did you not speak at the beginning when you planted*a* the earth—and that without help—and commanded the dust*b* ⁵ and it gave you Adam, a lifeless body? Yet he was the creation of your hands, and you breathed into him the breath of life, and he was made alive in your presence. ⁶ And you led him into the garden that your right hand had planted before the earth appeared. ⁷ And you laid upon him one commandment of yours; but he transgressed it, and immediately you appointed death for him and for his descendants. From him there sprang nations and tribes, peoples and clans without number. ⁸ And every nation walked after its own will; they did ungodly things in your sight and rejected your commands, and did not hinder them. ⁹ But again, in its time you brought the flood upon the inhabitants of the world and destroyed them. ¹⁰ And the same fate befell all of them: just as death came upon Adam, so the flood upon them. ¹¹ But you left one of them, Noah with his household, and all the righteous who have descended from him.

12 "When those who lived on earth began to multiply, they produced children and peoples and many nations, and again they began to be more ungodly than were their ancestors. ¹³ And when they were committing iniquity in your sight, you chose for yourself one of them, whose name was Abraham; ¹⁴ you loved him, and to him alone you revealed the end of the times, secretly by night. ¹⁵ You made an everlasting covenant with him, and promised him that you would never forsake his descendants; and you gave him Isaac, and to Isaac you gave Jacob and Esau. ¹⁶ You set apart Jacob for yourself, but Esau you rejected; and Jacob became a great multitude. ¹⁷ And when you led his descendants out of Egypt, you brought them to Mount Sinai. ¹⁸ You bent down the heavens and shook*c* the earth, and moved the world, and caused the depths to tremble, and troubled the times. ¹⁹ Your glory passed through the four gates of fire and earthquake and wind and ice, to give the law to the descendants of Jacob, and your commandment to the posterity of Israel.

20 "Yet you did not take away their evil heart from them, so that your law might produce fruit in them. ²¹ For the first Adam, burdened with an evil heart, transgressed and was overcome, as were also all who were descended from him. ²² Thus the disease became permanent; the law was in the hearts of the people along with the evil root; but what was good departed, and the evil remained. ²³ So the times passed and the years

---

a Other ancient authorities read *formed*   *b* Syr Ethiop: Lat *people* or *world*
c Syr Ethiop Arab 1 Georg: Lat *set fast*

3:1–5:20 The First Vision: Question about the Meaning of Evil

3:1a—The Setting: *Babylon* in 556 (**thirtieth year** of exile). Ezra was in bed at night.

3:4–35—Prayer before seeing vision. Cf. Dan. 9:4–19. Prayer remains crucial to disciples' understanding God's will and direction for them.

3:20–22 *Evil heart*—Cf. also *evil root* (v. 22). Jewish teaching spoke of two "inclinations" in humans, one an evil inclination, the other good. The so-called evil inclination consisted of characteristics humans share with animals: they eat and drink, void, sleep, and mate. The so-called good inclination consisted of characteristics that dis-

tinguish humans from animals: they walk erect, have eyes in the front of their heads, reason, and speak. Ideally, the good inclination would control the bad, but not eliminate it. Otherwise humanity would die out. The problem with humanity, as Ezra saw it, was that the evil inclination was out of control. Implicit in his finding of universal sin was the charge that God had made humans as they are and was, therefore, not without complicity. If so, Ezra was neither the first nor the last believer to question why God allows humans to sin. Yet human freedom stands at the heart of people's relationship to God.

3:23–26—Ezra jumps forward in time to the

were completed, and you raised up for yourself a servant, named David. **24** You commanded him to build a city for your name, and there to offer you oblations from what is yours. **25** This was done for many years; but the inhabitants of the city transgressed, **26** in everything doing just as Adam and all his descendants had done, for they also had the evil heart. **27** So you handed over your city to your enemies.

Babylon Compared with Zion

28 "Then I said in my heart, Are the deeds of those who inhabit Babylon any better? Is that why it has gained dominion over Zion? **29** For when I came here I saw ungodly deeds without number, and my soul has seen many sinners during these thirty years.*a* And my heart failed me, **30** because I have seen how you endure those who sin, and have spared those who act wickedly, and have destroyed your people, and protected your enemies, **31** and have not shown to anyone how your way may be comprehended.*b* Are the deeds of Babylon better than those of Zion? **32** Or has another nation known you besides Israel? Or what tribes have so believed the covenants as these tribes of Jacob? **33** Yet their reward has not appeared and their labor has borne no fruit. For I have traveled widely among the nations and have seen that they abound in wealth, though they are unmindful of your commandments. **34** Now therefore weigh in a balance our iniquities and those of the inhabitants of the world; and it will be found which way the turn of the scale will incline.

35 When have the inhabitants of the earth not sinned in your sight? Or what nation has kept your commandments so well? **36** You may indeed find individuals who have kept your commandments, but nations you will not find."

Limitations of the Human Mind

4 Then the angel that had been sent to me, whose name was Uriel, answered **2** and said to me, "Your understanding has utterly failed regarding this world, and do you think you can comprehend the way of the Most High?" **3** Then I said, "Yes, my lord." And he replied to me, "I have been sent to show you three ways, and to put before you three problems. **4** If you can solve one of them for me, then I will show you the way you desire to see, and will teach you why the heart is evil."

5 I said, "Speak, my lord."

And he said to me, "Go, weigh for me the weight of fire, or measure for me a blast*c* of wind, or call back for me the day that is past."

6 I answered and said, "Who of those that have been born can do that, that you should ask me about such things?"

7 And he said to me, "If I had asked you, 'How many dwellings are in the heart of the sea, or how many streams are at the source of the deep, or how many streams are above the firmament, or which are the exits of Hades, or which are the entrances*d* of paradise?' **8** perhaps you would have said to me, 'I never went down into the deep, nor as yet into

a Ethiop Arab 1 Arm: Lat Syr *in this thirtieth year*   *b* Syr; compare Ethiop: Lat *how this way should be forsaken*   *c* Syr Ethiop Arab 1 Arab 2 Georg *a measure*   *d* Syr Compare Ethiop Arab 2 Arm: Lat lacks *of Hades, or which are the entrances*

---

founding of the Davidic dynasty in the eleventh century (see 2 Sam.), but the evil inclination continued to prevail among the ancient Israelites.

3:28–36—Ezra questions the justice of God in allowing the Babylonians to capture Israel. He poses two questions. Were the Babylonians more moral than Israel? Did anyone besides Israel confess God as its deity? The implied answer to both questions is no. Disciples need to recognize that such questions are not sinful, but a natural part of faith development.

4:1–5:20—The angel Uriel uses various arguments to show Ezra that in time God will set things right. Apocalyptic literature is the product of people victimized by others, but it assures all faithful disciples that God ultimately will bring justice. That hope is basic to discipleship (cf. 1 Cor. 13:13).

4:1 *Uriel*—The name means "God is light" or "flame of God." He is identified as an archangel in 1 Enoch 9:1; 19:1; 20:2 and may have that same rank here.

Hades, neither did I ever ascend into heaven.' ⁹ But now I have asked you only about fire and wind and the day—things that you have experienced and from which you cannot be separated, and you have given me no answer about them." ¹⁰ He said to me, "You cannot understand the things with which you have grown up; ¹¹ how then can your mind comprehend the way of the Most High? And how can one who is already worn out*a* by the corrupt world understand incorruption?"*b* When I heard this, I fell on my face*c* ¹² and said to him, "It would have been better for us not to be here than to come here and live in ungodliness, and to suffer and not understand why."

Parable of the Forest and the Sea

13 He answered me and said, "I went into a forest of trees of the plain, and they made a plan ¹⁴ and said, 'Come, let us go and make war against the sea, so that it may recede before us and so that we may make for ourselves more forests.' ¹⁵ In like manner the waves of the sea also made a plan and said, 'Come, let us go up and subdue the forest of the plain so that there also we may gain more territory for ourselves.' ¹⁶ But the plan of the forest was in vain, for the fire came and consumed it; ¹⁷ likewise also the plan of the waves of the sea was in vain,*d* for the sand stood firm and blocked it. ¹⁸ If now you were a judge between them, which would you undertake to justify, and which to condemn?"

19 I answered and said, "Each made a foolish plan, for the land has been assigned to the forest, and the locale of the sea a place to carry its waves."

20 He answered me and said, "You have judged rightly, but why have you not judged so in your own case? ²¹ For as the land has been assigned to the forest and the sea to its waves, so also those who inhabit the earth can understand only what is on the earth, and he who is*e* above the heavens can understand what is above the height of the heavens."

The New Age Will Make All Things Clear

22 Then I answered and said, "I implore you, my lord, why*f* have I been endowed with the power of understanding? ²³ For I did not wish to inquire about the ways above, but about those things that we daily experience: why Israel has been given over to the Gentiles in disgrace; why the people whom you loved has been given over to godless tribes, and the law of our ancestors has been brought to destruction and the written covenants no longer exist. ²⁴ We pass from the world like locusts, and our life is like a mist,*g* and we are not worthy to obtain mercy. ²⁵ But what will he do for his*h* name that is invoked over us? It is about these things that I have asked."

26 He answered me and said, "If you are alive, you will see, and if you live long,*i* you will often marvel, because the age is hurrying swiftly to its end. ²⁷ It will not be able to bring the things that have been promised to the righteous in their appointed times, because this age is full of sadness and infirmities. ²⁸ For the evil about which*j* you ask me has been sown, but the harvest of it has not yet come. ²⁹ If therefore that which has been sown is not reaped, and if the place where the evil has been sown does not pass away, the field where the good has been sown will not come. ³⁰ For a grain of

---

a Meaning of Lat uncertain   *b* Syr Ethiop *the way of the incorruptible?*
c Syr Ethiop Arab 1: Meaning of Lat uncertain   *d* Lat lacks *was in vain*
e Or *those who are*   *f* Syr Ethiop Arm: Meaning of Lat uncertain   *g* Syr Ethiop Arab Georg: Lat *a trembling*   *h* Ethiop adds *holy*   *i* Syr: Lat *live*
j Syr Ethiop: Meaning of Lat uncertain

4:22–25—Ezra asks how the ungodly Babylonians could conquer Israel, who at least recognized and attempted to serve God.

4:26–32—Uriel advises Ezra not to jump to a premature conclusion. Time has not yet run its course; justice will prevail in the end. In a parable he reminds Ezra that one grain of seed will yield much fruit. In time, the seeds of the Babylonians will yield their fruit.

evil seed was sown in Adam's heart from the beginning, and how much ungodliness it has produced until now—and will produce until the time of threshing comes! **31** Consider now for yourself how much fruit of ungodliness a grain of evil seed has produced. **32** When heads of grain without number are sown, how great a threshing floor they will fill!"

When Will the New Age Come?

33 Then I answered and said, "How long?[a] When will these things be? Why are our years few and evil?" **34** He answered me and said, "Do not be in a greater hurry than the Most High. You, indeed, are in a hurry for yourself,[b] but the Highest is in a hurry on behalf of many. **35** Did not the souls of the righteous in their chambers ask about these matters, saying, 'How long are we to remain here?[c] And when will the harvest of our reward come?' **36** And the archangel Jeremiel answered and said, 'When the number of those like yourselves is completed;[d] for he has weighed the age in the balance, **37** and measured the times by measure, and numbered the times by number; and he will not move or arouse them until that measure is fulfilled.'"

38 Then I answered and said, "But, O sovereign Lord, all of us also are full of ungodliness. **39** It is perhaps on account of us that the time of threshing is delayed for the righteous—on account of the sins of those who inhabit the earth."

40 He answered me and said, "Go and ask a pregnant woman whether, when her nine months have been completed, her womb can keep the fetus within her any longer."

41 And I said, "No, lord, it cannot."

He said to me, "In Hades the chambers of the souls are like the womb. **42** For just as a woman who is in labor makes haste to escape the pangs of birth, so also do these places hasten to give back those things that were committed to them from the beginning. **43** Then the things that you desire to see will be disclosed to you."

How Much Time Remains?

44 I answered and said, "If I have found favor in your sight, and if it is possible, and if I am worthy, **45** show me this also: whether more time is to come than has passed, or whether for us the greater part has gone by. **46** For I know what has gone by, but I do not know what is to come."

47 And he said to me, "Stand at my right side, and I will show you the interpretation of a parable."

48 So I stood and looked, and lo, a flaming furnace passed by before me, and when the flame had gone by I looked, and lo, the smoke remained. **49** And after this a cloud full of water passed before me and poured down a heavy and violent rain, and when the violent rainstorm had passed, drops still remained in the cloud.[e]

50 He said to me, "Consider it for yourself; for just as the rain is more than the drops, and the fire is greater than the smoke, so the quantity that passed was far greater; but drops and smoke remained."

51 Then I prayed and said, "Do you

[a] Syr Ethiop: Meaning of Lat uncertain [b] Syr Ethiop Arab Arm: Meaning of Lat uncertain [c] Syr Ethiop Arab 2 Georg: Lat *How long do I hope thus?* [d] Syr Ethiop Arab 2: Lat *number of seeds is completed for you* [e] Lat *in it*

4:33—Ezra asks the perennial question of the apocalyptic seer: "How long will it be until the end?"

4:34–37—Uriel admonishes Ezra not to be so impatient; the world does not revolve around him. The end will come when all the righteous have committed to God. The admonition remains valid for modern disciples: patience is a virtue for them too.

4:51–52—Ezra asks whether he will live to see the end of days. Uriel says that he does not know. (The reader, of course, knows what Uriel did not: Ezra would not live that long.) Uriel does promise to answer Ezra's question about the signs. Since he has asked no such question, that sentence serves the literary function of introducing more disclosures in chap. 5.

think that I shall live until those days? Or who will be alive in those days?"

52 He answered me and said, "Concerning the signs about which you ask me, I can tell you in part; but I was not sent to tell you concerning your life, for I do not know.

Signs of the End

5 "Now concerning the signs: lo, the days are coming when those who inhabit the earth shall be seized with great terror,[a] and the way of truth shall be hidden, and the land shall be barren of faith. [2] Unrighteousness shall be increased beyond what you yourself see, and beyond what you heard of formerly. [3] And the land that you now see ruling shall be a trackless waste, and people shall see it desolate. [4] But if the Most High grants that you live, you shall see it thrown into confusion after the third period;[b]

and the sun shall suddenly begin to
　shine at night,
　and the moon during the day.
[5] Blood shall drip from wood,
　and the stone shall utter its voice;
　the peoples shall be troubled,
　and the stars shall fall.[c]

[6] And one shall reign whom those who inhabit the earth do not expect, and the birds shall fly away together; [7] and the Dead Sea[d] shall cast up fish; and one whom the many do not know shall make his voice heard by night, and all shall hear his voice.[e] [8] There shall be chaos also in many places, fire shall often break out, the wild animals shall roam beyond their haunts, and menstruous women shall bring forth monsters. [9] Salt waters shall be found in the sweet, and all friends shall conquer one another; then shall reason hide itself, and wisdom shall withdraw into its chamber, [10] and it shall be sought by many but shall not be found, and unrighteousness and unrestraint shall increase on earth. [11] One country shall ask its neighbor, 'Has righteousness, or anyone who does right, passed through you?' And it will answer, 'No.' [12] At that time people shall hope but not obtain; they shall labor, but their ways shall not prosper. [13] These are the signs that I am permitted to tell you, and if you pray again, and weep as you do now, and fast for seven days, you shall hear yet greater things than these."

Conclusion of the Vision

14 Then I woke up, and my body shuddered violently, and my soul was so troubled that it fainted. [15] But the angel who had come and talked with me held me and strengthened me and set me on my feet.

16 Now on the second night Phaltiel, a chief of the people, came to me and said, "Where have you been? And why is your face sad? [17] Or do you not know that Israel has been entrusted to you in the land of their exile? [18] Rise therefore and eat some bread, and do not forsake us, like a shepherd who leaves the flock in the power of savage wolves."

19 Then I said to him, "Go away from me and do not come near me for seven days; then you may come to me."

He heard what I said and left me. [20] So I fasted seven days, mourning and

---

[a] Syr Ethiop: Meaning of Lat uncertain　[b] Literally after the third; Ethiop after three months; Arm after the third vision; Georg after the third day　[c] Ethiop Compare Syr and Arab: Meaning of Lat uncertain　[d] Lat Sea of Sodom　[e] Cn: Lat fish; and it shall make its voice heard by night, which the many have not known, but all shall hear its voice.

5:3 *The land that you now see ruling*—Rome.

5:14–15—The aftereffects of the vision. Ezra says that he *woke up*, but the text never said he went to sleep. Apparently Ezra emerged from a trance state, but found Uriel still present.

5:16–20—The conclusion to the report of the first vision. Someone named *Phaltiel* visits Ezra the next night, emphasizes Ezra's role as the leader of the exiles, and pleads with him to rise and eat in order to fulfill his role. Ezra refuses and sends Phaltiel away until Ezra can complete his seven days of fasting. Disciples will notice that Ezra prepares for his experience with prayer and completes it with a fast. Such actions may assist them in their search for deeper experiences with God.

weeping, as the angel Uriel had commanded me.

Ezra's Second Prayer of Complaint

21 After seven days the thoughts of my heart were very grievous to me again. 22 Then my soul recovered the spirit of understanding, and I began once more to speak words in the presence of the Most High. 23 I said, "O sovereign Lord, from every forest of the earth and from all its trees you have chosen one vine, 24 and from all the lands of the world you have chosen for yourself one region,[a] and from all the flowers of the world you have chosen for yourself one lily, 25 and from all the depths of the sea you have filled for yourself one river, and from all the cities that have been built you have consecrated Zion for yourself, 26 and from all the birds that have been created you have named for yourself one dove, and from all the flocks that have been made you have provided for yourself one sheep, 27 and from all the multitude of peoples you have gotten for yourself one people; and to this people, whom you have loved, you have given the law that is approved by all. 28 And now, O Lord, why have you handed the one over to the many, and dishonored[b] the one root beyond the others, and scattered your only one among the many? 29 And those who opposed your promises have trampled on those who believed your covenants. 30 If you really hate your people, they should be punished at your own hands."

Response to Ezra's Complaints

31 When I had spoken these words, the angel who had come to me on a previous night was sent to me. 32 He said to me, "Listen to me, and I will instruct you; pay attention to me, and I will tell you more."

33 Then I said, "Speak, my lord." And he said to me, "Are you greatly disturbed in mind over Israel? Or do you love him more than his Maker does?"

34 I said, "No, my lord, but because of my grief I have spoken; for every hour I suffer agonies of heart, while I strive to understand the way of the Most High and to search out some part of his judgment."

35 He said to me, "You cannot." And I said, "Why not, my lord? Why then was I born? Or why did not my mother's womb become my grave, so that I would not see the travail of Jacob and the exhaustion of the people of Israel?"

36 He said to me, "Count up for me those who have not yet come, and gather for me the scattered raindrops, and make the withered flowers bloom again for me; 37 open for me the closed chambers, and bring out for me the winds shut up in them, or show me the picture of a voice; and then I will explain to you the travail that you ask to understand."[c]

38 I said, "O sovereign Lord, who is able to know these things except him whose dwelling is not with mortals? 39 As for me, I am without wisdom, and how can I speak concerning the things that you have asked me?"

40 He said to me, "Just as you cannot do one of the things that were mentioned, so you cannot discover my judgment, or the goal of the love that I have promised to my people."

Why Successive Generations Have Been Created

41 I said, "Yet, O Lord, you have charge of those who are alive at the end,

_____

[a] Ethiop: Lat *pit*   [b] Syr Ethiop Arab: Lat *prepared*   [c] Lat *see*

_____

5:21–6:34 The Second Vision: The Fate of Those Who Die before the End of the Present Age
5:23–30—Ezra's prayer.
5:31—Uriel reappears and converses with Ezra.
5:40 *My . . . I*—The angel speaks for God.

5:41–42—Ezra affirms that God will deal with people who are alive at the time of the end, but asks about people who die before then. Uriel answers that God does everything in due time. Again, disciples will note the necessity for patience.

but what will those do who lived before me, or we, ourselves, or those who come after us?"

42 He said to me, "I shall liken my judgment to a circle;*a* just as for those who are last there is no slowness, so for those who are first there is no haste."

43 Then I answered and said, "Could you not have created at one time those who have been and those who are and those who will be, so that you might show your judgment the sooner?"

44 He replied to me and said, "The creation cannot move faster than the Creator, nor can the world hold at one time those who have been created in it."

45 I said, "How have you said to your servant that you*b* will certainly give life at one time to your creation? If therefore all creatures will live at one time*c* and the creation will sustain them, it might even now be able to support all of them present at one time."

46 He said to me, "Ask a woman's womb, and say to it, 'If you bear ten*d* children, why one after another?' Request it therefore to produce ten at one time."

47 I said, "Of course it cannot, but only each in its own time."

48 He said to me, "Even so I have given the womb of the earth to those who from time to time are sown in it. 49 For as an infant does not bring forth, and a woman who has become old does not bring forth any longer, so I have made the same rule for the world that I created."

When and How Will the End Come?

50 Then I inquired and said, "Since you have now given me the opportunity, let me speak before you. Is our mother, of whom you have told me, still young? Or is she now approaching old age?"

51 He replied to me, "Ask a woman who bears children, and she will tell you. 52 Say to her, 'Why are those whom you have borne recently not like those whom you bore before, but smaller in stature?' 53 And she herself will answer you, 'Those born in the strength of youth are different from those born during the time of old age, when the womb is failing.' 54 Therefore you also should consider that you and your contemporaries are smaller in stature than those who were before you, 55 and those who come after you will be smaller than you, as born of a creation that already is aging and passing the strength of youth."

56 I said, "I implore you, O Lord, if I have found favor in your sight, show your servant through whom you will visit your creation."

6 He said to me, "At the beginning of the circle of the earth, before*e* the portals of the world were in place, and before the assembled winds blew, 2 and before the rumblings of thunder sounded, and before the flashes of lightning shone, and before the foundations of paradise were laid, 3 and before the beautiful flowers were seen, and before the powers of movements*f* were established, and before the innumerable hosts of angels were gathered together, 4 and before the heights of the air were lifted up, and before the measures of the firmaments were named, and before the footstool of Zion was established, 5 and before the present years were reckoned and before the imaginations of those who now sin were estranged, and before those who stored up treasures of faith

a Or *crown* *b* Syr Ethiop Arab 1: Meaning of Lat uncertain *c* Lat lacks *If... one time* *d* Syr Ethiop Arab 2 Arm: Meaning of Lat uncertain *e* Meaning of Lat uncertain: Compare Syr *The beginning by the hand of humankind, but the end by my own hands. For as before the land of the world existed there, and before;* Ethiop: *At first by the Son of Man, and afterwards I myself. For before the earth and the lands were created, and before* *f* Or *earthquakes*

5:43–49—Ezra asks why God did not create all people at once? Uriel answers that the world would not hold all its people at once, so God designed it to produce one generation at a time.

5:56–6:6—God alone had created the world; God alone would bring it to its end. This view of the sovereignty of God over time encourages disciples to work for God's glory while they have time.

were sealed— ⁶then I planned these things, and they were made through me alone and not through another; just as the end shall come through me alone and not through another."

The Dividing of the Times

7 I answered and said, "What will be the dividing of the times? Or when will be the end of the first age and the beginning of the age that follows?"

8 He said to me, "From Abraham to Isaac,ᵃ because from him were born Jacob and Esau, for Jacob's hand held Esau's heel from the beginning. ⁹Now Esau is the end of this age, and Jacob is the beginning of the age that follows. ¹⁰The beginning of a person is the hand, and the end of a person is the heel;ᵇ seek for nothing else, Ezra, between the heel and the hand, Ezra!"

More Signs of the End

11 I answered and said, "O sovereign Lord, if I have found favor in your sight, ¹²show your servant the last of your signs of which you showed me a part on a previous night."

13 He answered and said to me, "Rise to your feet and you will hear a full, resounding voice. ¹⁴And if the place where you are standing is greatly shaken ¹⁵while the voice is speaking, do not be terrified; because the word concerns the end, and the foundations of the earth will understand ¹⁶that the speech concerns them. They will tremble and be shaken, for they know that their end must be changed."

17 When I heard this, I got to my feet and listened; a voice was speaking, and its sound was like the sound of mightyᶜ waters. ¹⁸It said, "The days are coming when I draw near to visit the inhabitants of the earth, ¹⁹and when I require from the doers of iniquity the penalty of their iniquity, and when the humiliation of Zion is complete. ²⁰When the

seal is placed upon the age that is about to pass away, then I will show these signs: the books shall be opened before the face of the firmament, and all shall see my judgmentᵈ together. ²¹Children a year old shall speak with their voices, and pregnant women shall give birth to premature children at three and four months, and these shall live and leap about. ²²Sown places shall suddenly appear unsown, and full storehouses shall suddenly be found to be empty; ²³the trumpet shall sound aloud, and when all hear it, they shall suddenly be terrified. ²⁴At that time friends shall make war on friends like enemies, the earth and those who inhabit it shall be terrified, and the springs of the fountains shall stand still, so that for three hours they shall not flow.

25 "It shall be that whoever remains after all that I have foretold to you shall be saved and shall see my salvation and the end of my world. ²⁶And they shall see those who were taken up, who from their birth have not tasted death; and the heart of the earth'sᵉ inhabitants shall be changed and converted to a different spirit. ²⁷For evil shall be blotted out, and deceit shall be quenched; ²⁸faithfulness shall flourish, and corruption shall be overcome, and the truth, which has been so long without fruit, shall be revealed."

Conclusion of the Second Vision

29 While he spoke to me, little by little the place where I was standing began to rock to and fro.ᶠ ³⁰And he said to me, "I have come to show you these things this night.ᵍ ³¹If therefore you will pray again and fast again for seven days, I will again declare to you greater things than these,ʰ ³²because your voice has surely

---

ᵃ Other ancient authorities read *to Abraham* ᵇSyr: Meaning of Lat uncertain ᶜLat *many* ᵈSyr: Lat lacks *my judgment* ᵉSyr Compare Ethiop Arab 1 Arm: Lat lacks *earth's* ᶠSyr Ethiop Compare Arab Arm: Meaning of Lat uncertain ᵍSyr Compare Ethiop: Meaning of Lat uncertain ʰSyr Ethiop Arab 1 Arm: Lat adds *by day*

6:7–10—The two ages are the present age (symbolized by *Esau*) and the age to come (symbolized by *Jacob*). Just as Jacob seized Esau's

heel and was born immediately after him (Gen. 25:26), the age to come would follow immediately upon the present age.

been heard by the Most High; for the Mighty One has seen your uprightness and has also observed the purity that you have maintained from your youth. ³³ Therefore he sent me to show you all these things, and to say to you: 'Believe and do not be afraid! ³⁴ Do not be quick to think vain thoughts concerning the former times; then you will not act hastily in the last times.'"

The Third Vision

35 Now after this I wept again and fasted seven days in the same way as before, in order to complete the three weeks that had been prescribed for me. ³⁶ Then on the eighth night my heart was troubled within me again, and I began to speak in the presence of the Most High. ³⁷ My spirit was greatly aroused, and my soul was in distress.

God's Work in Creation

38 I said, "O Lord, you spoke at the beginning of creation, and said on the first day, 'Let heaven and earth be made,' and your word accomplished the work. ³⁹ Then the spirit was blowing, and darkness and silence embraced everything; the sound of human voices was not yet there.ᵃ ⁴⁰ Then you commanded a ray of light to be brought out from your storechambers, so that your works could be seen.

41 "Again, on the second day, you created the spirit of the firmament, and commanded it to divide and separate the waters, so that one part might move upward and the other part remain beneath.

42 "On the third day you commanded the waters to be gathered together in a seventh part of the earth; six parts you dried up and kept so that some of them might be planted and cultivated and be of service before you. ⁴³ For your word went forth, and at once the work was done. ⁴⁴ Immediately fruit came forth in endless abundance and of varied appeal to the taste, and flowers of inimitable color, and odors of inexpressible fragrance. These were made on the third day.

45 "On the fourth day you commanded the brightness of the sun, the light of the moon, and the arrangement of the stars to come into being; ⁴⁶ and you commanded them to serve humankind, about to be formed.

47 "On the fifth day you commanded the seventh part, where the water had been gathered together, to bring forth living creatures, birds, and fishes; and so it was done. ⁴⁸ The dumb and lifeless water produced living creatures, as it was commanded, so that therefore the nations might declare your wondrous works.

49 "Then you kept in existence two living creatures;ᵇ the one you called Behemothᶜ and the name of the other Leviathan. ⁵⁰ And you separated one from the other, for the seventh part where the water had been gathered together could not hold them both. ⁵¹ And you gave Behemothᶜ one of the parts that had been dried up on the third day, to live in it, where there are a thousand

ᵃ Syr Ethiop: Lat *was not yet from you*   ᵇ Syr Ethiop: Lat *two souls*   ᶜ Other Lat authorities read *Enoch*

6:35–9:25 The Third Vision: The Few Who Will Be Saved

6:35–37—The setting: Babylon, 557/556 (3:1), one week after the second vision (5:20), time spent in preparation by fasting.

6:38–59—Ezra reviews God's creation of the world.

6:49–52 *Behemoth*—Cf. Job 40:15, where it may have referred to the hippopotamus and *Leviathan* (cf. Job 3:8, 41:1; Ps. 74:14; Isa. 27:1). In Babylonian mythology they were originally

thought of as sea monsters. They were too big to share the seas, so the Behemoth went to a place where the waters had receded and mountains appeared, while Leviathan remained at sea. These verses remind modern believers that God did not create the world simply for humans. Rather, God created everything for its own place and God's own pleasure. Consequently, genuine disciples will seek to preserve all species, including those for which they see no value to humans.

mountains; [52] but to Leviathan you gave the seventh part, the watery part; and you have kept them to be eaten by whom you wish, and when you wish.

53 "On the sixth day you commanded the earth to bring forth before you cattle, wild animals, and creeping things; [54] and over these you placed Adam, as ruler over all the works that you had made; and from him we have all come, the people whom you have chosen.

Why Do God's People Suffer?

55 "All this I have spoken before you, O Lord, because you have said that it was for us that you created this world.[a] [56] As for the other nations that have descended from Adam, you have said that they are nothing, and that they are like spittle, and you have compared their abundance to a drop from a bucket. [57] And now, O Lord, these nations, which are reputed to be as nothing, domineer over us and devour us. [58] But we your people, whom you have called your firstborn, only begotten, zealous for you,[b] and most dear, have been given into their hands. [59] If the world has indeed been created for us, why do we not possess our world as an inheritance? How long will this be so?"

Response to Ezra's Questions

7 When I had finished speaking these words, the angel who had been sent to me on the former nights was sent to me again. [2] He said to me, "Rise, Ezra, and listen to the words that I have come to speak to you."

3 I said, "Speak, my lord." And he said to me, "There is a sea set in a wide expanse so that it is deep and vast, [4] but it has an entrance set in a narrow place, so that it is like a river. [5] If there are those who wish to reach the sea, to look at it or to navigate it, how can they come to the broad part unless they pass through the narrow part? [6] Another example: There is a city built and set on a plain, and it is full of all good things; [7] but the entrance to it is narrow and set in a precipitous place, so that there is fire on the right hand and deep water on the left. [8] There is only one path lying between them, that is, between the fire and the water, so that only one person can walk on the path. [9] If now the city is given to someone as an inheritance, how will the heir receive the inheritance unless by passing through the appointed danger?"

10 I said, "That is right, lord." He said to me, "So also is Israel's portion. [11] For I made the world for their sake, and when Adam transgressed my statutes, what had been made was judged. [12] And so the entrances of this world were made narrow and sorrowful and toilsome; they are few and evil, full of dangers and involved in great hardships. [13] But the entrances of the greater world are broad and safe, and yield the fruit of immortality. [14] Therefore unless the living pass through the difficult and futile experiences, they can never receive those things that have been reserved for them. [15] Now therefore why are you disturbed, seeing that you are to perish? Why are you moved, seeing that you are mortal?

[a] Syr Ethiop Arab 2: Lat *the firstborn world* Compare Arab 1 *first world*
[b] Meaning of Lat uncertain

6:55–58—Ezra says that God had created the world for Israel, while other nations fell outside God's concern. He thus misunderstood the idea of election. Genesis 12 emphasized that all nations could be blessed through Israel. Disciples will understand that God loves all peoples and seek to serve people in God's name.

7:1–9:25—In these chapters Uriel sets forth another program for God's salvation of the world, including the coming of the messiah, judgment, punishment, and eternal life. While not identical to the teachings of the New Testament, a Christian disciple will find much here to encourage faithful service to God.

7:1–16—Uriel's answer. Unless people pass through difficulty, they can never receive what is reserved for them (v. 14). Hence, the people of Israel could not rule in the world to come until they had passed through tribulation in this life. Similarly, disciples may encounter difficulties in their attempts to serve Christ, but can grow spiritually through them.

16 Why have you not considered in your mind what is to come, rather than what is now present?"

The Fate of the Ungodly

17 Then I answered and said, "O sovereign Lord, you have ordained in your law that the righteous shall inherit these things, but that the ungodly shall perish. 18 The righteous, therefore, can endure difficult circumstances while hoping for easier ones; but those who have done wickedly have suffered the difficult circumstances and will never see the easier ones."

19 He said to me, "You are not a better judge than the Lord,[a] or wiser than the Most High! 20 Let many perish who are now living, rather than that the law of God that is set before them be disregarded! 21 For the Lord[b] strictly commanded those who came into the world, when they came, what they should do to live, and what they should observe to avoid punishment. 22 Nevertheless they were not obedient, and spoke against him;

    they devised for themselves vain
        thoughts,
23   and proposed to themselves
        wicked frauds;
    they even declared that the Most
        High does not exist,
    and they ignored his ways.
24 They scorned his law,
    and denied his covenants;
    they have been unfaithful to his statutes,
    and have not performed his works.

25 That is the reason, Ezra, that empty things are for the empty, and full things are for the full.

The Temporary Messianic Kingdom

26 "For indeed the time will come, when the signs that I have foretold to you will come to pass, that the city that now is not seen shall appear,[c] and the land that now is hidden shall be disclosed. 27 Everyone who has been delivered from the evils that I have foretold shall see my wonders. 28 For my son the Messiah[d] shall be revealed with those who are with him, and those who remain shall rejoice four hundred years. 29 After those years my son the Messiah shall die, and all who draw human breath.[e] 30 Then the world shall be turned back to primeval silence for seven days, as it was at the first beginnings, so that no one shall be left. 31 After seven days the world that is not yet awake shall be roused, and that which is corruptible shall perish. 32 The earth shall give up those who are asleep in it, and the dust those who rest there in silence; and the chambers shall give up the souls that have been committed to them. 33 The Most High shall be revealed on the seat of judgment, and compassion shall pass away, and patience shall be withdrawn.[f] 34 Only judgment shall remain, truth shall stand, and faithfulness shall grow strong.

a Other ancient authorities read God; Ethiop Georg the only One b Other ancient authorities read God c Arm: Lat Syr that the bride shall appear, even the city appearing d Syr Arab 1: Ethiop my Messiah; Arab 2 the Messiah; Arm the Messiah of God; Lat my son Jesus e Arm all who have continued in faith and in patience f Lat shall gather together

---

7:26–29—The messianic kingdom. The messiah will return to rule four hundred years and then die. Unlike the death of Jesus, however, his death will have no power to save sinners.

7:26 *The city*—The future Jerusalem.

7:28 *My son the Messiah*—Other versions read "my Messiah" or "the Messiah (of God)." The words "my son" might be a Christian interpolation; cf. the Latin rendering "my son Jesus." However, they appear alone as a designation for the messiah in 13:32, 37, 52; 14:9. Psalm 2:7 conceived of the king as the adopted son of God, so perhaps the title is original in 2 Esdras.

Regardless, Christians confess Jesus as messiah and work toward Christ's rulership over the world. *Four hundred years*—One Arabic version reads "one thousand years," like the millennium in Rev. 20.

7:30–44—The end-time judgment. Seven days of silence will reverse the original creation (Gen. 1:1–2:4a). Then the immortal kingdom will emerge, and the dead will rise for judgment. Disciples will recognize that no one is beyond God's judgment, regardless of how powerful some people appear in this world.

35 Recompense shall follow, and the reward shall be manifested; righteous deeds shall awake, and unrighteous deeds shall not sleep.*a* **36** The pit*b* of torment shall appear, and opposite it shall be the place of rest; and the furnace of hell*c* shall be disclosed, and opposite it the paradise of delight. **37** Then the Most High will say to the nations that have been raised from the dead, 'Look now, and understand whom you have denied, whom you have not served, whose commandments you have despised. **38** Look on this side and on that; here are delight and rest, and there are fire and torments.' Thus he will*d* speak to them on the day of judgment— **39** a day that has no sun or moon or stars, **40** or cloud or thunder or lightning, or wind or water or air, or darkness or evening or morning, **41** or summer or spring or heat or winter*e* or frost or cold, or hail or rain or dew, **42** or noon or night, or dawn or shining or brightness or light, but only the splendor of the glory of the Most High, by which all shall see what has been destined. **43** It will last as though for a week of years. **44** This is my judgment and its prescribed order; and to you alone I have shown these things."

Only a Few Will Be Saved

45 I answered and said, "O sovereign Lord, I said then and*f* I say now: Blessed are those who are alive and keep your commandments! **46** But what of those for whom I prayed? For who among the living is there that has not sinned, or who is there among mortals that has not transgressed your covenant? **47** And now I see that the world to come will bring delight to few, but torments to many. **48** For an evil heart has grown up in us, which has alienated us from God,*g* and has brought us into corruption and the ways of death, and has shown us the paths of perdition and removed us far from life—and that not merely for a few but for almost all who have been created."

49 He answered me and said, "Listen to me, Ezra,*h* and I will instruct you, and will admonish you once more. **50** For this reason the Most High has made not one world but two. **51** Inasmuch as you have said that the righteous are not many but few, while the ungodly abound, hear the explanation for this.

52 "If you have just a few precious stones, will you add to them lead and clay?"*i* **53** I said, "Lord, how could that be?" **54** And he said to me, "Not only that, but ask the earth and she will tell you; defer to her, and she will declare it to you. **55** Say to her, 'You produce gold and silver and bronze, and also iron and lead and clay; **56** but silver is more abundant than gold, and bronze than silver, and iron than bronze, and lead than iron, and clay than lead.' **57** Judge therefore which things are precious and desirable, those that are abundant or those that are rare?"

58 I said, "O sovereign Lord, what is plentiful is of less worth, for what is more rare is more precious."

59 He answered me and said, "Consider within yourself*j* what you have thought, for the person who has what is hard to

---

a The passage from verse 36 to verse 105, formerly missing, has been restored to the text   *b* Syr Ethiop: Lat *place*   *c* Lat Syr Ethiop *Gehenna*   *d* Syr Ethiop Arab 1: Lat *you shall*   *e* Or *storm*   *f* Syr: Lat *And I answered, "I said then, O Lord, and*   *g* Cn: Lat Syr Ethiop *from these*   *h* Syr Arab 1 Georg: Lat Ethiop lack *Ezra*   *i* Arab 1: Meaning of Lat Syr Ethiop uncertain   *j* Syr Ethiop Arab 1: Meaning of Lat uncertain

---

7:36 *Pit of torment*—The future abode of the wicked. *Place of rest*—The future abode of the righteous.

[Note: Verses *36–105* appear in Arabic, Armenian, Ethiopic, and Syriac versions, but not in the Latin, possibly because vv. *102–105* reject intercession for the dead.]

7:45–48—Ezra objects that only a few people will be saved, and they too—like the wicked— have sinned, thus questioning the justice of God. Sensitive disciples today also question theological formulations that ignore either the justice or the grace of God. *Evil heart*—Cf. note at 3:20.

7:49–61—Uriel responds that that which is scarce is precious. In other words, a blessed future is not for the masses. Ezra is not to mourn for them.

get rejoices more than the person who has what is plentiful. ⁶⁰ So also will be the judgment^a that I have promised; for I will rejoice over the few who shall be saved, because it is they who have made my glory to prevail now, and through them my name has now been honored. ⁶¹ I will not grieve over the great number of those who perish; for it is they who are now like a mist, and are similar to a flame and smoke—they are set on fire and burn hotly, and are extinguished."

Lamentation of Ezra, with Response

62 I replied and said, "O earth, what have you brought forth, if the mind is made out of the dust like the other created things? ⁶³ For it would have been better if the dust itself had not been born, so that the mind might not have been made from it. ⁶⁴ But now the mind grows with us, and therefore we are tormented, because we perish and we know it. ⁶⁵ Let the human race lament, but let the wild animals of the field be glad; let all who have been born lament, but let the cattle and the flocks rejoice. ⁶⁶ It is much better with them than with us; for they do not look for a judgment, and they do not know of any torment or salvation promised to them after death. ⁶⁷ What does it profit us that we shall be preserved alive but cruelly tormented? ⁶⁸ For all who have been born are entangled in^b iniquities, and are full of sins and burdened with transgressions. ⁶⁹ And if after death we were not to come into judgment, perhaps it would have been better for us."

70 He answered me and said, "When the Most High made the world and Adam and all who have come from him, he first prepared the judgment and the things that pertain to the judgment. ⁷¹ But now, understand from your own words—for you have said that the mind grows with us. ⁷² For this reason, therefore, those who live on earth shall be tormented, because though they had understanding, they committed iniquity; and though they received the commandments, they did not keep them; and though they obtained the law, they dealt unfaithfully with what they received. ⁷³ What, then, will they have to say in the judgment, or how will they answer in the last times? ⁷⁴ How long the Most High has been patient with those who inhabit the world!—and not for their sake, but because of the times that he has foreordained."

State of the Dead before Judgment

75 I answered and said, "If I have found favor in your sight, O Lord, show this also to your servant: whether after death, as soon as everyone of us yields up the soul, we shall be kept in rest until those times come when you will renew the creation, or whether we shall be tormented at once?"

76 He answered me and said, "I will show you that also, but do not include yourself with those who have shown scorn, or number yourself among those who are tormented. ⁷⁷ For you have a treasure of works stored up with the Most High, but it will not be shown to you until the last times. ⁷⁸ Now concerning death, the teaching is: When the decisive decree has gone out from the Most High that a person shall die, as the spirit leaves the body to return again to him who gave it, first of all it adores the glory of the Most High. ⁷⁹ If it is one of those who have shown scorn and have not kept the way of the Most High, who have despised his law and hated those who fear God— ⁸⁰ such spirits shall not enter into habitations, but shall immediately wander about in torments, always griev-

^a Syr Arab 1: Lat *creation*   ^b Syr *defiled with*

7:70–74—Uriel reminds Ezra that humans are superior to animals because humans can choose to obey or disobey; hence, they are accountable to God. Even so, disciples will recognize that hu-man superiority is not grounds for human abuse of the animal kingdom.

7:75–105—The state of the dead before judgment.

ing and sad, in seven ways. **81** The first way, because they have scorned the law of the Most High. **82** The second way, because they cannot now make a good repentance so that they may live. **83** The third way, they shall see the reward laid up for those who have trusted the covenants of the Most High. **84** The fourth way, they shall consider the torment laid up for themselves in the last days. **85** The fifth way, they shall see how the habitations of the others are guarded by angels in profound quiet. **86** The sixth way, they shall see how some of them will cross over*a* into torments. **87** The seventh way, which is worse*b* than all the ways that have been mentioned, because they shall utterly waste away in confusion and be consumed with shame,*c* and shall wither with fear at seeing the glory of the Most High in whose presence they sinned while they were alive, and in whose presence they are to be judged in the last times.

88 "Now this is the order of those who have kept the ways of the Most High, when they shall be separated from their mortal body.*d* **89** During the time that they lived in it,*c* they laboriously served the Most High, and withstood danger every hour so that they might keep the law of the Lawgiver perfectly. **90** Therefore this is the teaching concerning them: **91** First of all, they shall see with great joy the glory of him who receives them, for they shall have rest in seven orders. **92** The first order, because they have striven with great effort to overcome the evil thought that was formed with them, so that it might not lead them astray from life into death. **93** The second order, because they see the perplexity in which the souls of the ungodly wander and the punishment that awaits them. **94** The third order, they see the witness that he who formed them bears concerning them, that throughout their life they kept the law with which they were entrusted. **95** The fourth order, they understand the rest that they now enjoy, being gathered into their chambers and guarded by angels in profound quiet, and the glory waiting for them in the last days. **96** The fifth order, they rejoice that they have now escaped what is corruptible and shall inherit what is to come; and besides they see the straits and toil*e* from which they have been delivered, and the spacious liberty that they are to receive and enjoy in immortality. **97** The sixth order, when it is shown them how their face is to shine like the sun, and how they are to be made like the light of the stars, being incorruptible from then on. **98** The seventh order, which is greater than all that have been mentioned, because they shall rejoice with boldness, and shall be confident without confusion, and shall be glad without fear, for they press forward to see the face of him whom they served in life and from whom they are to receive their reward when glorified. **99** This is the order of the souls of the righteous, as henceforth is announced;*f* and the previously mentioned are the ways of torment that those who would not give heed shall suffer hereafter."

100 Then I answered and said, "Will time therefore be given to the souls, after they have been separated from the bodies, to see what you have described to me?"

101 He said to me, "They shall have freedom for seven days, so that during these seven days they may see the things of which you have been told, and afterwards they shall be gathered in their habitations."

No Intercession for the Ungodly
102 I answered and said, "If I have

a Cn: Meaning of Lat uncertain *b* Lat Syr Ethiop greater *c* Syr Ethiop: Meaning of Lat uncertain *d* Lat the corruptible vessel *e* Syr Ethiop: Lat fullness *f* Syr: Meaning of Lat uncertain

7:102–105—Intercession for the dead is pointless. People will invariably reap after death what they have sown in this life. Just compensation stands at the heart of theodicy. If justice does not come in this life, it will in the next.

found favor in your sight, show further to me, your servant, whether on the day of judgment the righteous will be able to intercede for the ungodly or to entreat the Most High for them— *103* fathers for sons or sons for parents, brothers for brothers, relatives for their kindred, or friends for those who are most dear."

104 He answered me and said, "Since you have found favor in my sight, I will show you this also. The day of judgment is decisive[a] and displays to all the seal of truth. Just as now a father does not send his son, or a son his father, or a master his servant, or a friend his dearest friend, to be ill[b] or sleep or eat or be healed in his place, *105* so no one shall ever pray for another on that day, neither shall anyone lay a burden on another;[c] for then all shall bear their own righteousness and unrighteousness."

36 *106* I answered and said, "How then do we find that first Abraham prayed for the people of Sodom, and Moses for our ancestors who sinned in the desert, **37** *107* and Joshua after him for Israel in the days of Achan, **38** *108* and Samuel in the days of Saul,[d] and David for the plague, and Solomon for those at the dedication, **39** *109* and Elijah for those who received the rain, and for the one who was dead, that he might live, **40** *110* and Hezekiah for the people in the days of Sennacherib, and many others prayed for many? **41** *111* So if now, when corruption has increased and unrighteousness has multiplied, the righteous have prayed for the ungodly, why will it not be so then as well?"

42 *112* He answered me and said, "This present world is not the end; the full glory does not[e] remain in it;[f] therefore those who were strong prayed for the weak. **43** *113* But the day of judgment will be the end of this age and the beginning[g] of the immortal age to come, in which corruption has passed away, **44** *114* sinful indulgence has come to an end, unbelief has been cut off, and righteousness has increased and truth has appeared. **45** *115* Therefore no one will then be able to have mercy on someone who has been condemned in the judgment, or to harm[h] someone who is victorious."

Lamentation over the Fate of Most People

46 *116* I answered and said, "This is my first and last comment: it would have been better if the earth had not produced Adam, or else, when it had produced him, had restrained him from sinning. **47** *117* For what good is it to all that they live in sorrow now and expect punishment after death? **48** *118* O Adam, what have you done? For though it was you who sinned, the fall was not yours alone, but ours also who are your descendants. **49** *119* For what good is it to us, if an immortal time has been promised to us, but we have done deeds that bring death? **50** *120* And what good is it that an everlasting hope has been promised to us, but we have miserably failed? **51** *121* Or that safe and healthful habitations have been reserved for us, but we have lived wickedly? **52** *122* Or that the glory of the Most High will defend those who have led a pure life, but we have walked in the most wicked ways? **53** *123* Or that a paradise shall be revealed, whose fruit remains unspoiled and in which are abundance and healing, but we shall not enter it **54** *124* because we have lived in perverse ways?[i] **55** *125* Or that the faces of those who practiced self-control shall shine more than the stars, but our faces shall be blacker than darkness? **56** *126* For

---

[a] Lat bold   [b] Syr Ethiop Arm: Lat *to understand*   [c] Syr Ethiop: Lat lacks *on that… another*   [d] Syr Ethiop Arab 1: Lat Arab 2 Arm lack *in the days of Saul*   [e] Lat lacks *not*   [f] Or *the glory does not continuously abide in it*   [g] Syr Ethiop: Lat lacks *the beginning*   [h] Syr Ethiop: Lat *overwhelm*   [i] Cn: Lat Syr *places*

7:*112–115*—Uriel counsels that in this age, intercession is allowed. At judgment people must receive their due, so intercession is pointless.

Clearly disciples are to offer intercessory prayers for the living.

7:*116–139*—Lament over the fate of the wicked.

while we lived and committed iniquity we did not consider what we should suffer after death."

57 127 He answered and said, "This is the significance of the contest that all who are born on earth shall wage: **58 128** if they are defeated they shall suffer what you have said, but if they are victorious they shall receive what I have said.*a* **59 129** For this is the way of which Moses, while he was alive, spoke to the people, saying, 'Choose life for yourself, so that you may live!' **60 130** But they did not believe him or the prophets after him, or even myself who have spoken to them. **61 131** Therefore there shall not be*b* grief at their destruction, so much as joy over those to whom salvation is assured."

Ezra Appeals to God's Mercy

62 132 I answered and said, "I know, O Lord, that the Most High is now called merciful, because he has mercy on those who have not yet come into the world; **63 133** and gracious, because he is gracious to those who turn in repentance to his law; **64 134** and patient, because he shows patience toward those who have sinned, since they are his own creatures; **65 135** and bountiful, because he would rather give than take away;*c* **66 136** and abundant in compassion, because he makes his compassions abound more and more to those now living and to those who are gone and to those yet to come— **67 137** for if he did not make them abound, the world with those who inhabit it would not have life— **68 138** and he is called the giver, because if he did not give out of his goodness so that those who have committed iniquities might be relieved of them, not one ten-thousandth of humankind could have life; **69 139** and the judge,

because if he did not pardon those who were created by his word and blot out the multitude of their sins,*d* **70 140** there would probably be left only very few of the innumerable multitude."

8 He answered me and said, "The Most High made this world for the sake of many, but the world to come for the sake of only a few. ²But I tell you a parable, Ezra. Just as, when you ask the earth, it will tell you that it provides a large amount of clay from which earthenware is made, but only a little dust from which gold comes, so is the course of the present world. ³Many have been created, but only a few shall be saved."

Ezra Again Appeals to God's Mercy

4 I answered and said, "Then drink your fill of understanding,*e* O my soul, and drink wisdom, O my heart. ⁵For not of your own will did you come into the world,*f* and against your will you depart, for you have been given only a short time to live. ⁶O Lord above us, grant to your servant that we may pray before you, and give us a seed for our heart and cultivation of our understanding so that fruit may be produced, by which every mortal who bears the likeness*g* of a human being may be able to live. ⁷For you alone exist, and we are a work of your hands, as you have declared. ⁸And because you give life to the body that is now fashioned in the womb, and furnish it with members, what you have created is preserved amid fire and water, and for nine months the womb*h* endures your creature that has

---

a Syr Ethiop Arab 1: Lat *what I say*   *b* Syr: Lat *there was not*   *c* Or *he is ready to give according to requests*   *d* Lat *contempts*   *e* Syr: Lat *Then release understanding*   *f* Syr: Meaning of Lat uncertain   *g* Syr: Lat *place*   *h* Lat *what you have formed*

7:132–139—Ezra acknowledges the mercy, grace, patience, abundance, and compassion of God (cf. Exod. 34:6–7). With such characteristics, God cannot be blamed for human wickedness. The dialogue is moving Ezra (and the modern disciple) closer to a proper understanding of God.

8:4–36—Ezra asks God to be merciful (cf. 7:132) to humanity. To destroy almost all humans calls

into question their very creation (8:14), and by implication the worthiness of their creator. Then Ezra intercedes for Israel, including himself, again appealing to God's mercy toward sinners. Their salvation would come, if at all, as a function of God's nature, not human worthiness. His prayer constitutes a model for the prayers of disciples.

been created in it. ⁹ But that which keeps and that which is kept shall both be kept by your keeping.ᵃ And when the womb gives up again what has been created in it, ¹⁰ you have commanded that from the members themselves (that is, from the breasts) milk, the fruit of the breasts, should be supplied, ¹¹ so that what has been fashioned may be nourished for a time; and afterwards you will still guide it in your mercy. ¹² You have nurtured it in your righteousness, and instructed it in your law, and reproved it in your wisdom. ¹³ You put it to death as your creation, and make it live as your work. ¹⁴ If then you will suddenly and quick-lyᵇ destroy what with so great labor was fashioned by your command, to what purpose was it made? ¹⁵ And now I will speak out: About all humankind you know best; but I will speak about your people, for whom I am grieved, ¹⁶ and about your inheritance, for whom I lament, and about Israel, for whom I am sad, and about the seed of Jacob, for whom I am troubled. ¹⁷ Therefore I will pray before you for myself and for them, for I see the failings of us who inhabit the earth; ¹⁸ and now alsoᶜ I have heard of the swiftness of the judgment that is to come. ¹⁹ Therefore hear my voice and understand my words, and I will speak before you."

Ezra's Prayer

The beginning of the words of Ezra's prayer,ᵈ before he was taken up. He said: ²⁰ "O Lord, you who inhabit eternity,ᵉ whose eyes are exaltedᶠ and whose upper chambers are in the air, ²¹ whose throne is beyond measure and whose glory is beyond comprehension, before whom the hosts of angels stand trembling ²² and at whose command they are changed to wind and fire,ᵍ whose word is sure and whose utterances are certain, whose command is strong and whose ordinance is terrible, ²³ whose look dries up the depths and whose indignation makes the mountains melt away, and whose

truth is establishedʰ forever— ²⁴ hear, O Lord, the prayer of your servant, and give ear to the petition of your creature; attend to my words. ²⁵ For as long as I live I will speak, and as long as I have understanding I will answer. ²⁶ O do not look on the sins of your people, but on those who serve you in truth. ²⁷ Do not take note of the endeavors of those who act wickedly, but of the endeavors of those who have kept your covenants amid afflictions. ²⁸ Do not think of those who have lived wickedly in your sight, but remember those who have willingly acknowledged that you are to be feared. ²⁹ Do not will the destruction of those who have the ways of cattle, but regard those who have gloriously taught your law.ⁱ ³⁰ Do not be angry with those who are deemed worse than wild animals, but love those who have always put their trust in your glory. ³¹ For we and our ancestors have passed our lives in ways that bring death;ʲ but it is because of us sinners that you are called merciful. ³² For if you have desired to have pity on us, who have no works of righteousness, then you will be called merciful. ³³ For the righteous, who have many works laid up with you, shall receive their reward in consequence of their own deeds. ³⁴ But what are mortals, that you are angry with them; or what is a corruptible race, that you are so bitter against it? ³⁵ For in truth there is no one among those who have been born who has not acted wickedly; among those who have existedᵃ there is no one who has not done wrong. ³⁶ For in this, O Lord, your righteousness and goodness will be declared, when you are merciful to those who have no store of good works."

Response to Ezra's Prayer

37 He answered me and said, "Some things you have spoken rightly, and it

---

ᵃ Syr: Meaning of Lat uncertain ᵇ Syr: Lat will with a light command ᶜ Syr: Lat but ᵈ Syr Ethiop; Lat beginning of Ezra's words ᵉ Or you who abide forever ᶠ Another Lat text reads whose are the highest heavens ᵍ Syr: Lat they whose service takes the form of wind and fire ʰ Arab 2: Other authorities read truth bears witness ⁱ Syr have received the brightness of your law ʲ Syr Ethiop: Meaning of Lat uncertain

will turn out according to your words.
38 For indeed I will not concern myself
about the fashioning of those who have
sinned, or about their death, their judgment, or their destruction; **39** but I will
rejoice over the creation of the righteous, over their pilgrimage also, and
their salvation, and their receiving their
reward. **40** As I have spoken, therefore, so
it shall be.

41 "For just as the farmer sows many
seeds in the ground and plants a multitude of seedlings, and yet not all that
have been sown will come up[a] in due
season, and not all that were planted
will take root; so also those who have
been sown in the world will not all be
saved."

42 I answered and said, "If I have
found favor in your sight, let me speak.
43 If the farmer's seed does not come up,
because it has not received your rain in
due season, or if it has been ruined by
too much rain, it perishes.[b] **44** But people,
who have been formed by your hands
and are called your own image because
they are made like you, and for whose
sake you have formed all things—have
you also made them like the farmer's
seed? **45** Surely not, O Lord[c] above! But
spare your people and have mercy on
your inheritance, for you have mercy on
your own creation."

Ezra's Final Appeal for Mercy

46 He answered me and said, "Things
that are present are for those who live
now, and things that are future are for
those who will live hereafter. **47** For you
come far short of being able to love my
creation more than I love it. But you
have often compared yourself[d] to the
unrighteous. Never do so! **48** But even
in this respect you will be praiseworthy
before the Most High, **49** because you

have humbled yourself, as is becoming
for you, and have not considered yourself to be among the righteous. You will
receive the greatest glory, **50** for many
miseries will affect those who inhabit
the world in the last times, because they
have walked in great pride. **51** But think
of your own case, and inquire concerning the glory of those who are like yourself, **52** because it is for you that paradise
is opened, the tree of life is planted, the
age to come is prepared, plenty is provided, a city is built, rest is appointed,[e]
goodness is established and wisdom
perfected beforehand. **53** The root of evil[f]
is sealed up from you, illness is banished from you, and death[g] is hidden;
Hades has fled and corruption has been
forgotten;[h] **54** sorrows have passed away,
and in the end the treasure of immortality is made manifest. **55** Therefore do
not ask any more questions about the
great number of those who perish. **56** For
when they had opportunity to choose,
they despised the Most High, and were
contemptuous of his law, and abandoned his ways. **57** Moreover, they have
even trampled on his righteous ones,
58 and said in their hearts that there is no
God—though they knew well that they
must die. **59** For just as the things that I
have predicted await[i] you, so the thirst
and torment that are prepared await
them. For the Most High did not intend
that anyone should be destroyed; **60** but
those who were created have themselves
defiled the name of him who made them,
and have been ungrateful to him who
prepared life for them now. **61** Therefore
my judgment is now drawing near; **62** I

[a] Syr Ethiop *will live*; Lat *will be saved* [b] Cn: Compare Syr Arab 1 Arm
Georg 2: Meaning of Lat uncertain [c] Ethiop Arab Compare Syr: Lat
lacks *O Lord* [d] Syr Ethiop: Lat *brought yourself near* [e] Syr Ethiop: Lat
allowed [f] Lat lacks *of evil* [g] Syr Ethiop Arm: Lat lacks *death* [h] Syr: Lat
Hades and corruption have fled into oblivion; or *corruption has fled into Hades
to be forgotten* [i] Syr: Lat *will receive*

8:46–62—Uriel counsels that Ezra is not one
of the wicked; even his including of himself in
their number is a sign of his virtuous humility.
In addition, he tells Ezra to quit dwelling on the
fate of the wicked, who had the opportunity to

obey God, but did not. Instead, he should inquire
about the glory to come to him and other righteous people. This answer reminds all believers
that discipleship is a matter of choice.

have not shown this to all people, but only to you and a few like you."

Then I answered and said, **63** "O Lord, you have already shown me a great number of the signs that you will do in the last times, but you have not shown me when you will do them."

More about the Signs of the End

9 He answered me and said, "Measure carefully in your mind, and when you see that some of the predicted signs have occurred, **2** then you will know that it is the very time when the Most High is about to visit the world that he has made. **3** So when there shall appear in the world earthquakes, tumult of peoples, intrigues of nations, wavering of leaders, confusion of princes, **4** then you will know that it was of these that the Most High spoke from the days that were of old, from the beginning. **5** For just as with everything that has occurred in the world, the beginning is evident,*a* and the end manifest; **6** so also are the times of the Most High: the beginnings are manifest in wonders and mighty works, and the end in penalties*b* and in signs.

7 "It shall be that all who will be saved and will be able to escape on account of their works, or on account of the faith by which they have believed, **8** will survive the dangers that have been predicted, and will see my salvation in my land and within my borders, which I have sanctified for myself from the beginning. **9** Then those who have now abused my ways shall be amazed, and those who have rejected them with contempt shall live in torments. **10** For as many as did not acknowledge me in their lifetime,

though they received my benefits, **11** and as many as scorned my law while they still had freedom, and did not understand but despised it*c* while an opportunity of repentance was still open to them, **12** these must in torment acknowledge it*c* after death. **13** Therefore, do not continue to be curious about how the ungodly will be punished; but inquire how the righteous will be saved, those to whom the age belongs and for whose sake the age was made."*d*

The Argument Recapitulated

14 I answered and said, **15** "I said before, and I say now, and will say it again: there are more who perish than those who will be saved, **16** as a wave is greater than a drop of water."

17 He answered me and said, "As is the field, so is the seed; and as are the flowers, so are the colors; and as is the work, so is the product; and as is the farmer, so is the threshing floor. **18** For there was a time in this age when I was preparing for those who now exist, before the world was made for them to live in, and no one opposed me then, for no one existed; **19** but now those who have been created in this world, which is supplied both with an unfailing table and an inexhaustible pasture,*e* have become corrupt in their ways. **20** So I considered my world, and saw that it was lost. I saw that my earth was in peril because of the devices of those who*f* had come into it. **21** And I saw and spared some*g* with great difficulty, and saved for myself one

a Syr: Ethiop *is in the word; Meaning of Lat uncertain*   *b* Syr: Lat Ethiop *in effects*   *c* Or *me*   *d* Syr: Lat *saved, and whose is the age and for whose sake the age was made and when*   *e* Cn: Lat *law*   *f* Cn: Lat *devices that*   *g* Lat *them*

8:63–9:13—Uriel teaches that earthquakes, war, and political confusion will signal the beginning of the end. Then those who have performed good deeds will survive and see the salvation of the lands of Israel. By contrast, the wicked will endure torment. Neither a desire for rewards nor fear of punishment constitutes the highest moral grounds for discipleship, but 2 Esdras offers both emotions as reasons for disciples to serve God.

9:7—The phrase *on account of the faith by*

which they have believed sounds like a Christian interpolation. Nothing else in this vision suggests that people could be saved by faith.

9:14–22—Once more Ezra complains about how many more will perish than will be saved. Uriel replies that it is necessary for God to destroy the wicked, rather than allow them to ruin the righteous. Disciples will note that this verse does not authorize fallible humans to act to punish others in God's name.

grape out of a cluster, and one plant out of a great forest.*a* **22** So let the multitude perish that has been born in vain, but let my grape and my plant be saved, because with much labor I have perfected them.

23 "Now, if you will let seven days more pass—do not, however, fast during them, **24** but go into a field of flowers where no house has been built, and eat only of the flowers of the field, and taste no meat and drink no wine, but eat only flowers— **25** and pray to the Most High continually, then I will come and talk with you."

The Abiding Glory of the Mosaic Law

26 So I went, as he directed me, into the field that is called Ardat;*b* there I sat among the flowers and ate of the plants of the field, and the nourishment they afforded satisfied me. **27** After seven days, while I lay on the grass, my heart was troubled again as it was before. **28** Then my mouth was opened, and I began to speak before the Most High, and said, **29** "O Lord, you showed yourself among us, to our ancestors in the wilderness when they came out from Egypt and when they came into the untrodden and unfruitful wilderness; **30** and you said, 'Hear me, O Israel, and give heed to my words, O descendants of Jacob. **31** For I sow my law in you, and it shall bring forth fruit in you, and you shall be glorified through it forever.' **32** But though our ancestors received the law, they did not keep it and did not observe the*c* statutes; yet the fruit of the law did not perish— for it could not, because it was yours. **33** Yet those who received it perished, because they did not keep what had been sown in them. **34** Now this is the general rule that, when the ground has received seed, or the sea a ship, or any dish food or drink, and when it comes about that

what was sown or what was launched or what was put in is destroyed, **35** they are destroyed, but the things that held them remain; yet with us it has not been so. **36** For we who have received the law and sinned will perish, as well as our hearts that received it; **37** the law, however, does not perish but survives in its glory."

The Vision of a Weeping Woman

38 When I said these things in my heart, I looked around,*d* and on my right I saw a woman; she was mourning and weeping with a loud voice, and was deeply grieved at heart; her clothes were torn, and there were ashes on her head. **39** Then I dismissed the thoughts with which I had been engaged, and turned to her **40** and said to her, "Why are you weeping, and why are you grieved at heart?"

41 She said to me, "Let me alone, my lord, so that I may weep for myself and continue to mourn, for I am greatly embittered in spirit and deeply distressed."

42 I said to her, "What has happened to you? Tell me."

43 And she said to me, "Your servant was barren and had no child, though I lived with my husband for thirty years. **44** Every hour and every day during those thirty years I prayed to the Most High, night and day. **45** And after thirty years God heard your servant, and looked upon my low estate, and considered my distress, and gave me a son. I rejoiced greatly over him, I and my husband and all my neighbors;*e* and we gave great glory to the Mighty One. **46** And I brought him up with much care. **47** So when he grew up and I came to take a

---

a Syr Ethiop Arab 1: Lat *tribe*   *b* Syr Ethiop *Arpad*; Arm *Ardab*   *c* Lat *my*
d Syr Arab Arm: Lat *I looked about me with my eyes*   *e* Literally *all my citizens*

9:26–10:28 The Fourth Vision: A Woman Mourning over the Death of Her Only Son

9:26–28—The setting: An open field, outside a town (10:4), perhaps Babylon; seven days after the previous vision.

9:38–10:24—Ezra has a vision of an old woman, who turns out to be Mother Jerusalem.

wife for him, I set a day for the marriage feast.

10 "But it happened that when my son entered his wedding chamber, he fell down and died. ²So all of us put out our lamps, and all my neighbors[a] attempted to console me; I remained quiet until the evening of the second day. ³But when all of them had stopped consoling me, encouraging me to be quiet, I got up in the night and fled, and I came to this field, as you see. ⁴And now I intend not to return to the town, but to stay here; I will neither eat nor drink, but will mourn and fast continually until I die."

5 Then I broke off the reflections with which I was still engaged, and answered her in anger and said, ⁶"You most foolish of women, do you not see our mourning, and what has happened to us? ⁷For Zion, the mother of us all, is in deep grief and great distress. ⁸It is most appropriate to mourn now, because we are all mourning, and to be sorrowful, because we are all sorrowing; you are sorrowing for one son, but we, the whole world, for our mother.[b] ⁹Now ask the earth, and she will tell you that it is she who ought to mourn over so many who have come into being upon her. ¹⁰From the beginning all have been born of her, and others will come; and, lo, almost all go[c] to perdition, and a multitude of them will come to doom. ¹¹Who then ought to mourn the more, she who lost so great a multitude, or you who are grieving for one alone? ¹²But if you say to me, 'My lamentation is not like the earth's, for I have lost the fruit of my womb, which I brought forth in pain and bore in sorrow; ¹³but it is with the earth according to the way of the earth—the multitude that is now in it goes as it came'; ¹⁴then I say to you, 'Just as you brought forth in sorrow, so the earth also has from the beginning given her fruit, that is, humankind, to him who made her.' ¹⁵Now, therefore, keep your sorrow to yourself, and bear bravely the troubles that have come upon you. ¹⁶For if you acknowledge the decree of God to be just, you will receive your son back in due time, and will be praised among women. ¹⁷Therefore go into the town to your husband."

18 She said to me, "I will not do so; I will not go into the city, but I will die here."

19 So I spoke again to her, and said, ²⁰"Do not do that, but let yourself be persuaded—for how many are the adversities of Zion?—and be consoled because of the sorrow of Jerusalem. ²¹For you see how our sanctuary has been laid waste, our altar thrown down, our temple destroyed; ²²our harp has been laid low, our song has been silenced, and our rejoicing has been ended; the light of our lampstand has been put out, the ark of our covenant has been plundered, our holy things have been polluted, and the name by which we are called has been almost profaned; our children[d] have suffered abuse, our priests have been burned to death, our Levites have gone into exile, our virgins have been defiled, and our wives have been ravished; our righteous men[e] have been carried off, our little ones have been cast out, our young men have been enslaved and our strong men made powerless. ²³And, worst of all, the seal of Zion has been deprived of its glory, and given over into the hands of those that hate us. ²⁴Therefore shake off your great sadness and lay aside your many sorrows, so that the Mighty One may be merciful to you again, and the Most High may give you rest, a respite from your troubles."

---

a Literally *all my citizens*   *b* Compare Syr: Meaning of Lat uncertain   *c* Literally *walk*   *d* Ethiop *free men*   *e* Syr *our seers*

10:5–16—An angry Ezra tells the old woman to mourn the condition of the children of Mother Jerusalem instead. (In Ezra's day, Jerusalem still had no wall and few inhabitants.)

10:23 *Seal*—It is unclear whether Jerusalem would have had a physical seal. Sometimes the word is interpreted to mean "independence."

25 While I was talking to her, her face suddenly began to shine exceedingly; her countenance flashed like lightning, so that I was too frightened to approach her, and my heart was terrified. While[a] I was wondering what this meant, 26 she suddenly uttered a loud and fearful cry, so that the earth shook at the sound. 27 When I looked up, the woman was no longer visible to me, but a city was being built,[b] and a place of huge foundations showed itself. I was afraid, and cried with a loud voice and said, 28 "Where is the angel Uriel, who came to me at first? For it was he who brought me into this overpowering bewilderment; my end has become corruption, and my prayer a reproach."

Uriel's Interpretation of the Vision

29 While I was speaking these words, the angel who had come to me at first came to me, and when he saw me 30 lying there like a corpse, deprived of my understanding, he grasped my right hand and strengthened me and set me on my feet, and said to me, 31 "What is the matter with you? And why are you troubled? And why are your understanding and the thoughts of your mind troubled?"

32 I said, "It was because you abandoned me. I did as you directed, and went out into the field, and lo, what I have seen and can still see, I am unable to explain."

33 He said to me, "Stand up like a man, and I will instruct you."

34 I said, "Speak, my lord; only do not forsake me, so that I may not die before my time.[c] 35 For I have seen what I did not know, and I heard[d] what I do not understand 36 —or is my mind deceived, and my soul dreaming? 37 Now therefore I beg you to give your servant an explanation of this bewildering vision."

38 He answered me and said, "Listen to me, and I will teach you, and tell you about the things that you fear; for the Most High has revealed many secrets to you. 39 He has seen your righteous conduct, and that you have sorrowed continually for your people and mourned greatly over Zion. 40 This therefore is the meaning of the vision. 41 The woman who appeared to you a little while ago, whom you saw mourning and whom you began to console 42 (you do not now see the form of a woman, but there appeared to you a city being built)[e] 43 and who told you about the misfortune of her son—this is the interpretation: 44 The woman whom you saw is Zion, which you now behold as a city being built.[f] 45 And as for her telling you that she was barren for thirty years, the reason is that there were three thousand[g] years in the world before any offering was offered in it.[h] 46 And after three thousand[i] years Solomon built the city, and offered offerings; then it was that the barren woman bore a son. 47 And as for her telling you that she brought him up with much care, that was the period of residence in Jerusalem. 48 And as for her saying to you, 'My son died as he entered his wedding chamber,' and that misfortune had overtaken her,[j] this was the destruction that befell Jerusalem. 49 So you saw her like-

[a] Syr Ethiop Arab 1: Lat lacks I was too… terrified. While [b] Lat: Syr Ethiop Arab 1 Arab 2 Arm but there was an established city [c] Syr Ethiop Arab: Lat die to no purpose [d] Other ancient authorities read have heard [e] Lat: Syr Ethiop Arab 1 Arab 2 Arm an established city [f] Cn: Lat an established city [g] Most Lat Mss read three [h] Cn: Lat Syr Arab Arm her [i] Syr Ethiop Arab Arm: Lat three [j] Or him

---

10:29–57 Uriel's Interpretation of the Vision

10:45—The woman's *thirty years* of barrenness represented the first *three thousand years* of the earth's life, in which no one offered sacrifices in Jerusalem. In the chronology of 2 Esdras, those years began with creation (Gen. 1) and ended with the construction of Solomon's temple in the mid-tenth century (1 Kgs. 5 and 6). Though the identification is not explicit, the *son* (2 Esd. 10:46) seems to have represented the temple.

10:47—Her rearing of her son corresponded to the years the temple stood (ca. 950–586).

10:48—The death of her son symbolized the destruction of the temple and city by the Babylonians.

10:49—Ezra had seen the *likeness* of the city, the

ness, how she mourned for her son, and you began to console her for what had happened.*a* **50** For now the Most High, seeing that you are sincerely grieved and profoundly distressed for her, has shown you the brilliance of her glory, and the loveliness of her beauty. **51** Therefore I told you to remain in the field where no house had been built, **52** for I knew that the Most High would reveal these things to you. **53** Therefore I told you to go into the field where there was no foundation of any building, **54** because no work of human construction could endure in a place where the city of the Most High was to be revealed.

55 "Therefore do not be afraid, and do not let your heart be terrified; but go in and see the splendor or*b* the vastness of the building, as far as it is possible for your eyes to see it, **56** and afterward you will hear as much as your ears can hear. **57** For you are more blessed than many, and you have been called to be with*c* the Most High as few have been. **58** But tomorrow night you shall remain here, **59** and the Most High will show you in those dream visions what the Most High will do to those who inhabit the earth in the last days."

So I slept that night and the following one, as he had told me.

The Vision of the Eagle

11 On the second night I had a dream: I saw rising from the sea an eagle that had twelve feathered wings and three heads. **2** I saw it spread its wings over*d* the whole earth, and all the winds of heaven blew upon it, and the clouds were gathered around it.*e* **3** I saw that out of its wings there grew opposing wings; but they became little, puny wings. **4** But its heads were at rest; the middle head was larger than the other heads, but it too was at rest with them. **5** Then I saw that the eagle flew with its wings, and it reigned over the earth and over those who inhabit it. **6** And I saw how all things under heaven were subjected to it, and no one spoke against it—not a single creature that was on the earth. **7** Then I saw the eagle rise upon its talons, and it uttered a cry to its wings, saying, **8** "Do not all watch at the same time; let each sleep in its own place, and watch in its turn; **9** but let the heads be reserved for the last."

10 I looked again and saw that the voice did not come from its heads, but from the middle of its body. **11** I counted its rival wings, and there were eight of them. **12** As I watched, one wing on the right side rose up, and it reigned over all the earth. **13** And after a time its reign came to an end, and it disappeared, so that even its place was no longer visible. Then the next wing rose up and reigned, and it continued to reign a long time. **14** While it was reigning its end came also, so that it disappeared like the first. **15** And a voice sounded, saying to

a Most Lat Mss and Arab 1 add *These were the things to be opened to you* *b* Other ancient authorities read *and* *c* Or *been named by* *d* Arab 2 Arm: Lat Syr Ethiop *in* *e* Syr: Compare Ethiop Arab: Lat lacks *the clouds* and *around it*

---

future Jerusalem in heaven, awaiting its manifestation. The term "likeness" warned the reader not to take the language literally, because the reality under discussion was beyond verbal description.

11:1–12:3a The Fifth Vision: An Eagle Rising from the Sea

In this vision, Ezra learns that not even mighty Rome is beyond God's control. Disciples may conclude that neither are modern nations with nuclear weapons.

11:1—The setting: The same as for vision four, but following two nights of rest.

11:1 *Rising from the sea*—Cf. Dan. 7:3. The sea symbolized primordial chaos, opposed to God. The *eagle* symbolized the Roman Empire (cf. 2 Esd. 12:11–12), whose standards carried the emblem of an eagle. Its *wings* were its kings. Its three heads are often understood as the emperors Vespasian (69–79 CE), his eldest son Titus (79–81), and a younger son Domitian (81–96).

11:3 *Opposing wings*—Rebels desiring to be king or emperor. They *became little, puny wings*, which meant that they were defeated.

11:10–19—The kings reigned in succession, the second the longest of all. That king was possibly Caesar Augustus, who reigned the longest of any Roman emperor (31 BCE–14 CE).

it, [16] "Listen to me, you who have ruled the earth all this time; I announce this to you before you disappear. [17] After you no one shall rule as long as you have ruled, not even half as long."

18 Then the third wing raised itself up, and held the rule as the earlier ones had done, and it also disappeared. [19] And so it went with all the wings; they wielded power one after another and then were never seen again. [20] I kept looking, and in due time the wings that followed[a] also rose up on the right[b] side, in order to rule. There were some of them that ruled, yet disappeared suddenly; [21] and others of them rose up, but did not hold the rule.

22 And after this I looked and saw that the twelve wings and the two little wings had disappeared, [23] and nothing remained on the eagle's body except the three heads that were at rest and six little wings.

24 As I kept looking I saw that two little wings separated from the six and remained under the head that was on the right side; but four remained in their place. [25] Then I saw that these little wings[c] planned to set themselves up and hold the rule. [26] As I kept looking, one was set up, but suddenly disappeared; [27] a second also, and this disappeared more quickly than the first. [28] While I continued to look the two that remained were planning between themselves to reign together; [29] and while they were planning, one of the heads that were at rest (the one that was in the middle) suddenly awoke; it was greater than the other two heads. [30] And I saw how it allied the two heads with itself, [31] and how the head turned with those that were with it and devoured the two

little wings[c] that were planning to reign. [32] Moreover this head gained control of the whole earth, and with much oppression dominated its inhabitants; it had greater power over the world than all the wings that had gone before.

33 After this I looked again and saw the head in the middle suddenly disappear, just as the wings had done. [34] But the two heads remained, which also in like manner ruled over the earth and its inhabitants. [35] And while I looked, I saw the head on the right side devour the one on the left.

A Lion Roused from the Forest

36 Then I heard a voice saying to me, "Look in front of you and consider what you see." [37] When I looked, I saw what seemed to be a lion roused from the forest, roaring; and I heard how it uttered a human voice to the eagle, and spoke, saying, [38] "Listen and I will speak to you. The Most High says to you, [39] 'Are you not the one that remains of the four beasts that I had made to reign in my world, so that the end of my times might come through them? [40] You, the fourth that has come, have conquered all the beasts that have gone before; and you have held sway over the world with great terror, and over all the earth with grievous oppression; and for so long you have lived on the earth with deceit.[d] [41] You have judged the earth, but not with truth, [42] for you have oppressed the meek and injured the peaceable; you have hated those who tell the truth, and have loved liars; you have destroyed the homes of those who brought forth fruit, and have laid low the walls of those who

[a] Syr Arab 2 *the little wings* [b] Some Ethiop Mss read *left* [c] Syr: Lat *underwings* [d] Syr Arab Arm: Lat Ethiop *The fourth came, however, and conquered… and held sway… and for so long lived*

11:24–31—The identity of these *wings* is debated.

11:32–33—The *head* possibly is Vespasian, who died following a short illness. He treated Judah harshly after the first revolt in 67–72, possibly earning him the charge that he oppressed the world.

11:35—This seems to be a charge that Domitian (*the head on the right side*) had assassinated his older brother Titus, whose reign was conspicuously short.

did you no harm. **43** Your insolence has come up before the Most High, and your pride to the Mighty One. **44** The Most High has looked at his times; now they have ended, and his ages have reached completion. **45** Therefore you, eagle, will surely disappear, you and your terrifying wings, your most evil little wings, your malicious heads, your most evil talons, and your whole worthless body, **46** so that the whole earth, freed from your violence, may be refreshed and relieved, and may hope for the judgment and mercy of him who made it.'"

12 While the lion was saying these words to the eagle, I looked **2** and saw that the remaining head had disappeared. The two wings that had gone over to it rose up and*a* set themselves up to reign, and their reign was brief and full of tumult. **3** When I looked again, they were already vanishing. The whole body of the eagle was burned, and the earth was exceedingly terrified.

Then I woke up in great perplexity of mind and great fear, and I said to my spirit, **4** "You have brought this upon me, because you search out the ways of the Most High. **5** I am still weary in mind and very weak in my spirit, and not even a little strength is left in me, because of the great fear with which I have been terrified tonight. **6** Therefore I will now entreat the Most High that he may strengthen me to the end."

The Interpretation of the Vision

7 Then I said, "O sovereign Lord, if I have found favor in your sight, and if I have been accounted righteous before you beyond many others, and if my prayer has indeed come up before your face, **8** strengthen me and show me, your servant, the interpretation and meaning of this terrifying vision so that you may fully comfort my soul. **9** For you have judged me worthy to be shown the end of the times and the last events of the times."

10 He said to me, "This is the interpretation of this vision that you have seen: **11** The eagle that you saw coming up from the sea is the fourth kingdom that appeared in a vision to your brother Daniel. **12** But it was not explained to him as I now explain to you or have explained it. **13** The days are coming when a kingdom shall rise on earth, and it shall be more terrifying than all the kingdoms that have been before it. **14** And twelve kings shall reign in it, one after another. **15** But the second that is to reign shall hold sway for a longer time than any other one of the twelve. **16** This is the interpretation of the twelve wings that you saw.

17 "As for your hearing a voice that spoke, coming not from the eagle's*b* heads but from the midst of its body, this is the interpretation: **18** In the midst of*c* the time of that kingdom great struggles shall arise, and it shall be in danger of falling; nevertheless it shall not fall then, but shall regain its former power.*d* **19** As for your seeing eight little wings*e* clinging to its wings, this is the interpretation: **20** Eight kings shall arise in

a Ethiop: Lat lacks *rose up and* *b* Lat *his* *c* Syr Arm: Lat *After* *d* Ethiop Arab 1 Arm: Lat Syr *its beginning* *e* Syr: Lat *underwings*

12:1–3a—The disappearance of the third head probably symbolizes the death of Domitian (96 CE). The *two wings* apparently symbolize the last two usurpers of the eight. Nerva succeeded Domitian for a little over one year, and may have been the first. If the other is Nerva's successor Trajan, he hardly qualifies as a usurper who reigns but a short time, reigning as he did almost twenty years (98–117). Since the death of the second "wing" followed immediately, the apocalyptic writer may have turned to genuine prediction at this point and prophesied the destruction of the Roman Empire soon after the death of Domitian or of Nerva. If so, roughly 95–100 may have been the date for the writing of this vision, and perhaps for the whole of chaps. 3–14.

12:3b–39 The Interpretation of the Fifth Vision

12:11–12—God tells Ezra that the eagle is the fourth beast seen by Daniel (cf. Dan. 7:7), which is the Greek Empire. The eagle would refer to Rome now, however, since the fall of the Greek Empire did not usher in the kingdom of God.

it, whose times shall be short and their years swift; [21] two of them shall perish when the middle of its time draws near; and four shall be kept for the time when its end approaches, but two shall be kept until the end.

22 "As for your seeing three heads at rest, this is the interpretation: [23] In its last days the Most High will raise up three kings,[a] and they[b] shall renew many things in it, and shall rule the earth [24] and its inhabitants more oppressively than all who were before them. Therefore they are called the heads of the eagle, [25] because it is they who shall sum up his wickedness and perform his last actions. [26] As for your seeing that the large head disappeared, one of the kings[c] shall die in his bed, but in agonies. [27] But as for the two who remained, the sword shall devour them. [28] For the sword of one shall devour him who was with him; but he also shall fall by the sword in the last days.

29 "As for your seeing two little wings[d] passing over to[e] the head which was on the right side, [30] this is the interpretation: It is these whom the Most High has kept for the eagle's[f] end; this was the reign which was brief and full of tumult, as you have seen.

31 "And as for the lion whom you saw rousing up out of the forest and roaring and speaking to the eagle and reproving him for his unrighteousness, and as for all his words that you have heard, [32] this is the Messiah[g] whom the Most High has kept until the end of days, who will arise from the offspring of David, and will come and speak[h] with them. He will denounce them for their ungodli-

ness and for their wickedness, and will display before them their contemptuous dealings. [33] For first he will bring them alive before his judgment seat, and when he has reproved them, then he will destroy them. [34] But in mercy he will set free the remnant of my people, those who have been saved throughout my borders, and he will make them joyful until the end comes, the day of judgment, of which I spoke to you at the beginning. [35] This is the dream that you saw, and this is its interpretation. [36] And you alone were worthy to learn this secret of the Most High. [37] Therefore write all these things that you have seen in a book, put it[i] in a hidden place; [38] and you shall teach them to the wise among your people, whose hearts you know are able to comprehend and keep these secrets. [39] But as for you, wait here seven days more, so that you may be shown whatever it pleases the Most High to show you." Then he left me.

The People Come to Ezra

40 When all the people heard that the seven days were past and I had not returned to the city, they all gathered together, from the least to the greatest, and came to me and spoke to me, saying, [41] "How have we offended you, and what harm have we done you, that you have forsaken us and sit in this place? [42] For of all the prophets you alone are left to us, like a cluster of grapes from the vintage, and like a lamp in a dark place, and like a haven for a ship saved from a storm.

[a] Syr Ethiop Arab Arm: Lat *kingdoms*   [b] Syr Ethiop Arm: Lat *he*   [c] Lat *them*   [d] Arab 1: Lat *underwings*   [e] Syr Ethiop: Lat lacks *to*   [f] Lat *his*   [g] Literally *anointed one*   [h] Syr: Lat lacks *of days… and speak*   [i] Ethiop Arab 1 Arab 2 Arm: Lat Syr *them*

12:31–34—The *lion* is the Davidic messiah. He will judge the Romans and free the Israelites.

12:36–38—God deems Ezra alone worthy to receive this message, but instructs him to put it in writing and hide the book until a future, wise generation will be able to understand it. Obviously, that generation is the real author's own. By these verses the author explains why the book has remained unknown so long. While the hope that the demise of the Roman Empire would ush-

er in the kingdom of God proved premature, it still reminds the disciple that God will ultimately triumph over evil.

12:40–51 Epilogue: The People Search for Ezra

Worried at the prolonged absence of Ezra, the people search for and find him in the field outside the city, where he is waiting for the next vision. He assures them he has not abandoned them, but has interceded for Zion.

[43] Are not the disasters that have befallen us enough? [44] Therefore if you forsake us, how much better it would have been for us if we also had been consumed in the burning of Zion. [45] For we are no better than those who died there." And they wept with a loud voice.

Then I answered them and said, [46] "Take courage, O Israel; and do not be sorrowful, O house of Jacob; [47] for the Most High has you in remembrance, and the Mighty One has not forgotten you in your struggle. [48] As for me, I have neither forsaken you nor withdrawn from you; but I have come to this place to pray on account of the desolation of Zion, and to seek mercy on account of the humiliation of our[a] sanctuary. [49] Now go to your homes, every one of you, and after these days I will come to you." [50] So the people went into the city, as I told them to do. [51] But I sat in the field seven days, as the angel[b] had commanded me; and I ate only of the flowers of the field, and my food was of plants during those days.

The Man from the Sea

13 After seven days I dreamed a dream in the night. [2] And lo, a wind arose from the sea and stirred up[c] all its waves. [3] As I kept looking the wind made something like the figure of a man come up out of the heart of the sea. And I saw[d] that this man flew[e] with the clouds of heaven; and wherever he turned his face to look, everything under his gaze trembled, [4] and whenever his voice issued from his mouth, all who heard his voice melted as wax melts[f] when it feels the fire.

[5] After this I looked and saw that an innumerable multitude of people were gathered together from the four winds of heaven to make war against the man who came up out of the sea. [6] And I looked and saw that he carved out for himself a great mountain, and flew up on to it. [7] And I tried to see the region or place from which the mountain was carved, but I could not.

[8] After this I looked and saw that all who had gathered together against him, to wage war with him, were filled with fear, and yet they dared to fight. [9] When he saw the onrush of the approaching multitude, he neither lifted his hand nor held a spear or any weapon of war; [10] but I saw only how he sent forth from his mouth something like a stream of fire, and from his lips a flaming breath, and from his tongue he shot forth a storm of sparks.[g] [11] All these were mingled together, the stream of fire and the flaming breath and the great storm, and fell on the onrushing multitude that was prepared to fight, and burned up all of them, so that suddenly nothing was seen of the innumerable multitude but only the dust of ashes and the smell of smoke. When I saw it, I was amazed.

[12] After this I saw the same man come down from the mountain and call to himself another multitude that was peaceable. [13] Then many people[h] came to him, some of whom were joyful and some sorrowful; some of them were

---

[a] Syr Ethiop: Lat your   [b] Literally he   [c] Other ancient authorities read I saw a wind arise from the sea and stir up   [d] Syr: Lat lacks the wind … I saw   [e] Syr Ethiop Arab Arm: Lat grew strong   [f] Syr: Lat burned as the earth rests   [g] Meaning of Lat uncertain   [h] Lat Syr Arab 2 literally the faces of many people

---

13:1–20 The Sixth Vision: A Man Rising from the Sea

This vision portrays the Jews of the Diaspora returning to Israel. It can function to assure modern disciples that God will care for them wherever their service carries them.

13:3 *The figure of a man*—The messiah. *The heart of the sea*—The forces of chaos, opposed to God. In 2 Esd. 11:1, the antigodly Roman Empire emerged from the sea; here it is the messiah

(cf. 13:25–32). Contrast Dan. 7:13, where "one like a human being" simply appears in heaven. Here the messiah flies to heaven.

13:6—The messiah carves a mountain that turns out to be Zion (13:36). In Dan. 2, God carves from a mountain a rock representing the kingdom of God to replace the world empires.

13:13b–20—Ezra asks God to interpret the dream for the sake of the righteous people who will face these events.

bound, and some were bringing others as offerings.

The Interpretation of the Vision

Then I woke up in great terror, and prayed to the Most High, and said, [14] "From the beginning you have shown your servant these wonders, and have deemed me worthy to have my prayer heard by you; [15] now show me the interpretation of this dream also. [16] For as I consider it in my mind, alas for those who will be left in those days! And still more, alas for those who are not left! [17] For those who are not left will be sad [18] because they understand the things that are reserved for the last days, but cannot attain them. [19] But alas for those also who are left, and for that very reason! For they shall see great dangers and much distress, as these dreams show. [20] Yet it is better[a] to come into these things,[b] though incurring peril, than to pass from the world like a cloud, and not to see what will happen in the last days."

He answered me and said, [21] "I will tell you the interpretation of the vision, and I will also explain to you the things that you have mentioned. [22] As for what you said about those who survive, and concerning those who do not survive,[c] this is the interpretation: [23] The one who brings the peril at that time will protect those who fall into peril, who have works and faith toward the Almighty. [24] Understand therefore that those who are left are more blessed than those who have died.

[25] "This is the interpretation of the vision: As for your seeing a man come up from the heart of the sea, [26] this is he whom the Most High has been keeping for many ages, who will himself deliver his creation; and he will direct those who are left. [27] And as for your seeing wind and fire and a storm coming out of his mouth, [28] and as for his not holding a spear or weapon of war, yet destroying the onrushing multitude that came to conquer him, this is the interpretation: [29] The days are coming when the Most High will deliver those who are on the earth. [30] And bewilderment of mind shall come over those who inhabit the earth. [31] They shall plan to make war against one another, city against city, place against place, people against people, and kingdom against kingdom. [32] When these things take place and the signs occur that I showed you before, then my Son will be revealed, whom you saw as a man coming up from the sea.[d]

[33] "Then, when all the nations hear his voice, all the nations shall leave their own lands and the warfare that they have against one another; [34] and an innumerable multitude shall be gathered together, as you saw, wishing to come and conquer him. [35] But he shall stand on the top of Mount Zion. [36] And Zion shall come and be made manifest to all people, prepared and built, as you saw the mountain carved out without hands. [37] Then he, my Son, will reprove the assembled nations for their ungodliness (this was symbolized by the storm), [38] and will reproach them to their face with their evil thoughts and the torments with which they are to be tortured (which were symbolized by the flames), and will destroy them without effort by means of the law[e] (which was symbolized by the fire).

[39] "And as for your seeing him gather

---

[a] Ethiop Compare Arab 2: Lat *easier*   [b] Syr: Lat *this*   [c] Syr Arab 1: Lat lacks *and… not survive*   [d] Syr and most Lat Mss lack *from the sea*   [e] Syr: Lat *effort and the law*

13:21–55 God's Interpretation of the Dream

13:23—God, who sends the turmoil of the last days, will see the faithful through those times.

13:39–45—The tribes of northern Israel were conquered by the Assyrians. **Shalmaneser**, king of Assyria, sent some of the Israelites to other countries (2 Kgs. 17:24). Second Esdras has them deciding to escape to *a more distant region* (v. 41) *a year and a half*'s journey (v. 45) via *narrow passages of the Euphrates* (v. 43). The geography of this description is impossible to reconstruct.

to himself another multitude that was peaceable, **40** these are the nine*a* tribes that were taken away from their own land into exile in the days of King Hoshea, whom Shalmaneser, king of the Assyrians, made captives; he took them across the river, and they were taken into another land. **41** But they formed this plan for themselves, that they would leave the multitude of the nations and go to a more distant region, where no human beings had ever lived, **42** so that there at least they might keep their statutes that they had not kept in their own land. **43** And they went in by the narrow passages of the Euphrates river. **44** For at that time the Most High performed signs for them, and stopped the channels of the river until they had crossed over. **45** Through that region there was a long way to go, a journey of a year and a half; and that country is called Arzareth.*b*

46 "Then they lived there until the last times; and now, when they are about to come again, **47** the Most High will stop*c* the channels of the river again, so that they may be able to cross over. Therefore you saw the multitude gathered together in peace. **48** But those who are left of your people, who are found within my holy borders, shall be saved.*d* **49** Therefore when he destroys the multitude of the nations that are gathered together, he will defend the people who remain. **50** And then he will show them very many wonders."

51 I said, "O sovereign Lord, explain this to me: Why did I see the man coming up from the heart of the sea?"

52 He said to me, "Just as no one can explore or know what is in the depths of the sea, so no one on earth can see my Son or those who are with him, except in the time of his day.*e* **53** This is the interpretation of the dream that you saw. And you alone have been enlightened about this, **54** because you have forsaken your own ways and have applied yourself to mine, and have searched out my law; **55** for you have devoted your life to wisdom, and called understanding your mother. **56** Therefore I have shown you these things; for there is a reward laid up with the Most High. For it will be that after three more days I will tell you other things, and explain weighty and wondrous matters to you."

57 Then I got up and walked in the field, giving great glory and praise to the Most High for the wonders that he does*f* from time to time, **58** and because he governs the times and whatever things come to pass in their seasons. And I stayed there three days.

The Lord Commissions Ezra

14 On the third day, while I was sitting under an oak, suddenly a voice came out of a bush opposite me and said, "Ezra, Ezra!" **2** And I answered, "Here I am, Lord," and I rose to my feet. **3** Then he said to me, "I revealed myself in a bush and spoke to Moses when my people were in bondage in Egypt; **4** and I sent him and led*g* my people out of Egypt; and I led him up on Mount Sinai, where I kept him with me many days. **5** I told him many wondrous things, and

---

a Other Lat Mss *ten*; Syr Ethiop Arab 1 Arm *nine and a half*   *b* That is *Another Land*   *c* Syr: Lat *stops*   *d* Syr: Lat lacks *shall be saved*   *e* Syr: Ethiop *except when his time and his day have come*. Lat lacks *his*   *f* Lat *did*   *g* Syr Arab 1 Arab 2 *he led*

13:45 *Arzareth*—Hebrew word meaning "another land."

13:46–50—As God parted the Red Sea at the exodus (Exod. 14:21–22) and the Jordan River when Israel entered Canaan (Josh. 3:14–17), so also God parted the Euphrates when Israel went to Arzareth (2 Esd. 13:44) and will again when they return (v. 47).

13:52 *The time of his day*—The messiah will remain hidden from everyone except Ezra until he comes to begin his reign. That God already has the messiah in waiting, however, is "proof" that God will send him at the right time.

13:56–58— Ezra is instructed to wait three more days.

14:1–48 The Seventh Vision: Ezra Addressed by God

14:2–18—God reveals the end of the times.

showed him the secrets of the times and declared to him[a] the end of the times. Then I commanded him, saying, [6] 'These words you shall publish openly, and these you shall keep secret.' [7] And now I say to you: [8] Lay up in your heart the signs that I have shown you, the dreams that you have seen, and the interpretations that you have heard; [9] for you shall be taken up from among humankind, and henceforth you shall live with my Son and with those who are like you, until the times are ended. [10] The age has lost its youth, and the times begin to grow old. [11] For the age is divided into twelve parts, and nine[b] of its parts have already passed, [12] as well as half of the tenth part; so two of its parts remain, besides half of the tenth part.[c] [13] Now therefore, set your house in order, and reprove your people; comfort the lowly among them, and instruct those that are wise.[d] And now renounce the life that is corruptible, [14] and put away from you mortal thoughts; cast away from you the burdens of humankind, and divest yourself now of your weak nature; [15] lay to one side the thoughts that are most grievous to you, and hurry to escape from these times. [16] For evils worse than those that you have now seen happen shall take place hereafter. [17] For the weaker the world becomes through old age, the more shall evils be increased upon its inhabitants. [18] Truth shall go farther away, and falsehood shall come near. For the eagle[e] that you saw in the vision is already hurrying to come."

Ezra's Concern to Restore the Scriptures

19 Then I answered and said, "Let me speak[f] in your presence, Lord. [20] For I will go, as you have commanded me, and I will reprove the people who are now living; but who will warn those who will be born hereafter? For the world lies in darkness, and its inhabitants are without light. [21] For your law has been burned, and so no one knows the things which have been done or will be done by you. [22] If then I have found favor with you, send the holy spirit into me, and I will write everything that has happened in the world from the beginning, the things that were written in your law, so that people may be able to find the path, and that those who want to live in the last days may do so."

23 He answered me and said, "Go and gather the people, and tell them not to seek you for forty days. [24] But prepare for yourself many writing tablets, and take with you Sarea, Dabria, Selemia, Ethanus, and Asiel—these five, who are trained to write rapidly; [25] and you shall come here, and I will light in your heart the lamp of understanding, which shall not be put out until what you are about to write is finished. [26] And when you have finished, some things you shall make public, and some you shall deliver

[a] Syr Ethiop Arab Arm: Lat lacks *declared to him* [b] Cn: Lat Ethiop *ten* [c] Syr lacks verses 11, 12: Ethiop *For the world is divided into ten parts, and has come to the tenth, and half of the tenth remains. Now...* [d] Lat lacks *and... wise* [e] Syr Ethiop Arab Arm: Meaning of Lat uncertain [f] Most Lat Mss lack *Let me speak*

14:6—God told Moses to make part of the revelation on Mount Sinai public (the laws of the Pentateuch), and to keep the rest secret. He tells Ezra to keep secret the things God has just revealed to him, perhaps implying or even claiming that the contents of 2 Esdras originally were divulged to Moses.

14:9 *You shall be taken up*—Probably God means Ezra will die, but possibly the phrase means that Ezra will be transported to the hiding place of the messiah without dying. (Cf. Enoch in Gen. 5:21–24 and Elijah in 2 Kgs. 2:1–12.) The Syriac version of 2 Esdras ends with a note reporting that "Ezra was caught up, and taken to the place of those like him."

14:11–12—This age is divided into twelve parts (not necessarily equal in length), of which nine and a half have already passed. Hence, at the time Ezra lived, the world was already getting old. The time of the reader would be later, much closer to the end.

14:19–22—Ezra asks permission to write down what God had shown him.

14:23–26—God commissions Ezra to write. Like Moses, Ezra is to keep some of his writings secret.

in secret to the wise; tomorrow at this hour you shall begin to write."

Ezra's Last Words to the People

27 Then I went as he commanded me, and I gathered all the people together, and said, 28 "Hear these words, O Israel. 29 At first our ancestors lived as aliens in Egypt, and they were liberated from there 30 and received the law of life, which they did not keep, which you also have transgressed after them. 31 Then land was given to you for a possession in the land of Zion; but you and your ancestors committed iniquity and did not keep the ways that the Most High commanded you. 32 And since he is a righteous judge, in due time he took from you what he had given. 33 And now you are here, and your people*a* are farther in the interior.*b* 34 If you, then, will rule over your minds and discipline your hearts, you shall be kept alive, and after death you shall obtain mercy. 35 For after death the judgment will come, when we shall live again; and then the names of the righteous shall become manifest, and the deeds of the ungodly shall be disclosed. 36 But let no one come to me now, and let no one seek me for forty days."

The Restoration of the Scriptures

37 So I took the five men, as he commanded me, and we proceeded to the field, and remained there. 38 And on the next day a voice called me, saying, "Ezra, open your mouth and drink what I give you to drink." 39 So I opened my mouth, and a full cup was offered to me; it was full of something like water, but its color was like fire. 40 I took it and drank; and when I had drunk it, my heart poured forth understanding, and wisdom increased in my breast, for my spirit retained its memory, 41 and my mouth was opened and was no longer closed. 42 Moreover, the Most High gave understanding to the five men, and by turns they wrote what was dictated, using characters that they did not know.*c* They sat forty days; they wrote during the daytime, and ate their bread at night. 43 But as for me, I spoke in the daytime and was not silent at night. 44 So during the forty days, ninety-four*d* books were written. 45 And when the forty days were ended, the Most High spoke to me, saying, "Make public the twenty-four*e* books that you wrote first, and let the worthy and the unworthy read them; 46 but keep the seventy that were written last, in order to give them to the wise among your people. 47 For in them is the spring of understanding, the fountain of wisdom, and the river of knowledge." 48 And I did so.*f*

Vengeance on the Wicked

15 *g* Speak in the ears of my people the words of the prophecy that I will put in your mouth, says the Lord, 2 and cause them to be written on paper;

a Lat *brothers*   *b* Syr Ethiop Arm: Lat *are among you*   *c* Syr Compare Ethiop Arab 2 Arm: Meaning of Lat uncertain   *d* Syr Ethiop Arab 1 Arm: Meaning of Lat uncertain   *e* Syr Arab 1: Lat lacks *twenty-four*   *f* Syr adds *in the seventh year of the sixth week, five thousand years and three months and twelve days after creation. At that time Ezra was caught up, and taken to the place of those who are like him, after he had written all these things. And he was called the scribe of the knowledge of the Most High for ever and ever.* Ethiop Arab 1 Arm have a similar ending   *g* Chapters 15 and 16 (except 15.57–59, which has been found in Greek) are extant only in Lat

---

14:27–36—Ezra addresses Israel.

14:30 *Law of life*—The Pentateuch.

14:37–48—Ezra and five men write down God's words. The words will guide and inspire God's people through difficult times.

14:44 *Ninety-four books*—Twenty-four were the same as Hebrew Bible, the guide to faith and belief for disciples even today. The remaining seventy were to be kept hidden. The nature and even the identity of those seventy is unclear except for one: 2 Esdras.

15:1–16:78 Sixth Ezra

This Christian addition calls upon its readers to persevere in faith and service through all tribulations, including war.

15:1–4 God Directs a Prophet to Speak

15:2—The prophetic word is also to be put in writing because it will continue to be valid past the time of the prophets.

for they are trustworthy and true. ³ Do not fear the plots against you, and do not be troubled by the unbelief of those who oppose you. ⁴ For all unbelievers shall die in their unbelief.*ᵃ*

5 Beware, says the Lord, I am bringing evils upon the world, the sword and famine, death and destruction, ⁶ because iniquity has spread throughout every land, and their harmful doings have reached their limit. ⁷ Therefore, says the Lord, ⁸ I will be silent no longer concerning their ungodly acts that they impiously commit, neither will I tolerate their wicked practices. Innocent and righteous blood cries out to me, and the souls of the righteous cry out continually. ⁹ I will surely avenge them, says the Lord, and will receive to myself all the innocent blood from among them. ¹⁰ See, my people are being led like a flock to the slaughter; I will not allow them to live any longer in the land of Egypt, ¹¹ but I will bring them out with a mighty hand and with an uplifted arm, and will strike Egypt with plagues, as before, and will destroy all its land.

12 Let Egypt mourn, and its foundations, because of the plague of chastisement and castigation that the Lord will bring upon it. ¹³ Let the farmers that till the ground mourn, because their seed shall fail to grow*ᵇ* and their trees shall be ruined by blight and hail and by a terrible tempest. ¹⁴ Alas for the world and for those who live in it! ¹⁵ For the sword and misery draw near them, and nation shall rise up to fight against nation, with swords in their hands. ¹⁶ For there shall be unrest among people; growing strong against one another, they shall in their might have no respect for their king or the chief of their leaders. ¹⁷ For a person will desire to go into a city, and shall not be able to do so. ¹⁸ Because of their pride the cities shall be in confusion, the houses shall be destroyed, and people shall be afraid. ¹⁹ People shall have no pity for their neighbors, but shall make an assault upon*ᶜ* their houses with the sword, and plunder their goods, because of hunger for bread and because of great tribulation.

20 See how I am calling together all the kings of the earth to turn to me, says God, from the rising sun and from the south, from the east and from Lebanon; to turn and repay what they have given them. ²¹ Just as they have done to my elect until this day, so I will do, and will repay into their bosom. Thus says the Lord God: ²² My right hand will not spare the sinners, and my sword will not cease from those who shed innocent blood on earth. ²³ And a fire went forth from his wrath, and consumed the foundations of the earth and the sinners, like burnt straw. ²⁴ Alas for those who sin and do not observe my commandments, says the Lord;*ᵈ* ²⁵ I will not spare them. Depart, you faithless children! Do not pollute my sanctuary. ²⁶ For God*ᵉ* knows all who sin against him; therefore he will hand them over to death and slaughter. ²⁷ Already calamities have come upon the whole earth, and you shall remain in them; God*ᵉ* will not deliver you, because you have sinned against him.

ᵃ Other ancient authorities add *and all who believe shall be saved by their faith* *ᵇ* Lat lacks *to grow* *ᶜ* Cn: Lat *shall empty* *ᵈ* Other ancient authorities read *God* *ᵉ* Other ancient authorities read *the Lord*

15:5–19 God Is about to Punish the Wicked

15:5—Punishment will include typical apocalyptic catastrophes *sword, famine, death, destruction*.

15:11 *With a mighty hand and with an uplifted arm*—Typical description for the exodus from Egypt, used to assure Christians they would survive the catastrophes. *Plagues*—Cf. Exod. 7:8–11:10.

15:20–27 God Calls the Kings and Their People to Repent

Repentance is crucial for everyone, disciples as well as the ungodly.

15:25 *Pollute my sanctuary*—A reference to the destruction of the temple by Babylon (in 586 BCE) and Rome (in 70 CE).

A Terrifying Vision of Warfare

28 What a terrifying sight, appearing from the east! [29] The nations of the dragons of Arabia shall come out with many chariots, and from the day that they set out, their hissing shall spread over the earth, so that all who hear them will fear and tremble. [30] Also the Carmonians, raging in wrath, shall go forth like wild boars[a] from the forest, and with great power they shall come and engage them in battle, and with their tusks they shall devastate a portion of the land of the Assyrians with their teeth. [31] And then the dragons,[b] remembering their origin, shall become still stronger; and if they combine in great power and turn to pursue them, [32] then these shall be disorganized and silenced by their power, and shall turn and flee.[c] [33] And from the land of the Assyrians an enemy in ambush shall attack them and destroy one of them, and fear and trembling shall come upon their army, and indecision upon their kings.

Judgment on Babylon

34 See the clouds from the east, and from the north to the south! Their appearance is exceedingly threatening, full of wrath and storm. [35] They shall clash against one another and shall pour out a heavy tempest on the earth, and their own tempest;[d] and there shall be blood from the sword as high as a horse's belly [36] and a man's thigh and a camel's hock. [37] And there shall be fear and great trembling on the earth; those who see that wrath shall be horror-stricken, and they shall be seized with trembling.

[38] After that, heavy storm clouds shall be stirred up from the south, and from the north, and another part from the west. [39] But the winds from the east shall prevail over the cloud that was[e] raised in wrath, and shall dispel it; and the tempest[d] that was to cause destruction by the east wind shall be driven violently toward the south and west. [40] Great and mighty clouds, full of wrath and tempest, shall rise and destroy all the earth and its inhabitants, and shall pour out upon every high and lofty place[f] a terrible tempest, [41] fire and hail and flying swords and floods of water, so that all the fields and all the streams shall be filled with the abundance of those waters. [42] They shall destroy cities and walls, mountains and hills, trees of the forests, and grass of the meadows, and their grain. [43] They shall go on steadily to Babylon and blot it out. [44] They shall come to it and surround it; they shall pour out on it the tempest[d] and all its fury;[g] then the dust and smoke shall reach the sky, and all who are around it shall mourn for it. [45] And those who survive shall serve those who have destroyed it.

Judgment on Asia

46 And you, Asia, who share in the splendor of Babylon and the glory of her person— [47] woe to you, miserable wretch! For you have made yourself like her; you have decked out your daughters for prostitution to please and glory in your lovers, who have always lusted

a Other ancient authorities lack like wild boars   b Cn: Lat dragon   c Other ancient authorities read turn their face to the north   d Meaning of Lat uncertain   e Literally that he   f Or eminent person   g Other ancient authorities add until they destroy it to its foundations

---

15:28–63 War Will Engulf the Nations

15:28–30—May reflect the battles in 259–260 CE between the Persians (called the *Carmonians*) under their ruler Shapur I and the Romans under Emperor Valerian. In the course of the battles Shapur captured a number of cities in the Roman province of Syria, including Antioch. On their way back to Persia, they encountered fighters under Odenathus, leader of the Syrians (*the dragons of Arabia*), who chased them to the outskirts of their capital.

15:31–32—Verses anticipate an unsuccessful counterattack by the Persians.

15:34–45—Perhaps reflects continuing attacks upon the Romans (*Babylon*, v. 43) by Persians (*the east*) and Germans (*the north*). Emperor Valerian persecuted Christians, perhaps explaining the context for these verses.

15:46–63—Future punishment of Syria (*Asia*) for collaborating with Rome (*Babylon*).

after you. ⁴⁸ You have imitated that hateful one in all her deeds and devices.*ᵃ* Therefore God*ᵇ* says, ⁴⁹ I will send evils upon you: widowhood, poverty, famine, sword, and pestilence, bringing ruin to your houses, bringing destruction and death. ⁵⁰ And the glory of your strength shall wither like a flower when the heat shall rise that is sent upon you. ⁵¹ You shall be weakened like a wretched woman who is beaten and wounded, so that you cannot receive your mighty lovers. ⁵² Would I have dealt with you so violently, says the Lord, ⁵³ if you had not killed my chosen people continually, exulting and clapping your hands and talking about their death when you were drunk?

54 Beautify your face! ⁵⁵ The reward of a prostitute is in your lap; therefore you shall receive your recompense. ⁵⁶ As you will do to my chosen people, says the Lord, so God will do to you, and will hand you over to adversities. ⁵⁷ Your children shall die of hunger, and you shall fall by the sword; your cities shall be wiped out, and all your people who are in the open country shall fall by the sword. ⁵⁸ Those who are in the mountains and highlands*ᶜ* shall perish of hunger, and they shall eat their own flesh in hunger for bread and drink their own blood in thirst for water. ⁵⁹ Unhappy above all others, you shall come and suffer fresh miseries. ⁶⁰ As they pass by they shall crush the hateful*ᵈ* city, and shall destroy a part of your land and abolish a portion of your glory, when they return from devastated Babylon. ⁶¹ You shall be broken down by them like stubble,*ᵉ* and they shall be like fire to you. ⁶² They shall devour you and your cities, your land and your mountains; they shall burn with fire all your forests and your fruitful trees. ⁶³ They shall carry your children away captive, plunder your wealth, and mar the glory of your countenance.

Further Denunciations

16 Woe to you, Babylon and Asia! Woe to you, Egypt and Syria! ² Bind on sackcloth and cloth of goats' hair,*ᶠ* and wail for your children, and lament for them; for your destruction is at hand. ³ The sword has been sent upon you, and who is there to turn it back? ⁴ A fire has been sent upon you, and who is there to quench it? ⁵ Calamities have been sent upon you, and who is there to drive them away? ⁶ Can one drive off a hungry lion in the forest, or quench a fire in the stubble once it has started to burn?*ᵍ* ⁷ Can one turn back an arrow shot by a strong archer? ⁸ The Lord God sends calamities, and who will drive them away? ⁹ Fire will go forth from his wrath, and who is there to quench it? ¹⁰ He will flash lightning, and who will not be afraid? He will thunder, and who will not be terrified? ¹¹ The Lord will threaten, and who will not be utterly shattered at his presence? ¹² The earth and its foundations quake, the sea is churned up from the depths, and its waves and the fish with them shall be troubled at the presence of the Lord and the glory of his power. ¹³ For his right hand that bends the bow is strong, and his arrows that he shoots are sharp and when they are shot to the ends of the world will not miss once. ¹⁴ Calamities

---

ᵃ Other ancient authorities read *devices, and you have followed after that one about to gratify her magnates and leaders so that you may be made proud and be pleased by her fornications*   *ᵇ* Other ancient authorities read *the Lord*   *ᶜ* Gk: Lat omits *and highlands*   *ᵈ* Another reading is *idle* or *unprofitable*   *ᵉ* Other ancient authorities read *like dry straw*   *ᶠ* Other ancient authorities lack *cloth of goats' hair*   *ᵍ* Other ancient authorities read *fire when dry straw has been set on fire*

16:1–34 The War Will Be the Punishment of God

Scriptures sometimes portray warfare as the form God's punishment takes, but nations often are given to excess and must themselves be punished (cf. Isa. 10:5–19). Ultimately punishment belongs to God, who will punish with justice tempered by mercy. Disciples of Jesus are called to be peacemakers (Matt. 5:9).

16:1—*Babylon, Egypt*: Rome. *Asia, Syria*: Syria.

16:8—God sends the calamities; they are divine punishment for sinful actions, probably against Christians.

are sent forth and shall not return until they come over the earth. ¹⁵ The fire is kindled, and shall not be put out until it consumes the foundations of the earth. ¹⁶ Just as an arrow shot by a mighty archer does not return, so the calamities that are sent upon the earth shall not return. ¹⁷ Alas for me! Alas for me! Who will deliver me in those days?

The Horror of the Last Days

18 The beginning of sorrows, when there shall be much lamentation; the beginning of famine, when many shall perish; the beginning of wars, when the powers shall be terrified; the beginning of calamities, when all shall tremble. What shall they do, when the calamities come? ¹⁹ Famine and plague, tribulation and anguish are sent as scourges for the correction of humankind. ²⁰ Yet for all this they will not turn from their iniquities, or ever be mindful of the scourges. ²¹ Indeed, provisions will be so cheap upon earth that people will imagine that peace is assured for them, and then calamities shall spring up on the earth—the sword, famine, and great confusion. ²² For many of those who live on the earth shall perish by famine; and those who survive the famine shall die by the sword. ²³ And the dead shall be thrown out like dung, and there shall be no one to console them; for the earth shall be left desolate, and its cities shall be demolished. ²⁴ No one shall be left to cultivate the earth or to sow it. ²⁵ The trees shall bear fruit, but who will gather it? ²⁶ The grapes shall ripen, but who will tread them? For in all places there shall be great solitude; ²⁷ a person will long to see another human being, or even to hear a human voice. ²⁸ For ten shall be left out of a city; and two, out of the field, those who have hidden themselves

in thick groves and clefts in the rocks. ²⁹ Just as in an olive orchard three or four olives may be left on every tree, ³⁰ or just as, when a vineyard is gathered, some clusters may be left*ᵃ* by those who search carefully through the vineyard, ³¹ so in those days three or four shall be left by those who search their houses with the sword. ³² The earth shall be left desolate, and its fields shall be plowed up,*ᵇ* and its roads and all its paths shall bring forth thorns, because no sheep will go along them. ³³ Virgins shall mourn because they have no bridegrooms; women shall mourn because they have no husbands; their daughters shall mourn, because they have no help. ³⁴ Their bridegrooms shall be killed in war, and their husbands shall perish of famine.

God's People Must Prepare for the End

35 Listen now to these things, and understand them, you who are servants of the Lord. ³⁶ This is the word of the Lord; receive it and do not disbelieve what the Lord says.*ᶜ* ³⁷ The calamities draw near, and are not delayed. ³⁸ Just as a pregnant woman, in the ninth month when the time of her delivery draws near, has great pains around her womb for two or three hours beforehand, but when the child comes forth from the womb, there will not be a moment's delay, ³⁹ so the calamities will not delay in coming upon the earth, and the world will groan, and pains will seize it on every side.

40 Hear my words, O my people; prepare for battle, and in the midst of the calamities be like strangers on the earth. ⁴¹ Let the one who sells be like one who will flee; let the one who buys be like one who will lose; ⁴² let the one who does

---

ᵃ Other ancient authorities read *a cluster may remain exposed*   *ᵇ* Other ancient authorities read *be for briers*   *ᶜ* Cn: Lat *do not believe the gods of whom the Lord speaks*

16:35–50 The Righteous Should Remain Faithful until the End
The warfare ahead will affect them, but they will survive. This is the abiding message of 6 Ezra for disciples today.

16:40—It is not clear whether the author wants Christians to engage in the warfare. In any case, they are to prepare for the worst.

business be like one who will not make a profit; and let the one who builds a house be like one who will not live in it; ⁴³ let the one who sows be like one who will not reap; so also the one who prunes the vines, like one who will not gather the grapes; ⁴⁴ those who marry, like those who will have no children; and those who do not marry, like those who are widowed. ⁴⁵ Because of this, those who labor, labor in vain; ⁴⁶ for strangers shall gather their fruits, and plunder their goods, overthrow their houses, and take their children captive; for in captivity and famine they will produce their children.ᵃ ⁴⁷ Those who conduct business, do so only to have it plundered; the more they adorn their cities, their houses and possessions, and their persons, ⁴⁸ the more angry I will be with them for their sins, says the Lord. ⁴⁹ Just as a respectable and virtuous woman abhors a prostitute, ⁵⁰ so righteousness shall abhor iniquity, when she decks herself out, and shall accuse her to her face when he comes who will defend the one who searches out every sin on earth.

The Power and Wisdom of God

⁵¹ Therefore do not be like her or her works. ⁵² For in a very short time iniquity will be removed from the earth, and righteousness will reign over us. ⁵³ Sinners must not say that they have not sinned;ᵇ for Godᶜ will burn coals of fire on the head of everyone who says, "I have not sinned before God and his glory." ⁵⁴ The Lordᵈ certainly knows everything that people do; he knows their imaginations and their thoughts and their hearts. ⁵⁵ He said, "Let the earth be made," and it was made, and "Let the heaven be made," and it was made. ⁵⁶ At his word the stars were fixed in their places, and he knows the num-

ber of the stars. ⁵⁷ He searches the abyss and its treasures; he has measured the sea and its contents; ⁵⁸ he has confined the sea in the midst of the waters;ᵉ and by his word he has suspended the earth over the water. ⁵⁹ He has spread out the heaven like a dome and made it secure upon the waters; ⁶⁰ he has put springs of water in the desert, and pools on the tops of the mountains, so as to send rivers from the heights to water the earth. ⁶¹ He formed human beings and put a heart in the midst of each body, and gave each person breath and life and understanding ⁶² and the spiritᶠ of Almighty God,ᵍ who surely made all things and searches out hidden things in hidden places. ⁶³ He knows your imaginations and what you think in your hearts! Woe to those who sin and want to hide their sins! ⁶⁴ The Lord will strictly examine all their works, and will make a public spectacle of all of you. ⁶⁵ You shall be put to shame when your sins come out before others, and your own iniquities shall stand as your accusers on that day. ⁶⁶ What will you do? Or how will you hide your sins before the Lord and his glory? ⁶⁷ Indeed, Godʰ is the judge; fear him! Cease from your sins, and forget your iniquities, never to commit them again; so Godʰ will lead you forth and deliver you from all tribulation.

Impending Persecution of God's People

⁶⁸ The burning wrath of a great multitude is kindled over you; they shall drag some of you away and force you to eat what was sacrificed to idols. ⁶⁹ And those

---

ᵃ Other ancient authorities read *therefore those who are married may know that they will produce children for captivity and famine* ᵇ Other ancient authorities add *or the unjust done injustice* ᶜ Lat *for he* ᵈ Other ancient authorities read *Lord God* ᵉ Other ancient authorities read *confined the world between the waters and the waters* ᶠ Or *breath* ᵍ Other ancient authorities read *of the Lord Almighty* ʰ Other ancient authorities read *the Lord*

16:51–67 No One Can Hide from God
Hence, justice will ultimately prevail.

16:68–78 God's Elect Will Survive the Impending War
Hence, the readers should not fear. The book

ends on a word of encouragement: God is still in charge in this world, all appearances to the contrary notwithstanding. Disciples today need to hear that word too.

who consent to eat shall be held in derision and contempt, and shall be trampled under foot. 70 For in many places*a* and in neighboring cities there shall be a great uprising against those who fear the Lord. 71 They shall*b* be like maniacs, sparing no one, but plundering and destroying those who continue to fear the Lord.*c* 72 For they shall destroy and plunder their goods, and drive them out of house and home. 73 Then the tested quality of my elect shall be manifest, like gold that is tested by fire.

Promise of Divine Deliverance

74 Listen, my elect ones, says the Lord; the days of tribulation are at hand, but I will deliver you from them. 75 Do not fear or doubt, for God*d* is your guide. 76 You who keep my commandments and precepts, says the Lord God, must not let your sins weigh you down, or your iniquities prevail over you. 77 Woe to those who are choked by their sins and overwhelmed by their iniquities! They are like a field choked with underbrush and its path*e* overwhelmed with thorns, so that no one can pass through. 78 It is shut off and given up to be consumed by fire.

a Meaning of Lat uncertain *b* Other ancient authorities read *For people, because of their misfortunes, shall* *c* Other ancient authorities read *fear God* *d* Other ancient authorities read *the Lord* *e* Other ancient authorities read *seed*

The Book of
4 MACCABEES

D rawing upon 2 Maccabees 3–7 as its source, 4 Maccabees condenses to a minimum the history leading up to the Maccabean revolt and expands in gory, graphic detail the stories of the martyrs. Like 2 Maccabees, 4 Maccabees insists that martyrdom, not military might, defeats the Seleucid king. For more information about the Maccabean revolt, see the introduction to 1 Maccabees.

Fourth Maccabees and parts of the New Testament share the belief that the death of martyrs can also atone for sin. The martyr Eleazar declares: "Be merciful to your people, and let our punishment suffice for them" (6:28). The author argues that the martyrs have become "a ransom for the sin of our nation" and calls the blood of the devout "an atoning sacrifice" (17:21–22). Some early Christians use the same language to speak of Jesus' death, for example, Romans 3:25; 5:10; Matthew 20:28; Mark 10:45; 1 Corinthians 15:3. Bishop Ignatius of Antioch, who was martyred in 110 CE, uses ideas and terminology found in 4 Maccabees to speak of his own sacrificial death, and the *Martyrdom of Polycarp* (mid-second century CE) shows many parallels to the work; Origen and John Chrysostom also seem to know 4 Maccabees. Fourth Maccabees raises the question whether we mean what we say about our faith and are willing to "fight the sacred and noble battle for religion" (9:24).

It has been suggested that 4 Maccabees was composed as either a synagogue sermon, a funeral oration (encomium, eulogy), a commemorative address at the anniversary of martyrs' deaths, or as a discourse at the festival of Hanukkah (1 Macc. 4:36–39). Written in ornate Greek by an unknown author between 124 BCE and 150 CE (there is little consensus about the exact date), 4 Maccabees was perhaps composed in Antioch, where Christians celebrated a feast of the Maccabean martyrs, or Alexandria. Fourth Maccabees is found only as an appendix to some manuscripts in the Septuagint; it is not in the Vulgate, and therefore not in the Apocrypha.

Fourth Maccabees is divided into two parts: (1) 1:1–3:18—a philosophical discussion (diatribe) of the author's thesis that "devout reason is sovereign over the emotions," and (2) 3:19–18:24—stories about Eleazar, seven sons, and their mother, whose martyrdom proves this thesis. The two parts are tied together by 3:19 (see also 1:7–8). Part two revolves around the decree of Antiochus Epiphanes that the Jews must eat pork and food sacrificed to idols (5:2); this decree forces the confrontation between the martyrs and the king and results in their hideous tortures, which give them "an opportunity to show our endurance for the law" (11:12). The martyrs are presented as Jewish philosophers explaining their religious and political motivations in their extended dialogues with the king and his Greek philosophy.

While 2 Maccabees promotes the idea of bodily resurrection, 4 Maccabees embraces Greek (Platonic) ideas about the immortality of the soul (14:5; 16:13); the prize for which the martyrs contend is "immortality in endless life" (17:12). This difference may reflect a split between the lower classes, who felt disenfranchised by

Greco-Roman rule and clung to hope of bodily resurrection, and the upper classes, who embraced Greek culture and ideas like immortality and combined those ideas with Judaism. Similarly, differing relationships of Christians today to the dominant culture shape different beliefs about life after death.

Though written much later than the persecutions of Antiochus Epiphanes, 4 Maccabees aimed to persuade its Hellenized Jewish audience, by means of epideictic (demonstrative) Greek oratory, that a life lived in faithfulness to Torah (Jewish "instruction" or "guidance") is praiseworthy and honorable and should be imitated. Epideictic rhetoric affirms Jewish cultural values amid the pressures of the Hellenistic world and asks for commitment to those values. Such affirmation can inspire Christians struggling with their identity in the secular world today.

—**Denise Dombkowski Hopkins**

The Author's Definition of His Task

1 The subject that I am about to discuss is most philosophical, that is, whether devout reason is sovereign over the emotions. So it is right for me to advise you to pay earnest attention to philosophy. ² For the subject is essential to everyone who is seeking knowledge, and in addition it includes the praise of the highest virtue—I mean, of course, rational judgment. ³ If, then, it is evident that reason rules over those emotions that hinder self-control, namely, gluttony and lust, ⁴ it is also clear that it masters the emotions that hinder one from justice, such as malice, and those that stand in the way of courage, namely anger, fear, and pain. ⁵ Some might perhaps ask, "If reason rules the emotions, why is it not sovereign over forgetfulness and ignorance?" Their attempt at argument is ridiculous!ᵃ ⁶ For reason does not rule its own emotions, but those that are opposed to justice, courage, and self-control;ᵇ and it is not for the purpose of destroying them, but so that one may not give way to them.

⁷ I could prove to you from many and various examples that reasonᶜ is dominant over the emotions, ⁸ but I can dem-

onstrate it best from the noble bravery of those who died for the sake of virtue, Eleazar and the seven brothers and their mother. ⁹ All of these, by despising sufferings that bring death, demonstrated that reason controls the emotions. ¹⁰ On this anniversaryᵈ it is fitting for me to praise for their virtues those who, with their mother, died for the sake of nobility and goodness, but I would also call them blessed for the honor in which they are held. ¹¹ All people, even their torturers, marveled at their courage and endurance, and they became the cause of the downfall of tyranny over their nation. By their endurance they conquered the tyrant, and thus their native land was purified through them. ¹² I shall shortly have an opportunity to speak of this; but, as my custom is, I shall begin by stating my main principle, and then I shall turn to their story, giving glory to the all-wise God.

The Supremacy of Reason

13 Our inquiry, accordingly, is whether reason is sovereign over the emotions.

ᵃ Or *They are attempting to make my argument ridiculous!* ᵇ Other ancient authorities add *and rational judgment* ᶜ Other ancient authorities read *devout reason* ᵈ Gk *At this time*

1:1–3:18 Philosophical Discussion of Reason's Sovereignty over the Emotions

The author sets forth his thesis and defines his terms. Reason is wisdom that is acquired through education in the law (Torah); cf. Sirach in the Apocrypha (1:26; 19:20). This thesis that reason

trumps emotions plays out in American culture in terms of gender when women are stereotyped as weak and emotional and men as strong and rational.

1:8–9, 11–12—The martyrs offer the best demonstration of this thesis.

14 We shall decide just what reason is and what emotion is, how many kinds of emotions there are, and whether reason rules over all these. 15 Now reason is the mind that with sound logic prefers the life of wisdom. 16 Wisdom, next, is the knowledge of divine and human matters and the causes of these. 17 This, in turn, is education in the law, by which we learn divine matters reverently and human affairs to our advantage. 18 Now the kinds of wisdom are rational judgment, justice, courage, and self-control. 19 Rational judgment is supreme over all of these, since by means of it reason rules over the emotions. 20 The two most comprehensive types*a* of the emotions are pleasure and pain; and each of these is by nature concerned with both body and soul. 21 The emotions of both pleasure and pain have many consequences. 22 Thus desire precedes pleasure and delight follows it. 23 Fear precedes pain and sorrow comes after. 24 Anger, as a person will see by reflecting on this experience, is an emotion embracing pleasure and pain. 25 In pleasure there exists even a malevolent tendency, which is the most complex of all the emotions. 26 In the soul it is boastfulness, covetousness, thirst for honor, rivalry, and malice; 27 in the body, indiscriminate eating, gluttony, and solitary gormandizing.

28 Just as pleasure and pain are two plants growing from the body and the soul, so there are many offshoots of these plants,*b* 29 each of which the master cultivator, reason, weeds and prunes and ties up and waters and thoroughly irrigates, and so tames the jungle of habits and emotions. 30 For reason is the guide of the virtues, but over the emotions it is sovereign.

Observe now, first of all, that rational judgment is sovereign over the emotions by virtue of the restraining power of self-control. 31 Self-control, then, is dominance over the desires. 32 Some desires are mental, others are physical, and reason obviously rules over both. 33 Otherwise, how is it that when we are attracted to forbidden foods we abstain from the pleasure to be had from them? Is it not because reason is able to rule over appetites? I for one think so. 34 Therefore when we crave seafood and fowl and animals and all sorts of foods that are forbidden to us by the law, we abstain because of domination by reason. 35 For the emotions of the appetites are restrained, checked by the temperate mind, and all the impulses of the body are bridled by reason.

Compatibility of the Law with Reason

2 And why is it amazing that the desires of the mind for the enjoyment of beauty are rendered powerless? 2 It is for this reason, certainly, that the

a Or sources *b* Other ancient authorities read *these emotions*

1:16—This definition of wisdom was commonly shared in the Greco-Roman world.

1:18—The four kinds of wisdom are the four cardinal virtues of the Greco-Roman world, embraced by the Stoics, Philo, and Wis. (8:7). Contemporary society seems to reject these virtues in favor of self-gratification, hype, and excess.

1:26–27—A catalogue of vices, common in Greco-Roman literature. We scarcely speak of vices in contemporary culture because everyone is too busy doing their own thing. Clearly articulated norms of behavior are difficult to impose upon our pluralistic society.

1:30–35—Reason masters the emotions by means of self-control. The law checks cravings for forbidden food. Dietary laws were at the center of the struggle for Jewish identity in Greek culture. With the erosion of the Sabbath and the trivialization of religious commitment by law and politics, it is difficult to point to visible marks of Christian identity in our secular culture today.

2:1–3:18—Reason is compatible with the law, as the biblical examples of Joseph, Moses, and David show.

2:2–6—*Joseph* and Potiphar's wife, see Gen. 39:7–12. Joseph obeys the Torah prohibition against coveting (Exod. 20:17) by rejecting Potiphar's wife and thus achieves the virtue of temperance (self-control). In our contemporary society saturated with excess, self-control seems out of place.

temperate Joseph is praised, because by mental effort[a] he overcame sexual desire. [3] For when he was young and in his prime for intercourse, by his reason he nullified the frenzy[b] of the passions. [4] Not only is reason proved to rule over the frenzied urge of sexual desire, but also over every desire.[c] [5] Thus the law says, "You shall not covet your neighbor's wife or anything that is your neighbor's." [6] In fact, since the law has told us not to covet, I could prove to you all the more that reason is able to control desires.

Just so it is with the emotions that hinder one from justice. [7] Otherwise how could it be that someone who is habitually a solitary gormandizer, a glutton, or even a drunkard can learn a better way, unless reason is clearly lord of the emotions? [8] Thus, as soon as one adopts a way of life in accordance with the law, even though a lover of money, one is forced to act contrary to natural ways and to lend without interest to the needy and to cancel the debt when the seventh year arrives. [9] If one is greedy, one is ruled by the law through reason so that one neither gleans the harvest nor gathers the last grapes from the vineyard.

In all other matters we can recognize that reason rules the emotions. [10] For the law prevails even over affection for parents, so that virtue is not abandoned for their sakes. [11] It is superior to love for one's wife, so that one rebukes her when she breaks the law. [12] It takes precedence over love for children, so that one punishes them for misdeeds. [13] It is sovereign over the relationship of friends, so that one rebukes friends when they act wickedly.

[14] Do not consider it paradoxical when reason, through the law, can prevail even over enmity. The fruit trees of the enemy are not cut down, but one preserves the property of enemies from marauders and helps raise up what has fallen.[d]

15 It is evident that reason rules even[e] the more violent emotions: lust for power, vainglory, boasting, arrogance, and malice. [16] For the temperate mind repels all these malicious emotions, just as it repels anger—for it is sovereign over even this. [17] When Moses was angry with Dathan and Abiram, he did nothing against them in anger, but controlled his anger by reason. [18] For, as I have said, the temperate mind is able to get the better of the emotions, to correct some, and to render others powerless. [19] Why else did Jacob, our most wise father, censure the households of Simeon and Levi for their irrational slaughter of the entire tribe of the Shechemites, saying, "Cursed be their anger"? [20] For if reason could not control anger, he would not have spoken thus. [21] Now when God fashioned human beings, he planted in them emotions and inclinations, [22] but at the same time he enthroned the mind among the senses as a sacred governor over them all. [23] To the mind he gave the law; and one who lives subject to this will rule a kingdom that is temperate, just, good, and courageous.

24 How is it then, one might say, that if reason is master of the emotions, it does not control forgetfulness and ignorance? [1] But this argument is entirely ridiculous; for it is evident

3

[a] Other ancient authorities add *in reasoning*   [b] Or *gadfly*   [c] Or *all covetousness*   [d] Or *the beasts that have fallen*   [e] Other ancient authorities read *through*

2:8—Lending *without interest*, see Exod. 22:25; Lev. 25:35–37; Deut. 23:19–20.

2:17—*Dathan and Abiram*, see Num. 16:12–15, 23–35.

2:19—The rape of Dinah, see Gen. 34.

2:21–22; 3:5—Reason does not eliminate the passions but keeps them in check, since God created human beings with good and evil emotions, a theme in rabbinic literature.

2:23—Being a good Jew, obedient to Torah, makes virtue possible; cf. 1:7–8. Obedience is the equivalent of being "sovereign over the emotions," which is respected by Jew and Greek alike. Our society seems conflicted over the idea of self-control. On the one hand, we admire the tough guy who keeps a stiff upper lip; on the other hand, reality television shows encourage us to be voyeurs of emotional turmoil.

that reason rules not over its own emotions, but over those of the body. [2] No one of us[a] can eradicate that kind of desire, but reason can provide a way for us not to be enslaved by desire. [3] No one of us can eradicate anger from the mind, but reason can help to deal with anger. [4] No one of us can eradicate malice, but reason can fight at our side so that we are not overcome by malice. [5] For reason does not uproot the emotions but is their antagonist.

King David's Thirst

[6] Now this can be explained more clearly by the story of King David's thirst. [7] David had been attacking the Philistines all day long, and together with the soldiers of his nation had killed many of them. [8] Then when evening fell, he[b] came, sweating and quite exhausted, to the royal tent, around which the whole army of our ancestors had encamped. [9] Now all the rest were at supper, [10] but the king was extremely thirsty, and though springs were plentiful there, he could not satisfy his thirst from them. [11] But a certain irrational desire for the water in the enemy's territory tormented and inflamed him, undid and consumed him. [12] When his guards complained bitterly because of the king's craving, two staunch young soldiers, respecting[c] the king's desire, armed themselves fully, and taking a pitcher climbed over the enemy's ramparts. [13] Eluding the sentinels at the gates, they went searching throughout the enemy camp [14] and found the spring, and from it boldly brought the king a drink. [15] But David,[d] though he was burning with thirst, considered it an altogether fearful danger to his soul to drink what was regarded as equivalent to blood. [16] Therefore, opposing reason to desire, he poured out the drink as an offering to God. [17] For the temperate mind can conquer the drives of the emotions and quench the flames of frenzied desires; [18] it can overthrow bodily agonies even when they are extreme, and by nobility of reason spurn all domination by the emotions.

An Attempt on the Temple Treasury

[19] The present occasion now invites us to a narrative demonstration of temperate reason.

[20] At a time when our ancestors were enjoying profound peace because of their observance of the law and were prospering, so that even Seleucus Nicanor, king of Asia, had both appropriated money to them for the temple service and recognized their commonwealth— [21] just at that time certain persons attempted a revolution against the public harmony and caused many and various disasters.

4 Now there was a certain Simon, a political opponent of the noble and good man, Onias, who then held the high priesthood for life. When despite all manner of slander he was unable to injure Onias in the eyes of the nation, he fled the country with the purpose of betraying it. [2] So he came to Apollonius, governor of Syria, Phoenicia, and Cilicia, and said, [3] "I have come here because I am loyal to the king's government, to

---

[a] Gk you   [b] Other ancient authorities read *he hurried and*   [c] Or *embarrassed because of*   [d] Gk *he*

3:19–18:23 The Martyrs as Proof of the Author's Thesis

3:19–4:26 Simon, Onias, and Jason

3:19—The transitional link between parts one and two of the book.

3:20–4:26—The abbreviated historical context of the martyrs, based upon 2 Macc. 3:1–6:17. See the introduction to 1 Maccabees for a fuller account.

3:20—Peace and prosperity result from observing the law (*torah*, or instruction), a Deuteronomistic understanding of covenant.

3:21–4:14—Simon, the captain of the Jerusalem temple (see 2 Macc. 3:4), disturbs the peace by seeking favor from Seleucid officials. Onias III was the legitimate high priest.

report that in the Jerusalem treasuries there are deposited tens of thousands in private funds, which are not the property of the temple but belong to King Seleucus." ⁴ When Apollonius learned the details of these things, he praised Simon for his service to the king and went up to Seleucus to inform him of the rich treasure. ⁵ On receiving authority to deal with this matter, he proceeded quickly to our country accompanied by the accursed Simon and a very strong military force. ⁶ He said that he had come with the king's authority to seize the private funds in the treasury. ⁷ The people indignantly protested his words, considering it outrageous that those who had committed deposits to the sacred treasury should be deprived of them, and did all that they could to prevent it. ⁸ But, uttering threats, Apollonius went on to the temple. ⁹ While the priests together with women and children were imploring God in the temple to shield the holy place that was being treated so contemptuously, ¹⁰ and while Apollonius was going up with his armed forces to seize the money, angels on horseback with lightning flashing from their weapons appeared from heaven, instilling in them great fear and trembling. ¹¹ Then Apollonius fell down half dead in the temple area that was open to all, stretched out his hands toward heaven, and with tears begged the Hebrews to pray for him and propitiate the wrath of the heavenly army. ¹² For he said that he had committed a sin deserving of death, and that if he were spared he would praise the blessedness of the holy place before all people. ¹³ Moved by these words, the high priest Onias, although otherwise he had scruples about doing so, prayed for him so that King Seleucus would not suppose that Apollonius had been overcome by human treachery and not by divine justice. ¹⁴ So Apollonius,ᵃ having been saved beyond all expectations, went away to report to the king what had happened to him.

Antiochus's Persecution of the Jews

15 When King Seleucus died, his son Antiochus Epiphanes succeeded to the throne, an arrogant and terrible man, ¹⁶ who removed Onias from the priesthood and appointed Onias'sᵇ brother Jason as high priest. ¹⁷ Jasonᶜ agreed that if the office were conferred on him he would pay the king three thousand six hundred sixty talents annually. ¹⁸ So the king appointed him high priest and ruler of the nation. ¹⁹ Jasonᶜ changed the nation's way of life and altered its form of government in complete violation of the law, ²⁰ so that not only was a gymnasium constructed at the very citadelᵈ of our native land, but also the temple service was abolished. ²¹ The divine justice was angered by these acts and caused Antiochus himself to make war on them. ²² For when he was warring against Ptolemy in Egypt, he heard that a rumor of his death had spread and that the people of Jerusalem had rejoiced greatly. He speedily marched against them, ²³ and after he had plundered them he issued a decree that if any of them were found observing the ancestral law they should die. ²⁴ When, by means of his decrees, he had not been able in any way to put an

---

ᵃ Gk he　ᵇ Gk his　ᶜ Gk He　ᵈ Or high place

4:4—The temple served as a national treasury for private and public funds, as was common in the ancient world.

4:15–26—Jason also disturbs the peace by buying the high priesthood from the new king, Antiochus IV Epiphanes, and building a gymnasium (center for the Greek way of life) in Jerusalem. Judaism is outlawed and Antiochus issues a decree forcing people to eat defiling foods. The decree raises the twin issues of minority rights in a dominant culture and assimilation as an erosion of identity. Cf. 1 Macc. 1:11–15, 54–61; 2 Macc. 4:7–17; 6:1–11; 3 Macc. 3:31–33. These issues confront Christians continually today in our pluralistic society.

4:21—The Deuteronomistic understanding of covenant sees Jason's Hellenization as cause for divine anger and punishment, i.e., Antiochus's oppression of the Jews.

end to the people's observance of the law, but saw that all his threats and punishments were being disregarded [25]—even to the extent that women, because they had circumcised their sons, were thrown headlong from heights along with their infants, though they had known beforehand that they would suffer this— [26] when, I say, his decrees were despised by the people, he himself tried through torture to compel everyone in the nation to eat defiling foods and to renounce Judaism.

Antiochus's Encounter with Eleazar

5 The tyrant Antiochus, sitting in state with his counselors on a certain high place, and with his armed soldiers standing around him, [2] ordered the guards to seize each and every Hebrew and to compel them to eat pork and food sacrificed to idols. [3] If any were not willing to eat defiling food, they were to be broken on the wheel and killed. [4] When many persons had been rounded up, one man, Eleazar by name, leader of the flock, was brought[a] before the king. He was a man of priestly family, learned in the law, advanced in age, and known to many in the tyrant's court because of his philosophy.[b]

5 When Antiochus saw him he said, [6] "Before I begin to torture you, old man, I would advise you to save yourself by eating pork, [7] for I respect your age and your gray hairs. Although you have had them for so long a time, it does not seem to me that you are a philosopher when you observe the religion of the Jews. [8] When nature has granted it to us, why should you abhor eating the very excellent meat of this animal? [9] It is senseless not to enjoy delicious things that are not shameful, and wrong to spurn the gifts of nature. [10] It seems to me that you will do something even more senseless if, by holding a vain opinion concerning the truth, you continue to despise me to your own hurt. [11] Will you not awaken from your foolish philosophy, dispel your futile reasonings, adopt a mind appropriate to your years, philosophize according to the truth of what is beneficial, [12] and have compassion on your old age by honoring my humane advice? [13] For consider this: if there is some power watching over this religion of yours, it will excuse you from any transgression that arises out of compulsion."

14 When the tyrant urged him in this fashion to eat meat unlawfully, Eleazar asked to have a word. [15] When he had received permission to speak, he began to address the people as follows: [16] "We, O Antiochus, who have been persuaded to govern our lives by the divine law,

a Or was the first of the flock to be brought b Other ancient authorities read his advanced age

---

4:26—Since dietary laws are an important mark of Jewish identity, breaking them means renouncing Judaism. This reflects the Deuteronomistic understanding of covenant; keeping the dietary laws means keeping covenant. The marks of Christian covenant are not, perhaps, as readily apparent in today's culture.

5:1–38 Antiochus and Eleazar

This is the beginning of the story of the martyrdom of Eleazar, based upon 2 Macc. 6:18–31 but greatly expanded. Eleazar's confrontation with Antiochus mirrors the confrontation between Judaism and Greek culture that the audience faced daily. Christians today confront secular culture in less overt ways, often unconsciously, which may be more damaging to Christian identity in the long run.

5:1 Tyrant—Emphasizes Antiochus's unlimited and abusive power. Though the author thinks that Antiochus deserves this negative assessment, we must be careful today to recognize how we use similar terms to stereotype our cultural and political opponents undeservedly to protect our own interests.

5:5–13—Antiochus challenges Eleazar's philosophy, using Stoic arguments such as "living according to nature," which means following reason rather than the passions.

5:14–38—Eleazar replies to Antiochus by arguing for the superiority of Jewish philosophy, which teaches the four cardinal virtues. With a Jewish twist, piety (reverence for God) replaces rational judgment as the fourth virtue. Torah obedience means living according to nature. Eleazar models a response of resistance to assimilation both for the audience and for the contemporary reader.

think that there is no compulsion more powerful than our obedience to the law. [17] Therefore we consider that we should not transgress it in any respect. [18] Even if, as you suppose, our law were not truly divine and we had wrongly held it to be divine, not even so would it be right for us to invalidate our reputation for piety. [19] Therefore do not suppose that it would be a petty sin if we were to eat defiling food; [20] to transgress the law in matters either small or great is of equal seriousness, [21] for in either case the law is equally despised. [22] You scoff at our philosophy as though living by it were irrational, [23] but it teaches us self-control, so that we master all pleasures and desires, and it also trains us in courage, so that we endure any suffering willingly; [24] it instructs us in justice, so that in all our dealings we act impartially,[a] and it teaches us piety, so that with proper reverence we worship the only living God.

[25] "Therefore we do not eat defiling food; for since we believe that the law was established by God, we know that in the nature of things the Creator of the world in giving us the law has shown sympathy toward us. [26] He has permitted us to eat what will be most suitable for our lives,[b] but he has forbidden us to eat meats that would be contrary to this. [27] It would be tyrannical for you to compel us not only to transgress the law, but also to eat in such a way that you may deride us for eating defiling foods, which are most hateful to us. [28] But you shall have no such occasion to laugh at me, [29] nor will I transgress the sacred oaths of my ancestors concerning the keeping of the law, [30] not even if you gouge out my eyes and burn my entrails. [31] I am not so old and cowardly as not to be young in reason on behalf of piety. [32] Therefore get your torture wheels ready and fan the fire more

vehemently! [33] I do not so pity my old age as to break the ancestral law by my own act. [34] I will not play false to you, O law that trained me, nor will I renounce you, beloved self-control. [35] I will not put you to shame, philosophical reason, nor will I reject you, honored priesthood and knowledge of the law. [36] You, O king,[c] shall not defile the honorable mouth of my old age, nor my long life lived lawfully. [37] My ancestors will receive me as pure, as one who does not fear your violence even to death. [38] You may tyrannize the ungodly, but you shall not dominate my religious principles, either by words or through deeds."

Martyrdom of Eleazar

6 When Eleazar in this manner had made eloquent response to the exhortations of the tyrant, the guards who were standing by dragged him violently to the instruments of torture. [2] First they stripped the old man, though he remained adorned with the gracefulness of his piety. [3] After they had tied his arms on each side they flogged him, [4] while a herald who faced him cried out, "Obey the king's commands!" [5] But the courageous and noble man, like a true Eleazar, was unmoved, as though being tortured in a dream; [6] yet while the old man's eyes were raised to heaven, his flesh was being torn by scourges, his blood flowing, and his sides were being cut to pieces. [7] Although he fell to the ground because his body could not endure the agonies, he kept his reason upright and unswerving. [8] One of the cruel guards rushed at him and began to kick him in the side to make him get up again after he fell. [9] But he bore the pains and scorned the punishment and endured the tortures. [10] Like a noble

[a] Or so that we hold in balance all our habitual inclinations [b] Or souls
[c] Gk lacks O king

5:23—The martyrs repeatedly exhibit courage and self-control; cf. 13:16.
6:1–30 Eleazar's Tortures and Death (cf. 2 Macc. 6:28–29)

6:10—The contrast between the martyrs and their oppressors, between Jewish and Greek virtue, is expressed through athletic imagery. Often in our

athlete the old man, while being beaten, was victorious over his torturers; ¹¹ in fact, with his face bathed in sweat, and gasping heavily for breath, he amazed even his torturers by his courageous spirit.

12 At that point, partly out of pity for his old age, ¹³ partly out of sympathy from their acquaintance with him, partly out of admiration for his endurance, some of the king's retinue came to him and said, ¹⁴ "Eleazar, why are you so irrationally destroying yourself through these evil things? ¹⁵ We will set before you some cooked meat; save yourself by pretending to eat pork."

16 But Eleazar, as though more bitterly tormented by this counsel, cried out: ¹⁷ "Never may we, the children of Abraham,[a] think so basely that out of cowardice we feign a role unbecoming to us! ¹⁸ For it would be irrational if having lived in accordance with truth up to old age and having maintained in accordance with law the reputation of such a life, we should now change our course ¹⁹ and ourselves become a pattern of impiety to the young by setting them an example in the eating of defiling food. ²⁰ It would be shameful if we should survive for a little while and during that time be a laughingstock to all for our cowardice, ²¹ and be despised by the tyrant as unmanly by not contending even to death for our divine law. ²² Therefore, O children of Abraham, die nobly for your religion! ²³ And you, guards of the tyrant, why do you delay?"

24 When they saw that he was so courageous in the face of the afflictions, and that he had not been changed by their compassion, the guards brought him to the fire. ²⁵ There they burned him with maliciously contrived instruments, threw him down, and poured stinking liquids into his nostrils. ²⁶ When he was now burned to his very bones and about to expire, he lifted up his eyes to God and said, ²⁷ "You know, O God, that though I might have saved myself, I am dying in burning torments for the sake of the law. ²⁸ Be merciful to your people, and let our punishment suffice for them. ²⁹ Make my blood their purification, and take my life in exchange for theirs." ³⁰ After he said this, the holy man died nobly in his tortures; even in the tortures of death he resisted, by virtue of reason, for the sake of the law.

31 Admittedly, then, devout reason is sovereign over the emotions. ³² For if the emotions had prevailed over reason, we would have testified to their domination. ³³ But now that reason has conquered the emotions, we properly attribute to it the power to govern. ³⁴ It is right for us to acknowledge the dominance of reason when it masters even external agonies. It would be ridiculous to deny it.[b] ³⁵ I have proved not only that reason has mastered agonies, but also that it masters pleasures and in no respect yields to them.

An Encomium on Eleazar

7 For like a most skillful pilot, the reason of our father Eleazar steered the ship of religion over the sea of the

[a] Or O children of Abraham   [b] Syr: Meaning of Gk uncertain

---

culture, athletic contests promote political tension, for example, the Olympics.

6:11—The martyrs are admired by their captors for their endurance; cf. 1:11; 9:26; 17:17, 23–24.

6:16–23—Eleazar resists giving in because he must set a manly example for the young and because it would be cowardly and shameful to assimilate. He implicitly addresses the audience to do likewise.

6:28–29 *"Let our punishment suffice for them. Make my blood their purification"*—Eleazar

views his death as atonement for the sins of his people. See 17:22.

6:31–35—The author returns to his thesis, the sovereignty of reason over the emotions.

7:1–23 Praise for Eleazar in the Eulogy

Praise for the martyrs makes their choice to die desirable for the audience so that they might imitate that choice. The praise may also shame them, and us, for not being as courageous about our faith. These eulogies challenge us to reevaluate the heroes we worship in the contemporary

emotions, [2] and though buffeted by the stormings of the tyrant and overwhelmed by the mighty waves of tortures, [3] in no way did he turn the rudder of religion until he sailed into the haven of immortal victory. [4] No city besieged with many ingenious war machines has ever held out as did that most holy man. Although his sacred life was consumed by tortures and racks, he conquered the besiegers with the shield of his devout reason. [5] For in setting his mind firm like a jutting cliff, our father Eleazar broke the maddening waves of the emotions. [6] O priest, worthy of the priesthood, you neither defiled your sacred teeth nor profaned your stomach, which had room only for reverence and purity, by eating defiling foods. [7] O man in harmony with the law and philosopher of divine life! [8] Such should be those who are administrators of the law, shielding it with their own blood and noble sweat in sufferings even to death. [9] You, father, strengthened our loyalty to the law through your glorious endurance, and you did not abandon the holiness that you praised, but by your deeds you made your words of divine[a] philosophy credible. [10] O aged man, more powerful than tortures; O elder, fiercer than fire; O supreme king over the passions, Eleazar! [11] For just as our father Aaron, armed with the censer, ran through the multitude of the people and conquered the fiery[b] angel, [12] so the descendant of Aaron, Eleazar, though being consumed by the fire, remained unmoved in his reason. [13] Most amazing, indeed, though he was an old man, his body no longer tense and firm,[c] his muscles flabby, his

sinews feeble, he became young again [14] in spirit through reason; and by reason like that of Isaac he rendered the many-headed rack ineffective. [15] O man of blessed age and of venerable gray hair and of law-abiding life, whom the faithful seal of death has perfected!

16 If, therefore, because of piety an aged man despised tortures even to death, most certainly devout reason is governor of the emotions. [17] Some perhaps might say, "Not all have full command of their emotions, because not all have prudent reason." [18] But as many as attend to religion with a whole heart, these alone are able to control the passions of the flesh, [19] since they believe that they, like our patriarchs Abraham and Isaac and Jacob, do not die to God, but live to God. [20] No contradiction therefore arises when some persons appear to be dominated by their emotions because of the weakness of their reason. [21] What person who lives as a philosopher by the whole rule of philosophy, and trusts in God, [22] and knows that it is blessed to endure any suffering for the sake of virtue, would not be able to overcome the emotions through godliness? [23] For only the wise and courageous are masters of their emotions.

Seven Brothers Defy the Tyrant

8 For this is why even the very young, by following a philosophy in accordance with devout reason, have prevailed over the most painful instruments of torture. [2] For when the tyrant was conspicuously defeated in his first

---

[a] Other ancient authorities lack *divine*   [b] Other ancient authorities lack *fiery*   [c] Gk *the tautness of the body already loosed*

U.S. culture of hype, such as athletes, movie and rock stars, and corporate CEOs.

7:10 *O supreme king over the passions!*—Eleazar is the embodiment of the author's thesis that reason is sovereign over the emotions.

7:11—Aaron prevented a plague; see Num. 16:46–50.

7:19 *They . . . do not die to God, but live to God*—Those who are pious control passions and

live on with God like the patriarchs. Cf. 16:25; Mark 12:26–27; Rom. 6:10, 14:8; Gal. 2:19.

8:1–9:9 Speeches by Antiochus (8:5–11) and the Brothers (9:1–9)

A philosophical debate, expanding 2 Macc. 7:1–2.

8:2—Antiochus may control others but shows little self-control by ordering excessive torture of the martyrs; cf. 9:10–11. Consequently, he is

attempt, being unable to compel an aged man to eat defiling foods, then in violent rage he commanded that others of the Hebrew captives be brought, and that any who ate defiling food would be freed after eating, but if any were to refuse, they would be tortured even more cruelly.

3 When the tyrant had given these orders, seven brothers—handsome, modest, noble, and accomplished in every way—were brought before him along with their aged mother. ⁴ When the tyrant saw them, grouped about their mother as though a chorus, he was pleased with them. And struck by their appearance and nobility, he smiled at them, and summoned them nearer and said, ⁵ "Young men, with favorable feelings I admire each and every one of you, and greatly respect the beauty and the number of such brothers. Not only do I advise you not to display the same madness as that of the old man who has just been tortured, but I also exhort you to yield to me and enjoy my friendship. ⁶ Just as I am able to punish those who disobey my orders, so I can be a benefactor to those who obey me. ⁷ Trust me, then, and you will have positions of authority in my government if you will renounce the ancestral tradition of your national life. ⁸ Enjoy your youth by adopting the Greek way of life and by changing your manner of living. ⁹ But if by disobedience you rouse my anger, you will compel me to destroy each and every one of you with dreadful punishments through tortures. ¹⁰ Therefore take pity on yourselves. Even I, your enemy, have compassion for your youth and handsome appearance. ¹¹ Will you not consider this, that if you disobey, nothing remains for you but to die on the rack?"

12 When he had said these things, he ordered the instruments of torture to be brought forward so as to persuade them out of fear to eat the defiling food. ¹³ When the guards had placed before them wheels and joint-dislocators, rack and hooks[a] and catapults[b] and caldrons, braziers and thumbscrews and iron claws and wedges and bellows, the tyrant resumed speaking: ¹⁴ "Be afraid, young fellows; whatever justice you revere will be merciful to you when you transgress under compulsion."

15 But when they had heard the inducements and saw the dreadful devices, not only were they not afraid, but they also opposed the tyrant with their own philosophy, and by their right reasoning nullified his tyranny. ¹⁶ Let us consider, on the other hand, what arguments might have been used if some of them had been cowardly and unmanly. Would they not have been the following? ¹⁷ "O wretches that we are and so senseless! Since the king has summoned and exhorted us to accept kind treatment if we obey him, ¹⁸ why do we take pleasure in vain resolves and venture upon a disobedience that brings death? ¹⁹ O men and brothers, should we not fear the instruments of torture

---

[a] Meaning of Gk uncertain   [b] Here and elsewhere in 4 Macc an instrument of torture

---

shamed by the virtues of an old man, the seven brothers, and a woman (cf. Judith and the general Holofernes, Jdt. 9:10; 14:18; 16:15–16).

8:3–4—The beauty and skill of the brothers, an ideal in Greek culture, make them candidates for Greek success. Contemporary U.S. culture continues to place a premium on beauty, as the booming plastic surgery industry and television make-over programs illustrate.

8:5–14—This time, Antiochus attempts to persuade not with threats but with promises of his patronage; see *friendship* (v. 5b) and *benefac-*

tor (v. 6), suggesting that Hellenization has its economic and social advantages; see also 12:5. Jewish dietary restrictions kept social interaction to a minimum and made those advantages less attainable. Christian identity today is continually eroded in pursuit of prestige and advancement.

8:16–28—This imaginary speech has the brothers accepting Antiochus's argument, making their lives much easier (v. 26), and underscoring the temptations that their audience faces daily. What temptations do Christians face today from secular culture?

and consider the threats of torments, and give up this vain opinion and this arrogance that threatens to destroy us? [20] Let us take pity on our youth and have compassion on our mother's age; [21] and let us seriously consider that if we disobey we are dead! [22] Also, divine justice will excuse us for fearing the king when we are under compulsion. [23] Why do we banish ourselves from this most pleasant life and deprive ourselves of this delightful world? [24] Let us not struggle against compulsion[a] or take hollow pride in being put to the rack. [25] Not even the law itself would arbitrarily put us to death for fearing the instruments of torture. [26] Why does such contentiousness excite us and such a fatal stubbornness please us, when we can live in peace if we obey the king?"

27 But the youths, though about to be tortured, neither said any of these things nor even seriously considered them. [28] For they were contemptuous of the emotions and sovereign over agonies, [29] so that as soon as the tyrant had ceased counseling them to eat defiling food, all with one voice together, as from one mind, said:

9 "Why do you delay, O tyrant? For we are ready to die rather than transgress our ancestral commandments; [2] we are obviously putting our forebears to shame unless we should practice ready obedience to the law and to Moses[b] our counselor. [3] Tyrant and counselor of lawlessness, in your hatred for us do not pity us more than we pity ourselves.[c] [4] For we consider this pity of yours, which insures our safety through transgression of the law, to be more grievous than death itself. [5] You are trying to terrify us by threatening us with death by torture, as though a short time ago you learned nothing from Eleazar. [6] And if the aged men of the Hebrews because of their religion lived piously[d] while enduring torture, it would be even more fitting that we young men should die despising your coercive tortures, which our aged instructor also overcame. [7] Therefore, tyrant, put us to the test; and if you take our lives because of our religion, do not suppose that you can injure us by torturing us. [8] For we, through this severe suffering and endurance, shall have the prize of virtue and shall be with God, on whose account we suffer; [9] but you, because of your bloodthirstiness toward us, will deservedly undergo from the divine justice eternal torment by fire."

The Torture of the First and Second Brothers

10 When they had said these things, the tyrant was not only indignant, as at those who are disobedient, but also infuriated, as at those who are ungrateful. [11] Then at his command the guards brought forward the eldest, and having torn off his tunic, they bound his hands and arms with thongs on each side. [12] When they had worn themselves out beating him with scourges, without accomplishing anything, they placed him upon the wheel. [13] When the noble youth was stretched out around this, his limbs were dislocated, [14] and with every member disjointed he denounced the tyrant, saying, [15] "Most abominable tyrant, enemy of heavenly justice, savage of mind, you are mangling me in this manner, not because I am a murderer, or as one who acts impiously, but because I

---

[a] Or fate   [b] Other ancient authorities read knowledge   [c] Meaning of Gk uncertain   [d] Other ancient authorities read died

---

8:29–9:9—In the actual speech of the brothers, they absolutely reject giving in, since it would shame their ancestors. The imaginary and actual speeches side by side make clear the choice facing their audience.

9:8–9—Rewards and punishments unfold according to divine retribution.

9:10–12:19 The Martyrdom of the Seven Brothers
An expansion of 2 Macc. 7:1–40. The brothers endure for the sake of the divine law. The tortures are inflicted upon the sons in order, from oldest to youngest; for rhetorical effect, the first and last brothers endure the most elaborate tortures.

protect the divine law." [16] And when the guards said, "Agree to eat so that you may be released from the tortures," [17] he replied, "You abominable lackeys, your wheel is not so powerful as to strangle my reason. Cut my limbs, burn my flesh, and twist my joints; [18] through all these tortures I will convince you that children of the Hebrews alone are invincible where virtue is concerned." [19] While he was saying these things, they spread fire under him, and while fanning the flames[a] they tightened the wheel further. [20] The wheel was completely smeared with blood, and the heap of coals was being quenched by the drippings of gore, and pieces of flesh were falling off the axles of the machine. [21] Although the ligaments joining his bones were already severed, the courageous youth, worthy of Abraham, did not groan, [22] but as though transformed by fire into immortality, he nobly endured the rackings. [23] "Imitate me, brothers," he said. "Do not leave your post in my struggle[b] or renounce our courageous family ties. [24] Fight the sacred and noble battle for religion. Thereby the just Providence of our ancestors may become merciful to our nation and take vengeance on the accursed tyrant." [25] When he had said this, the saintly youth broke the thread of life.

26 While all were marveling at his courageous spirit, the guards brought in the next eldest, and after fitting themselves with iron gauntlets having sharp hooks, they bound him to the torture machine and catapult. [27] Before torturing him, they inquired if he were willing to eat, and they heard his noble decision.[c] [28] These leopard-like beasts tore out his sinews with the iron hands, flayed all his flesh up to his chin, and tore away his scalp. But he steadfastly endured this agony and said, [29] "How sweet is any kind

of death for the religion of our ancestors!" [30] To the tyrant he said, "Do you not think, you most savage tyrant, that you are being tortured more than I, as you see the arrogant design of your tyranny being defeated by our endurance for the sake of religion? [31] I lighten my pain by the joys that come from virtue, [32] but you suffer torture by the threats that come from impiety. You will not escape, you most abominable tyrant, the judgments of the divine wrath."

The Torture of the Third and Fourth Brothers

10 When he too had endured a glorious death, the third was led in, and many repeatedly urged him to save himself by tasting the meat. [2] But he shouted, "Do you not know that the same father begot me as well as those who died, and the same mother bore me, and that I was brought up on the same teachings? [3] I do not renounce the noble kinship that binds me to my brothers."[d] [5] Enraged by the man's boldness, they disjointed his hands and feet with their instruments, dismembering him by prying his limbs from their sockets, [6] and breaking his fingers and arms and legs and elbows. [7] Since they were not able in any way to break his spirit,[e] they abandoned the instruments[f] and scalped him with their fingernails in a Scythian fashion. [8] They immediately brought him to the wheel, and while his vertebrae were being dislocated by this, he saw his own flesh torn all around and drops of blood flowing from his entrails. [9] When he was about to die, he said, [10] "We, most abominable tyrant, are suffering because of our godly training and

---

[a] Meaning of Gk uncertain   [b] Other ancient authorities read *post forever*
[c] Other ancient authorities read *having heard his noble decision, they tore him to shreds*   [d] Other ancient authorities add verse 4, *So if you have any instrument of torture, apply it to my body; for you cannot touch my soul, even if you wish."*   [e] Gk *to strangle him*   [f] Other ancient authorities read *they tore off his skin*

9:23—The sons' encouragement of one another functions as a pep talk for the author's Diaspora Jewish audience; cf. 16:16, 19.

9:24 *"Fight the sacred and noble battle for religion"*—The theme of this section.

10:10–11—One of the main themes of the martyr

virtue, [11] but you, because of your impiety and bloodthirstiness, will undergo unceasing torments."

12 When he too had died in a manner worthy of his brothers, they dragged in the fourth, saying, [13] "As for you, do not give way to the same insanity as your brothers, but obey the king and save yourself." [14] But he said to them, "You do not have a fire hot enough to make me play the coward. [15] No—by the blessed death of my brothers, by the eternal destruction of the tyrant, and by the everlasting life of the pious, I will not renounce our noble family ties. [16] Contrive tortures, tyrant, so that you may learn from them that I am a brother to those who have just now been tortured." [17] When he heard this, the bloodthirsty, murderous, and utterly abominable Antiochus gave orders to cut out his tongue. [18] But he said, "Even if you remove my organ of speech, God hears also those who are mute. [19] See, here is my tongue; cut it off, for in spite of this you will not make our reason speechless. [20] Gladly, for the sake of God, we let our bodily members be mutilated. [21] God will visit you swiftly, for you are cutting out a tongue that has been melodious with divine hymns."

The Torture of the Fifth and Sixth Brothers

11 When he too died, after being cruelly tortured, the fifth leaped up, saying, [2] "I will not refuse, tyrant, to be tortured for the sake of virtue. [3] I have come of my own accord, so that by murdering me you will incur punishment from the heavenly justice for even more crimes. [4] Hater of virtue, hater of humankind, for what act of ours are you destroying us in this way? [5] Is it because[a] we revere the Creator of all things and live according to his virtuous law? [6] But these deeds deserve honors, not tortures."[b] [9] While he was saying these things, the guards bound him and dragged him to the catapult; [10] they tied him to it on his knees, and fitting iron clamps on them, they twisted his back[c] around the wedge on the wheel,[d] so that he was completely curled back like a scorpion, and all his members were disjointed. [11] In this condition, gasping for breath and in anguish of body, [12] he said, "Tyrant, they are splendid favors that you grant us against your will, because through these noble sufferings you give us an opportunity to show our endurance for the law."

13 When he too had died, the sixth, a mere boy, was led in. When the tyrant inquired whether he was willing to eat and be released, he said, [14] "I am younger in age than my brothers, but I am their equal in mind. [15] Since to this end we were born and bred, we ought likewise to die for the same principles. [16] So if you intend to torture me for not eating defiling foods, go on torturing!" [17] When he had said this, they led him to the wheel. [18] He was carefully stretched tight upon it, his back was broken, and he was roasted[e] from underneath. [19] To his back they applied sharp spits that had been heated in the fire, and pierced his ribs so that his entrails were burned

---

[a] Other ancient authorities read *Or does it seem evil to you that* [b] Other authorities add verses 7 and 8, [7] *If you but understood human feelings and had hope of salvation from God—* [8] *but, as it is, you are a stranger to God and persecute those who serve him.* [c] Gk *loins* [d] Meaning of Gk uncertain [e] Other ancient authorities add *by fire*

---

speeches is act/consequence or divine retribution, which dictates a markedly different end for the martyrs and the king; cf. 9:8–9, 31–32; 12:12–14, 17–18. When opponents are viewed as beyond redemption, we assume that there is no hope for them, making reconciliation impossible.

10:20—Suffering for God's sake; cf. the Suffering Servant in Isa. 53:10. When we think theologically about suffering, there is a desire to extract positive value from it. These efforts run the risk of glorifying suffering as intrinsically good and so distracting us from its causes.

11:12—Suffering as opportunity can give hope to those in pain but can also resign us to suffering without working to overcome it.

11:13—The sixth brother is a **mere boy**, an observation that increases our sympathy for the sons.

through. ²⁰ While being tortured he said, "O contest befitting holiness, in which so many of us brothers have been summoned to an arena of sufferings for religion, and in which we have not been defeated! ²¹ For religious knowledge, O tyrant, is invincible. ²² I also, equipped with nobility, will die with my brothers, ²³ and I myself will bring a great avenger upon you, you inventor of tortures and enemy of those who are truly devout. ²⁴ We six boys have paralyzed your tyranny. ²⁵ Since you have not been able to persuade us to change our mind or to force us to eat defiling foods, is not this your downfall? ²⁶ Your fire is cold to us, and the catapults painless, and your violence powerless. ²⁷ For it is not the guards of the tyrant but those of the divine law that are set over us; therefore, unconquered, we hold fast to reason."

The Torture of the Seventh Brother

12 When he too, thrown into the caldron, had died a blessed death, the seventh and youngest of all came forward. ² Even though the tyrant had been vehemently reproached by the brothers, he felt strong compassion for this child when he saw that he was already in fetters. He summoned him to come nearer and tried to persuade him, saying, ³ "You see the result of your brothers' stupidity, for they died in torments because of their disobedience. ⁴ You too, if you do not obey, will be miserably tortured and die before your time, ⁵ but if you yield to persuasion you will be my friend and a leader in the government of the kingdom." ⁶ When he had thus appealed to him, he sent for the boy's mother to show compassion on her who

had been bereaved of so many sons and to influence her to persuade the surviving son to obey and save himself. ⁷ But when his mother had exhorted him in the Hebrew language, as we shall tell a little later, ⁸ he said, "Let me loose, let me speak to the king and to all his friends that are with him." ⁹ Extremely pleased by the boy's declaration, they freed him at once. ¹⁰ Running to the nearest of the braziers, ¹¹ he said, "You profane tyrant, most impious of all the wicked, since you have received good things and also your kingdom from God, were you not ashamed to murder his servants and torture on the wheel those who practice religion? ¹² Because of this, justice has laid up for you intense and eternal fire and tortures, and these throughout all time*a* will never let you go. ¹³ As a man, were you not ashamed, you most savage beast, to cut out the tongues of men who have feelings like yours and are made of the same elements as you, and to maltreat and torture them in this way? ¹⁴ Surely they by dying nobly fulfilled their service to God, but you will wail bitterly for having killed without cause the contestants for virtue." ¹⁵ Then because he too was about to die, he said, ¹⁶ "I do not desert the excellent example*b* of my brothers, ¹⁷ and I call on the God of our ancestors to be merciful to our nation;*c* ¹⁸ but on you he will take vengeance both in this present life and when you are dead." ¹⁹ After he had uttered these imprecations, he flung himself into the braziers and so ended his life.*d*

a Gk throughout the whole age   *b* Other ancient authorities read the witness   *c* Other ancient authorities read my race   *d* Gk and so gave up; other ancient authorities read gave up his spirit or his soul

---

11:20–21—The torture is likened to an athletic contest.

11:24 *"We six boys have paralyzed your tyranny"*—See also 1:11–12; 8:15. Martyrdom, not military strength, defeats the king.

12:13 *You most savage beast*—Again and again, the brothers dehumanize Antiochus; he is a "tyrant" (9:1; 10:10; 11:12) and "bloodthirsty"

(9:9; 10:17). The opponents are irreconcilable opposites, fueled by an emotional rhetoric that leaves no room for middle ground or possible reconciliation. These caricatures challenge the use of dehumanizing language in international relations and social discourse, such as "axis of evil," because they can be roadblocks to peace.

Reason's Sovereignty in the Seven

13 Since, then, the seven brothers despised sufferings even unto death, everyone must concede that devout reason is sovereign over the emotions. [2] For if they had been slaves to their emotions and had eaten defiling food, we would say that they had been conquered by these emotions. [3] But in fact it was not so. Instead, by reason, which is praised before God, they prevailed over their emotions. [4] The supremacy of the mind over these cannot be overlooked, for the brothers[a] mastered both emotions and pains. [5] How then can one fail to confess the sovereignty of right reason over emotion in those who were not turned back by fiery agonies? [6] For just as towers jutting out over harbors hold back the threatening waves and make it calm for those who sail into the inner basin, [7] so the seven-towered right reason of the youths, by fortifying the harbor of religion, conquered the tempest of the emotions. [8] For they constituted a holy chorus of religion and encouraged one another, saying, [9] "Brothers, let us die like brothers for the sake of the law; let us imitate the three youths in Assyria who despised the same ordeal of the furnace. [10] Let us not be cowardly in the demonstration of our piety." [11] While one said, "Courage, brother," another said, "Bear up nobly," [12] and another reminded them, "Remember whence you came, and the father by whose hand Isaac would have submitted to being slain for the sake of religion." [13] Each of them and all of them together looking at one another, cheerful and undaunted, said, "Let us with all our hearts consecrate ourselves to God, who gave us our lives,[b] and let us

use our bodies as a bulwark for the law. [14] Let us not fear him who thinks he is killing us, [15] for great is the struggle of the soul and the danger of eternal torment lying before those who transgress the commandment of God. [16] Therefore let us put on the full armor of self-control, which is divine reason. [17] For if we so die,[c] Abraham and Isaac and Jacob will welcome us, and all the fathers will praise us." [18] Those who were left behind said to each of the brothers who were being dragged away, "Do not put us to shame, brother, or betray the brothers who have died before us."

19 You are not ignorant of the affection of family ties, which the divine and all-wise Providence has bequeathed through the fathers to their descendants and which was implanted in the mother's womb. [20] There each of the brothers spent the same length of time and was shaped during the same period of time; and growing from the same blood and through the same life, they were brought to the light of day. [21] When they were born after an equal time of gestation, they drank milk from the same fountains. From such embraces brotherly-loving souls are nourished; [22] and they grow stronger from this common nurture and daily companionship, and from both general education and our discipline in the law of God.

23 Therefore, when sympathy and brotherly affection had been so established, the brothers were the more sympathetic to one another. [24] Since they had been educated by the same law and trained in the same virtues and brought up in right living, they loved one another all the more. [25] A common zeal

[a] Gk they [b] Or souls [c] Other ancient authorities read suffer

---

13:1–14:10 A Return to the Opening Thesis
The seven brothers illustrate the validity of the thesis, that devout reason is sovereign over the emotions.

13:15—According to the Deuteronomistic understanding of covenant, transgressing the commandments can lead to **eternal torment**. In

contrast to an "anything goes" culture, this verse reminds readers to take seriously the consequences of their actions.

13:22–14:1—Education in Mosaic law cultivates virtue and overcomes brotherly love so that the brothers can encourage one another and die a noble death.

for nobility strengthened their goodwill toward one another, and their concord, [26] because they could make their brotherly love more fervent with the aid of their religion. [27] But although nature and companionship and virtuous habits had augmented the affection of family ties, those who were left endured for the sake of religion, while watching their brothers being maltreated and tortured to death.

14 Furthermore, they encouraged them to face the torture, so that they not only despised their agonies, but also mastered the emotions of brotherly love.

[2] O reason,[a] more royal than kings and freer than the free! [3] O sacred and harmonious concord of the seven brothers on behalf of religion! [4] None of the seven youths proved coward or shrank from death, [5] but all of them, as though running the course toward immortality, hastened to death by torture. [6] Just as the hands and feet are moved in harmony with the guidance of the mind, so those holy youths, as though moved by an immortal spirit of devotion, agreed to go to death for its sake. [7] O most holy seven, brothers in harmony! For just as the seven days of creation move in choral dance around religion, [8] so these youths, forming a chorus, encircled the sevenfold fear of tortures and dissolved it. [9] Even now, we ourselves shudder as we hear of the suffering of these young men; they not only saw what was happening, not only heard the direct word of threat, but also bore the sufferings patiently, and in agonies of fire at that. [10] What could be more excruciatingly painful than this? For the power of fire is intense and swift, and it consumed their bodies quickly.

An Encomium on the Mother of the Seven

[11] Do not consider it amazing that reason had full command over these men in their tortures, since the mind of woman despised even more diverse agonies, [12] for the mother of the seven young men bore up under the rackings of each one of her children.

[13] Observe how complex is a mother's love for her children, which draws everything toward an emotion felt in her inmost parts. [14] Even unreasoning animals, as well as human beings, have a sympathy and parental love for their offspring. [15] For example, among birds, the ones that are tame protect their young by building on the housetops, [16] and the others, by building at the tops of mountains and the depths of chasms, in holes of trees, and on tree-tops, hatch the nestlings and ward off the intruder. [17] If they are not able to keep the intruder[b] away, they do what they can to help their young by flying in circles around them in the anguish of love, warning them with their own calls. [18] And why is it necessary to demonstrate sympathy for children by the example of unreasoning animals, [19] since even bees at the time for making honeycombs defend themselves against intruders and, as though with an iron dart, sting those who approach their hive and defend it even to the death? [20] But sympathy for her children did not sway the mother of the young men; she was of the same mind as Abraham.

15 O reason of the children, tyrant over the emotions! O religion, more desirable to the mother than her children! [2] Two courses were open to this mother, that of religion, and that of pre-

[a] Or O minds　[b] Gk it

14:11–17:6 Eulogy for the Mother
This is meant to encourage imitation by those listening (cf. 7:1–15, the eulogy for Eleazar).

14:20 But sympathy for her children did not sway the mother—Her tortures were even more

painful since she had to overcome emotional natural maternal instincts greater than those of unreasoning animals (and of fathers; see 15:4); yet she encouraged her sons to die a noble death.

serving her seven sons for a time, as the tyrant had promised. ³ She loved religion more, the religion that preserves them for eternal life according to God's promise.ᵃ ⁴ In what manner might I express the emotions of parents who love their children? We impress upon the character of a small child a wondrous likeness both of mind and of form. Especially is this true of mothers, who because of their birth pangs have a deeper sympathy toward their offspring than do the fathers. ⁵ Considering that mothers are the weaker sex and give birth to many, they are more devoted to their children.ᵇ ⁶ The mother of the seven boys, more than any other mother, loved her children. In seven pregnancies she had implanted in herself tender love toward them, ⁷ and because of the many pains she suffered with each of them she had sympathy for them; ⁸ yet because of the fear of God she disdained the temporary safety of her children. ⁹ Not only so, but also because of the nobility of her sons and their ready obedience to the law, she felt a greater tenderness toward them. ¹⁰ For they were righteous and self-controlled and brave and magnanimous, and loved their brothers and their mother, so that they obeyed her even to death in keeping the ordinances.

11 Nevertheless, though so many factors influenced the mother to suffer with them out of love for her children, in the case of none of them were the various tortures strong enough to pervert her reason. ¹² But each child separately and all of them together the mother urged on to death for religion's sake. ¹³ O sa-

cred nature and affection of parental love, yearning of parents toward offspring, nurture and indomitable suffering by mothers! ¹⁴ This mother, who saw them tortured and burned one by one, because of religion did not change her attitude. ¹⁵ She watched the flesh of her children being consumed by fire, their toes and fingers scatteredᶜ on the ground, and the flesh of the head to the chin exposed like masks.

16 O mother, tried now by more bitter pains than even the birth pangs you suffered for them! ¹⁷ O woman, who alone gave birth to such complete devotion! ¹⁸ When the firstborn breathed his last, it did not turn you aside, nor when the second in torments looked at you piteously nor when the third expired; ¹⁹ nor did you weep when you looked at the eyes of each one in his tortures gazing boldly at the same agonies, and saw in their nostrils the signs of the approach of death. ²⁰ When you saw the flesh of children burned upon the flesh of other children, severed hands upon hands, scalped heads upon heads, and corpses fallen on other corpses, and when you saw the place filled with many spectators of the torturings, you did not shed tears. ²¹ Neither the melodies of sirens nor the songs of swans attract the attention of their hearers as did the voices of the children in torture calling to their mother. ²² How great and how many torments the mother then suffered as her sons were tortured on the wheel and with the hot irons! ²³ But devout reason,

ᵃ Gk according to God   ᵇ Or For to the degree that mothers are weaker and the more children they bear, the more they are devoted to their children.
ᶜ Or quivering

15:5—*Mothers are the weaker sex, more devoted to their children* than men, a belief commonly held in the ancient world. This observation is meant to underscore how extraordinary the mother's courage was in putting her religion above her sons' lives. Contemporary U.S. society reflects this belief in several ways: women are more often granted custody of children in divorce and are less likely to make it to the top of the corporate ladder or the political establishment.

15:23 *A man's courage*—Devout reason (Torah

obedience) gives the mother manly courage to overcome emotions and parental love; see v. 30; 16:14. The theme of the manly woman is widespread in the ancient world, found in Greco-Roman, Jewish, and early Christian texts, e.g., the *Martyrdom of Perpetua and Felicitas.* How ironic that a manly woman in today's culture is too often dismissed as aggressive and not a team player, yet "feminine" women are dismissed as too soft to make it in a man's world. Successful female politicians Margaret Thatcher and Golda

giving her heart a man's courage in the very midst of her emotions, strengthened her to disregard, for the time, her parental love.

24 Although she witnessed the destruction of seven children and the ingenious and various rackings, this noble mother disregarded all these[a] because of faith in God. 25 For as in the council chamber of her own soul she saw mighty advocates—nature, family, parental love, and the rackings of her children— 26 this mother held two ballots, one bearing death and the other deliverance for her children. 27 She did not approve the deliverance that would preserve the seven sons for a short time, 28 but as the daughter of God-fearing Abraham she remembered his fortitude.

29 O mother of the nation, vindicator of the law and champion of religion, who carried away the prize of the contest in your heart! 30 O more noble than males in steadfastness, and more courageous than men in endurance! 31 Just as Noah's ark, carrying the world in the universal flood, stoutly endured the waves, 32 so you, O guardian of the law, overwhelmed from every side by the flood of your emotions and the violent winds, the torture of your sons, endured nobly and withstood the wintry storms that assail religion.

16 If, then, a woman, advanced in years and mother of seven sons, endured seeing her children tortured to death, it must be admitted that devout reason is sovereign over the emotions. 2 Thus I have demonstrated not only that men have ruled over the emotions, but also that a woman has despised the fiercest tortures. 3 The lions surrounding Daniel were not so savage, nor was the raging fiery furnace of Mishael so intensely hot, as was her innate parental love, inflamed as she saw her seven sons tortured in such varied ways. 4 But the mother quenched so many and such great emotions by devout reason.

5 Consider this also: If this woman, though a mother, had been fainthearted, she would have mourned over them and perhaps spoken as follows: 6 "O how wretched am I and many times unhappy! After bearing seven children, I am now the mother of none! 7 O seven childbirths all in vain, seven profitless pregnancies, fruitless nurturings and wretched nursings! 8 In vain, my sons, I endured many birth pangs for you, and the more grievous anxieties of your upbringing. 9 Alas for my children, some unmarried, others married and without offspring.[b] I shall not see your children or have the happiness of being called grandmother. 10 Alas, I who had so many and beautiful children am a widow and alone, with many sorrows.[c] 11 And when I die, I shall have none of my sons to bury me."

12 Yet that holy and God-fearing mother did not wail with such a lament for any of them, nor did she dissuade any of them from dying, nor did she grieve as they were dying. 13 On the contrary, as though having a mind like adamant and giving rebirth for immortality to the whole number of her sons, she implored them and urged them on to death for the sake of religion. 14 O mother, sol-

---

[a] Other ancient authorities read *having bidden them farewell, surrendered them*   [b] Gk *without benefit*   [c] Or *much to be pitied*

Meir, for example, were known for their toughness.

15:28—The mother is likened to *Abraham*, who also overcame parental love and was willing to sacrifice his son for religion (Gen. 22); see 16:20; 17:6. She is even stronger than *Daniel* (16:3).

16:5–11—Imaginary speech of the mother if she had not had courage, emphasizing her sorrow and widowhood.

16:12–23—Actual courageous speech of the mother, which is purposely contrasted with her fainthearted imaginary words, making clear the choice before the audience.

16:14—The contrast between martyrs and their oppressors, between Jewish and Greek virtue, is expressed through military imagery. This language can promote triumphalism and victory at whatever price.

dier of God in the cause of religion, elder and woman! By steadfastness you have conquered even a tyrant, and in word and deed you have proved more powerful than a man. ¹⁵ For when you and your sons were arrested together, you stood and watched Eleazar being tortured, and said to your sons in the Hebrew language, ¹⁶ "My sons, noble is the contest to which you are called to bear witness for the nation. Fight zealously for our ancestral law. ¹⁷ For it would be shameful if, while an aged man endures such agonies for the sake of religion, you young men were to be terrified by tortures. ¹⁸ Remember that it is through God that you have had a share in the world and have enjoyed life, ¹⁹ and therefore you ought to endure any suffering for the sake of God. ²⁰ For his sake also our father Abraham was zealous to sacrifice his son Isaac, the ancestor of our nation; and when Isaac saw his father's hand wielding a knife[a] and descending upon him, he did not cower. ²¹ Daniel the righteous was thrown to the lions, and Hananiah, Azariah, and Mishael were hurled into the fiery furnace and endured it for the sake of God. ²² You too must have the same faith in God and not be grieved. ²³ It is unreasonable for people who have religious knowledge not to withstand pain."

24 By these words the mother of the seven encouraged and persuaded each of her sons to die rather than violate God's commandment. ²⁵ They knew also that those who die for the sake of God live to God, as do Abraham and Isaac and Jacob and all the patriarchs.

17 Some of the guards said that when she also was about to be

seized and put to death she threw herself into the flames so that no one might touch her body.

2 O mother, who with your seven sons nullified the violence of the tyrant, frustrated his evil designs, and showed the courage of your faith! ³ Nobly set like a roof on the pillars of your sons, you held firm and unswerving against the earthquake of the tortures. ⁴ Take courage, therefore, O holy-minded mother, maintaining firm an enduring hope in God. ⁵ The moon in heaven, with the stars, does not stand so august as you, who, after lighting the way of your star-like seven sons to piety, stand in honor before God and are firmly set in heaven with them. ⁶ For your children were true descendants of father Abraham.[b]

The Effect of the Martyrdoms

7 If it were possible for us to paint the history of your religion as an artist might, would not those who first beheld it have shuddered as they saw the mother of the seven children enduring their varied tortures to death for the sake of religion? ⁸ Indeed it would be proper to inscribe on their tomb these words as a reminder to the people of our nation:[c]

9 "Here lie buried an aged priest and an aged woman and seven sons, because of the violence of the tyrant who wished to destroy the way of life of the Hebrews. ¹⁰ They vindicated their nation, looking to God and enduring torture even to death."

11 Truly the contest in which they were engaged was divine, ¹² for on that day virtue gave the awards and tested

a Gk sword b Gk For your childbearing was from Abraham the father; other ancient authorities read For… Abraham the servant c Or as a memorial to the heroes of our people

---

16:19 *You ought to endure any suffering for the sake of God*—This belief has sometimes become a warrant for passivity and resignation in the face of evil. It can be twisted into an understanding that suffering is good for you, which can be used by those in power to maintain the status quo and keep groups "in their place." Positively, this thinking can help to make sense of suffering; suffering for God's sake gives it meaning.

17:7–18:5 The Purpose of the Martyrdoms
17:11–16—Martyrdom as athletic *contest* between Judaism and the Gentile world, with the prize being immortality. Jews could match anyone in the arena because of their Torah. This notion of competition may fuel the kind of rivalry today that supports civil wars and us-vs.-them mentality that can work against peace.

them for their endurance. The prize was immortality in endless life. [13] Eleazar was the first contestant, the mother of the seven sons entered the competition, and the brothers contended. [14] The tyrant was the antagonist, and the world and the human race were the spectators. [15] Reverence for God was victor and gave the crown to its own athletes. [16] Who did not admire the athletes of the divine[a] legislation? Who were not amazed?

[17] The tyrant himself and all his council marveled at their[b] endurance, [18] because of which they now stand before the divine throne and live the life of eternal blessedness. [19] For Moses says, "All who are consecrated are under your hands." [20] These, then, who have been consecrated for the sake of God,[c] are honored, not only with this honor, but also by the fact that because of them our enemies did not rule over our nation, [21] the tyrant was punished, and the homeland purified—they having become, as it were, a ransom for the sin of our nation. [22] And through the blood of those devout ones and their death as an atoning sacrifice, divine Providence preserved Israel that previously had been mistreated.

[23] For the tyrant Antiochus, when he saw the courage of their virtue and their endurance under the tortures, proclaimed them to his soldiers as an example for their own endurance, [24] and this made them brave and courageous for infantry battle and siege, and he ravaged and conquered all his enemies.

18 O Israelite children, offspring of the seed of Abraham, obey this law and exercise piety in every way, [2] knowing that devout reason is master of all emotions, not only of sufferings from within, but also of those from without.

[3] Therefore those who gave over their bodies in suffering for the sake of religion were not only admired by mortals, but also were deemed worthy to share in a divine inheritance. [4] Because of them the nation gained peace, and by reviving observance of the law in the homeland they ravaged the enemy. [5] The tyrant Antiochus was both punished on earth and is being chastised after his death. Since in no way whatever was he able to compel the Israelites to become pagans and to abandon their ancestral customs, he left Jerusalem and marched against the Persians.

The Mother's Address to Her Children

[6] The mother of seven sons expressed also these principles to her children: [7] "I was a pure virgin and did not go outside my father's house; but I guarded the rib from which woman was made.[d] [8] No seducer corrupted me on a desert plain, nor did the destroyer, the deceitful serpent, defile the purity of my virginity. [9] In the time of my maturity I remained with my husband, and when these sons had grown up their father died. A happy man was he, who lived out his life with good children, and did not have the grief of bereavement. [10] While he was still with you, he taught you the law and the prophets. [11] He read to you about Abel slain by Cain, and Isaac who was offered as a burnt offering, and about

---

[a] Other ancient authorities read *true*   [b] Other ancient authorities add *virtue and*   [c] Other ancient authorities lack *for the sake of God*   [d] Gk *the rib that was built*

17:20–22—Martyrdom as atoning sacrifice. See the introduction.

17:23–24—Even Antiochus holds up the martyrs as examples for his soldiers. Even one's enemies can respect such behavior.

18:1–5, 20–24 The Mother's Address to Her Children

The tyrant is punished and the martyrs are rewarded with immortality, in line with Deuteronomistic, act/consequence theology.

18:6–19 The Mother's Address to Her Children

Perhaps a later addition. The mother of "manly courage" is feminized once again, asserting her chastity and her husband's role in educating her sons. Some might suggest that she has paid a price for succeeding in a man's world, by being relegated to her traditional role at the end of the story.

Joseph in prison. ¹² He told you of the zeal of Phinehas, and he taught you about Hananiah, Azariah, and Mishael in the fire. ¹³ He praised Daniel in the den of the lions and blessed him. ¹⁴ He reminded you of the scripture of Isaiah, which says, 'Even though you go through the fire, the flame shall not consume you.' ¹⁵ He sang to you songs of the psalmist David, who said, 'Many are the afflictions of the righteous.' ¹⁶ He recounted to you Solomon's proverb, 'There is a tree of life for those who do his will.' ¹⁷ He confirmed the query of Ezekiel, 'Shall these dry bones live?' ¹⁸ For he did not forget to teach you the song that Moses taught, which says, ¹⁹ 'I kill and I make alive: this is your life and the length of your days.'"

20 O bitter was that day—and yet not bitter—when that bitter tyrant of the Greeks quenched fire with fire in his cruel caldrons, and in his burning rage brought those seven sons of the daughter of Abraham to the catapult and back again to more[a] tortures, ²¹ pierced the pupils of their eyes and cut out their tongues, and put them to death with various tortures. ²² For these crimes divine justice pursued and will pursue the accursed tyrant. ²³ But the sons of Abraham with their victorious mother are gathered together into the chorus of the fathers, and have received pure and immortal[b] souls from God, ²⁴ to whom be glory forever and ever. Amen.

[a] Other ancient authorities read *to all his* [b] Other ancient authorities read *victorious*

The NEW TESTAMENT

THE NEW COVENANT
COMMONLY CALLED
THE NEW TESTAMENT
OF OUR LORD AND SAVIOR
JESUS CHRIST

New Revised Standard Version

The Gospel according to
MATTHEW

The Gospel of Matthew is church-building literature. It is a blueprint for the establishment, sustenance, and encouragement of a struggling community of Jesus believers in the latter half of the first century. Written anonymously sometime around the year 85 CE, the evangelist who took the name Matthew attempts to nurture and strengthen the faith of those who believe that they represent Israel as God had come to intend it.

Even on first glance, a reader is struck by the Jewish style of the writing, imagery and argumentation. The formula quotations (1:22; 2:5, 15, 17, 23; 3:3; 4:14; 8:17; 12:17; 13:14, 35; 21:4; 26:56; 27:9) are a celebrated example. The way they proclaim that signal events in Jesus' life were the intended fulfillment of Old Testament prophecy reveals a sophisticated kind of *rabbinic* interpretative strategy.

This Jewish writing style and orientation to the Scriptures suggest much about the context of the Matthean community. Matthew was most likely part of a Jewish Christian community. Like other Jews, those who occupied his community were still reeling from the shock of Rome's annihilation of Jerusalem and the razing of its temple in 70 CE. The temple had been one of the premier symbols of the people's faith. Now that it had been lost, the people who had revered it, worshiped and sacrificed in it, and paid taxes to and for it struggled to find a satisfactory interpretative explanation. Three primary—and, in many ways, competing—conclusions were drawn. One was apocalyptic. Apocalyptic writers like 4 Ezra and 2 Baruch begged the question, "How could God allow this to happen to God's own people and their temple erected to the worship of that God?" The answer lay in the reality of the two ages. In this present age, evil triumphs. But in the final and more permanent age, God and God's people will be vindicated. Until that time God's people should be patient and should, in the absence now of the temple, live by the presence and power of the Torah.

Jewish Christianity, of which Matthew's Gospel is a prime representative, was a second response. Jewish Christians agreed with Jewish apocalyptic's understanding of the two ages, its stress on the Torah, and its longing for the future vindication of God's people. Matthew, however, adds a significant twist. He identifies Jesus as the messianic Son of Man who will usher in that new age. He also argues that the source of present guidance is not the Torah itself, particularly not as it has been traditionally understood, but Jesus' interpretation of it (see, for example the antitheses of 5:21–48: "You have heard it said . . . but *I* say . . .").

Such an interpretative position brought Matthew's Jewish Christians into direct opposition with the third, and clearly the strongest, Jewish response to the temple's demise: Pharisaic/rabbinic Judaism. Because their existence was not as tied to the life and structures of the temple, the Pharisees survived its loss by turning the people's symbolic affections more exclusively to the Law. Though they did not, at least in Jesus' time, have anywhere near the social and political power Matthew ascribes to

them, they were influential arbiters on matters of law and tradition. Their social and political authority crested in the aftermath of the temple's destruction, when competing groups like the Sadducees lost the authoritative footing that went with their symbiotic relationship to the temple. Matthew's identification, then, of the Pharisees as Jesus' primary opponents reveals as much about his own community's conflict with rabbinic Pharisaism as it does about Jesus' conflict with the leaders of his time. Matthew has artfully made his primary opponents Jesus' primary opponents, so that his community's fight with them over the proper way of interpreting the Torah in 85 CE would be seen as authorized by Jesus' comparable battle decades earlier. Jesus takes issue with Pharisaic traditions (15:20), attacks the Pharisees over particular issues like Sabbath observance (12:1–8), divorce (19:9), and taxes (22:15–22), and dismisses them as hypocrites whose concern for external ritual and status obliterates fidelity to God's original intent of a law based in mercy (chap. 23). Through such narration, Matthew grounds and thereby authorizes his community's actions and Torah interpretation in the words and actions of Jesus. Pharisaic faith, though exacting and showcased for all to see, was insufficient (5:20).

Matthew's intent was to build up a church where the proper righteousness was taught and lived. Obedience to the law in this community would not be driven by an obsession with external commands and legal detail, but would develop as a natural response to the realization that God had graciously brought the reality of the divine kingdom into their midst in the presence of Jesus. This radical, life-transforming act should generate in the believer an inner disposition toward God, a spirituality, that in turn should provoke the living response of an equally radical righteousness. That living response is laid out, not idealistically but realistically, in places like the Sermon on the Mount (chaps. 5–7), and the parables of the kingdom (chaps. 13, 24–25). This is why believers, ancient *and* contemporary, should "live" the expectations of the Sermon, not simply because they are mandated—that is to say, law—but because they are the proper transforming response to the theologically determined transformation that God has already christologically set in motion. Communally, believers respond to God properly when they live out this kind of Torah fidelity in the way they structure their community as *ecclesia* or church (16:18; chap. 18).

In the end, then, Matthew is "community-forming literature." He makes the necessary adjustments to his critical Markan source (of which he includes all but sixty verses) to speak to issues vital to the behavior (cf. 18:21–35) and operation (cf. 18:6–20) of an identifiable church and to increase the reliability and authority of its founding disciples (cf. 16:18). This emphasis is clearly on display at the Gospel's close, where the risen Jesus leaves his final instructions. The community is called upon to teach the Law as he has taught it, basing fidelity to the Law on the twin foundations of mercy and expectation of God's imminent reign. The community, ancient *and* contemporary, is to carry that teaching beyond Israel to all the nations, in the interests of making disciples and thereby widening the scope and impact of the church they compose and promote.

—**Brian K. Blount**

The Genealogy of Jesus the Messiah

1 An account of the genealogy[a] of Jesus the Messiah,[b] the son of David, the son of Abraham.

2 Abraham was the father of Isaac, and Isaac the father of Jacob, and Jacob the father of Judah and his brothers, 3 and Judah the father of Perez and Zerah by Tamar, and Perez the father of Hezron, and Hezron the father of Aram, 4 and Aram the father of Aminadab, and Aminadab the father of Nahshon, and Nahshon the father of Salmon, 5 and Salmon the father of Boaz by Rahab, and Boaz the father of Obed by Ruth, and Obed the father of Jesse, 6 and Jesse the father of King David.

And David was the father of Solomon by the wife of Uriah, 7 and Solomon the father of Rehoboam, and Rehoboam the father of Abijah, and Abijah the father of Asaph,[c] 8 and Asaph[c] the father of Jehoshaphat, and Jehoshaphat the father of Joram, and Joram the father of Uzziah, 9 and Uzziah the father of Jotham, and Jotham the father of Ahaz, and Ahaz the father of Hezekiah, 10 and Hezekiah the father of Manasseh, and Manasseh the father of Amos,[d] and Amos[d] the father of Josiah, 11 and Josiah the father of Jechoniah and his brothers, at the time of the deportation to Babylon.

12 And after the deportation to Babylon: Jechoniah was the father of Salathiel, and Salathiel the father of Zerubbabel, 13 and Zerubbabel the father of Abiud, and Abiud the father of Eliakim, and Eliakim the father of Azor, 14 and Azor the father of Zadok, and Zadok the father of Achim, and Achim the father of Eliud, 15 and Eliud the father of Eleazar, and Eleazar the father of Matthan, and Matthan the father of Jacob, 16 and Jacob the father of Joseph the husband of Mary, of whom Jesus was born, who is called the Messiah.[e]

17 So all the generations from Abraham to David are fourteen generations; and from David to the deportation to Babylon, fourteen generations; and from the deportation to Babylon to the Messiah,[e] fourteen generations.

The Birth of Jesus the Messiah

18 Now the birth of Jesus the Messiah[b] took place in this way. When his mother Mary had been engaged to Joseph, but before they lived together, she was found to be with child from the Holy Spirit. 19 Her husband Joseph, being a righteous man and unwilling to expose her to public disgrace, planned to dismiss her quietly. 20 But just when he had resolved to do this, an angel of the Lord appeared to him in a dream and said, "Joseph, son of

---

a Or *birth* *b* Or *Jesus Christ* *c* Other ancient authorities read *Asa* *d* Other ancient authorities read *Amon* *e* Or *the Christ*

1:1–17 Jesus' Family Line

1:1 *Messiah*—"Anointed one" or "Christ." *Son of David*—The title identifies Jesus as someone who heals persons of low and often objectionable status (cf., 9:27; 12:23; 15:22; 20:30, 31; 21:15). Followers of the man who strategically aligns himself with the powerless must adopt similar objectionable liaisons. *Son of Abraham*—What Jesus lacks as far as institutional status in the temple hierarchy, he more than makes up for by his direct and messianic relationship to David and Abraham. Similarly, what Jesus' followers lack in social and political pedigree, they more than make up for by their messianic relationship with Jesus, God's Son.

1:3–6—*Tamar* (Gen. 38), *Rahab* (Josh. 2), *Ruth, the wife of Uriah [Bathsheba]* (2 Sam. 11–12; 1 Kgs. 1)—These women are objectionable characters. Tamar dresses up like a harlot to have children by Judah. Rahab *is* a harlot. Ruth, a Moabite, is an ethnic outsider. Bathsheba is seduced by David and bears Solomon out of that illicit relationship. Jesus' heritage is as blemished as the status of the people he helps and leads his disciples to serve. Matthew's inclusion of these women is an encouragement for any disciple who feels socially ostracized; God can and will use anyone willing to respond to God's call.

1:18–25 The Birth of Jesus (Luke 1:26–2:40)

1:18 *Holy Spirit*—Because the Spirit of God effects the pregnancy, Jesus' sonship to God, not Joseph, takes precedence.

1:19 *Planned to dismiss her*—Like the four women mentioned in Jesus' genealogy, Mary's character appears to be blemished. God uses people whom "righteous" people would cast aside.

David, do not be afraid to take Mary as your wife, for the child conceived in her is from the Holy Spirit. ²¹ She will bear a son, and you are to name him Jesus, for he will save his people from their sins." ²² All this took place to fulfill what had been spoken by the Lord through the prophet:

²³ "Look, the virgin shall conceive and
　　　bear a son,
　　and they shall name him
　　　Emmanuel,"

which means, "God is with us." ²⁴ When Joseph awoke from sleep, he did as the angel of the Lord commanded him; he took her as his wife, ²⁵ but had no marital relations with her until she had borne a son;ᵃ and he named him Jesus.

The Visit of the Wise Men

2 In the time of King Herod, after Jesus was born in Bethlehem of Judea, wise menᵇ from the East came to Jerusalem, ² asking, "Where is the child who has been born king of the Jews? For we observed his star at its rising,ᶜ and have come to pay him homage." ³ When King Herod heard this, he was frightened, and all Jerusalem with him; ⁴ and calling together all the chief priests and scribes of the people, he inquired of them where the Messiahᵈ was to be born. ⁵ They told him, "In Bethlehem of Judea; for so it has been written by the prophet:

⁶ 'And you, Bethlehem, in the land of
　　　Judah,
　　are by no means least among the
　　　rulers of Judah;

for from you shall come a ruler
　　who is to shepherdᵉ my people
　　　Israel.' "

7 Then Herod secretly called for the wise menᵇ and learned from them the exact time when the star had appeared. ⁸ Then he sent them to Bethlehem, saying, "Go and search diligently for the child; and when you have found him, bring me word so that I may also go and pay him homage." ⁹ When they had heard the king, they set out; and there, ahead of them, went the star that they had seen at its rising,ᶜ until it stopped over the place where the child was. ¹⁰ When they saw that the star had stopped,ᶠ they were overwhelmed with joy. ¹¹ On entering the house, they saw the child with Mary his mother; and they knelt down and paid him homage. Then, opening their treasure chests, they offered him gifts of gold, frankincense, and myrrh. ¹² And having been warned in a dream not to return to Herod, they left for their own country by another road.

The Escape to Egypt

13 Now after they had left, an angel of the Lord appeared to Joseph in a dream and said, "Get up, take the child and his mother, and flee to Egypt, and remain there until I tell you; for Herod is about to search for the child, to destroy him." ¹⁴ Then Josephᵍ got up, took the child and his mother by night, and went to Egypt, ¹⁵ and remained there until the death of Herod. This was to fulfill what

---

ᵃ Other ancient authorities read *her firstborn son*　ᵇ Or *astrologers*; Gk *magi*　ᶜ Or *in the East*　ᵈ Or *the Christ*　ᵉ Or *rule*　ᶠ Gk *saw the star*　ᵍ Gk *he*

1:21 *Jesus*—The Greek form of Joshua: "The Lord/YHWH saves/helps."

1:22 *Fulfill*—Matthew composes "formula quotations" to demonstrate that Jesus' life fulfills Old Testament prophecy. See 2:5, 15, 17, 23; 3:3; 4:14; 8:17; 12:17; 13:14, 35; 21:4; 26:56; 27:9. As Jesus fulfills prophetic expectations, so must those who read this Gospel fulfill Jesus' radical expectations for discipleship (see Matt. 5–7).

1:23 *Emmanuel*—Cf. Isa. 7:14. Jesus brings humans back into relationship with God. His disciples must strive to do the same.

2:1–12 Jesus and Herod the Great

2:2 *King of the Jews*—Appointed by God, Jesus is the true earthly as well as heavenly sovereign. The title indicates that those who follow Jesus must be as politically engaged as he was.

2:6—Formula quotation: Cf. Mic. 5:2 and 2 Sam. 5:2. See note at Matt. 1:22.

2:13–23 Out of Egypt I Have Called My Son

2:15 *Death of Herod*—4 BCE. ***Out of Egypt*—**Formula quotation: Cf. Hos. 11:1. See note at Matt. 1:22. Matthew draws an explicit connec-

had been spoken by the Lord through the prophet, "Out of Egypt I have called my son."

The Massacre of the Infants

16 When Herod saw that he had been tricked by the wise men,*a* he was infuriated, and he sent and killed all the children in and around Bethlehem who were two years old or under, according to the time that he had learned from the wise men.*a* 17 Then was fulfilled what had been spoken through the prophet Jeremiah:

18 "A voice was heard in Ramah,
    wailing and loud lamentation,
  Rachel weeping for her children;
    she refused to be consoled,
        because they are no more."

The Return from Egypt

19 When Herod died, an angel of the Lord suddenly appeared in a dream to Joseph in Egypt and said, 20 "Get up, take the child and his mother, and go to the land of Israel, for those who were seeking the child's life are dead." 21 Then Joseph*b* got up, took the child and his mother, and went to the land of Israel. 22 But when he heard that Archelaus was ruling over Judea in place of his father Herod, he was afraid to go there. And after being warned in a dream, he went away to the district of Galilee. 23 There he made his home in a town called Nazareth, so that what had been spoken through the prophets might be fulfilled, "He will be called a Nazorean."

The Proclamation of John the Baptist

3 In those days John the Baptist appeared in the wilderness of Judea, proclaiming, 2 "Repent, for the kingdom of heaven has come near."*c* 3 This is the one of whom the prophet Isaiah spoke when he said,

  "The voice of one crying out in the
        wilderness:
  'Prepare the way of the Lord,
    make his paths straight.'"

4 Now John wore clothing of camel's hair with a leather belt around his waist, and his food was locusts and wild honey. 5 Then the people of Jerusalem and all Judea were going out to him, and all the region along the Jordan, 6 and they were baptized by him in the river Jordan, confessing their sins.

7 But when he saw many Pharisees and Sadducees coming for baptism, he said to them, "You brood of vipers! Who warned you to flee from the wrath to come? 8 Bear fruit worthy of repentance. 9 Do not presume to say to yourselves, 'We have Abraham as our ancestor'; for I tell you, God is able from these stones to raise up children to Abraham. 10 Even now the ax is lying at the root of the trees; every tree therefore that does not bear good fruit is cut down and thrown into the fire.

11 "I baptize you with*d* water for repentance, but one who is more powerful than I is coming after me; I am not worthy to carry his sandals. He will baptize

a Or astrologers; Gk magi   *b* Gk he   *c* Or is at hand   *d* Or in

---

tion between Moses, the liberator of the people, and Jesus, the one whose name means "YHWH saves." Jesus' ministry will be as socially and politically tinged as Moses'. The ministry of those who follow him cannot be otherwise.

2:18—Formula quotation: Cf. Jer. 31:15. See note at Matt. 1:22.

3:1–12 John the Baptist Prepares the Way (Mark 1:2–8; Luke 3:1–18; John 1:6–8, 19–28)

3:2 *Kingdom of heaven*—This Jewish formulation avoids the name "God." Matthew 4:23–25 and 9:35–38 connect the kingdom directly to the ministry of Jesus and his disciples, a ministry

dedicated to transforming social and physical as well as spiritual brokenness.

3:7 *Pharisees*—Mainly scribes, artisans, farmers, and merchants. According to the evangelist, they care more about ritual performance than God's desire for repentance and mercy (9:13; 12:7). Contemporary disciples must be careful that they do not allow their conscientious desire for proper religious observance to become more important than showing love, even to those who don't deserve it and even in situations that do not follow proper worship and religious protocol.

you with*a* the Holy Spirit and fire. ¹²His winnowing fork is in his hand, and he will clear his threshing floor and will gather his wheat into the granary; but the chaff he will burn with unquenchable fire."

The Baptism of Jesus

13 Then Jesus came from Galilee to John at the Jordan, to be baptized by him. ¹⁴John would have prevented him, saying, "I need to be baptized by you, and do you come to me?" ¹⁵But Jesus answered him, "Let it be so now; for it is proper for us in this way to fulfill all righteousness." Then he consented. ¹⁶And when Jesus had been baptized, just as he came up from the water, suddenly the heavens were opened to him and he saw the Spirit of God descending like a dove and alighting on him. ¹⁷And a voice from heaven said, "This is my Son, the Beloved,*b* with whom I am well pleased."

The Temptation of Jesus

4 Then Jesus was led up by the Spirit into the wilderness to be tempted by the devil. ²He fasted forty days and forty nights, and afterwards he was famished. ³The tempter came and said to him, "If you are the Son of God, command these stones to become loaves of bread." ⁴But he answered, "It is written,

'One does not live by bread alone,
    but by every word that comes from
        the mouth of God.'"

5 Then the devil took him to the holy city and placed him on the pinnacle of the temple, ⁶saying to him, "If you are the Son of God, throw yourself down; for it is written,

'He will command his angels
        concerning you,'
    and 'On their hands they will bear
        you up,
    so that you will not dash your foot
        against a stone.'"

⁷Jesus said to him, "Again it is written, 'Do not put the Lord your God to the test.'"

8 Again, the devil took him to a very high mountain and showed him all the kingdoms of the world and their splendor; ⁹and he said to him, "All these I will give you, if you will fall down and worship me." ¹⁰Jesus said to him, "Away with you, Satan! for it is written,

'Worship the Lord your God,
    and serve only him.'"

¹¹Then the devil left him, and suddenly angels came and waited on him.

Jesus Begins His Ministry in Galilee

12 Now when Jesus*c* heard that John had been arrested, he withdrew to Galilee. ¹³He left Nazareth and made his home in Capernaum by the sea, in the territory of Zebulun and Naphtali, ¹⁴so that what had been spoken through the prophet Isaiah might be fulfilled:

¹⁵ "Land of Zebulun, land of Naphtali,
        on the road by the sea, across
            the Jordan, Galilee of the
                Gentiles—
¹⁶   the people who sat in darkness
        have seen a great light,

a Or in *b* Or my beloved Son *c* Gk he

3:13–17 Jesus' Baptism (Mark 1:9–11; Luke 3:21–22; John 1:31–34)

3:15 *Righteousness*—Cf. 3:15; 5:6, 10, 20; 6:1, 33; 21:32. The kind of discipleship action necessary for entrance into the kingdom. It is radical behavior that pushes beyond what law and tradition require. Contemporary believers must do much more than obey the commandments; they must love beyond reason.

4:1–11 Jesus Is Tested by Satan (Mark 1:12–13; Luke 4:1–13; cf. Heb. 2:18; 4:15)

4:2 *Fasted*—Fasting represents dedication to God that rejects the temptation for human security and success. Jesus models this behavioral standard for the contemporary believer.

4:3 *Son of God*—Matthew's primary title for Jesus. As Son, Jesus dutifully represents God's presence, power, and authority (cf. 14:33; 26:36–46; 27:38–54). His actions model God's desires for the obedient behavior of God's people.

4:12–25 Jesus Begins His Ministry in Galilee (Mark 1:14–15; Luke 4:14–15)

4:14—Formula quotation: Cf. Isa. 9:1–2. See note at Matt. 1:22.

and for those who sat in the region
        and shadow of death
    light has dawned."
17 From that time Jesus began to proclaim, "Repent, for the kingdom of
heaven has come near."*a*

Jesus Calls the First Disciples

18 As he walked by the Sea of Galilee, he saw two brothers, Simon, who
is called Peter, and Andrew his brother,
casting a net into the sea—for they were
fishermen. **19** And he said to them, "Follow me, and I will make you fish for
people." **20** Immediately they left their
nets and followed him. **21** As he went
from there, he saw two other brothers,
James son of Zebedee and his brother
John, in the boat with their father Zebedee, mending their nets, and he called
them. **22** Immediately they left the boat
and their father, and followed him.

Jesus Ministers to Crowds of People

23 Jesus*b* went throughout Galilee,
teaching in their synagogues and proclaiming the good news*c* of the kingdom
and curing every disease and every sickness among the people. **24** So his fame
spread throughout all Syria, and they
brought to him all the sick, those who
were afflicted with various diseases and
pains, demoniacs, epileptics, and paralytics, and he cured them. **25** And great
crowds followed him from Galilee, the
Decapolis, Jerusalem, Judea, and from
beyond the Jordan.

The Beatitudes

5 When Jesus*d* saw the crowds, he
went up the mountain; and after
he sat down, his disciples came to him.
2 Then he began to speak, and taught
them, saying:

3 "Blessed are the poor in spirit, for
theirs is the kingdom of heaven.

4 "Blessed are those who mourn, for
they will be comforted.

5 "Blessed are the meek, for they will
inherit the earth.

6 "Blessed are those who hunger and
thirst for righteousness, for they will be
filled.

7 "Blessed are the merciful, for they
will receive mercy.

8 "Blessed are the pure in heart, for
they will see God.

9 "Blessed are the peacemakers, for
they will be called children of God.

10 "Blessed are those who are persecuted for righteousness' sake, for theirs
is the kingdom of heaven.

11 "Blessed are you when people
revile you and persecute you and utter
all kinds of evil against you falsely*e* on
my account. **12** Rejoice and be glad, for
your reward is great in heaven, for in the
same way they persecuted the prophets
who were before you.

Salt and Light

13 "You are the salt of the earth; but if
salt has lost its taste, how can its saltiness

*a Or is at hand b Gk He c Gk gospel d Gk he e Other ancient authorities
lack falsely*

4:17 *Kingdom of heaven*—See note at 3:2.

4:18–22—Mark 1:16–20; Luke 5:1–11; John
1:35–42.

4:23 *Their synagogues*—The frequent use of
"their" (9:35; 10:17; 12:9; 13:54) demonstrates
that a sectarian split had occurred within the
larger Jewish community where Matthew was
writing. The Matthean contingent felt ostracized.
Any disciple who follows Jesus in challenging
the status quo of worship, Torah interpretation,
and social convention will find himself or herself
similarly situated.

5:1–12 The Beatitudes (Luke 6:17, 20–23)

The next three chapters are known as the Sermon
on the Mount (Luke 6:17–38: Sermon on the

Plain), the first of five teaching discourses. See
also chaps. 10 (missionary teaching), 13 (parables
of the kingdom), 18 (ecclesiological teaching),
23–25 (teaching on the coming of the kingdom).

5:3 *Blessed*—Jesus' apocalyptic beatitudes
should be read imperatively. Be poor in spirit!
Mourn! Be meek! Hunger and thirst for righteousness! Be merciful (cf. 9:13; 12:7)! Be pure
in heart! Be peacemakers! The reward will be
the kingdom of heaven in the future and the
establishment of a community set apart to and for
the righteous work of God in the present (5:16).
Adherence to these *religious* beatitudes realizes a
practical, *social* benefit.

5:13–16 Discipleship in the Context of Torah

be restored? It is no longer good for anything, but is thrown out and trampled under foot.

14 "You are the light of the world. A city built on a hill cannot be hid. [15] No one after lighting a lamp puts it under the bushel basket, but on the lampstand, and it gives light to all in the house. [16] In the same way, let your light shine before others, so that they may see your good works and give glory to your Father in heaven.

The Law and the Prophets

17 "Do not think that I have come to abolish the law or the prophets; I have come not to abolish but to fulfill. [18] For truly I tell you, until heaven and earth pass away, not one letter,[a] not one stroke of a letter, will pass from the law until all is accomplished. [19] Therefore, whoever breaks[b] one of the least of these commandments, and teaches others to do the same, will be called least in the kingdom of heaven; but whoever does them and teaches them will be called great in the kingdom of heaven. [20] For I tell you, unless your righteousness exceeds that of the scribes and Pharisees, you will never enter the kingdom of heaven.

Concerning Anger

21 "You have heard that it was said to those of ancient times, 'You shall not murder'; and 'whoever murders shall be liable to judgment.' [22] But I say to you that if you are angry with a brother or sister,[c] you will be liable to judgment; and if you insult[d] a brother or sister,[e] you will be liable to the council; and if you say,

'You fool,' you will be liable to the hell[f] of fire. [23] So when you are offering your gift at the altar, if you remember that your brother or sister[g] has something against you, [24] leave your gift there before the altar and go; first be reconciled to your brother or sister,[g] and then come and offer your gift. [25] Come to terms quickly with your accuser while you are on the way to court[h] with him, or your accuser may hand you over to the judge, and the judge to the guard, and you will be thrown into prison. [26] Truly I tell you, you will never get out until you have paid the last penny.

Concerning Adultery

27 "You have heard that it was said, 'You shall not commit adultery.' [28] But I say to you that everyone who looks at a woman with lust has already committed adultery with her in his heart. [29] If your right eye causes you to sin, tear it out and throw it away; it is better for you to lose one of your members than for your whole body to be thrown into hell.[f] [30] And if your right hand causes you to sin, cut it off and throw it away; it is better for you to lose one of your members than for your whole body to go into hell.[f]

Concerning Divorce

31 "It was also said, 'Whoever divorces his wife, let him give her a certificate of divorce.' [32] But I say to you that anyone who divorces his wife, except on

[a] Gk one iota [b] Or annuls [c] Gk a brother; other ancient authorities add without cause [d] Gk say Raca to (an obscure term of abuse) [e] Gk a brother [f] Gk Gehenna [g] Gk your brother [h] Gk lacks to court

---

5:17–20 The Persistence of the Torah

5:17 Fulfill—Jesus' challenge is not to the law (cf. 12:2), but to the way rival leaders interpret (cf. 5:21–48) and/or live it (cf. 5:20; 23:1–3). Jesus fulfills the law by teaching others to live according to God's original intent, where deeds of righteousness are understood to be internally motivated responses (e.g., repentance, mercy, poverty of spirit) to a divinely initiated act (i.e., the drawing near of the kingdom). Likewise, contemporary disciples must focus more on fulfilling the law than merely obeying it.

5:20 Unless your righteousness exceeds—Matthean righteousness (see note at 3:15) is *qualitatively* greater/better because it operates from the premise of realizing God's original intent of mercy and love, not cultic obligation. It is not enough to go to church; the contemporary disciple must live a life that emulates Jesus' self-sacrificing love.

5:21–48 Six Antitheses

the ground of unchastity, causes her to commit adultery; and whoever marries a divorced woman commits adultery.

Concerning Oaths

33 "Again, you have heard that it was said to those of ancient times, 'You shall not swear falsely, but carry out the vows you have made to the Lord.' **34** But I say to you, Do not swear at all, either by heaven, for it is the throne of God, **35** or by the earth, for it is his footstool, or by Jerusalem, for it is the city of the great King. **36** And do not swear by your head, for you cannot make one hair white or black. **37** Let your word be 'Yes, Yes' or 'No, No'; anything more than this comes from the evil one.*a*

Concerning Retaliation

38 "You have heard that it was said, 'An eye for an eye and a tooth for a tooth.' **39** But I say to you, Do not resist an evil-doer. But if anyone strikes you on the right cheek, turn the other also; **40** and if anyone wants to sue you and take your coat, give your cloak as well; **41** and if anyone forces you to go one mile, go also the second mile. **42** Give to everyone who begs from you, and do not refuse anyone who wants to borrow from you.

Love for Enemies

43 "You have heard that it was said, 'You shall love your neighbor and hate your enemy.' **44** But I say to you, Love your enemies and pray for those who persecute you, **45** so that you may be children of your Father in heaven; for he makes his sun rise on the evil and on the good, and sends rain on the righteous and on the unrighteous. **46** For if you love those who love you, what reward do you have? Do not even the tax collectors do the same? **47** And if you greet only your brothers and sisters,*b* what more are you doing than others? Do not even the Gentiles do the same? **48** Be perfect, therefore, as your heavenly Father is perfect.

Concerning Almsgiving

6 "Beware of practicing your piety before others in order to be seen by them; for then you have no reward from your Father in heaven.

2 "So whenever you give alms, do not sound a trumpet before you, as the hypocrites do in the synagogues and in the streets, so that they may be praised by others. Truly I tell you, they have received their reward. **3** But when you give alms, do not let your left hand know what your right hand is doing, **4** so that your alms may be done in secret; and your Father who sees in secret will reward you.*c*

Concerning Prayer

5 "And whenever you pray, do not be like the hypocrites; for they love to stand and pray in the synagogues and at the street corners, so that they may

a Or evil   *b* Gk your brothers   *c* Other ancient authorities add openly

---

5:38 *An eye for an eye*—Cf. Exod. 21:23–24; Lev. 24:19–20; Deut. 19:21. Based on codes of human justice at the time, this was a liberalization of the law. It was aimed at limiting the excessive scope and magnitude of retribution often exacted when a wronged person or family took revenge on someone who had committed a crime against them. Likewise, contemporary disciples must strive to make the law work to encourage the best in people, not simply curb their worst.

5:44 *Love your enemies*—Only by following the radical expectations of this command can one break the cycles of violence and hatred that hold so many individuals, peoples, and nations hostage.

5:48 *Perfect*—Perfection is not a state of being; it is "blessed" historical existence that derives from an engagement of radical Torah interpretation (see note at v. 20). It is a better righteousness that has a potent social consequence; it creates a better community of faith.

6:1–18 How to Practice Righteousness: Three Examples of Piety

6:2 *Hypocrites*—"Hypocrite" originally referred to an actor who hid behind a mask. It came to mean someone who pretended to be something he or she was not, or who was showy or flashy, but without substance (v. 5). It defines the antithesis of Matthean discipleship (chap. 23). Contemporary disciples must not wear their faith like a disposable mask, but live it as a constant presence.

be seen by others. Truly I tell you, they have received their reward. 6 But whenever you pray, go into your room and shut the door and pray to your Father who is in secret; and your Father who sees in secret will reward you.*a*

7 "When you are praying, do not heap up empty phrases as the Gentiles do; for they think that they will be heard because of their many words. 8 Do not be like them, for your Father knows what you need before you ask him.

9 "Pray then in this way:
  Our Father in heaven,
    hallowed be your name.
10　Your kingdom come.
    Your will be done,
      on earth as it is in heaven.
11　Give us this day our daily bread.*b*
12　And forgive us our debts,
    as we also have forgiven our
      debtors.
13　And do not bring us to the time of
      trial,*c*
    but rescue us from the evil one.*d*
14 For if you forgive others their trespasses, your heavenly Father will also forgive you; 15 but if you do not forgive others, neither will your Father forgive your trespasses.

Concerning Fasting

16 "And whenever you fast, do not look dismal, like the hypocrites, for they disfigure their faces so as to show others that they are fasting. Truly I tell you, they have received their reward. 17 But when you fast, put oil on your head and wash your face, 18 so that your fasting may be seen not by others but by your Father who is in secret; and your Father who sees in secret will reward you.*a*

Concerning Treasures

19 "Do not store up for yourselves treasures on earth, where moth and rust*e* consume and where thieves break in and steal; 20 but store up for yourselves treasures in heaven, where neither moth nor rust*e* consumes and where thieves do not break in and steal. 21 For where your treasure is, there your heart will be also.

The Sound Eye

22 "The eye is the lamp of the body. So, if your eye is healthy, your whole body will be full of light; 23 but if your eye is unhealthy, your whole body will be full of darkness. If then the light in you is darkness, how great is the darkness!

Serving Two Masters

24 "No one can serve two masters; for a slave will either hate the one and love the other, or be devoted to the one and despise the other. You cannot serve God and wealth.*f*

Do Not Worry

25 "Therefore I tell you, do not worry about your life, what you will eat or what you will drink,*g* or about your body, what you will wear. Is not life more than food, and the body more than clothing? 26 Look at the birds of the air; they neither sow nor reap nor gather into barns, and yet your heavenly Father feeds them. Are you not of more value than they? 27 And can any of you by worrying add a single hour to your span of life?*h* 28 And why do you worry about clothing? Consider the lilies of the field, how they grow; they neither toil nor spin, 29 yet I tell you, even Solomon in all his glory was not clothed like one of these. 30 But if God so clothes the grass of the field, which is alive today

a Other ancient authorities add *openly*　*b* Or *our bread for tomorrow*　*c* Or *us into temptation*　*d* Or *from evil.* Other ancient authorities add, in some form, *For the kingdom and the power and the glory are yours forever. Amen.*　*e* Gk *eating*　*f* Gk *mammon*　*g* Other ancient authorities lack *or what you will drink*　*h* Or *add one cubit to your height*

6:9–15—The Lord's Prayer (Luke 11:2–4).

6:15 *Forgive others*—Humans are to live their lives with the expectation that the manner in which they treat others will become the yardstick by which God measures out divine treatment to them.

6:19–34 Teaching on Possessions (Luke 12:33–34; 11:34–36; 16:13; 12:22–31)

6:30 *Little faith*—See note at 8:26.

and tomorrow is thrown into the oven, will he not much more clothe you—you of little faith? [31] Therefore do not worry, saying, 'What will we eat?' or 'What will we drink?' or 'What will we wear?' [32] For it is the Gentiles who strive for all these things; and indeed your heavenly Father knows that you need all these things. [33] But strive first for the kingdom of God[a] and his[b] righteousness, and all these things will be given to you as well.

[34] "So do not worry about tomorrow, for tomorrow will bring worries of its own. Today's trouble is enough for today.

Judging Others

7 "Do not judge, so that you may not be judged. [2] For with the judgment you make you will be judged, and the measure you give will be the measure you get. [3] Why do you see the speck in your neighbor's[c] eye, but do not notice the log in your own eye? [4] Or how can you say to your neighbor,[d] 'Let me take the speck out of your eye,' while the log is in your own eye? [5] You hypocrite, first take the log out of your own eye, and then you will see clearly to take the speck out of your neighbor's[c] eye.

Profaning the Holy

6 "Do not give what is holy to dogs; and do not throw your pearls before swine, or they will trample them under foot and turn and maul you.

Ask, Search, Knock

7 "Ask, and it will be given you; search, and you will find; knock, and the door will be opened for you. [8] For everyone who asks receives, and everyone who searches finds, and for everyone who knocks, the door will be opened. [9] Is there anyone among you who, if your child asks for bread, will give a stone? [10] Or if the child asks for a fish, will give a snake? [11] If you then, who are evil, know how to give good gifts to your children, how much more will your Father in heaven give good things to those who ask him!

The Golden Rule

12 "In everything do to others as you would have them do to you; for this is the law and the prophets.

The Narrow Gate

13 "Enter through the narrow gate; for the gate is wide and the road is easy[e] that leads to destruction, and there are many who take it. [14] For the gate is narrow and the road is hard that leads to life, and there are few who find it.

A Tree and Its Fruit

15 "Beware of false prophets, who come to you in sheep's clothing but inwardly are ravenous wolves. [16] You will know them by their fruits. Are grapes gathered from thorns, or figs from thistles? [17] In the same way, every good tree bears good fruit, but the bad tree bears bad fruit. [18] A good tree cannot bear bad fruit, nor can a bad tree bear good fruit. [19] Every tree that does not bear good fruit is cut down and thrown into the fire. [20] Thus you will know them by their fruits.

Concerning Self-Deception

21 "Not everyone who says to me, 'Lord, Lord,' will enter the kingdom of heaven, but only the one who does the will of my Father in heaven. [22] On that day many will say to me, 'Lord, Lord, did we not prophesy in your name, and cast out demons in your name, and do many deeds of power in your name?' [23] Then I will declare to them, 'I never knew you; go away from me, you evildoers.'

[a] Other ancient authorities lack *of God*   [b] Or *its*   [c] Gk *brother's*
[d] Gk *brother*   [e] Other ancient authorities read *for the road is wide and easy*

7:1–29 Miscellaneous Community Imperatives

7:16 *Fruits*—Words are not enough; faith must be demonstrated socially, politically, and spiritually.

Hearers and Doers

24 "Everyone then who hears these words of mine and acts on them will be like a wise man who built his house on rock. 25 The rain fell, the floods came, and the winds blew and beat on that house, but it did not fall, because it had been founded on rock. 26 And everyone who hears these words of mine and does not act on them will be like a foolish man who built his house on sand. 27 The rain fell, and the floods came, and the winds blew and beat against that house, and it fell—and great was its fall!"

28 Now when Jesus had finished saying these things, the crowds were astounded at his teaching, 29 for he taught them as one having authority, and not as their scribes.

Jesus Cleanses a Leper

8 When Jesus*a* had come down from the mountain, great crowds followed him; 2 and there was a leper*b* who came to him and knelt before him, saying, "Lord, if you choose, you can make me clean." 3 He stretched out his hand and touched him, saying, "I do choose. Be made clean!" Immediately his leprosy*b* was cleansed. 4 Then Jesus said to him, "See that you say nothing to anyone; but go, show yourself to the priest, and offer the gift that Moses commanded, as a testimony to them."

Jesus Heals a Centurion's Servant

5 When he entered Capernaum, a centurion came to him, appealing to him 6 and saying, "Lord, my servant is lying at home paralyzed, in terrible distress." 7 And he said to him, "I will come and cure him." 8 The centurion answered, "Lord, I am not worthy to have you come under my roof; but only speak the word, and my servant will be healed. 9 For I also am a man under authority, with soldiers under me; and I say to one, 'Go,' and he goes, and to another, 'Come,' and he comes, and to my slave, 'Do this,' and the slave does it." 10 When Jesus heard him, he was amazed and said to those who followed him, "Truly I tell you, in no one*c* in Israel have I found such faith. 11 I tell you, many will come from east and west and will eat with Abraham and Isaac and Jacob in the kingdom of heaven, 12 while the heirs of the kingdom will be thrown into the outer darkness, where there will be weeping and gnashing of teeth." 13 And to the centurion Jesus said, "Go; let it be done for you according to your faith." And the servant was healed in that hour.

Jesus Heals Many at Peter's House

14 When Jesus entered Peter's house, he saw his mother-in-law lying in bed with a fever; 15 he touched her hand, and

a Gk *he* *b* The terms *leper* and *leprosy* can refer to several diseases *c* Other ancient authorities read *Truly I tell you, not even*

7:24 *Rock*—Cf. 4:18; 10:2; 16:18, where Simon is called Peter. The similar spelling and sounding of "rock" and Peter's name enhance Peter's discipleship role. He is the foundation upon which Jesus will build his church (16:18). Like Peter, contemporary disciples are expected to be steady and secure enough in their faith that God can build community around them.

8:1–17 Jesus Demonstrates the Power of the Kingdom

8:1–4—The healing of a leper (Mark 1:40–45; Luke 5:12–16).

8:3 *He . . . touched him*—Operating in direct contradiction of the Levitical code (cf. Lev. 13:45–46), Jesus touches the leper *before* healing him. Instead of becoming contaminated, Jesus infects him with wholeness. He not only over-turns a physical illness; he decimates a social and cultic norm, and thereby sets the pattern for a discipleship ministry that will engage in the same kinds of revolutionary behavior. Caring for broken people must always take higher precedence than fear of breaking the law.

8:5–13—Luke 7:1–10; 13:28–30.

8:5 *Centurion*—A Gentile. Jesus conducts his kingdom power across the most dramatic divide of all, ethnicity. This inclusive move establishes the boundary-breaking pattern expected of every disciple (28:19). Disciples must share their gifts and God's love across the lines of race, ethnicity, geography, and nationality.

8:14–17—Mark 1:29–34; Luke 4:38–41.

the fever left her, and she got up and began to serve him. ¹⁶ That evening they brought to him many who were possessed with demons; and he cast out the spirits with a word, and cured all who were sick. ¹⁷ This was to fulfill what had been spoken through the prophet Isaiah, "He took our infirmities and bore our diseases."

Would-Be Followers of Jesus

18 Now when Jesus saw great crowds around him, he gave orders to go over to the other side. ¹⁹ A scribe then approached and said, "Teacher, I will follow you wherever you go." ²⁰ And Jesus said to him, "Foxes have holes, and birds of the air have nests; but the Son of Man has nowhere to lay his head." ²¹ Another of his disciples said to him, "Lord, first let me go and bury my father." ²² But Jesus said to him, "Follow me, and let the dead bury their own dead."

Jesus Stills the Storm

23 And when he got into the boat, his disciples followed him. ²⁴ A windstorm arose on the sea, so great that the boat was being swamped by the waves; but he was asleep. ²⁵ And they went and woke him up, saying, "Lord, save us! We are perishing!" ²⁶ And he said to them, "Why are you afraid, you of little faith?" Then he got up and rebuked the winds and the sea; and there was a dead calm. ²⁷ They were amazed, saying, "What sort of man is this, that even the winds and the sea obey him?"

Jesus Heals the Gadarene Demoniacs

28 When he came to the other side, to the country of the Gadarenes,ᵃ two demoniacs coming out of the tombs met him. They were so fierce that no one could pass that way. ²⁹ Suddenly they shouted, "What have you to do with us, Son of God? Have you come here to torment us before the time?" ³⁰ Now a large herd of swine was feeding at some distance from them. ³¹ The demons begged him, "If you cast us out, send us into the herd of swine." ³² And he said to them, "Go!" So they came out and entered the swine; and suddenly, the whole herd rushed down the steep bank into the sea and perished in the water. ³³ The swineherds ran off, and on going into the town, they told the whole story about what had happened to the demoniacs. ³⁴ Then the whole town came out to

ᵃ Other ancient authorities read *Gergesenes*; others, *Gerasenes*

8:17 *He took our infirmities*—Formula quotation: Cf. Isa. 53:4. See note on Matt. 1:22. Jesus fulfills the work of the Suffering Servant of Isaiah. His ability to bear human weakness prefigures the passion where he bears "our" sins (cf. 26:28). His disciples must likewise be willing to take upon themselves and overturn the burdens of those struggling in the world.

8:18–22 **The Radical Nature of Discipleship** (Luke 9:57–60)

8:19 *Teacher*—A primary eschatological expectation was that the messiah would interpret the Torah definitively. Following in his footsteps and building upon his interpretative lead, contemporary followers must equip themselves to be teaching disciples.

8:20 *Son of Man*—Based on the figure from Dan. 7, it has the distinction of being the only title that Jesus uses to refer to himself. It is as Son of Man that Jesus will come as judge at the Parousia.

8:23–34 **Jesus Demonstrates the Power of the Kingdom**

8:23–27—Mark 4:35–41; Luke 8:22–25.

8:25 *Lord, save us*—While in Mark the disciples only protest that Jesus does not care that they are perishing, in Matthew they pray that he will save them. They recognize that Jesus has power to transform even this situation. The contemporary disciple should faithfully engage the social, religious, and political storms they face with the trust that, through Jesus' saving power, they will survive and even conquer.

8:26 *You of little faith*—In Mark, Jesus complains that the disciples do not yet have *any* faith. Here, even though their faith is small, it is present, and therefore can grow. Once again, they are models, particularly for those whose faith struggles in difficult circumstances like the one in which the disciples now find themselves (see 14:31). God can grow whatever faith one can muster.

8:28–34—Mark 5:1–20; Luke 8:26–39.

8:29 *Son of God*—See note at 4:3.

meet Jesus; and when they saw him, they begged him to leave their neighborhood.

9 ¹ And after getting into a boat he crossed the sea and came to his own town.

Jesus Heals a Paralytic

2 And just then some people were carrying a paralyzed man lying on a bed. When Jesus saw their faith, he said to the paralytic, "Take heart, son; your sins are forgiven." ³ Then some of the scribes said to themselves, "This man is blaspheming." ⁴ But Jesus, perceiving their thoughts, said, "Why do you think evil in your hearts? ⁵ For which is easier, to say, 'Your sins are forgiven,' or to say, 'Stand up and walk'? ⁶ But so that you may know that the Son of Man has authority on earth to forgive sins"—he then said to the paralytic—"Stand up, take your bed and go to your home." ⁷ And he stood up and went to his home. ⁸ When the crowds saw it, they were filled with awe, and they glorified God, who had given such authority to human beings.

The Call of Matthew

9 As Jesus was walking along, he saw a man called Matthew sitting at the tax booth; and he said to him, "Follow me." And he got up and followed him.

10 And as he sat at dinner*ᵃ* in the house, many tax collectors and sinners came and were sitting*ᵇ* with him and his disciples. ¹¹ When the Pharisees saw this, they said to his disciples, "Why does your teacher eat with tax collectors and sinners?" ¹² But when he heard this, he said, "Those who are well have no need of a physician, but those who are sick. ¹³ Go and learn what this means, 'I desire mercy, not sacrifice.' For I have come to call not the righteous but sinners."

The Question about Fasting

14 Then the disciples of John came to him, saying, "Why do we and the Pharisees fast often,*ᶜ* but your disciples do not fast?" ¹⁵ And Jesus said to them, "The wedding guests cannot mourn as long as the bridegroom is with them, can they? The days will come when the bridegroom is taken away from them, and then they will fast. ¹⁶ No one sews a piece of unshrunk cloth on an old cloak, for the patch pulls away from the cloak, and a worse tear is made. ¹⁷ Neither is new wine put into old wineskins; otherwise, the skins burst, and the wine is spilled, and the skins are destroyed; but new wine is put into fresh wineskins, and so both are preserved."

A Girl Restored to Life and a Woman Healed

18 While he was saying these things to them, suddenly a leader of the syna-

ᵃ Gk reclined   *ᵇ* Gk were reclining   *ᶜ* Other ancient authorities lack often

---

9:1–38 More Kingdom Power

9:2–8—Healing a paralytic (Mark 2:1–12; Luke 5:17–26).

9:6 Son of Man—See note at 8:20.

9:9–13—Calling and eating with tax collectors and sinners (Mark 2:14–17; Luke 5:27–32).

9:9 Matthew—Called Levi in Mark (2:14) and Luke (5:27).

9:10 Tax collectors—Because tax collectors often abused their clients and collaborated with Gentiles, many considered them socially degenerate and cultically impure. The frightening and revolutionary implication of Matthew's call is that even reprehensible social characters, those whose *intentional* conduct puts them on the societal margin, can, just as they are, become kingdom disciples.

9:13 I desire mercy, not sacrifice—Cf. Hos. 6:6. God cares more about human redemption than upholding arbitrary standards of cultic and social acceptability. So should Jesus' disciples.

9:14–17—Teaching on fasting (Mark 2:18–22; Luke 5:33–39).

9:17 New—Jesus' striking and dangerous Torah interpretation seems new only because it differs so radically from the "old" interpretative strategy of the Pharisaic/rabbinic leadership. Its focus on mercy returns to, and preserves, the original Torah intent. Contemporary disciples should see in the law a tool for conjuring acts of love and mercy, not simply a rule book for curbing acts of injustice.

9:18–26—Raising a girl and healing a woman (Mark 5:21–43; Luke 8:40–56).

gogue[a] came in and knelt before him, saying, "My daughter has just died; but come and lay your hand on her, and she will live." [19] And Jesus got up and followed him, with his disciples. [20] Then suddenly a woman who had been suffering from hemorrhages for twelve years came up behind him and touched the fringe of his cloak, [21] for she said to herself, "If I only touch his cloak, I will be made well." [22] Jesus turned, and seeing her he said, "Take heart, daughter; your faith has made you well." And instantly the woman was made well. [23] When Jesus came to the leader's house and saw the flute players and the crowd making a commotion, [24] he said, "Go away; for the girl is not dead but sleeping." And they laughed at him. [25] But when the crowd had been put outside, he went in and took her by the hand, and the girl got up. [26] And the report of this spread throughout that district.

Jesus Heals Two Blind Men

[27] As Jesus went on from there, two blind men followed him, crying loudly, "Have mercy on us, Son of David!" [28] When he entered the house, the blind men came to him; and Jesus said to them, "Do you believe that I am able to do this?" They said to him, "Yes, Lord." [29] Then he touched their eyes and said, "According to your faith let it be done to you." [30] And their eyes were opened. Then Jesus sternly ordered them, "See that no one knows of this." [31] But they went away and spread the news about him throughout that district.

Jesus Heals One Who Was Mute

[32] After they had gone away, a demoniac who was mute was brought to him. [33] And when the demon had been cast out, the one who had been mute spoke; and the crowds were amazed and said, "Never has anything like this been seen in Israel." [34] But the Pharisees said, "By the ruler of the demons he casts out the demons."[b]

The Harvest Is Great, the Laborers Few

[35] Then Jesus went about all the cities and villages, teaching in their synagogues, and proclaiming the good news of the kingdom, and curing every disease and every sickness. [36] When he saw the crowds, he had compassion for them, because they were harassed and helpless, like sheep without a shepherd. [37] Then he said to his disciples, "The harvest is plentiful, but the laborers are few; [38] therefore ask the Lord of the harvest to send out laborers into his harvest."

The Twelve Apostles

10 Then Jesus[c] summoned his twelve disciples and gave them authority over unclean spirits, to cast them out, and to cure every disease and every sickness. [2] These are the names of the twelve apostles: first, Simon, also known as Peter, and his brother Andrew; James

[a] Gk lacks of the synagogue [b] Other ancient authorities lack this verse [c] Gk he

---

9:20 *A woman who had been suffering from hemorrhages*—Probably menstrual bleeding. Leviticus 15:19–33 prescribes such a woman cultically unclean.

9:21 *Touch*—See note at 8:3. As with the leper, her contact with Jesus breaks ritual law since it occurs before her healing. Her faith pushes her beyond traditional law in search of Jesus' transformative power. This is surely the kind of faith Matthew wants his readers to emulate.

9:25 *Took her by the hand*—Again placing the demands of mercy first (v. 13), Jesus takes hold of one of the most cultically impure objects of all, a corpse (cf. Lev. 22:4; Num. 5:2–4).

9:27–38—More powerful kingdom acts.

9:27–31—Cf. 20:29–34; Mark 10:46–52.

9:27 *Son of David*—See note at 1:1.

9:35 *Their synagogues*—See note at 4:23.

10:1–42 The Missionary Discourse

10:1–4—Establishing the Twelve. Cf. Mark 3:13–19a; Luke 6:12–16.

10:1 *Jesus . . . gave them authority*—The true disciple not only follows; he or she leads by the content and authority of what he or she has been taught.

son of Zebedee, and his brother John; [3] Philip and Bartholomew; Thomas and Matthew the tax collector; James son of Alphaeus, and Thaddaeus;[a] [4] Simon the Cananaean, and Judas Iscariot, the one who betrayed him.

The Mission of the Twelve

5 These twelve Jesus sent out with the following instructions: "Go nowhere among the Gentiles, and enter no town of the Samaritans, [6] but go rather to the lost sheep of the house of Israel. [7] As you go, proclaim the good news, 'The kingdom of heaven has come near.'[b] [8] Cure the sick, raise the dead, cleanse the lepers,[c] cast out demons. You received without payment; give without payment. [9] Take no gold, or silver, or copper in your belts, [10] no bag for your journey, or two tunics, or sandals, or a staff; for laborers deserve their food. [11] Whatever town or village you enter, find out who in it is worthy, and stay there until you leave. [12] As you enter the house, greet it. [13] If the house is worthy, let your peace come upon it; but if it is not worthy, let your peace return to you. [14] If anyone will not welcome you or listen to your words, shake off the dust from your feet as you leave that house or town. [15] Truly I tell you, it will be more tolerable for the land of Sodom and Gomorrah on the day of judgment than for that town.

Coming Persecutions

16 "See, I am sending you out like sheep into the midst of wolves; so be wise as serpents and innocent as doves. [17] Beware of them, for they will hand you over to councils and flog you in their synagogues; [18] and you will be dragged before governors and kings because of me, as a testimony to them and the Gentiles. [19] When they hand you over, do not worry about how you are to speak or what you are to say; for what you are to say will be given to you at that time; [20] for it is not you who speak, but the Spirit of your Father speaking through you. [21] Brother will betray brother to death, and a father his child, and children will rise against parents and have them put to death; [22] and you will be hated by all because of my name. But the one who endures to the end will be saved. [23] When they persecute you in one town, flee to the next; for truly I tell you, you will not have gone through all the towns of Israel before the Son of Man comes.

24 "A disciple is not above the teacher, nor a slave above the master; [25] it is enough for the disciple to be like the teacher, and the slave like the master. If they have called the master of the house Beelzebul, how much more will they malign those of his household!

Whom to Fear

26 "So have no fear of them; for nothing is covered up that will not be uncovered, and nothing secret that will not become known. [27] What I say to you in the dark, tell in the light; and what you hear whispered, proclaim from the housetops. [28] Do not fear those who kill the body but cannot kill the soul; rather fear him who can destroy both soul and body in hell.[d] [29] Are not two sparrows sold for a penny? Yet not one of them will fall to the ground apart from your

---

[a] Other ancient authorities read *Lebbaeus,* or *Lebbaeus called Thaddaeus*
[b] Or *is at hand* [c] The terms *leper* and *leprosy* can refer to several diseases
[d] Gk *Gehenna*

10:5–15—A mission to Israel (Mark 6:8–11; 9:2–5).

10:5 *Go nowhere among the Gentiles*—Matthew is the only Synoptic writer who has Jesus initially restrict the mission of the disciples to the land of Israel. The risen Lord will end that restriction with a more universal charge in 28:19. That latter charge defines the scope of contemporary discipleship.

10:7 *The kingdom of heaven*—See note at 3:2.

10:16–25—The cost of kingdom preaching (Mark 13:9–13; Luke 21:12–17).

10:17 *Their synagogues*—See note at 4:23.

10:26–42—Miscellaneous instructions for mission and discipleship (Luke 12:2–9; 12:51–53; 14:26–27).

Father. **30** And even the hairs of your head are all counted. **31** So do not be afraid; you are of more value than many sparrows.

32 "Everyone therefore who acknowledges me before others, I also will acknowledge before my Father in heaven; **33** but whoever denies me before others, I also will deny before my Father in heaven.

Not Peace, but a Sword

34 "Do not think that I have come to bring peace to the earth; I have not come to bring peace, but a sword.

35 For I have come to set a man against his father,
    and a daughter against her mother,
    and a daughter-in-law against her mother-in-law;
36 and one's foes will be members of one's own household.

37 Whoever loves father or mother more than me is not worthy of me; and whoever loves son or daughter more than me is not worthy of me; **38** and whoever does not take up the cross and follow me is not worthy of me. **39** Those who find their life will lose it, and those who lose their life for my sake will find it.

Rewards

40 "Whoever welcomes you welcomes me, and whoever welcomes me welcomes the one who sent me. **41** Whoever welcomes a prophet in the name of a prophet will receive a prophet's reward; and whoever welcomes a righteous person in the name of a righteous person will receive the reward of the righteous; **42** and whoever gives even a cup of cold water to one of these little ones in the name of a disciple—truly I tell you, none of these will lose their reward."

11 Now when Jesus had finished instructing his twelve disciples, he went on from there to teach and proclaim his message in their cities.

Messengers from John the Baptist

2 When John heard in prison what the Messiah^a was doing, he sent word by his^b disciples **3** and said to him, "Are you the one who is to come, or are we to wait for another?" **4** Jesus answered them, "Go and tell John what you hear and see: **5** the blind receive their sight, the lame walk, the lepers^c are cleansed, the deaf hear, the dead are raised, and the poor have good news brought to them. **6** And blessed is anyone who takes no offense at me."

Jesus Praises John the Baptist

7 As they went away, Jesus began to speak to the crowds about John: "What did you go out into the wilderness to look at? A reed shaken by the wind? **8** What then did you go out to see? Someone^d dressed in soft robes? Look, those who wear soft robes are in royal palaces.

^{a} Or the Christ ^{b} Other ancient authorities read *two of his* ^{c} The terms *leper* and *leprosy* can refer to several diseases ^{d} Or *Why then did you go out? To see someone*

10:34 *Sword*—Jesus' kingdom message and the Torah interpretation that follows from it cause people to choose sides for or against him. The disciples who choose "for" must recognize early on the number and intensity of those who will choose "against." Discipleship means taking sides.

10:37–39—Cf. Mark 8:34–9:1.

10:38 *Take up the cross*—Those who would follow Jesus must preach the same radical, merciful Torah teaching that provokes hostile resistance from the Pharisaic/rabbinic leadership.

10:42 *Little ones*—A euphemism for those young or vulnerable in the faith in the Matthean community. One of the prime directives for a Matthean disciple is the care and nurture of novice disciples.

11:1–19 Jesus and John the Baptist (Luke 7:18–35)

11:2 *Messiah*—See note at 1:1.

11:5 *Go and tell*—The listing of miraculous activities parallels the work that Jesus performed in chaps. 8 and 9. It reminds the reader of 10:8. There the disciples performed the same catena of transformative spiritual, medical, social, and political acts. Jesus is not only a Christ who operates with kingdom power; he is a Christ who authorizes those who follow him to act with the same authority. Like messiahship, discipleship must always have a revolutionary focus.

⁹ What then did you go out to see? A prophet?ᵃ Yes, I tell you, and more than a prophet. ¹⁰ This is the one about whom it is written,

'See, I am sending my messenger
    ahead of you,
  who will prepare your way before
    you.'

¹¹ Truly I tell you, among those born of women no one has arisen greater than John the Baptist; yet the least in the kingdom of heaven is greater than he. ¹² From the days of John the Baptist until now the kingdom of heaven has suffered violence,ᵇ and the violent take it by force. ¹³ For all the prophets and the law prophesied until John came; ¹⁴ and if you are willing to accept it, he is Elijah who is to come. ¹⁵ Let anyone with earsᶜ listen!

16 "But to what will I compare this generation? It is like children sitting in the marketplaces and calling to one another,

¹⁷ 'We played the flute for you, and you
        did not dance;
    we wailed, and you did not
        mourn.'

¹⁸ For John came neither eating nor drinking, and they say, 'He has a demon'; ¹⁹ the Son of Man came eating and drinking, and they say, 'Look, a glutton and a drunkard, a friend of tax collectors and sinners!' Yet wisdom is vindicated by her deeds."ᵈ

Woes to Unrepentant Cities

20 Then he began to reproach the cities in which most of his deeds of power had been done, because they did not repent. ²¹ "Woe to you, Chora-zin! Woe to you, Bethsaida! For if the deeds of power done in you had been done in Tyre and Sidon, they would have repented long ago in sackcloth and ashes. ²² But I tell you, on the day of judgment it will be more tolerable for Tyre and Sidon than for you. ²³ And you, Capernaum,

  will you be exalted to heaven?
    No, you will be brought down to
        Hades.

For if the deeds of power done in you had been done in Sodom, it would have remained until this day. ²⁴ But I tell you that on the day of judgment it will be more tolerable for the land of Sodom than for you."

Jesus Thanks His Father

25 At that time Jesus said, "I thankᵉ you, Father, Lord of heaven and earth, because you have hidden these things from the wise and the intelligent and have revealed them to infants; ²⁶ yes, Father, for such was your gracious will.ᶠ ²⁷ All things have been handed over to me by my Father; and no one knows the Son except the Father, and no one knows the Father except the Son and anyone to whom the Son chooses to reveal him.

28 "Come to me, all you that are weary and are carrying heavy burdens, and I will give you rest. ²⁹ Take my yoke upon you, and learn from me; for I am gentle and humble in heart, and you will find rest for your souls. ³⁰ For my yoke is easy, and my burden is light."

ᵃ Other ancient authorities read *Why then did you go out? To see a prophet?* ᵇ *Or has been coming violently* ᶜ Other ancient authorities add *to hear* ᵈ Other ancient authorities read *children* ᵉ *Or praise* ᶠ *Or for so it was well-pleasing in your sight*

11:19 *Son of Man*—See note at 8:20.

11:20–30 Negative and Positive Responses to the Kingdom

11:20–24—Unrepentant cities (Luke 10:13–15).

11:24 *Sodom*—Jesus chides the Pharisaic/rabbinic community for refusing to believe in and respond to him, while Gentiles and Sodom sinners (Gen. 13:10–13; 14; 18; 19), to whom he did not himself minister directly, would have reacted positively. In matters of the kingdom, it is faithful and merciful (not legal) response (fruit), not lineage (of Israel, of the church) that matters. It should also be noted that, contrary to general opinion, the Gen. 19 account of an attempted rape of two angels by the men of Sodom is a condemnation of sexual violence, not a condemnation of what is today considered homosexuality.

11:25–27—Luke 10:21–22.

Plucking Grain on the Sabbath

12 At that time Jesus went through the grainfields on the sabbath; his disciples were hungry, and they began to pluck heads of grain and to eat. ² When the Pharisees saw it, they said to him, "Look, your disciples are doing what is not lawful to do on the sabbath." ³ He said to them, "Have you not read what David did when he and his companions were hungry? ⁴ He entered the house of God and ate the bread of the Presence, which it was not lawful for him or his companions to eat, but only for the priests. ⁵ Or have you not read in the law that on the sabbath the priests in the temple break the sabbath and yet are guiltless? ⁶ I tell you, something greater than the temple is here. ⁷ But if you had known what this means, 'I desire mercy and not sacrifice,' you would not have condemned the guiltless. ⁸ For the Son of Man is lord of the sabbath."

The Man with a Withered Hand

9 He left that place and entered their synagogue; ¹⁰ a man was there with a withered hand, and they asked him, "Is it lawful to cure on the sabbath?" so that they might accuse him. ¹¹ He said to them, "Suppose one of you has only one sheep and it falls into a pit on the sabbath; will you not lay hold of it and lift it out? ¹² How much more valuable is a human being than a sheep! So it is lawful to do good on the sabbath." ¹³ Then he said to the man, "Stretch out your hand." He stretched it out, and it was restored, as sound as the other. ¹⁴ But the Pharisees went out and conspired against him, how to destroy him.

God's Chosen Servant

15 When Jesus became aware of this, he departed. Many crowds[a] followed him, and he cured all of them, ¹⁶ and he ordered them not to make him known. ¹⁷ This was to fulfill what had been spoken through the prophet Isaiah:

¹⁸ "Here is my servant, whom I have
      chosen,
   my beloved, with whom my soul is
      well pleased.
I will put my Spirit upon him,
   and he will proclaim justice to the
      Gentiles.
¹⁹ He will not wrangle or cry aloud,
   nor will anyone hear his voice in
      the streets.
²⁰ He will not break a bruised reed
   or quench a smoldering wick
until he brings justice to victory.
²¹   And in his name the Gentiles will
      hope."

Jesus and Beelzebul

22 Then they brought to him a demoniac who was blind and mute; and he cured him, so that the one who had been mute could speak and see. ²³ All the crowds were amazed and said, "Can this be the Son of David?" ²⁴ But when the Pharisees heard it, they said, "It is only

[a] Other ancient authorities lack *crowds*

12:1–42 Jesus vs. the Pharisees

12:1–8—Plucking grain on the Sabbath (Mark 2:23–28; Luke 6:1–5).

12:2 *Pharisees*—See note at 3:7.

12:2 *What is not lawful*—Cf. Gen. 2:2; Exod. 16:26–30; 20:8–11; 23:12; 34:21. Despite their hunger, the disciples' actions, apparently reaping, were a violation of the Sabbath rest command. Like Jesus, though, they placed human need above legal observance. So must every Jesus disciple.

12:7 *I desire mercy and not sacrifice*—See note at 9:13.

12:8 *Son of Man*—See note at 8:20.

12:9–14—A healing on the Sabbath (Mark 3:1–6; Luke 6:6–11).

12:9 *Their synagogue*—See note at 4:23.

12:13 *Stretch out your hand*—Jesus goes out of his way to show that concern for human well-being (mercy) trumps devotion to legalism So must every Jesus disciple.

12:15–21—Jesus as God's servant for all people.

12:17—Formula quotation: Cf. Isa. 42:1–4. See note at Matt. 1:22.

12:22–37—The importance of words and deeds (Mark 3:23–30; Luke 11:17–23).

12:23 *Son of David*—See note at 1:1.

by Beelzebul, the ruler of the demons, that this fellow casts out the demons." 25 He knew what they were thinking and said to them, "Every kingdom divided against itself is laid waste, and no city or house divided against itself will stand. 26 If Satan casts out Satan, he is divided against himself; how then will his kingdom stand? 27 If I cast out demons by Beelzebul, by whom do your own exorcists[a] cast them out? Therefore they will be your judges. 28 But if it is by the Spirit of God that I cast out demons, then the kingdom of God has come to you. 29 Or how can one enter a strong man's house and plunder his property, without first tying up the strong man? Then indeed the house can be plundered. 30 Whoever is not with me is against me, and whoever does not gather with me scatters. 31 Therefore I tell you, people will be forgiven for every sin and blasphemy, but blasphemy against the Spirit will not be forgiven. 32 Whoever speaks a word against the Son of Man will be forgiven, but whoever speaks against the Holy Spirit will not be forgiven, either in this age or in the age to come.

A Tree and Its Fruit

33 "Either make the tree good, and its fruit good; or make the tree bad, and its fruit bad; for the tree is known by its fruit. 34 You brood of vipers! How can you speak good things, when you are evil? For out of the abundance of the heart the mouth speaks. 35 The good person brings good things out of a good treasure, and the evil person brings evil things out of an evil treasure. 36 I tell you, on the day of judgment you will have to give an account for every careless word you utter; 37 for by your words you will be justified, and by your words you will be condemned."

The Sign of Jonah

38 Then some of the scribes and Pharisees said to him, "Teacher, we wish to see a sign from you." 39 But he answered them, "An evil and adulterous generation asks for a sign, but no sign will be given to it except the sign of the prophet Jonah. 40 For just as Jonah was three days and three nights in the belly of the sea monster, so for three days and three nights the Son of Man will be in the heart of the earth. 41 The people of Nineveh will rise up at the judgment with this generation and condemn it, because they repented at the proclamation of Jonah, and see, something greater than Jonah is here! 42 The queen of the South will rise up at the judgment with this generation and condemn it, because she came from the ends of the earth to listen to the wisdom of Solomon, and see, something greater than Solomon is here!

The Return of the Unclean Spirit

43 "When the unclean spirit has gone out of a person, it wanders through waterless regions looking for a resting place, but it finds none. 44 Then it says, 'I will return to my house from which I came.' When it comes, it finds it empty, swept, and put in order. 45 Then it goes and brings along seven other spirits more evil than itself, and they enter and live there; and the last state of that person is worse than the first. So will it be also with this evil generation."

The True Kindred of Jesus

46 While he was still speaking to the crowds, his mother and his brothers

[a] Gk sons

12:32 *Son of Man*—See note at 8:20.

12:38–42—The sign of Jonah (Luke 11:29–32).

12:38 *Teacher*—See note at 8:19.

12:39 *Sign of the prophet Jonah*—Perhaps another reference to the Matthean community's Gentile mission. The reluctant prophet successfully preached repentance to a pagan Nineveh (Jonah 3:5). Jesus' disciples are called to the same boundary-breaking, universal task (28:19).

12:43–45 The Power of Regenerative Evil (Luke 11:24–26)

12:46–50 Jesus' True Family (Mark 3:31–35; Luke 8:19–25)

were standing outside, wanting to speak to him. [47] Someone told him, "Look, your mother and your brothers are standing outside, wanting to speak to you."[a] [48] But to the one who had told him this, Jesus[b] replied, "Who is my mother, and who are my brothers?" [49] And pointing to his disciples, he said, "Here are my mother and my brothers! [50] For whoever does the will of my Father in heaven is my brother and sister and mother."

The Parable of the Sower

13 That same day Jesus went out of the house and sat beside the sea. [2] Such great crowds gathered around him that he got into a boat and sat there, while the whole crowd stood on the beach. [3] And he told them many things in parables, saying: "Listen! A sower went out to sow. [4] And as he sowed, some seeds fell on the path, and the birds came and ate them up. [5] Other seeds fell on rocky ground, where they did not have much soil, and they sprang up quickly, since they had no depth of soil. [6] But when the sun rose, they were scorched; and since they had no root, they withered away. [7] Other seeds fell among thorns, and the thorns grew up and choked them. [8] Other seeds fell on good soil and brought forth grain, some a hundredfold, some sixty, some thirty. [9] Let anyone with ears[c] listen!"

The Purpose of the Parables

[10] Then the disciples came and asked him, "Why do you speak to them in parables?" [11] He answered, "To you it has been given to know the secrets[d] of the kingdom of heaven, but to them it has not been given. [12] For to those who have, more will be given, and they will have an abundance; but from those who have nothing, even what they have will be taken away. [13] The reason I speak to them in parables is that 'seeing they do not perceive, and hearing they do not listen, nor do they understand.' [14] With them indeed is fulfilled the prophecy of Isaiah that says:

'You will indeed listen, but never understand,
    and you will indeed look, but never perceive.
[15] For this people's heart has grown dull,
    and their ears are hard of hearing,
        and they have shut their eyes;
    so that they might not look with their eyes,
    and listen with their ears,
    and understand with their heart and turn—
    and I would heal them.'

[16] But blessed are your eyes, for they see, and your ears, for they hear. [17] Truly I tell you, many prophets and righteous people longed to see what you see, but did not see it, and to hear what you hear, but did not hear it.

The Parable of the Sower Explained

[18] "Hear then the parable of the sower. [19] When anyone hears the word of the kingdom and does not understand it, the evil one comes and snatches away what is sown in the heart; this is what

---

[a] Other ancient authorities lack verse 47 [b] Gk he [c] Other ancient authorities add to hear [d] Or mysteries

---

12:50 *Whoever does the will of my Father*—Words and deeds that are consistent with God's will as Jesus represents it are more important for inclusion in the kingdom family than either blood or geography or perhaps, for contemporary disciples, church membership.

13:1–54 The Parable Discourse

13:1–2—Introduction to the parable teaching about the kingdom (Mark 4:1–2; Luke 8:4).

13:3–9—The parable of the Sower (Mark 4:3–9; Luke 8:5–8).

13:3 *Parables*—A putting together of one thing alongside another by way of comparison or illustration. Jesus uses parables not only to teach, but to manage and, in some cases, inflame conflict (cf. vv. 10–17, 34–35).

13:10–17—An explanation for the use of parables (Mark 4:10–12; Luke 8:9–10).

13:11 *Kingdom of heaven*—See note at 3:2.

13:18–23—Jesus explains the parable of the Sower to the disciples (Mark 4:13–20; Luke 8:11–15).

was sown on the path. **20** As for what was sown on rocky ground, this is the one who hears the word and immediately receives it with joy; **21** yet such a person has no root, but endures only for a while, and when trouble or persecution arises on account of the word, that person immediately falls away.*a* **22** As for what was sown among thorns, this is the one who hears the word, but the cares of the world and the lure of wealth choke the word, and it yields nothing. **23** But as for what was sown on good soil, this is the one who hears the word and understands it, who indeed bears fruit and yields, in one case a hundredfold, in another sixty, and in another thirty."

The Parable of Weeds among the Wheat

24 He put before them another parable: "The kingdom of heaven may be compared to someone who sowed good seed in his field; **25** but while everybody was asleep, an enemy came and sowed weeds among the wheat, and then went away. **26** So when the plants came up and bore grain, then the weeds appeared as well. **27** And the slaves of the householder came and said to him, 'Master, did you not sow good seed in your field? Where, then, did these weeds come from?' **28** He answered, 'An enemy has done this.' The slaves said to him, 'Then do you want us to go and gather them?' **29** But he replied, 'No; for in gathering the weeds you would uproot the wheat along with them. **30** Let both of them grow together until the harvest; and at harvest time I will tell the reapers, Collect the weeds first and bind them in bundles to be burned, but gather the wheat into my barn.'"

The Parable of the Mustard Seed

31 He put before them another parable: "The kingdom of heaven is like a mustard seed that someone took and sowed in his field; **32** it is the smallest of all the seeds, but when it has grown it is the greatest of shrubs and becomes a tree, so that the birds of the air come and make nests in its branches."

The Parable of the Yeast

33 He told them another parable: "The kingdom of heaven is like yeast that a woman took and mixed in with*b* three measures of flour until all of it was leavened."

The Use of Parables

34 Jesus told the crowds all these things in parables; without a parable he told them nothing. **35** This was to fulfill what had been spoken through the prophet:*c*

"I will open my mouth to speak in
     parables;
I will proclaim what has been
     hidden from the foundation
     of the world."*d*

Jesus Explains the Parable of the Weeds

36 Then he left the crowds and went into the house. And his disciples approached him, saying, "Explain to us the parable of the weeds of the field." **37** He answered, "The one who sows the good seed is the Son of Man; **38** the field is the world, and the good seed

a Gk *stumbles* *b* Gk *hid in* *c* Other ancient authorities read *the prophet Isaiah* *d* Other ancient authorities lack *of the world*

13:24–52—Other parables of the kingdom.

13:24–30—The parable of the Weeds and the Wheat.

13:30 *At harvest time*—There will be a reckoning where the wheat and the weeds will be separated and the weeds will be consumed by fire. However, disciples must not attempt a premature apportionment. Believers must not determine who is right with God and who is not. This kind of judgment belongs to God alone.

13:31–32—The parable of the Mustard Seed (Mark 4:30–32; Luke 13:18–19).

13:35—Formula quotation: Cf. Ps. 78:2. See note at Matt. 1:22.

13:36–43—An explanation of the Weeds and the Wheat.

13:37 *Son of Man*—See note at 8:20.

are the children of the kingdom; the weeds are the children of the evil one, **39** and the enemy who sowed them is the devil; the harvest is the end of the age, and the reapers are angels. **40** Just as the weeds are collected and burned up with fire, so will it be at the end of the age. **41** The Son of Man will send his angels, and they will collect out of his kingdom all causes of sin and all evildoers, **42** and they will throw them into the furnace of fire, where there will be weeping and gnashing of teeth. **43** Then the righteous will shine like the sun in the kingdom of their Father. Let anyone with ears*a* listen!

Three Parables

44 "The kingdom of heaven is like treasure hidden in a field, which someone found and hid; then in his joy he goes and sells all that he has and buys that field.

45 "Again, the kingdom of heaven is like a merchant in search of fine pearls; **46** on finding one pearl of great value, he went and sold all that he had and bought it.

47 "Again, the kingdom of heaven is like a net that was thrown into the sea and caught fish of every kind; **48** when it was full, they drew it ashore, sat down, and put the good into baskets but threw out the bad. **49** So it will be at the end of the age. The angels will come out and separate the evil from the righteous **50** and throw them into the furnace of fire, where there will be weeping and gnashing of teeth.

Treasures New and Old

51 "Have you understood all this?" They answered, "Yes." **52** And he said to them, "Therefore every scribe who has been trained for the kingdom of heaven is like the master of a household who brings out of his treasure what is new and what is old." **53** When Jesus had finished these parables, he left that place.

The Rejection of Jesus at Nazareth

54 He came to his hometown and began to teach the people*b* in their synagogue, so that they were astounded and said, "Where did this man get this wisdom and these deeds of power? **55** Is not this the carpenter's son? Is not his mother called Mary? And are not his brothers James and Joseph and Simon and Judas? **56** And are not all his sisters with us? Where then did this man get all this?" **57** And they took offense at him. But Jesus said to them, "Prophets are not without honor except in their own country and in their own house." **58** And he did not do many deeds of power there, because of their unbelief.

The Death of John the Baptist

14 At that time Herod the ruler*c* heard reports about Jesus; **2** and he said to his servants, "This is John the Baptist; he has been raised from the dead, and for this reason these powers are at work in him." **3** For Herod had arrested John, bound him, and put him in prison on account of Herodias, his brother Philip's wife,*d* **4** because John had been telling him, "It is not lawful for you to have her." **5** Though Herod*e* wanted to put him to death, he feared the crowd, because they regarded him as a prophet. **6** But when Herod's birthday came, the daughter of Herodias danced before the company, and she pleased Herod **7** so much that he promised on oath to grant her whatever she might ask. **8** Prompted by her mother, she said, "Give me the head of John the Baptist here on a platter." **9** The king was grieved, yet out of regard for his oaths and for the guests, he commanded it to be given; **10** he sent

a Other ancient authorities add *to hear* *b* Gk *them* *c* Gk *tetrarch* *d* Other ancient authorities read *his brother's wife* *e* Gk *he*

13:44–50—Three more kingdom parables.
13:54–58—Jesus' rejection in his hometown (Mark 6:1–6; Luke 4:16–30; John 4:44).

13:54 *Their synagogue*—See note at 4:23.
14:1–12 The Death of John the Baptist (Mark 6:14–29)

and had John beheaded in the prison. **11** The head was brought on a platter and given to the girl, who brought it to her mother. **12** His disciples came and took the body and buried it; then they went and told Jesus.

Feeding the Five Thousand

13 Now when Jesus heard this, he withdrew from there in a boat to a deserted place by himself. But when the crowds heard it, they followed him on foot from the towns. **14** When he went ashore, he saw a great crowd; and he had compassion for them and cured their sick. **15** When it was evening, the disciples came to him and said, "This is a deserted place, and the hour is now late; send the crowds away so that they may go into the villages and buy food for themselves." **16** Jesus said to them, "They need not go away; you give them something to eat." **17** They replied, "We have nothing here but five loaves and two fish." **18** And he said, "Bring them here to me." **19** Then he ordered the crowds to sit down on the grass. Taking the five loaves and the two fish, he looked up to heaven, and blessed and broke the loaves, and gave them to the disciples, and the disciples gave them to the crowds. **20** And all ate and were filled; and they took up what was left over of the broken pieces, twelve baskets full. **21** And those who ate were about five thousand men, besides women and children.

Jesus Walks on the Water

22 Immediately he made the disciples get into the boat and go on ahead to the other side, while he dismissed the crowds. **23** And after he had dismissed the crowds, he went up the mountain by himself to pray. When evening came, he was there alone, **24** but by this time the boat, battered by the waves, was far from the land,*a* for the wind was against them. **25** And early in the morning he came walking toward them on the sea. **26** But when the disciples saw him walking on the sea, they were terrified, saying, "It is a ghost!" And they cried out in fear. **27** But immediately Jesus spoke to them and said, "Take heart, it is I; do not be afraid."

28 Peter answered him, "Lord, if it is you, command me to come to you on the water." **29** He said, "Come." So Peter got out of the boat, started walking on the water, and came toward Jesus. **30** But when he noticed the strong wind,*b* he became frightened, and beginning to sink, he cried out, "Lord, save me!" **31** Jesus immediately reached out his hand and caught him, saying to him, "You of little faith, why did you doubt?" **32** When they got into the boat, the wind ceased. **33** And those in the boat worshiped him, saying, "Truly you are the Son of God."

Jesus Heals the Sick in Gennesaret

34 When they had crossed over, they came to land at Gennesaret. **35** After the people of that place recognized him, they sent word throughout the region

a Other ancient authorities read *was out on the sea*   *b* Other ancient authorities read *the wind*

14:13–21 The Feeding of the Five Thousand (Mark 6:30–44; Luke 9:10–17; John 6:1–13)

14:16 *You give them something to eat*—The command is as figurative as it is literal. This is the essence of discipleship: to feed Jesus' "hungry" followers. Disciples feed Jesus' followers by teaching them in word and deed that care for human need (mercy) outweighs duty to law and tradition (sacrifice).

14:20 *All ate and were filled*—In this feeding the Jews are satisfied. Later, at 15:37, Jesus satisfies a Gentile multitude. Even if Jesus sent his disciples out only to the people of Israel (10:5–6),

the miraculous kingdom power and opportunity available in Jesus shatters the boundary between Jew and Gentile and makes itself available to all who seek it. Jesus' contemporary disciples must make themselves and their transformative gifts available to anyone, regardless of ethnicity or social standing.

14:22–36 Jesus Walks on the Water (Mark 6:45–52; John 6:16–21)

14:31 *Little faith*—See note at 8:26.

14:33 *Son of God*—See note at 4:3.

and brought all who were sick to him, ³⁶ and begged him that they might touch even the fringe of his cloak; and all who touched it were healed.

The Tradition of the Elders

15 Then Pharisees and scribes came to Jesus from Jerusalem and said, ² "Why do your disciples break the tradition of the elders? For they do not wash their hands before they eat." ³ He answered them, "And why do you break the commandment of God for the sake of your tradition? ⁴ For God said,[a] 'Honor your father and your mother,' and, 'Whoever speaks evil of father or mother must surely die.' ⁵ But you say that whoever tells father or mother, 'Whatever support you might have had from me is given to God,'[b] then that person need not honor the father.[c] ⁶ So, for the sake of your tradition, you make void the word[d] of God. ⁷ You hypocrites! Isaiah prophesied rightly about you when he said:

⁸ 'This people honors me with their lips,
    but their hearts are far from me;
⁹ in vain do they worship me,
    teaching human precepts as doctrines.'"

Things That Defile

¹⁰ Then he called the crowd to him and said to them, "Listen and understand: ¹¹ it is not what goes into the mouth that defiles a person, but it is what comes out of the mouth that defiles." ¹² Then the disciples approached and said to him, "Do you know that the Pharisees took offense when they heard what you said?" ¹³ He answered, "Every plant that my heavenly Father has not planted will be uprooted. ¹⁴ Let them alone; they are blind guides of the blind.[e] And if one blind person guides another, both will fall into a pit." ¹⁵ But Peter said to him, "Explain this parable to us." ¹⁶ Then he said, "Are you also still without understanding? ¹⁷ Do you not see that whatever goes into the mouth enters the stomach, and goes out into the sewer? ¹⁸ But what comes out of the mouth proceeds from the heart, and this is what defiles. ¹⁹ For out of the heart come evil intentions, murder, adultery, fornication, theft, false witness, slander. ²⁰ These are what defile a person, but to eat with unwashed hands does not defile."

[a] Other ancient authorities read *commanded, saying*   [b] Or *is an offering*   [c] Other ancient authorities add *or the mother*   [d] Other ancient authorities read *law*; others, *commandment*   [e] Other ancient authorities lack *of the blind*

15:1–20 Jesus, the Pharisees, and Scribes Argue about Tradition (Mark 7:1–23)

15:1 *Pharisees*—See note at 3:7.

15:2 *Your disciples*—Jesus' disciples are the ones charged with the boundary trespass. Their actions are as disruptive as his.

15:2 *Tradition of the elders*—This term most likely refers to the oral law which interpreted the written traditions of the Torah in light of contemporary circumstances. The Pharisees held that it was as authoritative as the written law. Jesus has been counseling his disciples to put mercy above allegiance to tradition. His disciples have been paying attention and changing the religious and political landscape as a result.

15:5 *Whatever support you might have had from me is given to God*—This consecration refers to a vow where a person "willed" his property and resources to the temple. While the person who willed it could still make use of it, he could not share it with anyone else, even his parents.

For Jesus, it was one more example where allegiance to the cultic letter of tradition superseded God's mercy and love. Here is a prime example where a believer can live by the law and still live against God's expectations. Contemporary disciples must realize that being "legal" is not the same thing as living out God's love.

15:7 *Hypocrites*—See note at 6:2.

15:11—Whereas Mark (7:19) uses this occasion to say that Jesus pronounced all foods clean, and thereby broke a major portion of the Jewish food laws, Matthew maintains the focus on the tradition of the elders regarding ritual washing and purification before meals. The law remains valid; Jesus challenges and overrides the human traditions that grew up inappropriately around the law and set the law over and against love and mercy. The warning is this: contemporary believers, in their zeal to live righteously, can legalize and thereby discredit the gospel.

The Canaanite Woman's Faith

21 Jesus left that place and went away to the district of Tyre and Sidon. [22] Just then a Canaanite woman from that region came out and started shouting, "Have mercy on me, Lord, Son of David; my daughter is tormented by a demon." [23] But he did not answer her at all. And his disciples came and urged him, saying, "Send her away, for she keeps shouting after us." [24] He answered, "I was sent only to the lost sheep of the house of Israel." [25] But she came and knelt before him, saying, "Lord, help me." [26] He answered, "It is not fair to take the children's food and throw it to the dogs." [27] She said, "Yes, Lord, yet even the dogs eat the crumbs that fall from their masters' table." [28] Then Jesus answered her, "Woman, great is your faith! Let it be done for you as you wish." And her daughter was healed instantly.

Jesus Cures Many People

29 After Jesus had left that place, he passed along the Sea of Galilee, and he went up the mountain, where he sat down. [30] Great crowds came to him, bringing with them the lame, the maimed, the blind, the mute, and many others. They put them at his feet, and he cured them, [31] so that the crowd was amazed when they saw the mute speaking, the maimed whole, the lame walking, and the blind seeing. And they praised the God of Israel.

Feeding the Four Thousand

32 Then Jesus called his disciples to him and said, "I have compassion for the crowd, because they have been with me now for three days and have nothing to eat; and I do not want to send them away hungry, for they might faint on the way." [33] The disciples said to him, "Where are we to get enough bread in the desert to feed so great a crowd?" [34] Jesus asked them, "How many loaves have you?" They said, "Seven, and a few small fish." [35] Then ordering the crowd to sit down on the ground, [36] he took the seven loaves and the fish; and after giving thanks he broke them and gave them to the disciples, and the disciples gave them to the crowds. [37] And all of them ate and were filled; and they took up the broken pieces left over, seven baskets full. [38] Those who had eaten were four thousand men, besides women and children. [39] After sending away the crowds, he got into the boat and went to the region of Magadan.[a]

The Demand for a Sign

16 The Pharisees and Sadducees came, and to test Jesus[b] they asked him to show them a sign from heaven. [2] He answered them, "When it is evening, you say, 'It will be fair weather, for the sky is red.' [3] And in the morning, 'It will be stormy today, for the sky is red and threatening.' You know how to interpret the appearance of the sky, but you cannot interpret the signs of the times.[c] [4] An evil and adulterous generation asks for a sign, but no sign will be given to it except the sign of Jonah." Then he left them and went away.

[a] Other ancient authorities read *Magdala* or *Magdalan*   [b] Gk *him*   [c] Other ancient authorities lack [2] *When it is . . . of the times*

15:21–28 The Canaanite Woman

15:22 *Son of David*—See note at 1:1.

15:27 *Even the dogs*—Despite the fact that Jesus' ministry was exclusively to the Jews, this Gentile woman convinces him to extend the transformative fruit of that ministry to her daughter and thus, symbolically, to her people. The woman's faith (v. 28) is a behavioral model for believers who encounter resistance to the boundary-breaking ways of the kingdom. Do not give up; God will respond.

15:29–31 More Healings

15:32–39 The Feeding of Four Thousand

15:37 *All of them ate and were filled*—See note at 14:20.

16:1–12 Conflict with the Pharisees and Sadducees (Mark 8:11–21)

16:1 *Pharisees*—See note at 3:7. *Sadducees*—Aristocratic, priestly party that served the temple. Unlike the Pharisees, they did not believe in the resurrection of the dead.

16:4 *Sign of Jonah*—See note at 12:39.

The Yeast of the Pharisees and Sadducees

5 When the disciples reached the other side, they had forgotten to bring any bread. 6 Jesus said to them, "Watch out, and beware of the yeast of the Pharisees and Sadducees." 7 They said to one another, "It is because we have brought no bread." 8 And becoming aware of it, Jesus said, "You of little faith, why are you talking about having no bread? 9 Do you still not perceive? Do you not remember the five loaves for the five thousand, and how many baskets you gathered? 10 Or the seven loaves for the four thousand, and how many baskets you gathered? 11 How could you fail to perceive that I was not speaking about bread? Beware of the yeast of the Pharisees and Sadducees!" 12 Then they understood that he had not told them to beware of the yeast of bread, but of the teaching of the Pharisees and Sadducees.

Peter's Declaration about Jesus

13 Now when Jesus came into the district of Caesarea Philippi, he asked his disciples, "Who do people say that the Son of Man is?" 14 And they said, "Some say John the Baptist, but others Elijah, and still others Jeremiah or one of the prophets." 15 He said to them, "But who do you say that I am?" 16 Simon Peter answered, "You are the Messiah,*a* the Son of the living God." 17 And Jesus answered him, "Blessed are you, Simon son of Jonah! For flesh and blood has not revealed this to you, but my Father in heaven. 18 And I tell you, you are Peter,*b* and on this rock*c* I will build my church, and the gates of Hades will not prevail against it. 19 I will give you the keys of the kingdom of heaven, and whatever you bind on earth will be bound in heaven, and whatever you loose on earth will be loosed in heaven." 20 Then he sternly ordered the disciples not to tell anyone that he was*d* the Messiah.*a*

Jesus Foretells His Death and Resurrection

21 From that time on, Jesus began to show his disciples that he must go to Jerusalem and undergo great suffering at the hands of the elders and chief priests and scribes, and be killed, and on the third day be raised. 22 And Peter took him aside and began to rebuke him, saying, "God forbid it, Lord! This must never happen to you." 23 But he turned and said to Peter, "Get behind me, Satan! You are a stumbling block to me; for you are setting your mind not on divine things but on human things."

The Cross and Self-Denial

24 Then Jesus told his disciples, "If any want to become my followers, let them

a Or the Christ *b* Gk Petros *c* Gk petra *d* Other ancient authorities add Jesus

---

16:8 *You of little faith*—See note at 8:26.

16:13–28 Peter's Confession and Jesus' First Passion Prediction (Mark 8:27–9:1; Luke 9:18–27)

16:13 *Son of Man*—See note at 8:20.

16:16 *Messiah*—See note at 1:1. *Son of…God*—See note at 4:3.

16:18 *Peter . . . rock*—See note at 7:24. *Church*—The term is used here and at 18:17 to refer to the Matthean community of believers. Matthew writes for the church's instruction and exhortation.

16:19 *Keys*—A symbol of authority (cf. Isa. 22:22). The use of this symbol, combined with the declaration of Peter's binding and loosing power, confirms that God's kingdom authority passes through Jesus to Jesus' disciples (cf. 10:1)

and then to the church built upon their foundation (cf. 18:18). Contemporary disciples should act with the fearful responsibility of knowing that they represent the reality and authority of God's kingdom in the world.

16:21—The first of three texts where Jesus predicts his passion. Cf. 17:22–23; 20:17–19.

16:23 *Get behind me, Satan*—Anyone who wishes to preserve an unhealthy status quo, even the status quo of messianic expectations that refuse the thought of a suffering messiah, cannot follow on the Lord's kingdom way. Likewise, anyone who is afraid to commit fully to the radically transformative way of Jesus' lordship that places mercy above law because of the suffering that such behavior will attract, cannot be a kingdom disciple.

16:24 *Take up their cross*—See note at 10:38.

deny themselves and take up their cross and follow me. 25 For those who want to save their life will lose it, and those who lose their life for my sake will find it. 26 For what will it profit them if they gain the whole world but forfeit their life? Or what will they give in return for their life?

27 "For the Son of Man is to come with his angels in the glory of his Father, and then he will repay everyone for what has been done. 28 Truly I tell you, there are some standing here who will not taste death before they see the Son of Man coming in his kingdom."

The Transfiguration

17 Six days later, Jesus took with him Peter and James and his brother John and led them up a high mountain, by themselves. 2 And he was transfigured before them, and his face shone like the sun, and his clothes became dazzling white. 3 Suddenly there appeared to them Moses and Elijah, talking with him. 4 Then Peter said to Jesus, "Lord, it is good for us to be here; if you wish, I*a* will make three dwellings*b* here, one for you, one for Moses, and one for Elijah." 5 While he was still speaking, suddenly a bright cloud overshadowed them, and from the cloud a voice said, "This is my Son, the Beloved;*c* with him I am well pleased; listen to him!" 6 When the disciples heard this, they fell to the ground and were overcome by fear. 7 But Jesus came and touched them, saying, "Get up and do not be afraid." 8 And when they looked up, they saw no one except Jesus himself alone.

9 As they were coming down the mountain, Jesus ordered them, "Tell no one about the vision until after the Son of Man has been raised from the dead." 10 And the disciples asked him, "Why, then, do the scribes say that Elijah must come first?" 11 He replied, "Elijah is indeed coming and will restore all things; 12 but I tell you that Elijah has already come, and they did not recognize him, but they did to him whatever they pleased. So also the Son of Man is about to suffer at their hands." 13 Then the disciples understood that he was speaking to them about John the Baptist.

Jesus Cures a Boy with a Demon

14 When they came to the crowd, a man came to him, knelt before him, 15 and said, "Lord, have mercy on my son, for he is an epileptic and he suffers terribly; he often falls into the fire and often into the water. 16 And I brought him to your disciples, but they could not cure him." 17 Jesus answered, "You faithless and perverse generation, how much longer must I be with you? How much longer must I put up with you? Bring him here to me." 18 And Jesus rebuked the demon,*d* and it*e* came out of him,

a Other ancient authorities read *we* *b* Or *tents* *c* Or *my beloved Son*
d Gk *it* or *him* *e* Gk *the demon*

16:27 Son of Man—See note at 8:20.

16:27 For what has been done—Right belief must be completed by repentant, kingdom-responsive behavior that places mercy above obligation to tradition.

17:1–8 The Transfiguration (Mark 9:2–8; Luke 9:28–36)

17:3 Moses and Elijah—Moses embodies the Law; Elijah represents the Prophets. Their presence with Jesus fits the Matthean theme that Jesus did not come to destroy the Law and the Prophets, but to fulfill them (cf. 5:17–20).

17:4 I will make three dwellings—Faced with the possibility of suffering, Peter elects to maintain the transfigured status quo that would keep Jesus, and, most importantly, those who believe in him, dwelling in a stationary and trouble-free, spiritual existence on the mountaintop. Matthew's unflattering account of Peter's generous offer suggests that disciples must not shelter themselves from the transformative imitation of Jesus' ministry, even if the hideout is a place and time of spiritual exaltation.

17:5 Listen to him—An exhortation to risky discipleship. Just as Jesus has been commissioned to a ministry where suffering is necessary (16:21–28), so have his followers.

17:9–13 Teaching about Elijah (Mark 9:9–13)

17:9 Son of Man—See note at 8:20.

17:14–20 Mustard Seed Faith (Mark 9:14–29; Luke 9:37–43)

and the boy was cured instantly. ¹⁹ Then the disciples came to Jesus privately and said, "Why could we not cast it out?" ²⁰ He said to them, "Because of your little faith. For truly I tell you, if you have faith the size of a*a* mustard seed, you will say to this mountain, 'Move from here to there,' and it will move; and nothing will be impossible for you."*b*

Jesus Again Foretells His Death and Resurrection

22 As they were gathering*c* in Galilee, Jesus said to them, "The Son of Man is going to be betrayed into human hands, ²³ and they will kill him, and on the third day he will be raised." And they were greatly distressed.

Jesus and the Temple Tax

24 When they reached Capernaum, the collectors of the temple tax*d* came to Peter and said, "Does your teacher not pay the temple tax?"*d* ²⁵ He said, "Yes, he does." And when he came home, Jesus spoke of it first, asking, "What do you think, Simon? From whom do kings of the earth take toll or tribute? From their children or from others?" ²⁶ When Peter*e* said, "From others," Jesus said to him, "Then the children are free. ²⁷ However, so that we do not give offense to them, go to the sea and cast a hook; take the first fish that comes up; and when you open its mouth, you will find a coin;*f* take that and give it to them for you and me."

True Greatness

18 At that time the disciples came to Jesus and asked, "Who is the greatest in the kingdom of heaven?" ²He called a child, whom he put among them, ³ and said, "Truly I tell you, unless you change and become like children, you will never enter the kingdom of heaven. ⁴ Whoever becomes humble like this child is the greatest in the kingdom of heaven. ⁵ Whoever welcomes one such child in my name welcomes me.

Temptations to Sin

6 "If any of you put a stumbling block before one of these little ones who believe in me, it would be better for you if a great millstone were fastened around your neck and you were drowned in the depth of the sea. ⁷ Woe to the world because of stumbling blocks! Occasions for stumbling are bound to come, but woe to the one by whom the stumbling block comes!

8 "If your hand or your foot causes you to stumble, cut it off and throw it away; it is better for you to enter life maimed or lame than to have two hands or two feet and to be thrown into the eternal fire. ⁹ And if your eye causes you to stumble, tear it out and throw it away; it is better for you to enter life with one eye than to have two eyes and to be thrown into the hell*g* of fire.

a Gk faith as a grain of *b* Other ancient authorities add verse 21, *But this kind does not come out except by prayer and fasting* *c* Other ancient authorities read *living* *d* Gk *didrachma* *e* Gk *he* *f* Gk *stater*; the stater was worth two didrachmas *g* Gk Gehenna

17:20 *Little faith*—See note at 8:26.

17:22–23 A Second Passion Prediction (Mark 9:30–32; Luke 9:43–45)

17:22—Cf. 16:21; 20:17–19. *Son of Man*—See note at 8:20.

17:24–27 The Temple Tax

18:1–35 The Ecclesiological Discourse

18:1–14—True greatness (Mark 9:33–37, 42–48; Luke 9:46–48; 17:1–2).

18:4 *Humble like this child*—Since a child had very little, if any, social status, Jesus' use of one as an object lesson immediately redirects the disciples' deliberation from thoughts of greatness to an image of humility. Only by assuming an identity and status of weakness can one appropriate the strength of the kingdom.

18:9—The body is a church metaphor (cf. 1 Cor. 12–14). The body parts are metaphors for those leaders or members of the community who by their pride and sense of self-importance cause the little ones to sin. The remedy for such an ecclesiological scandal is an ecclesiological act, excommunication, which prefigures eschatological judgment. Matthew pulls no punches where church leadership is concerned. In order to protect the sanctity of the larger community, the larger body, the transgressing member must be cut out or cut off. The disciple is challenged to weigh the good of the many over and against the faithlessness of the few.

The Parable of the Lost Sheep

10 "Take care that you do not despise one of these little ones; for, I tell you, in heaven their angels continually see the face of my Father in heaven.*a* 12 What do you think? If a shepherd has a hundred sheep, and one of them has gone astray, does he not leave the ninety-nine on the mountains and go in search of the one that went astray? 13 And if he finds it, truly I tell you, he rejoices over it more than over the ninety-nine that never went astray. 14 So it is not the will of your*b* Father in heaven that one of these little ones should be lost.

Reproving Another Who Sins

15 "If another member of the church*c* sins against you,*d* go and point out the fault when the two of you are alone. If the member listens to you, you have regained that one.*e* 16 But if you are not listened to, take one or two others along with you, so that every word may be confirmed by the evidence of two or three witnesses. 17 If the member refuses to listen to them, tell it to the church; and if the offender refuses to listen even to the church, let such a one be to you as a Gentile and a tax collector. 18 Truly I tell you, whatever you bind on earth will be bound in heaven, and whatever you loose on earth will be loosed in heaven. 19 Again, truly I tell you, if two of you agree on earth about anything you ask, it will be done for you by my Father in heaven. 20 For where two or three are gathered in my name, I am there among them."

Forgiveness

21 Then Peter came and said to him, "Lord, if another member of the church*f* sins against me, how often should I forgive? As many as seven times?" 22 Jesus said to him, "Not seven times, but, I tell you, seventy-seven*g* times.

The Parable of the Unforgiving Servant

23 "For this reason the kingdom of heaven may be compared to a king who wished to settle accounts with his slaves. 24 When he began the reckoning, one who owed him ten thousand talents*h* was brought to him; 25 and, as he could not pay, his lord ordered him to be sold, together with his wife and children and all his possessions, and payment to be made. 26 So the slave fell on his knees before him, saying, 'Have patience with me, and I will pay you everything.' 27 And out of pity for him, the lord of that slave released him and forgave him the debt. 28 But that same slave, as he went out, came upon one of his fellow slaves who owed him a hundred denarii;*i* and seizing him by the throat, he said, 'Pay what you owe.' 29 Then his fellow slave fell down and pleaded with him, 'Have patience with me, and I will pay you.' 30 But he refused; then he went and threw him into prison until he would pay the debt. 31 When his fellow slaves saw what had happened, they were greatly distressed, and they went and reported to their lord all that had taken place. 32 Then his lord summoned him and said to him, 'You wicked slave!

a Other ancient authorities add verse 11, *For the Son of Man came to save the lost*   *b* Other ancient authorities read *my*   *c* Gk *If your brother*   *d* Other ancient authorities lack *against you*   *e* Gk *the brother*   *f* Gk *if my brother*   *g* Or *seventy times seven*   *h* A talent was worth more than fifteen years' wages of a laborer   *i* The denarius was the usual day's wage for a laborer

---

18:10–14—The parable of the Lost Sheep (Luke 15:3–7).

18:12 *Shepherd*—The reality of sin in the community is acknowledged. Church leaders must be good shepherds who take particular care to win back those who have strayed from the proper path.

18:15–35—Matters of church discipline.

18:17 *Church*—See note at 16:18.

18:18 *Bind and loose*—See note at 16:19. The authority that passes from Jesus to Peter now passes to the church. Given the ecclesiological setting, it is most likely that Matthew means church leaders are given the authority to execute church discipline as either forgiveness or excommunication. When considering either decision, however, church leaders would also do well to remember the gospel directive that ultimate judgment belongs to God; they should therefore act with humility and great care.

I forgave you all that debt because you pleaded with me. ³³ Should you not have had mercy on your fellow slave, as I had mercy on you?' ³⁴ And in anger his lord handed him over to be tortured until he would pay his entire debt. ³⁵ So my heavenly Father will also do to every one of you, if you do not forgive your brother or sister*a* from your heart."

Teaching about Divorce

19 When Jesus had finished saying these things, he left Galilee and went to the region of Judea beyond the Jordan. ² Large crowds followed him, and he cured them there.

3 Some Pharisees came to him, and to test him they asked, "Is it lawful for a man to divorce his wife for any cause?" ⁴ He answered, "Have you not read that the one who made them at the beginning 'made them male and female,' ⁵ and said, 'For this reason a man shall leave his father and mother and be joined to his wife, and the two shall become one flesh'? ⁶ So they are no longer two, but one flesh. Therefore what God has joined together, let no one separate." ⁷ They said to him, "Why then did Moses command us to give a certificate of dismissal and to divorce her?" ⁸ He said to them, "It was because you were so hard-hearted that Moses allowed you to divorce your wives, but from the beginning it was not so. ⁹ And I say to you, whoever divorces his wife, except for unchastity, and marries another commits adultery."*b*

10 His disciples said to him, "If such is the case of a man with his wife, it is better not to marry." ¹¹ But he said to them, "Not everyone can accept this teaching, but only those to whom it is given. ¹² For there are eunuchs who have been so from birth, and there are eunuchs who have been made eunuchs by others, and there are eunuchs who have made themselves eunuchs for the sake of the kingdom of heaven. Let anyone accept this who can."

Jesus Blesses Little Children

13 Then little children were being brought to him in order that he might lay his hands on them and pray. The disciples spoke sternly to those who brought them; ¹⁴ but Jesus said, "Let the little children come to me, and do not stop them; for it is to such as these that the kingdom of heaven belongs." ¹⁵ And he laid his hands on them and went on his way.

The Rich Young Man

16 Then someone came to him and said, "Teacher, what good deed must I

a Gk brother *b* Other ancient authorities read *except on the ground of unchastity, causes her to commit adultery;* others add at the end of the verse *and he who marries a divorced woman commits adultery*

19:1–30 Discipleship Ethics

19:1–12—Another teaching on divorce (Mark 10:1–12).

19:6—Jesus argues that God's will for men and women in marriage must come first; any concessions to divorce made in the Mosaic law are secondary. See Deut. 24:1.

19:8 *From the beginning it was not so*—Operating from the principle of equanimity established at creation (cf. Gen. 1:27; 2:24), Jesus' radical response assures that the male will no longer be able to wield discretionary power over a marriage. His arbitrary ability to end it by certificate lost, he now finds himself as obligated as his mate to the preservation of the union. Obviously, the contemporary parameters of marriage are quite different from those in Jesus' time. Jesus' response is not aimed at a universal nullification of ending broken or distorted marriage, but is aimed at putting both marriage partners on firm, equal footing in every circumstance.

19:9 *Except for unchastity*—Unlike the case in the Markan parallel (10:1–12), Jesus here allows for divorce in the case of sexual unchastity. This so-called exception, however, is really not a liberalizing one at all. Adultery and unchastity were contaminants that destroyed marriage. The exception protects the indissolubility of marriage from contamination; it does not lessen the commitment to marriage.

19:13–15—Children and the kingdom (Mark 10:13–16; Luke 18:15–17).

19:13 *Children*—See note at 18:4.

19:16–30—Wealth and the kingdom (Mark 10:17–31; Luke 18:18–30).

19:16 *Teacher*—See note at 8:19. The man's question misses the point of the teaching

do to have eternal life?" ¹⁷ And he said to him, "Why do you ask me about what is good? There is only one who is good. If you wish to enter into life, keep the commandments." ¹⁸ He said to him, "Which ones?" And Jesus said, "You shall not murder; You shall not commit adultery; You shall not steal; You shall not bear false witness; ¹⁹ Honor your father and mother; also, You shall love your neighbor as yourself." ²⁰ The young man said to him, "I have kept all these;*a* what do I still lack?" ²¹ Jesus said to him, "If you wish to be perfect, go, sell your possessions, and give the money*b* to the poor, and you will have treasure in heaven; then come, follow me." ²² When the young man heard this word, he went away grieving, for he had many possessions.

23 Then Jesus said to his disciples, "Truly I tell you, it will be hard for a rich person to enter the kingdom of heaven. ²⁴ Again I tell you, it is easier for a camel to go through the eye of a needle than for someone who is rich to enter the kingdom of God." ²⁵ When the disciples heard this, they were greatly astounded and said, "Then who can be saved?" ²⁶ But Jesus looked at them and said, "For mortals it is impossible, but for God all things are possible."

27 Then Peter said in reply, "Look, we have left everything and followed you. What then will we have?" ²⁸ Jesus said to them, "Truly I tell you, at the renewal of all things, when the Son of Man is seated on the throne of his glory, you who have followed me will also sit on twelve thrones, judging the twelve tribes of Israel. ²⁹ And everyone who has left houses or brothers or sisters or father or mother or children or fields, for my name's sake, will receive a hundredfold,*c* and will inherit eternal life. ³⁰ But many

who are first will be last, and the last will be first.

The Laborers in the Vineyard

20 "For the kingdom of heaven is like a landowner who went out early in the morning to hire laborers for his vineyard. ² After agreeing with the laborers for the usual daily wage,*d* he sent them into his vineyard. ³ When he went out about nine o'clock, he saw others standing idle in the marketplace; ⁴ and he said to them, 'You also go into the vineyard, and I will pay you whatever is right.' So they went. ⁵ When he went out again about noon and about three o'clock, he did the same. ⁶ And about five o'clock he went out and found others standing around; and he said to them, 'Why are you standing here idle all day?' ⁷ They said to him, 'Because no one has hired us.' He said to them, 'You also go into the vineyard.' ⁸ When evening came, the owner of the vineyard said to his manager, 'Call the laborers and give them their pay, beginning with the last and then going to the first.' ⁹ When those hired about five o'clock came, each of them received the usual daily wage.*d* ¹⁰ Now when the first came, they thought they would receive more; but each of them also received the usual daily wage.*d* ¹¹ And when they received it, they grumbled against the landowner, ¹² saying, 'These last worked only one hour, and you have made them equal to us who have borne the burden of the day and the scorching heat.' ¹³ But he replied to one of them, 'Friend, I am doing you no wrong; did you not agree with me for the usual daily wage?*d* ¹⁴ Take what belongs to you and go; I choose to give to this last the same as I give to you.

a Other ancient authorities add *from my youth*   *b* Gk lacks *the money*
c Other ancient authorities read *manifold*   *d* Gk *a denarius*

---

throughout chap. 19. One does not do good things to earn placement in the kingdom. One does good as a response to the gift of the kingdom.

19:21 *Perfect*—See note at 5:48.

19:22 *He went away grieving*—The young man lacks a childlike recognition of God's kingdom and messiah that generates security not in one's possessions, but in one's relationship with God.

20:1–16 The Parable of the Day Laborers

¹⁵ Am I not allowed to do what I choose with what belongs to me? Or are you envious because I am generous?ᵃ ¹⁶ So the last will be first, and the first will be last."ᵇ

A Third Time Jesus Foretells His Death and Resurrection

17 While Jesus was going up to Jerusalem, he took the twelve disciples aside by themselves, and said to them on the way, ¹⁸ "See, we are going up to Jerusalem, and the Son of Man will be handed over to the chief priests and scribes, and they will condemn him to death; ¹⁹ then they will hand him over to the Gentiles to be mocked and flogged and crucified; and on the third day he will be raised."

The Request of the Mother of James and John

20 Then the mother of the sons of Zebedee came to him with her sons, and kneeling before him, she asked a favor of him. ²¹ And he said to her, "What do you want?" She said to him, "Declare that these two sons of mine will sit, one at your right hand and one at your left, in your kingdom." ²² But Jesus answered, "You do not know what you are asking. Are you able to drink the cup that I am about to drink?"ᶜ They said to him, "We are able." ²³ He said to them, "You will

indeed drink my cup, but to sit at my right hand and at my left, this is not mine to grant, but it is for those for whom it has been prepared by my Father."

24 When the ten heard it, they were angry with the two brothers. ²⁵ But Jesus called them to him and said, "You know that the rulers of the Gentiles lord it over them, and their great ones are tyrants over them. ²⁶ It will not be so among you; but whoever wishes to be great among you must be your servant, ²⁷ and whoever wishes to be first among you must be your slave; ²⁸ just as the Son of Man came not to be served but to serve, and to give his life a ransom for many."

Jesus Heals Two Blind Men

29 As they were leaving Jericho, a large crowd followed him. ³⁰ There were two blind men sitting by the roadside. When they heard that Jesus was passing by, they shouted, "Lord,ᵈ have mercy on us, Son of David!" ³¹ The crowd sternly ordered them to be quiet; but they shouted even more loudly, "Have mercy on us, Lord, Son of David!" ³² Jesus stood still and called them, saying, "What do you want me to do for you?" ³³ They said to him,

---

ᵃ Gk is your eye evil because I am good? ᵇ Other ancient authorities add for many are called but few are chosen ᶜ Other ancient authorities add or to be baptized with the baptism that I am baptized with? ᵈ Other ancient authorities lack Lord

---

20:16 *The last will be first*—Those who have been working from the beginning and have borne the burden of the day's heat in the Lord's vineyard (i.e., the disciples) will be eschatologically compensated. At the same time, however, Jesus defends God's sovereign liberty to reward others as God wills. Because no one can earn God's grace, a greater quantity of activity does not earn more of it. Everyone is equally capable of receiving God's grace. Contemporary disciples must accept that God, and not they, will decide how those whom they consider "good" and those whom they consider "bad" will be compensated.

20:17–19 A Third Passion Prediction (Mark 10:32–34; Luke 18:31–34)

The other passion predictions are recorded at 16:21 and 17:22–23.

20:18 *Son of Man*—See note at 8:20.

20:20–28 True Greatness Is Service (Mark 10:35–45)

20:21 *In your kingdom*—The request reveals status ambitions that are directly contrary to Jesus' servant identity. Disciples who seek positions of high status, even in the church, are moving against, not behind, Jesus.

20:22 *Cup*—See note at 26:28.

20:28 *Son of Man*—See note at 8:20. *Ransom for many*—Usually a payment to redeem someone from slavery or debt. The allusion is to the Suffering Servant figure in Isa. 53:11–12. Jesus gives his life in order that his followers may be able to live their lives in relationship to God. Jesus followers must yield their lives toward the same goal.

20:29–34 The Healing Power of the Son of David (Mark 10:46–42; Luke 18:31–34)

20:30 *Son of David*—See note at 1:1.

"Lord, let our eyes be opened." **34** Moved with compassion, Jesus touched their eyes. Immediately they regained their sight and followed him.

Jesus' Triumphal Entry into Jerusalem

21 When they had come near Jerusalem and had reached Bethphage, at the Mount of Olives, Jesus sent two disciples, **2** saying to them, "Go into the village ahead of you, and immediately you will find a donkey tied, and a colt with her; untie them and bring them to me. **3** If anyone says anything to you, just say this, 'The Lord needs them.' And he will send them immediately.*a*" **4** This took place to fulfill what had been spoken through the prophet, saying,
5 "Tell the daughter of Zion,
Look, your king is coming to you,
    humble, and mounted on a donkey,
        and on a colt, the foal of a
            donkey."
6 The disciples went and did as Jesus had directed them; **7** they brought the donkey and the colt, and put their cloaks on them, and he sat on them. **8** A very large crowd*b* spread their cloaks on the road, and others cut branches from the trees and spread them on the road. **9** The crowds that went ahead of him and that followed were shouting,
"Hosanna to the Son of David!
Blessed is the one who comes in
    the name of the Lord!
Hosanna in the highest heaven!"
10 When he entered Jerusalem, the whole city was in turmoil, asking, "Who is this?" **11** The crowds were saying, "This is the prophet Jesus from Nazareth in Galilee."

Jesus Cleanses the Temple

12 Then Jesus entered the temple*c* and drove out all who were selling and buying in the temple, and he overturned the tables of the money changers and the seats of those who sold doves. **13** He said to them, "It is written,
'My house shall be called a house of
    prayer';
    but you are making it a den of
        robbers."
14 The blind and the lame came to him in the temple, and he cured them. **15** But when the chief priests and the scribes saw the amazing things that he did, and heard*d* the children crying out in the temple, "Hosanna to the Son of David," they became angry **16** and said to him, "Do you hear what these are saying?" Jesus said to them, "Yes; have you never read,
'Out of the mouths of infants and
    nursing babies
you have prepared praise for
    yourself'?"
17 He left them, went out of the city to Bethany, and spent the night there.

Jesus Curses the Fig Tree

18 In the morning, when he returned to the city, he was hungry. **19** And seeing

---

a Or 'The Lord needs them and will send them back immediately.' *b* Or Most of the crowd *c* Other ancient authorities add of God *d* Gk lacks heard

---

21:1–11 Jesus' Entry into Jerusalem and Challenge to the Temple (Mark 11:1–10; Luke 19:28–38)

21:6 *The disciples went and did as Jesus had directed them*—The emphasis is on the willingness of the disciples to obey the humble and meek (cf. 21:5) Jesus. The message for the church leader is clear; humility and meekness are the qualities that command respect. There is an equally clear message for church members: faith must live itself out as obedience.

21:4—Formula quotation. See note at 1:22.

21:9 *Hosanna*—"Save now." Cf. Pss. 113–118. Jesus acts to save God's people from sin (1:21).

Jesus' followers as church must act as a body that will assist the risen Lord in the same task. *Son of David*—See note at 1:1.

21:12–27 Jesus' Challenge to the Temple (Mark 11:15–19; Luke 19:45–46; John 2:13–17)

21:13 *A house of prayer*—Quoting from both Isa. 56:7 and Jer. 7:11, Jesus condemns the temple for failing to live up to God's worship expectations.

21:14—Jesus fulfills God's original intent for the temple as a place of wholeness, physical as well as spiritual. This is the task of the church that follows him.

21:15 *Son of David*—See note at 1:1.

21:19 *Fig tree*—A metaphor for Israel in the Old

a fig tree by the side of the road, he went to it and found nothing at all on it but leaves. Then he said to it, "May no fruit ever come from you again!" And the fig tree withered at once. ²⁰ When the disciples saw it, they were amazed, saying, "How did the fig tree wither at once?" ²¹ Jesus answered them, "Truly I tell you, if you have faith and do not doubt, not only will you do what has been done to the fig tree, but even if you say to this mountain, 'Be lifted up and thrown into the sea,' it will be done. ²² Whatever you ask for in prayer with faith, you will receive."

The Authority of Jesus Questioned

23 When he entered the temple, the chief priests and the elders of the people came to him as he was teaching, and said, "By what authority are you doing these things, and who gave you this authority?" ²⁴ Jesus said to them, "I will also ask you one question; if you tell me the answer, then I will also tell you by what authority I do these things. ²⁵ Did the baptism of John come from heaven, or was it of human origin?" And they argued with one another, "If we say, 'From heaven,' he will say to us, 'Why then did you not believe him?' ²⁶ But if we say, 'Of human origin,' we are afraid of the crowd; for all regard John as a prophet." ²⁷ So they answered Jesus, "We do not know." And he said to them, "Neither will I tell you by what authority I am doing these things.

The Parable of the Two Sons

28 "What do you think? A man had two sons; he went to the first and said, 'Son, go and work in the vineyard today.' ²⁹ He answered, 'I will not'; but later he changed his mind and went. ³⁰ The father^a went to the second and said the same; and he answered, 'I go, sir'; but he did not go. ³¹ Which of the two did the will of his father?" They said, "The first." Jesus said to them, "Truly I tell you, the tax collectors and the prostitutes are going into the kingdom of God ahead of you. ³² For John came to you in the way of righteousness and you did not believe him, but the tax collectors and the prostitutes believed him; and even after you saw it, you did not change your minds and believe him.

The Parable of the Wicked Tenants

33 "Listen to another parable. There was a landowner who planted a vineyard, put a fence around it, dug a wine press in it, and built a watchtower. Then he leased it to tenants and went to another country. ³⁴ When the harvest time had come, he sent his slaves to the tenants to collect his produce. ³⁵ But the tenants seized his slaves and beat one, killed another, and stoned another. ³⁶ Again he sent other slaves, more than the first; and they treated them in the same way. ³⁷ Finally he sent his son to them, saying, 'They will respect my son.' ³⁸ But when the tenants saw the son, they said to themselves, 'This is the heir; come, let us kill him and get his inheritance.' ³⁹ So they seized him, threw him out of the vineyard, and killed him. ⁴⁰ Now when the owner of the vineyard comes, what will he do to those tenants?" ⁴¹ They said to him, "He will put those wretches to a miserable death, and lease the vineyard to other tenants who will give him the produce at the harvest time."

42 Jesus said to them, "Have you never read in the scriptures:

^{a} Gk He

Testament. Cf. Jer. 8:13; Isa. 28:3–4; Hos. 9:10, 16; Mic. 7:1; Joel 1:7, 12. The fruitful blossoming of the fig tree represented God's blessing; its withering connoted judgment and destruction.

21:27 *Neither will I tell you*—Jesus' victory has important implications for Matthew's church. Jesus' authority is the foundation of the church's

authority. Jesus' victory validates their authority to interpret the Torah not legalistically, as the rabbis interpret it, but mercifully, as Jesus interprets it.

21:28–46 Bearing Kingdom Fruit

21:33–46—Mark 12:1–12; Luke 20:9–19.

21:33 *Parable*—See note at 13:3.

'The stone that the builders rejected
has become the cornerstone;[a]
this was the Lord's doing,
and it is amazing in our eyes'?
[43] Therefore I tell you, the kingdom of
God will be taken away from you and
given to a people that produces the fruits
of the kingdom.[b] [44] The one who falls on
this stone will be broken to pieces; and it
will crush anyone on whom it falls."[c]

45 When the chief priests and the
Pharisees heard his parables, they realized that he was speaking about them.
[46] They wanted to arrest him, but they
feared the crowds, because they regarded
him as a prophet.

The Parable of the Wedding Banquet

22 Once more Jesus spoke to them
in parables, saying: [2] "The kingdom of heaven may be compared to a
king who gave a wedding banquet for
his son. [3] He sent his slaves to call those
who had been invited to the wedding
banquet, but they would not come.
[4] Again he sent other slaves, saying, 'Tell
those who have been invited: Look, I
have prepared my dinner, my oxen and
my fat calves have been slaughtered, and
everything is ready; come to the wedding banquet.' [5] But they made light of it
and went away, one to his farm, another
to his business, [6] while the rest seized his
slaves, mistreated them, and killed them.
[7] The king was enraged. He sent his

troops, destroyed those murderers, and
burned their city. [8] Then he said to his
slaves, 'The wedding is ready, but those
invited were not worthy. [9] Go therefore
into the main streets, and invite everyone you find to the wedding banquet.'
[10] Those slaves went out into the streets
and gathered all whom they found, both
good and bad; so the wedding hall was
filled with guests.

11 "But when the king came in to see
the guests, he noticed a man there who
was not wearing a wedding robe, [12] and
he said to him, 'Friend, how did you
get in here without a wedding robe?'
And he was speechless. [13] Then the king
said to the attendants, 'Bind him hand
and foot, and throw him into the outer
darkness, where there will be weeping
and gnashing of teeth.' [14] For many are
called, but few are chosen."

The Question about Paying Taxes

15 Then the Pharisees went and plotted to entrap him in what he said. [16] So
they sent their disciples to him, along
with the Herodians, saying, "Teacher,
we know that you are sincere, and teach
the way of God in accordance with
truth, and show deference to no one; for
you do not regard people with partiality.
[17] Tell us, then, what you think. Is it lawful to pay taxes to the emperor, or not?"
[18] But Jesus, aware of their malice, said,

---

[a] Or keystone [b] Gk the fruits of it [c] Other ancient authorities lack verse 44

**21:43 The kingdom of God will be taken away
. . . and given to a people**—The emphasis is
ecclesiological; Matthew reflects upon the incur-
sion of Gentiles into the kingdom movement (cf.
28:16–20). As was the case with the tax collectors and sinners, so it is with Gentiles; outward
status or identity is not as important as proper
response (bearing fruit—vv. 34, 41) to God's effort in the life and ministry of Jesus.

**22:1–14 The Parable of the Wedding Feast
(Luke 14:16–24)**

22:1 Parables—See note at 13:3.

22:10 Gathered all whom they found—The
implication is that because those who were
originally invited are unworthy and unprepared,
the invitation is spread to the roads going out of
the king's city. In other words, Gentiles are also

called. The implication for contemporary evangelism is clear; disciples must reach out beyond
their own social, ethnic, or political group.

22:11 Not wearing a wedding robe—Given the
unexpected nature of the call, it is surprising that
the king should be so concerned about lack of
proper dress. The concern is a warning for the
church; those who have not responded properly
to the kingdom by bearing the fruit of repentance, whether they are members or not, will be
rejected.

**22:15–22 A Hostile Question about Paying
Taxes to Caesar (Mark 12:13–17; Luke 20:20–26)**

22:15 Pharisees—See note at 3:7.

22:16 Teacher—See note at 8:19.

22:18 The test—A yes answer would incite the

"Why are you putting me to the test, you hypocrites? ¹⁹ Show me the coin used for the tax." And they brought him a denarius. ²⁰ Then he said to them, "Whose head is this, and whose title?" ²¹ They answered, "The emperor's." Then he said to them, "Give therefore to the emperor the things that are the emperor's, and to God the things that are God's." ²² When they heard this, they were amazed; and they left him and went away.

The Question about the Resurrection

23 The same day some Sadducees came to him, saying there is no resurrection;ᵃ and they asked him a question, saying, ²⁴ "Teacher, Moses said, 'If a man dies childless, his brother shall marry the widow, and raise up children for his brother.' ²⁵ Now there were seven brothers among us; the first married, and died childless, leaving the widow to his brother. ²⁶ The second did the same, so also the third, down to the seventh. ²⁷ Last of all, the woman herself died. ²⁸ In the resurrection, then, whose wife of the seven will she be? For all of them had married her."

29 Jesus answered them, "You are wrong, because you know neither the scriptures nor the power of God. ³⁰ For in the resurrection they neither marry nor are given in marriage, but are like angelsᵇ in heaven. ³¹ And as for the resurrection of the dead, have you not read what was said to you by God, ³² 'I am the God of Abraham, the God of Isaac, and the God of Jacob'? He is God not of the dead, but of the living." ³³ And when the crowd heard it, they were astounded at his teaching.

The Greatest Commandment

34 When the Pharisees heard that he had silenced the Sadducees, they gathered together, ³⁵ and one of them, a lawyer, asked him a question to test him. ³⁶ "Teacher, which commandment in the law is the greatest?" ³⁷ He said to him, " 'You shall love the Lord your God with all your heart, and with all your soul, and with all your mind.' ³⁸ This is the greatest and first commandment. ³⁹ And a second is like it: 'You shall love your neighbor as yourself.' ⁴⁰ On these two commandments hang all the law and the prophets."

The Question about David's Son

41 Now while the Pharisees were gathered together, Jesus asked them this question: ⁴² "What do you think of the Messiah?ᶜ Whose son is he?" They said to him, "The son of David." ⁴³ He said to them, "How is it then that David by the Spiritᵈ calls him Lord, saying,

⁴⁴ 'The Lord said to my Lord,
"Sit at my right hand,
until I put your enemies under
your feet" '?

ᵃ Other ancient authorities read *who say that there is no resurrection*   ᵇ Other ancient authorities add *of God*   ᶜ Or *Christ*   ᵈ Gk *in spirit*

---

anti-Roman crowd; a no would invite Roman anger. Jesus' clever response to the effort to *entrap him* (v. 15) operates from the Jewish premise that everything belongs to God. Since nothing really belongs to Caesar, one can faithfully give it to him. Believers will always be challenged by the demands government places upon time, energy, and resources. While fulfilling one's societal obligations, the believer must be sure always to put obligation to God first. Where commitment to God and commitment to government conflict, God has priority.

22:23–33 A Hostile Question about the Resurrection (Mark 12:18–27; Luke 20:27–40)

22:23 *Sadducees*—See note at 16:1.

22:24 *Teacher*—See note at 8:2.

22:34–40 A Question about the Law (Mark 12:28–34; Luke 10:25–28)

22:34 *Pharisees*—See note at 3:7.

22:36 *Teacher*—See note at 8:2.

22:39 *You shall love your neighbor as yourself*—Cf. Lev. 19:18. Jesus put the two commands in mutual relationship. Love of God finds its concrete expression in brotherly and sisterly love. Conversely, brotherly and sisterly love find their foundation in the love and support of God.

22:41–46 The Messiah and David's Son (Mark 12:35–37; Luke 20:41–44)

22:41 *Pharisees*—See note at 3:7.

22:42 *Son of David*—See note at 1:1.

⁴⁵ If David thus calls him Lord, how can he be his son?" ⁴⁶ No one was able to give him an answer, nor from that day did anyone dare to ask him any more questions.

Jesus Denounces Scribes and Pharisees

23 Then Jesus said to the crowds and to his disciples, ² "The scribes and the Pharisees sit on Moses' seat; ³ therefore, do whatever they teach you and follow it; but do not do as they do, for they do not practice what they teach. ⁴ They tie up heavy burdens, hard to bear,ᵃ and lay them on the shoulders of others; but they themselves are unwilling to lift a finger to move them. ⁵ They do all their deeds to be seen by others; for they make their phylacteries broad and their fringes long. ⁶ They love to have the place of honor at banquets and the best seats in the synagogues, ⁷ and to be greeted with respect in the marketplaces, and to have people call them rabbi. ⁸ But you are not to be called rabbi, for you have one teacher, and you are all students.ᵇ ⁹ And call no one your father on earth, for you have one Father—the one in heaven. ¹⁰ Nor are you to be called instructors, for you have one instructor, the Messiah.ᶜ ¹¹ The greatest among you will be your servant. ¹² All who exalt themselves will be humbled, and all who humble themselves will be exalted.

13 "But woe to you, scribes and Pharisees, hypocrites! For you lock people out of the kingdom of heaven. For you do not go in yourselves, and when others are going in, you stop them.ᵈ ¹⁵ Woe to you, scribes and Pharisees, hypocrites! For you cross sea and land to make a single convert, and you make the new convert twice as much a child of hellᵉ as yourselves.

16 "Woe to you, blind guides, who say, 'Whoever swears by the sanctuary is bound by nothing, but whoever swears by the gold of the sanctuary is bound by the oath.' ¹⁷ You blind fools! For which is greater, the gold or the sanctuary that has made the gold sacred? ¹⁸ And you say, 'Whoever swears by the altar is bound by nothing, but whoever swears by the gift that is on the altar is bound by the oath.' ¹⁹ How blind you are! For which is greater, the gift or the altar that makes the gift sacred? ²⁰ So whoever swears by the altar, swears by it and by everything on it; ²¹ and whoever swears by the sanctuary, swears by it and by the one who dwells in it; ²² and whoever swears by heaven, swears by the throne of God and by the one who is seated upon it.

23 "Woe to you, scribes and Pharisees, hypocrites! For you tithe mint, dill, and cummin, and have neglected the weightier matters of the law: justice and mercy and faith. It is these you ought to

ᵃ Other ancient authorities lack *hard to bear*   ᵇ Gk *brothers*   ᶜ Or *the Christ*   ᵈ Other authorities add here (or after verse 12) verse 14, *Woe to you, scribes and Pharisees, hypocrites! For you devour widows' houses and for the sake of appearance you make long prayers; therefore you will receive the greater condemnation*   ᵉ Gk *Gehenna*

23:1–39 Jesus' Critique of the Traditional Leadership (Luke 11:37–54)

23:2 *Pharisees*—See note at 3:7.

23:2 *Moses' seat*—Probably a metaphor for the teaching and ruling authority of the scribes and Pharisees.

23:3 *They do not practice what they teach*—This contradiction is the crux of their hypocrisy. See note at 6:2. The message for contemporary discipleship? Teach Jesus' way of love and mercy over and against the way of ritual and sacrifice. Then, practice what you teach.

23:6 *They love to have the place of honor*—Their desire for the prime dining spot next to the host and for the choice seat in the synagogue demon-

strates that the primary concern of the scribes and Pharisees is status. See note at 20:21. Christian leadership must be an antitype of this model. Leadership must be egalitarian, not hierarchical. Leaders must not indulge in status seeking or showy displays of authority, but must instead interpret the law in a way that embodies God's mercy and showcases a love of God that lives itself out in humble service of brother and sister.

23:13 *Pharisees*—See note at 3:7. *Hypocrites*—See note at 6:2.

23:23 *Tithe*—Cf. Lev. 27:30; Deut. 14:22–23. The leaders attend so much to making the one-tenth tax apply to even the most minuscule kind of harvest that they no longer attend to the larger

have practiced without neglecting the others. **24** You blind guides! You strain out a gnat but swallow a camel!

25 "Woe to you, scribes and Pharisees, hypocrites! For you clean the outside of the cup and of the plate, but inside they are full of greed and self-indulgence. **26** You blind Pharisee! First clean the inside of the cup,*a* so that the outside also may become clean.

27 "Woe to you, scribes and Pharisees, hypocrites! For you are like whitewashed tombs, which on the outside look beautiful, but inside they are full of the bones of the dead and of all kinds of filth. **28** So you also on the outside look righteous to others, but inside you are full of hypocrisy and lawlessness.

29 "Woe to you, scribes and Pharisees, hypocrites! For you build the tombs of the prophets and decorate the graves of the righteous, **30** and you say, 'If we had lived in the days of our ancestors, we would not have taken part with them in shedding the blood of the prophets.' **31** Thus you testify against yourselves that you are descendants of those who murdered the prophets. **32** Fill up, then, the measure of your ancestors. **33** You snakes, you brood of vipers! How can you escape being sentenced to hell?*b* **34** Therefore I send you prophets, sages, and scribes, some of whom you will kill and crucify, and some you will flog in your synagogues and pursue from town to town, **35** so that upon you may come all the righteous blood shed on earth, from the blood of righteous Abel to the blood of Zechariah son of Barachiah, whom you murdered between the sanctuary and the altar. **36** Truly I tell you, all this will come upon this generation.

The Lament over Jerusalem

37 "Jerusalem, Jerusalem, the city that kills the prophets and stones those who are sent to it! How often have I desired to gather your children together as a hen gathers her brood under her wings, and you were not willing! **38** See, your house is left to you, desolate.*c* **39** For I tell you, you will not see me again until you say, 'Blessed is the one who comes in the name of the Lord.'"

The Destruction of the Temple Foretold

24 As Jesus came out of the temple and was going away, his disciples came to point out to him the buildings of the temple. **2** Then he asked them, "You see all these, do you not? Truly I tell you, not one stone will be left here upon another; all will be thrown down."

Signs of the End of the Age

3 When he was sitting on the Mount of Olives, the disciples came to him privately, saying, "Tell us, when will this be, and what will be the sign of your coming and of the end of the age?" **4** Jesus answered them, "Beware that no one leads you astray. **5** For many will come in my name, saying, 'I am the Messiah!'*d* and they will lead many astray. **6** And you will hear of wars and rumors of wars; see that you are not alarmed; for this must take place, but the end is not yet. **7** For nation will rise against nation, and kingdom against kingdom, and there will be famines*e* and earthquakes in various places: **8** all this is but the beginning of the birth pangs.

a Other ancient authorities add *and of the plate* *b* Gk *Gehenna* *c* Other ancient authorities lack *desolate* *d* Or *the Christ* *e* Other ancient authorities add *and pestilences*

---

obligations of the law. They model the opposite of Christian leadership. Forcing compliance with statistical detail (even where tithing is concerned), at the cost of deemphasizing love and mercy, is not the way of Jesus discipleship.

23:24—Cf. Lev. 11:20–23. Again modeling the antitype of Christian leadership, the Pharisaic leaders are so attentive to minute impurities (*gnat*) that they allow larger and more grave un-

cleanness (*camel*). The implications for contemporary discipleship are clear. Focus on relationship building between God and humans, and humans and other humans, not on legalities.

23:34 *Your synagogues*—See note at 4:23.

24:1–51 The Apocalyptic Discourse (Mark 13:1–37; Luke 21:5–36)

24:5 *Messiah*—See note at 1:1.

Persecutions Foretold

9 "Then they will hand you over to be tortured and will put you to death, and you will be hated by all nations because of my name. [10] Then many will fall away,[a] and they will betray one another and hate one another. [11] And many false prophets will arise and lead many astray. [12] And because of the increase of lawlessness, the love of many will grow cold. [13] But the one who endures to the end will be saved. [14] And this good news[b] of the kingdom will be proclaimed throughout the world, as a testimony to all the nations; and then the end will come.

The Desolating Sacrilege

15 "So when you see the desolating sacrilege standing in the holy place, as was spoken of by the prophet Daniel (let the reader understand), [16] then those in Judea must flee to the mountains; [17] the one on the housetop must not go down to take what is in the house; [18] the one in the field must not turn back to get a coat. [19] Woe to those who are pregnant and to those who are nursing infants in those days! [20] Pray that your flight may not be in winter or on a sabbath. [21] For at that time there will be great suffering, such as has not been from the beginning of the world until now, no, and never will be. [22] And if those days had not been cut short, no one would be saved; but for the sake of the elect those days will be cut short. [23] Then if anyone says to you, 'Look! Here is the Messiah!'[c] or 'There he is!'—do not believe it. [24] For false messiahs[d] and false prophets will appear and produce great signs and omens, to lead astray, if possible, even the elect. [25] Take note, I have told you beforehand. [26] So, if they say to you, 'Look! He is in the wilderness,' do not go out. If they say, 'Look! He is in the inner rooms,' do not believe it. [27] For as the lightning comes from the east and flashes as far as the west, so will be the coming of the Son of Man. [28] Wherever the corpse is, there the vultures will gather.

The Coming of the Son of Man

29 "Immediately after the suffering of those days

the sun will be darkened,
    and the moon will not give its
        light;
the stars will fall from heaven,
    and the powers of heaven will be
        shaken.

[30] Then the sign of the Son of Man will appear in heaven, and then all the tribes of the earth will mourn, and they will see 'the Son of Man coming on the clouds of heaven' with power and great glory. [31] And he will send out his angels with a loud trumpet call, and they will gather his elect from the four winds, from one end of heaven to the other.

The Lesson of the Fig Tree

32 "From the fig tree learn its lesson: as soon as its branch becomes tender and puts forth its leaves, you know that

a Or stumble   b Or gospel   c Or the Christ   d Or christs

24:14 To all the nations—The goal of the preaching ministry, at least as it will ultimately be established, is to reach beyond the confines of Israel (cf. 28:19–20). The goal of contemporary preaching is to reach beyond all geographical, racial, and political boundaries.

24:15 The desolating sacrilege—Cf. Dan. 12:11, also Dan. 9:27 and 11:31. The term probably referred to the actions of Seleucid king Antiochus IV, who around 167 BCE attempted to install pagan imagery and worship in the temple. Closer to Matthew's own time (40 CE), the Roman emperor Caligula attempted, in direct defiance of the commandment against graven images, to set up a statue of himself in the temple. While the future orientation of Jesus' discourse suggests that Matthew is thinking of a prospective desecration, his choice of wording demonstrates that he believes the future provocation will be molded on such a past offense. Sanctuaries directed to God are always desecrated when human pride or monuments to human ability assume within them either a presence or a place.

24:27 Son of Man—See note at 8:20.

summer is near. [33] So also, when you see all these things, you know that he[a] is near, at the very gates. [34] Truly I tell you, this generation will not pass away until all these things have taken place. [35] Heaven and earth will pass away, but my words will not pass away.

The Necessity for Watchfulness

[36] "But about that day and hour no one knows, neither the angels of heaven, nor the Son,[b] but only the Father. [37] For as the days of Noah were, so will be the coming of the Son of Man. [38] For as in those days before the flood they were eating and drinking, marrying and giving in marriage, until the day Noah entered the ark, [39] and they knew nothing until the flood came and swept them all away, so too will be the coming of the Son of Man. [40] Then two will be in the field; one will be taken and one will be left. [41] Two women will be grinding meal together; one will be taken and one will be left. [42] Keep awake therefore, for you do not know on what day[c] your Lord is coming. [43] But understand this: if the owner of the house had known in what part of the night the thief was coming, he would have stayed awake and would not have let his house be broken into. [44] Therefore you also must be ready, for the Son of Man is coming at an unexpected hour.

The Faithful or the Unfaithful Slave

[45] "Who then is the faithful and wise slave, whom his master has put in charge of his household, to give the other slaves[d] their allowance of food at the proper time? [46] Blessed is that slave whom his master will find at work when he arrives. [47] Truly I tell you, he will put that one in charge of all his possessions. [48] But if that wicked slave says to himself, 'My master is delayed,' [49] and he begins to beat his fellow slaves, and eats and drinks with drunkards, [50] the master of that slave will come on a day when he does not expect him and at an hour that he does not know. [51] He will cut him in pieces[e] and put him with the hypocrites, where there will be weeping and gnashing of teeth.

The Parable of the Ten Bridesmaids

25 "Then the kingdom of heaven will be like this. Ten bridesmaids[f] took their lamps and went to meet the bridegroom.[g] [2] Five of them were foolish, and five were wise. [3] When the foolish took their lamps, they took no oil with them; [4] but the wise took flasks of oil with their lamps. [5] As the bridegroom was delayed, all of them became drowsy and slept. [6] But at midnight there was a

a Or *it*   *b* Other ancient authorities lack *nor the Son*   *c* Other ancient authorities read *at what hour*   *d* Gk *to give them*   *e* Or *cut him off*   *f* Gk *virgins*   *g* Other ancient authorities add *and the bride*

24:37 Son of Man—See note at 8:20.

24:40 One will be taken—Because the two people will be doing the same tasks, one will not be able to tell by outward appearances who is responding appropriately to the nearness of God's kingdom. God makes that discernment and thus receives one while forsaking the other. The counsel remains consistent with the Matthean theme throughout; concern should be placed not on exterior appearances or ritual observances, but on an inner orientation to God that provokes the proper kingdom response.

24:42 Keep awake—Be prepared. Jesus does not refer to a passive watching where one sits and awaits someone else's movement and activity; it refers to a preparatory waiting of repentant discipleship.

24:44 Son of Man—See note at 8:20.

24:46 Blessed—See note at 5:3. The blessed servant will be the one whose watchfulness lives itself out in deeds of faithful, repentant discipleship.

24:51 Hypocrites—See note at 6:2.

25:1–46 The Apocalyptic Discourse, Continued

25:1–13—The parable of the Ten Maidens.

25:1 Kingdom of heaven—See note at 3:2.

25:5 All of them became drowsy and slept—*None* of them demonstrates the *watchfulness* called for earlier; they *all* fall asleep (cf. 24:42–43). Perhaps there is here a message of God's graciousness for the church. The five wise maidens, because they have done the work of preparation, even though they do fall short, are viewed heroically. The same would no doubt hold true for the wise believers who do the work

shout, 'Look! Here is the bridegroom! Come out to meet him.' [7] Then all those bridesmaids[a] got up and trimmed their lamps. [8] The foolish said to the wise, 'Give us some of your oil, for our lamps are going out.' [9] But the wise replied, 'No! there will not be enough for you and for us; you had better go to the dealers and buy some for yourselves.' [10] And while they went to buy it, the bridegroom came, and those who were ready went with him into the wedding banquet; and the door was shut. [11] Later the other bridesmaids[a] came also, saying, 'Lord, lord, open to us.' [12] But he replied, 'Truly I tell you, I do not know you.' [13] Keep awake therefore, for you know neither the day nor the hour.[b]

The Parable of the Talents

14 "For it is as if a man, going on a journey, summoned his slaves and entrusted his property to them; [15] to one he gave five talents,[c] to another two, to another one, to each according to his ability. Then he went away. [16] The one who had received the five talents went off at once and traded with them, and made five more talents. [17] In the same way, the one who had the two talents made two more talents. [18] But the one who had received the one talent went off and dug a hole in the ground and hid his master's money. [19] After a long time the master of those slaves came and settled accounts with them. [20] Then the one who had received the five talents came forward, bringing five more talents, saying, 'Master, you handed over to me five talents; see, I have made five more talents.' [21] His master said to him, 'Well done, good and trustworthy slave; you have been trustworthy in a few things, I will put you in charge of many things; enter into the joy of your master.' [22] And the one with the two talents also came forward, saying, 'Master, you handed over to me two talents; see, I have made two more talents.' [23] His master said to him, 'Well done, good and trustworthy slave; you have been trustworthy in a few things, I will put you in charge of many things; enter into the joy of your master.' [24] Then the one who had received the one talent also came forward, saying, 'Master, I knew that you were a harsh man, reaping where you did not sow, and gathering where you did not scatter seed; [25] so I was afraid, and I went and hid your talent in the ground. Here you have what is yours.' [26] But his master replied, 'You wicked and lazy slave! You knew, did you, that I reap where I did not sow, and gather where I did not scatter? [27] Then you ought to have invested my money with the bankers, and on my return I would have received what was my own with interest. [28] So take the talent from him, and give it to the one with the ten talents. [29] For to all those who have, more will be given, and they will have an abundance; but from those who have nothing, even what they have will be taken away. [30] As for this worthless slave, throw him into the outer darkness, where there will be weeping and gnashing of teeth.'

[a] Gk virgins [b] Other ancient authorities add in which the Son of Man is coming [c] A talent was worth more than fifteen years' wages of a laborer

---

of faithful, repentant discipleship. Even if they fall short, because they have done the work of love and mercy, they can take comfort in knowing that God will respond mercifully.

25:14–30—The parable of the Talents (Luke 19:12–27).

25:15 *Talents*—A talent is both a sum of money and a description of someone's ability. Everyone is endowed with certain abilities (talents) to be put to use in the Lord's service. Everyone will be held responsible for developing (working; cf. v. 16) those abilities through their discipleship behavior.

25:25 *I was afraid*—Fear breeds inactivity. Could this too be a message for the discipleship community? They were just told in chap. 24 that they could expect harsh treatment because of their Jesus faith. Should this fear immobilize them, they would be not unlike the servant issued the single talent; they might try to protect their own faithful existence rather than attempt to extend it through the proper discipleship work of reaching out to all the nations (24:14; 28:19–20).

The Judgment of the Nations

31 "When the Son of Man comes in his glory, and all the angels with him, then he will sit on the throne of his glory. ³² All the nations will be gathered before him, and he will separate people one from another as a shepherd separates the sheep from the goats, ³³ and he will put the sheep at his right hand and the goats at the left. ³⁴ Then the king will say to those at his right hand, 'Come, you that are blessed by my Father, inherit the kingdom prepared for you from the foundation of the world; ³⁵ for I was hungry and you gave me food, I was thirsty and you gave me something to drink, I was a stranger and you welcomed me, ³⁶ I was naked and you gave me clothing, I was sick and you took care of me, I was in prison and you visited me.' ³⁷ Then the righteous will answer him, 'Lord, when was it that we saw you hungry and gave you food, or thirsty and gave you something to drink? ³⁸ And when was it that we saw you a stranger and welcomed you, or naked and gave you clothing? ³⁹ And when was it that we saw you sick or in prison and visited you?' ⁴⁰ And the king will answer them, 'Truly I tell you, just as you did it to one of the least of these who are members of my family,ᵃ you did it to me.' ⁴¹ Then he will say to those at his left hand, 'You that are accursed, depart from me into the eternal fire prepared for the devil and his angels; ⁴² for I was hungry and you gave me no food, I was thirsty and you gave me nothing to drink, ⁴³ I was a stranger and you did not welcome me, naked and you did not give me clothing, sick and in prison and you did not visit me.' ⁴⁴ Then they also will answer, 'Lord, when was it that we saw you hungry or thirsty or a stranger or naked or sick or in prison, and did not take care of you?' ⁴⁵ Then he will answer them, 'Truly I tell you, just as you did not do it to one of the least of these, you did not do it to me.' ⁴⁶ And these will go away into eternal punishment, but the righteous into eternal life."

The Plot to Kill Jesus

26 When Jesus had finished saying all these things, he said to his disciples, ² "You know that after two days the Passover is coming, and the Son of Man will be handed over to be crucified."

3 Then the chief priests and the elders of the people gathered in the palace of the high priest, who was called Caiaphas, ⁴ and they conspired to arrest Jesus by stealth and kill him. ⁵ But they said, "Not during the festival, or there may be a riot among the people."

The Anointing at Bethany

6 Now while Jesus was at Bethany in the house of Simon the leper,ᵇ ⁷ a woman came to him with an alabaster jar of

---

ᵃ Gk *these my brothers*   ᵇ The terms *leper* and *leprosy* can refer to several diseases

---

25:31–46—The judgment.

25:31 *Son of Man*—See note at 8:20.

25:32 *All the nations*—Anticipates 28:19, where the disciples are ordered by the risen Lord to make disciples of all the nations.

25:40 *Just as you did it to one of the least of these*—Gentiles may now find entrance into the kingdom by doing good works for those in need. An act of assistance for someone in need (v. 40) is in effect an act of assistance for the Son of Man. It is discipleship behavior—not status, race, or nationality—that makes one acceptable in God's sight.

26:1–16 Jesus' Anointing and Betrayal (Mark 14:1–11; Luke 22:1–6)

26:2 *Passover*—The Passover was a commemoration of the exodus intervention (cf. Exod. 12:14). The meal commemorates the redemption of the people from sociohistorical slavery. Its blood symbolizes sociopolitical liberation, on the one hand, and the realization of a sociohistorical covenant between God and Israel, on the other. Through this kind of "redemptive" lens Jesus wants his disciples to share the meal that remembers him.

26:3 *Caiaphas*—High priest 18–36 CE.

26:6 *Leper*—See note at 8:3.

very costly ointment, and she poured it on his head as he sat at the table. ⁸ But when the disciples saw it, they were angry and said, "Why this waste? ⁹ For this ointment could have been sold for a large sum, and the money given to the poor." ¹⁰ But Jesus, aware of this, said to them, "Why do you trouble the woman? She has performed a good service for me. ¹¹ For you always have the poor with you, but you will not always have me. ¹² By pouring this ointment on my body she has prepared me for burial. ¹³ Truly I tell you, wherever this good news*a* is proclaimed in the whole world, what she has done will be told in remembrance of her."

Judas Agrees to Betray Jesus

14 Then one of the twelve, who was called Judas Iscariot, went to the chief priests ¹⁵ and said, "What will you give me if I betray him to you?" They paid him thirty pieces of silver. ¹⁶ And from that moment he began to look for an opportunity to betray him.

The Passover with the Disciples

17 On the first day of Unleavened Bread the disciples came to Jesus, saying, "Where do you want us to make the preparations for you to eat the Passover?" ¹⁸ He said, "Go into the city to a certain man, and say to him, 'The Teacher says, My time is near; I will keep the Passover at your house with my disciples.'" ¹⁹ So the disciples did as Jesus had directed them, and they prepared the Passover meal.

20 When it was evening, he took his place with the twelve;*b* ²¹ and while they were eating, he said, "Truly I tell you, one of you will betray me." ²² And they became greatly distressed and began to say to him one after another, "Surely not I, Lord?" ²³ He answered, "The one who has dipped his hand into the bowl with me will betray me. ²⁴ The Son of Man goes as it is written of him, but woe to that one by whom the Son of Man is betrayed! It would have been better for that one not to have been born." ²⁵ Judas, who betrayed him, said, "Surely not I, Rabbi?" He replied, "You have said so."

The Institution of the Lord's Supper

26 While they were eating, Jesus took a loaf of bread, and after blessing it he broke it, gave it to the disciples, and said, "Take, eat; this is my body." ²⁷ Then

a Or *gospel*   *b* Other ancient authorities add *disciples*

26:10 *She has performed a good service*—The emphasis on service seems to point toward the Matthean community. She acts because she recognizes this moment as one of impending need and struggle for Jesus. Her faithful actions are the kind of work the church should emulate: the kinds of work that are pleasing and caring to the Lord in his moment of need. In 25:31–46, such work is described socially as feeding the hungry, giving drink to the thirsty, etc. Service to God includes much more than spiritual work.

26:15 *Thirty pieces of silver*—Only Matthew makes this accounting. In Exod. 21:32, it is the price of a slave; in Zech. 11:12–13, it is the amount the prophet uses to shame the temple authorities.

26:17–19 Preparing the Passover Meal (Mark 14:12–16; Luke 22:7–13)

26:17 *First day of Unleavened Bread . . . Passover*—See note at 26:2.

26:20–25 Jesus Predicts His Betrayal (Mark 14:17–21; Luke 22:21–23)

26:24 *Son of Man*—See note at 8:20.

26:25 *Surely, not I, Rabbi?*—Judas asks the same question that the other disciples ask in v. 22. Like them, the construction of his question expects a negative answer. Unlike them, he addresses Jesus as Rabbi instead of Lord. It is the same title he uses when betraying Jesus at v. 49. See also note at 8:19.

26:26–29 Jesus' Last Supper (Mark 14:22–25; Luke 22:14–20)

26:26 *Jesus took . . . after blessing . . . he broke it . . . gave it to his disciples*—Rekindles memory of Jesus' two most flamboyant kingdom preaching moments, the feeding of the five thousand (14:13–21) and the four thousand (15:32–39). God provided for *all* God's people. This political image of boundary-shattering, universal care, viewed through the liberating Passover lens (see note at 14:20), is the one Matthew wants in his readers' minds when they approach the Lord's table.

26:27, 28 *Cup . . . blood*—Matthew has already identified the cup with suffering (20:22, 23; cf.

he took a cup, and after giving thanks he gave it to them, saying, "Drink from it, all of you; ²⁸ for this is my blood of the^a covenant, which is poured out for many for the forgiveness of sins. ²⁹ I tell you, I will never again drink of this fruit of the vine until that day when I drink it new with you in my Father's kingdom."

30 When they had sung the hymn, they went out to the Mount of Olives.

Peter's Denial Foretold

31 Then Jesus said to them, "You will all become deserters because of me this night; for it is written,

'I will strike the shepherd,
and the sheep of the flock will be scattered.'
³² But after I am raised up, I will go ahead of you to Galilee." ³³ Peter said to him, "Though all become deserters because of you, I will never desert you." ³⁴ Jesus said to him, "Truly I tell you, this very night, before the cock crows, you will deny me three times." ³⁵ Peter said to him, "Even though I must die with you, I will not deny you." And so said all the disciples.

Jesus Prays in Gethsemane

36 Then Jesus went with them to a place called Gethsemane; and he said to his disciples, "Sit here while I go over there and pray." ³⁷ He took with him Peter and the two sons of Zebedee, and began to be grieved and agitated. ³⁸ Then he said to them, "I am deeply grieved, even to death; remain here, and stay awake with me." ³⁹ And going a little farther, he threw himself on the ground and prayed, "My Father, if it is possible,

let this cup pass from me; yet not what I want but what you want." ⁴⁰ Then he came to the disciples and found them sleeping; and he said to Peter, "So, could you not stay awake with me one hour? ⁴¹ Stay awake and pray that you may not come into the time of trial;^b the spirit indeed is willing, but the flesh is weak." ⁴² Again he went away for the second time and prayed, "My Father, if this cannot pass unless I drink it, your will be done." ⁴³ Again he came and found them sleeping, for their eyes were heavy. ⁴⁴ So leaving them again, he went away and prayed for the third time, saying the same words. ⁴⁵ Then he came to the disciples and said to them, "Are you still sleeping and taking your rest? See, the hour is at hand, and the Son of Man is betrayed into the hands of sinners. ⁴⁶ Get up, let us be going. See, my betrayer is at hand."

The Betrayal and Arrest of Jesus

47 While he was still speaking, Judas, one of the twelve, arrived; with him was a large crowd with swords and clubs, from the chief priests and the elders of the people. ⁴⁸ Now the betrayer had given them a sign, saying, "The one I will kiss is the man; arrest him." ⁴⁹ At once he came up to Jesus and said, "Greetings, Rabbi!" and kissed him. ⁵⁰ Jesus said to him, "Friend, do what you are here to do." Then they came and laid hands on Jesus and arrested him. ⁵¹ Suddenly, one of those with Jesus put his hand on his sword, drew it, and struck the slave of the high priest, cutting off his ear. ⁵² Then Jesus said to him, "Put your

^a Other ancient authorities add *new*   ^b Or *into temptation*

26:39). No wonder, then, that immediately after Jesus introduces the broken bread, which he uses to prefigure his crucified body, he warns his disciples that following him will lead to the same fate. By drinking out of the cup, they indicate their acceptance of this reality. Only in Matthew does Jesus also proclaim that the shedding of his blood will ensure the forgiveness of human sin.

26:30–56 Gethsemane (Mark 14:26–52; Luke 22:39–53)

26:39 *Cup*—See note at vv. 27–28.

26:41 *Stay awake*—See 24:42 and note at 25:5.

26:45 *Son of Man*—See note at 8:20.

26:49 *Rabbi*—See note at v. 25.

26:52 *Put your sword back into its place*—Jesus is faithful to the principles of nonviolence that he espoused in the Sermon on the Mount (cf. 5:38–48).

sword back into its place; for all who take the sword will perish by the sword. [53] Do you think that I cannot appeal to my Father, and he will at once send me more than twelve legions of angels? [54] But how then would the scriptures be fulfilled, which say it must happen in this way?" [55] At that hour Jesus said to the crowds, "Have you come out with swords and clubs to arrest me as though I were a bandit? Day after day I sat in the temple teaching, and you did not arrest me. [56] But all this has taken place, so that the scriptures of the prophets may be fulfilled." Then all the disciples deserted him and fled.

Jesus before the High Priest

[57] Those who had arrested Jesus took him to Caiaphas the high priest, in whose house the scribes and the elders had gathered. [58] But Peter was following him at a distance, as far as the courtyard of the high priest; and going inside, he sat with the guards in order to see how this would end. [59] Now the chief priests and the whole council were looking for false testimony against Jesus so that they might put him to death, [60] but they found none, though many false witnesses came forward. At last two came forward [61] and said, "This fellow said, 'I am able to destroy the temple of God and to build it in three days.'" [62] The high priest stood up and said, "Have you no answer? What is it that they testify against you?" [63] But Jesus was silent. Then the high priest said to him, "I put you under oath before the living God, tell us if you are the Messiah,[a] the Son of God." [64] Jesus said to him, "You have said so. But I tell you,

From now on you will see the Son of
  Man
seated at the right hand of Power
  and coming on the clouds of
    heaven."

[65] Then the high priest tore his clothes and said, "He has blasphemed! Why do we still need witnesses? You have now heard his blasphemy. [66] What is your verdict?" They answered, "He deserves death." [67] Then they spat in his face and struck him; and some slapped him, [68] saying, "Prophesy to us, you Messiah![a] Who is it that struck you?"

Peter's Denial of Jesus

[69] Now Peter was sitting outside in the courtyard. A servant-girl came to him and said, "You also were with Jesus the Galilean." [70] But he denied it before all of them, saying, "I do not know what you are talking about." [71] When he went out to the porch, another servant-girl saw him, and she said to the bystanders, "This man was with Jesus of Nazareth."[b] [72] Again he denied it with an oath, "I do not know the man." [73] After a little while the bystanders came up and said to Peter, "Certainly you are also one of them, for your accent betrays you." [74] Then he began to curse, and he swore an oath, "I do not know the man!" At that moment the cock crowed. [75] Then Peter remembered what Jesus had said: "Before the cock crows, you will deny me three times." And he went out and wept bitterly.

Jesus Brought before Pilate

27 When morning came, all the chief priests and the elders of the people conferred together against Jesus in order to bring about his death. [2] They

[a] Or *Christ*   [b] Gk *the Nazorean*

26:57–75 Jesus' Trial before the Sanhedrin and Peter's Denial (Mark 14:53–72; Luke 22:54–71; John 18:13–27)

26:57 *Caiaphas*—See note at v. 3.

26:58—While Jesus stands and witnesses courageously before the leaders, Peter breaks down and cowers before servants. The model for discipleship is clear.

26:63 *Messiah*—See note at 1:1. *Son of God*— See note at 4:3.

26:64—Cf. Dan. 7:13 and Ps. 110:1. *Son of Man*—See note at 8:20.

27:1–31 Jesus Is Condemned by Pilate (Mark 15:1–20; Luke 23:1–4; 17–25; John 18:28–19:16)

bound him, led him away, and handed him over to Pilate the governor.

The Suicide of Judas

3 When Judas, his betrayer, saw that Jesus[a] was condemned, he repented and brought back the thirty pieces of silver to the chief priests and the elders. 4 He said, "I have sinned by betraying innocent[b] blood." But they said, "What is that to us? See to it yourself." 5 Throwing down the pieces of silver in the temple, he departed; and he went and hanged himself. 6 But the chief priests, taking the pieces of silver, said, "It is not lawful to put them into the treasury, since they are blood money." 7 After conferring together, they used them to buy the potter's field as a place to bury foreigners. 8 For this reason that field has been called the Field of Blood to this day. 9 Then was fulfilled what had been spoken through the prophet Jeremiah,[c] "And they took[d] the thirty pieces of silver, the price of the one on whom a price had been set,[e] on whom some of the people of Israel had set a price, 10 and they gave[f] them for the potter's field, as the Lord commanded me."

Pilate Questions Jesus

11 Now Jesus stood before the governor; and the governor asked him, "Are you the King of the Jews?" Jesus said, "You say so." 12 But when he was accused by the chief priests and elders, he did not answer. 13 Then Pilate said to him, "Do you not hear how many accusations they make against you?" 14 But he gave him no answer, not even to a single charge, so that the governor was greatly amazed.

Barabbas or Jesus?

15 Now at the festival the governor was accustomed to release a prisoner for the crowd, anyone whom they wanted. 16 At that time they had a notorious prisoner, called Jesus[g] Barabbas. 17 So after they had gathered, Pilate said to them, "Whom do you want me to release for you, Jesus[g] Barabbas or Jesus who is called the Messiah?"[h] 18 For he realized that it was out of jealousy that they had handed him over. 19 While he was sitting on the judgment seat, his wife sent word to him, "Have nothing to do with that innocent man, for today I have suffered a great deal because of a dream about him." 20 Now the chief priests and the elders persuaded the crowds to ask for Barabbas and to have Jesus killed. 21 The governor again said to them, "Which of the two do you want me to release for you?" And they said, "Barabbas." 22 Pilate said to them, "Then what should I do with Jesus who is called the Messiah?"[h] All of them said, "Let him be crucified!" 23 Then he asked, "Why, what evil has he done?" But they shouted all the more, "Let him be crucified!"

Pilate Hands Jesus over to Be Crucified

24 So when Pilate saw that he could do nothing, but rather that a riot was beginning, he took some water and washed his hands before the crowd, saying, "I am innocent of this man's blood;[i] see to it yourselves." 25 Then the people as a whole answered, "His blood

---

[a] Gk he [b] Other ancient authorities read righteous [c] Other ancient authorities read Zechariah or Isaiah [d] Or I took [e] Or the price of the precious One [f] Other ancient authorities read I gave [g] Other ancient authorities lack Jesus [h] Or the Christ [i] Other ancient authorities read this righteous blood, or this righteous man's blood

---

27:2 Pilate—Prefect of Judea 26–36 CE.

27:3–10—This account of Judas's death is specific to Matthew. For an alternative account, see Acts 1:18–20.

27:9—Matthew's final formula quotation. Cf. Zech. 11:12–13. See note at Matt. 1:22.

27:11 King of the Jews—The fact that the Roman soldiers taunt him as a king (15:16–20) and that Pilate has the title affixed to the cross (15:26) suggest that it was upon this basis that he was

crucified. Jesus' activities were as threatening to the Roman maintenance of peace in the region as to the authoritative status of the Palestinian leadership. The implication is clear: discipleship that operates in Jesus' name will be as politically engaged as it is spiritually engaged.

27:17 Messiah—See note at 1:1.

27:25 His blood be on us—Tragically, this verse has been used across the centuries to fuel anti-Judaism. The imagery of fault for killing the Lord's

be on us and on our children!" **26** So he released Barabbas for them; and after flogging Jesus, he handed him over to be crucified.

The Soldiers Mock Jesus

27 Then the soldiers of the governor took Jesus into the governor's headquarters,[a] and they gathered the whole cohort around him. **28** They stripped him and put a scarlet robe on him, **29** and after twisting some thorns into a crown, they put it on his head. They put a reed in his right hand and knelt before him and mocked him, saying, "Hail, King of the Jews!" **30** They spat on him, and took the reed and struck him on the head. **31** After mocking him, they stripped him of the robe and put his own clothes on him. Then they led him away to crucify him.

The Crucifixion of Jesus

32 As they went out, they came upon a man from Cyrene named Simon; they compelled this man to carry his cross. **33** And when they came to a place called Golgotha (which means Place of a Skull), **34** they offered him wine to drink, mixed with gall; but when he tasted it, he would not drink it. **35** And when they had crucified him, they divided his clothes among themselves by casting lots;[b] **36** then they sat down there and kept watch over him. **37** Over his head they put the charge against him, which read, "This is Jesus, the King of the Jews."

38 Then two bandits were crucified with him, one on his right and one on his left. **39** Those who passed by derided[c] him, shaking their heads **40** and saying, "You who would destroy the temple and build it in three days, save yourself! If you are the Son of God, come down from the cross." **41** In the same way the chief priests also, along with the scribes and elders, were mocking him, saying, **42** "He saved others; he cannot save himself.[d] He is the King of Israel; let him come down from the cross now, and we will believe in him. **43** He trusts in God; let God deliver him now, if he wants to; for he said, 'I am God's Son.'" **44** The bandits who were crucified with him also taunted him in the same way.

The Death of Jesus

45 From noon on, darkness came over the whole land[e] until three in the afternoon. **46** And about three o'clock Jesus cried with a loud voice, "Eli, Eli, lema sabachthani?" that is, "My God, my God, why have you forsaken me?" **47** When some of the bystanders heard it, they said, "This man is calling for Elijah." **48** At once one of them ran and got a sponge, filled it with sour wine, put it on a stick, and gave it to him to drink. **49** But the others said, "Wait, let us see whether Elijah will come to save him."[f] **50** Then Jesus cried again with a loud voice and breathed his last.[g] **51** At that moment the

---

[a] Gk *the praetorium* [b] Other ancient authorities add *in order that what had been spoken through the prophet might be fulfilled, "They divided my clothes among themselves, and for my clothing they cast lots."* [c] Or *blasphemed* [d] Or *is he unable to save himself?* [e] Or *earth* [f] Other ancient authorities add *And another took a spear and pierced his side, and out came water and blood* [g] Or *gave up his spirit*

---

anointed comes from 2 Sam. 1:16 (cf. also Lev. 20:9–16; Josh. 2:19–20; 2 Sam. 14:9). *On our children*—The phrase limits the responsibility to the generation that follows Jesus' death.

27:29 *King of the Jews*—See note at v. 11.

27:32–54 The Death of Jesus (Mark 15:21–39; Luke 23:26–48; John 19:17–37)

27:32 *A man from Cyrene named Simon*—Cyrene is located in North Africa. Simon is an outsider from a distant part of the world who was probably characterized by outstanding ethnic physical traits. This outsider is driven (see note at

Mark 1:12) to take up the cross and follow Jesus (cf. 8:34). Being an "insider" is not what counts; what counts is how one responds to God's kingdom call.

27:37 *King of the Jews*—See note at v. 11.

27:51 *The curtain of the temple was torn*—The curtain, most likely the one that divided the Holy of Holies from the rest of the sanctuary complex, separated the people from the presence of God (cf. Exod. 26:31–33). The high priest was allowed in the Holy of Holies only on the Day of Atonement, when he sought forgiveness for

curtain of the temple was torn in two, from top to bottom. The earth shook, and the rocks were split. **52** The tombs also were opened, and many bodies of the saints who had fallen asleep were raised. **53** After his resurrection they came out of the tombs and entered the holy city and appeared to many. **54** Now when the centurion and those with him, who were keeping watch over Jesus, saw the earthquake and what took place, they were terrified and said, "Truly this man was God's Son!"*a*

55 Many women were also there, looking on from a distance; they had followed Jesus from Galilee and had provided for him. **56** Among them were Mary Magdalene, and Mary the mother of James and Joseph, and the mother of the sons of Zebedee.

The Burial of Jesus

57 When it was evening, there came a rich man from Arimathea, named Joseph, who was also a disciple of Jesus. **58** He went to Pilate and asked for the body of Jesus; then Pilate ordered it to be given to him. **59** So Joseph took the body and wrapped it in a clean linen cloth **60** and laid it in his own new tomb, which he had hewn in the rock. He then rolled a great stone to the door of the tomb and went away. **61** Mary Magdalene and the other Mary were there, sitting opposite the tomb.

The Guard at the Tomb

62 The next day, that is, after the day of Preparation, the chief priests and the Pharisees gathered before Pilate **63** and said, "Sir, we remember what that impostor said while he was still alive, 'After three days I will rise again.' **64** Therefore command the tomb to be made secure until the third day; otherwise his disciples may go and steal him away, and tell the people, 'He has been raised from the dead,' and the last deception would be worse than the first." **65** Pilate said to them, "You have a guard*b* of soldiers; go, make it as secure as you can."*c* **66** So they went with the guard and made the tomb secure by sealing the stone.

The Resurrection of Jesus

28 After the sabbath, as the first day of the week was dawning, Mary Magdalene and the other Mary went to see the tomb. **2** And suddenly there was a great earthquake; for an angel of the Lord, descending from heaven, came and rolled back the stone and sat on it. **3** His appearance was like lightning, and his clothing white as snow. **4** For fear of him the guards shook and became like dead men. **5** But the angel said to the women, "Do not be afraid; I know that you are looking for Jesus who was crucified. **6** He is not here; for he has been raised, as he said. Come, see the place where he*d* lay. **7** Then go quickly and tell his disciples, 'He has been raised from the dead,*e* and indeed he is going ahead of you to Galilee; there you will see him.'

a Or *a son of God*　*b* Or *Take a guard*　*c* Gk *you know how*　*d* Other ancient authorities read *the Lord*　*e* Other ancient authorities lack *from the dead*

---

the people's sins. The narrative symbolism seems clear; with Jesus' death, access to God need no longer be through the temple infrastructure, but can, through Jesus, be direct.

27:54 *God's Son*—See note at 4:3. While it is unclear in Mark whether the Gentile centurion is speaking sarcastically or reverently, Matthew assures his readers that the centurion recognized Jesus' true identity.

27:55–66 Jesus' Burial (Mark 15:40–47; Luke 23:49–56; John 19:28–42)

27:55 *Many women . . . followed Jesus . . . provided for him*—This is the language of disciple-ship. These women had been Jesus' disciples from the beginning of his ministry. In a world oriented around male disciples, Jesus' ministry broke new gender ground. When contemporary Christianity does not treat women as equals to men, it has diverted from the path Jesus set for his disciples.

27:62–66—Matthew is the only Gospel to record this account, probably as a way to refute the charges that the resurrection was a hoax hyped after Jesus' disciples secretly retrieved and hid his body.

28:1–15 The Empty Tomb

This is my message for you." [8] So they left the tomb quickly with fear and great joy, and ran to tell his disciples. [9] Suddenly Jesus met them and said, "Greetings!" And they came to him, took hold of his feet, and worshiped him. [10] Then Jesus said to them, "Do not be afraid; go and tell my brothers to go to Galilee; there they will see me."

The Report of the Guard

[11] While they were going, some of the guard went into the city and told the chief priests everything that had happened. [12] After the priests[a] had assembled with the elders, they devised a plan to give a large sum of money to the soldiers, [13] telling them, "You must say, 'His disciples came by night and stole him away while we were asleep.' [14] If this comes to the governor's ears, we will satisfy him and keep you out of trouble." [15] So they took the money and did as they were directed. And this story is still told among the Jews to this day.

The Commissioning of the Disciples

[16] Now the eleven disciples went to Galilee, to the mountain to which Jesus had directed them. [17] When they saw him, they worshiped him; but some doubted. [18] And Jesus came and said to them, "All authority in heaven and on earth has been given to me. [19] Go therefore and make disciples of all nations, baptizing them in the name of the Father and of the Son and of the Holy Spirit, [20] and teaching them to obey everything that I have commanded you. And remember, I am with you always, to the end of the age."[b]

[a] Gk they [b] Other ancient authorities add Amen

28:15—Like 27:62–66, these verses are recorded only in Matthew and are intended to counter the suggestion that Jesus' resurrection was a hoax perpetrated by his disciples.

28:16–20 The Commission from the Risen Jesus

28:18 All authority . . . has been given to me—Jesus accepts the due of the Son of Man as recorded at Dan. 7:14. Matthew's particular emphasis, of course, is that this authority has passed from Jesus to the church (cf. 16:19; 18:18).

28:19 Make disciples of all the nations—The declaration from the risen Jesus differs from the command of the earthly Jesus not to carry the ministry into Gentile land (10:5). However, the command is consistent with many of Jesus' own efforts that enriched the lives of Gentiles and prefigured the preaching of the gospel to all the nations.

28:20 I am with you—The promise of Jesus' name, Emmanuel, (1:23) is realized in Jesus' promise to remain always with his church. The church, by its living witness to Jesus' merciful and transformative ministry, can maintain the presence of Jesus in the world.

The Gospel according to
MARK

F irst-century apocalyptic literature aimed to reveal God's ultimate purpose for
human history. The Gospel of Mark is apocalyptic literature. The earliest of the
four Gospels was written anonymously in 70 CE, at the climax of the Jewish-
Roman War. The Romans were laying siege to Jerusalem in anticipation of utterly
destroying the city and the temple it harbored. The evangelist who claimed the name
Mark wrote to help his readers choose between the options that were available for
understanding the nature of God's revelation in that tragic time.

There were two primary competing Jewish impressions. The one laced with nationalistic fervor was the more popular. According to this assessment, God had moved
directly into historical time at the onset of hostilities between the two opposing,
strikingly uneven powers. The goliath Rome, armed with legions of pagan Gentiles,
did not believe in the power of the Hebrew God. They certainly did not believe that
power would be great enough to turn back their assault. But the patriotic, zealous
forces in charge of the revolt believed otherwise. Because it was a fight to rid God's
holy land and people from the interference and rule of foreign, impure, and hostile
powers, they were convicted in their belief that God would finish what they had
started. All true believers were therefore urged to join their fight and wage their war.

Mark wrote his Gospel in defense of a contrary position. His message countered the
suspicion that God was about to move militaristically in human history. His message
was that God had already moved, decades earlier, in the life of Jesus of Nazareth.
Most people, including God's people, had missed the power and opportunity of that
moment. His writing would give them another chance to hear the story of God's self-
revelation and what it disclosed about the meaning of the present and the possibilities
for the future. Though the past in which Jesus' life was lived was lost to them, there
remained an opportunity to seize its momentous vision. They could do so by reading
his Gospel and becoming a disciple to the cause its portrait of Jesus revealed.

Jesus reveals a God who breaks into human time in an effort to repair the breach
separating God from humans and humans from one another. God infiltrates through
Jesus' preaching ministry. That ministry represents the transformative power of God's
future kingdom in the present historical moment through three primary means: exorcism, miracle, and authoritative teaching. The revolutionary vision manifested by
these powerful preaching manifestations is the cause for which God's people should
fight.

The vision challenges the legal and cultic traditions of Israel, because they have
become socioreligious wedges that separate the "righteous" from those they have
declared impure and unholy: tax collectors, sinners, lepers, women, laborers, and
the diseased. Jesus' *teachings* counter the established understanding that one could
overcome one's sinful separation from God only by going through the established
structures and cultic institutions of the temple religion. Since God had broken directly

into human time through the life of Jesus, humans could now go directly through Jesus to God for restoration and reconnection (2:1–12). To make this clear, Jesus associated himself with tax collectors and sinners (2:15–17) and others of ill cultic repute in order to demonstrate that, through him, those whom society had ostracized were welcomed into God's kingdom reality. Jesus' *miracles* made the same point. From his forbidden touch of a leper (1:41) to his reception of a bleeding, impure woman's touch (5:28, 34), he used his healings as opportunities to demonstrate that when God broke into human time, God revealed a desire that humans use brokenness not as a reason to isolate, but as a motivation for reaching out and restoring wholeness. Jesus' *exorcisms* had the same objective. The incursions of divine power that operated in those moments when demonic forces were overwhelmed indicated that the conquest of evil harbored in religious (1:21–28), medical (9:14–29), social (7:24–30), and even political (5:1–20) structures had begun. It occurred through the preaching of Jesus and would continue to occur through the faithful re-presentation of that preaching by his disciples, not by the waging of holy war.

The greatest boundary Mark's Jesus encountered was the ethnic one that created a chasm between Jew and Gentile, the same chasm which had ignited the Jewish war with Rome. In this more volatile international arena, Mark's Jesus remained faithful to the boundary-breaking principle that characterized his transformative behavior within Israel. In an effort to demonstrate that God's future revelation disclosed a kingdom of Jew and Gentile linked together, Mark offered a Jesus whose present activity eventually focused on the task of sharing his exorcising, miracle-making, authoritative teaching power with Gentiles. From chapter 7's explosive comment that Jesus declared all foods clean, and thus all the people who ate such foods clean, to the narration of Jesus' delivery of God's kingdom bread to a Syrophoenician woman's daughter and 4,000 Gentiles hungry for God's physical and spiritual nourishment, Mark offers his readers a revelation that flies directly in the face of the militaristic fervor of the contrary, apocalyptic thinking of the time. While the leaders of the revolt were using the beleaguered temple as a staging ground for their campaign to drive the unholy Gentiles from their land, Mark offered a picture of Jesus cleansing the temple of that same parochial, ethnically limited perspective. Because this intended house of prayer for *all* the nations was determined to remain a citadel of cultic and ethnic exclusivity (11:17), Mark's Jesus predicted its demise, not its miraculous salvation (13:1, 2; 14:58; 15:29).

Such behavior brought Jesus into direct conflict with the leaders of his time, just as the espousal of one's faith in this Jesus would later bring Mark's community into direct conflict with the zealous leaders of his time. Mark therefore understood that Jesus' cross would also be carried by any who chose to walk his transformative, revolutionary path (8:34–9:1). Mark's story not only laments Jesus' tragic death; it forewarns his followers that those who follow his path will surely meet his end (13:9–13). Resistance to revolutionary revelation is always great.

Still, Mark's story is good news. It is good news not only because he believes that Jesus' story reveals God's ultimate intent for human history, but because he is sure that Jesus' life and ministry are vindicated by God. The empty tomb is full of the promise that, despite the anger it provokes and the fear it triggers, Jesus' way was God's way and thus remains *the* way that God's people should follow decades and centuries later. The contemporary discipleship commission is therefore clear. The con-

temporary disciple must be as focused on social and political transformation as he or she is focused on the spiritual conversion of God's people and world. Jesus' boundary breaking activities on behalf of lepers, sinners, tax collectors, children, women, and others of low social standing encourages similar acts that break down the barriers that segregate many in our world into low and demeaned social status. Perhaps even more importantly, Jesus' shattering of the ethnic boundaries that segregated Jew and Gentile from one another is a clarion call to every disciple who follows in his way. The task of discipleship is one that cuts across national, ethnic, geographical, and political boundaries in the interest of reaching out and opening up to everyone an equal access to God's merciful and just love.

—**Brian K. Blount**

The Proclamation of John the Baptist

1 The beginning of the good news*a* of Jesus Christ, the Son of God.*b*

2 As it is written in the prophet Isaiah,*c*

"See, I am sending my messenger
    ahead of you,*d*
who will prepare your way;
³ the voice of one crying out in the
    wilderness:
    'Prepare the way of the Lord,
    make his paths straight,' "

⁴ John the baptizer appeared*e* in the wilderness, proclaiming a baptism of repentance for the forgiveness of sins. ⁵ And people from the whole Judean countryside and all the people of Jerusalem were going out to him, and were baptized by him in the river Jordan, confessing their sins. ⁶ Now John was clothed with camel's hair, with a leather belt around his waist, and he ate locusts and wild honey. ⁷ He proclaimed, "The one who is more powerful than I is coming after me; I am not worthy to stoop down and untie the thong of his sandals. ⁸ I have baptized you with*f* water; but he will baptize you with*f* the Holy Spirit."

The Baptism of Jesus

9 In those days Jesus came from Nazareth of Galilee and was baptized by John in the Jordan. ¹⁰ And just as he was coming up out of the water, he saw the heavens

a Or gospel *b* Other ancient authorities lack *the Son of God* *c* Other ancient authorities read *in the prophets* *d* Gk *before your face* *e* Other ancient authorities read *John was baptizing* *f* Or *in*

1:1–3 The Beginning of the Good News (Matt. 3:1–3; Luke 3:1–6)

1:1 Good news—Good news? What's good about a story where the hero is misunderstood by his followers, opposed by the authorities, and eventually crucified? The news about Jesus is good, not because of what will happen *to* Jesus; it is good because Jesus' ministry makes powerfully transformative things happen *for* others. Mark's narrative will incite its readers to do the same. **Christ**—"Anointed one" or "Messiah." **Son of God**—The king is God's royal son. His authority is God's authority; his actions model God's desires for the behavior of God's people.

1:3—See Isa. 40:3. **Lord**—Parallels Jesus' activity to the activity of God. Jesus' way of social, political, and religious transformation is the way of the Lord that Mark challenges his readers to identify with and follow (see 2:1–3:6; see note at 8:3).

1:4–8 John the Baptizer (Matt. 3:4–12; Luke 3:10–18)

1:4 Baptism—John is interested in its moral, not its cultic significance. Baptism is not a ritual act that guarantees membership in the community of faith; it is instead a marker that identifies a believer's turn toward living life in accordance with God's expectation. **Proclaiming**—See note at v. 14.

1:9–13 Jesus' Baptism and Wilderness Experience (Matt. 3:13–17; 4:1–11; Luke 3:21–22; 4:1–13)

1:9 Galilee—The geographical headquarters of Jesus' ministry (vv. 14, 16, 28, 39; 3:7; 7:31; 9:30; 15:41). Jesus' identification with Galilee sets him in narrative opposition to the city center of Jerusalem. His story begins in Galilee and it will be resurrected there (14:28; 16:7). It is from the margins and on the margins that the believer will rise to the occasion of God's kingdom call.

1:10 Torn apart—God's divine demolition signals the initiation of Jesus' preaching ministry and sets its tone as a boundary-breaking one. God breaks

torn apart and the Spirit descending like a dove on him. ¹¹ And a voice came from heaven, "You are my Son, the Beloved;*a* with you I am well pleased."

The Temptation of Jesus

12 And the Spirit immediately drove him out into the wilderness. ¹³ He was in the wilderness forty days, tempted by Satan; and he was with the wild beasts; and the angels waited on him.

The Beginning of the Galilean Ministry

14 Now after John was arrested, Jesus came to Galilee, proclaiming the good news*b* of God,*c* ¹⁵ and saying, "The time is fulfilled, and the kingdom of God has come near;*d* repent, and believe in the good news."*b*

Jesus Calls the First Disciples

16 As Jesus passed along the Sea of Galilee, he saw Simon and his brother Andrew casting a net into the sea—for they were fishermen. ¹⁷ And Jesus said to them, "Follow me and I will make you fish for people." ¹⁸ And immediately they left their nets and followed him. ¹⁹ As he went a little farther, he saw James son of Zebedee and his brother John, who were in their boat mending the nets. ²⁰ Immediately he called them; and they left their father Zebedee in the boat with the hired men, and followed him.

The Man with an Unclean Spirit

21 They went to Capernaum; and when the sabbath came, he entered the synagogue and taught. ²² They were astounded at his teaching, for he taught them as one having authority, and not as the scribes. ²³ Just then there was in their synagogue a man with an unclean spirit,

a Or *my beloved Son* *b* Or *gospel* *c* Other ancient authorities read *of the kingdom* *d* Or *is at hand*

---

through the heavenly buffer that divides God and humans into separate zones. God's actions provide a blueprint of transformative behavior for the ministry of anyone who would follow God's Son. Discipleship becomes the business of tearing down the walls that separate God from humans, and humans from each other.

1:11 *My Son*—See note at v. 1.

1:12 *Drove him out*—The verb refers primarily to exorcism. As God drives Jesus, and Jesus teaches his disciples to drive out demons (3:15; 6:13), so Mark's narrative compels his readers to take up Jesus' apocalyptic cause and drive into submission the forces and people that haunt and oppress God's people.

1:13 *The angels waited on him*—This same verb ("waited," "provide for") describes Jesus' service as Son of Man (10:45). The only human characters worthy of being subjects to this verb are those whom society considers unworthy, women (1:31; 15:41). God values and uses those whom society devalues and casts aside.

1:14–15 Jesus Proclaims the Kingdom (Matt. 4:12–17)

1:14 *Galilee*—See note at 1:9. *Proclaiming*—Much more than verbal proclamation, it is the preaching act through which God's kingdom power erupts into the present. Jesus' preaching is boundary-breaking, socially and politically challenging behavior (e.g., 2:1–3:6). Contemporary believers who limit their preaching to pulpiteering follow rules of righteous rhetoric, but not

Mark's way of the Lord. *Good news*—See note at v. 1.

1:15 *Kingdom of God*—It is not a safe haven where disciples can escape the world's troubles. It is the forceful movement of God's future rule into the human present. Disciples are called to participate with its transformative movement and brave all the resistance it will incur (cf. 8:34–9:1).

1:16–20 The Call of the First Disciples (Matt. 4:18–22)

1:17, 18, 20 *Follow*—The response of these four men models the radical behavior expected from a Jesus disciple. Discipleship means placing one's trust in God's direction for living, rather than in one's material resources (10:17–22). It also means finding one's sense of family in a community bound solely by an allegiance to Jesus (3:31–35).

1:21–28 A Synagogue Cleansing (Matt. 7:28–29; Luke 4:31–37)

1:22 *Not as the scribes*—Jesus' teaching authority comes directly from God; he teaches neither from nor through the scribal traditions of the people. In fact, his teachings often run counter to them. To teach like Jesus means putting one's understanding of what God wants ahead of and instead of one's commitment to authorized ritual and institutional expectations.

1:23 *Their synagogue*—The possessive pronoun reinforces the hostility between Jesus and the leaders. Anyone who puts the desires of God's

²⁴ and he cried out, "What have you to do with us, Jesus of Nazareth? Have you come to destroy us? I know who you are, the Holy One of God." ²⁵ But Jesus rebuked him, saying, "Be silent, and come out of him!" ²⁶ And the unclean spirit, convulsing him and crying with a loud voice, came out of him. ²⁷ They were all amazed, and they kept on asking one another, "What is this? A new teaching—with authority! He*a* commands even the unclean spirits, and they obey him." ²⁸ At once his fame began to spread throughout the surrounding region of Galilee.

Jesus Heals Many at Simon's House

29 As soon as they*b* left the synagogue, they entered the house of Simon and Andrew, with James and John. ³⁰ Now Simon's mother-in-law was in bed with a fever, and they told him about her at once. ³¹ He came and took her by the hand and lifted her up. Then the fever left her, and she began to serve them.

32 That evening, at sunset, they brought to him all who were sick or possessed with demons. ³³ And the whole city was gathered around the door. ³⁴ And he cured many who were sick with various diseases, and cast out many demons; and he would not permit the demons to speak, because they knew him.

A Preaching Tour in Galilee

35 In the morning, while it was still very dark, he got up and went out to a deserted place, and there he prayed. ³⁶ And Simon and his companions hunted for him. ³⁷ When they found him, they said to him, "Everyone is searching for you." ³⁸ He answered, "Let us go on to the neighboring towns, so that I may proclaim the message there also; for that is what I came out to do." ³⁹ And he went throughout Galilee, proclaiming the message in their synagogues and casting out demons.

Jesus Cleanses a Leper

40 A leper*c* came to him begging him, and kneeling*d* he said to him, "If you choose, you can make me clean." ⁴¹ Moved with pity,*e* Jesus*f* stretched out his hand and touched him, and said to him, "I do choose. Be made clean!" ⁴² Immediately the leprosy*c* left him, and he was made clean. ⁴³ After sternly warning him he sent him away at once, ⁴⁴ saying to him, "See that you say nothing to anyone; but go, show yourself to the priest, and offer for your cleansing what Moses commanded, as a testimony to them." ⁴⁵ But he went out and began

a Or *A new teaching! With authority he*   *b* Other ancient authorities read *he*   *c* The terms *leper* and *leprosy* can refer to several diseases   *d* Other ancient authorities lack *kneeling*   *e* Other ancient authorities read *anger*   *f* Gk *he*

---

kingdom above his or her commitment to religious institution will often find that sanctuaries offer no sanctuary, but anger and hostility instead.

1:24 *The Holy One of God*—Since Jesus' ministry is devoted to "touching" and being "touched" (v. 41; 3:10; 5:28; 6:56; 8:22; 10:13) by the outcast and oppressed, holiness is redefined. Holy is no longer that which is set apart from brokenness, but that which reaches out to brokenness and makes it whole.

1:29–31 Healing Simon's Mother-in-Law (Matt. 8:14–15; Luke 4:38–39)

1:32–34 A Summary of Healings (Matt. 8:16–17; Luke 4:40–41)

1:35–38 Jesus Withdraws to Pray (Luke 4:42–43)

1:39–45 Jesus Heals a Leper (Matt. 8:1–4; Luke 5:12–16)

1:39 *Their synagogues*—See note at v. 23.

1:41 *Jesus . . . touched him*—Operating in direct contradiction of the Levitical code (cf. Lev. 13:45–46), Jesus touches the leper *before* healing him. Instead of becoming contaminated, Jesus infects the leper with wholeness. He not only overturns a physical illness; he decimates a social and cultic norm and thereby sets the pattern for a discipleship ministry that will engage in the same kinds of revolutionary, boundary-breaking activity. Caring for broken people must always be of higher priority than fear of breaking the law.

1:45 *Every quarter*—The scope of ministry has widened dramatically. Because of an unnamed leper's proclamation about Jesus' boundary-breaking behavior on his behalf, God's reach ("touch") knows neither cultic nor geographical bounds. One need not be a great figure with a great reputation like John the Baptizer to make a difference; it is the proclamation that matters, not the kind of person who makes it.

to proclaim it freely, and to spread the word, so that Jesus[a] could no longer go into a town openly, but stayed out in the country; and people came to him from every quarter.

Jesus Heals a Paralytic

2 When he returned to Capernaum after some days, it was reported that he was at home. [2] So many gathered around that there was no longer room for them, not even in front of the door; and he was speaking the word to them. [3] Then some people[b] came, bringing to him a paralyzed man, carried by four of them. [4] And when they could not bring him to Jesus because of the crowd, they removed the roof above him; and after having dug through it, they let down the mat on which the paralytic lay. [5] When Jesus saw their faith, he said to the paralytic, "Son, your sins are forgiven." [6] Now some of the scribes were sitting there, questioning in their hearts, [7] "Why does this fellow speak in this way? It is blasphemy! Who can forgive sins but God alone?" [8] At once Jesus perceived in his spirit that they were discussing these questions among themselves; and he said to them, "Why do you raise such questions in your hearts? [9] Which is easier, to say to the paralytic, 'Your sins are forgiven,' or to say, 'Stand up and take your mat and walk'? [10] But so that you may know that the Son of Man has authority on earth to forgive sins"—he said to the paralytic— [11] "I say to you, stand up, take your mat and go to your home." [12] And he stood up, and immediately took the mat and went out before all of them; so that they were all amazed and glorified God, saying, "We have never seen anything like this!"

Jesus Calls Levi

13 Jesus[c] went out again beside the sea; the whole crowd gathered around him, and he taught them. [14] As he was walking along, he saw Levi son of Alphaeus sitting at the tax booth, and he said to him, "Follow me." And he got up and followed him.

15 And as he sat at dinner[d] in Levi's[e] house, many tax collectors and sinners were also sitting[f] with Jesus and his disciples—for there were many who followed him. [16] When the scribes of[g] the Pharisees saw that he was eating with sinners and tax collectors, they said to his disciples, "Why does he eat[h] with tax collectors and sinners?" [17] When Jesus

[a] Gk he [b] Gk they [c] Gk He [d] Gk reclined [e] Gk his [f] Gk reclining [g] Other ancient authorities read and [h] Other ancient authorities add and drink

---

2:1–12 Jesus Heals a Paralytic (Matt. 9:1–8; Luke 5:17–26)

2:5 *Faith*—Mark labels the boundary-breaking initiative of the four, symbolized by their digging through the roof, faith. Their tenacity models the kind of discipleship Mark wants from his readers.

2:10 *Son of Man*—Based on Dan. 7, it has the distinction of being the only title that Jesus uses to refer to himself. Mark uses it most often in connection with Jesus' suffering and death (8:31; 9:12; 10:33, 45; 14:21, 41). Because that suffering is a direct result of the boundary-breaking preaching that causes conflict between Jesus and the priestly leadership, Jesus' role isn't a suffering one; it is a controversial preaching one. Jesus' disciples, then, are not called to suffer; they are called to emulate his kingdom preaching, despite the fact that doing so may lead to their suffering.

2:13–17 Eating with Tax Collectors and Sinners (Matt. 9:9–13; Luke 5:27–32)

2:15 *Tax collectors*—Because tax collectors often abused their clients and collaborated with Gentiles, many considered them socially degenerate and cultically impure. The frightening and revolutionary implication of Levi's call is that even reprehensible social characters, those whose *intentional* conduct puts them on the societal margin, can, just as they are, become kingdom disciples.

2:16 *Pharisees*—Mainly scribes, laymen, artisans, farmers, and merchants. According to Mark, they followed the commands of the Mosaic law so exactly that the law became more important than the people it had been crafted to serve. Anyone who becomes so enamored with the letter of the law that he or she no longer senses the merciful and communal reasons for which the law was first graciously given (v. 27), is in danger of falling into their Pharisaic trap.

heard this, he said to them, "Those who are well have no need of a physician, but those who are sick; I have come to call not the righteous but sinners."

The Question about Fasting

18 Now John's disciples and the Pharisees were fasting; and people[a] came and said to him, "Why do John's disciples and the disciples of the Pharisees fast, but your disciples do not fast?" 19 Jesus said to them, "The wedding guests cannot fast while the bridegroom is with them, can they? As long as they have the bridegroom with them, they cannot fast. 20 The days will come when the bridegroom is taken away from them, and then they will fast on that day.

21 "No one sews a piece of unshrunk cloth on an old cloak; otherwise, the patch pulls away from it, the new from the old, and a worse tear is made. 22 And no one puts new wine into old wineskins; otherwise, the wine will burst the skins, and the wine is lost, and so are the skins; but one puts new wine into fresh wineskins."[b]

Pronouncement about the Sabbath

23 One sabbath he was going through the grainfields; and as they made their way his disciples began to pluck heads of grain. 24 The Pharisees said to him, "Look, why are they doing what is not lawful on the sabbath?" 25 And he said to them, "Have you never read what David did when he and his companions were hungry and in need of food? 26 He entered the house of God, when Abia-

thar was high priest, and ate the bread of the Presence, which it is not lawful for any but the priests to eat, and he gave some to his companions." 27 Then he said to them, "The sabbath was made for humankind, and not humankind for the sabbath; 28 so the Son of Man is lord even of the sabbath."

The Man with a Withered Hand

3 Again he entered the synagogue, and a man was there who had a withered hand. 2 They watched him to see whether he would cure him on the sabbath, so that they might accuse him. 3 And he said to the man who had the withered hand, "Come forward." 4 Then he said to them, "Is it lawful to do good or to do harm on the sabbath, to save life or to kill?" But they were silent. 5 He looked around at them with anger; he was grieved at their hardness of heart and said to the man, "Stretch out your hand." He stretched it out, and his hand was restored. 6 The Pharisees went out and immediately conspired with the Herodians against him, how to destroy him.

A Multitude at the Seaside

7 Jesus departed with his disciples to the sea, and a great multitude from Galilee followed him; 8 hearing all that he was doing, they came to him in great numbers from Judea, Jerusalem, Idumea, beyond the Jordan, and the region around Tyre and Sidon. 9 He told his

---

[a] Gk they [b] Other ancient authorities lack *but one puts new wine into fresh wineskins*

2:18–22 The Old and the New (Matt. 9:14–17; Luke 5:33–39)

2:22 *New*—Jesus tears past the boundaries of cultic traditions like fasting, sin forgiveness, and avoidance of the ritually impure. This is the new way of discipleship. Commitment to God and devotion to the cause of changing the conditions of God's afflicted people are a disciple's highest priority.

2:23–28 Doing What Is Not Lawful on the Sabbath: Part I (Matt. 12:1–8; Luke 6:1–5)

2:24 *What is not lawful*—Cf. Gen. 2:2; Exod.

16:26–30; 20:8–11; 23:12; 34:21. Despite their hunger, the disciples' actions, apparently reaping, were a violation of the Sabbath rest command. Like Jesus, disciples place care for human need above adherence to the law.

3:1–6 Doing What Is Not Lawful on the Sabbath: Part II (Matt. 12:9–14; Luke 6:6–11)

3:4 *Is it lawful*—Jesus goes out of his way to show that concern for human well-being trumps obedience to the law (see note at 2:24).

3:7–12 A Summary of Jesus' Activities (Matt. 12:15–21; Luke 6:17–19)

disciples to have a boat ready for him because of the crowd, so that they would not crush him; ¹⁰ for he had cured many, so that all who had diseases pressed upon him to touch him. ¹¹ Whenever the unclean spirits saw him, they fell down before him and shouted, "You are the Son of God!" ¹² But he sternly ordered them not to make him known.

Jesus Appoints the Twelve

13 He went up the mountain and called to him those whom he wanted, and they came to him. ¹⁴ And he appointed twelve, whom he also named apostles,ᵃ to be with him, and to be sent out to proclaim the message, ¹⁵ and to have authority to cast out demons. ¹⁶ So he appointed the twelve:ᵇ Simon (to whom he gave the name Peter); ¹⁷ James son of Zebedee and John the brother of James (to whom he gave the name Boanerges, that is, Sons of Thunder); ¹⁸ and Andrew, and Philip, and Bartholomew, and Matthew, and Thomas, and James son of Alphaeus, and Thaddaeus, and Simon the Cananaean, ¹⁹ and Judas Iscariot, who betrayed him.

Jesus and Beelzebul

Then he went home; ²⁰ and the crowd came together again, so that they could not even eat. ²¹ When his family heard it, they went out to restrain him, for people were saying, "He has gone out of his mind." ²² And the scribes who came down from Jerusalem said, "He has Beelzebul, and by the ruler of the demons he casts out demons." ²³ And he called them to him, and spoke to them in parables, "How can Satan cast out Satan? ²⁴ If a kingdom is divided against itself, that kingdom cannot stand. ²⁵ And if a house is divided against itself, that house will not be able to stand. ²⁶ And if Satan has risen up against himself and is divided, he cannot stand, but his end has come. ²⁷ But no one can enter a strong man's house and plunder his property without first tying up the strong man; then indeed the house can be plundered.

28 "Truly I tell you, people will be forgiven for their sins and whatever blasphemies they utter; ²⁹ but whoever blasphemes against the Holy Spirit can never have forgiveness, but is guilty of an eternal sin"— ³⁰ for they had said, "He has an unclean spirit."

The True Kindred of Jesus

31 Then his mother and his brothers came; and standing outside, they sent to him and called him. ³² A crowd was sitting around him; and they said to him, "Your mother and your brothers and sistersᶜ are outside, asking for you." ³³ And he replied, "Who are my mother and my brothers?" ³⁴ And looking at those who sat around him, he said, "Here are my mother and my brothers! ³⁵ Whoever does the will of God is my brother and sister and mother."

ᵃ Other ancient authorities lack *whom he also named apostles* ᵇ Other ancient authorities lack *So he appointed the twelve* ᶜ Other ancient authorities lack *and sisters*

3:11 *Son of God*—See note at 1:1.

3:13–19a Jesus Appoints the Twelve (Matt. 10:1–4; Luke 6:12–16)

3:14 *He appointed twelve*—Jesus, rejected by traditional Israel (see v. 6; 11:18; 12:10), remakes Israel in his own contrary counterimage. *Proclaim*—See note at 1:14. Jesus commissions his disciples to preach with his disruptive, boundary-breaking force.

3:19b–35 Binding the Strong Man and Reconstituting Family (Matt. 12:22–32, 46–50; Luke 11:14–23; 12:10; 8:19–21)

3:23 *Parables*—A putting together of one thing alongside another by way of comparison or illustration. Jesus uses parables not only to teach but to manage—and in some cases, inflame—conflict (cf. 4:10–12).

3:35—Once again, Jesus shatters traditional boundaries. Like Israel (3:14), family is reconstituted. Relationship is not a matter of blood or geography (6:1–6a), but of commitment to the ways of God as represented in the boundary-breaking, kingdom-preaching ministry of Jesus. Disciples must seek community not with those who look like them, act like them, and come from similar backgrounds; they must seek community with those who look and act like Jesus.

The Parable of the Sower

4 Again he began to teach beside the sea. Such a very large crowd gathered around him that he got into a boat on the sea and sat there, while the whole crowd was beside the sea on the land. [2] He began to teach them many things in parables, and in his teaching he said to them: [3] "Listen! A sower went out to sow. [4] And as he sowed, some seed fell on the path, and the birds came and ate it up. [5] Other seed fell on rocky ground, where it did not have much soil, and it sprang up quickly, since it had no depth of soil. [6] And when the sun rose, it was scorched; and since it had no root, it withered away. [7] Other seed fell among thorns, and the thorns grew up and choked it, and it yielded no grain. [8] Other seed fell into good soil and brought forth grain, growing up and increasing and yielding thirty and sixty and a hundredfold." [9] And he said, "Let anyone with ears to hear listen!"

The Purpose of the Parables

10 When he was alone, those who were around him along with the twelve asked him about the parables. [11] And he said to them, "To you has been given the secret[a] of the kingdom of God, but for those outside, everything comes in parables; [12] in order that

'they may indeed look, but not
     perceive,
   and may indeed listen, but not
     understand;
   so that they may not turn again and
     be forgiven.'"

13 And he said to them, "Do you not understand this parable? Then how will you understand all the parables? [14] The sower sows the word. [15] These are the ones on the path where the word is sown: when they hear, Satan immediately comes and takes away the word that is sown in them. [16] And these are the ones sown on rocky ground: when they hear the word, they immediately receive it with joy. [17] But they have no root, and endure only for a while; then, when trouble or persecution arises on account of the word, immediately they fall away.[b] [18] And others are those sown among the thorns: these are the ones who hear the word, [19] but the cares of the world, and the lure of wealth, and the desire for other things come in and choke the word, and it yields nothing. [20] And these are the ones sown on the good soil: they hear the word and accept it and bear fruit, thirty and sixty and a hundredfold."

A Lamp under a Bushel Basket

21 He said to them, "Is a lamp brought in to be put under the bushel basket, or under the bed, and not on the lampstand? [22] For there is nothing hidden, except to be disclosed; nor is anything secret, except to come to light. [23] Let anyone with ears to hear listen!" [24] And he said to them, "Pay attention to what you hear; the measure you give will be the measure you get, and still more will be given you. [25] For to those who have, more will be given; and from those who have nothing, even what they have will be taken away."

[a] Or mystery [b] Or stumble

4:1–34 Teaching the Kingdom in Parables (Matt. 13:1–35; Luke 8:4–18; 13:18–19)

4:2 *Parables*—See note at 3:23.

4:5 *Rocky*—A play on the name Peter, which sounds like "rock" in Greek. The pun suggests that the faith of the disciples is not deep enough to weather the coming hardships (v. 40; 8:17). Believers should examine themselves to determine whether they are surface followers or are truly rooted by tenacious faith (see note at 2:5).

4:9 *Listen*—Mark is concerned that Jesus' followers pay attention and stay alert for opportunities to respond to and with kingdom power.

4:12—See Isa. 6:9–10.

4:23 *Let anyone . . . listen*—There are no restrictions. Neither blood, geography, cultic regulation, nor legal tradition can artificially separate someone from the mysterious offering of God's kingdom power in Jesus' preaching ministry.

The Parable of the Growing Seed

26 He also said, "The kingdom of God is as if someone would scatter seed on the ground, 27 and would sleep and rise night and day, and the seed would sprout and grow, he does not know how. 28 The earth produces of itself, first the stalk, then the head, then the full grain in the head. 29 But when the grain is ripe, at once he goes in with his sickle, because the harvest has come."

The Parable of the Mustard Seed

30 He also said, "With what can we compare the kingdom of God, or what parable will we use for it? 31 It is like a mustard seed, which, when sown upon the ground, is the smallest of all the seeds on earth; 32 yet when it is sown it grows up and becomes the greatest of all shrubs, and puts forth large branches, so that the birds of the air can make nests in its shade."

The Use of Parables

33 With many such parables he spoke the word to them, as they were able to hear it; 34 he did not speak to them except in parables, but he explained everything in private to his disciples.

Jesus Stills a Storm

35 On that day, when evening had come, he said to them, "Let us go across to the other side." 36 And leaving the crowd behind, they took him with them in the boat, just as he was. Other boats were with him. 37 A great windstorm arose, and the waves beat into the boat, so that the boat was already being swamped. 38 But he was in the stern, asleep on the cushion; and they woke him up and said to him, "Teacher, do you not care that we are perishing?" 39 He woke up and rebuked the wind, and said to the sea, "Peace! Be still!" Then the wind ceased, and there was a dead calm. 40 He said to them, "Why are you afraid? Have you still no faith?" 41 And they were filled with great awe and said to one another, "Who then is this, that even the wind and the sea obey him?"

Jesus Heals the Gerasene Demoniac

5 They came to the other side of the sea, to the country of the Gerasenes.[a] 2 And when he had stepped out of the boat, immediately a man out of the tombs with an unclean spirit met him. 3 He lived among the tombs; and no one could restrain him any more, even with a chain; 4 for he had often been restrained with shackles and chains, but the chains he wrenched apart, and the shackles he broke in pieces; and no one had the strength to subdue him. 5 Night and day among the tombs and on the mountains he was always howling and bruising himself with stones. 6 When he saw Jesus from a distance, he ran and bowed down before him; 7 and he shouted at the top of his voice, "What have you to do with me, Jesus, Son of the Most High God? I adjure you by God, do not torment me." 8 For he had said to him, "Come out of the man, you unclean spirit!" 9 Then Jesus[b] asked him, "What is your name?" He replied, "My name is Legion; for we are many." 10 He begged him earnestly not to send them out of the country. 11 Now there on the hillside a great herd of swine was feeding; 12 and the unclean spirits[c] begged him, "Send us into the swine; let us enter them." 13 So he gave them permission. And the unclean spirits came out

[a] Other ancient authorities read *Gergesenes*; others, *Gadarenes*   [b] Gk *he*   [c] Gk *they*

4:30 *Parable*—See note at 3:23.

4:35–41 Crossing the Sea (Matt. 8:23–27; Luke 8:22–25)

4:40 *Faith*—See note at 2:5.

5:1–20 Exorcising "Legion" (Matt. 8:28–34; Luke 8:26–39)

5:9 *Legion*—The demon shares the name of a Roman division. Jesus exorcises the evil within, not the Gentile himself.

and entered the swine; and the herd, numbering about two thousand, rushed down the steep bank into the sea, and were drowned in the sea.

14 The swineherds ran off and told it in the city and in the country. Then people came to see what it was that had happened. 15 They came to Jesus and saw the demoniac sitting there, clothed and in his right mind, the very man who had had the legion; and they were afraid. 16 Those who had seen what had happened to the demoniac and to the swine reported it. 17 Then they began to beg Jesus[a] to leave their neighborhood. 18 As he was getting into the boat, the man who had been possessed by demons begged him that he might be with him. 19 But Jesus[b] refused, and said to him, "Go home to your friends, and tell them how much the Lord has done for you, and what mercy he has shown you." 20 And he went away and began to proclaim in the Decapolis how much Jesus had done for him; and everyone was amazed.

A Girl Restored to Life and a Woman Healed

21 When Jesus had crossed again in the boat[c] to the other side, a great crowd gathered around him; and he was by the sea. 22 Then one of the leaders of the synagogue named Jairus came and, when he saw him, fell at his feet 23 and begged him repeatedly, "My little daughter is at the point of death. Come and lay your hands on her, so that she may be made well, and live." 24 So he went with him.

And a large crowd followed him and pressed in on him. 25 Now there was a woman who had been suffering from hemorrhages for twelve years. 26 She had endured much under many physicians, and had spent all that she had; and she was no better, but rather grew worse. 27 She had heard about Jesus, and came up behind him in the crowd and touched his cloak, 28 for she said, "If I but touch his clothes, I will be made well." 29 Immediately her hemorrhage stopped; and she felt in her body that she was healed of her disease. 30 Immediately aware that power had gone forth from him, Jesus turned about in the crowd and said, "Who touched my clothes?" 31 And his disciples said to him, "You see the crowd pressing in on you; how can you say, 'Who touched me?'" 32 He looked all around to see who had done it. 33 But the woman, knowing what had happened to her, came in fear and trembling, fell down before him, and told him the whole truth. 34 He said to her, "Daughter, your faith has made you well; go in peace, and be healed of your disease."

35 While he was still speaking, some people came from the leader's house to say, "Your daughter is dead. Why trouble the teacher any further?" 36 But overhearing[d] what they said, Jesus said

[a] Gk him   [b] Gk he   [c] Other ancient authorities lack in the boat
[d] Or ignoring; other ancient authorities read hearing

5:15 *Afraid*—The people do not trust this new circumstance of wholeness; they fear the disruptive power that brought it about. Change is threatening, even change for the better.

5:20 *Proclaim*—See note at 1:14. As was the case with the leper (1:45), the preaching of an ordinary person has profound, transformative impact.

5:21–43 Jesus Raises Jairus's Daughter and Heals a Hemorrhaging Woman (Matt. 9:18–26; Luke 8:40–56)

5:23 *Made well*—The Greek term Mark uses is "saved." The evangelist's choice of wording has dramatic implications for discipleship. Saving someone means transforming their social, physi-

cal, and political circumstance (cf. 3:4; 5:28, 34; 6:56; 10:52; 13:13,20; 15:30, 31) as surely as it means changing their spiritual relationship with God (cf. 8:35; 10:26; 13:13, 20).

5:25 *Hemorrhages for twelve years*—Probably menstrual bleeding. Leviticus 15:19–33 prescribes such a woman cultically unclean. As with the leper (see note at 1:41), her contact with Jesus breaks ritual law, since it occurs before her healing. Her faith pushes her beyond tradition and law in search of Jesus' transformative power. It is the kind of faith Mark expects his readers to emulate (see note at 2:5).

5:28 *Made well*—See note at v. 23.

to the leader of the synagogue, "Do not fear, only believe." ³⁷ He allowed no one to follow him except Peter, James, and John, the brother of James. ³⁸ When they came to the house of the leader of the synagogue, he saw a commotion, people weeping and wailing loudly. ³⁹ When he had entered, he said to them, "Why do you make a commotion and weep? The child is not dead but sleeping." ⁴⁰ And they laughed at him. Then he put them all outside, and took the child's father and mother and those who were with him, and went in where the child was. ⁴¹ He took her by the hand and said to her, "Talitha cum," which means, "Little girl, get up!" ⁴² And immediately the girl got up and began to walk about (she was twelve years of age). At this they were overcome with amazement. ⁴³ He strictly ordered them that no one should know this, and told them to give her something to eat.

The Rejection of Jesus at Nazareth

6 He left that place and came to his hometown, and his disciples followed him. ² On the sabbath he began to teach in the synagogue, and many who heard him were astounded. They said, "Where did this man get all this? What is this wisdom that has been given to him? What deeds of power are being done by his hands! ³ Is not this the carpenter, the son of Mary*ᵃ* and brother of James and Joses and Judas and Simon, and are

not his sisters here with us?" And they took offense*ᵇ* at him. ⁴ Then Jesus said to them, "Prophets are not without honor, except in their hometown, and among their own kin, and in their own house." ⁵ And he could do no deed of power there, except that he laid his hands on a few sick people and cured them. ⁶ And he was amazed at their unbelief.

The Mission of the Twelve

Then he went about among the villages teaching. ⁷ He called the twelve and began to send them out two by two, and gave them authority over the unclean spirits. ⁸ He ordered them to take nothing for their journey except a staff; no bread, no bag, no money in their belts; ⁹ but to wear sandals and not to put on two tunics. ¹⁰ He said to them, "Wherever you enter a house, stay there until you leave the place. ¹¹ If any place will not welcome you and they refuse to hear you, as you leave, shake off the dust that is on your feet as a testimony against them." ¹² So they went out and proclaimed that all should repent. ¹³ They cast out many demons, and anointed with oil many who were sick and cured them.

The Death of John the Baptist

14 King Herod heard of it, for Jesus'*ᶜ* name had become known. Some were*ᵈ* saying, "John the baptizer has been raised

---

ᵃ Other ancient authorities read *son of the carpenter and of Mary*   *ᵇ* Or *stumbled*   *ᶜ* Gk *his*   *ᵈ* Other ancient authorities read *He was*

5:41 *Took her by the hand*—Once again Jesus is operating outside the normal boundaries of cultic expectation. He takes hold of one of the most impure objects of all, a corpse. See notes at 1:41 and 5:25.

6:1–6a Jesus Is Rejected in His Hometown (Matt. 13:53–58)

6:1 *Hometown*—See note at 3:35.

6:3 *Son of Mary*—Jesus' home folk disrespect him with a social slur when they trace his lineage through his mother. Like the tax collectors and sinners he cavorts with, he finds himself the subject of ostracizing derision.

6b–13 Jesus Commissions the Twelve (Matt. 9:35; 10:1, 9–11, 14; Luke 9:1–6)

6:7 *He . . . began to send them*—Jesus' disciples are to be conduits of God's transformative, troublesome kingdom power. See note at 1:14.

6:14–29 The Death of John the Baptist (Matt. 14:1–12; Luke 9:7–9)

Mark frames the story of John's beheading with Jesus' sending and receiving of his disciples. The narrative move implies that discipleship which pushes people to live in God's kingdom image (see note at 1:14) will be met with hostility, persecution, and death. Many will be so addicted to tradition that they will prefer violence to change.

from the dead; and for this reason these powers are at work in him." ¹⁵ But others said, "It is Elijah." And others said, "It is a prophet, like one of the prophets of old." ¹⁶ But when Herod heard of it, he said, "John, whom I beheaded, has been raised."

17 For Herod himself had sent men who arrested John, bound him, and put him in prison on account of Herodias, his brother Philip's wife, because Herod*a* had married her. ¹⁸ For John had been telling Herod, "It is not lawful for you to have your brother's wife." ¹⁹ And Herodias had a grudge against him, and wanted to kill him. But she could not, ²⁰ for Herod feared John, knowing that he was a righteous and holy man, and he protected him. When he heard him, he was greatly perplexed;*b* and yet he liked to listen to him. ²¹ But an opportunity came when Herod on his birthday gave a banquet for his courtiers and officers and for the leaders of Galilee. ²² When his daughter Herodias*c* came in and danced, she pleased Herod and his guests; and the king said to the girl, "Ask me for whatever you wish, and I will give it." ²³ And he solemnly swore to her, "Whatever you ask me, I will give you, even half of my kingdom." ²⁴ She went out and said to her mother, "What should I ask for?" She replied, "The head of John the baptizer." ²⁵ Immediately she rushed back to the king and requested, "I want you to give me at once the head of John the Baptist on a platter." ²⁶ The king was deeply grieved; yet out of regard for his oaths and for the guests, he did not want to refuse her. ²⁷ Immediately the king sent a soldier of the guard with orders to bring John's*d* head. He went and beheaded him in the prison, ²⁸ brought his head on a platter, and gave it to the girl. Then the girl gave it to her mother. ²⁹ When his disciples heard about it, they came and took his body, and laid it in a tomb.

Feeding the Five Thousand

30 The apostles gathered around Jesus, and told him all that they had done and taught. ³¹ He said to them, "Come away to a deserted place all by yourselves and rest a while." For many were coming and going, and they had no leisure even to eat. ³² And they went away in the boat to a deserted place by themselves. ³³ Now many saw them going and recognized them, and they hurried there on foot from all the towns and arrived ahead of them. ³⁴ As he went ashore, he saw a great crowd; and he had compassion for them, because they were like sheep without a shepherd; and he began to teach them many things. ³⁵ When it grew late, his disciples came to him and said, "This is a deserted place, and the hour is now very late; ³⁶ send them away so that they may go into the surrounding country and villages and buy something for themselves to eat." ³⁷ But he answered them, "You give them something to eat." They said to him, "Are we to go and buy two hundred denarii*e* worth of bread, and give it to them to eat?" ³⁸ And he said to them, "How many loaves have you? Go and see." When they had found out, they said, "Five, and two fish." ³⁹ Then he ordered them to get all the people to sit down in groups on the green grass. ⁴⁰ So they sat down in groups of hundreds and of fifties. ⁴¹ Taking the five loaves and the two fish, he looked up to heaven, and blessed and broke the loaves, and gave them to his disciples to set before the people; and he divided the two fish among them all. ⁴² And all ate and were filled; ⁴³ and they took up

a Gk he *b* Other ancient authorities read *he did many things* *c* Other ancient authorities read *the daughter of Herodias herself* *d* Gk *his*
e The denarius was the usual day's wage for a laborer

6:30–44 Jesus Feeds Five Thousand in the Wilderness (Matt. 14:13–21; Luke 9:10–17)

6:42 *All . . . were filled*—The verb is next used in the story of the Syrophoenician woman (7:27),

where Jesus tells the Gentile woman that it is not right to give the children's bread to the dogs, i.e., Gentiles. The children (i.e., the Jews) must first be satisfied. In this feeding story, they are. Jesus not

twelve baskets full of broken pieces and of the fish. **44** Those who had eaten the loaves numbered five thousand men.

Jesus Walks on the Water

45 Immediately he made his disciples get into the boat and go on ahead to the other side, to Bethsaida, while he dismissed the crowd. **46** After saying farewell to them, he went up on the mountain to pray.

47 When evening came, the boat was out on the sea, and he was alone on the land. **48** When he saw that they were straining at the oars against an adverse wind, he came towards them early in the morning, walking on the sea. He intended to pass them by. **49** But when they saw him walking on the sea, they thought it was a ghost and cried out; **50** for they all saw him and were terrified. But immediately he spoke to them and said, "Take heart, it is I; do not be afraid." **51** Then he got into the boat with them and the wind ceased. And they were utterly astounded, **52** for they did not understand about the loaves, but their hearts were hardened.

Healing the Sick in Gennesaret

53 When they had crossed over, they came to land at Gennesaret and moored the boat. **54** When they got out of the boat, people at once recognized him,

55 and rushed about that whole region and began to bring the sick on mats to wherever they heard he was. **56** And wherever he went, into villages or cities or farms, they laid the sick in the marketplaces, and begged him that they might touch even the fringe of his cloak; and all who touched it were healed.

The Tradition of the Elders

7 Now when the Pharisees and some of the scribes who had come from Jerusalem gathered around him, **2** they noticed that some of his disciples were eating with defiled hands, that is, without washing them. **3** (For the Pharisees, and all the Jews, do not eat unless they thoroughly wash their hands,*a* thus observing the tradition of the elders; **4** and they do not eat anything from the market unless they wash it;*a* and there are also many other traditions that they observe, the washing of cups, pots, and bronze kettles.*c*) **5** So the Pharisees and the scribes asked him, "Why do your disciples not live*d* according to the tradition of the elders, but eat with defiled hands?" **6** He said to them, "Isaiah prophesied rightly about you hypocrites, as it is written,

'This people honors me with their
          lips,

a Meaning of Gk uncertain   *b* Other ancient authorities read *and when they come from the marketplace, they do not eat unless they purify themselves*   *c* Other ancient authorities add *and beds*   *d* Gk *walk*

---

only gives the woman the bread of his healing power; later, at 8:4 and 8:8, he fills a Gentile multitude with a similar miraculous feeding. The miraculous kingdom power available in Jesus shatters even the mighty boundaries of ethnicity and race. To follow Jesus is to maintain this disruptive path that shows no regard for racial divisiveness.

6:45–52 A Second Miracle at Sea (Matt. 14:22–33)

6:50 *It is I*—Reminiscent of Old Testament texts where God's self-identification is made in the same way (cf. Exod. 3:14; Deut. 32:39). Jesus' use of the term, particularly in such a difficult circumstance, reveals his identification with God and God's kingdom power to transform and save (see note at 5:23).

6:52 *Their hearts were hardened*—Hardness of

heart is a condition reserved for acute resistance to God's designs (Exod. 7:3, 14; Deut. 2:30; Josh. 11:20). Being a follower of Jesus is not enough; one must be able to see with faith and respond with courageous trust when the path he sets becomes tumultuous.

6:53–56 A Markan Summary: Jesus' Popularity Grows (Matt. 14:34–36)

6:56 *Were healed [made well]*—See note at 5:23.

7:1–23 Jesus and the Leaders Argue about Scripture and Tradition (Matt. 15:1–20)

7:1 *Jerusalem*—See note at 1:9.

7:5 *Your disciples*—Jesus' disciples are the ones charged with the boundary trespass. Their actions are as disruptive as his.

7:6–7—See Isa. 29:13 (LXX).

but their hearts are far from me;
7 in vain do they worship me,
     teaching human precepts as
        doctrines.'
8 You abandon the commandment of God and hold to human tradition."

9 Then he said to them, "You have a fine way of rejecting the commandment of God in order to keep your tradition! 10 For Moses said, 'Honor your father and your mother'; and, 'Whoever speaks evil of father or mother must surely die.' 11 But you say that if anyone tells father or mother, 'Whatever support you might have had from me is Corban' (that is, an offering to God*a*)— 12 then you no longer permit doing anything for a father or mother, 13 thus making void the word of God through your tradition that you have handed on. And you do many things like this."

14 Then he called the crowd again and said to them, "Listen to me, all of you, and understand: 15 there is nothing outside a person that by going in can defile, but the things that come out are what defile."*b*

17 When he had left the crowd and entered the house, his disciples asked him about the parable. 18 He said to them, "Then do you also fail to understand? Do you not see that whatever goes into a person from outside cannot defile, 19 since it enters, not the heart but the stomach, and goes out into the sewer?" (Thus he declared all foods clean.) 20 And he said, "It is what comes out of a person that defiles. 21 For it is from within, from the human heart, that evil intentions come: fornication, theft, murder, 22 adultery, avarice, wickedness, deceit, licentiousness, envy, slander, pride, folly. 23 All these evil things come from within, and they defile a person."

The Syrophoenician Woman's Faith

24 From there he set out and went away to the region of Tyre.*c* He entered a house and did not want anyone to know he was there. Yet he could not escape notice, 25 but a woman whose little daughter had an unclean spirit immediately heard about him, and she came and bowed down at his feet. 26 Now the woman was a Gentile, of Syrophoenician origin. She begged him to cast the demon out of her daughter. 27 He said to her, "Let the children be fed first, for it is not fair to take the children's food and throw it to the dogs." 28 But she answered him, "Sir,*d* even the dogs under the table eat the children's crumbs." 29 Then he said to her, "For saying that, you may go—the demon has left your daughter." 30 So she went home, found the child lying on the bed, and the demon gone.

Jesus Cures a Deaf Man

31 Then he returned from the region of Tyre, and went by way of Sidon

a Gk lacks to God *b* Other ancient authorities add verse 16, "Let anyone with ears to hear listen" *c* Other ancient authorities add and Sidon *d* Or Lord; other ancient authorities prefix Yes

---

7:10—Cf. Exod. 20:12; Deut. 5:16 ("Honor your father and mother") and Exod. 21:17; Lev. 20:9 ("Whoever speaks evil . . .").

7:11 *Corban*—"Gift to God." Refers to a vow where a person "willed" his property and resources to the temple. While the person who willed it could still make use of it, he could not share it with anyone else, even his parents. For Jesus, it was one more example where allegiance to the cultic letter of tradition superseded God's desire for mercy and love. Disciples must never allow concern for the law to supersede concern for human need.

7:19 *Thus he declared all foods clean*—Dietary restrictions were one way in which the ethnic boundary between Jew and Gentile was main-tained. This declaration removed that barrier and opened the door to Jewish-Gentile fraternization on a level heretofore unthinkable. See note at 6:42.

7:24–30 The Syrophoenician Woman (Matt. 15:21–28)

7:27 *Let the children be fed first*—See note at 6:42.

7:28 *Even the dogs . . .*—The woman's tenacity (see note at 2:5) is a behavioral model of faith for believers who encounter resistance to the boundary-breaking ways of the kingdom (see note at 6:42). Do not give up; God will respond.

7:31–37 The Healing of a Man Who Is Deaf and Mute (Matt. 15:29–31)

towards the Sea of Galilee, in the region of the Decapolis. ³² They brought to him a deaf man who had an impediment in his speech; and they begged him to lay his hand on him. ³³ He took him aside in private, away from the crowd, and put his fingers into his ears, and he spat and touched his tongue. ³⁴ Then looking up to heaven, he sighed and said to him, "Ephphatha," that is, "Be opened." ³⁵ And immediately his ears were opened, his tongue was released, and he spoke plainly. ³⁶ Then Jesus*a* ordered them to tell no one; but the more he ordered them, the more zealously they proclaimed it. ³⁷ They were astounded beyond measure, saying, "He has done everything well; he even makes the deaf to hear and the mute to speak."

Feeding the Four Thousand

8 In those days when there was again a great crowd without anything to eat, he called his disciples and said to them, ² "I have compassion for the crowd, because they have been with me now for three days and have nothing to eat. ³ If I send them away hungry to their homes, they will faint on the way—and some of them have come from a great distance." ⁴ His disciples replied, "How can one feed these people with bread here in the desert?" ⁵ He asked them, "How many loaves do you have?" They said, "Seven." ⁶ Then he ordered the crowd to sit down on the ground; and he took the seven loaves, and after giving thanks he broke them and gave them to his disciples to distribute; and they distributed them to the crowd. ⁷ They had also a few small fish; and after blessing them, he ordered

that these too should be distributed. ⁸ They ate and were filled; and they took up the broken pieces left over, seven baskets full. ⁹ Now there were about four thousand people. And he sent them away. ¹⁰ And immediately he got into the boat with his disciples and went to the district of Dalmanutha.*b*

The Demand for a Sign

11 The Pharisees came and began to argue with him, asking him for a sign from heaven, to test him. ¹² And he sighed deeply in his spirit and said, "Why does this generation ask for a sign? Truly I tell you, no sign will be given to this generation." ¹³ And he left them, and getting into the boat again, he went across to the other side.

The Yeast of the Pharisees and of Herod

14 Now the disciples*c* had forgotten to bring any bread; and they had only one loaf with them in the boat. ¹⁵ And he cautioned them, saying, "Watch out—beware of the yeast of the Pharisees and the yeast of Herod."*d* ¹⁶ They said to one another, "It is because we have no bread." ¹⁷ And becoming aware of it, Jesus said to them, "Why are you talking about having no bread? Do you still not perceive or understand? Are your hearts hardened? ¹⁸ Do you have eyes, and fail to see? Do you have ears, and fail to hear? And do you not remember? ¹⁹ When I broke the five loaves for the five thousand, how many baskets full of broken pieces did you collect?" They

a Gk he *b* Other ancient authorities read *Mageda* or *Magdala* *c* Gk *they* *d* Other ancient authorities read *the Herodians*

7:36 *Proclaimed*—See notes at 1:14 and 5:20. Even Gentiles can preach the kingdom in ways that have transformative impact. The power of God is *that* accessible.

8:1–9 Jesus Feeds Four Thousand in the Gentile Wilderness (Matt. 15:32–38)

8:3 *On the way*—A euphemism for kingdom discipleship (v. 27; 9:33, 34; 10:17, 32, 46, 52). By launching its use here, the evangelist makes a boundary-breaking narrative claim; the language

specific to kingdom discipleship includes, and indeed starts with, Gentiles. (See introduction and note at Matt. 14:20.)

8:8 *Were filled*—See note at 6:42.

8:10–12 The Pharisees Seek a Sign (Matt. 16:1–4; 12:38–39; Luke 11:16, 19)

8:13–21 The Disciples Misunderstand (Matt. 16:5–12; Luke 12:1)

8:17 *Hardened*—See note at 6:52.

said to him, "Twelve." [20] "And the seven for the four thousand, how many baskets full of broken pieces did you collect?" And they said to him, "Seven." [21] Then he said to them, "Do you not yet understand?"

Jesus Cures a Blind Man at Bethsaida

[22] They came to Bethsaida. Some people[a] brought a blind man to him and begged him to touch him. [23] He took the blind man by the hand and led him out of the village; and when he had put saliva on his eyes and laid his hands on him, he asked him, "Can you see anything?" [24] And the man[b] looked up and said, "I can see people, but they look like trees, walking." [25] Then Jesus[b] laid his hands on his eyes again; and he looked intently and his sight was restored, and he saw everything clearly. [26] Then he sent him away to his home, saying, "Do not even go into the village."[c]

Peter's Declaration about Jesus

[27] Jesus went on with his disciples to the villages of Caesarea Philippi; and on the way he asked his disciples, "Who do people say that I am?" [28] And they answered him, "John the Baptist; and others, Elijah; and still others, one of the prophets." [29] He asked them, "But who do you say that I am?" Peter answered him, "You are the Messiah."[d] [30] And he sternly ordered them not to tell anyone about him.

Jesus Foretells His Death and Resurrection

[31] Then he began to teach them that the Son of Man must undergo great suffering, and be rejected by the elders, the chief priests, and the scribes, and be killed, and after three days rise again. [32] He said all this quite openly. And Peter took him aside and began to rebuke him. [33] But turning and looking at his disciples, he rebuked Peter and said, "Get behind me, Satan! For you are setting your mind not on divine things but on human things."

[34] He called the crowd with his disciples, and said to them, "If any want to become my followers, let them deny themselves and take up their cross and follow me. [35] For those who want to save their life will lose it, and those who lose their life for my sake, and for the sake of the gospel,[e] will save it. [36] For what will it profit them to gain the whole world and forfeit their life? [37] Indeed, what can they give in return for their life? [38] Those who are ashamed of me and of my words[f] in this adulterous and sinful generation, of them the Son of Man will also be ashamed when he comes in the glory of his Father with the holy angels."

9 [1] And he said to them, "Truly I tell you, there are some standing here

---

[a] Gk They [b] Gk he [c] Other ancient authorities add *or tell anyone in the village* [d] Or *the Christ* [e] Other ancient authorities read *lose their life for the sake of the gospel* [f] Other ancient authorities read *and of mine*

8:22–26 Healing the Blind Man

8:27–33 Peter's Recognition and Misunderstanding of Jesus' Identity; Jesus' First Passion Prediction (Matt. 16:13–23; Luke 9:18–22)

8:27 *On the way*—See note at 8:3.

8:29 *Messiah*—See note at 1:1.

8:31 *Son of Man*—See note at 2:10.

8:31 *Must undergo great suffering*—Not satisfied with tearing down cultic and legal traditions that isolated Jews from one another (cf. 1:40–3:6), Jesus sets about dismantling the traditions and laws that separate Jew from Gentile (cf. note at 6:42). This kind of behavior makes trouble inevitable for him and those who emulate him (8:34; 13:9).

8:33 *Get behind me, Satan*—Anyone who

wishes to preserve an unhealthy status quo, even the status quo of messianic expectations that refuse the thought of a suffering messiah, cannot follow on the Lord's kingdom way. Likewise, anyone who is afraid to commit fully to the radically transformative way of Jesus' boundary-breaking lordship because of the suffering such behavior will attract, cannot be a kingdom disciple.

8:34–9:1 The High Cost of Discipleship (Matt. 16:24–28; Luke 9:23–27)

8:34 *Take up their cross*—Those who would follow Jesus must be willing to preach in the same kind of boundary-breaking, socially transformative, and therefore threatening way that often provokes hostile resistance from institutional authority.

who will not taste death until they see that the kingdom of God has come with[a] power."

The Transfiguration

2 Six days later, Jesus took with him Peter and James and John, and led them up a high mountain apart, by themselves. And he was transfigured before them, [3] and his clothes became dazzling white, such as no one[b] on earth could bleach them. [4] And there appeared to them Elijah with Moses, who were talking with Jesus. [5] Then Peter said to Jesus, "Rabbi, it is good for us to be here; let us make three dwellings,[c] one for you, one for Moses, and one for Elijah." [6] He did not know what to say, for they were terrified. [7] Then a cloud overshadowed them, and from the cloud there came a voice, "This is my Son, the Beloved;[d] listen to him!" [8] Suddenly when they looked around, they saw no one with them any more, but only Jesus.

The Coming of Elijah

9 As they were coming down the mountain, he ordered them to tell no one about what they had seen, until after the Son of Man had risen from the dead. [10] So they kept the matter to themselves, questioning what this rising from the dead could mean. [11] Then they asked him, "Why do the scribes say that Elijah must come first?" [12] He said to them, "Elijah is indeed coming first to restore all things. How then is it written about the Son of Man, that he is to go through many sufferings and be treated with contempt? [13] But I tell you that Elijah has come, and they did to him whatever they pleased, as it is written about him."

The Healing of a Boy with a Spirit

14 When they came to the disciples, they saw a great crowd around them, and some scribes arguing with them. [15] When the whole crowd saw him, they were immediately overcome with awe, and they ran forward to greet him. [16] He asked them, "What are you arguing about with them?" [17] Someone from the crowd answered him, "Teacher, I brought you my son; he has a spirit that makes him unable to speak; [18] and whenever it seizes him, it dashes him down; and he foams and grinds his teeth and becomes rigid; and I asked your disciples to cast it out, but they could not do so." [19] He answered them, "You faithless generation, how much longer must I be among you? How much longer must I put up with you? Bring him to me." [20] And they brought the boy[e] to him. When the spirit saw him, immediately it convulsed the boy,[e] and he fell on the ground and rolled about, foaming at the mouth. [21] Jesus[f] asked the father, "How long has this been happening to him?" And he said, "From childhood. [22] It has often cast him into the fire and into the water, to destroy him; but if you are able to do anything, have pity on us and help us." [23] Jesus said to him, "If you are able!—All things can be done for the one who believes." [24] Immediately the

[a] Or in [b] Gk no fuller [c] Or tents [d] Or my beloved Son [e] Gk him [f] Gk He

---

9:2–8 The Transfiguration (Matt. 17:1–8; Luke 9:28–36)

9:4 Elijah with Moses—Elijah represents the Prophets; Moses embodies the Law. Their presence with Jesus vindicates Jesus as the one sent by God and confirms Jesus' tradition trespassing behavior as being God directed.

9:5 Let us make three dwellings—Faced with the possibility of suffering, Peter elects to maintain the transfigured status quo that would keep Jesus—and, most importantly, those who believe in him—dwelling in a stationary and trouble-free, spiritual existence on the mountaintop. Mark's unflattering account of Peter's generous offer suggests that disciples must not shelter themselves from a transformative imitation of Jesus' ministry, even if the hideout is a place and time of spiritual exaltation.

9:9–13 Teaching about Elijah (Matt. 17:9–13)

9:9 Son of Man—See note at 2:10.

9:14–29 Healing a Child and Teaching about Prayer (Matt. 17:14–21; Luke 9:37–48)

father of the child cried out,[a] "I believe; help my unbelief!" 25 When Jesus saw that a crowd came running together, he rebuked the unclean spirit, saying to it, "You spirit that keeps this boy from speaking and hearing, I command you, come out of him, and never enter him again!" 26 After crying out and convulsing him terribly, it came out, and the boy was like a corpse, so that most of them said, "He is dead." 27 But Jesus took him by the hand and lifted him up, and he was able to stand. 28 When he had entered the house, his disciples asked him privately, "Why could we not cast it out?" 29 He said to them, "This kind can come out only through prayer."[b]

Jesus Again Foretells His Death and Resurrection

30 They went on from there and passed through Galilee. He did not want anyone to know it; 31 for he was teaching his disciples, saying to them, "The Son of Man is to be betrayed into human hands, and they will kill him, and three days after being killed, he will rise again." 32 But they did not understand what he was saying and were afraid to ask him.

Who Is the Greatest?

33 Then they came to Capernaum; and when he was in the house he asked them, "What were you arguing about on the way?" 34 But they were silent, for on the way they had argued with one another who was the greatest. 35 He sat down, called the twelve, and said to them, "Whoever wants to be first must be last of all and servant of all." 36 Then he took a little child and put it among them; and taking it in his arms, he said

to them, 37 "Whoever welcomes one such child in my name welcomes me, and whoever welcomes me welcomes not me but the one who sent me."

Another Exorcist

38 John said to him, "Teacher, we saw someone[c] casting out demons in your name, and we tried to stop him, because he was not following us." 39 But Jesus said, "Do not stop him; for no one who does a deed of power in my name will be able soon afterward to speak evil of me. 40 Whoever is not against us is for us. 41 For truly I tell you, whoever gives you a cup of water to drink because you bear the name of Christ will by no means lose the reward.

Temptations to Sin

42 "If any of you put a stumbling block before one of these little ones who believe in me,[d] it would be better for you if a great millstone were hung around your neck and you were thrown into the sea. 43 If your hand causes you to stumble, cut it off; it is better for you to enter life maimed than to have two hands and to go to hell,[e] to the unquenchable fire.[f] 45 And if your foot causes you to stumble, cut it off; it is better for you to enter life lame than to have two feet and to be thrown into hell.[e,f] 47 And if your eye causes you to stumble, tear it out; it is better for you to enter the kingdom of God with one eye than to have two eyes and to be thrown into hell,[e] 48 where their worm never dies, and the fire is never quenched.

[a] Other ancient authorities add *with tears*   [b] Other ancient authorities add *and fasting*   [c] Other ancient authorities add *who does not follow us*   [d] Other ancient authorities lack *in me*   [e] Gk *Gehenna*   [f] Verses 44 and 46 (which are identical with verse 48) are lacking in the best ancient authorities

---

9:30–37 Jesus' Second Passion Prediction and the Disciples' Misunderstanding (Matt. 17:22–23; 18:1–5; Luke 9:43–48)

9:31 *Son of Man*—See note at 2:10.

9:33 *On the way*—See note at 8:3.

9:38–41 A Matter of Membership (Luke 9:49–50)

9:38 *He was not following us*—The alarmed dis-

ciples are not concerned because the exorcist is not following Jesus; they are concerned because he does not follow *them*. Jesus' reply indicates that God is less concerned about matters of membership than about the liberative behavior one performs in God's name.

9:42–50 Miscellaneous Warnings about Life in Community (18:6–9; 5:13; Luke 17:1–2; 14:34–35)

49 "For everyone will be salted with fire.*a* **50** Salt is good; but if salt has lost its saltiness, how can you season it?*b* Have salt in yourselves, and be at peace with one another."

Teaching about Divorce

10 He left that place and went to the region of Judea and*c* beyond the Jordan. And crowds again gathered around him; and, as was his custom, he again taught them.

2 Some Pharisees came, and to test him they asked, "Is it lawful for a man to divorce his wife?" **3** He answered them, "What did Moses command you?" **4** They said, "Moses allowed a man to write a certificate of dismissal and to divorce her." **5** But Jesus said to them, "Because of your hardness of heart he wrote this commandment for you. **6** But from the beginning of creation, 'God made them male and female.' **7** 'For this reason a man shall leave his father and mother and be joined to his wife,*d* **8** and the two shall become one flesh.' So they are no longer two, but one flesh. **9** Therefore what God has joined together, let no one separate."

10 Then in the house the disciples asked him again about this matter. **11** He said to them, "Whoever divorces his wife and marries another commits adultery against her; **12** and if she divorces her husband and marries another, she commits adultery."

Jesus Blesses Little Children

13 People were bringing little children to him in order that he might touch them; and the disciples spoke sternly to them. **14** But when Jesus saw this, he was indignant and said to them, "Let the little children come to me; do not stop them; for it is to such as these that the kingdom of God belongs. **15** Truly I tell you, whoever does not receive the kingdom of God as a little child will never enter it." **16** And he took them up in his arms, laid his hands on them, and blessed them.

The Rich Man

17 As he was setting out on a journey, a man ran up and knelt before him, and asked him, "Good Teacher, what must I do to inherit eternal life?" **18** Jesus said to him, "Why do you call me good? No one is good but God alone. **19** You know the commandments: 'You shall not murder; You shall not commit adultery; You shall not steal; You shall not bear false witness; You shall not defraud; Honor your father and mother.' " **20** He said to him, "Teacher, I have kept all these since my youth." **21** Jesus, looking at him, loved him and said, "You lack one thing; go, sell what you own, and give the money*e* to the poor, and you will have treasure in heaven; then come, follow me." **22** When he heard this, he was shocked and went away grieving, for he had many possessions.

23 Then Jesus looked around and said to his disciples, "How hard it will be

---

a Other ancient authorities either add or substitute *and every sacrifice will be salted with salt* *b* Or *how can you restore its saltiness?* *c* Other ancient authorities lack *and* *d* Other ancient authorities lack *and be joined to his wife* *e* Gk lacks *the money*

10:1–12 Marriage and Divorce (Matt. 19:1–12)

10:2 *Pharisees*—See note at 2:16.

10:11–12—Operating from the principle of equanimity established at creation (cf. Gen. 1:27; 2:24), Jesus' radical response assures that the male will no longer be able to wield discretionary power over a marriage. His arbitrary ability to end it by certificate lost, the male now finds himself as obligated as his mate to the preservation of the union.

10:13–16 Jesus Blesses Children (Matt. 19:13–15; Luke 18:15–17)

10:14 *Kingdom of God*—See note at 1:15. *To such . . . the kingdom of God belongs*—Children represent persons of low social status. Jesus' words caution those of high status to reflect seriously on their relationship with God and to demonstrate greater care for the manner in which they relate to those who, while having less in the way of social and physical standing, hold title to God's coming reign.

10:17–31 A Rich Man (Matt. 19:16–30; Luke 18:18–30)

for those who have wealth to enter the kingdom of God!" [24] And the disciples were perplexed at these words. But Jesus said to them again, "Children, how hard it is[a] to enter the kingdom of God! [25] It is easier for a camel to go through the eye of a needle than for someone who is rich to enter the kingdom of God." [26] They were greatly astounded and said to one another,[b] "Then who can be saved?" [27] Jesus looked at them and said, "For mortals it is impossible, but not for God; for God all things are possible."

28 Peter began to say to him, "Look, we have left everything and followed you." [29] Jesus said, "Truly I tell you, there is no one who has left house or brothers or sisters or mother or father or children or fields, for my sake and for the sake of the good news,[c] [30] who will not receive a hundredfold now in this age—houses, brothers and sisters, mothers and children, and fields, with persecutions—and in the age to come eternal life. [31] But many who are first will be last, and the last will be first."

A Third Time Jesus Foretells His Death and Resurrection

32 They were on the road, going up to Jerusalem, and Jesus was walking ahead of them; they were amazed, and those who followed were afraid. He took the twelve aside again and began to tell them what was to happen to him, [33] saying, "See, we are going up to Jerusalem, and the Son of Man will be handed over to the chief priests and the scribes, and they will condemn him to death; then they will hand him over to the Gentiles;

[34] they will mock him, and spit upon him, and flog him, and kill him; and after three days he will rise again."

The Request of James and John

35 James and John, the sons of Zebedee, came forward to him and said to him, "Teacher, we want you to do for us whatever we ask of you." [36] And he said to them, "What is it you want me to do for you?" [37] And they said to him, "Grant us to sit, one at your right hand and one at your left, in your glory." [38] But Jesus said to them, "You do not know what you are asking. Are you able to drink the cup that I drink, or be baptized with the baptism that I am baptized with?" [39] They replied, "We are able." Then Jesus said to them, "The cup that I drink you will drink; and with the baptism with which I am baptized, you will be baptized; [40] but to sit at my right hand or at my left is not mine to grant, but it is for those for whom it has been prepared."

41 When the ten heard this, they began to be angry with James and John. [42] So Jesus called them and said to them, "You know that among the Gentiles those whom they recognize as their rulers lord it over them, and their great ones are tyrants over them. [43] But it is not so among you; but whoever wishes to become great among you must be your servant, [44] and whoever wishes to be first among you must be slave of all. [45] For the Son of Man came not to be served but to serve, and to give his life a ransom for many."

[a] Other ancient authorities add *for those who trust in riches*   [b] Other ancient authorities read *to him*   [c] Or *gospel*

10:32–45 Third Passion Prediction and Misunderstanding by the Disciples (Matt. 20:17–28; Luke 18:31–34; 22:24–27)

10:32 *On the road*—See note at 8:3.

10:37 *In your glory*—The request reveals status ambitions that are directly contrary to Jesus' servant identity. Jesus' obliteration of the barriers that isolate humans from each other and God will result not in status, but in rejection and death. Emulating that transformative effort is a disciple's glory.

10:45 *Son of Man*—See note at 2:10. *Serve*—See note at 1:13. *Ransom*—Usually a payment to redeem someone from slavery or debt, it has a connotation of liberation. In this context of apocalyptic struggle, Jesus ransoms the lives of those oppressed by various medical, spiritual, social, and political maladies by living in a way that brings transformative challenge to Israel's cultic, legal, and ethnic traditions.

The Healing of Blind Bartimaeus

46 They came to Jericho. As he and his disciples and a large crowd were leaving Jericho, Bartimaeus son of Timaeus, a blind beggar, was sitting by the roadside. 47 When he heard that it was Jesus of Nazareth, he began to shout out and say, "Jesus, Son of David, have mercy on me!" 48 Many sternly ordered him to be quiet, but he cried out even more loudly, "Son of David, have mercy on me!" 49 Jesus stood still and said, "Call him here." And they called the blind man, saying to him, "Take heart; get up, he is calling you." 50 So throwing off his cloak, he sprang up and came to Jesus. 51 Then Jesus said to him, "What do you want me to do for you?" The blind man said to him, "My teacher,ᵃ let me see again." 52 Jesus said to him, "Go; your faith has made you well." Immediately he regained his sight and followed him on the way.

Jesus' Triumphal Entry into Jerusalem

11 When they were approaching Jerusalem, at Bethphage and Bethany, near the Mount of Olives, he sent two of his disciples 2 and said to them, "Go into the village ahead of you, and immediately as you enter it, you will find tied there a colt that has never been ridden; untie it and bring it. 3 If anyone says to you, 'Why are you doing this?' just say this, 'The Lord needs it and will send it back here immediately.'" 4 They went away and found a colt tied near a door, outside in the street. As they were untying it, 5 some of the bystanders said to them, "What are you doing, untying the colt?" 6 They told them what Jesus had said; and they allowed them to take it. 7 Then they brought the colt to Jesus and threw their cloaks on it; and he sat on it. 8 Many people spread their cloaks on the road, and others spread leafy branches that they had cut in the fields. 9 Then those who went ahead and those who followed were shouting,

"Hosanna!
Blessed is the one who comes in
    the name of the Lord!
10   Blessed is the coming kingdom of
    our ancestor David!
Hosanna in the highest heaven!"

11 Then he entered Jerusalem and went into the temple; and when he had looked around at everything, as it was already late, he went out to Bethany with the twelve.

Jesus Curses the Fig Tree

12 On the following day, when they came from Bethany, he was hungry. 13 Seeing in the distance a fig tree in leaf, he went to see whether perhaps he would find anything on it. When he came to it, he found nothing but leaves, for it was not the season for figs. 14 He said to it, "May no one ever eat fruit from you again." And his disciples heard it.

Jesus Cleanses the Temple

15 Then they came to Jerusalem. And he entered the temple and began to drive out those who were selling and those who were buying in the temple, and he overturned the tables of the money changers and the seats of those who sold

ᵃ Aramaic *Rabbouni*

10:46–52 The Healing of Blind Bartimaeus (Matt. 20:29–34; Luke 18:35–43)

10:52 *Faith*—See note at 2:5. *Made you well*—See note at 5:23. *On the way*—See note at 8:3.

11:1–11 The Ride into Jerusalem (Matt. 21:1–10, 17; Luke 19:28–46)

11:9 *Hosanna*—"Save now." See Pss. 113–118. Jesus acts to save God's people from the domination of the cultic, legal, and ethnic status quo (see note at 5:23). So must the disciple who follows him.

11:12–26 A Challenge to the Temple and Its Traditions (Matt. 21:18–19, 12–16, 20–22; Luke 19:45–48)

11:13 *Fig tree*—A metaphor for Israel in the Old Testament. Cf. Isa. 28:3–4; Jer. 8:13; Hos. 9:10, 16; Joel 1:7, 12; Mic. 7:1. The fruitful blossoming of the fig tree represented God's blessing; its withering connoted judgment and destruction.

11:15 *Drive out*—See note at 1:12.

doves; [16] and he would not allow anyone to carry anything through the temple. [17] He was teaching and saying, "Is it not written,

'My house shall be called a house of
　　prayer for all the nations'?
But you have made it a den of
　　robbers.'"

[18] And when the chief priests and the scribes heard it, they kept looking for a way to kill him; for they were afraid of him, because the whole crowd was spellbound by his teaching. [19] And when evening came, Jesus and his disciples[a] went out of the city.

The Lesson from the Withered Fig Tree

20 In the morning as they passed by, they saw the fig tree withered away to its roots. [21] Then Peter remembered and said to him, "Rabbi, look! The fig tree that you cursed has withered." [22] Jesus answered them, "Have[b] faith in God. [23] Truly I tell you, if you say to this mountain, 'Be taken up and thrown into the sea,' and if you do not doubt in your heart, but believe that what you say will come to pass, it will be done for you. [24] So I tell you, whatever you ask for in prayer, believe that you have received[c] it, and it will be yours.

25 "Whenever you stand praying, forgive, if you have anything against anyone; so that your Father in heaven may also forgive you your trespasses."[d]

Jesus' Authority Is Questioned

27 Again they came to Jerusalem. As he was walking in the temple, the chief priests, the scribes, and the elders came to him [28] and said, "By what authority are you doing these things? Who gave you this authority to do them?" [29] Jesus said to them, "I will ask you one question; answer me, and I will tell you by what authority I do these things. [30] Did the baptism of John come from heaven, or was it of human origin? Answer me." [31] They argued with one another, "If we say, 'From heaven,' he will say, 'Why then did you not believe him?' [32] But shall we say, 'Of human origin'?"—they were afraid of the crowd, for all regarded John as truly a prophet. [33] So they answered Jesus, "We do not know." And Jesus said to them, "Neither will I tell you by what authority I am doing these things."

The Parable of the Wicked Tenants

12 Then he began to speak to them in parables. "A man planted a vineyard, put a fence around it, dug a pit for the wine press, and built a watchtower; then he leased it to tenants and went to another country. [2] When the season came, he sent a slave to the tenants to collect from them his share of the produce of the vineyard. [3] But they seized him, and beat him, and sent him away empty-handed. [4] And again he sent another slave to them; this one they beat over the head and insulted. [5] Then he sent another, and that one they killed. And so it was with many others; some they beat, and others they killed. [6] He

[a] Gk they: other ancient authorities read he　[b] Other ancient authorities read "If you have　[c] Other ancient authorities read are receiving　[d] Other ancient authorities add verse 26, "But if you do not forgive, neither will your Father in heaven forgive your trespasses."

11:17 *House of prayer for all the nations*—Cf. Isa. 56:7. The temple should be anyone's and everyone's house of worship and prayer. Because its leaders refuse to allow this to happen, Jesus condemns it. His followers must challenge any institution, no matter how important or powerful, that refuses acceptance to *all* of God's people. *Den of robbers*—Cf. Jer. 7:11. These robber bandits were armed marauders and insurrectionists. Caves ("den") were their hiding places of choice. Apparently, they also chose the temple. The intended house of international prayer became the staging ground for a nationalist war aimed at

ejecting Gentiles from the land. The disciple who follows Jesus' kingdom way must adopt a collision course with any institution that touts such an exclusivistic agenda.

11:22 *Faith*—See note at 2:5.

11:27–33 A Challenge to Jesus' Authority (Matt. 21:23–27; Luke 20:1–8)

12:1–12 The Parable of the Vineyard (Matt. 21:33–46; Luke 20:9–19)

12:1 *Parable*—See note at 3:23. *Vineyard*—Cf. Isa. 5:1–7 for Israel as a vineyard.

had still one other, a beloved son. Finally he sent him to them, saying, 'They will respect my son.' 7 But those tenants said to one another, 'This is the heir; come, let us kill him, and the inheritance will be ours.' 8 So they seized him, killed him, and threw him out of the vineyard. 9 What then will the owner of the vineyard do? He will come and destroy the tenants and give the vineyard to others. 10 Have you not read this scripture:

'The stone that the builders rejected
　　has become the cornerstone;*a*
11 this was the Lord's doing,
　　and it is amazing in our eyes'?"

12 When they realized that he had told this parable against them, they wanted to arrest him, but they feared the crowd. So they left him and went away.

The Question about Paying Taxes

13 Then they sent to him some Pharisees and some Herodians to trap him in what he said. 14 And they came and said to him, "Teacher, we know that you are sincere, and show deference to no one; for you do not regard people with partiality, but teach the way of God in accordance with truth. Is it lawful to pay taxes to the emperor, or not? 15 Should we pay them, or should we not?" But knowing their hypocrisy, he said to them, "Why are you putting me to the test? Bring me a denarius and let me see it." 16 And they brought one. Then he said to them, "Whose head is this, and whose title?" They answered, "The emperor's." 17 Jesus said to them, "Give to the emperor the things that are the emperor's, and to God the things that are God's." And they were utterly amazed at him.

The Question about the Resurrection

18 Some Sadducees, who say there is no resurrection, came to him and asked him a question, saying, 19 "Teacher, Moses wrote for us that if a man's brother dies, leaving a wife but no child, the man*b* shall marry the widow and raise up children for his brother. 20 There were seven brothers; the first married and, when he died, left no children; 21 and the second married the widow*c* and died, leaving no children; and the third likewise; 22 none of the seven left children. Last of all the woman herself died. 23 In the resurrection*d* whose wife will she be? For the seven had married her."

24 Jesus said to them, "Is not this the reason you are wrong, that you know neither the scriptures nor the power of God? 25 For when they rise from the dead, they neither marry nor are given in marriage, but are like angels in heaven. 26 And as for the dead being raised, have you not read in the book of Moses, in the story about the bush, how God said to him, 'I am the God of Abraham, the God of Isaac, and the God of Jacob'? 27 He is God not of the dead, but of the living; you are quite wrong."

The First Commandment

28 One of the scribes came near and heard them disputing with one another,

a Or keystone　*b* Gk his brother　*c* Gk her　*d* Other ancient authorities add when they rise

---

12:9–11 *Others*—Cf. Ps. 118:22–23. Given the context (see note at 11:17), one would expect the leadership of the new vineyard to be much more cultically and ethnically inclusive.

12:13–17 A Hostile Question about Paying Taxes (Matt. 22:15–22; Luke 20:20–26).

12:15 *The test*—A yes answer would incite the anti-Roman crowd; a no would invite Roman anger. Jesus' clever response to their efforts to *trap him* (v. 13) operates from the Jewish premise that everything belongs to God. Since nothing really belongs to Caesar, one can faithfully give it to him. Believers will always be challenged by

the demands government places upon their time, energy, and resources. While fulfilling their societal obligations, believers must be sure always to put obligation to God first. Where commitment to God and commitment to government conflict, God has priority.

12:18–27 A Hostile Question about the Resurrection (Matt. 22:23–33; Luke 20:27–40)

12:18 *Sadducees*—Aristocratic, priestly party that served the temple. Unlike the Pharisees, they did not believe in the resurrection of the dead.

12:28–34 A Question about the Law (Matt. 22:34–40; Luke 10:25–28)

and seeing that he answered them well, he asked him, "Which commandment is the first of all?" ²⁹ Jesus answered, "The first is, 'Hear, O Israel: the Lord our God, the Lord is one; ³⁰ you shall love the Lord your God with all your heart, and with all your soul, and with all your mind, and with all your strength.' ³¹ The second is this, 'You shall love your neighbor as yourself.' There is no other commandment greater than these." ³² Then the scribe said to him, "You are right, Teacher; you have truly said that 'he is one, and besides him there is no other'; ³³ and 'to love him with all the heart, and with all the understanding, and with all the strength,' and 'to love one's neighbor as oneself,'—this is much more important than all whole burnt offerings and sacrifices." ³⁴ When Jesus saw that he answered wisely, he said to him, "You are not far from the kingdom of God." After that no one dared to ask him any question.

The Question about David's Son

³⁵ While Jesus was teaching in the temple, he said, "How can the scribes say that the Messiah*a* is the son of David? ³⁶ David himself, by the Holy Spirit, declared,

'The Lord said to my Lord,
"Sit at my right hand,
until I put your enemies under
your feet."'

³⁷ David himself calls him Lord; so how can he be his son?" And the large crowd was listening to him with delight.

Jesus Denounces the Scribes

³⁸ As he taught, he said, "Beware of the scribes, who like to walk around in long robes, and to be greeted with respect in the marketplaces, ³⁹ and to have the best seats in the synagogues and places of honor at banquets! ⁴⁰ They devour widows' houses and for the sake of appearance say long prayers. They will receive the greater condemnation."

The Widow's Offering

⁴¹ He sat down opposite the treasury, and watched the crowd putting money into the treasury. Many rich people put in large sums. ⁴² A poor widow came and put in two small copper coins, which are worth a penny. ⁴³ Then he called his disciples and said to them, "Truly I tell you, this poor widow has put in more than all those who are contributing to the treasury. ⁴⁴ For all of them have contributed out of their abundance; but she out of her poverty has put in everything she had, all she had to live on."

The Destruction of the Temple Foretold

13 As he came out of the temple, one of his disciples said to him, "Look, Teacher, what large stones and what large buildings!" ² Then Jesus asked him, "Do you see these great buildings? Not one stone will be left here upon another; all will be thrown down."

³ When he was sitting on the Mount of Olives opposite the temple, Peter, James, John, and Andrew asked him privately, ⁴ "Tell us, when will this be, and what will

a Or the Christ

12:33—The scribe's answer reflects Jesus' belief that love for God and others takes precedence over allegiance to cultic, legal, and ethnic tradition.

12:35–37 The Messiah and David's Son (Matt. 22:41–46; Luke 20:41–44)

12:38–44 An Attack on the Scribes (Matt. 23:1–36; Luke 20:45–47; 21:1–4)

12:42 *A poor widow*—Like Jesus, the widow is willing to sacrifice all that she has in her commitment to God. She holds nothing back. Unlike Jesus, the directors of the temple treasury take

everything from her and other poor people like her, while allowing the wealthy to give what they desire. The story is as much a narrative of justice as it is one of stewardship. While God does desire a disciple's complete devotion, God's leaders must not use the traditional mandates of "sacrificial giving" to squeeze the life out of sincere followers who have little, while coddling those who *have more* and should thus be challenged to *give more*.

13:1–4 The Destruction of the Temple Foretold (Matt. 24:1–3; Luke 21:5–7)

be the sign that all these things are about to be accomplished?" ⁵ Then Jesus began to say to them, "Beware that no one leads you astray. ⁶ Many will come in my name and say, 'I am he!'ᵃ and they will lead many astray. ⁷ When you hear of wars and rumors of wars, do not be alarmed; this must take place, but the end is still to come. ⁸ For nation will rise against nation, and kingdom against kingdom; there will be earthquakes in various places; there will be famines. This is but the beginning of the birth pangs.

Persecution Foretold

9 "As for yourselves, beware; for they will hand you over to councils; and you will be beaten in synagogues; and you will stand before governors and kings because of me, as a testimony to them. ¹⁰ And the good newsᵇ must first be proclaimed to all nations. ¹¹ When they bring you to trial and hand you over, do not worry beforehand about what you are to say; but say whatever is given you at that time, for it is not you who speak, but the Holy Spirit. ¹² Brother will betray brother to death, and a father his child, and children will rise against parents and have them put to death; ¹³ and you will be hated by all because of my name. But the one who endures to the end will be saved.

The Desolating Sacrilege

14 "But when you see the desolating sacrilege set up where it ought not to be (let the reader understand), then those in Judea must flee to the mountains; ¹⁵ the one on the housetop must not go down or enter the house to take anything away; ¹⁶ the one in the field must not turn back to get a coat. ¹⁷ Woe to those who are pregnant and to those who are nursing infants in those days! ¹⁸ Pray that it may not be in winter. ¹⁹ For in those days there will be suffering, such as has not been from the beginning of the creation that God created until now, no, and never will be. ²⁰ And if the Lord had not cut short those days, no one would be saved; but for the sake of the elect, whom he chose, he has cut short those days. ²¹ And if anyone says to you at that time, 'Look! Here is the Messiah!'ᶜ or 'Look! There he is!'—do not believe it. ²² False messiahsᵈ and false prophets will appear and produce signs and omens, to lead astray, if possible, the elect. ²³ But be alert; I have already told you everything.

The Coming of the Son of Man

24 "But in those days, after that suffering,

the sun will be darkened,
    and the moon will not give its light,

ᵃ Gk I am   ᵇ Gk gospel   ᶜ Or the Christ   ᵈ Or christs

13:5–8 Only the Beginning, Not the End (Matt. 24:4–8; Luke 21:8–11)

13:5 *Beware*—The verb Mark uses is "see" or "watch." The "watch out" emphasis occurs as dramatically here (vv. 5, 9, 23, 34, 35, 37) as it did through the symbolism of listening in chap. 4 (cf., 4:3, 9, 23, 24, 33). See note at 4:9.

13:9–13 A Gospel Preached to All Nations (Matt. 24:9–14; Luke 21:12–19)

13:10 *To all nations*—Jesus' disciples must push God's kingdom preaching ministry beyond the boundaries of Israel (see note at 11:17). Mark prepares his readers for the consequences of such controversial behavior by bracketing this mandate with promises of persecution. Kingdom discipleship is a matter of calling people who are different into heterogeneous communities of faith despite the fact that such groundbreaking activity often sparks conflict and hurt.

13:13 *Save*—See note at 5:23.

13:14–23 A Historical Review of Destruction (Matt. 24:15–25; Luke 21:20–24)

13:14 *The desolating sacrilege*—Cf. Dan. 9:27; 11:31; 12:11. See note at Mark 11:17. The very attempt to purify the people by using the temple as a staging ground for war turns the temple into an "abomination of desolation" (KJV). It must be destroyed (13:1–2); another temple, not made with hands, will take its place (14:58; 15:29). That temple will gather its elect from everywhere (13:27). This is the kind of "temple" Mark wants his reading community, and, no doubt, the contemporary church, to become.

13:24–27 From Historical Review to Apocalyptic Vision (Matt. 24:29–31; Luke 21:25–28)

25 and the stars will be falling from
heaven,
and the powers in the heavens will
be shaken.
26 Then they will see 'the Son of Man
coming in clouds' with great power and
glory. 27 Then he will send out the angels,
and gather his elect from the four winds,
from the ends of the earth to the ends of
heaven.

The Lesson of the Fig Tree

28 "From the fig tree learn its lesson:
as soon as its branch becomes tender
and puts forth its leaves, you know that
summer is near. 29 So also, when you see
these things taking place, you know that
he*a* is near, at the very gates. 30 Truly I tell
you, this generation will not pass away
until all these things have taken place.
31 Heaven and earth will pass away, but
my words will not pass away.

The Necessity for Watchfulness

32 "But about that day or hour no one
knows, neither the angels in heaven, nor
the Son, but only the Father. 33 Beware,
keep alert;*b* for you do not know when
the time will come. 34 It is like a man
going on a journey, when he leaves
home and puts his slaves in charge, each
with his work, and commands the doorkeeper to be on the watch. 35 Therefore,
keep awake—for you do not know when
the master of the house will come, in
the evening, or at midnight, or at cock-
crow, or at dawn, 36 or else he may find
you asleep when he comes suddenly.
37 And what I say to you I say to all: Keep
awake."

The Plot to Kill Jesus

14 It was two days before the Passover and the festival of Unleavened Bread. The chief priests and the
scribes were looking for a way to arrest
Jesus*c* by stealth and kill him; 2 for they
said, "Not during the festival, or there
may be a riot among the people."

The Anointing at Bethany

3 While he was at Bethany in the
house of Simon the leper,*d* as he sat at
the table, a woman came with an alabaster jar of very costly ointment of nard,
and she broke open the jar and poured
the ointment on his head. 4 But some
were there who said to one another in
anger, "Why was the ointment wasted in
this way? 5 For this ointment could have
been sold for more than three hundred
denarii,*e* and the money given to the
poor." And they scolded her. 6 But Jesus
said, "Let her alone; why do you trouble
her? She has performed a good service
for me. 7 For you always have the poor
with you, and you can show kindness to
them whenever you wish; but you will
not always have me. 8 She has done what
she could; she has anointed my body
beforehand for its burial. 9 Truly I tell

a Or it *b* Other ancient authorities add *and pray* *c* Gk him *d* The terms *leper* and *leprosy* can refer to several diseases *e* The denarius was the usual day's wage for a laborer

---

13:26 Son of Man—See note at 2:10. See also 14:62; Dan. 7:13.

13:28–31 The Lesson of the Fig Tree (Matt. 24:32–35; Luke 21:29–33)

13:32–37 The Need for Watchfulness (Matt. 24:36; 24:42; 25:13)

13:33 Beware—See note at v. 5.

14:1–2 Viewing Jesus' Passion through the Lens of the Passover (Matt. 26:1–5; Luke 22:1–2)

14:1 Passover—See also v. 12. The Passover was a commemoration of the exodus intervention (cf. Exod. 12:14). The meal commemorates the redemption of the people from sociohistorical slavery. Its blood symbolizes sociopolitical liberation, on the one hand, and the realization of a sociohistorical covenant between God and Israel, on the other. Jesus wants his disciples to share the meal that remembers him through this kind of "redemptive" lens.

14:3–9 Jesus Is Anointed (Matt. 26:6–13)

14:3 Leper—See note at 1:41.

14:3 Poured the ointment on his head—Kings were customarily anointed by prophetic figures (cf. 1 Sam. 9:16). The fact that Jesus allows a woman to perform this function is one more boundary-breaking moment in a ministry full of them.

14:9 In the whole world—See notes at 11:17 and 13:10.

you, wherever the good news*a* is proclaimed in the whole world, what she has done will be told in remembrance of her."

Judas Agrees to Betray Jesus

10 Then Judas Iscariot, who was one of the twelve, went to the chief priests in order to betray him to them. **11** When they heard it, they were greatly pleased, and promised to give him money. So he began to look for an opportunity to betray him.

The Passover with the Disciples

12 On the first day of Unleavened Bread, when the Passover lamb is sacrificed, his disciples said to him, "Where do you want us to go and make the preparations for you to eat the Passover?" **13** So he sent two of his disciples, saying to them, "Go into the city, and a man carrying a jar of water will meet you; follow him, **14** and wherever he enters, say to the owner of the house, 'The Teacher asks, Where is my guest room where I may eat the Passover with my disciples?' **15** He will show you a large room upstairs, furnished and ready. Make preparations for us there." **16** So the disciples set out and went to the city, and found everything as he had told them; and they prepared the Passover meal.

17 When it was evening, he came with the twelve. **18** And when they had taken their places and were eating, Jesus said, "Truly I tell you, one of you will betray me, one who is eating with me." **19** They began to be distressed and to say to him one after another, "Surely, not I?" **20** He said to them, "It is one of the twelve, one who is dipping bread*b* into the bowl*c* with me. **21** For the Son of Man goes as it is written of him, but woe to that one by whom the Son of Man is betrayed! It would have been better for that one not to have been born."

The Institution of the Lord's Supper

22 While they were eating, he took a loaf of bread, and after blessing it he broke it, gave it to them, and said, "Take; this is my body." **23** Then he took a cup, and after giving thanks he gave it to them, and all of them drank from it. **24** He said to them, "This is my blood of the*d* covenant, which is poured out for many. **25** Truly I tell you, I will never again drink of the fruit of the vine until that day when I drink it new in the kingdom of God."

a Or gospel *b* Gk lacks bread *c* Other ancient authorities read *same bowl*
d Other ancient authorities add *new*

14:10–11 Judas Orchestrates Betrayal (Matt. 26:14–16; Luke 22:3–6)

14:12–16 Preparing the Passover (Matt. 26:17–19; Luke 22:7–13)

14:12 *Passover and Feast of Unleavened Bread*—See note at v. 1.

14:17–21 Jesus Predicts His Betrayal (Matt. 26:20–25; Luke 22:14, 21–23)

14:21 *Son of Man*—See note at 2:10.

14:22–25 Jesus' Last Supper (Matt. 26:26–29; Luke 22:15–20)

14:22 *He took . . . after blessing . . . he broke . . . gave it to them*—Rekindles memory of Jesus' two most flamboyant kingdom preaching moments, the feeding of the (Jewish) five thousand and (Gentile) four thousand (see note at 6:42). God provides for *all* God's people. This very political image of boundary-shattering, universal care, viewed through the liberating Passover lens (see note at 14:1), is the one Mark wants in his readers' minds when they approach the Lord's table.

Bread . . . body—See note at 6:42. On almost every occasion where Mark uses "bread," he does so in the context of a preaching moment that tears down a status quo cultic or legal tradition (2:26; 6:34–44 and 8:1–9; 7:1–23; 7:27). When disciples celebrate the breaking of the bread, they are also reaffirming themselves to Jesus' commission to break down the spiritual, social, and political boundaries that separate people from one another.

14:23, 24 *Cup . . . blood*—When God established a relationship with the "holy" people in Exod. 24:8, the sacrificial blood confirmed it. Jesus envisions a covenant between God and God's newly constituted "whole" people populated with lepers, tax collectors, sinners, impure women, and Gentiles. This covenant, established by his ministry, will be sealed with his blood. This is the kind of community his disciples must continue to foster and build.

14:25 *Kingdom of God*—See note at 1:15.

Peter's Denial Foretold

26 When they had sung the hymn, they went out to the Mount of Olives. 27 And Jesus said to them, "You will all become deserters; for it is written,

'I will strike the shepherd,
    and the sheep will be scattered.'

28 But after I am raised up, I will go before you to Galilee." 29 Peter said to him, "Even though all become deserters, I will not." 30 Jesus said to him, "Truly I tell you, this day, this very night, before the cock crows twice, you will deny me three times." 31 But he said vehemently, "Even though I must die with you, I will not deny you." And all of them said the same.

Jesus Prays in Gethsemane

32 They went to a place called Gethsemane; and he said to his disciples, "Sit here while I pray." 33 He took with him Peter and James and John, and began to be distressed and agitated. 34 And he said to them, "I am deeply grieved, even to death; remain here, and keep awake." 35 And going a little farther, he threw himself on the ground and prayed that, if it were possible, the hour might pass from him. 36 He said, "Abba,a Father, for you all things are possible; remove this cup from me; yet, not what I want, but what you want." 37 He came and found them sleeping; and he said to Peter, "Simon, are you asleep? Could you not keep awake one hour? 38 Keep awake and pray that you may not come into the time of trial;b the spirit indeed is willing, but the flesh is weak." 39 And again he went away and prayed, saying the same words. 40 And once more he came and found them sleeping, for their eyes were very heavy; and they did not know what to say to him. 41 He came a third time and said to them, "Are you still sleeping and taking your rest? Enough! The hour has come; the Son of Man is betrayed into the hands of sinners. 42 Get up, let us be going. See, my betrayer is at hand."

The Betrayal and Arrest of Jesus

43 Immediately, while he was still speaking, Judas, one of the twelve, arrived; and with him there was a crowd with swords and clubs, from the chief priests, the scribes, and the elders. 44 Now the betrayer had given them a sign, saying, "The one I will kiss is the man; arrest him and lead him away under guard." 45 So when he came, he went up to him at once and said, "Rabbi!" and kissed him. 46 Then they laid hands on him and arrested him. 47 But one of those who stood near drew his sword and struck the slave of the high priest, cutting off his ear. 48 Then Jesus said to them, "Have you come out with swords and clubs to arrest me as though I were a bandit? 49 Day after day I was with you in the temple teaching, and you did not arrest me. But let the scriptures be fulfilled." 50 All of them deserted him and fled.

51 A certain young man was following him, wearing nothing but a linen cloth. They caught hold of him, 52 but he left the linen cloth and ran off naked.

Jesus before the Council

53 They took Jesus to the high priest; and all the chief priests, the elders, and the scribes were assembled. 54 Peter had followed him at a distance, right into the courtyard of the high priest; and he was sitting with the guards, warming himself at the fire. 55 Now the chief priests and

a Aramaic for Father   b Or into temptation

14:26–52 Gethsemane (Matt. 26:30–56; Luke 22:39, 31–34; 40–53)

14:28 *Galilee*—See note at 1:9.

14:41 *Son of Man*—See note at 2:10.

14:53–72 Jesus' Trial before the Sanhedrin and Peter's Denial (Matt. 26:57–75; Luke 22:54–71)

14:54—While Jesus stands and witnesses courageously before the leaders, Peter breaks down and cowers before servants. The model for discipleship is clear.

the whole council were looking for testimony against Jesus to put him to death; but they found none. ⁵⁶ For many gave false testimony against him, and their testimony did not agree. ⁵⁷ Some stood up and gave false testimony against him, saying, ⁵⁸ "We heard him say, 'I will destroy this temple that is made with hands, and in three days I will build another, not made with hands.'" ⁵⁹ But even on this point their testimony did not agree. ⁶⁰ Then the high priest stood up before them and asked Jesus, "Have you no answer? What is it that they testify against you?" ⁶¹ But he was silent and did not answer. Again the high priest asked him, "Are you the Messiah,ᵃ the Son of the Blessed One?" ⁶² Jesus said, "I am; and

'you will see the Son of Man
seated at the right hand of the
Power,'
and 'coming with the clouds of
heaven.'"

⁶³ Then the high priest tore his clothes and said, "Why do we still need witnesses? ⁶⁴ You have heard his blasphemy! What is your decision?" All of them condemned him as deserving death. ⁶⁵ Some began to spit on him, to blindfold him, and to strike him, saying to him, "Prophesy!" The guards also took him over and beat him.

Peter Denies Jesus

66 While Peter was below in the courtyard, one of the servant-girls of the high priest came by. ⁶⁷ When she saw Peter warming himself, she stared at him and said, "You also were with Jesus, the man from Nazareth." ⁶⁸ But he denied it, saying, "I do not know or understand what you are talking about." And he went out into the forecourt.ᵇ Then the cock crowed.ᶜ ⁶⁹ And the servant-girl, on seeing him, began again to say to the bystanders, "This man is one of them." ⁷⁰ But again he denied it. Then after a little while the bystanders again said to Peter, "Certainly you are one of them; for you are a Galilean." ⁷¹ But he began to curse, and he swore an oath, "I do not know this man you are talking about." ⁷² At that moment the cock crowed for the second time. Then Peter remembered that Jesus had said to him, "Before the cock crows twice, you will deny me three times." And he broke down and wept.

Jesus before Pilate

15 As soon as it was morning, the chief priests held a consultation with the elders and scribes and the whole council. They bound Jesus, led him away, and handed him over to Pilate. ² Pilate asked him, "Are you the King of the Jews?" He answered him, "You say so." ³ Then the chief priests accused him of many things. ⁴ Pilate asked him again, "Have you no answer? See how many charges they bring against you." ⁵ But Jesus made no further reply, so that Pilate was amazed.

Pilate Hands Jesus over to Be Crucified

6 Now at the festival he used to release a prisoner for them, anyone for whom they asked. ⁷ Now a man called Barabbas was in prison with the rebels who had committed murder during the insurrection. ⁸ So the crowd came and began to

ᵃ Or the Christ ᵇ Or gateway ᶜ Other ancient authorities lack Then the cock crowed

---

14:61 *Messiah*—See note at 1:1.

14:62 *Son of Man*—See note at 2:10. Cf. Dan. 7:13 and Ps. 110:1.

15:1–15 Jesus Is Condemned by Pilate (Matt. 27:1–2, 11–26; Luke 23:1–5, 17–25)

15:1 *Pilate*—Prefect of Judea 26–36 CE.

15:2 *King of the Jews*—The fact that the Roman soldiers taunt him as a king (vv. 16–20) and that

Pilate has the title affixed to the cross (v. 26) suggest that it was upon this basis that Jesus was crucified. Jesus' boundary-breaking activities were as threatening to the Roman maintenance of peace in the region as to the authoritative status of the Palestinian leadership. The implication is clear: discipleship that operates in Jesus' name will be as politically engaged as it is spiritually engaged.

ask Pilate to do for them according to his custom. ⁹ Then he answered them, "Do you want me to release for you the King of the Jews?" ¹⁰ For he realized that it was out of jealousy that the chief priests had handed him over. ¹¹ But the chief priests stirred up the crowd to have him release Barabbas for them instead. ¹² Pilate spoke to them again, "Then what do you wish me to do*a* with the man you call*b* the King of the Jews?" ¹³ They shouted back, "Crucify him!" ¹⁴ Pilate asked them, "Why, what evil has he done?" But they shouted all the more, "Crucify him!" ¹⁵ So Pilate, wishing to satisfy the crowd, released Barabbas for them; and after flogging Jesus, he handed him over to be crucified.

The Soldiers Mock Jesus

16 Then the soldiers led him into the courtyard of the palace (that is, the governor's headquarters*c*); and they called together the whole cohort. ¹⁷ And they clothed him in a purple cloak; and after twisting some thorns into a crown, they put it on him. ¹⁸ And they began saluting him, "Hail, King of the Jews!" ¹⁹ They struck his head with a reed, spat upon him, and knelt down in homage to him. ²⁰ After mocking him, they stripped him of the purple cloak and put his own clothes on him. Then they led him out to crucify him.

The Crucifixion of Jesus

21 They compelled a passer-by, who was coming in from the country, to carry his cross; it was Simon of Cyrene, the father of Alexander and Rufus. ²² Then they brought Jesus*d* to the place called Golgotha (which means the place of a skull). ²³ And they offered him wine

mixed with myrrh; but he did not take it. ²⁴ And they crucified him, and divided his clothes among them, casting lots to decide what each should take.

25 It was nine o'clock in the morning when they crucified him. ²⁶ The inscription of the charge against him read, "The King of the Jews." ²⁷ And with him they crucified two bandits, one on his right and one on his left.*e* ²⁹ Those who passed by derided*f* him, shaking their heads and saying, "Aha! You who would destroy the temple and build it in three days, ³⁰ save yourself, and come down from the cross!" ³¹ In the same way the chief priests, along with the scribes, were also mocking him among themselves and saying, "He saved others; he cannot save himself. ³² Let the Messiah,*g* the King of Israel, come down from the cross now, so that we may see and believe." Those who were crucified with him also taunted him.

The Death of Jesus

33 When it was noon, darkness came over the whole land*h* until three in the afternoon. ³⁴ At three o'clock Jesus cried out with a loud voice, "Eloi, Eloi, lema sabachthani?" which means, "My God, my God, why have you forsaken me?"*i* ³⁵ When some of the bystanders heard it, they said, "Listen, he is calling for Elijah." ³⁶ And someone ran, filled a sponge with sour wine, put it on a stick, and gave it to him to drink, saying, "Wait, let us see whether Elijah will come to take him down." ³⁷ Then Jesus gave a loud cry and breathed his last. ³⁸ And the curtain

a Other ancient authorities read *what should I do* *b* Other ancient authorities lack *the man you call* *c* Gk *the praetorium* *d* Gk *him* *e* Other ancient authorities add verse 28, *And the scripture was fulfilled that says, "And he was counted among the lawless."* *f* Or *blasphemed* *g* Or *the Christ* *h* Or *earth* *i* Other ancient authorities read *made me a reproach*

15:16–41 The Death of Jesus (Matt. 27:27–56; Luke 23:26–49)

15:18 *King of the Jews*—See note at v. 2.

15:21 *Simon of Cyrene*—Cyrene is located in North Africa. Simon is an outsider from a distant part of the world, probably characterized by outstanding ethnic physical traits. This outsider is driven (see note at 1:12) to take up the cross and

follow Jesus (cf. 8:34). Being an "insider" is not what counts; what counts is how one responds to God's kingdom call.

15:26 *King of the Jews*—See note at v. 2.

15:34—Cf. Ps. 22.

15:38 *The curtain of the temple was torn*—See note at 1:10. The curtain was most likely the one

of the temple was torn in two, from top to bottom. [39] Now when the centurion, who stood facing him, saw that in this way he[a] breathed his last, he said, "Truly this man was God's Son!"[b]

40 There were also women looking on from a distance; among them were Mary Magdalene, and Mary the mother of James the younger and of Joses, and Salome. [41] These used to follow him and provided for him when he was in Galilee; and there were many other women who had come up with him to Jerusalem.

The Burial of Jesus

42 When evening had come, and since it was the day of Preparation, that is, the day before the sabbath, [43] Joseph of Arimathea, a respected member of the council, who was also himself waiting expectantly for the kingdom of God, went boldly to Pilate and asked for the body of Jesus. [44] Then Pilate wondered if he were already dead; and summoning the centurion, he asked him whether he had been dead for some time. [45] When he learned from the centurion that he was dead, he granted the body to Joseph. [46] Then Joseph[c] bought a linen cloth, and taking down the body,[d] wrapped it in the linen cloth, and laid it in a tomb that had been hewn out of the rock. He then rolled a stone against the door of the tomb. [47] Mary Magdalene and Mary the mother of Joses saw where the body[d] was laid.

The Resurrection of Jesus

16 When the sabbath was over, Mary Magdalene, and Mary the mother of James, and Salome bought spices, so that they might go and anoint him. [2] And very early on the first day of the week, when the sun had risen, they went to the tomb. [3] They had been saying to one another, "Who will roll away the stone for us from the entrance to the tomb?" [4] When they looked up, they saw that the stone, which was very large, had already been rolled back. [5] As they entered the tomb, they saw a young man, dressed in a white robe, sitting on the right side; and they were alarmed. [6] But he said to them, "Do not be alarmed; you are looking for Jesus of Nazareth, who was crucified. He has been raised; he is not here. Look, there is the place they laid him. [7] But go, tell his disciples and Peter that he is going ahead of you to Galilee; there you will see him, just as he told you." [8] So they went out and fled from the tomb, for terror and amazement had seized them; and they said nothing to anyone, for they were afraid.[e]

THE SHORTER ENDING OF MARK

[[And all that had been commanded them they told briefly to those around

a Other ancient authorities add *cried out* and b Or *a son of God* c Gk *he*
d Gk *it* e Some of the most ancient authorities bring the book to a close at the end of verse 8. One authority concludes the book with the shorter ending; others include the shorter ending and then continue with verses 9–20. In most authorities verses 9-20 follow immediately after verse 8, though in some of these authorities the passage is marked as being doubtful.

---

that divided the Holy of Holies from the rest of the sanctuary complex (cf. Exod. 26:31–33). The high priest was allowed in the Holy of Holies only on the Day of Atonement, when he sought forgiveness for the people's sins. With Jesus' death, access to God need no longer be through the temple infrastructure, but can, through Jesus' preaching ministry and its consequences, be direct (cf. 2:5).

15:39 *Son of God*—See note at 1:1. It is unclear whether the centurion meant the statement sympathetically or sarcastically.

15:41 *Used to follow him and provided for him*—The language of discipleship. See note at 1:13. The presence of women in Jesus' discipleship corps would have been yet one more controversial, boundary-breaking act.

15:42–47 Jesus' Burial (Matt. 27:57–61; Luke 23:50–56)

16:1–8 The Empty Tomb (Matt. 28:1–10; Luke 24:1–11)

16:7 *Galilee*—See note at 1:9.

16:8 *For they were afraid*—The narrative's striking ending suggests that there is no one left to tell the story. The implication is that if the story is to be told, since all the narrative characters fail to live up to the task, the reader must be the one to tell it.

The Shorter Ending

A brief ending written by a subsequent writer who hoped to give a stronger, more successful ending to the Gospel. Found mainly in a few late manuscripts.

Peter. And afterward Jesus himself sent out through them, from east to west, the sacred and imperishable proclamation of eternal salvation.[a]]]

The Longer Ending of Mark
Jesus Appears to Mary Magdalene

9 [[Now after he rose early on the first day of the week, he appeared first to Mary Magdalene, from whom he had cast out seven demons. 10 She went out and told those who had been with him, while they were mourning and weeping. 11 But when they heard that he was alive and had been seen by her, they would not believe it.

Jesus Appears to Two Disciples

12 After this he appeared in another form to two of them, as they were walking into the country. 13 And they went back and told the rest, but they did not believe them.

Jesus Commissions the Disciples

14 Later he appeared to the eleven themselves as they were sitting at the table; and he upbraided them for their lack of faith and stubbornness, because they had not believed those who saw him after he had risen.[b] 15 And he said

to them, "Go into all the world and proclaim the good news[c] to the whole creation. 16 The one who believes and is baptized will be saved; but the one who does not believe will be condemned. 17 And these signs will accompany those who believe: by using my name they will cast out demons; they will speak in new tongues; 18 they will pick up snakes in their hands,[d] and if they drink any deadly thing, it will not hurt them; they will lay their hands on the sick, and they will recover."

The Ascension of Jesus

19 So then the Lord Jesus, after he had spoken to them, was taken up into heaven and sat down at the right hand of God. 20 And they went out and proclaimed the good news everywhere, while the Lord worked with them and confirmed the message by the signs that accompanied it.[e]]]

a Other ancient authorities add *Amen* *b* Other ancient authorities add, in whole or in part, *And they excused themselves, saying, "This age of lawlessness and unbelief is under Satan, who does not allow the truth and power of God to prevail over the unclean things of the spirits. Therefore reveal your righteousness now"—thus they spoke to Christ. And Christ replied to them, "The term of years of Satan's power has been fulfilled, but other terrible things draw near. And for those who have sinned I was handed over to death, that they may return to the truth and sin no more, that they may inherit the spiritual and imperishable glory of righteousness that is in heaven."* *c* Or *gospel* *d* Other ancient authorities lack *in their hands* *e* Other ancient authorities add *Amen*

16:9–20 The Longer Ending

These verses were also not written by the Mark who penned the final draft of the manuscript up to v. 8. The style, vocabulary, and theology are quite different. The passage is missing in some of the earliest manuscripts, and in others it occurs only after the shorter ending. Most commentators agree that it was added later in an attempt to provide a more successful ending to the Gospel.

The Gospel according to
LUKE

The Gospel of Luke is particularly suited to contemporary readers already familiar with Jesus' story. Luke makes clear that his audience was not new to the teachings of the "Jesus movement." Whether written for a specific patron ("most excellent Theophilus," 1:3) or a more general, predominantly Gentile audience, the Gospel's intended reader had already "been instructed" (1:4) in the basic story of Jesus. Therefore Luke's Gospel is aimed not at gaining new proselytes, but at illumining and strengthening the faith of those already within the believing community. To those seeking better understanding of what it means to follow Jesus and participate in the reign of God that he inaugurated, Luke has much to say about Christian discipleship.

Luke's Gospel is the first installment of his two-volume composition, Luke–Acts. Probably written in the late first century by an anonymous author, The Gospel and the Acts of the Apostles tell the story of Jesus as the fulfillment of a divine plan that first unfolded in relation to the prophets of ancient Israel, reached its eschatological fulfillment in Jesus the Messiah, and continues in the ministry and mission of his followers. Several themes permeate the two volumes: (1) human history as the arena in which God's plan unfolds; (2) the visitation of God for the salvation of Jews and Gentiles that was intended since the covenant with Abraham; (3) the convention-busting reversal of values that characterizes God's reign; (4) the role of the Holy Spirit in God's unfolding plan; and (5) the understanding that Jesus is the eschatological prophet like Moses (Deut. 34:10–12; Acts 2:22–24) who announces and embodies God's visitation among all people. Like Moses (Acts 7:17–37) and all the prophets after him, Jesus is sent twice by God. During the first visitation, God's prophet comes in weakness and is rejected by the people out of ignorance. But the prophet returns a second time in power and offers salvation and liberation to those who will receive it. The Gospel narrates the story of Jesus' first visitation. Acts, with its emphasis on the Holy Spirit that the risen Lord sends to dwell among the people, tells the story of the second.

With this narrative framework established, the third Gospel includes several themes that convey Luke's understanding of discipleship. First, because the world matters, concrete human needs matter. True faith is expressed in word and deed in a kingdom that values the poor, the oppressed, and the outcast. There is no divide between the social and the spiritual in Luke's Gospel, so discipleship is an active, "fruit-bearing" enterprise. Second, because God's reign enacts the reversal of conventional values, disciples seek not only the liberation of the oppressed and relief for the poor, but also liberation for all from society's empty and false values. Luke's Gospel repeatedly condemns materialism, the accumulation of wealth and the unjust exercise of power. Finally, correction of human values is both a means and a sign of the salvation that has come to the lost. Thus repentance, limitless forgiveness, and abiding humility are hallmarks of the kingdom and characteristic of the community of disciples. Proclaiming the salvation that has come to a world that is lost and ignorant but nonetheless loved, the Gospel leaves little room for self-righteousness.

—Mary F. Foskett

Dedication to Theophilus

1 Since many have undertaken to set down an orderly account of the events that have been fulfilled among us, ² just as they were handed on to us by those who from the beginning were eyewitnesses and servants of the word, ³ I too decided, after investigating everything carefully from the very first,ᵃ to write an orderly account for you, most excellent Theophilus, ⁴ so that you may know the truth concerning the things about which you have been instructed.

The Birth of John the Baptist Foretold

5 In the days of King Herod of Judea, there was a priest named Zechariah, who belonged to the priestly order of Abijah. His wife was a descendant of Aaron, and her name was Elizabeth. ⁶ Both of them were righteous before God, living blamelessly according to all the commandments and regulations of the Lord. ⁷ But they had no children, because Elizabeth was barren, and both were getting on in years.

8 Once when he was serving as priest before God and his section was on duty, ⁹ he was chosen by lot, according to the custom of the priesthood, to enter the sanctuary of the Lord and offer incense. ¹⁰ Now at the time of the incense offering, the whole assembly of the people was praying outside. ¹¹ Then there appeared to him an angel of the Lord, standing at the right side of the altar of incense. ¹² When Zechariah saw him, he was terrified; and fear overwhelmed him. ¹³ But the angel said to him, "Do not be afraid, Zechariah, for your prayer has been heard. Your wife Elizabeth will bear you a son, and you will name him John. ¹⁴ You will have joy and gladness, and many will rejoice at his birth, ¹⁵ for he will be great in the sight of the Lord. He must never drink wine or strong drink; even before his birth he will be filled with the Holy Spirit. ¹⁶ He will turn many of the people of Israel to the Lord their God. ¹⁷ With the spirit and power

ᵃ Or for a long time

1:1–4 Prologue

Written like the prologues to Greek and Roman histories, Luke's opening emphasizes that the sequence and content of his Gospel convey precisely what he considers necessary for giving his readers greater assurance about the good news (v. 4).

1:3 An orderly account—Here Luke implies that his is a more effective rendering of the Gospel in terms of both narrative sequence and theology. He reminds us that storytelling is at the heart of the Christian witness and that even in its earliest decades, multiple stories of Jesus circulated among Christian communities (vv. 1–2). The gospel has never been univocal. This accords with the scholarly consensus that Luke probably drew on Mark's Gospel and other sources when he composed his Gospel. **Theophilus**—Theophilus may be the name of a patron or a general reference to Luke's reader as a "lover of God."

1:4 The truth—Luke suggests that his readers are in need of greater certainty or assurance concerning the gospel they already know. One of his chief aims is to emphasize various themes that are distinctive to his Gospel: according to the plan of God, Gentiles and Jews alike have a place in the kingdom of God; because the world matters, concrete human needs matter; disciple-

ship is an active "fruit-bearing" enterprise that not only seeks the liberation of the oppressed and relief for the poor, but counters conventional values such as the accumulation of wealth and the unjust use of power.

1:5–2:52 The Birth and Childhood of Jesus

These chapters set the stage for the remainder of the Gospel. In language, style, and content, they show that the story of Jesus is rooted in the story of Israel. To follow Jesus is to participate in the plan of God that began unfolding with the establishment of the covenant with Abraham (Gen. 12:1–3; cf. Acts 7:2–3).

1:5–25 The Announcement of John's Birth

1:7 No children—Zechariah and Elizabeth, both of priestly families (v. 5), are paragons of righteousness (v. 6). Yet all is not well with the aged couple, whose infertility is reminiscent of Abraham and Sarah and Elkanah and Hannah. Far from serving as a guarantee of a life free from hardship, righteousness is sometimes that which is demonstrated in the face of difficulty and even disgrace (cf. v. 25).

1:17 A people prepared—By turning the people to God (v. 16) and one another, John will ready the people for the way of peace (cf. v. 79) and the ruling of God, which is characterized by

of Elijah he will go before him, to turn the hearts of parents to their children, and the disobedient to the wisdom of the righteous, to make ready a people prepared for the Lord." **18** Zechariah said to the angel, "How will I know that this is so? For I am an old man, and my wife is getting on in years." **19** The angel replied, "I am Gabriel. I stand in the presence of God, and I have been sent to speak to you and to bring you this good news. **20** But now, because you did not believe my words, which will be fulfilled in their time, you will become mute, unable to speak, until the day these things occur."

21 Meanwhile the people were waiting for Zechariah, and wondered at his delay in the sanctuary. **22** When he did come out, he could not speak to them, and they realized that he had seen a vision in the sanctuary. He kept motioning to them and remained unable to speak. **23** When his time of service was ended, he went to his home.

24 After those days his wife Elizabeth conceived, and for five months she remained in seclusion. She said, **25** "This is what the Lord has done for me when he looked favorably on me and took away the disgrace I have endured among my people."

The Birth of Jesus Foretold

26 In the sixth month the angel Gabriel was sent by God to a town in Galilee called Nazareth, **27** to a virgin engaged to a man whose name was Joseph, of the house of David. The virgin's name was Mary. **28** And he came to her and said, "Greetings, favored one! The Lord is with you."*a* **29** But she was much perplexed by his words and pondered what sort of greeting this might be. **30** The angel said to her, "Do not be afraid, Mary, for you have found favor with God. **31** And now, you will conceive in your womb and bear a son, and you will name him Jesus. **32** He will be great, and will be called the Son of the Most High, and the Lord God will give to him the throne of his ancestor David. **33** He will reign over the house of Jacob forever, and of his kingdom there will be no end." **34** Mary said to the angel, "How can this be, since I am a virgin?"*b* **35** The

a Other ancient authorities add *Blessed are you among women* *b* Gk *I do not know a man*

---

social justice, compassion, forgiveness, and reconciliation.

1:19 *Gabriel*—The angel who visited Daniel (Dan. 9:20–27) appears here and in Luke 1:36, signaling God's activity in "the latter days." *Good news*—God's visitation among the people.

1:25 *Disgrace*—Elizabeth models the endurance of faith.

1:26–38 The Announcement of Jesus' Birth and the Commissioning of Mary

1:26 *Sixth month*—Here Luke draws a parallel between Elizabeth's and Mary's stories to emphasize the faith of both women. From the very beginning of this Gospel, women occupy central roles as witnesses and disciples. *Nazareth*—Nazareth, an obscure town in Galilee, stands in stark contrast to Jerusalem.

1:27 *A virgin engaged*—Luke's description implies that the couple are betrothed but not yet wed. *Mary*—The mother of Jesus, in Greek Mariam, bears the name of Miriam, the sister of Moses and the first woman prophet in Israel. The long-standing tradition of women bearing prophetic witness to the activity of the living God is one that Luke underscores for his audience and readers today.

1:28 *Greetings, favored one! The Lord is with you*—In contrast to Zechariah and Elizabeth, who are righteous and of priestly lineage, the cause for the divine favor that Mary receives is not evident. Luke says nothing of Mary's lineage, kin, social standing, or piety to distinguish her.

1:34 *How can this be . . . ?*—In contrast to the angel's response to Zechariah, whose doubt met only rebuke, the angel here tolerates and answers Mary's question. Unlike the priest, the circumstance of the young virgin has no biblical precedent.

1:35 *Holy Spirit*—In terms recalling the cloud of divine presence in Exod. 40:35, Mary will be overshadowed by the power and Spirit of God. Divine power will figure in Mary's extraordinary pregnancy and sustain her in difficult circumstances. Although Luke does not highlight the social implications of Mary's pregnancy (cf. Matt. 1:18–19), the public disgrace that the infertile Elizabeth endured prefigures that which the pregnant virgin is likely to face.

angel said to her, "The Holy Spirit will come upon you, and the power of the Most High will overshadow you; therefore the child to be born[a] will be holy; he will be called Son of God. 36 And now, your relative Elizabeth in her old age has also conceived a son; and this is the sixth month for her who was said to be barren. 37 For nothing will be impossible with God." 38 Then Mary said, "Here am I, the servant of the Lord; let it be with me according to your word." Then the angel departed from her.

Mary Visits Elizabeth

39 In those days Mary set out and went with haste to a Judean town in the hill country, 40 where she entered the house of Zechariah and greeted Elizabeth. 41 When Elizabeth heard Mary's greeting, the child leaped in her womb. And Elizabeth was filled with the Holy Spirit 42 and exclaimed with a loud cry, "Blessed are you among women, and blessed is the fruit of your womb. 43 And why has this happened to me, that the mother of my Lord comes to me? 44 For as soon as I heard the sound of your greeting, the child in my womb leaped for joy. 45 And blessed is she who believed that there would be[b] a fulfillment of what was spoken to her by the Lord."

Mary's Song of Praise

46 And Mary[c] said,
"My soul magnifies the Lord,
47   and my spirit rejoices in God my Savior,
48 for he has looked with favor on the lowliness of his servant.
Surely, from now on all generations will call me blessed;
49 for the Mighty One has done great things for me,
and holy is his name.
50 His mercy is for those who fear him from generation to generation.
51 He has shown strength with his arm; he has scattered the proud in the thoughts of their hearts.
52 He has brought down the powerful from their thrones, and lifted up the lowly;
53 he has filled the hungry with good things, and sent the rich away empty.
54 He has helped his servant Israel,

---

a Other ancient authorities add *of you*   b Or *believed, for there will be*   c Other ancient authorities read *Elizabeth*

1:36 *Sixth month*—Elizabeth's own surprising pregnancy and her liberation from public humiliation validate the angel's word. Thus Gabriel assures Mary that *nothing will be impossible with God* (v. 37). The convention-busting divine word is sure: a virgin will indeed conceive, and the reversal of social values and realities she celebrates in vv. 46–55 is certain.

1:38 *Here am I*—Mary's unsolicited consent to the divine word establishes her as a model disciple who discerns God's activity even in the midst of circumstances that place her precariously far outside of social convention.

1:39–45, 56 Mary and Elizabeth

1:45 *Blessed*—Elizabeth, *filled with the Holy Spirit* (v. 41), speaks prophetically to confirm that Mary is blessed because she has believed the divine word.

1:46–55 Mary's Song

It is impossible to overestimate the significance of Mary's hymn, the Magnificat. The only extended speech in all of Luke–Acts attributed to a female character, it casts Mary as a prophet. In the tradition of Hannah and her namesake, Miriam, Mary in song celebrates God's unfolding salvation of her people, Israel, and God's compassion for the lowly, represented here by the ordinary but exemplary Mary (v. 48). In so doing, Mary both embodies and introduces one of the Gospel's key themes, the reversal of the social order that exemplifies the ruling of God. She praises the God who *has brought down the powerful . . . and lifted up the lowly; . . . filled the hungry . . . and sent the rich away empty* (vv. 52–53). The vision of social justice that Mary prophesies here reappears at the center of Jesus' mission (cf. 4:18–19; 6:20–25), in Jesus' parables (cf. 16:19–31), and in Jesus' teaching on discipleship (cf. 18:18–27), where he reminds his hearers, "What is impossible for mortals is possible for God" (18:27). For Luke, discipleship is a life that embraces the gospel's call to justice and counters the widening gap between the rich and the poor, the powerful and the powerless.

in remembrance of his mercy,
55 according to the promise he made to
    our ancestors,
    to Abraham and to his
        descendants forever."

56 And Mary remained with her about three months and then returned to her home.

The Birth of John the Baptist

57 Now the time came for Elizabeth to give birth, and she bore a son. 58 Her neighbors and relatives heard that the Lord had shown his great mercy to her, and they rejoiced with her.

59 On the eighth day they came to circumcise the child, and they were going to name him Zechariah after his father. 60 But his mother said, "No; he is to be called John." 61 They said to her, "None of your relatives has this name." 62 Then they began motioning to his father to find out what name he wanted to give him. 63 He asked for a writing tablet and wrote, "His name is John." And all of them were amazed. 64 Immediately his mouth was opened and his tongue freed, and he began to speak, praising God. 65 Fear came over all their neighbors, and all these things were talked about throughout the entire hill country of Judea. 66 All who heard them pondered them and said, "What then will this child become?" For, indeed, the hand of the Lord was with him.

Zechariah's Prophecy

67 Then his father Zechariah was filled with the Holy Spirit and spoke this prophecy:

68 "Blessed be the Lord God of Israel,
    for he has looked favorably on his
        people and redeemed them.
69 He has raised up a mighty savior[a]
    for us
    in the house of his servant David,
70 as he spoke through the mouth of
        his holy prophets from of old,
71   that we would be saved from our
        enemies and from the hand of
        all who hate us.
72 Thus he has shown the mercy
        promised to our ancestors,
    and has remembered his holy
        covenant,
73 the oath that he swore to our
        ancestor Abraham,
    to grant us 74 that we, being
        rescued from the hands of our
        enemies,
    might serve him without fear, 75 in
        holiness and righteousness
    before him all our days.
76 And you, child, will be called the
        prophet of the Most High;
    for you will go before the Lord to
        prepare his ways,
77 to give knowledge of salvation to his
        people
    by the forgiveness of their sins.
78 By the tender mercy of our God,
    the dawn from on high will break
        upon[b] us,
79 to give light to those who sit in
        darkness and in the shadow of
        death,
    to guide our feet into the way of
        peace."

[a] Gk *a horn of salvation*   [b] Other ancient authorities read *has broken upon*

1:57–80 The Birth and Presentation of John

1:67—Again able to speak, Zechariah follows Mary's example and praises God. His song is vv. 68–79.

1:76 *Prophet*—John, the spokesperson for *the Most High*, goes before Jesus, the "Son of the Most High" (v. 32).

1:77 *Forgiveness*—Forgiveness is a means and sign of *salvation*. Throughout the Gospel, Luke teaches that disciples both experience forgiveness and extend it to others (cf. 4:19; 11:4).

1:78 *Tender mercy*—Salvation and forgiveness are owing to God's unlimited love and compassion. Discipleship is modeled after the pattern of divine compassion.

1:79 *Way of peace*—A concept that is social (v. 71) and spiritual (v. 77), the way of peace is here synonymous with the unobstructed ruling, or kingdom, of God. Kingdom discipleship is a comprehensive way of being that expresses justice, reconciliation, and peace.

80 The child grew and became strong in spirit, and he was in the wilderness until the day he appeared publicly to Israel.

The Birth of Jesus

2 In those days a decree went out from Emperor Augustus that all the world should be registered. ² This was the first registration and was taken while Quirinius was governor of Syria. ³ All went to their own towns to be registered. ⁴ Joseph also went from the town of Nazareth in Galilee to Judea, to the city of David called Bethlehem, because he was descended from the house and family of David. ⁵ He went to be registered with Mary, to whom he was engaged and who was expecting a child. ⁶ While they were there, the time came for her to deliver her child. ⁷ And she gave birth to her firstborn son and wrapped him in bands of cloth, and laid him in a manger, because there was no place for them in the inn.

The Shepherds and the Angels

8 In that region there were shepherds living in the fields, keeping watch over their flock by night. ⁹ Then an angel of the Lord stood before them, and the glory of the Lord shone around them, and they were terrified. ¹⁰ But the angel said to them, "Do not be afraid; for see—I am bringing you good news of great joy for all the people: ¹¹ to you is born this day in the city of David a Savior, who is the Messiah,ᵃ the Lord. ¹² This will be a sign for you: you will find a child wrapped in bands of cloth and lying in a manger." ¹³ And suddenly there was with the angel a multitude of the heavenly host,ᵇ praising God and saying,

¹⁴ "Glory to God in the highest heaven,
   and on earth peace among those
     whom he favors!"ᶜ

15 When the angels had left them and gone into heaven, the shepherds said to one another, "Let us go now to Bethlehem and see this thing that has taken place, which the Lord has made known to us." ¹⁶ So they went with haste and found Mary and Joseph, and the child lying in the manger. ¹⁷ When they saw this, they made known what had been told them about this child; ¹⁸ and all who heard it were amazed at what the shepherds told them. ¹⁹ But Mary treasured all these words and pondered them in her heart. ²⁰ The shepherds returned, glorifying and praising God for all they had heard and seen, as it had been told them.

Jesus Is Named

21 After eight days had passed, it was time to circumcise the child; and he was called Jesus, the name given by the angel before he was conceived in the womb.

Jesus Is Presented in the Temple

22 When the time came for their purification according to the law of Moses, they brought him up to Jerusalem to present him to the Lord ²³ (as it is written in the law of the Lord, "Every firstborn male shall be designated as holy to the Lord"), ²⁴ and they offered a sacrifice according to what is stated in the law of the Lord, "a pair of turtledoves or two young pigeons."

25 Now there was a man in Jerusalem whose name was Simeon;ᵈ this man

ᵃ Or the Christ ᵇ Gk army ᶜ Other ancient authorities read peace, goodwill among people ᵈ Gk Symeon

---

2:1–20 The Birth of Jesus

2:7 *No place*—Mary's son is born in humble surroundings, circumstances befitting a messiah who will proclaim God's favor for the world's majority of the poor.

2:17 *Made known what had been told them*— Having traveled to Bethlehem to see what had been *made known* to them (v. 15), the shepherds testify to what they have seen and heard. Public

testimony, in word and action, is characteristic of discipleship in Luke.

2:19 *Pondered*—The term (*symballo*, or "throwing together") is ambiguous. Having heard the shepherds' testimony, Mary carefully considers, but does not necessarily understand, what she is witnessing (cf. vv. 49–51).

2:21–40 The Circumcision and Presentation of Jesus

was righteous and devout, looking forward to the consolation of Israel, and the Holy Spirit rested on him. [26] It had been revealed to him by the Holy Spirit that he would not see death before he had seen the Lord's Messiah.[a] [27] Guided by the Spirit, Simeon[b] came into the temple; and when the parents brought in the child Jesus, to do for him what was customary under the law, [28] Simeon[c] took him in his arms and praised God, saying,

[29] "Master, now you are dismissing
           your servant[d] in peace,
           according to your word;
[30]   for my eyes have seen your salvation,
[31]   which you have prepared in the
           presence of all peoples,
[32]   a light for revelation to the Gentiles
           and for glory to your people
           Israel."

33 And the child's father and mother were amazed at what was being said about him. [34] Then Simeon[e] blessed them and said to his mother Mary, "This child is destined for the falling and the rising of many in Israel, and to be a sign that will be opposed [35] so that the inner thoughts of many will be revealed—and a sword will pierce your own soul too."

36 There was also a prophet, Anna[f] the daughter of Phanuel, of the tribe of Asher. She was of a great age, having lived with her husband seven years after her marriage, [37] then as a widow to the age of eighty-four. She never left the temple but worshiped there with fasting and prayer night and day. [38] At that moment she came, and began to praise God and to speak about the child[g] to all

who were looking for the redemption of Jerusalem.

The Return to Nazareth

39 When they had finished everything required by the law of the Lord, they returned to Galilee, to their own town of Nazareth. [40] The child grew and became strong, filled with wisdom; and the favor of God was upon him.

The Boy Jesus in the Temple

41 Now every year his parents went to Jerusalem for the festival of the Passover. [42] And when he was twelve years old, they went up as usual for the festival. [43] When the festival was ended and they started to return, the boy Jesus stayed behind in Jerusalem, but his parents did not know it. [44] Assuming that he was in the group of travelers, they went a day's journey. Then they started to look for him among their relatives and friends. [45] When they did not find him, they returned to Jerusalem to search for him. [46] After three days they found him in the temple, sitting among the teachers, listening to them and asking them questions. [47] And all who heard him were amazed at his understanding and his answers. [48] When his parents[h] saw him they were astonished; and his mother said to him, "Child, why have you treated us like this? Look, your father and I have been searching for you in great anxiety." [49] He said to them, "Why were you searching for me? Did you not know that I must be in my Father's house?"[i] [50] But they did

[a] Or the Lord's Christ [b] Gk In the Spirit, he [c] Gk he [d] Gk slave [e] Gk Symeon [f] Gk Hanna [g] Gk him [h] Gk they [i] Or be about my Father's interests?

2:32 *Glory*—In Jesus, God's active presence and power is made known to all peoples (v. 31). As in 3:4–6, Luke draws on the language and spirit of Isa. 40:3–5 (LXX) to indicate that Jesus the Savior (Luke 2:11) brings salvation to Jews and Gentiles alike.

2:34 *Falling and rising*—Simeon's prophecy recalls the theme of reversal that Mary underscored in 1:52–53. As *a sign that will be opposed*, Jesus' ministry will be cause for division and social change. Within such a framework, discipleship is far from an abstract ideal. Following this Jesus

calls for commitment, potential sacrifice, and openness to change.

2:35 *Inner thoughts*—The purposes and hidden thoughts of the people are revealed by their responses to Jesus' visitation. *Pierce*—In another ambiguous expression, Luke underscores the personal cost to Mary of Jesus' mission. Discipleship is not exclusive of hardship.

2:41–52 The Boy Jesus

2:49 *Did you not know . . . ?*—Even Jesus' par-

not understand what he said to them. ⁵¹ Then he went down with them and came to Nazareth, and was obedient to them. His mother treasured all these things in her heart.

52 And Jesus increased in wisdom and in years,*a* and in divine and human favor.

The Proclamation of John the Baptist

3 In the fifteenth year of the reign of Emperor Tiberius, when Pontius Pilate was governor of Judea, and Herod was ruler*b* of Galilee, and his brother Philip ruler*b* of the region of Ituraea and Trachonitis, and Lysanias ruler*b* of Abilene, ²during the high priesthood of Annas and Caiaphas, the word of God came to John son of Zechariah in the wilderness. ³He went into all the region around the Jordan, proclaiming a baptism of repentance for the forgiveness of sins, ⁴as it is written in the book of the words of the prophet Isaiah,

"The voice of one crying out in the wilderness:
'Prepare the way of the Lord,
make his paths straight.
⁵ Every valley shall be filled,
and every mountain and hill shall be made low,

and the crooked shall be made straight,
and the rough ways made smooth;
⁶ and all flesh shall see the salvation of God.'"

7 John said to the crowds that came out to be baptized by him, "You brood of vipers! Who warned you to flee from the wrath to come? ⁸Bear fruits worthy of repentance. Do not begin to say to yourselves, 'We have Abraham as our ancestor'; for I tell you, God is able from these stones to raise up children to Abraham. ⁹Even now the ax is lying at the root of the trees; every tree therefore that does not bear good fruit is cut down and thrown into the fire."

10 And the crowds asked him, "What then should we do?" ¹¹In reply he said to them, "Whoever has two coats must share with anyone who has none; and whoever has food must do likewise." ¹²Even tax collectors came to be baptized, and they asked him, "Teacher, what should we do?" ¹³He said to them, "Collect no more than the amount prescribed for you." ¹⁴Soldiers also asked him, "And we, what should we do?"

a Or *in stature*　*b* Gk *tetrarch*

---

ents cannot fully comprehend the events they are witnessing. Thus Luke shows that even the most faithful must grow in understanding and faith (cf. v. 17).

3:1–9:50 The Inauguration of the Kingdom of God

3:1–20 John the Baptizer

3:2 Word of God—As one who announces the divine word, John is God's prophet. As his prophetic career unfolds in the midst of a politically, socially, and religiously complex world, Luke reminds his readers that the gospel and its implications are never divorced from the concrete realities facing every generation of disciples (vv. 1–2).

3:3 Baptism . . . forgiveness—John's activity recalls 1:77. The forgiveness of sins exhibits the ruling, or way, of God.

3:8 Worthy of repentance—John challenges his hearers to remember that discipleship is demonstrated through deeds that evidence true repentance. Faith is action, not mere assent. Bearing

good fruit (v. 9) is an imperative of authentic faith.

3:10 What then should we do?—The question reiterates Luke's conviction that repentance and faith are real only when they are translated into action. The question, repeated throughout Luke–Acts, is a direct challenge to all of Luke's readers (cf. 10:25; 18:18; Acts 2:37).

3:11 Two coats—John introduces the importance of sharing possessions as another imperative of faith. Far from being a personal and private endeavor, faith is interpersonal, social, and public.

3:12–13 Tax collectors . . . soldiers—Tax collectors and soldiers were held in suspicion as Roman pawns, thieves, extortionists, and informants (vv. 13–14). Here Luke illustrates how repentance and forgiveness are possible for all persons, even those aligned with the powerful and oppressive. Repentance must be lived out on a daily basis, in concrete ways and in relation to every aspect of life, including one's work. Thus John responds with specific directives to tax collectors (v. 13) and soldiers (v. 14).

He said to them, "Do not extort money from anyone by threats or false accusation, and be satisfied with your wages."

15 As the people were filled with expectation, and all were questioning in their hearts concerning John, whether he might be the Messiah,*a* 16 John answered all of them by saying, "I baptize you with water; but one who is more powerful than I is coming; I am not worthy to untie the thong of his sandals. He will baptize you with*b* the Holy Spirit and fire. 17 His winnowing fork is in his hand, to clear his threshing floor and to gather the wheat into his granary; but the chaff he will burn with unquenchable fire."

18 So, with many other exhortations, he proclaimed the good news to the people. 19 But Herod the ruler,*c* who had been rebuked by him because of Herodias, his brother's wife, and because of all the evil things that Herod had done, 20 added to them all by shutting up John in prison.

The Baptism of Jesus

21 Now when all the people were baptized, and when Jesus also had been baptized and was praying, the heaven was opened, 22 and the Holy Spirit descended upon him in bodily form like a dove. And a voice came from heaven, "You are my Son, the Beloved;*d* with you I am well pleased."*e*

The Ancestors of Jesus

23 Jesus was about thirty years old when he began his work. He was the son (as was thought) of Joseph son of Heli, 24 son of Matthat, son of Levi, son of Melchi, son of Jannai, son of Joseph, 25 son of Mattathias, son of Amos, son of Nahum, son of Esli, son of Naggai, 26 son of Maath, son of Mattathias, son of Semein, son of Josech, son of Joda, 27 son of Joanan, son of Rhesa, son of Zerubbabel, son of Shealtiel,*f* son of Neri, 28 son of Melchi, son of Addi, son of Cosam, son of Elmadam, son of Er, 29 son of Joshua, son of Eliezer, son of Jorim, son of Matthat, son of Levi, 30 son of Simeon, son of Judah, son of Joseph, son of Jonam, son of Eliakim, 31 son of Melea, son of Menna, son of Mattatha, son of Nathan, son of David, 32 son of Jesse, son of Obed, son of Boaz, son of Sala,*g* son of Nahshon, 33 son of Amminadab, son of Admin, son of Arni,*h* son of Hezron, son of Perez, son of Judah, 34 son of Jacob, son of Isaac, son of Abraham, son of Terah, son of Nahor, 35 son of Serug, son of Reu, son of Peleg, son of Eber, son of Shelah, 36 son of Cainan, son of Arphaxad, son of Shem, son of Noah, son of Lamech, 37 son of Methuselah, son of Enoch, son of Jared, son of Mahalaleel, son of Cainan, 38 son of Enos, son of Seth, son of Adam, son of God.

The Temptation of Jesus

4 Jesus, full of the Holy Spirit, returned from the Jordan and was led by the

a Or the Christ   *b* Or in   *c* Gk tetrarch   *d* Or my beloved Son   *e* Other ancient authorities read You are my Son, today I have begotten you   *f* Gk Salathiel   *g* Other ancient authorities read Salmon   *h* Other ancient authorities read Amminadab, son of Aram; others vary widely

---

3:18 *Good news*—Cf. 1:19; 2:10.

3:21–4:13 Jesus the Son

3:22 *You are my Son*—Citing Ps. 2:7, the Holy Spirit anoints Jesus Messiah (cf. 1:32, 35).

3:38 *Son of Adam, son of God*—Tracing Jesus' lineage all the way to Adam, son of God, Luke portrays Jesus as a messiah who is related, by implication, to all humanity (cf. 2:32; 3:6) and to the God who created humankind.

4:1–13—Following Jesus' baptism and the divine confirmation of his identity as the Son of God, the devil challenges Jesus to prove himself through demonstrations of power and privilege

(vv. 3, 9). He not only tests Jesus (v. 12); he distorts the meaning of Jesus' identity as Son. By drawing on Deut. 8:3; 6:13; and 6:16 to refute the devil, Jesus fulfills the Mosaic ideal illustrated in Deut. 6:4–9. He thus demonstrates that he is the Son of God and clarifies what sonship really is. As ones yearning to be counted as "children of the Most High" (Luke 6:35), disciples are called to follow Jesus' example.

4:1 *Holy Spirit*—The same Spirit who anointed Jesus at his baptism empowers and leads him forth (cf. vv. 14, 18). Beginning with the sending of the Spirit at Pentecost (Acts 2:4), the Holy Spirit empowers the entire community of faith in

Spirit in the wilderness, ² where for forty days he was tempted by the devil. He ate nothing at all during those days, and when they were over, he was famished. ³ The devil said to him, "If you are the Son of God, command this stone to become a loaf of bread." ⁴ Jesus answered him, "It is written, 'One does not live by bread alone.'"

5 Then the devil*a* led him up and showed him in an instant all the kingdoms of the world. ⁶ And the devil*a* said to him, "To you I will give their glory and all this authority; for it has been given over to me, and I give it to anyone I please. ⁷ If you, then, will worship me, it will all be yours." ⁸ Jesus answered him, "It is written,

'Worship the Lord your God,
    and serve only him.'"

9 Then the devil*a* took him to Jerusalem, and placed him on the pinnacle of the temple, saying to him, "If you are the Son of God, throw yourself down from here, ¹⁰ for it is written,

'He will command his angels
        concerning you,
    to protect you,'

¹¹ and

'On their hands they will bear
        you up,
    so that you will not dash your foot
        against a stone.'"

¹² Jesus answered him, "It is said, 'Do not put the Lord your God to the test.'" ¹³ When the devil had finished every test, he departed from him until an opportune time.

The Beginning of the Galilean Ministry

14 Then Jesus, filled with the power of the Spirit, returned to Galilee, and a report about him spread through all the surrounding country. ¹⁵ He began to teach in their synagogues and was praised by everyone.

The Rejection of Jesus at Nazareth

16 When he came to Nazareth, where he had been brought up, he went to the synagogue on the sabbath day, as was his custom. He stood up to read, ¹⁷ and the scroll of the prophet Isaiah was given to him. He unrolled the scroll and found the place where it was written:

¹⁸ "The Spirit of the Lord is upon me,
    because he has anointed me
        to bring good news to the poor.
He has sent me to proclaim release
        to the captives
    and recovery of sight to the blind,
        to let the oppressed go free,
¹⁹   to proclaim the year of the Lord's
        favor."

²⁰ And he rolled up the scroll, gave it back to the attendant, and sat down. The eyes of all in the synagogue were fixed

a Gk *he*

Acts to speak boldly and to act upon the good news of the ruling of God and the visitation of God's prophet and Messiah, Jesus. It is by the power of the Spirit that the way of God, outlined in the teachings of Jesus and the prophetic speech of Mary (Luke 1:46–55), John (3:11–14), and others, will be realized.

4:13 *Until an opportune time*—The devil departs for the time being, only to return in 22:3, where Luke writes that "Satan entered into Judas." Readers are reminded of the persistent temptation to distort one's understanding of Jesus and discipleship to serve conventional norms and values, that is, kingdoms other than the ruling of God.

4:14–30 Jesus' Inaugural Sermon

4:18 *Spirit of the Lord*—Citing Isa. 61:1; 58:6; and 61:2, Jesus announces that he is empowered by the Spirit of God. In this way, Jesus' ministry

functions as a model for that of the believing community in Acts and beyond. *Good news to the poor*—The anointed Messiah inaugurates the ruling of God. At the heart of Jesus' mission is the proclamation of restoration, liberation, and forgiveness of debt (cf. 11:4). Jesus' inaugural sermon, consistent with Mary's song (1:52–53), expresses the divine interest in transforming the situation of the poor, the oppressed, and the outcast. Following this Messiah entails participation in this very concrete vision of social renewal.

4:19 *Year of the Lord's favor*—Jesus may have in mind the jubilee year (Lev. 25:8–12), that is, the "year of release" that occurred every fifty years to prevent the exploitation of the poor by legislating the return of family property to its original owners, the forgiveness of debts, and the release of indentured servants.

on him. ²¹ Then he began to say to them, "Today this scripture has been fulfilled in your hearing." ²² All spoke well of him and were amazed at the gracious words that came from his mouth. They said, "Is not this Joseph's son?" ²³ He said to them, "Doubtless you will quote to me this proverb, 'Doctor, cure yourself!' And you will say, 'Do here also in your hometown the things that we have heard you did at Capernaum.'" ²⁴ And he said, "Truly I tell you, no prophet is accepted in the prophet's hometown. ²⁵ But the truth is, there were many widows in Israel in the time of Elijah, when the heaven was shut up three years and six months, and there was a severe famine over all the land; ²⁶ yet Elijah was sent to none of them except to a widow at Zarephath in Sidon. ²⁷ There were also many lepers*a* in Israel in the time of the prophet Elisha, and none of them was cleansed except Naaman the Syrian." ²⁸ When they heard this, all in the synagogue were filled with rage. ²⁹ They got up, drove him out of the town, and led him to the brow of the hill on which their town was built, so that they might hurl him off the cliff. ³⁰ But he passed through the midst of them and went on his way.

The Man with an Unclean Spirit

³¹ He went down to Capernaum, a city in Galilee, and was teaching them on the sabbath. ³² They were astounded at his teaching, because he spoke with authority. ³³ In the synagogue there was a man who had the spirit of an unclean demon, and he cried out with a loud voice, ³⁴ "Let us alone! What have you to do with us, Jesus of Nazareth? Have you come to destroy us? I know who you are, the Holy One of God." ³⁵ But Jesus rebuked him, saying, "Be silent, and come out of him!" When the demon had thrown him down before them, he came out of him without having done him any harm. ³⁶ They were all amazed and kept saying to one another, "What kind of utterance is this? For with authority and power he commands the unclean spirits, and out they come!" ³⁷ And a report about him began to reach every place in the region.

Healings at Simon's House

³⁸ After leaving the synagogue he entered Simon's house. Now Simon's mother-in-law was suffering from a high fever, and they asked him about her. ³⁹ Then he stood over her and rebuked the fever, and it left her. Immediately she got up and began to serve them.

⁴⁰ As the sun was setting, all those who had any who were sick with various kinds of diseases brought them to him; and he laid his hands on each of them and cured them. ⁴¹ Demons also came out of many, shouting, "You are the Son of God!" But he rebuked them and would not allow them to speak, because they knew that he was the Messiah.*b*

Jesus Preaches in the Synagogues

⁴² At daybreak he departed and went into a deserted place. And the crowds were looking for him; and when they reached him, they wanted to prevent him from leaving them. ⁴³ But he said to them, "I must proclaim the good news of the kingdom of God to the other cities also; for I was sent for this purpose." ⁴⁴ So he continued proclaiming the message in the synagogues of Judea.*c*

Jesus Calls the First Disciples

5 Once while Jesus*d* was standing beside the lake of Gennesaret, and

---

a The terms *leper* and *leprosy* can refer to several diseases   *b* Or the *Christ*   *c* Other ancient authorities read *Galilee*   *d* Gk *he*

4:31–44 Proclaiming the Good News of the Kingdom

4:42 *Deserted place*—Jesus regularly withdraws from the crowds, balancing his very public time among the people with time alone, which is often time to pray (cf. 5:16; 9:28; 11:1). The effect underscores the necessity of making time for contemplative as well as active expressions of faith.

5:1–11 Calling Simon

the crowd was pressing in on him to hear the word of God, ² he saw two boats there at the shore of the lake; the fishermen had gone out of them and were washing their nets. ³ He got into one of the boats, the one belonging to Simon, and asked him to put out a little way from the shore. Then he sat down and taught the crowds from the boat. ⁴ When he had finished speaking, he said to Simon, "Put out into the deep water and let down your nets for a catch." ⁵ Simon answered, "Master, we have worked all night long but have caught nothing. Yet if you say so, I will let down the nets." ⁶ When they had done this, they caught so many fish that their nets were beginning to break. ⁷ So they signaled their partners in the other boat to come and help them. And they came and filled both boats, so that they began to sink. ⁸ But when Simon Peter saw it, he fell down at Jesus' knees, saying, "Go away from me, Lord, for I am a sinful man!" ⁹ For he and all who were with him were amazed at the catch of fish that they had taken; ¹⁰ and so also were James and John, sons of Zebedee, who were partners with Simon. Then Jesus said to Simon, "Do not be afraid; from now on you will be catching people." ¹¹ When they had brought their boats to shore, they left everything and followed him.

Jesus Cleanses a Leper

12 Once, when he was in one of the cities, there was a man covered with leprosy.ᵃ When he saw Jesus, he bowed with his face to the ground and begged him, "Lord, if you choose, you can make me clean." ¹³ Then Jesusᵇ stretched out his hand, touched him, and said, "I do choose. Be made clean." Immediately the leprosyᵃ left him. ¹⁴ And he ordered him to tell no one. "Go," he said, "and show yourself to the priest, and, as Moses commanded, make an offering for your cleansing, for a testimony to them." ¹⁵ But now more than ever the word about Jesusᶜ spread abroad; many crowds would gather to hear him and to be cured of their diseases. ¹⁶ But he would withdraw to deserted places and pray.

Jesus Heals a Paralytic

17 One day, while he was teaching, Pharisees and teachers of the law were sitting near by (they had come from every village of Galilee and Judea and from Jerusalem); and the power of the Lord was with him to heal.ᵈ ¹⁸ Just then some men came, carrying a paralyzed man on a bed. They were trying to bring him in and lay him before Jesus;ᶜ ¹⁹ but finding no way to bring him in because of the crowd, they went up on the roof and let him down with his bed through the tiles into the middle of the crowdᵉ in front of Jesus. ²⁰ When he saw their faith, he said, "Friend,ᶠ your sins are forgiven you." ²¹ Then the scribes and the Pharisees began to question, "Who is this who is speaking blasphemies? Who can forgive sins but God alone?" ²² When Jesus perceived their questionings, he answered them, "Why do you raise such questions in your hearts? ²³ Which is easier, to say, 'Your sins are forgiven you,' or to say, 'Stand up and walk'? ²⁴ But so that

ᵃ The terms *leper* and *leprosy* can refer to several diseases   ᵇ Gk *he*
ᶜ Gk *him*   ᵈ Other ancient authorities read *was present to heal them*
ᵉ Gk *into the midst*   ᶠ Gk *Man*

5:8 *A sinful man*—In a statement of profound humility, itself a mark of discipleship, Peter acknowledges both his sinfulness and his awe at being in Jesus' presence. Discipleship is participation in and recognition of God's limitless and life-giving compassion.

5:11 *Left everything*—Their response expresses the essence of discipleship, a willingness to drop everything in order to follow Jesus (cf. v. 27).

5:12–26 Two Healings

5:20 *Their faith*—The determination, certainty, and trust exhibited by the paralyzed man and his friends exemplifies the faith that Luke expects of disciples.

5:24 *Authority . . . to forgive sins*—The theme of forgiveness (1:77) reoccurs here, with Jesus being identified as one who has divine authority to forgive sins. The liberating redemption that Jesus extends is mirrored by the physical changes he accomplishes for the two whom he heals.

you may know that the Son of Man has authority on earth to forgive sins"—he said to the one who was paralyzed—"I say to you, stand up and take your bed and go to your home." 25 Immediately he stood up before them, took what he had been lying on, and went to his home, glorifying God. 26 Amazement seized all of them, and they glorified God and were filled with awe, saying, "We have seen strange things today."

Jesus Calls Levi

27 After this he went out and saw a tax collector named Levi, sitting at the tax booth; and he said to him, "Follow me." 28 And he got up, left everything, and followed him.

29 Then Levi gave a great banquet for him in his house; and there was a large crowd of tax collectors and others sitting at the table*a* with them. 30 The Pharisees and their scribes were complaining to his disciples, saying, "Why do you eat and drink with tax collectors and sinners?" 31 Jesus answered, "Those who are well have no need of a physician, but those who are sick; 32 I have come to call not the righteous but sinners to repentance."

The Question about Fasting

33 Then they said to him, "John's disciples, like the disciples of the Pharisees, frequently fast and pray, but your disciples eat and drink." 34 Jesus said to them, "You cannot make wedding guests fast while the bridegroom is with them, can you? 35 The days will come when the bridegroom will be taken away from them, and then they will fast in those days." 36 He also told them a parable: "No one tears a piece from a new garment and sews it on an old garment; otherwise the new will be torn, and the piece from the new will not match the old. 37 And no one puts new wine into old wineskins; otherwise the new wine will burst the skins and will be spilled, and the skins will be destroyed. 38 But new wine must be put into fresh wineskins. 39 And no one after drinking old wine desires new wine, but says, 'The old is good.'"*b*

The Question about the Sabbath

6 One sabbath*c* while Jesus*d* was going through the grainfields, his disciples plucked some heads of grain, rubbed them in their hands, and ate them. 2 But some of the Pharisees said, "Why are you doing what is not lawful*e* on the sabbath?" 3 Jesus answered, "Have you not read what David did when he and his companions were hungry? 4 He entered the house of God and took and ate the bread of the Presence, which it is not lawful for any but the priests to eat, and gave some to his companions?" 5 Then he said to them, "The Son of Man is lord of the sabbath."

The Man with a Withered Hand

6 On another sabbath he entered the synagogue and taught, and there was a man there whose right hand was withered. 7 The scribes and the Pharisees

---

a Gk *reclining* *b* Other ancient authorities read *better*; others lack verse 39 *c* Other ancient authorities read *On the second first sabbath* *d* Gk *he* *e* Other ancient authorities add *to do*

5:27–39 Authorizing Community

5:27 *Follow me*—Cf. v. 11.

5:29 *Tax collectors*—Jesus enjoys the intimacy of table fellowship even with those who were often loathed as instruments of the imperial government. Here Jesus models the inclusive commensality that distinguishes the believing community.

5:32 *Not the righteous but sinners*—Here and throughout Luke, the call to repentance is a call to change. It is, by definition, open to everyone, especially sinners.

5:36–39 *New . . . old*—The new and old are mutually exclusive. Jesus' proclamation of God's radical concern for, and inclusion of, the poor and the marginalized cannot be reconciled with conventional values.

6:1–11 Sabbath Controversies

6:2 *Sabbath*—Because keeping the Sabbath holy is itself an act of faithfulness (Exod. 20:8–11; Deut. 5:12–15), concern for what was lawful on the Sabbath (cf. Luke 6:9) is well-attested in ancient Judaism.

watched him to see whether he would cure on the sabbath, so that they might find an accusation against him. 8 Even though he knew what they were thinking, he said to the man who had the withered hand, "Come and stand here." He got up and stood there. 9 Then Jesus said to them, "I ask you, is it lawful to do good or to do harm on the sabbath, to save life or to destroy it?" 10 After looking around at all of them, he said to him, "Stretch out your hand." He did so, and his hand was restored. 11 But they were filled with fury and discussed with one another what they might do to Jesus.

Jesus Chooses the Twelve Apostles

12 Now during those days he went out to the mountain to pray; and he spent the night in prayer to God. 13 And when day came, he called his disciples and chose twelve of them, whom he also named apostles: 14 Simon, whom he named Peter, and his brother Andrew, and James, and John, and Philip, and Bartholomew, 15 and Matthew, and Thomas, and James son of Alphaeus, and Simon, who was called the Zealot, 16 and Judas son of James, and Judas Iscariot, who became a traitor.

Jesus Teaches and Heals

17 He came down with them and stood on a level place, with a great crowd of his disciples and a great multitude of people from all Judea, Jerusalem, and the coast of Tyre and Sidon. 18 They had come to hear him and to be healed of their dis-

eases; and those who were troubled with unclean spirits were cured. 19 And all in the crowd were trying to touch him, for power came out from him and healed all of them.

Blessings and Woes

20 Then he looked up at his disciples and said:

"Blessed are you who are poor,
    for yours is the kingdom of God.
21 "Blessed are you who are hungry now,
    for you will be filled.
"Blessed are you who weep now,
    for you will laugh.

22 "Blessed are you when people hate you, and when they exclude you, revile you, and defame you[a] on account of the Son of Man. 23 Rejoice in that day and leap for joy, for surely your reward is great in heaven; for that is what their ancestors did to the prophets.

24 "But woe to you who are rich,
    for you have received your
        consolation.
25 "Woe to you who are full now,
    for you will be hungry.
"Woe to you who are laughing now,
    for you will mourn and weep.

26 "Woe to you when all speak well of you, for that is what their ancestors did to the false prophets.

Love for Enemies

27 "But I say to you that listen, Love your enemies, do good to those who

a Gk cast out your name as evil

6:9 To do good or to do harm—Jesus reminds his hearers of the moral and ethical purposes served by the law. The challenge for disciples is to focus not on scriptural teachings or principles alone, as if they exist in a vacuum, but on the values they uphold and express.

6:12–19 Commissioning the Twelve

6:12 In prayer—Luke continues to stress the necessity of prayer that joins contemplation and action.

6:13 Apostles—As a small group that is specially commissioned, or sent out, by Jesus (cf. 9:2, 10), the twelve remind us that discipleship is expressed through a variety of vocations.

6:20–49 The Sermon on the Plain

6:20–26 The Beatitudes and Woes—In contrast to Matthew, Luke resists spiritualizing the beatitudes and includes a series of warnings (vv. 24–26) that stand in stark contrast to the blessings that precede them. Together they confirm the theme of reversal that Mary introduced in her hymn (1:52–53). The poor, the hungry, and the grieving will be blessed and included among the restored people of God, but the rich, the well fed, and the mirthfully haughty will be excluded.

6:27–36 Loving one's enemies—Consistent with Jesus' emphasis on action, his radical demand to **love your enemies** (v. 27) is followed by the

hate you, ²⁸ bless those who curse you, pray for those who abuse you. ²⁹ If anyone strikes you on the cheek, offer the other also; and from anyone who takes away your coat do not withhold even your shirt. ³⁰ Give to everyone who begs from you; and if anyone takes away your goods, do not ask for them again. ³¹ Do to others as you would have them do to you.

³² "If you love those who love you, what credit is that to you? For even sinners love those who love them. ³³ If you do good to those who do good to you, what credit is that to you? For even sinners do the same. ³⁴ If you lend to those from whom you hope to receive, what credit is that to you? Even sinners lend to sinners, to receive as much again. ³⁵ But love your enemies, do good, and lend, expecting nothing in return.ᵃ Your reward will be great, and you will be children of the Most High; for he is kind to the ungrateful and the wicked. ³⁶ Be merciful, just as your Father is merciful.

Judging Others

³⁷ "Do not judge, and you will not be judged; do not condemn, and you will not be condemned. Forgive, and you will be forgiven; ³⁸ give, and it will be given to you. A good measure, pressed down, shaken together, running over, will be put into your lap; for the measure you give will be the measure you get back."

³⁹ He also told them a parable: "Can a blind person guide a blind person? Will not both fall into a pit? ⁴⁰ A disciple is not above the teacher, but everyone who is fully qualified will be like the teacher. ⁴¹ Why do you see the speck in your neighbor'sᵇ eye, but do not notice the log in your own eye? ⁴² Or how can you say to your neighbor,ᶜ 'Friend,ᶜ let me take out the speck in your eye,' when you yourself do not see the log in your own eye? You hypocrite, first take the log out of your own eye, and then you will see clearly to take the speck out of your neighbor'sᵇ eye.

A Tree and Its Fruit

⁴³ "No good tree bears bad fruit, nor again does a bad tree bear good fruit; ⁴⁴ for each tree is known by its own fruit. Figs are not gathered from thorns, nor are grapes picked from a bramble bush. ⁴⁵ The good person out of the good treasure of the heart produces good, and the evil person out of evil treasure produces evil; for it is out of the abundance of the heart that the mouth speaks.

The Two Foundations

⁴⁶ "Why do you call me 'Lord, Lord,' and do not do what I tell you? ⁴⁷ I will show you what someone is like who comes to me, hears my words, and acts on them. ⁴⁸ That one is like a man build-

ᵃ Other ancient authorities read *despairing of no one*   ᵇ Gk *brother's*
ᶜ Gk *brother*

---

command to **do good to those who hate you** (v. 27). Such acts of good are spelled out in vv. 28–30 and summarized in v. 31, **Do to others as you would have them do to you**. A paraphrase of Lev. 19:18, "Love your neighbor as yourself," v. 31 illumines how 6:27–36 recalls the concrete demonstrations of moral holiness that God demands of Israel in Lev. 19:1–18. Jesus' message appears radically new when compared to the convention of inflicting violence upon one's enemies, but it is rooted in ancient Jewish tradition.

6:35 Love your enemies, do good, and lend, expecting nothing in return—Jesus outlines the concrete expressions of love and the absence of self-interest that he expects of his followers. **Children of the Most High**—Those who follow

Jesus' example and teaching will themselves be regarded as children of God.

6:36 Be merciful—The demand to love unconditionally recalls the logic of Lev. 19:2, "You shall be holy, for I the Lᴏʀᴅ your God am holy."

6:37 Do not judge, and you will not be judged—Jesus inverts the logic of the previous section. Just as his disciples, like all human beings, are to reflect God's own being in their regard for others (cf. Gen. 1:27; Lev. 19:2), so will their experience of God reflect their relationship to their neighbors.

6:43–45 Bear good fruit . . . treasure of the heart—Just as love and faith must be expressed in action (cf. v. 47), one's actions reveal the inner person (cf. Simeon's prophecy, 2:35).

ing a house, who dug deeply and laid the foundation on rock; when a flood arose, the river burst against that house but could not shake it, because it had been well built.*a* **49** But the one who hears and does not act is like a man who built a house on the ground without a foundation. When the river burst against it, immediately it fell, and great was the ruin of that house."

Jesus Heals a Centurion's Servant

7 After Jesus*b* had finished all his sayings in the hearing of the people, he entered Capernaum. **2** A centurion there had a slave whom he valued highly, and who was ill and close to death. **3** When he heard about Jesus, he sent some Jewish elders to him, asking him to come and heal his slave. **4** When they came to Jesus, they appealed to him earnestly, saying, "He is worthy of having you do this for him, **5** for he loves our people, and it is he who built our synagogue for us." **6** And Jesus went with them, but when he was not far from the house, the centurion sent friends to say to him, "Lord, do not trouble yourself, for I am not worthy to have you come under my roof; **7** therefore I did not presume to come to you. But only speak the word, and let my servant be healed. **8** For I also am a man set under authority, with soldiers under me; and I say to one, 'Go,' and he goes, and to another, 'Come,' and he comes, and to my slave, 'Do this,' and the slave does it." **9** When Jesus heard this he was amazed at him, and turning to the crowd that followed him, he said, "I tell you, not even in Israel have I found such faith." **10** When those who had been sent returned to the house, they found the slave in good health.

Jesus Raises the Widow's Son at Nain

11 Soon afterwards*c* he went to a town called Nain, and his disciples and a large crowd went with him. **12** As he approached the gate of the town, a man who had died was being carried out. He was his mother's only son, and she was a widow; and with her was a large crowd from the town. **13** When the Lord saw her, he had compassion for her and said to her, "Do not weep." **14** Then he came forward and touched the bier, and the bearers stood still. And he said, "Young man, I say to you, rise!" **15** The dead man sat up and began to speak, and Jesus*d* gave him to his mother. **16** Fear seized all of them; and they glorified God, saying, "A great prophet has risen among us!" and "God has looked favorably on his people!" **17** This word about him spread throughout Judea and all the surrounding country.

Messengers from John the Baptist

18 The disciples of John reported all these things to him. So John summoned two of his disciples **19** and sent them to the Lord to ask, "Are you the one who is to come, or are we to wait for another?" **20** When the men had come to him, they said, "John the Baptist has sent us to you to ask, 'Are you the one who is to come, or are we to wait for another?'" **21** Jesus*d* had just then cured many people of diseases, plagues, and evil spirits, and had given sight to many who were blind. **22** And he answered them, "Go and tell John what you have seen and heard: the blind receive their sight, the lame walk, the lepers*e* are cleansed, the deaf hear, the dead are raised, the poor have good news brought to them. **23** And blessed is anyone who takes no offense at me."

a Other ancient authorities read *founded upon the rock* *b* Gk *he* *c* Other ancient authorities read *Next day* *d* Gk *He* *e* The terms *leper* and *leprosy* can refer to several diseases

---

7:1–35 Jesus the Prophet and Messiah

7:12 *His mother's only son*—The story illustrates Jesus' compassion for the poor, as her son would have been the widow's only secure source of economic support.

7:16 *God has looked favorably on his people!*—

Lit. "God has visited his people." God's presence is made known in Jesus (cf. 1:68; 19:44).

7:22 *The blind . . . the poor*—Jesus' concern for the poor and marginalized is illustrated here. Note that the raising of the dead is equal to, not greater than, the bringing of good news to the poor.

24 When John's messengers had gone, Jesus[a] began to speak to the crowds about John:[b] "What did you go out into the wilderness to look at? A reed shaken by the wind? 25 What then did you go out to see? Someone[c] dressed in soft robes? Look, those who put on fine clothing and live in luxury are in royal palaces. 26 What then did you go out to see? A prophet? Yes, I tell you, and more than a prophet. 27 This is the one about whom it is written,

'See, I am sending my messenger
      ahead of you,
who will prepare your way before
      you.'

28 I tell you, among those born of women no one is greater than John; yet the least in the kingdom of God is greater than he." 29 (And all the people who heard this, including the tax collectors, acknowledged the justice of God,[d] because they had been baptized with John's baptism. 30 But by refusing to be baptized by him, the Pharisees and the lawyers rejected God's purpose for themselves.)

31 "To what then will I compare the people of this generation, and what are they like? 32 They are like children sitting in the marketplace and calling to one another,

'We played the flute for you, and you
      did not dance;
we wailed, and you did not weep.'

33 For John the Baptist has come eating no bread and drinking no wine, and you say, 'He has a demon'; 34 the Son of Man has come eating and drinking, and you say, 'Look, a glutton and a drunkard, a friend of tax collectors and sinners!' 35 Nevertheless, wisdom is vindicated by all her children."

A Sinful Woman Forgiven

36 One of the Pharisees asked Jesus[b] to eat with him, and he went into the Pharisee's house and took his place at the table. 37 And a woman in the city, who was a sinner, having learned that he was eating in the Pharisee's house, brought an alabaster jar of ointment. 38 She stood behind him at his feet, weeping, and began to bathe his feet with her tears and to dry them with her hair. Then she continued kissing his feet and anointing them with the ointment. 39 Now when the Pharisee who had invited him saw it, he said to himself, "If this man were a prophet, he would have known who and what kind of woman this is who is touching him—that she is a sinner." 40 Jesus spoke up and said to him, "Simon, I have something to say to you." "Teacher," he replied, "speak." 41 "A certain creditor had two debtors; one owed five hundred denarii,[e] and the other fifty. 42 When they could not pay, he canceled the debts for both of them. Now which of them will love him more?" 43 Simon answered, "I suppose the one for whom he canceled the greater debt." And Jesus[a] said to him, "You have judged rightly." 44 Then turning toward the woman, he said to Simon, "Do you see this woman? I entered your house; you gave me no water for my feet, but she has bathed my feet with her tears and dried them with her hair. 45 You gave me no kiss, but from the time I came in she has not stopped kissing my feet. 46 You did not anoint my head with oil, but she has anointed my feet with ointment. 47 Therefore, I tell you, her sins, which were many, have been forgiven; hence she has shown great love. But the one to whom little is forgiven, loves little." 48 Then he said to her, "Your sins are forgiven." 49 But those who were at the table with him began to say among themselves, "Who is this who even forgives sins?" 50 And he said

a Gk he   b Gk him   c Or Why then did you go out? To see someone
d Or praised God   e The denarius was the usual day's wage for a laborer

---

7:36–50 Forgiving Sins

7:50 Your faith has saved you; go in peace—The woman's love expresses her faith in Jesus and acknowledges the forgiveness he has extended to her (v. 47). Jesus' words recall Luke's emphasis on the connection between forgiveness, salvation, and peace (cf. 1:77–79).

to the woman, "Your faith has saved you; go in peace."

Some Women Accompany Jesus

8 Soon afterwards he went on through cities and villages, proclaiming and bringing the good news of the kingdom of God. The twelve were with him, ² as well as some women who had been cured of evil spirits and infirmities: Mary, called Magdalene, from whom seven demons had gone out, ³ and Joanna, the wife of Herod's steward Chuza, and Susanna, and many others, who provided for them[a] out of their resources.

The Parable of the Sower

4 When a great crowd gathered and people from town after town came to him, he said in a parable: ⁵ "A sower went out to sow his seed; and as he sowed, some fell on the path and was trampled on, and the birds of the air ate it up. ⁶ Some fell on the rock; and as it grew up, it withered for lack of moisture. ⁷ Some fell among thorns, and the thorns grew with it and choked it. ⁸ Some fell into good soil, and when it grew, it produced a hundred-fold." As he said this, he called out, "Let anyone with ears to hear listen!"

The Purpose of the Parables

9 Then his disciples asked him what this parable meant. ¹⁰ He said, "To you it has been given to know the secrets[b] of the kingdom of God; but to others I speak[c] in parables, so that

'looking they may not perceive,
  and listening they may not
      understand.'

The Parable of the Sower Explained

11 "Now the parable is this: The seed is the word of God. ¹² The ones on the path are those who have heard; then the devil comes and takes away the word from their hearts, so that they may not believe and be saved. ¹³ The ones on the rock are those who, when they hear the word, receive it with joy. But these have no root; they believe only for a while and in a time of testing fall away. ¹⁴ As for what fell among the thorns, these are the ones who hear; but as they go on their way, they are choked by the cares and riches and pleasures of life, and their fruit does not mature. ¹⁵ But as for that in the good soil, these are the ones who, when they hear the word, hold it fast in an honest and good heart, and bear fruit with patient endurance.

A Lamp under a Jar

16 "No one after lighting a lamp hides it under a jar, or puts it under a bed, but puts it on a lampstand, so that those who enter may see the light. ¹⁷ For nothing is hidden that will not be disclosed, nor is anything secret that will not become known and come to light. ¹⁸ Then pay attention to how you listen; for to those who have, more will be given; and from those who do not have, even what they seem to have will be taken away."

The True Kindred of Jesus

19 Then his mother and his brothers came to him, but they could not reach him because of the crowd. ²⁰ And he was told, "Your mother and your brothers are standing outside, wanting to see you." ²¹ But he said to them, "My mother and my brothers are those who hear the word of God and do it."

---

[a] Other ancient authorities read *him*   [b] Or *mysteries*   [c] Gk lacks *I speak*

8:1–21 The Mysteries of the Kingdom

8:2 *As well as some women*—As in the previous scene, the activity of the women disciples conveys their faith.

8:15 *Good soil*—The description here is consistent with Jesus' emphasis on good deeds as the irrefutable evidence of authentic faith. True disciples keep the word *in an honest and good heart, and bear fruit with patient endurance.*

8:21 *My mother and my brothers*—The bonds of discipleship surpass those of ordinary familial relations. Jesus' kin are those who embody the good soil (cf. v. 15).

Jesus Calms a Storm

22 One day he got into a boat with his disciples, and he said to them, "Let us go across to the other side of the lake." So they put out, 23 and while they were sailing he fell asleep. A windstorm swept down on the lake, and the boat was filling with water, and they were in danger. 24 They went to him and woke him up, shouting, "Master, Master, we are perishing!" And he woke up and rebuked the wind and the raging waves; they ceased, and there was a calm. 25 He said to them, "Where is your faith?" They were afraid and amazed, and said to one another, "Who then is this, that he commands even the winds and the water, and they obey him?"

Jesus Heals the Gerasene Demoniac

26 Then they arrived at the country of the Gerasenes,*a* which is opposite Galilee. 27 As he stepped out on land, a man of the city who had demons met him. For a long time he had worn*b* no clothes, and he did not live in a house but in the tombs. 28 When he saw Jesus, he fell down before him and shouted at the top of his voice, "What have you to do with me, Jesus, Son of the Most High God? I beg you, do not torment me"— 29 for Jesus*c* had commanded the unclean spirit to come out of the man. (For many times it had seized him; he was kept under guard and bound with chains and shackles, but he would break the bonds and be driven by the demon into the wilds.) 30 Jesus then asked him, "What is your name?" He said, "Legion"; for many demons had entered him. 31 They begged him not to order them to go back into the abyss.

32 Now there on the hillside a large herd of swine was feeding; and the demons*d* begged Jesus*e* to let them enter these. So he gave them permission. 33 Then the demons came out of the man and entered the swine, and the herd rushed down the steep bank into the lake and was drowned.

34 When the swineherds saw what had happened, they ran off and told it in the city and in the country. 35 Then people came out to see what had happened, and when they came to Jesus, they found the man from whom the demons had gone sitting at the feet of Jesus, clothed and in his right mind. And they were afraid. 36 Those who had seen it told them how the one who had been possessed by demons had been healed. 37 Then all the people of the surrounding country of the Gerasenes*a* asked Jesus*e* to leave them; for they were seized with great fear. So he got into the boat and returned. 38 The man from whom the demons had gone begged that he might be with him; but Jesus*c* sent him away, saying, 39 "Return to your home, and declare how much God has done for you." So he went away, proclaiming throughout the city how much Jesus had done for him.

A Girl Restored to Life and a Woman Healed

40 Now when Jesus returned, the crowd welcomed him, for they were all waiting for him. 41 Just then there came a man named Jairus, a leader of the synagogue. He fell at Jesus' feet and begged him to come to his house, 42 for he had an only daughter, about twelve years old, who was dying.

As he went, the crowds pressed in on him. 43 Now there was a woman who had been suffering from hemorrhages for twelve years; and though she had spent

a Other ancient authorities read *Gadarenes*; others, *Gergesenes*   *b* Other ancient authorities read *a man of the city who had had demons for a long time met him. He wore*   *c* Gk *he*   *d* Gk *they*   *e* Gk *him*

8:22–56 The Authority of the Messiah
The stories of the storm on the lake and the Gerasene demoniac illustrate the fear with which even disciples struggle. Sometimes fear arises not only in times of great need (v. 24), but in response to needs being met (vv. 25, 37). The radical change brought about by the ruling of God is not always easy to accept. Discipleship calls for the courage to embrace change.

all she had on physicians,[a] no one could cure her. ⁴⁴ She came up behind him and touched the fringe of his clothes, and immediately her hemorrhage stopped. ⁴⁵ Then Jesus asked, "Who touched me?" When all denied it, Peter[b] said, "Master, the crowds surround you and press in on you." ⁴⁶ But Jesus said, "Someone touched me; for I noticed that power had gone out from me." ⁴⁷ When the woman saw that she could not remain hidden, she came trembling; and falling down before him, she declared in the presence of all the people why she had touched him, and how she had been immediately healed. ⁴⁸ He said to her, "Daughter, your faith has made you well; go in peace."

49 While he was still speaking, someone came from the leader's house to say, "Your daughter is dead; do not trouble the teacher any longer." ⁵⁰ When Jesus heard this, he replied, "Do not fear. Only believe, and she will be saved." ⁵¹ When he came to the house, he did not allow anyone to enter with him, except Peter, John, and James, and the child's father and mother. ⁵² They were all weeping and wailing for her; but he said, "Do not weep; for she is not dead but sleeping." ⁵³ And they laughed at him, knowing that she was dead. ⁵⁴ But he took her by the hand and called out, "Child, get up!" ⁵⁵ Her spirit returned, and she got up at once. Then he directed them to give her something to eat. ⁵⁶ Her parents were astounded; but he ordered them to tell no one what had happened.

The Mission of the Twelve

9 Then Jesus[c] called the twelve together and gave them power and authority over all demons and to cure diseases, ² and he sent them out to proclaim the kingdom of God and to heal. ³ He said to them, "Take nothing for your journey, no staff, nor bag, nor bread, nor money—not even an extra tunic. ⁴ Whatever house you enter, stay there, and leave from there. ⁵ Wherever they do not welcome you, as you are leaving that town shake the dust off your feet as a testimony against them." ⁶ They departed and went through the villages, bringing the good news and curing diseases everywhere.

Herod's Perplexity

7 Now Herod the ruler[d] heard about all that had taken place, and he was perplexed, because it was said by some that John had been raised from the dead, ⁸ by some that Elijah had appeared, and by others that one of the ancient prophets had arisen. ⁹ Herod said, "John I beheaded; but who is this about whom I hear such things?" And he tried to see him.

Feeding the Five Thousand

10 On their return the apostles told Jesus[e] all they had done. He took them with him and withdrew privately to a city called Bethsaida. ¹¹ When the crowds found out about it, they followed him; and he welcomed them, and spoke to them about the kingdom of God, and healed those who needed to be cured.

12 The day was drawing to a close, and the twelve came to him and said, "Send the crowd away, so that they may go into the surrounding villages and countryside, to lodge and get provisions; for we are here in a deserted place." ¹³ But he said to them, "You give them something to eat." They said, "We have no more than

---

[a] Other ancient authorities lack *and though she had spent all she had on physicians* [b] Other ancient authorities add *and those who were with him* [c] Gk *he* [d] Gk *tetrarch* [e] Gk *him*

9:1–17 Following the Messiah

9:1–6 The sending forth of the Twelve—Authorized and empowered by Jesus to proclaim the reign of God and to cure diseases and exorcise demons, the Twelve share in Jesus' ministry and mission. They are to minister wherever they are, as long as they are well received. Should they be rejected, they are released from obligation and given permission to move on (vv. 4–5). Ministers and disciples are compelled to announce good news, not to enforce its acceptance.

9:13 *Give them something to eat*—As ones proclaiming the kingdom of God, it is the disciples' responsibility to feed the crowd.

five loaves and two fish—unless we are to go and buy food for all these people." [14] For there were about five thousand men. And he said to his disciples, "Make them sit down in groups of about fifty each." [15] They did so and made them all sit down. [16] And taking the five loaves and the two fish, he looked up to heaven, and blessed and broke them, and gave them to the disciples to set before the crowd. [17] And all ate and were filled. What was left over was gathered up, twelve baskets of broken pieces.

Peter's Declaration about Jesus

[18] Once when Jesus[a] was praying alone, with only the disciples near him, he asked them, "Who do the crowds say that I am?" [19] They answered, "John the Baptist; but others, Elijah; and still others, that one of the ancient prophets has arisen." [20] He said to them, "But who do you say that I am?" Peter answered, "The Messiah[b] of God."

Jesus Foretells His Death and Resurrection

[21] He sternly ordered and commanded them not to tell anyone, [22] saying, "The Son of Man must undergo great suffering, and be rejected by the elders, chief priests, and scribes, and be killed, and on the third day be raised."

[23] Then he said to them all, "If any want to become my followers, let them deny themselves and take up their cross daily and follow me. [24] For those who want to save their life will lose it, and those who lose their life for my sake will save it. [25] What does it profit them if they gain the whole world, but lose or forfeit themselves? [26] Those who are ashamed of me and of my words, of them the Son of Man will be ashamed when he comes in his glory and the glory of the Father and of the holy angels. [27] But truly I tell you, there are some standing here who will not taste death before they see the kingdom of God."

The Transfiguration

[28] Now about eight days after these sayings Jesus[a] took with him Peter and John and James, and went up on the mountain to pray. [29] And while he was praying, the appearance of his face changed, and his clothes became dazzling white. [30] Suddenly they saw two men, Moses and Elijah, talking to him. [31] They appeared in glory and were speaking of his departure, which he was about to accomplish at Jerusalem. [32] Now Peter and his companions were weighed down with sleep; but since they had stayed awake,[c] they saw his glory and the two men who stood with him. [33] Just as they were leaving him, Peter said to Jesus, "Master, it is good for us to be here; let us make three dwellings,[d] one for you, one for Moses, and one for Elijah"—not knowing what he said. [34] While he was saying this, a cloud came and overshadowed them; and they were terrified as they entered the cloud. [35] Then from the cloud came a voice that said, "This is my Son, my Chosen;[e] listen to him!" [36] When the voice had spoken, Jesus was found alone. And they kept silent and in those days told no one any of the things they had seen.

Jesus Heals a Boy with a Demon

[37] On the next day, when they had come down from the mountain, a great

[a] Gk he [b] Or The Christ [c] Or but when they were fully awake [d] Or tents [e] Other ancient authorities read my Beloved

---

9:18–36 The Way of the Messiah and the Way of Discipleship

9:20 But who do you say that I am?—Deciding for oneself who Jesus is requires one to actively and comprehensively engage the gospel. Doing so can be itself an act of discipleship.

9:24 Those who want to save their life will lose it—Following the revelation of his impending suf-

fering and death, Jesus reveals that true discipleship is patterned after the Messiah. Paradoxically, the way of salvation defies conventional norms and practices of self-interest and self-preservation. It is shaped instead by the ethics and morality of Jesus' teachings on the ruling of God.

9:37–50 The Challenges of Discipleship

crowd met him. [38] Just then a man from the crowd shouted, "Teacher, I beg you to look at my son; he is my only child. [39] Suddenly a spirit seizes him, and all at once he[a] shrieks. It convulses him until he foams at the mouth; it mauls him and will scarcely leave him. [40] I begged your disciples to cast it out, but they could not." [41] Jesus answered, "You faithless and perverse generation, how much longer must I be with you and bear with you? Bring your son here." [42] While he was coming, the demon dashed him to the ground in convulsions. But Jesus rebuked the unclean spirit, healed the boy, and gave him back to his father. [43] And all were astounded at the greatness of God.

Jesus Again Foretells His Death

While everyone was amazed at all that he was doing, he said to his disciples, [44] "Let these words sink into your ears: The Son of Man is going to be betrayed into human hands." [45] But they did not understand this saying; its meaning was concealed from them, so that they could not perceive it. And they were afraid to ask him about this saying.

True Greatness

[46] An argument arose among them as to which one of them was the greatest. [47] But Jesus, aware of their inner thoughts, took a little child and put it by his side, [48] and said to them, "Whoever welcomes this child in my name welcomes me, and whoever welcomes me welcomes the one who sent me; for the least among all of you is the greatest."

Another Exorcist

[49] John answered, "Master, we saw someone casting out demons in your name, and we tried to stop him, because he does not follow with us." [50] But Jesus said to him, "Do not stop him; for whoever is not against you is for you."

A Samaritan Village Refuses to Receive Jesus

[51] When the days drew near for him to be taken up, he set his face to go to Jerusalem. [52] And he sent messengers ahead of him. On their way they entered a village of the Samaritans to make ready for him; [53] but they did not receive him, because his face was set toward Jerusalem. [54] When his disciples James and John saw it, they said, "Lord, do you want us to command fire to come down from heaven and consume them?"[b] [55] But he turned and rebuked them. [56] Then[c] they went on to another village.

Would-Be Followers of Jesus

[57] As they were going along the road, someone said to him, "I will follow you wherever you go." [58] And Jesus said to him, "Foxes have holes, and birds of the air have nests; but the Son of Man has nowhere to lay his head." [59] To another he said, "Follow me." But he said, "Lord, first let me go and bury my father." [60] But Jesus[d] said to him, "Let the dead bury their own dead; but as for you, go and proclaim the kingdom of God." [61] Another said, "I will follow you, Lord; but let me first say farewell to those at my home." [62] Jesus said to him, "No one who puts a hand to the plow and looks back is fit for the kingdom of God."

[a] Or it [b] Other ancient authorities add as Elijah did [c] Other ancient authorities read rebuked them, and said, "You do not know what spirit you are of, 56 for the Son of Man has not come to destroy the lives of human beings but to save them." Then [d] Gk he

---

9:41 *Faithless and perverse generation*—Jesus charges that the disciples, who are falling short of their commission, are untrustworthy.

9:51–19:27 *Following Jesus on the Way*
This large section of the Gospel, the "travel narrative," chronicles Jesus' journey to Jerusalem. Along the way, Jesus instructs his disciples, engages the crowd, and encounters opposition.

9:51–62 The Priority of the Kingdom

9:55 *Rebuked them*—In Luke, rejection due to ignorance is not to be met with vengeance or wrath. According to some manuscripts, on the cross Jesus prays that even his executioners will be forgiven (23:34).

9:62 *Fit for the kingdom of God*—Discipleship calls for a complete and uncompromising commitment to the ruling, or way, of God.

The Mission of the Seventy

10 After this the Lord appointed seventy[a] others and sent them on ahead of him in pairs to every town and place where he himself intended to go. [2] He said to them, "The harvest is plentiful, but the laborers are few; therefore ask the Lord of the harvest to send out laborers into his harvest. [3] Go on your way. See, I am sending you out like lambs into the midst of wolves. [4] Carry no purse, no bag, no sandals; and greet no one on the road. [5] Whatever house you enter, first say, 'Peace to this house!' [6] And if anyone is there who shares in peace, your peace will rest on that person; but if not, it will return to you. [7] Remain in the same house, eating and drinking whatever they provide, for the laborer deserves to be paid. Do not move about from house to house. [8] Whenever you enter a town and its people welcome you, eat what is set before you; [9] cure the sick who are there, and say to them, 'The kingdom of God has come near to you.'[b] [10] But whenever you enter a town and they do not welcome you, go out into its streets and say, [11] 'Even the dust of your town that clings to our feet, we wipe off in protest against you. Yet know this: the kingdom of God has come near.'[c] [12] I tell you, on that day it will be more tolerable for Sodom than for that town.

Woes to Unrepentant Cities

[13] "Woe to you, Chorazin! Woe to you, Bethsaida! For if the deeds of power done in you had been done in Tyre and Sidon, they would have repented long ago, sitting in sackcloth and ashes. [14] But at the judgment it will be more tolerable for Tyre and Sidon than for you. [15] And you, Capernaum,

will you be exalted to heaven?
No, you will be brought down to Hades.

[16] "Whoever listens to you listens to me, and whoever rejects you rejects me, and whoever rejects me rejects the one who sent me."

The Return of the Seventy

[17] The seventy[a] returned with joy, saying, "Lord, in your name even the demons submit to us!" [18] He said to them, "I watched Satan fall from heaven like a flash of lightning. [19] See, I have given you authority to tread on snakes and scorpions, and over all the power of the enemy; and nothing will hurt you. [20] Nevertheless, do not rejoice at this, that the spirits submit to you, but rejoice that your names are written in heaven."

Jesus Rejoices

[21] At that same hour Jesus[d] rejoiced in the Holy Spirit[e] and said, "I thank[f] you, Father, Lord of heaven and earth, because you have hidden these things from the wise and the intelligent and have revealed them to infants; yes, Father, for such was your gracious will.[g] [22] All things have been handed over to me by my Father; and no one knows who the Son is except the Father, or who the Father is except the Son and anyone to whom the Son chooses to reveal him."

[23] Then turning to the disciples, Jesus[d] said to them privately, "Blessed are the eyes that see what you see! [24] For I tell you that many prophets and kings desired to see what you see, but did not see it, and to hear what you hear, but did not hear it."

[a] Other ancient authorities read *seventy-two* [b] Or *is at hand for you* [c] Or *is at hand* [d] Gk *he* [e] Other authorities read *in the spirit* [f] Or *praise* [g] Or *for so it was well-pleasing in your sight*

10:1–24 Sending Forth the Seventy
The story recalls 9:1–6 and 9:52.

10:1 *Seventy*—Jesus sends forth his disciples (seventy or seventy-two) in pairs to proclaim the kingdom, cure the sick (v. 9), and prepare

the way for Jesus (v. 1). The conditions (vv. 4, 7, 10–11) are similar to those outlined in 9:1–6.

10:3 *Lambs into the midst of wolves*—Discipleship can be dangerous. Thus the seventy are dissuaded from greeting anyone *on the road* (v. 4), which was known for its dangers.

The Parable of the Good Samaritan

25 Just then a lawyer stood up to test Jesus.[a] "Teacher," he said, "what must I do to inherit eternal life?" 26 He said to him, "What is written in the law? What do you read there?" 27 He answered, "You shall love the Lord your God with all your heart, and with all your soul, and with all your strength, and with all your mind; and your neighbor as yourself." 28 And he said to him, "You have given the right answer; do this, and you will live."

29 But wanting to justify himself, he asked Jesus, "And who is my neighbor?" 30 Jesus replied, "A man was going down from Jerusalem to Jericho, and fell into the hands of robbers, who stripped him, beat him, and went away, leaving him half dead. 31 Now by chance a priest was going down that road; and when he saw him, he passed by on the other side. 32 So likewise a Levite, when he came to the place and saw him, passed by on the other side. 33 But a Samaritan while traveling came near him; and when he saw him, he was moved with pity. 34 He went to him and bandaged his wounds, having poured oil and wine on them. Then he put him on his own animal, brought him to an inn, and took care of him. 35 The next day he took out two denarii,[b] gave them to the innkeeper, and said, 'Take care of him; and when I come back, I will repay you whatever more you spend.' 36 Which of these three, do you think, was a neighbor to the man who fell into the hands of the robbers?" 37 He said, "The one who showed him mercy." Jesus said to him, "Go and do likewise."

Jesus Visits Martha and Mary

38 Now as they went on their way, he entered a certain village, where a woman named Martha welcomed him into her home. 39 She had a sister named Mary, who sat at the Lord's feet and listened to what he was saying. 40 But Martha was distracted by her many tasks; so she came to him and asked, "Lord, do you not care that my sister has left me to do all the work by myself? Tell her then to help me." 41 But the Lord answered her, "Martha, Martha, you are worried and distracted by many things; 42 there is need of only one thing.[c] Mary has chosen the better part, which will not be taken away from her."

The Lord's Prayer

11 He was praying in a certain place, and after he had finished, one of

[a] Gk *him*   [b] The denarius was the usual day's wage for a laborer   [c] Other ancient authorities read *few things are necessary, or only one*

10:25–11:13 The Way of the Kingdom

10:25–37 On being a neighbor—The lawyer cites the Shema (Deut. 6:4–9) and Lev. 19:18, the same verse to which Jesus alluded in 6:31.

10:30–33—The ancient and long-standing social and religious tensions between the Jews and the Samaritans is well documented. Here the *priest* (v. 31) and *Levite* (v. 32) represent those with an expected place in the kingdom, whereas the *Samaritan* (v. 33) symbolizes those for whom no place is anticipated (cf. the Samaritan rejection of Jesus in 9:53). Yet, in this parable infused with biting social and religious commentary, it is the Samaritan who fulfills the Scripture cited by the lawyer (10:27) by demonstrating love for his neighbor.

10:36 *Which of these . . . was a neighbor?*— Jesus' parable turns the lawyer's question around so that the operative issue is no longer *Who is my neighbor?* (v. 29) but, rather, "How may I be a neighbor?" The way of discipleship is one of "kingdom neighborliness." It focuses not on discerning one's neighbors but on being a neighbor to all.

10:38–42 On listening—The contrast between Mary and Martha revolves around the importance of listening to the word of the prophet, which is the *better part* (v. 42) that Mary has chosen.

10:41 *Worried and distracted*—A theme that reoccurs in 12:26. Luke counters Martha's anxiety with Mary's single-mindedness. The first is futile, but the latter will bear fruit.

11:1–13 On prayer—The prayer that Jesus teaches his disciples brings together key elements of his mission with its presumption of intimate fellowship with God, desire for the unfettered ruling of God, genuine concern for basic human needs, focus on forgiveness as central to the kingdom, and request to be protected from the kind of testing that Jesus endured. The prayer therefore functions as a summary outline of the life of discipleship.

his disciples said to him, "Lord, teach us to pray, as John taught his disciples." [2] He said to them, "When you pray, say:

Father,[a] hallowed be your name.
    Your kingdom come.[b]
[3]   Give us each day our daily bread.[c]
[4]   And forgive us our sins,
        for we ourselves forgive
            everyone indebted to us.
        And do not bring us to the time of
            trial."[d]

Perseverance in Prayer

5 And he said to them, "Suppose one of you has a friend, and you go to him at midnight and say to him, 'Friend, lend me three loaves of bread; [6] for a friend of mine has arrived, and I have nothing to set before him.' [7] And he answers from within, 'Do not bother me; the door has already been locked, and my children are with me in bed; I cannot get up and give you anything.' [8] I tell you, even though he will not get up and give him anything because he is his friend, at least because of his persistence he will get up and give him whatever he needs.

9 "So I say to you, Ask, and it will be given you; search, and you will find; knock, and the door will be opened for you. [10] For everyone who asks receives, and everyone who searches finds, and for everyone who knocks, the door will be opened. [11] Is there anyone among you who, if your child asks for[e] a fish, will give a snake instead of a fish? [12] Or if the child asks for an egg, will give a scorpion? [13] If you then, who are evil, know how to give good gifts to your children,

how much more will the heavenly Father give the Holy Spirit[f] to those who ask him!"

Jesus and Beelzebul

14 Now he was casting out a demon that was mute; when the demon had gone out, the one who had been mute spoke, and the crowds were amazed. [15] But some of them said, "He casts out demons by Beelzebul, the ruler of the demons." [16] Others, to test him, kept demanding from him a sign from heaven. [17] But he knew what they were thinking and said to them, "Every kingdom divided against itself becomes a desert, and house falls on house. [18] If Satan also is divided against himself, how will his kingdom stand? —for you say that I cast out the demons by Beelzebul. [19] Now if I cast out the demons by Beelzebul, by whom do your exorcists[g] cast them out? Therefore they will be your judges. [20] But if it is by the finger of God that I cast out the demons, then the kingdom of God has come to you. [21] When a strong man, fully armed, guards his castle, his property is safe. [22] But when one stronger than he attacks him and overpowers him, he takes away his armor in which he trusted and divides his plunder. [23] Whoever is not with me is against me, and whoever does not gather with me scatters.

[a] Other ancient authorities read *Our Father in heaven*   [b] A few ancient authorities read *Your Holy Spirit come upon us and cleanse us.* Other ancient authorities add *Your will be done, on earth as in heaven*   [c] Or *our bread for tomorrow*   [d] Or *us into temptation.* Other ancient authorities add *but rescue us from the evil one* (or *from evil*)   [e] Other ancient authorities add *bread, will give a stone; or if your child asks for*   [f] Other ancient authorities read *the Father give the Holy Spirit from heaven*   [g] Gk *sons*

11:1 *Teach us to pray*—The question is particularly apt in Luke, where Jesus often withdraws to pray.

11:2 *Father*—The prayer implies that the intimacy of the Messiah's relationship with God extends to all of God's children (cf. 6:35). *Your kingdom come*—The realization of God's unfettered ruling over and among all things is the center of Jesus' proclamation and the primary concern of the disciples' prayer.

11:3 *Our daily bread*—Provision for concrete human needs is integral to Jesus' vision. Social

justice does not supplement ministry and discipleship. It is evidence of its authenticity.

11:4 *For we ourselves forgive*—Suggesting that our experience of God reflects our relations with other persons, the prayer recalls 6:37–38. *Time of trial*—The prayer asks for protection from those powers that oppose the reign of God (cf. 8:13; 22:3, 28, 31, 40, 46).

11:8 *Persistence*—As Mary demonstrated faith in the divine word (1:45), persistence expresses faith in God's response to human need.

11:14–36 Discerning Opposition

The Return of the Unclean Spirit

24 "When the unclean spirit has gone out of a person, it wanders through waterless regions looking for a resting place, but not finding any, it says, 'I will return to my house from which I came.' 25 When it comes, it finds it swept and put in order. 26 Then it goes and brings seven other spirits more evil than itself, and they enter and live there; and the last state of that person is worse than the first."

True Blessedness

27 While he was saying this, a woman in the crowd raised her voice and said to him, "Blessed is the womb that bore you and the breasts that nursed you!" 28 But he said, "Blessed rather are those who hear the word of God and obey it!"

The Sign of Jonah

29 When the crowds were increasing, he began to say, "This generation is an evil generation; it asks for a sign, but no sign will be given to it except the sign of Jonah. 30 For just as Jonah became a sign to the people of Nineveh, so the Son of Man will be to this generation. 31 The queen of the South will rise at the judgment with the people of this generation and condemn them, because she came from the ends of the earth to listen to the wisdom of Solomon, and see, something greater than Solomon is here! 32 The people of Nineveh will rise up at the judgment with this generation and condemn it, because they repented at the proclamation of Jonah, and see, something greater than Jonah is here!

The Light of the Body

33 "No one after lighting a lamp puts it in a cellar,*a* but on the lampstand so that those who enter may see the light. 34 Your eye is the lamp of your body. If your eye is healthy, your whole body is full of light; but if it is not healthy, your body is full of darkness. 35 Therefore consider whether the light in you is not darkness. 36 If then your whole body is full of light, with no part of it in darkness, it will be as full of light as when a lamp gives you light with its rays."

Jesus Denounces Pharisees and Lawyers

37 While he was speaking, a Pharisee invited him to dine with him; so he went in and took his place at the table. 38 The Pharisee was amazed to see that he did not first wash before dinner. 39 Then the Lord said to him, "Now you Pharisees clean the outside of the cup and of the dish, but inside you are full of greed and wickedness. 40 You fools! Did not the one who made the outside make the inside also? 41 So give for alms those things that are within; and see, everything will be clean for you.

42 "But woe to you Pharisees! For you tithe mint and rue and herbs of all kinds, and neglect justice and the love of God; it is these you ought to have practiced, without neglecting the others. 43 Woe to you Pharisees! For you love to have the seat of honor in the synagogues and to be greeted with respect in the market-places. 44 Woe to you! For you are like unmarked graves, and people walk over them without realizing it."

45 One of the lawyers answered him, "Teacher, when you say these things, you insult us too." 46 And he said, "Woe also to you lawyers! For you load people with burdens hard to bear, and you yourselves do not lift a finger to ease

a Other ancient authorities add *or under the bushel basket*

11:28—Jesus again stresses that discipleship is not simply about belief, but about action. Those who would be followers of Jesus are the ones who *hear the word* and *obey it*.

11:35 *The light in you*—Discerning light from darkness is key in a Gospel that asks readers to rethink conventional values and practices.

11:37–54 Woes and Judgments
Here Luke portrays the Pharisees as ones who fail to fulfill the ethic of servant leadership expected of Jesus' disciples (22:24–27).

them. **47** Woe to you! For you build the tombs of the prophets whom your ancestors killed. **48** So you are witnesses and approve of the deeds of your ancestors; for they killed them, and you build their tombs. **49** Therefore also the Wisdom of God said, 'I will send them prophets and apostles, some of whom they will kill and persecute,' **50** so that this generation may be charged with the blood of all the prophets shed since the foundation of the world, **51** from the blood of Abel to the blood of Zechariah, who perished between the altar and the sanctuary. Yes, I tell you, it will be charged against this generation. **52** Woe to you lawyers! For you have taken away the key of knowledge; you did not enter yourselves, and you hindered those who were entering."

53 When he went outside, the scribes and the Pharisees began to be very hostile toward him and to cross-examine him about many things, **54** lying in wait for him, to catch him in something he might say.

A Warning against Hypocrisy

12 Meanwhile, when the crowd gathered by the thousands, so that they trampled on one another, he began to speak first to his disciples, "Beware of the yeast of the Pharisees, that is, their hypocrisy. **2** Nothing is covered up that will not be uncovered, and nothing secret that will not become known. **3** Therefore whatever you have said in the dark will be heard in the light, and what you have whispered behind closed doors will be proclaimed from the housetops.

Exhortation to Fearless Confession

4 "I tell you, my friends, do not fear those who kill the body, and after that can do nothing more. **5** But I will warn you whom to fear: fear him who, after he has killed, has authority*a* to cast into hell.*b* Yes, I tell you, fear him! **6** Are not five sparrows sold for two pennies? Yet not one of them is forgotten in God's sight. **7** But even the hairs of your head are all counted. Do not be afraid; you are of more value than many sparrows.

8 "And I tell you, everyone who acknowledges me before others, the Son of Man also will acknowledge before the angels of God; **9** but whoever denies me before others will be denied before the angels of God. **10** And everyone who speaks a word against the Son of Man will be forgiven; but whoever blasphemes against the Holy Spirit will not be forgiven. **11** When they bring you before the synagogues, the rulers, and the authorities, do not worry about how*c* you are to defend yourselves or what you are to say; **12** for the Holy Spirit will teach you at that very hour what you ought to say."

The Parable of the Rich Fool

13 Someone in the crowd said to him, "Teacher, tell my brother to divide the family inheritance with me." **14** But he said to him, "Friend, who set me to be a judge or arbitrator over you?" **15** And he said to them, "Take care! Be on your guard against all kinds of greed; for one's life does not consist in the abundance of possessions." **16** Then he told them a parable: "The land of a rich man produced abundantly. **17** And he thought to himself, 'What should I do, for I have no place to store my crops?' **18** Then he said, 'I will do this: I will pull down my barns and build larger ones, and there I will store all my grain and my goods. **19** And I

---

a Or *power* *b* Gk *Gehenna* *c* Other ancient authorities add *or what*

12:1–13:21 Discerning the Way of the Kingdom

12:1–12 On boldness—True discipleship is expressed not by private belief but by bold speech and action.

12:13–34 On material needs and spiritual discernment—This section starts with the first in a

series of parables where Jesus underscores the dangers of accruing and misusing wealth (cf. 16:1–9; 18:1–8). The stories warn against material accumulation and confirm God's concern for the poor (cf. 1:53; 4:18; 6:20–21, 24–25).

will say to my soul, Soul, you have ample goods laid up for many years; relax, eat, drink, be merry.' 20 But God said to him, 'You fool! This very night your life is being demanded of you. And the things you have prepared, whose will they be?' 21 So it is with those who store up treasures for themselves but are not rich toward God."

Do Not Worry

22 He said to his disciples, "Therefore I tell you, do not worry about your life, what you will eat, or about your body, what you will wear. 23 For life is more than food, and the body more than clothing. 24 Consider the ravens: they neither sow nor reap, they have neither storehouse nor barn, and yet God feeds them. Of how much more value are you than the birds! 25 And can any of you by worrying add a single hour to your span of life?[a] 26 If then you are not able to do so small a thing as that, why do you worry about the rest? 27 Consider the lilies, how they grow: they neither toil nor spin;[b] yet I tell you, even Solomon in all his glory was not clothed like one of these. 28 But if God so clothes the grass of the field, which is alive today and tomorrow is thrown into the oven, how much more will he clothe you—you of little faith! 29 And do not keep striving for what you are to eat and what you are to drink, and do not keep worrying. 30 For it is the nations of the world that strive after all these things, and your Father knows that you need them. 31 Instead, strive for his[c] kingdom, and these things will be given to you as well.

32 "Do not be afraid, little flock, for it is your Father's good pleasure to give you the kingdom. 33 Sell your possessions, and give alms. Make purses for yourselves that do not wear out, an unfailing treasure in heaven, where no thief comes near and no moth destroys. 34 For where your treasure is, there your heart will be also.

Watchful Slaves

35 "Be dressed for action and have your lamps lit; 36 be like those who are waiting for their master to return from the wedding banquet, so that they may open the door for him as soon as he comes and knocks. 37 Blessed are those slaves whom the master finds alert when he comes; truly I tell you, he will fasten his belt and have them sit down to eat, and he will come and serve them. 38 If he comes during the middle of the night, or near dawn, and finds them so, blessed are those slaves.

39 "But know this: if the owner of the house had known at what hour the thief was coming, he[d] would not have let his house be broken into. 40 You also must be ready, for the Son of Man is coming at an unexpected hour."

The Faithful or the Unfaithful Slave

41 Peter said, "Lord, are you telling this parable for us or for everyone?" 42 And the Lord said, "Who then is the faithful and prudent manager whom his master will put in charge of his slaves, to give them

[a] Or add a cubit to your stature [b] Other ancient authorities read Consider the lilies; they neither spin nor weave [c] Other ancient authorities read God's [d] Other ancient authorities add would have watched and

---

12:20 *Fool*—The rich man resembles "the lost" in Luke, but this parable leaves his story unresolved.

12:22 *Do not worry*—Consistent with the Gospel's social concern, the aim is not to belittle such anxiety, but to meet it.

12:31 *Strive for his kingdom*—The kingdom meets human needs. Living collectively in accordance with Jesus' socially relevant teachings will ensure that the basic needs of God's children are met.

12:33—*Sell your possessions*—The kingdom

teachings that encourage almsgiving and highlight the needs of the poor also counter conventional practices of acquisition and accumulation.

12:35–59 On watchfulness—Jesus' disciples are called to anticipate and show themselves prepared, by word and deed, for the full manifestation of God's reign.

12:37 *Serve them*—With the master becoming a servant to his slaves, Jesus' examples illustrate the ethic of servanthood that characterizes the kingdom (cf. 22:27).

their allowance of food at the proper time? **43** Blessed is that slave whom his master will find at work when he arrives. **44** Truly I tell you, he will put that one in charge of all his possessions. **45** But if that slave says to himself, 'My master is delayed in coming,' and if he begins to beat the other slaves, men and women, and to eat and drink and get drunk, **46** the master of that slave will come on a day when he does not expect him and at an hour that he does not know, and will cut him in pieces,*a* and put him with the unfaithful. **47** That slave who knew what his master wanted, but did not prepare himself or do what was wanted, will receive a severe beating. **48** But the one who did not know and did what deserved a beating will receive a light beating. From everyone to whom much has been given, much will be required; and from the one to whom much has been entrusted, even more will be demanded.

Jesus the Cause of Division

49 "I came to bring fire to the earth, and how I wish it were already kindled! **50** I have a baptism with which to be baptized, and what stress I am under until it is completed! **51** Do you think that I have come to bring peace to the earth? No, I tell you, but rather division! **52** From now on five in one household will be divided, three against two and two against three; **53** they will be divided:

father against son
  and son against father,
mother against daughter
  and daughter against mother,
mother-in-law against her
    daughter-in-law
  and daughter-in-law against
    mother-in-law."

Interpreting the Time

54 He also said to the crowds, "When you see a cloud rising in the west, you immediately say, 'It is going to rain'; and so it happens. **55** And when you see the south wind blowing, you say, 'There will be scorching heat'; and it happens. **56** You hypocrites! You know how to interpret the appearance of earth and sky, but why do you not know how to interpret the present time?

Settling with Your Opponent

57 "And why do you not judge for yourselves what is right? **58** Thus, when you go with your accuser before a magistrate, on the way make an effort to settle the case,*b* or you may be dragged before the judge, and the judge hand you over to the officer, and the officer throw you in prison. **59** I tell you, you will never get out until you have paid the very last penny."

Repent or Perish

13 At that very time there were some present who told him about the Galileans whose blood Pilate had mingled with their sacrifices. **2** He asked them, "Do you think that because these Galileans suffered in this way they were worse sinners than all other Galileans? **3** No, I tell you; but unless you repent, you will all perish as they did. **4** Or those eighteen who were killed when the tower of Siloam fell on them—do you think that they were worse offenders than all the others living in Jerusalem? **5** No, I tell you; but unless you repent, you will all perish just as they did."

The Parable of the Barren Fig Tree

6 Then he told this parable: "A man had a fig tree planted in his vineyard; and he came looking for fruit on it and found none. **7** So he said to the gardener, 'See here! For three years I have come looking for fruit on this fig tree, and still I find none. Cut it down! Why should

a Or *cut him off* *b* Gk *settle with him*

12:48 *Even more will be demanded*—Living out the ethic of servanthood is demanded of all of Jesus' followers, especially those in positions of leadership.

13:1–9 On repentance—The parable illustrates Luke's conviction that God graciously allows those hearing the word ample time (*one more year*, v. 8) for repentance and response.

it be wasting the soil?' ⁸He replied, 'Sir, let it alone for one more year, until I dig around it and put manure on it. ⁹If it bears fruit next year, well and good; but if not, you can cut it down.'"

Jesus Heals a Crippled Woman

10 Now he was teaching in one of the synagogues on the sabbath. ¹¹And just then there appeared a woman with a spirit that had crippled her for eighteen years. She was bent over and was quite unable to stand up straight. ¹²When Jesus saw her, he called her over and said, "Woman, you are set free from your ailment." ¹³When he laid his hands on her, immediately she stood up straight and began praising God. ¹⁴But the leader of the synagogue, indignant because Jesus had cured on the sabbath, kept saying to the crowd, "There are six days on which work ought to be done; come on those days and be cured, and not on the sabbath day." ¹⁵But the Lord answered him and said, "You hypocrites! Does not each of you on the sabbath untie his ox or his donkey from the manger, and lead it away to give it water? ¹⁶And ought not this woman, a daughter of Abraham whom Satan bound for eighteen long years, be set free from this bondage on the sabbath day?" ¹⁷When he said this, all his opponents were put to shame; and the entire crowd was rejoicing at all the wonderful things that he was doing.

The Parable of the Mustard Seed

18 He said therefore, "What is the kingdom of God like? And to what should I compare it? ¹⁹It is like a mustard seed that someone took and sowed in the garden; it grew and became a tree, and the birds of the air made nests in its branches."

The Parable of the Yeast

20 And again he said, "To what should I compare the kingdom of God? ²¹It is like yeast that a woman took and mixed in with*ᵃ* three measures of flour until all of it was leavened."

The Narrow Door

22 Jesus*ᵇ* went through one town and village after another, teaching as he made his way to Jerusalem. ²³Someone asked him, "Lord, will only a few be saved?" He said to them, ²⁴"Strive to enter through the narrow door; for many, I tell you, will try to enter and will not be able. ²⁵When once the owner of the house has got up and shut the door, and you begin to stand outside and to knock at the door, saying, 'Lord, open to us,' then in reply he will say to you, 'I do not know where you come from.' ²⁶Then you will begin to say, 'We ate and drank with you, and you taught in our streets.' ²⁷But he will say, 'I do not know where you come from; go away from me, all you evildoers!' ²⁸There will be weeping and gnashing of teeth when you see Abraham and Isaac and Jacob and all the prophets in the kingdom of God, and you yourselves thrown out. ²⁹Then people will come from east and west, from north and south, and will eat in the kingdom of God. ³⁰Indeed, some are last who will be first, and some are first who will be last."

ᵃ Gk hid in *ᵇ* Gk He

13:10–17 Another Sabbath controversy—In keeping with Jesus' inaugural sermon, Luke continues to cast Jesus' healing ministry as an expression of liberation (*set free*, v. 12).

13:18–21 Parables of the kingdom—These two stories emphasize the enlivening and expansive dimensions of the kingdom that Jesus proclaims.

13:22–30 The Last and the First

13:26 *Ate and drank with you*—The protest conveys the speaker's expectation that previous table fellowship should have guaranteed privilege (cf. 14:1–35).

13:27 *Go away from me*—Citing Ps. 6:8, Luke returns to the theme of status reversal. As in the psalm, the evildoers are turned away, but the *Lord* (v. 25) hears the supplications of the suffering righteous. Thus *some are last who will be first, and some are first who will be last* (v. 30).

The Lament over Jerusalem

31 At that very hour some Pharisees came and said to him, "Get away from here, for Herod wants to kill you." ³²He said to them, "Go and tell that fox for me,ᵃ 'Listen, I am casting out demons and performing cures today and tomorrow, and on the third day I finish my work. ³³Yet today, tomorrow, and the next day I must be on my way, because it is impossible for a prophet to be killed outside of Jerusalem.' ³⁴Jerusalem, Jerusalem, the city that kills the prophets and stones those who are sent to it! How often have I desired to gather your children together as a hen gathers her brood under her wings, and you were not willing! ³⁵See, your house is left to you. And I tell you, you will not see me until the time comes whenᵇ you say, 'Blessed is the one who comes in the name of the Lord.'"

Jesus Heals the Man with Dropsy

14 On one occasion when Jesusᶜ was going to the house of a leader of the Pharisees to eat a meal on the sabbath, they were watching him closely. ²Just then, in front of him, there was a man who had dropsy. ³And Jesus asked the lawyers and Pharisees, "Is it lawful to cure people on the sabbath, or not?" ⁴But they were silent. So Jesusᶜ took him and healed him, and sent him away. ⁵Then he said to them, "If one of you has a childᵈ or an ox that has fallen into a well, will you not immediately pull it out on a sabbath day?" ⁶And they could not reply to this.

Humility and Hospitality

7 When he noticed how the guests chose the places of honor, he told them a parable. ⁸"When you are invited by someone to a wedding banquet, do not sit down at the place of honor, in case someone more distinguished than you has been invited by your host; ⁹and the host who invited both of you may come and say to you, 'Give this person your place,' and then in disgrace you would start to take the lowest place. ¹⁰But when you are invited, go and sit down at the lowest place, so that when your host comes, he may say to you, 'Friend, move up higher'; then you will be honored in the presence of all who sit at the table with you. ¹¹For all who exalt themselves will be humbled, and those who humble themselves will be exalted."

12 He said also to the one who had invited him, "When you give a luncheon or a dinner, do not invite your friends or your brothers or your relatives or rich neighbors, in case they may invite you in return, and you would be repaid. ¹³But when you give a banquet, invite the poor, the crippled, the lame, and the blind. ¹⁴And you will be blessed, because they cannot repay you, for you will be repaid at the resurrection of the righteous."

The Parable of the Great Dinner

15 One of the dinner guests, on hearing this, said to him, "Blessed is anyone who will eat bread in the kingdom of God!" ¹⁶Then Jesusᶜ said to him, "Someone gave a great dinner and invited many. ¹⁷At the time for the dinner he sent his slave to say to those who had been invited, 'Come; for everything is ready

ᵃ Gk lacks *for me*　ᵇ Other ancient authorities lack *the time comes when*
ᶜ Gk *he*　ᵈ Other ancient authorities read *a donkey*

13:31–35 Lament over Jerusalem

13:34 *Jerusalem, Jerusalem*—As Jesus continues towards *the city that kills the prophets*, readers are reminded that discipleship involves walking in the footsteps of a Messiah who will be rejected at the hands of the ignorant.

14:1–35 Table Fellowship and the Kingdom

In Judaism and early Christianity, the banquet was a metaphor for the heavenly or messianic feast. Sharing the meal table was also an im-

portant expression of hospitality. In this section, table fellowship is a metaphor for inclusion at the banquet over which the Lord presides. Special attention is given to the invitation extended to the marginalized, represented here as *the poor, the crippled, the lame, and the blind* (vv. 13, 21).

14:14 *They cannot repay you*—Genuine acts of hospitality and kindness are those that carry no expectation of reciprocity (cf. v. 12).

now.' ¹⁸ But they all alike began to make excuses. The first said to him, 'I have bought a piece of land, and I must go out and see it; please accept my regrets.' ¹⁹ Another said, 'I have bought five yoke of oxen, and I am going to try them out; please accept my regrets.' ²⁰ Another said, 'I have just been married, and therefore I cannot come.' ²¹ So the slave returned and reported this to his master. Then the owner of the house became angry and said to his slave, 'Go out at once into the streets and lanes of the town and bring in the poor, the crippled, the blind, and the lame.' ²² And the slave said, 'Sir, what you ordered has been done, and there is still room.' ²³ Then the master said to the slave, 'Go out into the roads and lanes, and compel people to come in, so that my house may be filled. ²⁴ For I tell you,^a none of those who were invited will taste my dinner.'"

The Cost of Discipleship

25 Now large crowds were traveling with him; and he turned and said to them, ²⁶ "Whoever comes to me and does not hate father and mother, wife and children, brothers and sisters, yes, and even life itself, cannot be my disciple. ²⁷ Whoever does not carry the cross and follow me cannot be my disciple. ²⁸ For which of you, intending to build a tower, does not first sit down and estimate the cost, to see whether he has enough to complete it? ²⁹ Otherwise, when he has laid a foundation and is not able to finish, all who see it will begin to ridicule him, ³⁰ saying, 'This fellow began to build and was not able to finish.' ³¹ Or what king, going out to wage war against another king, will not sit down first and consider whether he is able with ten thousand to

oppose the one who comes against him with twenty thousand? ³² If he cannot, then, while the other is still far away, he sends a delegation and asks for the terms of peace. ³³ So therefore, none of you can become my disciple if you do not give up all your possessions.

About Salt

34 "Salt is good; but if salt has lost its taste, how can its saltiness be restored?^b ³⁵ It is fit neither for the soil nor for the manure pile; they throw it away. Let anyone with ears to hear listen!"

The Parable of the Lost Sheep

15 Now all the tax collectors and sinners were coming near to listen to him. ² And the Pharisees and the scribes were grumbling and saying, "This fellow welcomes sinners and eats with them."

3 So he told them this parable: ⁴ "Which one of you, having a hundred sheep and losing one of them, does not leave the ninety-nine in the wilderness and go after the one that is lost until he finds it? ⁵ When he has found it, he lays it on his shoulders and rejoices. ⁶ And when he comes home, he calls together his friends and neighbors, saying to them, 'Rejoice with me, for I have found my sheep that was lost.' ⁷ Just so, I tell you, there will be more joy in heaven over one sinner who repents than over ninety-nine righteous persons who need no repentance.

The Parable of the Lost Coin

8 "Or what woman having ten silver coins,^c if she loses one of them, does not light a lamp, sweep the house, and

^a The Greek word for *you* here is plural ^b Or *how can it be used for seasoning?* ^c Gk *drachmas,* each worth about a day's wage for a laborer

---

14:24 None . . . invited—Overly occupied by less significant concerns, the invited guests fail to acknowledge and accept the invitation to participate in the kingdom. The parable warns against getting caught up in conventional and tragically misguided preoccupations.

15:1–32 Repentance and Rejoicing

In this series of parables, the joy of finding the lost is as extravagant as concern for the lost is excessive (v. 4, the sheep; v. 8, the coin). The parables underscore the abundant compassion that characterizes the kingdom of God and that Jesus' disciples are to emulate.

search carefully until she finds it? [9] When she has found it, she calls together her friends and neighbors, saying, 'Rejoice with me, for I have found the coin that I had lost.' [10] Just so, I tell you, there is joy in the presence of the angels of God over one sinner who repents."

The Parable of the Prodigal and His Brother

[11] Then Jesus[a] said, "There was a man who had two sons. [12] The younger of them said to his father, 'Father, give me the share of the property that will belong to me.' So he divided his property between them. [13] A few days later the younger son gathered all he had and traveled to a distant country, and there he squandered his property in dissolute living. [14] When he had spent everything, a severe famine took place throughout that country, and he began to be in need. [15] So he went and hired himself out to one of the citizens of that country, who sent him to his fields to feed the pigs. [16] He would gladly have filled himself with[b] the pods that the pigs were eating; and no one gave him anything. [17] But when he came to himself he said, 'How many of my father's hired hands have bread enough and to spare, but here I am dying of hunger! [18] I will get up and go to my father, and I will say to him, "Father, I have sinned against heaven and before you; [19] I am no longer worthy to be called your son; treat me like one of your hired hands."' [20] So he set off and went to his father. But while he was still far off, his father saw him and was filled with compassion; he ran and put his arms around him and kissed him. [21] Then the son said to him, 'Father, I have sinned against heaven and before you; I am no longer worthy to be called your son.'[c] [22] But the father said to his slaves, 'Quickly, bring out a robe—the

best one—and put it on him; put a ring on his finger and sandals on his feet. [23] And get the fatted calf and kill it, and let us eat and celebrate; [24] for this son of mine was dead and is alive again; he was lost and is found!' And they began to celebrate.

[25] "Now his elder son was in the field; and when he came and approached the house, he heard music and dancing. [26] He called one of the slaves and asked what was going on. [27] He replied, 'Your brother has come, and your father has killed the fatted calf, because he has got him back safe and sound.' [28] Then he became angry and refused to go in. His father came out and began to plead with him. [29] But he answered his father, 'Listen! For all these years I have been working like a slave for you, and I have never disobeyed your command; yet you have never given me even a young goat so that I might celebrate with my friends. [30] But when this son of yours came back, who has devoured your property with prostitutes, you killed the fatted calf for him!' [31] Then the father[a] said to him, 'Son, you are always with me, and all that is mine is yours. [32] But we had to celebrate and rejoice, because this brother of yours was dead and has come to life; he was lost and has been found.'"

The Parable of the Dishonest Manager

16 Then Jesus[a] said to the disciples, "There was a rich man who had a manager, and charges were brought to him that this man was squandering his property. [2] So he summoned him and said to him, 'What is this that I hear about you? Give me an accounting of your management, because you cannot be my manager any longer.' [3] Then

[a] Gk he [b] Other ancient authorities read *filled his stomach with* [c] Other ancient authorities add *Treat me like one of your hired servants*

15:32 *Celebrate and rejoice*—The ability to rejoice at the inclusion of the penitent and real change in the lives of others is a sign of true discipleship (cf. vv. 6, 9).

16:1–31 On Wealth, the Law, and the Prophets

the manager said to himself, 'What will I do, now that my master is taking the position away from me? I am not strong enough to dig, and I am ashamed to beg. **4** I have decided what to do so that, when I am dismissed as manager, people may welcome me into their homes.' **5** So, summoning his master's debtors one by one, he asked the first, 'How much do you owe my master?' **6** He answered, 'A hundred jugs of olive oil.' He said to him, 'Take your bill, sit down quickly, and make it fifty.' **7** Then he asked another, 'And how much do you owe?' He replied, 'A hundred containers of wheat.' He said to him, 'Take your bill and make it eighty.' **8** And his master commended the dishonest manager because he had acted shrewdly; for the children of this age are more shrewd in dealing with their own generation than are the children of light. **9** And I tell you, make friends for yourselves by means of dishonest wealth*a* so that when it is gone, they may welcome you into the eternal homes.*b*

10 "Whoever is faithful in a very little is faithful also in much; and whoever is dishonest in a very little is dishonest also in much. **11** If then you have not been faithful with the dishonest wealth,*a* who will entrust to you the true riches? **12** And if you have not been faithful with what belongs to another, who will give you what is your own? **13** No slave can serve two masters; for a slave will either hate the one and love the other, or be devoted to the one and despise the other. You cannot serve God and wealth."*a*

The Law and the Kingdom of God

14 The Pharisees, who were lovers of money, heard all this, and they ridiculed him. **15** So he said to them, "You are those who justify yourselves in the sight of others; but God knows your hearts; for what is prized by human beings is an abomination in the sight of God.

16 "The law and the prophets were in effect until John came; since then the good news of the kingdom of God is proclaimed, and everyone tries to enter it by force.*c* **17** But it is easier for heaven and earth to pass away, than for one stroke of a letter in the law to be dropped.

18 "Anyone who divorces his wife and marries another commits adultery, and whoever marries a woman divorced from her husband commits adultery.

The Rich Man and Lazarus

19 "There was a rich man who was dressed in purple and fine linen and who feasted sumptuously every day. **20** And at his gate lay a poor man named Lazarus, covered with sores, **21** who longed to satisfy his hunger with what fell from the rich man's table; even the dogs would come and lick his sores. **22** The poor man died and was carried away by the angels to be with Abraham.*d* The rich man also died and was buried. **23** In Hades, where he was being tormented, he looked up and saw Abraham far away with Lazarus by his side.*e* **24** He called out, 'Father Abraham, have mercy on me, and send Lazarus to dip the tip of his finger in water and cool my tongue; for I am in agony in these flames.' **25** But Abraham said, 'Child, remember that during your lifetime you received your good things, and Lazarus in like manner evil things; but now he is comforted here, and you are in agony. **26** Besides all this, between you and us a great chasm has been fixed, so that those who might want to pass from here to you cannot do so, and no one can cross from there to us.' **27** He

---

a Gk mammon *b* Gk tents *c* Or everyone is strongly urged to enter it *d* Gk to Abraham's bosom *e* Gk in his bosom

---

16:15 *Prized by human beings*—Jesus' words recall 12:21 and 34. One's greatest commitments, intentions, and values are reflected in the "treasures" that one accumulates. Jesus' reference to *abomination* underscores the opposition between human values and those of the kingdom.

16:25 *During your lifetime . . . but now*—The parable illustrates previous statements about the inversion of human circumstances that accompanies the dawning of the kingdom.

said, 'Then, father, I beg you to send him to my father's house— [28] for I have five brothers—that he may warn them, so that they will not also come into this place of torment.' [29] Abraham replied, 'They have Moses and the prophets; they should listen to them.' [30] He said, 'No, father Abraham; but if someone goes to them from the dead, they will repent.' [31] He said to him, 'If they do not listen to Moses and the prophets, neither will they be convinced even if someone rises from the dead.'"

Some Sayings of Jesus

17 Jesus[a] said to his disciples, "Occasions for stumbling are bound to come, but woe to anyone by whom they come! [2] It would be better for you if a millstone were hung around your neck and you were thrown into the sea than for you to cause one of these little ones to stumble. [3] Be on your guard! If another disciple[b] sins, you must rebuke the offender, and if there is repentance, you must forgive. [4] And if the same person sins against you seven times a day, and turns back to you seven times and says, 'I repent,' you must forgive."

[5] The apostles said to the Lord, "Increase our faith!" [6] The Lord replied, "If you had faith the size of a[c] mustard seed, you could say to this mulberry tree, 'Be uprooted and planted in the sea,' and it would obey you.

[7] "Who among you would say to your slave who has just come in from plowing or tending sheep in the field, 'Come here at once and take your place at the table'? [8] Would you not rather say to him, 'Prepare supper for me, put on your apron and serve me while I eat and drink; later you may eat and drink'? [9] Do you thank the slave for doing what was commanded? [10] So you also, when you have done all that you were ordered to do, say, 'We are worthless slaves; we have done only what we ought to have done!'"

Jesus Cleanses Ten Lepers

[11] On the way to Jerusalem Jesus[a] was going through the region between Samaria and Galilee. [12] As he entered a village, ten lepers[d] approached him. Keeping their distance, [13] they called out, saying, "Jesus, Master, have mercy on us!" [14] When he saw them, he said to them, "Go and show yourselves to the priests." And as they went, they were made clean. [15] Then one of them, when he saw that he was healed, turned back, praising God with a loud voice. [16] He prostrated himself at Jesus'[e] feet and thanked him. And he was a Samaritan. [17] Then Jesus asked, "Were not ten made clean? But the other nine, where are they? [18] Was none of them found to return and give praise to God except this foreigner?" [19] Then he said to him, "Get up and go on your way; your faith has made you well."

The Coming of the Kingdom

[20] Once Jesus[f] was asked by the Pharisees when the kingdom of God was coming, and he answered, "The kingdom of God is not coming with things that can be observed; [21] nor will they say, 'Look,

---

aGk He bGk your brother cGk faith as a grain of dThe terms leper and leprosy can refer to several diseases eGk his fGk he

---

16:31—Jesus' proclamation, mission, rejection, and resurrection are consistent with the traditions of *Moses and the prophets*.

17:1–10 Lessons to Jesus' Disciples

17:1–4—Jesus underscores the interdependence and reciprocity of the community of disciples. Discipleship consists of caring for one another, holding one another mutually accountable, and extending forgiveness (vv. 2–4).

17:10 *What we ought to have done*—Kingdom

ethics reflect the purposes for which humans were originally created. Jesus' followers should not seek reward for doing what is expected.

17:11–19 The Faith of the Samaritan

17:19 *Your faith has made you well*—Here again, a *Samaritan* (v. 16), or *foreigner* (v. 18) serves as the exemplar of faith.

17:20–37 The Coming Kingdom

17:21 *Among you*—The presence of the kingdom

here it is!' or 'There it is!' For, in fact, the kingdom of God is among*a* you."

22 Then he said to the disciples, "The days are coming when you will long to see one of the days of the Son of Man, and you will not see it. 23 They will say to you, 'Look there!' or 'Look here!' Do not go, do not set off in pursuit. 24 For as the lightning flashes and lights up the sky from one side to the other, so will the Son of Man be in his day.*b* 25 But first he must endure much suffering and be rejected by this generation. 26 Just as it was in the days of Noah, so too it will be in the days of the Son of Man. 27 They were eating and drinking, and marrying and being given in marriage, until the day Noah entered the ark, and the flood came and destroyed all of them. 28 Likewise, just as it was in the days of Lot: they were eating and drinking, buying and selling, planting and building, 29 but on the day that Lot left Sodom, it rained fire and sulfur from heaven and destroyed all of them 30 —it will be like that on the day that the Son of Man is revealed. 31 On that day, anyone on the housetop who has belongings in the house must not come down to take them away; and likewise anyone in the field must not turn back. 32 Remember Lot's wife. 33 Those who try to make their life secure will lose it, but those who lose their life will keep it. 34 I tell you, on that night there will be two in one bed; one will be taken and the other left. 35 There will be two women grinding meal together; one will be taken and the other left."*c* 37 Then they asked him, "Where, Lord?" He said to them, "Where the corpse is, there the vultures will gather."

The Parable of the Widow and the Unjust Judge

18 Then Jesus*d* told them a parable about their need to pray always and not to lose heart. 2 He said, "In a certain city there was a judge who neither feared God nor had respect for people. 3 In that city there was a widow who kept coming to him and saying, 'Grant me justice against my opponent.' 4 For a while he refused; but later he said to himself, 'Though I have no fear of God and no respect for anyone, 5 yet because this widow keeps bothering me, I will grant her justice, so that she may not wear me out by continually coming.'"*e* 6 And the Lord said, "Listen to what the unjust judge says. 7 And will not God grant justice to his chosen ones who cry to him day and night? Will he delay long in helping them? 8 I tell you, he will quickly grant justice to them. And yet, when the Son of Man comes, will he find faith on earth?"

The Parable of the Pharisee and the Tax Collector

9 He also told this parable to some who trusted in themselves that they were righteous and regarded others with contempt: 10 "Two men went up to the temple to pray, one a Pharisee and the other a tax collector. 11 The Pharisee, standing by himself, was praying thus, 'God, I thank you that I am not like other people: thieves, rogues, adulterers, or even like this tax collector. 12 I fast twice a week; I give a tenth of all my income.' 13 But the tax collector, standing far off, would not even look up to heaven, but

a Or within *b* Other ancient authorities lack *in his day* *c* Other ancient authorities add verse 36, *"Two will be in the field; one will be taken and the other left."* *d* Gk *he* *e* Or *so that she may not finally come and slap me in the face*

---

is perceived not by physical observation (v. 20), but by spiritual discernment and receptivity (cf. 2:35; 14:15–24).

17:32 *Lot's wife*—There is no "looking back" for Jesus' followers.

18:1–8 The Unjust Judge

18:3—The example of the *widow* again underscores concern for the marginalized.

18:9–17 On Humility

The parable of the Pharisee and the tax collector (vv. 10–14) and Jesus' reception of the children (vv. 16–17) teach against self-righteous disdain and dismissal of others.

was beating his breast and saying, 'God, be merciful to me, a sinner!' [14] I tell you, this man went down to his home justified rather than the other; for all who exalt themselves will be humbled, but all who humble themselves will be exalted."

Jesus Blesses Little Children

15 People were bringing even infants to him that he might touch them; and when the disciples saw it, they sternly ordered them not to do it. [16] But Jesus called for them and said, "Let the little children come to me, and do not stop them; for it is to such as these that the kingdom of God belongs. [17] Truly I tell you, whoever does not receive the kingdom of God as a little child will never enter it."

The Rich Ruler

18 A certain ruler asked him, "Good Teacher, what must I do to inherit eternal life?" [19] Jesus said to him, "Why do you call me good? No one is good but God alone. [20] You know the commandments: 'You shall not commit adultery; You shall not murder; You shall not steal; You shall not bear false witness; Honor your father and mother.' " [21] He replied, "I have kept all these since my youth." [22] When Jesus heard this, he said to him, "There is still one thing lacking. Sell all that you own and distribute the money[a] to the poor, and you will have treasure in heaven; then come, follow me." [23] But when he heard this, he became sad; for he was very rich. [24] Jesus looked at him and said, "How hard it is for those who have wealth to enter the kingdom of God! [25] Indeed, it is easier for a camel to go through the eye of a needle than for someone who is rich to enter the kingdom of God."

26 Those who heard it said, "Then who can be saved?" [27] He replied, "What is impossible for mortals is possible for God."

28 Then Peter said, "Look, we have left our homes and followed you." [29] And he said to them, "Truly I tell you, there is no one who has left house or wife or brothers or parents or children, for the sake of the kingdom of God, [30] who will not get back very much more in this age, and in the age to come eternal life."

A Third Time Jesus Foretells His Death and Resurrection

31 Then he took the twelve aside and said to them, "See, we are going up to Jerusalem, and everything that is written about the Son of Man by the prophets will be accomplished. [32] For he will be handed over to the Gentiles; and he will be mocked and insulted and spat upon. [33] After they have flogged him, they will kill him, and on the third day he will rise again." [34] But they understood nothing about all these things; in fact, what he said was hidden from them, and they did not grasp what was said.

Jesus Heals a Blind Beggar Near Jericho

35 As he approached Jericho, a blind man was sitting by the roadside begging. [36] When he heard a crowd going by, he asked what was happening. [37] They told him, "Jesus of Nazareth[b] is passing by." [38] Then he shouted, "Jesus, Son of David, have mercy on me!" [39] Those who were in front sternly ordered him to be quiet; but he shouted even more loudly, "Son of David, have mercy on me!" [40] Jesus stood still and ordered the man to be brought to him; and when he

---

[a] Gk lacks *the money*   [b] Gk *the Nazorean*

18:18–27 The Problem of Possessions (cf. 10:25–37)

Jesus reinforces that wealth is a serious stumbling block, for the accumulation of possessions is antithetical to meeting the needs of the poor and indicative of values that run counter to those of the kingdom. Worldly wealth and heavenly treasure (cf. v. 22) are mutually exclusive.

18:27 *What is impossible for mortals is possible for God*—Reminiscent of 1:37. Salvation of those laden with riches is as extraordinary as Mary's pregnancy, but nonetheless possible and equally owing to God's initiative.

18:28–19:10 On Following Jesus

came near, he asked him, [41] "What do you want me to do for you?" He said, "Lord, let me see again." [42] Jesus said to him, "Receive your sight; your faith has saved you." [43] Immediately he regained his sight and followed him, glorifying God; and all the people, when they saw it, praised God.

Jesus and Zacchaeus

19 He entered Jericho and was passing through it. [2] A man was there named Zacchaeus; he was a chief tax collector and was rich. [3] He was trying to see who Jesus was, but on account of the crowd he could not, because he was short in stature. [4] So he ran ahead and climbed a sycamore tree to see him, because he was going to pass that way. [5] When Jesus came to the place, he looked up and said to him, "Zacchaeus, hurry and come down; for I must stay at your house today." [6] So he hurried down and was happy to welcome him. [7] All who saw it began to grumble and said, "He has gone to be the guest of one who is a sinner." [8] Zacchaeus stood there and said to the Lord, "Look, half of my possessions, Lord, I will give to the poor; and if I have defrauded anyone of anything, I will pay back four times as much." [9] Then Jesus said to him, "Today salvation has come to this house, because he too is a son of Abraham. [10] For the Son of Man came to seek out and to save the lost."

The Parable of the Ten Pounds

11 As they were listening to this, he went on to tell a parable, because he was near Jerusalem, and because they supposed that the kingdom of God was to appear immediately. [12] So he said, "A nobleman went to a distant country to get royal power for himself and then return. [13] He summoned ten of his slaves, and gave them ten pounds,[a] and said to them, 'Do business with these until I come back.' [14] But the citizens of his country hated him and sent a delegation after him, saying, 'We do not want this man to rule over us.' [15] When he returned, having received royal power, he ordered these slaves, to whom he had given the money, to be summoned so that he might find out what they had gained by trading. [16] The first came forward and said, 'Lord, your pound has made ten more pounds.' [17] He said to him, 'Well done, good slave! Because you have been trustworthy in a very small thing, take charge of ten cities.' [18] Then the second came, saying, 'Lord, your pound has made five pounds.' [19] He said to him, 'And you, rule over five cities.' [20] Then the other came, saying, 'Lord, here is your pound. I wrapped it up in a piece of cloth, [21] for I was afraid of you, because you are a harsh man; you take what you did not deposit, and reap what you did not sow.' [22] He said to him, 'I will judge you by your own words, you wicked slave! You knew, did you, that I was a harsh man, taking what I did not deposit and reaping what I did not sow? [23] Why then did you not put my money into the bank? Then when I returned, I could have collected it with interest.' [24] He said to the bystanders, 'Take the pound from him and give it to the one who has ten pounds.' [25] (And they said to him, 'Lord, he has ten pounds!') [26] 'I tell you, to all those who have, more will be given; but from those who have nothing, even what they have will be taken away. [27] But as for these enemies of mine

[a] The mina, rendered here by *pound*, was about three months' wages for a laborer

---

19:1–10—A *chief tax collector* who *was rich* (v. 2), Zacchaeus, a foil to the rich men in 16:19–31 and 18:18–27, demonstrates that "nothing is impossible with God" (1:37; 18:27). Like Lazarus, he is counted a son of Abraham (19:9).

19:11–27 On Stewardship
Following the statement that Jesus' disciples ex-pected the imminent arrival of the kingdom, Jesus tells the parable of the nobleman. The disciples are to remain good stewards, no matter how long their wait for the kingdom may be. Far from being a means to an end, the faithful use of God's resources is itself an act of discipleship.

who did not want me to be king over them—bring them here and slaughter them in my presence.'"

Jesus' Triumphal Entry into Jerusalem

28 After he had said this, he went on ahead, going up to Jerusalem.

29 When he had come near Bethphage and Bethany, at the place called the Mount of Olives, he sent two of the disciples, [30] saying, "Go into the village ahead of you, and as you enter it you will find tied there a colt that has never been ridden. Untie it and bring it here. [31] If anyone asks you, 'Why are you untying it?' just say this, 'The Lord needs it.'" [32] So those who were sent departed and found it as he had told them. [33] As they were untying the colt, its owners asked them, "Why are you untying the colt?" [34] They said, "The Lord needs it." [35] Then they brought it to Jesus; and after throwing their cloaks on the colt, they set Jesus on it. [36] As he rode along, people kept spreading their cloaks on the road. [37] As he was now approaching the path down from the Mount of Olives, the whole multitude of the disciples began to praise God joyfully with a loud voice for all the deeds of power that they had seen, [38] saying,

"Blessed is the king
　who comes in the name of the
　　Lord!
Peace in heaven,
　and glory in the highest heaven!"

[39] Some of the Pharisees in the crowd said to him, "Teacher, order your disciples to stop." [40] He answered, "I tell you, if these were silent, the stones would shout out."

Jesus Weeps over Jerusalem

41 As he came near and saw the city, he wept over it, [42] saying, "If you, even you, had only recognized on this day the things that make for peace! But now they are hidden from your eyes. [43] Indeed, the days will come upon you, when your enemies will set up ramparts around you and surround you, and hem you in on every side. [44] They will crush you to the ground, you and your children within you, and they will not leave within you one stone upon another; because you did not recognize the time of your visitation from God."[a]

Jesus Cleanses the Temple

45 Then he entered the temple and began to drive out those who were selling things there; [46] and he said, "It is written,

'My house shall be a house of
　prayer';
but you have made it a den of
　robbers.'"

47 Every day he was teaching in the temple. The chief priests, the scribes, and the leaders of the people kept looking for a way to kill him; [48] but they did not find anything they could do, for all the people were spellbound by what they heard.

The Authority of Jesus Questioned

20 One day, as he was teaching the people in the temple and telling the good news, the chief priests and the scribes came with the elders [2] and said to him, "Tell us, by what authority are you doing these things? Who is

a Gk lacks from God

19:28–21:38 Jesus in Jerusalem

19:28–40 Jesus' Entry into Jerusalem

The royal procession depicted here, reminiscent of Zech. 9:9, illustrates Jesus' messianic identity in a manner befitting the Son of David (Luke 18:38).

19:39 Some of the Pharisees—Not all the Pharisees wished for Jesus' followers to cease. Together with references to the *whole multitude of the disciples* (v. 37), the story presents the

picture of a people divided in their responses to Jesus (cf. 2:35).

19:41–48 Opposition in Jerusalem

19:42 Things that make for peace—Despite its pattern of rejecting God's prophets (13:34), Jesus longs for Jerusalem to recognize "the way of peace" of which Zechariah spoke in 1:79 and which, according to Luke, is fully revealed only after the resurrection.

20:1–21:4 Opposition at the Temple

it who gave you this authority?" ³ He answered them, "I will also ask you a question, and you tell me: ⁴ Did the baptism of John come from heaven, or was it of human origin?" ⁵ They discussed it with one another, saying, "If we say, 'From heaven,' he will say, 'Why did you not believe him?' ⁶ But if we say, 'Of human origin,' all the people will stone us; for they are convinced that John was a prophet." ⁷ So they answered that they did not know where it came from. ⁸ Then Jesus said to them, "Neither will I tell you by what authority I am doing these things."

The Parable of the Wicked Tenants

9 He began to tell the people this parable: "A man planted a vineyard, and leased it to tenants, and went to another country for a long time. ¹⁰ When the season came, he sent a slave to the tenants in order that they might give him his share of the produce of the vineyard; but the tenants beat him and sent him away empty-handed. ¹¹ Next he sent another slave; that one also they beat and insulted and sent away empty-handed. ¹² And he sent still a third; this one also they wounded and threw out. ¹³ Then the owner of the vineyard said, 'What shall I do? I will send my beloved son; perhaps they will respect him.' ¹⁴ But when the tenants saw him, they discussed it among themselves and said, 'This is the heir; let us kill him so that the inheritance may be ours.' ¹⁵ So they threw him out of the vineyard and killed him. What then will the owner of the vineyard do to them? ¹⁶ He will come and destroy those tenants and give the vineyard to others." When they heard this, they said, "Heaven forbid!" ¹⁷ But he looked at them and said, "What then does this text mean:

'The stone that the builders rejected
    has become the cornerstone'?ᵃ
¹⁸ Everyone who falls on that stone will be broken to pieces; and it will crush anyone on whom it falls." ¹⁹ When the scribes and chief priests realized that he had told this parable against them, they wanted to lay hands on him at that very hour, but they feared the people.

The Question about Paying Taxes

20 So they watched him and sent spies who pretended to be honest, in order to trap him by what he said, so as to hand him over to the jurisdiction and authority of the governor. ²¹ So they asked him, "Teacher, we know that you are right in what you say and teach, and you show deference to no one, but teach the way of God in accordance with truth. ²² Is it lawful for us to pay taxes to the emperor, or not?" ²³ But he perceived their craftiness and said to them, ²⁴ "Show me a denarius. Whose head and whose title does it bear?" They said, "The emperor's." ²⁵ He said to them, "Then give to the emperor the things that are the emperor's, and to God the things that are God's." ²⁶ And they were not able in the presence of the people to trap him by what he said; and being amazed by his answer, they became silent.

The Question about the Resurrection

27 Some Sadducees, those who say there is no resurrection, came to him ²⁸ and asked him a question, "Teacher, Moses wrote for us that if a man's brother dies, leaving a wife but no children, the manᵇ shall marry the widow and raise up children for his brother. ²⁹ Now there were seven brothers; the first married, and died childless; ³⁰ then the second ³¹ and the third married her, and so in

ᵃ Or keystone ᵇ Gk his brother

20:9–19—Jesus' parable is in keeping with a tradition of prophetic judgments against those who fail to recognize or attend to God's prophets. Far from an indictment of the whole Jewish people, the parable is a critique of those religious professionals who oppose Jesus.

20:20–44—In meeting a series of challenges, Jesus frustrates the efforts of those religious leaders seeking to corner him publicly and turn him over to the Roman authorities (vv. 26, 40).

the same way all seven died childless. ³²Finally the woman also died. ³³In the resurrection, therefore, whose wife will the woman be? For the seven had married her."

34 Jesus said to them, "Those who belong to this age marry and are given in marriage; ³⁵but those who are considered worthy of a place in that age and in the resurrection from the dead neither marry nor are given in marriage. ³⁶Indeed they cannot die anymore, because they are like angels and are children of God, being children of the resurrection. ³⁷And the fact that the dead are raised Moses himself showed, in the story about the bush, where he speaks of the Lord as the God of Abraham, the God of Isaac, and the God of Jacob. ³⁸Now he is God not of the dead, but of the living; for to him all of them are alive." ³⁹Then some of the scribes answered, "Teacher, you have spoken well." ⁴⁰For they no longer dared to ask him another question.

The Question about David's Son

41 Then he said to them, "How can they say that the Messiah*a* is David's son? ⁴²For David himself says in the book of Psalms,

'The Lord said to my Lord,
"Sit at my right hand,
⁴³   until I make your enemies your
            footstool."'

⁴⁴David thus calls him Lord; so how can he be his son?"

Jesus Denounces the Scribes

45 In the hearing of all the people he said to the*b* disciples, ⁴⁶"Beware of the scribes, who like to walk around in long robes, and love to be greeted with respect in the marketplaces, and to have the best seats in the synagogues and places of honor at banquets. ⁴⁷They

devour widows' houses and for the sake of appearance say long prayers. They will receive the greater condemnation."

The Widow's Offering

21 He looked up and saw rich people putting their gifts into the treasury; ²he also saw a poor widow put in two small copper coins. ³He said, "Truly I tell you, this poor widow has put in more than all of them; ⁴for all of them have contributed out of their abundance, but she out of her poverty has put in all she had to live on."

The Destruction of the Temple Foretold

5 When some were speaking about the temple, how it was adorned with beautiful stones and gifts dedicated to God, he said, ⁶"As for these things that you see, the days will come when not one stone will be left upon another; all will be thrown down."

Signs and Persecutions

7 They asked him, "Teacher, when will this be, and what will be the sign that this is about to take place?" ⁸And he said, "Beware that you are not led astray; for many will come in my name and say, 'I am he!'*c* and, 'The time is near!'*d* Do not go after them.

9 "When you hear of wars and insurrections, do not be terrified; for these things must take place first, but the end will not follow immediately." ¹⁰Then he said to them, "Nation will rise against nation, and kingdom against kingdom; ¹¹there will be great earthquakes, and in various places famines and plagues; and there will be dreadful portents and great signs from heaven.

12 "But before all this occurs, they will arrest you and persecute you; they

---

a Or the Christ   *b* Other ancient authorities read his   *c* Gk I am   *d* Or at hand

---

21:4 *Abundance . . . poverty*—The widow's gift surpasses the offerings of the rich because it expresses greater commitment and sacrifice. Since her gift is no cause for public honor, neither is it diluted by self-interest.

21:5–38 Warning
21:8 *Led astray*—In other words, don't be fooled!

will hand you over to synagogues and prisons, and you will be brought before kings and governors because of my name. ¹³ This will give you an opportunity to testify. ¹⁴ So make up your minds not to prepare your defense in advance; ¹⁵ for I will give you words*a* and a wisdom that none of your opponents will be able to withstand or contradict. ¹⁶ You will be betrayed even by parents and brothers, by relatives and friends; and they will put some of you to death. ¹⁷ You will be hated by all because of my name. ¹⁸ But not a hair of your head will perish. ¹⁹ By your endurance you will gain your souls.

The Destruction of Jerusalem Foretold

20 "When you see Jerusalem surrounded by armies, then know that its desolation has come near.*b* ²¹ Then those in Judea must flee to the mountains, and those inside the city must leave it, and those out in the country must not enter it; ²² for these are days of vengeance, as a fulfillment of all that is written. ²³ Woe to those who are pregnant and to those who are nursing infants in those days! For there will be great distress on the earth and wrath against this people; ²⁴ they will fall by the edge of the sword and be taken away as captives among all nations; and Jerusalem will be trampled on by the Gentiles, until the times of the Gentiles are fulfilled.

The Coming of the Son of Man

25 "There will be signs in the sun, the moon, and the stars, and on the earth distress among nations confused by the roaring of the sea and the waves. ²⁶ People will faint from fear and foreboding of what is coming upon the world, for the powers of the heavens will be shaken. ²⁷ Then they will see 'the Son of Man coming in a cloud' with power and great glory. ²⁸ Now when these things begin to take place, stand up and raise your heads, because your redemption is drawing near."

The Lesson of the Fig Tree

29 Then he told them a parable: "Look at the fig tree and all the trees; ³⁰ as soon as they sprout leaves you can see for yourselves and know that summer is already near. ³¹ So also, when you see these things taking place, you know that the kingdom of God is near. ³² Truly I tell you, this generation will not pass away until all things have taken place. ³³ Heaven and earth will pass away, but my words will not pass away.

Exhortation to Watch

34 "Be on guard so that your hearts are not weighed down with dissipation and drunkenness and the worries of this life, and that day does not catch you unexpectedly, ³⁵ like a trap. For it will come upon all who live on the face of the whole earth. ³⁶ Be alert at all times, praying that you may have the strength to escape all these things that will take place, and to stand before the Son of Man."

37 Every day he was teaching in the temple, and at night he would go out and spend the night on the Mount of Olives, as it was called. ³⁸ And all the people would get up early in the morning to listen to him in the temple.

The Plot to Kill Jesus

22 Now the festival of Unleavened Bread, which is called the Passover, was near. ² The chief priests and the scribes were looking for a way to put Jesus*c* to death, for they were afraid of the people.

3 Then Satan entered into Judas called

---

a Gk *a mouth*   *b* Or *is at hand*   *c* Gk *him*

21:13 *Opportunity to testify*—Bold speech expresses faith and divine guidance (cf. vv. 14–15).
22:1–23:56 *The Death of Jesus*
22:1–6 Betrayal

22:3 *Satan*—The "opportune time" (4:13) for Satan arrives. Disciples must be prepared for persistent opposition to the ways of the kingdom.

Iscariot, who was one of the twelve; [4] he went away and conferred with the chief priests and officers of the temple police about how he might betray him to them. [5] They were greatly pleased and agreed to give him money. [6] So he consented and began to look for an opportunity to betray him to them when no crowd was present.

The Preparation of the Passover

[7] Then came the day of Unleavened Bread, on which the Passover lamb had to be sacrificed. [8] So Jesus[a] sent Peter and John, saying, "Go and prepare the Passover meal for us that we may eat it." [9] They asked him, "Where do you want us to make preparations for it?" [10] "Listen," he said to them, "when you have entered the city, a man carrying a jar of water will meet you; follow him into the house he enters [11] and say to the owner of the house, 'The teacher asks you, "Where is the guest room, where I may eat the Passover with my disciples?"' [12] He will show you a large room upstairs, already furnished. Make preparations for us there." [13] So they went and found everything as he had told them; and they prepared the Passover meal.

The Institution of the Lord's Supper

[14] When the hour came, he took his place at the table, and the apostles with him. [15] He said to them, "I have eagerly desired to eat this Passover with you before I suffer; [16] for I tell you, I will not eat it[b] until it is fulfilled in the kingdom of God." [17] Then he took a cup, and after giving thanks he said, "Take this and divide it among yourselves; [18] for I tell you that from now on I will not drink of the fruit of the vine until the kingdom of God comes." [19] Then he took a loaf of bread, and when he had given thanks, he broke it and gave it to them, saying, "This is my body, which is given for you. Do this in remembrance of me." [20] And he did the same with the cup after supper, saying, "This cup that is poured out for you is the new covenant in my blood.[c] [21] But see, the one who betrays me is with me, and his hand is on the table. [22] For the Son of Man is going as it has been determined, but woe to that one by whom he is betrayed!" [23] Then they began to ask one another which one of them it could be who would do this.

The Dispute about Greatness

[24] A dispute also arose among them as to which one of them was to be regarded as the greatest. [25] But he said to them, "The kings of the Gentiles lord it over them; and those in authority over them are called benefactors. [26] But not so with you; rather the greatest among you must become like the youngest, and the leader like one who serves. [27] For who is greater, the one who is at the table or the one who serves? Is it not the one at the table? But I am among you as one who serves.

[28] "You are those who have stood by me in my trials; [29] and I confer on you, just as my Father has conferred on me, a kingdom, [30] so that you may eat and drink at my table in my kingdom, and you will sit on thrones judging the twelve tribes of Israel.

[a] Gk he [b] Other ancient authorities read *never eat it again* [c] Other ancient authorities lack, in whole or in part, verses 19b-20 (*which is given . . . in my blood*)

22:5 *Money*—The lure of wealth is implicated in Judas's betrayal of Jesus.

22:7–38 The Passover Table

22:22 *As it has been determined*—The rejection of the Son of Man unfolds according to the divine plan that also determined the way of a long line of prophets who, having first been rejected out of ignorance, returned for a second visitation among the people. For Luke, human ignorance is tragic but unremarkable in human history. What is remarkable is the persistent compassion and mercy God repeatedly visits upon the people through God's prophets.

22:28 *Stood by me in my trials*—Having patiently endured with Jesus and borne the fruit of faith, the disciples' place in the kingdom is assured (v. 30; cf. 8:12, 15). Faith is never in vain.

22:30 *My table*—Jesus fulfills the promise of continued table fellowship in 24:36–43.

Jesus Predicts Peter's Denial

31 "Simon, Simon, listen! Satan has demanded[a] to sift all of you like wheat, 32 but I have prayed for you that your own faith may not fail; and you, when once you have turned back, strengthen your brothers." 33 And he said to him, "Lord, I am ready to go with you to prison and to death!" 34 Jesus[b] said, "I tell you, Peter, the cock will not crow this day, until you have denied three times that you know me."

Purse, Bag, and Sword

35 He said to them, "When I sent you out without a purse, bag, or sandals, did you lack anything?" They said, "No, not a thing." 36 He said to them, "But now, the one who has a purse must take it, and likewise a bag. And the one who has no sword must sell his cloak and buy one. 37 For I tell you, this scripture must be fulfilled in me, 'And he was counted among the lawless'; and indeed what is written about me is being fulfilled." 38 They said, "Lord, look, here are two swords." He replied, "It is enough."

Jesus Prays on the Mount of Olives

39 He came out and went, as was his custom, to the Mount of Olives; and the disciples followed him. 40 When he reached the place, he said to them, "Pray that you may not come into the time of trial."[c] 41 Then he withdrew from them about a stone's throw, knelt down, and prayed, 42 "Father, if you are willing, remove this cup from me; yet, not my will but yours be done." [[43 Then an angel from heaven appeared to him and gave him strength. 44 In his anguish he prayed more earnestly, and his sweat became like great drops of blood falling down on the ground.]][d] 45 When he got up from prayer, he came to the disciples and found them sleeping because of grief, 46 and he said to them, "Why are you sleeping? Get up and pray that you may not come into the time of trial."[c]

The Betrayal and Arrest of Jesus

47 While he was still speaking, suddenly a crowd came, and the one called Judas, one of the twelve, was leading them. He approached Jesus to kiss him; 48 but Jesus said to him, "Judas, is it with a kiss that you are betraying the Son of Man?" 49 When those who were around him saw what was coming, they asked, "Lord, should we strike with the sword?" 50 Then one of them struck the slave of the high priest and cut off his right ear. 51 But Jesus said, "No more of this!" And he touched his ear and healed him. 52 Then Jesus said to the chief priests, the officers of the temple police, and the elders who had come for him, "Have you come out with swords and clubs as if I were a bandit? 53 When I was with you day after day in the temple, you did not lay hands on me. But this is your hour, and the power of darkness!"

Peter Denies Jesus

54 Then they seized him and led him away, bringing him into the high priest's house. But Peter was following at a distance. 55 When they had kindled a fire in the middle of the courtyard and sat down together, Peter sat among them. 56 Then a servant-girl, seeing him in the

---

[a] Or has obtained permission [b] Gk He [c] Or into temptation [d] Other ancient authorities lack verses 43 and 44

22:32 *Prayed*—Jesus prays for those whom *Satan* (v. 31) tests. He neither abandons his disciples to temptation, nor forgets them when they fail. Rather, he encourages them to turn back and *strengthen* others.

22:38 *Enough*—The only reason for the swords is the fulfillment of Scripture (vv. 37–38).

22:39–53 On the Mount of Olives

22:40 *Time of trial*—Jesus' admonition to the disciples is reminiscent of his prayer in 11:4. The model of obedience for his disciples, he then prays, *Not my will, but yours be done* (v. 42).

22:51 *Healed him*—Even now, Jesus opposes violence and extends forgiveness to his enemies. At *the time of trial* (v. 40), Jesus embodies the way of God.

22:54–65 Peter's Denial

firelight, stared at him and said, "This man also was with him." [57] But he denied it, saying, "Woman, I do not know him." [58] A little later someone else, on seeing him, said, "You also are one of them." But Peter said, "Man, I am not!" [59] Then about an hour later still another kept insisting, "Surely this man also was with him; for he is a Galilean." [60] But Peter said, "Man, I do not know what you are talking about!" At that moment, while he was still speaking, the cock crowed. [61] The Lord turned and looked at Peter. Then Peter remembered the word of the Lord, how he had said to him, "Before the cock crows today, you will deny me three times." [62] And he went out and wept bitterly.

The Mocking and Beating of Jesus

63 Now the men who were holding Jesus began to mock him and beat him; [64] they also blindfolded him and kept asking him, "Prophesy! Who is it that struck you?" [65] They kept heaping many other insults on him.

Jesus before the Council

66 When day came, the assembly of the elders of the people, both chief priests and scribes, gathered together, and they brought him to their council. [67] They said, "If you are the Messiah,[a] tell us." He replied, "If I tell you, you will not believe; [68] and if I question you, you will not answer. [69] But from now on the Son of Man will be seated at the right hand of the power of God." [70] All of them asked, "Are you, then, the Son of God?" He said to them, "You say that I am." [71] Then they said, "What further testimony do we need? We have heard it ourselves from his own lips!"

Jesus before Pilate

23 Then the assembly rose as a body and brought Jesus[b] before Pilate. [2] They began to accuse him, saying, "We found this man perverting our nation, forbidding us to pay taxes to the emperor, and saying that he himself is the Messiah, a king."[c] [3] Then Pilate asked him, "Are you the king of the Jews?" He answered, "You say so." [4] Then Pilate said to the chief priests and the crowds, "I find no basis for an accusation against this man." [5] But they were insistent and said, "He stirs up the people by teaching throughout all Judea, from Galilee where he began even to this place."

Jesus before Herod

6 When Pilate heard this, he asked whether the man was a Galilean. [7] And when he learned that he was under Herod's jurisdiction, he sent him off to Herod, who was himself in Jerusalem at that time. [8] When Herod saw Jesus, he was very glad, for he had been wanting to see him for a long time, because he had heard about him and was hoping to see him perform some sign. [9] He questioned him at some length, but Jesus[d] gave him no answer. [10] The chief priests and the scribes stood by, vehemently accusing him. [11] Even Herod with his soldiers treated him with contempt and mocked him; then he put an elegant robe on him, and sent him back to Pilate. [12] That same day Herod and Pilate

[a] Or the Christ [b] Gk him [c] Or is an anointed king [d] Gk he

---

22:61 *Word of the Lord*—Peter is indicted by Jesus' words in v. 34.

22:66–71 Jesus Before the Assembly

The *council* focuses on the royal titles for Jesus, *Messiah* (v. 67) and *Son of God* (v. 70). By not calling himself Messiah (vv. 67–68), Jesus remains innocent of the charge for which he is killed (23:38, 47).

23:1–25 Jesus before Pilate and Herod

23:3 *King of the Jews*—Pilate, the Roman gov-ernor, focuses on the specific charge for which Jesus will be killed.

23:5 *Stirs up the people*—The crowds and leaders who are present accuse Jesus of creating an atmosphere of unrest and potential insurrection.

23:12 *Friends*—The newly established friendship of former enemies, Pilate and the tetrarch, Herod Antipas, underscores their shared culpability (cf. Acts 4:26–27).

became friends with each other; before this they had been enemies.

Jesus Sentenced to Death

13 Pilate then called together the chief priests, the leaders, and the people, [14] and said to them, "You brought me this man as one who was perverting the people; and here I have examined him in your presence and have not found this man guilty of any of your charges against him. [15] Neither has Herod, for he sent him back to us. Indeed, he has done nothing to deserve death. [16] I will therefore have him flogged and release him."[a]

18 Then they all shouted out together, "Away with this fellow! Release Barabbas for us!" [19] (This was a man who had been put in prison for an insurrection that had taken place in the city, and for murder.) [20] Pilate, wanting to release Jesus, addressed them again; [21] but they kept shouting, "Crucify, crucify him!" [22] A third time he said to them, "Why, what evil has he done? I have found in him no ground for the sentence of death; I will therefore have him flogged and then release him." [23] But they kept urgently demanding with loud shouts that he should be crucified; and their voices prevailed. [24] So Pilate gave his verdict that their demand should be granted. [25] He released the man they asked for, the one who had been put in prison for insurrection and murder, and he handed Jesus over as they wished.

The Crucifixion of Jesus

26 As they led him away, they seized a man, Simon of Cyrene, who was coming from the country, and they laid the cross on him, and made him carry it behind Jesus. [27] A great number of the people followed him, and among them were women who were beating their breasts and wailing for him. [28] But Jesus turned to them and said, "Daughters of Jerusalem, do not weep for me, but weep for yourselves and for your children. [29] For the days are surely coming when they will say, 'Blessed are the barren, and the wombs that never bore, and the breasts that never nursed.' [30] Then they will begin to say to the mountains, 'Fall on us'; and to the hills, 'Cover us.' [31] For if they do this when the wood is green, what will happen when it is dry?"

32 Two others also, who were criminals, were led away to be put to death with him. [33] When they came to the place that is called The Skull, they crucified Jesus[b] there with the criminals, one on his right and one on his left. [[[34] Then Jesus said, "Father, forgive them; for they do not know what they are doing."]][c] And they cast lots to divide his clothing. [35] And the people stood by, watching; but the leaders scoffed at him, saying, "He saved others; let him save himself if he is the Messiah[d] of God, his chosen one!" [36] The soldiers also mocked him,

[a] Here, or after verse 19, other ancient authorities add verse 17, *Now he was obliged to release someone for them at the festival* [b] Gk *him* [c] Other ancient authorities lack the sentence *Then Jesus . . . what they are doing* [d] Or the *Christ*

23:25—Although he presents Pilate as acting according to the crowd's wishes, Luke places responsibility for sentencing Jesus to death squarely at the feet of the Roman governor. The immorality of Pilate's action is highlighted by the fact that he thrice declares Jesus innocent (vv. 4, 15, 22). Jesus' tragic death is that of an innocent man (cf. v. 47), thus it fulfills the prophetic pattern that frames Luke's entire two-volume narrative.

23:26–56 Jesus' Death

23:26–27 *Simon*—As one who carries the cross for Jesus, Simon, a Jew from Cyrene, embodies the image of discipleship of which Jesus spoke in 9:23.

23:34 *Father, forgive them; for they do not know what they are doing*—Jesus' prayer reminds the reader that those who contributed to and participated in the death of Jesus did so out of ignorance, which, though tragic, is unremarkable in human history. What is remarkable is God's forgiveness and compassion. Thus the theme of forgiveness, so central to the gospel, reaches its fullest expression here. Discipleship is cast, then, not as a badge of honor over and against others, but as participation in and recognition of God's limitless and life-giving compassion.

coming up and offering him sour wine, [37] and saying, "If you are the King of the Jews, save yourself!" [38] There was also an inscription over him,[a] "This is the King of the Jews."

39 One of the criminals who were hanged there kept deriding[b] him and saying, "Are you not the Messiah?[c] Save yourself and us!" [40] But the other rebuked him, saying, "Do you not fear God, since you are under the same sentence of condemnation? [41] And we indeed have been condemned justly, for we are getting what we deserve for our deeds, but this man has done nothing wrong." [42] Then he said, "Jesus, remember me when you come into[d] your kingdom." [43] He replied, "Truly I tell you, today you will be with me in Paradise."

The Death of Jesus

44 It was now about noon, and darkness came over the whole land[e] until three in the afternoon, [45] while the sun's light failed;[f] and the curtain of the temple was torn in two. [46] Then Jesus, crying with a loud voice, said, "Father, into your hands I commend my spirit." Having said this, he breathed his last. [47] When the centurion saw what had taken place, he praised God and said, "Certainly this man was innocent."[g] [48] And when all the crowds who had gathered there for this spectacle saw what had taken place, they returned home, beating their breasts. [49] But all his acquaintances, including the women who had followed him from Galilee, stood at a distance, watching these things.

The Burial of Jesus

50 Now there was a good and righteous man named Joseph, who, though a member of the council, [51] had not agreed to their plan and action. He came from the Jewish town of Arimathea, and he was waiting expectantly for the kingdom of God. [52] This man went to Pilate and asked for the body of Jesus. [53] Then he took it down, wrapped it in a linen cloth, and laid it in a rock-hewn tomb where no one had ever been laid. [54] It was the day of Preparation, and the sabbath was beginning.[h] [55] The women who had come with him from Galilee followed, and they saw the tomb and how his body was laid. [56] Then they returned, and prepared spices and ointments.

On the sabbath they rested according to the commandment.

The Resurrection of Jesus

24 But on the first day of the week, at early dawn, they came to the tomb, taking the spices that they had prepared. [2] They found the stone rolled away from the tomb, [3] but when they went in, they did not find the body.[i] [4] While they were perplexed about this, suddenly two men in dazzling clothes stood beside them. [5] The women[j] were terrified and bowed their faces to the ground, but the men[k] said to them, "Why do you look for the living among the dead? He is not here, but has risen.[l] [6] Remember how he told you, while he was still in Galilee, [7] that the Son of Man must be handed over to sinners, and be crucified, and on the third day

---

a Other ancient authorities add *written in Greek and Latin and Hebrew* (that is, *Aramaic*) b Or *blaspheming* c Or *the Christ* d Other ancient authorities read *in* e Or *earth* f Or *the sun was eclipsed.* Other ancient authorities read *the sun was darkened* g Or *righteous* h Gk *was dawning* i Other ancient authorities add *of the Lord Jesus* j Gk *They* k Gk *but they* l Other ancient authorities lack *He is not here, but has risen*

23:37–38 *King of the Jews*—The charge for which Jesus was unjustly condemned.

23:41 *Nothing wrong*—The criminal also declares Jesus' innocence.

23:42–43 *Your kingdom . . . Paradise*—The criminal's example makes clear that the essence of the kingdom Jesus has preached and embodies is restoration and forgiveness.

23:47 *Innocent*—The centurion's declaration, unique to Luke, confirms Jesus' innocence. Like all the prophets before him, Jesus is rejected out of tragic ignorance.

23:50 *Joseph*—Joseph of Arimathea is an important example of a *good and righteous . . . member of the council.*

24:1–53 The Risen Jesus

24:1–12 The Empty Tomb

rise again." [8] Then they remembered his words, [9] and returning from the tomb, they told all this to the eleven and to all the rest. [10] Now it was Mary Magdalene, Joanna, Mary the mother of James, and the other women with them who told this to the apostles. [11] But these words seemed to them an idle tale, and they did not believe them. [12] But Peter got up and ran to the tomb; stooping and looking in, he saw the linen cloths by themselves; then he went home, amazed at what had happened.[a]

The Walk to Emmaus

13 Now on that same day two of them were going to a village called Emmaus, about seven miles[b] from Jerusalem, [14] and talking with each other about all these things that had happened. [15] While they were talking and discussing, Jesus himself came near and went with them, [16] but their eyes were kept from recognizing him. [17] And he said to them, "What are you discussing with each other while you walk along?" They stood still, looking sad.[c] [18] Then one of them, whose name was Cleopas, answered him, "Are you the only stranger in Jerusalem who does not know the things that have taken place there in these days?" [19] He asked them, "What things?" They replied, "The things about Jesus of Nazareth,[d] who was a prophet mighty in deed and word before God and all the people, [20] and how our chief priests and leaders handed him over to be condemned to death and crucified him. [21] But we had hoped that he was the one to redeem Israel.[e] Yes, and besides all this, it is now the third day since these things took place. [22] Moreover, some women of our group astounded us. They were at the tomb early this morning, [23] and when they did not find his body there, they came back and told us that they had indeed seen a vision of angels who said that he was alive. [24] Some of those who were with us went to the tomb and found it just as the women had said; but they did not see him." [25] Then he said to them, "Oh, how foolish you are, and how slow of heart to believe all that the prophets have declared! [26] Was it not necessary that the Messiah[f] should suffer these things and then enter into his glory?" [27] Then beginning with Moses and all the prophets, he interpreted to them the things about himself in all the scriptures.

28 As they came near the village to which they were going, he walked ahead as if he were going on. [29] But they urged him strongly, saying, "Stay with us, because it is almost evening and the day is now nearly over." So he went in to stay with them. [30] When he was at the table with them, he took bread, blessed and broke it, and gave it to them. [31] Then their eyes were opened, and they recognized him; and he vanished from their sight. [32] They said to each other, "Were not our hearts burning within us[g] while he was talking to us on the road, while he was opening the scriptures

[a] Other ancient authorities lack verse 12   [b] Gk *sixty stadia;* other ancient authorities read *a hundred sixty stadia*   [c] Other ancient authorities read *walk along, looking sad?"*   [d] Other ancient authorities read *Jesus the Nazorean*   [e] Or *to set Israel free*   [f] Or *the Christ*   [g] Other ancient authorities lack *within us*

24:8–9 *Remembered . . . told*—By remembering Jesus' words and telling what they have witnessed, the women are ideal disciples.

24:13–35 Fellowship with the Risen Lord

24:25 *Slow of heart*—Slowness of heart is characteristic of many.

24:26 *Necessary that the Messiah should suffer all these things and then enter into his glory*—All that has happened has unfolded according to the plan of God.

24:27 *Beginning with Moses and all the*

prophets—In terms of both his ministry and his rejection and later acceptance, Jesus' mission is rooted in Israel's prophetic tradition (cf. v. 25; 16:31; 24:44).

24:30 *At the table*—The scene fulfills Jesus' promise in 22:30.

24:31 *Their eyes were opened*—Jesus is made known through the Scriptures and the intimacy of table fellowship (vv. 27, 32, 35, 44–45). A hallmark of the believing community, Jesus' presence is made known in commensality.

to us?" **33** That same hour they got up and returned to Jerusalem; and they found the eleven and their companions gathered together. **34** They were saying, "The Lord has risen indeed, and he has appeared to Simon!" **35** Then they told what had happened on the road, and how he had been made known to them in the breaking of the bread.

Jesus Appears to His Disciples

36 While they were talking about this, Jesus himself stood among them and said to them, "Peace be with you."*a* **37** They were startled and terrified, and thought that they were seeing a ghost. **38** He said to them, "Why are you frightened, and why do doubts arise in your hearts? **39** Look at my hands and my feet; see that it is I myself. Touch me and see; for a ghost does not have flesh and bones as you see that I have." **40** And when he had said this, he showed them his hands and his feet.*b* **41** While in their joy they were disbelieving and still wondering, he said to them, "Have you anything here to eat?" **42** They gave him a piece of broiled fish, **43** and he took it and ate in their presence.

44 Then he said to them, "These are my words that I spoke to you while I was still with you—that everything written about me in the law of Moses, the prophets, and the psalms must be fulfilled." **45** Then he opened their minds to understand the scriptures, **46** and he said to them, "Thus it is written, that the Messiah*c* is to suffer and to rise from the dead on the third day, **47** and that repentance and forgiveness of sins is to be proclaimed in his name to all nations, beginning from Jerusalem. **48** You are witnesses*d* of these things. **49** And see, I am sending upon you what my Father promised; so stay here in the city until you have been clothed with power from on high."

The Ascension of Jesus

50 Then he led them out as far as Bethany, and, lifting up his hands, he blessed them. **51** While he was blessing them, he withdrew from them and was carried up into heaven.*e* **52** And they worshiped him, and*f* returned to Jerusalem with great joy; **53** and they were continually in the temple blessing God.*g*

a Other ancient authorities lack *and said to them, "Peace be with you."*
b Other ancient authorities lack verse 40　*c* Or *the Christ*　*d* Or *nations. Beginning from Jerusalem* **48** *you are witnesses*　*e* Other ancient authorities lack *and was carried up into heaven*　*f* Other ancient authorities lack *worshiped him, and*　*g* Other ancient authorities add *Amen*

24:36–53 Commissioning the Disciples

24:36 *Peace*—Since the beginning of the Gospel, the proclamation of peace has remained central to Jesus' purpose (cf. 1:79; 2:14, 29; 7:50; 8:48; 19:38, 42).

24:44–45 *The law of Moses, the prophets, and the psalms . . . the scriptures*—The teaching reflects the early Christian understanding of Jesus as the fulfillment of and key to understanding the Scriptures (cf. vv. 27, 32, 35). One of the most significant lessons in Luke, the story of the risen Jesus and the Jesus movement's experience of him serves as the norm for faith, practice, and scriptural interpretation. This understanding paves the way for the full inclusion of the Gentiles in Acts.

24:47 *Repentance and forgiveness*—Following Jesus' resurrection and ascension, his disciples will continue proclaiming the kingdom and announcing God's forgiveness of the penitent, whose eyes too may now be opened. *Jerusalem*—The city from whom the way of peace had been hidden becomes the starting point for the disciples' ministry (cf. 19:42).

24:49 *Sending*—Ascending to the right hand of God, Jesus promises to be continually present among the disciples through the sending of the Holy Spirit, who will empower and embolden them to proclaim God's kingdom and minister in Jesus' name. The story continues in the Acts of the Apostles.

The Gospel according to

JOHN

Discipleship in John's Gospel is a consequence of and shaped by the Gospel's presentation of Jesus as the revealer of God (1:18). Jesus is "the Word" that communicates God's purposes and actions among people (1:14). This revelation is grounded in the intimate relationship that Jesus and God share from "the beginning" (1:1). Their relationship is marked by mutual love (14:31; 15:9), oneness of will (10:30), and Jesus' submission to the Father (4:34; 5:19).

God sends Jesus as God's agent or son to make God known. The Gospel constantly reiterates Jesus' origin from God, from heaven, from above, to underline the authority and nature of his revelation. Jesus' words and works are those of God who sent him (14:7–11). To know Jesus is to know God. Some believe in or accept or receive Jesus and thereby share in the very life and purposes of God. Jesus empowers those who accept his revelation—believers—to enter into the relationship that he shares with God (1:12). This relationship comprises eternal life or life of the age (17:3) wherein believers know intimate relationship with God and a life that manifests God's life-giving purposes (5:24).

Not all receive Jesus' revelation. Discipleship takes place in the context of division and resistance to Jesus' revelation. In chapters 1–12, Jesus frequently is in conflict with a group called "the Ioudaioi," a term awkwardly translated sometimes as the Judeans or "the Jews." The term does not include all Jews, since Jesus and his disciples are Jews, and in chapter 11 people identified as "Jews" comfort the grieving Mary and Martha (11:19, 31) and believe in Jesus (11:45). The opposing Ioudaioi are probably best understood from references such as 1:19; 2:18; and 3:1 as an alliance of Judean leaders, the elite based in Jerusalem who exercised considerable religious, sociopolitical, and economic power as allies of the occupying Romans. They plot to kill Jesus (5:18; 11:45–57).

Their opposition centers on Jesus' claims that he comes from God (5:16–18; 10:33) and that he reveals God's purposes. His actions confront their power (2:13–21) and their maintenance and sanction of a hierarchical society for their own benefit, in which many are sick and lack food. Jesus, anticipating the completion of God's life-giving and saving purposes, provides physical wholeness (4:46–54; 5:1–18; chap. 9), plentiful food (chap. 6; Isa. 25:6–10; 35:5–6), and encounter with God's life-giving purposes. In this world, disciples are to continue Jesus' mission empowered, guided, and taught by the Spirit, or Paraclete (14:26; 15:26; 20:21).

Opposition also involves the Ioudaioi's allies, the Roman Empire. Jesus and Pilate, the Roman governor, collide over claims to sovereignty over the world. Jesus is crucified as king of the Jews, representing God's claim to creation and human society while denying Pilate such power (18:28–19:16). Jesus' resurrection shows that Rome's power is limited and subordinate to God's power.

This opposition is also referred to with the term "the world." This term denotes

those who, though loved by God (3:16), reject God's purposes manifested in Jesus (1:10). The world hates Jesus and his disciples (15:18). It is allied with and marked by death, darkness, sin, falseness, and the devil. The Gospel thus presents a strong dualistic divide between the world and the disciples. Considerable antagonism marks this antithesis. Disciples abide in union with God and Jesus (15:1–11), knowing God (17:3), loving one another (13:34–35; 15:12–17), and doing greater works of life-giving service than Jesus did (14:12) until Jesus returns to take them to be with God (14:2–3).

There has been much debate about the situation of the disciples addressed and shaped by the Gospel. Some have pointed to three references that seem to indicate that John's group has been recently expelled from a synagogue for their commitment to Jesus (9:22; 12:42; 16:2). But others are not persuaded that it is possible to reconstruct such a historical setting from a text that is so polemical and dualistic. Rather than reflect tension and conflict, perhaps the text seeks to create division and distance from the world because it thinks its audience is too societally comfortable and accommodated, not taking its commitment to the Jesus crucified by the Roman Empire's elite seriously enough.

Whatever the situation, the Gospel probably reached its final form after the fall of Jerusalem and its temple in 70 CE (2:13–22; 11:47–53), perhaps in the 80s–90s CE in an unknown place (traditionally Ephesus). Its writer is traditionally understood as John son of Zebedee, though there is little evidence for this identification.

Contemporary disciples—or believers as the Gospel prefers—find puzzling and life-giving material in this Gospel. Discerning the meaning of John's distinctive vocabulary is important. The word "life," for example, means knowing God (17:3). Also important is recognizing that the Gospel envisions God's life-giving purposes as shaping human society in ways that often conflict with conventional cultural values. Problematic is the term "the Jews/*Ioudaioi*" and the presentation of them as children of the devil (8:44). This term does not refer to all Jewish people for all time. The ancient conflict with Jesus does not permit contemporary Christians to continue hostility toward Jewish people.

—**Warren Carter**

The Word Became Flesh

1 In the beginning was the Word, and the Word was with God, and the Word was God. ²He was in the beginning with God. ³All things came into being through him, and without him not one thing came into being. What has come into being ⁴in him was life,*ᵃ*

and the life was the light of all people. ⁵The light shines in the darkness, and the darkness did not overcome it.

6 There was a man sent from God, whose name was John. ⁷He came as a witness to testify to the light, so that all

ᵃ Or ³through him. And without him not one thing came into being that has come into being. ⁴In him was life

---

1:1–51 Prologue and Setting the Stage

1:1–18—The prologue, invoking Wisdom traditions (Prov. 8; Wis. 7; Sir. 24), introduces important perspectives that shape discipleship. Jesus, the Word, is God's self-expression or revelation, the means by which disciples know God. Coming from God, Jesus takes human form (*flesh*) to reveal God's power and presence (*glory*, v. 14) among humans. His revelation is authorita-

tive because Jesus exists from the beginning, in intimate relationship with God. Jesus empowers those who accept or believe him to enter the same intimate relationship with God (vv. 12–13). But most, identified as *the world* (v. 10), do not accept him. Jesus' revelation, witnessed to by John the Baptist, continues previous revelations of God's loving kindness and faithfulness in the law given by Moses (vv. 15–17).

might believe through him. [8] He himself was not the light, but he came to testify to the light. [9] The true light, which enlightens everyone, was coming into the world.[a]

10 He was in the world, and the world came into being through him; yet the world did not know him. [11] He came to what was his own,[b] and his own people did not accept him. [12] But to all who received him, who believed in his name, he gave power to become children of God, [13] who were born, not of blood or of the will of the flesh or of the will of man, but of God.

14 And the Word became flesh and lived among us, and we have seen his glory, the glory as of a father's only son,[c] full of grace and truth. [15] (John testified to him and cried out, "This was he of whom I said, 'He who comes after me ranks ahead of me because he was before me.'") [16] From his fullness we have all received, grace upon grace. [17] The law indeed was given through Moses; grace and truth came through Jesus Christ. [18] No one has ever seen God. It is God the only Son,[d] who is close to the Father's heart,[e] who has made him known.

The Testimony of John the Baptist

19 This is the testimony given by John when the Jews sent priests and Levites from Jerusalem to ask him, "Who are you?" [20] He confessed and did not deny it, but confessed, "I am not the Messiah."[f] [21] And they asked him, "What then? Are you Elijah?" He said, "I am not." "Are you the prophet?" He answered, "No." [22] Then they said to him, "Who are you? Let us have an answer for those who sent us. What do you say about yourself?" [23] He said,

"I am the voice of one crying out in the wilderness,
'Make straight the way of the Lord,'"
as the prophet Isaiah said.

24 Now they had been sent from the Pharisees. [25] They asked him, "Why then are you baptizing if you are neither the Messiah,[f] nor Elijah, nor the prophet?" [26] John answered them, "I baptize with water. Among you stands one whom you do not know, [27] the one who is coming after me; I am not worthy to untie the thong of his sandal." [28] This took place in Bethany across the Jordan where John was baptizing.

The Lamb of God

29 The next day he saw Jesus coming toward him and declared, "Here is the Lamb of God who takes away the sin of the world! [30] This is he of whom I said, 'After me comes a man who ranks ahead of me because he was before me.' [31] I myself did not know him; but I came baptizing with water for this reason, that he might be revealed to Israel." [32] And John testified, "I saw the Spirit descending from heaven like a dove, and it remained on him. [33] I myself did not know him, but the one who sent me to baptize with water said to me, 'He on whom you see the Spirit descend and remain is the one who baptizes with the Holy Spirit.' [34] And I myself have seen and have testified that this is the Son of God."[g]

The First Disciples of Jesus

35 The next day John again was standing with two of his disciples, [36] and as he

---

a Or He was the true light that enlightens everyone coming into the world   *b* Or to his own home   *c* Or the Father's only Son   *d* Other ancient authorities read It is an only Son, God, or It is the only Son   *e* Gk bosom   *f* Or the Christ   *g* Other ancient authorities read is God's chosen one

---

1:19–34—John models an important task for disciples, to bear witness to Jesus (vv. 6–8, 15). His witness has content: Jesus is God's Son (v. 34) or obedient agent in intimate relationship with God (v. 18) who takes away sin (vv. 29, 35). John's witness poses a challenge. The world is not ordered according to God's life-giving purposes. Those who benefit from the status quo, the powerful leaders or elite, based in the Jerusalem temple (vv. 19–24), suspect and monitor John's threatening testimony to God's transforming action. Witness requires courage.

1:35–51—John's witness produces disciples, the church (vv. 35–39). Discipleship begins when people trust themselves to God's gracious

watched Jesus walk by, he exclaimed, "Look, here is the Lamb of God!" [37] The two disciples heard him say this, and they followed Jesus. [38] When Jesus turned and saw them following, he said to them, "What are you looking for?" They said to him, "Rabbi" (which translated means Teacher), "where are you staying?" [39] He said to them, "Come and see." They came and saw where he was staying, and they remained with him that day. It was about four o'clock in the afternoon. [40] One of the two who heard John speak and followed him was Andrew, Simon Peter's brother. [41] He first found his brother Simon and said to him, "We have found the Messiah" (which is translated Anointed[a]). [42] He brought Simon[b] to Jesus, who looked at him and said, "You are Simon son of John. You are to be called Cephas" (which is translated Peter[c]).

Jesus Calls Philip and Nathanael

43 The next day Jesus decided to go to Galilee. He found Philip and said to him, "Follow me." [44] Now Philip was from Bethsaida, the city of Andrew and Peter. [45] Philip found Nathanael and said to him, "We have found him about whom Moses in the law and also the prophets wrote, Jesus son of Joseph from Nazareth." [46] Nathanael said to him, "Can anything good come out of Nazareth?" Philip said to him, "Come and see." [47] When Jesus saw Nathanael coming toward him, he said of him, "Here is truly an Israelite in whom there is no deceit!" [48] Nathanael asked him, "Where did you get to know me?" Jesus answered, "I saw you under the fig tree before Philip called you." [49] Nathanael replied, "Rabbi, you are the Son of God! You are the King of Israel!" [50] Jesus answered, "Do you believe because I told you that I saw you under the fig tree? You will see greater things than these." [51] And he said to him, "Very truly, I tell you,[d] you will see heaven opened and the angels of God ascending and descending upon the Son of Man."

The Wedding at Cana

2 On the third day there was a wedding in Cana of Galilee, and the mother of Jesus was there. [2] Jesus and his disciples had also been invited to the wedding. [3] When the wine gave out, the mother of Jesus said to him, "They have no wine." [4] And Jesus said to her, "Woman, what concern is that to you and to me? My hour has not yet come." [5] His mother said to the servants, "Do whatever he tells you." [6] Now standing there were six stone water jars for the Jewish rites of purification, each holding twenty or thirty gallons. [7] Jesus said to them, "Fill the jars with water." And they filled them up to the brim. [8] He said to them, "Now draw some out, and take it to the chief steward." So they took it. [9] When the steward tasted the water that had become wine, and did not know where it came from (though the ser-

---

[a] Or Christ   [b] Gk him   [c] From the word for *rock* in Aramaic (*kepha*) and Greek (*petra*), respectively   [d] Both instances of the Greek word for *you* in this verse are plural

---

invitation manifested in Jesus (vv. 38, 43). Discipleship involves activity (following Jesus, vv. 37, 43), "seeing" or discerning his identity and role, and remaining/abiding with him (vv. 39, 46; cf. 15:1–11). It means bearing witness (vv. 40, 44–46), new identity (v. 42), and growing understandings (vv. 44–49, 51). Disciples form a new community.

2:1–4:54 Jesus' Revelation

2:1–12—Turning water into wine enacts God's purposes for fertility and life to which Jesus is committed (v. 4; cf. 4:34). Until his "hour," when Jesus shows God's power and presence in his death and return to God (12:23; 13:1–3), Jesus reveals God's purposes in words and actions. The steward cannot understand the "new and improved" wine according to social customs (vv. 8–10). But for disciples, the "sign" points to God's saving presence at work in Jesus (*glory*, v. 11). The wedding (Isa. 62:1–5) and abundant wine (Amos 9:13–14; *2 Bar.* 29:5) picture the world of joy, fertility, and abundant provision that God seeks to establish. To believe is to discern God at work in Jesus and to follow Jesus by participating in God's life-giving purposes.

vants who had drawn the water knew), the steward called the bridegroom ¹⁰ and said to him, "Everyone serves the good wine first, and then the inferior wine after the guests have become drunk. But you have kept the good wine until now." ¹¹ Jesus did this, the first of his signs, in Cana of Galilee, and revealed his glory; and his disciples believed in him.

12 After this he went down to Capernaum with his mother, his brothers, and his disciples; and they remained there a few days.

Jesus Cleanses the Temple

13 The Passover of the Jews was near, and Jesus went up to Jerusalem. ¹⁴ In the temple he found people selling cattle, sheep, and doves, and the money changers seated at their tables. ¹⁵ Making a whip of cords, he drove all of them out of the temple, both the sheep and the cattle. He also poured out the coins of the money changers and overturned their tables. ¹⁶ He told those who were selling the doves, "Take these things out of here! Stop making my Father's house a marketplace!" ¹⁷ His disciples remembered that it was written, "Zeal for your house will consume me." ¹⁸ The Jews then said to him, "What sign can you show us for doing this?" ¹⁹ Jesus answered them,

"Destroy this temple, and in three days I will raise it up." ²⁰ The Jews then said, "This temple has been under construction for forty-six years, and will you raise it up in three days?" ²¹ But he was speaking of the temple of his body. ²² After he was raised from the dead, his disciples remembered that he had said this; and they believed the scripture and the word that Jesus had spoken.

23 When he was in Jerusalem during the Passover festival, many believed in his name because they saw the signs that he was doing. ²⁴ But Jesus on his part would not entrust himself to them, because he knew all people ²⁵ and needed no one to testify about anyone; for he himself knew what was in everyone.

Nicodemus Visits Jesus

3 Now there was a Pharisee named Nicodemus, a leader of the Jews. ² He came to Jesus*a* by night and said to him, "Rabbi, we know that you are a teacher who has come from God; for no one can do these signs that you do apart from the presence of God." ³ Jesus answered him, "Very truly, I tell you, no one can see the kingdom of God without being born from above."*b* ⁴ Nicodemus said to him, "How can anyone be born after

a Gk him *b* Or born anew

2:13–22—Passover celebrates liberation from foreign control (Exod. 12:1–13:10). Jesus, like previous prophets (Isa. 1; Jer. 7), attacks the temple elite's unjust political, economic, and religious power, maintained in alliance with Rome. Disrupting the purchase of sacrifices threatens the temple's operation and the elite's wealth, and provokes the elite's opposition (John 2:17–18). Rome's destruction of the temple in 70 CE is viewed as judgment. Jesus is the new temple, in whom believers encounter God's presence and salvation (vv. 19–22). Power used by any elite against the poor and for death is always contrary to God's purposes.

2:23–25—Jesus' actions challenge people to discern God's saving presence and power at work in him. Trustworthy discipleship encounters and embraces God's purposes.

3:1–2—Nicodemus is a leader among the elite, *the Jews*/Judeans. This problematic term does not designate an ethnic group but the powerful elite

allied with Rome whose sociopolitical and religious power is centered on the Jerusalem temple (1:19; 2:18). Jesus' conflicts with "the Jews" involve his claims to manifest God's presence and will for a world that differs greatly from their unjust social structures.

3:3–15—Discipleship begins as God's Spirit enables receptive people to start a new life centered on discerning and encountering God's saving presence (**enter the kingdom of God**, v. 5). The Greek word emphasizes that it is not so much a matter of being "born again" (Nicodemus's partial misunderstanding) as entering into new life in relationship to God (**born from above**) according to God's purposes revealed in Jesus. The Spirit enables Jesus to continue to be present with disciples when he is physically no longer present (7:37–39; 14:16–17). Nicodemus typifies the elite's lack of receptiveness to God's purposes manifested in Jesus.

having grown old? Can one enter a second time into the mother's womb and be born?" [5] Jesus answered, "Very truly, I tell you, no one can enter the kingdom of God without being born of water and Spirit. [6] What is born of the flesh is flesh, and what is born of the Spirit is spirit.[a] [7] Do not be astonished that I said to you, 'You[b] must be born from above.'[c] [8] The wind[d] blows where it chooses, and you hear the sound of it, but you do not know where it comes from or where it goes. So it is with everyone who is born of the Spirit." [9] Nicodemus said to him, "How can these things be?" [10] Jesus answered him, "Are you a teacher of Israel, and yet you do not understand these things?

[11] "Very truly, I tell you, we speak of what we know and testify to what we have seen; yet you[e] do not receive our testimony. [12] If I have told you about earthly things and you do not believe, how can you believe if I tell you about heavenly things? [13] No one has ascended into heaven except the one who descended from heaven, the Son of Man.[f] [14] And just as Moses lifted up the serpent in the wilderness, so must the Son of Man be lifted up, [15] that whoever believes in him may have eternal life.[g]

[16] "For God so loved the world that he gave his only Son, so that everyone who believes in him may not perish but may have eternal life. [17] "Indeed, God did not send the Son into the world to condemn the world, but in order that the world might be saved through him. [18] Those who believe in him are not condemned; but those who do not believe are condemned already, because they have not believed in the name of the only Son of God. [19] And this is the judgment, that the light has come into the world, and people loved darkness rather than light because their deeds were evil. [20] For all who do evil hate the light and do not come to the light, so that their deeds may not be exposed. [21] But those who do what is true come to the light, so that it may be clearly seen that their deeds have been done in God."[g]

Jesus and John the Baptist

[22] After this Jesus and his disciples went into the Judean countryside, and he spent some time there with them and baptized. [23] John also was baptizing at Aenon near Salim because water was abundant there; and people kept coming and were being baptized [24] —John, of course, had not yet been thrown into prison.

[25] Now a discussion about purification arose between John's disciples and a Jew.[h] [26] They came to John and said to him, "Rabbi, the one who was with you across the Jordan, to whom you testified, here he is baptizing, and all are going to him." [27] John answered, "No one can receive anything except what has been given from heaven. [28] You yourselves are my witnesses that I said, 'I am not the Messiah,[i] but I have been sent ahead of him.' [29] He who has the bride is the bridegroom. The friend of the bridegroom, who stands and hears him, rejoices greatly at the bridegroom's voice. For this reason my joy has been fulfilled. [30] He must increase, but I must decrease."[j]

The One Who Comes from Heaven

[31] The one who comes from above is above all; the one who is of the earth belongs to the earth and speaks about

---

[a] The same Greek word means both *wind* and *spirit*　[b] The Greek word for *you* here is plural　[c] Or *anew*　[d] The same Greek word means both *wind* and *spirit*　[e] The Greek word for *you* here and in verse 12 is plural　[f] Other ancient authorities add *who is in heaven*　[g] Some interpreters hold that the quotation concludes with verse 15　[h] Other ancient authorities read *the Jews*　[i] Or *the Christ*　[j] Some interpreters hold that the quotation continues through verse 36

3:16–21—Jesus manifests God's salvation, reveals God's love, and offers disciples *eternal life* lived in intimate relationship with God (17:3), free from sin and death (5:24), and encountered now through believing (3:16–18; 1:12). God's offer reveals people's commitments and origin. To reject God's salvation (*light*, v. 19) is to condemn oneself. Disciples choose to believe Jesus' offer.

3:22–30—John witnesses (see 1:6–8, 15, 19–34).

3:31–36—Verse 36 sums up what is at stake in responding to Jesus. For believers, this decision

earthly things. The one who comes from heaven is above all. [32] He testifies to what he has seen and heard, yet no one accepts his testimony. [33] Whoever has accepted his testimony has certified[a] this, that God is true. [34] He whom God has sent speaks the words of God, for he gives the Spirit without measure. [35] The Father loves the Son and has placed all things in his hands. [36] Whoever believes in the Son has eternal life; whoever disobeys the Son will not see life, but must endure God's wrath.

Jesus and the Woman of Samaria

4 Now when Jesus[b] learned that the Pharisees had heard, "Jesus is making and baptizing more disciples than John" [2]—although it was not Jesus himself but his disciples who baptized— [3] he left Judea and started back to Galilee. [4] But he had to go through Samaria. [5] So he came to a Samaritan city called Sychar, near the plot of ground that Jacob had given to his son Joseph. [6] Jacob's well was there, and Jesus, tired out by his journey, was sitting by the well. It was about noon.

[7] A Samaritan woman came to draw water, and Jesus said to her, "Give me a drink." [8] (His disciples had gone to the city to buy food.) [9] The Samaritan woman said to him, "How is it that you, a Jew, ask a drink of me, a woman of Samaria?" (Jews do not share things in common with Samaritans.)[c] [10] Jesus answered her, "If you knew the gift of God, and who it is that is saying to you, 'Give me a drink,' you would have asked him, and he would have given you living water." [11] The woman said to him, "Sir, you have no bucket, and the well is deep. Where do you get that living water? [12] Are you greater than our ancestor Jacob, who gave us the well, and with his sons and his flocks drank from it?" [13] Jesus said to her, "Everyone who drinks of this water will be thirsty again, [14] but those who drink of the water that I will give them will never be thirsty. The water that I will give will become in them a spring of water gushing up to eternal life." [15] The woman said to him, "Sir, give me this water, so that I may never be thirsty or have to keep coming here to draw water."

[16] Jesus said to her, "Go, call your husband, and come back." [17] The woman answered him, "I have no husband." Jesus said to her, "You are right in saying, 'I have no husband'; [18] for you have had five husbands, and the one you have now is not your husband. What you have said is true!" [19] The woman said to him, "Sir, I see that you are a prophet. [20] Our ancestors worshiped on this mountain, but you[d] say that the place where people must worship is in Jerusalem." [21] Jesus said to her, "Woman,

[a] Gk set a seal to   [b] Other ancient authorities read the Lord   [c] Other ancient authorities lack this sentence   [d] The Greek word for you here and in verses 21 and 22 is plural

---

or commitment defines human existence as life lived in intimate relationship with God. To reject the witness is not to know this life.

4:1–42—In contrast to the elite male Nicodemus, the culturally and socioeconomically marginal Samaritan woman responds positively to Jesus' revelation. God's life-giving purposes are not restricted by ethnicity, gender, or social status.

4:1–6—Jesus' route through Samaria (v. 4) is theologically but not geographically necessary. It reveals God's inclusive love for all.

4:7–15—Jewish-Samaritan animosity was long-standing. Jesus' request for a drink (vv. 7–9) crosses religious, ethnic, and gender boundaries, foreshadowing a different human community that shares God's life. The community of disciples is to overcome conventional divisions. Jesus' reference to *living water* (v. 10) creates ambiguity, typical of John's narratives (3:3–9). Jesus refers to his revelation of God's purposes, but she thinks of literal water (vv. 13–15). Discipleship requires a process of growing understanding and faith.

4:16–30—Jesus' revelation (not condemnation) of her relationships increases her understanding (*prophet*, v. 19), enabling him to manifest himself as the Messiah/Christ anointed to reveal God's faithful salvation (vv. 23–26). Jesus uses *I am*, a formula that reveals God's salvation of the people from Egypt (Exod. 3:13–14) and Babylonian exile (Isa. 43:10–13, 25; 51:12). God's saving purposes form the basis of the inclusive community of disciples.

believe me, the hour is coming when you will worship the Father neither on this mountain nor in Jerusalem. **22** You worship what you do not know; we worship what we know, for salvation is from the Jews. **23** But the hour is coming, and is now here, when the true worshipers will worship the Father in spirit and truth, for the Father seeks such as these to worship him. **24** God is spirit, and those who worship him must worship in spirit and truth." **25** The woman said to him, "I know that Messiah is coming" (who is called Christ). "When he comes, he will proclaim all things to us." **26** Jesus said to her, "I am he,*a* the one who is speaking to you."

27 Just then his disciples came. They were astonished that he was speaking with a woman, but no one said, "What do you want?" or, "Why are you speaking with her?" **28** Then the woman left her water jar and went back to the city. She said to the people, **29** "Come and see a man who told me everything I have ever done! He cannot be the Messiah,*b* can he?" **30** They left the city and were on their way to him.

31 Meanwhile the disciples were urging him, "Rabbi, eat something." **32** But he said to them, "I have food to eat that you do not know about." **33** So the disciples said to one another, "Surely no one has brought him something to eat?" **34** Jesus said to them, "My food is to do the will of him who sent me and to complete his work. **35** Do you not say, 'Four months more, then comes the harvest'? But I tell you, look around you, and see how the fields are ripe for harvesting.

36 The reaper is already receiving*c* wages and is gathering fruit for eternal life, so that sower and reaper may rejoice together. **37** For here the saying holds true, 'One sows and another reaps.' **38** I sent you to reap that for which you did not labor. Others have labored, and you have entered into their labor."

39 Many Samaritans from that city believed in him because of the woman's testimony, "He told me everything I have ever done." **40** So when the Samaritans came to him, they asked him to stay with them; and he stayed there two days. **41** And many more believed because of his word. **42** They said to the woman, "It is no longer because of what you said that we believe, for we have heard for ourselves, and we know that this is truly the Savior of the world."

Jesus Returns to Galilee

43 When the two days were over, he went from that place to Galilee **44** (for Jesus himself had testified that a prophet has no honor in the prophet's own country). **45** When he came to Galilee, the Galileans welcomed him, since they had seen all that he had done in Jerusalem at the festival; for they too had gone to the festival.

Jesus Heals an Official's Son

46 Then he came again to Cana in Galilee where he had changed the water into wine. Now there was a royal official whose son lay ill in Capernaum. **47** When he heard that Jesus had come from Judea to Galilee, he went and begged him to

a Gk I am *b* Or the Christ *c* Or 35. . . . the fields are already ripe for harvesting. 36 The reaper is receiving

---

4:31–38—Jesus describes his mission to do God's will (v. 34). Disciples share the same mission (vv. 35–38).

4:39–42—The woman models the transformation that comes with discipleship. She began her meeting with Jesus surprised, perplexed, but questioning (vv. 9–12). Increasingly receptive to his teaching, she grows in understanding and faith (vv. 15–26). Bravely she testifies to her emerging relationship and insight (vv. 28–30), enabling others in her village to encounter Jesus

and believe Jesus' words for themselves (vv. 39–42).

4:43–54—Jesus' second sign in Cana (2:1–11) displays God's life-giving power. His healing of the believing official's son reveals and anticipates God's salvation, in which physical wholeness (along with abundant fertility) reverses present suffering and injustice (Isa. 35:5–10; *2 Bar.* 29, 73). Disciples participate in God's life-giving purposes.

come down and heal his son, for he was at the point of death. **48** Then Jesus said to him, "Unless you*a* see signs and wonders you will not believe." **49** The official said to him, "Sir, come down before my little boy dies." **50** Jesus said to him, "Go; your son will live." The man believed the word that Jesus spoke to him and started on his way. **51** As he was going down, his slaves met him and told him that his child was alive. **52** So he asked them the hour when he began to recover, and they said to him, "Yesterday at one in the afternoon the fever left him." **53** The father realized that this was the hour when Jesus had said to him, "Your son will live." So he himself believed, along with his whole household. **54** Now this was the second sign that Jesus did after coming from Judea to Galilee.

Jesus Heals on the Sabbath

5 After this there was a festival of the Jews, and Jesus went up to Jerusalem.

2 Now in Jerusalem by the Sheep Gate there is a pool, called in Hebrew*b* Bethzatha,*c* which has five porticoes. **3** In these lay many invalids—blind, lame, and paralyzed.*d* **5** One man was there who had been ill for thirty-eight years. **6** When Jesus saw him lying there and knew that he had been there a long time, he said to him, "Do you want to be made well?" **7** The sick man answered him, "Sir, I have no one to put me into the pool when the water is stirred up; and while I am making my way, someone else steps

down ahead of me." **8** Jesus said to him, "Stand up, take your mat and walk." **9** At once the man was made well, and he took up his mat and began to walk.

Now that day was a sabbath. **10** So the Jews said to the man who had been cured, "It is the sabbath; it is not lawful for you to carry your mat." **11** But he answered them, "The man who made me well said to me, 'Take up your mat and walk.'" **12** They asked him, "Who is the man who said to you, 'Take it up and walk'?" **13** Now the man who had been healed did not know who it was, for Jesus had disappeared in*e* the crowd that was there. **14** Later Jesus found him in the temple and said to him, "See, you have been made well! Do not sin any more, so that nothing worse happens to you." **15** The man went away and told the Jews that it was Jesus who had made him well. **16** Therefore the Jews started persecuting Jesus, because he was doing such things on the sabbath. **17** But Jesus answered them, "My Father is still working, and I also am working." **18** For this reason the Jews were seeking all the more to kill him, because he was not only breaking the sabbath, but was also calling God his own Father, thereby making himself equal to God.

The Authority of the Son

19 Jesus said to them, "Very truly, I tell you, the Son can do nothing on his own,

a Both instances of the Greek word for *you* in this verse are plural   *b* That is, *Aramaic*   *c* Other ancient authorities read *Bethesda*, others *Bethsaida*   *d* Other ancient authorities add, wholly or in part, *waiting for the stirring of the water;* **4** *for an angel of the Lord went down at certain seasons into the pool, and stirred up the water; whoever stepped in first after the stirring of the water was made well from whatever disease that person had.*   *e* Or *had left because of*

5:1–12:50 Increasing Opposition
As happens to disciples (17:14), Jesus' revelation encounters increasing opposition. Jewish festivals celebrating God's salvific acts provide the context.

5:1–18—Back in Jerusalem (2:13–22) for a festival, Jesus associates with the numerous human casualties of the hierarchical society structured by the Jerusalem leaders and their Roman allies (5:3). Jesus reveals God's life-giving salvation in healing a paralyzed man (see 4:43–54). God's purposes transform physical and sociopolitical dimensions of human existence. Jesus' action

precipitates a dispute over how to honor the Sabbath (5:9b–10; Gen. 2:2–3; Deut. 5:12–15), whether by rest or by transformative action. Jesus claims to manifest God's life-giving actions (5:17; 4:34), provoking the leaders (*the Jews*/Judean leaders, see note at 3:1–2) to seek, for the first time, to kill him for blasphemy or dishonoring God. They reject his claim to reveal God's purposes for a different human society. Disciples continue his work with similar opposition from vested interests.

5:19–30—Jesus does the work that God gives him (vv. 19–20). This work defines human identity. He

but only what he sees the Father doing; for whatever the Father*a* does, the Son does likewise. **20** The Father loves the Son and shows him all that he himself is doing; and he will show him greater works than these, so that you will be astonished. **21** Indeed, just as the Father raises the dead and gives them life, so also the Son gives life to whomever he wishes. **22** The Father judges no one but has given all judgment to the Son, **23** so that all may honor the Son just as they honor the Father. Anyone who does not honor the Son does not honor the Father who sent him. **24** Very truly, I tell you, anyone who hears my word and believes him who sent me has eternal life, and does not come under judgment, but has passed from death to life.

25 "Very truly, I tell you, the hour is coming, and is now here, when the dead will hear the voice of the Son of God, and those who hear will live. **26** For just as the Father has life in himself, so he has granted the Son also to have life in himself; **27** and he has given him authority to execute judgment, because he is the Son of Man. **28** Do not be astonished at this; for the hour is coming when all who are in their graves will hear his voice **29** and will come out—those who have done good, to the resurrection of life, and those who have done evil, to the resurrection of condemnation.

Witnesses to Jesus

30 "I can do nothing on my own. As I hear, I judge; and my judgment is just, because I seek to do not my own will but the will of him who sent me.

31 "If I testify about myself, my testimony is not true. **32** There is another who testifies on my behalf, and I know that his testimony to me is true. **33** You sent messengers to John, and he testified to the truth. **34** Not that I accept such human testimony, but I say these things so that you may be saved. **35** He was a burning and shining lamp, and you were willing to rejoice for a while in his light. **36** But I have a testimony greater than John's. The works that the Father has given me to complete, the very works that I am doing, testify on my behalf that the Father has sent me. **37** And the Father who sent me has himself testified on my behalf. You have never heard his voice or seen his form, **38** and you do not have his word abiding in you, because you do not believe him whom he has sent.

39 "You search the scriptures because you think that in them you have eternal life; and it is they that testify on my behalf. **40** Yet you refuse to come to me to have life. **41** I do not accept glory from human beings. **42** But I know that you do not have the love of God in*b* you. **43** I have come in my Father's name, and you do not accept me; if another comes in his own name, you will accept him. **44** How can you believe when you accept glory from one another and do not seek the glory that comes from the one who alone is God? **45** Do not think that I will accuse you before the Father; your accuser is Moses, on whom you have set your hope. **46** If you believed Moses, you would believe me, for he wrote about me. **47** But if you do not believe what he wrote, how will you believe what I say?"

Feeding the Five Thousand

6 After this Jesus went to the other side of the Sea of Galilee, also called the Sea of Tiberias.*c* **2** A large crowd kept fol-

a Gk that one *b* Or among *c* Gk of Galilee of Tiberias

---

gives life and effects judgment through people's responses of acceptance or resistance (3:16–21; 5:21–27). Believers live eternal life now, in intimate relationship with God (17:3) unrestricted by sin and death (5:24) and marked by doing God's will. The future resurrection will complete God's saving purposes (vv. 28–29) at Jesus' return (14:1–3).

5:31–47—Five witnesses sustain Jesus' claims to reveal God's purposes: *John* the Baptist (vv. 33–35), Jesus' *works* (v. 36), God (vv. 37–38), the *scriptures* (vv. 39–40), *Moses* (vv. 41–47).

6:1–15—In the first-century Roman world, adequate food supply was a challenge for many, as in our world. The elite removed people's

lowing him, because they saw the signs that he was doing for the sick. ³ Jesus went up the mountain and sat down there with his disciples. ⁴ Now the Passover, the festival of the Jews, was near. ⁵ When he looked up and saw a large crowd coming toward him, Jesus said to Philip, "Where are we to buy bread for these people to eat?" ⁶ He said this to test him, for he himself knew what he was going to do. ⁷ Philip answered him, "Six months' wages[a] would not buy enough bread for each of them to get a little." ⁸ One of his disciples, Andrew, Simon Peter's brother, said to him, ⁹ "There is a boy here who has five barley loaves and two fish. But what are they among so many people?" ¹⁰ Jesus said, "Make the people sit down." Now there was a great deal of grass in the place; so they[b] sat down, about five thousand in all. ¹¹ Then Jesus took the loaves, and when he had given thanks, he distributed them to those who were seated; so also the fish, as much as they wanted. ¹² When they were satisfied, he told his disciples, "Gather up the fragments left over, so that nothing may be lost." ¹³ So they gathered them up, and from the fragments of the five barley loaves, left by those who had eaten, they filled twelve baskets. ¹⁴ When the people saw the sign that he had done, they began to say, "This is indeed the prophet who is to come into the world."

¹⁵ When Jesus realized that they were about to come and take him by force to make him king, he withdrew again to the mountain by himself.

Jesus Walks on the Water

¹⁶ When evening came, his disciples went down to the sea, ¹⁷ got into a boat, and started across the sea to Capernaum. It was now dark, and Jesus had not yet come to them. ¹⁸ The sea became rough because a strong wind was blowing. ¹⁹ When they had rowed about three or four miles,[c] they saw Jesus walking on the sea and coming near the boat, and they were terrified. ²⁰ But he said to them, "It is I;[d] do not be afraid." ²¹ Then they wanted to take him into the boat, and immediately the boat reached the land toward which they were going.

The Bread from Heaven

²² The next day the crowd that had stayed on the other side of the sea saw that there had been only one boat there. They also saw that Jesus had not got into the boat with his disciples, but that his disciples had gone away alone. ²³ Then some boats from Tiberias came near the place where they had eaten the bread after the Lord had given thanks.[e] ²⁴ So when the crowd saw that neither Jesus nor his disciples were there, they

[a] Gk *Two hundred denarii*; the denarius was the usual day's wage for a laborer [b] Gk *the men* [c] Gk *about twenty-five or thirty stadia* [d] Gk *I am* [e] Other ancient authorities lack *after the Lord had given thanks*

---

food with taxes and tributes. Scenes depicting God's final and just salvation often celebrate an abundant food supply to which all have fair access (Isa. 25:6–10; *2 Bar.* 29:4–8). Jesus' feeding enacts and anticipates God's saving purposes (vv. 11–13; cf. 2:1–11) and calls disciples to work for this sort of world. *Passover* (v. 4) recalls God's faithfulness in providing food after the exodus from Egypt (Exod. 16).

6:16–21—Jesus reveals God's presence by manifesting God's rule over the sea (Job 9:9; Pss. 77:16–20; 107:23–32; Isa. 43:16; Exod. 14–15; Gen. 1:6–10). Jesus speaks God's words of revelation ("I am," 4:16–30) and reassurance (6:20 "do not be afraid," Gen. 15:1; Isa. 41:10–13). Even in the midst of stormy chaos, disciples know God's transforming presence in Jesus.

6:22–59—Jesus interprets Passover as God's salvific action manifested through him. His words, like bread, are life giving for disciples. They reveal his origin and authority from God to reveal life that shares in the very being of God (vv. 22–33). He is therefore trustworthy, the one in whom people encounter eternal life and God's salvation (vv. 34–40, 51–59) revealed in Jesus' actions (vv. 1–21) and words (vv. 22–71). As "I am" (see note at 4:16–30), he is sent from God to reveal God's life (vv. 41–51). Disciples entrust themselves to this revelation (v. 69) and know its life-giving power (6:68), yet as Jesus warns, disciples are not immune from betrayal and falseness (vv. 66–71).

themselves got into the boats and went to Capernaum looking for Jesus.

25 When they found him on the other side of the sea, they said to him, "Rabbi, when did you come here?" 26 Jesus answered them, "Very truly, I tell you, you are looking for me, not because you saw signs, but because you ate your fill of the loaves. 27 Do not work for the food that perishes, but for the food that endures for eternal life, which the Son of Man will give you. For it is on him that God the Father has set his seal." 28 Then they said to him, "What must we do to perform the works of God?" 29 Jesus answered them, "This is the work of God, that you believe in him whom he has sent." 30 So they said to him, "What sign are you going to give us then, so that we may see it and believe you? What work are you performing? 31 Our ancestors ate the manna in the wilderness; as it is written, 'He gave them bread from heaven to eat.'" 32 Then Jesus said to them, "Very truly, I tell you, it was not Moses who gave you the bread from heaven, but it is my Father who gives you the true bread from heaven. 33 For the bread of God is that which*a* comes down from heaven and gives life to the world." 34 They said to him, "Sir, give us this bread always."

35 Jesus said to them, "I am the bread of life. Whoever comes to me will never be hungry, and whoever believes in me will never be thirsty. 36 But I said to you that you have seen me and yet do not believe. 37 Everything that the Father gives me will come to me, and anyone who comes to me I will never drive away; 38 for I have come down from heaven, not to do my own will, but the will of him who sent me. 39 And this is the will of him who sent me, that I should lose nothing of all that he has given me, but raise it up on the last day. 40 This is indeed the will of my Father, that all who see the Son and believe in him may have eternal life; and I will raise them up on the last day."

41 Then the Jews began to complain about him because he said, "I am the bread that came down from heaven." 42 They were saying, "Is not this Jesus, the son of Joseph, whose father and mother we know? How can he now say, 'I have come down from heaven'?" 43 Jesus answered them, "Do not complain among yourselves. 44 No one can come to me unless drawn by the Father who sent me; and I will raise that person up on the last day. 45 It is written in the prophets, 'And they shall all be taught by God.' Everyone who has heard and learned from the Father comes to me. 46 Not that anyone has seen the Father except the one who is from God; he has seen the Father. 47 Very truly, I tell you, whoever believes has eternal life. 48 I am the bread of life. 49 Your ancestors ate the manna in the wilderness, and they died. 50 This is the bread that comes down from heaven, so that one may eat of it and not die. 51 I am the living bread that came down from heaven. Whoever eats of this bread will live forever; and the bread that I will give for the life of the world is my flesh."

52 The Jews then disputed among themselves, saying, "How can this man give us his flesh to eat?" 53 So Jesus said to them, "Very truly, I tell you, unless you eat the flesh of the Son of Man and drink his blood, you have no life in you. 54 Those who eat my flesh and drink my blood have eternal life, and I will raise them up on the last day; 55 for my flesh is true food and my blood is true drink. 56 Those who eat my flesh and drink my blood abide in me, and I in them. 57 Just as the living Father sent me, and I live because of the Father, so whoever eats me will live because of me. 58 This is the bread that came down from heaven, not like that which your ancestors ate, and they died. But the one who eats this bread will live forever." 59 He said these things while he was teaching in the synagogue at Capernaum.

a Or *he who*

The Words of Eternal Life

60 When many of his disciples heard it, they said, "This teaching is difficult; who can accept it?" 61 But Jesus, being aware that his disciples were complaining about it, said to them, "Does this offend you? 62 Then what if you were to see the Son of Man ascending to where he was before? 63 It is the spirit that gives life; the flesh is useless. The words that I have spoken to you are spirit and life. 64 But among you there are some who do not believe." For Jesus knew from the first who were the ones that did not believe, and who was the one that would betray him. 65 And he said, "For this reason I have told you that no one can come to me unless it is granted by the Father."

66 Because of this many of his disciples turned back and no longer went about with him. 67 So Jesus asked the twelve, "Do you also wish to go away?" 68 Simon Peter answered him, "Lord, to whom can we go? You have the words of eternal life. 69 We have come to believe and know that you are the Holy One of God."*a* 70 Jesus answered them, "Did I not choose you, the twelve? Yet one of you is a devil." 71 He was speaking of Judas son of Simon Iscariot,*b* for he, though one of the twelve, was going to betray him.

The Unbelief of Jesus' Brothers

7 After this Jesus went about in Galilee. He did not wish*c* to go about in Judea because the Jews were looking for an opportunity to kill him. 2 Now the Jewish festival of Booths*d* was near. 3 So his brothers said to him, "Leave here and go to Judea so that your disciples also may see the works you are doing; 4 for no one who wants*e* to be widely known acts in secret. If you do these things, show yourself to the world." 5 (For not even his brothers believed in him.) 6 Jesus said to them, "My time has not yet come, but your time is always here. 7 The world cannot hate you, but it hates me because I testify against it that its works are evil. 8 Go to the festival yourselves. I am not*f* going to this festival, for my time has not yet fully come." 9 After saying this, he remained in Galilee.

Jesus at the Festival of Booths

10 But after his brothers had gone to the festival, then he also went, not publicly but as it were*g* in secret. 11 The Jews were looking for him at the festival and saying, "Where is he?" 12 And there was considerable complaining about him among the crowds. While some were saying, "He is a good man," others were saying, "No, he is deceiving the crowd." 13 Yet no one would speak openly about him for fear of the Jews.

14 About the middle of the festival Jesus went up into the temple and began to teach. 15 The Jews were astonished at it, saying, "How does this man have such learning,*h* when he has never been

a Other ancient authorities read *the Christ, the Son of the living God*
b Other ancient authorities read *Judas Iscariot son of Simon;* others, *Judas son of Simon from Karyot* (Kerioth) *c* Other ancient authorities read *was not at liberty* *d* Or *Tabernacles* *e* Other ancient authorities read *wants it* *f* Other ancient authorities add *yet* *g* Other ancient authorities lack *as it were* *h* Or *this man know his letters*

7:1–13—From John 7:1 to 10:21 Jesus is in Jerusalem for the fall Festival of *Booths* or Tabernacles (Sukkoth; 7:2). This festival commemorated God's salvific care in providing food in the wilderness and in the annual harvest. It anticipated the establishment of God's salvation (Zech. 14). Jesus, the new temple (2:18–22), reinterprets its central symbols of water (7:37–39) and light (8:12; 9:5) to announce his revelation of God's salvation.

Jesus' announcement of God's salvation challenges the elite's power and way of organizing society, so they oppose him and seek to kill him (7:1, 7; cf. 3:1–2; 5:18). Close to home, his own brothers do not believe him either (7:5). The assertion of God's purposes, whether by Jesus or by disciples, requires everyone to decide whether to embrace or resist God's purposes.

7:14–31—Hostility from the Jerusalem elite increases (vv. 1, 7–13, 19–20, 25, 30–32, 44), and division grows as Jesus again declares the origin of his teaching (vv. 16–17), and *his* own origin and authority with God (vv. 27–29). Contemporary disciples must be careful not to adopt a similar stance of complacency, being closed to God's continuing and disruptive presence in their lives.

taught?" [16] Then Jesus answered them, "My teaching is not mine but his who sent me. [17] Anyone who resolves to do the will of God will know whether the teaching is from God or whether I am speaking on my own. [18] Those who speak on their own seek their own glory; but the one who seeks the glory of him who sent him is true, and there is nothing false in him.

[19] "Did not Moses give you the law? Yet none of you keeps the law. Why are you looking for an opportunity to kill me?" [20] The crowd answered, "You have a demon! Who is trying to kill you?" [21] Jesus answered them, "I performed one work, and all of you are astonished. [22] Moses gave you circumcision (it is, of course, not from Moses, but from the patriarchs), and you circumcise a man on the sabbath. [23] If a man receives circumcision on the sabbath in order that the law of Moses may not be broken, are you angry with me because I healed a man's whole body on the sabbath? [24] Do not judge by appearances, but judge with right judgment."

Is This the Christ?

[25] Now some of the people of Jerusalem were saying, "Is not this the man whom they are trying to kill? [26] And here he is, speaking openly, but they say nothing to him! Can it be that the authorities really know that this is the Messiah?[a] [27] Yet we know where this man is from; but when the Messiah[a] comes, no one will know where he is from." [28] Then Jesus cried out as he was teaching in the temple, "You know me, and you know where I am from. I have not come on my own. But the one who sent me is true, and you do not know

him. [29] I know him, because I am from him, and he sent me." [30] Then they tried to arrest him, but no one laid hands on him, because his hour had not yet come. [31] Yet many in the crowd believed in him and were saying, "When the Messiah[a] comes, will he do more signs than this man has done?"[b]

Officers Are Sent to Arrest Jesus

[32] The Pharisees heard the crowd muttering such things about him, and the chief priests and Pharisees sent temple police to arrest him. [33] Jesus then said, "I will be with you a little while longer, and then I am going to him who sent me. [34] You will search for me, but you will not find me; and where I am, you cannot come." [35] The Jews said to one another, "Where does this man intend to go that we will not find him? Does he intend to go to the Dispersion among the Greeks and teach the Greeks? [36] What does he mean by saying, 'You will search for me and you will not find me' and 'Where I am, you cannot come'?"

Rivers of Living Water

[37] On the last day of the festival, the great day, while Jesus was standing there, he cried out, "Let anyone who is thirsty come to me, [38] and let the one who believes in me drink. As[c] the scripture has said, 'Out of the believer's heart[d] shall flow rivers of living water.' " [39] Now he said this about the Spirit, which believers in him were to receive; for as yet there was no Spirit,[e] because Jesus was not yet glorified.

[a] Or the Christ [b] Other ancient authorities read is doing [c] Or come to me and drink. [38] The one who believes in me, as [d] Gk out of his belly [e] Other ancient authorities read for as yet the Spirit (others, Holy Spirit) had not been given

---

7:32–36—Even the elite's continuing efforts to kill Jesus and to protect their world and power exist within God's purposes. By reinterpreting his imminent death as a return to God via his resurrection and ascension, Jesus declares a victory over the elite's opposition. Nothing can thwart God's purposes and the worst of circumstances cannot separate believers from God's loving presence.

7:37–39—Even his death cannot remove Jesus' presence from disciples. Jesus' ascension means the gift of the Spirit to continue God's saving work through disciples. The Spirit brings birth from above (3:3–15), accompanies and instructs disciples (14:15–17), and convicts the world of sin (16:8–11; 7:7).

Division among the People

40 When they heard these words, some in the crowd said, "This is really the prophet." **41** Others said, "This is the Messiah."*a* But some asked, "Surely the Messiah*a* does not come from Galilee, does he? **42** Has not the scripture said that the Messiah*a* is descended from David and comes from Bethlehem, the village where David lived?" **43** So there was a division in the crowd because of him. **44** Some of them wanted to arrest him, but no one laid hands on him.

The Unbelief of Those in Authority

45 Then the temple police went back to the chief priests and Pharisees, who asked them, "Why did you not arrest him?" **46** The police answered, "Never has anyone spoken like this!" **47** Then the Pharisees replied, "Surely you have not been deceived too, have you? **48** Has any one of the authorities or of the Pharisees believed in him? **49** But this crowd, which does not know the law—they are accursed." **50** Nicodemus, who had gone to Jesus*b* before, and who was one of them, asked, **51** "Our law does not judge people without first giving them a hearing to find out what they are doing, does it?" **52** They replied, "Surely you are not also from Galilee, are you? Search and you will see that no prophet is to arise from Galilee."

The Woman Caught in Adultery

8 [[**53** Then each of them went home, **1** while Jesus went to the Mount of Olives. **2** Early in the morning he came again to the temple. All the people came to him and he sat down and began to teach them. **3** The scribes and the Pharisees brought a woman who had been caught in adultery; and making her stand before all of them, **4** they said to him, "Teacher, this woman was caught in the very act of committing adultery. **5** Now in the law Moses commanded us to stone such women. Now what do you say?" **6** They said this to test him, so that they might have some charge to bring against him. Jesus bent down and wrote with his finger on the ground. **7** When they kept on questioning him, he straightened up and said to them, "Let anyone among you who is without sin be the first to throw a stone at her." **8** And once again he bent down and wrote on the ground.*c* **9** When they heard it, they went away, one by one, beginning with the elders; and Jesus was left alone with the woman standing before him. **10** Jesus straightened up and said to her, "Woman, where are they? Has no one condemned you?" **11** She said, "No one, sir."*d* And Jesus said, "Neither do I condemn you. Go your way, and from now on do not sin again."]]*e*

Jesus the Light of the World

12 Again Jesus spoke to them, saying, "I am the light of the world. Whoever

---

a Or the Christ *b* Gk him *c* Other ancient authorities add *the sins of each of them* *d* Or Lord *e* The most ancient authorities lack 7.53—8.11; other authorities add the passage here or after 7.36 or after 21.25 or after Luke 21.38, with variations of text; some mark the passage as doubtful.

7:40–52—Claims about Jesus' identity and origin continue to divide people. The elite try but fail to arrest him (vv. 30, 32, 44). Jesus *gives* his life in God's timing (10:15–18; 12:23). Disciples trust one who is not defeated but in control. They must also trust one who accomplishes God's purposes in God's own timing and in God's ways.

7:53–8:11—Earliest manuscripts lack this story. In giving the woman life and the new start of forgiveness, Jesus displays his God-given authority (5:19–30) over the condemning leaders (8:3–9).

8:12–59—Conflict between Jesus and the Jerusalem leaders over his identity and authority to reveal God's will continues (v. 25). Jesus empha-

sizes his unity with, origin from, and departure to his Father (vv. 14, 26–27, 58). The leaders' nonacceptance of his claims reveals their origin and identity (vv. 41–47). They do not come from God (v. 23). Nor do they come from Abraham (vv. 31–59), who welcomed God's word and with whom God covenanted to bless all people (Gen. 12:1–3). Abraham's real descendants would imitate Abraham in welcoming God's messengers and words (Gen. 18). Their attempts to kill Jesus show that they come from the devil (John 8:20, 37, 42–47, 59; 10:20, 31), but God thwarts their efforts (8:20, 59; 10:15–18). The regrettable, mutual accusations of belonging to the devil

follows me will never walk in darkness but will have the light of life." [13] Then the Pharisees said to him, "You are testifying on your own behalf; your testimony is not valid." [14] Jesus answered, "Even if I testify on my own behalf, my testimony is valid because I know where I have come from and where I am going, but you do not know where I come from or where I am going. [15] You judge by human standards;[a] I judge no one. [16] Yet even if I do judge, my judgment is valid; for it is not I alone who judge, but I and the Father[b] who sent me. [17] In your law it is written that the testimony of two witnesses is valid. [18] I testify on my own behalf, and the Father who sent me testifies on my behalf." [19] Then they said to him, "Where is your Father?" Jesus answered, "You know neither me nor my Father. If you knew me, you would know my Father also." [20] He spoke these words while he was teaching in the treasury of the temple, but no one arrested him, because his hour had not yet come.

Jesus Foretells His Death

21 Again he said to them, "I am going away, and you will search for me, but you will die in your sin. Where I am going, you cannot come." [22] Then the Jews said, "Is he going to kill himself? Is that what he means by saying, 'Where I am going, you cannot come'?" [23] He said to them, "You are from below, I am from above; you are of this world, I am not of this world. [24] I told you that you would die in your sins, for you will die in your sins unless you believe that I am he."[c] [25] They said to him, "Who are you?" Jesus said to them, "Why do I speak to you at all?[d] [26] I have much to say about you and much to condemn; but the one who sent me is true, and I declare to the world what I have heard from him." [27] They did not understand that he was speaking to them about the Father. [28] So Jesus said, "When you have lifted up the Son of Man, then you will realize that I am he,[c] and that I do nothing on my own, but I speak these things as the Father instructed me. [29] And the one who sent me is with me; he has not left me alone, for I always do what is pleasing to him." [30] As he was saying these things, many believed in him.

True Disciples

31 Then Jesus said to the Jews who had believed in him, "If you continue in my word, you are truly my disciples; [32] and you will know the truth, and the truth will make you free." [33] They answered him, "We are descendants of Abraham and have never been slaves to anyone. What do you mean by saying, 'You will be made free'?"

34 Jesus answered them, "Very truly, I tell you, everyone who commits sin is a slave to sin. [35] The slave does not have a permanent place in the household; the son has a place there forever. [36] So if the Son makes you free, you will be free indeed. [37] I know that you are descendants of Abraham; yet you look for an opportunity to kill me, because there is no place in you for my word. [38] I declare what I have seen in the Father's presence; as for you, you should do what you have heard from the Father."[e]

Jesus and Abraham

39 They answered him, "Abraham is our father." Jesus said to them, "If you were Abraham's children, you would be doing[f] what Abraham did, [40] but now you are trying to kill me, a man who has told you the truth that I heard from God. This is not what Abraham did. [41] You are indeed doing what your father does."

[a] Gk according to the flesh   [b] Other ancient authorities read he   [c] Gk I am   [d] Or What I have told you from the beginning   [e] Other ancient authorities read you do what you have heard from your father   [f] Other ancient authorities read If you are Abraham's children, then do

---

(7:20; 8:44, 48) are typical of ancient rhetorical exchanges between opposing groups. They reflect specific disputes over diverse claims and practices. They do not permit contemporary followers of Jesus to continue practices or rhetoric that are hateful toward Jewish, or any, people.

They said to him, "We are not illegitimate children; we have one father, God himself." ⁴²Jesus said to them, "If God were your Father, you would love me, for I came from God and now I am here. I did not come on my own, but he sent me. ⁴³Why do you not understand what I say? It is because you cannot accept my word. ⁴⁴You are from your father the devil, and you choose to do your father's desires. He was a murderer from the beginning and does not stand in the truth, because there is no truth in him. When he lies, he speaks according to his own nature, for he is a liar and the father of lies. ⁴⁵But because I tell the truth, you do not believe me. ⁴⁶Which of you convicts me of sin? If I tell the truth, why do you not believe me? ⁴⁷Whoever is from God hears the words of God. The reason you do not hear them is that you are not from God."

48 The Jews answered him, "Are we not right in saying that you are a Samaritan and have a demon?" ⁴⁹Jesus answered, "I do not have a demon; but I honor my Father, and you dishonor me. ⁵⁰Yet I do not seek my own glory; there is one who seeks it and he is the judge. ⁵¹Very truly, I tell you, whoever keeps my word will never see death." ⁵²The Jews said to him, "Now we know that you have a demon. Abraham died, and so did the prophets; yet you say, 'Whoever keeps my word will never taste death.' ⁵³Are you greater than our father Abraham, who died? The prophets also died. Who do you claim to be?" ⁵⁴Jesus answered, "If I glorify myself, my glory is nothing. It is my Father who glorifies me, he of whom you say, 'He is our God,' ⁵⁵though you do not know him. But I know him; if I would say that I do

not know him, I would be a liar like you. But I do know him and I keep his word. ⁵⁶Your ancestor Abraham rejoiced that he would see my day; he saw it and was glad." ⁵⁷Then the Jews said to him, "You are not yet fifty years old, and have you seen Abraham?"*a* ⁵⁸Jesus said to them, "Very truly, I tell you, before Abraham was, I am." ⁵⁹So they picked up stones to throw at him, but Jesus hid himself and went out of the temple.

A Man Born Blind Receives Sight

9 As he walked along, he saw a man blind from birth. ²His disciples asked him, "Rabbi, who sinned, this man or his parents, that he was born blind?" ³Jesus answered, "Neither this man nor his parents sinned; he was born blind so that God's works might be revealed in him. ⁴We*b* must work the works of him who sent me*c* while it is day; night is coming when no one can work. ⁵As long as I am in the world, I am the light of the world." ⁶When he had said this, he spat on the ground and made mud with the saliva and spread the mud on the man's eyes, ⁷saying to him, "Go, wash in the pool of Siloam" (which means Sent). Then he went and washed and came back able to see. ⁸The neighbors and those who had seen him before as a beggar began to ask, "Is this not the man who used to sit and beg?" ⁹Some were saying, "It is he." Others were saying, "No, but it is someone like him." He kept saying, "I am the man." ¹⁰But they kept asking him, "Then how were your eyes opened?" ¹¹He answered, "The man called Jesus made mud, spread it on my eyes, and said to me, 'Go to Siloam and wash.' Then I went and

a Other ancient authorities read *has Abraham seen you?* *b* Other ancient authorities read *I* *c* Other ancient authorities read *us*

9:1–12—Jesus manifests God's salvation (*light*, v. 5; Ps. 27:1; Isa. 9:1–7) by healing a blind beggar. As with Jesus' previous miracles (4:46–54; 5:1–18), this healing enacts God's life-giving purposes even among physically restricted and socially despised folks. The event challenges people to discern Jesus' identity, the significance of

his action, and the transforming nature of God's purposes. Through the chapter, various people try to understand what Jesus has done. The healed man begins with a simple report that *the man called Jesus* (v. 11) healed him but journeys to faith and insight, often in the face of hostility and opposition.

washed and received my sight." [12] They said to him, "Where is he?" He said, "I do not know."

The Pharisees Investigate the Healing

13 They brought to the Pharisees the man who had formerly been blind. [14] Now it was a sabbath day when Jesus made the mud and opened his eyes. [15] Then the Pharisees also began to ask him how he had received his sight. He said to them, "He put mud on my eyes. Then I washed, and now I see." [16] Some of the Pharisees said, "This man is not from God, for he does not observe the sabbath." But others said, "How can a man who is a sinner perform such signs?" And they were divided. [17] So they said again to the blind man, "What do you say about him? It was your eyes he opened." He said, "He is a prophet."

18 The Jews did not believe that he had been blind and had received his sight until they called the parents of the man who had received his sight [19] and asked them, "Is this your son, who you say was born blind? How then does he now see?" [20] His parents answered, "We know that this is our son, and that he was born blind; [21] but we do not know how it is that now he sees, nor do we know who opened his eyes. Ask him; he is of age. He will speak for himself." [22] His parents said this because they were afraid of the Jews; for the Jews had already agreed that anyone who confessed Jesus[a] to be the Messiah[b] would be put out of the synagogue. [23] Therefore his parents said, "He is of age; ask him."

24 So for the second time they called the man who had been blind, and they said to him, "Give glory to God! We know that this man is a sinner." [25] He answered, "I do not know whether he is a sinner. One thing I do know, that though I was blind, now I see." [26] They said to him, "What did he do to you? How did he open your eyes?" [27] He answered them, "I have told you already, and you would not listen. Why do you want to hear it again? Do you also want to become his disciples?" [28] Then they reviled him, saying, "You are his disciple, but we are disciples of Moses. [29] We know that God has spoken to Moses, but as for this man, we do not know where he comes from." [30] The man answered, "Here is an astonishing thing! You do not know where he comes from, and yet he opened my eyes. [31] We know that God does not listen to sinners, but he does listen to one who worships him and obeys his will. [32] Never since the world began has it been heard that anyone opened the eyes of a person born blind. [33] If this man were not from God, he could do nothing." [34] They answered him, "You were born entirely in sins, and are you trying to teach us?" And they drove him out.

[a] Gk him   [b] Or the Christ

9:13–17—Members of the elite, the Pharisees (1:19, 24; 3:1), conclude that healing on the Sabbath proves Jesus is not from God. They exemplify the very human response of opposing that which challenges their sense of how the world should be ordered. They remain oblivious to God's merciful, transforming work that brings inclusion and wholeness to the healed man. His growing understanding of Jesus' identity is reflected in his new confession of Jesus' identity (v. 17).

9:18–23—The elite (called *Jews*/Judeans; see note at 3:1–2) question his parents, who confirm he was blind but, because of fear, say nothing about Jesus. Many interpreters see v. 22 (also 12:42; 16:2) as reflecting a situation of alienation between John's community and a synagogue over Jesus' identity and mission.

9:24–34—The healed man models characteristics of discipleship. Disciples know pressure and opposition from the elite opposed to Jesus (v. 24). Without giving in, he bears witness as he challenges them to become disciples (v. 27). He confesses Jesus' origin from God (v. 33). Recognizing Jesus' identity (vv. 24–25) and origin (vv. 29–33) are central affirmations for disciples. He suffers the social consequences as the leaders, committed to Moses as God's revealer (9:29; 5:45–47) *drove him out* (v. 34, cf. v. 22). The man's insight and faithful witness grow through pressure, opposition, and social exclusion.

Spiritual Blindness

35 Jesus heard that they had driven him out, and when he found him, he said, "Do you believe in the Son of Man?"[a] 36 He answered, "And who is he, sir?[b] Tell me, so that I may believe in him." 37 Jesus said to him, "You have seen him, and the one speaking with you is he." 38 He said, "Lord,[b] I believe." And he worshiped him. 39 Jesus said, "I came into this world for judgment so that those who do not see may see, and those who do see may become blind." 40 Some of the Pharisees near him heard this and said to him, "Surely we are not blind, are we?" 41 Jesus said to them, "If you were blind, you would not have sin. But now that you say, 'We see,' your sin remains.

Jesus the Good Shepherd

10 "Very truly, I tell you, anyone who does not enter the sheepfold by the gate but climbs in by another way is a thief and a bandit. 2 The one who enters by the gate is the shepherd of the sheep. 3 The gatekeeper opens the gate for him, and the sheep hear his voice. He calls his own sheep by name and leads them out. 4 When he has brought out all his own, he goes ahead of them, and the sheep follow him because they know his voice. 5 They will not follow a stranger, but they will run from him because they do not know the voice of strangers." 6 Jesus used this figure of speech with them, but they did not understand what he was saying to them.

7 So again Jesus said to them, "Very truly, I tell you, I am the gate for the sheep. 8 All who came before me are thieves and bandits; but the sheep did not listen to them. 9 I am the gate. Whoever enters by me will be saved, and will come in and go out and find pasture. 10 The thief comes only to steal and kill and destroy. I came that they may have life, and have it abundantly.

11 "I am the good shepherd. The good shepherd lays down his life for the sheep. 12 The hired hand, who is not the shepherd and does not own the sheep, sees the wolf coming and leaves the sheep and runs away—and the wolf snatches them and scatters them. 13 The hired hand runs away because a hired hand does not care for the sheep. 14 I am the good shepherd. I know my own and my own know me, 15 just as the Father knows me and I know the Father. And I

---

a Other ancient authorities read *the Son of God*   *b* *Sir* and *Lord* translate the same Greek word

---

9:35–38—Like a model disciple, the man responds to Jesus' revelation as *Son of Man* (God's revealer linking heaven and earth, 1:51; 3:13–14) with faith and worship (cf. v. 11).

9:39–41—The blindness of the elite denotes not seeing/discerning Jesus' identity. Contemporary disciples can similarly be so committed to certain doctrines, ecclesial practices, cultural mind-sets, or social roles that they remain blind to God's larger purposes.

10:1–6—Jesus employs the figure of the *shepherd* to reveal his role in God's purposes among God's people in contrast to the false leaders exposed in chap. 9 for not receiving God's revelation or living faithfully to it. Jesus is, like God, a shepherd who cares and provides for the *sheep*/disciples (Ps. 23). The image "shepherd" commonly refers to rulers and leaders. Bad shepherds refuse to listen to God's agenda, misuse power to rob people of basic resources, and threaten their existence, contrary to God's purposes (see Ezek. 34). They forfeit their leadership, cease to be shepherds, and become *thieves*, *bandits* (v. 8), and *strangers* (v. 5; see Jer. 7:8–11). Jesus' life-giving mission means continued conflict with the ruling elite's very different understanding of human society. Disciples who lead other disciples need to imitate Jesus' shepherding.

10:7–18—In contrast to "bad" shepherds, Jesus the gate leads disciples to God's salvation (see 3:16–21), in which there is abundant life (10:10), physical wholeness (9:1–12), plentiful food (see 4:43–54; 6:1–15), and intimate encounter with God (17:3). Jesus the good shepherd reveals God's good rule (Ps. 23). Jesus knows the sheep, and they know his voice (John 10:14; see 5:24). This close relationship, the center of discipleship, reflects Jesus' relationship with God (10:15) and is made possible because Jesus willingly and lovingly dies and rises (vv. 15–18). Disciples, the sheep, know he dies for their benefit, enabling a relationship with God and one another marked by mutual love.

lay down my life for the sheep. **16** I have other sheep that do not belong to this fold. I must bring them also, and they will listen to my voice. So there will be one flock, one shepherd. **17** For this reason the Father loves me, because I lay down my life in order to take it up again. **18** No one takes*a* it from me, but I lay it down of my own accord. I have power to lay it down, and I have power to take it up again. I have received this command from my Father."

19 Again the Jews were divided because of these words. **20** Many of them were saying, "He has a demon and is out of his mind. Why listen to him?" **21** Others were saying, "These are not the words of one who has a demon. Can a demon open the eyes of the blind?"

Jesus Is Rejected by the Jews

22 At that time the festival of the Dedication took place in Jerusalem. It was winter, **23** and Jesus was walking in the temple, in the portico of Solomon. **24** So the Jews gathered around him and said to him, "How long will you keep us in suspense? If you are the Messiah,*b* tell us plainly." **25** Jesus answered, "I have told you, and you do not believe. The works that I do in my Father's name testify to me; **26** but you do not believe, because you do not belong to my sheep. **27** My sheep hear my voice. I know them, and they follow me. **28** I give them eternal life, and they will never perish. No one will snatch them out of my hand. **29** What my Father has given me is greater than all else, and no one can snatch it out of the Father's hand.*c* **30** The Father and I are one."

31 The Jews took up stones again to stone him. **32** Jesus replied, "I have shown you many good works from the Father. For which of these are you going to stone me?" **33** The Jews answered, "It is not for a good work that we are going to stone you, but for blasphemy, because you, though only a human being, are making yourself God." **34** Jesus answered, "Is it not written in your law,*d* 'I said, you are gods'? **35** If those to whom the word of God came were called 'gods'—and the scripture cannot be annulled— **36** can you say that the one whom the Father has sanctified and sent into the world is blaspheming because I said, 'I am God's Son'? **37** If I am not doing the works of my Father, then do not believe me. **38** But if I do them, even though you do not believe me, believe the works, so that you may know and understand*e* that the Father is in me and I am in the Father." **39** Then they tried to arrest him again, but he escaped from their hands.

40 He went away again across the Jordan to the place where John had been baptizing earlier, and he remained there. **41** Many came to him, and they were saying, "John performed no sign, but everything that John said about this man was true." **42** And many believed in him there.

The Death of Lazarus

11 Now a certain man was ill, Lazarus of Bethany, the village of

a Other ancient authorities read *has taken* *b* Or *the Christ* *c* Other ancient authorities read *My Father who has given them to me is greater than all, and no one can snatch them out of the Father's hand* *d* Other ancient authorities read *in the law* *e* Other ancient authorities lack *and understand*; others read *and believe*

10:19–21—Jesus' revelation always causes division.

10:22–42—Another festival (see note at 7:1–13), commemorating the Jerusalem temple's rededication in 164 BCE, provides the setting. Jesus is the new temple after Rome destroyed the temple in 70 CE (2:18–22; 11:48). Jesus' loving unity of will with God (10:30; 1:1–3) attests that God has *sanctified* or commissioned or set apart Jesus (10:36) to reveal God's loving and life-giving presence in his actions (vv. 37–38). Disciples

see/discern (9:36–38) God's power and presence in Jesus, believe, and live in ways that manifest God's good purposes.

11:1–16—Lazarus dies. Jesus acts in his own time (2:4; 7:1–10) to demonstrate God's powerful presence in and power over death in raising Lazarus (3:16–21). Jesus' life-giving action that manifests God's purposes (10:30) takes place in the midst of the elite's continued hostility and rejection (11:7–8, 16).

Mary and her sister Martha. [2] Mary was the one who anointed the Lord with perfume and wiped his feet with her hair; her brother Lazarus was ill. [3] So the sisters sent a message to Jesus,[a] "Lord, he whom you love is ill." [4] But when Jesus heard it, he said, "This illness does not lead to death; rather it is for God's glory, so that the Son of God may be glorified through it." [5] Accordingly, though Jesus loved Martha and her sister and Lazarus, [6] after having heard that Lazarus[b] was ill, he stayed two days longer in the place where he was.

[7] Then after this he said to the disciples, "Let us go to Judea again." [8] The disciples said to him, "Rabbi, the Jews were just now trying to stone you, and are you going there again?" [9] Jesus answered, "Are there not twelve hours of daylight? Those who walk during the day do not stumble, because they see the light of this world. [10] But those who walk at night stumble, because the light is not in them." [11] After saying this, he told them, "Our friend Lazarus has fallen asleep, but I am going there to awaken him." [12] The disciples said to him, "Lord, if he has fallen asleep, he will be all right." [13] Jesus, however, had been speaking about his death, but they thought that he was referring merely to sleep. [14] Then Jesus told them plainly, "Lazarus is dead. [15] For your sake I am glad I was not there, so that you may believe. But let us go to him." [16] Thomas, who was called the Twin,[c] said to his fellow disciples, "Let us also go, that we may die with him."

Jesus the Resurrection and the Life

[17] When Jesus arrived, he found that Lazarus[b] had already been in the tomb four days. [18] Now Bethany was near Jerusalem, some two miles[d] away, [19] and many of the Jews had come to Martha and Mary to console them about their brother. [20] When Martha heard that Jesus was coming, she went and met him, while Mary stayed at home. [21] Martha said to Jesus, "Lord, if you had been here, my brother would not have died. [22] But even now I know that God will give you whatever you ask of him." [23] Jesus said to her, "Your brother will rise again." [24] Martha said to him, "I know that he will rise again in the resurrection on the last day." [25] Jesus said to her, "I am the resurrection and the life.[e] Those who believe in me, even though they die, will live, [26] and everyone who lives and believes in me will never die. Do you believe this?" [27] She said to him, "Yes, Lord, I believe that you are the Messiah,[f] the Son of God, the one coming into the world."

Jesus Weeps

[28] When she had said this, she went back and called her sister Mary, and told her privately, "The Teacher is here and is calling for you." [29] And when she heard it, she got up quickly and went to him. [30] Now Jesus had not yet come to the village, but was still at the place where Martha had met him. [31] The Jews who were with her in the house, consoling her, saw Mary get up quickly and go out. They followed her because they thought that she was going to the tomb to weep there. [32] When Mary came where Jesus was and saw him, she knelt at his feet and said to him, "Lord, if you had been here, my brother would not have died." [33] When Jesus saw her weeping, and the Jews who came with her also weeping,

[a] Gk him [b] Gk he [c] Gk Didymus [d] Gk fifteen stadia [e] Other ancient authorities lack and the life [f] Or the Christ

---

11:17–45—Martha, comforted by local Jews/Judeans, rebukes Jesus for doing nothing (vv. 21–23). She understands Jesus' assurance to mean Lazarus will be raised in the future resurrection (Dan. 12:1–3; 2 Macc. 7; John 5:28–29). But Jesus' raising of Lazarus displays God's loving power over death, at work even now in the present. Martha models the response of all disciples who trust God to continue to overcome death's work (11:25–27). Mary's grief moves Jesus (vv. 32–34). He remains forever present to people's pain. Jesus' word gives life to Lazarus (5:24) as it does to all believers.

he was greatly disturbed in spirit and deeply moved. [34] He said, "Where have you laid him?" They said to him, "Lord, come and see." [35] Jesus began to weep. [36] So the Jews said, "See how he loved him!" [37] But some of them said, "Could not he who opened the eyes of the blind man have kept this man from dying?"

Jesus Raises Lazarus to Life

38 Then Jesus, again greatly disturbed, came to the tomb. It was a cave, and a stone was lying against it. [39] Jesus said, "Take away the stone." Martha, the sister of the dead man, said to him, "Lord, already there is a stench because he has been dead four days." [40] Jesus said to her, "Did I not tell you that if you believed, you would see the glory of God?" [41] So they took away the stone. And Jesus looked upward and said, "Father, I thank you for having heard me. [42] I knew that you always hear me, but I have said this for the sake of the crowd standing here, so that they may believe that you sent me." [43] When he had said this, he cried with a loud voice, "Lazarus, come out!" [44] The dead man came out, his hands and feet bound with strips of cloth, and his face wrapped in a cloth. Jesus said to them, "Unbind him, and let him go."

The Plot to Kill Jesus

45 Many of the Jews therefore, who had come with Mary and had seen what Jesus did, believed in him. [46] But some of them went to the Pharisees and told them what he had done. [47] So the chief priests and the Pharisees called a meeting of the council, and said, "What are we to do? This man is performing many signs. [48] If we let him go on like this, everyone will believe in him, and the Romans will come and destroy both our holy place[a] and our nation." [49] But one of them, Caiaphas, who was high priest that year, said to them, "You know nothing at all! [50] You do not understand that it is better for you to have one man die for the people than to have the whole nation destroyed." [51] He did not say this on his own, but being high priest that year he prophesied that Jesus was about to die for the nation, [52] and not for the nation only, but to gather into one the dispersed children of God. [53] So from that day on they planned to put him to death.

54 Jesus therefore no longer walked about openly among the Jews, but went from there to a town called Ephraim in the region near the wilderness; and he remained there with the disciples.

55 Now the Passover of the Jews was near, and many went up from the country to Jerusalem before the Passover to purify themselves. [56] They were looking for Jesus and were asking one another as they stood in the temple, "What do you think? Surely he will not come to the festival, will he?" [57] Now the chief priests and the Pharisees had given orders that anyone who knew where Jesus[b] was should let them know, so that they might arrest him.

Mary Anoints Jesus

12 Six days before the Passover Jesus came to Bethany, the home of Lazarus, whom he had raised from the dead. [2] There they gave a dinner for him. Martha served, and Lazarus was one of those at the table with him. [3] Mary took a pound of costly perfume made of pure nard, anointed Jesus' feet, and wiped

[a] Or our temple; Greek our place   [b] Gk he

11:46–57—The elite, unable to match Jesus' gift of new life and opposed to God's life-giving purposes for a new world, plot against him (vv. 53, 57) because his presence threatens their control (vv. 47–48). John interprets Rome's destruction of Jerusalem and its temple in 70 CE as judgment on the elite for not believing in Jesus! Caiaphas, appointed chief priest by the Romans, suggests an expedient political action (Jesus' death), but ironically describes God's purposes that Jesus' death offers life to all (vv. 50–52; 3:14–16; 12:32).

12:1–11—Mary's action displays qualities that are hallmarks of disciples: self-giving love and recognition of Jesus' identity as the one who manifests God's life through his death.

them[a] with her hair. The house was filled with the fragrance of the perfume. [4] But Judas Iscariot, one of his disciples (the one who was about to betray him), said, [5] "Why was this perfume not sold for three hundred denarii[b] and the money given to the poor?" [6] (He said this not because he cared about the poor, but because he was a thief; he kept the common purse and used to steal what was put into it.) [7] Jesus said, "Leave her alone. She bought it[c] so that she might keep it for the day of my burial. [8] You always have the poor with you, but you do not always have me."

The Plot to Kill Lazarus

[9] When the great crowd of the Jews learned that he was there, they came not only because of Jesus but also to see Lazarus, whom he had raised from the dead. [10] So the chief priests planned to put Lazarus to death as well, [11] since it was on account of him that many of the Jews were deserting and were believing in Jesus.

Jesus' Triumphal Entry into Jerusalem

[12] The next day the great crowd that had come to the festival heard that Jesus was coming to Jerusalem. [13] So they took branches of palm trees and went out to meet him, shouting,

"Hosanna!

Blessed is the one who comes in the
　　　name of the Lord—
　　the King of Israel!"

[14] Jesus found a young donkey and sat on it; as it is written:

[15] "Do not be afraid, daughter of Zion.
　Look, your king is coming,
　　sitting on a donkey's colt!"

[16] His disciples did not understand these things at first; but when Jesus was glorified, then they remembered that these things had been written of him and had been done to him. [17] So the crowd that had been with him when he called Lazarus out of the tomb and raised him from the dead continued to testify.[d] [18] It was also because they heard that he had performed this sign that the crowd went to meet him. [19] The Pharisees then said to one another, "You see, you can do nothing. Look, the world has gone after him!"

Some Greeks Wish to See Jesus

[20] Now among those who went up to worship at the festival were some Greeks. [21] They came to Philip, who was from Bethsaida in Galilee, and said to him, "Sir, we wish to see Jesus." [22] Philip went and told Andrew; then Andrew and Philip went and told Jesus. [23] Jesus answered them, "The hour has come for the Son of Man to be glorified. [24] Very truly, I tell you, unless a grain of wheat falls into the earth and dies, it remains just a single grain; but if it dies, it bears much fruit. [25] Those who love their life lose it, and those who hate their life in this world will keep it for eternal life. [26] Whoever serves me must follow me, and where I am, there will my servant be also. Whoever serves me, the Father will honor.

Jesus Speaks about His Death

[27] "Now my soul is troubled. And what should I say—'Father, save me

[a] Gk his feet　[b] Three hundred denarii would be nearly a year's wages for a laborer　[c] Gk lacks She bought it　[d] Other ancient authorities read with him began to testify that he had called . . . from the dead

---

12:12–19—Jesus enters Jerusalem, revealing not the dominating and death-bringing kingship of a conquering human empire, but God's life-giving reign that will soon be established in full. See Ps. 118:25–26; Zech. 9:9; Zeph. 3:15. The postresurrection perspective is the same as that of contemporary disciples and celebrates Jesus' self-giving love in exhibiting God's purposes (John 12:16).

12:20–26—The appearance of some Gentiles (*Greeks*) means Jesus' hour to die has arrived

(11:51–53; 2:4; 7:30). As non-Jews, they represent the Gentile world that is also included in God's love and purposes. Jesus' life-giving death embraces all people, restores relationship with God, produces the inclusive church, and requires a life of service (12:24–26).

12:27–36—Without the struggle portrayed in Mark 14:32–42, Jesus affirms his death and destiny as part of his life's mission. To confront the elite by revealing God's alternative purposes

from this hour'? No, it is for this reason that I have come to this hour. [28] Father, glorify your name." Then a voice came from heaven, "I have glorified it, and I will glorify it again." [29] The crowd standing there heard it and said that it was thunder. Others said, "An angel has spoken to him." [30] Jesus answered, "This voice has come for your sake, not for mine. [31] Now is the judgment of this world; now the ruler of this world will be driven out. [32] And I, when I am lifted up from the earth, will draw all people[a] to myself." [33] He said this to indicate the kind of death he was to die. [34] The crowd answered him, "We have heard from the law that the Messiah[b] remains forever. How can you say that the Son of Man must be lifted up? Who is this Son of Man?" [35] Jesus said to them, "The light is with you for a little longer. Walk while you have the light, so that the darkness may not overtake you. If you walk in the darkness, you do not know where you are going. [36] While you have the light, believe in the light, so that you may become children of light."

The Unbelief of the People

After Jesus had said this, he departed and hid from them. [37] Although he had performed so many signs in their presence, they did not believe in him. [38] This was to fulfill the word spoken by the prophet Isaiah:

"Lord, who has believed our
    message,
  and to whom has the arm of the
    Lord been revealed?"

[39] And so they could not believe, because Isaiah also said,

[40] "He has blinded their eyes
      and hardened their heart,
  so that they might not look with
      their eyes,
  and understand with their heart
      and turn—
  and I would heal them."

[41] Isaiah said this because[c] he saw his glory and spoke about him. [42] Nevertheless many, even of the authorities, believed in him. But because of the Pharisees they did not confess it, for fear that they would be put out of the synagogue; [43] for they loved human glory more than the glory that comes from God.

Summary of Jesus' Teaching

44 Then Jesus cried aloud: "Whoever believes in me believes not in me but in him who sent me. [45] And whoever sees me sees him who sent me. [46] I have come as light into the world, so that everyone who believes in me should not remain in the darkness. [47] I do not judge anyone who hears my words and does not keep them, for I came not to judge the world, but to save the world. [48] The one who rejects me and does not receive my word has a judge; on the last day the word that I have spoken will serve as judge, [49] for I have not spoken on my own, but the Father who sent me has himself given me a commandment about what to say and what to speak. [50] And I know that his commandment is eternal life. What I speak, therefore, I speak just as the Father has told me."

Jesus Washes the Disciples' Feet

13 Now before the festival of the Passover, Jesus knew that his hour had come to depart from this

[a] Other ancient authorities read *all things*   [b] Or *the Christ*   [c] Other ancient witnesses read *when*

---

inevitably means death. But his being *lifted up* (v. 34) includes not only his death, but also his resurrection and ascension (13:1–3; 3:14; 8:28). It reveals God's power and presence (*glorify*, v. 28), expresses judgment on those who reject him, and offers salvation and life to all people (vv. 24, 31–32). Jesus' death, which embodies these realities, shapes the life of discipleship.

12:37–50—Jesus' ministry ends with a scriptural explanation recognizing that God's purposes are often rejected, and a summary of important themes in Jesus' teaching, including the necessity for a response of believing. Contemporary disciples are challenged to make the same believing response. Nothing—social status, ecclesial role, busy and lengthy service, numerous worthy works—can substitute for it.

world and go to the Father. Having loved his own who were in the world, he loved them to the end. ²The devil had already put it into the heart of Judas son of Simon Iscariot to betray him. And during supper ³Jesus, knowing that the Father had given all things into his hands, and that he had come from God and was going to God, ⁴got up from the table,ᵃ took off his outer robe, and tied a towel around himself. ⁵Then he poured water into a basin and began to wash the disciples' feet and to wipe them with the towel that was tied around him. ⁶He came to Simon Peter, who said to him, "Lord, are you going to wash my feet?" ⁷Jesus answered, "You do not know now what I am doing, but later you will understand." ⁸Peter said to him, "You will never wash my feet." Jesus answered, "Unless I wash you, you have no share with me." ⁹Simon Peter said to him, "Lord, not my feet only but also my hands and my head!" ¹⁰Jesus said to him, "One who has bathed does not need to wash, except for the feet,ᵇ but is entirely clean. And youᶜ are clean, though not all of you." ¹¹For he knew who was to betray him; for this reason he said, "Not all of you are clean."

12 After he had washed their feet, had put on his robe, and had returned to the table, he said to them, "Do you know what I have done to you? ¹³You call me Teacher and Lord—and you are right, for that is what I am. ¹⁴So if I, your Lord and Teacher, have washed your feet, you also ought to wash one another's feet. ¹⁵For I have set you an example, that you also should do as I have done to you. ¹⁶Very truly, I tell you, servantsᵈ are not greater than their master, nor are messengers greater than the one who sent them. ¹⁷If you know these things, you are blessed if you do them. ¹⁸I am not speaking of all of you; I know whom I have chosen. But it is to fulfill the scripture, 'The one who ate my breadᵉ has lifted his heel against me.' ¹⁹I tell you this now, before it occurs, so that when it does occur, you may believe that I am he.ᶠ ²⁰Very truly, I tell you, whoever receives one whom I send receives me; and whoever receives me receives him who sent me."

Jesus Foretells His Betrayal

21 After saying this Jesus was troubled in spirit, and declared, "Very truly, I tell you, one of you will betray me." ²²The disciples looked at one another, uncertain of whom he was speaking. ²³One of his disciples—the one whom Jesus loved—was reclining next to him; ²⁴Simon Peter therefore motioned to him to ask Jesus of whom he was speaking.

ᵃGk from supper   ᵇOther ancient authorities lack except for the feet   ᶜThe Greek word for you here is plural   ᵈGk slaves   ᵉOther ancient authorities read ate bread with me   ᶠGk I am

---

13:1–17:26 Farewell Discourse
Jesus' Farewell Discourse or final testament (cf. Gen. 48–49; Deut.) instructs his disciples about maintaining faithful discipleship when he is not physically present.

13:1–3—Jesus' imminent death marks not his defeat but his faithfulness to his identity and mission. Jesus' death comes about through various factors: a betraying disciple and Satan's opposition (v. 27), God's will (12:27–32), Jesus' self-giving (10:15–18), and the hostile elite's actions (11:45–57).

13:4–11—Jesus' conversation with the uncomfortable Peter explains one aspect of the footwashing. In this intimate service Jesus lovingly offers himself. Being washed by Jesus is to choose to participate in his work of revealing God's saving love. It recognizes the intimate relationship with God that is the foundation of Jesus' ministry and the life of discipleship.

13:12–20—Footwashing also invites disciples into relationships of self-giving love with each other. These relationships embody faithfulness to God's love and sustain disciples in their witness.

13:21–38—Jesus' command to disciples to love one another expresses a consequence of their dwelling in the loving union he shares with God, and faithfully expresses their identity as God's children (1:12). The experience of God's love is neither self-centered nor static. The community of disciples of course does not always live in and out of loving, self-giving relationships with God and each other. Sometimes it lives falsely against God's love in betrayal and faithlessness.

25 So while reclining next to Jesus, he asked him, "Lord, who is it?" 26 Jesus answered, "It is the one to whom I give this piece of bread when I have dipped it in the dish."*a* So when he had dipped the piece of bread, he gave it to Judas son of Simon Iscariot.*b* 27 After he received the piece of bread,*c* Satan entered into him. Jesus said to him, "Do quickly what you are going to do." 28 Now no one at the table knew why he said this to him. 29 Some thought that, because Judas had the common purse, Jesus was telling him, "Buy what we need for the festival"; or, that he should give something to the poor. 30 So, after receiving the piece of bread, he immediately went out. And it was night.

The New Commandment

31 When he had gone out, Jesus said, "Now the Son of Man has been glorified, and God has been glorified in him. 32 If God has been glorified in him,*d* God will also glorify him in himself and will glorify him at once. 33 Little children, I am with you only a little longer. You will look for me; and as I said to the Jews so now I say to you, 'Where I am going, you cannot come.' 34 I give you a new commandment, that you love one another. Just as I have loved you, you also should love one another. 35 By this everyone will know that you are my disciples, if you have love for one another."

Jesus Foretells Peter's Denial

36 Simon Peter said to him, "Lord, where are you going?" Jesus answered, "Where I am going, you cannot follow me now; but you will follow afterward." 37 Peter said to him, "Lord, why can I not follow you now? I will lay down my life for you." 38 Jesus answered, "Will you lay down your life for me? Very truly, I tell you, before the cock crows, you will have denied me three times.

Jesus the Way to the Father

14 "Do not let your hearts be troubled. Believe*e* in God, believe also in me. 2 In my Father's house there are many dwelling places. If it were not so, would I have told you that I go to prepare a place for you?*f* 3 And if I go and prepare a place for you, I will come again and will take you to myself, so that where I am, there you may be also. 4 And you know the way to the place where I am going."*g* 5 Thomas said to him, "Lord, we do not know where you are going. How can we know the way?" 6 Jesus said to him, "I am the way, and the truth, and the life. No one comes to the Father except through me. 7 If you know me, you will know*h* my Father also. From now on you do know him and have seen him."

8 Philip said to him, "Lord, show us the Father, and we will be satisfied." 9 Jesus said to him, "Have I been with you all this time, Philip, and you still do not know me? Whoever has seen me has seen the Father. How can you say, 'Show us the Father'? 10 Do you not believe that I am in the Father and the Father is in me? The words that I say to you I do not speak on my own; but the Father who dwells in me does his works. 11 Believe me that I am in the Father and the Father is in me; but if you do not, then believe me because of the works themselves. 12 Very truly, I tell you, the one who believes in me will also do the works that I do and, in fact, will do greater works than these, because I am going to the Father. 13 I will do whatever you ask in my name, so that the Father

a Gk dipped it   *b* Other ancient authorities read *Judas Iscariot son of Simon*; others, *Judas son of Simon from Karyot* (Kerioth)   *c* Gk *After the piece of bread*   *d* Other ancient authorities lack *If God has been glorified in him*   *e* Or *You believe*   *f* Or *If it were not so, I would have told you; for I go to prepare a place for you*   *g* Other ancient authorities read *Where I am going you know, and the way you know*   *h* Other ancient authorities read *If you had known me, you would have known*

14:1–14—Jesus' life (words and actions) and death reveal God's saving presence in the midst of human experience now (especially encountered in prayer) and anticipate the full experience of that relationship in God's future. Disciples know Jesus as *the way*, the embodiment of and access to God's presence.

may be glorified in the Son. ¹⁴ If in my name you ask me^a for anything, I will do it.

The Promise of the Holy Spirit

15 "If you love me, you will keep^b my commandments. ¹⁶ And I will ask the Father, and he will give you another Advocate,^c to be with you forever. ¹⁷ This is the Spirit of truth, whom the world cannot receive, because it neither sees him nor knows him. You know him, because he abides with you, and he will be in^d you.

18 "I will not leave you orphaned; I am coming to you. ¹⁹ In a little while the world will no longer see me, but you will see me; because I live, you also will live. ²⁰ On that day you will know that I am in my Father, and you in me, and I in you. ²¹ They who have my commandments and keep them are those who love me; and those who love me will be loved by my Father, and I will love them and reveal myself to them." ²² Judas (not Iscariot) said to him, "Lord, how is it that you will reveal yourself to us, and not to the world?" ²³ Jesus answered him, "Those who love me will keep my word, and my Father will love them, and we will come to them and make our home with them. ²⁴ Whoever does not love me does not keep my words; and the word

that you hear is not mine, but is from the Father who sent me.

25 "I have said these things to you while I am still with you. ²⁶ But the Advocate,^c the Holy Spirit, whom the Father will send in my name, will teach you everything, and remind you of all that I have said to you. ²⁷ Peace I leave with you; my peace I give to you. I do not give to you as the world gives. Do not let your hearts be troubled, and do not let them be afraid. ²⁸ You heard me say to you, 'I am going away, and I am coming to you.' If you loved me, you would rejoice that I am going to the Father, because the Father is greater than I. ²⁹ And now I have told you this before it occurs, so that when it does occur, you may believe. ³⁰ I will no longer talk much with you, for the ruler of this world is coming. He has no power over me; ³¹ but I do as the Father has commanded me, so that the world may know that I love the Father. Rise, let us be on our way.

Jesus the True Vine

15 "I am the true vine, and my Father is the vinegrower. ² He removes every branch in me that bears no fruit. Every branch that bears fruit he prunes^e to make it bear more fruit.

^a Other ancient authorities lack *me*   ^b Other ancient authorities read *me, keep*   ^c Or *Helper*   ^d Or *among*   ^e The same Greek root refers to pruning and cleansing

---

14:15–17—*The Spirit* (lit. "Paraclete") is the mode of Jesus' continuing presence in his physical absence. The Spirit remains with disciples (not with the hostile world; 1:10; 15:18) as an agent of God's truth or faithful, loving, salvific action. The word "paraclete" denotes several dimensions of the Spirit's work, present among disciples as companion, counselor, adviser, one who strengthens, and advocate. Discipleship consists of love for Jesus and instruction and obedience through the ever-present Spirit.

14:18–24—Jesus promises to return to disciples to complete the loving union of Father, Son, and disciples (v. 20). Until then, he is present through the Spirit. Love and obedience mark discipleship.

14:25–31—The Paraclete teaches and guides disciples. Jesus comforts disciples by again promising to return (vv. 1–7, 18–20). His death reveals God's will. The *ruler of this world* (v. 30) is usu-

ally understood to be Satan, but the language of "ruler" may also refer to the elite (3:1; 7:26), and Jesus is about to confront the Roman governor, Pilate (chaps. 18–19).

15:1–11—Jesus pictures his intimate ("abiding") relationship with disciples as *branches* growing from a *vine*. The vine often represented Israel's covenant relationship with God (Isa. 5:1–7). God the faithful *vinegrower* holds the branches accountable, tending and pruning this community (John 15:2, 6). Jesus exhorts disciples to abide in him in a mutual relationship (v. 4) marked by oneness of will, prayer, fruitful or productive service, and obedience. Discipleship is not a private, individualistic relationship with God, but membership in a community with relationships and responsibilities. Love for Jesus reciprocates the love of Father and Son (3:35; 5:20).

3 You have already been cleansed[a] by the word that I have spoken to you. 4 Abide in me as I abide in you. Just as the branch cannot bear fruit by itself unless it abides in the vine, neither can you unless you abide in me. 5 I am the vine, you are the branches. Those who abide in me and I in them bear much fruit, because apart from me you can do nothing. 6 Whoever does not abide in me is thrown away like a branch and withers; such branches are gathered, thrown into the fire, and burned. 7 If you abide in me, and my words abide in you, ask for whatever you wish, and it will be done for you. 8 My Father is glorified by this, that you bear much fruit and become[b] my disciples. 9 As the Father has loved me, so I have loved you; abide in my love. 10 If you keep my commandments, you will abide in my love, just as I have kept my Father's commandments and abide in his love. 11 I have said these things to you so that my joy may be in you, and that your joy may be complete.

12 "This is my commandment, that you love one another as I have loved you. 13 No one has greater love than this, to lay down one's life for one's friends. 14 You are my friends if you do what I command you. 15 I do not call you servants[c] any longer, because the servant[d] does not know what the master is doing; but I have called you friends, because I have made known to you everything that I have heard from my Father. 16 You did not choose me but I chose you. And I appointed you to go and bear fruit, fruit that will last, so that the Father will give you whatever you ask him in my name. 17 I am giving you these commands so that you may love one another.

The World's Hatred

18 "If the world hates you, be aware that it hated me before it hated you. 19 If you belonged to the world,[e] the world would love you as its own. Because you do not belong to the world, but I have chosen you out of the world—therefore the world hates you. 20 Remember the word that I said to you, 'Servants[f] are not greater than their master.' If they persecuted me, they will persecute you; if they kept my word, they will keep yours also. 21 But they will do all these things to you on account of my name, because they do not know him who sent me. 22 If I had not come and spoken to them, they would not have sin; but now they have no excuse for their sin. 23 Whoever hates me hates my Father also. 24 If I had not done among them the works that no one else did, they would not have sin. But now they have seen and hated both me and my Father. 25 It was to fulfill the word that is written in their law, 'They hated me without a cause.'

26 "When the Advocate[g] comes, whom I will send to you from the Father, the Spirit of truth who comes from the Father, he will testify on my behalf. 27 You also are to testify because you have been with me from the beginning.

16 "I have said these things to you to keep you from stumbling. 2 They

a The same Greek root refers to pruning and cleansing b Or be c Gk slaves d Gk slave e Gk were of the world f Gk Slaves g Or Helper

---

15:12–17—The mutual love between Father and Son creates a community of love among disciples that embodies God's love (vv. 12, 17). The measure of this love is not one's prominent place or power over others, but self-giving service like Jesus' (v. 13; 10:15–18), active obedience to Jesus' teaching (15:14), fruitfulness, and prayer (v. 16). Fruitfulness requires active discipleship that in service and love works for a world that embodies God's life-giving purposes for all creation (as depicted in Jesus' miracles or signs). Disciples who have chosen to receive Jesus' revelation of God are Jesus' friends, an image that describes wisdom's recipients (v. 15; Wis. 7:27).

15:18–16:4a—Intimate abiding with Jesus (15:1–11) and love for one another (15:12–17) sustain faithful discipleship in a society opposed to God's purposes. Because "the world" (see 1:10) rejects Jesus' revelation, disciples can expect rejection. But harassment does not allow retreat. The Paraclete/Spirit enables disciples to bear witness (15:26–27).

will put you out of the synagogues. Indeed, an hour is coming when those who kill you will think that by doing so they are offering worship to God. ³ And they will do this because they have not known the Father or me. ⁴ But I have said these things to you so that when their hour comes you may remember that I told you about them.

The Work of the Spirit

"I did not say these things to you from the beginning, because I was with you. ⁵ But now I am going to him who sent me; yet none of you asks me, 'Where are you going?' ⁶ But because I have said these things to you, sorrow has filled your hearts. ⁷ Nevertheless I tell you the truth: it is to your advantage that I go away, for if I do not go away, the Advocate*a* will not come to you; but if I go, I will send him to you. ⁸ And when he comes, he will prove the world wrong about*b* sin and righteousness and judgment: ⁹ about sin, because they do not believe in me; ¹⁰ about righteousness, because I am going to the Father and you will see me no longer; ¹¹ about judgment, because the ruler of this world has been condemned.

12 "I still have many things to say to you, but you cannot bear them now. ¹³ When the Spirit of truth comes, he will guide you into all the truth; for he will not speak on his own, but will speak whatever he hears, and he will declare to you the things that are to come. ¹⁴ He will glorify me, because he will take what is mine and declare it to you. ¹⁵ All that the Father has is mine. For this reason I

said that he will take what is mine and declare it to you.

Sorrow Will Turn into Joy

16 "A little while, and you will no longer see me, and again a little while, and you will see me." ¹⁷ Then some of his disciples said to one another, "What does he mean by saying to us, 'A little while, and you will no longer see me, and again a little while, and you will see me'; and 'Because I am going to the Father'?" ¹⁸ They said, "What does he mean by this 'a little while'? We do not know what he is talking about." ¹⁹ Jesus knew that they wanted to ask him, so he said to them, "Are you discussing among yourselves what I meant when I said, 'A little while, and you will no longer see me, and again a little while, and you will see me'? ²⁰ Very truly, I tell you, you will weep and mourn, but the world will rejoice; you will have pain, but your pain will turn into joy. ²¹ When a woman is in labor, she has pain, because her hour has come. But when her child is born, she no longer remembers the anguish because of the joy of having brought a human being into the world. ²² So you have pain now; but I will see you again, and your hearts will rejoice, and no one will take your joy from you. ²³ On that day you will ask nothing of me.*c* Very truly, I tell you, if you ask anything of the Father in my name, he will give it to you.*d* ²⁴ Until now you have not asked for anything in my name. Ask and you will receive, so that your joy may be complete.

a Or *Helper* *b* Or *convict the world of* *c* Or *will ask me no question* *d* Other ancient authorities read *Father, he will give it to you in my name*

16:4b–15—Jesus' departure by death and ascension is good news because he will send the Spirit to disciples (v. 7; 14:16–17, 26; 15:26). Disciples live with the Spirit, who continues Jesus' work, exposing the *world*'s sin of not believing in Jesus (16:8–9; 3:19–21), upholding Jesus' revelation (16:10), and effecting judgment (v. 11; 3:18; 5:19–30). The Spirit continues the presence and revelatory mission of Jesus among the community of disciples, enacting God's saving faithfulness (*truth*, v. 13) and guiding them in faithful living.

God's loving work is not limited by space, time, or individual failings.

16:16–24—For a while disciples grieve Jesus' absence (vv. 20–22a). His promised return (vv. 16–18), though, will be a time of joy and unity with God as God's salvation, known already in the present, is finally completed (vv. 22b–24). Disciples live actively in the light of and toward this goal.

Peace for the Disciples

25 "I have said these things to you in figures of speech. The hour is coming when I will no longer speak to you in figures, but will tell you plainly of the Father. [26] On that day you will ask in my name. I do not say to you that I will ask the Father on your behalf; [27] for the Father himself loves you, because you have loved me and have believed that I came from God.[a] [28] I came from the Father and have come into the world; again, I am leaving the world and am going to the Father."

29 His disciples said, "Yes, now you are speaking plainly, not in any figure of speech! [30] Now we know that you know all things, and do not need to have anyone question you; by this we believe that you came from God." [31] Jesus answered them, "Do you now believe? [32] The hour is coming, indeed it has come, when you will be scattered, each one to his home, and you will leave me alone. Yet I am not alone because the Father is with me. [33] I have said this to you, so that in me you may have peace. In the world you face persecution. But take courage; I have conquered the world!"

Jesus Prays for His Disciples

17 After Jesus had spoken these words, he looked up to heaven and said, "Father, the hour has come; glorify your Son so that the Son may glorify you, [2] since you have given him authority over all people,[b] to give eternal life to all whom you have given him. [3] And this is eternal life, that they may know you, the only true God, and Jesus Christ whom you have sent. [4] I glorified you on earth by finishing the work that you gave me to do. [5] So now, Father, glorify me in your own presence with the glory that I had in your presence before the world existed.

6 "I have made your name known to those whom you gave me from the world. They were yours, and you gave them to me, and they have kept your word. [7] Now they know that everything you have given me is from you; [8] for the words that you gave to me I have given to them, and they have received them and know in truth that I came from you; and they have believed that you sent me. [9] I am asking on their behalf; I am not asking on behalf of the world, but on behalf of those whom you gave me, because they are yours. [10] All mine are yours, and yours are mine; and I have been glorified in them. [11] And now I am no longer in the world, but they are in the world, and I am coming to you. Holy Father, protect them in your name that you have given me, so that they may be one,

[a] Other ancient authorities read *the Father*　[b] Gk *flesh*

16:25–33—Now is a time of veiled revelation. Jesus' return will be a time of plain speech (v. 25), of direct relationship with the God of love whom Jesus reveals and to whom he returns (vv. 26–28). The disciples mistakenly think that time is now (vv. 29–30). Instead, Jesus warns that discipleship now means pressure, faithlessness, testing (vv. 31–32a). But God's presence is faithful (v. 32b), and God's victory over the hostile world is sure. Disciples in the meantime must show *courage* (v. 33).

17:1–8—Discipleship involves not only the realities identified in chaps. 13–16, but also membership in a community for whom Jesus prays. Jesus entrusts this community to God's grace now that Jesus' *hour* to depart to the Father through his death has come (12:23; 13:1–3). This death, like his life, is his glorification, namely the revelation of God's power and presence. God has authorized Jesus' mission to give *eternal life* or intimate mutual relationship with God (17:2–4). Disciples attest that Jesus has faithfully carried out this mission because they know this life, this relationship, by trusting themselves to God's purposes revealed in Jesus (vv. 6–8).

17:9–19—Jesus' prayer emphasizes important aspects of discipleship. They live in a hostile world under Satan's influence, so Jesus prays that God will *protect* them (vv. 11, 14–15; 15:18–16:4). There are pressures for division, so Jesus prays that God will preserve their unity that reflects and embodies the unity of Father and Son (17:11). They must not be distracted from their identity and mission as a community set apart (*sanctify*) to serve God's saving purposes (*truth*, v. 17) and to continue Jesus' tasks of revealing God's loving, life-giving power and presence (v. 18).

as we are one. **12** While I was with them, I protected them in your name that[a] you have given me. I guarded them, and not one of them was lost except the one destined to be lost,[b] so that the scripture might be fulfilled. **13** But now I am coming to you, and I speak these things in the world so that they may have my joy made complete in themselves.[c] **14** I have given them your word, and the world has hated them because they do not belong to the world, just as I do not belong to the world. **15** I am not asking you to take them out of the world, but I ask you to protect them from the evil one.[d] **16** They do not belong to the world, just as I do not belong to the world. **17** Sanctify them in the truth; your word is truth. **18** As you have sent me into the world, so I have sent them into the world. **19** And for their sakes I sanctify myself, so that they also may be sanctified in truth.

20 "I ask not only on behalf of these, but also on behalf of those who will believe in me through their word, **21** that they may all be one. As you, Father, are in me and I am in you, may they also be in us,[e] so that the world may believe that you have sent me. **22** The glory that you have given me I have given them, so that they may be one, as we are one, **23** I in them and you in me, that they

may become completely one, so that the world may know that you have sent me and have loved them even as you have loved me. **24** Father, I desire that those also, whom you have given me, may be with me where I am, to see my glory, which you have given me because you loved me before the foundation of the world.

25 "Righteous Father, the world does not know you, but I know you; and these know that you have sent me. **26** I made your name known to them, and I will make it known, so that the love with which you have loved me may be in them, and I in them."

The Betrayal and Arrest of Jesus

18 After Jesus had spoken these words, he went out with his disciples across the Kidron valley to a place where there was a garden, which he and his disciples entered. **2** Now Judas, who betrayed him, also knew the place, because Jesus often met there with his disciples. **3** So Judas brought a detachment of soldiers together with police from the chief priests and the Pharisees, and they came there with lanterns and torches and weapons. **4** Then Jesus,

[a] Other ancient authorities read *protected in your name those whom*
[b] Gk *except the son of destruction*   [c] Or *among themselves*   [d] Or *from evil*
[e] Other ancient authorities read *be one in us*

17:20–26—Jesus prays that in being one, disciples will participate in the loving unity of Jesus and God (vv. 21–23; cf. v. 11), bring other believers into this relationship and community, and be present with Jesus in the eschatological completion of God's life-giving purposes (vv. 24–26). The divided state of contemporary Christianity, dominated by denominations and independent groups, seems far from this vision of a unified people. Unity, of course, can be expressed in numerous ways, and patterns of organization or solemn declarations from official committees do not guarantee it. Nor does unity negate diversity. But the prayer spells out the goal for believers of unity in the very life of God, a purpose that God, to whom Jesus entrusts the church in this prayer, has not yet completed.

18:1–19:42 The Passion Narrative

The transition from Jesus' instructions for disciples to Jesus' "trial" and crucifixion is sudden.

The world (esp. the political-religious elite) rejects Jesus. God's power and presence are revealed in raising Jesus and in Jesus' return to God (also called his hour [2:4; 12:23; 13:1–3], lifting up [12:32–33], and glorification, [17:1–5]).

18:1–12—Judas, though close to Jesus, betrays him and allies himself with the elite's soldiers (12:1–8; 13:1–30). Why? Not for greed as in Matt. 26:14–16, but because he comes under the cosmic power of Satan, the opponent of God's purposes (13:2, 27). As contemporary disciples know, discipleship is always brittle and vulnerable, despite Jesus' prayer, to betrayal through false commitments and alliances, decisions that counter God's purposes, inactivity, indifference, etc. But God's purposes are not thwarted by Judas's act. Jesus gives himself to die willingly (10:15–18; 18:4), and, as always, reveals God's presence (*I am*, 18:5–8).

knowing all that was to happen to him, came forward and asked them, "Whom are you looking for?" [5] They answered, "Jesus of Nazareth."[a] Jesus replied, "I am he."[b] Judas, who betrayed him, was standing with them. [6] When Jesus[c] said to them, "I am he,"[b] they stepped back and fell to the ground. [7] Again he asked them, "Whom are you looking for?" And they said, "Jesus of Nazareth."[a] [8] Jesus answered, "I told you that I am he.[b] So if you are looking for me, let these men go." [9] This was to fulfill the word that he had spoken, "I did not lose a single one of those whom you gave me." [10] Then Simon Peter, who had a sword, drew it, struck the high priest's slave, and cut off his right ear. The slave's name was Malchus. [11] Jesus said to Peter, "Put your sword back into its sheath. Am I not to drink the cup that the Father has given me?"

Jesus before the High Priest

12 So the soldiers, their officer, and the Jewish police arrested Jesus and bound him. [13] First they took him to Annas, who was the father-in-law of Caiaphas, the high priest that year. [14] Caiaphas was the one who had advised the Jews that it was better to have one person die for the people.

Peter Denies Jesus

15 Simon Peter and another disciple followed Jesus. Since that disciple was known to the high priest, he went with Jesus into the courtyard of the high priest, [16] but Peter was standing outside at the gate. So the other disciple, who was known to the high priest, went out, spoke to the woman who guarded the gate, and brought Peter in. [17] The woman said to Peter, "You are not also one of this man's disciples, are you?" He said, "I am not." [18] Now the slaves and the police had made a charcoal fire because it was cold, and they were standing around it and warming themselves. Peter also was standing with them and warming himself.

The High Priest Questions Jesus

19 Then the high priest questioned Jesus about his disciples and about his teaching. [20] Jesus answered, "I have spoken openly to the world; I have always taught in synagogues and in the temple, where all the Jews come together. I have said nothing in secret. [21] Why do you ask me? Ask those who heard what I said to them; they know what I said." [22] When he had said this, one of the police standing nearby struck Jesus on the face, saying, "Is that how you answer the high priest?" [23] Jesus answered, "If I have spoken wrongly, testify to the wrong. But if I have spoken rightly, why do you strike me?" [24] Then Annas sent him bound to Caiaphas the high priest.

Peter Denies Jesus Again

25 Now Simon Peter was standing and warming himself. They asked him, "You are not also one of his disciples, are you?" He denied it and said, "I am not." [26] One of the slaves of the high priest, a relative of the man whose ear Peter had cut off, asked, "Did I not see you in the garden with him?" [27] Again Peter denied it, and at that moment the cock crowed.

Jesus before Pilate

28 Then they took Jesus from Caiaphas to Pilate's headquarters.[d] It was early in the morning. They themselves

[a] Gk the Nazorean [b] Gk I am [c] Gk he [d] Gk the praetorium

---

18:13–27—The Jerusalem leaders investigate Jesus' supporters and teaching (v. 19) and with violence (v. 22) reject his claims, sending him to Pilate, the Roman governor, for the death penalty. Peter, like Judas, denies allegiance to Jesus (vv. 15–18, 25–27), as Jesus reliably but sadly predicted (13:38). Disciples always face the difficult challenges and consequences of choosing loyalty to God rather than cultural norms, social acceptability, and certain success.

18:28–19:16 Jesus' "Trial"
Jesus' "trial" before Pilate comprises seven sub-scenes as Pilate shuttles between his Jerusalem allies and Jesus. The governor represents and protects Rome's political-economic interests against

did not enter the headquarters,[a] so as to avoid ritual defilement and to be able to eat the Passover. 29 So Pilate went out to them and said, "What accusation do you bring against this man?" 30 They answered, "If this man were not a criminal, we would not have handed him over to you." 31 Pilate said to them, "Take him yourselves and judge him according to your law." The Jews replied, "We are not permitted to put anyone to death." 32 (This was to fulfill what Jesus had said when he indicated the kind of death he was to die.)

33 Then Pilate entered the headquarters[a] again, summoned Jesus, and asked him, "Are you the King of the Jews?" 34 Jesus answered, "Do you ask this on your own, or did others tell you about me?" 35 Pilate replied, "I am not a Jew, am I? Your own nation and the chief priests have handed you over to me. What have you done?" 36 Jesus answered, "My kingdom is not from this world. If my kingdom were from this world, my followers would be fighting to keep me from being handed over to the Jews. But as it is, my kingdom is not from here." 37 Pilate asked him, "So you are a king?" Jesus answered, "You say that I am a king. For this I was born, and for this I came into the world, to testify to the truth. Everyone who belongs to the truth listens to my voice." 38 Pilate asked him, "What is truth?"

Jesus Sentenced to Death

After he had said this, he went out to the Jews again and told them, "I find no case against him. 39 But you have a custom that I release someone for you at the Passover. Do you want me to release for you the King of the Jews?" 40 They shouted in reply, "Not this man, but Barabbas!" Now Barabbas was a bandit.

19 Then Pilate took Jesus and had him flogged. 2 And the soldiers wove a crown of thorns and put it on his head, and they dressed him in a purple robe. 3 They kept coming up to him, saying, "Hail, King of the Jews!" and striking him on the face. 4 Pilate went out again and said to them, "Look, I am bringing him out to you to let you know that I find no case against him." 5 So Jesus came out, wearing the crown of thorns and the purple robe. Pilate said to them, "Here is the man!" 6 When the chief priests and the police saw him, they shouted, "Crucify him! Crucify him!" Pilate said to them, "Take him yourselves and crucify him; I find no case against him." 7 The Jews answered him, "We have a law, and according to that law he ought to die because he has claimed to be the Son of God."

8 Now when Pilate heard this, he was more afraid than ever. 9 He entered his headquarters[a] again and asked Jesus,

[a] Gk the praetorium

Jesus' vision for a different society. The trial occurs in the headquarters of Roman occupation (*praetorium*, v. 28 NRSV footnote) ironically during Passover's celebration of God's liberation of the people from Pharaoh, who also opposed God's purposes (v. 28).

18:29–32—The Jerusalem elite, opponents of Jesus throughout, cannot recognize him as God's Son or agent. They accuse Jesus of "doing evil," the literal translation of *criminal* (v. 30). Though it is Jesus' trial, they condemn themselves (3:18; 12:46–50).

18:33–40—Pilate rejects Jesus. His question about Jesus' identity accuses him of being a political rebel. Jesus is not a typical "king" in violently imposing his will for his own benefit, but in his healings, feedings, and teaching (3:3,

5; 18:36) he reveals God's life-giving reign. Jesus testifies to *truth*, God's saving purposes (v. 37), but Pilate can't "hear" Jesus' words. In offering Barabbas's release, Pilate ironically provides a choice between violent or nonviolent opposition to Rome. Jesus' commitment to nonviolence rejects the usual violent way of doing business and challenges disciples to live accordingly.

19:1–7—Physical violence and humiliation express the elite's decision against Jesus. After Pilate had Jesus whipped, Pilate's claim to find *no case* (v. 4) may be a sarcastic taunt at his Jerusalem allies. They reject Jesus and God's purposes while ironically defending God's honor in charging *Jesus* with dishonoring God (blasphemy, Lev. 24:16).

19:8–11—Pilate asks the key question, which

"Where are you from?" But Jesus gave him no answer. [10] Pilate therefore said to him, "Do you refuse to speak to me? Do you not know that I have power to release you, and power to crucify you?" [11] Jesus answered him, "You would have no power over me unless it had been given you from above; therefore the one who handed me over to you is guilty of a greater sin." [12] From then on Pilate tried to release him, but the Jews cried out, "If you release this man, you are no friend of the emperor. Everyone who claims to be a king sets himself against the emperor."

13 When Pilate heard these words, he brought Jesus outside and sat[a] on the judge's bench at a place called The Stone Pavement, or in Hebrew[b] Gabbatha. [14] Now it was the day of Preparation for the Passover; and it was about noon. He said to the Jews, "Here is your King!" [15] They cried out, "Away with him! Away with him! Crucify him!" Pilate asked them, "Shall I crucify your King?" The chief priests answered, "We have no king but the emperor." [16] Then he handed him over to them to be crucified.

The Crucifixion of Jesus

So they took Jesus; [17] and carrying the cross by himself, he went out to what is called The Place of the Skull, which in Hebrew[a] is called Golgotha. [18] There they crucified him, and with him two others, one on either side, with Jesus between them. [19] Pilate also had an inscription written and put on the cross.

It read, "Jesus of Nazareth,[c] the King of the Jews." [20] Many of the Jews read this inscription, because the place where Jesus was crucified was near the city; and it was written in Hebrew,[b] in Latin, and in Greek. [21] Then the chief priests of the Jews said to Pilate, "Do not write, 'The King of the Jews,' but, 'This man said, I am King of the Jews.'" [22] Pilate answered, "What I have written I have written." [23] When the soldiers had crucified Jesus, they took his clothes and divided them into four parts, one for each soldier. They also took his tunic; now the tunic was seamless, woven in one piece from the top. [24] So they said to one another, "Let us not tear it, but cast lots for it to see who will get it." This was to fulfill what the scripture says,

"They divided my clothes among themselves,
and for my clothing they cast lots."

[25] And that is what the soldiers did.

Meanwhile, standing near the cross of Jesus were his mother, and his mother's sister, Mary the wife of Clopas, and Mary Magdalene. [26] When Jesus saw his mother and the disciple whom he loved standing beside her, he said to his mother, "Woman, here is your son." [27] Then he said to the disciple, "Here is your mother." And from that hour the disciple took her into his own home.

28 After this, when Jesus knew that all was now finished, he said (in order to fulfill the scripture), "I am thirsty." [29] A jar full of sour wine was standing there.

[a] Or seated him   [b] That is, Aramaic   [c] Gk the Nazorean

---

Jesus has already answered (18:36–37). Jesus relativizes Pilate's threat and boast by testifying to God's greater purposes.

19:12–16—The Jerusalem leaders' allegiance to Rome, not to God, is exposed. Not for the last time in human history, political expediency and protection of their own interests, against God's life-giving work, seem to win. Pilate condemns Jesus (*king*) as a threat to the status quo.

19:17–42 Jesus' Crucifixion and Burial

19:17–22—Rome used painful and shameful crucifixion to eliminate those who threatened its control, and to deter others. Pilate, ironically,

proclaims Jesus' identity as revealer of God's reign for all to know.

19:23–30—Casting *lots* (Ps. 22:18) and Jesus' thirst (Ps. 69:21) present Jesus as the righteous one who in lament psalms like Pss. 22 and 69 suffers at the hands of enemies and is vindicated by God. Jesus finishes the work of revealing God's life (John 17:4) and love (3:16) amidst brutal hatred and resistance to God's purposes. This is the world in and to which disciples are called to bear witness. To be a disciple is to recognize that one does not want to live according to the ways of the status quo, but according to God's purposes.

So they put a sponge full of the wine on a branch of hyssop and held it to his mouth. ³⁰ When Jesus had received the wine, he said, "It is finished." Then he bowed his head and gave up his spirit.

Jesus' Side Is Pierced

31 Since it was the day of Preparation, the Jews did not want the bodies left on the cross during the sabbath, especially because that sabbath was a day of great solemnity. So they asked Pilate to have the legs of the crucified men broken and the bodies removed. ³² Then the soldiers came and broke the legs of the first and of the other who had been crucified with him. ³³ But when they came to Jesus and saw that he was already dead, they did not break his legs. ³⁴ Instead, one of the soldiers pierced his side with a spear, and at once blood and water came out. ³⁵ (He who saw this has testified so that you also may believe. His testimony is true, and he knows*a* that he tells the truth.) ³⁶ These things occurred so that the scripture might be fulfilled, "None of his bones shall be broken." ³⁷ And again another passage of scripture says, "They will look on the one whom they have pierced."

The Burial of Jesus

38 After these things, Joseph of Arimathea, who was a disciple of Jesus, though a secret one because of his fear of the Jews, asked Pilate to let him take away the body of Jesus. Pilate gave him permission; so he came and removed his body. ³⁹ Nicodemus, who had at first come to Jesus by night, also came, bringing a mixture of myrrh and aloes, weighing about a hundred pounds. ⁴⁰ They took the body of Jesus and wrapped it with the spices in linen cloths, according to the burial custom of the Jews. ⁴¹ Now there was a garden in the place where he was crucified, and in the garden there was a new tomb in which no one had ever been laid. ⁴² And so, because it was the Jewish day of Preparation, and the tomb was nearby, they laid Jesus there.

The Resurrection of Jesus

20 Early on the first day of the week, while it was still dark, Mary Magdalene came to the tomb and saw that the stone had been removed from the tomb. ² So she ran and went to Simon Peter and the other disciple, the one whom Jesus loved, and said to them, "They have taken the Lord out of the tomb, and we do not know where they have laid him." ³ Then Peter and the other disciple set out and went toward the tomb. ⁴ The two were running together, but the other disciple outran Peter and reached the tomb first. ⁵ He bent down to look in and saw the linen wrappings lying there, but he did not go in. ⁶ Then Simon Peter came, following him, and went into the tomb. He saw the linen wrappings lying there, ⁷ and the cloth that had been on Jesus' head, not lying with the linen wrappings but rolled up in a place by itself. ⁸ Then the other disciple, who reached the tomb first, also went in, and he saw

a Or there is one who knows

19:31–37—*Blood and water* (v. 34) confirm Jesus' death, from which flows life for all (6:53–55; 7:37–38).

19:38–42—Joseph and Nicodemus (3:1–5) honor Jesus with a burial—and enough spices to keep someone dead forever! Jesus has already indicated that God will "lift him up" (3:14; 8:28; 12:32) from death in the resurrection and ascension. Despite all appearances to the contrary, God's purposes for life are being worked out.

20:1–21:25 The Resurrection

20:1–18—Jesus' resurrection reveals the limits of the elite's power, their sinful opposition to God's life-giving purposes, and their commitment to death. Resurrection was expected when God's reign was established in full (Dan. 12:1–3), so Jesus' resurrection anticipates the completion of God's purposes. The grieving Mary encounters the risen Jesus. She, a woman, is the first to witness and proclaim that Jesus is ascending to *my God and your God* (v. 17). Believers share in the intimate loving relationship that God and Jesus enjoy.

and believed; [9] for as yet they did not understand the scripture, that he must rise from the dead. [10] Then the disciples returned to their homes.

Jesus Appears to Mary Magdalene

[11] But Mary stood weeping outside the tomb. As she wept, she bent over to look[a] into the tomb; [12] and she saw two angels in white, sitting where the body of Jesus had been lying, one at the head and the other at the feet. [13] They said to her, "Woman, why are you weeping?" She said to them, "They have taken away my Lord, and I do not know where they have laid him." [14] When she had said this, she turned around and saw Jesus standing there, but she did not know that it was Jesus. [15] Jesus said to her, "Woman, why are you weeping? Whom are you looking for?" Supposing him to be the gardener, she said to him, "Sir, if you have carried him away, tell me where you have laid him, and I will take him away." [16] Jesus said to her, "Mary!" She turned and said to him in Hebrew,[b] "Rabbouni!" (which means Teacher). [17] Jesus said to her, "Do not hold on to me, because I have not yet ascended to the Father. But go to my brothers and say to them, 'I am ascending to my Father and your Father, to my God and your God.'" [18] Mary Magdalene went and announced to the disciples, "I have seen the Lord"; and she told them that he had said these things to her.

Jesus Appears to the Disciples

[19] When it was evening on that day, the first day of the week, and the doors of the house where the disciples had met were locked for fear of the Jews, Jesus came and stood among them and said, "Peace be with you." [20] After he said this, he showed them his hands and his side. Then the disciples rejoiced when they saw the Lord. [21] Jesus said to them again, "Peace be with you. As the Father has sent me, so I send you." [22] When he had said this, he breathed on them and said to them, "Receive the Holy Spirit. [23] If you forgive the sins of any, they are forgiven them; if you retain the sins of any, they are retained."

Jesus and Thomas

[24] But Thomas (who was called the Twin[c]), one of the twelve, was not with them when Jesus came. [25] So the other disciples told him, "We have seen the Lord." But he said to them, "Unless I see the mark of the nails in his hands, and put my finger in the mark of the nails and my hand in his side, I will not believe."

[26] A week later his disciples were again in the house, and Thomas was with them. Although the doors were shut, Jesus came and stood among them and said, "Peace be with you." [27] Then he said to Thomas, "Put your finger here and see my hands. Reach out your hand and put it in my side. Do not doubt but believe." [28] Thomas answered him, "My Lord and my God!" [29] Jesus said to him, "Have you believed because you have seen me? Blessed are those who have not seen and yet have come to believe."

The Purpose of This Book

[30] Now Jesus did many other signs in the presence of his disciples, which are not written in this book. [31] But these are written so that you may come to

a Gk lacks to look   b That is, Aramaic   c Gk Didymus

20:19–23—Jesus appears to the disciples who fear that Jesus' fate will be theirs too. Jesus' *peace* (vv. 19, 21; see 14:27) expresses God's saving work. True to his word, Jesus gives them the promised *Spirit* (v. 22; see 14:26; 15:26) to guide and empower them in their mission work to announce God's salvation.

20:24–29—Thomas does not believe the proclamation (v. 25). Jesus' gracious appearance elicits

his recognition of God's work. Jesus blesses subsequent generations who believe John's gospel story that makes Jesus present.

20:30–31—Addressed to the Gospel's audience, these verses sum up Jesus' ministry, state the Gospel's purpose of affirming continuing belief in Jesus as God's revelation, and name *life*, intimate relationship with God, as Jesus' gift.

believe[a] that Jesus is the Messiah,[b] the Son of God, and that through believing you may have life in his name.

Jesus Appears to Seven Disciples

21 After these things Jesus showed himself again to the disciples by the Sea of Tiberias; and he showed himself in this way. ² Gathered there together were Simon Peter, Thomas called the Twin,[c] Nathanael of Cana in Galilee, the sons of Zebedee, and two others of his disciples. ³ Simon Peter said to them, "I am going fishing." They said to him, "We will go with you." They went out and got into the boat, but that night they caught nothing.

4 Just after daybreak, Jesus stood on the beach; but the disciples did not know that it was Jesus. ⁵ Jesus said to them, "Children, you have no fish, have you?" They answered him, "No." ⁶ He said to them, "Cast the net to the right side of the boat, and you will find some." So they cast it, and now they were not able to haul it in because there were so many fish. ⁷ That disciple whom Jesus loved said to Peter, "It is the Lord!" When Simon Peter heard that it was the Lord, he put on some clothes, for he was naked, and jumped into the sea. ⁸ But the other disciples came in the boat, dragging the net full of fish, for they were not far from the land, only about a hundred yards[d] off.

9 When they had gone ashore, they saw a charcoal fire there, with fish on it, and bread. ¹⁰ Jesus said to them, "Bring some of the fish that you have just caught." ¹¹ So Simon Peter went aboard and hauled the net ashore, full of large fish, a hundred fifty-three of them; and though there were so many, the net was not torn. ¹² Jesus said to them, "Come and have breakfast." Now none of the disciples dared to ask him, "Who are you?" because they knew it was the Lord. ¹³ Jesus came and took the bread and gave it to them, and did the same with the fish. ¹⁴ This was now the third time that Jesus appeared to the disciples after he was raised from the dead.

Jesus and Peter

15 When they had finished breakfast, Jesus said to Simon Peter, "Simon son of John, do you love me more than these?" He said to him, "Yes, Lord; you know that I love you." Jesus said to him, "Feed my lambs." ¹⁶ A second time he said to him, "Simon son of John, do you love me?" He said to him, "Yes, Lord; you know that I love you." Jesus said to him, "Tend my sheep." ¹⁷ He said to him the third time, "Simon son of John, do you love me?" Peter felt hurt because he said to him the third time, "Do you love me?" And he said to him, "Lord, you know everything; you know that I love you." Jesus said to him, "Feed my sheep. ¹⁸ Very truly, I tell you, when you were younger, you used to fasten your own belt and to go wherever you wished. But when you grow old, you will stretch out your hands, and someone else will fasten a belt around you and take you where you do not wish to go." ¹⁹ (He said this to indicate the kind of death by which he would glorify God.) After this he said to him, "Follow me."

---

[a] Other ancient authorities read *may continue to believe*   [b] Or *the Christ*   [c] Gk *Didymus*   [d] Gk *two hundred cubits*

21:1–14—This chapter, perhaps added sometime later, makes an awkward sequence after 20:30–31. The chapter provides further appearance stories and in restoring Peter points to the community's future in Jesus' absence (so chaps. 13–17).

Jesus is revealed in the large catch of fish. The large number (153) may anticipate the disciples' effective mission work or may symbolize the abundant food and fertility of God's new age (wine in 2:1–11; bread in chap. 6).

21:15–23—Jesus' threefold questions to Peter recall his threefold denial in 18:17–27. Love for Jesus is the appropriate response to the love shared by Father and Son (3:35) and exhibited by Jesus to the world (3:16) and to disciples (15:9). Peter is commissioned, as are all disciples, to continue Jesus' work as shepherd (chap. 10). Martyrdom, the giving of his life, is Peter's destiny (21:18–19), but not that of the beloved disciple (vv. 20–23).

Jesus and the Beloved Disciple

20 Peter turned and saw the disciple whom Jesus loved following them; he was the one who had reclined next to Jesus at the supper and had said, "Lord, who is it that is going to betray you?" 21 When Peter saw him, he said to Jesus, "Lord, what about him?" 22 Jesus said to him, "If it is my will that he remain until I come, what is that to you? Follow me!" 23 So the rumor spread in the community*a* that this disciple would not die. Yet Jesus did not say to him that he would not die, but, "If it is my will that he remain until I come, what is that to you?"*b*

24 This is the disciple who is testifying to these things and has written them, and we know that his testimony is true. 25 But there are also many other things that Jesus did; if every one of them were written down, I suppose that the world itself could not contain the books that would be written.

a Gk *among the brothers*   *b* Other ancient authorities lack *what is that to you*

21:24–25—This second conclusion legitimates the Gospel's claim. The Gospel is true in faithfully bearing witness to God's loving, life-giving, saving purposes that are to shape the lives and witness of all disciples.

The ACTS
of the Apostles

T he Acts of the Apostles is one of the most exciting and challenging books in
the Christian Bible. For those interested in knowing what became of the "Jesus
movement" following the death and departure of its founder, this is the first
book to which they turn. Here is told an evocative story of the church's roots that
traces its beginnings in the final days of the risen Jesus and the Pentecostal arrival of
his Father's promised Spirit to the concluding story of an imprisoned Paul's undeterred
mission in downtown Rome. The various episodes narrated in between relate the missions of Jesus' prophetic successors to the entire house of Israel (chaps. 3–8) and then
to the nations (chaps. 9–28). Acts renders this historical phenomenon within a theological framework as the fulfillment of God's redemptive plans according to Israel's
Scriptures (2:17–21; 15:16–18; 28:26–27; cf. Luke 1:1).

Careful study of Acts is guided by four interpretive questions. If raised in chronological order, the first asks about the book's origins: *What circumstances occasioned the
writing of Acts?* Acts is an anonymous book addressed to "Theophilus" (1:1; cf. Luke
1:3–4), who is otherwise unknown to us. If the likely narrator is the third Gospel's
Luke, inferences drawn from both writings suggest he was a well-educated Gentile
convert to Judaism, whose theological outlook was cultivated by a careful study of
Israel's Scriptures and who after converting to Jesus became Paul's traveling companion (cf. Acts 16:10–17; 20:5–16; 21:1–18; 27:1–28:16).

Some have speculated that Theophilus's name, which in Greek means "dear to
God," is a metaphor for new converts seeking theological instruction—the implied
audience of his compositions. Yet if identified by his honorific title, "most excellent"
(Luke 1:3), Theophilus was likely the wealthy patron who provided sufficient funds
for Luke to write his story for public consumption. In any case, in his Gospel's preface, Luke implies that Theophilus requires a more secure understanding of his faith
(Acts 1:4), suggesting he is a new believer with questions still unanswered. If so, then
he has much in common with any disciple with unanswered questions who seeks
after the security of an informed faith.

Several of these "questions" may be broadly inferred from the narrative's most
important themes:

1. The persistent struggle to maintain Christian unity in the face of intramural conflict (5:1–11; 6:1–11; 11:1–18; 15:1–29) may suggest that Acts was written to consolidate the faith communions within an increasingly international church. Moreover,
when first read within a Roman world riddled with class conflict, the portraits of a
faith community that resolved conflict with "one heart and soul" (4:32) embody an
important line of evidence for the unifying power of God's love (4:33; cf. 2:42–47).

2. The ambivalent depiction of Rome (and of Paul's Roman citizenship) may intend
to define the church's relations with secular authority as ambivalent. While the Paul
of Acts is a Roman citizen, his obligations to Rome are secondary and never compromise his obedience to God. If Theophilus has political standing in his community,

Acts would remind him that his principal loyalty is to God's kingdom rather than to Caesar's Rome!

3. If Acts is written to secure the fragile faith of believers such as Theophilus (cf. Luke 1:3–4), Luke may have intended his story to provide a catechism by which new converts might learn of God while locating themselves in a religious movement traced back to the risen Jesus himself. The illustrations of the community's "resurrection practices" (e.g., sharing possessions with the needy, hospitality to strangers, apostolic teaching, "street" evangelism, conflict resolution, public worship) are formative of a bold counterculture, which would have been especially challenging for the church's growing urban middle class of Roman society.

4. Most importantly, Acts responds to a theological crisis. The rousing success of Paul's urban mission among non-Jews, coupled with his relative lack of success among Jews, may have prompted some believers to wonder whether the church's Jewish legacy had lost its relevance. This question may be especially relevant for Theophilus, if he was first a convert to Judaism—or at least a non-Jewish "God-fearer"—before becoming a disciple of Jesus. The story of Acts makes clear the continuity between Israel and the church, and the continuing importance of Jewish traditions, especially of Israel's Scriptures (our Old Testament), in cultivating Christian faith and witness.

A second interpretive question asks, *How did Luke compose the story of Acts?* Most students begin their literary analysis of Acts by simply noting that its plotline continues from Luke's Gospel. But Acts is not the Gospel's kind of book: Luke's Gospel is more like ancient biographical literature, which tells the story of an important person's life and career—that is, Jesus' messianic career. Acts, on the other hand, sketches the origins of a religious movement similar to historical monographs of antiquity. Acts is best read, then, as ancient *historiography*.

Since Luke was not an eyewitness to much of what he recounts, he must depend upon unnamed sources for his information (cf. Luke 1:1–2). From these sources, he selects certain events, which he then crafts into a coherent literary composition. Acts tells how the promise of God's redemption is realized for "all the families of earth" (Acts 3:21). Toward this end, Jesus' farewell prophecy (1:8) plots the progress of salvation beginning in Jerusalem (chaps. 1–7), beyond Jerusalem into the neighboring provinces of Samaria and Judea (chap. 8), before journeying into other nations and peoples beyond Palestine (chaps. 9–28).

The many speeches of Acts are especially important because they often signal plot movements while providing summaries of the narrator's core theological commitments. The most important of these speeches serve "missionary" ends: Peter's Pentecost sermon (2:14–41), the inaugural sermon of Paul's mission to the nations at Pisidian Antioch (13:16–41), and his sharply stated Socratic retort at the Athenian Areopagus (17:22–31) are good examples of public discourse that serve to persuade readers to Luke's understanding of the gospel. While not set in missionary settings, Paul's "farewell" (20:17–35) and defense (22:1–21; 24:10–21; 26:2–23; 28:17–20) speeches serve to define his spiritual authority in a way that frames his personal importance for the church's future. For this reason, believers continue to take important lessons from the Pauline letters that follow Acts in the New Testament.

A third question asks, *What does Acts teach us about God?* The plotline of Acts gives expression to Luke's core convictions:

1. Even though *God* is not a stated character of Luke's narrative world, narrated events occur as a "divine necessity" (1:16; 3:18; 5:38; 13:27; 27:24).

2. *Jesus* is God's Messiah whose divine appointment as the world's Savior is at God's direction (2:22–23, 36; 10:34–43).

3. All those who hear this word proclaimed are sharply divided into two groups: those who repent and become *disciples* of Jesus and those who do not.

4. The *Spirit* of Acts is the source of divine "power" that empowers the disciples' witness to their risen Lord (1:4–8). However, the powerful influence of the Spirit now extends to all believers and increasingly reflects the characteristics of a personal deity: it speaks (8:29; 10:19; 13:2) and guides (13:4; 15:28; 16:6–7); and people can lie to (5:3), test (5:9), and resist (7:51) it. The Spirit is not external to those it influences (however, 11:15) but is "poured out" to "fill up" (2:4; 4:8, 31; 6:3, 5; 7:55; 9:17; 11:24; 13:9) believers in preparation for ministry to continue the salvation the risen Jesus has begun.

5. The *church* of Acts is a community of shared goods. The community's "resurrection practices" include economic, spiritual, religious, and social actions. As an economic *koinonia*, the community reorders its possessions so that its generosity toward the needy reciprocates God's generosity in the gift of salvation (2:44–45; 4:32–35; 4:36–5:11; 6:1–6; 11:27–30). Likewise, the Holy Spirit is shared property among all disciples, so that its Pentecostal coming upon repentant Jews is repeated on repentant Gentiles (10:44; cf. 11:17; 15:9). The spiritual dimension of the community's solidarity is expressed most profoundly by the prohibition, "abstain from things polluted by idols" (15:20, 29; 21:25), which today might include possessions, careers, nationalism, or anything else that displaces God as the disciple's central devotion. The concern of Acts is not only the inward, spiritual purification of individual believers, but also the social purity of the entire community's public identity (cf. 15:22–29).

6. Pentecost begins Israel's "last days" (2:17); and every episode of Acts is understood against this *future* horizon. The outpouring of the Holy Spirit and the Lord's return (1:10–11; 3:19–21) are the events that bracket the "last days" of Israel's history in which believers are called by God to live and work according to God's redemptive purposes.

A final interpretive question regards, *What role does Acts continue to perform within the New Testament?* When the church formed the New Testament during the early centuries of the common era, the arrangement of its different parts intended their sequential use—the Old Testament in preparation of the New Testament, the fourfold Gospel in preparation for Acts, and Acts in preparation for the letters and then finally Revelation as the Bible's conclusion. Not only will there be evident continuity between what Jesus began to do and say according to the Gospel (1:1) and what his apostles did according to Acts, but their portraits in Acts will commend their religious and moral authority in advance of using their letters for Christian instruction. In fact, the unity of these different apostles in Acts commends an approach that seeks to explain rather than temper the theological diversity found among their New Testament letters. Today's church, which confesses continuity with the apostles, should embrace a rich pluralism of faith and practice, even if such a diversity results on occasion in internal controversy and conflict. What is achieved at the Jerusalem council (chap. 15; cf. Gal. 2:1–10) is Christian unity rather than theological uniformity.

—**Robert W. Wall**

The Promise of the Holy Spirit

1 In the first book, Theophilus, I wrote about all that Jesus did and taught from the beginning ² until the day when he was taken up to heaven, after giving instructions through the Holy Spirit to the apostles whom he had chosen. ³ After his suffering he presented himself alive to them by many convincing proofs, appearing to them during forty days and speaking about the kingdom of God. ⁴ While staying*ᵃ* with them, he ordered them not to leave Jerusalem, but to wait there for the promise of the Father. "This," he said, "is what you have heard from me; ⁵ for John baptized with water, but you will be baptized with*ᵇ* the Holy Spirit not many days from now."

The Ascension of Jesus

6 So when they had come together, they asked him, "Lord, is this the time when you will restore the kingdom to Israel?" ⁷ He replied, "It is not for you to know the times or periods that the Father has set by his own authority. ⁸ But you will receive power when the Holy Spirit has come upon you; and you will be my witnesses in Jerusalem, in all Judea and Samaria, and to the ends of the earth." ⁹ When he had said this, as they were watching, he was lifted up, and a cloud took him out of their sight. ¹⁰ While he was going and they were gazing up toward heaven, suddenly two men in white robes stood by them. ¹¹ They said, "Men of Galilee, why do you stand looking up toward heaven? This Jesus, who has been taken up from you into heaven, will come in the same way as you saw him go into heaven."

Matthias Chosen to Replace Judas

12 Then they returned to Jerusalem from the mount called Olivet, which is near Jerusalem, a sabbath day's journey away. ¹³ When they had entered the city, they went to the room upstairs where they were staying, Peter, and John, and James, and Andrew, Philip and Thomas, Bartholomew and Matthew, James son of Alphaeus, and Simon the Zealot, and Judas son of*ᶜ* James. ¹⁴ All these were constantly devoting themselves to prayer, together with certain women, including Mary the mother of Jesus, as well as his brothers.

15 In those days Peter stood up among the believers*ᵈ* (together the crowd num-

ᵃ Or eating   *ᵇ* Or by   *ᶜ* Or the brother of   *ᵈ* Gk brothers

---

1:1–2 The Preface

1:1 *First book*—The reader who attempts to learn from Acts without first reading the gospel story of Jesus will have missed what is essential for doing so: *all that Jesus did and taught from the beginning*. *Theophilus*—Meaning "lover of God" (cf. Luke 1:3), is probably Luke's literary patron.

1:2—*Apostles*, from a Greek verb, "to send," are chosen by God to carry God's word to others (cf. Luke 6:12–16). Luke seems to distinguish the Twelve from other disciples who succeeded Jesus and were granted special authority by him to lead the restored Israel (cf. Luke 22:28–30).

1:3–14 The Succession of Jesus

1:3—The opening sentence of Acts is followed by a brief summary of what Jesus does between his resurrection and ascension. Luke adds *during forty days* since "forty" is an Old Testament symbol for a season of preparation (cf. Luke 24:36–53). *Kingdom of God*—Luke brackets Acts by this phrase (see Acts 28:31). An important theme of Jesus' teaching, God's "kingdom" refers to both the location of God's presence and the various activities by which a benevolent God rules over God's people. The sociology, economic patterns, and politics of God's kingdom, embodied in the life and ministry of Jesus, now reorder the common life of his disciples.

1:5 *Spirit*—Jesus predicts the baptism of God's Spirit (vv. 4–5; cf. 2:1–13) will empower the community's global witness (1:8; cf. 13:44–47) through which God's promise of faithful Israel's restoration will finally be realized (1:6).

1:8 *Witnesses*—The Lord's "Great Commission" defines the church's vocation as a prophecy, which Acts then narrates as fulfilled.

1:14 *All these*—The solidarity of the faith community is exhibited by its devotion to *prayer* and by the inclusiveness of its membership, which included *certain women* who had witnessed Jesus' crucifixion (Luke 23:49; John 19:25) and to whom the risen Jesus had first appeared (Matt. 28:8–10).

1:15–26 Restoration of the Twelve

bered about one hundred twenty persons) and said, [16] "Friends,[a] the scripture had to be fulfilled, which the Holy Spirit through David foretold concerning Judas, who became a guide for those who arrested Jesus— [17] for he was numbered among us and was allotted his share in this ministry." [18] (Now this man acquired a field with the reward of his wickedness; and falling headlong,[b] he burst open in the middle and all his bowels gushed out. [19] This became known to all the residents of Jerusalem, so that the field was called in their language Hakeldama, that is, Field of Blood.) [20] "For it is written in the book of Psalms,

'Let his homestead become desolate,
    and let there be no one to live
        in it';
and

'Let another take his position of
        overseer.'

[21] So one of the men who have accompanied us during all the time that the Lord Jesus went in and out among us, [22] beginning from the baptism of John until the day when he was taken up from us—one of these must become a witness with us to his resurrection." [23] So they proposed two, Joseph called Barsabbas, who was also known as Justus, and Matthias. [24] Then they prayed and said, "Lord, you know everyone's heart. Show us which

one of these two you have chosen [25] to take the place[c] in this ministry and apostleship from which Judas turned aside to go to his own place." [26] And they cast lots for them, and the lot fell on Matthias; and he was added to the eleven apostles.

The Coming of the Holy Spirit

2 When the day of Pentecost had come, they were all together in one place. [2] And suddenly from heaven there came a sound like the rush of a violent wind, and it filled the entire house where they were sitting. [3] Divided tongues, as of fire, appeared among them, and a tongue rested on each of them. [4] All of them were filled with the Holy Spirit and began to speak in other languages, as the Spirit gave them ability.

5 Now there were devout Jews from every nation under heaven living in Jerusalem. [6] And at this sound the crowd gathered and was bewildered, because each one heard them speaking in the native language of each. [7] Amazed and astonished, they asked, "Are not all these who are speaking Galileans? [8] And how is it that we hear, each of us, in our own native language? [9] Parthians, Medes, Elamites, and residents of Mesopotamia,

[a] Gk Men, brothers [b] Or swelling up [c] Other ancient authorities read the share

---

1:16 Had to be fulfilled—Luke's account of Judas's demise (cf. Matt. 27:1–10) follows God's "script" of salvation: Peter argues from Scripture that Judas's disaffection and death had been prophesied by Pss. 69:26 and 109:8.

1:24 Show us which one—There is hardly a more important numerical symbol in Scripture than twelve, which stands for a restored Israel (= twelve tribes) as God's covenant people. Matthias's selection to replace Judas and restore the circle of Twelve symbolizes God's sovereign intention to restore Israel according to Scripture's promise (v. 6).

1:26 Cast lots—Widely used in the ancient world to select one among equals; also recalls a biblical pattern for determining God's will (cf. Josh. 14:1–5; 1 Sam. 14:36–44).

2:1–13 The Baptism of God's Spirit
2:1—The day of Pentecost falls on the fiftieth

day after Passover, when Jewish pilgrims gather in Jerusalem to celebrate God's gracious provisions of harvested food, land, and Torah.

2:2–4 Filled with the Holy Spirit—The Spirit's dramatic arrival fulfills Jesus' prophecy (1:4–5), enabling the entire community to communicate God's word to the household of Israel. "Filling" is the idiom of prophetic inspiration, which empowers believers to speak to others persuasively and also to interpret Scripture according to God's intended meaning.

2:8—The miracle of xenolalia, speaking in foreign languages, must be distinguished from Paul's spiritual gift of "speaking in tongues" (cf. 1 Cor. 12–14). Unlike Paul's definition, which concerns a Christian congregation's worship practices, this expression of the Spirit's power is evangelistic and enables communication of the gospel to nonbelievers in their own languages.

Judea and Cappadocia, Pontus and Asia, [10] Phrygia and Pamphylia, Egypt and the parts of Libya belonging to Cyrene, and visitors from Rome, both Jews and proselytes, [11] Cretans and Arabs—in our own languages we hear them speaking about God's deeds of power." [12] All were amazed and perplexed, saying to one another, "What does this mean?" [13] But others sneered and said, "They are filled with new wine."

Peter Addresses the Crowd

14 But Peter, standing with the eleven, raised his voice and addressed them, "Men of Judea and all who live in Jerusalem, let this be known to you, and listen to what I say. [15] Indeed, these are not drunk, as you suppose, for it is only nine o'clock in the morning. [16] No, this is what was spoken through the prophet Joel:

[17] 'In the last days it will be, God declares,
   that I will pour out my Spirit upon all flesh,
      and your sons and your daughters shall prophesy,
   and your young men shall see visions,
      and your old men shall dream dreams.
[18] Even upon my slaves, both men and women,
      in those days I will pour out my Spirit;

and they shall prophesy.
[19] And I will show portents in the heaven above
      and signs on the earth below,
         blood, and fire, and smoky mist.
[20] The sun shall be turned to darkness
      and the moon to blood,
         before the coming of the Lord's great and glorious day.
[21] Then everyone who calls on the name of the Lord shall be saved.'

22 "You that are Israelites,[a] listen to what I have to say: Jesus of Nazareth,[b] a man attested to you by God with deeds of power, wonders, and signs that God did through him among you, as you yourselves know— [23] this man, handed over to you according to the definite plan and foreknowledge of God, you crucified and killed by the hands of those outside the law. [24] But God raised him up, having freed him from death,[c] because it was impossible for him to be held in its power. [25] For David says concerning him,

'I saw the Lord always before me,
   for he is at my right hand so that I will not be shaken;
[26] therefore my heart was glad, and my tongue rejoiced;
   moreover my flesh will live in hope.

[a] Gk Men, Israelites   [b] Gk the Nazorean   [c] Gk the pains of death

---

2:10 *Proselytes*—Non-Jews who convert to Judaism who demonstrated their faith in Israel's God by receiving instruction in Israel's Scriptures, undergoing circumcision, and observing Jewish traditions.

Excursus on Peter's Pentecost Sermon (2:14–36)

More than one-third of Acts consists of speeches. Like other speeches in Acts that address a Jewish audience, Peter's Pentecost sermon is a midrash (or "commentary") on Israel's Scripture. Peter carefully crafts it into a persuasive speech that deals with the immediate crisis of Israel's skepticism. Faith is the *logical* response to Peter's persuasive speech (v. 41), since truth expects to dispel Israel's ignorance. John Wesley, the founder of Methodism, called gospel preaching

an "awakening experience." Good preaching compels people to deeper reflection and courageous action, and under the aegis of the Spirit can even transform scoffers into believers.

2:14–41 Peter Responds to Perplexed Israel

2:17 *In the last days*—Luke adds this phrase to the Greek version (Septuagint/LXX) of Joel's prophecy (2:28–32) to interpret the Spirit's outpouring "upon all flesh . . . both men and women" at Pentecost as the inaugural event of a final epoch in the history of God's salvation. The Spirit enables *sons* and *daughters* to *prophesy*— not to predict the future but to relate the meaning of Israel's Scriptures to contemporary events in persuasive ways. Peter's speech is an example of prophetic speaking.

²⁷ For you will not abandon my soul to
  Hades,
    or let your Holy One experience
      corruption.
²⁸ You have made known to me the
      ways of life;
    you will make me full of gladness
      with your presence.'

29 "Fellow Israelites,^a I may say to
you confidently of our ancestor David
that he both died and was buried, and
his tomb is with us to this day. ³⁰ Since
he was a prophet, he knew that God
had sworn with an oath to him that he
would put one of his descendants on his
throne. ³¹ Foreseeing this, David^b spoke
of the resurrection of the Messiah,^c
saying,

  'He was not abandoned to Hades,
    nor did his flesh experience
      corruption.'

³² This Jesus God raised up, and of that
all of us are witnesses. ³³ Being therefore exalted at^d the right hand of God,
and having received from the Father
the promise of the Holy Spirit, he has
poured out this that you both see and
hear. ³⁴ For David did not ascend into
the heavens, but he himself says,

  'The Lord said to my Lord,
    "Sit at my right hand,
³⁵   until I make your enemies your
        footstool."'

³⁶ Therefore let the entire house of Israel
know with certainty that God has made
him both Lord and Messiah,^e this Jesus
whom you crucified."

The First Converts

37 Now when they heard this, they
were cut to the heart and said to Peter
and to the other apostles, "Brothers,^a
what should we do?" ³⁸ Peter said to
them, "Repent, and be baptized every
one of you in the name of Jesus Christ so
that your sins may be forgiven; and you
will receive the gift of the Holy Spirit.
³⁹ For the promise is for you, for your
children, and for all who are far away,
everyone whom the Lord our God calls
to him." ⁴⁰ And he testified with many
other arguments and exhorted them,
saying, "Save yourselves from this corrupt generation." ⁴¹ So those who welcomed his message were baptized, and
that day about three thousand persons
were added. ⁴² They devoted themselves
to the apostles' teaching and fellowship, to the breaking of bread and the
prayers.

Life among the Believers

43 Awe came upon everyone, because
many wonders and signs were being
done by the apostles. ⁴⁴ All who believed
were together and had all things in common; ⁴⁵ they would sell their possessions
and goods and distribute the proceeds^f
to all, as any had need. ⁴⁶ Day by day, as
they spent much time together in the
temple, they broke bread at home^g and
ate their food with glad and generous^h
hearts, ⁴⁷ praising God and having the
goodwill of all the people. And day by

^a Gk Men, brothers ^b Gk he ^c Or the Christ ^d Or by ^e Or Christ
^f Gk them ^g Or from house to house ^h Or sincere

2:38 *Repent*—To repent is to reorient one's
way of thinking and living according to "all that
Jesus did and taught" (1:1). Repentance is the
single condition of forgiveness of sin by which
the believer is initiated into new life with God.
The *baptism* of new believers, a purity practice
followed by "devout Jews" (2:5; cf. Luke 7:16),
marks out publicly those who repent as members
of a community covenanted with God for new
life (cf. Acts 2:42–47).

2:42–47 The Community of Goods
The early chapters of Acts include several important summaries—snapshots—of the community's

life and mission in Jerusalem (e.g., 4:32–5:16;
6:1–7). These snapshots are touched up by Luke
to form a portfolio of "resurrection practices" that
remain paradigmatic of the church's corporate witness in the world. Sharing possessions,
learning the gospel truth, enjoying one another's
company, and worshiping together (so 2:42)
forge a compelling testimony to the risen Jesus.
These summaries form a biblical reminder that a
congregation's life together should nurture "one
heart and soul" (4:32) that seeks to meet the
material and spiritual needs of its members as a
public witness to God's "great grace" (4:33).

day the Lord added to their number those who were being saved.

Peter Heals a Crippled Beggar

3 One day Peter and John were going up to the temple at the hour of prayer, at three o'clock in the afternoon. [2] And a man lame from birth was being carried in. People would lay him daily at the gate of the temple called the Beautiful Gate so that he could ask for alms from those entering the temple. [3] When he saw Peter and John about to go into the temple, he asked them for alms. [4] Peter looked intently at him, as did John, and said, "Look at us." [5] And he fixed his attention on them, expecting to receive something from them. [6] But Peter said, "I have no silver or gold, but what I have I give you; in the name of Jesus Christ of Nazareth,[a] stand up and walk." [7] And he took him by the right hand and raised him up; and immediately his feet and ankles were made strong. [8] Jumping up, he stood and began to walk, and he entered the temple with them, walking and leaping and praising God. [9] All the people saw him walking and praising God, [10] and they recognized him as the one who used to sit and ask for alms at the Beautiful Gate of the temple; and they were filled with wonder and amazement at what had happened to him.

Peter Speaks in Solomon's Portico

[11] While he clung to Peter and John, all the people ran together to them in the portico called Solomon's Portico, utterly astonished. [12] When Peter saw it, he addressed the people, "You Israelites,[b] why do you wonder at this, or why do you stare at us, as though by our own power or piety we had made him walk? [13] The God of Abraham, the God of Isaac, and the God of Jacob, the God of our ancestors has glorified his servant[c] Jesus, whom you handed over and rejected in the presence of Pilate, though he had decided to release him. [14] But you rejected the Holy and Righteous One and asked to have a murderer given to you, [15] and you killed the Author of life, whom God raised from the dead. To this we are witnesses. [16] And by faith in his name, his name itself has made this man strong, whom you see and know; and the faith that is through Jesus[d] has given him this perfect health in the presence of all of you.

[a] Gk the Nazorean [b] Gk Men, Israelites [c] Or child [d] Gk him

---

Summary of 3:1–8:3, "You Will Be My Witnesses in Jerusalem"

Increasing conflicts face the church in Jerusalem between the apostles and the priests of "official" Judaism (4:5–22; 5:17–39; 6:8–8:3) and also within the faith community over the distribution of goods (4:32–5:16; 6:1–2). God's faithfulness and the spiritual authority of the apostles are two predominant themes of this narrative. Both themes are easily detected by a common literary pattern that shapes each episode of the church's Jerusalem mission since Pentecost: (1) God initiates the church's mission by "deeds of power" (2:1–12; 3:1–8; 4:5–12; 5:17–23; 6:8–10). (2) Unbelieving Jews are puzzled by what they observe because of their ignorance of the gospel (2:13–16; 3:9–11; 4:13–18; 5:24–28; 6:11–7:1). (3) The apostles respond to their puzzlement by interpreting the Spirit's "signs and wonders" from personal experience and Scripture (2:14–40; 3:12–26; 4:19–20; 5:29–32; 7:2–53). (4) Yet Israel remains divided because of Jesus—some repent, others do not (2:41–47; 4:1–4, 21–31; 5:33–42; 7:54–8:3; cf. Luke 2:34).

3:1–4:4 The Lame Man Is Healed in Jesus' Name

3:1—The apostles were devout Jews (cf. 2:46). The time (*three o'clock in the afternoon*) and place (*the gate of the temple called the Beautiful Gate*) of this story agrees with Torah's command that those who love God offer daily sacrifices to the Lord (Exod. 29:38–39; Lev. 6:20).

3:2—God's salvation is embodied in the healing of those *lame from birth* (Luke 5:17–26; 7:22).

3:6—Peter and John *have no silver or gold* since they had given up their wealth to help fund the community's welfare (see 2:45).

3:14—Peter's claim that Jesus is the *Righteous One* (7:52; 22:14; cf. Luke 23:47) recalls Isaiah's prophecy of a Suffering Servant (Isa. 53:11) whose sacrificial obedience to God purifies and makes others "righteous" before God—such as Joseph of Arimathea (Luke 23:50) and Cornelius (Acts 10:22).

17 "And now, friends,a I know that you acted in ignorance, as did also your rulers. 18 In this way God fulfilled what he had foretold through all the prophets, that his Messiahb would suffer. 19 Repent therefore, and turn to God so that your sins may be wiped out, 20 so that times of refreshing may come from the presence of the Lord, and that he may send the Messiahc appointed for you, that is, Jesus, 21 who must remain in heaven until the time of universal restoration that God announced long ago through his holy prophets. 22 Moses said, 'The Lord your God will raise up for you from your own peopled a prophet like me. You must listen to whatever he tells you. 23 And it will be that everyone who does not listen to that prophet will be utterly rooted out of the people.' 24 And all the prophets, as many as have spoken, from Samuel and those after him, also predicted these days. 25 You are the descendants of the prophets and of the covenant that God gave to your ancestors, saying to Abraham, 'And in your descendants all the families of the earth shall be blessed.' 26 When God raised up his servant,a he sent him first to you, to bless you by turning each of you from your wicked ways."

Peter and John before the Council

4 While Peter and Johne were speaking to the people, the priests, the captain of the temple, and the Sadducees came to them, 2 much annoyed because they were teaching the people and proclaiming that in Jesus there is the resurrection of the dead. 3 So they arrested them and put them in custody until the next day, for it was already evening. 4 But many of those who heard the word believed; and they numbered about five thousand.

5 The next day their rulers, elders, and scribes assembled in Jerusalem, 6 with Annas the high priest, Caiaphas, John,f and Alexander, and all who were of the high-priestly family. 7 When they had made the prisonersg stand in their midst, they inquired, "By what power or by what name did you do this?" 8 Then Peter, filled with the Holy Spirit, said to them, "Rulers of the people and elders, 9 if we are questioned today because of a good deed done to someone who was sick and are asked how this man has been healed, 10 let it be known to all of you, and to all the people of Israel, that this man is standing before you in good health by the name of Jesus Christ of Nazareth,h whom you crucified, whom God raised from the dead. 11 This Jesusi is

'the stone that was rejected by you,
        the builders;
    it has become the cornerstone.'j

12 There is salvation in no one else, for there is no other name under heaven given among mortals by which we must be saved."

a Gk brothers b Or his Christ c Or the Christ d Or child e Gk While they f Other ancient authorities read Jonathan g Gk them h Gk the Nazorean i Gk This j Or keystone

---

3:17—In Acts, humanity's spiritual crisis is *ignorance* about God's redemptive plan (see 17:30).

4:1 *Sadducees*—Opposition to the apostles comes primarily from the Sadducees, who were influential members of the Jerusalem's priestly establishment. Religiously conservative, their opposition to the church is rooted in their belief that Torah does not predict Israel's resurrection and that Israel's purity before God is conditioned upon observing Torah and the temple practices Moses prescribes, rather than believing in a word about a suffering and resurrected messiah (cf. 3:18–19).

4:4 *Five thousand*—Luke does not intend this large number to be a precise count of converts but rather a symbol of the extraordinary success of the church's Jerusalem mission following Pentecost.

4:5–31 The Apostles vs. the Sanhedrin, Round One

4:7–8—The political battle waged over the exercise of power is finally won by those who are *filled with the Holy Spirit* and are empowered to mediate God's salvation.

4:8—Spiritual and physical healing is a resurrection practice because it signals the arrival and embodies the character of God's salvation. God's grace makes disciples whole again both spiritually (3:8) and physically (4:10, 16).

13 Now when they saw the boldness of Peter and John and realized that they were uneducated and ordinary men, they were amazed and recognized them as companions of Jesus. 14 When they saw the man who had been cured standing beside them, they had nothing to say in opposition. 15 So they ordered them to leave the council while they discussed the matter with one another. 16 They said, "What will we do with them? For it is obvious to all who live in Jerusalem that a notable sign has been done through them; we cannot deny it. 17 But to keep it from spreading further among the people, let us warn them to speak no more to anyone in this name." 18 So they called them and ordered them not to speak or teach at all in the name of Jesus. 19 But Peter and John answered them, "Whether it is right in God's sight to listen to you rather than to God, you must judge; 20 for we cannot keep from speaking about what we have seen and heard." 21 After threatening them again, they let them go, finding no way to punish them because of the people, for all of them praised God for what had happened. 22 For the man on whom this sign of healing had been performed was more than forty years old.

The Believers Pray for Boldness

23 After they were released, they went to their friends[a] and reported what the chief priests and the elders had said to them. 24 When they heard it, they raised their voices together to God and said, "Sovereign Lord, who made the heaven and the earth, the sea, and everything in them, 25 it is you who said by the Holy Spirit through our ancestor David, your servant:[b]

'Why did the Gentiles rage,
   and the peoples imagine vain
      things?
26   The kings of the earth took their
      stand,
   and the rulers have gathered
      together
      against the Lord and against his
         Messiah.'[c]

27 For in this city, in fact, both Herod and Pontius Pilate, with the Gentiles and the peoples of Israel, gathered together against your holy servant[b] Jesus, whom you anointed, 28 to do whatever your hand and your plan had predestined to take place. 29 And now, Lord, look at their threats, and grant to your servants[d] to speak your word with all boldness, 30 while you stretch out your hand to heal, and signs and wonders are performed through the name of your holy servant[b] Jesus." 31 When they had prayed, the place in which they were gathered together was shaken; and they were all filled with the Holy Spirit and spoke the word of God with boldness.

The Believers Share Their Possessions

32 Now the whole group of those who believed were of one heart and soul, and no one claimed private ownership of any

a Gk their own b Or child c Or his Christ d Gk slaves

4:13—Even though they are **uneducated and ordinary** and therefore unprepared to lead Israel by conventional standards, the apostles are schooled by God's Spirit, who "fills" them (v. 8) to speak with a prophet's **boldness** and persuasion (cf. vv. 29–31; 9:27–28; 13:46; 26:26). Not only does the presence of God's Spirit empower disciples to engage in a productive ministry; the Spirit also provides the assurance of God's triumph that makes them courageous in their obedience to God.

4:19–20—Peter and John's courageous response to the council frames the church's position toward secular authority: while acknowledging the council's verdict as legally binding, the apostles must respond in obedience to God, whatever the consequence.

4:23–31—Praying together is another resurrection practice of a people belonging to God. Petitions are rooted in the belief that the Creator cares. God's provident care is reflected in God's **plan** (v. 28) to heal what sin has broken. God has **predestined** salvation **to take place** (v. 28) according to Israel's Scriptures.

4:32–5:16 One Holy and Apostolic Church

4:32—The spiritual hallmarks of the Lord's disciples are corporate. Disciples form communities

possessions, but everything they owned was held in common. ³³ With great power the apostles gave their testimony to the resurrection of the Lord Jesus, and great grace was upon them all. ³⁴ There was not a needy person among them, for as many as owned lands or houses sold them and brought the proceeds of what was sold. ³⁵ They laid it at the apostles' feet, and it was distributed to each as any had need. ³⁶ There was a Levite, a native of Cyprus, Joseph, to whom the apostles gave the name Barnabas (which means "son of encouragement"). ³⁷ He sold a field that belonged to him, then brought the money, and laid it at the apostles' feet.

Ananias and Sapphira

5 But a man named Ananias, with the consent of his wife Sapphira, sold a piece of property; ² with his wife's knowledge, he kept back some of the proceeds, and brought only a part and laid it at the apostles' feet. ³ "Ananias," Peter asked, "why has Satan filled your heart to lie to the Holy Spirit and to keep back part of the proceeds of the land? ⁴ While it remained unsold, did it not remain your own? And after it was sold, were not the proceeds at your disposal? How is it that you have contrived this deed in your heart? You did not lie to us[a] but to God!" ⁵ Now when Ananias heard these words, he fell down and died. And great fear seized all who heard of it. ⁶ The young men came and wrapped up his body,[b] then carried him out and buried him.

⁷ After an interval of about three hours his wife came in, not knowing what had happened. ⁸ Peter said to her, "Tell me whether you and your husband sold the land for such and such a price." And she said, "Yes, that was the price." ⁹ Then Peter said to her, "How is it that you have agreed together to put the Spirit of the Lord to the test? Look, the feet of those who have buried your husband are at the door, and they will carry you out." ¹⁰ Immediately she fell down at his feet and died. When the young men came in they found her dead, so they carried her out and buried her beside her husband. ¹¹ And great fear seized the whole church and all who heard of these things.

The Apostles Heal Many

12 Now many signs and wonders were done among the people through the apostles. And they were all together in Solomon's Portico. ¹³ None of the rest dared to join them, but the people held them in high esteem. ¹⁴ Yet more than ever believers were added to the Lord, great numbers of both men and women, ¹⁵ so that they even carried out the sick into the streets, and laid them on cots and mats, in order that Peter's shadow might fall on some of them as he came by. ¹⁶ A great number of people would also gather from the towns around Jerusalem, bringing the sick and those tormented by unclean spirits, and they were all cured.

---

[a] Gk to men [b] Meaning of Gk uncertain

---

whose solidarity is witnessed publicly by sharing their goods with those believers in need of them (cf. 2:42–47; 20:32–35; 28:10).

4:34–35—Possessions are *laid at the apostles' feet* (cf. v. 37; 5:2) to acknowledge their spiritual authority in continuity with Jesus.

4:36–5:11—The contrast between *Barnabas* (4:36–37) and *Ananias and Sapphira* (5:1–11) underscores the importance of sharing one's possessions as a barometer of the disciple's relationship with God's Spirit.

5:3—Peter's question may allude to Scripture's story of humankind's "original sin" in which the serpent (= Satan) deceived Adam (= Ananias) and Eve (= Sapphira) to make self-centered choices that subverted their relationship with God.

5:12–16—The performance of *signs and wonders . . . among the people* reconfirms Joel's prophecy (cf. 2:19) that the "last days" of salvation's history have arrived. Since this epoch of salvation history concludes with the return of Jesus to complete his messianic mission, today's church still lives in these "last days," when the performance of the Spirit's signs and wonders testify to the presence of God's reign in the world.

The Apostles Are Persecuted

17 Then the high priest took action; he and all who were with him (that is, the sect of the Sadducees), being filled with jealousy, **18** arrested the apostles and put them in the public prison. **19** But during the night an angel of the Lord opened the prison doors, brought them out, and said, **20** "Go, stand in the temple and tell the people the whole message about this life." **21** When they heard this, they entered the temple at daybreak and went on with their teaching.

When the high priest and those with him arrived, they called together the council and the whole body of the elders of Israel, and sent to the prison to have them brought. **22** But when the temple police went there, they did not find them in the prison; so they returned and reported, **23** "We found the prison securely locked and the guards standing at the doors, but when we opened them, we found no one inside." **24** Now when the captain of the temple and the chief priests heard these words, they were perplexed about them, wondering what might be going on. **25** Then someone arrived and announced, "Look, the men whom you put in prison are standing in the temple and teaching the people!" **26** Then the captain went with the temple police and brought them, but without violence, for they were afraid of being stoned by the people.

27 When they had brought them, they had them stand before the council. The high priest questioned them, **28** saying, "We gave you strict orders not to teach in this name,*a* yet here you have filled Jerusalem with your teaching and you are determined to bring this man's blood on us." **29** But Peter and the apostles answered, "We must obey God rather than any human authority.*b* **30** The God of our ancestors raised up Jesus, whom you had killed by hanging him on a tree. **31** God exalted him at his right hand as Leader and Savior that he might give repentance to Israel and forgiveness of sins. **32** And we are witnesses to these things, and so is the Holy Spirit whom God has given to those who obey him."

33 When they heard this, they were enraged and wanted to kill them. **34** But a Pharisee in the council named Gamaliel, a teacher of the law, respected by all the people, stood up and ordered the men to be put outside for a short time. **35** Then he said to them, "Fellow Israelites,*c* consider carefully what you propose to do to these men. **36** For some time ago Theudas rose up, claiming to be somebody, and a number of men, about four hundred, joined him; but he was killed, and all who followed him were dispersed and disappeared. **37** After him Judas the Galilean rose up at the

a Other ancient authorities read *Did we not give you strict orders not to teach in this name?* *b* Gk *than men* *c* Gk *Men, Israelites*

5:17–42 The Apostles vs. the Sanhedrin, Round Two

5:17—In Acts, Christianity is a sect (or communion) within Judaism (cf. 24:5, 14; 28:22). Typically, opponents of the church's mission, principally the Sadducees, are *filled with jealousy* rather than by God's Spirit (cf. 4:8). They therefore act in ways contrary to God's purpose. In the Greco-Roman world, jealousy is a well-known vice that undermines responsible leadership.

5:19—Stories of miraculous jailbreaks in Acts (12:1–11; 16:26–31) remind readers that God's redemptive purpose survives malicious opposition to it.

5:20—The apostles are instructed to return to *the temple*, a place sanctified for Israel's instruction

and worship. The sarcastic portrait of Judaism's ruling elite in the following episode underwrites the apostles' legitimacy as Israel's divinely approved leaders (cf. Luke 22:38–40).

5:29–32—Obedience to *God rather than any human authority* motivates the community's ministry—with which the high priest, a dedicated monotheist, would surely agree!

5:34—Although the Sanhedrin was led by its majority Sadducean cohort, a *Pharisee in the council named Gamaliel* addressed his colleagues. In Acts, Pharisees are regarded more positively than Sadducees because they share a belief in the resurrection and a future new creation. Later in Acts, Paul introduces himself to this very council as a Pharisee and as Gamaliel's student (23:3).

time of the census and got people to follow him; he also perished, and all who followed him were scattered. **38** So in the present case, I tell you, keep away from these men and let them alone; because if this plan or this undertaking is of human origin, it will fail; **39** but if it is of God, you will not be able to overthrow them—in that case you may even be found fighting against God!"

They were convinced by him, **40** and when they had called in the apostles, they had them flogged. Then they ordered them not to speak in the name of Jesus, and let them go. **41** As they left the council, they rejoiced that they were considered worthy to suffer dishonor for the sake of the name. **42** And every day in the temple and at home*a* they did not cease to teach and proclaim Jesus as the Messiah.*b*

Seven Chosen to Serve

6 Now during those days, when the disciples were increasing in number, the Hellenists complained against the Hebrews because their widows were being neglected in the daily distribution of food. **2** And the twelve called together the whole community of the disciples and said, "It is not right that we should neglect the word of God in order to wait on tables.*c* **3** Therefore, friends,*d* select from among yourselves seven men of good standing, full of the Spirit and of wisdom, whom we may appoint to this task, **4** while we, for our part, will devote ourselves to prayer and to serving the word." **5** What they said pleased the whole community, and they chose Stephen, a man full of faith and the Holy Spirit, together with Philip, Prochorus, Nicanor, Timon, Parmenas, and Nicolaus, a proselyte of Antioch. **6** They had these men stand before the apostles, who prayed and laid their hands on them.

7 The word of God continued to spread; the number of the disciples increased greatly in Jerusalem, and a great many of the priests became obedient to the faith.

The Arrest of Stephen

8 Stephen, full of grace and power, did great wonders and signs among the people. **9** Then some of those who belonged to the synagogue of the Freedmen (as it

a Or from house to house   *b* Or the Christ   *c* Or keep accounts   *d* Gk brothers

---

5:38–39—Gamaliel's advice to *keep away from these men* is ironically rooted in the same theological belief that orders the plotline of Acts: *if it is of God, you will not be able to overthrow them!* The motive of Gamaliel's speech remains unclear. Either he is a peacekeeper whose argument sets the apostles free, or he is a troublemaker who reduces Jesus to the same level as well-known revolutionaries whose movements failed and were executed by Rome.

6:1–7 Conflict Resolution in the Community of Goods

6:1—*Hellenists* refers to Jews from the Diaspora who speak Greek (rather than Aramaic) and maintain their ethnic customs. Because their neighborhoods were isolated from those where the *Hebrews* lived with the apostles and a growing majority of believers, their most vulnerable members, the *widows*, were neglected. The rapid growth in church membership also strained the administration of *daily distribution of food* to a breaking point. The urgency of this internal crisis goes to the heart of the community's public identity, since God's presence is indicated by the practice of sharing goods with those in need (4:34).

6:2—This social crisis within the community also occasioned *the twelve* apostles to reconsider their prophetic vocation, which finally was not to *wait on tables* but to pray and boldly proclaim *the word* of God (cf. 4:31; 6:4).

6:3—The community resolves its crisis by selecting *from among yourselves seven men of good standing*, following Jesus' pattern of sending out seventy after sending out twelve (cf. Luke 9).

6:7—The extent of the success of the apostles' prophetic ministry in Jerusalem is indicated by Luke's remarkable summary that *a great number of the priests became obedient to the faith*. Although indicating inroads into the priestly establishment of Jerusalem, these "priests" probably came from among the thousands of earnest Jews, typically from lower social classes, who lived and worked as volunteers in the Jerusalem temple.

6:8–8:3 Stephen, a Prophet Mighty in Word and Deed

was called), Cyrenians, Alexandrians, and others of those from Cilicia and Asia, stood up and argued with Stephen. ¹⁰ But they could not withstand the wisdom and the Spirit*a* with which he spoke. ¹¹ Then they secretly instigated some men to say, "We have heard him speak blasphemous words against Moses and God." ¹² They stirred up the people as well as the elders and the scribes; then they suddenly confronted him, seized him, and brought him before the council. ¹³ They set up false witnesses who said, "This man never stops saying things against this holy place and the law; ¹⁴ for we have heard him say that this Jesus of Nazareth*b* will destroy this place and will change the customs that Moses handed on to us." ¹⁵ And all who sat in the council looked intently at him, and they saw that his face was like the face of an angel.

Stephen's Speech to the Council

7 Then the high priest asked him, "Are these things so?" ² And Stephen replied:

"Brothers*c* and fathers, listen to me. The God of glory appeared to our ancestor Abraham when he was in Mesopotamia, before he lived in Haran, ³ and said to him, 'Leave your country and your relatives and go to the land that I will show you.' ⁴ Then he left the country of the Chaldeans and settled in Haran. After his father died, God had him move from there to this country in which you are now living. ⁵ He did not give him any of it as a heritage, not even a foot's length, but promised to give it to him as his possession and to his descendants after him, even though he had no child. ⁶ And God spoke in these terms, that his descendants would be resident aliens in a country belonging to others, who would enslave them and mistreat them during four hundred years. ⁷ 'But I will judge the nation that they serve,' said God, 'and after that they shall come out and worship me in this place.' ⁸ Then he gave him the covenant of circumcision. And so Abraham*d* became the father of Isaac and circumcised him on the eighth day; and Isaac became the father of Jacob, and Jacob of the twelve patriarchs.

9 "The patriarchs, jealous of Joseph, sold him into Egypt; but God was with him, ¹⁰ and rescued him from all his afflictions, and enabled him to win favor and to show wisdom when he stood before Pharaoh, king of Egypt, who appointed him ruler over Egypt and over all his household. ¹¹ Now there came a famine throughout Egypt and Canaan, and great suffering, and our ancestors could find no food. ¹² But when Jacob heard that there was grain in Egypt, he sent our ancestors there on their first

a Or *spirit*   *b* Gk *the Nazorean*   *c* Gk *Men, brothers*   *d* Gk *he*

6:11—*The synagogue of the Freedmen* (v. 9) is an assembly of Roman Jews who, freed from slavery, had settled in Jerusalem out of religious devotion.

6:13–14—Luke's reference to *false witnesses* is ironical, since they correctly report that Stephen teaches Jews that Jesus has replaced Torah and temple as the central symbols of Israel's covenant keeping with God. They are "false" only because they claim something to be false that is actually true—an inference that Luke's readers would surely have understood, since he wrote Acts after Rome had destroyed the Jerusalem temple in 70 CE.

6:15—Stephen's transfiguration echoes the story of Moses on Mount Sinai (cf. Exod. 34:29), thereby indicating that his teaching does not "blaspheme Moses" (cf. Acts 6:11) but stands in continuity with him. Acts opposes the religious supersessionism that claims the church has replaced Israel and that Israel's Scriptures (= Old Testament) have no role in forming the faith of Christian disciples.

7:1–53—Stephen's speech retells the biblical story of God's relations with an unrepentant Israel (cf. Neh. 9:5–37) in a manner that is Jewish in both literary form and religious function.

7:2—*The God of glory* is the principal character of Scripture's story of Israel and of Stephen's speech.

7:2–16—The story of *the twelve patriarchs* (= twelve apostles) (v. 8) centers on God's promise of land to Abraham (vv. 2–8), which God realizes through the prophetic work of Joseph (vv. 9–16).

visit. ¹³ On the second visit Joseph made himself known to his brothers, and Joseph's family became known to Pharaoh. ¹⁴ Then Joseph sent and invited his father Jacob and all his relatives to come to him, seventy-five in all; ¹⁵ so Jacob went down to Egypt. He himself died there as well as our ancestors, ¹⁶ and their bodies*a* were brought back to Shechem and laid in the tomb that Abraham had bought for a sum of silver from the sons of Hamor in Shechem.

17 "But as the time drew near for the fulfillment of the promise that God had made to Abraham, our people in Egypt increased and multiplied ¹⁸ until another king who had not known Joseph ruled over Egypt. ¹⁹ He dealt craftily with our race and forced our ancestors to abandon their infants so that they would die. ²⁰ At this time Moses was born, and he was beautiful before God. For three months he was brought up in his father's house; ²¹ and when he was abandoned, Pharaoh's daughter adopted him and brought him up as her own son. ²² So Moses was instructed in all the wisdom of the Egyptians and was powerful in his words and deeds.

23 "When he was forty years old, it came into his heart to visit his relatives, the Israelites.*b* ²⁴ When he saw one of them being wronged, he defended the oppressed man and avenged him by striking down the Egyptian. ²⁵ He supposed that his kinsfolk would understand that God through him was rescuing them, but they did not understand. ²⁶ The next day he came to some of them as they were quarreling and tried to reconcile them, saying, 'Men, you are brothers; why do you wrong each other?' ²⁷ But the man who was wronging his neighbor pushed Moses*c* aside, saying, 'Who made you a ruler and a judge over us? ²⁸ Do you

want to kill me as you killed the Egyptian yesterday?' ²⁹ When he heard this, Moses fled and became a resident alien in the land of Midian. There he became the father of two sons.

30 "Now when forty years had passed, an angel appeared to him in the wilderness of Mount Sinai, in the flame of a burning bush. ³¹ When Moses saw it, he was amazed at the sight; and as he approached to look, there came the voice of the Lord: ³² 'I am the God of your ancestors, the God of Abraham, Isaac, and Jacob.' Moses began to tremble and did not dare to look. ³³ Then the Lord said to him, 'Take off the sandals from your feet, for the place where you are standing is holy ground. ³⁴ I have surely seen the mistreatment of my people who are in Egypt and have heard their groaning, and I have come down to rescue them. Come now, I will send you to Egypt.'

35 "It was this Moses whom they rejected when they said, 'Who made you a ruler and a judge?' and whom God now sent as both ruler and liberator through the angel who appeared to him in the bush. ³⁶ He led them out, having performed wonders and signs in Egypt, at the Red Sea, and in the wilderness for forty years. ³⁷ This is the Moses who said to the Israelites, 'God will raise up a prophet for you from your own people*d* as he raised me up.' ³⁸ He is the one who was in the congregation in the wilderness with the angel who spoke to him at Mount Sinai, and with our ancestors; and he received living oracles to give to us. ³⁹ Our ancestors were unwilling to obey him; instead, they pushed him aside, and in their hearts they turned back to Egypt, ⁴⁰ saying to Aaron, 'Make gods for us who will lead the way for us;

a Gk they *b* Gk his brothers, the sons of Israel *c* Gk him *d* Gk your brothers

7:20–43—Stephen considers Moses God's prototypical prophet, who establishes the pattern of bringing God's word to Israel. Jesus is a prophet like Moses (cf. v. 37; 3:22), and his prophetic ministry is followed by his apostles and their disciples. According to this pattern, God allows two chances to hear and respond to the prophet's word. If those who hear fail to repent, *God turn(s) away from them* (v. 42; see, e.g., 13:42–47).

as for this Moses who led us out from the land of Egypt, we do not know what has happened to him.' [41] At that time they made a calf, offered a sacrifice to the idol, and reveled in the works of their hands. [42] But God turned away from them and handed them over to worship the host of heaven, as it is written in the book of the prophets:

'Did you offer to me slain victims
   and sacrifices
forty years in the wilderness,
   O house of Israel?
[43] No; you took along the tent of
      Moloch,
   and the star of your god Rephan,
   the images that you made to
      worship;
so I will remove you beyond
   Babylon.'

[44] "Our ancestors had the tent of testimony in the wilderness, as God[a] directed when he spoke to Moses, ordering him to make it according to the pattern he had seen. [45] Our ancestors in turn brought it in with Joshua when they dispossessed the nations that God drove out before our ancestors. And it was there until the time of David, [46] who found favor with God and asked that he might find a dwelling place for the house of Jacob.[b] [47] But it was Solomon who built a house for him. [48] Yet the Most High does not dwell in houses made with human hands;[c] as the prophet says,

[49] 'Heaven is my throne,
   and the earth is my footstool.
What kind of house will you build
   for me, says the Lord,

or what is the place of my
   rest?
[50] Did not my hand make all these
   things?'

[51] "You stiff-necked people, uncircumcised in heart and ears, you are forever opposing the Holy Spirit, just as your ancestors used to do. [52] Which of the prophets did your ancestors not persecute? They killed those who foretold the coming of the Righteous One, and now you have become his betrayers and murderers. [53] You are the ones that received the law as ordained by angels, and yet you have not kept it."

The Stoning of Stephen

[54] When they heard these things, they became enraged and ground their teeth at Stephen.[d] [55] But filled with the Holy Spirit, he gazed into heaven and saw the glory of God and Jesus standing at the right hand of God. [56] "Look," he said, "I see the heavens opened and the Son of Man standing at the right hand of God!" [57] But they covered their ears, and with a loud shout all rushed together against him. [58] Then they dragged him out of the city and began to stone him; and the witnesses laid their coats at the feet of a young man named Saul. [59] While they were stoning Stephen, he prayed, "Lord Jesus, receive my spirit." [60] Then he knelt down and cried out in a loud voice, "Lord, do not hold this sin against them." When he had said this, he died.[e]

8 [1] And Saul approved of their killing him.

a Gk he *b* Other ancient authorities read *for the God of Jacob* *c* Gk with hands *d* Gk him *e* Gk fell asleep

---

7:51–53—God's care of Israel is not bounded by a particular place of worship but rather by a particular Messiah.

7:58–60—Saul is introduced to readers as a willing participant in the mob that illegally stones Stephen to death (8:1a). Following the example of Jesus (cf. Luke 23:34), Stephen requests of the Lord, *do not hold this sin against them*, including Saul, whose subsequent conversion to Jesus is his favorable response to Stephen's petition for forgiveness.

8:1–3—Because the Hellenist believers, led at one time by Stephen and now by Philip, are persecuted, they leave Jerusalem and scatter *throughout the countryside of Judea and Samaria*, thereby fulfilling Jesus' prophecy (1:8). This Christian Diaspora eventually settles in Syrian Antioch (cf. 11:19–20), where they become the base of missionary operations for Saul, their former persecutor (cf. 13:1–4).

Saul Persecutes the Church

That day a severe persecution began against the church in Jerusalem, and all except the apostles were scattered throughout the countryside of Judea and Samaria. [2] Devout men buried Stephen and made loud lamentation over him. [3] But Saul was ravaging the church by entering house after house; dragging off both men and women, he committed them to prison.

Philip Preaches in Samaria

4 Now those who were scattered went from place to place, proclaiming the word. [5] Philip went down to the city[a] of Samaria and proclaimed the Messiah[b] to them. [6] The crowds with one accord listened eagerly to what was said by Philip, hearing and seeing the signs that he did, [7] for unclean spirits, crying with loud shrieks, came out of many who were possessed; and many others who were paralyzed or lame were cured. [8] So there was great joy in that city.

9 Now a certain man named Simon had previously practiced magic in the city and amazed the people of Samaria, saying that he was someone great. [10] All of them, from the least to the greatest, listened to him eagerly, saying, "This man is the power of God that is called Great." [11] And they listened eagerly to him because for a long time he had amazed them with his magic. [12] But when they believed Philip, who was proclaiming the good news about the kingdom of God and the name of Jesus Christ, they were baptized, both men and women. [13] Even Simon himself believed. After being baptized, he stayed constantly with Philip and was amazed when he saw the signs and great miracles that took place.

14 Now when the apostles at Jerusalem heard that Samaria had accepted the word of God, they sent Peter and John to them. [15] The two went down and prayed for them that they might receive the Holy Spirit [16] (for as yet the Spirit had not come[c] upon any of them; they had only been baptized in the name of the Lord Jesus). [17] Then Peter and John[d] laid their hands on them, and they received the Holy Spirit. [18] Now when Simon saw that the Spirit was given through the laying on of the apostles' hands, he offered them money, [19] saying, "Give me

[a] Other ancient authorities read *a city*   [b] Or *the Christ*   [c] Gk *fallen*
[d] Gk *they*

Summary of 8:4–40, "In All Judea and Samaria"

The narrative of mission in Acts is shaped by a geographical conception of salvation's progress (1:8); Jerusalem is now in the reader's rearview mirror—always in sight but left behind (8:1b). This next section of Acts tells the story of Philip, the successor to Stephen and like him a charismatic prophet like Jesus from the ranks of the seven (6:5). His inspired ministry carries the word of God into new territories beyond Jerusalem and establishes a new pattern for those who come after him, first Peter (9:32–11:18; cf. 8:14–25) and then Paul (13:1–28:31; cf. 21:7–14). Despite its strategic importance in Acts, only two episodes of Philip's mission are narrated—in a Samaritan city (8:4–25) and to an Ethiopian pilgrim (8:26–39). Both are surprising converts, since both are marginal Jews, even more removed from Israel's promised blessings than their geographical separation from Jerusalem suggests. Their conversion stories complete the church's mission to the *whole* household of Israel, from mainstream Jews in Palestine to marginal Jews from the Diaspora, to prepare readers for the story of yet another Jew whom the risen Jesus will call to a ministry beyond Israel as a "light to the nations" (13:47; cf. 9:15).

8:4–25 Philip's Mission in Samaria

8:5—Philip arrives at *the city of Samaria*. In Acts, the church's mission is urban, located in the most important cities of the Roman world. Luke does not consider Samaritans proto-Gentiles, but from among "the lost sheep of Israel"—religious renegades and racially "impure," according to more traditional Jewish teaching and practices.

8:7—This new stage of Christian mission beyond Jerusalem is symbolized by reference to a new resurrection practice: exorcism of *unclean spirits*.

8:19—*Simon's* spiritual failure is his unwarranted desire for political *power*. God gave Peter authority to distribute the Spirit to Samaritan believers, including Simon (vv. 14–18); and now Simon wants this same office for himself. The Protestant Reformation of Roman Catholicism was initiated,

also this power so that anyone on whom I lay my hands may receive the Holy Spirit." ²⁰ But Peter said to him, "May your silver perish with you, because you thought you could obtain God's gift with money! ²¹ You have no part or share in this, for your heart is not right before God. ²² Repent therefore of this wickedness of yours, and pray to the Lord that, if possible, the intent of your heart may be forgiven you. ²³ For I see that you are in the gall of bitterness and the chains of wickedness." ²⁴ Simon answered, "Pray for me to the Lord, that nothing of what you*a* have said may happen to me."

25 Now after Peter and John*b* had testified and spoken the word of the Lord, they returned to Jerusalem, proclaiming the good news to many villages of the Samaritans.

Philip and the Ethiopian Eunuch

26 Then an angel of the Lord said to Philip, "Get up and go toward the south*c* to the road that goes down from Jerusalem to Gaza." (This is a wilderness road.) ²⁷ So he got up and went. Now there was an Ethiopian eunuch, a court official of the Candace, queen of the Ethiopians, in charge of her entire treasury. He had

come to Jerusalem to worship ²⁸ and was returning home; seated in his chariot, he was reading the prophet Isaiah. ²⁹ Then the Spirit said to Philip, "Go over to this chariot and join it." ³⁰ So Philip ran up to it and heard him reading the prophet Isaiah. He asked, "Do you understand what you are reading?" ³¹ He replied, "How can I, unless someone guides me?" And he invited Philip to get in and sit beside him. ³² Now the passage of the scripture that he was reading was this:
"Like a sheep he was led to the
     slaughter,
   and like a lamb silent before its
     shearer,
   so he does not open his mouth.
³³ In his humiliation justice was denied
     him.
   Who can describe his generation?
     For his life is taken away from
       the earth."
³⁴ The eunuch asked Philip, "About whom, may I ask you, does the prophet say this, about himself or about someone else?" ³⁵ Then Philip began to speak, and starting with this scripture, he proclaimed to

a The Greek word for *you* and the verb *pray* are plural   *b* Gk *after they*
c Or *go at noon*

---

in part, to overturn the church's practice of appointing the wealthy to religious offices in exchange for money, rather than because of spiritual gifts and personal maturity—a practice that became known as "simony," taking Simon's name.

8:25—Peter and John *returned to Jerusalem*, retracing Philip's mission since his departure from Jerusalem (vv. 4–5) in support of *the good news* about the kingdom of God (cf. v. 12).

8:26–40 The Conversion of the Ethiopian Eunuch

8:26—The *angel of the Lord* is a Jewish euphemism for God's *Spirit* (cf. v. 29), who enables Philip to facilitate God's redemptive purposes (cf. 1:8).

8:27—The object of God's interest is an *Ethiopian eunuch,* a Jewish proselyte who *had come to Jerusalem to worship* God. But he is returning from his pilgrimage with questions left unanswered (vv. 30–31). His outsider status is indicated both geographically (he is a foreigner from Ethiopia) and religiously (he is a eunuch whose

castration in service of a pagan ruler excludes him from pious Israel, according to Deut. 23:1–2 and Lev. 21:17–21). God's acceptance of him symbolizes Israel's hope that even its religious outcasts—"foreigners and eunuchs"—will be restored when God's reign is restored in Israel (so Isa. 56:1–8; cf. Ps. 67:32; Acts 1:6).

8:30–31—In the initial exchange between the Ethiopian and Philip, Luke underscores the importance of a Spirit-filled teacher who is able to explain the meaning of Scripture for those in search of God.

8:32–33—Even though rarely used by Jesus, Isaiah's prophecy of God's Suffering Servant, portrayed in this quotation of Isa. 53:7–8, became central in the church's proclamation about Jesus' costly obedience to God.

8:34–35—The Ethiopian's question indicates his dissatisfaction with current interpretations of this prophecy within Israel. Philip's prophetic rereading of Isa. 53 implies that his response is not his own; he *began to speak* by inspiration of God's Spirit (cf. 2 Pet. 1:20–21).

him the good news about Jesus. **36** As they were going along the road, they came to some water; and the eunuch said, "Look, here is water! What is to prevent me from being baptized?"*a* **38** He commanded the chariot to stop, and both of them, Philip and the eunuch, went down into the water, and Philip*b* baptized him. **39** When they came up out of the water, the Spirit of the Lord snatched Philip away; the eunuch saw him no more, and went on his way rejoicing. **40** But Philip found himself at Azotus, and as he was passing through the region, he proclaimed the good news to all the towns until he came to Caesarea.

The Conversion of Saul

9 Meanwhile Saul, still breathing threats and murder against the disciples of the Lord, went to the high priest **2** and asked him for letters to the synagogues at Damascus, so that if he found any who belonged to the Way, men or women, he might bring them bound to Jerusalem. **3** Now as he was going along and approaching Damascus, suddenly a light from heaven flashed around him. **4** He fell to the ground and heard a voice saying to him, "Saul, Saul, why do you

a Other ancient authorities add all or most of verse 37, *And Philip said, "If you believe with all your heart, you may." And he replied, "I believe that Jesus Christ is the Son of God."* *b* Gk *he*

8:39–40—Leaving no doubt that the eunuch's controversial conversion accords with God's plan, Acts reports that the Spirit "deposits" Philip in *Azotus*, which is north of Gaza, where he continues his mission until finally settling with his family in *Caesarea* (cf. 21:8).

Summary of 9:1–28:31, "And to the Ends of the Earth"

The story of Acts not only unfolds geographically from Jerusalem to the "ends of the earth" (1:8) but as a succession of prophetic leaders. The central character of this third and final narrative movement is Paul. The continuity of the word he proclaims with those who preceded him ensures the solidarity of the community's witness across space and time in an unbroken testimony to the faithfulness of God embodied in what Jesus "did and taught from the beginning" (1:1). But Paul is instructed by Jesus "to bring my name before Gentiles (= non-Jews)" (9:15; cf. 2:21), which clearly indicates the universal scope of God's love and redemptive plan. While his urban mission often begins in a synagogue (or "meeting place"), where religious Jews would assemble for worship and instruction, Paul's programmatic success extends to those God-fearing Gentiles associated with the synagogues, and then even to idol-worshiping pagans (14:8–10). His interpretation of Israel's Scripture would provoke sharp conflict among traditional Jews, even within the church (14:27–15:5; cf. 11:1–2). Yet even when breaking from Jewish tradition, Paul never deviates from his prophetic vocation or from the pattern of mission established during his first evangelistic crusade in Asia (chaps. 13–14). Later, in Europe, his secular work as a "tentmaker" in Corinth would come to symbolize God's work that Amos prophesied, to repair and rebuild "the tent of David" (15:16–18). His second mission westward to Macedonia (15:30–17:15) and then

southward to Greece (17:16–18:17) includes Athens as the intellectual center of Paul's world (see 17:16–34) and Corinth among the wealthiest cities of the day (see 18:1–17). Luke's narrative of Paul's third mission (18:18–21:16) considers his evangelistic crusade in a single city, the mighty Ephesus, which would become a pivotal center of Paul's mission when Acts is written (see 20:17–38). Paul finally returns to Jerusalem as a religious pilgrim (20:16), but faces increasing hostilities there within both the Jewish church (21:16–26) and Judaism (21:27–31; cf. 20:22–23; 21:11–14). Rome, not Jerusalem, is the city of Paul's destiny, however; for it is there, at the mythic "ends of the earth," that Paul realizes the terms of Jesus' commission to the church (1:8; cf. 19:21; 23:11; 27:24).

9:1–31 The Conversion and Commission of Saul

9:1–2—Saul is introduced as a minor player at Stephen's execution (7:58). Although his participation in this treachery is cleverly relativized by Stephen's petition for divine forgiveness (7:59–60), Saul's solidarity with the church's opponents in Jerusalem (8:1) is immediately evident by his persecution of the very community that Stephen once led (8:3). When his story resumes, the reader is left to puzzle over how the Lord will cash Stephen's promissory note. Meanwhile, Philip's successful mission "to all the towns" (8:40) extends the gospel's influence north toward Syria, which explains why Saul travels to Damascus in search of *any who belonged to the Way.*

9:3–4—The *light from heaven* Saul sees and the divine audition he hears recall biblical images of divine appearances, notably when God calls a prophet into service (cf. Exod. 3:4–10; Ezek. 1:28; Dan. 10:6). The importance of his experience is indicated by its three different accounts in Acts, here in the narrator's voice and twice again in Paul's voice (Acts 22:3–16; 26:4–23).

persecute me?" ⁵He asked, "Who are you, Lord?" The reply came, "I am Jesus, whom you are persecuting. ⁶But get up and enter the city, and you will be told what you are to do." ⁷The men who were traveling with him stood speechless because they heard the voice but saw no one. ⁸Saul got up from the ground, and though his eyes were open, he could see nothing; so they led him by the hand and brought him into Damascus. ⁹For three days he was without sight, and neither ate nor drank.

10 Now there was a disciple in Damascus named Ananias. The Lord said to him in a vision, "Ananias." He answered, "Here I am, Lord." ¹¹The Lord said to him, "Get up and go to the street called Straight, and at the house of Judas look for a man of Tarsus named Saul. At this moment he is praying, ¹²and he has seen in a vision[a] a man named Ananias come in and lay his hands on him so that he might regain his sight." ¹³But Ananias answered, "Lord, I have heard from many about this man, how much evil he has done to your saints in Jerusalem; ¹⁴and here he has authority from the chief priests to bind all who invoke your name." ¹⁵But the Lord said to him, "Go, for he is an instrument whom I have chosen to bring my name before Gentiles and kings and before the people of Israel; ¹⁶I myself will show him how much he must suffer for the sake of my name." ¹⁷So Ananias went and entered the house. He laid his hands on Saul[b] and said, "Brother Saul, the Lord Jesus, who appeared to you on your way here, has sent me so that you may regain your sight and be filled with the Holy Spirit." ¹⁸And immediately something like scales fell from his eyes, and his sight was restored. Then he got up and was baptized, ¹⁹and after taking some food, he regained his strength.

Saul Preaches in Damascus

For several days he was with the disciples in Damascus, ²⁰and immediately he began to proclaim Jesus in the synagogues, saying, "He is the Son of God." ²¹All who heard him were amazed and said, "Is not this the man who made havoc in Jerusalem among those who invoked this name? And has he not come here for the purpose of bringing them bound before the chief priests?" ²²Saul became increasingly more powerful and confounded the Jews who lived in Damascus by proving that Jesus[c] was the Messiah.[d]

Saul Escapes from the Jews

23 After some time had passed, the Jews plotted to kill him, ²⁴but their plot became known to Saul. They were watching the gates day and night so that they might kill him; ²⁵but his disciples

[a] Other ancient authorities lack *in a vision* [b] Gk *him* [c] Gk *that this* [d] Or *the Christ*

9:5–6—The risen Jesus continues to work on God's behalf by appearing to Saul to provoke his repentance, and then to his disciple Ananias (vv. 10–14) to commission Saul to his prophetic vocation (vv. 15–16).

9:8–9—The radical change in Saul is seen in the contrast between the purposeful persecutor who comes to Damascus *breathing threats and murder against the disciples of the Lord* (v. 1) and the helpless man who can *see nothing* and needs assistance from others, who *led him by the hand* into the city.

9:15–16—Saul's turn toward the risen Jesus climaxes with his prophetic calling. Acts plots his mission to *Gentiles and kings and before the people of Israel*, and relates how he suffers *for the sake of my name* because of his obedience

to his calling. Acts defines discipleship by its missionary tasks and also by the personal costs exacted on those who obey God.

9:17–18—Saul was *filled with the Holy Spirit*, at which time *his sight was restored*, to symbolize God's confirmation of both his forgiveness (cf. 2:38; 7:58–60) and his prophetic calling to be a "light for the Gentiles, so that you may bring salvation to the ends of the earth" (13:47; cf. 9:15).

9:20—Saul proclaims Jesus first to the Jews and thereby establishes the pattern of his mission, which according to Acts is centered in urban synagogues. His message that Jesus *is the Son of God* is rooted in the Jewish expectation of a Davidic messiah to broker God's promise of a restored Israel (see 13:32–37; cf. 2 Sam. 7:12–16).

took him by night and let him down through an opening in the wall,*a* lowering him in a basket.

Saul in Jerusalem

26 When he had come to Jerusalem, he attempted to join the disciples; and they were all afraid of him, for they did not believe that he was a disciple. 27 But Barnabas took him, brought him to the apostles, and described for them how on the road he had seen the Lord, who had spoken to him, and how in Damascus he had spoken boldly in the name of Jesus. 28 So he went in and out among them in Jerusalem, speaking boldly in the name of the Lord. 29 He spoke and argued with the Hellenists; but they were attempting to kill him. 30 When the believers*b* learned of it, they brought him down to Caesarea and sent him off to Tarsus.

31 Meanwhile the church throughout Judea, Galilee, and Samaria had peace and was built up. Living in the fear of the Lord and in the comfort of the Holy Spirit, it increased in numbers.

The Healing of Aeneas

32 Now as Peter went here and there among all the believers,*c* he came down also to the saints living in Lydda. 33 There he found a man named Aeneas, who had been bedridden for eight years, for he was paralyzed. 34 Peter said to him, "Aeneas, Jesus Christ heals you; get up and make your bed!" And immediately he got up. 35 And all the residents of Lydda and Sharon saw him and turned to the Lord.

Peter in Lydda and Joppa

36 Now in Joppa there was a disciple whose name was Tabitha, which in Greek is Dorcas.*d* She was devoted to good works and acts of charity. 37 At that time she became ill and died. When they had washed her, they laid her in a room upstairs. 38 Since Lydda was near Joppa, the disciples, who heard that Peter was there, sent two men to him with the request, "Please come to us without delay." 39 So Peter got up and went with them; and when he arrived, they took him to the room upstairs. All the widows stood beside him, weeping and showing tunics and other clothing that Dorcas had made while she was with them. 40 Peter put all of them outside, and then he knelt down and prayed. He turned to the body and said, "Tabitha, get up." Then she opened her eyes, and seeing Peter, she sat up. 41 He gave her his hand and helped her up. Then calling the saints and widows, he showed her to be alive. 42 This became known throughout Joppa, and many believed in the Lord. 43 Meanwhile he stayed in Joppa for some time with a certain Simon, a tanner.

Peter and Cornelius

10 In Caesarea there was a man named Cornelius, a centurion

a Gk through the wall *b* Gk brothers *c* Gk all of them *d* The name Tabitha in Aramaic and the name Dorcas in Greek mean a *gazelle*

9:29–30—Jesus' prophecy of Saul's suffering is realized at the hands of *the Hellenists*, who are Diaspora Jews living in Jerusalem and probably connected to the same group that had earlier opposed the ministry of Stephen (6:9–10) and which Saul, himself a Hellenist Jew, may have once led (see 8:3; 9:1–2). These snapshots of a converted Saul illustrate the transforming effect of God's grace!

9:32–11:18 Peter's Mission beyond Jerusalem

9:36–42—Luke's use of *disciple* as a feminine noun emphasizes the role of women within the community of goods where Tabitha's *good works and acts of charity* (cf. 2:42) are the public marks of covenant keeping.

9:43—The repeated reference to the city of *Joppa* connects the subsequent story of Peter's mission to the "unclean" household of an uncircumcised Gentile, Cornelius, with the biblical story of Jonah, who also departed from Joppa on an earlier mission to another unclean place, the city-state of Nineveh. In both stories, the unexpected occurs: unclean non-Jews repent and are forgiven by Israel's God.

10:1–2—*Cornelius* is a Roman *centurion* who leads a garrison of 100 soldiers within a *cohort* of 600. He is considered a *devout* man because he *feared God . . . gave alms generously . . . and prayed constantly to God*. Certain non-Jews are called God-fearers in Acts because while they

of the Italian Cohort, as it was called. [2] He was a devout man who feared God with all his household; he gave alms generously to the people and prayed constantly to God. [3] One afternoon at about three o'clock he had a vision in which he clearly saw an angel of God coming in and saying to him, "Cornelius." [4] He stared at him in terror and said, "What is it, Lord?" He answered, "Your prayers and your alms have ascended as a memorial before God. [5] Now send men to Joppa for a certain Simon who is called Peter; [6] he is lodging with Simon, a tanner, whose house is by the seaside." [7] When the angel who spoke to him had left, he called two of his slaves and a devout soldier from the ranks of those who served him, [8] and after telling them everything, he sent them to Joppa.

9 About noon the next day, as they were on their journey and approaching the city, Peter went up on the roof to pray. [10] He became hungry and wanted something to eat; and while it was being prepared, he fell into a trance. [11] He saw the heaven opened and something like a large sheet coming down, being lowered to the ground by its four corners. [12] In it were all kinds of four-footed creatures and reptiles and birds of the air. [13] Then he heard a voice saying, "Get up, Peter; kill and eat." [14] But Peter said, "By no means, Lord; for I have never eaten anything that is profane or unclean." [15] The voice said to him again, a second time, "What God has made clean, you must not call profane." [16] This happened three times, and the thing was suddenly taken up to heaven.

17 Now while Peter was greatly puzzled about what to make of the vision that he had seen, suddenly the men sent by Cornelius appeared. They were asking for Simon's house and were standing by the gate. [18] They called out to ask whether Simon, who was called Peter, was staying there. [19] While Peter was still thinking about the vision, the Spirit said to him, "Look, three[a] men are searching for you. [20] Now get up, go down, and go with them without hesitation; for I have sent them." [21] So Peter went down to the men and said, "I am the one you are looking for; what is the reason for your coming?" [22] They answered, "Cornelius, a centurion, an upright and God-fearing man, who is well spoken of by the whole Jewish nation, was directed by a holy angel to send for you to come to his house and to hear what you have to say." [23] So Peter[b] invited them in and gave them lodging.

The next day he got up and went with them, and some of the believers[c] from Joppa accompanied him. [24] The following day they came to Caesarea. Cornelius was expecting them and had called together his relatives and close friends. [25] On Peter's arrival Cornelius met him, and falling at his feet, worshiped him. [26] But Peter made him get up, saying, "Stand up; I am only a mortal." [27] And as he talked with him, he went in and found that many had assembled; [28] and

[a] One ancient authority reads *two*; others lack the word   [b] Gk *he*
[c] Gk *brothers*

---

worship with Jews they are not yet converts to Judaism. From Peter's perspective as a religious Jew, uncircumcised God-fearers such as Cornelius are still "unclean" and a potential threat to his covenant relations with God and other pious Jews (vv. 28–29).

10:11–14—According to Levitical law (Lev. 11), faithful Jews demonstrate their love for God by abstaining from unclean foods outlawed by Torah, including *reptiles and birds of the air* (Lev. 11:13–19, 29–38).

10:15–17—*Three times* symbolizes importance:

God now accepts what is formerly *unclean* (= nonproselyte Gentiles such as Cornelius). As a traditional Jew who observes the kosher rules stipulated by Torah, Peter remains *greatly puzzled about what to make of the vision* and requires more evidence before converting to God's way of salvation.

10:19—Conversion to God's way sometimes follows a process of rethinking our old beliefs in light of new evidence *the Spirit* supplies.

10:28–29—Peter's hesitancy in meeting with Cornelius is not racial but religious: Cornelius is

he said to them, "You yourselves know that it is unlawful for a Jew to associate with or to visit a Gentile; but God has shown me that I should not call anyone profane or unclean. ²⁹ So when I was sent for, I came without objection. Now may I ask why you sent for me?"

30 Cornelius replied, "Four days ago at this very hour, at three o'clock, I was praying in my house when suddenly a man in dazzling clothes stood before me. ³¹ He said, 'Cornelius, your prayer has been heard and your alms have been remembered before God. ³² Send therefore to Joppa and ask for Simon, who is called Peter; he is staying in the home of Simon, a tanner, by the sea.' ³³ Therefore I sent for you immediately, and you have been kind enough to come. So now all of us are here in the presence of God to listen to all that the Lord has commanded you to say."

Gentiles Hear the Good News

34 Then Peter began to speak to them: "I truly understand that God shows no partiality, ³⁵ but in every nation anyone who fears him and does what is right is acceptable to him. ³⁶ You know the message he sent to the people of Israel, preaching peace by Jesus Christ—he is Lord of all. ³⁷ That message spread throughout Judea, beginning in Galilee after the baptism that John announced: ³⁸ how God anointed Jesus of Nazareth with the Holy Spirit and with power; how he went about doing good and healing all who were oppressed by the devil, for God was with him. ³⁹ We are witnesses to all that he did both in Judea and in Jerusalem. They put him to death by hanging him on a tree; ⁴⁰ but God raised him on the third day and allowed him to appear, ⁴¹ not to all the people but to us who were chosen by God as witnesses, and who ate and drank with him after he rose from the dead. ⁴² He commanded us to preach to the people and to testify that he is the one ordained by God as judge of the living and the dead. ⁴³ All the prophets testify about him that everyone who believes in him receives forgiveness of sins through his name."

Gentiles Receive the Holy Spirit

44 While Peter was still speaking, the Holy Spirit fell upon all who heard the word. ⁴⁵ The circumcised believers who had come with Peter were astounded that the gift of the Holy Spirit had been poured out even on the Gentiles, ⁴⁶ for they heard them speaking in tongues and extolling God. Then Peter said, ⁴⁷ "Can anyone withhold the water for baptizing these people who have received the Holy Spirit just as we have?" ⁴⁸ So he ordered them to be baptized in the name of Jesus Christ. Then they invited him to stay for several days.

Peter's Report to the Church at Jerusalem

11 Now the apostles and the believers*a* who were in Judea heard that the Gentiles had also accepted the

a Gk brothers

---

still **unclean** because he is not yet circumcised and identified with the covenant community according to Torah's rule. He is a God-fearing (v. 2) but not a proselyte Gentile (cf. 2:10; 6:5).

10:34–35—Peter's lesson concerns God's impartiality, which he knows from Scripture (Deut. 10:17). He now realizes that the church's mission beyond Israel is international and multiethnic.

10:44—Even though the "double vision" that has brought Peter together with Cornelius implies the apostle's spiritual authority to interpret the importance of Jesus for others, God assumes ultimate responsibility for saving them and interrupts Peter

to give the **Spirit** to those who had received the **word**.

10:46—The phenomenon of **speaking in tongues** provides conclusive evidence of God's forgiveness (cf. 2:38), since their experience appears similar to what occurred on the Day of Pentecost (cf. 2:4).

11:1–2—Peter's decision to baptize Cornelius and his household **in the name of Jesus Christ** (10:48) provokes criticism among the **circumcised believers** of Judea, including **the apostles** who had not observed what Peter had (see 10:45).

word of God. ² So when Peter went up to Jerusalem, the circumcised believers*a* criticized him, ³ saying, "Why did you go to uncircumcised men and eat with them?" ⁴ Then Peter began to explain it to them, step by step, saying, ⁵ "I was in the city of Joppa praying, and in a trance I saw a vision. There was something like a large sheet coming down from heaven, being lowered by its four corners; and it came close to me. ⁶ As I looked at it closely I saw four-footed animals, beasts of prey, reptiles, and birds of the air. ⁷ I also heard a voice saying to me, 'Get up, Peter; kill and eat.' ⁸ But I replied, 'By no means, Lord; for nothing profane or unclean has ever entered my mouth.' ⁹ But a second time the voice answered from heaven, 'What God has made clean, you must not call profane.' ¹⁰ This happened three times; then everything was pulled up again to heaven. ¹¹ At that very moment three men, sent to me from Caesarea, arrived at the house where we were. ¹² The Spirit told me to go with them and not to make a distinction between them and us.*b* These six brothers also accompanied me, and we entered the man's house. ¹³ He told us how he had seen the angel standing in his house and saying, 'Send to Joppa and bring Simon, who is called Peter; ¹⁴ he will give you a message by which you and your entire household will be saved.' ¹⁵ And as I began to speak, the Holy Spirit fell upon them just as it had upon us at the beginning. ¹⁶ And I remembered the word of the Lord, how

he had said, 'John baptized with water, but you will be baptized with the Holy Spirit.' ¹⁷ If then God gave them the same gift that he gave us when we believed in the Lord Jesus Christ, who was I that I could hinder God?" ¹⁸ When they heard this, they were silenced. And they praised God, saying, "Then God has given even to the Gentiles the repentance that leads to life."

The Church in Antioch

19 Now those who were scattered because of the persecution that took place over Stephen traveled as far as Phoenicia, Cyprus, and Antioch, and they spoke the word to no one except Jews. ²⁰ But among them were some men of Cyprus and Cyrene who, on coming to Antioch, spoke to the Hellenists*c* also, proclaiming the Lord Jesus. ²¹ The hand of the Lord was with them, and a great number became believers and turned to the Lord. ²² News of this came to the ears of the church in Jerusalem, and they sent Barnabas to Antioch. ²³ When he came and saw the grace of God, he rejoiced, and he exhorted them all to remain faithful to the Lord with steadfast devotion; ²⁴ for he was a good man, full of the Holy Spirit and of faith. And a great many people were brought to the Lord. ²⁵ Then Barnabas went to Tarsus to look for Saul, ²⁶ and when he had found him, he brought him to Antioch. So it was that for an entire year they met with*d* the

a Gk lacks *believers* *b* Or *not to hesitate* *c* Other ancient authorities read *Greeks* *d* Or *were guests of*

11:13–14—In retelling the events of Acts 10, Peter adds the angelic annunciation to Cornelius that *your entire household will be saved* to clarify that God (not Peter) has taken responsibility for Cornelius's salvation (cf. 11:18).

11:18—To *praise God* symbolizes agreement with Peter's interpretation of Gentile conversion (cf. 3:8). The full implication of their verdict awaits a subsequent meeting in Jerusalem, when another council of church leaders convenes to discuss the stunning results and implications of Paul's mission to the nations (see 15:4–21).

11:19–12:25 The Succession of the Twelve

11:19–20—Syrian *Antioch* is one of the largest and most important cities in the Roman Empire.

11:22–24—*Barnabas* enjoys good relations with the Jerusalem church and the apostolate (4:36–37; 9:27). In Acts, his virtuous character identifies him as someone with whom God can do business (cf. 10:1–2).

11:25–26—Barnabas's protégé is *Saul* (9:27), whose teaching in Antioch forges a new public identity: *the disciples were first called "Christians."* Their mixed membership and beliefs about the resurrected Jesus were distinct from other messianic movements within Judaism.

church and taught a great many people, and it was in Antioch that the disciples were first called "Christians."

27 At that time prophets came down from Jerusalem to Antioch. 28 One of them named Agabus stood up and predicted by the Spirit that there would be a severe famine over all the world; and this took place during the reign of Claudius. 29 The disciples determined that according to their ability, each would send relief to the believers[a] living in Judea; 30 this they did, sending it to the elders by Barnabas and Saul.

James Killed and Peter Imprisoned

12 About that time King Herod laid violent hands upon some who belonged to the church. 2 He had James, the brother of John, killed with the sword. 3 After he saw that it pleased the Jews, he proceeded to arrest Peter also. (This was during the festival of Unleavened Bread.) 4 When he had seized him, he put him in prison and handed him over to four squads of soldiers to guard him, intending to bring him out to the people after the Passover. 5 While Peter was kept in prison, the church prayed fervently to God for him.

Peter Delivered from Prison

6 The very night before Herod was going to bring him out, Peter, bound with two chains, was sleeping between two soldiers, while guards in front of the door were keeping watch over the prison. 7 Suddenly an angel of the Lord appeared and a light shone in the cell. He tapped Peter on the side and woke him, saying, "Get up quickly." And the chains fell off his wrists. 8 The angel said to him, "Fasten your belt and put on your sandals." He did so. Then he said to him, "Wrap your cloak around you and follow me." 9 Peter[b] went out and followed him; he did not realize that what was happening with the angel's help was real; he thought he was seeing a vision. 10 After they had passed the first and the second guard, they came before the iron gate leading into the city. It opened for them of its own accord, and they went outside and walked along a lane, when suddenly the angel left him. 11 Then Peter came to himself and said, "Now I am sure that the Lord has sent his angel and rescued me from the hands of Herod and from all that the Jewish people were expecting."

12 As soon as he realized this, he went to the house of Mary, the mother of John whose other name was Mark, where many had gathered and were praying. 13 When he knocked at the outer gate, a maid named Rhoda came to answer. 14 On recognizing Peter's voice, she was so overjoyed that, instead of opening the gate, she ran in and announced that Peter was standing at the gate. 15 They said to her, "You are out of your mind!" But she insisted that it was so. They said, "It is his angel." 16 Meanwhile Peter continued knocking; and when they

[a] Gk brothers   [b] Gk He

11:27–30—In continuity with Jerusalem, *disciples* in Antioch formed a community of goods, which *determined that according to their ability, each would send relief to the believers living in Judea* (cf. 2:42–47; 4:32–35).

12:2–3—*King Herod* Agrippa I is related to Herod Antipas, who shared responsibility for the execution of Jesus during an earlier *festival of Unleavened Bread* (Luke 23:7–15). *James, the brother of John*, was a close friend of Jesus and one of his apostolic successors (Acts 1:13). He is executed while Peter is arrested; these two tragic events break apart the church's apostolate, which is not restored to Twelve as before (cf. 1:15–26),

thus requiring a succession to a second generation of Christian leaders led by James, the brother of Jesus (12:17), and Paul.

12:4–11—Stories of jailbreaks in Acts, facilitated by divine intervention (cf. 5:19; 16:26), are thematic of God's triumph over evil. The Passover setting of Peter's escape (12:3) anticipates an ironical story of God's *rescue* (v. 11), not of a captive Israel but of an apostle held captive by Herod.

12:12–17—Luke uses similar images to narrate the story of Jesus' appearance to his disciples following his resurrection (cf. Luke 24:13–35).

opened the gate, they saw him and were amazed. [17] He motioned to them with his hand to be silent, and described for them how the Lord had brought him out of the prison. And he added, "Tell this to James and to the believers."[a] Then he left and went to another place.

18 When morning came, there was no small commotion among the soldiers over what had become of Peter. [19] When Herod had searched for him and could not find him, he examined the guards and ordered them to be put to death. Then he went down from Judea to Caesarea and stayed there.

The Death of Herod

20 Now Herod[b] was angry with the people of Tyre and Sidon. So they came to him in a body; and after winning over Blastus, the king's chamberlain, they asked for a reconciliation, because their country depended on the king's country for food. [21] On an appointed day Herod put on his royal robes, took his seat on the platform, and delivered a public address to them. [22] The people kept shouting, "The voice of a god, and not of a mortal!" [23] And immediately, because he had not given the glory to God, an angel of the Lord struck him down, and he was eaten by worms and died.

24 But the word of God continued to advance and gain adherents. [25] Then after completing their mission Barnabas and Saul returned to[c] Jerusalem and brought with them John, whose other name was Mark.

Barnabas and Saul Commissioned

13 Now in the church at Antioch there were prophets and teachers: Barnabas, Simeon who was called Niger, Lucius of Cyrene, Manaen a member of the court of Herod the ruler,[d] and Saul. [2] While they were worshiping the Lord and fasting, the Holy Spirit said, "Set apart for me Barnabas and Saul for the work to which I have called them." [3] Then after fasting and praying they laid their hands on them and sent them off.

The Apostles Preach in Cyprus

4 So, being sent out by the Holy Spirit, they went down to Seleucia; and from there they sailed to Cyprus. [5] When they arrived at Salamis, they proclaimed the word of God in the synagogues of the Jews. And they had John also to assist them. [6] When they had gone through the whole island as far as Paphos, they met a certain magician, a Jewish false prophet, named Bar-Jesus. [7] He was with the proconsul, Sergius Paulus, an intelligent man, who summoned Barnabas and Saul and wanted to hear the word of God. [8] But the magician Elymas (for that is the translation of his name) opposed them and tried to turn the proconsul away from the faith. [9] But Saul, also known as Paul, filled with the Holy Spirit, looked intently at him [10] and said,

[a] Gk brothers [b] Gk he [c] Other ancient authorities read from [d] Gk tetrarch

---

12:24—The irrepressible progress of *the word of God* (= gospel) from Jerusalem to the "ends of the earth" (= Rome) is an important theme of Acts (cf. 4:4, 31; 6:2, 7; 11:1; 13:5; 15:35; 18:11; 19:20).

13:1–14:26 Paul's Mission to the Nations

13:1—Luke's story of Paul and Barnabas's first mission is bracketed by references to the *church at Antioch* (v. 1; 14:21–26), which has replaced Jerusalem as the center of the church's mission to the nations. The ethnic mix of its membership embodies the universal scope of Paul's missionary vocation (9:15).

13:3–4—Unlike Jesus' apostolic successors, all of whom knew him personally (1:21–22) and were chosen and sent out by him (1:2, 8), Paul and Barnabas are *sent off* by the leaders of the Antiochene church. In Acts, Barnabas is Paul's silent partner (14:12), even as earlier John was Peter's.

13:5—*Synagogue* refers to any quorum of Jews assembled to worship and receive religious instruction. Often they met in the living room of a middle-class home.

13:6–12—Paul's conflict with a *Jewish false prophet, named Bar-Jesus* ("son of Joshua"), anticipates and typifies his ongoing battles with unrepentant Jews who seek to subvert his mission. As a representative of Israel's spiritual blindness, he is temporarily made *blind*.

"You son of the devil, you enemy of all righteousness, full of all deceit and villainy, will you not stop making crooked the straight paths of the Lord? [11] And now listen—the hand of the Lord is against you, and you will be blind for a while, unable to see the sun." Immediately mist and darkness came over him, and he went about groping for someone to lead him by the hand. [12] When the proconsul saw what had happened, he believed, for he was astonished at the teaching about the Lord.

Paul and Barnabas in Antioch of Pisidia

13 Then Paul and his companions set sail from Paphos and came to Perga in Pamphylia. John, however, left them and returned to Jerusalem; [14] but they went on from Perga and came to Antioch in Pisidia. And on the sabbath day they went into the synagogue and sat down. [15] After the reading of the law and the prophets, the officials of the synagogue sent them a message, saying, "Brothers, if you have any word of exhortation for the people, give it." [16] So Paul stood up and with a gesture began to speak:

"You Israelites,[a] and others who fear God, listen. [17] The God of this people Israel chose our ancestors and made the people great during their stay in the land of Egypt, and with uplifted arm he led them out of it. [18] For about forty years he put up with[b] them in the wilderness. [19] After he had destroyed seven nations in the land of Canaan, he gave them their land as an inheritance [20] for about four hundred fifty years. After that he gave them judges until the time of the prophet Samuel. [21] Then they asked for a king; and God gave them Saul son of Kish, a man of the tribe of Benjamin, who reigned for forty years. [22] When he had removed him, he made David their king. In his testimony about him he said, 'I have found David, son of Jesse, to be a man after my heart, who will carry out all my wishes.' [23] Of this man's posterity God has brought to Israel a Savior, Jesus, as he promised; [24] before his coming John had already proclaimed a baptism of repentance to all the people of Israel. [25] And as John was finishing his work, he said, 'What do you suppose that I am? I am not he. No, but one is coming after me; I am not worthy to untie the thong of the sandals[c] on his feet.'

26 "My brothers, you descendants of Abraham's family, and others who fear God, to us[d] the message of this salvation has been sent. [27] Because the residents of Jerusalem and their leaders did not recognize him or understand the words of the prophets that are read every sabbath, they fulfilled those words by condemning him. [28] Even though they found no cause for a sentence of death, they asked Pilate to have him killed. [29] When they had carried out everything that was written about him, they took him down from the tree and laid him in a tomb. [30] But God raised him from the dead; [31] and for many days he appeared to those who came up with him from Galilee to Jerusalem, and they are now his witnesses to the people. [32] And we bring you the good news that what God promised to our ancestors [33] he has fulfilled for us, their children, by raising Jesus; as also it is written in the second psalm,

[a] Gk Men, Israelites   [b] Other ancient authorities read cared for   [c] Gk untie the sandals   [d] Other ancient authorities read you

---

13:14—The Paul of Acts is portrayed as an observant Jew and teacher of Israel, and so routinely keeps *the sabbath day*.

13:16–41—Paul's *word of exhortation* is the basis of every other missionary speech he gives in Acts, and it continues many of the same themes voiced earlier by both Peter and Stephen. In the first part of his speech (vv. 16–25), Paul retells the biblical story of Israel as a story about God. The second section (vv. 26–37) concerns Jesus who is Israel's *Savior* (v. 23) but was rejected by *the residents of Jerusalem and their leaders* (v. 27). Paul's ministry beyond Jerusalem in the Diaspora, then, is to proclaim that God's promises to Israel according to Scripture have been fulfilled because of Jesus, and to give Jews first of all a new opportunity to accept this good news.

'You are my Son;
today I have begotten you.'
³⁴ As to his raising him from the dead,
no more to return to corruption, he has
spoken in this way,
'I will give you the holy promises
made to David.'
³⁵ Therefore he has also said in another
psalm,
'You will not let your Holy One
experience corruption.'
³⁶ For David, after he had served the
purpose of God in his own generation,
died,ᵃ was laid beside his ancestors, and
experienced corruption; ³⁷ but he whom
God raised up experienced no corruption. ³⁸ Let it be known to you therefore,
my brothers, that through this man forgiveness of sins is proclaimed to you; ³⁹ by
this Jesusᵇ everyone who believes is set
free from all those sinsᶜ from which you
could not be freed by the law of Moses.
⁴⁰ Beware, therefore, that what the prophets said does not happen to you:
⁴¹ 'Look, you scoffers!
Be amazed and perish,
for in your days I am doing a work,
a work that you will never believe,
even if someone tells you.' "

42 As Paul and Barnabasᵈ were going
out, the people urged them to speak
about these things again the next sabbath. ⁴³ When the meeting of the synagogue broke up, many Jews and devout
converts to Judaism followed Paul and
Barnabas, who spoke to them and urged
them to continue in the grace of God.

44 The next sabbath almost the whole
city gathered to hear the word of the
Lord.ᵉ ⁴⁵ But when the Jews saw the
crowds, they were filled with jealousy;
and blaspheming, they contradicted
what was spoken by Paul. ⁴⁶ Then both

Paul and Barnabas spoke out boldly,
saying, "It was necessary that the word
of God should be spoken first to you.
Since you reject it and judge yourselves
to be unworthy of eternal life, we are
now turning to the Gentiles. ⁴⁷ For so the
Lord has commanded us, saying,
'I have set you to be a light for the
Gentiles,
so that you may bring salvation to
the ends of the earth.' "
48 When the Gentiles heard this, they
were glad and praised the word of the
Lord; and as many as had been destined
for eternal life became believers. ⁴⁹ Thus
the word of the Lord spread throughout
the region. ⁵⁰ But the Jews incited the
devout women of high standing and the
leading men of the city, and stirred up
persecution against Paul and Barnabas,
and drove them out of their region. ⁵¹ So
they shook the dust off their feet in protest against them, and went to Iconium.
⁵² And the disciples were filled with joy
and with the Holy Spirit.

Paul and Barnabas in Iconium

14 The same thing occurred in Iconium, where Paul and Barnabasᵈ
went into the Jewish synagogue and
spoke in such a way that a great number
of both Jews and Greeks became believers. ² But the unbelieving Jews stirred up
the Gentiles and poisoned their minds
against the brothers. ³ So they remained
for a long time, speaking boldly for
the Lord, who testified to the word of
his grace by granting signs and wonders to be done through them. ⁴ But the
residents of the city were divided; some
sided with the Jews, and some with the
apostles. ⁵ And when an attempt was

ᵃ Gk fell asleep ᵇ Gk this ᶜ Gk all ᵈ Gk they ᵉ Other ancient authorities
read God

13:42–45—The division among those Jews who
hear Paul's message fulfills Simeon's prophecy
that Jesus will divide the household of Israel (cf.
Luke 2:34; Acts 28:26–27; Isa. 6:9–10).

13:46—Paul's *turning to the Gentiles* of Pisidian Antioch (vv. 48–49) does not reflect God's
retribution against unrepentant Jews, but merely

recognizes that, having given them two chances
to repent (see note at 7:20–43), his ministry
among the Jews of Antioch had ended.

13:47—Paul's ministry personifies the sacred
vocation of restored Israel to *bring salvation to
the end of the earth* (Isa. 49:6) in obedience to
the risen Lord (cf. 1:8).

made by both Gentiles and Jews, with their rulers, to mistreat them and to stone them, [6] the apostles[a] learned of it and fled to Lystra and Derbe, cities of Lycaonia, and to the surrounding country; [7] and there they continued proclaiming the good news.

Paul and Barnabas in Lystra and Derbe

[8] In Lystra there was a man sitting who could not use his feet and had never walked, for he had been crippled from birth. [9] He listened to Paul as he was speaking. And Paul, looking at him intently and seeing that he had faith to be healed, [10] said in a loud voice, "Stand upright on your feet." And the man[b] sprang up and began to walk. [11] When the crowds saw what Paul had done, they shouted in the Lycaonian language, "The gods have come down to us in human form!" [12] Barnabas they called Zeus, and Paul they called Hermes, because he was the chief speaker. [13] The priest of Zeus, whose temple was just outside the city,[c] brought oxen and garlands to the gates; he and the crowds wanted to offer sacrifice. [14] When the apostles Barnabas and Paul heard of it, they tore their clothes and rushed out into the crowd, shouting, [15] "Friends,[d] why are you doing this? We are mortals just like you, and we bring you good news, that you should turn from these worthless things to the living God, who made the heaven and the earth and the sea and all that is in them. [16] In past generations he allowed all the nations to follow their own ways; [17] yet he has not left himself without a witness in doing good—giving you rains from heaven and fruitful seasons, and filling you with food and your hearts with joy." [18] Even with these words, they scarcely restrained the crowds from offering sacrifice to them.

[19] But Jews came there from Antioch and Iconium and won over the crowds. Then they stoned Paul and dragged him out of the city, supposing that he was dead. [20] But when the disciples surrounded him, he got up and went into the city. The next day he went on with Barnabas to Derbe.

The Return to Antioch in Syria

[21] After they had proclaimed the good news to that city and had made many disciples, they returned to Lystra, then on to Iconium and Antioch. [22] There they strengthened the souls of the disciples and encouraged them to continue in the faith, saying, "It is through many persecutions that we must enter the kingdom of God." [23] And after they had appointed elders for them in each church, with prayer and fasting they entrusted them to the Lord in whom they had come to believe.

[24] Then they passed through Pisidia and came to Pamphylia. [25] When they had spoken the word in Perga, they went down to Attalia. [26] From there they sailed back to Antioch, where they had been commended to the grace of God for the work[e] that they had completed. [27] When they arrived, they called the church

[a] Gk they [b] Gk he [c] Or The priest of Zeus-Outside-the-City [d] Gk Men
[e] Or committed in the grace of God to the work

14:8–18—The mission of Paul and Barnabas to Zeus worshipers in the Roman colony of Lystra moves them beyond the synagogues of the Diaspora to bring good news to pagans.

14:8–10—The literary parallels between this healing story of a man *crippled from birth* and the earlier story of 3:1–10 link Paul's religious authority with Peter's and the church's mission to Israel with this mission to pagans: the healing effect of God's salvation extends to all people.

14:12 *Zeus . . . Hermes*—According to Greek mythology, Hermes is the divine messenger for a pantheon of gods led by Zeus.

14:15–17—This speech is the first in Acts to Gentiles outside of a synagogue setting who have no knowledge of Israel's God or Scriptures (cf. 17:22–31). Repentance from Zeus worship is invited based upon the universal authority of Israel's God, who is Creator of all things.

14:23—Following the pattern of Diaspora synagogues, Paul and Barnabas *appointed elders . . . in each church* (cf. Titus 1:5–6).

14:27–15:35 Conflict Reconvenes the Jerusalem Council

together and related all that God had done with them, and how he had opened a door of faith for the Gentiles. **28** And they stayed there with the disciples for some time.

The Council at Jerusalem

15 Then certain individuals came down from Judea and were teaching the brothers, "Unless you are circumcised according to the custom of Moses, you cannot be saved." **2** And after Paul and Barnabas had no small dissension and debate with them, Paul and Barnabas and some of the others were appointed to go up to Jerusalem to discuss this question with the apostles and the elders. **3** So they were sent on their way by the church, and as they passed through both Phoenicia and Samaria, they reported the conversion of the Gentiles, and brought great joy to all the believers.*a* **4** When they came to Jerusalem, they were welcomed by the church and the apostles and the elders, and they reported all that God had done with them. **5** But some believers who belonged to the sect of the Pharisees stood up and said, "It is necessary for them to be circumcised and ordered to keep the law of Moses."

6 The apostles and the elders met together to consider this matter. **7** After there had been much debate, Peter stood up and said to them, "My brothers,*b* you know that in the early days God made a choice among you, that I should be the one through whom the Gentiles would hear the message of the good news and become believers. **8** And God, who knows the human heart, testified to them by giving them the Holy Spirit, just as he did to us; **9** and in cleansing their hearts by faith he has made no distinction between them and us. **10** Now therefore why are you putting God to the test by placing on the neck of the disciples a yoke that neither our ancestors nor we have been able to bear? **11** On the contrary, we believe that we will be saved through the grace of the Lord Jesus, just as they will."

12 The whole assembly kept silence, and listened to Barnabas and Paul as they told of all the signs and wonders that God had done through them among the Gentiles. **13** After they finished speaking, James replied, "My brothers,*b* listen to me. **14** Simeon has related how God

a Gk brothers　*b* Gk Men, brothers

15:1–2—Paul and Barnabas's missionary report provokes *no small dissension and debate* with their opponents from the Judean church. Their presence in Antioch is unauthorized (v. 24) and recalls the earlier debate following Cornelius's conversion that the church's leaders have already settled (11:1–18). Readers of Acts know that a repentant Gentile, even though uncircumcised and unclean, can be saved without being circumcised by "calling upon the name of the Lord" (2:21).

15:4–5—A new and important question raised by *believers who belonged to the sect of the Pharisees* asks whether Christian fellowship is possible between traditional Jews and "unclean" Gentiles (cf. Gal. 2:11–15)—a question that is made more urgent as Paul's mission carries his gospel well beyond Jerusalem and into the pagan precincts of Roman cities.

15:6–9—In responding to the Pharisees' commitment to maintain purity within the church's Diaspora congregations, Peter rehearses for a second time the story of Cornelius's conversion (cf. 11:3–18), adding that God purifies human hearts without distinction in response to their faith. The

heart symbolizes a person's internal spiritual apparatus, where a disciple's life with God is freely chosen and cultivated.

15:10–11—Peter concludes his speech with words reminiscent of both Moses (Deut. 10:16; 30:6) and Paul (Rom. 2:25–29) that covenanting with God results from a purity of heart rather than circumcision of flesh.

15:12—Luke's summary of the testimony of Barnabas and Paul echoes Joel's prophecy and recalls the preface to Peter's Pentecost sermon about Jesus (2:22): the Spirit's presence *among the Gentiles* is indicated by the *signs and wonders* performed *through them* (cf. 2:19, 22; 14:3); what began with Jesus within Israel now continues with Paul and Barnabas among Gentiles beyond Israel.

15:13—*James*, the brother of Jesus, is now the leader of the Jerusalem congregation, whose membership is comprised of more traditional Jews.

15:14–15—James summarizes the hard evidence presented by trusted witnesses that a covenant

first looked favorably on the Gentiles, to take from among them a people for his name. [15] This agrees with the words of the prophets, as it is written,

[16] 'After this I will return,
and I will rebuild the dwelling of David, which has fallen;
from its ruins I will rebuild it,
and I will set it up,
[17] so that all other peoples may seek the Lord—
even all the Gentiles over whom my name has been called.
Thus says the Lord, who has been making these things
[18] known from long ago.'[a]

[19] Therefore I have reached the decision that we should not trouble those Gentiles who are turning to God, [20] but we should write to them to abstain only from things polluted by idols and from fornication and from whatever has been strangled[b] and from blood. [21] For in every city, for generations past, Moses has had those who proclaim him, for he has been read aloud every sabbath in the synagogues."

The Council's Letter to Gentile Believers

22 Then the apostles and the elders, with the consent of the whole church, decided to choose men from among their members[c] and to send them to Antioch with Paul and Barnabas. They sent Judas called Barsabbas, and Silas, leaders among the brothers, [23] with the following letter: "The brothers, both the apostles and the elders, to the believers[d] of Gentile origin in Antioch and Syria and Cilicia, greetings. [24] Since we have heard that certain persons who have gone out from us, though with no instructions from us, have said things to disturb you and have unsettled your minds,[e] [25] we have decided unanimously to choose representatives[f] and send them to you, along with our beloved Barnabas and Paul, [26] who have risked their lives for the sake of our Lord Jesus Christ. [27] We have therefore sent Judas and Silas, who themselves will tell you the same things by word of mouth. [28] For it has seemed good to the Holy Spirit and to us to impose on you no further burden than these essentials: [29] that you abstain from what has been sacrificed to idols and from blood and from what is strangled[g] and from fornication. If you keep yourselves from these, you will do well. Farewell."

30 So they were sent off and went down to Antioch. When they gathered the congregation together, they delivered the letter. [31] When its members[h] read it, they rejoiced at the exhortation.

[a] Other ancient authorities read *things*. [18]*Known to God from of old are all his works.'* [b] Other ancient authorities lack *and from whatever has been strangled* [c] Gk *from among them* [d] Gk *brothers* [e] Other ancient authorities add *saying, 'You must be circumcised and keep the law,'* [f] Gk *men* [g] Other ancient authorities lack *and from what is strangled* [h] Gk *When they*

---

people for [God's] name now includes uncircumcised *Gentiles*; and this new reality agrees with Israel's Scriptures that supply the script of God's redemptive plan.

15:16–18—According to LXX Amos 9:11–12, the rebuilding of *the dwelling of David* (= Jerusalem's temple; cf. Jer. 12:16–17; Zech. 2:11–12) marks the moment and location of the conversion of all nations. According to Acts, this prophecy has already been fulfilled symbolically at the resurrection of Jesus (cf. Acts 6:11–14; 3:18–26).

15:19–21—Rabbi James offers his commentary (midrash) on the Amos prophecy that retrieves a meaning relevant to the question under discussion (see v. 5). While James agrees with Peter that God cleanses the hearts of unclean Gentiles because of their faith in Jesus and so *we should*

not trouble those Gentiles who are turning to God (see vv. 9–10), he is unwilling to authorize a Christian mission that sets aside the purity practices that publicly mark out a covenant *people for [God's] name* (v. 14). As the Letter of James instructs, "faith apart from works is dead" (Jas. 2:17, 20, 26). Repentant Gentiles, therefore, must *abstain from what has been sacrificed to idols and from [sexual] fornication* (15:29; 21:25), following Moses who is *read aloud every sabbath in the synagogues* (cf. Lev. 17–18).

15:22–29—James's commentary on Amos is inscribed as a pastoral *letter* and sent to Antiochene believers with a coalition of leaders from both congregations, including *Silas*, who will later replace Barnabas as Paul's partner (vv. 36–41).

32 Judas and Silas, who were themselves prophets, said much to encourage and strengthen the believers.*a* 33 After they had been there for some time, they were sent off in peace by the believers*a* to those who had sent them.*b* 35 But Paul and Barnabas remained in Antioch, and there, with many others, they taught and proclaimed the word of the Lord.

Paul and Barnabas Separate

36 After some days Paul said to Barnabas, "Come, let us return and visit the believers*a* in every city where we proclaimed the word of the Lord and see how they are doing." 37 Barnabas wanted to take with them John called Mark. 38 But Paul decided not to take with them one who had deserted them in Pamphylia and had not accompanied them in the work. 39 The disagreement became so sharp that they parted company; Barnabas took Mark with him and sailed away to Cyprus. 40 But Paul chose Silas and set out, the believers*a* commending him to the grace of the Lord. 41 He went through Syria and Cilicia, strengthening the churches.

Timothy Joins Paul and Silas

16 Paul*c* went on also to Derbe and to Lystra, where there was a disciple named Timothy, the son of a Jewish woman who was a believer; but his father was a Greek. 2 He was well spoken of by the believers*a* in Lystra and Iconium. 3 Paul wanted Timothy to accompany him; and he took him and had him circumcised because of the Jews who were in those places, for they all knew that his father was a Greek. 4 As they went from town to town, they delivered to them for observance the decisions that had been reached by the apostles and elders who were in Jerusalem. 5 So the churches were strengthened in the faith and increased in numbers daily.

Paul's Vision of the Man of Macedonia

6 They went through the region of Phrygia and Galatia, having been forbidden by the Holy Spirit to speak the word in Asia. 7 When they had come opposite Mysia, they attempted to go into Bithynia, but the Spirit of Jesus did not allow them; 8 so, passing by Mysia, they went down to Troas. 9 During the night Paul had a vision: there stood a man of Macedonia pleading with him and saying, "Come over to Macedonia and help us." 10 When he had seen the vision, we immediately tried to cross over to Macedonia, being convinced that God had called us to proclaim the good news to them.

The Conversion of Lydia

11 We set sail from Troas and took a straight course to Samothrace, the following day to Neapolis, 12 and from there to Philippi, which is a leading city of the district*d* of Macedonia and

a Gk brothers   *b* Other ancient authorities add verse 34, *But it seemed good to Silas to remain there*   *c* Gk He   *d* Other authorities read *a city of the first district*

15:36–16:10 Paul's Mission beyond Roman Asia

15:38–39—Paul interprets John Mark's earlier departure (13:13) as "desertion" (in religious terms, apostasy) and will have nothing more to do with him.

15:40–41—In Luke's narrative world, mission is typically by pairs (cf. Luke 10:1). Paul's new partner is *Silas*.

16:3—Paul *had [Timothy] circumcised because of the Jews* (cf. Gal. 2:2). Since he is the "son of a Jewish woman" (16:1), Judaism considers Timothy Jewish, and circumcision merely confirms his birthright. Yet Paul's decision to do so responds to James' earlier exhortation that his mission in the Diaspora should retain those religious practices

that forge solidarity with the church's Jewish heritage (cf. 15:19–21, 29).

16:7—*The Spirit of Jesus* is the Holy Spirit, who continues to direct the church's mission.

16:9 *Paul had a vision*—In Acts, God's commission is often communicated by vision to underscore divine agency when the church is redirected in a radically new direction (cf. 9:3–6, 10–16; 10:3–8, 9–16). *Macedonia* is a remote area in northern Greece, far removed from Paul's home.

16:10–17—The first of four *we* passages in Acts (20:5–15; 21:1–18; 27:12–28:16), locating the narrator within the narrated story to give it added credibility and dramatic color.

16:11–40 Paul's Mission in Roman Philippi

a Roman colony. We remained in this city for some days. ¹³ On the sabbath day we went outside the gate by the river, where we supposed there was a place of prayer; and we sat down and spoke to the women who had gathered there. ¹⁴ A certain woman named Lydia, a worshiper of God, was listening to us; she was from the city of Thyatira and a dealer in purple cloth. The Lord opened her heart to listen eagerly to what was said by Paul. ¹⁵ When she and her household were baptized, she urged us, saying, "If you have judged me to be faithful to the Lord, come and stay at my home." And she prevailed upon us.

Paul and Silas in Prison

16 One day, as we were going to the place of prayer, we met a slave-girl who had a spirit of divination and brought her owners a great deal of money by fortune-telling. ¹⁷ While she followed Paul and us, she would cry out, "These men are slaves of the Most High God, who proclaim to you*a* a way of salvation." ¹⁸ She kept doing this for many days. But Paul, very much annoyed, turned and said to the spirit, "I order you in the name of Jesus Christ to come out of her." And it came out that very hour.

19 But when her owners saw that their hope of making money was gone, they seized Paul and Silas and dragged them into the marketplace before the authorities. ²⁰ When they had brought them before the magistrates, they said, "These men are disturbing our city; they are Jews ²¹ and are advocating customs that are not lawful for us as Romans to adopt or observe." ²² The crowd joined in attacking them, and the magistrates had them stripped of their clothing and ordered them to be beaten with rods. ²³ After they had given them a severe flogging, they threw them into prison and ordered the jailer to keep them securely. ²⁴ Following these instructions, he put them in the innermost cell and fastened their feet in the stocks.

25 About midnight Paul and Silas were praying and singing hymns to God, and the prisoners were listening to them. ²⁶ Suddenly there was an earthquake, so violent that the foundations of the prison were shaken; and immediately all the doors were opened and everyone's chains were unfastened. ²⁷ When the jailer woke up and saw the prison doors wide open, he drew his sword and was about to kill himself, since he supposed that the prisoners had escaped. ²⁸ But Paul shouted in a loud voice, "Do not harm yourself, for we are all here." ²⁹ The jailer*b* called for lights, and rushing in, he fell down trembling before

a Other ancient authorities read *to us* *b* Gk *He*

16:13—A *place of prayer* is a makeshift synagogue for religious Jews visiting Roman *Philippi*, such as Paul and Silas. It is *outside the gate* to make clear that the city itself is hostile toward Jews (cf. vv. 20–21) and is populated by those interested in material rather than spiritual gain (cf. vv. 16–18).

16:14—*Lydia* is the female equivalent of Cornelius (cf. chap. 10): she is a middle-class non-Jew, professionally successful, who worships the God of Israel (cf. 10:2) and is saved by listening to the proclaimed gospel (cf. 10:34–44).

16:15—In Acts, a person's hospitality indicates the capacity to respond to the truth of God's word (vv. 33–34; 28:10).

16:16—*Spirit of divination* (lit. "spirit of a python") alludes to a famous myth about the dragon (= python) that guarded the Delphi oracle at Mount Parnassus where people sought to learn about their future success. In Luke's day, its name was used of those with clairvoyant powers. The sharp contrast between the greedy owners of a *slave-girl* who oppose Paul and Lydia who embraces Paul's message represents the nature of the conflict occasioned by Paul's European mission.

16:19–20—Not only are Paul's missionary practices Jewish; the legal accusation leveled against him and Silas by their unscrupulous opponents is *These men . . . are Jews*, even though their anti-Semitism disguises their real motive: the loss of financial profit.

16:23—In Acts, God acts to liberate those unjustly imprisoned to illustrate the gospel message.

16:26—As does the "angel of the Lord" (cf. 5:19; 12:7), the *earthquake* signals God's presence (cf. Matt. 27:54; 28:2).

Paul and Silas. [30] Then he brought them outside and said, "Sirs, what must I do to be saved?" [31] They answered, "Believe on the Lord Jesus, and you will be saved, you and your household." [32] They spoke the word of the Lord[a] to him and to all who were in his house. [33] At the same hour of the night he took them and washed their wounds; then he and his entire family were baptized without delay. [34] He brought them up into the house and set food before them; and he and his entire household rejoiced that he had become a believer in God.

35 When morning came, the magistrates sent the police, saying, "Let those men go." [36] And the jailer reported the message to Paul, saying, "The magistrates sent word to let you go; therefore come out now and go in peace." [37] But Paul replied, "They have beaten us in public, uncondemned, men who are Roman citizens, and have thrown us into prison; and now are they going to discharge us in secret? Certainly not! Let them come and take us out themselves." [38] The police reported these words to the magistrates, and they were afraid when they heard that they were Roman citizens; [39] so they came and apologized to them. And they took them out and asked them to leave the city. [40] After leaving the prison they went to Lydia's home; and when they had seen and encouraged the brothers and sisters[b] there, they departed.

The Uproar in Thessalonica

17 After Paul and Silas[c] had passed through Amphipolis and Apollonia, they came to Thessalonica, where there was a synagogue of the Jews. [2] And Paul went in, as was his custom, and on three sabbath days argued with them from the scriptures, [3] explaining and proving that it was necessary for the Messiah[d] to suffer and to rise from the dead, and saying, "This is the Messiah,[d] Jesus whom I am proclaiming to you." [4] Some of them were persuaded and joined Paul and Silas, as did a great many of the devout Greeks and not a few of the leading women. [5] But the Jews became jealous, and with the help of some ruffians in the marketplaces they formed a mob and set the city in an uproar. While they were searching for Paul and Silas to bring them out to the assembly, they attacked Jason's house. [6] When they could not find them, they dragged Jason and some believers[b] before the city authorities,[e] shouting, "These people who have been turning the world upside down have come here

[a] Other ancient authorities read *word of God*　[b] Gk *brothers*　[c] Gk *they*
[d] Or *the Christ*　[e] Gk *politarchs*

16:30–31—The warden fears his own execution for allowing prisoners to escape during his watch. His question recalls the one asked by devout Jews of Peter earlier in Acts (2:37) in response to his claim that God resurrected Jesus as proof that he is Lord and Messiah (2:36). Paul's ironical response to the warden's question carries a similar meaning: God's salvation, whether to liberate one from the threat of execution or from the deadening effects of sin, results from trusting *the Lord Jesus* (cf. 2:21, 38; 13:38–39).

16:37–38—The stunning reversal of Paul's political situation results from mention of his Roman citizenship for the first time in Acts. To flog and imprison a Roman citizen without a trial is illegal; for these magistrates to do so is a criminal offense under Roman law, which made them *afraid* and resulted in their public apology.

16:40—A congregation of *brothers and sisters* is now hosted and led by Lydia within Philippi's city limits (cf. v. 13).

17:1–15 Paul's Mission among Diaspora Jews

17:1–3—The Jewish conventions of Paul's urban mission are summarized: he enters a *synagogue* on successive *sabbath days* where he *argues from the scriptures* that Jesus is the savior of the world. The phrase *it was necessary* translates the Greek word *dei* and is used frequently in Acts to express the belief that Israel's Scriptures "script" God's redemptive plan (see notes at 19:21; 23:11).

17:1—Acts follows Paul's travel itinerary along the Via Egnatia from Philippi to *Thessalonica*, the most important city of Macedonia.

17:4–5—Conflict within the synagogue is always over whether the suffering and resurrected Jesus is God's Messiah (v. 7; cf. 28:25–28; Luke 2:34; 1 Sam. 2:20–21; Isa. 6:9–10), and never over whether Paul is an observant Jew.

also, ⁷ and Jason has entertained them as guests. They are all acting contrary to the decrees of the emperor, saying that there is another king named Jesus." ⁸ The people and the city officials were disturbed when they heard this, ⁹ and after they had taken bail from Jason and the others, they let them go.

Paul and Silas in Beroea

10 That very night the believers[a] sent Paul and Silas off to Beroea; and when they arrived, they went to the Jewish synagogue. ¹¹ These Jews were more receptive than those in Thessalonica, for they welcomed the message very eagerly and examined the scriptures every day to see whether these things were so. ¹² Many of them therefore believed, including not a few Greek women and men of high standing. ¹³ But when the Jews of Thessalonica learned that the word of God had been proclaimed by Paul in Beroea as well, they came there too, to stir up and incite the crowds. ¹⁴ Then the believers[a] immediately sent Paul away to the coast, but Silas and Timothy remained behind. ¹⁵ Those who conducted Paul brought him as far as Athens; and after

receiving instructions to have Silas and Timothy join him as soon as possible, they left him.

Paul in Athens

16 While Paul was waiting for them in Athens, he was deeply distressed to see that the city was full of idols. ¹⁷ So he argued in the synagogue with the Jews and the devout persons, and also in the marketplace[b] every day with those who happened to be there. ¹⁸ Also some Epicurean and Stoic philosophers debated with him. Some said, "What does this babbler want to say?" Others said, "He seems to be a proclaimer of foreign divinities." (This was because he was telling the good news about Jesus and the resurrection.) ¹⁹ So they took him and brought him to the Areopagus and asked him, "May we know what this new teaching is that you are presenting? ²⁰ It sounds rather strange to us, so we would like to know what it means." ²¹ Now all the Athenians and the foreigners living there would spend their time in nothing but telling or hearing something new.

22 Then Paul stood in front of the

[a] Gk brothers   [b] Or civic center; Gk agora

17:7—The claim that *there is another king named Jesus* is politically charged, since in a Roman city the only legitimate ruler is the Caesar.

17:11—The evidence that Beroean Jews *were more receptive than those in Thessalonica* is their eagerness to examine Scripture with Paul (cf. vv. 2–3; 8:30–31). A person's character, whether virtuous or not, plays a role in one's ability to receive truth—an important ideal of Greek philosophy and probably in today's world as well.

17:16–34 Paul's Mission in Athens

17:16—While no longer politically important in Paul's day, *Athens* remained an educational and cultural center.

17:17–18—When Paul expands his mission to the *marketplace*, he engages *Epicurean and Stoic philosophers* in collegial debate much like a Christian Socrates. Paul and both philosophical schools share a critical view of idolatry (v. 16), although for different reasons: atheistic Epicureans taught that religious observance displaced humanistic sources of happiness, while pantheistic Stoics taught that contentment resulted from a shared belief in a deity that exists in all living things.

17:18—The philosophers question Paul's intellectual competence when calling him a *babbler* of new but irrelevant ideas, and of civic treachery by lobbying to introduce *foreign* beliefs into Athenian life. The former charge is a threat to Paul's career as a teacher, but the latter is a capital offense according to Athenian law and threatens Paul's life.

17:19—*They took him* may mean that Paul is arrested, inferring that Paul's subsequent speech is a legal defense. The *Areopagus*, which means "hill of Ares" (the Greek god of warfare, = Roman Mars), is the site where the city's law court met and legal briefs were heard and verdicts rendered.

17:22–31—Paul's defense speech is among the most important in Acts because it illustrates the working principles of communicating the gospel to thoughtful "secular humanists." Here again Paul moves God's word across another cultural boundary that has long separated people from God's salvation. A disciple should not avoid society's intellectuals but should seek to challenge them with thoughtful conversation that relates the gospel's claims to the best of current research and contemporary thought.

Areopagus and said, "Athenians, I see how extremely religious you are in every way. ²³ For as I went through the city and looked carefully at the objects of your worship, I found among them an altar with the inscription, 'To an unknown god.' What therefore you worship as unknown, this I proclaim to you. ²⁴ The God who made the world and everything in it, he who is Lord of heaven and earth, does not live in shrines made by human hands, ²⁵ nor is he served by human hands, as though he needed anything, since he himself gives to all mortals life and breath and all things. ²⁶ From one ancestor*a* he made all nations to inhabit the whole earth, and he allotted the times of their existence and the boundaries of the places where they would live, ²⁷ so that they would search for God*b* and perhaps grope for him and find him—though indeed he is not far from each one of us. ²⁸ For 'In him we live and move and have our being'; as even some of your own poets have said,

'For we too are his offspring.'

²⁹ Since we are God's offspring, we ought not to think that the deity is like gold, or silver, or stone, an image formed by the art and imagination of mortals. ³⁰ While God has overlooked the times of human ignorance, now he commands all people everywhere to repent, ³¹ because he has fixed a day on which he will have the world judged in righteousness by a man whom he has appointed, and of this he has given assurance to all by raising him from the dead."

32 When they heard of the resurrection of the dead, some scoffed; but others said, "We will hear you again about this." ³³ At that point Paul left them. ³⁴ But some of them joined him and became believers, including Dionysius the Areopagite and a woman named Damaris, and others with them.

Paul in Corinth

18 After this Paul*c* left Athens and went to Corinth. ² There he found a Jew named Aquila, a native of Pontus, who had recently come from Italy with his wife Priscilla, because Claudius had ordered all Jews to leave Rome. Paul*d* went to see them, ³ and, because he was of the same trade, he stayed with them, and they worked together—by trade they were tentmakers. ⁴ Every sabbath

a Gk *From one*; other ancient authorities read *From one blood* *b* Other ancient authorities read *the Lord* *c* Gk *he* *d* Gk *He*

17:24–25—Paul's central religious claims are Jewish: there is but one *God*, who has *made the world* and takes responsibility for its salvation.

17:27–28—Paul quotes unnamed (probably Stoic) poets to defend his belief that human life depends upon a benevolent God after whom creatures *search . . . grope . . . find* and in whom *we live and move and have our being*.

17:30—*Human ignorance* of the gospel threatens the world's future (cf. 3:17; 13:27; 14:16); in Acts the church's mission is motivated in response to this spiritual crisis.

17:31—The *fixed day* refers to God's final judgment, which Paul claims will be rendered *in righteousness*—that is, fairly but without the legal practices of the Aeropagus!

17:32–33—Paul's concluding allusion to a risen Messiah who will broker God's righteous judgment of every nation divides the Aeropagus, even as it has already divided the synagogue. Salvation is a matter of neither ethnicity nor education; it is conditioned upon the risky response of faith to the claim that God has raised *a man whom [God] has appointed* (v. 31) to judge the world in righteousness.

18:1–23 Paul's Corinthian Mission

18:1—*Corinth* was the capital city of Roman Achaia and a commercial hub overlooking two ports, thereby allowing easy access to the Aegean and Ionian seas, and the world beyond. Its many important civic and religious buildings were well known and frequently visited.

18:2—The edict of *Claudius* in 49 CE ordered activist Jews to leave Rome as a peacekeeping move. Among these Jews were *Aquila* and *Priscilla*.

18:3–4—By religious training, Pharisees were bivocational (cf. 1 Cor. 4:12; 1 Thess. 2:9): during the week Paul worked as a *tentmaker* (or leather worker), which provided for his financial support and deepened his friendship with Aquila and Priscilla, and then on *every sabbath he would argue in the synagogue to convince Jews and Greeks* (cf. 17:1–3).

he would argue in the synagogue and would try to convince Jews and Greeks.

5 When Silas and Timothy arrived from Macedonia, Paul was occupied with proclaiming the word,[a] testifying to the Jews that the Messiah[b] was Jesus. [6] When they opposed and reviled him, in protest he shook the dust from his clothes[c] and said to them, "Your blood be on your own heads! I am innocent. From now on I will go to the Gentiles." [7] Then he left the synagogue[d] and went to the house of a man named Titius[e] Justus, a worshiper of God; his house was next door to the synagogue. [8] Crispus, the official of the synagogue, became a believer in the Lord, together with all his household; and many of the Corinthians who heard Paul became believers and were baptized. [9] One night the Lord said to Paul in a vision, "Do not be afraid, but speak and do not be silent; [10] for I am with you, and no one will lay a hand on you to harm you, for there are many in this city who are my people." [11] He stayed there a year and six months, teaching the word of God among them.

12 But when Gallio was proconsul of Achaia, the Jews made a united attack on Paul and brought him before the tribunal. [13] They said, "This man is persuading people to worship God in ways that are contrary to the law." [14] Just as Paul was about to speak, Gallio said to the Jews, "If it were a matter of crime or serious villainy, I would be justified in accepting the complaint of you Jews; [15] but since it is a matter of questions about words and names and your own law, see to it yourselves; I do not wish to be a judge of these matters." [16] And he dismissed them from the tribunal. [17] Then all of them[f] seized Sosthenes, the official of the synagogue, and beat him in front of the tribunal. But Gallio paid no attention to any of these things.

Paul's Return to Antioch

18 After staying there for a considerable time, Paul said farewell to the believers[g] and sailed for Syria, accompanied by Priscilla and Aquila. At Cenchreae he had his hair cut, for he was under a vow. [19] When they reached Ephesus, he left them there, but first he himself went into the synagogue and had a discussion with the Jews. [20] When they asked him to stay longer, he declined; [21] but on taking leave of them, he said, "I[h] will return to you, if God wills." Then he set sail from Ephesus.

22 When he had landed at Caesarea, he went up to Jerusalem[i] and greeted the church, and then went down to Antioch. [23] After spending some time there he departed and went from place to place through the region of Galatia[j] and Phrygia, strengthening all the disciples.

[a] Gk with the word   [b] Or the Christ   [c] Gk reviled him, he shook out his clothes   [d] Gk left there   [e] Other ancient authorities read Titus   [f] Other ancient authorities read all the Greeks   [g] Gk brothers   [h] Other ancient authorities read I must at all costs keep the approaching festival in Jerusalem, but I   [i] Gk went up   [j] Gk the Galatian region

18:5–6—The central property of Paul's missionary work is **proclaiming the word . . . that the Messiah was Jesus**; and the response to this word remains opposition among those who **revile him**. Paul's gesture of protest is the prophet's response to an unbelieving Israel (cf. Josh. 2:19; 2 Sam. 1:16; 1 Kgs. 2:32). The refrain, **from now on I will go to the Gentiles**, pertains only to his mission in Corinth (cf. Acts 13:46; 28:28), which he moves from the synagogue to the house of a Gentile believer, Titius Justus (v. 7).

18:9–11—In Acts, visionary experiences confirm God's presence and define the scope of God's salvation and thus of the church's mission (cf. 9:15; 16:9; 27:23–24).

18:12–17—The case brought before **Gallio**, proconsul over Roman Achaia, is paradigmatic of Rome's neutrality toward the church's mission in Acts: according to him, the conflict between Paul and his opponents in Corinth is a religious matter that should be settled among Jews and does not concern Rome.

18:18–19:7 Paul Begins His Third Mission in Ephesus

18:18—The narrative of Paul's third mission is bracketed by ritual acts of purification, probably to maintain a Nazirite vow of consecrated ministry (cf. Num. 6:1–21): his haircut and the prescribed "rite of purification" at the Jerusalem temple (Acts 21:26) complete a vow that underscores his commitment to maintain the traditions of his ancestral religion.

Ministry of Apollos

24 Now there came to Ephesus a Jew named Apollos, a native of Alexandria. He was an eloquent man, well-versed in the scriptures. 25 He had been instructed in the Way of the Lord; and he spoke with burning enthusiasm and taught accurately the things concerning Jesus, though he knew only the baptism of John. 26 He began to speak boldly in the synagogue; but when Priscilla and Aquila heard him, they took him aside and explained the Way of God to him more accurately. 27 And when he wished to cross over to Achaia, the believers[a] encouraged him and wrote to the disciples to welcome him. On his arrival he greatly helped those who through grace had become believers, 28 for he powerfully refuted the Jews in public, showing by the scriptures that the Messiah[b] is Jesus.

Paul in Ephesus

19 While Apollos was in Corinth, Paul passed through the interior regions and came to Ephesus, where he found some disciples. 2 He said to them, "Did you receive the Holy Spirit when you became believers?" They replied, "No, we have not even heard that there is a Holy Spirit." 3 Then he said, "Into what then were you baptized?" They answered, "Into John's baptism." 4 Paul said, "John baptized with the baptism of repentance, telling the people to believe in the one who was to come after him, that is, in Jesus." 5 On hearing this, they were baptized in the name of the Lord Jesus. 6 When Paul had laid his hands on them, the Holy Spirit came upon them, and they spoke in tongues and prophesied— 7 altogether there were about twelve of them.

8 He entered the synagogue and for three months spoke out boldly, and argued persuasively about the kingdom of God. 9 When some stubbornly refused to believe and spoke evil of the Way before the congregation, he left them, taking the disciples with him, and argued daily in the lecture hall of Tyrannus.[c] 10 This continued for two years, so that all the residents of Asia, both Jews and Greeks, heard the word of the Lord.

[a] Gk brothers [b] Or the Christ [c] Other ancient authorities read of a certain Tyrannus, from eleven o'clock in the morning to four in the afternoon

18:25—Acts introduces readers to *Apollos* (v. 24) before his fruitful ministry in Achaia begins (cf. 1 Cor. 1:12; 3:5–9; 4:6–13). While evidently well trained and gifted, Apollos *knew only the baptism of John* and needed more instruction so that he could more accurately teach others about *the Way of God* (v. 26).

18:26—By reordering their names, *Priscilla and Aquila* (cf. v. 2), Luke suggests that Priscilla was Apollos's principal instructor.

Excursus on Priscilla's Story

The story of Priscilla in Acts provides an important check-and-balance in the history of interpreting Scripture's teaching about women in ministry. Acts continues the gospel witness of Jesus' relations with women disciples (e.g., Luke 10:38–42) and provides a narrative setting for Paul's statement in Gal. 3:28 that "there is no longer male nor female; for all of you are one in Christ Jesus." Christian women form equitable partnerships with their husbands in both the workplace (Acts 18:2) and local congregation (v. 26), even taking the lead in these efforts (v. 18). Moreover, Christian women can instruct men more accurately in the way of the Lord (v. 26). The consequence of women in ministry is a more powerful performance of God's word in the world (vv. 27–28).

19:1—*Ephesus* was a great Roman city and strategically situated within the empire; in due time its church would become the center of Pauline Christianity.

19:2–5—The problem with the twelve disciples Paul encounters in Ephesus upon his arrival is similar to the problem with Apollos's incomplete faith: while participating in John's revival among Jews (cf. 18:25; Luke 3:3), they had not yet heard the gospel message about the risen Jesus.

19:6—Although not a consistent pattern of conversion in Acts, the disciples' reception of *the Spirit* as a sign of their forgiveness (cf. 2:38) is indicated by speaking *in tongues*. What is clear in Acts is that conversion makes concrete changes in a person's public life.

19:8–41 Paul's Mission in Ephesus

19:10—The universal scope of God's salvation is reflected by Paul's audience, since *both Jews and Greeks* listen to his message (cf. v. 20).

The Sons of Sceva

11 God did extraordinary miracles through Paul, [12] so that when the handkerchiefs or aprons that had touched his skin were brought to the sick, their diseases left them, and the evil spirits came out of them. [13] Then some itinerant Jewish exorcists tried to use the name of the Lord Jesus over those who had evil spirits, saying, "I adjure you by the Jesus whom Paul proclaims." [14] Seven sons of a Jewish high priest named Sceva were doing this. [15] But the evil spirit said to them in reply, "Jesus I know, and Paul I know; but who are you?" [16] Then the man with the evil spirit leaped on them, mastered them all, and so overpowered them that they fled out of the house naked and wounded. [17] When this became known to all residents of Ephesus, both Jews and Greeks, everyone was awestruck; and the name of the Lord Jesus was praised. [18] Also many of those who became believers confessed and disclosed their practices. [19] A number of those who practiced magic collected their books and burned them publicly; when the value of these books[a] was calculated, it was found to come to fifty thousand silver coins. [20] So the word of the Lord grew mightily and prevailed.

The Riot in Ephesus

21 Now after these things had been accomplished, Paul resolved in the Spirit to go through Macedonia and Achaia, and then to go on to Jerusalem. He said, "After I have gone there, I must also see Rome." [22] So he sent two of his helpers, Timothy and Erastus, to Macedonia, while he himself stayed for some time longer in Asia.

23 About that time no little disturbance broke out concerning the Way. [24] A man named Demetrius, a silversmith who made silver shrines of Artemis, brought no little business to the artisans. [25] These he gathered together, with the workers of the same trade, and said, "Men, you know that we get our wealth from this business. [26] You also see and hear that not only in Ephesus but in almost the whole of Asia this Paul has persuaded and drawn away a considerable number of people by saying that gods made with hands are not gods. [27] And there is danger not only that this trade of ours may come into disrepute but also that the temple of the great goddess Artemis will be scorned, and she will be deprived of her majesty that brought all Asia and the world to worship her."

28 When they heard this, they were enraged and shouted, "Great is Artemis of the Ephesians!" [29] The city was filled with the confusion; and people[b] rushed together to the theater, dragging with them Gaius and Aristarchus, Macedonians who were Paul's travel companions. [30] Paul wished to go into the crowd, but the disciples would not let him; [31] even some officials of the province of Asia,[c] who were friendly to him, sent him a message urging him not to venture into the theater. [32] Meanwhile, some

[a] Gk them   [b] Gk they   [c] Gk some of the Asiarchs

19:18–20—The *extraordinary miracles* (v. 11) performed by Paul contrast with the magical practices that are contrary to *the word of the Lord* and must be purged to maintain the community's covenant with God.

19:21—Luke's use of *must* (Gk. *dei*) indicates that *Rome* (not Ephesus or Jerusalem) is Paul's city of destiny according to the divine script. And so it is in Rome that his story in Acts concludes (28:16–31).

19:24–27—The local shrine to the Greek fertility goddess, *Artemis* (= Rome's Diana), attracted thousands of pilgrims to Ephesus from Roman

Asia every year in search of good fortune and new life. Silver trinkets were fabricated for use in their worship of Artemis, which was an important business interest of Ephesian artisans and merchants. As in Philippi (cf. 16:19), the loss of potential profit is a principal reason for conflict between Paul's message and his pagan audience.

19:32—The repeated description of the lynch mob's *confusion* suggests the hostile reaction to Paul's message is nonrational, prompted by devotion to a civic shrine in opposition to Israel's God (cf. v. 34) and by love of money.

were shouting one thing, some another; for the assembly was in confusion, and most of them did not know why they had come together. ³³ Some of the crowd gave instructions to Alexander, whom the Jews had pushed forward. And Alexander motioned for silence and tried to make a defense before the people. ³⁴ But when they recognized that he was a Jew, for about two hours all of them shouted in unison, "Great is Artemis of the Ephesians!" ³⁵ But when the town clerk had quieted the crowd, he said, "Citizens of Ephesus, who is there that does not know that the city of the Ephesians is the temple keeper of the great Artemis and of the statue that fell from heaven?ᵃ ³⁶ Since these things cannot be denied, you ought to be quiet and do nothing rash. ³⁷ You have brought these men here who are neither temple robbers nor blasphemers of ourᵇ goddess. ³⁸ If therefore Demetrius and the artisans with him have a complaint against anyone, the courts are open, and there are proconsuls; let them bring charges there against one another. ³⁹ If there is anything furtherᶜ you want to know, it must be settled in the regular assembly. ⁴⁰ For we are in danger of being charged with rioting today, since there is no cause that we can give to justify this commotion." ⁴¹ When he had said this, he dismissed the assembly.

Paul Goes to Macedonia and Greece

20 After the uproar had ceased, Paul sent for the disciples; and after encouraging them and saying farewell, he left for Macedonia. ² When he had gone through those regions and had given the believersᵈ much encouragement, he came to Greece, ³ where he stayed for three months. He was about to set sail for Syria when a plot was made against him by the Jews, and so he decided to return through Macedonia. ⁴ He was accompanied by Sopater son of Pyrrhus from Beroea, by Aristarchus and Secundus from Thessalonica, by Gaius from Derbe, and by Timothy, as well as by Tychicus and Trophimus from Asia. ⁵ They went ahead and were waiting for us in Troas; ⁶ but we sailed from Philippi after the days of Unleavened Bread, and in five days we joined them in Troas, where we stayed for seven days.

Paul's Farewell Visit to Troas

7 On the first day of the week, when we met to break bread, Paul was holding a discussion with them; since he intended to leave the next day, he continued speaking until midnight. ⁸ There were many lamps in the room upstairs where we were meeting. ⁹ A young man named Eutychus, who was sitting in the window, began to sink off into a deep sleep while Paul talked still longer. Overcome by sleep, he fell to the ground three floors below and was picked up dead. ¹⁰ But Paul went down, and bending over him took him in his arms, and said, "Do not be alarmed, for his life is in him." ¹¹ Then Paul went upstairs, and after he had broken bread and eaten, he continued to converse with them until dawn; then he left. ¹² Meanwhile they had taken the boy away alive and were not a little comforted.

The Voyage from Troas to Miletus

13 We went ahead to the ship and set sail for Assos, intending to take Paul on board there; for he had made this arrangement, intending to go by land himself. ¹⁴ When he met us in Assos, we took him on board and went to Mitylene. ¹⁵ We sailed from there, and on the following day we arrived oppo-

ᵃ Meaning of Gk uncertain   ᵇ Other ancient authorities read *your*   ᶜ Other ancient authorities read *about other matters*   ᵈ Gk *given them*

20:1–16 Paul's Pilgrimage to Jerusalem
20:6—Paul's travel itinerary is regulated by the liturgical calendar of his Jewish faith: *the days of Unleavened Bread* refers to Passover.

20:7–12—The story of Eutychus's resuscitation may be included to explain why Christians now gather for worship *on the first day of the week* rather than on the more traditional Sabbath.

site Chios. The next day we touched at Samos, and[a] the day after that we came to Miletus. [16] For Paul had decided to sail past Ephesus, so that he might not have to spend time in Asia; he was eager to be in Jerusalem, if possible, on the day of Pentecost.

Paul Speaks to the Ephesian Elders

[17] From Miletus he sent a message to Ephesus, asking the elders of the church to meet him. [18] When they came to him, he said to them:

"You yourselves know how I lived among you the entire time from the first day that I set foot in Asia, [19] serving the Lord with all humility and with tears, enduring the trials that came to me through the plots of the Jews. [20] I did not shrink from doing anything helpful, proclaiming the message to you and teaching you publicly and from house to house, [21] as I testified to both Jews and Greeks about repentance toward God and faith toward our Lord Jesus. [22] And now, as a captive to the Spirit,[b] I am on my way to Jerusalem, not knowing what will happen to me there, [23] except that the Holy Spirit testifies to me in every city that imprisonment and persecutions are waiting for me. [24] But I do not count my life of any value to myself, if only I may finish my course and the ministry that I received from the Lord Jesus, to testify to the good news of God's grace.

[25] "And now I know that none of you, among whom I have gone about proclaiming the kingdom, will ever see my face again. [26] Therefore I declare to you this day that I am not responsible for the blood of any of you, [27] for I did not shrink from declaring to you the whole purpose of God. [28] Keep watch over yourselves and over all the flock, of which the Holy Spirit has made you overseers, to shepherd the church of God[c] that he obtained with the blood of his own Son.[d] [29] I know that after I have gone, savage wolves will come in among you, not sparing the flock. [30] Some even from your own group will come distorting the truth in order to entice the disciples to follow them. [31] Therefore be alert, remembering that for three years I did not cease night or day to warn everyone with tears. [32] And now I commend you to God and to the message of his grace, a message that is able to build you up and to give you the inheritance among all who are sanctified. [33] I coveted no one's silver or gold or clothing. [34] You know for yourselves that I worked with my own hands to support myself and my companions. [35] In all this I have given you an example that by such work we must support the weak, remembering the words of the Lord Jesus, for he himself said, 'It is more blessed to give than to receive.'"

[36] When he had finished speaking,

---

[a] Other ancient authorities add *after remaining at Trogyllium* [b] Or *And now, bound in the spirit* [c] Other ancient authorities read *of the Lord*
[d] Or *with his own blood*; Gk *with the blood of his Own*

20:16—On *Pentecost*, Jewish pilgrims travel to Jerusalem to celebrate God's goodness to Israel as a public act of their devotion (cf. 2:1, 5–11). A central characteristic of Paul's portrait in Acts is reflected here: an unwavering loyalty to Israel's God.

20:17–38 Paul's Speech of Succession in Miletus

20:17—Paul's speech to *the elders of the church* is among the most important in Acts. His summary of his European mission to Christian leaders commissions them to succeed him, while anticipating the rest of his story according to Acts.

20:21–25—Paul's prediction of his *imprisonment and persecutions* (v. 23) in Jerusalem echoes Jesus' passion story; however, Paul also knows

that Rome, not Jerusalem, is his destination (cf. 19:21).

20:28–35—Paul commissions the elders to care for the church in a manner that imitates his ministry among them. Consistent with the other prophetic exemplars of Acts, this example includes proclaiming a message of truth and forming a community of goods. Discipleship is prophetic in Acts, since both these practices are essential identifying marks of a community belonging to the risen Lord (cf. 2:42–47).

20:35—Although the canonical Gospels do not include this saying, its plain sense reflects Jesus' teaching about wealth (cf. Luke 6:27–36).

he knelt down with them all and prayed. [37] There was much weeping among them all; they embraced Paul and kissed him, [38] grieving especially because of what he had said, that they would not see him again. Then they brought him to the ship.

Paul's Journey to Jerusalem

21 When we had parted from them and set sail, we came by a straight course to Cos, and the next day to Rhodes, and from there to Patara.[a] [2] When we found a ship bound for Phoenicia, we went on board and set sail. [3] We came in sight of Cyprus; and leaving it on our left, we sailed to Syria and landed at Tyre, because the ship was to unload its cargo there. [4] We looked up the disciples and stayed there for seven days. Through the Spirit they told Paul not to go on to Jerusalem. [5] When our days there were ended, we left and proceeded on our journey; and all of them, with wives and children, escorted us outside the city. There we knelt down on the beach and prayed [6] and said farewell to one another. Then we went on board the ship, and they returned home.

[7] When we had finished[b] the voyage from Tyre, we arrived at Ptolemais; and we greeted the believers[c] and stayed with them for one day. [8] The next day we left and came to Caesarea; and we went into the house of Philip the evangelist, one of the seven, and stayed with him. [9] He had four unmarried daughters[d] who had the gift of prophecy. [10] While we were staying there for several days, a prophet named Agabus came down from Judea. [11] He came to us and took Paul's belt, bound his own feet and hands with it, and said, "Thus says the Holy Spirit, 'This is the way the Jews in Jerusalem will bind the man who owns this belt and will hand him over to the Gentiles.'" [12] When we heard this, we and the people there urged him not to go up to Jerusalem. [13] Then Paul answered, "What are you doing, weeping and breaking my heart? For I am ready not only to be bound but even to die in Jerusalem for the name of the Lord Jesus." [14] Since he would not be persuaded, we remained silent except to say, "The Lord's will be done."

[15] After these days we got ready and started to go up to Jerusalem. [16] Some of the disciples from Caesarea also came along and brought us to the house of Mnason of Cyprus, an early disciple, with whom we were to stay.

Paul Visits James at Jerusalem

[17] When we arrived in Jerusalem, the brothers welcomed us warmly. [18] The next day Paul went with us to visit James; and all the elders were present. [19] After greeting them, he related one by one the things that God had done among the Gentiles through his ministry. [20] When

---

[a] Other ancient authorities add *and Myra* [b] Or *continued* [c] Gk *brothers* [d] Gk *four daughters, virgins,*

21:1–16 Paul Arrives in Jerusalem

21:4—*The Spirit* has told other prophets what it has told Paul: he will suffer in Jerusalem (vv. 10–12). In previous episodes, Paul heeds similar advice and avoids persecution (cf. 9:23–30; 17:10; 20:3); he is no masochist! But here he disagrees and proceeds on to Jerusalem since he is under orders from God (cf. 21:13–14).

21:7–12—Passing references to *Philip the evangelist* (v. 8; cf. 8:4–40) and *a prophet named Agabus* (v. 10; cf. 11:27–30) link these concluding snapshots of Paul's mission to earlier missionary stories in Acts.

21:13—Paul's ironical response to his friends in Caesarea (including Luke!) that he is prepared *to die in Jerusalem for the name of the Lord Jesus* is an expression of unswerving devotion to his vocation (9:16), since he will not die in Jerusalem but "must also see Rome" (19:21). His refusal to follow their advice is also an expression of his religious authority, since he has received more "inside information" from God than they have.

21:17–26 Paul Meets with James

21:18–21—On the day following his safe arrival in the Holy City, Paul visits the leaders of the Jerusalem church, including James (vv. 17–19). The topic of their conversation turns to a rumor heard among Judea's more traditional Jews that Paul's ministry to the Jews of the Diaspora included instructions to abandon those practices that forged a Jewish identity in the world. Readers of Paul's story in Acts know this rumor is false.

they heard it, they praised God. Then they said to him, "You see, brother, how many thousands of believers there are among the Jews, and they are all zealous for the law. [21] They have been told about you that you teach all the Jews living among the Gentiles to forsake Moses, and that you tell them not to circumcise their children or observe the customs. [22] What then is to be done? They will certainly hear that you have come. [23] So do what we tell you. We have four men who are under a vow. [24] Join these men, go through the rite of purification with them, and pay for the shaving of their heads. Thus all will know that there is nothing in what they have been told about you, but that you yourself observe and guard the law. [25] But as for the Gentiles who have become believers, we have sent a letter with our judgment that they should abstain from what has been sacrificed to idols and from blood and from what is strangled[a] and from fornication." [26] Then Paul took the men, and the next day, having purified himself, he entered the temple with them, making public the completion of the days of purification when the sacrifice would be made for each of them.

Paul Arrested in the Temple

27 When the seven days were almost completed, the Jews from Asia, who had seen him in the temple, stirred up the whole crowd. They seized him, [28] shouting, "Fellow Israelites, help! This is the man who is teaching everyone everywhere against our people, our law, and this place; more than that, he has actually brought Greeks into the temple and has defiled this holy place." [29] For they had previously seen Trophimus the Ephesian with him in the city, and they supposed that Paul had brought him into the temple. [30] Then all the city was aroused, and the people rushed together. They seized Paul and dragged him out of the temple, and immediately the doors were shut. [31] While they were trying to kill him, word came to the tribune of the cohort that all Jerusalem was in an uproar. [32] Immediately he took soldiers and centurions and ran down to them. When they saw the tribune and the soldiers, they stopped beating Paul. [33] Then the tribune came, arrested him, and ordered him to be bound with two chains; he inquired who he was and what he had done. [34] Some in the crowd shouted one thing, some another; and as he could not learn the facts because of the uproar, he ordered him to be brought into the barracks. [35] When Paul[b] came to the steps, the violence of the mob was so great that he had to be carried by the

---

[a] Other ancient authorities lack *and from what is strangled*   [b] Gk *he*

21:23–24—To prove his commitment to the traditional practices of his Jewish faith, Paul agrees to join with other Jewish believers in fulfilling a Nazirite **rite of purification** (cf. Num. 6:1–21). He even agrees to pay the various fees associated with the vow, which demonstrates his commitment to the Jewish church.

21:25—This is the third mention of James's purity code instituted at the Jerusalem council (cf. 15:20, 29). Luke adds it here to underwrite a more traditional definition of purity that includes both inward cleansing of the heart by the Holy Spirit (15:8–11) and public practices of a holy life (15:20; 21:26). Discipleship must always integrate a purified heart with public actions that demonstrate loyalty to the ways of God.

21:27–39 Paul Is Arrested

21:28—The specific charge that Paul **brought**

Greeks into the temple brings together all three accusations that he is **against our people, our law, and this place** (cf. 6:11–14), all formative of Israel's religious identity. The reader of Acts knows these accusations are frivolous and false: true Christianity continues (rather than subverts) those beliefs and practices that maintain Israel's covenant with God.

21:30—The image of dragging Paul outside the temple gates, which are then slammed shut, symbolizes the division within Israel over Paul's Jesus (cf. Luke 2:34).

21:33—The Roman tribune who intervenes to save Paul is Claudius Lysias (cf. 23:26), who commands a garrison of thousand soldiers guarding the temple precinct. Paul is **arrested** and **bound with two chains** (cf. 21:10–12) to protect him from the lynch mob that threatens to destroy him.

soldiers. **36** The crowd that followed kept shouting, "Away with him!"

Paul Defends Himself

37 Just as Paul was about to be brought into the barracks, he said to the tribune, "May I say something to you?" The tribune[a] replied, "Do you know Greek? **38** Then you are not the Egyptian who recently stirred up a revolt and led the four thousand assassins out into the wilderness?" **39** Paul replied, "I am a Jew, from Tarsus in Cilicia, a citizen of an important city; I beg you, let me speak to the people." **40** When he had given him permission, Paul stood on the steps and motioned to the people for silence; and when there was a great hush, he addressed them in the Hebrew[b] language, saying:

22 "Brothers and fathers, listen to the defense that I now make before you."

2 When they heard him addressing them in Hebrew,[b] they became even more quiet. Then he said:

3 "I am a Jew, born in Tarsus in Cilicia, but brought up in this city at the feet of Gamaliel, educated strictly according to our ancestral law, being zealous for God, just as all of you are today. **4** I persecuted this Way up to the point of death by binding both men and women and putting them in prison, **5** as the high priest and the whole council of elders can testify about me. From them I also received letters to the brothers in Damascus, and I went there in order to bind those who were there and to bring them back to Jerusalem for punishment.

Paul Tells of His Conversion

6 "While I was on my way and approaching Damascus, about noon a great light from heaven suddenly shone about me. **7** I fell to the ground and heard a voice saying to me, 'Saul, Saul, why are you persecuting me?' **8** I answered, 'Who are you, Lord?' Then he said to me, 'I am Jesus of Nazareth[c] whom you are persecuting.' **9** Now those who were with me saw the light but did not hear the voice of the one who was speaking to me. **10** I asked, 'What am I to do, Lord?' The Lord said to me, 'Get up and go to Damascus; there you will be told everything that has been assigned to you to

a Gk He *b* That is, *Aramaic* *c* Gk *the Nazorean*

21:40—In Acts, different languages are spoken in order to communicate truth to an international audience (cf. 2:5–11). Paul uses Greek to identify himself to Lysias as a Diaspora Jew (21:37) and *the Hebrew language* (= Aramaic) when defending himself to Jews.

Excursus on Paul's Roman "Trials" (22:1–26:32)

Acts narrates four integral episodes in which Paul defends himself against accusations leveled against him by his opponents (22:1–21; 22:30–23:11; 24:1–21; 26:1–23; cf. 21:28). When read as a whole, these speeches (apologia) defend his importance for the church and prepare readers for his New Testament letters. Paul's most important claim is his opening assertion that *"I am a Jew"* (22:3) according to which readers better understand the substance of his mission and message in Acts. His commitment to Israel's future is observed by the interplay between Paul's first (22:1–21) and final (26:1–23) speeches that enclose the entire narrative of Paul's legal problems. Both speeches are focused by different rehearsals of his Damascus road experience (22:6–16; 26:12–18; cf. 9:1–19a), which has defined his

prophetic vocation (22:17–21; 26:19–23; cf. 13:47). His Jewish roots frame his persona and sacred calling: he is no criminal, no maverick, no madman, no seller of snake oil, no intellectual lightweight or religious mediocre. The Paul of Acts is a prophet of God whose personal intentions are above reproach, whose confession of faith is thoroughly orthodox, whose religious practices are pure, and whose proclamation is concentrated on Israel's hope in the resurrection of the dead (22:30–23:11). So Acts remains disinterested in Rome's verdict of Paul's guilt and therefore concludes without legal closure, portraying him in Rome as elsewhere—whether free or bound— engaged in his prophetic vocation (28:30–31).

22:1–23:10 Paul Defends Himself before Jews

22:3–5—Paul's Jewish identity is rooted in his Pharisaic piety, which equates a strict observance of *our ancestral law* (Moses) with *being zealous for God*.

22:8—Paul's accounting of his Damascus road experience (cf. 9:1–9) provides additional commentary on his initial assertion that "I am a Jew" (22:3).

do.' **11** Since I could not see because of the brightness of that light, those who were with me took my hand and led me to Damascus.

12 "A certain Ananias, who was a devout man according to the law and well spoken of by all the Jews living there, **13** came to me; and standing beside me, he said, 'Brother Saul, regain your sight!' In that very hour I regained my sight and saw him. **14** Then he said, 'The God of our ancestors has chosen you to know his will, to see the Righteous One and to hear his own voice; **15** for you will be his witness to all the world of what you have seen and heard. **16** And now why do you delay? Get up, be baptized, and have your sins washed away, calling on his name.'

Paul Sent to the Gentiles

17 "After I had returned to Jerusalem and while I was praying in the temple, I fell into a trance **18** and saw Jesus*a* saying to me, 'Hurry and get out of Jerusalem quickly, because they will not accept your testimony about me.' **19** And I said, 'Lord, they themselves know that in every synagogue I imprisoned and beat those who believed in you. **20** And while the blood of your witness Stephen was shed, I myself was standing by, approving and keeping the coats of those who killed him.' **21** Then he said to me, 'Go, for I will send you far away to the Gentiles.'"

Paul and the Roman Tribune

22 Up to this point they listened to him, but then they shouted, "Away with such a fellow from the earth! For he should not be allowed to live." **23** And while they were shouting, throwing off their cloaks, and tossing dust into the air, **24** the tribune directed that he was to be brought into the barracks, and ordered him to be examined by flogging, to find out the reason for this outcry against him. **25** But when they had tied him up with thongs,*b* Paul said to the centurion who was standing by, "Is it legal for you to flog a Roman citizen who is uncondemned?" **26** When the centurion heard that, he went to the tribune and said to him, "What are you about to do? This man is a Roman citizen." **27** The tribune came and asked Paul,*a* "Tell me, are you a Roman citizen?" And he said, "Yes." **28** The tribune answered, "It cost me a large sum of money to get my citizenship." Paul said, "But I was born a citizen." **29** Immediately those who were about to examine him drew back from him; and the tribune also was afraid, for he realized that Paul was a Roman citizen and that he had bound him.

Paul before the Council

30 Since he wanted to find out what Paul*c* was being accused of by the Jews, the next day he released him and ordered the chief priests and the entire council to meet. He brought Paul down and had him stand before them.

23 While Paul was looking intently at the council he said, "Brothers,*d* up to this day I have lived my life with

a Gk him *b* Or up for the lashes *c* Gk he *d* Gk Men, brothers

---

22:12–14—*Ananias* (cf. 9:10–19) is characterized as *a devout man according to the law* in support of Paul's testimony that his ministry is undertaken on behalf of *the God of our ancestors*.

22:17–21—The story of Paul's temple *trance* is added here probably to link his prophetic calling with Isaiah's (cf. Isa. 6) and his prophecy that God *will send* faithful Israel *far away to the Gentiles* (cf. Isa. 57:19; 49:6; Acts 13:47; 1:8). In this setting of fulfilled prophecy, then, Paul's mission to the Gentiles is directly stated for the first time.

22:25–29—Only in Acts does Paul identify himself as a Roman citizen, and only to end Roman mistreatment of him (16:35–40; 25:10–12). Citizenship, which Lysias had purchased for *a large sum of money*, is not an important element of Paul's identity, and probably for this reason is not mentioned in his letters.

23:1—Paul's testimony before the Sanhedrin asserts his *clear conscience before God*, the result of completing the "days of purification" in the temple (21:26) and observing the commands of Torah.

a clear conscience before God." ²Then the high priest Ananias ordered those standing near him to strike him on the mouth. ³At this Paul said to him, "God will strike you, you whitewashed wall! Are you sitting there to judge me according to the law, and yet in violation of the law you order me to be struck?" ⁴Those standing nearby said, "Do you dare to insult God's high priest?" ⁵And Paul said, "I did not realize, brothers, that he was high priest; for it is written, 'You shall not speak evil of a leader of your people.'"

6 When Paul noticed that some were Sadducees and others were Pharisees, he called out in the council, "Brothers, I am a Pharisee, a son of Pharisees. I am on trial concerning the hope of the resurrection*a* of the dead." ⁷When he said this, a dissension began between the Pharisees and the Sadducees, and the assembly was divided. ⁸(The Sadducees say that there is no resurrection, or angel, or spirit; but the Pharisees acknowledge all three.) ⁹Then a great clamor arose, and certain scribes of the Pharisees' group stood up and contended, "We find nothing wrong with this man. What if a spirit or an angel has spoken to him?" ¹⁰When the dissension became violent, the tribune, fearing that they would tear Paul to pieces, ordered the soldiers to go down, take him by force, and bring him into the barracks.

11 That night the Lord stood near him and said, "Keep up your courage! For just as you have testified for me in Jeru-salem, so you must bear witness also in Rome."

The Plot to Kill Paul

12 In the morning the Jews joined in a conspiracy and bound themselves by an oath neither to eat nor drink until they had killed Paul. ¹³There were more than forty who joined in this conspiracy. ¹⁴They went to the chief priests and elders and said, "We have strictly bound ourselves by an oath to taste no food until we have killed Paul. ¹⁵Now then, you and the council must notify the tribune to bring him down to you, on the pretext that you want to make a more thorough examination of his case. And we are ready to do away with him before he arrives."

16 Now the son of Paul's sister heard about the ambush; so he went and gained entrance to the barracks and told Paul. ¹⁷Paul called one of the centurions and said, "Take this young man to the tribune, for he has something to report to him." ¹⁸So he took him, brought him to the tribune, and said, "The prisoner Paul called me and asked me to bring this young man to you; he has something to tell you." ¹⁹The tribune took him by the hand, drew him aside privately, and asked, "What is it that you have to report to me?" ²⁰He answered, "The Jews have agreed to ask you to bring Paul down to the council tomorrow, as though they were going to inquire more thoroughly into his case. ²¹But do not be persuaded

a Gk concerning hope and resurrection

23:3—The exchange between Ananias and Paul replays the earlier conflict between the apostles and council in Jerusalem (chaps. 4–5). Paul's *insult* (23:4) is based on Deut. 28:22 to delineate faithful (Paul) from unfaithful (council) Israel.

23:6—Paul notes that the conflict provoked by his mission is the same that divides the council between its Sadducean and Pharisaic membership: *hope of the resurrection of the dead*, in which Pharisees believe (although about a future Israel rather than a past Messiah!) but the more conservative Sadducees do not.

23:11–35 Jewish Opposition to Paul Increases

23:11—Luke uses *dei* once again to indicate a scripted element of God's redemptive plan: *you must [dei] bear witness also in Rome*. Divine necessity shapes the disciple's credulity toward any plot to undermine the church's ministry by God's enemies in the world. Paul would not die in Jerusalem because God intends him to bear witness in Rome.

23:16—The *son of Paul's sister* plays the role of Paul's helper. The Jerusalem church remains strangely quiet throughout Paul's trials.

by them, for more than forty of their men are lying in ambush for him. They have bound themselves by an oath neither to eat nor drink until they kill him. They are ready now and are waiting for your consent." 22 So the tribune dismissed the young man, ordering him, "Tell no one that you have informed me of this."

Paul Sent to Felix the Governor

23 Then he summoned two of the centurions and said, "Get ready to leave by nine o'clock tonight for Caesarea with two hundred soldiers, seventy horsemen, and two hundred spearmen. 24 Also provide mounts for Paul to ride, and take him safely to Felix the governor." 25 He wrote a letter to this effect:

26 "Claudius Lysias to his Excellency the governor Felix, greetings. 27 This man was seized by the Jews and was about to be killed by them, but when I had learned that he was a Roman citizen, I came with the guard and rescued him. 28 Since I wanted to know the charge for which they accused him, I had him brought to their council. 29 I found that he was accused concerning questions of their law, but was charged with nothing deserving death or imprisonment. 30 When I was informed that there would be a plot against the man, I sent him to you at once, ordering his accusers also to state before you what they have against him.a"

31 So the soldiers, according to their instructions, took Paul and brought him during the night to Antipatris. 32 The next day they let the horsemen go on with him, while they returned to the barracks. 33 When they came to Caesarea and delivered the letter to the governor, they presented Paul also before him. 34 On reading the letter, he asked what province he belonged to, and when he learned that he was from Cilicia, 35 he said, "I will give you a hearing when your accusers arrive." Then he ordered that he be kept under guard in Herod's headquarters.b

Paul before Felix at Caesarea

24 Five days later the high priest Ananias came down with some elders and an attorney, a certain Tertullus, and they reported their case against Paul to the governor. 2 When Paulc had been summoned, Tertullus began to accuse him, saying:

"Your Excellency,d because of you we have long enjoyed peace, and reforms have been made for this people because of your foresight. 3 We welcome this in every way and everywhere with utmost gratitude. 4 But, to detain you no further, I beg you to hear us briefly with your customary graciousness. 5 We have, in fact, found this man a pestilent fellow, an agitator among all the Jews throughout the world, and a ringleader of the sect of the Nazarenes.e 6 He even tried to profane the temple, and so we seized him.f 8 By examining him yourself you will be able to learn from him concerning everything of which we accuse him."

9 The Jews also joined in the charge by asserting that all this was true.

Paul's Defense before Felix

10 When the governor motioned to him to speak, Paul replied:

a Other ancient authorities add *Farewell*   b Gk *praetorium*   c Gk *he*
d Gk lacks *Your Excellency*   e Gk *Nazoreans*   f Other ancient authorities
add *and we would have judged him according to our law.* 7 *But the chief captain
Lysias came and with great violence took him out of our hands,* 8 *commanding
his accusers to come before you.*

23:27—Paul's status as **a Roman citizen** secures Lysias's help in moving him from harm's way in Jerusalem to Caesarea.

23:33—*Caesarea* is a Roman territory with a diminished threat from Paul's Jewish opposition.

24:1–27 Paul's Roman Trial in Caesarea

24:1—The Latin surname, *Tertullus*, suggests that Paul's Jewish opposition has hired a non-Jewish lawyer to adapt their legal case against him before the region's Roman governor, Felix.

24:5–6—The prosecutorial speech portrays Paul as a religious and political subversive. Labeling Christianity **sect** (or "party"; cf. 15:5) **of the Nazarenes** locates Paul's mission **among all the Jews throughout the world**.

"I cheerfully make my defense, knowing that for many years you have been a judge over this nation. ¹¹ As you can find out, it is not more than twelve days since I went up to worship in Jerusalem. ¹² They did not find me disputing with anyone in the temple or stirring up a crowd either in the synagogues or throughout the city. ¹³ Neither can they prove to you the charge that they now bring against me. ¹⁴ But this I admit to you, that according to the Way, which they call a sect, I worship the God of our ancestors, believing everything laid down according to the law or written in the prophets. ¹⁵ I have a hope in God—a hope that they themselves also accept—that there will be a resurrection of both[a] the righteous and the unrighteous. ¹⁶ Therefore I do my best always to have a clear conscience toward God and all people. ¹⁷ Now after some years I came to bring alms to my nation and to offer sacrifices. ¹⁸ While I was doing this, they found me in the temple, completing the rite of purification, without any crowd or disturbance. ¹⁹ But there were some Jews from Asia—they ought to be here before you to make an accusation, if they have anything against me. ²⁰ Or let these men here tell what crime they had found when I stood before the council, ²¹ unless it was this one sentence that I called out while standing before them, 'It is about the resurrection of the dead that I am on trial before you today.'"

22 But Felix, who was rather well informed about the Way, adjourned the hearing with the comment, "When Lysias the tribune comes down, I will decide your case." ²³ Then he ordered the centurion to keep him in custody, but to let him have some liberty and not to prevent any of his friends from taking care of his needs.

Paul Held in Custody

24 Some days later when Felix came with his wife Drusilla, who was Jewish, he sent for Paul and heard him speak concerning faith in Christ Jesus. ²⁵ And as he discussed justice, self-control, and the coming judgment, Felix became frightened and said, "Go away for the present; when I have an opportunity, I will send for you." ²⁶ At the same time he hoped that money would be given him by Paul, and for that reason he used to send for him very often and converse with him.

27 After two years had passed, Felix was succeeded by Porcius Festus; and since he wanted to grant the Jews a favor, Felix left Paul in prison.

Paul Appeals to the Emperor

25 Three days after Festus had arrived in the province, he went up from Caesarea to Jerusalem ² where the chief priests and the leaders of the Jews gave him a report against Paul. They appealed to him ³ and requested, as a favor to them against Paul,[b] to have him transferred to Jerusalem. They were, in fact, planning an ambush to kill him along the way. ⁴ Festus replied that Paul was being kept at Caesarea, and that he himself intended to go there shortly. ⁵ "So," he said, "let those of you who have the authority come down with

[a] Other ancient authorities read *of the dead, both of* [b] Gk *him*

24:14–16—Since the case against Paul is cast in religious terms, the heart of his defense speech catalogs his spiritual credentials and shared beliefs: Paul came to Jerusalem as a Jewish pilgrim not only to **worship God** with other observant Jews but also to purify himself in preparation for a ministry to which Israel's Messiah had called him. The clarity and certainty of Paul's mission, even in the face of hostile opposition, is exemplary of every disciple's sense of sacred calling.

25:1–12 Paul Appeals to Caesar

25:1—Emperor Nero's appointment of *Festus* around 60 CE as procurator of Judea signals an important shift in the politics of the region: Festus was a cunning and intelligent man whose administration was characterized by fairness toward the Jews.

me, and if there is anything wrong about the man, let them accuse him."

6 After he had stayed among them not more than eight or ten days, he went down to Caesarea; the next day he took his seat on the tribunal and ordered Paul to be brought. 7 When he arrived, the Jews who had gone down from Jerusalem surrounded him, bringing many serious charges against him, which they could not prove. 8 Paul said in his defense, "I have in no way committed an offense against the law of the Jews, or against the temple, or against the emperor." 9 But Festus, wishing to do the Jews a favor, asked Paul, "Do you wish to go up to Jerusalem and be tried there before me on these charges?" 10 Paul said, "I am appealing to the emperor's tribunal; this is where I should be tried. I have done no wrong to the Jews, as you very well know. 11 Now if I am in the wrong and have committed something for which I deserve to die, I am not trying to escape death; but if there is nothing to their charges against me, no one can turn me over to them. I appeal to the emperor." 12 Then Festus, after he had conferred with his council, replied, "You have appealed to the emperor; to the emperor you will go."

Festus Consults King Agrippa

13 After several days had passed, King Agrippa and Bernice arrived at Caesarea to welcome Festus. 14 Since they were staying there several days, Festus laid Paul's case before the king, saying, "There is a man here who was left in prison by Felix. 15 When I was in Jeru-salem, the chief priests and the elders of the Jews informed me about him and asked for a sentence against him. 16 I told them that it was not the custom of the Romans to hand over anyone before the accused had met the accusers face to face and had been given an opportunity to make a defense against the charge. 17 So when they met here, I lost no time, but on the next day took my seat on the tribunal and ordered the man to be brought. 18 When the accusers stood up, they did not charge him with any of the crimes*a* that I was expecting. 19 Instead they had certain points of disagreement with him about their own religion and about a certain Jesus, who had died, but whom Paul asserted to be alive. 20 Since I was at a loss how to investigate these questions, I asked whether he wished to go to Jerusalem and be tried there on these charges.*b* 21 But when Paul had appealed to be kept in custody for the decision of his Imperial Majesty, I ordered him to be held until I could send him to the emperor." 22 Agrippa said to Festus, "I would like to hear the man myself." "Tomorrow," he said, "you will hear him."

Paul Brought before Agrippa

23 So on the next day Agrippa and Bernice came with great pomp, and they entered the audience hall with the military tribunes and the prominent men of the city. Then Festus gave the order and Paul was brought in. 24 And Festus said, "King Agrippa and all here present with us, you see this man about whom the whole Jewish community petitioned me,

a Other ancient authorities read *with anything*   *b* Gk *on them*

25:10–11—A frustrated Paul sees through Festus's political strategy, which promises a further delay, and therefore ends the legal proceeding by *appeal to the emperor* as a privilege of his Roman citizenship.

25:13–27 Festus Reviews Paul's Case

25:13—*King Agrippa and Bernice* are members of the Herodian family that populate the Gospel and Acts narratives, typically as political enemies of God's redemptive plan (Matt. 2:1–12; Luke 3:19; 13:31; 23:11; Acts 12). Luke introduces Agrippa II as king, recalling Jesus' prophecy to Ananias that Paul would preach to kings (cf. 9:15), which soon is realized (see 26:1–23).

25:15–20—Festus embodies a secular Rome that views Paul with theological ignorance and political self-interest, which in combination safeguard him from the treachery of his religiously motivated opponents.

both in Jerusalem and here, shouting that he ought not to live any longer. ²⁵ But I found that he had done nothing deserving death; and when he appealed to his Imperial Majesty, I decided to send him. ²⁶ But I have nothing definite to write to our sovereign about him. Therefore I have brought him before all of you, and especially before you, King Agrippa, so that, after we have examined him, I may have something to write— ²⁷ for it seems to me unreasonable to send a prisoner without indicating the charges against him."

Paul Defends Himself
before Agrippa

26 Agrippa said to Paul, "You have permission to speak for yourself." Then Paul stretched out his hand and began to defend himself:

2 "I consider myself fortunate that it is before you, King Agrippa, I am to make my defense today against all the accusations of the Jews, ³ because you are especially familiar with all the customs and controversies of the Jews; therefore I beg of you to listen to me patiently. 4 "All the Jews know my way of life from my youth, a life spent from the beginning among my own people and in Jerusalem. ⁵ They have known for a long time, if they are willing to testify, that I have belonged to the strictest sect of our religion and lived as a Pharisee. ⁶ And now I stand here on trial on account of my hope in the promise made by God to our ancestors, ⁷ a promise that our twelve tribes hope to attain, as they earnestly worship day and night. It is for this hope, your Excellency,ᵃ that I

am accused by Jews! ⁸ Why is it thought incredible by any of you that God raises the dead?

9 "Indeed, I myself was convinced that I ought to do many things against the name of Jesus of Nazareth.ᵇ ¹⁰ And that is what I did in Jerusalem; with authority received from the chief priests, I not only locked up many of the saints in prison, but I also cast my vote against them when they were being condemned to death. ¹¹ By punishing them often in all the synagogues I tried to force them to blaspheme; and since I was so furiously enraged at them, I pursued them even to foreign cities.

Paul Tells of His Conversion

12 "With this in mind, I was traveling to Damascus with the authority and commission of the chief priests, ¹³ when at midday along the road, your Excellency,ᵃ I saw a light from heaven, brighter than the sun, shining around me and my companions. ¹⁴ When we had all fallen to the ground, I heard a voice saying to me in the Hebrewᶜ language, 'Saul, Saul, why are you persecuting me? It hurts you to kick against the goads.' ¹⁵ I asked, 'Who are you, Lord?' The Lord answered, 'I am Jesus whom you are persecuting. ¹⁶ But get up and stand on your feet; for I have appeared to you for this purpose, to appoint you to serve and testify to the things in which you have seen meᵈ and to those in which I will appear to you. ¹⁷ I will rescue you from your people and from the Gentiles—to whom I am sending

ᵃ Gk O king ᵇ Gk the Nazorean ᶜ That is, Aramaic ᵈ Other ancient authorities read *the things that you have seen*

26:1–32 Paul Defends Himself before King Agrippa

26:4–5—See note at 22:3–5.

26:8—Paul's ironical defense of the resurrection is to suspect the credibility of any deity unable to *raise the dead*.

26:9–11—Paul expands on his activities as a persecutor (cf. 9:1–2). His emphatic use of *I myself was convinced* interprets his activities as self-motivated rather than incited by Israel's God.

26:14—A popular Greek aphorism that expresses the futility of seeking to subvert the divine purpose.

26:16—Paul's second testimony of his Damascus road christophany does not mention his blindness or pious Ananias (cf. 22:11–16). The risen Jesus appears *to appoint [Paul] to serve and testify* to God, which is the work of any disciple but in Acts is exemplified by the Lord's apostolic successors.

you [18] to open their eyes so that they may turn from darkness to light and from the power of Satan to God, so that they may receive forgiveness of sins and a place among those who are sanctified by faith in me.'

Paul Tells of His Preaching

19 "After that, King Agrippa, I was not disobedient to the heavenly vision, [20] but declared first to those in Damascus, then in Jerusalem and throughout the countryside of Judea, and also to the Gentiles, that they should repent and turn to God and do deeds consistent with repentance. [21] For this reason the Jews seized me in the temple and tried to kill me. [22] To this day I have had help from God, and so I stand here, testifying to both small and great, saying nothing but what the prophets and Moses said would take place: [23] that the Messiah[a] must suffer, and that, by being the first to rise from the dead, he would proclaim light both to our people and to the Gentiles."

Paul Appeals to Agrippa to Believe

24 While he was making this defense, Festus exclaimed, "You are out of your mind, Paul! Too much learning is driving you insane!" [25] But Paul said, "I am not out of my mind, most excellent Festus, but I am speaking the sober truth. [26] Indeed the king knows about these things, and to him I speak freely; for I am certain that none of these things has escaped his notice, for this was not done in a corner. [27] King Agrippa, do you believe the prophets? I know that you believe." [28] Agrippa said to Paul, "Are you so quickly persuading me to become a Christian?"[b] [29] Paul replied,

"Whether quickly or not, I pray to God that not only you but also all who are listening to me today might become such as I am—except for these chains."

30 Then the king got up, and with him the governor and Bernice and those who had been seated with them; [31] and as they were leaving, they said to one another, "This man is doing nothing to deserve death or imprisonment." [32] Agrippa said to Festus, "This man could have been set free if he had not appealed to the emperor."

Paul Sails for Rome

27 When it was decided that we were to sail for Italy, they transferred Paul and some other prisoners to a centurion of the Augustan Cohort, named Julius. [2] Embarking on a ship of Adramyttium that was about to set sail to the ports along the coast of Asia, we put to sea, accompanied by Aristarchus, a Macedonian from Thessalonica. [3] The next day we put in at Sidon; and Julius treated Paul kindly, and allowed him to go to his friends to be cared for. [4] Putting out to sea from there, we sailed under the lee of Cyprus, because the winds were against us. [5] After we had sailed across the sea that is off Cilicia and Pamphylia, we came to Myra in Lycia. [6] There the centurion found an Alexandrian ship bound for Italy and put us on board. [7] We sailed slowly for a number of days and arrived with difficulty off Cnidus, and as the wind was against us, we sailed under the lee of Crete off Salmone. [8] Sailing past it with difficulty, we came to a place called Fair Havens, near the city of Lasea.

9 Since much time had been lost and

[a] Or the Christ   [b] Or Quickly you will persuade me to play the Christian

---

26:18—Summary of spiritual results from turning to God in repentance (cf. 2:38; 3:19; 5:31; 10:43; 13:38, 46; 20:32).

26:24–32—God's favorable verdict of Paul's service is not rendered in terms of his political innocence but rather by the salvation of those who are prospective beneficiaries of divine grace "to the ends of the earth," represented here by a

pagan governor and Jewish king. Not only does God's plan to save the world dismantle divisions of race and nation but divisions between the powerful and powerless. All stand before God equal in their need for salvation.

27:1–44 Paul Sails toward Rome

27:9—*Paul advised* the sailors based upon his

sailing was now dangerous, because even the Fast had already gone by, Paul advised them, [10] saying, "Sirs, I can see that the voyage will be with danger and much heavy loss, not only of the cargo and the ship, but also of our lives." [11] But the centurion paid more attention to the pilot and to the owner of the ship than to what Paul said. [12] Since the harbor was not suitable for spending the winter, the majority was in favor of putting to sea from there, on the chance that somehow they could reach Phoenix, where they could spend the winter. It was a harbor of Crete, facing southwest and northwest.

The Storm at Sea

13 When a moderate south wind began to blow, they thought they could achieve their purpose; so they weighed anchor and began to sail past Crete, close to the shore. [14] But soon a violent wind, called the northeaster, rushed down from Crete.[a] [15] Since the ship was caught and could not be turned head-on into the wind, we gave way to it and were driven. [16] By running under the lee of a small island called Cauda[b] we were scarcely able to get the ship's boat under control. [17] After hoisting it up they took measures[c] to undergird the ship; then, fearing that they would run on the Syrtis, they lowered the sea anchor and so were driven. [18] We were being pounded by the storm so violently that on the next day they began to throw the cargo overboard, [19] and on the third day with their own hands they threw the ship's tackle overboard. [20] When neither sun nor stars appeared for many days, and no small tempest raged, all hope of our being saved was at last abandoned.

21 Since they had been without food for a long time, Paul then stood up among them and said, "Men, you should have listened to me and not have set sail from Crete and thereby avoided this damage and loss. [22] I urge you now to keep up your courage, for there will be no loss of life among you, but only of the ship. [23] For last night there stood by me an angel of the God to whom I belong and whom I worship, [24] and he said, 'Do not be afraid, Paul; you must stand before the emperor; and indeed, God has granted safety to all those who are sailing with you.' [25] So keep up your courage, men, for I have faith in God that it will be exactly as I have been told. [26] But we will have to run aground on some island."

27 When the fourteenth night had come, as we were drifting across the sea of Adria, about midnight the sailors suspected that they were nearing land. [28] So they took soundings and found twenty fathoms; a little farther on they took soundings again and found fifteen fathoms. [29] Fearing that we might run on the rocks, they let down four anchors from the stern and prayed for day to come. [30] But when the sailors tried to escape from the ship and had lowered the boat into the sea, on the pretext of putting out anchors from the bow, [31] Paul said to the centurion and the soldiers, "Unless these men stay in the ship, you cannot be saved." [32] Then the soldiers cut away the ropes of the boat and set it adrift.

33 Just before daybreak, Paul urged all of them to take some food, saying, "Today is the fourteenth day that you have been in suspense and remaining without food, having eaten nothing. [34] Therefore I urge you to take some food, for it will help you survive; for none of you will lose a hair from your heads." [35] After he had said this, he took bread;

a Gk *it*   *b* Other ancient authorities read *Clauda*   *c* Gk *helps*

---

knowledge of the Mediterranean travel. In doing so, he refers to **the Fast**, Israel's Day of Atonement. This combination of secular with sacred is characteristic of Paul's mission.

27:24 *must*—See note at 17:1–3.

27:30–31—The sailors *cannot be saved* if they *escape from the ship*, since God promises safety only *to all those who are sailing with [Paul]* (v. 24) as another testimony to his spiritual authority.

27:35—Paul's meal blessing echoes the Lord's

and giving thanks to God in the presence of all, he broke it and began to eat. **36** Then all of them were encouraged and took food for themselves. **37** (We were in all two hundred seventy-six*a* persons in the ship.) **38** After they had satisfied their hunger, they lightened the ship by throwing the wheat into the sea.

The Shipwreck

39 In the morning they did not recognize the land, but they noticed a bay with a beach, on which they planned to run the ship ashore, if they could. **40** So they cast off the anchors and left them in the sea. At the same time they loosened the ropes that tied the steering-oars; then hoisting the foresail to the wind, they made for the beach. **41** But striking a reef,*b* they ran the ship aground; the bow stuck and remained immovable, but the stern was being broken up by the force of the waves. **42** The soldiers' plan was to kill the prisoners, so that none might swim away and escape; **43** but the centurion, wishing to save Paul, kept them from carrying out their plan. He ordered those who could swim to jump overboard first and make for the land, **44** and the rest to follow, some on planks and others on pieces of the ship. And so it was that all were brought safely to land.

Paul on the Island of Malta

28 After we had reached safety, we then learned that the island was called Malta. **2** The natives showed us unusual kindness. Since it had begun to rain and was cold, they kindled a fire and welcomed all of us around it. **3** Paul

had gathered a bundle of brushwood and was putting it on the fire, when a viper, driven out by the heat, fastened itself on his hand. **4** When the natives saw the creature hanging from his hand, they said to one another, "This man must be a murderer; though he has escaped from the sea, justice has not allowed him to live." **5** He, however, shook off the creature into the fire and suffered no harm. **6** They were expecting him to swell up or drop dead, but after they had waited a long time and saw that nothing unusual had happened to him, they changed their minds and began to say that he was a god.

7 Now in the neighborhood of that place were lands belonging to the leading man of the island, named Publius, who received us and entertained us hospitably for three days. **8** It so happened that the father of Publius lay sick in bed with fever and dysentery. Paul visited him and cured him by praying and putting his hands on him. **9** After this happened, the rest of the people on the island who had diseases also came and were cured. **10** They bestowed many honors on us, and when we were about to sail, they put on board all the provisions we needed.

Paul Arrives at Rome

11 Three months later we set sail on a ship that had wintered at the island, an Alexandrian ship with the Twin Brothers as its figurehead. **12** We put in at Syracuse and stayed there for three days; **13** then we weighed anchor and came to

---

a Other ancient authorities read *seventy-six*; others, *about seventy-six*
b Gk *place of two seas*

Supper: the food the sailors eat will strengthen them for their prospective salvation from the sea (vv. 43–44).

28:1–15 Paul's Mission in Malta

28:2—The Maltese are called *natives* (*barbaroi*) because they are superstitious, with only their instincts to guide their religious devotion (cf. Rom. 2:12–16).

28:4—*Justice* is the name of an avenging deity responsible for a person's fate.

28:6—See note at 14:8–18.

28:8—Healing is a featured element of Paul's prophetic ministry in Acts (14:8–10; 19:11–12; 20:9–10) in continuity with Jesus (cf. Luke 4:38–44) and his apostolic successors (Acts 3:12–16; 6:6–8; 9:36–42), demonstrating the triumph and presence of God's reign.

28:10—On the community of goods, see 2:43–47; 4:32–35; 11:27–30.

Rhegium. After one day there a south wind sprang up, and on the second day we came to Puteoli. ¹⁴There we found believers*a* and were invited to stay with them for seven days. And so we came to Rome. ¹⁵The believers*a* from there, when they heard of us, came as far as the Forum of Appius and Three Taverns to meet us. On seeing them, Paul thanked God and took courage.

16 When we came into Rome, Paul was allowed to live by himself, with the soldier who was guarding him.

Paul and Jewish Leaders in Rome

17 Three days later he called together the local leaders of the Jews. When they had assembled, he said to them, "Brothers, though I had done nothing against our people or the customs of our ancestors, yet I was arrested in Jerusalem and handed over to the Romans. ¹⁸When they had examined me, the Romans*b* wanted to release me, because there was no reason for the death penalty in my case. ¹⁹But when the Jews objected, I was compelled to appeal to the emperor—even though I had no charge to bring against my nation. ²⁰For this reason therefore I have asked to see you and speak with you,*c* since it is for the sake of the hope of Israel that I am bound with this chain." ²¹They replied, "We have received no letters from Judea about you, and none of the brothers coming here has reported or spoken anything evil about you. ²²But we would like to hear from you what you think, for with regard to this sect we know that everywhere it is spoken against."

Paul Preaches in Rome

23 After they had set a day to meet with him, they came to him at his lodgings in great numbers. From morning until evening he explained the matter to them, testifying to the kingdom of God and trying to convince them about Jesus both from the law of Moses and from the prophets. ²⁴Some were convinced by what he had said, while others refused to believe. ²⁵So they disagreed with each other; and as they were leaving, Paul made one further statement: "The Holy Spirit was right in saying to your ancestors through the prophet Isaiah,

²⁶ 'Go to this people and say,
You will indeed listen, but never
    understand,
and you will indeed look, but
    never perceive.
²⁷ For this people's heart has grown
    dull,
and their ears are hard of hearing,
    and they have shut their eyes;
    so that they might not look with
    their eyes,
and listen with their ears,
and understand with their heart and
    turn—
and I would heal them.'
²⁸Let it be known to you then that this

a Gk brothers *b* Gk they *c* Or I have asked you to see me and speak with me

---

28:16–28 "We Came into Rome"

28:16—Paul *came into Rome* under house arrest but free to *proclaim the kingdom of God and teach about the Lord Jesus Christ* (v. 31). While Jerusalem is located at the epicenter of Luke's narrative universe, drawn by biblical prophecy, Rome is at "the ends of the earth" (1:8), where the gospel's "light" has now come (cf. 13:47).

28:17—Following the pattern of his urban missions, Paul's Roman mission begins with the Jewish leadership of Rome.

28:17–20—Final summary of Paul's defense (cf. 22:3–21; 23:6; 24:10–21; 26:2–23) to Jewish objections of his ministry (cf. 21:28; 24:5–6).

28:22—On Christianity as a *sect* (or party) within Judaism, see notes at 5:17; 15:4–5; 24:5–6.

28:23—Final summary of Paul's prophetic ministry: he argues from Israel's Scripture that the resurrected Jesus is the Messiah (cf. 17:2–4) by whom God's promise to restore God's kingdom to Israel is realized (cf. 1:6).

28:28—For a third and final time, Paul's gospel ministry divides Diaspora Israel according to its Scriptures (cf. vv. 26–27, 23), thereby inclining Paul's attention toward *the Gentiles* of Rome because *they will listen* to the gospel (cf. 13:42–47; 18:4–7). While Paul's ministry continues among Jews who seek him out, his mission in Rome will now include Gentiles (see 28:30–31).

salvation of God has been sent to the Gentiles; they will listen."[a]

30 He lived there two whole years at his own expense[b] and welcomed all who came to him, [31] proclaiming the kingdom of God and teaching about the Lord Jesus Christ with all boldness and without hindrance.

[a] Other ancient authorities add verse 29, *And when he had said these words, the Jews departed, arguing vigorously among themselves*   [b] Or *in his own hired dwelling*

28:30–31 The Curious Ending of Acts

While in Rome, Paul paid his own rent, and this allowed him to receive guests *without hindrance*. Luke's reference to *all who came to him* implies a mixed audience that included Jew and Gentile. In the Greco-Roman world, to *welcome* guests into one's home was considered a virtue and demonstrated the capacity to give and receive the truth (cf. 16:14–15; Luke 19:6). For some it may seem surprising that Luke does not mention the outcome of Paul's meeting with the Roman Caesar; however, Luke's concern is not with Rome but with God. And at the end of Acts, Paul is simply being Paul in compliance with his sacred vocation. And so it should be with every disciple.

The Book of
ROMANS

R omans is not a summary of Paul's missionary message. It presupposes that its readers are seasoned Christians who already know much about Jesus, and it pursues questions that only relatively mature believers would be likely to raise or care about:

> 1. How is the gospel about Jesus related to God's creation and government of the world and the justice people expect from God?
>
> 2. How is Christian faith related to the Jewish Scriptures, particularly the law of Moses? How should Jewish and Gentile Christians relate to one another?
>
> 3. What are God's future intentions, not only regarding persons inside the church, but also for people on the outside and even for the nonhuman creation?
>
> 4. How should Christians understand their ongoing encounters with sin and death?
>
> 5. How ought Christians to go about their daily lives vis-à-vis other Christians as well as non-Christians (including representatives of a non-Christian government)? Can disagreements and doubts be part of the life of faith?

Paul wrote his letter to the Roman Christians sometime between 55 and 58 CE, probably from Corinth. Toward the end of the letter the apostle says he expects to make his first visit to Rome as a stopover on his way to open a new mission field in Spain. Before coming to Rome, however, he says that he will go to Jerusalem to deliver to its struggling Christian community money he has collected from Gentile churches he has founded (15:23–29).

We do not know when or how the Christian community in Rome was founded. The Roman historian Suetonius reports that Jewish conflicts connected with a certain "Chrestus" caused the emperor Claudius to expel Jews from Rome (*Life of Claudius* 25:4). This expulsion may have involved a considerable number of Jewish Christians (Acts 18:2). Romans itself indicates that the Roman Christian community at the time Paul wrote included both Jews and Gentiles (e.g., Rom. 1:5–6; 11:13). The letter's frequent Old Testament quotations and allusions, plus the lengthy discussion of Israel's future in chapters 9–11, suggest that many Roman Christians cared deeply about Judaism and the Jewish people.

One of Paul's purposes in writing the letter is to introduce himself and his message to the believers in Rome. He writes in a way suggesting that the Romans already know something about his preaching and have heard criticisms of it (3:5–8; 6:1, 15; 9:1). He hopes they will accept his interpretation of the gospel and seeks their prayers both for his journey to Jerusalem and for his new mission to Spain. Most of Romans is shaped by Paul's central convictions about the gospel rather than any specific problems in Rome. Chapter 13, however, addresses a question about obeying the govern-

ment that may have been pressing in Rome, and chapter 14 may refer to a particular controversy between "weak" and "strong" believers there.

Modern readers need to be attentive to the special meanings Paul gives to key terms as the letter progresses. The "righteousness of God" is both God's own integrity and the divine power working through the gospel to bring the world into a valid relationship with God (1:16–17; 3:24–26; 10:9–10). "Faith" regularly implies a spiritual union with Christ, and even the discussion of Abraham's faith is linked with Jesus' death and resurrection (4:22–25). Paul often speaks of "sin" as a hostile personal power that can take control of people's lives, turning them away from God and authentic living (e.g., 5:20–21; 6:12–14; 7:11). "Flesh" usually connotes wrongful desires (as in 7:14; 8:5), whereas "body" often has positive associations (8:23; 12:5).

After its opening section (1:1–17), the letter begins with a major statement of humanity's spiritual need (1:18–3:20) and the dimensions of salvation through Christ (3:21–8:39). Chapters 9–11 offer a complex argument about the situation of Jews who have rejected the gospel. Then comes an extended presentation of teachings about the Christian life, mainly in the form of pithy exhortations (12:1–15:13). Finally, Paul explains his plans for visiting Jerusalem and Rome (15:14–33). The letter's conclusion emphasizes greetings to numerous friends and colleagues in ministry (chap. 16).

Prior to the Nazi Holocaust, many readers of Romans tended to regard chapters 9–11 as a relatively unimportant appendix to the argument of chapters 1–8. Today many regard these three chapters as crucial for grasping Paul's overall message and for rethinking Christian attitudes toward Jews and other non-Christians.

Although it does not discuss all topics, the letter to the Romans is the New Testament's most systematic and comprehensive interpretation of the Christian message. It emphasizes the universal effects of God's work in Christ, interpreting the gospel as a message addressed to all peoples and offering hope to all of God's creation.

The letter has had an immense impact on later generations of ordinary believers as well as on revolutionary Christian thinkers like Augustine, Martin Luther, John Calvin, and Karl Barth. Calvin wrote that anyone who understands Romans has a key to understanding "all the most hidden treasures of Scripture."

Centered as it is on the claim that the message about Christ reveals the justice of God (1:17), the letter to the Romans largely consists of a series of arguments responding to questions or doubts about that justice raised in Christian minds by the gospel itself. The questions embedded in Paul's text (e.g., 2:3–4, 17; 3:3; 4:1; 6:1, 15; 7:7, 13; 8:31; 9:14; 10:18; 11:1) are not mere literary devices. The apostle is trying to answer actual objections. Like the book of Job, Romans assumes that doubts must be faced in the life of faith, not denied or swept under the carpet.

At the same time Romans is an eloquent expression of Paul's driving certainties. The message about Jesus' life, death, and resurrection is a word of divine welcome to all humanity, intended to unite everyone (Jews and Gentiles alike) beneath the canopy of God's judgment and mercy. Through the power of the Spirit, believers are already able to live with genuine holiness and tolerance. Without having arrived at moral perfection, they are able to love God and other people, patiently endure present sufferings, and look to the future with invincible hope.

—David Hay

Salutation

1 Paul, a servant[a] of Jesus Christ, called to be an apostle, set apart for the gospel of God, [2] which he promised beforehand through his prophets in the holy scriptures, [3] the gospel concerning his Son, who was descended from David according to the flesh [4] and was declared to be Son of God with power according to the spirit[b] of holiness by resurrection from the dead, Jesus Christ our Lord, [5] through whom we have received grace and apostleship to bring about the obedience of faith among all the Gentiles for the sake of his name, [6] including yourselves who are called to belong to Jesus Christ,

[7] To all God's beloved in Rome, who are called to be saints:

Grace to you and peace from God our Father and the Lord Jesus Christ.

Prayer of Thanksgiving

[8] First, I thank my God through Jesus Christ for all of you, because your faith is proclaimed throughout the world. [9] For God, whom I serve with my spirit by announcing the gospel[c] of his Son, is my witness that without ceasing I remember you always in my prayers, [10] asking that by God's will I may somehow at last succeed in coming to you. [11] For I am longing to see you so that I may share with you some spiritual gift to strengthen you— [12] or rather so that we may be mutually encouraged by each other's faith, both yours and mine. [13] I want you to know, brothers and sisters,[d] that I have often intended to come to you (but thus far have been prevented), in order that I may reap some harvest among you as I have among the rest of the Gentiles. [14] I am a debtor both to Greeks and to barbarians, both to the wise and to the foolish [15] —hence my eagerness to proclaim the gospel to you also who are in Rome.

The Power of the Gospel

[16] For I am not ashamed of the gospel; it is the power of God for salvation to everyone who has faith, to the Jew first and also to the Greek. [17] For in it the righteousness of God is revealed through faith for faith; as it is written, "The one who is righteous will live by faith."[e]

The Guilt of Humankind

[18] For the wrath of God is revealed from heaven against all ungodliness and wickedness of those who by their wickedness suppress the truth. [19] For what can be known about God is plain to them, because God has shown it to them. [20] Ever since the creation of the world his eternal power and divine nature, invisible though they are, have been understood and seen through the things he has made. So they are without excuse; [21] for though they knew God, they did not honor him as God or give thanks to him, but they became futile in their thinking, and their senseless minds were darkened. [22] Claiming to be wise, they became fools; [23] and they exchanged the glory of the immortal God for images resembling a mortal human being or birds or four-footed animals or reptiles.

[24] Therefore God gave them up in the lusts of their hearts to impurity, to the

---

[a] Gk slave   [b] Or Spirit   [c] Gk my spirit in the gospel   [d] Gk brothers   [e] Or The one who is righteous through faith will live

---

1:1–17 Letter Introduction

1:16–17—Like an expert orator, Paul announces concisely the main theme of his letter: the message of Christ makes manifest the power and righteousness of God.

1:18–3:20 Why Christ's Coming Was Necessary

The gospel includes a warning that no one is exempt from God's impartial judgment (2:16; cf. 14:10).

1:18–32 The Error of People Who Suppress Their Own Knowledge of God

The sins described here stem from refusal to honor the one God worshiped by Jews and Christians. Hence the wrongdoers chiefly in view must be persons who believe in many divine beings—or in none at all.

degrading of their bodies among themselves, [25] because they exchanged the truth about God for a lie and worshiped and served the creature rather than the Creator, who is blessed forever! Amen.

26 For this reason God gave them up to degrading passions. Their women exchanged natural intercourse for unnatural, [27] and in the same way also the men, giving up natural intercourse with women, were consumed with passion for one another. Men committed shameless acts with men and received in their own persons the due penalty for their error.

28 And since they did not see fit to acknowledge God, God gave them up to a debased mind and to things that should not be done. [29] They were filled with every kind of wickedness, evil, covetousness, malice. Full of envy, murder, strife, deceit, craftiness, they are gossips, [30] slanderers, God-haters,[a] insolent, haughty, boastful, inventors of evil, rebellious toward parents, [31] foolish, faithless, heartless, ruthless. [32] They know God's decree, that those who practice such things deserve to die— yet they not only do them but even applaud others who practice them.

The Righteous Judgment of God

2 Therefore you have no excuse, whoever you are, when you judge others; for in passing judgment on another you condemn yourself, because you, the judge, are doing the very same things. [2] You say,[b] "We know that God's judgment on those who do such things is in accordance with truth." [3] Do you imagine, whoever you are, that when you judge those who do such things and yet do them yourself, you will escape the judgment of God? [4] Or do you despise the riches of his kindness and forbearance and patience? Do you not realize that God's kindness is meant to lead you to repentance? [5] But by your hard and impenitent heart you are storing up wrath for yourself on the day of wrath, when God's righteous judgment will be revealed. [6] For he will repay according to each one's deeds: [7] to those who by patiently doing good seek for glory and honor and immortality, he will give eternal life; [8] while for those who are self-seeking and who obey not the truth but wickedness, there will be wrath and fury. [9] There will be anguish and distress for everyone who does evil, the Jew first and also the Greek, [10] but glory and honor and peace for everyone who does good, the Jew first and also the Greek. [11] For God shows no partiality.

12 All who have sinned apart from the law will also perish apart from the law, and all who have sinned under the law will be judged by the law. [13] For it is not the hearers of the law who are righteous in God's sight, but the doers of the law who will be justified. [14] When Gentiles, who do not possess the law, do instinctively what the law requires, these, though not having the law, are a law to themselves. [15] They show that what the law requires is written on their hearts, to which their own conscience also bears witness; and their conflicting thoughts will accuse or perhaps excuse them [16] on the day when, according to my gospel,

[a] Or God-hated   [b] Gk lacks You say

1:26–27 *Exchanged natural intercourse for unnatural*—This is one of the few biblical passages dealing with homosexuality, and the only one that mentions lesbianism. Paul probably assumes that all homosexual activity is wrong (following Jewish tradition—Lev. 18:22; 20:13; Wis. 14:26; Philo, *Abraham* 135–37; *Testament of Naphtali* 3:4), but he mentions it mainly to illustrate how false religion leads to false living. Modern debates on the topic should not overlook the apostle's assertions that sin is universal (Rom.

3:23) and that the chief duty of Christians is not to condemn their neighbors but to love them (13:8; 14:10).

2:1–16 Gentiles and Jews Will All Be Judged by God's Law

2:14–16—Even people unfamiliar with the writings of Moses sometimes act in accord with God's law, showing that every human conscience has some awareness of divine requirements.

God, through Jesus Christ, will judge the secret thoughts of all.

The Jews and the Law

17 But if you call yourself a Jew and rely on the law and boast of your relation to God [18] and know his will and determine what is best because you are instructed in the law, [19] and if you are sure that you are a guide to the blind, a light to those who are in darkness, [20] a corrector of the foolish, a teacher of children, having in the law the embodiment of knowledge and truth, [21] you, then, that teach others, will you not teach yourself? While you preach against stealing, do you steal? [22] You that forbid adultery, do you commit adultery? You that abhor idols, do you rob temples? [23] You that boast in the law, do you dishonor God by breaking the law? [24] For, as it is written, "The name of God is blasphemed among the Gentiles because of you."

25 Circumcision indeed is of value if you obey the law; but if you break the law, your circumcision has become uncircumcision. [26] So, if those who are uncircumcised keep the requirements of the law, will not their uncircumcision be regarded as circumcision? [27] Then those who are physically uncircumcised but keep the law will condemn you that have the written code and circumcision but break the law. [28] For a person is not a Jew who is one outwardly, nor is true circumcision something external and physical. [29] Rather, a person is a Jew who is one inwardly, and real circumcision is a matter of the heart—it is spiritual and not literal. Such a person receives praise not from others but from God.

3 Then what advantage has the Jew? Or what is the value of circumcision? [2] Much, in every way. For in the first place the Jews[a] were entrusted with the oracles of God. [3] What if some were unfaithful? Will their faithlessness nullify the faithfulness of God? [4] By no means! Although everyone is a liar, let God be proved true, as it is written,

"So that you may be justified in your words,
    and prevail in your judging."[b]

[5] But if our injustice serves to confirm the justice of God, what should we say? That God is unjust to inflict wrath on us? (I speak in a human way.) [6] By no means! For then how could God judge the world? [7] But if through my falsehood God's truthfulness abounds to his glory, why am I still being condemned as a sinner? [8] And why not say (as some people slander us by saying that we say), "Let us do evil so that good may come"? Their condemnation is deserved!

None Is Righteous

9 What then? Are we any better off?[c] No, not at all; for we have already charged that all, both Jews and Greeks, are under the power of sin, [10] as it is written:

"There is no one who is righteous,
    not even one;
[11]   there is no one who has
        understanding,

[a] Gk they [b] Gk when you are being judged [c] Or at any disadvantage?

2:17–29 Jews Also Are under Judgment

Now Paul addresses the Jews, who know the Mosaic law and rely on being God's chosen people (v. 17). Paul does not say that all Jews have committed the specific sins mentioned in v. 22, but finds in Isa. 52:5 (LXX) proof that Jewish wrongdoing has led Gentiles to blaspheme God (v. 24). By implication Christians, who also often understand themselves to be God's people, should beware of spiritual arrogance and judgmentalism.

3:1–8 Answers to Possible Objections

Paul briefly identifies possible or actual criticisms of his teaching. Jewish wrongdoing does not nullify the religious advantages of the Jews as recipients of God's truth (vv. 1–4), nor does grace encourage sin (vv. 5–8). Paul responds to these criticisms (in reverse order) in chaps. 6–8 and 9–11.

3:9–20 All Are Sinners

A series of Old Testament quotations demonstrates that all Jews and Gentiles alike are sinners. Recognition that even the best people are alienated from God and other persons is the negative backdrop for understanding why God sent Christ into the world (see 4:5; 5:6–8).

there is no one who seeks God.
¹² All have turned aside, together they
    have become worthless;
    there is no one who shows
      kindness,
    there is not even one."
¹³ "Their throats are opened graves;
    they use their tongues to deceive."
    "The venom of vipers is under their
      lips."
¹⁴   "Their mouths are full of cursing
    and bitterness."
¹⁵ "Their feet are swift to shed blood;
¹⁶   ruin and misery are in their paths,
¹⁷ and the way of peace they have not
    known."
¹⁸   "There is no fear of God before
    their eyes."

19 Now we know that whatever the
law says, it speaks to those who are
under the law, so that every mouth may
be silenced, and the whole world may
be held accountable to God. **20** For "no
human being will be justified in his
sight" by deeds prescribed by the law,
for through the law comes the knowledge of sin.

Righteousness through Faith

21 But now, apart from law, the righteousness of God has been disclosed,
and is attested by the law and the prophets, **22** the righteousness of God through
faith in Jesus Christ[a] for all who believe.
For there is no distinction, **23** since all
have sinned and fall short of the glory
of God; **24** they are now justified by his
grace as a gift, through the redemption
that is in Christ Jesus, **25** whom God put

forward as a sacrifice of atonement[b] by
his blood, effective through faith. He did
this to show his righteousness, because
in his divine forbearance he had passed
over the sins previously committed; **26** it
was to prove at the present time that he
himself is righteous and that he justifies
the one who has faith in Jesus.[c]

27 Then what becomes of boasting? It
is excluded. By what law? By that of
works? No, but by the law of faith. **28** For
we hold that a person is justified by
faith apart from works prescribed by
the law. **29** Or is God the God of Jews
only? Is he not the God of Gentiles also?
Yes, of Gentiles also, **30** since God is one;
and he will justify the circumcised on
the ground of faith and the uncircumcised through that same faith. **31** Do we
then overthrow the law by this faith? By
no means! On the contrary, we uphold
the law.

The Example of Abraham

4 What then are we to say was gained
by[d] Abraham, our ancestor according to the flesh? **2** For if Abraham was
justified by works, he has something to
boast about, but not before God. **3** For
what does the scripture say? "Abraham
believed God, and it was reckoned to
him as righteousness." **4** Now to one who
works, wages are not reckoned as a gift
but as something due. **5** But to one who
without works trusts him who justifies
the ungodly, such faith is reckoned as
righteousness. **6** So also David speaks

^a Or through the faith of Jesus Christ   ^b Or a place of atonement   ^c Or who has
the faith of Jesus   ^d Other ancient authorities read say about

---

**3:20 Through the law comes the knowledge
of sin**—How this happens will be explained in
5:13–14 and 7:7–8:4.

**3:21–8:39 The Dimensions of Salvation
through Christ**

3:21–26 A Brief Summary of the Gospel
Paul interprets Christ's death as the event through
which God demonstrates his righteousness to the
world and makes righteous (justifies) everyone who
has faith in Christ. Some scholars think that the
faith of Jesus Christ (NRSV footnote) mentioned in

vv. 22, 26 refers to Christ's own faithful obedience
to God.

**4:1–25 The Jewish Scriptures, Rightly
Interpreted, Teach Justification by Faith**
Paul proceeds to argue that the Old Testament
supports his doctrine of justification (3:31). Abraham, the father of the Jewish nation, was justified
by faith as a gift (according to Gen. 15:6) well
before God commanded that he be circumcised
(Gen. 17:10–14). By implication, all ritual and
moral actions should be seen as responses to
God's grace, not deeds that earn it.

of the blessedness of those to whom God reckons righteousness apart from works:

[7] "Blessed are those whose iniquities
        are forgiven,
    and whose sins are covered;
[8] blessed is the one against whom the
        Lord will not reckon sin."

9 Is this blessedness, then, pronounced only on the circumcised, or also on the uncircumcised? We say, "Faith was reckoned to Abraham as righteousness." [10] How then was it reckoned to him? Was it before or after he had been circumcised? It was not after, but before he was circumcised. [11] He received the sign of circumcision as a seal of the righteousness that he had by faith while he was still uncircumcised. The purpose was to make him the ancestor of all who believe without being circumcised and who thus have righteousness reckoned to them, [12] and likewise the ancestor of the circumcised who are not only circumcised but who also follow the example of the faith that our ancestor Abraham had before he was circumcised.

God's Promise Realized through Faith

13 For the promise that he would inherit the world did not come to Abraham or to his descendants through the law but through the righteousness of faith. [14] If it is the adherents of the law who are to be the heirs, faith is null and the promise is void. [15] For the law brings wrath; but where there is no law, neither is there violation.

16 For this reason it depends on faith, in order that the promise may rest on grace and be guaranteed to all his descendants, not only to the adherents of the law but also to those who share the faith of Abraham (for he is the father of all of us, [17] as it is written, "I have made you the father of many nations")—in the presence of the God in whom he believed, who gives life to the dead and calls into existence the things that do not exist. [18] Hoping against hope, he believed that he would become "the father of many nations," according to what was said, "So numerous shall your descendants be." [19] He did not weaken in faith when he considered his own body, which was already[a] as good as dead (for he was about a hundred years old), or when he considered the barrenness of Sarah's womb. [20] No distrust made him waver concerning the promise of God, but he grew strong in his faith as he gave glory to God, [21] being fully convinced that God was able to do what he had promised. [22] Therefore his faith[b] "was reckoned to him as righteousness." [23] Now the words, "it was reckoned to him," were written not for his sake alone, [24] but for ours also. It will be reckoned to us who believe in him who raised Jesus our Lord from the dead, [25] who was handed over to death for our trespasses and was raised for our justification.

Results of Justification

5 Therefore, since we are justified by faith, we[c] have peace with God through our Lord Jesus Christ, [2] through whom we have obtained access[d] to this grace in which we stand; and we[e] boast in our hope of sharing the glory of God. [3] And not only that, but we[e] also boast

[a] Other ancient authorities lack *already* [b] Gk *Therefore it* [c] Other ancient authorities read *let us* [d] Other ancient authorities add *by faith* [e] Or *let us*

4:16–21—Abraham is a model of resisting doubt and trusting God in an apparently hopeless situation. He believed that God's promises would be fulfilled, though Isaac's conception seemed as impossible as a resurrection from the dead (vv. 17–21).

4:24–25—Like Abraham, Christians gain a right relationship with God solely through personal faith, though their faith is a response to God's gracious prior action in Jesus' death and resurrection (see also 10:9–10).

5:1–11 Results of Justification

5:1–5—Believers are now at peace with God through Christ, and this enables them to grow in genuine fortitude, hope, and love (see 8:28; 15:13).

in our sufferings, knowing that suffering produces endurance, [4] and endurance produces character, and character produces hope, [5] and hope does not disappoint us, because God's love has been poured into our hearts through the Holy Spirit that has been given to us.

6 For while we were still weak, at the right time Christ died for the ungodly. [7] Indeed, rarely will anyone die for a righteous person—though perhaps for a good person someone might actually dare to die. [8] But God proves his love for us in that while we still were sinners Christ died for us. [9] Much more surely then, now that we have been justified by his blood, will we be saved through him from the wrath of God.[a] [10] For if while we were enemies, we were reconciled to God through the death of his Son, much more surely, having been reconciled, will we be saved by his life. [11] But more than that, we even boast in God through our Lord Jesus Christ, through whom we have now received reconciliation.

Adam and Christ

12 Therefore, just as sin came into the world through one man, and death came through sin, and so death spread to all because all have sinned— [13] sin was indeed in the world before the law, but sin is not reckoned when there is no law. [14] Yet death exercised dominion from Adam to Moses, even over those whose sins were not like the transgression of Adam, who is a type of the one who was to come.

15 But the free gift is not like the trespass. For if the many died through the one man's trespass, much more surely have the grace of God and the free gift in the grace of the one man, Jesus Christ, abounded for the many. [16] And the free gift is not like the effect of the one man's sin. For the judgment following one trespass brought condemnation, but the free gift following many trespasses brings justification. [17] If, because of the one man's trespass, death exercised dominion through that one, much more surely will those who receive the abundance of grace and the free gift of righteousness exercise dominion in life through the one man, Jesus Christ.

18 Therefore just as one man's trespass led to condemnation for all, so one man's act of righteousness leads to justification and life for all. [19] For just as by the one man's disobedience the many were made sinners, so by the one man's obedience the many will be made righteous. [20] But law came in, with the result that the trespass multiplied; but where sin increased, grace abounded all the more, [21] so that, just as sin exercised dominion in death, so grace might also exercise dominion through justification[b] leading to eternal life through Jesus Christ our Lord.

Dying and Rising with Christ

6 What then are we to say? Should we continue in sin in order that grace

[a] Gk the wrath　[b] Or righteousness

5:6–8—Jesus' death is now interpreted as a demonstration of God's love, a statement that clarifies the meaning of the divine righteousness (3:24–26) and looks forward to promises of security in 8:31–39. Paul's words about sinners and enemies undercut any Christian pretensions to superiority over other groups, races, and religious communities.

5:12–21 Adam and Christ

The general meaning of this "typological" argument seems clear: human history is essentially determined by the relationship that everyone has to both Adam and Christ. Through Adam (the *type*, v. 14), all are entangled in sin, alienation

from God, and death. Through Christ, who more than counterbalances Adam, God's grace triumphs over sin, drawing everyone toward *righteousness* and eternal *life* (v. 18). The universalistic hope implied here is echoed in 11:32.

5:12 *So death spread to all because all have sinned*—Paul's brief statement does not explain how he understands the spread of sin and death to have occurred (cf. 2 Esd. 7:48 [*118*]). Later theologians like Augustine worked out a detailed doctrine of original sin based partly on this New Testament verse.

may abound? ² By no means! How can we who died to sin go on living in it? ³ Do you not know that all of us who have been baptized into Christ Jesus were baptized into his death? ⁴ Therefore we have been buried with him by baptism into death, so that, just as Christ was raised from the dead by the glory of the Father, so we too might walk in newness of life.

5 For if we have been united with him in a death like his, we will certainly be united with him in a resurrection like his. ⁶ We know that our old self was crucified with him so that the body of sin might be destroyed, and we might no longer be enslaved to sin. ⁷ For whoever has died is freed from sin. ⁸ But if we have died with Christ, we believe that we will also live with him. ⁹ We know that Christ, being raised from the dead, will never die again; death no longer has dominion over him. ¹⁰ The death he died, he died to sin, once for all; but the life he lives, he lives to God. ¹¹ So you also must consider yourselves dead to sin and alive to God in Christ Jesus.

12 Therefore, do not let sin exercise dominion in your mortal bodies, to make you obey their passions. ¹³ No longer present your members to sin as instruments^a of wickedness, but present yourselves to God as those who have been brought from death to life, and present your members to God as instruments^a of righteousness. ¹⁴ For sin will have no dominion over you, since you are not under law but under grace.

Slaves of Righteousness

15 What then? Should we sin because we are not under law but under grace?

By no means! ¹⁶ Do you not know that if you present yourselves to anyone as obedient slaves, you are slaves of the one whom you obey, either of sin, which leads to death, or of obedience, which leads to righteousness? ¹⁷ But thanks be to God that you, having once been slaves of sin, have become obedient from the heart to the form of teaching to which you were entrusted, ¹⁸ and that you, having been set free from sin, have become slaves of righteousness. ¹⁹ I am speaking in human terms because of your natural limitations.^{b} For just as you once presented your members as slaves to impurity and to greater and greater iniquity, so now present your members as slaves to righteousness for sanctification.

20 When you were slaves of sin, you were free in regard to righteousness. ²¹ So what advantage did you then get from the things of which you now are ashamed? The end of those things is death. ²² But now that you have been freed from sin and enslaved to God, the advantage you get is sanctification. The end is eternal life. ²³ For the wages of sin is death, but the free gift of God is eternal life in Christ Jesus our Lord.

An Analogy from Marriage

7 Do you not know, brothers and sisters^c—for I am speaking to those who know the law—that the law is binding on a person only during that person's lifetime? ² Thus a married woman is bound by the law to her husband as long as he lives; but if her husband dies, she is discharged from the law concerning the husband. ³ Accordingly, she will

^{a} Or weapons ^{b} Gk the weakness of your flesh ^{c} Gk brothers

6:1–23 Freedom from Sin through Union with Christ

Paul responds to critics who say that his preaching of salvation as God's free gift (4:4–5; 5:17) encourages church members to be morally irresponsible (6:1, 15).

6:2–11—Christians are united with Christ through faith and baptism. This union means that they must consider themselves dead to sin, no longer

under the sway of their passions, and pursue Christlike living in anticipation of a future resurrection (vv. 5–8).

6:16–23—True freedom comes from seeking God's will in all of one's private and public decisions.

7:1–6 An Analogy from Marriage

Through Christ's death Christians have died not only to sin (6:2) but also to any effort to use the law to save themselves (7:6; cf. 8:9).

be called an adulteress if she lives with another man while her husband is alive. But if her husband dies, she is free from that law, and if she marries another man, she is not an adulteress.

4 In the same way, my friends,[a] you have died to the law through the body of Christ, so that you may belong to another, to him who has been raised from the dead in order that we may bear fruit for God. [5] While we were living in the flesh, our sinful passions, aroused by the law, were at work in our members to bear fruit for death. [6] But now we are discharged from the law, dead to that which held us captive, so that we are slaves not under the old written code but in the new life of the Spirit.

The Law and Sin

7 What then should we say? That the law is sin? By no means! Yet, if it had not been for the law, I would not have known sin. I would not have known what it is to covet if the law had not said, "You shall not covet." [8] But sin, seizing an opportunity in the commandment, produced in me all kinds of covetousness. Apart from the law sin lies dead. [9] I was once alive apart from the law, but when the commandment came, sin revived [10] and I died, and the very commandment that promised life proved to be death to me. [11] For sin, seizing an opportunity in the commandment, deceived me and through it killed me. [12] So the law is holy, and the commandment is holy and just and good.

13 Did what is good, then, bring death to me? By no means! It was sin, working death in me through what is good, in order that sin might be shown to be sin, and through the commandment might become sinful beyond measure.

The Inner Conflict

14 For we know that the law is spiritual; but I am of the flesh, sold into slavery under sin.[b] [15] I do not understand my own actions. For I do not do what I want, but I do the very thing I hate. [16] Now if I do what I do not want, I agree that the law is good. [17] But in fact it is no longer I that do it, but sin that dwells within me. [18] For I know that nothing good dwells within me, that is, in my flesh. I can will what is right, but I cannot do it. [19] For I do not do the good I want, but the evil I do not want is what I do. [20] Now if I do what I do not want, it is no longer I that do it, but sin that dwells within me.

21 So I find it to be a law that when I want to do what is good, evil lies close at hand. [22] For I delight in the law of God in my inmost self, [23] but I see in my members another law at war with the law of my mind, making me captive to the law of sin that dwells in my members. [24] Wretched man that I am! Who will rescue me from this body of death? [25] Thanks be to God through Jesus Christ our Lord!

So then, with my mind I am a slave to the law of God, but with my flesh I am a slave to the law of sin.

Life in the Spirit

8 There is therefore now no condemnation for those who are in Christ

[a] Gk brothers [b] Gk sold under sin

7:7–25 The Law Cannot Help the Divided Self
Since Adam human nature has been dominated by the power of sin and "fleshly" desires, which the law of Moses (as an external standard of right and wrong) cannot overcome (cf. 3:19–20; 5:13). Knowledge of the law's prohibitions actually stirs up sinful desires, even though the law in itself is *holy and just and good* (7:12). When we aspire to do all that God's law requires, our sinful nature can trick us into imagining that we can perfectly do God's will on the basis of our own power, thereby earning the right to condemn or mistreat

other, "less perfect" people (cf. Luke 18:9–14). Self-righteousness is a destructive temptation for churches and nations as well as individuals.

8:1–8 Now No Condemnation
Jesus' death overcame the power of sin, and the Spirit enables Christians to fulfill God's law without arrogance (vv. 3–4; 13:8). This, however, is not a magical or automatic process. Believers must steadily choose to think and live in accord with God's Spirit, resisting temptations of *the flesh* (vv. 5–8).

Jesus. [2] For the law of the Spirit[a] of life in Christ Jesus has set you[b] free from the law of sin and of death. [3] For God has done what the law, weakened by the flesh, could not do: by sending his own Son in the likeness of sinful flesh, and to deal with sin,[c] he condemned sin in the flesh, [4] so that the just requirement of the law might be fulfilled in us, who walk not according to the flesh but according to the Spirit.[a] [5] For those who live according to the flesh set their minds on the things of the flesh, but those who live according to the Spirit[a] set their minds on the things of the Spirit.[a] [6] To set the mind on the flesh is death, but to set the mind on the Spirit[a] is life and peace. [7] For this reason the mind that is set on the flesh is hostile to God; it does not submit to God's law—indeed it cannot, [8] and those who are in the flesh cannot please God.

[9] But you are not in the flesh; you are in the Spirit,[a] since the Spirit of God dwells in you. Anyone who does not have the Spirit of Christ does not belong to him. [10] But if Christ is in you, though the body is dead because of sin, the Spirit[a] is life because of righteousness. [11] If the Spirit of him who raised Jesus from the dead dwells in you, he who raised Christ[d] from the dead will give life to your mortal bodies also through[e] his Spirit that dwells in you.

[12] So then, brothers and sisters,[f] we are debtors, not to the flesh, to live according to the flesh— [13] for if you live according to the flesh, you will die; but if by the Spirit you put to death the deeds of the body, you will live. [14] For all who are led by the Spirit of God are children of God. [15] For you did not receive a spirit of slavery to fall back into fear, but you have received a spirit of adoption. When we cry, "Abba![g] Father!" [16] it is that very Spirit bearing witness[h] with our spirit that we are children of God, [17] and if children, then heirs, heirs of God and joint heirs with Christ—if, in fact, we suffer with him so that we may also be glorified with him.

Future Glory

[18] I consider that the sufferings of this present time are not worth comparing with the glory about to be revealed to us. [19] For the creation waits with eager longing for the revealing of the children of God; [20] for the creation was subjected to futility, not of its own will but by the will of the one who subjected it, in hope [21] that the creation itself will be set free from its bondage to decay and will obtain the freedom of the glory of the children of God. [22] We know that the whole creation has been groaning in labor pains until now; [23] and not only the creation, but we ourselves, who have the first fruits of the Spirit, groan inwardly while we wait for adoption, the redemption of our bodies. [24] For in[i] hope we were saved. Now hope that is seen is not hope. For who hopes[j] for what is seen? [25] But if we hope for what we do not see, we wait for it with patience.

[26] Likewise the Spirit helps us in our weakness; for we do not know how to pray as we ought, but that very Spirit intercedes[k] with sighs too deep for

[a] Or spirit [b] Here the Greek word you is singular number; other ancient authorities read me or us [c] Or and as a sin offering [d] Other ancient authorities read the Christ or Christ Jesus or Jesus Christ [e] Other ancient authorities read on account of [f] Gk brothers [g] Aramaic for Father [h] Or [15]a spirit of adoption, by which we cry, "Abba! Father!" [16]The Spirit itself bears witness [i] Or by [j] Other ancient authorities read awaits [k] Other ancient authorities add for us

---

8:9–39 Living by the Spirit Brings Freedom from Anxiety about the Future

8:15–16—Christians know they are God's children because the Spirit inspires them to pray to God as their Father, just as Jesus did (see also Gal. 4:6; Mark 14:36).

8:18–25—Believers can endure present-time suffering and persecution (vv. 17, 35–36) because they have a glorious hope. All living things are subject to decay and death (cf. 5:12; 1 Cor. 15:21–22; Gen. 3:19). Yet faith looks forward to a day when all God's creatures will be set free from death (cf. 1 Cor. 15:54–55). Their hope for universal deliverance lies beyond the horizon of the human efforts (cf. 1 Cor. 2:9).

words. ²⁷ And God,*a* who searches the heart, knows what is the mind of the Spirit, because the Spirit*b* intercedes for the saints according to the will of God.*c*

28 We know that all things work together for good*d* for those who love God, who are called according to his purpose. ²⁹ For those whom he foreknew he also predestined to be conformed to the image of his Son, in order that he might be the firstborn within a large family.*e* ³⁰ And those whom he predestined he also called; and those whom he called he also justified; and those whom he justified he also glorified.

God's Love in Christ Jesus

31 What then are we to say about these things? If God is for us, who is against us? ³² He who did not withhold his own Son, but gave him up for all of us, will he not with him also give us everything else? ³³ Who will bring any charge against God's elect? It is God who justifies. ³⁴ Who is to condemn? It is Christ Jesus, who died, yes, who was raised, who is at the right hand of God, who indeed intercedes for us.*f* ³⁵ Who will separate us from the love of Christ? Will hardship, or distress, or persecution, or famine, or nakedness, or peril, or sword? ³⁶ As it is written,

> "For your sake we are being killed all day long;
> we are accounted as sheep to be slaughtered."

³⁷ No, in all these things we are more than conquerors through him who loved us. ³⁸ For I am convinced that neither death, nor life, nor angels, nor rulers, nor things present, nor things to come, nor powers, ³⁹ nor height, nor depth, nor anything else in all creation, will be able to separate us from the love of God in Christ Jesus our Lord.

God's Election of Israel

9 I am speaking the truth in Christ—I am not lying; my conscience confirms it by the Holy Spirit— ² I have great sorrow and unceasing anguish in my heart. ³ For I could wish that I myself were accursed and cut off from Christ for the sake of my own people,*g* my kindred according to the flesh. ⁴ They are Israelites, and to them belong the adoption, the glory, the covenants, the giving of the law, the worship, and the promises; ⁵ to them belong the patriarchs, and from them, according to the flesh, comes the Messiah,*h* who is over all, God blessed forever.*i* Amen.

6 It is not as though the word of God had failed. For not all Israelites truly belong to Israel, ⁷ and not all of Abraham's children are his true descendants; but "It is through Isaac that descendants shall be named for you." ⁸ This means that it is not the children of the flesh who are the children of God, but the children of the promise are counted as descendants. ⁹ For this is what the

---

a Gk the one *b* Gk he or it *c* Gk according to God *d* Other ancient authorities read God makes all things work together for good, or in all things God works for good *e* Gk among many brothers *f* Or Is it Christ Jesus . . . for us? *g* Gk my brothers *h* Or the Christ *i* Or Messiah, who is God over all, blessed forever; or Messiah. May he who is God over all be blessed forever

---

8:31–39—Not only in his death but also in his resurrection, Christ is the firmest possible assurance to believers that God's all-conquering love will always be with them (cf. 5:6–8). People committed to Christ's cause must expect suffering and defeats, but they will never be defeated.

8:38—The hostile *angels* and *powers* refer to supernatural forces opposing God and threatening human beings. Some scholars think they should be interpreted in relation to impersonal institutions, ideologies, and systems of prejudice that encourage injustice and hopelessness (cf. 16:20; 1 Cor. 2:8; Gal. 4:3, 8; Eph. 6:12; Col. 2:15).

9:1–11:36 Israel in Relation to the Gospel

How should Christians think about the fact that most Jews do not recognize Jesus as the Messiah? Paul writes out of profound concern both for his non-Christian brothers, his **kindred according to the flesh** (9:3), and for the reliability of God's gifts and promises presented in the Jewish Scriptures as well as in Jesus Christ (9:4, 6, 14; 11:29; cf. 8:31–39).

9:6–29 First Stage of Paul's Argument

The Jewish Scriptures themselves show that membership in Israel is based not on physical descent but on God's free grace (as in 4:16; 8:29–30).

promise said, "About this time I will return and Sarah shall have a son." [10] Nor is that all; something similar happened to Rebecca when she had conceived children by one husband, our ancestor Isaac. [11] Even before they had been born or had done anything good or bad (so that God's purpose of election might continue, [12] not by works but by his call) she was told, "The elder shall serve the younger." [13] As it is written,

"I have loved Jacob,
but I have hated Esau."

14 What then are we to say? Is there injustice on God's part? By no means! [15] For he says to Moses,

"I will have mercy on whom I have
mercy,
and I will have compassion on
whom I have compassion."

[16] So it depends not on human will or exertion, but on God who shows mercy. [17] For the scripture says to Pharaoh, "I have raised you up for the very purpose of showing my power in you, so that my name may be proclaimed in all the earth." [18] So then he has mercy on whomever he chooses, and he hardens the heart of whomever he chooses.

God's Wrath and Mercy

19 You will say to me then, "Why then does he still find fault? For who can resist his will?" [20] But who indeed are you, a human being, to argue with God? Will what is molded say to the one who molds it, "Why have you made me like this?" [21] Has the potter no right over the clay, to make out of the same lump one object for special use and another for ordinary use? [22] What if God, desiring to show his wrath and to make known his power, has endured with much patience the objects of wrath that are made for destruction; [23] and what if he has done so in order to make known the riches of his glory for the objects of mercy, which he has prepared beforehand for glory— [24] including us whom he has called, not from the Jews only but also from the Gentiles? [25] As indeed he says in Hosea,

"Those who were not my people I
will call 'my people,'
and her who was not beloved I will
call 'beloved.' "
[26] "And in the very place where it was
said to them, 'You are not my
people,'
there they shall be called children
of the living God."

27 And Isaiah cries out concerning Israel, "Though the number of the children of Israel were like the sand of the sea, only a remnant of them will be saved; [28] for the Lord will execute his sentence on the earth quickly and decisively."[a] [29] And as Isaiah predicted,

"If the Lord of hosts had not left
survivors[b] to us,
we would have fared like Sodom
and been made like Gomorrah."

Israel's Unbelief

30 What then are we to say? Gentiles, who did not strive for righteousness, have attained it, that is, righteousness through faith; [31] but Israel, who did strive for the righteousness that is based on the law, did not succeed in fulfilling that law. [32] Why not? Because they did not strive for it on the basis of faith, but

[a] Other ancient authorities read *for he will finish his work and cut it short in righteousness, because the Lord will make the sentence shortened on the earth*   [b] Or *descendants*; Gk *seed*

9:14–23—Paul's main point is that human evil does not undermine God's righteousness (vv. 3–4). Later interpreters sometimes detected here a rigid doctrine of predestination (see also vv. 17–18). The apostle emphasizes God's ultimate purpose of mercy (v. 16).

9:30–10:21 Second Stage of Paul's Argument

God has made faith in Christ the path of salvation for everyone.

9:31–10:4—Christians and Jews both pursue the righteousness of God, and Christ is the goal to which the law of Moses points (10:4). From Paul's Jewish-Christian perspective, non-Christian Jews are to be honored for their devotion to God, although they have not yet grasped the significance of Jesus (cf. Phil. 3:4–11).

as if it were based on works. They have stumbled over the stumbling stone, [33] as it is written,

> "See, I am laying in Zion a stone that
> will make people stumble, a
> rock that will make them fall,
> and whoever believes in him[a] will
> not be put to shame."

10 Brothers and sisters,[b] my heart's desire and prayer to God for them is that they may be saved. [2] I can testify that they have a zeal for God, but it is not enlightened. [3] For, being ignorant of the righteousness that comes from God, and seeking to establish their own, they have not submitted to God's righteousness. [4] For Christ is the end of the law so that there may be righteousness for everyone who believes.

Salvation Is for All

[5] Moses writes concerning the righteousness that comes from the law, that "the person who does these things will live by them." [6] But the righteousness that comes from faith says, "Do not say in your heart, 'Who will ascend into heaven?'" (that is, to bring Christ down) [7] "or 'Who will descend into the abyss?'" (that is, to bring Christ up from the dead). [8] But what does it say?

> "The word is near you,
> on your lips and in your heart"

(that is, the word of faith that we proclaim); [9] because[c] if you confess with your lips that Jesus is Lord and believe in your heart that God raised him from the dead, you will be saved. [10] For one believes with the heart and so is justified, and one confesses with the mouth and so is saved. [11] The scripture says, "No one who believes in him will be put to shame." [12] For there is no distinction between Jew and Greek; the same Lord is Lord of all and is generous to all who call on him. [13] For, "Everyone who calls

on the name of the Lord shall be saved."

[14] But how are they to call on one in whom they have not believed? And how are they to believe in one of whom they have never heard? And how are they to hear without someone to proclaim him? [15] And how are they to proclaim him unless they are sent? As it is written, "How beautiful are the feet of those who bring good news!" [16] But not all have obeyed the good news;[d] for Isaiah says, "Lord, who has believed our message?" [17] So faith comes from what is heard, and what is heard comes through the word of Christ.[e]

[18] But I ask, have they not heard? Indeed they have; for

> "Their voice has gone out to all the
> earth,
> and their words to the ends of the
> world."

[19] Again I ask, did Israel not understand? First Moses says,

> "I will make you jealous of those
> who are not a nation;
> with a foolish nation I will make
> you angry."

[20] Then Isaiah is so bold as to say,

> "I have been found by those who did
> not seek me;
> I have shown myself to those who
> did not ask for me."

[21] But of Israel he says, "All day long I have held out my hands to a disobedient and contrary people."

Israel's Rejection Is Not Final

11 I ask, then, has God rejected his people? By no means! I myself am an Israelite, a descendant of Abraham, a member of the tribe of Benjamin. [2] God has not rejected his people whom he foreknew. Do you not know what the scripture says of Elijah, how he pleads

---

[a] Or trusts in it   [b] Gk Brothers   [c] Or namely, that   [d] Or gospel   [e] Or about Christ; other ancient authorities read of God

---

10:8—Paul's distinctly Christian reading of Moses' words finds in them a prophecy that God's righteousness will be realized through faith in Jesus' resurrection and lordship (vv. 9–10)

11:1–10 The Third Stage of Paul's Argument
Some Jews (like Paul) have already become Christians, thereby showing that a part of Israel is already in a right relationship with God.

with God against Israel? [3] "Lord, they have killed your prophets, they have demolished your altars; I alone am left, and they are seeking my life." [4] But what is the divine reply to him? "I have kept for myself seven thousand who have not bowed the knee to Baal." [5] So too at the present time there is a remnant, chosen by grace. [6] But if it is by grace, it is no longer on the basis of works, otherwise grace would no longer be grace.[a]

[7] What then? Israel failed to obtain what it was seeking. The elect obtained it, but the rest were hardened, [8] as it is written,

"God gave them a sluggish spirit,
    eyes that would not see
    and ears that would not hear,
down to this very day."
[9] And David says,
"Let their table become a snare and
        a trap,
    a stumbling block and a
        retribution for them;
[10] let their eyes be darkened so that
        they cannot see,
    and keep their backs forever
        bent."

The Salvation of the Gentiles

[11] So I ask, have they stumbled so as to fall? By no means! But through their stumbling[b] salvation has come to the Gentiles, so as to make Israel[c] jealous. [12] Now if their stumbling[b] means riches for the world, and if their defeat means riches for Gentiles, how much more will their full inclusion mean!

[13] Now I am speaking to you Gentiles. Inasmuch then as I am an apostle to the Gentiles, I glorify my ministry [14] in order to make my own people[d] jeal-

ous, and thus save some of them. [15] For if their rejection is the reconciliation of the world, what will their acceptance be but life from the dead! [16] If the part of the dough offered as first fruits is holy, then the whole batch is holy; and if the root is holy, then the branches also are holy.

[17] But if some of the branches were broken off, and you, a wild olive shoot, were grafted in their place to share the rich root[e] of the olive tree, [18] do not boast over the branches. If you do boast, remember that it is not you that support the root, but the root that supports you. [19] You will say, "Branches were broken off so that I might be grafted in." [20] That is true. They were broken off because of their unbelief, but you stand only through faith. So do not become proud, but stand in awe. [21] For if God did not spare the natural branches, perhaps he will not spare you.[f] [22] Note then the kindness and the severity of God: severity toward those who have fallen, but God's kindness toward you, provided you continue in his kindness; otherwise you also will be cut off. [23] And even those of Israel,[g] if they do not persist in unbelief, will be grafted in, for God has the power to graft them in again. [24] For if you have been cut from what is by nature a wild olive tree and grafted, contrary to nature, into a cultivated olive tree, how much more will these natural branches be grafted back into their own olive tree.

[a] Other ancient authorities add *But if it is by works, it is no longer on the basis of grace, otherwise work would no longer be work* [b] Gk *transgression* [c] Gk *them* [d] Gk *my flesh* [e] Other ancient authorities read *the richness* [f] Other ancient authorities read *neither will he spare you* [g] Gk lacks *of Israel*

11:11–32 The Fourth Stage of Paul's Argument
The present-time unbelief of most non-Christian Jews is only temporary and it gives the church a special responsibility to witness to Gentiles (cf. Acts 13:46–48; 28:26–28).

11:11—God intends the conversion of Gentiles to prompt non-Christian Jews to move toward Christian faith (see also vv. 13–14). Neither here nor elsewhere, however, does Paul call for a spe-

cial Christian campaign to convert Jews. In later centuries, the refusal of Jews to accept Christian faith has often triggered Christian animosity and anti-Semitic actions.

11:20—Paul uses a rather awkward agricultural analogy in vv. 17–24 to argue that God can remove and graft in **branches** at will. Hence Gentiles presently inside the church dare not despise Jews on the outside.

All Israel Will Be Saved

25 So that you may not claim to be wiser than you are, brothers and sisters,[a] I want you to understand this mystery: a hardening has come upon part of Israel, until the full number of the Gentiles has come in. 26 And so all Israel will be saved; as it is written,

"Out of Zion will come the Deliverer;
    he will banish ungodliness from
        Jacob."
27 "And this is my covenant with them,
    when I take away their sins."
28 As regards the gospel they are enemies of God[b] for your sake; but as regards election they are beloved, for the sake of their ancestors; 29 for the gifts and the calling of God are irrevocable. 30 Just as you were once disobedient to God but have now received mercy because of their disobedience, 31 so they have now been disobedient in order that, by the mercy shown to you, they too may now[c] receive mercy. 32 For God has imprisoned all in disobedience so that he may be merciful to all.

33 O the depth of the riches and wisdom and knowledge of God! How unsearchable are his judgments and how inscrutable his ways!
34 "For who has known the mind of the
        Lord?
    Or who has been his counselor?"
35 "Or who has given a gift to him,
    to receive a gift in return?"
36 For from him and through him and to him are all things. To him be the glory forever. Amen.

The New Life in Christ

12 I appeal to you therefore, brothers and sisters,[a] by the mercies of God, to present your bodies as a living sacrifice, holy and acceptable to God, which is your spiritual[d] worship. 2 Do not be conformed to this world,[e] but be transformed by the renewing of your minds, so that you may discern what is the will of God—what is good and acceptable and perfect.[f]

3 For by the grace given to me I say to everyone among you not to think of yourself more highly than you ought to think, but to think with sober judgment, each according to the measure of faith that God has assigned. 4 For as in one body we have many members, and not all the members have the same function, 5 so we, who are many, are one body in Christ, and individually we are members one of another. 6 We have gifts that differ according to the grace given to us: prophecy, in proportion to faith; 7 ministry, in ministering; the teacher, in teaching; 8 the exhorter, in exhortation; the giver, in generosity; the leader, in diligence; the compassionate, in cheerfulness.

Marks of the True Christian

9 Let love be genuine; hate what is evil, hold fast to what is good; 10 love one

a Gk brothers b Gk lacks of God c Other ancient authorities lack now
d Or reasonable e Gk age f Or what is the good and acceptable and perfect will of God

---

11:26—Paul solemnly prophesies that *all Israel* will ultimately be brought into a true relationship with God, in fulfillment of Old Testament promises (vv. 28–32; cf. 16:26). Many interpreters have assumed that Paul expects that all Jews will become Christians at the end of the world (cf. v. 23), but the apostle does not say this explicitly. On the other hand, he nowhere speaks of a right relationship with God apart from recognition of Jesus as the Christ.

11:33–36 God's Salvation Exceeds Human Comprehension
People of faith must remember that they cannot grasp all mysteries. Paul ends his long argument with a doxology praising the God who alone rules events and shapes the future of all persons, Christians and non-Christians alike.

12:1–15:13 Guidelines for Christian Living
12:1–21 Introduction

12:1–2—The entire existence of believers should be sacrificial worship of God, in response to the sacrifice of God's Son (3:24–26). This requires choosing to be *transformed* in mind by the Spirit of God (8:14; 1 Cor. 2:12) rather than conforming to "what everyone else does."

12:4—The church is Christ's body, and its members are required to use their gifts with humility for the good of the whole community (cf. 1 Cor. 12).

another with mutual affection; outdo one another in showing honor. [11] Do not lag in zeal, be ardent in spirit, serve the Lord.[a] [12] Rejoice in hope, be patient in suffering, persevere in prayer. [13] Contribute to the needs of the saints; extend hospitality to strangers.

14 Bless those who persecute you; bless and do not curse them. [15] Rejoice with those who rejoice, weep with those who weep. [16] Live in harmony with one another; do not be haughty, but associate with the lowly;[b] do not claim to be wiser than you are. [17] Do not repay anyone evil for evil, but take thought for what is noble in the sight of all. [18] If it is possible, so far as it depends on you, live peaceably with all. [19] Beloved, never avenge yourselves, but leave room for the wrath of God;[c] for it is written, "Vengeance is mine, I will repay, says the Lord." [20] No, "if your enemies are hungry, feed them; if they are thirsty, give them something to drink; for by doing this you will heap burning coals on their heads." [21] Do not be overcome by evil, but overcome evil with good.

Being Subject to Authorities

13 Let every person be subject to the governing authorities; for there is no authority except from God, and those authorities that exist have been instituted by God. [2] Therefore whoever resists authority resists what God has appointed, and those who resist will incur judgment. [3] For rulers are not a terror to good conduct, but to bad. Do you wish to have no fear of the authority? Then do what is good, and you will receive its approval; [4] for it is God's servant for your good. But if you do what is wrong, you should be afraid, for the authority[d] does not bear the sword in vain! It is the servant of God to execute wrath on the wrongdoer. [5] Therefore one must be subject, not only because of wrath but also because of conscience. [6] For the same reason you also pay taxes, for the authorities are God's servants, busy with this very thing. [7] Pay to all what is due them—taxes to whom taxes are due, revenue to whom revenue is due, respect to whom respect is due, honor to whom honor is due.

Love for One Another

8 Owe no one anything, except to love one another; for the one who loves another has fulfilled the law. [9] The commandments, "You shall not commit adultery; You shall not murder; You shall not steal; You shall not covet"; and any other commandment, are summed up in this word, "Love your neighbor as yourself." [10] Love does no wrong to a neighbor; therefore, love is the fulfilling of the law.

An Urgent Appeal

11 Besides this, you know what time it is, how it is now the moment for you to

---

[a] Other ancient authorities read *serve the opportune time*   [b] Or *give yourselves to humble tasks*   [c] Gk *the wrath*   [d] Gk *it*

12:14–21—Paul's words about blessing persecutors may intentionally echo Jesus' teaching (Matt. 5:11–12, 43–48). The instruction about heaping **burning coals** (v. 20) recalls Prov. 25:21–22. Christians are to be peacemakers whenever possible. Plainly Paul's instructions do not cover the situations faced since his time by some Christians who have held political power or public office as police officers or judges.

13:1–7 Political Obligations

Paul counsels obedience without qualification to government authorities as a matter of conscience, since **there is no authority except from God** (v. 1). God works through even a government of nonbelievers to establish some justice and restrain evildoers (v. 4). Paul's words about paying **taxes** may allude to special revenue problems in Rome in his day (vv. 6–7). Revelation 13 takes a radically different view of government at a later time when representatives of the Roman Empire persecuted some Christians. Paul's teaching applies to more normal periods when governments do not pressure believers to violate their consciences.

13:8–10 Love One Another

Christians can and must fulfill the Mosaic law by loving their neighbors (see 8:4–8; Gal. 5:14).

13:11–14 The End Is Near

Paul assumes that the end of the world is near

wake from sleep. For salvation is nearer to us now than when we became believers; [12] the night is far gone, the day is near. Let us then lay aside the works of darkness and put on the armor of light; [13] let us live honorably as in the day, not in reveling and drunkenness, not in debauchery and licentiousness, not in quarreling and jealousy. [14] Instead, put on the Lord Jesus Christ, and make no provision for the flesh, to gratify its desires.

Do Not Judge Another

14 Welcome those who are weak in faith,[a] but not for the purpose of quarreling over opinions. [2] Some believe in eating anything, while the weak eat only vegetables. [3] Those who eat must not despise those who abstain, and those who abstain must not pass judgment on those who eat; for God has welcomed them. [4] Who are you to pass judgment on servants of another? It is before their own lord that they stand or fall. And they will be upheld, for the Lord[b] is able to make them stand.

[5] Some judge one day to be better than another, while others judge all days to be alike. Let all be fully convinced in their own minds. [6] Those who observe the day, observe it in honor of the Lord. Also those who eat, eat in honor of the Lord, since they give thanks to God; while those who abstain, abstain in honor of the Lord and give thanks to God.

[7] We do not live to ourselves, and we do not die to ourselves. [8] If we live, we live to the Lord, and if we die, we die to the Lord; so then, whether we live or whether we die, we are the Lord's. [9] For to this end Christ died and lived again, so that he might be Lord of both the dead and the living.

[10] Why do you pass judgment on your brother or sister?[c] Or you, why do you despise your brother or sister?[c] For we will all stand before the judgment seat of God.[d] [11] For it is written,

"As I live, says the Lord, every knee
    shall bow to me,
  and every tongue shall give praise
    to[e] God.'"

[12] So then, each of us will be accountable to God.[f]

Do Not Make Another Stumble

[13] Let us therefore no longer pass judgment on one another, but resolve instead never to put a stumbling block or hindrance in the way of another.[g] [14] I know and am persuaded in the Lord Jesus that nothing is unclean in itself; but it is unclean for anyone who thinks it unclean. [15] If your brother or sister[c] is

---

a Or *conviction* b Other ancient authorities read *for God* c Gk *brother* d Other ancient authorities read *of Christ* e Or *confess* f Other ancient authorities lack *to God* g Gk *of a brother*

(e.g., 1 Cor. 15:51–52). This makes it all the more urgent that believers live now wholly in accord with God's will (cf. 14:10–12), putting on (like clothing) their identification with Jesus Christ (cf. 6:3–11; 8:9–11; Gal. 2:20; 3:27) and repudiating immorality and injustice.

14:1–23 Distinguishing Essentials from Nonessentials

Serious disputes sometimes arise in churches over matters seemingly as minor as food and calendar observances (see Gal. 2:11–14; 1 Cor. 8, 10; Col. 2:16–23). Evidently Paul knows of strife in the Roman community between **weak** (14:1) believers, who insist on honoring certain days and practicing vegetarianism, and **strong** (15:1) ones, who reject such demands. Food issues might have been particularly important for Jewish Christians, though the law of Moses did not mandate vegetarianism (14:2). Paul particularly urges that the "strong" show love toward those who are "weak," lest they stumble in their faith.

14:5—When believers differ on such issues, each should act with sincerity (see also vv. 22–23)

14:7—A second fundamental principle is that believers belong to God and the Lord Jesus and hence should not live to please themselves or insist that their opinions are the only right ones.

14:15—A third principle is to pursue peace in the church by not judging or acting with regard to nonessentials like food and special days in a way that injures other members. Each new generation must learn to accept diversity within the church and to tolerate honest disagreements over personal and social values. Yet individual Christians and congregations must be true to what they believe to be God's will (vv. 22–23).

being injured by what you eat, you are no longer walking in love. Do not let what you eat cause the ruin of one for whom Christ died. [16] So do not let your good be spoken of as evil. [17] For the kingdom of God is not food and drink but righteousness and peace and joy in the Holy Spirit. [18] The one who thus serves Christ is acceptable to God and has human approval. [19] Let us then pursue what makes for peace and for mutual upbuilding. [20] Do not, for the sake of food, destroy the work of God. Everything is indeed clean, but it is wrong for you to make others fall by what you eat; [21] it is good not to eat meat or drink wine or do anything that makes your brother or sister[a] stumble.[b] [22] The faith that you have, have as your own conviction before God. Blessed are those who have no reason to condemn themselves because of what they approve. [23] But those who have doubts are condemned if they eat, because they do not act from faith;[c] for whatever does not proceed from faith[c] is sin.[d]

Please Others, Not Yourselves

15 We who are strong ought to put up with the failings of the weak, and not to please ourselves. [2] Each of us must please our neighbor for the good purpose of building up the neighbor. [3] For Christ did not please himself; but, as it is written, "The insults of those who insult you have fallen on me." [4] For whatever was written in former days was written for our instruction, so that by steadfastness and by the encouragement of the scriptures we might have hope. [5] May the God of steadfastness and encouragement grant you to live in harmony with one another, in accordance

with Christ Jesus, [6] so that together you may with one voice glorify the God and Father of our Lord Jesus Christ.

The Gospel for Jews and Gentiles Alike

7 Welcome one another, therefore, just as Christ has welcomed you, for the glory of God. [8] For I tell you that Christ has become a servant of the circumcised on behalf of the truth of God in order that he might confirm the promises given to the patriarchs, [9] and in order that the Gentiles might glorify God for his mercy. As it is written,

"Therefore I will confess[e] you among
     the Gentiles,
   and sing praises to your name";
[10] and again he says,
"Rejoice, O Gentiles, with his
     people";
[11] and again,
"Praise the Lord, all you Gentiles,
   and let all the peoples praise him";
[12] and again Isaiah says,
"The root of Jesse shall come,
   the one who rises to rule the
     Gentiles;
   in him the Gentiles shall hope."
[13] May the God of hope fill you with all joy and peace in believing, so that you may abound in hope by the power of the Holy Spirit.

Paul's Reason for Writing So Boldly

14 I myself feel confident about you, my brothers and sisters,[f] that you yourselves are full of goodness, filled with all knowledge, and able to instruct one another. [15] Nevertheless on some points I have written to you rather boldly by way of reminder, because of the grace

[a] Gk brother   [b] Other ancient authorities add *or be upset or be weakened*
[c] Or *conviction*   [d] Other authorities, some ancient, add here 16.25-27
[e] Or *thank*   [f] Gk *brothers*

15:1–13 Conclusion: Welcome One Other as Christ Welcomed You

Church members should treat one another with respect and love, just as Christ did not please himself but lived and died to confirm God's promises to Israel and extend salvation to Gentiles (vv. 9–11).

15:14–16:27 Plans and Greetings

15:14–33 Paul's Plans to Visit Jerusalem, Rome, and Spain

Paul explains his intention to extend his missionary labors to Spain, with preliminary visits to Jerusalem and Rome. He asks for the prayers and support of the Roman believers.

given me by God [16] to be a minister of Christ Jesus to the Gentiles in the priestly service of the gospel of God, so that the offering of the Gentiles may be acceptable, sanctified by the Holy Spirit. [17] In Christ Jesus, then, I have reason to boast of my work for God. [18] For I will not venture to speak of anything except what Christ has accomplished[a] through me to win obedience from the Gentiles, by word and deed, [19] by the power of signs and wonders, by the power of the Spirit of God,[b] so that from Jerusalem and as far around as Illyricum I have fully proclaimed the good news[c] of Christ. [20] Thus I make it my ambition to proclaim the good news,[c] not where Christ has already been named, so that I do not build on someone else's foundation, [21] but as it is written,

"Those who have never been told of
    him shall see,
and those who have never heard of
    him shall understand."

Paul's Plan to Visit Rome

22 This is the reason that I have so often been hindered from coming to you. [23] But now, with no further place for me in these regions, I desire, as I have for many years, to come to you [24] when I go to Spain. For I do hope to see you on my journey and to be sent on by you, once I have enjoyed your company for a little while. [25] At present, however, I am going to Jerusalem in a ministry to the saints; [26] for Macedonia and Achaia have been pleased to share

their resources with the poor among the saints at Jerusalem. [27] They were pleased to do this, and indeed they owe it to them; for if the Gentiles have come to share in their spiritual blessings, they ought also to be of service to them in material things. [28] So, when I have completed this, and have delivered to them what has been collected,[d] I will set out by way of you to Spain; [29] and I know that when I come to you, I will come in the fullness of the blessing[e] of Christ.

30 I appeal to you, brothers and sisters,[f] by our Lord Jesus Christ and by the love of the Spirit, to join me in earnest prayer to God on my behalf, [31] that I may be rescued from the unbelievers in Judea, and that my ministry[g] to Jerusalem may be acceptable to the saints, [32] so that by God's will I may come to you with joy and be refreshed in your company. [33] The God of peace be with all of you.[h] Amen.

Personal Greetings

16 I commend to you our sister Phoebe, a deacon[i] of the church at Cenchreae, [2] so that you may welcome her in the Lord as is fitting for the saints, and help her in whatever she may require from you, for she has been a benefactor of many and of myself as well.

3 Greet Prisca and Aquila, who work

[a] Gk speak of those things that Christ has not accomplished   [b] Other ancient authorities read of the Spirit or of the Holy Spirit   [c] Or gospel   [d] Gk have sealed to them this fruit   [e] Other ancient authorities add of the gospel   [f] Gk brothers   [g] Other ancient authorities read my bringing of a gift   [h] One ancient authority adds 16.25-27 here   [i] Or minister

---

15:16—Paul's apostleship is directed primarily to Gentiles, though he interprets this work as intrinsically linked with God's plan to save Israel (cf. vv. 8–12, 25–32; 1:16; 11:13–27).

15:25–28—Paul has organized a collection of money from various Gentile churches to benefit the Jewish Christians in Jerusalem, thereby demonstrating and encouraging Jewish-Gentile spiritual unity (see 1 Cor. 16:1–4; 2 Cor. 8–9; Gal. 2:10). Sharing financially with persons in need in and beyond one's local church is an indispensable expression of Christian love.

16:1–16 Greetings to Individuals

This is the longest set of personal greetings and

commendations in the Pauline letters. Churches are not faceless entities. They are made up of individuals whose faith decisions make a difference. Many of the persons Paul names are women, so this passage provides vital evidence of the importance of women as leaders in the churches of his time.

16:3–4 *Prisca and Aquila*—The first persons named are missionary associates of Paul (Acts 18:2, 18, 26; 1 Cor. 16:19; 2 Tim. 4:19). Since Prisca is named first, she probably was a more important leader than her husband.

with me in Christ Jesus, [4] and who risked their necks for my life, to whom not only I give thanks, but also all the churches of the Gentiles. [5] Greet also the church in their house. Greet my beloved Epaenetus, who was the first convert[a] in Asia for Christ. [6] Greet Mary, who has worked very hard among you. [7] Greet Andronicus and Junia,[b] my relatives[c] who were in prison with me; they are prominent among the apostles, and they were in Christ before I was. [8] Greet Ampliatus, my beloved in the Lord. [9] Greet Urbanus, our co-worker in Christ, and my beloved Stachys. [10] Greet Apelles, who is approved in Christ. Greet those who belong to the family of Aristobulus. [11] Greet my relative[d] Herodion. Greet those in the Lord who belong to the family of Narcissus. [12] Greet those workers in the Lord, Tryphaena and Tryphosa. Greet the beloved Persis, who has worked hard in the Lord. [13] Greet Rufus, chosen in the Lord; and greet his mother—a mother to me also. [14] Greet Asyncritus, Phlegon, Hermes, Patrobas, Hermas, and the brothers and sisters[e] who are with them. [15] Greet Philologus, Julia, Nereus and his sister, and Olympas, and all the saints who are with them. [16] Greet one another with a holy kiss. All the churches of Christ greet you.

Final Instructions

17 I urge you, brothers and sisters,[e] to keep an eye on those who cause dissensions and offenses, in opposition to the teaching that you have learned; avoid them. [18] For such people do not serve our Lord Christ, but their own appetites,[f]

and by smooth talk and flattery they deceive the hearts of the simple-minded. [19] For while your obedience is known to all, so that I rejoice over you, I want you to be wise in what is good and guileless in what is evil. [20] The God of peace will shortly crush Satan under your feet. The grace of our Lord Jesus Christ be with you.[g]

21 Timothy, my co-worker, greets you; so do Lucius and Jason and Sosipater, my relatives.[c]

22 I Tertius, the writer of this letter, greet you in the Lord.[h]

23 Gaius, who is host to me and to the whole church, greets you. Erastus, the city treasurer, and our brother Quartus, greet you.[i]

Final Doxology

25 Now to God[j] who is able to strengthen you according to my gospel and the proclamation of Jesus Christ, according to the revelation of the mystery that was kept secret for long ages [26] but is now disclosed, and through the prophetic writings is made known to all the Gentiles, according to the command of the eternal God, to bring about the obedience of faith— [27] to the only wise God, through Jesus Christ, to whom[k] be the glory forever! Amen.[l]

[a] Gk first fruits   [b] Or Junias; other ancient authorities read Julia
[c] Or compatriots   [d] Or compatriot   [e] Gk brothers   [f] Gk their own belly
[g] Other ancient authorities lack this sentence   [h] Or I Tertius, writing this letter in the Lord, greet you   [i] Other ancient authorities add verse 24, The grace of our Lord Jesus Christ be with all of you. Amen.   [j] Gk the one   [k] Other ancient authorities lack to whom. The verse then reads, to the only wise God be the glory through Jesus Christ forever. Amen.   [l] Other ancient authorities lack 16.25-27 or include it after 14.23 or 15.33; others put verse 24 after verse 27

16:7—Junia is a woman's name. She is the only woman given the title "apostle" in the New Testament.

16:17–20 Warning against Unspecified False Teachers

16:21–23 Greetings from Paul's Co-workers

16:23—Since he was able to host Paul and prob-

ably the entire Corinthian church, Gaius must be a person of comparatively high status and wealth. The same must be true of Erastus, the city treasurer.

16:25–27 Closing Doxology

Discrepancies among the manuscripts suggest that a later writer added this doxology.

The Book of
1 CORINTHIANS

Corinth was a major commercial center located on the isthmus between the northern and southern parts of Greece. Paul himself founded the Christian community there. Acts 18:12 mentions that Gallio was the local governor when Paul was in the city, and the modern discovery of an inscription naming Gallio indicates that Paul's first visit to Corinth was probably in 51 or 52 CE. Most of the Corinthian believers were former pagans (1 Cor. 12:2). Nonetheless, Paul frequently argues on the basis of the Jewish Scriptures, implying that members of the Corinthian church know and revere them. While some of the Corinthian believers were relatively wealthy or of high social status (see Rom. 16:23), most were not (1 Cor. 1:26).

The letter illustrates Paul's sense of responsibility for the churches he founded, and his methods of staying in contact with them. After founding the church in Corinth and moving on to other places, he remained in touch, partly through return visits of his own, partly through visits by authorized associates, and partly through letters. He has written an earlier letter we do not have, which the Corinthians misunderstood (5:9). The church has sent at least one letter requesting his guidance (e.g., 7:1), and Paul has received reports especially from "Chloe's people" about other problems and church divisions (1:11). First Corinthians must have been written around 55 CE, when Paul was making final arrangements for funds his Gentile churches had collected to be sent to Jerusalem (16:1–4). Probably Paul writes from Ephesus (16:8). He anticipates making a lengthy return visit to Corinth (16:7) and apparently has no inkling of major rebellions against his authority. Yet he is unsure how the church will receive his co-worker Timothy (16:10–11), whose visit is probably meant to prepare the way for Paul's.

First Corinthians is a unified letter addressing a remarkable variety of issues, some touching on the interface between believers and nonbelievers. There are factions within the church identifying themselves with different missionary leaders (Paul, Apollos, Cephas [Peter], 1:12). Some in the church promote sexual license (5:1; 6:15–16); others think believers should avoid sexual relationships altogether (7:1). There are questions about divorce and widows who want to remarry (7:8–16). Some in the church have no qualms about eating food associated with pagan gods, while others feel contaminated by it (8:1–7; 10:19–33). There are conflicts about church worship in relation to woman prophets (11:2–16), the Lord's Supper (11:17–34), and the diversity of gifts and offices in the church (chaps. 12–14). Chapter 15 indicates that some church members were skeptical about resurrection.

The letter shows an overall concern to heal divisions among the Corinthian believers. Associated with those divisions were claims of at least some that they had attained to extraordinary heights of spiritual wisdom and maturity (3:18). Perhaps they imagined they were already living a kind of heavenly existence (4:8). Paul affirms that the Corinthians have indeed received all kinds of spiritual gifts (1:7; chaps. 12 and

14). Yet he deflates their euphoria by warning that the present order of things is transitory (7:29–31) and that the fullness of salvation will come only in the future (e.g., 1:7–8; 4:5; 6:2; 13:10; 15:20–28).

Modern readers are likely to find many of the specific problems addressed in the letter and some of Paul's solutions dated and irrelevant. How many of today's church members would defend incest or prostitution or, by contrast, notions that all sexual activity is sinful? How many worry about appeals to secular courts, meat offered to idols, women's head coverings, and speaking in tongues? Paul's arguments based on assuming that the world's end is very near (7:29–31; 15:51), his confident pronouncements about proper hairstyles for men and women (11:13–15), and some of his other judgments may impress moderns as merely interesting.

On the other hand, congregational conflicts are still all too common, and we still struggle with defining sexual responsibility, religious authority, appropriate standards for worship (including the question of women's leadership in worship), and how to affirm life after death without becoming irresponsibly otherworldly. Most of Paul's principles have continuing power to inspire or stimulate, even if all of his concrete "answers" cannot be simplistically appropriated. Above all, what he has to say about love in chapter 13 is so imbued with the spirit of Jesus that it has probably influenced more thinking about Christian ethics than any other passage in the Bible outside the Gospels.

Paul envisions the church as an "alternative society," a very self-conscious minority group living by distinctive standards, yet not turning its back on the outside world. Pagan religiosity is sternly rejected, but some believers have pagan spouses, and non-Christians apparently are made welcome even in worship services. The church is no perfectionist utopia, but a community of fallible persons called to model both freedom and holiness, both humility and confidence, both tolerance of differences and such a unified articulation of truth that the conscience of a visiting outsider might lead her to confess "God is really among you" (14:25).

Above all, Paul seeks to interpret the wisdom of God revealed in Christ (1:30). The Corinthians know the basic apostolic message and possess outstanding spiritual gifts, but they lack humility and insight into the bearing of that wisdom on their own circumstances and decisions. Often a brief but telling reference to Christ is found at the heart of a chapter or argument (e.g. 1:17; 2:2; 3:11; 4:5; 5:7; 6:20; 7:35; 8:11; 9:12; 10:21; 11:23–27; 12:3; 15:3–5, 20–28, 45–49; 16:22). The unity and peace of the church require that believers hold fast to Christ and demonstrate maturity when new problems arise (3:1–4; 10:15; 11:13; 14:20; 15:34).

—David Hay

Salutation

1 Paul, called to be an apostle of Christ Jesus by the will of God, and our brother Sosthenes,

2 To the church of God that is in Corinth, to those who are sanctified in Christ Jesus, called to be saints, together with all those who in every place call on the name of our Lord Jesus Christ, both their Lord*a* and ours:

3 Grace to you and peace from God our Father and the Lord Jesus Christ.

4 I give thanks to my*b* God always for you because of the grace of God that has been given you in Christ Jesus, *5* for in every way you have been enriched in him, in speech and knowledge of every kind— *6* just as the testimony of*c* Christ has been strengthened among you— *7* so that you are not lacking in any spiritual gift as you wait for the revealing of our Lord Jesus Christ. *8* He will also strengthen you to the end, so that you may be blameless on the day of our Lord Jesus Christ. *9* God is faithful; by him you were called into the fellowship of his Son, Jesus Christ our Lord.

Divisions in the Church

10 Now I appeal to you, brothers and sisters,*d* by the name of our Lord Jesus Christ, that all of you be in agreement and that there be no divisions among you, but that you be united in the same mind and the same purpose. *11* For it has been reported to me by Chloe's people that there are quarrels among you, my brothers and sisters.*e* *12* What I mean is that each of you says, "I belong to Paul," or "I belong to Apollos," or "I belong to Cephas," or "I belong to Christ." *13* Has Christ been divided? Was Paul crucified for you? Or were you baptized in the name of Paul? *14* I thank God*f* that I baptized none of you except Crispus and Gaius, *15* so that no one can say that you were baptized in my name. *16* (I did baptize also the household of Stephanas; beyond that, I do not know whether I baptized anyone else.) *17* For Christ did not send me to baptize but to proclaim the gospel, and not with eloquent wisdom, so that the cross of Christ might not be emptied of its power.

Christ the Power and Wisdom of God

18 For the message about the cross is foolishness to those who are perishing, but to us who are being saved it is the power of God. *19* For it is written,

"I will destroy the wisdom of the
    wise,
   and the discernment of the
     discerning I will thwart."

20 Where is the one who is wise? Where is the scribe? Where is the debater of this age? Has not God made foolish the wisdom of the world? *21* For since, in the wisdom of God, the world did not know God through wisdom, God decided, through the foolishness of our proclamation, to save those who believe. *22* For Jews demand signs and Greeks desire

---

a Gk theirs   *b* Other ancient authorities lack *my*   *c* Or *to*   *d* Gk brothers   *e* Gk *my brothers*   *f* Other ancient authorities read *I am thankful*

1:1–10 Letter Opening

1:4–9—This paragraph of thanksgiving emphasizes that, while the Corinthians already are blessed with all kinds of spiritual gifts, they remain dependent on God.

1:10 *That you be united in the same mind and the same purpose*—Paul announces the major theme of the letter: church unity, despite differences in individual gifts and opinions.

1:11–4:21 Church Divisions

1:11–17 Divisions Based on Loyalty to Various Leaders

1:12—*Apollos* was a Christian missionary who came from Alexandria (Acts 18:24; 19:1; Titus 3:13) and had gained a strong following in Corinth (1 Cor. 3:4–6, 22; 4:6; 16:12). *Cephas* or Peter (see note at Gal. 1:18–19) was also well known to the church (see 1 Cor. 3:22; 9:5; 15:5). On Paul's perspective, see also 3:1–4.

1:18–2:16 The Divine Wisdom in Christ's Cross

God's wisdom revealed in Christ's cross undercuts any claims to wisdom that might encourage some believers to feel superior to others.

1:22–23—*Jews* and *Greeks* are here conceived of as the two basic groups comprising humanity (as in Rom. 1:16).

wisdom, 23 but we proclaim Christ cru-cified, a stumbling block to Jews and foolishness to Gentiles, 24 but to those who are the called, both Jews and Greeks, Christ the power of God and the wisdom of God. 25 For God's foolish-ness is wiser than human wisdom, and God's weakness is stronger than human strength.

26 Consider your own call, brothers and sisters:ª not many of you were wise by human standards,ᵇ not many were powerful, not many were of noble birth. 27 But God chose what is foolish in the world to shame the wise; God chose what is weak in the world to shame the strong; 28 God chose what is low and despised in the world, things that are not, to reduce to nothing things that are, 29 so that no oneᶜ might boast in the pres-ence of God. 30 He is the source of your life in Christ Jesus, who became for us wisdom from God, and righteousness and sanctification and redemption, 31 in order that, as it is written, "Let the one who boasts, boast inᵈ the Lord."

Proclaiming Christ Crucified

2 When I came to you, brothers and sisters,ª I did not come proclaim-ing the mysteryᵉ of God to you in lofty words or wisdom. 2 For I decided to know nothing among you except Jesus Christ, and him crucified. 3 And I came to you in weakness and in fear and in much trembling. 4 My speech and my proclamation were not with plausible words of wisdom,ᶠ but with a demon-stration of the Spirit and of power, 5 so that your faith might rest not on human wisdom but on the power of God.

The True Wisdom of God

6 Yet among the mature we do speak wisdom, though it is not a wisdom of this age or of the rulers of this age, who are doomed to perish. 7 But we speak God's wisdom, secret and hidden, which God decreed before the ages for our glory. 8 None of the rulers of this age understood this; for if they had, they would not have crucified the Lord of glory. 9 But, as it is written,

"What no eye has seen,
　nor ear heard, nor the human
　　heart conceived,
what God has prepared for those
　who love him"—

10 these things God has revealed to us through the Spirit; for the Spirit searches everything, even the depths of God. 11 For what human being knows what is truly human except the human spirit that is within? So also no one comprehends what is truly God's except the Spirit of God. 12 Now we have received not the spirit of the world, but the Spirit that is from God, so that we may understand

ª Gk brothers ᵇ Gk according to the flesh ᶜ Gk no flesh ᵈ Or of ᵉ Other ancient authorities read testimony ᶠ Other ancient authorities read the persuasiveness of wisdom

---

1:24 *Christ the power of God and the wisdom of God*—Paul begins his main argument by asserting that the crucified Christ is the key to understanding God's way of salvation (cf. Rom. 3:21–31; 2 Cor. 5:14–16; John 1:18).

1:26—Most of the Corinthian Christians were not "high class" by worldly standards. This should make them not ashamed but thankful for God's amazing grace. Those who know that God has established a personal relationship with them (v. 9) will not be obsessed with outward prestige and success.

2:2—Jesus' death as the essential expression of God's love was central to Paul's mission-ary preaching (e.g., 11:23–26; 15:3–5; 2 Cor. 5:14–21; Rom. 5:6–8, 8:31–39; Gal. 2:20). Much of this letter aims at helping believers discern

how they should respond to God's love by loving other persons with insight and humility (cf. 4:21; 8:1; 13:1–14:1; 16:14).

2:5 *So that your faith might rest not on human wisdom but on the power of God*—Faith should not be tied to the personal qualities of preachers.

2:8—By *rulers of this age*, Paul probably means human rulers like Pilate and perhaps supernatural powers influencing them. Despite Rom. 13:1–7, Paul assumes that political authorities can be spiritually blind.

2:9 *As it is written*—Christian wisdom hopes for a life of unimaginable glory after death (13:12; cf. Isa. 64:4; 52:15).

2:10–16—All Christians have received true wis-dom from God.

the gifts bestowed on us by God. ¹³ And we speak of these things in words not taught by human wisdom but taught by the Spirit, interpreting spiritual things to those who are spiritual.ᵃ

14 Those who are unspiritualᵇ do not receive the gifts of God's Spirit, for they are foolishness to them, and they are unable to understand them because they are spiritually discerned. ¹⁵ Those who are spiritual discern all things, and they are themselves subject to no one else's scrutiny.

¹⁶ "For who has known the mind of the Lord

so as to instruct him?"

But we have the mind of Christ.

On Divisions in the Corinthian Church

3 And so, brothers and sisters,ᶜ I could not speak to you as spiritual people, but rather as people of the flesh, as infants in Christ. ² I fed you with milk, not solid food, for you were not ready for solid food. Even now you are still not ready, ³ for you are still of the flesh. For as long as there is jealousy and quarreling among you, are you not of the flesh, and behaving according to human inclinations? ⁴ For when one says, "I belong to Paul," and another, "I belong to Apollos," are you not merely human?

5 What then is Apollos? What is Paul? Servants through whom you came to believe, as the Lord assigned to each. ⁶ I planted, Apollos watered, but God gave the growth. ⁷ So neither the one who plants nor the one who waters is anything, but only God who gives the growth. ⁸ The one who plants and the one who waters have a common purpose, and each will receive wages according to the labor of each. ⁹ For we are God's servants, working together; you are God's field, God's building.

10 According to the grace of God given to me, like a skilled master builder I laid a foundation, and someone else is building on it. Each builder must choose with care how to build on it. ¹¹ For no one can lay any foundation other than the one that has been laid; that foundation is Jesus Christ. ¹² Now if anyone builds on the foundation with gold, silver, precious stones, wood, hay, straw— ¹³ the work of each builder will become visible, for the Day will disclose it, because it will be revealed with fire, and the fire will test what sort of work each has done. ¹⁴ If what has been built on the foundation survives, the builder will receive a reward. ¹⁵ If the work is burned up, the builder will suffer loss; the builder will be saved, but only as through fire.

16 Do you not know that you are God's temple and that God's Spirit dwells in you?ᵈ ¹⁷ If anyone destroys God's temple, God will destroy that person. For God's temple is holy, and you are that temple.

18 Do not deceive yourselves. If you think that you are wise in this age, you should become fools so that you may become wise. ¹⁹ For the wisdom of this world is foolishness with God. For it is written,

"He catches the wise in their craftiness,"

ᵃ Or *interpreting spiritual things in spiritual language,* or *comparing spiritual things with spiritual*   ᵇ Or *natural*   ᶜ Gk *brothers*   ᵈ In verses 16 and 17 the Greek word for *you* is plural

---

2:16 *The mind of Christ*—The church might be defined as the community of those who truly know Christ, the Spirit, and God the Father because they have accepted the message about the cross (1:5, 18; cf. Phil. 2:5). Paul does not say, however, that any Christians have total knowledge (13:8–12).

3:1–23 Divisions in the Church

3:1–4—Taking sides around one church leader or another is proof of immaturity, not of wisdom.

3:5–15—Christ is the *foundation* (v. 11) of all church growth and development. What will count in the end is how God, judging by the standard of the crucified Christ, assesses the work of everyone who has labored for the fellowship of believers.

3:16–23—The church must realize that it is the holy community of *God's Spirit* (v. 16; cf. 6:19). Members' only concern should be to discover and respond to God's will.

20 and again,

"The Lord knows the thoughts of the
wise,
that they are futile."

21 So let no one boast about human leaders. For all things are yours, 22 whether Paul or Apollos or Cephas or the world or life or death or the present or the future—all belong to you, 23 and you belong to Christ, and Christ belongs to God.

The Ministry of the Apostles

4 Think of us in this way, as servants of Christ and stewards of God's mysteries. 2 Moreover, it is required of stewards that they be found trustworthy. 3 But with me it is a very small thing that I should be judged by you or by any human court. I do not even judge myself. 4 I am not aware of anything against myself, but I am not thereby acquitted. It is the Lord who judges me. 5 Therefore do not pronounce judgment before the time, before the Lord comes, who will bring to light the things now hidden in darkness and will disclose the purposes of the heart. Then each one will receive commendation from God.

6 I have applied all this to Apollos and myself for your benefit, brothers and sisters,a so that you may learn through us the meaning of the saying, "Nothing beyond what is written," so that none of you will be puffed up in favor of one

against another. 7 For who sees anything different in you?b What do you have that you did not receive? And if you received it, why do you boast as if it were not a gift?

8 Already you have all you want! Already you have become rich! Quite apart from us you have become kings! Indeed, I wish that you had become kings, so that we might be kings with you! 9 For I think that God has exhibited us apostles as last of all, as though sentenced to death, because we have become a spectacle to the world, to angels and to mortals. 10 We are fools for the sake of Christ, but you are wise in Christ. We are weak, but you are strong. You are held in honor, but we in disrepute. 11 To the present hour we are hungry and thirsty, we are poorly clothed and beaten and homeless, 12 and we grow weary from the work of our own hands. When reviled, we bless; when persecuted, we endure; 13 when slandered, we speak kindly. We have become like the rubbish of the world, the dregs of all things, to this very day.

Fatherly Admonition

14 I am not writing this to make you ashamed, but to admonish you as my beloved children. 15 For though you might have ten thousand guardians in Christ, you do not have many fathers. Indeed, in Christ Jesus I became your

a Gk brothers   b Or Who makes you different from another?

3:21 *All things are yours*—Because they *belong to Christ* (v. 23) and God, believers have dominion over all things (cf. Gen. 1:28; Ps. 8:6–8; Rom. 8:37–39). They are also set free from absolutizing any human authority.

4:1–7 All Persons Are under God's Judgment

Ministers like Paul and Apollos are simply *stewards* of the divine *mysteries*. Believers should avoid pronouncing God's judgment on other people.

4:7 *What do you have that you did not receive?*—Divine grace, not human achievement, accounts for the wealth of spiritual gifts church members enjoy (1:4–7). Such gifts are no basis for boasting or divisiveness.

4:8–21 An Appeal to Accept Paul's Leadership

4:8–13—This description of Paul's seeming foolishness and genuine suffering, in ironic contrast to the apparent "success" of the Corinthian church, recalls what was said about the message of the cross (1:17–25). Christians should be suspicious of preachers who say God wants them to concentrate on pursuing outward success and material prosperity.

4:14–21—Paul as the founder of the Corinthian church claims a unique right to guide its members in Christ's ways. Faithful ministers must teach and warn, and their congregations must have the humility to listen.

father through the gospel. [16] I appeal to you, then, be imitators of me. [17] For this reason I sent[a] you Timothy, who is my beloved and faithful child in the Lord, to remind you of my ways in Christ Jesus, as I teach them everywhere in every church. [18] But some of you, thinking that I am not coming to you, have become arrogant. [19] But I will come to you soon, if the Lord wills, and I will find out not the talk of these arrogant people but their power. [20] For the kingdom of God depends not on talk but on power. [21] What would you prefer? Am I to come to you with a stick, or with love in a spirit of gentleness?

Sexual Immorality Defiles the Church

5 It is actually reported that there is sexual immorality among you, and of a kind that is not found even among pagans; for a man is living with his father's wife. [2] And you are arrogant! Should you not rather have mourned, so that he who has done this would have been removed from among you?

3 For though absent in body, I am present in spirit; and as if present I have already pronounced judgment [4] in the name of the Lord Jesus on the man who has done such a thing.[b] When you are assembled, and my spirit is present with the power of our Lord Jesus, [5] you are to hand this man over to Satan for the destruction of the flesh, so that his spirit may be saved in the day of the Lord.[c]

6 Your boasting is not a good thing. Do you not know that a little yeast leavens the whole batch of dough? [7] Clean out the old yeast so that you may be a new batch, as you really are unleavened. For our paschal lamb, Christ, has been sacrificed. [8] Therefore, let us celebrate the festival, not with the old yeast, the yeast of malice and evil, but with the unleavened bread of sincerity and truth.

Sexual Immorality Must Be Judged

9 I wrote to you in my letter not to associate with sexually immoral persons— [10] not at all meaning the immoral of this world, or the greedy and robbers, or idolaters, since you would then need to go out of the world. [11] But now I am writing to you not to associate with anyone who bears the name of brother or sister[d] who is sexually immoral or greedy, or is an idolater, reviler, drunkard, or robber. Do not even eat with such a one. [12] For what have I to do with judging those outside? Is it not those who are inside that you are to judge? [13] God will judge those outside. "Drive out the wicked person from among you."

[a] Or am sending   [b] Or on the man who has done such a thing in the name of the Lord Jesus   [c] Other ancient authorities add Jesus   [d] Gk brother

---

5:1–7:40 Sexual and Legal Controversies Related to Boundaries between the Church and the Outside World

5:1–13 A Case of Incest and the Problem of Church Purity

Paul has learned that someone in the congregation is in a sexual relationship with his stepmother (*his father's wife*, v. 1). Such behavior violated the moral standards of both pagans and Jews (see Lev. 18:8).

5:2—Paul is particularly incensed because Corinthian believers proudly tolerate this incestuous behavior. They evidently interpret Christian freedom to mean anything goes. Paul has a very different view (cf. 6:12; 8:9; 10:29; Gal. 5:1, 13).

5:3–5—Paul insists that the man practicing incest cannot remain in the church. Verse 5 is unclear on how the man's expulsion will lead to his physical death, but it clearly expresses Paul's hope for the man's ultimate salvation at God's final judgment. Like Acts 5:1–11, this passage stresses the necessity of truthfulness within the community of faith. Churches continue to wrestle with defining the boundary between acceptable and unacceptable behavior.

5:6–8—As the Jewish Passover, with its lamb and unleavened bread, recalled the liberation of Israelite slaves from Egypt (see 10:1–11), Christ's sacrificial death brought freedom or redemption to all believers (cf. 1:30; 6:20; 7:22–23). *Yeast* here is a symbol of moral corruption, which the church must avoid.

5:9–13—Paul clarifies a statement he had made in an earlier letter. Believers must live with holiness and integrity, but they are not to avoid non-Christians (cf. Matt. 5:16).

Lawsuits among Believers

6 When any of you has a grievance against another, do you dare to take it to court before the unrighteous, instead of taking it before the saints? ²Do you not know that the saints will judge the world? And if the world is to be judged by you, are you incompetent to try trivial cases? ³Do you not know that we are to judge angels—to say nothing of ordinary matters? ⁴If you have ordinary cases, then, do you appoint as judges those who have no standing in the church? ⁵I say this to your shame. Can it be that there is no one among you wise enough to decide between one believer*a* and another, ⁶but a believer*a* goes to court against a believer*a*—and before unbelievers at that?

7 In fact, to have lawsuits at all with one another is already a defeat for you. Why not rather be wronged? Why not rather be defrauded? ⁸But you yourselves wrong and defraud—and believers*b* at that.

9 Do you not know that wrongdoers will not inherit the kingdom of God? Do not be deceived! Fornicators, idolaters, adulterers, male prostitutes, sodomites, ¹⁰thieves, the greedy, drunkards, revilers, robbers—none of these will inherit the kingdom of God. ¹¹And this is what some of you used to be. But you were washed, you were sanctified, you were justified in the name of the Lord Jesus Christ and in the Spirit of our God.

Glorify God in Body and Spirit

12 "All things are lawful for me," but not all things are beneficial. "All things are lawful for me," but I will not be dominated by anything. ¹³"Food is meant for the stomach and the stomach for food,"*c* and God will destroy both one and the other. The body is meant not for fornication but for the Lord, and the Lord for the body. ¹⁴And God raised the Lord and will also raise us by his power. ¹⁵Do you not know that your bodies are members of Christ? Should I therefore take the members of Christ and make them members of a prostitute? Never! ¹⁶Do you not know that whoever is united to a prostitute becomes one body with her? For it is said, "The two shall be one flesh." ¹⁷But anyone united to the Lord becomes one spirit with him. ¹⁸Shun fornication! Every sin that a person commits is outside the body; but the fornicator sins against the body itself. ¹⁹Or do you not know that your body is a temple*d* of the Holy Spirit within you, which you have from God, and that you are not your own? ²⁰For you were bought with a price; therefore glorify God in your body.

a Gk brother *b* Gk brothers *c* The quotation may extend to the word other *d* Or sanctuary

---

6:1–11 A Second Problem Area: Christians Suing One Another in Pagan Courts

6:2—Paul anticipates that believers will take part in God's final judgment (cf. Matt. 19:28). They should be capable of resolving disputes within the church community.

6:7—Christians should not lightly appeal to the power of governmental courts to pursue claims against others, even when the courts are in "Christian" nations and even when they believe their claims are justified.

6:9–11 Believers are called to purity—Paul conceives of the church as a kind of hospital for recovering sinners. Some of the Corinthian believers formerly practiced the particular vices listed in vv. 9–10 (cf. Rom. 1:29–31 and Gal. 5:19–21), but all Christians have sinned and all have been **washed** and purified through Christ (6:11; 15:3; 2 Cor. 5:19). The terms translated *male prostitutes* and *sodomites* may refer to passive and active partners in male homosexual activity, but scholars still debate their meanings. Cf. Rom. 1:26–27.

6:12–20 A Third Problem Area: Believers Using Prostitutes

6:12 *"All things are lawful for me"*—Paul quotes a slogan evidently popular with some Corinthian believers. Apparently they tended to compartmentalize their religion, supposing it had nothing to do with their bodily activities, particularly sexual relationships.

6:15—The physical bodies of believers belong to Christ and are *temples of the Holy Spirit* (see v. 19 and 3:17). Sexual choices matter.

Directions concerning Marriage

7 Now concerning the matters about which you wrote: "It is well for a man not to touch a woman." ² But because of cases of sexual immorality, each man should have his own wife and each woman her own husband. ³ The husband should give to his wife her conjugal rights, and likewise the wife to her husband. ⁴ For the wife does not have authority over her own body, but the husband does; likewise the husband does not have authority over his own body, but the wife does. ⁵ Do not deprive one another except perhaps by agreement for a set time, to devote yourselves to prayer, and then come together again, so that Satan may not tempt you because of your lack of self-control. ⁶ This I say by way of concession, not of command. ⁷ I wish that all were as I myself am. But each has a particular gift from God, one having one kind and another a different kind.

8 To the unmarried and the widows I say that it is well for them to remain unmarried as I am. ⁹ But if they are not practicing self-control, they should marry. For it is better to marry than to be aflame with passion.

10 To the married I give this command—not I but the Lord—that the wife should not separate from her husband ¹¹ (but if she does separate, let her remain unmarried or else be reconciled to her husband), and that the husband should not divorce his wife.

12 To the rest I say—I and not the Lord—that if any believer[a] has a wife who is an unbeliever, and she consents to live with him, he should not divorce her. ¹³ And if any woman has a husband who is an unbeliever, and he consents to live with her, she should not divorce him. ¹⁴ For the unbelieving husband is made holy through his wife, and the unbelieving wife is made holy through her husband. Otherwise, your children would be unclean, but as it is, they are holy. ¹⁵ But if the unbelieving partner separates, let it be so; in such a case the brother or sister is not bound. It is to peace that God has called you.[b] ¹⁶ Wife, for all you know, you might save your husband. Husband, for all you know, you might save your wife.

The Life that the Lord Has Assigned

17 However that may be, let each of you lead the life that the Lord has assigned, to which God called you. This is my rule in all the churches. ¹⁸ Was anyone at the time of his call already circumcised? Let him not seek to remove the marks of circumcision. Was anyone at the time of his call uncircumcised? Let him not seek circumcision. ¹⁹ Circumcision is nothing, and uncircumcision is nothing; but

[a] Gk brother   [b] Other ancient authorities read *us*

7:1–9 Sexuality within Marriage

7:1 *"It is well for a man not to touch a woman."*—Paul refers to a letter the Corinthian church sent to him and quotes a slogan popular with some of its members. They were inclined to consider all sexual activity sinful.

7:2–4—Paul indicates that sex within marriage is a good safeguard against sin (cf. v. 9). Given the usual assumptions of male domination in the Greco-Roman world, vv. 2–4 are remarkable for addressing wives and husbands as equals (cf. vv. 10–11, 12–16, 32–35).

7:7—Paul would prefer that everyone were celibate like himself, but celibacy demands a capacity for self-control that God does not give to everyone (including apostles—cf. 9:5). Both marriage and the single life are legitimate choices

for believers, who should seek to recognize their individual gifts.

7:10–16 Separation and Divorce

7:10—One of Paul's rare direct references to the teaching of Jesus (see Mark 10:1–12; Luke 16:18; Matt. 5:31–32; 19:3–9; cf. 1 Cor. 9:14).

7:12–16—Paul permits divorce in the case of a religiously mixed marriage when the non-Christian spouse wants to end it. He points out that Jesus did not say this (implying that he does not consider Jesus' rejection of divorce to be a rigid law for the church).

7:17–24 The Life that the Lord Has Assigned

Christian conversion and serving God do not depend on a person's social position (cf. vv. 26–27).

obeying the commandments of God is everything. ²⁰ Let each of you remain in the condition in which you were called.

21 Were you a slave when called? Do not be concerned about it. Even if you can gain your freedom, make use of your present condition now more than ever.ᵃ ²² For whoever was called in the Lord as a slave is a freed person belonging to the Lord, just as whoever was free when called is a slave of Christ. ²³ You were bought with a price; do not become slaves of human masters. ²⁴ In whatever condition you were called, brothers and sisters,ᵇ there remain with God.

The Unmarried and the Widows

25 Now concerning virgins, I have no command of the Lord, but I give my opinion as one who by the Lord's mercy is trustworthy. ²⁶ I think that, in view of the impendingᶜ crisis, it is well for you to remain as you are. ²⁷ Are you bound to a wife? Do not seek to be free. Are you free from a wife? Do not seek a wife. ²⁸ But if you marry, you do not sin, and if a virgin marries, she does not sin. Yet those who marry will experience distress in this life,ᵈ and I would spare you that. ²⁹ I mean, brothers and sisters,ᵇ the appointed time has grown short; from now on, let even those who have wives be as though they had none, ³⁰ and those who mourn as though they were not mourning, and those who rejoice as though they were not rejoicing, and those who buy as though they had no possessions, ³¹ and those who deal with the world as though they had no deal-

ings with it. For the present form of this world is passing away.

32 I want you to be free from anxieties. The unmarried man is anxious about the affairs of the Lord, how to please the Lord; ³³ but the married man is anxious about the affairs of the world, how to please his wife, ³⁴ and his interests are divided. And the unmarried woman and the virgin are anxious about the affairs of the Lord, so that they may be holy in body and spirit; but the married woman is anxious about the affairs of the world, how to please her husband. ³⁵ I say this for your own benefit, not to put any restraint upon you, but to promote good order and unhindered devotion to the Lord.

36 If anyone thinks that he is not behaving properly toward his fiancée,ᵉ if his passions are strong, and so it has to be, let him marry as he wishes; it is no sin. Let them marry. ³⁷ But if someone stands firm in his resolve, being under no necessity but having his own desire under control, and has determined in his own mind to keep her as his fiancée,ᵉ he will do well. ³⁸ So then, he who marries his fiancéeᵉ does well; and he who refrains from marriage will do better.

39 A wife is bound as long as her husband lives. But if the husband dies,ᶠ she is free to marry anyone she wishes, only in the Lord. ⁴⁰ But in my judgment she is more blessed if she remains as she is. And I think that I too have the Spirit of God.

ᵃ Or avail yourself of the opportunity ᵇ Gk brothers ᶜ Or present ᵈ Gk in the flesh ᵉ Gk virgin ᶠ Gk falls asleep

---

7:21 *Make use of your present condition*—The language is ambiguous. Paul may mean that Christian slaves should use any opportunity they have to gain their freedom, or he may mean that they should serve God despite their condition as slaves.

7:25–40 Marriage Is Good but Celibacy Is Better

Paul argues that single Christians should not seek marriage in view of the near end of the world (vv. 29–31). Marital responsibilities create divided loyalties.

7:32–35—Paul distinguishes sharply between serving the Lord and a marriage partner. He does not consider the possibility that husbands and wives might serve God by caring for one another.

7:36–38—This much-discussed passage may allude to a special Corinthian institution of "spiritual marriage" in which persons were married and lived together without sexual relations (cf. v. 1). Or it may refer to couples who became engaged but did not marry and remained sexually inactive.

Food Offered to Idols

8 Now concerning food sacrificed to idols: we know that "all of us possess knowledge." Knowledge puffs up, but love builds up. [2] Anyone who claims to know something does not yet have the necessary knowledge; [3] but anyone who loves God is known by him.

[4] Hence, as to the eating of food offered to idols, we know that "no idol in the world really exists," and that "there is no God but one." [5] Indeed, even though there may be so-called gods in heaven or on earth—as in fact there are many gods and many lords— [6] yet for us there is one God, the Father, from whom are all things and for whom we exist, and one Lord, Jesus Christ, through whom are all things and through whom we exist.

[7] It is not everyone, however, who has this knowledge. Since some have become so accustomed to idols until now, they still think of the food they eat as food offered to an idol; and their conscience, being weak, is defiled. [8] "Food will not bring us close to God."[a] We are no worse off if we do not eat, and no better off if we do. [9] But take care that this liberty of yours does not somehow become a stumbling block to the weak. [10] For if others see you, who possess knowledge, eating in the temple of an idol, might they not, since their conscience is weak, be encouraged to the point of eating food sacrificed to idols? [11] So by your knowledge those weak believers for whom Christ died are destroyed.[b] [12] But when you thus sin against members of your family,[c] and wound their conscience when it is weak, you sin against Christ. [13] Therefore, if food is a cause of their falling,[d] I will never eat meat, so that I may not cause one of them[e] to fall.

The Rights of an Apostle

9 Am I not free? Am I not an apostle? Have I not seen Jesus our Lord? Are you not my work in the Lord? [2] If I am not an apostle to others, at least I am to you; for you are the seal of my apostleship in the Lord.

[3] This is my defense to those who would examine me. [4] Do we not have the right to our food and drink? [5] Do we not have the right to be accompanied by a believing wife,[f] as do the other apostles and the brothers of the Lord and Cephas? [6] Or is it only Barnabas and I who have no right to refrain from working for a living? [7] Who at any time pays the expenses for doing military service? Who plants a vineyard and does not eat any of its fruit? Or who tends a flock and does not get any of its milk?

[8] Do I say this on human authority? Does not the law also say the same? [9] For it is written in the law of Moses, "You shall not muzzle an ox while it is treading out the grain." Is it for oxen that God is concerned? [10] Or does he not speak entirely for our sake? It was indeed written for our sake, for whoever

---

a The quotation may extend to the end of the verse *b* Gk *the weak brother . . . is destroyed* *c* Gk *against the brothers* *d* Gk *my brother's falling* *e* Gk *cause my brother* *f* Gk *a sister as wife*

8:1–11:1 Rights and Responsibilities

8:1–13 Problems Related to Eating Meat Offered to Idols

In a Gentile city like Corinth, meat for domestic consumption would ordinarily come from animals that had been ritually slaughtered in honor of pagan gods (*idols*). Church members disagreed about whether they could eat such meat.

8:1 *Knowledge puffs up, but love builds up*—Every Christian should "know" that there is only *one God* and *one Lord* (v. 6). Yet valid religious knowledge without loving consideration for other church members can breed destructive pride.

8:7—Some former pagans in the church still thought that pagan gods were real and their Christian faith might be shaken if they saw other church members eat food offered to those deities. Modern believers need to consider how their daily choices, however well-intentioned, may look to other Christians.

9:1–27 Paul as a Model of Giving Love Priority over Freedom and Rights

9:1—Paul's claim to the title of *apostle* rests on his vision of the risen Christ (15:8–10; Gal. 1:15–16) and on his effective work in establishing churches like the one in Corinth (cf. 2 Cor. 3:1–3).

plows should plow in hope and whoever threshes should thresh in hope of a share in the crop. ¹¹ If we have sown spiritual good among you, is it too much if we reap your material benefits? ¹² If others share this rightful claim on you, do not we still more?

Nevertheless, we have not made use of this right, but we endure anything rather than put an obstacle in the way of the gospel of Christ. ¹³ Do you not know that those who are employed in the temple service get their food from the temple, and those who serve at the altar share in what is sacrificed on the altar? ¹⁴ In the same way, the Lord commanded that those who proclaim the gospel should get their living by the gospel.

15 But I have made no use of any of these rights, nor am I writing this so that they may be applied in my case. Indeed, I would rather die than that— no one will deprive me of my ground for boasting! ¹⁶ If I proclaim the gospel, this gives me no ground for boasting, for an obligation is laid on me, and woe to me if I do not proclaim the gospel! ¹⁷ For if I do this of my own will, I have a reward; but if not of my own will, I am entrusted with a commission. ¹⁸ What then is my reward? Just this: that in my proclamation I may make the gospel free of charge, so as not to make full use of my rights in the gospel.

19 For though I am free with respect to all, I have made myself a slave to all, so that I might win more of them. ²⁰ To the Jews I became as a Jew, in order to win Jews. To those under the law I became as one under the law (though I myself am not under the law) so that I might win those under the law. ²¹ To those outside the law I became as one outside the law (though I am not free from God's law but am under Christ's law) so that I might win those outside the law. ²² To the weak I became weak, so that I might win the weak. I have become all things to all people, that I might by all means save some. ²³ I do it all for the sake of the gospel, so that I may share in its blessings.

24 Do you not know that in a race the runners all compete, but only one receives the prize? Run in such a way that you may win it. ²⁵ Athletes exercise self-control in all things; they do it to receive a perishable wreath, but we an imperishable one. ²⁶ So I do not run aimlessly, nor do I box as though beating the air; ²⁷ but I punish my body and enslave it, so that after proclaiming to others I myself should not be disqualified.

Warnings from Israel's History

10 I do not want you to be unaware, brothers and sisters,ᵃ that our ancestors were all under the cloud, and all passed through the sea, ² and all were baptized into Moses in the cloud and in the sea, ³ and all ate the same spiritual food, ⁴ and all drank the same spiritual drink. For they drank from the spiritual rock that followed them, and the rock was Christ. ⁵ Neverthe-

ᵃ Gk brothers

9:12—Paul's main point is that he does not stand on his rights, lest this create an obstacle to the faith of others (cf. 8:13). Financial arrangements should serve, not control, the work of the church (cf. 2 Cor. 12:13–16; 1 Thess. 2:9).

9:21 *Under Christ's law*—Paul's general practice as an apostle is governed by his commission from God to draw as many persons as possible to Christ. Christian witnesses must present the gospel faithfully and flexibly to make it meaningful to different audiences (cf. 10:32–33).

9:24–27—The Christian life is like an athletic competition in the sense that believers must ex-

ercise lifelong self-discipline, not least by putting the good of others ahead of their own rights.

10:1–13 Israel in the Wilderness: A Lesson about Temptation

10:1 *Our ancestors*—Though the Corinthian Christians were mainly Gentiles (12:2), Paul implies that the Old Testament Israelites were their spiritual parents, who received similar blessings (including baptism and *spiritual food* and *drink*, 10:3–4) and faced similar trials.

10:4—Paul reads the story of Exod. 17:6 and Num. 20:11 as symbolically referring to Christ as the source of salvation.

less, God was not pleased with most of them, and they were struck down in the wilderness.

6 Now these things occurred as examples for us, so that we might not desire evil as they did. [7] Do not become idolaters as some of them did; as it is written, "The people sat down to eat and drink, and they rose up to play." [8] We must not indulge in sexual immorality as some of them did, and twenty-three thousand fell in a single day. [9] We must not put Christ[a] to the test, as some of them did, and were destroyed by serpents. [10] And do not complain as some of them did, and were destroyed by the destroyer. [11] These things happened to them to serve as an example, and they were written down to instruct us, on whom the ends of the ages have come. [12] So if you think you are standing, watch out that you do not fall. [13] No testing has overtaken you that is not common to everyone. God is faithful, and he will not let you be tested beyond your strength, but with the testing he will also provide the way out so that you may be able to endure it.

14 Therefore, my dear friends,[b] flee from the worship of idols. [15] I speak as to sensible people; judge for yourselves what I say. [16] The cup of blessing that we bless, is it not a sharing in the blood of Christ? The bread that we break, is it not a sharing in the body of Christ? [17] Because there is one bread, we who are many are one body, for we all partake of the one bread. [18] Consider the people of Israel;[c] are not those who eat the sacrifices partners in the altar? [19] What do I imply then? That food sacrificed to idols is anything, or that an idol is anything? [20] No, I imply that what pagans sacrifice, they sacrifice to demons and not to God. I do not want you to be partners with demons. [21] You cannot drink the cup of the Lord and the cup of demons. You cannot partake of the table of the Lord and the table of demons. [22] Or are we provoking the Lord to jealousy? Are we stronger than he?

Do All to the Glory of God

23 "All things are lawful," but not all things are beneficial. "All things are lawful," but not all things build up. [24] Do not seek your own advantage, but that of the other. [25] Eat whatever is sold in the meat market without raising any question on the ground of conscience, [26] for "the earth and its fullness are the Lord's." [27] If an unbeliever invites you to a meal and you are disposed to go, eat whatever is set before you without raising any question on the ground of conscience. [28] But if someone says to you, "This has been offered in sacrifice," then do not eat it, out of consideration for the one who informed you, and for the sake of conscience— [29] I mean the other's conscience, not your own. For why should my liberty be subject to the judgment of someone else's conscience? [30] If I partake with thankfulness, why should I be denounced because of that for which I give thanks?

31 So, whether you eat or drink, or whatever you do, do everything for the glory of God. [32] Give no offense to Jews or to Greeks or to the church of God, [33] just as I try to please everyone

[a] Other ancient authorities read the Lord [b] Gk my beloved [c] Gk Israel according to the flesh

---

10:11–13—Paul's main point is that Christians, like ancient Israelites, continually face temptation and must maintain discipline (cf. 9:24–27).

10:14–11:1 Responsibility in Relation to Food Linked with Paganism

10:25–29—Believers are free to eat food offered to idols when sold in the marketplace or even in the homes of unbelievers (v. 27). When, however, their eating may disturb the faith of other Christians, they must abstain. Freedom must be exercised with loving consideration of how others will interpret one's actions (cf. 8:13).

10:32 *Give no offense*—Believers must avoid giving *unnecessary offense* to the consciences of outsiders or fellow believers. They need simply to be loyal to the offense-generating message about Christ's cross (1:18–25) and its implications for unselfish love (cf. 13:4–5).

in everything I do, not seeking my own advantage, but that of many, so that they may be saved. ¹Be imitators of me, as I am of Christ.

11

Head Coverings

2 I commend you because you remember me in everything and maintain the traditions just as I handed them on to you. ³But I want you to understand that Christ is the head of every man, and the husband*a* is the head of his wife,*b* and God is the head of Christ. ⁴Any man who prays or prophesies with something on his head disgraces his head, ⁵but any woman who prays or prophesies with her head unveiled disgraces her head—it is one and the same thing as having her head shaved. ⁶For if a woman will not veil herself, then she should cut off her hair; but if it is disgraceful for a woman to have her hair cut off or to be shaved, she should wear a veil. ⁷For a man ought not to have his head veiled, since he is the image and reflection*c* of God; but woman is the reflection*c* of man. ⁸Indeed, man was not made from woman, but woman from man. ⁹Neither was man created for the sake of woman, but woman for the sake of man. ¹⁰For this reason a woman ought to have a symbol of*d* authority on her head,*e* because of the angels. ¹¹Nevertheless, in the Lord woman is not independent of man or man independent of woman. ¹²For just as woman came from man, so man comes through woman; but all things come from God. ¹³Judge for yourselves: is it proper for a woman to pray to God with her head unveiled? ¹⁴Does not nature itself teach you that if a man wears long hair, it is degrading to him, ¹⁵but if a woman has long hair, it is her glory? For her hair is given to her for a covering. ¹⁶But if anyone is disposed to be contentious—we have no such custom, nor do the churches of God.

Abuses at the Lord's Supper

17 Now in the following instructions I do not commend you, because when you come together it is not for the better but for the worse. ¹⁸For, to begin with, when you come together as a church, I hear that there are divisions among you; and to some extent I believe it. ¹⁹Indeed, there have to be factions among you, for only so will it become clear who among you are genuine. ²⁰When you come together, it is not really to eat the Lord's supper. ²¹For when the time comes to eat, each of you goes ahead with your own supper, and one goes hungry and another becomes drunk. ²²What! Do you not have homes to eat and drink

a The same Greek word means *man or husband*   *b* Or *head of the woman*   *c* Or *glory*   *d* Gk lacks *a symbol of*   *e* Or *have freedom of choice regarding her head*

11:1—As the church's spiritual parent, Paul feels he must preach by example, following the example of Christ (cf. 4:16–17).

11:2–14:40 Worship and Spiritual Gifts

11:2–16 A Controversy about Women's Head Coverings

Paul assumes that women can lead worship, but he wants them to cover their heads while doing so. Some of his arguments are unclear, however.

11:3—Somehow Paul sees a connection between the head-covering issue and the subordination of wives to husbands. Despite Gal. 3:28 and the egalitarian tendencies of 1 Cor. 7:2–4 (see note), Paul here implies that gender distinctions remain important in the church. Consider the tension between vv. 8–9 and 11–12.

11:4–5—Prophecy here does not refer mainly to predicting the future but to leading public worship with prayer and preaching (see 14:3). Paul assumes that the church has both male and female worship leaders. His concern is that the sexes be clearly distinguishable in head covering: women should cover their heads.

11:13–15—Paul speaks of *nature* teaching that women must wear their hair long and men keep theirs short. Modern believers might more readily speak of culture and customs, which merit respect but need not be followed slavishly.

11:17–34 Observing the Lord's Supper in a Worthy Manner

11:18–22—Paul is particularly concerned about divisions between rich and poor church members that appear even in communion services, which may not be sharply distinguished from fellowship meals.

in? Or do you show contempt for the church of God and humiliate those who have nothing? What should I say to you? Should I commend you? In this matter I do not commend you!

The Institution of the Lord's Supper

23 For I received from the Lord what I also handed on to you, that the Lord Jesus on the night when he was betrayed took a loaf of bread, 24 and when he had given thanks, he broke it and said, "This is my body that is for*a* you. Do this in remembrance of me." 25 In the same way he took the cup also, after supper, saying, "This cup is the new covenant in my blood. Do this, as often as you drink it, in remembrance of me." 26 For as often as you eat this bread and drink the cup, you proclaim the Lord's death until he comes.

Partaking of the Supper Unworthily

27 Whoever, therefore, eats the bread or drinks the cup of the Lord in an unworthy manner will be answerable for the body and blood of the Lord. 28 Examine yourselves, and only then eat of the bread and drink of the cup. 29 For all who eat and drink*b* without discerning the body,*c* eat and drink judgment against themselves. 30 For this reason many of you are weak and ill, and some have died.*d* 31 But if we judged ourselves, we would not be judged. 32 But when we are judged by the Lord, we are disciplined*e* so that we may not be condemned along with the world.

33 So then, my brothers and sisters,*f* when you come together to eat, wait for one another. 34 If you are hungry, eat at home, so that when you come together, it will not be for your condemnation. About the other things I will give instructions when I come.

Spiritual Gifts

12 Now concerning spiritual gifts,*g* brothers and sisters,*f* I do not want you to be uninformed. 2 You know that when you were pagans, you were enticed and led astray to idols that could not speak. 3 Therefore I want you to understand that no one speaking by the Spirit of God ever says "Let Jesus be cursed!" and no one can say "Jesus is Lord" except by the Holy Spirit.

4 Now there are varieties of gifts, but the same Spirit; 5 and there are varieties of services, but the same Lord; 6 and there are varieties of activities, but it is the same God who activates all of them in everyone. 7 To each is given the manifestation of the Spirit for the common good. 8 To one is given through the Spirit the utterance of wisdom, and to another the utterance of knowledge according to the same Spirit, 9 to another faith by the same Spirit, to another gifts of healing by the one Spirit, 10 to another the working of miracles, to another prophecy, to another the discernment of spirits, to another various kinds of tongues, to another the interpretation of tongues. 11 All these are activated by one and the same Spirit, who allots to each one individually just as the Spirit chooses.

a Other ancient authorities read *is broken for* *b* Other ancient authorities add *in an unworthy manner*, *c* Other ancient authorities read *the Lord's body* *d* Gk *fallen asleep* *e* Or *When we are judged, we are being disciplined by the Lord* *f* Gk *brothers* *g* Or *spiritual persons*

11:27–32—To share in the Lord's Supper requires recognition that the church, as Christ's body, is constituted by his death and continuing lordship. When church members discriminate against other members on the basis of income or social position, they dishonor the Lord who brings them together.

12:1–31 The Diversity of Gifts and the Oneness of the Church

Another source of dissension at Corinth was boasting over individual spiritual gifts.

12:3 *No one can say*—The confession of Jesus as Lord, which unites all believers (see Rom. 10:9), is itself a gift of the *Spirit*.

12:7—Each believer receives a gift, which is to be used for the good of the whole community. As a gift, it is not something to boast about (cf. 4:7).

One Body with Many Members

12 For just as the body is one and has many members, and all the members of the body, though many, are one body, so it is with Christ. [13] For in the one Spirit we were all baptized into one body—Jews or Greeks, slaves or free—and we were all made to drink of one Spirit.

14 Indeed, the body does not consist of one member but of many. [15] If the foot would say, "Because I am not a hand, I do not belong to the body," that would not make it any less a part of the body. [16] And if the ear would say, "Because I am not an eye, I do not belong to the body," that would not make it any less a part of the body. [17] If the whole body were an eye, where would the hearing be? If the whole body were hearing, where would the sense of smell be? [18] But as it is, God arranged the members in the body, each one of them, as he chose. [19] If all were a single member, where would the body be? [20] As it is, there are many members, yet one body. [21] The eye cannot say to the hand, "I have no need of you," nor again the head to the feet, "I have no need of you." [22] On the contrary, the members of the body that seem to be weaker are indispensable, [23] and those members of the body that we think less honorable we clothe with greater honor, and our less respectable members are treated with greater respect; [24] whereas our more respectable members do not need this. But God has so arranged the body, giving the greater honor to the inferior member, [25] that there may be no dissension within the body, but the members may have the same care for one another. [26] If one member suffers, all suffer together with it; if one member is honored, all rejoice together with it.

27 Now you are the body of Christ and individually members of it. [28] And God has appointed in the church first apostles, second prophets, third teachers; then deeds of power, then gifts of healing, forms of assistance, forms of leadership, various kinds of tongues. [29] Are all apostles? Are all prophets? Are all teachers? Do all work miracles? [30] Do all possess gifts of healing? Do all speak in tongues? Do all interpret? [31] But strive for the greater gifts. And I will show you a still more excellent way.

The Gift of Love

13 If I speak in the tongues of mortals and of angels, but do not have love, I am a noisy gong or a clanging cymbal. [2] And if I have prophetic powers, and understand all mysteries and all knowledge, and if I have all faith, so as to remove mountains, but do not have love, I am nothing. [3] If I give away all my possessions, and if I hand over my body so that I may boast,[a] but do not have love, I gain nothing.

4 Love is patient; love is kind; love is

[a] Other ancient authorities read body to be burned

12:13 *For in the one Spirit we were all baptized into one body—Jews or Greeks, slaves or free*—Paul probably alludes to an early church baptismal formula which implies the equality of all persons in Christ (as in Gal. 3:28 and Col. 3:11).

12:25—Church members should not despise or envy each other's gifts but be thankful that all contribute to the well-being of the community. They should also *care* about each other, recognizing God's intention that they be interdependent rather than isolated individuals.

12:27 *Now you are the body of Christ*—The church is not equated with Christ, but it belongs to Christ, who is its Lord (cf. Col. 1:18; 2:19; Eph. 4:15; 5:23).

12:28 *And God has appointed in the church*— Corresponding to the variety of gifts (vv. 8–10) is the diversity of church offices or responsibilities in Christ's body (vv. 28–30). Each gift is also a divine commission.

13:1–13 Love Makes All the Difference

13:1–3—The possession of any spiritual gift or the practice of the most extreme self-sacrifice is pointless without *love*. Mother Teresa of Calcutta said that what everyone needs most of all is a sense of being valued and loved.

13:1—The *I* in this chapter stands for Paul and all believers (as in Gal. 2:20).

13:4–7—Some positive characteristics of love, which Paul conceives as outward action as well

not envious or boastful or arrogant [5] or rude. It does not insist on its own way; it is not irritable or resentful; [6] it does not rejoice in wrongdoing, but rejoices in the truth. [7] It bears all things, believes all things, hopes all things, endures all things.

8 Love never ends. But as for prophecies, they will come to an end; as for tongues, they will cease; as for knowledge, it will come to an end. [9] For we know only in part, and we prophesy only in part; [10] but when the complete comes, the partial will come to an end. [11] When I was a child, I spoke like a child, I thought like a child, I reasoned like a child; when I became an adult, I put an end to childish ways. [12] For now we see in a mirror, dimly,[a] but then we will see face to face. Now I know only in part; then I will know fully, even as I have been fully known. [13] And now faith, hope, and love abide, these three; and the greatest of these is love.

Gifts of Prophecy and Tongues

14 Pursue love and strive for the spiritual gifts, and especially that you may prophesy. [2] For those who speak in a tongue do not speak to other people but to God; for nobody understands them, since they are speaking mysteries in the Spirit. [3] On the other hand, those who prophesy speak to other people for their upbuilding and encouragement and consolation. [4] Those who speak in a tongue build up themselves, but those who prophesy build up the church. [5] Now I would like all of you to speak in tongues, but even more to prophesy. One who prophesies is greater than one who speaks in tongues, unless someone interprets, so that the church may be built up.

6 Now, brothers and sisters,[b] if I come to you speaking in tongues, how will I benefit you unless I speak to you in some revelation or knowledge or prophecy or teaching? [7] It is the same way with lifeless instruments that produce sound, such as the flute or the harp. If they do not give distinct notes, how will anyone know what is being played? [8] And if the bugle gives an indistinct sound, who will get ready for battle? [9] So with yourselves; if in a tongue you utter speech that is not intelligible, how will anyone know what is being said? For you will be speaking into the air. [10] There are doubtless many different kinds of sounds in the world, and nothing is without sound. [11] If then I do not know the meaning of a sound, I will be a foreigner to the speaker and the speaker a foreigner to me. [12] So with

[a] Gk in a riddle [b] Gk brothers

---

as inward mind-set. Loving persons *rejoice* when justice is done and *believe all things* promised by God (cf. Rom. 8:28).

13:8–13—Love will never become obsolete, though other spiritual gifts will pass away when Christ returns (1:7).

13:12 *Then we will see face to face*—Paul's end-time hope is for existence in the immediate presence of God and Christ, whose love is the source and template of believers' love (see 2:9; 8:3; 16:22; 2 Cor. 5:14; Rom. 5:5; Phil. 1:23; 1 John 4:19).

14:1–40 Spiritual Gifts in the Setting of Worship
The passage implies that the Corinthians were seriously divided over the relative value of spiritual gifts (as in chap. 12), especially speaking in tongues and prophesying in corporate worship.

14:2 *Those who speak in a tongue*—Apparently Paul refers to glossolalia, a religious phenomenon (not limited to Christianity) involving ecstatic *speaking* with sounds that are not part of any language system (cf. 12:10, 28; Acts 10:46). In modern times the gift of tongues is emphasized by Pentecostal churches, but often ignored by others.

14:3–5—For the meaning of "prophecy," see note at 11:4–5. Paul values both speaking in tongues and prophecy as genuine gifts of the Spirit, but rates prophecy higher because it directly benefits other church members.

14:12—Although Paul himself speaks in tongues and approves of it as a desirable gift (vv. 5, 18), he urges the Corinthians to give priority to love and building up the community through intelligible and mature communications (vv. 20–22). Believers, especially in worship, should prefer clear messages that actually help people rather than sensational ones that do not.

yourselves; since you are eager for spiritual gifts, strive to excel in them for building up the church.

13 Therefore, one who speaks in a tongue should pray for the power to interpret. ¹⁴ For if I pray in a tongue, my spirit prays but my mind is unproductive. ¹⁵ What should I do then? I will pray with the spirit, but I will pray with the mind also; I will sing praise with the spirit, but I will sing praise with the mind also. ¹⁶ Otherwise, if you say a blessing with the spirit, how can anyone in the position of an outsider say the "Amen" to your thanksgiving, since the outsider does not know what you are saying? ¹⁷ For you may give thanks well enough, but the other person is not built up. ¹⁸ I thank God that I speak in tongues more than all of you; ¹⁹ nevertheless, in church I would rather speak five words with my mind, in order to instruct others also, than ten thousand words in a tongue.

20 Brothers and sisters,ᵃ do not be children in your thinking; rather, be infants in evil, but in thinking be adults. ²¹ In the law it is written,

"By people of strange tongues
    and by the lips of foreigners
I will speak to this people;
    yet even then they will not listen
        to me,"

says the Lord. ²² Tongues, then, are a sign not for believers but for unbelievers, while prophecy is not for unbelievers but for believers. ²³ If, therefore, the whole church comes together and all speak in tongues, and outsiders or unbelievers enter, will they not say that you are out of your mind? ²⁴ But if all prophesy, an unbeliever or outsider who enters is reproved by all and called to account by all. ²⁵ After the secrets of the unbeliever's heart are disclosed, that person will bow down before God and worship him, declaring, "God is really among you."

Orderly Worship

26 What should be done then, my friends?ᵃ When you come together, each one has a hymn, a lesson, a revelation, a tongue, or an interpretation. Let all things be done for building up. ²⁷ If anyone speaks in a tongue, let there be only two or at most three, and each in turn; and let one interpret. ²⁸ But if there is no one to interpret, let them be silent in church and speak to themselves and to God. ²⁹ Let two or three prophets speak, and let the others weigh what is said. ³⁰ If a revelation is made to someone else sitting nearby, let the first person be silent. ³¹ For you can all prophesy one by one, so that all may learn and all be encouraged. ³² And the spirits of prophets are subject to the prophets, ³³ for God is a God not of disorder but of peace.

(As in all the churches of the saints, ³⁴ women should be silent in the churches. For they are not permitted to speak, but should be subordinate, as the law also says. ³⁵ If there is anything they desire to know, let them ask their husbands at home. For it is shameful for a woman to speak in church.ᵇ ³⁶ Or did the word of God originate with you? Or are you the only ones it has reached?)

37 Anyone who claims to be a prophet, or to have spiritual powers, must acknowledge that what I am writing to you is a command of the Lord. ³⁸ Anyone who does not recognize this is not to be recognized. ³⁹ So, my friends,ᶜ be eager to prophesy, and do not forbid speaking in tongues; ⁴⁰ but all things should be done decently and in order.

ᵃ Gk brothers ᵇ Other ancient authorities put verses 34-35 after verse 40
ᶜ Gk my brothers

14:24–25—Genuine worship should prick consciences so that even unbelievers become aware of God's presence.

14:33b–36—In striking contrast to 11:2–16, this passage seems to forbid women to speak at all in worship. The passage's contents and certain manuscript discrepancies make it probable that these words are not from Paul but were added by a later writer (one who essentially agreed with 1 Tim. 2:8–15).

The Resurrection of Christ

15 Now I would remind you, brothers and sisters,[a] of the good news[b] that I proclaimed to you, which you in turn received, in which also you stand, 2 through which also you are being saved, if you hold firmly to the message that I proclaimed to you—unless you have come to believe in vain.

3 For I handed on to you as of first importance what I in turn had received: that Christ died for our sins in accordance with the scriptures, 4 and that he was buried, and that he was raised on the third day in accordance with the scriptures, 5 and that he appeared to Cephas, then to the twelve. 6 Then he appeared to more than five hundred brothers and sisters[a] at one time, most of whom are still alive, though some have died.[c] 7 Then he appeared to James, then to all the apostles. 8 Last of all, as to one untimely born, he appeared also to me. 9 For I am the least of the apostles, unfit to be called an apostle, because I persecuted the church of God. 10 But by the grace of God I am what I am, and his grace toward me has not been in vain. On the contrary, I worked harder than any of them—though it was not I, but the grace of God that is with me. 11 Whether then it was I or they, so we proclaim and so you have come to believe.

The Resurrection of the Dead

12 Now if Christ is proclaimed as raised from the dead, how can some of you say there is no resurrection of the dead? 13 If there is no resurrection of the dead, then Christ has not been raised; 14 and if Christ has not been raised, then our proclamation has been in vain and your faith has been in vain. 15 We are even found to be misrepresenting God, because we testified of God that he raised Christ—whom he did not raise if it is true that the dead are not raised. 16 For if the dead are not raised, then Christ has not been raised. 17 If Christ has not been raised, your faith is futile and you are still in your sins. 18 Then those also who have died[c] in Christ have perished. 19 If for this life only we have hoped in Christ, we are of all people most to be pitied.

20 But in fact Christ has been raised from the dead, the first fruits of those who have died.[c] 21 For since death came through a human being, the resurrection of the dead has also come through a human being; 22 for as all die in Adam, so all will be made alive in Christ. 23 But each in his own order: Christ the first fruits, then at his coming those who belong to Christ. 24 Then comes the end,[d] when he hands over the kingdom to God

a Gk brothers b Or gospel c Gk fallen asleep d Or Then come the rest

---

15:1–58 Faith in Resurrections Past and Future Determines the Present Life of Believers

At least some Corinthians doubted their own future resurrection and perhaps also Jesus' resurrection. Perhaps some thought they were already living a resurrection life (cf. 4:8–10; 2 Tim. 2:18).

15:1–19 The Church Is Founded on Faith in Jesus' Saving Death and Resurrection (cf. Rom. 10:9–10)

15:1–11—Paul argues that Christians' faith is centered on Jesus' resurrection as well as his death (cf. 2:2). He evidently quotes from an early church credal formulation (15:3–5) and adds a list of witnesses to whom the risen Christ appeared.

15:12–19—For Paul, the gospel is a message that Jesus' death and resurrection together bring deliverance from the domination of sin and the finality of death (cf. Rom. 4:24–25). To affirm Jesus' death without his resurrection would therefore make Christian faith futile.

15:20–34 Jesus' Resurrection Is the Decisive First Step toward the Defeat of All That Opposes God, Including Death

15:22—Through *Adam*, sin and death (as a punishment for sin) came into the world (cf. v. 56; Gen. 3). *Christ*, the last Adam, brings resurrection and life to others (see 1 Cor. 15:45–49; Rom. 5:12–21).

15:23–28—Christians live in a world of conflict, widespread opposition to God, and death. They have the assurance, however, that the risen Christ already reigns invisibly as Lord to overcome all the opposing forces, including death. In the end, all persons and powers will submit to the sovereignty of God.

the Father, after he has destroyed every ruler and every authority and power. [25] For he must reign until he has put all his enemies under his feet. [26] The last enemy to be destroyed is death. [27] For "God[a] has put all things in subjection under his feet." But when it says, "All things are put in subjection," it is plain that this does not include the one who put all things in subjection under him. [28] When all things are subjected to him, then the Son himself will also be subjected to the one who put all things in subjection under him, so that God may be all in all.

29 Otherwise, what will those people do who receive baptism on behalf of the dead? If the dead are not raised at all, why are people baptized on their behalf?

30 And why are we putting ourselves in danger every hour? [31] I die every day! That is as certain, brothers and sisters,[b] as my boasting of you—a boast that I make in Christ Jesus our Lord. [32] If with merely human hopes I fought with wild animals at Ephesus, what would I have gained by it? If the dead are not raised,

"Let us eat and drink,
    for tomorrow we die."

[33] Do not be deceived:

"Bad company ruins good morals."

[34] Come to a sober and right mind, and sin no more; for some people have no knowledge of God. I say this to your shame.

The Resurrection Body

35 But someone will ask, "How are the dead raised? With what kind of body do they come?" [36] Fool! What you sow does not come to life unless it dies. [37] And as for what you sow, you do not sow the body that is to be, but a bare seed, perhaps of wheat or of some other grain. [38] But God gives it a body as he has chosen, and to each kind of seed its own body. [39] Not all flesh is alike, but there is one flesh for human beings, another for animals, another for birds, and another for fish. [40] There are both heavenly bodies and earthly bodies, but the glory of the heavenly is one thing, and that of the earthly is another. [41] There is one glory of the sun, and another glory of the moon, and another glory of the stars; indeed, star differs from star in glory.

42 So it is with the resurrection of the dead. What is sown is perishable, what is raised is imperishable. [43] It is sown in dishonor, it is raised in glory. It is sown in weakness, it is raised in power. [44] It is sown a physical body, it is raised a spiritual body. If there is a physical body, there is also a spiritual body. [45] Thus it is written, "The first man, Adam, became a living being"; the last Adam became a life-giving spirit. [46] But it is not the spiritual that is first, but the physical, and then the spiritual. [47] The first man was from the earth, a man of dust; the second man is[c] from heaven. [48] As was the man of dust, so are those who are of the dust; and as is the man of heaven, so are those who are of heaven. [49] Just as we have borne the image of the man of dust, we will[d] also bear the image of the man of heaven.

50 What I am saying, brothers and

[a] Gk he   [b] Gk brothers   [c] Other ancient authorities add the Lord   [d] Other ancient authorities read let us

15:29–34—Christian living in the present depends on the hope of a greater life to come (cf. Rom. 6:5–11). Paul evidently refers to a special practice current in the Corinthian church whereby some persons were baptized vicariously for relatives or friends who had already died. The practice would be ridiculous if they had no hope that the deceased would live again.

15:35–57 The Resurrection Body Will Be Spiritual, Not Material

Against Corinthian skeptics, Paul uses a series of metaphors to argue for the reality of a future existence fundamentally different from the present world of flesh and blood (cf. Rom. 8:18–23).

15:49—Paul explains that the best way to conceive of the *spiritual body* (v. 44) is to realize that those who are raised will resemble the risen Christ (cf. Rom. 8:29; Phil. 3:21).

sisters,[a] is this: flesh and blood cannot inherit the kingdom of God, nor does the perishable inherit the imperishable. [51] Listen, I will tell you a mystery! We will not all die,[b] but we will all be changed, [52] in a moment, in the twinkling of an eye, at the last trumpet. For the trumpet will sound, and the dead will be raised imperishable, and we will be changed. [53] For this perishable body must put on imperishability, and this mortal body must put on immortality. [54] When this perishable body puts on imperishability, and this mortal body puts on immortality, then the saying that is written will be fulfilled:

"Death has been swallowed up in victory."

[55] "Where, O death, is your victory?
Where, O death, is your sting?"

[56] The sting of death is sin, and the power of sin is the law. [57] But thanks be to God, who gives us the victory through our Lord Jesus Christ.

[58] Therefore, my beloved,[c] be steadfast, immovable, always excelling in the work of the Lord, because you know that in the Lord your labor is not in vain.

The Collection for the Saints

16 Now concerning the collection for the saints: you should follow the directions I gave to the churches of Galatia. [2] On the first day of every week, each of you is to put aside and save whatever extra you earn, so that collections need not be taken when I come. [3] And when I arrive, I will send any whom you approve with letters to take your gift to Jerusalem. [4] If it seems advisable that I should go also, they will accompany me.

Plans for Travel

[5] I will visit you after passing through Macedonia—for I intend to pass through Macedonia— [6] and perhaps I will stay with you or even spend the winter, so that you may send me on my way, wherever I go. [7] I do not want to see you now just in passing, for I hope to spend some time with you, if the Lord permits. [8] But I will stay in Ephesus until Pentecost, [9] for a wide door for effective work has opened to me, and there are many adversaries.

[10] If Timothy comes, see that he has nothing to fear among you, for he is doing the work of the Lord just as I am; [11] therefore let no one despise him. Send him on his way in peace, so that he may come to me; for I am expecting him with the brothers.

[12] Now concerning our brother Apollos, I strongly urged him to visit you with the other brothers, but he was not at all willing[d] to come now. He will come when he has the opportunity.

Final Messages and Greetings

[13] Keep alert, stand firm in your faith, be courageous, be strong. [14] Let all that you do be done in love.

[15] Now, brothers and sisters,[a] you know that members of the household of Stephanas were the first converts in Achaia, and they have devoted themselves to the service of the saints; [16] I urge you to put yourselves at the service of such people, and of everyone who works and toils with them. [17] I rejoice at the coming of Stephanas and Fortunatus and Achaicus, because they have made

---

[a] Gk brothers   [b] Gk fall asleep   [c] Gk beloved brothers   [d] Or it was not at all God's will for him

---

15:51—Paul assumes that the end of the present world and Christ's return will occur before everyone in his own generation dies (cf. 7:29; 1 Thess. 4:15).

15:58—Faith in God's future leads to meaningful work in the present world (cf. vv. 29–34; 2 Cor. 5:8–10).

16:1–24 Letter Closing

16:1–4—Paul gives practical instructions about his *collection* for the impoverished believers (*saints*) in Jerusalem (see Rom. 15:25–27).

16:9—Christians should not be surprised when *effective* evangelism arouses opposition.

16:13–14—A brief summary of Christian responsibilities: watchfulness, steadiness in faith, courage, strength, and, above all, *love*.

up for your absence; [18] for they refreshed my spirit as well as yours. So give recognition to such persons.

19 The churches of Asia send greetings. Aquila and Prisca, together with the church in their house, greet you warmly in the Lord. [20] All the brothers and sisters[a] send greetings. Greet one another with a holy kiss.

21 I, Paul, write this greeting with my own hand. [22] Let anyone be accursed who has no love for the Lord. Our Lord, come![b] [23] The grace of the Lord Jesus be with you. [24] My love be with all of you in Christ Jesus.[c]

[a] Gk brothers [b] Gk Marana tha. These Aramaic words can also be read Maran atha, meaning Our Lord has come [c] Other ancient authorities add Amen

---

16:22 *Let anyone be accursed who has no love for the Lord*—The church is simply the community of those who believe in and love Christ (cf. 2:9; Gal. 1:6–9; Eph. 6:24; John 21:15–17).

The Book of
2 CORINTHIANS

Whereas 1 Corinthians deals with a variety of topics, some raised by prior communications between Paul and the Christian community in Corinth, 2 Corinthians deals in more concentrated fashion with criticisms of Paul's apostolic ministry in relation to the gospel. It is arguably the letter that most fully reveals Paul as an individual: passionate, brilliant, earnest, ironical, practical, determined to explain the depths of the meaning of the gospel when his apostleship is under sharp attack and people for whose welfare he feels deeply responsible are near the edge of spiritual catastrophe.

The primary theme running through most of 2 Corinthians is Paul's own ministry. He has to defend it against a variety of implied criticisms raised or entertained by at least some members of the Corinthian church. For example, it is said that Paul is inconsistent (1:17), that he is cunning and underhanded (4:2), that he doesn't really care about the Corinthians (2:4; 11:11), that he was wrong to refuse their offers of financial support (11:7), that he is inferior as a speaker or in other respects to some "super-apostles" who have visited Corinth since Paul was there (11:5).

To answer such criticisms, Paul employs a wide range of arguments. He frequently cites or alludes to the Old Testament (e.g., 1:20; 3:6–16; 4:13; 6:2, 16–18; 9:9). He displays a sophisticated mastery of Greco-Roman rhetoric, using with ease and distinctiveness such devices as direct self-praise (e.g., 2:14–3:4) and an ironic "fool's speech" (11:16–12:11). Above all, Paul defends his apostleship by stressing (a) that he does not preach himself but Christ and (b) there is an appropriate correlation between Christ's death and resurrection and the suffering and power present in his own ministry (4:10–11). Paul uses "we" more often in chaps. 1–9 than in his other letters (in chaps. 10–13, he mainly uses "I" rather than "we," probably because he is countering attacks centered on himself). This emphasis on "we" suggests that other ministers and believers share Paul's personal experiences of Christ's death and resurrection life.

Although some other Pauline letters draw attention to how Christians participate in the death and resurrection of Christ (e.g., Rom. 6:1–11; Gal. 2:20; Phil. 3:8–11), this concept is developed with special intensity in 2 Corinthians. Though on the surface it is concerned largely with vindicating Paul's own ministry, the letter urges believers of all times and circumstances to see how their own lives conform to the model of Christ's love, death, and resurrection. Paul—and other Christians as well—participates in Jesus' death through patient suffering and burden bearing (1:8–10; 4:7–12), through renouncing self-centeredness and accepting God's forgiveness and reconciliation through Christ's death (5:14–21), through giving of resources for the good of others (8:9), and through accepting various experiences of weakness according to the will of Christ (12:9). Believers like Paul look forward to a future life free from the trials and frustrations of present bodily existence (4:16–5:10). Yet they can already see

and verify the power of Jesus' resurrection life in such present-time experiences as observing Paul's consistent witnessing that no amount of suffering can deter (1:18–22; 6:4–10) and recognizing the triumphant work of God in the spread of the gospel (2:14–16) and the changes in their own lives as they are being transformed "from one degree of glory to another" (3:18). Although Paul speaks of a future judgment of works (5:10) and boasts about his own missionary achievements (3:1–4; 10:14; 11:23), he repeatedly concludes that everything depends on God's grace (1:12; 3:5; 4:15; 8:9; 9:14; 12:9). To recognize divine power and mercy in such present-time experiences, however, requires a new way of seeing (5:16).

Despite the pervasiveness of the theme of the integrity of Paul's ministry, many modern scholars consider 2 Corinthians not a single letter but a combination of two or more letters written by Paul to the Christian community in Corinth around the same general time period, the mid-50s of the first Christian century, but addressing different situations. The following historical hypothesis (there are others!) attempts to outline how the apostle's relationship with the Corinthians developed and how 1 and 2 Corinthians are connected with those developments. Around 51 CE Paul founded the church at Corinth and then moved on to establish other churches. Some years later, while a resident in Ephesus, he wrote 1 Corinthians in response to specific questions and a general problem of disunity in the church. Trouble broke out, however. Paul made a hurried second visit to Corinth, where he encountered sharp opposition led by an unnamed church member (2 Cor. 2:5). He subsequently sent his co-worker, Titus, who found the church members sorry for the estrangement from Paul and eager for reconciliation. He then wrote 2 Corinthians 1–9, sending this letter with Titus and some other church delegates whom he authorized to receive the church's contribution to the collection for the Jerusalem church (2 Cor. 8:16–24). Despite these efforts, a major rebellion now erupted in the Corinthian church, triggered especially by the arrival of other Christian missionaries who claimed to be better apostles than Paul (2 Cor. 11:4–6, 12–15). In response, Paul made plans for a third visit (2 Cor. 13:1), sending in advance a letter containing a most vehement defense of his apostleship, now found in 2 Corinthians 10–13. We have no direct information about how well that third visit went, but the completion of the collection in Greece (Rom. 15:26) and the subsequent preservation of some of Paul's letters to Corinth suggest that his authority was restored in the church.

Modern theories about the sequence of events and the literary unity or composite character of 2 Corinthians are important, and scholarly debates about them will continue. Most readers, however, will find the entire letter to be a profound and often eloquent exploration of the ways in which human hearts, like clay jars, can be touched and then reshaped by the message of God's love in Christ. Those who seek to serve others for Christ's sake, ordained ministers and lay persons alike, can expect that other church members will sometimes misconstrue their actions and motives. In their labors, difficulties, and anxieties they will learn, as Paul obviously did, to rely ever more fully on the unwavering comfort and transforming power of God.

—**David Hay**

Salutation

1 Paul, an apostle of Christ Jesus by the will of God, and Timothy our brother,

To the church of God that is in Corinth, including all the saints throughout Achaia:

2 Grace to you and peace from God our Father and the Lord Jesus Christ.

Paul's Thanksgiving after Affliction

3 Blessed be the God and Father of our Lord Jesus Christ, the Father of mercies and the God of all consolation, ⁴who consoles us in all our affliction, so that we may be able to console those who are in any affliction with the consolation with which we ourselves are consoled by God. ⁵For just as the sufferings of Christ are abundant for us, so also our consolation is abundant through Christ. ⁶If we are being afflicted, it is for your consolation and salvation; if we are being consoled, it is for your consolation, which you experience when you patiently endure the same sufferings that we are also suffering. ⁷Our hope for you is unshaken; for we know that as you share in our sufferings, so also you share in our consolation.

8 We do not want you to be unaware, brothers and sisters,ᵃ of the affliction we experienced in Asia; for we were so utterly, unbearably crushed that we despaired of life itself. ⁹Indeed, we felt that we had received the sentence of death so that we would rely not on ourselves but on God who raises the dead. ¹⁰He who rescued us from so deadly a peril will continue to rescue us; on him we have ᵇset our hope that he will rescue us again, ¹¹as you also join in helping us by your prayers, so that many will give thanks on ourᵇ behalf for the blessing granted us through the prayers of many.

The Postponement of Paul's Visit

12 Indeed, this is our boast, the testimony of our conscience: we have behaved in the world with franknessᶜ and godly sincerity, not by earthly wisdom but by the grace of God—and all the more toward you. ¹³For we write you nothing other than what you can read and also understand; I hope you will understand until the end— ¹⁴as you have already understood us in part—that on the day of the Lord Jesus we are your boast even as you are our boast.

15 Since I was sure of this, I wanted to come to you first, so that you might have a double favor;ᵈ ¹⁶I wanted to visit you on my way to Macedonia, and to come back to you from Macedonia and have you send me on to Judea. ¹⁷Was I vacillating when I wanted to do this? Do I make my plans according to ordinary human standards,ᵉ ready to say "Yes, yes" and "No, no" at the same time? ¹⁸As surely as God is faithful, our word to you has not been "Yes and No." ¹⁹For the Son of God, Jesus Christ, whom we proclaimed among you, Silvanus and Timothy and I, was not "Yes and No"; but in him it is always "Yes." ²⁰For in him every one of God's promises is a "Yes." For this

---

ᵃ Gk *brothers*　ᵇ Other ancient authorities read *your*　ᶜ Other ancient authorities read *holiness*　ᵈ Other ancient authorities read *pleasure*　ᵉ Gk *according to the flesh*

1:1–11 Letter Opening

1:1–2—Paul writes to the Corinthian church, who are to remember their spiritual oneness with other believers in *Achaia* (the Roman province of Greece).

1:3–7—This initial blessing indicates that a primary theme of Paul's letter is the *consolation* of God known in Christ, a consolation which the apostle and the Corinthians share together with *suffering*.

1:8–11—Without going into details, Paul mentions a recent crisis in Asia Minor, one in which he despaired of life but learned afresh to trust in God

1:12–7:16 Paul's Concern for Corinth

1:12–2:13 Paul's Sincerity despite Appearances to the Contrary

1:18 *Our word to you has not been "Yes and No"*—The trustworthiness of ministers and other believers depends on their consistent witness to God's message in Christ, which is one of unchanging love (cf. 5:18–19).

reason it is through him that we say the "Amen," to the glory of God. ²¹ But it is God who establishes us with you in Christ and has anointed us, ²² by putting his seal on us and giving us his Spirit in our hearts as a first installment.

23 But I call on God as witness against me: it was to spare you that I did not come again to Corinth. ²⁴ I do not mean to imply that we lord it over your faith; rather, we are workers with you for your joy, because you stand firm in the faith.

2 ¹ So I made up my mind not to make you another painful visit. ² For if I cause you pain, who is there to make me glad but the one whom I have pained? ³ And I wrote as I did, so that when I came, I might not suffer pain from those who should have made me rejoice; for I am confident about all of you, that my joy would be the joy of all of you. ⁴ For I wrote you out of much distress and anguish of heart and with many tears, not to cause you pain, but to let you know the abundant love that I have for you.

Forgiveness for the Offender

5 But if anyone has caused pain, he has caused it not to me, but to some extent— not to exaggerate it—to all of you. ⁶ This punishment by the majority is enough for such a person; ⁷ so now instead you should forgive and console him, so that he may not be overwhelmed by excessive sorrow. ⁸ So I urge you to reaffirm your love for him. ⁹ I wrote for this reason: to test you and to know whether you are obedient in everything. ¹⁰ Any-

one whom you forgive, I also forgive. What I have forgiven, if I have forgiven anything, has been for your sake in the presence of Christ. ¹¹ And we do this so that we may not be outwitted by Satan; for we are not ignorant of his designs.

Paul's Anxiety in Troas

12 When I came to Troas to proclaim the good news of Christ, a door was opened for me in the Lord; ¹³ but my mind could not rest because I did not find my brother Titus there. So I said farewell to them and went on to Macedonia.

14 But thanks be to God, who in Christ always leads us in triumphal procession, and through us spreads in every place the fragrance that comes from knowing him. ¹⁵ For we are the aroma of Christ to God among those who are being saved and among those who are perishing; ¹⁶ to the one a fragrance from death to death, to the other a fragrance from life to life. Who is sufficient for these things? ¹⁷ For we are not peddlers of God's word like so many;^a but in Christ we speak as persons of sincerity, as persons sent from God and standing in his presence.

Ministers of the New Covenant

3 Are we beginning to commend ourselves again? Surely we do not need, as some do, letters of recommendation to you or from you, do we? ² You yourselves are our letter, written on our^b hearts, to be known and read by all;

^a Other ancient authorities read *like the others*   ^b Other ancient authorities read *your*

2:1—Sometime after sending 1 Corinthians, Paul visited Corinth and encountered hostility and rejection. Afterwards, to spare everyone's feelings, he decided **not to make . . . another painful visit** as he had earlier planned. Instead he wrote an emotional "letter of tears," expressing both his continuing love for the Corinthians and the pain he felt because of the conflict (v. 4). See introduction.

2:10–11—Paul forgives and seeks the restoration of the person who led the opposition to himself. Refusing to **forgive** would only serve Satan's purposes.

2:14–17 God's Triumphal Procession

Paul and his fellow ministers simply and honestly preach the message of Christ. How people respond them to them depends on their reaction to the message.

3:1–6 Letters of Recommendation

The Corinthians should not require letters of recommendation about Paul, to whom they owe their faith. They cannot question his apostleship without calling into doubt their own faith.

³and you show that you are a letter of Christ, prepared by us, written not with ink but with the Spirit of the living God, not on tablets of stone but on tablets of human hearts.

4 Such is the confidence that we have through Christ toward God. ⁵Not that we are competent of ourselves to claim anything as coming from us; our competence is from God, ⁶who has made us competent to be ministers of a new covenant, not of letter but of spirit; for the letter kills, but the Spirit gives life.

7 Now if the ministry of death, chiseled in letters on stone tablets,ᵃ came in glory so that the people of Israel could not gaze at Moses' face because of the glory of his face, a glory now set aside, ⁸how much more will the ministry of the Spirit come in glory? ⁹For if there was glory in the ministry of condemnation, much more does the ministry of justification abound in glory! ¹⁰Indeed, what once had glory has lost its glory because of the greater glory; ¹¹for if what was set aside came through glory, much more has the permanent come in glory!

12 Since, then, we have such a hope, we act with great boldness, ¹³not like Moses, who put a veil over his face to keep the people of Israel from gazing at the end of the glory thatᵇ was being set aside. ¹⁴But their minds were hardened. Indeed, to this very day, when they hear the reading of the old covenant, that same veil is still there, since only in Christ is it set aside. ¹⁵Indeed, to this very day

whenever Moses is read, a veil lies over their minds; ¹⁶but when one turns to the Lord, the veil is removed. ¹⁷Now the Lord is the Spirit, and where the Spirit of the Lord is, there is freedom. ¹⁸And all of us, with unveiled faces, seeing the glory of the Lord as though reflected in a mirror, are being transformed into the same image from one degree of glory to another; for this comes from the Lord, the Spirit.

Treasure in Clay Jars

4 Therefore, since it is by God's mercy that we are engaged in this ministry, we do not lose heart. ²We have renounced the shameful things that one hides; we refuse to practice cunning or to falsify God's word; but by the open statement of the truth we commend ourselves to the conscience of everyone in the sight of God. ³And even if our gospel is veiled, it is veiled to those who are perishing. ⁴In their case the god of this world has blinded the minds of the unbelievers, to keep them from seeing the light of the gospel of the glory of Christ, who is the image of God. ⁵For we do not proclaim ourselves; we proclaim Jesus Christ as Lord and ourselves as your slaves for Jesus' sake. ⁶For it is the God who said, "Let light shine out of darkness," who has shone in our hearts to give the light of the knowledge of the glory of God in the face of Jesus Christ.

ᵃ Gk on stones   ᵇ Gk of what

3:5 Our competence is from God—Believers must rely from first to last on God rather than on themselves.

3:7–18 The New Covenant

The **old covenant** God gave through Moses provided God's people with a true knowledge of right and wrong and God's inevitable condemnation of sin. That covenant points forward to the new covenant given through Christ (see 1 Cor. 11:25), which brought reconciliation with God through the overcoming of sin (see 2 Cor. 5:18–21; Rom. 5:12–8:6). Those who participate in the new covenant live by **the Spirit** rather than a written law (vv. 3, 6; Rom. 6:14–15), and they

grow in **glory** as God's image in Christ reconfigures their lives (v. 18; 4:4–6; Rom. 8:29–30).

4:1–6 Not Proclaiming Ourselves

Faithful ministers proclaim Christ rather than themselves (cf. 1 Cor. 3:5–15).

4:3—Discerning a further meaning in Moses' veil (3:13), Paul indicates that persons who fail to see in Christ the image of God have been spiritually blinded by a demonic power (**the god of this world**, v. 4).

7 But we have this treasure in clay jars, so that it may be made clear that this extraordinary power belongs to God and does not come from us. **8** We are afflicted in every way, but not crushed; perplexed, but not driven to despair; **9** persecuted, but not forsaken; struck down, but not destroyed; **10** always carrying in the body the death of Jesus, so that the life of Jesus may also be made visible in our bodies. **11** For while we live, we are always being given up to death for Jesus' sake, so that the life of Jesus may be made visible in our mortal flesh. **12** So death is at work in us, but life in you.

13 But just as we have the same spirit of faith that is in accordance with scripture—"I believed, and so I spoke"—we also believe, and so we speak, **14** because we know that the one who raised the Lord Jesus will raise us also with Jesus, and will bring us with you into his presence. **15** Yes, everything is for your sake, so that grace, as it extends to more and more people, may increase thanksgiving, to the glory of God.

Living by Faith

16 So we do not lose heart. Even though our outer nature is wasting away, our inner nature is being renewed day by day. **17** For this slight momentary affliction is preparing us for an eternal weight of glory beyond all measure, **18** because we look not at what can be seen but at what cannot be seen; for what can be seen is temporary, but what cannot be seen is eternal.

5 For we know that if the earthly tent we live in is destroyed, we have a building from God, a house not made with hands, eternal in the heavens. **2** For in this tent we groan, longing to be clothed with our heavenly dwelling— **3** if indeed, when we have taken it off*a* we will not be found naked. **4** For while we are still in this tent, we groan under our burden, because we wish not to be unclothed but to be further clothed, so that what is mortal may be swallowed up by life. **5** He who has prepared us for this very thing is God, who has given us the Spirit as a guarantee.

6 So we are always confident; even though we know that while we are at home in the body we are away from the Lord— **7** for we walk by faith, not by sight. **8** Yes, we do have confidence, and we would rather be away from the body and at home with the Lord. **9** So whether we are at home or away, we make it our aim to please him. **10** For all of us must appear before the judgment seat of Christ, so that each may receive recompense for what has been done in the body, whether good or evil.

The Ministry of Reconciliation

11 Therefore, knowing the fear of the Lord, we try to persuade others; but we ourselves are well known to God, and I hope that we are also well known to your consciences. **12** We are not commending ourselves to you again, but giving you an opportunity to boast about us, so that you may be able to answer those who boast in outward appearance and not in the heart. **13** For if we are beside ourselves, it is

a Other ancient authorities read *put it on*

4:7–5:10 The Glory of God in Christ, Concealed within the Sufferings of Paul and Other Believers

Such suffering prepares Paul and all Christians for future glory (cf. Rom. 5:2–5). In addition, the light and life of God already appear in their lives (cf. Phil. 2:15).

4:10—Believers like Paul understand their sufferings in the service of God as an experience of common fellowship in the sufferings of Jesus. They also encounter the power of Jesus' resur-

rection as God sustains them in the midst of hardships (vv. 8–9).

4:13—Paul affirms that he and the Corinthians share the same Spirit-given *faith*, a faith that also speaks in the Jewish Scriptures.

5:9–10—Confidence about future glory does not mean indifference to the present life. Rather, believers expect that after death God will judge how they have use their opportunities in this world.

5:11–6:13 Reconciliation with God and with Paul

for God; if we are in our right mind, it is for you. ¹⁴ For the love of Christ urges us on, because we are convinced that one has died for all; therefore all have died. ¹⁵ And he died for all, so that those who live might live no longer for themselves, but for him who died and was raised for them.

16 From now on, therefore, we regard no one from a human point of view;ᵃ even though we once knew Christ from a human point of view,ᵃ we know him no longer in that way. ¹⁷ So if anyone is in Christ, there is a new creation: everything old has passed away; see, everything has become new! ¹⁸ All this is from God, who reconciled us to himself through Christ, and has given us the ministry of reconciliation; ¹⁹ that is, in Christ God was reconciling the world to himself,ᵇ not counting their trespasses against them, and entrusting the message of reconciliation to us. ²⁰ So we are ambassadors for Christ, since God is making his appeal through us; we entreat you on behalf of Christ, be reconciled to God. ²¹ For our sake he made him to be sin who knew no sin, so that in him we might become the righteousness of God.

6 As we work together with him,ᶜ we urge you also not to accept the grace of God in vain. ² For he says,

"At an acceptable time I have
      listened to you,
   and on a day of salvation I have
      helped you."

See, now is the acceptable time; see, now is the day of salvation! ³ We are putting no obstacle in anyone's way, so that no fault may be found with our ministry, ⁴ but as servants of God we have commended ourselves in every way: through great endurance, in afflictions, hardships, calamities, ⁵ beatings, imprisonments, riots, labors, sleepless nights, hunger; ⁶ by purity, knowledge, patience, kindness, holiness of spirit, genuine love, ⁷ truthful speech, and the power of God; with the weapons of righteousness for the right hand and for the left; ⁸ in honor and dishonor, in ill repute and good repute. We are treated as impostors, and yet are true; ⁹ as unknown, and yet are well known; as dying, and see—we are alive; as punished, and yet not killed; ¹⁰ as sorrowful, yet always rejoicing; as poor, yet making many rich; as having nothing, and yet possessing everything.

11 We have spoken frankly to you Corinthians; our heart is wide open to you. ¹² There is no restriction in our affections, but only in yours. ¹³ In return—I

ᵃ Gk according to the flesh   ᵇ Or God was in Christ reconciling the world to himself   ᶜ Gk As we work together

---

5:14—Christ's love was expressed in his death for others, and he now lives in believers who are committed to him unconditionally (cf. Gal. 2:20; Phil. 1:21).

5:16—Believers must think and live by the radically unconventional norm of Christ and his cross (cf. 1 Cor. 1:18–25).

5:19—The entire message of the apostles and the church is one of peace between God and the cosmos (cf. Rom. 5:10–11). In Christ's death God established a peace that people who believe can enter and so become God's righteous peacemakers in the world. Christians should concentrate not on keeping a rigorous tally of other people's sins but on the message of the *reconciliation* initiated by God.

5:21—In his sacrificial death Jesus identified with sinful humanity and brought former sinners into a right relationship with God (cf. Rom. 5:15–21;

8:3; 1 Cor. 15:3; Gal. 3:13). Paul nowhere elaborates a detailed atonement theory (if he had one), but he stresses that Jesus' death was God's chosen means of restoration, by which the barrier of human sin and distrust of God is overcome.

6:1—Even persons who have responded in faith to the message of God's reconciling work must continue making choices in keeping with that message. That includes accepting the witness of ministers like Paul.

6:3–10—This new "tribulations catalog" re-emphasizes the rectitude of Paul's conduct and paradoxically affirms that God brings new life through various deathlike experiences of believers (cf. 4:8–9).

6:10—Paul does not say that physical poverty in itself is good, but that spiritual wealth is independent of it and is the condition of "enriching" others (cf. 8:9; Phil. 4:12–13; Luke 12:21).

speak as to children—open wide your hearts also.

The Temple of the Living God

14 Do not be mismatched with unbelievers. For what partnership is there between righteousness and lawlessness? Or what fellowship is there between light and darkness? 15 What agreement does Christ have with Beliar? Or what does a believer share with an unbeliever? 16 What agreement has the temple of God with idols? For we[a] are the temple of the living God; as God said,

"I will live in them and walk among
    them,
and I will be their God,
and they shall be my people.
17 Therefore come out from them,
    and be separate from them, says
        the Lord,
and touch nothing unclean;
    then I will welcome you,
18 and I will be your father,
    and you shall be my sons and
        daughters,
says the Lord Almighty."

7 Since we have these promises, beloved, let us cleanse ourselves from every defilement of body and of spirit, making holiness perfect in the fear of God.

Paul's Joy at the Church's Repentance

2 Make room in your hearts[b] for us; we have wronged no one, we have corrupted no one, we have taken advantage of no one. 3 I do not say this to condemn you, for I said before that you are in our hearts, to die together and to live together. 4 I often boast about you; I have great pride in you; I am filled with consolation; I am overjoyed in all our affliction.

5 For even when we came into Macedonia, our bodies had no rest, but we were afflicted in every way—disputes without and fears within. 6 But God, who consoles the downcast, consoled us by the arrival of Titus, 7 and not only by his coming, but also by the consolation with which he was consoled about you, as he told us of your longing, your mourning, your zeal for me, so that I rejoiced still more. 8 For even if I made you sorry with my letter, I do not regret it (though I did regret it, for I see that I grieved you with that letter, though only briefly). 9 Now I rejoice, not because you were grieved, but because your grief led to repentance; for you felt a godly grief, so that you were not harmed in any way by us. 10 For godly grief produces a repentance that leads to salvation and brings no regret, but worldly grief produces death. 11 For see what earnestness this godly grief has produced in you, what eagerness to clear yourselves, what indignation, what alarm, what longing, what zeal, what punishment! At every point you have proved yourselves guiltless in the matter. 12 So although I wrote to you, it was not on account of the one who did the wrong, nor on account of the one who was wronged, but in order that your zeal for us might be made known to you before God. 13 In this we find comfort.

[a] Other ancient authorities read you [b] Gk lacks in your hearts

---

6:14–7:1 Separation from Unbelievers
This passage agrees with Paul's teachings elsewhere about the holiness of the church and individual believers (e.g., Rom. 12:1; 1 Cor. 1:2; 3:17; 6:19; 2 Cor. 1:1; 1 Thess. 3:13). It does not fit well in its present context, however, and may be an excerpt from another Pauline letter (possibly the one mentioned in 1 Cor. 5:9).

6:15—In the light of 1 Cor. 5:9–13, Paul must mean that believers are not to accept conduct or beliefs contrary to Christ. Yet they are not to avoid contacts with non-Christians. Each new genera-

tion of believers is challenged to discern how to combine holiness and existence in a pluralistic world (cf. 1 Cor. 9:24–27).

7:2–16 An Appeal for Continuing Reconciliation and Mutual Affection

7:3 *You are in our hearts, to die together and to live together*—At the climax of his appeal for deeper loyalty, Paul assures the Corinthians of his enduring love for them.

7:10—Paul does not endorse depression or all kinds of grieving. Yet healthy *repentance* may result from painful recognition of past wrongdoing.

In addition to our own consolation, we rejoiced still more at the joy of Titus, because his mind has been set at rest by all of you. **14** For if I have been somewhat boastful about you to him, I was not disgraced; but just as everything we said to you was true, so our boasting to Titus has proved true as well. **15** And his heart goes out all the more to you, as he remembers the obedience of all of you, and how you welcomed him with fear and trembling. **16** I rejoice, because I have complete confidence in you.

Encouragement to Be Generous

8 We want you to know, brothers and sisters,*a* about the grace of God that has been granted to the churches of Macedonia; **2** for during a severe ordeal of affliction, their abundant joy and their extreme poverty have overflowed in a wealth of generosity on their part. **3** For, as I can testify, they voluntarily gave according to their means, and even beyond their means, **4** begging us earnestly for the privilege*b* of sharing in this ministry to the saints— **5** and this, not merely as we expected; they gave themselves first to the Lord and, by the will of God, to us, **6** so that we might urge Titus that, as he had already made a beginning, so he should also complete this generous undertaking*c* among you. **7** Now as you excel in everything—in faith, in speech, in knowledge, in utmost eagerness, and in our love for you*d*—so we want you to excel also in this generous undertaking.*c*

8 I do not say this as a command, but I am testing the genuineness of your love against the earnestness of others. **9** For you know the generous act*e* of our Lord Jesus Christ, that though he was rich, yet for your sakes he became poor, so that by his poverty you might become rich. **10** And in this matter I am giving my advice: it is appropriate for you who began last year not only to do something but even to desire to do something— **11** now finish doing it, so that your eagerness may be matched by completing it according to your means. **12** For if the eagerness is there, the gift is acceptable according to what one has—not according to what one does not have. **13** I do not mean that there should be relief for others and pressure on you, but it is a question of a fair balance between **14** your present abundance and their need, so that their abundance may be for your need, in order that there may be a fair balance. **15** As it is written,

> "The one who had much did not
> have too much,
> and the one who had little did not
> have too little."

Commendation of Titus

16 But thanks be to God who put in the heart of Titus the same eagerness for you that I myself have. **17** For he not only accepted our appeal, but since he is more eager than ever, he is going to you of his own accord. **18** With him we are sending

a Gk brothers   *b* Gk grace   *c* Gk this grace   *d* Other ancient authorities read your love for us   *e* Gk the grace

---

7:15—Faith involves reverence for a holy God's message and messengers (cf. Phil. 2:12; 1 Thess. 2:13; 2 Cor. 6:3–6; 7:1).

8:1–9:15 Appeals and Instructions about the Collection for the Saints
Giving money to people in need is a prime expression of Christian faith and love.

8:1–5 The good example of the Macedonian churches—In a time of affliction and great poverty, these churches contributed eagerly and extravagantly to Paul's collection for the impoverished Jewish Christians of Jerusalem (see Rom. 15:25–32; 1 Cor. 16:1–4).

8:9—The supreme model of giving is Christ, who gave up the "wealth" of divine rank to become human and through the **poverty** of his sacrificial life and death enriched the world (cf. 5:14–15; 6:10; Phil. 2:6–8). His followers should likewise share themselves and their resources, whatever the cost in hardship and self-denial.

8:14—Those who give to others should be generous without condescension.

8:18–21—Paul has taken steps to make sure that no one can justifiably accuse him of misusing the funds gathered for the collection (cf. 5:11; 12:17–18). If a church leader's honesty is open to doubt,

the brother who is famous among all the churches for his proclaiming the good news;[a] [19] and not only that, but he has also been appointed by the churches to travel with us while we are administering this generous undertaking[b] for the glory of the Lord himself[c] and to show our goodwill. [20] We intend that no one should blame us about this generous gift that we are administering, [21] for we intend to do what is right not only in the Lord's sight but also in the sight of others. [22] And with them we are sending our brother whom we have often tested and found eager in many matters, but who is now more eager than ever because of his great confidence in you. [23] As for Titus, he is my partner and co-worker in your service; as for our brothers, they are messengers[d] of the churches, the glory of Christ. [24] Therefore openly before the churches, show them the proof of your love and of our reason for boasting about you.

The Collection for Christians at Jerusalem

9 Now it is not necessary for me to write you about the ministry to the saints, [2] for I know your eagerness, which is the subject of my boasting about you to the people of Macedonia, saying that Achaia has been ready since last year; and your zeal has stirred up most of them. [3] But I am sending the brothers in order that our boasting about you may not prove to have been empty in this case, so that you may be ready, as I said you would be; [4] otherwise, if some Macedonians come with me and find that you are not ready, we would be humiliated—to say nothing of you—in this undertak-ing.[e] [5] So I thought it necessary to urge the brothers to go on ahead to you, and arrange in advance for this bountiful gift that you have promised, so that it may be ready as a voluntary gift and not as an extortion.

[6] The point is this: the one who sows sparingly will also reap sparingly, and the one who sows bountifully will also reap bountifully. [7] Each of you must give as you have made up your mind, not reluctantly or under compulsion, for God loves a cheerful giver. [8] And God is able to provide you with every blessing in abundance, so that by always having enough of everything, you may share abundantly in every good work. [9] As it is written,

"He scatters abroad, he gives to the poor;
   his righteousness[f] endures forever."

[10] He who supplies seed to the sower and bread for food will supply and multiply your seed for sowing and increase the harvest of your righteousness.[f] [11] You will be enriched in every way for your great generosity, which will produce thanksgiving to God through us; [12] for the rendering of this ministry not only supplies the needs of the saints but also overflows with many thanksgivings to God. [13] Through the testing of this ministry you glorify God by your obedience to the confession of the gospel of Christ and by the generosity of your sharing with them and with all others, [14] while they long for you and pray for you because of the surpassing grace of God that he has given you. [15] Thanks be to God for his indescribable gift!

a Or the gospel b Gk this grace c Other ancient authorities lack himself d Gk apostles e Other ancient authorities add of boasting f Or benevolence

---

not least in money matters, the whole community may be injured.

9:6–10—Believers should trust that *God* will *provide* for them as they give to others.

9:11–15—Paul concludes by explaining that the Corinthians' sharing in the collection will lead to multiple blessings. They themselves will be spiritually enriched as they match their confession of faith with generous action. The recipients of the gift will praise God with prayers for the Corinthians. Paul and his ministerial colleagues will thank God for the gift. Finally, Paul probably also thinks of the spiritual oneness of Jews and Gentiles in the church, which the gift will attest and support (see Rom. 15:25–27). Such gift giving will be an appropriate response to God's indescribably great gift of Christ (8:9; 9:14–15).

Paul Defends His Ministry

10 I myself, Paul, appeal to you by the meekness and gentleness of Christ—I who am humble when face to face with you, but bold toward you when I am away!— ²I ask that when I am present I need not show boldness by daring to oppose those who think we are acting according to human standards.*a* ³Indeed, we live as human beings,*b* but we do not wage war according to human standards;*a* ⁴for the weapons of our warfare are not merely human,*c* but they have divine power to destroy strongholds. We destroy arguments ⁵and every proud obstacle raised up against the knowledge of God, and we take every thought captive to obey Christ. ⁶We are ready to punish every disobedience when your obedience is complete.

7 Look at what is before your eyes. If you are confident that you belong to Christ, remind yourself of this, that just as you belong to Christ, so also do we. ⁸Now, even if I boast a little too much of our authority, which the Lord gave for building you up and not for tearing you down, I will not be ashamed of it. ⁹I do not want to seem as though I am trying to frighten you with my letters. ¹⁰For they say, "His letters are weighty and strong, but his bodily presence is weak, and his speech contemptible." ¹¹Let such people understand that what we say by letter when absent, we will also do when present.

12 We do not dare to classify or compare ourselves with some of those who commend themselves. But when they measure themselves by one another, and compare themselves with one another, they do not show good sense. ¹³We, however, will not boast beyond limits, but will keep within the field that God has assigned to us, to reach out even as far as you. ¹⁴For we were not overstepping our limits when we reached you; we were the first to come all the way to you with the good news*d* of Christ. ¹⁵We do not boast beyond limits, that is, in the labors of others; but our hope is that, as your faith increases, our sphere of action among you may be greatly enlarged, ¹⁶so that we may proclaim the good news*d* in lands beyond you, without boasting of work already done in someone else's sphere of action. ¹⁷"Let the one who boasts, boast in the Lord." ¹⁸For it is not those who commend themselves that are approved, but those whom the Lord commends.

Paul and the False Apostles

11 I wish you would bear with me in a little foolishness. Do bear with me! ²I feel a divine jealousy for you, for I promised you in marriage to one husband, to present you as a chaste virgin to Christ. ³But I am afraid that as the serpent deceived Eve by its cunning, your

a Gk *according to the flesh*   *b* Gk *in the flesh*   *c* Gk *fleshly*   *d* Or *the gospel*

10:1–13:10 Paul Defends His Apostleship

10:1–6 An Appeal

Paul declares that he will defend his apostolic ministry according to the norm of Christ, whose death and resurrection disclose weakness and omnipotence (cf. 12:9, 19; 13:3–4).

10:7–18 Paul Boasts about His Apostleship

10:8—Paul claims God has bestowed on him a Jeremiah-like authority to destroy false ideas, not persons (see Jer. 1:10; 2 Cor. 10:4–5; 12:19; 13:10).

10:17–18—The only proper boasting for believers is about what God has done in Christ (see 1 Cor. 1:31, which also refers to Jer. 9:24).

11:1–33 Paul and the "Super-Apostles"

11:1 *A little foolishness*—Paul begins to use the ironic device of speaking like a fool to make the Corinthians realize their genuine foolishness (see also vv. 16–21; 12:11). The test of a valid Christian witness is conformity to Christ, whose way of the cross is bound to appear weak or foolish by worldly standards (cf. 1 Cor. 1:18–25).

11:3—The *serpent* persuaded *Eve* that she would gain wisdom by disobeying God's command (Gen. 3:5–6). Similarly, the Corinthians are in danger of betraying their bridelike commitment to Christ by listening to *super-apostles* (v. 5) who preach *another Jesus* (v. 4) and insinuate that Paul and his message are contemptible (see 13:5; Gal. 1:6–9).

thoughts will be led astray from a sincere and pure*a* devotion to Christ. **4** For if someone comes and proclaims another Jesus than the one we proclaimed, or if you receive a different spirit from the one you received, or a different gospel from the one you accepted, you submit to it readily enough. **5** I think that I am not in the least inferior to these super-apostles. **6** I may be untrained in speech, but not in knowledge; certainly in every way and in all things we have made this evident to you.

7 Did I commit a sin by humbling myself so that you might be exalted, because I proclaimed God's good news*b* to you free of charge? **8** I robbed other churches by accepting support from them in order to serve you. **9** And when I was with you and was in need, I did not burden anyone, for my needs were supplied by the friends*c* who came from Macedonia. So I refrained and will continue to refrain from burdening you in any way. **10** As the truth of Christ is in me, this boast of mine will not be silenced in the regions of Achaia. **11** And why? Because I do not love you? God knows I do!

12 And what I do I will also continue to do, in order to deny an opportunity to those who want an opportunity to be recognized as our equals in what they boast about. **13** For such boasters are false apostles, deceitful workers, disguising themselves as apostles of Christ. **14** And no wonder! Even Satan disguises himself as an angel of light. **15** So it is not strange if his ministers also disguise themselves as ministers of righteousness. Their end will match their deeds.

Paul's Sufferings as an Apostle

16 I repeat, let no one think that I am a fool; but if you do, then accept me as a fool, so that I too may boast a little. **17** What I am saying in regard to this boastful confidence, I am saying not with the Lord's authority, but as a fool; **18** since many boast according to human standards,*d* I will also boast. **19** For you gladly put up with fools, being wise yourselves! **20** For you put up with it when someone makes slaves of you, or preys upon you, or takes advantage of you, or puts on airs, or gives you a slap in the face. **21** To my shame, I must say, we were too weak for that!

But whatever anyone dares to boast of—I am speaking as a fool—I also dare to boast of that. **22** Are they Hebrews? So am I. Are they Israelites? So am I. Are they descendants of Abraham? So am I. **23** Are they ministers of Christ? I am talking like a madman—I am a better one: with far greater labors, far more imprisonments, with countless floggings, and often near death. **24** Five times I have received from the Jews the forty lashes minus one. **25** Three times I was beaten with rods. Once I received a stoning. Three times I was shipwrecked; for a night and a day I was adrift at sea; **26** on frequent journeys, in danger from rivers, danger from bandits, danger from my own people, danger from Gentiles, danger in the city, danger in the wilderness, danger at sea, danger from false brothers and sisters;*c* **27** in toil and hardship, through many a sleepless night, hungry and thirsty, often without food, cold and naked. **28** And, besides other things, I am under daily pressure because of my anxiety for all the churches. **29** Who is weak, and I am not weak? Who is made to stumble, and I am not indignant?

a Other ancient authorities lack *and pure*   *b* Gk *the gospel of God*
c Gk *brothers*   *d* Gk *according to the flesh*

11:7—Some in Corinth blamed Paul for not taking money from the church (see also 12:14–18; cf. 1 Cor. 9:15–18). Even the best-intentioned financial policies can arouse suspicion.

11:11—A fundamental issue for both apostle and congregation was whether Paul, often physically separated from his converts, really cared about the Corinthians (cf. 12:14–15; 13:7).

11:23—The quality of genuine apostles is publicly shown in their missionary labors, successes, and sufferings for Christ's sake (cf. 1 Cor. 4:9–13; 2 Cor. 4:8–12; 6:3–10; Gal. 6:17; Col. 1:24).

30 If I must boast, I will boast of the things that show my weakness. 31 The God and Father of the Lord Jesus (blessed be he forever!) knows that I do not lie. 32 In Damascus, the governor*a* under King Aretas guarded the city of Damascus in order to*b* seize me, 33 but I was let down in a basket through a window in the wall,*c* and escaped from his hands.

Paul's Visions and Revelations

12 It is necessary to boast; nothing is to be gained by it, but I will go on to visions and revelations of the Lord. 2 I know a person in Christ who fourteen years ago was caught up to the third heaven—whether in the body or out of the body I do not know; God knows. 3 And I know that such a person—whether in the body or out of the body I do not know; God knows— 4 was caught up into Paradise and heard things that are not to be told, that no mortal is permitted to repeat. 5 On behalf of such a one I will boast, but on my own behalf I will not boast, except of my weaknesses. 6 But if I wish to boast, I will not be a fool, for I will be speaking the truth. But I refrain from it, so that no one may think better of me than what is seen in me or heard from me, 7 even considering the exceptional character of the revelations. Therefore, to keep*d* me from being too elated, a thorn was given me in the flesh, a messenger of Satan to torment me, to keep me from being too elated.*e* 8 Three times I appealed to the Lord about this, that it would leave me, 9 but he said to me, "My grace is sufficient for you, for power*f* is made perfect in weakness." So, I will boast all the more gladly of my weaknesses, so that the power of Christ may dwell in me. 10 Therefore I am content with weaknesses, insults, hardships, persecutions, and calamities for the sake of Christ; for whenever I am weak, then I am strong.

Paul's Concern for the Corinthian Church

11 I have been a fool! You forced me to it. Indeed you should have been the ones commending me, for I am not at all inferior to these super-apostles, even though I am nothing. 12 The signs of a true apostle were performed among you with utmost patience, signs and wonders and mighty works. 13 How have you been worse off than the other churches, except that I myself did not burden you? Forgive me this wrong!

14 Here I am, ready to come to you this third time. And I will not be a burden, because I do not want what is yours but you; for children ought not to lay up

a Gk ethnarch *b* Other ancient authorities read *and wanted to* *c* Gk *through the wall* *d* Other ancient authorities read *To keep* *e* Other ancient authorities lack *to keep me from being too elated* *f* Other ancient authorities read *my power*

11:30 *My weakness*—Paul takes up the accusation of weakness (10:10) and turns it around: his willingness to suffer and endure anxiety and shame as an apostle (e.g., 11:28–33) attests his integrity.

12:1–4 Paul Boasts about a Heavenly Revelation He Cannot Reveal

12:2—Most interpreters assume that Paul is talking about himself, but he describes this extraordinary experience with great reserve.

12:5–10 Paul Boasts about a Prayer Request God Did Not Grant

12:7—The exact nature of Paul's *thorn in the flesh*, probably a physical ailment, has been endlessly debated.

12:9 *"My grace is sufficient for you, for power is made perfect in weakness"*—God's power was revealed in the Lord's death and continues to work through human weakness (13:4). Believers who follow in Paul's footsteps will accept their experiences of limitation and suffering, trusting in the divine power that won victory through a cross.

12:11–13 Paul's Boasting, Nonsense Made Necessary by the Corinthians' Accusations

12:11—Paul's humility is not abject. He defends his authority and probity as an apostle because it is in the best interests of the church that he do so (v. 19) and because this is a way of defending the truth of the gospel. Yet he knows that he and his ministry are *nothing* apart from God's grace. Cf. 4:5; 12:9; Rom. 15:17–18; 1 Cor. 3:5–7; 15:9–10.

12:14–21 Everything to Build Up the Church

for their parents, but parents for their children. [15] I will most gladly spend and be spent for you. If I love you more, am I to be loved less? [16] Let it be assumed that I did not burden you. Nevertheless (you say) since I was crafty, I took you in by deceit. [17] Did I take advantage of you through any of those whom I sent to you? [18] I urged Titus to go, and sent the brother with him. Titus did not take advantage of you, did he? Did we not conduct ourselves with the same spirit? Did we not take the same steps?

19 Have you been thinking all along that we have been defending ourselves before you? We are speaking in Christ before God. Everything we do, beloved, is for the sake of building you up. [20] For I fear that when I come, I may find you not as I wish, and that you may find me not as you wish; I fear that there may perhaps be quarreling, jealousy, anger, selfishness, slander, gossip, conceit, and disorder. [21] I fear that when I come again, my God may humble me before you, and that I may have to mourn over many who previously sinned and have not repented of the impurity, sexual immorality, and licentiousness that they have practiced.

Further Warning

13 This is the third time I am coming to you. "Any charge must be sustained by the evidence of two or three witnesses." [2] I warned those who sinned previously and all the others, and I warn them now while absent, as I did when present on my second visit, that if I come again, I will not be lenient— [3] since you desire proof that Christ is speaking in me. He is not weak in dealing with you, but is powerful in you. [4] For he was crucified in weakness, but lives by the power of God. For we are weak in him,[a] but in dealing with you we will live with him by the power of God.

5 Examine yourselves to see whether you are living in the faith. Test yourselves. Do you not realize that Jesus Christ is in you?—unless, indeed, you fail to meet the test! [6] I hope you will find out that we have not failed. [7] But we pray to God that you may not do anything wrong—not that we may appear to have met the test, but that you may do what is right, though we may seem to have failed. [8] For we cannot do anything against the truth, but only for the truth. [9] For we rejoice when we are weak and you are strong. This is what we pray for, that you may become perfect. [10] So I write these things while I am away from you, so that when I come, I may not have to be severe in using the authority that the Lord has given me for building up and not for tearing down.

Final Greetings and Benediction

11 Finally, brothers and sisters,[b] farewell.[c] Put things in order, listen to my appeal,[d] agree with one another, live in peace; and the God of love and peace will be with you. [12] Greet one another with a holy kiss. All the saints greet you.

13 The grace of the Lord Jesus Christ, the love of God, and the communion of[e] the Holy Spirit be with all of you.

[a] Other ancient authorities read *with him* [b] Gk *brothers* [c] Or *rejoice*
[d] Or *encourage one another* [e] Or *and the sharing in*

12:20–21—As the church's founder, Paul would be humiliated if he found the Corinthians torn by quarrels over false apostleship and by immorality (cf. 3:2; 4:14; 9:4; 1 Cor. 3:10–15).

13:1–10 Paul's Plans for a Third Visit

13:5–7—The proof of genuine Christian community is the presence of Christ. Church members must continually *examine* their values and actions to see if they are in line with Jesus' love, crucifixion, and resurrection.

13:9—The Greek term rendered *become perfect* here could also be translated "become mature."

Paul prays that the church may return to a true understanding of Christian faith, not that its members be absolutely faultless.

13:11–14 Letter Closing: Summary Instructions, Greetings, Blessing

13:12—The Corinthian Christians must remember that they belong to a worldwide community (*all the saints*), whose members pray for their welfare and care about their decisions. Awareness of other believers should both encourage them and heighten their sense of responsibility.

The Book of
GALATIANS

Paul wrote his letter to the Galatian churches in a situation of extreme crisis. The letter expresses his passionate concern for the welfare of these churches and presents some of his most profound thoughts about Christian freedom.

The letter gives valuable historical information about Paul's perspectives on his life before and after his conversion (1:13–24), the apostolic council in Jerusalem (2:1–10—almost certainly the same one described in rather different fashion in Acts 15), and a heated argument between himself and Peter in Antioch (2:11–14). Many scholars have supposed that Galatians was written fairly soon after the council (perhaps in 49 or 50 CE), but some date it to the middle 50s since what it says about faith, the Jewish law, and the Spirit make Galatians appear like a first draft of the letter to the Romans.

The letter does not say exactly where the Galatian churches were located, but Galatia must refer to a region in central Asia Minor (modern Turkey). Paul had converted the persons he addresses, but they were now on the brink of disowning him and his gospel. Evidently they did not realize they were in danger of abandoning Christ, and Paul writes to wake them up to the fact (1:6–9; 5:4).

Four developments in the early history of the Galatian churches may be inferred from the letter. A physical infirmity of some kind led to Paul's initial preaching in the region (4:13). The Galatians (who had formerly worshiped pagan gods—4:8) at first responded to Paul with great devotion (4:15) and experienced various signs of the power of God's Spirit (3:2–5). Sometime after the apostle left to preach elsewhere, other Christian missionaries appeared in the region and began to persuade the new converts that Paul had misled them by not making it clear that they needed to be circumcised (and, perhaps, to accept the entire Jewish law)—in effect, that they had to become Jews before they could be real Christians. (Paul never names these persons, and we shall refer to them simply as "the opponents.") When Paul learned about this new turn of events, he wrote the letter we have, denouncing the opponents as perverters of the gospel (1:7) and earnestly defending his apostleship and his understanding of Christian freedom.

Paul argues vehemently that Christ has given genuine liberty, a liberty that believers must steadfastly maintain in defiance of every assertion that Christ's work is insufficient (5:2–4). Salvation or justification hinges on trusting exclusively in what God has accomplished in Christ (2:19–21), a position of faith bound up with experiences of God's Spirit (5:5). Some of the nuances of meaning that Paul gives to the term "faith" in Galatians are debated, but a bond with Christ is essential (3:22–26). While Christians are not "under" the law (5:18), they are obligated to love their neighbors (5:13–14) and reject all temptations of the "flesh" (which include the temptation to seek to justify themselves through works of the law). The freedom of the children of God precludes reliance on the Jewish law just as much as it forbids returning to pagan superstitions (4:1–11).

Galatians powerfully affirms that authentic Christian ministry depends on God's calling and that the truth of the good news in Jesus is finally independent of human religious authorities. The gospel offers liberation from all the evil elements in the world and in ourselves, including legalism and discriminatory classifications of people by racial or religious background, economic and social status, and gender (3:28). The "present evil age" (1:4) displays the propensity of individuals and groups to imagine themselves superior to others. The letter celebrates a freedom God gives to persons who identify through faith with the crucified Christ (2:20), thereby entering a new spiritual world marked by peace and unselfish love of others (6:14–15).

—David Hay

Salutation

1 Paul an apostle—sent neither by human commission nor from human authorities, but through Jesus Christ and God the Father, who raised him from the dead— [2] and all the members of God's family[a] who are with me,

To the churches of Galatia:

3 Grace to you and peace from God our Father and the Lord Jesus Christ, [4] who gave himself for our sins to set us free from the present evil age, according to the will of our God and Father, [5] to whom be the glory forever and ever. Amen.

There Is No Other Gospel

6 I am astonished that you are so quickly deserting the one who called you in the grace of Christ and are turning to a different gospel— [7] not that there is another gospel, but there are some who are confusing you and want to pervert the gospel of Christ. [8] But even if we or an angel[b] from heaven should proclaim to you a gospel contrary to what we proclaimed to you, let that one be accursed! [9] As we have said before, so now I repeat, if anyone proclaims to you a gospel contrary to what you received, let that one be accursed!

10 Am I now seeking human approval, or God's approval? Or am I trying to please people? If I were still pleasing people, I would not be a servant[c] of Christ.

Paul's Vindication of His Apostleship

11 For I want you to know, brothers and sisters,[d] that the gospel that was proclaimed by me is not of human origin; [12] for I did not receive it from a human source, nor was I taught it, but I received it through a revelation of Jesus Christ.

13 You have heard, no doubt, of my earlier life in Judaism. I was violently persecuting the church of God and was trying to destroy it. [14] I advanced in Juda-

[a] Gk all the brothers   [b] Or a messenger   [c] Gk slave   [d] Gk brothers

---

1:1–9 Letter Opening

Paul briefly identifies himself and the churches he is addressing. He also indicates two primary themes of the letter: the direct calling from Christ and God that is the basis of his apostleship, and the liberating nature of the Christian message.

1:4 *The present evil age*—Jesus, acting in obedience to God, died as a sacrifice for our sins *to set us free* from all that is evil in the present world order (cf. 3:13–14; 5:1; 1 Cor. 15:3).

1:6–9—Paul is writing to counter unnamed opponents who have told the Galatians that what Paul preached was false or inadequate. In fact there is only one true gospel, and people who try to "improve" it lead their listeners away from both Christ and salvation (cf. 5:4).

1:10–2:21 A Defense of Paul's Apostleship as Both Independent and Valid

Paul argues that his apostleship rests on divine calling rather than human appointment (1:13–24) and that he has consistently maintained the *truth of the gospel* (2:5) regarding the terms of the conversion of Gentiles.

1:10–24 Paul's Divine Calling

1:13–16—The event of Paul's conversion and appointment as an apostle was a special demonstration of God's miraculous grace made known in Christ. It was not the result of Paul's personal

ism beyond many among my people of the same age, for I was far more zealous for the traditions of my ancestors. [15] But when God, who had set me apart before I was born and called me through his grace, was pleased [16] to reveal his Son to me,[a] so that I might proclaim him among the Gentiles, I did not confer with any human being, [17] nor did I go up to Jerusalem to those who were already apostles before me, but I went away at once into Arabia, and afterwards I returned to Damascus.

[18] Then after three years I did go up to Jerusalem to visit Cephas and stayed with him fifteen days; [19] but I did not see any other apostle except James the Lord's brother. [20] In what I am writing to you, before God, I do not lie! [21] Then I went into the regions of Syria and Cilicia, [22] and I was still unknown by sight to the churches of Judea that are in Christ; [23] they only heard it said, "The one who formerly was persecuting us is now proclaiming the faith he once tried to destroy." [24] And they glorified God because of me.

Paul and the Other Apostles

2 Then after fourteen years I went up again to Jerusalem with Barnabas, taking Titus along with me. [2] I went up in response to a revelation. Then I laid before them (though only in a private meeting with the acknowledged leaders) the gospel that I proclaim among the Gentiles, in order to make sure that I was not running, or had not run, in vain. [3] But even Titus, who was with me, was not compelled to be circumcised, though he was a Greek. [4] But because of false believers[b] secretly brought in, who slipped in to spy on the freedom we have in Christ Jesus, so that they might enslave us— [5] we did not submit to them even for a moment, so that the truth of the gospel might always remain with you. [6] And from those who were supposed to be acknowledged leaders (what they actually were makes no difference to me; God shows no partiality)—those leaders contributed nothing to me. [7] On the contrary, when they saw that I had been entrusted with the gospel for the uncircumcised, just as Peter had been entrusted with the gospel for the circumcised [8] (for he who worked through Peter making him an apostle to the circumcised also worked through me in sending me to the Gentiles), [9] and when James and Cephas and John, who were acknowledged pillars, recognized the grace that had been given to me, they gave to Barnabas and me the right hand of fellowship, agreeing that we should go to the Gentiles and they to the circumcised. [10] They asked only one thing, that we remember the poor, which was actually what I was[c] eager to do.

[a] Gk in me [b] Gk false brothers [c] Or had been

---

worthiness (he had been persecuting God's church) or authorization from other apostles. People turn to God when God speaks to them, and his call requires full and immediate commitment to the service of God's people.

1:18–19—*Cephas* is the Aramaic name of Peter (cf. 1 Cor. 1:12). *James* is the **brother** of Jesus, who became a leader of the Jerusalem church (see 2:9, 12; 1 Cor. 15:7; Mark 6:3).

2:1–14 Agreements and Disagreements with Leaders of the Jerusalem Church

2:1–10—This apostolic conference at **Jerusalem** was evidently the same one described in Acts 15. It occurred about 49 CE.

2:4 The freedom we have in Christ Jesus—The presenting issue at the conference was whether Gentile Christians had to be **circumcised** (and so, at least in principle, become Jews—see Acts 15:1). Paul defended the truth of the gospel and the **freedom** it gives to all believers. If a right relationship with God comes through faith in Christ, the church dare not add extra requirements such as circumcision or American middle-class values.

2:6–10—Paul is glad to report that the chief *pillars* of the Jerusalem church (James, Peter, and John) gave their approval to his missionary work with **Gentiles**. They added no conditions but acknowledged that God was at work in that mission.

Paul Rebukes Peter at Antioch

11 But when Cephas came to Antioch, I opposed him to his face, because he stood self-condemned; [12] for until certain people came from James, he used to eat with the Gentiles. But after they came, he drew back and kept himself separate for fear of the circumcision faction. [13] And the other Jews joined him in this hypocrisy, so that even Barnabas was led astray by their hypocrisy. [14] But when I saw that they were not acting consistently with the truth of the gospel, I said to Cephas before them all, "If you, though a Jew, live like a Gentile and not like a Jew, how can you compel the Gentiles to live like Jews?"[a]

Jews and Gentiles Are Saved by Faith

15 We ourselves are Jews by birth and not Gentile sinners; [16] yet we know that a person is justified[b] not by the works of the law but through faith in Jesus Christ.[c] And we have come to believe in Christ Jesus, so that we might be justified by faith in Christ,[d] and not by doing the works of the law, because no one will be justified by the works of the law. [17] But if, in our effort to be justified in Christ, we ourselves have been found to be sinners, is Christ then a servant of sin? Certainly not! [18] But if I build up again the very things that I once tore down, then I demonstrate that I am a transgressor. [19] For through the law I died to the law, so that I might live to God. I have been crucified with Christ; [20] and it is no longer I who live, but it is Christ who lives in me. And the life I now live in the flesh I live by faith in the Son of God,[e] who loved me and gave himself for me. [21] I do not nullify the grace of God; for if justification[f] comes through the law, then Christ died for nothing.

Law or Faith

3 You foolish Galatians! Who has bewitched you? It was before your eyes that Jesus Christ was publicly exhibited as crucified! [2] The only thing I want to learn from you is this: Did you receive the Spirit by doing the works of the law or by believing what you heard? [3] Are you so foolish? Having started with the Spirit, are you now ending with the flesh? [4] Did you experience so much for nothing?—if it really was for nothing. [5] Well then, does God[g] supply you with the Spirit and work miracles among you by your doing the works of the law, or by your believing what you heard?

6 Just as Abraham "believed God, and

[a] Some interpreters hold that the quotation extends into the following paragraph　[b] Or reckoned as righteous; and so elsewhere　[c] Or the faith of Jesus Christ　[d] Or the faith of Christ　[e] Or by the faith of the Son of God　[f] Or righteousness　[g] Gk he

---

2:11–12—The church of *Antioch* in Syria was an early center of the Christian movement with both Jewish and Gentile members (Acts 11:19–26). Peter, prodded by James, thought that Old Testament dietary laws required that Jewish Christians separate themselves from Gentile Christians at meals (presumably including observances of the Lord's Supper). Paul's opposition to Peter and the others stemmed from his conviction that the church is not a club in which certain members can discriminate against others (cf. Gal. 3:28).

2:15–21 Summary of the Issues at Stake

Paul defines the fundamental issue both at Antioch and in Galatia: justification as God's gift given through Christ-centered faith, not a human accomplishment based on observing the Jewish law (including the dietary requirements).

2:19–20 *I died to the law*—The *I* here is Paul and, by implication, every Christian. Faith oriented to Christ means dying to the law—that is, giving up every effort to earn God's approval through one's own achievements. It also means finding in Christ the inner foundation and truth of one's own existence, without confusing oneself with Christ (cf. 2 Cor. 4:7–12; Phil. 1:21; 3:7–11; Col. 1:27; 3:3).

3:1–6:10 The Gospel Means Freedom from Both Legalism and Self-Indulgence

3:1–5 The Coming of the Spirit

People need to ponder their own experiences of God. Paul asks if the Galatians were inspired to the point of conversion by their own good deeds or by hearing the story of Christ.

3:6–29 Justification by Faith Based on a Christian Reading of the Jewish Scriptures

Paul is probably responding to an argument from the opponents to the effect that salvation (or justification) requires both faith (like Abraham's) and fulfilling the entire law of Moses.

it was reckoned to him as righteousness," [7] so, you see, those who believe are the descendants of Abraham. [8] And the scripture, foreseeing that God would justify the Gentiles by faith, declared the gospel beforehand to Abraham, saying, "All the Gentiles shall be blessed in you." [9] For this reason, those who believe are blessed with Abraham who believed.

10 For all who rely on the works of the law are under a curse; for it is written, "Cursed is everyone who does not observe and obey all the things written in the book of the law." [11] Now it is evident that no one is justified before God by the law; for "The one who is righteous will live by faith."[a] [12] But the law does not rest on faith; on the contrary, "Whoever does the works of the law[b] will live by them." [13] Christ redeemed us from the curse of the law by becoming a curse for us—for it is written, "Cursed is everyone who hangs on a tree"— [14] in order that in Christ Jesus the blessing of Abraham might come to the Gentiles, so that we might receive the promise of the Spirit through faith.

The Promise to Abraham

15 Brothers and sisters,[c] I give an example from daily life: once a person's will[d] has been ratified, no one adds to it or annuls it. [16] Now the promises were made to Abraham and to his offspring;[e] it does not say, "And to offsprings,"[f] as of many; but it says, "And to your offspring,"[e] that is, to one person, who is Christ. [17] My point is this: the law, which came four hundred thirty years later, does not annul a covenant previously ratified by God, so as to nullify the promise. [18] For if the inheritance comes from the law, it no longer comes from the promise; but God granted it to Abraham through the promise.

The Purpose of the Law

19 Why then the law? It was added because of transgressions, until the offspring[e] would come to whom the promise had been made; and it was ordained through angels by a mediator. [20] Now a mediator involves more than one party; but God is one.

21 Is the law then opposed to the promises of God? Certainly not! For if a law had been given that could make alive, then righteousness would indeed come through the law. [22] But the scripture has imprisoned all things under the power of sin, so that what was promised through faith in Jesus Christ[g] might be given to those who believe.

23 Now before faith came, we were imprisoned and guarded under the law until faith would be revealed. [24] Therefore the law was our disciplinarian until Christ came, so that we might be justified by faith. [25] But now that faith has come, we are no longer subject to a disciplinarian, [26] for in Christ Jesus you are all children of God through faith. [27] As many of you as were baptized into Christ have clothed yourselves with Christ. [28] There is no longer Jew or Greek, there is no longer slave or free, there is no longer male and female; for

---

a Or *The one who is righteous through faith will live* b Gk *does them* c Gk *Brothers* d Or *covenant* (as in verse 17) e Gk *seed* f Gk *seeds* g Or *through the faith of Jesus Christ*

3:6–9—Scripture declares that *Abraham* was justified *by faith*, as are all his spiritual descendants (both Jews and Gentiles).

3:10–14—A legalistic religion is one in which people trust themselves to fulfill everything God commands, thereby earning salvation. Such religion is incompatible with radical trust in God (or Christ).

3:21–22—The *law* of Moses is not contrary to God's *promises* of salvation through faith. God never intended the law to do more than define right and wrong and show humans how far short of perfection they have fallen (cf. Rom. 3:19–23).

3:23–29—Although Abraham demonstrated genuine faith in the pre-Christian era, the coming of Jesus Christ made faith possible for everyone. Those united to Christ *through faith* and baptism are all equal *children of God*. Here differences of sex, social and economic position, nationality or even religious background no longer matter (v. 28). Christian faith affirms the essential equality of all persons before God.

all of you are one in Christ Jesus. [29] And if you belong to Christ, then you are Abraham's offspring,[a] heirs according to the promise.

4 My point is this: heirs, as long as they are minors, are no better than slaves, though they are the owners of all the property; [2] but they remain under guardians and trustees until the date set by the father. [3] So with us; while we were minors, we were enslaved to the elemental spirits[b] of the world. [4] But when the fullness of time had come, God sent his Son, born of a woman, born under the law, [5] in order to redeem those who were under the law, so that we might receive adoption as children. [6] And because you are children, God has sent the Spirit of his Son into our[c] hearts, crying, "Abba![d] Father!" [7] So you are no longer a slave but a child, and if a child then also an heir, through God.[e]

Paul Reproves the Galatians

8 Formerly, when you did not know God, you were enslaved to beings that by nature are not gods. [9] Now, however, that you have come to know God, or rather to be known by God, how can you turn back again to the weak and beggarly elemental spirits?[f] How can you want to be enslaved to them again? [10] You are observing special days, and months, and seasons, and years. [11] I am afraid that my work for you may have been wasted.

12 Friends,[g] I beg you, become as I am, for I also have become as you are. You have done me no wrong. [13] You know that it was because of a physical infirmity that I first announced the gospel to you; [14] though my condition put you to the test, you did not scorn or despise me, but welcomed me as an angel of God, as Christ Jesus. [15] What has become of the goodwill you felt? For I testify that, had it been possible, you would have torn out your eyes and given them to me. [16] Have I now become your enemy by telling you the truth? [17] They make much of you, but for no good purpose; they want to exclude you, so that you may make much of them. [18] It is good to be made much of for a good purpose at all times, and not only when I am present with you. [19] My little children, for whom I am again in the pain of childbirth until Christ is formed in you, [20] I wish I were present with you now and could change my tone, for I am perplexed about you.

The Allegory of Hagar and Sarah

21 Tell me, you who desire to be subject to the law, will you not listen to the law? [22] For it is written that Abraham had two sons, one by a slave woman and the other by a free woman. [23] One, the child of the slave, was born according to the flesh; the other, the child of the free woman, was born through the promise.

[a] Gk seed   [b] Or the rudiments   [c] Other ancient authorities read your
[d] Aramaic for Father   [e] Other ancient authorities read an heir of God through Christ   [f] Or beggarly rudiments   [g] Gk Brothers

---

4:1–11 Living as Mature Children of God

4:2–3 The elemental spirits—This phrase probably refers to pagan divinities (see v. 8; Col. 2:8, 20). People without faith in God are driven by superstitious assumptions about what they have to do and what powers govern the world.

4:6 Abba! Father—Christians' use of "Abba" (Aramaic for "father") to address God is inspired by the Holy Spirit and confirms that they are God's children (cf. Rom. 8:15–16).

4:12–20 A Personal Appeal Recalling Previous Affection and Respect

4:19 Childbirth—Paul compares himself to a loving mother (cf. 1 Thess. 2:7). Although he asks the Galatians to become as I am (Gal. 4:12), his goal is for Christ to be formed in them (cf. 2:20). Their calling is not to become Paul look-alikes, but mature children of God (see 3:26; 4:6; Rom. 8:28–29).

4:21–31 A Final Argument against Legalism

Paul now interprets Hagar and Sarah, Abraham's wives, as allegorical symbols of slavery and freedom. He is attacking not Judaism as such but the position of his Christian opponents in Galatia. Here Hagar symbolizes the "fleshly" idea that Christians are bound like slaves to a legalistic observance of the law of Moses. Sarah represents a Spirit-directed reliance on God's promises.

24 Now this is an allegory: these women are two covenants. One woman, in fact, is Hagar, from Mount Sinai, bearing children for slavery. 25 Now Hagar is Mount Sinai in Arabia[a] and corresponds to the present Jerusalem, for she is in slavery with her children. 26 But the other woman corresponds to the Jerusalem above; she is free, and she is our mother. 27 For it is written,

"Rejoice, you childless one, you who
bear no children,
burst into song and shout, you
who endure no birth pangs;
for the children of the desolate
woman are more numerous
than the children of the one who is
married."

28 Now you,[b] my friends,[c] are children of the promise, like Isaac. 29 But just as at that time the child who was born according to the flesh persecuted the child who was born according to the Spirit, so it is now also. 30 But what does the scripture say? "Drive out the slave and her child; for the child of the slave will not share the inheritance with the child of the free woman." 31 So then, friends,[c] we are children, not of the slave but of the free woman. 1 For freedom Christ has set us free. Stand firm, therefore, and do not submit again to a yoke of slavery.

The Nature of Christian Freedom

2 Listen! I, Paul, am telling you that if you let yourselves be circumcised, Christ will be of no benefit to you. 3 Once again I testify to every man who lets himself be circumcised that he is obliged to obey the entire law. 4 You who want to be justified by the law have cut yourselves off from Christ; you have fallen away from grace. 5 For through the Spirit, by faith, we eagerly wait for the hope of righteousness. 6 For in Christ Jesus neither circumcision nor uncircumcision counts for anything; the only thing that counts is faith working[d] through love.

7 You were running well; who prevented you from obeying the truth? 8 Such persuasion does not come from the one who calls you. 9 A little yeast leavens the whole batch of dough. 10 I am confident about you in the Lord that you will not think otherwise. But whoever it is that is confusing you will pay the penalty. 11 But my friends,[c] why am I still being persecuted if I am still preaching circumcision? In that case the offense of the cross has been removed. 12 I wish those who unsettle you would castrate themselves!

13 For you were called to freedom, brothers and sisters;[c] only do not use your freedom as an opportunity for self-indulgence,[e] but through love become slaves to one another. 14 For the whole law is summed up in a single commandment, "You shall love your neighbor as yourself." 15 If, however, you bite and

[a] Other ancient authorities read For Sinai is a mountain in Arabia [b] Other ancient authorities read we [c] Gk brothers [d] Or made effective [e] Gk the flesh

---

5:1 For Freedom Christ Has Set Us Free

Paul concludes the allegorical argument of 4:21–31 by exhorting the Galatians to hold fast to their *freedom*. They are free from all obligations except to serve Christ and God (cf. 1 Cor. 3:21–23).

5:2–12 A Final Appeal to Maintain Freedom in Christ

5:2–4 *Christ will be of no benefit to you*—The opponents' insistence on circumcision implies that salvation hinges on their keeping the entire Mosaic *law*. That, Paul says, means rejecting what God has accomplished through Christ (cf. 2:21; 3:21).

5:5–6—The triad of *faith*, *hope*, and *love* sums up the Christian life (cf. 1 Thess. 1:3; 5:8; 1 Cor. 13:13).

5:13–6:10 General Moral Exhortations: Life in the Spirit

Cf. Rom. 13:1–15:13; 1 Thess. 4:1–5:22; Col. 3:1–4:6; Eph. 4:1–6:18.

5:13 *Through love become slaves to one another*—The *freedom* of the Spirit means freedom from *self-indulgence* through loving others as you love yourself. Appropriate love of neighbor and self-love hinge on the love of God known in Christ (2:20). Such love fulfills the law (vv. 14, 18, 23; Rom. 8:4; 13:8–10; cf. Mark 12:28–34) without making human effort the basis of salvation.

devour one another, take care that you are not consumed by one another.

The Works of the Flesh

16 Live by the Spirit, I say, and do not gratify the desires of the flesh. [17] For what the flesh desires is opposed to the Spirit, and what the Spirit desires is opposed to the flesh; for these are opposed to each other, to prevent you from doing what you want. [18] But if you are led by the Spirit, you are not subject to the law. [19] Now the works of the flesh are obvious: fornication, impurity, licentiousness, [20] idolatry, sorcery, enmities, strife, jealousy, anger, quarrels, dissensions, factions, [21] envy,[a] drunkenness, carousing, and things like these. I am warning you, as I warned you before: those who do such things will not inherit the kingdom of God.

The Fruit of the Spirit

22 By contrast, the fruit of the Spirit is love, joy, peace, patience, kindness, generosity, faithfulness, [23] gentleness, and self-control. There is no law against such things. [24] And those who belong to Christ Jesus have crucified the flesh with its passions and desires. [25] If we live by the Spirit, let us also be guided by the Spirit. [26] Let us not become conceited, competing against one another, envying one another.

Bear One Another's Burdens

6 My friends,[b] if anyone is detected in a transgression, you who have received the Spirit should restore such a one in a spirit of gentleness. Take care

that you yourselves are not tempted. [2] Bear one another's burdens, and in this way you will fulfill[c] the law of Christ. [3] For if those who are nothing think they are something, they deceive themselves. [4] All must test their own work; then that work, rather than their neighbor's work, will become a cause for pride. [5] For all must carry their own loads.

6 Those who are taught the word must share in all good things with their teacher.

7 Do not be deceived; God is not mocked, for you reap whatever you sow. [8] If you sow to your own flesh, you will reap corruption from the flesh; but if you sow to the Spirit, you will reap eternal life from the Spirit. [9] So let us not grow weary in doing what is right, for we will reap at harvest time, if we do not give up. [10] So then, whenever we have an opportunity, let us work for the good of all, and especially for those of the family of faith.

Final Admonitions and Benediction

11 See what large letters I make when I am writing in my own hand! [12] It is those who want to make a good showing in the flesh that try to compel you to be circumcised—only that they may not be persecuted for the cross of Christ. [13] Even the circumcised do not themselves obey the law, but they want you to be circumcised so that they may boast about your flesh. [14] May I never boast of anything except the cross of our Lord Jesus Christ, by which[d] the world has

[a] Other ancient authorities add *murder*　[b] Gk *Brothers*　[c] Other ancient authorities read *in this way fulfill*　[d] Or *through whom*

5:19 *The works of the flesh*—A list of typical vices in vv. 19–21 supplies a working definition of the "flesh." Most involve self-centeredness or malice toward other people.

5:22–23 *The fruit of the Spirit*—God's Spirit can be recognized by the fruit it bears in believers' lives: habits of virtue that support love of others.

6:2 *The law of Christ*—An unusual expression, probably implying living by the Spirit (5:16, 25) and the law of love (5:14; cf. 1 Cor. 9:21).

6:10 *The family of faith*—Believers must seek

the good of all, including outsiders. Emphasis on the church community suggests practical concentration on loving one's "nearest neighbors."

6:11–18 *Letter Closing, Briefly Recalling Major Themes in the Letter*

6:14 *May I never boast*—Believers should place confidence not in their own accomplishments but in the death of Christ, which reveals his love and contradicts the values of the ordinary world (cf. 1:4; 2:19; Phil. 3:7–11).

been crucified to me, and I to the world. [15] For[a] neither circumcision nor uncircumcision is anything; but a new creation is everything! [16] As for those who will follow this rule—peace be upon them, and mercy, and upon the Israel of God.

[17] From now on, let no one make trouble for me; for I carry the marks of Jesus branded on my body.

[18] May the grace of our Lord Jesus Christ be with your spirit, brothers and sisters.[b] Amen.

[a] Other ancient authorities add *in Christ Jesus*   [b] Gk *brothers*

6:17 *The marks of Jesus*—Paul's fidelity as a servant and ambassador of Christ is shown by his scars, perhaps the result of beatings (cf. 5:11; 2 Cor. 11:23–25). The crucified Jesus is well represented by persons whose lives bear signs of costly discipleship.

The Book of
EPHESIANS

The sublime rhetoric of this letter affirms convictions and practices that make possible a church both unified and resistant to the threats posed by the fallen powers of the world. Ephesians depicts the Christian life as a battle against cosmic and worldly powers (6:10–18) that enslave humankind and darken our awareness and understanding (4:17–24). Christ has overcome these forces and now rules the cosmos, though not yet in a way that is evident to all. The first three chapters describe the new reality that has come into being in Christ, especially the reconciliation that has taken place between Jew and Gentile, making one new humanity. These chapters begin and end with liturgical materials (1:3–23 and 3:14–21) that function rhetorically to dislocate audiences from life in the everyday world and relocate them "in Christ" and "in the heavenly places" (1:3). The last three chapters (4–6) employ a variety of exhortations to call forth practices that distinguish this alternative community from the world and nurture its inner unity.

Theological and literary considerations, especially its extraordinarily long sentences and distinctive use of vocabulary, distinguish Ephesians from the undisputed letters of Paul, leading many scholars to conclude that it was written by one of Paul's disciples. Ephesians shares an abundance of material with Colossians, but lacks the specificity that distinguishes the argument of that letter. Rather than addressing the needs of a particular congregation, as did Colossians, Ephesians may have been written for more general circulation among churches across Asia Minor. It is thus more like a sermon, the kind one could deliver in town after town, than a personal letter. It should be read with attention not only to the ways it might influence an audience both emotionally and intellectually, but to the ways it uses language to captivate and transform their imagination.

Ephesians was one of the most influential statements of Christian discipleship in early Christianity and remains a deep well of theological and spiritual resources today. Its depiction of Christian life as a battle against hostile forces, its call to unity and harmony within the church, and its prayer that believers might be filled with the fullness of God all continue to appeal to diverse branches of the church today. The image Ephesians holds forth as the appropriate model for relationships among members of the Christian household (5:21–6:9) serves for some as a timeless ideal, but strikes others as a capitulation to the patriarchal culture of the first-century Mediterranean world. Whatever one makes of such controversies, readers should not be distracted from the central message of the letter: discipleship in Ephesians entails leaving behind the practices of alienation and hostility taught by the world and embodying the vision of reconciliation, peace, and human unity that is the accomplishment of Christ's death on the cross and the continuing manifestation of his comprehensive reign as Lord of heaven and earth.

—**Stanley Saunders**

Salutation

1 Paul, an apostle of Christ Jesus by the will of God,

To the saints who are in Ephesus and are faithful[a] in Christ Jesus:

2 Grace to you and peace from God our Father and the Lord Jesus Christ.

Spiritual Blessings in Christ

3 Blessed be the God and Father of our Lord Jesus Christ, who has blessed us in Christ with every spiritual blessing in the heavenly places, [4] just as he chose us in Christ[b] before the foundation of the world to be holy and blameless before him in love. [5] He destined us for adoption as his children through Jesus Christ, according to the good pleasure of his will, [6] to the praise of his glorious grace that he freely bestowed on us in the Beloved. [7] In him we have redemption through his blood, the forgiveness of our trespasses, according to the riches of his grace [8] that he lavished on us. With all wisdom and insight [9] he has made known to us the mystery of his will, according to his good pleasure that he set forth in Christ, [10] as a plan for the fullness of time, to gather up all things in him, things in heaven and things on earth. [11] In Christ we have also obtained an inheritance,[c] having been destined according to the purpose of him who accomplishes all things according to his counsel and will, [12] so that we, who were the first to set our hope on Christ, might live for the praise of his glory. [13] In him you also, when you had heard the word of truth, the gospel of your salvation, and had believed in him, were marked with the seal of the promised Holy Spirit; [14] this[d] is the pledge of our inheritance toward redemption as God's own people, to the praise of his glory.

Paul's Prayer

15 I have heard of your faith in the Lord Jesus and your love[e] toward all the saints, and for this reason [16] I do not cease to give thanks for you as I remember you in my prayers. [17] I pray that the God of our Lord Jesus Christ, the Father of glory, may give you a spirit of wisdom and revelation as you come to know him, [18] so that, with the eyes of your heart enlightened, you may know what is the hope to which he has called you, what are the riches of his glorious inheritance among the saints, [19] and what is the immeasurable greatness of his power for us who believe, according to the working of his great power. [20] God[f] put this

---

[a] Other ancient authorities lack *in Ephesus*, reading *saints who are also faithful* [b] Gk *in him* [c] Or *been made a heritage* [d] Other ancient authorities read *who* [e] Other ancient authorities lack *and your love* [f] Gk *He*

1:1 Address

The ascription *in Ephesus* is not found in some early manuscripts. The letter lacks references to the specific issues of any particular congregation; see introduction.

1:3–14 A "Eulogy" Celebrating God's Blessings in Christ

In the Greek, these verses comprise one long sentence, with clauses arranged in stair-step fashion, designed to displace readers from everyday consciousness and reorient them to the altered realities of life *in Christ* and *in the heavenly places* (v. 3). The language of these verses is very doxological; modern readers may find themselves lost in the rarified atmosphere of divine praise and adoration, especially when the book is read aloud. By evoking the experience of worship, the writer elevates the audience into a new setting, from which it may be possible both to glimpse the *mystery* of God's *plan for the fullness of*

time (vv. 9–10) and begin to realize the dimensions of life "in him." Renewed imagination leads to transformed relationships.

1:15–23 Thanksgiving and a Prayer for Enlightenment

These verses declare God's majesty and Christ's unlimited and unsurpassed dominion. Again, these verses are a single sentence in the Greek, designed to evoke a sense not only of divine power, but of the power now available to the church as it gathers to give witness to God's reconciling presence in the world.

1:18—*Eyes of your heart enlightened* establishes a contrast to the darkened imagination of those who are alienated from God (4:18).

1:20—*At his right hand* alludes to Ps. 110, which describes God's judgment against worldly rulers. The leaders of this world exercise only transitory power.

power to work in Christ when he raised him from the dead and seated him at his right hand in the heavenly places, [21] far above all rule and authority and power and dominion, and above every name that is named, not only in this age but also in the age to come. [22] And he has put all things under his feet and has made him the head over all things for the church, [23] which is his body, the fullness of him who fills all in all.

From Death to Life

2 You were dead through the trespasses and sins [2] in which you once lived, following the course of this world, following the ruler of the power of the air, the spirit that is now at work among those who are disobedient. [3] All of us once lived among them in the passions of our flesh, following the desires of flesh and senses, and we were by nature children of wrath, like everyone else. [4] But God, who is rich in mercy, out of the great love with which he loved us [5] even when we were dead through our trespasses, made us alive together with Christ[a]—by grace you have been saved— [6] and raised us up with him and seated us with him in the

heavenly places in Christ Jesus, [7] so that in the ages to come he might show the immeasurable riches of his grace in kindness toward us in Christ Jesus. [8] For by grace you have been saved through faith, and this is not your own doing; it is the gift of God— [9] not the result of works, so that no one may boast. [10] For we are what he has made us, created in Christ Jesus for good works, which God prepared beforehand to be our way of life.

One in Christ

11 So then, remember that at one time you Gentiles by birth,[b] called "the uncircumcision" by those who are called "the circumcision"—a physical circumcision made in the flesh by human hands— [12] remember that you were at that time without Christ, being aliens from the commonwealth of Israel, and strangers to the covenants of promise, having no hope and without God in the world. [13] But now in Christ Jesus you who once were far off have been brought near by the blood of Christ. [14] For he is our peace; in his flesh he has made both groups into one and has broken down

[a] Other ancient authorities read *in Christ*   [b] Gk *in the flesh*

1:21—*Rule and authority* refers to forces hostile to God that dominate and exploit humankind. These forces may take a variety of forms—spiritual, institutional, personal, political, economic, and cultural.

1:22–23—The church is not merely a collection of individuals or limited to local assemblies, but an organic, universal whole. Christ is the single person in whom all Christians across history and space are incorporated.

2:1–10 The Old Life (vv. 1–3) and the New Life in Christ (vv. 4–10)

2:2 *The ruler of the power of the air*—Evil is represented here not as an abstraction, but as living forces that exert their will in defiance of God and seek dominion over humankind. *Air* is the realm close at hand, all around us, in which this dominating force exercises its power.

2:3—All those born under the alienating forces of disobedience—all humans—are tainted by sin in every dimension of life and are subject to God's judgment. In a fallen world the abnormal conditions of sin, death, alienation, and disobedience appear normal and "natural." Discipleship entails

recognition of the ways reality is distorted in the fallen creation.

2:4–5—The shift from the realm of sin and death to life with Christ is not a matter of human volition or action, but God's loving and merciful accomplishment. Recognition of this new reality provides the foundation for transformed perception and practices of discipleship.

2:6—Those who are in Christ are already exalted with him in power (cf. 1:3, 20). The *heavenly places* are not a realm separate from the earth, but the realm of God's new creation in Christ, which does not stand under the limitations of human notions of time or space. Disciples are set free from the tyranny of modern notions of time and from social constructions that disrupt or limit our relationships with one another.

2:11–22 One New Humanity

This section affirms the changed reality of Gentiles, now made one with *the commonwealth of Israel* (v. 12).

2:14—Christ's death and resurrection not only accomplish the redemption of individual believ-

the dividing wall, that is, the hostility between us. **15** He has abolished the law with its commandments and ordinances, that he might create in himself one new humanity in place of the two, thus making peace, **16** and might reconcile both groups to God in one body*a* through the cross, thus putting to death that hostility through it.*b* **17** So he came and proclaimed peace to you who were far off and peace to those who were near; **18** for through him both of us have access in one Spirit to the Father. **19** So then you are no longer strangers and aliens, but you are citizens with the saints and also members of the household of God, **20** built upon the foundation of the apostles and prophets, with Christ Jesus himself as the cornerstone.*c* **21** In him the whole structure is joined together and grows into a holy temple in the Lord; **22** in whom you also are built together spiritually*d* into a dwelling place for God.

Paul's Ministry to the Gentiles

3 This is the reason that I Paul am a prisoner for*e* Christ Jesus for the sake of you Gentiles— **2** for surely you have already heard of the commission of God's grace that was given me for you, **3** and how the mystery was made known to me by revelation, as I wrote above in a few words, **4** a reading of which will enable you to perceive my understanding of the mystery of Christ. **5** In former generations this mystery*f* was not made known to humankind, as it has now been revealed to his holy apostles and prophets by the Spirit: **6** that is, the Gentiles have become fellow heirs, members of the same body, and sharers in the promise in Christ Jesus through the gospel.

7 Of this gospel I have become a servant according to the gift of God's grace that was given me by the working of his power. **8** Although I am the very least of all the saints, this grace was given to me to bring to the Gentiles the news of the boundless riches of Christ, **9** and to make everyone see*g* what is the plan of the mystery hidden for ages in*h* God who created all things; **10** so that through the church the wisdom of God in its rich variety might now be made known to the rulers and authorities in the heavenly places. **11** This was in accordance with the eternal purpose that he has carried out in Christ Jesus our Lord, **12** in whom we have access to God in boldness and confidence through faith in him.*i* **13** I pray therefore that you*j* may not lose heart over my sufferings for you; they are your glory.

Prayer for the Readers

14 For this reason I bow my knees before the Father,*k* **15** from whom every family*l* in heaven and on earth takes its

a Or reconcile both of us in one body for God   *b* Or in him, or in himself   *c* Or keystone   *d* Gk in the Spirit   *e* Or of   *f* Gk it   *g* Other ancient authorities read to bring to light   *h* Or by   *i* Or the faith of him   *j* Or I   *k* Other ancient authorities add of our Lord Jesus Christ   *l* Gk fatherhood

---

ers, but fundamentally alter the condition of sinful, fallen creation, making real peace a possibility for the first time. Where sin, death, and fallen powers no longer dominate, alienation and war are no longer necessary or inevitable conditions.

2:19–22—As the embodiment of God's reconciling mercy, the church is sacred and living space, within which God dwells. The church is not defined by or limited to buildings, programs, or offices, but exists wherever disciples give witness to God's reconciling presence in human experience. God creates this space—the *household of God*, a *holy temple in the Lord*—by means of transformed relationships, relationships that would be inconceivable in the worldly ordering of space.

3:1–13 Paul's Commission to Reveal the Mystery of Christ to the Nations

3:10—The church's witness to the rulers and authorities is by proclamation and by its very nature as a reconciled body.

3:13—Paul's *sufferings* and imprisonment (cf. v. 1) are not disconfirming or shaming conditions, but the means by which Christians participate in Christ's glory (cf. 2 Cor. 1:5–6, 4:7–12; Phil. 1:12–14). As Christ suffered for the sake of humankind, so also Paul's suffering is *for you*, the readers of the letter. Paul is not affirming any and all suffering, but suffering endured for the sake of those around us, suffering in consequence of the world's resistance to God's purposes.

3:14–21 A Prayer

A prayer for strength, faith, and love (v. 17), and for comprehension of Christ's incomprehensible

name. [16] I pray that, according to the riches of his glory, he may grant that you may be strengthened in your inner being with power through his Spirit, [17] and that Christ may dwell in your hearts through faith, as you are being rooted and grounded in love. [18] I pray that you may have the power to comprehend, with all the saints, what is the breadth and length and height and depth, [19] and to know the love of Christ that surpasses knowledge, so that you may be filled with all the fullness of God.

[20] Now to him who by the power at work within us is able to accomplish abundantly far more than all we can ask or imagine, [21] to him be glory in the church and in Christ Jesus to all generations, forever and ever. Amen.

Unity in the Body of Christ

[4] I therefore, the prisoner in the Lord, beg you to lead a life worthy of the calling to which you have been called, [2] with all humility and gentleness, with patience, bearing with one another in love, [3] making every effort to maintain the unity of the Spirit in the bond of peace. [4] There is one body and one Spirit, just as you were called to the one hope of your calling, [5] one Lord, one faith, one baptism, [6] one God and Father of all, who is above all and through all and in all.

[7] But each of us was given grace according to the measure of Christ's gift.

[8] Therefore it is said,
"When he ascended on high he
    made captivity itself a captive;
    he gave gifts to his people."
[9] (When it says, "He ascended," what does it mean but that he had also descended[a] into the lower parts of the earth? [10] He who descended is the same one who ascended far above all the heavens, so that he might fill all things.) [11] The gifts he gave were that some would be apostles, some prophets, some evangelists, some pastors and teachers, [12] to equip the saints for the work of ministry, for building up the body of Christ, [13] until all of us come to the unity of the faith and of the knowledge of the Son of God, to maturity, to the measure of the full stature of Christ. [14] We must no longer be children, tossed to and fro and blown about by every wind of doctrine, by people's trickery, by their craftiness in deceitful scheming. [15] But speaking the truth in love, we must grow up in every way into him who is the head, into Christ, [16] from whom the whole body, joined and knit together by every ligament with which it is equipped, as each part is working properly, promotes the body's growth in building itself up in love.

The Old Life and the New

[17] Now this I affirm and insist on in the Lord: you must no longer live as the Gentiles live, in the futility of their

---

[a] Other ancient authorities add *first*

---

love (vv. 18–19). This prayer marks the close of the first half of the book, establishing an *inclusio* with the prayers and liturgical materials that begin the letter. As in those prayers, disciples are called to participate with the writer in worship, the foundational practice of Christian discipleship. To worship is to participate in and comprehend what is beyond human comprehension (vv. 18–20).

4:1–16 An Appeal for Unity amid Diversity

The letter shifts to the practical, ethical, and communal implications of the vision set forth in chaps. 1–3.

4:7–10—Christ's distribution of gifts to his people expresses his lordship over the powers.

4:11–16—The nurture of Christ's body requires the full functioning of this diverse array of gifts, which are not limited to any professional class and do not serve to distinguish disciples hierarchically, but enable Christians to resist human cunning and deceit (v. 14), as well as build up the church *in love* (v. 16). The body imagery used to describe the church points to the essential, organic, interdependent nature of those who are growing up *into Christ*—a difficult concept for those who experience church primarily as a loose collection of individual believers.

4:17–24 Learning Christ

These verses draw yet another contrast between the imagination and social practices of humans

minds. ¹⁸They are darkened in their understanding, alienated from the life of God because of their ignorance and hardness of heart. ¹⁹They have lost all sensitivity and have abandoned themselves to licentiousness, greedy to practice every kind of impurity. ²⁰That is not the way you learned Christ! ²¹For surely you have heard about him and were taught in him, as truth is in Jesus. ²²You were taught to put away your former way of life, your old self, corrupt and deluded by its lusts, ²³and to be renewed in the spirit of your minds, ²⁴and to clothe yourselves with the new self, created according to the likeness of God in true righteousness and holiness.

Rules for the New Life

25 So then, putting away falsehood, let all of us speak the truth to our neighbors, for we are members of one another. ²⁶Be angry but do not sin; do not let the sun go down on your anger, ²⁷and do not make room for the devil. ²⁸Thieves must give up stealing; rather let them labor and work honestly with their own hands, so as to have something to share with the needy. ²⁹Let no evil talk come out of your mouths, but only what is useful for building up,ᵃ as there is need, so that your words may give grace to those who hear. ³⁰And do not grieve the Holy Spirit of God, with which you were marked with a seal for the day of redemption. ³¹Put away from you all bitterness and wrath and anger and wrangling and slander, together with all malice, ³²and be kind to one another, tenderhearted, forgiving one

another, as God in Christ has forgiven you.ᵇ ¹Therefore be imitators of God, as beloved children, ²and live in love, as Christ loved usᶜ and gave himself up for us, a fragrant offering and sacrifice to God.

Renounce Pagan Ways

3 But fornication and impurity of any kind, or greed, must not even be mentioned among you, as is proper among saints. ⁴Entirely out of place is obscene, silly, and vulgar talk; but instead, let there be thanksgiving. ⁵Be sure of this, that no fornicator or impure person, or one who is greedy (that is, an idolater), has any inheritance in the kingdom of Christ and of God.

6 Let no one deceive you with empty words, for because of these things the wrath of God comes on those who are disobedient. ⁷Therefore do not be associated with them. ⁸For once you were darkness, but now in the Lord you are light. Live as children of light— ⁹for the fruit of the light is found in all that is good and right and true. ¹⁰Try to find out what is pleasing to the Lord. ¹¹Take no part in the unfruitful works of darkness, but instead expose them. ¹²For it is shameful even to mention what such people do secretly; ¹³but everything exposed by the light becomes visible, ¹⁴for everything that becomes visible is light. Therefore it says,

"Sleeper, awake!
Rise from the dead,
and Christ will shine on you."

ᵃ Other ancient authorities read building up faith ᵇ Other ancient authorities read us ᶜ Other ancient authorities read you

alienated from God and those who have put on a new self in baptism. Baptism marks a new birth and, with it, new ways of discerning reality.

4:17–19—The powers arrayed against God sow confusion and darkness; social practices reflecting alienation arise naturally from this state.

4:20—As with learning a language or a culture, "learning Christ" comprehends both intellect and practice.

4:25–5:14 Admonitions for Life in the Christian Community

5:1–2—A call to imitate Christ's love and self-sacrifice for the sake of others (cf. v. 25; Phil. 2:1–11).

5:3–7—Because language both represents and shapes our views of the world, *thanksgiving* (v. 4) is the right kind of speech for Christians, for it gives witness to the reality of God's sustaining and reconciling presence in the world.

5:11—Christians are not only to avoid *works of darkness*, but to expose them. Resistance to the powers requires unmasking their false claims.

15 Be careful then how you live, not as unwise people but as wise, ¹⁶ making the most of the time, because the days are evil. ¹⁷ So do not be foolish, but understand what the will of the Lord is. ¹⁸ Do not get drunk with wine, for that is debauchery; but be filled with the Spirit, ¹⁹ as you sing psalms and hymns and spiritual songs among yourselves, singing and making melody to the Lord in your hearts, ²⁰ giving thanks to God the Father at all times and for everything in the name of our Lord Jesus Christ.

The Christian Household

21 Be subject to one another out of reverence for Christ.

22 Wives, be subject to your husbands as you are to the Lord. ²³ For the husband is the head of the wife just as Christ is the head of the church, the body of which he is the Savior. ²⁴ Just as the church is subject to Christ, so also wives ought to be, in everything, to their husbands.

25 Husbands, love your wives, just as Christ loved the church and gave himself up for her, ²⁶ in order to make her holy by cleansing her with the washing of water by the word, ²⁷ so as to present the church to himself in splendor, without a spot or wrinkle or anything of the kind—yes, so that she may be holy and without blemish. ²⁸ In the same way, husbands should love their wives as they do their own bodies. He who loves his wife loves himself. ²⁹ For no one ever hates his own body, but he nourishes and tenderly cares for it, just as Christ does for the church, ³⁰ because we are members of his body.^a ³¹ "For this reason a man will leave his father and mother and be joined to his wife, and the two will become one flesh." ³² This is a great mystery, and I am applying it to Christ and the church. ³³ Each of you, however, should love his wife as himself, and a wife should respect her husband.

Children and Parents

6 Children, obey your parents in the Lord,^b for this is right. ² "Honor your father and mother"—this is the first commandment with a promise: ³ "so that it may be well with you and you may live long on the earth."

4 And, fathers, do not provoke your children to anger, but bring them up in the discipline and instruction of the Lord.

Slaves and Masters

5 Slaves, obey your earthly masters with fear and trembling, in singleness of heart, as you obey Christ; ⁶ not only while being watched, and in order to please them, but as slaves of Christ, doing the will of God from the heart.

^a Other ancient authorities add *of his flesh and of his bones*　^b Other ancient authorities lack *in the Lord*

5:15–6:9 Worship and Life in Christian Households

The instructions in 5:22–6:9 (cf. Col. 3:18–4:1) follow a common form of moral instruction in Mediterranean antiquity, the "household code," which focuses on proper relationships between the patron and various members of the household.

5:21 *Be subject*—Lit. "being subject . . ." The syntax of vv. 18–21 coordinates the instructions to the members of the household with instructions regarding worship in vv. 18–20. Here again, the writer uses worship as the foundation and framework for Christian practice. Life in Christian community and the daily lives of Christians in the world are as much an expression of worship as thanksgiving and song.

The call for mutual subordination stands in irresolvable tension with the patriarchal character of the ancient household, which was oriented around the interests of the patron. Because these verses presume the cultural structures of the ancient Mediterranean world, including patriarchal marriages and the widespread practice of slavery, the instructions here should not be idealized as a timeless model for family life. It is rather the call to mutual subordination, love, and respect, and the repeated appeal to Christ as the definitive model for Christian life that are normative.

5:22–32—Christ is the model for the behavior of both wives (vv. 23–24) and husbands (vv. 25, 29).

6:5–9—Both *slaves* and *masters* are to understand themselves as servants of God, having the same master, who is impartial. God does not respect or affirm human social constructions rooted in hierarchy, domination, and exploitation.

[7] Render service with enthusiasm, as to the Lord and not to men and women, [8] knowing that whatever good we do, we will receive the same again from the Lord, whether we are slaves or free.

9 And, masters, do the same to them. Stop threatening them, for you know that both of you have the same Master in heaven, and with him there is no partiality.

The Whole Armor of God

10 Finally, be strong in the Lord and in the strength of his power. [11] Put on the whole armor of God, so that you may be able to stand against the wiles of the devil. [12] For our[a] struggle is not against enemies of blood and flesh, but against the rulers, against the authorities, against the cosmic powers of this present darkness, against the spiritual forces of evil in the heavenly places. [13] Therefore take up the whole armor of God, so that you may be able to withstand on that evil day, and having done everything, to stand firm. [14] Stand therefore, and fasten the belt of truth around your waist, and put on the breastplate of righteousness. [15] As shoes for your feet put on whatever will make you ready to proclaim the gospel of peace. [16] With all

of these,[b] take the shield of faith, with which you will be able to quench all the flaming arrows of the evil one. [17] Take the helmet of salvation, and the sword of the Spirit, which is the word of God.

18 Pray in the Spirit at all times in every prayer and supplication. To that end keep alert and always persevere in supplication for all the saints. [19] Pray also for me, so that when I speak, a message may be given to me to make known with boldness the mystery of the gospel,[c] [20] for which I am an ambassador in chains. Pray that I may declare it boldly, as I must speak.

Personal Matters and Benediction

21 So that you also may know how I am and what I am doing, Tychicus will tell you everything. He is a dear brother and a faithful minister in the Lord. [22] I am sending him to you for this very purpose, to let you know how we are, and to encourage your hearts.

23 Peace be to the whole community,[d] and love with faith, from God the Father and the Lord Jesus Christ. [24] Grace be with all who have an undying love for our Lord Jesus Christ.[e]

[a] Other ancient authorities read *your* [b] Or *In all circumstances* [c] Other ancient authorities lack *of the gospel* [d] Gk *to the brothers* [e] Other ancient authorities add *Amen*

6:10–20 The Tools and Disciplines of Spiritual Warfare
Cf. Isa. 11:4–5, 59:17. Proclamation of the gospel (v. 17) is the only offensive device named in this list. These verses do not condone human warfare, but depict the Christian life as part of the cosmic struggle between God and the forces of fallen creation. The war against the forces that seek to dominate and destroy God's creation is fought not with the traditional tools of battle, which destroy life, but with weapons that build community and nurture reconciled relationships.

The Book of
PHILIPPIANS

P hilippi was a flourishing administrative and commercial center in Macedonia, a northern province of Greece, and the site of an important military victory for Caesar Augustus, who granted the colony full privileges of Roman cities. Monuments celebrating imperial power were set amid shrines and temples dedicated to various deities, including the emperor himself. In a world where the emperor was proclaimed "savior," and offered "salvation" in exchange for "faith," Paul announces the "good news" of the lordship not of Caesar but of the crucified Galilean, Jesus the Christ.

Paul himself is in prison, under Roman custody and possibly at risk of his own life, as he writes to the Philippian Christians. He uses these circumstances, however, both to affirm the power of the gospel and as a model of the cruciform life. Paul writes especially to counter threats to church unity arising from continued adherence to the social values and practices of the Roman world. Where the competitive quest for honor, hierarchical social relationships, and economic arrangements based on self-interested patronage intruded into the life of the community, its unity was under attack. He reminds the Philippians that their partnership in the gospel makes them citizens of another order and overturns the assumptions that shape social, political, and economic interactions in the first century. By conforming their thinking and practices to Christ, as well as to the models of Paul, Timothy, and Epaphroditus, the Philippians will preserve their unity and shine as lights in the world. The discipleship Paul envisions rejoices even in apparently disconfirming circumstances and is sustained in practices that build up the community. At the heart of this discipleship is a provocative theological vision, expressed most clearly in the Christ hymn in 2:6–11. The one who is now exalted as Lord and whose name is above every name is the very one who emptied himself of his divine power in order to live in solidarity with the least ones of this world, even to the point of death on the cross. The New Testament contains no more powerful expression of the nature of Christian discipleship and the basis of Christian unity.

—**Stanley Saunders**

Salutation

1 Paul and Timothy, servants[a] of Christ Jesus,

To all the saints in Christ Jesus who are in Philippi, with the bishops[b] and deacons:[c]

2 Grace to you and peace from God our Father and the Lord Jesus Christ.

Paul's Prayer for the Philippians

3 I thank my God every time I remem-

[a] Gk slaves [b] Or overseers [c] Or overseers and helpers

1:1–2 Salutation
Paul's self-designation suggests a prominent theme of the letter, servanthood. By calling themselves slaves (NRSV *servants*) of Christ Jesus, Paul and Timothy identify themselves with the least powerful members of the household of

Christ. *Bishops and deacons* were not yet church offices; terms suggesting function—overseers and servants—may be preferable.

1:3–11 Paul's Prayer of Thanksgiving
This prayer for the Philippians' *sharing* (or

ber you, [4] constantly praying with joy in every one of my prayers for all of you, [5] because of your sharing in the gospel from the first day until now. [6] I am confident of this, that the one who began a good work among you will bring it to completion by the day of Jesus Christ. [7] It is right for me to think this way about all of you, because you hold me in your heart,[a] for all of you share in God's grace[b] with me, both in my imprisonment and in the defense and confirmation of the gospel. [8] For God is my witness, how I long for all of you with the compassion of Christ Jesus. [9] And this is my prayer, that your love may overflow more and more with knowledge and full insight [10] to help you to determine what is best, so that in the day of Christ you may be pure and blameless, [11] having produced the harvest of righteousness that comes through Jesus Christ for the glory and praise of God.

Paul's Present Circumstances

[12] I want you to know, beloved,[c] that what has happened to me has actually helped to spread the gospel, [13] so that it has become known throughout the whole imperial guard[d] and to everyone else that my imprisonment is for Christ; [14] and most of the brothers and sisters,[c] having been made confident in the Lord by my imprisonment, dare to speak the word[e] with greater boldness and without fear.

[15] Some proclaim Christ from envy and rivalry, but others from goodwill. [16] These proclaim Christ out of love, knowing that I have been put here for the defense of the gospel; [17] the others proclaim Christ out of selfish ambition, not sincerely but intending to increase my suffering in my imprisonment. [18] What does it matter? Just this, that Christ is proclaimed in every way, whether out of false motives or true; and in that I rejoice.

Yes, and I will continue to rejoice, [19] for I know that through your prayers and the help of the Spirit of Jesus Christ this will turn out for my deliverance. [20] It is my eager expectation and hope that I will not be put to shame in any way, but that by my speaking with all boldness, Christ will be exalted now as always in my body, whether by life or by death. [21] For to me, living is Christ and dying is gain. [22] If I am to live in the flesh, that means fruitful labor for me; and I do not know which I prefer. [23] I am hard pressed between the two: my desire is to depart and be with Christ, for that is far better; [24] but to remain in the flesh is more necessary for you. [25] Since I am convinced of this, I know that I will remain and continue with all of you for your progress and joy in faith, [26] so that I may share abundantly in your boasting in Christ Jesus when I come to you again.

[27] Only, live your life in a manner

[a] Or because I hold you in my heart   [b] Gk in grace   [c] Gk brothers   [d] Gk whole praetorium   [e] Other ancient authorities read word of God

---

partnership, fellowship) *in the gospel* (v. 5) emphasizes expressions of mutual concern. The gospel is embodied not merely in salvation of the individual, but in the life of Christian community.

1:12–26 The Surprising Results of Paul's Incarceration

Mediterranean culture focused on honor and shame as primary measures of human power and worth. The gospel turns these values on their head. While some would see Paul's imprisonment as a source of shame, in fact the gospel is boldly being spread (vv. 12–14). Even apparently negative circumstances provide opportunities for witness.

1:27–2:4 The Encouragement of Unity

By living *in a manner worthy of the gospel of Christ* (1:27), the Philippians secure their unity, resist their opponents, and participate in Christ's suffering (1:29–30). *Be of the same mind* (2:2, 5) does not imply complete agreement in all matters, nor forced conformity of thought and practice. Christian unity is not founded on uniformity or homogeneity or top-down management strategies. As the hymn that follows makes clear, the *same mind* (2:2) entails not only a common attitude and focus (on Christ), but the willingness to set aside self-promotion, embrace as equals even the most humble, and place the *interests of others* before one's own (2:3–4).

worthy of the gospel of Christ, so that, whether I come and see you or am absent and hear about you, I will know that you are standing firm in one spirit, striving side by side with one mind for the faith of the gospel, ²⁸ and are in no way intimidated by your opponents. For them this is evidence of their destruction, but of your salvation. And this is God's doing. ²⁹ For he has graciously granted you the privilege not only of believing in Christ, but of suffering for him as well— ³⁰ since you are having the same struggle that you saw I had and now hear that I still have.

Imitating Christ's Humility

2 If then there is any encouragement in Christ, any consolation from love, any sharing in the Spirit, any compassion and sympathy, ² make my joy complete: be of the same mind, having the same love, being in full accord and of one mind. ³ Do nothing from selfish ambition or conceit, but in humility regard others as better than yourselves. ⁴ Let each of you look not to your own interests, but to the interests of others. ⁵ Let the same mind be in you that was*a* in Christ Jesus,

⁶ who, though he was in the form
        of God,

did not regard equality with God
        as something to be exploited,
⁷ but emptied himself,
        taking the form of a slave,
        being born in human likeness.
    And being found in human form,
⁸   he humbled himself
        and became obedient to the point
                of death—
        even death on a cross.

⁹ Therefore God also highly exalted
                him
        and gave him the name
        that is above every name,
¹⁰ so that at the name of Jesus
        every knee should bend,
        in heaven and on earth and under
                the earth,
¹¹ and every tongue should confess
        that Jesus Christ is Lord,
        to the glory of God the Father.

Shining as Lights in the World

12 Therefore, my beloved, just as you have always obeyed me, not only in my presence, but much more now in my absence, work out your own salvation with fear and trembling; ¹³ for it is God who is at work in you, enabling you both to will and to work for his good pleasure.

a Or that you have

2:5–11 The Christ Hymn
A provocative hymn, which Paul could be certain the Philippians already knew, describes the central focus and one mind of which Paul speaks, the mind of Christ. This hymn both narrates the gospel story of salvation in Christ and provides the definitive model for discipleship and Christian mission. The hymn calls not only individuals, but the Christian community as a whole, to life in conformity with the story of Jesus' self-emptying and crucifixion.

2:6–7—*The form of God* and *the form of a slave* designate distinguishable categories of being (e.g., animals vs. plants, or apes vs. humans). Christ not only appeared to be like God, but was God; he not only took on the appearance of a slave, but emptied himself of his essential privileges and powers as God, and took on the essence of what it is to be a servant or slave.

2:8—*He humbled himself* means that he placed

himself in full solidarity with those who are humiliated. He was *obedient* to God by conforming his life wholly to God's will, even to the point of crucifixion, the dishonoring form of execution reserved for slaves and enemies of the Roman state.

2:9–11—*Every knee should bend* and ***every tongue should confess*** are drawn from Isa. 45:23, part of an oracle that speaks of both Israel's salvation and the redemption of the nations. The hymn thus points to the unified worshiping community and universal mission that arise in consequence of the gospel story.

2:12–13 Work Out Your Own Salvation
Work out your own salvation in fear and trembling (that is, in reverence before God) suggests that in any circumstance—whether imprisoned or free, in suffering and hope—disciples conform themselves to the mind of Christ (v. 5).

14 Do all things without murmuring and arguing, 15 so that you may be blameless and innocent, children of God without blemish in the midst of a crooked and perverse generation, in which you shine like stars in the world. 16 It is by your holding fast to the word of life that I can boast on the day of Christ that I did not run in vain or labor in vain. 17 But even if I am being poured out as a libation over the sacrifice and the offering of your faith, I am glad and rejoice with all of you— 18 and in the same way you also must be glad and rejoice with me.

Timothy and Epaphroditus

19 I hope in the Lord Jesus to send Timothy to you soon, so that I may be cheered by news of you. 20 I have no one like him who will be genuinely concerned for your welfare. 21 All of them are seeking their own interests, not those of Jesus Christ. 22 But Timothy's*a* worth you know, how like a son with a father he has served with me in the work of the gospel. 23 I hope therefore to send him as soon as I see how things go with me; 24 and I trust in the Lord that I will also come soon.

25 Still, I think it necessary to send to you Epaphroditus—my brother and co-worker and fellow soldier, your messen-ger*b* and minister to my need; 26 for he has been longing for*c* all of you, and has been distressed because you heard that he was ill. 27 He was indeed so ill that he nearly died. But God had mercy on him, and not only on him but on me also, so that I would not have one sorrow after another. 28 I am the more eager to send him, therefore, in order that you may rejoice at seeing him again, and that I may be less anxious. 29 Welcome him then in the Lord with all joy, and honor such people, 30 because he came close to death for the work of Christ,*d* risking his life to make up for those services that you could not give me.

3 Finally, my brothers and sisters,*e* rejoice*f* in the Lord.

Breaking with the Past

To write the same things to you is not troublesome to me, and for you it is a safeguard.

2 Beware of the dogs, beware of the evil workers, beware of those who mutilate the flesh!*g* 3 For it is we who are the circumcision, who worship in the Spirit of God*h* and boast in Christ Jesus and have no confidence in the flesh— 4 even though I, too, have reason for confidence in the flesh.

---

a Gk *his* *b* Gk *apostle* *c* Other ancient authorities read *longing to see*
d Other ancient authorities read *of the Lord* *e* Gk *my brothers* *f* Or *farewell*
g Gk *the mutilation* *h* Other ancient authorities read *worship God in spirit*

2:14–18 Shining as Lights
Obedient conformity to the pattern of Christ will establish communities that stand in contrast to their surrounding cultures—shining *like stars in the world* (v. 15).

2:19–3:1 Travel Plans
The travel itineraries for Timothy (2:19–24) and Epaphroditus (2:25–30) also serve to present them as models of Christian obedience and service, even at the risk of their lives. Rejoicing, a dominant theme in this letter (1:18, 2:2, 2:17–18, 4:4), is a consequence and expression of full participation in the gospel story. Rejoicing is not an individually cultivated virtue, but is nurtured in Christian community.

3:2–4:1 Boasting in Christ vs. Confidence in the Flesh
With an abrupt shift in tone, Paul takes up the threat to Christian unity posed by practices such as circumcision, a central element of Jewish identity (Gen. 17:9–14). Paul's focus, however, is not on rejection of Judaism or the Jewish people, but on the ways people, especially religious people, mark distinctions and create hierarchies within their communities. Circumcision is the example that lies closest at hand for Paul and that poses the most immediate threat to his churches. The gospel does away with all distinctions based on human action or achievement. Even religious and spiritual accomplishments, whatever their apparent merit, may be turned into individual virtues that threaten to destroy the church's unity.

3:4–6—Paul's résumé is an impressive demonstration that he, if anyone, had reason to place confidence in his own status and accomplishments.

If anyone else has reason to be confident in the flesh, I have more: [5] circumcised on the eighth day, a member of the people of Israel, of the tribe of Benjamin, a Hebrew born of Hebrews; as to the law, a Pharisee; [6] as to zeal, a persecutor of the church; as to righteousness under the law, blameless.

[7] Yet whatever gains I had, these I have come to regard as loss because of Christ. [8] More than that, I regard everything as loss because of the surpassing value of knowing Christ Jesus my Lord. For his sake I have suffered the loss of all things, and I regard them as rubbish, in order that I may gain Christ [9] and be found in him, not having a righteousness of my own that comes from the law, but one that comes through faith in Christ,[a] the righteousness from God based on faith. [10] I want to know Christ[b] and the power of his resurrection and the sharing of his sufferings by becoming like him in his death, [11] if somehow I may attain the resurrection from the dead.

Pressing toward the Goal

[12] Not that I have already obtained this or have already reached the goal;[c] but I press on to make it my own, because Christ Jesus has made me his own. [13] Beloved,[d] I do not consider that I have made it my own;[e] but this one thing I do: forgetting what lies behind and straining forward to what lies ahead, [14] I press on toward the goal for the prize of the heavenly[f] call of God in Christ Jesus. [15] Let those of us then who are mature be of the same mind; and if you think differently about anything, this too God will reveal to you. [16] Only let us hold fast to what we have attained.

[17] Brothers and sisters,[d] join in imitating me, and observe those who live according to the example you have in us. [18] For many live as enemies of the cross of Christ; I have often told you of them, and now I tell you even with tears. [19] Their end is destruction; their god is the belly; and their glory is in their shame; their minds are set on earthly things. [20] But our citizenship[g] is in heaven, and it is from there that we are expecting a Savior, the Lord Jesus Christ. [21] He will transform the body of our humiliation[h] that it may be conformed to the body of his glory,[i] by the power that also enables him to make all things subject to himself. [1] Therefore, my brothers and sisters,[j] whom I love and long for, my joy and crown, stand firm in the Lord in this way, my beloved.

Exhortations

[2] I urge Euodia and I urge Syntyche to be of the same mind in the Lord. [3] Yes, and I ask you also, my loyal companion,[k] help these women, for they have struggled beside me in the work of the gospel, together with Clement and the rest of my co-workers, whose names are in the book of life.

[a] Or through the faith of Christ   [b] Gk him   [c] Or have already been made perfect   [d] Gk Brothers   [e] Other ancient authorities read my own yet   [f] Gk upward   [g] Or commonwealth   [h] Or our humble bodies   [i] Or his glorious body   [j] Gk my brothers   [k] Or loyal Syzygus

---

3:7–9—Paul moves his entire résumé to the *loss* side of the ledger and now boasts in the *righteousness* that comes through the faithfulness of Christ. In doing so, he reverses the values with which he had grown up and subverts the paradigms by which humans measure personal merit and accomplishment.

3:10–11—These clauses form an inverted parallelism (a/b/b/a), firmly correlating the "fellowship" of *suffering* with the glory of the *resurrection*. For Paul, the life of discipleship entails exposing both the church and individuals to the risk of suffering for the sake of the gospel, as Paul himself does throughout his missionary journeys.

The same correlation of suffering and exaltation expressed in the Christ hymn (2:6–11) is at work here. The path to resurrection always lies through the cross.

3:17–4:1—*Our citizenship is in heaven* (3:20) reminds the Philippians that their Lord is not Caesar, but Christ.

4:2–9 A Summary of the Letter's Key Themes

Paul sounds again the key themes of the letter, focusing first on unity (vv. 2–3), then rejoicing, *prayer* and *thanksgiving*, and the promise of God's *peace*.

4 Rejoice[a] in the Lord always; again I will say, Rejoice.[a] 5 Let your gentleness be known to everyone. The Lord is near. 6 Do not worry about anything, but in everything by prayer and supplication with thanksgiving let your requests be made known to God. 7 And the peace of God, which surpasses all understanding, will guard your hearts and your minds in Christ Jesus.

8 Finally, beloved,[b] whatever is true, whatever is honorable, whatever is just, whatever is pure, whatever is pleasing, whatever is commendable, if there is any excellence and if there is anything worthy of praise, think about[c] these things. 9 Keep on doing the things that you have learned and received and heard and seen in me, and the God of peace will be with you.

Acknowledgment of the Philippians' Gift

10 I rejoiced[d] in the Lord greatly that now at last you have revived your concern for me; indeed, you were concerned for me, but had no opportunity to show it.[e] 11 Not that I am referring to being in need; for I have learned to be content with whatever I have. 12 I know what it is to have little, and I know what it is to have plenty. In any and all circumstances I have learned the secret of being well-fed and of going hungry, of having plenty and of being in need. 13 I can do all things through him who strengthens me. 14 In any case, it was kind of you to share my distress.

15 You Philippians indeed know that in the early days of the gospel, when I left Macedonia, no church shared with me in the matter of giving and receiving, except you alone. 16 For even when I was in Thessalonica, you sent me help for my needs more than once. 17 Not that I seek the gift, but I seek the profit that accumulates to your account. 18 I have been paid in full and have more than enough; I am fully satisfied, now that I have received from Epaphroditus the gifts you sent, a fragrant offering, a sacrifice acceptable and pleasing to God. 19 And my God will fully satisfy every need of yours according to his riches in glory in Christ Jesus. 20 To our God and Father be glory forever and ever. Amen.

Final Greetings and Benediction

21 Greet every saint in Christ Jesus. The friends[b] who are with me greet you. 22 All the saints greet you, especially those of the emperor's household.

23 The grace of the Lord Jesus Christ be with your spirit.[f]

---

[a] Or Farewell [b] Gk brothers [c] Gk take account of [d] Gk I rejoiced [e] Gk lacks to show it [f] Other ancient authorities add Amen

---

4:8–9—Paul affirms consideration of the virtues listed in v. 8, but emphasizes the practice of what he himself has modeled (v. 9).

4:10–20 Paul's Contract with the Philippians
While acknowledging the Philippians' gifts to him, Paul seeks to remove both himself and the Philippians from the entrapments of obligation that characterized the patronage-based economy of the empire. The Philippians gave their gift not from obligation to him, but as *a fragrant offering ... to God* (v. 18) that now accumulates profit to their account. Only when it becomes clear that positive actions toward others are motivated by love, not by self-interest or in expectation of some return, is it possible to establish relationships of genuine unity and solidarity, that is, to become partners in the gospel. As Paul says in Rom. 13:8, after encouraging the payment of all taxes (even unfair taxes), "owe no one anything but love."

The Book of
COLOSSIANS

What must humans do to secure a positive relationship with God? People today continue to seek answers to this question, as humans have throughout history, for the sense of alienation and uncertainty that lies beneath it is one of the consequences of the fall from grace. Paul addressed this question, which arose in various forms, throughout his correspondence with the churches he founded. He persistently affirmed both the faithfulness of God toward humankind and the certainty that Jesus Christ had already accomplished all that was necessary for full reconciliation between God and humankind. Baptism marked the transition from the old life, shaped by alienation, uncertainty, and death, to a new life in Christ, where the powers of the fallen world no longer held believers in captivity and darkness.

The Gentile Christians who made up the church in Colossae may have been especially susceptible to uncertainty about their status before the God of Israel. The church apparently faced threats arising from various expressions of social and religious intimidation, or at least from suggestions that they might improve their status before God by observing particular rituals, by following certain esoteric teachings, or by relying on angelic mediators, for example (2:8–23). At the heart of this crisis were doubts about what Christ had really accomplished in his death and resurrection, especially whether he had really set believers free from the powers of this world. In response, this letter reminds its readers of both the unsurpassed authority of Christ (1:15–20) and the fundamental change in the created order that has taken place through Christ (1:21–28). This altered reality in turn leads to transformed relationships and practices that distinguish the life together of the Christian community (3:1–4:1). While the information in 2:8–23 regarding the threats facing the Colossian Christians is not enough for us to identify any single group, religion, or philosophy, the letter takes clear aim at human traditions and spiritualities, whatever their apparent merit, that effectively deny or displace singular dependence on Christ and life in Christ.

The church in Colossae, located east of Ephesus in the Roman province of Asia Minor, was not founded by Paul but by Epaphras, whose ministry is affirmed in 1:7–8. The primary author, perhaps Timothy (1:1) or another of Paul's disciples, draws heavily on early Christian liturgical materials (e.g., 1:15–20) and traditional forms of moral discourse (e.g., 3:18–4:1) to shape and flavor the argument. In form, content, and language, Colossians stands close to Ephesians, with which it shares a deep conviction about the power of worship to shape Christian imagination and practice. The roots of discipleship lie in the convictions, confessions, and life together of the Christian community in worship, where Christ's saving and reconciling power is discerned, tested, and embodied. The discipleship evoked in this letter does not consist in the heroic or virtuous practices of individuals, but in the nurture of communities that manifest the realities of God's new creation in Christ.

—Stanley Saunders

Salutation

1 Paul, an apostle of Christ Jesus by the will of God, and Timothy our brother,

2 To the saints and faithful brothers and sisters*a* in Christ in Colossae:

Grace to you and peace from God our Father.

Paul Thanks God for the Colossians

3 In our prayers for you we always thank God, the Father of our Lord Jesus Christ, ⁴for we have heard of your faith in Christ Jesus and of the love that you have for all the saints, ⁵because of the hope laid up for you in heaven. You have heard of this hope before in the word of the truth, the gospel ⁶that has come to you. Just as it is bearing fruit and growing in the whole world, so it has been bearing fruit among yourselves from the day you heard it and truly comprehended the grace of God. ⁷This you learned from Epaphras, our beloved fellow servant.*b* He is a faithful minister of Christ on your*c* behalf, ⁸and he has made known to us your love in the Spirit.

9 For this reason, since the day we heard it, we have not ceased praying for you and asking that you may be filled with the knowledge of God's*d* will in all spiritual wisdom and understanding, ¹⁰so that you may lead lives worthy of the Lord, fully pleasing to him, as you bear fruit in every good work and as you grow in the knowledge of God. ¹¹May you be made strong with all the strength that comes from his glorious power, and may you be prepared to endure everything with patience, while joyfully ¹²giving thanks to the Father, who has enabled*e* you *f* to share in the inheritance of the saints in the light. ¹³He has rescued us from the power of darkness and transferred us into the kingdom of his beloved Son, ¹⁴in whom we have redemption, the forgiveness of sins.*h*

The Supremacy of Christ

15 He is the image of the invisible God, the firstborn of all creation; ¹⁶for in*h* him all things in heaven and on earth were created, things visible and

a Gk brothers *b* Gk slave *c* Other ancient authorities read our *d* Gk his *e* Other ancient authorities read called *f* Other ancient authorities read us *g* Other ancient authorities add through his blood *h* Or by

1:1–2 Greeting and Address
The addressees are named *brothers and sisters in Christ*, an affirmation of their full inclusion within the family of God's people.

1:3–20 Paul's Prayer for the Colossians

1:3–8 Thanksgiving—The thanksgiving focuses on the Colossians' foundational experiences of Christian life, especially their faith, love, and hope, a common triad in the writings of Paul. *Faith* has to do with our primary orientation, either toward or away from God. More specifically, faith is the expression of our trust in and reliance upon Christ, as well as our conformity to the pattern of his life, which comes to fruition especially in practices of *love* toward others (cf. 1:24, 3:12–17). *Hope* is the dimension of faith that is oriented toward realization of the coming power and glory of God in Christ, where the believers' lives are hidden (3:1–4), in the transformed life of the community. Hope is the faithful imagination of the coming reign of Christ, which allows us already to discern and name Christ's reign in the present order.

1:9–14—The primary qualities of the spiritual life (vv. 9–12) are gifts from God rather than virtues cultivated by humans themselves. Because God has transferred Christ's followers *from the power of darkness* into Christ's reign, where they have a full inheritance, no other spiritual accomplishments are required.

1:15–20 The Christ Hymn—The prayer continues with an early Christian hymn that affirms Christ as creator and lord. His lordship comprehends not only the church, but *all creation*, all space and all time. Christ is the very embodiment of God (vv. 15, 19), the one in whom all the mediating powers of creation, including those that would pretend to mediate between humankind and God, *were created* (v. 16), Christ is also the origin and source of the new creation, in which reconciliation and redemption from death are normative (vv. 18b–20). The hymn thus affirms the complete sufficiency of Christ and what he has accomplished not only for humankind, but the whole creation. This is the foundation for the community's response to challenges and threats (cf. 2:8–23).

invisible, whether thrones or dominions or rulers or powers—all things have been created through him and for him. [17] He himself is before all things, and in[a] him all things hold together. [18] He is the head of the body, the church; he is the beginning, the firstborn from the dead, so that he might come to have first place in everything. [19] For in him all the fullness of God was pleased to dwell, [20] and through him God was pleased to reconcile to himself all things, whether on earth or in heaven, by making peace through the blood of his cross.

21 And you who were once estranged and hostile in mind, doing evil deeds, [22] he has now reconciled[b] in his fleshly body[c] through death, so as to present you holy and blameless and irreproachable before him— [23] provided that you continue securely established and steadfast in the faith, without shifting from the hope promised by the gospel that you heard, which has been proclaimed to every creature under heaven. I, Paul, became a servant of this gospel.

Paul's Interest in the Colossians

24 I am now rejoicing in my sufferings for your sake, and in my flesh I am completing what is lacking in Christ's afflictions for the sake of his body, that is, the church. [25] I became its servant according to God's commission that was given to me for you, to make the word of God fully known, [26] the mystery that has been hidden throughout the ages and generations but has now been revealed to his saints. [27] To them God chose to make known how great among the Gentiles are the riches of the glory of this mystery, which is Christ in you, the hope of glory. [28] It is he whom we proclaim, warning everyone and teaching everyone in all wisdom, so that we may present everyone mature in Christ. [29] For this I toil and struggle with all the energy that he powerfully inspires within me.

2 For I want you to know how much I am struggling for you, and for those in Laodicea, and for all who have not seen me face to face. [2] I want their hearts to be encouraged and united in love, so that they may have all the riches of assured understanding and have the knowledge of God's mystery, that is, Christ himself,[d] [3] in whom are hidden all the treasures of wisdom and knowledge. [4] I am saying this so that no one may deceive you with plausible arguments. [5] For though I am absent in body, yet I am with you in spirit, and I rejoice to see your morale and the firmness of your faith in Christ.

Fullness of Life in Christ

6 As you therefore have received Christ Jesus the Lord, continue to live your lives[e] in him, [7] rooted and built up in him and established in the faith, just as you were taught, abounding in thanksgiving.

8 See to it that no one takes you captive through philosophy and empty deceit, according to human tradition,

---

[a] Or by [b] Other ancient authorities read you have now been reconciled [c] Gk in the body of his flesh [d] Other ancient authorities read of the mystery of God, both of the Father and of Christ [e] Gk to walk

---

1:21–23 The New Status of Believers

An affirmation of the new status of the believers—reconciled with God and with those who once were strangers or enemies—and a warning not to depart from the gospel hope of reconciliation.

1:24–2:7 Paul's Calling and the Mystery of Christ

By naming Christ as the *mystery…revealed to his saints* (v. 26; 2:2–4), the author prepares to displace the human philosophies and traditions named in the next section.

2:6–7—A summary of the whole letter.

2:8–23 The Errors Threatening the Colossians

2:8–15—An extended christological argument reiterates material, especially from the Christ hymn in 1:15–20, and counters the threat of human philosophies and traditions. In *baptism*, believers already participate not only in Christ's death but his resurrection (vv. 11–14). Burial and resurrec-

according to the elemental spirits of the universe,[a] and not according to Christ. [9] For in him the whole fullness of deity dwells bodily, [10] and you have come to fullness in him, who is the head of every ruler and authority. [11] In him also you were circumcised with a spiritual circumcision,[b] by putting off the body of the flesh in the circumcision of Christ; [12] when you were buried with him in baptism, you were also raised with him through faith in the power of God, who raised him from the dead. [13] And when you were dead in trespasses and the uncircumcision of your flesh, God[c] made you[d] alive together with him, when he forgave us all our trespasses, [14] erasing the record that stood against us with its legal demands. He set this aside, nailing it to the cross. [15] He disarmed[e] the rulers and authorities and made a public example of them, triumphing over them in it.

[16] Therefore do not let anyone condemn you in matters of food and drink or of observing festivals, new moons, or sabbaths. [17] These are only a shadow of what is to come, but the substance belongs to Christ. [18] Do not let anyone disqualify you, insisting on self-abasement and worship of angels, dwelling[f] on visions,[g] puffed up without cause by a human way of thinking,[h] [19] and not holding fast to the head, from whom the whole body, nourished and held together by its ligaments and sinews, grows with a growth that is from God.

Warnings against False Teachers

[20] If with Christ you died to the elemental spirits of the universe,[i] why do you live as if you still belonged to the world? Why do you submit to regulations, [21] "Do not handle, Do not taste, Do not touch"? [22] All these regulations refer to things that perish with use; they are simply human commands and teachings. [23] These have indeed an appearance of wisdom in promoting self-imposed piety, humility, and severe treatment of the body, but they are of no value in checking self-indulgence.[j]

The New Life in Christ

3 So if you have been raised with Christ, seek the things that are above, where Christ is, seated at the right

[a] Or the rudiments of the world [b] Gk a circumcision made without hands [c] Gk he [d] Other ancient authorities read made us; others, made [e] Or divested himself of [f] Other ancient authorities read not dwelling [g] Meaning of Gk uncertain [h] Gk by the mind of his flesh [i] Or the rudiments of the world [j] Or are of no value, serving only to indulge the flesh

---

tion with Christ in baptism erase the record that keeps humankind alienated from God (v. 14) and disarm all the powers of this world (v. 15). Again, recognition of this reality fundamentally undermines the need for and claims of any other supposed mediation—whether by means of angels, priests or pastors, pious actions and rituals, good deeds or spiritual accomplishments—between humankind and God.

2:16–23—Paul's language suggests that experiences of religious intimidation and coercion are threatening the Colossians' experience of the gospel. By not joining in the practices being imposed upon them, they risk condemnation and disqualification. Such practices threaten not only to undermine the Colossians' faith, but also to tear the social fabric of the community itself. Human attempts to establish and control the terms of mediation between humankind and God inevitably result in distinctions that rupture the oneness of the church. The individual's own spiritual and social interests displace awareness of God's presence in nourishing and growing the community (v. 19). But if the Colossians have already truly died with Christ to the powers of this world, why continue to act as if these powers still have force in their lives? The *elemental spirits* (v. 20) designate forces that seek to dominate and exploit human life in the fallen creation. They may take on spiritual, institutional, personal, political, economic, or cultural forms, and often come to expression in "common sense." They are the forces that cause people to accept as truth or "the ways things are" what are in fact merely human social constructions (e.g., homelessness, the disparity between rich and poor, or the necessity of violence and domination to preserve peace and order). Life in thrall of the elemental spirits means acceptance of fallen creation as normative.

3:1–4:6 Exhortations for the Christian Life

3:1–4—The roots of Christian practice lie in recognition of the new reality that is life in Christ.

hand of God. [2] Set your minds on things that are above, not on things that are on earth, [3] for you have died, and your life is hidden with Christ in God. [4] When Christ who is your[a] life is revealed, then you also will be revealed with him in glory.

5 Put to death, therefore, whatever in you is earthly: fornication, impurity, passion, evil desire, and greed (which is idolatry). [6] On account of these the wrath of God is coming on those who are disobedient.[b] [7] These are the ways you also once followed, when you were living that life.[c] [8] But now you must get rid of all such things—anger, wrath, malice, slander, and abusive[d] language from your mouth. [9] Do not lie to one another, seeing that you have stripped off the old self with its practices [10] and have clothed yourselves with the new self, which is being renewed in knowledge according to the image of its creator. [11] In that renewal[e] there is no longer Greek and Jew, circumcised and uncircumcised, barbarian, Scythian, slave and free; but Christ is all and in all!

12 As God's chosen ones, holy and beloved, clothe yourselves with compassion, kindness, humility, meekness, and patience. [13] Bear with one another and, if anyone has a complaint against another, forgive each other; just as the Lord[f] has forgiven you, so you also must forgive. [14] Above all, clothe yourselves with love, which binds everything together in perfect harmony. [15] And let the peace of Christ rule in your hearts, to which indeed you were called in the one body. And be thankful. [16] Let the word of Christ[g] dwell in you richly; teach and admonish one another in all wisdom; and with gratitude in your hearts sing psalms, hymns, and spiritual songs to God.[h] [17] And whatever you do, in word or deed, do everything in the name of the Lord Jesus, giving thanks to God the Father through him.

Rules for Christian Households

18 Wives, be subject to your husbands, as is fitting in the Lord. [19] Husbands, love your wives and never treat them harshly.

20 Children, obey your parents in everything, for this is your acceptable duty in the Lord. [21] Fathers, do not provoke your children, or they may lose heart. [22] Slaves, obey your earthly masters[i] in everything, not only while being watched and in order to please them, but wholeheartedly, fearing the Lord. [i]

[a] Other authorities read our   [b] Other ancient authorities lack on those who are disobedient (Gk the children of disobedience)   [c] Or living among such people   [d] Or filthy   [e] Gk its creator, [11] where   [f] Other ancient authorities read just as Christ   [g] Other ancient authorities read of God, or of the Lord   [h] Other ancient authorities read to the Lord   [i] In Greek the same word is used for master and Lord

---

3:5–17—Baptismal images in vv. 9b–11 reaffirm the transformation that has already taken place among the Colossians, making it possible for them to leave behind the ways of living that mark human existence apart from Christ in favor of the practices that nurture Christian community.

3:11—In Christ, the fundamental distinctions and polarities that determine human relationships have been overturned (cf. Gal. 3:28). Within the Christian community, there is but one head, Christ, and all the members are servants of Christ, and thus of one another. This teaching undermines the ways by which humans typically establish distinctions of status and privilege within community, including the use of piety, doctrine, office, or spiritual practices to establish status distinctions within the church.

3:12–17—Christian practices attain their power as expressions of what Christians have already

experienced in Christ: forgiveness, *love*, the *peace of Christ*, and the *word of Christ*. All of this constitutes Christian worship and mission.

3:18–4:1 Rules for relationships in the household—These verses adopt a conventional form of moral argumentation, the "household code," to exhort the members of households regarding their relationships with the patron of the house (cf. Eph. 5:21–6:9, 1 Pet. 2:18–3:7). The code aims to preserve harmony by calling forth conformity with predetermined social roles and patterns. Because it presumes the patriarchal focus of the ancient Mediterranean household, including the practice of slavery, the code should not be read as a timeless ideal, applicable to all people in all times and places, but rather as a case study in the ways Christian ideals intersected, for better or worse, with prevailing cultural norms.

²³ Whatever your task, put yourselves into it, as done for the Lord and not for your masters,ᵃ ²⁴ since you know that from the Lord you will receive the inheritance as your reward; you serveᵇ the Lord Christ. ²⁵ For the wrongdoer will be paid back for whatever wrong has been done, and there is no partiality.

4 ¹ Masters, treat your slaves justly and fairly, for you know that you also have a Master in heaven.

Further Instructions

2 Devote yourselves to prayer, keeping alert in it with thanksgiving. ³ At the same time pray for us as well that God will open to us a door for the word, that we may declare the mystery of Christ, for which I am in prison, ⁴ so that I may reveal it clearly, as I should.

5 Conduct yourselves wisely toward outsiders, making the most of the time.ᶜ ⁶ Let your speech always be gracious, seasoned with salt, so that you may know how you ought to answer everyone.

Final Greetings and Benediction

7 Tychicus will tell you all the news about me; he is a beloved brother, a faithful minister, and a fellow servantᵈ in the Lord. ⁸ I have sent him to you for this very purpose, so that you may know how we areᵉ and that he may encourage your hearts; ⁹ he is coming with Onesimus, the faithful and beloved brother, who is one of you. They will tell you about everything here.

10 Aristarchus my fellow prisoner greets you, as does Mark the cousin of Barnabas, concerning whom you have received instructions—if he comes to you, welcome him. ¹¹ And Jesus who is called Justus greets you. These are the only ones of the circumcision among my co-workers for the kingdom of God, and they have been a comfort to me. ¹² Epaphras, who is one of you, a servantᵈ of Christ Jesus, greets you. He is always wrestling in his prayers on your behalf, so that you may stand mature and fully assured in everything that God wills. ¹³ For I testify for him that he has worked hard for you and for those in Laodicea and in Hierapolis. ¹⁴ Luke, the beloved physician, and Demas greet you. ¹⁵ Give my greetings to the brothers and sistersᶠ in Laodicea, and to Nympha and the church in her house. ¹⁶ And when this letter has been read among you, have it read also in the church of the Laodiceans; and see that you read also the letter from Laodicea. ¹⁷ And say to Archippus, "See that you complete the task that you have received in the Lord."

18 I, Paul, write this greeting with my own hand. Remember my chains. Grace be with you.ᵍ

ᵃ Gk not for men ᵇ Or you are slaves of, or be slaves of ᶜ Or opportunity ᵈ Gk slave ᵉ Other authorities read that I may know how you are ᶠ Gk brothers ᵍ Other ancient authorities add Amen

---

4:2–6—Final exhortations focus on the mission of Paul and the Colossians toward outsiders.

The Book of
1 THESSALONIANS

Thessalonica was a prosperous center of trade, located at the juncture of sea and land routes on the northwest shore of the Aegean Sea. As the capital of the Roman province of Macedonia, Thessalonica was not only the seat of Roman political interests, but a locus of worship for Greek and Roman deities, including the imperial cult, in which members of the imperial household were worshiped as gods. Rome claimed to offer "peace and security" (5:3), "justice" (or "righteousness"), "unity," and "salvation" to its subject peoples, but demanded loyalty ("faith") in return. Rome adopted an urbane, benevolent posture and advocated conservative social values that preserved the traditional order, thereby serving the interests of the dominant classes. Roman advocacy of the rule of law—alongside intimidation, violence, and a steep social hierarchy—served the same interests. Religious tolerance was also the rule; as long as subject peoples continued to bow the knee before the emperor, they were free to worship other deities, as well.

It should come as no surprise, then, that the exclusive devotion Christians manifested toward the God of Jesus Christ put them at extreme risk in Roman imperial society. Their refusal to bow before imperial images or confess Caesar as Lord and Savior and their withdrawal from the worship of other deities implicated them in antisocial and anti-Roman behavior. In its confessions, its worship, and the character of its life together, the Thessalonian church would have stood in contrast to the political and economic arrangements of the day, placing the Christians at risk of rejection or persecution. Paul writes this letter to confirm and encourage the continued embodiment of a faithful, Christ-centered alternative to Roman imperial culture. Within this gathering, the death and resurrection of Jesus sustains life and community, rather than the patronage and domination of the Roman elites. While it strikes many modern readers as benign religious encouragement, 1 Thessalonians affirms the Christian faith not merely as an alternative religion among many, but as a singular alternative to the assumptions, motivations, values, and social and political order of empire. Given the fact that many people around the world today regard the global economy as the most powerful expression of empire the world has yet seen, Paul's argument in 1 Thessalonians challenges us to think critically and faithfully about the church's complicity in systems of domination that many of us take for granted.

Paul successfully established the gospel among predominantly Gentile households in Thessalonica, but then was forced to flee. After his own attempts to return were frustrated, Paul sent Timothy back to check on the Christian movement in this city. A positive report from Timothy gave rise to this letter, probably the earliest surviving document in the New Testament. As Paul confirms the Thessalonians' faithful participation in and witness to the gospel, he also calls forth behavior that will continue to distinguish the Christians from their neighbors yet leave the doors open for continuing witness.

—**Stanley Saunders**

Salutation

1 Paul, Silvanus, and Timothy,
To the church of the Thessalonians in God the Father and the Lord Jesus Christ:
Grace to you and peace.

The Thessalonians' Faith and Example

2 We always give thanks to God for all of you and mention you in our prayers, constantly ³remembering before our God and Father your work of faith and labor of love and steadfastness of hope in our Lord Jesus Christ. ⁴For we know, brothers and sisters*a* beloved by God, that he has chosen you, ⁵because our message of the gospel came to you not in word only, but also in power and in the Holy Spirit and with full conviction; just as you know what kind of persons we proved to be among you for your sake. ⁶And you became imitators of us and of the Lord, for in spite of persecution you received the word with joy inspired by the Holy Spirit, ⁷so that you became an example to all the believers in Macedonia and in Achaia. ⁸For the word of the Lord has sounded forth from you not only in Macedonia and Achaia, but in every place your faith in God has become known, so that we have no need to speak about it. ⁹For the people of those regions*b* report about us

what kind of welcome we had among you, and how you turned to God from idols, to serve a living and true God, ¹⁰and to wait for his Son from heaven, whom he raised from the dead—Jesus, who rescues us from the wrath that is coming.

Paul's Ministry in Thessalonica

2 You yourselves know, brothers and sisters,*a* that our coming to you was not in vain, ²but though we had already suffered and been shamefully mistreated at Philippi, as you know, we had courage in our God to declare to you the gospel of God in spite of great opposition. ³For our appeal does not spring from deceit or impure motives or trickery, ⁴but just as we have been approved by God to be entrusted with the message of the gospel, even so we speak, not to please mortals, but to please God who tests our hearts. ⁵As you know and as God is our witness, we never came with words of flattery or with a pretext for greed; ⁶nor did we seek praise from mortals, whether from you or from others, ⁷though we might have made demands as apostles of Christ. But we were gentle*c* among you, like a nurse tenderly caring for her own children. ⁸So deeply do we care for you that we are determined to share

---

a Gk brothers *b* Gk For they *c* Other ancient authorities read *infants*

1:1–10 Salutation and Thanksgiving
The thanksgiving (vv. 2–10) sounds the key themes that will dominate the letter. The triad of faith, love, and hope (v. 3; cf. 5:8) is a common motif in Paul's letters (cf. Rom. 5:1–5, 1 Cor. 13:13, Gal. 5:5–6). *Faith* is the foundational orientation of trust toward God, expressed most clearly in the faithfulness of Christ, even to the point of death on the cross, in obedience to God and in love toward humankind. *Love* is the social manifestation of faith; trusting God who frees us from the constraints of sin, death, and alienation, so that we can serve one another. *Hope* is the aspect of faith that looks, with both certainty and anticipation, toward the culmination of God's redemption and restoration of the world. Faith, love, and hope are the primary forces by which the church as an alternative community is sustained.

1:5–10—Paul recalls his relationship with the Thessalonian Christians, especially the way they became *imitators of us and of the Lord* (v. 6), despite *persecution* (cf. 2:14). Their story and faithful witness have subsequently been made known throughout Greece. Paul continues to affirm this witness throughout the letter.

2:1–3:13 The Character of Christian Witness

2:1–12—*Courage* and integrity in the face of opposition characterized Paul's ministry in Thessalonica, never *deceit* or the quest for human approval, which were typical of Greco-Roman culture. He uses both maternal (vv. 7–8) and paternal (vv. 11–12) images to describe the care that marked his relationship with them. Mutuality and solidarity, rather than patronage and domination, characterize his relationship with them and establish the foundational model for discipleship, even today.

with you not only the gospel of God but also our own selves, because you have become very dear to us.

9 You remember our labor and toil, brothers and sisters;[a] we worked night and day, so that we might not burden any of you while we proclaimed to you the gospel of God. [10] You are witnesses, and God also, how pure, upright, and blameless our conduct was toward you believers. [11] As you know, we dealt with each one of you like a father with his children, [12] urging and encouraging you and pleading that you lead a life worthy of God, who calls you into his own kingdom and glory.

13 We also constantly give thanks to God for this, that when you received the word of God that you heard from us, you accepted it not as a human word but as what it really is, God's word, which is also at work in you believers. [14] For you, brothers and sisters,[a] became imitators of the churches of God in Christ Jesus that are in Judea, for you suffered the same things from your own compatriots as they did from the Jews, [15] who killed both the Lord Jesus and the prophets,[b] and drove us out; they displease God and oppose everyone [16] by hindering us from speaking to the Gentiles so that they may be saved. Thus they have constantly been filling up the measure of their sins; but God's wrath has overtaken them at last.[c]

Paul's Desire to Visit the Thessalonians Again

17 As for us, brothers and sisters,[a] when, for a short time, we were made orphans by being separated from you— in person, not in heart—we longed with great eagerness to see you face to face. [18] For we wanted to come to you—certainly I, Paul, wanted to again and again—but Satan blocked our way. [19] For what is our hope or joy or crown of boasting before our Lord Jesus at his coming? Is it not you? [20] Yes, you are our glory and joy!

3 Therefore when we could bear it no longer, we decided to be left

[a] Gk brothers [b] Other ancient authorities read *their own prophets*
[c] Or *completely* or *forever*

2:13–16—The Thessalonians' experience of suffering establishes them as imitators of the *churches in Judea*, who also **suffered** opposition from their own people on account of the gospel. Especially in its embrace of suffering for the sake of the other, Christian witness always leaves itself open to ridicule and increased hostility. This vulnerability is a hallmark of genuine mission, an expression of identification with Christ, and a parody of the power and patterns of domination associated with empire. Suffering remains a reality for many Christians in the world today; its relative absence in the life of most North American congregations may suggest the degree to which the witness of the contemporary church is muted, isolated, or has been accommodated to the patterns of empire in our own day.

2:17–19—Paul turns again to familial language (*orphans*) to describe his frustration at having been **separated** from and prevented from visiting the Christians in Thessalonica. When he speaks of **boasting**, Paul takes up common Greco-Roman social values in order to invest them with new associations. Boasting had to do with social expressions of honor, the often ostentatious display of one's status and worth vis-à-vis others, not unlike the use of dress, homes, or cars to display wealth and status today. In contrast, Paul here speaks of the Thessalonians themselves as the focus of Paul's boasting. He is advocating community—relationships of love, mutuality, and genuine compassion—as the focus of his boasting when the Lord comes.

3:1–13—Despite facing persecution, Paul decided to send Timothy to **encourage** the church. Paul reminds them that he had predicted the suffering he would endure, yet expresses concern that they would see this suffering, despite their preparation, as disconfirming the power of the gospel (vv. 3–5). In vv. 6–10 Paul offers reassurance that he has heard from Timothy that they are standing firm in **faith and love**. The point here is not only that suffering is always a likely consequence of faithful proclamation of the gospel (vv. 3–4, 7), but that Christians require an alternative set of values—a fundamentally different way of making sense of the world—in order to rightly discern both the nature of suffering and the way of the gospel in the world. Paul's words of reassurance also confirm the sustaining power of solidarity in community amidst suffering, even across time and the distances that separate them from him. Neither suffering nor the gospel witness can long be sustained apart from Christian community.

alone in Athens; [2] and we sent Timothy, our brother and co-worker for God in proclaiming[a] the gospel of Christ, to strengthen and encourage you for the sake of your faith, [3] so that no one would be shaken by these persecutions. Indeed, you yourselves know that this is what we are destined for. [4] In fact, when we were with you, we told you beforehand that we were to suffer persecution; so it turned out, as you know. [5] For this reason, when I could bear it no longer, I sent to find out about your faith; I was afraid that somehow the tempter had tempted you and that our labor had been in vain.

Timothy's Encouraging Report

[6] But Timothy has just now come to us from you, and has brought us the good news of your faith and love. He has told us also that you always remember us kindly and long to see us—just as we long to see you. [7] For this reason, brothers and sisters,[b] during all our distress and persecution we have been encouraged about you through your faith. [8] For we now live, if you continue to stand firm in the Lord. [9] How can we thank God enough for you in return for all the joy that we feel before our God because of you? [10] Night and day we pray most earnestly that we may see you face to face and restore whatever is lacking in your faith.

[11] Now may our God and Father himself and our Lord Jesus direct our way to you. [12] And may the Lord make you increase and abound in love for one another and for all, just as we abound in love for you. [13] And may he so strengthen your hearts in holiness that you may be blameless before our God and Father at the coming of our Lord Jesus with all his saints.

A Life Pleasing to God

4 Finally, brothers and sisters,[b] we ask and urge you in the Lord Jesus that, as you learned from us how you ought to live and to please God (as, in fact, you are doing), you should do so more and more. [2] For you know what instructions we gave you through the Lord Jesus. [3] For this is the will of God, your sanctification: that you abstain from fornication; [4] that each one of you know how to control your own body[c] in holiness and honor, [5] not with lustful passion, like the Gentiles who do not know God; [6] that no one wrong or exploit a brother or sister[d] in this matter, because the Lord is an avenger in all these things, just as we have already told you beforehand and solemnly warned you. [7] For God did not call us to impurity but in holiness. [8] Therefore whoever rejects this rejects not human authority but God, who also gives his Holy Spirit to you.

[9] Now concerning love of the brothers and sisters,[b] you do not need to have anyone write to you, for you yourselves have been taught by God to love one another; [10] and indeed you do love all the brothers and sisters[b] throughout Macedonia. But we urge you, beloved,[b] to do so more and more, [11] to aspire to live quietly, to mind your own affairs, and to work with your hands, as we directed you, [12] so that you may behave properly toward outsiders and be dependent on no one.

[a] Gk lacks proclaiming [b] Gk brothers [c] Or how to take a wife for himself [d] Gk brother

---

4:1–12 Relations with Insiders and Outsiders
Paul returns to the motif of imitation in v. 1, then enumerates practices that are to define the Christians in relation both to one another and to *the Gentiles who do not know God* (v. 5). Paul calls for mutual love, sexual self-control, and avoidance of exploitive relationships. While these may sound benignly conventional to modern ears, they were not, in fact, normative in the world of Roman imperial politics. The politics of domination, in whatever era, inevitably entails manipulation, exploitation, and interpersonal expressions of license and abuse. The good news of God's solidarity with humankind, however, puts an end to the social hierarchies and patterns of aggrandizement and denigration that are commonplace in the fallen creation.

The Coming of the Lord

13 But we do not want you to be uninformed, brothers and sisters,*a* about those who have died,*b* so that you may not grieve as others do who have no hope. 14 For since we believe that Jesus died and rose again, even so, through Jesus, God will bring with him those who have died.*b* 15 For this we declare to you by the word of the Lord, that we who are alive, who are left until the coming of the Lord, will by no means precede those who have died.*b* 16 For the Lord himself, with a cry of command, with the archangel's call and with the sound of God's trumpet, will descend from heaven, and the dead in Christ will rise first. 17 Then we who are alive, who are left, will be caught up in the clouds together with them to meet the Lord in the air; and so we will be with the Lord forever. 18 Therefore encourage one another with these words.

5 Now concerning the times and the seasons, brothers and sisters,*a* you do not need to have anything written to you. 2 For you yourselves know very well that the day of the Lord will come like a thief in the night. 3 When they say, "There is peace and security," then sudden destruction will come upon them, as labor pains come upon a pregnant woman, and there will be no escape! 4 But you, beloved,*a* are not in darkness, for that day to surprise you like a thief; 5 for you are all children of light and children of the day; we are not of the night or of darkness. 6 So then let us not fall asleep as others do, but let us keep awake and be sober; 7 for those who sleep sleep at night, and those who are drunk get drunk at night. 8 But since we belong to the day, let us be sober, and put on the breastplate of faith and love, and for a helmet the hope of salvation. 9 For God has destined us not for wrath but for obtaining salvation through our Lord Jesus Christ, 10 who died for us, so that whether we are awake or asleep we may live with him. 11 Therefore encourage one another and build up each other, as indeed you are doing.

Final Exhortations, Greetings, and Benediction

12 But we appeal to you, brothers and sisters,*a* to respect those who labor among you, and have charge of you in the Lord and admonish you; 13 esteem them very highly in love because of their work. Be at peace among yourselves. 14 And we urge you, beloved,*a* to admonish the idlers, encourage the fainthearted, help the weak, be patient with all of them. 15 See that none of you repays evil for evil, but always seek to do good to one another and to all. 16 Rejoice always, 17 pray without ceasing, 18 give thanks in all circumstances; for this is the will of God in Christ Jesus for you. 19 Do not quench the Spirit. 20 Do not

a Gk brothers   *b* Gk fallen asleep

4:13–5:11 Teaching concerning the Coming of the Lord

4:13–18—Paul addresses concerns about what will happen when Christ returns, including the fate of those who have already died in Christ.

5:1–11—The reminder that *the day of the Lord will come like a thief in the night* calls forth watchfulness. Wariness regarding claims of *peace and security* (v. 3) helps resist Roman imperial propaganda and the claims of all human empires. Apocalyptic consciousness is wakeful and sober, i.e., resistant to the delusions and numbness of life in the fallen world.

5:8—See 1:3 and note at 1:1–10.

5:12–22 Exhortations for Christian Community

These varied appeals aim both to secure the inner life of the community and to facilitate ongoing mission. Paul worked hard to enable his congregations to live faithfully in the world, to preserve their distinctive calling and identity while remaining open to outsiders and newcomers. *Idlers* (v. 14) is probably better translated as "troublemakers," i.e., those whose behavior, for whatever reason, is disruptive. Paul does not suggest the removal of such persons, but constructive engagement with them. The admonitions in vv. 12–19 together affirm the importance within the faith community of relationships characterized by integrity, honesty, and mutual encouragement.

despise the words of prophets,*a* [21] but test everything; hold fast to what is good; [22] abstain from every form of evil.

[23] May the God of peace himself sanctify you entirely; and may your spirit and soul and body be kept sound*b* and blameless at the coming of our Lord Jesus Christ. [24] The one who calls you is faithful, and he will do this.

[25] Beloved,*c* pray for us.

[26] Greet all the brothers and sisters*d* with a holy kiss. [27] I solemnly command you by the Lord that this letter be read to all of them.*e*

[28] The grace of our Lord Jesus Christ be with you.*f*

a Gk despise prophecies   *b* Or complete   *c* Gk Brothers   *d* Gk brothers   *e* Gk to all the brothers   *f* Other ancient authorities add Amen

2 THESSALONIANS

When Paul and other early Christian missionaries preached the gospel, they drew heavily on Jewish, Greek, and Roman traditions that focused on the direction and goal of human history, an area of speculation that we often call eschatology (the study of the end times). The early Christians held strong convictions that they were living in the "last days," when God was fulfilling the promises made to Israel, gathering and restoring the chosen people, and pouring out the Holy Spirit on the faithful. Second Thessalonians focuses on issues arising from the eschatological convictions and expectations of the early Christians.

While modern Christians often find the eschatological elements in the New Testament hard to understand, for the early Christians, convictions about the last days were a crucial element of faith itself, instilling hope and fueling imagination that allowed them to discern the presence of the risen Christ and experience the power of the Spirit in their midst, transforming their relationships with one another. But for first-century as for twenty-first-century Christians, eschatological conviction was ripe for misunderstanding and misappropriation. In general, the writings of the New Testament encourage watchful, vigilant expectation, even as they caution against unbridled speculation about the future or the events leading up to the end. Rather than fueling expectation of flight from the world, writers like Paul persistently articulate eschatological convictions that encourage responsible engagement with the world as they await its full redemption. This too is the primary goal of 2 Thessalonians.

Both of the New Testament letters addressed to the church in Thessalonica address concerns arising from eschatological convictions, but do so in apparently divergent ways. Whereas 1 Thessalonians claims that "the day of the Lord will come like a thief in the night" (5:2), 2 Thessalonians includes an extensive and, for many readers, bewildering description of the events leading up to the end. The claim in 2 Thessalonians that God will both vindicate those who have suffered and inflict vengeance on opponents of the gospel (1:6–10) lends this letter a harsher tone.

Apart from the differences in their approaches to questions about the end, the two letters share remarkable formal and thematic similarities. Both letters encourage churches under threat of persecution, affirm imitation of the apostolic witness (2 Thess. 3:7; 1 Thess. 1:6; 2:14; 4:1), and address concerns about "idleness" (lit. "disorderliness"; 2 Thess. 3:6–13; 1 Thess. 5:14). Both letters presume the crucial connection between the recipients' eschatological perspectives and the character of their life together. For those who are concerned about Christian witness today, the eschatological dimensions of faith should not be seen as mere curiosities, but as foundational for our sense of where history is headed, how God is involved in human experience, and what faithful, hope-filled disciples are to be about as we await the fulfillment of God's work in the world.

—**Stanley Saunders**

Salutation

1 Paul, Silvanus, and Timothy,
To the church of the Thessalonians in God our Father and the Lord Jesus Christ:

2 Grace to you and peace from God our*a* Father and the Lord Jesus Christ.

Thanksgiving

3 We must always give thanks to God for you, brothers and sisters,*b* as is right, because your faith is growing abundantly, and the love of every one of you for one another is increasing. 4 Therefore we ourselves boast of you among the churches of God for your steadfastness and faith during all your persecutions and the afflictions that you are enduring.

The Judgment at Christ's Coming

5 This is evidence of the righteous judgment of God, and is intended to make you worthy of the kingdom of God, for which you are also suffering. 6 For it is indeed just of God to repay with affliction those who afflict you, 7 and to give relief to the afflicted as well as to us, when the Lord Jesus is revealed from heaven with his mighty angels 8 in flaming fire, inflicting vengeance on those who do not know God and on those who do not obey the gospel of our Lord Jesus. 9 These will suffer the punishment of eternal destruction, separated from the presence of the Lord and from the glory of his might, 10 when he comes to be glorified by his saints and to be marveled at on that day among all who have believed, because our testimony to you was believed. 11 To this end we always pray for you, asking that our God will make you worthy of his call and will fulfill by his power every good resolve and work of faith, 12 so that the name of our Lord Jesus may be glorified in you, and you in him, according to the grace of our God and the Lord Jesus Christ.

The Man of Lawlessness

2 As to the coming of our Lord Jesus Christ and our being gathered together to him, we beg you, brothers

a Other ancient authorities read *the*   *b* Gk *brothers*

1:3–4 A Prayer
Thanksgiving for steadfastness amid affliction.

1:5–10 Apocalyptic Reassurance
The claim that God will both vindicate those who have suffered for the kingdom of God (vv. 5–7) and wreak vengeance against those who have afflicted the community (vv. 8–9) sounds common apocalyptic tones, but more harshly than is typical of Paul. Whereas much modern, popular eschatological speculation focuses on scenarios of destruction and divine vengeance, not unlike the sentiments expressed here, New Testament writers—and Paul especially—are generally more concerned with God's redemption and restoration of creation.

2:1–12 Unmasking False Eschatologies
While many details in this portion of the letter resist precise explanation, the passage clearly warns against the deceptions of humans who wrap themselves in religious rhetoric and eschatological ideologies. The identity of **the lawless one** (v. 3) is not clear, nor even whether he is a historical figure or a literary construction. **Lawlessness** (v. 7) refers probably to refusal to recognize God's sovereignty and to stand in obedience to the one true God. The lawless one functions in ways that first-century readers would have associated with imperial ideology, by declaring himself to be God, for example (v. 4). The Roman imperial cult customarily made claims about the divinity of the emperors and their families that were widely accepted in the religious and political atmosphere of the day. Roman imperial self-understanding also came to expression in forms of realized eschatology, the claim that divine power is already embodied historically in human institutions, such as empires. Four points emerge from this for readers today. First, evil is a powerful reality in the world, both dominating and deluding humankind. Second, eschatology is not merely a matter of religious fantasy, but a tool that can be used (and still is used today) to cloak political and economic interests in divine garb. No human political or economic systems, especially those that rely on domination or violence to enforce their aims, can legitimately claim to represent or enjoy the blessing of the God of Jesus Christ. Third, Christians must recognize the **powerful delusion** and deceit associated with imperial expressions of power (vv. 10–12) and their claims to represent divine will. Finally, the coming of the Lord Jesus means the complete destruction of such pretensions (v. 8) as well

and sisters,[a] [2] not to be quickly shaken in mind or alarmed, either by spirit or by word or by letter, as though from us, to the effect that the day of the Lord is already here. [3] Let no one deceive you in any way; for that day will not come unless the rebellion comes first and the lawless one[b] is revealed, the one destined for destruction.[c] [4] He opposes and exalts himself above every so-called god or object of worship, so that he takes his seat in the temple of God, declaring himself to be God. [5] Do you not remember that I told you these things when I was still with you? [6] And you know what is now restraining him, so that he may be revealed when his time comes. [7] For the mystery of lawlessness is already at work, but only until the one who now restrains it is removed. [8] And then the lawless one will be revealed, whom the Lord Jesus[d] will destroy[e] with the breath of his mouth, annihilating him by the manifestation of his coming. [9] The coming of the lawless one is apparent in the working of Satan, who uses all power, signs, lying wonders, [10] and every kind of wicked deception for those who are perishing, because they refused to love the truth and so be saved. [11] For this reason God sends them a powerful delusion, leading them to believe what is false, [12] so that all who have not believed the truth but took pleasure in unrighteousness will be condemned.

Chosen for Salvation

13 But we must always give thanks to God for you, brothers and sisters[a] beloved by the Lord, because God chose you as the first fruits[f] for salvation through sanctification by the Spirit and through belief in the truth. [14] For this purpose he called you through our proclamation of the good news,[g] so that you may obtain the glory of our Lord Jesus Christ. [15] So then, brothers and sisters,[a] stand firm and hold fast to the traditions that you were taught by us, either by word of mouth or by our letter.

16 Now may our Lord Jesus Christ himself and God our Father, who loved us and through grace gave us eternal comfort and good hope, [17] comfort your hearts and strengthen them in every good work and word.

Request for Prayer

3 Finally, brothers and sisters,[a] pray for us, so that the word of the Lord may spread rapidly and be glorified everywhere, just as it is among you, [2] and that we may be rescued from wicked and evil people; for not all have faith. [3] But the Lord is faithful; he will strengthen you and guard you from the evil one.[h] [4] And we have confidence in the Lord concerning you, that you are doing and will go on doing the things that we command. [5] May the Lord direct your hearts to the love of God and to the steadfastness of Christ.

Warning against Idleness

6 Now we command you, beloved,[a] in the name of our Lord Jesus Christ, to keep away from believers who are[i] living in idleness and not according to

---

[a] Gk brothers　[b] Gk the man of lawlessness; other ancient authorities read the man of sin　[c] Gk the son of destruction　[d] Other ancient authorities lack Jesus　[e] Other ancient authorities read consume　[f] Other ancient authorities read from the beginning　[g] Or through our gospel　[h] Or from evil　[i] Gk from every brother who is

---

as the systems of domination they support. The realization of Christian hope entails the end of human political, economic, and social arrangements, whatever their apparent power, longevity, or inevitability.

2:13–17 Prayers of Thanksgiving and Encouragement

3:1–15 Instructions to the Community

The argument against *idleness* in vv. 6–11

highlights the apostle's own work and economic independence, which he pursued in order to prevent the growth of exploitive dependencies in the community. Paul is concerned not about laziness per se, but the economic vulnerability and social disruption that accompany the lack of work. The community discipline described in vv. 14–15 seeks the ultimate restoration of those who cause trouble.

the tradition that they[a] received from us. 7 For you yourselves know how you ought to imitate us; we were not idle when we were with you, 8 and we did not eat anyone's bread without paying for it; but with toil and labor we worked night and day, so that we might not burden any of you. 9 This was not because we do not have that right, but in order to give you an example to imitate. 10 For even when we were with you, we gave you this command: Anyone unwilling to work should not eat. 11 For we hear that some of you are living in idleness, mere busybodies, not doing any work. 12 Now such persons we command and exhort in the Lord Jesus Christ to do their work quietly and to earn their own living. 13 Brothers and sisters,[b] do not be weary in doing what is right.

14 Take note of those who do not obey what we say in this letter; have nothing to do with them, so that they may be ashamed. 15 Do not regard them as enemies, but warn them as believers.[c]

Final Greetings and Benediction

16 Now may the Lord of peace himself give you peace at all times in all ways. The Lord be with all of you.

17 I, Paul, write this greeting with my own hand. This is the mark in every letter of mine; it is the way I write. 18 The grace of our Lord Jesus Christ be with all of you.[d]

[a] Other ancient authorities read you [b] Gk Brothers [c] Gk a brother
[d] Other ancient authorities add Amen

Introduction to the Pastoral Epistles:
1 TIMOTHY, 2 TIMOTHY, AND TITUS

This collection of letters, usually called the Pastoral Epistles, occupies a shadowy but important place in the development of the canon of early Christian Scripture. The shadows surround the precise date and authorship of the letters. While they are written in the name of Paul, a significant number of scholars argue that they are not genuinely from Paul of Tarsus but were composed a few generations after his death. Matters of style, vocabulary, and content separate the letters from what are considered the "authentic" Pauline writings (Romans, 1 and 2 Corinthians, Galatians, Philippians, 1 Thessalonians, Philemon). The Pastoral Epistles are regarded as examples of pseudepigrapha, reflecting an ancient Greek rhetorical practice of writing in the name of a revered teacher or mentor. In terms of their importance for understanding the themes of Christian discipleship and issues of social concern, 1 Timothy, 2 Timothy, and Titus represent a pivotal moment in the life of the church. In them we can discern a struggle in the early church to interpret the legacy of Paul's gospel and what it means for the social organization of church and the relationship of the church to the broader society.

For many contemporary Christians, the suggestion that biblical writings are falsely ascribed to an author is threatening to their understanding of the authority of Scripture. How can writings that are deceptive regarding their authorship be understood as "true," or "God's word"? Such queries must be placed within the context of the ancient practices of letter writing. The device was common and offered this writer a means of defining and perpetuating his community's understanding of the Pauline tradition. While the letters may not afford a glimpse of the "real" Paul, they offer an example of how a particular church in the late first and early second century interpreted the teachings of Paul and understood the mission of the church.

Beyond the challenge of authorship, other contemporary readers are troubled by the content of the letters. Proscriptions in them regarding women's leadership in the church (e.g., 1 Tim. 2:8–15) and exhortations for slaves to honor their believing masters (e.g., 1 Tim. 6:1–2) offend more inclusive notions of church life that many hold today. Such dissonance has led to disregard of the letters particularly within "old line" Protestant churches. They have been characterized as examples of culturally accommodated religion and represented as the domestication of Paul. While somewhat understandable, this characterization lacks contextual sensitivity. The statements of the letter writer must be read alongside statements in other early Christian writings that interpret the legacy of Paul differently. The letter writer's proscriptions of women's leadership and standards for clergy are a part of an ancient argument about the social reality of the church in light of the gospel of Jesus Christ. Marcionites, Montanists, Gnostics, and many other groups understood Paul's writings to be authoritative and

yet held varying understandings of the structure and social situation of the church. In this plurality of interpretations regarding Paul, the expressions in these letters convey one part of that ancient argument. A critical appreciation of these writings, namely, in light of other early Christian texts and their historical context, provides the contemporary church a resource for the study of the church in the late first century and early second century. While demanding what is "correct," they witness to a context of contentious diversity in early Christian faith and practice that is remarkably similar to our own.

—**Deborah Krause**

The Book of

1 TIMOTHY

The letter is addressed to one of Paul's closest companions, who is cited in several of his letters as a co-sender (e.g., 2 Cor. 1:1, Phil. 1:1; and Phlm. 1). Throughout Paul's letters Timothy is named as a trustworthy co-worker and someone who is often sent by Paul to preach the gospel in his stead (Phil. 2:22, 1 Cor. 4:17, 1 Thess. 3:1–6). By naming Timothy as the addressee, this letter provides a setting for the most intimate and thereby dependable disclosure of Paul's teaching. For the writer of the letter, the convention provides a means for revealing Paul's least guarded and most direct address.

Despite the genre of intimate address, the content of the letter is far from personal. Rather it primarily concerns the maintenance of order in the church and its offices, alongside a thoroughgoing concern with protecting doctrine from influences and practices that are considered outside of the true faith. In this sense, the writing seems to bear the marks of an official ecclesiastical document more than those of a private communication.

—Deborah Krause

Salutation

1 Paul, an apostle of Christ Jesus by the command of God our Savior and of Christ Jesus our hope,

2 To Timothy, my loyal child in the faith:

Grace, mercy, and peace from God the Father and Christ Jesus our Lord.

Warning against False Teachers

3 I urge you, as I did when I was on my way to Macedonia, to remain in Ephesus so that you may instruct certain people not to teach any different doctrine, 4 and not to occupy themselves with myths and endless genealogies that promote speculations rather than the divine

---

1:3a *I urge you, as I did when I was on my way to Macedonia, to remain in Ephesus*—These place names support the theory that 1 Timothy, 2 Timothy, and Titus were written in Asia Minor. However, such a focus also places the writing in the traditional center of Paul's mission in Greece, Ephesus. The letter writer's portrayal of "homespun" Paul is also served by the place name. In relation to other extant early Christian literature, Asia Minor was indeed a place of contention and dissension for the church. From Paul's own struggles with the church in Galatia to the venomous barbs of John of Patmos to several Asia Minor churches in Rev. 1–3 (e.g., Smyrna, Pergamum, and Laodicea), the literature reflects tension with regard to the beliefs, practices, and social situations of the churches there. In this sense, Asia Minor provides a fitting backdrop for the struggles evident in the Pastoral Epistles writer's rhetoric toward those who are "outside" the church as he defines it.

1:3b–4 *Not to teach any different doctrine, and not to occupy themselves with myths and endless genealogies*—This establishes the central concern of the entire Pastoral Epistles corpus, right instruction and its maintenance against "different" (Gk. "heretical") teachings. The precise content of the "heresies" is difficult to pin down. Commentators dispute whether Gnosticism is present or certain forms of Jewish Christianity. The characterization of these "different" teachings is a part of the writer's rhetorical work. Discerning his doctrinal agenda, therefore, should come from what he describes as *sincere faith* (v. 5) as much as from what he disparages as "different." For the letter writer, faith is characterized by conformity to the social structure of the community and trust in the sovereign provision of God as befits works of generosity and care within the community. Such commitment to social order may strain Western and modern conceptions of individuality and human freedom, but that is

training*a* that is known by faith. [5] But the aim of such instruction is love that comes from a pure heart, a good conscience, and sincere faith. [6] Some people have deviated from these and turned to meaningless talk, [7] desiring to be teachers of the law, without understanding either what they are saying or the things about which they make assertions.

8 Now we know that the law is good, if one uses it legitimately. [9] This means understanding that the law is laid down not for the innocent but for the lawless and disobedient, for the godless and sinful, for the unholy and profane, for those who kill their father or mother, for murderers, [10] fornicators, sodomites, slave traders, liars, perjurers, and whatever else is contrary to the sound teaching [11] that conforms to the glorious gospel of the blessed God, which he entrusted to me.

Gratitude for Mercy

12 I am grateful to Christ Jesus our Lord, who has strengthened me, because he judged me faithful and appointed me to his service, [13] even though I was formerly a blasphemer, a persecutor, and a man of violence. But I received mercy because I had acted ignorantly in unbelief, [14] and the grace of our Lord overflowed for me with the faith and love that are in Christ Jesus. [15] The saying is sure and worthy of full acceptance, that Christ Jesus came into the world to save sinners—of whom I am the foremost. [16] But for that very reason I received mercy, so that in me, as the foremost, Jesus Christ might display the utmost patience, making me an example to those who would come to believe in him for eternal life. [17] To the King of the ages, immortal, invisible, the only God, be honor and glory forever and ever.*b* Amen.

18 I am giving you these instructions, Timothy, my child, in accordance with the prophecies made earlier about you, so that by following them you may fight the good fight, [19] having faith and a good conscience. By rejecting conscience, certain persons have suffered shipwreck in the faith; [20] among them are Hymenaeus and Alexander, whom I have turned over to Satan, so that they may learn not to blaspheme.

Instructions concerning Prayer

2 First of all, then, I urge that supplications, prayers, intercessions, and thanksgivings be made for everyone, [2] for kings and all who are in high positions, so that we may lead a quiet and peaceable life in all godliness and dignity. [3] This is right and is acceptable in the sight of God our Savior, [4] who desires everyone to be saved and to come to the knowledge of the truth. [5] For

there is one God;
    there is also one mediator between
      God and humankind,
    Christ Jesus, himself human,
[6]   who gave himself a ransom for all

—this was attested at the right time. [7] For this I was appointed a herald and an apostle (I am telling the truth,*c* I am not lying), a teacher of the Gentiles in faith and truth.

8 I desire, then, that in every place the men should pray, lifting up holy hands without anger or argument; [9] also that the women should dress themselves modestly and decently in suitable clothing, not with their hair braided, or with gold, pearls, or expensive clothes, [10] but with good works, as is proper for women who profess reverence for God. [11] Let a woman*d* learn in silence with full

a Or plan *b* Gk to the ages of the ages *c* Other ancient authorities add *in Christ* *d* Or wife

---

precisely the challenge these letters present to contemporary understandings of discipleship. While the church may perennially articulate faith in Jesus Christ as the goal of the Christian life, discerning how such a confession shapes everyday life and how that faith is measured in the life of Christian community is the particular call of each church in every place and time.

submission. [12] I permit no woman[a] to teach or to have authority over a man;[b] she is to keep silent. [13] For Adam was formed first, then Eve; [14] and Adam was not deceived, but the woman was deceived and became a transgressor. [15] Yet she will be saved through childbearing, provided they continue in faith and love and holiness, with modesty.

Qualifications of Bishops

3 The saying is sure:[c] whoever aspires to the office of bishop[d] desires a noble task. [2] Now a bishop[e] must be above reproach, married only once,[f] temperate, sensible, respectable, hospitable, an apt teacher, [3] not a drunkard, not violent but gentle, not quarrelsome, and not a lover of money. [4] He must manage his own household well, keeping his children submissive and respectful in every way— [5] for if someone does not know how to manage his own household, how can he take care of God's church? [6] He must not be a recent convert, or he may be puffed up with conceit and fall into the condemnation of the devil. [7] Moreover, he must be well thought of by outsiders, so that he may not fall into disgrace and the snare of the devil.

Qualifications of Deacons

[8] Deacons likewise must be serious, not double-tongued, not indulging in much wine, not greedy for money; [9] they must hold fast to the mystery of the faith with a clear conscience. [10] And let them first be tested; then, if they prove themselves blameless, let them serve as deacons. [11] Women[g] likewise must be serious, not slanderers, but temperate, faithful in all things. [12] Let deacons be married only once,[h] and let them manage their children and their households well; [13] for those who serve well as dea-

---

[a] Or *wife* [b] Or *her husband* [c] Some interpreters place these words at the end of the previous paragraph. Other ancient authorities read *The saying is commonly accepted* [d] Or *overseer* [e] Or *an overseer* [f] Gk *the husband of one wife* [g] Or *Their wives,* or *Women deacons* [h] Gk *be husbands of one wife*

2:12 *I permit no woman to teach or have authority over a man; she is to keep silent*—This proscription of women's leadership within the church is situated in the context of instruction on prayer. The letter writer bases his claim in an interpretation of Gen. 2:4–3:18, the story of Adam and Eve. The interpretation reveals the writer's commitment to establishing a clear division of roles within the community along gender lines. Other Pauline writings reveal a very different social structure within the church. Paul himself in Gal. 3:28 quotes an ancient baptismal formula that holds out the abolition of gender divisions in the church. In addition, the stories of Thecla, within the early Christian apocryphal work the *Acts of Paul,* lionize a woman's quest to be an apostle. Furthermore, Marcion, a fervent interpreter of Paul, did not proscribe women's leadership roles within his churches. In this larger field of claims about women's leadership within the church, the letter writer's harsh rhetoric can be seen as prescriptive, rather than representative of the reality of the church in his time. Clearly women were active in leadership in the church. Women's speech was prevalent enough for the letter writer to demand their silence! The proscription and its exegetical justification can be seen as an attempt on the part of the letter writer to steer the interpretation of Paul from more socially egalitarian forms of community to those more accommodated to existing Greco-Roman modes of hierarchical and patriarchal social practice. While such an understanding does not apologize for the position of the writer, it does provide a lens through which to appreciate his rhetoric as one voice in a larger debate within the church about the role of women in church leadership and society.

3:5 *For if someone does not know how to manage his own household, how can he take care of God's church?*—This piece of proverbial wisdom appears in a section delineating the ideal character and qualifications of bishops in the church. This section and the one that follows in vv. 8–13 regarding deacons are the basis for the "pastoral" description of the letter collection. This particular saying reveals the extent to which traditional Greco-Roman piety and values of the patriarchal household have become normative for the letter writer's understanding of the church. In contrast to Paul's socially revolutionary claim in 1 Cor. 7 that both men and women should seek to live celibate lives outside of the commitments of marriage, this writer requires church leaders to be the husband of one wife. The writer assumes that the positions of bishop and deacon are open only to men, and marriage has moved from what in Paul's thought was a secondary allowance (a kind of necessary evil) to a requirement for positions of highest leadership.

cons gain a good standing for themselves and great boldness in the faith that is in Christ Jesus.

The Mystery of Our Religion

14 I hope to come to you soon, but I am writing these instructions to you so that, [15] if I am delayed, you may know how one ought to behave in the household of God, which is the church of the living God, the pillar and bulwark of the truth. [16] Without any doubt, the mystery of our religion is great:

He[a] was revealed in flesh,
    vindicated[b] in spirit,[c]
    seen by angels,
proclaimed among Gentiles,
    believed in throughout the world,
    taken up in glory.

False Asceticism

4 Now the Spirit expressly says that in later[d] times some will renounce the faith by paying attention to deceitful spirits and teachings of demons, [2] through the hypocrisy of liars whose consciences are seared with a hot iron. [3] They forbid marriage and demand abstinence from foods, which God created to be received with thanksgiving by those who believe and know the truth. [4] For everything created by God is good, and nothing is to be rejected, provided it is received with thanksgiving; [5] for it is sanctified by God's word and by prayer.

A Good Minister of Jesus Christ

6 If you put these instructions before the brothers and sisters,[e] you will be a good servant[f] of Christ Jesus, nourished on the words of the faith and of the sound teaching that you have followed. [7] Have nothing to do with profane myths and old wives' tales. Train yourself in godliness, [8] for, while physical training is of some value, godliness is valuable in every way, holding promise for both the present life and the life to come. [9] The saying is sure and worthy of full acceptance. [10] For to this end we toil and struggle,[g] because we have our hope set on the living God, who is the Savior of all people, especially of those who believe.

11 These are the things you must insist on and teach. [12] Let no one despise your youth, but set the believers an example in speech and conduct, in love, in faith, in purity. [13] Until I arrive, give attention to the public reading of scripture,[h] to exhorting, to teaching. [14] Do not neglect the gift that is in you, which was given to you through prophecy with the laying on of hands by the council of elders.[i] [15] Put these things into practice, devote yourself to them, so that all may see your progress. [16] Pay close attention to yourself and to your teaching; continue in these things, for in doing this you will save both yourself and your hearers.

Duties toward Believers

5 Do not speak harshly to an older man,[j] but speak to him as to a father, to younger men as brothers, [2] to older women as mothers, to younger women as sisters—with absolute purity.

3 Honor widows who are really widows. [4] If a widow has children or grandchildren, they should first learn their religious duty to their own family and make some repayment to their parents; for this is pleasing in God's sight. [5] The real widow, left alone, has set her hope on God and continues in supplications and prayers night and day; [6] but the widow[k] who lives for pleasure is dead even while she lives. [7] Give these commands as well, so that they may be above reproach. [8] And whoever does not provide for relatives, and especially for family members, has denied the faith and is worse than an unbeliever.

9 Let a widow be put on the list if she is not less than sixty years old and has been married only once;[l] [10] she must be well attested for her good works, as one

---

[a] Gk *Who;* other ancient authorities read *God;* others, *Which*   [b] Or *justified*   [c] Or *by the Spirit*   [d] Or *the last*   [e] Gk *brothers*   [f] Or *deacon*   [g] Other ancient authorities read *suffer reproach*   [h] Gk *to the reading*   [i] Gk *by the presbytery*   [j] Or *an elder,* or *a presbyter*   [k] Gk *she*   [l] Gk *the wife of one husband*

who has brought up children, shown hospitality, washed the saints' feet, helped the afflicted, and devoted herself to doing good in every way. **11** But refuse to put younger widows on the list; for when their sensual desires alienate them from Christ, they want to marry, **12** and so they incur condemnation for having violated their first pledge. **13** Besides that, they learn to be idle, gadding about from house to house; and they are not merely idle, but also gossips and busybodies, saying what they should not say. **14** So I would have younger widows marry, bear children, and manage their households, so as to give the adversary no occasion to revile us. **15** For some have already turned away to follow Satan. **16** If any believing woman[a] has relatives who are really widows, let her assist them; let the church not be burdened, so that it can assist those who are real widows.

17 Let the elders who rule well be considered worthy of double honor,[b] especially those who labor in preaching and teaching; **18** for the scripture says, "You shall not muzzle an ox while it is treading out the grain," and, "The laborer deserves to be paid." **19** Never accept any accusation against an elder except on the evidence of two or three witnesses. **20** As for those who persist in sin, rebuke them in the presence of all, so that the rest also may stand in fear. **21** In the presence of God and of Christ Jesus and of the elect angels, I warn you to keep these instructions without prejudice, doing nothing on the basis of partiality. **22** Do not ordain[c] anyone hastily, and do not participate in the sins of others; keep yourself pure.

23 No longer drink only water, but take a little wine for the sake of your stomach and your frequent ailments.

24 The sins of some people are conspicuous and precede them to judgment, while the sins of others follow them there. **25** So also good works are conspicuous; and even when they are not, they cannot remain hidden.

6 Let all who are under the yoke of slavery regard their masters as worthy of all honor, so that the name of God and the teaching may not be blasphemed. **2** Those who have believing masters must not be disrespectful to them on the ground that they are members of the church;[d] rather they must serve them all the more, since those who benefit by their service are believers and beloved.[e]

[a] Other ancient authorities read *believing man or woman*; others, *believing man*   [b] Or *compensation*   [c] Gk *Do not lay hands on*   [d] Gk *are brothers*   [e] Or *since they are believers and beloved, who devote themselves to good deeds*

6:1–2 *Let all who are under the yoke of slavery regard their masters as worthy of all honor, so that the name of God and the teaching may not be blasphemed. Those who have believing masters must not be disrespectful to them on the ground that they are members of the church; rather they must serve them all the more, since those who benefit by their service are believers and beloved*—As with the proscription of women's speech and leadership in 2:11–15, this call for the submission of slaves, particularly to "believing masters," is difficult to reconcile with the early Christian baptismal formulae in Gal. 3:28 and 1 Cor. 12:13. If Christian community is represented by a unity of Jew and Gentile, slave and free, male and female, how are some called to submission and service, while others are given power and privilege? Clear in these verses are the social stratification of the church and its propensity to exploit the class differences within the Christian community for the benefit of some at the cost of others. These verses are a part of a long, sad legacy within the church—that continues to the present—of complicity with human rights abuses. One might argue that such claims ought to be expunged from the canon of Christian Scripture. Their presence in the canon, however, can be viewed as evidence to a crime for which the church must continually be held to account. Moreover the verses can be seen as a witness to the voices of slaves (much like the voices of women) who were called to submission, precisely because there were some who refused to submit. Such implicit witnesses to the divinely created sanctity of each human being continue to this day in acts of defiance of human degradation and demands for human liberation. This is Christian discipleship in action. A part of the social mission of the church is discerning the places where these witnesses are coming forth and listening to these voices.

False Teaching and True Riches

Teach and urge these duties. [3] Whoever teaches otherwise and does not agree with the sound words of our Lord Jesus Christ and the teaching that is in accordance with godliness, [4] is conceited, understanding nothing, and has a morbid craving for controversy and for disputes about words. From these come envy, dissension, slander, base suspicions, [5] and wrangling among those who are depraved in mind and bereft of the truth, imagining that godliness is a means of gain.[a] [6] Of course, there is great gain in godliness combined with contentment; [7] for we brought nothing into the world, so that[b] we can take nothing out of it; [8] but if we have food and clothing, we will be content with these. [9] But those who want to be rich fall into temptation and are trapped by many senseless and harmful desires that plunge people into ruin and destruction. [10] For the love of money is a root of all kinds of evil, and in their eagerness to be rich some have wandered away from the faith and pierced themselves with many pains.

The Good Fight of Faith

[11] But as for you, man of God, shun all this; pursue righteousness, godliness, faith, love, endurance, gentleness. [12] Fight the good fight of the faith; take hold of the eternal life, to which you were called and for which you made[c] the good confession in the presence of many witnesses. [13] In the presence of God, who gives life to all things, and of Christ Jesus, who in his testimony before Pontius Pilate made the good confession, I charge you [14] to keep the commandment without spot or blame until the manifestation of our Lord Jesus Christ, [15] which he will bring about at the right time—he who is the blessed and only Sovereign, the King of kings and Lord of lords. [16] It is he alone who has immortality and dwells in unapproachable light, whom no one has ever seen or can see; to him be honor and eternal dominion. Amen.

[17] As for those who in the present age are rich, command them not to be haughty, or to set their hopes on the uncertainty of riches, but rather on God who richly provides us with everything for our enjoyment. [18] They are to do good, to be rich in good works, generous, and ready to share, [19] thus storing up for themselves the treasure of a good foundation for the future, so that they may take hold of the life that really is life.

Personal Instructions and Benediction

[20] Timothy, guard what has been entrusted to you. Avoid the profane chatter and contradictions of what is falsely called knowledge; [21] by professing it some have missed the mark as regards the faith.

Grace be with you.[d]

---

[a] Other ancient authorities add *Withdraw yourself from such people*
[b] Other ancient authorities read *world—it is certain that*   [c] Gk *confessed*
[d] The Greek word for *you* here is plural; in other ancient authorities it is singular. Other ancient authorities add *Amen*

2 TIMOTHY

Many commentators have noted how 2 Timothy differs from 1 Timothy and Titus. Paul is portrayed writing the letter from prison (1:8). In addition, the letter bears elements of a last testament of Paul to Timothy, recalling his life, his endurance of suffering, his service as an example of Christian faith for Timothy and all who would read the letter (4:7–8). Because of its different form, some scholars have posited that 2 Timothy was originally intended to close the Pastoral Epistle corpus, with Titus preceding 1 Timothy. The letter draws upon the life of Paul as a means of defining Christian faith and calling all Christians to "suffer for the gospel and rely on the power of God" (1:8).

—Deborah Krause

Salutation

1 Paul, an apostle of Christ Jesus by the will of God, for the sake of the promise of life that is in Christ Jesus,

2 To Timothy, my beloved child:

Grace, mercy, and peace from God the Father and Christ Jesus our Lord.

Thanksgiving and Encouragement

3 I am grateful to God—whom I worship with a clear conscience, as my ancestors did—when I remember you constantly in my prayers night and day. [4] Recalling your tears, I long to see you so that I may be filled with joy. [5] I am reminded of your sincere faith, a faith that lived first in your grandmother Lois and your mother Eunice and now, I am sure, lives in you. [6] For this reason I remind you to rekindle the gift of God that is within you through the laying on of my hands; [7] for God did not give us a spirit of cowardice, but rather a spirit of power and of love and of self-discipline.

8 Do not be ashamed, then, of the testimony about our Lord or of me his prisoner, but join with me in suffering for the gospel, relying on the power of God, [9] who saved us and called us with a holy calling, not according to our works but according to his own purpose and grace. This grace was given to us in Christ Jesus before the ages began, [10] but it has now been revealed through the appearing of our Savior Christ Jesus, who abolished death and brought life and immortality to light through the gospel. [11] For this gospel I was appointed a herald and an apostle and a teacher,[a] [12] and for this reason I suffer as I do. But I am not ashamed, for I know the one in whom I have put my trust, and I am sure that he is able to guard until that day what I have entrusted to him.[b] [13] Hold to the standard of sound teaching that you have heard from me, in the faith and love that are in Christ Jesus. [14] Guard the good treasure entrusted to you, with the help of the Holy Spirit living in us.

15 You are aware that all who are in Asia have turned away from me, including Phygelus and Hermogenes. [16] May the Lord grant mercy to the household of Onesiphorus, because he often refreshed me and was not ashamed of my chain; [17] when he arrived in Rome, he eagerly[c] searched for me and found me [18]—may the Lord grant that he will find mercy from the Lord on that day!

[a] Other ancient authorities add *of the Gentiles* [b] Or *what has been entrusted to me* [c] Or *promptly*

And you know very well how much service he rendered in Ephesus.

A Good Soldier of Christ Jesus

2 You then, my child, be strong in the grace that is in Christ Jesus; [2] and what you have heard from me through many witnesses entrust to faithful people who will be able to teach others as well. [3] Share in suffering like a good soldier of Christ Jesus. [4] No one serving in the army gets entangled in everyday affairs; the soldier's aim is to please the enlisting officer. [5] And in the case of an athlete, no one is crowned without competing according to the rules. [6] It is the farmer who does the work who ought to have the first share of the crops. [7] Think over what I say, for the Lord will give you understanding in all things.

[8] Remember Jesus Christ, raised from the dead, a descendant of David—that is my gospel, [9] for which I suffer hardship, even to the point of being chained like a criminal. But the word of God is not chained. [10] Therefore I endure everything for the sake of the elect, so that they may also obtain the salvation that is in Christ Jesus, with eternal glory. [11] The saying is sure:

If we have died with him, we will
     also live with him;
[12] if we endure, we will also reign with
     him;
if we deny him, he will also deny us;
[13] if we are faithless, he remains
     faithful—
for he cannot deny himself.

A Worker Approved by God

[14] Remind them of this, and warn them before God[a] that they are to avoid wrangling over words, which does no good but only ruins those who are listening. [15] Do your best to present yourself to God as one approved by him, a worker who has no need to be ashamed, rightly explaining the word of truth. [16] Avoid profane chatter, for it will lead people into more and more impiety,

[17] and their talk will spread like gangrene. Among them are Hymenaeus and Philetus, [18] who have swerved from the truth by claiming that the resurrection has already taken place. They are upsetting the faith of some. [19] But God's firm foundation stands, bearing this inscription: "The Lord knows those who are his," and, "Let everyone who calls on the name of the Lord turn away from wickedness."

20 In a large house there are utensils not only of gold and silver but also of wood and clay, some for special use, some for ordinary. [21] All who cleanse themselves of the things I have mentioned[b] will become special utensils, dedicated and useful to the owner of the house, ready for every good work. [22] Shun youthful passions and pursue righteousness, faith, love, and peace, along with those who call on the Lord from a pure heart. [23] Have nothing to do with stupid and senseless controversies; you know that they breed quarrels. [24] And the Lord's servant[c] must not be quarrelsome but kindly to everyone, an apt teacher, patient, [25] correcting opponents with gentleness. God may perhaps grant that they will repent and come to know the truth, [26] and that they may escape from the snare of the devil, having been held captive by him to do his will.[d]

Godlessness in the Last Days

3 You must understand this, that in the last days distressing times will come. [2] For people will be lovers of themselves, lovers of money, boasters, arrogant, abusive, disobedient to their parents, ungrateful, unholy, [3] inhuman, implacable, slanderers, profligates, brutes, haters of good, [4] treacherous, reckless, swollen with conceit, lovers of pleasure rather than lovers of God, [5] holding to the outward form of godliness but denying its power. Avoid them! [6] For among

---

[a] Other ancient authorities read *the Lord*   [b] Gk *of these things*   [c] Gk *slave*
[d] Or *by him, to do his* (that is, God's) *will*

them are those who make their way into households and captivate silly women, overwhelmed by their sins and swayed by all kinds of desires, [7] who are always being instructed and can never arrive at a knowledge of the truth. [8] As Jannes and Jambres opposed Moses, so these people, of corrupt mind and counterfeit faith, also oppose the truth. [9] But they will not make much progress, because, as in the case of those two men,[a] their folly will become plain to everyone.

Paul's Charge to Timothy

[10] Now you have observed my teaching, my conduct, my aim in life, my faith, my patience, my love, my steadfastness, [11] my persecutions, and my suffering the things that happened to me in Antioch, Iconium, and Lystra. What persecutions I endured! Yet the Lord rescued me from all of them. [12] Indeed, all who want to live a godly life in Christ Jesus will be persecuted. [13] But wicked people and impostors will go from bad to worse, deceiving others and being deceived. [14] But as for you, continue in what you have learned and firmly believed, knowing from whom you learned it, [15] and how from childhood you have known the sacred writings that are able to instruct you for salvation through faith in Christ Jesus. [16] All scripture is inspired by God and is[b] useful for teaching, for reproof, for correction, and for training in righteousness, [17] so that everyone who belongs to God may be proficient, equipped for every good work.

4 In the presence of God and of Christ Jesus, who is to judge the living and the dead, and in view of his appearing and his kingdom, I solemnly urge you: [2] proclaim the message; be persistent whether the time is favorable or unfavorable; convince, rebuke, and encourage, with the utmost patience in teaching. [3] For the time is coming when people will not put up with sound doctrine, but having itching ears, they will accumulate for themselves teachers to suit their own desires, [4] and will turn away from listening to the truth and wander away to myths. [5] As for you, always be sober, endure suffering, do the work of an evangelist, carry out your ministry fully.

[6] As for me, I am already being poured out as a libation, and the time of my departure has come. [7] I have fought the good fight, I have finished the race,

---

[a] Gk lacks two men   [b] Or Every scripture inspired by God is also

---

3:10–11 *Now you have observed my teaching, my conduct, my aim in life, my faith, my patience, my love, my steadfastness, my persecutions, and my suffering the things that happened to me in Antioch, Iconium, and Lystra. What persecutions I endured! Yet the Lord rescued me from all of them*—Here the letter writer reflects on Paul's life and charges Timothy to remain faithful to his mission. In this section, the writer draws upon biographical traditions regarding Paul, much like the material found in Luke's Acts of the Apostles. In the closing of 2 Timothy, the writer refers to Paul's brush with the lion's mouth (4:17). Here the material of the early Christian apocryphal literature (e.g., the *Acts of Paul*) seems to be in view. The persecutions and sufferings of Paul form the basis for his witness to God's faithfulness and the encouragement to Timothy to forge on in his proclamation of the gospel to the Gentiles. In his own letters Paul frequently calls on his churches to imitate him as he imitates Christ. For Paul, however, this imitation takes the form of debasement and suffering as a paradoxical display of the power and wisdom of God revealed in Christ (e.g., 2 Cor. 11:16–12:10). In this sense, the Pastoral Epistles writer has idealized Paul's biography as exemplary of Christian discipleship in a way that Paul does not. For Paul, suffering is redemptive because it reveals the mysteries of God's wisdom and power in Jesus Christ. For the writer of the Pastoral Epistles, suffering is redemptive because it bears proof that one is actually being faithful to the "godly life in Christ" (2 Tim. 3:12). In the first sense, suffering promises a bond with the experience of God's power; in the second sense, it embodies a particular idealized version of the Christian life. Martyrdom as such has shifted from a vehicle of religious experience that bears hope for those who indeed suffer, to a prototype of faithful living. Such a shift seems to reveal a church preoccupied less with mystical religious experience and its extension of hope to those who suffer, and more with its own preservation through the regulation of the religious practice and belief of its members.

I have kept the faith. **8** From now on there is reserved for me the crown of righteousness, which the Lord, the righteous judge, will give me on that day, and not only to me but also to all who have longed for his appearing.

Personal Instructions

9 Do your best to come to me soon, **10** for Demas, in love with this present world, has deserted me and gone to Thessalonica; Crescens has gone to Galatia,*a* Titus to Dalmatia. **11** Only Luke is with me. Get Mark and bring him with you, for he is useful in my ministry. **12** I have sent Tychicus to Ephesus. **13** When you come, bring the cloak that I left with Carpus at Troas, also the books, and above all the parchments. **14** Alexander the coppersmith did me great harm; the Lord will pay him back for his deeds. **15** You also must beware of him, for he strongly opposed our message.

16 At my first defense no one came to my support, but all deserted me. May it not be counted against them! **17** But the Lord stood by me and gave me strength, so that through me the message might be fully proclaimed and all the Gentiles might hear it. So I was rescued from the lion's mouth. **18** The Lord will rescue me from every evil attack and save me for his heavenly kingdom. To him be the glory forever and ever. Amen.

Final Greetings and Benediction

19 Greet Prisca and Aquila, and the household of Onesiphorus. **20** Erastus remained in Corinth; Trophimus I left ill in Miletus. **21** Do your best to come before winter. Eubulus sends greetings to you, as do Pudens and Linus and Claudia and all the brothers and sisters.*b*

22 The Lord be with your spirit. Grace be with you.*c*

a Other ancient authorities read *Gaul* *b* Gk *all the brothers* *c* The Greek word for *you* here is plural. Other ancient authorities add *Amen*

The Book of

TITUS

While quite similar in content to portions of 1 Timothy, this letter bears the name of Titus as its addressee. In Paul's letters, Titus is a Gentile traveling companion who according to Paul resisted circumcision as a demonstration of the gospel of freedom from the law in the midst of the Jerusalem church leadership (Gal. 2:3). In this context he appears as a trusted delegate of Paul's authority in a church on the island of Crete. Much as with Timothy, the choice of Titus as the addressee of the letter denotes a private and trustworthy communication between the apostle Paul and one of his closest companions in ministry.

—Deborah Krause

Salutation

1 Paul, a servant*a* of God and an apostle of Jesus Christ, for the sake of the faith of God's elect and the knowledge of the truth that is in accordance with godliness, ² in the hope of eternal life that God, who never lies, promised before the ages began— ³ in due time he revealed his word through the proclamation with which I have been entrusted by the command of God our Savior,

4 To Titus, my loyal child in the faith we share:

Grace*b* and peace from God the Father and Christ Jesus our Savior.

Titus in Crete

5 I left you behind in Crete for this reason, so that you should put in order what remained to be done, and should appoint elders in every town, as I directed you: ⁶ someone who is blameless, married only once,*c* whose children are believers, not accused of debauchery and not rebellious. ⁷ For a bishop,*d* as God's steward, must be blameless; he must not be arrogant or quick-tempered or addicted to wine or violent or greedy for gain; ⁸ but he must be hospitable, a lover of goodness, prudent, upright, devout, and self-controlled. ⁹ He must have a firm grasp of the word that is trustworthy in accordance with the teaching, so that he may be able both to preach with sound doctrine and to refute those who contradict it.

10 There are also many rebellious people, idle talkers and deceivers, especially those of the circumcision; ¹¹ they must be silenced, since they are upsetting whole families by teaching for sordid gain what it is not right to teach. ¹² It was one of them, their very own prophet, who said,

"Cretans are always liars, vicious
  brutes, lazy gluttons."

¹³ That testimony is true. For this reason rebuke them sharply, so that they may become sound in the faith, ¹⁴ not paying attention to Jewish myths or to commandments of those who reject the truth. ¹⁵ To the pure all things are pure, but to the corrupt and unbelieving nothing is pure. Their very minds and consciences are corrupted. ¹⁶ They profess to know God, but they deny him by their actions. They are detestable, disobedient, unfit for any good work.

Teach Sound Doctrine

2 But as for you, teach what is consistent with sound doctrine. ² Tell the

a Gk *slave* *b* Other ancient authorities read *Grace, mercy,* *c* Gk *husband of one wife* *d* Or *an overseer*

2:1 *Sound doctrine*—As a whole, 1 Timothy, 2 Timothy, and Titus are concerned with "sound" or

older men to be temperate, serious, prudent, and sound in faith, in love, and in endurance.

3 Likewise, tell the older women to be reverent in behavior, not to be slanderers or slaves to drink; they are to teach what is good, [4] so that they may encourage the young women to love their husbands, to love their children, [5] to be self-controlled, chaste, good managers of the household, kind, being submissive to their husbands, so that the word of God may not be discredited.

6 Likewise, urge the younger men to be self-controlled. [7] Show yourself in all respects a model of good works, and in your teaching show integrity, gravity, [8] and sound speech that cannot be censured; then any opponent will be put to shame, having nothing evil to say of us.

9 Tell slaves to be submissive to their masters and to give satisfaction in every respect; they are not to talk back, [10] not to pilfer, but to show complete and perfect fidelity, so that in everything they may be an ornament to the doctrine of God our Savior.

11 For the grace of God has appeared, bringing salvation to all,[a] [12] training us to renounce impiety and worldly passions, and in the present age to live lives that are self-controlled, upright, and godly, [13] while we wait for the blessed hope and the manifestation of the glory of our great God and Savior,[b] Jesus Christ. [14] He it is who gave himself for us that he might redeem us from all iniquity and purify for himself a people of his own who are zealous for good deeds.

15 Declare these things; exhort and reprove with all authority.[c] Let no one look down on you.

Maintain Good Deeds

3 Remind them to be subject to rulers and authorities, to be obedient, to

[a] Or has appeared to all, bringing salvation [b] Or of the great God and our Savior [c] Gk commandment

---

"right" teaching and doctrine. Such a concern reflects a context of contention about the "true" church in the generations following Paul. Paul's own letters reflect intramural arguments about the nature of his authority and the relationship of law to gospel in the emerging Gentile mission of the church. These letters assume the validity of the Gentile mission, but reflect other intramural arguments about the doctrines and teachings of the church and how these beliefs are to be lived in practice. They represent the church defining itself as "the church," and attempting to protect a store of imparted doctrine from the perceived threat of other competing beliefs and practices. In this sense, the letters represent how matters of discipleship and social justice can seem to become secondary to the church's maintenance of its own structure, beliefs, and practices. As such, the Pastoral Epistles must continually be seen as only a part of the puzzle of what made up the church and its mission in the late first and second centuries CE. It is certain that contemporary Christians would not wish to have their church's faithfulness judged on the basis of a few slim ecclesiastical documents or proclamations.

3:1–2 *Remind them to be subject to rulers and authorities, to be obedient, to be ready for every good work, to speak evil of no one, to avoid quarreling, to be gentle, and to show every courtesy to everyone*—The charge to show deference for those in positions of civil authority echoes a similar call in Rom. 13:1–7. Indeed, the verses in Titus appear as an abbreviated version of Paul's thoughts short of his theological justification for the expectation. One could likely surmise that Paul's elaborate apologia for civil authority bespoke existing tensions and rebellion among those in the church in Rome. In contrast, the call in Titus makes no argument as to why such submission to authority is essential, and calls for an almost idealized form of conduct on the part of those in the church. What does it really mean to speak evil of no one, avoid quarreling, and to show courtesy to everyone? In many senses one might well wonder if such an expression of the church has or ever could exist. The idealized expectation of good behavior is particularly interesting in light of the preceding list of commands regarding the temperance of older men (2:2), the reverence of older women (2:3), the chasteness of younger women (2:5), the respectability of younger men (2:6), and the submissiveness of slaves (2:9), which are all capped off with a call that Titus let no one "look down on" him (2:15). The expectations for hierarchical authority are high, but in light of such a stratified and tense social situation they seem to represent a desire more than a reality of control. In this sense the church of the Pastoral Epistles can perhaps be best viewed between the lines of the writer's rhetoric. In between these lines there are tensions of rhetoric

be ready for every good work, [2] to speak evil of no one, to avoid quarreling, to be gentle, and to show every courtesy to everyone. [3] For we ourselves were once foolish, disobedient, led astray, slaves to various passions and pleasures, passing our days in malice and envy, despicable, hating one another. [4] But when the goodness and loving kindness of God our Savior appeared, [5] he saved us, not because of any works of righteousness that we had done, but according to his mercy, through the water[a] of rebirth and renewal by the Holy Spirit. [6] This Spirit he poured out on us richly through Jesus Christ our Savior, [7] so that, having been justified by his grace, we might become heirs according to the hope of eternal life. [8] The saying is sure.

I desire that you insist on these things, so that those who have come to believe in God may be careful to devote themselves to good works; these things are excellent and profitable to everyone. [9] But avoid stupid controversies, genealogies, dissensions, and quarrels about the law, for they are unprofitable and worthless. [10] After a first and second admonition, have nothing more to do with anyone who causes divisions, [11] since you know that such a person is perverted and sinful, being self-condemned.

Final Messages and Benediction

[12] When I send Artemas to you, or Tychicus, do your best to come to me at Nicopolis, for I have decided to spend the winter there. [13] Make every effort to send Zenas the lawyer and Apollos on their way, and see that they lack nothing. [14] And let people learn to devote themselves to good works in order to meet urgent needs, so that they may not be unproductive.

[15] All who are with me send greetings to you. Greet those who love us in the faith.

Grace be with all of you.[b]

a Gk washing b Other ancient authorities add Amen

---

and reality that bespeak the real struggles of Christians to live as faithful disciples of Jesus Christ. These same tensions are evident between rhetoric and reality today as our denominations declare themselves "multicultural," "open and affirming," and "pro children" and yet continue to participate within and even perpetuate socially entrenched injustices regarding age, race, gender, and class.

The Book of

PHILEMON

This letter is occasioned by Paul's incarceration. He was not free to work with his colleague Philemon in the ministry of the Christian assembly that met in the latter's house. In chains, Paul dispatched a surrogate, Philemon's brother Onesimus. Paul was well aware that the two brothers were estranged, perhaps due to some past wrongdoing or debt for which Onesimus had failed to compensate Philemon. Knowing the seriousness of the estrangement, and that it threatened Paul's attempt to minister to Philemon and his congregation by proxy, Paul writes a diplomatic letter of reintroduction for Onesimus. Paul writes that he loves Onesimus as a son and has sent him to Philemon and his community as a substitute to work in his stead. Paul insists that Philemon receive Onesimus as he would receive Paul himself: Onesimus is to be Paul's virtual presence in Philemon's assembly. Paul further insists that Philemon receive Onesimus as his brother both in the flesh and in the Lord: the two, Philemon and Onesimus, are brothers in the same family as well as brothers in the Lord. To strengthen his appeal, Paul promises Philemon that he Paul will repay any and all debts that Onesimus has incurred or will incur. Paul closes with his own signature and the veiled threat that he will come to Philemon himself at some yet-to-be-determined time in the near future to inspect Philemon's compliance and hospitality.

The traditional interpretation of this letter is that it is an epistolary intercession that Paul writes to an irate slave master on behalf of his repentant runaway slave. But the names of Philemon and Onesimus are not connected in a possessive construction: nowhere does Onesimus appear to "belong to" Philemon. Paul does not refer to Philemon as a "lord" or a "master." Nor is Onesimus necessarily a slave name, as some modern commentators have asserted. The weight of the identification of Onesimus as a slave falls to verse 16a: "[receive him] no longer as a slave but more than a slave." The key word in this verse, however, is not "slave," but "as," which indicates a virtual and not an actual state of affairs. Paul uses the word with precisely this sense in the next verse when he exhorts Philemon to receive Onesimus "as you would welcome me."

Many commentaries claim that Onesimus is a fugitive, though there is no indication of his flight anywhere in the epistle. Paul does not so much as hint at a reason for Onesimus's departure. It is in the hypothesis or argument of the late-fourth-century Greek exegete John Chrysostom that we encounter the first full treatment of the epistle to Philemon as a letter reconciling slave and master. He proposes that Onesimus was a fugitive slave on whose behalf Paul writes to Philemon. Nothing in his words suggests that Chrysostom is drawing on an interpretation either current or traditional. He is offering, on the eve of the fifth century, a novel interpretation and argues for its validity. From Paul's epistle to Philemon, John Chrysostom derives an exegesis treating slavery, an issue of great moment in his own time. He was concerned that "many are reduced to blasphemy, and of saying Christianity has been

introduced into life for the subversion of everything, masters having their servants taken from them, and it is a matter of violence." "But . . . this epistle was sent upon necessary matters. Observe therefore how many things are rectified thereby." According to Chrysostom, the letter affirms most importantly "that we ought not to withdraw slaves from their masters." Apparently the reputation of the Christian community was being ruined by libertarian extremists in its midst who were challenging slavery, an institution of signal importance to the Roman imperial regime. Chrysostom is the earliest of the prodigious efforts and wide, authoritative circulation of late fourth- and early fifth-century interpreters, sympathetic to the imperial Roman order and conservative in their views toward slaves and other subordinated persons, who assert that Onesimus was a fugitive slave.

In the first half of the nineteenth century, American proslavery advocates referred to the epistle to Philemon as "the Pauline Mandate," a biblical sanction of American slavery. Because they understood Onesimus to be a runaway, they cited it in support of the Fugitive Slave Law, which required the return of runaway slaves to their masters under penalty of law, even when the slaves had absconded to free states. But abolitionist exegetes insisted on an alternative interpretation. According to them, the letter says nothing of Onesimus's servile status. In calling Onesimus a "beloved brother . . . both in the flesh and in the Lord," Paul suggests that Onesimus is not Philemon's slave, but his brother by blood, that is, "in the flesh," and by faith, "in the Lord." Their alternative hypothesis takes into account the epistle's important elements: the familial vocabulary that Paul uses to describe his relationship to Philemon and Onesimus and their relationship to each other; Paul's diplomatic tone in addressing Philemon; and the apostle's determined, self-sacrificial concern for the reconciliation of the estranged brothers.

Thus the letter has little to tell us about slavery or Paul's attitude toward it. At issue here are family, ministry and, as the prose of the epistle itself stresses, love. All come together in the relationship between Paul and the two brothers: Paul cannot do the work of the gospel that he seeks to realize in Philemon's assembly without reconciling them.

Nor is this text about forgiveness. Paul addresses the possibility of his emissary's wrongdoing by offering remedy, concrete remedy for wrongdoing. Paul does this at his own expense, signing off on the debt that Onesimus may owe his brother. Paul's intervention suggests a radical experiment in peacemaking. He insists that the love between those in the Lord cannot be fulfilled when love has grown cold between those who are brothers in the flesh. The crisis of familial strife is not merely a concern of the church: it is itself a crisis of the church. And Paul has anticipated that the crisis makes ministry impossible.

Like charity, justice must begin at home, as it were. Paul is willing to subsidize justice—that is, underwrite costs and damages—because without justice there is no peace, and without peace between the brethren there can be no ministry. Unless and until justice is served, God cannot be served. Insistence on forgiveness in the face of injustice is special pleading for cheap grace. Thus we find no language of forgiveness here. To effect justice, appeals to forgiveness—even God's forgiveness—will not do. The debt must be paid, and Paul, without appeal to forgiveness or admission of guilt on the part of any of the principals, offers to pay it.

—Allen Callahan

Salutation

1 Paul, a prisoner of Christ Jesus, and Timothy our brother,*a*

To Philemon our dear friend and co-worker, 2 to Apphia our sister,*b* to Archippus our fellow soldier, and to the church in your house:

3 Grace to you and peace from God our Father and the Lord Jesus Christ.

Philemon's Love and Faith

4 When I remember you*c* in my prayers, I always thank my God 5 because I hear of your love for all the saints and your faith toward the Lord Jesus. 6 I pray that the sharing of your faith may become effective when you perceive all the good that we*d* may do for Christ. 7 I have indeed received much joy and encouragement from your love, because the hearts of the saints have been refreshed through you, my brother.

Paul's Plea for Onesimus

8 For this reason, though I am bold enough in Christ to command you to do your duty, 9 yet I would rather appeal to you on the basis of love— and I, Paul, do this as an old man, and now also as a prisoner of Christ Jesus.*e* 10 I am appealing to you for my child, Onesimus, whose father I have become during my imprisonment. 11 Formerly he was useless to you, but now he is indeed useful*f* both to you and to me. 12 I am sending him, that is, my own heart, back to you. 13 I wanted to keep him with me, so that he might be of service to me in your place during my imprisonment for the gospel; 14 but I preferred to do nothing without your consent, in order that your good deed might be voluntary and not something forced. 15 Perhaps this is the reason he was separated from you for a while, so that you might have him back forever, 16 no longer as a slave but more

a Gk the brother *b* Gk the sister *c* From verse 4 through verse 21, you is singular *d* Other ancient authorities read you (plural) *e* Or as an ambassador of Christ Jesus, and now also his prisoner *f* The name Onesimus means useful or (compare verse 20) beneficial

---

1 *Prisoner of Christ Jesus*—Paul so identifies himself here, in contrast to his customary self-presentation as "apostle of Jesus Christ." In the undisputed letters, see 1 Cor. 1:1, 2; 2 Cor. 1:1; Gal. 1:1; in the so-called deutero-Paulines, Eph. 1:1; Col. 1:1; and in the Pastoral Epistles, 1 Tim. 1:1; 2 Tim. 1:1. See also Eph. 3:1, "prisoner of Christ Jesus," and 2 Tim. 1:8, "his [i.e., the Lord's] prisoner." *Timothy our brother*—Presumably identical with the man Paul calls "my co-worker" in Rom. 16:21, traditionally identified with the junior colleague who accompanied Paul in Greece (see Acts 16) and the recipient of two pastoral letters in the New Testament that bear his name. As here, Paul joins Timothy's name to his own in the opening greetings of 2 Corinthians, Philippians, and Colossians. *Philemon*—The name appears only here in the entire corpus of Paul's letters, and only in this verse of the epistle.

2 *Apphia our sister*—Like Philemon, she is a figure of influence in the assembly, and so is addressed directly in the letter's opening. *Archippus*—Perhaps the same person mentioned in Col. 4:17, and one of several names common to Paul's epistles to Philemon and Colossians. *The church in your house*—Not merely the structure in which the assembly met, but those who lived together in it, that is, the extended family. Households were associated with several assemblies of the Pauline mission. An assembly met in the house of Prisca and Aquila (Rom. 16:3–5; 1 Cor. 16:19b), presumably in Ephesus (see Acts 18:2), and the Laodicean assembly met at Nympha's house (Col. 4:15).

6 *Sharing*—Often translated "liberality" or "fellowship," the word may signify partnership, joint ownership, the act or object of shared possession, or, as here, generosity.

9—According to the first-century Judean philosopher Philo (citing the ancient Greek physician Hippocrates), an "elder" (NRSV *old man*) is a man between fifty and fifty-six years of age. But an alternative reading, "ambassador," is consonant with the diplomatic tone of the letter and Paul's ambassadorial self-presentation elsewhere, (see 2 Cor. 5:20; also Eph. 6:20).

As in v. 1, Paul invokes his status as one who suffers incarceration for the sake of Christ. Early Christians were exhorted to extend care and concern for those in prison (e.g., Matt. 25:36; Heb. 10:34; 13:3).

10 *My child*—Of individuals other than Onesimus, Paul speaks only of Timothy as his child (1 Cor. 4:17; Phil. 2:22). *Onesimus*—Likely the same as the "faithful and beloved brother" of Col. 4:9.

16 *No longer as a slave*—"As" here has the force of "as if," "as though." Just as Paul says that the Galatians are no longer slaves but sons in the

than a slave, a beloved brother—especially to me but how much more to you, both in the flesh and in the Lord.

17 So if you consider me your partner, welcome him as you would welcome me. [18] If he has wronged you in any way, or owes you anything, charge that to my account. [19] I, Paul, am writing this with my own hand: I will repay it. I say nothing about your owing me even your own self. [20] Yes, brother, let me have this benefit from you in the Lord! Refresh my heart in Christ. [21] Confident of your obedience, I am writing to you, knowing that you will do even more than I say.

22 One thing more—prepare a guest room for me, for I am hoping through your prayers to be restored to you.

Final Greetings and Benediction

23 Epaphras, my fellow prisoner in Christ Jesus, sends greetings to you,[a] [24] and so do Mark, Aristarchus, Demas, and Luke, my fellow workers.

25 The grace of the Lord Jesus Christ be with your spirit.[b]

[a] Here you is singular   [b] Other ancient authorities add Amen

---

family of God (Gal. 4:7), so Paul insists here that Onesimus be received no longer as though he were a slave but a brother in Philemon's family of faith. To be a "slave of God" was an honorific of the ancient servants of God: Abraham (Ps. 104:42), Jacob (Isa. 48:20), and David (Ps. 88:3) are God's slaves, as are martyrs past and present (see Rev. 1:7; 19:2). Paul refers to himself as a slave of Christ in several of his letters (Rom. 1:1; Phil. 1:1; see Titus 1:1), as do other early Christian authors (Jas. 1:1; 2 Pet. 1:1, etc.). But in Greek the term "slave" also signifies subjugation, powerlessness, and dishonor. Paul trades on both meanings here. Paul would not suffer Onesimus to suffer dishonor and disrespect at Philemon's hands, for whatever reason. And just as Paul sends Onesimus to serve Philemon's assembly, Onesimus has been dispatched in service to the gospel and is thus a "slave of God." But he is more: he is entitled to Philemon's love, honor, and respect as a beloved brother *in the flesh and in the Lord*, that is, by blood as well as by faith.

17—By calling him a *partner* Paul suggests a close, interdependent working relationship with Philemon, such as that he enjoys with Titus, whom he describes as "my partner" (2 Cor. 8:23).

18—Paul speaks of Onesimus's wrongdoing in a conditional clause: Onesimus's debt is a troubling possibility, not a fact.

19—Like many letter writers in antiquity, Paul no doubt dictated his letters to an amanuensis. But this and similar notices in Gal. 6:11, Col. 4:18, and 2 Thess. 3:17 indicate that Paul wrote the greetings in his letters himself to endorse their authenticity.

20—Paul underscores his request with an oblique pun on Onesimus's name. The name "Onesimus" and the verb "to *benefit*" are derived from the same root.

23 *Epaphras*—Perhaps the same person mentioned in Col. 1:7 as "our beloved fellow servant" and in Col. 4:12 as "a servant of Christ Jesus." *Greetings to you*—The personal pronoun "you" is singular. Philemon alone is addressed.

24—Paul mentions several other comrades, thus underscoring by implication the importance of collegiality and teamwork in his ministry.

25—A characteristically Pauline benediction. See Gal. 6:18, Phil. 4:23. The personal pronoun *your* is plural: Paul addresses the closing benediction to all the recipients. The letter opened with the grace that is God's gift, and ends with the *grace* of God's character, a grace which Paul hopes and prays will be manifest in Philemon and his assembly as they prepare to receive their beloved brother Onesimus.

The Book of
HEBREWS

The letter to the Hebrews is one of the more difficult books in the New Testament to study: its linguistic style is the most erudite in the New Testament; its densely woven argument is complex and sustained; its imagery of priesthood and sacrificial ritual emerges from an ancient world of thought that is quite foreign to our own. Yet those who wrestle with it will find in Hebrews a powerful presentation of the Christian message. Moreover, that message turns out to be strikingly contemporary in its relevance to our situation.

Hebrews addresses people who have been Christians for some time, but who find that their earlier enthusiasm has faded and that their faith commitment is on the wane (see 2:1–3; 3:12; 6:1–6; 6:11–12; 10:23–25; 12:12). They have grown "sluggish," and are in danger of "drifting" and "falling away." Many have stopped attending the Christian assembly altogether. Moreover, they have ceased to grow in their understanding of the Christian faith (see 5:11–14). They are in a state of arrested development as Christians! One would not have expected this to be the case, for their earlier history was exemplary. Indeed, they had willingly endured public abuse, even "the plundering of [their] possessions" for their Christian confession, all the while supporting their fellow Christians in the midst of suffering (see 10:32–36). New threats of persecution (see 12:3–13; 13:13–14) may well have given rise to the community's weariness and discouragement. Whatever the reason for their lethargy, Hebrews addresses fatigued and beleagured Christians on the verge of abandoning Christian faith. It speaks a word of grace to them and to Christians of all times and places who find themselves drooping in their Christian pilgrimage and in need of encouragement, revitalization, and renewed commitment to the faith.

Hebrews' prescription for this malady is a heavy dose of theological reflection. People in this condition need more than a pep talk. They need a deepened understanding of the person and work of Jesus Christ. Hebrews goes beyond "the basic teaching about Christ" (6:1) to instruct its readers with a creative reinterpretation of the traditions about Jesus. By means of innovative, intellectually challenging food for thought, Hebrews aims to rekindle their vision. If they can catch a glimpse of what God has accomplished and made available in him, there will be no thought of drifting from the faith.

The major purpose of Hebrews is thus to encourage, strengthen, and motivate its readers—to call them to faithfulness. The author seeks to achieve this purpose by means of two central themes: *priesthood* and *pilgrimage*. First, Hebrews sets forth a new presentation of Jesus as high priest and enthroned Son, through whom faithful Christians have direct access to God. In the New Testament only Hebrews explores the significance of Jesus' work by means of the priestly image. Like the priests of old, Jesus is a mediator between the human and divine realms, a boundary crosser who opens access to the holy. He cleanses our conscience, effectively removes our sin,

and intercedes for us before the throne of grace. His completed work as high priest brings us into the very presence of God and makes possible our own lives of covenant faithfulness.

Second, the theme of pilgrimage is also central. In his priestly, boundary-crossing role, Jesus is a trailblazer, a pioneer, who leads us to faith's destination—who draws us toward our home with God. Thus Christians are urged to look "to Jesus the pioneer and perfecter of our faith" and to "run with perseverance the race that is set before" them (12:2). Hebrews envisions the Christian life as a journey, in which we follow Christ's example of faithful service and live as he did, even in the midst of persecution. Christians are to be a pilgrim people, on the move, sojourners in this world, who seek their home in the city "whose architect and builder is God" (11:10). Thus Hebrews urges its readers to "get the lead out," to keep moving, to get on with their marching toward the goal. By rekindling their vision of what God has accomplished in Jesus Christ and by reminding them of the great personal resources available to them through Jesus' completed work, the author of Hebrews seeks to rejuvenate weary readers of every age for the pilgrimage of faith.

Two further observations about the character of Hebrews will help orient us to it. First, Hebrews takes the form of a sermon rather than a letter. To be sure, it presents weighty theological reflection, but it is by no means abstract. It is geared to the very specific situation described above and betrays a clear pastoral orientation. This is apparent in the author's own designation of his work in 13:22 as a "word of exhortation." Thus the theological insights of Hebrews are presented not for their own sake, but rather for the purpose of exhorting and encouraging readers to live effective lives of discipleship.

That Hebrews' word of exhortation is sermonic in form can be observed from the fact that it alternates between exposition and application. First, the author expounds on the significance of Christ, usually on the basis of a biblical text. Then, he moves to apply his christological insights to the life situation of his audience by means of a practical exhortation. This pattern is repeated throughout Hebrews and is the kind of speech we recognize on Sunday mornings as a sermon. Even though Hebrews ends like a letter in 13:19–25, with a benediction and concluding greetings, we may surmise that it is an extended sermon sent as a letter to a distant congregation.

A second notable characteristic of Hebrews is its strong emphasis on both the continuity and discontinuity between Judaism and Christianity. This is apparent in its opening line: "Long ago God spoke to our ancestors in many and various ways by the prophets, but in these last days [God] has spoken to us by a Son" (1:1–2). Continuity is apparent, for God has spoken with authority in the past, and the events Hebrews describes are to be viewed within the context of the history of God's dealings with Israel. Discontinuity, however, is apparent as well, for that which takes place in Jesus Christ, God's new agent of speaking, is decisive and incomparable.

Judaism and Christianity in Hebrews

Because the relationship between Judaism and Christianity is marked by continuity and discontinuity, we find in Hebrews both a strikingly Jewish ethos and a strong insistence on the "superiority" of Christianity over Judaism. On the one hand, one is immediately struck by the decidedly Jewish ethos of Hebrews. Its argument draws heavily on the imagery of priesthood and on presuppositions of Israel's sacrificial

system. Indeed, the Day of Atonement (Yom Kippur) ceremonies in particular and the high priest's role in them provide the central language and imagery by which Hebrews articulates the work of Christ as eternal priest and perfect sacrifice. Moreover, Old Testament Scripture plays a prominent role in the argument of Hebrews. There are thirty actual citations of Scripture, and more than double that number of allusions. Hebrews also makes use of a Jewish method of Scripture interpretation called midrash, a form of imaginative interpretation that seeks to demonstrate both the authority and the relevance of a biblical passage for the community in its present situation.

On the other hand, for all its "Jewishness," one is also struck by Hebrews' notable emphasis on the superiority of Christianity to Judaism. Indeed, Hebrews is distinguished by constant comparisons between the two. The word "superior" or "better" turns out to be a key word in the argument: Christ as Son is better than the angels (1:5–14), than Moses (3:1–6), than Aaron (5:1–10), and the Levitical priests (7:1–28). His sacrifice is better than their sacrifices (9:1–14), and the covenant that he inaugurated is better than the first (8:7–13; 9:15–22; 12:24). Moreover, Hebrews does not simply celebrate the superiority of Christianity; it also denigrates ancient Israelite religion and practices, declaring them ineffectual. Indeed, Hebrews claims that the covenant between God and Israel has been "abolished," and replaced by the "better" covenant established in the sacrifice of Jesus Christ (see 8:6–7, 13 and 10:9).

What are we to make of this emphasis on the continuity and discontinuity between Christianity and Judaism? In particular, what are we to make of the striking and denigrating comparisons? Traditionally, commentators have supposed that Hebrews addresses Jewish Christians who are mightily tempted to abandon Christian faith in order to return to the synagogue and Judaism. The comparisons and polemic therefore aim to prevent any such retreat, by persuading readers of the inherent superiority of Christianity to Judaism. While there are interpreters who still hold to some version of this thesis, it has increasingly been called into question, for it can be observed that the comparisons and statements of superiority appear in the expository sections of Hebrews, rather than in the exhortations. In the exhortations, which get down to practical matters and apply the author's christological insights to realities facing the life of the congregation, the author makes no differentiation between the two faiths and no effort to dissuade them of the attractions of Judaism.

Whether or not Hebrews seeks to prevent a retreat into Judaism, we may reasonably assume that Hebrews was originally addressed to a Jewish Christian audience, who would have understood and appreciated the author's use of Scripture and Jewish presuppositions. Furthermore, it is important for us to remember that the first Christians were Jews. Hebrews no doubt reflects a period in the early church's life when Christians and Jews had not yet reached a parting of the ways, and when Christians were in the midst of a process of self-definition and differentiation. In the midst of such a process, it would have been natural for Christians to claim superiority for their beliefs over the beliefs of their parent faith and chief competitor. Thus, the comparisons and claims of superiority in Hebrews are understandable within a first-century context of differentiation and self-definition.

However, we no longer live in such a context. While the author of Hebrews and his audience still found themselves enmeshed in Judaism, in our day Christianity and Judaism have long since gone their separate ways. Thus, many of Hebrews' claims

and comparisons present a problem for contemporary Christian interpretation. Claims that Christianity has "replaced" Judaism and rendered it "obsolete" are no longer appropriate in our historical context—indeed, such claims are deeply offensive to our Jewish neighbors. Such claims represent supercessionist theology, that is, a theology that holds that Christians have replaced or superceded Israel in the purposes and affections of God. This kind of theology, which draws heavily from Hebrews, has had an unfortunate use and misuse in the history of Christian interpretation. It has long been employed to denigrate and discredit Judaism, and thus has had a disastrous and tragic effect on the attitudes of many Christians and consequently on the fate of many Jews. Contemporary Christians must therefore exercise sensitivity and caution in their interpretation and appropriation of Hebrews.

Certainly we can appreciate and appropriate Hebrews' powerful witness to God's decisive and sure word in Jesus Christ and its profound theology of access without any accompanying denigration of Judaism. Moreover, it is well for us to remember that other New Testament writers, such as Paul, present a different view of the relationship between Christianity and Judaism. As Paul notes in Romans, God's covenant with Israel has by no means been rendered obsolete, nor have Christians replaced Israel in the purposes of God. Instead, he speaks of Christians as "wild" olive branches that have been "grafted" onto Israel's "cultivated olive tree" (see Rom. 11:17–24). Similarly, the prominent theologian Karl Barth affirmed of the people Israel that we Christians are "guests in their house, . . . new wood grafted onto their old tree" (*Against the Stream*). If we bear this in mind, we will interpret Hebrews in ways that are consistent with the gospel of God's gracious love extended to all people in Jesus Christ.

Hebrews on Repentance and Apostasy

The severe words of warning in 6:4–6; 10:26–31; and 12:15–17 are the most disturbing words in all of Hebrews and call for special comment, for they have often been held to deny the possibility of forgiveness for any sin committed after baptism or conversion. They led Martin Luther, the Protestant reformer, to an intense dislike of Hebrews and to a relegation of it (along with James, the Revelation, and Jude) to a later and less authoritative section of the canon. They have even led some Christians to put off baptism until their deathbeds.

Three things are critical in any assessment of these severe warnings. First, it is important to note that Hebrews does not speak of sin in general, but rather of the specific and extreme sin of apostasy: that is, continuing, public, and defiant repudiation of Christ by one who has experienced God's forgiveness and newness of life. It is impossible to restore such a one to repentance, for they have cut themselves off from the one who is the source of forgiveness. There is no other means of salvation available than that which they have rejected.

Second, it is important to recall Hebrews' decidedly pastoral orientation. In 6:4–6, the author addresses a serious pastoral crisis, greatly fearing that his weary readers are on the verge of abandoning Christian faith. They must be made to see the gravity of their situation—the seriousness of what they are contemplating. Thus, this is not the best time for a reassuring affirmation that God's mercy is everlasting, though this be true.

Finally, the Christians addressed have not yet reached the point of apostasy (see 6:9). Hebrews holds before them the dire consequences of a course of action they may be considering in order to dissuade them from it. These are words of warning

rather than condemnation. Warning has an appropriate place in the life of the Christian community.

Day of Atonement; Shadow and Reality; New Covenant

The imagery of Hebrews emerges from an ancient world of thought and may require explanation. Three images in particular play a central role.

Day of Atonement. The Day of Atonement ceremony and the high priest's role in it provide the central imagery by which Hebrews conveys the significance of Christ's person and work. Only Hebrews in the New Testament draws an explicit connection between the Day of Atonement ceremony and Christ's sacrifice. The Day of Atonement (Yom Kippur) is the holiest day of the Jewish calendar, a day of fasting, prayer, and self-examination that seeks the reconciliation—the "at-one-ment"—of God and the people. In ancient times it was also the occasion for an extraordinary ritual, described in Leviticus 16. Once a year on this day, after he had made sacrifices for himself and for the people, the high priest entered alone into the inner sanctum or Holy of Holies of the desert tabernacle (and later the temple). In so doing, he crossed a boundary into holy space—into the presence of God. There he performed an act of cleansing with the sacrificial blood that purified the altar and sanctuary, the meeting place between the people and God. The annual act of cleansing thus eliminated obstacles to the relationship between God and Israel by removing the barrier of sin. The author of Hebrews does not explain why it is that sacrificial blood effects cleansing and atonement, and the ancient logic is not clear to us; he simply shares with his Jewish contemporaries the assumption that it does (9:22). The sacrificial rituals and the Day of Atonement are accepted as means of grace—as the God-given way of dealing with sin and of maintaining the purity required of the place of rendezvous between the people and God.

The work of Jesus Christ both corresponds to, and contrasts with, the work of the Levitical high priest on this annual occasion: Christ too enters God's own presence with a blood sacrifice for sins—but with a difference. He enters "once for all" and with his own blood. This kind of supreme sacrifice can be made only once, for it entails Christ's death, and one cannot die repeatedly. Jesus' self-sacrifice is thus a final, sufficient, fully effective sacrifice for sin (9:26). From Hebrews' perspective, Christ brings the sacrificial system to an end, for his extraordinary self-sacrifice completely and finally removes the barrier created by sin and opens direct access to God.

Shadow and reality. The concept of shadow and reality is borrowed from Greek philosophy, which held that visible things of this earth are mere shadows or copies of the true realities that exist on the heavenly plane. Hebrews draws upon this concept to convey that the work of the Levitical priesthood foreshadowed the priestly work of Jesus Christ that is of ultimate significance. The Levitical priests exercise their ministry in "an earthly sanctuary" (9:1); Jesus exercises his priestly ministry in a heavenly sanctuary. His is clearly a "more excellent ministry" (8:6), for his priestly boundary crossing takes place on a cosmic plane, as through death and resurrection he passes into the holiest place of all—the eternal realm of God. The significance of what he accomplished cannot be fully contained within a dualistic framework of earthly shadow and heavenly reality, for paradoxically, Christ's heavenly sacrifice was decidedly earthly as well. It touched time and history and involved Christ's own body on a cross (see 10:5–10, 20).

New covenant. Christ's death is not only an atoning sacrifice, but also a covenant-inaugurating sacrifice. As an atoning sacrifice, it deals with past sins; as a covenant-inaugurating sacrifice, it establishes a new and lasting relationship between God and God's people for the future. Hebrews maintains that Jesus' sacrifice fulfills the prediction of a new covenant found in Jeremiah 31:31–34 (quoted in full in Heb. 8:8–12—the longest Old Testament quotation in the New Testament). The new and better covenant differs from the old covenant in two respects: (1) it is an interior covenant that involves our innermost being; and (2) sins are effectively forgiven. Though the prophet Jeremiah did not specify how the new covenant was to be established and forgiveness of sins effected, the author of Hebrews discerns a clear connection between the new covenant and the sacrifice of Jesus Christ (9:15–22), taking advantage of the fact that the Greek word for "covenant" (*diathēkē*) can also mean "last will and testament." Hebrews declares that the new covenant is now in force, ratified by the blood of Jesus Christ. We now stand in a new and lasting relationship with the living God.

A covenant relationship entails obligations for both parties entering into it. For God, it entails an irrevocable commitment to remember our sins no more. And since God's will for us in this new and enduring relationship is for our perfection and sanctification (10:14)—a reference not to moral perfection or saintliness but to growth in grace—the covenant entails on our part a commitment to live so as to fulfill God's will for our lives. Hebrews turns to this topic in its closing chapters.

In our day, it would be a misuse of Hebrews—and grossly insensitive as well—to declare to our Jewish neighbors that our experience of the grace of God in Jesus Christ renders their religion and their covenant with God obsolete. Still, we may rejoice with Hebrews that the reality of human sin has been finally and effectively dealt with by the perfect sacrifice of Jesus Christ. We need not be paralyzed by its guilt and power. We too may approach God through Jesus Christ, find our consciences cleansed, and experience forgiveness at the deepest level of who we are. God both forgives and forgets, thereby freeing us to grow in grace—to get on with the business of living in faithfulness to God's purposes for human life.

Who wrote Hebrews? Though Paul's name has long been associated with Hebrews, neither the apostle's name nor reference to his experience can be found in it. Moreover, it would appear that both the author and his addressees are one generation removed from those who encountered Jesus directly. They are second-generation Christians (see 2:3). Finally, both the style and theological perspective of Hebrews have long been recognized as uncharacteristic of Paul. The style of Hebrews is the most sophisticated in the New Testament, and quite dissimilar to Paul's. Most importantly, the theological differences between Hebrews and Paul's letters are considerable. Hebrews' presentation of Jesus as high priest is unique in the New Testament; and central Pauline emphases (for example, justification by faith, the church as the body of Christ, the resurrection of Christ) are not to be found in Hebrews. In addition, Hebrews and Paul present different twists on the meaning of "faith." Paul speaks of faith as a passive reality: it is trusting acceptance of Christ's saving work as a gift from God. What Hebrews intends by "faith," however, is closer in meaning to "faithfulness." It speaks of faith as active in obedience. For all of these reasons, Hebrews is widely regarded as an anonymous writing. Many are content to accept the verdict

of Origen of Alexandria (185–254 CE), the greatest scriptural scholar of the ancient church, on its authorship: "Only God knows"!

The recipients of the "letter," though not identified within the document itself, have traditionally been designated as "the Hebrews." This designation has no doubt been made on the basis of the document's contents, for Jewish-Christian readers would have been able to appreciate the author's use of Scripture, as well as the language and imagery of Israel's sacrificial system and priesthood.

But where were they located? One might presume that these Hebrews would be Palestinian Jews. However, it is more likely that the recipients were Diaspora Jews, that is, Jews who lived outside Palestine, scattered among the nations. They were clearly Greek-speaking, for the author's quotations of Scripture are from the Septuagint (LXX), the Greek translation of the Hebrew Scriptures. Both the author and his audience appear to have been nurtured upon the Scripture and traditions of Hellenistic Judaism—that is, the form of Judaism that emerged in urban centers throughout the Greek-speaking world. And while we cannot be sure where, specifically, they were located, the traditional and best guess continues to be Rome. Our only geographical clue is found in 13:24, where the author appears to convey greetings from fellow Italians back to the home congregation. To be sure, this clue is ambiguous. However, the first extrabiblical mention of Hebrews is found in the writings of the ancient church leader Clement of Rome, who in the year 95 CE quotes Hebrews extensively. Moreover, the persecution that the recipients are said to have endured (see 10:32–36) may well have been the temporary expulsion from Rome of Jews (and thus Jewish Christians) during the reign of the emperor Claudius in 49 CE. The persecution referred to is not thought to be the violent and fiery one that occurred under the emperor Nero in 64 CE, for the author notes that the Hebrews "have not yet resisted to the point of shedding [their] blood" (12:4). All of these factors make it possible that Hebrews is addressed to second-generation Jewish Christians who were perhaps associated with the larger church at Rome. If so, the letter may be dated in the early 60s, after Claudius's expulsion from Rome of Jews and Jewish Christians and their subsequent return, but before Nero's persecution in 64 CE. This would also place the composition of Hebrews before the year 70 CE, when the Jerusalem temple was destroyed by the Romans and Israel's sacrificial cult came to an end. It must be admitted, however, that we are entirely in the realm of speculation. Fortunately, neither a precise identification of the author and recipients nor an accurate date is required for us to appreciate the message of Hebrews.

—**Frances Taylor Gench**

God Has Spoken by His Son

1 Long ago God spoke to our ancestors in many and various ways by the prophets, ²but in these last days he has spoken to us by a Son,ᵃ whom he appointed heir of all things, through whom he also created the worlds. ³He is the reflection of God's glory and the exact imprint of God's very being, and he sustainsᵇ all things by his powerful word. When he had made purification for sins, he sat down at the right hand of the Majesty on high, ⁴having become as much superior to angels as the name he has inherited is more excellent than theirs.

The Son Is Superior to Angels

5 For to which of the angels did God ever say,

"You are my Son;
    today I have begotten you"?

Or again,

"I will be his Father,
    and he will be my Son"?

⁶ And again, when he brings the firstborn into the world, he says,

"Let all God's angels worship him."

⁷ Of the angels he says,

"He makes his angels winds,
    and his servants flames of fire."

⁸ But of the Son he says,

"Your throne, O God, isᶜ forever and
    ever,
and the righteous scepter is the
    scepter of yourᵈ kingdom.

⁹ You have loved righteousness and
    hated wickedness;

therefore God, your God, has
    anointed you
with the oil of gladness beyond
    your companions."

¹⁰ And,

"In the beginning, Lord, you
    founded the earth,
and the heavens are the work of
    your hands;

¹¹ they will perish, but you remain;
    they will all wear out like clothing;

¹² like a cloak you will roll them up,
    and like clothingᵉ they will be
        changed.
But you are the same,
    and your years will never end."

¹³ But to which of the angels has he ever said,

"Sit at my right hand
    until I make your enemies a
        footstool for your feet"?

¹⁴ Are not all angelsᶠ spirits in the divine service, sent to serve for the sake of those who are to inherit salvation?

Warning to Pay Attention

2 Therefore we must pay greater attention to what we have heard, so that we do not drift away from it. ²For if the message declared through angels was valid, and every transgression or disobedience received a just penalty, ³how can we escape if we neglect so great a salvation? It was declared at first through the Lord, and it was attested to

ᵃ Or the Son ᵇ Or bears along ᶜ Or God is your throne ᵈ Other ancient authorities read his ᵉ Other ancient authorities lack like clothing ᶠ Gk all of them

---

1:1–4 A Cosmic Panorama

God is one who speaks, who has continually reached out to the creation, who is present to be experienced and known—decisively, finally, and fully *by a Son*. God's Son stands at both the beginning and end of God's purpose for the world, and his sustaining power continues to uphold and preserve it. His cross and death deal decisively with human sin.

1:5–2:18 So Great a Salvation

1:5–14 The Son's superiority to angels—Hebrews affirms the preeminent status and role of the Son in the purposes of God. Angels, though important

creatures of God, cannot compare with God's Son.

2:1–4 Warning not to neglect so great a salvation—A key word in Hebrews is **therefore** (see 2:1; 3:1, 7; 4:1, 11, 16; 6:1; 10:19; 12:1, 12, 28). Christian living is always a "therefore" kind of living. God's demonstration of love for us in Jesus Christ calls for an appropriate response. It is unthinkable that God's precious gift should be neglected or taken lightly. Often it is "drifting" or neglect, rather than outright rejection, that most jeopardizes Christian faith.

us by those who heard him, ⁴ while God added his testimony by signs and wonders and various miracles, and by gifts of the Holy Spirit, distributed according to his will.

Exaltation through Abasement

5 Now God^a did not subject the coming world, about which we are speaking, to angels. ⁶ But someone has testified somewhere,

"What are human beings that you
        are mindful of them,^b
    or mortals, that you care for them?^c
⁷   You have made them for a little
        while lower^d than the angels;
    you have crowned them with glory
        and honor,^e
⁸   subjecting all things under their
        feet."

Now in subjecting all things to them, God^a left nothing outside their control. As it is, we do not yet see everything in subjection to them, ⁹ but we do see Jesus, who for a little while was made lower^f than the angels, now crowned with glory and honor because of the suffering of death, so that by the grace of God^g he might taste death for everyone.

10 It was fitting that God,^a for whom and through whom all things exist, in bringing many children to glory, should make the pioneer of their salvation perfect through sufferings. ¹¹ For the one who sanctifies and those who are sanctified all have one Father.^h For this reason Jesus^a is not ashamed to call them brothers and sisters,ⁱ ¹² saying,

"I will proclaim your name to my
        brothers and sisters,ⁱ
    in the midst of the congregation I
        will praise you."

¹³ And again,
    "I will put my trust in him."
And again,
    "Here am I and the children whom
        God has given me."

14 Since, therefore, the children share flesh and blood, he himself likewise shared the same things, so that through death he might destroy the one who has the power of death, that is, the devil, ¹⁵ and free those who all their lives were held in slavery by the fear of death. ¹⁶ For it is clear that he did not come to help angels, but the descendants of Abraham. ¹⁷ Therefore he had to become like his brothers and sistersⁱ in every respect, so that he might be a merciful and faithful high priest in the service of God, to make a sacrifice of atonement for the sins of the people. ¹⁸ Because he himself was tested by what he suffered, he is able to help those who are being tested.

Moses a Servant, Christ a Son

3 Therefore, brothers and sisters,ⁱ holy partners in a heavenly calling, consider that Jesus, the apostle and high priest of our confession, ² was faithful to the one who appointed him, just as Moses also "was faithful in all^j God's^k house." ³ Yet Jesus^l is worthy of more glory than Moses, just as the builder of a house has more honor than the house itself. ⁴ (For every house is built by someone, but the builder of all things is God.) ⁵ Now Moses was faithful in all God's^k house as a servant, to testify to

^a Gk he ^b Gk What is man that you are mindful of him? ^c Gk or the son of man that you care for him? In the Hebrew of Psalm 8.4-6 both man and son of man refer to all humankind ^d Or them only a little lower ^e Other ancient authorities add and set them over the works of your hands ^f Or who was made a little lower ^g Other ancient authorities read apart from God ^h Gk are all of one ⁱ Gk brothers ^j Other ancient authorities lack all ^k Gk his ^l Gk this one

---

2:5–18—Jesus, *for a little while . . . lower than the angels* (v. 9). These verses are perhaps the most profound statement of Jesus' humanity and solidarity with us in the New Testament. So complete is his identification with us that he is family (vv. 11–17), and thus qualified to be our merciful and faithful high priest, for he knows our struggles and identifies with us completely.

3:1–4:13 A Call to Faithfulness

3:1–6 Jesus and Moses: examples of faithfulness—Jesus is designated as both *apostle* and *high priest*. Only here in the New Testament is Jesus referred to as an apostle (Gk. *apostellō*, "to send out"). Hebrews views Jesus as one sent from God, who represents God to humanity (1:1–4). At the same time, he is high priest, in that he also represents humanity to God.

the things that would be spoken later. [6] Christ, however, was faithful over God's[a] house as a son, and we are his house if we hold firm[b] the confidence and the pride that belong to hope.

Warning against Unbelief

7 Therefore, as the Holy Spirit says,
"Today, if you hear his voice,
[8] do not harden your hearts as in the
        rebellion,
    as on the day of testing in the
        wilderness,
[9] where your ancestors put me to the
        test,
    though they had seen my works
            [10] for forty years.
    Therefore I was angry with that
        generation,
    and I said, 'They always go astray in
        their hearts,
    and they have not known my ways.'
[11] As in my anger I swore,
    'They will not enter my rest.'"

[12] Take care, brothers and sisters,[c] that none of you may have an evil, unbelieving heart that turns away from the living God. [13] But exhort one another every day, as long as it is called "today," so that none of you may be hardened by the deceitfulness of sin. [14] For we have become partners of Christ, if only we hold our first confidence firm to the end. [15] As it is said,
"Today, if you hear his voice,
    do not harden your hearts as in the
        rebellion."

[16] Now who were they who heard and yet were rebellious? Was it not all those who left Egypt under the leadership of Moses? [17] But with whom was he angry forty years? Was it not those who sinned, whose bodies fell in the wilderness? [18] And to whom did he swear that they would not enter his rest, if not to those who were disobedient? [19] So we see that they were unable to enter because of unbelief.

The Rest That God Promised

[4] Therefore, while the promise of entering his rest is still open, let us take care that none of you should seem to have failed to reach it. [2] For indeed the good news came to us just as to them; but the message they heard did not benefit them, because they were not united by faith with those who listened.[d] [3] For we who have believed enter that rest, just as God[e] has said,
"As in my anger I swore,
    'They shall not enter my rest,'"
though his works were finished at the foundation of the world. [4] For in one place it speaks about the seventh day as follows, "And God rested on the seventh day from all his works." [5] And again in this place it says, "They shall not enter my rest." [6] Since therefore it remains open for some to enter it, and those who formerly received the good news failed to enter because of disobedience, [7] again he sets a certain day—"today"—saying through David much later, in the words already quoted,
"Today, if you hear his voice,
    do not harden your hearts."
[8] For if Joshua had given them rest, God[e] would not speak later about another day. [9] So then, a sabbath rest still remains for the people of God; [10] for those who enter God's rest also cease from their labors as God did from his. [11] Let us therefore make every effort to enter that rest, so that no one may fall through such disobedience as theirs.

[a] Gk his [b] Other ancient authorities add to the end [c] Gk brothers [d] Other ancient authorities read it did not meet with faith in those who listened [e] Gk he

---

3:7–4:13 A history lesson on faithfulness—A minisermon presents a call to faithfulness, highlighting three themes: (1) faithfulness vs. faithlessness; (2) God's promise of *rest* (a symbol for the whole process of salvation, a journey initiated in baptism and completed on the last day); and (3) the daily challenge of Christian life.

Every day of our lives presents opportunities for faithfulness—for responding in obedience to the promises of God. Faithfulness is far more than intellectual assent; it involves fidelity and perseverance as we seek to follow in the path that Christ has set before us and to embody God's purposes for human life.

12 Indeed, the word of God is living and active, sharper than any two-edged sword, piercing until it divides soul from spirit, joints from marrow; it is able to judge the thoughts and intentions of the heart. 13 And before him no creature is hidden, but all are naked and laid bare to the eyes of the one to whom we must render an account.

Jesus the Great High Priest

14 Since, then, we have a great high priest who has passed through the heavens, Jesus, the Son of God, let us hold fast to our confession. 15 For we do not have a high priest who is unable to sympathize with our weaknesses, but we have one who in every respect has been tested*a* as we are, yet without sin. 16 Let us therefore approach the throne of grace with boldness, so that we may receive mercy and find grace to help in time of need.

5 Every high priest chosen from among mortals is put in charge of things pertaining to God on their behalf, to offer gifts and sacrifices for sins. 2 He is able to deal gently with the ignorant and wayward, since he himself is subject to weakness; 3 and because of this he must offer sacrifice for his own sins as well as for those of the people. 4 And one does not presume to take this honor, but takes it only when called by God, just as Aaron was.

5 So also Christ did not glorify himself in becoming a high priest, but was appointed by the one who said to him,

"You are my Son,
today I have begotten you";
6 as he says also in another place,
"You are a priest forever,
according to the order of
Melchizedek."

7 In the days of his flesh, Jesus*b* offered up prayers and supplications, with loud cries and tears, to the one who was able to save him from death, and he was heard because of his reverent submission. 8 Although he was a Son, he learned obedience through what he suffered; 9 and having been made perfect, he became the source of eternal salvation for all who obey him, 10 having been designated by God a high priest according to the order of Melchizedek.

Warning against Falling Away

11 About this*c* we have much to say that is hard to explain, since you have become dull in understanding. 12 For though by this time you ought to be teachers, you need someone to teach you again the basic elements of the oracles of God. You need milk, not solid food; 13 for everyone who lives on milk, being still an infant, is unskilled in the word of righteousness. 14 But solid food is for the mature, for those whose faculties have been trained by practice to distinguish good from evil.

The Peril of Falling Away

6 Therefore let us go on toward perfection,*d* leaving behind the basic

a Or tempted   *b* Gk he   *c* Or him   *d* Or toward maturity

---

4:14–6:20 A Call to Maturity

4:14–5:10 Jesus, the sympathetic high priest—The life of faithfulness does not depend on our own strength, determination, or subjective state. It depends on Jesus Christ, our **great high priest**, who enables Christians to remain faithful (vv. 14–16). Because he is intimately related to God, he leads us into God's own presence. Because he is genuinely human, he is sympathetically linked to us. His priesthood combines both divine sonship and humanity, and in this way his priesthood is truly unique.

5:11–6:8 A word of warning—These exasperated words may serve as a reminder of the importance

of continued nurture and growth to the vitality of Christian faith, lest we assume that "Christian education" is necessary only for children. Continued growth occurs throughout our lives in a variety of ways: as we carefully study the Scriptures; as we listen to the "great cloud of witnesses" who speak to us through the confessions, hymns, and tradition of the church; as we join together with other Christians in worship, service, study, and fellowship; as we stretch our minds with programs of reading and Christian education; and as we reflect together on issues that face us in this world and seek to embody God's purposes for human life.

teaching about Christ, and not laying again the foundation: repentance from dead works and faith toward God, [2] instruction about baptisms, laying on of hands, resurrection of the dead, and eternal judgment. [3] And we will do[a] this, if God permits. [4] For it is impossible to restore again to repentance those who have once been enlightened, and have tasted the heavenly gift, and have shared in the Holy Spirit, [5] and have tasted the goodness of the word of God and the powers of the age to come, [6] and then have fallen away, since on their own they are crucifying again the Son of God and are holding him up to contempt. [7] Ground that drinks up the rain falling on it repeatedly, and that produces a crop useful to those for whom it is cultivated, receives a blessing from God. [8] But if it produces thorns and thistles, it is worthless and on the verge of being cursed; its end is to be burned over.

9 Even though we speak in this way, beloved, we are confident of better things in your case, things that belong to salvation. [10] For God is not unjust; he will not overlook your work and the love that you showed for his sake[b] in serving the saints, as you still do. [11] And we want each one of you to show the same diligence so as to realize the full assurance of hope to the very end, [12] so that you may not become sluggish, but imitators of those who through faith and patience inherit the promises.

The Certainty of God's Promise

13 When God made a promise to Abraham, because he had no one greater by whom to swear, he swore by himself, [14] saying, "I will surely bless you and multiply you." [15] And thus Abraham,[c] having patiently endured, obtained the promise. [16] Human beings, of course, swear by someone greater than themselves, and an oath given as confirmation puts an end to all dispute. [17] In the same way, when God desired to show even more clearly to the heirs of the promise the unchangeable character of his purpose, he guaranteed it by an oath, [18] so that through two unchangeable things, in which it is impossible that God would prove false, we who have taken refuge might be strongly encouraged to seize the hope set before us. [19] We have this hope, a sure and steadfast anchor of the soul, a hope that enters the inner shrine behind the curtain, [20] where Jesus, a forerunner on our behalf, has entered, having become a high priest forever according to the order of Melchizedek.

The Priestly Order of Melchizedek

7 This "King Melchizedek of Salem, priest of the Most High God, met Abraham as he was returning from defeating the kings and blessed him"; [2] and to him Abraham apportioned "one-tenth of everything." His name, in the first place, means "king of righteousness"; next he is also king of Salem, that is, "king of peace." [3] Without father, without mother, without genealogy, having neither beginning of days nor end of life, but resembling the Son of God, he remains a priest forever.

4 See how great he is! Even[d] Abraham the patriarch gave him a tenth of the spoils. [5] And those descendants of Levi who receive the priestly office have

---

[a] Other ancient authorities read let us do　[b] Gk for his name　[c] Gk he
[d] Other ancient authorities lack Even

6:9–20—A word of encouragement.

7:1–10:18 The High Priesthood of Jesus Christ
This central section of Hebrews is an extended exposition of the high priesthood of Jesus Christ.

7:1–10—The priestly order of *Melchizedek*. According to the law of Moses (Exod. 32:25–29; Deut. 33:8–11), priests were supposed to descend from the tribe of Levi. Jesus descended

from the tribe of Judah (v. 14). How, then, can he be said to be a priest? The mysterious figure of Melchizedek makes only two appearances in the Old Testament (Ps. 110:4; Gen. 14:17–20), and the author of Hebrews finds in these passages God's own prediction of a new order of priesthood, superior to the Levitical line, and a foreshadowing of the priesthood of Jesus Christ.

a commandment in the law to collect tithes*a* from the people, that is, from their kindred,*b* though these also are descended from Abraham. ⁶ But this man, who does not belong to their ancestry, collected tithes*a* from Abraham and blessed him who had received the promises. ⁷ It is beyond dispute that the inferior is blessed by the superior. ⁸ In the one case, tithes are received by those who are mortal; in the other, by one of whom it is testified that he lives. ⁹ One might even say that Levi himself, who receives tithes, paid tithes through Abraham, ¹⁰ for he was still in the loins of his ancestor when Melchizedek met him.

Another Priest, Like Melchizedek

11 Now if perfection had been attainable through the levitical priesthood—for the people received the law under this priesthood—what further need would there have been to speak of another priest arising according to the order of Melchizedek, rather than one according to the order of Aaron? ¹² For when there is a change in the priesthood, there is necessarily a change in the law as well. ¹³ Now the one of whom these things are spoken belonged to another tribe, from which no one has ever served at the altar. ¹⁴ For it is evident that our Lord was descended from Judah, and in connection with that tribe Moses said nothing about priests.

15 It is even more obvious when another priest arises, resembling Melchizedek, ¹⁶ one who has become a priest, not through a legal requirement concerning physical descent, but through the power of an indestructible life. ¹⁷ For it is attested of him,

"You are a priest forever,
    according to the order of
        Melchizedek."

¹⁸ There is, on the one hand, the abrogation of an earlier commandment because it was weak and ineffectual ¹⁹ (for the law made nothing perfect); there is, on the other hand, the introduction of a better hope, through which we approach God.

20 This was confirmed with an oath; for others who became priests took their office without an oath, ²¹ but this one became a priest with an oath, because of the one who said to him,

"The Lord has sworn
    and will not change his mind,
'You are a priest forever' "—

²² accordingly Jesus has also become the guarantee of a better covenant.

23 Furthermore, the former priests were many in number, because they were prevented by death from continuing in office; ²⁴ but he holds his priesthood permanently, because he continues forever. ²⁵ Consequently he is able for all time to save*c* those who approach God through him, since he always lives to make intercession for them.

26 For it was fitting that we should have such a high priest, holy, blameless, undefiled, separated from sinners, and exalted above the heavens. ²⁷ Unlike the other*d* high priests, he has no need to offer sacrifices day after day, first for his own sins, and then for those of the people; this he did once for all when he offered himself. ²⁸ For the law appoints as high priests those who are subject to weakness, but the word of the oath, which came later than the law, appoints a Son who has been made perfect forever.

Mediator of a Better Covenant

8 Now the main point in what we are saying is this: we have such a high

a Or a tenth *b* Gk brothers *c* Or able to save completely *d* Gk lacks other

---

7:11–28 Implications of Christ's eternal priesthood—There would have been no need for God to establish a new order of priesthood, had the old one been effective. The whole religious system of Israel, grounded in the law, falls under indictment. There is a permanent and unchang-ing reality on which we can rely: Jesus Christ, who through resurrection lives to represent our concerns before God forever.

8:1–10:18 A perfect sacrifice—The sacrificial act that is central to Christ's work as high priest

priest, one who is seated at the right hand of the throne of the Majesty in the heavens, [2] a minister in the sanctuary and the true tent[a] that the Lord, and not any mortal, has set up. [3] For every high priest is appointed to offer gifts and sacrifices; hence it is necessary for this priest also to have something to offer. [4] Now if he were on earth, he would not be a priest at all, since there are priests who offer gifts according to the law. [5] They offer worship in a sanctuary that is a sketch and shadow of the heavenly one; for Moses, when he was about to erect the tent,[a] was warned, "See that you make everything according to the pattern that was shown you on the mountain." [6] But Jesus[b] has now obtained a more excellent ministry, and to that degree he is the mediator of a better covenant, which has been enacted through better promises. [7] For if that first covenant had been faultless, there would have been no need to look for a second one.

[8] God[c] finds fault with them when he says:

"The days are surely coming, says the Lord,
    when I will establish a new covenant with the house of Israel
    and with the house of Judah;
[9] not like the covenant that I made with their ancestors,
    on the day when I took them by the hand to lead them out of the land of Egypt;
for they did not continue in my covenant,
    and so I had no concern for them, says the Lord.
[10] This is the covenant that I will make with the house of Israel
    after those days, says the Lord:
I will put my laws in their minds,
    and write them on their hearts,
and I will be their God,
    and they shall be my people.
[11] And they shall not teach one another or say to each other, 'Know the Lord,'
    for they shall all know me,
    from the least of them to the greatest.
[12] For I will be merciful toward their iniquities,
    and I will remember their sins no more."

[13] In speaking of "a new covenant," he has made the first one obsolete. And what is obsolete and growing old will soon disappear.

The Earthly and the Heavenly Sanctuaries

9 Now even the first covenant had regulations for worship and an earthly sanctuary. [2] For a tent[a] was constructed, the first one, in which were the lampstand, the table, and the bread of the Presence;[d] this is called the Holy Place. [3] Behind the second curtain was a tent[a] called the Holy of Holies. [4] In it stood the golden altar of incense and the ark of the covenant overlaid on all sides with gold, in which there were a golden urn holding the manna, and Aaron's rod that budded, and the tablets of the covenant; [5] above it were the cherubim of glory overshadowing the mercy seat.[e] Of these things we cannot speak now in detail.

[6] Such preparations having been made, the priests go continually into the first tent[a] to carry out their ritual duties; [7] but only the high priest goes into the second, and he but once a year, and not without taking the blood that he

[a] Or tabernacle [b] Gk he [c] Gk He [d] Gk the presentation of the loaves [e] Or the place of atonement

---

is clearly **the main point** (8:1) of Hebrews. This book is not the first to speak of Christ's death as a self-sacrifice for sins; other New Testament witnesses also make this claim (see Rom. 3:25, 8:3; Gal. 2:20; Eph. 5:2; 1 Tim. 2:5–6; 1 Pet. 2:24;

1 John 2:2; Mark 10:45). It is the first, however, to infer that the sacrificial act must have been performed by a priest. Thus Christ is presented in a double role as both mediating priest and sacrificial victim.

offers for himself and for the sins committed unintentionally by the people. [8] By this the Holy Spirit indicates that the way into the sanctuary has not yet been disclosed as long as the first tent[a] is still standing. [9] This is a symbol[b] of the present time, during which gifts and sacrifices are offered that cannot perfect the conscience of the worshiper, [10] but deal only with food and drink and various baptisms, regulations for the body imposed until the time comes to set things right.

[11] But when Christ came as a high priest of the good things that have come,[c] then through the greater and perfect[d] tent[a] (not made with hands, that is, not of this creation), [12] he entered once for all into the Holy Place, not with the blood of goats and calves, but with his own blood, thus obtaining eternal redemption. [13] For if the blood of goats and bulls, with the sprinkling of the ashes of a heifer, sanctifies those who have been defiled so that their flesh is purified, [14] how much more will the blood of Christ, who through the eternal Spirit[e] offered himself without blemish to God, purify our[f] conscience from dead works to worship the living God!

[15] For this reason he is the mediator of a new covenant, so that those who are called may receive the promised eternal inheritance, because a death has occurred that redeems them from the transgressions under the first covenant.[g] [16] Where a will[g] is involved, the death of the one who made it must be established. [17] For a will[g] takes effect only at death, since it is not in force as long as the one who made it is alive. [18] Hence not even the first covenant was inaugurated without blood. [19] For when every commandment had been told to all the people by Moses in accordance with the law, he took the blood of calves and goats,[h] with water and scarlet wool and hyssop, and sprinkled both the scroll itself and all the people, [20] saying, "This is the blood of the covenant that

God has ordained for you." [21] And in the same way he sprinkled with the blood both the tent[a] and all the vessels used in worship. [22] Indeed, under the law almost everything is purified with blood, and without the shedding of blood there is no forgiveness of sins.

Christ's Sacrifice Takes Away Sin

[23] Thus it was necessary for the sketches of the heavenly things to be purified with these rites, but the heavenly things themselves need better sacrifices than these. [24] For Christ did not enter a sanctuary made by human hands, a mere copy of the true one, but he entered into heaven itself, now to appear in the presence of God on our behalf. [25] Nor was it to offer himself again and again, as the high priest enters the Holy Place year after year with blood that is not his own; [26] for then he would have had to suffer again and again since the foundation of the world. But as it is, he has appeared once for all at the end of the age to remove sin by the sacrifice of himself. [27] And just as it is appointed for mortals to die once, and after that the judgment, [28] so Christ, having been offered once to bear the sins of many, will appear a second time, not to deal with sin, but to save those who are eagerly waiting for him.

Christ's Sacrifice Once for All

10 Since the law has only a shadow of the good things to come and not the true form of these realities, it[i] can never, by the same sacrifices that are continually offered year after year, make perfect those who approach. [2] Otherwise, would they not have ceased being offered, since the worshipers, cleansed once for all, would no longer have any consciousness of sin? [3] But in these sacrifices there is a reminder of sin year

---

[a] Or tabernacle　[b] Gk parable　[c] Other ancient authorities read good things to come　[d] Gk more perfect　[e] Other ancient authorities read Holy Spirit　[f] Other ancient authorities read your　[g] The Greek word used here means both covenant and will　[h] Other ancient authorities lack and goats　[i] Other ancient authorities read they

after year. [4] For it is impossible for the blood of bulls and goats to take away sins. [5] Consequently, when Christ[a] came into the world, he said,

"Sacrifices and offerings you have not desired,
  but a body you have prepared for me;
[6] in burnt offerings and sin offerings you have taken no pleasure.
[7] Then I said, 'See, God, I have come to do your will, O God'
  (in the scroll of the book[b] it is written of me)."

[8] When he said above, "You have neither desired nor taken pleasure in sacrifices and offerings and burnt offerings and sin offerings" (these are offered according to the law), [9] then he added, "See, I have come to do your will." He abolishes the first in order to establish the second. [10] And it is by God's will[c] that we have been sanctified through the offering of the body of Jesus Christ once for all.

11 And every priest stands day after day at his service, offering again and again the same sacrifices that can never take away sins. [12] But when Christ[d] had offered for all time a single sacrifice for sins, "he sat down at the right hand of God," [13] and since then has been waiting "until his enemies would be made a footstool for his feet." [14] For by a single offering he has perfected for all time those who are sanctified. [15] And the Holy Spirit also testifies to us, for after saying,

[16] "This is the covenant that I will make with them
  after those days, says the Lord:
  I will put my laws in their hearts,

and I will write them on their minds,"
[17] he also adds,
  "I will remember[e] their sins and their lawless deeds no more."
[18] Where there is forgiveness of these, there is no longer any offering for sin.

A Call to Persevere

19 Therefore, my friends,[f] since we have confidence to enter the sanctuary by the blood of Jesus, [20] by the new and living way that he opened for us through the curtain (that is, through his flesh), [21] and since we have a great priest over the house of God, [22] let us approach with a true heart in full assurance of faith, with our hearts sprinkled clean from an evil conscience and our bodies washed with pure water. [23] Let us hold fast to the confession of our hope without wavering, for he who has promised is faithful. [24] And let us consider how to provoke one another to love and good deeds, [25] not neglecting to meet together, as is the habit of some, but encouraging one another, and all the more as you see the Day approaching.

26 For if we willfully persist in sin after having received the knowledge of the truth, there no longer remains a sacrifice for sins, [27] but a fearful prospect of judgment, and a fury of fire that will consume the adversaries. [28] Anyone who has violated the law of Moses dies without mercy "on the testimony of two or three witnesses." [29] How much worse punishment do you think will be deserved by those who have spurned

a Gk he b Meaning of Gk uncertain c Gk by that will d Gk this one e Gk on their minds and I will remember f Gk Therefore, brothers

---

10:19–12:2 The Endurance of Faith

10:19–39 A call to persevere—The author attempts, in four different ways, to motivate and rejuvenate weary Christians for the pilgrimage of faith. First, in vv. 19–25, he reminds them of what Christ has accomplished in their behalf, and urges them to take advantage of it. He has made available access to God! This appeal highlights the three great virtues of *faith, hope, and love* (vv. 22, 23, 24–25). One of the primary ways

in which we can stir up and demonstrate love for our fellow Christians is by *not neglecting to meet together* (v. 25)—by church attendance. Second, a stern warning in vv. 26–31 repeats the dire warning in 6:4–8 (see introduction: Hebrews on Repentance and Apostasy). Third, in vv. 32–39, he calls to their remembrance their earlier history, which was exemplary. Fourth, he parades before them a "great cloud of witnesses" whose lives bear witness to the power of faith (chap. 11).

the Son of God, profaned the blood of the covenant by which they were sanctified, and outraged the Spirit of grace? [30] For we know the one who said, "Vengeance is mine, I will repay." And again, "The Lord will judge his people." [31] It is a fearful thing to fall into the hands of the living God.

32 But recall those earlier days when, after you had been enlightened, you endured a hard struggle with sufferings, [33] sometimes being publicly exposed to abuse and persecution, and sometimes being partners with those so treated. [34] For you had compassion for those who were in prison, and you cheerfully accepted the plundering of your possessions, knowing that you yourselves possessed something better and more lasting. [35] Do not, therefore, abandon that confidence of yours; it brings a great reward. [36] For you need endurance, so that when you have done the will of God, you may receive what was promised. [37] For yet

"in a very little while,
  the one who is coming will come
    and will not delay;
[38] but my righteous one will live by
    faith.
  My soul takes no pleasure in
    anyone who shrinks back."

[39] But we are not among those who shrink back and so are lost, but among those who have faith and so are saved.

The Meaning of Faith

11 Now faith is the assurance of things hoped for, the conviction of things not seen. [2] Indeed, by faith[a] our ancestors received approval. [3] By faith we understand that the worlds were prepared by the word of God, so that what is seen was made from things that are not visible.[b]

The Examples of Abel, Enoch, and Noah

4 By faith Abel offered to God a more acceptable[c] sacrifice than Cain's. Through this he received approval as righteous, God himself giving approval to his gifts; he died, but through his faith[d] he still speaks. [5] By faith Enoch was taken so that he did not experience death; and "he was not found, because God had taken him." For it was attested before he was taken away that "he had pleased God." [6] And without faith it is impossible to please God, for whoever would approach him must believe that he exists and that he rewards those who seek him. [7] By faith Noah, warned by God about events as yet unseen, respected the warning and built an ark

a Gk by this b Or was not made out of visible things c Gk greater
d Gk through it

11:1–12:2 The great cloud of witnesses—Hebrews speaks of faith more than any other book in the New Testament, but highlights an aspect of it different from that stressed by other New Testament witnesses. What Hebrews intends by "faith" is close in meaning to "faithfulness." It speaks of faith as active in obedience. That characteristic of the Christian life enables one both to endure—to persevere—even in the midst of difficult circumstances, and also to step out into the unknown with courage and to live in a risky and vigorous way, confident that God's redemptive purpose in the world will not fail to be achieved, despite all appearances to the contrary.

Hebrews views life on this earth as a pilgrimage to a heavenly *homeland* (11:14). Believers are always *strangers and foreigners on the earth* (11:13), resident aliens who are "in the world," but "not of the world" (John 17:14–18). We seek to embody the life pattern of God's eternal world, which is our ultimate destination, and so make it real in the here and now.

Faith does not guarantee prosperity or success by the world's standards (11:23ff.). Nor does it guarantee deliverance or shelter believers from suffering (11:32–39). As believers are guided in this world by the vision and standards of God's eternal world, they inevitably encounter opposition and maltreatment; for the world is threatened by those who do not share its values and lashes out at them. Faith sustains believers and enables them to persevere, because they know that their ultimate destiny is in the hands of the unseen God whose promises are sure, and because they know that God's saving purposes will not fail to be achieved, despite all appearances to the contrary.

to save his household; by this he condemned the world and became an heir to the righteousness that is in accordance with faith.

The Faith of Abraham

8 By faith Abraham obeyed when he was called to set out for a place that he was to receive as an inheritance; and he set out, not knowing where he was going. 9 By faith he stayed for a time in the land he had been promised, as in a foreign land, living in tents, as did Isaac and Jacob, who were heirs with him of the same promise. 10 For he looked forward to the city that has foundations, whose architect and builder is God. 11 By faith he received power of procreation, even though he was too old—and Sarah herself was barren—because he considered him faithful who had promised.a 12 Therefore from one person, and this one as good as dead, descendants were born, "as many as the stars of heaven and as the innumerable grains of sand by the seashore."

13 All of these died in faith without having received the promises, but from a distance they saw and greeted them. They confessed that they were strangers and foreigners on the earth, 14 for people who speak in this way make it clear that they are seeking a homeland. 15 If they had been thinking of the land that they had left behind, they would have had opportunity to return. 16 But as it is, they desire a better country, that is, a heavenly one. Therefore God is not ashamed to be called their God; indeed, he has prepared a city for them.

17 By faith Abraham, when put to the test, offered up Isaac. He who had received the promises was ready to offer up his only son, 18 of whom he had been told, "It is through Isaac that descendants shall be named for you." 19 He considered the fact that God is able even to raise someone from the dead—and figuratively speaking, he did receive him back. 20 By faith Isaac invoked blessings for the future on Jacob and Esau. 21 By faith Jacob, when dying, blessed each of the sons of Joseph, "bowing in worship over the top of his staff." 22 By faith Joseph, at the end of his life, made mention of the exodus of the Israelites and gave instructions about his burial.b

The Faith of Moses

23 By faith Moses was hidden by his parents for three months after his birth, because they saw that the child was beautiful; and they were not afraid of the king's edict.c 24 By faith Moses, when he was grown up, refused to be called a son of Pharaoh's daughter, 25 choosing rather to share ill-treatment with the people of God than to enjoy the fleeting pleasures of sin. 26 He considered abuse suffered for the Christd to be greater wealth than the treasures of Egypt, for he was looking ahead to the reward. 27 By faith he left Egypt, unafraid of the king's anger; for he persevered as thoughe he saw him who is invisible. 28 By faith he kept the Passover and the sprinkling of blood, so that the destroyer of the firstborn would not touch the firstborn of Israel.f

The Faith of Other Israelite Heroes

29 By faith the people passed through the Red Sea as if it were dry land, but when the Egyptians attempted to do so they were drowned. 30 By faith the walls of Jericho fell after they had been encircled for seven days. 31 By faith Rahab the prostitute did not perish with those who were disobedient,g because she had received the spies in peace.

32 And what more should I say? For time would fail me to tell of Gideon, Barak, Samson, Jephthah, of David and Samuel and the prophets— 33 who through faith conquered kingdoms, administered justice, obtained promises, shut the mouths of lions, 34 quenched rag-

a Or By faith Sarah herself, though barren, received power to conceive, even when she was too old, because she considered him faithful who had promised. b Gk his bones c Other ancient authorities add By faith Moses, when he was grown up, killed the Egyptian, because he observed the humiliation of his people (Gk brothers) d Or the Messiah e Or because f Gk would not touch them g Or unbelieving

ing fire, escaped the edge of the sword, won strength out of weakness, became mighty in war, put foreign armies to flight. [35] Women received their dead by resurrection. Others were tortured, refusing to accept release, in order to obtain a better resurrection. [36] Others suffered mocking and flogging, and even chains and imprisonment. [37] They were stoned to death, they were sawn in two,[a] they were killed by the sword; they went about in skins of sheep and goats, destitute, persecuted, tormented— [38] of whom the world was not worthy. They wandered in deserts and mountains, and in caves and holes in the ground.

39 Yet all these, though they were commended for their faith, did not receive what was promised, [40] since God had provided something better so that they would not, apart from us, be made perfect.

The Example of Jesus

12 Therefore, since we are surrounded by so great a cloud of witnesses, let us also lay aside every weight and the sin that clings so closely,[b] and let us run with perseverance the race that is set before us, [2] looking to Jesus the pioneer and perfecter of our faith, who for the sake of[c] the joy that was set before him endured the cross, disregarding its shame, and has taken his seat at the right hand of the throne of God.

3 Consider him who endured such hostility against himself from sinners,[d] so that you may not grow weary or lose heart. [4] In your struggle against sin you have not yet resisted to the point of shedding your blood. [5] And you have forgotten the exhortation that addresses you as children—

"My child, do not regard lightly the
　　discipline of the Lord,
　or lose heart when you are
　　punished by him;
[6]　for the Lord disciplines those whom
　　he loves,
　and chastises every child whom he
　　accepts."

[7] Endure trials for the sake of discipline. God is treating you as children; for what child is there whom a parent does not discipline? [8] If you do not have that discipline in which all children share, then you are illegitimate and not his children. [9] Moreover, we had human parents to discipline us, and we respected them. Should we not be even more willing to be subject to the Father of spirits and live? [10] For they disciplined us for a short time as seemed best to them, but he disciplines us for our good, in order that we may share his holiness. [11] Now, discipline always seems painful rather than pleasant at the time, but later it yields the peaceful fruit of righteousness to those who have been trained by it.

a Other ancient authorities add *they were tempted* *b* Other ancient authorities read *sin that easily distracts* *c* Or *who instead of* *d* Other ancient authorities read *such hostility from sinners against themselves*

12:3–13:25 Concluding Exhortations

12:3–12 A perspective on suffering—Hebrews is distinguished by the attention that it gives both to the sufferings of Jesus and to the sufferings of God's people. In this section, a clear connection is drawn between the suffering of Jesus and that of God's people. Suffering and being a child of God go hand in hand, because those who are guided in this world by the vision and standards of God's eternal world inevitably encounter opposition and maltreatment. In particular, those who witness to God's call for justice and who work for change in this world can expect sharp opposition. In many instances, suffering comes our way not in spite of the fact that we are disciples, but precisely because of it. The example of Jesus' endurance in the face of hostility can inspire Christians to face bravely their own experiences of reproach and rejection.

Moreover, Christians can learn and grow through experiences of suffering (see 5:8), which are not signs of divine displeasure. They are to be viewed as divine discipline and training, and as such, signs of God's love and acceptance. Hebrews speaks not of suffering in general, but rather of suffering that comes our way as a direct result of obedient discipleship and Christian witness in the world—as a direct result of our commitment to Jesus Christ. Those who suffer for their identification with Christ can emerge from trying circumstances even stronger in faith and witness.

12 Therefore lift your drooping hands and strengthen your weak knees, 13 and make straight paths for your feet, so that what is lame may not be put out of joint, but rather be healed.

Warnings against Rejecting God's Grace

14 Pursue peace with everyone, and the holiness without which no one will see the Lord. 15 See to it that no one fails to obtain the grace of God; that no root of bitterness springs up and causes trouble, and through it many become defiled. 16 See to it that no one becomes like Esau, an immoral and godless person, who sold his birthright for a single meal. 17 You know that later, when he wanted to inherit the blessing, he was rejected, for he found no chance to repent,*a* even though he sought the blessing*b* with tears.

18 You have not come to something*c* that can be touched, a blazing fire, and darkness, and gloom, and a tempest, 19 and the sound of a trumpet, and a voice whose words made the hearers beg that not another word be spoken to them. 20 (For they could not endure the order that was given, "If even an animal touches the mountain, it shall be stoned to death." 21 Indeed, so terrifying was the sight that Moses said, "I tremble with fear.") 22 But you have come to Mount Zion and to the city of the living God, the heavenly Jerusalem, and to innumerable angels in festal gathering, 23 and to the assembly*d* of the firstborn who are enrolled in heaven, and to God the judge of all, and to the spirits of the righteous made perfect, 24 and to Jesus, the mediator of a new covenant, and to the sprinkled blood that speaks a better word than the blood of Abel.

25 See that you do not refuse the one who is speaking; for if they did not escape when they refused the one who warned them on earth, how much less will we escape if we reject the one who warns from heaven! 26 At that time his voice shook the earth; but now he has promised, "Yet once more I will shake not only the earth but also the heaven." 27 This phrase, "Yet once more," indicates the removal of what is shaken—that is, created things—so that what cannot be shaken may remain. 28 Therefore, since we are receiving a kingdom that cannot be shaken, let us give thanks, by which we offer to God an acceptable worship with reverence and awe; 29 for indeed our God is a consuming fire.

Service Well-Pleasing to God

13 Let mutual love continue. 2 Do not neglect to show hospitality

a Or no chance to change his father's mind b Gk it c Other ancient authorities read a mountain d Or angels, and to the festal gathering 23 and assembly

---

12:14–29 Final warning against rejecting God's grace—Hebrews issues one last warning of the dangers of apostasy (see introduction: Hebrews on Repentance and Apostasy). It also provides a climactic summary of the benefits of Christ's work that takes the form of a final, grand comparison between Mount Sinai and Mount Zion—or, in effect, between Judaism and Christianity, between the old covenant and the new (see introduction: Judaism and Christianity in Hebrews).

The gift that God has provided is secure. In the midst of a complex and changing world, Christians have something secure on which to base their lives and hopes: the reign of God (an "unshakable" kingdom), which has come into their midst in Jesus Christ, and will one day be established in fullness on the earth (v. 28).

13:1–19 Contours of the Christian life—Hebrews sketches the contours of life under God's rule, which touches our lives with amazing comprehensiveness. It is embodied in the *mutual love* that Christians extend to one another (v. 1); in acts of graciousness and hospitality that reflect God's love and testify to God's presence; in solidarity with prisoners (v. 3); in marriages characterized by fidelity (v. 4); and when lives are kept *free from the love of money* (v. 5).

The source of our ultimate security and the object of our ultimate allegiance is articulated clearly in v. 8, which sums up the message of Hebrews. *Yesterday*, as our great high priest, *Jesus Christ* presented himself as a sacrifice on our behalf; *today*, Christ intercedes for us before the throne of God; and in the future, he will return to bring the saving purposes of God to their fulfillment. Christ's great faithfulness to us is unchanging, and upon it we may rely.

Leaders, both lay and ordained, who have

to strangers, for by doing that some have entertained angels without knowing it. **3** Remember those who are in prison, as though you were in prison with them; those who are being tortured, as though you yourselves were being tortured.*a* **4** Let marriage be held in honor by all, and let the marriage bed be kept undefiled; for God will judge fornicators and adulterers. **5** Keep your lives free from the love of money, and be content with what you have; for he has said, "I will never leave you or forsake you." **6** So we can say with confidence,

"The Lord is my helper;
   I will not be afraid.
What can anyone do to me?"

7 Remember your leaders, those who spoke the word of God to you; consider the outcome of their way of life, and imitate their faith. **8** Jesus Christ is the same yesterday and today and forever. **9** Do not be carried away by all kinds of strange teachings; for it is well for the heart to be strengthened by grace, not by regulations about food,*b* which have not benefited those who observe them. **10** We have an altar from which those who officiate in the tent*c* have no right to eat. **11** For the bodies of those animals whose blood is brought into the sanctuary by the high priest as a sacrifice for sin are burned outside the camp. **12** Therefore Jesus also suffered outside the city gate in order to sanctify the people by his own blood. **13** Let us then go to him outside the camp and bear the abuse he endured. **14** For here we have no lasting city, but we are looking for the city that

is to come. **15** Through him, then, let us continually offer a sacrifice of praise to God, that is, the fruit of lips that confess his name. **16** Do not neglect to do good and to share what you have, for such sacrifices are pleasing to God.

17 Obey your leaders and submit to them, for they are keeping watch over your souls and will give an account. Let them do this with joy and not with sighing—for that would be harmful to you.

18 Pray for us; we are sure that we have a clear conscience, desiring to act honorably in all things. **19** I urge you all the more to do this, so that I may be restored to you very soon.

Benediction

20 Now may the God of peace, who brought back from the dead our Lord Jesus, the great shepherd of the sheep, by the blood of the eternal covenant, **21** make you complete in everything good so that you may do his will, working among us*d* that which is pleasing in his sight, through Jesus Christ, to whom be the glory forever and ever. Amen.

Final Exhortation and Greetings

22 I appeal to you, brothers and sisters,*e* bear with my word of exhortation, for I have written to you briefly. **23** I want you to know that our brother Timothy has been set free; and if he comes in time, he will be with me when I see you. **24** Greet all your leaders and all the saints. Those from Italy send you greetings. **25** Grace be with all of you.*f*

a Gk were in the body *b* Gk not by foods *c* Or tabernacle *d* Other ancient authorities read you *e* Gk brothers *f* Other ancient authorities add Amen

---

been entrusted with oversight of the church at denominational, regional, and local levels need the support, prayers, and partnership of the whole Christian community as they carry out their tasks (vv. 7, 17, 18).

The striking admonition in vv. 10–16 borrows one last motif from the Day of Atonement ceremonies. By means of it, Hebrews suggests that our Christian pilgrimages are not to be confined to holy space—to the safety of the sanctuary. Rather, we are to follow Christ *outside the camp* (v. 13) into all the secular spaces of our world,

where we may well invite the world's hostility and share Christ's suffering as we embody God's intentions for human life. Christ's death outside the camp made every secular space potentially holy, and those who follow him are to claim every arena of life as God's own and subject to God's rule.

13:20–25 Benediction and farewell—The God who was able to raise Jesus *from the dead* can surely bring us, too, through the most trying of circumstances.

The Book of

JAMES

T he letter of James has often been regarded as the junk mail in the New Testament, thanks in large part to Martin Luther, the great Protestant reformer, who denounced it as an "epistle of straw." Luther was concerned, as others too have been, about the glaring absence of reference to central tenets of Christian faith in James. In particular, one looks in vain for any reference to the life and ministry of Jesus or to his death and resurrection. There are, in fact, only two brief references to Jesus in the whole letter (1:1; 2:1). Moreover, the letter is short on grace and long on works, and thus has had the misfortune of appearing to contradict the New Testament's preeminent apostle, Paul, who maintained that we are saved by grace through faith *apart* from works of the law (Rom. 3:28). For all of these reasons, Luther complained that James has "nothing of the nature of the gospel about it."

Misgivings about the letter are laid to rest, however, when one understands an important fact about its nature: it is *paraenesis*, or ethical exhortation, in the form of a letter. "Paraenesis" is derived from the Greek word *parainesis,* which means "advice," "counsel," "exhortation." It is instruction concerning how one ought to live. This insight is crucial for one's reading and interpretation of the letter; James is not trying to evangelize the world. The letter is instead challenging its readers to live the Christian life. It does not present the whole of Christian truth, for it is addressed to readers who have already heard the gospel and embraced it and who are very familiar with the central tenets of Christian faith. Its aim is to help believers see the implications of Christian faith for individual and communal behavior—for how they live their lives.

In five short chapters, the letter of James discerns (among other things) the relevance of Christian faith to our speech, to our economic pursuits and business practices, to our experiences of trial and temptation, to our responses to discrimination and to people in need, and to our life together in the Christian community. James deals almost exclusively with the social and practical aspects of Christianity. It reminds us of the everyday problems with which we struggle and maintains that Christian faith touches every aspect of life, transforming routine pursuits into opportunities for discipleship.

Above all, the letter challenges us to be persons of integrity, that is, people who are consistent in all we see, say, believe, and do. Throughout the letter, by way of negative example, the author draws our attention to the "double-minded" person (see 1:8; 4:8)—the person beset by double vision, double talk, double face—and expresses a hope that we, by contrast, will manifest integrity of faith. From the first verse to the last, James calls us to behavior consistent with our convictions and inspires us to *live* our faith.

Moreover, the letter assists us in discerning how we might order and maintain every aspect of our lives in the light of God's sovereignty. Indeed, every aspect of Christian life of which James speaks is related to the God who is creator, sustainer, savior, and

judge (see, for example, 3:9; 2:2–6; 4:13–17). It is important to recognize the decid-edly theocentric or God-centered nature of James's ethical exhortation. Why? Because the Christian life that James describes is demanding and could not be pursued on our own strength. This is the good news: It is God's own gracious presence and power and wisdom that makes it possible for Christians to live as James describes.

Who is the author who speaks to us through this challenging letter? We do not know! "James" is one of the most common of Jewish and Christian names. Though church tradition has attributed the letter to the brother of the Lord and leader of the early Christian community in Jerusalem, the author nowhere identifies himself as a leader of the church or as a relative of Jesus. We may surmise that the author was an early Christian teacher (see 3:1), one who was responsible for guiding the early Christian community in many aspects of its life. In fact, the letter of James may serve as an example of the work of early Christian teachers.

Neither can we say with certainty to whom the letter of James was first addressed. It is regarded as one of the General or Catholic (that is, universal) Epistles, which is to say that it is addressed to Christians in general rather than to a specific commu-nity at a particular place. But though it is intended for wide distribution and speaks of general rather than particular situations, it indicates those areas of life in the early Christian community that the author found to be most urgently in need of direction and regulation. Interestingly, the areas of Christian life to which James devotes atten-tion continue to be areas that are urgently in need of direction and regulation today. For this reason, this first-century letter is startlingly relevant in our century, and those who study it closely will find within its "straw" much nourishing grain.

Does James Contradict Paul?

James has been accused frequently of standing in direct contradiction to the apostle Paul and to the very heart of Christian faith. In Rom. 3:28, Paul states quite emphati-cally that "we hold that a person is justified by faith apart from works prescribed by the law." This affirmation, that we are brought into right relationship with God by God's grace alone and not by meritorious works, sparked the Protestant Reformation in the sixteenth century and is central to both Protestant and modern Roman Catholic faith. Thus, when the author of James insists that "a person is justified by works and not by faith alone" (2:24), is he not proposing a new way of salvation? Is he not distorting the very heart of Christian faith? Before jumping to this conclusion, it is important to note that Paul and James are addressing very different struggles and intend quite different things by "works."

Paul, on the one hand, addresses the starting point of faith—the question of how one is brought into right relationship with God. He battles the notion that one must perform meritorious works to earn God's acceptance and approval. The works to which he refers are "works of the law" and include such matters as compliance with food laws, circumcision, purification rites, and ritual prescriptions. None of these matters, Paul argues, are requirements for salvation, for salvation is a gracious gift of God, to be accepted by faith alone, apart from any such works of the law.

The letter of James, on the other hand, does not address the initial experience of acceptance by God, but the continuing life of the believer. It does not speak of works as meritorious deeds aimed to win God's approval, but rather as the fruit of Christian faith (see also Matt. 12:33). Moreover, when James speaks of works, it refers not to

works of the law such as legal observances, but rather to acts of love in the neighbor's behalf. Therefore, for James, works include such matters as the care of widows and orphans, respect for the poor, feeding the hungry, clothing the naked, and control of the tongue. From James's viewpoint, genuine faith cannot exist without producing this kind of works as the fruit of obedience.

Thus, while their emphases differ, Paul and James do not stand as directly in opposition to each other as they might appear to at first glance. Most interpreters agree that James is not responding directly to Paul at all, but rather to an area of the church in which Paul's slogan of "justification by faith" was being used and distorted to argue that "faith alone" was all that counted, without any accompanying moral fruit or transformation of life. Moreover, both Paul and James are needed to keep Christian faith in perspective. Paul forcefully reminds us that there is nothing we can do to "earn" God's grace and forgiveness. We can only accept it. James, however, forcefully reminds us that works are intrinsically related to faith and are, in fact, its proper expression. Thus Paul guards against "works righteousness" and James guards against "cheap grace."

Rich and Poor in James

James speaks vigorously and repeatedly about economic realities (1:9–11, 27; 2:1–7, 15–16; 4:13–5:6). It may be no coincidence that James's first reference to poverty and riches is juxtaposed with words about experiences of trial (1:9–11), for a close reading of the letter suggests that economic hardship may have been among the chief trials with which James's first readers struggled.

There may be no doubt, in fact, about the author's animosity toward the rich, especially in 5:1–6, where he unleashes his fury in fierce denunciations, announcing the disasters that surely await them on the judgment day. Two specific charges are leveled against the rich. First, James declares them guilty of oppression. They have abused their position of power as employers, exploiting the poor by withholding the wages of laborers (see Deut. 24:14–15). Day laborers depended completely on their meager pay. To withhold their wages was to attack their very lives—it was in fact gradually to kill them, an accusation that is made directly in 5:6. For this reason, James strikingly depicts wages as the very blood of the workers crying out in protest against injustice and declares that these cries, along with the cries of the exploited laborers themselves, "have reached the ears of the Lord of hosts." Second, James censures the rich for their pampered lives. The hardship they have inflicted on others stands in sharp contrast to the softness of their own living. James explicitly notes that this self-indulgent state of affairs will not last forever.

Is James attacking wealthy members of the Christian community? Interpreters tend to agree that James is probably not attacking rich Christians. It is doubtful that "the rich people" censured were actually Christians, for in the three passages in which "the rich" are mentioned (1:9–11; 2:6–7; 5:1–6), they appear to be regarded as "outsiders"—people who are not members of the Christian community. There is no attempt to influence the rich. The condemnation is absolute. There is no call to repentance.

More than likely, the Christian communities with which the author was most closely associated were largely from the lower end of the economic spectrum. There were some people of means within these congregations. Small merchants, for exam-

ple, appear to be addressed in 4:13–17 (though they are not designated as "the rich"). Moreover, rich visitors were beginning to frequent worship services (2:1–13)—indeed, they were being fawned over, and the author also feared this development.

James's words continue to be good news to the poor of this world to this day. They announce that there will come a day when the poor will be lifted up and when the rich will be held accountable for injustice.

—Frances Taylor Gench

Salutation

1 James, a servant[a] of God and of the Lord Jesus Christ,

To the twelve tribes in the Dispersion:

Greetings.

Faith and Wisdom

2 My brothers and sisters,[b] whenever you face trials of any kind, consider it nothing but joy, [3] because you know that the testing of your faith produces endurance; [4] and let endurance have its full effect, so that you may be mature and complete, lacking in nothing.

5 If any of you is lacking in wisdom, ask God, who gives to all generously and ungrudgingly, and it will be given you. [6] But ask in faith, never doubting, for the one who doubts is like a wave of the sea, driven and tossed by the wind; [7, 8] for the doubter, being double-minded and unstable in every way, must not expect to receive anything from the Lord.

Poverty and Riches

9 Let the believer[c] who is lowly boast in being raised up, [10] and the rich in being brought low, because the rich will disappear like a flower in the field. [11] For the sun rises with its scorching heat and withers the field; its flower falls, and its beauty perishes. It is the same way with the rich; in the midst of a busy life, they will wither away.

Trial and Temptation

12 Blessed is anyone who endures temptation. Such a one has stood the test and will receive the crown of life that the Lord[d] has promised to those who love him. [13] No one, when tempted, should say, "I am being tempted by God"; for God cannot be tempted by evil and he himself tempts no one. [14] But one is tempted by one's own desire, being lured and enticed by it; [15] then, when that desire has conceived, it gives birth to sin, and that sin, when it is fully grown, gives birth to death. [16] Do not be deceived, my beloved.[e]

17 Every generous act of giving, with every perfect gift, is from above, coming down from the Father of lights, with whom there is no variation or shadow due to change.[f] [18] In fulfillment of his own purpose he gave us birth by the word of truth, so that we would become a kind of first fruits of his creatures.

[a] Gk slave   [b] Gk brothers   [c] Gk brother   [d] Gk he; other ancient authorities read God   [e] Gk my beloved brothers   [f] Other ancient authorities read variation due to a shadow of turning

---

1:2–18 Trials and Temptations

1:2–4—The various trials we encounter—experiences of pain, loss, injury, or oppression—are not occasions of joy in and of themselves. The joy of which James speaks results from the growth trials can bring. In the midst of them, we can be drawn closer to God, experience God's sustaining power, and grow in faith and maturity. Just as exercising one's muscles, putting them under duress, makes them stronger, not weaker, so too can experiences of trial strengthen faith. *Endur-*ance connotes active steadfastness in the face of trial, not passive resignation.

1:9–11—Economic hardship may have been among the chief trials with which James's first readers struggled. See the note at 5:1–6.

1:12–18—*Temptation* is not to be blamed on God. God's constant, unchanging will for us is not trial or temptation, but life—a life of steadfast faith and wholeness and, in the end, life eternal—a life of constancy and integrity modeled on the constancy and integrity of God.

Hearing and Doing the Word

19 You must understand this, my beloved:[a] let everyone be quick to listen, slow to speak, slow to anger; 20 for your anger does not produce God's righteousness. 21 Therefore rid yourselves of all sordidness and rank growth of wickedness, and welcome with meekness the implanted word that has the power to save your souls.

22 But be doers of the word, and not merely hearers who deceive themselves. 23 For if any are hearers of the word and not doers, they are like those who look at themselves[b] in a mirror; 24 for they look at themselves and, on going away, immediately forget what they were like. 25 But those who look into the perfect law, the law of liberty, and persevere, being not hearers who forget but doers who act— they will be blessed in their doing.

26 If any think they are religious, and do not bridle their tongues but deceive their hearts, their religion is worthless. 27 Religion that is pure and undefiled before God, the Father, is this: to care for orphans and widows in their distress, and to keep oneself unstained by the world.

Warning against Partiality

2 My brothers and sisters,[c] do you with your acts of favoritism really believe in our glorious Lord Jesus Christ?[d] 2 For if a person with gold rings and in fine clothes comes into your assembly, and if a poor person in dirty clothes also comes in, 3 and if you take notice of the one wearing the fine clothes and say, "Have a seat here, please," while to the one who is poor you say, "Stand there," or, "Sit at my feet,"[e] 4 have you not made distinctions among yourselves, and become judges with evil thoughts? 5 Listen, my beloved brothers and sisters.[f] Has not God chosen the poor in the world to be rich in faith and to be heirs of the kingdom that he has promised to those who love him? 6 But you have dishonored the poor. Is it not the rich who oppress you? Is it not they who drag you into court? 7 Is it not they who blaspheme the excellent name that was invoked over you?

8 You do well if you really fulfill the royal law according to the scripture, "You shall love your neighbor as yourself." 9 But if you show partiality, you commit sin and are convicted by the law as transgressors. 10 For whoever keeps the whole law but fails in one point has become accountable for all of it. 11 For the one who said, "You shall not commit adultery," also said, "You shall not mur-

a Gk my beloved brothers   b Gk at the face of his birth   c Gk My brothers
d Or hold the faith of our glorious Lord Jesus Christ without acts of favoritism
e Gk Sit under my footstool   f Gk brothers

1:19–27 Hear and Do the Word

1:19–21—The *implanted word* is God's word to us of mercy, power, and renewal in Jesus Christ. One of our primary and ongoing tasks as Christians is to engage that word as it comes to us in preaching and the sacraments, in teaching, in tradition, and in careful study of the Scriptures.

1:22–25—James does not contrast *hearers* and *doers*, but two kinds of hearers: those who act upon what they have heard and those who do not. *The word* is referred to as *law*, because once received, it implies commitment and obedience. The law is the will of God for our lives as revealed in the Old Testament and in the life and teaching of Jesus Christ.

1:26–27—For James, the test of genuine *religion* is not orthodoxy (right belief) but orthopraxy (right practice). Christians are to be engaged in the world, but they are to hold a different understanding of reality and a different set of values, informed by their experience of the grace of God in Jesus Christ.

2:1–13 Beware of Discrimination

2:1–4—James provides the strongest castigation of discrimination in the New Testament—any discrimination based on outward appearance. The discrimination depicted entails evident differences in socioeconomic class. However, discrimination can also be linked to evidence of race or ethnicity, gender, disability, or sexual orientation. The fact that James refers to *acts of favoritism* in the plural form suggests that discrimination can manifest itself in the Christian community in a variety of ways.

2:5–13—All will be accountable to God for their words and deeds on the judgment day. Our practice of indiscriminate love toward all people will reveal whether we have allowed the grace and power of God to produce a transformation in our lives.

der." Now if you do not commit adultery but if you murder, you have become a transgressor of the law. ¹²So speak and so act as those who are to be judged by the law of liberty. ¹³For judgment will be without mercy to anyone who has shown no mercy; mercy triumphs over judgment.

Faith without Works Is Dead

14 What good is it, my brothers and sisters,*ᵃ* if you say you have faith but do not have works? Can faith save you? ¹⁵If a brother or sister is naked and lacks daily food, ¹⁶and one of you says to them, "Go in peace; keep warm and eat your fill," and yet you do not supply their bodily needs, what is the good of that? ¹⁷So faith by itself, if it has no works, is dead.

18 But someone will say, "You have faith and I have works." Show me your faith apart from your works, and I by my works will show you my faith. ¹⁹You believe that God is one; you do well. Even the demons believe—and shudder. ²⁰Do you want to be shown, you senseless person, that faith apart from works is barren? ²¹Was not our ancestor Abraham justified by works when he offered his son Isaac on the altar? ²²You see that faith was active along with his works, and faith was brought to completion by the works. ²³Thus the scripture was fulfilled that says, "Abraham believed God, and it was reckoned to him as righteousness," and he was called the friend of God. ²⁴You see that a person is justified by works and not by faith alone. ²⁵Likewise, was not Rahab the prostitute also justified by works when she welcomed the messengers and sent them out by another road? ²⁶For just as the body without the spirit is dead, so faith without works is also dead.

Taming the Tongue

3 Not many of you should become teachers, my brothers and sisters,*ᵃ* for you know that we who teach will be judged with greater strictness. ²For all of us make many mistakes. Anyone who makes no mistakes in speaking is perfect, able to keep the whole body in check with a bridle. ³If we put bits into the mouths of horses to make them obey us, we guide their whole bodies. ⁴Or look at ships: though they are so large that it takes strong winds to drive them, yet they are guided by a very small rudder wherever the will of the pilot directs. ⁵So also the tongue is a small member, yet it boasts of great exploits.

How great a forest is set ablaze by a small fire! ⁶And the tongue is a fire. The tongue is placed among our members as a world of iniquity; it stains the whole body, sets on fire the cycle of nature,*ᵇ* and is itself set on fire by hell.*ᶜ* ⁷For every species of beast and bird, of reptile and sea creature, can be tamed and has been tamed by the human species, ⁸but no one can tame the tongue—a restless evil, full of deadly poison. ⁹With it we bless the Lord and Father, and with

*ᵃ*Gk brothers   *ᵇ*Or wheel of birth   *ᶜ*Gk Gehenna

2:14–26 Faith and Works

James insists on the inseparable connection between *faith* and *works*. At no point does James contrast faith and works. Instead, the contrast is between two kinds of faith: genuine faith (of which works are a sign) and counterfeit faith (which finds no expression in works and thus cannot really be faith at all). Faith, when it is genuine, is inseparable from works, which are its proper expression.

3:1–12 Taming the Tongue

3:1–5a—While all people make mistakes, *teachers* are at special risk, for *the tongue*, the teacher's chief tool of trade, is a powerful and dangerous instrument.

3:5b–8—James graphically portrays the destructive effect of undisciplined speech for all believers. The imagery is severe and exaggerated to impress upon us the dangerous potential of uncontrolled speech.

3:9–12—The tongue's potential for evil can also include silence. Sometimes failure to speak can damage our family, church, or community relationships. Indeed, James does not counsel us to zipper the tongue, but to *bridle* it (1:26; 3:2). The bridle does not stop the horse from running;

it we curse those who are made in the likeness of God. [10] From the same mouth come blessing and cursing. My brothers and sisters,[a] this ought not to be so. [11] Does a spring pour forth from the same opening both fresh and brackish water? [12] Can a fig tree, my brothers and sisters,[b] yield olives, or a grapevine figs? No more can salt water yield fresh.

Two Kinds of Wisdom

13 Who is wise and understanding among you? Show by your good life that your works are done with gentleness born of wisdom. [14] But if you have bitter envy and selfish ambition in your hearts, do not be boastful and false to the truth. [15] Such wisdom does not come down from above, but is earthly, unspiritual, devilish. [16] For where there is envy and selfish ambition, there will also be disorder and wickedness of every kind. [17] But the wisdom from above is first pure, then peaceable, gentle, willing to yield, full of mercy and good fruits, without a trace of partiality or hypocrisy. [18] And a harvest of righteousness is sown in peace for[c] those who make peace.

Friendship with the World

4 Those conflicts and disputes among you, where do they come from? Do they not come from your cravings that are at war within you? [2] You want something and do not have it; so you commit murder. And you covet[d] something and cannot obtain it; so you engage in disputes and conflicts. You do not have, because you do not ask. [3] You ask and do not receive, because you ask wrongly, in order to spend what you get on your pleasures. [4] Adulterers! Do you not know that friendship with the world is enmity with God? Therefore whoever wishes to be a friend of the world becomes an enemy of God. [5] Or do you suppose that it is for nothing that the scripture says, "God[e] yearns jealously for the spirit that he has made to dwell in us"? [6] But he gives all the more grace; therefore it says,

> "God opposes the proud,
> 　but gives grace to the humble."

[7] Submit yourselves therefore to God. Resist the devil, and he will flee from you. [8] Draw near to God, and he will draw near to you. Cleanse your hands, you sinners, and purify your hearts, you double-minded. [9] Lament and mourn and weep. Let your laughter be turned into mourning and your joy into dejection. [10] Humble yourselves before the Lord, and he will exalt you.

Warning against Judging Another

11 Do not speak evil against one another, brothers and sisters.[f] Whoever speaks evil against another or judges another, speaks evil against the law and judges the law; but if you judge the law, you are not a doer of the law but a judge. [12] There is one lawgiver and judge who is able to save and to destroy. So who, then, are you to judge your neighbor?

Boasting about Tomorrow

13 Come now, you who say, "Today or tomorrow we will go to such and such a town and spend a year there, doing

---

[a] Gk My brothers　[b] Gk my brothers　[c] Or by　[d] Or you murder and you covet　[e] Gk He　[f] Gk brothers

---

it helps the horse run in a more disciplined direction.

3:13–4:12 Friendship with God

3:13–18—True *wisdom* has little to do with intellectual brilliance or schooling. It is entirely a gift of God and consists of knowledge of how to live according to God's ways. It is manifested in one's conduct—in a manner of life that is, above all, *peaceable*.

4:1–6—It is not possible to share the attitudes, values, and perceptions of *God* and *the world* simultaneously.

4:7–12—We are called away from uncommitted double-mindedness to single-minded devotion to God. Right relationship with God also bears implications for our relationship to others.

4:13–5:6 Wealth and Poverty

4:13–17—James rebukes the arrogant assumption that life consists of *doing business and making money*, that human calculation can

business and making money." **14** Yet you do not even know what tomorrow will bring. What is your life? For you are a mist that appears for a little while and then vanishes. **15** Instead you ought to say, "If the Lord wishes, we will live and do this or that." **16** As it is, you boast in your arrogance; all such boasting is evil. **17** Anyone, then, who knows the right thing to do and fails to do it, commits sin.

Warning to Rich Oppressors

5 Come now, you rich people, weep and wail for the miseries that are coming to you. **2** Your riches have rotted, and your clothes are moth-eaten. **3** Your gold and silver have rusted, and their rust will be evidence against you, and it will eat your flesh like fire. You have laid up treasure*a* for the last days. **4** Listen! The wages of the laborers who mowed your fields, which you kept back by fraud, cry out, and the cries of the harvesters have reached the ears of the Lord of hosts. **5** You have lived on the earth in luxury and in pleasure; you have fattened your hearts in a day of slaughter. **6** You have condemned and murdered the righteous one, who does not resist you.

Patience in Suffering

7 Be patient, therefore, beloved,*b* until the coming of the Lord. The farmer waits for the precious crop from the earth, being patient with it until it receives the early and the late rains. **8** You also must be patient. Strengthen your hearts, for the coming of the Lord is near.*c* **9** Beloved,*d* do not grumble against one another, so that you may not be judged. See, the Judge is standing at the doors! **10** As an example of suffering and patience, beloved,*b* take the prophets who spoke in the name of the Lord. **11** Indeed we call blessed those who showed endurance. You have heard of the endurance of Job, and you have seen the purpose of the Lord, how the Lord is compassionate and merciful.

12 Above all, my beloved,*b* do not swear, either by heaven or by earth or by any other oath, but let your "Yes" be yes and your "No" be no, so that you may not fall under condemnation.

The Prayer of Faith

13 Are any among you suffering? They should pray. Are any cheerful? They should sing songs of praise. **14** Are any among you sick? They should call for the elders of the church and have them pray over them, anointing them with oil in the name of the Lord. **15** The prayer of faith will save the sick, and the Lord will raise them up; and anyone who has committed sins will be forgiven. **16** Therefore confess your sins to one another, and pray for one another, so that you may be healed. The prayer of the righteous is powerful and effective.

a Or will eat your flesh, since you have stored up fire *b* Gk brothers *c* Or is at hand *d* Gk Brothers

---

secure the future. In everything, we are utterly dependent on the living God. God is sovereign over all of life, and our business pursuits, like all the activities of our lives, are to be informed and transformed by God's presence, power, and intentions.

5:1–6—The rich are declared guilty of oppression, and their pampered lives stand in sharp contrast to the hardship they have inflicted upon others. These harsh words of condemnation aim to give comfort and consolation to those who had experienced hardship at the hands of the rich. (See "Rich and Poor in James" in the introduction.) These words are no less relevant for those who are not poor, for they serve as a warning of the danger of riches. They also serve as a reminder that God wills justice for the poor and that God hears the cries of the oppressed. Those who are not poor are thereby called to repentance—to redress the crippling inequities and injustice with which so many daily contend.

5:7–20 Final Words of Counsel for the Christian Community

5:7–11—We are to wait patiently and to live in hope of Christ's return.

5:12–18—All of the circumstances of our lives are circumstances for *prayer*. Prayer is not only personal, it is also communal.

[17] Elijah was a human being like us, and he prayed fervently that it might not rain, and for three years and six months it did not rain on the earth. [18] Then he prayed again, and the heaven gave rain and the earth yielded its harvest.

19 My brothers and sisters,[a] if anyone among you wanders from the truth and is brought back by another, [20] you should know that whoever brings back a sinner from wandering will save the sinner's[b] soul from death and will cover a multitude of sins.

[a] Gk My brothers   [b] Gk his

5:19–20—Christians are not to give up on each other, and have a responsibility for brothers and sisters who wander from the community. James focuses not on the person who sins, but on the responsibility incumbent upon other Christians to seek actively to restore the sinner.

The Book of

1 PETER

How is the church to relate to the society in which it finds itself? To what extent does Christian identity demand distinction from that society? And how are believers to understand and endure the suffering that may come their way as a result of Christian identity and vocation? The letter of 1 Peter provides a rich resource for reflection on these perennial questions, for it bears witness to the struggle of early Christian communities to maintain their identity, their fellowship, and their mission in the midst of vigorous social opposition.

Every church in this world lives out its life in the midst of non-Christian society, even those in Western countries where it is often assumed that Christian values and national values are one and the same. Indeed, Christians who do not experience opposition in their social context may be prompted by 1 Peter to reflect on the integrity of their Christian identity. Are we bearing public witness to Christian values, which are profoundly countercultural? Is not authentic witness to them likely to evoke vigorous social opposition in our own day? Have we succumbed to pressures for conformity in ways that compromise Christian life and witness? In short, 1 Peter challenges believers of every age to reflect on their own negotiation of distinctive Christian identity on the one hand and societal participation on the other.

First Peter is one of the General or Catholic Epistles, for it is addressed not to a particular church but to a group of churches in five Roman provinces of Asia Minor (modern Turkey). Still, they share a common experience: they bear the name "Christian" (4:16) and find that wearing that name entails social ostracism and persecution. For this reason, they are addressed as "exiles of the Dispersion" in 1:1 and as "exiles and aliens" in 2:11 (see also 1:17). These striking metaphors recall the history of the Jews living outside Palestine and away from home, scattered among pagan nations, and suggest that the letter's intended readers now share a similar experience of alienation. Some would argue that the language of exile and alienation reflects actual legal and social status as well as a spiritual state; perhaps they are literally "resident aliens," foreigners working in communities where they have no citizenship or power. Whatever the case may be, it is clear that those to whom the letter is addressed are not fully at home in the world. They are outsiders in an increasingly hostile environment. Indeed, the language of suffering pervades the letter.

The exact nature of their suffering has been debated. At one time, full-scale Roman persecution was supposed, perhaps under the emperors Nero, Domitian, or Trajan. More recently, scholars have been inclined to view the persecution as unofficial and local in nature, inflicted by fellow citizens rather than the government. It clearly included verbal abuse, for 1 Peter indicates that Christians are "blasphemed" (4:4) and "reviled" (4:14), "maligned" as "evildoers" (2:12). They have ceased to participate in traditional religious and social practices (4:3–4) and are regarded as antisocial, even a threat perhaps, for adherents of new foreign religions might well be

subversive of domestic and political order. In fact, some Christian women and slaves defy custom by worshiping a different God from their husbands and masters (2:18–3:6). The Christians addressed do not appear to be in mortal danger, for martyrdom is not in view. But they face vigorous hostility from neighbors who cannot understand the change in lifestyle that the gospel has produced in their lives. And there is no doubt that persecution and ostracism are profoundly demoralizing and debilitating realities. Could they be blamed for wondering if Christian identity and commitment were worth the price?

First Peter is thus addressed to suffering, alienated Christians who are no longer "at home" in their world and are mightily tempted to succumb to external pressures—to relinquish Christian identity and vocation and conform to societal expectations. The letter's expressed aim is to "encourage" and strengthen such readers—to urge them to "stand fast" in the "true grace of God" (5:12). In so doing, it provides a profound exploration of the meaning of Jesus Christ's life, death, and resurrection for Christian suffering and for the church's life in society.

Readers are given to understand that through the events of Christ's passion, God has acted to change the structure of reality and to create a new people who are connected both to the cosmos and to society in a profoundly new way. With extraordinary words of assurance, 1 Peter affirms their new birth, their divinely conferred dignity and status, and their responsibility in the world as the elect and holy people of God. They are "a chosen race, a royal priesthood, a holy nation, God's own people" (2:9)— all the pride of the Israelites as special people of God is appropriated to describe their new vocation. The distinctly obedient and holy way of life that they embody manifests God's plan for the whole world and God's own presence. Indeed, Christian conduct in the world has evangelistic power.

First Peter acknowledges that Christian identity and vocation does entail suffering, and thus also articulates christological and ecclesiological perspectives to enable its beleaguered readers to understand and endure it. The unique christological affirmation that it makes is that suffering unites believers with their Lord, who suffered for doing good and on their behalf, leaving them "an example," so that they might "follow in his steps" (2:21). But Jesus Christ is more than an example or model; he also provided the means by which they are empowered to endure suffering. His vicarious suffering broke the power of sin and gave them a new life of righteousness, and his resurrection and glorification is a sure sign of the new and glorious future that awaits them too. The pattern of his life thus indicates that suffering is a necessary moment on the journey to salvation. Believers are thereby encouraged to hold fast to their faith despite their present suffering, for it is the only path to the glorious future that awaits them—a future that will transform their present condition just as surely as their present condition as God's elect and holy people represents a transformation from their past (2:10).

If suffering unites believers with their Lord, it also unites them with each other and with "brothers and sisters in all the world" who are "undergoing the same kinds of suffering" (5:9). Indeed, the unique ecclesiological affirmation that 1 Peter articulates for its alienated and exiled readers is that they have a home in the household of God. As commentator John Elliott has so eloquently put it, the Christian community provides "a home for the homeless"—a place of belonging. The new life that is God's gift in Christ is life in community and entails shared identity and vocation. Thus,

1 Peter endeavors to build up the life and cohesion of the household of God which have been threatened by present trials, promoting the solidarity of believers with each other. It also urges its readers to preserve the distinctive communal identity that is so central to their mission in the world, for it is in confrontation with it that outsiders are drawn to God in Christ. To this end, as noted above, the glorious appellations once used to describe Israel's collective identity and vocation are appropriated to articulate the church's unique mission in the world as elect and holy people of God (2:9–10) and to foster a proud sense of belonging.

The Household Code in 1 Peter

The "household code" in 1 Peter 2:18–3:12 is one of five domestic codes that appear in the New Testament (see Eph. 5:21–6:9; Col. 3:18–4:1; 1 Tim. 2–3; Titus 2:1–10), all of which draw on a standard pattern of ethical instruction among both Jews and Greeks. Such codes consisted of instructions to various members of the household (husbands and wives, parents and children, masters and slaves) and were commonplace in ethical reflection, for the stability of the Greco-Roman household was held to be foundational for the stability of the state.

The household code found in 1 Peter is a much-discussed and controversial aspect of the letter, for it reflects many of the values of patriarchal Greco-Roman culture. Indeed, the basic structure of the ancient household is not questioned or transformed. Slaves, for example, are exhorted to accept "with all deference" the authority of their masters, even abusive ones (2:18–25). Wives are told to accept the authority of their husbands, receive advice on proper dress and coiffure, and are urged to exhibit a "gentle and quiet spirit" (3:1–6). Slave owners, on the other hand, are not addressed at all, and husbands are advised, briefly, to "show consideration" for their wives, "paying honor to the woman as the weaker sex" (3:7). Many regard these admonitions as examples of ecclesial accommodation to patriarchal cultural values, a failure of nerve, and there is some truth to this. No attention is given to changing the existing social or domestic order, even when abusive or unjust, and the burden of alleviating tensions between the Christian community and Greco-Roman culture falls on women and slaves, who are urged to conform to societal expectations. Contemporary Christians would do well to discern points at which failure of nerve and ecclesial accommodation to prevailing cultural values may be compromising the church's life and public witness today.

Others, however, emphasize that the household code tradition is not adopted uncritically. The wife of an unbeliever, for example, does not have to give up her faith for her husband's religion, as would have been the norm. And slaves, usually the lowest rung on the social ladder and the last to be addressed, are addressed first in this code, and it is only to their admonitions that a christological rationale is appended in 2:21–25. The admonitions to slaves thus play a central role within the strategy of the whole letter, for the role of the suffering slave or servant, exemplified by Jesus Christ, is held up as a model for all Christian conduct—a model reflected also in the teaching of Jesus in the Synoptic Gospels (see Mark 10:42–45 and parallels). Moreover, slaves are vulnerable to abusive masters, just as Christians are vulnerable to the hostile society in which they find themselves. Their role is thus a paradigmatic one.

Ambiguities abound, and contemporary use of the New Testament household codes remains a critical and debated matter of interpretation. Like the Christians to whom

1 Peter was first addressed, we too must wrestle with the tensions involved in establishing a working relationship with our culture on the one hand, while remaining true to our identity and vocation as people of God on the other. We too must discern appropriate points of connection and disconnection, for the sake of both our well-being and our witness. First Peter may not give us conclusive guidance in these matters. But it affirms the importance of embodying a distinctly obedient and holy way of life in society, even when suffering is the cost, in order that others may encounter the one who called us out of darkness into marvelous light. And it points us to the household of God, which continues to be a place of belonging, where together we seek what it means to be faithful in our world to the God who has "given us a new birth into a living hope through the resurrection of Jesus Christ" (1:3).

Finally, was the letter written by the apostle Peter, as it purports? The high quality of the Greek implies an educated author, one unlikely to have been a Galilean fisherman. Moreover, Petrine authorship would presume that Christianity spread quite rapidly to Asia Minor before Peter's martyrdom in Rome (64–67 CE). The letter's complete lack of reference to any Jewish debate over Mosaic law, along with signs of rudimentary structures of church leadership (5:1–5), reflect circumstances that are more likely to have existed after Peter's death. The letter was probably written from Rome, which was cryptically referred to as "Babylon" (5:13) after the Roman destruction of Jerusalem in 70 CE. Thus most scholars suspect that the letter dates to the latter part of the first century (70–90 CE), after Peter's death, emerging from his circle of influence. It may well represent a pastoral effort on the part of the Roman church to provide oversight of Christian communities taking root in the northern reaches of the Roman Empire.

—**Frances Taylor Gench**

Salutation

1 Peter, an apostle of Jesus Christ,
To the exiles of the Dispersion in Pontus, Galatia, Cappadocia, Asia, and Bithynia, ²who have been chosen and destined by God the Father and sanctified by the Spirit to be obedient to Jesus Christ and to be sprinkled with his blood:
May grace and peace be yours in abundance.

A Living Hope

3 Blessed be the God and Father of our Lord Jesus Christ! By his great mercy he has given us a new birth into a living hope through the resurrection of Jesus Christ from the dead, ⁴and into an inheritance that is imperishable, undefiled, and unfading, kept in heaven for you, ⁵who are being protected by the power of God through faith for a salvation ready to be revealed in the last time. ⁶In this you rejoice,ᵃ even if now for a little while you have had to suffer various trials, ⁷so that the genuineness of your faith—being more precious than gold that, though perishable, is

ᵃ Or *Rejoice in this*

tested by fire—may be found to result in praise and glory and honor when Jesus Christ is revealed. [8] Although you have not seen[a] him, you love him; and even though you do not see him now, you believe in him and rejoice with an indescribable and glorious joy, [9] for you are receiving the outcome of your faith, the salvation of your souls.

10 Concerning this salvation, the prophets who prophesied of the grace that was to be yours made careful search and inquiry, [11] inquiring about the person or time that the Spirit of Christ within them indicated when it testified in advance to the sufferings destined for Christ and the subsequent glory. [12] It was revealed to them that they were serving not themselves but you, in regard to the things that have now been announced to you through those who brought you good news by the Holy Spirit sent from heaven—things into which angels long to look!

A Call to Holy Living

13 Therefore prepare your minds for action;[b] discipline yourselves; set all your hope on the grace that Jesus Christ will bring you when he is revealed. [14] Like obedient children, do not be conformed to the desires that you formerly had in ignorance. [15] Instead, as he who called you is holy, be holy yourselves in all your conduct; [16] for it is written, "You shall be holy, for I am holy."

17 If you invoke as Father the one who judges all people impartially according to their deeds, live in reverent fear during the time of your exile. [18] You know that you were ransomed from the futile ways inherited from your ancestors, not with perishable things like silver or gold, [19] but with the precious blood of Christ, like that of a lamb without defect or blemish. [20] He was destined before the foundation of the world, but was revealed at the end of the ages for your sake. [21] Through him you have come to trust in God, who raised him from the dead and gave him glory, so that your faith and hope are set on God.

22 Now that you have purified your souls by your obedience to the truth[c] so that you have genuine mutual love, love one another deeply[d] from the heart.[e] [23] You have been born anew, not of perishable but of imperishable seed, through the living and enduring word of God.[f] [24] For

"All flesh is like grass
　　and all its glory like the flower of
　　　　grass.
The grass withers,
　　and the flower falls,
[25]　but the word of the Lord endures
　　　　forever."

That word is the good news that was announced to you.

The Living Stone and a Chosen People

2 Rid yourselves, therefore, of all malice, and all guile, insincerity, envy, and all slander. [2] Like newborn infants, long for the pure, spiritual milk, so that by it you may grow into salvation— [3] if indeed you have tasted that the Lord is good.

4 Come to him, a living stone, though rejected by mortals yet chosen and precious in God's sight, and [5] like living stones, let yourselves be built[g] into a

---

[a] Other ancient authorities read *known*　[b] Gk *gird up the loins of your mind*　[c] Other ancient authorities add *through the Spirit*　[d] Or *constantly*　[e] Other ancient authorities read *a pure heart*　[f] Or *through the word of the living and enduring God*　[g] Or *you yourselves are being built*

1:13–2:3—Believers are called to a distinctly obedient and holy way of life. To be **holy** (1:15–16) is to be set apart for God's purposes, and thus to live in a way that reflects the priorities and character of God. The calling is not a solitary one, for the new life that is God's gift in Christ is life in community.

2:1–10—A number of Old Testament texts are woven together to give expression to the new communal vocation of God's people (Isa. 28:16, Ps. 118:22, Isa. 3:14). Priestly status and dignity is conferred upon all believers. All are made holy by baptism and minister before God, offering **spiritual sacrifices** (v. 5) which consist, in part, of good conduct that will bear witness before nonbelievers (see v. 12).

spiritual house, to be a holy priesthood, to offer spiritual sacrifices acceptable to God through Jesus Christ. [6] For it stands in scripture:

"See, I am laying in Zion a stone,
    a cornerstone chosen and precious;
and whoever believes in him[a] will
      not be put to shame."

[7] To you then who believe, he is precious; but for those who do not believe,

"The stone that the builders rejected
    has become the very head of the
      corner,"

[8] and

"A stone that makes them stumble,
    and a rock that makes them fall."

They stumble because they disobey the word, as they were destined to do.

[9] But you are a chosen race, a royal priesthood, a holy nation, God's own people,[b] in order that you may proclaim the mighty acts of him who called you out of darkness into his marvelous light.

[10] Once you were not a people,
    but now you are God's people;
once you had not received mercy,
    but now you have received mercy.

Live as Servants of God

[11] Beloved, I urge you as aliens and exiles to abstain from the desires of the flesh that wage war against the soul. [12] Conduct yourselves honorably among the Gentiles, so that, though they malign you as evildoers, they may see your honorable deeds and glorify God when he comes to judge.[c]

[13] For the Lord's sake accept the authority of every human institution,[d] whether of the emperor as supreme, [14] or of governors, as sent by him to punish those who do wrong and to praise those who do right. [15] For it is God's will that by doing right you should silence the ignorance of the foolish. [16] As servants[e] of God, live as free people, yet do not use your freedom as a pretext for evil. [17] Honor everyone. Love the family of believers.[f] Fear God. Honor the emperor.

The Example of Christ's Suffering

[18] Slaves, accept the authority of your masters with all deference, not only those who are kind and gentle but also those who are harsh. [19] For it is a credit to you if, being aware of God, you endure pain while suffering unjustly. [20] If you endure when you are beaten for

[a] Or it   [b] Gk a people for his possession   [c] Gk God on the day of visitation   [d] Or every institution ordained for human beings   [e] Gk slaves   [f] Gk Love the brotherhood

---

2:11–3:12 Christian Conduct within the Structures of Society

Christian conduct has evangelistic power. Thus, though believers are *aliens and exiles* (2:11), they are not advised to withdraw from society, but neither are they urged to reform it. Instead, they are to exhibit true goodness within it. They are to conduct themselves in public and domestic spheres in ways that bear witness to God.

2:11–17—Honorable conduct may draw unbelievers (*Gentiles*) to God. First Peter's neutral reference to governmental authorities may be distinguished from the positive view of Rom. 13:1–7, but also from the thoroughly negative view that appears later in the Revelation to John (see Rev. 12–18). The government is not identified as a servant of God, as in Romans. Christians are God's *servants* (2:16). They are to *honor everyone* (v. 17), including the *emperor*, and to accept governmental *authority* (vv. 13, 17), but reverent awe or *fear* is reserved for God alone (1:17; 2:17).

2:18–3:12—To articulate appropriate conduct in the domestic sphere, 1 Peter draws on a standard pattern of ethical instruction among both Jews and Greeks, commonly called a "table of household duties" or "household code" (see introduction). Christian modifications of the standard pattern can be observed, but regrettably, 1 Peter goes farther than other household codes in the New Testament in exhorting slaves to accept unjust suffering without complaint, and slave owners are nowhere addressed. It also promotes regrettable silencing of women's voices—voices that need to be heard in public profession and within the community of faith. To deflect social criticism of the church, slaves and wives bear the burden of conforming to societal expectations. The code is misappropriated by contemporary Christians when it is used to exhort passivity on the part of wives, especially those trapped within cycles of domestic violence, as it was once used to exhort passivity on the part of African American slaves.

doing wrong, what credit is that? But if you endure when you do right and suffer for it, you have God's approval. ²¹ For to this you have been called, because Christ also suffered for you, leaving you an example, so that you should follow in his steps.

²² "He committed no sin,
    and no deceit was found in his
        mouth."
²³ When he was abused, he did not return abuse; when he suffered, he did not threaten; but he entrusted himself to the one who judges justly. ²⁴ He himself bore our sins in his body on the cross,ᵃ so that, free from sins, we might live for righteousness; by his woundsᵇ you have been healed. ²⁵ For you were going astray like sheep, but now you have returned to the shepherd and guardian of your souls.

Wives and Husbands

3 Wives, in the same way, accept the authority of your husbands, so that, even if some of them do not obey the word, they may be won over without a word by their wives' conduct, ² when they see the purity and reverence of your lives. ³ Do not adorn yourselves outwardly by braiding your hair, and by wearing gold ornaments or fine clothing; ⁴ rather, let your adornment be the inner self with the lasting beauty of a gentle and quiet spirit, which is very precious in God's sight. ⁵ It was in this way long ago that the holy women who

hoped in God used to adorn themselves by accepting the authority of their husbands. ⁶ Thus Sarah obeyed Abraham and called him lord. You have become her daughters as long as you do what is good and never let fears alarm you.

7 Husbands, in the same way, show consideration for your wives in your life together, paying honor to the woman as the weaker sex,ᶜ since they too are also heirs of the gracious gift of life—so that nothing may hinder your prayers.

Suffering for Doing Right

8 Finally, all of you, have unity of spirit, sympathy, love for one another, a tender heart, and a humble mind. ⁹ Do not repay evil for evil or abuse for abuse; but, on the contrary, repay with a blessing. It is for this that you were called— that you might inherit a blessing. ¹⁰ For

"Those who desire life
    and desire to see good days,
let them keep their tongues from evil
    and their lips from speaking
        deceit;
¹¹ let them turn away from evil and do
        good;
    let them seek peace and pursue it.
¹² For the eyes of the Lord are on the
        righteous,
    and his ears are open to their
        prayer.
But the face of the Lord is against
        those who do evil."

13 Now who will harm you if you are

ᵃ Or carried up our sins in his body to the tree ᵇ Gk bruise ᶜ Gk vessel

---

3:13–5:11 Christian Conduct in the Midst of Suffering

Suffering in general is not in view—that is, suffering that comes one's way as a result of disease, accident, or natural disaster. The suffering of which 1 Peter speaks comes one's way as a direct result of Christian identity and vocation.

3:13–22—Christians are to defend their faith when challenged, actively but gently, with sensitivity and compassion, in hopes that adversaries will be brought by word and example to belief in God.

In vv. 18–22, the author sets Christian suffering in theological perspective, by connecting it with Christ's own unjust suffering and by scanning the

cosmic horizon of God's redemptive activity in him. Verse 19 is one of the most puzzling verses in the New Testament. Some take it as a reference to a descent by Christ into hell during the period between his death and resurrection, along the lines of the Apostles' Creed. Others envision an ascending Christ, who preaches to demonic spirits as he passes through the heavens on his way to exaltation (after the manner of Enoch; see *1 En.* 6–11, 12–21). Though the literary allusion is lost to us, the image undoubtedly points to the cosmic and universal extent of Christ's redemptive activity. To such an extent does grace abound!

eager to do what is good? **14** But even if you do suffer for doing what is right, you are blessed. Do not fear what they fear,*a* and do not be intimidated, **15** but in your hearts sanctify Christ as Lord. Always be ready to make your defense to anyone who demands from you an accounting for the hope that is in you; **16** yet do it with gentleness and reverence.*b* Keep your conscience clear, so that, when you are maligned, those who abuse you for your good conduct in Christ may be put to shame. **17** For it is better to suffer for doing good, if suffering should be God's will, than to suffer for doing evil. **18** For Christ also suffered*c* for sins once for all, the righteous for the unrighteous, in order to bring you*d* to God. He was put to death in the flesh, but made alive in the spirit, **19** in which also he went and made a proclamation to the spirits in prison, **20** who in former times did not obey, when God waited patiently in the days of Noah, during the building of the ark, in which a few, that is, eight persons, were saved through water. **21** And baptism, which this prefigured, now saves you—not as a removal of dirt from the body, but as an appeal to God for*e* a good conscience, through the resurrection of Jesus Christ, **22** who has gone into heaven and is at the right hand of God, with angels, authorities, and powers made subject to him.

Good Stewards of God's Grace

4 Since therefore Christ suffered in the flesh,*f* arm yourselves also with the same intention (for whoever has suffered in the flesh has finished with sin), **2** so as to live for the rest of your earthly life*g* no longer by human desires but by the will of God. **3** You have already spent enough time in doing what the Gentiles like to do, living in licentiousness, passions, drunkenness, revels, carousing, and lawless idolatry. **4** They are surprised that you no longer join them in the same excesses of dissipation, and so they blaspheme.*h* **5** But they will have to give an accounting to him who stands ready to judge the living and the dead. **6** For this is the reason the gospel was proclaimed even to the dead, so that, though they had been judged in the flesh as everyone is judged, they might live in the spirit as God does.

7 The end of all things is near;*i* therefore be serious and discipline yourselves for the sake of your prayers. **8** Above all, maintain constant love for one another, for love covers a multitude of sins. **9** Be hospitable to one another without complaining. **10** Like good stewards of the manifold grace of God, serve one another with whatever gift each of you has received. **11** Whoever speaks must do so as one speaking the very words of God; whoever serves must do so with the strength that God supplies, so that God may be glorified in all things through Jesus Christ. To him belong the glory and the power forever and ever. Amen.

Suffering as a Christian

12 Beloved, do not be surprised at the fiery ordeal that is taking place among you to test you, as though something strange were happening to you. **13** But rejoice insofar as you are sharing Christ's sufferings, so that you may also be glad and shout for joy when his glory is revealed. **14** If you are reviled for the name of Christ, you are blessed, because the spirit of glory,*j* which is the Spirit of God, is resting on you.*k* **15** But let none

a Gk their fear   *b* Or respect   *c* Other ancient authorities read died   *d* Other ancient authorities read us   *e* Or a pledge to God from   *f* Other ancient authorities add for us; others, for you   *g* Gk rest of the time in the flesh   *h* Or they malign you   *i* Or is at hand   *j* Other ancient authorities add and of power   *k* Other ancient authorities add On their part he is blasphemed, but on your part he is glorified

---

4:1–19—This section provides our clearest picture of the historical situation to which the letter responds. It describes conduct in accordance with *the will of God* (v. 2), detailing what new life in Christ means for patterns of behavior among former friends and within their culture (vv. 1–6) and also within the new Christian fellowship (vv. 7–11).

of you suffer as a murderer, a thief, a criminal, or even as a mischief maker. [16] Yet if any of you suffers as a Christian, do not consider it a disgrace, but glorify God because you bear this name. [17] For the time has come for judgment to begin with the household of God; if it begins with us, what will be the end for those who do not obey the gospel of God? [18] And

> "If it is hard for the righteous to be saved,
>   what will become of the ungodly
>   and the sinners?"

[19] Therefore, let those suffering in accordance with God's will entrust themselves to a faithful Creator, while continuing to do good.

Tending the Flock of God

5 Now as an elder myself and a witness of the sufferings of Christ, as well as one who shares in the glory to be revealed, I exhort the elders among you [2] to tend the flock of God that is in your charge, exercising the oversight,[a] not under compulsion but willingly, as God would have you do it[b]—not for sordid gain but eagerly. [3] Do not lord it over those in your charge, but be examples to the flock. [4] And when the chief shepherd appears, you will win the crown of glory that never fades away. [5] In the same way, you who are younger must accept the authority of the elders.[c] And all of you must clothe yourselves with humility in your dealings with one another, for

> "God opposes the proud,
>   but gives grace to the humble."

[6] Humble yourselves therefore under the mighty hand of God, so that he may exalt you in due time. [7] Cast all your anxiety on him, because he cares for you. [8] Discipline yourselves, keep alert.[d] Like a roaring lion your adversary the devil prowls around, looking for someone to devour. [9] Resist him, steadfast in your faith, for you know that your brothers and sisters[e] in all the world are undergoing the same kinds of suffering. [10] And after you have suffered for a little while, the God of all grace, who has called you to his eternal glory in Christ, will himself restore, support, strengthen, and establish you. [11] To him be the power forever and ever. Amen.

Final Greetings and Benediction

[12] Through Silvanus, whom I consider a faithful brother, I have written this short letter to encourage you and to testify that this is the true grace of God. Stand fast in it. [13] Your sister church[f] in Babylon, chosen together with you, sends you greetings; and so does my son Mark. [14] Greet one another with a kiss of love.

Peace to all of you who are in Christ.[g]

[a] Other ancient authorities lack *exercising the oversight*   [b] Other ancient authorities lack *as God would have you do it*   [c] Or *of those who are older*   [d] Or *be vigilant*   [e] Gk *your brotherhood*   [f] Gk *She who is*   [g] Other ancient authorities add *Amen*

5:12–14 Final Exhortation and Greetings
The final exhortation captures the purpose of the whole letter: to encourage believers to **stand fast** in the **true grace of God**. The letter to suffering Christians concludes, most appropriately, with a wish for **peace**.

The Book of
2 PETER

Possibly the latest writing in the New Testament, the Second Letter of Peter provides a window onto a critical transition in the early church from the apostolic to the postapostolic age. Moreover, it is multicultural in approach, adapting the Christian faith, with its Jewish apocalyptic origins, to the language and culture of the Hellenistic world. It thus provides important food for thought for subsequent Christian generations, which also face the task of adapting and interpreting the Christian faith with integrity in new times and places. It also emphasizes the integral connection between theology and morality—between what we believe and how we live. For all of these reasons, this much-neglected letter repays careful study.

Second Peter is presented as the apostle Peter's "farewell speech" or dying "testament" in the form of a letter. In keeping with the testamentary genre, it both "predicts" and "reminds": it anticipates future difficulties the community will face and provides an authoritative, final summary of Peter's religious and ethical teaching (1:3–11, 12–15; 2:1–3a; 3:1–4). Though attributed to the apostle Peter (1:1, 14, 16–18), most scholars believe that it was written in Peter's name after his death (64–67 CE) in order to defend the apostolic tradition against false teaching.

Several things point to origin in the second Christian generation, rather than the first. For one thing, the "fathers" or "ancestors" have died, and believers are contending with disappointment and doubt about the second coming of Christ in glory, which had been anticipated during the lifetime of the first Christian generation (3:3–4). For another thing, a collection of Pauline letters is in circulation (3:15–16). In fact, an unusual feature of 2 Peter is its explicit reference to other normative writings. In addition to Paul's letters, a "first" letter of Peter is noted (3:1) along with the tradition of Jesus' transfiguration recorded in the Synoptic Gospels (1:16–18). Moreover, a close relationship with the letter of Jude has long been recognized. Most scholars believe that 2 Peter is dependent upon it, adapting nineteen of Jude's twenty-five verses in the service of its own argument (in 2:1–18 and 3:1–3). Finally, 2 Peter is decidedly Hellenistic in hue, sophisticated (even grandiose) in vocabulary and style, written by someone well versed in the conventions of Greco-Roman rhetoric. All of these factors point to a second-generation Christian author, a highly literate custodian of treasured materials and traditions, who embraces and integrates Jewish-Christian and Greco-Roman worlds of thought. He cloaks himself in the mantle of Peter's authority in an effort to defend and mediate the Petrine tradition in a new day.

We do not know where the letter was written, though Rome, where Peter was martyred and revered, is a possibility. Its destination and recipients are not identified (1:1), but a specific community and urgent crisis are clearly addressed. While the apostle Peter is presented as predicting the future emergence of false teachers, no doubt they are already on the scene, disrupting the life and faith of the community addressed, for future-tense predictions are juxtaposed to present-tense polemics against them. Indeed, 2 Peter is largely polemical and argumentative in tone. It aims

primarily to refute the false teachers and to stabilize the faithful by reminding them of the need to hold fast to foundational beliefs.

Interestingly, the false teachers appear to be insiders rather than outsiders or interlopers. They are members of the community who probably thought of themselves as interpreters of the Christian tradition for the non-Jewish world rather than opponents or corrupters of it. The author of 2 Peter also believes that the gospel needs to be interpreted and adapted for new audiences, for he combines Jewish-Christian and Greco-Roman traditions in his own cross-cultural presentation of the Christian faith. However, the false teachers have lost a great deal in translation, compromising fundamental Christian beliefs.

In terms of eschatology (doctrine of the end times), the false teachers have relieved themselves of what they viewed as an embarrassing, archaic doctrine: the second coming of God in Christ in judgment and cosmic renewal (1:16; 3:3–7). The delay of the Parousia or second coming probably steered them in this direction. But they may also have been influenced by popularized forms of Epicureanism, a rationalistic philosophy in vogue that emphasized the complete transcendence of the deity, denying any dramatic intervention of God in the world, past, present, or future.

In terms of ethics, therefore, the false teachers promised "freedom" from any supposed threat of divine retribution or final judgment (2:19), thereby relieving themselves also of the ethical rigor that characterized the apostolic tradition. Eschatological skepticism was thus accompanied by moral libertinism. By means of these innovations, the false teachers no doubt sought to translate and adapt the gospel for new audiences—to rid it of archaic Jewish-Christian notions and render it tenable in the larger, more permissive Greco-Roman world. In the author's view, however, these innovations had gone too far, compromising foundational beliefs and eroding the community's ethical mores. Furthermore, they had undermined the community's confidence, cohesion, and public witness (2:2).

Given the nature of the crisis addressed, 2 Peter places far more emphasis on the sovereignty and providence of God than on the person and work of Jesus Christ, for false teaching called into question the presence and participation of God in human history. Second Peter affirms that the world is in fact in the hands of the living God, who created it, who continues to sustain it and shape it in accordance with the divine will, and who will ultimately judge it and transform it, establishing "new heavens and a new earth, where righteousness is at home" (3:13). The one event in Jesus' life that plays a role in this argument is his transfiguration, which foreshadowed the Parousia and proved that Jesus possesses divine glory and will one day exercise God's universal rule (1:16–18).

Second Peter also emphasizes that theology and ethics are integrally related—that what we believe shapes how we live. Thus, if we believe that the world is dependent upon God, the very source of all reality, then we live in accordance with that reality. This might suggest, for example, that the abundant material resources with which a gracious Creator has blessed the creation are not to be amassed and hoarded, by individuals or nations, but they are to be available to all of God's people to nourish and sustain the fullness of life that is God's will for all. In fact, 2 Peter describes the Christian life as participation in the very nature of God (1:3–4), for by the grace of God the righteous are called and empowered to share in God's glory. Moreover, if we believe that on a day of final judgment we will be held accountable for our deeds, we

conduct our lives in the interim with ethical integrity, "leading lives of holiness and godliness" (3:11).

Because eschatology and ethical motivation are so clearly connected, 2 Peter offers the most sustained defense in the New Testament of the second coming of the Lord (3:1–13). Second Peter vigorously reasserts that, though delayed, it will surely come, as promised by prophets and apostles and the Lord himself, and anticipates its imminent arrival. The delay is attributed to the generous patience of God, who does not want "any to perish, but all to come to repentance" (3:9).

In sum, 2 Peter affirms that the second coming of God in Christ, both in judgment and cosmic renewal, is a sure promise foundational to Christian life and faith in every age. Indeed, that future horizon shapes discipleship in the present as we strive to be now what we hope to be then, attending individually and corporately to the "sort of persons" we ought to be (3:11).

—**Frances Taylor Gench**

Salutation

1 Simeon[a] Peter, a servant[b] and apostle of Jesus Christ,

To those who have received a faith as precious as ours through the righteousness of our God and Savior Jesus Christ:[c]

2 May grace and peace be yours in abundance in the knowledge of God and of Jesus our Lord.

The Christian's Call and Election

3 His divine power has given us everything needed for life and godliness, through the knowledge of him who called us by[d] his own glory and goodness. [4] Thus he has given us, through these things, his precious and very great promises, so that through them you may escape from the corruption that is in the world because of lust, and may become participants of the divine nature. [5] For this very reason, you must make every effort to support your faith with goodness, and goodness with knowledge, [6] and knowledge with self-control, and self-control with endurance, and endurance with godliness, [7] and godliness with mutual[e] affection, and mutual[e] affection with love. [8] For if these things are yours and are increasing among you, they keep you from being ineffective and unfruitful in the knowledge of our Lord Jesus Christ. [9] For anyone who lacks these things is short-sighted and blind, and is forgetful of the cleansing of past sins. [10] Therefore, brothers and sisters,[f] be all the more eager to confirm your call and election, for if you do this, you will never stumble. [11] For in this

[a] Other ancient authorities read *Simon*   [b] Gk *slave*   [c] Or *of our God and the Savior Jesus Christ*   [d] Other ancient authorities read *through*
[e] Gk *brotherly*   [f] Gk *brothers*

1:1–2 Salutation

Faith is a gift of God bestowed equally on all believers. There are no second-class Christians; all have *received a faith as precious* as that of the apostles themselves. The knowledge of God and Jesus Christ is not merely intellectual in nature, but entails life-transforming power.

1:3–11 A Summary of Peter's Teaching

Second Peter places extraordinary emphasis on the importance of moral endeavor and growth in grace, but divine gifts equip and empower believers for the Christian life (vv. 3–4). We then *make every effort* to respond to God's initiative and grace with lives of moral integrity, marked by the quality of God's own holiness. This effort confirms our *call and election* and guarantees entrance into God's *eternal kingdom* (vv. 5–11).

A notable feature of this summary is the use of Greco-Roman concepts to convey the gospel message (e.g., the ideal of *godliness* [v. 7], and the notion of escaping the corruption [v. 4] of the world and sharing in the divine nature [v. 4]). But this terminology is employed within a decidedly Christian frame of reference. Contemporary Christians must also engage the task of interpreting the gospel message in ways that connect with ideals and aspirations in their own cultural context, and yet also honor the foundational beliefs that have oriented Christian life through the ages.

way, entry into the eternal kingdom of our Lord and Savior Jesus Christ will be richly provided for you.

12 Therefore I intend to keep on reminding you of these things, though you know them already and are established in the truth that has come to you. [13] I think it right, as long as I am in this body,[a] to refresh your memory, [14] since I know that my death[b] will come soon, as indeed our Lord Jesus Christ has made clear to me. [15] And I will make every effort so that after my departure you may be able at any time to recall these things.

Eyewitnesses of Christ's Glory

16 For we did not follow cleverly devised myths when we made known to you the power and coming of our Lord Jesus Christ, but we had been eyewitnesses of his majesty. [17] For he received honor and glory from God the Father when that voice was conveyed to him by the Majestic Glory, saying, "This is my Son, my Beloved,[c] with whom I am well pleased." [18] We ourselves heard this voice come from heaven, while we were with him on the holy mountain.

19 So we have the prophetic message more fully confirmed. You will do well to be attentive to this as to a lamp shining in a dark place, until the day dawns and the morning star rises in your hearts. [20] First of all you must understand this, that no prophecy of scripture is a matter of one's own interpretation, [21] because no prophecy ever came by human will, but men and women moved by the Holy Spirit spoke from God. [d]

False Prophets and Their Punishment

2 But false prophets also arose among the people, just as there will be false teachers among you, who will secretly bring in destructive opinions. They will even deny the Master who bought them—bringing swift destruction on themselves. [2] Even so, many will follow their licentious ways, and because of these teachers[e] the way of truth will be maligned. [3] And in their greed they will exploit you with deceptive words. Their condemnation, pronounced against them long ago, has not been idle, and their destruction is not asleep.

[a] Gk tent [b] Gk the putting off of my tent [c] Other ancient authorities read my beloved Son [d] Other ancient authorities read but moved by the Holy Spirit saints of God spoke [e] Gk because of them

---

1:12–15 Peter's Testament
The letter is presented as Peter's dying testament and thus as a trustworthy, abiding witness to the apostolic foundations of Christian faith. Every Christian generation must ensure that succeeding generations have had the opportunity to hear and understand the fundamentals of Christian faith, that they too may be *established* (v. 12) and "stabilized" in their practice of the Christian life (3:16–17). Christian education is thus of utmost importance, as is responsible preaching.

1:16–21 Confirmation of the Truth of Christ's Second Coming
The chief doctrine defended in the letter is that of the second coming of Christ in power, glory, and judgment. Both apostolic (vv. 16–18) and prophetic (vv. 19–21) testimony confirm the truth of this future reality.

2:1–22 Tirade against False Teachers
Ironically, though the false teachers consider divine judgment a "myth," they will be subject to it for their destructive teaching and behavior.
Key affirmations about the life of discipleship

emerge in the midst of the tirade: (1) Discipleship is a life of obedience and service to our *Master*, Jesus Christ, who purchased our freedom from sin (v. 1). One responds with a life of gratitude and loyalty that honors the Master, rather than shames him. (2) Human beings are not autonomous; they are always subject to some master. (3) What we believe effects how we live. Thus deviant teaching goes hand in hand with deviant conduct. Christian faith entails a Christian lifestyle (vv. 2, 21) that involves living in accordance with God's will and commandment. (4) Christian conduct is an important part of public witness, for deviant conduct can bring disrepute upon the gospel and dissuade others from coming to the knowledge of God in Christ (v. 2). (5) How human beings live is a matter of utmost importance, and all will be held accountable for their deeds before the living God.

One may question the bombastic, insulting manner in which the author of 2 Peter writes. Can more gracious, constructive ways be found to confront false teachings and lifestyles in our day?

4 For if God did not spare the angels when they sinned, but cast them into hell[a] and committed them to chains[b] of deepest darkness to be kept until the judgment; 5 and if he did not spare the ancient world, even though he saved Noah, a herald of righteousness, with seven others, when he brought a flood on a world of the ungodly; 6 and if by turning the cities of Sodom and Gomorrah to ashes he condemned them to extinction[c] and made them an example of what is coming to the ungodly;[d] 7 and if he rescued Lot, a righteous man greatly distressed by the licentiousness of the lawless 8 (for that righteous man, living among them day after day, was tormented in his righteous soul by their lawless deeds that he saw and heard), 9 then the Lord knows how to rescue the godly from trial, and to keep the unrighteous under punishment until the day of judgment 10—especially those who indulge their flesh in depraved lust, and who despise authority.

Bold and willful, they are not afraid to slander the glorious ones,[e] 11 whereas angels, though greater in might and power, do not bring against them a slanderous judgment from the Lord.[f] 12 These people, however, are like irrational animals, mere creatures of instinct, born to be caught and killed. They slander what they do not understand, and when those creatures are destroyed,[g] they also will be destroyed, 13 suffering[h] the penalty for doing wrong. They count it a pleasure to revel in the daytime. They are blots and blemishes, reveling in their dissipation[i] while they feast with you. 14 They have eyes full of adultery, insatiable for sin. They entice unsteady souls. They have hearts trained in greed. Accursed children! 15 They have left the straight road and have gone astray, following the road of Balaam son of Bosor,[j] who loved the wages of doing wrong, 16 but was rebuked for his own transgression; a speechless donkey spoke with a human voice and restrained the prophet's madness.

17 These are waterless springs and mists driven by a storm; for them the deepest darkness has been reserved. 18 For they speak bombastic nonsense, and with licentious desires of the flesh they entice people who have just[k] escaped from those who live in error. 19 They promise them freedom, but they themselves are slaves of corruption; for people are slaves to whatever masters them. 20 For if, after they have escaped the defilements of the world through the knowledge of our Lord and Savior Jesus Christ, they are again entangled in them and overpowered, the last state has become worse for them than the first. 21 For it would have been better for them never to have known the way of righteousness than, after knowing it, to turn back from the holy commandment that was passed on to them. 22 It has happened to them according to the true proverb,

"The dog turns back to its own
    vomit,"

and,

"The sow is washed only to wallow
    in the mud."

The Promise of the Lord's Coming

3 This is now, beloved, the second letter I am writing to you; in them I am trying to arouse your sincere in-

[a] Gk *Tartaros*   [b] Other ancient authorities read *pits*   [c] Other ancient authorities lack *to extinction*   [d] Other ancient authorities read *an example to those who were to be ungodly*   [e] Or *angels*; Gk *glories*   [f] Other ancient authorities read *before the Lord*; others lack the phrase   [g] Gk *in their destruction*   [h] Other ancient authorities read *receiving*   [i] Other ancient authorities read *love-feasts*   [j] Other ancient authorities read *Beor*   [k] Other ancient authorities read *actually*

3:1–13 The Promise of the Lord's Coming
The Parousia, though delayed, will most assuredly come. However, finite humans cannot presume to calculate the time of the second coming; human lives are too brief to comprehend the plans of the infinite God. Moreover, the delay of the second coming is attributed to divine intentionality—to the merciful patience of God, who wants no one *to perish, but all to come to repentance* (v. 9).

Those who anticipate life in Christ's eternal kingdom, where *righteousness* will be *at*

tention by reminding you ²that you should remember the words spoken in the past by the holy prophets, and the commandment of the Lord and Savior spoken through your apostles. ³First of all you must understand this, that in the last days scoffers will come, scoffing and indulging their own lusts ⁴and saying, "Where is the promise of his coming? For ever since our ancestors died,ᵃ all things continue as they were from the beginning of creation!" ⁵They deliberately ignore this fact, that by the word of God heavens existed long ago and an earth was formed out of water and by means of water, ⁶through which the world of that time was deluged with water and perished. ⁷But by the same word the present heavens and earth have been reserved for fire, being kept until the day of judgment and destruction of the godless.

8 But do not ignore this one fact, beloved, that with the Lord one day is like a thousand years, and a thousand years are like one day. ⁹The Lord is not slow about his promise, as some think of slowness, but is patient with you,ᵇ not wanting any to perish, but all to come to repentance. ¹⁰But the day of the Lord will come like a thief, and then the heavens will pass away with a loud noise, and the elements will be dissolved with fire, and the earth and everything that is done on it will be disclosed.ᶜ

11 Since all these things are to be dissolved in this way, what sort of persons ought you to be in leading lives of holiness and godliness, ¹²waiting for and hasteningᵈ the coming of the day of God, because of which the heavens will be set ablaze and dissolved, and the elements will melt with fire? ¹³But, in accordance with his promise, we wait for new heavens and a new earth, where righteousness is at home.

Final Exhortation and Doxology

14 Therefore, beloved, while you are waiting for these things, strive to be found by him at peace, without spot or blemish; ¹⁵and regard the patience of our Lord as salvation. So also our beloved brother Paul wrote to you according to the wisdom given him, ¹⁶speaking of this as he does in all his letters. There are some things in them hard to understand, which the ignorant and unstable twist to their own destruction, as they do the other scriptures. ¹⁷You therefore, beloved, since you are forewarned, beware that you are not carried away with the error of the lawless and lose your own stability. ¹⁸But grow in the grace and knowledge of our Lord and Savior Jesus Christ. To him be the glory both now and to the day of eternity. Amen.ᵉ

ᵃ Gk our fathers fell asleep ᵇ Other ancient authorities read on your account ᶜ Other ancient authorities read will be burned up ᵈ Or earnestly desiring ᵉ Other ancient authorities lack Amen

---

home (v. 13), must live in ways that reflect that righteousness in the present. For 2 Peter at least, the second coming is the primary motivation for Christian living.

3:14–18 Final Exhortation to Stability
Waiting for the final coming of the Lord is by no means a passive endeavor. It entails active striving (v. 14) to embody the righteousness of the eternal kingdom and growth (v. 18) in the grace and knowledge of . . . Jesus Christ. This striving and growth safeguards stability (v. 17) in the faith, rendering believers immune to the destructive influence of false, unstable teachers (v. 16). False teachers can twist the Scriptures to suit their purposes. However, interpreting Scripture by Scripture, taking the whole canonical witness into account, can provide a corrective perspective when we are faced with unfaithful biblical interpretation.

The Book of
1 JOHN

Faithful discipleship is under pressure in this letter. Written a decade or so after John's Gospel, there has been, sadly, a schism within the community over christological and ethical issues (2:18–19). As far as the writer is concerned, those who have left denied that Jesus was God's commissioned agent or Son, the Messiah, and that he was a human being (2:22–23; 4:2–3). They did not love (2:9–11) and claimed to be sinless (1:6–10). The letter explains the separation of the groups and affirms the faithfulness of those who remain. The separation shows, so the letter explains, that some never truly belonged to the community (2:19), to God (2:4), or to the faith (4:6). Separation reveals that they really belong to the world, that which is opposed to God and the believing community (3:1; 4:4–6). They are "antichrists" (2:18) belonging to the devil (3:8). The schism shows that the "last days" are here (2:18–19).

The letter affirms the community's identity as faithful to the teaching they have heard "from the beginning" (1:1–4). Disciples are God's beloved children or covenant people ("little children," 2:1; 3:2). They belong to God and Jesus (2:20–25; 3:19–21; 5:19), who protect (2:26–27; 5:18) and empower them (2:14; 4:4–6). It exhorts them as disciples to confess, not deny, their sin (1:6–10), to obey the commandments (2:3–6), to love one another (2:8–10; 3:11–18, 23; 4:7–12;), to do right (3:4–10), to maintain the confession of Jesus as God's Christ or anointed agent (3:23–4:2; 5:1–12, 19–21), to test other teachings (4:1–6), to resist the "world" (4:4; 5:4–5), to pray (5:14–17). They will have no fear in the judgment (2:28; 4:13–18) and are assured of eternal life (5:13, 20).

The place of the letter's writing is uncertain, as is the identity of its author(s). The date is likely to be a decade or so after John's Gospel (the problem is now an internal schism), perhaps around 100 CE.

The letter articulates important matters for disciples of all times. It underlines central affirmations and practices for faithful discipleship. It shows the importance of working to maintain the unity of the Christian community. It also raises the troubling issue of how to handle disagreements. Are there limits to diversity? Are there litmus tests for Christian identity? In what circumstances is separation the best solution?

—Warren Carter

The Word of Life

1 We declare to you what was from the beginning, what we have heard, what we have seen with our eyes, what we have looked at and touched with our hands, concerning the word of life— ² this life was revealed, and we have seen it and testify to it, and declare to you the eternal life that was with the Father and was revealed to us— ³ we declare to you what we have seen and heard so that you also may have fellowship with us; and truly our fellowship is with the Father and with his Son Jesus Christ. ⁴ We are writing these things so that our*ᵃ* joy may be complete.

God Is Light

5 This is the message we have heard from him and proclaim to you, that God is light and in him there is no darkness at all. ⁶ If we say that we have fellowship with him while we are walking in darkness, we lie and do not do what is true; ⁷ but if we walk in the light as he himself is in the light, we have fellowship with one another, and the blood of Jesus his Son cleanses us from all sin. ⁸ If we say that we have no sin, we deceive ourselves, and the truth is not in us. ⁹ If we

confess our sins, he who is faithful and just will forgive us our sins and cleanse us from all unrighteousness. ¹⁰ If we say that we have not sinned, we make him a liar, and his word is not in us.

Christ Our Advocate

2 My little children, I am writing these things to you so that you may not sin. But if anyone does sin, we have an advocate with the Father, Jesus Christ the righteous; ² and he is the atoning sacrifice for our sins, and not for ours only but also for the sins of the whole world.

3 Now by this we may be sure that we know him, if we obey his commandments. ⁴ Whoever says, "I have come to know him," but does not obey his commandments, is a liar, and in such a person the truth does not exist; ⁵ but whoever obeys his word, truly in this person the love of God has reached perfection. By this we may be sure that we are in him: ⁶ whoever says, "I abide in him," ought to walk just as he walked.

A New Commandment

7 Beloved, I am writing you no new commandment, but an old commandment that you have had from the

ᵃ Other ancient authorities read your

1:1–4—This opening prologue echoes language and themes from the prologue of John's Gospel (John 1:1–18). It emphasizes a tradition of teaching personally witnessed to (hearing, seeing, touching) and proclaimed by the community's teachers (*we*). This tradition concerns *the word of life*, namely Jesus, who reveals eternal life, encounter or relationship with God the Father (John 17:3) and with Jesus as God's commissioned one (*Christ*) and agent (*Son*, 1 John 5:20). Disciples are grounded in this confession, experience, and community.

1:5–2:11—This section, introduced and closed by references to *light*, elaborates the revelation of God in Jesus the light (John 8:12; 9:5), an image of salvation (Ps. 27:1; Isa. 9:1–4). But salvation is not just about relationship with God; it creates an ethical way of life that manifests God's saving presence (1 John 1:6–7a). To *walk* denotes lives faithful to God's will (Deut. 30:15–16) lived in loving fellowship with other believers (1 John 1:7b). Salvation also involves truthfully confessing sin and receiving forgiveness through Jesus'

death (*blood*) from a *faithful and just* God (1:7c–10). The phrase *If we say* (1:6, 8, 10) suggests the opponents were making these misleading claims expressed in each verse. Discipleship demands a unity of confession in words and deeds, and active commitment to a community of believers.

2:1–2—Forgiveness occurs through Jesus, the *atoning sacrifice*. John's Gospel presents Jesus' death more in terms of a revelation of God's life-giving purposes. John's tradition encompasses diverse images of Jesus' death. This diversity warns contemporary disciples against thinking there is only one "orthodox" understanding, and celebrates the richness of God's act in Jesus.

2:3–6—Obedience to God's will revealed and lived by Jesus marks faithful discipleship. *Whoever says* in vv. 4, 6, 9 suggests the correction of further false teaching and practices.

2:7–11—Love for other believers, as difficult and demanding as this can be, manifests God's light or salvation.

beginning; the old commandment is the word that you have heard. **8** Yet I am writing you a new commandment that is true in him and in you, because*a* the darkness is passing away and the true light is already shining. **9** Whoever says, "I am in the light," while hating a brother or sister,*b* is still in the darkness. **10** Whoever loves a brother or sister*c* lives in the light, and in such a person*d* there is no cause for stumbling. **11** But whoever hates another believer*e* is in the darkness, walks in the darkness, and does not know the way to go, because the darkness has brought on blindness.

12   I am writing to you, little children,
          because your sins are forgiven on
               account of his name.
13   I am writing to you, fathers,
          because you know him who is
               from the beginning.
     I am writing to you, young people,
          because you have conquered the
               evil one.
14   I write to you, children,
          because you know the Father.
     I write to you, fathers,
          because you know him who is
               from the beginning.
     I write to you, young people,
          because you are strong
          and the word of God abides
               in you,
               and you have overcome the
               evil one.
     15 Do not love the world or the things

in the world. The love of the Father is not in those who love the world; **16** for all that is in the world—the desire of the flesh, the desire of the eyes, the pride in riches—comes not from the Father but from the world. **17** And the world and its desire*f* are passing away, but those who do the will of God live forever.

Warning against Antichrists

18 Children, it is the last hour! As you have heard that antichrist is coming, so now many antichrists have come. From this we know that it is the last hour. **19** They went out from us, but they did not belong to us; for if they had belonged to us, they would have remained with us. But by going out they made it plain that none of them belongs to us. **20** But you have been anointed by the Holy One, and all of you have knowledge.*g* **21** I write to you, not because you do not know the truth, but because you know it, and you know that no lie comes from the truth. **22** Who is the liar but the one who denies that Jesus is the Christ?*h* This is the antichrist, the one who denies the Father and the Son. **23** No one who denies the Son has the Father; everyone who confesses the Son has the Father also. **24** Let what you heard from the beginning abide in you. If what you heard from the beginning abides in you, then you will abide in the Son and in the Father.

a Or that   *b* Gk hating a brother   *c* Gk loves a brother   *d* Or in it   *e* Gk hates a brother   *f* Or the desire for it   *g* Other ancient authorities read you know all things   *h* Or the Messiah

---

2:12–14—The author addresses the community (*children*) and perhaps groups within it (*fathers, young people*), affirming their faithful discipleship in the difficult context of division and confusion over basic beliefs and ethical requirements.

2:15–17—Disciples are distinguished from the world that has not received or entrusted itself to God's loving and life-giving purposes. Its commitments and aspirations (e.g., wealth, power) are opposed to God's will. The world is under judgment (*passing away*). Such a distinction can entice disciples to view themselves as superior, to consider "the rest" with disdain, and to disengage from actively manifesting God's love to such a world. But such a perspective and passivity would comprise false, not true, discipleship.

2:18–29—Christology was central to the split in the community. Some denied Jesus as God's anointed one (*Christ*, v. 22) in intimate relationship with God. They departed from the community (v. 19) and from relationship with God (v. 23). The enemy, the *antichrist* expected at the end of the age, is at work in them (vv. 18, 22). The community is exhorted to abide (John 15:1–11) in what they have been taught (1 John 2:26–27) so that they will not be condemned in the judgment at Jesus' return (vv. 28–29). Continuing doctrinal divisions among disciples require both a respectful recognition of legitimate diversity within the Christian tradition and continued efforts at genuine understanding and reconciliation.

25 And this is what he has promised us,[a] eternal life.

26 I write these things to you concerning those who would deceive you. 27 As for you, the anointing that you received from him abides in you, and so you do not need anyone to teach you. But as his anointing teaches you about all things, and is true and is not a lie, and just as it has taught you, abide in him.[b]

28 And now, little children, abide in him, so that when he is revealed we may have confidence and not be put to shame before him at his coming.

Children of God

29 If you know that he is righteous, you may be sure that everyone who does right has been born of him. 1 See what love the Father has given us, that we should be called children of God; and that is what we are. The reason the world does not know us is that it did not know him. 2 Beloved, we are God's children now; what we will be has not yet been revealed. What we do know is this: when he[b] is revealed, we will be like him, for we will see him as he is. 3 And all who have this hope in him purify themselves, just as he is pure.

4 Everyone who commits sin is guilty of lawlessness; sin is lawlessness. 5 You know that he was revealed to take away sins, and in him there is no sin. 6 No one who abides in him sins; no one who sins has either seen him or known him. 7 Little children, let no one deceive you. Everyone who does what is right is righteous, just as he is righteous. 8 Everyone who commits sin is a child of the devil; for the devil has been sinning from

the beginning. The Son of God was revealed for this purpose, to destroy the works of the devil. 9 Those who have been born of God do not sin, because God's seed abides in them;[c] they cannot sin, because they have been born of God. 10 The children of God and the children of the devil are revealed in this way: all who do not do what is right are not from God, nor are those who do not love their brothers and sisters.[d]

Love One Another

11 For this is the message you have heard from the beginning, that we should love one another. 12 We must not be like Cain who was from the evil one and murdered his brother. And why did he murder him? Because his own deeds were evil and his brother's righteous. 13 Do not be astonished, brothers and sisters,[e] that the world hates you. 14 We know that we have passed from death to life because we love one another. Whoever does not love abides in death. 15 All who hate a brother or sister[d] are murderers, and you know that murderers do not have eternal life abiding in them. 16 We know love by this, that he laid down his life for us—and we ought to lay down our lives for one another. 17 How does God's love abide in anyone who has the world's goods and sees a brother or sister[f] in need and yet refuses help?

18 Little children, let us love, not in word or speech, but in truth and action. 19 And by this we will know that we are from the truth and will reassure our

---

a Other ancient authorities read you b Or it c Or because the children of God abide in him d Gk his brother e Gk brothers f Gk brother

---

3:1–10—Believers are God's children, **born** of God (2:29; John 3:3–5), loved by God but rejected by the world (1 John 3:1). Jesus' return will complete their transformation into his likeness (v. 3). In the meantime they should imitate him, doing God's will and not sinning.

3:11–18—Children of God *love one another* (v. 11), unlike children of the devil (v. 10), who hate and destroy like Cain (Gen. 4:1–16). The experience of God's salvation is confirmed by

the world's hatred (1 John 3:13) but evidenced in love for other believers (vv. 14–18). Love imitates Jesus' self-giving for the other's good, including ensuring access to necessary economic resources. Love is not sentimental or inactive, but like God's love experienced in Jesus, it is freely and actively manifested among all people in self-giving actions.

3:19–24—A lifestyle of obedient, practical, relational, mutual love provides assurance to

hearts before him ²⁰ whenever our hearts condemn us; for God is greater than our hearts, and he knows everything. ²¹ Beloved, if our hearts do not condemn us, we have boldness before God; ²² and we receive from him whatever we ask, because we obey his commandments and do what pleases him.

23 And this is his commandment, that we should believe in the name of his Son Jesus Christ and love one another, just as he has commanded us. ²⁴ All who obey his commandments abide in him, and he abides in them. And by this we know that he abides in us, by the Spirit that he has given us.

Testing the Spirits

4 Beloved, do not believe every spirit, but test the spirits to see whether they are from God; for many false prophets have gone out into the world. ² By this you know the Spirit of God: every spirit that confesses that Jesus Christ has come in the flesh is from God, ³ and every spirit that does not confess Jesus*ᵃ* is not from God. And this is the spirit of the antichrist, of which you have heard that it is coming; and now it is already in the world. ⁴ Little children, you are from God, and have conquered them; for the one who is in you is greater than the one who is in the world. ⁵ They are from the world; therefore what they say is from the world, and the world listens

to them. ⁶ We are from God. Whoever knows God listens to us, and whoever is not from God does not listen to us. From this we know the spirit of truth and the spirit of error.

God Is Love

7 Beloved, let us love one another, because love is from God; everyone who loves is born of God and knows God. ⁸ Whoever does not love does not know God, for God is love. ⁹ God's love was revealed among us in this way: God sent his only Son into the world so that we might live through him. ¹⁰ In this is love, not that we loved God but that he loved us and sent his Son to be the atoning sacrifice for our sins. ¹¹ Beloved, since God loved us so much, we also ought to love one another. ¹² No one has ever seen God; if we love one another, God lives in us, and his love is perfected in us.

13 By this we know that we abide in him and he in us, because he has given us of his Spirit. ¹⁴ And we have seen and do testify that the Father has sent his Son as the Savior of the world. ¹⁵ God abides in those who confess that Jesus is the Son of God, and they abide in God. ¹⁶ So we have known and believe the love that God has for us.

God is love, and those who abide in love abide in God, and God abides in

ᵃ Other ancient authorities read does away with Jesus (Gk dissolves Jesus)

---

believers in their innermost being (**hearts**, v. 19) that they have experienced God's loving, saving work (**truth**, v. 19). Relational love among believers manifests the loving relationship that God and Jesus share. Answered prayer is another assurance (v. 22). Verses 23–24 sum up the letter's central affirmations. Christian existence is an abiding, intimate, mutual relationship with God and Jesus through the Spirit marked by doing God's will of love in and through a community of disciples.

4:1–6—Inspired prophetic proclamation must be tested to discern if it is **from God** or from the antichrist and **the world** (vv. 1, 3, 5–6). The proclamation's content must confess Jesus as truly human and from God. These affirmations provide disciples with criteria for discerning claims to speak about God's purposes. Response to proc-

lamation reveals people's origins and commitments, either to God (like the community) or to the world opposed to God (vv. 4–6). This dualistic understanding that a person is loyal either to God or to the world interprets and confirms the group's social experience of hostility and rejection (2:18–19; 3:1, 13).

4:7–16—God's love is active and powerful; it is God's saving work among humans, initiated by God (v. 10) and revealed in Jesus, especially in his self-giving death (vv. 9–10, 14–16). God's love seeks mutual relationship between a believer and God (vv. 15–16), but also among believers in a community of mutual love that embodies the love shared between Jesus and God (vv. 7, 11–12). God's **Spirit** dwells among this loving (v. 12) and confessing (vv. 14–16) community.

them. [17] Love has been perfected among us in this: that we may have boldness on the day of judgment, because as he is, so are we in this world. [18] There is no fear in love, but perfect love casts out fear; for fear has to do with punishment, and whoever fears has not reached perfection in love. [19] We love[a] because he first loved us. [20] Those who say, "I love God," and hate their brothers or sisters,[b] are liars; for those who do not love a brother or sister[c] whom they have seen, cannot love God whom they have not seen. [21] The commandment we have from him is this: those who love God must love their brothers and sisters[b] also.

Faith Conquers the World

5 Everyone who believes that Jesus is the Christ[d] has been born of God, and everyone who loves the parent loves the child. [2] By this we know that we love the children of God, when we love God and obey his commandments. [3] For the love of God is this, that we obey his commandments. And his commandments are not burdensome, [4] for whatever is born of God conquers the world. And this is the victory that conquers the world, our faith. [5] Who is it that conquers the world but the one who believes that Jesus is the Son of God?

Testimony concerning the Son of God

6 This is the one who came by water and blood, Jesus Christ, not with the water only but with the water and the blood. And the Spirit is the one that testifies, for the Spirit is the truth. [7] There are three that testify:[e] [8] the Spirit and the water and the blood, and these three agree. [9] If we receive human testimony, the testimony of God is greater; for this is the testimony of God that he has testified to his Son. [10] Those who believe in the Son of God have the testimony in their hearts. Those who do not believe in God[f] have made him a liar by not believing in the testimony that God has given concerning his Son. [11] And this is the testimony: God gave us eternal life, and this life is in his Son. [12] Whoever has the Son has life; whoever does not have the Son of God does not have life.

Epilogue

13 I write these things to you who believe in the name of the Son of God,

[a] Other ancient authorities add *him*; others add *God*   [b] Gk *brothers*   [c] Gk *brother*   [d] Or *the Messiah*   [e] A few other authorities read (with variations) [7] *There are three that testify in heaven, the Father, the Word, and the Holy Spirit, and these three are one.* [8] *And there are three that testify on earth:*   [f] Other ancient authorities read *in the Son*

4:17–18—Talk of *judgment* often disturbs disciples. The acceptance of God's revealed love manifested in a believing, loving life provides confidence for the judgment in which disciples are held accountable to God.

4:19–21—God's loving initiative and human responsiveness are again emphasized. The opponents are again quoted and condemned (2:18–19). Their separation from and lack of love for believers confirms they have not encountered God's saving love.

5:1–5—Belief in Jesus as the one commissioned (*the Christ*) by God, the practice of love, and obedience constitute discipleship. This lived faith is not overcome by but overcomes the hostile world with its false commitments and rejection of God's purposes (2:15–17). The letter underlines that discipleship is not just about actions. Appropriate actions derive from and embody an adequate understanding of God's purposes for the world.

5:6–12—Recognition of (*believing*, trusting, v. 10) Jesus' role as God's Son or agent who reveals God's purposes is crucial for this understanding. Jesus' baptism (*water*) and death (*blood*, v. 6) demonstrate his role. The promised *Spirit* (John 14:16–17, 26) dwells with and instructs believers (1 John 4:13; 5:7–9). To reject Jesus is to reject God. To believe Jesus is to know intimate mutual relationship with God not interrupted by sin and death. This is *eternal life* (v. 11; John 5:24; 17:3) lived in a community of disciples that actively demonstrates God's love.

5:13–21—The letter's conclusion declares its pastoral purpose to confirm and strengthen belief in God's Son as the means of encountering *eternal life* or union with God (v. 13). Intimate relationship with Jesus and God means answered prayer, including prayer for believers who are sinning but not committing apostasy in denying the community's beliefs and practices (vv. 14–17; 2:18–19). Three final affirmations of communal belief (*we know*, vv. 18, 19, 20) affirm union with God and Jesus that is stronger than sin, the world, and the devil that oppose this union. Faithful living embodies this union.

so that you may know that you have eternal life.

14 And this is the boldness we have in him, that if we ask anything according to his will, he hears us. **15** And if we know that he hears us in whatever we ask, we know that we have obtained the requests made of him. **16** If you see your brother or sister*a* committing what is not a mortal sin, you will ask, and God*b* will give life to such a one—to those whose sin is not mortal. There is sin that is mortal; I do not say that you should pray about that. **17** All wrongdoing is sin, but there is sin that is not mortal.

18 We know that those who are born of God do not sin, but the one who was born of God protects them, and the evil one does not touch them. **19** We know that we are God's children, and that the whole world lies under the power of the evil one. **20** And we know that the Son of God has come and has given us understanding so that we may know him who is true;*c* and we are in him who is true, in his Son Jesus Christ. He is the true God and eternal life.

21 Little children, keep yourselves from idols.*d*

a Gk your brother *b* Gk he *c* Other ancient authorities read *know the true God* *d* Other ancient authorities add *Amen*

The Book of
2 JOHN

The schism visible in 1 John (1 John 2:18–19) provides the letter's context. Two themes, prominent in 1 John, summarize discipleship here: confessing Jesus' humanity and expressing faith in love. Those who do not share these emphases are to be denied hospitality (2 John 7–11) so as to reduce their destructive influence. When discipleship is under attack, one strategy is to reestablish appropriate boundaries.

—**Warren Carter**

Salutation

1 The elder to the elect lady and her children, whom I love in the truth, and not only I but also all who know the truth, ²because of the truth that abides in us and will be with us forever:

3 Grace, mercy, and peace will be with us from God the Father and from*a* Jesus Christ, the Father's Son, in truth and love.

Truth and Love

4 I was overjoyed to find some of your children walking in the truth, just as we have been commanded by the Father. ⁵But now, dear lady, I ask you, not as though I were writing you a new commandment, but one we have had from the beginning, let us love one another. ⁶And this is love, that we walk according to his commandments; this is the commandment just as you have heard it from the beginning—you must walk in it.

7 Many deceivers have gone out into the world, those who do not confess that Jesus Christ has come in the flesh; any such person is the deceiver and the antichrist! ⁸Be on your guard, so that you do not lose what we*b* have worked for, but may receive a full reward. ⁹Everyone who does not abide in the teaching of Christ, but goes beyond it, does not have God; whoever abides in the teaching has both the Father and the Son. ¹⁰Do not receive into the house or welcome anyone who comes to you and does not bring this teaching; ¹¹for to welcome is to participate in the evil deeds of such a person.

Final Greetings

12 Although I have much to write to you, I would rather not use paper and ink; instead I hope to come to you and talk with you face to face, so that our joy may be complete.

13 The children of your elect sister send you their greetings.*c*

a Other ancient authorities add *the Lord* *b* Other ancient authorities read *you* *c* Other ancient authorities add *Amen*

1–3—The unidentified *elder*, perhaps one of the leaders referred to in 1 John by "we," carries out pastoral leadership by means of the letter. The *elect lady* may be the congregation (v. 5) or perhaps the congregation's woman leader, with the *children* being the congregation or family of believers. The writer appeals to *love*, a term that in the Johannine tradition evokes the intimate relationship of God and Jesus in which disciples participate and that disciples manifest in relationships with other disciples. *Truth* (five times in vv. 1–4) denotes God's saving faithfulness manifested in Jesus' life and death.

4–6—*Walking in the truth* is to live according to God's saving, loving purposes (Deut. 30:15–16)

incarnated in Jesus, God's agent. Disciples are to embody that self-giving love. Salvation includes relationship with God and ethical living.

7–11—Those who have left the community (1 John 2:18–19) denied Jesus' humanity as God's agent and show themselves to be "antichrist," not belonging to or commissioned by God. The writer urges the faithful to be wary of these people, since they have the capacity to cause believers to lose their salvation. Refusing them hospitality prevents them from deceiving disciples with false teaching and protects the church. Discipleship is always vulnerable. Faithfulness needs daily renewal by attention to its foundational union with Jesus and active expression in loving actions.

The Book of
3 JOHN

This letter may assume the schism of 1–2 John or may reflect a different situation. There is a struggle over the authority of leaders and conflict in the community between two individuals, Diotrephes and Gaius. The letter commends Gaius and discredits Diotrephes. In doing so, it offers disciples some guidance about appropriate leadership styles and ways of participating in the church, particularly in offering hospitality to strangers.

—Warren Carter

Salutation

1 The elder to the beloved Gaius, whom I love in truth.

Gaius Commended for His Hospitality

2 Beloved, I pray that all may go well with you and that you may be in good health, just as it is well with your soul. [3] I was overjoyed when some of the friends[a] arrived and testified to your faithfulness to the truth, namely how you walk in the truth. [4] I have no greater joy than this, to hear that my children are walking in the truth.

5 Beloved, you do faithfully whatever you do for the friends,[a] even though they are strangers to you; [6] they have testified to your love before the church. You will do well to send them on in a manner worthy of God; [7] for they began their journey for the sake of Christ,[b] accepting no support from non-believers.[c] [8] Therefore we ought to support such people, so that we may become co-workers with the truth.

Diotrephes and Demetrius

9 I have written something to the church; but Diotrephes, who likes to put himself first, does not acknowledge our authority. [10] So if I come, I will call attention to what he is doing in spreading false charges against us. And not content with those charges, he refuses to welcome the friends,[a] and even prevents those who want to do so and expels them from the church.

11 Beloved, do not imitate what is evil but imitate what is good. Whoever does good is from God; whoever does evil has not seen God. [12] Everyone has testified favorably about Demetrius, and so has the truth itself. We also testify for him,[d] and you know that our testimony is true.

Final Greetings

13 I have much to write to you, but I would rather not write with pen and ink; [14] instead I hope to see you soon, and we will talk together face to face.

15 Peace to you. The friends send you their greetings. Greet the friends there, each by name.

[a] Gk brothers [b] Gk for the sake of the name [c] Gk the Gentiles [d] Gk lacks for him

1–8—*Gaius*, the *elder*'s ally, has shown commendable hospitality to visiting teachers.

9–11—But there is conflict with *Diotrephes*, who is prominent in the congregation and whose behavior disrupts it. He asserts his authority and *likes to put himself first*, contrary to the command to love others (v. 9a; John 13:34–35). He opposes the letter's writer (v. 9b), spreads *false* stories (v. 10a), *refuses* hospitality (v. 10b), and *expels* those who disagree with him from the church (v. 10c). Disciples are not to imitate this sort of empire-building behavior. Actions reveal the heart's commitments.

12–15—The elder commends *Demetrius*, perhaps the letter carrier, and hopes to visit. Divisions within congregations require disciples to discern situations and personalities that might sustain discipleship and those that might destroy it. Hospitality to strangers is a valuable action because it manifests God's welcoming love.

The Book of JUDE

The brief letter of Jude is one of the most unusual writings in the New Testament and among the most neglected. Apparently expressions of outrage do not always make for appealing reading. Jude is largely combative in tone, harsh and bitter in denouncing its opponents, if colorful in its invective. Furthermore, its use of noncanonical texts (such as *1 Enoch* and the *Testament of Moses*) often renders it unfamiliar and obscure. Still, Jude bears abiding witness to the integral connection between Christian faith and moral obedience to Christ. Christian behavior, no less than Christian belief, is a mark of authentic, apostolic faith.

False teachers apparently infiltrated the church Jude addressed (v. 4). These itinerant charismatics rejected the moral authority of the Mosaic law and of Jesus Christ himself and advocated libertine beliefs and practices. Visionary experiences led them to believe that freedom in Christ relieved them of moral obligations. As a result, Christian freedom became a license for self-indulgence and found expression in immorality, especially sexual misbehaviors. This false teaching and practice gained a following in the church addressed, disrupting and corrupting its life (even the love-feasts at the heart of the community's fellowship, v. 12), and dividing the congregation.

The crisis at hand was thus a serious one, which explains the urgent tone of the letter. In its author's view, the false teachers jeopardized the salvation of persons under their influence, who would surely face divine judgment and destruction for immoral deeds when Christ returned on the judgment day. The letter of Jude aims to warn its readers of this grave danger, to build up the life of a divided church, to encourage behavior befitting disciples of Jesus Christ, and to restore the faith of those led astray. It also seeks to enlist its readers in the struggle to defend the apostolic faith (v. 4).

So that there may be no doubt about the danger represented by the belief and practice of the intruders, Jude engages in sustained denunciation of them. Indeed, the bulk of the letter (vv. 4–19) is devoted to substantiation of the claim that they are "people who long ago were designated for this condemnation as ungodly" (v. 4). In an elaborate commentary on Scripture, Jude compares them to notorious sinners of the past who were punished by God (vv. 5–13) and reviews both ancient and apostolic prophecies of judgment regarding the ungodly (vv. 14–19). Some of the examples are unfamiliar, as they are drawn from noncanonical sources (the *Testament of Moses* in v. 9, and *1 Enoch* in vv. 6, 14–15), but their common point is plain. These historical and prophetic illustrations expose the character and fate of Jude's opponents, who are but the latest in a long line of ungodly persons whose fate and judgment have been determined by God long ago. In fact, their appearance on the scene, as predicted by the apostles, is taken as a sign that the return of Christ as judge is near at hand (vv. 17–18).

While harsh denunciation constitutes the bulk of the letter (vv. 4–19), it is important to note that this is framed by positive exhortation and affirmation of God's action on

behalf of believers (vv. 1–3, 20–25). While the ungodly will face divine destruction when Christ returns, the righteous may look forward to the mercy and eternal life that will be their appointed destiny. Indeed, the author of Jude expresses confidence that his "called" and "beloved" readers are "kept safe for Jesus Christ" (v. 1), by the power of God "who is able to keep" them "from falling" (v. 24). At the same time, they are exhorted to "keep" themselves in the love of God (v. 21). Two important realities of Christian life thus find expression. On the one hand, the very power of God is at work to protect and preserve the faithful. On the other hand, believers have a responsibility to respond to their calling and to remain in grace by living in obedience to Jesus Christ. Embodied Christian behavior, no less than Christian belief, is a mark of authentic discipleship.

In sum, the letter of Jude is decidedly pastoral in orientation. It seeks not so much to debate the false teachers, but rather to instruct and exhort the faithful, to restore their faith, and to defend the apostolic witness that affirmed the inseparability of Christian belief and Christian behavior. Proactive engagement in the Christian life and growth in grace will safeguard believers against the destructive influence of false teaching and practice, as will the protective power of God.

Very little is known of the letter's author or destination. It is attributed to Jude (Judas), the brother of James and Jesus, who was not a believer during the lifetime of Jesus but later became a recognized leader and missionary in the Jewish Christian community in Palestine (Mark 6:3; Matt. 13:55; John 7:3–5; Acts 1:14; 1 Cor. 9:5). Some scholars find authorship by Jude plausible and thus consider it one of the earliest writings in the New Testament, emerging in the 50s from Palestine. However, the letter's highly literate Greek style and unusual vocabulary suggest to many other scholars that it was written in Jude's name toward the end of the first century (90–100) in a Hellenistic environment outside Palestine. Reference to the "predictions of the apostles" (v. 17) further implies that the author writes in the postapostolic generation. The letter's destination is unknown, but assumed familiarity with Jewish Scripture and tradition suggests that its recipients are Jewish Christians.

—**Frances Taylor Gench**

Salutation

1 Jude,[a] a servant[b] of Jesus Christ and brother of James,

To those who are called, who are beloved[c] in[d] God the Father and kept safe for[d] Jesus Christ:

2 May mercy, peace, and love be yours in abundance.

Occasion of the Letter

3 Beloved, while eagerly preparing to write to you about the salvation we share, I find it necessary to write and appeal to you to contend for the faith that was once for all entrusted to the saints. 4 For certain intruders have sto-

[a] Gk *Judas*   [b] Gk *slave*   [c] Other ancient authorities read *sanctified*   [d] Or *by*

1–2 Salutation

God's calling of believers entails moral and ethical responsibility on their part. Jude begins and ends with a promise: God's love will protect and sustain (**keep**) believers in their practice of the Christian life until the day when Christ returns as judge (vv. 2, 24–25).

3–4 Contend for the Faith

Contending for the apostolic faith involves more than verbal argument. It entails a lifestyle that embodies the gospel, explicated in vv. 20–23. The troublemakers teach that Christian freedom means freedom from moral constraint, and thereby deny the lordship of Jesus Christ, to whom believers owe allegiance and moral obedience.

len in among you, people who long ago were designated for this condemnation as ungodly, who pervert the grace of our God into licentiousness and deny our only Master and Lord, Jesus Christ.[a]

Judgment on False Teachers

5 Now I desire to remind you, though you are fully informed, that the Lord, who once for all saved[b] a people out of the land of Egypt, afterward destroyed those who did not believe. [6] And the angels who did not keep their own position, but left their proper dwelling, he has kept in eternal chains in deepest darkness for the judgment of the great day. [7] Likewise, Sodom and Gomorrah and the surrounding cities, which, in the same manner as they, indulged in sexual immorality and pursued unnatural lust,[c] serve as an example by undergoing a punishment of eternal fire.

8 Yet in the same way these dreamers also defile the flesh, reject authority, and slander the glorious ones.[d] [9] But when the archangel Michael contended with the devil and disputed about the body of Moses, he did not dare to bring a condemnation of slander[e] against him, but said, "The Lord rebuke you!" [10] But these people slander whatever they do not understand, and they are destroyed by those things that, like irrational animals, they know by instinct. [11] Woe to them! For they go the way of Cain, and abandon themselves to Balaam's error for the sake of gain, and perish in Korah's rebellion. [12] These are blemishes[f] on your love-feasts, while they feast with you without fear, feeding themselves.[g] They are water-less clouds carried along by the winds; autumn trees without fruit, twice dead, uprooted; [13] wild waves of the sea, casting up the foam of their own shame; wandering stars, for whom the deepest darkness has been reserved forever.

14 It was also about these that Enoch, in the seventh generation from Adam, prophesied, saying, "See, the Lord is coming[h] with ten thousands of his holy ones, [15] to execute judgment on all, and to convict everyone of all the deeds of ungodliness that they have committed in such an ungodly way, and of all the harsh things that ungodly sinners have spoken against him." [16] These are grumblers and malcontents; they indulge their own lusts; they are bombastic in speech, flattering people to their own advantage.

Warnings and Exhortations

17 But you, beloved, must remember the predictions of the apostles of our Lord Jesus Christ; [18] for they said to you, "In the last time there will be scoffers, indulging their own ungodly lusts." [19] It is these worldly people, devoid of the Spirit, who are causing divisions. [20] But you, beloved, build yourselves up on your most holy faith; pray in the Holy Spirit; [21] keep yourselves in the love of God; look forward to the mercy of our Lord Jesus Christ that leads to[i] eternal life. [22] And have mercy on some who are wavering; [23] save others by snatching them out of the fire; and have mercy

---

[a] Or the only Master and our Lord Jesus Christ [b] Other ancient authorities read though you were once for all fully informed, that Jesus (or Joshua) who saved [c] Gk went after other flesh [d] Or angels; Gk glories [e] Or condemnation for blasphemy [f] Or reefs [g] Or without fear. They are shepherds who care only for themselves [h] Gk came [i] Gk Christ to

---

5–19 God's Judgment of the Ungodly: History and Prophecy

The intruders are compared to notorious sinners of the past, who showcase a variety of ungodly behaviors. Both history (vv. 5–13) and prophecy (vv. 14–19) confirm that God's judgment of the ungodly is sure.

20–23 Final Exhortation: How to Contend for the Faith

Jude provides explicit instruction in the kind of proactive Christian living that will strengthen the communal life of the faithful and enable them to resist and counter the dangerous influence of false teaching. The hope of restoration to faithfulness is left open, and believers are to extend themselves in mercy and rescue to those

on still others with fear, hating even the tunic defiled by their bodies.[a]

Benediction

24 Now to him who is able to keep you from falling, and to make you stand without blemish in the presence of his glory with rejoicing, 25 to the only God our Savior, through Jesus Christ our Lord, be glory, majesty, power, and authority, before all time and now and forever. Amen.

[a] Gk by the flesh. The Greek text of verses 22-23 is uncertain at several points

---

who are led astray. Christians are to look out for each other's welfare and to take direct action in its behalf.

24–25 Closing Doxology

The Book of
REVELATION

Revelation receives its name from its opening words, "the revelation of Jesus Christ." The Greek word for "revelation" is *apokalypsis*, from which the English words "apocalyptic" and "apocalypse" derive. Contrary to popular usage, the primary meaning of apocalypse is not "the cataclysmic end of the world," but revelation, or more literally, "unveiling." What is unveiled in Revelation is the way the affairs of the world look when viewed through the eyes of God as spoken by a prophet, John (1:3, 9–10). Revelation shares much with the prophetic books of the Old Testament—not a foretelling of the future, but a "forth" telling of God's vision of and for the world. John, like those earlier prophets on whom he draws so heavily in Revelation, is commissioned to tell forth where and how the faith community and the world run counter to God's justice and peace.

John was a common name in New Testament times; and the John of Revelation identifies himself to his readers based solely on his own experience as a prophet and witness to the word of God in Jesus. While it may be tempting to equate this John with the author of the Gospel, the epistles, or some other John known elsewhere in the New Testament, there is not enough data to do so, nor is his extratextual identity of fundamental importance. John's authority comes from his vocation as a prophet and his experience of the word and spirit of God. John writes this book while in exile on Patmos, a small island in the Aegean Sea. John identifies his testimony about Jesus as the cause of his exile, and while John has often been portrayed as in prison, he says nothing about that himself. Revelation was probably written at the end of the first century CE, during the reign of the Roman emperor Domitian.

Revelation is first and foremost a pastoral letter, sent to seven churches in Asia Minor (1:4, chaps. 2–3; modern Turkey), which was then part of the Roman Empire. Although the traditional view of Revelation was that it was written to churches undergoing severe persecution, the historical data does not support a view of widespread persecution during the reign of Domitian. The imperial cult was pervasive in Asia Minor in the first century—temples and shrines to the Roman emperors in the major cities—but the punishment for not participating in the emperor cult was rarely death. The penalties were actually much more subtle—social ostracism, reduced economic opportunities. For the city dwellers to whom Revelation is addressed, participation in the emperor cult, alongside their participation in Christian worship, seemed harmless enough as a way of ensuring their economic livelihood. While a few of the churches named here (Pergamum and Philadelphia) faced some persecution and so receive from John encouragement to persevere, most did not. Instead, for most of the readers of Revelation, John is trying to encourage resistance to the pull of the empire. The problem is not persecution by the empire, but accommodation to the empire.

John's prophetic commission in Revelation is to give the churches new eyes through which to see themselves—to unveil the Roman Empire for what it is and to show that

its claim on the churches' lives is not innocuous, but actually violates all that is true about God. For John, the choices for the churches are clear—resist the pull of empire, even if that resistance may result ultimately in death, or else be consumed by the empire. John's churches and today's churches are easily lulled into thinking that human empires and human power have the answers and that there is no cost to participating in the systems of the empire. Empires often act as if their power is the same as God's power, and so they can speak about their goals and God's goals as if they are one and the same. As a prophet, John knows that this is a lie. The only truth and power lie with God, not with any human empire. All human actions that participate in the false power of the empire—idolatry, violence, and acts based in falsehood and deceit— need to end. There is no middle ground for John, which is why Revelation is such a disorienting book to read. The empire embodies and enacts evil, not good.

The need to unveil the truth about empire explains much about the language and structure of Revelation. From beginning to end, Revelation is symbolic and deeply imagistic, because John is trying to get his readers to see the power and pull of empire with new eyes. John's prophetic experience draws on all the senses—hearing, sight, taste, smell, touch. The best way to read Revelation is to allow oneself to experience along with John, to move with his images and to enter the world that he creates. Revelation is like a large, bold painting. The total effect, not the deciphering of each individual detail, gives meaning. Revelation consists of many cyclical series, the seven seals, seven trumpets, seven bowls, as well as many complementary visions of the church and of the power of evil. The cyclical patterning of Revelation conveys that these visionary series are not a literal mapping of the future but provide a way of viewing human history from the perspective of the kingdom of God. John's primary concern is the present, not the future, as he uses his images to reveal the values that underlie unexamined practices of empire—injustice, violence, and oppression. Babylon is the primary symbol for Rome and for all empire, and the goal of Revelation is to invite the churches to move out of Babylon and into the grace of the city of God.

Is there an "end of the world" emphasis to Revelation, as so much popular usage suggests? Yes and no. Revelation envisions the end of evil, not the end of the world. The dramatic battle scenes and the images of death and destruction portray what the world is like and will be like when the power of evil is allowed to run unchecked. Human power as an agent of destruction has no place in Revelation. Human power as the power to resist the pull of empire, to offer allegiance to God and not the state, to work for justice against the injustice of political empires, to resist the lure of economic reward when the cost is participation in empire—this form of human power has a large place in Revelation. For John, power is defined not by which empire has the largest army or gross national product, but by the model of the Lamb who was slaughtered and yet still lives (5:6). The only true power is the power of God "unveiled" in the crucifixion and resurrection of Jesus. If John's "unveiling" of empire and the nature of power were to catch hold, then there would be an end of the world as we know it, because we would begin to live uncompromisingly according to the model of the Lamb—power in weakness, justice instead of injustice, liberation instead of oppression.

—**Gail R. O'Day**

Introduction and Salutation

1 The revelation of Jesus Christ, which God gave him to show his servants[a] what must soon take place; he made[b] it known by sending his angel to his servant[c] John, **2** who testified to the word of God and to the testimony of Jesus Christ, even to all that he saw.

3 Blessed is the one who reads aloud the words of the prophecy, and blessed are those who hear and who keep what is written in it; for the time is near.

4 John to the seven churches that are in Asia:

Grace to you and peace from him who is and who was and who is to come, and from the seven spirits who are before his throne, **5** and from Jesus Christ, the faithful witness, the firstborn of the dead, and the ruler of the kings of the earth.

To him who loves us and freed[d] us from our sins by his blood, **6** and made[b] us to be a kingdom, priests serving[e] his God and Father, to him be glory and dominion forever and ever. Amen.

7　Look! He is coming with the clouds;
　　every eye will see him,
　even those who pierced him;
　　and on his account all the tribes of
　　　the earth will wail.
So it is to be. Amen.

8 "I am the Alpha and the Omega," says the Lord God, who is and who was and who is to come, the Almighty.

A Vision of Christ

9 I, John, your brother who share with you in Jesus the persecution and the kingdom and the patient endurance, was on the island called Patmos because of the word of God and the testimony of Jesus.[f] **10** I was in the spirit[g] on the Lord's day, and I heard behind me a loud voice like a trumpet **11** saying, "Write in a book what you see and send it to the seven churches, to Ephesus, to Smyrna, to Pergamum, to Thyatira, to Sardis, to Philadelphia, and to Laodicea."

12 Then I turned to see whose voice it was that spoke to me, and on turning I saw seven golden lampstands, **13** and in the midst of the lampstands I saw one like the Son of Man, clothed with a long robe and with a golden sash across his chest. **14** His head and his hair were white as white wool, white as snow; his eyes were like a flame of fire, **15** his feet were like burnished bronze, refined as in a furnace, and his voice was like the sound of many waters. **16** In his right hand he held seven stars, and from his mouth came a sharp, two-edged sword, and his face was like the sun shining with full force.

17 When I saw him, I fell at his feet as though dead. But he placed his right hand on me, saying, "Do not be afraid;

a Gk slaves　*b* Gk and he made　*c* Gk slave　*d* Other ancient authorities read washed　*e* Gk priests to　*f* Or testimony to Jesus　*g* Or in the Spirit

---

1:1–16 Introduction

1:1–3 Prologue

1:1–2—John communicates to others what is given to him by God through Jesus Christ.

1:3—The words of this book were written to be read aloud in a community worship service. It is not a private or secret communication, intended only for a select group. It is a word intended to be shared, not secreted away or feared today.

1:9–16 John's First Vision

1:9—As in Paul's letters, the author identifies himself by name. His self-description is a definition of discipleship—in fellowship with others, a witness to God and Jesus.

1:10–11—*In the spirit* identifies John as a prophet.

1:12–16—John's description of the risen Christ uses imagery from the Old Testament (Ezekiel, Daniel). As a prophet, John sees Jesus through the lens of his tradition and invites others to see Jesus that way.

1:17–3:22 The Messages of the Risen Christ to Seven Churches

These cities were cultural and economic centers. The real threat to discipleship was the appeal of the wealth and power of the Roman Empire, not widespread persecution (see introduction). This threat remains for contemporary churches who are attracted to the power and privilege of governments and the market economy. Therefore the messages contain warnings from Jesus for the churches as well as promises. The *angel* to whom each message is delivered represents the church's

I am the first and the last, [18] and the living one. I was dead, and see, I am alive forever and ever; and I have the keys of Death and of Hades. [19] Now write what you have seen, what is, and what is to take place after this. [20] As for the mystery of the seven stars that you saw in my right hand, and the seven golden lampstands: the seven stars are the angels of the seven churches, and the seven lampstands are the seven churches.

The Message to Ephesus

2 "To the angel of the church in Ephesus write: These are the words of him who holds the seven stars in his right hand, who walks among the seven golden lampstands:

2 "I know your works, your toil and your patient endurance. I know that you cannot tolerate evildoers; you have tested those who claim to be apostles but are not, and have found them to be false. [3] I also know that you are enduring patiently and bearing up for the sake of my name, and that you have not grown weary. [4] But I have this against you, that you have abandoned the love you had at first. [5] Remember then from what you have fallen; repent, and do the works you did at first. If not, I will come to you and remove your lampstand from its place, unless you repent. [6] Yet this is to your credit: you hate the works of the Nicolaitans, which I also hate. [7] Let anyone who has an ear listen to what the Spirit is saying to the churches. To everyone who conquers, I will give permission to eat from the tree of life that is in the paradise of God.

The Message to Smyrna

8 "And to the angel of the church in Smyrna write: These are the words of the first and the last, who was dead and came to life:

9 "I know your affliction and your poverty, even though you are rich. I know the slander on the part of those who say that they are Jews and are not, but are a synagogue of Satan. [10] Do not fear what you are about to suffer. Beware, the devil is about to throw some of you into prison so that you may be tested, and for ten days you will have affliction. Be faithful until death, and I will give you the crown of life. [11] Let anyone who has an ear listen to what the Spirit is saying to the churches. Whoever conquers will not be harmed by the second death.

The Message to Pergamum

12 "And to the angel of the church in Pergamum write: These are the words of him who has the sharp two-edged sword:

13 "I know where you are living, where Satan's throne is. Yet you are holding fast to my name, and you did not deny your

---

collective identity. Then as now, a church is recognized by more than its individual members.

1:17–20—John is the scribe for the messages, but Jesus is the author. The words of the risen Jesus enable a church to look at itself through Jesus' eyes.

2:1–7 The First Message

2:1–3—This message begins with praise, but moves to judgment.

2:4–5—This church has become complacent about the life of faith (*abandoned the love [it] had at first*). Contemporary churches are in danger of doing the same thing.

2:6—The *Nicolaitans* taught that it was acceptable to participate in worship services to other gods of the Roman Empire (vv. 14–15). One of the challenges for contemporary discipleship is to recognize that we also are tempted to worship many gods—success, money, possessions—and discipleship requires resistance to this pull of empire.

2:8–11 The Second Message

2:9—*Smyrna* models faithful discipleship because it endures hardship and embraces poverty in the face of wealth. *Synagogue of Satan* relates to the strong conflicts among the many different religions in the cities of the Roman Empire (see vv. 13, 24), including competing communities of Jewish background. It has nothing to do with present-day relationships between Jews and Christians. The risen Jesus has only praise, no judgment, for Smyrna (cf. Philadelphia, 3:7–13).

2:12–17 The Third Message

2:13—*Pergamum* competed with Ephesus to be

faith in me*a* even in the days of Antipas my witness, my faithful one, who was killed among you, where Satan lives. ¹⁴ But I have a few things against you: you have some there who hold to the teaching of Balaam, who taught Balak to put a stumbling block before the people of Israel, so that they would eat food sacrificed to idols and practice fornication. ¹⁵ So you also have some who hold to the teaching of the Nicolaitans. ¹⁶ Repent then. If not, I will come to you soon and make war against them with the sword of my mouth. ¹⁷ Let anyone who has an ear listen to what the Spirit is saying to the churches. To everyone who conquers I will give some of the hidden manna, and I will give a white stone, and on the white stone is written a new name that no one knows except the one who receives it.

The Message to Thyatira

18 "And to the angel of the church in Thyatira write: These are the words of the Son of God, who has eyes like a flame of fire, and whose feet are like burnished bronze:

19 "I know your works—your love, faith, service, and patient endurance. I know that your last works are greater than the first. ²⁰ But I have this against you: you tolerate that woman Jezebel, who calls herself a prophet and is teaching and beguiling my servants*b* to practice fornication and to eat food sacrificed to idols. ²¹ I gave her time to repent, but she refuses to repent of her fornication. ²² Beware, I am throwing her on a bed, and those who commit adultery with her I am throwing into great distress, unless they repent of her doings; ²³ and I will strike her children dead. And all the churches will know that I am the one who searches minds and hearts, and I will give to each of you as your works deserve. ²⁴ But to the rest of you in Thyatira, who do not hold this teaching, who have not learned what some call 'the deep things of Satan,' to you I say, I do not lay on you any other burden; ²⁵ only hold fast to what you have until I come. ²⁶ To everyone who conquers and continues to do my works to the end,

I will give authority over the nations;
²⁷ to rule*c* them with an iron rod,

as when clay pots are shattered—
²⁸ even as I also received authority from my Father. To the one who conquers I will also give the morning star. ²⁹ Let anyone who has an ear listen to what the Spirit is saying to the churches.

The Message to Sardis

3 "And to the angel of the church in Sardis write: These are the words of him who has the seven spirits of God and the seven stars:

"I know your works; you have a name of being alive, but you are dead. ² Wake up, and strengthen what remains and is on the point of death, for I have not found your works perfect in the sight of my God. ³ Remember then what you

a Or *deny my faith*   *b* Gk *slaves*   *c* Or *to shepherd*

---

recognized as the center of the cult that worshiped the Roman emperor. *Satan's throne* refers to the imperial temple. This church has experienced persecution (*Antipas*).

2:14–15—Some members of this church engage in the practices of the imperial cult (see v. 6). There is no middle ground—to participate even a little in the empire is to participate in evil. Discipleship involves repentance and resistance. This imperative was difficult for the Christians of Pergamum, who did not automatically think that Rome was evil, and is difficult for many contemporary Christians who do not think that they live in an empire.

2:18–29 The Fourth Message

2:19, 24–25—Discipleship is seen in works of *love* and *service*.

2:20–23—*Jezebel*, like the Nicolaitans, stands for participation in the practices of the imperial cult. *Fornication* and *adultery* symbolize idolatry. A true disciple remains faithful to the one God, and belief in that one God presupposes political and social choices.

3:1–6 The Fifth Message

Sardis is hypocritical in its faith commitments. It rests on its reputation for faithfulness instead of doing new acts of service.

received and heard; obey it, and repent. If you do not wake up, I will come like a thief, and you will not know at what hour I will come to you. ⁴ Yet you have still a few persons in Sardis who have not soiled their clothes; they will walk with me, dressed in white, for they are worthy. ⁵ If you conquer, you will be clothed like them in white robes, and I will not blot your name out of the book of life; I will confess your name before my Father and before his angels. ⁶ Let anyone who has an ear listen to what the Spirit is saying to the churches.

The Message to Philadelphia

7 "And to the angel of the church in Philadelphia write:

These are the words of the holy one,
　the true one,
who has the key of David,
who opens and no one will shut,
who shuts and no one opens:

8 "I know your works. Look, I have set before you an open door, which no one is able to shut. I know that you have but little power, and yet you have kept my word and have not denied my name. ⁹ I will make those of the synagogue of Satan who say that they are Jews and are not, but are lying—I will make them come and bow down before your feet, and they will learn that I have loved you. ¹⁰ Because you have kept my word of patient endurance, I will keep you from the hour of trial that is coming on the whole world to test the inhabitants of the earth. ¹¹ I am coming soon; hold fast to what you have, so that no one may seize your crown. ¹² If you conquer, I will make you a pillar in the temple of my God; you will never go out of it. I will write on you the name of my God, and the name of the city of my God, the new Jerusalem that comes down from my God out of heaven, and my own new name. ¹³ Let anyone who has an ear listen to what the Spirit is saying to the churches.

The Message to Laodicea

14 "And to the angel of the church in Laodicea write: The words of the Amen, the faithful and true witness, the origin[a] of God's creation:

15 "I know your works; you are neither cold nor hot. I wish that you were either cold or hot. ¹⁶ So, because you are lukewarm, and neither cold nor hot, I am about to spit you out of my mouth. ¹⁷ For you say, 'I am rich, I have prospered, and I need nothing.' You do not realize that you are wretched, pitiable, poor, blind, and naked. ¹⁸ Therefore I counsel you to buy from me gold refined by fire so that you may be rich; and white robes to clothe you and to keep the shame of your nakedness from being seen; and salve to anoint your eyes so that you may see. ¹⁹ I reprove and discipline those whom I love. Be earnest, therefore, and repent. ²⁰ Listen! I am standing at the door, knocking; if you hear my voice and open the door, I will come in to you and eat with you, and you with me. ²¹ To the one who conquers I will give a place with me on my throne, just as I myself conquered and sat down with my Father on his throne. ²² Let anyone who has an ear listen to what the Spirit is saying to the churches."

[a] Or beginning

3:7–13 The Sixth Message

3:8—As with Smyrna, the risen Jesus has only praise, no judgment, for *Philadelphia*. The two churches who receive only praise are churches that are marginalized either through poverty (Smyrna) or powerlessness (Philadelphia).

3:10—The challenge to faith here is persecution, not accommodation.

3:14–22 The Seventh Message

3:15–16—*Laodicea* has become *lukewarm* because it no longer stands for anything.

3:17–18—The church prides itself on its wealth and prosperity and does not see how these interfere with the call to discipleship. Laodicea has a contemporary parallel in church communities who pride themselves on finding the safe middle ground and on being economically successful.

The Heavenly Worship

4 After this I looked, and there in heaven a door stood open! And the first voice, which I had heard speaking to me like a trumpet, said, "Come up here, and I will show you what must take place after this." ²At once I was in the spirit,ᵃ and there in heaven stood a throne, with one seated on the throne! ³And the one seated there looks like jasper and carnelian, and around the throne is a rainbow that looks like an emerald. ⁴Around the throne are twenty-four thrones, and seated on the thrones are twenty-four elders, dressed in white robes, with golden crowns on their heads. ⁵Coming from the throne are flashes of lightning, and rumblings and peals of thunder, and in front of the throne burn seven flaming torches, which are the seven spirits of God; ⁶and in front of the throne there is something like a sea of glass, like crystal.

Around the throne, and on each side of the throne, are four living creatures, full of eyes in front and behind: ⁷the first living creature like a lion, the second living creature like an ox, the third living creature with a face like a human face, and the fourth living creature like a flying eagle. ⁸And the four living creatures, each of them with six wings, are full of eyes all around and inside. Day and night without ceasing they sing,

"Holy, holy, holy,
  the Lord God the Almighty,
    who was and is and is to come."

⁹And whenever the living creatures give glory and honor and thanks to the one who is seated on the throne, who lives forever and ever, ¹⁰the twenty-four elders fall before the one who is seated on the throne and worship the one who lives forever and ever; they cast their crowns before the throne, singing,

¹¹ "You are worthy, our Lord and God,
  to receive glory and honor and
    power,
  for you created all things,
    and by your will they existed and
      were created."

The Scroll and the Lamb

5 Then I saw in the right hand of the one seated on the throne a scroll written on the inside and on the back, sealedᵇ with seven seals; ²and I saw a mighty angel proclaiming with a loud voice, "Who is worthy to open the scroll and break its seals?" ³And no one in heaven or on earth or under the earth was able to open the scroll or to look into it. ⁴And I began to weep bitterly because no one was found worthy to open the scroll or to look into it. ⁵Then one of the elders said to me, "Do not weep. See, the Lion of the tribe of Judah, the Root

ᵃOr *in the Spirit* ᵇOr *written on the inside, and sealed on the back*

4:1–5:14 Two Visions of Heaven

4:1–11 The Vision of the Heavenly Throne Room

4:1—The open door evokes communication between heaven and earth.

4:2–3—This *throne* room scene shows that God has the only real power, not any earthly king, governor, or other political leader.

4:4—*Elders* are figures of political and religious significance in John's time. Their worship of God (see v. 10) signifies the subordination of all forms of earthly power to God.

4:6—A glasslike *sea* symbolizes God's control over chaos (see Ps. 29:10). Chaos is often not a sea of water but the frightening and unpredictable aspects of our lives and world. Yet God, not chaos, has the last word.

4:7—See Ezek. 1 and Isa. 6. All of God's *creatures*—wild beast, domestic animal, human being, and bird—surround the throne of God.

4:8–11—Heaven is alive with hymns of praise. The heavenly throne room models the life of faith—unceasing and joyful praise and worship of God.

5:1–14 The Vision of the Lamb

5:1—Like the spoken word of God at creation, the words of God written in the *scroll* will set everything in motion.

5:2–4—A *seal* was an imprint made in clay or wax that signified a document's authenticity and importance. The revealing of God's word is not a casual matter.

5:5—Traditional political and messianic language drawn from the history of Israel. The elder

of David, has conquered, so that he can open the scroll and its seven seals."

6 Then I saw between the throne and the four living creatures and among the elders a Lamb standing as if it had been slaughtered, having seven horns and seven eyes, which are the seven spirits of God sent out into all the earth. [7] He went and took the scroll from the right hand of the one who was seated on the throne. [8] When he had taken the scroll, the four living creatures and the twenty-four elders fell before the Lamb, each holding a harp and golden bowls full of incense, which are the prayers of the saints. [9] They sing a new song:

"You are worthy to take the scroll
    and to open its seals,
for you were slaughtered and by your
        blood you ransomed for God
    saints from[a] every tribe and
        language and people and nation;
[10]   you have made them to be a
        kingdom and priests serving[b]
        our God,
    and they will reign on earth."

11 Then I looked, and I heard the voice of many angels surrounding the throne and the living creatures and the elders; they numbered myriads of myriads and thousands of thousands, [12] singing with full voice,

"Worthy is the Lamb that was
        slaughtered

to receive power and wealth and
        wisdom and might
    and honor and glory and blessing!"
[13] Then I heard every creature in heaven and on earth and under the earth and in the sea, and all that is in them, singing,

"To the one seated on the throne and
        to the Lamb
be blessing and honor and glory and
        might
    forever and ever!"
[14] And the four living creatures said, "Amen!" And the elders fell down and worshiped.

The Seven Seals

6 Then I saw the Lamb open one of the seven seals, and I heard one of the four living creatures call out, as with a voice of thunder, "Come!"[c] [2] I looked, and there was a white horse! Its rider had a bow; a crown was given to him, and he came out conquering and to conquer.

3 When he opened the second seal, I heard the second living creature call out, "Come!"[c] [4] And out came[d] another horse, bright red; its rider was permitted to take peace from the earth, so that people would slaughter one another; and he was given a great sword.

5 When he opened the third seal, I heard the third living creature call out, "Come!"[c] I looked, and there was a black

[a] Gk ransomed for God from   [b] Gk priests to   [c] Or "Go!"   [d] Or went

---

assesses worthiness according to conventional categories of power and conquest.

5:6–7—Instead of the conquering lion he expected, John sees a *Lamb standing as if it had been slaughtered*. *Seven horns* and eyes evoke the perfection of the Lamb's power and knowledge. What we define as weakness is strength in the eyes of God.

5:8–10—The *new song* celebrates the Lamb's death as the source of his power (cf. chap. 4). All political and religious power (*kingdoms and priests*) is redefined by Jesus' death. Any other basis for power is false.

6:1–8:1 The Opening of the Seven Seals

The Lamb who is worthy because of his life and death opens the seals and makes God's word available.

6:1–8 The First Four Seals

The four *horses* and their *riders* describe the destruction that humanity already visits on itself and do not predict God's future punishment of the earth.

6:1–2—The destruction of war. Rome's most feared invaders were the Parthians, whose cavalry were archers on *white horses*. The *crown* symbolizes false power.

6:3–4—Internal conflicts that rob a society of peace. The *sword* symbolizes the propensity of humans to fight one another.

6:5–6—Economic exploitation. The *scales* symbolize human injustice. *Wheat* and *barley*, food staples needed by the poor, are exorbitantly priced, while the delicacies of the rich (see list of merchandise at 18:13) are unaffected.

horse! Its rider held a pair of scales in his hand, **⁶**and I heard what seemed to be a voice in the midst of the four living creatures saying, "A quart of wheat for a day's pay,*a* and three quarts of barley for a day's pay,*a* but do not damage the olive oil and the wine!"

7 When he opened the fourth seal, I heard the voice of the fourth living creature call out, "Come!"*b* **⁸**I looked and there was a pale green horse! Its rider's name was Death, and Hades followed with him; they were given authority over a fourth of the earth, to kill with sword, famine, and pestilence, and by the wild animals of the earth.

9 When he opened the fifth seal, I saw under the altar the souls of those who had been slaughtered for the word of God and for the testimony they had given; **¹⁰**they cried out with a loud voice, "Sovereign Lord, holy and true, how long will it be before you judge and avenge our blood on the inhabitants of the earth?" **¹¹**They were each given a white robe and told to rest a little longer, until the number would be complete both of their fellow servants*c* and of their brothers and sisters,*d* who were soon to be killed as they themselves had been killed.

12 When he opened the sixth seal, I looked, and there came a great earthquake; the sun became black as sackcloth, the full moon became like blood, **¹³**and the stars of the sky fell to the earth as the fig tree drops its winter fruit when shaken by a gale. **¹⁴**The sky vanished like a scroll rolling itself up, and every mountain and island was removed from its place. **¹⁵**Then the kings of the earth and the magnates and the generals and the rich and the powerful, and everyone, slave and free, hid in the caves and among the rocks of the mountains, **¹⁶**calling to the mountains and rocks, "Fall on us and hide us from the face of the one seated on the throne and from the wrath of the Lamb; **¹⁷**for the great day of their wrath has come, and who is able to stand?"

The 144,000 of Israel Sealed

7 After this I saw four angels standing at the four corners of the earth, holding back the four winds of the earth so that no wind could blow on earth or sea or against any tree. **²**I saw another angel ascending from the rising of the sun, having the seal of the living God, and he called with a loud voice to the four angels who had been given power to damage earth and sea, **³**saying, "Do not damage the earth or the sea or the trees, until we have marked the servants*c* of our God with a seal on their foreheads."

*a*Gk *a denarius* *b*Or "Go!" *c*Gk *slaves* *d*Gk *brothers*

6:7–8—The raw power of death and destruction. Humanity then and now is numb to its self-destructive practices. We act as if there are no realistic alternatives to war and injustice, but the path humanity is on leads to death, not life.

6:9–11 The Fifth Seal

6:9—Those *under the altar* may include all the martyred prophets in Israel's history, as well as first-century Christian martyrs. Their deaths exemplify humanity's destructive bent.

6:10—*"How long?"* echoes Israel's lament psalms (e.g., Ps. 79).

6:11—God answers the martyr's plea for vengeance with an alternative form of justice. God's holy ones, whether martyrs or everyday disciples, cannot dictate God's justice.

6:12–16 The Sixth Seal

6:12–14—See Joel 2:30–31, Matt. 24:29 for similar language of cosmic upheaval. Humanity's actions have an environmental cost.

6:15–17—The *wrath* of God is a biblical expression for God's judgment. Many contemporary Christians are uncomfortable with judgment language, but it is a reminder that our actions have consequences.

7:1–17 Interlude: Hope for the Church

This vision gives the churches hope for their future, by identifying the source of their strength.

7:1–3—Baptism is the seal of Christians' identity as servants of God. Servanthood contradicts the popular notion of individual achievement, but it defines discipleship here.

4 And I heard the number of those who were sealed, one hundred forty-four thousand, sealed out of every tribe of the people of Israel:

5 From the tribe of Judah twelve thousand sealed,

from the tribe of Reuben twelve thousand,

from the tribe of Gad twelve thousand,

6 from the tribe of Asher twelve thousand,

from the tribe of Naphtali twelve thousand,

from the tribe of Manasseh twelve thousand,

7 from the tribe of Simeon twelve thousand,

from the tribe of Levi twelve thousand,

from the tribe of Issachar twelve thousand,

8 from the tribe of Zebulun twelve thousand,

from the tribe of Joseph twelve thousand,

from the tribe of Benjamin twelve thousand sealed.

The Multitude from Every Nation

9 After this I looked, and there was a great multitude that no one could count, from every nation, from all tribes and peoples and languages, standing before the throne and before the Lamb, robed in white, with palm branches in their hands. 10 They cried out in a loud voice, saying,

"Salvation belongs to our God who
　　is seated on the throne, and to
　　the Lamb!"

11 And all the angels stood around the throne and around the elders and the four living creatures, and they fell on their faces before the throne and worshiped God, 12 singing,

"Amen! Blessing and glory and
　　wisdom
and thanksgiving and honor
and power and might
be to our God forever and ever!
　　Amen."

13 Then one of the elders addressed me, saying, "Who are these, robed in white, and where have they come from?" 14 I said to him, "Sir, you are the one that knows." Then he said to me, "These are they who have come out of the great ordeal; they have washed their robes and made them white in the blood of the Lamb.

15 For this reason they are before the
　　throne of God,
and worship him day and night
　　within his temple,
and the one who is seated on the
　　throne will shelter them.
16 They will hunger no more, and thirst
　　no more;
the sun will not strike them,
nor any scorching heat;
17 for the Lamb at the center of the
　　throne will be their shepherd,
and he will guide them to springs
　　of the water of life,
and God will wipe away every tear
　　from their eyes."

The Seventh Seal
and the Golden Censer

8 When the Lamb opened the seventh seal, there was silence in heaven for

---

7:4–8—A multiple of 12 tribes x 12 apostles, 144,000 symbolically represents the totality of God's people. Disciples are not citizens and participants of the Roman Empire; they are citizens of God's Israel. Loyalty to nation and God are not the same thing.

7:9—This vision of the church complements vv. 5–8—both represent the totality of God's people. There is an innumerable throng to be saved, not

a limited number. The Roman Empire has no real power over the churches because in the future there are no national distinctions.

7:13–17—The church's victory is not in a demonstration of power or self-vindication, but in the unceasing praise of God and the Lamb.

7:16–17—See Ps. 23; Isa. 25:8; 49:10.

8:1 The Seventh Seal

What we thought would be an ending is actually

about half an hour. [2] And I saw the seven angels who stand before God, and seven trumpets were given to them.

3 Another angel with a golden censer came and stood at the altar; he was given a great quantity of incense to offer with the prayers of all the saints on the golden altar that is before the throne. [4] And the smoke of the incense, with the prayers of the saints, rose before God from the hand of the angel. [5] Then the angel took the censer and filled it with fire from the altar and threw it on the earth; and there were peals of thunder, rumblings, flashes of lightning, and an earthquake.

The Seven Trumpets

6 Now the seven angels who had the seven trumpets made ready to blow them.

7 The first angel blew his trumpet, and there came hail and fire, mixed with blood, and they were hurled to the earth; and a third of the earth was burned up, and a third of the trees were burned up, and all green grass was burned up.

8 The second angel blew his trumpet, and something like a great mountain, burning with fire, was thrown into the sea. [9] A third of the sea became blood, a third of the living creatures in the sea died, and a third of the ships were destroyed.

10 The third angel blew his trumpet, and a great star fell from heaven, blazing like a torch, and it fell on a third of the rivers and on the springs of water. [11] The name of the star is Wormwood. A third of the waters became wormwood, and many died from the water, because it was made bitter.

12 The fourth angel blew his trumpet, and a third of the sun was struck, and a third of the moon, and a third of the stars, so that a third of their light was darkened; a third of the day was kept from shining, and likewise the night.

13 Then I looked, and I heard an eagle crying with a loud voice as it flew in midheaven, "Woe, woe, woe to the inhabitants of the earth, at the blasts of the other trumpets that the three angels are about to blow!"

9 And the fifth angel blew his trumpet, and I saw a star that had fallen from heaven to earth, and he was given the key to the shaft of the bottomless pit; [2] he opened the shaft of the bottomless pit, and from the shaft rose smoke like the smoke of a great furnace, and the sun and the air were darkened with the smoke from the shaft. [3] Then from

---

a new beginning (v. 2). Revelation envisions the world's ongoing relationship with God, not its ending.

8:2–11:19 The Seven Trumpets

The trumpet plagues mirror the exodus plagues (Exod. 7:14–12:32) and share in an ongoing story of social and communal liberation, not vengeance. The God of exodus justice is also the God of Revelation. Then in 10:1–11:14 we see an alternative picture of the faith community as powerful, not powerless in the face of the empire (cf. 7:1–17).

8:2–5 Worship Scene

Again, all action originates in worship (cf. chaps. 4 and 5). The *incense* symbolizes two-way communication between earth and heaven.

8:6–12 The First Four Trumpets

8:6—In ancient Israel, a *trumpet* was sounded to announce a battle or to call the community to worship. A trumpet (shofar) was blown at Yom Kippur as a call to communal repentance.

8:7—See Exod. 9:13–35.

8:8–9—See Exod. 7:14–25.

8:10–11—This plague has no exodus parallel. Each trumpet's damage will be limited to one-third of a given area. The goal is awakening and repentance, not total devastation.

8:12—See Exod. 10:21–28.

8:13–9:19 The Fifth and Sixth Trumpets

The battle imagery highlights that even the seemingly all-powerful Roman Empire is not invincible. Many in John's audience were seduced by Roman power, as many Christians today are seduced by false notions of power.

9:1–12—The *fifth* trumpet. See Exod. 10:1–20 and Joel 2:1–11.

9:3–5—*Locusts* are an agricultural plague, yet the plants are left alone. The goal is to alter human behavior.

the smoke came locusts on the earth, and they were given authority like the authority of scorpions of the earth. [4] They were told not to damage the grass of the earth or any green growth or any tree, but only those people who do not have the seal of God on their foreheads. [5] They were allowed to torture them for five months, but not to kill them, and their torture was like the torture of a scorpion when it stings someone. [6] And in those days people will seek death but will not find it; they will long to die, but death will flee from them.

[7] In appearance the locusts were like horses equipped for battle. On their heads were what looked like crowns of gold; their faces were like human faces, [8] their hair like women's hair, and their teeth like lions' teeth; [9] they had scales like iron breastplates, and the noise of their wings was like the noise of many chariots with horses rushing into battle. [10] They have tails like scorpions, with stingers, and in their tails is their power to harm people for five months. [11] They have as king over them the angel of the bottomless pit; his name in Hebrew is Abaddon,[a] and in Greek he is called Apollyon.[b]

[12] The first woe has passed. There are still two woes to come.

[13] Then the sixth angel blew his trumpet, and I heard a voice from the four[c] horns of the golden altar before God, [14] saying to the sixth angel who had the trumpet, "Release the four angels who are bound at the great river Euphrates." [15] So the four angels were released, who had been held ready for the hour, the day, the month, and the year, to kill a third of humankind. [16] The number of the troops of cavalry was two hundred million; I heard their number. [17] And this was how I saw the horses in my vision: the riders wore breastplates the color of fire and of sapphire[d] and of sulfur; the heads of the horses were like lions' heads, and fire and smoke and sulfur came out of their mouths. [18] By these three plagues a third of humankind was killed, by the fire and smoke and sulfur coming out of their mouths. [19] For the power of the horses is in their mouths and in their tails; their tails are like serpents, having heads; and with them they inflict harm.

[20] The rest of humankind, who were not killed by these plagues, did not repent of the works of their hands or give up worshiping demons and idols of gold and silver and bronze and stone and wood, which cannot see or hear or walk. [21] And they did not repent of their murders or their sorceries or their fornication or their thefts.

The Angel with the Little Scroll

10 And I saw another mighty angel coming down from heaven, wrapped in a cloud, with a rainbow over his head; his face was like the sun, and his legs like pillars of fire. [2] He held a little scroll open in his hand. Setting his right foot on the sea and his left foot on the land, [3] he gave a great shout, like a lion roaring. And when he shouted, the seven thunders sounded. [4] And when the seven thunders had sounded, I was

[a] That is, *Destruction*   [b] That is, *Destroyer*   [c] Other ancient authorities lack four   [d] Gk *hyacinth*

9:7–11—The locusts are given human attributes in order to parody Rome's pretension of power. *Apollyon*, "the one who destroys," parodies the power of the god Apollo and the Roman emperor's identification with him.

9:13–19—The *sixth* trumpet. The unleashing of the demonic cavalry parodies Rome's military might. Cf. 6:1–2.

9:20–21 The Absence of Repentance

John's audience, then and now, is called to turn away from the falsehoods of the empire and re-

claim their identity as a people shaped by God's power for liberation and justice. Cf. Exod. 8:15, 19; 9:27–35.

10:1–11 John as Prophet and Witness Cf. 1:1

10:2–4—Traditional Old Testament symbols of God's presence—rainbow, pillars of fire, lion's roar, thunder. The source of prophetic power and insight is God, not the prophet or leader's personality.

10:4—See Dan. 12:5–13. *Seal up*—John's words provide a glimpse into God's will and hope for

about to write, but I heard a voice from heaven saying, "Seal up what the seven thunders have said, and do not write it down." ⁵ Then the angel whom I saw standing on the sea and the land

　　raised his right hand to heaven
⁶　　and swore by him who lives
　　　　forever and ever,

who created heaven and what is in it, the earth and what is in it, and the sea and what is in it: "There will be no more delay, ⁷ but in the days when the seventh angel is to blow his trumpet, the mystery of God will be fulfilled, as he announced to his servants*a* the prophets."

8 Then the voice that I had heard from heaven spoke to me again, saying, "Go, take the scroll that is open in the hand of the angel who is standing on the sea and on the land." ⁹ So I went to the angel and told him to give me the little scroll; and he said to me, "Take it, and eat; it will be bitter to your stomach, but sweet as honey in your mouth." ¹⁰ So I took the little scroll from the hand of the angel and ate it; it was sweet as honey in my mouth, but when I had eaten it, my stomach was made bitter.

11 Then they said to me, "You must prophesy again about many peoples and nations and languages and kings."

The Two Witnesses

11 Then I was given a measuring rod like a staff, and I was told,

"Come and measure the temple of God and the altar and those who worship there, ² but do not measure the court outside the temple; leave that out, for it is given over to the nations, and they will trample over the holy city for forty-two months. ³ And I will grant my two witnesses authority to prophesy for one thousand two hundred sixty days, wearing sackcloth."

4 These are the two olive trees and the two lampstands that stand before the Lord of the earth. ⁵ And if anyone wants to harm them, fire pours from their mouth and consumes their foes; anyone who wants to harm them must be killed in this manner. ⁶ They have authority to shut the sky, so that no rain may fall during the days of their prophesying, and they have authority over the waters to turn them into blood, and to strike the earth with every kind of plague, as often as they desire.

7 When they have finished their testimony, the beast that comes up from the bottomless pit will make war on them and conquer them and kill them, ⁸ and their dead bodies will lie in the street of the great city that is prophetically*b* called Sodom and Egypt, where also their Lord was crucified. ⁹ For three and a half days members of the peoples and tribes and languages and nations will gaze at their dead bodies and refuse to let them be

a Gk slaves　*b* Or allegorically; Gk spiritually

---

the world, but are not the sum total of the words God has for the world.

10:6 No . . . delay—The present moment is God's time. One cannot be casual in the way one meets the challenges of faithful living.

10:8–10—See Ezek. 2:8–3:3. The good news is often also hard news.

10:11—John is to continue to tell the story of the empire as it looks through God's eyes. The commitment to truth telling can be costly.

11:1–14 The Two Witnesses

11:1–2—To *measure* indicates protection; see Ezek. 40:3–42:20, Zech. 2:1–5. The *temple* stands for the people of God. Adversity will not be avoided (*trample*), but God is with God's people in their turmoil.

11:3–4—*Two witnesses* are required for testimony to be valid (Deut. 17:6, 19:15; Matt. 18:16); the two witnesses here symbolize the prophetic witness of the whole church. See Zech. 4:1–14 for *olive tree* and *lampstand* as symbols of Joshua the priest and Zerubbabel the king. Lampstands are also churches (1:20). The whole church, not simply individual leaders, is God's kingdom and priesthood (1:6).

11:5–6—Cf. Moses (Exod. 7:14–25) and Elijah (1 Kgs. 17:1, 2 Kgs. 1:10–12).

11:7–10—The church will suffer because of its faithful witness. *The beast* (see chap. 13) symbolizes all that is opposed to the truth. The word of God appears to be no match for the powers of the empire.

placed in a tomb; [10] and the inhabitants of the earth will gloat over them and celebrate and exchange presents, because these two prophets had been a torment to the inhabitants of the earth.

11 But after the three and a half days, the breath[a] of life from God entered them, and they stood on their feet, and those who saw them were terrified. [12] Then they[b] heard a loud voice from heaven saying to them, "Come up here!" And they went up to heaven in a cloud while their enemies watched them. [13] At that moment there was a great earthquake, and a tenth of the city fell; seven thousand people were killed in the earthquake, and the rest were terrified and gave glory to the God of heaven.

14 The second woe has passed. The third woe is coming very soon.

The Seventh Trumpet

15 Then the seventh angel blew his trumpet, and there were loud voices in heaven, saying,

"The kingdom of the world has
    become the kingdom of our
    Lord
  and of his Messiah,[c]
and he will reign forever and ever."

16 Then the twenty-four elders who sit on their thrones before God fell on their faces and worshiped God, [17] singing,

"We give you thanks, Lord God
    Almighty,
  who are and who were,
for you have taken your great power
  and begun to reign.

18 The nations raged,
  but your wrath has come,
  and the time for judging the dead,
for rewarding your servants,[d] the
    prophets
  and saints and all who fear your
    name,
  both small and great,
and for destroying those who
    destroy the earth."

19 Then God's temple in heaven was opened, and the ark of his covenant was seen within his temple; and there were flashes of lightning, rumblings, peals of thunder, an earthquake, and heavy hail.

The Woman and the Dragon

12 A great portent appeared in heaven: a woman clothed with the sun, with the moon under her feet, and on her head a crown of twelve stars. [2] She was pregnant and was crying out in birth pangs, in the agony of giving birth. [3] Then another portent appeared in heaven: a great red dragon, with seven heads and ten horns, and seven diadems on his heads. [4] His tail swept down a third of the stars of heaven and threw them to the earth. Then the dragon stood before the woman who was about to bear a child, so that he might devour her child as soon as it was born. [5] And she gave birth to a son, a male child, who is to rule[e] all the nations with a rod of iron. But her child was snatched away and taken to God and to his throne; [6] and the

---

[a] Or *the spirit*   [b] Other ancient authorities read *I*   [c] Gk *Christ*   [d] Gk *slaves*
[e] Or *to shepherd*

11:11–12—See Ezek. 37. The false powers of the empire cannot triumph over the life-giving powers of God.

11:13 *A great earthquake*—A sign of the eschatological age. A choice is required of disciples: to side with empire or to risk everything in order to witness to the scandal of the gospel.

11:15–19 The Seventh Trumpet

The third woe is not recounted (cf. v. 14; 8:1). The beginning of the reign of God is announced and celebrated in heavenly worship.

12:1–13:18 The Mythic Battle of Good and Evil

John attempts to move his readers out of the everyday and into the realm of the mythic in order to show what is at stake in the decisions they make about human empires.

12:1–6 A Woman Clothed like a Sun

12:1 *Portent*—A sign or symbol.

12:3—The monster from the sea embodies the power of chaos and everything that is anti-God. Cf. Isa. 27:1, Dan. 7:7–8.

12:2–6—Evokes thoughts of the birth of Apollo, a well-known story to John's readers, the nativity of Jesus, and the symbolic birth of the people of God. *Wilderness* is God's place of refuge (cf. Exodus tradition).

woman fled into the wilderness, where she has a place prepared by God, so that there she can be nourished for one thousand two hundred sixty days.

Michael Defeats the Dragon

7 And war broke out in heaven; Michael and his angels fought against the dragon. The dragon and his angels fought back, **8** but they were defeated, and there was no longer any place for them in heaven. **9** The great dragon was thrown down, that ancient serpent, who is called the Devil and Satan, the deceiver of the whole world—he was thrown down to the earth, and his angels were thrown down with him.

10 Then I heard a loud voice in heaven, proclaiming,

"Now have come the salvation and
     the power
  and the kingdom of our God
  and the authority of his Messiah,*a*
for the accuser of our comrades*b* has
     been thrown down,
  who accuses them day and night
     before our God.
11 But they have conquered him by the
     blood of the Lamb
  and by the word of their testimony,
  for they did not cling to life even in
     the face of death.
12 Rejoice then, you heavens
  and those who dwell in them!

But woe to the earth and the sea,
  for the devil has come down to
     you
  with great wrath,
     because he knows that his time is
        short!"

The Dragon Fights Again on Earth

13 So when the dragon saw that he had been thrown down to the earth, he pursued*c* the woman who had given birth to the male child. **14** But the woman was given the two wings of the great eagle, so that she could fly from the serpent into the wilderness, to her place where she is nourished for a time, and times, and half a time. **15** Then from his mouth the serpent poured water like a river after the woman, to sweep her away with the flood. **16** But the earth came to the help of the woman; it opened its mouth and swallowed the river that the dragon had poured from his mouth. **17** Then the dragon was angry with the woman, and went off to make war on the rest of her children, those who keep the commandments of God and hold the testimony of Jesus.

The First Beast

18 Then the dragon*d* took his stand on
13 the sand of the seashore. **1** And I saw a beast rising out of the sea,

a Gk Christ *b* Gk brothers *c* Or persecuted *d* Gk Then he; other ancient authorities read Then I stood

---

12:7–12 The War in Heaven

New characters depict the side of good (**Michael and his angels**), but evil (**the dragon**) remains the same.

12:9—The true identity of the dragon is made clear.

12:10–12—A hymn of praise to the source of these victories.

12:11—Power to defeat the dragon comes from the life-giving death of Jesus and the churches' testimony to it. Disciples share in this awesome power and the attendant responsibility to fight evil. Discipleship is not something to be taken lightly or to be timid about.

12:13–17 The Dragon Pursues the Woman Again

12:14–16—The earth actively sides with the

woman against the dragon. The woman's children should reflect on the ways that they have repaid the earth.

12:17—The dragon now turns against the people of God. The churches' current situation is seen as part of this cosmic story. Evil is resilient, and yet its defeat is sure.

12:18–13:18 The Two Beasts

The dragon, the power of chaos and evil, is a pale imitation of God the Creator. The two beasts parody, respectively, the Lamb and the power of the Spirit as known in prophets and witnesses. The first beast is pictured in 12:18–13:10, the second in 13:11–16.

13:1–2—Combines the chaos sea monster (see 12:3) with all four beasts of Dan. 7:1–8. Chaos and evil are lodged in the beast of historical

having ten horns and seven heads; and on its horns were ten diadems, and on its heads were blasphemous names. [2] And the beast that I saw was like a leopard, its feet were like a bear's, and its mouth was like a lion's mouth. And the dragon gave it his power and his throne and great authority. [3] One of its heads seemed to have received a death-blow, but its mortal wound[a] had been healed. In amazement the whole earth followed the beast. [4] They worshiped the dragon, for he had given his authority to the beast, and they worshiped the beast, saying, "Who is like the beast, and who can fight against it?"

5 The beast was given a mouth uttering haughty and blasphemous words, and it was allowed to exercise authority for forty-two months. [6] It opened its mouth to utter blasphemies against God, blaspheming his name and his dwelling, that is, those who dwell in heaven. [7] Also it was allowed to make war on the saints and to conquer them.[b] It was given authority over every tribe and people and language and nation, [8] and all the inhabitants of the earth will worship it, everyone whose name has not been written from the foundation of the world in the book of life of the Lamb that was slaughtered.[c]

9 Let anyone who has an ear listen:

[10]   If you are to be taken captive,
        into captivity you go;
   if you kill with the sword,

with the sword you must be killed. Here is a call for the endurance and faith of the saints.

The Second Beast

11 Then I saw another beast that rose out of the earth; it had two horns like a lamb and it spoke like a dragon. [12] It exercises all the authority of the first beast on its behalf, and it makes the earth and its inhabitants worship the first beast, whose mortal wound[d] had been healed. [13] It performs great signs, even making fire come down from heaven to earth in the sight of all; [14] and by the signs that it is allowed to perform on behalf of the beast, it deceives the inhabitants of earth, telling them to make an image for the beast that had been wounded by the sword[e] and yet lived; [15] and it was allowed to give breath[f] to the image of the beast so that the image of the beast could even speak and cause those who would not worship the image of the beast to be killed. [16] Also it causes all, both small and great, both rich and poor, both free and slave, to be marked on the right hand or the forehead, [17] so that no one can buy or sell who does not have the mark, that is, the name of the beast or the number of its name. [18] This calls for wisdom: let anyone with understanding calculate the number of the beast, for it

[a] Gk the plague of its death   [b] Other ancient authorities lack this sentence
[c] Or written in the book of life of the Lamb that was slaughtered from the foundation of the world   [d] Gk whose plague of its death   [e] Or that had received the plague of the sword   [f] Or spirit

---

empires. For John's original readers, that empire was Rome.

13:2—Just as God gives power to the Lamb, the *dragon* gives power to the beast.

13:3—The beast's wounds parody the wounds of the Lamb (5:6). May allude to the emperor Nero, who was reputed to have survived a death blow.

13:4—Emperor worship was a mark of the imperial cult. Faithful disciples pledge their allegiance only to God and the Lamb, not to the state.

13:5–8—All the beast's activities are a distortion of the work of the Lamb.

13:11–12—Just as true prophets are in the image of the Lamb, the false prophet is in the image of the first beast.

13:13–15—The false prophet looks like a genuine prophet (cf. 1 Kgs. 18:20–39), but leads people with deception instead of true witness (cf. Rev. 11:4–13).

13:16–17—The true prophet helps the people resist empire (cf. chaps. 2 and 3), but the false prophet leads the people into economic dependence on the empire.

13:18—*It is the number of a person* means that evil will not always be as easily recognizable as is a mythological beast. The number 666 may have suggested a particular individual to John's original readers, but decoding this number is not the point. The challenge for faithful discipleship is to recognize the face of evil in the everyday and to resist its pull.

is the number of a person. Its number is six hundred sixty-six.[a]

The Lamb and the 144,000

14 Then I looked, and there was the Lamb, standing on Mount Zion! And with him were one hundred forty-four thousand who had his name and his Father's name written on their foreheads. 2 And I heard a voice from heaven like the sound of many waters and like the sound of loud thunder; the voice I heard was like the sound of harpists playing on their harps, 3 and they sing a new song before the throne and before the four living creatures and before the elders. No one could learn that song except the one hundred forty-four thousand who have been redeemed from the earth. 4 It is these who have not defiled themselves with women, for they are virgins; these follow the Lamb wherever he goes. They have been redeemed from humankind as first fruits for God and the Lamb, 5 and in their mouth no lie was found; they are blameless.

The Messages of the Three Angels

6 Then I saw another angel flying in midheaven, with an eternal gospel to proclaim to those who live[b] on the earth—to every nation and tribe and language and people. 7 He said in a loud voice, "Fear God and give him glory, for the hour of his judgment has come; and worship him who made heaven and earth, the sea and the springs of water."

8 Then another angel, a second, followed, saying, "Fallen, fallen is Babylon the great! She has made all nations drink of the wine of the wrath of her fornication."

9 Then another angel, a third, followed them, crying with a loud voice, "Those who worship the beast and its image, and receive a mark on their foreheads or on their hands, 10 they will also drink the wine of God's wrath, poured unmixed into the cup of his anger, and they will be tormented with fire and sulfur in the presence of the holy angels and in the presence of the Lamb. 11 And the smoke of their torment goes up forever and ever. There is no rest day or night for those who worship the beast and its image and for anyone who receives the mark of its name."

12 Here is a call for the endurance of the saints, those who keep the commandments of God and hold fast to the faith of[c] Jesus.

13 And I heard a voice from heaven saying, "Write this: Blessed are the dead who from now on die in the Lord." "Yes," says the Spirit, "they will rest from their labors, for their deeds follow them."

Reaping the Earth's Harvest

14 Then I looked, and there was a white cloud, and seated on the cloud was

a Other ancient authorities read *six hundred sixteen*   b Gk *sit*   c Or *to their faith in*

14:1–20 Visions of the Church's Future

14:1–5 The Redeemed Community

14:1—Cf. 7:1–8.

14:3–4—*Redeemed*, or purchased, means that the Lamb's life and death, not any human action, ultimately create the community of disciples.

14:2–5—Disciples respond to the Lamb's redeeming act with worship and by living lives of truth instead of deceit.

14:6–20 God Is the Only True Judge

14:6–7—Judgment rests with God, not the dragon and its beasts.

14:8—Anticipates chaps. 17 and 18.

14:9–13—This vision of judgment is directed toward church members who are tempted to receive the *mark* of the *beast* (cf. 13:16–17). Accommodation with the empire brings economic and social advantages; this vision reveals the true cost of alignment with the empire. Verses 12–13, the alternative to accommodation.

14:14 *Son of Man*—See Dan. 7:13. Traditional figure of judgment, see Rev. 1:13.

14:14–20—*Harvest* and *wine press* are traditional images of judgment in the Old Testament (Joel 3:13; Hos. 6:11; Isa. 63:1–3) and New Testament (Matt. 13:36–43; Rev. 19:15). This vision is not intended to make community members feel superior to those "outsiders" who will feel God's wrath, but to awaken disciples to the cosmic scale of their own decisions about empire.

one like the Son of Man, with a golden crown on his head, and a sharp sickle in his hand! ¹⁵ Another angel came out of the temple, calling with a loud voice to the one who sat on the cloud, "Use your sickle and reap, for the hour to reap has come, because the harvest of the earth is fully ripe." ¹⁶ So the one who sat on the cloud swung his sickle over the earth, and the earth was reaped.

17 Then another angel came out of the temple in heaven, and he too had a sharp sickle. ¹⁸ Then another angel came out from the altar, the angel who has authority over fire, and he called with a loud voice to him who had the sharp sickle, "Use your sharp sickle and gather the clusters of the vine of the earth, for its grapes are ripe." ¹⁹ So the angel swung his sickle over the earth and gathered the vintage of the earth, and he threw it into the great wine press of the wrath of God. ²⁰ And the wine press was trodden outside the city, and blood flowed from the wine press, as high as a horse's bridle, for a distance of about two hundred miles.ᵃ

The Angels with the Seven Last Plagues

15 Then I saw another portent in heaven, great and amazing: seven angels with seven plagues, which are the last, for with them the wrath of God is ended.

2 And I saw what appeared to be a sea of glass mixed with fire, and those who had conquered the beast and its image and the number of its name, standing beside the sea of glass with harps of God in their hands. ³ And they sing the song of Moses, the servantᵇ of God, and the song of the Lamb:

"Great and amazing are your deeds,
    Lord God the Almighty!
Just and true are your ways,
    King of the nations!ᶜ
⁴ Lord, who will not fear
    and glorify your name?
For you alone are holy.
    All nations will come
    and worship before you,
for your judgments have been
     revealed."

5 After this I looked, and the temple of the tentᵈ of witness in heaven was opened, ⁶ and out of the temple came the seven angels with the seven plagues, robed in pure bright linen,ᵉ with golden sashes across their chests. ⁷ Then one of the four living creatures gave the seven angels seven golden bowls full of the wrath of God, who lives forever and ever; ⁸ and the temple was filled with smoke from the glory of God and from his power, and no one could enter the temple until the seven plagues of the seven angels were ended.

The Bowls of God's Wrath

16 Then I heard a loud voice from the temple telling the seven angels, "Go and pour out on the earth the seven bowls of the wrath of God."

2 So the first angel went and poured his bowl on the earth, and a foul and painful sore came on those who had the mark of the beast and who worshiped its image.

3 The second angel poured his bowl into the sea, and it became like the blood

---

ᵃ Gk one thousand six hundred stadia ᵇ Gk slave ᶜ Other ancient authorities read the ages ᵈ Or tabernacle ᵉ Other ancient authorities read stone

---

15:1–16:21 The Seven Plagues
These mirror the exodus plagues (see also 8:2–11:19). The destruction of a past empire (Egypt) anticipates the fall of the current empire (Rome). Yet the battle against the pervasive power of empire is ongoing throughout history, as the repeating series of seals, trumpets, and bowls show.

15:2–8 Heavenly Worship (cf. 4:1–11; 8:2–5)

15:3–4—Songs of Moses and the Lamb—see Exod. 15. The faithful worship in the confidence of God's justice and do not celebrate vengeance or destruction.

16:1–21 The Pouring Out of the Seven Bowls
16:2—See Exod. 9:8–12.
16:3—See Exod. 7:14–25.

of a corpse, and every living thing in the sea died.

4 The third angel poured his bowl into the rivers and the springs of water, and they became blood. **5** And I heard the angel of the waters say,

"You are just, O Holy One, who are and were,
for you have judged these things;
6 because they shed the blood of saints and prophets,
you have given them blood to drink.
It is what they deserve!"

7 And I heard the altar respond,

"Yes, O Lord God, the Almighty,
your judgments are true and just!"

8 The fourth angel poured his bowl on the sun, and it was allowed to scorch people with fire; **9** they were scorched by the fierce heat, but they cursed the name of God, who had authority over these plagues, and they did not repent and give him glory.

10 The fifth angel poured his bowl on the throne of the beast, and its kingdom was plunged into darkness; people gnawed their tongues in agony, **11** and cursed the God of heaven because of their pains and sores, and they did not repent of their deeds.

12 The sixth angel poured his bowl on the great river Euphrates, and its water was dried up in order to prepare the way for the kings from the east. **13** And I saw three foul spirits like frogs coming from

the mouth of the dragon, from the mouth of the beast, and from the mouth of the false prophet. **14** These are demonic spirits, performing signs, who go abroad to the kings of the whole world, to assemble them for battle on the great day of God the Almighty. **15** ("See, I am coming like a thief! Blessed is the one who stays awake and is clothed,*a* not going about naked and exposed to shame.") **16** And they assembled them at the place that in Hebrew is called Harmagedon.

17 The seventh angel poured his bowl into the air, and a loud voice came out of the temple, from the throne, saying, "It is done!" **18** And there came flashes of lightning, rumblings, peals of thunder, and a violent earthquake, such as had not occurred since people were upon the earth, so violent was that earthquake. **19** The great city was split into three parts, and the cities of the nations fell. God remembered great Babylon and gave her the wine-cup of the fury of his wrath. **20** And every island fled away, and no mountains were to be found; **21** and huge hailstones, each weighing about a hundred pounds,*b* dropped from heaven on people, until they cursed God for the plague of the hail, so fearful was that plague.

The Great Whore and the Beast

17 Then one of the seven angels who had the seven bowls came

a Gk and keeps his robes   *b* Gk weighing about a talent

16:4–7—See Exod. 7:14–25. These plagues are God's judgment against the presence and power of evil. John's readers, like many contemporary Christians, discount the power of evil, but John calls the community to see that evil is resilient and always the enemy of God's justice.

16:8–9—Unlike the effect of the seals and trumpets, the destruction of the first four plagues is for the entire cosmos, not a fraction of it. The resilience of evil is seen in the lack of repentance (cf. 9:20–21 and Exod. 9:27–35; 10:24–28).

16:10–11—See Exod. 10:21–23; 9:8–11. The plagues now shift to the beast and his empire.

16:12–16—See Exod. 8:3–6; Josh. 3:1–4:8; Exod. 14:21–22. This plague envisions the arrival of Rome's enemies (cf. 6:2; 9:7–19). The actual

battle is not fought, because God is the agent of justice, not human armies.

16:15—Cf. Matt. 24:42–44; Luke 12:39–40; 1 Thess. 5:12.

16:17–21—See Exod. 9:23–25. *Babylon* stands for Rome, as the true object of God's justice is named.

16:21—God is the author of justice. Human agents are completely absent. Disciples are called to declare themselves on the side of God's justice and not on the side of the empire that works against justice.

17:1–18:24 The Fall of Babylon

Idolatry and faithlessness, violence, economic exploitation, and arrogance evoke the judgment

and said to me, "Come, I will show you the judgment of the great whore who is seated on many waters, ²with whom the kings of the earth have committed fornication, and with the wine of whose fornication the inhabitants of the earth have become drunk." ³So he carried me away in the spirit*ᵃ* into a wilderness, and I saw a woman sitting on a scarlet beast that was full of blasphemous names, and it had seven heads and ten horns. ⁴The woman was clothed in purple and scarlet, and adorned with gold and jewels and pearls, holding in her hand a golden cup full of abominations and the impurities of her fornication; ⁵and on her forehead was written a name, a mystery: "Babylon the great, mother of whores and of earth's abominations." ⁶And I saw that the woman was drunk with the blood of the saints and the blood of the witnesses to Jesus.

When I saw her, I was greatly amazed. ⁷But the angel said to me, "Why are you so amazed? I will tell you the mystery of the woman, and of the beast with seven heads and ten horns that carries her. ⁸The beast that you saw was, and is not, and is about to ascend from the bottomless pit and go to destruction. And the inhabitants of the earth, whose names have not been written in the book of life from the foundation of the world, will be amazed when they see the beast, because it was and is not and is to come. ⁹"This calls for a mind that has wisdom: the seven heads are seven moun-

tains on which the woman is seated; also, they are seven kings, ¹⁰of whom five have fallen, one is living, and the other has not yet come; and when he comes, he must remain only a little while. ¹¹As for the beast that was and is not, it is an eighth but it belongs to the seven, and it goes to destruction. ¹²And the ten horns that you saw are ten kings who have not yet received a kingdom, but they are to receive authority as kings for one hour, together with the beast. ¹³These are united in yielding their power and authority to the beast; ¹⁴they will make war on the Lamb, and the Lamb will conquer them, for he is Lord of lords and King of kings, and those with him are called and chosen and faithful."

15 And he said to me, "The waters that you saw, where the whore is seated, are peoples and multitudes and nations and languages. ¹⁶And the ten horns that you saw, they and the beast will hate the whore; they will make her desolate and naked; they will devour her flesh and burn her up with fire. ¹⁷For God has put it into their hearts to carry out his purpose by agreeing to give their kingdom to the beast, until the words of God will be fulfilled. ¹⁸The woman you saw is the great city that rules over the kings of the earth."

The Fall of Babylon

18 After this I saw another angel coming down from heaven, having great authority; and the earth was

ᵃ Or in the Spirit

---

that has been anticipated from the opening of the first seal (6:1).

17:1–18 The Identity of Babylon

17:1–2—*Whore* symbolizes an idolatrous city, whose power seduces people away from God's truth and justice; see Isa. 23:16–18; Nah. 3:1–7.

17:3–6—Many symbols describe the corrupt empire—power and domination (v. 3), excessive wealth (v. 4), violence (v. 6).

17:7—Even John is impressed by what Babylon has to offer. The appeal of empire is very strong.

17:9–11—*Seven mountains* and the series of *kings* made clear to John's original readers that

Babylon stands for Rome. The challenge has never been to decode the symbols, but to recognize that John's presentation of Rome communicates the truth about empire.

17:12–14—Roman emperors only have power from the *beast*. The power of evil cannot stand against the power in weakness of the *Lamb*.

17:15–17—Evil is by definition self-destructive (cf. 6:3–4).

17:18—The whore is Rome.

18:1–24 Response to the Fall of Babylon

The fall of Babylon is not narrated directly, but takes place off stage. The reader experiences

made bright with his splendor. ²He called out with a mighty voice,

> "Fallen, fallen is Babylon the great!
> It has become a dwelling place of
>   demons,
> a haunt of every foul spirit,
>   a haunt of every foul bird,
>   a haunt of every foul and hateful
>   beast.ᵃ
> ³ For all the nations have drunkᵇ
>   of the wine of the wrath of her
>   fornication,
> and the kings of the earth have
>   committed fornication with
>   her,
>   and the merchants of the earth
>   have grown rich from the
>   powerᶜ of her luxury."

4 Then I heard another voice from heaven saying,

> "Come out of her, my people,
>   so that you do not take part in her
>   sins,
> and so that you do not share in her
>   plagues;
> ⁵ for her sins are heaped high as
>   heaven,
>   and God has remembered her
>   iniquities.
> ⁶ Render to her as she herself has
>   rendered,
>   and repay her double for her
>   deeds;
>   mix a double draught for her in
>   the cup she mixed.
> ⁷ As she glorified herself and lived
>   luxuriously,
>   so give her a like measure of
>   torment and grief.

> Since in her heart she says,
>   'I rule as a queen;
> I am no widow,
>   and I will never see grief,'
> ⁸ therefore her plagues will come in a
>   single day—
>   pestilence and mourning and
>   famine—
> and she will be burned with fire;
>   for mighty is the Lord God who
>   judges her."

9 And the kings of the earth, who committed fornication and lived in luxury with her, will weep and wail over her when they see the smoke of her burning; ¹⁰ they will stand far off, in fear of her torment, and say,

> "Alas, alas, the great city,
>   Babylon, the mighty city!
> For in one hour your judgment has
>   come."

11 And the merchants of the earth weep and mourn for her, since no one buys their cargo anymore, ¹²cargo of gold, silver, jewels and pearls, fine linen, purple, silk and scarlet, all kinds of scented wood, all articles of ivory, all articles of costly wood, bronze, iron, and marble, ¹³cinnamon, spice, incense, myrrh, frankincense, wine, olive oil, choice flour and wheat, cattle and sheep, horses and chariots, slaves—and human lives.ᵈ

> ¹⁴ "The fruit for which your soul
>   longed
>   has gone from you,

ᵃ Other ancient authorities lack the words *a haunt of every foul beast* and attach the words *and hateful* to the previous line so as to read *She has made a haunt of every foul and hateful bird* ᵇ Other ancient authorities read *She has made all nations drink* ᶜ Or *resources* ᵈ Or *chariots, and human bodies and souls*

---

the fall through the responses of others. Verses 1–8 give heavenly responses, 9–19 laments over Babylon, and 21–24 Babylon's defeat. Cf. the oracles against the nations, Isa. 23–24; Jer. 50–51; Ezek. 26–27.

18:2—Cf. Isa. 29:1.

18:3—Abuse of power and wealth cause Babylon's fall.

18:4—Cf. Jer. 50:8; 51, 6, 45; Isa. 48:20. To *come out* of Babylon is not to shift geographical locale, but to renounce all that empire stands for.

A difficult command, because many people in the church like what empire has to offer—stability, economic profit, social status, etc.

18:5–8—Sins are public acts of injustice, oppression, arrogance (v. 7), and faithlessness that inevitably evoke God's judgment.

18:9–10—The loss of power.

18:11–17a—The loss of wealth and profit.

18:13–14—Everything is a commodity to the empire, including human bodies and souls.

and all your dainties and your splendor
    are lost to you,
       never to be found again!"

15 The merchants of these wares, who gained wealth from her, will stand far off, in fear of her torment, weeping and mourning aloud,

16 "Alas, alas, the great city,
    clothed in fine linen,
       in purple and scarlet,
    adorned with gold,
       with jewels, and with pearls!
17 For in one hour all this wealth has
       been laid waste!"

And all shipmasters and seafarers, sailors and all whose trade is on the sea, stood far off 18 and cried out as they saw the smoke of her burning,

  "What city was like the great city?"
19 And they threw dust on their heads, as they wept and mourned, crying out,

  "Alas, alas, the great city,
    where all who had ships at sea
    grew rich by her wealth!
For in one hour she has been laid
    waste."

20 Rejoice over her, O heaven, you saints and apostles and prophets! For God has given judgment for you against her.

21 Then a mighty angel took up a stone like a great millstone and threw it into the sea, saying,

  "With such violence Babylon the
      great city
  will be thrown down,
  and will be found no more;
22 and the sound of harpists and
      minstrels and of flutists and
      trumpeters

will be heard in you no more;
  and an artisan of any trade
  will be found in you no more;
and the sound of the millstone
  will be heard in you no more;
23 and the light of a lamp
  will shine in you no more;
and the voice of bridegroom and
    bride
  will be heard in you no more;
for your merchants were the
    magnates of the earth,
  and all nations were deceived by
    your sorcery.
24 And in you[a] was found the blood of
    prophets and of saints,
  and of all who have been
    slaughtered on earth."

The Rejoicing in Heaven

19 After this I heard what seemed to be the loud voice of a great multitude in heaven, saying,
  "Hallelujah!
Salvation and glory and power to
    our God,
2   for his judgments are true and
    just;
he has judged the great whore
  who corrupted the earth with her
    fornication,
and he has avenged on her the blood
    of his servants."[b]
3 Once more they said,
  "Hallelujah!
The smoke goes up from her forever
    and ever."
4 And the twenty-four elders and the four living creatures fell down and wor-

[a] Gk her   [b] Gk slaves

18:17b–19—The end of commerce.

18:20—Another difficult command (cf. v. 4). Many members of the church benefit from the power and wealth of the empire and do not automatically rejoice at its defeat.

18:21—Cf. Jer. 51:63–64.

18:22–24—The evil and injustice of empire compromise everything. To be a disciple one must resist the allure of empire completely or share in its judgment.

19:1–10 Heavenly Worship
See 4:1–10; 8:2–5; 15:2–8.

19:1–5—God's justice and righteousness are praised (**Hallelujah** occurs only here in the entire New Testament); death and destruction are not celebrated. The establishment of God's kingdom is the focus.

shiped God who is seated on the throne, saying,

"Amen. Hallelujah!"

5 And from the throne came a voice saying,

"Praise our God,
   all you his servants,[a]
and all who fear him,
   small and great."

6 Then I heard what seemed to be the voice of a great multitude, like the sound of many waters and like the sound of mighty thunderpeals, crying out,

"Hallelujah!
For the Lord our God
   the Almighty reigns.
7 Let us rejoice and exult
   and give him the glory,
for the marriage of the Lamb has
     come,
   and his bride has made herself
     ready;
8 to her it has been granted to be
     clothed
   with fine linen, bright and pure"—

for the fine linen is the righteous deeds of the saints.

9 And the angel said[b] to me, "Write this: Blessed are those who are invited to the marriage supper of the Lamb." And he said to me, "These are true words of God." 10 Then I fell down at his feet to worship him, but he said to me, "You must not do that! I am a fellow servant[c] with you and your comrades[d] who hold the testimony of Jesus.[e] Worship God! For the testimony of Jesus[e] is the spirit of prophecy."

The Rider on the White Horse

11 Then I saw heaven opened, and there was a white horse! Its rider is called Faithful and True, and in righteousness he judges and makes war. 12 His eyes are like a flame of fire, and on his head are many diadems; and he has a name inscribed that no one knows but himself. 13 He is clothed in a robe dipped in[f] blood, and his name is called The Word of God. 14 And the armies of heaven, wearing fine linen, white and pure, were following him on white horses. 15 From his mouth comes a sharp sword with which to strike down the nations, and he will rule[g] them with a rod of iron; he will tread the wine press of the fury of the wrath of God the Almighty. 16 On his robe and on his thigh he has a name inscribed, "King of kings and Lord of lords."

The Beast and Its Armies Defeated

17 Then I saw an angel standing in the sun, and with a loud voice he called to all the birds that fly in midheaven, "Come, gather for the great supper of God, 18 to eat the flesh of kings, the flesh of captains, the flesh of the mighty, the flesh of horses and their riders—flesh

a Gk slaves   *b* Gk he said   *c* Gk slave   *d* Gk brothers   *e* Or to Jesus   *f* Other ancient authorities read *sprinkled with*   *g* Or will shepherd

---

19:6–10—The church is invited to a new identity, no longer part of empire but the *bride of the Lamb*. The bride embodies everything that empire was not—fidelity, covenant, and justice.

19:11–22:21 Visions of the Establishment of God's Justice on Earth

John does not present a blueprint for the end of the world but a series of visions that each try to evoke the coming of God's reign and destruction of the obstacles to its coming.

19:11–16 Christ the Conqueror

The conquering Messiah is the Lamb who has been slaughtered.

19:11—Cf. 1:5; 3:14; 6:1.

19:12—Cf. 1:14–15.

19:13—Christ's own *blood*, cf. 5:6, 9; 7:14. *The Word of God*, cf. John 1; 1 John 1:1.

19:14—*White linen*, 6:11; 7:14. The armies' strength comes from the power in Christ's death, not from conventional military might.

19:15—Christ's sword is the *sword* of *his mouth* (1:16, v. 21). *Rule*, to shepherd (Ps. 23; Rev. 7:17). The battle is won by Christ's life and death.

19:17–21 The Last Battle (cf. Ezek. 38–39)

No actual fighting is narrated (cf. 6:1–7; 9:7–19), because God's victory in the life and death of the Lamb has already taken place.

19:17–18—A reversal of the eschatological banquet (cf. Ezek. 39:4, 17–20). As in the prophets, the question for the churches is whether they will be a guest at this banquet or served as its food.

of all, both free and slave, both small and great." ¹⁹ Then I saw the beast and the kings of the earth with their armies gathered to make war against the rider on the horse and against his army. ²⁰ And the beast was captured, and with it the false prophet who had performed in its presence the signs by which he deceived those who had received the mark of the beast and those who worshiped its image. These two were thrown alive into the lake of fire that burns with sulfur. ²¹ And the rest were killed by the sword of the rider on the horse, the sword that came from his mouth; and all the birds were gorged with their flesh.

The Thousand Years

20 Then I saw an angel coming down from heaven, holding in his hand the key to the bottomless pit and a great chain. ² He seized the dragon, that ancient serpent, who is the Devil and Satan, and bound him for a thousand years, ³ and threw him into the pit, and locked and sealed it over him, so that he would deceive the nations no more, until the thousand years were ended. After that he must be let out for a little while.

4 Then I saw thrones, and those seated on them were given authority to judge. I also saw the souls of those who had been beheaded for their testimony to Jesusᵃ and for the word of God. They had not worshiped the beast or its image and had not received its mark on their foreheads or their hands. They came to life and reigned with Christ a thousand years. ⁵ (The rest of the dead did not come to life until the thousand years were ended.) This is the first resurrection. ⁶ Blessed and holy are those who share in the first resurrection. Over these the second death has no power, but they will be priests of God and of Christ, and they will reign with him a thousand years.

Satan's Doom

7 When the thousand years are ended, Satan will be released from his prison ⁸ and will come out to deceive the nations at the four corners of the earth, Gog and Magog, in order to gather them for battle; they are as numerous as the sands of the sea. ⁹ They marched up over the breadth of the earth and surrounded the camp of the saints and the beloved city. And fire came down from heavenᵇ and consumed them. ¹⁰ And the devil who had deceived them was thrown into the lake of fire and sulfur, where the beast and the false prophet were, and they will be tormented day and night forever and ever.

The Dead Are Judged

11 Then I saw a great white throne and the one who sat on it; the earth and the heaven fled from his presence, and no place was found for them.

ᵃ Or for the testimony of Jesus   ᵇ Other ancient authorities read from God, out of heaven, or out of heaven from God

---

19:19–21—Cf. 13:1–18. The minions of evil are the first to lose power, as God's justice breaks into the world.

20:1–3 The Imprisonment of the Dragon

20:1 *Bottomless pit*—Cf. Isa. 24:21–22.

20:2—See 12:3, 9.

20:3 *Thousand years*—See vv. 4–6. *Must be let out for a little while*—Even when evil seems to have been neutralized, one cannot be casual about its power.

20:4–6 The Millennial Reign

A thousand years is a symbolic number, not a literal counting of time; see Ps. 90:4. The time of the future will be according to God's reckoning, not ours. Ironically, 1000 years has been turned into a tool in human timekeeping. The challenge for discipleship is to be open to the rhythms of God's time, instead of trying to dictate it.

20:7–10 The Defeat of Satan (cf. Ezek 38–39)

God's victory over Satan has never been in doubt.

20:7—Corporate acts, not private temptations to evil, are the real expression of evil's power.

20:10—The *devil* shares the same fate as his agents.

20:11–15 The Last Judgment

20:11—See 4:1–11.

[12] And I saw the dead, great and small, standing before the throne, and books were opened. Also another book was opened, the book of life. And the dead were judged according to their works, as recorded in the books. [13] And the sea gave up the dead that were in it, Death and Hades gave up the dead that were in them, and all were judged according to what they had done. [14] Then Death and Hades were thrown into the lake of fire. This is the second death, the lake of fire; [15] and anyone whose name was not found written in the book of life was thrown into the lake of fire.

The New Heaven and the New Earth

21 Then I saw a new heaven and a new earth; for the first heaven and the first earth had passed away, and the sea was no more. [2] And I saw the holy city, the new Jerusalem, coming down out of heaven from God, prepared as a bride adorned for her husband. [3] And I heard a loud voice from the throne saying,

"See, the home*a* of God is among mortals.
He will dwell*b* with them;
they will be his peoples,*c*
and God himself will be with them;*d*
[4] he will wipe every tear from their eyes.
Death will be no more;
mourning and crying and pain will be no more,

for the first things have passed away."

[5] And the one who was seated on the throne said, "See, I am making all things new." Also he said, "Write this, for these words are trustworthy and true." [6] Then he said to me, "It is done! I am the Alpha and the Omega, the beginning and the end. To the thirsty I will give water as a gift from the spring of the water of life. [7] Those who conquer will inherit these things, and I will be their God and they will be my children. [8] But as for the cowardly, the faithless,*e* the polluted, the murderers, the fornicators, the sorcerers, the idolaters, and all liars, their place will be in the lake that burns with fire and sulfur, which is the second death."

Vision of the New Jerusalem

[9] Then one of the seven angels who had the seven bowls full of the seven last plagues came and said to me, "Come, I will show you the bride, the wife of the Lamb." [10] And in the spirit*f* he carried me away to a great, high mountain and showed me the holy city Jerusalem coming down out of heaven from God. [11] It has the glory of God and a radiance like a very rare jewel, like jasper, clear as crystal. [12] It has a great, high wall with twelve gates, and at the gates twelve

a Gk *the tabernacle*   *b* Gk *will tabernacle*   *c* Other ancient authorities read *people*   *d* Other ancient authorities add *and be their God*   *e* Or *the unbelieving*   *f* Or *in the Spirit*

20:12—The *books* symbolize the records of all human actions. The *book of life* is the book of grace that counterbalances human actions.

20:12–15 *According to what they had done*—Judgment is self-judgment. Not the judgment of outsiders to the faith community, because all the dead are judged. The "last" judgment, because *Death and Hades* themselves are judged and destroyed.

21:1–8 The New Heaven and the New Earth (cf. Isa. 65:17; 66:22)

The destruction of evil clears the way for the establishment of God's reign of justice on earth.

21:1—The end of the sea, the end of the power of chaos and death on earth (cf. 4:6).

21:1–2—The *new Jerusalem* descends to the

earth. The city of the Lamb replaces the city of the beast. This is not a vision of a future in heaven, but of a new life with God on earth.

21:3–5—See 7:16–17; Isa. 49:10.

21:7–8—Definitions of the two communities, those who share in God's covenant (v. 7) and those who choose to exclude themselves from this covenant by their actions of falsehood and deceit. In the new earth, as in the first, people still need to choose whether they will be on the side of God's covenant or not.

21:9–22:5 The New Jerusalem

21:9–21—See Ezek. 40–48.

21:9—John has been shown two cities; cf. 17:1. The community of disciples must decide in which city they want to live.

angels, and on the gates are inscribed the names of the twelve tribes of the Israelites; ¹³ on the east three gates, on the north three gates, on the south three gates, and on the west three gates. ¹⁴ And the wall of the city has twelve foundations, and on them are the twelve names of the twelve apostles of the Lamb.

15 The angel*a* who talked to me had a measuring rod of gold to measure the city and its gates and walls. ¹⁶ The city lies foursquare, its length the same as its width; and he measured the city with his rod, fifteen hundred miles;*b* its length and width and height are equal. ¹⁷ He also measured its wall, one hundred forty-four cubits*c* by human measurement, which the angel was using. ¹⁸ The wall is built of jasper, while the city is pure gold, clear as glass. ¹⁹ The foundations of the wall of the city are adorned with every jewel; the first was jasper, the second sapphire, the third agate, the fourth emerald, ²⁰ the fifth onyx, the sixth carnelian, the seventh chrysolite, the eighth beryl, the ninth topaz, the tenth chrysoprase, the eleventh jacinth, the twelfth amethyst. ²¹ And the twelve gates are twelve pearls, each of the gates is a single pearl, and the street of the city is pure gold, transparent as glass.

22 I saw no temple in the city, for its temple is the Lord God the Almighty and the Lamb. ²³ And the city has no need of sun or moon to shine on it, for the glory of God is its light, and its lamp is the Lamb. ²⁴ The nations will walk by its light, and the kings of the earth will bring their glory into it. ²⁵ Its gates will never be shut by day—and there will be no night there. ²⁶ People will bring into it the glory and the honor of the nations. ²⁷ But nothing unclean will enter it, nor anyone who practices abomination or falsehood, but only those who are written in the Lamb's book of life.

The River of Life

22 Then the angel*d* showed me the river of the water of life, bright as crystal, flowing from the throne of God and of the Lamb ² through the middle of the street of the city. On either side of the river is the tree of life*e* with its twelve kinds of fruit, producing its fruit each month; and the leaves of the tree are for the healing of the nations. ³ Nothing accursed will be found there any more. But the throne of God and of the Lamb will be in it, and his servants*f* will worship him; ⁴ they will see his face, and his name will be on their foreheads. ⁵ And there will be no more night; they need no light of lamp or sun, for the Lord God will be their light, and they will reign forever and ever.

6 And he said to me, "These words are trustworthy and true, for the Lord, the God of the spirits of the prophets, has sent his angel to show his servants*f* what must soon take place."

7 "See, I am coming soon! Blessed is the one who keeps the words of the prophecy of this book."

Epilogue and Benediction

8 I, John, am the one who heard and

a Gk He *b* Gk twelve thousand stadia *c* That is, almost seventy-five yards *d* Gk he *e* Or the Lamb. 2 In the middle of the street of the city, and on either side of the river, is the tree of life *f* Gk slaves

---

21:18–21 *Jewel*—See Exod. 28:17–21; 39:10–14; Isa. 54:11–17.

21:22—Unlike Ezek. 40–48, **no temple** is needed in the city, because the city itself contains the presence of God and the Lamb.

21:24—Nations and kings are inhabitants, not enemies of the city.

21:25—The city is always open. The city of God is not a sectarian possession or refuge. Its gifts and grace are available to all.

21:27—The only way to be excluded from the city is to choose to practice falsehood and deceit, which by definition do not belong to the city of God (cf. v. 8; 22:3).

22:1–5—See Gen. 2:9–10.

22:2—New life is available to all **the nations**, not to a select minority.

22:6–21 Conclusion

22:6—Cf. 1:1.

22:7—Cf. 1:3.

22:8–9—Cf. 1:9–11.

saw these things. And when I heard and saw them, I fell down to worship at the feet of the angel who showed them to me; [9] but he said to me, "You must not do that! I am a fellow servant[a] with you and your comrades[b] the prophets, and with those who keep the words of this book. Worship God!"

10 And he said to me, "Do not seal up the words of the prophecy of this book, for the time is near. [11] Let the evildoer still do evil, and the filthy still be filthy, and the righteous still do right, and the holy still be holy."

12 "See, I am coming soon; my reward is with me, to repay according to everyone's work. [13] I am the Alpha and the Omega, the first and the last, the beginning and the end."

14 Blessed are those who wash their robes,[c] so that they will have the right to the tree of life and may enter the city by the gates. [15] Outside are the dogs and sorcerers and fornicators and murderers and idolaters, and everyone who loves and practices falsehood.

16 "It is I, Jesus, who sent my angel to you with this testimony for the churches. I am the root and the descendant of David, the bright morning star."
[17]   The Spirit and the bride say, "Come."
      And let everyone who hears say,
         "Come."
      And let everyone who is thirsty
         come.
      Let anyone who wishes take the
         water of life as a gift.

18 I warn everyone who hears the words of the prophecy of this book: if anyone adds to them, God will add to that person the plagues described in this book; [19] if anyone takes away from the words of the book of this prophecy, God will take away that person's share in the tree of life and in the holy city, which are described in this book.

20 The one who testifies to these things says, "Surely I am coming soon." Amen. Come, Lord Jesus!

21 The grace of the Lord Jesus be with all the saints. Amen.[d]

[a] Gk slave [b] Gk brothers [c] Other ancient authorities read do his commandments [d] Other ancient authorities lack all; others lack the saints; others lack Amen

---

22:10–11—The prophecy is kept open, so that all readers can be reminded of the consequences of their choices and their actions.

22:16–17—An invitation to participate in the grace that is offered by this book.

22:21—Ends like a letter; see 1:4–5.

Chronology

C. 2000–1500 BCE	TIME OF THE ANCESTORS
C. 1280? BCE	EXODUS
C. 1250–1200 BCE	ISRAELITE CONQUEST OF THE PROMISED LAND
C. 1200–1020 BCE	TIME OF THE JUDGES
C. 1020–1000 BCE	SAUL, KING OF JUDAH
C. 1000–961 BCE	DAVID, KING OF JUDAH AND ISRAEL
C. 961–922 BCE	SOLOMON, KING OF ISRAEL AND JUDAH
C. 950 BCE	CONSTRUCTION OF FIRST TEMPLE
922 BCE	DIVISION OF ISRAEL AND JUDAH INTO SEPARATE KINGDOMS
922–721 BCE	ISRAEL AS SEPARATE KINGDOM
922–587 BCE	JUDAH AS SEPARATE KINGDOM
C. 750 BCE	AMOS
C. 750 BCE	HOSEA
C. 740 BCE	ISAIAH
C. 630 BCE	JEREMIAH
C. 590 BCE	EZEKIEL
587 BCE	FALL OF JERUSALEM AND DESTRUCTION OF FIRST TEMPLE
587–539 BCE	BABYLONIAN EXILE
539 BCE	BABYLONIAN JEWS BEGIN MIGRATION TO JERUSALEM
522 BCE	CONSTRUCTION OF SECOND TEMPLE
539–333 BCE	PERSIAN EMPIRE
C. 450–400 BCE	MISSIONS OF EZRA AND NEHEMIAH
330–63 BCE	HELLENISTIC PERIOD
C. 300–200 BCE	PTOLEMAIC RULE OF JUDAH
C. 200–167	SELEUCID RULE OF JUDAH
167	DESECRATION OF JERUSALEM TEMPLE
166–160	JUDAS MACCABEUS RULER OF JERUSALEM
164	REDEDICATION OF SECOND TEMPLE
63 BCE–324 CE	ROMAN PERIOD
40–4 BCE	HEROD, KING OF JUDAH
20–19 BCE	HEROD'S RECONSTRUCTION OF THE JERUSALEM TEMPLE
4 BCE–39 CE	HEROD ANTIPAS, RULER OF GALILEE
4 BCE?	BIRTH OF JESUS OF NAZARETH
26–36 CE	PONTIUS PILATE, GOVERNOR OF JUDAH
C. 30 CE	CRUCIFIXION OF JESUS OF NAZARETH
33 CE	MARTYRDOM OF STEPHEN
34 CE	CONVERSION OF SAUL (PAUL) OF TARSUS
C. 44 CE	PETER LEAVES JERUSALEM
C. 45–64 CE	MISSIONS OF PAUL
C. 70 CE	DESTRUCTION OF SECOND TEMPLE

Concordance

The following abbreviations are used for the Canonical Books:

1Ch	1 Chronicles	Ecc	Ecclesiastes	La	Lamentations
1Co	1 Corinthians	Eph	Ephesians	Lev	Leviticus
1Jn	1 John	Est	Esther	Lk	Luke
1Ki	1 Kings	Ex	Exodus	Mal	Malachi
1Pe	1 Peter	Eze	Ezekiel	Mic	Micah
1Sa	1 Samuel	Ezr	Ezra	Mk	Mark
1Th	1 Thessalonians	Gal	Galatians	Mt	Matthew
1Ti	1 Timothy	Ge	Genesis	Na	Nahum
2Ch	2 Chronicles	Hab	Habakkuk	Ne	Nehemiah
2Co	2 Corinthians	Hag	Haggai	Nu	Numbers
2Jn	2 John	Heb	Hebrews	Ob	Obadiah
2Ki	2 Kings	Hos	Hosea	Phm	Philemon
2Pe	2 Peter	Isa	Isaiah	Php	Philippians
2Sa	2 Samuel	Jas	James	Pr	Proverbs
2Th	2 Thessalonians	Jdg	Judges	Ps	Psalms
2Ti	2 Timothy	Jer	Jeremiah	Rev	Revelation
3Jn	3 John	Jn	John	Ro	Romans
Ac	Acts	Jnh	Jonah	Ru	Ruth
Am	Amos	Job	Job	SS	Song of Solomon
Col	Colossians	Joel	Joel	Tit	Titus
Da	Daniel	Jos	Joshua	Zec	Zechariah
Dt	Deuteronomy	Jude	Jude	Zep	Zephaniah

The following abbreviations are used for the Deuterocanonical Books:

AdE	Additions to Esther	1Mc	1 Maccabees
Aza	Prayer of Azariah	2Mc	2 Maccabees
Bar	Baruch	3Mc	3 Maccabees
Bel	Bel and the Dragon	4Mc	4 Maccabees
1Es	1 Esdras	Pm	Psalm 151
2Es	2 Esdras	Sir	Sirach
Jdt	Judith	Sus	Susanna
LtJ	Letter of Jeremiah	Tob	Tobit
Man	Prayer of Manasseh	Wis	Wisdom

Other abbreviations and special symbols used:

S   Shorter ending of Mark

T   Psalm titles

Pr: Sirach Prologue

*   Entries followed by an asterisk (e.g., ABBA*) contain every reference in the NRSV

†   A dagger distinguishes LORD and GOD from Lord and God in Hebrew Bible references

→   An arrow following an entry heading points to related words for additional study

=   An equals sign marks an alternate proper name for additional study (e.g., ISRAEL =JACOB)

[[ ]]   Contexts in double brackets are from passages that are similarly bracketed in the NRSV (e.g., John 7:53—8:11)

For further study consult *The Concise Concordance to the New Revised Standard Version* (Oxford University Press, 1993) and *The NRSV Concordance Unabridged* (Zondervan, 1991).

—John R. Kohlenberger III

AARON

Genealogy (Ex 6:16-20; Jos 21:4, 10; 1Ch 6:3-15). Priesthood of (Ex 28:1; Nu 17; Heb 5:1-4; 7), vestments of (Ex 28; 39), consecration of (Ex 29), ordination of (Lev 8).

Spokesman for Moses (Ex 4:14-16, 27-31; 7:1-2). Supported Moses' hands in battle (Ex 17:8-13). Built golden calf (Ex 32; Dt 9:20). Spoke against Moses (Nu 12). Priesthood opposed (Nu 16); staff budded (Nu 17). Forbidden to enter the promised land (Nu 20:1-12). Death of (Nu 20:22-29; 33:38-39). Praise of (Sir 45:6-22).

ABANDON → ABANDONED

Nu   32:15   will again a them in the wilderness;
Dt   4:31   will neither a you nor destroy you;
2Ch 15: 2   but if you a him, he will a you.
Mk   7: 8   You a the commandment of God
Ac   2:27   For you will not a my soul to Hades
Heb 10:35   Do not, therefore, a that confidence

ABANDONED → ABANDON

Dt   29:25   they a the covenant of the LORD,
Jdg   2:13   a the LORD, and worshiped Baal
2Ch 12: 5   You a me, so I have a you
Isa   54: 7   For a brief moment I a you,
Sir   49: 4   for they a the law of the Most High;

ABBA*

Mk 14:36   "A, Father, for you all things are
                    possible;
Ro   8:15   When we cry, "A! Father!"
Gal   4: 6   into our hearts, crying, "A! Father!"

ABEDNEGO* → =AZARIAH

Deported to Babylon with Daniel (Da 1:1-6). Name changed from Azariah (Da 1:7). Refused defilement by food (Da 1:8-20). Refused idol worship (Da 3:1-12); saved from furnace (Da 3:13-30).

ABEL

Second son of Adam (Ge 4:2). Offered acceptable sacrifice (Ge 4:4; Heb 11:4; 12:24). Murdered by Cain (Ge 4:8; Mt 23:35; Lk 11:51; 1Jn 3:12).

ABHOR → ABHORRENT

Lev 26:11   and I shall not a you.

ABHORRENT → ABHOR

Dt   14: 3   You shall not eat any a thing.
       18: 9   not learn to imitate the a practices

ABIATHAR

High priest in days of Saul and David (1Sa 22; 2Sa 15; 1Ki 1-2; Mk 2:26). Escaped Saul's slaughter of priests (1Sa 22:18-23). Supported David in Absalom's revolt (2Sa 15:24-29). Supported Adonijah (1Ki 1:7-42); deposed by Solomon (1Ki 2:22-35; cf. 1Sa 2:31-35).

ABIDE → ABIDES, ABODE

Ge   6: 3   My spirit shall not a in mortals
                    forever,
Ps   15: 1   O LORD, who may a in your tent?
       91: 1   a in the shadow of the Almighty,
Jn   15: 4   A in me as I a in you.
1Co 13:13   faith, hope, and love a, these three;
1Jn   2:28   And now, little children, a in him,
Wis   3: 9   the faithful will a with him in love,

ABIDES → ABIDE

Hag   2: 5   My spirit a among you; do not fear.
1Jn   3:14   Whoever does not love a in death.

ABIGAIL

1. Sister of David (1Ch 2:16-17).
2. Wife of Nabal (1Sa 25:30); pled for his life with David (1Sa 25:14-35). Became David's wife after Nabal's death (1Sa 25:36-42).

ABIHU

Son of Aaron (Ex 6:23; 24:1, 9); killed for offering illicit fire (Lev 10; Nu 3:2-4; 1Ch 24:1-2).

ABIJAH

1. Second son of Samuel (1Ch 6:28); a corrupt judge (1Sa 8:1-5).
2. An Aaronic priest (1Ch 24:10; Lk 1:5).
3. Son of Jeroboam I; died as prophesied by Ahijah (1Ki 14:1-18).
4. Son of Rehoboam, also called Abijam; king of Judah who fought Jeroboam I attempting to reunite Israel (1Ki 14:31-15:8; 2Ch 12:16-14:1).

ABILITY → ABLE

Ex   31: 3   filled him with divine spirit, with a,
Mt   25:15   to each according to his a.
Ac   2: 4   as the Spirit gave them a.

ABIMELECH

1. King of Gerar who took Abraham's wife Sarah, believing her to be his sister (Ge 20). Covenanted with Abraham (Ge 21:22-33).
2. King of Gerar who took Isaac's wife Rebekah, believing her to be his sister (Ge 26:1-11). Covenanted with Isaac (Ge 26:12-31).
3. Son of Gideon (Jdg 8:31). Attempted to become king (Jdg 9).

ABIRAM

Sided with Dathan in rebellion against Moses and Aaron (Nu 16; 26:9; Dt 11:6; Sir 45:18).

ABISHAI

Son of Zeruiah, David's sister (1Sa 26:6; 1Ch 2:16). One of David's chief warriors (1Ch 11:15-21): against Edom (1Ch 18:12-13), Ammon (2Sa 10), Absalom (2Sa 18), Sheba (2Sa 20). Wanted to kill Saul (1Sa 26), killed Abner (2Sa 2:18-27; 3:22-39).

ABLE → ABILITY

Ex   18:25   Moses chose a men from all Israel
Jos   1: 5   No one shall be a to stand against
       23: 9   no one has been a to withstand you
Da   3:17   God whom we serve is a to deliver
Mt   9:28   "Do you believe that I am a to do
Mk 10:38   you a to drink the cup that I drink,
Ro   14: 4   the Lord is a to make them stand.
2Co   9: 8   God is a to provide you with every
Eph   6:11   a to stand against the wiles of the
                    devil.
2Ti   1:12   he is a to guard until that day
Heb   2:18   a to help those who are being tested.
         5: 2   is a to deal gently with the ignorant
         7:25   he is a for all time to save
Rev   5: 3   a to open the scroll or to look into it.
Jdt   11:18   of them will be a to withstand you.

ABNER

Cousin of Saul and commander of his army (1Sa 14:50; 17:55-57; 26). Made Ish-Bosheth king after Saul (2Sa 2:8-10), but later defected to David (2Sa 3:6-21). Killed Asahel (2Sa 2:18-32), for which he was killed by Joab and Abishai (2Sa 3:22-39).

ABODE → ABIDE

Ps   68:16   mount that God desired for his a,
Pr   3:33   but he blesses the a of the righteous.

ABOLISH → ABOLISHED

Da   11:31   shall a the regular burnt offering
Mt   5:17   I have not come to a but to fulfill.

ABOLISHED → ABOLISH

Eph   2:15   a the law with its commandments
2Ti   1:10   who a death and brought life

ABOMINABLE → ABOMINATION

2Ch 28: 3   the a practices of the nations
Eze   7:20   they made their a images,
1Mc   1:48   to make themselves a by everything

ABOMINATION → ABOMINABLE, ABOMINATIONS

Pr   6:16   seven that are an a to him:
Da   9:27   shall be an a that desolates,
Rev 21:27   anyone who practices a or falsehood
Sir   1:25   but godliness is an a to a sinner.

1Mc   6: 7   that they had torn down the a
                    that

ABOMINATIONS → ABOMINATION

Lev 18:27   committed all of these a,
1Ki 14:24   all the a of the nations that the LORD
Eze 44: 7   broken my covenant with all your a.
Rev 17: 5   mother of whores and of earth's a."

ABOUND → ABOUNDED, ABOUNDING

Dt   28:11   LORD will make you a in prosperity,
Ro   6: 1   in sin in order that grace may a?

ABOUNDED → ABOUND

Ro   5:20   sin increased, grace a all the more,

ABOUNDING → ABOUND

Ex   34: 6   a in steadfast love and faithfulness,
Ps   86: 5   a in steadfast love to all who call on
Joel   2:13   to anger, and a in steadfast love,
Jnh   4: 2   to anger, and a in steadfast love,

ABOVE

Dt   4:39   the LORD is God in heaven a
Jn   3: 7   'You must be born from a.'
Php   2: 9   the name that is a every name,
Col   3: 2   Set your minds on things that are a,

ABRAHAM

Abram, son of Terah (Ge 11:26-27), husband of Sarah (Ge 11:29).

Covenant relation with the LORD (Ge 12:1-3; 13:14-17; 15; 17; 22:15-18; Ex 2:24; Ne 9:8; Ps 105; Mic 7:20; Lk 1:68-75; Ro 4; Heb 6:13-15).

Called from Ur, via Haran, to Canaan (Ge 12:1; Ac 7:2-4; Heb 11:8-10). Moved to Egypt, nearly lost Sarah to Pharoah (Ge 12:10-20). Divided the land with Lot; settled in Hebron (Ge 13). Saved Lot from four kings (Ge 14:1-16); blessed by Melchizedek (Ge 14:17-20; Heb 7:1-17). Declared righteous by faith (Ge 15:6; Ro 4:3; Gal 3:6-9; 1Mc 2:52). Fathered Ishmael by Hagar (Ge 16).

Name changed from Abram (Ge 17:5; Ne 9:7). Circumcised (Ge 17; Ro 4:9-12). Entertained three visitors (Ge 18); promised a son by Sarah (Ge 18:9-15; 17:16). Questioned destruction of Sodom and Gomorrah (Ge 18:16-33). Moved to Gerar; nearly lost Sarah to Abimelech (Ge 20). Fathered Isaac by Sarah (Ge 21:1-7; Ac 7:8; Heb 11:11-12); sent away Hagar and Ishmael (Ge 21:8-21; Gal 4:22-30). Covenant with Abimelech (Ge 21:22-32). Tested by offering Isaac (Ge 22; Heb 11:17-19; Jas 2:21-24). Sarah died; bought field of Ephron for burial (Ge 23). Secured wife for Isaac (Ge 24). Fathered children by Keturah (Ge 25:1-6; 1Ch 1:32-33). Death (Ge 25:7-11).

Called servant of God (Ge 26:24), friend of God (2Ch 20:7; Isa 41:8; Jas 2:23), prophet (Ge 20:7), father of Israel (Ex 3:15; Isa 51:2; Mt 3:9; Jn 8:39-58). Praised (Sir 44:19-45:1).

ABSALOM

Son of David by Maacah (2Sa 3:3; 1Ch 3:2). Killed Amnon for rape of his sister Tamar; banished by David (2Sa 13). Returned to Jerusalem; received by David (2Sa 14). Rebelled against David (2Sa 15-17). Killed (2Sa 18).

ABSENT

1Co   5: 3   a in body, I am present in spirit;
Col   2: 5   For though I am a in body,

ABUNDANCE → ABUNDANTLY

Lk   6:45   a of the heart that the mouth speaks.
       12:15   one's life does not consist in the a
2Co   9: 8   provide you with every blessing in a

ABUNDANTLY → ABUNDANCE

Jn   10:10   that they may have life, and have
                    it a.
Eph   3:20   to accomplish a far more than all

ABYSS

Lk   8:31   to order them to go back into the a.
Ro   10: 7   'Who will descend into the a?'"

ACCEPT → ACCEPTABLE, ACCEPTED
Pr   19:20 Listen to advice and **a** instruction,
Jer 32:33 would not listen and **a** correction,
Mt 19:11 "Not everyone can **a** this teaching,
Jn   1:11 his own people did not **a** him.

ACCEPTABLE → ACCEPT
Ps 19:14 meditation of my heart be **a** to you,
    51:17 sacrifice **a** to God is a broken spirit;
Ro 12: 1 a living sacrifice, holy and **a** to God,

ACCEPTED → ACCEPT
Ge   4: 7 If you do well, will you not be **a?**
Lk   4:24 no prophet is **a** in the prophet's
          hometown.

ACCESS
Ro   5: 2 we have obtained **a** to this grace
Eph 2:18 have **a** in one Spirit to the Father.

ACCOMPLISH → ACCOMPLISHED
Isa 55:11 but it shall **a** that which I purpose,
Eze 17:24 I the LORD have spoken; I will **a** it.

ACCOMPLISHED → ACCOMPLISH
Mt   5:18 will pass from the law until all is **a.**

ACCORDING
Ps 28: 4 Repay them **a** to their work,
  119: 9 By guarding it **a** to your word.
Mt   9:29 "**A** to your faith let it be done to you
Ro   8: 4 not **a** to the flesh but **a** to the Spirit.
Heb 2: 4 Holy Spirit, distributed **a** to his will.
1Jn 5:14 that if we ask anything **a** to his will,
Rev 20:12 dead were judged **a** to their works,
Sir 16:12 he judges a person **a** to one's deeds.

ACCOUNT → ACCOUNTABLE
Mt 12:36 judgment you will have to give an **a**
Heb 4:13 to whom we must render an **a.**

ACCOUNTABLE → ACCOUNT
Ro 14:12 each of us will be **a** to God.

ACCURSED → CURSE
Ro   9: 3 I could wish that I myself were **a**
Rev 22: 3 Nothing **a** will be found there any

ACCUSATION → ACCUSE
Lk 23: 4 no basis for an **a** against this man."

ACCUSE → ACCUSATION, ACCUSER
Ps 103: 9 He will not always **a,**
Zec 3: 1 Satan standing at his right hand to **a**
Mt 12:10 so that they might **a** him.

ACCUSER → ACCUSE
Jn   5:45 your **a** is Moses,
Rev 12:10 the **a** of our comrades has been
          thrown

ACHAN
    Sinned at Jericho; stoned (Jos 7; 22:20; 1Ch 2:7).

ACHISH
    King of Gath before whom David feigned insanity (1Sa 21:10-15). Later "ally" of David (2Sa 27-29).

ACKNOWLEDGE
Dt   4:35 you would **a** that the LORD is God;
Pr   3: 6 In all your ways **a** him,
Mt 10:32 I also will **a** before my Father in
Ro   1:28 since they did not see fit to **a** God,

ACT → ACTED, ACTIVE, ACTS
Ps 37: 5 trust in him, and he will **a.**
Ro 14:23 because they do not **a** from faith;
Jas   1:25 hearers who forget but doers who **a**

ACTED → ACT
Eze 20: 9 But I **a** for the sake of my name,
Ac   3:17 I know that you **a** in ignorance,
1Ti 1:13 mercy because I had **a** ignorantly

ACTIVE → ACT
Heb 4:12 the word of God is living and **a,**
Jas 2:22 faith was **a** along with his works,

ACTS → ACT
Ex   6: 6 outstretched arm and with mighty **a**
Ps 71:15 mouth will tell of your righteous **a,**
Mt   7:24 hears these words of mine and **a**

ADAM
    First man (Ge 1:26-2:25; Ro 5:14; 1Ti 2:13; Tob 8:6). Sin of (Ge 3; Hos 6:7 [note]; Ro 5:12-21; 2Es 3:21; 7:70-140). Children of (Ge 4:1-5:5). Death of (Ge 5:5; Ro 5:12-21; 1Co 15:22).

ADD → ADDED
Dt   4: 2 You must neither **a** anything
Pr 30: 6 Do not **a** to his words, or else
Lk 12:25 by worrying **a** a single hour to your

ADDED → ADD
Ecc 3:14 nothing can be **a** to it, nor anything
Sir 42:21 Nothing can be **a** or taken away,

ADDICTED*
Tit   1: 7 or quick-tempered or **a** to wine

ADMONISH → ADMONITION
Col 3:16 and **a** one another in all wisdom;

ADMONITION → ADMONISH
Pr 15: 5 one who heeds **a** is prudent.

ADONIJAH
    1. Son of David by Haggith (2Sa 3:4; 1Ch 3:2). Attempted to be king after David; killed at Solomon's order (1Ki 1-2).
    2. Levite; teacher of the Law (2Ch 17:8).

ADOPTION
Ro   8:23 groan inwardly while we wait for **a,**
Gal   4: 5 that we might receive **a** as children.

ADORNED → ADORNMENT
Lk 21: 5 how it was **a** with beautiful stones
Rev 17: 4 **a** with gold and jewels and pearls,
    21: 2 as a bride **a** for her husband.

ADORNMENT → ADORNED, ADORNS
Pr   3:22 for your soul and **a** for your neck.
1Pe 3: 4 let your **a** be the inner self with the

ADORNS → ADORNMENT
Isa 61:10 as a bride **a** herself with her jewels.

ADULT* → ADULTS
1Co 13:11 an **a,** I put an end to childish ways.

ADULTERERS → ADULTERY
Jer 23:10 For the land is full of **a;**
1Co 6: 9 idolaters, **a,** male prostitutes,

ADULTERESS → ADULTERY
Lev 20:10 the **a** shall be put to death.
Pr   2:16 from the **a** with her smooth words,

ADULTERY → ADULTERERS, ADULTERESS
Ex 20:14 You shall not commit **a.**
Jer   3: 9 committing **a** with stone and tree.
Mt   5:28 committed **a** with her in his heart.
Lk 16:18 and marries another commits **a,**
Jn   8: 3 [[a woman who had been caught
          in **a;**]]

ADULTS* → ADULT
1Co 14:20 infants in evil, but in thinking be **a.**

ADVANTAGE
Ecc 7:12 **a** of knowledge is that wisdom gives
Ro   3: 1 Then what **a** has the Jew?
1Co 10:24 Do not seek your own **a,** but that of

ADVERSARIES → ADVERSARY
Dt 32:41 I will take vengeance on my **a,**
2Sa 22:49 you exalted me above my **a,**

ADVERSARY → ADVERSARIES
1Ti 5:14 give the **a** no occasion to revile us.
1Pe 5: 8 roaring lion your **a** the devil prowls

ADVERSITY → ADVERSARY
Dt 30:15 life and prosperity, death and **a.**
Isa 48:10 I have tested you in the furnace of **a.**

ADVICE → ADVISERS
2Ch 10:13 rejected the **a** of the older men;
Ps   1: 1 do not follow the **a** of the wicked,
Pr   8:14 I have good **a** and sound wisdom;
Tob 4:18 Seek **a** from every wise person
Sir 37:11 pay no attention to any **a** they
          give.

ADVISERS → ADVICE
Pr 15:22 but with many **a** they succeed.

ADVOCATE
Jn 14:26 But the **A,** the Holy Spirit,
    15:26 the **A** comes, whom I will send
1Jn 2: 1 we have an **a** with the Father,

AFFLICT → AFFLICTED, AFFLICTION, AFFLICTIONS, AFFLICTS
2Sa 7:10 evildoers shall **a** them no more,
La   3:33 for he does not willingly **a**
2Th 1: 6 repay with affliction those who **a**

AFFLICTED → AFFLICT
Dt 26: 6 Egyptians treated us harshly and **a**
Na   1:12 Though I have **a** you, I will afflict
2Co 4: 8 are **a** in every way, but not crushed;

AFFLICTION → AFFLICT
Dt 16: 3 bread with it—the bread of **a**—
Ps 25:18 Consider my **a** and my trouble,
Isa 30:20 of adversity and the water of **a,**
La   1: 9 "O LORD, look at my **a,**
2Co 4:17 this slight momentary **a** is preparing

AFFLICTIONS → AFFLICT
Ps 34:19 Many are the **a** of the righteous,

AFFLICTS* → AFFLICT
Tob 13: 2 For he **a,** and he shows mercy;

AFRAID → FEAR
Ge   3:10 and I was **a,** because I was naked;
    15: 1 not be **a,** Abram, I am your shield;
Ex   3: 6 his face, for he was **a** to look at God.
Lev 26: 6 and no one shall make you **a;**
Dt 20: 3 Do not lose heart, or be **a,**
Ps   3: 6 I am not **a** of ten thousands
    27: 1 of whom shall I be **a?**
    56:11 in God I trust; I am not **a.**
Isa 12: 2 I will trust, and will not be **a,**
Eze 2: 6 do not be **a** of their words,
Mt 10:31 So do not be **a;** you are of more
    28:10 Jesus said to them, "Do not be **a;**
Lk 12:32 "Do not be **a,** little flock,
Heb 13: 6 Lord is my helper; I will not be **a.**

AGABUS*
    A Christian prophet (Ac 11:28; 21:10).

AGAG
    King of Amalekites; not killed by Saul (1Sa 15).

AGAIN
Job 14:14 If mortals die, will they live **a?**
Ecc 3:20 and all turn to dust **a.**
Mk 8:31 and after three days rise **a.**
Jn 14: 3 I will come **a** and will take you to
Heb 6: 6 they are crucifying the Son of God
     9:25 Nor was it to offer himself **a** and **a,**

AGE → AGES
Ge 21: 2 bore Abraham a son in his old **a,**
Mt 28:20 with you always, to the end of the **a."**
Gal   1: 4 to set us free from the present evil **a,**

AGES → AGE
Dt   4:32 For ask now about former **a,**
1Co 2: 7 decreed before the **a** for our glory.
Col 1:26 has been hidden throughout the **a**
1Ti 1:17 To the King of the **a,** immortal,

AGREE
Mt 18:19 if two of you **a** on earth about
Mk 14:56 and their testimony did not **a.**
1Jn 5: 8 and the blood, and these three **a.**

AGRIPPA

Descendant of Herod; king before whom Paul argued his case in Caesarea (Ac 25:13-26:32).

AHAB

1. Son of Omri; king of Israel (1Ki 16:28-22:40), husband of Jezebel (1Ki 16:31). Promoted Baal worship (1Ki 16:31-33); opposed by Elijah (1Ki 17:1; 18; 21), a prophet (1Ki 20:35-43), Micaiah (1Ki 22:1-28). Defeated Ben-Hadad (1Ki 20). Killed for failing to kill Ben-Hadad and for murder of Naboth (1Ki 20:35-21:40).

2. A false prophet (Jer 29:21-22).

AHASUERUS → =ARTAXERXES

King of Persia (Ezr 4:6), husband of Esther. Deposed Vashti; replaced her with Esther (Est 1-2). Sealed Haman's edict to annihilate the Jews (Est 3). Received Esther without having called her (Est 5:1-8). Honored Mordecai (Est 6). Hanged Haman (Est 7). Issued edict allowing Jews to defend themselves (Est 8). Promoted Mordecai (Est 8:1-2, 15; 9:4; 10). Called Artaxerxes in the Additions to Esther.

AHAZ

Son of Jotham; king of Judah, (2Ki 16; 2Ch 28; Mt 1:9). Idolatry of (2Ki 16:3-4, 10-18; 2Ch 28:1-4, 22-25). Defeated by Aram and Israel (2Ki 16:5-6; 2Ch 28:5-15). Sought help from Assyria rather than the LORD (2Ki 16:7-9; 2Ch 28:16-21; Isa 7).

AHAZIAH → =JEHOAHAZ

1. Son of Ahab; king of Israel (1Ki 22:51-2Ki 1:18; 2Ch 20:35-37). Made an unsuccessful alliance with Jehoshaphat (2Ch 20:35-37). Died for seeking Baal rather than the LORD (2Ki 1).

2. Son of Jehoram; king of Judah (2Ki 8:25-29; 9:14-29), also called Jehoahaz (2Ch 21:17-22:9; 25:23). Killed by Jehu while visiting Joram (2Ki 9:14-29; 2Ch 22:1-9).

AHEAD

Mt 11:10 sending my messenger **a** of you,
Php 3:13 straining forward to what lies **a**,"
Heb 11:26 for he was looking to the reward.

AHIJAH

1. Priest during Saul's reign (1Sa 14:3,18).
2. Prophet of Shiloh (1Ki 11:29-39; 14:1-18).

AHIKAM

Father of Gedaliah (2Ki 25:22), protector of Jeremiah (Jer 26:24).

AHIMAAZ

1. Father-in-law of Saul (1Sa 14:50).
2. Son of Zadok, the high priest, loyal to David (2Sa 15:27,36; 17:17-20; 18:19-33).

AHIMELECH

1. Priest who helped David in his flight from Saul (1Sa 21-22).
2. One of David's warriors (1Sa 26:6).

AHITHOPHEL

One of David's counselors who sided with Absalom (2Sa 15:12, 31-37; 1Ch 27:33-34); committed suicide when his advice was ignored (2Sa 16:15-17:23).

AI

Jos 7:4 and they fled before the men of **A.**

AIR

Eph 2:2 the ruler of the power of the **a**,
1Th 4:17 to meet the Lord in the **a**;
Rev 16:17 angel poured his bowl into the **a**,

ALARMED

Mk 13:7 and rumors of wars, do not be **a**;
2Th 2:2 to be quickly shaken in mind or **a**,

ALERT

Lk 12:37 slaves whom the master finds **a**
1Co 16:13 Keep **a**, stand firm in your faith,
Eph 6:18 keep **a** and always persevere
1Pe 5:8 Discipline yourselves, keep **a.**

ALEXANDER

1Mc 1:1 **A** son of Philip, the Macedonian,

ALIEN → ALIENS

Ex 2:22 an **a** residing in a foreign land."
Lev 19:34 you shall love the **a** as yourself,
Dt 24:17 You shall not deprive a resident **a**

ALIENS → ALIEN

Ge 15:13 your offspring shall be **a** in a land
Eph 2:19 you are no longer strangers and **a**,
1Pe 1:1 I urge you as **a** and exiles to abstain
1Mc 2:7 the sanctuary given over to **a**?

ALIVE → LIVE

Ge 6:19 to keep them **a** with you;
Dt 32:39 I kill and I make **a**; I wound and I heal;
Ac 1:3 suffering he presented himself **a**
Ro 6:11 dead to sin and **a** to God
Eph 2:5 made us **a** together with Christ—
1Th 4:17 Then we who are **a**, who are left,
Rev 1:18 I am **a** forever and ever;
19:20 were thrown **a** into the lake of fire

ALL

Ge 6:13 to make an end of **a** flesh,
Dt 6:5 You shall love the LORD your God with **a** your heart, and with **a** your soul, and with **a** your might.
Ps 1:3 In **a** that they do, they prosper.
Jer 29:13 if you seek me with **a** your heart,
Lk 10:27 love the Lord your God with **a** your
Ro 3:23 have sinned and fall short of the
6:10 he died to sin, once for **a**;
1Co 6:12 "**A** things are lawful for me,"
15:51 not **a** die, but we will **a** be changed,
Eph 1:23 the fullness of him who fills **a** in **a.**
Php 4:13 I can do **a** things through him
2Ti 3:16 **A** scripture is inspired by God
2Pe 3:9 but **a** to come to repentance.
Rev 21:5 "See, I am making **a** things new."
Sir 7:29 With **a** your soul fear the Lord,

ALMIGHTY → MIGHT

Ge 17:1 "I am God **A**; walk before me,
Ex 6:3 Isaac, and Jacob as God **A**,
Ps 91:1 who abide in the shadow of the **A**,
Rev 1:8 who was and who is to come, the **A.**
21:22 its temple is the Lord God the **A**
Bar 3:1 O Lord **A**, God of Israel,
Man 1:1 O Lord **A**, God of our ancestors,

ALMS

Mt 6:2 "So whenever you give **a**,
Tob 12:8 better to give **a** than to lay up gold.
Sir 7:10 do not neglect to give **a.**

ALONE → LONELY

Ge 2:18 not good that the man should be **a**;
Dt 6:4 The LORD is our God, the LORD **a.**
Isa 2:11 Lord **a** will be exalted in that day.
Mk 2:7 Who can forgive sins but God **a**?"
10:18 No one is good but God **a.**
Jas 2:24 justified by works and not by faith **a**

ALPHA

Rev 1:8 "I am the **A** and the Omega,"
22:13 I am the **A** and the Omega,

ALTAR → ALTARS

Ge 22:9 Isaac, and laid him on the **a**,
Ex 27:1 shall make the **a** of acacia wood,
30:1 an **a** on which to offer incense;
Ezr 3:2 to build the **a** of the God of Israel,
Mt 5:24 leave your gift there before the **a**
Heb 13:10 We have an **a** from which those
Jas 2:21 he offered his son Isaac on the **a**?
Rev 6:9 I saw under the **a** the souls of those
Jdt 4:12 even draped the **a** with sackcloth
1Mc 1:54 a desolating sacrilege on the **a** of
4:47 built a new **a** like the former one.

ALTARS → ALTAR

Ex 34:13 You shall tear down their **a**,

Nu 3:31 the table, the lampstand, the **a**,
1Mc 2:45 went around and tore down the **a**;

ALWAYS

Mt 28:20 And remember, I am with you **a**,
Lk 18:1 to pray **a** and not to lose heart.
Php 4:4 Rejoice in the Lord **a**; again I will

AMALEK

Ex 17:8 Then **A** came and fought with Israel
1Sa 15:3 attack **A**, and utterly destroy all

AMASA

Nephew of David (1Ch 2:17). Commander of Absalom's forces (2Sa 17:24-27). Returned to David (2Sa 19:13). Killed by Joab (2Sa 20:4-13).

AMAZED → AMAZING

Mt 8:27 **a**, saying, "What sort of man is this,
Mk 6:6 And he was **a** at their unbelief.
Ac 2:7 **A** and astonished, they asked,

AMAZIAH

1. Son of Joash; king of Judah (2Ki 14; 2Ch 25). Defeated Edom (2Ki 14:7; 2Ch 25:5-13); defeated by Israel for worshiping Edom's gods (2Ki 14:8-14; 2Ch 25:14-24).

2. Idolatrous priest; opposed Amos (Am 7:10-17).

AMAZING → AMAZED

Mk 12:11 and it is **a** in our eyes'?"
Rev 15:3 "Great and **a** are your deeds,

AMBASSADOR* → AMBASSADORS

Eph 6:20 for which I am an **a** in chains.

AMBASSADORS → AMBASSADOR

2Co 5:20 So we are **a** for Christ,

AMBITION

Php 2:3 Do nothing from selfish **a** or conceit
Jas 3:14 envy and selfish **a** in your hearts,

AMEN

Dt 27:15 people shall respond, saying, "**A**!"
2Co 1:20 through him that we say the "**A**,"
Rev 3:14 The words of the **A**, the faithful and

AMMONITE → AMMONITES

Dt 23:3 No **A** or Moabite shall be admitted

AMMONITES → AMMONITE

Ge 19:38 the ancestor of the **A** to this day.
Jer 49:6 I will restore the fortunes of the **A**,

AMNON

Firstborn of David (2Sa 3:2; 1Ch 3:1). Killed by Absalom for raping his sister Tamar (2Sa 13).

AMON

1. Son of Manasseh; king of Judah (2Ki 21:18-26; 1Ch 3:14; 2Ch 33:21-25).

2. Ruler of Samaria (1Ki 22:26; 2Ch 18:25).

AMORITES

Ge 15:16 iniquity of the **A** is not yet complete
Nu 21:31 Israel settled in the land of the **A.**

AMOS

Prophet from Tekoa (Am 1:1; 7:10-17; Tob 2:6).

ANANIAS

1. Early disciple; died for lying to God (Ac 5:1-11).

2. Disciple who baptized Saul (Ac 9:10-19).

3. High priest at Paul's arrest (Ac 22:30-24:1).

ANCESTOR → ANCESTORS

Dt 26:5 "A wandering Aramean was my **a**;
Mt 3:9 'We have Abraham as our **a**';

ANCESTORS → ANCESTOR

Ex 3:13 'The God of your **a** has sent me to
Dt 4:31 not forget the covenant with your **a**
La 5:7 Our **a** sinned; they are no more,
Ac 5:30 The God of our **a** raised up Jesus,
Heb 1:1 Long ago God spoke to our **a** in

ANCHOR

Heb 6:19 a sure and steadfast **a** of the soul,

ANCIENT

Ps   24: 7 and be lifted up, O a doors!
Jer   6:16 ask for the a paths, where the good
Da   7: 9 and an A One took his throne,
Mic   5: 2 origin is from of old, from a days.
Rev   20: 2 He seized the dragon, that a serpent,

ANDREW*

Apostle; brother of Simon Peter (Mt 4:18; 10:2;
Mk 1:16-18, 29; 3:18; 13:3; Lk 6:14; Jn 1:35-44;
6:8-9; 12:22; Ac 1:13).

ANGEL → ANGELS, ARCHANGEL, ARCHANGEL'S

Ge   22:11 the a of the LORD called to him
Ex   3: 2 the a of the LORD appeared to him
     23:20 going to send an a in front of you,
Nu   22:22 the a of the LORD took his stand in
1Ch 21:15 sent an a to Jerusalem to destroy it;
Ps   34: 7 The a of the LORD encamps
Isa 37:36 the a of the LORD set out and struck
Da   3:28 who has sent his a and delivered
      6:22 God sent his a and shut the lions'
Mt   an a of the Lord appeared to him in
Lk   1:26 In the sixth month the a Gabriel
Ac   5:19 during the night an a of the Lord
     23: 8 say that there is no resurrection,
            or a,
2Co 11:14 Satan disguises himself as an a of
            light.
Gal   1: 8 if we or an a from heaven should
Tob   5: 4 the a Raphael standing in front of
Sir 48:21 and his a wiped them out.
LtJ   6: 7 For my a is with you,
Aza   1:26 But the a of the Lord came down
Sus   1:59 a of God is waiting with his sword
Bel   1:34 the a of the Lord said to Habakkuk,
1Mc   7:41 your a went out and struck
2Es   2:44 Then I asked an a, "Who are these,

ANGELS → ANGEL

Ge   19: 1 The two a came to Sodom in the
     28:12 a of God were ascending and
Ps 103:20 Bless the LORD, O you his a,
Mk   12:25 but are like a in heaven.
Lk   4:10 command his a concerning you,
Jn   1:51 and the a of God ascending and
Ro   8:38 that neither death, nor life, nor a,
1Co   6: 3 not know that we are to judge a—
Col   2:18 on self-abasement and worship of a,
Heb   2: 7 for a little while lower than the a;
1Pe   1:12 things into which a long to look!
2Pe   2: 4 not spare the a when they sinned,
Rev   1:20 stars are the a of the seven churches,
      7: 1 After this I saw four a standing at
     21:12 and at the gates twelve a,
Tob 11:14 and blessed be all his holy a.

ANGER → ANGRY

Ex   32:19 the dancing, Moses' a burned hot,
     34: 6 merciful and gracious, slow to a,
Dt   32:22 For a fire is kindled by my a,
Jdg   2:12 and they provoked the LORD to a.
1Ki 16:13 God of Israel to a with their idols.
Ps   30: 5 For his a is but for a moment;
Pr   12:16 Fools show their a at once,
Ecc   7: 9 Do not be quick to a,
Isa 48: 9 For my name's sake I defer my a,
Joel 2:13 slow to a, and abounding in
Jnh   4: 2 slow to a, and abounding in
Mk   3: 5 He looked around at them with a;
Eph   4:26 not let the sun go down on your a,
Jas   1:19 slow to speak, slow to a;
Rev 14:10 unmixed into the cup of his a,
Sir   5: 4 for the Lord is slow to a.

ANGRY → ANGER

Ge   4: 5 So Cain was very a, and his
Jer   3:12 I will not be a forever.
Mt   5:22 that if you are a with a brother or

ANGUISH

Isa 53:11 Out of his a he shall see light;
Da   12: 1 There shall be a time of a,

Zep   1:15 a day of distress and a,
Lk   22:44 [[In his a he prayed more
            earnestly,]]

ANIMAL → ANIMALS

Ge   2:19 God formed every a of the field
      9: 2 dread of you shall rest on every a of
Ps   50:10 every wild a of the forest is mine,

ANIMALS → ANIMAL

Ge   3:14 cursed are you among all a
Lev 26: 6 remove dangerous a from the land,
Ps   36: 6 save humans and a alike, O LORD.

ANNA

1. Prophetess; spoke of the child Jesus (Lk
2:36-38).
2. Wife of Tobit (Tob 1:20; 2:1, 11).

ANNAS*

High priest C.E. 6-15 (Lk 3:2; Jn 18:13, 24; Ac
4:6).

ANNOUNCED → ANNOUNCING

Isa 48: 5 before they came to pass I a them
1Pe   1:25 the good news that was a to you.

ANNOUNCES → ANNOUNCING

Isa 52: 7 feet of the messenger who a peace,

ANNOUNCING* → ANNOUNCED, ANNOUNCES

Isa 63: 1 I, a vindication, mighty to save."
Ro   1: 9 serve with my spirit by a the gospel

ANNULLED

Jn   10:35 and the scripture cannot be a—

ANOINT → ANOINTED, ANOINTING

Ex   30:30 You shall a Aaron and his sons,
1Sa 15: 1 "The LORD sent me to a you king
Ps   23: 5 you a my head with oil; my cup
Da   9:24 and to a a most holy place.

ANOINTED → ANOINT

1Sa   2:10 and exalt the power of his a."
     26: 9 raise his hand against the LORD's a,
1Ch 16:22 "Do not touch my a ones;
Ps   2: 2 against the LORD and his a, saying,
Isa 61: 1 because the LORD has a me;
Eze 28:14 With an a cherub as guardian
Da   9:26 an a one shall be cut off and
Zec   4:14 These are the two a ones who stand
Lk   4:18 he has a me to bring good news to
Jn   1:41 Messiah" (which is translated A).

ANOINTING → ANOINT

Ex   30:25 it shall be a holy a oil.
Jas   5:14 a them with oil in the name of the
            Lord
1Jn   2:27 as his a teaches you about all things,

ANOTHER

Pr   27: 2 Let a praise you, and not your own
Isa 48:11 My glory I will not give to a.
Jn   14:16 and he will give you a Advocate,
Gal   1: 7 not that there is a gospel,

ANSWER → ANSWERED

1Ki 18:37 A me, O LORD, a me,
Job 30:20 I cry to you and you do not a me;
Ps   65: 2 O you who a prayer!
Pr   15: 1 A soft a turns away wrath,
Isa 65:24 Before they call I will a,
Lk   23: 9 but Jesus gave him no a.

ANSWERED → ANSWER

1Ch 21:26 and he a him with fire from heaven
Ps 118:21 I thank you that you have a me

ANT*

Pr   6: 6 Go to the a, you lazybones;

ANTICHRIST*

1Jn   2:18 As you have heard that a is coming,
      2:22 the a, the one who denies the Father
      4: 3 And this is the spirit of the a,
2Jn   1: 7 person is the deceiver and the a!

ANTIOCH

Ac   11:26 in A that the disciples were first
            called "Christians."
     13: 1 the church at A there were prophets
Gal   2:11 But when Cephas came to A,

ANTIOCHUS

Antiochus IV Epiphanes, king of the Syrian
Greeks B.C.E. 175-164 (1Mc 1:10-19). Plundered
the temple in Jerusalem (1Mc 1:20-28). Attempted
to force the Hellenization of the Jewish people
(1Mc 1:41-53), including defiling the altar and
holy place (1Mc 1:54-64). His policies sparked the
Maccabean revolt.

ANXIETIES → ANXIETY

1Co   7:32 I want you to be free from a.

ANXIETY → ANXIETIES

Ecc 11:10 Banish a from your mind,
1Pe   5: 7 Cast all your a on him, because he

ANYTHING

Ge   18:14 Is a too wonderful for the LORD?
Jer 32:27 is a too hard for me?
Mt   18:19 if two of you agree on earth about a
Jn   16:23 if you ask a of the Father in my
            name,

APART → PART

Jn   15: 5 a from me you can do nothing.
Ro   3:21 a from law, the righteousness of
Jas   2:20 that faith a from works is barren?

APOLLOS

Christian from Alexandria, learned in the
Scriptures; instructed by Aquila and Priscilla (Ac
18:24-28). At Corinth (Ac 19:1; 1Co 1:12; 3; Tit
3:13).

APOSTASIES → APOSTASY

Jer   2:19 and your a will convict you.
Eze 37:23 I will save them from all the a

APOSTASY* → APOSTASIES

1Mc   2:15 officers who were enforcing the a

APOSTLE → APOSTLES

Ro   11:13 as I am an a to the Gentiles,
1Co   9: 1 Am I not an a?
2Co 12:12 signs of a true a were performed
Heb   3: 1 a and high priest of our confession,

APOSTLES → APOSTLE

See also Andrew, Bartholomew, Barnabas,
James, John, Judas, Matthew, Matthias, Nathanael,
Paul, Peter, Philip, Simon, Thaddaeus, Thomas.
Mt   10: 2 the names of the twelve a:
Ac   2:43 and signs were being done by the a.
1Co 12:28 has appointed in the church first a,
Eph   2:20 foundation of the a and prophets,
      4:11 he gave were that some would be a,
Rev 21:14 are the twelve names of the twelve a

APPEAL

Mt   26:53 think that I cannot a to my Father,
Ac   25:11 I a to the emperor."
2Co   5:20 God is making his a through us;
Phm   1: 9 rather a to you on the basis of love
1Pe   3:21 an a to God for a good conscience,

APPEAR → APPEARANCE, APPEARANCES, APPEARED, APPEARING

Mt   24:30 the sign of the Son of Man will a in
Mk   13:22 messiahs and false prophets will a
2Co   5:10 a before the judgment seat of Christ,
Heb   9:28 a a second time, not to deal with sin,

APPEARANCE → APPEAR

Ex   24:17 Now the a of the glory of the LORD
1Sa 16: 7 not look on his a or on the height
2Co   5:12 those who boast in outward a
Jdt 11:23 You are not only beautiful in a,
AdE   2: 7 The girl was beautiful in a.
Sir 19:29 A person is known by his a,

APPEARANCES → APPEAR
Jn   7:24 not judge by a, but judge with right

APPEARED → APPEAR
Jn   21:14 that Jesus a to the disciples after he
1Co 15: 5 he a to Cephas, then to the twelve.
Heb 9:26 a once for all at the end of the age

APPEARING → APPEAR
Ac   1: 3 a to them during forty days and
2Ti   4: 8 to all who have longed for his a.

APPETITES
Ro 16:18 our Lord Christ, but their own a,
Sir 18:30 base desires, but restrain your a.

APPLE
Dt 32:10 guarded him as the a of his eye.
Zec 2: 8 touches you touches the a of my eye

APPOINT → APPOINTED
1Sa   8: 5 a for us, then, a king to govern us,
Isa 60:17 I will a Peace as your overseer

APPOINTED → APPOINT
Lev 23: 2 the a festivals of the Lord
Ecc 3:17 for he has a a time for every matter,
Hab 2: 3 there is still a vision for the a time;
Mk   3:16 So he a the twelve: Simon (to whom
Ac   3:20 that he may send the Messiah a for
Heb 1: 2 whom he a heir of all things,
         9:27 just as it is a for mortals to die once,

APPORTIONED → PORTION
Dt   32: 8 When the Most High a the nations,
Jos 18:10 Joshua a the land to the Israelites.

APPROACH
Heb 4:16 a the throne of grace with boldness,
        11: 6 whoever would a him must believe
Sir 1:28 do not a him with a divided mind.

APPROVAL → APPROVED
Gal   1:10 I now seeking human a, or God's a?
Heb 11: 2 by faith our ancestors received a.
1Pe 2:20 and suffer for it, you have God's a.

APPROVED → APPROVAL
1Th   2: 4 but just as we have been a by God
2Ti   2:15 to present yourself to God as one a

AQUILA*
Husband of Priscilla; co-worker with Paul,
instructor of Apollos (Ac 18; Ro 16:3; 1Co 16:19;
2Ti 4:19).

ARABS
Ne   4: 7 and the A and the Ammonites
1Mc 5:39 also have hired A to help them,

ARAM → ARAMAIC, ARAMEAN
Jdg 10: 6 the gods of A, the gods of Sidon,
2Ch 16: 7 you relied on the king of A,

ARAMAIC → ARAM
2Ki 18:26 to your servants in the A language,
Ezr   4: 7 the letter was written in A and
Da   2: 4 Chaldeans said to the king (in A),

ARAMEAN → ARAM
Dt 26: 5 "A wandering A was my ancestor;

ARARAT
Ge   8: 4 ark came to rest on the mountains
         of A.

ARAUNAH → =ORNAN
2Sa 24:16 the threshing floor of A the Jebusite.

ARCHANGEL* → ANGEL
Jude 1: 9 a Michael contended with the devil
2Es   4:36 the a Jeremiel answered and said,

ARCHANGEL'S* → ANGEL
1Th   4:16 a call and with the sound of God's

ARCHITECT*
Heb 11:10 whose a and builder is God.

AREOPAGUS
Ac 17:22 Then Paul stood in front of the A

**ARGUE → ARGUES, ARGUMENT,
      ARGUMENTS**
Job 13: 3 and I desire to a my case with God.
Isa   1:18 now, let us a it out, says the Lord;
Ac 18: 4 Every sabbath he would a in the
Ro   9:20 a human being, to a with God?

ARGUES* → ARGUE
Job 40: 2 who a with God must respond."

ARGUMENT → ARGUE
Lk   9:46 An a arose among them as to which
1Ti   2: 8 up holy hands without anger or a;

ARGUMENTS → ARGUE
2Co 10: 4 destroy strongholds. We destroy a
Col   2: 4 may deceive you with plausible a.

ARIMATHEA
Jn 19:38 After these things, Joseph of A,

ARISE → RISE
SS   2:10 "A, my love, my fair one, and
Isa 60: 1 A, shine; for your light has come,
Mt 24:11 false prophets will a and lead many
1Mc 14:41 until a trustworthy prophet
         should a,

ARK
Ge   6:14 Make yourself an a of cypress wood
Ex 25:10 shall make an a of acacia wood;
1Sa 4:11 The a of God was captured;
1Ki 8: 9 There was nothing in the a except
1Pe 3:20 during the building of the a,
Rev 11:19 the a of his covenant was seen
2Mc 2: 4 that the tent and the a should follow
2Es 10:22 the a of our covenant has been

ARM → ARMIES, ARMOR, ARMS, ARMY
Ex   6: 6 redeem you with an outstretched a
Dt   7:19 mighty hand and the outstretched a
2Ch 32: 8 With him is an a of flesh;
Job 40: 9 Have you an a like God,
Ps 98: 1 his holy a have gotten him victory.
Isa 53: 1 the a of the Lord been revealed?
Jn 12:38 the a of the Lord been revealed?"

ARMIES → ARM
1Sa 17:36 defied the a of the living God."
Lk 21:20 you see Jerusalem surrounded by a,
Rev 19:14 the a of heaven, wearing fine linen,

ARMOR → ARM
1Sa 17:38 Saul clothed David with his a;
Ro 13:12 and put on the a of light;
Eph 6:11 Put on the whole a of God,
Wis 5:17 will take his zeal as his whole a,

ARMS → ARM
Pr 31:17 and makes her a strong.
Hos 11: 3 I took them up in my a;
Mk 10:16 And he took them up in his a,

ARMY → ARM
Ex 15: 4 and his a he cast into the sea;
Jos 5:14 as commander of the a of the Lord
Ps 27: 3 Though an a encamp against me,
        33:16 A king is not saved by his great a;
Rev 19:19 rider on the horse and against his a.

AROMA
2Co 2:15 For we are the a of Christ to God

ARRESTED
Jer 37:14 and a Jeremiah and brought him to
Mt 14: 3 For Herod had a John, bound him,
        26:50 and laid hands on Jesus and a him.
Ac   5:18 a the apostles and put them in the
        28:17 yet I was a in Jerusalem and handed

ARROGANCE → ARROGANT
Pr   8:13 Pride and a and the way of evil
Eze 7:24 put an end to the a of the strong,
Jdt   9:10 their a by the hand of a woman.
Sir 10: 7 A is hateful to the Lord and to
1Mc 1:24 much blood, and spoke with great a.

ARROGANT → ARROGANCE
Ps 73: 3 For I was envious of the a;
Da   7:11 a words that the horn was speaking.
1Co 13: 4 love is not envious or boastful or a

ARROW → ARROWS
Ps 64: 7 But God will shoot his a at them;
Isa 49: 2 he made me a polished a,

ARROWS → ARROW
1Sa 20:20 I will shoot three a to the side of it,
Eph 6:16 quench all the flaming a of the evil

ARTAXERXES → =AHASUERUS
1. King of Persia; allowed rebuilding of temple
under Ezra (Ezr 4; 7), and of walls of Jerusalem
under his cupbearer Nehemiah (Ne 2; 5:14; 13:6).
2. See Ahasuerus.

ARTEMIS
Ac 19:27 the temple of the great goddess A

ASA
King of Judah (1Ki 15:8-24; 1Ch 3:10; 2Ch
14-16). Godly reformer (2Ch 15); in later years
defeated Israel with help of Aram, not the Lord
(1Ki 15:16-22; 2Ch 16).

ASAHEL
Nephew of David, one of his warriors (2Sa
23:24; 1Ch 2:16; 11:26; 27:7). Killed by Abner (2Sa
2); avenged by Joab (2Sa 3:22-39).

ASAPH
1. Recorder to Hezekiah (2Ki 18:18, 37; Isa
36:3, 22).
2. Levitical musician (1Ch 6:39; 15:17-19;
16:4-7, 37), seer (2Ch 29:30). Sons of (1Ch 25;
2Ch 5:12; 20:14; 29:13; 35:15; Ezr 2:41; 3:10; Ne
7:44; 11:17; 12:27-47). Psalms of (2Ch 29:30; Ps
50; 73-83).

**ASCEND → ASCENDED, ASCENDING,
      ASCENTS**
Ps 139: 8 If I a to heaven, you are there;
Isa 14:13 in your heart, "I will a to heaven;
Ac   2:34 David did not a into the heavens,
Ro 10: 6 'Who will a into heaven?'"
2Es 4: 8 neither did I ever a into heaven.'

ASCENDED → ASCEND
2Ki 2:11 Elijah a in a whirlwind into heaven.
Jn   3:13 No one has a into heaven except

ASCENDING → ASCEND
Ge 28:12 the angels of God were a and
Jn   1:51 the angels of God a and descending

ASCENTS → ASCEND
Songs of ascents (Ps 120-134).

ASCRIBE
Dt 32: 3 a greatness to our God!
1Ch 16:29 A to the Lord the glory due his
Ps 68:34 A power to God,
Sir 39:15 A majesty to his name
Bar 2:17 not a glory or justice to the Lord;

ASHAMED → SHAME
Ge   2:25 were both naked, and were not a.
Ps   6:10 All my enemies shall be a and
Isa 29:22 No longer shall Jacob be a,
Mk   8:38 who are a of me and of my words
Ro   1:16 For I am not a of the gospel;
2Ti   2:15 a worker who has no need to be a,
Heb 2:11 Jesus is not a to call them brothers
        11:16 God is not a to be called their God;

ASHER
Son of Jacob by Zilpah (Ge 30:13; 35:26; 46:17;
Ex 1:4; 1Ch 2:2). Tribe of blessed (Ge 49:20; Dt
33:24-25), numbered (Nu 1:40-41; 26:44-47),
allotted land (Jos 10:24-31; Eze 48:2), failed to
fully possess (Jdg 1:31-32), failed to support
Deborah (Jdg 5:17), supported Gideon (Jdg 6:35;
7:23) and David (1Ch 12:36), 12,000 from (Rev
7:6).

ASHERAH → ASHERAHS, ASTARTE
1Ki 18:19 and the four hundred prophets of A,
2Ch 15:16 made an abominable image for A.

ASHERAHS* → ASHERAH
Jdg 3: 7 and worshiping the Baals and the A.

ASHES
Ge 18:27 I who am but dust and a.
Est 4: 1 and put on sackcloth and a,
Job 42: 6 and repent in dust and a."
Jnh 3: 6 himself with sackcloth, and sat in a.
Mt 11:21 long ago in sackcloth and a.
Jdt 4:11 the temple and put a on their heads
Sir 17:32 but all human beings are dust and a.

ASIA
Ac 16: 6 Holy Spirit to speak the word in A.
Rev 1: 4 to the seven churches that are in A:

ASIDE → SIDE
Ex 32: 8 quick to turn a from the way that I
Dt 28:14 if you do not turn a from any of the
Jer 5:23 they have turned a and gone away.
Da 9: 5 turning a from your commandments
Ro 3:12 All have turned a, together they
Heb 12: 1 also lay a every weight and the sin

ASK
Ps 2: 8 A of me, and I will make the nations
Isa 65: 1 sought out by those who did not a,
Mt 6: 8 knows what you need before you a
7: 7 "A, and it will be given you;
Jn 16:24 A and you will receive,
Jas 4: 3 You a and do not receive, because
you a wrongly,
1Jn 5:14 we a anything according to his will,

ASLEEP → SLEEP
Jnh 1: 5 had lain down, and was fast a.
Mt 8:24 by the waves; but he was a.
1Th 5: 6 So then let us not fall a as others do,

ASSEMBLE → ASSEMBLY
1Ki 18:19 all Israel a for me at Mount Carmel,
Zep 3: 8 to gather nations, to a kingdoms,
Rev 16:14 to a them for battle on the great day

ASSEMBLY → ASSEMBLE
Ne 8: 2 Ezra brought the law before the a,
Ps 149: 1 his praise in the a of the faithful.
Heb 12:23 the a of the firstborn who are

ASSIGNED
Ro 12: 3 the measure of faith that God has a.
1Co 3: 5 as the Lord a to each.
7:17 lead the life that the Lord has a,

ASSURANCE
Dt 28:66 in dread, with no a of your life.
Heb 6:11 so as to realize the full a of hope
11: 1 faith is the a of things hoped for,

ASSYRIA
Ge 10:11 From that land he went into A,
2Ki 18:11 of A carried the Israelites away to A,
Jer 50:18 as I punished the king of A.

ASTARTE → ASHERAH, ASTARTES
1Ki 11: 5 Solomon followed A the goddess

ASTARTES → ASTARTE
Jdg 2:13 and worshiped Baal and the A.

ASTONISHED
Isa 52:14 there were many who were a at him
Lk 2:48 his parents saw him they were a;
Gal 1: 6 a that you are so quickly deserting

ASTRAY → STRAY
Dt 30:17 are led a to bow down to other gods
Isa 53: 6 All we like sheep have gone a;
Jer 50: 6 their shepherds have led them a,
Mt 18:12 go in search of the one that went a?
1Pe 2:25 For you were going a like sheep,

ATE → EAT
Ge 3: 6 she took of its fruit and a;
Ex 16:35 The Israelites a manna forty years,

Ps 78:25 Mortals a of the bread of angels;
Eze 3: 3 I a it; and in my mouth it was as
Mt 14:20 And all a were filled;
15:37 And all of them a and were filled;
Rev 10:10 from the hand of the angel and a it;

ATHALIAH
Granddaughter of Omri; wife of Jehoram and mother of Ahaziah; encouraged their evil ways (2Ki 8:18, 27; 2Ch 22:2). At death of Ahaziah she made herself queen, killing all his sons but Joash (2Ki 11:1-3; 2Ch 22:10-12); killed six years later when Joash revealed (2Ki 11:4-16; 2Ch 23:1-15).

ATHLETE → ATHLETES
2Ti 2: 5 And in the case of an a,

ATHLETES → ATHLETE
1Co 9:25 A exercise self-control in all things;

ATONE → ATONEMENT
Da 9:24 an end to sin, and to a for iniquity,
Sir 3: 3 who honor their father a for sins,

ATONED* → ATONEMENT
Pr 16: 6 and faithfulness iniquity is a for,

ATONEMENT → ATONE, ATONED, ATONING
Ex 29:36 a bull as a sin offering for a.
30:10 Aaron shall perform the rite of a
32:30 perhaps I can make a for your sin."
Lev 23:28 for it is a day of a,
Ro 3:25 God put forward as a sacrifice of a
Heb 2:17 to make a sacrifice of a for the sins

ATONING → ATONEMENT
1Jn 2: 2 and he is the a sacrifice for our sins,
4:10 sent his Son to be the a sacrifice for
Sir 28: 5 will make an a sacrifice for his sins?

ATTAIN → ATTAINED
Ps 139: 6 it is so high that I cannot a it.
Pr 8:12 and I a knowledge and discretion.
Da 12:12 those who persevere and a
Php 3:11 a the resurrection from the dead.

ATTAINED → ATTAIN
Ro 9:30 not strive for righteousness, have a
Php 3:16 let us hold fast to what we have a.

ATTENTION
Nu 16:15 "Pay no a to their offering.
Job 24:12 yet God pays no a to their prayer.
Heb 2: 1 greater a to what we have heard,

ATTESTED
Ac 2:22 a man a to you by God with deeds
Ro 3:21 and is a by the law and the prophets,

AUTHOR*
Ac 3:15 and you killed the A of life,
Wis 13: 3 for the a of beauty created them.

AUTHORITIES → AUTHORITY
Ro 13: 1 be subject to the governing a;
Col 2:15 He disarmed the rulers and a and

AUTHORITY → AUTHORITIES
Ge 41:45 Thus Joseph gained a over the land
Pr 29: 2 When the righteous are in a,
Mk 1:27 A new teaching—with a!
Lk 5:24 Son of Man has a on earth to forgive
Ac 5:29 obey God rather than any human a.
Ro 13: 1 for there is no a except from God,
1Co 11:10 woman ought to have a symbol of a
Col 2:10 who is the head of every ruler and a.
1Ti 2:12 no woman to teach or to have a over
Rev 12:10 and the a of his Messiah,
20: 4 on them were given a to judge.

AVENGE → VENGEANCE
Dt 32:43 he will a the blood of his children,
Joel 3:21 I will a their blood, and I will not
Ro 12:19 Beloved, never a yourselves,
Rev 6:10 and a our blood on the inhabitants
1Mc 2:67 a the wrong done to your people.

AVENGER → VENGEANCE
Nu 35:12 shall be for you a refuge from the a,
Ps 8: 2 to silence the enemy and the a.
1Th 4: 6 the Lord is an a in all these things,

AVENGING → VENGEANCE
Na 1: 2 A jealous and a God is the Lord,

AVOID → AVOIDS
2Ti 2:16 A profane chatter, for it will lead
Tit 3: 9 But a stupid controversies,

AVOIDS → AVOID
Pr 16: 6 by the fear of the Lord one a evil.

AWAKE
Ps 44:23 A, do not cast us off forever!
57: 8 A, my soul! A, O harp and lyre!
Isa 51: 9 A, a, put on strength, O arm of the
Lord!
Da 12: 2 in the dust of the earth shall a,
Mk 14:37 Could you not keep a one hour?
Eph 5:14 "Sleeper, a! Rise from the dead,
1Th 5: 6 but let us keep a and be sober;
Rev 16:15 Blessed is the one who stays a and

AWE → AWESOME
Ps 119:161 my heart stands in a of your words.
Isa 29:23 will stand in a of the God of Israel.
Mt 9: 8 saw it, they were filled with a,
Ac 2:43 A came upon everyone, because
Ro 11:20 do not become proud, but stand
in a.

AWESOME → AWE
Ex 15:11 majestic in holiness, a in splendor,
Dt 6:22 before our eyes great and a signs
10:17 the great God, mighty and a,
Ne 1: 5 and a God who keeps covenant
Ps 47: 2 For the Lord, the Most High, is a,
65: 5 By a deeds you answer us with
68:35 A is God in his sanctuary,
Da 9: 4 saying, "Ah, Lord, great and a God,
Sir 43:29 A is the Lord and very great,

AX
2Ki 6: 5 his a head fell into the water;
Mt 3:10 Even now the a is lying at the root

AZARIAH → =ABEDNEGO, =UZZIAH
1. King of Judah; see Uzziah (2Ki 15:1-7).
2. Prophet (2Ch 15:1-8).
3. Opponent of Jeremiah (Jer 43:2).
4. Jewish exile; see Abednego (Da 1:6-19).

AZAZEL
Lev 16: 8 for the Lord and the other lot for A.

B

BAAL → BAALS
Nu 25: 3 Israel yoked itself to the B of Peor,
Jdg 2:13 and worshiped B and the Astartes.
1Ki 18:25 Elijah said to the prophets of B,
19:18 the knees that have not bowed to B,
Jer 2: 8 the prophets prophesied by B,
Hos 2:16 no longer will you call me, "My B."
Ro 11: 4 not bowed the knee to B."

BAALS → BAAL
Jdg 2:13 worshiping the B and the Asherahs;
1Sa 7: 4 So Israel put away the B and the

BAASHA
King of Israel (1Ki 15:16-16:7; 2Ch 16:1-6).

BABEL → BABYLON
Ge 11: 9 Therefore it was called B,

BABES → BABIES
Ps 8: 2 Out of the mouths of b and infants
Isa 3: 4 and b shall rule over them.

BABIES → BABES
Mt 21:16 the mouths of infants and nursing b

BABYLON → BABEL
2Ki 24:15 into captivity from Jerusalem to B.
Ps 137: 1 By the rivers of B—there we sat

Isa   14: 4   this taunt against the king of **B**:
        21: 9   he responded, "Fallen, fallen is **B**;
Jer   25:11   serve the king of **B** seventy years.
1Pe   5:13   Your sister church in **B**, chosen
Rev   14: 8   "Fallen, fallen is **B** the great!
Bel   1:36   he set him down in **B**,

BACK → BACKSLIDING
Ge   19:26   Lot's wife, behind him, looked **b**,
2Ki   20:11   he brought the shadow **b** the ten
Lk   9:62   puts a hand to the plow and looks **b**

BACKSLIDING* → BACK
Jer   8: 5   people turned away in perpetual **b**?

BAD
Pr   20:14   "**B, b**," says the buyer, then goes
Mt   7:17   but the tree bears **b** fruit.
1Co   15:33   "**B** company ruins good morals."

BALAAM
Prophet who attempted to curse Israel (Nu 22-24; Dt 23:4-5; 2Pe 2:15; Jude 11; Rev 2:14). Killed in Israel's vengeance on Midianites (Nu 31:8; Jos 13:22).

BALAK
Moabite king who hired Balaam to curse Israel (Nu 22-24; Jos 24:9; Mic 6:5).

BALANCE → BALANCES
Job   31: 6   let me be weighed in a just **b**,
Isa   40:12   in scales and the hills in a **b**?

BALANCES → BALANCE
Lev   19:36   shall have honest **b**, honest weights,
Pr   16:11   Honest **b** and scales are the LORD's;
Sir   28:25   make **b** and scales for your words.

BALM
Jer   8:22   Is there no **b** in Gilead?

BANDIT
Mt   26:55   to arrest me as though I were a **b**?
Jn   10: 1   in by another way is a thief
                and a **b**.

BANISH
Ecc   11:10   **B** anxiety from your mind,
Ro   11:26   he will **b** ungodliness from Jacob."

BANNER
Ex   17:15   and called it, The LORD is my **b**.

BAPTISM → BAPTIZE
Mk   1: 4   proclaiming a **b** of repentance for
       10:38   be baptized with the **b** that I am
Lk   20: 4   the **b** of John come from heaven,
Ac   18:25   though he knew only the **b** of John.
       19: 3   They answered, "Into John's **b**."
Ro   6: 4   buried with him by **b** into death,
1Co   15:29   receive **b** on behalf of the dead?
Eph   4: 5   one Lord, one faith, one **b**,
Col   2:12   when you were buried with him
                in **b**,
1Pe   3:21   **b**, which this prefigured, now saves

BAPTISMS* → BAPTIZE
Heb   6: 2   about **b**, laying on of hands,
        9:10   with food and drink and various **b**,

BAPTIST → BAPTIZE
Mt   3: 1   In those days John the **B** appeared
       11:11   has arisen greater than John the **B**;
       14: 8   the head of John the **B** here on a
       16:14   they said, "Some say John the **B**,

BAPTIZE → BAPTISM, BAPTISMS, BAPTIST, BAPTIZED, BAPTIZING
Mt   3:11   "I **b** you with water for repentance,
Lk   3:16   He will **b** you with the Holy Spirit
1Co   1:17   For Christ did not send me to **b** but

BAPTIZED → BAPTIZE
Mt   3:13   to John at the Jordan, to be **b**
Ac   1: 5   John **b** with water, but you will be **b**
                with the Holy
        2:38   "Repent, and be **b** every one of you
Ro   6: 3   **b** into Christ Jesus were **b** into his

1Co   10: 2   all were **b** into Moses in the cloud
       12:13   one Spirit we were all **b** into one

BAPTIZING* → BAPTIZE
Mt   28:19   **b** them in the name of the Father
Jn   4: 1   "Jesus is making and **b** more

BARABBAS*
Prisoner released by Pilate instead of Jesus (Mt 27:16-26; Mk 15:7-15; Lk 23:18-19; Jn 18:40).

BARAK*
Judge who fought with Deborah against Canaanites (Jdg 4-5; 1Sa 12:11; Heb 11:32).

BARBARIAN → BARBARIANS
Col   3:11   circumcised and uncircumcised, **b**,

BARBARIANS* → BARBARIAN
Ro   1:14   am a debtor both to Greeks and to **b**,

BARBS*
Nu   33:55   let remain shall be as **b** in your eyes

BARE → BARED
Ps   18:15   were laid **b** at your rebuke,
Heb   4:13   all are naked and laid **b** to the eyes

BARED* → BARE
Isa   52:10   The LORD has **b** his holy arm

BARN → BARNS
Lk   12:24   they have neither storehouse nor **b**,

BARNABAS* → =JOSEPH
Disciple, originally Joseph (Ac 4:36), prophet (Ac 13:1), apostle (Ac 14:14). Brought Paul to apostles (Ac 9:27), Antioch (Ac 11:22-29; Gal 2:1-13), on the first missionary journey (Ac 13-14). Together at Jerusalem Council, they separated over John Mark (Ac 15). Later co-workers (1Co 9:6; Col 4:10).

BARNS* → BARN
Dt   28: 8   the blessing upon you in your **b**,
Ps   144:13   May our **b** be filled, with produce
Lk   12:18   pull down my **b** and build larger

BARREN → BARRENNESS
Ge   11:30   Now Sarai was **b**; she had no child.
Ex   23:26   No one shall miscarry or be **b** in
1Sa   2: 5   The **b** has borne seven, but she who
Ps   113: 9   He gives the **b** woman a home,
Isa   54: 1   Sing, O **b** one who did not bear;
Lk   1: 7   because Elizabeth was **b**,
Heb   11:11   too old—and Sarah herself was **b**—

BARRENNESS* → BARREN
Dt   7:14   neither sterility nor **b** among you
Ro   4:19   considered the **b** of Sarah's womb.

BARTHOLOMEW* → =NATHANAEL?
Apostle (Mt 10:3; Mk 3:18; Lk 6:14; Ac 1:13). Possibly also called Nathanael (Jn 1:45-49; 21:2).

BARUCH*
Jeremiah's secretary (Jer 32:12-16; 36; 43:1-6; 45:1-2). Deuterocanonical book ascribed to (Bar 1:1, 3, 8).

BARZILLAI
1. Gileadite who aided David during Absalom's revolt (2Sa 17:27; 19:31-39).
2. Son-in-law of 1. (Ezr 2:61; Ne 7:63).

BASED*
Ro   9:31   righteousness that is **b** on the law,
        9:32   but as if it were **b** on works.
Php   3: 9   righteousness from God **b** on faith.

BASHAN
Nu   21:33   King Og of **B** came out against
Ps   22:12   strong bulls of **B** surround me;
Mic   7:14   let them feed in **B** and Gilead as in

BASIN
Ex   30:18   You shall make a bronze **b** with a
1Ki   7:30   four corners were supports for a **b**.
Jn   13: 5   **b** and began to wash the disciples'

BASIS
Lk   23: 4   "I find no **b** for an accusation
Phm   1: 9   rather appeal to you on the **b** of love

BASKET
Ex   2: 3   she got a papyrus **b** for him,
Mt   5:15   a lamp puts it under the bushel **b**,
Ac   9:25   in the wall, lowering him in a **b**.

BATHING
2Sa   11: 2   he saw from the roof a woman **b**;

BATHSHEBA*
Wife of Uriah; committed adultery with and married David (2Sa 11; Ps 51), mother of Solomon (2Sa 12:24; 1Ki 1-2; 1Ch 3:5).

BATTLE
1Sa   17:47   the **b** is the LORD's and he will give
2Ch   20:15   for the **b** is not yours but God's.
Ps   24: 8   and mighty, the LORD, mighty in **b**.
Ecc   9:11   nor the **b** to the strong, nor bread to
Rev   16:14   them for **b** on the great day of God
       20: 8   Magog, in order to gather them
                for **b**;
1Mc   3:19   the army that victory in **b** depends,

BEAR → BEARS, BIRTH, BIRTHRIGHT, BORE, BORN, CHILDBEARING, FIRSTBORN
Ge   4:13   punishment is greater than I can **b**!
       17:19   your wife Sarah shall **b** you a son,
Isa   7:14   is with child and shall **b** a son,
Mt   1:23   virgin shall conceive and **b** a son,
        7:18   A good tree cannot **b** bad fruit,
Lk   11:46   load people with burdens hard to **b**,
Jn   15: 2   he prunes to make it **b** more fruit.
Gal   6: 2   **B** one another's burdens,
Col   3:13   **B** with one another and,
Heb   9:28   offered once to **b** the sins of many,
Rev   12: 4   woman who was about to **b** a child,

BEARS → BEAR
Ps   68:19   Blessed be the Lord, who daily **b** us
1Co   13: 7   It **b** all things, believes all things,

BEAST → BEASTS
Rev   11: 7   **b** that comes up from the bottomless
                pit
       13:18   calculate the number of the **b**,
       16: 2   who had the mark of the **b**
       19:20   who had received the mark of the **b**

BEASTS → BEAST
Da   7: 3   four great **b** came up out of the sea,
Mk   1:13   and he was with the wild **b**;

BEAT → BEATEN, BEATING
Isa   2: 4   shall **b** their swords into plowshares,
Joel   3:10   **B** your plowshares into swords,
Lk   22:63   began to mock him and **b** him;

BEATEN → BEAT
2Co   11:25   Three times I was **b** with rods.
1Pe   2:20   If you endure when you are **b** for

BEATING → BEAT
Ex   2:11   He saw an Egyptian **b** a Hebrew,
1Co   9:26   nor do I box as though **b** the air;

BEAUTIFUL → BEAUTY
Ge   12:11   you are a woman **b** in appearance,
1Sa   25: 3   The woman was clever and **b**,
Est   2: 7   the girl was fair and **b**,
Job   42:15   no women so **b** as Job's daughters;
Ps   48: 2   **b** in elevation, is the joy of all
SS   1: 5   I am black and **b**, O daughters of
Isa   4: 2   the branch of the LORD shall be **b**
       52: 7   How **b** upon the mountains are the
Ac   3: 2   the temple called the **B** Gate so that
Ro   10:15   **b** are the feet of those who bring
Tob   6:12   girl is sensible, brave, and very **b**,
Jdt   8: 7   She was **b** in appearance,
Wis   7:29   She is more **b** than the sun,
Sir   25: 1   and they are **b** in the sight of God
Sus   1: 2   very **b** woman and one who feared

BEAUTY → BEAUTIFUL
2Sa 14:25 so much for his **b** as Absalom;
Ps 27: 4 to behold the **b** of the LORD,
Pr 6:25 Do not desire her **b** in your heart,
31:30 Charm is deceitful, and **b** is vain,
1Pe 3: 4 with the lasting **b** of a gentle
Jdt 16: 9 her **b** captivated his mind,
Wis 13: 3 for the author of **b** created them.
Sir 14: 8 not gaze at **b** belonging to another;
Sus 1:56 **b** has beguiled you and lust has
1Mc 2:12 And see, our holy place, our **b**,

BED → BEDS
Ge 47:31 bowed himself on the head of his **b**.
Ps 139: 8 if I make my **b** in Sheol, you are
Lk 5:19 let him down with his **b** through the
Heb 13: 4 let the marriage **b** be kept undefiled;

BEDS → BED
Ps 36: 4 They plot mischief while on their **b**;
Mic 2: 1 and evil deeds on their **b**!

BEE* → BEES
Isa 7:18 the **b** that is in the land of Assyria.
Sir 11: 3 The **b** is small among flying

BEER-SHEBA
Ge 21:31 Therefore that place was called **B**;
1Sa 3:20 And all Israel from Dan to **B** knew

BEES → BEE
Jdg 14: 8 a swarm of **b** in the body of the lion,

BEFORE
Ex 20: 3 you shall have no other gods **b** me.
33: 2 I will send an angel **b** you,
Isa 43:10 **B** me no god was formed,
65:24 **B** they call I will answer,
Mal 3: 1 my messenger to prepare the way **b**
Mt 6: 8 Father knows what you need **b** you
Lk 22:61 "**B** the cock crows today,
Heb 12: 2 sake of the joy that was set **b** him

BEGGAR → BEGS
Mk 10:46 son of Timaeus, a blind **b**,
Jn 9: 8 who had seen him before as a **b**

BEGINNING
Ge 1: 1 In the **b** when God created the
Ps 111:10 fear of the LORD is the **b** of wisdom;
Pr 1: 7 The fear of the LORD is the **b** of
8:22 The LORD created me at the **b** of his
Ecc 7: 8 Better is the end of a thing than its **b**
Isa 40:21 Has it not been told you from the **b**?
Mt 24: 8 this is but the **b** of the birth pangs.
Jn 1: 1 In the **b** was the Word,
1Jn 1: 1 declare to you what was from the **b**,
2Jn 1: 6 as you have heard it from the **b**—
Rev 21: 6 and the Omega, the **b** and the end.
Wis 6:17 The **b** of wisdom is the most sincere
Sir 1:14 To fear the Lord is the **b** of wisdom;

BEGOTTEN
Ps 2: 7 You are my son; today I have **b** you.
Ac 13:33 are my Son; today I have **b** you.'
Heb 1: 5 are my Son; today I have **b** you"?
2Es 6:58 have called your firstborn, only **b**,

BEGS → BEG
Lk 6:30 Give to everyone who **b** from you;

BEHEADED → HEAD
Lk 9: 9 Herod said, "John I **b**;
Rev 20: 4 the souls of those who had been **b**

BEHEMOTH
Job 40:15 "Look at **B**, which I made just as I
2Es 6:49 the one you called **B** and the name

BEHIND
Isa 38:17 have cast all my sins **b** your back.
Mt 16:23 said to Peter, "Get me **b**, Satan!
Php 3:13 forgetting what lies **b** and straining

BEING
Ge 2: 7 and the man became a living **b**.
Nu 23:19 God is not a human **b**,
Da 7:13 one like a human **b** coming with the

Jn 1: 3 All things came into **b** through him,
1Co 15:45 Adam, became a living **b**";
Heb 1: 3 the exact imprint of God's very **b**,

BEL*
Babylonian deity (Isa 46:1; Jer 50:2; 51:44; LtJ 6:40; Bel 1:3-28).

BELIEF → BELIEVE
2Th 2:13 the Spirit and through **b** in the truth.

BELIEVE → BELIEF, BELIEVED, BELIEVER, BELIEVERS, BELIEVES, BELIEVING
Ex 4: 5 that they may **b** that the LORD,
Nu 14:11 long will they refuse to **b** in me,
2Ki 17:14 did not **b** in the LORD their God.
Ps 119:66 for I **b** in your commandments.
Pr 14:15 The simple **b** everything,
Jer 12: 6 do not **b** them, though they speak
Hab 1: 5 you would not **b** if you were told.
Mt 18: 6 one of these little ones who **b** in me,
24:23 or 'There he is!'—do not **b** it.
Mk 1:15 repent, and **b** in the good news."
9:24 "I **b**; help my unbelief!"
Lk 24:25 How slow of heart to **b** all that the
Jn 1: 7 so that all might **b** through him.
3:18 who **b** in him are not condemned;
5:46 believed Moses, you would **b** me,
6:29 you **b** in him whom he has sent."
10:38 you do not **b** me, **b** the works,
14: 1 **B** in God, **b** also in me.
17:20 will **b** in me through their word,
20:29 not seen and yet have come to **b**."
Ac 16:31 answered, "**B** on the Lord Jesus,
28:24 while others refused to **b**.
Ro 3:22 faith in Jesus Christ for all who **b**.
10: 9 **b** in your heart that God raised him
1Co 15: 2 unless you have come to **b** in vain.
Gal 3: 9 this reason, those who **b** are blessed
1Th 4:14 For since we **b** that Jesus died and
Heb 11: 6 would approach him must **b**
Jas 2:19 Even the demons **b**—and shudder.
1Pe 1: 8 you do not see him now, you **b**
1Jn 4: 1 Beloved, do not **b** every spirit,
Jude 1: 5 destroyed those who did not **b**.
Sir 19:15 so do not **b** everything you hear.

BELIEVED → BELIEVE
Ge 15: 6 And he **b** the LORD;
Ex 14:31 **b** in the LORD and in his servant
Isa 53: 1 Who has **b** what we have heard?
Jn 1:12 received him, who **b** in his name,
12:38 "Lord, who has **b** our message,
20: 8 also went in, and he saw and **b**;
Ac 2:44 All who **b** were together and had all
Ro 4: 3 "Abraham **b** God, and it was
10:16 "Lord, who has **b** our message?"
2Co 4:13 "I **b**, and so I spoke"—
Gal 3: 6 Just as Abraham "**b** God,
1Ti 3:16 **b** in throughout the world, taken up
Heb 4: 3 For we who have **b** enter that rest,
Jas 2:23 that says, "Abraham **b** God,
Jdt 14:10 had done, he **b** firmly in God.
1Mc 2:59 **b** and were saved from the flame.

BELIEVER → BELIEVE
1Co 6: 6 but a **b** goes to court against a **b**—
7:12 **b** has a wife who is an unbeliever,
2Co 6:15 Or what does a **b** share with an

BELIEVERS → BELIEVE
1Co 14:22 a sign not for **b** but for unbelievers,
Gal 2: 4 because of false **b** secretly brought
2Th 3: 6 keep away from **b** who are living in
1Pe 2:17 Love the family of **b**.

BELIEVES → BELIEVE
Jn 3:15 whoever **b** in him may have eternal
11:26 everyone who lives and **b** in me
Ro 9:33 whoever **b** in him will not be put to
10:10 **b** with the heart and so is justified,
1Co 13: 7 It bears all things, **b** all things,

BELIEVING → BELIEVE
Jn 20:31 through **b** you may have life in his
Gal 3: 5 or by your **b** what you heard?

BELLY
Ge 3:14 upon your **b** you shall go,
Lev 11:42 Whatever moves on its **b**,
Jnh 1:17 and Jonah was in the **b** of the fish
Mt 12:40 three days and three nights in the **b**
Php 3:19 is destruction; their god is the **b**;

BELONG → BELONGS
Dt 29:29 The secret things **b** to the LORD our God, but the revealed things **b** to us
Ps 82: 8 for all the nations **b** to you!
Da 9: 9 To the Lord our God **b** mercy and
Jn 10:16 sheep that do not **b** to this fold.
15:19 Because you do not **b** to the world,
Ro 9: 6 not all Israelites truly **b** to Israel,
1Co 3:23 you **b** to Christ, and Christ belongs
12:15 I do not **b** to the body,"
1Jn 2:19 out from us, but they did not **b** to us;

BELONGS → BELONG
Ps 22:28 For dominion **b** to the LORD,
62:11 I heard this: that power **b** to God,
Jnh 2: 9 Deliverance **b** to the LORD!"
Rev 7:10 "Salvation **b** to our God who is

BELOVED → LOVE
SS 2:16 My **b** is mine and I am his;
Mt 3:17 heaven said, "This is my Son, the **B**,
12:18 my **b**, with whom my soul is well
17: 5 "This is my Son, the **B**;
Col 3:12 As God's chosen ones, holy and **b**,
Rev 20: 9 camp of the saints and the **b** city.

BELSHAZZAR*
King of Babylon (Da 5; Bar 1:11-12).

BELT
1Sa 18: 4 his sword and his bow and his **b**.
Isa 11: 5 Righteousness shall be the **b** around
Mk 1: 6 with a leather **b** around his waist,
Eph 6:14 the **b** of truth around your waist,

BELTESHAZZAR → See DANIEL

BEN-HADAD*
1. King of Syria in time of Asa (1Ki 15:18-20; 2Ch 16:2-4).
2. King of Syria in time of Ahab (1Ki 20; 2Ki 6:24; 8:7-15).
3. King of Syria in time of Jehoahaz (2Ki 13:3, 24-25; Jer 49:27; Am 1:4).

BENAIAH
A commander of David's army (2Sa 8:18; 20:23; 23:20-30); loyal to Solomon (1Ki 1:8-2:46; 4:4).

BEND → BENT
Php 2:10 name of Jesus every knee should **b**,
Man 1:11 And now I **b** the knee of my heart,

BENEFICIAL → BENEFIT
1Co 6:12 but not all things are **b**.
10:23 lawful," but not all things are **b**.

BENEFIT → BENEFICIAL, BENEFITS
Gal 5: 2 Christ will be of no **b** to you.
Phm 1:20 have this **b** from you in the Lord!
Heb 4: 2 message they heard did not **b** them,

BENEFITS → BENEFIT
Ps 103: 2 and do not forget all his **b**—
1Co 9:11 if we reap your material **b**?

BENJAMIN → BENJAMINITE
Twelfth son of Jacob by Rachel (Ge 35:16-24; 46:19-21; 1Ch 2:2). Jacob refused to send him to Egypt, but relented (Ge 42-45). Tribe of blessed (Ge 49:27; Dt 33:12), numbered (Nu 1:37; 26:41), allotted land (Jos 18:11-28; Eze 48:23), failed to fully possess (Jdg 1:21), nearly obliterated (Jdg 20-21), sided with Ish-Bosheth (2Sa 2), but turned to David (1Ch 12:2, 29). 12,000 from (Rev 7:8).

BENJAMINITE → BENJAMIN
Jdg   3:15   the **B**, a left-handed man.
1Sa   9:21   Saul answered, "I am only a **B**,

BENT → BEND
Hos   11: 4   I **b** down to them and fed them.
Jn   8: 6   [[Jesus **b** down and wrote with his]]
      20: 5   He **b** down to look in and saw

BEREAVE → BEREAVES
Lev   26:22   they shall **b** you of your children
Eze   36:12   No longer shall you **b** them of

BEREAVES* → BEREAVE
La   1:20   In the street the sword **b**;

BESIDES
Dt   32:39   there is no god **b** me.
Ps   18:31   And who is a rock **b** our God?—
Isa   45:21   There is no other god **b** me,
Wis   12:13   For neither is there any god **b** you,
Bel   1:41   there is no other **b** you!"

BEST → GOOD
Dt   33:21   He chose the **b** for himself,
Mk   12:39   the **b** seats in the synagogues and
2Ti   2:15   your **b** to present yourself to God

BETHANY
Mt   26: 6   Jesus was at **B** in the house of
Jn   11: 1   a certain man was ill, Lazarus of **B**,

BETHEL
Ge   12: 8   the east of **B**, and pitched his tent,
     28:19   He called that place **B**;
1Sa   7:16   a circuit year by year to **B**, Gilgal,

BETHLEHEM
Ru   4:11   and bestow a name in **B**;
1Sa   17:12   David was the son of an Ephrathite
         of **B**
Mic   5: 2   But you, O **B** of Ephrathah,
Mt   2: 1   after Jesus was born in **B** of Judea,
Lk   2:15   "Let us go now to **B** and see this

BETRAY → BETRAYED
Mt   10:21   Brother will **b** brother to death,
Mk   14:11   to look for an opportunity to **b** him.
Jn   13:11   For he knew who was to **b** him;

BETRAYED → BETRAY
Lk   21:16   You will be **b** even by parents and
1Co   11:23   Jesus on the night when he was **b**

BETTER → GOOD
1Sa   15:22   Surely, to obey is **b** than sacrifice,
Ps   63: 3   your steadfast love is **b** than life,
Pr   15:16   **B** is a little with the fear of
     27: 5   **B** is open rebuke than hidden love.
Ecc   2:24   There is nothing **b** for mortals than
      9: 4   a living dog is **b** than a dead lion.
SS   1: 2   For your love is **b** than wine,
Da   1:20   he found them ten times **b** than all
Mt   5:29   it is **b** for you to lose one of your
Mk   14:21   It would have been **b** for that one
Jn   11:50   **b** for you to have one man die for
Ro   14: 5   Some judge one day to be **b** than
Php   1:23   and be with Christ, for that is far **b**;
      2: 3   in humility regard others as **b** than
Heb   7:22   the guarantee of a **b** covenant.
      9:23   need **b** sacrifices than these.
1Pe   3:17   For it is **b** to suffer for doing good,
Tob   12: 8   A little with righteousness is **b** than
Sir   40:26   the fear of the Lord is **b** than either.

BETWEEN
Ge   3:15   put enmity **b** you and the woman,
      9:13   a sign of the covenant **b** me and
     16: 5   the LORD judge **b** you and me!"
Isa   2: 4   He shall judge **b** the nations,
Eze   34:17   I shall judge **b** sheep and sheep, **b**
         rams and goats:
Jn   19:18   on either side, with Jesus **b** them.
Ro   10:12   no distinction **b** Jew and Greek;
Eph   2:14   dividing wall, that is, the hostility **b**
1Ti   2: 5   one mediator **b** God and
         humankind

BEWARE
Ecc   12:12   anything beyond these, my child, **b**.
Mt   6: 1   "**B** of practicing your piety before
Php   3: 2   **B** of the dogs, **b** of the evil workers,

BEYOND
Ps   147: 5   his understanding is **b** measure.
2Co   4:17   an eternal weight of glory **b** all
2Jn   1: 9   but goes **b** it, does not have God;
Sir   3:23   not meddle in matters that are **b** you

BEZALEL
     Judahite craftsman in charge of building the
tabernacle (Ex 31:1-11; 35:30-39:31).

BILDAD*
     One of Job's friends (Job 2:11; 8; 18; 25; 42:9).

BILHAH
     Servant of Rachel, mother of Jacob's sons Dan
and Naphtali (Ge 30:1-7; 35:25; 46:23-25).

BIND → BINDS
Dt   6: 8   **B** them as a sign on your hand,
Pr   6:21   **B** them upon your heart always;
Isa   61: 1   to **b** up the brokenhearted,
Mt   16:19   whatever you **b** on earth will be

BINDS → BIND
Job   5:18   For he wounds, but he **b** up;
Col   3:14   **b** everything together in perfect

BIRD → BIRDS
Ge   1:21   and every winged **b** of every kind.
Lev   20:25   the unclean **b** and the clean;

BIRDS → BIRD
Ge   1:22   and let **b** multiply on the earth."
      7: 3   and seven pairs of the **b** of the air
Ps   50:11   I know all the **b** of the air,
Jer   7:33   be food for the **b** of the air, and for
Mt   6:26   Look at the **b** of the air;
Rev   19:21   the **b** were gorged with their flesh.

BIRTH → BEAR
Dt   32:18   you forgot the God who gave you **b**.
Ps   22:10   On you I was cast from my **b**,
Mt   24: 8   is but the beginning of the **b** pangs.
Jas   1:18   he gave us **b** by the word of truth,
1Pe   1: 3   given us a new **b** into a living hope

BIRTHRIGHT → BEAR, RIGHT
Ge   25:34   Thus Esau despised his **b**.
Heb   12:16   who sold his **b** for a single meal.

BISHOP
1Ti   3: 1   whoever aspires to the office of **b**
Tit   1: 7   For a **b**, as God's steward, must be

BIT → BITE, BITS
Nu   21: 9   and whenever a serpent **b** someone,
Ps   32: 9   temper must be curbed with **b** and

BITE* → BIT
Gal   5:15   If, however, you **b** and devour one
Sir   21: 2   if you approach sin, it will **b** you.

BITS → BIT
Jas   3: 3   we put **b** into the mouths of horses

BITTER → BITTERNESS
Ex   1:14   made their lives **b** with hard service
     12: 8   with unleavened bread and **b** herbs.
     15:23   water of Marah because it was **b**.
Ru   1:13   it has been far more **b** for me than
Rev   8:11   the water, because it was made **b**.

BITTERNESS → BITTER
Nu   5:18   the water of **b** that brings the curse.
Pr   14:10   The heart knows its own **b**,
Ro   3:14   mouths are full of cursing and **b**."
Eph   4:31   Put away from you all **b** and wrath

BLACK
SS   1: 5   I am **b** and beautiful, O daughters
Zec   6: 2   the second chariot **b** horses,
Mt   5:36   cannot make one hair white or **b**.
Rev   6: 5   I looked, and there was a **b** horse!

BLAMELESS
Ge   17: 1   walk before me, and be **b**.
2Sa   22:26   with the **b** you show yourself **b**;
Job   1: 1   That man was **b** and upright,
Ps   37:18   The LORD knows the days of the **b**,
Pr   11:20   but those of **b** ways are his delight.
Eph   1: 4   holy and **b** before him in love.
Php   2:15   so that you may be **b** and innocent,
1Th   5:23   and **b** at the coming of our Lord
Tit   1: 7   bishop, as God's steward, must be **b**
Heb   7:26   **b**, undefiled, separated from sinners,
Rev   14: 5   mouth no lie was found; they are **b**.
1Mc   4:42   chose **b** priests devoted to the law,

BLASPHEME → BLASPHEMED,
     BLASPHEMER, BLASPHEMES,
     BLASPHEMIES, BLASPHEMOUS
Ac   26:11   I tried to force them to **b**;
1Ti   1:20   so that they may learn not to **b**.

BLASPHEMED → BLASPHEME
Eze   20:27   In this again your ancestors **b** me,
Mt   26:65   tore his clothes and said, "He has **b**!

BLASPHEMER → BLASPHEME
1Ti   1:13   even though I was formerly a **b**,
Sir   3:16   forsakes a father is like a **b**,

BLASPHEMES → BLASPHEME
Lev   24:16   One who **b** the name of the LORD
Lk   12:10   whoever **b** against the Holy Spirit

BLASPHEMIES → BLASPHEME
Mk   3:28   their sins and whatever **b** they utter;
Rev   13: 6   its mouth to utter **b** against God,
1Mc   2: 6   He saw the **b** being committed in

BLASPHEMOUS → BLASPHEME
Ac   6:11   "We have heard him speak **b** words
Rev   13: 1   and on its heads were **b** names.

BLAZING
Ex   3: 2   he looked, and the bush was **b**,
Dt   4:11   the mountain was **b** up to the very
Heb   12:18   a **b** fire, and darkness, and gloom,

BLEMISH → BLEMISHED
Ex   12: 5   Your lamb shall be without **b**,
Lev   22:20   not offer anything that has a **b**,
Eph   5:27   that she may be holy and without **b**.
Heb   9:14   offered himself without **b** to God,
1Pe   1:19   that of a lamb without defect or **b**.
Jude   1:24   to make you stand without **b** in the

BLEMISHED* → BLEMISH
Mal   1:14   yet sacrifices to the Lord what is **b**;
Sir   34:21   ill-gotten goods, the offering is **b**;

BLESS → BLESSED, BLESSING, BLESSINGS
Ge   12: 2   I will **b** you, and make your name
     17:16   I will **b** her, and moreover I will
     22:17   I will indeed **b** you, and I will make
     26: 3   I will be with you, and will **b** you;
     32:26   not let you go, unless you **b** me."
Ex   20:24   I will come to you and **b** you.
Nu   6:24   The LORD **b** you and keep you;
     23:20   See, I received a command to **b**;
Dt   7:13   he will love you, **b** you,
     30:16   the LORD your God will **b** you in
1Ch   29:20   "**B** the LORD your God."
Ps   5:12   For you **b** the righteous, O LORD;
     29:11   the LORD **b** his people with peace!
     34: 1   I will **b** the LORD at all times;
    103: 1   **B** the LORD, O my soul,
   109:28   Let them curse, but you will **b**.
Hag   2:19   From this day on I will **b** you.
Lk   6:28   **b** those who curse you, pray
Ro   12:14   **B** those who persecute you;
1Co   4:12   When reviled, we **b**;
Jas   3: 9   With it we **b** the Lord and Father,
Tob   4:19   At all times **b** the Lord God,
Sir   32:13   But above all **b** your Maker,

BLESSED → BLESS
Ge   1:22   God **b** them, saying, "Be fruitful
     2: 3   So God **b** the seventh day and

BLESSED (cont.)

Ge	14:19	He **b** him and said, "**B** be Abram
Nu	24: 9	**B** is everyone who blesses you,
Job	1:21	be the name of the LORD."
	42:12	The LORD **b** the latter days
Ps	118:26	**B** is the one who comes in the name
Isa	30:18	**b** are all those who wait for him.
Jer	17: 7	**B** are those who trust in the LORD,
Mt	5: 3	"**B** are the poor in spirit,
Mk	10:16	laid his hands on them, and **b** them.
Lk	1:42	"**B** are you among women,
	6:20	"**B** are you who are poor,
Jn	12:13	**B** is the one who comes in the name
	20:29	**B** are those who have not seen and
Ac	20:35	It is more **b** to give than to receive.
Gal	3: 8	"All the Gentiles shall be **b** in you."
Eph	1: 3	who has **b** us in Christ
1Pe	3:14	for doing what is right, you are **b.**
Rev	1: 3	**B** is the one who reads aloud the
	22: 7	**B** is the one who keeps the words of
Tob	3:11	she prayed and said, "**B** are you,
Jdt	13:17	one accord, "**B** are you our God,
Aza	1: 3	"**B** are you, O Lord, God of our
Sus	1:60	raised a great shout and **b** God,

BLESSING → BLESS

Ge	12: 2	so that you will be a **b.**
	22:18	the nations of the earth gain **b** for
	27:36	now he has taken away my **b.**"
Dt	11:26	before you today a **b** and a curse:
	23: 5	your God turned the curse into a **b**
Ne	13: 2	our God turned the curse into a **b.**
Eze	34:26	they shall be showers of **b.**
Mal	3:10	for you an overflowing **b.**
Mk	14:22	of bread, and after **b** it broke it,
Lk	24:51	While he was **b** them, he withdrew
1Co	10:16	The cup of **b** that we bless,
Gal	3:14	in Christ Jesus the **b** of Abraham
Eph	1: 3	every spiritual **b** in the heavenly
Rev	5:12	might and honor and glory and **b!**"
	7:12	**B** and glory and wisdom and
Tob	8:15	you, O God, with every pure **b;**
Sir	34:20	he gives health and life and **b.**

BLESSINGS → BLESS

Dt	28: 2	all these **b** shall come upon you
Jos	8:34	the words of the law, the **b** and curses,
Ps	21: 6	You bestow on him **b** forever;
	144:15	Happy are the people to whom such **b**
Pr	10: 6	**B** are on the head of the righteous,
Mal	2: 2	and I will curse your **b;**
Ro	15:27	come to share in their spiritual **b,**

BLIND → BLINDED, BLINDNESS

Ex	4:11	mute or deaf, seeing or **b?**
Dt	27:18	misleads a **b** person on the road."
Ps	146: 8	the LORD opens the eyes of the **b.**
Isa	35: 5	the eyes of the **b** shall be opened,
	42:19	Who is **b** but my servant,
Mt	11: 5	**b** receive their sight, the lame walk,
Lk	6:39	"Can a **b** person guide a **b** person?
Jn	9:25	though I was **b,** now I see."
Ro	2:19	sure that you are a guide to the **b,**
2Pe	1: 9	**b,** and is forgetful of the cleansing
Tob	2:10	until I became completely **b.**
LtJ	6:37	They cannot restore sight to the **b;**

BLINDED → BLIND

Zec	11:17	withered, his right eye utterly **b!**
Jn	12:40	"He has **b** their eyes and hardened
2Co	4: 4	has **b** the minds of the unbelievers,

BLINDNESS → BLIND

Ge	19:11	And they struck with **b** the men
Dt	28:28	will afflict you with madness, **b,**
1Jn	2:11	the darkness has brought on **b.**

BLOCK → BLOCKS

Isa	44:19	I fall down before a **b** of wood?"
Eze	14: 7	their iniquity as a stumbling **b**
Mt	16:23	You are a stumbling **b** to me;
Ro	11: 9	a stumbling **b** and a retribution for
1Co	1:23	stumbling **b** to Jews and foolishness

Sir	31: 7	It is a stumbling **b** to those who are

BLOCKS → BLOCK

Jer	6:21	before this people stumbling **b**
Mt	18: 7	the world because of stumbling **b!**

BLOOD → BLOODSHED

Ge	4:10	your brother's **b** is crying out to me
	9: 6	sheds the **b** of a human, by a human shall that person's **b** be shed;
Ex	7:17	and it shall be turned to **b.**
	12:13	when I see the **b,** I will pass over
	24: 8	the **b** of the covenant that the LORD
Lev	1: 5	the priests shall offer the **b,**
	3:17	you must not eat any fat or any **b.**
	17:11	it is the **b** that makes atonement.
Nu	35:33	for **b** pollutes the land,
Ps	72:14	and precious is their **b** in his sight.
Isa	1:11	I do not delight in the **b** of bulls,
Eze	33: 4	**b** shall be upon their own heads.
Joel	2:30	**b** and fire and columns of smoke.
Mt	27: 8	field has been called the Field of **B**
Mk	14:24	"This is my **b** of the covenant,
Lk	22:44	[[sweat became like great drops of **b**]]
Jn	1:13	who were born, not of **b**
	6:53	of the Son of Man and drink his **b,**
	19:34	and at once **b** and water came out.
Ac	2:20	to darkness and the moon to **b,**
Ro	5: 9	that we have been justified by his **b,**
1Co	11:25	cup is the new covenant in my **b.**
Eph	1: 7	we have redemption through his **b,**
	6:12	not against enemies of **b** and flesh,
Heb	9:12	the **b** of goats and calves, but with his own **b,**
	9:22	without the shedding of **b** there is no
1Jn	5: 6	the one who came by water and **b,**
Rev	1: 5	and freed us from our sins by his **b,**
	5: 9	by your **b** you ransomed for God
	6:12	the full moon became like **b,**
	8: 9	A third of the sea became **b,**
	12:11	conquered him by the **b** of the Lamb

BLOODSHED → BLOOD, SHED

Isa	5: 7	he expected justice, but saw **b;**
Eze	35: 6	you did not hate **b, b** shall pursue
Hab	2: 8	because of human **b,** and violence

BLOSSOMS

Ex	25:33	three cups shaped like almond **b,**
Nu	17: 8	It put forth buds, produced **b,**

BLOT

Ge	6: 7	"I will **b** out from the earth
Ex	32:32	**b** me out of the book that you have
Ps	51: 1	mercy **b** out my transgressions.
Rev	3: 5	not **b** your name out of the book of

BLOW → BLOWING

Joel	2: 1	**B** the trumpet in Zion; sound the
Rev	8: 6	the seven trumpets made ready to **b**

BOAST → BOASTERS, BOASTFUL, BOASTING

Ps	34: 2	My soul makes its **b** in the LORD;
Pr	27: 1	Do not **b** about tomorrow,
Jer	9:24	but let those who **b b** in this,
Ro	2:23	You that **b** in the law,
1Co	1:31	the one who boasts, **b** in the Lord."
2Co	11:30	If I must **b,** I will **b** of the things that
Gal	6:14	never **b** of anything except the cross
Eph	2: 9	of works, so that no one may **b.**
Sir	25: 6	and their **b** is the fear of the Lord.

BOASTERS* → BOAST

2Co	11:13	For such **b** are false apostles,
2Ti	3: 2	**b,** arrogant, abusive, disobedient to

BOASTFUL → BOAST

Ps	5: 5	The **b** will not stand before your
1Co	13: 4	love is not envious or **b** or arrogant

BOASTING → BOAST

1Co	5: 6	Your **b** is not a good thing.
1Th	2:19	or crown of **b** before our Lord Jesus

BOAZ

Bethlehemite who showed favor to Ruth (Ru 2), married her (Ru 4). Ancestor of David (Ru 4:18-22; 1Ch 2:12-15), Jesus (Mt 1:5-16; Lk 3:23-32).

BODIES → BODY

Ro	12: 1	present your **b** as a living sacrifice,
1Co	6:15	that your **b** are members of Christ?
Heb	10:22	and our **b** washed with pure water.

BODILY → BODY

Lk	3:22	upon him in **b** form like a dove.
Col	2: 9	the whole fullness of deity dwells **b,**

BODY → BODIES, BODILY

2Sa	7:12	who shall come forth from your **b,**
Mic	6: 7	fruit of my **b** for the sin of my soul?
Mt	6:22	"The eye is the lamp of the **b.**
Mk	14:22	and said, "Take; this is my **b.**"
Lk	12: 4	do not fear those who kill the **b,**
Jn	2:21	speaking of the temple of his **b.**
Ro	7:24	will rescue me from this **b** of death?
1Co	6:13	**b** is meant not for fornication but
	15:44	It is sown a physical **b,** it is raised a spiritual **b.**
2Co	5: 8	from the **b** and at home with the Lord.
Eph	4: 4	There is one **b** and one Spirit,

BOLD → BOLDNESS

Dt	31: 6	Be strong and **b;** have no fear
Pr	28: 1	but the righteous are as **b** as a lion.

BOLDNESS → BOLD

Eph	3:12	whom we have access to God in **b**
Heb	4:16	approach the throne of grace with **b,**
1Jn	4:17	may have **b** on the day of judgment,

BONE → BONES

Ge	2:23	"This at last is **b** of my bones and
Eze	37: 7	the bones came together, **b** to its **b.**

BONES → BONE

Ex	12:46	and you shall not break any of its **b.**
Ps	34:20	He keeps all their **b;** not one of
Jn	19:36	"None of his **b** shall be broken."

BOOK → BOOKS

Ex	17:14	"Write this as a reminder in a **b** and
Dt	31:24	writing down in a **b** the words of
Jos	1: 8	This **b** of the law shall not depart
Ps	69:28	be blotted out of the **b** of the living;
Rev	1:11	"Write in a **b** what you see and
	21:27	who are written in the Lamb's **b**
1Mc	1:57	possessing the **b** of the covenant,

BOOKS → BOOK

Ecc	12:12	Of making many **b** there is no end,
Da	7:10	in judgment, and the **b** were opened.
Jn	21:25	world itself could not contain the **b**
Rev	20:12	the throne, and **b** were opened.
1Mc	1:56	The **b** of the law that they found
2Es	14:44	ninety-four **b** were written.

BOOTHS

Lev	23:34	the festival of **b** to the LORD.
Ezr	3: 4	kept the festival of **b,** as prescribed,
Zec	14:16	and to keep the festival of **b.**

BORE → BEAR

Isa	53:12	yet he **b** the sin of many,
Mt	8:17	our infirmities and **b** our diseases."
1Pe	2:24	He himself **b** our sins in his body

BORN → BEAR

Ecc	3: 2	a time to be **b,** and a time to die;
Isa	9: 6	For a child has been **b** for us,
	66: 8	Shall a land be **b** in one day?
Lk	2:11	is **b** this day in the city of David
Jn	3: 7	'You must be **b** from above.'
1Co	15: 8	Last of all, as to one untimely **b,**
1Pe	1: 3	You have been **b** anew,
1Jn	4: 7	everyone who loves is **b** of God

BORROW → BORROWER

Dt	28:12	to many nations, but you will not **b.**
Ps	37:21	The wicked **b,** and do not pay back,
Mt	5:42	anyone who wants to **b** from you.

BORROWER → BORROW
Pr　22:　7　and the **b** is the slave of the lender.

BOUGHT → BUY
1Co　6:20　For you were **b** with a price;
2Pe　2:　1　even deny the Master who **b** them—

BOW → BOWED, RAINBOW
Ge　9:13　I have set my **b** in the clouds,
Ex　20:　5　You shall not **b** down to them or
Ps　95:　6　O come, let us worship and **b** down,
Isa　45:23　"To me every knee shall **b**,
Ro　14:11　every knee shall **b** to me,

BOWED → BOW
Ps　146:　8　The LORD lifts up those who are **b**
Jn　19:30　he **b** his head and gave up his spirit.

BOWLS
Rev　16:　1　the seven **b** of the wrath of God."

BOY → BOYS
Jer　1:　7　to me, "Do not say, 'I am only a **b**';
Lk　2:43　**b** Jesus stayed behind in Jerusalem,

BOYS → BOY
Ex　1:18　and allowed the **b** to live?"
2Ki　2:24　and mauled forty-two of the **b**.

BRANCH → BRANCHES
Isa　4:　2　On that day the **b** of the LORD
　　　　　　shall
　　11:　1　and a **b** shall grow out of his roots.
Jer　23:　5　raise up for David a righteous **B**,
Zec　3:　8　going to bring my servant the **B**.
Jn　15:　2　every **b** in me that bears no fruit.

BRANCHES → BRANCH
Ro　11:21　if God did not spare the natural **b**,

BREAD
Ge　3:19　sweat of your face you shall eat **b**
Ex　12:　8　with unleavened **b** and bitter herbs.
　　25:30　set the **b** of the Presence on the table
Dt　8:　3　that one does not live by **b** alone,
Ecc　11:　1　Send out your **b** upon the waters,
Mt　6:11　Give us this day our daily **b**.
Lk　4:　4　'One does not live by **b** alone.'"
Jn　6:35　Jesus said to them, "I am the **b** of
　　　　　　life.
Ac　2:42　to the breaking of **b** and the prayers.
1Co　11:26　For as often as you eat this **b** and
Wis　16:20　from heaven with **b** ready to eat,
Sir　15:　3　will feed him with the **b** of learning.

BREAK → BREAKING, BROKEN,
　　　　　　BROKENHEARTED
Ps　2:　9　You shall **b** them with a rod of iron,
Mt　6:19　where thieves **b** in and steal;
Jn　19:33　they did not **b** his legs.

BREASTPIECE → BREASTPLATE
Ex　28:15　You shall make a **b** of judgment,

BREASTPLATE → BREASTPIECE
Isa　59:17　He put on righteousness like a **b**,
Eph　6:14　and put on the **b** of righteousness.
Wis　5:18　he will put on righteousness as a **b**,

BREATH
Ge　2:　7　into his nostrils the **b** of life;
　　6:17　all flesh in which is the **b** of life,
Job　7:　7　"Remember that my life is a **b**;
Ecc　12:　7　the **b** returns to God who gave it.
2Th　2:　8　will destroy with the **b** of his mouth,

BRIBE
Dt　16:19　for a **b** blinds the eyes of the wise
Pr　6:35　and refuses a **b** no matter how great.

BRIDE → BRIDEGROOM
Isa　62:　5　the bridegroom rejoices over the **b**,
Rev　21:　9　the **b**, the wife of the Lamb."

BRIDEGROOM → BRIDE
Mt　9:15　as long as the **b** is with them,
Jn　3:29　He who has the bride is the **b**.

BRIDLE
Ps　32:　9　must be curbed with bit and **b**,
Jas　3:　2　the whole body in check with a **b**.

BRIGHT → BRIGHTNESS
Mt　17:　5　suddenly a **b** cloud overshadowed
Rev　15:　6　robed in pure **b** linen,
　　22:16　of David, the **b** morning star."

BRIGHTNESS → BRIGHT
Da　12:　3　wise shall shine like the **b** of the sky
Am　5:20　not light, and gloom with no **b** in it?

BRING → BRINGS, BROUGHT
Ge　6:19　**b** two of every kind into the ark,
Ecc　12:14　will **b** every deed into judgment,
Jer　24:　6　and I will **b** them back to this land.
Mt　10:34　not come to **b** peace, but a sword.
Ro　10:15　the feet of those who **b** good news!"

BRINGS → BRING
1Sa　2:　6　The LORD kills and **b** to life;
Jas　5:20　that whoever **b** back a sinner

BROKE → BREAK
Ex　32:19　tablets from his hands and **b** them
2Ch　36:19　**b** down the wall of Jerusalem,
Jer　31:32　a covenant that they **b**,
Mt　14:19　and blessed and **b** the loaves,
1Co　11:24　he **b** it and said, "This is my body
1Mc　3:　5　and pursued those who **b** the law;

BROKEN → BREAK
Ne　1:　3　the wall of Jerusalem is **b** down,
Ps　51:17　acceptable to God is a **b** spirit;
Mt　15:37　they took up the **b** pieces left over,
Lk　20:18　who falls on that stone will be **b**
Ro　11:20　were **b** off because of their unbelief,

BROKENHEARTED → BREAK, HEART
Ps　147:　3　He heals the **b**, and binds up their
Isa　61:　1　the oppressed, to bind up the **b**,

BRONZE
Nu　21:　9　look at the serpent of **b** and live.
Dt　28:23　The sky over your head shall be **b**,
Da　10:　6　legs like the gleam of burnished **b**,
Rev　1:15　his feet were like burnished **b**,

BROOD
Mt　3:　7　he said to them, "You **b** of vipers!
Lk　13:34　a hen gathers her **b** under her wings,

BROTHER → BROTHER'S, BROTHER-IN-
　　　　　　LAW, BROTHERS
Ge　4:　8　Cain rose up against his **b** Abel,
Mt　5:24　first be reconciled to your **b** or
　　10:21　**B** will betray **b** to death,

BROTHER'S → BROTHER
Dt　25:　7　has no desire to marry his **b** widow,
Mk　6:18　lawful for you to have your **b** wife."

BROTHER-IN-LAW* → BROTHER
Ge　38:　8　and perform the duty of a **b** to her;

BROTHERS → BROTHER
Ge　9:25　lowest of slaves shall he be to his **b**.
　　37:11　So his **b** were jealous of him,
Mk　3:33　"Who are my mother and my **b?**"
Lk　22:32　turned back, strengthen your **b**."
Heb　2:11　not ashamed to call them **b** and

BROUGHT → BRING
Ge　15:　7　**b** you from Ur of the Chaldeans,
Jdg　2:　1　"I **b** you up from Egypt, and **b** you
　　　　　　into
2Ch　36:18　all these he **b** to Babylon.
Ezr　6:　5　**b** back to the temple in Jerusalem,
Ro　6:13　who have been **b** from death to life,
1Ti　6:　7　for we **b** nothing into the world,

BUILD → BUILDER, BUILDERS, BUILDING,
　　　　　　BUILDS, BUILT, REBUILD
Ge　11:　4　"Come, let us **b** ourselves a city,
Dt　6:10　fine, large cities that you did not **b**,
Ps　127:　1　those who **b** it labor in vain.
Isa　57:14　said, "**B** up, **b** up, prepare the way,

BUILDER → BUILD
Heb　3:　4　but the **b** of all things is God.)
　　11:10　whose architect and **b** is God.

BUILDERS → BUILD
Ps　118:22　The stone that the **b** rejected has
Mk　12:10　'The stone that the **b** rejected has
1Pe　2:　7　"The stone that the **b** rejected has

BUILDING → BUILD
1Co　3:　9　you are God's field, God's **b**.
2Co　5:　1　we have a **b** from God,
Eph　4:12　for **b** up the body of Christ,

BUILDS → BUILD
Ps　127:　1　Unless the LORD **b** the house,
Pr　14:　1　The wise woman **b** her house,
1Co　8:　1　Knowledge puffs up, but love **b** up.

BUILT → BUILD
1Ki　6:14　Solomon **b** the house, and finished
Ne　7:　1　the wall had been **b** and I had set up
Pr　9:　1　Wisdom has **b** her house,
Da　9:25　sixty-two weeks it shall be **b** again
Eph　2:20　**b** upon the foundation of the
Tob　13:16　Jerusalem will be **b** as his house for
1Mc　4:47　**b** a new altar like the former one.

BULL → BULLS
Ps　50:　9　will not accept a **b** from your house,

BULLS → BULL
1Ch　29:21　a thousand **b**, a thousand rams,
Ps　22:12　**b** encircle me, strong **b** of Bashan
Isa　1:11　I do not delight in the blood of **b**,
Heb　10:　4　it is impossible for the blood of **b**

BURDEN → BURDENS, BURDENSOME
Ps　55:22　Cast your **b** on the LORD,
Mt　11:30　my yoke is easy, and my **b** is light."
2Co　5:　4　in this tent, we groan under our **b**,

BURDENS → BURDEN
Ex　6:　6　free you from the **b** of the Egyptians
Lk　11:46　you load people with **b** hard to bear,
Gal　6:　2　Bear one another's **b**, and

BURDENSOME → BURDEN
1Jn　5:　3　And his commandments are not **b**,

BURIED → BURY
Ro　6:　4　have been **b** with him by baptism.
1Co　15:　4　he was **b**, and that he was raised on

BURN → BURNED, BURNING, BURNT
Ex　21:25　**b** for **b**, wound for wound,
Ps　79:　5　Will your jealous wrath **b** like fire?
Jer　7:31　to **b** their sons and their daughters
Mal　4:　1　the day that comes shall **b** them up,
Lk　3:17　but the chaff he will **b** with

BURNED → BURN
Ex　3:　3　and see why the bush is not **b** up."
Jn　15:　6　thrown into the fire, and **b**.
1Co　3:15　If the work is **b** up, the builder will

BURNING → BURN
Lk　24:32　"Were not our hearts **b** within us

BURNT → BURN
Ex　40:　6　You shall set the altar of **b** offering
Lev　1:　3　If the offering is a **b** offering from
1Sa　15:22　LORD as great delight in **b** offerings
Ps　51:16　if I were to give a **b** offering,
Da　8:11　it took the regular **b** offering away
Hos　6:　6　the knowledge of God rather than **b**
Mic　6:　6　Shall I come before him with **b**
Mk　12:33　more important than all whole **b**
1Mc　1:45　to forbid **b** offerings and sacrifices
　　4:56　and joyfully offered **b** offerings;

BURY → BURIED
Lk　9:60　"Let the dead **b** their own dead;

BUSH

Ex　　3: 2　he looked, and the **b** was blazing,
Jnh　 4: 6　The LORD God appointed a **b**,

BUY → BOUGHT, BUYS

Pr　 23:23　**B** truth, and do not sell it;
Isa　 55: 1　**b** wine and milk without money
Rev　 3:18　to **b** from me gold refined by fire so

BUYS → BUY

Pr　 31:16　She considers a field and **b** it;
Mt　 13:44　sells all that he has and **b** that field.

BYWORD → WORD

Dt　 28:37　and **b** among all the peoples where
Job　 17: 6　He has made me a **b** of the peoples,
Ps　 44:14　made us a **b** among the nations,

C

CAESAREA

Mt　 16:13　came into the district of **C** Philippi,
Ac　 10: 1　**C** there was a man named Cornelius
　　 25: 4　that Paul was being kept at **C**,

CAIAPHAS*

　　High priest at trial of Jesus (Mt 26:3, 57; Lk 3:2;
Jn 11:49; 18:13-28); at trial of disciples (Ac 4:6).

CAIN*

　　Firstborn of Adam (Ge 4:1), murdered brother
Abel (Ge 4:1-25; Heb 11:4; 1Jn 3:12; Jude 11; 4Mc
18:11).

CALAMITIES → CALAMITY

1Sa　 10:19　who saves you from all your **c** and
2Co　 6: 4　in afflictions, hardships, **c**,
　　 12:10　and **c** for the sake of Christ;

CALAMITY → CALAMITIES

Pr　　1:26　I also will laugh at your **c**;
Da　　9:13　all this **c** has come upon us.
Hab　 3:16　wait quietly for the day of **c** to come

CALEB

　　Judahite who spied out Canaan (Nu 13:6);
allowed to enter land (Nu 13:30-14:38; Dt 1:36;
Sir 46:7-9; 1Mc 2:56). Given Hebron (Jos 14:6-
15:19).

CALF → CALVES

Ex　 32: 4　and cast an image of a **c**;
Lk　 15:23　And get the fatted **c** and kill it,

CALL → CALLED, CALLING

Dt　　4:26　I **c** heaven and earth to witness
1Sa　　3: 5　But he said, "I did not **c**; lie down
1Ki　 18:24　you **c** on the name of your god and I
　　　　　　will **c** on the name of the LORD;
1Ch　 16: 8　thanks to the LORD, **c** on his name,
Ps　 61: 2　From the end of the earth I **c** to you,
Pr　　8: 1　Does not wisdom **c**, and does
Isa　 65:24　Before they **c** I will answer,
Mt　　9:13　to **c** not the righteous but sinners."
Lk　　6:46　"Why do you **c** me 'Lord, Lord,'
Jn　 15:15　I do not **c** you servants any longer,
Ro　 10:12　and is generous to all who **c** on him.
Php　 3:14　goal for the prize of the heavenly **c**

CALLED → CALL

2Sa　 22: 7　In my distress I **c** upon the LORD;
Isa　 43: 1　I have **c** you by name, you are mine.
Mt　 23: 8　But you are not to be **c** rabbi,
1Co　 7:15　It is to peace that God has **c** you.
Eph　 1:18　the hope to which he has **c** you,
1Jn　 3: 1　that we should be **c** children of God;

CALLING → CALL

Ro　 11:29　and the **c** of God are irrevocable.
Eph　 4: 1　lead a life worthy of the **c** to which

CALVES → CALF

1Ki　 12:28　and made two **c** of gold.
Mal　 4: 2　go out leaping like **c** from the stall.

CAMEL

Mt　 23:24　strain out a gnat but swallow a **c**!
Mk　 10:25　**c** to go through the eye of a needle

CANA

Jn　　2: 1　there was a wedding in **C**

CANAAN → CANAANITE, CANAANITES

Ge　　9:25　"Cursed be **C**; lowest of slaves
Nu　 13: 2　"Send men to spy out the land of **C**,
1Ch　 16:18　"To you I will give the land of **C**

CANAANITE → CANAAN

Ge　 28: 1　not marry one of the **C** women.
Mt　 15:22　a **C** woman from that region came

CANAANITES → CANAAN

Ex　 33: 2　I will drive out the **C**, the Amorites
Jdg　　3: 5　So the Israelites lived among the **C**,

CAPERNAUM

Mt　　4:13　and made his home in **C** by the sea,
Jn　　6:59　was teaching in the synagogue at **C**.

CAPTIVE → CAPTIVITY

2Ki　 15:29　he carried the people **c** to Assyria.
　　 24:16　king of Babylon brought **c** to
Ro　　7:23　making me **c** to the law of sin
Eph　 4: 8　he made captivity itself a **c**;

CAPTIVITY → CAPTIVE

Dt　 28:41　for they shall go into **c**.
Ezr　　8:35　those who had come from **c**,

CARE → CAREFUL, CARELESS, CARES, CARING

Ps　　8: 4　mortals that you **c** for them?
Heb　 2: 6　or mortals, that you **c** for them?
Jas　　1:27　to **c** for orphans and widows in

CAREFUL → CARE

Dt　　4:23　So be **c** not to forget the covenant
Jos　　1: 8　you may be **c** to act in accordance
Eph　 5:15　Be **c** then how you live,

CARELESS* → CARE

Pr　 14:16　the fool throws off restraint and is **c**.
Mt　 12:36　to give an account for every **c** word

CARES → CARE

Lk　　8:14　they are choked by the **c** and riches
1Pe　　5: 7　on him, because he **c** for you.

CARMEL

1Ki　 18:20　assembled the prophets at Mount **C**.

CARPENTER'S*

Mt　 13:55　Is not this the **c** son?

CARRY

Ps　 28: 9　their shepherd, and **c** them forever.
Isa　 40:11　and **c** them in his bosom,
Lk　 14:27　does not **c** the cross and follow me

CASE

Job　 13: 3　and I desire to argue my **c** with God.
Isa　 41:21　Set forth your **c**, says the LORD;
Lk　 12:58　make an effort to settle the **c**,
Jn　 18:38　"I find no **c** against him.

CAST

Ex　 34:17　You shall not make **c** idols.
Est　　9:24　Jews to destroy them, and had **c** Pur
Ps　 22:18　and for my clothing they **c** lots.
　　 55:22　**C** your burden on the LORD,
Pr　 16:33　The lot is **c** into the lap,
Mk　　3:23　"How can Satan **c** out Satan?
Jn　 19:24　and for my clothing they **c** lots."
1Pe　　5: 7　**C** all your anxiety on him,

CATTLE

Ge　　1:25　and the **c** of every kind,
Ps　 50:10　the **c** on a thousand hills.

CAUGHT

2Co　 12: 2　was **c** up to the third heaven—
1Th　　4:17　be **c** up in the clouds together with

CAUSE

Job　　5: 8　and to God I would commit my **c**.
Ps　　9: 4　For you have maintained my just **c**;
　　 140:12　LORD maintains the **c** of the needy,
Jn　 15:25　'They hated me without a **c**.'

CAVE

Ge　 23: 9　he may give me the **c** of Machpelah,
1Sa　 22: 1　and escaped to the **c** of Adullam;
　　 24: 3　in the innermost parts of the **c**.
1Ki　 18: 4　hid them fifty to a **c**,

CEASE

Ge　　8:22　winter, day and night, shall not **c**."
Jer　 31:36　If this fixed order were ever to **c**
1Co　 13: 8　as for tongues, they will **c**;

CEDAR

2Sa　　7: 2　See now, I am living in a house of **c**,
Ps　 92:12　and grow like a **c** in Lebanon.

CELEBRATE

Lev　 23:37　shall **c** as times of holy convocation,
1Co　　5: 8　Therefore, let us **c** the festival,

CENSER

Lev　 10: 1　Nadab and Abihu, each took his **c**,
Eze　　8:11　Each had his **c** in his hand,
Rev　　8: 3　Another angel with a golden **c** came

CENSUS

Nu　　1: 2　Take a **c** of the whole congregation
2Sa　 24: 2　and take a **c** of the people,

CENTURION

Mt　　8: 5　he entered Capernaum, a **c** came to
Lk　 23:47　the **c** saw what had taken place,
Ac　 10: 1　a man named Cornelius, a **c**

CEPHAS* → =PETER

　　Name given to the apostle Peter (Jn 1:42; 1Co
1:12; 3:22; 9:5; 15:5; Gal 1:18; 2:9, 11, 14).

CERTIFICATE

Dt　 24: 1　and so he writes her a **c** of divorce,
Mt　　5:31　let him give her a **c** of divorce.'
Mk　 10: 4　a man to write a **c** of dismissal

CHAFF

Ps　　1: 4　are like **c** that the wind drives away.
Lk　　3:17　**c** he will burn with unquenchable

CHAINED* → CHAINS

2Ti　　2: 9　the point of being **c** like a criminal.
　　　　　　But the word of God is not **c**.

CHAINS → CHAINED

Eph　　6:20　for which I am an ambassador in **c**;
Heb　 11:36　and even **c** and imprisonment.
2Pe　　2: 4　them to **c** of deepest darkness

CHALDEANS

Ge　 15: 7　who brought you from Ur of the **C**,
Da　　1: 4　the literature and language of the **C**.

CHANGE → CHANGED, CHANGERS

Ex　 32:12　**c** your mind and do not bring
Nu　 23:19　a mortal, that he should **c** his mind.
1Sa　 15:29　will not recant or **c** his mind;
Ps　 46: 2　not fear, though the earth should **c**,
Jer　 18: 8　I will **c** my mind about the disaster
Jas　　1:17　is no variation or shadow due to **c**.

CHANGED → CHANGE

1Co　 15:51　will not all die, but we will all be **c**,
Heb　 1:12　and like clothing they will be **c**.

CHANGERS → CHANGE

Mk　 11:15　overturned the tables of the money **c**
Jn　　2:15　poured out the coins of the money **c**

CHARACTER

Ro　　5: 4　endurance produces **c**, and **c**
　　　　　　produces

CHARGE

Mt　 25:21　I will put you in **c** of many things;
Mk　 15:26　The inscription of the **c** against him
Ro　　8:33　will bring any **c** against God's elect?
1Co　　9:18　I may make the gospel free of **c**,

CHARIOT → CHARIOTS

2Ki　　2:11　a **c** of fire and horses of fire
Ps　 104: 3　you make the clouds your **c**,

CHARIOTS → CHARIOT

Ex   14:28 waters returned and covered the **c**
Zec   6: 1 and saw four **c** coming out from

CHARM

Pr   31:30 **C** is deceitful, and beauty is vain,
Sir   7:19 for her **c** is worth more than gold.
       26:15 A modest wife adds **c** to **c**,

CHASTISEMENT → CHASTISES

La   4: 6 the **c** of my people has been greater
Sir   16:12 Great as his mercy, so also is his **c**;

CHASTISES* → CHASTISEMENT

Heb   12: 6 and **c** every child whom he accepts.

CHEEK

Ps   3: 7 you strike all my enemies on the **c**;
Mt   5:39 if anyone strikes you on the right **c**,

CHEERFUL

Pr   15:13 A glad heart makes a **c** countenance,
       17:22 A **c** heart is a good medicine,
2Co   9: 7 for God loves a **c** giver.
Jas   5:13 Are any **c**? They should sing songs

CHEMOSH

1Ki   11: 7 Solomon built a high place for **C**
Jer   48: 7 **C** shall go out into exile,

CHERUB → CHERUBIM

2Ch   3:11 touched the wing of the other **c**;
Ps   18:10 He rode on a **c**, and flew;
Eze   10:14 the first face was that of the **c**,
       28:14 an anointed **c** as guardian I placed

CHERUBIM → CHERUB

Ge   3:24 the garden of Eden he placed the **c**,
Ex   25:18 You shall make two **c** of gold;
Ps   80: 1 You who are enthroned upon the **c**,
Heb   9: 5 the **c** of glory overshadowing the

CHIEF

Ps   118:22 has become the **c** cornerstone.
Mk   15: 3 the **c** priests accused him of many
1Pe   5: 4 And when the **c** shepherd appears,

CHILD → CHILDBEARING, CHILDISH,
        CHILDREN

Ge   17:17 **c** be born to a man who is a hundred
1Ki   3: 7 although I am only a little **c**
Isa   11: 6 and a little **c** shall lead them.
       49:15 Can a woman forget her nursing **c**,
Hos   11: 1 When Israel was a **c**, I loved him,
Mt   1:18 with **c** from the Holy Spirit.
Mk   10:15 the kingdom of God as a little **c**
Lk   2:12 you will find a **c** wrapped in bands
1Co   13:11 When I was a **c**, I spoke like a **c**,
Gal   4: 7 So you are no longer a slave but a **c**,
Rev   12: 4 that he might devour her **c** as soon

CHILDBEARING* → CHILD, BEAR

Ge   3:16 greatly increase your pangs in **c**;
1Ti   2:15 Yet she will be saved through **c**,

CHILDISH* → CHILD

1Co   13:11 an adult, I put an end to **c** ways.

CHILDREN → CHILD

Ex   12:26 And when your **c** ask you,
Dt   6: 7 Recite them to your **c** and talk about
       11:19 Teach them to your **c**, talking about
Pr   22: 6 Train **c** in the right way, and when
Mt   3: 9 stones to raise up **c** to Abraham.
Lk   18:16 "Let the little **c** come to me,
Jn   1:12 he gave power to become **c** of God,
Ro   8:14 by the Spirit of God are **c** of God.
1Co   14:20 do not be **c** in your thinking;
Eph   6: 4 do not provoke your **c** to anger,
Heb   12: 7 God is treating you as **c**;
1Jn   3:10 The **c** of God and the **c** of the devil
Sir   30: 1 CONCERNING **C** He who loves his son

CHOOSE → CHOOSES, CHOSE, CHOSEN

Dt   12:14 at the place that the LORD will **c**
       30:19 **C** life so that you and your
Jos   24:15 **c** this day whom you will serve,
Jn   15:16 You did not **c** me but I chose you.

CHOOSES → CHOOSE

Ro   9:18 he has mercy on whomever he **c**,

CHOSE → CHOOSE

Dt   4:37 he **c** their descendants after them.
Ne   9: 7 God who **c** Abram and brought him
Mk   13:20 for the sake of the elect, whom he **c**,
1Co   1:27 God **c** what is foolish in the world

CHOSEN → CHOOSE

Isa   42: 1 my servant, whom I uphold, my **c**,
Mt   22:14 For many are called, but few are **c**."
Ro   11: 5 there is a remnant, **c** by grace.
1Pe   2: 6 a cornerstone **c** and precious;
       2: 9 you are a **c** race, a royal priesthood,

CHRIST → CHRIST'S, CHRISTIAN,
        CHRISTIANS, MESSIAH

Jn   4:25 Messiah is coming" (who is
             called **C**).
Ro   5: 6 right time **C** died for the ungodly.
       8:35 will separate us from the love of **C**?
       10: 4 For **C** is the end of the law so that
1Co   1:23 but we proclaim **C** crucified,
       3:11 that foundation is Jesus **C**.
       11: 1 Be imitators of me, as I am of **C**.
       15: 3 **C** died for our sins in accordance
Gal   5: 1 For freedom **C** has set us free.
Eph   4:15 into him who is the head, into **C**,
Php   1:21 to me, living is **C** and dying is gain.
       2:11 should confess that Jesus **C** is Lord,
Col   1:27 **C** in you, the hope of glory.
Rev   20: 4 reigned with **C** a thousand years.

CHRIST'S → CHRIST

Col   1:24 what is lacking in **C** afflictions
1Pe   4:13 as you are sharing **C** sufferings,

CHRISTIAN* → CHRIST

Ac   26:28 persuading me to become a **C**?"
1Pe   4:16 Yet if any of you suffers as a **C**,

CHRISTIANS* → CHRIST

Ac   11:26 the disciples were first called "**C**."

CHURCH

Mt   16:18 and on this rock I will build my **c**,
Ac   8: 1 persecution began against the **c**
1Co   12:28 has appointed in the **c** first apostles,
       14: 4 those who prophesy build up the **c**.
Col   1:18 He is the head of the body, the **c**;

CIRCUMCISE → CIRCUMCISED,
        CIRCUMCISION

Ge   17:11 shall **c** the flesh of your foreskins;
Dt   10:16 **C**, then, the foreskin of your heart,
Lk   1:59 the eighth day they came to **c** the
Jn   7:22 and you **c** a man on the sabbath.

CIRCUMCISED → CIRCUMCISE

Ge   17:10 Every male among you shall be **c**.
Ac   15: 1 according to the custom of Moses,
Gal   6:13 **c** do not themselves obey the law,
Col   2:11 also you were **c** with a spiritual
1Mc   1:60 the women who had their
             children **c**,

CIRCUMCISION → CIRCUMCISE

Ro   2:29 and real **c** is a matter of the heart—
Gal   5: 6 For in Christ Jesus neither **c**

CISTERN

Pr   5:15 Drink water from your own **c**,
Jer   38: 6 Jeremiah and threw him into the **c**

CITIES → CITY

Ge   19:25 and he overthrew those **c**,
Jos   20: 2 'Appoint the **c** of refuge,
Rev   16:19 and the **c** of the nations fell.

CITIZENSHIP

Php   3:20 But our **c** is in heaven,

CITY → CITIES

1Ch   11: 7 it was called the **c** of David.
Ps   127: 1 Unless the LORD guards the **c**,
Pr   31:31 her works praise her in the **c** gates.
La   1: 1 lonely sits the **c** that once was full

Da   9:24 for your people and your holy **c**:
Mt   5:14 A **c** built on a hill cannot be hid.
Heb   12:22 Zion and to the **c** of the living God,
Rev   21: 2 I saw the holy **c**, the new Jerusalem,

CLAP

Ps   47: 1 **C** your hands, all you peoples;
Isa   55:12 all the trees of the field shall **c** their

CLAY

Isa   45: 9 Does the **c** say to the one who
Jer   18: 6 Just like the **c** in the potter's hand,
Da   2:33 its feet partly of iron and partly of **c**.
Ro   9:21 Has the potter no right over the **c**,
2Co   4: 7 But we have this treasure in **c** jars,
2Ti   2:20 and silver but also of wood and **c**,

CLEAN → CLEANSE, CLEANSING

Ge   7: 2 seven pairs of all **c** animals,
Lev   10:10 and between the unclean and the **c**;
Ps   51: 7 with hyssop, and I shall be **c**;
Mk   7:19 (Thus he declared all foods **c**.)
Jn   13:10 you are **c**, though not all of you."
Ac   10:15 "What God has made **c**,
Heb   10:22 with our hearts sprinkled **c** from

CLEANSE → CLEAN

Ps   51: 2 and **c** me from my sin.
1Jn   1: 9 **c** us from all unrighteousness.
Sir   38:10 and **c** your heart from all sin.

CLEANSING → CLEAN

Eph   5:26 by **c** her with the washing of water
2Pe   1: 9 and is forgetful of the **c** of past sins.

CLEAR → CLEARING

Ps   19: 8 the commandment of the LORD is **c**,
Na   1: 3 LORD will by no means **c** the guilty.
1Ti   3: 9 of the faith with a **c** conscience.
Rev   21:18 the city is pure gold, **c** as glass.

CLEARING* → CLEAR

Ex   34: 7 yet by no means **c** the guilty,

CLEFT

Ex   33:22 I will put you in a **c** of the rock,
Dt   14: 6 the hoof and has the hoof **c** in two,

CLINGS

Ge   2:24 and his mother and **c** to his wife,
Ps   119:25 My soul **c** to the dust;
Heb   12: 1 weight and the sin that **c** so closely,

CLOAK

Ex   4: 6 "Put your hand inside your **c**."
       22:26 you take your neighbor's **c** in pawn,
1Sa   24: 4 cut off a corner of Saul's **c**.
Mk   15:17 And they clothed him in a purple **c**;
Heb   1:12 like a **c** you will roll them up,

CLOTH → SACKCLOTH

Isa   64: 6 righteous deeds are like a filthy **c**.
Lk   2: 7 and wrapped him in bands of **c**,

CLOTHE → CLOTHED, CLOTHES,
        CLOTHING

Col   3:14 Above all, **c** yourselves with love,
1Pe   5: 5 you must **c** yourselves with humility

CLOTHED → CLOTHE

2Co   5: 2 longing to be **c** with our heavenly
Gal   3:27 have **c** yourselves with Christ.
Rev   12: 1 a woman **c** with the sun,

CLOTHES → CLOTHE

Zec   3: 3 Joshua was dressed with filthy **c** as
Lk   8:44 and touched the fringe of his **c**,

CLOTHING → CLOTHE

Ps   22:18 and for my **c** they cast lots.
Mt   25:36 I was naked and you gave me **c**,
Jn   19:24 and for my **c** they cast lots."

CLOUD → CLOUDS

Ex   13:21 went in front of them in a pillar of **c**
1Ki   8:10 a **c** filled the house of the LORD,
       18:44 a little **c** no bigger than a person's
Eze   10: 4 the house was filled with the **c**,
Mk   9: 7 Then a **c** overshadowed them,

CLOUD (cont.)
Lk 21:27 'the Son of Man coming in a **c**'
Heb 12: 1 by so great a **c** of witnesses,
Rev 14:14 on the **c** was one like the Son of Man,
Ge 9:13 I have set my bow in the **c**,
Da 7:13 being coming with the **c** of heaven.
Mt 24:30 'the Son of Man coming on the **c** of
1Th 4:17 be caught up in the **c** together with
Rev 1: 7 He is coming with the **c**;
2Es 13: 3 this man flew with the **c** of heaven;

CLUSTER
Nu 13:23 from there a branch with a single **c**

COALS
Ps 11: 6 On the wicked he will rain **c** of fire
Pr 25:22 will heap **c** of fire on their heads,
Ro 12:20 will heap burning **c** on their heads."

CODE*
Ro 2:27 condemn you that have the written **c**
7: 6 slaves not under the old written **c**

COIN*
Mt 17:27 open its mouth, you will find a **c**;
22:19 Show me the **c** used for the tax."
Lk 15: 9 I have found the **c** that I had lost.'

COLD
Zec 14: 6 that day there shall not be either **c**
Mt 24:12 the love of many will grow **c**.
Rev 3:16 lukewarm, and neither **c** nor hot,

COLLECTOR → COLLECTORS
Mt 10: 3 Thomas and Matthew the tax **c**;
Lk 18:10 one a Pharisee and the other a tax **c**.
19: 2 he was a chief tax **c** and was rich.

COLLECTORS → COLLECTOR
Mt 5:46 Do not even the tax **c** do the same?
11:19 a friend of tax **c** and sinners!'

COLT
Ge 49:11 his donkey's **c** to the choice vine,
Zec 9: 9 and riding on a donkey, on a **c**,
Jn 12:15 coming, sitting on a donkey's **c**!"

COME → COMES, COMING
Ps 144: 5 your heavens, O LORD, and **c** down;
Isa 59:20 And he will **c** to Zion as Redeemer,
Zec 14: 5 Then the LORD my God will **c**,
Mt 6:10 Your kingdom **c**. Your will be done,
Lk 7:20 'Are you the one who is to **c**,
Jn 6:37 the Father gives me will **c** to me,
1Co 16:22 Our Lord, **c**!
Rev 1: 4 who is and who was and who is to **c**,
22:20 Amen. **C**, Lord Jesus!

COMES → COME
Ps 118:26 one who **c** in the name of the LORD.
Lk 19:38 "Blessed is the king who **c** in the
Jn 14: 6 No one **c** to the Father except through

COMFORT → COMFORTED, COMFORTER, COMFORTERS, COMFORTS
Ps 23: 4 your rod and your staff—they **c** me.
Isa 40: 1 **C**, O **c** my people, says your God.

COMFORTED → COMFORT
Ps 86:17 LORD, have helped me and **c** me.
Isa 49:13 For the LORD has **c** his people,
Jer 31:15 she refuses to be **c** for her children,
Mt 5: 4 those who mourn, for they will be **c**.

COMFORTER* → COMFORT
La 1:16 for a **c** is far from me,

COMFORTERS → COMFORT
Job 16: 2 miserable **c** are you all.
Ps 69:20 and for **c**, but I found none.

COMFORTS → COMFORT
Isa 66:13 As a mother **c** her child, so I will

COMING → COME
Mal 3: 2 But who can endure the day of his **c**,
Heb 10:37 is **c** will come and will not delay;

2Pe 3: 4 "Where is the promise of his **c**?
Rev 22:20 "Surely I am **c** soon."

COMMAND → COMMANDED, COMMANDING, COMMANDMENT, COMMANDMENTS
Ex 34:11 Observe what I **c** you today.
Dt 1:26 rebelled against the **c** of the LORD
Jdg 2: 2 But you have not obeyed my **c**.

COMMANDED → COMMAND
Ge 7: 5 Noah did all that the LORD had **c**
Ex 40:32 as the LORD had **c** Moses.
Jos 1:16 "All that you have **c** us we will do,
Mt 28:20 to obey everything that I have **c** you.
Jn 14:31 but I do as the Father has **c** me,

COMMANDING → COMMAND
Dt 4:40 **c** you today for your own well-being
30:11 **c** you today is not too hard for you,

COMMANDMENT → COMMAND
Dt 6: 1 Now this is the **c**—the statutes
Ps 19: 8 of the LORD is clear,
Mt 22:38 This is the greatest and first **c**.
Ro 7:12 and the **c** is holy and just and good.
Gal 5:14 law is summed up in a single **c**,
1Jn 3:23 this is his **c**, that we should believe

COMMANDMENTS → COMMAND
Ex 20: 6 those who love me and keep my **c**.
Dt 4:13 to observe, that is, the ten **c**;
Ps 119:66 for I believe in your **c**.
Pr 10: 8 The wise of heart will heed **c**,
Ecc 12:13 Fear God, and keep his **c**;
Mt 22:40 On these two **c** hang all the law and
Jn 14:15 If you love me, you will keep my **c**.
1Co 7:19 obeying the **c** of God is everything.
1Jn 5: 3 And his **c** are not burdensome,
Rev 14:12 those who keep the **c** of God and
Sir 1:26 If you desire wisdom, keep the **c**,
1Mc 2:19 and have chosen to obey his **c**,

COMMENDABLE* → COMMENDATION
Php 4: 8 whatever is pleasing, whatever is **c**,

COMMENDATION* → COMMENDABLE, COMMENDED
1Co 4: 5 each one will receive **c** from God.

COMMENDED → COMMENDATION
2Co 6: 4 but as servants of God we have **c**
Heb 11:39 though they were **c** for their faith,

COMMIT → COMMITS
Dt 5:18 Neither shall you **c** adultery.
2Ki 17:21 and made them **c** great sin.
Ps 31: 5 Into your hand I **c** my spirit;
Pr 16: 3 **C** your work to the LORD,
Mt 5:27 'You shall not **c** adultery.'

COMMITS → COMMIT
Jn 8:34 who **c** sin is a slave to sin.
Jas 4:17 to do and fails to do it, **c** sin.

COMMON
Lev 10:10 between the holy and the **c**,
Eze 22:26 between the holy and the **c**,
Ac 2:44 and had all things in **c**;
1Co 10:13 has overtaken you that is not **c**
12: 7 of the Spirit for the **c** good.

COMMUNION*
2Co 13:13 the **c** of the Holy Spirit be with all

COMPANY
1Co 15:33 "Bad **c** ruins good morals."

COMPARE → COMPARING
Pr 8:11 all that you may desire cannot **c**
Isa 40:18 or what likeness will **c** with him?
Lk 7:31 I **c** the people of this generation,

COMPARING* → COMPARE
Ro 8:18 of this present time are not worth **c**

COMPASSION → COMPASSIONATE
Dt 32:36 will vindicate his people, have **c**
Ps 103:13 As a father has **c** for his children,

Isa 54: 8 with everlasting love I will have **c**
Jer 12:15 I will again have **c** on them,
Hos 11: 8 my **c** grows warm and tender.
Mt 14:14 had **c** for them and cured their sick.
Ro 9:15 I will have **c** on whom I have **c**."
Col 3:12 clothe yourselves with **c**, kindness,
Sir 18:13 the **c** of the Lord is for every living

COMPASSIONATE → COMPASSION
Ex 22:27 I will listen, for I am **c**.
Jas 5:11 how the Lord is **c** and merciful.
Sir 2:11 For the Lord is **c** and merciful;

COMPETE → COMPETING, COMPETITION
Jer 12: 5 how will you **c** with horses?
1Co 9:24 that in a race the runners all **c**,

COMPETING* → COMPETE
Gal 5:26 **c** against one another, envying one
2Ti 2: 5 is crowned without **c** according to

COMPLAIN → COMPLAINING, COMPLAINT
Nu 14:27 shall this wicked congregation **c**
Jer 2:29 Why do you **c** against me?
1Co 10:10 And do not **c** as some of them did,

COMPLAINING → COMPLAIN
Ex 16: 7 has heard your **c** against the LORD.
1Pe 4: 9 hospitable to one another without **c**.

COMPLAINT → COMPLAIN
Job 10: 1 I will give free utterance to my **c**;
Ps 142: 2 I pour out my **c** before him;
Hab 2: 1 he will answer concerning my **c**.
Col 3:13 if anyone has a **c** against another,

COMPLETE → COMPLETED, COMPLETION
Ge 15:16 iniquity of the Amorites is not yet **c**
Lev 23: 3 seventh day is a sabbath of **c** rest,
Jn 4:34 him who sent me and to **c** his work.
Rev 6:11 until the number would be **c**

COMPLETED → COMPLETE
Jer 25:12 Then after seventy years are **c**,
Da 11:36 until the period of wrath is **c**,

COMPLETION → COMPLETE
Php 1: 6 work among you will bring it to **c**
Jas 2:22 faith was brought to **c** by the works.

CONCEALED
Lk 9:45 its meaning was **c** from them,
Sir 11: 4 his works are **c** from humankind.

CONCEIT → CONCEITED
Php 2: 3 nothing from selfish ambition or **c**,
1Ti 3: 6 he may be puffed up with **c** and fall
Sir 3:24 For their **c** has led many astray,

CONCEITED* → CONCEIT
Gal 5:26 Let us not become **c**, competing
1Ti 6: 4 is **c**, understanding nothing,

CONCEIVE → CONCEIVED
Mt 1:23 the virgin shall **c** and bear a son,
Lk 1:31 you will **c** in your womb and bear

CONCEIVED → CONCEIVE
1Co 2: 9 ear heard, nor the human heart **c**,
Jas 1:15 desire has **c**, it gives birth to sin,

CONDEMN → CONDEMNATION, CONDEMNED
Job 10: 2 I will say to God, Do not **c** me;
Ps 109:31 save them from those who would **c**
Lk 11:31 of this generation and **c** them,
Jn 3:17 not send the Son into the world to **c**
Ro 8:34 Who is to **c**?
1Jn 3:21 Beloved, if our hearts do not **c** us,

CONDEMNATION → CONDEMN
Mk 12:40 They will receive the greater **c**."
Ro 5:18 one man's trespass led to **c** for all,
1Ti 3: 6 fall into the **c** of the devil.
Jas 5:12 so that you may not fall under **c**.

CONDEMNED → CONDEMN
Mt 12:37 and by your words you will be **c**."
Lk 24:20 handed him over to be **c** to death
Jn   3:18 Those who believe in him are not **c**.
     16:11 the ruler of this world has been **c**.
1Co 11:32 disciplined so that we may not be **c**.

CONDUCT
Eze 22:31 returned their **c** upon their heads,
Ro 13: 3 For rulers are not a terror to good **c**,
1Pe 1:15 be holy yourselves in all your **c**;
Tob 4:14 and discipline yourself in all your **c**.
Sir 37:17 The mind is the root of all **c**;

CONFESS → CONFESSES, CONFESSION
Lev   5: 5 you shall **c** the sin that you have
     16:21 **c** over it all the iniquities of the
Ps 38:18 **c** my iniquity; I am sorry for my sin.
Php 2:11 should **c** that Jesus Christ is Lord,
1Jn 1: 9 If we **c** our sins, he who is faithful
Rev 3: 5 will **c** your name before my Father
Sir 4:26 Do not be ashamed to **c** your sins,

CONFESSES → CONFESS
Ro 10:10 **c** with the mouth and so is saved.
1Jn 2:23 who **c** the Son has the Father also.

CONFESSION → CONFESS
Da   9: 4 to the LORD my God and made **c**.
1Ti 6:12 for which you made the good **c** in
Heb 4:14 let us hold fast to our **c**.

CONFIDENCE
Ps 118: 8 in the LORD than to put **c** in mortals.
Php 3: 3 and have no **c** in the flesh—
Heb 10:19 we have **c** to enter the sanctuary

CONFIRM → CONFIRMED
2Sa 7:25 **c** it forever; do as you have
Ps 119:38 **C** to your servant your promise,
Ro 15: 8 that he might **c** the promises given

CONFIRMED → CONFIRM
Ps 105:10 which he **c** to Jacob as a statute,
2Pe 1:19 the prophetic message more fully **c**.

CONFORMED*
Ro   8:29 predestined to be **c** to the image of
     12: 2 Do not be **c** to this world,
Php 3:21 may be **c** to the body of his glory,
1Pe 1:14 do not be **c** to the desires that you

CONFUSE → CONFUSION
Ge 11: 7 go down, and **c** their language there,

CONFUSION → CONFUSE
Ex 23:27 and will throw into **c** all the people
Dt 28:28 blindness, and **c** of mind;
Ps 44: 7 and have put to **c** those who hate us.

CONGREGATION
Lev 4:13 **c** of Israel errs unintentionally
Nu   1: 2 a census of the whole **c** of Israelites,
Ps   1: 5 nor sinners in the **c** of the righteous;
Heb 2:12 the midst of the **c** I will praise you."

CONQUER → CONQUERED, CONQUERORS, CONQUERS
Rev 17:14 and the Lamb will **c** them,
     21: 7 who **c** will inherit these things,

CONQUERED → CONQUER
Jn 16:33 take courage; I have **c** the world!"
Heb 11:33 who through faith **c** kingdoms,
1Jn 2:13 because you have **c** the evil one.
Rev 15: 2 who had **c** the beast and its image

CONQUERORS → CONQUER
Ro 8:37 all these things we are more than **c**

CONQUERS → CONQUER
1Jn 5: 4 victory that **c** the world, our faith.
Rev 2: 7 To everyone who **c**, I will give

CONSCIENCE
Ro 2:15 their own **c** also bears witness;
1Co 8: 7 and their **c**, being weak, is
           defiled.
1Ti 1: 5 a good **c**, and sincere faith.

Heb 9:14 purify our **c** from dead works to
1Pe 3:21 as an appeal to God for a good **c**,

CONSECRATE → CONSECRATED
Ex 13: 2 **C** to me all the firstborn;
     40: 9 and **c** it and all its furniture,

CONSECRATED → CONSECRATE
Lev 8:30 Thus he **c** Aaron and his vestments,
2Ch 7:16 now I have chosen and **c** this house
Ne   3: 1 They **c** it and set up its doors;
1Mc 4:48 of the temple, and **c** the courts.

CONSIDER → CONSIDERED
Ex 33:13 **C** too that this nation is your people.
1Sa 12:24 for **c** what great things he has done
Ps 107:43 and **c** the steadfast love of the LORD.
Lk 12:27 **C** the lilies, how they grow:
Ro   6:11 must **c** yourselves dead to sin
Jas   1: 2 of any kind, **c** it nothing but joy,

CONSIDERED → CONSIDER
Pr 17:28 fools who keep silent are **c** wise;
Heb 11:11 he **c** him faithful who had promised.

CONSOLATION
Lk   2:25 looking forward to the **c** of Israel,
2Co 1: 3 of mercies and the God of all **c**,

CONSPIRACY → CONSPIRE
Isa 8:12 not call **c** all that this people calls **c**,

CONSPIRE → CONSPIRACY, CONSPIRED
Ps   2: 1 Why do the nations **c**,
     83: 5 They **c** with one accord;

CONSPIRED → CONSPIRE
Da   6: 6 So the presidents and satraps **c**
Mt 26: 4 and they **c** to arrest Jesus by stealth

CONSULT → CONSULTED
1Sa 28: 8 And he said, "**C** a spirit for me,
Isa 31: 1 Holy One of Israel or **c** the LORD!
     40:14 did he **c** for his enlightenment,
Sir 8:17 Do not **c** with fools, for they cannot

CONSULTED → CONSULT
1Ch 10:13 had a **c** medium, seeking guidance,
Eze 20: 3 Lord GOD, I will not be **c** by you.

CONSUME → CONSUMED, CONSUMING
Ex 32:12 **c** them from the face of the earth'?
Nu 16:21 so that I may **c** them in a moment.
Mt   6:19 where moth and rust **c** and where
Jn   2:17 "Zeal for your house will **c** me."

CONSUMED → CONSUME
Ex   3: 2 bush was blazing, yet it was not **c**.
Ps 69: 9 zeal for your house that has **c** me;
     90: 7 For we are **c** by your anger;
Zep 3: 8 all the earth shall be **c**.
Gal 5:15 that you are not **c** by one another.

CONSUMING → CONSUME
Heb 12:29 for indeed our God is a **c** fire.

CONTAIN
2Ch 2: 6 even highest heaven, cannot **c** him?
Jn 21:25 world itself could not **c** the books

CONTEMPT
Da 12: 2 some to shame and everlasting **c**.
Mk 9:12 sufferings and be treated with **c**?
Heb 6: 6 and are holding him up to **c**.

CONTEND
Isa 49:25 I will **c** with those who **c** with you,
Jude 1: 3 to **c** for the faith that was once for

CONTENT → CONTENTMENT
2Co 12:10 Therefore I am **c** with weaknesses,
Php 4:11 learned to be **c** with whatever I have
Heb 13: 5 and be **c** with what you have;
Sir 29:23 Be **c** with little or much,

CONTENTMENT* → CONTENT
1Ti 6: 6 gain in godliness combined with **c**;

CONTINUE
1Ch 17:27 that it may **c** forever before you.

Jn   8:31 "If you **c** in my word,
Ac 13:43 urged them to **c** in the grace of God.
1Th 3: 8 if you **c** to stand firm in the Lord.
Heb 8: 9 for they did not **c** in my covenant,

CONTRARY
Gal 1: 8 a gospel **c** to what we proclaimed to
1Ti 1:10 else is **c** to the sound teaching

CONTRIBUTE* → CONTRIBUTING
Ro 12:13 **C** to the needs of the saints;

CONTRIBUTING* → CONTRIBUTE
Dt 16:10 **c** a freewill offering in proportion to
Mk 12:43 all those who are **c** to the treasury.

CONTRITE
Ps 51:17 broken and **c** heart, O God, you wil
Isa 57:15 who are **c** and humble in spirit,

CONVERT
Mt 23:15 sea and land to make a single **c**,
1Ti 3: 6 He must not be a recent **c**,

CONVICT → CONVICTION
Dt 19:15 to **c** a person of any crime
Jude 1:15 to **c** everyone of all the deeds of

CONVICTION → CONVICT
Heb 11: 1 the **c** of things not seen.

CONVINCE → CONVINCED, CONVINCING
Ac 28:23 and trying to **c** them about Jesus
2Ti 4: 2 **c**, rebuke, and encourage,

CONVINCED → CONVINCE
Lk 16:31 neither will they be **c** even if
Ro   8:38 For I am **c** that neither death, nor
2Co 5:14 we are **c** that one has died for all;

CONVINCING* → CONVINCE
Ac   1: 3 to them by many **c** proofs,

CONVOCATIONS
Lev 23: 2 that you shall proclaim as holy **c**,

COPPER
Lev 26:19 like iron and your earth like **c**.
Mk 12:42 and put in two small **c** coins,

COPY
Dt 17:18 he shall have a **c** of this law written
Heb 9:24 a mere **c** of the true one,

CORDS
2Sa 22: 6 the **c** of Sheol entangled me,
Hos 11: 4 led them with **c** of human kindness,

CORNELIUS*
   First Gentile Christian (Ac 10).

CORNER → CORNERSTONE
Pr   1:21 At the busiest **c** she cries out;
1Pe 2: 7 has become the very head of the **c**,"

CORNERSTONE → CORNER, STONE
Ps 118:22 rejected has become the chief **c**.
Isa 28:16 a tested stone, a precious **c**, a sure
Zec 10: 4 Out of them shall come the **c**,
Lk 20:17 builders rejected has become
           the **c**'?
Eph 2:20 with Christ Jesus himself as the **c**.
1Pe 2: 6 laying in Zion a stone, a **c** chosen

CORRECT → CORRECTING, CORRECTION
Ps 141: 5 let the faithful **c** me.
Jer 10:24 **C** me, O LORD, but in just measure;
Sir 42: 8 Do not be ashamed to **c** the stupid

CORRECTING* → CORRECT
2Ti 2:25 **c** opponents with gentleness.

CORRECTION → CORRECT
Jer 5: 3 but they refused to take **c**.
2Ti 3:16 **c**, and for training in righteousness,

CORRUPT → CORRUPTION
Ge   6:11 Now the earth was **c** in God's sight,
Ac 2:40 yourselves from this **c** generation."
Eph 4:22 your old self, **c** and deluded

CORRUPTION → CORRUPT
Ac 2:31 nor did his flesh experience c.
2Pe 1: 4 you may escape from the c

COST
1Ch 21:24 burnt offerings that c me nothing."
Lk 14:28 not first sit down and estimate the c,

COUNCIL → COUNCILS
Jer 23:18 who has stood in the c of the LORD
Mt 26:59 the whole c were looking for false

COUNCILS* → COUNCIL
Mk 13: 9 for they will hand you over to c;

COUNSEL → COUNSELOR, COUNSELORS
Job 38: 2 that darkens c by words without
Ps 2: 2 and the rulers take c together,
33:11 The c of the LORD stands forever,
Isa 28:29 he is wonderful in c, and excellent

COUNSELOR → COUNSEL
Isa 9: 6 and he is named Wonderful C,
Ro 11:34 Or who has been his c?"
Sir 42:21 and he needs no one to be his c.

COUNSELORS → COUNSEL
Pr 11:14 in an abundance of c there is safety.
24: 6 in abundance of c there is victory.

COUNT → COUNTED, COUNTS
Ge 13:16 if one can c the dust of the earth,
1Ch 21: 1 incited David to c the people of
Ps 90:12 So teach us to c our days

COUNTED → COUNT
Ecc 1:15 and what is lacking cannot be c.
Mt 10:30 even the hairs of your head are all c.

COUNTENANCE
Nu 6:26 the LORD lift up his c upon you,
Ps 89:15 O LORD, in the light of your c;
Pr 15:13 A glad heart makes a cheerful c,

COUNTRY
Ge 12: 1 "Go from your c and your kindred
Jer 31:17 shall come back to their own c.
Jn 4:44 has no honor in the prophet's own c).
Heb 11:16 they desire a better c, that is,

COURAGE → COURAGEOUS
1Ch 22:13 Be strong and of good c.
Jn 16:33 But take c; I have conquered

COURAGEOUS → COURAGE
Jos 1: 6 Be strong and c; for you shall put
Da 10:19 Be strong and c!"
1Co 16:13 stand firm in your faith, be c,
1Mc 2:64 be c and grow strong in the law,

COURT → COURTS
Ex 27: 9 shall make the c of the tabernacle.
Pr 25: 8 do not hastily bring into c;
Da 7:10 c sat in judgment, and the books
Mt 5:25 while you are on the way to c
1Co 6: 6 believer goes to c against a believer

COURTS → COURT
Ps 84:10 in your c is better than a thousand
96: 8 an offering, and come into his c.

COVENANT → COVENANTS
Ge 6:18 But I will establish my c with you;
9: 9 I am establishing my c with you
15:18 the LORD made a c with Abram,
Ex 2:24 remembered his c with Abraham,
19: 5 you obey my voice and keep my c,
24: 7 Then he took the book of the c,
40: 3 put in it the ark of the c,
Lev 26:42 will I remember my c with Jacob;
Jdg 2: 1 'I will never break my c with you.
1Ki 8:23 keeping c and steadfast love
Ezr 10: 3 now let us make a c with our God
Job 31: 1 "I have made a c with my eyes;
Ps 105: 8 He is mindful of his c forever,
Isa 61: 8 I will make an everlasting c with
Jer 31:31 when I will make a new c with

COVENANTS → COVENANT
Ro 9: 4 the adoption, the glory, the c,
Gal 4:24 an allegory: these women are two c.

COVER
Ex 33:22 I will c you with my hand
Ps 139:11 "Surely the darkness shall c me,
Isa 11: 9 as the waters the c the sea.
Jas 5:20 and will c a multitude of sins.

COVET
Ex 20:17 shall not c your neighbor's house;
Ro 7: 7 had not said, "You shall not c."
Jas 4: 2 you c something and cannot obtain

CRAFTINESS → CRAFTY
Ro 1:29 of envy, murder, strife, deceit, c,
1Co 3:19 "He catches the wise in their c,"

CRAFTY → CRAFTINESS
Ge 3: 1 serpent was more c than any other
2Co 12:16 (you say) since I was c, I took you

CRAVING*
Nu 11: 4 rabble among them had a strong c;
Ps 78:30 But before they had satisfied their c,

CREATE → CREATED, CREATION, CREATOR
Ps 51:10 C in me a clean heart, O God,
Isa 65:17 to c new heavens and a new earth;
Eph 2:15 c in himself one new humanity

CREATED → CREATE
Ge 1: 1 In the beginning when God c the
1:27 So God c humankind in his image,
Dt 32: 6 Is not he your father, who c you,
Pr 8:22 The LORD c me at the beginning of
Mal 2:10 Has not one God c us?
1Co 11: 9 Neither was man c for the sake of
Eph 2:10 c in Christ Jesus for good works,
Col 1:16 all things have been c through him
1Ti 4: 4 For everything c by God is good,
Rev 4:11 for you c all things, and by your will
Jdt 13:18 who c the heavens and the earth,
Wis 2:23 for God c us for incorruption,
Sir 1: 4 Wisdom was c before all other

CREATION → CREATE
Ge 2: 3 all the work that he had done in c.
Mk 10: 6 But from the beginning of c,
Ro 8:19 the c waits with eager longing for
2Co 5:17 anyone is in Christ, there is a new c:
Col 1:15 invisible God, the firstborn of all c;
2Pe 3: 4 they were from the beginning of c!"

CREATOR → CREATE
Ecc 12: 1 Remember your c in the days of
Ro 1:25 served the creature rather than the C
Col 3:10 according to the image of its c.
1Pe 4:19 to a faithful C,

CREATURE → CREATURES
Ge 2:19 the man called every living c,
Ro 1:25 worshiped and served the c rather

CREATURES → CREATURE
Lev 11: 2 these are the c that you may eat.
Ps 104:24 the earth is full of your c.
Eze 1: 5 was something like four living c.
Rev 4: 6 are four living c, full of eyes
19: 4 elders and the four living c fell

CREDIT → CREDITED
Lk 6:33 what c is that to you?
1Pe 2:20 for doing wrong, what c is that?

CREDITED → CREDIT
Lev 7:18 nor shall it be c to the one who

CREEPING
Ge 1:24 cattle and c things and wild animals
Ps 148:10 c things and flying birds!

CRIED → CRY
Ex 2:23 under their slavery, and c out.
Nu 20:16 when we c to the LORD, he heard
Jdg 3: 9 the Israelites c out to the LORD,
Ps 22: 5 To you they c, and were saved;
Mt 27:46 Jesus c with a loud voice,

CRIMINAL → CRIMINALS
Jn 18:30 "If this man were not a c,
2Ti 2: 9 the point of being chained like a c.
1Pe 4:15 suffer as a murderer, a thief, a c,

CRIMINALS → CRIMINAL
Lk 23:32 Two others also, who were c,

CRIMSON
Ex 25: 4 purple, and c yarns and fine linen,
Lev 14: 4 cedarwood and c yarn and hyssop
Jos 2:21 she tied the c cord in the window.

CROOKED
Dt 32: 5 a perverse and c generation.
Ps 18:26 the c you show yourself perverse.
Ecc 1:15 What is c cannot be made straight,
Lk 3: 5 and the c shall be made straight,
Php 2:15 in the midst of a c and perverse

CROSS → CROSSROADS
Dt 31: 3 your God himself will c over before
Mk 15:30 and come down from the c!"
Lk 14:27 the c and follow me cannot be my
1Co 1:18 the c is foolishness to those who are
Gal 6:14 never boast of anything except the c
Php 2: 8 of death—even death on a c.
Col 1:20 peace through the blood of his c.
Heb 12: 2 was set before him endured the c,

CROSSROADS* → CROSS, ROAD
Pr 8: 2 at the c she takes her stand;
Jer 6:16 Stand at the c, and look, and ask for

CROW*
Lk 22:34 the cock will not c this day,

CROWD → CROWDS
Mk 8: 2 "I have compassion for the c,
14:43 a c with swords and clubs,

CROWDS → CROWD
Mt 7:28 c were astounded at his teaching,

CROWN → CROWNED, CROWNS
Lev 8: 9 the golden ornament, the holy c,
Pr 4: 9 will bestow on you a beautiful c."
La 5:16 The c has fallen from our head;
Jn 19: 2 soldiers wove a c of thorns and put
Php 4: 1 my joy and c, stand firm in the Lord
2Ti 4: 8 there is reserved for me the c
1Pe 5: 4 the c of glory that never fades away.
Rev 6: 2 Its rider had a bow; a c was given
14:14 with a golden c on his head,
Sir 1:18 fear of the Lord is the c of wisdom,

CROWNED → CROWN
Ps 8: 5 and c them with glory and honor.
2Ti 2: 5 no one is c without competing
Heb 2: 9 now c with glory and honor

CROWNS → CROWN
Rev 4:10 they cast their c before the throne,

CRUCIFIED → CRUCIFY
Mt 27:22 All of them said, "Let him be c!"
Lk 24: 7 c, and on the third day rise again."
Ac 4:10 whom you c, whom God raised
Ro 6: 6 We know that our old self was c
1Co 1:23 but we proclaim Christ c,
Gal 2:19 I have been c with Christ;

CRUCIFY → CRUCIFIED, CRUCIFYING
Lk	23:21	they kept shouting, "C, c him!"
Jn	19:15	asked them, "Shall I c your King?"

CRUCIFYING* → CRUCIFY
Heb	6: 6	they are c again the Son of God

CRUSH → CRUSHED
Job	6: 9	that it would please God to c me,
Isa	53:10	it was the will of the LORD to c him
Da	2:40	it shall c and shatter all these.
Mt	21:44	it will c anyone on whom it falls."
Ro	16:20	will shortly c Satan under your feet.

CRUSHED → CRUSH
Ps	34:18	and saves the c in spirit.
2Co	4: 8	afflicted in every way, but not c;

CRY → CRIED, CRYING
Ex	2:23	Out of the slavery their c for help
Ps	5: 2	Listen to the sound of my c,
	130: 1	Out of the depths I c to you,
Hab	1: 2	how long shall I c for help,
Mk	15:37	Then Jesus gave a loud c

CRYING → CRY
Ge	4:10	your brother's blood is c out to me
Mk	1: 3	the voice of one c out in the
Rev	21: 4	c and pain will be no more,

CRYSTAL
Eze	1:22	shining like c, spread out above
Rev	22: 1	river of the water of life, bright as c,

CUP
Ps	23: 5	my head with oil; my c overflows.
Jer	25:15	my hand this c of the wine of wrath,
Mt	10:42	gives even a c of cold water to one
	26:39	if it is possible, let this c pass from
Mk	10:38	you able to drink the c that I drink,
Lk	22:17	he took a c, and after giving thanks
1Co	11:25	c is the new covenant in my blood.
Rev	14:10	unmixed into the c of his anger,

CURE → CURED
Hos	5:13	But he is not able to c you or heal

CURED → CURE
Mt	8:16	and c all who were sick.
Ac	5:16	and they were all c.

CURSE → ACCURSED, CURSED, CURSES
Ge	8:21	"I will never again c the ground
	12: 3	and the one who curses you I will c;
Nu	22:12	not c the people, for they are blessed
Dt	21:23	hung on a tree is under God's c.
	23: 5	God turned the c into a blessing
Job	2: 9	C God, and die."
Ps	109:28	Let them c, but you will bless.
Mal	4: 6	come and strike the land with a c.
Mk	14:71	he began to c, and he swore an oath,
Lk	6:28	bless those who c you, pray
Ro	12:14	bless and do not c them.
Gal	3:13	Christ redeemed us from the c of the
		law by becoming a c for us—
Sir	4: 5	and give no one reason to c you;

CURSED → CURSE
Ge	3:17	c is the ground because of you;
	9:25	"C be Canaan; lowest of slaves
	27:29	C be everyone who curses you,
Nu	23: 8	can I curse whom God has not c?
Job	3: 1	Job opened his mouth and c the day
Mk	11:21	fig tree that you c has withered."
Gal	3:10	"C is everyone who does not
Heb	6: 8	and on the verge of being c;
Rev	16: 9	but they c the name of God,

CURSES → CURSE
Lev	24:15	who c God shall bear the sin.
2Ch	34:24	all the c that are written in the book

CURTAIN
Ex	26:31	You shall make a c of blue, purple,
2Ch	3:14	And Solomon made the c of blue
Lk	23:45	the c of the temple was torn in two.
Heb	10:20	that he opened for us through the c

CUSTOM → CUSTOMS
Est	9:23	Jews adopted as a c
Jn	18:39	But you have a c that I release

CUSTOMS → CUSTOM
2Ki	17: 8	the c of the nations whom the LORD
Ac	16:21	advocating c that are not lawful for
1Mc	1:42	all should give up their particular c.

CUT
Ge	9:11	never again shall all flesh be c off
Ps	37: 9	For the wicked shall be c off,
Isa	53: 8	c off from the land of the living,
Da	2:45	a stone was c from the mountain
Mt	3:10	does not bear good fruit is c down
Mk	9:43	hand causes you to stumble, c it off;
Ro	11:22	otherwise you also will be c off.

CYMBAL* → CYMBALS
1Co	13: 1	I am a noisy gong or a clanging c,

CYMBALS → CYMBAL
2Sa	6: 5	tambourines and castanets and c.
Ne	12:27	and with singing, with c,
Ps	150: 7	Praise him with clanging c;

CYRUS
Persian king who allowed exiles to return (2Ch 36:22-Ezr 1:8), to rebuild temple (Ezr 5:13-6:14), as appointed by the LORD (Isa 44:28-45:13).

D

DAGON
Jdg	16:23	a great sacrifice to their god D,
1Sa	5: 2	and brought it into the house of D

DAILY → DAY
Mt	6:11	Give us this day our d bread.
Lk	9:23	take up their cross d and follow me.

DAMASCUS
Ac	9: 3	was going along and approaching D,

DAN
1. Son of Jacob by Bilhah (Ge 30:4-6; 35:25; 46:23). Tribe of blessed (Ge 49:16-17; Dt 33:22), numbered (Nu 1:39; 26:43), allotted land (Jos 19:40-48; Eze 48:1), failed to fully possess (Jdg 1:34-35), failed to support Deborah (Jdg 5:17), possessed Dan (Jdg 18).
2. Northernmost city in Israel (Ge 14:14; Jdg 18; 20:1).

DANCE → DANCED
Ps	150: 4	Praise him with tambourine and d;
Ecc	3: 4	a time to mourn, and a time to d;
Lk	7:32	the flute for you, and you did not d;

DANCED → DANCE
2Sa	6:14	David d before the LORD with all
Mt	14: 6	the daughter of Herodias d before

DANIEL → =BELTESHAZZAR
1. Hebrew exile to Babylon, name changed to Belteshazzar (Da 1:6-7). Refused to eat unclean food (Da 1:8-21). Interpreted Nebuchadnezzar's dreams (Da 2; 4), writing on the wall (Da 5). Thrown into lion's den (Da 6). Visions of (Da 7-12). In deuterocanonical books of Bel and the Dragon, Susanna.
2. Son of David (1Ch 3:1).

DARE
Mt	22:46	d to ask him any more questions.
Ro	5: 7	someone might actually d to die.

DARIUS
1. King of Persia (Ezr 4:5), allowed rebuilding of temple (Ezr 5-6).
2. Mede who conquered Babylon (Da 5:31).

DARK → DARKEST, DARKNESS
Ps	139:12	even the darkness is not d to you;
Lk	12: 3	whatever you have said in the d will
2Pe	1:19	as to a lamp shining in a d place,

DARKEST* → DARK
Ps	23: 4	though I walk through the d valley,

DARKNESS → DARK
Ge	1: 2	the earth was a formless void and d
Ex	10:22	was dense d in all the land of Egypt
Dt	5:23	you heard the voice out of the d,
Isa	9: 2	walked in d have seen a great light;
Joel	2:31	The sun shall be turned to d,
Zep	1:15	a day of d and gloom,
Mt	4:16	who sat in d have seen a great light,
	6:23	light in you is d, how great is the d!
Jn	1: 5	light shines in the d, and the d did not
Eph	5: 8	For once you were d, but now in
Col	1:13	from the power of d and transferred
1Jn	1: 5	God is light and in him there is no d

DATHAN*
Involved in Korah's rebellion against Moses and Aaron (Nu 16:1-27; 26:9; Dt 11:6; Ps 106:17; Sir 45:18; 4Mc 2:17).

DAUGHTER → DAUGHTERS
Ex	2: 5	d of Pharaoh came down to bathe at
Est	2: 7	Mordecai adopted her as his own d.
Ps	9:14	and, in the gates of d Zion;
La	2: 1	in his anger has humiliated d Zion!
Mic	7: 6	the d rises up against her mother,
Zec	9: 9	Rejoice greatly, O d Zion!
Mt	14: 6	the d of Herodias danced before the
Lk	12:53	against d and d against mother,
Jdt	10:12	replied, "I am a d of the Hebrews,

DAUGHTERS → DAUGHTER
Ge	6: 4	of God went in to the d of humans,
	19:36	the d of Lot became pregnant by their
Nu	27: 1	the d of Zelophehad came forward.
Dt	12:31	even burn their sons and their d in
Job	42:15	no women so beautiful as Job's d;
Joel	2:28	sons and your d shall prophesy,
Ac	2:17	sons and your d shall prophesy,
2Co	6:18	and you shall be my sons and d,
1Pe	3: 6	You have become her d as long

DAVID
Son of Jesse (Ru 4:17-22; 1Ch 2:13-15), ancestor of Jesus (Mt 1:1-17; Lk 3:31). Wives and children (1Sa 18; 25:39-44; 2Sa 3:2-5; 5:13-16; 11:27; 1Ch 3:1-9).

Anointed king by Samuel (1Sa 16:1-13). Musician to Saul (1Sa 16:14-23; 18:10). Killed Goliath (1Sa 17). Relation with Jonathan (1Sa 18:1-4; 19-20; 23:16-18; 2Sa 1). Disfavor of Saul (1Sa 18:6-23:29). Spared Saul's life (1Sa 24; 26). Among Philistines (1Sa 21:10-14; 27-30). Lament for Saul and Jonathan (2Sa 1).

Anointed king of Judah (2Sa 2:1-11). Conflict with house of Saul (2Sa 2-4). Anointed king of Israel (2Sa 5:1-4; 1Ch 11:1-3). Conquered Jerusalem (2Sa 5:6-10; 1Ch 11;4-9). Brought ark to Jerusalem (2Sa 6; 1Ch 13; 15-16). The LORD promised eternal dynasty (2Sa 7; 1Ch 17; Ps 132). Showed kindness to Mephibosheth (2Sa 9). Adultery with Bathsheba, murder of Uriah (2Sa 11-12). Son Amnon raped daughter Tamar; killed by Absalom (2Sa 13). Absalom's revolt (2Sa 14-17); death (2Sa 18). Sheba's revolt (2Sa 20). Victories: Philistines (2Sa 5:17-25; 21:15-22; 1Ch 14:8-17; 20:4-8), Ammonites (2Sa 10; 1Ch 19), various (2Sa 8; 1Ch 18). Mighty men (2Sa 23:8-39; 1Ch 11-12). Punished for numbering army (2Sa 24; 1Ch 21). Appointed Solomon king (1Ki 1:28-2:9). Prepared for building of temple (1Ch 22-29). Last words (2Sa 23:1-7). Death (1Ki 2:10-12; 1Ch 29:28).

Psalmist (Mt 22:43-45), musician (Am 6:5), prophet (2Sa 23:2-7; Ac 1:16; 2:30).

Psalms of: 2 (Ac 4:25), 3-32, 34-41, 51-65, 68-70, 86, 95 (Heb 4:7), 101, 103, 108-110, 122, 124, 131, 133, 138-145. Deuterocanonical Ps 151 ascribed to.

DAWN → DAWNS
Isa 14:12 from heaven, O Day Star, son of D!
Hos   6: 3 his appearing is as sure as the **d**;

DAWNS → DAWN
Ps 97:11 Light **d** for the righteous,
2Pe 1:19 until the day **d** and the morning star

DAY → DAILY, DAYS
Ge   1: 5 God called the light **D**, and
     8:22 **d** and night, shall not cease.”
Ex 13:21 of them in a pillar of cloud by **d**,
    20: 8 Remember the sabbath **d**, and keep
Jos   1: 8 you shall meditate on it **d** and night,
Ps   1: 2 his law they meditate **d** and night.
  118:24 is the **d** that the LORD has made;
Isa 66: 8 Shall a land be born in one **d**?
Joel 1:15 For the **d** of the LORD is near,
Zec 14: 1 See, a **d** is coming for the LORD,
Mal   3: 2 who can endure the **d** of his coming,
Mt 25:13 you know neither the **d** nor the hour.
Lk 11: 3 Give us each **d** our daily bread.
  24:46 to rise from the dead on the third **d**,
Jn   6:40 I will raise them up on the last **d**.”
Ro 14: 5 Some judge one **d** to be better than
2Co 6: 2 see, now is the **d** of salvation!
1Th 5: 2 very well that the **d** of the Lord
2Pe 3: 8 the Lord one **d** is like a thousand years,
   3:10 **d** of the Lord will come like a thief,
1Jn 4:17 have boldness on the **d** of judgment,
Rev 1:10 I was in the spirit on the Lord's **d**,
  16:14 for battle on the great **d** of God

DAYS → DAY
Ge   1:14 and for seasons and for **d** and years,
   7: 4 rain on the earth for forty **d** and forty
Ex 24:18 on the mountain for forty **d** and
1Ki 19: 8 that food forty **d** and forty nights
Ps 90:10 The **d** of our life are seventy years,
Mk 1:13 He was in the wilderness forty **d**,
Eph 5:16 of the time, because the **d** are evil.
2Ti 3: 1 in the last **d** distressing times will
Heb 1: 2 last **d** he has spoken to us by a Son,
1Mc 4:56 dedication of the altar for eight **d**,
2Es 14:42 They sat forty **d**; they wrote

DEACON* → DEACONS
Ro 16: 1 a **d** of the church at Cenchreae,

DEACONS → DEACON
1Ti 3: 8 **D** likewise must be serious, not

DEAD → DEATH, DIE, DIED, DYING
Nu 16:48 stood between the **d** and the living;
Dt 18:11 or who seeks oracles from the **d**.
Ps 115:17 The **d** do not praise the LORD,
Ecc 9: 4 a living dog is better than a **d** lion.
Mt 8:22 and let the **d** bury their own **d**.”
Mk 12:27 God not of the **d**, but of the living;
Lk 24: 5 look for the living among the **d**?
Ro 6:11 must consider yourselves **d** to sin
Eph 2: 1 You were **d** through the trespasses
Col 1:18 the firstborn from the **d**,
1Pe 4: 5 ready to judge the living and the **d**.
Rev 1: 5 witness, the firstborn of the **d**,
  20:12 And the **d** were judged according to

DEAF
Ex 4:11 Who makes them mute or **d**,
Isa 29:18 On that day the **d** shall hear the
Lk 7:22 the lepers are cleansed, the **d** hear,

DEATH → DEAD
Dt 30:19 that I have set before you life and **d**,
Ru 1:17 if even **d** parts me from you!”
Ps 22:15 you lay me in the dust of **d**.
Pr 18:21 **D** and life are in the power of the
SS 8: 6 for love is strong as **d**,
Isa 25: 7 he will swallow up **d** forever.
Hos 13:14 O **d**, where are your plagues?
Mt 16:28 standing here who will not taste **d**
Lk 1:79 in darkness and in the shadow of **d**,

Jn 5:24 but has passed from **d** to life.
Ro 4:25 handed over to **d** for our trespasses
1Co 15:55 “Where, O **d**, is your victory?
2Co 2:16 to the one a fragrance from **d** to **d**,
Heb 2:14 through **d** he might destroy the one who has the power of **d**,
1Jn 3:14 that we have passed from **d** to life
Rev 1:18 I have the keys of **D** and of Hades.
  20:14 **D** and Hades were thrown into the lake
  21: 4 **D** will be no more;
Sir 15:17 Before each person are life and **d**,

DEBAUCHERY
Ro 13:13 not in **d** and licentiousness,
Eph 5:18 drunk with wine, for that is **d**;

DEBORAH
Prophetess; led victory over Canaanites (Jdg 4-5).

DEBT → DEBTS, INDEBTED
Mt 18:27 released him and forgave him the **d**.

DEBTS → DEBT
Dt 15: 1 you shall grant a remission of **d**.
Mt 6:12 And forgive us our **d**, as we

DECEIT → DECEITFUL, DECEIVE, DECEIVED, DECEIVERS
Dt 32: 4 A faithful God, without **d**,
Isa 53: 9 and there was no **d** in his mouth.
Ro 1:29 Full of envy, murder, strife, **d**,
1Pe 2:22 and no **d** was found in his mouth.”

DECEITFUL → DECEIT
Ps 35:20 but they conceive **d** words
Zep 3:13 nor shall a **d** tongue be found
1Ti 4: 1 by paying attention to **d** spirits

DECEIVE → DECEIT
Eph 5: 6 Let no one **d** you with empty words,
1Jn 1: 8 that we have no sin, we **d** ourselves,
Rev 20: 8 to **d** the nations at the four corners

DECEIVED → DECEIT
Gal 6: 7 Do not be **d**; God is not mocked,
1Ti 2:14 was not **d**, but the woman was **d**

DECEIVERS* → DECEIT
Tit 1:10 rebellious people, idle talkers and **d**,
2Jn 1: 7 Many **d** have gone out into the

DECISION
Pr 16:33 but the **d** is the LORD's alone.
Joel 3:14 multitudes, in the valley of **d**!

DECLARE → DECLARED
Ps 50: 6 The heavens **d** his righteousness,
Col 4: 3 that we may **d** the mystery of Christ,

DECLARED → DECLARE
Isa 41:26 Who **d** it from the beginning,
Mk 7:19 (Thus he **d** all foods clean.)
Ro 1: 4 and was **d** to be Son of God

DECREASE
Jn 3:30 He must increase, but I must **d**.”

DECREE → DECREED, DECREES
Ps 2: 7 I will tell of the **d** of the LORD:
Lk 2: 1 **d** went out from Emperor Augustus

DECREED → DECREE
Da 9:24 “Seventy weeks are **d** for your

DECREES → DECREE
Dt 6: 2 and keep all his **d** and his
Ps 19: 7 the **d** of the LORD are sure,
  119: 2 Happy are those who keep his **d**,

DEDICATED → DEDICATION
1Ki 8:63 all the people of Israel **d** the house
Lk 21: 5 beautiful stones and gifts **d** to God,

DEDICATION → DEDICATED
2Ch 7: 9 the **d** of the altar seven days and
Ezr 6:16 the **d** of this house of God with joy.
1Mc 4:56 the **d** of the altar for eight days,

DEED → DEEDS
Ecc 12:14 will bring every **d** into judgment,
Jer 32:10 I signed the **d**, sealed it,
Mt 19:16 good **d** must I do to have eternal life
Col 3:17 And whatever you do, in word or **d**,

DEEDS → DEED
Dt 3:24 in heaven or on earth can perform **d**
Ps 9: 1 I will tell of all your wonderful **d**.
Jer 50:29 Repay her according to her **d**;
Ob 1:15 your **d** shall return on your own
Lk 23:41 getting what we deserve for our **d**,
Ro 2: 6 repay according to each one's **d**:
Rev 15: 3 “Great and amazing are your **d**,
  19: 8 the righteous **d** of the saints.

DEEP → DEPTH, DEPTHS
Ge 1: 2 darkness covered the face of the **d**,
  7:11 the fountains of the great **d** burst
Ro 8:26 with sighs too **d** for words.

DEFECT
1Pe 1:19 like that of a lamb without **d** or

DEFEND
Ps 72: 4 May he **d** the cause of the poor of
Pr 31: 9 **d** the rights of the poor and needy,
Jdt 5:21 for their Lord and God will **d** them,

DEFILE → DEFILED
Lev 11:43 you shall not **d** yourselves
Nu 35:34 You shall not **d** the land
Mk 7:15 things that come out are what **d**.”

DEFILED → DEFILE
Ps 79: 1 they have **d** your holy temple;
1Mc 1:37 they even **d** the sanctuary.

DEFRAUD*
Lev 19:13 You shall not **d** your neighbor;
Mk 10:19 You shall not **d**;
1Co 6: 8 you yourselves wrong and **d**—

DEITY
Col 2: 9 whole fullness of **d** dwells bodily,

DELAY
Dt 7:10 He does not **d** but repays
Ps 70: 5 my deliverer; O LORD, do not **d**!
Heb 10:37 will come and will not **d**;

DELIGHT → DELIGHTS
1Sa 15:22 “Has the LORD as great **d** in burnt
Ps 1: 2 but their **d** is in the law of the LORD,
  40: 8 I **d** to do your will, O my God;
Pr 8:30 I was daily his **d**, rejoicing before
Ro 7:22 For I **d** in the law of God in my
Sir 1:27 fidelity and humility are his **d**.

DELIGHTS → DELIGHT
Ps 5: 4 not a God who **d** in wickedness,
Isa 42: 1 chosen, in whom my soul **d**;

DELILAH*
Philistine who betrayed Samson (Jdg 16:4-22).

DELIVER → DELIVERANCE, DELIVERED, DELIVERER, DELIVERS
Ex 3: 8 to **d** them from the Egyptians,
Dt 32:39 and no one can **d** from my hand.
Da 3:17 able to **d** us from the furnace
  6:20 able to **d** you from the lions?”
Mt 27:43 let God **d** him now,

DELIVERANCE → DELIVER
Ex 14:13 and see the **d** that the LORD will
Est 4:14 **d** will rise for the Jews from another
Ps 3: 8 **D** belongs to the LORD;
Php 1:19 this will turn out for my **d**.
Jdt 8:17 while we wait for his **d**,

DELIVERED → DELIVER
Isa 66: 8 Shall a nation be **d** in one moment?
Da 12: 1 at that time your people shall be **d**,

DELIVERER → DELIVER
Ps 140: 7 O LORD, my Lord, my strong **d**,
Ro 11:26 “Out of Zion will come the **D**;

DEMON → DEMONIACS, DEMONIC, DEMONS
Mt　11:18　and they say, 'He has a **d**';
　　17:18　Jesus rebuked the **d**, and it came out
Jn　8:48　you are a Samaritan and have a **d**?"
　　10:21　not the words of one who has a **d**.
Tob　3: 8　the wicked Asmodeus had killed
　　6: 8　of a man or woman afflicted by a **d**

DEMONIACS → DEMON
Mt　4:24　**d**, epileptics, and paralytics, and he
　　8:28　two **d** coming out of the tombs met

DEMONIC* → DEMON
Rev　16:14　These are **d** spirits, performing signs

DEMONS → DEMON
Dt　32:17　They sacrificed to **d**, not God,
Ps　106:37　and their daughters to the **d**;
Lk　11:18　that I cast out the **d** by Beelzebul.
1Co　10:20　not want you to be partners with **d**.
1Ti　4: 1　deceitful spirits and teachings of **d**,
Jas　2:19　Even the **d** believe—and shudder.
Rev　9:20　their hands or give up worshiping **d**
Bar　4: 7　by sacrificing to **d** and not

DEN
Jer　7:11　a **d** of robbers in your sight?
Da　6: 7　shall be thrown into a **d** of lions.
Mk　11:17　you have made it a **d** of robbers."

DENARIUS
Mk　12:15　Bring me a **d** and let me see it."

DENIED → DENY
Mt　26:70　But he **d** it before all of them,
1Ti　5: 8　has **d** the faith and is worse than an
Rev　3: 8　my word and have not **d** my name.

DENIES → DENY
Lk　12: 9　but whoever **d** me before others
1Jn　2:22　the liar but the one who **d** that Jesus

DENY → DENIED, DENIES
Lev　16:29　you shall **d** yourselves,
　　23:27　you shall **d** yourselves
Mt　16:24　let them **d** themselves and take up
2Ti　2:12　if we **d** him, he will also **d** us;
2Pe　2: 1　**d** the Master who bought them—

DEPART → DEPARTED
Ge　49:10　The scepter shall not **d** from Judah,
Jos　1: 8　law shall not **d** out of your mouth;
Ps　34:14　**D** from evil, and do good;
Php　1:23　my desire is to **d** and be with Christ,

DEPARTED → DEPART
1Sa　4:21　"The glory has **d** from Israel,"

DEPRAVED → DEPRAVITY
1Ti　6: 5　among those who are **d** in mind
2Pe　2:10　who indulge their flesh in **d** lust,

DEPRAVITY → DEPRAVED
Lev　20:14　that there may be no **d** among you.

DEPRIVE
Dt　24:17　not **d** a resident alien or an orphan
1Co　7: 5　not **d** one another except perhaps

DEPTH → DEEP
Mt　13: 5　since they had no **d** of soil.
Ro　11:33　O the **d** of the riches and wisdom
Eph　3:18　and length and height and **d**,

DEPTHS → DEEP
Ps　130: 1　Out of the **d** I cry to you, O LORD.
1Co　2:10　even the **d** of God.

DESCENDANTS
Ge　15:18　saying, "To your **d** I give this land,
Dt　4:37　he chose their **d** after them.
Isa　44: 3　I will pour my spirit upon your **d**,
Ro　9: 7　Abraham's children are his true **d**;
Gal　3: 7　who believe are the **d** of Abraham.

DESCENDED → DESCENDING
Ex　34: 5　LORD **d** in the cloud and stood
Jn　3:13　except the one who **d** from heaven,

DESCENDING → DESCENDED
Ge　28:12　angels of God were ascending and **d**
Mk　1:10　and the Spirit **d** like a dove
Jn　1:51　the angels of God ascending and **d**

DESERT → DESERTED
Ps　106:14　and put God to the test in the **d**;
Isa　40: 3　make straight in the **d** a highway
Mk　8: 4　with bread here in the **d**?"

DESERTED → DESERT
Mt　26:56　all the disciples **d** him and fled.

DESERVE
Pr　14:14　and the good, what their deeds **d**.
Lk　23:15　he has done nothing to **d** death,
Ac　26:31　man is doing nothing to **d** death
Rev　2:23　give to each of you as your works **d**.

DESIRE → DESIRED, DESIRES
Ge　3:16　your **d** shall be for your husband,
Ps　20: 4　May he grant you your heart's **d**,
Pr　3:15　nothing you **d** can compare with her
Hos　6: 6　I **d** steadfast love and not sacrifice,
Mt　9:13　learn what this means, 'I **d** mercy,
Jas　1:14　But one is tempted by one's own **d**,
1Jn　2:16　the **d** of the flesh, the **d** of the eyes,

DESIRED → DESIRE
Ps　19:10　More to be **d** are they than gold,
Lk　22:15　I have eagerly **d** to eat this Passover

DESIRES → DESIRE
Ps　37: 4　he will give you the **d** of your heart.
Gal　5:16　do not gratify the **d** of the flesh.
1Ti　2: 4　who **d** everyone to be saved
2Ti　4: 3　teachers to suit their own **d**,
Sir　18:30　Do not follow your base **d**,

DESOLATE → DESOLATES, DESOLATING
Ex　23:29　or the land would become **d** and
Da　11:31　the abomination that makes **d**.
Mt　23:38　See, your house is left to you, **d**.
1Mc　1:39　sanctuary became **d** like a desert;

DESOLATES → DESOLATE
Da　9:27　shall be an abomination that **d**,

DESOLATING → DESOLATE
Mk　13:14　the **d** sacrilege set up where it ought
1Mc　1:54　erected a **d** sacrilege on the altar

DESPAIR → DESPAIRED
2Co　4: 8　perplexed, but not driven to **d**;

DESPAIRED* → DESPAIR
2Co　1: 8　crushed that we **d** of life itself.

DESPISE → DESPISED
Job　5:17　not **d** the discipline of the Almighty.
Ps　51:17　contrite heart, O God, you will not **d**
Pr　1: 7　fools **d** wisdom and instruction.
Lk　16:13　devoted to the one and **d** the other.

DESPISED → DESPISE
Isa　53: 3　He was **d** and rejected by others;
1Co　1:28　God chose what is low and **d** in the

DESTINED
Eph　1: 5　He **d** us for adoption as his children
1Th　5: 9　For God has **d** us not for wrath but
1Pe　1:11　to the sufferings **d** for Christ

DESTROY → DESTROYED, DESTROYER, DESTRUCTION
Ge　6:13　to **d** them along with the earth.
Est　3: 6　Haman plotted to **d** all the Jews,
Mt　10:28　rather fear him who can **d** both soul
Jn　10:10　comes only to steal and kill and **d**.
Jas　4:12　who is able to save and to **d**.
1Jn　3: 8　to **d** the works of the devil.

DESTROYED → DESTROY
Da　6:26　His kingdom shall never be **d**,
1Co　15:26　The last enemy to be **d** is death.
2Co　5: 1　if the earthly tent we live in is **d**,

DESTROYER → DESTROY
Ex　12:23　not allow the **d** to enter your houses
1Co　10:10　and were destroyed by the **d**.

DESTRUCTION → DESTROY
Pr　16:18　Pride goes before **d**, and a haughty
Mt　7:13　and the road is easy that leads to **d**,
Ro　9:22　objects of wrath that are made for **d**;
2Pe　3:16　and unstable twist to their own **d**,

DEVIL
Mt　4: 1　wilderness to be tempted by the **d**.
Lk　8:12　**d** comes and takes away the word
Jn　8:44　You are from your father the **d**,
Eph　4:27　and do not make room for the **d**.
　　6:11　to stand against the wiles of the **d**.
1Ti　3: 6　fall into the condemnation of the **d**.
Heb　2:14　the power of death, that is, the **d**,
Jas　4: 7　Resist the **d**, and he will flee from
1Pe　5: 8　lion your adversary the **d** prowls
1Jn　3: 8　to destroy the works of the **d**.
Jude　1: 9　Michael contended with the **d**
Rev　12: 9　who is called the **D** and Satan,
　　20: 2　that ancient serpent, who is the **D**

DEVOTED
Ps　86: 2　Preserve my life, for I am **d** to you;
Mt　6:24　**d** to the one and despise the other.

DEVOUR → DEVOURING
Gal　5:15　you bite and **d** one another,
1Pe　5: 8　looking for someone to **d**.
Rev　12: 4　that he might **d** her child

DEVOURING → DEVOUR
Ex　24:17　glory of the LORD was like a **d** fire
Dt　9: 3　crosses over before you as a **d** fire;

DEW
Jdg　6:37　if there is **d** on the fleece alone,

DICTATED*
Jer　36:18　"He **d** all these words to me,
2Es　14:42　and by turns they wrote what was **d**,

DIE → DEAD
Ge　2:17　eat of it you shall **d**."
　　3: 4　to the woman, "You will not **d**;
Ex　11: 5　firstborn in the land of Egypt shall **d**
Ru　1:17　Where you **d**, I will **d**—
Job　2: 9　Curse God, and **d**."
Pr　10:21　but fools **d** for lack of sense.
Ecc　3: 2　a time to be born, and a time to **d**;
Isa　22:13　eat and drink, for tomorrow we **d**."
Jer　31:30　But all shall **d** for their own sins;
Mt　26:35　"Even though I must **d** with you,
Jn　11:26　and believes in me will never **d**.
Ro　14: 8　if we **d**, we **d** to the Lord;
1Co　15:32　eat and drink, for tomorrow we **d**."
Heb　9:27　it is appointed for mortals to **d** once,

DIED → DEAD
Ro　5: 6　right time Christ **d** for the ungodly.
1Co　15: 3　Christ **d** for our sins in accordance
Gal　2:19　the law I **d** to the law,

DIFFERENT
2Co　11: 4　or a **d** gospel from the one you
Gal　1: 6　and are turning to a **d** gospel—

DIFFICULT
Da　4: 9　and that no mystery is too **d**
Jn　6:60　teaching is **d**; who can accept it?"

DILIGENCE → DILIGENTLY
Ro　12: 8　the leader, in **d**;
Heb　6:11　each one of you to show the same **d**

DILIGENTLY → DILIGENCE
Dt　4: 6　You must observe them **d**,
Pr　8:17　and those who seek me **d** find me.

DINAH*
　Only daughter of Jacob, by Leah (Ge 30:21; 46:15). Raped by Shechem; avenged by Simeon and Levi (Ge 34).

DIRECT → DIRECTS
Ps 119:128 I **d** my steps by all your precepts;
2Th 3: 5 the Lord **d** your hearts to the love

DIRECTS → DIRECT
Pr 16: 9 but the LORD **d** the steps.
Jas 3: 4 wherever the will of the pilot **d**.

DISAPPOINT*
Ro 5: 5 and hope does not **d** us,

DISASTER
Ex 32:12 your mind and do not bring **d**
Dt 28:20 The LORD will send upon you **d**,
Jer 18: 8 I will change my mind about the **d**
Eze 7: 5 Thus says the Lord GOD: **D** after **d**!

DISCERNED → DISCERNMENT
1Co 2:14 because they are spiritually **d**.

DISCERNING → DISCERNMENT
Dt 4: 6 nation is a wise and **d** people!"
Pr 1: 5 in learning, and the **d** acquire skill,
1Co 1:19 discernment of the **d** I will thwart."
Sir 1:19 knowledge and **d** comprehension,

DISCERNMENT → DISCERNED, DISCERNING
1Ki 4:29 Solomon very great wisdom, **d**,
1Co 12:10 prophecy, to another the **d** of spirits,

DISCIPLE → DISCIPLES
Mt 10:24 "A **d** is not above the teacher,
Lk 14:26 even life itself, cannot be my **d**.

DISCIPLES → DISCIPLE
Isa 8:16 seal the teaching among my **d**.
Mt 26:56 all the **d** deserted him and fled.
  28:19 therefore and make **d** of all nations,
Lk 6:13 he called his **d** and chose twelve of
Jn 8:31 in my word, you are truly my **d**;
Ac 11:26 the **d** were first called "Christians."

DISCIPLINE → DISCIPLINED
Job 5:17 not despise the **d** of the Almighty.
Ps 94:12 Happy are those whom you **d**,
Pr 5:23 They die for lack of **d**,
Jer 7:28 their God, and did not accept **d**;
Eph 6: 4 in the **d** and instruction of the Lord.
Heb 12: 5 not regard lightly the **d** of the Lord,
1Pe 5: 8 **D** yourselves, keep alert.
Sir 1:27 fear of the Lord is wisdom and **d**,

DISCIPLINED → DISCIPLINE
1Co 11:32 **d** so that we may not be condemned
Wis 3: 5 Having been **d** a little, they will

DISEASE → DISEASES
Mt 4:23 of the kingdom and curing every **d**
  9:35 curing every **d** and every sickness.

DISEASES → DISEASE
Ex 15:26 **d** that I brought upon the Egyptians;
Ps 103: 3 your iniquity, who heals all your **d**,
Isa 53: 4 our infirmities and carried our **d**;
Mt 8:17 took our infirmities and bore our **d**."

DISGRACE
Jos 5: 9 I have rolled away from you the **d**
Pr 11: 2 When pride comes, then comes **d**;
Mt 1:19 unwilling to expose her to public **d**,
1Pe 4:16 do not consider it a **d**,
1Mc 4:58 the **d** brought by the Gentiles was

DISGUISES
2Co 11:14 Satan **d** himself as an angel of light.

DISHONEST
Jer 22:17 and heart are only on your **d** gain,
Lk 16:10 is **d** in a very little is **d** also in much.
Sir 5: 8 Do not depend on **d** wealth,

DISHONOR
Jn 8:49 I honor my Father, and you **d** me.
Ac 5:41 considered worthy to suffer **d** for
1Co 15:43 It is sown in **d**, it is raised in glory.

DISMAYED
Dt 1:21 do not fear or be **d**."

Jos 1: 9 do not be frightened or **d**,
Jer 17:18 them be **d**, but do not let me be **d**;

DISOBEDIENT → DISOBEY
Ne 9:26 they were **d** and rebelled
Ro 10:21 I have held out my hands to a **d**
  11:30 as you were once **d** to God but have
Tit 3: 3 ourselves were once foolish, **d**, led

DISOBEY → DISOBEDIENT
Lev 26:27 But if, despite this, you **d** me,
1Pe 2: 8 stumble because they **d** the word,
Sir 1:28 Do not **d** the fear of the Lord;

DISPERSION
Jn 7:35 Does he intend to go to the **D**

DISQUALIFIED* → DISQUALIFY
1Co 9:27 to others I myself should not be **d**.

DISQUALIFY* → DISQUALIFIED
Col 2:18 Do not let anyone **d** you,

DISSENSION → DISSENSIONS
1Co 12:25 there may be no **d** within the body,
1Ti 6: 4 From these come envy, **d**, slander,

DISSENSIONS → DISSENSION
Gal 5:20 strife, jealousy, anger, quarrels, **d**,
Tit 3: 9 stupid controversies, genealogies, **d**,

DISTINCTION → DISTINCTIONS
Ex 8:23 I will make a **d** between my people
Lev 11:47 make a **d** between the unclean and
Eze 22:26 have made no **d** between the holy
Ro 3:22 For there is no **d**,

DISTINCTIONS* → DISTINCTION
Jas 2: 4 you not made **d** among yourselves,

DISTRESS → DISTRESSED
Dt 4:30 In your **d**, when all these things
Jdg 2:15 and they were in great **d**.
2Sa 22: 7 In my **d** I called upon the LORD;
Ps 81: 7 In **d** you called, and I rescued you;
Jer 30: 7 it is a time of **d** for Jacob;
Lk 21:23 For there will be great **d** on the earth
Ro 8:35 Will hardship, or **d**, or persecution,
Sir 2:11 and saves in time of **d**.

DISTRESSED → DISTRESS
La 1:20 See, O LORD, how **d** I am;

DISTRIBUTED
Jos 13:32 the inheritances that Moses **d**
Ps 112: 9 They have **d** freely,
Ac 4:35 it was **d** to each as any had need.
Heb 2: 4 gifts of the Holy Spirit, **d** according

DIVIDE → DIVIDED
Ex 14:16 your hand over the sea and **d** it,
Ps 22:18 **d** my clothes among themselves,
Lk 23:34 And they cast lots to **d** his clothing.

DIVIDED → DIVIDE
Lev 11: 3 Any animal that has **d** hoofs
Ps 136:13 who **d** the Red Sea in two,
Lk 11:18 If Satan also is **d** against himself,

DIVINATION → DIVINE
Dt 18:10 who practices **d**, or is a soothsayer,
1Sa 15:23 For rebellion is no less a sin than **d**,
2Ki 17:17 they used **d** and augury;

DIVINE → DIVINATION
Ro 1:20 his eternal power and **d** nature,
2Pe 1: 4 become participants of the **d** nature.

DIVORCE → DIVORCED
Dt 24: 1 so he writes her a certificate of **d**,
Isa 50: 1 Where is your mother's bill of **d**
Jer 3: 8 sent her away with a decree of **d**;
Mal 2:16 For I hate **d**, says the LORD,
Mt 5:31 let him give her a certificate of **d**.'
  19: 3 a man to **d** his wife for any cause?"
1Co 7:11 the husband should not **d** his wife.
Sir 7:26 Do not **d** her;

DIVORCED → DIVORCE
Lev 21: 7 neither shall they marry a woman **d**
Mt 5:32 whoever marries a **d** woman

DOCTOR*
Lk 4:23 this proverb, '**D**, cure yourself!'

DOCTRINE → DOCTRINES
Eph 4:14 blown about by every wind of **d**,
1Ti 1: 3 not to teach any different **d**,
2Ti 4: 3 people will not put up with sound **d**,
Tit 1: 9 able both to preach with sound **d**

DOCTRINES → DOCTRINE
Mk 7: 7 teaching human precepts as **d**.'

DOEG*
  Edomite; Saul's chief shepherd; murdered 85 priests at Nob (1Sa 21:7; 22:6-23; Ps 52).

DOERS → DOES, DONE
Jas 1:22 But be **d** of the word,

DOES → DOERS
Ps 135: 6 Whatever the LORD pleases he **d**,
Ecc 3:14 whatever God **d** endures forever;
Mk 3:35 **d** the will of God is my brother

DOG → DOGS
Jdg 7: 5 as a **d** laps, you shall put to one side
Pr 26:11 Like a **d** that returns to its vomit
2Pe 2:22 "The **d** turns back to its own vomit,"

DOGS → DOG
Mt 7: 6 "Do not give what is holy to **d**;
  15:26 children's food and throw it to the **d**
Php 3: 2 Beware of the **d**, beware of the evil
Rev 22:15 Outside are the **d** and sorcerers

DOMINION
Ge 1:26 and let them have **d** over
Ps 22:28 For **d** belongs to the LORD,
Da 7:14 His **d** is an everlasting **d**
Ro 6:14 for sin will have no **d** over you,
Rev 1: 6 to him be glory and **d** forever

DONE → DOERS
Mt 6:10 Your will be **d**, on earth as it is in
  26:42 unless I drink it, your will be **d**."
Rev 16:17 from the throne, saying, "It is **d**!"
  21: 6 Then he said to me, "It is **d**!

DONKEY
Nu 22:30 But he **d** said to Balaam,
Jdg 15:15 he found a fresh jawbone of a **d**,
Zec 9: 9 humble and riding on a **d**,
Mt 21: 5 humble, and mounted on a **d**,

DOOM → DOOMED
Dt 32:35 their **d** comes swiftly.
Ps 81:15 and their **d** would last forever.

DOOMED → DOOM
Ps 102:20 to set free those who were **d** to die;
1Co 2: 6 of this age, who are **d** to perish.

DOOR → DOORPOSTS
Mt 7: 7 knock, and the **d** will be opened for
Lk 13:24 Strive to enter through the narrow **d**
Rev 3:20 I am standing at the **d**, knocking;

DOORPOSTS → DOOR
Ex 12: 7 the blood and put it on the two **d**

DORCAS*
  Disciple; raised from the dead (Ac 9:36-43).

DOUBLE → DOUBLE-TONGUED
Ex 22: 7 then the thief, if caught, shall pay **d**.
Dt 21:17 giving him a **d** portion of all that he
1Sa 1: 5 but to Hannah he gave a **d** portion,
2Ki 2: 9 me inherit a **d** share of your spirit."
Rev 18: 6 and repay her **d** for her deeds;

DOUBLE-TONGUED → DOUBLE, TONGUE
1Ti 3: 8 likewise must be serious, not **d**,
Sir 5:14 Do not be called **d** and do not

DOUBT → DOUBTED, DOUBTING
Mt 14:31 of little faith, why did you **d**?"
Jn 20:27 Do not **d** but believe."

DOUBTED* → DOUBT
Mt 28:17 they worshiped him; but some **d**.

DOUBTING* → DOUBT
Jas 1: 6 But ask in faith, never **d**,

DOUGH
Ex 12:39 **d** that they had brought out of Egypt
Gal 5: 9 yeast leavens the whole batch of **d**.

DOVE
Ge 8: 8 Then he sent out the **d** from him,
Mk 1:10 Spirit descending like a **d** on him.

DRAGON
Isa 27: 1 and he will kill the **d** that
Rev 12: 3 a great red **d**, with seven heads and
      20: 2 seized the **d**, that ancient serpent,
Bel 1:23 in that place there was a great **d**,

DRANK → DRINK
Ex 24:11 beheld God, and they ate and **d**.
Mk 14:23 and all of them **d** from it.
1Co 10: 4 and all **d** the same spiritual drink.

DRAW
Jn 12:32 will **d** all people to myself."
Jas 4: 8 **D** near to God, and he will **d** near

DREAM → DREAMED, DREAMER,
DREAMS
1Ki 3: 5 LORD appeared to Solomon in a **d**
Da 7: 1 Daniel had a **d** and visions of his
Joel 2:28 your old men shall **d** dreams,
Mt 1:20 of the Lord appeared to him in a **d**
Ac 2:17 and your old men shall **d** dreams.

DREAMED → DREAM
Ge 28:12 he **d** that there was a ladder set up
      41: 1 Pharaoh **d** that he was standing by
Da 2: 1 Nebuchadnezzar **d** such dreams
2Es 13: 1 After seven days I **d** a dream in the

DREAMER* → DREAM
Ge 37:19 to one another, "Here comes this **d**.

DREAMS → DREAM
Nu 12: 6 I speak to them in **d**.
1Sa 28: 6 LORD did not answer him, not by **d**,
Sir 34: 7 For **d** have deceived many,

DRIED → DRY
Ge 8:13 the waters were **d** up from the earth;
Jos 5: 1 had **d** up the waters of the Jordan
Isa 51:10 Was it not you who **d** up the sea,

DRINK → DRANK, DRUNK, DRUNKARD,
DRUNKENNESS
Ge 19:33 So they made their father **d** wine
Ex 32: 6 the people sat down to eat and **d**,
Ecc 9: 7 and **d** your wine with a merry heart;
Isa 22:13 eat and **d**, for tomorrow we die."
Mt 20:22 to **d** the cup that I am about to **d**?"
Jn 18:11 not to **d** the cup that the Father has
Ro 14:17 kingdom of God is not food and **d**
1Co 12:13 we were all made to **d** of one Spirit.
Rev 14:10 also **d** the wine of God's wrath,

DRIVE → DROVE
Ex 23:30 Little by little I will **d** them out
Nu 33:52 you shall **d** out all the inhabitants of
Jos 13:13 Yet the Israelites did not **d** out the
Mk 11:15 to **d** out those who were selling
Jn 6:37 comes to me I will never **d** away;

DROSS
Ps 119:119 wicked of the earth you count as **d**;
Isa 1:25 I will smelt away your **d** as with lye
Eze 22:18 house of Israel has become **d** to me;

DROVE → DRIVE
Jos 24:18 the LORD **d** out before us all the
Mk 1:12 Spirit immediately **d** him out into

DRUNK → DRINK
Ge 9:21 some of the wine and became **d**,
1Sa 1:13 therefore Eli thought she was **d**.
SS 5: 1 drink, and be **d** with love.
Jn 2:10 after the guests have become **d**.
Ac 2:15 these are not **d**, as you suppose,
Eph 5:18 Do not get **d** with wine,
Jdt 13: 2 on his bed, for he was dead **d**.

DRUNKARD → DRINK
Pr 23:21 for the **d** and the glutton will come
Mt 11:19 they say, 'Look, a glutton and a **d**,
1Co 5:11 is an idolater, reviler, **d**, or robber.
1Ti 3: 3 not a **d**, not violent but gentle,

DRUNKENNESS → DRINK
Ecc 10:17 for strength, and not for **d**!
Gal 5:21 **d**, carousing, and things like these.
Tob 4:15 to excess or let **d** go with you

DRY → DRIED
Ge 1: 9 and let the **d** land appear."
Ex 14:16 may go into the sea on **d** ground,
Jos 3:17 were crossing over on **d** ground,
Jdg 6:37 and it is **d** on all the ground,
Eze 37: 4 **d** bones, hear the word of the LORD.

DUE
1Ch 16:29 Ascribe to the LORD the glory **d** his
Ps 28: 4 render them their **d** reward.
Mal 1: 6 a father, where is the honor **d** me?
Ro 13: 7 Pay to all what is **d** them—

DULL
Isa 6:10 Make the mind of this people **d**,
      59: 1 nor his ear too **d** to hear.
Mt 13:15 For this people's heart has grown **d**,

DUST
Ge 2: 7 LORD God formed man from the **d**
      3:14 and **d** you shall eat all the days of
      3:16 offspring like the **d** of the earth;
1Sa 2: 8 He raises up the poor from the **d**;
Ps 103:14 he remembers that we are **d**.
Ecc 3:20 from the **d**, and all turn to **d** again.
Na 1: 3 and the clouds are the **d** of his feet.
Mt 10:14 shake off the **d** from your feet
1Co 15:47 man was from the earth, a man of **d**;

DWELL → DWELLING, DWELLS
Ex 25: 8 so that I may **d** among them.
1Ki 8:27 But will God indeed **d** on the earth?
Ps 23: 6 and I shall **d** in the house of
Eph 3:17 that Christ may **d** in your hearts
Col 1:19 fullness of God was pleased to **d**,
Rev 21: 3 He will **d** with them as their God;

DWELLING → DWELL
Lev 26:11 I will place my **d** in your midst,
Dt 12:11 will choose as a **d** for his name:
Ps 90: 1 our **d** place in all generations.
Jn 14: 2 my Father's house there are many **d**
2Co 5: 2 to be clothed with our heavenly **d**—
Eph 2:22 spiritually into a **d** place for God.

DWELLS → DWELL
Jn 14:10 but the Father who **d** in me
Ro 7:17 but sin that **d** within me.
1Co 3:16 and that God's Spirit **d** in you?
Col 2: 9 the whole fullness of deity **d** bodily,

DYING → DEAD
2Co 6: 9 as **d**, and see—we are alive;
Php 1:21 living is Christ and **d** is gain.

E

EAGLE → EAGLES, EAGLES'
Eze 1:10 the left side, and the face of an **e**;
      17: 3 A great **e**, with great wings and long
Rev 4: 7 fourth living creature like a flying **e**.
2Es 11: 1 an **e** that had twelve feathered wings

EAGLES → EAGLE
Isa 40:31 shall mount up with wings like **e**,

EAGLES' → EAGLE
Ex 19: 4 and how I bore you on **e** wings
Da 7: 4 like a lion and had **e** wings.

EAR → EARS
Isa 64: 4 has heard, no **e** has perceived,
Lk 22:51 he touched his **e** and healed him.
1Co 2: 9 "What no eye has seen, nor **e** heard,
Rev 2: 7 Let anyone who has an **e** listen

EARLY
Dt 11:14 the **e** rain and the later rain,
Lk 24:22 were at the tomb **e** this morning,
Jas 5: 7 receives the **e** and the late rains.

EARS → EAR
Dt 29: 4 or eyes to see, or **e** to hear.
Isa 35: 5 and the **e** of the deaf unstopped;
Mt 11:15 Let anyone with **e** listen!
2Ti 4: 3 sound doctrine, but having
            itching **e**,

EARTH → EARTHLY, EARTHQUAKE,
EARTHQUAKES
Ge 1: 1 God created the heavens and the **e**,
      6:11 the **e** was corrupt in God's sight,
Ex 19: 5 Indeed, the whole **e** is mine,
Ps 47: 2 a great king over all the **e**.
Isa 6: 3 the whole **e** is full of his glory."
      65:17 to create new heavens and a new **e**;
Jer 23:24 Do I not fill heaven and **e**?
Mt 5: 5 the meek, for they will inherit the **e**.
      24:35 Heaven and **e** will pass away,
Lk 5:24 has authority on **e** to forgive sins"—
2Pe 3:13 wait for new heavens and a new **e**,
Rev 21: 1 I saw a new heaven and a new **e**;
Sir 40:11 All that is of **e** returns to **e**,

EARTHLY → EARTH
Jn 3:12 If I have told you about **e** things
2Co 5: 1 if the **e** tent we live in is destroyed,

EARTHQUAKE → EARTH, QUAKE
1Ki 19:11 but the LORD was not in the **e**;
Mt 28: 2 And suddenly there was a great **e**;
Ac 16:26 Suddenly there was an **e**,
Rev 6:12 I looked, and there came a great **e**;
2Es 3:19 four gates of fire and wind

EARTHQUAKES → EARTH, QUAKE
Mt 24: 7 be famines and **e** in various places:
2Es 9: 3 there shall appear in the world **e**,

EASIER → EASY
Mt 9: 5 is **e**, to say, 'Your sins are forgiven,'
Lk 16:17 it is **e** for heaven and earth to pass
      18:25 **e** for a camel to go through the eye

EAST
Ge 2: 8 planted a garden in Eden, in the **e**;
Ps 103:12 as far as the **e** is from the west,
Mt 2: 1 wise men from the **E** came to

EASY → EASIER
Mt 7:13 road is **e** that leads to destruction,
      11:30 For my yoke is **e**, and my burden is

EAT → ATE, EATING, EATS
Ge 2:16 freely **e** of every tree of the garden;
Ex 12:11 This is how you shall **e** it:
Lev 3:17 not **e** any fat or any blood.
      11: 4 you shall not **e** the following:
Ecc 2:24 nothing better for mortals than to **e**
Mt 26:26 to the disciples, and said, "Take, **e**;
Ac 10:13 "Get up, Peter; kill and **e**."
1Co 10:31 whether you **e** or drink, or whatever
Rev 3:20 I will come in to you and **e** with you

EATING → EAT
Lk 7:34 the Son of Man has come and **e** and
Ro 14: 2 Some believe in **e** anything,
1Co 8: 4 as to the **e** of food offered to idols,

EATS → EAT
Jn 6:51 **e** of this bread will live forever;
1Co 11:27 **e** the bread or drinks the cup of the

EDEN
Ge	2: 8	a garden in **E**, in the east;
Isa	51: 3	and will make her wilderness like **E**,
Eze	28:13	You were in **E**, the garden of God;

EDOM → =ESAU
Ge	25:30	(Therefore he was called **E**.)
Nu	20:18	But **E** said to him, "You shall not
Ob	1: 1	says the Lord GOD concerning **E**:
Mal	1: 4	If **E** says, "We are shattered but we

EFFORT
Gal	2:17	in our **e** to be justified in Christ,
Eph	4: 3	every **e** to maintain the unity of the
Heb	4:11	make every **e** to enter that rest,
2Pe	1: 5	make every **e** to support your faith

EGYPT
Ge	12:10	So Abram went down to **E** to reside
	37:28	And they took Joseph to **E**.
	47:27	Thus Israel settled in the land of **E**,
Ex	1: 8	Now a new king arose over **E**,
	12:40	in **E** was four hundred thirty years.
Jos	15:47	to the Wadi of **E**, and the Great Sea
Ne	9:18	God who brought you up out of **E**,'
Ps	78:51	He struck all the firstborn in **E**,
Hos	11: 1	and out of **E** I called my son.
Mt	2:15	"Out of **E** I have called my son."
Rev	11: 8	prophetically called Sodom and **E**,

EHUD
Judge of Israel (Jdg 3:12-30).

ELAH
1. Son of Baasha; king of Israel (1Ki 16:6-14).
2. Valley in which David fought Goliath (1Sa 17:2, 19; 21:9).

ELDER → ELDERS
Ge	25:23	the **e** shall serve the younger."
Ro	9:12	"The **e** shall serve the younger."
1Ti	5:19	any accusation against an **e** except
1Pe	5: 1	as an **e** myself and a witness of the

ELDERS → ELDER
Ex	24: 1	and seventy of the **e** of Israel,
Jdg	2: 7	days of the **e** who outlived Joshua,
Isa	3:14	enters into judgment with the **e**
Mt	27:12	accused by the chief priests and **e**,
Mk	7: 3	thus observing the tradition of the **e**;
1Ti	5:17	the **e** who rule well be considered
Jas	5:14	**e** of the church and have them pray
1Pe	5: 5	must accept the authority of the **e**.
Rev	4: 4	on the thrones are twenty-four **e**,
Sus	1:61	they took action against the two **e**,

ELEAZAR
1. Third son of Aaron (Ex 6:23-25). Succeeded Aaron as high priest (Nu 20:26; Dt 10:6). Allotted land to tribes (Jos 14:1). Death (Jos 24:33).
2. Brother of Judas Maccabeus (1Mc 2:5; 6:43-46).

ELECT → ELECTION
Mt	24:22	sake of the **e** those days will be cut
Mk	13:22	to lead astray, if possible, the **e**.
Wis	3:14	grace and mercy are with his **e**,
2Es	16:73	Then the tested quality of my **e**

ELECTION* → ELECT
Ro	9:11	God's purpose of **e** might continue,
	11:28	but as regards **e** they are beloved,
2Pe	1:10	eager to confirm your call and **e**,

ELEMENTS
Heb	5:12	the basic **e** of the oracles of God.
2Pe	3:10	and the **e** will be dissolved with fire,

ELEVEN
Mt	28:16	Now the **e** disciples went to Galilee,
Ac	1:26	and he was added to the **e** apostles.

ELI
1. High priest in youth of Samuel (1Sa 1-4). Blessed Hannah (1Sa 1:12-18); raised Samuel (1Sa 2:11-26). Prophesied against because of wicked sons (1Sa 2:27-36). Death of Eli and sons (1Sa 4:11-22).
2. "Eli, Eli, lema sabachthani?" (Mt 27:46).

ELIAKIM → =JEHOIAKIM
1. Original name of Jehoiakim (2Ki 23:34; 2Ch 36:4).
2. Hezekiah's palace administrator (2Ki 18:17-37; 19:2; Isa 36:1-22; 37:2).

ELIEZER
1. Servant of Abraham (Ge 15:2).
2. Son of Moses (Ex 18:4; 1Ch 23:15-17).

ELIHU
A friend of Job (Job 32-37).

ELIJAH
Prophet; predicted famine in Israel (1Ki 17:1; Jas 5:17). Fed by ravens (1Ki 17:2-6). Raised Sidonian widow's son (1Ki 17:7-24). Defeated prophets of Baal at Carmel (1Ki 18:16-46). Ran from Jezebel (1Ki 19:1-9). Prophesied death of Azariah (2Ki 1). Succeeded by Elishah (1Ki 19:19-21; 2Ki 2:1-18). Taken to heaven in whirlwind (2Ki 2:11-12; Sir 48:1-12; 1Mc 2:58).
Return prophesied (Mal 4:5-6); equated with John the Baptist (Mt 17:9-13; Mk 9:9-13; Lk 1:17). Appeared with Moses in transfiguration of Jesus (Mt 17:1-8; Mk 9:1-8).

ELIMELECH
Ru	1: 3	But **E**, the husband of Naomi, died,

ELIPHAZ
A friend of Job (Job 4-5; 15; 22; 42:7, 9).

ELISHA
Prophet; successor of Elijah (1Ki 19:16-21; Sir 48:12-14); inherited his mantle (2Ki 2:1-18). Purified bad water (2Ki 2:19-22). Cursed young men (2Ki 2:23-25). Aided Israel's defeat of Moab (2Ki 3). Provided widow with oil (2Ki 4:1-7). Raised Shunammite woman's son (2Ki 4:8-37). Purified food (2Ki 4:38-41). Fed 100 men (2Ki 4:42-44). Healed Naaman's leprosy (2Ki 5). Made axhead float (2Ki 6:1-7). Captured Arameans (2Ki 6:8-23). Political adviser to Israel (2Ki 6:24-8:6; 9:1-3; 13:14-19), Aram (2Ki 8:7-15). Death (2Ki 13:20).

ELIZABETH*
Mother of John the Baptist (Lk 1:5-58).

ELKANAH
Husband of Hannah, father of Samuel (1Sa 1-2).

EMMANUEL* → =IMMANUEL
Mt	1:23	and they shall name him **E**,"

EMMAUS
Lk	24:13	were going to a village called **E**,

EMPEROR
Mt	22:17	Is it lawful to pay taxes to the **e**, or
Jn	19:12	you are no friend of the **e**.

EMPTIED → EMPTY
1Co	1:17	cross of Christ might not be **e** of its
Php	2: 7	but **e** himself, taking the form of

EMPTY → EMPTIED, EMPTY-HANDED
Ru	1:21	the LORD has brought me back **e**;
Isa	55:11	it shall not return to me **e**,
Mt	6: 7	do not heap up **e** phrases
Eph	5: 6	no one deceive you with **e** words,

EMPTY-HANDED → EMPTY, HAND
Ex	23:15	No one shall appear before me **e**.
Ru	3:17	not go back to your mother-in-law **e**."

EN-GEDI
1Sa	23:29	and lived in the strongholds of **E**.

ENCOURAGE → ENCOURAGEMENT
1Th	4:18	**e** one another with these words.
1Pe	5:12	written this short letter to **e** you

ENCOURAGEMENT → ENCOURAGE
Ac	4:36	Barnabas (which means "son of **e**").
Ro	15: 5	God of steadfastness and **e** grant
Php	2: 1	If then there is any **e** in Christ,

END → ENDS
Ge	6:13	determined to make an **e** of all flesh,
Pr	14:12	but its **e** is the way to death.
Ecc	12:12	making many books there is no **e**,
Mt	24:13	But the one who endures to the **e**
	28:20	always, to the **e** of the age."
Jn	13: 1	he loved them to the **e**.
Ro	10: 4	For Christ is the **e** of the law so that
Rev	22:13	the beginning and the **e**."

ENDOR*
1Sa	28: 7	"There is a medium at **E**."

ENDS → END
Ps	2: 8	the **e** of the earth your possession.
Isa	40:28	the Creator of the **e** of the earth.
Ro	10:18	their words to the **e** of the world."
1Co	13: 8	Love never **e**. But as for prophecies,

ENDURANCE → ENDURE
Lk	8:15	and bear fruit with patient **e**.
Ro	5: 3	knowing that suffering produces **e**,
1Ti	6:11	godliness, faith, love, **e**,
Heb	10:36	For you need **e**, so that when you
Jas	1: 3	the testing of your faith produces **e**;
2Pe	1: 6	and self-control with **e**, and **e** with
Rev	1: 9	and the kingdom and the patient **e**,

ENDURE → ENDURANCE, ENDURED, ENDURES
Ps	89:29	his throne as long as the heavens **e**.
Mal	3: 2	who can **e** the day of his coming,
1Co	10:13	out so that you may be able to **e** it.
2Ti	2:12	if we **e**, we will also reign with him;

ENDURED → ENDURE
Heb	12: 2	that was set before him **e** the cross,

ENDURES → ENDURE
1Ch	16:41	for his steadfast love **e** forever.
Mt	13:21	but **e** only for a while,
Jn	6:27	for the food that **e** for eternal life,
1Co	13: 7	hopes all things, **e** all things.
1Pe	1:25	but the word of the Lord **e** forever."
Sir	40:17	and almsgiving **e** forever.
Bar	4: 1	the law that **e** forever.

ENEMIES → ENEMY
Ex	23:22	be an enemy to your **e** and a foe to
Est	9: 5	the Jews struck down all their **e**
Ps	110: 1	until I make your **e** your footstool."
Mt	5:44	But I say to you, Love your **e** and
Lk	20:43	until I make your **e** your footstool."
Ro	5:10	For if while we were **e**,
	12:20	"if your **e** are hungry, feed them;
Jdt	8:35	to take vengeance on our **e**."
1Mc	4:36	said, "See, our **e** are crushed;

ENEMY → ENEMIES, ENMITY
Mt	13:39	the **e** who sowed them is the devil;
1Co	15:26	The last **e** to be destroyed is death.
Jas	4: 4	of the world becomes an **e** of God.

ENGAGED
Mt	1:18	mother Mary had been **e** to Joseph,

ENJOY → ENJOYMENT
Ecc	3:22	that all should **e** their work,
	9: 9	**E** life with the wife whom you love,

ENJOYMENT → ENJOY
Ecc	8:15	So I commend **e**, for there is nothing
1Ti	6:17	with everything for our **e**.

ENLIGHTENED → LIGHT
Ro	10: 2	have a zeal for God, but it is not **e**.
Eph	1:18	with the eyes of your heart **e**,
Heb	6: 4	those who have once been **e**,

ENLIGHTENS* → LIGHT
Jn	1: 9	The true light, which **e** everyone,

ENMITY → ENEMY
Ge   3:15   put e between you and the woman,
Jas   4: 4   with the world is e with God?

ENOCH
   Walked with God and taken by him (Ge 5:18-24; Heb 11:5; Sir 44:16). Prophet (Jude 14).

ENSLAVE → SLAVE
1Co   9:27   but I punish my body and e it,
Gal   2: 4   so that they might e us—

ENSLAVED → SLAVE
Ro   6: 6   and we might no longer be e to sin.
Gal   4: 9   want to be e to them again?

ENTER → ENTRY
Ex   40:35   Moses was not able to e the tent
Nu   20:24   not e the land that I have given to
Ps   95:11   I swore, "They shall not e my rest."
Mt   5:20   will never e the kingdom of heaven.
      7:13   "E through the narrow gate;
Mk   10:15   as a little child will never e it."
Jn   3: 5   no one can e the kingdom of God
Heb   3:11   "They will not e my rest.'"
      10:19   have confidence to e the sanctuary
Rev   21:27   But nothing unclean will e it,

ENTHRONED → THRONE
1Ch   13: 6   the LORD, who is e on the cherubim,
Ps   9: 7   But the LORD sits e forever,

ENTRUST → TRUST
Jn   2:24   Jesus on his part would not e
1Pe   4:19   e themselves to a faithful Creator,

ENTRUSTED → TRUST
Lk   12:48   the one to whom much has been e,
2Ti   1:12   guard until that day what I have e to
Jude   1: 3   the faith that was once for all e to

ENVY
Pr   23:17   Do not let your heart e sinners,
Mk   7:22   deceit, licentiousness, e, slander,
Ro   1:29   Full of e, murder, strife, deceit,
Jas   3:16   For where there is e and selfish

EPHOD
Ex   28: 6   They shall make the e of gold,
Jdg   8:27   Gideon made an e of it and put it in

EPHRAIM
   1. Second son of Joseph (Ge 41:52; 46:20). Blessed as firstborn by Jacob (Ge 48). Tribe of numbered (Nu 1:33; 26:37), blessed (Dt 33:17), allotted land (Jos 16:4-9; Eze 48:5), failed to fully possess (Jos 16:10; Jdg 1:29).
   2. Term for the Northern Kingdom (Isa 7:17; Hos 5).

EQUAL → EQUALITY
Isa   40:25   you compare me, or who is my e?
      46: 5   will you liken me and make me e,
Jn   5:18   thereby making himself e to God.

EQUALITY* → EQUAL
Php   2: 6   not regard e with God as something

ERROR
Lev   5:18   for the e that you committed
Ro   1:27   the due penalty for their e.
1Jn   4: 6   the spirit of truth and the spirit of e.
Wis   1:12   Do not invite death by the e of your

ESAU → =EDOM
   Firstborn of Isaac, twin of Jacob (Ge 25:21-26). Also called Edom (Ge 25:30). Sold Jacob his birthright (Ge 25:29-34); lost blessing (Gen 27). Married Hittites (Ge 26:34), Ishmaelites (Ge 28:6-9). Reconciled to Jacob (Gen 33). Genealogy (Ge 36). The LORD chose Jacob over Esau (Mal 1:2-3), but gave Esau land (Dt 2:2-12). Descendants eventually obliterated (Ob 1-21; Jer 49:7-22).

ESCAPE
Ge   7: 7   went into the ark to e the waters of
Ps   68:20   the Lord, belongs e from death.
Ro   2: 3   you will e the judgment of God?

1Th   5: 3   and there will be no e!
Heb   12:25   how much less will we e if we reject
2Pe   1: 4   you may e from the corruption

ESTABLISH → ESTABLISHED
Ge   6:18   But I will e my covenant with you;
Dt   28: 9   LORD will e you as his holy people,
Ps   89: 4   'I will e your descendants forever,
Eze   16:60   e with you an everlasting covenant.
Ro   10: 3   and seeking to e their own,
Heb   8: 8   when I will e a new covenant with

ESTABLISHED → ESTABLISH
2Sa   7:16   your throne shall be e forever.
Ps   89: 2   your steadfast love is e forever;
      103:19   The LORD has e his throne in the
Jer   10:12   who e the world by his wisdom,
2Pe   1:12   you know them already and are e in

ESTHER
   Jewess, originally named Hadassah, who lived in Persia; cousin of Mordecai (Est 2:7). Chosen queen of Xerxes (Est 2:8-18). Persuaded by Mordecai to foil Haman's plan to exterminate the Jews (Est 3-4). Revealed Haman's plans to Xerxes, resulting in Haman's death (Est 7), the Jews' preservation (Est 8-9), Mordecai's exaltation (Est 8:15; 9:4; 10). Decreed celebration of Purim (Est 9:18-32). See Additions to Esther.

ETERNAL → ETERNITY
Mt   25:46   but the righteous into e life."
Mk   10:17   what must I do to inherit e life?"
Jn   3:16   may not perish but may have e life.
      10:28   I give them e life, and they will
Ro   5:21   e life through Jesus Christ our Lord.
2Co   4:17   an e weight of glory beyond all
Heb   5: 9   the source of e salvation for all who
1Jn   5:13   may know that you have e life.

ETERNITY → ETERNAL
Isa   57:15   high and lofty one who inhabits e,
2Pe   3:18   glory both now and to the day of e.
Wis   2:23   made us in the image of his own e,
Sir   42:21   he is from all e one and the same.

ETHIOPIANS
Jer   13:23   Can E change their skin

EUNUCH → EUNUCHS
Jer   38: 7   Ebed-melech the Ethiopian, a e
Ac   8:27   Now there was an Ethiopian e,

EUNUCHS → EUNUCH
Isa   56: 4   To the e who keep my sabbaths,
Mt   19:12   made themselves e for the sake of the

EUPHRATES
Ge   2:14   And the fourth river is the E.
      15:18   Egypt to the great river, the river E,
Rev   16:12   poured his bowl on the great river E

EUTYCHUS*
Ac   20: 9   A young man named E,

EVANGELIST* → EVANGELISTS
Ac   21: 8   went into the house of Philip the e,
2Ti   4: 5   do the work of an e, carry out your

EVANGELISTS* → EVANGELIST
Eph   4:11   some e, some pastors and teachers,

EVE*
Ge   3:20   The man named his wife E,
      4: 1   Now the man knew his wife E,
2Co   11: 3   afraid that as the serpent deceived E
1Ti   2:13   For Adam was formed first, then E;
Tob   8: 6   his wife E as a helper and support.

EVENING
Ge   1: 5   there was e and there was morning,
Ecc   11: 6   at e do not let your hands be idle;
Zec   14: 7   for at e time there shall be light.

EVERLASTING → LAST
Ge   9:16   remember the e covenant between
Ps   90: 2   from e to e you are God.

Isa   9: 6   God, E Father, Prince of Peace.
      40:28   The LORD is the e God,
Jer   31: 3   I have loved you with an e love;
Da   4: 3   His kingdom is an e kingdom,

EVERY → EVERYTHING
Ge   7:23   He blotted out e living thing that
Ex   11: 5   E firstborn in the land of Egypt
Dt   8: 3   e word that comes from the mouth
Ecc   12:14   God will bring e deed into judgment
Isa   45:23   "To me e knee shall bow,
Mt   12:25   "E kingdom divided against itself
Ro   14:11   e knee shall bow to me, and e tongue
Php   2:10   at the name of Jesus e knee should
2Ti   3:17   equipped for e good work.
1Jn   4: 1   Beloved, do not believe e spirit,
Rev   21: 4   he will wipe e tear from their eyes.

EVERYTHING → EVERY
Ge   1:31   God saw e that he had made,
Ex   19: 8   "E that the LORD has spoken we will
Ecc   3: 1   For e there is a season,
1Co   10:31   do e for the glory of God.
1Ti   4: 4   For e created by God is good,
2Pe   1: 3   divine power has given us e needed

EVIDENCE
Dt   17: 6   On the e of two or three witnesses
Mt   18:16   by the e of two or three witnesses.
Sus   1:43   men have given false e against me.

EVIL → EVILDOER, EVILDOERS
Ge   2: 9   tree of the knowledge of good and e.
      3: 5   be like God, knowing good and e."
      6: 5   their hearts was only e continually.
Ex   32:22   the people, that they are bent on e.
Dt   13: 5   So you shall purge the e from your
Jdg   2:11   Then the Israelites did what was e
Ps   23: 4   the darkest valley, I fear no e;
Pr   8:13   The fear of the LORD is hatred of e.
Ecc   12:14   secret thing, whether good or e.
Isa   5:20   you who call e good and good e,
Mt   6:13   but rescue us from the e one.
      12:35   e person brings e things out of an e
Lk   11:13   who are e, know how to give good
Jn   17:15   to protect them from the e one.
Ro   12:17   Do not repay anyone e for e,
Eph   5:16   of the time, because the days are e.
1Ti   6:10   of money is a root of all kinds of e,
1Pe   2:16   use your freedom as a pretext for e.
1Jn   5:18   and the e one does not touch them.
2Jn   1:11   to welcome is to participate in the e
3Jn   1:11   do not imitate what is e but imitate
Tob   12: 7   Do good and e will not overtake
Sir   7: 1   Do no e, and e will never overtake

EVILDOER → EVIL
Ps   52: 6   and will laugh at the e, saying,
Mt   5:39   But I say to you, Do not resist an e.

EVILDOERS → EVIL
2Sa   7:10   and e shall afflict them no more,
Ps   34:16   The face of the LORD is against e,
Lk   13:27   go away from me, all you e!'
1Pe   2:12   though they malign you as e,

EXALT → EXALTED, EXALTS
Ex   15: 2   my father's God, and I will e him.
Pr   4: 8   Prize her highly, and she will e you;
Isa   25: 1   I will e you, I will praise your name;
Lk   14:11   who e themselves will be humbled,
Jas   4:10   before the Lord, and he will e you.

EXALTED → EXALT
Ps   57: 5   Be e, O God, above the heavens.
      97: 9   you are e far above all gods.
Isa   2:11   the LORD alone will be e in that day.
Php   2: 9   highly e him and gave him the name

EXALTS → EXALT
Pr   14:34   Righteousness e a nation,
Sir   7:11   for there is One who humbles and e.

EXAMINE
1Co   11:28   E yourselves, and only then eat of

EXAMINE (cont.)
2Co 13: 5 **E** yourselves to see whether you
Sir 18:20 Before judgment comes, **e** yourself;

EXAMPLE → EXAMPLES
Jn 13:15 For I have set you an **e**,
Php 3:17 according to the **e** you have in us.

EXAMPLES → EXAMPLE
1Co 10: 6 these things occurred as **e** for us,
1Pe 5: 3 but be **e** to the flock.

EXCEL → EXCELLENCE, EXCELLENT
1Co 14:12 strive to **e** in them for building up
Sir 33:23 **E** in all that you do;

EXCELLENCE → EXCEL
Php 4: 8 if there is any **e** and if there is

EXCELLENT → EXCEL
Isa 28:29 in counsel, and **e** in wisdom.
1Co 12:31 I will show you a still more **e** way.
Heb 1: 4 the name he has inherited is more **e**

EXCEPT
2Sa 22:32 And who is a rock, **e** our God?
Mt 11:27 no one knows the Son **e** the Father,
Lk 11:29 be given to it **e** the sign of Jonah.
Jn 14: 6 No one comes to the Father **e**

EXCHANGED
Ps 106:20 They **e** the glory of God for the
Ro 1:23 **e** the glory of the immortal God

EXCUSE
Jn 15:22 but now they have no **e** for their sin.
Ro 1:20 So they are without **e**;

EXHORT
Tit 2:15 **e** and reprove with all authority.
Heb 3:13 But **e** one another every day,

EXILE → EXILES
2Ki 25:11 carried into **e** the rest of the people
Ezr 6:21 of Israel who had returned from **e**,

EXILES → EXILE
1Pe 2:11 I urge you as aliens and **e**

EXIST → EXISTED, EXISTS
1Co 8: 6 are all things and for whom we **e**,
Heb 2:10 and through whom all things **e**,

EXISTED → EXIST
2Pe 3: 5 the word of God heavens **e** long ago
Rev 4:11 by your will they **e** and were created

EXISTS → EXIST
Ps 119:89 The LORD **e** forever;
Heb 11: 6 that he **e** and that he rewards those

EXPECTING
Lk 6:35 and lend, **e** nothing in return.
Php 3:20 that we are **e** a Savior,

EXPLAIN → EXPLAINED, EXPLAINING
2Ch 9: 2 Solomon that he could not **e** to her.
Da 5:12 to interpret dreams, **e** riddles,

EXPLAINED → EXPLAIN
Mk 4:34 but he **e** everything in private to his

EXPLAINING → EXPLAIN
2Ti 2:15 rightly **e** the word of truth.

EXPOSE → EXPOSED
Mt 1:19 unwilling to **e** her to public disgrace
Eph 5:11 of darkness, but instead **e** them.

EXPOSED → EXPOSE
Jn 3:20 so that their deeds may not be **e**.
Eph 5:13 everything **e** by the light becomes
Heb 10:33 sometimes being publicly **e** to abuse

EYE → EYES, EYEWITNESSES
Ex 21:24 **e** for **e**, tooth for tooth,
Ps 17: 8 Guard me as the apple of the **e**;
Mt 5:29 If your right **e** causes you to sin,
5:38 An **e** for an **e** and a tooth for a tooth.
7: 3 see the speck in your neighbor's **e**,
Mk 10:25 to go through the **e** of a needle

1Co 15:52 in the twinkling of an **e**, at the last
Rev 1: 7 the clouds; every **e** will see him,

EYES → EYE
Ge 3: 7 Then the **e** of both were opened,
Dt 29: 4 or **e** to see, or ears to hear.
2Ch 16: 9 **e** of the LORD range throughout the
Ps 121: 1 I lift up my **e** to the hills—
Pr 3: 7 Do not be wise in your own **e**;
22:12 The **e** of the LORD keep watch over
Isa 11: 3 He shall not judge by what his **e** see,
Jer 9: 1 and my **e** a fountain of tears,
Eze 1:18 rims of all four were full of **e** all
Da 10: 6 lightning, his **e** like flaming torches,
Zec 4:10 "These seven are the **e** of the LORD,
Mt 9:30 And their **e** were opened.
13:15 that they might not look with their **e**,
Lk 24:31 their **e** were opened, and they
Eph 1:18 with the **e** of your heart enlightened,
1Pe 3:12 **e** of the Lord are on the righteous,
1Jn 2:16 of the flesh, the desire of the **e**,
Rev 1:14 his **e** were like a flame of fire,
4: 6 full of **e** in front and behind:
21: 4 he will wipe every tear from their **e**.

EYEWITNESSES* → EYE, WITNESS
Lk 1: 2 who from the beginning were **e**
2Pe 1:16 but we had been **e** of his majesty.

EZEKIEL
Priest called to be prophet to the exiles (Eze 1-3; Sir 49:8). Symbolically acted out destruction of Jerusalem (Eze 4-5; 12; 24).

EZRA
Priest and teacher of the Law who led a return of exiles to Israel to reestablish temple and worship (Ezr 7-8). Corrected intermarriage of priests (Ezr 9-10; 1Es 8-9). Read Law at celebration of Feast of Tabernacles (Ne 8; 1Es 9:37-55). Participated in dedication of Jerusalem's walls (Ne 12).

F

FACE → FACES
Ge 1: 2 darkness covered the **f** of the deep,
32:30 saying, "For I have seen God **f** to **f**,
Ex 3: 6 Moses hid his **f**, for he was afraid to
34:30 the skin of his **f** was shining,
Nu 6:25 LORD make his **f** to shine upon you,
12: 8 With him I speak **f** to **f**—
Ps 4: 6 Let the light of your **f** shine on us,
Isa 54: 8 wrath for a moment I hid my **f**
Eze 39:29 I will never again hide my **f** from
Lk 9:29 the appearance of his **f** changed,
2Co 3: 7 not gaze at Moses' **f** because of the glory
Rev 1:16 his **f** was like the sun shining with

FACES → FACE
Eze 1: 6 Each had four **f**, and each
2Co 3:18 And all of us, with unveiled **f**,
Rev 9: 7 their **f** were like human **f**,

FACTIONS*
1Co 11:19 there have to be **f** among you,
Gal 5:20 anger, quarrels, dissensions, **f**,

FADE → FADES
Ps 37: 2 for they will soon **f** like the grass,
Isa 64: 6 We all **f** like a leaf,

FADES → FADE
Isa 40: 7 The grass withers, the flower **f**,
1Pe 5: 4 crown of glory that never **f** away.

FAIL → FAILED
Dt 31: 6 he will not **f** you or forsake you."
Jos 1: 5 I will not **f** you or forsake you.
Eze 47:12 will not wither nor their fruit **f**,
Mk 8:18 Do you have eyes, and **f** to see?

FAILED → FAIL
Jos 23:14 pass for you, not one of them has **f**.

1Ki 8:56 not one word has **f** of all his good
Ro 9: 6 not as though the word of God had **f**

FAINT
Ps 142: 3 When my spirit is **f**, you know my
Isa 40:31 they shall walk and not **f**.

FAITH → FAITHFUL, FAITHFULNESS, FAITHLESS
Ps 146: 6 in them; who keeps **f** forever;
Isa 7: 9 If you do not stand firm in **f**,
Hab 2: 4 but the righteous live by their **f**.
Mt 17:20 have **f** the size of a mustard seed,
Mk 2: 5 When Jesus saw their **f**, he said to
Lk 7:50 the woman, "Your **f** has saved you;
18: 8 comes, will he find **f** on earth?"
Ac 3:16 and the **f** that is through Jesus
Ro 1:17 one who is righteous will live by **f**."
3:28 that a person is justified by **f** apart
1Co 13:13 And now **f**, hope, and love abide,
Gal 3:11 one who is righteous will live by **f**."
Eph 4: 5 one Lord, one **f**, one baptism,
Php 3: 9 righteousness from God based on **f**.
1Ti 6:11 pursue righteousness, godliness, **f**,
2Ti 4: 7 finished the race, I have kept the **f**.
Heb 11: 1 **f** is the assurance of things hoped
12: 2 the pioneer and perfecter of our **f**,
Jas 2:17 **f** by itself, if it has no works, is dead
2Pe 1: 1 a **f** as precious as ours through the
1Jn 5: 4 that conquers the world, our **f**.
Jude 1: 3 the **f** that was once for all entrusted
Rev 2:13 and you did not deny your **f** in me
Sir 40:12 but good **f** will last forever.

FAITHFUL → FAITH
Dt 32: 4 A **f** God, without deceit, just and
Ps 4: 3 LORD has set apart the **f** for himself;
116:15 is the death of his **f** ones.
Mic 7: 2 The **f** have disappeared from the
Zec 8: 3 Jerusalem shall be called the **f** city,
Mt 24:45 "Who then is the **f** and wise slave,
1Co 10:13 God is **f**, and he will not let you be
1Th 5:24 The one who calls you is **f**,
Heb 10:23 for he who has promised is **f**.
1Pe 4:19 to a **f** Creator,
1Jn 1: 9 is **f** and just will forgive us our sins
Rev 1: 5 **f** witness, the firstborn of the dead,
19:11 Its rider is called **F** and True,
Wis 3: 9 the **f** will abide with him in love,
Sir 4:16 If they remain **f**, they will inherit

FAITHFULNESS → FAITH
Ex 34: 6 abounding in steadfast love and **f**,
Jos 24:14 and serve him in sincerity and in **f**;
Ps 26: 3 and I walk in **f** to you.
36: 5 to the heavens, your **f** to the clouds.
Pr 16: 6 By loyalty and **f** iniquity is atoned
Isa 11: 5 and **f** the belt around his loins.
Jer 31: 3 I have continued my **f** to you.
La 3:23 new every morning; great is your **f**.
Hos 4: 1 There is no **f** or loyalty, and no
Ro 3: 3 faithlessness nullify the **f** of God?
Gal 5:22 patience, kindness, generosity, **f**,

FAITHLESS → FAITH
Jer 3:14 Return, O **f** children, says the LORD,
Mt 17:17 "You **f** and perverse generation,
2Ti 2:13 if we are **f**, he remains faithful—
Rev 21: 8 But as for the cowardly, the **f**,

FALL → FALLEN, FALLING, FELL
Ps 91: 7 A thousand may **f** at your side,
Pr 16:18 and a haughty spirit before a **f**.
Lk 10:18 "I watched Satan **f** from heaven like
Ro 9:33 a rock that will make them **f**,
1Co 10:12 watch out that you do not **f**.
Heb 10:31 a fearful thing to **f** into the hands of
Sir 28:23 Those who forsake the Lord will **f**

FALLEN → FALL
2Sa 1:19 How the mighty have **f**!
Isa 14:12 **f** from heaven, O Day Star,
21: 9 he responded, "**F**, **f** is Babylon;

Rev 9: 1   I saw a star that had **f** from heaven
18: 2   "**F, f** is Babylon the great!

FALLING → FALL
Lk 22:44   [[like great drops of blood **f** down]]
Jude 1:24   him who is able to keep you from **f,**

FALSE
Dt 5:20   Neither shall you bear **f** witness
2Ki 17:15   went after **f** idols and became **f;**
Mt 7:15   "Beware of **f** prophets, who come to
Mk 13:22   **F** messiahs and **f** prophets will
Heb 6:18   impossible that God would prove **f,**
2Pe 2: 1   there will be **f** teachers among you,
Rev 16:13   and from the mouth of the **f** prophet.
20:10   where the beast and the **f** prophet
LtJ 6: 8   but they are **f** and cannot speak.
Sus 1:61   convicted them of bearing **f** witness;

FAMILIES → FAMILY
Ac 3:25   all the **f** of the earth shall be blessed.
Tit 1:11   are upsetting whole **f** by teaching

FAMILY → FAMILIES
Pr 6:19   and one who sows discord in a **f.**
Gal 6:10   especially for those of the **f** of faith.
Eph 3:15   from whom every **f** in heaven and
1Pe 2:17   Love the **f** of believers.

FAMINE
Ge 12:10   Now there was a **f** in the land.
41:27   They are seven years of **f.**
Ru 1: 1   there was a **f** in the land,
Ps 37:19   in the days of **f** they have abundance
Am 8:11   not a **f** of bread, or a thirst for water,
Ac 11:28   there would be a severe **f** over all
Ro 8:35   or distress, or persecution, or **f,**

FAR
Nu 16: 3   "You have gone too **f!**
1Sa 7:12   "Thus **f** the LORD has helped us."
Isa 57:19   Peace, peace, to the **f** and the near,
Jer 23:23   and not a God **f** off?
Mk 7: 6   but their hearts are **f** from me;
12:34   are not **f** from the kingdom of God."

FAST → FASTED, FASTING
Isa 58: 5   Is such the **f** that I choose,
Mt 6:16   "And whenever you **f,**
Lk 18:12   I **f** twice a week; I give

FASTED → FAST
Mt 4: 2   He **f** forty days and forty nights,

FASTING → FAST
Mt 6:16   so as to show others that they are **f.**

FATHER → FATHER'S
Ge 2:24   a man leaves his **f** and his mother
Ex 20:12   Honor your **f** and your mother,
21:15   Whoever strikes **f** or mother shall
2Sa 7:14   I will be a **f** to him, and he shall be
Ps 89:26   cry to me, 'You are my **F,** my God,
Pr 28:24   Anyone who robs **f** or mother and
Isa 8: 4   child knows how to call "My **f**" or
9: 6   Mighty God, Everlasting **F,** Prince
Jer 3:19   I thought you would call me, My **F,**
Mal 1: 6   If then I am a **f,** where is the honor
Mt 6: 9   Our **F** in heaven, hallowed be your
28:19   the name of the **F** and of the Son and
Lk 18:20   Honor your **f** and mother.'"
Jn 5:18   but was also calling God his own **F,**
8:44   You are from your **f** the devil,
14: 6   comes to the **F** except through me.
Ro 8:15   When we cry, "Abba! **F!**"
Gal 4: 6   into our hearts, crying, "Abba! **F!**"
Eph 6: 2   "Honor your **f** and mother"—
Heb 1: 5   be his **F,** and he will be my Son"?
12: 9   to be subject to the **F** of spirits
Jas 1:17   coming down from the **F** of lights,
Rev 3: 5   confess your name before my **F**
Wis 2:16   and boasts that God is his **f.**
Sir 3: 3   who honor their **f** atone for sins,

FATHER'S → FATHER
Lk 2:49   that I must be in my **F** house?"
Jn 1:14   the glory as of a **f** only son,
2:16   making my **F** house a marketplace!"
10:29   can snatch it out of the **F** hand.
14: 2   **F** house there are many dwelling

FAULT
Ro 9:19   "Why then does he still find **f**?
Sir 11: 7   Do not find **f** before you investigate;

FAVOR → FAVORITISM
Ge 6: 8   Noah found **f** in the sight of the
Ex 33:12   you have also found **f** in my sight.'
Ps 30: 5   his **f** is for a lifetime.
Isa 49: 8   In a time of **f** I have answered you,
Zec 11: 7   I named **F,** the other I named Unity,
Lk 4:19   proclaim the year of the Lord's **f.**"

FAVORITISM* → FAVOR**
Jas 2: 1   with your acts of **f** really believe

FEAR → AFRAID, FEARED, FEARFULLY, FEARS
Ge 22:12   for now I know that you **f** God,
Dt 6:13   The LORD your God you shall **f;**
Ps 19: 9   the **f** of the LORD is pure, enduring
23: 4   the darkest valley, I **f** no evil;
27: 1   and my salvation; whom shall I **f**?
Pr 1: 7   **f** of the LORD is the beginning of
Ecc 12:13   **F** God, and keep his commandments
Mt 10:28   rather **f** him who can destroy both
Mk 5:36   "Do not **f,** only believe."
Php 2:12   work out your own salvation with **f**
1Pe 3:14   Do not **f** what they **f,**
1Jn 4:18   but perfect love casts out **f;**
Rev 14: 7   "**F** God and give him glory,
Sir 1:11   The **f** of the Lord is glory

FEARED → FEAR
Ex 14:31   the people **f** the LORD and believed
Job 1: 1   **f** God and turned away from evil.
Hag 1:12   and the people **f** the LORD.

FEARFULLY* → FEAR**
Ps 139:14   I am **f** and wonderfully made.

FEARS → FEAR
Ps 34: 4   and delivered me from all my **f.**
Pr 31:30   a woman who **f** the LORD is to be
Jdt 16:16   whoever **f** the Lord is great forever.
Sir 15: 1   Whoever **f** the Lord will do this,

FED → FEED
Dt 8:16   **f** you in the wilderness with manna
Ps 80: 5   have **f** them with the bread of tears,
Eze 34: 8   but the shepherds have **f** themselves,

FEED → FED
Isa 40:11   He will **f** his flock like a shepherd;
65:25   wolf and the lamb shall **f** together,
Jn 21:15   Jesus said to him, "**F** my lambs."
Ro 12:20   "if your enemies are hungry, **f** them;

FEET → FOOT
Ps 8: 6   you have put all things under their **f,**
119:105   Your word is a lamp to my **f**
Da 2:33   its **f** partly of iron and partly of clay.
Mt 22:44   I put your enemies under your **f**'"?
Lk 24:39   Look at my hands and my **f;**
Jn 13: 5   and began to wash the disciples' **f**
Ro 16:20   shortly crush Satan under your **f.**
1Co 15:25   put all his enemies under his **f.**
Heb 1:13   enemies a footstool for your **f**"?
Rev 1:15   his **f** were like burnished bronze,

FELLOWSHIP
Ac 2:42   to the apostles' teaching and **f,**
2Co 6:14   Or what **f** is there between light and
1Jn 1: 3   and truly our **f** is with the Father and

FEMALE
Ge 1:27   male and **f** he created them.
Mk 10: 6   'God made them male and **f.'**
Gal 3:28   there is no longer male and **f;**

FESTIVAL → FESTIVALS
Ex 23:14   in the year you shall hold a **f** for me.
1Co 5: 8   Therefore, let us celebrate the **f,**

FESTIVALS → FESTIVAL
Lev 23: 2   are the appointed **f** of the LORD
Ne 10:33   the new moons, the appointed **f,**
Col 2:16   of food and drink or of observing **f,**

FEVER
Dt 28:22   will afflict you with consumption, **f,**
Mk 1:30   mother-in-law was in bed with a **f,**

FEW
Ps 105:12   When they were **f** in number,
Ecc 5: 2   therefore let your words be **f.**
Mt 22:14   many are called, but **f** are chosen."
Lk 13:23   "Lord, will only a **f** be saved?"

FIELD → FIELDS
Pr 31:16   She considers a **f** and buys it;
Mt 6:28   Consider the lilies of the **f,** how
13:44   is like treasure hidden in a **f,**
24:40   Then two will be in the **f;**
1Co 3: 9   you are God's **f,** God's building.

FIELDS → FIELD
Lk 2: 8   there were shepherds living in the **f,**
Jn 4:35   see how the **f** are ripe for harvesting.

FIG → FIGS
Ge 3: 7   and they sewed **f** leaves together
Hab 3:17   Though the **f** tree does not blossom,
Mt 24:32   "From the **f** tree learn its lesson:
Lk 13: 6   "A man had a **f** tree planted in his

FIGHT → FOUGHT
Ex 14:14   The LORD will **f** for you,
Ps 35: 1   **f** against those who **f** against me!
1Ti 1:18   you may **f** the good **f,**
2Ti 4: 7   I have fought the good **f,**

FIGS → FIG
Jer 24: 1   LORD showed me two baskets of **f**
Lk 6:44   **F** are not gathered from thorns,

FILL → FILLED, FULL, FULLNESS
Ge 1:28   and **f** the earth and subdue it;
9: 1   fruitful and multiply, and **f** the earth.
Ps 72:19   may his glory **f** the whole earth.
Jer 23:24   Do I not **f** heaven and earth?
Eph 4:10   so that he might **f** all things.)

FILLED → FILL
Ex 1: 7   so that the land was **f** with them.
40:34   glory of the LORD **f** the tabernacle.
1Ki 8:11   glory of the LORD **f** the house of the
Eze 43: 5   the glory of the LORD **f** the temple.
Lk 1:15   he will be **f** with the Holy Spirit.
Ac 2: 4   were **f** with the Holy Spirit and
Eph 5:18   but be **f** with the Spirit,

FILTHY
Isa 64: 6   righteous deeds are like a **f** cloth.
Zec 3: 3   Joshua was dressed with **f** clothes
Rev 22:11   and the **f** still be **f,**

FIND → FINDS, FOUND
Nu 32:23   and be sure your sin will **f** you out.
Dt 4:29   you will **f** him if you search after
Jer 29:13   you search for me, you will **f** me;
Mt 11:29   and you will **f** rest for your souls.
16:25   lose their life for my sake will **f** it.
Lk 11: 9   search, and you will **f;**

FINDS → FIND
Pr 8:35   For whoever **f** me **f** life and obtains
18:22   He who **f** a wife **f** a good thing,

FINGER
Ex 8:19   "This is the **f** of God!"
Dt 9:10   tablets written with the **f** of God;
Mt 23: 4   themselves are unwilling to lift a **f**
Lk 11:20   if it is by the **f** of God that I cast out

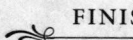
FINISHED
Ge	2: 2	on the seventh day God **f** the work
Ex	40:33	So Moses **f** the work.
Jn	19:30	received the wine, he said, "It is **f**."
Sir	38: 8	God's works will never be **f**;

FIRE → FIERY
Ex	3: 2	appeared to him in a flame of **f** out
	13:21	and in a pillar of **f** by night, to give
Lev	9:24	**F** came out from the LORD and
Nu	11: 1	the **f** of the LORD burned against
Dt	4:24	the LORD your God is a devouring **f**,
1Ki	19:12	but the LORD was not in the **f**;
2Ki	2:11	a chariot of **f** and horses of **f** separated
2Ch	7: 1	**f** came down from heaven and
Isa	66:24	their **f** shall not be quenched,
Da	3:25	walking in the middle of the **f**,
Zec	2: 5	For I will be a wall of **f** all around it,
Mal	3: 2	For he is like a refiner's **f** and like
Mt	3:11	baptize you with the Holy Spirit and **f**.
Mk	9:43	to go to hell, to the unquenchable **f**.
Ac	2: 3	Divided tongues, as of **f**, appeared
1Co	3:13	the **f** will test what sort of work each
Heb	12:29	indeed our God is a consuming **f**.
Jas	3: 6	And the tongue is a **f**.
2Pe	3:10	elements will be dissolved with **f**,
Rev	20:14	the second death, the lake of **f**;
Sir	7:17	punishment of the ungodly is **f** and

FIRM → FIRMLY
Ex	14:13	"Do not be afraid, stand **f**,
Isa	7: 9	If you do not stand **f** in faith,
2Co	1:24	because you stand **f** in the faith.
Eph	6:13	having done everything, to stand **f**.
Heb	3: 6	if we hold **f** the confidence

FIRMAMENT
Ps	19: 1	and the **f** proclaims his handiwork.
	150: 1	praise him in his mighty **f**!

FIRMLY → FIRM
Ps	119:89	your word is **f** fixed in heaven.
Ecc	12:11	like nails **f** fixed are the collected

FIRST → FIRSTBORN
Ge	1: 5	and there was morning, the **f** day.
Nu	18:15	The issue of the womb of all
Pr	8:22	the **f** of his acts of long ago.
Isa	41: 4	I, the LORD, am **f**,
Mt	6:33	But strive **f** for the kingdom of God
Mk	10:31	But many who are **f** will be last, and the last will be **f**."
	16: 2	very early on the **f** day of the week,
Jn	2:11	Jesus did this, the **f** of his signs,
Ac	11:26	disciples were **f** called "Christians."
Ro	1:16	to the Jew **f** and also to the Greek.
1Co	15:45	it is written, "The **f** man, Adam,
1Th	4:16	and the dead in Christ will rise **f**.
1Jn	4:19	We love because he **f** loved us.
Rev	1:17	I am the **f** and the last,
	20: 5	This is the **f** resurrection.
	21: 1	the **f** heaven and the **f** earth

FIRSTBORN → BEAR, FIRST
Ex	4:22	'Thus says the LORD: Israel is my **f**
	12:29	the LORD struck down all the **f**
	13: 2	Consecrate to me all the **f**;
Ps	78:51	He struck all the **f** in Egypt,
Zec	12:10	as one weeps over a **f**.
Lk	2: 7	And she gave birth to her **f** son and
Col	1:15	invisible God, the **f** of all creation;
Heb	1: 6	when he brings the **f** into the world,
Rev	1: 5	faithful witness, the **f** of the dead,
Sir	36:17	whom you have named your **f**,
2Es	6:58	whom you have called your **f**,

FISH
Ge	1:26	have dominion over the **f** of the sea,
Jnh	2: 1	his God from the belly of the **f**,
Mt	7:10	Or if the child asks for a **f**, will give
Jn	6: 9	has five barley loaves and two **f**.

FIVE
1Sa	17:40	chose **f** smooth stones from the wadi
Mt	14:19	Taking the **f** loaves and the two fish,
1Co	14:19	church I would rather speak **f** words

FLAME
Ex	3: 2	in a **f** of fire out of a bush;
Isa	10:17	and his Holy One a **f**;
Rev	19:12	His eyes are like a **f** of fire,
Aza	1:26	drove the fiery **f** out of the furnace,

FLED → FLEE
Ex	2:15	But Moses **f** from Pharaoh.
1Sa	19:18	Now David **f** and escaped;
Mk	14:50	All of them deserted him and **f**,
Rev	12: 6	the woman **f** into the wilderness,
	20:11	and the heaven **f** from his presence,

FLEE → FLED
Ps	11: 1	"**F** like a bird to the mountains;
	139: 7	where can I **f** from your presence?
Isa	30:17	A thousand shall **f** at the threat of
1Co	10:14	**f** from the worship of idols.
Jas	4: 7	Resist the devil, and he will **f** from

FLESH
Ge	2:23	is bone of my bones and **f** of my **f**;
	2:24	and they become one **f**.
Job	19:26	then in my **f** I shall see God,
Eze	36:26	of stone and give you a heart of **f**.
Mt	16:17	For **f** and blood has not revealed this
	26:41	but the **f** is weak."
Jn	1:14	the Word became **f** and lived among
	3: 6	What is born of the **f** is **f**,
Ro	8: 4	to the **f** but according to the Spirit.
2Co	12: 7	a thorn was given me in the **f**,
Gal	5:19	Now the works of the **f** are obvious:
Eph	6:12	not against enemies of blood and **f**,
1Pe	1:24	"All **f** is like grass and all its glory
1Jn	4: 2	that Jesus Christ has come in the **f**

FLOCK
Isa	40:11	He will feed his **f** like a shepherd;
Eze	34:22	I will save my **f**, and they shall no
Mt	26:31	the sheep of the **f** will be scattered.'
Lk	12:32	"Do not be afraid, little **f**,
Jn	10:16	So there will be one **f**, one shepherd.
1Pe	5: 3	but be examples to the **f**.

FLOGGED
Jn	19: 1	Pilate took Jesus and had him **f**.
Ac	5:40	the apostles, they had them **f**.

FLOOD
Ge	7: 7	the ark to escape the waters of the **f**.
	9:15	waters shall never again become a **f**
Ps	29:10	The LORD sits enthroned over the **f**;
2Pe	2: 5	a **f** on a world of the ungodly;
Sir	40:10	and on their account the **f** came.

FLOW → FLOWING, FLOWS
Zec	14: 8	waters shall **f** out from Jerusalem,
Jn	7:38	'Out of the believer's heart shall **f**

FLOWER
Isa	40: 7	The grass withers, the **f** fades,
1Pe	1:24	The grass withers, and the **f** falls,

FLOWING → FLOW
Ex	3: 8	a land **f** with milk and honey,
Jos	5: 6	a land **f** with milk and honey.
Eze	47: 1	water was **f** from below the
Rev	22: 1	**f** from the throne of God and

FOE
Ex	23:22	and a **f** to your foes.
Ps	60:11	O grant us help against the **f**,

FOLLOW → FOLLOWED
Ex	16: 4	whether they will **f** my instruction
Dt	6:14	Do not **f** other gods, any of the gods
1Ki	18:21	If the LORD is God, **f** him;
Ps	23: 6	mercy shall **f** me all the days of my
Lk	9:23	take up their cross daily and **f** me.
Jn	10:27	I know them, and they **f** me.
Rev	14: 4	these **f** the Lamb wherever he goes.

FOLLOWED → FOLLOW
Jdg	2:12	they **f** other gods, from among the
Jer	9:14	have stubbornly **f** their own hearts
Mk	1:18	they left their nets and **f** him.
Rev	13: 3	the whole earth **f** the beast.

FOLLY → FOOL
Pr	13:16	but the fool displays **f**.
	26: 4	not answer fools according to their **f**
Ecc	2:13	that wisdom excels **f** as light excels
Mk	7:22	envy, slander, pride, **f**.

FOOD → FOODS
Ge	1:30	I have given every green plant for **f**.
	9: 3	thing that lives shall be **f** for you;
Ps	136:25	who gives **f** to all flesh,
Mt	6:25	Is not life more than **f**,
Jn	6:55	for my flesh is true **f** and my blood
1Co	8: 8	"**F** will not bring us close to God."
1Mc	1:63	to die rather than to be defiled by **f**

FOODS → FOOD
Mk	7:19	(Thus he declared all **f** clean.)
1Ti	4: 3	and demand abstinence from **f**,

FOOL → FOLLY, FOOLISH, FOOLISHNESS, FOOLS
Pr	15: 5	A **f** despises a parent's instruction,
	20: 3	but every **f** is quick to quarrel.
Mt	5:22	'You **f**,' you will be liable to the
2Co	11:21	I am speaking as a **f**—I also dare to

FOOLISH → FOOL
Pr	17:25	**F** children are a grief to their father
Jer	5:21	O **f** and senseless people,
Mt	7:26	like a **f** man who built his house
	25: 2	Five of them were **f**, and five were
1Co	1:20	Has not God made **f** the wisdom of
Gal	3: 1	**f** Galatians! Who has bewitched
Tit	3: 3	For we ourselves were once **f**,

FOOLISHNESS → FOOL
1Co	1:18	cross is **f** to those who are perishing,
	3:19	wisdom of this world is **f** with God.

FOOLS → FOOL
Ps	14: 1	**f** say in their hearts, "There is no God."
Pr	1: 7	**f** despise wisdom and instruction.
	10:21	but **f** die for lack of sense.
Ecc	5: 4	for he has no pleasure in **f**.
Ro	1:22	Claiming to be wise, they became **f**;
1Co	4:10	We are **f** for the sake of Christ,

FOOT → FEET, FOOTSTOOL
Ps	91:12	will not dash your **f** against a stone.
Mt	18: 8	or your **f** causes you to stumble,
Lk	4:11	not dash your **f** against a stone.'"

FOOTSTOOL → FOOT
Ps	110: 1	until I make your enemies your **f**."
Isa	66: 1	is my throne and the earth is my **f**;
Heb	10:13	until his enemies would be made a **f**

FORCES
Mt	5:41	and if anyone **f** you to go one mile,
Eph	6:12	spiritual **f** of evil in the heavenly

FOREHEAD → FOREHEADS
Ex	13: 9	and as a reminder on your **f**,
1Sa	17:49	and struck the Philistine on his **f**;
Rev	13:16	marked on the right hand or the **f**,

FOREHEADS → FOREHEAD
Eze	9: 4	and put a mark on the **f** of those
Rev	7: 3	of our God with a seal on their **f**."
	20: 4	not received its mark on their **f**

FOREIGN → FOREIGNER, FOREIGNERS
Jos	24:23	"Then put away the **f** gods that are
Ps	81: 9	you shall not bow down to a **f** god.

FOREIGNER → FOREIGN
Ex	12:43	no **f** shall eat of it,
1Co	14:11	and the speaker a **f** to me.

FOREIGNERS → FOREIGN
1Co	14:21	by the lips of **f** I will speak to this

Heb 11:13 were strangers and **f** on the
earth,

FOREKNEW* → KNOW
Ro   8:29 whom he **f** he also predestined to
     11: 2 not rejected his people whom he **f.**

FORERUNNER* → RUN
Heb   6:20 a **f** on our behalf, has entered,

FORESEEING* → SEE
Ac   2:31 **F** this, David spoke of the
Gal   3: 8 **f** that God would justify the Gentiles

FORESKIN
Ge   17:14 circumcised in the flesh of his **f**
Dt   10:16 Circumcise, then, the **f** of your heart

FORETOLD → TELL
Isa   43: 9 and **f** to us the former things?
Ac   3:18 this way God fulfilled what he had **f**

FOREVER
Ge   3:22 the tree of life, and eat, and live **f"**
     6: 3 spirit shall not abide in mortals **f,**
Ex   3:15 This is my name **f,** and this my title
2Sa   7:13 the throne of his kingdom **f.**
1Ch 16:15 Remember his covenant **f,**
Ps   19: 9 fear of the LORD is pure, enduring **f;**
     110: 4 "You are a priest **f** according to the
     117: 2 faithfulness of the LORD endures **f.**
Ecc   3:14 that whatever God does endures **f;**
Isa   40: 8 the word of our God will stand **f.**
     51: 6 but my salvation will be **f,**
Jn   6:51 eats of this bread will live **f;**
     14:16 another Advocate, to be with you **f.**
Heb   5: 6 "You are a priest **f,** according to the
     13: 8 the same yesterday and today and **f.**
1Pe   1:25 but the word of the Lord endures **f."**
Rev   1:18 I am alive **f** and ever;
     11:15 and he will reign **f** and ever."
     22: 5 and they will reign **f** and ever.
Wis   5:15 But the righteous live **f,**

FORFEIT
Mk   8:36 the whole world and **f** their life?

FORGAVE → FORGIVE
Ps   32: 5 and you **f** the guilt of my sin.
     85: 2 You **f** the iniquity of your people;
Col   2:13 when he **f** us all our trespasses,

FORGET → FORGOT, FORGOTTEN
Dt   4:23 So be careful not to **f** the covenant
     6:12 take care that you do not **f** the LORD,
Ps   137: 5 If I **f** you, O Jerusalem, let my right
Pr   4: 5 Get wisdom; get insight: do not **f,**
Isa   49:15 these may I, yet I will not **f** you.

FORGIVE → FORGAVE, FORGIVEN,
     FORGIVENESS, FORGIVING
Ge   18:26 **f** the whole place for their sake."
Ex   32:32 But now, if you will only **f** their sin
Nu   14:20 the LORD said, "I do **f,**
1Ki   8:30 your dwelling place; heed and **f.**
Ne   9:17 But you are a God ready to **f,**
Ps   79: 9 and **f** our sins, for your name's sake.
Eze   16:63 when I **f** you all that you have done,
Da   9:19 O Lord, hear; O Lord, **f;**
Mt   6:12 And **f** us our debts, as we
Lk   5:24 has authority on earth to **f** sins"—
1Jn   1: 9 is faithful and just will **f** us oursins
Sir   5: 6 he will **f** the multitude of my sins,"
Man   1:13 **f** me, O Lord, **f** me!

FORGIVEN → FORGIVE
Lev   4:20 for them, and they shall be **f.**
Ps   32: 1 are those whose transgression is **f,**
Mt   6:12 as we also have **f** our debtors.
     12:31 against the Spirit will not be **f.**
Mk   2: 9 to the paralytic, 'Your sins are **f,'**
Ac   2:38 so that your sins may be **f,**
Ro   4: 7 are those whose iniquities are **f,**
Eph   4:32 as God in Christ has **f** you.

FORGIVENESS → FORGIVE
Mk   1: 4 a baptism of repentance for the **f**

Mk   3:29 against the Holy Spirit can never
have **f,**
Col   1:14 we have redemption, the **f** of sins.
Heb   9:22 the shedding of blood there is no **f**

FORGIVING → FORGIVE
Ex   34: 7 **f** iniquity and transgression and sin,
Ps   86: 5 For you, O Lord, are good and **f,**
Eph   4:32 **f** one another, as God in Christ has

FORGOT → FORGET
Dt   32:18 you **f** the God who gave you birth.
Jer   23:27 just as their ancestors **f** my name
Hos   2:13 and went after her lovers, and **f** me,
Bar   4: 8 You **f** the everlasting God,

FORGOTTEN → FORGET
Ps   77: 9 Has God **f** to be gracious?
Isa   49:14 forsaken me, my Lord has **f** me."
Heb   12: 5 And you have **f** the exhortation

FORM → FORMED, FORMLESS
Ex   20: 4 in the **f** of anything that is in heaven
Lk   3:22 descended upon him in bodily **f**

FORMED → FORM
Ge   2: 7 the LORD God **f** man from the dust
Ps   139:13 you who **f** my inward parts;
Gal   4:19 until Christ is **f** in you,

FORMLESS* → FORM
Ge   1: 2 the earth was a **f** void and darkness
Wis   11:17 created the world out of **f** matter,

FORNICATION → FORNICATOR,
     FORNICATORS
Mk   7:21 that evil intentions come: **f,**
1Co   6:13 meant not for **f** but for the Lord,
Gal   5:19 works of the flesh are obvious: **f,**
Rev   19: 2 who corrupted the earth with her **f,**

FORNICATOR* → FORNICATION
1Co   6:18 but the **f** sins against the body itself.
Eph   5: 5 that no **f** or impure person,
Sir   23:17 To a **f** all bread is sweet;

FORNICATORS → FORNICATION
1Ti   1:10 **f,** sodomites, slave traders, liars,
Rev   22:15 and sorcerers and **f** and murderers

FORSAKE → FORSAKEN
Dt   31: 6 he will not fail you or **f** you."
Jos   1: 5 I will not fail you or **f** you.
Jer   17:13 All who **f** you shall be put to shame;
Heb   13: 5 "I will never leave you or **f** you."

FORSAKEN → FORSAKE
Ps   9:10 O LORD, have not **f** those who seek
     22: 1 my God, why have you **f** me?
Mt   27:46 my God, why have you **f** me?"
2Co   4: 9 persecuted, but not **f;**

FORTRESS
2Sa   22: 2 The LORD is my rock, my **f,** and my
Ps   71: 3 for you are my rock and my **f.**

FORTUNES
Dt   30: 3 LORD your God will restore your **f**
Jer   32:44 I will restore their **f,** says the LORD.

FORTY
Ge   7: 4 rain on the earth for **f** days and **f**
Nu   14:34 **f** days, for every day a year,
1Ki   19: 8 **f** days and **f** nights to Horeb
Jnh   3: 4 And he cried out, "**F** days more,
Mt   4: 2 He fasted **f** days and **f** nights,
Heb   3:17 with whom was he angry **f** years?
2Es   14:42 They sat **f** days; they wrote

FOUGHT → FIGHT
Jos   10:42 the LORD God of Israel **f** for Israel.
2Ti   4: 7 I have **f** the good fight,
Rev   12: 7 and his angels **f** against the dragon.

FOUND → FIND
Isa   55: 6 Seek the LORD while he may be **f,**
     65: 1 be **f** by those who did not seek me.
Lk   15:24 he was lost and is **f!'**
Ro   10:20 **f** by those who did not seek me;

Rev   20:15 not **f** written in the book of life was

FOUNDATION → FOUNDATIONS
1Ki   6:37 **f** of the house of the LORD was laid,
Ezr   3: 6 **f** of the temple of the LORD was not
Isa   28:16 See, I am laying in Zion a **f** stone,
1Co   3:11 that **f** is Jesus Christ.
Eph   2:20 built upon the **f** of the apostles and
2Ti   2:19 But God's firm **f** stands,

FOUNDATIONS → FOUNDATION
Heb   11:10 looked forward to the city that has **f,**
Rev   21:14 the wall of the city has twelve **f,**

FOUNTAIN
Ps   36: 9 For with you is the **f** of life;
Pr   16:22 Wisdom is a **f** of life to one who
Jer   9: 1 and my eyes a **f** of tears,
Joel   3:18 a **f** shall come forth from the house
Zec   13: 1 a **f** shall be opened for the house of

FOUR
Eze   1: 5 something like **f** living creatures.
     10:14 Each one had **f** faces:
Rev   4: 6 are **f** living creatures,

FOXES
Jdg   15: 4 went and caught three hundred **f,**
Lk   9:58 Jesus said to him, "**F** have holes,

FRAGRANCE → FRAGRANT
2Co   2:14 spreads in every place the **f**

FRAGRANT → FRAGRANCE
Ex   25: 6 anointing oil and for the **f** incense,
Eph   5: 2 a **f** offering and sacrifice to God.

FRANKINCENSE → INCENSE
Isa   60: 6 They shall bring gold and **f,**
Mt   2:11 gifts of gold, **f,** and myrrh.

FREE → FREED, FREEDOM, FREEWILL
Ex   21: 2 in the seventh he shall go out a **f**
Ps   146: 7 The LORD sets the prisoners **f;**
Jn   8:32 and the truth will make you **f."**
Ro   6:23 but the **f** gift of God is eternal life
1Co   9:21 not **f** from God's law but am under
Gal   3:28 there is no longer slave or **f,**
Eph   6: 8 whether we are slaves or **f.**

FREED → FREE
Ac   2:24 having **f** him from death,
Rev   1: 5 **f** us from our sins by his blood,

FREEDOM → FREE
2Co   3:17 the Spirit of the Lord is, there is **f.**
Gal   5: 1 For **f** Christ has set us free.
1Pe   2:16 not use your **f** as a pretext for evil.

FREEWILL → FREE, WILL
Ex   35:29 as a **f** offering to the LORD.
Ps   54: 6 With a **f** offering I will sacrifice to

FRIEND → FRIENDS, FRIENDSHIP
Ex   33:11 as one speaks to a **f.**
Pr   17:17 A **f** loves at all times,
     18:24 but a true **f** sticks closer than one's
Mt   11:19 a **f** of tax collectors and sinners!'
Jas   2:23 and he was called the **f** of God.
     4: 4 a **f** of the world becomes an enemy
Sir   7:18 Do not exchange a **f** for money,

FRIENDS → FRIEND
Job   2:11 when Job's three **f** heard of all
Jn   15:13 to lay down one's life for one's **f.**
Sir   6:15 Faithful **f** are beyond price;

FRIENDSHIP → FRIEND
Ps   25:14 The **f** of the LORD is for those who
Jas   4: 4 know that **f** with the world is enmity

FRINGES*
Nu   15:38 to make **f** on the corners of their
Mt   23: 5 phylacteries broad and their **f** long.

FRUIT → FRUITFUL, FRUITLESS, FRUITS
Ge   3: 6 she took of its **f** and ate;
Dt   28: 4 Blessed shall be the **f** of your womb,
Ps   1: 3 which yield their **f** in its season,

FRUIT (cont.)

Pr   8:19 My f is better than gold,
Eze 47:12 will not wither nor their f fail,
Hos 14: 2 and we will offer the f of our lips.
Mt   3: 8 Bear f worthy of repentance.
Lk   6:44 for each tree is known by its own f.
Jn   15: 2 branch that bears f he prunes to make it bear more f.
Col   1:10 as you bear f in every good work
Heb 13:15 the f of lips that confess his name.
Rev 22: 2 tree of life with its twelve kinds of f,

FRUITFUL → FRUIT

Ge   1:22 Be f and multiply and fill the waters
      9: 1 said to them, "Be f and multiply,
Ex   1: 7 the Israelites were f and prolific;

FRUITS → FRUIT

Ex   23:16 of the first f of your labor,
Pr   3: 9 with the first f of all your produce;
Mt   7:16 You will know them by their f.
Ro   8:23 who have the first f of the Spirit,
1Co 15:23 in his own order: Christ the first f,
Rev 14: 4 as first f for God and the Lamb.

FULFILL → FULFILLED, FULFILLING

Ps   20: 5 May the LORD f all your petitions.
Ecc   5: 4 F what you vow.
Mt   5:17 I have come not to abolish but to f.
Gal   6: 2 way you will f the law of Christ.
Jas   2: 8 really f the royal law according to

FULFILLED → FULFILL

Mk   1:15 "The time is f, and the kingdom
Lk   24:44 prophets, and the psalms must be f."
Ro   8: 4 requirement of the law might be f

FULFILLING → FULFILL

Ro   9:31 did not succeed in f that law.
     13:10 love is the f of the law.

FULL → FILL

Isa   6: 3 the whole earth is f of his glory."
Eze 10:12 were f of eyes all around.
     37: 1 it was f of bones.
Mt   6:22 your whole body will be f of light;
Jn   1:14 f of grace and truth.
Rev   4: 6 f of eyes in front and behind:
Sir 42:16 work of the Lord is f of his glory.

FULLNESS → FILL

Jn   1:16 From his f we have all received,
1Co 10:26 "the earth and its f are the Lord's."
Gal   4: 4 But when the f of time had come,
Eph   3:19 may be filled with all the f of God.
Col   1:19 in him all the f of God was pleased

FURNACE

Isa 48:10 have tested you in the f of adversity.
Da   3: 6 be thrown into a f of blazing fire."
Mt   13:42 will throw them into the f of fire,
Aza   1:26 of the Lord came down into the f

FURNITURE

Ex   25: 9 the tabernacle and of all its f,

FURY

Ps   2: 5 and terrify them in his f,
La   2: 4 he has poured out his f like fire.
Ro   2: 8 there will be wrath and f.
Rev 16:19 the wine-cup of the f of his wrath.

FUTILE

Ro   1:21 but they became f in their thinking,
1Co   3:20 thoughts of the wise, that they are f.

FUTURE

Pr   24:20 for the evil have no f;
Jer 31:17 hope for your f, says the LORD:
1Co   3:22 life or death or the present or the f—
1Ti   6:19 of a good foundation for the f,

G

GABRIEL*

Angel who interpreted Daniel's visions (Da 8:16-26; 9:20-27); announced births of John (Lk 1:11-20), Jesus (Lk 1:26-38).

GAD

1. Son of Jacob by Zilpah (Ge 30:9-11; 35:26; 1Ch 2:2). Tribe of blessed (Ge 49:19; Dt 33:20-21), numbered (Nu 1:25; 26:18), allotted land east of the Jordan (Nu 32; 34:14; Jos 18:7; 22), west (Eze 48:27-28), 12,000 from (Rev 7:5).

2. Prophet; seer of David (1Sa 22:5; 2Sa 24:11-19; 1Ch 29:29).

GAIN

Ecc   1: 3 What do people g from all the toil
Lk   9:25 if they g the whole world,
Php   1:21 living is Christ and dying is g.
      3: 8 in order that I may g Christ
1Ti   6: 5 that godliness is a means of g.

GALILEAN → GALILEE

Mt   26:69 "You also were with Jesus the G."

GALILEANS → GALILEE

Ac   2: 7 not all these who are speaking G?

GALILEE → GALILEAN, GALILEANS

Isa   9: 1 beyond the Jordan, G of the nations.
Mt   4:15 across the Jordan, G of the Gentiles
Jn   7:41 the Messiah does not come from G,

GAMALIEL

Pharisee (Ac 5:34-39), teacher of Paul (Ac 22:5).

GARDEN

Ge   2: 8 the LORD God planted a g in Eden,
Eze 28:13 You were in Eden, the g of God;
Jn   19:41 and in the g there was a new tomb

GARMENT → GARMENTS

Ge   39:12 she caught hold of his g,
Dt   22: 5 nor shall a man put on a woman's g;
Ps 102:26 they will all wear out like a g.
Lk   5:36 a new g and sews it on an old g;

GARMENTS → GARMENT

Ge   3:21 the LORD God made g of skins for
Isa 61:10 clothed me with the g of salvation,

GATE → GATES

Mt   7:13 "Enter through the narrow g;
Jn   10: 7 I am the g for the sheep.
Heb 13:12 Jesus also suffered outside the city g

GATES → GATE

Ge   24:60 offspring gain possession of the g
Dt   6: 9 of your house and on your g.
Ps 100: 4 Enter his g with thanksgiving,
Mt   16:18 and the g of Hades will not prevail
Rev 21:21 And the twelve g are twelve pearls,

GATH

1Sa 17: 4 Goliath, of G, whose height was six
2Sa   1:20 Tell it not in G, proclaim it not in

GATHER → GATHERED, INGATHERING

Ex   16: 4 and g enough for that day.
Ru   2: 7 and g among the sheaves behind
Isa 11:12 and g the dispersed of Judah from
Mt   12:30 does not g with me scatters.
Lk   13:34 to g your children together as

GATHERED → GATHER

Mt   18:20 two or three are g in my name,
2Th   2: 1 Christ and our being g together
Rev 14:19 and g the vintage of the earth,

GAVE → GIVE

Ge   28: 4 land that God g to Abraham."
Ex   31:18 he g him the two tablets of the
1Ki   4:29 God g Solomon very great wisdom,
Ne   9:15 you g them bread from heaven,
Ecc 12: 7 the breath returns to God who g it.
Mt   25:35 for I was hungry and you g me food,
Jn   1:12 g power to become children of God,
      3:16 loved the world that he g his only Son,
Ro   8:32 but g him up for all of us,
Eph   4:11 The gifts he g were that some would
1Ti   2: 6 who g himself a ransom

GEDALIAH

Governor of Judah (2Ki 25:22-26; Jer 39-41).

GEHAZI*

Servant of Elisha (2Ki 4:12-5:27; 8:4-5).

GENEALOGIES → GENEALOGY

1Ch   9: 1 So all Israel was enrolled by g;
Ne   7:64 among those enrolled in the g,

GENEALOGY → GENEALOGIES

Mt   1: 1 of the g of Jesus the Messiah,

GENERATION → GENERATIONS

Ge   15:16 come back here in the fourth g;
Ex   20: 6 steadfast love to the thousandth g
     34: 7 to the third and the fourth g."
Da   4:34 his kingdom endures from g to g.
Mt   12:39 evil and adulterous g asks for a sign,
Lk   21:32 this g will not pass away

GENERATIONS → GENERATION

Isa 51: 8 and my salvation to all g.
Lk   1:48 now on all g will call me blessed;

GENEROSITY → GENEROUS

Ro   12: 8 the giver, in g;
Gal   5:22 joy, peace, patience, kindness, g,

GENEROUS → GENEROSITY

Ro   10:12 and is g to all who call on him.
Jas   1:17 Every g act of giving,

GENTILE → GENTILES

Mt   18:17 as a G and a tax collector.
Gal   2:14 live like a G and not like a Jew,
1Mc   1:14 according to G custom,

GENTILES → GENTILE

Lk   21:24 until the times of the G are fulfilled.
Ac   15:19 those G who are turning to God,
Ro   3:29 Is he not the God of G also?
Gal   3: 8 God would justify the G by faith,
Eph   4:17 must no longer live as the G live,
Tob   1:11 from eating the food of the G.
1Mc   1:11 and make a covenant with the G
2Es   4:23 Israel has been given over to the G

GENTLE → GENTLENESS

Pr   15: 4 A g tongue is a tree of life,
Mt   11:29 for I am g and humble in heart,
1Pe   3: 4 with the lasting beauty of a g

GENTLENESS → GENTLE

Gal   5:23 g, and self-control. There is no law
Php   4: 5 Let your g be known to everyone.
1Ti   6:11 godliness, faith, love, endurance, g.

GETHSEMANE

Mk   14:32 They went to a place called G;

GHOST

Mt   14:26 were terrified, saying, "It is a g!"
Lk   24:39 for a g does not have flesh and

GIANT → GIANTS

Sir 47: 4 In his youth did he not kill a g,

GIANTS → GIANT

1Ch 20: 4 was one of the descendants of the g;
Sir 16: 7 He did not forgive the ancient g

GIBEON

Jos 10:12 "Sun, stand still at G, and Moon, in
1Ki   3: 5 G the LORD appeared to Solomon

GIDEON → =JERUBBAAL

Judge, also called Jerubbaal; freed Israel from Midianites (Jdg 6-8; Heb 11:32). The fleece (Jdg 8:36-40).

GIFT → GIFTS

Nu   18: 7 I give your priesthood as a g;
Ecc   5:19 this is the g of God.
Mt   5:23 So when you are offering your g at
Jn   4:10 "If you knew the g of God,
Ac   2:38 will receive the g of the Holy Spirit.
Ro   6:23 but the free g of God is eternal life
1Co   7: 7 each has a particular g from God,
Jas   1:17 with every perfect g, is from above,

Rev 21: 6 the thirsty I will give water as
a **g**

GIFTS → GIFT

Dt 12: 6 and your donations, your votive **g**,
Mt 2:11 offered him **g** of gold, frankincense,
Lk 11:13 how to give good **g** to your children.
Ro 11:29 for the **g** and the calling of God are
1Co 12: 1 Now concerning spiritual **g**,
Eph 4: 8 he gave **g** to his people."
Sir 32:13 who fills you with his good **g**.

GILGAL

Jos 5: 9 so that place is called **G** to this day.
1Sa 7:16 a circuit year by year to Bethel, **G**,

GIRL

Ex 1:16 but if it is a **g**, she shall live."
Mk 5:41 which means, "Little **g**, get up!"

GIVE → GAVE, GIVEN, GIVER, GIVES

Ge 9: 3 the green plants, I **g** you everything.
12: 7 your offspring I will **g** this land."
1Ki 3: 5 said, "Ask what I should **g** you."
Pr 25:21 If your enemies are hungry, **g** them
30:15 leech has two daughters; **"G, g,"**
Eze 36:26 A new heart I will **g** you,
Mt 6:11 **G** us this day our daily bread.
7: 6 "Do not **g** what is holy to dogs;
Mk 10:45 to **g** his life a ransom for many."
Jn 10:28 I **g** them eternal life, and they will
Ac 20:35 more blessed to **g** than to receive."
Tob 12: 9 who **g** alms will enjoy a full life,
Sir 7:10 do not neglect to **g** alms.

GIVEN → GIVE

Mt 7: 7 "Ask, and it will be **g** you;
Mk 4:25 to those who have, more will be **g**;
Lk 22:19 "This is my body, which is **g** for
Ro 5: 5 the Holy Spirit that has been **g**
to us.
Sir 35:12 Give to the Most High as he has **g**

GIVER → GIVE

Ro 12: 8 the **g**, in generosity;
2Co 9: 7 for God loves a cheerful **g**.

GIVES → GIVE

2Co 3: 6 the letter kills, but the Spirit **g** life.
Jas 4: 6 But he **g** all the more grace;

GLAD → GLADNESS

Ps 16: 9 Therefore my heart is **g**, and my
90:15 Make us **g** as many days as you
Pr 10: 1 A wise child makes a **g** father,
Mt 5:12 and be **g**, for your reward is great in
Ac 2:26 heart was **g**, and my tongue rejoiced

GLADNESS → GLAD

Ps 100: 2 Worship the LORD with **g**;
Pr 10:28 The hope of the righteous ends in **g**,
Isa 16:10 Joy and **g** are taken away from the
Jer 31:13 and give them **g** for sorrow.
Zep 3:17 he will rejoice over you with **g**,
Heb 1: 9 has anointed you with the oil of **g**

GLASS

Rev 4: 6 there is something like a sea of **g**,
21:18 the city is pure gold, clear as **g**.

GLEAN

Dt 24:21 do not **g** what is left;
Ru 2: 2 Let me go to the field and **g** among

GLOOM

Isa 9: 1 there will be no **g** for those who
Joel 2: 2 a day of darkness and **g**,
Heb 12:18 and darkness, and **g**, and a tempest,

GLORIFIED → GLORY

Lev 10: 3 before all the people I will be **g**.'"
Jn 13:31 "Now the Son of Man has been **g**,
17: 4 **g** you on earth by finishing the work
Ac 3:13 has **g** his servant Jesus,
Ro 8:30 those whom he justified he also **g**.

GLORIFY → GLORY

Ps 86:12 and I will **g** your name forever.

Jn 17: 1 **g** your Son so that the Son may **g**
you,
1Co 6:20 therefore **g** God in your body.
2Co 9:13 you **g** God by your obedience to
Rev 15: 4 who will not fear and **g** your name?
Sir 43:30 **G** the Lord and exalt him as much

GLORIOUS → GLORY

Jas 2: 1 in our **g** Lord Jesus Christ?
Jdt 16:13 O Lord, you are great and **g**,
Aza 1: 3 and **g** is your name forever!

GLORY → GLORIFIED, GLORIFY, GLORIOUS

Ex 24:16 The **g** of the LORD settled on Mount
33:18 Moses said, "Show me your **g**,
40:34 **g** of the LORD filled the tabernacle.
1Sa 4:21 "The **g** has departed from Israel,"
1Ki 8:11 **g** of the LORD filled the house of the
Ps 8: 5 crowned them with **g** and honor.
19: 1 heavens are telling the **g** of God;
24: 7 that the King of **g** may come in.
Isa 6: 3 the whole earth is full of his **g**."
40: 5 the **g** of the LORD shall be revealed,
Eze 11:23 **g** of the LORD ascended from the
44: 4 **g** of the LORD filled the temple of
Hos 4: 7 they changed their **g** into shame.
Mt 25:31 the Son of Man comes in his **g**,
Lk 2:14 "**G** to God in the highest heaven,
Jn 1:14 and we have seen his **g**,
12:41 Isaiah said this because he saw his **g**
Ro 3:23 sinned and fall short of the **g** of God;
8:18 not worth comparing with the **g**
9: 4 the **g**, the covenants, the giving of
1Co 10:31 do everything for the **g** of God.
2Co 4:17 for an eternal weight of **g** beyond
Heb 1: 3 reflection of God's **g** and the exact
2Pe 1:17 conveyed to him by the Majestic **G**,
Rev 4:11 to receive **g** and honor and power,
21:23 for the **g** of God is its light,
Sir 1:11 The fear of the Lord is **g** and
Bar 5: 4 "Righteous Peace, Godly **G**."
1Mc 1:40 dishonor now grew as great as her **g**

GLUTTON

Pr 23:21 and the **g** will come to poverty,
Mt 11:19 they say, 'Look, a **g** and a drunkard,

GNASHING

Mt 8:12 will be weeping and **g** of teeth."
25:30 will be weeping and **g** of teeth.'

GNAT*

Mt 23:24 strain out a **g** but swallow a camel!

GO

Ex 5: 1 the God of Israel, 'Let my people **g**,
Jos 1: 9 God is with you wherever you **g**."
Ru 1:16 Where you **g**, I will **g**;
Mt 28:19 **G** therefore and make disciples of
Jn 14: 3 if I **g** and prepare a place for you,

GOAT → GOATS

Lev 16: 9 Aaron shall present the **g** on which
Da 8:21 The male **g** is the king of Greece,

GOATS → GOAT

Ps 50:13 or drink the blood of **g**?
Mt 25:32 separates the sheep from the **g**,
Heb 10: 4 for the blood of bulls and **g**

GOD → GOD'S, GODDESS, GODLESS, GODLINESS, GODLY, GODS

Ge 1: 1 In the beginning when **G** created
1:27 So **G** created humankind in his
image,
3: 5 be like **G**, knowing good and evil."
6: 2 sons of **G** saw that they were fair;
17: 1 and said to him, "I am **G** Almighty,"
Ex 3: 4 **G** called to him out of the bush,
15: 2 this is my **G**, and I will praise him,
20: 5 I the LORD your **G** am a jealous **G**,
34: 6 a **G** merciful and gracious, slow to
Nu 23:19 **G** is not a human being,
Dt 4: 7 a **g** so near to it as the LORD our **G**

6: 5 love the LORD your **G** with all your
Jos 22:34 between us that the LORD is **G**."
1Sa 2: 2 there is no Rock like our **G**.
1Ki 8:27 will **G** indeed dwell on the earth?
18:24 the **g** who answers by fire is
indeed **G**.
2Ki 17: 7 sinned against the LORD their **G**,
2Ch 2: 5 for our **G** is greater than other gods.
Ezr 6:16 the dedication of this house of **G**
Ne 8:18 read from the book of the law of **G**.
Ps 19: 1 heavens are telling the glory of **G**,
22: 1 My **G**, my **G**, why have you forsaken
46: 1 **G** is our refuge and strength,
46:10 "Be still, and know that I am **G**!
47: 7 For **G** is the king of all the earth;
53: 1 Fools say in their hearts, "There is
no **G**."
68:20 Our **G** is a **G** of salvation,
90: 2 everlasting to everlasting you are **G**.
136: 2 O give thanks to the **G** of gods,
145: 1 I will extol you, my **G** and King,
Ecc 12:13 Fear **G**, and keep his
Isa 9: 6 Wonderful Counselor, Mighty **G**,
12: 2 Surely **G** is my salvation;
40:28 The LORD is the everlasting **G**,
44: 6 besides me there is no **g**.
Jer 10:10 But the LORD is the true **G**;
Eze 28: 2 proud and you have said, "I am
a **g**;
Hos 12: 6 But as for you, return to your **G**,
Am 4:12 prepare to meet your **G**,
Mic 6: 8 and to walk humbly with your **G**?
Hab 3:18 I will exult in the **G** of my salvation.
Mal 2:10 Has not one **G** created us?
Mt 1:23 which means, "**G** is with us."
4: 4 that comes from the mouth of **G**.'"
4: 7 not put the Lord your **G** to the test.'
4:10 written, 'Worship the Lord your **G**,
6:24 You cannot serve **G** and wealth.
27:40 If you are the Son of **G**,
Mk 1: 1 news of Jesus Christ, the Son of **G**.
2: 7 Who can forgive sins but **G** alone?"
10: 9 what **G** has joined together, let no
12:30 the Lord your **G** with all your heart,
Lk 2:14 "Glory to **G** in the highest heaven,
18:19 No one is good but **G** alone.
22:70 "Are you, then, the Son of **G**?"
Jn 1: 1 was with **G**, and the Word was **G**.
1:18 It is **G** the only Son,
3:16 **G** so loved the world that he gave his
only Son,
5:18 calling **G** his own Father, thereby
making himself equal to **G**.
20:28 "My Lord and my **G**!"
Ac 5:29 "We must obey **G** rather than any
Ro 4: 3 "Abraham believed **G**, and it was
6:23 gift of **G** is eternal life in Christ
8:31 If **G** is for us, who is against us?
1Co 10:31 do everything for the glory of **G**.
2Co 4: 4 Christ, who is the image of **G**.
6:16 we are the temple of the living **G**;
Eph 4: 6 one **G** and Father of all,
Php 2: 6 though he was in the form of **G**,
Col 1:19 fullness of **G** was pleased to dwell,
Tit 2:13 of our great **G** and Savior, Jesus
Heb 4:12 the word of **G** is living and active,
10:31 to fall into the hands of the living **G**.
12:29 indeed our **G** is a consuming fire.
Jas 2:23 "Abraham believed **G**,
4: 8 Draw near to **G**, and he will draw
1Jn 1: 5 **G** is light and in him there is no
4:16 **G** is love, and those who abide
5: 2 love **G** and obey his commandments
Jude 1:21 keep yourselves in the love of **G**;
Rev 4: 8 "Holy, holy, holy, the Lord **G**
19:13 his name is called **The** Word of **G**.
22: 5 for the Lord **G** will be their light,
Tob 4:19 At all times bless the Lord **G**,
Sir 32:14 seeks **G** will accept his discipline,
Bar 4: 8 You forgot the everlasting **G**,
Bel 1: 4 But Daniel worshiped his own **G**.

GOD (cont.)

Man	1: 1	Lord Almighty, **G** of our ancestors,
2Es	16:67	Indeed, **G** is the judge; fear him!

†GOD → †LORD

Ge	15: 2	But Abram said, "O Lord **G**,
2Sa	7:18	"Who am I, O Lord **G**,
Isa	25: 8	Lord **G** will wipe away the tears
	61: 1	The spirit of the Lord **G** is upon me,

GOD'S → GOD

Mt	27:43	for he said, 'I am **G** Son.'"
	27:54	"Truly this man was **G** Son!"
Ro	2: 4	that **G** kindness is meant to lead you
1Co	3: 9	you are **G** field, **G** building.
	3:16	you are **G** temple and that **G** Spirit
Heb	1: 3	reflection of **G** glory and the exact
		imprint of **G**
1Jn	3: 2	Beloved, we are **G** children now;

GODDESS → GOD

1Ki	11: 5	Astarte the **g** of the Sidonians,
Ac	19:27	the temple of the great **g** Artemis

GODLESS → GOD

Job	8:13	the hope of the **g** shall perish.
Ps	119:122	do not let the **g** oppress me.
1Ti	1: 9	for the **g** and sinful,
2Pe	3: 7	judgment and destruction of the **g**.

GODLINESS → GOD

1Ti	4: 7	Train yourself in **g**,
	6: 5	imagining that **g** is a means of gain.
2Ti	3: 5	outward form of **g** but denying its
Tit	1: 1	truth that is in accordance with **g**,
2Pe	1: 3	everything needed for life and **g**,
Wis	10:12	**g** is more powerful than anything

GODLY → GOD

Mal	2:15	the one God desire? **G** offspring.
2Co	7:10	For **g** grief produces a repentance
2Ti	3:12	to live a **g** life in Christ Jesus will
Tit	2:12	are self-controlled, upright, and **g**,
2Pe	2: 9	how to rescue the **g** from trial,
Sir	37:12	But associate with a **g** person
Bar	5: 4	"Righteous Peace, **G** Glory."

GODS → GOD

Ge	31:19	stole her father's household **g**.
Ex	12:12	**g** of Egypt I will execute judgments:
	20: 3	you shall have no other **g** before me.
Jdg	2:17	they lusted after other **g** and bowed
2Ki	17: 7	They had worshiped other **g**
Jn	10:34	in your law, 'I said, you are **g'?**
1Co	8: 5	so-called **g** in heaven or on earth—

GOG

Eze	38:18	**G** comes against the land of Israel,
Rev	20: 8	**G** and Magog, in order to gather

GOLD

Ex	20:23	make for yourselves gods of **g**.
	25:17	shall make a mercy seat of pure **g**;
	25:31	shall make a lampstand of pure **g**.
	28: 6	They shall make the ephod of **g**, of
	32:31	have made for themselves gods of **g**
1Ki	6:21	the inside of the house with pure **g**,
Job	28:15	It cannot be gotten for **g**,
Ps	119:127	love your commandments more
		than **g**,
Isa	60:17	Instead of bronze I will bring **g**,
Ac	3: 6	Peter said, "I have no silver or **g**,
1Pe	1: 7	being more precious than **g** that,
Rev	21:21	and the street of the city is pure **g**,
Tob	12: 8	better to give alms than to lay up **g**.
Sir	31: 5	who loves **g** will not be justified;

GOLGOTHA

Mt	27:33	**G** (which means Place of a Skull),

GOLIATH

Giant killed by David (1Sa 17; 21:9; Sir 47:4).

GOMORRAH

Ge	19:24	LORD rained on Sodom and **G** sulfur
Isa	1: 9	like Sodom, and become like **G**.
Jude	1: 7	Sodom and **G** and the surrounding

GOOD → BEST, BETTER, GOODNESS

Ge	1:31	and indeed, it was very **g**.
	2: 9	tree of the knowledge of **g** and evil.
	3:22	become like one of us, knowing **g**
	50:20	to me, God intended it for **g**,
Dt	6:18	Do what is right and **g** in the sight
2Ch	7: 3	"For he is **g**, for his steadfast love
Ps	14: 1	there is no one who does **g**.
	34: 8	O taste and see that the LORD is **g**;
	84:11	No **g** thing does the LORD withhold
Pr	18:22	He who finds a wife finds a **g** thing,
Ecc	12:14	every secret thing, whether **g** or evil.
Isa	52: 7	who brings **g** news, who announces
Mt	5:45	his sun rise on the evil and on the **g**,
	13: 8	Other seeds fell on **g** soil and
	25:21	'Well done, **g** and trustworthy slave;'
Mk	10:18	No one is **g** but God alone.
Lk	2:10	I am bringing you **g** news of great
	6:43	"No **g** tree bears bad fruit,
Jn	10:11	"I am the **g** shepherd.
Ro	7:16	I agree that the law is **g**.
	12: 2	is **g** and acceptable and perfect.
	12:21	but overcome evil with **g**.
Eph	2:10	created in Christ Jesus for **g** works,
1Ti	4: 4	For everything created by God is **g**,
Heb	10: 1	the law has only a shadow of the **g**
1Pe	3:17	For it is better to suffer for doing **g**,
Tob	4: 9	laying up a **g** treasure for yourself
Aza	1:67	to the Lord, for he is **g**,

GOODNESS → GOOD

Ex	33:19	will make all my **g** pass before you,
Ps	23: 6	Surely **g** and mercy shall follow me
Heb	6: 5	tasted the **g** of the word of God and
2Pe	1: 5	support your faith with **g**, and **g**

GOSHEN

Ge	45:10	You shall settle in the land of **G**,
Ex	8:22	day I will set apart the land of **G**,

GOSPEL

Mk	8:35	and for the sake of the **g**,
Ro	1:16	For I am not ashamed of the **g**;
1Co	9:16	woe to me if I do not proclaim the **g**
2Co	4: 3	And even if our **g** is veiled,
Gal	1: 6	and are turning to a different **g**—
Php	1:27	life in a manner worthy of the **g**
Rev	14: 6	an eternal **g** to proclaim to those

GOSSIP

Pr	11:13	A **g** goes about telling secrets,
2Co	12:20	selfishness, slander, **g**, conceit,

GRACE → GRACIOUS

Jn	1:14	father's only son, full of **g** and truth.
	1:16	we have all received, **g** upon **g**.
Ac	15:11	that we will be saved through the **g**
Ro	3:24	are now justified by his **g** as a gift,
	6: 1	in sin in order that **g** may abound?
	6:14	you are not under law but under **g**.
	11: 6	otherwise **g** would no longer be **g**.
2Co	12: 9	"My **g** is sufficient for you,
Gal	5: 4	you have fallen away from **g**.
Eph	2: 5	by **g** you have been saved—
2Th	2:16	through **g** gave us eternal comfort
Tit	2:11	For the **g** of God has appeared,
Heb	4:16	approach the throne of **g** with
Jas	4: 6	But he gives all the more **g**;
1Pe	5:10	the God of all **g**,
Jude	1: 4	who pervert the **g** of our God into
Rev	22:21	The **g** of the Lord Jesus be with all
Wis	3: 9	**g** and mercy are upon his holy ones,
2Es	2:32	and my **g** will not fail."

GRACIOUS → GRACE

Ex	34: 6	the LORD, a God merciful and **g**,
Nu	6:25	to shine upon you, and be **g** to you;
Ezr	8:22	of our God is **g** to all who seek him,
Ne	9:31	for you are a **g** and merciful God.
Ps	77: 9	Has God forgotten to be **g?**
	116: 5	**G** is the LORD, and righteous;
Col	4: 6	Let your speech always be **g**,

GRAFTED

Ro	11:17	were **g** in their place to share the

GRAIN

Lev	2: 1	presents a **g** offering to the LORD,
Dt	25: 4	an ox while it is treading out the **g**.
Mk	2:23	disciples began to pluck heads of **g**.
1Ti	5:18	an ox while it is treading out the **g**,"

GRAPES

Nu	13:23	a branch with a single cluster of **g**,
Isa	5: 2	to yield **g**, but it yielded wild **g**.
Jer	31:29	"The parents have eaten sour **g**,
Mt	7:16	Are **g** gathered from thorns, or figs
Rev	14:18	vine of the earth, for its **g** are ripe."

GRASS

Isa	40: 6	All people are **g**, their constancy is
Mt	6:30	if God so clothes the **g** of the field,
1Pe	1:24	"All flesh is like **g** and all its glory

GRATIFY*

Ro	13:14	for the flesh, to **g** its desires.
Gal	5:16	do not **g** the desires of the flesh.

GRAVE → GRAVES

Ps	49:14	straight to the **g** they descend,
Isa	53: 9	They made his **g** with the wicked

GRAVES → GRAVE

Eze	37:12	and bring you up from your **g**,
Lk	11:44	For you are like unmarked **g**,

GRAY

Pr	16:31	**g** hair is a crown of glory;
Sir	6:18	**g** hair you will still find wisdom.

GREAT → GREATER, GREATEST

Ge	1:16	God made the two **g** lights—
	12: 2	I will make of you a **g** nation,
Ex	32:11	**g** power and with a mighty hand?
Dt	10:17	the **g** God, mighty and awesome,
Ne	8: 6	Ezra blessed the LORD, the **g** God,
Ps	95: 3	the LORD is a **g** God, and a **g** King
Jer	10: 6	you are **g**, and your name is **g**
La	3:23	**g** is your faithfulness.
Da	9: 4	"Ah, Lord, **g** and awesome God,
Joel	2:11	Truly the day of the LORD is **g**;
Mt	4:16	sat in darkness have seen a **g** light,
	13:46	on finding one pearl of **g** value,
	20:26	whoever wishes to be **g** among you
Eph	2: 4	the **g** love with which he loved us
Tit	2:13	of the glory of our **g** God and Savior
Heb	2: 3	if we neglect so **g** a salvation?
	12: 1	by so **g** a cloud of witnesses,
	13:20	the **g** shepherd of the sheep,
Rev	12: 9	The **g** dragon was thrown down,
	14: 8	"Fallen, fallen is Babylon the **g**!
	20:11	I saw a **g** white throne and the one
Jdt	16:13	O Lord, you are **g** and glorious,
Sir	17:29	How **g** is the mercy of the Lord,

GREATER → GREAT

Ex	18:11	that the LORD is **g** than all gods,
Mt	12: 6	something **g** than the temple is here.
Mk	12:31	no other commandment **g** than
		these
Jn	14:12	in fact, will do **g** works than these,
	15:13	No one has **g** love than this,
1Jn	4: 4	for the one who is in you is **g** than

GREATEST → GREAT

Mt	22:38	the **g** and first commandment.
Lk	9:48	the least among all of you is the **g**."
1Co	13:13	and the **g** of these is love.

GREECE → GREEK, GREEKS

Da	8:21	The male goat is the king of **G**,
1Mc	1: 1	had previously become king of **G**.)

GREED → GREEDY

Mt	23:25	but inside they are full of **g**
Lk	12:15	on your guard against all kinds of **g**;
Col	3: 5	evil desire, and **g** (which is idolatry)

GREEDY → GREED

Pr	28:25	The **g** person stirs up strife,

1Co 6:10 the **g**, drunkards, revilers, robbers—
Tit 1: 7 to wine or violent or **g** for gain;

GREEK → GREECE
Jn 19:20 in Hebrew, in Latin, and in **G**.
Ro 1:16 to the Jew first and also to the **G**.
Gal 3:28 There is no longer Jew or **G**,

GREEKS → GREECE
1Co 1:22 demand signs and **G** desire wisdom,

GREEN
Ge 1:30 I have given every **g** plant for food."
Ps 23: 2 makes me lie down in **g** pastures;

GREW → GROW
1Sa 2:21 boy Samuel **g** up in the presence of
Isa 53: 2 he **g** up before him like a young
Lk 1:80 child **g** and became strong in spirit,
     2:40 child **g** and became strong, filled

GRIEF → GRIEVE, GRIEVED
La 3:32 causes **g**, he will have compassion
2Co 7: 9 your **g** led to repentance;

GRIEVE → GRIEF
Eph 4:30 do not **g** the Holy Spirit of God,
1Th 4:13 not **g** as others do who have no hope

GRIEVED → GRIEF
Isa 63:10 they rebelled and **g** his holy spirit;
Mt 26:38 "I am deeply **g**, even to death;

GRINDING
Lk 17:35 will be two women **g** meal together;

GROAN → GROANING
Ro 8:23 **g** inwardly while we wait for
2Co 5: 2 For in this tent we **g**, longing to be
2Es 16:39 and the world will **g**,

GROANING → GROAN
Ex 2:24 heard their **g**, and God remembered
Jdg 2:18 would be moved to pity by their **g**
Ps 22: 1 from the words of my **g**?

GROUND
Ge 2: 7 formed man from the dust of the **g**,
     3:17 cursed is the **g** because of you;
Ex 3: 5 which you are standing is holy **g**."
Isa 53: 2 and like a root out of dry **g**;
Mt 13: 5 Other seeds fell on rocky **g**,
Sir 33:10 All human beings come from the **g**,

GROW → GREW, GROWTH
Isa 11: 1 and a branch shall **g** out of his roots.
Eze 47:12 will **g** all kinds of trees for food.
Col 1:10 as you **g** in the knowledge of God.
2Pe 3:18 But **g** in the grace and knowledge of

GROWTH → GROW
1Co 3: 7 but only God who gives the **g**.
Col 2:19 grows with a **g** that is from God.

GUARANTEE → GUARANTEED
2Co 5: 5 who has given us the Spirit as a **g**.
Heb 7:22 Jesus has also become the **g** of a

GUARANTEED* → GUARANTEE
Ro 4:16 promise may rest on grace and be **g**
Heb 6:17 he **g** it by an oath,

GUARD → GUARDIAN, GUARDS
Pr 2:11 and understanding will **g** you.
2Th 3: 3 and **g** you from the evil one.
2Ti 1:12 to **g** until that day what I have

GUARDIAN → GUARD
1Pe 2:25 to the shepherd and **g** of your souls.
Sir 51:12 *Give thanks to the **g** of Israel,*

GUARDS → GUARD
Ps 127: 1 Unless the LORD **g** the city,
Mt 28: 4 the **g** shook and became like dead

GUIDANCE → GUIDE
Pr 11:14 Where there is no **g**, a nation falls,

GUIDE → GUIDANCE
Ps 48:14 He will be our **g** forever.
Isa 58:11 The LORD will **g** you continually,

Lk 6:39 Can a blind person **g** a blind person?
Jn 16:13 he will **g** you into all the truth;

GUILT → GUILTY
Lev 5:15 as your **g** offering to the LORD,
Ps 32: 5 and you forgave the **g** of my sin.
Hos 14: 2 say to him, "Take away all **g**;
Zec 3: 9 I will remove the **g** of this land

GUILTY → GUILT
Ex 23: 7 for I will not acquit the **g**.
Nu 14:18 but by no means clearing the **g**,
Mk 3:29 but is **g** of an eternal sin"—
Sus 1:53 the innocent and acquitting the **g**,

H

HABAKKUK
Prophet to Judah (Hab 1:1; 3:1; Bel 1:33-39).

HADASSAH → See ESTHER

HADES
Mt 16:18 and the gates of **H** will not prevail
Ac 2:27 not abandon my soul to **H**,
Rev 1:18 I have the keys of Death and of **H**.
     20:14 **H** were thrown into the lake of fire.
Sir 21:10 but at its end is the pit of **H**.

HAGAR
Servant of Sarah, wife of Abraham, mother of Ishmael (Ge 16:1-6; 25:12). Driven away by Sarah while pregnant (Ge 16:5-16); after birth of Isaac (Ge 21:9-21; Gal 4:21-31).

HAGGAI*
Post-exilic prophet who encouraged rebuilding of the temple (Ezr 5:1; 6:14; Hag 1-2; 1Es 6:1; 7:3; 2Es 1:40).

HAIL → HAILSTONES
Ex 9:19 will die when the **h** comes down
Rev 8: 7 came **h** and fire, mixed with blood,

HAILSTONES → HAIL
Jos 10:11 of the **h** than the Israelites killed
Rev 16:21 and huge **h**, each weighing about

HAIR → HAIRS
Jdg 16:22 **h** of his head began to grow again
Lk 7:44 her tears and dried them with her **h**.
1Co 11: 6 for a woman to have her **h** cut off
1Ti 2: 9 not with their **h** braided, or with

HAIRS → HAIR
Ps 40:12 more than the **h** of my head,
Mt 10:30 the **h** of your head are all counted.

HALF
Est 5: 3 even to the **h** of my kingdom."
Mk 6:23 give you, even **h** of my kingdom."
Lk 19: 8 of my possessions, Lord, I will

HALLELUJAH
Rev 19: 1 multitude in heaven, saying, "**H**!
Tob 13:17 and all her houses will cry, '**H**!

HALLOWED
Ge 2: 3 blessed the seventh day and **h** it,
Mt 6: 9 Father in heaven, **h** be your name.

HAM
Son of Noah (Ge 5:32; 1Ch 1:4), father of Canaan (Ge 9:18; 10:6-20; 1Ch 1:8-16). Saw Noah's nakedness (Ge 9:20-27).

HAMAN
Agagite nobleman honored by Xerxes (Est 3:1-2). Plotted to exterminate the Jews because of Mordecai (Est 3:3-15). Forced to honor Mordecai (Est 5-6). Plot exposed by Esther (Est 5:1-8; 7:1-8). Hanged (Est 7:9-10). See also Additions to Esther.

HANANIAH → =SHADRACH
1. False prophet; adversary of Jeremiah (Jer 28).
2. Original name of Shadrach (Da 1:6-19; 2:17).

HAND → EMPTY-HANDED, HANDED, HANDS
Ex 3:19 unless compelled by a mighty **h**.
     15: 6 Your right **h**, O LORD, glorious in
Dt 19:21 tooth for tooth, **h** for **h**, foot for foot
1Ki 18:44 cloud no bigger than a person's **h** is
Ps 16: 8 he is at my right **h**, I shall not be
     98: 1 right **h** and his holy arm have gotten
     110: 1 says to my lord, "Sit at my right **h**
Pr 3:16 Long life is in her right **h**;
Isa 5:25 and his **h** is stretched out still.
Da 5: 5 the fingers of a human **h** appeared
Hab 2:16 The cup in the LORD's right **h** will
Mt 3:12 His winnowing fork is in his **h**,
Mk 9:43 If your **h** causes you to stumble, cut
Lk 20:42 said to my Lord, "Sit at my right **h**,
Jn 10:28 will snatch them out of my **h**.
Ro 8:34 raised, who is at the right **h** of God,
1Co 12:15 would say, "Because I am not a **h**,
Heb 10:12 "he sat down at the right **h** of God,"
Rev 1:16 In his right **h** he held seven stars,
     5: 1 saw in the right **h** of the one seated
Jdt 9:10 by the **h** of a woman.

HANDED → HAND
Mt 27:26 he **h** him over to be crucified.
Ro 4:25 **h** over to death for our trespasses

HANDS → HAND
Ps 24: 4 who have clean **h** and pure hearts,
     115: 7 They have **h**, but do not feel;
Ecc 11: 6 at evening do not let your **h** be idle;
Isa 49:16 inscribed you on the palms of my **h**;
Da 2:45 was cut from the mountain not by **h**,
Lk 23:46 into your **h** I commend my spirit."
     24:40 he showed them his **h** and his feet.
Jn 3:35 has placed all things in his **h**.
Ac 8:18 the laying on of the apostles' **h**,
Ro 10:21 "All day long I have held out my **h**
Heb 6: 2 laying on of **h**, resurrection of the
     10:31 to fall into the **h** of the living God.

HANNAH*
Wife of Elkanah, mother of Samuel (1Sa 1). Prayer at dedication of Samuel (1Sa 2:1-10). Blessed (1Sa 2:18-21).

HAPPY
Ps 1: 1 **H** are those who do not follow the
     33:12 **H** is the nation whose God is the LORD,
     84:12 **h** is everyone who trusts in you.
Pr 3:13 **H** are those who find wisdom,
Ecc 3:12 nothing better for them than to be **h**
Tob 13:14 **H** are those who love you,
Sir 1:13 who fear the Lord will have a **h** end;

HARD → HARD-HEARTED, HARDEN, HARDENED, HARDENING, HARDSHIP, HARDSHIPS
Ex 1:14 made their lives bitter with **h** service
Jer 32:17 Nothing is too **h** for you.
Mt 7:14 the road is **h** that leads to life,
     19:23 **h** for a rich person to enter the

HARD-HEARTED* → HARD, HEART
Dt 15: 7 do not be **h** or tight-fisted toward
Pr 28:14 one who is **h** will fall into calamity.
Mt 19: 8 you were so **h** that Moses allowed

HARDEN → HARD
Ex 4:21 but I will **h** his heart,
Ps 95: 8 Do not **h** your hearts, as at Meribah,
Heb 3: 8 not **h** your hearts as in the rebellion,

HARDENED → HARD
Ex 10:20 But the LORD **h** Pharaoh's heart,
Mk 8:17 Are your hearts **h**?
Ro 11: 7 elect obtained it, but the rest were **h**,
2Co 3:14 But their minds were **h**.

HARDENING* → HARD
Ro 11:25 a **h** has come upon part of Israel,

HARDSHIP → HARD
Ro 8:35 Will **h**, or distress, or persecution,

HARDSHIPS → HARD
2Co 12:10 content with weaknesses, insults, **h,**

HARM
Ge 50:20 though you intended to do **h** to me,
Ne 6: 2 But they intended to do me **h.**
Pr 12:21 No **h** happens to the righteous,
Jer 29:11 plans for your welfare and not for **h,**
1Pe 3:13 who will **h** you if you are eager

HARP → HARPS
Ps 150: 3 praise him with lute and **h!**
Rev 5: 8 each holding a **h** and golden bowls

HARPS → HARP
1Ch 15:16 on **h** and lyres and cymbals,
Ne 12:27 with cymbals, **h,** and lyres.
Ps 137: 2 the willows there we hung up our **h.**

HARSHLY
Dt 26: 6 When the Egyptians treated us **h**
Col 3:19 your wives and never treat them **h.**
1Ti 5: 1 Do not speak **h** to an older man,

HARVEST → HARVESTING
Ge 8:22 the earth endures, seedtime and **h,**
Ex 23:16 You shall observe the festival of **h,**
Mt 13:39 **h** is the end of the age, and the
Lk 10: 2 He said to them, "The **h** is plentiful,
Rev 14:15 the **h** of the earth is fully ripe."

HARVESTING* → HARVEST
Jn 4:35 and see how the fields are ripe for **h.**

HASTENING*
Zep 1:14 day of the LORD is near, near and **h**
2Pe 3:12 and **h** the coming of the day of God,

HATE → HATED, HATING
Ps 45: 7 righteousness and **h** wickedness.
     97:10 The LORD loves those who **h** evil;
Pr 13: 5 The righteous **h** falsehood,
Ecc 3: 8 a time to love, and a time to **h;**
Am 5:15 **H** evil and love good, and establish
Mal 2:16 For I **h** divorce, says the LORD,
Mt 5:43 your neighbor and **h** your enemy.'
Lk 6:27 do good to those who **h** you,
Jn 7: 7 The world cannot **h** you, but it hates
Ro 7:15 but I do the very thing I **h.**

HATED → HATE
Jn 15:18 aware that it **h** me before it **h** you.
Ro 9:13 loved Jacob, but I have **h** Esau."

HATES → HATE
Dt 16:22 things that the LORD your God **h.**
Pr 6:16 six things that the LORD **h,**
Jn 15:23 Whoever **h** me **h** my Father also.
Sir 15:13 The Lord **h** all abominations;

HAUGHTY
Pr 6:17 **h** eyes, a lying tongue, and hands
     16:18 and a **h** spirit before a fall.
1Ti 6:17 command them not to be **h,**

HAY*
1Co 3:12 precious stones, wood, **h,** straw—

HEAD → BEHEADED, HEADS
Isa 59:17 and a helmet of salvation on his **h;**
Mt 8:20 of Man has nowhere to lay his **h."**
Mk 6:28 brought his **h** on a platter,
1Co 11: 3 Christ is the **h** of every man, and the
       husband is the **h** of his wife,
Eph 1:22 has made him the **h** over all things

HEADS → HEAD
Eze 11:21 bring their deeds upon their own **h,**
Rev 12: 3 a great red dragon, with seven **h**

HEAL → HEALED, HEALING, HEALS,
     HEALTH, HEALTHY
Dt 32:39 and I make alive; I wound and I **h;**
Ecc 3: 3 a time to kill, and a time to **h;**
Isa 57:19 says the LORD; and I will **h** them.
Jer 3:22 I will **h** your faithlessness.
Hos 14: 4 I will **h** their disloyalty; I will love
Jn 12:40 and turn—and I would **h** them."

HEALED → HEAL
Isa 6:10 their minds, and turn and be **h."**
     53: 5 and by his bruises we are **h.**
Hos 11: 3 but they did not know that I **h** them.
Jas 5:16 one another, so that you may be **h.**
1Pe 2:24 by his wounds you have been **h.**

HEALING → HEAL
Pr 12:18 but the tongue of the wise brings **h.**
Eze 47:12 for food, and their leaves for **h."**
Mal 4: 2 shall rise, with **h** in its wings.
1Co 12: 9 another gifts of **h** by the one Spirit,
Rev 22: 2 leaves of the tree are for the **h** of
Sir 38: 2 gift of **h** comes from the Most High,

HEALS → HEAL
Ex 15:26 for I am the LORD who **h** you."
Ps 103: 3 iniquity, who **h** all your diseases,
Wis 16:12 your word, O Lord, that **h** all people

HEALTH → HEAL
3Jn 1: 2 and that you may be in good **h,**
Sir 30:15 **H** and fitness are better than any

HEALTHY → HEAL
Lk 11:34 If your eye is **h,** your whole body

HEAR → HEARD, HEARERS, HEARING,
     HEARS
Dt 6: 4 **H,** O Israel: The LORD is our God,
     31:13 may **h** and learn to fear the LORD
1Ki 8:30 O **h** in heaven your dwelling place;
Isa 59: 1 nor his ear too dull to **h.**
Jer 5:21 who have ears, but do not **h.**
Eze 37: 4 dry bones, **h** the word of the LORD.
Mt 13:17 to **h** what you **h,** but did not **h** it.
Mk 12:29 answered, "The first is, '**H,** O Israel:
Lk 7:22 the lepers are cleansed, the deaf **h,**
Heb 3: 7 says, "Today, if you **h** his voice,
Sir 5:11 Be quick to **h,** but deliberate in

HEARD → HEAR
Isa 40:21 not known? Have you not **h?**
1Co 2: 9 "What no eye has seen, nor ear **h,**
1Jn 1: 3 to you what we have seen and **h** so
Rev 22: 8 I, John, am the one who **h** and saw

HEARERS → HEAR
Ro 2:13 For it is not the **h** of the law who
Jas 1:22 merely **h** who deceive themselves.

HEARING → HEAR
Pr 18:13 one gives answer before **h,**
Am 8:11 but of **h** the words of the LORD.
1Co 12:17 If the whole body were **h,**

HEARS → HEAR
Ps 69:33 For the LORD **h** the needy,
Pr 15:29 but he **h** the prayer of the righteous.
Mt 7:24 then who **h** these words of mine
Jn 5:24 I tell you, anyone who **h** my word
1Jn 5:14 according to his will, he **h** us.
Rev 22:18 I warn everyone who **h** the words

HEART → BROKENHEARTED, HARD-
     HEARTED, HEART'S, HEARTLESS,
     HEARTS, TENDERHEARTED
Ge 6: 6 and it grieved him to his **h.**
Ex 4:21 but I will harden his **h,**
     14: 4 I will harden Pharaoh's **h,**
Dt 6: 5 the LORD your God with all your **h,**
     30:14 in your mouth and in your **h** for you
Jos 22: 5 all your **h** and with all your soul."
1Sa 16: 7 but the LORD looks on the **h."**
Ps 19:14 meditation of my **h** be acceptable to
     51:10 Create in me a clean **h,** O God,
Pr 3: 5 Trust in the LORD with all your **h,**
     7: 3 write them on the tablet of your **h.**
Jer 9:26 of Israel is uncircumcised in **h.**
Eze 36:26 A new **h** I will give you,
Mt 5: 8 "Blessed are the pure in **h,** for they
     5:28 adultery with her in his **h.**
Mk 12:30 the Lord your God with all your **h,**
Lk 12:34 treasure is, there your **h** will be also.
Ro 2:29 circumcision is a matter of the **h**—
     10: 9 believe in your **h** that God raised

Heb 10:22 let us approach with a true **h** in full
Sir 1:12 The fear of the Lord delights the **h,**
Aza 1:16 Yet with a contrite and
Man 1:11 And now I bend the knee of my **h,**

HEART'S → HEART
Ps 20: 4 May he grant you your **h** desire,
Ro 10: 1 my **h** desire and prayer to God for

HEARTLESS* → HEART
Ro 1:31 foolish, faithless, **h,** ruthless.

HEARTS → HEART
Ps 95: 8 not harden your **h,** as at Meribah,
Jer 31:33 and I will write it on their **h;**
Mk 7: 6 but their **h** are far from me;
Jn 14: 1 "Do not let your **h** be troubled.
Ro 2:15 law requires is written on their **h,**
Eph 3:17 Christ may dwell in your **h** through
Col 3:15 the peace of Christ rule in your **h,**
Heb 3: 8 do not harden your **h** as in the
     10:16 I will put my laws in their **h,**
2Pe 1:19 and the morning star rises in your **h.**
1Jn 3:20 for God is greater than our **h,**
Rev 2:23 the one who searches minds and **h,**

HEAVEN → HEAVENLY, HEAVENS
Ge 14:19 by God Most High, maker of **h** and
     28:12 the top of it reaching to **h;**
Ex 16: 4 "I am going to rain bread from **h**
Dt 30:12 "Who will go up to **h** for us,
     31:28 and call **h** and earth to witness
1Ki 8:27 **h** and the highest **h** cannot contain
Job 16:19 now, in fact, my witness is in **h,**
Ecc 3: 1 and a time for every matter under **h:**
Isa 14:12 you are fallen from **h,** O Day Star,
Jer 23:24 Do I not fill **h** and earth?
Mt 3: 2 "Repent, for the kingdom of **h** has
     6: 9 Father in **h,** hallowed be your name.
     24:35 **H** and earth will pass away,
     26:64 and coming on the clouds of **h."**
Mk 10:21 and you will have treasure in **h;**
Lk 10:18 "I watched Satan fall from **h** like a
     19:38 Peace in **h,** and glory in the
       highest **h!"**
     24:51 and was carried up into **h.**
Jn 3:13 No one has ascended into **h** except
       the one who descended from **h,**
Ac 1:11 same way as you saw him go into **h.**
Ro 10: 6 'Who will ascend into **h?'"**
2Co 12: 2 was caught up to the third **h**—
Php 3:20 But our citizenship is in **h,**
1Th 1:10 to wait for his Son from **h,**
Heb 9:24 but he entered into **h** itself,
2Pe 1:18 heard this voice come from **h,**
Rev 4: 1 and there in **h** a door stood open!
     21: 1 I saw a new **h** and a new earth;

HEAVENLY → HEAVEN
Mt 5:48 as your **h** Father is perfect.
2Co 5: 2 longing to be clothed with our **h**
Eph 1: 3 spiritual blessing in the **h** places,
Heb 3: 1 holy partners in a **h** calling,

HEAVENS → HEAVEN
Ge 1: 1 when God created the **h** and
     11: 4 and a tower with its top in the **h,**
Dt 10:14 the heaven of **h** belong to the LORD
Ps 57: 5 Be exalted, O God, above the **h.**
     115:16 The **h** are the LORD's **h,**
Isa 65:17 to create new **h** and a new earth;
Jer 10:11 The gods who did not make the **h**
Eph 4:10 who ascended far above all the **h,**
Heb 4:14 priest who has passed through the **h,**
2Pe 3:10 the **h** will pass away with a loud

HEAVY
Mt 23: 4 They tie up **h** burdens, hard to bear,
Mk 14:40 for their eyes were very **h;**

HEBREW → HEBREWS
Jnh 1: 9 "I am a **H,**" he replied.
Jn 19:20 and it was written in **H,** in Latin,
Php 3: 5 of Benjamin, a **H** born of Hebrews;

HEBREWS → HEBREW

Ex 3:18 The Lord, the God of the **H**, has
2Co 11:22 Are they **H**? So am I.
Jdt 10:12 "I am a daughter of the **H**,

HEBRON

Ge 13:18 the oaks of Mamre, which are at **H**;
2Sa 2:11 The time that David was king in **H**

HEEL

Ge 3:15 your head, and you will strike his **h**.
25:26 with his hand gripping Esau's **h**;
Ps 41: 9 has lifted the **h** against me,
Jn 13:18 has lifted his **h** against me.'

HEIGHT → HIGH

Ro 8:39 nor **h**, nor depth, nor anything else
Eph 3:18 and length and **h** and depth,

HEIGHTS → HIGH

Ps 148: 1 the heavens; praise him in the **h**!
Hab 3:19 and makes me tread upon the **h**.

HEIR → HEIRS

Ge 15: 4 "This man shall not be your **h**;
Gal 4: 7 then also an **h**, through God.
Heb 1: 2 whom he appointed **h** of all things,

HEIRS → HEIR

Ro 8:17 **h**, **h** of God and joint **h** with
Christ—
Eph 3: 6 the Gentiles have become fellow **h**,
1Pe 3: 7 also **h** of the gracious gift of life—

HELL

Mt 10:28 both soul and body in **h**.
Mk 9:43 to have two hands and to go to **h**,
2Pe 2: 4 cast them into **h** and committed
2Es 2:29 so that your children may not
see **h**.

HELMET

Isa 59:17 and a **h** of salvation on his head;
Eph 6:17 Take the **h** of salvation, and the

HELP → HELPED, HELPER, HELPS

Ex 18: 4 "The God of my father was my **h**,
Ps 33:20 he is our **h** and shield.
46: 1 a very present **h** in trouble.
Mk 9:24 "I believe; **h** my unbelief!"
Heb 2:18 able to **h** those who are being tested.
4:16 receive mercy and find grace to **h**
Jdt 6:21 called on the God of Israel for **h**.
Sir 2: 6 Trust in him, and he will **h** you;

HELPED → HELP

1Sa 7:12 "Thus far the Lord has **h** us."
Ps 118:13 I was falling, but the Lord **h** me.
Isa 49: 8 on a day of salvation I have **h** you;

HELPER → HELP

Ge 2:18 I will make him a **h** as his partner."
Ps 30:10 O Lord, be my **h**!"
Heb 13: 6 Lord is my **h**; I will not be afraid.
Tob 8: 6 Eve as a **h** and support.

HELPS → HELP

Ps 37:40 The Lord **h** them and rescues them;
Ro 8:26 the Spirit **h** us in our weakness;

HERBS

Ex 12: 8 with unleavened bread and bitter **h**.

HERMON

Dt 3: 8 from the Wadi Arnon to Mount **H**
Ps 133: 3 It is like the dew of **H**,

HEROD → HERODIANS

1. King of Judea; tried to kill Jesus (Mt 2; Lk 1:5).
2. Son of 1. Tetrarch of Galilee who arrested and beheaded John the Baptist (Mt 14:1-12; Mk 6:14-29; Lk 3:1, 19-20; 9:7-9); tried Jesus (Lk 23:6-15).
3. Grandson of 1. King of Judea who killed James (Ac 12:2); arrested Peter (Ac 12:3-19). Death (Ac 12:19-23).

HERODIANS → HEROD

Mk 3: 6 immediately conspired with the **H**
12:13 some **H** to trap him in what he said.

HERODIAS*

Wife of Herod the Tetrarch who persuaded her daughter to ask for John the Baptist's head (Mt 14:1-12; Mk 6:14-29; Lk 3:19).

HEWN

Ex 20:25 do not build it of **h** stones;
Mk 15:46 laid it in a tomb that had been **h**

HEZEKIAH

King of Judah (Sir 48:17-25). Restored the temple and worship (2Ch 29-31). Sought the Lord for help against Assyria (2Ki 18-19; 2Ch 32:1-23; Isa 36-37). Illness healed (2Ki 20:1-11; 2Ch 32:24-26; Isa 38). Judged for showing Babylonians his treasures (2Ki 20:12-21; 2Ch 32:31; Isa 39).

HID → HIDE

Ge 3: 8 and his wife **h** themselves from the
Ex 2: 2 a fine baby, she **h** him three months.
3: 6 Moses **h** his face, for he was afraid
Jos 2: 6 live because she **h** the messengers
1Ki 18:13 **h** a hundred of the Lord's prophets
Isa 49: 2 in the shadow of his hand he **h** me;
54: 8 wrath for a moment I **h** my face
Mt 25:25 and **h** your talent in the ground.

HIDDEN → HIDE

Ps 19:12 Clear me from **h** faults.
Pr 2: 4 and search for it as for **h** treasures—
Isa 40:27 "My way is **h** from the Lord,
Mt 13:44 is like treasure **h** in a field,
Mk 4:22 nothing **h**, except to be disclosed;
Col 3: 3 your life is **h** with Christ in God.
Rev 2:17 the **h** manna, and I will give a white
Sir 42:20 and nothing is **h** from him.

HIDE → HID, HIDDEN

Dt 31:17 I will forsake them and **h** my face
Ps 13: 1 How long will you **h** your face
17: 8 **h** me in the shadow of your wings,

HIGH → HEIGHT, HEIGHTS, HIGHER, HIGHEST, HIGHLY

Ge 14:18 he was priest of God Most **H**.
1Ki 3: 2 were sacrificing at the **h** places,
Ps 91: 1 live in the shelter of the Most **H**,
Mt 4: 8 a very **h** mountain and showed him
17: 1 and led them up a **h** mountain,
Mk 5: 7 Jesus, Son of the Most **H** God?
Eph 4: 8 "When he ascended on **h** he made
Heb 2:17 a merciful and faithful **h** priest
7:26 that we should have such a **h** priest,

HIGHER → HIGH

Ps 61: 2 Lead me to the rock that is **h** than I;
Isa 55: 9 so are my ways **h** than your ways

HIGHEST → HIGH

1Ki 8:27 the **h** heaven cannot contain you,
Mt 21: 9 Hosanna in the **h** heaven!"
Lk 2:14 "Glory to God in the **h** heaven,

HIGHLY → HIGH

Ps 47: 9 to God; he is **h** exalted.
Ro 12: 3 not to think of yourself more **h** than

HILL → HILLS

Ps 15: 1 Who may dwell on your holy **h**?
Isa 40: 4 every mountain and **h** be made low;
Mt 5:14 A city built on a **h** cannot be hid.
Lk 3: 5 mountain and **h** shall be made low,

HILLS → HILL

1Ki 20:23 "Their gods are gods of the **h**,
Ps 50:10 the cattle on a thousand **h**.

HINDER

1Sa 14: 6 nothing can **h** the Lord from saving
Isa 43:13 I work and who can **h** it?
1Pe 3: 7 so that nothing may **h** your prayers.

HIP

Ge 32:25 Jacob's **h** was put out of joint

HIRAM

King of Tyre; helped David build his palace (2Sa 5:11-12; 1Ch 14:1); helped Solomon build the temple (1Ki 5; 2Ch 2) and his navy (1Ki 9:10-27; 2Ch 8).

HITTITE → HITTITES

Ge 23:10 Ephron the **H** answered Abraham
2Sa 11: 3 the wife of Uriah the **H**."

HITTITES → HITTITE

Dt 20:17 **H** and the Amorites, the Canaanites
Ezr 9: 1 Canaanites, the **H**, the Perizzites,

HOLD → HOLDS

Ps 73:23 you **h** my right hand.
Isa 41:13 I, the Lord your God, **h** your right
Jn 20:17 Jesus said to her, "Do not **h** on to
Col 1:17 and in him all things **h** together.

HOLDS → HOLD

Ps 37:24 for the Lord **h** us by the hand.
Rev 2: 1 who **h** the seven stars in his right
Wis 1: 7 which **h** all things together

HOLES

Hag 1: 6 to put them into a bag with **h**.
Mt 8:20 Jesus said to him, "Foxes have **h**,

HOLINESS → HOLY

Ex 15:11 Who is like you, majestic in **h**,
Dt 32:51 by failing to maintain my **h** among
Ps 89:35 and for all I have sworn by my **h**;
Ro 1: 4 according to the spirit of **h** by
2Co 6: 6 kindness, **h** of spirit, genuine love,
1Ti 2:15 continue in faith and love and **h**,
Heb 12:14 **h** without which no one will see the

HOLOFERNES

Assyrian general (Jdt 2:4). Beguiled and beheaded by Judith (Jdt 10-13).

HOLY → HOLINESS

Ex 3: 5 which you are standing is **h** ground.
20: 8 the sabbath day, and keep it **h**.
26:33 the **h** place from the most **h**.
29:37 the altar shall be most **h**;
Lev 11:44 and be **h**, for I am **h**.
Jos 5:15 for the place where you stand is **h**."
1Sa 2: 2 "There is no **H** One like the Lord,
Ps 2: 6 set my king on Zion, my **h** hill."
11: 4 The Lord is in his **h** temple;
Isa 6: 3 "**H**, **h**, **h** is the Lord of hosts;
40:25 who is my equal? says the **H** One.
Da 9:24 and to anoint a most **h** place.
Mt 1:18 to be with child from the **H** Spirit.
3:11 baptize you with the **H** Spirit and
24:15 sacrilege standing in the **h** place,
Mk 1:24 who you are, the **H** One of God."
3:29 against the **H** Spirit can never have
Lk 3:22 the **H** Spirit descended upon him in
11:13 heavenly Father give the **H** Spirit
Jn 14:26 But the Advocate, the **H** Spirit,
Ac 2: 4 were filled with the **H** Spirit and
2:27 your **H** One experience corruption.
5: 3 your heart to lie to the **H** Spirit
Ro 12: 1 living sacrifice, **h** and acceptable to
Eph 1: 4 to be **h** and blameless
4:30 do not grieve the **H** Spirit of God,
Heb 6: 4 and have shared in the **H** Spirit,
1Pe 1:16 "You shall be **h**, for I am **h**."
1Jn 2:20 have been anointed by the **H** One,
Jude 1:14 with ten thousands of his **h** ones,
Rev 4: 8 **H**, **h**, **h**, the Lord God the Almighty
21: 2 I saw the **h** city, the new Jerusalem,
Wis 4:15 he watches over his **h** ones.
1Mc 1:15 and abandoned the **h** covenant.
2Es 14:22 send the **h** spirit into me,

HOME → HOMELESS, HOMETOWN

Dt 6: 7 when you are at **h** and when you
Ps 68: 6 God gives the desolate a **h**
Jn 14:23 to them and make our **h** with them.
2Co 5: 8 the body and at **h** with the Lord.

HOMELESS* → HOME
Isa 58: 7 the **h** poor into your house;
1Co 4:11 poorly clothed and beaten and **h**,

HOMETOWN → HOME, TOWN
Mk 6: 4 not without honor, except in their **h**,

HONEST
Lev 19:36 have **h** balances, **h** weights,
Pr 16:11 **H** balances and scales are the

HONEY
Ex 3: 8 a land flowing with milk and **h**,
Jdg 14: 8 bees in the body of the lion, and **h**.
1Sa 14:26 honeycomb, the **h** was dripping out;
Ps 19:10 sweeter also than **h**, and drippings
Mt 3: 4 and his food was locusts and wild **h**.

**HONOR → HONORABLE, HONORED,
        HONORS**
Dt 5:16 **H** your father and your mother,
1Ch 29:12 Riches and **h** come from you,
Ps 8: 5 and crowned them with glory and **h**.
Ecc 10: 1 little folly outweighs wisdom and **h**.
Isa 29:13 and **h** me with their lips,
Mal 1: 6 a father, where is the **h** due me?
Mt 13:57 not without **h** except in their own
  15: 4 For God said, 'H your father and
Jn 12:26 serves me, the Father will **h**.
Ro 13: 7 **h** to whom **h** is due.
Eph 6: 2 "H your father and mother"—
1Ti 5:17 considered worthy of double **h**,
Heb 2: 7 crowned them with glory and **h**,
Rev 4:11 to receive glory and **h** and power,
Tob 4: 3 **H** your mother and do not

HONORABLE → HONOR
Php 4: 8 whatever is true, whatever is **h**,

HONORED → HONOR
Hag 1: 8 I may take pleasure in it and be **h**,
1Co 12:26 if one member is **h**, all rejoice

HONORS → HONOR
Mal 1: 6 A son **h** his father, and servants
Mt 15: 8 'This people **h** me with their lips,

HOOFS
Lev 11: 3 Any animal that has divided **h**

HOOK → HOOKS
Mt 17:27 go to the sea and cast a **h**;

HOOKS → HOOK
Isa 2: 4 and their spears into pruning **h**;
Joel 3:10 and your pruning **h** into spears;

HOPE → HOPED, HOPES
Job 17:15 where then is my **h**?
Ps 62: 5 for my **h** is from him.
  146: 5 whose **h** is in the LORD their God,
Pr 23:18 and your **h** will not be cut off.
Isa 8:17 and I will **h** in him.
Jer 14: 8 O **h** of Israel, its savior in time of
La 3:21 and therefore I have **h**:
Mt 12:21 in his name the Gentiles will **h**."
Ro 5: 5 and **h** does not disappoint us,
  12:12 Rejoice in **h**, be patient in suffering,
1Co 13:13 And now faith, **h**, and love abide,
Col 1:27 Christ in you, the **h** of glory.
1Th 5: 8 and for a helmet the **h** of salvation.
Heb 6:19 this **h**, a sure and steadfast anchor
  7:19 the introduction of a better **h**,
1Pe 1: 3 a living **h** through the resurrection
1Jn 3: 3 all who have this **h** in him purify
Sir 34:15 their **h** is in him who saves them.
Sus 1:60 who saves those who **h** in him.

HOPED → HOPE
Heb 11: 1 faith is the assurance of things **h**
          for,
1Pe 3: 5 the holy women who **h** in God

HOPES → HOPE
1Co 13: 7 believes all things, **h** all things,

HOREB → =SINAI
Ex 3: 1 came to **H**, the mountain of God.

Dt 5: 2 God made a covenant with us at **H**.
1Ki 19: 8 forty days and forty nights to **H**

HORN → HORNS
Ps 18: 2 and the **h** of my salvation,
Da 7: 8 when another **h** appeared,
  8: 5 The goat had a **h** between its eyes.

HORNS → HORN
Ge 22:13 caught in a thicket by its **h**.
Ex 27: 2 make **h** for it on its four corners;
Da 7: 7 that preceded it, and it had ten **h**.
  8: 3 Both **h** were long, but one
Zec 1:18 And I looked up and saw four **h**.
Rev 5: 6 having seven **h** and seven eyes,
  9:13 from the four **h** of the golden altar
  17: 3 and it had seven heads and ten **h**.

HORSE → HORSES
Ex 15: 1 **h** and rider he has thrown into the
Ps 33:17 The war **h** is a vain hope for victory,
Zec 1: 8 I saw a man riding on a red **h**!
Rev 6: 2 I looked, and there was a white **h**!
  19:11 and there was a white **h**!

HORSES → HORSE
2Ki 2:11 a chariot of fire and **h** of fire
Ps 20: 7 pride in chariots, and some in **h**,
Joel 2: 4 They have the appearance of **h**,
Rev 9: 7 appearance the locusts were like **h**
  19:14 following him on white **h**.

HOSANNA
Mk 11:10 **H** in the highest heaven!"
Jn 12:13 went out to meet him, shouting, "H!

HOSEA
Prophet whose wife and family pictured the
unfaithfulness of Israel (Hos 1-3).

HOSHEA → =JOSHUA
1. Original name of Joshua (Nu 13:8, 16).
2. Last king of Israel (2Ki 15:30; 17:1-6).

HOSPITABLE* → HOSPITALITY
1Ti 3: 2 temperate, sensible, respectable, **h**,
Tit 1: 8 but he must be **h**, a lover
1Pe 4: 9 Be **h** to one another without

HOSPITALITY* → HOSPITABLE
Ro 12:13 of the saints; extend to strangers,
1Ti 5:10 has brought up children, shown **h**,
Heb 13: 2 not neglect to show **h** to strangers,

HOST → HOSTS
Dt 4:19 all the **h** of heaven,
2Ki 17:16 worshiped all the **h** of heaven
Lk 2:13 angel a multitude of the heavenly **h**,

HOSTILE → HOSTILITY
Ro 8: 7 that is set on the flesh is **h** to God;
Col 1:21 once estranged and **h** in mind,

HOSTILITY → HOSTILE
Eph 2:14 the dividing wall, that is, the **h**
Heb 12: 3 Consider him who endured such **h**

HOSTS → HOST
1Sa 1: 3 and to sacrifice to the LORD of **h**
Ps 46: 7 The LORD of **h** is with us;
Isa 48: 2 the LORD of **h** is his name.

HOT
Rev 3:15 you are neither cold nor **h**.

HOUR
Mt 6:27 by worrying add a single **h** to your
  24:36 about that day and **h** no one knows,
Jn 2: 4 My **h** has not yet come."
  17: 1 "Father, the **h** has come;
Rev 3:10 I will keep you from the **h** of trial
  14: 7 for the **h** of his judgment has come;

**HOUSE → HOUSEHOLD, HOUSES,
        HOUSETOP, HOUSETOPS,
        STOREHOUSE**
Ex 20:17 shall not covet your neighbor's **h**;
2Sa 7:11 that the LORD will make you a **h**.
1Ch 22: 1 "Here shall be the **h** of the LORD

Ezr 1: 5 rebuild the **h** of the LORD in
Ps 69: 9 zeal for your **h** that has consumed
  127: 1 Unless the LORD builds the **h**,
Pr 9: 1 Wisdom has built her **h**, she has
Isa 56: 7 my **h** shall be called a **h** of prayer
Mt 7:24 like a wise man who built his **h**
  21:13 'My **h** shall be called a **h** of prayer';
Mk 3:25 And if a **h** is divided against itself,
Jn 2:17 "Zeal for your **h** will consume me."
  14: 2 In my Father's **h** there are many
1Pe 2: 5 be built into a spiritual **h**,

HOUSEHOLD → HOUSE
Jos 24:15 and my **h**, we will serve the LORD."
Mic 7: 6 enemies are members of your own **h**
Mt 10:36 will be members of one's own **h**.
1Ti 3: 4 He must manage his own **h** well,
Tit 2: 5 good managers of the **h**, kind,
1Pe 4:17 judgment to begin with the **h** of God

HOUSES → HOUSE
Ex 12:27 passed over the **h** of the Israelites in
Mt 19:29 everyone who has left **h** or brothers

HOUSETOP → HOUSE
Mt 24:17 the one on the **h** must not go down

HOUSETOPS → HOUSE
Mt 10:27 whispered, proclaim from the **h**.

HULDAH*
Prophetess inquired by Hilkiah for Josiah (2Ki
22; 2Ch 34:14-28).

HUMAN → HUMANKIND
Ge 6: 7 blot out from the earth the **h** beings
Ps 8: 4 are **h** beings that you are mindful
Da 2:34 a stone was cut out, not by **h** hands,
  5: 5 the fingers of a **h** hand appeared
Hos 11: 4 I led them with cords of **h** kindness,
Mt 15: 9 teaching **h** precepts as doctrines.'"
Ac 5:29 obey God rather than any **h**
1Co 2:13 in words not taught by **h** wisdom
Php 2: 7 being born in **h** likeness.
Rev 4: 7 with a face like a **h** face,
Jdt 8:16 for God is not like a **h** being,

HUMANKIND → HUMAN
Ge 1:26 "Let us make **h** in our image,
Mk 2:27 "The sabbath was made for **h**,
1Ti 2: 5 one mediator between God and **h**,

**HUMBLE → HUMBLED, HUMBLY,
        HUMILITY**
Nu 12: 3 Now the man Moses was very **h**,
Dt 8:16 to **h** you and to test you,
Ps 25: 9 He leads the **h** in what is right,
  149: 4 he adorns the **h** with victory.
Isa 57:15 to revive the spirit of the **h**,
Zep 2: 3 Seek the LORD, all you **h** of the land
Mt 11:29 for I am gentle and **h** in heart,
  21: 5 **h**, and mounted on a donkey,
Jas 4:10 **H** yourselves before the Lord,
1Pe 5: 5 but gives grace to the **h**."
Sir 3:20 but by the **h** he is glorified.

HUMBLED → HUMBLE
Ps 119:71 It is good for me that I was **h**,
Lk 14:11 all who exalt themselves will be **h**,
Php 2: 8 he **h** himself and became obedient

HUMBLY* → HUMBLE
Mic 6: 8 and to walk **h** with your God?

HUMILITY → HUMBLE
Pr 15:33 and **h** goes before honor.
Zep 2: 3 seek righteousness, seek **h**;
Php 2: 3 but in **h** regard others as better than
Col 3:12 with compassion, kindness, **h**,
1Pe 5: 5 must clothe yourselves with **h**
Sir 1:27 fidelity and **h** are his delight.

HUNDRED
Ge 17:17 born to a man who is a **h** years old?
Isa 65:20 one who dies at a **h** years will be
Ro 4:19 (for he was about a **h** years old),

HUNG
Dt   21:23 **h** on a tree is under God's curse.
Ps 137: 2 the willows there we **h** up our harps.
Mk   9:42 if a great millstone were **h** around

HUNGER → HUNGRY
Dt   8: 3 He humbled you by letting you **h,**
Mt   5: 6 "Blessed are those who **h** and thirst
Rev 7:16 will **h** no more, and thirst no more;

HUNGRY → HUNGER
Ps 50:12 "If I were **h,** I would not tell you,
    146: 7 who gives food to the **h.**
Pr 25:21 If your enemies are **h,** give them
Mt 12: 1 his disciples were **h,** and they began
Jn   6:35 comes to me will never be **h,**
Ro 12:20 "if your enemies are **h,** feed them;

HUSBAND → HUSBANDS
Ge   3: 6 and she also gave some to her **h,**
    3:16 yet your desire shall be for your **h,**
Pr 31:28 her **h** too, and he praises her:
Isa 54: 5 For your Maker is your **h,**
Jer 31:32 they broke, though I was their **h,**
Hos 2:16 the Lord, you will call me, "My **h,**"
1Co 7:10 wife should not separate from her **h**
Eph 5:23 **h** is the head of the wife just as
Rev 21: 2 as a bride adorned for her **h.**
Sir 26: 1 Happy is the **h** of a good wife;

HUSBANDS → HUSBAND
Jn   4:18 for you have had five **h,**
Eph 5:25 **H,** love your wives, just as Christ
Col 3:18 Wives, be subject to your **h,**
Tit   2: 4 the young women to love their **h,**
1Pe 3: 7 **H,** in the same way, show

HUSHAI
    Wise man of David; foiled Absalom's revolt
(2Sa 15:32-37; 16:15-17:16).

HYMN → HYMNS
Mt 26:30 When they had sung the **h,**
Sir 44: 1 **H** in honor of our ancestors

HYMNS → HYMN
Eph 5:19 psalms and **h** and spiritual songs
Col 3:16 in your hearts sing psalms, **h,**
Aza 1: 1 singing **h** to God and blessing the

HYPOCRISY → HYPOCRITE, HYPOCRITES
Mt 23:28 but inside you are full of **h** and
Mk 12:15 knowing their **h,** he said to them,
Lk 12: 1 of the Pharisees, that is, their **h.**
Jas 3:17 without a trace of partiality or **h.**

HYPOCRITE → HYPOCRISY
Lk   6:42 You **h,** first take the log out of your
Sir 1:29 Do not be a **h** before others,

HYPOCRITES → HYPOCRISY
Mt   6: 5 you pray, do not be like the **h;**
    23:13 to you, scribes and Pharisees, **h!**
Mk   7: 6 prophesied rightly about you **h,**

HYSSOP
Ex 12:22 a bunch of **h,** dip it in the blood that
Nu 19: 6 The priest shall take cedarwood, **h,**
Ps 51: 7 Purge me with **h,** and I shall be
Jn 19:29 full of the wine on a branch of **h**

I

I AM
Ex   3:14 God said to Moses, "**I am who I**
         am."
Isa 44: 6 **I am** the first and **I am** the last;
Mt 28:20 **I am** with you always, to the end of
Mk 8:29 "But who do you say that **I am?**"
Jn   6:35 to them, "**I am** the bread of life.
    8:12 "**I am** the light of the world.
    8:58 before Abraham was, **I am.**"
    9: 5 **I am** the light of the world."
   10: 7 **I am** the gate for the sheep.
  10:11 **I am** the good shepherd.
  11:25 "**I am** the resurrection and the life.
  14: 6 "**I am** the way, and the truth, and

Jn 15: 1 "**I am** the true vine, and my Father
Rev 1: 8 "**I am** the Alpha and the Omega,"
  22:20 "Surely **I am** coming soon."

IDLE
Ecc 11: 6 evening do not let your hands be **i;**
2Th 3: 7 were not **i** when we were with you,

IDOL → IDOLS
Ex 20: 4 shall not make for yourself an **i,**
Isa 40:19 An **i?**—A workman casts it,
1Co 10:19 or that an **i** is anything?

IDOLS → IDOL
Ex 34:17 You shall not make cast **i.**
2Ki 17:15 went after false **i** and became false;
Ps 115: 4 Their **i** are silver and gold,
1Co 8: 1 concerning food sacrificed to **i:**
1Mc 1:43 they sacrificed to **i** and profaned the

IGNORANCE → IGNORANT
Ac 17:30 overlooked the times of human **i,**
1Pe 2:15 silence the **i** of the foolish.

IGNORANT → IGNORANCE
Heb 5: 2 He is able to deal gently with the **i**
2Pe 3:16 the **i** and unstable twist to their own

ILL → ILLNESS
1Co 11:30 many of you are weak and **i,**

ILLEGITIMATE
Jn   8:41 said to him, "We are not **i** children;
Heb 12: 8 then you are **i** and not his children.

ILLNESS → ILL
Dt   7:15 will turn away from you every **i;**
Ps 41: 3 their **i** you heal all their infirmities.

IMAGE → IMAGES
Ge   1:26 "Let us make humankind in our **i,**
Dt 27:15 who makes an idol or casts an **i,**
1Co 15:49 the **i** of the man of heaven.
Col 1:15 He is the **i** of the invisible God,
Rev 20: 4 not worshiped the beast or its **i** and
Sir 17: 3 and made them in his own **i.**

IMAGES → IMAGE
Nu 33:52 destroy all their cast **i,**
Ps 97: 7 All worshipers of **i** are put to shame,

IMITATE → IMITATORS
Heb 13: 7 their way of life, and **i** their faith.
3Jn 1:11 not **i** what is evil but **i** what is good.

IMITATORS → IMITATE
1Co 11: 1 Be **i** of me, as I am of Christ.
Eph 5: 1 be **i** of God, as beloved children,

IMMANUEL* → =EMMANUEL
Isa 7:14 bear a son, and shall name him **I.**
  8: 8 fill the breadth of your land, O **I.**

IMMORAL → IMMORALITY
1Co   5: 9 not to associate with sexually **i**
Heb 12:16 an **i** and godless person,

IMMORALITY → IMMORAL
2Co 12:21 sexual **i,** and licentiousness
Jude 1: 7 indulged in sexual **i** and pursued
Sir 41:17 Be ashamed of sexual **i,**

IMMORTAL → IMMORTALITY
Ro   1:23 the glory of the **i** God for images
1Ti 1:17 To the King of the ages, **i,** invisible,

IMMORTALITY → IMMORTAL
1Co 15:53 and this mortal body must put on **i.**
1Ti 6:16 It is he alone who has **i** and dwells

IMPERISHABLE
1Co 9:25 a perishable wreath, but we an **i** one.
  15:52 and the dead will be raised **i,**
1Pe 1: 4 and into an inheritance that is **i,**

IMPORTANCE* → IMPORTANT
1Co 15: 3 of first **i** what I in turn had received:

IMPORTANT → IMPORTANCE
Mk 12:33 much more **i** than all whole burnt

IMPOSSIBLE
Zec 8: 6 should it also seem **i** to me,
Mt 17:20 and nothing will be **i** for you."
Mk 10:27 "For mortals it is **i,** but not for God;
Heb 11: 6 without faith it is **i** to please God,

IMPURE* → IMPURITY
Eph 5: 5 that no fornicator or **i** person,
1Th 2: 3 not spring from deceit or **i** motives

IMPURITY → IMPURE
Zec 13: 1 to cleanse them from sin and **i.**
Gal 5:19 fornication, **i,** licentiousness,
1Th 4: 7 did not call us to **i** but in holiness.

INCENSE → FRANKINCENSE
Ex 25: 6 anointing oil and for the fragrant **i,**

INCLINATION
Ge   6: 5 and that every **i** of the thoughts
Ecc 11: 9 Follow the **i** of your heart and

INCREASE → INCREASED
Ge   3:16 greatly **i** your pangs in childbearing;
Lk 17: 5 said to the Lord, "**I** our faith!"
Jn   3:30 He must **i,** but I must decrease."

INCREASED → INCREASE
Ro 5:20 but where sin **i,** grace abounded all

INDEBTED* → DEBT
Lk 11: 4 forgive everyone **i** to us.

INDEPENDENT*
1Co 11:11 not **i** of man or man **i** of woman.

INFANTS
Ps   8: 2 Out of the mouths of babes and **i**
Mt 21:16 'Out of the mouths of **i** and nursing
1Co 14:20 **i** in evil, but in thinking be adults.

INFIRMITIES
Isa 53: 4 borne our **i** and carried our diseases;
Mt   8:17 took our **i** and bore our diseases."

INGATHERING → GATHER
Ex 23:16 You shall observe the festival of **i**

INHERIT → INHERITANCE
Lev 20:24 You shall **i** their land,
Ps 37:11 But the meek shall **i** the land,
Zec 2:12 The Lord will **i** Judah as his portion
Lk 10:25 "what must I do to **i** eternal life?"
1Co 6: 9 wrongdoers will not **i** the kingdom
Heb 1:14 sake of those who are to **i** salvation?

INHERITANCE → INHERIT
Ex 34: 9 and take us for your **i.**"
Eph 1:11 In Christ we have also obtained an **i,**
Heb 9:15 the promised eternal **i,**

INIQUITIES → INIQUITY
Lev 16:22 goat shall bear on itself all their **i**
Ps 103:10 nor repay us according to our **i.**
Isa 53:11 and he shall bear their **i.**
Ro   4: 7 are those whose **i** are forgiven,
Rev 18: 5 and God has remembered her **i.**

INIQUITY → INIQUITIES
Ex 34: 7 forgiving **i** and transgression and sin
Ps 103: 3 who forgives all your **i,**
Isa 53: 6 Lord has laid on him the **i** of us all.
Tit 2:14 that he might redeem us from all **i**

INJURY
Lev 24:20 the **i** inflicted is the **i** to be suffered.

INJUSTICE
Hos 10:13 wickedness, you have reaped **i,**
Ro 9:14 Is there **i** on God's part?

INN*
Lk   2: 7 there was no place for them in the **i.**
  10:34 brought him to an **i,** and took care

INNER → INWARDLY
Mt 24:26 He is in the **i** rooms,' do not believe
2Co 4:16 our **i** nature is being renewed day
1Pe 3: 4 let your adornment be the **i** self

INNOCENCE → INNOCENT
Ps   26: 6   I wash my hands in i,
Hos   8: 5   long will they be incapable of i?

INNOCENT → INNOCENCE
Pr   6:17   tongue, and hands that shed i blood,
Mt   10:16   be wise as serpents and i as doves.
     27:24   "I am i of this man's blood;

INQUIRE → INQUIRED
Dt   12:30   do not i concerning their gods,

INQUIRED → INQUIRE
Zep   1: 6   not sought the LORD or i of him.

INSCRIBED → INSCRIPTION
Da   10:21   what is i in the book of truth.
Rev   19:12   he has a name i that no one

INSCRIPTION → INSCRIBED
Mk   15:26   The i of the charge against him read,
2Ti   2:19   foundation stands, bearing this i:

INSIGHT
Pr   3: 5   and do not rely on your own i.
Eph   1: 8   With all wisdom and i
Sir   6:37   It is he who will give i to your mind,

INSPIRED
Ex   35:34   And he has i him to teach,
2Ti   3:16   All scripture is i by God and is

INSTITUTED → INSTITUTION
Ro   13: 1   that exist have been i by God.

INSTITUTION* → INSTITUTED
Nu   10: 8   this shall be a perpetual i for you
1Pe   2:13   the authority of every human i,

INSTRUCT → INSTRUCTED,
     INSTRUCTION, INSTRUCTOR
Dt   17:10   observing everything they i you.
Ne   9:20   You gave your good spirit to i them,
Ro   15:14   and able to i one another.
1Co   14:19   in order to i others also,

INSTRUCTED → INSTRUCT
Isa   40:13   or as his counselor has i him?
Jn   8:28   these things as the Father i me.

INSTRUCTION → INSTRUCT
Pr   8:10   Take my i instead of silver,
Mic   4: 2   For out of Zion shall go forth i,
Ro   15: 4   in former days was written for our i,
1Ti   1: 5   But the aim of such i is love
Sir   51:26   and let your souls receive i;

INSTRUCTOR → INSTRUCT
Mt   23:10   for you have one i, the Messiah.

INSULTS
Ps   69: 9   the i of those who insult you have
Lk   22:65   heaping many other i on him.
2Co   12:10   I am content with weaknesses, i,

INTEGRITY
Job   27: 5   until I die I will not put away my i
Pr   14:32   the righteous find a refuge in their i.
Tit   2: 7   and in your teaching show i, gravity,

INTELLIGENCE → INTELLIGENT
Pr   8: 5   acquire i, you who lack it.
Sir   22:11   fool, for he has left i behind.

INTELLIGENT → INTELLIGENCE
Pr   11:12   but an i person remains silent.
Ecc   9:11   nor riches to the i,

INTENDED → INTENTIONS
Ge   50:20   i to do harm to me, God i it for
     good,
Jer   18:10   the good that I had i to do to it.

INTENTIONS → INTENDED
Mk   7:21   the human heart, that evil i come:
Heb   4:12   judge the thoughts and i of the
     heart.

INTERCEDES → INTERCESSION
Ro   8:26   Spirit i with sighs too deep for

INTERCESSION* → INTERCEDES
1Sa   2:25   against the LORD, who can make i?
Isa   53:12   and made i for the transgressors.
Heb   7:25   he always lives to make i for them.

INTERMARRY → MARRIAGE
Dt   7: 3   Do not i with them, giving your

INTERPRET → INTERPRETATION,
     INTERPRETATIONS
Ge   41:15   no one who can i it.
Mt   16: 3   cannot i the signs of the times.
1Co   12:30   Do all speak in tongues? Do all i?

INTERPRETATION → INTERPRET
Da   2: 4   and we will reveal the i."
1Co   12:10   to another the i of tongues.
2Pe   1:20   scripture is a matter of one's own i,
2Es   12:10   "This is the i of this vision

INTERPRETATIONS → INTERPRET
Ge   40: 8   to them, "Do not i belong to God?

INVADE → INVADED
La   1:10   the nations i her sanctuary,
Na   1:15   never again shall the wicked i you;

INVADED → INVADE
2Ki   17: 5   the king of Assyria i all the land

INVISIBLE
Col   1:15   He is the image of the i God,
1Ti   1:17   To the King of the ages, immortal, i,

INVITE → INVITED, INVITES
Lk   14:13   when you give a banquet, i the poor,

INVITED → INVITE
Rev   19: 9   Blessed are those who are i to

INVITES → INVITE
1Co   10:27   If an unbeliever i you to a meal
Sir   13: 9   When an influential person i you,

INVOKE
Ex   23:13   Do not i the names of other gods;
1Pe   1:17   If you i as Father the one who

INWARDLY → INNER
Ro   2:29   a person is a Jew who is one i,
     8:23   groan i while we wait for adoption,

IRON
Ps   2: 9   shall break them with a rod of i,
Pr   27:17   I sharpens i, and one person
Da   2:33   its legs of i, its feet partly of i
Rev   19:15   he will rule them with a rod of i;

IRREVOCABLE
Ro   11:29   gifts and the calling of God are i.

ISAAC
Son of Abraham by Sarah (Ge 17:19; 21:1-7; 1Ch 1:28). Abrahamic covenant perpetuated with (Ge 17:21; 26:2-5). Offered up by Abraham (Ge 22; Heb 11:17-19). Rebekah taken as wife (Ge 24). Inherited Abraham's estate (Ge 25:5). Father of Esau and Jacob (Ge 25:19-26; 1Ch 1:34). Nearly lost Rebekah to Abimelech (Ge 26:1-11). Covenant with Abimelech (Ge 26:12-31). Tricked into blessing Jacob (Ge 27). Death (Ge 35:27-29). Father of Israel (Ex 3:6; Dt 29:13; Ro 9:10).

ISAIAH
Prophet to Judah (Isa 1:1). Called by the LORD (Isa 6). Announced judgment to Ahaz (Isa 7), deliverance from Assyria to Hezekiah (2Ki 19; Isa 36-37), deliverance from death to Hezekiah (2Ki 20:1-11; Isa 38). Chronicler of Judah's history (2Ch 26:22; 32:32).

ISCARIOT
Mt   10: 4   Judas I, the one who betrayed him.
Lk   22: 3   Satan entered into Judas called I,

ISHBAAL*
Son of Saul; would-be king (2Sa 2:8-4:12).

ISHMAEL
Son of Abraham by Hagar (Ge 16; 1Ch 1:28).

Blessed, but not son of covenant (Ge 17:18-21; Gal 4:21-31). Sent away by Sarah (Ge 21:8-21). Children (Ge 25:12-18; 1Ch 1:29-31). Death (Ge 25:17).

ISRAEL → ISRAELITE, ISRAELITES,
     =JACOB
     1. Name given to Jacob (Ge 32:28; 35:10).
     2. Corporate name of Jacob's descendants; often specifically Northern Kingdom.
Ge   49:28   All these are the twelve tribes of I,
Ex   28:11   with the names of the sons of I;
Nu   24:17   and a scepter shall rise out of I;
Dt   6: 4   Hear, O I: The LORD is our God,
Ps   125: 5   Peace be upon I!
Jer   31:31   a new covenant with the house of I
Hos   11: 1   When I was a child, I loved him,
Mt   2: 6   who is to shepherd my people I.'"
Mk   12:29   answered, "The first is, 'Hear, O I:
Lk   22:30   judging the twelve tribes of I.
Ac   1: 6   you will restore the kingdom to I?"
Ro   9: 6   not all Israelites truly belong to I,
Heb   8: 8   a new covenant with the house of I
Rev   7: 4   out of every tribe of the people of I:
Sir   17:17   but I is the Lord's own portion.

ISRAELITE → ISRAEL
Jn   1:47   an I in whom there is no deceit!"
Ro   11: 1   I myself am an I, a descendant of

ISRAELITES → ISRAEL
Ex   2:23   The I groaned under their slavery,
     29:45   I will dwell among the I, and I will

ISSACHAR
Son of Jacob by Leah (Ge 30:18; 35:23; 1Ch 2:1). Tribe of blessed (Ge 49:14-15; Dt 33:18-19), numbered (Nu 1:29; 26:25), allotted land (Jos 19:17-23; Eze 48:25), assisted Deborah (Jdg 5:15), 12,000 from (Rev 7:7).

ITCHING
2Ti   4: 3   sound doctrine, but having i ears,

J

JACOB → =ISRAEL
     1. Son of Isaac, younger twin of Esau (Ge 26:21-26; 1Ch 1:34). Bought Esau's birthright (Ge 26:29-34); tricked Isaac into blessing him (Ge 27:1-37). Fled to Haran (Ge 28:1-5). Abrahamic covenant perpetuated through (Ge 28:13-15; Mal 1:2). Vision at Bethel (Ge 28:10-22). Served Laban for Rachel and Leah (Ge 29:1-30). Children (Ge 29:31-30:24; 35:16-26; 1Ch 2-9). Flocks increased (Ge 30:25-43). Returned to Canaan (Ge 31). Wrestled with God; name changed to Israel (Ge 32:22-32). Reconciled to Esau (Ge 33). Returned to Bethel (Ge 35:1-15). Favored Joseph (Ge 37:3). Sent sons to Egypt during famine (Ge 42-43). Settled in Egypt (Ge 46). Blessed Ephraim and Manasseh (Ge 48). Blessed sons (Ge 49:1-28; Heb 11:21). Death (Ge 49:29-33). Burial (Ge 50:1-14).
     2. Corporate name of Jacob's descendants; often specifically Northern Kingdom.
Ps   135: 4   the LORD has chosen J for himself,
Mic   7:20   You will show faithfulness to J
Ro   9:13   "I have loved J,
1Mc   1:28   house of J was clothed with shame.

JAEL*
Woman who killed the Canaanite general, Sisera (Jdg 4:17-22; 5:6, 24-27).

JAIRUS
Synagogue ruler whose daughter Jesus raised (Mk 5:22-43; Lk 8:41-56).

JAMES
     1. Apostle; brother of John (Mt 4:21-22; 10:2; Mk 3:17; Lk 5:1-10). At transfiguration (Mt 17:1-13; Mk 9:1-13; Lk 9:28-36). Killed by Herod (Ac 12:2).
     2. Apostle (Mt 10:3; Mk 3:18; Lk 6:15).
     3. Brother of Jesus (Mt 13:55; Mk 6:3; Lk 24:10;

Gal 1:19) and Judas (Jude 1). With believers before Pentecost (Ac 1:13). Leader of church at Jerusalem (Ac 12:17; 15; 21:18; Gal 2:9, 12). Author of epistle (Jas 1:1).

JAPHETH

Son of Noah (Ge 5:32; 1Ch 1:4-5). Blessed (Ge 9:18-28). Sons of (Ge 10:2-5).

JAR → JARS

1Ki	17:14	The j of meal will not be emptied
Mk	14: 3	alabaster j of very costly ointment
Lk	22:10	man carrying a j of water will meet

JARS → JAR

| Jn | 2: 6 | there were six stone water j for |
| 2Co | 4: 7 | But we have this treasure in clay j, |

JEALOUS

Ex	34:14	whose name is J, is a j God).
Dt	4:24	God is a devouring fire, a j God.
	32:16	They made him j with strange gods,
Eze	39:25	and I will be j for my holy name.
Ro	10:19	"I will make you j of those

JEBUSITES

| Ex | 3: 8 | the Perizzites, the Hivites, and the J. |
| Jos | 15:63 | Judah could not drive out the J, |

JECONIAH → See JEHOIACHIN

JEHOAHAZ

1. Son of Jehu; king of Israel (2Ki 13:1-9).

2. Son of Josiah; king of Judah (2Ki 23:31-34; 2Ch 36:1-4).

JEHOASH → =JOASH

1. Son of Ahaziah, king of Judah (2Ki 12). See Joash, 1.

2. Son of Jehoahaz; king of Israel. Defeat of Aram prophesied by Elisha (2Ki 13:10-25). Defeated Amaziah in Jerusalem (2Ki 14:1-16). See Joash, 2.

JEHOIACHIN → =CONIAH, =JECONIAH

Son of Jehoiakim; king of Judah exiled by Nebuchadnezzar (2Ki 24:8-17; 2Ch 36:8-10; Eze 1:2). Status improved (2Ki 25:27-30; Jer 52:31-34).

JEHOIADA

Priest who sheltered Joash from Athaliah (2Ki 11-12; 2Ch 22:11-24:16).

JEHOIAKIM → =ELIAKIM

Son of Josiah; made king of Judah by Nebuchadnezzar (2Ki 23:34-24:6; 2Ch 36:4-8; Jer 22:18-23). Burned scroll of Jeremiah's prophecies (Jer 36).

JEHORAM → =JORAM

1. Son of Jehoshaphat; king of Judah. Prophesied against by Elijah; killed by the LORD (2Ch 21). See Joram, 1.

2. Son of Ahab; king of Israel (2Ch 22:5). Joined Jehoshaphat against Moab (2Ki 3). See Joram, 2.

JEHOSHAPHAT

1. Son of Asa; king of Judah. Strengthened his kingdom (2Ch 17). Joined with Ahab against Aram (2Ki 22; 2Ch 18). Established judges (2Ch 19). Joined Joram against Moab (2Ki 3; 2Ch 20).

2. Valley of judgment (Joel 3:2, 12).

JEHU

1. Prophet against Baasha (2Ki 16:1-7).

2. King of Israel. Anointed by Elijah to obliterate house of Ahab (1Ki 19:16-17); anointed by servant of Elisha (2Ki 9:1-13). Killed Joram and Ahaziah (2Ki 9:14-29; 2Ch 22:7-9), Jezebel (2Ki 9:30-37), relatives of Ahab (2Ki 10:1-17; Hos 1:4), ministers of Baal (2Ki 10:18-29). Death (2Ki 10:30-36).

JEPHTHAH

Judge from Gilead who delivered Israel from Ammon (Jdg 10:6-12:7). Made rash vow concerning his daughter (Jdg 11:30-40).

JEREMIAH

Prophet to Judah (Jer 1:1-3). Called by the LORD (Jer 1). Put in stocks (Jer 20:1-3). Threatened for prophesying (Jer 11:18-23; 26). Opposed by Hananiah (Jer 28). Scroll burned (Jer 36). Imprisoned (Jer 37). Thrown into cistern (Jer 38). Forced to Egypt with those fleeing Babylonians (Jer 43).

JERICHO

Jos	6: 2	"See, I have handed J over to you,
1Ki	16:34	In his days Hiel of Bethel built J;
Lk	18:35	As he approached J, a blind man

JEROBOAM

1. Official of Solomon; rebelled to become first king of Israel (1Ki 11:26-40; 12:1-20; 2Ch 10). Idolatry (1Ki 12:25-33; Tob 1:5; Sir 47:23); judgment for (1Ki 13-14; 2Ch 13).

2. Son of Jehoash; king of Israel (1Ki 14:23-29).

JERUSALEM

2Sa	5: 5	and at J he reigned over all Israel
	15:29	carried the ark of God back to J,
2Ki	25:10	broke down the walls around J.
Ezr	2: 1	they returned to J and Judah,
Ne	2:17	Come, let us rebuild the wall of J,
Isa	40: 2	Speak tenderly to J,
La	1: 8	J sinned grievously, so she has
Da	9:25	went out to restore and rebuild J
Joel	3: 1	I restore the fortunes of Judah and J,
Mic	4: 2	and the word of the LORD from J.
Zec	1:14	I am very jealous for J and for Zion.
	14: 8	living waters shall flow out from J,
Mt	23:37	"J, J, the city that kills the prophets
Lk	4: 9	Then the devil took him to J,
Gal	4:25	corresponds to the present J,
Heb	12:22	of the living God, the heavenly J,
Rev	21: 2	And I saw the holy city, the new J,
1Mc	1:29	and he came to J with a large force.

JESSE

Father of David (Ru 4:17-22; 1Sa 16; 1Ch 2:12-17).

JESUS

1. Jesus the Messiah.

LIFE: Genealogy (Mt 1:1-17; Lk 3:21-37). Birth announced (Mt 1:18-25; Lk 1:26-45). Birth (Mt 2:1-12; Lk 2:1-40). Escape to Egypt (Mt 2:13-23). As a boy in the temple (Lk 2:41-52). Baptism (Mt 3:13-17; Mk 1:9-11; Lk 3:21-22; Jn 1:32-34). Temptation (Mt 4:1-11; Mk 1:12-13; Lk 4:1-13). Ministry in Galilee (Mt 4:12-18:35; Mk 1:14-9:50; Lk 4:14-13:9; Jn 1:35-2:11; 4; 6), Transfiguration (Mt 17:1-8; Mk 9:2-8; Lk 9:28-36), on the way to Jerusalem (Mt 19-20; Mk 10; Lk 13:10-19:27), in Jerusalem (Mt 21-25; Mk 11-13; Lk 19:28-21:38; Jn 2:12-3:36; 5; 7-12). Last supper (Mt 26:17-35; Mk 14:12-31; Lk 22:1-38; Jn 13-17). Arrest and trial (Mt 26:36-27:31; Mk 14:43-15:20; Lk 22:39-23:25; Jn 18:1-19:16). Crucifixion (Mt 27:32-66; Mk 15:21-47; Lk 23:26-55; Jn 19:28-42). Resurrection and appearances (Mt 28; Mk 16; Lk 24; Jn 20-21; Ac 1:1-11; 7:56; 9:3-6; 1Co 15:1-8; Rev 1:1-20).

MIRACLES. Healings: official's son (Jn 4:43-54), demoniac in Capernaum (Mk 1:23-26; Lk 4:33-35), Peter's mother-in-law (Mt 8:14-17; Mk 1:29-31; Lk 4:38-39), leper (Mt 8:2-4; Mk 1:40-45; Lk 5:12-16), paralytic (Mt 9:1-8; Mk 2:1-12; Lk 5:17-26), cripple (Jn 5:1-9), shriveled hand (Mt 12:10-13; Mk 3:1-5; Lk 6:6-11), centurion's servant (Mt 8:5-13; Lk 7:1-10), widow's son raised (Lk 7:11-17), demoniac (Mt 12:22-23; Lk 11:14), Gadarene demoniacs (Mt 8:28-34; Mk 5:1-20; Lk 8:26-39), woman's bleeding and Jairus' daughter (Mt 9:18-26; Mk 5:21-43; Lk 8:40-56), blind man (Mt 9:27-31), mute man (Mt 9:32-33), Canaanite woman's daughter (Mt 15:21-28; Mk 7:24-30), deaf man (Mk 7:31-37), blind man (Mk 8:22-26), demoniac boy (Mt 17:14-18; Mk 9:14-29; Lk 9:37-

43), ten lepers (Lk 17:11-19), man born blind (Jn 9:1-7), Lazarus raised (Jn 11), crippled woman (Lk 13:11-17), man with dropsy (Lk 14:1-6), two blind men (Mt 20:29-34; Mk 10:46-52; Lk 18:35-43), Malchus' ear (Lk 22:50-51). *Other Miracles:* water to wine (Jn 2:1-11), catch of fish (Lk 5:1-11), storm stilled (Mt 8:23-27; Mk 4:37-41; Lk 8:22-25), 5,000 fed (Mt 14:15-21; Mk 6:35-44; Lk 9:10-17; Jn 6:1-14), walking on water (Mt 14:25-33; Mk 6:48-52; Jn 6:15-21), 4,000 fed (Mt 15:32-39; Mk 8:1-9), money from fish (Mt 17:24-27), fig tree cursed (Mt 21:18-22; Mk 11:12-14), catch of fish (Jn 21:1-14).

MAJOR TEACHING: Sermon on the Mount (Mt 5-7; Lk 6:17-49), to Nicodemus (Jn 3), to Samaritan woman (Jn 4), Bread of Life (Jn 6:22-59), at Feast of Tabernacles (Jn 7-8), woes to Pharisees (Mt 23; Lk 11:37-54), Good Shepherd (Jn 10:1-18), Olivet Discourse (Mt 24-25; Mk 13; Lk 21:5-36), Upper Room Discourse (Jn 13-16).

PARABLES: Sower (Mt 13:3-23; Mk 4:3-25; Lk 8:5-18), seed's growth (Mk 4:26-29), wheat and weeds (Mt 13:24-30, 36-43), mustard seed (Mt 13:31-32; Mk 4:30-32), yeast (Mt 13:33; Lk 13:20-21), hidden treasure (Mt 13:44), valuable pearl (Mt 13:45-46), net (Mt 13:47-51), house owner (Mt 13:52), good Samaritan (Lk 10:25-37), unmerciful servant (Mt 18:15-35), lost sheep (Mt 18:10-14; Lk 15:4-7), lost coin (Lk 15:8-10), prodigal son (Lk 15:11-32), dishonest manager (Lk 16:1-13), rich man and Lazarus (Lk 16:19-31), persistent widow (Lk 18:1-8), Pharisee and tax collector (Lk 18:9-14), payment of workers (Mt 20:1-16), tenants and the vineyard (Mt 21:28-46; Mt 12:1-12; Lk 20:9-19), wedding banquet (Mt 22:1-14), faithful servant (Mt 24:45-51), ten virgins (Mt 25:1-13), talents (Mt 25:1-30; Lk 19:12-27).

DISCIPLES see APOSTLES. Call (Jn 1:35-51; Mt 4:18-22; 9:9; Mk 1:16-20; 2:13-14; Lk 5:1-11, 27-28). Named Apostles (Mk 3:13-19; Lk 6:12-16). Twelve sent out (Mt 10; Mk 6:7-11; Lk 9:1-5). Seventy sent out (Lk 10:1-24). Defection of (Jn 6:60-71; Mt 26:56; Mk 14:50-52). Final commission (Mt 28:16-20; Jn 21:15-23; Ac 1:3-8).

Ac	9: 5	"I am J, whom you are persecuting.
1Co	8: 6	and one Lord, J Christ,
Php	2:10	name of J every knee should bend,
2Th	2: 1	the coming of our Lord J Christ
1Ti	1:15	J came into the world to save
Heb	12: 2	to J the pioneer and perfecter of our
	13: 8	J Christ is the same yesterday and
1Jn	1: 7	the blood of J his Son cleanses us
Rev	1: 1	The revelation of J Christ,
	22:20	Amen. Come, Lord J!

2. Disciple, also called Justus (Col 4:11).

3. Writer of Sirach (Sir Pr:1; 50:27; 51:1).

JETHRO

Father-in-law and adviser of Moses (Ex 3:1; 4:18; 18). Also known as Reuel (Ex 2:18).

JEW → JEWS, JUDAISM

Est	10: 3	Mordecai the J was next in rank to
Zec	8:23	shall take hold of a J,
Ro	1:16	to the J first and also to the Greek.
	2:29	a person is a J who is one inwardly,
1Co	9:20	To the Jews I became as a J,
Col	3:11	there is no longer Greek and J,

JEWEL → JEWELS

| Pr | 20:15 | by knowledge are a precious j. |
| Rev | 21:19 | of the city are adorned with every j; |

JEWELS → JEWEL

Pr	3:15	She is more precious than j,
Isa	54:12	your gates of j, and all your wall
Rev	17: 4	adorned with gold and j and pearls,

JEWS → JEW

Ne	4: 1	enraged, and he mocked the J,
Est	3:13	to kill, and to annihilate all J,
Mt	2: 2	who has been born king of the J?

JEWS (cont.)

Mt 27:11 "Are you the King of the **J**?"
Jn 4:22 for salvation is from the **J**.
Ro 3:29 Or is God the God of **J** only?

JEZEBEL*

Sidonian wife of Ahab (1Ki 16:31). Promoted Baal worship (1Ki 16:32-33). Killed prophets of the LORD (1Ki 18:4, 13). Opposed Elijah (1Ki 19:1-2). Had Naboth killed (1Ki 21). Death (1Ki 21:17-24; 2Ki 9:30-37). Metaphor of immorality (Rev 2:20).

JEZREEL

2Ki 10: 7 in baskets and sent them to him at **J**.
Hos 1: 4 the LORD said to him, "Name him **J**;

JOAB

Nephew of David (1Ch 2:16). Commander of his army (2Sa 8:16). Victorious over Ammon (2Sa 10; 1Ch 19), Rabbah (2Sa 11; 1Ch 20), Jerusalem (1Ch 11:6), Absalom (2Sa 18), Sheba (2Sa 20). Killed Abner (2Sa 3:22-39), Amasa (2Sa 20:1-13). Numbered David's army (2Sa 24; 1Ch 21). Sided with Adonijah (1Ki 1:17, 19). Killed by Benaiah (1Ki 2:5-6, 28-35).

JOASH → **=JEHOASH**

1. Son of Ahaziah; king of Judah. Sheltered from Athaliah by Jehoiada (2Ki 11; 2Ch 22:10-23:21). Repaired temple (2Ch 24). See Jehoash, 1.
2. Son of Jehoahaz, king of Israel (2Ki 13; 2Ch 25:17-25). See Jehoash, 2.

JOB

Wealthy man from Uz; feared God (Job 1:1-5). Integrity tested by disaster (Job 1:6-22), personal affliction (Job 2). Maintained innocence in debate with three friends (Job 3-31), Elihu (Job 32-37). Rebuked by the LORD (Job 38-41). Vindicated and restored to greater stature by the LORD (Job 42). Example of righteousness (Eze 14:14, 20; Sir 49:9).

JOEL

1. Son of Samuel (1Sa 8:2; 1Ch 6:28).
2. Prophet (Joel 1:1; Ac 2:16).

JOHANAN

1. First high priest in the temple (1Ch 6:9-10).
2. Jewish leader who tried to save Gedaliah from assassination (Jer 40:13-14); took Jews, including Jeremiah, to Egypt (Jer 40-43).

JOHN

1. Son of Zechariah and Elizabeth (Lk 1). Called the Baptist (Mt 3:1-12; Mk 1:2-8). Witness to Jesus (Mt 3:11-12; Mk 1:7-8; Lk 3:15-18; Jn 1:6-35; 3:27-30; 5:33-36). Doubts about Jesus (Mt 11:2-6; Lk 7:18-23). Arrest (Mt 4:12; Mk 1:14). Execution (Mt 14:1-12; Mk 6:14-29; Lk 9:7-9). Ministry compared to Elijah (Mt 11:7-19; Mk 9:11-13; Lk 7:24-35).
2. Apostle; brother of James (Mt 4:21-22; 10:2; Mk 3:17; Lk 5:1-10). At transfiguration (Mt 17:1-13; Mk 9:1-13; Lk 9:28-36). Desire to be greatest (Mk 10:35-45). Leader of church at Jerusalem (Ac 4:1-3; Gal 2:9). Elder who wrote epistles (2Jn 1; 3Jn 1). Prophet who wrote Revelation (Rev 1:1; 22:8).
3. Cousin of Barnabas, co-worker with Paul, (Ac 12:12-13:13; 15:37; see Mark).
4. Son of Simon Maccabeus (1Mc 13:53; 16).

JOIN → **JOINED**

Eze 37:17 and **j** them together into one stick,
2Ti 1: 8 **j** with me in suffering for the gospel

JOINED → **JOIN**

Mt 19: 6 what God has **j** together, let no one
Eph 2:21 the whole structure is **j** together and

JOINT → **JOINTS**

Ge 32:25 and Jacob's hip was put out of **j**
Ps 22:14 and all my bones are out of **j**;
Ro 8:17 heirs of God and **j** heirs with Christ

JOINTS → **JOINT**

Heb 4:12 soul from spirit, **j** from marrow;

JONAH

Prophet in days of Jeroboam II (2Ki 14:25). Called to Nineveh; fled to Tarshish (Jnh 1:1-3). Cause of storm; thrown into sea (Jnh 1:4-16). Swallowed by fish (Jnh 1:17). Prayer (Jnh 2). Preached to Nineveh (Jnh 3). Attitude reproved by the LORD (Jnh 4). Sign of (Mt 12:39-41; Lk 11:29-32).

JONATHAN

1. Son of Saul (1Sa 13:16; 1Ch 8:33). Valiant warrior (1Sa 13-14). Relation to David (1Sa 18:1-4; 19-20; 23:16-18). Killed at Gilboa (1Sa 31). Mourned by David (2Sa 1).
2. Brother and successor of Judas Maccabeus (1Mc 2:5; 9:28-31).

JOPPA

Jnh 1: 3 down to **J** and found a ship going
Ac 9:43 he stayed in **J** for some time with

JORAM → **=JEHORAM**

1. Son of Jehoshaphat; king of Judah (2Ki 8:16-24). See Jehoram, 1.
2. Son of Ahab; king of Israel. Killed with Ahaziah by Jehu (2Ki 8:25-29; 9:14-26; 2Ch 22:5-9). See Jehoram, 2.

JORDAN

Ge 13:10 the plain of the **J** was well watered
Nu 34:12 the boundary shall go down to the **J**,
Jos 3:17 dry ground in the middle of the **J**,
Mt 3: 6 were baptized by him in the river **J**,

JOSEPH → **=BARNABAS, =BARSABBAS**

1. Son of Jacob by Rachel (Ge 30:24; 1Ch 2:2). Favored by Jacob, hated by brothers (Ge 37:3-4). Dreams (Ge 37:5-11). Sold by brothers (Ge 37:12-36). Served Potiphar; imprisoned by false accusation (Ge 39). Interpreted dreams of Pharaoh's servants (Ge 40), of Pharaoh (Ge 41:4-40). Made greatest in Egypt (Ge 41:41-57). Sold grain to brothers (Ge 42-45). Brought Jacob and sons to Egypt (Ge 46-47). Sons Ephraim and Manasseh blessed (Ge 48). Blessed (Ge 49:22-26; Dt 33:13-17). Death (Ge 50:22-26; Ex 13:19; Heb 11:22). 12,000 from (Rev 7:8).
2. Husband of Mary mother of Jesus (Mt 1:16-24; 2:13-19; Lk 1:27; 2; Jn 1:45).
3. Disciple from Arimathea; buried Jesus in his tomb (Mt 27:57-61; Mk 15:43-47; Lk 24:50-52).
4. Original name of Barnabas (Ac 4:36).

JOSHUA → **=HOSHEA, =JESHUA**

1. Son of Nun; name changed from Hoshea (Nu 13:8, 16; 1Ch 7:27). Fought Amalekites under Moses (Ex 17:9-14). Servant of Moses on Sinai (Ex 24:13; 32:17). Spied Canaan (Nu 13). With Caleb, allowed to enter land (Nu 14:6, 30). Succeeded Moses (Dt 1:38; 31:1-8; 34:9). Charged Israel to conquer Canaan (Jos 1). Crossed Jordan (Jos 3-4). Circumcised sons of wilderness wanderings (Jos 5). Conquered Jericho (Jos 6), Ai (Jos 7-8), five kings at Gibeon (Jos 10:1-28), southern Canaan (Jos 10:29-43), northern Canaan (Jos 11-12). Defeated at Ai (Jos 7). Deceived by Gibeonites (Jos 9). Renewed covenant (Jos 8:30-35; 24:1-27). Divided land among tribes (Jos 13-22). Last words (Jos 23). Death (Jos 24:28-31).
2. High priest during rebuilding of temple (Hag 1-2; Zec 3:1-9; 6:11). See Jeshua.

JOSIAH

Son of Amon; king of Judah (2Ki 21:26; 1Ch 3:14). Prophesied (1Ki 13:2). Book of the Law discovered during his reign (2Ki 22; 2Ch 34:14-31). Reforms (2Ki 23:1-25; 2Ch 34:1-13; 35:1-19; Sir 49:1-4). Killed in battle (2Ki 23:29-30; 2Ch 35:20-27).

JOTHAM

1. Son of Gideon (Jdg 9).
2. Son of Azariah (Uzziah); king of Judah (2Ki 15:32-38; 2Ch 26:21-27:9).

JOY → **JOYFUL**

Ne 8:10 the **j** of the LORD is your strength."
Job 20: 5 **j** of the godless is but for a moment?
Ps 51:12 Restore to me the **j** of your salvation
Pr 21:15 When justice is done, it is a **j** to the
Isa 12: 3 With **j** you will draw water from
35:10 everlasting **j** shall be upon their
La 2:15 of beauty, the **j** of all the earth?"
Mt 28: 8 tomb quickly with fear and great **j**,
Mk 4:16 they immediately receive it with **j**.
Lk 1:44 the child in my womb leaped for **j**.
2:10 bringing you good news of great **j**
Jn 16:22 no one will take your **j** from you.
Ro 14:17 but righteousness and peace and **j** in
Gal 5:22 the fruit of the Spirit is love, **j**,
Php 4: 1 I love and long for, my **j** and crown,
Heb 12: 2 **j** that was set before him endured
Jas 1: 2 consider it nothing but **j**,
Tob 13:17 Jerusalem will sing hymns of **j**,
Bar 5: 9 For God will lead Israel with **j**,

JOYFUL → **JOY**

Ps 98: 4 Make a **j** noise to the LORD,
Jdt 14: 9 and made a **j** noise in their town.

JUBILEE

Lev 25:10 It shall be a **j** for you:
Nu 36: 4 when the **j** of the Israelites comes,

JUDAH → **JUDEA**

1. Son of Jacob by Leah (Ge 29:35; 35:23; 1Ch 2:1). Did not want to kill Joseph (Ge 37:26-27). Among Canaanites, fathered Perez by Tamar (Ge 38). Tribe of blessed as ruling tribe (Ge 49:8-12; Dt 33:7), numbered (Nu 1:27; 26:22), allotted land (Jos 15; Eze 48:7), failed to fully possess (Jos 15:63; Jdg 1:1-20).
2. Name used for Southern Kingdom.

2Sa 2: 4 David king over the house of **J**.
La 1: 3 **J** has gone into exile with suffering
Joel 3: 1 when I restore the fortunes of **J** and
Mic 5: 2 who are one of the little clans of **J**,
Mt 2: 6 least among the rulers of **J**;
Heb 7:14 our Lord was descended from **J**,
Rev 5: 5 See, the Lion of the tribe of **J**,

JUDAISM → **JEW**

Ac 13:43 devout converts to **J** followed Paul
Gal 1:13 no doubt, of my earlier life in **J**.

JUDAS → **=BARSABBAS, =JUDE, =THADDAEUS, MACCABEUS**

1. Apostle; son of James (Lk 6:16; Jn 14:22; Ac 1:13). Probably also called Thaddaeus (Mt 10:3; Mk 3:18).
2. Brother of James and Jesus (Mt 13:55; Mk 6:3), also called Jude (Jude 1).
3. Christian prophet (Ac 15:22-32).
4. Apostle, also called Iscariot, who betrayed Jesus (Mt 10:4; 26:14-56; Mk 3:19; 14:10-50; Lk 6:16; 22:3-53; Jn 6:71; 12:4; 13:2-30; 18:2-11). Suicide of (Mt 27:3-5; Ac 1:16-25).
5. Leader of the Maccabean revolt (1Mc 2:4, 66). Recaptured Jerusalem and rededicated the temple and altar (1Mc 4:36-61). Death of (1Mc 9).

JUDE → See **JUDAS**, 2

JUDEA → **JUDAH**

Mt 2: 1 Jesus was born in Bethlehem of **J**,
Lk 3: 1 Pontius Pilate was governor of **J**,
Ac 1: 8 my witnesses in Jerusalem, in all **J**

JUDGE → **JUDGED, JUDGES, JUDGMENT, JUDGMENTS**

Ge 16: 5 the LORD **j** between you and me!"
Ex 2:14 made you a ruler and **j** over us?
1Sa 2:10 LORD will **j** the ends of the earth;
Ps 96:13 for he is coming to **j** the earth.

Isa 11: 3 He shall not **j** by what his eyes see,
Jer 11:20 O Lord of hosts, who **j** righteously,
Eze 34:17 I **j** between sheep and sheep,
Lk 6:37 not **j**, and you will not be judged;
Jn 7:24 Do not **j** by appearances,
18:31 "Take him yourselves and **j** him
Ac 4:19 rather than to God, you must **j**;
Ro 3: 6 then how could God **j** the world?
1Co 6: 2 that the saints will **j** the world?
2Ti 4: 1 who is to **j** the living and the dead,
Heb 12:23 and to God the **j** of all,
Jas 5: 9 See, the **J** is standing at the doors!
Rev 20: 4 on them were given authority to **j**
Sir 35:15 for the Lord is the **j**,

JUDGED → JUDGE
Mt 7: 1 not judge, so that you may not be **j**.
1Co 11:31 if we **j** ourselves, we would not be **j**.
Jas 3: 1 know that we who teach will be **j**
Rev 20:12 dead were **j** according to their works

JUDGES → JUDGE
Jdg 2:16 Then the Lord raised up **j**,
Lk 11:19 Therefore they will be your **j**.
Jas 4:11 evil against the law and **j** the law;
Rev 19:11 righteousness he **j** and makes war.
Sir 16:12 **j** a person according to one's deeds.

JUDGMENT → JUDGE
Ex 6: 6 arm and with mighty acts of **j**.
Ps 1: 5 wicked will not stand in the **j**,
Ps 119:66 Teach me good **j** and knowledge,
Ecc 12:14 God will bring every deed into **j**,
Jer 25:31 he is entering into **j** with all flesh,
Da 7:22 **j** was given for the holy ones of the
Mal 3: 5 Then I will draw near to you for **j**;
Mt 11:24 day of **j** it will be more tolerable for
Jn 16:11 about **j**, because the ruler
Ro 14:10 we will all stand before the **j** seat of
2Co 5:10 all of us must appear before the **j**
Heb 9:27 to die once, and after that the **j**,
10:27 but a fearful prospect of **j**,
Jas 2:13 mercy triumphs over **j**.
1Pe 4:17 for **j** to begin with the household of
1Jn 4:17 may have boldness on the day of **j**,
Rev 18:10 For in one hour your **j** has come."
Wis 12:12 Or will resist your **j**?
Sir 18:20 Before **j** comes, examine yourself;
2Es 7:70 the things that pertain to the **j**.

JUDGMENTS → JUDGE
Ps 119:75 Lord, that your **j** are right,
Ro 11:33 How unsearchable are his **j** and
Rev 19: 2 for his **j** are true and just;

JUDITH
Virtuous widow and heroine of the deutero-canonical book of Judith (Jdt 8-16).

JUST → JUSTICE, JUSTIFICATION, JUSTIFIED, JUSTIFY
Ge 18:25 Judge of all the earth do what is **j**?"
Dt 32: 4 without deceit, **j** and upright is he;
Ps 111: 7 works of his hands are faithful and **j**
Eze 33:17 "The way of the Lord is not **j**,"
Ro 7:12 the commandment is holy and **j** and
1Jn 1: 9 he who is faithful and **j** will forgive
Rev 15: 3 **J** and true are your ways, King of
Tob 3: 2 O Lord, and all your deeds are **j**;
Sir 18: 2 the Lord alone is **j**.

JUSTICE → JUST
Ex 23: 6 not pervert the **j** due to your poor
1Ki 7: 7 pronounce judgment, the Hall of **J**,
Job 19: 7 I call aloud, but there is no **j**.
37:23 he is great in power and **j**,
Ps 33: 5 He loves righteousness and **j**;
106: 3 Happy are those who observe **j**,
Pr 21:15 **j** is done, it is a joy to the righteous,
Isa 30:18 For the Lord is a God of **j**;
42: 4 until he has established **j** in the earth
Jer 9:24 I act with steadfast love, **j**,
Hos 12: 6 to your God, hold fast to love and **j**,
Am 5:24 But let **j** roll down like waters,

Mal 2:17 by asking, "Where is the God of **j**?"
Lk 11:42 and neglect **j** and the love of God;

JUSTIFICATION → JUST
Ro 4:25 trespasses and was raised for our **j**.
2Co 9: 9 more does the ministry of **j** abound
Gal 2:21 for if **j** comes through the law,

JUSTIFIED → JUST
Job 32: 2 he **j** himself rather than God;
Mt 12:37 for by your words you will be **j**,
Ro 3:24 they are now **j** by his grace as a gift,
5: 1 Therefore, since we are **j** by faith,
10:10 believes with the heart and so is **j**,
Gal 2:16 that we might be **j** by faith in Christ,
Jas 2:24 is **j** by works and not by faith alone.

JUSTIFY → JUST
Ro 3:30 and he will **j** the circumcised on the
Gal 3: 8 that God would **j** the Gentiles

K

KADESH → KADESH-BARNEA
Nu 20: 1 and the people stayed in **K**.
Dt 1:46 you had stayed at **K** as many days

KADESH-BARNEA → KADESH
Nu 32: 8 sent them from **K** to see the land.

KEEP → KEEPER, KEEPS, KEPT
Ge 17: 9 for you, you shall **k** my covenant,
Ex 19: 5 obey my voice and **k** my covenant,
Nu 6:24 The Lord bless you and **k** you;
Dt 5:10 love me and **k** my commandments.
Ne 1: 5 love him and **k** his commandments;
Pr 7: 2 **k** my commandments and live,
Ecc 3: 6 time to **k**, and a time to throw away;
12:13 Fear God, and **k** his commandments
Lk 17:33 those who lose their life will **k** it.
Jude 1:24 Now to him who is able to **k** you
Rev 22: 9 those who **k** the words of this book.
Sir 1:26 wisdom, **k** the commandments,

KEEPER → KEEP
Ge 4: 9 am I my brother's **k**?"
Ps 121: 5 The Lord is your **k**;

KEEPS → KEEP
Ps 121: 3 he who **k** you will not slumber.
Jas 2:10 whoever **k** the whole law but fails

KEPT → KEEP
Mt 19:20 said to him, "I have **k** all these;
Jn 17: 6 and they have **k** your word.
2Ti 4: 7 finished the race, I have **k** the faith.

KEY → KEYS
Isa 22:22 on his shoulder the **k** of the house
Lk 11:52 taken away the **k** of knowledge;
Rev 3: 7 true one, who has the **k** of David,

KEYS* → KEY
Mt 16:19 you the **k** of the kingdom of heaven,
Rev 1:18 I have the **k** of Death and of Hades.

KIDNAPS*
Ex 21:16 Whoever **k** a person, whether

KIDRON
2Sa 15:23 the king crossed the Wadi **K**,
Jn 18: 1 his disciples across the **K** valley

KILL → KILLED, KILLS
Ex 4:23 now I will **k** your firstborn son.'"
Ecc 3: 3 a time to **k**, and a time to heal;
Mt 10:28 not fear those who **k** the body but cannot **k** the soul;
Mk 14: 1 to arrest Jesus by stealth and **k** him;

KILLED → KILL
Mk 9:31 after being **k**, he will rise again."
Ac 3:15 and you **k** the Author of life,
Ro 7:11 deceived me and through it **k** me.
2Co 6: 9 as punished, and yet not **k**;

KILLS → KILL
1Sa 2: 6 The Lord **k** and brings to life;
2Co 3: 6 the letter **k**, but the Spirit gives life.

KIND → KINDNESS, KINDS
Ge 6:20 two of every **k** shall come in to you,
Ps 145:17 and **k** in all his doings.
1Co 13: 4 Love is patient; love is **k**;
Eph 4:32 and be **k** to one another,

KINDNESS → KIND
Pr 31:26 teaching of **k** is on her tongue.
Hos 11: 4 I led them with cords of human **k**,
Ro 2: 4 **k** is meant to lead you to repentance
Gal 5:22 joy, peace, patience, **k**, generosity,

KINDS → KIND
Lev 19:19 not sow your field with two **k** of
1Co 12:10 to another various **k** of tongues,
1Ti 6:10 of money is a root of all **k** of evil,

KING → KINGDOM, KINGS
Ex 1: 8 Now a new **k** arose over Egypt,
Dt 17:14 and you say, "I will set a **k** over me,
1Sa 8: 7 rejected me from being **k** over them.
2Sa 2: 4 there they anointed David **k** over
Ps 2: 6 set my **k** on Zion, my holy hill."
10:16 The Lord is **k** forever and ever;
Isa 6: 5 have seen the **K**, the Lord of hosts!
Jer 10:10 living God and the everlasting **K**.
Mt 2: 2 who has been born **k** of the Jews?
27:37 "This is Jesus, the **K** of the Jews."
Lk 19:38 "Blessed is the **k** who comes in the
Jn 1:49 You are the **K** of Israel!"
1Ti 1:17 To the **K** of the ages, immortal,
Rev 19:16 "**K** of kings and Lord of lords."
Tob 10:13 Lord of heaven and earth, **K** over all
Jdt 9:12 **K** of all your creation,

KINGDOM → KING
Ex 19: 6 you shall be for me a priestly **k** and
2Sa 7:12 and I will establish his **k**.
1Ki 11:31 "See, I am about to tear the **k**
Ps 145:13 Your **k** is an everlasting **k**,
Da 4: 3 His **k** is an everlasting **k**,
Mt 4:17 "Repent, for the **k** of heaven has
5: 3 for theirs is the **k** of heaven.
6:10 Your **k** come. Your will be done,
13:24 "The **k** of heaven may be compared
Mk 6:23 I will give you, even half of my **k**."
10:24 how hard it is to enter the **k** of God!
12:34 You are not far from the **k** of God."
13: 8 and **k** against **k**;
Lk 17:21 in fact, the **k** of God is among you."
22:16 not eat it until it is fulfilled in the **k**
Jn 18:36 "My **k** is not from this world.
Ac 1: 6 you will restore the **k** to Israel?"
Ro 14:17 the **k** of God is not food and drink
1Co 6: 9 wrongdoers will not inherit the **k**
Eph 5: 5 any inheritance in the **k** of Christ
Col 1:13 transferred us into the **k** of his
1Th 2:12 calls you into his own **k** and glory.
Heb 12:28 receiving a **k** that cannot be shaken,
2Pe 1:11 entry into the eternal **k** of our Lord
Rev 11:15 world has become the **k** of our Lord
Wis 10:10 she showed him the **k** of God,

KINGS → KING
Ge 17: 6 and **k** shall come from you.
Ps 2: 2 The **k** of the earth set themselves,
138: 4 All the **k** of the earth shall praise
Pr 8:15 By me **k** reign, and rulers decree
Isa 52:15 **k** shall shut their mouths because of
Da 7:24 of this kingdom ten **k** shall arise,
Ac 4:26 The **k** of the earth took their stand,
1Ti 6:15 the King of **k** and Lord of lords.
Rev 19:16 "King of **k** and Lord of lords."
Sir 51:12 *Give thanks to the King of the* **k** *of* **k**,

KISS
Ps 2:12 **k** his feet, or he will be angry,
SS 1: 2 Let him **k** me with the kisses of his
Mt 26:48 "The one I will **k** is the man; arrest
2Co 13:12 Greet one another with a holy **k**.

KNEE → KNEES
Isa 45:23 "To me every **k** shall bow,

KNEE (cont.)

Ro 14:11 says the Lord, every **k** shall bow to
Php 2:10 at the name of Jesus every **k** should

KNEEL → KNELT

Ps 95: 6 let us **k** before the Lord, our Maker

KNEES → KNEE

1Ki 19:18 the **k** that have not bowed to Baal,
Eph 3:14 I bow my **k** before the Father,

KNELT → KNEEL

2Ch 6:13 he **k** on his knees in the presence of
Lk 22:41 about a stone's throw, **k** down,

KNEW → KNOW

Dt 34:10 whom the Lord **k** face to face.
Jer 1: 5 I formed you in the womb I **k** you,
Mt 7:23 will declare to them, 'I never **k** you;
Ro 1:21 they **k** God, they did not honor him

KNOCK → KNOCKING

Lk 11: 9 **k**, and the door will be opened for

KNOCKING → KNOCK

Rev 3:20 I am standing at the door, **k**;

KNOW → FOREKNEW, KNEW, KNOWING, KNOWLEDGE, KNOWN, KNOWS

Ge 22:12 for now I **k** that you fear God,
Ex 6: 7 **k** that I am the Lord your God,
1Ki 8:39 only you **k** what is in every human
Job 19:25 For I **k** that my Redeemer lives,
Ps 46:10 "Be still, and **k** that I am God!
Ecc 8:16 I applied my mind to **k** wisdom,
Isa 1: 3 Israel does not **k**, my people do not
Jer 31:34 "K the Lord," for they shall all **k**
Mt 6: 3 left hand **k** what your right hand is
24:42 do not **k** on what day your Lord is
Lk 11:13 how to give good gifts to your
22:34 denied three times that you **k** me."
Jn 10:14 I **k** my own and my own **k** me,
13:35 will **k** that you are my disciples,
21:24 and we **k** that his testimony is true.
Ac 1: 7 **k** the times or periods that the
Ro 8:28 We **k** that all things work together
1Co 8: 2 Anyone who claims to **k** something
13:12 I **k** only in part; then I will **k** fully,
Eph 3:19 the love of Christ that surpasses
Php 3:10 to **k** Christ and the power of his
Tit 1:16 profess to **k** God, but they deny him
Heb 8:11 'K the Lord,' for they shall all **k** me,
1Jn 2: 4 Whoever says, "I have come to **k**
3:16 **k** love by this, that he laid down his
Rev 3: 3 not **k** at what hour I will come to

KNOWING → KNOW

Ge 3:22 like one of us, **k** good and evil;
Jn 18: 4 Jesus, **k** all that was to happen to
Php 3: 8 surpassing value of **k** Christ Jesus
Heb 13: 2 have entertained angels without **k** it.

KNOWLEDGE → KNOW

Ge 2: 9 the tree of the **k** of good and evil.
Job 21:22 Will any teach God **k**,
Pr 1: 7 of the Lord is the beginning of **k**;
8:10 and **k** rather than choice gold;
Ecc 1:18 who increase **k** increase sorrow.
Isa 11: 2 spirit of **k** and the fear of the Lord.
Hos 4: 6 people are destroyed for lack of **k**;
Lk 11:52 you have taken away the key of **k**;
Ro 11:33 riches and wisdom and **k** of God!
1Co 8: 1 K puffs up, but love builds up.
Eph 3:19 the love of Christ that surpasses **k**,
Col 2: 3 the treasures of wisdom and **k**
1Ti 6:20 of what is falsely called **k**;
2Pe 1: 5 goodness, and goodness with **k**,
1Jn 2:20 and all of you have **k**.
Sir 3:25 without **k** there is no wisdom.

KNOWN → KNOW

Ps 139: 1 you have searched me and **k** me.
Lk 6:44 for each tree is **k** by its own fruit.
Jn 1:18 Father's heart, who has made him **k**.
Ro 7: 7 I would not have **k** sin.
1Co 2:16 For who has **k** the mind of the Lord
Eph 1: 9 made **k** to us the mystery of his will,

KNOWS → KNOW

Ps 94:11 The Lord **k** our thoughts,
103:14 For he **k** how we were made;
Mt 6: 8 your Father **k** what you need before
24:36 about that day and hour no one **k**,
Ro 8:27 **k** what is the mind of the Spirit,
2Ti 2:19 "The Lord **k** those who are his,"
1Jn 4: 7 loves is born of God and **k** God.
Sir 42:18 Most High **k** all that may be known;

KORAH → KORAHITES

Levite; led rebels against Moses (Nu 16; Jude 11).

KORAHITES → KORAH

Psalms of: Pss 42; 44-49; 84; 85; 87; 88.

L

LABAN

Brother of Rebekah (Ge 24:29), father of Rachel and Leah (Ge 29:16). Received Abraham's servant (Ge 24:29-51). Provided daughters as wives for Jacob in exchange for Jacob's service (Ge 29:1-30). Provided flocks for Jacob's service (Ge 30:25-43). Pursued and covenanted with Jacob (Ge 31).

LABOR → LABORER

Ex 1:11 to oppress them with forced **l**.
20: 9 Six days you shall **l** and do all your
Jn 4:38 reap that for which you did not **l**.

LABORER → LABOR

Lev 19:13 the wages of a **l** until morning.
Lk 10: 7 for the **l** deserves to be paid.
1Ti 5:18 and, "The **l** deserves to be paid."

LACKED → LACKING

Dt 2: 7 with you; you have **l** nothing."

LACKING → LACKED

Ecc 1:15 and what is **l** cannot be counted.
Lk 18:22 "There is still one thing **l**.
Col 1:24 completing what is **l** in Christ's

LADDER

Ge 28:12 that there was a **l** set up on the earth,

LAID → LAY

Isa 53: 6 the Lord has **l** on him the iniquity
Mk 16: 6 Look, there is the place they **l** him.
1Jn 3:16 that he **l** down his life for us—

LAKE

Rev 19:20 were thrown alive into the **l** of fire
20:14 This is the second death, the **l** of fire

LAMB → LAMBS

Ge 22: 8 "God himself will provide the **l** for
Ex 12:21 and slaughter the passover **l**.
Isa 53: 7 like a **l** that is led to the slaughter,
Mk 14:12 when the Passover **l** is sacrificed,
Jn 1:29 L of God who takes away the sin of
1Co 5: 7 For our paschal **l**, Christ, has been
1Pe 1:19 like that of a **l** without defect or
Rev 5:12 the L that was slaughtered to
21:23 and its lamp is the L.

LAMBS → LAMB

Isa 40:11 he will gather the **l** in his arms,
Jn 21:15 Jesus said to him, "Feed my **l**."

LAME

Isa 35: 6 then the **l** shall leap like a deer,
Zep 3:19 And I will save the **l** and gather the
Mt 11: 5 the **l** walk, the lepers are cleansed,

LAMENTATION

La 2: 5 in daughter Judah mourning and **l**.

LAMP → LAMPS, LAMPSTAND, LAMPSTANDS

1Ki 11:36 servant David may always have a **l**
Ps 18:28 It is you who light my **l**;
119:105 Your word is a **l** to my feet and a
Mt 5:15 lighting a **l** puts it under the bushel
6:22 "The eye is the **l** of the body.
Rev 22: 5 they need no light of **l** or sun,

LAMPS → LAMP

Ex 25:37 You shall make the seven **l** for it;
Mt 25: 1 Ten bridesmaids took their **l** and

LAMPSTAND → LAMP

Ex 25:31 You shall make a **l** of pure gold.
Zec 4: 2 And I said, "I see a **l** all of gold,
1Mc 4:50 and lit the lamps on the **l**,

LAMPSTANDS → LAMP

Rev 1:20 the seven **l** are the seven churches.
11: 4 the two **l** that stand before the Lord

LAND

Ge 1:10 God called the dry **l** Earth,
12: 7 your offspring I will give this **l**."
Ex 3: 8 a **l** flowing with milk and honey,
20: 2 brought you out of the **l** of Egypt,
Nu 13: 2 to spy out the **l** of Canaan,
Jos 11:23 So Joshua took the whole **l**,
Jdg 1:27 Canaanites continued to live in that **l**
2Ki 17: 5 the king of Assyria invaded all the **l**
25:21 So Judah went into exile out of its **l**.
2Ch 7:14 will forgive their sin and heal their **l**.
Ps 37:11 But the meek shall inherit the **l**,
Jer 22:29 O **l, l, l**, hear the word of the Lord!
Da 11:41 He shall come into the beautiful **l**,
Mal 4: 6 come and strike the **l** with a curse.

LANGUAGE

Ge 11: 9 Lord confused the **l** of all the earth;
Ac 2: 6 speaking in the native **l** of each.

LAP

Jdg 7: 5 who **l** the water with their tongues,
Pr 16:33 The lot is cast into the **l**,

LASHES

Dt 25: 3 Forty **l** may be given but not more;
2Co 11:24 from the Jews the forty **l** minus one.

LAST → EVERLASTING

2Sa 23: 1 Now these are the **l** words of David:
Isa 44: 6 I am the first and I am the **l**;
Mt 19:30 first will be **l**, and the **l** will be first.
Mk 9:35 first must be **l** of all and servant of
1Co 15:26 **l** enemy to be destroyed is death.
15:52 twinkling of an eye, at the **l** trumpet.
2Ti 3: 1 that in the **l** days distressing times
Heb 1: 2 **l** days he has spoken to us by a Son,
1Jn 2:18 Children, it is the **l** hour!
Rev 1:17 I am the first and the **l**,

LAUGH → LAUGHINGSTOCK, LAUGHTER

Ge 18:13 said to Abraham, "Why did Sarah **l**,
Ecc 3: 4 a time to weep, and a time to **l**;
Lk 6:21 you who weep now, for you will **l**.

LAUGHINGSTOCK → LAUGH

Ps 44:14 the nations, a **l** among the peoples.
La 3:14 have become the **l** of all my people,

LAUGHTER → LAUGH

Ps 126: 2 Then our mouth was filled with **l**,
Jas 4: 9 Let your **l** be turned into mourning

LAW → LAWFUL, LAWLESSNESS

Dt 1: 5 Moses undertook to expound this **l**
31: 9 Then Moses wrote down this **l**,
Jos 1: 8 book of the **l** shall not depart out of
Ps 1: 2 their delight is in the **l** of the Lord,
119:97 Oh, how I love your **l**!
Jer 31:33 I will put my **l** within them,
Mt 5:17 come to abolish the **l** or the prophets
23:23 the weightier matters of the **l**:
Lk 24:44 written about me in the **l** of Moses,
Jn 1:17 indeed was given through Moses;
Ro 6:14 you are not under **l** but under grace.
10: 4 For Christ is the end of the **l** so that
Gal 2:19 through the **l** I died to the **l**,
Heb 10: 1 Since the **l** has only a shadow of the
Jas 2:10 For whoever keeps the whole **l** but
1Mc 2:48 They rescued the **l** out of the hands

LAWFUL → LAW

Mt 12:12 So it is **l** to do good on the sabbath."

1Co　6:12　"All things are **l** for me,"
　　10:23　"All things are **l**," but

LAWLESSNESS → LAW
2Th　2: 7　the mystery of **l** is already at work,
1Jn　3: 4　commits sin is guilty of **l**; sin is **l**.
Sir　21: 3　All **l** is like a two-edged sword;

LAY → LAID
Mt　8:20　of Man has nowhere to **l** his head."
　　28: 6　Come, see the place where he **l**.
Jn　10:15　And I **l** down my life for the sheep.
1Co　3:11　no one can **l** any foundation other

LAZARUS*
　1. Poor man in Jesus' parable (Lk 16:19-31).
　2. Brother of Mary and Martha whom Jesus
raised from the dead (Jn 11:1-12:19).

LAZY
Ex　5:17　He said, "You are **l, l**;
Pr　13: 4　The appetite of the **l** craves,

LEAD → LEADER, LEADERS, LEADS, LED
Ex　32:34　**l** the people to the place
Ps　61: 2　**L** me to the rock that is higher than
Isa　11: 6　and a little child shall **l** them.
Mk　13:22　to **l** astray, if possible, the elect.
Ro　2: 4　meant to **l** you to repentance?

LEADER → LEAD
1Ch　28: 4　for he chose Judah as **l**,
Ro　12: 8　the **l**, in diligence;

LEADERS → LEAD
Isa　3:12　O my people, your **l** mislead you,
Lk　19:47　the **l** of the people kept looking for
Heb　13: 7　Remember your **l**, those who spoke

LEADS → LEAD
Ps　23: 2　he **l** me beside still waters;
Mk　13: 5　"Beware that no one **l** you astray.
Ro　6:16　obedience, which **l** to righteousness

LEAH
　Wife of Jacob (Ge 29:16-30); bore six sons and
one daughter (Ge 29:31-30:21; 34:1; 35:23; Ru
4:11).

LEAPING
1Ch　15:29　and saw King David **l** and dancing;
Ac　3: 8　walking and **l** and praising God.

LEARN → LEARNED, LEARNING
Dt　4:10　that they may **l** to fear me as long as
Isa　1:17　**l** to do good; seek justice,
1Ti　2:11　Let a woman **l** in silence with full

LEARNED → LEARN
Jn　6:45　**l** from the Father comes to me.
Php　4:11　I have **l** to be content with whatever

LEARNING → LEARN
Jn　7:15　"How does this man have such **l**,
Ac　26:24　Too much **l** is driving you insane!"

LEAST → LESS
Mt　2: 6　are by no means **l** among the rulers
　　5:19　called **l** in the kingdom of heaven;
Lk　9:48　**l** among all of you is the greatest."

LEAVE → LEFT
Nu　11:20　'Why did we ever **l** Egypt?'"
Mk　10: 7　this reason a man shall **l** his father
Jn　14:18　not **l** you orphaned; I am coming
　　　　to
Heb　13: 5　said, "I will never **l** you or forsake

LEAVEN → LEAVENS
Ex　12:15　on the first day you shall remove **l**

LEAVENS → LEAVEN
Gal　5: 9　A little yeast **l** the whole batch of

LEAVES
Ge　3: 7　and they sewed fig **l** together
Eze　47:12　and their **l** for healing."
Rev　22: 2　**l** of the tree are for the healing of

LEBANON
Dt　11:24　from the wilderness to the **L** and
Isa　40:16　**L** would not provide fuel enough,

LED → LEAD
Isa　53: 7　like a lamb that is **l** to the slaughter,
Jer　50: 6　their shepherds have **l** them astray,
Hos　11: 4　**l** them with cords of human
Mt　4: 1　Then Jesus was **l** up by the Spirit
　　27:31　they **l** him away to crucify him.
Lk　21: 8　"Beware that you are not **l** astray;
Ro　8:14　For all who are **l** by the Spirit

LEFT → LEAVE
Dt　28:14　either to the right or to the **l**,
Mt　6: 3　your **l** hand know what your right
　　25:33　his right hand and the goats at
　　　　the **l**.
Lk　17:34　one will be taken and the other **l**.

LEGION
Lk　8:30　He said, "**L**"; for many demons

LEGS
Da　10: 6　**l** like the gleam of burnished bronze
Jn　19:33　they did not break his **l**.
Rev　10: 1　and his **l** like pillars of fire.

LENDER
Pr　22: 7　the borrower is the slave of the **l**.

LEPER → LEPROUS
Mt　8: 2　and there was a **l** who came to him
　　26: 6　in the house of Simon the **l**,

LEPERS → LEPROUS
Lk　7:22　the lame walk, the **l** are cleansed,

LEPROUS → LEPER, LEPERS
Ex　4: 6　he took it out, his hand was **l**,
Nu　12:10　Miriam had become **l**,

LESS → LEAST
Ex　30:15　and the poor shall not give **l**,
Ezr　9:13　punished us **l** than our iniquities

LETTER
Mt　5:18　not one **l**, not one stroke of a **l**,
2Co　3: 6　the **l** kills, but the Spirit gives life.

LEVI → LEVITES, LEVITICAL, =MATTHEW
　1. Son of Jacob by Leah (Ge 29:34; 46:11; 1Ch
2:1). With Simeon avenged rape of Dinah (Ge 34).
Tribe of blessed (Ge 49:5-7; Dt 33:8-11), chosen
as priests (Nu 3-4), numbered (Nu 3:39; 26:62),
given cities, but not land (Nu 18; 35; Dt 10:9; Jos
13:14; 21), land (Eze 48:8-22), 12,000 from (Rev
7:7).
　2. See Matthew.

LEVIATHAN
Job　41: 1　you draw out **L** with a fishhook,
Ps　74:14　You crushed the heads of **L**;
2Es　6:49　and the name of the other **L**.

LEVITES → LEVI
Nu　1:53　**L** shall camp around the tabernacle
Jos　14: 4　no portion was given to the **L** in the
Ne　8: 9　**L** who taught the people said to all

LEVITICAL → LEVI
Heb　7:11　attainable through the **l** priesthood

LIAR → LIE
Pr　19:22　and it is better to be poor than a **l**.
Jn　8:44　for he is a **l** and the father of lies.
Ro　3: 4　Although everyone is a **l**,
1Jn　2:22　**l** but the one who denies that Jesus

LIARS → LIE
1Ti　1:10　sodomites, slave traders, **l**, perjurers,
Rev　21: 8　the sorcerers, the idolaters, and all **l**,

LIBERTY
Lev　25:10　shall proclaim **l** throughout the land
Isa　41: 1　to proclaim **l** to the captives,
1Co　8: 9　this **l** of yours does not somehow

LICENTIOUSNESS
Mk　7:22　avarice, wickedness, deceit, **l**, envy,

LIE → LIAR, LIARS, LIES, LYING
Nu　23:19　that he should **l**, or a mortal,
Ps　23: 2　makes me **l** down in green pastures;
Isa　11: 6　leopard shall **l** down with the kid,
Ac　5: 3　your heart to **l** to the Holy Spirit
1Jn　2:21　know that no **l** comes from the
　　　　truth.

LIES → LIE
Ps　5: 6　You destroy those who speak **l**;
Php　3:13　forgetting what **l** behind and
　　　　straining forward to what **l** ahead,

LIFE → LIVE
Ge　2: 7　into his nostrils the breath of **l**;
　　2: 9　the tree of **l** also in the midst of the
　　9: 5　require a reckoning for human **l**.
Ex　21:23　then you shall give **l** for **l**,
Dt　12:23　for the blood is the **l**,
　　30:19　Choose **l** so that you and your
Ps　34:12　Which of you desires **l**, and covets
Pr　18:21　Death and **l** are in the power of the
　　　　tongue,
Ecc　7:12　that wisdom gives **l** to the one who
Isa　53:10　you make his **l** an offering for sin,
Da　12: 2　shall awake, some to everlasting **l**,
Mt　7:14　and the road is hard that leads to **l**,
　　10:39　Those who find their **l** will lose it,
　　20:28　to give his **l** a ransom for many."
Mk　10:30　and in the age to come eternal **l**.
Lk　12:25　a single hour to your span of **l**?
Jn　1: 4　in him was **l**, and the **l** was the light
　　3:15　believes in him may have eternal **l**.
　　6:35　said to them, "I am the bread of **l**.
　　11:25　"I am the resurrection and the **l**.
　　14: 6　"I am the way, and the truth, and
　　　　the **l**.
Ac　3:15　and you killed the Author of **l**,
Ro　5:21　eternal **l** through Jesus Christ our
　　8:38　convinced that neither death, nor **l**,
2Co　3: 6　the letter kills, but the Spirit gives **l**.
Eph　4: 1　to lead a **l** worthy of the calling
Php　4: 3　whose names are in the book of **l**.
1Jn　3:14　that we have passed from death to **l**
　　5:20　He is the true God and eternal **l**.
Rev　2: 8　who was dead and came to **l**:
　　20: 4　came to **l** and reigned with Christ
　　20:12　book was opened, the book of **l**.
　　22: 2　the tree of **l** with its twelve kinds
Sir　4:12　Whoever loves her loves **l**,
2Es　8:52　the tree of **l** is planted,

LIFTED
Isa　52:13　he shall be exalted and **l** up,
Jn　3:14　so must the Son of Man be **l** up,

LIGHT → ENLIGHTENED, ENLIGHTENS,
　　LIGHTS
Ge　1: 3　"Let there be **l**"; and there was **l**.
Ex　13:21　pillar of fire by night, to give them **l**,
Ps　27: 1　The Lord is my **l** and my salvation;
Pr　4:18　the path of the righteous is like the **l**
Ecc　2:13　that wisdom excels folly as **l** excels
Isa　9: 2　in darkness have seen a great **l**;
　　42: 6　as a covenant to the people, a **l**
　　60: 1　Arise, shine; for your **l** has come,
Mt　4:16　in darkness have seen a great **l**,
　　5:14　"You are the **l** of the world.
　　11:30　my yoke is easy, and my burden is **l**.
Jn　1: 9　true **l**, which enlightens everyone,
　　8:12　saying, "I am the **l** of the world.
Ro　13:12　and put on the armor of **l**;
2Co　11:14　Satan disguises himself as an angel
　　　　of **l**.
1Pe　2: 9　of darkness into his marvelous **l**.
1Jn　1: 7　walk in the **l** as he himself is in the **l**
Rev　22: 5　for the Lord God will be their **l**,

LIGHTNING
Ex　19:16　third day there was thunder and **l**,
Da　10: 6　body was like beryl, his face like **l**,

LIGHTNING (cont.)
Lk   10:18   from heaven like a flash of l.
Rev   4: 5   from the throne are flashes of l,

LIGHTS → LIGHT
Ge   1:16   God made the two great l—
Jas   1:17   coming down from the Father of l,

LIKE → LIKENESS
Ge   3: 5   be l God, knowing good and evil."
Ex   15:11 "Who is l you, O LORD, among the
2Sa   7:22   for there is no one l you,
Ps   113: 5 Who is l the LORD our God,
Isa   46: 9   I am God, and there is no one l me,
Jer   10: 6   There is none l you, O LORD;
Lk   13:18   "What is the kingdom of God l?
1Co   13:11 When I was a child, I spoke l a child
Rev   1:13   I saw one l the Son of Man,
      10: 1   l his face was l the sun,
      16:15   ("See, I am coming l a thief!

LIKENESS → LIKE
Ge   1:26   in our image, according to our l;
Ro   8: 3   his own Son in the l of sinful flesh,
Php   2: 7   of a slave, being born in human l.

LILIES
Lk   12:27 Consider the l, how they grow:

LINE
Isa   28:10 l upon l, l upon l, here a little,
Am   7: 7   with a plumb l in his hand.

LINEN
Ex   26: 1   with ten curtains of fine twisted l,
Da   10: 5   and saw a man clothed in l,
Rev   19: 8   for the fine l is the righteous deeds

LION → LION'S, LIONS
1Sa   17:34 and whenever a l or a bear came,
Ecc   9: 4   a living dog is better than a dead l.
Isa   11: 7   and the l shall eat straw like the ox.
Da   7: 4   first was like a l and had eagles'
Rev   4: 7   the first living creature like a l,
      5: 5   See, the L of the tribe of Judah,

LION'S → LION
2Ti   4:17   So I was rescued from the l mouth.

LIONS → LION
Da   6:20   able to deliver you from the l?"

LIPS
Dt   23:23 Whatever your l utter you must
Job   2:10   Job did not sin with his l.
Isa   6: 5   am lost, for I am a man of unclean l,
Mt   15: 8   with their l, but their hearts are far
Heb   13:15 the fruit of l that confess his name.

LISTEN → LISTENS
Ex   23:22 But if you l attentively to his voice
2Ki   17:40 They would not l, however,
Ps   5: 2   L to the sound of my cry, my King
Pr   4: 1   L, children, to a father's instruction,
Ecc   5: 1   l is better than the sacrifice offered
Mk   9: 7   my Son, the Beloved; l to him!"
Lk   16:31 'If they do not l to Moses and the
Ac   3:22   You must l to whatever he tells you.
Jas   1:19   be quick to l, slow to speak,
Sir   11: 8   Do not answer before you l,

LISTENS → LISTEN
Jn   18:37 Everyone who belongs to the truth l
1Jn   4: 6   Whoever knows God l to us,

LITTLE
Ex   16:18 who gathered l had no shortage;
Ps   8: 5   have made them a l lower than God,
Pr   15:16 Better is a l with the fear of
Mt   8:26   "Why are you afraid, you of l faith?
      19:14 "Let the l children come to me,
2Co   8:15   one who had l did not have too l."
Gal   5: 9   A l yeast leavens the whole batch of
Rev   10: 2   He held a l scroll open in his hand.
Sir   29:23 Be content with l or much,

LIVE → ALIVE, LIFE, LIVED, LIVES, LIVING
Ge   3:22   and eat, and l forever"—
Ex   1:16   but if it is a girl, she shall l."

Ex   33:20 for no one shall see me and l."
Lev   18: 5   by doing so one shall l:
Dt   8: 3   one does not l by bread alone,
Ps   91: 1   l in the shelter of the Most High,
Hab   2: 4   but the righteous l by their faith.
Mt   4: 4   'One does not l by bread alone,
Jn   11:25 even though they die, will l,
Ro   1:17   one who is righteous will l by faith."
      14: 8   If we l, we l to the Lord,
2Co   5:15   those who l might l no longer for
Gal   3:12   does works of the law will l
Wis   5:15   But the righteous l forever,
Sir   34:14 those who fear the Lord will l,

LIVED → LIVE
Ro   14: 9   to this end Christ died and l again,

LIVES → LIVE
Job   19:25 For I know that my Redeemer l,
Ps   18:46 The LORD l! Blessed be my rock,
Jn   11:26 and everyone who l and believes
Ro   6:10   but the life he l, he l to God.
1Jn   3:16   to lay down our l for one another.
Rev   15: 7   of God, who l forever and ever;
Tob   13: 1   "Blessed be God who l forever,

LIVING → LIVE
Ge   2: 7   and the man became a l being.
      3:20   because she was the mother of all l.
      6:19   And of every l thing, of all flesh,
Dt   5:26   the voice of the l God speaking out
Jer   2:13   forsaken me, the fountain of l water,
Zec   14: 8   that day l waters shall flow out from
Mt   16:16 the Messiah, the Son of the l God."
Jn   4:10   he would have given you l water."
      6:51   I am the l bread that came down
Ro   12: 1   present your bodies as a l sacrifice,
2Co   6:16   For we are the temple of the l God;
Heb   4:12   the word of God is l and active,
1Pe   2: 8   l stone, though rejected by mortals

LOAVES
Mk   6:41   Taking the five l and the two fish,
      8: 6   and he took the seven l,

LOCK
Mt   23:13 you l people out of the kingdom of

LOCUST → LOCUSTS
2Ch   6:28   if there is plague, blight, mildew, l,
Joel 2:25   years that the swarming l has eaten,

LOCUSTS → LOCUST
Ex   10: 4   I will bring l into your country.
Mt   3: 4   and his food was l and wild honey.
Rev   9: 3   from the smoke came l on the earth,

LOG
Mt   7: 3   do not notice the l in your own eye?

LONELY → ALONE
Ps   25:16 for I am l and afflicted.
La   1: 1   How l sits the city that once was full

LONG → LONGING
Ex   20:12 that your days may be l in the land
Ps   13: 1   How l, O LORD?
Pr   3:16   L life is in her right hand;
1Co   11:14 that if a man wears l hair,
1Pe   1:12   things into which angels l to look!
      2: 2   Like newborn infants, l for the pure,
Rev   6:10   how l will it be before you judge

LONGING → LONG
Ro   8:19   the creation waits with eager l for
2Co   5: 2   l to be clothed with our heavenly

LOOK → LOOKED, LOOKS
Ex   3: 6   for he was afraid to l at God.
Ps   8: 3   When I l at your heavens,
      80:14 l down from heaven, and see;
Lk   24:39 L at my hands and my feet;

LOOKED → LOOK
Ge   19:26 But Lot's wife, behind him, l back,
Ex   2:25   God l upon the Israelites,
Sir   16:29 Then the Lord l upon the earth,

LOOKS → LOOK
1Sa   16: 7   the LORD l on the heart."
Ps   14: 2   The LORD l down from heaven
Mt   5:28   who l at a woman with lust

LORD → LORD'S, LORDS
Ge   18:27 take it upon myself to speak to the L
Ex   4:10   Moses said to the LORD, "O my L,
Dt   10:17 God is God of gods and L of lords,
Ps   16: 2   I say to the LORD, "You are my L;
      110: 1 The LORD says to my l,
Isa   6: 1   I saw the L sitting on a throne, high
Da   2:47   God is God of gods and L of kings
Mic   1: 2   the L from his holy temple.
Mt   7:22   many will say to me, 'L, L,
      9:38   the L of the harvest to send out
      12: 8   the Son of Man is l of the sabbath."
Mk   1: 3   'Prepare the way of the L,
      12:29 the L our God, the L is one;
Lk   2:11   who is the Messiah, the L.
      10:27 "You shall love the L your God
      19:38 who comes in the name of the L!
Jn   13:13 You call me Teacher and L—
      20:28 "My L and my God!"
Ac   2:34   'The L said to my L, "Sit at my
Ro   4:24   in him who raised Jesus our L
      10:12 the same L is L of all and
1Co   2:16   who has known the mind of the L
      8: 6   and one L, Jesus Christ,
2Co   3:17   Now the L is the Spirit,
Eph   4: 5   one L, one faith, one baptism,
Php   2:11   that Jesus Christ is L, to the glory
      4: 5   The L is near.
Col   3:13   just as the L has forgiven you,
1Th   4:15   are left until the coming of the L,
1Ti   6:15   the King of kings and L of lords.
Heb   12:14 without which no one will see the L.
Jas   4:10   Humble yourselves before the L,
1Pe   3:15   in your hearts sanctify Christ as L.
2Pe   3: 9   The L is not slow about his promise,
Jude 1: 4   and deny our only Master and L,
Rev   4: 8   "Holy, holy, holy, the L God
      19:16 "King of kings and L of lords."
      22:20 Amen. Come, L Jesus!
Jdt   6:19   L God of heaven, see their
Wis   8: 3   and the L of all loves her.
Sir   1: 1   All wisdom is from the L,
Aza   1:35   Bless the L, all you works of the L;
Sus   1: 2   and one who feared the L.

†LORD → †GOD, †LORD'S
Ge   2: 7   L God formed man from the dust of
      6: 6   the L was sorry that he had made
      13: 4   Abram called on the name of the L.
      18:14 that place "The L will provide";
      22:14 that place "The L will provide";
Ex   3:15   shall say to the Israelites, 'The L,
      5: 2   But Pharaoh said, "Who is the L,
      6: 7   know that I am the L your God,
      15: 3   The L is a warrior; the L is his name.
      34: 6   and proclaimed, "The L, the L,
Lev   19: 2   for I the L your God am holy.
Nu   6:24   The L bless you and keep you;
      14:18 'The L is slow to anger,
Dt   6: 4   The L is our God, the L alone.
Jos   24:15 my household, we will serve the L."
1Sa   2: 2   "There is no Holy One like the L,
1Ki   8:11   of the L filled the house of the L.
      18:21 If the L is God, follow him;
1Ch   16:11 Seek the L and his strength,
Ezr   7:10   his heart to study the law of the L,
Ne   8:10   the joy of the L is your strength."
Job   1:21   the L gave, and the L has taken
      42:12 The L blessed the latter days
Ps   1: 2   their delight is in the law of the L,
      10:16 The L is king forever and ever;
      18: 1 I love you, O L, my strength.
      23: 1 The L is my shepherd, I shall not
      33:12 Happy is the nation whose God is the L
      84:11 For the L God is a sun and shield;
      110: 1 The L says to my lord,

Ps　113: 5　Who is like the **L** our God,
　　　125: 2　so the **L** surrounds his people,
　　　128: 1　Happy is everyone who fears the **L**,
　　　145:18　The **L** is near to all who call on him,
　　　150: 6　that breathes praise the **L**!
Pr　　1: 7　fear of the **L** is the beginning of
　　　　3: 5　Trust in the **L** with all your heart,
　　　19:23　The fear of the **L** is life indeed;
　　　21: 2　but the **L** weighs the heart.
Isa　　2:11　**L** alone will be exalted in that day.
　　　　6: 3　"Holy, holy, holy is the **L** of hosts;
　　　33:22　the **L** is our judge, the **L** is our ruler,
　　　53: 6　the **L** has laid on him the iniquity
　　　64: 8　Yet, O **L**, you are our Father;
Jer　　4: 4　Circumcise yourselves to the **L**,
　　　31:34　"Know the **L**," for they shall all
　　　32:27　I am the **L**, the God of all flesh;
La　　3:25　The **L** is good to those who wait for
Eze　3:23　and the glory of the **L** stood there,
　　　10:18　the glory of the **L** went out from
　　　37: 4　O dry bones, hear the word of the **L**.
　　　44: 4　glory of the **L** filled the temple
　　　48:35　time on shall be, The **L** is There.
Hos　14: 1　Return, O Israel, to the **L** your God,
Joel　1:15　For the day of the **L** is near,
Am　5: 6　Seek the **L** and live,
Ob　1:15　the day of the **L** is near against all
Na　1: 3　The **L** is slow to anger but great in
Zep　1:14　The great day of the **L** is near,
Zec　14: 9　the **L** will be one and his name one.
Mal　3: 6　For I the **L** do not change;
　　　4: 5　and terrible day of the **L** comes.

LORD'S → LORD
Mk　12:11　was the **L** doing, and it is amazing
Lk　4:19　to proclaim the year of the **L** favor."
Ro　14: 8　or whether we die, we are the **L**,
1Co　10:26　the earth and its fullness are the **L**."
Sir　17:17　but Israel is the **L** own portion.

†LORD'S → †LORD
Nu　11:23　"Is the **L** power limited?
Dt　32: 9　the **L** own portion was his people,
Ps　24: 1　The earth is the **L** and all that is in it
Isa　59: 1　the **L** hand is not too short to save,
Ob　1:21　and the kingdom shall be the **L**.

LORDS → LORD
Dt　10:17　God is God of gods and Lord of **l**,
Ps　136: 3　O give thanks to the Lord of **l**,
1Co　8: 5　there are many gods and many **l**—
Rev　19:16　"King of kings and Lord of **l**."

LOSE → LOSS, LOST
Mk　8:35　who **l** their life for my sake,
Jn　12:25　Those who love their life **l** it,
2Co　4: 1　in this ministry, we do not **l** heart.
Heb　12: 3　you may not grow weary or **l** heart.
2Jn　1: 8　do not **l** what we have worked for,

LOSS → LOSE
1Co　3:15　burned up, the builder will suffer **l**;
Php　3: 8　I regard everything as **l** because of
Sir　32:24　who trusts the Lord will not suffer **l**.

LOST → LOSE
Ps　119:176　I have gone astray like a **l** sheep;
Jer　50: 6　My people have been **l** sheep;
Eze　34:16　I will seek the **l**, and I will bring
Mt　10: 6　to the **l** sheep of the house of Israel.
Lk　15: 6　I have found my sheep that was **l**."
　　　19:10　came to seek out and to save the **l**."

LOT → LOT'S, LOTS
　　　1. Nephew of Abraham (Ge 11:27; 12:5). Chose to live in Sodom (Ge 13). Rescued from four kings (Ge 14). Rescued from Sodom (Ge 19:1-29; 2Pe 2:7). Fathered Moab and Ammon (Ge 19:30-38).
　　　2. Object cast to make decisions.
Nu　33:54　You shall apportion the land by **l**
Est　3: 7　they cast Pur—which means "the **l**"
Pr　16:33　The **l** is cast into the lap,
Jnh　1: 7　cast lots, and the **l** fell on Jonah.
Ac　1:26　and the **l** fell on Matthias;

LOT'S → LOT, 1
Ge　19:26　**L** wife, behind him, looked back,
Lk　17:32　Remember **L** wife.

LOTS → LOT, 2
Ps　22:18　and for my clothing they cast **l**.
Mt　27:35　among themselves by casting **l**;

LOVE → BELOVED, LOVED, LOVER, LOVERS, LOVES
Ex　20: 6　but showing steadfast **l** to the
　　　34: 6　and abounding in steadfast **l** and
Lev　19:18　shall **l** your neighbor as yourself:
Nu　14:18　and abounding in steadfast **l**,
Dt　6: 5　You shall **l** the LORD your God
2Sa　7:15　not take my steadfast **l** from him,
1Ki　11: 2　Solomon clung to these in **l**.
2Ch　6:42　Remember your steadfast **l**
Ezr　3:11　his steadfast **l** endures forever
Ne　1: 5　steadfast **l** with those who **l** him
Ps　18: 1　I **l** you, O LORD, my strength.
　　　86: 5　abounding in steadfast **l** to all who
　　　116: 1　I **l** the LORD, because he has heard
　　　119:97　Oh, how I **l** your law!
　　　136: 1　for his steadfast **l** endures forever.
Pr　5:19　you be intoxicated always by her **l**.
　　　8:17　I **l** those who **l** me,
　　　19: 8　To get wisdom is to **l** oneself;
Ecc　3: 8　a time to **l**, and a time to hate;
SS　1: 2　For your **l** is better than wine,
　　　8: 6　for **l** is strong as death,
Isa　54: 8　but with everlasting **l** I will have
La　3:22　steadfast **l** of the LORD never ceases,
Da　9: 4　steadfast **l** with those who **l** you
Hos　6: 4　Your **l** is like a morning cloud,
　　　11: 4　of human kindness, with bands of **l**.
　　　14: 4　heal their disloyalty; I will **l** them
Joel　2:13　and abounding in steadfast **l**,
Jnh　4: 2　and abounding in steadfast **l**,
Mt　5:44　**L** your enemies and pray
　　　6:24　either hate the one and **l** the other,
Mk　12:31　shall **l** your neighbor as yourself.'
Lk　6:32　For even sinners **l** those who **l** them.
　　　10:27　"You shall **l** the Lord your God
Jn　12:25　Those who **l** their life lose it,
　　　13:34　new commandment, that you **l** one
　　　14:15　"If you **l** me, you will keep my
　　　15:13　No one has greater **l** than this,
　　　21:16　"Simon son of John, do you **l** me?"
Ro　5: 8　But God proves his **l** for us in that
　　　12: 9　Let **l** be genuine; hate what is evil,
　　　13: 8　anything, except to **l** one another;
1Co　8: 1　Knowledge puffs up, but **l** builds up.
　　　13: 4　**L** is patient; **l** is kind;
　　　13:13　and the greatest of these is **l**.
Gal　5: 6　is faith working through **l**.
　　　5:22　the fruit of the Spirit is **l**, joy,
Eph　3:19　**l** of Christ that surpasses knowledge
　　　5:25　Husbands, **l** your wives,
Col　3:14　Above all, clothe yourselves with **l**,
1Th　5: 8　put on the breastplate of faith and **l**,
1Ti　6:10　For the **l** of money is a root of all
Tit　2: 2　in faith, in **l**, and in endurance.
Heb　10:24　provoke one another to **l** and good
　　　13: 5　your lives free from the **l** of money,
Jas　2: 8　shall **l** your neighbor as yourself."
1Pe　1: 8　you have not seen him, you **l** him;
2Pe　1: 7　and mutual affection with **l**.
1Jn　2:15　not **l** the world or the things in the
　　　3: 1　See what the Father has given us,
　　　3:16　We know **l** by this, that he laid
　　　5: 3　For the **l** of God is this,
2Jn　1: 6　And this is **l**, that we walk according
Jude　1:21　keep yourselves in the **l** of God;
Rev　2: 4　abandoned the **l** you had at first.
Sir　2:15　and those who **l** him keep his ways.
　　　7:30　With all your might **l** your Maker,
Bel　1:38　have not forsaken those who **l** you."
1Mc　4:33　with the sword of those who **l** you,

LOVED → LOVE
Dt　4:37　And because he **l** your ancestors,

Jer　31: 3　have **l** you with an everlasting love;
Hos　11: 1　When Israel was a child, I **l** him,
Mal　1: 2　I have **l** you, says the LORD.
Jn　3:16　God so **l** the world that he gave his
　　　13: 1　he **l** them to the end.
　　　15: 9　the Father has, so I have **l** you;
　　　15:12　love one another as I have **l** you.
Gal　2:20　who **l** me and gave himself for me.
Eph　5: 2　Christ **l** us and gave himself up for
1Jn　4:19　We love because he first **l** us.

LOVER → LOVE
Ps　99: 4　Mighty King, **l** of justice,
Ecc　5:10　**l** of money will not be satisfied with
1Ti　3: 3　quarrelsome, and not a **l** of money.

LOVERS → LOVE
Jer　3: 1　have played the whore with many **l**;
La　1: 2　all her **l** she has no one to comfort
Hos　2: 5　For she said, "I will go after my **l**;
Lk　16:14　Pharisees, who were **l** of money,
2Ti　3: 2　For people will be **l** of themselves,

LOVES → LOVE
Ps　33: 5　He **l** righteousness and justice;
Pr　3:12　for the LORD reproves the one he **l**,
　　　17:17　A friend **l** at all times,
Mt　10:37　Whoever **l** father or mother more
Lk　7:47　to whom little is forgiven, **l** little."
Ro　13: 8　who **l** another has fulfilled the law.
Eph　5:28　He who **l** his wife **l** himself.
Heb　12: 6　Lord disciplines those whom he **l**,
1Jn　4: 7　who **l** is born of God and knows
Rev　1: 5　who **l** us and freed us from our sins
Wis　8: 3　and the Lord of all **l** her.
Sir　4:12　Whoever **l** her **l** life,

LOW → LOWER, LOWLY
Ps　136:23　who remembered us in our **l** estate,
Isa　40: 4　every mountain and hill be made **l**;
Lk　3: 5　mountain and hill shall be made **l**,

LOWER → LOW
Ps　8: 5　have made them a little **l** than God,
Heb　2: 7　made them for a little while **l** than

LOWLY → LOW
Pr　16:19　It is better to be of a **l** spirit
Lk　1:52　their thrones, and lifted up the **l**;
Ro　12:16　but associate with the **l**;
Jdt　9:11　But you are the God of the **l**,

LOYAL → LOYALTY
2Sa　22:26　With the **l** you show yourself **l**;
Da　11:32　who are **l** to their God

LOYALTY → LOYAL
Dt　7: 9　God who maintains covenant **l**
Ru　3:10　this last instance of your **l**
Ps　101: 1　I will sing of **l** and of justice;
Hos　4: 1　There is no faithfulness or **l**,

LUKE*
　　　Associate of Paul (Col 4:14; 2Ti 4:11; Phm 24).

LUKEWARM*
Rev　3:16　because you are **l**, and neither cold

LUST → LUSTS
Mt　5:28　looks at a woman with **l** has already
2Pe　1: 4　that is in the world because of **l**,

LUSTS → LUST
Ro　1:24　gave them up in the **l** of their hearts
Eph　4:22　old self, corrupt and deluded by its **l**
2Pe　3: 3　scoffing and indulging their own **l**

LYDIA
Ac　16:14　named **L**, a worshiper of God,

LYING → LIE
1Ki　22:23　a **l** spirit in the mouth of all these
Pr　6:17　a **l** tongue, and hands that shed
Hos　4: 2　Swearing, **l**, and murder,
Wis　1:11　and a **l** mouth destroys the soul.

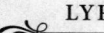
LYRE

1Sa 18:10 while David was playing the **l,**
Ps 33: 2 Praise the Lord with the **l;**
Da 3: 5 pipe, **l,** trigon, harp, drum,

M

MACCABEUS → JUDAS

1Mc 2:66 Judas **M** has been a mighty warrior

MACEDONIA

Ac 16: 9 a man of **M** pleading with him and

MADE → MAKE

Ge 1:31 God saw everything that he had **m,**
   2:22 he **m** into a woman and brought her
   3:21 the Lord God **m** garments of skins
   6: 6 was sorry that he had **m** humankind
   15:18 the Lord **m** a covenant with Abram,
Ex 20:11 For in six days the Lord **m** heaven
   36: 8 the workers **m** the tabernacle with
Ps 8: 5 have **m** them a little lower than God
   118:24 This is the day that the Lord has **m;**
   139:14 I am fearfully and wonderfully **m.**
Jer 27: 5 outstretched arm have **m** the earth,
Mk 2:27 "The sabbath was **m** for humankind,
Ac 2:36 that God has **m** him both Lord and
Eph 2: 5 **m** us alive together with Christ—
Rev 14: 7 and worship him who **m** heaven
Sir 43:33 For the Lord has **m** all things,

MADNESS

Dt 28:28 The Lord will afflict you with **m,**
Ecc 9: 3 **m** is in their hearts while they live,

MAGDALENE

Mt 27:56 Among them were Mary **M,**

MAGICIANS

Ex 7:11 and they also, the **m** of Egypt,
Da 2: 2 So the king commanded that the **m,**

MAGNIFIES* → MAGNIFY

Lk 1:46 Mary said, "My soul **m** the Lord,

MAGNIFY → MAGNIFIES

Ps 34: 3 O **m** the Lord with me,

MAJESTIC → MAJESTY

Ex 15:11 Who is like you, **m** in holiness,
Ps 8: 1 how **m** is your name in all the earth!
2Pe 1:17 conveyed to him by the **M** Glory,

MAJESTY → MAJESTIC

1Ch 29:11 the glory, the victory, and the **m;**
Ps 93: 1 The Lord is king, he is robed in **m;**
Isa 53: 2 or **m** that we should look at him,
Heb 1: 3 sat down at the right hand of the **M**
2Pe 1:16 we had been eyewitnesses of his **m.**

MAKE → MADE, MAKER

Ge 1:26 "Let us **m** humankind in our image,
   2:18 will **m** him a helper as his partner."
   12: 2 I will **m** of you a great nation,
Ex 20: 4 You shall not **m** for yourself an
        idol,
   32: 1 "Come, **m** gods for us, who shall go
Nu 6:25 Lord **m** his face to shine upon you,
Isa 61: 8 I will **m** an everlasting covenant
   66:22 and the new earth, which I will **m,**
Jer 31:31 when I will **m** a new covenant with
Mt 28:19 and **m** disciples of all nations,
Mk 1:17 and I will **m** you fish for people."

MAKER → MAKE

Ge 14:19 God Most High, **m** of heaven and
Job 4:17 beings be pure before their **M?**
Ps 95: 6 kneel before the Lord, our **M!**
Isa 54: 5 For your **M** is your husband,
Sir 7:30 With all your might love your **M,**

MALACHI*

Post-exilic prophet (Mal 1:1; 2Es 1:40).

MALE

Ge 1:27 **m** and female he created them.
   17:10 **m** among you shall be circumcised.
Lev 20:13 If a man lies with a **m** as with a

Mt 19: 4 'made them **m** and female,'
Rev 12: 5 she gave birth to a son, a **m** child,

MALICE

Ro 1:29 wickedness, evil, covetousness, **m.**
1Co 5: 8 the old yeast, the yeast of **m** and

MAN → MEN

Ge 2: 7 Lord God formed **m** from the dust
   2:18 not good that the **m** should be
        alone;
   32:24 **m** wrestled with him until daybreak.
1Sa 13:14 sought out a **m** after his own heart;
Mt 9: 6 Son of **M** has authority on earth to
Lk 6: 5 The Son of **M** is lord of the sabbath.
Jn 9:35 "Do you believe in the Son of **M?**"
1Co 11: 3 that Christ is the head of every **m,**
Rev 1:13 I saw one like the Son of **M,**
   14:14 cloud was one like the Son of **M,**

MANAGE → MANAGERS

1Ti 3: 4 He must **m** his own household well,
   5:14 children, and **m** their households,

MANAGERS* → MANAGE

Tit 2: 5 chaste, good **m** of the household,

MANASSEH

1. Firstborn of Joseph (Ge 41:51; 46:20). Blessed by Jacob but not as firstborn (Ge 48). Tribe of blessed (Dt 33:17), numbered (Nu 1:35; 26:34), half allotted land east of Jordan (Nu 32; Jos 13:8-33), half west (Jos 16; Eze 48:4), failed to fully possess (Jos 17:12-13; Jdg 1:27), 12,000 from (Rev 7:6).
2. Son of Hezekiah; king of Judah (2Ki 21:1-18; 2Ch 33:1-20). Judah exiled for his detestable sins (2Ki 21:10-15). Repented (2Ch 33:12-19; Man 1-15).

MANGER

Lk 2:12 in bands of cloth and lying in a **m."**

MANNA

Ex 16:31 The house of Israel called it **m;**
Jos 5:12 The **m** ceased on the day they ate
Jn 6:49 ate the **m** in the wilderness,
Rev 2:17 I will give some of the hidden **m,**

MANNER

1Co 11:27 cup of the Lord in an unworthy **m**
Php 1:27 life in a **m** worthy of the gospel

MANTLE

1Ki 19:19 and threw his **m** over him.
2Ki 2: 8 Elijah took his **m** and rolled it up,

MANY

Isa 53:12 yet he bore the sin of **m,**
Mt 22:14 **m** are called, but few are chosen."
Mk 10:45 and to give his life a ransom for **m."**
Jn 20:30 Now Jesus did **m** other signs in the
Ro 12: 5 who are **m,** are one body in Christ,

MARAH

Ex 15:23 That is why it was called **M.**

MARK → MARKED, MARKS

1. Cousin of Barnabas (Ac 12:12; 15:37-39; Col 4:10; 2Ti 4:11; Phm 24; 1Pe 5:13), see John.
2. Brand or symbol:
Ge 4:15 And the Lord put a **m** on Cain,
Eze 9: 6 but touch no one who has the **m.**
Rev 14: 9 receive a **m** on their foreheads or
   19:20 who had received the **m** of the beast

MARKED → MARK

Hab 1:12 you have **m** them for judgment;
Eph 1:13 **m** with the seal of the promised

MARKET → MARKETPLACE

Mk 7: 4 not eat anything from the **m** unless
1Co 10:25 Eat whatever is sold in the meat **m**

MARKETPLACE → MARKET

Jn 2:16 Stop making my Father's house a **m**

MARKS → MARK

1Co 7:18 to remove the **m** of circumcision.

Gal 6:17 I carry the **m** of Jesus branded on
1Mc 1:15 and removed the **m** of circumcision,

MARRIAGE → INTERMARRY, MARRIED, MARRIES

Mt 22:30 are given in **m,** but are like angels
Heb 13: 4 Let **m** be held in honor by all,
Rev 19: 7 for the **m** of the Lamb has come,

MARRIED → MARRIAGE

Mal 2:11 has **m** the daughter of a foreign god.
Mk 12:23 For the seven had **m** her."
1Ti 3: 2 be above reproach, **m** only once,
Tit 1: 6 **m** only once, whose children are

MARRIES → MARRIAGE

Mk 10:11 and **m** another commits adultery
Ro 7: 3 if she **m** another man, she is not an
1Co 7:28 and if a virgin **m,** she does not sin.

MARTHA*

Sister of Mary and Lazarus (Lk 10:38-42; Jn 11; 12:2).

MARVELOUS

Ps 98: 1 for he has done **m** things.
   131: 1 things too great and too **m** for me.
Sir 39:20 and nothing is too **m** for him.

MARY

1. Mother of Jesus (Mt 1:16-25; Lk 1:27-56; 2:1-40). With Jesus at temple (Lk 2:41-52), at the wedding in Cana (Jn 2:1-5), questioning his sanity (Mk 3:21), at the cross (Jn 19:25-27). Among disciples (Ac 1:14).
2. Magdalene; former demoniac (Lk 8:2). Helped support Jesus' ministry (Lk 8:1-3). At the cross (Mt 27:56; Mk 15:40; Jn 19:25), burial (Mt 27:61; Mk 15:47). Saw angel after resurrection (Mt 28:1-10; Mk 16:1-9; Lk 24:1-12); also Jesus (Jn 20:1-18).
3. Sister of Martha and Lazarus (Jn 11). Washed Jesus' feet (Jn 12:1-8).
4. Mother of James and Joses; witnessed crucifixion (Mt 27:56; Mk 15:40) and empty tomb (Mk 16:1; Lk 24:10).

MASTER → MASTERS, TASKMASTERS

Ge 4: 7 desire is for you, but you must **m** it.
Mal 1: 6 if I am a **m,** where is the respect due
Mt 25:21 enter into the joy of your **m.'**
Jn 15:20 Servants are not greater than their **m**
2Pe 2: 1 deny the **M** who bought them—

MASTERS → MASTER

Mt 6:24 "No one can serve two **m;**

MATTANIAH → See ZEDEKIAH

MATTATHIAS

Priest who started the Maccabean revolt (1Mc 2).

MATTER

Ecc 3: 1 a time for every **m** under heaven:
   12:13 end of the **m;** all has been heard.

MATTHEW* → =LEVI

Apostle; former tax collector (Mt 9:9-13; 10:3; Mk 3:18; Lk 6:15; Ac 1:13). Also called Levi (Mk 2:14-17; Lk 5:27-32).

MATTHIAS

Disciple chosen to replace Judas (Ac 1:23-26).

MATURE → MATURITY

1Co 2: 6 among the **m** we do speak wisdom,
Php 3:15 who are **m** be of the same mind;
Col 4:12 you may stand **m** and fully assured
Heb 5:14 But solid food is for the **m,**

MATURITY → MATURE

Eph 4:13 to **m,** to the measure of the full

MEAN → MEANING, MEANS

Ex 12:26 What do you **m** by this observance?
Jos 4: 6 'What do those stones **m** to you?'

MEANING → MEAN
Ge 40: 5 and each dream with its own **m**.
Dt 6:20 "What is the **m** of the decrees

MEANS → MEAN
Mt 9:13 learn what this **m**, 'I desire mercy,
1Co 9:22 that I might by all **m** save some.

MEASURE
Dt 25:15 have only a full and honest **m**,
Mk 4:24 **m** you give will be the **m** you get,
Lk 6:38 A good **m**, pressed down, shaken
Jn 3:34 for he gives the Spirit without **m**.

MEAT
Ex 16:12 'At twilight you shall eat **m**,
Ro 14:21 not to eat **m** or drink wine or do

MEDIA
Da 8:20 these are the kings of M and Persia.

MEDIATOR
Gal 3:19 ordained through angels by a **m**.
1Ti 2: 5 **m** between God and humankind,
Heb 8: 6 he is the **m** of a better covenant,

MEDICINE
Pr 17:22 A cheerful heart is a good **m**,
Sir 6:16 Faithful friends are life-saving **m**;

MEDITATE → MEDITATION
Jos 1: 8 you shall **m** on it day and night,
Ps 1: 2 on his law they **m** day and night.
119:15 I will **m** on your precepts,
Wis 12:22 we may **m** upon your goodness,
Sir 6:37 and **m** at all times on his

MEDITATION → MEDITATE
Ps 19:14 of my mouth and the **m** of my heart
119:97 It is my **m** all day long.

MEDIUM
Lev 20:27 A man or a woman who is a **m**
1Ch 10:13 moreover, he had consulted a **m**,

MEEK → MEEKNESS
Ps 37:11 But the **m** shall inherit the land,
Mt 5: 5 "Blessed are the **m**, for they will

MEEKNESS → MEEK
Col 3:12 kindness, humility, **m**, and patience.
Jas 1:21 with **m** the implanted word

MEET → MEETING
Ex 30:36 tent of meeting where I shall **m** with
Am 4:12 prepare to **m** your God,
1Th 4:17 together with them to **m** the Lord

MEETING → MEET
Ex 27:21 In the tent of **m**, outside the curtain
40:34 the cloud covered the tent of **m**,

MELCHIZEDEK
Ge 14:18 King M of Salem brought out bread
Ps 110: 4 forever according to the order of M."
Heb 7: 1 This "King M of Salem, priest of

MELT
Dt 1:28 made our hearts **m** by reporting,
Ps 97: 5 The mountains **m** like wax before
2Pe 3:12 and the elements will **m** with fire?

MEMBERS
Ro 7:23 I see in my **m** another law at war
1Co 6:15 that your bodies are **m** of Christ?
12:18 God arranged the **m** in the body,

MEMORIAL
Lev 5:12 a handful of it as its **m** portion,
Jos 4: 7 stones shall be to the Israelites a **m**

MEN → MAN
Ge 18: 2 and saw three **m** standing near him.
Da 3:25 "But I see four **m** unbound,
Mt 2: 1 wise **m** from the East came to
Lk 9:30 they saw two **m**, Moses and Elijah,
Sir 44: 1 now sing the praises of famous **m**,

MENAHEM*
King of Israel (2Ki 15:14-23).

MENE
Da 5:25 inscribed: M, M, TEKEL, and PARSIN.

MEPHIBOSHETH
Son of Jonathan shown kindness by David (2Sa 4:4; 9; 21:7). Accused of siding with Absalom (2Sa 16:1-4; 19:24-30).

MERCIES → MERCY
La 3:22 his **m** never come to an end;
2Co 1: 3 the Father of **m** and the God of all

MERCIFUL → MERCY
Dt 4:31 the LORD your God is a **m** God,
Ps 111: 4 the LORD is gracious and **m**.
Jer 3:12 not look on you in anger, for I am **m**
Mt 5: 7 "Blessed are the **m**, for they will
Lk 6:36 Be **m**, just as your Father is **m**.
Heb 2:17 be a **m** and faithful high priest
Sir 2:11 the Lord is compassionate and **m**;

MERCY → MERCIES, MERCIFUL
Ex 25:17 make a **m** seat of pure gold;
1Ch 21:13 of the LORD, for his **m** is very great;
Ps 40:11 Do not, O LORD, withhold your **m**
Da 9: 9 To the Lord our God belong **m**
Hab 3: 2 in wrath may you remember **m**.
Zec 1:12 will you withhold **m** from Jerusalem
Mt 9:13 learn what this means, 'I desire **m**,
23:23 of the law: justice and **m** and faith.
Ro 9:15 "I will have **m** on whom I have **m**,
Eph 2: 4 But God, who is rich in **m**,
1Ti 1:13 **m** because I had acted ignorantly
Tit 3: 5 had done, but according to his **m**,
Heb 4:16 so that we may receive **m** and find
Jas 2:13 **m** triumphs over judgment.
Sir 2:17 for equal to his majesty is his **m**,

MERIBAH
Ex 17: 7 He called the place Massah and M,
Ps 95: 8 Do not harden your hearts, as at M,

MESHACH → =MISHAEL
Hebrew exiled to Babylon; name changed from Mishael (Da 1:6-7). Refused defilement by food (Da 1:8-20). Refused to worship idol (Da 3:1-18); saved from furnace (Da 3:19-30).

MESSAGE → MESSENGER
Jn 12:38 "Lord, who has believed our **m**,
1Co 1:18 the **m** about the cross is foolishness
2Co 5:19 entrusting the **m** of reconciliation to

MESSENGER → MESSAGE
Isa 42:19 or deaf like my **m** whom I send?
Mt 11:10 I am sending my **m** ahead of you,
2Co 12: 7 a **m** of Satan to torment me,

MESSIAH → CHRIST, MESSIAHS
Mt 16:16 Peter answered, "You are the M,
Lk 2:11 a Savior, who is the M, the Lord.
Ac 2:36 God has made him both Lord and M
Ro 9: 5 according to the flesh, comes the M,
Rev 11:15 kingdom of our Lord and of his M,
2Es 7:28 For my son the M shall be revealed

MESSIAHS → MESSIAH
Mk 13:22 False **m** and false prophets will

MICAH
1. Idolater from Ephraim (Jdg 17-18).
2. Prophet from Moresheth (Jer 26:18-19; Mic 1:1).

MICAIAH
Prophet of the LORD who spoke against Ahab (1Ki 22:1-28; 2Ch 18:1-27).

MICHAEL
Archangel (Jude 9); warrior in angelic realm, protector of Israel (Da 10:13, 21; 12:1; Rev 12:7).

MICHAL*
Daughter of Saul, wife of David (1Sa 14:49; 18:20-28). Warned David of Saul's plot (1Sa 19). Saul gave her to Paltiel (1Sa 25:44); David

retrieved her (2Sa 3:13-16). Criticized David for dancing before the ark (2Sa 6:16-23; 1Ch 15:29).

MIDDLE
Ge 3: 3 tree that is in the **m** of the garden,
Rev 22: 2 the **m** of the street of the city.

MIDIAN → MIDIANITES
Ex 18: 1 Jethro, the priest of M, Moses'

MIDIANITES → MIDIAN
Ge 37:36 the M had sold him in Egypt to
Nu 31: 2 "Avenge the Israelites on the M;

MIDWIVES
Ex 1:17 But the **m** feared God; they did not

MIGHT → ALMIGHTY, MIGHTY
2Ch 6:41 you and the ark of your **m**.
20: 6 In your hand are power and **m**,
Ps 54: 1 and vindicate me by your **m**.
Ecc 9:10 hand finds to do, do with your **m**;
Zec 4: 6 **m**, nor by power, but by my spirit,
Sir 7:30 With all your **m** love your Maker,

MIGHTY → MIGHT
Ge 49:24 by the hands of the M One of Jacob,
Ex 6: 1 by a **m** hand he will let them go;
Dt 5:15 a **m** hand and an outstretched arm;
2Sa 1:19 How the **m** have fallen!
Ps 99: 4 M King, lover of justice, you have
Isa 9: 6 Wonderful Counselor, M God,
Lk 1:49 the M One has done great things
Rev 18: 8 for **m** is the Lord God who judges

MILE
Mt 5:41 one **m**, go also the second **m**.

MILK
Ex 3: 8 a land flowing with **m** and honey,
Heb 5:12 You need **m**, not solid food;
1Pe 2: 2 long for the pure, spiritual **m**,

MILLSTONE → STONE
Lk 17: 2 better for you if a **m** were hung

MIND → MINDFUL, MINDS
Nu 23:19 mortal, that he should change his **m**.
1Ch 28: 9 for the LORD searches every **m**,
Ps 110: 9 sworn and will not change his **m**,
Jnh 3: 9 God may relent and change his **m**,
Mt 22:37 all your soul, and with all your **m**.'
Ro 1:28 God gave them up to a debased **m**
8: 6 but to set the **m** on the Spirit is life
1Co 2:16 who has known the **m** of the Lord
Php 2: 5 same **m** be in you that was in Christ
Heb 7:21 sworn and will not change his **m**,
Sir 37:17 The **m** is the root of all conduct;

MINDFUL → MIND
Ps 8: 4 beings that you are **m** of them,
111: 5 he is ever **m** of his covenant.
Heb 2: 6 beings that you are **m** of them,

MINDS → MIND
2Co 4: 4 blinded the **m** of the unbelievers,
Eph 4:23 be renewed in the spirit of your **m**,
Php 4: 7 guard your hearts and your **m**

MINISTER → MINISTERS, MINISTRY
Ex 28:43 to **m** in the holy place;
Ps 101: 6 that is blameless shall **m** to me.

MINISTERS → MINISTER
2Co 3: 6 to be **m** of a new covenant,
11:15 if his **m** also disguise themselves as **m**

MINISTRY → MINISTER
2Co 5:18 has given us the **m** of reconciliation;
Eph 4:12 equip the saints for the work of **m**,
Heb 8: 6 now obtained a more excellent **m**,

MIRACLES → See also JESUS: MIRACLES
Ps 78:11 and the **m** that he had shown them.
Ac 19:11 did extraordinary **m** through Paul,
1Co 12:29 Are all teachers? Do all work **m**?
Heb 2: 4 signs and wonders and various **m**,

MIRIAM
Sister of Moses and Aaron (Nu 26:59). Led dancing at Red Sea (Ex 15:20-21). Struck with leprosy for criticizing Moses (Nu 12). Death (Nu 20:1).

MIRROR
1Co 13:12 For now we see in a **m**, dimly,
2Co 3:18 as though reflected in a **m**,
Jas 1:23 who look at themselves in a **m**;

MISHAEL → See MESHACH

MISUSES
Ex 20: 7 not acquit anyone who **m** his name.

MOAB → MOABITE
Ge 19:37 bore a son, and named him **M**;
Ru   1: 1 went to live in the country of **M**,
Isa 15: 1 An oracle concerning **M**.

MOABITE → MOAB
Dt 23: 3 **M** shall be admitted to the assembly

MOCK → MOCKED
Ps 22: 7 All who see me **m** at me;
Mk 10:34 they will **m** him, and spit upon him,

MOCKED → MOCK
1Ki 18:27 At noon Elijah **m** them, saying,
Gal 6: 7 God is not **m**, for you reap

MOLECH
Lev 18:21 to sacrifice them to **M**,

MOMENT → MOMENTARY
Ex 33: 5 single **m** I should go up among you,
Ps 30: 5 For his anger is but for a **m**;
Isa 54: 7 For a brief **m** I abandoned you,
    66: 8 a nation be delivered in one **m**?
1Co 15:52 in a **m**, in the twinkling of an eye,

MOMENTARY* → MOMENT
2Co 4:17 this slight **m** affliction is preparing

MONEY
Ecc 10:19 and **m** meets every need.
Mk 11:15 the tables of the **m** changers
1Ti 3: 3 quarrelsome, and not a lover of **m**.
     6:10 love of **m** is a root of all kinds
Heb 13: 5 your lives free from the love of **m**,

MONTH
Ex 12: 2 be the first **m** of the year for you.
Eze 47:12 they will bear fresh fruit every **m**,
Rev 22: 2 producing its fruit each **m**;

MOON → MOONS
Ge 37: 9 the sun, the **m**, and eleven stars
Dt 17: 3 the sun or the **m** or any of the host
Jos 10:13 sun stood still, and the **m** stopped,
Joel 2:31 to darkness, and the **m** to blood,
Ac   2:20 to darkness and the **m** to blood,
Rev 6:12 the full **m** became like blood,
    21:23 no need of sun or **m** to shine on it,

MOONS → MOON
2Ch 8:13 the new **m**, and the three annual
Col 2:16 or of observing festivals, new **m**,

MORALS*
1Co 15:33 "Bad company ruins good **m**."

MORDECAI
Benjamite exile who raised Esther (Est 2:5-15). Exposed plot to kill Xerxes (Est 2:19-23). Refused to honor Haman (Est 3:1-6; 5:9-14). Charged Esther to foil Haman's plot against the Jews (Est 4). Xerxes forced Haman to honor Mordecai (Est 6). Mordecai exalted (Est 8-10). Established Purim (Est 9:18-32). See also Additions to Esther.

MORE → MOST
Ps 19:10 **M** to be desired are they than gold,
    69:31 will please the LORD **m** than an ox
Ecc 6:11 The **m** words, the **m** vanity,
Mk   4:25 to those who have, **m** will be given;
Lk 12:23 For life is **m** than food,
Ro   8:37 things we are **m** than conquerors

1Co 12:31 a still **m** excellent way.
Jas 4: 6 But he gives all the **m** grace;
Rev 7:16 will hunger no **m**, and thirst no **m**;
    21: 4 Death will be no **m**;

MORIAH*
Ge 22: 2 you love, and go to the land of **M**,
2Ch 3: 1 the LORD in Jerusalem on Mount **M**,

MORNING
Ge   1: 5 and there was **m**, the first day.
Ps 30: 5 but joy comes with the **m**.
La   3:23 every **m**; great is your faithfulness.
Lk 24:22 They were at the tomb early this **m**,
2Pe 1:19 the day dawns and the **m** star rises
Rev 22:16 of David, the bright **m** star."

MORTAL
Nu 23:19 **m**, that he should change his mind.
1Sa 15:29 **m**, that he should change his mind."
1Co 15:53 **m** body must put on immortality.
2Co 5: 4 is **m** may be swallowed up by life.

MOSES
Levite; brother of Aaron (Ex 6:20; 1Ch 6:3). Put in basket into Nile; discovered and raised by Pharaoh's daughter (Ex 2:1-10). Fled to Midian after killing Egyptian (Ex 2:11-15). Married to Zipporah, fathered Gershom (Ex 2:16-22).
Called by the LORD to deliver Israel (Ex 3-4). Pharaoh's resistance (Ex 5). Ten plagues (Ex 7-11). Passover and Exodus (Ex 12-13). Led Israel through Red Sea (Ex 14). Song of deliverance (Ex 15:1-21). Brought water from rock (Ex 17:1-7). Raised hands to defeat Amalekites (Ex 17:8-16). Delegated judges (Ex 18; Dt 1:9-18).
Received Law at Sinai (Ex 19-23; 25-31; Jn 1:17). Announced Law to Israel (Ex 19:7-8; 24; 35). Broke tablets because of golden calf (Ex 32; Dt 9). Saw glory of the LORD (Ex 33-34). Supervised building of tabernacle (Ex 36-40). Set apart Aaron and priests (Lev 8-9). Numbered tribes (Nu 1-4; 26). Opposed by Aaron and Miriam (Nu 12). Sent spies into Canaan (Nu 13). Announced forty years of wandering for failure to enter land (Nu 14). Opposed by Korah (Nu 16). Forbidden to enter land for striking rock (Nu 20:1-13; Dt 1:37). Lifted bronze snake for healing (Nu 21:4-9; Jn 3:14). Final address to Israel (Dt 1-33). Succeeded by Joshua (Nu 27:12-23; Dt 34). Death and burial by God (Dt 34:5-12). Praise of (Sir 45).
Law of (1Ki 2:3; Ezr 3:2; Mk 12:26; Lk 24:44). Book of (2Ch 25:12; Ne 13:1). Song of (Ex 15:1-21; Rev 15:3). Prayer of (Ps 90).

MOST → MORE
Ge 14:18 he was priest of God **M** High.
Ex 26:33 the holy place from the **m** holy.
Ps 91: 1 live in the shelter of the **M** High,
Mk   5: 7 Jesus, Son of the **M** High God?
Col 4: 5 making the **m** of the time.
Jude 1:20 yourselves up on your **m** holy faith;

MOTH
Ps 39:11 consuming like a **m** what is dear to
Mt   6:19 where **m** and rust consume and

MOTHER → MOTHER'S, MOTHERS
Ge   2:24 a man leaves his father and his **m**
     3:20 because she was the **m** of all living.
Ex 20:12 Honor your father and your **m**,
Jdg 5: 7 Deborah, arose as a **m** in Israel.
Pr 31: 1 An oracle that his **m** taught him:
Isa 66:13 As a **m** comforts her child, so I will
Mt 10:37 loves father or **m** more than me is
Lk 14:26 and does not hate father and **m**,
Jn 19:27 to the disciple, "Here is your **m**."
Eph 5:31 a man will leave his father and **m**
Rev 17: 5 **m** of whores and of earth's
Tob 4: 3 Honor your **m** and do not abandon
Sir 3: 6 who honor their **m** obey the Lord;

MOTHER'S → MOTHER
Job 1:21 "Naked I came from my **m** womb,

Pr   1: 8 and do not reject your **m** teaching;
Jn   3: 4 a second time into the **m** womb and

MOTHERS → MOTHER
Pr 15:20 but the foolish despise their **m**.
Mk 10:30 brothers and sisters, **m** and children,

MOUNT → MOUNTAIN, MOUNTAINS
Ge 22:14 "On the **m** of the LORD it shall be
Ex 19:20 the LORD descended upon **M** Sinai,
Dt 11:29 blessing on **M** Gerizim and the curse
Ps 78:68 **M** Zion, which he loves.
Mic 4: 7 will reign over them in **M** Zion
Zec 14: 4 the **M** of Olives shall be split in two
Mk 13: 3 he was sitting on the **M** of Olives
Heb 12:22 But you have come to **M** Zion and
Rev 14: 1 the Lamb, standing on **M** Zion!

MOUNTAIN → MOUNT
Ex   3: 1 and came to Horeb, the **m** of God.
    24:18 on the **m** for forty days and forty
Isa 2: 2 the **m** of the LORD's house shall be
Da   2:45 saw that a stone was cut from the **m**
Mt   4: 8 a very high **m** and showed him all
    17:20 you will say to this **m**, 'Move from
2Pe 1:18 we were with him on the holy **m**.

MOUNTAINS → MOUNT
Ge   7:20 the waters swelled above the **m**,
Ps 125: 2 As the **m** surround Jerusalem,
Isa 52: 7 beautiful upon the **m** are the feet of
1Co 13: 2 have all faith, so as to remove **m**,
Rev 16:20 and no **m** were to be found;

MOURN → MOURNFUL, MOURNING
Ecc 3: 4 a time to **m**, and a time to dance;
Zec 12:10 they shall **m** for him,
Mt   5: 4 "Blessed are those who **m**,
Sir 7:34 but **m** with those who **m**.

MOURNING → MOURN
Ps 30:11 You have turned my **m** into dancing
Isa 61: 3 the oil of gladness instead of **m**,
Rev 21: 4 **m** and crying and pain will be no

MOUTH → MOUTHS
Ex   4:12 Now go, and I will be with your **m**
Dt   8: 3 that comes from the **m** of the LORD.
Ps 19:14 Let the words of my **m** and
Ecc 5: 2 Never be rash with your **m**,
Isa 49: 2 He made my **m** like a sharp sword,
Mt   4: 4 every word that comes from the **m**
    15:11 it is not what goes into the **m**
Jas 3:10 From the same **m** come blessing and
Rev 19:15 From his **m** comes a sharp sword
Sir 28:25 and a bolt for your **m**.

MOUTHS → MOUTH
Ps 115: 5 They have **m**, but do not speak;
Da   6:22 sent his angel and shut the lions' **m**

MUCH
Ps 19:10 they than gold, even **m** fine gold;
Ecc 12:12 **m** study is a weariness of the flesh.
Lk 12:48 to whom **m** has been given, **m** will be required;
Jn 12:24 but if it dies, it bears **m** fruit.
1Jn 4:11 since God loved us so **m**,

MUD
Jn   9: 6 and spread the **m** on the man's eyes,
2Pe 2:22 washed only to wallow in the **m**."

MULTIPLY
Ge   1:28 to them, "Be fruitful and **m**,
     9: 7 And you, be fruitful and **m**,
Dt   6: 3 that you may **m** greatly in a land

MULTITUDE → MULTITUDES
Jas 5:20 and will cover a **m** of sins.
1Pe 4: 8 for love covers a **m** of sins.

MULTITUDES → MULTITUDE
Joel 3:14 **M**, in the valley of decision!
Rev 17:15 are peoples and **m** and nations

MURDER → MURDERER, MURDERERS
Ex 20:13 You shall not **m**.

Hos 4: 2 lying, and **m**, and stealing and
Mt 5:21 of ancient times, 'You shall not **m**';

MURDERER → MURDER
Nu 35:16 the **m** shall be put to death.
Jn 8:44 He was a **m** from the beginning

MURDERERS → MURDER
1Jn 3:15 who hate a brother or sister are **m**,
Rev 21: 8 the faithless, the polluted, the **m**,

MUSIC
1Sa 19: 9 while David was playing **m**.
Ps 92: 3 to the **m** of the lute and the harp,

MUSTARD
Mt 17:20 have faith the size of a **m** seed,
Mk 4:31 It is like a **m** seed, which,

MUTUAL
Ro 12:10 love one another with **m** affection;
Heb 13: 1 Let **m** love continue.

MYRRH
Mt 2:11 gifts of gold, frankincense, and **m**.
Mk 15:23 offered him wine mixed with **m**;

MYSTERY
Da 2:19 **m** was revealed to Daniel in a vision
Ro 11:25 I want you to understand this **m**:
1Co 15:51 Listen, I will tell you a **m**!
Eph 3: 4 my understanding of the **m** of Christ
1Ti 3: 9 must hold fast to the **m** of the faith
Rev 17: 5 a name, a **m**: "Babylon the great,

MYTHS
2Pe 1:16 did not follow cleverly devised **m**

N

NAAMAN
Aramean general whose leprosy was cleansed by Elisha (2Ki 5; Lk 4:27).

NABAL
Wealthy Carmelite the LORD killed for refusing to help David (1Sa 25). David married Abigail, his widow (1Sa 25:39-42).

NABOTH
Jezreelite killed for his vineyard (1Ki 21). Ahab's family punished (1Ki 21:17-24; 2Ki 9:21-37).

NADAB
1. Firstborn of Aaron (Ex 6:23); killed with Abihu for offering unauthorized fire (Lev 10; Nu 3:4).
2. Son of Jeroboam I; king of Israel (1Ki 15:25-32).

NAHUM
Prophet against Nineveh (Na 1:1; Tob 14:4).

NAILING* → NAILS
Col 2:14 He set this aside, **n** it to the cross.

NAILS → NAILING
Ecc 12:11 like **n** firmly fixed are the collected
Jn 20:25 put my finger in the mark of the **n**

NAKED → NAKEDNESS
Ge 2:25 the man and his wife were both **n**,
Job 1:21 "**N** I came from my mother's womb, and **n** shall
2Co 5: 3 taken it off we will not be found **n**.

NAKEDNESS → NAKED
Ro 8:35 or persecution, or famine, or **n**,

NAME → NAME'S, NAMES
Ge 2:19 every living creature, that was its **n**.
4:26 people began to invoke the **n** of
12: 2 bless you, and make your **n** great,
Ex 3:15 my **n** forever, and this my title
20: 7 wrongful use of the **n** of the LORD
34: 5 and proclaimed the **n**, "The LORD."
Nu 17: 2 Write each man's **n** on his staff,
Dt 11:5 as a dwelling for his **n**:
Ps 9:10 know your **n** put their trust in you,
Pr 18:10 The **n** of the LORD is a strong tower;

Isa 42: 8 I am the LORD, that is my **n**;
Eze 20: 9 But I acted for the sake of my **n**,
Joel 2:32 on the **n** of the LORD shall be saved;
Zec 14: 9 the LORD will be one and his **n** one.
Mt 1:21 a son, and you are to **n** him Jesus,
6: 9 Father in heaven, hallowed be your **n**.
28:19 baptizing them in the **n** of the Father
Jn 1:12 received him, who believed in his **n**,
20:31 believing you may have life in his **n**.
Ac 4:12 for there is no other **n** under heaven
Php 2: 9 gave him the **n** that is above every **n**
Rev 13:17 **n** of the beast or the number of its **n**,
19:13 his **n** is called The Word of God.
22: 4 and his **n** will be on their foreheads.
Sir 2:17 and equal to his **n** are his works.

NAME'S → NAME
Ps 23: 3 in right paths for his **n** sake.

NAMES → NAME
Ge 2:20 The man gave **n** to all cattle,
Ex 28: 9 engrave on them the **n** of the sons
Mt 10: 2 are the **n** of the twelve apostles:
Rev 21:14 the twelve **n** of the twelve apostles

NAOMI*
Wife of Elimelech, mother-in-law of Ruth (Ru 1:2, 4). Left Bethlehem for Moab during famine (Ru 1:1). Returned a widow, with Ruth (Ru 1:6-22). Advised Ruth to seek marriage with Boaz (Ru 2:17-3:4). Cared for Ruth's son Obed (Ru 4:13-17).

NAPHTALI
Son of Jacob by Bilhah (Ge 30:8; 35:25; 1Ch 2:2). Tribe of blessed (Ge 49:21; Dt 33:23), numbered (Nu 1:43; 26:50), allotted land (Jos 19:32-39; Eze 48:3), failed to fully possess (Jdg 1:33), supported Deborah (Jdg 4:10; 5:18), David (1Ch 12:34), 12,000 from (Rev 7:6).

NARROW
Lk 13:24 "Strive to enter through the **n** door;

NATHAN
Prophet and chronicler of Israel's history (1Ch 29:29; 2Ch 9:29). Announced the Davidic covenant (2Sa 7; 1Ch 17). Denounced David's sin with Bathsheba (2Sa 12). Supported Solomon (1Ki 1).

NATHANAEL → =BARTHOLOMEW?
Apostle (Jn 1:45-49; 21:2). Probably also called Bartholomew (Mt 10:3).

NATION → NATIONS
Ge 12: 2 I will make of you a great **n**, and
Ex 32:10 and of you I will make a great **n**."
Ps 33:12 Happy is the **n** whose God is the LORD
Pr 14:34 Righteousness exalts a **n**,
Isa 2: 4 **n** shall not lift up sword against **n**,
66: 8 a **n** be delivered in one moment?
Mt 24: 7 For **n** will rise against **n**,
1Pe 2: 9 a holy **n**, God's own people,

NATIONS → NATION
Ge 18:18 the **n** of the earth shall be blessed in
2Ki 17:15 followed the **n** that were around
Ps 47: 8 God is king over the **n**;
Isa 2: 2 all the **n** shall stream to it.
42: 1 he will bring forth justice to the **n**.
Am 9:12 and all the **n** who are called
Mt 28:19 and make disciples of all **n**,
Mk 11:17 a house of prayer for all the **n**'?
Ro 4:18 become "the father of many **n**,"
Rev 22: 2 the tree are for the healing of the **n**.

NATURAL → NATURE
Nu 16:29 If these people die a **n** death,
Ro 11:21 if God did not spare the **n** branches,

NATURE → NATURAL
Ro 1:20 his eternal power and divine **n**,
2Pe 1: 4 become participants of the divine **n**.

NAZARETH
Mt 2:23 made his home in a town called **N**,
Jn 1:46 Can anything good come out of **N**?
19:19 "Jesus of **N**, the King of the Jews."

NAZIRITE
Nu 6: 2 make a special vow, the vow of a **n**,
Jdg 13: 5 boy shall be a **n** to God from birth.

NEAR → NEARSIGHTED
Dt 4: 7 has a god so **n** to it as the LORD
30:14 No, the word is very **n** to you;
Isa 55: 6 call upon him while he is **n**;
Zep 1:14 The great day of the LORD is **n**,
Lk 10: 9 'The kingdom of God has come **n**
Jas 4: 8 Draw **n** to God, and he will draw **n** to
Rev 22:10 of this book, for the time is **n**.

NEARSIGHTED* → NEAR, SEE
2Pe 1: 9 lacks these things is **n** and blind,

NEBUCHADNEZZAR
Babylonian king, also spelled Nebuchadrezzar. Subdued and exiled Judah (2Ki 24-25; 2Ch 36; Jer 39). Dreams interpreted by Daniel (Da 2; 4). Worshiped God (Da 3:28-29; 4:34-37).

NECK → STIFF-NECKED
Pr 3:22 your soul and adornment for your **n**.
Mt 18: 6 were fastened around your **n**

NECO
Pharaoh who killed Josiah (2Ki 23:29-30; 2Ch 35:20-22), deposed Jehoahaz (2Ki 23:33-35; 2Ch 36:3-4).

NEED → NEEDY
Mt 6: 8 for your Father knows what you **n**
1Co 12:21 to the hand, "I have no **n** of you,"
Heb 4:16 and find grace to help in time of **n**.
1Jn 2:27 you do not **n** anyone to teach you.

NEEDLE
Lk 18:25 a camel to go through the eye of a **n**

NEEDY → NEED
1Sa 2: 8 he lifts the **n** from the ash heap,
Job 29:16 I was a father to the **n**,
Ps 113: 7 and lifts the **n** from the ash heap,

NEGLECT
Lk 11:42 and **n** justice and the love of God;
1Ti 4:14 Do not **n** the gift that is in you,
Heb 2: 3 escape if we **n** so great a salvation?

NEHEMIAH
Cupbearer of Artaxerxes (Ne 2:1); governor of Israel (Ne 8:9). Returned to Jerusalem to rebuild walls (Ne 2-6). With Ezra, reestablished worship (Ne 8). Prayer confessing nation's sin (Ne 9). Dedicated wall (Ne 12). Story of the miraculous fire (2Mc 1).

NEIGHBOR
Lev 19:18 shall love your **n** as yourself:
Dt 5:20 bear false witness against your **n**.
Mt 19:19 You shall love your **n** as yourself."
Jas 2: 8 "You shall love your **n** as yourself."

NESTS
Mt 8:20 and birds of the air have **n**;
Lk 13:19 made **n** in its branches."

NEVER
Ps 15: 5 do these things shall **n** be moved.
La 3:22 steadfast love of the LORD **n** ceases,
Da 2:44 will set up a kingdom that shall **n**
Mt 7:23 will declare to them, 'I **n** knew you;
Jn 10:28 eternal life, and they will **n** perish.
1Co 13: 8 Love **n** ends. But as for prophecies,
Heb 13: 5 he has said, "I will **n** leave you or

NEW
Ex 1: 8 Now a **n** king arose over Egypt,
Ps 33: 3 Sing to him a **n** song;
Ecc 1: 9 there is nothing **n** under the sun.
Isa 43:19 I am about to do a **n** thing;

NEW *(cont.)*

Isa   65:17   create **n** heavens and a **n** earth;
Jer   31:31   I will make a **n** covenant with the
La   3:23   they are **n** every morning;
Eze   36:26   A **n** heart I will give you,
Mt   9:17   is **n** wine put into old wineskins;
Mk   1:27   A **n** teaching—with authority!
Lk   22:20   is the **n** covenant in my blood.
Jn   13:34   I give you a **n** commandment,
2Co   3: 6   to be ministers of a **n** covenant,
Col   3:10   clothed yourselves with the **n** self,
Heb   8: 8   when I will establish a **n** covenant
1Pe   1: 3   mercy he has given us a **n** birth into
2Pe   3:13   we wait for **n** heavens and a **n** earth,
1Jn   2: 7   writing you no **n** commandment,
Rev   21: 1   I saw a **n** heaven and a **n** earth;
     21: 2   I saw the holy city, the **n** Jerusalem,
     21: 5   "See, I am making all things **n**."

NEWS

Isa   52: 7   who brings good **n**, who announces
Mt   11: 5   the poor have good **n** brought to
Mk   1:15   repent, and believe in the good **n**."

NICODEMUS

Pharisee who visted Jesus at night (Jn 3). Argued for fair treatment of Jesus (Jn 7:50-52). With Joseph, prepared Jesus for burial (Jn 19:38-42).

NIGHT → NIGHTS

Ge   1: 5   and the darkness he called **N**.
Ex   13:21   a pillar of fire by **n**, to give them
Jos   1: 8   you shall meditate on it day and **n**,
Mt   24:43   part of the **n** the thief was coming,
1Th   5: 2   Lord will come like a thief in the **n**.
Rev   22: 5   And there will be no more **n**;

NIGHTS → NIGHT

Ge   7:12   on the earth forty days and forty **n**.
Ex   24:18   mountain for forty days and forty **n**.
1Ki   19: 8   of that food forty days and forty **n**
Jnh   1:17   of the fish three days and three **n**.
Mt   4: 2   He fasted forty days and forty **n**,
     12:40   for three days and three **n** the Son

NILE

Ex   7:17   will strike the water that is in the **N**,

NINEVEH

Jnh   1: 2   "Go at once to **N**, that great city,
Na   1: 1   An oracle concerning **N**.
Mt   12:41   The people of **N** will rise up at the

NOAH

Righteous man (Eze 14:14, 20) called to build ark (Ge 6-8; Heb 11:7; 1Pe 3:20; 2Pe 2:5). God's covenant with (Ge 9:1-17). Drunkenness of (Ge 9:18-23). Blessed sons, cursed Canaan (Ge 9:24-27). Praised (Sir 44:17-18).

NOISE

Ex   32:17   "There is a **n** of war in the camp."
Ps   66: 1   Make a joyful **n** to God, all the earth
2Pe   3:10   will pass away with a loud **n**,

NOON

Am   8: 9   I will make the sun go down at **n**,
Mk   15:33   When it was **n**, darkness came over

NORTH

Jer   4: 6   I am bringing evil from the **n**,
Da   11: 6   come to the king of the **n** to ratify

NOTHING

Ecc   1: 9   there is **n** new under the sun.
Jer   32:17   **N** is too hard for you.
Mt   17:20   and **n** will be impossible for you."
Jn   15: 5   apart from me you can do **n**.
1Co   13: 2   but do not have love, I am **n**.
Sir   39:20   and **n** is too marvelous for him.

NULLIFY

Ro   3: 3   **n** the faithfulness of God?
Gal   2:21   I do not **n** the grace of God;

NUMBER → NUMBERED, NUMEROUS

Nu   1:45   So the whole **n** of the Israelites,
     26:51   the **n** of the Israelites enrolled:
Ro   11:25   until the full **n** of the Gentiles has
Rev   13:18   Its **n** is six hundred sixty-six.

NUMBERED → NUMBER

2Sa   24:10   because he had **n** the people.

NUMEROUS → NUMBER

Ge   17: 2   and will make you exceedingly **n**."
Ex   1: 9   the Israelite people are more **n**
Zec   10: 8   shall be as **n** as they were before.

NURSING

Isa   49:15   Can a woman forget her **n** child,

O

OATH

Dt   7: 8   and kept the **o** that he swore to your
Ne   13:25   them take an **o** in the name of God,
Ps   132:11   a sure **o** from which he will not turn
Heb   7:20   This was confirmed with an **o**;

OBADIAH

1. Believer who sheltered 100 prophets from Jezebel (1Ki 18:1-16).
2. Prophet against Edom (Ob 1; 2Es 1:39).

OBEDIENCE → OBEY

Ro   5:19   so by the one man's **o** the many will
Heb   5: 8   learned **o** through what he suffered;

OBEDIENT → OBEY

Ex   24: 7   spoken we will do, and we will be **o**.
Php   2: 8   and became **o** to the point of death

OBEY → OBEDIENCE, OBEDIENT, OBEYED

Ex   19: 5   if you **o** my voice and keep my
Dt   12:28   Be careful to **o** all these words that
Jos   24:24   we will serve, and him we will **o**."
Mt   28:20   **o** everything that I have commanded
Ac   5:29   "We must **o** God rather than any
Eph   6: 1   Children, **o** your parents in the Lord,
1Jn   5: 3   love of God is this, that we **o** his

OBEYED → OBEY

Jer   3:13   have not **o** my voice, says the LORD.
Heb   11: 8   By faith Abraham **o** when he was

OBSERVE

Lev   20: 8   Keep my statutes, and **o** them;
Ps   119: 8   I will **o** your statutes;

OBSTACLE

1Co   9:12   **o** in the way of the gospel of Christ.
2Co   6: 3   are putting no **o** in anyone's way,

OBTAIN → OBTAINED

Ro   11: 7   Israel failed to **o** what it was seeking
2Ti   2:10   that they may also **o** the salvation

OBTAINED → OBTAIN

Php   3:12   Not that I have already **o** this
Heb   8: 6   Jesus has now **o** a more excellent

ODOR

Ge   8:21   the LORD smelled the pleasing **o**,
Ex   29:18   it is a pleasing **o**, an offering

OFFENSE

Mk   6: 3   And they took **o** at him.
Gal   5:11   **o** of the cross has been removed.

OFFER → OFFERING, OFFERINGS

Ps   4: 5   **O** right sacrifices, and put your trust
Hos   14: 2   and we will **o** the fruit of our lips.
Heb   9:25   Nor was it to **o** himself again and

OFFERING → OFFER

Ge   4: 4   LORD had regard for Abel and his **o**,
     22: 8   will provide the lamb for a burnt **o**,
2Ch   7: 1   heaven and consumed the burnt **o**
Ps   40: 6   Sacrifice and **o** you do not desire,
Da   11:31   shall abolish the regular burnt **o**
Eph   5: 2   a fragrant **o** and sacrifice to God.
Heb   10:14   For by a single **o** he has perfected

1Mc   4:44   what to do about the altar of burnt **o**,

OFFERINGS → OFFER

1Sa   15:22   the LORD as great delight in burnt **o**
Hos   6: 6   of God rather than burnt **o**.
Mk   12:33   important than all whole burnt **o**
1Mc   1:45   to forbid burnt **o** and sacrifices

OFFSPRING

Ge   3:15   and between your **o** and hers;
     12: 7   "To your **o** I will give this land."
2Sa   7:12   I will raise up your **o** after you,

OHOLIAB

Craftsman who worked on the tabernacle (Ex 31:6; 35:34; 36:1-2; 38:23).

OIL

Ex   25: 6   **o** for the lamps, spices for the anointing **o**
Dt   14:23   your wine, and your **o**, as well
Ps   23: 5   you anoint my head with **o**;
Heb   1: 9   with the **o** of gladness beyond your
Jas   5:14   anointing them with **o** in the name

OLD

Ge   21: 7   I have borne him a son in his **o** age."
Ps   74:12   Yet God my King is from of **o**,
Mk   2:22   puts new wine into **o** wineskins;
Ro   4:19   he was about a hundred years **o**),
Eph   4:22   your **o** self, corrupt and deluded by

OLIVE → OLIVES

Zec   4: 3   And by it there are two **o** trees,
Ro   11:17   and you, a wild **o** shoot,
Rev   11: 4   two **o** trees and the two lampstands

OLIVES → OLIVE

Zec   14: 4   Mount of **O** shall be split in two
Mt   24: 3   he was sitting on the Mount of **O**,

OMEGA

Rev   1: 8   "I am the Alpha and the **O**,"

OMRI

King of Israel (1Ki 16:21-26).

ONCE → ONE

Ex   30:10   **O** a year Aaron shall perform the
Ro   6:10   he died, he died to sin, **o** for all;
Heb   7:27   this he did **o** for all when he offered
     9:27   it is appointed for mortals to die **o**,

ONE → FIRST, ONCE

Ge   2:24   and they become **o** flesh.
Zec   14: 9   the LORD will be **o** and his name **o**.
Mk   12:29   the Lord our God, the Lord is **o**;
Jn   10:30   The Father and I are **o**."
1Co   12:13   For in the **o** Spirit we were all baptized
Eph   4: 5   **o** Lord, **o** faith, **o** baptism,

ONLY

Ge   22: 2   "Take your son, your **o** son Isaac,
1Ki   18:22   "I, even I **o**, am left a prophet
Jn   1:14   the glory as of a father's **o** son,
     3:16   that he gave his **o** Son,
1Ti   1:17   the **o** God, be honor and glory
1Jn   4: 9   God sent his **o** Son into the world so

OPEN → OPENED, OPENS

Isa   53: 7   so he did not **o** his mouth.
Rev   5: 2   "Who is worthy to **o** the scroll

OPENED → OPEN

Ge   3: 7   Then the eyes of both were **o**,
Da   7:10   in judgment, and the books were **o**.
Zec   13: 1   a fountain shall be **o** for the house
Lk   11: 9   knock, and the door will be **o** for
Heb   10:20   new and living way that he **o** for us
Rev   20:12   book was **o**, the book of life.

OPENS → OPEN

Rev   3: 7   who **o** and no one will shut,

OPPORTUNITY

Mt   26:16   began to look for an **o** to betray him.
Gal   5:13   not use your freedom as an **o** for

OPPRESSED → OPPRESSION
Ge   15:13 shall be o for four hundred years;
Ex   1:12 But the more they were o,
Ps 146: 7 who executes justice for the o;
Isa   53: 7 He was o, and he was afflicted,
Jdt   9:11 God of the lowly, helper of the o,

OPPRESSION → OPPRESSED
Jer   9: 6 O upon o, deceit upon deceit!
Eze 45: 9 Put away violence and o,

ORACLES
Ro   3: 2 entrusted with the o of God.

ORDAIN → ORDINANCE, ORDINANCES
Ex   29: 9 shall then o Aaron and his sons.
1Ti   5:22 Do not o anyone hastily,

ORDER
Ps 110: 4 according to the o of Melchizedek.
Heb   5:10 according to the o of Melchizedek.

ORDINANCE → ORDAIN
Ex   12:17 your generations as a perpetual o.
      29: 9 shall be theirs by a perpetual o.

ORDINANCES → ORDAIN
Ps   19: 9 o of the LORD are true and righteous

ORIGIN
Mt   21:26 But if we say, 'Of human o,'
Ac   5:38 or this undertaking is of human o,

ORNAMENTS
Ex   33: 6 stripped themselves of their o,
1Pe   3: 3 by wearing gold o or fine clothing;

ORPHAN → ORPHANED, ORPHANS
Ex   22:22 You shall not abuse any widow or o.
Hos 14: 3 In you the o finds mercy."

ORPHANED → ORPHAN
Jn   14:18 will not leave you o; I am coming

ORPHANS → ORPHAN
Jas   1:27 to care for o and widows in their
Sir   4:10 Be a father to o, and be like a

OTHER → OTHERS
Ex   20: 3 you shall have no o gods before me.
Jdg   2:19 following o gods,
2Ki 17: 7 They had worshiped o gods
Isa   45: 5 I am the LORD, and there is no o;
Mt   6:24 to the one and despise the o.

OTHERS → OTHER
Lk   6:31 Do to o as you would have them do
Php   2: 3 but in humility regard o as better

OTHNIEL
      Nephew of Caleb (Jos 15:15-19; Jdg 1:12-15).
Judge who freed Israel from Aram (Jdg 3:7-11).

OUTSIDE
Lk   11:39 Pharisees clean the o of the cup
             and
Heb 13:12 Jesus also suffered o the city gate in
Rev 22:15 O are the dogs and sorcerers and

OUTSTRETCHED → STRETCH
Ex   6: 6 I will redeem you with an o arm
Ps 136:12 an o arm, for his steadfast love
Jer 27: 5 by my great power and my o arm

OUTWARD
1Sa 16: 7 they look on the o appearance,
2Co   5:12 those who boast in o appearance
2Ti   3: 5 the o form of godliness but denying

OVERCOME
Jn   1: 5 and the darkness did not o it.
Ro   12:21 Do not be o by evil, but o evil with
1Jn   2:14 and you have o the evil one.

OVERSHADOW* → OVERSHADOWED
Lk   1:35 power of the Most High will o you;

OVERSHADOWED → OVERSHADOW
Lk   9:34 a cloud came and o them;

OWE → OWES
Mt   18:28 he said, 'Pay what you o.'
Ro   13: 8 O no one anything, except to love

OWN
Isa   53: 6 we have all turned to our o way,
Jer 31:30 But all shall die for their o sins;
Jn   1:11 He came to what was his o, and his o
             people did not accept him.
      10:18 but I lay it down of my o accord.
1Co   6:19 and that you are not your o?

OX → OXEN
Dt   25: 4 not muzzle an o while it is treading
Isa 65:25 the lion shall eat straw like the o;
Eze   1:10 the face of an o on the left side,
1Ti   5:18 not muzzle an o while it is treading
Rev   4: 7 the second living creature like an o,

P

PAGANS
1Co   5: 1 that is not found even among p;
      12: 2 You know that when you were p,

PAIN → PAINS
Ge   3:16 in p you shall bring forth children,
1Pe   2:19 endure p while suffering unjustly.
Rev 21: 4 and crying and p will be no more,

PAINS → PAIN
Ro   8:22 creation has been groaning in
             labor p
1Th   5: 3 as labor p come upon a pregnant

PALM → PALMS
Jn   12:13 So they took branches of p trees
Rev   7: 9 robed in white, with p branches in

PALMS → PALM
Isa 49:16 I have inscribed you on the p of my

PANGS
Ge   3:16 increase your p in childbearing;
Mk   13: 8 but the beginning of the birth p.
Rev 12: 2 and was crying out in birth p,

PARABLE → PARABLES
Ps   78: 2 I will open my mouth in a p;
Mt   13:18 "Hear then the p of the sower.

PARABLES → PARABLE; See also JESUS: PARABLES
Mt   13:35 I will open my mouth to speak in p;
Sir 39: 2 penetrates the subtleties of p;

PARADISE
Lk   23:43 today you will be with me in P."
2Co 12: 4 was caught up into P and heard
Rev   2: 7 tree of life that is in the p of God.
2Es   8:52 for you that p is opened,

PARALYTIC → PARALYZED
Mt   9: 2 saw their faith, he said to the p,

PARALYZED → PARALYTIC
Jn   5: 3 many invalids—blind, lame, and p.
Ac   8: 7 who were p or lame were cured.

PARCHMENTS*
2Ti   4:13 also the books, and above all the p.

PARDON
Ex   34: 9 p our iniquity and our sin,
Isa 55: 7 our God, for he will abundantly p.

PARENT → PARENTS
Dt   8: 5 that as a p disciplines a child
Eze 18:20 nor a p suffer for the iniquity of a

PARENTS → PARENT
Mal   4: 6 turn the hearts of p to their children
Lk   1:17 turn the hearts of p to their children,
Eph   6: 1 Children, obey your p in the Lord,
Sir 48:10 turn the hearts of p to their children,

PART → APART
1Co 13: 9 For we know only in p, and we
             prophesy only in p;

PARTAKE
1Co 10:17 for we all p of the one bread.

PARTIALITY
Dt   16:19 distort justice; you must not show p;
Pr   24:23 P in judging is not good.
Ro   2:11 For God shows no p.
Jas   3:17 without a trace of p or hypocrisy.
Sir 35:15 and with him there is no p.

PARTICIPANTS → PARTICIPATE
2Pe   1: 4 may become p of the divine nature.

PARTICIPATE* → PARTICIPANTS
1Ti   5:22 and do not p in the sins of others;
2Jn   1:11 for to welcome is to p in the evil

PARTNER → PARTNERS, PARTNERSHIP
Pr   2:17 who forsakes the p of her youth
1Co   7:15 But if the unbelieving p separates,

PARTNERS → PARTNER
1Co 10:20 not want you to be p with demons.
Heb   3: 1 holy p in a heavenly calling,

PARTNERSHIP* → PARTNER
2Co   6:14 p is there between righteousness

PASHHUR
      Priest; opponent of Jeremiah (Jer 20:1-6).

PASS → PASSED, PASSING
Ex   12:13 when I see the blood, I will p over
      33:19 make all my goodness p before you,
Am   5:17 I will p through the midst of you,
Mt   24:35 Heaven and earth will p away, but
             my words will not p away.
2Pe   3:10 then the heavens will p away

PASSED → PASS
Ge   15:17 torch p between these pieces.
Ex   12:27 he p over the houses of the Israelites
      33:22 with my hand until I have p by;
2Co   5:17 everything old has p away;
1Jn   3:14 that we have p from death to life
Rev 21: 4 for the first things have p away."

PASSING → PASS
1Co   7:31 present form of this world is p away
1Jn   2:17 the world and its desire are p away,

PASSIONS
Gal   5:24 have crucified the flesh with its p
2Ti   2:22 Shun youthful p and pursue

PASSOVER
Ex   12:11 It is the p of the LORD.
Dt   16: 1 the month of Abib by keeping the p
Mk   14:12 when the P lamb is sacrificed,

PASTORS*
Eph   4:11 evangelists, some p and teachers,

PASTURE → PASTURES
Ps 100: 3 his people, and the sheep of his p.
Jer 50: 7 the LORD, the true p, the LORD,

PASTURES → PASTURE
Ps   23: 2 He makes me lie down in green p;

PATH → PATHS
Ps   16:11 You show me the p of life.
     119:105 lamp to my feet and a light to my p.
Mt   13: 4 he sowed, some seeds fell on the p,

PATHS → PATH
Ps   23: 3 in right p for his name's sake.
Pr   3: 6 and he will make straight your p.
Mt   3: 3 of the Lord, make his p straight.'"
Heb 12:13 and make straight p for your feet,

PATIENCE → PATIENT
Mic   2: 7 Is the LORD's p exhausted?
Ro   2: 4 his kindness and forbearance and p?
Gal   5:22 fruit of the Spirit is love, joy,
             peace, p,
2Pe   3:15 regard the p of our Lord as salvation

PATIENT → PATIENCE
Lk   8:15 and bear fruit with p endurance.

PATIENT *(cont.)*
Ro 12:12 Rejoice in hope, be **p** in suffering,
1Co 13: 4 Love is **p**; love is kind;
2Pe 3: 9 as some think of slowness, but is **p**

PATTERN
Ex 25:40 make them according to the **p** for
Heb 8: 5 make everything according to the **p**

PAUL → =SAUL
Also called Saul (Ac 13:9). Pharisee from Tarsus (Ac 9:11; Php 3:5). Apostle (Gal 1). At stoning of Stephen (Ac 8:1). Persecuted Church (Ac 9:1-2; Gal 1:13). Vision of Jesus on road to Damascus (Ac 9:4-9; 26:12-18). In Arabia (Gal 1:17). Preached in Damascus; escaped death through the wall in a basket (Ac 9:19-25). In Jerusalem; back to Tarsus (Ac 9:26-30).
Brought to Antioch by Barnabas (Ac 11:22-26). First missionary journey to Cyprus and Galatia (Ac 13-14). Stoned at Lystra (Ac 14:19-20). At Jerusalem council (Ac 15). Split with Barnabas over Mark (Ac 15:36-41).
Second missionary journey with Silas (Ac 16-20). Called to Macedonia (Ac 16:6-10). Freed from prison in Philippi (Ac 16:16-40). In Thessalonica (Ac 17:1-9). Speech in Athens (Ac 17:16-33). In Corinth (Ac 18). In Ephesus (Ac 19). Return to Jerusalem (Ac 20). Farewell to Ephesian elders (Ac 20:13-38). Arrival in Jerusalem (Ac 21:1-26). Arrested (Ac 21:27-36). Addressed crowds (Ac 22), Sanhedrin (Ac 23:1-11). Sent to Caesarea (Ac 23:12-35). Trial before Felix (Ac 24), Festus (Ac 25:1-12). Before Agrippa (Ac 25:13-26:32). Voyage to Rome; shipwreck (Ac 27). Arrival in Rome (Ac 28).

PAVEMENT
Ex 24:10 his feet there was something like a **p**
Jn 19:13 bench at a place called The Stone **P,**

PAY → REPAY
Ex 22: 4 the thief shall **p** double.
Dt 24:15 You shall **p** them their wages daily
Mt 22:17 lawful to **p** taxes to the emperor, or
Ro 13: 7 **P** to all what is due them—

PEACE → PEACEMAKERS
Lev 26: 6 And I will grant **p** in the land,
Ps 122: 6 Pray for the **p** of Jerusalem:
Isa 26: 3 in **p** because they trust in you.
    57:19 **P, p,** to the far and the near,
    57:21 no **p,** says my God, for the wicked.
Jer 6:14 saying, "**P, p,**" when there is no **p.**
Mic 5: 5 and he shall be the one of **p.**
Lk   2:14 on earth **p** among those whom he
Jn 14:27 **P** I leave with you; my **p** I give
Ro 16:20 God of **p** will shortly crush Satan
1Co 14:33 is a God not of disorder but of **p.**
Gal 5:22 the fruit of the Spirit is love, joy, **p,**
Eph 4: 3 unity of the Spirit in the bond of **p.**
Php 4: 7 the **p** of God, which surpasses all
2Ti 2:22 righteousness, faith, love, and **p,**

PEACEMAKERS* → PEACE
Mt   5: 9 "Blessed are the **p,** for they will be

PEARL* → PEARLS
Mt 13:46 on finding one **p** of great value,
Rev 21:21 each of the gates is a single **p,**

PEARLS → PEARL
Mt   7: 6 do not throw your **p** before swine,

PEKAH*
King of Israel (2Ki 15:25-31; 2Ch 28:6; Isa 7:1).

PEKAHIAH*
Son of Menahem; king of Israel (2Ki 15:22-26).

PENALTY
Ro   1:27 in their own persons the due **p**
2Pe 2:13 suffering the **p** for doing wrong.

PENTECOST
Ac   2: 1 When the day of **P** had come,

PEOPLE → PEOPLES
Ex   5: 1 the God of Israel, 'Let my **p** go,
    33:13 that this nation is your **p.**"
Dt   4:20 a **p** of his very own possession,
    32: 9 the LORD's own portion was his **p,**
Ru   1:16 your **p** shall be my **p,**
2Sa 5: 2 shall be shepherd of my **p** Israel,
Ps 29:11 the LORD bless his **p** with peace!
   125: 2 so the LORD surrounds his **p,**
Isa 40: 1 Comfort, O comfort my **p,** says
    42: 6 given you as a covenant to the **p,**
    53: 8 for the transgression of my **p.**
Jer 50: 6 My **p** have been lost sheep;
La   1: 1 sits the city that once was full of **p!**
Da   9:24 "Seventy weeks are decreed for your **p**
Zec 13: 9 I will say, "They are my **p**";
Mt   1:21 he will save his **p** from their sins."
Jn 11:50 the **p** than to have the whole nation
    18:14 to have one person die for the **p.**
Ro   9:25 not my **p** I will call 'my **p,**'
Heb 8:10 their God, and they shall be my **p.**
1Pe 2: 9 a holy nation, God's own **p,**

PEOPLES → PEOPLE
Ge 17:16 kings of **p** shall come from her."
Dt   7: 7 for you were the fewest of all **p.**
Ps 117: 1 Extol him, all you **p!**
Rev 21: 3 they will be his **p,** and God himself

PERFECT → PERFECTED, PERFECTER, PERFECTION
Lev 22:21 to be acceptable it must be **p;**
2Sa 22:31 This God—his way is **p;**
Ps 19: 7 The law of the LORD is **p,** reviving
Mt   5:48 Be **p,** therefore, as your heavenly Father is **p.**
Ro 12: 2 what is good and acceptable and **p.**
2Co 12: 9 for power is made **p** in weakness."
Heb 7:19 (for the law made nothing **p**);
1Jn 4:18 in love, but **p** love casts out fear;

PERFECTED → PERFECT
Heb 10:14 For by a single offering he has **p**
1Jn 4:12 God lives in us, and his love is **p** in

PERFECTER* → PERFECT
Heb 12: 2 Jesus the pioneer and **p** of our faith,

PERFECTION → PERFECT
Heb 6: 1 Therefore let us go on toward **p,**
1Jn 2: 5 the love of God has reached **p.**

PERISH → PERISHABLE
Lev 26:38 You shall **p** among the nations,
Jos 23:13 until you **p** from this good land that
Est 4:16 and if I **p, I p.**"
Ps   1: 6 but the way of the wicked will **p.**
Lk 21:18 But not a hair of your head will **p.**
Jn   3:16 who believes in him may not **p**
2Pe 3: 9 with you, not wanting any to **p,**

PERISHABLE → PERISH
1Co 9:25 they do it to receive a **p** wreath,
    15:42 What is sown is **p,** what is raised is
1Pe 1:23 not of **p** but of imperishable seed,

PERMANENT → PERMANENTLY
2Co 3:11 much more has the **p** come in glory!

PERMANENTLY* → PERMANENT
Heb 7:24 but he holds his priesthood **p,**

PERSECUTE → PERSECUTED, PERSECUTION
Mt   5:44 and pray for those who **p** you,
Ac   9: 4 "Saul, Saul, why do you **p** me?"
Ro 12:14 Bless those who **p** you; bless

PERSECUTED → PERSECUTE
Ps 119:86 I am **p** without cause; help me!
Jn 15:20 they **p** me, they will persecute you;
2Co 4: 9 **p,** but not forsaken; struck down,
2Ti 3:12 godly life in Christ Jesus will be **p.**

PERSECUTION → PERSECUTE
Mt 13:21 or **p** arises on account of the word,

Ro   8:35 Will hardship, or distress, or **p,** or
Heb 10:33 publicly exposed to abuse and **p,**

PERSEVERANCE* → PERSEVERE
Heb 12: 1 let us run with **p** the race that is set

PERSEVERE → PERSEVERANCE
Da 12:12 Happy are those who **p**
Ro 12:12 be patient in suffering, **p** in prayer.

PERSIA → PERSIANS
Ezr 1: 1 the spirit of King Cyrus of **P**
Da   8:20 these are the kings of Media and **P.**

PERSIANS → PERSIA
Da   6:15 a law of the Medes and **P** that

PESTILENCE
Dt 32:24 burning consumption, bitter **p.**
Ps 91: 6 or the **p** that stalks in darkness,

PETER → =CEPHAS, =SIMON
Apostle, brother of Andrew, also called Simon (Mt 10:2; Mk 3:16; Lk 6:14; Ac 1:13), and Cephas (Jn 1:42). Confession of Christ (Mt 16:13-20; Mk 8:27-30; Lk 9:18-27). At transfiguration (Mt 17:1-8; Mk 9:2-8; Lk 9:28-36; 2Pe 1:16-18). Caught fish with coin (Mt 17:24-27). Denial of Jesus predicted (Mt 26:31-35; Mk 14:27-31; Lk 22:31-34; Jn 13:31-38). Denied Jesus (Mt 26:69-75; Mk 14:66-72; Lk 22:54-62; Jn 18:15-27). Commissioned by Jesus to shepherd his flock (Jn 21:15-23).
Speech at Pentecost (Ac 2). Healed beggar (Ac 3:1-10). Speech at temple (Ac 3:11-26), before Sanhedrin (Ac 4:1-22). In Samaria (Ac 8:14-25). Sent by vision to Cornelius (Ac 10). Announced salvation of Gentiles in Jerusalem (Ac 11; 15). Freed from prison (Ac 12). Inconsistency at Antioch (Gal 2:11-21). At Jerusalem Council (Ac 15).

PHARAOH → PHARAOH'S
Ge 41:14 Then **P** sent for Joseph,
Ex   3:11 "Who am I that I should go to **P,**
    14:17 I will gain glory for myself over **P**
Ro   9:17 For the scripture says to **P,**

PHARAOH'S → PHARAOH
Ex   7: 3 But I will harden **P** heart,
Heb 11:24 refused to be called a son of **P**

PHARISEE → PHARISEES
Lk 11:37 a **P** invited him to dine with him;
Jn   3: 1 a **P** named Nicodemus,
Ac   5:34 a **P** in the council named Gamaliel,
Php 3: 5 as to the law, a **P;**

PHARISEES → PHARISEE
Mt   5:20 that of the scribes and **P,**
    16: 6 beware of the yeast of the **P** and
    23:13 "But woe to you, scribes and **P,**

PHILEMON*
Phm 1: 1 To **P** our dear friend and co-worker,

PHILIP
1. Apostle (Mt 10:3; Mk 3:18; Lk 6:14; Jn 1:43-48; 14:8; Ac 1:13).
2. Deacon (Ac 6:1-7); evangelist in Samaria (Ac 8:4-25), to Ethiopian (Ac 8:26-40).

PHILISTINE → PHILISTINES
1Sa 17:37 save me from the hand of this **P.**"
Pm 151: 6 I went out to meet the **P,**

PHILISTINES → PHILISTINE
Ge 26: 1 Gerar, to King Abimelech of the **P.**
1Sa 5: 1 the **P** captured the ark of God,
    17: 1 the **P** gathered their armies for battle
2Sa 8: 1 David attacked the **P** and subdued
Am   1: 8 the remnant of the **P** shall perish,

PHILOSOPHERS* → PHILOSOPHY
Ac 17:18 Epicurean and Stoic **p** debated with

PHILOSOPHY → PHILOSOPHERS
Col 2: 8 no one takes you captive through **p**

PHINEHAS
1. Grandson of Aaron (Ex 6:25; Jos 22:30-32).
Zeal for the LORD (Nu 25:7-13; Ps 106:30).
2. A wicked priest (1Sa 1:3; 2:12-17; 4:1-19).

PHOEBE*
Ro   16: 1   I commend to you our sister **P,**

PHYSICAL
1Co 15:44   It is sown a **p** body, it is raised a
1Ti   4: 8   while **p** training is of some value,

PHYSICIAN → PHYSICIANS
Mt   9:12   who are well have no need of a **p,**
Col   4:14   Luke, the beloved **p,** and Demas

PHYSICIANS → PHYSICIAN
Job 13: 4   all of you are worthless **p.**
Mk   5:26   had endured much under many **p,**

PIECES
Ge   15:17   torch passed between these **p.**
Mt   14:20   what was left over of the broken **p,**
    15:37   they took up the broken **p** left over,
Lk   20:18   on that stone will be broken to **p;**

PIERCED
Zec 12:10   look on the one whom they have **p,**
Jn   19:37   look on the one whom they have **p."**
Rev   1: 7   even those who **p** him;

PIG
Dt   14: 8   the **p,** because it divides the hoof

PILATE
Governor of Judea. Questioned Jesus (Mt 27:1-26; Mk 15:15; Lk 22:66-23:25; Jn 18:28-19:16); sent him to Herod (Lk 23:6-12); consented to his crucifixion when crowds chose Barabbas (Mt 27:15-26; Mk 15:6-15; Lk 23:13-25; Jn 19:1-10).

PILLAR → PILLARS
Ge   19:26   back, and she became a **p** of salt.
Ex   13:21   and in a **p** of fire by night,

PILLARS → PILLAR
Jdg 16:29   Samson grasped the two middle **p**
1Ki   7:15   He cast two **p** of bronze.
Pr   9: 1   she has hewn her seven **p.**

PIONEER*
Heb   2:10   make the **p** of their salvation perfect
    12: 2   Jesus the **p** and perfecter of our faith

PIT
Rev 20: 3   into the **p,** and locked and sealed it
Sir 21:10   but at its end is the **p** of Hades.

PITY
Dt   7:16   showing them no **p;**
Hos   1: 6   for I will no longer have **p**
    2:23   And I will have **p** on Lo-ruhamah,

PLACE → PLACES
Ge   28:16   "Surely the LORD is in this **p—**
Ex   26:33   shall separate for you the holy **p**
Ps   24: 3   And who shall stand in his holy **p?**
    32: 7   You are a hiding **p** for me;
Jn   14: 3   And if I go and prepare a **p** for you,

PLACES → PLACE
Lev 26:30   I will destroy your high **p**
Ps   78:58   him to anger with their high **p;**

PLAGUE → PLAGUES
Ex   32:35   the LORD sent a **p** on the people,
Nu   25: 8   So the **p** was stopped among the
Zec 14:12   the **p** with which the LORD will
Rev 11: 6   strike the earth with every kind of **p,**

PLAGUES → PLAGUE
Hos 13:14   O Death, where are your **p?**
Rev 15: 1   seven angels with seven **p,** which
    22:18   God will add to that person the **p**

PLAIN
Ge   13:12   among the cities of the **P** and
Isa   40: 4   and the rough places a **p.**

PLANNED
Ex   32:14   his mind about the disaster that he **p**
Isa 46:11   I have **p,** and I will do it.

PLANT → PLANTED
Ge   1:29   I have given you every **p** yielding
Ecc   3: 2   time to **p,** and a time to pluck up

PLANTED → PLANT
Ge   2: 8   the LORD God **p** a garden in Eden,
Ps   1: 3   like trees **p** by streams of water,
1Co   3: 6   I **p,** Apollos watered, but God gave

PLEA
1Ki   8:28   your servant's prayer and his **p,**
La   3:56   heard my **p,** "Do not close your ear

PLEASE → PLEASED, PLEASES, PLEASING, PLEASURE
Ps   69:31   will **p** the LORD more than an ox
Ro   8: 8   who are in the flesh cannot **p** God.
    15: 3   For Christ did not **p** himself;
1Co 10:33   as I try to **p** everyone in everything
1Th   4: 1   how you ought to live and to **p** God
Heb 11: 6   without faith it is impossible to **p** God,
Sir   2:16   Those who fear the Lord seek to **p**

PLEASED → PLEASE
Ps   40:13   Be **p,** O LORD, to deliver me;
Mic   6: 7   Will the LORD be **p** with thousands
Mt   3:17   Beloved, with whom I am well **p."**
Col   1:19   the fullness of God was **p** to dwell,
2Pe   1:17   Beloved, with whom I am well **p."**

PLEASES → PLEASE
Ps   115: 3   the heavens; he does whatever he **p.**
1Jn   3:22   commandments and do what **p** him.

PLEASING → PLEASE
Ps 104:34   May my meditation be **p** to him,
Eph   5:10   to find out what is **p** to the Lord.
Php   4:18   a sacrifice acceptable and **p** to God.

PLEASURE → PLEASE
Pr   21:17   Whoever loves **p** will suffer want;
Eze 18:32   I have no **p** in the death of anyone,
Eph   1: 5   according to the good **p** of his will,
2Ti   3: 4   lovers of **p** rather than lovers of God

PLENTIFUL → PLENTY
Lk   10: 2   He said to them, "The harvest is **p,**

PLENTY → PLENTIFUL
Php   4:12   and I know what it is to have **p.**

PLOT → PLOTTED
Ps   2: 1   and the peoples **p** in vain?
Na   1: 9   Why do you **p** against the LORD?

PLOTTED → PLOT
Est   9:24   **p** against the Jews to destroy them,

PLOWSHARES
Isa   2: 4   they shall beat their swords into **p,**
Joel   3:10   Beat your **p** into swords, and your

PLUNDER
Ex   3:22   and so you shall **p** the Egyptians."
Est   9:10   but they did not touch the **p.**
Eze 39:10   and **p** those who plundered them,

POISON
Ps   69:21   They gave me **p** for food,
Jas   3: 8   a restless evil, full of deadly **p.**

POLE → POLES
Nu   21: 8   poisonous serpent, and set it on a **p;**
Dt   16:21   not plant any tree as a sacred **p**

POLES → POLE
2Ki 17:10   for themselves pillars and sacred **p**

POLLUTED → POLLUTES
Ac   15:20   from things **p** by idols and from
Rev 21: 8   the cowardly, the faithless, the **p,**

POLLUTES* → POLLUTED
Nu   35:33   blood **p** the land, and no expiation

POOR → POVERTY
Ex   23: 6   not pervert the justice due to your **p**
1Sa   2: 8   He raises up the **p** from the dust;
Ps   113: 7   He raises the **p** from the dust,
Pr   19:22   and it is better to be **p** than a liar.
Mt   5: 3   "Blessed are the **p** in spirit,
Mk 10:21   own, and give the money to the **p,**
    12:42   **p** widow came and put in two small
Jn   12: 8   You always have the **p** with you,
2Co   6:10   as **p,** yet making many rich;
    8: 9   yet for your sakes he became **p,**
Jas   2: 5   Has not God chosen the **p** in the

PORTION → APPORTIONED
Dt   32: 9   the LORD's own **p** was his people,
Jos   18: 7   The Levites have no **p** among you,
Ps   142: 5   my **p** in the land of the living."
La   3:24   "The LORD is my **p,**" says my soul,
Sir 17:17   Israel is the Lord's own **p.**

POSSESS → POSSESSED, POSSESSION, POSSESSIONS
Dt   28:21   the land that you are entering to **p.**
Ezr   9:11   that you are entering to **p** is a land
Isa 60:21   they shall **p** the land forever.

POSSESSED → POSSESS
Mt   8:16   many who were **p** with demons;
Heb 10:34   you yourselves **p** something better

POSSESSION → POSSESS
Ex   19: 5   treasured **p** out of all the peoples.
Jos   1:11   to go in to take **p** of the land that
Ps   2: 8   and the ends of the earth your **p.**

POSSESSIONS → POSSESS
Lk   12:15   not consist in the abundance of **p.**
1Co 13: 3   If I give away all my **p,**

POSSIBLE
Mt   19:26   but for God all things are **p."**
    26:39   if it is **p,** let this cup pass from me;

POTIPHAR*
Egyptian who bought Joseph (Ge 37:36; 39:1-6), sent him to prison (Ge 39:7-30).

POTTER → POTTER'S
Isa   64: 8   we are the clay, and you are our **p;**
Ro   9:21   Has the **p** no right over the clay,
Sir 33:13   Like clay in the hand of the **p,**

POTTER'S → POTTER
Jer   18: 2   go down to the **p** house,
Mt   27: 7   to buy the **p** field as a place to bury

POUR → POURED
Dt   12:16   **p** it out on the ground like water.
Isa   44: 3   I will **p** my spirit upon your
Eze 39:29   I **p** out my spirit upon the house of
Joel   2:28   I will **p** out my spirit on all flesh;
Ac   2:17   I will **p** out my Spirit upon all flesh,
Rev 16: 1   **p** out on the earth the seven bowls

POURED → POUR
Mt   26:28   is **p** out for many for the forgiveness
Ac   2:33   he has **p** out this that you both see
Tit   3: 6   This Spirit he **p** out on us richly

POVERTY → POOR
Pr   30: 8   give me neither **p** nor riches;
Mk 12:44   out of her **p** has put in everything
2Co   8: 9   by his **p** you might become rich.
Sir 11:14   **p** and wealth, come from the Lord.

POWER → POWERFUL, POWERS
Ex   9:16   show you my **p,** and to make
    15: 6   right hand, O LORD, glorious in **p—**
1Ch 29:11   O LORD, are the greatness, the **p,**
Ps   68:34   Ascribe **p** to God, whose majesty is
Pr   18:21   and life are in the **p** of the tongue,
Isa 40:29   He gives **p** to the faint,
Zec   4: 6   by might, nor by **p,** but by my spirit,
Mt   22:29   the scriptures nor the **p** of God.
Mk 13:26   coming in clouds' with great **p** and
Ro   1:20   creation of the world his eternal **p**

POWER (cont.)

1Co	1:17	might not be emptied of its **p**.
	15:24	and every authority and **p**.
Eph	1:19	the immeasurable greatness of his **p**
Php	3:10	Christ and the **p** of his resurrection
2Ti	3: 5	form of godliness but denying its **p**.
2Pe	1: 3	divine **p** has given us everything
Rev	19: 1	and glory and **p** to our God,
	20: 6	these the second death has no **p**,
Jdt	9:14	the God of all **p** and might,
Sir	39:18	and none can limit his saving **p**.

POWERFUL → POWER

Mk	1: 7	one who is more **p** than I is coming
1Co	1:26	not many were **p**,
Heb	1: 3	he sustains all things by his **p** word.

POWERS → POWER

Ro	8:38	present, nor things to come, nor **p**,
Eph	6:12	against the cosmic **p** of this present

PRACTICE → PRACTICES

Mt	23: 3	for they do not **p** what they teach.
Sir	50:29	For if they put them into **p**,

PRACTICES → PRACTICE

Ex	23:24	or worship them, or follow their **p**,
Col	3: 9	stripped off the old self with its **p**

PRAISE → PRAISED, PRAISES

Ex	15: 2	this is my God, and I will **p** him,
Dt	10:21	He is your **p**; he is your God,
Ps	56: 4	whose word I **p**, in God I trust;
	150: 6	that breathes **p** the Lord!
Pr	27: 2	Let another **p** you, and not your own
	31:31	let her works **p** her in the city gates.
Mt	21:16	nursing babies you have prepared **p**
1Co	14:15	but I will sing **p** with the mind also.
Rev	19: 5	"**P** our God, all you his servants,
Tob	12: 6	Bless and sing **p** to his name.
Sir	24: 1	the **P** of wisdom Wisdom praises

PRAISED → PRAISE

Ps	48: 1	is the Lord and greatly to be **p**
Lk	23:47	what had taken place, he **p** God and

PRAISES → PRAISE

Ps	47: 6	Sing **p** to God, sing **p**;

PRAY → PRAYED, PRAYER, PRAYERS

1Sa	12:23	against the Lord by ceasing to **p**
2Ch	7:14	humble themselves, **p**, seek my face
Ps	5: 2	King and my God, for to you I **p**.
	122: 6	**P** for the peace of Jerusalem:
Jer	7:16	As for you, do not **p** for this people,
Mt	5:44	and **p** for those who persecute you,
	6: 5	you **p**, do not be like the hypocrites;
Lk	11: 1	teach us to **p**, as John taught his
Ro	8:26	do not know how to **p** as we ought,
1Co	14:15	but I will **p** with the mind also;
1Th	5:17	**p** without ceasing,
Jas	5:16	and **p** for one another, so that you
Sir	37:15	But above all **p** to the Most High

PRAYED → PRAY

Mk	1:35	to a deserted place, and there he **p**.
	14:35	threw himself on the ground and **p**

PRAYER → PRAY

Ps	6: 9	the Lord accepts my **p**.
Pr	15:29	but he hears the **p** of the righteous.
Isa	56: 7	house shall be called a house of **p**
Mt	21:13	house shall be called a house of **p'**;
Mk	11:24	I tell you, whatever you ask for in **p**,
Ro	12:12	patient in suffering, persevere in **p**,
Jas	5:16	The **p** of the righteous is powerful

PRAYERS → PRAY

Mk	12:40	the sake of appearance say long **p**.
Heb	5: 7	Jesus offered up **p** and supplications
Rev	5: 8	which are the **p** of the saints.

PREACH → PREACHING

Tit	1: 9	able both to **p** with sound doctrine

PREACHING → PREACH

1Ti	5:17	those who labor in **p** and teaching;

PRECEPT → PRECEPTS

Isa	28:10	For it is **p** upon **p**, **p** upon **p**,

PRECEPTS → PRECEPT

Ps	19: 8	the **p** of the Lord are right,
	119:15	I will meditate on your **p**,
Mt	15: 9	teaching human **p** as doctrines.'"

PRECIOUS

Ps	72:14	and **p** is their blood in his sight.
Pr	3:15	She is more **p** than jewels,
Isa	28:16	a tested stone, a **p** cornerstone,
1Pe	1:19	but with the **p** blood of Christ,
	2: 6	a cornerstone chosen and **p**;
2Pe	1: 1	received a faith as **p** as ours

PREDESTINED

Ro	8:30	those whom he **p** he also called;

PREDICTION* → PREDICTIONS

Isa	44:26	and fulfills the **p** of his messengers;

PREDICTIONS* → PREDICT

Jude	1:17	the **p** of the apostles of our Lord

PREPARE → PREPARED

Ps	23: 5	You **p** a table before me in the
Mal	3: 1	sending my messenger to **p** the way
Mt	3: 3	'**P** the way of the Lord, make his
Jn	14: 2	I have told you that I go to **p** a place

PREPARED → PREPARE

Lk	1:17	make ready a people **p** for the Lord.
1Co	2: 9	God has **p** for those who love him"

PRESENCE → PRESENT

Ex	25:30	the bread of the **P** on the table
	33:14	He said, "My **p** will go with you,
Ps	51:11	Do not cast me away from your **p**,
	139: 7	Or where can I flee from your **p**?
Jn	17: 5	with the glory that I had in your **p**
Heb	9:24	now to appear in the **p** of God

PRESENT → PRESENCE

Ro	6:13	but **p** yourselves to God as
1Co	3:22	or death or the **p** or the future—
Eph	5:27	**p** the church to himself in splendor,
2Ti	2:15	**p** yourself to God as one approved

PRESS → PRESSED

Php	3:14	I **p** on toward the goal for the prize

PRESSED → PRESS

Lk	6:38	A good measure, **p** down, shaken
Php	1:23	I am hard **p** between the two:

PREVAIL → PREVAILED

1Sa	2: 9	for not by might does one **p**.

PREVAILED → PREVAIL

Ge	32:28	God and with humans, and have **p**."
Hos	12: 4	He strove with the angel and **p**,

PRICE

Mt	27: 9	the one on whom a **p** had been set,
1Co	6:20	For you were bought with a **p**;

PRIDE → PROUD

Ps	20: 7	our **p** is in the name of the Lord
Pr	16:18	**P** goes before destruction,
Mk	7:22	licentiousness, envy, slander, **p**,
1Jn	2:16	the desire of the eyes, the **p** in riches
Sir	10:13	For the beginning of **p** is sin,

PRIEST → PRIESTHOOD, PRIESTS

Ge	14:18	he was **p** of God Most High.
Ex	2:16	**p** of Midian had seven daughters.
Ne	8: 9	and Ezra the **p** and scribe,
Ps	110: 4	"You are a **p** forever according to
Mk	14:63	Then the high **p** tore his clothes and
Heb	3: 1	apostle and high **p** of our confession
	7: 3	the Son of God, he remains a **p**
	10:21	since we have a great **p** over the

PRIESTHOOD → PRIEST

Ex	29: 9	the **p** shall be theirs by a perpetual
Heb	7:24	but he holds his **p** permanently,
1Pe	2: 5	a holy **p**, to offer spiritual sacrifices

PRIESTS → PRIEST

Ex	28: 1	the Israelites, to serve me as **p**—
Dt	31: 9	this law, and gave it to the **p**,
Mic	3:11	its **p** teach for a price, its prophets
Mk	15: 3	the chief **p** accused him of many
Heb	7:27	Unlike the other high **p**, he has no
Rev	20: 6	they will be **p** of God and of Christ,

PRINCE → PRINCES

Isa	9: 6	Everlasting Father, **P** of Peace.
Eze	37:25	David shall be their **p** forever.
Da	10:21	princes except Michael, your **p**.

PRINCES → PRINCE

1Sa	2: 8	to make them sit with **p** and inherit
Da	8:25	even rise up against the Prince of **p**.

PRISCILLA*

Wife of Aquila, also called Prisca; co-worker with Paul (Ac 18; Ro 16:3; 1Co 16:19; 2Ti 4:19); instructor of Apollos (Ac 18:24-28).

PRISON → PRISONER, PRISONERS

Ge	39:20	he remained there in **p**.
Mt	14:10	and had John beheaded in the **p**.
Ac	12: 5	While Peter was kept in **p**,
	16:26	foundations of the **p** were shaken;

PRISONER → PRISON

Mk	15: 6	at the festival he used to release a **p**
Eph	3: 1	that I Paul am a **p** for Christ Jesus

PRISONERS → PRISON

Ps	146: 7	The Lord sets the **p** free;
Isa	61: 1	to the captives, and release to the **p**;

PRIZE

1Co	9:24	but only one receives the **p**?
Php	3:14	the **p** of the heavenly call of God in

PROCLAIM → PROCLAIMED

Ex	33:19	**p** before you the name, 'The Lord';
Ps	97: 6	The heavens **p** his righteousness;
Mt	10:27	whispered, **p** from the housetops.
Lk	4:19	to **p** the year of the Lord's favor."
Ro	10: 8	the word of faith that we **p**);

PROCLAIMED → PROCLAIM

Mk	13:10	the good news must first be **p** to all
Col	1:23	which has been **p** to every creature

PRODUCE → PRODUCES

Nu	18:12	choice **p** that they give to the Lord,
Jos	5:11	they ate the **p** of the land,
Pr	3: 9	with the first fruits of all your **p**;

PRODUCES → PRODUCE

2Co	7:10	For godly grief **p** a repentance that
Jas	1: 3	testing of your faith **p** endurance;

PROFANE

Lev	22:32	You shall not **p** my holy name,
1Mc	1:45	to **p** sabbaths and festivals,

PROFIT

Mt	16:26	For what will it **p** them if they gain
Sir	29:11	and it will **p** you more than gold.

PROMISE → PROMISED, PROMISES

Ps	105:42	For he remembered his holy **p**,
Ac	2:39	the **p** is for you, for your children,
Eph	2:12	and strangers to the covenants of **p**,
1Ti	4: 8	holding **p** for both the present life
2Pe	3: 9	The Lord is not slow about his **p**,

PROMISED → PROMISE

Dt	1:11	and bless you, as he has **p** you!
2Sa	7:28	**p** this good thing to your servant;
Lk	24:49	sending upon you what my Father **p**
Ac	13:23	to Israel a Savior, Jesus, as he **p**;
Eph	1:13	with the seal of the **p** Holy Spirit;
Heb	10:23	for he who has **p** is faithful.

PROMISES → PROMISE

Jos	21:45	the good **p** that the Lord had made
Ps	12: 6	**p** of the Lord are **p** that are pure,
2Co	1:20	every one of God's **p** is a "Yes."
Heb	8: 6	has been enacted through better **p**.

PROOFS* → PROVE
Isa 41:21 bring your **p**, says the King of Jacob
Ac 1: 3 to them by many convincing **p**,

PROPHECIES → PROPHESY
1Co 13: 8 as for **p**, they will come to an end;

PROPHECY → PROPHESY
Ac 21: 9 daughters who had the gift of **p**.
1Co 12:10 to another a **p**, to another
2Pe 1:20 that no **p** of scripture is a matter
Rev 22:18 who hears the words of the **p**

PROPHESY → PROPHECIES, PROPHECY,
PROPHET, PROPHETS
Joel 2:28 sons and your daughters shall **p**,
Mt 7:22 Lord, did we not **p** in your name,
1Co 13: 9 only in part, and we **p** only in part;
Rev 11: 3 my two witnesses authority to **p**

PROPHET → PROPHESY
Ex 7: 1 your brother Aaron shall be your **p**.
Dt 18:18 a **p** like you from among their own
Mal 4: 5 the **p** Elijah before the great and
Lk 4:24 no **p** is accepted in the prophet's
20: 6 are convinced that John was a **p**."
Rev 16:13 and from the mouth of the false **p**.
20:10 where the beast and the false **p** were
1Mc 4:46 until a **p** should come to tell what

PROPHETS → PROPHESY
Nu 11:29 that all the LORD's people were **p**,
1Ki 18:40 said to them, "Seize the **p** of Baal;
Ps 105:15 anointed ones; do my **p** no harm."
Mt 5:17 come to abolish the law or the **p**;
22:40 hang all the law and the **p**."
Lk 24:44 **p**, and the psalms must be fulfilled."
1Co 12:28 the church first apostles, second **p**,
Eph 2:20 the foundation of the apostles and **p**,
4:11 some **p**, some evangelists,
Rev 11:10 these two **p** had been a torment to
18:20 you saints and apostles and **p**!
1Mc 9:27 that **p** ceased to appear among them.

PROSPER → PROSPERING, PROSPERITY,
PROSPEROUS
Ge 39: 3 LORD caused all that he did to **p**
Ps 1: 3 In all that they do, they **p**.
Isa 53:10 the will of the LORD shall **p**.

PROSPERING → PROSPER
Dt 30: 9 will again take delight in **p** you,

PROSPERITY → PROSPER
Dt 30:15 have set before you today life and **p**,
Ps 73: 3 I saw the **p** of the wicked.
Isa 48:18 your **p** would have been like a river,

PROSPEROUS → PROSPER
Jos 1: 8 For then you shall make your way **p**

PROSTITUTE → PROSTITUTES
Ex 34:15 they **p** themselves to their gods
Jos 2: 1 a **p** whose name was Rahab,
1Co 6:15 and make members of a **p**?
Heb 11:31 By faith Rahab the **p** did not perish

PROSTITUTES → PROSTITUTE
Mt 21:31 the **p** are going into the kingdom of
1Co 6: 9 idolaters, adulterers, male **p**,
Sir 9: 6 Do not give yourself to **p**,

PROTECT → PROTECTS
Ps 91:14 I will **p** those who know my name.
Jn 17:11 **p** them in your name that you have

PROTECTS → PROTECT
Ps 116: 6 The LORD **p** the simple;
Jdt 9:14 no other who **p** the people of Israel

PROUD → PRIDE
Ps 94: 2 give to the **p** what they deserve!
Pr 21: 4 Haughty eyes and a **p** heart—
Jas 4: 6 God opposes the **p**, but gives grace
Sir 10: 9 How can dust and ashes be **p**?

PROVE → PROOFS, PROVED
Heb 6:18 impossible that God would **p** false,

PROVED → PROVE
Ro 3: 4 let God be **p** true,

PROVERBS
1Ki 4:32 He composed three thousand **p**,
Pr 1: 1 The **p** of Solomon son of David,
Ecc 12: 9 and studying and arranging many **p**,
Sir 39: 3 seeks out the hidden meanings of **p**

PROVIDE → PROVIDES
Ge 22: 8 "God himself will **p** the lamb for
1Co 10:13 testing he will also **p** the way out

PROVIDES → PROVIDE
Ps 111: 5 He **p** food for those who fear him;
1Ti 6:17 who richly **p** us with everything

PROVOKE → PROVOKED
Dt 32:21 **p** them with a foolish nation.
Jer 25: 6 not **p** me to anger with the work of
Heb 10:24 how to **p** one another to love

PROVOKED → PROVOKE
Ps 78:41 and **p** the Holy One of Israel.

PROWLS*
1Pe 5: 8 your adversary the devil **p** around,

PRUNES
Jn 15: 2 he **p** to make it bear more fruit.

PSALM → PSALMS
Ps 47: 7 sing praises with a **p**.
Jdt 16: 1 Raise to him a new **p**;

PSALMS → PSALM
Lk 24:44 and the **p** must be fulfilled."
Eph 5:19 you sing **p** and hymns and spiritual

PUBLIC
Mt 1:19 to expose her to **p** disgrace,
Col 2:15 and made a **p** example of them,
1Ti 4:13 to the **p** reading of scripture,

PUFFED → PUFFS
Col 2:18 **p** up without cause by a human way
1Ti 3: 6 or he may be **p** up with conceit

PUFFS* → PUFFED
1Co 8: 1 Knowledge **p** up, but love builds up.

PUNISH → PUNISHING, PUNISHMENT
Ex 32:34 I will **p** them for their sin."
2Sa 7:14 I will **p** him with a rod such as
Jer 21:14 I will **p** you according to the fruit of
1Pe 2:14 by him to **p** those who do wrong

PUNISHING → PUNISH
Dt 5: 9 **p** children for the iniquity of parents
Joel 2:13 in steadfast love, and relents from **p**.

PUNISHMENT → PUNISH
Ge 4:13 "My **p** is greater than I can bear!
Isa 53: 5 was the **p** that made us whole,
Mt 25:46 these will go away into eternal **p**,
1Jn 4:18 for fear has to do with **p**,

PURE → PURIFICATION, PURIFIED,
PURIFY, PURITY
2Sa 22:27 with the **p** you show yourself **p**,
Ps 19: 9 the fear of the LORD is **p**, enduring
119: 9 can young people keep their way **p**?
Hab 1:13 Your eyes are too **p** to behold evil,
Mt 5: 8 "Blessed are the **p** in heart, for they
Php 4: 8 whatever is **p**, whatever is pleasing,
Tit 1:15 To the **p** all things are **p**,
1Jn 3: 3 purify themselves, just as he is **p**.

PURIFICATION → PURE
Jn 2: 6 water jars for the Jewish rites of **p**,
Heb 1: 3 When he had made **p** for sins,

PURIFIED → PURE
Da 12:10 Many shall be **p**, cleansed, and
1Pe 1:22 your souls by your obedience to

PURIFY → PURE
Tit 2:14 **p** for himself a people of his own
Heb 9:14 **p** our conscience from dead works

PURIM
Est 9:26 are called P, from the word Pur.

PURITY → PURE
2Co 6: 6 by **p**, knowledge, patience, kindness
1Pe 3: 2 the **p** and reverence of your lives.

PURPLE
Ex 25: 4 **p**, and crimson yarns and fine linen,
Mk 15:17 And they clothed him in a **p** cloak;

PURPOSE
Ps 57: 2 to God who fulfills his **p** for me.
Isa 46:10 saying, "My **p** shall stand,
Ro 8:28 who are called according to his **p**.
Eph 3:11 was in accordance with the eternal **p**
2Ti 1: 9 works but according to his own **p**

PURSUE → PURSUED, PURSUES
Ps 34:14 and do good; seek peace, and **p** it.
Ro 14:19 Let us then **p** what makes for peace
1Ti 6:11 righteousness, godliness, faith,
Sir 27: 8 If you **p** justice, you will attain it

PURSUED → PURSUE
Ex 14:23 Egyptians **p**, and went into the sea
Ps 18:37 I **p** my enemies and overtook them;

PURSUES → PURSUE
Pr 21:21 Whoever **p** righteousness
Sir 31: 5 **p** money will be led astray by it.

PUT
Isa 42: 1 I have **p** my spirit upon him;
Eze 36:27 I will **p** my spirit within you,
Mt 12:18 I will **p** my Spirit upon him,
Eph 6:11 **P** on the whole armor of God,

Q

QUAILS
Ex 16:13 In the evening **q** came up
Nu 11:31 and it brought **q** from the sea and

QUARRELED → QUARRELSOME
Ex 17: 7 the Israelites **q** and tested the LORD,
Nu 20: 3 The people **q** with Moses and said,

QUARRELSOME* → QUARRELED
1Ti 3: 3 not **q**, and not a lover of money.
2Ti 2:24 the Lord's servant must not be **q**

QUEEN
1Ki 10: 1 the **q** of Sheba heard of the fame of
Est 2:17 and made her **q** instead of Vashti.
Mt 12:42 The **q** of the South will rise up at
Rev 18: 7 in her heart she says, 'I rule as a **q**;

QUESTIONS
2Ch 9: 1 to Jerusalem to test him with hard **q**,
Mt 22:46 anyone dare to ask him any more **q**.

QUICK → QUICKLY
Jas 1:19 be **q** to listen, slow to speak,
Sir 5:11 Be **q** to hear, but deliberate

QUICKLY → QUICK
Jn 13:27 "Do **q** what you are going to do."
Ro 9:28 execute his sentence on the earth **q**
Gal 1: 6 so **q** deserting the one who called

QUIET
1Ti 2: 2 **q** and peaceable life in all godliness
1Pe 3: 4 beauty of a gentle and **q** spirit,

QUIVER
Ps 127: 5 Happy is the man who has his **q**
full of
Isa 49: 2 in his **q** he hid me away.

R

RABBI
Mt 23: 8 But you are not to be called **r**,
Jn 1:38 "**R**" (which translated means
Teacher),

RACE
Ecc 9:11 the sun the **r** is not to the swift,
1Co 9:24 that in a **r** the runners all compete,

RACE (*cont.*)
Heb 12: 1 let us run with perseverance the **r**
1Pe 2: 9 But you are a chosen **r**, a royal

RACHEL
  Daughter of Laban (Ge 29:16); wife of Jacob (Ge 29:28); bore two sons (Ge 30:22-24; 35:16-24; 46:19). Stole Laban's gods (Ge 31:19, 32-35). Death (Ge 35:19-20).

RAHAB
  Prostitute who hid Israelite spies (Jos 2; 6:22-25; Heb 11:31; Jas 2:25). Mother of Boaz (Mt 1:5).

RAIN → RAINBOW, RAINED, RAINS
Ge   7: 4 For in seven days I will send **r** on
1Ki 17: 1 neither dew nor **r** these years,
Isa 45: 8 let the skies **r** down righteousness;
Mt   5:45 sends **r** on the righteous and on the
Rev 11: 6 so that no **r** may fall during the days

RAINBOW → BOW
Rev 4: 3 the throne is a **r** that looks like an

RAINED → RAIN
Ge 19:24 **r** on Sodom and Gomorrah sulfur
Ex   9:23 LORD **r** hail on the land of Egypt;

RAINS → RAIN
Lev 26: 4 I will give you your **r** in their season
Jas   5: 7 receives the early and the late **r**.

RAISE → RISE
Dt 18:15 God will **r** up for you a prophet
Jn   2:19 and in three days I will **r** it up."
2Co 4:14 who raised the Lord Jesus will **r** us

RAISED → RISE
Mt 17:23 and on the third day he will be **r**."
Ac   2:24 God **r** him up, having freed him
Ro   4:25 and was **r** for our justification.
1Co 15: 4 **r** on the third day in accordance

RAM → RAMS
Ge 22:13 and took the **r** and offered it up as
Ex 29:22 (for it is a **r** of ordination),
Da   8: 3 saw a **r** standing beside the river.

RAMS → RAM
1Sa 15:22 and to heed than the fat of **r**.

RANSOM → RANSOMED
Ps 49: 8 For the **r** of life is costly, and can
Mt 20:28 and to give his life a **r** for many."
1Ti   2: 6 who gave himself a **r** for all

RANSOMED → RANSOM
Isa 35:10 And the **r** of the LORD shall return,
Rev 5: 9 by your blood you **r** for God saints

RAVENS
1Ki 17: 6 **r** brought him bread and meat in
Lk 12:24 Consider the **r**: they neither sow

READ → READING
Ex 24: 7 and **r** it in the hearing of the people;
Jos   8:34 he **r** all the words of the law,
Ne   8: 8 they **r** from the book, from the law
Lk   4:16 as was his custom. He stood up to **r**,
2Co 3:15 this very day whenever Moses is **r**,

READING → READ
Ac   8:30 you understand what you are **r**?"

READY
Lk   1:17 **r** a people prepared for the Lord."
Rev 19: 7 and his bride has made herself **r**;

REAP
Gal 6: 7 for you **r** whatever you sow.
Rev 14:15 for the hour to **r** has come,

REBEKAH
  Sister of Laban, secured as bride for Isaac (Ge 24). Mother of Esau and Jacob (Ge 25:19-26). Taken by Abimelech as sister of Isaac; returned (Ge 26:1-11). Encouraged Jacob to trick Isaac out of blessing (Ge 27:1-17).

REBEL → REBELLED, REBELLION
Ex 23:21 do not **r** against him, for he will
1Sa 12:14 not **r** against the commandment

REBELLED → REBEL
Nu 20:24 because you **r** against my command
Ne   9:26 they were disobedient and **r**

REBELLION → REBEL
1Sa 15:23 For **r** is no less a sin than divination,
2Th 2: 3 the **r** comes first and the lawless one

REBUILD → BUILD
Ezr 1: 3 and **r** the house of the LORD,
Ne   2:17 let us **r** the wall of Jerusalem,
Da   9:25 went out to restore and **r** Jerusalem
Ac 15:16 and I will **r** the dwelling of David,

REBUKE
Ps   6: 1 O LORD, do not **r** me in your anger,
Pr 27: 5 Better is open **r** than hidden love.
Zec 3: 2 said to Satan, "The LORD **r** you,
Mk 8:32 Peter took him aside and began to **r**
2Ti 4: 2 convince, **r**, and encourage,

RECEIVE → RECEIVED
Jn 16:24 Ask and you will **r**, so that your joy
Ac   2:38 you will **r** the gift of the Holy Spirit.
  20:35 'It is more blessed to give than to **r**.'
Rev 4:11 to **r** glory and honor and power,

RECEIVED → RECEIVE
Mt   6: 2 I tell you, they have **r** their reward.
Jn   1:12 But to all who **r** him, who believed
1Co 11:23 I **r** from the Lord what I also handed

RECKONED → RECKONING
Ge 15: 6 LORD **r** it to him as righteousness.
Ro   4: 3 it was **r** to him as righteousness."

RECKONING → RECKONED
Ge   9: 5 I will require a **r** for human life.
Sir 2:14 you do when the Lord's **r** comes?

RECONCILE → RECONCILED, RECONCILIATION
Ac   7:26 were quarreling and tried to **r** them,
Col 1:20 God was pleased to **r** to himself all

RECONCILED → RECONCILE
Mt   5:24 first be **r** to your brother or sister,
1Co 7:11 let her remain unmarried or else be **r**

RECONCILIATION → RECONCILE
Ro   5:11 whom we have now received **r**.
2Co 5:18 and has given us the ministry of **r**;

RED
Ex 15: 4 officers were sunk in the R Sea.
Mt 16: 3 for the sky is **r** and threatening.'
Rev 12: 3 a great **r** dragon, with seven heads

REDEEM → REDEEMED, REDEEMER, REDEMPTION
Ex   6: 6 I will **r** you with an outstretched
2Sa 7:23 whose God went to **r** it as a people,
Gal 4: 5 to **r** those who were under the law,

REDEEMED → REDEEM
Dt 15:15 and the LORD your God **r** you;
Ps 107: 2 Let the **r** of the LORD say so,

REDEEMER → REDEEM
Job 19:25 For I know that my R lives,
Ps 19:14 O LORD, my rock and my **r**.
Isa 48:17 Thus says the LORD, your R,

REDEMPTION → REDEEM
Lk 21:28 because your **r** is drawing near."
Eph 1: 7 In him we have **r** through his blood,
Heb 9:12 own blood, thus obtaining eternal **r**.

REFINE → REFINED
Jer 9: 7 I will now **r** and test them,
Zec 13: 9 **r** them as one refines silver,

REFINED → REFINE
Da 12:10 shall be purified, cleansed, and **r**,

REFLECTED → REFLECTION
2Co 3:18 though **r** in a mirror,

REFLECTION → REFLECTED
1Co 11: 7 since he is the image and **r** of God;
Heb 1: 3 He is the **r** of God's glory

REFUGE
Nu 35:11 select cities to be cities of **r** for you,
Ps   2:12 Happy are all who take **r** in him.
Pr 30: 5 a shield to those who take **r** in him.
Jer 16:19 my **r** in the day of trouble,

REFUSE
Ex   8: 2 If you **r** to let them go,
Eze 3:27 and let those who **r** to hear, **r**;
Heb 12:25 do not **r** the one who is speaking;

REGARD
Isa 8:13 of hosts, him you shall **r** as holy;
Php 2: 6 did not **r** equality with God as
   3: 7 these I have come to **r** as loss
Heb 12: 5 not **r** lightly the discipline of the

REGULATIONS
Col 2:20 Why do you submit to **r**,
Heb 9:10 **r** for the body imposed until the

REHOBOAM
  Son of Solomon (1Ki 11:43; 1Ch 3:10). Harsh treatment of subjects caused divided kingdom (1Ki 12:1-24; 14:21-31; 2Ch 10-12).

REIGN → REIGNS
Ex 15:18 The LORD will **r** forever and ever."
Ps 146:10 The LORD will **r** forever,
1Co 15:25 **r** until he has put all his enemies
2Ti   2:12 we will also **r** with him;
Rev 11:15 and he will **r** forever and ever."
  22: 5 and they will **r** forever and ever.

REIGNS → REIGN
Isa 52: 7 who says to Zion, "Your God **r**."
Rev 19: 6 the Lord our God the Almighty **r**.

REJECT → REJECTED
Ex 20: 5 generation of those who **r** me,
Isa 30:12 Because you **r** this word,

REJECTED → REJECT
1Sa 8: 7 but they have **r** me from being king
Ps 60: 1 O God, you have **r** us, broken our
  118:22 The stone that the builders **r**
Isa 53: 3 He was despised and **r** by others;
Mt 21:42 'The stone that the builders **r**
1Pe 2: 4 though **r** by mortals yet chosen and

REJOICE → REJOICING
Ps   5:11 But let all who take refuge in you **r**;
  118:24 let us **r** and be glad in it.
Isa 62: 5 so shall your God **r** over you.
Zep 3:17 he will **r** over you with gladness,
Lk   6:23 R in that day and leap for joy,
Php 4: 4 R in the Lord always; again I will say, R.

REJOICING → REJOICE
2Sa 6:12 to the city of David with **r**;
Ne   8:17 And there was very great **r**.
2Co 6:10 as sorrowful, yet always **r**;

RELEASE
Isa 61: 1 liberty to the captives, and **r** to
Mt 27:15 the governor was accustomed to **r**

RELENT → RELENTED
Eze 24:14 I will not spare, I will not **r**.
Joel 2:14 whether he will not turn and **r**,
Jnh 3: 9 God may **r** and change his mind;

RELENTED → RELENT
1Ch 21:15 LORD took note and **r** concerning
Jer 4:28 I have not **r** nor will I turn back.

RELIGION
Jas 1:27 R that is pure and undefiled before

RELY
2Ch 14:11 O LORD our God, for we **r** on you,

Pr 3: 5 and do not **r** on your own insight.
Gal 3:10 all who **r** on the works of the law
Sir 5: 1 Do not **r** on your wealth,

REMAIN → REMAINS
1Co 7:20 Let each of you **r** in the condition
Heb 1:11 they will perish, but you **r;**

REMAINS → REMAIN
Jos 13: 2 This is the land that still **r:**
Heb 7: 3 Son of God, he **r** a priest forever.
10:26 there no longer **r** a sacrifice for sins,

REMEMBER → REMEMBERED,
REMEMBRANCE
Ge 9:15 I will **r** my covenant that is between
Ex 20: 8 **R** the sabbath day, and keep it holy.
Dt 8:18 But **r** the LORD your God,
Job 10: 9 **R** that you fashioned me like clay;
Ecc 12: 1 **R** your creator in the days of your
Jer 31:34 and **r** their sin no more.
2Ti 2: 8 **R** Jesus Christ, raised from the dead
Heb 8:12 and I will **r** their sins no more."
Sir 23:18 The Most High will not **r** sins."

REMEMBERED → REMEMBER
Ex 2:24 God **r** his covenant with Abraham,
Ps 78:35 They **r** that God was their rock,
106:45 For their sake he **r** his covenant,
Rev 16:19 God **r** great Babylon and gave her

REMEMBRANCE → REMEMBER
Lk 22:19 Do this in **r** of me."

REMNANT
Ge 45: 7 before you to preserve for you a **r**
Isa 10:21 A **r** will return, the **r** of Jacob,
Jer 50:20 will pardon the **r** that I have spared.
Ro 9:27 only a **r** of them will be saved;

REMOVE
Eze 36:26 **r** from your body the heart of stone
Lk 22:42 if you are willing, **r** this cup from

RENEW → RENEWAL, RENEWED,
RENEWING
Isa 40:31 for the LORD shall **r** their strength,
La 5:21 **r** our days as of old—

RENEWAL → RENEW
Mt 19:28 I tell you, at the **r** of all things,
Col 3:11 In that **r** there is no longer Greek

RENEWED → RENEW
2Co 4:16 inner nature is being **r** day by day.
Eph 4:23 to be **r** in the spirit of your minds,

RENEWING* → RENEW
Ro 12: 2 transformed by the **r** of your minds,

REPAY → PAY
Ps 28: 4 **R** them according to their work,
Isa 59:18 to their deeds, so will he **r;**
Ro 12:17 Do not **r** anyone evil for evil,
Rev 18: 6 and **r** her double for her deeds;

REPENT → REPENTANCE
1Ki 8:47 **r,** and plead with you in the land
Job 42: 6 and **r** in dust and ashes."
Mt 3: 2 "**R,** for the kingdom of heaven has
Ac 2:38 "**R,** and be baptized every one of
Rev 16: 9 they did not **r** and give him glory.
Sir 18:21 and when you have sinned, **r.**

REPENTANCE → REPENT
Mk 1: 4 a baptism of **r** for the forgiveness
Lk 3: 8 Bear fruits worthy of **r.**
Ro 2: 4 kindness is meant to lead you to **r?**
2Co 7:10 **r** that leads to salvation and brings
2Pe 3: 9 any to perish, but all to come to **r.**

REPROVE
Pr 19:25 **r** the intelligent, and they will gain
Tit 2:15 exhort and **r** with all authority.
Rev 3:19 **r** and discipline those whom I love.

REQUIRE
Dt 10:12 does the LORD your God **r** of you?
Mic 6: 8 the LORD **r** of you but to do justice,

RESCUE → RESCUED, RESCUES
Ps 22: 8 him **r** the one in whom he delights!"
Mt 6:13 but **r** us from the evil one.
2Pe 2: 9 the Lord knows how to **r** the godly

RESCUED → RESCUE
Col 1:13 has **r** us from the power of darkness
Sir 51:12 and **r** me in time of trouble.

RESCUES → RESCUE
Ps 37:40 The LORD helps them and **r** them;
Da 6:27 and **r,** he works signs and wonders
1Th 1:10 Jesus, who **r** us from the wrath that

RESIST
Mt 5:39 I say to you, Do not **r** an evildoer.
Ro 9:19 For who can **r** his will?"
Jas 4: 7 **R** the devil, and he will flee from

RESPECT
Mal 1: 6 if I am a master, where is the **r** due
Ro 13: 7 **r** to whom **r** is due,

REST → RESTED, RESTS
Ex 31:15 seventh day is a sabbath of solemn **r**
2Sa 7:11 give you **r** from all your enemies.
Ps 95:11 swore, "They shall not enter my **r.**"
Mt 11:28 and I will give you **r.**
Heb 4:10 those who enter God's **r** also cease

RESTED → REST
Ge 2: 2 he **r** on the seventh day from all the
Ex 20:11 all that is in them, but **r** the seventh

RESTORE → RESTORES
Dt 30: 3 LORD your God will **r** your fortunes
Ps 51:12 **R** to me the joy of your salvation,
Da 9:25 the word went out to **r** and rebuild
Mt 17:11 "Elijah is indeed coming and will **r**

RESTORES → RESTORE
Ps 23: 3 he **r** my soul. He leads me in right

RESTS → REST
Ps 16: 9 my body also **r** secure.
Pr 19:23 one **r** secure and suffers no harm.

RESURRECTION
Mt 22:30 For in the **r** they neither marry nor
Mk 12:18 Sadducees, who say there is no **r,**
Jn 11:25 said to her, "I am the **r** and the life.
1Co 15:12 you say there is no **r** of the dead?
Php 3:10 know Christ and the power of his **r**
Rev 20: 5 This is the first **r.**
2Es 2:23 will give you the first place in my **r.**

RETURN
Ge 3:19 you are dust, and to dust you shall **r.**
Dt 30: 2 and **r** to the LORD your God,
Ps 116:12 What shall I **r** to the LORD
Hos 14: 1 **R,** O Israel, to the LORD your God,
Mal 3: 7 **R** to me, and I will **r** to you,

REUBEN
Firstborn of Jacob by Leah (Ge 29:32; 46:8;
1Ch 2:1). Attempted to rescue Joseph (Ge 37:21-
30). Lost birthright for sleeping with Bilhah (Ge
35:22; 49:4). Tribe of blessed (Ge 49:3-4; Dt 33:6),
numbered (Nu 1:21; 26:7), allotted land east of
Jordan (Nu 32; 34:14; Jos 13:15), west (Eze 48:6),
failed to help Deborah (Jdg 5:15-16), supported
David (1Ch 12:37), 12,000 from (Rev 7:5).

REVEAL → REVEALED, REVELATION,
REVELATIONS
Mt 11:27 to whom the Son chooses to **r** him.

REVEALED → REVEAL
Isa 40: 5 the glory of the LORD shall be **r,**
Mt 16:17 flesh and blood has not **r** this to
you
Lk 17:30 on the day that the Son of Man is **r.**
Ro 1:17 in it the righteousness of God is **r**
2Th 1: 7 the Lord Jesus is **r** from heaven
1Jn 3: 2 we do know is this: when he is **r,**

REVELATION → REVEAL
1Co 14: 6 some **r** or knowledge or prophecy

Eph 3: 3 was made known to me by **r,**
Rev 1: 1 The **r** of Jesus Christ, which God

REVELATIONS → REVEAL
2Co 12: 1 but I will go on to visions and **r** of

REVERE → REVERENCE
Jos 24:14 "Now therefore **r** the LORD,
Mal 4: 2 But for you who **r** my name the sun
Tob 4: 5 "**R** the Lord all your days,

REVERENCE → REVERE
Eph 5:21 subject to one another out of **r** for
1Pe 3: 2 see the purity and **r** of your lives.

REVILE → REVILED
Ex 22:28 You shall not **r** God, or curse
Mt 5:11 people **r** you and persecute you

REVILED → REVILE
1Co 4:12 When **r,** we bless;
1Pe 4:14 If you are **r** for the name of Christ,

REWARD → REWARDED
Ps 19:11 in keeping them there is great **r.**
Isa 40:10 **r** is with him, and his recompense
Mt 6: 5 I tell you, they have received their **r.**
Lk 6:23 for surely your **r** is great in heaven;
Heb 11:26 for he was looking ahead to the **r.**
Rev 22:12 I am coming soon; my **r** is with me,

REWARDED → REWARD
2Sa 22:21 The LORD **r** me according to my

RIB
Ge 2:22 **r** that the LORD God had taken from

RICH → RICHES
Pr 23: 4 Do not wear yourself out to get **r;**
Mt 19:23 hard for a **r** person to enter the
Lk 12:21 but are not **r** toward God."
2Co 8: 9 by his poverty you might become **r.**
Eph 2: 4 But God, who is **r** in mercy,
1Ti 6:18 to do good, to be **r** in good works,
Jas 1:10 and the **r** in being brought low,

RICHES → RICH
Ps 62:10 if **r** increase, do not set your heart
Pr 30: 8 give me neither poverty nor **r;**
Lk 8:14 they are choked by the cares and **r**
Ro 11:33 O the depth of the **r** and wisdom
1Jn 2:16 the desire of the eyes, the pride in **r**
Sir 13:24 **R** are good if they are free from sin;

RID
Col 3: 8 But now you must get **r** of all such
1Pe 2: 1 **R** yourselves, therefore, of all

RIDER → RIDES, RIDING
Rev 19:11 Its **r** is called Faithful and True,

RIDES → RIDER
Dt 33:26 **r** through the heavens to your help,
Ps 68: 4 a song to him who **r** upon the clouds

RIDING → RIDER
Zec 9: 9 humble and **r** on a donkey,

RIGHT → BIRTHRIGHT
Ex 15: 6 Your **r** hand, O LORD, glorious in
Dt 6:18 Do what is **r** and good in the sight
Job 42: 7 have not spoken of me what is **r,**
Ps 110: 1 says to my lord, "Sit at my **r** hand
Pr 14:12 a way that seems **r** to a person,
Mt 25:33 sheep at his **r** hand and the goats at
Ac 2:34 said to my Lord, "Sit at my **r** hand,
Heb 1:13 "Sit at my **r** hand until I make your
1Pe 3:14 if you do suffer for doing what is **r,**

RIGHTEOUS → RIGHTEOUSNESS
Ge 18:23 "Will you indeed sweep away the **r**
Job 4:17 'Can mortals be **r** before God?
Ps 11: 7 For the LORD is **r;** he loves **r** deeds;
Pr 10: 6 Blessings are on the head of the **r,**
11:23 desire of the **r** ends only in good;
15:29 but he hears the prayer of the **r.**
Jer 23: 5 I will raise up for David a **r** Branch,
Eze 3:20 if the **r** turn from their righteousness
Hab 2: 4 but the **r** live by their faith.

RIGHTEOUS *(cont.)*
Mt   5:45 rain on the *r* and on the
          unrighteous.
Mk   2:17 come to call not the *r* but sinners."
Ro   1:17 one who is *r* will live by faith."
     5:19 the many will be made *r.*
Heb 10:38 but my *r* one will live by faith.
1Jn 2: 1 with the Father, Jesus Christ the *r*;
Rev 19: 8 the fine linen is the *r* deeds of the
Wis 5:15 *r* live forever, and their reward
Sir 35:22 and does justice for the *r,*

RIGHTEOUSNESS → RIGHTEOUS
Ge 15: 6 the Lord reckoned it to him as *r.*
Ps   9: 8 He judges the world with *r*;
Pr 12:28 In the path of *r* there is life,
Ecc 7:15 people who perish in their *r,*
Isa 11: 5 **R** shall be the belt around his waist,
Jer 23: 6 be called: "The Lord is our *r.*"
Da   9:24 to bring in everlasting *r,*
    12: 3 and those who lead many to *r,*
Hos 10:12 Sow for yourselves *r*; reap steadfast
Mt   5: 6 those who hunger and thirst for *r,*
Jn 16: 8 about sin and *r* and judgment;
Ro   5:18 act of *r* leads to justification
    10: 4 be *r* for everyone who believes.
Gal 3: 6 and it was reckoned to him as *r,*"
Eph 6:14 and put on the breastplate of *r.*
1Pe 2:24 free from sins, we might live for *r*;
2Pe 3:13 heavens and a new earth, where *r* is
Rev 19:11 and in *r* he judges and makes war.

RIPE
Joel 3:13 Put in the sickle, for the harvest is *r.*
Jn   4:35 how the fields are *r* for harvesting.
Rev 14:15 the harvest of the earth is fully *r.*"

RISE → ARISE, RAISE, RAISED, ROSE
Nu 24:17 and a scepter shall *r* out of Israel;
Ps 94: 2 **R** up, O judge of the earth;
Da 12:13 shall *r* for your reward at the end of
Mal 4: 2 the sun of righteousness shall *r,*
Mt 27:63 'After three days I will *r* again.'
Eph 5:14 **R** from the dead, and Christ will
1Th 4:16 and the dead in Christ will *r* first.

RIVER → RIVERS
Ps 46: 4 a *r* whose streams make glad the
Isa 48:18 prosperity would have been like a *r,*
Eze 47:12 On the banks, on both sides of the *r,*
Mt   3: 6 baptized by him in the *r* Jordan,
Rev 22: 1 showed me the *r* of the water of life,

RIVERS → RIVER
Ps 137: 1 By the *r* of Babylon—there we sat
Rev 8:10 it fell on a third of the *r* and on the

ROAD → CROSSROADS
Mt   7:13 and the *r* is easy that leads to

ROAR → ROARING, ROARS
Ps 46: 3 though its waters *r* and foam,
Jer 25:30 The Lord will *r* from on high,

ROARING → ROAR
1Pe 5: 8 a *r* lion your adversary the devil

ROARS → ROAR
Hos 11:10 the Lord, who *r* like a lion;
Joel 3:16 The Lord *r* from Zion,

ROB → ROBBER, ROBBERS
Mal 3: 8 anyone *r* God? Yet you are robbing

ROBBER → ROB
1Co 5:11 an idolater, reviler, drunkard, or *r.*

ROBBERS → ROB
Jer 7:11 become a den of *r* in your sight?
Mt 21:13 but you are making it a den of *r.*"

ROBE → ROBED, ROBES
Ge 37: 3 had made him a long *r* with sleeves.
Ex 28: 4 a breastpiece, an ephod, a *r,*
Jn 19: 5 crown of thorns and the purple *r,*
Rev 6:11 They were each given a white *r* and
    19:13 He is clothed in a *r* dipped in blood,

ROBED → ROBE
Ps 93: 1 Lord is king, he is *r* in majesty;
Rev 15: 6 *r* in pure bright linen,

ROBES → ROBE
Mk 12:38 who like to walk around in long *r,*
Rev 22:14 Blessed are those who wash their *r,*

ROCK
Ex 17: 6 Strike the *r,* and water will come
Nu 20: 8 you shall bring water out of the *r*
1Sa 2: 2 there is no **R** like our God.
Ps 19:14 O Lord, my *r* and my redeemer.
Isa 44: 8 There is no other *r*; I know not one.
Mt 16:18 and on this *r* I will build my church,
Mk 15:46 that had been hewn out of the *r.*
1Pe 2: 8 and a *r* that makes them fall."

ROD
2Sa 7:14 I will punish him with a *r* such as
Ps   2: 9 shall break them with a *r* of iron,
    23: 4 your *r* and your staff—they comfort
Pr 13:24 who spare the *r* hate their children,
Heb 9: 4 and Aaron's *r* that budded,
Rev 2:27 to rule them with an iron *r,*

ROLL
Am   5:24 But let justice *r* down like waters,
Mk 16: 3 "Who will *r* away the stone for us

ROOF
Jos 2: 6 to the *r* and hidden them
2Sa 11: 2 he saw from the *r* a woman bathing;
Mk   2: 4 they removed the *r* above him;

ROOM
Mk 14:15 He will show you a large *r* upstairs,
Ro 12:19 but leave *r* for the wrath of God;
Eph 4:27 and do not make *r* for the devil.

ROOT → ROOTED
Isa 11:10 On that day the *r* of Jesse
    53: 2 and like a *r* out of dry ground;
Ro 15:12 "The *r* of Jesse shall come,
1Ti 6:10 For the love of money is a *r* of all
Rev 5: 5 the tribe of Judah, the **R** of David,

ROOTED → ROOT
Eph 3:17 are being *r* and grounded in love.

ROSE → RISE
SS   2: 1 I am a *r* of Sharon, a lily
1Th 4:14 believe that Jesus died and *r* again,

ROUGH
Isa 40: 4 and the *r* places a plain.
Lk   3: 5 and the *r* ways made smooth;

ROYAL
Jas 2: 8 if you really fulfill the *r* law
1Pe 2: 9 are a chosen race, a *r* priesthood,

RUBBISH
1Co 4:13 have become like the *r* of the world,
Php 3: 8 and I regard them as *r,*

RUIN → RUINS
Eze 21:27 A *r,* a *r,* a *r*—I will make it!
Zep 1:15 a day of *r* and devastation,

RUINS → RUIN
Ezr 9: 9 the house of our God, to repair its *r,*
Ne   2:17 Jerusalem lies in *r* with its gates
Ac 15:16 from its *r* I will rebuild it,
1Co 15:33 "Bad company *r* good morals."
1Mc 3:43 "Let us restore the *r* of our people,

RULE → RULER, RULER'S, RULERS, RULES
Ge   3:16 husband, and he shall *r* over you."
Ps 110: 2 **R** in the midst of your foes.
Eph 1:21 far above all *r* and authority and
Col 3:15 the peace of Christ *r* in your hearts,
Rev 19:15 he will *r* them with a rod of iron;

RULER → RULE
Ex   2:14 made you a *r* and judge over us?
Mt   2: 6 a *r* who is to shepherd my people
1Co 15:24 after he has destroyed every *r*
Rev 1: 5 and the *r* of the kings of the earth.

RULER'S → RULE
Ge 49:10 the *r* staff from between his feet,

RULERS → RULE
Ps   2: 2 and the *r* take counsel together,
Isa 40:23 makes the *r* of the earth as nothing.
Eph 6:12 against the *r,* against the authorities,

RULES → RULE
Ps 66: 7 who *r* by his might forever,
Isa 40:10 and his arm *r* for him;
2Ti 2: 5 competing according to the *r.*

RUMORS
Mt 24: 6 you will hear of wars and *r* of wars;

RUN → FORERUNNER, RUNNERS
Isa 40:31 they shall *r* and not be weary,
Gal 2: 2 or had not *r,* in vain.
Heb 12: 1 let us *r* with perseverance the race

RUNNERS* → RUN
1Co 9:24 that in a race the *r* all compete,

RUST
Mt   6:19 where moth and *r* consume
LtJ 6:12 cannot save themselves from *r*

RUTH
Moabitess; widow who went to Bethlehem with
mother-in-law Naomi (Ru 1). Gleaned in field of
Boaz; shown favor (Ru 2). Proposed marriage to
Boaz (Ru 3). Married (Ru 4:1-12); bore Obed,
ancestor of David (Ru 4:13-22), Jesus (Mt 1:5).

S

SABBATH
Ex 20: 8 Remember the *s* day, and keep it
          holy.
2Ch 36:21 the days that it lay desolate it kept *s,*
Mt 12: 1 through the grainfields on the *s*;
Mk   2:28 Son of Man is lord even of the *s.*"
1Mc 1:43 to idols and profaned the *s.*

SACKCLOTH → CLOTH
Da   9: 3 supplication with fasting and *s* and
Mt 11:21 would have repented long ago in *s*

SACRED
Ex 28: 2 You shall make *s* vestments for
    34:13 and cut down their *s* poles

SACRIFICE → SACRIFICED, SACRIFICES
Ex 12:27 'It is the passover *s* to the Lord,
Lev 3: 1 If the offering is a *s* of well-being,
1Sa 15:22 Surely, to obey is better than *s,*
Ps 40: 6 **S** and offering you do not desire,
Pr 15: 8 *s* of the wicked is an abomination
Da   9:27 he shall make *s* and offering cease;
Hos 6: 6 For I desire steadfast love and not *s,*
Mt   9:13 this means, 'I desire mercy, not *s.*'
Ro   3:25 put forward as a *s* of atonement
Php 4:18 a *s* acceptable and pleasing to God.
Heb 13:15 let us continually offer a *s* of praise
1Jn 2: 2 and he is the atoning *s* for our sins,

SACRIFICED → SACRIFICE
1Co 5: 7 our paschal lamb, Christ, has been *s.*
     8: 1 Now concerning food *s* to idols;

SACRIFICES → SACRIFICE
Mk 12:33 all whole burnt offerings and *s.*"
Heb 7:27 has no need to offer *s* day after day,

SADDUCEES
Mt 16: 6 the yeast of the Pharisees and **S**."
Mk 12:18 **S,** who say there is no resurrection,

SAFE → SAFETY
Ps 37:28 righteous shall be kept *s* forever,
Pr 18:10 the righteous run into it and are *s.*

SAFETY → SAFE
Dt 12:10 around so that you live in *s,*
Eze 34:28 they shall live in *s,*

SAINTS
Ps 31:23 Love the Lord, all you his *s.*

Ro   8:27   the Spirit intercedes for the **s**
1Co   6: 2   that the **s** will judge the world?
Eph   4:12   equip the **s** for the work of ministry,
Rev   5: 9   by your blood you ransomed for
            God **s**

SALT
Ge   19:26   back, and she became a pillar of **s**.
Mt   5:13   "You are the **s** of the earth;

SALVATION → SAVE
Ex   15: 2   and he has become my **s**;
Ps   27: 1   The LORD is my light and my **s**;
      51:12   Restore to me the joy of your **s**,
Isa   12: 3   draw water from the wells of **s**.
      52: 7   brings good news, who announces **s**,
La   3:26   one should wait quietly for the **s**
Hab   3:18   I will exult in the God of my **s**.
Lk   3: 6   all flesh shall see the **s** of God.'"
Ac   4:12   There is **s** in no one else,
2Co   6: 2   see, now is the day of **s**!
Php   2:12   work out your own **s** with fear
Heb   2: 3   escape if we neglect so great a **s**?
2Pe   3:15   regard the patience of our Lord as **s**.
Rev   19: 1   **S** and glory and power to our God,
Bar   4:29   everlasting joy with your **s**.

SAMARIA → SAMARITAN
1Ki   16:24   and called the city that he built, **S**,
2Ki   17: 6   the king of Assyria captured **S**;
Jn   4: 4   But he had to go through **S**.
Ac   1: 8   in all Judea and **S**, and to the ends

SAMARITAN → SAMARIA
Lk   10:33   But a **S** while traveling came near
Jn   4: 7   A **S** woman came to draw water,

SAME
Ro   10:12   the **s** Lord is Lord of all
1Co   12: 4   varieties of gifts, but the **s** Spirit;
Heb   13: 8   Jesus Christ is the **s** yesterday and

SAMSON*
Danite judge. Birth promised (Jdg 13). Married a Philistine, but his wife given away (Jdg 14). Vengeance on the Philistines (Jdg 15). Betrayed by Delilah (Jdg 16:1-22). Death (Jdg 16:23-31). Feats of strength: killed lion (Jdg 14:6), 30 Philistines (Jdg 14:19), 1,000 Philistines with jawbone (Jdg 15:13-17), carried off gates of Gaza (Jdg 16:3), pushed down temple of Dagon (Jdg 16:25-30; Heb 11:32).

SAMUEL
Ephraimite judge and prophet (Heb 11:32). Birth prayed for (1Sa 1:10-18). Dedicated to temple by Hannah (1Sa 1:21-28). Raised by Eli (1Sa 2:11, 18-26). Called as prophet (1Sa 3). Led Israel to victory over Philistines (1Sa 7). Asked by Israel for a king (1Sa 8). Anointed Saul as king (1Sa 9-10). Farewell speech (1Sa 12). Rebuked Saul for sacrifice (1Sa 13). Announced rejection of Saul (1Sa 15). Anointed David as king (1Sa 16). Protected David from Saul (1Sa 19:18-24). Death (1Sa 25:1). Returned from dead to condemn Saul (1Sa 28).

SANCTIFICATION → SANCTIFY
Ro   6:19   as slaves to righteousness for **s**.
1Th   4: 3   For this is the will of God, your **s**;

SANCTIFIED → SANCTIFY
Ex   29:43   and it shall be **s** by my glory;
Jn   17:19   so that they also may be **s** in truth.
1Co   6:11   But you were washed, you were **s**,

SANCTIFY → SANCTIFICATION, SANCTIFIED
Lev   11:44   **s** yourselves therefore, and be holy,
Heb   13:12   to **s** the people by his own blood.

SANCTUARY
Ex   25: 8   And have them make me a **s**,
1Ch   22:19   build the **s** of the LORD God
Eze   37:26   and will set my **s** among them
Da   9:26   shall destroy the city and the **s**.

Heb   9:24   Christ did not enter a **s** made by
1Mc   1:21   He arrogantly entered the **s**
      4:36   cleanse the **s** and dedicate it."

SAND
Ge   22:17   as the stars of heaven and as the **s**
Hos   1:10   Israel shall be like the **s** of the sea,
Mt   7:26   foolish man who built his house
            on **s**.

SANDALS
Ex   3: 5   Remove the **s** from your feet,
Mt   3:11   I am not worthy to carry his **s**.

SARAH
Wife of Abraham, originally named Sarai; barren (Ge 11:29-31; 1Pe 3:6). Taken by Pharaoh as Abraham's sister; returned (Ge 12:10-20). Gave Hagar to Abraham; sent her away in pregnancy (Ge 16). Name changed; Isaac promised (Ge 17:15-21; 18:10-15; Heb 11:11). Taken by Abimelech as Abraham's sister; returned (Ge 20). Isaac born; Hagar and Ishmael sent away (Ge 21:1-21; Gal 4:21-31). Death (Ge 23).

SAT → SIT
Heb   10:12   "he **s** down at the right hand of God,
Rev   3:21   and **s** down with my Father

SATAN
1Ch   21: 1   **S** stood up against Israel,
Job   1: 6   and **S** also came among them.
Zec   3: 2   "The LORD rebuke you, O **S**!
Mt   4:10   Jesus said to him, "Away with you, **S**!
      12:26   If **S** casts out **S**, he is divided
      16:23   said to Peter, "Get behind me, **S**!
2Co   11:14   **S** disguises himself as an angel of
            light.
Rev   12: 9   who is called the Devil and **S**,
      20: 7   **S** will be released from his prison

SATISFIED → SATISFY
Ps   17:15   I shall be **s**, beholding your likeness.
Joel   2:26   You shall eat in plenty and be **s**,

SATISFY → SATISFIED
Isa   55: 2   labor for that which does not **s**?
Jer   31:25   I will **s** the weary, and all who are

SAUL → =PAUL
1. Benjamite; anointed by Samuel as first king of Israel (1Sa 9-10). Defeated Ammonites (1Sa 11). Rebuked for offering sacrifice (1Sa 13:1-15). Defeated Philistines (1Sa 14). Rejected as king for failing to annihilate Amalekites (1Sa 15). Soothed from evil spirit by David (1Sa 16:14-23). Sent David against Goliath (1Sa 17). Jealousy and attempted murder of David (1Sa 18:1-11). Gave David Michal as wife (1Sa 18:12-30). Second attempt to kill David (1Sa 19). Anger at Jonathan (1Sa 20:26-34). Pursued David: killed priests at Nob (1Sa 22), went to Keilah and Ziph (1Sa 23), life spared by David at En Gedi (1Sa 24) and in his tent (1Sa 26). Rebuked by Samuel's spirit for consulting witch at Endor (1Sa 28). Wounded by Philistines; took his own life (1Sa 31; 1Ch 10). Lamented by David (2Sa 1:17-27). Children (1Sa 14:49-51; 1Ch 8).
2. See Paul.

SAVE → SALVATION, SAVED, SAVIOR
Ps   54: 1   **S** me, O God, by your name,
Isa   59: 1   LORD's hand is not too short to **s**,
Jer   15:20   for I am with you to **s** you
Mt   1:21   he will **s** his people from their sins."
      16:25   who want to **s** their life will lose it,
Lk   19:10   came to seek out and to **s** the lost."
Heb   7:25   to **s** those who approach God

SAVED → SAVE
Isa   45:22   Turn to me and be **s**,
Joel   2:32   on the name of the LORD shall be **s**;
Mt   10:22   who endures to the end will be **s**.
Mk   15:31   He **s** others; he cannot save himself.
Lk   13:23   "Lord, will only a few be **s**?"
Ac   2:21   on the name of the Lord shall be **s**.'

Ac   16:30   "Sirs, what must I do to be **s**?"
Ro   10:13   on the name of the Lord shall be **s**."
Eph   2: 8   For by grace you have been **s**

SAVIOR → SAVE
Ps   106:21   They forgot God, their **S**,
Isa   49:26   know that I am the LORD your **S**,
Hos   13: 4   and besides me there is no **s**.
Lk   2:11   this day in the city of David a **S**,
Ac   13:23   to Israel a **S**, Jesus, as he promised;
1Ti   4:10   who is the **S** of all people,
Tit   2:13   of the glory of our great God and **S**,
2Pe   3:18   knowledge of our Lord and **S** Jesus

SCARLET
Isa   1:18   your sins are like **s**, they shall be
Mt   27:28   stripped him and put a **s** robe on
            him

SCATTER → SCATTERED
Dt   4:27   LORD will **s** you among the peoples;
Jer   9:16   I will **s** them among nations that

SCATTERED → SCATTER
Dt   30: 3   the LORD your God has **s** you.
Jer   31:10   "He who **s** Israel will gather him,
Mk   14:27   the shepherd, and the sheep will
            be **s**.'

SCEPTER
Ge   49:10   The **s** shall not depart from Judah;
Nu   24:17   and a **s** shall rise out of Israel;
Heb   1: 8   righteous **s** is the **s** of your kingdom.

SCOFFED → SCOFFERS
Lk   23:35   but the leaders **s** at him, saying,

SCOFFERS → SCOFFED
Ps   1: 1   or sit in the seat of **s**;
Pr   19:29   Condemnation is ready for **s**,
2Pe   3: 3   that in the last days **s** will come,

SCRIBES
Mt   7:29   having authority, and not as their **s**.
      23:13   "But woe to you, **s** and Pharisees,

SCRIPTURE → SCRIPTURES
Lk   4:21   "Today this **s** has been fulfilled in
Jn   10:35   and the **s** cannot be annulled—
1Ti   4:13   attention to the public reading of **s**,
2Ti   3:16   All **s** is inspired by God and is useful

SCRIPTURES → SCRIPTURE
Mt   22:29   know neither the **s** nor the power
Lk   24:45   their minds to understand the **s**,
Jn   5:39   "You search the **s** because you think
1Co   15: 3   our sins in accordance with the **s**,

SCROLL
Lk   4:17   the **s** of the prophet Isaiah was given
Rev   5: 2   to open the **s** and break its seals?"

SEA
Ge   1:26   have dominion over the fish of the **s**,
Ex   15: 1   and rider he has thrown into the **s**.
Dt   30:13   Neither is it beyond the **s**, that you
Ps   95: 5   The **s** is his, for he made it,
Da   7: 3   great beasts came up out of the **s**,
Mic   7:19   all our sins into the depths of the **s**.
Rev   4: 6   there is something like a **s** of glass,
      13: 1   a beast rising out of the **s** having
      21: 1   and the **s** was no more.

SEAL → SEALS
Da   8:26   As for you, **s** up the vision,
2Co   1:22   by putting his **s** on us and giving us
Eph   1:13   the **s** of the promised Holy Spirit;
Rev   7: 3   our God with a **s** on their foreheads.
      22:10   not **s** up the words of the prophecy

SEALS → SEAL
Rev   5: 2   to open the scroll and break its **s**?"

SEARCH → SEARCHES
Dt   4:29   if you **s** after him with all your heart
Ps   139:23   **S** me, O God, and know my heart;
Eze   34:11   I myself will **s** for my sheep,

SEARCHES → SEARCH
Ro　8:27　And God, who **s** the heart,
1Co　2:10　the Spirit **s** everything,

SEASON → SEASONS
Ps　1: 3　which yield their fruit in its **s,**
Ecc　3: 1　For everything there is a **s,**

SEASONS → SEASON
Ge　1:14　let them be for signs and for **s** and
Gal　4:10　and months, and **s,** and years.
1Th　5: 1　Now concerning the times and the **s,**

SEAT → SEATED
Ex　25:17　make a mercy **s** of pure gold;
Ps　1: 1　or sit in the **s** of scoffers;
Ro　14:10　stand before the judgment **s** of God.
2Co　5:10　must appear before the judgment **s**

SEATED → SEAT
Lk　22:69　the Son of Man will be **s** at the right
Eph　1:20　and **s** him at his right hand
Rev　4: 4　**s** on the thrones are twenty-four
　　　　　elders,
　　19: 4　and worshiped God who is **s** on

SECOND → TWO
Mt　22:39　And a **s** is like it:
Rev　20:14　This is the **s** death, the lake of fire;

SECRET
Dt　29:29　The **s** things belong to the LORD
Ro　2:16　will judge the **s** thoughts of all.

SECURITY → SECURE
Pr　12: 3　No one finds **s** by wickedness,
1Th　5: 3　they say, "There is peace and **s,"**

**SEE → FORESEEING, NEAR-SIGHTED,
　　　　SEEN, SEES, SIGHT**
Ex　12:13　when I **s** the blood, I will pass over
　　33:20　for no one shall **s** me and live."
Ps　115: 5　eyes, but do not **s.**
Jn　9:25　that though I was blind, now I **s."**
1Co　13:12　we **s** in a mirror, dimly,
1Jn　3: 2　for we will **s** him as he is.
Rev　1: 7　the clouds; every eye will **s** him,

SEED → SEEDS, SEEDTIME
Isa　6:13　The holy **s** is its stump.
Mt　17:20　have faith the size of a mustard **s,**
1Pe　1:23　of perishable but of imperishable **s,**

SEEDS → SEED
Mt　13: 8　Other **s** fell on good soil
Mk　4:31　the smallest of all the **s** on earth;

SEEK
1Ch　28: 9　If you **s** him, he will be found by
Ps　34:10　those who **s** the LORD lack no good
　　119:10　With my whole heart I **s** you;
Isa　55: 6　**S** the LORD while he may be found,
　　65: 1　found by those who did not **s** me.
Lk　19:10　came to **s** out and to save
Heb　11: 6　that he rewards those who **s** him.
Sir　2:16　who fear the Lord **s** to please him,

SEEMS
Pr　16:25　there is a way that **s** to be right,
Heb　12:11　discipline always **s** painful rather

SEEN → SEE
Jn　1:18　No one has ever **s** God.
　　14: 9　Whoever has **s** me has **s** the Father.
　　20:29　Blessed are those who have not **s**
1Pe　1: 8　you have not **s** him, you love him;

SELF-CONTROL → SELF-CONTROLLED
1Co　7: 5　tempt you because of your lack of **s.**
2Pe　1: 6　with **s,** and **s** with endurance,

SELF-CONTROLLED → SELF-CONTROL
Tit　1: 8　prudent, upright, devout, and **s.**
　　2: 5　to be **s,** chaste, good managers

SELFISH → SELFISHNESS
Ps　119:36　to your decrees, and not to **s** gain.
Php　1:17　proclaim Christ out of **s** ambition,
Jas　3:14　if you have bitter envy and **s**

SELFISHNESS* → SELFISH
2Co　12:20　anger, **s,** slander, gossip, conceit,

SELL
Pr　23:23　Buy truth, and do not **s** it;
Mk　10:21　**s** what you own, and give the money

SEND → SENT
Ex　33: 2　I will **s** an angel before you,
Isa　6: 8　And I said, "Here am I; **s** me!"
Jn　3:17　God did not **s** the Son into the
　　　　　world to
　　14:26　whom the Father will **s** in my name,

SENNACHERIB
　　Assyrian king; siege of Jerusalem was overthrown by the LORD following prayer of Hezekiah and Isaiah (2Ki 18:13-19:37; 2Ch 32:1-21;
Isa 36-37).

SENT → SEND
Ex　3:14　'I AM has **s** me to you.'"
Lk　10:16　rejects me rejects the one who **s** me.
Jn　17:18　As you have **s** me into the world,
　　20:21　the Father has **s** me, so I send you."
1Jn　4:10　and **s** his Son to be the atoning

SEPARATE → SEPARATED
Mt　19: 6　joined together, let no one **s."**
Ro　8:35　will **s** us from the love of Christ?
1Co　7:10　wife should not **s** from her husband

SEPARATED → SEPARATE
Lev　20:24　I have **s** you from the peoples.
Heb　7:26　**s** from sinners, and exalted above

SERPENT → SERPENTS
Ge　3: 1　the **s** was more crafty than any other
Nu　21: 9　Moses made a **s** of bronze,
2Co　11: 3　the **s** deceived Eve by its cunning,
Rev　20: 2　He seized the dragon, that ancient **s,**

SERPENTS → SERPENT
Mt　10:16　wise as **s** and innocent as doves.

SERVANT → SERVANTS
Ps　19:11　Moreover by them is your **s** warned;
Isa　42: 1　Here is my **s,** whom I uphold,
　　43:10　and my **s** whom I have chosen,
　　53:11　my **s,** shall make many righteous,
Zec　3: 8　going to bring my **s** the Branch.
Lk　1:38　"Here am I, the **s** of the Lord;
Ac　3:13　has glorified his **s** Jesus,
2Ti　2:24　Lord's **s** must not be quarrelsome
Heb　3: 5　faithful in all God's house as a **s,**

SERVANTS → SERVANT
2Ki　17:23　as he had foretold through all his **s**
Jn　15:15　I do not call you **s** any longer,
1Pe　2:16　As **s** of God, live as free people,
Rev　7: 3　marked the **s** of our God with a
　　　　　seal

SERVE
Jos　24:15　my household, we will **s** the LORD."
1Sa　12:20　but **s** the LORD with all your heart;
Mt　6:24　You cannot **s** God and wealth.
Mk　10:45　Son of Man came not to be served
　　　　　but to **s,**
1Pe　4:10　**s** one another with whatever gift

SETH
Ge　4:25　she bore a son and named him **S,**

SETTLE
Ge　26: 2　**s** in the land that I shall show you.
Nu　33:53　possession of the land and **s** in it,

SEVEN → SEVENTH
Ge　7: 2　with you **s** pairs of all clean animals,
Ex　25:37　You shall make the **s** lamps for it;
Jos　6: 4　march around the city **s** times,
Da　9:25　prince, there shall be **s** weeks;
Mt　18:22　"Not **s** times, but, I tell you, seventy-
　　　　　seven
Rev　1:12　turning I saw **s** golden lampstands,
　　5: 1　and on the back, sealed with **s** seals;
　　8: 2　I saw the **s** angels who stand before

SEVENTH → SEVEN
Ge　2: 2　on the **s** day God finished the work
Ex　20:10　the **s** day is a sabbath to the LORD
　　23:11　but the **s** year you shall let it rest
Heb　4: 4　God rested on the **s** day from all his

SEVENTY → SEVENTY-SEVEN
Ge　46:27　who came into Egypt were **s.**
2Ch　36:21　it kept sabbath, to fulfill **s** years.
Jer　25:12　Then after **s** years are completed,
Da　9:24　**S** weeks are decreed for your people

SEVENTY-SEVEN → SEVENTY
Mt　18:22　"Not seven times, but, I tell you, **s**

SEXUAL
1Co　10: 8　not indulge in **s** immorality as some

SHADOW
2Ki　20:11　brought the **s** back the ten intervals,
Ps　17: 8　hide me in the **s** of your wings,
　　91: 1　who abide in the **s** of the Almighty,
Mt　4:16　and **s** of death light has dawned."
Col　2:17　are only a **s** of what is to come,

SHADRACH → =HANANIAH
　　Hebrew exiled to Babylon; name changed from
Hananiah (Da 1:6-7). Refused defilement by food
(Da 1:8-20). Refused to worship idol (Da 3:1-18);
saved from furnace (Da 3:19-30).

SHALLUM
　　King of Israel (2Ki 15:10-16).

SHALMANESER
　　King of Assyria; conquered and deported Israel
(2Ki 17:3-4; 18:9; Tob 1:2).

SHAME → ASHAMED, SHAMEFUL
Ps　69: 6　who hope in you be put to **s** because
Eze　39:26　They shall forget their **s,** and all
Da　12: 2　some to **s** and everlasting contempt.
1Co　1:27　foolish in the world to **s** the wise;
Heb　12: 2　endured the cross, disregarding its **s,**
1Jn　2:28　be put to **s** before him at his coming.

SHAMEFUL → SHAME
2Co　4: 2　We have renounced the **s** things
Eph　5:12　For it is **s** even to mention

SHAMGAR*
　　Judge; killed 600 Philistines (Jdg 3:31; 5:6).

SHARE
Nu　18:20　I am your **s** and your possession
Lk　3:11　"Whoever has two coats must **s**
Ro　15:27　for if the Gentiles have come to **s**
Col　1:12　to **s** in the inheritance of the saints
Heb　12:10　in order that we may **s** his holiness.
Jude　1: 3　to you about the salvation we **s,**

SHARP → SHARPENS, SHARPER
Pr　5: 4　**s** as a two-edged sword,
Rev　19:15　a **s** sword with which to strike down

SHARPENS → SHARP
Pr　27:17　Iron **s** iron, and one person **s**

SHARPER* → SHARP
Heb　4:12　**s** than any two-edged sword,

SHEBA
　　1. Benjamite; rebelled against David (2Sa 20).
　　2. Queen of Sheba (1Ki 10; 2Ch 9; Mt 12:42;
Lk 11:31).

SHECHEM
　　1. Raped Jacob's daughter Dinah; killed (Ge
34).
　　2. City where Joshua renewed the covenant (Jos
24). Abimelech as king (Jdg 9).

SHED → BLOODSHED, SHEDDING
Ge　9: 6　shall that person's blood be **s;**
Pr　6:17　and hands that **s** innocent blood,
Mt　23:35　may come all the righteous blood **s**
Rev　16: 6　**s** the blood of saints and prophets,

SHEDDING → SHED
Heb	9:22	without the **s** of blood there is no
	12: 4	resisted to the point of **s** your blood.

SHEEP
1Ki	22:17	like **s** that have no shepherd;
Ps	100: 3	people, and the **s** of his pasture.
Isa	53: 6	All we like **s** have gone astray;
Eze	34:15	myself will be the shepherd of my **s**,
Zec	13: 7	shepherd, that the **s** may be scattered;
Mt	9:36	like **s** without a shepherd.
Lk	15: 4	a hundred **s** and losing one of them,
Jn	10: 7	I am the gate for the **s**.
	10:15	And I lay down my life for the **s**.
Heb	13:20	the great shepherd of the **s**,
1Pe	2:25	For you were going astray like **s**,

SHELTER
Ps	91: 1	who live in the **s** of the Most High,
Rev	7:15	is seated on the throne will **s** them.

SHEM
Son of Noah (Ge 5:32; 6:10). Blessed (Ge 9:26). Descendants (Ge 10:21-31; 11:10-32; Lk 3:36).

SHEOL
Nu	16:30	and they go down alive into **S**,
Job	26: 6	**S** is naked before God,
Ps	139: 8	if I make my bed in **S**, you are there.
Isa	28:15	and with **S** we have an agreement;
Hos	13:14	O **S**, where is your destruction?

SHEPHERD → SHEPHERDS
2Sa	7: 7	whom I commanded to **s** my people
Ps	23: 1	The LORD is my **s**, I shall not want.
Ecc	12:11	sayings that are given by one **s**.
Isa	40:11	He will feed his flock like a **s**;
Mt	2: 6	ruler who is to **s** my people Israel.'"
	26:31	strike the **s**, and the sheep of the flock
Jn	10:11	"I am the good **s**.
Heb	13:20	the great **s** of the sheep,
1Pe	5: 4	And when the chief **s** appears,

SHEPHERDS → SHEPHERD
Eze	34: 2	prophesy against the **s** of Israel:
Lk	2: 8	there were **s** living in the fields,

SHIELD
Ge	15: 1	I am your **s**; your reward shall be
Ps	7:10	God is my **s**, who saves the upright
Eph	6:16	With all of these, take the **s** of faith,

SHILOH
1Sa	1:24	to the house of the LORD at **S**;

SHIMEI
Cursed David (2Sa 16:5-14); spared (2Sa 19:16-23). Killed by Solomon (1Ki 2:8-9, 36-46).

SHINE → SHINES, SHINING
Nu	6:25	LORD make his face to **s** upon you,
Ps	4: 6	light of your face **s** on us, O LORD!"
Isa	60: 1	**s**; for your light has come,
Da	12: 3	Those who are wise shall **s** like the
Mt	5:16	let your light **s** before others,
Eph	5:14	the dead, and Christ will **s** on you."

SHINES → SHINE
Jn	1: 5	The light **s** in the darkness,

SHINING → SHINE
2Pe	1:19	to this as to a lamp **s** in a dark place,
1Jn	2: 8	and the true light is already **s**.

SHORT
Isa	59: 1	the LORD's hand is not too **s** to save,
Mt	24:22	if those days had not been cut **s**,
Ro	3:23	sinned and fall **s** of the glory of God;

SHOUT
Ps	47: 1	**s** to God with loud songs of joy.
Zec	9: 9	**S** aloud, O daughter Jerusalem!
Lk	19:40	were silent, the stones would **s** out."

SHOW → SHOWED
Ge	12: 1	to the land that I will **s** you.

Ex	33:18	Moses said, "**S** me your glory,
Ps	85: 7	**S** us your steadfast love, O LORD.
Jn	14: 8	said to him, "Lord, **s** us the Father,
1Co	12:31	will **s** you a still more excellent way
Rev	4: 1	I will **s** you what must take place

SHOWED → SHOW
Dt	34: 1	the LORD **s** him the whole land:
Jn	20:20	he **s** them his hands and his side.

SHOWERS
Dt	32: 2	rain on grass, like **s** on new growth.
Eze	34:26	they shall be **s** of blessing.

SHUT
Isa	22:22	he shall open, and no one shall **s**;
Da	6:22	God sent his angel and **s** the lions'
Rev	3: 7	who opens and no one will **s**,

SICK → SICKNESS
Mt	8:16	and cured all who were **s**.
	9:12	of a physician, but those who are **s**.
Jas	5:14	Are any among you **s**?

SICKLE
Joel	3:13	Put in the **s**, for the harvest is ripe.
Rev	14:14	and a sharp **s** in his hand!

SICKNESS → SICK
Ex	23:25	I will take **s** away from among you.
Mt	4:23	and curing every disease and every **s**

SIDE → ASIDE
Ps	91: 7	A thousand may fall at your **s**,
	124: 1	the LORD who was on our **s**
Jn	19:34	soldiers pierced his **s** with a spear,

SIFT
Isa	30:28	to **s** the nations with the sieve of
Lk	22:31	Satan has demanded to **s** all of you

SIGHT → SEE
Ge	6:11	the earth was corrupt in God's **s**,
Ps	72:14	and precious is their blood in his **s**.
Mt	11: 5	blind receive their **s**, the lame walk,
2Co	5: 7	for we walk by faith, not by **s**.
1Pe	3: 4	which is very precious in God's **s**.

SIGN → SIGNS
Ge	9:12	the **s** of the covenant that I make
	17:11	a **s** of the covenant between me
Isa	7:14	the Lord himself will give you a **s**.
Mt	24: 3	the **s** of your coming and of the end
Mk	8:12	does this generation ask for a **s**?

SIGNS → SIGN
Ge	1:14	be for **s** and for seasons and for days
Ex	7: 3	I will multiply my **s** and wonders in
Da	6:27	he works **s** and wonders in heaven
Mt	16: 3	cannot interpret the **s** of the times.
Jn	20:30	Jesus did many other **s** in the
1Co	1:22	Jews demand **s** and Greeks desire
Rev	16:14	demonic spirits, performing **s**,

SILAS
Prophet (Ac 15:22-32); co-worker with Paul on second missionary journey (Ac 16-18; 2Co 1:19). Co-writer with Paul (1Th 1:1; 2Th 1:1); Peter (1Pe 5:12).

SILENT
Isa	53: 7	a sheep that before its shearers is **s**,
Zep	1: 7	Be **s** before the Lord GOD!
Mk	14:61	But he was **s** and did not answer.
1Co	14:34	women should be **s** in the churches.

SILVER
Ps	66:10	you have tried us as **s** is tried.
Pr	8:10	Take my instruction instead of **s**,
Isa	48:10	I have refined you, but not like **s**;
Zec	13: 9	refine them as one refines **s**,
Mt	26:15	They paid him thirty pieces of **s**.
Ac	3: 6	But Peter said, "I have no **s** or gold,
1Co	3:12	on the foundation with gold, **s**,

SIMEON → =SIMON
1. Son of Jacob by Leah (Ge 29:33; 35:23; 1Ch 2:1). With Levi killed Shechem for rape of Dinah

(Ge 34:25-29). Held hostage by Joseph in Egypt (Ge 42:24-43:23). Tribe of blessed (Ge 49:5-7), numbered (Nu 1:23; 26:14), allotted land (Jos 19:1-9; Eze 48:24), 12,000 from (Rev 7:7).

2. Godly Jew who blessed the infant Jesus (2:25-35).

3. See Peter (Ac 15:14; 2Pe 1:1).

SIMON → =PETER, =SIMEON
1. See Peter.

2. Apostle; the Zealot (Mt 10:4; Mk 3:18; Lk 6:15; Ac 1:13).

3. Samaritan sorcerer (Ac 8:9-24).

SIMPLE
Ps	19: 7	are sure, making wise the **s**;
Pr	1:22	O **s** ones, will you love being **s**?
	14:15	The **s** believe everything,

SIN → SINFUL, SINNED, SINNER, SINNERS, SINS
Ge	4: 7	not do well, **s** is lurking at the door;
Ex	32:32	if you will only forgive their **s**—
Nu	32:23	and be sure your **s** will find you out.
1Ki	8:46	"If they **s** against you—
2Ch	7:14	forgive their **s** and heal their land.
Ps	119:11	so that I may not **s** against you.
Isa	53:12	yet he bore the **s** of many,
Mt	5:29	If your right eye causes you to **s**,
Jn	1:29	who takes away the **s** of the world!
Ro	6:23	For the wages of **s** is death,
2Co	5:21	made him to be **s** who knew no **s**,
Heb	4:15	tested as we are, yet without **s**.
1Jn	1: 7	Jesus his Son cleanses us from all **s**.
Tob	12:10	but those who commit **s**
Wis	10:13	but delivered him from **s**.
Sir	3:30	so almsgiving atones for **s**.

SINAI → =HOREB
Ex	19:20	the LORD descended upon Mount **S**,
Ps	68:17	the Lord came from **S** into the holy
Gal	4:25	Now Hagar is Mount **S** in Arabia

SINFUL → SIN
Lk	5: 8	from me, Lord, for I am a **s** man!"
Ro	8: 3	Son in the likeness of **s** flesh,
1Mc	1:10	From them came forth a **s** root,

SING → SINGERS, SONG, SONGS, SUNG
Ex	15: 1	"I will **s** to the LORD,
Ps	47: 6	**S** praises to God, **s** praises;
Isa	5: 1	**s** for my beloved my love-song
1Co	14:15	I will **s** praise with the spirit,
Col	3:16	gratitude in your hearts **s** psalms,
Rev	5: 9	They **s** a new song:
Jdt	16:13	I will **s** to my God a new song:
Aza	1:35	**s** praise to him and highly exalt him

SINGERS → SING
1Ch	15:16	to appoint their kindred as the **s**
Ezr	2:70	and the **s**, the gatekeepers,

SINGLE
Mt	6:27	worrying add a **s** hour to your span
Rev	21:21	each of the gates is a **s** pearl,

SINNED → SIN
Nu	14:40	LORD has promised, for we have **s**."
Ps	51: 4	Against you, you alone, have I **s**,
La	5: 7	Our ancestors **s**; they are no more,
Ro	3:23	all have **s** and fall short of the glory of God;
1Jn	1:10	If we say that we have not **s**,
Sir	18:21	and when you have **s**, repent.

SINNER → SIN
Lk	15: 7	over one **s** who repents than
Jas	5:20	that whoever brings back a **s**

SINNERS → SIN
Ps	1: 1	or take the path that **s** tread,
Pr	23:17	Do not let your heart envy **s**,
Lk	6:33	For even **s** do the same.
Ro	5: 8	we still were **s** Christ died for us.
1Ti	1:15	Jesus came into the world to save **s**

SINS → SIN
1Sa 2:25 but if someone **s** against the LORD,
Ps 103:10 not deal with us according to our **s**,
Isa 1:18 your **s** are like scarlet, they shall be
Eze 18: 4 only the person who **s** that shall die.
Mic 7:19 cast all our **s** into the depths of the
Mt 9: 6 has authority on earth to
forgive **s**"—
Mk 1: 5 the river Jordan, confessing their **s**.
Lk 11: 4 forgive us our **s**, for we ourselves
Ac 3:19 to God so that your **s** may be wiped
1Co 15: 3 Christ died for our **s** in accordance
Heb 9:28 offered once to bear the **s** of many,
1Jn 1: 9 If we confess our **s**, he who is
faithful
Rev 1: 5 loves us and freed us from our **s**
Sir 2:11 he forgives **s** and saves

SISTER
Ge 12:13 Say you are my **s**, so that it may go
20: 2 of his wife Sarah, "She is my **s**."
Pr 7: 4 Say to wisdom, "You are my **s**,"
Mk 3:35 the will of God is my brother and **s**

SIT → SAT, SITS
Ps 1: 1 or **s** in the seat of scoffers;
110: 1 says to my lord, "**S** at my right hand
Jer 33:17 never lack a man to **s** on the throne
Mt 20:23 to **s** at my right hand and at my left,
Heb 1:13 "**S** at my right hand until I make

SITS → SIT
Ps 2: 4 He who **s** in the heavens laughs;
Isa 28: 6 to the one who **s** in judgment,

SIX
Ex 20: 9 **S** days you shall labor and do all
Pr 6:16 are **s** things that the LORD hates,
Isa 6: 2 above him; each had **s** wings:
Rev 4: 8 each of them with **s** wings,

SKILL
Ex 28: 3 whom I have endowed with **s**,
1Ki 7:14 he was full of **s**, intelligence,

SKIN
Job 2: 4 Satan answered the LORD, "**S** for s!
19:26 after my **s** has been thus destroyed,
Jer 13:23 Can Ethiopians change their **s**

SKULL
2Ki 9:35 they found no more of her than the **s**
Mt 27:33 Golgotha (which means Place of a **S**)

SKY
Dt 28:23 **s** over your head shall be bronze,
Mt 16: 3 to interpret the appearance of the **s**,
Rev 6:14 The **s** vanished like a scroll rolling

SLANDER → SLANDERED
Ps 15: 3 who do not **s** with their tongue,
Pr 10:18 and whoever utters **s** is a fool.
Mt 15:19 fornication, theft, false witness, **s**.
1Pe 2: 1 all guile, insincerity, envy, and all **s**.

SLANDERED → SLANDER
1Co 4:13 when **s**, we speak kindly.

SLAUGHTER → SLAUGHTERED
Pr 7:22 and goes like an ox to the **s**,
Isa 53: 7 like a lamb that is led to the **s**,
Zec 11: 4 a shepherd of the flock doomed to **s**.
Ac 8:32 "Like a sheep he was led to the **s**,

SLAUGHTERED → SLAUGHTER
Rev 5: 6 a Lamb standing as if it had been **s**,
6: 9 who had been **s** for the word of God

SLAVE → ENSLAVE, ENSLAVED, SLAVERY, SLAVES
Ge 21:10 Cast out this **s** woman with her son;
Mk 10:44 first among you must be **s** of all.
Jn 8:34 who commits sin is a **s** to sin.
Gal 3:28 there is no longer **s** or free,

SLAVERY → SLAVE
Ex 20: 2 out of the house of **s**;
Ro 7:14 of the flesh, sold into **s** under sin.

Gal 5: 1 do not submit again to a yoke
of **s**.

SLAVES → SLAVE
Ro 6:16 are **s** of the one whom you obey,
2Pe 2:19 people are **s** to whatever masters

SLEEP → ASLEEP, SLEEPER, SLEEPING
Ge 2:21 God caused a deep **s** to fall upon
15:12 a deep **s** fell upon Abram,
Ps 121: 4 keeps Israel will neither slumber
nor **s**.
Da 12: 2 Many of those who **s** in the dust of

SLEEPER → SLEEP
Eph 5:14 "**S**, awake! Rise from the dead,

SLEEPING → SLEEP
Mt 9:24 for the girl is not dead but **s**."
26:40 to the disciples and found them **s**;

SLING
1Sa 17:50 over the Philistine with a **s** and a
stone,

SLIP
Dt 32:35 for the time when their foot shall **s**;
Ps 37:31 their steps do not **s**.

SLOW → SLOWNESS
Ex 34: 6 merciful and gracious, **s** to anger,
Nu 14:18 The LORD is **s** to anger,
Ps 145: 8 **s** to anger and abounding in
Na 1: 3 The LORD is **s** to anger but great in
Lk 24:25 and how **s** of heart to believe all that
2Pe 3: 9 The Lord is not **s** about his promise,
Tob 12: 6 Do not be **s** to acknowledge him.
Sir 5: 4 for the Lord is **s** to anger.

SLOWNESS → SLOW
2Pe 3: 9 think of **s**, but is patient with you,

SMALL → SMALLEST
Jas 3: 5 So also the tongue is a **s** member,

SMALLEST → SMALL
Mk 4:31 is the **s** of all the seeds on earth;

SMOKE → SMOKING
Ex 19:18 Now Mount Sinai was wrapped in **s**,
Isa 6: 4 and the house filled with **s**.
Joel 2:30 blood and fire and columns of **s**.
Rev 15: 8 with **s** from the glory of God and

SMOKING → SMOKE
Ge 15:17 **s** fire pot and a flaming torch passed
Ex 20:18 of the trumpet, and the mountain **s**,

SNAKE
Ex 4: 3 and it became a **s**; and Moses drew
Lk 11:11 will give a **s** instead of a fish?

SNARE
Ex 23:33 it will surely be a **s** to you.
Jdg 2: 3 their gods shall be a **s** to you."

SNOW
Ps 51: 7 and I shall be whiter than **s**.
Isa 1:18 sins are like scarlet, they shall be
like **s**;
Da 7: 9 his clothing was white as **s**,
Rev 1:14 as white wool, white as **s**;

SOBER
1Th 5: 6 but let us keep awake and be **s**;
2Ti 4: 5 always be **s**, endure suffering,

SODOM
Ge 19:24 rained on **S** and Gomorrah sulfur
Isa 1: 9 we would have been like **S**,
Lk 10:12 it will be more tolerable for **S** than
Rev 11: 8 city that is prophetically called **S**

SOLDIERS
Mt 28:12 give a large sum of money to the **s**,
Jn 19:23 When the **s** had crucified Jesus,

SOLID
1Co 3: 2 I fed you with milk, not **s** food,
Heb 5:14 But **s** food is for the mature,

SOLOMON
Son of David by Bathsheba; king of Judah (2Sa 12:24; 1Ch 3:5, 10). Appointed king by David (1Ki 1); adversaries Adonijah, Joab, Shimei killed by Benaiah (1Ki 2). Asked for wisdom (1Ki 3; 2Ch 1). Judged between two prostitutes (1Ki 3:16-28). Built temple (1Ki 5-7; 2Ch 2-5); prayer of dedication (1Ki 8; 2Ch 6). Visited by Queen of Sheba (1Ki 10; 2Ch 9). Wives turned his heart from God (1Ki 11:1-13). Jeroboam rebelled against (1Ki 11:26-40). Death (1Ki 11:41-43; 2Ch 9:29-31).
Proverbs of (1Ki 4:32; Pr 1:1; 10:1; 25:1); psalms of (Ps 72; 127); song of (SS 1:1).

SON → SONS
Ge 21: 2 conceived and bore Abraham a **s**
Ex 4:23 now I will kill your firstborn **s**.'"
2Sa 7:14 and he shall be a **s** to me.
Ps 2: 7 He said to me, "You are my **s**;
Isa 7:14 is with child and shall bear a **s**,
Mt 1:23 virgin shall conceive and bear a **s**,
2:15 "Out of Egypt I have called my **s**."
3:17 from heaven said, "This is my **S**,
12: 8 the **S** of Man is lord of the sabbath."
16:16 the Messiah, the **S** of the living God."
Mk 10:45 **S** of Man came not to be served
but to
Lk 1:35 he will be called **S** of God.
20:44 so how can he be his **s**?"
Jn 1:34 testified that this is the **S** of God."
3:16 loved the world that he gave his
only **S**,
Ro 8:29 be conformed to the image of his **S**,
1Th 1:10 to wait for his **S** from heaven,
Heb 1: 2 last days he has spoken to us by a **S**,
1: 5 my **S**; today I have begotten you"?
2Pe 1:17 saying, "This is my **S**, my Beloved,
1Jn 4: 9 God sent his only **S** into the world
Rev 12: 5 she gave birth to a **s**, a male child,
14:14 the cloud was one like the **S** of Man,
Sir 4:10 be like a **s** of the Most High,
2Es 13:32 then my **S** will be revealed,

SONG → SING
Ex 15: 1 sang this **s** to the LORD:
Dt 31:21 **s** will confront them as a witness,
Ps 40: 3 He put a new **s** in my mouth,
Rev 5: 9 They sing a new **s**: "You are worthy
15: 3 and the **s** of the Lamb:

SONGS → SING
1Ki 4:32 his **s** numbered a thousand and five.
Ps 137: 3 "Sing us one of the **s** of Zion!"
Col 3:16 hymns, and spiritual **s** to God.

SONS → SON
Ge 6: 2 the **s** of God saw that they were fair;
35:22 Now the **s** of Jacob were twelve.
Dt 7: 3 giving your daughters to their **s**
Ac 2:17 **s** and your daughters shall prophesy,
2Co 6:18 you shall be my **s** and daughters,

SOON
Isa 56: 1 for **s** my salvation will come,
Rev 22:20 says, "Surely I am coming **s**."

SORCERERS → SORCERY
Rev 22:15 Outside are the dogs and **s** and

SORCERY → SORCERERS
Gal 5:20 **s**, enmities, strife, jealousy, anger,
Rev 18:23 all nations were deceived by your **s**.

SORROW → SORROWFUL
Est 9:22 turned for them from **s** into gladness
Ecc 1:18 who increase knowledge increase **s**.
Isa 35:10 and **s** and sighing shall flee away.

SORROWFUL → SORROW
2Co 6:10 as **s**, yet always rejoicing;

SOUL → SOULS
Dt 6: 5 all your **s**, and with all your might.
Jos 22: 5 all your heart and with all your **s**."
Ps 16: 9 heart is glad, and my **s** rejoices;

Ps   25: 1 To you, O LORD, I lift up my **s**.
      42: 1 so my **s** longs for you, O God.
Mic   6: 7 fruit of my body for the sin of
          my **s**?"
Mt 10:28 fear him who can destroy both **s** and
Heb 4:12 piercing until it divides **s** from spirit
Jas 5:20 will save the sinner's **s** from death
3Jn 1: 2 just as it is well with your **s**.
Sir 7:29 With all your **s** fear the Lord,

SOULS → SOUL
Jer 6:16 walk in it, and find rest for your **s**.
Mt 11:29 and you will find rest for your **s**.
1Pe 2:25 the shepherd and guardian of your **s**.

SOUND
Eze 1:24 like the **s** of mighty waters,
1Co 15:52 For the trumpet will **s**, and the dead
2Ti 4: 3 will not put up with **s** doctrine,
Tit 1: 9 able both to preach with **s** doctrine
Rev 1:15 voice was like the **s** of many waters.

SOUR
Jer 31:29 "The parents have eaten **s** grapes,
Mk 15:36 filled a sponge with **s** wine,

SOVEREIGN → SOVEREIGNTY
1Ki 4:21 Solomon was **s** over all the
Rev 6:10 "**S** Lord, holy and true, how long

SOVEREIGNTY → SOVEREIGN
Da 4:34 For his **s** is an everlasting **s**,

SOW → SOWED, SOWS
Ex 23:10 For six years you shall **s** your land
Ecc 11: 6 In the morning **s** your seed,
Hos 10:12 **S** for yourselves righteousness;
Mt 13: 3 A sower went out to **s**.
1Co 15:36 **s** does not come to life unless it dies.

SOWED → SOW
Mt 13:24 to someone who **s** good seed
Lk 13:19 took and **s** in the garden;

SOWS → SOW
Jn 4:37 'One **s** and another reaps.'
2Co 9: 6 who **s** sparingly will also reap

SPAN
Isa 40:12 marked off the heavens with a **s**,
Mt 6:27 add a single hour to your **s** of life?

SPARE
Ro 11:21 perhaps he will not **s** you.
2Pe 2: 4 if God did not **s** the angels when

SPARROWS
Lk 12: 7 you are of more value than many **s**.

SPEAK → SPEAKING, SPEECH, SPOKE
Ge 18:27 take it upon myself to **s** to the Lord,
Nu 12: 8 With him I **s** face to face—
Dt 18:20 presumes to **s** in my name a word
Job 13: 3 But I would **s** to the Almighty,
Ecc 3: 7 time to keep silence, and a time to **s**;
Mt 13:13 The reason I **s** to them in parables is
Ac 2: 4 began to **s** in other languages,
1Co 12:30 Do all **s** in tongues?
Jas 1:19 be quick to listen, slow to **s**,
Sir 4:25 Never **s** against the truth,

SPEAKING → SPEAK
1Co 14:39 and do not forbid **s** in tongues;
Eph 4:15 But **s** the truth in love,

SPEAR → SPEARS
1Sa 19:10 to pin David to the wall with the **s**;
Jn 19:34 the soldiers pierced his side with a **s**,

SPEARS → SPEAR
Joel 3:10 and your pruning hooks into **s**;
Mic 4: 3 and their **s** into pruning hooks;

SPECK
Mt 7: 4 'Let me take the **s** out of your eye,'

SPECTACLE
1Co 4: 9 we have become a **s** to the world,

SPEECH → SPEAK
Ex 4:10 I am slow of **s** and slow of tongue."
Ps 19: 3 There is no **s**, nor are there words;
1Ti 4:12 set the believers an example in **s**
1Jn 3:18 let us love, not in word or **s**,
Sir 4:29 Do not be reckless in your **s**,

SPICES
Ex 25: 6 **s** for the anointing oil and for
Jn 19:40 wrapped it with the **s** in linen cloths,

SPIES → SPY
Nu 13:32 we have gone through as **s**
Jos 2: 1 two men secretly from Shittim as **s**,

SPIRIT → SPIRITS, SPIRITUAL
Ge 6: 3 My **s** shall not abide in mortals
          forever,
Nu 11:25 **s** rested upon them, they
          prophesied.
2Ki 2: 9 inherit a double share of your **s**."
Ne 9:20 You gave your good **s** to instruct
Job 33: 4 The **s** of God has made me,
Ps 31: 5 Into your hand I commit my **s**;
     51:17 acceptable to God is a broken **s**;
Pr 16:18 and a haughty **s** before a fall.
Isa 42: 1 I have put my **s** upon him;
Eze 36:26 and a new **s** I will put within you;
Joel 2:28 I will pour out my **s** on all flesh;
Mt 1:18 to be with child from the Holy **S**.
      5: 3 "Blessed are the poor in **s**,
    12:31 against the **S** will not be forgiven.
    26:41 the **s** indeed is willing, but the flesh
Mk 1: 8 will baptize you with the Holy **S**."
Jn 3: 5 without being born of water and **S**.
      4:24 God is **s**, and those who worship
          him must worship in **s** and truth."
      6:63 It is the **s** that gives life;
   14:26 But the Advocate, the Holy **S**,
Ac 2: 4 of them were filled with the Holy **S**
Ro 8: 9 not in the flesh; you are in the **S**,
      8:26 the **S** helps us in our weakness;
1Co 6:19 your body is a temple of the Holy **S**
    12: 4 are varieties of gifts, but the same **S**;
2Co 3: 6 the letter kills, but the **S** gives life.
Gal 5:22 the fruit of the **S** is love, joy, peace,
Eph 1:13 the seal of the promised Holy **S**;
      4:30 do not grieve the Holy **S** of God,
      5:18 but be filled with the **S**,
1Th 5:19 Do not quench the **S**.
Heb 4:12 piercing until it divides soul from **s**,
1Pe 3: 4 lasting beauty of a gentle and quiet **s**
1Jn 4: 1 Beloved, do not believe every **s**,
Rev 1:10 I was in the **s** on the Lord's day,

SPIRITS → SPIRIT
Nu 16:22 the God of the **s** of all flesh,
Dt 18:11 or who consults ghosts or **s**,
Lk 4:36 power he commands the unclean **s**,
1Co 12:10 to another the discernment of **s**,
Gal 4: 9 we were enslaved to the elemental **s**
Rev 1: 4 seven **s** who are before his throne,

SPIRITUAL → SPIRIT
Ro 7:14 For we know that the law is **s**;
1Co 2:13 interpreting **s** things to those who
          are **s**.
    12: 1 Now concerning **s** gifts,
    14: 1 Pursue love and strive for the **s** gifts,
    15:46 the **s** that is first, but the physical,
Eph 1: 3 every **s** blessing in the heavenly
Col 1: 9 of God's will in all **s** wisdom
1Pe 2: 2 infants, long for the pure, **s** milk,
      2: 5 yourselves be built into a **s** house,

SPIT
Mk 14:65 began to **s** on him, to blindfold him,
Rev 3:16 am about to **s** you out of my mouth.

SPLENDOR
1Ch 16:29 Worship the LORD in holy **s**;
Eph 5:27 to present the church to himself in **s**,

SPOKE → SPEAK
Mk 4:33 many such parables he **s** the word

SPOT
1Co 13:11 When I was a child, I **s** like a child,
Heb 1: 1 Long ago God **s** to our ancestors in
2Pe 1:21 moved by the Holy Spirit **s** from

SPOT
Eph 5:27 without a **s** or wrinkle or anything
2Pe 3:14 at peace, without **s** or blemish;

SPRING
Isa 45: 8 earth open, that salvation may **s** up,
Jn 4:14 a **s** of water gushing up to eternal
          life."
Rev 21: 6 from the **s** of the water of life.

SPRINKLE → SPRINKLED
Nu 8: 7 **s** the water of purification on them,
Eze 36:25 I will **s** clean water upon you,

SPRINKLED → SPRINKLE
Lev 8:11 He **s** some of it on the altar seven
Heb 10:22 with our hearts **s** clean from an evil
1Pe 1: 2 and to be **s** with his blood:

SPY → SPIES
Nu 13: 2 men to **s** out the land of Canaan,
Jos 6:25 whom Joshua sent to **s** out Jericho.

STAFF
Ge 49:10 the ruler's **s** from between his feet,
Ex 4: 4 and it became a **s** in his hand—
Nu 17: 6 the **s** of Aaron was among theirs.
Ps 23: 4 your rod and your **s**—they comfort
          me.
Zec 11:10 I took my Favor and broke it,

STAND → STANDING
Ex 14:13 "Do not be afraid, **s** firm,
Job 19:25 at the last he will **s** upon the earth;
Ps 1: 5 wicked will not **s** in the judgment,
Isa 7: 9 If you do not **s** firm in faith,
Mt 12:25 house divided against itself will **s**.
Ro 14: 4 for the Lord is able to make them **s**.
    14:10 all **s** before the judgment seat of
          God.
Eph 6:11 may be able to **s** against the wiles of

STANDARDS
Jn 8:15 You judge by human **s**; I judge no
1Co 1:26 of you were wise by human **s**,

STANDING → STAND
1Co 10:12 So if you think you are **s**,
Jas 5: 9 See, the Judge is a **s** the doors!
Rev 3:20 I am **s** at the door, knocking;

STAR → STARS
Nu 24:17 a **s** shall come out of Jacob,
Isa 14:12 are fallen from heaven, O Day **S**,
Mt 2: 2 For we observed his **s** at its rising,
2Pe 1:19 day dawns and the morning **s** rises
Rev 9: 1 saw a **s** that had fallen from heaven
    22:16 of David, the bright morning **s**."

STARS → STAR
Ge 1:16 to rule the night—and the **s**.
Job 38: 7 when the morning **s** sang together
Ps 148: 3 praise him, all you shining **s**!
Da 12: 3 like the **s** forever and ever.
Php 2:15 you shine like **s** in the world.
Rev 1:16 In his right hand he held seven **s**,
    12: 4 a third of the **s** of heaven and threw

STATUE
Da 2:31 there was a great **s**.

STATUTE → STATUTES
Lev 16:29 This shall be a **s** to you forever:
Nu 19:21 It shall be a perpetual **s** for them.

STATUTES → STATUTE
Ge 26: 5 commandments, my **s**, and my laws.
Dt 4: 1 give heed to the **s** and ordinances
Ne 9:13 good **s** and commandments,
Ps 119: 8 I will observe your **s**;

STEADFAST
Ex 34: 6 abounding in **s** love and faithfulness
Nu 14:18 and abounding in **s** love,

STEADFAST (cont.)

2Sa 7:15 I will not take my **s** love from him,
Ps 57: 7 My heart is **s**, O God, my heart is **s**.
136: 1 for his **s** love endures forever.
Heb 6:19 a sure and **s** anchor of the soul,
1Pe 5: 9 Resist him, **s** in your faith,

STEAL

Ex 20:15 You shall not **s**.
Mt 6:19 and where thieves break in and **s**;
Jn 10:10 The thief comes only to **s** and kill

STEPHEN*

Early church leader (Ac 6:5). Arrested (Ac 6:8-
15). Speech to Sanhedrin (Ac 7). Stoned (Ac 7:54-
60; 8:2; 11:19; 22:20).

STEPS

Pr 16: 9 but the LORD directs the **s**.
1Pe 2:21 so that you should follow in his **s**.

STIFF-NECKED → NECK

Ex 32: 9 "I have seen this people, how **s**
Ac 7:51 "You **s** people, uncircumcised in

STILL

Ex 14:14 and you have only to keep **s**."
Jos 10:13 sun stood **s**, and the moon stopped,
Ps 46:10 "Be **s**, and know that I am God!
Mk 4:39 said to the sea, "Peace! Be **s**!"
Ro 5: 8 we **s** were sinners Christ died for us.
Heb 11: 4 but through his faith he **s** speaks.

STING

1Co 15:55 Where, O death, is your **s**?"

STONE → CORNERSTONE, MILLSTONE, STONED, STONES

Ge 28:18 the **s** that he had put under his head
Ex 28:10 six of their names on the one **s**,
31:18 tablets of **s**, written with the finger of
1Sa 17:50 the Philistine with a sling and a **s**,
Ps 118:22 The **s** that the builders rejected has
Isa 28:16 in Zion a foundation **s**, a tested **s**,
Eze 36:26 from your body the heart of **s**
Mt 4: 6 will not dash your foot against a **s**.'"
Mk 12:10 'The **s** that the builders rejected has
16: 3 "Who will roll away the **s** for us
Ro 9:32 have stumbled over the stumbling **s**,
2Co 3: 3 not on tablets of **s** but on tablets
1Pe 2: 4 living **s**, though rejected by mortals
Rev 2:17 and I will give a white **s**,

STONED → STONE

2Ch 24:21 by command of the king they **s** him
Ac 14:19 Then they **s** Paul and dragged him
Heb 11:37 **s** to death, they were sawn in two,

STONES → STONE

Ex 28:21 twelve **s** with names corresponding
Jos 4: 3 'Take twelve **s** from here out of the
1Sa 17:40 chose five smooth **s** from the wadi,
Mt 3: 9 God is able from these **s** to raise
Lk 19:40 were silent, the **s** would shout out"
1Co 3:12 precious **s**, wood, hay, straw—
1Pe 2: 5 like living **s**, let yourselves be built

STORE → STOREHOUSE, STORING

Pr 7: 1 and **s** up my commandments
Mt 6:19 Do not **s** up for yourselves treasures

STOREHOUSE → HOUSE, STORE

Dt 28:12 LORD will open for you his rich **s**,
Mal 3:10 Bring the full tithe into the **s**,

STORING* → STORE

Ro 2: 5 you are **s** up wrath for yourself
1Ti 6:19 **s** up for themselves the treasure of

STRAIGHT

Pr 3: 6 and he will make **s** your paths.
Isa 40: 3 **s** in the desert a highway for our God.
Mt 3: 3 way of the Lord, make his paths **s**.'"
Ac 9:11 Get up and go to the street called **S**,
Sir 2: 6 make your ways **s**, and hope in him.

STRANGE → STRANGER, STRANGERS

Dt 32:16 They made him jealous with **s** gods,
1Co 14:21 "By people of **s** tongues and by the

STRANGER → STRANGE

Dt 10:19 You shall also love the **s**,
Mt 25:35 I was a **s** and you welcomed me,

STRANGERS → STRANGE

Dt 10:19 for you were **s** in the land of Egypt.
Ro 12:13 extend hospitality to **s**.
Eph 2:12 and **s** to the covenants of promise,
Heb 11:13 They confessed that they were **s**

STRAW

Ex 5:10 says Pharaoh, 'I will not give you **s**.
1Co 3:12 precious stones, wood, hay, **s**—

STRAY → ASTRAY

Ps 119:10 not let me **s** from your commandments.
Pr 22: 6 and when old, they will not **s**.

STREAM → STREAMS

Isa 2: 2 all the nations shall **s** to it.
Am 5:24 righteousness like an ever-flowing **s**

STREAMS → STREAM

Ps 1: 3 like trees planted by **s** of water,
42: 1 As a deer longs for flowing **s**,

STREET

Pr 1:20 Wisdom cries out in the **s**;
Mt 6: 5 the synagogues and at the **s** corners,
Rev 21:21 and the **s** of the city is pure gold,

STRENGTH → STRONG

Ex 15: 2 The LORD is my **s** and my might,
1Ch 16:11 Seek the LORD and his **s**,
Ne 8:10 for the joy of the LORD is your **s**."
Ps 46: 1 God is our refuge and **s**,
Pr 31:25 **S** and dignity are her clothing,
Isa 40:31 for the LORD shall renew their **s**,
Mk 12:30 all your mind, and with all your **s**.'
1Co 1:25 God's weakness is stronger than human **s**.
Jdt 9:11 your **s** does not depend on numbers,
1Mc 3:19 but **s** comes from Heaven.

STRENGTHEN → STRONG

Jdg 16:28 and **s** me only this once, O God,
Ps 119:28 **s** me according to your word.
Lk 22:32 have turned back, **s** your brothers."
Heb 12:12 hands and **s** your weak knees,

STRENGTHENS → STRONG

Isa 40:29 to the faint, and **s** the powerless.
Php 4:13 do all things through him who **s** me.

STRETCH → OUTSTRETCHED, STRETCHED

Ex 14:16 and **s** out your hand over the sea
Mk 3: 5 to the man, "**S** out your hand."

STRETCHED → STRETCH

2Sa 24:16 angel **s** out his hand toward Jerusalem
Isa 5:25 and his hand is **s** out still.

STRIFE → STRIVE

Pr 23:29 Who has sorrow? Who has **s**?
Ro 1:29 Full of envy, murder, **s**, deceit,
Gal 5:20 enmities, **s**, jealousy, anger,

STRIKE

Ge 3:15 he will **s** your head, and you will **s**
Ex 17: 6 **S** the rock, and water will come out
Zec 13: 7 **S** the shepherd, that the sheep may
Mal 4: 6 come and **s** the land with a curse.
Mk 14:27 'I will **s** the shepherd, and the sheep
Rev 19:15 to **s** down the nations,

STRIVE → STRIFE

Mt 6:33 But **s** first for the kingdom of God
1Co 12:31 But **s** for the greater gifts.
2Pe 3:14 **s** to be found by him at peace,

STRONG → STRENGTH, STRENGTHEN, STRENGTHENS, STRONGHOLD

Dt 31: 6 Be **s** and bold; have no fear
Jos 1: 6 Be **s** and courageous; for you shall
Ps 140: 7 O LORD, my Lord, my **s** deliverer,
Pr 18:10 The name of the LORD is a **s** tower;
Ecc 9:11 nor the battle to the **s**, nor bread to
SS 8: 6 for love is **s** as death, passion fierce
Ro 15: 1 We who are **s** ought to put up with
1Co 1:27 in the world to shame the **s**;
2Co 12:10 whenever I am weak, then I am **s**.
Eph 6:10 be **s** in the Lord and in the strength

STRONGHOLD → STRONG

Ps 9: 9 The LORD is a **s** for the oppressed,
Na 1: 7 a **s** in a day of trouble;

STRUGGLE

Eph 6:12 our **s** is not against enemies of
Heb 12: 4 In your **s** against sin you have not yet

STUBBORN

Dt 9: 6 for you are a **s** people.
Hos 4:16 Like a **s** heifer, Israel is **s**;

STUDY

Ezr 7:10 Ezra had set his heart to **s** the law
Ecc 12:12 much **s** is a weariness of the flesh.

STUMBLE → STUMBLING

Ps 37:24 we **s**, we shall not fall headlong,
Pr 4:12 and if you run, you will not **s**.
Mt 18: 9 And if your eye causes you to **s**,
Ro 9:33 a stone that will make people **s**,
1Pe 2: 8 **s** because they disobey the word,

STUMBLING → STUMBLE

Eze 14: 3 placed their iniquity as a **s** block
Mt 16:23 You are a **s** block to me;
Ro 11: 9 a **s** block and a retribution for them;
1Co 8: 9 not somehow become a **s** block to

STUMP

Isa 6:13 The holy seed is its **s**.
11: 1 shall come out from the **s** of Jesse,

SUBDUE

Ge 1:28 and fill the earth and **s** it;
1Ch 17:10 and I will **s** all your enemies.

SUBJECT → SUBJECTED

Ro 13: 1 be **s** to the governing authorities;
Gal 4:21 who desire to be **s** to the law,
Eph 5:21 **s** to one another out of reverence

SUBJECTED → SUBJECT

Ro 8:20 for the creation was **s** to futility,
1Co 15:28 When all things are **s** to him,

SUBMISSION* → SUBMIT

1Ti 2:11 a woman learn in silence with full **s**.
Heb 5: 7 was heard because of his reverent **s**.

SUBMISSIVE → SUBMIT

1Ti 3: 4 keeping his children **s** and respectful
Tit 2: 5 kind, being **s** to their husbands,

SUBMIT → SUBMISSION, SUBMISSIVE

Ps 81:11 Israel would not **s** to me.
Gal 5: 1 do not **s** again to a yoke of slavery.
Heb 13:17 Obey your leaders and **s** to them,

SUCCEED → SUCCESS, SUCCESSFUL

Pr 15:22 but with many advisers they **s**.
Ecc 10:10 but wisdom helps one to **s**.

SUCCESS → SUCCEED

Ps 118:25 O LORD, we beseech you, give us **s**!
Sir 10: 5 Human **s** is in the hand of the Lord,

SUCCESSFUL → SUCCEED

Jos 1: 7 that you may be **s** wherever you go.

SUDDENLY

Mal 3: 1 Lord whom you seek will **s** come to
Mk 13:36 find you asleep when he comes **s**.

SUFFER → SUFFERED, SUFFERING,
SUFFERINGS, SUFFERS
Lk   22:15   this Passover with you before I s;
      24:46   the Messiah is to s and to rise from
Heb   9:26   then he would have had to s again
1Pe   3:17   For it is better to s for doing good,

SUFFERED → SUFFER
Php   3: 8   For his sake I have s the loss of all
1Pe   2:21   because Christ also s for you,

SUFFERING → SUFFER
Job   2:13   they saw that his s was very great.
Isa   53: 3   a man of s and acquainted with
Mk   8:31   Son of Man must undergo great s,
Ro   12:12   Rejoice in hope, be patient in s,

SUFFERINGS → SUFFER
Ro   8:18   the s of this present time are not
1Pe   4:13   insofar as you are sharing Christ's s,

SUFFERS → SUFFER
1Co   12:26   If one member s, all suffer together

SUFFICIENT
2Co   12: 9   "My grace is s for you,

SULFUR
Ge   19:24   rained on Sodom and Gomorrah s
Ps   11: 6   he will rain coals of fire and s;
Rev   21: 8   in the lake that burns with fire and s,

SUMMED*
Ro   13: 9   commandment, are s up in this
             word
Gal   5:14   the whole law is s up in a single

SUN
Jos   10:13   And the s stood still,
Ps   84:11   For the LORD God is a s and shield;
Ecc   1: 9   there is nothing new under the s.
Joel   2:31   The s shall be turned to darkness,
Mal   4: 2   the s of righteousness shall rise,
Mt   5:45   he makes his s rise on the evil and
Ac   2:20   The s shall be turned to darkness
Rev   1:16   his face was like the s shining with
      19:17   I saw an angel standing in the s,
      22: 5   they need no light of lamp or s,

SUPERIOR
Heb   1: 4   having become as much s to angels
      7: 7   that the inferior is blessed by the s.

SUPPER
Lk   22:20   he did the same with the cup after s,
Rev   19: 9   to the marriage s of the Lamb."

SUPPLICATION → SUPPLICATIONS
Ps   6: 9   The LORD has heard my s;
Zec   12:10   a spirit of compassion and s
Eph   6:18   at all times in every prayer and s.

SUPPLICATIONS → SUPPLICATION
1Ti   2: 1   then, I urge that s, prayers,
Heb   5: 7   Jesus offered up prayers and s,

SUPPORT
Ps   18:18   but the LORD was my s.
Ro   11:18   that it is not you that s the root,

SURE
Nu   32:23   and be s your sin will find you out.
Ps   19: 7   the decrees of the LORD are s,
Isa   28:16   a s foundation: "One who trusts
Heb   6:19   a s and steadfast anchor of the soul,

SURPASSES → SURPASSING
Eph   3:19   the love of Christ that s knowledge,
Php   4: 7   the peace of God, which s all
Sir   25:11   Fear of the Lord s everything;

SURPASSING → SURPASSES
Ps   150: 2   according to his s greatness!
2Co   9:14   pray for you because of the s grace

SURPRISE → SURPRISED
1Th   5: 4   for that day to s you like a thief;

SURPRISED → SURPRISE
1Pe   4:12   do not be s at the fiery ordeal that is

SURROUNDED → SURROUNDS
Lk   21:20   you see Jerusalem s by armies,
Heb   12: 1   s by so great a cloud of witnesses,
Rev   20: 9   of the earth and s the camp of

SURROUNDS → SURROUNDED
Ps   89: 8   Your faithfulness s you.
      125: 2   so the LORD s his people,

SURVIVORS
Isa   1: 9   of hosts had not left us a few s,
Eze   14:22   Yet, s shall be left in it,

SUSA
Ne   1: 1   while I was in S the capital,
Est   1: 2   his royal throne in the citadel of S,

SUSANNA
     Righteous woman wrongly accused of
immorality (Sus 1:1-44); vindicated by Daniel
(Sus 1:45-64).

SUSTAINS
Ps   3: 5   for the LORD s me.
Heb   1: 3   he s all things by his powerful word.

SWALLOW → SWALLOWED
Jnh   1:17   provided a large fish to s up Jonah;
Mt   23:24   You strain out a gnat but s a camel!

SWALLOWED → SWALLOW
Ge   41: 7   The thin ears s up the seven plump
Nu   16:32   earth opened its mouth and s them
1Co   15:54   "Death has been s up in victory."

SWEAR → SWORE, SWORN
Dt   10:20   and by his name you shall s.
Ps   24: 4   and do not s deceitfully.
Mt   5:34   Do not s at all, either by heaven,

SWEAT
Ge   3:19   By the s of your face you shall eat
Lk   22:44   [[s became like great drops of
             blood]]

SWEET → SWEETER
Ex   15:25   the water, and the water became s.
Ps   119:103   How s are your words to my taste,
Eze   3: 3   in my mouth it was as s as honey.
Rev   10:10   it was s as honey in my mouth,

SWEETER → SWEET
Jdg   14:18   "What is s than honey?
Ps   19:10   s also than honey, and drippings of

SWIFT
Ecc   9:11   the race is not to the s, nor the battle
2Pe   2: 1   bringing s destruction on
             themselves

SWINE
Mt   7: 6   do not throw your pearls before s,
Mk   5:12   "Send us into the s;
1Mc   1:47   sacrifice s and other unclean
             animals,

SWORD → SWORDS
Ge   3:24   and a s flaming and turning to guard
1Sa   17:47   LORD does not save by s and spear;
1Ch   21:30   he was afraid of the s of the angel
Isa   2: 4   shall not lift up s against nation,
      49: 2   He made my mouth like a sharp s,
Hos   2:18   and I will abolish the bow, the s,
Mt   10:34   not come to bring peace, but a s.
Eph   6:17   the s of the Spirit, which is the word
Heb   4:12   sharper than any two-edged s,
Rev   1:16   mouth came a sharp, two-edged s,
      19:15   a sharp s with which to strike down
Sir   21: 3   All lawlessness is like a two-edged s

SWORDS → SWORD
Isa   2: 4   shall beat their s into plowshares,
Joel   3:10   Beat your plowshares into s,

SWORE → SWEAR
Ex   6: 8   the land that I s to give to Abraham,
      32:13   how you s to them by your own self,
Ps   132:11   The LORD s to David a sure oath
Heb   6:13   by whom to swear, he s by himself,

SWORN → SWEAR
Ge   22:16   "By myself I have s, says the LORD:
Ps   110: 4   The LORD has s and will not change
Heb   7:21   "The Lord has s and will not change

SYMPATHIZE* → SYMPATHIZE
Heb   4:15   unable to s with our weaknesses,

SYMPATHY → SYMPATHIZE
Php   2: 1   any compassion and s,
1Pe   3: 8   all of you, have unity of spirit, s,

SYNAGOGUE → SYNAGOGUES
Lk   4:16   he went to the s on the sabbath day,
      8:41   man named Jairus, a leader of the s,
Ac   18:26   He began to speak boldly in the s;

SYNAGOGUES → SYNAGOGUE
Mt   4:23   teaching in their s and proclaiming
Jn   18:20   always taught in s and in the temple,

T

TABERNACLE
Ex   25: 9   concerning the pattern of the t
      40:34   the glory of the LORD filled the t.
1Ch   6:48   for all the service of the t of the
             house

TABITHA* → See DORCAS

TABLE → TABLES
Ex   25:23   You shall make a t of acacia wood,
Ps   23: 5   a t before me in the presence of my

TABLES → TABLE
Mk   11:15   overturned the t of the money
             changers

TABLET → TABLETS
Pr   3: 3   write them on the t of your heart.

TABLETS → TABLET
Ex   31:18   gave him the two t of the covenant,
2Co   3: 3   not on t of stone but on t of human
             hearts.

TAKE → TAKEN, TAKES
Dt   12:32   do not add to it or t anything from
Mt   11:29   T my yoke upon you, and learn
Mk   8:34   deny themselves and t up their cross

TAKEN → TAKE
Ecc   3:14   added to it, nor anything t from it;
Heb   11: 5   By faith Enoch was t so that he did
Sir   44:16   Enoch pleased the Lord and was t

TAKES → TAKE
Jn   1:29   t away the sin of the world!
      10:18   No one t it from me,
Rev   22:19   if anyone t away from the words of

TALENT
Mt   25:25   and hid your t in the ground.

TAMAR
     1. Wife of Judah's sons Er and Onan (Ge 38:1-
10). Children by Judah (Ge 38:11-30; Mt 1:3).
     2. Daughter of David, raped by Amnon (2Sa
13).

TASTE → TASTED
Ps   34: 8   O t and see that the LORD is good;
Mt   16:28   not t death before they see the Son
Col   2:21   not handle, Do not t, Do not touch"?

TASTED → TASTE
Heb   6: 4   and have t the heavenly gift,
1Pe   2: 3   you have t that the Lord is good.

TAUGHT → TEACH
Isa   40:14   Who t him knowledge,
Jn   6:45   'And they shall all be t by God.'

TAX → TAXES
Mt   11:19   a friend of t collectors and sinners!'
Lk   18:10   Pharisee and the other a t collector.

TAXES → TAX
Mt   22:17   Is it lawful to pay t to the emperor,
Ro   13: 7   t to whom t are due,

TEACH → TAUGHT, TEACHER, TEACHERS, TEACHING

Dt 6: 1 to t you to observe in the land that
Ps 90:12 So t us to count our days that we
Jer 31:34 No longer shall they t one another,
Jn 14:26 will t you everything,
Col 3:16 t and admonish one another in all
1Ti 2:12 I permit no woman to t or
1Jn 2:27 so you do not need anyone to t you.

TEACHER → TEACH

Ecc 1: 1 words of the T, the son of David,
Mt 10:24 "A disciple is not above the t,
Jn 1:38 "Rabbi" (which translated means T)
1Ti 3: 2 respectable, hospitable, an apt t,

TEACHERS → TEACH

Ps 119:99 more understanding than all my t,
1Co 12:28 second prophets, third t;
Eph 4:11 evangelists, some pastors and t,
Jas 3: 1 Not many of you should become t,

TEACHING → TEACH

Mk 1:27 A new t—with authority!
Tit 1:11 by t for sordid gain what it is not right
2Jn 1: 9 who does not abide in the t of Christ,

TEAR → TORN

Mk 2:21 from the old, and a worse t is made.
Rev 7:17 God will wipe away every t from

TEETH → TOOTH

Mt 8:12 will be weeping and gnashing of t."

TEKEL

Da 5:27 T, you have been weighed on the scales

TELL → FORETOLD

Ps 50:12 "If I were hungry, I would not t you,
105: 2 t of all his wonderful works.
1Co 15:51 Listen, I will t you a mystery!

TEMPERATE

1Ti 3: 2 married only once, t, sensible,
Tit 2: 2 Tell the older men to be t, serious,

TEMPLE

1Sa 3: 3 Samuel was lying down in the t of the
2Ch 2:12 who will build a t for the LORD,
Ps 11: 4 The LORD is in his holy t;
Mt 4: 5 placed him on the pinnacle of the t,
12: 6 something greater than the t is here.
Jn 2:21 was speaking of the t of his body.
1Co 3:16 you are God's t and that God's Spirit
Eph 2:21 and grows into a holy t in the Lord;
Rev 21:22 its t is the Lord God the Almighty and
1Mc 4:48 sanctuary and the interior of the t,

TEMPTATION* → TEMPTED, TEMPTER

1Ti 6: 9 who want to be rich into t and
Jas 1:12 Blessed is anyone who endures t.

TEMPTED → TEMPTATION

Mk 1:13 wilderness forty days, t by Satan;
Gal 6: 1 care that you yourselves are not t.

TEMPTER* → TEMPTATION

Mt 4: 3 The t came and said to him,
1Th 3: 5 that somehow the t had tempted you

TEN → TENTH

Ex 34:28 the covenant, the t commandments.
Da 7:24 out of this kingdom t kings shall arise,
Mt 25: 1 T bridesmaids took their lamps and
Rev 17:12 the t horns that you saw are t kings

TENDER → TENDERHEARTED

Hos 11: 8 my compassion grows warm and t.
Lk 1:78 By the t mercy of our God,

TENDERHEARTED* → HEART, TENDER

Eph 4:32 t, forgiving one another,

TENT

Ex 27:21 the t of meeting, outside the curtain
2Sa 7: 2 but the ark of God stays in a t."
2Co 5: 1 the earthly t we live in is destroyed,

TENTH → TEN

Ge 14:20 Abram gave him one t of everything
Isa 6:13 Even if a t part remain in it,

TERROR

Ex 23:27 I will send my t in front of you,
Ps 91: 5 You will not fear the t of the night,
Ro 13: 3 rulers are not a t to good conduct,

TEST → TESTED, TESTING

Dt 6:16 not put the LORD your God to the t,
Lk 4:12 not put the Lord your God to the t.'
10:25 then a lawyer stood up to t Jesus.
2Co 13: 5 indeed, you fail to meet the t!
1Jn 4: 1 t the spirits to see whether they are
Sir 37:27 My child, t yourself while you live;

TESTED → TEST

Ge 22: 1 After these things God t Abraham.
Ps 78:41 They t God again and again,
Heb 4:15 been t as we are, yet without sin.

TESTIFIED → TESTIFY

Jn 1:15 (John t to him and cried out,
1Pe 1:11 it t in advance to the sufferings

TESTIFIES → TESTIFY

1Jn 5: 6 Spirit is the one that t,

TESTIFY → TESTIFIED, TESTIFIES, TESTIMONY

Jn 15:26 he will t on my behalf.
1Jn 5: 7 There are three that t:

TESTIMONY → TESTIFY

Nu 35:30 put to death on the t of a single
Mk 14:59 on this point their t did not agree.
Rev 1: 9 the word of God and the t of Jesus.

TESTING → TEST

1Co 10:13 No t has overtaken you that is not
Jas 1: 3 t of your faith produces endurance;

THADDAEUS* → =JUDAS

Apostle (Mt 10:3; Mk 3:18); probably also known as Judas son of James (Lk 6:16; Ac 1:13).

THANK → THANKS, THANKSGIVING

2Ch 29:31 bring sacrifices and t offerings to
Ps 52: 9 I will t you forever,
Sir 35: 4 gives alms sacrifices a t offering.

THANKS → THANK

1Ch 16: 8 give t to the LORD, call on his name,
Ps 107: 1 O give t to the LORD, for he is good;
Ro 1:21 not honor him as God or give t to
1Co 11:24 and when he had given t,
2Co 9:15 T be to God for his indescribable
Rev 4: 9 give glory and honor and t to

THANKSGIVING → THANK

Lev 7:12 If you offer it for t,
Ps 50:14 Offer to God a sacrifice of t,
Php 4: 6 with t let your requests be made known
Rev 7:12 glory and wisdom and t and honor

THEFT → THIEF

Mt 15:19 fornication, t, false witness, slander.

THEFTS* → THIEF

Rev 9:21 or their fornication or their t.

THIEF → THEFT, THEFTS, THIEVES

Ex 22: 1 The t shall make restitution,
Jn 10:10 The t comes only to steal and kill
1Th 5: 2 day of the Lord will come like a t in
Rev 16:15 ("See, I am coming like a t!

THIEVES → THIEF

Mt 6:19 and where t break in and steal;
Eph 4:28 T must give up stealing;

THINK → THINKING, THOUGHT, THOUGHTS

Ro 12: 3 not to t of yourself more highly than
1Co 10:12 So if you t you are standing,

THINKING → THINK

Ro 1:21 but they became futile in their t,
1Co 14:20 infants in evil, but in t be adults.

THIRD → THREE

Hos 6: 2 on the t day he will raise us up,
Mt 26:44 and prayed for the t time,
Lk 18:33 and on the t day he will rise again."
2Co 12: 2 was caught up to the t heaven—

THIRST → THIRSTY

Mt 5: 6 who hunger and t for righteousness,
Rev 7:16 will hunger no more, and t no more;

THIRSTY → THIRST

Mt 25:35 I was t and you gave me something
Jn 6:35 believes in me will never be t.
Rev 22:17 And let everyone who is t come.

THOMAS*

Apostle (Mt 10:3; Mk 3:18; Lk 6:15; Jn 11:16; 14:5; 21:2; Ac 1:13). Doubted resurrection (Jn 20:24-28).

THORN → THORNS

2Co 12: 7 a t was given me in the flesh,

THORNS → THORN

Ge 3:18 t and thistles it shall bring forth for
Mt 13: 7 Other seeds fell among t,
Jn 19: 2 the soldiers wove a crown of t and

THOUGHT → THINK

1Co 13:11 I spoke like a child, I t like a child,
2Co 10: 5 take every t captive to obey Christ.

THOUGHTS → THINK

Isa 55: 8 For my t are not your t,
1Co 3:20 "The Lord knows the t of the wise,
Heb 4:12 judge the t and intentions of the heart.

THOUSAND → THOUSANDS

Ps 50:10 the cattle on a t hills.
90: 4 t years in your sight are like yesterday
2Pe 3: 8 one day is like a t years, and a t years
Rev 20: 4 and reigned with Christ a t years.

THOUSANDS → THOUSAND

1Sa 18: 7 has killed his t, and David his ten t."
Da 7:10 A thousand t served him,
Rev 5:11 myriads of myriads and t of t,

THREE → THIRD

Ge 18: 2 and saw t men standing near him.
Ex 23:14 T times in the year you shall hold a
Mt 18:20 two or t are gathered in my name,
26:34 you will deny me t times."
Mk 8:31 be killed, and after t days rise again.
2Co 12: 8 T times I appealed to the Lord
1Jn 5: 7 There are t that testify:

THRONE → THRONES

2Sa 7:13 the t of his kingdom forever.
Ps 45: 6 Your t, O God, endures forever
Isa 6: 1 I saw the Lord sitting on a t, high
Jer 33:21 not have a son to reign on his t,
Mt 19:28 the Son of Man is seated on the t
Heb 4:16 approach the t of grace with boldness;
12: 2 his seat at the right hand of the t
Rev 4:10 they cast their crowns before the t,
20:11 I saw a great white t and the one

THRONES → THRONE

Da 7: 9 t were set in place,
Rev 4: 4 Around the throne are twenty-four t,

THROW → THROWN

Ex 1:22 Hebrews you shall t into the Nile,
Mt 7: 6 do not t your pearls before swine,

THROWN → THROW
Ex   15: 1   horse and rider he has **t** into the sea.
Da   3:21   **t** into the furnace of blazing fire.
         6:12   shall be **t** into a den of lions?"
Rev 20:10   **t** into the lake of fire and sulfur,

THUMMIM
Ex   28:30   you shall put the Urim and the **T**,

THUNDER → THUNDERS
Ex   9:23   and the LORD sent **t** and hail,
Rev   4: 5   and rumblings and peals of **t**,

THUNDERS → THUNDER
Rev 10: 3   he shouted, the seven **t** sounded.

TIBNI*
     King of Israel (1Ki 16:21-22).

TIE
Pr   6:21   **t** them around your neck.
Mt   23: 4   **t** up heavy burdens, hard to bear,

TIME → TIMES
Est   4:14   dignity for just such a **t** as this."
Ecc   3: 1   a **t** for every matter under heaven:
Da   7:25   for a **t**, two times, and half a **t**.
Ro   5: 6   the right **t** Christ died for the
                   ungodly.
2Co   6: 2   See, now is the acceptable **t**;
Gal   4: 4   when the fullness of **t** had come,
Col   4: 5   making the most of the **t**.
Rev 12:14   for a **t**, and times, and half a **t**.
        22:10   of this book, for the **t** is near.

TIMES → TIME
Jos   6: 4   march around the city seven **t**,
Mt   16: 3   cannot interpret the signs of the **t**.
        18:22   seven **t**, but, I tell you, seventy-
                   seven **t**.
Mk   14:30   you will deny me three **t**."
Sir   20:12   but pay for it seven **t** over.

TIMOTHY
     Believer from Lystra (Ac 16:1). Joined Paul on
second missionary journey (Ac 16-20). Sent to
settle problems at Corinth (1Co 4:17; 16:10). Led
church at Ephesus (1Ti 1:3). Co-writer with Paul
(1Th 1:1; 2Th 1:1; Phm 1).

TITHE
Dt   12:17   the **t** of your grain, your wine, and
Mal   3:10   Bring the full **t** into the storehouse,

TITUS
     Gentile co-worker of Paul (Gal 2:1-3; 2Ti 4:10);
sent to Corinth (2Co 2:13; 7-8; 12:18), Crete (Tit
1:4-5).

TOBIAH
     Enemy of Nehemiah (Ne 2:10-19; 4; 6; 13:4-9).

TOBIT
Tob   1: 1   This book tells the story of **T**

TODAY
Dt   30:15   set before you **t** life and prosperity,
Ps   2: 7   my son; **t** I have begotten you.
Lk   23:43   **t** you will be with me in Paradise."
Heb   1: 5   my Son; **t** I have begotten you"?
        13: 8   Christ is the same yesterday and **t**
                   and

TOGETHER
Mt   19: 6   God has joined **t**, let no one
                   separate."
Eph   2: 5   made us alive **t** with Christ—

TOLA
     A judge of Israel (Jdg 10:1-2).

TOMB
Mk   15:46   laid it in a **t** that had been hewn out
Lk   24: 2   the stone rolled away from the **t**,

TOMORROW
Isa   22:13   "Let us eat and drink, for **t** we die."
Mt   6:34   "So do not worry about **t**,
Jas   4:14   do not even know what **t** will bring.

TONGUE → DOUBLE-TONGUED,
        TONGUES
Ex   4:10   I am slow of speech and slow of **t**."
Ps   139: 4   before a word is on my **t**, O LORD,
Pr   18:21   Death and life are in the power of
                   the **t**,
Isa   45:23   shall bow, every **t** shall swear."
1Co 14:19   than ten thousand words in a **t**.
Php   2:11   every **t** should confess that Jesus
                   Christ
Jas   3: 8   but no one can tame the **t**—
Sir   20:18   is better than a slip of the **t**;
        23: 7   DISCIPLINE OF THE **T**

TONGUES → TONGUE
Ac   2: 3   Divided **t**, as of fire, appeared
1Co 12:10   of **t**, to another the interpretation
                   of **t**.
        14: 5   in **t**, unless someone interprets,

TOOTH → TEETH
Ex   21:24   **t** for **t**, hand for hand, foot for foot,
Mt   5:38   'An eye for an eye and a **t** for a **t**.'

TORCHES
Da   10: 6   lightning, his eyes like flaming **t**,
Rev   4: 5   of the throne burn seven flaming **t**,

TORMENTED
Rev 20:10   they will be **t** day and night forever

TORN → TEAR
1Sa 28:17   has **t** the kingdom out of your hand,
Lk   23:45   curtain of the temple was **t** in two.

TORTURED
Mt   18:34   handed him over to be **t** until
Heb 11:35   were **t**, refusing to accept release,

TOUCH
Ge   3: 3   nor shall you **t** it, or you shall die.'"
Mt   9:21   only **t** his cloak, I will be made well.
Lk   24:39   **T** me and see;
Col   2:21   not handle, Do not taste, Do not **t**"?

TOWER
Ge   11: 4   and a **t** with its top in the heavens,
Pr   18:10   The name of the LORD is a strong **t**;

TRADITION
Mt   15: 2   disciples break the **t** of the elders?
Col   2: 8   empty deceit, according to human **t**,

TRAIN → TRAINING
Pr   22: 6   **T** children in the right way, and
1Ti   4: 7   **T** yourself in godliness,

TRAINING → TRAIN
1Ti   4: 8   while physical **t** is of some value,
2Ti   3:16   and for **t** in righteousness,

TRAITOR
Lk   6:16   and Judas Iscariot, who became a **t**.

TRANSFIGURED
Mt   17: 2   And he was **t** before them,

TRANSFORM* → TRANSFORMED
Php   3:21   will **t** the body of our humiliation

TRANSFORMED → TRANSFORM
Ro   12: 2   be **t** by the renewing of your minds,
2Co   3:18   are being **t** into the same image

TRANSGRESSION → TRANSGRESSIONS,
        TRANSGRESSORS
Ex   23:21   for he will not pardon your **t**;
Da   9:24   to finish the **t**, to put an end to sin,
Gal   6: 1   if anyone is detected in a **t**,

TRANSGRESSIONS → TRANSGRESSION
Ps   103:12   so far he removes our **t** from us.
Isa   53: 5   But he was wounded for our **t**,

TRANSGRESSORS → TRANSGRESSION
Ps   51:13   Then I will teach **t** your ways,
Isa   53:12   and was numbered with the **t**;

TRAP
Lk   20:20   in order to **t** him by what he said,

Ro   11: 9   their table become a snare
                   and a **t**,

TREAD → TREADING
Mic   7:19   he will **t** our iniquities under foot.
Rev 19:15   he will **t** the wine press of the fury

TREADING → TREAD
Dt   25: 4   not muzzle an ox while it is **t** out
1Co   9: 9   not muzzle an ox while it is **t** out

TREASURE → TREASURED, TREASURES
Ps   119:11   I **t** your word in my heart,
Mt   6:21   where your **t** is, there your heart
2Co   4: 7   But we have this **t** in clay jars,
2Ti   1:14   Guard the good **t** entrusted
                   to you,

TREASURED → TREASURE
Ex   19: 5   be my **t** possession out of all the

TREASURES → TREASURE
Col   2: 3   are hidden all the **t** of wisdom

TREE → TREES
Ge   3:24   to guard the way to the **t** of life.
Dt   21:23   hung on a **t** is under God's curse.
Mt   12:33   for the **t** is known by its fruit.
Ac   5:30   had killed by hanging him on a **t**.
Ro   11:24   grafted back into their own olive **t**.
Rev 22: 2   the **t** of life with its twelve kinds

TREES → TREE
Ps   96:12   all the **t** of the forest sing for joy
Zec   4:11   "What are these two olive **t** on the
Rev 11: 4   two olive **t** and the two lampstands

TREMBLE → TREMBLED, TREMBLING
Ps   114: 7   **T**, O earth, at the presence of the
                   LORD
Hab   3: 6   he looked and made the nations **t**.

TREMBLED → TREMBLE
Ex   20:18   they were afraid and **t** and stood at

TREMBLING → TREMBLE
Ps   2:11   Serve the LORD with fear, with **t**
Php   2:12   your own salvation with fear and **t**;

TRESPASS → TRESPASSES
Ro   5:15   But the free gift is not like the **t**.

TRESPASSES → TRESPASS
Mt   6:14   For if you forgive others their **t**,
2Co   5:19   not counting their **t** against them,

TRIAL → TRIALS
Lk   11: 4   do not bring us to the time of **t**."
2Pe   2: 9   knows how to rescue the godly
                   from **t**,
Rev   3:10   I will keep you from the hour of **t**

TRIALS → TRIAL
Jas   1: 2   whenever you face **t** of any kind,
1Pe   1: 6   you have had to suffer various **t**,

TRIBE → TRIBES
Nu   1: 4   A man from each **t** shall be with you
Ps   78:68   but he chose the **t** of Judah,
Rev   5: 5   See, the Lion of the **t** of Judah,

TRIBES → TRIBE
Ge   49:28   All these are the twelve **t** of Israel,
Ex   24: 4   to the twelve **t** of Israel.
Mt   19:28   judging the twelve **t** of Israel.
Rev 21:12   inscribed the names of the twelve **t**

TRIUMPH → TRIUMPHAL, TRIUMPHS
Ps   112: 8   they will look in **t** on their foes.
Pr   28:12   the righteous **t**, there is great glory,

TRIUMPHAL* → TRIUMPH
2Co   2:14   Christ always leads us in **t**
                   procession,

TRIUMPHS → TRIUMPH
Jas   2:13   mercy **t** over judgment.

TROUBLE → TROUBLED
Job 14: 1   few of days and full of **t**,
Ps   9: 9   a stronghold in times of **t**.

TROUBLE (cont.)

Pr   11: 8   The righteous are delivered from t,
Isa   33: 2   our salvation in the time of t.
Mt   6:34   Today's t is enough for today.
Sir   51:10   do not forsake me in the days of t,

TROUBLED → TROUBLE

Jn   14: 1   "Do not let your hearts be t.

TRUE → TRUTH

Ps   119:151   and all your commandments are t.
Jn   1: 9   The t light, which enlightens
    21:24   and we know that his testimony is t.
Ro   3: 4   everyone is a liar, let God be
             proved t,
1Jn   5:20   He is the t God and eternal life.
Rev   3:14   the Amen, the faithful and t witness,
    19:11   Its rider is called Faithful and T,
    22: 6   "These words are trustworthy and t,

TRUMPET → TRUMPETS

Ex   19:16   a blast of a t so loud that all the
Joel   2:15   Blow the t in Zion; sanctify a fast;
1Co   15:52   twinkling of an eye, at the last t.
1Th   4:16   and with the sound of God's t,

TRUMPETS → TRUMPET

Nu   10: 2   Make two silver t; you shall make
Rev   8: 2   and seven t were given to them.

TRUST → ENTRUST, ENTRUSTED, TRUSTED, TRUSTEES, TRUSTS, TRUSTWORTHY

Ps   9:10   know your name put their t in you,
    37: 3   T in the LORD, and do good;
    119:42   for I t in your word.
Pr   3: 5   T in the LORD with all your heart,
Isa   12: 2   Surely God is my salvation; I will t,
Jer   17: 7   Blessed are those who t in the LORD,
Heb   2:13   And again, "I will put my t in him."
Sir   2: 6   T in him, and he will help you;

TRUSTED → TRUST

Ps   22: 4   they t, and you delivered them.
Da   3:28   delivered his servants who t in him.
    6:23   because he had t in his God.
Sus   1:35   for her heart t in the Lord.

TRUSTS → TRUST

Ps   86: 2   save your servant who t in you.
Mt   27:43   He t in God; let God deliver him

TRUSTWORTHY → TRUST

Ps   111: 7   and just; all his precepts are t.
Rev   22: 6   "These words are t and true,
1Mc   14:41   until a t prophet should arise,

TRUTH → TRUE

Ps   25: 5   Lead me in your t, and teach me,
    119:142   and your law is the t.
Pr   23:23   Buy t, and do not sell it;
Jn   1:17   grace and t came through Jesus
            Christ.
    4:23   worship the Father in spirit and t,
    8:32   and the t will make you free."
    14: 6   "I am the way, and the t, and the life.
    14:17   This is the Spirit of t,
Eph   4:15   But speaking the t in love,
2Ti   2:15   rightly explaining the word of t.
Tob   3: 2   all your ways are mercy and t;

TUNIC

Lk   9: 3   nor money—not even an extra t.
Jn   19:23   t was seamless, woven in one piece

TURN → TURNED

Ex   32:12   T from your fierce wrath;
Jos   1: 7   do not t from it to the right hand or
Isa   6:10   and t and be healed."
    45:22   T to me and be saved,
Mal   4: 6   He will t the hearts of parents to their
Lk   1:17   t the hearts of parents to their children

TURNED → TURN

Dt   23: 5   your God the curse into a blessing
Isa   53: 6   we have all t to our own way,
Ro   3:12   All have t aside, together they have

TWELVE

Ge   49:28   All these are the t tribes of Israel,
Ex   24: 4   the mountain, and set up t pillars,
Jos   4: 3   Take t stones from here out of the
Mt   10: 1   Jesus summoned his t disciples
Lk   9:17   t baskets of broken pieces.
Rev   21:12   inscribed the names of the t tribes
    22: 2   tree of life with its t kinds of fruit,

TWINKLING*

1Co   15:52   in the t of an eye, at the last trumpet

TWO → TWICE, TWO-EDGED

Ge   1:16   God made the t great lights—
    6:19   bring t of every kind into the ark,
Ex   31:18   the t tablets of the covenant,
Dt   17: 5   of t or three witnesses the death
Mt   6:24   "No one can serve t masters;
    19: 5   and the t shall become one flesh?

TWO-EDGED → TWO

Heb   4:12   sharper than any t sword,
Rev   1:16   his mouth came a sharp, t sword,

TYRE

1Ki   5: 1   King Hiram of T sent his servants to
Eze   28:12   a lamentation over the king of T,
Mt   11:22   be more tolerable for T and Sidon

U

UNBELIEF → UNBELIEVER, UNBELIEVERS

Mk   6: 6   And he was amazed at their u.
    9:24   cried out, "I believe; help my u!"
Ro   11:20   were broken off because of their u,
1Ti   1:13   because I had acted ignorantly in u,

UNBELIEVER → UNBELIEF

1Co   10:27   If an u invites you to a meal and
2Co   6:15   does a believer share with an u?

UNBELIEVERS → UNBELIEF

2Co   6:14   Do not be mismatched with u.
2Es   15: 4   For all u shall die in their unbelief.

UNCHASTITY*

Mt   5:32   except on the ground of u,
    19: 9   divorces his wife, except for u,

UNCIRCUMCISED → UNCIRCUMCISION

Ex   12:48   But no u person shall eat of it;
Ac   7:51   people, u in heart and ears,
Ro   4:11   he had by faith while he was still u.
Col   3:11   circumcised and u, barbarian,
1Mc   1:48   and to leave their sons u.

UNCIRCUMCISION → UNCIRCUMCISED

1Co   7:19   Circumcision is nothing, and u is
Gal   5: 6   neither circumcision nor u counts

UNCLEAN → UNCLEANNESS

Lev   5: 2   when any of you touch any u thing
Isa   52:11   Touch no u thing;
Mk   3:11   Whenever the u spirits saw him,
Rev   21:27   But nothing u will enter it,

UNDER

Ps   8: 6   you have put all things u their feet,
Ac   4:12   for there is no other name u heaven
Ro   6:14   since you are not u law but u grace.
Eph   1:22   And he has put all things u his feet

UNDERSTAND → UNDERSTANDING

Job   42: 3   I have uttered what I did not u,
Pr   2: 5   then you will u the fear of the LORD
Hos   14: 9   Those who are wise u these things;
Mt   13:15   and u with their heart and turn—
Lk   24:45   opened their minds to u the
            scriptures.
Ac   8:30   "Do you u what you are reading?"
Eph   5:17   but u what the will of the Lord is.

UNDERSTANDING → UNDERSTAND

Ex   36: 1   has given skill and u to know how
Pr   2: 6   from his mouth come knowledge
            and u
Isa   40:14   and showed him the way of u?
Lk   2:47   heard him were amazed at his u

Php   4: 7   peace of God, which surpasses all u,
2Ti   2: 7   Lord will give you u in all things.

UNEXPECTED

Mt   24:44   Son of Man is coming at an u hour.

UNFAITHFUL → UNFAITHFULNESS

Ro   3: 3   What if some were u?

UNFAITHFULNESS → UNFAITHFUL

1Ch   9: 1   exile in Babylon because of their u.

UNGODLY

Ro   5: 6   the right time Christ died for the u.
2Pe   2: 6   example of what is coming to the u;
Sir   12: 5   but do not give to the u;

UNINTENTIONALLY

Lev   4: 2   When anyone sins u in any of
Nu   15:22   if you u fail to observe all these

UNITY

Ps   133: 1   when kindred live together in u!
Eph   4: 3   to maintain the u of the Spirit in the

UNJUST

Ro   3: 5   That God is u to inflict wrath on us?
Heb   6:10   For God is not u; he will

UNLEAVENED

Ex   12:17   shall observe the festival of u bread,
Mt   26:17   first day of U Bread the disciples

UNPRODUCTIVE*

1Co   14:14   my spirit prays but my mind is u.
Tit   3:14   so that they may not be u.

UNRIGHTEOUS → UNRIGHTEOUSNESS

Mt   5:45   rain on the righteous and on the u.
2Pe   2: 9   u under punishment until the day

UNRIGHTEOUSNESS → UNRIGHTEOUS

Ps   92:15   and there is no u in him.
1Jn   1: 9   and cleanse us from all u.

UPHOLD

Isa   42: 1   my servant, whom I u, my chosen,
Ro   3:31   On the contrary, we u the law.

UPRIGHT

Job   1: 1   That man was blameless and u,
Ps   7:10   God is my shield, who saves the u
Tit   1: 8   a lover of goodness, prudent, u,

UR

Ge   15: 7   LORD who brought you from U of

URIAH

Hittite husband of Bathsheba, killed (2Sa 11).

URIM

Ex   28:30   of judgment you shall put the U

USE → USEFUL

Ex   20: 7   not make wrongful u of the name of
Gal   5:13   only do not u your freedom as an
2Ti   2:20   for special u, some for ordinary.

USEFUL → USE

Eph   4:29   but only what is u for building up,
2Ti   3:16   scripture is inspired by God and is u

UZZIAH → =AZARIAH

Son of Amaziah; king of Judah also known as Azariah (2Ki 15:1-7; 1Ch 6:24; 2Ch 26). Struck with leprosy because of pride (2Ch 26:16-23).

V

VAIN → VANITY

Lev   26:16   You shall sow your seed in v,
Ps   2: 1   and the peoples plot in v?
Mt   15: 9   in v do they worship me,
Php   2:16   that I did not run in v or labor in v.

VALLEY

Ps   23: 4   through the darkest v, I fear no evil;
Isa   40: 4   Every v shall be lifted up,
Joel   3:14   multitudes, in the v of decision!
Lk   3: 5   Every v shall be filled, and every

VALUE
Mt   13:46 on finding one pearl of great **v**,
Ro   3: 1 Or what is the **v** of circumcision?
1Ti   4: 8 while physical training is of some **v**,

VANITY → VAIN
Ecc   1: 2 **v** of vanities! All is **v**.
     12: 8 **V** of vanities, says the Teacher; all
             is **v**.

VASHTI
     Persian queen replaced by Esther (Est 1-2; AdE
1-2).

VEIL
Ex   34:33 he put a **v** on his face;
2Co   3:15 a **v** lies over their minds;

VENGEANCE → AVENGE, AVENGER,
AVENGING
Ps   94: 1 O LORD, you God of **v**,
Isa 34: 8 For the LORD has a day of **v**,
Na   1: 2 the LORD takes **v** on his adversaries

VICTORY
Pr   21:31 but the **v** belongs to the LORD.
1Co 15:54 Death has been swallowed up in **v**."
1Jn   5: 4 the **v** that conquers the world, our
             faith.

VINDICATE → VINDICATED
Ps   26: 1 **V** me, O LORD, for I have walked
    135:14 For the LORD will **v** his people,

VINDICATED → VINDICATE
Job 13:18 I know that I shall be **v**.
Mt   11:19 Yet wisdom is **v** by her deeds."
1Ti   3:16 He was revealed in flesh, **v** in spirit,

VINE → VINEYARD
Ps   80: 8 You brought a **v** out of Egypt;
Jer   2:21 Yet I planted you as a choice **v**,
Jn   15: 1 "I am the true **v**, and my Father is
Rev 14:18 gather the clusters of the **v** of the

VINEYARD → VINE
1Ki 21: 1 Naboth the Jezreelite had a **v** in
Isa   5: 1 had a **v** on a very fertile hill.
Mt   21:33 a landowner who planted a **v**,

VIOLENCE → VIOLENT
Ge   6:11 and the earth was filled with **v**.
Isa 53: 9 although he had done no **v**,
Hab   2:17 because of human bloodshed and **v**

VIOLENT → VIOLENCE
1Ti   3: 3 not **v** but gentle, not quarrelsome,
Tit   1: 7 or addicted to wine or **v** or greedy

VIPERS
Mt   23:33 You snakes, you brood of **v**!
Ro   3:13 venom of **v** is under their lips."

VIRGIN
Jer 31:21 Return, O **v** Israel, return to these
Mt   1:23 the **v** shall conceive and bear a son,
Lk   1:34 "How can this be, since I am a **v**?"
2Co 11: 2 present you as a chaste **v** to Christ.

VISION → VISIONS
Isa 22: 1 oracle concerning the valley of **v**.
Da   8:26 As for you, seal up the **v**,
Ac   26:19 not disobedient to the heavenly **v**,

VISIONS → VISION
Nu   12: 6 make myself known to them in **v**;
Eze   1: 1 were opened, and I saw **v** of God.
Da   1:17 Daniel also had insight into all **v**
Joel 2:28 and your young men shall see **v**.
Ac   2:17 and your young men shall see **v**,

VOICE
Isa 40: 3 A **v** cries out: "In the wilderness
Jn   1:23 **v** of one crying out in the wilderness
     10: 3 and the sheep hear his **v**.
Heb   3: 7 says, "Today, if you hear his **v**,
Rev   3:20 if you hear my **v** and open the door,

VOID
Ge   1: 2 the earth was a formless **v**
Mt   15: 6 you make **v** the word of God.

VOW → VOWS
Ecc   5: 4 Fulfill what you **v**.
Sir 18:23 Before making a **v**, prepare yourself

VOWS → VOW
Ps   22:25 my **v** I will pay before those who fear

W

WAGES
Ro   6:23 For the **w** of sin is death,

WAIT → WAITS
Ps   27:14 **W** for the LORD; be strong,
La   3:26 should **w** quietly for the salvation of
Hab   2: 3 If it seems to tarry, **w** for it;
Ro   8:23 while we **w** for adoption,
1Th   1:10 to **w** for his Son from heaven,
Sir   2: 7 fear the Lord, **w** for his mercy;

WAITS → WAIT
Ps 130: 6 my soul **w** for the Lord more than
Ro   8:19 the creation **w** with eager longing

WALK → WALKED
Ge   17: 1 **w** before me, and be blameless.
Dt   10:12 to **w** in all his ways, to love him,
Ps   23: 4 I **w** through the darkest valley, I
             fear no
Isa   2: 5 let us **w** in the light of the LORD!
     40:31 they shall **w** and not faint.
Jer   6:16 **w** in it, and find rest for your souls.
Jn   8:12 follows me will never **w** in darkness
2Co   5: 7 for we **w** by faith, not by sight.
Rev 21:24 The nations will **w** by its light,

WALKED → WALK
Ge   5:24 Enoch **w** with God; then he was no

WALL
Jos   6:20 shout, and the **w** fell down flat;
Ne   2:17 let us rebuild the **w** of Jerusalem;
Zec   2: 5 I will be a **w** of fire all around it,
Eph   2:14 has broken down the dividing **w**,

WANT → WANTING
Ps   23: 1 LORD is my shepherd, I shall not **w**.
Php   3:10 I **w** to know Christ and the power

WANTING → WANT
2Pe   3: 9 not **w** any to perish, but all to
             come to

WAR → WARRIOR, WARS
Ecc   3: 8 a time for **w**, and a time for peace.
Da   9:26 and to the end there shall be **w**.
Ro   7:23 in my members another law at **w**
Rev 19:11 righteousness he judges and
             makes **w**.

WARRIOR → WAR
Ex   15: 3 LORD is a **w**; the LORD is his name.

WARS → WAR
Mt   24: 6 you will hear of **w** and rumors of **w**;

WASH → WASHED
Ps   51: 7 **w** me, and I shall be whiter than
             snow.
Jn   13: 5 and began to **w** the disciples' feet
Rev 22:14 Blessed are those who **w** their robes,

WASHED → WASH
1Co   6:11 you were **w**, you were sanctified,
2Pe   2:22 sow is **w** only to wallow in the mud.

WATCH → WATCHES
Lk   2: 8 keeping **w** over their flock by night.
Heb 13:17 they are keeping **w** over your souls

WATCHES → WATCH
Ps   1: 6 LORD **w** over the way of the
             righteous,
Wis   3: 9 and he **w** over his elect.

WATER → WATERS
Ex   17: 1 no **w** for the people to drink.
Nu   20: 2 there was no **w** for the congregation;
Jer   2:13 the fountain of living **w**,
Eze 36:25 I will sprinkle clean **w** upon you,
Mk   1: 8 I have baptized you with **w**;
Jn   2: 9 tasted the **w** that had become wine,
      3: 5 without being born of **w** and Spirit,
      4:10 he would have given you living **w**."
1Jn   5: 6 the one who came by **w** and blood,
Rev 22: 1 showed me the river of the **w** of life,

WATERS → WATER
Ge   7: 7 the ark to escape the **w** of the flood.
Ex   14:21 dry land; and the **w** were divided.
Ecc 11: 1 Send out your bread upon the **w**,
Isa 55: 1 who thirsts, come to the **w**;

WAVERING
Heb 10:23 confession of our hope without **w**,
Jude 1:22 have mercy on some who are **w**;

WAY → WAYS
Ps   1: 6 watches over the **w** of the righteous,
     86:11 Teach me your **w**, O LORD,
Pr   12:15 Fools think their own **w** is right,
     22: 6 Train children in the right **w**,
Isa 40: 3 wilderness prepare the **w** of the
             LORD,
Mal   3: 1 sending my messenger to prepare
             the **w**
Mt   3: 3 'Prepare the **w** of the Lord,
Jn   14: 6 "I am the **w**, and the truth, and the
             life.
Ac   9: 2 found any who belonged to the **W**,
1Co 12:31 show you a still more excellent **w**.
Heb 10:20 the new and living **w** that he opened

WAYS → WAY
Dt   10:12 to walk in all his **w**, to love him,
Hos 14: 9 For the **w** of the LORD are right,
Rev 15: 3 Just and true are your **w**, King of
Sir   2:15 who love him keep his **w**.

WEAK → WEAKNESS, WEAKNESSES
Mt   26:41 indeed is willing, but the flesh is **w**."
Ro   14: 1 Welcome those who are **w** in faith,
1Co   1:27 God chose what is **w** in the world
2Co 12:10 whenever I am **w**, then I am strong.

WEAKNESS → WEAK
Ro   8:26 the Spirit helps us in our **w**;
1Co 15:43 It is sown in **w**, it is raised in power.

WEAKNESSES → WEAK
2Co 12:10 I am content with **w**, insults,
Heb   4:15 to sympathize with our **w**,

WEALTH
Ps   49: 6 those who trust in their **w** and boast
Pr   19: 4 **W** brings many friends,
Mt   13:22 and the lure of **w** choke
Rev   5:12 receive power and **w** and wisdom
Sir   5: 1 Do not rely on your **w**,

WEAPONS
Ecc   9:18 Wisdom is better than **w** of war,
2Co   6: 7 the **w** of righteousness for the right

WEAR
Isa 51: 6 the earth will **w** out like a garment,
Mt   6:31 or 'What will we **w**?'

WEARY
Isa 40:31 they shall run and not be **w**,
Heb 12: 3 you may not grow **w** or lose heart.

WEDDING
Jn   2: 1 there was a **w** in Cana of Galilee,

WEEKS
Ex   34:22 You shall observe the festival of **w**,
Lev 23:15 you shall count off seven **w**;
Da   9:24 "Seventy **w** are decreed for your

WEEP → WEEPING
Ecc   3: 4 a time to **w**, and a time to laugh;
Ro   12:15 **w** with those who **w**.

WEEPING → WEEP
Ps 30: 5 **W** may linger for the night,
Mt 2:18 Rachel **w** for her children;
8:12 will be **w** and gnashing of teeth."

WEIGHED
1Sa 2: 3 and by him actions are **w**.
Da 5:27 you have been **w** on the scales

WELL
Dt 6: 3 so that it may go **w** with you,
Mt 3:17 with whom I am **w** pleased."
17: 5 I am **w** pleased; listen to him!"
2Pe 1:17 with whom I am **w** pleased."

WEST
Ps 103:12 as far as the east is from the **w**,
Isa 43: 5 and from the **w** I will gather you;

WHEAT
Mt 13:25 and sowed weeds among the **w**,
Lk 22:31 demanded to sift all of you like **w**,
Jn 12:24 grain of **w** falls into the earth and dies,

WHIRLWIND → WIND
2Ki 2:11 Elijah ascended in a **w** into heaven.
Na 1: 3 His way is in **w** and storm,

WHITE → WHITER
Da 7: 9 his clothing was **w** as snow,
Mt 5:36 cannot make one hair **w** or black.
Rev 1:14 his hair were **w** as **w** wool, **w** as snow;
20:11 a great **w** throne and the one who sat

WHITER → WHITE
Ps 51: 7 wash me, and I shall be **w** than snow.

WICKED → WICKEDNESS
Ge 13:13 Now the people of Sodom were **w**,
18:23 the righteous with the **w**?
Ps 1: 5 the **w** will not stand in the judgment,
73: 3 I saw the prosperity of the **w**.
Isa 48:22 no peace," says the LORD, "for the **w**."
Eze 18:23 any pleasure in the death of the **w**,
Da 12:10 None of the **w** shall understand,

WICKEDNESS → WICKED
Ge 6: 5 The LORD saw that the **w** of
Ps 45: 7 you love righteousness and hate **w**.
Lk 11:39 inside you are full of greed and **w**.

WIDE
Mt 7:13 the gate is **w** and the road is easy

WIDOW → WIDOWS
Ex 22:22 shall not abuse any **w** or orphan.
Ps 146: 9 he upholds the orphan and the **w**,
1Ti 5: 4 If a **w** has children or grandchildren,
Rev 18: 7 I am no **w**, and I will never see grief

WIDOWS → WIDOW
1Ti 5: 3 Honor **w** who are really **w**.
Jas 1:27 to care for orphans and **w** in their

WIFE → WIVES
Ge 2:24 and his mother and clings to his **w**,
Ex 20:17 shall not covet your neighbor's **w**,
Pr 18:22 who finds a **w** finds a good thing,
Mt 5:32 that anyone who divorces his **w**,
19: 3 to divorce his **w** for any cause?"
Eph 5:28 He who loves his **w** loves himself.
Rev 21: 9 the bride, the **w** of the Lamb."
Tob 8: 6 his **w** Eve as a helper and support.
Sir 26: 3 A good **w** is a great blessing;

WILD
Ex 32:25 saw that the people were running **w**
Mk 1:13 and he was with the **w** beasts;
Ro 11:17 a **w** olive shoot,

WILDERNESS
Isa 40: 3 the **w** prepare the way of the LORD,
Mt 3: 3 voice of one crying out in the **w**:

WILL → FREEWILL, WILLING
40: 8 I delight to do your **w**, O my God;

Ps 143:10 Teach me to do your **w**,
Isa 53:10 it was the **w** of the LORD to crush him
Mt 6:10 Your **w** be done, on earth as it is in
Lk 22:42 yet, not my **w** but yours be done."
Jn 4:34 "My food is to do the **w** of him who
Ro 9:19 For who can resist his **w**?"
Eph 6: 6 doing the **w** of God from the heart.
1Jo 5:14 if we ask anything according to his **w**,

WILLING → WILL
Mt 26:41 spirit indeed is **w**, but the flesh is weak.
Lk 22:42 if you are **w**, remove this cup from

WIND → WHIRLWIND
1Ki 19:11 but the LORD was not in the **w**;
Ps 1: 4 like chaff that the **w** drives away.
Ecc 1:14 all is vanity and a chasing after **w**.
Jn 3: 8 The **w** blows where it chooses,
Ac 2: 2 a sound like the rush of a violent **w**,

WINE
Dt 7:13 your grain and your **w** and your oil,
Ps 104:15 and **w** to gladden the human heart,
Pr 20: 1 **W** is a mocker, strong drink a
SS 1: 2 For your love is better than **w**,
Mt 9:17 is new **w** put into old wineskins;
Jn 2: 9 tasted the water that had become **w**,
Eph 5:18 Do not get drunk with **w**, for that is
Rev 18: 3 have drunk of the **w** of the wrath
Sir 40:20 **W** and music gladden the heart,

WINGS
Ex 19: 4 and how I bore you on eagles' **w**
Ps 17: 8 hide me in the shadow of your **w**,
Mal 4: 2 shall rise, with healing in its **w**.
Lk 13:34 hen gathers her brood under her **w**,

WIPE → WIPED
Isa 25: 8 God will **w** away the tears from all faces,
Rev 21: 4 he will **w** every tear from their eyes.

WIPED → WIPE
Ac 3:19 so that your sins may be **w** out,

WISDOM → WISE
Dt 4: 6 will show your **w** and discernment
1Ki 4:29 God gave Solomon very great **w**,
Job 11: 6 the secrets of **w**! For **w** is many-sided.
Pr 1:20 **W** cries out in the street;
9:10 fear of the LORD is the beginning of **w**,
Ecc 1:13 to search out by **w** all that is done
Jer 9:23 Do not let the wise boast in their **w**,
Mt 13:54 this man get this **w** and these deeds
Lk 2:52 Jesus increased in **w** and in years,
Ro 11:33 the depth of the riches and **w** and
1Co 1:19 "I will destroy the **w** of the wise,
Col 2: 3 whom are hidden all the treasures of **w**
Jas 3:17 But the **w** from above is first pure,
Rev 5:12 wealth and **w** and might and honor
Wis 6:12 **W** is radiant and unfading,
Sir 1: 1 All **w** is from the Lord,
24: 1 THE PRAISE OF **W**

WISE → WISDOM
Dt 4: 6 great nation is a **w** and discerning
Ps 19: 7 are sure, making **w** the simple;
Pr 3: 7 Do not be **w** in your own eyes;
13:20 walks with the **w** becomes **w**,
Ecc 12:11 The sayings of the **w** are like goads,
Da 12: 3 are **w** shall shine like the brightness
Mt 25: 2 were foolish, and five were **w**.
1Co 1:26 not many of you were **w** by human
Eph 5:15 not as unwise people but as **w**,

WITHER → WITHERED, WITHERS
Ps 1: 3 and their leaves do not **w**.
Eze 47:12 Their leaves will not **w** nor their

WITHERED → WITHER
Mt 13: 6 since they had no root, they **w** away.
21:19 And the fig tree **w** at once.

WITHERS → WITHER
Jn 15: 6 is thrown away like a branch and **w**;
1Pe 1:24 The grass **w**, and the flower falls,

WITHHOLD
Ps 84:11 No good thing does the LORD **w** from
Ro 8:32 He who did not **w** his own Son,

WITHOUT
2Ch 18:16 like sheep **w** a shepherd;
Pr 19: 2 Desire **w** knowledge is not good,
Mt 9:36 helpless, like sheep **w** a shepherd.
Jn 3:34 for he gives the Spirit **w** measure.
Eph 2:12 no hope and **w** God in the world.
Heb 4:15 tested as we are, yet **w** sin.

WITNESS → EYEWITNESSES, WITNESSES
Dt 19:15 single **w** shall not suffice to convict
Job 16:19 in fact, my **w** is in heaven,
Ro 2:15 their own conscience also bears **w**;
Rev 1: 5 faithful **w**, the firstborn of the dead,

WITNESSES → WITNESS
Mt 26:60 though many false **w** came forward.
Heb 12: 1 surrounded by so great a cloud of **w**,
Rev 11: 3 my two **w** authority to prophesy

WIVES → WIFE
1Ki 11: 3 and his **w** turned away his heart.
Eph 5:22 **W**, be subject to your husbands as
1Pe 3: 1 **W**, in the same way, accept the

WOE
Mt 23:13 "But **w** to you, scribes and Pharisees
Rev 8:13 "**W**, **w**, **w** to the inhabitants of the

WOLF → WOLVES
Isa 11: 6 The **w** shall live with the lamb,
Jn 10:12 sees the **w** coming and leaves the sheep

WOLVES → WOLF
Mt 7:15 but inwardly are ravenous **w**.

WOMAN → WOMEN
Ge 2:22 he made into a **w** and brought her to
3:15 enmity between you and the **w**,
Ps 113: 9 He gives the barren **w** a home,
Pr 11:16 A gracious **w** gets honor,
31:30 **w** who fears the LORD is to be praised.
Isa 54: 1 of the desolate **w** will be more than
Rev 12: 1 a **w** clothed with the sun,
Jdt 16: 5 foiled them by the hand of a **w**.
Sus 1: 2 a very beautiful **w** and one who feared

WOMB
Job 1:21 Naked I came from my mother's **w**,
Ps 139:13 knit me together in my mother's **w**.
Lk 1:44 the child in my **w** leaped for joy.

WOMEN → WOMAN
Ezr 10: 2 married foreign **w** from the peoples
Mt 24:41 Two **w** will be grinding meal
Lk 1:42 "Blessed are you among **w**,
23:55 **w** who had come with him from
1Pe 3: 5 that the holy **w** who hoped in God

WONDERFUL → WONDERS
Ge 18:14 Is anything too **w** for the LORD?
Jdg 13:18 do you ask my name? It is too **w**."
Ps 107: 8 for his **w** works to humankind.
Isa 9: 6 named **W** Counselor, Mighty God,

WONDERS → WONDERFUL
Ex 3:20 and strike Egypt with all my **w** that
Ps 136: 4 who alone does great **w**,
Jn 4:48 signs and **w** you will not believe."
2Th 2: 9 who uses all power, signs, lying **w**,

WOOD
Dt   28:64   serve other gods, of **w** and stone,
1Co   3:12   silver, precious stones, **w,** hay,

WORD → BYWORD, WORDS
Dt   30:14   No, the **w** is very near to you;
1Ki   8:56   not one **w** has failed of all his good
Ps   56: 4   In God, whose **w** I praise,
    119:105   Your **w** is a lamp to my feet and
Pr   30: 5   Every **w** of God proves true;
Isa   40: 8   the **w** of our God will stand forever.
   55:11   my **w** be that goes out from my
           mouth;
Mk   4:14   The sower sows the **w.**
Jn   1: 1   In the beginning was the **W,** and the
           W was with God, and the **W** was
           God.
   1:14   the **W** became flesh and lived among
  17:17   in the truth; your **w** is truth.
Ro   9: 6   as though the **w** of God had failed.
2Ti   2:15   rightly explaining the **w** of truth.
Jas   1:22   But be doers of the **w,**
1Jn   2: 5   but whoever obeys his **w,**
Rev   19:13   his name is called The **W** of God.

WORDS → WORD
Ex   20: 1   Then God spoke all these **w:**
Dt   11:18   put these **w** of mine in your heart
Ps   5: 1   Give ear to my **w,** O LORD;
Pr   30: 6   not add to his **w,** or else he will
           rebuke
Hos   6: 5   killed them by the **w** of my mouth,
Mt   24:35   but my **w** will not pass away.
Lk   6:47   hears my **w,** and acts on them.
1Co   2:13   in **w** not taught by human wisdom
Rev   22:19   takes away from the **w** of the book

WORK → WORKS
Ge   2: 2   the seventh day God finished the **w**
Ex   20:10   you shall not do any **w**—
Ps   8: 3   heavens, the **w** of your fingers,
Jn   6:27   Do not **w** for the food that perishes,
Php   1: 6   who began a good **w** among you will
   2:12   **w** out your own salvation with fear
2Ti   3:17   equipped for every good **w.**

WORKS → WORK
Ps   8: 6   given them dominion over the **w**
   92: 5   How great are your **w,** O LORD!
Gal   2:16   and not by doing the **w** of the law,
   5:19   the **w** of the flesh are obvious:
Eph   2: 9   not the result of **w,** so that no one
           may
1Ti   6:18   to do good, to be rich in good **w,**

WORLD
Ps   9: 8   He judges the **w** with righteousness;
Mt   5:14   "You are the light of the **w.**
   16:26   gain the whole **w** but forfeit their
           life?
Jn   1:10   yet the **w** did not know him.
   3:16   loved the **w** that he gave his only
           Son,
   8:12   saying, "I am the light of the **w.**
   16:33   courage; I have conquered the **w!**"
1Ti   6: 7   we brought nothing into the **w,**
Jas   4: 4   friend of the **w** becomes an enemy of
1Jn   2: 2   but also for the sins of the whole **w.**
   2:15   not love the **w** or the things in the **w.**
Rev   11:15   kingdom of the **w** has become the

WORM
Ps   22: 6   But I am a **w,** and not human;
Mk   9:48   where their **w** never dies,

WORRY
Mt   6:25   do not **w** about your life,
   10:19   not **w** about how you are to speak

WORSHIP → WORSHIPED
Ex   20: 5   not bow down to them or **w** them;
Ps   100: 2   **W** the LORD with gladness;
Mt   4: 9   if you will fall down and **w** me."
Jn   4:24   who **w** him must **w** in spirit and
           truth."

Ro   12: 1   which is your spiritual **w.**
Rev   22: 3   and his servants will **w** him;
Sir   35:10   Be generous when you **w** the Lord,

WORSHIPED → WORSHIP
Mt   28: 9   took hold of his feet, and **w** him.
Rev   5:14   And the elders fell down and **w.**

WORTHY
2Sa   22: 4   LORD, who is **w** to be praised,
Mt   10:38   and follow me is not **w** of me.
Eph   4: 1   to lead a life **w** of the calling
Heb   3: 3   Jesus is **w** of more glory than Moses
Rev   4:11   "You are **w,** our Lord and God,
   5:12   **W** is the Lamb that was slaughtered

WOUND → WOUNDS
Ex   21:25   burn for burn, **w** for **w,** stripe for
Rev   13: 3   but its mortal **w** had been healed.

WOUNDS → WOUND
Ps   147: 3   brokenhearted, and binds up
           their **w.**
1Pe   2:24   by his **w** you have been healed.

WRAPPED
Mk   15:46   the body, **w** it in the linen cloth,
Lk   2: 7   **w** him in bands of cloth,

WRATH
Nu   16:46   For **w** has gone out from the LORD;
Ps   2: 5   Then he will speak to them in his **w,**
   6: 1   or discipline me in your **w.**
Pr   15: 1   A soft answer turns away **w,**
Jer   25:15   my hand this cup of the wine of **w,**
La   4:11   The LORD gave full vent to his **w;**
Zep   1:15   That day will be a day of **w,**
Mt   3: 7   you to flee from the **w** to come?
Ro   1:18   **w** of God is revealed from heaven
1Th   1:10   rescues us from the **w** that is coming
Rev   6:17   the great day of their **w** has come,
Sir   16:11   For mercy and **w** are with the Lord;

WRESTLED
Ge   32:24   a man **w** with him until daybreak.

WRITE → WRITING, WRITTEN, WROTE
Ex   34:27   LORD said to Moses: **W** these
           words;
Nu   17: 2   **W** each man's name on his staff,
Dt   6: 9   **w** them on the doorposts of your
           house
Pr   7: 3   **w** them on the tablet of your heart.
Jer   31:33   and I will **w** it on their hearts;
Heb   8:10   and **w** them on their hearts,
Rev   21: 5   "**W** this, for these words are
           trustworthy

WRITING → WRITE
Ex   32:16   and the **w** was the **w** of God,
Da   5: 7   "Whoever can read this **w**
2Es   14:24   prepare for yourself many **w** tablets,

WRITTEN → WRITE
Jos   23: 6   to observe and do all that is **w** in
Da   12: 1   who is found **w** in the book.
Lk   24:44   everything **w** about me in the law
Jn   21:25   if every one of them were **w** down,
Rev   21:27   are **w** in the Lamb's book of life.
2Es   14:44   forty days, ninety-four books
           were **w.**

WRONG → WRONGDOING, WRONGED
Nu   5: 7   shall make full restitution for the **w,**
Lk   23:41   but this man has done nothing **w.**"
Ac   23: 9   "We find nothing **w** with this man.
Ro   13:10   Love does no **w** to a neighbor;

WRONGDOING → DO, WRONG
Ex   23: 2   You shall not follow a majority in **w**
1Jn   5:17   All **w** is sin, but there is sin that is
           not

WRONGED → WRONG
1Co   6: 7   Why not rather be **w?**

WROTE → WRITE
Ex   24: 4   And Moses **w** down all the words

Ex   34:28   he **w** on the tablets the words of the
Jn   5:46   believe me, for he **w** about me.

Y

YEAR → YEARS
Ex   23:14   Three times in the **y** you shall hold
Heb   10: 1   continually offered **y** after **y,**

YEARS → YEAR
Ge   1:14   and for seasons and for days and **y,**
Ex   12:40   in Egypt was four hundred thirty **y.**
Nu   14:34   forty **y,** and you shall know my
2Ch   36:21   it kept sabbath, to fulfill seventy **y.**
Ps   90: 4   For a thousand **y** in your sight are
           like
Jer   25:12   Then after seventy **y** are completed,
Da   9: 2   of Jerusalem, namely, seventy **y.**
Gal   4:10   and months, and seasons, and **y.**
2Pe   3: 8   the Lord one day is like a
           thousand **y,**
Rev   20: 2   and bound him for a thousand **y,**

YEAST
Mt   16: 6   beware of the **y** of the Pharisees and
Gal   5: 9   A little **y** leavens the whole batch of

YESTERDAY
Heb   13: 8   Jesus Christ is the same **y** and today

YOKE
Mt   11:30   my **y** is easy, and my burden is light."
Gal   5: 1   not submit again to a **y** of slavery.

YOUNG → YOUTH
Ps   119: 9   can **y** people keep their way pure?
Joel   2:28   and your **y** men shall see visions.
Ac   2:17   and your **y** men shall see visions,

YOUTH → YOUNG
Ps   71: 5   my trust, O LORD, from my **y.**
Ecc   12: 1   Remember your creator in the days
           of your **y,**

Z

ZACCHAEUS
Lk   19: 2   A man was there named **Z;**

ZEAL → ZEALOUS
Ps   69: 9   **z** for your house that has
           consumed me
Isa   37:32   The **z** of the LORD of hosts will do
           this.
Jn   2:17   "**Z** for your house will consume me.
Ro   10: 2   testify that they have a **z** for God,
Php   3: 6   as to **z,** a persecutor of the church;
1Mc   2:26   Thus he burned with **z** for the law,

ZEALOUS → ZEAL
Nu   25:13   because he was **z** for his God,
1Ki   19:10   "I have been very **z** for the LORD,

ZEBULUN
     Son of Jacob by Leah (Ge 30:20; 35:23; 1Ch 2:1). Tribe of blessed (Ge 49:13; Dt 33:18-19), numbered (Nu 1:31; 26:27), allotted land (Jos 19:10-16; Eze 48:26), failed to fully possess (Jdg 1:30), supported Deborah (Jdg 4:6-10; 5:14, 18), David (1Ch 12:33), 12,000 from (Rev 7:8).

ZECHARIAH
     1. Son of Jeroboam II; king of Israel (2Ki 15:8-12).
     2. Post-exilic prophet who encouraged rebuilding of temple (Ezr 5:1; 6:14; Zec 1:1).

ZEDEKIAH → =MATTANIAH
     1. False prophet (1Ki 22:11-24; 2Ch 18:10-23).
     2. Mattaniah, son of Josiah (1Ch 3:15), made king of Judah by Nebuchadnezzar (2Ki 24:17-25:7; 2Ch 36:10-14; Jer 37-39; 52:1-11).

ZEPHANIAH
     Prophet; descendant of Hezekiah (Zep 1:1).

ZERUBBABEL
     Descendant of David (1Ch 3:19; Mt 1:3). Led

ZERUBBABEL *(cont.)*
return from exile (Ezr 2:2; Ne 7:7). Governor of Israel; helped rebuild temple (Ezr 3; Hag 1-2; Zec 4).

ZIMRI
King of Israel (1Ki 16:9-20).

ZION
2Sa   5: 7   David took the stronghold of **Z**,

Ps   2: 6   I have set my king on **Z**, my holy hill.
      48: 2   is the joy of all the earth, Mount **Z**,
      78:68   Mount **Z**, which he loves.
Isa 28:16   I am laying in **Z** a foundation stone,
Mic   4: 2   For out of **Z** shall go forth instruction,
Zec   9: 9   Rejoice greatly, O daughter **Z!**
Mt   21: 5   "Tell the daughter of **Z,**

Ro   11:26   "Out of **Z** will come the Deliverer;
1Pe   2: 6   "See, I am laying in **Z** a stone,
Rev 14: 1   the Lamb, standing on Mount **Z!**

ZIPPORAH*
Daughter of Reuel; wife of Moses (Ex 2:21-22; 4:20-26; 18:1-6).

ZOPHAR*
One of Job's friends (Job 2:11; 11; 20; 42:9).

ISRAEL AT THE TIME
OF THE PATRIARCHS

MOAB Kingdoms
ARAM Areas

0   10   20 Miles
0   10   20 Kilometers

A   B   C   D

1   1

THE
GREAT
SEA

2   2

3   3

4   4

5   5

6   6

THE GREAT SEA

Sidon
PHOENECIA
DAMASCUS
ARAM
(SYRIA)
Ijon
Mt. Hermon
Tyre
Uzu
Kanah
Abel   Beth-rehob
Dan (Laish)
MACCAH
Beth-anath?
Kedesh
Rehob?
Achzib   Janoah
HAZOR   Aduru
Merom   GESHUR   ARGOB
Acco   Capernaum   BASHAN
Chinnereth   Karnaim
Magdala   Ashtaroth
Mt. Carmel   Hannathon   Madon   Beth-yerah
Achshaph?   Hammath   (Philoteria)   Golan   Jarmuk R.
Jokneam   Shimron   Mt. Tabor   Yanoam   HAVVOTH-JAIR
Dor   Japhia   Endor   Anaharath   Edrei
Megiddo   Shunem   Ramoth-gilead
Aruna   Taanach   Beth-shean   Ham
Beth-haggan   Mt. Gilboa   Rehob
Migdal   Arubboth   Ibleam   Pehel (Pella)   GILEAD
Gath of Sharon   Dothan
Yehem
Socoh   Samaria   Tirzah
Mt. Ebal   SHECHEM   Succoth   Penuel   TRANSJORDAN
Mt. Gerazim   Jabbok R.
Aphek   Hill Country   Mahanaim
of Israel
Joppa   Shiloh   Gilead   Jogbehah
Beth-dagon   Ono   Jazer   AMMON
Lod   Bethel   Beth-nimrah   PHILADELPHIA
Beth-   (Luz)   (RABBAH)
horon   Ai   Gilgal   Shittim   Elealeh
Gezer   GIBEON   Jericho   Ghassul   Heshbon
Aijalon   Beth-   Bezer
Ekron   JERUSALEM   jeshimoth   Mt. Nebo   Medeba
Ashdod   Beth-shemesh   (SALEM)   Mt. Pisgah   Kiriathaim
Gath   Socoh   Bethlehem   Beth-baal-meon
Ashkelon   Timnah   (Ephrath)   Mattanah
Adullam   Ataroth   Kedemoth
Chezib   Keilah   Dibon
Lachish   Mamre   Aroer
Eglon   Beth-tappuah   Hebron
Gaza   (Kiriath-arba)   Arnon R.
Beth-eglaim   Debir   En-gedi   Salt
Yurza   Sea
Gerar   Ziklag   Bab ed-Dra'
Sharuhen   ARAD   Ar
Beer-sheba   Moladah   Arad?   MOAB
Tel Abu Matar   Hormah
Hormah   Numeira
Adadah (Aroer)
Rehoboth   Es-Safi
Ziph   Zoer   Feifa   Zered Brook
The Negeb   EDOM
ARABAH

N

©2008 CHK America www.mapsusa.com

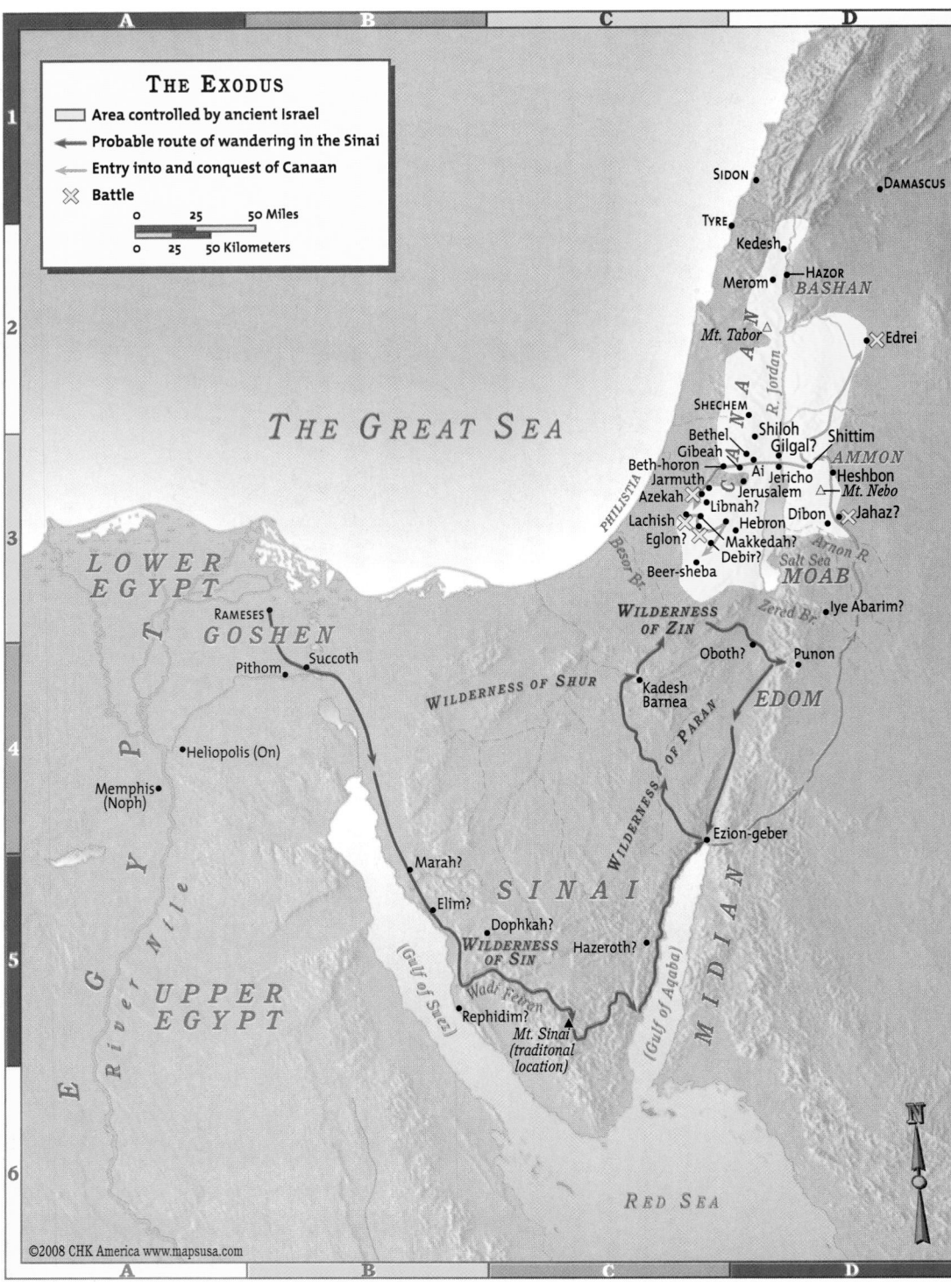

THE EXODUS

- Area controlled by ancient Israel
- Probable route of wandering in the Sinai
- Entry into and conquest of Canaan
- ⊠ Battle

0   25   50 Miles
0   25   50 Kilometers

THE GREAT SEA

SIDON

DAMASCUS

TYRE

Kedesh

Merom   HAZOR
BASHAN

Mt. Tabor △

Edrei ⊠

SHECHEM

R. Jordan

Bethel   Shiloh   Shittim
Gibeah   Gilgal?   AMMON
Beth-horon   Ai   Jericho   Heshbon
Jarmuth   Jerusalem   △ *Mt. Nebo*
Azekah   Libnah?   Dibon   Jahaz? ⊠
Lachish   Hebron
Eglon?   Makkedah?   Arnon R.
Debir?   MOAB
Beer-sheba   Salt Sea

PHILISTIA

Besor Br.

WILDERNESS OF ZIN

Zered Br.   Iye Abarim?

Oboth?   Punon

LOWER EGYPT

GOSHEN

RAMESES

Pithom   Succoth

Kadesh Barnea

EDOM

WILDERNESS OF SHUR

WILDERNESS OF PARAN

Heliopolis (On)

Memphis (Noph)

Ezion-geber

Marah?

SINAI

Elim?

Dophkah?
WILDERNESS OF SIN   Hazeroth?

UPPER EGYPT

River Nile

Wadi Feiran

Rephidim?

Mt. Sinai (traditonal location) ▲

MIDIAN

(Gulf of Suez)

(Gulf of Aqaba)

N

RED SEA

©2008 CHK America www.mapsusa.com

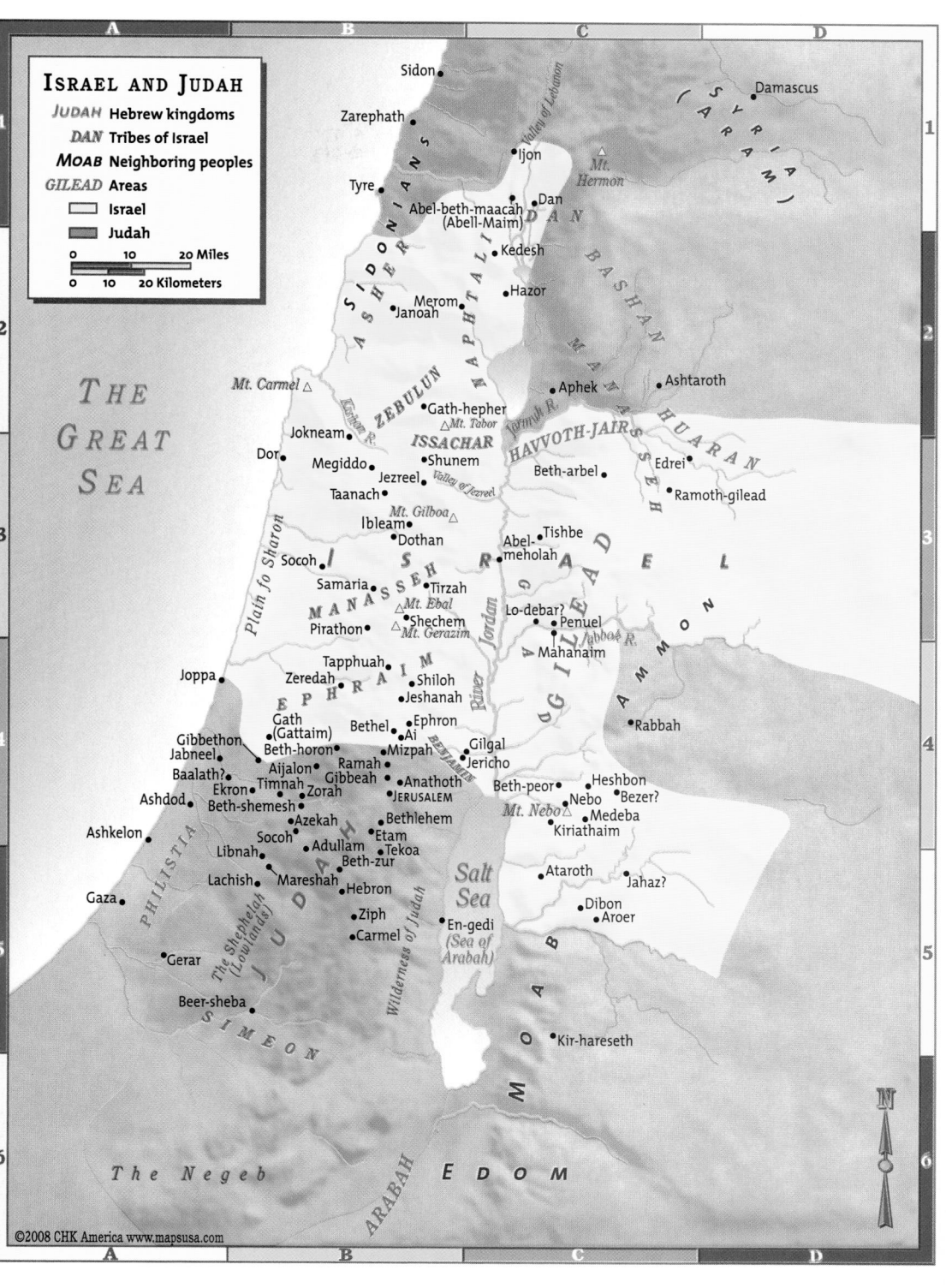

ISRAEL AND JUDAH

JUDAH Hebrew kingdoms
DAN Tribes of Israel
MOAB Neighboring peoples
GILEAD Areas

Israel
Judah

0   10   20 Miles
0   10   20 Kilometers

THE
GREAT
SEA

THE NEGEB

©2008 CHK America www.mapsusa.com

Sidon
Zarephath
Ijon
Tyre
Abel-beth-maacah
(Abell-Maim)
Kedesh
Merom
Janoah
Hazor
Damascus

SIDONIANS
NAPHTALI
DAN
Valley of Lebanon
Mt. Hermon
SYRIA (ARAM)
BASHAN

Mt. Carmel
ZEBULUN
Gath-hepher
Mt. Tabor
ISSACHAR
Aphek
Ashtaroth
HAVVOTH-JAIR
HAURAN

Jokneam
Dor
Megiddo
Jezreel
Shunem
Beth-arbel
Edrei
Ramoth-gilead
Taanach
Valley of Jezreel
Mt. Gilboa
Ibleam
Dothan
Tishbe
Abel-meholah
GILEAD

Plain fo Sharon
Socoh
Samaria
Tirzah
MANASSEH
Mt. Ebal
Pirathon
Shechem
Mt. Gerazim
Lo-debar?
Penuel
Mahanaim
Jabbok R.
AMMON

Joppa
Tapphuah
Zeredah
Shiloh
Jeshanah
Gath
(Gattaim)
Bethel
Ephron
Ai
Gilgal
Jericho
Rabbah
EPHRAIM
River Jordan

Gibbethon
Beth-horon
Jabneel
Mizpah
Ramah
Baalath?
Aijalon
Gibbeah
Anathoth
Beth-peor
Heshbon
Ekron
Timnah
Zorah
JERUSALEM
Nebo
Bezer?
Ashdod
Beth-shemesh
Bethlehem
Mt. Nebo
Medeba
Azekah
Kiriathaim
Ashkelon
Socoh
Adullam
Etam
Tekoa
Libnah
Beth-zur
Ataroth
Jahaz?
Lachish
Mareshah
Hebron
Dibon
Aroer
Gaza
Ziph
Carmel
En-gedi
PHILISTIA
The Shephelah
(Lowlands)
JUDAH
Wilderness of Judah
Salt Sea
(Sea of Arabah)

Gerar
Beer-sheba
SIMEON
Kir-hareseth
MOAB

ARABAH
EDOM

N

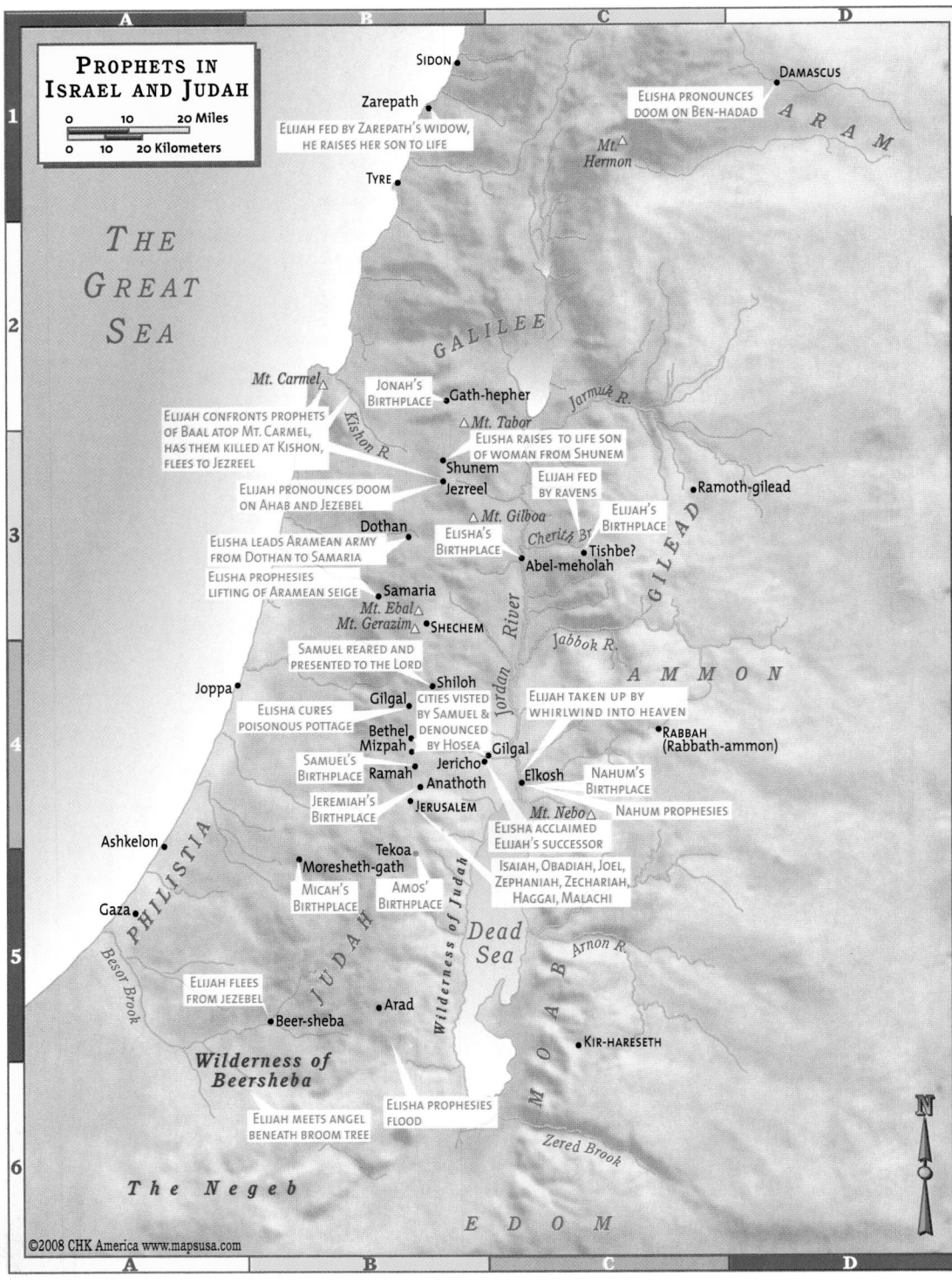

PROPHETS IN ISRAEL AND JUDAH

0 10 20 Miles
0 10 20 Kilometers

A **B** **C** **D**

SIDON

Zarepath

DAMASCUS

ELISHA PRONOUNCES
DOOM ON BEN-HADAD

A R A M

ELIJAH FED BY ZAREPATH'S WIDOW,
HE RAISES HER SON TO LIFE

TYRE

Mt.
Hermon

1

THE
GREAT
SEA

GALILEE

2

Mt. Carmel

JONAH'S
BIRTHPLACE

Gath-hepher

Jarmuk R.

ELIJAH CONFRONTS PROPHETS
OF BAAL ATOP MT. CARMEL,
HAS THEM KILLED AT KISHON,
FLEES TO JEZREEL

Mt. Tabor

ELISHA RAISES TO LIFE SON
OF WOMAN FROM SHUNEM

Kishon R.

Shunem

ELIJAH FED
BY RAVENS

Ramoth-gilead

ELIJAH PRONOUNCES DOOM
ON AHAB AND JEZEBEL

Jezreel

Mt. Gilboa

ELIJAH'S
BIRTHPLACE

Dothan

ELISHA'S
BIRTHPLACE

Cherith Br.

Tishbe?

G I L E A D

ELISHA LEADS ARAMEAN ARMY
FROM DOTHAN TO SAMARIA

Abel-meholah

ELISHA PROPHESIES
LIFTING OF ARAMEAN SEIGE

Samaria

Jabbok R.

Mt. Ebal
Mt. Gerazim

SHECHEM

A M M O N

SAMUEL REARED AND
PRESENTED TO THE LORD

Shiloh

Joppa

Gilgal

CITIES VISTED
BY SAMUEL &
DENOUNCED
BY HOSEA

ELIJAH TAKEN UP BY
WHIRLWIND INTO HEAVEN

ELISHA CURES
POISONOUS POTTAGE

Bethel

Gilgal

RABBAH
(Rabbath-ammon)

Mizpah

SAMUEL'S
BIRTHPLACE

Ramah

Jericho

Elkosh

NAHUM'S
BIRTHPLACE

Anathoth

JEREMIAH'S
BIRTHPLACE

JERUSALEM

Mt. Nebo

NAHUM PROPHESIES

Ashkelon

ELISHA ACCLAIMED
ELIJAH'S SUCCESSOR

Tekoa

ISAIAH, OBADIAH, JOEL,
ZEPHANIAH, ZECHARIAH,
HAGGAI, MALACHI

Moresheth-gath

Gaza

MICAH'S
BIRTHPLACE

AMOS'
BIRTHPLACE

Dead
Sea

P H I L I S T I A

Arnon R.

5

ELIJAH FLEES
FROM JEZEBEL

J U D A H

Arad

Wilderness of Judah

M O A B

Kir-hareseth

Beer-sheba

Wilderness of
Beersheba

N

ELIJAH MEETS ANGEL
BENEATH BROOM TREE

ELISHA PROPHESIES
FLOOD

Zered Brook

6

The Negeb

E D O M

©2008 CHK America www.mapsusa.com

A **B** **C** **D**

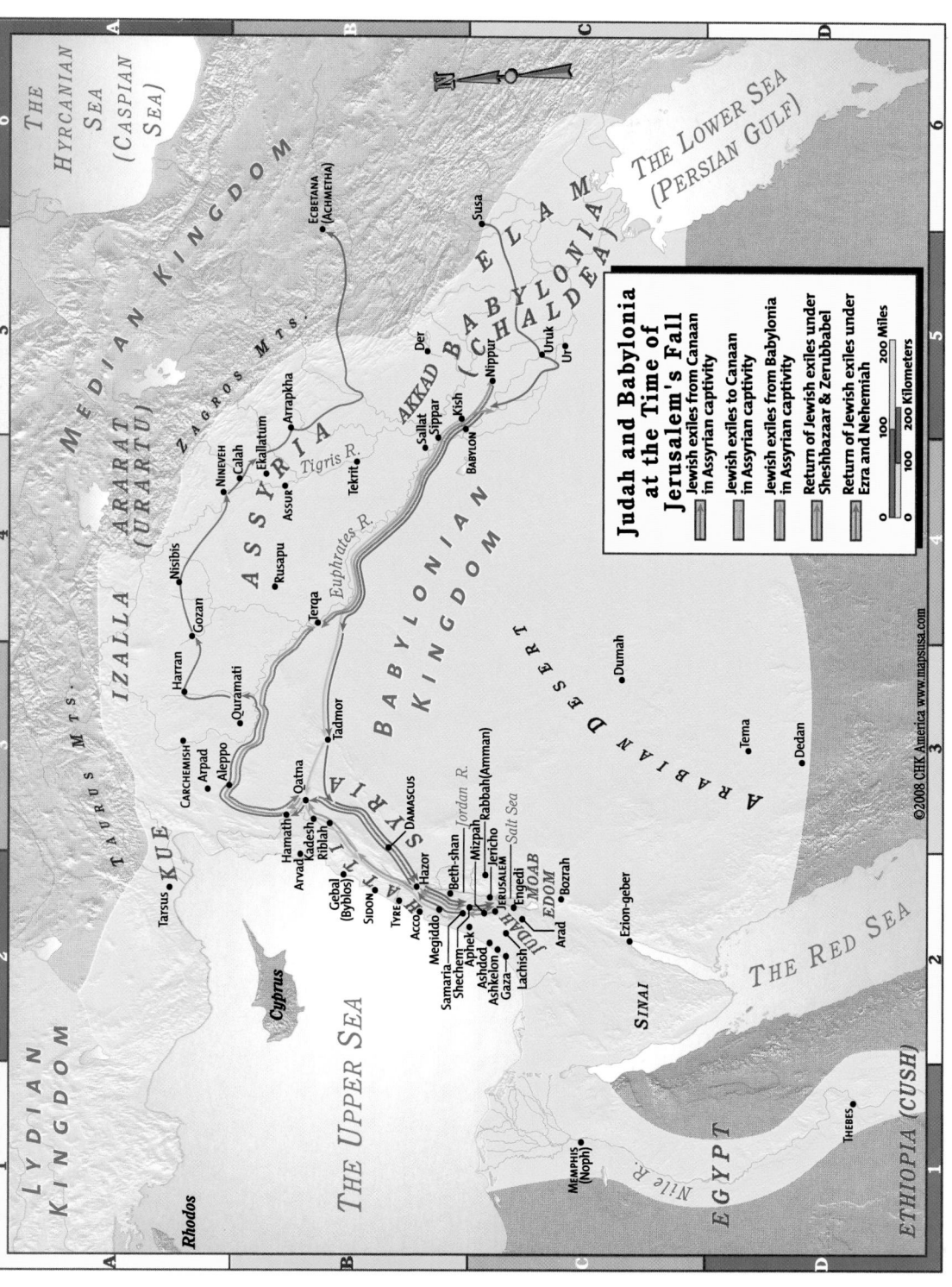

Judah and Babylonia at the Time of Jerusalem's Fall

Jewish exiles from Canaan in Assyrian captivity

Jewish exiles to Canaan in Assyrian captivity

Jewish exiles from Babylonia in Assyrian captivity

Return of Jewish exiles under Sheshbazzar & Zerubbabel

Return of Jewish exiles under Ezra and Nehemiah

0   100   200 Miles
0   100   200 Kilometers

©2008 CHK America www.mapsusa.com

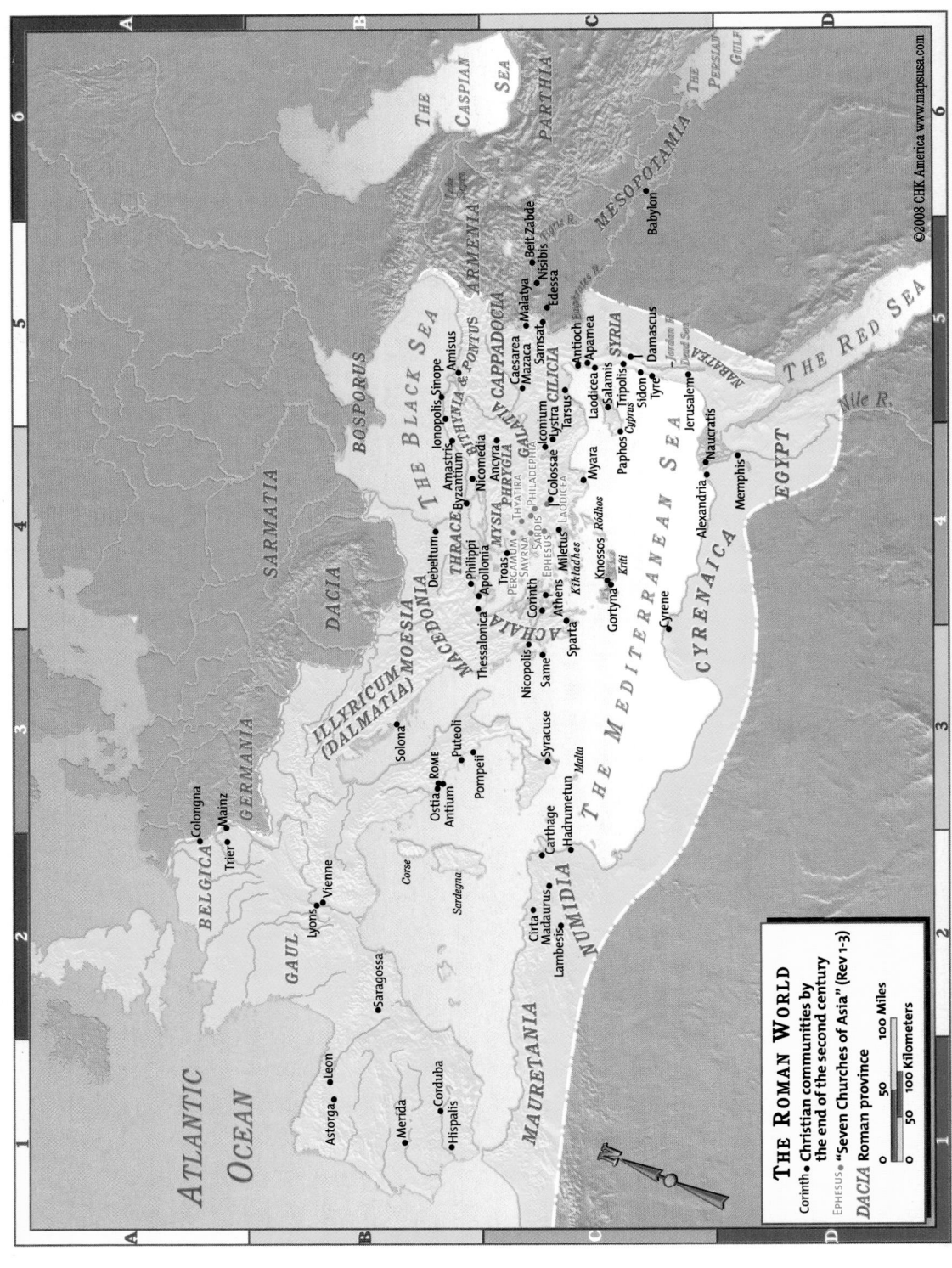

THE ROMAN WORLD

Corinth ● Christian communities by the end of the second century

EPHESUS ● "Seven Churches of Asia" (Rev 1-3)

DACIA Roman province

©2008 CHK America www.mapsusa.com